REFERENCE ENCYCLOPEDIA

OF THE
AMERICAN INDIAN

11TH EDITION

BARRY T. KLEIN

REFERENCE ENCYCLOPEDIA OF THE AMERICAN INDIAN

11th Edition

TODD PUBLICATIONS
P.O.Box 635
Nyack, New York 10960
(914) 907-9790
E-mail: toddpub@aol.com

ISBN 0-915344-77-7

Contents

Contents (Cont'd)

Section Two
Canadian Section

Section Three
Bibliography

Section Four
Biographies

Introduction

According to figures released by the 2000 U.S. Census, there are approximately 4,500,000 American Indians, Eskimos and Aleuts in the United States. The most populous states in terms of Indians is California with approximately 500,000, Oklahoma, 400,000, Arizona, 450,000, and New Mexico, 400,000; Alaska has more than 100,000 Eskimos and Aleuts. Population figures have been increasing at a rate of more than 70% per decade since 1960. There is no one Federal or tribal definition that establishes a person's identity as Indian. Government Agencies use different criteria for determining who is an Indian. Similarly, tribal groups have varying requirements for determining tribal membership.

There are now 562 federally recognized tribes and groups including about 200 Alaskan Native village groups; and about 200 state recognized groups in the United States. An Indian reservation is an area of land reserved for Indian use. The name comes from the early days of Indian-white relations when Indian tribes relinquished land through treaties, reserving a portion for their own use. Congressional acts, Executive orders, and agreements have also created reservations. Many reservations today, however, have some non-Indian residents and non-Indian landowners. Tribe among the North American Indians originally meant a body of persons bound together by blood ties who were socially, politically, and religiously organized, and who lived together, occupying a definite territory and speaking a common language or dialect. With the relegation of Indians to reservations, the word tribe developed a number of different meanings. Today, it can be a distinct group within an Indian village or community, a large number of communities, several different groups or villages speaking different languages but sharing a common government, or a widely scattered number of villages with a common language but no common government. According to a 2000 estimate by the Bureau of Indian Affairs, about 1.5 million Indians live on or adjacent to reservations. The remaining 3 million American Indians reside in cities and suburbs across the country.

A special U.S. Senate committee charged with investigating fraud and mismanagement in the Bureau of Indian Affairs has recommended adoption of what it calls *"A New Federalism,"'* in which the federal government would abolish the BIA and transfer annual federal appropriations directly to tribal governments. The committee said new agreements are needed between the federal governments and the tribes "that both allow American Indians to run their own affairs and pledge permanent federal support for tribal governments." These new agreements would not affect any existing treaty rights or alter the legal status of tribal governments. An Office of Federal-Tribal Relations (OFTR) would be created within the executive office of the President. The OFTR would be responsible for negotiating and overseeing implementation of formal agreements with federally recognized Indian tribes. "The agreements will allow any tribe that so chooses to exit the current bureaucracy of federal Indian programs and to receive and use at its own discretion a proportional share of the federal Indian budget." The committee proposes that funding be allocated to tribal governments based solely on population figures. The special committee also recommended that each House of Congress create a permanent full committee on Indian affairs, with additional staff specifically assigned to perform oversight and investigations.

The U.S., upon ratification of an agreement by both a tribe and the federal government, would provide the tribe with an annual Tribal Self-Governance Grant (TSGG), equalling its fair share of the current federal Indian budget. The size of the grant would be proportional to the population base of the tribe. Each grant would be supplemented by an annual cost-of-living allowance. Equally important, there would be a transfer from the BIA and Indian Health Service and any other federal agency with Indian-related programs to the contracting tribes, such assets as necessary for the tribe to carry out their new responsibilities under the agreement.

This 11th Edition of *Reference Encyclopedia of the American Indian* is divided into four main sections. The *first section* contains source listings. Each listing gives address, phone number, contact and, in most cases, a brief description of activities and pertinent information. Listings are arranged either alphabetically or alpha-geographically. At the beginning of each section there is an explanatory note detailing the type of sources listed and the manner in which they are arranged. The length of each listing reflects the amount of material received from each source. Material has been researched directly from questionnaires or has been gathered from other reliable sources. For further information on any listed source, it is suggested that the reader write to the address or call the number given in the listing. The *second section* is solely Canadian listings; the *third section* of the book is a bibliography of approximately 6,000 in-print books. Listed alphabetically, each book gives basic bibliographic information. The alphabetical section is broken down into a subject categories section with corresponding titles listed for each category. A publishers index is provided at the end giving the publishers' addresses and phone numbers. The *fourth section* contains approximately 2,500 biographical sketches of prominent Native Americans involved in Indian Affairs, education, healthcare, business, the arts and professions, as well as non-Indians active in Indian affairs, history, art, anthropology, archaeology, etc., and the many fields to which the subject of the American Indian is related.

All changes and additions to the listings in this book should be directed to me at the address given on the copyright page. Thank you.

Barry Klein
Editor

REFERENCE ENCYCLOPEDIA OF THE AMERICAN INDIAN

As of this printing there are 562 federally recognized American Indian reservations and communities. These groups are entitled to U.S. legal protections of tribal self-government and rights to tribally owned land. Included are approximately 200 Alaskan Native groups. Also listed are about 175 state recognized and non-recognized Indian communities who have not signed treaties or, who have not had regular legal relations with the U.S. Government.

Listed in this section are reservation tribal councils, organizations, and governing bodies, which handle tribal and/or reservation affairs and which represent the tribes and create policy on land, enrollment, etc. Listings are arranged alphabetically within states.

The U.S. Dept. of the Interior, Bureau of Indian Affairs (BIA) is the agency that identifies and recognizes Indian tribal entities for establishing and maintaining federal government to government relations with Indians. Those tribes, bands and groups that have been recognized by the BIA are listed below, with the BIA agency or area office of jurisdiction indicated for each.

ALABAMA

MOWA BAND OF CHOCTAW INDIANS
1080 W. Red Fox Rd. • Mt. Vernon, AL 36560
(251) 829-5500 Fax 829-6328
Wilford "Longhair" Taylor, Chief
E-mail: chieftaylor@mowachoctaw
Kesler Weaver, Sr., Council Chairperson
Reservation served: Choctaw Indian Reservation. *Tribe*: Choctaw. *In Residence*: 5,500. *Acreage*: 600. *Geographic Boundaries*: North Mobile County & South Washington County. *Tribal Councilpersons*: Washington County - Verma Reed, Kesler Weaver, Sr., Donell Orso, Cleve Reed, Addie Odom. Mobile County - John A. Byrd, Sr., Alex Hopkins, Sr., Claudette Snow, Cherry Smith. *Tribal Judge*: Samuel Hill. *Activities*: Annual pow wow, 3rd weekend in June; Cultural Festival - last weekend in September. Operates two elementary school; Mowa Choctaw Dancers; operates two Indian schools. Museum & Culture Center. *Publication*: "Chata" quarterly newsletter. Choctaw Agency.

POARCH BAND OF CREEK INDIANS
5811 Jack Springs Rd. • Atmore, AL 36502
(251) 368-9136 Fax 368-1026
Eddie L. Tullis, Chairperson
Website: www.poarchcreekindians.org
Tribe served: Creek. Choctaw Agency-Eastern Regional Office.

ALASKA

NATIVE VILLAGE OF AFOGNAK
P.O. Box 968 • Kodiak, AK 99615
(907) 486-6357 Fax 486-6529
Roger Malutin, Chairperson
E-mail: john@afognak.net
West-Central Alaska Field Office

AGDAAGUX TRIBE OF KING COVE
P.O. Box 249, King Cove, AK 99612
(907) 497-2648 Fax 497-2803
Marvin Hoff, Sr., President
E-mail: atc@arctic.net
West-Central Alaska Field Office

NATIVE VILLAGE OF AKHIOK
P.O. Box 5050, Akhiok, AK 99615
(907) 836-2313 Fax 836-2345
Speridon M. Simeonoff, Sr., President
Tribe: Eskimo. *In residence*: 90.
West-Central Alaska Field Office

AKIACHAK NATIVE COMMUNITY
P.O. Box 70, Akiachak, AK 99551

(907) 825-4626 Fax 825-4029
Samuel J. George, Chief
Tribe: Yup'ik Eskimo. *In residence*: 500. *Area*: 115,600 acres. Cooperatively manage community library with the school district. West-Central Alaska Field Office.

AKIAK NATIVE COMMUNITY
P.O. Box 52127, Akiak, AK 99552
(907) 765-7112 Fax 765-7512
Moses Owen, Chief
E-mail: akiak@aol.com
Tribe: Eskimo. *In residence*: 225.
West-Central Alaska Field Office.

NATIVE VILLAGE OF AKUTAN
Akutan Traditional Council
P.O. Box 89, Akutan, AK 99553
(907) 698-2300 Fax 698-2301
Jacob Stepetin, President
Self-Gov: Aleutian/Pribilof Islands Association
West-Central Alaska Field Office

VILLAGE OF ALAKANUK
P.O. Box 149, Alakanuk, AK 99554
(907) 238-3419 Fax 238-3429
Patrick Phillips, President
Self-Gov: Association of Village Council President
West-Central Alaska Field Office

ALATNA VILLAGE TRIBAL OFFICE
P.O. Box 70, Allakaket, Alatna, AK 99720
(907) 968-2304 Fax 968-2305
Harding Sam, Chief
Self-Gov: Tanana Chiefs
Fairbanks Field Office.

NATIVE VILLAGE OF ALEKNAGIK
P.O. Box 115, Aleknagik, AK 99555
(907) 842-2080 Fax 842-2081
Kay M. Gorman, President
E-mail: alnilutsik@hotmail.com
Self-Gov: Bristol Bay Native Association, Inc.
Tribe: Athapascan. *In residence*: 175.
West-Central Alaska Field Office.

ALGAACIQ NATIVE VILLAGE
P.O. Box 48, St. Mary's, AK 99658
(907) 438-2932 Fax 438-2227
Moses Paukan, Sr., President
Self-Gov: Association of Village Council Presidents
Tribe: Eskimo. *In residence*: 125.
West-Central Alaska Field Office.

ALLAKAKET VILLAGE
P.O. Box 30, Allakaket, AK 99720
(907) 968-2237 Fax 968-2233
Gilbert Vent, First Chief
Self-Gov: Tanana Chiefs
Tribe: Athapascan. *In residence*: 120.
Fairbanks Field Office.

NATIVE VILLAGE OF AMBLER
P.O. Box 47, Ambler, AK 99786
(907) 445-2196 Fax 445-2181
Truman Cleveland, Sr., Chief
Self-Gov: Maniilaq Consortium.
Fairbanks Field Office.

VILLAGE OF ANAKTUVUK PASS
P.O. Box 21065, Anaktuvuk Pass, AK 99721
(907) 661-2575 Fax 661-2576
Thomas Rulland, President
Tribe: Eskimo. *In residence*: 100.
Fairbanks Field Office.

YUPIIT OF ANDREAFSKI
P.O. Box 88, St. Mary's, AK 99658
(907) 438-2312 Fax 438-2512
Gail Alstrom, President
Tribe: Yupiit. *Membership*:150. *Publication*: Andreafsky Tribal Newsletter. *Activities*: Meetings are held 1st Wednesday of each month. West-Central Alaska Field Office.

ANGOON COMMUNITY ASSOCIATION
P.O. Box 188, Angoon, AK 99820
(907) 788-3411 Fax 788-3412
Wally Frank, Sr., President
Self-Gov: Central Council of Tlingit-Haida
West-Central Alaska Field Office

VILLAGE OF ANIAK
P.O. Box 349, Aniak, AK 99557
(907) 675-4349 Fax 675-4513
Ruth Birky, President
Tribe: Eskimo. *In residence*: 150.
West-Central Alaska Field Office.

ANVIK VILLAGE
P.O. Box 10, Anvik, AK 99558
(907) 663-6322 Fax 663-6357
Carl Jerue, Chief
E-mail: anviktribal@hotmail.com
Self-Gov: Tanana Chiefs
Tribe: Eskimo. *In residence*: 150.
Fairbanks Field Office.

VILLAGE OF ARCTIC VILLAGE
P.O. Box 22069, Arctic Village, AK 99722
(907) 587-5990 Fax 587-5900
Evon Peter, First Chief
E-mail: nativemovement@hotmail.com
Tribe: Athapascan. Fairbanks Field Office.

ASA'CARSARMIUT TRIBE
P.O. Box 32249, Mountain Village, AK 99632
(907) 591-2814 Fax 591-2811
James C. Landlord, First Chief
Tribe: Eskimo. *In residence*: 275.
West-Central Alaska Field Office.

NATIVE VILLAGE OF ATKA
P.O. Box 47030, Atka, AK 99547
(907) 839-2229 Fax 839-2269
Mark Snigaroff, President
E-mail: atka@aitc.org
Self-Gov: Aleutian/Pribilof Islands Association, Inc.
West-Central Alaska Field Office.

VILLAGE OF ATMAUTLUAK
P.O. Box 6568, Atmautluak, AK 99559
(907) 553-5610 Fax 553-5216
Daniel A. Waska, President
E-mail: atmautlu@unicorn-alaska.com
West-Central Alaska Field Office.

NATIVE VILLAGE OF ATQASUK
P.O. Box 91108, Atqasuk, AK 99791
(907) 633-2575 Fax 633-2576
Herman Kignak, Sr., President
E-mail: jkakpik@hotmail.com
Fairbanks Field Office.

NATIVE VILLAGE OF BARROW
Inupiat Traditional Government
6970 Almaogak St.
P.O. Box 1130, Barrow, AK 99723
(907) 852-4411 Fax 852-8844
Percy Nusunginya, President
Tribe: Inupiat. *In residence*: 3,000.
Fairbanks Field Office.

BEAVER VILLAGE
P.O. Box 24029, Beaver, AK 99724
(907) 628-6126 Fax 628-6815
Charlene Fisher, Chief
Self-Gov: Tanana Chiefs
Tribes: Eskimo, Athapascan, Indian.
In residence: 150. Fairbanks Field Office.

NATIVE VILLAGE OF BELKOFSKY
P.O. Box 57, King Cove, AK 99612
(907) 497-3122 Fax 497-3123
Jeff Kenezuroff, President
E-mail: bert@artic.net
Self-Gov: Aleutian/Pribilof Islands Association, Inc.
Tribe: Aleut. *In residence*: 200. West-Central Alaska Field Office.

VILLAGE OF BILL MOORE'S SLOUGH
P.O. Box 20288, Kotlik, AK 99620
(907) 899-4232 Fax 899-4461
Joseph Aparezuk, Tribal Chairperson
Self-Gov: Association of Village Council Presidents
West-Central Alaska Field Office.

BIRCH CREEK TRIBE
P.O. Box KBC, Fort Yukon, AK 99701
(907) 221-2211 Fax 221-2312
Winston James, First Chief
E-mail: e_itta@hotmail.com

Self-Gov: Tanana Chiefs
Fairbanks Field Office.

NATIVE VILLAGE OF BREVIG MISSION
P.O. Box 85039, Brevig Mission, AK 99785
(907) 642-4301 Fax 642-2099
Gilbert Tocktoo, President
E-mail: ada@kawerak.org
Self-Gov: Kawerak
Fairbanks Field Office.

NATIVE VILLAGE OF BUCKLAND (IRA)
P.O. Box 67, Buckland, AK 99727
(907) 494-2171 Fax 494-2217
Percy Ballot, Sr., President
E-mail: erweber@maniilaq.org
Self-Gov: Maniilaq Consortium
Fairbanks Field Office.

NATIVE VILLAGE OF CANTWELL
P.O. Box 94, Cantwell, AK 99729
(907) 768-2591 Fax 768-1111
Veronica Nicholas, President
E-mail: hallvc@yahoo.com
Self-Gov: Copper River Native Association, Inc.
Tribe: Athapascan. West-Central Alaska Field Office.

**CENTRAL COUNCIL OF TLINGIT &
HAIDA INDIAN TRIBES OF ALASKA**
320 W. Willoughby Ave., Suite 300
Juneau, AK 99801
(907) 586-1432 Fax 586-8970
Edward K. Thomas, President
Tribes: Tlingit & Haida

CHALKYITSIK VILLAGE
P.O. Box 57, Chalkyitsik, AK 99788
(907) 848-8117 Fax 848-8986
James Nathaniel, Sr., First Chief
E-mail: cik_vig_coun@email.com
Self-Gov: Tanana Chiefs
Fairbanks Field Office.

CHEESH-NA TRIBAL COUNCIL
P.O. Box 241, Gakona, AK 99586
(907) 822-3503 Fax 822-5179
Marilynn Beeter, President
E-mail: esinyon@tribalnet.org
West-Central Alaska Field Office

VILLAGE OF CHEFORNAK
P.O. Box 110, Chefornak, AK 99561
(907) 867-8850 Fax 867-8711
Oscar Wassillie, President
Self-Gov: Association of Village Council Presidents
Tribe: Eskimo. In residence: 175.
West-Central Alaska Field Office.

NATIVE VILLAGE OF CHENEGA
623 Cato St., P.O. Box 8079
Chenega Bay, AK 99574
(907) 573-5132 Fax 573-5120
Larry Evanoff, President
E-mail: chenegaira@aol.com
Self-Gov: Chugachmiut, Inc.
West-Central Alaska Field Office.

CHEVAK NATIVE VILLAGE
P.O. Box 140, Chevak, AK 99563
(907) 858-7428 Fax 858-7812
Peter Tuluk, Chairperson
E-mail: chevaktc@unicom-alaska.com
Self-Gov: Association of Village Council Presidents
Tribe: Eskimo. In residence: 400.
West-Central Alaska Field Office.

CHICKALOON NATIVE VILLAGE
P.O. Box 1105, Chickaloon, AK 99674
(907) 745-0707 Fax 746-7154
Gary Harrison, Chairperson
E-mail: cvadmin@chickaloon.org
Website: www.chickaloon.org
Maintains school. Publication: "Traditional Stories About Values" by Katherine Wade. West-Central Alaska Field Office.

NATIVE VILLAGE OF CHIGNIK
P.O. Box 50, Chignik, AK 99564
(907) 749-2445 Fax 749-2423
Minnie Skonberg, President

E-mail: cbaytc@aol.com
Self-Gov: Bristol Bay Native Association, Inc.
Tribe: Eskimo. In residence: 385.
West-Central Alaska Field Office.

NATIVE VILLAGE OF CHIGNIK LAGOON
P.O. Box 09, Chignik Lagoon, AK 99565
(907) 840-2281 Fax 840-2217
Laura Stepanoff, President
E-mail: clvc101@aol.com
Self-Gov: Bristol Bay Native Association, Inc.
Tribe: Eskimo. West-Central Alaska Field Office.

CHIGNIK LAKE VILLAGE
P.O. Box 33, Chignik Lake, AK 99548
(907) 845-2212 Fax 845-2217
John Lind, President
Self-Gov: Bristol Bay Native Association, Inc.
Tribe: Eskimo. West-Central Alaska Field Office.

CHILKAT INDIAN VILLAGE (KLUKWAN)
32 Chilkat Ave.
P.O. Box 210, Klukwan, AK 99827
(907) 767-5505 Fax 767-5518
Jones P. Hotch, Jr., President
E-mail: klukwan@wytbear.com
West-Central Alaska Field Office.

CHILKOOT INDIAN ASSOCIATION (IRA)
207 Main St., Suite 2
P.O. Box 490, Haines, AK 99827
(907) 766-2323 Fax 766-2365
Lee E. Clayton, President
E-mail: chilkoot@wytbear.com
Self-Gov: Central Council of Tlingit-Haida
Tribe: Chilkoot. West-Central Alaska Field Office.

CHINIK ESKIMO COMMUNITY (aka Golovin)
P.O. Box 62020, Golovin, AK 99762
(907) 779-2214 Fax 779-2829
Frank Amarok, President
Self-Gov: Kawerak
Tribe: Eskimo. In residence: 140.
Fairbanks Field Office.

NATIVE VILLAGE OF CHISTOCHINA
P.O. Box 241, Gakona, AK 99586
(907) 822-3503 Fax 822-5179
Karen Eskilda, President
Tribe: Athapascan. West-Central Alaska Field Office.

NATIVE VILLAGE OF CHITINA
P.O. Box 31, Chitina, AK 99566
(907) 823-2215 Fax 823-2233
Harry Billum, President
West-Central Alaska Field Office.

NATIVE VILLAGE OF CHUATHBALUK
P.O. Box CHU, Chuathbaluk, AK 99557
(907) 467-4313 Fax 467-4113
William O. Nesbit, Chairperson
West-Central Alaska Field Office.

CHULOONAWICK NATIVE VILLAGE
P.O. Box 245, Chuloonawick, AK 99581
(907) 949-1345 Fax 949-1346
Bill Akers, President
West-Central Alaska Field Office.

CIRCLE NATIVE COMMUNITY (IRA)
P.O. Box 89, Circle, AK 99733
(907) 733-2822 Fax 773-2823
Larry Nathaniel, 1st Chief
Self Gov: Tanana Chiefs
Tribe: Athapascan. In residence: 115.
Fairbanks Field Office.

NATIVE VILLAGE OF CLARK'S POINT
P.O. Box 90, Clark's Point, AK 99569
(907) 236-1435 Fax 236-1428
Esther J. Floresta, President
Self-Gov: Bristol Bay Native Association, Inc.
West-Central Alaska Field Office.

NATIVE VILLAGE OF NOME COUNCIL
P.O. Box 2050, Nome, AK 99762
(907) 443-7649 Fax 443-5965
Barbara Gray, Acting President
Self-Gov: Kawerak
Fairbanks Field Office

CRAIG COMMUNITY ASSOCIATION
1330 Craig/Klawock Hwy.
P.O. Box 828, Craig, AK 99921
(907) 826-3996 Fax 826-3997
A. Millie Stevens, President
E-mail: cgtribe@aptalaska.net
Self-Gov: Central Council of Tlingit-Haida
West-Central Alaska Field Office.

NATIVE VILLAGE OF CROOKED CREEK
P.O. Box 69, Crooked Creek, AK 99575
(907) 432-2200 Fax 432-2201
Johnny John, Jr., President
Self-Gov: Kuskokwim Native Association
Tribe: Athapascan. West-Central Alaska Field Office.

CURYUNG TRIBAL COUNCIL
134 - 1st Ave. West
P.O. Box 216, Dillingham, AK 99576
(907) 842-2384 Fax 842-4510
Rose Heyano, Chief
E-mail: curyungh@nutshtel.com
Self-Gov: Bristol Bay Native Association, Inc.
Tribes: Athapascan and Indian. In residence: 450.
West-Central Alaska Field Office.

NATIVE VILLAGE OF DEERING
P.O. Box 36089, Deering, AK 99736
(907) 363-2138 Fax 363-2195
Emerson Moto, Jr., President
E-mail: rrmoto@maniilaq.org
Self-Gov: Maniilaq Consortium
Tribe: Eskimo. In residence: 250.
Fairbanks Field Office.

NATIVE VILLAGE OF DIOMEDE (IRA) (aka Inalik)
P.O. Box 7079, Diomede, AK 99762
(907) 686-2175 Fax 686-2203
Eric Iyapana, President
Self-Gov: Kawerak. Fairbanks Field Office.

VILLAGE OF DOT LAKE
P.O. Box 2279, Dot Lake, AK 99737
(907) 882-2695 Fax 882-5558
William J. Miller, President
E-mail: dotlake@aitc.org.
Self-Gov: Tanana Chiefs. Fairbanks Field Office.

DOUGLAS INDIAN ASSOCIATION
918 3rd St., Juneau, AK 99824
(907) 364-2916 Fax 364-2917
Dorothy Owen, President
West-Central Alaska Field Office.

NATIVE VILLAGE OF EAGLE (IRA)
P.O. Box 19, Eagle, AK 99738
(907) 547-2271 Fax 547-2318
Joanne Beck, First Chief
Self-Gov: Tanana Chiefs
Tribes: Eskimo & Indian. Fairbanks Field Office.

NATIVE VILLAGE OF EEK
P.O. Box 87, Eek, AK 99578
(907) 536-5128 Fax 536-5711
Nick A. Carter, President
Self-Gov: Association of Village Council Presidents
Tribe: Eskimo. In residence: 190.
West-Central Alaska Field Office.

EGEGIK TRIBAL COUNCIL
289 Airport Rd.
P.O. Box 29, Egegik, AK 99579
(907) 233-2211 Fax 233-2312
Lawrence Abalama, President
E-mail: evc233@aol.com
Self-Gov: Bristol Bay Native Association, Inc.
Tribes: Eskimo & Indian. In residence: 140.
West-Central Alaska Field Office.

EKLUTNA NATIVE VILLAGE
26339 Eklutna Village Rd., Chugiak, AK 99567
(907) 688-6020 Fax 688-6021
Dorothy Cook, President
E-mail: nve@ak.net
Tribe: Athapascan. West-Central Alaska Field Office.

NATIVE VILLAGE OF EKUK
300 Main St., P.O. Box 530
Dillingham, AK 99576
(907) 842-3842 Fax 842-3843

Robert Heyano, President
Self-Gov: Bristol Bay Native Association, Inc.
West-Central Alaska Field Office.

EKWOK VILLAGE COUNCIL
100 Main St.
P.O. Box 70, Ekwok, AK 99580
(907) 464-3336 Fax 464-3378
Carol J. Nicoli, President
E-mail: ekwokvill@aol.com
Website: www.bbna.com
Self-Gov: Bristol Bay Native Association, Inc.
West-Central Alaska Field Office.

NATIVE VILLAGE OF ELIM
P.O. Box 70, Elim, AK 99739
(907) 890-3737 Fax 890-3738
Robert A. Keith, President
E-mail: colleen@kawerak.org
Self-Gov: Kawerak
Tribe: Eskimo. *In residence*: 225.
Fairbanks Field Office.

EMMONAK VILLAGE
P.O. Box 126, Emmonak, AK 99581
(907) 949-1720 Fax 949-1384
Billy A. Charles, President
E-mail: etcadmin@unicom-alaska.com
Self-Gov: Association of Village Council Presidents
West-Central Alaska Field Office.

EVANSVILLE VILLAGE
101 Hickle Hwy., P.O. Box 26025
Bettles Field, AK 99726
(907) 692-5005 Fax 692-5006
Rhonda Musser, Chief
E-mail: evansville@aitc.org.
Self-Gov: Tanana Chiefs
Tribes: Eskimo & Indian. *In residence*: 65.
Fairbanks Field Office.

NATIVE VILLAGE OF EYAK
P.O. Box 1388, Cordova, AK 99574
(907) 424-7738 Fax 424-7739
Robert Henrichs, President
Self-Gov: Chugachmiut, Inc.
West-Central Alaska Field Office.

NATIVE VILLAGE OF FALSE PASS
P.O. Box 29, False Pass, AK 99583
(907) 548-2227 Fax 548-2256
Gilda M. Shellikoff, President
West-Central Alaska Field Office.

NATIVE VILLAGE OF FORT YUKON (IRA)
P.O. Box 286, Fort Yukon, AK 99740
(907) 662-2581 Fax 662-2222
Adlai R. Alexander, President
Self-Gov: Tanana Chiefs
Tribes: Athapascan & Indian.
In residence: 600. Fairbanks Field Office.

NATIVE VILLAGE OF GAKONA
P.O. Box H, Copper Center, AK 99573
(907) 822-5241 Fax 822-8801
Linda Tyone, President
Self-Gov: Copper River Native Association, Inc.
West-Central Alaska Field Office.

NATIVE VILLAGE OF GAMBELL
P.O. Box 90, Gambell, AK 99742
(907) 985-5346 Fax 985-5014
Edmond Apassingok, President
E-mail: nvgmillennium@aol.com
Self Gov: Gambell. Fairbanks Field Office.

NATIVE VILLAGE OF GEORGETOWN
1400 Virginia Court, Anchorage, AK 99501
(907) 274-2195 Fax 274-2196
Glenn W. Fredericks, President
E-mail: gtc@gci.net
West-Central Alaska Field Office.

NATIVE VILLAGE OF GOODNEWS BAY
P.O. Box 03, Goodnews Bay, AK 99589
(907) 697-8929 Fax 967-8330
James M. Smith, President
Self-Gov: Association of Village Council Presidents
West-Central Alaska Field Office.

ORGANIZED VILLAGE OF GRAYLING (IRA)
General Delivery, Grayling, AK 99590
(907) 453-5116 Fax 453-5146
Henry Deacon, President
Self-Gov: Tanana Chiefs. Fairbanks Field Office.

GULKANA VILLAGE COUNCIL
P.O. Box 254, Gakona, AK 99586
(907) 822-3746 Fax 822-3976
Eileen L. Ewan, President
E-mail: lclaw@gulkanacouncil.org
Website: www.gulkanacouncil.org
Self Gov: Copper River Native Association, Inc.
Tribe: Athapascan. West-Central Alaska Field Office.

NATIVE VILLAGE OF HAMILTON
P.O. Box 20248, Kotlik, AK 99620
(907) 899-4252 Fax 899-4202
George A.E. Williams, President
Self-Gov: Association of Village Council Presidents
West-Central Alaska Field Office.

HEALY LAKE VILLAGE
P.O. Box 60300, Fairbanks, AK 99706
(907) 876-5018 Fax 876-5013
Fred Kirsteatler, President
Self-Gov: Tanana Chiefs. Fairbanks Field Office.

HOLY CROSS VILLAGE
P.O. Box 89, Holy Cross, AK 99602
(907) 476-7124 Fax 476-7132
Eugene J. Paul, First Chief
Self-Gov: Tanana Chiefs
Tribes: Eskimo and Athapascan.
In residence: 220. Fairbanks Field Office.

HOONAH INDIAN ASSOCIATION (IRA)
P.O. Box 602, Hoonah, AK 99829
(907) 945-3545 Fax 945-3703
Frank Wright, Jr., President
Self-Gov: Central Council of Tlingit-Haida
West-Central Alaska Field Office.

NATIVE VILLAGE OF HOOPER BAY
P.O. Box 69, Hooper Bay, AK 99604
(907) 758-4915 Fax 758-4066
Patrick Lake, I, President
Tribe: Eskimo. *In residence*: 450. Self-Gov: Association
of Village Council Presidents. West-Central Alaska Field
Office.

HUGHES VILLAGE
P.O. Box 45029, Hughes, AK 99745
(907) 899-2239 Fax 889-2252
Ella D. Sam, First Chief
E-mail: janet.bifelt@tananachiefs.org
Tribe: Athapascan. Self Gov: Tanana Chiefs.
Fairbanks Field Office.

HUSLIA VILLAGE COUNCIL
P.O. Box 70, Huslia, AK 99746
(907) 829-2294 Fax 829-2214
Jack Wholecheese, First Chief
Tribe served: Huslia Athabascan. *Activities*: Owns and
operates Athabasca Cultural Journeys, tourism project
located at P.O. Box 10, Huslia, AK 99746 (800) 423-
0094 Fax (907) 452-8148. Self-Gov: Tanana Chiefs.
Fairbanks Field Office.

HYDABURG COOPERATIVE ASSOCIATION
P.O. Box 349, Hydaburg, AK 99922
(907) 285-3666 Fax 285-3667
Becky Frank, President
E-mail: jjcarle@aptalaska.net
Self-Gov: Central Council of Tlingit-Haida
West-Central Alaska Field Office.

IGIUGIG VILLAGE
P.O. Box 4008, Iguigig, AK 99613
(907) 533-3211 Fax 533-3217
Michael Andrew, Jr., President
Self-Gov: Bristol Bay Native Association, Inc.
West-Central Alaska Field Office.

NATIVE VILLAGE OF ILIAMNA
P.O. Box 286, Iliamna, AK 99606
(907) 571-1246 Fax 571-1256
Harvey Anelon, President
Tribes: Athapascan and Indian.
West-Central Alaska Field Office.

INUPIAT COMMUNITY OF ARCTIC SLOPE
P.O. Box 934, Barrow, AK 99723
(907) 852-4227 Fax 852-4246
Arnold Brower, Jr., President
E-mail: aib@co.north-slope.ak.us
Fairbanks Field Office.

IQURMIUT TRIBE
P.O. Box 09, Russian Mission, AK 99657
(907) 584-5511 Fax 584-5593
Liza R. Busch, President
Tribe: Iqurmiut (Eskimo).
West-Central Alaska Field Office.

IVANOFF BAY VILLAGE
P.O. Box 500, Perryville, AK 99648
(907) 669-2200 Fax 669-2207
Glenn Kalmakoff, Sr., President
Self-Gov: Bristol Bay Native Association, Inc.
West-Central Alaska Field Office.

KAGUYAK VILLAGE
1400 W. Benson Blvd., Suite 350
Anchorage, AK 99503
(907) 561-0604 Fax 561-0608
Ralph Eluska, President
E-mail: kaguyak@smtp..ak.bia.gov
West-Central Alaska Field Office.

ORGANIZED VILLAGE OF KAKE (IRA)
541 Keku Rd.
P.O. Box 316, Kake, AK 99830
(907) 785-6471 Fax 785-4902
Casimero A. Aceveda, President
E-mail: keexkwaan@starband.net
Self Gov: Kake. West-Central Alaska Field Office.

KAKTOVIK VILLAGE
P.O. Box 130, Kaktovik, AK 99747
(907) 640-6120 Fax 640-6217
Isaac A. Akootchook, President
Fairbanks Field Office.

NATIVE VILLAGE OF KALSKAG
P.O. Box 50, Kalskag, AK 99607
(907) 471-2207 Fax 471-2399
Henry Alousius, President
Self-Gov: Association of Village Council Presidents
Tribe: Eskimo. *In residence*: 225.
West-Central Alaska Field Office.

VILLAGE OF KALTAG
P.O. Box 129, Kaltag, AK 99748
(907) 534-2224 Fax 534-2299
John F. Madros, First Chief
Self-Gov: Tanana Chiefs. Fairbanks Field Office.

NATIVE VILLAGE OF KANATAK
490 N. Main St., Box 139
Wasilla, AK 99654
(907) 376-7271 Fax 376-7203
James Shanigan, President
E-mail: kanatak@mtaonline.net
Website: www.kanatak.org
Self-Gov: Bristol Bay Native Association, Inc.
Tribe: Kanatak. *Goal*: To improve living conditions of
tribal members and to protect and preserve our culture.
West-Central Alaska Field Office.

NATIVE VILLAGE OF KARLUK
P.O. Box 22, Karluk, AK 99608
(907) 241-2218 Fax 241-2208
Alicia L. Reft, President
E-mail: a96lynn@aol.com
Tribe: Aleut. *In resdidence*: 225.
West-Central Alaska Field Office.

ORGANIZED VILLAGE OF KASAAN
P.O. Box 26 - Kasaan, KetchikanAK 99950
(907) 542-2230 Fax 542-3006
Richard J. Peterson, President
Self-Gov: Central Council of Tlingit-Haida
West-Central Alaska Field Office.

NATIVE VILLAGE OF KASIGLUK
P.O. Box 19, Kasigluk, AK 99609
(907) 477-6405 Fax 477-6212
Yeako Slim, President
Tribe: Eskimo. *In residence*: 175.
West-Central Alaska Field Office.

KENAITZE INDIAN TRIBE (IRA)
255 N. Ames Rd., P.O. Box 988, Kenai, AK 99611
(907) 283-3633 Fax 283-3052
  Rosalie Tepp, Chairperson
E-mail: kenaitze@alaska.net
West-Central Alaska Field Office.

KETCHIKAN INDIAN CORPORATION
2960 Tongass Ave., Ketchikan, AK 99901
(907) 225-5158 Fax 247-0429
  Charles W. White, President
E-mail: medenso@kictribe.org
West-Central Alaska Field Office.

NATIVE VILLAGE OF KIANA
117 Kozak St., P.O. Box 69, Kiana, AK 99749
(907) 475-2109 Fax 475-2180
  Charles A. Curtis, President
Self-Gov: Maniilaq Consortium.
Tribe: Eskimo. *In residence*: 220.
Fairbanks Field Office.

KING ISLAND NATIVE COMMUNITY (IRA)
P.O. Box 992, Nome, AK 99762
(907) 443-5494 Fax 443-3620
  Carmelita Nattanguk, Chief
Self-Gov: Kawerak. Fairbanks Field Office.

KING SALMON TRIBE
P.O. Box 68, King Salmon, AK 99613
(907) 246-3553 Fax 246-3449
  Ralph Angasan, Sr., President
E-mail: kstvc@bristolbay.com
West-Central Alaska Field Office.

NATIVE VILLAGE OF KIPNUK
P.O. Box 57, Kipnuk, AK 99614
(907) 896-5515 Fax 896-5240
  Howard Paul, President
West-Central Alaska Field Office.

NATIVE VILLAGE OF KIVALINA (IRA)
P.O. Box 50051, Kivalina, AK 99750
(907) 645-2153 Fax 645-2193
  Jerry R. Norton, Sr., President
E-mail: kivalina@aitc.org
Self-Gov: Maniilaq Consortium
Tribe: Inupiat of Kivalina. *In residence*: 360. *Council members*: Fred Swan and Oscar Sage, Sr. *Activities*: New Years Day traditional activities celebration; cultural enrichment Summer Youth Camp
Fairbanks Field Office.

KLAWOCK COOPERATIVE ASSOCIATION
P.O. Box 430, Klawock, AK 99925
(907) 755-2265 Fax 755-8800
  Leonard Kato, President
E-mail: iralg@aptalaska.net
Self-Gov: Central Council of Tlingit-Haida
West-Central Alaska Field Office.

**NATIVE VILLAGE OF KLUTI-KAAH
(aka COPPER CENTER)**
P.O. Box 68, Copper Center, AK 99573
(907) 822-5541 Fax 822-5130
  Carl Pete, President
Self-Gov: Copper River Native Association, Inc.
Tribe: Athapascan. *In residence*: 115.
West-Central Alaska Field Office.

KNIK TRIBAL COUNCIL
P.O. Box 871565, Wasilla, AK 99687
(907) 373-7991 Fax 373-2161
  Carol M. Theodore, President
E-mail: kniktribe@matonline.net
West-Central Alaska Field Office.

NATIVE VILLAGE OF KOBUK
P.O. Box 51039, Kobuk, AK 99751
(907) 948-2203 Fax 948-2123
  Johnetta Cleveland, President
Self-Gov: Maniilaq Consortium
Tribe: Eskimo. Fairbanks Field Office.

KOKHANOK VILLAGE
P.O. Box 1007, Kokhanok, AK 99606
(907) 282-2202 Fax 282-2264
  Roy Andrews, President
Self-Gov: Bristol Bay Native Association, Inc.
Tribe: Aleut. West-Central Alaska Field Office.

NATIVE VILLAGE OF KONGIGANAK
P.O. Box 5069, Kongiganak, AK 99559
(907) 557-5226 Fax 557-5224
  Tommy Phillip, Sr., President
E-mail: kongiganak@aitc.org
Self-Gov: Association of Village Council Presidents
West-Central Alaska Field Office.

NATIVE VILLAGE OF KOTLIK
P.O. Box 20210, Kotlik, AK 99620
(907) 899-4326 Fax 899-4790
  Joseph P. Mike, President
E-mail: pakaran@avcp.org
Self-Gov: Association of Village Council Presidents
Tribe: Eskimo. West-Central Alaska Field Office.

NATIVE VILLAGE OF KOTZEBUE (IRA)
333 Shore Ave.
P.O. Box 296, Kotzebue, AK 99752
(907) 442-3467 Fax 442-2162
  Eugene Smith, Chairperson
E-mail: kcruthers@maniilaq.org
Website: www.kotzebueira.org
Self-Gov: Maniilaq Consortium
Tribe: Eskimo. *In residence*: 1,900. *Activities*: Northwest Alaska Native Trade Fair. Fairbanks Field Office.

NATIVE VILLAGE OF KOYUK (IRA)
P.O. Box 53030, Koyuk, AK 99753
(907) 963-3651 Fax 963-2353
  Merlin Henry, President
E-mail: arlene@kawerak.org
Self-Gov: Kawerak. *Tribe*: Eskimo.
In residence: 190. Fairbanks Field Office.

KOYUKUK NATIVE VILLAGE
300 Vista Rd., P.O. Box 109
Koyukuk, AK 99754
  (907) 927-2253 Fax 927-2220
  Percy Lolnitz, 1st Chief
Self-Gov: Tanana Chiefs
Tribe: Athapascan. *In residence*: 115.
Fairbanks Field Office.

ORGANIZED VILLAGE OF KWETHLUK (IRA)
P.O. Box 129, Kwethluk, AK 99621
(907) 757-6714 Fax 757-6328
  Chariton A. Epchook, President
E-mail: kwtira@unicom-alaska.com
Tribe: Eskimo. *In residence*: 350.
West-Central Alaska Field Office.

KWIGILLINGOK IRA COUNCIL
P.O. Box 49, Kwigillingok, AK 99622
(907) 588-8114 Fax 588-8429
  Mary Ann Wilkinson, President
Self-Gov: Association of Village Council Presidents
Tribe: Eskimo. *In residence*: 350.
West-Central Alaska Field Office.

NATIVE VILLAGE OF KWINHAGAK (IRA)
P.O. BOX 149, Quinhagak, AK 99655
(907) 556-8165 FAX 556-8166
  Wassillie Bavilla, President
Self-Gov: Association of Village Council Presidents
Tribe: Yup'ik Eskimo. *In residence*: 600. *Total acreage*: 120,000. *Council members*: Marie Smith, Grace Friendly, Paul Beebe, Willard Church, Annie Cleveland, and Charles Evans. West-Central Alaska Field Office.

NATIVE VILLAGE OF LARSEN BAY
P.O. Box 35, Larsen Bay, AK 99624
(907) 847-2207 Fax 847-2307
  Brad Aga, Jr., President
Tribe: Eskimo. Anchorage Agency.

LESNOI VILLAGE
326 Center Ave., Suite 204
P.O. Box 9009, Kodiak, AK 99615
(907) 486-2821 Fax 486-2738
  Gordon Pullar, PhD, President
E-mail: twitc@ptialaska.net
West-Central Alaska Field Office.

LEVELOCK VILLAGE
P.O. Box 70, Levelock, AK 99625
(907) 287-3030 Fax 287-3032
  Peter Apokedak, Sr., President
Self-Gov: Bristol Bay Native Association, Inc.
Tribe: Aleut. West-Central Alaska Field Office.

LIME VILLAGE
General Delivery, Lime Village, AK 99627
(907) 526-5236 Fax 526-5235
  Evan Bobby, Sr., President
West-Central Alaska Field Office.

LOUDEN TRIBAL COUNCIL
P.O. Box 244, Galena, AK 99741
(907) 656-1711 Fax 656-1716
  Peter Captain, Sr., First Chief
Self Gov: Tanana Chiefs. Fairbanks Field Office.

VILLAGE OF LOWER KALSKAG
P.O. Box 27, Lower Kalskag, AK 99626
(907) 471-2379 Fax 471-2378
  Phyllis Evan, President
Tribe: Eskimo. *In residence*: 175.
West-Central Alaska Field Office.

MANLEY HOT SPRINGS VILLAGE
P.o. Box 105, Manley Hot Springs, AK 99756
(907) 672-3177 Fax 672-3200
  Frank Guther, President
Self-Gov: Tanana Chiefs. Fairbanks Field Office.

MANOKOTAK VILLAGE
P.O. Box 169, Manokotak, AK 99628
(907) 289-2150 Fax 289-1061
  Michael Gloka, Sr., President
Self-Gov: Bristol Bay Native Association, Inc.
Tribes: Eskimo and Indian. *In residence*: 190.
West-Central Alaska Field Office.

**NATIVE VILLAGE OF MARSHALL
(aka FORTUNA LEDGE)**
P.O. Box 110, Fortuna Ledge, AK 99585
(907) 679-6302 Fax 679-6187
  Benjamin Francis, President
Tribe: Eskimo. *In residence*: 115.
West-Central Alaska Field Office.

MARY'S IGLOO TRADITIONAL COUNCIL
P.O. Box 629, Teller, AK 99778
(907) 642-3731 Fax 642-2189
  Nathan Topkok, President
Self-Gov: Kawerak. Fairbanks Field Office.

McGRATH NATIVE VILLAGE COUNCIL
P.O. Box 134, McGrath, AK 99627
(907) 524-3024 Fax 524-3899
  Michael Fleagle, First Chief
E-mail: mnvc@mcgrathalaska.net
Self-Gov: Tanana Chiefs
Tribes: Athapascan, Indian and Eskimo.
In residence: 125. Fairbanks Field Office.

NATIVE VILLAGE OF MEKORYUK
100 Chase Rd., P.O. Box 66
Mekoryuk, AK 99630
  (907) 827-8828 Fax 827-8133
  Howard T. Amos, President
E-mail: mekoryukira@aol.com
Tribe: Eskimo. *In residence*: 220.
West-Central Alaska Field Office.

MENTASTA LAKE TRIBAL COUNCIL
P.O. Box 6019, Mentasta Lake, AK 99780
(907) 291-2319 Fax 291-2305
  Lisa Wolf, First Chief
E-mail: kmartin@tribalnet.com
West-Central Alaska Field Office

METLAKATLA INDIAN COMMUNITY COUNCIL
P.O. Box 8, Metlakatla, AK 99926
(907) 886-4441 Fax 886-3338
  Tim F. Gilmarten, Mayor
Northwest Regional Office. Head Start Program.

NATIVE VILLAGE OF MINTO
P.O. Box 58026, Minto, AK 99758
(907) 798-7112 Fax 798-7627
  Roy Charles, Chief
Self Gov: Tanana Chiefs
Tribes: Athapascan and Indian.
In residence: 225. Fairbanks Field Office.

NAKNEK NATIVE VILLAGE
P.O. Box 106, Naknek, AK 99633
(907) 246-4210 Fax 246-3563
  Norman Anderson, President

Self-Gov: Bristol Bay Native Association, Inc.
Tribes: Aleut & Indian. Anchorage Agency.

**NATIVE VILLAGE OF NANWALEK
(aka ENGLISH BAY)**
P.O. Box 8028, English Bay, AK 99603
(907) 281-2274 Fax 281-2252
Emilie Swenning, Chief
Self-Gov: Chugachmiut, Inc.
Tribe: Eskimo. *In residence*: 115.
West-Central Alaska Field Office.

NATIVE VILLAGE OF NAPAIMUTE
P.O. Box 1301, Bethel, AK 99559
(907) 543-2887 Fax 543-2892
Marcie Sherer, President
E-mail: napaimute@avcp.org
Website: www.napaimute.org
Self-Gov: Association of Village Council Presidents
West-Central Alaska Field Office.

NATIVE VILLAGE OF NAPAKIAK
P.O. Box 69, Napakiak, AK 99634
(907) 589-2135 Fax 589-2136
Carl Matgin, President
E-mail: napakiak@unicom-alaska.com
Self-Gov: Association of Village Council Presidents
Tribe: Eskimo. *In residence*: 200.
West-Central Alaska Field Office.

NATIVE VILLAGE OF NAPASKIAK
P.O. Box 6009, Napaskiak, AK 99559
(907) 737-7364 Fax 737-7039
Chris G. Larson, President
E-mail: pnicholai@avcp.org
Self-Gov: Association of Village Council Presidents
Tribe: Eskimo. *In residence*: 175.
West-Central Alaska Field Office.

NELSON LAGOON TRIBAL COUNCIL
P.O. Box 13 - N.L.C., Nelson Lagoon, AK 99571
(907) 989-2204 Fax 989-2233
Harold D. Johnson, Sr., President
Self-Gov: Aleutian/Pribilof Islands Association, Inc.
West-Central Alaska Field Office.

NENANA NATIVE ASSOCIATION
P.O. Box 356, Nenana, AK 99760
(907) 832-5461 Fax 832-1077
Mitch Demientieff, First Chief
Self-Gov: Tanana Chiefs
Tribes: Athapascan & Indian. *In residence*: 175.
Fairbanks Field Office.

NEW KOLIGANEK VILLAGE COUNCIL
P.O. Box 5057, Koliganek, AK 99576
(907) 596-3434 Fax 596-3462
Herman Nelson, Sr., President
Tribes: Athapascan and Indian. *In residence*: 205. Council members: Gust Tunguing, Sr., Gust Tunguing, Jr., Blunka Ishnook, Jr., Betty Lee, and Edward Kapatak.
West-Central Alaska Field Office.

NEW STUYAHOK VILLAGE
P.O. Box 49, New Stuyahok, AK 99636
(907) 693-3173 Fax 693-3179
Wally Gust, President
Self-Gov: Bristol Bay Native Association, Inc.
Tribe: Athapascan. *In residence*: 140.
West-Central Alaska Field Office.

NEWHALEN VILLAGE
P.O. Box 207 - Iliamna
Newhalen, AK 99606
(907) 571-1410 Fax 571-1537
Raymond Wassillie, President
E-mail: newhalentribal@starband.net
Self-Gov: Bristol Bay Native Association, Inc.
Tribes: Aleut & Indian. West-Central Alaska Field Office.

NEWTOK TRADITIONAL COUNCIL
P.O. Box 5545, Newtok, AK 99559
(907) 237-2314 Fax 237-2428
Moses Carl, President
West-Central Alaska Field Office.

NIGHTMUTE TRADITIONAL COUNCIL
P.O. Box 90021, Nightmute, AK 99690
(907) 647-6215 Fax 647-6112

Joseph Post, President
Tribe: Eskimo. West-Central Alaska Field Office.

NIKOLAI VILLAGE
P.O. Box 9105, Nikolai, AK 99691
(907) 293-2311 Fax 293-2481
Ignatti Petruska, First Chief
Self Gov: Tanana Chiefs
Tribes: Athapascans & Indian.
In residence: 145. Fairbanks Field Office.

NATIVE VILLAGE OF NIKOLSKI
P.o. Box 105, Nikolski, AK 99638
(907) 576-2225 Fax 576-2205
Charlene Shapsnikoff, President
E-mail: nvnikolski@yahoo.com
Self-Gov: Aleutian/Pribilof Islands Association, Inc.
West-Central Alaska Field Office.

NINILCHIK TRADITIONAL COUNCIL
15910 Sterling Hwy.
P.O. Box 39070, Ninilchik, AK 99639
(907) 567-3313 Fax 567-3308
Bruce E. Oskolkoff, President
E-mail: nintribe@ptialaska.net
Tribe: Kenaitse. *In residence*: 120.
West-Central Alaska Field Office.

NATIVE VILLAGE OF NOATAK
P.O. Box 89, Noatak, AK 99761
(907) 485-2173 Fax 485-2137
Elmer Howarth, President
Self-Gov: Maniilaq Consortium
Tribes: Eskimo and Indian. *In residence*: 550.
Fairbanks Field Office.

NOME ESKIMO COMMUNITY
P.O. Box 1090, Nome, AK 99762
(907) 443-2246 Fax 443-3539
Andrew Miller, Jr., President
E-mail: barengo@nome.net
Self-Gov: Kawerak
Tribes: Eskimo and Indian. *In residence*: 1,750.
Fairbanks Field Office.

NONDALTON VILLAGE COUNCIL
P.O. Box 49, Nondalton, AK 99640
(907) 294-2220 Fax 294-2234
William Trefon, Sr., President
Tribe: Athapascan. *In residence*: 175.
West-Central Alaska Field Office.

NOORVIK NATIVE COMMUNITY
P.O. Box 209, Noorvik, AK 99763
(907) 636-2144 Fax 636-2284
Lonnie Tebbits, President
E-mail: fsmith@maniilaq.org
Self-Gov: Maniilaq Consortium
Tribe: Eskimo. *In residence*: 450. Nome Agency.

NORTHWAY VILLAGE
P.O. Box 516, Northway, AK 99764
(907) 778-2287 Fax 778-2220
Lorraine Titus, President
Tribe: Athapascan. *In residence*: 150.
Fairbanks Field Office.

NATIVE VILLAGE OF NUIQSUT
P.O. Box 112, Nuiqsut, AK 99723
(907) 480-3010 Fax 480-3011
Leonard Lampe, President
Tribe: Athapascan. *In residence*: 125.
Fairbanks Field Office.

NULATO TRIBAL COUNCIL
P.O. Box 65049, Nulato, AK 99765
(907) 898-2339 Fax 898-2207
Michael J. Stickman, First Chief
E-mail: nulatotribe@aol.com
Tribe: Athapascan. *In residence*: 250.
Fairbanks Field Office.

NUNAKAUYAK TRADITIONAL COUNCIL
P.O. Box 37048, TOKSOOK BAY, AK 99637
(907) 427-7114 Fax 427-7714
David B. Tim, Chairperson
E-mail: toksookbay@aitc.org
Tribe: Eskimo. West-Central Alaska Field Office.

NATIVE VILLAGE OF NUNAPITCHUK (IRA)
P.O. Box 130, Nunapitchuk, AK 99641
(907) 527-5705 Fax 527-5711
Jimmy P. Stevens, Sr., President
E-mail: elijwass@unicom-alask.com
Self-Gov: Association of Village Council Presidents
Tribe: Eskimo. *In residence*: 200.
West-Central Alaska Field Office.

VILLAGE OF OHOGAMIUT
P.O. Box 49, Marshall, AK 99585
(907) 679-6517 Fax 679-6516
Jacob W. Isaac, President
West-Central Alaska Field Office.

VILLAGE OF OLD HARBOR
P.O. Box 62, Old Harbor, AK 99643
(907) 286-2215 Fax 286-2277
Tony Azuyak, Sr., President
Tribe: Eskimo. *In residence*: 200.
West-Central Alaska Field Office.

ORUTSARARMUIT NATIVE COUNCIL
835 Ridgecrest Dr.
P.O. Box 927, Bethel, AK 99559
(907) 543-2608 Fax 543-2639
Henry J. Hunter, Sr., President
Population served: Bethel Native Corporation Shareholders. *Programs*: Social Services; Vocational Training; Higher Education grants; Energy Assistance; Housing Improvement; among others. West-Central Alaska Field Office.

OSCARVILLE TRIBAL COUNCIL
P.O. Box 6129, Oscarville, AK 99559
(907) 737-7099 Fax 737-7428
Ignati Jacob, President
Self-Gov: Association of Village Council Presidents
Tribes: Indian and Eskimo.
West-Central Alaska Field Office.

NATIVE VILLLAGE OF OUZINKIE
P.O. Box 130, Ouzinkie, AK 99644
(907) 680-2259 Fax 680-2214
Paul Panamarioff, President
West-Central Alaska Field Office.

NATIVE VILLAGE OF PAIMIUT
P.O. BOX 100193, Anchorage, AK 99510
(907) 561-9878 Fax 563-5398
Franklin I. Napoleon, President
E-mail: e.thompson-hale@worldnet.att.net
West-Central Alaska Field Office.

NATIVE VILLAGE OF PAIMIUT
P.O. BOX 230, Hooper Bay, AK 99604
(907) 758-4002 Fax 758-4024
Franklin I. Napoleon, President
E-mail: e.thompson-hale@worldnet.att.net
West-Central Alaska Field Office.

PAULOFF HARBOR VILLAGE
P.O. Box 194, Sand Point, AK 99661
(907) 383-6075 Fax 383-6094
Paul Gundersen, President
West-Central Alaska Field Office.

PEDRO BAY VILLAGE COUNCIL
P.O. Box 47020, Pedro Bay, AK 99647
(907) 850-2225 Fax 850-2221
Keith Jensen, President
E-mail: thecouncil@pedrobay.com
Website: www.pedrobay.com
Tribe: Athapascan. West-Central Alaska Field Office.

NATIVE VILLAGE OF PERRYVILLE (IRA)
P.O. Box 101, Perryville, AK 99648
(907) 853-2203 Fax 853-2230
Gerald Kosbruk, President
Self-Gov: Bristol Bay Native Association, Inc.
Tribe: Eskimo. *In residence*: 175.
West-Central Alaska Field Office.

PETERSBURG INDIAN ASSOCIATION (IRA)
P.O. Box 1418, Petersburg, AK 99833
(907) 772-3636 Fax 772-3637
Jeanette Ness, President
E-mail: mfrentz@mitkof.net
Self-Gov: Central Council of Tlingit-Haida
West-Central Alaska Field Office.

PILOT POINT TRADITIONAL COUNCIL
P.O. Box 449, Pilot Point, AK 99649
(907) 797-2208 Fax 797-2258
Suzanne Evanoff, President
Self-Gov: Bristol Bay Native Association, Inc.
West-Central Alaska Field Office.

PILOT STATION TRADITIONAL COUNCIL
P.O. Box 5119, Pilot Station, AK 99650
(907) 549-3373 Fax 549-3301
Wassillie Myers, President
Self-Gov: Association of Village Council Presidents
Tribe: Eskimo. West-Central Alaska Field Office.

NATIVE VILLAGE OF PITKA'S POINT
P.O. Box 127, St. Mary's, AK 99658
(907) 438-2833 Fax 438-2569
Maureen Sipary, President
Tribe: Eskimo. West-Central Alaska Field Office.

PLATINUM TRADITIONAL VILLAGE COUNCIL
P.O. Box 8, Platinum, AK 99651
(907) 979-8220 Fax 979-8178
Henry S. Williams, President
Tribe: Eskimo. West-Central Alaska Field Office.

NATIVE VILLAGE OF POINT HOPE (IRA)
P.O. Box 109, Point Hope, AK 99766
(907) 368-2330 Fax 368-2332
Rex Tuzroyluk, Jr., President
Tribe: Eskimo. *In residence*: 385.
Fairbanks Field Office.

NATIVE VILLAGE OF POINT LAY (IRA)
P.O. Box 101, Point Lay, AK 99759
(907) 833-2319 Fax 833-2528
Willard Neakok, Village Coordinator
Tribe: Eskimo. *In residence*: 125.
Fairbanks Field Office.

PORT GRAHAM VILLAGE COUNCIL
P.O. Box 5510, Port Graham, AK 99603
(907) 284-2227 Fax 284-2222
Eleanor McMullen, President
E-mail: f.norman@worldnet.att.net
Self-Gov: Chugachmiut, Inc.
Tribe: Eskimo. *In residence*: 115.
West-Central Alaska Field Office.

NATIVE VILLAGE OF PORT HEIDEN
P.O. Box 49007, Port Heiden, AK 99549
(907) 837-2296 Fax 837-2297
Laura Christensen, Chairperson
Self-Gov: Bristol Bay Native Association, Inc.
West-Central Alaska Field Office.

NATIVE VILLAGE OF PORT LIONS
P.O. Box 69, Port Lions, AK 99550
(907) 454-2234 Fax 454-2434
Marilyn R. Wagner, President
E-mail: portlions@aitc.org
West-Central Alaska Field Office.

PORTAGE CREEK VILLAGE COUNCIL
P.O. Box PCA, Portage Creek, AK 99576
(907) 842-5257 Fax 842-5932
Maryanne Johnson, President
Self-Gov: Bristol Bay Native Association, Inc.
West-Central Alaska Field Office.

**QAGAN TAYAGUNGIN TRIBE
OF SAND POINT VILLAGE**
100 Municipal Bldg., Rm. 7A
P.O. Box 447, Sand Point, AK 99661
(907) 383-5616 Fax 383-5814
David O. Osterback, President
E-mail: qagantayagungin.aitc.org
Tribe: Qagun Tayagungin (Aleut).
Self-Gov: Aleutian/Pribilof Islands Association, Inc.
West-Central Alaska Field Office.

QAWALANGIN TRIBE OF UNALASKA
205 Broadway, P.O. Box 334
Unalaska, AK 99685
(907) 581-2920 Fax 581-3644
janice Kruloff, President
Self-Gov: Aleutian/Pribilof Islands Association, Inc.
West-Central Alaska Field Office.

RAMPART VILLAGE
P.O. Box 29, Rampart, AK 99767
(907) 358-3312 Fax 358-3115
James Arrison, President
Self-Gov: Tanana Chiefs
Tribe: Athapascan. *In residence*: 140.
Fairbanks Field Office.

VILLAGE OF RED DEVIL
P.O. Box 61, Red Devil, AK 99656
(907) 447-3223 Fax 447-3224
Tommy Willis, President
Self-Gov: Association of Village Council Presidents
West-Central Alaska Field Office.

RUBY TRIBAL COUNCIL
P.O. Box 210, Ruby, AK 99768
(907) 468-4479 Fax 468-4474
Patrick McCarty, First Chief
Self-Gov: Tanana Chiefs
Tribe: Athapascan. *In residence*: 150.
Fairbanks Field Office.

ST. GEORGE ISLAND
P.O. Box 940, St. George Island, AK 99591
(907) 859-2205 Fax 859-2242
Gilbert Kashevarof, President
Self-Gov: Aleutian/Pribilof Islands Association, Inc.
West-Central Alaska Field Office.

NATIVE VILLAGE OF ST. MICHAEL
P.O. Box 59058, St. Michael, AK 99659
(907) 923-2304 Fax 923-2406
Pius Washington, President
E-mail: ksmkira@aol.com
Self-Gov: Kawerak. Fairbanks Field Office.

ALEUT COMMUNITY OF ST. PAUL ISLAND
P.O. Box 86, St. Paul Island, AK 99660
(907) 546-2211 Fax 546-2407
Richard Zacharof, President
Tribe: Aleut. Self-Gov: Aleutian/Pribilof Islands
Association, Inc. West-Central Alaska Field Office.

VILLAGE OF SALAMANTOF
P.O. Box 2682, Kenai, AK 99611
(907) 283-7864 Fax 283-6470
Penny Carty, President
E-mail: salamaantoff@smtp.ak.bia.gov
West-Central Alaska Field Office.

NATIVE VILLAGE OF SAVOONGA
P.O. Box 120, Savoonga, AK 99769
(907) 984-6414 Fax 984-6027
Fritz Waghiyi, President
Self-Gov: Kawerak
Tribe: Eskimo. *In residence*: 330.
Fairbanks Field Office.

ORGANIZED VILLAGE OF SAXMAN (IRA)
Route 2, Box 2 - Saxman, Ketchikan, AK 99901
(907) 247-2502 Fax 247-2504
Joe Williams, President
E-mail: saxman@smtp.ak.bia.gov
Self-Gov: Central Council of Tlingit-Haida
West-Central Alaska Field Office.

NATIVE VILLAGE OF SCAMMON BAY
P.O. Box 110, Scammon Bay, AK 99662
(907) 558-5425 Fax 558-5134
Andrew Kasayuli, Sr., President
E-mail: scammonbay@aitc.org
Self-Gov: Association of Village Council Presidents
West-Central Alaska Field Office.

NATIVE VILLAGE OF SELAWIK
P.O. Box 59, Selawik, AK 99770
(907) 484-2165 Fax 484-2226
Marvin Ramoth, President
E-mail: selawik@smtp.ak.bia.gov
Self-Gov: Manillaq Consortium
Fairbanks Field Office.

SELDOVIA VILLAGE TRIBE
328 Main St., P.O. Drawer L
Seldovia, AK 99663
(907) 234-7898 Fax 234-7637
Don Kashevaroff, President
E-mail: svt@svt.org; Website: www.svt.org
West-Central Alaska Field Office.

SHAGELUK NATIVE VILLAGE (IRA)
P.O. Box 109, Shageluk, AK 99665
(907) 473-8239 Fax 473-8295
Kathy Workman, Chief
Self-Gov: Tanana Chiefs
Tribe: Athapascan. *In residence*: 150.
Fairbanks Field Office.

NATIVE VILLAGE OF SHAKTOOLIK
P.O. Box 100, Shaktoolik, AK 99771
(907) 955-3701 Fax 955-2352
Simon Dekoalok President
E-mail: shaktoolik@smtp.ak.bia.gov
Self-Gov: Kawerak. Fairbanks Field Office.

**NATIVE VILLAGE OF SHELDON'S POINT
Nunam Iqua Tribal Council**
P.O. Box 27, Sheldon's Point, AK 99666
(907) 498-4184 Fax 498-4185
Edward J. Adams, Sr., President
Self-Gov: Association of Village Council Presidents
West-Central Alaska Field Office.

NATIVE VILLAGE OF SHISHMAREF
P.O. Box 72110, Shishmaref, AK 99772
(907) 649-3821 Fax 649-2104
Darlene Turner, President
Self-Gov: Kawerak
Tribe: Eskimo. *In residence*: 200.
Fairbanks Field Office.

SHOONAQ' TRIBE OF KODIAK
713 E. Rezanof Dr. #B, Kodiak, AK 99615
(907) 486-4449 Fax 486-3361
Leonard Heitman, Chairperson
E-mail: tribe@ptialaska.net
West-Central Alaska Field Office.

NATIVE VILLAGE OF SHUNGNAK (IRA)
P.O. Box 64, Shungnak, AK 99773
(907) 437-2163 Fax 437-2183
Frederick Sun, President
E-mail: shungnak@smtp.ak.bia.gov
Self-Gov: Manilaq Consortium
Tribe: Eskimo. *In residence*: 200.
Fairbanks Field Office.

SITKA TRIBE OF ALASKA
456 Katlian St., Sitka, AK 99835
(907) 747-3207 Fax 747-4915
Lawrence A. Widmark, President
E-mail: widmarkw@mail.ssd.k12..ak.us
Tribe: Sitka. West-Central Alaska Field Office.

SKAGWAY VILLAGE
P.O. Box 1157, Skagway, AK 99840
(907) 983-4068 FAX 983-3068
Lance A. Twitchell, President
Self-Gov: Central Council of Tlingit-Haida
West-Central Alaska Field Office.

SLEETMUTE TRADITIONAL COUNCIL
P.O. Box 109, Sleetmute, AK 99668
(907) 449-4205 Fax 449-4203
Pete Mellick, President
Self-Gov: Association of Village Council Presidents
Tribes: Athapascan and Indian. *In residence*: 175.
West-Central Alaska Field Office.

SOLOMON TRADITIONAL COUNCIL
P.O. Box 2053, Solomon, AK 99762
(907) 443-4985 Fax 443-5189
Joseph Curran, President
E-mail: solomon@smtp.ak.bia.gov
Self-Gov: Kawerak. Fairbanks Field Office.

NATIVE VILLAGE OF SOUTH NAKNEK
P.O. Box 70029, South Naknek, AK 99670
(907) 246-8614 Fax 246-8613
Donald F. Nielsen, President
E-mail: southnaknek@smtp..ak.bia.gov
Self-Gov: Bristol Bay Native Association, Inc.
West-Central Alaska Field Office.

STEBBINS COMMUNITY ASSOCIATION
P.O. Box 71002, Stebbins, AK 99671
(907) 934-3561 Fax 934-3560
Morris Nashoanak, Sr., President
E-mail: stebbins@smtp.ak.bia.gov
Self-Gov: Kawerak

Tribe: Eskimo. *In residence*: 175.
Fairbanks Field Office.

NATIVE VILLAGE OF STEVENS (IRA)
P.O. Box 74012, Stevens Village, AK 99774
(907) 478-7228 Fax 478-7229
Randy Mayo, First Chief
E-mail: stevens@smtp.ak.bia.gov
Self-Gov: Tanana Chiefs
Tribe: Athapascan. *In residence*: 125.
Fairbanks Field Office.

VILLAGE OF STONY RIVER
P.O. Box SRV, Stoney River, AK 99557
(907) 537-3253 Fax 537-3254
Mary L. Willis, President
E-mail: stonyriver@smtp.ak.bia.gov
Self-Gov: Association of Village Council Presidents
West-Central Alaska Field Office.

TAKOTNA VILLAGE
P.O. Box TYC, Takotna, AK 99675
(907) 298-2212 Fax 298-2314
Carol Abraham, Chief
E-mail: takotna@smtp.ak.bia.gov
Self-Gov: Tanana Chiefs
Tribes: Eskimo & Indian. Fairbanks Field Office.

NATIVE VILLAGE OF TANACROSS
P.O. Box 76009, Tanacross, AK 99776
(907) 883-5024 Fax 883-4497
Jerry Isaac, President
E-mail: tanacross@smtp.ak.bia.gov
Self-Gov: Tanana Chiefs
Tribe: Athapascan. *In residence*: 150.
Fairbanks Field Office.

NATIVE VILLAGE OF TANANA
P.O. Box 130, Tanana, AK 99777
(907) 366-7160 Fax 366-7195
Faith Peters, President
Self-Gov: Tanana IRA Native Council
Tribes: Athapascan & Indian.
In residence: 225. Fairbanks Field Office.

NATIVE VILLAGE OF TATITLEK
P.O. Box 171, Tatitlek, AK 99677
(907) 325-2311 Fax 325-2298
Gary Kompkoff, President
Self-Gov: Chugachmiut, Inc.
Tribe: Aleut. *In residence*: 150.
West-Central Alaska Field Office.

NATIVE VILLAGE OF TAZLINA
P.O. Box 87, Glenallen, AK 99588
(907) 822-4375 Fax 822-5865
Gloria Stickwan, President
E-mail: tazlina@cvinternet.net
Self-Gov: Copper River Native Association, Inc.
West-Central Alaska Field Office.

TELIDA VILLAGE
P.O. Box 32, Telida, AK 99627
Mike Feagle First Chief
(907) 524-3550 Fax 524-3163
E-mail: kuskoyim@aol.com
Self-Gov: Tanana Chiefs
Fairbanks Field Office.

TELLER TRADITIONAL COUNCIL
P.O. Box 567, Teller, AK 99778
(907) 642-3381 Fax 642-2072
Isaac Okleasik, President
Self-Gov: Kawerak
Tribe: Eskimo. *In residence*: 200.
Fairbanks Field Office.

NATIVE VILLAGE OF TETLIN (IRA)
P.O. Box TTL, Tetlin, AK 99779
(907) 324-2130 Fax 324-2131
Donald Adams, President
E-mail: tetlin@earthlink.net
Self-Gov: Tanana Chiefs
Tribe: Athapascan. *In residence*: 125.
Fairbanks Field Office.

**CENTRAL COUNCIL OF TLINGIT &
HAIDA INDIAN TRIBES OF ALASKA**
320 W. Willoughby Ave., Suite 300
Juneau, AK 99801

(907) 586-1432 Fax 586-8970
Edward K. Thomas, President
West-Central Alaska Field Office.

TRADITIONAL VILLAGE OF TOGIAK
P.O. Box 310, Togiak, AK 99678
(907) 493-5004 Fax 493-5005
Frank Logusak, President
E-mail: togiak@aitc.org
Self-Gov: Bristol Bay Native Association, Inc.
Tribe: Eskimo. *In residence*: 175.
West-Central Alaska Field Office.

TULUKSAK NATIVE COMMUNITY
P.O. Box 95, Tuluksak, AK 99679
(907) 695-6420 Fax 695-6932
John Napoka, Jr., President
E-mail: tuluksak@aitc.org
Tribe: Eskimo. *In residence*: 200.
West-Central Alaska Field Office.

NATIVE VILLAGE OF TUNTUTULIAK
P.O. Box 8086, Tuntutuliak, AK 99680
(907) 256-2128 Fax 256-2080
Nick Frank, President
E-mail: tuntutuliak@aitc.org
Self-Gov: Association of Village Council Presidents
Tribe: Eskimo. *In residence*: 120.
West-Central Alaska Field Office.

NATIVE VILLAGE OF TUNUNAK (IRA)
P.O. Box 77, Tununak, AK 99681
(907) 652-6527 Fax 652-6011
Felix Albert, President
Self-Gov: Association of Village Council Presidents
West-Central Alaska Field Office.

TWIN HILLS VILLAGE COUNCIL
P.O. Box TWA, Twin Hills, AK 99576
(907) 525-4821 Fax 525-4822
John W. Sharp, President
E-mail: twinhills@aitc.org
Self-Gov: Bristol Bay Native Association, Inc.
West-Central Alaska Field Office.

NATIVE VILLAGE OF TYONEK (IRA)
P.O. Box 82009, Tyonek, AK 99682
(907) 583-2271 Fax 583-2442
Peter Merryman, President
E-mail: tyonek@aitc.org
Tribe: Athapascan. *In residence*: 200.
West-Central Alaska Field Office.

UGASHIK TRADITIONAL VILLAGE COUNCIL
206 E. Fireweed Ln #204
Anchorage, AK 99503
(907) 338-7611 Fax 338-7659
Fred A. Matsuno, President
E-mail: ugashik@gci.net
Tribes: Eskimo and Indian.
Self-Gov: Bristol Bay Native Association, Inc.
West-Central Alaska Field Office.

UMKUMIUT NATIVE VILLAGE
General Delivery, Nightmute, AK 99690
(907) 647-6145 Fax 647-6146
Simon Agnus, President
West-Central Alaska Field Office.

NATIVE VILLAGE OF UNALAKLEET (IRA)
P.O. Box 270, Unalakleet, AK 99684
(907) 624-3190 Fax 624-3402
William Johnson, President
E-mail: unkira@unalakleet.net
Website: www.unalakleet.net
Self-Gov: Kawerak
Tribes: Eskimo and Indian. *In residence*: 850. *Total acreage*: 258. *Council members*: Paul Katchatag, Ruth Blatchford, and Eleanor Bahr. *Activities*: Operates a clinic. Fairbanks Field Office.

NATIVE VILLAGE OF UNGA
P.O. Box 508, Sand Point, AK 99661
(907) 383-5215 Fax 383-5553
John A. Foster, President
Self-Gov: Aleutian/Pribilof Islands Association, Inc.
West-Central Alaska Field Office.

**NATIVE VILLAGE OF VENETIE
TRIBAL GOVERNMENT (IRA)**
P.O. Box 81080, Venetie, AK 99781
(907) 849-8165 Fax 849-8097
Mary R. Gamboa, First Chief
E-mail: venetietribal@hotmail.com
Tribe: Athapascan. *In residence*: 125.
Fairbanks Field Office.

VENETIE VILLAGE COUNCIL
P.O. Box 81119, Venetie, AK 99781
(907) 849-8212 Fax 849-8149
Bobby J. Tritt, First Chief
Tribe: Athapascan. *In residence*: 125.
Fairbanks Field Office.

VILLAGE OF WAINWRIGHT
P.O. Box 184, Wainwright, AK 99783
(907) 763-2726 Fax 763-2536
George Agnassage, President
Tribe: Eskimo. *In residence*: 335.
Fairbanks Field Office.

NATIVE VILLAGE OF WALES (IRA)
P.O. Box 549, Wales, AK 99783
(907) 664-3062 (phone & fax)
Luther C. Komonaseak, President
E-mail: kareno@kawerak.org
Website: www.kawerak.org
Tribe: Eskimo. *In residence*: 225.
Fairbanks Field Office.

NATIVE VILLAGE OF WHITE MOUNTAIN
P.O. Box 84082, White Mountain, AK 99784
(907) 638-3651 Fax 638-3652
Mary D. Charles, President
E-mail: roya@kawerak.org
Self-Gov: Kawerak
Tribes: Eskimo & Indian. *In residence*: 200.
Fairbanks Field Office.

WRANGELL COOPERATIVE ASSN (IRA)
P.O. Box 868, Wrangell, AK 99929
(907) 874-3481 Fax 874-2918
John Feller, President
Self-Gov: Central Council of Tlingit-Haida
West-Central Alaska Field Office.

YAKUTAT TLINGIT TRIBE
716 Ocean Cape Rd.
P.O. Box 418, Yakutat, AK 99689
(907) 784-3238 Fax 784-3595
Bert Adams, Sr., President
E-mail: yttorg@ptialaska.net
Self Gov: Yakutat Tlingit Tribe
Tribes: Tlingit & Haida. West-Central
Alaska Field Office.

ARIZONA

BIRD SPRINGS RESERVATION
Tribe: Navajo. Western Navajo Agency

BLUE GAP RESERVATION
Tribe: Navajo. Chinle Agency

CAMERON RESERVATION
Cameron, AZ 86020
Tribe: Navajo. Western Navajo Agency.

CAMP VERDE RESERVATION
Yavapai-Apache Community Council
2400 W. Datsi • Camp Verde, AZ 86322
(520) 567-3649 Fax 567-3994
Vincent Randall, Chairperson
Fred Sanchez, Vice Chairperson
Website: www.yavapai-apache-nation.com
Tribe served: Yavapai-Apache. *In residence*: 600. *Area*: 500 acres. *Council members*: David Kwail, Norman Smith, Charles Bonnaha, Lorna Hazelwood, Darlene Rubio, Aaron Russell, Donna Nightpipe. Truxton Canon Agency.

CHILCHINBETO RESERVATION
c/o Western Navajo Agency
Tribe: Navajo. Located in Arizona and Utah.
See listing under Utah.

CHINLE RESERVATION
Tribe: Navajo. Chinle Agency.

COALMINE RESERVATION
Tribe: Navajo. Western Navajo Agency.

COCOPAH RESERVATION
Cocopah Tribal Council
County 15 & Ave. G, Somerton, AZ 85350
  (928) 627-2102 Fax 627-3173
  Sherry Cordova, Chairperson
Tribe served: Cocopah. *In residence*: 550.
Head Start Program. Fort Yuma Field Office.

COLORADO RIVER INDIAN TRIBES
Colorado River Tribal Council
Route 1, Box 23-B, Parker, AZ 85344
  (928) 669-9211 Fax 669-1216
  Daniel Eddy, Jr., Chairperson
  Russell Welsh, Vice Chairperson
  LaWanda Laffoon, Secretary; Eldred Enas, Treasurer
Tribes served: Mohave, Chemehuevi, Hopi, and Navajo.
Tribal enrollment: 3,100. *Area*: Located along the Colorado River in Arizona and southeast California. 286,691 acres (244,000 acres in Arizona, and 42,700 acres in California). *Council members*: Herman Laffoon, Jr., Conner Byestewa, Jr., Fernando Flores, Sr., Dennis Patch, and Rayford Patch. *Tribal services*: Tribal police, courts, museum and library; also, departments: fish and game, education, health and social services, recreation, manpower, building and zoning, fire, housing. *Local attractions*: Colorado River; Old Mohave Presbyterian Church, National Historic Site; archaeological excavations and ruins of La Paz, a former gold mining town; Tribal Museum and Library. *Activities*: National Indian Day, Mohave Day, All-Indian Rodeo, 4th of July Celebration; Annual Thanksgiving and Christmas Program. *Facilities*: Lodging, and camping. *Publication*: CRIT Newsletter, quarterly. Head Start Program. Colorado River Agency.

COPPER MINE RESERVATION
Tribe: Navajo. Western Navajo Agency.

CORNFIELDS RESERVATION
Tribe: Navajo. Fort Defiance Agency.

COYOTE CANYON RESERVATION
Tribe: Navajo. Fort Defiance Agency.

CRYSTAL RESERVATION
Tribe: Navajo. Fort Defiance Agency. Located in Arizona and New Mexico. See listing under New Mexico.

DENNEHOTSO RESERVATION
Dennehotso, AZ 86535
Tribe: Navajo. Western Navajo Agency.

DILKON COMMUNITY
Winslow, AZ 86047
Tribe: Navajo. *In residence*: 1,000.
Western Navajo Agency.

FOREST LAKE RESERVATION
Heber, AZ 85928
Tribe: Navajo. Chinle Agency.

FORT APACHE INDIAN RESERVATION
White Mountain Apache Tribal Council
P.O. Box 700, Whiteriver, AZ 85941
  (928) 338-4346 Fax 338-4778
  Dallas Massey, Sr., Chairperson
  John Endfield, Vice Chairperson
Tribe: White Mountain Apache. *In residence*: 8,500.
Area: 1,664,872 acres. *Local attraction*: Apache Cultural Center and Museum. Head Start Program. Fort Apache Agency.

FORT DEFIANCE RESERVATION
Tribe: Navajo. Fort Defiance Agency.
Located in Arizona and New Mexico.
See listing under New Mexico.

FORT McDOWELL RESERVATION
Fort McDowell Yavapai Tribal Council
P.O. Box 17779, Fountain Hills, AZ 85268
  (480) 837-5121 Fax 837-1630
  Clinton Pattea, President
Tribes: Mohave-Apache. *In residence*: 550. *Area*: 24,680 acres; located twenty miles northeast of Phoenix on the

Verde River. *Local attractions*: Roosevelt Dam and Reservoir; Bartlett Reservoir. Salt River Field Office.

FORT MOHAVE RESERVATION
Fort Mohave, AZ 86427
Tribe: Mohave. Located in Arizona, California and Nevada. See listings under California and Nevada. Colorado River Agency.

FORT YUMA RESERVATION
Quechan Tribal Council
P.O. Box 1899, Yuma, AZ 85366
  (760) 572-0213 Fax 572-2102
  Mike Jackson, Sr., President
Tribe: Quechan. Located in Arizona & California.
Fort Yuma Field Office.

GANADO RESERVATION
P.O. Box 188, Ganado, AZ 86505
Tribe: Navajo. Fort Defiance Agency.

GILA BEND RESERVATION
P.O. Box GG, Gila Bend, AZ 85337
Tribe: Papago. *In residence*: 300. *Area*: 10,000 acres. Located four miles north of Gila Bend. *Local attractions*: Kitt Peak National Observatory on San Xavier Reservation. Papago Agency.

GILA RIVER RESERVATION
Gila River Indian Community Council
P.O. Box 97, Sacaton, AZ 85247
  (520) 562-6000 Fax 562-6010
  Donald R. Antone, Sr., Governor
  Website: www.gric.nsn.us
Tribes: Pima-Maricopa. *In residence*: 9,750. *Area*: 370,000 acres. *Activities*: Operates a casino. Head Start Program. Pima Agency.

GREASEWOOD RESERVATION
Greasewood, AZ 86505
Tribe: Navajo. Fort Defiance Agency.

HAVASUPAI RESERVATION
Havasupai Tribal Council
P.O. Box 10, Supai, AZ 86435
  (928) 448-2961 Fax 448-2551
  Augustine Hanna, Chairperson
Tribe: Havasupai. *In residence*: 650. *Area*: 188,058 acres. Located in Cataract Canyon, within the Grand Canyon. *Facilities*: Tribal lodge. Head Start Program. Truxton Canon Field Office.

HOPI RESERVATION
Hopi Tribal Council
· P.O. Box 123, Kykotsmovi, AZ 86039
  (928) 734-2441 Fax 734-6665
  Wayne Taylor, Jr., Chairperson
  Caleb Johnson, Vice Chairperson
  Website: www.hopi.nsn.us/
Tribes: Hopi and Tewa. *In residence*: 8,500. *Area*: 1,565,376 acres. *Facilities*: Hopi Cultural Center; arts and crafts shops; tribal museum; motels and restaurants. Head Start Program. Hopi Agency.

HOUCK RESERVATION
Houck, AZ 86506
Tribe: Navajo. Fort Defiance Agency.

HUALAPAI RESERVATION
Hualapai Tribal Council
P.O. Box 179, Peach Springs, AZ 86434
  (928) 769-2216 Fax 769-2343
  Louise Benson, Chairperson
Tribe: Hualapai. *In residence*: 1,200. *Area*: 995,000 acres. Head Start Program. Truxton Canon Field Office.

INSCRIPTION HOUSE RESERVATION
Tribe: Navajo. Western Navajo Agency.

JEDDITO RESERVATION
Tribe: Navajo. Fort Defiance Agency.

KAIBAB RESERVATION
Kaibab Paiute Tribal Council
HC65, Box 2, Fredonia, AZ 86022
  (928) 643-7245 Fax 643-7260
  Carmen Bradley, Chairperson
Tribe: Paiute. *In residence*: 250. Located in Arizona and Utah. Southern Paiute Field Station.

KAIBITO RESERVATION
Kaibito, AZ 86053
Tribe: Navajo. Western Navajo Agency.

KAYENTA RESERVATION
Kayenta, AZ 86033
Tribe: Navajo. Western Navajo Agency.

KINLICHEE RESERVATION
Tribe: Navajo. Fort Defiance Agency

KLAGETOH RESERVATION
Tribe: Navajo. Fort Defiance Agency

LECHEE RESERVATION
Tribe: Navajo. Western Navajo Agency

LEUPP RESERVATION
Leupp, AZ 86035
Tribe: Navajo. Western Navajo Agency.

LOW MOUNTAIN RESERVATION
Tribe: Navajo. Fort Defiance Agency

LUKACHUKAI RESERVATION
Lukachukai, AZ 86507
Tribe: Navajo. Chinle Agency.

LUPTON RESERVATION
Lupton, AZ 86508
Tribe: Navajo. Fort Defiance Agency.

MANY FARMS RESERVATION
Many Farms, AZ 86538
Tribe: Navajo. Chinle Agency.

MARICOPA RESERVATION
Ak Chin Indian Community Council
42507 W. Peters & Nall Rd.
Maricopa, AZ 85239
  (520) 568-2227 Fax 568-4566
  Delia M. Carlyle, Chairperson
Tribes: Papago and Pima. *In residence*: 450. *Area*: 21,500 acres. *Activities*: Operates a casino. Pima Agency.

MEXICAN SPRINGS RESERVATION
Tribe: Navajo. Fort Defiance Agency

MEXICAN WATERS RESERVATION
Tribe: Navajo. Located in Arizona, New Mexico and Utah. See listings under New Mexico and Utah. Shiprock Agency

NASCHITTI RESERVATION
Tribe: Navajo. Fort Defiance Agency

NAVAJO MOUNTAIN RESERVATION
Tribe: Navajo. Located in Arizona & Utah.
See listing in Utah. Western Navajo Agency

NAVAJO-DINE NATION
P.O. Box 9000, Window Rock, AZ 86515
  (928) 871-6352 Fax 871-4025
  Joe Shirley, Jr., President
Tribe served: Navajo of Arizona, New Mexico & Utah. *In residence*: 185,000. *Area*: 16 million acres. Located in northern Arizona, northwest New Mexico, and southern Utah. *Local attractions*: Navajo Nation Fair (September); summer & winter ceremonials (each week); Office of Navajo Veterans Affairs: P.O. Box 430; (602) 871-6597 Ext. 6598. Museum and library. *Head Start Program*: Division of Child Development, Box 260, Fort Defiance, AZ 86505 (602) 729-5360. Tribal council. Navajo Area Office.

NAZLINI RESERVATION
Tribe: Navajo. Chinle Agency

OAK SPRINGS RESERVATION
Tribe: Navajo. Fort Defiance Agency

OLJATOH RESERVATION
Tribe: Navajo. Located in Arizona and Utah. Western Navajo Agency. See listing under Utah.

PASCUA YAQUI INDIAN COMMUNITY
Pascua Yaqui Tribal Council
7474 S. Camino De Oeste, Tucson, AZ 85746
  (520) 883-5000 Fax 883-5014

Robert Valencia, Chairperson
Tribe served: Pascua Yaqui. Head Start Program.
Salt River Field Office.

PINON RESERVATION
Pinon, AZ86510
Tribe: Navajo. Chinle Agency.

RED LAKE RESERVATION
Tribe: Navajo. Fort Defiance Agency

RED LAKE RSERVATION
Tribe: Navajo. Western Navajo Agency

RED MESA RESERVATION
Tribe: Navajo. Located in Arizona, New Mexico and Utah.
Shiprock Agency. See listings in New Mexico and Utah.

RED ROCK RESERVATION
Tribe: Navajo. Located in Arizona and New Mexico.
See listing under New Mexico. Shiprock Agency

ROUGH ROCK RESERVATION
Tribe: Navajo. Chinle Agency

ROUND ROCK RESERVATION
Tribe: Navajo. Chinle Agency

ST. MICHAELS RESERVATION
Tribe: Navajo. Fort Defiance Agency

SALT RIVER RESERVATION
Salt River Pima-Maricopa
Indian Community Council
10005 E. Osborn, Scottsdale, AZ 85256
(480) 850-8000 Fax 850-8014
Ivan Makil, President
Robert K. Chiago, Tribal Planner
Website: www.saltriver-pima-maricopa.nsn.us
Tribes: Pima-Maricopa. *In residence*: 3,500. *Area*:
46,619 acres. Located in Salt River Valley, adjacent to
Phoenix. Head Start Program. Salt River Field Office.

SAN CARLOS APACHE RESERVATION
San Carlos Tribal Council
P.O. Box 0, San Carlos, AZ 85550
(928) 475-2361 Fax 475-2567
Kathleen W. Kitcheyan, Chairperson
Tribe: Apache. *In residence*: 10,800. Area: 1,877,216
acres. Council members: Rupert Alden, Leo Natsyn,
John Wesley, Leroy Kitcheyan, Ned Anderson, Lambert
Noline, Eugene Duncan, William Belvado, Rhyne
Dosela. *Local attractions*: Coolidge Dam; Tonto National
Forest. *Activities*: Apache Tribal Fair (November); In-
dian Round-up (May & November); Apache Gold Ca-
sino; Self-Governance *Programs*. The tribe recently
opened a Cultural Center featuring and displaying arti-
facts of the Apaches in the early 1800's & modern artwork in basketry, beadwork, traditional clothing/attire with
an information center. P*ublication*: San Carlos Apache
Moccasin newspaper featuring news about the San
Carlos Apache people and its tribal government. Head
Start Program. San Carlos Agency.

SAN JUAN SOUTHERN PAIUTE COUNCIL
P.O. Box 1989, Tuba City, AZ 86045-1989
(928) 283-4589 Fax 283-5761
Evelyn James, President
Tribes served: Paiute-Navajo. *Population served*: 265.
Federally recognized in March 1990. *Tribal Officials*:
Camilla Younker, Clyde Whiskers, Grace Lehi, Mabel
Lehi, & Mary Tillman. A*ctivities*: Annual pow-wow in June.
Publications: Sands to the Mountains; The Paiute Indi-
ans of North America. Southern Paiute Field Office. Li-
brary.

SELLS RESERVATION
Tohono O'Odham Nation Council
P.O. Box 837, Sells, AZ 85634
(520) 383-2028 Fax 383-2087
Edward Manuel, Chairperson
Tribe: Papago. *In residence*: 7,700. *Reservations
served*: Sells, San Xavier, and Gila Bend. *Area*:
2,774,000 acres. Located 25 miles west of Tucson.
Papago Agency.

SAN XAVIER RESERVATION
San Xavier, AZ 85640
Tribe: Papago. *In residence*: 1,000.
Area: 71,000 acres. Papago Agency.

SANOTSEE RESERVATION
Tribe: Navajo. Located in Arizona and New Mexico.
Shiprock Agency. See listing under New Mexico.

SAWMILL RESERVATION
Tribe: Navajo. Fort Defiance Agency

SHONTO RESERVATION
Shonto, AZ 86054
Tribe: Navajo. Located in Arizona and Utah.
Western Navajo Agency. See listing under Utah.

STEAMBOAT RESERVATION
Tribe: Navajo. Fort Defiance Agency

TEECNOSPOS RESERVATION
Tribe: Navajo. Located in Arizona, New Mexico and Utah.
Shiprock Agency. See listings under New Mexico and
Utah.

TEESTO RESERVATION
Tribe: Navajo. Fort Defiance Agency

TOHATCHI RESERVATION
Tribe: Navajo. Fort Defiance Agency

TOLANI LAKE RESERVATION
Tribe: Navajo. Western Navajo Agency

TONTO APACHE RESERVATION
Tonto Apache Tribal Council
#30 Tonto Reservation, Payson, AZ 85541
(928) 474-5000 Fax 474-9125
Vivian L. Burdette, Chairperson
Tribe served: Tonto Apache. Truxton Canon Agency.

TSAILE-WHEATFIELDS RESERVATION
Tsaile, AZ 86556
Tribe: Navajo. Located in Arizona & New Mexico.
Chinle Agency. See listing under New Mexico.

TSELANI RESERVATION
Tribe: Navajo. Chinle Agency

TUBA CITY RESERVATION
Tuba City, AZ 86045
Tribe: Navajo. Western Navajo Agency.

TWIN LAKES RESERVATION
Tribe: Navajo. Fort Defiance Agency

WHITE CONE RESERVATION
Tribe: Navajo. Fort Defiance Agency

WIDE RUINS RESERVATION
Wide Ruins, AZ 86502
Tribe: Navajo. Fort Defiance Agency.

YAVAPAI-PRESCOTT RESERVATION
Yavapai-Prescott Board of Directors
530 E. Merritt St., Prescott, AZ 86301
(928) 445-8790 Fax 778-9445
Stan Rice, Jr., President
Tribe: Yavapai. *In residence*: 175. Area: 1,402 acres.
Special program: Pow-wow; 10-K. *Publication*: Viola
Jimulla, The Indian Chieftess. Library. Truxton Canon
Agency.

CALIFORNIA

AGUA CALIENTE RESERVATION
Agua Caliente Band of Cahuilla Indians
600 E. Tahquitz Canyon Way
Palm Springs, CA 92262 (800) 790-3398
(760) 325-3400 Fax 325-0593
Website: www.aguacaliente.org
Richard M. Milanovich, Chairperson
Barbara Gonzales-Lyons, Vice Chairperson
Moraino J. Patencio, Secretary/Treasurer
Jeanette Prieto-Dodd, Councilperson
Tribe: Agua Caliente Band of Cahuilla Indians. *In resi-
dence*: 250. *Area*: 52,000 acres of which 6,700 acres
lie within the Palm Springs city limits. The area includes
the Palm, Murray, Andreas, Tahquitz and Chino Can-
yons. *Facilities*: Spa Resort Casino; Agua Caliente Ca-
sino, Museum & Reference Library. Palm Springs Field
Office.

ALPINE WASHOE RESERVATION
Woodfords Community Council
96 Washoe Blvd. • Markleeville, CA 96120
(775) 883-1446; Willard Bennett, Chairperson
Tribe served: Component Band of the Washoe Tribe.
Western Nevada Agency.

ALTURAS RANCHERIA
P.O. Box 340 • Alturas, CA 96101
(530) 233-5571 Fax 233-4165
Paul Del Rosa, Chairperson
Tribe served: Pit River. *In residence*: 15. Area: 20 acres.
Tribal Council. Northern California Field Office.

AUGUSTINE BAND OF MISSION INDIANS
P.O. Box 846 • Coachella, CA 92236
(760) 398-4722 Fax 398-4922
Mary Ann Martin, Chairperson
Tribe: Cahuilla. Unoccupied. *Area*: 500 acres.
Southern California Agency.

BARONA RESERVATION
Barona General Business Council
1095 Barona Rd. • Lakeside, CA 92040
(619) 443-6612 Fax 443-0681
Clifford M. LaChappa, Sr., Chairperson
Tribe: Diegueno (Barona Band of Mission Indians).
In residence: 330. Area: 5,000 acres. *Resources*: Barona
Indian Museum. Southern California Agency.

BENTON PAIUTE RESERVATION
Utu Utu Gwaitu Paiute Tribal Council
567 Yellow Jacket Rd. • Benton, CA 93512
(760) 933-2321 Fax 933-2412
Rose Marie Saulque, Chairperson
Tribe: Utu Utu Gwaitu Paiute. *In residence*: 70. Area:
160 acres. Located in Mono County, in Blind Springs
Valley about three miles from Benton Hot Springs. *Activity*: Annual Meeting. Central California Agency.

BERRY CREEK RANCHERIA
5 Tyme Way • Oroville, CA 95966
(530) 534-3859 Fax 534-1151
James Edwards, Chairperson
Tribe: Tyme Maidu. In residence: 275. Area: 66 acres.
Facility: Operates the Gold Country Casino (see Ca-
sino section). *Publication*: Monthly tribal newsletter.
Tribal Council. Central California Agency.

BIG LAGOON RANCHERIA
P.O. Drawer 3060 • Trinidad, CA 95570
(707) 826-2079 Fax 826-0459
Virgil Moorehead, Chairperson
Tribes: Yurok & Tolowa. *In residence*: 12. *Area*: 9 acres.
General council. Northern California Field Office.

BIG PINE RESERVATION
P.O. Box 700 • Big Pine, CA 93513
(760) 938-2003 Fax 938-2942
Cheryl Levine, Chairperson-
Tribes: Paiute & Shoshone. In residence: 110.
Population served: 450. *Area*: 280 acres.
General council. Central California Agency.

BIG SANDY RANCHERIA
P.O. Box 337 • Auberry, CA 93602
(559) 855-4003 Fax 855-4129
Wilbur Beecher, Chairperson
Tribe: Mono. *In residence*: 55. *Area*: 8 acres.
Facilities: Operates the Mono Wind Casino.
Tribal council. Central California Agency.

BIG VALLEY RANCHERIA
2726 Mission Rancheria Rd.
Lakeport, CA 95453
(707) 263-3924 Fax 263-3977
Anthony Jack, Chairperson
Central California Agency.

BISHOP RESERVATION
Bishop Indian Tribal Council
50 Tu Su Lane • Bishop, CA 93514
(760) 873-3584 Fax 873-4143
Monty Bengochia, Chairperson
Doug Vega, Vice-Chairperson
E-mail: admin4@qnet.com
Tribes: Paiute & Shoshone. *In residence*: 1,075. *Area*:
875 acres. *Tribal council members*: Tina Stone, Ron Barr,
Gerald Kane. *Facilities*: Culture Center & museum; ca-
sino; gas station. *Special programs*: Toiyabe Indian

health project; career development; housing; education center (teaching of the Paiute language); headstart/daycare; elders program. *Activities*: Annual Pow Wow in July. *Memberships*: Intertribal Council of California; National Congress of American Indians; California Indian Manpower Consortium; California National Indian Gaming Association. *Publication*: Bishop Tribal Newsletter, bi-monthlyCentral California Agency.

BLUE LAKE RANCHERIA
P.O. Box 428 • Blue Lake, CA 95525
(707) 668-5615 Fax 668-4272
   Claudia Brundin, Chairperson
Tribes served: Wiyot, Yurok, Cherokee, Warm Springs, Black Foot, Towala. *In residence*: 35. *Area*: 31 acres. Business council. Northern California Field Office.

BRIDGEPORT INDIAN COLONY
P.O. Box 37 • Bridgeport, CA 93517
(760) 932-7083 Fax 932-7846
   Herb Glazier, Chairperson
Tribe: Paiute. *In residence*: 100. General council.
Central California Agency.

BUENA VISTA RANCHERIA
4650 Coalmine Rd. • Ione, CA 95640
(209) 274-6512 Fax 274-6514
   Donnamarie Potts, Spokesperson
Tribe served: Mewuk. Central California Agency.

CABAZON BAND OF MISSION INDIANS
Cabazon Tribal Business Committee
84-245 Indio Spring Dr. • Indio, CA 92201
(760) 342-2593 Fax 347-7880
   John A. James, Chairperson
   Brenda Soulliere, 1st Vice Chair
   Charles Welmas, 2nd Vice Chair
   Mark Nichols, CEO; Duff Wenz, COO
   Judy Stapp, Cultural Affairs Director
   Patrick Schoonover, Legal Affairs Director
   Greg Cervantes, Public Affairs Director
   Joan Kite, Public Information Officer
Tribe served: Cabazon Band of Mission Indians. *In residence*: 38. *Total acreage*: 1,700 acres located in Coachella Valley, Riverside County. *Activities*: PowWows (Spring & Thanksgiving); operates Cahuilla Child Development Center; Cabazon Cultural Museum; Cabazon Tribal Reference Library; Fantasy Springs Casino (See Casino section). *Publications*: Cabazon Circle Newsletter; Code of Cabazon Band of Mission Indians, and Return of the Buffalo-The Explosion of Indian Gaming. Southern California Agency.

CAHUILLA BAND OF MISSION INDIANS
P.O. Box 391760 • Anza, CA 92539
(909) 763-5549 Fax 763-2808
   LeeAnn Salgado, Spokesperson
Tribe: Cahuilla. *In residence*: 175. *Area*: 18,270 acres. General council. Southern California Agency.

CAMPO BAND OF MISSION INDIANS
36190 Church Rd., #1 • Campo, CA 91906
(619) 478-9046 Fax 478-5818
   Ralph Goff, Chairperson
Tribe: Diegueno (Campo Band of Mission Indians). *In residence*: 225. *Area*: 15,000 acres. General council. Southern California Agency.

CAPITAN GRANDE RESERVATION
Lakeside, CA
Tribe: Diegueno (Capitan Grande Band of Mission Indians). Southern California Agency.

CEDARVILLE RANCHERIA
200 S. Howard St. • Altura, CA 96101
(530) 233-3969 Fax 233-4776
   Virginia Lash, Chairperson
   Georgianna DeGarmo, Secretary
   Cherie Lash, Housing Chairperson
Tribe: Paiute. *In residence*: 22. *Area*: 17 acres. Community council. Northern California Field Office.

CHEMEHUEVI RESERVATION
P.O. Box 1976 • Havasu Lake, CA 92363
(760) 858-4301 Fax 858-5400
   Edward Smith, Chairperson
Tribe: Chemehuevi. *In residence*: 135. *Facility*: Havasu Landing Resort & Casino. Tribal council. Located in California and Arizona. Colorado River Agency.

CHICKEN RANCH RANCHERIA
P.O. Box 1159 • Jamestown, CA 95327
(209) 984-4806 Fax 984-5606
   Llyod Mathieson, Chairperson
Central California Agency.

CHUMASH RESERVATION
SANTA YNEZ BAND OF MISSION INDIANS
P.O. Box 517 • Santa Ynez, CA 93440
(805) 688-7997 Fax 686-9578
   Vincent Armenta, Chairperson
Tribe: Chumash (Santa Ynez Band of Chumash Mission Indians). *In residence*: 100. *Population served*: 200. *Area*: 126 acres. *Activities*: Annual meeting in September; Elders Council (P.O. Box 365 (805) 688-8446 Fax 693-1768. E-mail: elders@synth.com). Casino. Business committee. Southern California Agency.

CLOVERDALE RANCHERIA COUNCIL
555 S. Cloverdale Blvd. #1
Cloverdale, CA 95425
(707) 894-5775 Fax 894-5727
   Patricia Hermosillo, Chairperson
Central California Agency.

COLD SPRINGS RANCHERIA
P.O. Box 209 • Tollhouse, CA 93667
(559) 855-5043 Fax 855-4445
   Lonnie Bill, Chairperson
Tribe: Mono. *In residence*: 235. *Area*: 98 acres. Tribal council. Central California Agency.

COLORADO RIVER RESERVATION
About 50,000 acres in southwest California and 245,000 in southeast Arizona. (See listing under Arizona.)

COLUSA RANCHERIA
50 Wintun Rd., Dept. D • Colusa, CA 95932
(530) 458-8231 Fax 458-4186
   Wayne Mitchum, Chairperson
Tribe: Cachil DeHe Band of Wintun Indians. *In residence*: 55. *Area* 300 acres. Community council. Central California Agency.

CORTINA RANCHERIA
P.O. Box 1630 • Williams, CA 95987
(530) 473-3274 Fax 473-3301
   Elaine Patterson, Chairperson
Tribe: Wintun. *In residence*: 90. *Area*: 640 acres. General council. Central California Agency.

COYOTE VALLEY RESERVATION
P.O. Box 39 • Redwood Valley, CA 95470
(707) 485-8723 Fax 485-1247
   Priscilla Hunter, Chairperson
Tribe served: Pomo. Central California Agency.

CUYAPAIPE GENERAL COUNCIL
4054 Willows Rd., P.O. Box 2250
Alpine, CA 91903-2250
(619) 455-6315 Fax 445-9126
   Tony J. Pinto, Chairperson
Tribe: Diegueno (Campo Band of Mission Indians). *In residence*: 30. *Area*: 4,100 acres. General council. Southern California Agency.

DRY CREEK RANCHERIA
P.O. Box 607 • Geyserville, CA 95441
(707) 431-2388 Fax 431-2615
   Michael Racho, Chairperson
Tribe served: Pomo. *Population served*: 135. *Area*: 75 acres. General council. Central California Agency.

ELK VALLEY RANCHERIA
Elk Valley Rancheria Tribal Council
P.O. Box 1042, 440 Mathews St.
Crescent City, CA 95531
(707) 464-4680 Fax 464-4519
   Dale A. Miller, Chairperson
   Richard Warner, Vice-Chairperson
   Donna Crook, Secretary
   Robert Loez, Treasurer
   Website: www.elkvalleyrancheria.com
   E-mail: wgreen@elk-valley.com
Tribes served: Tolowa/Yurok. *Area*: 400 acres.
Council members: Lotea Stinchcomb, John W. Green, Sean McClaflin, Linda Martin, Frank Postillo. *Resources*: Small library. Northern California Agency.

ENTERPRISE RANCHERIA
1940 Feather River Blvd., Suite B
Oroville, CA 95965
(530) 532-9214 Fax 532-1768
   Harvey Angle, Chairperson
Central California Agency.

FORT BIDWELL RESERVATION
Fort Bidwell Community Council
P.O. Box 129 • Fort Bidwell, CA 96112
(530) 279-6310 Fax 279-2233
   Denise Pollard, Chairperson
Tribe: Paiute. *In residence*: 200. *Area*: 3,330 acres.
Activity: PowWows. Tribal council. Northern California Field Office.

FORT INDEPENDENCE RESERVATION
Fort Independence Paiute Tribal Council
P.O. Box 67 • Independence, CA 93526
(760) 878-2126 Fax 878-2311
   Vernon Miller, Chairperson
   John Bracken, Vice Chairperson
Tribes: Paiute. *In residence*: 110. *Area*: 360 acres.
Publication: Quarterly newsletter. Central California Agency.

FORT MOJAVE RESERVATION
Fort Mojave Tribal Council
500 Merriman Ave. • Needles, CA 92363
(760) 629-4591 Fax 629-2468
   Nora McDowell, Chairperson
Tribe served: Mojave. *Population served*: 600. *Area*: 48,000 acres. Located in California, Arizona, and Nevada. Colorado River Agency. *Activities*: Operates a Avi Resort & Casino; PowWow in February; Mojave Days in October. *School*: Aha MacCav High School.

FORT YUMA RESERVATION
Located in Arizona & California. Fort Yuma Agency. See listing under Arizona.

GRATON RANCHERIA
P.O. Box 481 • Novato, CA 94948
(707) 763-6143 Fax (415) 883-3051
   Greg Sarris, Spokesperson
Community council. Central California Agency.

GREENVILLE RANCHERIA
P.O. Box 279 • Greenville, CA 95947
(530) 284-7990 Fax 284-6612
   Lorie James, Chairperson
Community council. Central California Agency.

GRINDSTONE RANCHERIA
P.O. Box 63 • Elk Creek, CA 95939
(530) 968-5365 Fax 968-5366
   Dudley Burrows, Chairperson
Tribe served: Wintun. *Population served*: 185.
Area: 80 acres. General council. Central California Agency.

GUIDIVILLE RANCHERIA
P.O. Box 339 • Talmadge, CA 95481
(707) 462-3682 Fax 462-9183
   Merlene Sanchez, Chairperson
Tribe served: Pomo. *Population served*: 100.
Northern California Agency.

HOOPA EXTENSION RESERVATION
Weitchpec, CA 95546
Tribe: Yurok. *In residence*: 300. *Area*: 6,800 acres.
Northern California Agency.

HOOPA VALLEY INDIAN RESERVATION
Hooper Valley Tribal Council
P.O. Box 1348 • Hoopa, CA 95546
(530) 625-4211 Fax 625-4594
   Duane Sherman, Sr., Chairperson
Tribe served: Hoopa. *In residence*: 2,200. *Area*: 86,042 acres. *Location*: Located along Trinity River, 35 miles northeast of Eureka, California. *Facilities*: Operates Lucky Bear Casino & Bingo. *Program*: Head Start. Northern California Field Office.

HOPLAND RESERVATION
Hopland Tribal Council
P.O. Box 610 • Hopland, CA 95449
(707) 744-1647 Fax 744-1506
   Sandra Sigala, Sr., Chairperson
   E-mail: sigala@hoplandtribe.com

Website: www.shokawah.com/tribal.html
Tribe: Sho-ka-wah Band of Pomo Indians. *Elected officials*: William Elliott, Secretary; Sandra Sigala, Treasurer; Council members: Orval Elliott, Sr., Beverly Rodriguez, Kenneth Arnold, Sr. *In residence*: 150. *Area*: 2,070 acres. *Activities*: Operates an early child development school, 3-5 years old; publishes monthly newsletter. Tribal council. Central California Agency.

INAJA-COSMIT RESERVATION
1040 E. Valley Pkwy., Unit A
Escondido, CA 92025
(760) 747-8581 Fax 747-8568
Rebecca Maxcy, Chairperson
Tribe: Diegueno. *In residence*: 15.
Area: 880 acres. Southern California Agency.

**INDIAN CANYON MUTSUN
BAND OF COSTANOAN INDIANS**
P.O. Box 28, Hollister, CA 95024
Ann-Marie Sayers, Chairperson
Land recently revived to trust.

IONE BAND OF MIWOK INDIANS
P.O. Box 1190 • Ione, CA 95640
(209) 274-6753 Fax 274-6636
Kathy Ramey, Chairperson
Central California Agency.

JACKSON RANCHERIA
P.O. Box 1090 • Jackson, CA 95642
(209) 223-1935 Fax 223-5366
Margaret Dalton, Chairperson
Tribe: Me-Wuk (Miwok). *Area*: 330 acres.
Interim council. Central California Agency.

JAMUL INDIAN VILLAGE
P.O. Box 612 • Jamul, CA 91935
(619) 669-4785 Fax 669-4817
Kenneth A. Meza, Chairperson
Carlene Chamberlain, Vice Chair
Veronica Thing, Sec./Treasurer
Tribe: Kumeyaay. *Area*: 6.4 acres. *Council members*: William Meza, Adolph Thing, Erica Pinto. Southern California Agency.

KARUK TRIBE OF CALIFORNIA
P.O. Box 1016 • Happy Camp, CA 96039
(530) 493-5305 Fax 493-5322
Alvis Johnson, Chairperson
Tribe: Karuk. Interim committee.
Northern California Field Office.

LA JOLLA BAND OF LUISENO INDIANS
22000 Hwy. 76 • Pauma Valley, CA 92061
(760) 742-3771 Fax 742-1704
Jack Musick, Chairperson
Tribe served: Luiseno. *Population served*: 235.
General council. Southern California Agency.

LA POSTA BAND OF MISSION INDIANS
P.O. Box 1048 • Boulevard, CA 91905
(619) 478-2113 Fax 561-3114
Gwendolyn Parada, Chairperson
Tribe: Diegueno (La Posta Band of Mission Indians).
Unoccupied. *Area*: 3,600 acres. General council. Southern California Agency.

LAYTONVILLE RANCHERIA
P.O. Box 1239 • Laytonville, CA 95454
(707) 984-6197 Fax 984-6201
Genevieve Campbell, Chairperson
Tribe: Cahto-Pomo. *In residence*: 150. *Area*: 200 acres.
General council. Central California Agency.

LONE PINE RESERVATION
P.O. Box 757 • Lone Pine, CA 93545
(760) 876-1034 Fax 876-8302
Racheal Joseph, Chairperson
Tribe served: Paiute-Shoshone. *Population served*: 225.
Area: 237 acres. Tribal council. Central California Agency.

LOS COYOTES RESERVATION
P.O. Box 189 • Warner Springs, CA 92086
(760) 782-0711 Fax 782-2701
Catherine Saubel, Spokesperson
Tribe: Luiseno. *In residence*: 195. *Area*: 25,000 acres.
General council. Southern California Agency.

LOWER LAKE RANCHERIA
131 Lincoln St. • Healdsburg, CA 95448
Daniel D. Beltran, Chairperson
Tribe served: Pomo Central California Agency.

LYTTON RANCHERIA
1250 Coddingtown Center, Suite 1
Santa Rosa, CA 95401
(707) 575-5917 Fax 575-6974
Marjorie Mejia, Chairperson
Tribe served: Yurok. *Population served*: 100.
Central California Agency.

MANCHESTER - PORT ARENA RANCHERIA
P.O. Box 623 • Point Arena, CA 95468
(707) 882-2788 Fax 882-3417
Jose, Oropeza, Chairperson
Tribe served: Pomo. *Population served*: 100. *Area*: 364 acres. Community council. Central California Agency.

MANZANITA BAND OF MISSION INDIANS
P.O. Box 1302 • Boulevard, CA 91905
(619) 766-4930 Fax 766-4957
Leroy J. Elliott, Chairperson
Tribe served: Diegueno. *Population served*: 20. *In residence*: 22. *Area*: 3,579 acres. *Activities*: Economic Development Project. General council. Southern California Agency.

**MECHOOPDA INDIAN TRIBE
OF CHICO RANCHERIA**
125 Mission Ranch Blvd. • Chico, CA 95926
(530) 899-8922 Fax 899-8517
Website: www.mechoopda.nsn.us
Steve C. Santos, Chairperson
Barbara Rose, Vice-Chairperson
Tammi Carruth, Treasurer
Sandra Knight, Secretary
Members at large: Rodney Clements and Jessie Kai.

MESA GRANDE BAND OF MISSION INDIANS
P.O. Box 270 • Santa Ysabel, CA 92070
(760) 782-3818 Fax 782-9029
Howard K. Marcy, Chairperson
Michael Linton, Vice Chairperson
E-mail: mesagrandeband@msn.com
Tribe served: Diegueno (Mesa Grande Band of Mission Indians). *In residence*: 70. *Area*: 1,800 acres.
Councilmembers: Manuel La Chappa, Jr., Darrel Langley, Yvonne La Chappa. *Special program*: Buffalo Project. Tribal library. Business Committee. Southern California Agency.

MIDDLETOWN RANCHERIA
Middletown, CA 95461
Jose Simon, III, Chairperson
(707) 987-3670 Fax 987-9091
Tribe served: Pomo. *Population served*: 65. *Area*: 109 acres. Interim council. Central California Agency.

MOORETOWN RANCHERIA
1 Alverda Dr. • Oroville, CA 95966
(530) 533-3625 Fax 533-3680
Shirley Prusia, Chairperson
Tribes served: Concow, Maidu. *Area*: 35 acres in trust; 20 acres in fee land. Tribal Council. School. Library. Central California Agency.

MORONGO BAND OF MISSION INDIANS
11581 Potrero Rd. • Banning, CA 92220
(909) 849-4697 Fax 849-4425
Maurice Lyons, Chairperson
Tribe: Cahuilla. *In residence*: 375. *Population served*: 750. *Area*: 32,250 acres. Activities: Owns & operates the new Morongo Casino, Resort & Spa. General Council. Southern California Agency.

NORTH FORK RANCHERIA
P.O. Box 929 • North Fork, CA 93643
(559) 877-2461 Fax 877-2467
Delores Roberts, Chairperson
Juanita Williams, Vice Chairperson
Elected officials: Ron Roberts, Treasurer; Barbara Coleman, Secretary; Patrick Beihn, Member-at-Large.
Tribe served: Mono. *Facility*: Library. *Published works*: "Nu Qwah Neum," quarterly newsletter. Central California Agency.

PALA BAND OF MISSION INDIANS
P.O. Box 50 • Pala, CA 92059
(760) 742-3784 Fax 742-1411
Robert Smith, Chairperson
Tribe served: Cupa. *In residence*: 395. *Population served*: 580. *Area*: 11,000 acres. *Activities*: Cupa Day (May); Museum. *Publication*: Pala Mumalki, newsletter. Southern California Agency.

PASKENTA BAND OF NOMLAKI INDIANS
P.O. Box 398 • Orland, CA 95963
(530) 865-3119 Fax 865-2345
Everett Freeman, Chairperson
Tribe served: Nomlaki. Central California Agency.

PAUMA-YUIMA BAND OF MISSION INDIANS
P.O. Box 369 • Pauma Valley, CA 92061
(760) 742-1289 Fax 742-3422
Christobal C. Devers, Sr., Chairperson
Tribe served: Luiseno (Pauma Band of Mission Indians.)
Reservation served: Pauma & Yuima Reservation.
Population served: 35. *Area*: 5,750 acres. *Activities*: education center; memorial celebration. Tribal Council. Southern California Agency.

PECHANGA BAND OF LUISENO INDIANS
P.O. Box 1477 • Temecula, CA 92593
(909) 676-2768 Fax 695-1778
Mark A. Macarro, Chairperson
Tribe served: Luiseno. *Population served*: 450. Tribal Council. *Publication*: Indian Gaming newsletter (Internet) www.pechanga.net. Southern California Agency.

PICAYUNE RANCHERIA OF CHUKCHANSI INDIANS
46575 Road 417 • Coarsegold, CA 93614
(559) 683-6633 Fax 683-0599
Dixie Jackson, Chairperson
Tribe served: Chuckchansi. *In residence*: 65. *Area*: 78 acres, located from the San Joaquin River to the south to Yosemite National Park to the north, North Fork to the east to Chowchilla to the west. *Elected officials*: Armanda Ramirez, Treasurer; Nancy Ayala, Secretary; Holly Wyatt & Louie Ramirez, Jr. *Special activity*: Pow-Wow. Library. Tribal council. Central California Agency.

PINOLEVILLE RESERVATION
367 N. State St. #204 • Ukiah, CA 95482
(707) 463-1454 Fax 463-6601
Leona Williams, Chairperson
Central California Agency.

PIT RIVER TRIBE
37014 Main St. • Burney, CA 96013
(530) 335-5421 Fax 335-3140
Angel Winn, Chairperson
Tribe served: Pit River (consists of 11 autonomous bands in several locations organized as one tribe). *Area*: 9,242 acres. *Facility*: Ownes the Pit River Casino. Tribal Council. Northern California Field Office.

POTTER VALLEY RANCHERIA
112 N. School St. • Ukiah, CA 95482
(707) 485-5115
Salvador Rosales, Chairperson
Tribe served: Pomo. Central California Agency.

QUARTZ VALLEY RESERVATION
P.O. Box 24 • Fort Jones, CA 96032
(530) 468-5907 Fax 468-5908
Roy Lincoln, Chairperson
Tribes served: Karuk & Shasta. *Membership*: 250. *Area*: Legal boundaries encompass 640 acres in Quartz Valley - all tribal land was lost to termination process. *Facility*: Library. *Publication*: Quartz Valley Indian News, newsletter. Northern California Field Office.

RAMONA BAND OF MISSION INDIANS
P.O. Box 391670 • Anza, CA 92539
(909) 763-4105 Fax 763-4325
Manuel Hamilton, Representative
Tribe: Cahuilla. *Area*: 560 acres. *Officials*: Joseph D. Hamilton, General Council; Jessica S. Hamilton, Secretary. Southern California Agency.

REDDING RANCHERIA
2000 Rancheria Rd. • Redding, CA 96001
(530) 225-8979 Fax 241-1879
Tracy Edwards, Chairperson
Tribes served: Pit River, Wintun, Yana. *Elected officials*: Hope Wilkes, Treasurer; Mac Hayward, Secretary; Bar-

bara Murphy, Bob Foreman & Carla Maslin, council members. *Area*: 31 acres. *Activities*: Stillwater Pow-wow; Health fair. *Publications*: Redding Rancheria Times (newsletter); Redding Rancheria Indian Health Service (newsletter). Library. Northern California Field Office.

REDWOOD VALLEY RESERVATION
3250 Road I • Redwood Valley, CA 95470
(707) 485-0361 Fax 485-5726
Elizabeth Hansen, Chairperson
Tribe served: Pomo. Central California Agency.

RESIGHINI RANCHERIA
Coast Indian Community Council
P.O. Box 529 • Klamath, CA 95548
(707) 482-2431 Fax 482-3425
William J. Scott, Chairperson
Tribe served: Yurok. *Population served*: 110.
Area: 230 acres. Northern California Agency.

RINCON BAND OF MISSION INDIANS
P.O. Box 68 • Valley Center, CA 92082
(760) 749-1051 Fax 749-8901
John Currier, Chairperson
Tribe served: Luiseno. *Population served*: 275.
In residence: 150. Business Committee. Southern California Agency.

ROBINSON RANCHERIA
1545 E. Highway 20 • Nice, CA 95464
(707) 275-0527 Fax 275-0235
Clara Wilson, Chairperson
Tribe served: Pomo. Central California Agency.

BEAR RIVER BAND OF
ROHNERVILLE RANCHERIA
32 Bear River Dr. • Loleta, CA 95551
(888) 733-1900 Fax (707) 733-1972
James W. Moon, Jr., Chairperson
Tribe served: Wiyot-Mattole. Northern California Agency.

ROUND VALLEY RESERVATION
Covelo Indian Community Council
P.O. Box 448 • Covelo, CA 95428
(707) 983-6126 Fax 983-6128
John Azbill, President
Tribes: Wailaki, Yuki, Nomlacki, Pomo, Concow, Pit River, Little Lake. *In residence*: 1,300. *Area*: 33,000 acres one mile north of Covelo. *Activities*: Operates health center, career center, education center, senior center, and tribal library; California Indian Days, annually, 3rd weekend in September; All Indian Rodeo Spring & Fall Festivals. *Publication*: Poekan Tribal Newsletter/ Newspaper. Central California Agency.

RUMSEY RANCHERIA
P.O. Box 18 • Brooks, CA 95606
(530) 796-3400 Fax 796-2143
Paula Lorenzo, Chairperson
Tribe: Wintun. *Population served*: 50. *Area*: 67 acres. Community Council. Central California Agency.

SAN MANUEL BAND OF MISSION INDIANS
P.O. Box 266 • Patton, CA 92369
(909) 864-8933 Fax 864-3370
Deron Marquez, Chairperson
Tribe served: Serrano (San Manuel Band of Serrano Mission Indians). *In residence*: 55. *Population served*: 90. *Area*: 820 acres in San Bernardino County. General Council. Southern California Agency.

SAN PASQUAL BAND OF DIEGUENO INDIANS
P.O. Box 365 • Valley Center, CA 92082
(760) 749-3200 Fax 749-3876
Allen E. Lawson, Jr., Chairperson
Tribe served: Diegueno. *Population served*: 350. *Area*: 1,380 acres. Tribal Council. Southern California Agency.

SANTA ROSA RANCHERIA
P.O. Box 8 • Lemoore, CA 93245
(559) 924-1278 Fax 924-3583
Michael Sisco Chairperson
Tribe served: Tache Yokut. *In residence*: 135. *Population served*: 275. *Area*: 170 acres. General Council. Central California Agency.

SANTA ROSA BAND OF MISSION INDIANS
P.O. Box 390611 • Anza, CA 92539
(909) 849-4761 Fax 849-5612
Vivian Scribner, Spokesperson

Tribe: Cahuilla. *In residence*: 110. *Area*: 11,000 acres. General Council. Southern California Agency.

SANTA YSABEL BAND OF MISSION INDIANS
P.O. Box 130 • Santa Ysabel, CA 92070
(760) 765-0846 Fax 765-0320
Ben Scerato, Chairperson
Tribe: Diegueno (Santa Ysabel Band of Mission Indians). *In residence*: 325. *Population served*: 900. *Area*: 15,500 acres. General Council. Southern California Agency.

SCOTTS VALLEY RANCHERIA
Lakeport, CA 95453
(707) 263-4771 Fax 263-4773
Donald Arnold, Chairperson
Tribe served: Pomo. *Population served*: 100. General Council. Central California Agency.

SHEEP RANCH RANCHERIA
Tracy, CA 95376
(209) 834-0197 Fax 834-0318
Silvia Burley, Chairperson
Tribe served: California Valley Miwok Tribe. Central California Agency.

SHERWOOD VALLEY RANCHERIA
190 Sherwood Hill Dr. • Willits, CA 95490
(707) 459-9690 Fax 459-6936
Allen Wright, Chairperson
Tribe served: Pomo. *Population served*: 175. General Council. Central California Agency.

SHINGLE SPRINGS RANCHERIA
P.O. Box 1340 • Shingle Springs, CA 95682
(530) 676-8010 Fax 676-8033
Nick Fonseco Chairperson
Tribe served: Me-Wuk. Unoccupied.
Area: 160 acres. Central California Agency.

SMITH RIVER RANCHERIA
250 N. Indian Rd. • Smith River, CA 95567
(707) 487-9255 Fax 487-0930
Karen L. Miller, Chairperson
Tribe served: Tolowa. *In residence*: 175. *Area*: 161 acres. *Facilities*: Operates the Lucky 7 Casino. Northern California Agency.

SOBOBA BAND OF LUISENO INDIANS
23904 Soboba Rd. • San Jacinto, CA 92583
Soboba Tribal Council
P.O. Box 487 • San Jacinto, CA 92581
(909) 654-2765 Fax 654-4198
Robert J. Salgado, Sr., Spokesperson
Tribe served: Luiseno. *Population served*: 725. *Area*: 5,000 acres. *Activities*: Annual Pow wow in September; Operates a pre-school, Noli Indian School (Grades 6-12); D-Q University. Southern California Agency.

STEWARTS POINT RANCHERIA
Kashia Business Committee
1420 Guerneville Rd., Suite 3
Santa Rosa, CA 95403
(707) 591-0580 Fax 591-0583
Lester Pinola, Chairperson
Barry Parriah, Vice Chairperson
Audrey Guerrero, Treasurer
Betsy Cobarrubia, Secretary
Tribe served: Kashia Pomo. *In residence*: 100.
Population served: 375. *Area*: 40 acres. Central California Agency.

SULPHUR BANK RANCHERIA
Elem Indian Colony Council
P.O. Box 618 • Clearlake Oaks, CA 95423
(707) 995-2853 Fax 995-2805
Stephen Brown, Chairperson
Tribe served: Elem Indian Colony of Pomo Indians.
In residence: 55. *Population served*: 165. Central California Agency.

SUSANVILLE INDIAN RANCHERIA
P.O. Drawer U • Susanville, CA 96130
(530) 257-6264 Fax 257-7986
Dwight Lowry, Chairperson
Tribes: Paiute, Maidu, and Pit River. *In residence*: 350. *Area*: 140 acres. Business Council. Northern California Field Office.

SYCUAN BAND OF KUMEYAAY NATION
5459 Dehesa Rd. • El Cajon, CA 92021
(619) 445-2613 Fax 445-1927
Daniel Tucker, Chairperson
Tribe: Kumeyaay. *In residence*: 70. *Area*: 640 acres. Business Committee. Southern California Agency.

TABLE BLUFF RANCHERIA
1000 Wiyot Dr. • Loleta, CA 95551
(707) 733-5055 Fax 733-5601
Cheryl A. Seidner, Chairperson
Tribe served: Wiyot. *In residence*: 218.
Area: 102 acres. Northern California Field Office.

TABLE MOUNTAIN RANCHERIA
P.O. Box 410 • Friant, CA 93626
(559) 822-2587 Fax 822-2693
Leanne Walker-Grant, Chairperson
Tribe served: Yokut. Central California Agency.

TIMBI-SHA SHOSHONE TRIBE
P.O. Box 206 • Death Valley, CA 92328
(760) 786-2374 Fax 786-2376
Pauline Esteves, Chairperson
E-Mail Address: Timbisha@aol.com
Tribe: Timbisha Shoshone. *Council members*: Leroy Jackson, Grace Goad, Gayle Johnson, Joann Rogers. *Area*: 40 acres. *Publication*: "The Timbisha Shoshone Tribe and Their Living Valley", by the Timbisha Preservation Committee. Central California Agency.

TORRES-MARTINEZ
DESERT CAHUILLA INDIANS
P.O. Box 1160 • Thermal, CA 92274
(760) 397-8144 Fax 397-8146
Mary E. Belardo, Chairperson
Tribe: Cahuilla. *In residence*: 90. *Area*: 25,000 acres. Business Committee. Southern California Agency.

TRINIDAD RANCHERIA
P.O. Box 630 • Trinidad, CA 95570
(707) 677-0211 Fax 677-3921
Carol Ervin, Chairperson
Tribe served: Yurok. *Elected officials*: Shirley Laos, Secretary/Treasurer; Fred Lamberson, Jr. & Nicole VanMeter, Council members. *Population served*: 75. *Area*: 91.5 acres. *Activities*: Own/operate the Cher-Ae Heights Bingo & Casino. Tribal library for people on rancheria. Northern California Field Office.

TULE RIVER RESERVATION
P.O. Box 589 • Porterville, CA 93258
(559) 781-4271 Fax 781-4610
Duane Garfield, Chairperson
Tribe served: Yokut. *In residence*: 550. *Area*: 54,000 acres. Tribal Council. Central California Agency.

TUOLUMNE RANCHERIA
P.O. Box 699 • Tuolumne, CA 95379
(209) 928-3475 Fax 928-1677
Kevin Day, Chairperson
Tribe: Me-Wuk (Miwok). *Population served*: 285.
Area: 325 acres. Community Council. Central California Agency.

TWENTY NINE PALMS
BAND OF LUISENO INDIANS
46-200 Harrison St. • Coachella, CA 92236
(760) 775-5566 Fax 775-4639
Dean Mike, Chairperson
Tribe: Luiseno. Unoccupied. *Area*: 160 acres. Southern California Agency.

UNITED AUBURN RANCHERIA
661 Newcastle Rd., Suite 1 • Newcastle, CA 95658
(916) 663-3720 Fax 663-3727
Jessica Travares, Chairperson
David Keyser, Vice-Chairperson
Website: www.auburnindians.com
Tribes: Miwok & Maidu. Central California Agency.

UPPER LAKE RANCHERIA (HABEMATOLEL)
P.O. Box 516 • Upper Lake, CA 95485
(707) 275-0737 Fax 275-0757
Leora J. Treppa-Diego, Chairperson
Carmella Icay-Johnson, Secretary
E-mail: habematolel@saber.net
Tribe served: Pomo. *Executive council members*: Sheila Diego, Michael Icay, Georgeanne Mareks. Central California Agency.

VIEJAS INDIAN RESERVATION
Viejas Tribal Council
P.O. Box 308• Alpine, CA 91903
(619) 445-3810 Fax 445-5337
Anthony R. Pico, Chairperson
Website: www.viejasbandofkumeyaay.org
Tribe: Viejas Band of Kumeyaay Indians. *In residence*: 195. *Area*: 1,609 acres. *Special programs*: Birdsingers Gathering; Summer Cultural Program. Viejas has a tribal education center that offers academic & cultural programs for Viejas Tribal members and their children. Library. Southern California Agency.

YUROK RESERVATION
1034 Sixth St. • Eureka, CA 95501
(707) 444-0433 Fax 444-0437
Susan M. Masten, Chairperson
Howard McConnell, Vice Chairperson
Tribe served: Yurok. Councilpersons: Larry Hendrix, Orick District; Bonnie Green, South District; Walt Lara, Jr., Requa District; Marjorie Buckskin, North District; Sid Nix, Weitchpec District; Richard Myers, Pecwan District. Tribal council. Northern California Field Office.

COLORADO

SOUTHERN UTE TRIBE
P.O. Box 737 • Ignacio, CO 81137
(970) 563-0100 Fax 563-0396
Leonard C. Burch, Chairperson
Tom Shipps, Tribal Attorney
Website: www.southern-ute.nsn.us/index.html
Tribe served: Southern Ute. *In residence*: 1,200. *Area*: 307,000 acres located along the Colorado—New Mexico border. *Activities*: Sun Dance, Bear Dance, and Ute Fair. *Publication*: "Ute Drum" , newspaper. Library. *Head Start Program*: P.O. Box 400 (303) 563-4566. Cheryl Clay, Director - provides comprehensive early childhood development services to 95 children & their families in the reservation area. Tribal council. Southern Ute Agency.

UTE MOUNTAIN RESERVATION
Ute Mountain Ute Tribal Council
General Delivery • Towaoc, CO 81334
(970) 565-3751 Fax 565-7412
Ernest House, Chairperson
Tribe: Ute Mountain Ute. *In residence*: 1,600. *Area*: 590,000 acres. Located in Colorado, New Mexico, and Utah. Ute Mountain Field Office.

CONNECTICUT

GOLDEN HILL INDIAN RESERVATION
Trumbull, CT 06611
(203) 377-4410; (207) 738-2051
Big Eagle (Aurelius H. Piper, Sr.), Tribal Chief
Quiet Hawk (Aurelius H. Piper, Jr.), Council Chief
Tribe served: Pequonock Indians. *In residence*: 5. *Population served*: 80. *Area*: 1/4 acre, 1 house; 107 acres in Colchester, CT. *Program*: Sweatlodge; White Buffalo Society. *Publications*: Quarter Acre of Heartache, and Red Man in Red Square. Eastern Regional Office.

MASHANTUCKET PEQUOT TRIBAL NATION
P.O. Box 3060, 1 Matts Path
Mashantucket, CT 06338
(860) 396-6500 Fax 396-6540
Michael J. Thomas, Chairperson
Kenneth M. Reels, Vice-Chairperson
Richard A. (Skip) Hayward, Vice-Chairperson
John Guevremont, Chief Operation Officer
Pedro Johnson, Treasurer; Gary Carter, Secretary
Terry Bell, Director-PR & Cultural Resources
Charlene Jones, Tribal Librarian
Bruce MacDonald, *Pequot Times* Editor
Tribe served: Mashantucket Pequot. *Area*: 1,220 acres (trust). *Tribal council members*: Jo-Ann Isaac, Richard F. Sebastian, Michael Thomas. *Activity*: Foxwoods Resort & Casino; Library; Museum & Research Center being built and will open mid 1998. *Publications*: The Pequot Times, monthly tribal newspaper; and sells the book, "The Pequots in Southern New England: The Fall and Rise of an American Indian Nation." Eastern Regional Office.

MOHEGAN INDIAN TRIBE
5 Crow Hill Rd. • Uncasville, CT 06382
(860) 862-6100 Fax 862-6162
Mark F. Brown, Chairperson
Peter J. Schultz, Vice Chairperson
Ralph Sturges, Chief
E-mail: ctodd@moheganmail.com
Website: www.mohegan.nsn.us
Recognized as a tribe by the Federal Government in March of 1994. The Tribe has bought 244 acres for a reservation on the Thames River in Uncasville (land taken into Trust). The Tribal government and Mohegan Sun Casino are located on this reservation. The state has returned the 116-acre Fort Shantok State Park to the tribe for which the tribe paid $3 million. Shantok, which overlooks the Thames River, is the site of the Mohegans' only active burial ground. *Special program*: Wigwam Festival (3rd weekend in August). *Publication*: NiYaYo (newspaper) is available free of charge by subscription. Books are available for purchase through our web site. Eastern Regional Office.

SCHAGHTICOKE TRIBAL NATION OF KENT, INC.
Schaghticoke Tribal Council
Schaghticoke Rd., Kent, CT 06757
(860) 459-2531 Fax 459-2535
Richard Velky, Chairperson
Paulette S. Crone-Morange, Vice Chair
Tribe: Schaghticoke. *In residence*: 300. *Area*: 400 acres. Located in Kent, CT, Litchfield Co. Eastern Area Office.

FLORIDA

BIG CYPRESS RESERVATION
6075 Stirling Rd. • Hollywood, FL 33024
David Cypress, Big Cypress Representative
Tribe: Miccosukee Seminole. In residence: 450. Area: 42,700. Located in southern Florida.

BRIGHTON RESERVATION
6075 Stirling Rd. • Hollywood, FL 33024
Roger Smith, Brighton Representative
Tribe: Cow Creek. *In residence*: 440. *Area*: 35,800 acres located in south-central Florida.

MICCOSUKEE INDIAN TRIBE
Miccosukee Business Committee
Box 440021, Tamiami Sta. • Miami, FL 33144
(305) 223-8380/3 Fax 223-1011
Billy Cypress, Chairperson
Tribe served: Miccosukee-Creek. *Tribe*: Creek. *In residence*: 495. *Area*: 333 acres located on Tamiami Trail, 40 miles west of Miami. *Activities*: Ownes and operates Miccosukee Indian Gaming in Miami. Business Committee. Head Start Program. Eastern Regional Office.

SEMINOLE RESERVATION
6300 Stirling Rd. • Hollywood, FL 33024
(800) 683-7800; (954) 966-6300 Fax 967-3486
Mitchell Cypress, Chairperson & Vice-President
Moses B. Osceola, Jr., President & Vice-Chairperson
Max B. Osceola, Hollywood Representative
E-mail: tribune@semtribe.com
Website: www.semtribe.com
Tribe: Seminole. *In residence*: 500. *Population served*: 1,450. *Area*: 480 acres. Located on U.S. 441, in the Fort Lauderdale—Miami area. *Local attractions*: Seminole Indian Village featuring typical village life and customs, native arts and crafts, native animal exhibits. *Activities*: Indian ceremonials held in mid-July. Ownes and operated the Seminole Casinos in Brighton, Immokalee, Hollywood, Coconut Creek & Tampa. Museum & Library. *Publication*: "Seminole Tribune," tribal newspaper. Tribal council. Head Start Program. Seminole Agency.

IDAHO

COEUR D'ALENE RESERVATION
Coeur D'Alene Tribal Council
850 A St., P.O. Box 408 • Plummer, ID 83851
(208) 686-1800 Fax 686-1182
Ernest L. Stensgar, Chairperson
Tribe: Coeur D'Alene (Skitswish). Enrolled members: 1,250. *In residence*: 850. *Area*: 69,300 acres located

about 33 miles south of Coeur D'Alene, Idaho.
Tribal Council. Coeur d'Alene Tribe BIA Field Office.

FORT HALL RESERVATION
Fort Hall Business Council
P.O. Box 306 • Fort Hall, ID 83203
(208) 238-3700 Fax 237-0797
Lionel Boyer, Chairperson
Tribes: Shoshone-Bannock. *In residence*: 4,000. *Area*: 523,917 acres. Located near Pocatello, Idaho, east and south of the Snake River. *Local attractions*: Annual Shoshone-Bannock Indian Festival; Trading Post; Museum & Library; Fishing & Hunting in the "Bottoms area of Reservation; High Stakes Bingo; American Falls. Head Start Program. Fort Hall Agency.

KOOTENAI RESERVATION
Kootenai Tribal Council
P.O. Box 1269 • Bonners Ferry, ID 83805
(208) 267-3519 Fax 267-2960
Velma Bahe, Chairperson
Tribe: Kootenai. *In residence*: 150. *Area*: 2,680 acres. Located in Boundary County, near Mirror Lake and the Canadian border. Tribal Council. Northern Idaho Agency.

NEZ PERCE RESERVATION
Nez Perce Tribal Executive Committee
P.O. Box 305 • Lapwai, ID 83540
(208) 843-2253 Fax 843-7354
Anthony Johnson, Chairperson
Tribe: Nez Perce. *In residence*: 2,200. *Area*: 92,685 acres located a few miles from the city of Lewiston in Nez Perce, Lewis, Clearwater & Idaho Counties. *Activities*: Owns & operates the Nez Perze Tribal Gaming Enterprise which operates two casinos, the Clearwater River Casino in Lewiston, & It'Se-Ye-Ye Bingo & Casino in Kamiah. Head Start. Northern Idaho Agency.

NORTHWESTERN BAND OF SHOSHONI NATION
427 N. Main, Suite 101 • Blackfoot, ID 83204
(208) 478-5712 Fax 478-5713
Gwen Davis, Chairperson
Tribe served: Shoshoni. Located in Iowa and Utah. Tribal council. Fort Hall Agency.

INDIANA

INDIANA MIAMI COUNCIL
641 Buchanan St., Huntington, IN 46750
Not yet federally recognized as of date of publication.

MIAMI NATION OF INDIANS OF INDIANA COUNCIL
P.O. Box 41, Peru, IN 46970 (317) 473-9631
Not yet federally recognized as of date of publication.

UPPER KISPOKO BAND OF SHAWNEE NATION
Kokomo, IN
Not yet federally recognized as of date of publication.

IOWA

OMAHA RESERVATION
Omaha Tribal Council
P.O. Box 368 • Macy, NE 68039
(402) 837-5391 Fax 878-2943
Doran L. Morris, Chairperson
Tribe: Omaha. Located in Iowa & Nebraska. Winnebago Agency. See listing under Nebraska.

SAC & FOX TRIBE OF THE MISSISSIPPI IN IOWA
349 Meskwaki Rd. • Tama, IA 52339
(515) 484-4678 Fax 484-5424
Talbert Davenport, Chairperson
Tribe served: Sac & Fox. *Population served*: 700. *Area*: 10 acres. Midwest Regional Office.

WINNEBAGO RESERVATION
Winnebago Tribal Council
P.O. Box 687 • Winnebago, NE 68071
(402) 878-2272 Fax 878-2963
John Blackhawk, Chairperson
Website: winnebagotribe.com
Tribe: Winnebago. Located in Nebraska and Iowa (off-reservation lands in Iowa.) Winnebago Agency. See listing under Nebraska.

KANSAS

IOWA RESERVATION
Iowa Tribe of Kans. & Neb. Executive Committee
2340 - 330th St. • White Cloud, KS 66094
(785) 595-3258 Fax 595-6610
  Louis DeRoin, Chairperson
Tribe: Iowa. *In residence*: 310. Located in Kansas and
Nebraska. Tribal Council. (See listing under Nebraska.)
Horton Field Office.

KICKAPOO RESERVATION
Kickapoo of Kansas Tribal Council
P.O. Box 271 • Horton, KS 66439
(785) 486-2131 Fax 486-2801
  Nancy Bear, Chairperson
Tribe served: Kickapoo. *Population served*: 600.
Head Start Program. Horton Field Office.

PRAIRIE BAND POTAWATOMI RESERVATION
Prairie Band Potawatomi Tribal Council
16281 Q Road • Mayetta, KS 66509
(785) 966-4000 Fax 966-4002
  Badger Wahwasuck, Chairperson
Tribe served: Prairie Brand Potawatomi.
Population served: 1,350. Horton Field Office.

SAC & FOX NATION OF MISSOURI
Sac & Fox of Missouri Tribal Council
305 N. Main St. • Reserve, KS 66434
(785) 742-7471 Fax 742-3785
  Sandra Keo, Chairperson
Tribe served: Sac & Fox of Kansas & Nebraska.
Activities: Pow-wow, last week in August. Tribal Museum.
Horton Field Office.

SHAWNEE RESERVE
Shawnee Tribe Business Committee
P.O. Box 106 • DeSoto, KS 66018
P.O. Box 189 • Miami, OK 74355
(918) 542-2441 Fax 542-2922
  Website: shawnee-tribe.org
  E-mail: shawneetribe@neok.com
  Ron Sparkman, Chairperson
  Barry Kerr, Vice Chairperson
  Georgie Honey, Treasurer
  Shirley Staubus, Secretary
Committee members: Carolyn Smith, Roberta Coombs,
Barbara Wisdom, Tony Booth, Tommie Buchfink, Kenny
Daugherty, Roy Baldridge. *Tribe*: Shawnee. *Total acre-
age*: 210,000 acres In Oklahoma & Kansas. *Programs*:
Numerous social service programs & community activi-
ties; annual pow-wow in August or September each year.
Maintains a small library for historial and genealogical
research. *Publication*: Shawnee Journal, quarterly news-
letter. Miami Field Office.

LOUISIANA

CHITIMACHA TRIBE OF LOUISIANA
Chitimacha Tribal Council
P.O. Box 661 • Charenton, LA 70523
(337) 923-4973 Fax 923-6848
  Alton D. LeBlanc, Jr., Chairperson
  E-mail: aleblanc@chitimacha.gov
Tribe: Chitimacha. *In residence*: 310. *Area*: 283 acres.
Activities: Chitimacha Tribal Fair (Fourth of July Week-
end). *Publication*: The Chitimacha People, by Herbert
T. Hoover (part of the tribal series.) Museum and library.
Eastern Regional Office.

COUSHATTA INDIAN TRIBE
Coushatta Tribal Council
P.O. Box 818 • Elton, LA 70532
(337) 584-2261 Fax 584-2998
  Lovelin Poncho, Chairperson
Tribe: Coushatta. *In residence*: 295.
Eastern Regional Office.

UNITED HOUMA NATION
20986 Hwy. 1 • Golden Meadow, LA 70357
(504) 475-6640
  Brenda Dardar Robichaux, Chairperson
Tribe: Houma. *Members*: 15,000. Located in southeast
Louisiana, including Terrebonne, Lafourche, St. Mary's,
and Jefferson Parishes. No corporate land base.

JENA BAND OF CHOCTAW INDIANS
P.O. Box 14 • Jena, LA 71342
(318) 992-2717 Fax 992-8244
  Christine Norris, Prinicpal Chief
Eastern Regional Office

TUNICA-BILOXI INDIAN TRIBE
151 Melacon Dr., Box 1589 • Marksville, LA 71351
(318) 253-9767 Fax 253-9791
  Earl J. Barbry, Sr., Chairperson
  E-mail: pat_foster@tunica.org
  Website: www.tunica.org
Tribe served: Tunica-Biloxi. Eastern Area Office.

MAINE

AROOSTOOK BAND OF MICMACS
P.O. Box 772 • Presque Island, ME 04769
(207) 764-1972 Fax 764-7667
  William Phillips, Chief
Tribe served: Micmac. *Population served*: 485. The total Micmac population is approximately 15,000, most of
whom live in Canada. Between 550 and 700 Micmacs
live in Maine and are the most traditional Indians in the
eastern U.S. Eastern Regional Office.

HOULTON BAND OF MALISEET INDIANS
88 Bell Rd. • Littleton, ME 04730
(207) 532-4273 Fax 532-2660
  Brenda Commander, Tribal Chief
  E-mail: tribal-chief@maliseets.com
Tribe served: Maliseet. *Population served*: 300.
Councilmembers: Tony Tomah, Gloria Tomah, Suzanne
Desiderio, Susanna Wright, David Lindsay, Linda
Raymond. Activities: Maliseet Recognition Day, Octo-
ber 10. Eastern Regional Office.

PASSAMAQUODDY TRIBE
INDIAN TOWNSHIP RESERVATION
Indian Township Passamaquoddy Tribal Council
P.O. Box 301 • Princeton, ME 04668
(207) 796-2301 Fax 796-5256
  Robert Newell, Tribal Governor
Website: www.peopleofthedawn.com
Tribe: Passamaquoddy. *In residence*: 395. *Area*: 18,000
acres. Indian communities at Peter Dana Point and The
Strip. Eastern Regional Office.

PENOBSCOT NATION RESERVATION
Penobscot Indian Nation Tribal Council
Community Bldg. - Indian Island
6 River Rd. • Indian Island, ME 04468
(207) 827-7776 Fax 827-6042
  Barry Dana, Tribal Governor
  E-mail: bkimball@penobscotnation.org
Tribe: Penobscot. *In residence*: 1,150. *Area*: 4,400 acres
located on Indian Island. Eastern Regional Office.

PLEASANT POINT RESERVATION
Pleasant Point Passamaquoddy Tribal Council
P.O. Box 343 • Perry, ME 04667
(207) 853-2600 Fax 853-6039
  Melvin Francis, Tribal Governor
  E-mail: rickd@wabanaki.com
  Website: www.wabanaki.com
Tribe served: Passamaquoddy. *In residence*: 880. En-
rollment: 1,850. *Area*: 141,000 acres. Council Members:
Margaret Dana, Fred Francis, Louis Paul, Peter Clem-
ent, George Bassett, Lorene Homan. *Activities*: Annual
Indian Day Ceremonies-2nd weekend in Aug; operates
Beatrice Rafferty School & Waponahki Museum & Re-
source Center. Publications. Eastern Regional Office.

MASSACHUSETTS

WAMPANOAG RESERVATION
Wampanoag Tribe of Gay Head (Aquinnah)
20 Black Brook Rd. • Aquinnah, MA 02535
(508) 645-9265 Fax 645-3790
  Beverly M. Wright, Chairperson
  E-Mail: chairprs@wampanoagtribe.net
  Website: www.wampanoagtribe.net
Tribe: Aquinnah Wampanoag. *In residence*: 260; off is-
land residence, 540. *Area*: 500 acres on Island of
Martha's Vineyard.. Eastern Area Office.

MICHIGAN

BAY MILLS INDIAN COMMUNITY OF MICHIGAN
Bay Mills Executive Council
12140 W. Lakeshore Dr. • Brimley, MI 49715
(906) 248-3241 Fax 248-3283
  Jeffrey D. Parker, Chairperson
  Website: www.4baymills.com
Tribe: Chippewa (Bay Mills and Sault Ste. Marie Bands.)
In residence: 475. *Area*: 2,200 acres. *Activities*: Owns
and operates the Bay Mills Resort and Casino, and the
Kings Club Casino, both in Brimley, Michigan. Execu-
tive Council. Michigan Field Office.

GRAND TRAVERSE BAND OF
OTTAWA & CHIPPEWA INDIANS
Peshawbestown Community Center
2605 N.W. Bayshore Dr. • Suttons Bay, MI 49682
(231) 271-3538 Fax 271-4861
  E-mail: gbennett@gtbindians.com
  Robert Kewaygoshkum, Chairperson
Tribes served: Ottawa (mostly), few Chippewa. *Elected
officials*: Jaime Barrientoz, Lou Scott & John Concannon,
council members. *Area*: 1,400 acres. *Activities*: Annual
"Peshawbestown Pow-Wow" held 3rd weekend in August; Health Fair Friday before pow-wow; active Elder's
group; annual Education Banquet; Fall Festival; operates tribal school & library. *Activities*: Owns and operates the Leelanau Sands Casino Resort in Suttons Bay,
and Turtle Creek Casino in Williamsburg, Michigan.
Publication: Monthly newsletter. Michigan Field Office.

HANNAHVILLE INDIAN
COMMUNITY OF MICHIGAN
N14911 Hannahville B1 Rd. • Wilson, MI 49896
(906) 466-2934 Fax 466-2933
  Kenneth Meshigaud, Chairperson
Tribe served: Potawatomi. *In residence*: 375. *Area*: 2,850
acres. Tribal Council. Michigan Field Office.

HURON POTAWATOMI, INC.
2221 - 1.5 Mile Rd. • Fulton, MI 49502
(616) 729-5151 Fax 729-5920
  Laura Spurr, Chairperson
Tribe: Nottawaseppi Band of Huron Potawatomi. *In resi-
dence*: 600. *Area*: 120 acres. Located in Calhoun
County's Athens Township. *Activities*: Casino being built.
Michigan Field Office.

L'ANSE RESERVATION
KEWEENAW BAY INDIAN
COMMUNITY OF MICHIGAN
107 Beartown Rd. • Baraga, MI 49908
(906) 353-6623 Fax 353-7540
  Richard Shalifoe, President
  Website: www.ojibwa.com
Tribe: Chippewa (Keewenah Bay, L'Anse, and
Ontonagon Bands.) *In residence*: 950. *Area*: 10,000
acres. *Activities*: Owns and operates the Ojibwa Ca-
sino Resort and Big Bucks Bingo, and Ojibwa Casino
Marquette. Michigan Field Office.

LAC VIEUX DESERT BAND
OF LAKE SUPERIOR CHIPPEWA
P.O. Box 249 - Choate Rd. • Watersmeet, MI 49969
(906) 358-4577 Fax 358-4785
  Richard McGeshick, Sr., Chairperson
  Website: www.lacvieuxdesert.com
Tribe: Chippewa (Lac Vieux Desert Band). *Activities*:
Owns and operates the Lac Vieux Desert Casino Re-
sort Complex. Library. Michigan Field Office.

LITTLE RIVER BAND OF OTTAWA INDIANS
375 River St. • Manistee, MI 49660-2729
(616) 723-8288 Fax 723-8761
  Bob Guenthardt, Chairperson
Tribe: Ottawa. Michigan Field Office. *Activities*:
Owns and operates the Little River Casino.

LITTLE TRAVERSE BAY BANDS
OF ODAWA INDIANS
7500 Odawa Cir. • Harbor Springs, MI 49740
(231) 242-1400 Fax 242-1414
  Frank D. Ettawageshik, Chairperson
  E-mail: chairman@tbbodawa.org
  Website: www.tbbodawa.org
Tribe: Odawa. *Area*: 336 square miles. Councilors:
Beatrice A. Law, Janet Shomin & Rita Shananaquet.
Activities: Technology training; Annual Odawa Home

Coming Pow Wow in August. *Activities*: Owns and operates the Victories Casino and Hotel in Petoskey, Michigan. *Publication*: Odawa Trails. Michigan Field Office.

MATCH-E-BE-NASH-SHE-WISH
BAND OF POTTAWATOMI INDIANS
1743 142nd Ave.
P.O. Box 218 • Dorr, MI 49323
(616) 681-8830 Fax 681-8836
David K. Sprague, Chairperson
Tribe: Pottawatomi. Michigan Field Office.

POKAGON BAND OF POTAWATOMI INDIANS
P.O. Box 180, 901 Spruce St. • Dowagiac, MI 49047
(616) 782-8998 Fax 782-6882
John Miller, Chairperson
Tribe: Potawatomi. Michigan Field Office.

SAGINAW-CHIPPEWA INDIAN TRIBE
ISABELLA RESERVATION
7070 E. Broadway • Mt. Pleasant, MI 48858
(517) 775-4000 Fax 772-3508
Audrey Falcon, Chief
Website: www.sagchip.org/government/index.htm
Tribe: Saginaw-Chippewa. *In residence*: 450. *Area*: 1,125 acres. *Activities*: Owns and operates the Soaring Eagle Casino and Bingo Hall. Michigan Field Office.

SAULT STE. MARIE TRIBE OF CHIPPEWA INDIANS
523 Ashmun St., Sault Ste. Marie, MI 49783
(906) 635-6050 Fax 635-4969
Bernard Bouschor, Chairperson
Website: www.sootribe.org
Tribe served: Sault Ste. Marie Chippewa. *Reservations served*: St. Ignace, Manistique, Munising, Michigan. *In residence*: 2,500. *Area*: 242 acres. *Activities*: Tribal powwows (two each summer, July 4th (Sault Ste. Marie), and first week in August (St. Ignace.) Owns and operates the Kewadin Casinos in Sault Ste. Marie, St. Ignace, Manistique, Christmas and Hessel, Michigan *Publication*: Nisasotowen, Tribal newspaper. Michigan Field Office.

MINNESOTA

BOIS FORTE RESERVATION
Bois Forte Tribal Business Committee
P.O. Box 16 • Nett Lake, MN 55772
(218) 757-3261 Fax 757-3312
Gary W. Donald, Chairperson
Tribe served: Ojibwe (Chippewa-Deer Creek). *In residence*: 1,250. *Area*: 41,750 acres. Head Start Program. Component reservation of Minnesota Chippewa Tribe. Minnesota Agency.

FOND DU LAC RESERVATION
Business Committee
105 University Rd. • Cloquet, MN 55720
(218) 879-4593 Fax 879-4146
Robert "Sonny" Peacock, Chairperson
Peter J. Defoe, Secretary/Treasurer
Tribe: Lake Superior Chippewa. *In residence*: 1,750. *Area*: 100,000 acres. *Activities*: Ni-mi-win pow wow; Mash-ka-wisen pow wow. Operates Fond du Lac Ojibway School (Library); operates Black Bear Casino & Hotel, and Fond-De-Luth Casino. Head Start Program. Component reservation of the Minnesota Chippewa Tribe. Minnesota Agency.

GRAND PORTAGE RESERVATION
Business Committee
P.O. Box 428 • Grand Portage, MN 55605
(218) 475-2277 Fax 475-2284
Norman DesChampe, Chairperson
Tribe: Ojibwe (Chippewa). *In residence*: 325. *Area*: 43,836 acres located near Lake Superior, adjacent to the Canadian border. *Activities*: Operates hotel, bingo & casino facility. Head Start Program. Component reservation of Minnesota Ojibwe (Chippewa) Tribe. Minnesota Agency.

LEECH LAKE RESERVATION
Business Committee
Route 3, Box 100 • Cass Lake, MN 56633
(218) 335-8200 Fax 335-8309
Eli O. Hunt, Chairperson
Linda Johnston, Secreaty/Treasurer
Tribe served: Minnesota Ojibwe (Mississippi & Pillanger Bands.) *In residence*: 5,200. *Area*: 27,760 acres. *Tribal representatives*: Pete White, District I; Lymon Losh, District II; Richard Robinson, Jr., District III. *Activities*: Five annual pow-wows: Spring, Fourth of July, Labor Day, Veterans Day, and Winter; operates Chief Bug-O-Nay-Ge-Shig School & Leech Lake Tribal College; operates The Palace Bingo & Casino, and Northern Lights Casino & Bingo Hall. Head Start Program. *Publication*: Monthly newspaper titled, "De-Bah-Ji-Mon"; Leech Lake Reservation Fact Sheet. Component reservation of Minnesota Chippewa Tribe. Minnesota Agency.

LOWER SIOUX INDIAN COMMUNITY OF MN
Lower Sioux Indian Community Council
RR 1, Box 308 • Morton, MN 56270
(507) 697-6185 Fax 637-4380
Roger Prescott, Chairperson
Tribe served: Mdewakanton Sioux. *In residence*: 230. *Area*: 1,750 acres. Midwest Regional Office.

MILLE LACS RESERVATION
Business Committee
43408 Oodena Dr. • Onamia, MN 56359
(320) 532-4181 ext. 7486 Fax 532-4209
Melanie A. Benjamin, Chief Executive
E-mail: louised@millelacsojibwe.nsn.us
Web site: www.millelacsojibwe.org/
Tribe served: Mille Lacs Band of Ojibwe (Chippewa). *In residence*: 950. *Area*: Covers a total of approximately 61,000 square acres in Mille Lacs, Pine, Crow Wing, and Atkin counties. About 3,500 acres are held in trust for the Bands, and the Band owns about 3,000 acres. *Tribal reps*: Marvin Bruneau and Harry Davis. *Special programs and activities*: Americorps Program; Annual Grand Celebration Powwow and Rodeo in Hinckley; Annual Powwow in Mille Lacs; Community Youth Services; Operates Grand Casino Mille Lacs, Grand Casino Hinckley and Bingo Hall; Head Start Program. Mille Lacs Indian Museum. Runs two schools: Nay Ah Shing Abinoojiiyag School, grades K-4; and The Nay Ah Shing Upper School, grades 5-12. Library located in the Nay Ah Shing Upper School. *Publications*: Ojibwe Inaajimowin, monthly band newspaper; Woodland Voice, quarterly newsletter; and Mille Lacs Progress, bi-annual newspaper. Component reservation of Minnesota Chippewa Tribe. Minnesota Agency.

MINNESOTA CHIPPEWA TRIBE
Tribal Executive Committee
P.O. Box 217 • Cass Lake, MN 56633
(218) 335-8581 Fax 335-6562
Peter J. Defoe, President
E-Mail: metpr@mail.paulbunyan.net
Tribe served: Ojibwe (Chippewa). *Reservations served*: Nett Lake, Fond du Lac, Grand Portage, Leech Lake, Mille Lacs, White Earth. Minnesota Agency.

PRAIRIE ISLAND INDIAN COMMUNITY
5636 Sturgeon Lake Rd. • Welch, MN 55089
(651) 385-2554 Fax 388-1576
Audrey Kohnen, President
Tribe served: Mdewakanton Sioux. *In residence*: 135. *Area*: 534 acres. *Activities*: Operates Treasure Island Casino & Bingo Hall. Midwest Regional Office.

RED LAKE BAND OF CHIPPEWA INDIANS
Red Lake Tribal Council
P.O. Box 550 • Red Lake, MN 56671
(218) 679-3341 Fax 679-3378
Bobby Whitefeather, Chairperson
Tribe served: Red Lake Band of Ojibwe (Chippewa). *In residence*: 4,850. *Area*: 564,364 acres located along lower Red Lake, 30 miles north of Bemidji, Minnesota. *Activities*: Operates three casinos. Head Start Program. Red Lake Agency.

SHAKOPEE MDEWAKANTON SIOUX COMMUNITY
2330 Sioux Trail, NW • Prior Lake, MN 55372
(612) 445-8900 Fax 445-8906
Stanley R. Crooks, Chairperson
E-mail: bcadmin@ccsmdc.org
Website: www.ccsmdc.org
Tribe served: Mdewakanton Sioux. *In residence*: 110. *Activity*: Operates Mystic Lake Casino & Bingo Hall. Midwest Regional Office.

UPPER SIOUX COMMUNITY OF MINNESOTA
Upper Sioux Board of Trustees
P.O. Box 147 • Granite Falls, MN 56241
(320) 564-2360 Fax 564-3264
Helen Blue-Redner, Chairperson
Tribe served: Dakota. *Elected officials*: Jeanette Marlow, Treasurer; L. Alan Olson, Secretary; Tom Ross, Board of Trustees, Member-At-Large. *Membership*: 414. *In residence*: 170. *Area*: 1,250 acres. *Activities*: Owns & operates Prairie's Edge Casino & Resort. Midwest Regional Office.

WHITE EARTH RESERVATION
Business Committee
P.O. Box 418 • White Earth, MN 56591
(218) 983-3285 Fax 983-3641
Erma Vizenor, Chairperson
Eugene McArthur, Jr., Anthony Wadena
& Irene Auginarish-Turney, District Reps
Web site: www.whiteearth.com
Tribe served: Ojibwe (Chippewa). *Population served*: 28,000. *Area*: 27,560 acres. *Activities*: Operates Shooting Star Casino in Mahnomen, Minnesota. Head Start Program. *Publication*: "Anishinaabeg Today," newsletter. Member of the six reservation Minnesota Chippewa Tribe. Minnesota Agency.

MISSISSIPPI

MISSISSIPPI BAND OF CHOCTAW INDIANS
Tribal Council of the Mississippi Band of Choctaws
P.O. Box 6010 • Choctaw, MS 39350
(601) 650-1500 Fax 656-1992
Phillip Martin, Tribal Chief
Tribe served: Mississippi Band of Choctaws. *Membership*: 6,000. *In residence*: 5,500. *Area*: 21,000 acres located in nine east-central Mississippi counties centering on eight distinct Indian communities. *Tribal services*: Education - operates six grammar schools, a middle school, and a high school; Adult Education Program; Health Care - tribe manages a 43 bed hospital; Choctaw Housing Authority - manages over 500 housing units. *Economic Activities and Resources*: Chahta Enterprise; Choctaw Electronics Enterprise; Choctaw Manufacturing Enterprise; Choctaw Greetings Enterprise; First American Printing & Direct Mail Enterprise; Choctaw Residential Center Enterprise; Choctaw Shopping Enterprise; Choctaw-Creek Technologies; Chata Development Co.; Choctaw Transit Authority; and Operates Choctaw Resort & Casino. Tribal enterprises employ 1,700 workers & generates over $60 million in annual sales. *Communication*: tribe operates local station WHTV. *Activities*: Annual Choctaw Indian Fair (July). Museum. Library. *Publications*: Choctaw Community News, monthly newspaper. Head Start Program. Choctaw Field Office.

MISSOURI

EASTERN SHAWNEE TRIBE OF OKLAHOMA
Eastern Shawnee Tribal Council
P.O. Box 350 • Seneca, MO 64865
(918) 666-2435 Fax 666-3325
Charles D. Enyart, Chief
Danny Captain, Second Chief
Glenna Wallace, Secretary
Betty Sullivan, Treasurer
Councilpersons: Shawn King, Cliff Carpenter, and Perry Hauser. *Tribe*: Eastern Shawnee. *In residence*: 400. *Area*: 210 acres. *Special activity*: Traditional Indian beading classes. Owns and operates Border Town Bingo & Casino. *Publication*: "Shooting Star," Tribal newsletter. Library. Miami Field Station.

MONTANA

BLACKFEET RESERVATION
Blackfeet Tribal Business Council
P.O. Box 850 • Browning, MT 59417
(406) 338-7276 Fax 338-7716
Earl Old Person, Chairperson
Tribe served: Blackfeet. *In residence*: 7,000. *Area*: 955,241 acres. Located west of Glacier National Park, south of the Canadian border. *Local attraction*: Museum of the Plains Indians. *Activities*: Annual Blackfeet Medi-

cine Lodge Ceremonial and Sun Dance (July.) Owns the Blackfeet National Bank. Head Start Program. Blackfeet Agency.

CROW INDIAN RESERVATION
Crow Tribal Council
P.O. Box 400 • Crow Agency, MT 59022
(406) 638-2601 Fax 638-2380
Clifford Birdinground, Chairperson
Tribe: Crow. *In residence*: 9,000 (enrolled). *Total acreage*: 2.1 million acres located in south eastern Montana within Big Horn County, 15 miles southeast of Hardin, Montana. Occupies a total of 408,444 acres of trust land. *Activities*: Annual Crow Fair and Rodeo Celebration, 3rd week-end in August; pow-wow at New Years; operates tribal college and library, "Little Bighorn College. *Local attraction*: Custer Battlefield National Monument and Museum. *Publication*: The Crow Briefs, monthly tribal newsbrief. *Head Start Program*: Crow Central Education Commission, P.O. Box 249 (406) 638-2697. Crow Agency.

FLATHEAD INDIAN RESERVATION
Tribal Council of the Confederated
Salish & Kootenai Tribes
P.O. Box 278 • Pablo, MT 59855
(406) 675-2700 Fax 675-2806
Fred Matt, Chairperson
E-Mail: csktadmn@ronan.net
Web site: http://www.ronan.net/~csktadmn
Tribe served: Confederated Salish & Kootenai. *In residence*: 3,500. *Area*: 1.316 million acres. *Activities*: 4th of July Celebration in Arlee, and the Standing Arrow Pow-wow in Elmo; owns and operates The Peoples Center Museum, the Salish & Kootenai College, and the Two Eagle River School. Head Start Program. Flathead Field Office.

FORT BELKNAP RESERVATION
Fort Belknap Community Council
RR 1, Box 66 • Harlem, MT 59526
(406) 353-2205 Fax 353-2886
Darrell Martin, President
Tribes: Gros Ventre & Assiniboine. *In residence*: 2,500. *Area*: 708,602 acres. Located in north central Montana, 35 miles east of Havre. *Council members*: Joseph B. Fox, Randall E. Wing, Ronald G. Speakthunder, William T. Main. *Activities*: Mid-Winter Fair (February); Milk River Indian Days (3rd weekend of July); Hays X-Mas Pow-wow; Hays Fair & Radio (July); Hays Pow-wow (July); Chief Joseph Celebration (October). Fort Belknap College (2-year instituion of higher education). *Publications*: Community newsletter; Circle Speaker (environmental newsletter); Hays newsletter (Hays community newsletter). Head Start Program. Fort Belknap Agency.

FORT PECK RESERVATION
Fort Peck Tribal Executive Board
P.O. Box 1027 • Poplar, MT 59255
(406) 768-5155 Fax 768-3405
Arlyn Headdress, Chairperson
Tribe: Assiniboine & Sioux. *In residence*: 5,500. *Area*: 981,144 acres. Loctaed 20 miles south of the Canadian border. Head Start Program. Fort Peck Agency.

NORTHERN CHEYENNE RESERVATION
Northern Cheyenee Tribal Council
P.O. Box 128 • Lame Deer, MT 59043
(406) 477-6284 Fax 477-8324
Jerri Small, President
Tribe served: Northern Cheyenne. *In residence*: 3,300. *Area*: 425,000 acres. Head Start Program. Northern Cheyenne Agency.

ROCKY BOY'S RESERVATION
Chippewa-Cree Business Committee
RR 1, Box 544 • Box Elder, MT 59521
(406) 395-4282 Fax 395-4497
Alvin Windy Boy, Chairperson
Tribes served: Chippewa & Cree. *Reservation served*: Rocky Boy's Reservation. *Population served*: 1,950. *Area*: 107,532 acres located in Bear Paw Mountains, north-central Montana. Head Start Program. Rocky Boy's Field Office.

NEBRASKA

IOWA RESERVATION
Tribe: Iowa. Located in Kansas & Nebraska.
See listing under Kansas.

OMAHA RESERVATION
Omaha Tribal Council
P.O. Box 368 • Macy, NE 68039
(402) 837-5391 Fax 837-5308
Elmer Blackbird, Chairperson
Tribe: Omaha. *In residence*: 1,500. *Area*: 27,700 acres. Located in Nebraska and Iowa. Head Start Program. Winnebago Agency.

PINE RIDGE RESERVATION
Tribe: Oglala Sioux. Located 60 miles east of the Black Hills, extending into Nebraska. See listing under South Dakota.

PONCA TRIBE OF NEBRASKA
P.O. Box 288 • Niobrara, NE 68760
(402) 857-3391 Fax 857-3736
Fred LeRoy, Chairperson
Located in Nebraska & South Dakota.
Winnebago Agency.

SAC & FOX NATION OF MISSOURI
Located in Nebraska & Kansas.
See listing under Kansas.

SANTEE SIOUX RESERVATION
Santee Sioux Tribal Council
Route 2 • Niobrara, NE 68760
(402) 857-2302 Fax 857-2307
Roger Trudell, Chairperson
Tribe served: Santee Sioux. *In residence*: 425. *Area*: 3,600 acres. Head Start Program. Winnebago Agency.

WINNEBAGO RESERVATION
Winnebago Tribal Council
P.O. Box 687 • Winnebago, NE 68071
(402) 878-2272 Fax 878-2963
John Blackhawk, Chairperson
Website: www.winnebagotribe.com
Tribe served: Winnebago. *In residence*: 1,100. *Area*: 27,000 acres located in Neb. & Iowa (off-reservation lands in Iowa.) Head Start Program. Winnebago Agency.

NEVADA

BATTLE MOUNTAIN RESERVATION
Battle Mountain Band Council
37 Mountain View Dr. #C
Battle Mountain, NV 89820
(775) 635-2004 Fax 635-8016
Stanford Knight, Chairperson
Tribe: Te-Moak Band of Western Shoshone. A constituent band of the Te-Moak Tribe of Western Shoshone Indians. *Area*: 700 acres. Eastern Nevada Agency.

CARSON INDIAN COLONY
Carson Community Council
2900 S. Curry St. • Carson City, NV 89703
(775) 883-6459
Daniel F. Bender, Chairperson
Tribe: Washoe. A component band of the Washoe Tribe. *Area*: 150 acres. Western Nevada Agency.

DRESSLERVILLE INDIAN COLONY
Dresslerville Community Council
c/o Washoe Tribe, 919 Hwy. 395 South
Gardnerville, NV 89410
(775) 883-1446 Fax 265-6240
Anthony Smokey, Chairperson
Tribe: Washoe. A component band of the Washoe Tribe. *Area*: 40 acres. Western Nevada Agency.

DUCK VALLEY RESERVATION
Shoshone Paiute Business Council
P.O. Box 219 • Owyhee, NV 89832
(775) 757-3161 Fax 757-2219
James Paiva, Chairperson
Tribes: Shoshone-Paiute. *In residence*: 1,100. *Area*: 145,000 acres. Located in Nevada and Idaho. Eastern Nevada Agency.

DUCKWATER RESERVATION
Duckwater Shoshone Tribal Council
P.O. Box 140068 • Duckwater, NV 89314
(775) 863-0227 Fax 863-0301
Henry Michael Blackeye, Jr., Chairperson
E-mail: mike@duckwater.org
Website: www.duckwater.org
Tribe: Shoshone. *In residence*: 150. *Area*: 800 acres. Activities: Duckwater Festival; operates Dickwater Shoshone Elementary School (K-8th grade). Eastern Nevada Field Office.

ELKO BAND COUNCIL
511 Sunset St. • Elko, NV 89803
(775) 738-8889 Fax 753-5439
Fermina Stevens, Chairperson
Tribe: Te-Moak Band of Western Shoshone.
Area: 15,000 acres. Business Council.
Eastern Nevada Field Office.

ELY COLONY TRIBAL COUNCIL
16 Shoshone Circle • Ely, NV 89301
(775) 289-3013 Fax 289-3156
Alfred Stanton, Chairperson
Tribe: Shoshone. *Population served*: 250.
Area: 111 acres. Eastern Nevada Field Office.

FALLON PAIUTE & SHOSHONE TRIBE
Fallon Business Council
8955 Mission Rd. • Fallon, NV 89406
(775) 423-6075 Fax 423-5202
Website: www.fpst.org
E-mail: chairman@fpst.org
Alvin Moyle, Chairperson
Len George, Vice Chairperson
Susan Willie, Secretary
Nevada Iverson, Treasurer
Council members: Rochanne Downs, Steven Frank, and Daniel Allen. *Tribes*: Paiute & Shoshone. *In residence*: 700. *Area*: 8,200 acres. *Activities*: Nevada Indian Days, rodeo & powwow, 3rd weekend in July. *Publication*: "Nuhmuh News," tribal newsletter. Western Nevada Agency.

FORT McDERMITT RESERVATION
Fort McDermitt Tribal Council
P.O. Box 457 • McDermitt, NV 89421
(775) 532-8259 Fax 532-8903
Dennis Smartt, Chairperson
Tribes: Shoshone and Paiute. *In residence*: 710. *Area*: 16,400 acres located in Nevada & Oregon. Western Nevada Agency.

FORT MOHAVE RESERVATION
Tribe: Mohave. Located in Arizona, California & Nevada. See listing under Arizona.

LAS VEGAS INDIAN COLONY
Las Vegas Tribal Council
One Paiute Dr. • Las Vegas, NV 89106
(702) 386-3926 Fax 383-4019
Curtis Anderson, Chairperson
Tribe: Paiute. *In residence*: 125. *Area*: 10 acres.
Southern Paiute Field Office.

LOVELOCK INDIAN COLONY
Lovelock Tribal Council
P.O. Box 878 • Lovelock, NV 89419
(775) 273-7861 Fax 273-1144
Allen W. Ambler, Chairperson
Tribe: Lovelock Paiute. *In residence*: 175. *Area*: 20 acres. *Publication*: Tribal newsletter. Western Nevada Agency.

MOAPA RIVER INDIAN RESERVATION
Moapa Business Council
P.O. Box 340 • Moapa, NV 89025
(702) 865-2787 Fax 865-2875
Eugene Tom, Interim Chairperson
Tribe: Moapa Band of Paiute Indians (Southern Paiute). *In residence*: 295. *Area*: 73,258 acres. Southern Paiute Field Office.

PYRAMID LAKE RESERVATION
Pyramid Lake Paiute Tribal Council
P.O. Box 256 • Nixon, NV 89424
(775) 574-1000 Fax 574-1008
Keith Alan Mandell Chairperson
Tribe: Paiute. *In residence*: 850. *Area*: 1,195,000 acres. Western Nevada Agency.

RENO-SPARKS INDIAN COLONY
Reno-Sparks Tribal Council
98 Colony Rd. • Reno, NV 89502
(775) 329-2936 Fax 359-9501
 Arlan Melendez, Chairperson
Tribes: Washoe & Paiute. *Population served*: 625.
Western Nevada Agency.

RUBY VALLEY (TE-MOAK) RESERVATION
Tribal Council of the Te-Moak Western
Shoshone Indians of Nevada
525 Sunset St. • Elko, NV 89801
(702) 738-9251 Fax 738-2345
 Elwood Mose, Chairperson
Tribe: Te-Moak Band of Western Shoshone. *Area*:
15,000 acres. Business Council. Eastern Nevada
Agency.

SOUTH FORK INDIAN COLONY
South Fork Band Council
HC 30, Box B-13 - Lee
Spring Creek, NV 89815
(775) 744-4273 Fax 744-4523
 Larson Bill, Chairperson
Tribe: Te-Moak Band of Western Shoshone. A constitu-
ent band of the Te-Moak Tribe of Western Shoshone
Indians. *Area*: 15,000 acres. Eastern Nevada Field Of-
fice.

STEWART INDIAN COLONY
Stewart Community Council
5352 Dat-So-La-Lee Way
Carson City, NV 89701
(775) 883-1446
 Jacqueline Steele, Chairperson
Tribe: Washoe. A component band of the Washoe Tribe.
Western Nevada Agency.

SUMMIT LAKE RESERVATION
Summit Lake Paiute Council
655 Anderson St. • Winnemucca, NV 89445
(775) 623-5151 Fax 623-0558
 Robyn Burdette, Chairperson
Tribe: Paiute. *Area*: 10,500 acres.
Western Nevada Agency.

TE-MOAK TRIBE OF WESTERN
SHOSHONE COUNCIL
525 Sunset St. • Elko, NV 89801
(775) 738-9251 Fax 738-2345
 Felix Ike, Chairperson
Tribe: Te-Moak Tribe of Western Shoshone. A constitu-
ent band of the Te-Moak Tribe of Western Shoshone
Indians. *Area*: 200 acres. Eastern Nevada Agency.

WALKER RIVER RESERVATION
Walker River Paiute Tribal Council
P.O. Box 220 • Schurz, NV 89427
(775) 773-2306 Fax 773-2585
 Robert W. Quintero, Chairperson
Tribe: Paiute. *In residence*: 1,100. *Area*: 320,000 acres.
in Schurz, Mineral County, and in Churchill and Lyon
Counties. *Activities*: Tribal health center (775) 773-2005.
Western Nevada Agency.

WASHOE TRIBE OF NEVADA & CALIFORNIA
Washoe Tribal Council
919 U.S. Hwy. 395 S.
Gardnerville, NV 89410
(775) 883-1446 Fax 265-6240
 A. Brian Wallace, Chairperson
 Lenora Kizer, Vice Chair
Tribe served: Washoe. *In residence*: 1,380. Total acre-
age: 4,300 acres; plus over 60,000 acres of ten
noncontiguous parcels and numerous public domain
allotments. *Colonies served*: Dresslerville, Woodfords,
Carson Colony, and Stewart Colony. *Activities*: Annual
Tribal Picnic. Library and Archives being established at
Stewart Colony; Washoe Cultural Center in progress at
Lake Tahoe. *Publication*: Washoe Newsletter. Western
Nevada Agency.

WELLS INDIAN COLONY
Wells Indian Colony Band Council
P.O. Box 809 • Wells, NV 89835
(775) 752-3045 Fax 752-2186
 Willie Johnny, Chairperson
Tribe: Te-Moak Tribe of Western Shoshone. A constitu-
ent band of the Te-Moak Tribe of Western Shoshone
Indians. Eastern Nevada Field Office.

WINNEMUCCA INDIAN COLONY
Winnemucca Colony Council
P.O. Box 1370 • Winnemucca, NV 89446
(775) 623-0888 (phone & fax)
 Allen W. Ambler, Chairperson
 Charlene F. Dressler, Vice-Chairperson
 Linda Ayer, Secretary
 Clorinda A. George, Treasurer
 Lovelle Brown, Councilperson
Tribe: Paiute. *In residence*: 110. *Area*: 360 acres.
Tribal Council. Western Nevada Agency.

YERRINGTON INDIAN COLONY
Yerrington Paiute Tribal Council
171 Campbell Lane • Yerington, NV 89447
(775) 463-3301 Fax 463-2416
 Elwood L. Emm, Jr., Chairperson
Tribe: Yerrington Paiute. *In residence*: 430. *Area*: 1,160
acres. *Council Members*: Linda Howard, Lawrence
Conway, Raynese Salas, Cecelia Emm, and Victor Sam.
Western Nevada Agency.

YOMBA RESERVATION
Yomba Tribal Council
HC61, Box 6275 • Austin, NV 89310
(775) 964-2463 Fax 964-2443
 James Birchum, Chairperson
Tribe: Shoshone. *In residence*: 135. *Area*: 4,700 acres.
Western Nevada Agency.

NEW MEXICO

PUEBLO OF ACOMA
Pueblo of Acoma Tribal Council
P.O. Box 309 • Acomita, NM 87034
(505) 552-6604 Fax 552-7204
 Cyrus J. Chino, Governor
Tribe: Acoma. *In residence*: 3,000. *Area*: 431,664 acres
located 50 miles west of Albuquerque. *Activities*: Annual Feast of San Estevan at Old Acoma on Sept. 2nd
of every year. Maintains small community library, Tourist Visitors Center which houses a small museum;
Acoma Community School. Head Start Program. *Publication*: Acoma: Pueblo in the Sky, by Ward Alan Minge.
Southern Pueblos Agency.

ANETH RESERVATION
Tribe: Navajo. Shiprock Agency.

BACA RESERVATION
Tribe: Navajo. Eastern Navajo Agency.

BECENTI RESERVATION
Tribe: Navajo. Eastern Navajo Agency.

BECLABITO RESERVATION
Tribe: Navajo. Shiprock Agency.

BREAD SPRINGS RESERVATION
Tribe: Navajo. Eastern Navajo Agency.

BURNHAM RESERVATION
Tribe: Navajo. Shiprock Agency.

CANONCITO RESERVATION
Tribe: Navajo. Eastern Navajo Agency.

CASAMERO LAKE RESERVATION
Tribe: Navajo. Eastern Navajo Agency.

CHEECHILGEETHO RESERVATION
Tribe: Navajo. Eastern Navajo Agency.

CHURCH ROCK RESERVATION
Tribe: Navajo. Eastern Navajo Agency.

PUEBLO OF COCHITI
Cochiti Pueblo Council
P.O. Box 70 • Cochiti, NM 87072
(505) 465-2244 Fax 465-1135
 Regis Pecos, Governor
Tribe: Pueblo. *In residence*: 975. *Area*: 28,000 acres
located in Sandoral County near U.S. 85 on the west
bank of the Rio Grande River. Southern Pueblos Agency.

CROWNPOINT RESERVATION
Tribe: Navajo. Eastern Navajo Agency.

CRYSTAL RIVER RESERVATION
Tribe: Navajo. Located in Arizona and New Mexico.
(See listing under Arizona.)

DALTON PASS RESERVATION
Tribe: Navajo. Eastern Navajo Agency.

FORT DEFIANCE RESERVATION
Tribe: Navajo. Located in Arizona and New Mexico.
See listing under Arizona.

HUERFANO RESERVATION
Tribe: Navajo. Eastern Navajo Agency.

PUEBLO OF ISLETA
Isleta Pueblo Council
P.O. Box 1270 • Isleta, NM 87022
(505) 869-3111 Fax 869-4236
 Alvino Lucero, Governor
Tribe: Pueblo. *In residence*: 3,500. *Area*: 209,000 acres.
Library. Health Center. Head Start Program. Southern
Pueblos Agency.

PUEBLO OF JEMEZ
Jemez Pueblo Council
P.O. Box 100 • Jemez, NM 87024
(505) 834-7359 Fax 834-7331
 Joe Cajero, Governor
Tribe: Pueblo. *In residence*: 2,000. *Area*: 88,500 acres
located 44 miles north of Albuquerque. Southern Pueb-
los Agency.

IYANBIT RESERVATION
Tribe: Navajo. Eastern Navajo Agency.

JICARILLA APACHE RESERVATION
Jicarilla Apache Tribal Council
P.O. Box 507 • Dulce, NM 87528
(505) 759-3242 Fax 759-3005
 Claudia J. Vigil-Muniz, President
Website: www.ausbcomp.com/redman/jicarilla.htm
Tribe: Jicarilla Apache. *In residence*: 2,600. *Area*:
742,303 acres located about two miles northwest of Al-
buquerque. Jicarilla Agency.

PUEBLO OF LAGUNA
Laguna Pueblo Council
P.O. Box 194 • Laguna, NM 87026
(505) 552-6654 Fax 552-6941
 Harry D. Early, Governor
Tribe: Pueblo. *In residence*: 4,250. *Area*: 420,000 acres
located 40 miles west of Albuquerque, on U.S. 66. Head
Start Program. Laguna Agency.

LAKE VALLEY RESERVATION
Tribe: Navajo. Eastern Navajo Agency.

LITTLE WATER RESERVATION
Tribe: Navajo. Eastern Navajo Agency.

MANUELITO RESERVATION
Tribe: Navajo. Eastern Navajo Agency.

MARIANO RESERVATION
Tribe: Navajo. Eastern Navajo Agency.

MESCALERO APACHE RESERVATION
Mescalero Apache Tribal Council
P.O. Box 227 • Mescalero, NM 88340
(505) 464-4494 Fax 464-9191
 Sara Misquez, President
Tribe: Mescalero Apache. *In residence*: 2,750. *Area*:
460,173 acres located 30 miles northeast of
Alamagordo, New Mexico. Head Start Program.
Mescalero Agency.

MEXICAN WATER RESERVATION
Tribe: Navajo. Located in AZ & Utah. Shiprock Agency.

NAGEEZI RESERVATION
Tribe: Navajo. Eastern Navajo Agency.

PUEBLO OF NAMBE
Nambe Pueblo Council
Route 1, Box 117-BB • Santa Fe, NM 87501
(505) 455-2036 Fax 455-2038
 David A. Perez, Governor
Tribe: Pueblo. *In residence*: 400. *Area*: 19,000 acres
located five miles east of Pojoaque, New Mexico, on
Highway 285. Northern Pueblos Agency.

NENAHNEZAD RESERVATION
Tribe: Navajo. Shiprock Agency.

OJO ENCINO RESERVATION
Tribe: Navajo. Eastern Navajo Agency.

PUEBLO OF PICURIS
Picuris Pueblo Council
P.O. Box 127 • Penasco, NM 87553
  (505) 587-2519 Fax 587-1071
  Clarence Chile, Governor
Tribe: Pueblo. *In residence*: 200. *Area*: 1,500 acres located east of the Rio Grande River, 20 miles south of Taos, New Mexico. Northern Pueblos Agency.

PINEDALE RESERVATION
Tribe: Navajo. Eastern Navajo Agency.

PUEBLO OF POJOAQUE
Pojoaque Pueblo Council
39 Camino del Rincon #1
Santa Fe, NM 87501
  (505) 455-2278 Fax 455-3363
  Jacob Viarrial, Governor
Tribe: Pueblo. *In residence*: 175. *Area*: 11,500 acres.
Activities: Annual Feast Day (December). Northern Pueblos Agency.

PUEBLO PLAINTADO RESERVATION
Tribe: Navajo. Eastern Navajo Agency.

PUERTOCITO (ALAMO) RESERVATION
Tribe: Navajo. Eastern Navajo Agency.

RAMAH NAVAJO RESERVATION
Ramah Navajo Chapter Council
Rte. 2, Box 13 • Ramah, NM 87321
  (505) 775-7130 Fax 775-3538
  Leo L. Pino, President
Tribe: Navajo. Ramah-Navajo Agency.

RED LAKE RESERVATION
Tribe: Navajo. Located in Arizona & New Mexico. Western Navajo Agency

RED MESA RESERVATION
Tribe: Navajo. Located in New Mexico, Arizona & Utah. Shiprock Agency.

RED ROCK RESERVATION
Tribe: Navajo. Located in Arizona & New Mexico. Shiprock Agency.

ROCK POINT RESERVATION
Tribe: Navajo. Shiprock Agency.

ROCK SPRINGS RESERVATION
Tribe: Navajo. Eastern Navajo Agency.

PUEBLO OF SAN FELIPE
San Felipe Pueblo Council
P.O. Box 4339 • San Felipe Pueblo, NM 87001
  (505) 867-3381 Fax 867-3383
  Lawrence Troncosa, Governor
Tribe: Pueblo. *In residence*: 2,200. *Area*: 49,000 acres located ten miles north of Bernalillo, off U.S. 85. Head Start Program. Southern Pueblos Agency.

PUEBLO OF SAN ILDEFONSO
San Ildefonso Tribal Council
Rte. 5, Box 315-A • Santa Fe, NM 87501
  (505) 455-2273 Fax 455-7351
  Perry Martinez, Governor
Tribe: San Ildefonso Tewa. *In residence*: 600. *Area*: 26,000 acres located 20 miles northwest of Santa Fe, off Highway 285. *Activities*: Annual Feast Day (January 23). Operates small museum and library. Northern Pueblos Agency.

PUEBLO OF SAN JUAN
San Juan Pueblo Council
P.O. Box 1099 • San Juan Pueblo, NM 87566
  (505) 852-4400 Fax 852-4820
  Wilfred Garcia, Governor
Tribe: Pueblo. *In residence:* 1,500. *Area*: 12,000 acres located five miles north of Espanola, near Highway 64. Northern Pueblos Agency.

PUEBLO OF SANDIA
Sandia Tribal Council
P.O. Box 6008 • Bernalillo, NM 87004
  (505) 867-3317 Fax 867-9235
  Stuwart Paisano, Governor
Tribe: Pueblo. *In residence*: 320. *Area*: 23,000 acres located 14 miles north of Albuquerque, on U.S. 85. Southern Pueblos Agency.

SANOSTEE RESERVATION
Tribe: Navajo. Shiprock Agency.

PUEBLO OF SANTA ANA
Santa Ana Pueblo Council
2 Dove Rd. • Bernalillo, NM 87004
  (505) 867-3301 Fax 867-3395
  Leonard Armijo, Governor
Tribe: Pueblo. *In residence*: 550. *Area*: 4,200 acres located near Jemez Creek, eight miles from Bernalillo. *Activities*: Owns & operates Santa Ana Star Casino, and Santa Ana Golf Course. Southern Pueblos Agency.

PUEBLO OF SANTA CLARA
Santa Clara Pueblo Council
P.O. Box 580 • Espanola, NM 87532
  (505) 753-7330 Fax 753-5375
  Denny Gutierrez, Governor
Tribe: Santa Clara Pueblo. *In residence*: 1,350. *Area*: 45,744 acres located 25 miles northwest of Santa Fe. *Activities*: Annual Feasts, June & August. Operates small library. *Publication*: Monthly newsletter. Northern Pueblos Agency.

PUEBLO OF SANTO DOMINGO
Santo Domingo Pueblo Council
P.O. Box 99 • Santo Domingo Pueblo, NM 87052
  (505) 465-2214 Fax 465-2688
  Ramon Garcia, Governor
Tribe: Pueblo. *In residence*: 2,750. *Area*: 70,000 acres located in Sandoval County, ten miles east of the Rio Grande River. Head Start Program. So Pueblos Agency.

SHEEP SPRINGS RESERVATION
Tribe: Navajo. Shiprock Agency.

SHIPROCK RESERVATION
Tribe: Navajo. c/o Shiprock Agency.

SMITH LAKE RESERVATION
Tribe: Navajo. Eastern Navajo Agency.

STANDING ROCK RESERVATION
Tribe: Navajo. Eastern Navajo Agency.

SWEETWATER RESERVATION
Tribe: Navajo. Shiprock Agency.

PUEBLO OF TAOS
Taos Pueblo Council
P.O. Box 1846 • Taos, NM 87571
  (505) 758-9593 Fax 758-4604
  Nelson Cordova, Governor
Tribe: Pueblo. *In residence*: 1,750. *Area*: 75,000 acres. Northern Pueblos Agency.

TEECNOSPOS RESERVATION
Tribe: Navajo. Located in Arizona, Utah and New Mexico. Shiprock Agency.

PUEBLO OF TESUQUE
Tesuque Pueblo Council
Rte. 5, Box 360-T • Santa Fe, NM 87501
  (505) 983-2667 Fax 983-2331
  Charlie Dorame, Governor
Tribe: Pueblo. *In residence*: 325. *Area*: 17,000 acres located ten miles north of Santa Fe. Tribal Council. Northern Pueblos Agency.

THOREAU RESERVATION
Tribe: Navajo. Eastern Navajo Agency.

TORREON & STAR LAKE RESERVATION
Tribe: Navajo. Eastern Navajo Agency.

TSAYATOH RESERVATION
Tribe: Navajo. Eastern Navajo Agency.

TSAILE-WHEATFIELDS RESERVATION
Tribe: Navajo. Located in Arizona and New Mexico. See listing under Arizona.

TWO GREY HILLS RESERVATION
Tribe: Navajo. Shiprock Agency.

UPPER FRUITLAND RESERVATION
Tribe: Navajo. Shiprock Agency.

UTE MOUNTAIN RESERVATION
Tribe: Ute. Located in Colorado, Utah and New Mexico. (See listing under Colorado.)

WHITE ROCK RESERVATION
Tribe: Navajo. Eastern Navajo Agency.

WHITEHORSE LAKE RESERVATION
Tribe: Navajo. Eastern Navajo Agency.

PUEBLO OF ZIA
Zia Pueblo Tribal Council
135 Capitol Square Dr.
Zia Pueblo, NM 87053
  (505) 867-3304 Fax 867-3308
  William Toribio, Governor
Tribe: Zia Pueblo. *In residence*: 650. *Area*: 112,000 acres located 16 miles northwest of Bernalillo. Cultural Center/Library. Southern Pueblos Agency.

PUEBLO OF ZUNI
Zuni Pueblo Tribal Council
P.O. Box 339 • Zuni, NM 87327
  (505) 782-4481 Fax 782-2700
  Malcolm Bowekaty, Governor
Tribe: Zuni Pueblo. *In residence*: 7,450. *Area*: 407,247 acres located 40 miles south of Gallup, New Mexico, on the Arizona border. *Population served*: 7,100. Head Start Program. Zuni Agency.

NEW YORK

SENECA NATION OF INDIANS
Seneca Nation Tribal Council
1490 Rte. 438 • Irving, New York 14081
  (716) 532-4900 Fax 532-6272
  Rickey L. Armstrong, Sr., President
  Website: www.sni.org; www.honorindiantreaties.org
Tribe served: Seneca. *Reservations served*: Allegany & Cattaraugus. *Population served*: 6,500. *In residence*: 3,500. *Area*: 30,469 acres located along Route 438. *Activities*: Seneca Fall Festival (2nd weekend in September); Allegany Indian Fair (late August); Spring and Christmas Bazaars. Operates Seneca-Iroquois National Museum in Salamanca; Seneca Nation Library (branches for both Allegany & Cattaraugus Reservation); Seneca Nation Bingo at Irving; and Seneca Sports Arena located at the Cattaraugus Reservation. *Publication*: Tribal Newsletter. Head Start Program. Museum & Library. New York Field Office.

CAYUGA INDIAN NATION
Cayuga Nation Tribal Council
P.O. Box 11 • Versailles, NY 14168
  (716) 532-4847 Fax 532-5417
  Vernon Isaac, Chief
Tribe: Cayuga. *In residence*: 110. Tribal Council. New York Field Office.

OIL SPRINGS CORNERS RESERVATION
P.O. Box 146 • Kill Buck, NY 14748-0040
Tribe: Seneca. *Area*: 640 acres. Located near Cuba Lake in Allegheny County. New York Field Office.

ONEIDA INDIAN NATION OF NEW YORK
Genessee St., Ames Plaza • Oneida, NY 13421
5218 Patrick Rd. • Verona, NY 13498
  (315) 361-7633 Fax 361-7619
  Council address: P.O. Box 1 • Vernon, NY 13476
  (315) 361-6300 Fax 361-6333
  Ray Halbritter, Nation Representative
  E-mail: sbarbano@oneida-nation.org
  Website: www.oneida-nation.net
Tribe: (Six Nations) Oneida. *In residence*: 1,100. *Area*: 32 acres. Located three miles south of the city of Oneida in Madison County in Central New York. *Programs*: Health Center; educational scholarship incentives; youth corps; elderly meals program; housing development. *Activities*: Operates the Turning Stone Casino in Verona, NY; Bingo Hall; Lacrosse Box; Pool/Recreation Center; Traditional ceremonies held in Council House. Museum-

Shako:wi Cultural Center located on territory open Tues-Sunday 9 am - 5 pm. Developing library. *Publication*: Oneida Nation Newsletter. New York Field Office.

ONONDAGA RESERVATION
Onondaga Nation Tribal Council
RR 1, Box 319-B • Nedrow, NY 13120
(315) 492-4210; Irving Powless, Jr., Chief
Tribes: Onondaga, Oneida and Cayuga. *In residence*: 1,500. *Area*: 7,300 acres. Located near Nedrow, six miles south of Syracuse. Tribal Council. New York Field Office.

POOSPATUCK RESERVATION
P.O. Box 86 • Mastic, NY 11950
(516) 281-6464
Tribe: Unkechauge Nation (Poospatuck). *In residence*: 100. *Area*: 60 acres. Located on Mastic River near Brookhaven, L.I., NY. Eastern Area Office.

ST. REGIS MOHAWK INDIAN RESERVATION
St. Regis Mohawk Council
Akwesasne Community Bldg.
412 State Rte. 37 • Akwesasne, NY 13655
(518) 358-2272 Fax 358-4519
Website: www.akwesasnemohawk.com
Paul O. Thompson, Chief
Tribe: St. Regis Mohawk. *In residence*: 6,500. *Area*: 14,640 acres located in Franklin County on Route 37. Straddles the Canadian border; portion lies within Quebec and Ontario. *Facilities*: Museum. Library; St. Regis Mohawk School; St. Regis Casino, a 50,000 sq. ft. facility. *Publication*: Kariwenhawi, monthly newsletter. New York Field Office.

TONAWANDA RESERVATION
Tonawanda Band of Senecas Council
7027 Meadville Rd. • Basom, NY 14013
(716) 542-4244 Fax 542-4244
Emerson Webster, Chief
Tribe: Tonawanda Band of Seneca Indians. *In residence*: 675. *Area*: 7,550 acres. Located on Route 267, near Batavia, NY. Council of Chiefs. New York Field Office.

TUSCARORA RESERVATION
Tuscarora Indian Nation
2006 Mt. Hope Rd. • Lewiston, NY 14092
(716) 297-3995 Fax 297-7355
Leo R. Henry, Chief (716) 622-7061
Arnold Hewitt, Chief ; Kenneth Patterson, Chief
Tribe: Tuscarora. *In residence*: 775. *Area*: 5,700 acres. Located in Niagara County near Sanborn and Lewiston on Upper Mountain Rd. New York Field Office. *Activities*: Tuscarora Field Day 2nd Saturday of July and Tuscarora Community Fair in October.

NORTH CAROLINA

EASTERN BAND OF CHEROKEE INDIANS
Eastern Band Cherokee Tribal Council
Qualla Boundary, P.O. Box 455
Cherokee, NC 28719
(828) 497-2771 Fax 497-7007
Mitchell Hicks, Chairperson
Leon Jones, Principal Chief
Website: www.cherokee-nc.com
Tribe: Eastern Band of Cherokee. *In residence*: 8,800. *Area*: 56,572 acres located 50 miles west of Asheville, North Carolina. *Activities*: Operates school and hospital. *Local attractions*: Replica of an Oconaluftee Indian Village; Museum of the Cherokee; Qualla Arts & Crafts Cooperative; Casino. *Special activity*: Annual Cherokee Fall Festival. Tribal Council. Cherokee Agency.

NORTH DAKOTA

FORT BERTHOLD RESERVATION
Three Affiliated Tribes Business Council
HC 3, Box 2 • New Town, ND 58763
(701) 627-4781 Fax 627-3805
Tex Hall, Chairperson
Tribes: Three Affiliated Tribes - Mandan, Hidatsa and Arikara. *In residence*: 4,000. *Area*: 980,000 acres. Located above Garrison Dam on the Missouri River, southwest of Minot, North Dakota. *Special activity*: Community Pow-Wows through the summer months. Operates schools at Mandaree, White Shield and Twin Buttes, ND; Museum at 4-Bears complex new New Town, ND; and Library at Fort Berthold Community College. *Publication*: Mandan, Hidatsa & Arikara Times, tribal newspaper. Head Start Program. Fort Berthold Agency.

OJIBWA OF THE RED RIVER
Tribe: Ojibwa (Chippewa). *In residence*: 850. Located in northeast North Dakota.

SPIRIT LAKE SIOUX RESERVATION
Spirit Lake Sioux Tribal Council
P.O. Box 359 • Fort Totten, ND 58335
(701) 766-4221 Fax 766-4126
Phillip "Skip" Longie, Chairperson
Tribe: Sisseton-Wahpeton Sioux. *In residence*: 3,500. *Area*: 185,045 acres located along the Cheyenne River. *Activities*: Annual Fort Totten Days Pow-Wow (July). Tribal Council. Fort Totten Agency.

STANDING ROCK RESERVATION
Standing Rock Sioux Tribal Council
P.O. Box D • Fort Yates, ND 58538
(701) 854-7202 Fax 854-7299
Charles W. Murphy, Chairperson
Tribe: Sioux. *In residence*: 9,500 (4,500 Yankton Sioux in North Dakota, and 5,000 Teton Sioux in South Dakota.) *Area*: 306,000 acres (ND); 540,000 acres (SD). Located 60 miles south of Bismarck, N.D., in North and South Dakota. Head Start Program. Standing Rock Agency.

TRENTON INDIAN SERVICE AREA
Board of Directors
P.O. Box 210 • Trenton, ND 58853
(701) 572-8316 Fax 572-0124
Cynthia LaCounte, Chairperson
Turtle Mountain Agency.

TURTLE MOUNTAIN RESERVATION
Turtle Mountain Tribal Council
P.O. Box 900 • Belcourt, ND 58316
(701) 477-0470 Fax 477-6836
Richard A. Monette, Chairperson
Tribe: Chippewa. *In residence*: 8,950. *Area*: 34,528 acres. Located west of the Canadian border. Head Start Program. Turtle Mountain Agency.

OKLAHOMA

NOTE: There are no reservations in Oklahoma. Rather, there are land holdings by the various Oklahoma Indian tribes.

ABSENTEE-SHAWNEE TRIBE OF OKLAHOMA
Absentee-Shawnee Executive Committee
2025 S. Gordon Cooper Dr. • Shawnee, OK 74801
(580) 275-4030 Fax 275-5637
James Lee Edwards, Jr., Governor
Tribe: Absentee-Shawnee. *Elected officials*: Jennifer Makaseah, Secretary; Marvin Wilson, Rep. *Population served*: 1,500. *Area*: 33 acres. Shawnee Field Office.

ALABAMA-QUASSARTE TRIBAL TOWN
Alabama-Quassarte Governing Committee
P.O. Box 87 • Wetumka, OK 74883
(918) 683-2388 Fax 683-3818
Tarpie Yargee, Chief
Zerndorff Billy, Chairperson
Tribes: Alabamas & Quassartes. *Area*: 878 acres. *Activities*: Annual Retreat, 3rd weekend in September. Library. Okmulgee Field Station.

APACHE TRIBE OF OKLAHOMA
Apache Business Committee
P.O. Box 1220 • Anadarko, OK 73005
(405) 247-9493 Fax 247-3153
Gene Maroquin, Chairperson
Amos Pewenofkit, Sr., Vice-Chairperson
Tribe: Apache & Kiowa. *Population served*: 550. Anadarko Agency.

CADDO TRIBE OF OKLAHOMA
Caddo Tribal Council
P.O. Box 487 • Binger, OK 73009
(405) 656-2344 Fax 656-2892
LaRue Parker, Chairperson

Tribe: Caddo. *Population served*: 1,250. Anadarko Agency.

CHEROKEE NATION OF OKLAHOMA
P.O. Box 948 • Tahlequah, OK 74465
(918) 456-0671 Fax 458-5580
Chadwick 'Corntassel' Smith, Principal Chief
Joseph Grayson, Jr., Deputy Principal Chief
E-mail: csmith@cherokee.org
E-mail: cnwo@cherokee. org
Website: www.cherokee.org
Washington, DC office:
1000 Connecticut Ave., NW #309
Washington, DC 20036
Tribe: Cherokee of Oklahoma. *Population served*: 45,000. Head Start Program. Eastern Oklahoma Regional Office.

CHEYENNE & ARAPAHO TRIBES OF OKLAHOMA
Cheyenne-Arapaho Business Committee
P.O. Box 38 • Concho, OK 73022
(800) 247-4612; (405) 262-0345 Fax 422-1184
Robert Tabor, Chairperson
William J. Blind, Vice Chairperson
Website: www.cheyenne-arapaho.nsn.us
Tribes: Cheyenne & Arapaho. *Cheyenne & Arapaho population*: 11,000. Cheyenne & Arapaho *population in service area*: 5,000. *Other Indian population*: 5,000. *Tribal Trust Property Area*: 10,200 acres; *Individual Trust Property Area*: 70,000 acres. *Activities*: Annual Summerfest in August. *Publication*: Monthly tribal newsletter. Concho Field Office.

CHICKASAW NATION
P.O. Box 1548 • Ada, OK 74821
(580) 436-2603 Fax 436-4287
Website: www.chickasaw.net
E-mail: support@chickasaw.net
The Chickasaw Tribal Legislature
P.O. Box 2669 • Ada, OK 74821
(580) 436-1460 Fax 436-4287
Bill Anoatubby, Governor
Tribe: Chickasaw. *Population served*: 35,000 in U.S.; 12,000+ in residence. *Area*: 7,648 square miles inside boundary; 2,000+ acres owned by the Chickasaw Nation. *Special activitiy*: Chickasaw Festival and Annual Meeting in Tishomingo, OK in September/October. Operates Carter Seminary in Ardmore, Chickasaw Council House Museum in Tishomingo; and Tribal Museum and Library in Ada. *Publications*: Chickasaw Times, monthly tribal newspaper; Chickasaw Dictionary. Head Start Program. Chickasaw Agency.

CHOCTAW NATION OF OKLAHOMA
P.O. Drawer 1210 • Durant, OK 74702
(580) 924-8280 Fax 924-1150
Gregory E. Pyle, Chief
Tribe: Choctaw. *Population served*: 83,500. Geographic boundaries include 10.5 counties in southeastern Oklahoma. *Activities*: Annual commemorative "Trail of Tears" Walk, Skullyville, OK; annual Labor Day Festival, Tuskahoma, OK. Maintains museum. *Publication*: "Bishinik," monthly newspaper. Head Start Program. Talihina Field Office.

CITIZEN BAND POTAWATOMI TRIBE
Citizen Band Potawatomi Business Committee
1901 S. Gordon Cooper Dr. • Shawnee, OK 74801
(405) 275-3121 Fax 275-0198
John A. Barrett, Chairperson
Tribe: Citizen Band Potawatomi. *Population served*: 4,500 in Oklahoma; 12,500 nationwide. Acts on behalf of the tribe on all matters except claims and treaties. *Area*: 300 acres (in trust). *Facilities*: Tribal Museum and Trading Post. *Publications*: HowNikan, tribal newsletter; Grandfather, Tell Me A Story, oral history book. Under jurisdiction of Southern Plains Regional Office.

COMANCHE INDIAN TRIBE OF OKLAHOMA
Comanche Tribal Business Committee
P.O. Box 908 • Lawton, OK 73502
(580) 492-4988 Fax 492-3796
Johnny C. Wauqua, Chairperson
Tribe: Comanche. *Population served*: 4,000. Anadarko Agency.

DELAWARE TRIBE OF INDIANS
Delaware Trust Board
220 NW Virginia Ave. • Bartlesville, OK 74003
(918) 336-5272 Fax 336-5513

Larry Joe Brooks, Chief
Raymond Cline, Trust Board Chairperson
Website: www.delawaretribeofindians.nsn.us
Tribe: Delaware. Eastern Oklahoma Regional Office.

DELAWARE NATION
Delaware Executive Committee
P.O. Box 825 • Anadarko, OK 73005
(405) 247-2448 Fax 247-9393
Lawrence F. Snake, President
Website: www.westerndelaware.nsn.us/
Tribe: Delaware. *Population served*: 950. *Area*: 2,400 acres held jointly with the Wichita and Caddo Tribes. *Publications*: Cooley's Traditional Stories of the Delaware, and Turtle Tales: Oral Traditions of the Delaware of Western Oklahoma, both edited by Duane Hale. Library. Anadarko Agency.

EASTERN SHAWNEE TRIBE OF OKLAHOMA
P.O. Box 350 • Seneca, MO 64865
(918) 666-2435 Fax 666-2186
Charles D. Enyart, Chief
Tribe: Eastern Shawnee. Miami Field Station.
See listing under Missouri.

FORT SILL APACHE TRIBE OF OKLAHOMA
Fort Sill Apache Business Committee
Rt. 2, Box 121 • Apache, OK 73006
(580) 588-2298 Fax 588-3133
Ruey Darrow, Chairperson
Tribe: Fort Sill Apache. *Population served*: 375.
Anadarko Agency.

IOWA TRIBE OF OKLAHOMA
Iowa Tribe Business Committee
Rt. 1, Box 721 • Perkins, OK 74059
(405) 547-2402 Fax 547-5294
Lawrence P. Murray, Chairperson
Tribe: Iowa. All tribes living within jurisdiction. *Population served*: 6,000. *Programs*: Social Services; Higher Education; Law Enforcement; Direct Employment Assistance; Substance Abuse. Small reference library. Shawnee Field Office.

KAW NATION
Kaw Business Committee
Drawer 50 • Kaw City, OK 74641
(580) 269-2552 Fax 269-2301
Wanda Stone, Chairperson
Tribe: Kaw. *Population served*: 1,200. Located at the northeast section of Kay County, Oklahoma. *Activities*: Tribal Pow-Wow (2nd Thurs. of Aug.). Pawnee Agency.

KIALAGEE TRIBAL TOWN
P.O. Box 332 • Wetumka, OK 74883
(405) 452-3262 Fax 452-3413
Lowell Wesley, Town King
Tribe: Creek. Okmulgee Field Station.

KICKAPOO TRIBE OF OKLAHOMA
Kickapoo of Oklahoma Business Committee
P.O. Box 70 • McLoud, OK 74851
(405) 964-2075 Fax 964-2745
Danny Kaskaske, Chairperson
Tribe: Kickapoo. *Population served*: 800.
Head Start Program. Shawnee Field Office.

KIOWA INDIAN TRIBE OF OKLAHOMA
Kiowa Business Committee
P.O. Box 369 • Carnegie, OK 73015
(580) 654-2300 Fax 654-2188
Billy Evans Horse, Chairperson
Tribe: Kiowa. *Membership*: 10,000. Operates Kiowa Tribal Museum which exhibits the new Kiowa Murals. *Publication*: Kiowa Indian News. Head Start Program. Anadarko Agency.

MIAMI TRIBE OF OKLAHOMA
Miami Business Committee
P.O. Box 1326 • Miami, OK 74355
(918) 542-1445 Fax 542-7260
Floyd E. Leonard, Chief
Tribe: Miami. *Membership*: 2,678. Library.
Miami Field Station.

MODOC TRIBE OF OKLAHOMA
515 G St. SE • Miami, OK 74354
(918) 542-1190 Fax 542-5415
Bill Gene Follis, Chief
Tribe: Modoc. Miami Field Station.

MUSCOGEE (CREEK) NATION OF OKLAHOMA
P.O. Box 580 • Okmulgee, OK 74447
(918) 756-8700 Fax 756-2911
R. Perry Beaver, Principal Chief
Tribe served: Muscogee Creek. *Population served*: 30,000. *Area*: 6,000 acres located in an eight county area in northeastern Oklahoma—bounded on the north at Admiral St. in the city of Tulsa, and on the south by the Canadian River. *Activities*: Green Corn, Creek Festival, and Creek Rodeo. Museum. Library. Head Start Program. Okmulgee Field Station.

OSAGE TRIBE OF OKLAHOMA
Osage Tribal Council
P.O. Box 779 • Pawhuska, OK 74056
(918) 287-1085 Fax 287-2257
Jim Roan Gray, Principal Chief
Tribe: Osage. *Population served*: 6,000.
Head Start Program. Osage Agency.

OTOE-MISSOURIA TRIBE OF INDIANS
Otoe-Missouria Tribal Council
8151 Highway 77 • Red Rock, OK 74651
(580) 723-4434 Fax 723-4273
James E. Grant, Chairperson
Tribe: Otoe-Missouria. *Population served*: 1,250.
Pawnee Agency.

OTTAWA TRIBE OF OKLAHOMA
P.O. Box 110 • Miami, OK 74355
(918) 540-1536 Fax 542-3214
Charles Todd, Chief
Tribe: Ottawa. Miami Field Station.

PAWNEE NATION OF OKLAHOMA
Pawnee Business Committee
P.O. Box 470 • Pawnee, OK 74058
(918) 762-3621 Fax 762-6446
Robert Chapman, President
Tribe: Pawnee. *Population served*: 2,500.
Program: Education & Training "Te-Tu-Koo"
Resources: (918) 762-2541 Fax 762-4643;
E-mail: adedheid@aol.com. Pawnee Agency.

PEORIA TRIBE OF INDIANS OF OKLAHOMA
P.O. Box 1527 • Miami, OK 74355
(918) 540-2535 Fax 540-2538
John P. Froman, Chief
E-mail: jfroman@peoriatribe.com
Web site: www. peoriatribe.com
Tribe: Peoria. *Council persons*: Claude Landers, Emmett Ellis, Don Giles. *Activities*: Peoria Pow Wow. Peoria Stomp Dance. Library. *Publication*: Quarterly newsletter. Miami Field Station.

PONCA TRIBE OF OKLAHOMA
Ponca Business Committee
20 White Eagle Dr. • Ponca City, OK 74601
(580) 762-8104 Fax 762-2743
Mark Peniska, Chairperson
Tribe: Ponca. *Population served*: 2,500.
Pawnee Agency.

QUAPAW TRIBE OF OKLAHOMA
Quapaw Tribal Business Committee
P.O. Box 765 • Quapaw, OK 74363
(918) 542-1853 Fax 542-4694
John Berrey, Chairperson
E-mail: jberrey@quapawtribe.org
Website: www.quapawtribe.org
Tribe: Quapaw. *Population served*: 1,450.
Total acreage: 13,000+ acres. *Activities*: Annual pow-wow held on July 4. Miami Field Station.

SAC & FOX NATION OF OKLAHOMA
Sac & Fox Business Committee
Rt. 2, Box 246 • Stroud, OK 74079
(918) 968-3526 Fax 968-3887
Don Abney, Principal Chief
Tribe: Sac and Fox. *Membership*: 2,300. *Total acreage*: 800 acres. *Activities*: Pow-wow. *Publications*: Sac and Fox News, monthly newspaper; Sac and Fox Nation Welcomes You to Capitol (historical & tourism brochure); Sac and Fox Court: Justice for a Nation (court brochure). Pawnee Agency.

SEMINOLE NATION OF OKLAHOMA
P.O. Box 1498 • Wewoka, OK 74884
(405) 257-6287 Fax 257-6205
Kenneth Chambers, Principal Chief

Tribe: Seminole. *Population served*: 4,500.
Program: Head Start. Wewoka Agency.

SENECA-CAYUGA TRIBE OF OKLAHOMA
Seneca-Cayuga Business Committee
P.O. Box 1283 • Miami, OK 74355
(918) 542-6609 Fax 542-3684
LeRoy Howard, Chief
Tribes: Seneca & Cayuga. *Population served*: 750.
Miami Field Station.

SHAWNEE RESERVE
Shawnee Tribe Business Committee
P.O. Box 189 • Miami, OK 74355
(918) 542-2441 Fax 542-2922
P.O. Box 106 • DeSoto, KS 66018
Website: shawnee-tribe.org
E-mail: shawneetribe@neok.com
Ron Sparkman, Chairperson
Barry Kerr, Vice Chairperson
Georgie Honey, Treasurer
Shirley Staubus, Secretary
Committee members: Carolyn Smith, Roberta Coombs, Barbara Wisdom, Tony Booth, Tommie Buchfink, Kenny Daugherty, Roy Baldridge. *Tribe*: Shawnee. *Total acreage*: 210,000 acres in Oklahoma & Kansas. *Programs*: Numerous social service programs & community activities; annual pow-wow in August or September each year. Maintains a small library for historical and genealogical research. *Publication*: Shawnee Journal, quarterly newsletter. Miami Field Office.

THLOPTHLOCCO TRIBAL TOWN
P.O. Box 188 • Okemah, OK 74859
(918) 623-2620 Fax 623-0419
Bryan McGertt, Town King
Tribe: Creek. Tribal Town Council.
Okmulgee Field Station.

TONKAWA TRIBE OF INDIANS OF OKLAHOMA
Tonkawa Business Committee
P.O. Box 70 • Tonkawa, OK 74653
(580) 628-2561 Fax 628-3375
Donald Patterson, President
Tribe: Tonkawa. *Population served*: 1,500.
Pawnee Agency.

UNITED KEETOOWAH BAND
OF CHEROKEE INDIANS
United Keetoowah Band Tribal Council
P.O. Box 746 • Tahlequah, OK 74465
(918) 431-1818 Fax 431-1873
Dallas Proctor, Chief
Tribe: United Keetoowah Band of Cherokee. *Membership*: 7,700. *Council members*: Emma Sue Holland, Allogan Slagle, Adalene Smith, Jim Proctor, Richard Manus, Roberta Smoke, Charlie Bird, Susan Adair, and Mose Killer. *Activities*: Annual Tribal Celebration (1st Saturday in October). Library. Eastern Oklahoma Regional Office.

WICHITA & AFFILIATED TRIBES OF OKLAHOMA
Wichita & Affiliated Tribes Executive Committee
P.O. Box 729 • Anadarko, OK 73005
(405) 247-2425 Fax 247-2430
Gary McAdams, President
E-mail: wtep@tanet.net
Website: www.wichita.nsn.us
Tribe: Wichita. *Population served*: 700.
Anadarko Agency.

WYANDOTTE NATION
Wyandotte Business Committee
P.O. Box 250 • Wyandotte, OK 74370
(918) 678-2297 Fax 678-2944
Leaford Bearskin, Chief
Tribe: Wyandotte. *Population served*: 500.
Miami Field Station.

YUCHI TRIBE
P.O. Box 10 • Sapulpa, OK 74067
(918) 224-3605 Fax 224-3140
Andrew Skeeter, Chairperson
Tribe: Yuchi.

OREGON

BURNS PAIUTE TRIBE
Burns Paiute General Council
HC 71, 100 PaSiGo St. • Burns, OR 97720
(541) 573-2088 Fax 573-2323
Albert Teeman, Chairperson
Tribe: Paiute. *In residence*: 220. *Area*: 11,944 acres located in Harney Basin, Harney County. Tribal Council. Warm Springs Agency.

CONFEDERATED TRIBES OF COOS,
LOWER UMPQUA & SUISLAW INDIANS
1245 Fulton Ave. • Coos Bay, OR 97420
(541) 888-9577 Fax 888-5388
Ron Brainard, Chairperson
Tribes: Umpqua & Suislaw. Siletz Field Office.

GRAND RONDE INDIAN
COMMUNITY OF OREGON
Conferedated Tribes of the
Grand Ronde Tribal Council
9615 Grand Ronde Rd.
Grand Ronde, OR 97347
(503) 879-5211 Fax 879-5964
Cheryl Kennedy, Chairperson
Reyn Leno, Vice-Chairperson
June Sell Sherer, Secretary
Website: www.grandronde.org
Tribes: Five main Confederated Tribes: Rogue River, Chasta, Molalla, Umpqua and Kalapuya. Councilpersons: Val Grout, Ed Larsen, Ed Pearsall, Jan Reibach, Bob Haller, Butch LaBonte. Located in northwest Oregon. *In residence*: 650. Tribal Council. *Activites*: November - Restoration Celebration; August - Annual Pow wow; July - Veterans Pow Wow; May/June - Education Honor & Recognition Celebration. Library - Education Division which contains a small collection of books and materials, Internet access; special programs currently being established. Siletz Field Office.

COQUILLE INDIAN TRIBE
P.O. Box 783, 3050 Tremont St.
North Bend, OR 97549
(541) 756-0904 Fax 756-0847
Edward L. Metcalf, Chairperson
Tribes: Upper & Lower Coquilles. *Population served*: 630. *Area*: 6 acres (planning stages of land acquisition for economic and community development) located on the southern coast of Oregon, primarily in Coos County. *Activity*: Annual Restoration Celebration and Salmon Bake, last weekend in June. Tribe restored 1989. Siletz Field Office.

COW CREEK BAND OF UMPQUA INDIANS
2371 N.E. Stevens, Suite 100
Roseburg, OR 97470
(541) 672-9405 Fax 673-0432
Sue M. Shaffer, Chairperson
Tribe: Umpqua. Siletz Field Office.

FORT McDERMITT RESERVATION
Tribes: Paiute and Shoshone. Located in Oregon & Nevada. See listing under Nevada.

KLAMATH RESERVATION
Klamath General Council
P.O. Box 436 • Chiloquin, OR 97624
(541) 783-2219 Fax 783-2029
Allen Foreman, Chairperson
Tribe: Klamath. Under jurisdiction of Northwest Regional Office.

SILETZ RESERVATION
Siletz Tribal Council
P.O. Box 549, Siletz, OR 97380
(800) 922-1399
(541) 444-2532 Fax 444-2307
Delores Pigsley, Chairperson
Tribes: Confederated Tribes. *Enrolled members*: 3,025. *In residence*: 800. *Population served*: 1,800. *Area*: 3,669 acres of timber lands in Lincoln County located on the northwest Oregon coast, as well as several parcels of land purchased by the Tribe. *Activities*: Memorial Day and Restoration Day Celebrations in May and November respectively; pow wow in August. Museum/Archive currently being established. Siletz Field Office. Head Start Program.

CONFEDERATED TRIBES OF
THE UMATILLA RESERVATION
Umatilla Board of Trustees
P.O. Box 638 • Pendleton, OR 97801
(541) 276-3165 Fax 276-3095
Antone C. Minthorn, Chairperson
Tribes: Umatilla, Cayuse, and Walla Walla. *In residence*: 1,750. *Population served*: 1,500. *Area*: 95,273 acres. Located in Umatilla County, adjacent to Pendleton and west of Umatilla National Forest. Umatilla Agency.

CONFEDERATED TRIBES OF THE
WARM SPRINGS RESERVATION
Confederated Tribes Tribal Council
P.O. Box C, Warm Springs, OR 97761
(541) 553-1161 Fax 553-1924
Olney Patt, Jr., Chairperson
Tribes: Warm Springs, Wasco, Paiute, Walla Walla, and Waco. *In residence*: 2,750. *Area*: 563,916 acres. Located in Jefferson & Wasco Counties, east of the Cascade Mountains. Tribal Council. Head Start Program. Warm Springs Agency.

PUERTO RICO

TAINO NATION OF THE ANTILLES
New York office: P.O. Box 883
New York, NY 10025-0883
(212) 866-4573 (718) 287-4853
Rene Cibanakan Marcano Quinones, Chief
Governed by Council of Chiefs. *Goal*: Reclaim right to aboriginal identity, restore tribal government, acquire lands at home for tribal purposes, restore culture, language, customs, traditions and heritage. *Activities*: The Wanakan, Inc. Cultural Center located at 252 E. 4th St., New York, NY 10009 (212) 844-0097 and (718) 485-0467, Eric Tihuibo, Director. Assists the Taino people in cultural reconstruction and overseas presentations of indigenous music, song, and dance. *Publication*: Bi-monthly newsletter in Spanish and English.

RHODE ISLAND

NARRAGANSETT INDIAN TRIBE
P.O. Box 268 • Charleston, RI 02813
(401) 364-1100 Fax 364-1104
Matthew Thomas, Chief Sachem
E-mail: mattslaw61@hotmail.com
Tribe: Narragansett. Eastern Regional Office.

SOUTH CAROLINA

CATAWBA INDIAN TRIBE
P.O. Box 188 • Catawba, SC 29704
(803) 366-4792 Fax 366-9150
Gilbert Blue, Chairperson
E-mail: catawbaone@aol.com
Tribe: Catawba. Eastern Area Office.

SOUTH DAKOTA

CHEYENNE RIVER RESERVATION
Cheyenne River Sioux Tribal Council
P.O. Box 590 • Eagle Butte, SD 57625
(605) 964-4155 Fax 964-4151
Harold C. Frazier, Chairperson
Website: www.sioux.org
E-mail: crstchrm@rapidnet.com
Tribe: Cheyenne River Sioux. *In residence*: 5,500. *Area*: 2,811,480 acres. Located in Dewey and Zeibach Counties. *Programs*: Human Services; Health; Education-Head Start; Environmental; Economic Development. Cheyenne River Agency.

CROW CREEK RESERVATION
Crow Creek Sioux Tribal Council
P.O. Box 50 • Fort Thompson, SD 57339
(605) 245-2221 Fax 245-2470
Roxanne Sazue, Chairperson
Tribe: Crow Creek Sioux. *In residence*: 2,500. *Area*:

125,000 acres. Head Start Program. Crow Creek Agency.

FLANDREAU SANTEE SIOUX RESERVATION
Flandreau Santee-Sioux Executive Committee
P.O. Box 283 • Flandreau, SD 57028
(605) 997-3891 Fax 997-3878
Thomas Ranfranz, President
Tribe: Santee Sioux. *In residence*: 440. *Area*: 2,180 acres. *Activities*: Runs Royal River Casino. Great Plains Regional Office.

LOWER BRULE RESERVATION
Lower Brule Sioux Tribal Council
P.O. Box 187 • Lower Brule, SD 57548
(605) 473-5561 Fax 473-5606
Michael B. Jandreau, Chairperson
Tribe: Lower Brule Sioux. *In residence*: 1,100. *Area*: 114,500 acres. Head Start Program. Lower Brule Agency.

PINE RIDGE RESERVATION
Oglala Lakotah Tribal Council
P.O. Box H • Pine Ridge, SD 57770
(605) 867-2244 Fax 867-2609
John Yellow Bird Steele, President
Tribe: Oglala Sioux. *In residence*: 14,500. *Area*: 1,560,196 acres (SD) and 90,000 acres (Nebraska), located 60 miles east of the Black Hills, extending into Nebraska. *Activities*: Plans to open a casino in the near future. The Lakota Fund, P.O. Box 340, Kyle, SD 57750 (605) 455-2500, Elsie Meeks, Executive Director - formed to help build a private sector economy on the Reservation by providing loans and technical assistance & business training; and arts & crafts marketing assistance tribal members. *Local attractions*: Wounded Knee Battlefield (15 miles northeast of Pine Ridge); Badlands National Monument. *Activities*: Annual Oglala Sioux Sun Dance (Aug.). Head Start Program. Pine Ridge Agency.

PONCA TRIBE OF NEBRASKA
Located in Nebraska and South Dakota. See listing under Nebraska.

ROSEBUD RESERVATION
Rosebud Sioux Tribal Council
P.O. Box 430 • Rosebud, SD 57570
(605) 747-2381 Fax 747-2243
Charles Colombe, President
Tribe: Rosebud Sioux. *In residence*: 9,900. *Area*: 964,778 acres located in south-central South Dakota, adjoining the Nebraska State line. *Local attraction*: Crazy Horse Canyon Park (tribe-operated); St. Francis Mission; Sioux Indian Museum. Head Start Program. Rosebud Agency.

SISSETON-WAHPETON RESERVATION
Sisseton-Wahpeton Dakota Tribal Council
P.O. Box 509 • Agency Village, SD 57262
(605) 698-3911 Fax 698-7907
J.C. Crawford, Chairperson
Website: www.swcc.cc.sd.us
Tribe: Sisseton-Wahpeton Sioux. *In residence*: 4,000. *Area*: 105,000 acres located in North and South Dakota (only a minor portion in North Dakota.) Tribal Council. Sisseton Agency.

STANDING ROCK RESERVATION
Tribes: Teton Sioux (SD) and Yankton Sioux (ND). Located in North & South Dakota. See listing under North Dakota.

YANKTON SIOUX RESERVATION
Yankton Sioux Tribal Business Committee
P.O. Box 248 • Marty, SD 57361
(605) 384-3804 Fax 384-5687
Madonna Archambeau, Chairperson
Website: www.yanktonsiouxtribe.org/index.html
Tribe: Yankton Sioux. *In residence*: 2,600. *Area*: 35,000 acres. Yankton Agency.

TEXAS

ALABAMA-COUSHATTA TRIBE OF TEXAS
Alabama-Coushatta Tribal Council
571 State Park Rd. 56 • Livingston, TX 77351
(936) 563-1100 Fax 563-4397

McClamroch Battise, Chairperson
Morris Bullock, Vice Chairperson
Sharon Miller, Public Information Officer
E-mail: sawa@actribe.org
Website: www.alabama-coushatta.com
Tribe: Alabama-Coushatta of Texas. *Area*: 4,600 acres.
Council members: Oscola Clayton "Smiley" Sylestine,
1st Chief; Colab III Clem Sylestine, 2nd Chief; Edwin
Battise, Treasurer; Melinda Sylestine, Secretary;
Othelda Williams; Darrel Battise; MacClamroch Battise.
Programs: Chief Kina Health Clinic (phone: 563-2058/
9); WIA Employment & Training; Head Start (phone: 563-
1300); Social Services (Richard Cordes, Director -
phone: 563-5215); Education (Janie Rhinesmith, Direc-
tor - phone: 563-1280); Youth; Environmental (Cecilia
Flores, Specialist). *Activities*: Annual powwow 1st weekend in June. Library. Under jurisdiction of Southern
Plains Regional Office.

KICKAPOO TRADITIONAL TRIBE OF TEXAS
HC 1, Box 9700 • Eagle Pass, TX 78852
(830) 773-2105 Fax 757-9228
Raul Garza, Chairperson
Tribe served: Kickapoo. Under jurisdiction
of Southern Plains Regional Office.

YSLETA DEL SUR PUEBLO
Ysleta Del Sur Pueblo Council
P.O. Box 17579, Ysleta Sta.
El Paso, TX 79917
(915) 859-7913 Fax 859-2988
Albert Alvidrez Governor
Tribe served: Tigua. Southern Pueblos Agency.

UTAH

CHILCHINBETO RESERVATION
Tribe: Navajo. Located in Utah & Arizona.
See listing under Arizona.

DENNEHOTSO RESERVATION
Tribe: Navajo. Located in Utah & Arizona.
See listing under Arizona.

DUCK VALLEY RESERVATION
Shoshone Paiute Business Council
P.O. Box 219 • Owyhee, NV 89832
(208) 759-3100 Fax 759-3102
Marvin Cota, Chairperson
Tribes: Shoshone and Paiute. Located in Idaho
and Nevada. Eastern Nevada Field Office

GOSHUTE RESERVATION
Goshute Business Council
P.O. Box 6104 • Ibapah, UT 84034
(435) 234-1138 Fax 234-1162
Rupert Steele, Chairperson
Tribe: Goshute. *In residence*: 200. *Population served*:
380. *Area*: 113,000 acres. Located in Utah and Nevada.
Eastern Nevada Field Office.

KAYENTA RESERVATION
Tribe: Navajo. Located in Utah and Arizona.
See listing under Arizona.

MEXICAN WATER RESERVATION
Tribe: Navajo. Located in Utah and Arizona.
See listing under New Mexico.

NAVAJO MOUNTAIN RESERVATION
Tribe: Navajo. Located in Utah and Arizona.
See listing under Arizona.

OLJATOH RESERVATION
Tribe: Navajo. Located in Utah & Arizona.
See listing under Arizona.

PAIUTE INDIAN TRIBE OF UTAH
Paiute Indian Tribe of Utah Tribal Council
440 N. Paiute Dr. • Cedar City, UT 84720
(435) 586-1112 Fax 586-7388
Lora E. Tom, Chairperson
Phil Pikyavit, Vice-Chairperson
Tribe: Paiute (Cedar Band, Indian Peaks Band, Kanosh
Band, Koosharem Band, and Shivwits Band). *Elected
officials*: Cyndi Charles, Kooharem Band Chair; Glen
Rogers, Shivwits Band Chair; Anthonia Tom, Indian

Peaks Chair; Travis Parashonts, Cedar Band Chair. *In
residence*: 600. *Area*: Southwestern Utah. *Special activity*: Paiute Restoration Gathering and Pow Wow in
June. Library. Southern Paiute Field Office.

RED MESA RESERVATION
Tribe: Navajo. Located in Utah and Arizona.
(See listing under New Mexico.)

SHONTO RESERVATION
Tribe: Navajo. Located in Utah and Arizona.
(See listing under Arizona.)

SKULL VALLEY BAND OF GOSHUTE INDIANS
Skull Valley Executive Committee
3359 S. Main St. #808 • Salt Lake City UT 84115
(801) 484-4422 Fax 484-5511
Leon D. Bear, Chairperson
Website: www.skullvalleygoshutes.org
Tribe: Skull Valley Band of Goshute. *In residence*: 85.
AREA: 18,000 acres. Library and cultural center cur-
rently being developed. Uintah & Ouray Agency.

TEECNOSPOS RESERVATION
Tribe: Navajo. Located in Utah, Arizona & New Mexico.
See listing under New Mexico.

UINTAH & OURAY RESERVATION
Uintah & Ouray Tribal Business Council
P.O. Box 190 • Fort Duchesne, UT 84026
(801) 722-5141 Fax 722-2374
Ruby Atwine, Chairperson
Tribe: Ute. *In residence*: 2,000. *Area*: 852,411. Located
in the Uintah Basin in northeast Utah. Head Start Pro-
gram. Uintah & Ouray Agency.

UTE MOUNTAIN RESERVATION
Tribe: Ute. Located in Utah, New Mexico & Colorado.
See listing under Colorado.

WASHAKIE RESERVATION
Tribe: Northwest Band of Shoshone of Utah.
Located in Utah. See listing under Idaho.

VIRGINIA

CHEROKEE TRIBE OF VIRGINIA
Cherokee of Virginia Tribal Council
address unknown
Samuel W. Beeler, Sr., Principal Chief
Samuel W. Beeler, Jr., Vice Principal Chief
Tribe: Cherokee Tribe of Virginia. *Population served*:
150. *Activities*: Traditional Cherokee holidays, festivals,
and ceremonies. Library. Eastern Area Office.

PAMUNKEY INDIAN RESERVATION
Pamunkey Tribal Council
Rt. 1, Box 2220 • King William, VA 23086
(804) 843-3526
William P. Miles, Chief
Tribe: Pamunkey. *In residence*: 90. *Area*: 1,250 acres.
Council: Raymond Bosh, Walter Hill, Robert Grey, Tom
Dennis, William P. Miles, Ivy Bradley. Museum.

WASHINGTON

CONFEDERATED TRIBES OF
THE CHEHALIS RESERVATION
Chehalis Community Council
P.O. Box 536 • Oakville, WA 98568
(360) 273-5911 Fax 273-5914
David Youckton, Chairperson
Tribe: Chehalis. *In residence*: 750 (525 enrolled mem-
bers). *Area*: 4,225 acres located in the southeastern
corner of Grays Harbor County bordering Thurston
County, southeast of Oakville. Head Start Program.
Olympic Peninsula Agency.

COLVILLE RESERVATION
Colville Business Committee
P.O. Box 150 • Nespelem, WA 99155
(509) 634-2200 Fax 634-4116
Colleen Cawston, Chairperson
Tribes: Confederated Tribes (Colville, Okanogan, Lakes,
San Poil, Methow, Nespelem, Entiat, Wenatchee,

Moses, Nez Perce, Palouse.) *In residence*: 3,750 (Tribal
rolls: 6,200). *Area*: 1,087,271 acres located in Okanogan
& Ferry Counties. *Local attractions*: Grand Coulee Dam;
Old Fort Okanogan; burial place of Nez Perce, Chief
Joseph. *Activities*: Operates a Casino. Head Start.
Colville Agency.

HOH RESERVATION
Hoh Tribal Business Committee
2464 Lower Hoh Rd. • Forks, WA 98331
(360) 374-6582 Fax 374-9788
Alvin Penn, Chairperson
Tribe: Hoh. *In residence*: 75. *Area*: 443 acres located at
Cape Flattery in Jefferson County. Olympic Peninsula
Agency.

JAMESTOWN S'KLALLAM RESERVATION
Jamestown S'Klallem Tribal Council
1033 Old Blyn Hwy. • Sequim, WA 98382
(360) 683-1109 Fax 681-4643
William Ron Allen, Chairperson
Tribe: Jamestown Band of S'Klallem Indians. *In resi-
dence*: 250. *Area*: 18 acres in Clallam County. *Tribal
Officers*: Sandy Ehrhorn, Vice Chairperson; Ann Balch,
Secretary; Jerry Allen, Treasurer. *Programs*: Childrens
Cultural Program; and annual gathering called,
"S'Klallam Qwen Seyu." Library. Olympic Peninsula
Agency.

KALISPEL RESERVATION
Kalispel Business Committee
P.O. Box 39 • Usk, WA 99180
(509) 445-1147 Fax 455-1705
Glen Nenema, Chairperson
Tribe: Kalispel. *In residence*: 250. Located
in Pend Oreille County. Spokane Agency.

LOWER ELWHA RESERVATION
Lower Elwha Tribal Council
2851 Lower Elwha Rd. • Port Angeles, WA 98362
(360) 452-8471 Fax 452-3428
Russell J. Hepfer, Chairperson
Tribe served: Lower Elwha Band of S'Klallam Indians
(main membership). *In residence*: 470. *Area*: 430 acres
located in Clallam County. *Activities*: Substance abuse
program; health clinic; housing department; hatchery-
fisheries department; higher adult-vocational education
department. Olympic Peninsula Agency.

LUMMI NATION RESERVATION
Lummi Indian Business Council
2616 Kwina Rd. • Bellingham, WA 98226
(360) 384-1489 Fax 380-1850
Darrell Hillaire, Chairperson
William E. Jones, Sr., Vice Chairperson
Gerald I. James, Treasurer
Sheri Williams, Secretary
Tribe: Lummi. *In residence*: 3,300. *Area*: 12 acres (trib-
ally-owned); 7,073 acres (allotted). Located in Whatcom
County. *Activities*: Lummi Water Stommish Festival; op-
erates middle school, high school, and Northwest In-
dian College; ownes & operates the Silver Reef Casino.
Program: Head Start. *Publication*: Bi-weekly commu-
nity newsletter. Puget Sound Field Office.

MAKAH RESERVATION
Makah Indian Tribal Council
P.O. Box 115 • Neah Bay, WA 98357
(360) 645-2201 Fax 645-2788
Greig W. Arnold, Chairperson
Tribe: Makah. *In residence*: 1,250. *Area*: 27,012 acres
located on the Pacific Ocean & Straits of Juan De Fuca
in Clallam County. Head Start Program. Olympic Peninsula Agency.

MUCKLESHOOT RESERVATION
Muckleshoot Tribal Council
39015 172nd St. SE • Auburn, WA 98092
(253) 939-3311 Fax 939-5311
John Daniels, Jr., Chairperson
Tribe: Muckleshoot. *In residence*: 2,500. *Area*: 1,959
acres located in King County. *Activities*: Muckleshoot
Indian Casino. *Program*: Head Start. Puget Sound Field
Office.

NISQUALLY INDIAN COMMUNITY
4820 She-Nah-Num Dr. SE • Olympia, WA 98513
(360) 456-5221 Fax 438-8618
John Simmons, Chairperson
Tribe: Nisqually. *In residence*: 1,400. *Area*: 941 acres

located in Thurston County. Head Start Program. Puget Sound Field Office.

NOOKSACK RESERVATION
Nooksack Indian Tribal Council
P.O. Box 157 • Deming, WA 98244
 (360) 592-5176 Fax 592-2125
 Art George, Chairperson
Tribe: Nooksack. *In residence*: 750. *Area*: 2,906 acres located in Whatcom County. *Activities*: Owns and operates the Nooksack River Casino. *Program*: Head Start. Puget Sound Field Office.

PORT GAMBLE INDIAN COMMUNITY
Port Gamble S'Klallam Tribal Council
31912 Little Boston Rd. NE • Kingston, WA 98346
 (360) 297-2646 Fax 297-7097
 Ronald G. Charles, Chairperson
Tribe: Port Gamble Band of S'Klallam Indians. *Enrolled members*: 950. *In residence*: 650. *Area*: 1,341 acres located in the northern end of the Kitsap Peninsula in Kitsap County in Washington State. The land on the Reservation is held in trust for the tribe. *Local attractions*: Library; Owns and operates the Point No Point Casino & Bingo. *Program*: Head Start. Puget Sound Field Office.

PORT MADISON RESERVATION
Suquamish Tribal Council
P.O. Box 498 • Suquamish, WA 98392
 (360) 598-3311 Fax 598-6295
 Bennie J. Armstrong, Chairperson
Website: www.suquamish.nsn.us
Tribe: Suquamish. *In residence*: 480. *Area*: 8,000 acres located in Kitsap County. *Population served*: 650. *Activities*: Chief Seattle Day (annual traditional tribal celebration, held in August). *Local attractions*: Totem Poles throughout the Reservation; Suquamish Museum; Photographic Archives and Oral History Collection. *Publications*: Dsub'Wub'Siatsub (Suquamish News), tribal newsletter; A Guide to Oral History in the Native American Community; Suquamish Tribal *Photographic Archives Project*: A Case Study; Suquamish Today; and The Eyes of Chief Seattle (exhibit catalog.) Library. Puget Sound Field Office.

PUYALLUP RESERVATION
Puyallup Tribal Council
1850 E. Alexander Ave.
Tacoma, WA 98421-4105
 (253) 597-6200 Fax 593-0197
 Herman Dillon, Sr., Chairperson
Tribes: Puyallup, Nisqually, Muckleshoot, Skwawksnamish, and Steilacoom. *Population served*: 6,500. *Area*: 33 acres located in Pierce County. *Activities*: Owns and operates the Emerald Queen Riverboat Casino. Tribal Council. Puget Sound Field Office.

QUILEUTE RESERVATION
Quileute Tribal Council
P.O. Box 279 • LaPush, WA 98350
 (360) 374-6163 Fax 374-6311
 Russell Woodruff, Sr., Chairperson
Tribe: Quileute. *Population served*: 300. *Area*: 1 square mile located on the Pacific Ocean in Clallam County. *Program*: Head Start. *Activities*: Quileute Days (July); Elders Week Celebration (May); operates tribal school serving K-8. *Publication*: Quileute Indian News, monthly; The Quileute of La Push, book. Olympic Peninsula Agency.

QUINAULT RESERVATION
Quinault Indian Nation Business Committee
P.O. Box 189 • Taholah, WA 98587
 (360) 276-8211 Fax 276-8256
 Pearl Capoeman-Baller, President
 E-mail: pballer@quinault.org
 Website: www.quinault.org
Tribe: Quinault. *In residence*: 2,200. *Area*: 136,456 acres located 40 miles north of Hoquiam, on the Pacific Ocean in Grays Harbor County. *Activities*: Annual celebration in July; owns and operates the Quinault Beach Resort & Casino. *Local attraction*: Indian village. Head Start Program. Olympic Peninsula Agency.

SAMISH INDIAN NATION
P.O. Box 217, 1618 D Ave.
Anacortes, WA 98221
 (360) 293-6404 Fax 299-0790
 Ken Hansen, Chairperson

Tom Wooten, Vice Chairperson
Located in Skagit County. Puget Sound Field Office.

SAUK-SUIATTLE INDIAN RESERVATION
Sauk-Suiattle Tribal Council
5318 Chief Brown Ln. • Darrington, WA 98241
 (360) 436-0131 Fax 436-0242
 Jason L. Joseph, Chairperson
Tribe: Sauk-Suiattle. *In residence*: 215. *Area*: 23 acres located in Skagit County. *Activities*: Annual Huckleberry Festival (September); Annual Yo-Buch Days (July). Library. Tribal Council. Puget Sound Field Office.

SHOALWATER BAY RESERVATION
Shoalwater Bay Tribal Council
P.O. Box 130 • Tokeland, WA 98590
 (360) 267-6766 Fax 267-6778
 Herbert "Ike" Whitish, Chairperson
 James Anderson, Vice-Chairperson
Tribe: Shoalwater. *In residence*: 100. *Area*: 335 acres located in Pacific County, near Tokeland. Olympic Peninsula Agency.

SKOKOMISH INDIAN RESERVATION
Skokomish Tribal Council
N. 80 Tribal Center Rd. • Shelton, WA 98584
 (360) 426-4232 Fax 877-5943
 Denny Hurtado, Chairperson
Tribe: Skokomish. *In residence*: 350. *Population served*: 1,000. *Area*: 6,300 acres located in Mason County. *Council members*: Pat and Denise Laclair. *Activities*: 1st Plant Ceremony (April); 1st Salmon Ceremony (August); 1st Elk Ceremony (October). Small museum and library. *Publication*: Portrait of a Tribe: An Intro to the Skokomish. Head Start Program. Olympic Peninsula Agency.

SNOQUALMIE RESERVATION
Snoqualmie Tribal Organization
P.O. Box 670 • Fall City, WA 98024
 (425) 222-6900 Fax 222-7798
 Joseph Mullen, Chairperson
Tribe: Snoqualmie. Puget Sound Field Office.

SPOKANE RESERVATION
Spokane Business Council
P.O. Box 100 • Wellpinit, WA 99040
 (509) 258-4581 Fax 258-9243
 Alfred Peone, Chairperson
Tribe: Spokane. *In residence*: 1,200 (tribal roll, 2,500). *Area*: 138,750 acres located in the southwest corner of Stevens County. *Local attractions*: Old Fort Spokane; Tsimshian Mission (1838). Owns and operates the Two Rivers Casino in Davenport, WA. Spokane Agency.

SQUAXIN ISLAND RESERVATION
Squaxin Island Tribal Council
SE 70, Squaxin Lane • Shelton, WA 98584
 (360) 426-9781 Fax 426-6577
 David Lopeman, Chairman
Tribes: Squaxin Island, Nisqually, Steilacoom, and others. *In residence*: 1,000. *Location*: Mason County. Olympic Peninsula Agency.

STILLAGUAMISH RESERVATION
Stillaquamish Board of Directors
P.O. Box 277 • Arlington, WA 98223
 (360) 652-7362 Fax 435-7689
 Edward L. Goodridge, Sr., Chairperson
Tribe served: Stillaguamish. *Enrolled members*: 250 with a service population of about 1,500. *Location*: In northern Snohomish County near Arlington, WA between the Cascade Mountains and Puget Sound. Puget Sound Field Office.

SWINOMISH INDIAN TRIBAL COMMUNITY
Swinomish Indian Senate
P.O. Box 817 • LaConnor, WA 98257
 (360) 466-3163 Fax 466-5309
 M. Brian Cladoosby, Chairperson
Tribes: Swinomish, Samish, Lower Skagit, and Kikiallus. *Elected officials*: Susan Wilbur, Vice-Chair; Lydia Charles, Secretary; Barbara James, Treasurer. *In residence*: 750. *Area*: 7,000 acres located in Skagit County. *Activities*: "Treaty Day Celebration" (January); "All My Relations Pow Wow" (June). *Publication*: "A Gathering of Wisdoms." Library. Puget Sound Field Office.

TULALIP RESERVATION
Tulalip Board of Directors
6700 Totem Beach Rd. • Marysville, WA 98271

 (360) 651-4000 Fax 651-4032
 Herman A. Williams, Jr., Chairperson
Website: www.tulalip.nsn.us
Tribe: Tulalip (Snohomish, Snoqualmie, Skagit, Suiattle, Samish, and allied bands). *In residence*: 950. *Area*: 22,000 acres located in Snohomish County. *Activities*: Operates Tulalip Casino. Puget Sound Field Office.

UPPER SKAGIT INDIAN RESERVATION
Upper Skagit Tribal Council
25944 Community Plaza
Sedro Woolley, WA 98284
 (360) 856-5501 Fax 856-3175
 Marilyn Scott, Chairperson
Tribe: Upper Skagit. *In residence*: 200. *Area*: 99 acres located in Skagit County. Puget Sound Field Office.

YAKAMA RESERVATION
Yakama Tribal Council
P.O. Box 151 • Toppenish, WA 98948
 (509) 865-5121 Fax 865-5528
 Lonnie Selam, Sr., Chairperson
Tribe: Yakama. *In residence*: 9,000. *Area*: 1,134,830 acres located in Yakama & Klickitat Counties. *Activities*: All-Indian Rodeo (June); Annual Pow-Wow (July); Huckleberry Feast (August). Head Start Program. Yakama Agency.

WISCONSIN

BAD RIVER RESERVATION
**Bad River Band of Lake
Superior Tribe of Ojibwe
Tribal Council**
P.O. Box 39 • Odanah, WI 54861
 (715) 682-7111 Fax 682-7118
 Eugene Bigboy, Sr., Chairperson
Tribe: Bad River Band of Lake Superior Band of (Ojibwe) Chippewa. *In residence*: 1,550. *Area*: 125,000 acres. Located on Lake Superior, southeast of Duluth, Minnesota. *Special activity*: Annual Minomin Wild Rice Powwow in August. *Council members*: Robert Bender, Charles Wiggins, and Matt O'Claire. Library. Head Start. Great Lakes Agency.

FOREST COUNTY POTAWATOMI COMMUNITY
Executive Council
P.O. Box 340 • Crandon, WI 54520
 (715) 478-2903 Fax 478-5280
 Harold Frank, Chairperson
Tribe: Forest County Potawatomi. *In residence*: 450. *Area*: 10,000 acres. Great Lakes Agency.

HO CHUNK (WINNEBAGO) NATION
Business Committee
P.O. Box 667 • Black River Falls, WI 54615
 (800) 294-9343; (715) 284-9343 Fax 284-9805
 Website: www.ho-chunk.com
 George R. Lewis, President
 Gary Lonetree, Jr., Executive Administrative Officer
 Melissa Pettibone, Executive Secretary
 Ed Littlejohn, Jr., Public Relations Officer
Tribe: Wisconsin Ho Chunk. *In residence*: 1350. *Population served*: 1,850. *Area*: 4,100 acres. *Activity*: Casino. Head Start Program. Great Lakes Agency.

LAC COURTE OREILLES RESERVATION
Lac Courte Oreilles Tribal Governing Board
13394 W. Trapania Rd., Bldg. No. 1
Hayward, WI 54843
 (715) 634-8934 Fax 634-4797
 Alfred Trepania, Chairperson
Tribe served: Lac Courte Oreilles Band of Lake Superior Chippewa. *In residence*: 2,000. *Area*: 70,000 acres. Located within Sawyer County. *Special programs*: Head Start - Cathy Barber, Program Director. Provides comprehensive child development services to 94 LCO children and their families; K-12 school system; Community College; cultural center/museum. *Activities*: Annuall Contest Powwow, May/June; Annual Honor the Earth Powwow, 3rd weekend in July; Annual Veterans Day Powwow, Nov. 11th; Annual New Years Eve Sobriety Powwow, Dec. 31st. *Publication*: LCO Ojibwe Early Childhood Curriculum. Library. Great Lakes Agency.

LAC DU FLAMBEAU CHIPPEWA RESERVATION
Lac du Flambeau Tribal Council
P.O. Box 67 • Lac du Flambeau, WI 54538

(715) 588-3303 Fax 588-7930
Henry St. Germaine, Sr., President
E-mail: museum@ojibwe.com
Website: www.ojibwe.com
Tribe: Lac du Flambeau Band of Lake Superior Chippewa. *In residence*: 2,400. *Area*: 144 square miles. *Activities*: Annual Bear River Pow Wow; Weekly Pow wows; 4th of July Pow wow; Art shows; Craft classes. Museum & Cultural Center. Library. Head Start. *Publication*: Reflections of Lac du Flambeau (book); "The Messenger," bi-annual newsletter. Under jurisidiction of Great Lakes Agency.

MENOMINEE INDIAN RESERVATION
Menominee Tribal Legislature
P.O. Box 910, Keshena, WI 54135
(715) 799-5100 Fax 799-3373
Joan Delabreau, Chairperson
Website: www.menominee.nsn.us
Tribe: Menominee. *In residence*: 3,750. Located off Hwy. 47, 55 Tribal Office Loop Rd. *Area*: 233,800 acres. *Council members*: Frieda Bergeon, Lisa Waukau, Louis Dixon, Llewellyn Boyd, Margaret Snow & Robert Deer. *Activities*: Annual Pow-wow, 1st weekend in August; Restoration Day, Dec. 22nd. Operates Menominee Tribal School in Neopit, WI and College of the Menominee Nation in Keshena, WI. Head Start Program (awarded grant for family literacy). Midwest Regional Office. *Publication*: "Menominee Nation News," twice monthly.

ONEIDA NATION OF WI RESERVATION
Oneida Tribal Council
P.O. Box 365, Oneida, WI 54155
(920) 869-2214 (4040)Fax 869-2194
Tina Danforth, Chairperson
Kathy Hughes, Vice Chairperson
William Gollnick, General Manager
Tribe: Oneida. *In residence*: 2,700 (tribal roll: 3,800). *Area*: 2,600 acres. *Elected officials*: Cristina Danforth, Vice-chair; Judy Cornelius, Treasurer; Julie Barton, Secretary. *Council members*: Sandy Ninham, Paul Ninham, Vince Delardsa, David Bischoff, Eugene Metoxen. *Activities*: Owns & operates the Oneida Bingo & Casino and the Oneida Radisson Inn-Green Bay, WI; Oneida pow-wow (4th of July weekend); Oneida has its own library as well as Oneida Nation elementary school and high school. Head Start Program. *Published work*: Kalihwisaks (bi-weekly) newspaper. Great Lakes Agency.

RED CLIFF RESERVATION
Red Cliff Tribal Council
P.O. Box 529 • Bayfield, WI 54814
(715) 779-3700 Fax 779-3704
Jean Buffalo-Reyes, Chairperson
Tribe: Red Cliff Band of Lake Superior Chippewa. *In residence*: 1,500. *Area*: 7,311 acres. Extends over Lake Superior, about 25 miles northwest of Ashland, Wisc. Great Lakes Agency.

ST. CROIX CHIPPEWA INDIANS
P.O. Box 287 • Hertel, WI 54845
(715) 349-2195 Fax 349-5768
David Merrill, Chairperson
Tribe: St. Croix Chippewa. *In residence*: 1,100. *Area*: 2,230 acres. Great Lakes Agency.

SOKAOGON CHIPPEWA
(MOLE LAKE) COMMUNITY
Sokaogon Chippewa Tribal Council
3086 State Hwy. 55 • Crandon, WI 54520
(715) 478-7500 Fax 478-5275
Sandra L. Rachal, Chairperson
Tribe: Mole Lake Chippewa. *In residence*: 275. *Area*: 1,700 acres. Great Lakes Agency.

STOCKBRIDGE-MUNSEE COMMUNITY
Stockbridge-Munsee Tribal Council
N8476 Mo He Con Nuck Rd.
Bowler, WI 54416
(715) 793-4111 Fax 793-1307
Robert Chicks, President
Tribe: Stockbridge-Munsee Band of Mohicans. Council members: Leah Johnson, Greg Miller, Joseph Miller, Dave Koeller. *In residence*: 900 (tribal enrollment: 1,500). *Area*: Towns of Bartelme & Red Springs...64,000 acres (17,000 in trust). *Activity*: Runs annual veterans pow-wow, 2nd weekend in August each year. Mohican North Star Casino open daily. *Publication*: "Mohican News", biweekly. Library/Museum. Great Lakes Agency.

WYOMING

WIND RIVER RESERVATION
Arapaho Business Council
P.O. Box 396 • Fort Washakie, WY 82514
(307) 332-6120 Fax 332-7543
Anthony Addison, Chairperson
Tribe served: Wind River Arapaho. *In residence*: 5,500 (combined Arapaho & Shoshone). *Population served*: 8,000. *Area*: 1,887,372 acres. Located in east-central Wyoming. *Program*: Head Start - Karen King, Director. *Goals*: To provide comprehensive child care services to low-income children and families in the areas of education, health, nutrition, social services and parent involvement. *Publications*: Social Service Directory, handbooks and pamphlets. Library. Wind River Agency.

WIND RIVER RESERVATION
Shoshone Business Council
P.O. Box 217 • Fort Washakie, WY 82514
(307) 332-3532 Fax 332-3055
Ivan Posey, Chairperson
Tribe served: Wind River Shoshone. *In residence*: 5,500 (combined Shoshone & Arapaho). *Population served*: 8,000. *Area*: 1,887,372 acres. Located in east-central Wyoming. *Program*: Head Start - Karen King, Director. *Goals*: To provide comprehensive child care services to low-income children and families in the areas of education, health, nutrition, social services and parent involvement. *Publications*: Social Service Directory, handbooks and pamphlets. Library. Wind River Agency.

OTHER INDIAN TRIBES & GROUPS

This section lists Indian tribes, groups, and bands who represent the interests of their members, They are, in most cases, landless, recognized by the various states, but not yet federally recognized.

ALABAMA

CHEROKEES OF NORTHEAST ALABAMA
located near Collinsville, AL

CHEROKEES OF SOUTHEAST ALABAMA
2221 Rocky Ridge Rd. • Hoover, AL 35216
(205) 979-7019

ECHOTA CHEROKEE TRIBE OF ALABAMA
located near Birmingam, AL
Serves Cherokees in the Maylene region.

MACHIS LOWER ALABAMA
CREEK INDIAN TRIBE
708 South John St. • New Brockton, AL 36351

PRINCIPAL CREEK INDIAN NATION
EAST OF THE MISSISSIPPI
Florala, AL 36442

STAR CLAN OF MUSKOGEE CREEK
TRIBE OF PIKE COUNTY
P.O. Box 126 • Goshen, AL 36035

UNITED CHEROKEE TRIBE OF ALABAMA
Route 1, Box 8 • Daleville, AL 36322

ARIZONA

BARRIO PASCUA
San Ignacio Yaqui Council, Inc.
2256 North Calle Central • Tucson, AZ 85705

GUADALUPE ORGANIZATIONS
8810 South 56th St. • Guadalupe, AZ 85705

SAN IGNACIO YAQUI COUNCIL
Tucson, AZ 85705

SAN JUAN NORTHERN PAIUTE
P.O. Box 2656 • Tuba City, AZ 86045

ARKANSAS

OUACHITA INDIANS OF ARKANSAS & AMERICA
Revived Ouachita Indian Grand Council
Story, AR (no address since last edition)
Chief John "Lone Elk" Woodall, Grand Head Chief
Cletus "Songbird" Jones, Grand Head Vice Chief
Tribe: Ouachita Indians of Arkansas and America. *Programs*: Health, Social Service, Housing, Employment and Education in Indian traditions and customs; and environmental concerns of Mother Earth. *Activities*: Annual Native American Indian Pow-Wow and Crafts Fair; personal appearances of Chief Lone Elk and members for school children and organizations. Organized in 1981.

CALIFORNIA

ACJACHMEN NATION (JUANENO)
31742 Via Belardes
San Juan Capistrano, CA 92675
(714) 493-4933
David Belardes, Contact

AMAH BAND OF MUTSUN-OHLONE/
COSTANOAN TRIBE OF SANTA CLARA CO.
789 Canada Rd. • Woodside, CA 94062
(415) 851-7747
Irene Zwierlein, Contact

AMERICAN INDIAN COUNCIL OF
MARIPOSA CO. (a.k.a. YOSEMITE)
P.O. Box 1200 • Mariposa, CA 95338
(209) 966-4296

ANTELOPE VALLEY INDIAN COMMUNITY
P.O. Box 168 • Coleville, CA 96107

ATAHUN SHOSHONES OF
SAN JUAN CAPISTRANO
2352 Bahia Dr. • La Jolla, CA 92037

BIG MEADOWS LODGE TRIBE
P.O. Box 362 • Chester, CA 96020

BO-CAH AMA COUNCIL
P.O. Box 1387 • Mendocino, CA 95460
Tribe: Coastal Pomo

BUTTE TRIBAL COUNCIL
3300 Spencer Ave. • Oroville, CA95965

CALAVERAS CO. BAND OF MI-WUK INDIANS
579 Ball Mountain Rd.
West Point, CA 95255
Gloria Greene, Contact

CENTRAL CALIFORNIA INDIAN TRIBAL COUNCIL
1425 S. Center St. • Stockton, CA 95206
(209) 466-0201

CHEROKEES OF CALIFORNIA
9643 Kent St. • Elk Grove, CA 95624

CHOINUMNI TRIBAL COUNCIL
Fresno, CA (209) 233-9781
Mae Davidian, Contact

CHUKCHANSI YOKOTCH TRIBE
P.O. Box 269 • Coarsegold, CA 95614
Linda Shaw, Contact

CHUKCHANSI YOKOTCH TRIBE OF MARIPOSA
4962 Watt Rd. • Mariposa, CA 95338-9743
(209) 742-7060
Lynda Appling, Contact

COASTAL BAND OF CHUMASH NATION
Santa Barbara Urban Indian Health
610 Del Monte Ave.
Santa Barbara, CA 93101

**COSTANOAN BAND OF
CARMEL MISSION INDIANS**
P.O. Box 1657 • Monroavia, CA 91016
Anthony Miranda, Contact

COSTANOAN OHLONE INDIAN COUNCIL
922 N. Lassen Ave. • Ontario, CA 91764

COSTANOAN-RUMSEN CARMEL TRIBE
3929 Riverside Dr. • Chino, CA 91710
(909) 622-1564
Tony Cerda, Contact

DUNLAP BAND OF MONO INDIANS
P.O. Box 126 • Dunlap, CA 93621

ESSELEN TRIBE OF MONTEREY COUNTY
38655 Tassajara Rd.
Carmel Valley, CA 93924
(408) 659-2153
Jim Barker, Tom Little Bear Nason, Contacts

FEDERATED COAST MIWOK TRIBE
P.O. Box 481 • Novato, CA 94948
Greg Sarris, Contact

FERNANDENO/TATAVIAM TRIBAL COUNCIL
11640 Rincon Ave. • Sylmar, CA 91342-5455
(818) 361-0860
Edward Ortega, Contact

GABRIELINO/TONGVA NATION
P.O. Box 693 • San Gabriel, CA 91778
Martin Alcala, Contact

**HAYFORK BAND OF
NOR-EL-MUK WINTU INDIANS**
P.O. Box 673 • Hayfork, CA 96041
(916) 628-5175
Raymond Patton, Contact

HOWNONQUET COMMUNITY ASSOCIATION
address unknown (located near Smith River, CA)

**INDIAN CANYON BAND OF COSTANOAN/
MUTSUN INDIANS OF CALIFORNIA**
address unknown (located near Hollister, CA)

JAMUL BAND
P.O. Box 353 • Jamul, CA 92035

JUANENO BAND OF MISSION INDIANS
31742 Via Belardes
San Juan Capistrano, CA 92675
(714) 493-4933

KERN VALLEY INDIAN COMMUNITY
P.O. Box 168 • Kernville, CA 93238
(619) 376-4240
Ron Wermuth, Contact

LIKELY RANCHERIA
P.O. Drawer 1570 • Burney, CA 96013
(916) 335-5421
Tribe served: Pit River.

MAIDU NATION
P.O. Box 204 • Susanville, CA 96130

MELOCHUNDUM BAND OF TOLOWA INDIANS
P.O. Box 388 • Fort Dick, CA 95538

MONO LAKE INDIAN COMMUNITY
P.O. Box 237 • Lee Vining, CA 93541
Jerry Andrews, Contact

MONO TRIBAL COUNCIL AT DUNLAP
P.O. Box 344 • Dunlap, CA 93621
(209) 338-2842
Dock & Florence Dick, Contacts
Tribe served: Mono.

MONTGOMERY CREEK RANCHERIA
P.O. Drawer 1570 • Burney, CA 96013
(619) 335-5421
Tribe served: Pit River.

NOR-EL-MUK WINTU INDIANS
P.O. Box 3027 • Weaverville, CA 96093-3027
(916) 628-5175

NORTH FORK BAND OF MONO INDIANS
P.O. Box 49 • North Fork, CA 93643
(209) 299-3729 Ron Goode, Contact

NORTHERN MAIDU TRIBE
516 Grand Ave. • Susanville, CA 9613

OAKBROOK CHUMASH PEOPLE
3290 Long Ranch Pkwy.
Thousand Oaks, CA 91362
Paul Varela, Contact

OHLONE/COSTANOAN MUWEKMA TRIBE
San Jose, CA area (408) 441-6473
Rosemary Cambra, Chairperson
E-mail: web@muwekma.org
Website: www.muwekma.org/index.html
Tribal members: 400.

OHLONE/COSTANOAN-ESSELEN NATION
P.O.Box 464, Palo Alto, CA 94302
(408) 455-8315 Loretta Escobar-Wyer, Contact

PAJARO VALLEY OHLONE INDIAN COUNCIL
110 Dick Phelps Rd. • Watsonville, CA 95076
(408) 728-8471 Patrick Orozco, Contact

PLUMAS COUNTY INDIANS, INC.
P.O.Box 102, Taylorsville, CA 95947
Tommy Merino, Contact

ROARING CREEK RANCHERIA
Montgomery Creek • Shasta, CA 96065
Tribe: Pit River

SALINAN NATION
P.O. Box 33 • Greenfield, CA 93927
(800) 997-8999
Robert Duckworth, Contact

SAN LUIS REY BAND OF MISSION INDIANS
Mission Indians Bands Paralegal Consortium
360 N. Midway, Suite 301 • Escondido, CA 92027
(619) 741-1996 Carmen Mojado, Contact

SHASTA NATION
P.O. Box 1054, Yreka, CA 96097
(916) 842-5654 Roy Hall, Jr., Contact

SHEEP RANCH RANCHERIA
Sheep Ranch, CA 95250
Tribe served: Me-Wuk.

SHIVWITS BAND OF PAIUTES
located near Santa Clara, CA

TEHATCHAPI TRIBE
219 East H St., Tehatchapi, CA 93561

TENA COUNCIL
located near Greenfield, CA
(408) 659-5812 • Teresa Candelaria, Chair

THREE RIVERS INDIAN LODGE
13505 Union Rd., Manteca, CA
(209) 858-2421

**TINOQUI-CHALOLI COUNCIL OF KITANEMUK
& YOWLUMNI TEJON INDIANS**
981 N. Virginia, Covina, CA 91722
Dee Dominguez

TOLOWA NATION
P.O. Box 213, Fort Dick, CA 95538
(707) 464-7332 • Charlene Storr, Contact

TSNUNGWE TRIBE
P.O. Box 373, Salyer, CA95563
(916) 629-3356 • John Ammon, Contact

UNITED LUMBEE NATION OF N.C. & AMERICA
P.O. Box 512, Fall River Mills, CA 96028
(530) 336-6701
Eva Silver Star Reed, Chief
Areba Elnora Bailey, Vice-Chief
Chirstyne Dyer, Secretary
Billy Reed, Treasurer
Gary Bromley, Director of R&D
Tribe served: United Lumbee Nation. *Council Elders:*
Elmer "Shorty" Gray, Benton Screaming Eagle Bailey,

Gary Bear Paw Ledbetter, Patty Flaming Star Ledbetter,
and Helyn Burnt Willow Taylor. Pow-wow. *Publications:*
United Lumbee Nation Times, 3x/year newspaper;
"United Lumbee Ceremonies," 1982, "Over the Cook-
ing Fires," 1982, and "United Lumbee's Deer Clan Cook
Book," 1988, all by Princess Silver Star Reed; and "A
Message to Our People," by Frank Chilcote & Princess
Silver Star Reed. Northern California Agency.

UNITED MAIDU NATION
P.O. Box 204, Susanville, CA 96130
(916) 257-9691
Clara LeCompte, Chairperson
Rhonda Rupert, Council Member

WADATKUHT BAND OF NORTHERN PAIUTES
Honey Lake Valley • P.O. Box 541
Susanville, CA 96134

WASHOE/PAIUTE OF ANTELOPE VALLEY
@ Coleville, CA 96107

WILTON RANCHERIA
Wilton, CA
(currently seeking restoration of trust status)

WINTU TRIBE OF N. CALIFORNIA
P.O. Box 1036, Project City, CA 96079
(916) 878-4428 • Gene Malone, Contact

WINTU TRIBE OF SASHTA COUNTY
7480 Dr Creek Rd., Redding, CA 96003

WUKCHUMNI COUNCIL
Clovis, CA (209) 323-9817
Martha Tapleras, Contact

YOKAYO POMO RANCHERIA
1114 Helen Ave., Ukiah, CA 95482
Doreen Mitchell, Chairperson

COLORDO

**MUNSEE THAMES RIVER
DELAWARE TRIBAL COUNCIL**
Manitou Springs, CO

CONNECTICUT

GOLDEN HILL PAUGUSSETT TRIBE
P.O. Box 120 • Trumbull, CT 06611
(203) 377-4410
Reservation - Stanavage Rd., Colchester, CT

**PAUCATUCK EASTERN PEQUOT
INDIAN RESERVATION**
640 Lantern Hill Rd., P.O. Box 370
North Stonington, CT 06359
(860) 448-0492 Fax 448-0715
E-mail: pepitn@aol.com
Web site: www.paucatuck.org
Marcia Jones Flowers, Chairperson
James L. Williams, Sr. (Chief Screaming Eagle),
Grand Chief Sachem
Tribe served: Paucatuck Eastern Pequot. *Elected offi-
cials:* Francis M. Young (Songbird), Vice-Chairperson;
James A. Cunha, Jr. (Growling Bear), Tribal Chief/Trea-
surer; Gina M. Hogan (Sunflower), Tribal Secretary;
Brenda L. Geer, Councilperson; Bertha Brown (Neese
Maha), Beverly A. Kilpatrick (Lone Feather), Agnes
Cunha (White Dove) and James L. Williams, Sr. (Grand
Chief Screaming Eagle), are elders. *Area:* 225 acres.
Activities: Harvest Moon Powwow every Columbus Day
weekend in October. Library (for use by tribal members
only). *Publications:* Pow-wow books at annual pow-wow,
and "The Pequot Tribe," by Allison Lassieur.

DELAWARE

NANTICOKE INDIAN ASSOCIATION
Rte. 4, Box 107-A, Millsboro, DE 19966
(302) 945-3400 (phone & fax)

Kenneth S. Clark, Sr., Chief
Programs: JTPA, Indian Elders (CHEER). *Activities*:
Operates Indian Museum; and runs annual Powwow in
September.

FLORIDA

THE APALACHICOLA BAND OF CREEK INDIANS
c/o Mary Blount, Chairwoman
104 West 4th Ave. • Tallahassee, FL 32303

CREEKS EAST OF THE MISSISSIPPI
c/o Thornley, 7701 Ennon School Rd.
Walnut Hill, FL 32568 (904) 587-2116

ECHOTA CHEROKEE TRIBE OF FLORIDA
P.O. Box 325 • Sneads, FL 32460
(904) 593-5176

FLORIDA TRIBE OF EASTERN CREEK INDIANS
P.O. Box 3028 • Bruce, FL 32455
(904) 835-2078 (phone & fax)
John C.B. Thomas, Chairperson
Kenneth McKenzie, Vice-Chairperson
Chief Andrew Ramsey
Ceremonies: Pine Arbor Tribal Town; Berry, Green Corn,
Little Green Corn, Harvest. The Museum (Blountstown,
FL); Library. *Publication*: The Florida Muskogee (Creek)
News.

**NORTH BAY CLAN OF LOWER
CREEK MUSCOGEE TRIBE**
P.O. Box 687, Lynn Haven, FL 32444
(904) 265-3345
Lonzo Woods, Chief

OCKLEHUVA BAND OF SEMINOLE-YAMASEE
P.O. Box 521 • Orange Springs, FL 32812
(904) 546-1386

TOPACHULA TRIBAL COUNCIL
Pine Arbor Tribal Town, @ Tallahassee

**TUSCOLA UNITED CHEROKEE
TRIBE OF FLORIDA & ALABAMA**
P.O. Box 49, Geneva, FL 32732

GEORGIA

**CANE BREAK BAND OF EASTERN
CHEROKEES TRIBAL COUNCIL**
Rte. 3, Box 750 • Dahlonega, GA 30533
(706) 864-6010

CHEROKEE NATION OF GEORGIA
P.O. Box 1324 • Clayton, GA 30525
(706) 746-2448

**GEORGIA TRIBE OF EASTERN
CHEROKEES TRIBAL COUNCIL**
Rt. 3, Box 3162 • Dawsonville, GA 30534
(706) 427-8299

**LOWER MUSKOGEE CREEK TRIBE-
EAST OF THE MISSISSIPPI**
Tama Reservation • Cairo, GA

AMERICAN CHEROKEE CONFEDERACY
619 Pine Cone Rd. • Albany, GA 31705-6906
(229) 787-5722
William Rattlesnale Jackson, Principal Chief
Michael Black Hawk Willeford, Principal Vice Chief
William R. Robertson, Tribal Attorney
David Wind Walker Willeford, Orator/Parliamentor
Activities: Special Chiefs of Council meeting in March;
annual meeting for membership in September. Indian
library. *Publication*: Quarterly newsletter.

**TENNESSEE RIVER BAND
OF CHICKAMAUGA CHEROKEE**
address unknown (located near Flintstone, GA)
David Q. Brown, Raven, Chairperson
Robert T. Murray, Chief
Tribes served: Metis Cherokee of TN, GA, and AL.
Publication: Voices of the Council Fire, newsletter.

IDAHO

DELAWARES OF IDAHO TRIBAL COUNCIL
address unknown @ Boise

INDIANA

**INDIANA MIAMI INDIAN
ORGANIZATIONAL COUNCIL**
641 Buchanan St., Huntington, IN 46750

UPPER KISPOKO BAND OF SHAWNEE
@ Kokomo, IN 46901

WEA INDIAN TRIBE
715 Park Ave. • Lafayette, IN 47904
Terry Stuff, Sr, Chief
Brenda (Mahkoonsahkwa) Lindley, Administrator
E-mail: weatribe@wea-indian-tribe.com
Website: www.wea-indian-tribe.com

KANSAS

DELAWARE-MUNCIE TRIBAL COUNCIL
P.O. Box 274, Pomona, KS 66076

**KAWEAH INDIAN NATION OF
WESTERN USA & MEXICO**
located near Hutchinson, KS
(316) 665-3614
Chief Thunderbird Webber, Grand Chief
Tribe: Kawia Shoshone. *Publication*: "Itza Voice."

SWAN CREEK & BLACK RIVER CHIPPEWAS
519 Willow St., Ottawa, KS 66067

LOUISIANA

**CHOCTAW-APACHE COMMUNITY OF EBARB
Choctaw-Apache Tribal Council**
P.O. Box 858, Zwolle, LA 71486
(318) 645-2744
Tommy Bolton, Chief
Victor Sepulvado, Vice Chief
Sheli Lafitte, Treasurer
Tribe: Choctaw and Lipan Apache. *In residence*: 900.
Location: West Central Sabine Parish. *Activities*: Annual
Pow-wow, last weekend in May. Maintains school - only
officially recognized "Indian School" in the state of Loui-
siana.

CLIFTON CHOCTAW INDIANS TRIBAL COUNCIL
P.O. Box 32, Gardner, LA 71431 (318) 793-8796

HOUMA NATION TRIBAL COUNCIL
Star Rte., Box 95-A, Golden Meadow, LA 70357
(504) 475-6640

MARYLAND

PISCATAWAY INDIAN NATION COUNCIL
P.O. Box 312, Port Tobacco, MD 20677
(301) 932-0808

MASSACHUSETTS

GAY HEAD WAMPANOAG TRIBE
State Rd. RFD Box 137 • Gay Head, MA 02535
(508) 645-9265

**MASHPEE-WAMPANOAG
INDIAN TRIBAL COUNCIL**
Route 1048 • Mashpee, MA 02649 (617) 477-0208

**NEW ENGLAND COASTAL
SCHAGTICOKE INDIAN ASSOCIATION**
P.O. Box 551 • Avon, MA 02322
(617) 961-1346
Laurence "Swift Tide" Shanks, Chief

NIPMUC NATION
Grafton Reservation
Hassanamisco Reservation, Sutton, MA
Frances Richardson Garnett, Chairperson
Rae Gould, Tribal Historic Preservation Officer
Cheryl Stedtler, Webmaster
State-recognized; waiting for federal recognition.
Museum & Cultural Center being planned for
Worcester, Mass.

MICHIGAN

**BURT LAKE BAND OF OTTAWA
& CHIPPEWA INDIANS COUNCIL**
P.O. Box 206 • Brutus, MI 49716
(616) 529-6113

**GRAND RIVER BAND OF THE
OTTAWA NATION COUNCIL**
c/o Mark Kok, 200 Peach Ave. • Hart, MI 49420

**LAKE SUPERIOR CHIPPEWA
OF MARQUETTE TRIBAL COUNCIL**
P.O. Box 1071 • Marquette, MI 49855
(906) 249-3969

LES CHENEAUX TRIBE
P.O Box 267 • Hessel, MI49862 (906) 484-3574

NORTHERN MICHIGAN OTTAWA TRIBE
1391 Terrace St. • Muskegon, MI 49441

**POTAWATOMI INDIAN TRIBE
OF INDIANA & MICHIGAN**
Route 6, Box 526 • Dowagiac, MI 49047

MISSOURI

**NORTHERN CHEROKEE NATION
OF THE OLD LOUISIANA TERRITORY**
1502 E. Broadway #201 • Columbia, MO 65201

MONTANA

**LITTLE SHELL TRIBE OF CHIPPEWA
INDIANS OF MONTANA**
P.O. Box 1384 • Great Falls, MT 59403-1384
(406) 265-2741

SWAN CREEK & BLACK RIVER CHIPPEWA
Dixon, MT

NEW JERSEY

**NANTICOKE LENNI-LENAPE
INDIANS OF NJ, INC.**
18 E. Commerce St. • Bridgeton, NJ 08302
(609) 455-8210/6910
Mark M. Gould, Chairperson
Programs: Cultural Center - job training/employment,
drug/alcohol/cigarette abuse program; AIDS education
program; elders program; referral service; cultural-danc-
ing, singing & drumming; annual pow-wow. Maintains
museum and library.

CHEROKEE NATION OF NEW JERSEY
1164 Stuyvesant Ave. • Irvington, NJ 07111
(973) 351-1210 (phone & fax)
Carl Watson Longbow, Principal Chief
Katherine Buffalo Woman Ferrante, Chief Assistant
Edward Sunwolf, Chief Speaker
Activities: Actively involved with the habitat and environmental matters of Mother Earth. *Programs*: Performances for senior citizens and schools. Maintains mini
museum, library and trading post.

NATIVE DELAWARE INDIANS
c/o New Jersey Indian Office
300 Main St., Suite 3F • Orange, NJ 07050
(201) 675-0694

POWHATAN RENAPE NATION
RANKOKUS RESERVATION
P.O. Box 225 • Rancocas, NJ 08073
(609) 261-4747
Chief Nemattanew (Roy Crazy Horse)
Description: Located near Mt. Holly, NJ, the reservation consists of the Powhatan ancestral village with a conference center, heritage museum and art gallery, library, gift shop, and nature trails. *Special programs:* Crafts - Indian artists demonstrate their skills; cultural programs; audio-visual presentations; and classes and meetings in Powhatan language and traditions are held. Annual Arts Festival.

RAMAPOUGH MOUNTAIN INDIANS
19 Mountain Rd. • Mahwah, NJ 07430 (201) 529-5750

NEW MEXICO

PUEBLO OF SAN JUAN DE GUADALUPE
Piro/Manso/Tiwa Indian Tribal Council
P.O. Box 16243 • Las Cruces, NM 88004
(505) 647-5372 (Phone & Fax)
Louis Roybal, Governor
Edward Roybal, Sr., Casique
Carlos Sanchez, Lt. Governor
Andrew Roybal, 1st War Captain
Location: A non-federally recognized Tribe with over 200 enrolled members is situated within an urban city near the Rio Grande River in the Mesilla Valley in southern New Mexico. *Tribes served:* Piro, Manso and Tiwa. *Population served:* 350. *Project:* Establishing a tribal cultural center. *Activities:* Tribal religious ceremonies and feast days occur four times a year in March, June, September and December. State recognized. Federal recognition is pending.

TIWA INDIAN TRIBE
4028 San Ysidro Rd. • San Ysidro, NM 88005
a.k.a. San Juan de Guadalupe Tiwa

NEW YORK

ABENAKI INDIAN VILLAGE
Lake George, NY 12845

MONTAUK INDIAN TRIBE
Hempstead Dr. • Sag Harbor, NY 11963

POOSPATUCK TRIBE
Unkechauge Nation Council
Poospetuck Reservation
198 Poospetuck Ln., P.O. Box 86
Mastic, NY 11950 (516) 399-3843; 281-6464
Howard E. Treadwell, Chief

SHINNECOCK TRIBE
P.O. Box 59 • Southampton, NY 11968
(516) 283-1643
Brad Smith, Kevin Eleazer,
James Eleazer, Jr., Trustees
Tribe: Shinnecock. *In residence:* 375. *Area:* 400 acres. Located in Suffolk County, NY, near Southampton.

NORTH CAROLINA

CHEROKEE INDIANS OF HOKE CITY
Rt. 1, Box 129-C, Lumber Bridge, NC 28357
(919) 975-0222

CHEROKEE INDIANS OF ROBESON
& ADJOINING COUNTIES
Rte. 2, P.O. Box 272-A, Red Springs, NC 28377

CHEROKEE-POWHATTAN INDIAN ASSOCIATION
P.O. Box 3265, Roxboro, NC 27573
(919) 599-6448

COHAIRIE INDIAN TRIBE - Clinton, NC area

FAIRCLOTH INDIAN TRIBE
P.O. Box 161, Atlantic, NC 28511

HALIWA-SAPONI TRIBE
P.O. Box 99, Hollister, NC 27844

(919) 586-4017 Fax 586-3918
Joseph Richardson, Chairperson
Michael Mills, Vice Chairperson
W.R. Richardson, Chief
Barry Richardson, Administrator
Tribe: Haliva-Saponi. *Activities:* Pow-wow (3rd Saturday in April). Small museum & library.

HATTADARE INDIAN TRIBE
Rte. 1, Box 85-B, Bunnlevel, NC 28323
(919) 893-2512

KAWEAH INDIAN NATION, INC.
address unknown @ Oriental

LUMBEE REGIONAL DEVELOPMENT ASSOCIATION, INC.
East Main St., Box 68, Pembroke, NC 28372
(919) 521-8602

MEHERRIN INDIAN TRIBE
P.O. Box 508, Winton, NC 27986
(252) 398-3321 Fax 396-0334
Calvin S. Hall, Chief
Thomas Lewis, Chairperson
E-mail: meherrin@inteliport.com
Tribe: Meherrin. *Area:* 46.9 acres. *Council:* Thomas Lewis, Wayne Brown, Ernest Poole, Phyllis Bibb, Dorothy Melton, Paige Archer, Dorothy Lee, Curtis Garrett. *Activities:* Annual Pow-Wow in Oct.; Family & Friends Day in May; Festivals; Thanksgiving Celebration. *Publication:* Quarterly newsletter for tribal members.

NEW RIVER TRIBE OF METIS
P.O. Box 126, Laurel Springs, NC 28644
(910) 657-8891 Fax 359-8834
Wayne (Guardian Bear) Rodgers, Chief
Mary Nichols, Vice-Chief
Brian Hampton, Peace Chief
Sally Meachum, Sec/Treas.
Activities: Annual Pow-Wow, Homecoming Festival; Teaching Weekends, Medicine Weekends; Red Fox Warrior Society; Phoenix Rising Women's Society. Developing funding for the Western North Carolina Center for Metis Education and presently providing a speakers bureau making presentations at schools and business organizations. *Publication:* "The Drumbeat," tribal information journal.

NORTHERN TSALAGI INDIAN TRIBE OF SOUTHWEST VIRGINIA
1813 Chandler St. • Burlington, NC 27217
(919) 584-4834

TUSCARORA INDIAN TRIBE
Drowning Creek Reservation
Maxton, NC 28364 (919) 844-3827
Chief Wise Owl

WACCAMAW SIOUAN TRIBE
P.O. Box 221, Bolton, NC 28423

NORTH DAKOTA

CHRISTIAN PEMBINA CHIPPEWA INDIANS
P.O. Box 727, Dunseith, ND 58329

LITTLE SHELL BAND OF CHIPPEWA
Dunseith, ND 58329

OHIO

ALLEGHENNY TRIBAL COUNCIL
Canton, OH (216) 453-6224 Fax 453-2867
Sakim, Chief (lifetime)
Tribe: Alleghenny Lenape. *Membership:* 17,000 (nationwide). *Activities:* Annual Festival in June; crafts, dancing and medicine ceremonies.

SHAWNEE NATION UNITED REMNANT BAND
P.O. Box 162, Dayton, OH 45401

OKLAHOMA

CHICKAMAUGA CHEROKEE INDIAN NATION OF ARKANSAS & MISSOURI
@ Miami, OK
(918) 540-1492 Fax 540-1630

YUCHI TRIBAL ORGANIZATION
located near Sapulpa, OK

OREGON

CHETCO TRIBE
564 Fern St., Brookings, OR 97415

CHINOOK TRIBE
5621 Altamont Dr., Klamath Falls, OR 97603

CONFEDERATED TRIBES OF COOS,
LOWER UMPQUAH & SIUSLAW INDIANS
338 Wallace Ave., Coos Bay, OR 97420-3100

KLAMATH TRIBE
P.O. Box 436, Chiloquin, OR 97624

NORTHWEST CHEROKEE WOLF BAND OF THE
SOUTHEASTERN CHEROKEE CONFEDERACY
address unknown @ Talent

TCHINOUK INDIANS (CHINOOK)
5621 Altamont Dr., Klamath Falls, OR 97601

SOUTH CAROLINA

FOUR HOLE INDIAN ORGANIZATION
Edisto Tribal Council, Ridgeville, SC 29472
(803) 871-2126

LOWER CHEROKEE NATION
OF SOUTH CAROLINA
Simpsonville, SC - Gene Norris, Chief

SANTEE INDIAN ORGANIZATION
675 Bayview St. • Holly Hill, SC 29059
(803) 496-3399 Fax 496-3246
Oscar Pratt, Sr., Chief; T.L. Scott, Vice-Chief

WACCAMAW-SIOUAN INDIANS OF SC
Conway, SC 29544
Harold Hatcher, Principal Chief
Tribe: Waccamaw. Organized in 1992 under the laws of the state of South Carolina. *Purpose:* To perpetuate the cultural heritage of the Waccamaw Indian people as well as all other indigenous peoples of South Carolina; to act as an international bridge between Indians and non-Indians. *Facility:* The Education and Cultural Center. *Activities:* Offers programs in traditional crafts, spirituality, traditional medicines, & foods, as well as children's programs; Sweat Lodges. *Goals:* To develop the South Carolina Museum & Library of Native American History.

TENNESSEE

ETOWAH CHEROKEE NATION
Cleveland, TN; Hugh Gibbs, Chief
Tribes served: Upper towns, Cherokee and descendants. *In residence:* 150. *Total acreage:* 1.5 Historic-Council grounds area. Historic home range - Upper towns-Ohio River Valley to Tennessee River Valley; contemporary home range - Tennessee and tributaries River Valleys. *Activities:* School/public presentations; 7 Cherokee ceremonials. Museum & Library specializing in Upper towns material. *Publications:* My People The Cherokee by Hu Gibbs.
RED CLAY INTER-TRIBAL INDIAN BAND OF
SOUTHEASTERN CHEROKEE CONFEDERACY
7703 Georgetown Rd., Ooltewah, TN 37363

TEXAS

ALABAMA-COUSHATTA TRIBES OF TEXAS
Alabama-Coushatta Reservation
Route 3, Box 640, Livingston, TX 77351

TIGUA (TIWA) TRIBE
P.O. Box 17579, Ysleta Sta. • El Paso, TX 79917

UTAH

KOOSHAHEN BAND OF PAIUTES
P.O. Box 454 • Richfield, UT 84701

NORTHEASTERN BAND OF SHOSHONE INDIANS
660 S. 200 W. • Brigham City, UT 84302

WHITE MESA UTE COUNCIL
P.O. Box 340 • Blanding, UT 84511
(801) 678-3397

VERMONT

ABENAKI TRIBAL COUNCIL
P.O. Box 276, Swanton, VT 05488
(802) 868-7146; Homer St. Francis, Chief
Tribe: St. Francis/Sokoki Band of Abenakis of Vermont.

VIRGINIA

CHICKAHOMINY INDIAN TRIBE
Providence Forge, VA 23140
(804) 829-2186
Arthur L. (Lone Wolf) Adkins, Chief
Population: @1,000. Located in Charles City County.

EASTERN CHICKAHOMINY INDIAN TRIBE
12111 Indian Hill Lane, Providence Forge, VA 23140
(804) 966-2719 • Marvin (Strong Oak) Bradby, Chief
Population: 150. Located in New Kent County, 25 miles
east of Richmond.

MATTAPONI TRIBE
Rte. 2, Box 255, West Point, VA 23181
(804) 769-2194
Webster (Little Eagle) Custalow, Chief
Tribe: Mattaponi. Population: 75. Located in King William County along the Mattaponi River off Rt. 30 at Rt.
626. Operates a museum, trading post and craft shop.

MONACAN NATION
Monacan Tribal Council
P.O. Box 1136, Madison Heights, VA 24572
(804) 946-0389; Kenneth Branham, Chief
E-mail: mnation538@aol.com
Web site: http://11members.tripod.com/monacannation
Tribe: Monacan. *In residence*: 500. *Total acreage*: 110
acres located on Bear Mountain, 10 miles northwest of
Lynchburg, VA. *Elected officials*: Johnny Johns, Assistant Chief; Karenne Wood, Secretary. *Activities*: Annual
Pow-wow; Homecoming Festival; Scholarship Auction;
Land Recovery Project; Museum; Bear Mountain Indian
Mission School - a National Historic Landmark. *Publication*: Monthly newsletter. Received state recognition
in 1989.

NANSEMOND INDIAN TRIBAL ASSOCIATION
P.O. Box 9293, 3429 Galberry Rd. (Chief)
3316 Fietz Dr. (Asst. Chief), Chesapeake, VA 23321
(804) 487-5116
Earl (Running Deer) Bass, Chief
William K. Langston (Strong Bear), Asst. Chief
Tribe: Nansemond. *Population*: 300. The area of Reeds
Ferry and Chuckatuck in Suffolk was the original preserve of the Nansemonds. Today members are stretched
across Norfolk, Chesapeake, Virginia Beach, and Portsmouth. *Councilmen*: Alvin L. Bond; Kenneth P. Bass,
Sr. (Iron Horse); Barry W. Bass (Big Buck); Charles T.
Bond; Gary F. Bond (Red Hawk).

PAMUNKEY RESERVATION
Rte. 1, Box 987, King William, VA 23086
(804) 843-2851 or 843-4792
William P. (Swift Water) Miles, Chief
Tribe: Pamunkey. Located in King William County, off
Rt. 30 and Rt. 133 along the Pamunkey River. Operates a museum. *Council Members*: Raymond Bosh,
Walter Hill, Robert Grey, Tom Dennis, William P. Miles,
Ivy Bradley. The burial site of Chief Powhatan; Museum.

UNITED RAPPAHANNOCK TRIBE
Richmond County @ Indian Neck, VA
(804) 769-4767

Captain (Chaawanta) Nelson, Chief
Population: 750. Located in King & Queen County.
Activities: Rappahannock Tribal Dancers.

UPPER MATTAPONI INDIAN TRIBE
P.O. Box 182, King William, VA 23086
(804) 769-0041 • Edmund S. Adams, Chief
Located in King William County. A new cultural village
site is being developed on Rt. 30, known as the
Pamunkey-Mattaponi Trail.

WASHINGTON

CHINOOK INDIAN NATION
P.O. Box 228, Chinook, WA 98614
(360) 777-8303
Gary C. Johnson, Chairperson
Enrollment: 2,304. Located in Pacific County.
Does not yet have a permanent reservation.

COWLITZ INDIAN TRIBE
P.O. Box 2547, Longview, WA 98632
(360) 577-8140 Fax 577-7432
John Barnett, Chairperson
Located in Cowlitz County.

DUWAMISH TRIBAL COUNCIL
Renton, WA (206) 226-5185 Fax 226-5240
Cecile Hansen, Chairperson (lifetime term)
Cindy Williams, Secretary/Treasurer
E-Mail: Duwamish@nwrain.com
Tribe served: Duwamish. *Membership*: 460. Located in
King County, Seattle metro area. *Council members*:
James Rasmussen, Jolene Williams, Mary Jane
Holmes, William Conklin, Sr., Barbara Droettboom. *Activities*: Annual meeting in June; river restoration;
fundraising events. *Publications*: Tribal newsletter;
Washington's "Landless" Tribes: Our Quest for Federal
Tribal Recognition.

KIKIALLUS INDIAN NATION
3933 Bagley Ave. N. • Seattle, WA 98103
Paul Lavan, Chief
Located in King County

MARIETTA BAND OF NOOKSACK TRIBE
1827 Marine Dr. • Bellingham, WA 98226
Robert Davis, Jr., Chairperson

SNOHOMISH TRIBAL COUNCIL - Arlington, WA
William E. Matheson, Chairperson
Michael C. Evans, Vice-Chair
Tribe: Snohomish. *Programs*: Governance Leadership
Development. *Activities*: Annual Canoe Activity Project
for tribal youth; Annual September Gathering; Annual
Treaty Celebration in January. *Publications*: Quarterly
newsletter; "The Snohomish Sound," in-house cookbook
of tribal members' family recipes. Located in Skagit Co.

SNOQUALMIE TRIBE
P.O. Box 280 • Carnation, WA 98014
(206) 333-6551 Fax 333-6553
Andy de los Angeles, Chairperson
Located in Kings County.

SNOQUALMOO TRIBE OF WHIDBEY
Couperville, WA (206) 221-8301
Lon J. Posenjak, Chairperson
Located in Island County.

STEILACOOM INDIAN TRIBE
P.O. Box 419, Steilacoom, WA 98388
(206) 584-6308; Joan K. Ortez, Chairperson
Located in Pierce County. As of May 1994, this tribe did
not yet have a permanent reservation. *Tribal membership*: approximately 650.

WISCONSIN

BROTHERTON INDIANS OF WISCONSIN
2848 Witches Lake Rd., Arbor Vitae, WI 54568
(715) 542-3913
June Ezold, Chairperson
Phyllis Mattern, Vice President
Leo Tousey, Treasurer Sandra Pawlacyk, Secretary

Tribe: Brotherton. *Council members*: Bernard Sampson,
Irene Shady, Cyrus Welch, Anne Walters, and George
Wentz. *Activities*: Annual picnic in July, and annual
homecoming pow-wows selling crafts in October. Archives held at Adams House, Fond du Lac Historical
Society, WI. *Publications*: "The Brotherton Indian Nation of Wisconsin: A Brief History", brochure; A Man
Called Sampson by Will & Rudi Ottery; and Families of
Ettink and Welch by Joan Waldvogel.

WYOMING

NORTHWESTERN BAND OF SHOSHONE NATION
Rock Springs, WY

FEDERALLY RECOGNIZED
TRIBES & BANDS

**ABSENTEE-SHAWNEE TRIBE OF INDIANS
OF OKLAHOMA**

ALABAMA-COUSHATTA TRIBES OF TEXAS

ALABAMA-QUASSARTE TRIBAL TOWN, OKLAHOMA

ALASKAN NATIVES
Aleuts, Eskimos, and Indians (Athapascans)

APACHE
Apache Tribe of Oklahoma
Camp Verde Reservation, Arizona
Fort Apache Reservation (White Mountain), Arizona
Fort Sill Apache Tribe of Oklahoma
Fort McDowell Reservation, Arizona
Jicarilla Apache Reservation, New Mexico
Mescalero Apache Reservation, New Mexico
San Carlos Reservation, Arizona
Tonto Apache Tribe of Arizona

ARAPAHOE
Arapahoe Tribe of Oklahoma
Wind River Reservation, Wyoming

**AROOSTOOK BAND OF MICMACS OF MAINE
ASSINIBOINE & SIOUX TRIBES**
Fort Peck Reservation, Montana

BANNOCK (SHOSHONE-BANNOCK)
Fort Hall Reservation, Idaho

BLACKFEET
Blackfeet Reservation, Montana

CADDO
Caddo Indian Tribe of Oklahoma

CAHUILLA
Agua Caliente Indian Reservation, California
Augustine Reservation, California
Cabazon Reservation, California
Cahuilla Reservation, California
Los Coyotes Reservation, California
Morongo Reservation, California
Ramona Reservation, California
Santa Rosa Reservation, California
Torres Martinez Reservation, California

CAYUGA
Cayuga Nation of New York
Cayuga Tribe of Oklahoma

CHEHALIS
Confederated Tribes of the Chehalis Reservation, WA

CHEMEHUEVI
Chemehuevi Reservation, California

CHEROKEE
Cherokee Nation of Oklahoma
Eastern Band of Cherokee, North Carolina
United Keetoowah Band of Cherokee Indians, Okla.
United Cherokee of Alabama
Echota Cherokee of Alabama
Cherokees of Northeast Alabama

Cherokees of Southeast Alabama
Cherokees of Jackson City, Alabama
Southeastern Cherokee Confederacy, Georgia (ST)
Georgia Tribe of Cherokees, Georgia
Cherokee Tribe of Robeson & Adjoining Cos, NC
Cherokee Indians of Hoke County, North Carolina
Northwest Wolf Band of the South Eastern
  Cherokee Confederacy, Oregon
Red Clay Inter Tribal Band of the South Eastern
  Cherokee Confederacy, Tennessee
Cherokee Tribe of Virginia

CHEYENNE
Cheyenne Tribe of Oklahoma
Northern Cheyenne Tribe of Montana

CHICKASAW
Chickasaw Nation of Oklahoma

CHIPPEWA (OJIBWE)
Bay Mills Reservation (Sault Ste. Marie Band), Mich.
Grande Traverse Band of Chippewa, Michigan
Isabella Reservation (Saginaw Chippewa), Michigan
L'Anse Reservation, Michigan
Lake Superior Band of Chippewa:
  Bad River Reservation, Wisconsin
  Lac Courte Oreilles Reservation, Wisconsin
  Lac du Flambeau Reservation, Wisconsin
  Red Cliff Reservation, Wisconsin
Minnesota Chippewa Tribe (six reservations):
  Nett Lake (Boise Forte) Reservation
  Fond du Lac Reservation
  Grand Portage Reservation
  Leech Lake Reservation
  Mill Lac Reservation
  White Earth Reservation
Red Lake Reservation, Minnesota
Rocky Boy's Reservation, Montana
Sault Ste. Marie Reservation, Michigan
St. Croix Reservation, Wisconsin
Sokoagon Chippewa (Mole Lake Band), Wisconsin
Turtle Mountain Reservation, North Dakota

CHITIMACHA
Chitimacha Tribe of Louisiana

CHOCTAW
Choctaw Nation of Oklahoma
Mississippi Band of Choctaw, Mississippi

CHUMASH (MISSION INDIANS)
Santa Ynez Reservation, California

COCOPAH
Cocopah Tribe of Arizona

COEUR D' ALENE
Coeur D' Alene Reservation, Idaho

COLORADO RIVER
Colorado River Reservation, Arizona and California

COLVILLE
Confederated Tribes of the Colville Reservation, WA

COMANCHE
Comanche Indian Tribe of Oklahoma

COUSHATTA
Coushatta Tribe of Louisiana

CREE
Cree Indians of Rocky Boy's Reservation, Montana

CREEK
Alabama-Quassarte Tribal Town of Creek Nation, Okla.
Creek Nation of Oklahoma
Kialegee Tribal Town of the Creek Nation, Oklahoma
Thlopthlocco Tribal Town of the Creek Nation, Oklahoma

CROW
Crow Tribe of Montana

DELAWARE
Delaware Tribes of Western Oklahoma

DIEGUENO (MISSION INDIANS)
Barona Reservation, California
Campo Reservation, California
Capitan Grande Reservation, California

Cuyapaipe Reservation, California
Inaga and Cosmit Reservations, California
LaPosta Reservation, California
Manzanita Reservation, California
Mesa Grande Reservation, California
San Pasqual Reservation, California
Santa Ysabel, Reservation, California
Sycuan Reservation, California
Viejas Reservtion, California

FORT BELKNAP INDIAN COMMUNITY
OF FORT BELKNAP RESERVATION, MONT.

GOSHUTE
Confederated Tribes-Goshute Reservation, NV & UT
Skull Valley Band of the Goshute Indians of Utah

GROS VENTRE
Fort Belknap Reservation, Montana

HAVASUPAI
Havasupai Tribe of Arizona

HOH
Hoh Reservation, Washington

HOOPA
Hoopa Valley Reservation, California

HOPI
Hopi Tribe of Arizona

HUALAPAI
Hualapai Reservation, Arizona

IOWA
Iowa Tribe of Oklahoma
Iowa Reservation, Nebraska and Kansas

KALISPEL
Kalispel Reservation, Washington

KAROK
Karok Tribe of California

KAW
Kaw Indian Tribe of Oklahoma

KICKAPOO
Kickapoo Reservation, Kansas
Kickapoo Tribe of Oklahoma

KIOWA
Kiowa Tribe of Oklahoma

KLALLAM
Jamestown Band of Klallam Indians, Washington
Lower Elwha Reservation, Washington
Port Gamble Reservation, Washington
KOOTENAI
Kootenai Tribe of Idaho

LUISENO (MISSION INDIANS)
La Jolla Reservation, California
Pala Reservation, California
Pauma and Yuima Reservation, California
Pechanga Reservation, California
Rincon Reservation, California
Soboba Reservation, California
Twenty-Nine Palms Reservation, California

LUMMI
Lummi Reservation, Washington

MAIDU
Berry Creek Rancheria, California
Enterprise Rancheria, California
Round Valley Reservation (Covelo Community), CA
Susanville Indian Rancheria, California

MAKAH
Makah Reservation, Washington

MARICOPA
Gila River Reservation, Arizona
Salt River Reservation, Arizona

ME-WUK (MIWOK)
Jackson Rancheria, California
Sheep Ranch Rancheria, California

Shingle Springs Band of Me-Wuk Indians of California
Trinidad Rancheria (Cher-Ae Heights Indian
  Community), California
Tuolumne Band of Me-Wuk Indians of California

MENOMINEE
Menominee Reservation, Wisconsin
MIAMI
Miami Tribe of Oklahoma

MICCOSUKEE
Miccosukkee Tribe of Florida

MODOC
Modoc Tribe of Oklahoma

MOHAVE
Fort McDowell Reservation, Arizona

MOHAWK
St. Regis Band of Mohawk, New York

MONO
Cold Springs Rancheria, California

MUCKLESHOOT
Muckleshoot Reservation, Washington

NARRAGANSETT INDIAN TRIBE OF R.I.

NAVAJO
Navajo Reservation, Arizona, New Mexico and Utah

NEZ PERCE
Nez Perce Reservation, Idaho

NISQUALLY
Nisqually Reservation, Washington

NOOKSACK
Nooksack Indian Tribe of Washington

OMAHA
Omaha Tribe of Nebraska

ONEIDA
Oneida Nation of New York
Oneida Tribe of Wisconsin

ONONDAGA
Onondaga Nation of New York

OSAGE
Osage Tribe of Oklahoma

OTOE-MISSOURIA
Otoe-Missouria of Oklahoma

OTTAWA
Grande Traverse Band, Michigan
Ottawa Tribe of Oklahoma

PAIUTE
Benton (Utu Utu Gwaitu) Paiute Reservation, CA
Big Pine Reservation, California
Bishop Colony, California
Bridgeport Indian Colony, California
Burns Paiute Indian Colony, Oregon
Cedarville Rancheria, California
Duck Valley Reservation, Nevada
Fallon Reservation and Colony, Nevada
Fort Bidwell Reservation, California
Fort Independence Reservation, California
Fort McDermitt Reservation, Nevada
Kaibab Reservation, Arizona
Las Vegas Indian Colony, Nevada
Lone Pine Reservation, California
Lovelock Indian Colony, Nevada
Moapa River Reservation, Nevada
Pyramid Lake Reservation, Nevada
Reno-Sparks Indian Colony, Nevada
Summit Lake Reservation, Nevada
Utah: Cedar City, Indian Peaks, Kanosh,
  Koosharen and Shivwite
Walker River Reservation, Nevada
Winnemucca Indian Colony, Nevada
Yerington Colony and Campbell Ranch, Nevada

PASQUA YAQUI
Pascua Yaqui Tribe of Arizona

PASSAMAQUODDY
Passamaquoddy Tribe of Maine

PAWNEE
Pawnee Indian Tribe of Oklahoma

PENOBSCOT
Penobscot Tribe of Maine

PEORIA
Peoria Tribe of Oklahoma

PIT RIVER
Alturas Indian Rancheria, California
Big Bend Rancheria, California
Lookout Rancheria, California
Montgomery Creek Rancheria, California
Roaring Creek Rancheria, California
Susanville Indian Rancheria, California
XL Ranch Reservation, California

POMO
Coyote Valley Band, California
Dry Creek Rancheria, California
Hopland Rancheria (Hopland Band), California
Laytonville Rancheria (Cahto Indian Tribe), CA
Manchester—Point Arena Rancheria, California
Middletown Rancheria, California
Robinson Rancheria. California
Sherwood Valley Rancheria, California
Stewarts Point Rancheria (Kashia Band), CA
Sulphur Bank Rancheria (Elem Indian Colony), CA
Upper Lake Band, California

PONCA
Ponca Tribe of Nebraska
Ponca Tribe of Oklahoma

POTAWATOMI
Citizen Band Potawatomi Indians of Oklahoma
Forest County Potawatomi Community of Wisconsin
Hannahville Indian Community of Michigan
Prairie Band of Potawatomi of Kansas

PUEBLO (NEW MEXICO)
Pueblo of Acoma
Pueblo of Cochiti
Pueblo of Jemez
Pueblo of Ildefonso
Pueblo of Isleta
Pueblo of Laguna
Pueblo of Nambe
Pueblo of Picuris
Pueblo of Pojoaque
Pueblo of San Felipe
Pueblo of San Juan
Pueblo of Sandia
Pueblo of Santa Ana
Pueblo of Santa Clara
Pueblo of Santo Domingo
Pueblo of Taos
Pueblo of Tesuque
Pueblo of Zia
Zuni Reservation (Zuni Tribe)

PUYALLUP
Puyallup Reservation, Washington

QUAPAW
Quapaw Tribe of Oklahoma

QUECHAN
Fort Yuma Reservation (Yuma), California

QUILEUTE
Quileute Reservation, Washington

QUINAULT
Quinault Reservation, Washington

SAC AND FOX
Sac and Fox Reservation (Sac and Fox of the
    Missouri), Kansas and Nebraska
Sac and Fox Tribe of the Mississippi, Iowa
Sac and Fox Tribe of Oklahoma

SALISH & KOOTENAI
Flathead Reservation (Confederated Tribes), Montana

SAUK-SUIATTLE
Sauk-Suiattle Tribe of Washington

SEMINOLE
Seminole Nation of Oklahoma
Seminole Tribe of Florida

SENECA
Seneca-Cayuga Tribe of Oklahoma
Seneca Nation of New York
Tonawanda Band, New York

SERRANO
San Manual (Band) Reservation, California

SHAWNEE
Absentee Shawnee of Oklahoma
Eastern Shawnee Tribe of Oklahoma

SHOALWATER
Shoalwater Bay Reservation, Washington

SHOSHONE
Battle Mountain Colony (Te-Moak Band), Nevada
Big Pines Band (Owens Valley), California
Duck Valley Reservation, Nevada
Duckwater Reservation, Nevada
Elko Colony (Te-Moak Band), Nevada
Ely Indian Colony, Nevada
Fallon Reservation and Colony, Nevada
Fort McDermitt Reservation, Nevada
Lone Pine Reservation, California
Northwestern Band, Utah
South Fork Colony, Nevada
Wind River Reservation, Wyoming
Yomba Shoshone Tribe of Nevada

SILETZ
Confederated Tribes of the Siletz Reservation, OR

SIOUX
Cheyenne River Reservation, South Dakota
Crow Creek Reservation, South Dakota
Devils Lake Reservation, North Dakota
Flandreau Santee Sioux Reservation, South Dakota
Fort Peck Reservation (Assiniboine & Sioux), SD
Lower Brule Sioux Reservation, South Dakota
Lower Sioux Community (Mdewakanton), Minnesota
Pine Ridge Reservation (Oglala), South Dakota
Prairie Island Reservation (Mdewakanton), MN
Rosebud Reservation, South Dakota
Santee Sioux Reservation, Nebraksa
Shakopee Mdewakanton Sioux Community, Minnesota
Sisseton-Wahpeton Sioux Reservation, South Dakota
Standing Rock Reservation, North and South Dakota
Upper Sioux Reservation, Minnesota
Yankton Sioux Tribe of South Dakota

SKAGIT
Upper Skagit Indian Tribe of Washington

SKOKOMISH
Skokomish Reservation, Washington

SMITH RIVER
Big Lagoon Rancheria, California

SPOKANE
Spokane Tribe of Washington

SQUAXIN ISLAND
Squaxin Island Reservation, Washington

STILLAGUAMISH
Stillaguamish Tribe of Washington

STOCKBRIDGE-MUNSEE
Stockbridge-Munsee Community of Mohican Indians,
    Wisconsin

SWINOMISH
Swinomish Reservation, Washington

SUQUAMISH
Port Madison Reservation, Washington

TACHE
Santa Rosa Rancheria, California

THREE AFFILIATED TRIBES
  (GROSS VENTRE, HIDATSA, MANDAN)
Three Affiliated Tribes of Fort Berthold, ND

TOHONO O'ODHAM - PIMA/PAPAGO
Ak Chin Indian Community of the
   Maricopa Indian Reservation, Arizona
Gila Bend Reservation, Arizona
Gila River Reservation, Arizona
Salt River Reservation, Arizona
San Xavier Reservation, Arizona
Sells Reservation, Arizona

TOLOWA
Cher-Ae Heights Community, Trinidad Rancheria, CA

TONKAWA
Tonawa Tribe of Oklahoma

TULALIP
Tule River Reservation, California

TUSCARORA
Tuscarora Nation of New York

UMATILLA
Confederated Tribes of the Umatilla Reservation, OR

UTE
Southern Ute Reservation, Colorado
Uintah and Ouray Reservation, Utah
Ute Mountain Reservation, CO, UT & NM

WYANDOTTE
Wyandotte Tribe of Oklahoma

WARM SPRINGS
Confederated Tribes of the Warm Springs
   Reservation   (Walla Walla and Cayuga), Oregon

WASHOE
Carson Colony, Nevada
Dresslerville Rancheria, Nevada
Reno-Sparks Indian Colony, Nevada
Susanville Indian Rancheria, California
Washoe Rancheria, Nevada

WICHITA
Wichita Tribe of Oklahoma

WINNEBAGO
Winnebago Tribe of Nebraska
Winnebago Tribe of Wisconsin

WINTUN
Colusa Rancheria (Cachil DeHe Band), California
Cortina Indian Rancheria, California
Grindstone Indian Rancheria (Wintun-Wailaki),
   California
Rumsey Indian Rancheria, California

WIYOT
Table Bluff Rancheria of California

YAKAMA
Yakama Reservation (Confederated Tribes),
   Washington

YAVAPAI
Camp Verde Reservation, Arizona
Yavapai-Prescott Tribe of Arizona

YOKUT
Santa Rosa Rancheria, California
Table Mountain Rancheria, California

YUROK
Berry Creek Reservation, California
Hoopa Valley Reservation, California
Resighini Rancheria, California
Trinidad Rancheria (Cher-Ae Heights), California

This section is an alpha-geographical listing of government agencies—regional and state, mainly—concerned in various ways with the American Indian and his affairs. The principal federal agency in this area is the Bureau of Indian Affairs of the U.S. Department of the Interior. The following is a description of the activities of the Bureau, with a directory of its Central (Washington, DC) Office. The geographical listings follow.

U.S. DEPT. OF THE INTERIOR
BUREAU OF INDIAN AFFAIRS
1849 C St., NW - MS 4140-MIB
WASHINGTON, DC 20240-0001
(202) 208-7163 Fax 208-5320
David W. Anderson, Ass't. Secretary of the Interior-Indian Affairs
Aurene Martin, Deputy Ass't Secretary of the Interior-Indian Affairs
Ross Swimmer, Special Trustee
Joe Kahklen, Alaska Liaison Officer 208-5819
Nedra Darling, Director-Public Affairs 208-3711

Website: http://www.doi.gov/bureau-Indian-affairs.html

Description: Established in 1824, the Bureau of Indian Affairs (BIA) is an agency of the U.S. Department of the Interior. Its original function was the trusteeship of Indian lands—which now number some 54 million acres of land held in trust by the U.S. for various Indian tribes and individuals. Though most trust land is reservation land, all reservation land is not trust land. The Secretary of the Interior functions on behalf of the U.S. as the trustee, with many of the more routine responsibilities delegated to the Bureau of Indian Affairs officials. The Assistant Secretary-Indian Affairs has the responsibilies to individual and tribal trust beneficiaries, as well as promoting tribal self-determination, self-governance, and economic development for the nation's 562 federally recognized American Indian & Alaska Native tribes and their members. The Assistant Secretary also overseas the BIA, that provides services to individual American Indians and Alaska Natives from the federally recognized tribes; the Office of Federal Acknowledgement, which administers the Federal Acknowledgement Process; and the BIA school system which serves almost 50,000 American Indian & Alaska Native children located on or near 63 reservations in 23 states, .

The BIA is responsible for the administration of federal programs for federally recognized tribes, and for promoting Indian self-determination. In addition, the Bureau has a trust responsibility emanating from treaties and other agreements with Native groups, The mission of the Bureau is to enhance the quality of life, to promote economic opportunity, and to carry out the responsibility to protect and improve the trust assets of Indian tribes and Alaska Natives. The BIA provides the kind of services one expects from a local, city, county, State, or the Federal Government. This includes, but is not limited to, law enforcement, social services, education, housing improvements, loan opportunities for Indian businesses, and leasing of land. The Indian Health Service, an agency within the Dept. of Health and Human Services, provides health care for American Indians and Alaska Natives.

The BIA currently provides federal services to approximately 1.5 million American Indians and Alaska Natives who are members of 562 federally recognized Indian tribes in the 48 contiguous U.S. and in Alaska. The Bureau administers 54 million acres of land held in trust status of which 43.4 million are tribally-owned, 10.2 million individually-owned, and .4 million acres are federally-owned.

The BIA is headed by an Assistant Secretary-Indian Affairs, who is responsible for BIA policy, but operationally the BIA is a bifurcated organization directed by (1) a Depty Commissioner of Indian Affairs, who has line authority over Area Offices, Agency Offices, sub-agencies, field stations, and irrigation project offices; the Director of the Office of Indian Education, who has authority over education line offices.

The BIA funds approximately 200 elementary, secondary and post-secondary Indian schools, many of them operated by tribal governments or organizations under contract with the Bureau. Other programs provide assistance for Indian college students, for vocational training, and for adult education.

Budget — The Bureau receives approximately 2 billion dollars per year for its programs & projects. The budget includes money for education, Indian services which include law enforcement, social service programs and other local governmental programs; economic development and employment programs; natural resources development; trust responsibilities; facilities management; general administration; construction; for Indian loan guarantees and insurance fund; the BIA receives additional money for reservation road construction through the Department of Transportation, under provisions of the Highway Improvement Act of 1982.

In accordance with the policy of Indian Self-Determination, the Bureau encourages tribes to operate their own reservation programs under contract with the Bureau. Almost one half of the total BIA budget is transmitted directly to tribal governments for the operation of such contracted programs.

Appropriations for other federal Indian Agencies: Indian Health Service in the Department of Health and Human Services; Indian Education Office in the Department of Education. Other federal agencies, such as Agriculture, Commerce and HUD, also receive funding specifically designated for Indian programs.

Education — There are approximately 300,000 Indian children of school age, the majority of whom are enrolled in public schools. Legislation: In recent years, two major laws have resulted in a restructuring of the entire Bureau education program. In 1975, the passage of P.L. 93-638, The Indian Self Determination and Education Assistance Act, greatly facilitated contracting for the operation of education programs by tribal groups. The passage of P.L. 95-561, The Indian Education Act, in 1978, mandated a major change in the operation of both Bureau-operated and tribally contracted schools. The implementation of P.L. 95-561 resulted in decision-making powers for Indian school boards, local hiring of teachers and staff, direct funding to the schools, and increased authority for the Director of Indian Education Programs within the Bureau.

Federal Schools: In 2004, the BIA will fund a approximately 200 school facilities, of which about half are contracted out and operated directly by Indian tribes. These include day schools, on-reservation boarding schools, off-reservation boarding schools, tribally contracted schools, and dormitories. Dormitories are operated by the Bureau to facilitate public school attendance for Indian students.

Public School Assistance (Johnson O'Malley Program): The B.I.A. provides funds under the Johnson-O'Malley Act of 1934 to meet the special needs of Indian students in public schools. These funds, which are largely administered through contracts with tribal organizations, public school districts and state departments of education, enable the contractors to provide supplemental programs for Indian students. Approximately 200,000 Indian students in 26 states receive assistance from JOM funds. The Bureau has JOM contracts for administration and development of programs with about 250 tribal organizations, numerous public schools and a number of state departments of education. There are more than 800 Indian parent committees working with these contractors.

Indians in College: In 2000, there were approximately 40,000 Indian students on BIA, IHS, and ED scholarships and fellowships. In 2000, more than 2,500 Indian students at the graduate and undergraduate levels earned degrees. About 500 students receiving BIA assistance are in law school, medical school, and other graduate programs. Total appropriations provided through the BIA for Indian higher education were about $50 million in 2000.

Tribally Controlled Colleges: The BIA provides grants for the operation of more than 30 tribally controlled colleges. There are approximately 20,000 Indian students (half of them part time) enrolled in these community colleges. Tribal colleges must pass a stringent feasibility study in order to be eligible for grants under the Tribally Controlled College Assistance Act of 1978.

B.I.A. Post-Secondary Schools: The BIA operates three post-secondary schools. They are Haskell Indian Nations University in Lawrence, Kansas with an enrollment of about 800 students; Institute of American Indian Arts at Santa Fe, New Mexico with about 200 students; and Southwestern Indian Polytechnic Institute at Albuquerque, New Mexico with about 500 students.

Handicapped Children's Program: Under the Handicapped Children's Act, P.L. 94-142, the Bureau provides financial support for the educational costs of handicapped Indian children. An average of 200 children are served annually in about 25 different facilities.

Substance/Alcohol Abuse Education Programs: The objective of BIA educational programs in substance and alcohol abuse is to provide Bureau-funded schools with curriculum materials and technical assistance in developing and implementing alcohol and substance abuse programs in areas of identification, assessment, prevention, and crisis intervention through the use of referrals and additional counselors at the schools.

Health — Indian Health Service: An agency of the Department of Health & Human Services and the primary federal health resource for approximately 1.5 million eligible American Indians and Alaskan Natives.

Housing — In cooperation with the Department of Housing and Urban Development (HUD) tribes are treated as local government units with authority to establish local housing authorities, the instruments through which Indians may obtain low-income housing from the Federal Government. More than 200 tribes have established such housing authorities.

Water Rights — The Office of Indian Water Rights, established in 1972, is designed to protect the water rights of reservation Indians. Since its formation, water allocation studies have been made on many reservations, and legal suits have been filed to protect Indian water.

Forestry — Established in 1910 to bring about order in the management of Indian owned forest property. Some objectives of management are to preserve the property in perpetuity by providing effective protection services, by applying sound economic principles to the harvesting of forest crops, and by making adequate provisions for the continuity in growth of forest crops.

Employment with the BIA — The Bureau employs approximately 10,000 people. Native Americans make up more than 75% of that work force. Only about 400 work in the Washington central office. (Preference in employment with the B.I.A. has been granted for some years to Indians who are members of Federally recognized tribes or are one-half or more degree Indian blood.) Native Americans hold most of the top management positions in the Bureau's Central & Area offices & constitutes most of the positions in the Bureau's federally operated schools of which many are teachers, teacher's aides, administrators & workmen.

* * *

The following is a directory of the Central (Washington, DC) Office (zip code 20245) of the Bureau of Indian Affairs and its various offices & divisions. Listings of B.I.A. area & field offices & agencies may be found under specific states in the geographical part of this section which follows Independent Agencies.

Office of the Assistant Secretary-Indian Affairs: Room, 4160 MS: 4140-MIB (202) 208-7163 • David W. Anderson, Assistant Secretary; M. Sharon Blackwell & Dominic Nessi, Special Assistants.

Alaska Liaison Officer: Joe Kahklen (202) 208-5819

Office of Indian Education Programs: Rm. 3510; MS 3512-MIB. William Mehojah, Director (202) 208-6123; Joy Martin, Chief - Branch of Administrative Services (202) 208-4555; Jim Womack, Chief, Branch of Management Information Services (202) 208-7111; Dr. Dennis Fox, Chief-Division of Education Programs (202) 208-7388; Charles Geboe, Chief - Branch of Elementary & Secondary Education (202) 208-1129; Garry Martin, Chief-Branch of Post Secondary Education (202) 208-4871; Kenneth Whitehorn, Acting Chief-Branch of Exceptional Education (202) 208-6675; Sharon Wells, Chief - Branch of Supplemental Services (202) 208) 6364; Dr. James Martin, Director - Planning, Oversight and Evaluation (202) 208-3550; Keener Cobb, Chief-Branch of Planning (202) 219-1131; Dalton Henry, Chief, Branch of Research & Policy Analysis (202) 208-3562; Sandra Fox, Supervisory Education Specialist (202) 273-2339; Albuquerque Field Office - Dr. Kenneth Ross, Rodney Young, Dr. Benjamin Atencio and Cecilia Baca (505) 766-3850. Provides quality education opportunities from early childhood through life for enrolled members of federally recognized Indian tribes and Alaska Natives.

Office of Tribal Services: MS 4603-MIB. Deborah J. Maddox, Director (202) 208-3463; Harry Rainbolt, Jr., Budget & Program Officer; Betti Delrow, Child Protection Coordinator (202) 208-6858. Works directly with tribal governments and in partnership with them, provides for housing, social services, tribal enrollment, judicial systems, and police protection.

Division of Tribal Government Services: MS: 4641-MIB. Lathal Duffield, Chief - Branch of Tribal Enrollment (202) 208-2472; Holly Reckford, Chief - Branch of Acknowledgement and Research (202) 208-4686; Daisy West, Chief - Branch of Tribal Relations (202) 208-2475; Bettie Rushing, Chief - Branch of Judicial Services (202) 208-4400; Larry Blair, Chief-Division of Social Services (202) 208-2479; June Henkel, Chief-Division of Housing Services; James Thomas, Chief-Division of Self-Determination Services (202) 208-5727.

Division of Law Enforcement Services: MS: 4443-MIB. Harry DeLashmutt, Law Enforcement Specialist (208-3485); Mark Mullins, Criminal Investigator (208) 5039; *Central Office, Albuquerque*, P.O. Box 66, Albuquerque, NM 87103; 505-248-7939 Fax 248-7905 - Theodore R. Quasula, Chief; Ed Naranjo, Supervisory Criminal Investigator; Monte Daney, Director of Internal Affairs Section. *Indian Police Academy*, 1300 W. Richey, Artesia, NM 88210; 505-748-8151 Fax 748-8162 - Joseph W. Wright, Director of Training Section; C. Leon Glenn, Director of Drug Enforcement Section (748-8148).

Office of Management & Administration: MS 4613-MIB. Deborah J. Maddox, Acting Director (202) 208-4174; Anthony Howard, Chief - Division of Contracts & Grants (202) 208-2825. Responsible for the recommendation and formulation of policy to the Deputy Commissioner. Functions include personnel management, contracts and grants administration, property management, data systems, and the Equal Employment Opportunity office.

Office of Trust Responsibilities: MS 4513-MIB. Terry Virden, Director (208-5831); Glenda Brokeshoulder, Supervisor - Program Analysis Officer & Staff Coordinator(208-7216); Dan Thayer, Acting Chief - Branch of Environmental Services (208-3606); Ross Mooney, Acting Chief - Division of Water & Land Resources (208-4004); Larry Scrivner, Chief - Division of Real Estate Services (202) 208-7737; Quentin "Mike" Jones, Chief - Branch of Land Titles & Records; John Dibble, Acting Chief - Branch of Forest Resources Planning (Portland, OR - (503) 231-6799); Joe Bonga, Acting Chief - Division of Transportation (Albuquerque, NM - (505) 766-8560); William J. Bonner, Chief - Branch of Geographic Information Systems (303) 231-5100; Richard Wilson, Chief - Division of Energy & Minerals (Golden, CO - (303) 231-5070. Provides administrative direction, policy development, planning and management of renewable natural resources of Indian owned land on Federal reservations including wildlife and parks, water resources, agriculture, range, irrigation, and forestry.

Office of Economic Development: Rm. 2529; MS: 2061-MIB. Dominic (Dom) Nessi, Acting Director (202) 208-5324. Enhances reservation economies and services to Indians & Alaska Native people by developing and recommending policies, standards and procedures to assist Bureau management and Indian tribes and individuals in the development and implementation of economic development projects.

Office of Audit & Evaluation:
Rm. 2559; MS: 2472-MIB.
Linda L. Richardson, Director (202) 208-1916

Office of Public Affairs: Nedra Darling, Director (202) 219-4150

Office of American Indian Trust: MS: 2471-MIB. Elizabeth Homer, Director (202) 208-3338

Office of Self-Governance: Rm. 2550; MS: 2548-MIB. William (Bill) Sinclair, Director (202) 219-0240

Office of Congressional & Legislative Affairs: Rm. 1340; MS:1340-MIB. Jacquelyn M. (Jackie) Cheek, Director (202) 208-5706; Marge Wilkins, Legislative Coordinator

Office of the Special Trustee for American Indians: MS: 5140-MIB. (202) 208-4866. Ross Swimmer, Special Trustee

Office of Trust Funds Management (Albuquerque, NM): Donna Erwin, Director (505) 248-5723

Office of Equal Opportunity Programs: Room 4561; MS: 4559-MIB. John C. Nicholas, Director (208-3600).

Office of Indian Gaming Management Staff: Rm. 2070; MS: 2070-MIB. (202) 219-4066

Office of Alcohol & Substance Abuse Prevention: Director (202) 208-6179; Ella Lankford, Indian Youth Program Specialist

Indian Arts & Crafts Board: (Rm. 2058 MIB) (888) 278-3253; (202) 208-3773

Office of Facilities Management (Albuquerque, NM): Bill Collier, Director (505) 766-2805

* * *

The following are federal offices that direct special programs for Indians and related other federal and congressional offices.

EXECUTIVE BRANCH

The White House
1600 Pennsylvania Ave., NW
Washington, DC 20500
Personnel: George W. Bush, President; Loretta Avent, Special Assistant to the President for Intergovernment Affairs, Old Executive Office Bldg., Rm. 122, 17th & Pennsylvania Ave., NW, Washington, DC 20503 (202) 456-2896. Staff Specialists: New Executive Office Bldg., Washington, DC 20503 - Indian Affairs (202) 395-4993; Indian Education (202) 395-5880; Indian Health Service (202) 395-4926

U.S. Department of Agriculture
14th and Independence Ave., SW
Washington, DC 20250
Personnel: Elwood H. "Woody" Patawa, Director of Native American Programs - Office of Intergovernmental Affairs, Rm. 102-A, Administration Bldg. (202) 720-3805; Ronald P. Andrade, Equal Opportunity Specialist, Indian Affairs, Rm. 2305, Auditor's Bldg. (202) 720-7370; Douglas V. Sellars, Liaison for Indian Assistance, Rural Development Staff, Soil Conservation Service, Rm. 6103, South Bldg., P.O. Box 2890, Washington, DC 20013 (202) 720-7690.

U.S. Department of Commerce
U.S. Small Business Administration
Office of Native American Affairs
Washington, DC 20230
Personnel: Don Evans, Secretary; Pete Homer, Jr., Director

Bureau of the Census
Federal Center • Suitland, MD 20233
Liaison for American Indians & Alaska Natives (301) 763-2607 Fax 763-3862

U.S. Department of Education
Office of Indian Education
Rm. 3W200, Federal Office Bldg. 6
400 Maryland Ave., SW
Washington, DC 20202
(202) 260-3774 Fax 260-7779
Dr. Rod Paige, Secretary of Education
Dr. Aaron Shedd, Director, Indian Education
Programs: Educational Personnel Development Program; Educational Services Program; Formula Grant Program; Indian-Controlled Schools Enrichment Program; Indian Fellowship Program (202) 401-1916; Indian Gifted and Talented Pilot Program (202) 401-1916; and Planning, Pilot, and Demonstration Program. Office of the Assistant Secretary for Elementary and Secondary Education (202) 401-1342 - Native Hawaiian Model Curriculum Development, and School Improvement Program-Native Hawaiian Gifted and Talented; and Native Hawaiian Family-Based Education Centers. Office of the Assistant Secretary for Vocational and Adult Education, Division of National Programs, Vocational Education - Indian and Hawaiian Natives. Office of Special Education and Rehabilitative Services, 330 C St., SW, Rm. 4072, Switzer Bldg., Washington, DC 20202 (202) 732-1353, Fax (202) 732-3897

Funds six regional Indian Education Technical Assistance Centers (IETACs) which serves educators of Native students within specific geographical regions (see Indian Education Section). Also funds ten Regional Educational Laboratories which have joined together to form the Native American Education Initiative whose purpose is to improve the access of educators serving Native students to the many resources available through the various laboratories (see Indian Education Section).

U.S. Department of Energy
Denver Support Office
2801 Youngfield, Suite 380
Golden, CO 80401 (303) 231-5750
Program: Indian Energy Resource Development.

U.S. Department of Health & Human Services
Humphrey Bldg., 200 Independence Ave., SW
Washington, DC 20201
Room 615 F (202) 690-7000 Fax 245-3380; Gary Niles Kimble, Commissioner - Administration for Native Americans (202) 690-7776 (Established to provide economic and social self-sufficiency among American Indians, Native Hawaiians, and Alaskan Natives. Provides grants to achieve goals); Sharon McCully, Executive Director - Intra-Departmental Council on Indian Affairs (202) 690-6546; Fred Luhmann, Associate Commissioner - American Indian, Alaskan Native & Native Hawaiian Programs, 330 Independence Ave., SW, Washington, DC 20201 (202) 619-2957 or 619-0641; Dr. Michael H. Trujillo, M.D., Director - Indian Health Service, Room 5A-55, Parklawn Bldg., 5600 Fishers Lane, Rockville, MD 20857 (301) 443-1083; Martin Seneca, Program Specialist, Head Start Bureau, American Indian Program Branch, Room 2116, 330 C St., SW, Washington, DC 20202 (202) 205-8457

U.S. Department of Housing
& Urban Development (HUD)
451 7th St., SW
Washington, DC 20410
(202) 708-0417 Fax 755-0299
Special Assistant to the Secretary for Indian & Alaska Native Programs, Room 10222 (202) 708-0420; Assistant Secretary for Public and Indian Housing, Room 4100 (202) 708-0950; Office of Indian Housing, Room 4232 (202) 708-1015.

U.S. Department of the Interior
1849 C St., NW • Washington, DC 20240
(202) 208-7351 Fax 208-6956
Personnel: Gale Norton, Secretary; Aurene Martin, Assistant Secretary for Indian Affairs, Room 4160 (202) 208-7163; Meredith Z. Stanton, Director - Indian Arts & Crafts Board, Rm. 2058 MIB (202) 208-3773.

U.S. Dept. of the Interior
National Park Service
American Indian Liaison Office
1849 C St., NW, Rm. 3410
Washington, DC 20240
(202) 208-5475/6; Fax 273-0870

Emogene A. Bevitt, Program Specialist
Ronald M. Greenberg, Editor CRM
E-Mail: Ron_Greenberg@nps.gov
Purpose: To improve relationships between American Indian tribes, Alaska Natives, Native Hawaiians and the National Park Service through consultation, outreach, technical assistance, education, and advisory services. Office created in February 1995.

U.S. Department of Justice
10th & Constitution Ave., NW
Washington, DC 20530
(202) 514-2001
Personnel: John Ashcroft, Attorney General; Office of Tribal Justice; James Brookshire, Chief - Indian Claims Section, Land and Natural Resources Division, Room 648, 550 11th St., N.W., Washington, D.C. 20530 (202) 724-7375; Hank Meshorer, Chief - Indian Resources Section, Land and Natural Resources Division, Room 624 (202) 724-7156.

U.S. Department of Labor
200 Constitution Ave., NW
Washington, DC 20210
(202) 219-8271
Division of Indian and Native American Programs, Employment & Training Administration (202) 219-6827

U.S. Department of Transportation
400 7th St., SW • Washington, DC 20590
(202) 366-1111
Director - American Indian Nations, National Highway Traffic Safety Administration, (817) 334-4300.

LEGISLATIVE BRANCH
U.S. CONGRESS

SENATE

U.S. Senate Committee on Indian Affairs
838 Hart Senate Office Bldg. •
Washington, DC 20510
(202) 224-2251 Fax 228-2589
Website: www.indian.senate.gov
Ben Nighthorse Campbell (Northern Cheyenne)
(R-CO), Chair
Daniel Inouye (D-HI), Vice Chair

As of January 2005, Sen. Campbell will be retiring from the U.S. Senate and Sen. Inouye will be stepping down from the Committee. Next in line for leadership of the Committee will be John McCain (R) and either Daniel Akaka (D-HI) or Tim Johnson (D-SD).

Committee members:
John McCain (R-AZ)
Lisa Murkowski (R-AK)
Craig Thomas (R-WY)
Orrin G. Hatch (R-UT)
Jame M. Inhofe (R-OK)
Pete V. Domenici (R-NM)
Gordon Smith (R-OR)

Daniel K. Akaka (D-HI)
Kent Conrad (D-ND)
Harry Reid (D-NV)
Byron L. Dorgan (D-ND)
Tim Johnson (D-SD)
Maria Cantwell (D-WA)

Paul Moorehead, Majority Staff
  Director & Chief Counsel
Lee Frazier, Majority Professional Staff
David Mullon, Majority Senior Counsel
Jim Hall, Majority Counsel
Rhonda Harjo, & John Tahsuda,
  Senior Counsel to the Majority
Morgan Litchfield, Majority Executive Assistant

Patricia Zell, Minority Staff Director & Chief Counsel
Carl Christensen & Colin Kippen,
  Senior Counsel to the Minority
Janet Erickson & Diana Kupchella,
  Counsel to the Minority

Has full jurisdiction over all proposed legislation and other matters relating to American Indian affairs, including Indian education at all levels.

HOUSE OF REPRESENTATIVES
House Resources Committee
Subcommittee on Native American Affairs
1522 Longworth House Office Bldg.
New Jersey & Independence Ave., SE
Washington, DC 20515
(202) 226-7736 Fax 226-0522
  Rep. Richard W. Pombo (CA), Chair
Has legislative and oversight jurisdiction over measures related to the care and management of Indians and the federal government's management of Indian programs.

BUREAU OF INDIAN AFFAIRS

AREA OFFICES

ALASKA REGIONAL OFFICE
Bureau of Indian Affairs
P.O. Box 25520 • JUNEAU, AK 99802
(800) 645-8397; (907) 586-7177 Fax 586-7252
  Niles C. Caesar, Regional Director
Administers all BIA services within the State of Alaska. *Responsible for the following agencies*: Anchorage, Fairbanks, and Bethel Field Office. *Tribes served*: Eskimo, Aleut, and Alaska Indians. *Total population served*: 75,000.

EASTERN OKLAHOMA REGIONAL OFFICE
Bureau of Indian Affairs
3100 W. Peak Blvd.
P.O. Box 8002 • MUSKOGEE, OK 74401
(918) 781-4600 Fax 781-4604
  Jeanette Hanna, Regional Director
Administers BIA programs for regions of Oklahoma. *Responsible for the following agencies*: Ardmore, Okmulgee, Osage, Miami, Tahlequah, Talihina, and Wewoka. *Tribes served*: Cherokee, Chickasaw, Choctaw, Creek, Seminole, Osage, Seneca-Cayuga, Keetowah, Eastern Shawnee, Quapaw, Wyandotte, Miami, Peoria, Ottawa, Cherokee-Shawnee, and Modoc. *Total population served*: 75,000.

EASTERN REGIONAL OFFICE
Bureau of Indian Affairs
711 Stewarts Ferry Pike
NASHVILLE, TN 37214-2751
(615) 467-1700 Fax 467-1701
  Franklin Keel, Regional Director
Tribes served: Aroostook Band of Micmacs, Catawba Tribe, Cayuga Nation, Chitimacha Tribe, Coushatta Tribe, Eastern Band of Cherokee, Houlton Band of Maliseets, Jena Band of Choctaws, Mashantucket Pequots, Miccosukee Tribe, Mississippi Band of Choctaw, Mohegan Tribe, Narragansett Tribe, Oneida Nation, Onondaga Nation, Passamaquoddy Tribe-Indian Township & Pleasant Point, Penobscot Nation, Poarch Band of Creek Tribe, St. Regis Mohawk Tribe, Seminole Tribe of Florida, Seneca Nation, Tonawanda Band of Seneca, Tunica-Biloxi Tribe, Tuscarora Nation, Wampanoag Tribe of Gay Head. *Administers BIA programs through the following agencies*: Cherokee Agency, Seminole Agency, South & Eastern States Education Agency, Choctaw Field Office, and New York Field Office.

GREAT PLAINS REGIONAL OFFICE
Bureau of Indian Affairs
Federal Bldg., 115 4th Ave., SE
ABERDEEN, SD 57401
(605) 226-7343 Fax 226-7446
  Website: www.doi.gov/bia/aberdeen
  Alice Harwood, Acting Regional Director
  Robert Ecoffey, Deputy Regional Director
Administers BIA programs for regions of North and South Dakota, and Nebraska. *Responsible for the following agencies and schools*: Cheyenne River Agency, Crow Creek Agency, Flandreau Indian School, Fort Berthold Agency, Fort Totten Agency, Lower Brule Agency, Pine Ridge Agency, Rosebud Agency, Sisseton Agency, Standing Rock Agency, Turtle Mountain Agency, Wahpeton Indian School, Winnebago Agency, and Yankton Agency.

MIDWEST REGIONAL OFFICE
Bureau of Indian Affairs
One Federal Dr., Rm. 550
FORT SNELLING, MN 55111-4007

(612) 713-4400 Fax 713-4401
Larry Morrin, Regional Director
Website: www.na.fs.fed.us/spfo/bia/index.htm
Administers BIA programs in the State of Iowa, Michigan, Minnesota, and Wisconsin. *Responsible for the following agencies and field offices*: Great Lakes Agency, Michigan Field Office, Minnesota Agency, and Red Lake Field Office. Total population served: 22,000.

NAVAJO REGIONAL OFFICE
Bureau of Indian Affairs
P.O. Box 1060 • GALLUP, NM 87305
(505) 863-8314 Fax 863-8324
  Elouise Chicharello, Regional Director
Tribe served: Navajo (in Arizona, New Mexico and Utah.) *Total population served*: 200,000. *Programs*: Natural Resources; Forestry; Roads Construction & Maintenance; Irrigation Project. Museum. *Responsible for the following agencies*: Navajo Area Office (Administration), Chinle, Eastern Navajo, Fort Defiance, Navajo Irrigation Project, Shiprock, and Western Navajo.

NORTHWEST REGIONAL OFFICE
Bureau of Indian Affairs
911 NE 11th Ave. • PORTLAND, OR 97232
(503) 231-6702 Fax 231-2201
  Stanley M. Speaks, Regional Director
Administers BIA programs for regions of Oregon, Washington, and Idaho. *Responsible for the following agencies, projects and stations*: Coeur d'Alene Tribe BIA Field Office, Colville Agency, Fort Hall Agency, Flathead Field Office, Makah Field Office, Metlakatla Field Office, Northern Idaho Agency, Olympic Peninsula Agency, Puget Sound Agency, Siletz Field Office, Spokane Agency, Taholah Field Office, Umatilla Agency, Wapato Irrigation Project, Warm Springs Agency, and Yakima Agency.

PACIFIC REGIONAL OFFICE
Bureau of Indian Affairs
2800 Cottage Way • SACRAMENTO, CA 95825
(916) 978-6000 Fax 978-6099
  William Benjamin, Acting Regional Director
Administers BIA programs through the following agencies: Central California Agency, Northern California Agency, Southern California Agency, and Palm Springs Field Office. Total population served: 45,000.

ROCKY MOUNTAIN REGIONAL OFFICE
Bureau of Indian Affairs
316 N. 26th St. • BILLINGS, MT 59101
(406) 247-7943 Fax 247-7976
  Keith Beartusk, Regional Director
Administers BIA programs for the region of Montana and Wyoming. *Responsible for the following agencies*: Blackfeet, Crow, Fort Belknap, Fort Peck, Northern Cheyenne, Rocky Boy's, and Wind River. *Tribes served*: Blackfeet, Crow, Gros-Ventre and Assiniboine, Sioux and Assiniboine, Northern Cheyenne, Chippewa Cree, and Shoshone and Arapahoe. *Total population served*: 48,000.

SOUTHERN PLAINS REGIONAL OFFICE
Bureau of Indian Affairs
W.C.D. Office Complex
P.O. Box 368 • ANADARKO, OK 73005
(405) 247-6673 Fax 247-5611
  Dan Deerinwater, Regional Director
Administers BIA programs for regions of Oklahoma, Kansas, Missouri and Texas. *Tribes served*: 24 Oklahoma tribes - Apache, Caddo, Comanche, Delaware, Ft. Sill Apache, Kiowa, Wichita and Affiliated, Cheyenne-Arapaho, Kaw, Otoe-Missouria, Pawnee, Ponca, Tonkawa, Absentee-Shawnee, Citizen Band Potawatomi, Iowa, Kickapoo, Sac & Fox; Kansas tribes - Iowa, Kickapoo, Prairie Band Potawatomi, Sac & Fox of Missouri; Texas tribes - Alabama-Coushatta, and Kickapoo Traditional. Responsible for the following agencies, schools, and offices: Anadarko, Concho, Horton, Pawnee, Shawnee, Concho Indian School, Riverside Indian School, Fort Sill Maintenance & Security Detachment, Chilocco Maintenance & Security Detachment, & Haskell Indian Junior College. *Population served*: 36,310. *Programs*: Provides services to support tribal governments & protect Indian land.

SOUTHWEST REGIONAL OFFICE
Bureau of Indian Affairs
P.O. Box 26567 • ALBUQUERQUE, NM 87125
(505) 346-7590 Fax 346-7517

Website: www.swr-hq.nm.bia.gov
Robert Baracker, Regional Director
Administers BIA programs for regions of Colorado and New Mexico. *Responsible for the following agencies:* Jicarilla, Laguna, Mescalero, Northern Pueblos, Ramah Navajo, Southern Pueblo, Southern Ute, Ute Mountain Ute, and Zuni. *Programs:* Full range of BIA land and human resource programs. *Total population served:* 55,000.

WESTERN REGIONAL OFFICE
Bureau of Indian Affairs
P.O. Box 10 • PHOENIX, AZ 85001
(602) 379-6600 Fax 379-4413
Website: www.phxao.az.bia.gov
Wayne Nordwall, Regional Director
Website: www.phxao.az.bia.gov
Administers BIA programs for regions of Arizona, California, Nevada and Utah. *Responsible for the following agencies:* Colorado River, Eastern Nevada, Fort Apache, Fort Yuma, Hopi, Papago, Pima, Salt River, San Carlos, San Carlos Irrigation Project, Southern Paiute Field Station, Truxton Canon, Uintah and Ouray, and Western Nevada.

BIA AGENCY OFFICES

ALASKA REGION

WEST-CENTRAL ALASKA FIELD OFFICE
Bureau of Indian Affairs
3601 C St., Suite 1100
ANCHORAGE, AK 99503
(907) 271-4088 Fax 271-4083
Charles F. Bunch, Field Rep.
Area served: Southwestern Alaska—Calista Region. Responsible for six Indian regional cooperative schools, and the maintenance of plant facilities for an additional 21 schools; active in numerous other projects and functions related to regional problems. *Tribes served:* Eskimo, Athapascan, Aleut. *Total population served:* 75,000. *Programs:* All BIA programs—grants, natural resources, realty, social services, housing, etc. Under jurisdiction of Alaska Regional Office.

FAIRBANKS FIELD OFFICE
Bureau of Indian Affairs
Federal Bldg. & Courthouse
101 12th Ave., Rm. 168
FAIRBANKS, AK 99701
(907) 456-0222 Fax 456-0225
Kathy B. Wilson, Field Rep.
Reservations served: Interior Alaska and the North Slope Area. *Tribes served:* Eskimo, Athapascan. *Total population served:* 12,000. *Programs:* BIA Enrollment, Realty and Contracts & Grants. Under jurisdiction of Alaska Regional Office.

METLAKATLA FIELD OFFICE
Bureau of Indian Affairs
P.O. Box 450 • METLAKATLA, AK 99926
(907) 886-3791 Fax 886-7738
Edward W. Gunyah, Field Rep.
Under jurisdiction of Northwest Regional Office.

ARIZONA

CHINLE AGENCY
Bureau of Indian Affairs
P.O. Box 7H • CHINLE, AZ 86503
(505) 863-8314 Fax 863-8324
Elouise Chicharello, Regional Director
Tribe served: Navajo. *Reservation served:* Navajo. There are 10 schools within Chinle Agency. Six are BIA, three are contract and one is grant. Under jurisdiction of Navajo Area Office.

SAN CARLOS IRRIGATION PROJECT
Bureau of Indian Affairs
P.O. Box 250 • COOLIDGE, AZ 85228
(520) 723-5439 Fax 723-5770
Bob Carolin, Project Manager
Under jurisdiction of Western Regional Office.

FORT DEFIANCE AGENCY
Bureau of Indian Affairs
P.O. Box 619 • FORT DEFIANCE, AZ 86504
(505) 863-8314 Fax 863-8324
Elouise Chicharello, Regional Director
Tribe served: Navajo. Under jurisdiction of Navajo Area Office.

HOPI AGENCY
Bureau of Indian Affairs
P.O. Box 158 • KEAMS CANYON, AZ 86034
(928) 738-2228 Fax 738-5187
Wendell Honanie, Supt.
Website: www.phx.az.bia.gov/agencies/ hopi/h63000.html
Tribes served: Hopi & Paiute. *Total population served:* 7,500. Under jurisdiction of Western Regional Office.

COLORADO RIVER AGENCY
Bureau of Indian Affairs
Route 1, Box 9-C • PARKER, AZ 85344
(928) 669-7111 Fax 669-7187
Allen J. Anspach, Supt.
Website: www.phxao.az.bia.gov/agencies/ coloriv/h51000.html
Tribes served: Chemehuevi, Colorado River (in Arizona and California), Mohave (in Arizona, California and Nevada.) *Total population served:* 6,500. Under jurisdiction of Western Regional Office.

PIMA AGENCY
Bureau of Indian Affairs
P.O. Box 8 • SACATON, AZ 85247
(520) 562-3326 Fax 562-3543
Davis F. Pecusa, Supt.
Website: www.phxao.az.bia.gov/agencies/pima/ h54000.html
Tribes served: Papago, Pima, and Maricopa. *Total population served:* 10,000. Under jurisdiction of Western Regional Office.

SAN CARLOS AGENCY
Bureau of Indian Affairs
P.O. Box 209 • SAN CARLOS, AZ 85550
(928) 475-2321 Fax 475-2783
Janice Staudte, Supt.
Website: www.phzao.az.bia.gov/agencies/ sancarlos/h55000.html
Tribe served: San Carlos Apache. *Population served:* 10,500. *Programs:* Administrative/Tribal Operations; Employment Assistance; Law Enforcement & Social Services; Indian Self-Determination Services; Natural Resources; Facilities & Fire Management; Soil & Moisture; Real Estate Services; Credit & Finance; Roads. Under jurisdiction of Western Regional Office.

SALT RIVER FIELD OFFICE
Bureau of Indian Affairs
10000 E. McDowell Rd.
SCOTTSDALE, AZ 85256
(480) 421-0807 Fax 421-0814
Veronica L. Homer, Supt.
Website: www.phxao.az.bia.gov/agencies/ saltriver/h55000.html
Tribes served: Pima, Maricopa, Mohave, and Apache. *Population served:* 3,500. Under jurisdiction of Western Regional Office.

PAPAGO AGENCY
Bureau of Indian Affairs
P.O. Box 578 • SELLS, AZ 85634
(520) 383-3286 Fax 383-2087
Nina Siquieros, Supt.
Website: www.phxao.az.bia.gov/agencies/ papago/h54000.html
Tribe served: Tohono O'odham. *Population served:* 17,500. Under jurisdiction of Western Regional Office.

WESTERN NAVAJO AGENCY
Bureau of Indian Affairs
P.O. Box 127 • TUBA CITY, AZ 86045
(928) 863-8314 Fax 863-8324
Elouise Chicharello, Regional Director
Tribe served: Navajo. *Total population served:* 4,555. Under jurisdiction of Navajo Area Office.

TRUXTON CANON AGENCY
Bureau of Indian Affairs
P.O. Box 37 • VALENTINE, AZ 86434
(928) 769-2286 Fax 769-2444

Robert R. McNichols, Supt.
E-mail: rmcnichols@bia.gov
Website: www.doi.gov
Tribes served: Hualapai Nation, Havasupai Tribe, Yavapai-Apache Nation, Yavapai-Prescott Tribe, and Tonto-Apache Tribe. *Total population served:* 3,975. *Special programs:* Economic Development, Community Development, Real Estate Services, Natural Resources Development, Tribal Government Services. *Activities:* Runs Havasupai Reservation School, Grades K-8, Supai, AZ. Under jurisdiction of Western Regional Office.

FORT APACHE AGENCY
Bureau of Indian Affairs
P.O. Box 560 • WHITERIVER, AZ 85941
(928) 338-5353 Fax 338-5383
Benjamin H. Nuvamsa, Supt.
Website: www.phxao.bia.gov/agencies/ftapa
Tribe served: Apache. *Total population served:* 7,000. Under jurisdiction of Western Regional Office.

FORT YUMA FIELD OFFICE
Bureau of Indian Affairs
P.O. Box 11000 • YUMA, AZ 85366
(928) 782-1202 Fax 782-1266
Website:www.phxo.az.gov/agencies/ ftyuma.h63000.html
Samuel Rideshorse, Supt.
Tribes served: Cocopah and Quechan tribes (in Arizona and California) *Total population served:* 1,800. Under jurisdiction of Western Regional Office.

CALIFORNIA

PALM SPRINGS FIELD OFFICE
Bureau of Indian Affairs
650 E. Tahquitz Canyon Way, Suite A
P.O. Box 2245 • PALM SPRINGS, CA 92262
(760) 416-2133 Fax 416-2687
Don Magee, Director
Under jurisdiction of Pacific Regional Office.

NORTHERN CALIFORNIA AGENCY
Bureau of Indian Affairs
1900 Churn Creek Rd., Suite 300
REDDING, CA 96002-0292
(530) 246-5141 Fax 246-5167
Dr. Virgil Akins, Supt.
Under jurisdiction of Pacific Regional Office.

SOUTHERN CALIFORNIA AGENCY
Bureau of Indian Affairs
2038 Iowa Ave., Suite 101
RIVERSIDE, CA 92507
(909) 276-6624 Fax 276-6641
Virgil Townsend, Supt.
Serves the Mission area in southern California. Under jurisdiction of Pacific Regional Office.

CENTRAL CALIFORNIA AGENCY
Bureau of Indian Affairs
1824 Tribute Rd., Suite J
SACRAMENTO, CA 95815
(916) 566-7121 Fax 566-7510
Dale Risling, Sr. , Supt.
Under jurisdiction of Pacific Regional Office.

COLORADO

SOUTHERN UTE AGENCY
Bureau of Indian Affairs
P.O. Box 315 • IGNACIO 81137
(970) 563-4511 Fax 563-9321
Mike Stancampiano, Supt.
Tribe served: Ute. *Total population served:* 1,000. Under jurisdiction of Albuquerque Area Office.

UTE MOUNTAIN UTE FIELD OFFICE
Bureau of Indian Affairs
P.O. Box KK • TOWAOC 81334
(970) 565-8473 Fax 565-8906
Priscilla Bancroft, Acting Supt.
Tribe served: Ute. *Total population served:* 1,750. Under jurisdiction of Albuquerque Area Office.

DISTRICT OF COLUMBIA

BUREAU OF INDIAN AFFAIRS
1951 Constitution Ave., N.W.
WASHINGTON 20245
See Central Office listing at the beginning
of this section.

INDIAN ARTS & CRAFTS BOARD
U.S. Dept. of the Interior
1849 C. St., NW MS 2058-MIB
WASHINGTON 20240 (888) 278-3253
(202) 208-3773 Fax 208-5196
E-mail: iacb@os.doi.gov
Website: www.iacb.doi.gov
Meredith Z. Stanton, Director
Purpose: To promote the development of American
Indians and Alaska Natives of federally recognized
tribes through the expansion of the Indian arts and
crafts market. *Activities*: Provides promotional oppor-
tunities, general business advice, and information on
the Indian Arts & Crafts Act to Native American artists,
craftspeople, businesses, museums, and cultural centers of federally recognized tribes. Additionally, the
Board operates three regional museums, including the
Museum of the Plains Indian, Browning, MT; Sioux
Indian Museum, Rapid City, SD; and Southern Plains
Indian Museum, Anadarko, OK. The Board conducts
a promotional museum exhibition program, produces
a "Source Directory, and oversees the implementation of the Indian Arts & Crafts Act (the Act). *Publication*: Source Directory of Americn Indian and Alaska
Native Owned and Operated Arts & Crafts Businesses.
Established 1935.

FLORIDA

SEMINOLE AGENCY
Bureau of Indian Affairs
6075 Stirling Rd.
HOLLYWOOD, FL 33024
(954) 581-7050 Fax 792-7340
Joe Frank, Acting Supt.
Tribe served: Seminole. *Total population served*: 1,750.
Under jurisdiction of Eastern Regional Office.

IDAHO

FORT HALL AGENCY
Bureau of Indian Affairs
P.O. Box 220 • FORT HALL, ID 83203
(208) 238-2301 Fax 237-0466
Eric J. LaPointe, Supt.
Tribes served: Shoshone & Bannock. *Total population
served*: 4,000. Under jurisdiction of Northwest Regional
Office.

NORTHERN IDAHO AGENCY
Bureau of Indian Affairs
P.O. Box 277 • LAPWAI, ID 83540
(208) 843-2300 Fax 843-7142
Sharon Yepa, Acting Supt.
Tribes served: Coeur d'Alene, Kootenai, and Nez
Perce. *Total population served*: 2,200. *Programs*: Law
Enforcement & Social Services; Real Estate Services;
Finance & Economic Development; Education; Aid to
Tribal Governments. Under jurisdiction of Northwest
Regional Office.

COEUR D'ALENE TRIBE BIA FIELD OFFICE
850 A ST., P.O. Box 408 • PLUMMER, ID 83851
(208) 686-1887 Fax 686-1903
John Abraham, Field Rep.
Tribe served: Coeur d'Alene. Under jurisdiction
of Northwest Regional Office.

KANSAS

HORTON FIELD OFFICE
Bureau of Indian Affairs
P.O. Box 31 • HORTON 66439
(785) 486-2161 Fax 486-2515

Galen Hubbard, Field Rep.
Tribes served:: Iowa, Kickapoo of Kansas, Sac and
Fox of Missouri, and Prairie Band Potawatomi of Kansas. *Total population served*: 1,500. Under jurisdiction of Southern Plains Regional Office.

MICHIGAN

MICHIGAN FIELD OFFICE
Bureau of Indian Affairs
Federal Square Office Plaza
2901.5 I-75 Business Spur
SAULT STE. MARIE, MI 49783
(906) 632-6809 Fax 632-0689
Anne E. Bolton, Supt.
E-mail: annebolton@bia.gov
Website: www.na.fs.fed.us/spfo/bia/mao/agy/miapa
Tribes served: Bay Mills, Grand Traverse, Hannahville,
Keweenaw Bay, Lac Vieux Desert, Saginaw Chippewa,
and Sault Ste. Marie. Under jurisdiction of Midwest
Regional Office.

MINNESOTA

MINNESOTA AGENCY
Bureau of Indian Affairs
Federal Bldg., Rm. 418
522 Minnesota Ave., NW
BEMIDJI, MN 56601
(218) 751-2011 Fax 751-4367
Joel D. Smith, Supt.
E-mail: joelsmith@bia.gov
Website: www.na.fs.fed.us/spfo/bia/mao/agy/webd
Tribes served: Chippewa and Sioux. *Total population
served*: 12,000. Under jurisdiction of Midwest Regional
Office.

RED LAKE FIELD OFFICE
Bureau of Indian Affairs
RED LAKE, MN 56671
(218) 679-3361 Fax 679-3691
Francis Brun, Supt.
Website: www.na.fs.fed.us/spfo/bia/mao/agy/webd
Tribe served: Chippewa (Red Lake Band.) *Total popu-
lation served*: 4,500. Contracted by Tribe. Under juris-
diction of Midwest Regional Office.

MISSISSIPPI

CHOCTAW FIELD OFFICE
Bureau of Indian Affairs
421 Powell St. • PHILADELPHIA, MS 39350
(601) 656-1521 Fax 656-2350
Ray Thomas, Field Rep.
E-mail: raythomas@bia.gov
Tribe served: Mississippi Band of Choctaw. *Total popu-
lation served*: 5,500. Museum. Library. *Publications*:
Choctaw Community News; Choctaw Drummer. Un-
der jurisdiction of Eastern Regional Office.

MONTANA

ROCKY BOY'S FIELD OFFICE
Bureau of Indian Affairs
RR 1, Box 542 • BOX ELDER, MT 59521
(406) 395-4476 Fax 395-4382
James Montes, Field Rep.
Tribe served: Chippewa Cree. *Reservation served*:
Rocky Boy's. *Total population served*: 3,150. Under
jurisdiction of Rocky Mountain Regional Office.

BLACKFEET AGENCY
Bureau of Indian Affairs
P.O. Box 880 • BROWNING, MT 59417
(406) 338-7544 Fax 338-7761
Ross Denny, Supt.
Tribe served: Blackfeet. *Total population served*:
7,000. Under jurisdiction of Rocky Mountain
Regional Office.

CROW AGENCY
Bureau of Indian Affairs
CROW AGENCY, MT 59022
(406) 638-2672 Fax 638-2380
Gordon Jackson, Supt.
Tribe served: Crow. *Total population served*: 5,000.
Under jurisdiction of Rocky Mountain Regional Office.

FORT BELKNAP AGENCY
Bureau of Indian Affairs
RR 1, Box 980 • HARLEM, MT, 59526
(406) 353-2901 Ext 23 Fax 353-2886
Cleo Hamilton, Supt.
Tribes served:: Assiniboine & Gros Ventre. *Total popu-
lation served*: 2,200. Under jurisdiction of Rocky Moun-
tain Regional Office.

FORT PECK AGENCY
Bureau of Indian Affairs
P.O. Box 637 • POPLAR, MT 59255
(406) 768-5312 Fax 768-3405
Dennis Whiteman, Supt.
Tribes served: Sioux and Assiniboine. *Total popula-
tion served*: 5,000. Under jurisdiction of Rocky Moun-
tain Regional Office.

FLATHEAD FIELD OFFICE
Bureau of Indian Affairs
P.O. Box 40 • PABLO, MT 59855
(406) 675-2700 Fax 675-2805
Ernest T. Moran, Supt.
E-mail: biafa2@ronan.net
Tribes served: Salish & Kootenai. *Total population
served*: 6,000. Under jurisdiction of Northwest Regional
Office.

NORTHERN CHEYENNE AGENCY
Bureau of Indian Affairs
P.O. Box 40 • LAME DEER, MT 59043
(406) 477-8242 Fax 477-6636
Marjorie Eagleman, Supt.
Tribe served: Northern Cheyenne. *Total population
served*: 8,100. *Programs*: Natural Resources, Real Es-
tate Services, Facilities, Transportation, Social Ser-
vices, Economic Development, Fire Management; Law
Enforcement; Administrative Services; Forestry, Indian
Self Determination, Property Management. Under ju-
risdiction of Rocky Mountain Regional Office.

NEBRASKA

WINNEBAGO AGENCY
Bureau of Indian Affairs
P.O. Box 18 • WINNEBAGO, NE 68071
(402) 878-2502 Fax 878-2943
Michael Hackett, Supt.
Tribes served: Omaha, Winnebago, and Santee Sioux
of Nebraska. *Total population served*: 5,100; total Indians enrolled, 10,000. *Programs*: Administrative Services; Tribal Government; Social Services; Law Enforcement; Forestry & Land Operations; among others. Under jurisdiction of Great Plains Reg. Office.

NEVADA

WESTERN NEVADA AGENCY
Bureau of Indian Affairs
1677 Hot Springs Rd.
CARSON CITY, NV 89706
(775) 887-3500 Fax 702-3531
Robert L. Hunter, Supt.
Website: www.phxao.az.bia.gov/agencies/
wnevada/h61000.html
Tribes served: Shoshone, Paiute, Washoe, and
Goshute. *Total population served*: 6,500. Under juris-
diction of Western Regional Office.

EASTERN NEVADA FIELD OFFICE
Bureau of Indian Affairs
1555 Shoshone Cir. • ELKO, NV 89801
(775) 738-0569 Fax 738-4710
Paul Young, Supt.
Website: www.phxao.az.bia.gov/agencies/
nevada/h64000.html
Reservations served: Duck Valley, Te-Moak Bands—
Western Shoshone, Battle Mountain Colony, Elko

Colony, South Fork, Ruby Valley Allotments, Odgers Ranch, Goshute, Ely Colony, and Duck Water. *Total population served:* 3,500. Under jurisdiction of Western Regional Office.

NEW MEXICO

OFFICE OF FACILITIES MANAGEMENT
Bureau of Indian Affairs
500 Gold Ave. SW, 8th Fl.
P.O. Box 1248 • ALBUQUERQUE 87103
  (505) 766-2825
  Virgil Pochop, Supt.

OFFICE OF INDIAN EDUCATION PROGRAMS
Bureau of Indian Affairs
500 Gold Ave. SW, Rm. 7C
P.O. Box 769 • ALBUQUERQUE, NM 87103
  (505) 248-6965 Fax 248-6997

SOUTHERN PUEBLOS AGENCY
Bureau of Indian Affairs
P.O. Box 1667 • ALBUQUERQUE, NM 87103
  (505) 346-2423 Fax 346-2426
  Florene L. Gutierrez, Supt.
Pueblos served: Acoma, Cochiti, Isleta, Jemez, Sandia, San Felipe, Santa Ana, Santo Domingo, Ysleta del Sur, and Zia. *Total population served:* 17,500. Under jurisdiction of Southwest Regional Office.

EASTERN NAVAJO AGENCY
Bureau of Indian Affairs
P.O. Box 328 • CROWNPOINT, NM 87313
  (505) 863-8314 Fax 863-8324
  Elouise Chicharello, Acting Area Director
Tribe served: Navajo (in Arizona, New Mexico & Utah.)
Under jurisdiction of Navajo Area Office.

JICARILLA AGENCY
Bureau of Indian Affairs
P.O. Box 167 • DULCE, NM 87528
  (505) 759-3951 Fax 759-3948
  Sherryl J. Vigil, Supt.
Tribe served: Jicarilla Apache. *Total population served:* 2,500. Under jurisdiction of Albuquerque Area Office.

NORTHERN PUEBLOS AGENCY
Bureau of Indian Affairs
Box 4269, Fairview Station
ESPANOLA, NM 87533
  (505) 753-1400 Fax 753-1404
  Cameron Martinez, Supt.
Tribes served: Nambe Pueblo, Picuris Pueblo, Pojoaque Pueblo, San Ildefonso Pueblo, San Juan Pueblo, Santa Clara Pueblo, Taos & Tesuque Pueblo. *Programs:* All BIA programs; adult education & social services. *Total population served:* 6,500. Under jurisdiction of Southwest Regional Office.

LAGUNA AGENCY
Bureau of Indian Affairs
P.O. Box 1448 • LAGUNA, NM 87026
  (505) 552-6001 Fax 552-7497
  Yamie Leeds, Supt.
Tribe served: Pueblo of Laguna. *Population served:* 4,000 on reservation; 3,000 off reservation. *Programs:* Administrative Services, Property & Supply; Natural Resources; Roads, Real Estate Services; Law Enforcement & Social Services. Under jurisdiction of Southwest Regional Office.

MESCALERO AGENCY
Bureau of Indian Affairs
P.O. Box 189 • MESCALERO, NM 88340
  (505) 464-4202 Fax 464-4215
  Robert G. Toya, Supt.
Tribe served: Mescalero Apache. *Population served:* 3,800. *Programs:* BIA programs; Rehab Center; Wildlife Conservation; Tribal Court; Forestry; Natural Resources; operates school (K-12 grant school to tribe). Under jurisdiction of Southwest Regional Office.

RAMAH-NAVAJO AGENCY
Bureau of Indian Affairs
Route 2, Box 13 • RAMAH, NM 87321
  (505) 775-7130 Fax 775-3538
  William P. Leeds, Supt.
Tribe served: Navajo (in Arizona, New Mexico & Utah.)

Population served: 1,750. Under jurisdiction of Southwest Regional Office.

SHIPROCK AGENCY
Bureau of Indian Affairs
P.O. Box 3538 • SHIPROCK, NM 87420
  (505) 863-8314 Fax 863-8324
  Elouise Chicharello, Regional Director
Tribe served: Navajo (in Arizona, New Mexico & Utah.)
Under jurisdiction of Navajo Area Office.

ZUNI AGENCY
Bureau of Indian Affairs
P.O. Box 369 • ZUNI, NM 87327
  (505) 782-5591 Fax 782-5715
  Clayton Seoutewa, Supt.
Tribe served: Zuni. *Total population served:* 6,000. Under jurisdiction of Southwest Regional Office.

NEW YORK

NEW YORK FIELD OFFICE
Bureau of Indian Affairs
P.O. Box 7366 • SYRACUSE, NY 13261
  (315) 448-0620 Fax 448-0624
  Dean A. White, Field Rep.
  E-mail: deanwhite@bia.gov
Tribes served: Seneca Reservations (Allegany, Cattaraugus, Oil Springs), Cayuga, St. Regis Mohawk, Onondaga, Poosepatuck, Oneida, Tuscarora, Tonawanda Seneca. *Total population served:* 15,000. Activities: Administers BIA programs for reservations and tribes in New York State. Under jurisdiction of Eastern Regional Office.

NORTH CAROLINA

CHEROKEE AGENCY
Bureau of Indian Affairs
CHEROKEE, NC 28719
  (828) 497-9131 Fax 497-6715
  Dean White, Acting Supt.
Tribe served: Cherokee. *Total population served:* 6,000. Under jurisdiction of Eastern Regional Office.

NORTH DAKOTA

TURTLE MOUNTAIN AGENCY
Bureau of Indian Affairs
P.O. Box 60 • BELCOURT, ND 58316
  (701) 477-3191 Fax 477-6628
  Patrick J. Hemmy, Supt.
Tribe served: Chippewa. *Total population served:* 9,000. Under jurisdiction of Great Plains Regional Office.

FORT TOTTEN AGENCY
Bureau of Indian Affairs
P.O. Box 270 • FORT TOTTEN, ND 58335
  (701) 766-4545 Fax 766-4117
  Warren D. LeBeau, Supt.
Tribe served: Devils Lake Sioux. *Population served:* 3,500. *Programs:* Law Enforcement & Social Services; Property/Procurement; Agriculture; Realty; Road Maintenance and Facilty Management. Under jurisdiction of Great Plains Regional Office.

STANDING ROCK AGENCY
Bureau of Indian Affairs
P.O. Box E • FORT YATES, ND 58538
  (701) 854-3433 Fax 854-7184
  Carmen Jacobs, Acting Supt.
Tribe served: Sioux (in North and South Dakota.) *Total population served:* 6,000. Under jurisdiction of Great Plains Regional Office.

FORT BERTHOLD AGENCY
Bureau of Indian Affairs
P.O. Box 370 • NEW TOWN, ND 58763
  (701) 627-4707 Fax 627-3601
  Paige J. Baker, Supt.
Tribes served:: Arikara, Mandan, and Hidatsa. *Total population served:* 8,500. Under jurisdiction of Great Plains Regional Office.

OKLAHOMA

ANADARKO AGENCY
Bureau of Indian Affairs
P.O. Box 309 • ANADARKO, OK 73005
  (405) 247-6677 Fax 247-9232
  Betty Tippeconnie, Supt.
Tribes served:: Apache of Oklahoma, Kiowa, Comanche, Caddo of Oklahoma, Delaware of Western Oklahoma, Wichita and Affiliated Tribes, and Fort Sill Apache of Oklahoma. *Population served :* 29,000. Under jurisdiction of Southern Plains Regional Office.

CHICKASAW AGENCY
Bureau of Indian Affairs
1500 N. Country Club Rd.
P.O. Box 2240 • ADA, OK 74821
  (580) 436-0784 Fax 436-3215
  Traile G. Glory, Supt.
Tribe served: Chickasaw. *Total population served:* 7,000. Under jurisdiction of Eastern Oklahoma Regional Office.

CONCHO FIELD OFFICE
Bureau of Indian Affairs
P.O. Box 68 • EL RENO, OK 73005
  (405) 262-7481 Fax 262-3140
  Galila Johnson, Field Rep.
Tribes served: Cheyenne-Arapaho of Oklahoma. *Total population served:* 7,000. Under jurisdiction of Southern Plains Regional Office.

MIAMI FIELD STATION
Bureau of Indian Affairs
P.O. Box 391 • MIAMI, OK 74355
  (918) 542-3396 Fax 542-7202
  Charles Head, Field Rep.
Tribes served: Shawnee, Miami, Seneca-Cayuga, and Quapaw. Under jurisdiction of Eastern Oklahoma Regional Office.

OKMULGEE FIELD STATION
Bureau of Indian Affairs
P.O. Box 370 • OKMULGEE, OK 74447
  (918) 756-3950 Fax 756-9626
  Floyd Waters, Field Rep.
Tribe served: Creek. *Total population served:* 16,000. Under jurisdiction of Eastern Okla. Regional Office.

OSAGE AGENCY
Bureau of Indian Affairs
P.O. Box 1539 • PAWHUSKA, OK 74056
  (918) 287-1032 Fax 287-4320
  Jim Fields, Supt.
Tribe served: Osage. *Total population served:* 13,000. *Programs:* Tribal Social Services; Tribal Court; Law Enforcement; Finance & Administration. Under jurisdiction of Eastern Oklahoma Regional Office.

PAWNEE AGENCY
Bureau of Indian Affairs
P.O. Box 440 • PAWNEE, OK 74058
  (918) 762-2585 Fax 762-3201
  Julia M. Langan, Supt.
  E-mail: julialangan@bia.gov
Tribes served: Kaw, Pawnee, Ponca, Otoe-Missouria, and Tonkawa. Under jurisdiction of Southern Plains Regional Office.

SHAWNEE FIELD OFFICE
Bureau of Indian Affairs
824 W. Independence #114
SHAWNEE, OK 74801
  (405) 273-0317 Fax 273-0072
  Robert Jones, Field Rep.
Tribes served: Kickapoo of Oklahoma and Texas, Iowa Tribe of Oklahoma, Citizen Band Potawatomi, Sac and Fox, and Absentee- Shawnee. *Total population served:* 15,000. *Programs:* Tribal Government, Social Services, Higher Education, Law Enforcement, Natural Resources, and Real Estate Management. Under jurisdiction of Southern Plains Regional Office.

TAHLEQUAH AGENCY
Bureau of Indian Affairs
P.O. Box 828 • TAHLEQUAH, OK 74465
  (918) 456-6146; Dennis Wickliffe, Supt.
Tribe served: Cherokee. *Total population served:* 14,000. Contracted by Tribe.

TALIHINA FIELD STATION
Bureau of Indian Affairs
P.O. Drawer 8 • TALIHINA, OK 74571
(918) 567-2207 Fax 567-2061
Larry W. Mings, Field Rep.
Tribe served: Choctaw. *Total population served*:
83,500. Operates Jones Academy at Hartshorne, Okla.
Under jurisdiction of Eastern Oklahoma Regional Office.

WEWOKA AGENCY
Bureau of Indian Affairs
P.O. Box 1060 • WEWOKA, OK 74884
(405) 257-6259 Fax 257-6748
Gloria Spybuck, Supt.
Tribe served: Seminole Nation of Oklahoma.
Total population served: 6,500. Under jurisdiction
of Eastern Oklahoma Regional Office.

OREGON

UMATILLA AGENCY
Bureau of Indian Affairs
P.O. Box 520 • PENDLETON, OR 97801
(541) 278-3786 Fax 278-3791
Philip Sanchez, Supt.
Tribes served: Cayuse, Umatilla, and Walla Walla.
Total population served: 2,000. Under jurisdiction
of Northwest Regional Office.

SILETZ FIELD OFFICE
Bureau of Indian Affairs
P.O. Box 569 • SILETZ, OR 97380
(541) 444-2679 Fax 444-2513
Ronald D. Kortlever, Supt.
Website: www.ctsi.nsn.us
Reservations served: Coos, Cow Creek, Coquille,
Grand Ronde and Siletz. Under jurisdiction of Northwest Regional Office.

WARM SPRINGS AGENCY
Bureau of Indian Affairs
P.O. Box 1239 • WARM SPRINGS, OR 97761
(541) 553-2411 Fax 553-2426
Cheryl Lohman, Acting Supt.
Tribes served: Paiute, Walla Walla, Chinook, Cayuse,
and Wasco. T*otal population served*: 2,750. Under jurisdiction of Northwest Regional Office.

SOUTH DAKOTA

CHEYENNE RIVER AGENCY
Bureau of Indian Affairs
P.O. Box 325 • EAGLE BUTTE, SD 57625
(605) 964-6611 Fax 964-4060
Russell J. McClure, Supt.
Tribe served: Sioux. *Total population served*: 5,000.
Under jurisdiction of Great Plains Regional Office.

CROW CREEK AGENCY
Bureau of Indian Affairs
P.O. Box 139 • FORT THOMPSON, SD 57339
(605) 245-2311 Fax 245-2343
Steve McLaughlin, Supt.
Tribe served: Crow Creek Sioux. *Total population
served*: 2,900. *Programs*: Social services; Land Operations; Law Enforcement; Facilities Management;
Realty; Property & Supply. Library. Under jurisdiction
of Great Plains Regional Office.

LOWER BRULE AGENCY
Bureau of Indian Affairs
P.O. Box 190 • LOWER BRULE, SD 57548
(605) 473-5512 Fax 473-5491
Cleve Her Many Horses, Supt.
Tribe served: Sioux. *Total population served*: 1,200.
Under jurisdiction of Great Plains Regional Office.

PINE RIDGE AGENCY
Bureau of Indian Affairs
P.O. Box 1203 • PINE RIDGE, SD 57770
(605) 867-5125 Fax 867-1141
Larry Bodin, Acting Supt.
Tribe served: Oglala Sioux (in South Dakota and Nebraska. *Total population served*: 13,500. Under jurisdiction of Great Plains Regional Office.

ROSEBUD AGENCY
Bureau of Indian Affairs
P.O. Box 550 • ROSEBUD, SD 57570
(605) 747-2224 Fax 747-2805
JoAnn Young, Acting Supt.
Tribe served: Rosebud Sioux. *Total population served*:
12,000. Under jurisdiction of Great Plains Regional
Office.

SISSETON AGENCY
Bureau of Indian Affairs
P.O. Box 688
AGENCY VILLAGE, SD 57262
(605) 698-3001 Fax 698-7784
Lois Jackson, Acting Supt.
Tribe served: Sisseton-Wahpeton Sioux (in North &
South Dakota.) *Reservation served*: Lake Traverse.
Total population served: 9,000. Under jurisdiction of
Great Plains Regional Office.

YANKTON AGENCY
Bureau of Indian Affairs
P.O. Box 577 • WAGNER, SD 57380
(605) 384-3651 Fax 384-3876
Timothy C. Lake, Supt.
Tribe served: Yankton Sioux and Ponca Tribe of Nebraska. *Total population served*: 4,000. Under jurisdiction of Great Plains Regional Office.

TENNESSEE

SOUTH & EASTERN STATES EDUCATION AGENCY
Bureau of Indian Affairs
51 Century Blvd., Suite 307
NASHVILLE, TN 37214
(615) 695-4100 Fax 695-4104
Carol Gipp, Acting Education Line Officer
Under jurisdiction of Eastern Regional Office

UTAH

UINTAH & OURAY AGENCY
Bureau of Indian Affairs
988 South 7500 East
P.O. Box 130 • FORT DUCHESNE, UT 84026
(435) 722-4300 Fax 722-2323
David L. Allison, Supt.
Tribes served: Ute and Goshute. *Total population
served*: 2,000. *Publication*: Ute Bulletin. Under jurisdiction of Western Regional Office.

SOUTHERN PAIUTE FIELD OFFICE
Bureau of Indian Affairs
P.O. Box 720 • ST. GEORGE, UT 84771
(435) 674-9720 Fax 674-9714
Ben Burshin, Field Rep.
Website: phxao.az.bia.gov/agencies/
sopaiute/h69000.html
Tribes served: Paiute Indian Tribe of Utah, Kaibab
Paiute Tribe, Moapa Band of Paiute Indians, San Juan
Southern Paiute Tribe, and Las Vegas Paiute Indian
Tribe. Under jurisdiction of Western Regional Office.

WASHINGTON

OLYMPIC PENINSULA AGENCY
Bureau of Indian Affairs
P.O. Box 48 • ABERDEEN, WA 98550
(360) 533-9100 Fax 533-9141
Raymond Maldonado, Supt.
Under jurisdiction of Northwest Regional Office.

PUGET SOUND FIELD OFFICE
Bureau of Indian Affairs
2707 Colby Ave., Suite 1101
EVERETT, WA 98201
(425) 258-2651 Fax 258-1254
Judy Joseph, Acting Supt.
Tribes served: Lummi, Muckleshoot, Nisqually,
Nooksack, Port Gamble, Puyallup, Sauk-Suiattle,
Stillaguamish, Suquamish, Swinomish, Tulalip, Upper
Skagit, and Snoqualmie. *Population served*: 15,500.
Programs: Tribal Administration/Operation; Contracts

& Grants; Social Services, Realty; Law Enforcement;
Education. Under jurisdiction of Northwest Regional
Office.

MAKAH FIELD OFFICE
Bureau of Indian Affairs
P.O. Box 115 • NEAH BAY, WA 98357
(360) 645-3232 Fax 645-2788
Greg Argel, Self-Governance Specialist
Under jurisdiction of Northwest Regional Office.

COLVILLE AGENCY
Bureau of Indian Affairs
P.O. Box 111 • NESPELEM, WA 99155
(509) 634-2316 Fax 634-2355
William E. (Gene) Nicholson, Supt.
Tribes served: Columbia, Colville, Lakes, Nespelem,
and Nez Perce. *Total population served*: 3,500. Under
jurisdiction of Northwest Regional Office.

TAHOLAH FIELD OFFICE
Bureau of Indian Affairs
P.O. Box 39 • TAHOLAH, WA 98587
(360) 276-4850 Fax 276-4853
Neil Eldridge, Acting Trust Officer
Under jurisdiction of Northwest Regional Office.

YAKAMA AGENCY
Bureau of Indian Affairs
P.O. Box 632 • TOPPENISH, WA 98948
(509) 865-2255 Fax (865-2049
Acey Oberly, Jr., Supt.
Tribe served: Confederated tribes and bands of the
Yakama Nation. *Total population served*: 9,900. Under jurisdiction of Northwest Regional Office.

WAPATO IRRIGATION PROJECT
Bureau of Indian Affairs
P.O. Box 220 • WAPATO, WA 98951
(509) 877-3155 Fax 877-3478
Under jurisdiction of Northwest Regional Office.

SPOKANE AGENCY
Bureau of Indian Affairs
P.O. Box 389 • WELLPINIT, WA 99040
(509) 258-4561 Fax 258-7542
Marcella L. Teters, Acting Supt.
Tribe served: Spokane & Kalispel. T*otal population
served*: 2,633. Under jurisdiction of Northwest Regional
Office.

WISCONSIN

GREAT LAKES AGENCY
Bureau of Indian Affairs
615 W. Main St. • ASHLAND, WI 54806
(715) 682-4527 Fax 682-8897
Robert R. Jaeger, Supt.
E-mail: robertjaeger@bia.gov
Reservations served: Bad River, Oneida, Forest
County Potawatomi, Lac Courte Oreilles, Lac du Flambeau, Red Cliff, St. Croix, Sokaogon, Stockbridge-
Munsee, Ho-Chunk. *Total population served*: 40,000.
Under jurisdiction of Midwest Regional Office.

WYOMING

WIND RIVER AGENCY
Bureau of Indian Affairs
FORT WASHAKIE, WY 82514
(307) 332-7810 Fax 332-4578
Perry Baker, Supt.
Tribes served:: Arapaho & Shoshone. *Total population served*: 5,500. Under jurisdiction of Rocky Mountain Regional Office.

This section lists national associations, societies, and organizations active in Indian affairs; also, religious, charitable, and philanthropic associations. Listings are arranged alphabetically.

AMERICAN ACADEMY OF PEDIATRICS
Committee on Native American Child Health
141 Northwest Point Blvd.
Elk Grove Village, IL 60007
(800) 433-9016 ext. 4739; (847) 981-4739
Joe M. Sanders, Jr., MD, Executive Director
Ana Garcia, MPA, Community Health Liaison
David Grossman, MD, MPH, Chairperson
E-Mail: nativeamerican@aap.org
Purpose: To provide leadership in the development of medical policies and initiatives that promote the health of Native American children, particularly those that are underserved (such as urban Indians) and/or geographically isolated. *Activities*: Conduct pediatric consultation visits and continuing medical education presentations to chosen areas within the Indian Health Service (IHS); stengthen ties with Indian tribes, especially those responsible for their own health care; survey IHS sites to determine pediatric locum tenens opportunities and share this information with interested pediatricians; presents an annual Native American Child Health Advocacy award to individuals who have made a significant contribution to improving the health of Native American children. *Publications*: Catalogue available. Library. Established 1965.

AMERICAN ANTHROPOLOGICAL ASSOCIATION
4350 N. Fairfax Dr. # 640 • Arlington, VA 22203
(703) 528-1902
Eugene L. Sterud, Executive Director
Membership: 10,000. Professional society of anthropologists, educators, students and others interested in the biological and cultural origin and development of mankind. *Activities*: Sponsors visiting lecturers, congressional fellowship, and departmental services programs. Maintains speaker's bureau, consultants' bureau, and placement service. Sponsors competitions; bestows awards; conducts research programs and compiles statistics. *Full-time staff*: David Givens, PhD (Director of Information Services, Editor, Anthropology Newsletter; and Judith Lisansky, PhD (Director, External Affairs). *Publications*: Special Publications, periodic monograph series; American Anthropologist, quarterly journal; Anthropology and Education Quarterly journal; Anthropology Newsletter, 9x/year; Cultural Anthropology, quarterly journal; Guide to Departments of Anthropology, annual. Established in 1902.

AMERICAN ANTIQUARIAN SOCIETY
185 Salisbury St. • Worcester, MA 01609
(617) 755-5221; Ellen S. Dunlap, President
Nancy H. Burkett, Librarian
Membership: 560. *Purpose*: To collect, preserve and encourage serious study of the materials of American history and life through 1876. Library. Newsletter. Established in 1812.

AMERICAN ETHNOLOGICAL SOCIETY
c/o Nancy McDowell, Ph.D., Sec.
Dept. of Anthropology, Franklin & Marshall College
Lancaster, PA 17604 (717) 291-4193
Membership: 2,500. A division of American Anthropological Association. Includes anthropologists and others interested in the field of ethnology and social anthropology. *Activities*: Conducts symposia. *Publications*: American Ethnologist, quarterly journal; Monograph Series, periodic; Unit News in Anthropology Newsletter, monthly; Proceedings, The Development of Political Organization in Native North America. Annual conference in conjunction with AAA. Founded 1942.

AMERICAN FRIENDS SERVICE COMMITTEE
Native American Affairs
1501 Cherry St. • Philadelphia, PA 19102
(215) 241-7000
Asia A. Bennett, Executive Secretary
Description: One of the corporate expressions of Quaker faith and practice. *Purpose*: To conduct programs with U.S. communities on the problem of minority groups—housing, employment and denial of legal rights. Founded 1917.

AMERICAN HISTORICAL ASSOCIATION
400 A St., S.E. • Washington, D.C. 20003
(202) 544-2422
Samuel R. Gamnon, Executive Director
Membership: 13,000. Professional historians, educators, and others interested in promoting historical studies and collecting and preserving historical manuscripts. *Publications*: American Historical Review, 5/yr. Library. Founded 1884.

AMERICAN INDIAN ADOPTION RESOURCE EXCHANGE
Council of Three Rivers American Indian Center, Inc.
200 Charles St. • Pittsburgh, PA 15238
(412) 782-4457
Description: This organization maintains registers of prospective Indian adoption homes and Indian children who are available for placement. Although not an adoption agency, the exchange provides information on the adoption of Indian children.

AMERICAN INDIAN & ALASKA NATIVE PROGRAMS
University of Colorado Health Sciences Center
Dept. of Psychiatry
Nighthorse Campbell Native Health Bldg.
P.O. Box 6508, Mail Stop F800
Aurora, CO 80045-0508
(303) 724-1414 Fax 724-1474
Website: www.uchsc.edu/sm/psych/dept/research/aianp.htm
Spero M. Manson, PhD, Program Director
Candace Fleming, PhD, Program Co-Director
Jan Beals, PhD, Director for Research
Christina Mitchell, PhD, Director for Prevention Research
Douglas Novins, MD, Director of CoCETAC
Tana Quintana, CoCETAC Program Specialist
Purpose: To increase knowledge and understanding of psychological dysfunction and psychotic illness among American Indian and Alaska natives. Comprised of six centers: The National Center for American Indian & Alaska Native American Health Research; The National Program Office of the Healthy Nations Initiative; The Native Elder Health Care Resource Center; Resource Center for Minority Aging Research; Center for Native American TeleHealth & TeleEducation; and The Circles of Care Initiative-Evaluation Techical Assistance Center (CoCETAC) supports American Indian and Alaska Native communities who are developing initial health service programs for children with serious emotional disturbances (SED) Website: www. samhsa.gov/programs. *Activities*: Research, training, information dissemination, and limited technical assistance. *Publications*: Research Journal; special reports; and annual journal.

AMERICAN INDIAN & ALASKA NATIVE PERIODICALS RESEARCH CLEARINGHOUSE
Stabler Hall 502, University of Arkansas
33rd & University Ave. • Little Rock, AR 72204
Purpose: To help identify and take advantage of periodicals produced by and for Native Americans.

AMERICAN INDIAN ANTI-DEFAMATION COUNCIL
215 W. Fifth Ave. • Denver, CO 80204
(303) 892-7011; Russell Means, Chair
Purpose: To combat racism by countering negative images of Native Americans in academia, the arts, film, and literature. *Activities*: Engages in public education, direct action, and selective litigation. *Membership*: Open to all, $25/year. Organization announcements and updates.

AMERICAN INDIAN ARCHAEOLOGICAL INSTITUTE
Curtis Rd., Box 1260 • Washington, CT 06793
(203) 868-0518
Susan F. Payne, Director
Purpose: To discover, preserve, and interpret information about the lifeways of the first peoples of the Northeast Woodlands area of the U.S., and to enhance appreciation for their cultures and achievements. *Activities*: Conducts archaeological surveys and excavations; provides indoor and outdoor exhibits; sponsors archaeological training sessions, teacher workshops, craft workshops, summer youth programs-educational programs to school groups. *Publication*: Artifacts, quarterly magazine; annual research report; bibliography and educational resource pamphlets. Annual

conference, with symposium - always November, Lowell, MA. Museum. Library. Established in 1971.

AMERICAN INDIAN ARTISTS, INC. (AMERINDA)
c/o AFSC, 15 Waverly Pl. • New York, NY 10003
(212) 598-0968 Fax 529-4603
Diane Fraher Thornton, Director
E-mail: amerinda@amerinda.org
Website: www.amerinda.org
Purpose: American Indian Artists works to empower Native Americans, break down barriers, and foster understanding and appreciation for Native culture. Through a variety of arts programs, productions and services to artists, AMERINDA supports Native artists who embody the traditional practices and values that define Indian culture. AMERINDA also promotes the indigenous perspective in the arts to a wide audience through mainstream art forms—visual, performing, literary and media arts. *Publication*: "Talking Stick," Native arts quarterly. Established in 1987.

AMERICAN INDIAN ARTS COUNCIL
725 Preston Forest Shopping Center, Suite B
Dallas, TX 75230 (214) 891-9640 Fax 891-0221
Ms. Joel C. Olson, President
Pat Peterson, Executive Director
E-mail: aiac@flash.net
Website: www.americanindianartsfestival.org
Purpose: To increase the awareness of the American Indian community; to enhance the quality of life by making American Indian art and cultural activities accessible to both the art community and the community- at-large; to educate the public, thereby enhancing an appreciation of the tribal heritage, art, culture, history, traditions, and contributions of American Indians to our culturally diverse community; to foster, promote, and showcase American Indian visual and performing arts. *Activities*: sponsor & produce an annual American Indian Art Festival & Market (Fall); create and sustain an Academic Scholarship Fund for Native American students enrolled in institutions of higher learning; develop a Museum of American Indian Arts and Culture; community exhibits; Cultural Presenters Program; Speakers Bureau. *Publication*: Quarterly newsletter; general information brochure and special event advertising supplement. Resource library.

AMERICAN INDIAN BAR ASSOCIATION
6017 Franconia Forest Ln.
Alexandria, VA 22310
(202) 714-3874
Approximately 150 member Native American attorneys concerned with improving the status of Native American peoples.

AMERICAN INDIAN COLLEGE FUND
8333 Greenwood Blvd. • Denver, CO 80221
P.O. Box 172449 • Denver, CO 80217
(800) 776-3863; (303) 426-8900 Ext. 308
Dr. David Gipp, Chairperson
Richard Williams, President
Cheryl Cadue, Public Information
E-mail: cadue@collegefund.org
Website: www.collegefund.org
Purpose: To raise funds to support the 34 member colleges of the American Indian Higher Education Consortium that are located in the U.S. *Activities*: Disbursements made directly to member colleges. *Publication*: Annual report. Established in 1989.

AMERICAN INDIAN COUNCIL OF ARCHITECTS & ENGINEERS
P.O. Box 15096 • Portland, OR 97215
(503) 235-4402 Fax 228-2058

AMERICAN INDIAN CULTURE RESEARCH CENTER
P.O. Box 98 • Marvin, SD 57251
(605) 398-9200 Fax 398-9201
Rev. Stanislaus Maudlin, Executive Director
E-mail: abbey@bluecloud.org
Website: www.bluecloud.org
Purpose: To support Indian leaders, and educators in their ambitions for rebuilding the Indian community; aids in teaching the non-Indian public of the culture & philosophy of the Indian. *Programs*: Compiled oral history & photographic collection; distributes films, records, and tapes; conducts workshops & seminars; maintains speakers bureau. Library. Established in 1967.

AMERICAN INDIAN DANCE THEATRE
223 East 61st St. • New York, NY 10021
Barb Schwei, Founder
Hanay Geiogamah, Director
The group has 20 dancers, representing various tribes across the country, including Zuni, Ute, Apache, Cheyenne & Creek. They perform dances of different tribes touring the U.S. and Europe. Founded 1987.

AMERICAN INDIAN DEVELOPMENT FOUNDATION
American Indian Science & Engineering Society
P.O. Box 9828 • Albuquerque, NM 87119-9828
(505) 765-1052 Fax 765-5608
Norbert S. Hill, Jr., Executive Director
Purpose: To encourage Native American Indian students to pursue their educational goals. Scholarships available.

AMERICAN INDIAN DISABILITY LEGISLATION: TOWARD THE DEVELOPMENT OF A PROCESS THAT RESPECTS SOVEREIGNTY & CULTURAL DIVERSITY
52 Corbin Hall, University of Montana
Missoula, MT 59801 (406) 243-5467
Julie Clay, Coordinator
Description: New project funded by the Office of Special Education and Rehabilitation, of the Dept. of Education. *Goal*: To develop and test methods for fostering the adoption of disability legislation by American Indian tribes that is consistent with principles established within the American With Disabilities Act and are respectful of tribal sovereignty & cultural diversity.

AMERICAN INDIAN EDUCATION ADVISORY COUNCIL
900 Grant St., Rm. 400 • Denver, CO 80203
(303) 764-3579; Phyl Ogden, Contact

AMERICAN INDIAN EDUCATION FOUNDATION
P.O. Box 27491 • Albuquerque, NM 87125
(866) 866-8642 Fax (503) 641-0495
Malinda Griffith, Program Coordinator
E-mail: info@aiefprograms.org
Website: www.aiefprograms.org
Purpose: To help Native American people improve the quality of their lives by providing opportunities for them to bring about positive changes in their communities. *Activities/Programs*: A non-profit organization whose mission is to give American Indian students the tools and opportunities to learn. The programs include: purchasing essential school supplies and curriculum materials, supporting student incentive programs, funding repair of structural deterioration in schools and awarding grants to American Indian students for tuition and living expenses. *Publication*: Quarterly newsletter. Established in 1998.

AMERICAN INDIAN EDUCATION POLICY CENTER
Penn. State University, 320 Rackley Bldg.
University Park, PA 16803 (814) 865-1489
Dr. L.A. Napier, Director
Program: American Indian Leadership Program. Goal: To train qualified leaders for service to Indian nations by providing graduate degrees in educational administration & certification credentials in principal ship and superintendency. Fellowships. Library. Founded 1970.

AMERICAN INDIAN FILM INSTITUTE
333 Valencia St. #322 • San Francisco, CA 94103
(415) 554-0525 Fax 554-0542
Website: www.aifisf.com
Mike Smith, Director
Activities: Annual Silver Star Pow-wow & Indian Market.

AMERICAN INDIAN GRADUATE CENTER
4520 Montgomery Blvd., NE, Suite 1-B
Albuquerque, NM 87109 (505) 881-4584
Website: www.aigc.com
Ada Pecos-Melton, President of Board
Louis Baca, Vice President of Board
Norbert S. Hill, Jr., Executive Director
Molly Tovar, Chief Operating Officer
Purpose: To help open doors to graduate education for American Indian and Alaska Native college graduates. *Activities*: Has awarded more than 10,000 fellowships to qualified Native American and Alaska Native students (from federally recognized tribes) pursuing master's, doctoral and professional degrees in all fields of study. Established 1969.

AMERICAN INDIAN GRADUATE STUDENT NETWORK
317 Ingraham Hall - University of Wisconsin
1155 Observatory Dr. • Madison, WI 53706
(608) 263-3106 Fax 262-7137; E-Mail: AISPC

AMERICAN INDIAN HEAD START QUALITY IMPROVEMENT CENTER
American Indian Institute
College of Continuing Education
The University of Oklahoma
555 Constitution St., Suite 228
Norman, OK 73072-7820 (800) 379-3869
(405) 325-4129 Fax 325-7319
Anita Chisholm, Executive Director
Pattie Howell, Project Director
E-mail: phowell@ou.edu
Website: www.aihsqic.ou.edu
Publication: Native Horizons, quarterly newsletter. Resource Center - catalog. *Alaska Satellite*: Prevention Associates, 101 E. 9th Ave., Suite 7-A, Anchorage, AK 99501 (907) 272-6925 Fax 272-6946.

AMERICAN INDIAN HEALTH CARE ASSOCIATION
address unknown
Michael Arfsten, Executive Director
Joan Myrick, AIDS Education Coordinator
Membership: Approximately 40 Indian health programs and 50 staff and support persons. *Purpose*: A national organization that provides technical assistance and training to urban Indian health program clinics funded by Indian Health Service. Technical assistance includes administration, financial and clinical development. Bestows awards and recognition for Indian health care achievements. *Publications*: Newsbriefs, quarterly newsletter; AIDS Briefs, quarterly newsletter; Summary Program Publication, annual; Diabetes Surveillance Survey, periodic; directory of programs and World Health Day materials which are Indian specific; AIDS education comic books (aimed at 5-16 year olds). Annual Urban Indian Health Care Management Conference. Established in 1975.

AMERICAN INDIAN HERITAGE FOUNDATION
6051 Arlington Blvd. • Falls Church, VA 22044
(703) 237-7500 Fax 532-1921
Princess Pale Moon, President
Dr. Wil Rose, Chief Executive Officer
E-mail: webmaster@indians.org
Website: www.indians.org
Donors: 25,000+. Corporate and individual donors.
Purpose: To inform and educate non-Indians concerning the culture and heritage of the American Indian; to be responsive to the felt needs of Indian people both at the tribal and urban levels; to introduce a positive Indian presence into every strata of society where it is appropriate; and to initiate creative programs to actively share the diverse Indian culture in many creative ways. *Activities/Programs*: Meets emergency needs, distributes gifts-in-kind; promotes an Outstanding Achievement Youth Role Model Program; sponsors the National Miss Indian USA Pageant; and promotes the National American Indian Heritage Month. *Publication*: Occasional bulletins. Museum and Library. Established in 1973.

AMERICAN INDIAN HIGHER EDUCATION CONSORTIUM (AIHEC)
121 Oronoco St. • Alexandria, VA 22314
(703) 838-0400 Fax 838-0388
Gerald Gipp, Executive Director
Diane L. Cullo, Director, Development, Communications
E-Mail: ggipp@aihec.org; dcullo@aihec.org
Website: www.aihec.org
Purpose: To promote higher education opportunities for this nation's 30 tribal colleges. Activities: Represents 30 tribally-controlled colleges in the U.S. to the Congress, federal agencies, and other national organizations, in an effort to acquire funds, support programs, and growth; to build a satellite network linking the 30 tribal colleges; technical assistance; research. *Publications*: Tribal College; Journal of American Indian Education, quarterly. Library. Established in 1978.

AMERICAN INDIAN HORSE REGISTRY
9028 State Park Rd. • Lockhart, TX 78644
(512) 398-6642; Nanci Falley, President
E-mail: nanci@indianhorse.com
Website: www.indianhorse.com

Membership: 1,200. Persons who own or desire to own American Indian horses. *Purpose*: To collect, record, and preserve the pedigrees of American Indian horses. *Activities*: National Indian Horse Show each September; awards programs for members. Maintains Indian Horse Hall of Fame Museum. *Publications*: American Indian Horse Studbook, annual; quarterly newsletter. Library. Established 1961.

AMERICAN INDIAN INSTITUTE
555 Constitution Ave., Suite 237
Norman, OK 73072-7820
(405) 325-4127 Fax 325-7757
Anita Chisholm, Executive Director
E-Mail: aii@cce.occe.ou.edu
Purpose: To promote Indian education and research, training and career development opportunities, the development of human and natural resources; the perpetuation of tribal/band cultures and traditions and their histories; and to facilitate the utilization of University of Oklahoma resources by Indian tribes, bands, organizations and groups. *Activities*: Historical/cultural research design and methodology; cultural resource identification and development; substance abuse training for schools and communities; cultural curriculum development for schools and tribal/band education departments; annual Early Childhood Intervention Conference; annual National American Indian Conference on Child Abuse and Neglect; annual National Conference on Gifted and Talented Education for Native People; annual National Native American, Alaska Native, First Nations Cultural Curriculum Development Workshop; arts & crafts cultural workshops and exchanges. *Publications*: Conference Proceedings; Cultural lessons: cultural curriculum, gifted & talented, math & science, and drug & alcohol. Resource library. Established in 1951.

AMERICAN INDIAN LAW CENTER
P.O. Box 4456, Station A, 1117 Stanford, N.E.
Albuquerque, NM 87196 (505) 277-5462
Philip S. Deloria, Executive Director
Description: Staff of 12 Indian law graduates and attorneys; located at the University of New Mexico, School of Law. *Purpose*: To render services, primarily research and training, of a broad legal and governmental nature; and, to assist tribes in making legal decisions when assistance is necessary. *Programs*: Helped found and currently provides staff support to the Commission on State-Tribal Relations; provides individualized training for tribal judges and tribal prosecutors; administers the Special Scholarship Program in Law for American Indians through which students receive admission advice, financial assistance, tutorial aid, and job placement services; provides assistance to Alaskan natives; sponsors conferences and seminars. *Publications*: American Indian Law Newsletter, bimonthly; manuals for tribal judges and prosecutors, and on Indian criminal court procedures. Library. Established in 1967.

AMERICAN INDIAN LAW & POLICY CENTER
University of Oklahoma College of Law
300 Timberdell Rd. • Norman, OK 73019
(405) 325-4676
Prof. Rennard Strickland, Director
Jan Young, Secretary

AMERICAN INDIAN LAWYER TRAINING PROGRAM, INC.
American Indian Resource Institute
319 MacArthur Blvd. • Oakland, CA 94610
(510) 834-9333 Fax 834-3836
Purpose: To strengthen and enhance the development of tribal institutions by providing programs and services that improve access to the vast and complex legal developments that affect Indian tribes and their members; promote communication and cooperation among and between members of the Indian legal community; and develop the skilss of members of the Indian legal community. *Projects*: Indian attorney fellowship program; summer internships; law associate program; tribal court advocate training project; and working seminars and conferences. *Publication*: The Indian Law Reporter.

AMERICAN INDIAN LIBERATION CRUSADE, INC.
4009 S. Halldale Ave. • Los Angeles, CA 90062
(323) 299-1810
Basil M. Gaynor, President

Membership: 4,000. *Purpose*: To transform the negative stereotypical thinking of both Indians and White people, while facilitating self-sufficiency and self-determination for the American Indian. *Activities*: Support ministry to Indian churches and organizations on the Indian Reservations across the nation. Assist with relief, education, emergency situations, and provide a network of talents and resources; sends Indian children to summer Bible Camp; maintain a radio broadcast making known the needs and hopes of the First Americans. *Publication*: "The Indian Crusader," quarterly newsletter; "The Four Directions'; "A Warrior's Greatest Honor" and other publications. Established in 1952.

AMERICAN INDIAN LIBRARIANS
c/o Janice Beaudin - U. of Wisconsin Library
600 N. Park St. • Madison, WI 53706
    (608) 262-3193
Purpose: To unite librarians of American Indian origin.

AMERICAN INDIAN LIBRARY ASSOCIATION (AILA)
620-U Hillman Library, University of Pittsburgh
Pittsburgh, PA 15260 (412) 648-7780
    Victor Schill, President
    c/o Lisa Mitten, Social Sceinces Bibliographer
    E-mail: lmitten@pitt.edu
    Web site: www.nativeculture.com/lmitten/aila.html
    c/o SLIS, 401 W. Brooks, U. of Oklahoma
Norman, OK 73019 (405) 325-3921 Fax 325-7648
    Dr. Rhonda Taylor, Editor
    E-Mail: rtaylor@uoknor.edu
Purpose: To promote the development, maintenance, and improvement of libraries, library systems, and cultural and information services on reservations and in communities of Native Americans and Native Alaskans. *Publication*: AILA Newsletter, quarterly, $10/year-indidivuals, $25/year-organizations; $5/yearstudents. Annual conference program during American Library Association annual conference in June. Established in 1979.

AMERICAN INDIAN MOVEMENT
Minneapolis, MN (Address unknown)
    Dennis Banks, Clyde Bellecourt et al,
    Founding members
Membership: 5,000. Primary objective is to encourage self-determination among American Indians and to establish international recognition of American Indian treaty rights. Founded Heart of the Earth Survival School which enrolls 600 students from preschool to adult programs. Maintains historical archives and speakers' bureau; conducts research. *Publication*: Survival News, quarterly. Annual meeting. Established in 1968.

AMERICAN INDIAN PROFESSIONAL TRAINING PROGRAM IN SPEECH-LANGUAGE PATHOLOGY & AUDIOLOGY
University of Arizona
Dept. of Speech & Hearing Sciences
Tucson, AZ 85721 (520) 621-1969/1644
    Dr. Theodore Glattke, Director
    Betty D. Nunnery, Program Coordinator
    Pamela R. Wood, Clinical Supervisor, Audiologist
Objectives: To recruit, retain, and provide education to American Indian men and women in the fields of speech-language pathology or audiology. *Goals*: To qualify students for a Master's degree in speech-language pathology or audiology; to integrate the study of Indian languages and cultures into the training program; to develop therapy programs sensitive to Indian cultural needs; to establish a professional work force to serve American Indians who have communication disorders both on and off reservations. *Activities/Programs*: Speech & hearing clinics operated on two reservation sites. Scholarship recipients receive a tuition waiver and a stipend. *Publications*: Directory of Native Americans in Speech-Language Pathology & Audiology; newsletter, Desert Connections, a network publication for Native American speech-language pathologists & audiologists. Library. Established in 1978.

AMERICAN INDIAN RADIO ON SATELLITE
P.O. Box 83111 • Lincoln, NE 68501
    (800) 571-6885; (402) 472-9333 Fax 472-8675
    Susan Braine, Manager
Goal: To distribute programs that address political, social, economic, health, artistic, and spiritual concerns and issues of Native American communities. *Activity*:

To inventory Native American content radio programs for the public radio system.

AMERICAN INDIAN REHABILITATION RESEARCH & TRAINING CENTER
Institute for Human Development
Northern Arizona University, CU Box 5630
Flagstaff, AZ 86011
    (520) 523-4791 Fax 523-9127
    Dr. Timothy Thomason, Director
Web site: http://www.nav.edu/~ihd
Purpose: To improve the lives of American Indians with disabilities. *Publications*: Quarterly newsletter; "Hotline" bimonthly newsletter; AITRRTC Catalog - publications, reports, papers, etc. offered by the center.

AMERICAN INDIAN RELIEF COUNCIL
P.O. Box 6200 • Rapid City, SD 57709
    (800) 370-0872; (605) 399-9905 Fax 399-9908
    Brian Brown, President
    Elora Antoine, Program Coordinator
    E-mail: info@airc.org; Website: www.airc.org
Purpose: A member of the National Relief Charities, the Council was organized to help Native American people improve the quality of their lives by providing opportunities for them to bring about positive changes in their communities. *Activities/Programs*: A non-profit organization which develops self-help programs and emergency relief services for Native Americans on reservations in ND, SD, NE, MT and WY. These services include: emergency food distribution, clothing and shoe distributions, winterization of homes, fuel assistance programs, school supplies, holiday dinners, gifts and stockings for children at Christmas and Easter, baby baskets for new mothers and incentive programs for seniors, adult volunteers and children. *Publication*: Quarterly newsletter. Established in 1988.

AMERICAN INDIAN RELIGIOUS RIGHTS (AIRR)
1017 Lincoln Ave. • College Station, TX 77840
    (409) 268-9008 Fax 758-1187
    Alex Montana, Council Chairperson
Purpose: To secure and protect the religious rights of American Indian prisoners.

AMERICAN INDIAN RESEARCH & DEVELOPMENT
2233 W. Lindsey St., Suite 118
Norman, OK 73069-4054
    (405) 364-0656 Fax 364-5464
    Stuart A. Tonemah, President
Description: Educational service organization which seeks to improve the quality of education for gifted and talented Native American students. *Activities*: Provides training and technical assistance to local and state education agencies, tribes, and other Native American organizations; offers summer and weekend programs; leadership enrichment programs for gifted and talented American and Alaska Native students; conducts research; develops curriculum and teaching materials; maintains speaker's bureau; sponsors competitions; and compiles statistics. *Publications*: American Indian Gifted and Talented Assessment Model; and Elementary American Indian Gifted and Talented Assessment Model. Established 1982.

AMERICAN INDIAN RESEARCH OPPORUNITIES
307 Culbertson Hall, Montana State University
Bozeman, MT 59715 (406) 994-5567
Web site: www.montana.edu/~wwwai
Purpose: Operates a number of programs, including a minority apprenticeship program (MAP), a minority biomedical research support program (MBRS), and a minority access-to-research careers program.

AMERICAN INDIAN RESOURCES INSTITUTE
319 MacArthur Blvd. • Oakland, CA 94610
    (510) 834-9333
Purpose: To design and implement programs to promote tribal sovereignty and self-determination through provision of training resources to Indian attorneys, law students, and advocates committed to serving the legal needs of Indian people. *Program*: American Indian Lawyer Training Program. Founded 1973.

AMERICAN INDIAN RITUAL OBJECT REPATRIATION FOUNDATION
463 E. 57th St. • New York, NY 10128
    (212) 980-9441 Fax 421-2746

Elizabeth Sackler, Founder/President
Anne W. Cassidy, Executive Director
Pilar Montalvo, Repatriation Coordinator
E-Mail: circle@repatriationfoundation.org
Wibe site: www.repatriationfoundation.org
Purpose: An intercultural organization committed to assisting in the return of ceremonial objects to American Indian Nations and to educating the public about the importance of repatriation. *Activities*: Assist in the repatriation of ceremonial objects by acting as a liaison between collectors, dealers, auction houses and Native representatives; provide collectors who currently possess ritual objects with information about the cultural significance of the object; locate & contact American Indian individuals needed to authenticate and/or escort home sacred objects identified for repatriation; provide information about federal and other repatriation policies; sponsor workshops addressing the repatriation process and the significance of sacred material culture to American Indian communities; collect information regarding repatriation activities. *Publications*: Biannual newsletter; "Mending the Circle: A Native American Repatriation Guide."

AMERICAN INDIAN SCIENCE & ENGINEERING SOCIETY (AISES)
P.O. Box 9828
Albuquerque, NM 87119-9828
    (505) 765-1052 Fax 765-5608
    Norbert S. Hill, Jr., Executive Director
Membership: 1,500. American Indian and non-Indian students and professionals in science, technology, and engineering fields. *Purpose*: To increase the number of American Indian scientists and engineers in the nation; seeks to motivate and encourage students to pursue graduate studies in science, engineering and technology; and the ultimate goal is to serve as a catalyst for the advancement of American Indians to become more self-reliant members of society. *Activities*: American Indian Science and Education Center - provides training and educational opportunities to American Indian college students and tribal leaders; teacher-training programs; sponsors internships nationwide & specially designed workshops; curriculum materials development; conducts research and community-affiliated programs; sponsors scholarship; bestows awards; maintains speakers bureau and job placement service. AISES Environmental Institute - camp for about 35 kids, ages 11-17, for 1-2 week sessions to experience nature and to put together the best of modern science with traditional American Indian values and teachings. Located in Pike Mountain National Forest, about 50 miles southwest of Denver; American Indian Development Foundation - to encourage Native American Indian students to pursue their educational goals. Scholarships available. *Publications*: Journal, biennial; Winds of Change, quarterly magazine; Science Education Newsletter, quarterly; Annual Report. Annual conference. Library. Established in 1977.

AMERICAN INDIAN STUDIES CENTER
University of California, Los Angeles
3220 Campbell Hall, Box 951548
LOS ANGELES 90095-1548
    (310) 825-7315 Fax 206-7060
    E-mail: aisc@ucla.edu
    Web site: www.sscnet.ucla.edu/indian/
    Duane Champagne, Director
    Paul V. Kroskrity, Chair (IDP Program)
Description: The Center ranks among the top research centers of its kind in the country serving the educational and cultural needs of the American Indian community. *Activities*: Sponsors research and administers competetive grants; offers a minor, masters and a concurrent law program; publishes books; encourages the development of new courses, addresses recruitment of American Indian students and faculty; offers a forum for scholarly exchange for American Indian students, the community and alumni; and sponsors an annual Pow Wow in the Spring quarter. *Facilities*: The Museum of Cultural History; Library; the publications unit produces numerous books, bibliographies, monographs. *Publication*: "American Indian Culture and Research Journal."

AMERICAN INDIAN STUDIES RESEARCH INSTITUTE
Indiana University • Bloomington, IN 47405
    (812) 855-1203 Raymond J. De Mallie, Director

AMERICAN INDIAN VETERANS ASSOCIATION, INC.
P.O. Box 543 • Isleta, NM 87022
(505) 869-9284
Description: Organized for the benevolence of American Indian veterans of the Armed Forces of the U.S. Established in 1977.

AMERICAN INDIAN YOUTH RUNNING STRONG
8815 Telegraph Rd. • Lorton, VA 22079
(703) 550-2123 Fax 550-2473
Lauren Haas, Executive Director
E-mail: info@indianyouth.org
Website: www.indianyouth.org
Purpose: To help American Indian people meet their immediate survival needs - food, water and shelter - while implementing and supporting programs designed to create opportunities for self-sufficiency and self-esteem, particularly for tribal youth. *Activities/programs*: Long-term development programs such as organic gardening, housing, water resource development, nutrition, health care and youth programs. *Publications*: Quarterly newsletter; annual reports. Established in 1986.

AMERICAN INDIANS IN FILM & TELEVISION
65 N. Allen Ave. #105 • Pasadena, CA 91106
(818) 578-0344
Sonny Skyhawk, CEO & Founder

AMERICAN NATIVE PRESS ARCHIVES & RESEARCH ASSOCIATION
American Indian and Alaska Native
Periodicals Research Clearinghouse
502 Stabler Hall, University of Arkansas
33rd & University Ave.
Little Rock, AR 72204 (501) 569-3160
Johnye E. Strickland, Sec.-Treas.
Purpose: To promote and foster academic research concerning the American native press, those involved in it, and American native periodical literature as a whole; disseminate research results; refine methodologies. Annual Meeting. Established in 1984.

AMERICAN SOCIETY FOR ETHNOHISTORY
Dept. of Anthropology, 265 McGraw Hall
Cornell University • Ithaca, NY 14853
(607) 277-0109
Frederic W. Gleach, Sec/Treas.
E-Mail: fwg1@cornell.edu
Membership: 1,400. Anthropologists, historians, geographers, etc. *Purpose*: To promote the educational and scientific study of world societies and cultures, cultural change, and history; and to foster the study of ethnohistory worldwide. *Awards*: Robert F. Heizer Award, annual for best article concerning ethnohistory; and Erminie Wheeler-Voegel Award, annual for best book-length work in ethnohistory. Library of copies of Ethnohistory and Society's archives. *Publication*: Ethnohistory, (quarterly journal) by Duke University Press. Annual Meeting. Established in 1954.

AMERICANS FOR INDIAN OPPORTUNITY (AIO)
681 Juniper Hill Rd. • Bernalillo, NM 87004
(505) 867-0278 Fax 867-0441
LaDonna Harris (Comanche), Founder/President
Laura Harris (Comanche), Executive Director
E-mail: aio@aio.org. Web site: www.aio.org
Description: Americans for Indian Opportunity catalyzes and facilitates culturally appropriate initiatives and opportunities that enrich the cultural, political and economic lives of Indigenous peoples. *Purpose*: AIO draws upon traditional Indigenous values to foster enlightened and responsible leadership, inspires stakeholder-driven solutions, and convenes visionary leaders to probe contemporary issues and address challenges of the new century. *Activities*: AIO's acclaimed initiative, the American Indian Ambassadors Program, is a Native American community capacity-building, leadership development effort that AIO has been operating since 1993. The program is designed to help early to mid-career Native American professionals strengthen, within an Indigenous cultural context, their ability to improve the well-being and growth of their communities. In addition, AIO projects and initiatives include: partnering with Indigenous communities worldwide through the newly formed international organization, the Advancement of Global Indigeneity, which is an outgrowth of a partnership with the Advancement of Maori Opportunity (AMO), New Zealand;

developing solutions through consensus building methodology, as a developer and facilitator of the Indigenous Leadership Interactive System (ILIS™); enhancing intergovernmental relations and acting as a resource and facilitation center. *Publication*: The Ambassador: Newsletter of the American Indian Ambassadors Program. Established in 1970.

THE AMERIND FOUNDATION, INC.
P.O. Box 400 • Dragoon, AZ 85609-0400
(520) 586-3666 Fax 586-4679
John A. Ware, PhD, Director
E-mail: amerind@amerind.org
Website: www.amerind.org
Description: A nonprofit archaeological research institution and museum specializing in the Native American cultures of the Americas. *Activities*: Archaeological field research in the Greater Southwest; advanced seminar programs; research library; anthropology museum and art gallery. Publishes monograph series on archaeology of the Southwest and Northern Mexico. Museum. Library. Semiannual meeting in May & November. Established in 1937.

AMERIND RISK MANAGEMENT CORP.
6201 Uptown Blvd., Suite 100
Albuquerque, NM 87110 (800) 352-3496
(505) 837-2290 Fax 837-2053
Kent E. Paul, CEO; Rod Crawley, COO
Description: A consortium of tribes and tribal housing authorities throughout the U.S. working together to protect themselves and their tribal families from disasters. Represented by nine regions with each region electing a representative to serve on the Board of Directors. *Activities*: Provides risk management consulting services and insurance products to Native American & Alaska Native Housing Authorities, Tribal Designated Housing Entities, Tribal organizations and their tribal members. primary focus has been the management of a risk sharing pool providing property & casualty protection for Indian housing...curently 220 members (representing 400+ tribes).

ANTHROPOLOGY FILM CENTER FOUNDATION
Santa Fe, NM 87594
(505) 983-4127 Joan S. Williams, Director
Purpose: To further scholarship, research and practice in visual anthropology through consultation and research services, seminars, publications, teaching, equipment outfitting and specialized facilities. *Program*: Intensive 9 month filmmaking program stressing cultural factors in documentary film production. American Indian graduates: Larry Littlebird, Rain Parrish, George Burdeau, and Ron Sarracino, and others. *Publication*: Filmography for American Indian Education. Library-Archives. Established in 1971.

ANTI-YUN'WIYA SOCIETY
3601 Wenatchee Ave. • Bakersfield, CA 93306
(805) 871-2977 Dick Hutchinson, Contact
Purpose: To perpetuate the culture and tradition of the indigenous people; to help them regain their Indian heritage; to help them keep their Native language alive; to inform them of any change in Indian affairs that arise; and to help the general public learn more about the Native American Indian people and their way of life. *Activities*: Annual pow wow; research and registration into Native tribes; monthly meetings. *Publications*: Newsletter. Established in 1979.

APPLIED EARTHWORKS, INC.
5090 N. Fruit Ave. #101 • Fresno, CA 93711
(559) 229-1856 Fax 229-2019
E-mail: ae93711@aol.com
Susan K. Goldberg, Chairperson
A California corporation, AE performs contract-supported research in archaeology and allied sciences for many governmental and private agencies. Native American consultation; Navajo WPA architecture

ARCHAEOLOGICAL CONSERVANCY
5301 Central Ave. NE, Suite 1218
Albuquerque, NM 87108 (505) 266-1540
Mark Michel, President
Membership: 17,000. People interested in preserving prehistoric and historic sites for interpretive or research purposes. *Purpose*: To acquire for permanent preservation the ruins of past American cultures, primarily those of American Indians. *Publication*: "American Archaeology" (quarterly magazine). Established 1979.

ARCHAEOLOGICAL INSTITUTE OF AMERICA
656 Beacon St. • Boston, MA 02215
(617) 353-9361 Fax 353-6550
Mark J. Meister, Executive Director
E-mail: aia@bu.edu
Web site: www.archaeological.org
Membership: 11,000. Educational and scientific society of archaeologists and others interested in archaeological study and research. *Publication*: Archaeology, bimonthly; Dig Magazine, bimonthly (children's magazine); American Journal of Archaeology, quarterly; Archaeological Fieldwork Opportunities Bulletin, annual. Annual meeting. Established in 1879.

ARROW, INC. (AMERICANS FOR THE RESTITUTION & RIGHTING OF OLD WRONGS)
Washington, DC 20036 (888) ARROW10
(202) 296-0685 Fax 659-4377
Dolores Bronson Tidrick, President
Hazel E. Elbert, Executive Director
Membership: 2,200. *Purpose*: The betterment of American Indian health and education. *Activities*: Programs on alcohol, drug and child abuse; recruits physicians and RN's from the private sector to help fill shortages at Indian hospitals; and offers graduate scholarships. Annual meeting. Established in 1949.

ASSOCIATED COMMITTEE OF FRIENDS ON INDIAN AFFAIRS (QUAKER)
P.O. Box 2326 • Richmond, IN 47375
(765) 935-0801
H. Keith Kendall, Executive Secretary
E-mail: kjkendall@earthlink.net
Website: www.acfiaquaker.org
Description: Missionary project of the Religious Society of Friends (Quakers.) Purpose: To bear testimony to the Christian faith and teachings by word and deed; to persist in calling for integrity in all phases of the administration of Indian affairs; to encourage pride of all Indians in their heritage; to assist those with whom the ACFIA works to build a strong sense of community & personal responsibility. Activities: Runs an academy in Alabama among the Mowa-Choctaws; church meetings; runs youth/children programs in Oklahoma (Wyandotte, Seneca-Cayuga, Kickapoo and Osage) and in Iowa (Mesquakie); social welfare assistance at all centers; school in Alabama for 2004-05 year (only pre-K and Kindergarten class). *Publication*: Indian Progress, quarterly newsletter. Established in 1869.

ASSOCIATION FOR COMMUNITY TRIBAL SCHOOLS
616 4th Ave. W. • Sisseton, SD 57262
(605) 698-3953 Fax 698-7686
Dr. Roger Bordeaux, Executive Director
E-mail: roger@wambdi.bia.edu
Membership: 30. American Indian controlled schools organized under the Indian Self-Determination Education Assistance Act and Tribally Controlled Schools Act. Publication: Quarterly newsletter. Established 1982.

ASSOCIATION FOR THE STUDY OF AMERICAN INDIAN LITERATURES
P.O. Box 112 • Richmond, VA 23173
(804) 289-8311 Fax 289-8313
Robert M. Nelson, Director
E-Mail: melson@richmond.edu
Membership: Primarily academic, and those involved one way or another with the study of or creation of Native American literatures (oral as well as print, old time as well as contemporary). *Publication*: Studies in American Indian Literatures, quarterly scholarly journal focusing exclusively on American Indian literatures.

ASSOCIATION OF AMERICAN INDIAN & ALASKA NATIVE SOCIAL WORKERS
1220 South Third Ave.
Portland, OR 97204 (503) 231-2641
Membership: Indian social workers concerned with the social welfare of Indian people. *Purpose*: To meet the unique needs of Indians according to their customs, traditions, life style and values. Established in 1970.

ASSOCIATION OF AMERICAN INDIAN LAW SCHOOLS
Center for the Study of American Indian Law & Policy
University of Oklahoma-College of Law
300 W. Timberdell Rd. • Norman, OK 73019
(405) 325-4699; Prof. Rennard Strickland, President

**ASSOCIATION OF AMERICAN
INDIAN PHYSICIANS**
1225 Sovereign Row, Suite 103
Oklahoma City, OK 73108
(405) 946-7072 Fax 946-7651
Matthew Kauley, Executive Director
Website: www.aaip.com
Membership: 235. Physicians (M.D. or D.O.) of 1/8 American Indian descent or more. *Purpose*: To encourage and recruit American Indians into the health professions; to provide a forum for the interchange of ideas and information of mutual interest between physicians; to make recommendations to government agencies regarding the health of American Indians and Alaska Natives; to enter into contracts with these agencies to provide consultation and other expert opinions regarding health care of American Indians and Alaska Natives. *Program*: The National Native American Youth Initiative - A Health, Biomedical Research, and Policy Development Program for Native American high school students between the ages of 16 and 18. To motivate them to remain in the academic pipeline and to pursue a career in the health professions and/or biomedical research; and prepares students for admission to college & professional schools. *Activities*: Seeks scholarship funds for Indian professional students; conducts seminars for students interested in health careers. *Publications*: Quarterly newsletter; American Indian Health Careers Handbook. Annual conference. Founded 1971.

**ASSOCIATION OF NATIVE AMERICAN
MEDICAL STUDENTS**
1225 Sovereign Row, 103
Oklahoma City, OK 73159
(405) 677-1468; Laurie McLemore, MD, Director
Publication: AIDS Regional Directory: Resources in Indian Country.

ASSOCIATION ON AMERICAN INDIAN AFFAIRS
966 Hungerford Dr., Suite 12-B
Rockville, MD 20850
(240) 314-7155 Fax 314-7159
Jack F. Trope, Executive Director
E-mail: general.aaia@verizon.net
Web site: www.indian-affairs.org
Board of Directors: Brad Keeler, President; Alfred R. Ketzler, Sr., Vice-President; Joy Hanley, Treasurer; Owanah Anderson, Secretary; Wathene Young, John Echohawk, David Risling, DeeAnn DeRoin, MD, and James Hena, Jerry Flute, Tom Acevedo. *Membership*: 30,000. *Purpose*: To sustain and perpetuate Indian cultures and languages; to protect their sovereignty, constitutional, legal and human rights, and natural resources; and to improve their health, education, economic and community development. *Programs*: Sacred Land Protection; Repatriation; Language Preservation; Health - Diabetes Education; Scholarships; Youth Camps; Sovereignty; Child Welfare. Also, programs in Indian community development, education, legal defense; religious freedom, and public education. Aids Indian tribes in mobilizing all available resources—federal, state and private—for a coordinated attack on the problems of poverty and injustice, and protects the constitutional and treaty rights of Native peoples, as well as their special aboriginal rights; the Adolph Van Pelt Special Fund for Indian Scholarships offers scholarships to undergraduate and graduate students in amounts ranging from $500 to $800; the Sequoyah Graduate Fellowship Program provides a one-year $1,500 unrestricted stipend paid in two equal installments; the Emergency Aid Scholarship Program provides grants of $100 to $400 to American Indian & Alaska Native students; Florence Young Grauate Fellowship, $5,000 for Art Majors; Emilie Hesemeyer Memorial Scholarship-Cintinuity Scholarship $1,500 per year; Allogan Slagle Scholarship for students from tribes that are state recognized or seeking federal recognition. *Publications*: Indian Affairs, Biannual newsletter; 1996 Proceedings of the National Sacred Sites Caucus. Archives are held at Princeton University Mudd Library. Library. Established in 1922.

**ATLATL, INC. NATIONAL SERVICE ORGANIZATION
FOR NATIVE AMERICAN ARTS**
P.O. Box 34090 • Phoenix, AZ 85067-4090
(602) 277-3711 Fax 277-3690
Carla A. Roberts, Executive Director
E:Mail: atlatl@artswire.org or atlatl@atlatl.org
Description: A non-profit Native American arts service

organization founded as a national advocate for Native American art. *Goals*: To heighten awareness of indigenous aesthetics and modes of expression; to promote the vitality of contemporary Native American art through self determination in cultural expression; to create an informational network between Native American artists and arts; and provide training opportunities and economic development for Native American artists. *Activities*: Traveling Exhibit Service; technical assistance and consulting services; sponsors annual workshops; hosts a national biennial conference for Native artists and administrators (Native Arts Network) ; and maintains resource files on Native artists and art organizations; international exchange program with aboriginal Australians, the Maori of New Zealand, and indigenous peoples of Mexico; maintains a slide, video tape and audio tape resource center; distributes audio-visual materials by and about Native Americans; *Publications*: Native Arts Update, quarterly newsletter; From Village, Clan and City (poetry & short stories); Directory of Native American Performing Artists; maintains a National Registry of Native American artists; periodic special reports (Survey of State Arts Agency Support of Native Arts Programs); exhibition catalogs. Founded 1977.

BEAR TRIBE MEDICINE SOCIETY
3750A Airport Blvd. #223
Mobile, AL 36608-1618 (509) 326-6561
Sun Bear, Founder; Wabun James, Exec. Director
Description: An educational organization. *Purpose*: To teach people respect for the earth as the giver and sustainer of life. It uses the Native American ways of viewing the earth to help people find their connection with the earth so that people will begin to think about the effects of their actions on the earth. Activities: Educational workshops, lectures, tours, survival camps, visitor programs; operates a bookstore/mail order business; offers a barter or trade system for people who want to take their programs but cannot afford them—they offer their skills in return for the programs. *Publications*: The Path of Power; The Medicine Wheel Book; Buffalo Hearts; The Self-Reliance Book. Founded 1971.

BUREAU OF CATHOLIC INDIAN MISSIONS
2021 H St., NW • Washington, DC 20006
(202) 331-8542
Msgr. Paul A. Lenz, Executive Director
Purpose: The support of Catholic Indian missions, parishes, schools, centers, and activities; the advocacy for national legislation for the benefit of all American Indian tribes, pueblos, nations. *Activities*: Participation in the Tekakwitha Conference; testimony to congressional committees on legislation affecting Indian groups; presentations on Indian issues to organizations; grants to Catholic Indian organizations through the diocese in which they are located. *Publication*: Monthly newsletter. Archives—located in the library at Marquette University, Milwaukee, Wisconsin. Established 1874.

CATCHING THE DREAM
8200 Mountain Rd., NE #203
Albuquerque, NM 87110
(505) 262-2351 Fax 262-0534
E-mail: nscholarsh@aol.com
Dr. Dean Chavers, Director
James Lujan, President
Darrell Jeanotte, VP
Membership: 600. Native Americans and others working to ensure that Native American college students prepare adequately for college, enroll, graduate, and return to their tribes as doctors, nurses, teachers, engineers, business entrpreneurs, dentists, and computer programmers. Also advocates for school improvement for reservation schools. Operates six grant programs for school improvement. *Publication*: Newsletter; annual report in September. Publisher of a dozen books on Indian education, exemplary programs, proposal writing, and management. Holds an annual Exemplary Institute featuring successful Indian education program. Established in 1987.

CENTER FOR AMERICAN ARCHAEOLOGY
P.O. Box 366 • Kampsville, IL 62053
(618) 653-4316 Fax 653-4232
Jane E. Buikstra, President
Cynthia Sutton, Executive Director
E-mail: caa@caa-archaeology.org

Web site: www.caa-archaeology.org
Membership: 500. Institutions, professional and amateur archaeologists, students and others interested in archaeology in the U.S. *Activities*: Conducts archaeological research and disseminates the results; excavates, analyzes, and conserves archaeological sites and artifacts; sponsors tours, lectures, and educational and outreach programs; conducts teachers workshops; maintains speaker's bureau and library; and operated Kampsville Archaeological Museum. *Publications*: Quarterly newsletter; research series and technical reports; monographs; annual report. Founded 1958.

CENTER FOR INDIGENOUS ARTS & CULTURES
Div. of Southwest Learning Centers, Inc.
P.O. Box 8627 • Santa Fe, NM 87504-8627
(505) 473-5375 Fax 424-1025
Gregory Schaaf, PhD, Director
E-mail: indians@nets.com
Website: www.indianartbooks.com
Purpose: To provide services to American Indians and communities, as well as providing educational materials for the general public. CIACPress is a non-profit publishing company that produces books, videotapes, CDs and other forms of media. Monthly seminars are offered related to American Indian art and cultural activities. CIAC will help any American Indian artist develop their biography free of charge. *Activities/Programs*: "The American Indian Art Series," is a planned 20-volume series of volumes featuring American Indian artist biographical profiles grouped by art form. Five volumes are now available: Vol. 1 - Hopi-Tewa Pottery: 500 Artist Biographies; Vol. 2 - Pueblo Indian Pottery: 750 Artist Biographies; Vol. 3 - American Indian Textiles: 2,000 Artist Biographies; Vol. 4 - Southern Pueblo Pottery: 2,000 Artist Biographies; Vol. 5 - American Indian Jewelry: 2,000 Artist Biographies. The 6th volume, American Indian Basketry," is planned for Fall 2003. Future volumes will profile American Indian painters, sculptors, beadworkers, dollmakers, musical instrument makers, clothing designers and more. The last three volumes will be the native artists of Mexico, Central and South America. Once completed the series will embrace over 30,000 artists throughout the Western Hemisphere. Features a small museum with over 3,000 objects in the collection. There is a small library and archives featuring over 100,000 documents. Publications: Beyond the "American Indian Art Series," CIAC also distributes other works by Dr. Gregory Schaaf.

**CENTER FOR INDIGENOUS
STUDIES IN THE AMERICAS**
1121 North 2nd St.
Phoenix, AZ 85004 (602) 253-4938
Cory Dale Breternitz, President
Established to promote archaeological and anthropological research of indigenous peoples and national history of the Americas. *Goal*: To contribute to a better and fuller knowledge of the archaeology, ethnology, and arts of the Native American. The focus of the organization is the anthropology of Native Americans. *Staff*: Michael S. Foster, Douglas R. Mitchell, Christine K. Robinson, Adrian S. White. *Activities*: Archaeological tours; research facilities (office and lab); publications. Library.

**CENTER FOR THE STUDY OF
AMERICAN INDIAN LAW & POLICY**
University of Oklahoma-College of Law
300 W. Timberdell Rd.
Norman, OK 73072 (405) 325-4699
Prof. Rennard Strickland, Director
Publication: The Handbook of Federal Indian Law.

**CENTER FOR THE STUDY
OF THE FIRST AMERICANS**
Oregon State University
Corvallis, OR 97331 (503) 737-4515
Robson Bonnichsen, PhD, Director

**CENTER FOR SUPPORT & PROTECTION OF
INDIAN RELIGIONS & INDIGENOUS TRADITIONS**
National Congress of American Indians
2010 Massachusetts Ave., NW, 2nd Floor
Washington, DC 20036
(202) 466-7767 Fax 466-7797
John Lavelle, Director
CENTER OF AMERICAN INDIAN

& MINORITY HEALTH

School of Medicine, 10 University Dr.
Duluth, MN 55812-2487
(218) 726-7235 Fax 726-6235
Dr. Gerald Hill, Director
Purpose: To offer today's American Indian students a pathway to achieve a successful career in health or science related careers.

CHEROKEE INDIAN RECORDS

P.O. Box 41 • Boaz, AL 35957
(205) 593-7336; Robert Morrison, President
Purpose: Provides individual and family heritage charts for Cherokees nationally. The charge is $25 to search 43 records, 7 of them are of the Cherokee in the Civil War. The fee is for all the information on the records from 1817-1924.

CHEROKEE LANGUAGE & CULTURE

4158 E. 48 Place • Tulsa, OK 74135-4739
(918) 749-3082
Prentice & Willena Robinson, Owners
E-mail: prenticewillena@aol.com
Website: www.cherokeemadeeasy.com
Purpose: To keep the Cherokee language and history alive and as accurate as possible. *Programs*: Lectures on language and/or history. *Publications*: Book & tapes - Cherokee Made Easy. Study course - workbook and tape (language study); hymns/history book; Your Name in Cherokee book; picture associated Syllabary Flash Cards; national award winning videos on Cherokee history & Native American artists. Established in 1974.

CHEROKEE NATIONAL HISTORICAL SOCIETY

P.O. Box 515 • Tahlequah, OK 74465
(918) 456-6007 Fax 456-6165
Ellen Meredith, Acting Director
E-mail: info@cherokeeheritage.org
Website: www.leftmoon.com/cnhs
Description: Persons and organizations interested in preserving the history and traditions of the Cherokee Indian Nation. *Purpose*: To interest the public in Cherokee history; to mark locations of historic significance to the Cherokees. *Activities/Programs*: Sponsors educational, charitable, and benevolent activities for Cherokees and their descendents; operated Cherokee Heritage Center, which includes the Cherokee National Museum, and Cherokee Arboretum and Herb Garden; maintains a "living" Indian Village, circa 1700-50 and a Rural Cherokee Museum Village, circa 1875-90; annually presents the Trail of Tears, an outdoor symphonic drama; maintains Cherokee Hall of Fame for persons of Cherokee descent; also maintains the Ho-Chee-Nee Trail of Tears Memorial Chapel; annual Trail of Tears Art Show; lecture series on Cherokee history & culture. *Publications*: The Columns, 4/year newsletter; Trail of Tears Drama Program, annual. Library.

CLOSEUP FOUNDATION

44 Canal Center Plaza
Alexandria, VA 22314 (703) 706-3661
Karen Melick, Outreach Specialist

COMANCHE LANGUAGE & CULTURAL PRESERVATION COMMITTEE

P.O. Box 3610 • Lawton, OK 73502
(877) 492-4988 Fax (580) 353-6322
Ronald Red Elk, President
Barbara Goodin, Coordinator
Website: www.comanchelanguage.org
E-mail: clcpc@comanchelanguage.org
Purpose: To revive the Comanche language into a "living language" once again; to foster a cooperative relationship among federal, state and tribal agencies, schools, parents and others for the preservation and promotion of the Comanche language and culture; to change the direction of the Comanche language—from near extinction—and to take our language into the future. *Activities*: Developed Comanche dictionary, flash cards, picture dictionary, language lessons, hymn book and college work books; administered immersion programs, children's camps, community language classes, and language workshops; provide teachers for daycare and pre-schools; certified two speakers to teach in the Comanche Nation College. *Publications*: Quarterly language newsletter; Comanche dictionary, picture dictionary, flash cards, hymn book, language lessons; cassettes & CDs. Established 1993.

x2COMMISSION FOR MULTICULTURAL MINISTRIES OF ELCA

Native American Program
8765 W. Higgens Rd. • Chicago, IL 60631
(302) 380-2700; Rose Robinson, Director
Description: Consists of a nine member board of American Indians and Alaskan natives. A program of the Evangelical Lutheran Church in America. Acts as an advocate and consultant to Lutheran churches on behalf of the needs of Indian communities. Supports American Indian and Alaskan native rights. Supersedes the National Indian Lutheran Board (founded 1970). Biennial conference. Established 1987.

COMMITTEE FOR ACTION FOR RURAL INDIANS (CARI)

1235 Hazelton • Petoskey, MI 49770
(616) 347-0059; Martin J. King, Chairman
Purpose: To promote the welfare of Indian who do not live on reservations. *Programs*: Referrral services; alcohol and substance abuse programs.

CONCERNED AMERICAN INDIAN PARENTS

CUHCC Clinic • 3624 - 13th Ave. So.
Minneapolis, MN 55407 (612) 729-0850
Fred Veileux, Contact
Description: Serves as a network for American Indian parents and others interested in abolishing symbols that are degrading to American Indians, such as the Redskins, Braves, Indians, etc. logos adopted by sports teams in the U.S. Seeks to make the future easier for native American children by educating the public about racial messages inherent in such symbols. Established in 1987.

CONSORTIA OF ADMINISTRATORS FOR NATIVE AMERICAN REHABILITATION (CANAR)

Institute for Human Development
Northern Arizona University
P.O. Box 5630 • Flagstaff, AZ 86011
(928) 523-4791 Fax 523-1695
Website: www.nau.edu/ihd.canar/
Description: Works to advance and improve rehabilitation services for Native Americans.

CONTINENTAL CONFEDERATION OF ADOPTED INDIANS

960 Walhonding Ave. • Logan, OH 43138
(740) 385-7136 Fax 385-9093
Leland L. Connor, Chief
E-mail: lelandconner@webtv.net
Membership: 150. *Description*: Non-Indians who have been presented with honorary tribal chieftainship, an official Indian name, or recipients of any other Indian-oriented awards. Membership also open to blooded Indians. *Activities*: Maintains Indian Lore Hall of Fame; maintains speakers bureau; bestows annual National Catlin Peace Pipe Achievement Award; study, interpret, teach Indian lore; help people trace their Indian ancestry. *Publication*: Sunlodge Buffalo Tales, quarterly; annual newsletter. Research Library. Established in 1950.

CORPORATE RESOURCE CONSULTANTS

P.O. Box 22583 • Kansas City, MO 64113
(800) 268-2059; (816) 361-2059 Fax 361-2115
Phyllis A. Meiners, President
E-Mail: crcpub@coop.crn.org/crcpub@aol.com
Purpose: To assist Native American tribes and organizations to access corporate, foundation, and religious sector grants and loans for projects which help indigenous peoples to become independent. *Activities*: Conducts seminars, publish books and list rentals which specialize in private sector grant making, non-profit management, and project development for multicultural charitable organizations; Sponsors the Corporate Resource Center library which houses thousands of grant maker research profiles for sale to the public; CRC Publishing Co. published the following books: "The National Directory of Philanthropy for Native Americans"; "Corporate & Foundation Fundraising Manual for Native Americans"; and "Church Philanthropy for Native Americans & Other Minorities: A Guide to Multicultural Funding from Religious Sources."

THE COUNCIL FOR INDIAN EDUCATION

1240 Burlington Ave.• Billings, MT 59102-4224
(406) 248-3465 (Phone & Fax)
Website: www.cie-mt.org

E-mail: cie@cie-mt.org
Editorial Office: Manuscripts only
2032 Woody Dr. • Billings, MT 59102-2852
(406) 625-7598 Fax 652-0536
Dr. Hap Gilliland, President
Membership: 100. *Purpose*: To improve and secure higher standards of education for American Indian children. *Activities*: Provides in-service training for teachers working on Indian reservations to help them better meet the needs of their Native American students by equipping the teachers with information on Native American culture and traditions and on ways in which their instruction can be adapted to the needs of their Native American students; promotes quality children's literature on Indian culture; publishes authentic books about American Indian life; conducts in-service education of teachers. Established 1970.

COUNCIL FOR NATIVE AMERICAN INDIANS

280 Broadway, Suite 316
New York, NY 10007 (212) 732-0485
Walter S. James, Jr., Executive Director
Membership: 850. Individuals interested in the holistic philosophies and teachings of the earlier indigenous groups of North and Central America. Conducts research between the indigenous groups and the 16th century settlers in New York City and Long Island, NY. *Publications*: Earth Walk and Four Directions for Peace and Medicine Lodge, both newsletters. Annual meeting. Established 1974.

COUNCIL OF ENERGY RESOURCE TRIBES (CERT)

695 S. Colorado Blvd., Suite 10
Denver, CO 80202
(303) 282-7576 Fax 282-7584
Carmen Bradley, Chairperson
A. David Lester, Executive Director
E-mail: cert1975@aol.com
Website: www.certredearth.com
Membership: 57. American Indian Tribes owning energy resources. *Purpose*: To promote the general welfare of members through the protection, conservation, control and prudent management of their oil, coal, natural gas, uranium, and other resources. *Activities*: Provides on-site, technical assistance to Tribes in energy resource management; conducts programs to enhance Tribal planning and management capacities; sponsors workshops. Established in 1975.

COUNCIL OF INDIAN NATIONS

P.O. Box 1800 • Apache Junction, AZ 85217
(800) 811-6955 Fax (480) 281-0708
Lovena B. Lee, Chairperson
Lisa Begay, Program Coordinator
E-mail: info@cinprograms.org
Website: www.cinprograms.org
Purpose: To help Native American people improve the quality of their lives by providing opportunities for them to bring about positive changes in their communities. *Activities/Programs*: A non-profit organization which develops self-help programs and emergency relief services for Native Americans on reservations in the Southwest. These services include: emergency food distribution, clothing and shoe distributions, winterization of homes, school supplies, holiday dinners, gifts and stockings for children at Christmas and Easter, baby baskets for new mothers and incentive programs for seniors, adult volunteers and children. *Publication*: Quarterly newsletter. Established in 1995.

CRAZY HORSE MEMORIAL FOUNDATION

The Black Hills, Avenue of the Chiefs
Crazy Horse, SD 57730
(605) 673-4681 Fax 673-2185
Ruth Ziolkowski, Chairperson
Anne Ziolkowski, Director
Purpose: To carve a mountain (Thunderhead Mountain) into the memorial statue of the Sioux Chief Crazy Horse, astride his pony, pointing to the lands of his people (563' high and 641' long.) Carved from Thunderhead Mountains in South Dakota by sculptor Korczak Ziolkowski, 1908-1982; and to build and maintain a university, museum, and medical center for Native Americans. *Activities*: Operates the Indian Museum of North America and Crazy Horse Memorial; offers scholarships to Native Americans. *Publications*: Crazy Horse Progress, quarterly newsletter; Korczak: Storyteller in Stone (biography); Crazy Horse and Korczak; and Korczak, Saga of Sitting Bull's Bones

and Crazy Horse Memorial 40th Anniversary Booklet. Library. Annual meeting. Established in 1948.

CREEK INDIAN MEMORIAL ASSOCIATION
106 W. 6th • Okmulgee, OK 74447
Nolan Crowley, President
E-mail: creekmuseum@prodigy.net

CULTURAL SURVIVAL
96 Mt. Auburn St. • Cambridge, MA 02138
(617) 441-5400 Fax 441-5417
E-mail: csinc@cs.org
Web site: www.cs.org
Maria Tocco, Managing Director
International advocate for the human rights of indigenous peoples. *Publication*: Quarterly newsletter.

DAKOTA WOMEN OF ALL RED NATIONS
P.O. Box 69 • Fort Yates, ND 58538
(701) 854-7592
Description: Grass roots organization of American Indian women seeking to advance the Native American movement. *Activities*: Establishes local chapters to work on issues of concern such as women's health, adoption and foster-care abuse, community education, legal and juvenile justice problems; supports leadership roles for American Indian women. Publishes reports on health problems of American Indian women. Annual conference. Formerly Women of All Red Nations. Established in 1978.

EAGLE VISION EDUCATIONAL NETWORK
8657 Bronson Dr. • Granite Bay, CA 95746
(916) 791-7910 (phone & fax)
Cathy White Eagle, Director
E-Mail: evision@quiknet.com
Web site: http://www.quiknet.com/~evision/index.html
Purpose: To present in an accurate manner the history, philosophy and concept of "Earth Stewardship of the American Indian Nations" for the general public. *Activities*: Community cultural powwow; interactive presentations for elementary schools; lecture series; cultural scholarships and youth camps for American Indian children. Museum. Library. *Publications*: Quarterly newsletter; Matter of Fact Educational Sheets for the classroom; teacher in-service workbooks on accurate history and current issues. Established in 1992.

EARLY SITES RESEARCH SOCIETY
c/o James Whittall, Long Hill • Rowley, MA 01969
(508) 948-2410; James P. Whittall, Director
Membership: 220. *Purpose*: To research and record unknown stonework, petroglyphs, artifacts, and other unexplained antiquities in the U.S. *Activities*: Archaeological Field School; research awards, and art/archaeological grant; video material. *Publications*: Newsletter; bulletin; other occasional publications. Museum. Library. Established in 1973.

THE EDUCATION FOR PARENTS OF INDIAN CHILDREN WITH SPECIAL NEEDS (EPICS) PROJECT
Southwest Communication Resources, Inc.
P.O. Box 788 • Bernalillo, NM 87004
(800) 765-7320; (505) 867-3396
Norman Segel, Executive Director
Purpose: To provide services to parents of children with special needs and professionals who serve them. EPICS conducts workshops and provides individual assistance to parents. The staff provides input to state and national advisory boards on issues affecting Indian families that have children with special needs. Library. Established in 1985.

THE EDUCATIONAL FOUNDATION OF AMERICA
35 Church Lane • Westport, CT 06880
(203) 226-6498
Diane M. Allison, Executive Director
Goal: The availability of quality education to all. *Activities*: Provides educational grants—aid for Native Americans. Ettinger Scholarships.

ERIC CLEARINGHOUSE ON RURAL EDUCATION & SMALL SCHOOLS (ERIC/CRESS)
Appalachia Educational Laboratory
P.O. Box 1348 • Charleston, WV 25325
(800) 624-9120; Fax (304) 347-0487
Timothy Collins, Director
E-mail: ericrc@ael.org
Web site: www.ael.org/eric/

Purpose: To provide information about education to all who request it and to build a bibliographic database on the education of American Indians, Alaskan Natives, Mexican-Americans & migrants, and on rural education, outdoor education and small schools. *Activities*: Build database, provide free searches, publish free research summaries; develop ERIC microfiche collection. Library. *Publications*: ERIC/CRESS Bulletin; ERIC Digests; books. Established in 1966.

THE FALMOUTH INSTITUTE, INC.
3702 Pender Dr. #300 • Fairfax, VA 22030
(800) 992-4489; (703) 352-2250 Fax 352-2323
Richard Phelps, Director
Website: www.falmouthinstitute.com
Purpose: To provide quality training, technical assistance, and consulting to the American Indian and Alaska native communities. *Activities/programs*: Training programs and workshops - quarterly brochure. *Scholarships*: Awarded to an American Indian who is a member of a federally recognized tribe and is a high school senior accepted to an accredited college. *Publications*: American Indian Report, monthly subscription magazine; Native American Law Digest, monthly; various course manuals. Library. Established in 1985.

FEDERAL BAR ASSOCIATION
2215 M St., NW • Washington, DC 20037
(202) 785-1614 Fax 785-1568
E-mail: fba@fedbar.org
Website: www.fedbar.org
Lawrence R. Baca, Chairperson
John G. Blanche, III, Executive Director
Indian Law Section. *Committees include*: Indian Law Development, Public Education, Tribal Justice, and Legislation. *Purpose*: To participate as amicus in important Indian law cases, comment on developing Indian legislation, and offer expertise and advice to developing tribal court systems. *Activities*: Annual Indian Law Conference. The Conference is an aggregate of lawyers, law students, law professors, and federal, state, and tribal personnel - Indians and non-Indians - serving as speakers and listeners. It focuses on putting in perspective the court decisions and legislative action and analyzing how they impact the exercise of tribal sovereignty and other Indian rights. Makes available for purchase the proceedings of Indian Law conferences. Offers a limited number of partial scholarships to individuals from law schools, public interest and other organizations unable to allocate funds for the full Conference registration fee. Publications. Indian Law Section established in 1990.

FIRST NATIONS DEVELOPMENT INSTITUTE
2300 Fall Hill Ave., Suite 412
Fredericksburg, VA 22401
(540) 371-5615 Fax 371-3505
Website: www.firstnations.org
E-mail: info@firstnations.org
Rebecca L. Adamson, President & Founder
Sherry Salway Black, Vice President
Purpose: To assist American Indian tribes and communities obtain economic self-sufficiency through the promotion of culturally appropriate economic development activities and efforts. *Programs*: The Eagle Staff Fund provides grants for reservation-based economic development projects to tribes and Native nonprofits; The Oweesta Program re-lends capital to reservation-based micro-enterprise loan funds, revolving loan funds, and Native owned banks and credit unions. In addition to these two programs, First Nations also engages in various research-oriented projects through its Strengthening Native American Philanthropy programs. Research programs: Native Assets Research Center; The Census Information Center. Publication: CRA Manual; Investment Series; et al. Annual board meeting. Founded in 1980.

FOURTH WORLD CENTER FOR THE STUDY OF INDIGENOUS LAW & POLITICS
University of Colorado, Dept. of Political Science
Campus Box 190, P.O. Box 173364
Denver, CO 80217 (303) 556-2850
Glenn T. Morris, Executive Director
Purpose: Seeks to promote peaceful change through dissemination of information and ideas. *Activities*: Develops academic courses, compiles and publishes literature and documentation, and presents a public forum and arbitration in the political arena.

FRIENDS COMMITTEE ON NATIONAL LEGISLATION
245 Second St., NE
Washington, DC 20002
(800) 630-1330
(202) 547-6000 Fax 547-6019
E-mail: indian@fcnl.org
Web site: www.fcnl.org
Joe E. Volk, Executive Director
Description: A Quaker lobbying organization seeking to impact public policy and the Congress on issues of concern, among which are Native American rights including the upholding of treaty rights, the self-determination of Indian communities, and the Federal trusteeship responsibility. FCNL has specifically advocated, along with tribes and Indian organizations, on land and water rights. Federal Indian programs, health care, education, economic development, fishing rights, and self-determination. *Publication*: Indian Report, quarterly newsletter. Established in 1943.

GATHERING OF NATIONS
3301 Coors Blvd. NW #R300
Albuquerque, NM 87120-1292
(505) 836-2810 Fax 839-0475
Derek Mathews, Director
E-mail: melaniemathews@gatheringofnations.com
Web site: www.gatheringofnations.com
Purpose: To promote the traditions and culture of the American Indian, in the most positive manor possible; to dispel stereotypes created about the American Indian; to provide Indian people the opportunity to participate, practice, teach, and exchange tribal traditions and costumes among all the tribes; and to enlighten the non-Indian about the history and culture of America's first inhabitants. Does not offer scholarships. *Activities*: Academic support for Indian students in college; development instructional materials on Indian history and culture for elementary and secondary schools; sponsors periodic song, dance, and Miss Indian World competitions; bestows awards. Annual Powwow, 4th weekend in April (North America's biggest powwow, the largest annual gathering of Native Americans in the world). *Publications*: Annual magazine; program book; Video Lesson Plans - Elementary & Secondary Schools. Established in 1984.

GREAT PLAINS INDIAN GAMING ASSOCIATION (GPIGA)
P.O. Box 1983 • Bismarck, ND 59502-1983
(701) 255-9275 Fax 255-9281
J. Kurt Luger, Executive Director
Website: www.gpiga.org
E-mail: gpiga@btinet.net
Description: Currently composed of 28 tribal members. *Purpose*: To bring together and provide information and services to all the federally recognized Tribal Nations in the Great Plains region, including the states of North & South Dakota, Nebraska, Iowa, Kansas, Wyoming & Montana, who are operating gaming enterprises; also, to develop common strategies and positions concerning issue affecting all gaming tribes, and to promote tribal economic development and its positive impacts within the Great Plains. *Activities*: Annual Great Plains/Midwest Indian Gaming Trade Show & Conference. Founded in 1997.

GREENFIELD REVIEW PRESS
23 Middle Grove Rd., P.O. Box 308
Greenfield Center, NY 12833
(518) 584-1728; 583-1440 Fax 583-9741
James Bruchac, Owner
E-Mail: asban@aol.com
Web site: nativeauthors.com or nativeresources.com
Description: Publishes books of folklore & multicultural literature, especially Native American works. Conducts various projects aimed at education and continuation of Native American culture. *Special Programs*: "The North American Native Authors Project" - a free 50-page catalog of books and cassettes by native American writers and performers; The Ndakinna Wilderness Project - teaching of wilderness and cultural understanding from a Native American perspective, servicing northeastern U.S. and southeastern Canada; "The Abenaki Heritage Day Tape" - live recording of the 1993 Heritage Day performance. "The Dawn Land Singers" - a combination of traditional and contemporary music in both Abenaki and English, all with Native American themes. Good Mind Records. Established in 1971.

GEORGE BIRD GRINNELL AMERICAN INDIAN CHILDREN'S FUND

11602 Montague Court • Potomac, MD 20854
(301) 424-2440 fax 424-8281
Dr. Paula Mintzies, President
Scott Meyer, Vice President
Purpose: Provides support to organizations that: improve educational opportunities for American Indians; expand cultural, recreational and social services available to Native children and their families; empower American Indian children, families, communities and nations; promote understanding of and respect for American Indian nations. *Programs*: Provide scholarships; support Circle of Life Essay Program; provide financial support to other organizations as well as establish programs e.g. learning programs in partnership with other organizations. Established in 1988.

HERITAGE INSTITUTE

383 Inverness Pkwy., Suite 330
Englewood, CO 80112-5863
(303) 221-7410 Fax 221-7412
J. Mark Hannifan, COO
E-mail: hannifan@heritageinstitute.org
Website: www.heritageinstitute.org/
Dscription: Provides technical, policy, educational, financial assistance to American Indian tribes to pursue sustainable, environmentally sound economic development. *Programs*: InCompass Education; InCompass Energy. annual Native American Science Bowl - competition, for students in high schools in Indian communities. *Publication*: InCompass Energy News.

HOBBS, STRAUS, DEAN & WALKER, LLP

2120 L St., NW, Suite 700
Washington, DC 20037
(202) 822-8282 Fax 296-8834
Website: www.hsdwdc.com
Charles A. Hobbs (chobbs@hsdwdc.com)
Jerry C. Straus (jstraus@hsdwdc.com)
S. Bobo Dean (sdean@hsdwdc.com)
Hans Walker, Jr. (hwalker@hsdwdc.com)
Branch locations: Portland, OR (806 SW Broadway, Suite 900, Portland, OR 97205 (503) 242-1745 Fax 242-1072); Oklahoma City, OK (117 Park Ave., 2nd Floor, Oklahoma City, OK 73102 (405) 602-9425 Fax 602-9426). *Description*: Dedicated to providing high quality legal services, including advocacy before federal, state and local governments, agencies and courts, to Indian and Alaska Native tribes and tribal organizations throughout the U.S. D.C. home office opened in 1982. Current clients include tribes, tribal organizations, and individual Indians in all regions of the U.S., including Alaska. Also provide legal and legislative sevices to national Indian organizations such as the National Congress of American Indians and Americans for Indian Opportunity, as well as to national & regional; Indian organizations reprsenting the education, housing, health, child welfare, and gaming interests of Indian tribes & Indian people. *Staff*: **DC office** - Carol L. Barbero, Marsha K. Schmidt, Michael L. Roy, Christopher T. Stearns, Joseph H. Webster, M. Frances Ayer, Jennifer P. Hughes, Lisa F. Ryan, Elliott A. Milhollin, Eric D. Lement, Heidi J.Frechette, S. Nicole Bazan. **Portland, OR office** - Geoffrey D. Strommer, Edmund C. Goodman, Starla K. Roels, Lee K. Shannon, Steven D. Osborne. **Oklahoma City, OK office** - james M. Burson, Staci D. Coleman, Kirke Kickingbird, William R. Norman, Jr., Susan L. Work.

HONOR, INC. (HONOR OUR NEIGHBORS ORIGINS & RIGHTS)

6435 Wiesner Rd. • Omro, WI 54963
(414) 582-7142; Jeff Smith, President
DiAnne Wyss (Washington, DC satellite office)
Description: A coalition of church, citizen and Native American groups focusing on Native American human rights issues. *Purpose*: To seek justice on critical concerns facing Native Americans today. *Activities*: Efforts include advocacy, action, education, and communication; devoted entirely to issues affecting & relating to Indian country (through satellite office in Washington, DC (DiAnne Wyss (202) 338-7851). Established 1988.

INDIAN ARTS & CRAFTS ASSOCIATION

4010 Carlisle NE, Suite C
Albuquerque, NM 87107
(505) 265-9149 Fax 265-8251
George "ShuKata" Willis, Executive Director

E-mail: info@iaca.com; Website: www.iaca.com
Membership: 700. Indian crafts people and artists, museums, retailer and wholesalers, and collectors. *Purpose*: To promote, preserve, and protect the handmade creations of the Native American Indian. *Activities*: Semi-annual wholesale markets for retailers only; marketing information; educational seminars; Native American Art; Artist of the Year Prints. *Award*: Artist of the Year Award, annually, $1,500. *Publications*: Monthly newsletter; annual directory; brochures for point-of-purchase distribution. Semiannual wholesale trade shows. Small library. Established in 1974.

INDIAN ARTS & CRAFTS BOARD - HEADQUARTERS OFFICE

U.S. Department of the Interior
1849 C St., NW - MS #4004-MIB
Washington, DC 20240
(202) 208-3773 Fax 208-5196
Meridith Z. Stanton, Director
Rosemary Ellison, Chief Curator
E-mail: iacb@os.doi.gov
Website: www.iacb.doi.gov
Description: The Indian Arts & Crafts Board was created by Congress in 1935 to promote American Indian & Alaska Native economic development through the expansion of the Indian arts and crafts market. In support of this mission, the Board: implements the Indian Arts & Crafts Act of 1990, Public Law 101-644; increases the participation of Native Americans in the growing $1 billion a year Native American fine arts and crafts business; assists emerging artists entering the market; and assists Native American cultural leaders who are developing institutional frameworks for supporting the evolution and preservation of tribal cultural activities. The Board operates three museums: the Museum of the Plains Indian in Browning, MT; the Sioux Indian Museum in Rapid City, SD; and the Southern Plains Indian Museum in Anadarko, OK. *Publications*: Source Directory: American Indian and Alaska Native Owned & Operated Arts & Crafts Businesses (serves as a marketing link betweenn about 180 Native American owned & operated arts & crafts enterprises and over 40,000 consumers); The Indian Arts & Crafts Act brochure & Know the Law brochure.

INDIAN CHOIR

Bacone College • Muskogee, OK 74401
(918) 683-4581 Dr. Marlene Smith
Description: Music sung in several Indian languages as well as English. Tours around country.

INDIAN EDUCATORS FEDERATION

2301 Yale Blvd. SE, Suite E-1
Albuquerque, NM 87106
(505) 243-4088 Fax 243-4098
Website: www.ief-aft.org
E-mail: ief@ief-aft.org
Patrick Carr, President
Peter Camp, Executive Vice President
Membership: 750 professional educators employed in federal schools operated by the Bureau of Indian Affairs in the Albuquerque-Navajo areas. *Purpose*: To meet the unique needs and interests of teachers within the BIA's Office of Indian Education Programs. An affiliate of the American Federation of Teachers. Supports programs and projects that will improve the entire educational program in BIA schools. *Publication*: Newsletter. Annual meeting. Established in 1967.

INDIAN DEFENSE LEAGUE OF AMERICA (IDLA)

c/o Joseph Rickard, Sr., President
P.O. Box 305 • Niagara Falls, NY 14302
Website: www.tuscaroras.com/idla/
Description: Works to guarantee unrestricted passage on the North American continent for Indian people/

INDIAN HEALTH SERVICE

U.S. Department of Health and Human Services
5600 Fishers Lane, Parklawn Bldg.
Rockville, MD 20857 (301) 443-1083
Michael H. Trujillo, M.D., Director
Goals: To raise the status of health of American Indians to the highest levels possible. *Programs*: Provides a full range of curative, preventive, and rehabilitative services for approximately 1.4 million eligible American Indians and Alaskan Natives. *Publication*: Trends in Indian Health, annual. Established 1955. See Indian Health Service section for names and locations of facilities across the U.S.

INDIAN HERITAGE COUNCIL

P.O. Box 752 • McCall, ID 83638
(423) 277-1103
Louis Hooban, CEO
Purpose: To promote Native American writers and literature, customs and beliefs. *Activities*: Conducts research and educational programs; cultural events; sponsors charitable events; operates speaker's bureau; and sponsors an annual National Powwow in October, in Townsend, Tennessee; monthly conference. *Award*: Native American Literary Award, annual. *Publication*: Quarterly newsletter; books - Crazy Horse's Philosophy of Riding Rainbows; Great American Indian Bible; Indian Drug Usage; Native American Play; Native American Poetry; Native American Poets' Anthology; Native American Prophecies; Native Letters to the People; Vision Quest. Library. Established 1988.

INDIAN LAW RESOURCE CENTER

602 N. Ewing St. • Helena MT 59601-3603
(406) 449-2006 Fax 449-2031
Robert T. Coulter, Executive Director
E-mail: ilrc@mt.net; Website: www.indianlaw.org
District Office: 601 E St., SE
Washington, DC 20003
(202) 547-2800 Fax 547-2803
Steve Tullberg, Director of the DC office
Purpose: To provide a legal, educational and research service for American Indians and other Indian tribes and nations and other indigenous peoples in the Western Hemisphere; seeks to enable Indian people to survive as distinct peoples with unique living cultures; to combat discrimination and injustice in the law; and protection of the environment. *Activities*: Engages in human rights advocacy on behalf of Indians at the U.N.; and offers free legal help to tribes. *Publications*: Indian Rights-Human Rights (handbook); quarterly newsletter; annual report, articles and reprints. Established in 1978.

INDIAN LIFE MINISTRIES

Intertribal Christian Communications
P.O. Box 32 • Pembina, ND 58271
(204) 661-9333 Fax 661-3982
Tim Nielsen, General Director
Publication: Indian Life: Christian Media for Native North Americans.

INDIAN RIGHTS ASSOCIATION

c/o Janney Montgomery Scott
1801 Market St. • Philadelphia, PA 19103
(215) 665-4523 Fax 977-8612
E. Morris Davis, Treasurer
Membership: 700. Individuals interested in protection of the legal and human rights of American Indians and promotion of their welfare. *Publications*: Indian Truth, bimonthly newsletter (presently inactive); Annual Meeting. Established in 1882.

INDIAN YOUTH OF AMERICA

609 Badgerow Bldg., 4th & Jackson
P.O. Box 2786 • Sioux City, IA 51106
(712) 252-3230 Fax 252-3712
Patricia Trudell Gordon, Executive Director
E-mail: ptgordon@hotmail.com
Purpose: To improve the lives of Indian children; to inform families, social service agencies, and courts on the rights of Indian people under the Indian Child Welfare Act. *Program*: The American Indian Child Service Program—attempts to prevent the distressful effects brought on by the breakup of Indian families. *Facility*: Resource Center. *Publications*: Brochures. *Activities*: Conducts summer camp for Indian children ages 10-14; distributes information through its Resource Center and has a college scholarship program. Locally, staff provides referrals, advocacy and consultation services to Native American families and children; and sponsors an afterschool program for children ages 8-13. also holds meetings and annual Substance Abuse and Indian Child Welfare Act Workshops. Established in 1978.

INDIANS FOR UNITED SOCIAL ACTION

Englewood, CO 80110 (303) 762-6579
Dr. Gregory W. Frazier, Executive Director
Purpose: To provide a viable vehicle for American Indian and Alaska Native communities and people; to carry out projects and programs designed to reduce unemployment in our communities; to serve as a cata-

lyst to improve the social and economic condition of American Indian and Alaska Native communities; to create bridges through communication between the Native American community and other minority communities to the community at large; to discharge and distribute information to the community at large; to engage in projects for the betterment of Indian communities; and to provide information to the general public through the publication and distribution of printed materials. *Activities*: National Indian Writers Project; National Indian Business Information Center; Indian Consultant Provider; Speakers' Bureau; Indian/Alaska Technical Assistance Center assistance. Established in 1989.

INDIANS INTO MEDICINE
University of North Dakota
School of Medicine & Health Sciences
P.O. Box 9037 • Grand Forks, ND 58202
(701) 777-3037 Fax 777-3277
Gene DeLorme, J.D., Director
E-mail: inmed@mail.med.und.nodak.edu
Web site: www.med.und.nodak.edu/
　　　depts/inmed/home.htm
Purpose: To assist American Indian students preparing for health careers; provide summer academic enrichment sessions at the junior high, high school, college and pre-medical levels; provide academic year support for college and professional students; to increase the awareness of and interest in health care professions among young American Indians. *Services*: Referral and counseling services; tutoring; financial aid; minority medical education program (for college students); and Med Prep (for students preparing for medical school). The INMED director is a coordinator for Indian Health Service scholarships; provides short term emergency loans to participating students. *Publications*: Indians Into Medicine (recruitment book); Healthy Games and Teasers (activity book); Good Medicine for Our People (coloring book); Serpent, Staff and Drum (quarterly newsletter). Library-The INMED Learning Resource Center includes a variety of books and journals to assist students in their courses and in preparing for health careers entrance exams; distributes recruitment publications. Periodic educational conferences. Established in 1973.

INDIGENOUS COMMUNICATIONS ASSOCIATION
P.O. Box 953 • Hogansburg, NY 13655-0953
(518) 358-4185; Ray Cook, Executive Director
Description: Native American owned and/or operated radio stations in the U.S. *Purpose*: To help develop the Native American Public Radio Satellite Network in conjunction the Native American Public Broadcasting Consortium to provide programming to Native-controlled public radio stations.

INDIGENOUS ENVIRONMENTAL NETWORK
P.O. Box 485 • Bemidji, MN 56601
(218) 679-3959; Tom Goldtooth

INDIGENOUS PEOPLE'S NETWORK
226 Blackman Hill Rd. • Berkshire, NY 13736
(607) 657-8413; John Mohawk, Co-Director
Membership: 75. Indigenous, human rights and energy-conscious organizations. *Purpose*: To provide communications services and information to people in remote areas that have little access to public media; to disseminate information on threats to the existence of indigenous people; seeks to raise the consciousness of people in North America and Western Europe. *Activities*: Documentation missions; indigenous refugee project; Radio Network which features taped interviews with indigenous leaders and community elders; maintains speakers bureau. *Publications*: Congressional Indian Report, weekly; IPN Weekly Report; Federal Register and Environmental Report, weekly; and Native Peoples in Struggle (book); emergency bulletins. Established in 1983.

INSTITUTE FOR THE DEVELOPMENT OF INDIAN LAW
Oklahoma City University-School of Law
2501 N. Blackwelder • Oklahoma City, OK 73106
(405) 521-5337 Fax 521-5185
K. Blue Clark, Executive Director
E-mail: bclark@okcu.edu
Description: A research training center on federal Indian law, with special emphasis on Indian sovereignty, self-confidence and self-government, and clarification

of historical and legal foundations of modern Indian rights. *Activities*: Research and analysis; training and technical assistance; dissemination of educational materials relating to federal Indian law, Indian Treaties, curriculum and community development. *Programs*: American Indian Legal Studies; American Indian Life Coping Skills; Indian Legal Curriculum & Training; holds seminars. *Publications*: American Indian Journal, quarterly; Publications and Materials List, semiannual; Annual Publications Catalog; The Indians and U.S. Constitution (book, brochure and videotape); distributed films, videotapes and filmstrips. Library. Established in 1971.

INSTITUTE FOR NATIVE AMERICAN DEVELOPMENT (INAD)
Native American Studies Dept., U. of New Mexico
1812 Las Lomas Dr., NE • Albuquerque, NM 87131
(505) 277-3917; Ted Jojola, Director
Alison Freese, Information Specialist
Purpose: To advocate and develop research for and with Native Americans and their communities. *Activities*: Varies from year-to-year; sponsors lecture series, specialized seminars and conferences; regular course offerings. Publications. Library. Established in 1980.

INSTITUTE FOR THE STUDY OF AMERICAN CULTURES
233 12th St. #500, P.O. Box 2707
Columbus, GA 31902
(706) 243-6218 Fax 322-7747
Carole Sides, Contact
E-mail: webmaster@isacnet.org
Website: www.isacnet.org
Purpose: To support and promote unbiased research into the origin and history of the American Indians and their pre-Columbian ancestors. Promotes a revisionist examination of the discovering of America by Columbus. Uses research technology in the fields of archaeology, anthropology, linguistics, epigraphy, music, and history to determine the "truth and relevancy of new discoveries without allegiance to any historical or ethnological paradigm." *Activities*: Sponsors projects; maintains library; Award - The Root Cutter Award, annual, for recognition. *Published works*: Columbus, the Man; Dene and NaDene Indian Migration 1233 A.D., Escape from Genghis Khan to America; ISAC Report, quarterly newsletter. Established in 1983.

INSTITUTE FOR THE STUDY OF NATURAL SYSTEMS
P.O. Box 637 • Mill Valley, CA 94942
(415) 383-5064
James A. Swan, PhD, President
Purpose: To promote solutions to environmental problems from a cross-cultural perspective. *Activities*: Coordinates fundraising activities for Native Americans working to restore buffalo herds. The Buffalo Tour-a series of concerts to support bison restoration on Indian reservations-will begin in 1992 and will culminate in the first annual Buffalo Festival, which will be held in late July 1993, in the LaCrosse, Wisconsin area in cooperation with the first International Bison Conference; sponsors symposia; conducts research, charitable, and educational programs. *Publication*: In Harmony, bi-annual newsletter; books, Sacred Places, The Power of Place, and Nature As Teacher and Healer, all by James Swan. Established in 1987.

INSTITUTE FOR THE STUDY OF TRADITIONAL AMERICAN INDIAN ARTS
P.O. Box 66124 • Portland, OR 97290
(503) 233-8131; John M. Gogol, President
Purpose: To promote traditional Native American arts through publications, lectures, & seminars. Conducts research. *Publication*: American Indian Basketry and Other Native Arts, quarterly magazine. Established in 1982.

INSTITUTE FOR TRIBAL ENVIRONMENTAL PROFESSIONALS (ITEP)
Northern Arizona University
P.O. Box 15004 • Flagstaff, AZ 86011
(928) 523-9651; Virgil Masayesva, Director
E-mail: itep@nau.edu
Website: www.www4.nau.edu/itep/
Description: Works to assist Indian tribes in the management of environmental resources through training and education programs. *Programs*: Student internships; scholarships.

INSTITUTE OF AMERICAN INDIAN ARTS
83 Avan Nu Po Rd. • Santa Fe, NM 87505
(800) 804-6422; (505) 424-2300 Fax 424-4500
Della C. Warrior, President
E-mail: dwarrior@iaiancad.org
Web site: www.iaiancad.org
Description: A federally chartered private institution offering learning opportunities in the arts and culture to American Indian and Alaska Native youth. Emphasis is placed upon Indian traditions as the basis for creative expression in the fine arts. *Activities*: Sponsors Indian arts-oriented Junior College offering Associate of Fine Arts degrees in various fields as well as seminars, and exhibition program, and traveling exhibits; maintains extensive library, museum, and biographical archives. Established in 1962.

INSTITUTE OF EARLY AMERICAN HISTORY & CULTURE
P.O. Box 8781 • Williamsburg, VA 23187
(804) 221-1110; Ronald Hoffman, Director
Purpose: To encourage study and research in American history before 1820, especially but not exclusively, through book and periodical publications, conferences, etc. *Programs*: Do not deal exclusively with American Indian history, but has been significantly represented in its recent activities; book publishing in conjunction with UNC Press. *Award*: Two-Year Postdoctoral Fellowships, annually—research topics on American Indian history, 1500-1820 are eligible. *Publications*: The William and Mary Quarterly. Library. Established in 1943.

INSTITUTE OF THE GREAT PLAINS
Museum of the Great Plains
601 Ferris, Elmer Thomas Park
P.O. Box 68 • Lawton, OK 73502
(405) 353-5675 Steve Wilson, Director
Membership: 825. *Purpose*: To further the study and understanding of the history, ecology, anthropology, archaeology, and sociology of the Great Plains of North America. *Activities*: Conducts research; maintains the Museum of the Great Plains, the Great Plains Archives, and Library. *Publications*: Great Plains Journal, annual; Irregular newsletter; books for sale. Established in 1961.

INTER-AMERICAN INDIAN INSTITUTE
Av. Insurgentes Sur 1690
Col. Florida • Mexico D.F. 01030 MEXICO
(905) 660-0007/660-0132
Dr. Oscar Arze Quintanilla, Director
Activities: Conducts development programs for Indian communities in the Americas; trains technical personnel; investigates culture of extinct Indian groups; provides information services. *Publications*: America Indigena; quarterly journal; books. Library. Established in 1940.

INTER-TRIBAL INDIAN CEREMONIAL ASSOCIATION
226 W. Coal Ave.• Gallup, NM 87301
(800) 233-4528
(505) 863-3896 Fax 722-5158
Laurance D. Linford, Executive Director
E-mail: fmncvb@cyberport.com
Website: www.ceremonial.org
Membership: 350. *Description*: Indian people, businessmen, dealers in Indian arts and crafts, and other individuals interested in the annual Inter-Tribal Indian Ceremonial. *Goals*: The preservation and promotion of American Indian culture, with an emphasis on the handmade arts and crafts. *Activities*: Annual Inter-Tribal Indian Ceremonial, a four day Indian exposition of dances, sports, crafts, rituals and a rodeo, held each August in Gallup, New Mexico; Summer Indian Dance Program; the Indian Country Guide Service; bestows awards; conducts specialized educational and children's services; maintains biographical archives; plans a Hall of Fame; publishes educational materials on Indian crafts for teachers; color slides of Indian ceremonials available. Closely associated with the Red Rock Museum, which houses the majority of Association's collections. *Scholarships*: Indian art scholarships to accredited colleges and universities beginning in 1995. *Publications*: Inter-Tribal America Magazine, quarterly newsletter; A Measure of Excellence, annual; "So You Want to Buy A Navajo Rug?" information pamphlet. Library. Annual meeting in Gallup, NM in November. Established in 1922.

**INTERNATIONAL ASSOCIATION
OF NATIVE AMERICAN STUDIES**
P.O. Box 325 • Biddeford, ME 04005-0325
(207) 839-8004 (phone & fax)
Lemeul Berry, Jr., Director
E-mail: l.berry@morehead-st.edu
Website: www.naaas.org
Publication: Journal of Intercultural Disciplines,
semiannual.

INTERNATIONAL INDIAN TREATY COUNCIL (IITC)
2390 Mission St., Suite 301
San Francisco, CA 94110
(415) 641-4482 Fax 641-1298
Andrea Carmen, Executive Director
Sherri Norris, Bay Area Youth Program Coordinator
E-mail: iitc@sbcglobal.net
Website: www.treatycouncil.org
Description: "An organization of Indigenous Peoples
from North, Central, South America, and the Pacific
working for the sovereignty and self-determination of
Indigenous peoples working for the recognition and
protection of Indigenous rights, traditional cultures and
sacred lands. In 1977, the IITC became the first organization of Indigenous Peoples to be recognized as a
non-governmental organization (NGO) with consultative status to the United Nations Economic and Social
Council." *Programs*: IITC's Bay Area Indian Youth
Mentorship Program, initiated in 1996, provides high
school and college youth with experiences in community organizing, advocacy and activism, building leadership and capacity and links between urban and rural Indian communities in California, nationally and
internationally. In 2003, IITC initiated the Tribal Health
and Mercury Education project in partnership withg
the Pit River Indian Nation to address the widespread
yet largely unknown health and environmental crisis
of the mercury contamination in San Francisco and
Northern California. *Activities*: Makes regular presentations to the U.N. Commission on Human Rights.
Maintains a research and documentation center in
South Dakota and an Information Center in New York
City. *Publication*: Treaty Council News, quarterly. Annual conference. Founded in 1974.

INTERTRIBAL AGRICULTURAL COUNCIL
100 North 27th St. #500 • Billings, MT 59101
(406) 259-3525 Robert Miller, President
Greg Smitman, Executive Director
Purpose: To pursue and promote the conservation, development and use of Indian resources for the betterment of Indian people. *Activities*: Annual Indian Agriculture Symposium. *Publications*: National Indian Agriculture Profile; Indian Borrowers Guide to Agriculture Lending Programs of the FmHA and BIA; Indian
Guide to Farmer Programs of the Soil Conservation
Service, USDA, and the Indian Guide on the use of
the "Made by American Indians" trademark. Established in 1987.

INTERTRIBAL BISON COOPERATIVE
1560 Concourse Dr. • Rapid City, SD 57703
(605) 394-9730 Fax 394-7742
Fred DuBray, President
Mark Heckert, Executive Director
Description: A consortium of 27 tribes. *Purpose*: To
re-establish buffalo herds on Indian lands in a man-
ner that promotes economic development, cultural en-
hancement, ecological restoration, and spiritual revi-
talization. *Member tribes*: Blackfeet, MT; Cheyenne
River Sioux, SD; Choctaw Nation, OK; Confederated
Salish & Kootenai, MT; Crow, MT; Crow Creek Sioux,
SD; Ft. Sill Apache, OK; Gros Ventre & Assiniboine,
MT; Kalispel, WA; Lower Brule Sioux, SD; Modoc of
OK; Nez Perce, ID; Northern Cheyenne, MT; Oglala
Sioux, SD; Oneida of WI; Picuris Pueblo, NM; Round
Valley, CA; Santee Sioux, NE; Shoshone-Bannock, ID;
Sisseton-Wahpeton Dakota Nation, SD; Southern Ute,
CO; Standing Rock Sioux, ND; Taos Pueblo, NM; Ute,
UT; Winnebago of NE; WI Winnebago; Yankton Sioux,
SD. *Activities*: Education & training; Native American
Bison Refuge; Yellowstone Project; Elementary Buf-
falo Curriculum; Public Education; Tribal Advocacy.
Library. *Publications*: Quarterly newsletter; Annual
Report. Established in 1992.

**INTERTRIBAL COUNCIL OF
AMERICAN INDIANS, INC.**
1765 Woodchuck Ave.
Pensacola, FL 32504 (904) 484-9292

William Irontail McCay, Executive Director
Web site: www.itcnet.org
Purpose: To preserve the heritage, culture and crafts
of all Indian people regardless of their original nation;
to develop community health, educational and economic programs. *Activities*: Pow wows, corn roasts,
lecture, multi-media events, scholarships, health programs. Museum. Library. Established in 1976.

INTERTRIBAL TIMBER COUNCIL
4370 NE Halsey St.
Portland, OR 97213-1566
(503) 282-4296 Fax 282-1274
Purpose: To promote sound, economic management
of natural resources so as to sustain Indian forests
and dependent economies in accordance with tribal
goals and objectives for the benefit of Indian people.
Activities: Annual National Indian Timber Symposium;
annual scholarship awards for Native American &
Native Alaskan students pursuing a higher education
in Natural Resources. Established in 1979.

IROQUOIS STUDIES ASSOCIATION
28 Zevan Rd. • Johnson City, NY 13790
(607) 729-0016 Fax 770-9610
E-mail: isa@tier.net
Website: www.tier.net/isa

THE JACOBSON FOUNDATION
609 Chautauqua Ave. • Norman, OK 73069
(405) 366-1667; John Parrish, Director
Description: A non-profit educational foundation concerned with the understanding and preservation of Native American arts and culture. *Goals*: To preserve the
historic Jacobson House (a resource center for Native Americans) and to showcase American Indian fine
art and culture. *Programs*: Art exhibits of material culture, cultural events, classes teaching American Indian arts & crafts. Museum & Library. Established in
1986.

**JOHNS HOPKINS CENTER
FOR AMERICAN INDIAN HEALTH**
Johns Hopkins University
Johns Hopkins Bloomburg School of Public Health
615 N. Wolfe St. E8132 • Baltimore, MD 21205
(410) 955-3952 Fax 614-1419
Mathuram Santosham, MD, MPH, Director
E-mail: msantosh@jhsph.edu
Website: www.jhsph.edu/caih
Founded in 1991 based on two decades of collaboration between Hopkins health experts and Indian communities. The center's mission is to work in partnership with tribes to research, design, implement, and
evaluate interventions to raise the health & well-being
of American Indians to the highest possible level. *Facilities & Personnel*: The placement within the Johns
Hopkins Medical Institutions allows the Center to draw
on vast intellectual resources and multi-disciplined approaches to address tribes' priority health & social
problems. The Center curently operates 11 health stations on the Navajo (AZ/NM), White Mountain Apache
(AZ), and Wind River (WY) Reservations, whose combined populations represent about one-fourth of American Indians living on reservations in the U.S. Over the
past five years, the Center has conducted additional
projects with tribes in North Carolina, California, South
Dakota, Alaska, Michigan, Wisconsin, and Oklahoma.
More than half of the Center's 70-person staff is American Indian, including an American Indian physician,
more than 30 Native outreach workers, and 4 field-
based project coordinators. *Programs*: All programs
are crafted to increase the skill and capacity of tribes.
Each initiative includes a training and employment
component to ensure that indigenous workers carry
out the work. For the NATIVEVISION program
(www.nativevision.org), the Center provides ongoing
technical expertise to Native communities to support
all aspects of the planning, design, implementation and
evaluation of the NATIVEVISION progams. Johns
Hopkins employs local program coordinators to oversee the day-to-day operations of the NATIVEVISION
on the reservations involved. Activities: Operates an
annual Sports Camp which is helped funded by the
NFL (National Football league) Players Association
(www.nflpa.org). It also helps with the management
of the camp by recruiting pro athletes from various
sports to adopt and routinely visit the NATIVE VISION
communities across the America. The Nick Lowery (an
ex-NFL player) Foundation (www.nicklowery.com),

assists with youth development strategies, as well as
recruitment of athletes and Native American role models, and development of financial resources.

KROEBER ANTHROPOLOGICAL SOCIETY
c/o University of California
Dept. of Anthropology
232 Kroeber Hall
Berkeley, CA 94720
(415) 642-6932
Description: Professional anthropologists, students, interested laymen and institutional members (200 major universities and anthropological institutions. *Publications*: Papers, annual. Annual conference. Established in 1949.

**LABRIOLA NATIONAL AMERICAN
INDIAN DATA CENTER**
Dept. of Archives & Manuscripts
University Libraries
Box 871006, ASU
Tempe, AZ 85287-1006
(602) 965-6490 Fax 965-0776
E-mail: patricia.etter@asu.edu
Web site: http://www.asu.edu/lib/archives/labriola.htm
Patricia A. Etter, Curator
Description: A research collection containing and dis-
seminating information on Native American and Alas-
kan Native tribes. It provides access to the informa-
tion through the use of computer databases, the
Internet, and CD-ROM. The collection is national in
scope and brings together in one location current and
historic information on government, culture, religion,
social life, customs, tribal history, and information on
individuals from the U.S., Canada, & Sonora, Mexico.

LEONARD PELTIER DEFENSE COMMITTEE
P.O. Box 583
Lawrence, KS 66044
(785) 842-5774 Fax 842-5796
Leonard Peltier, Director
E-mail: lpdc@idir.net
Web site: http://members.xoom.com/
freepeltier/index.html
Purpose: To obtain justice for Leonard Peltier and all
political prisoners; equality under the law; sovereignty;
economic, health care, and educational reform. *Activities*: Public education; lobbying; Prisoner art program; pilot program with Dr. Jeffrey Timmons (Harvard)
on economic reform on Pine Ridge; Dr. Stuart Selkin
(NY) on health care reform on Rosebud; year round
food and clothing drive. *Publication*: Spirit of Crazy
Horse, bimonthly newspaper.

**MARQUETTE LEAGUE FOR
CATHOLIC INDIAN MISSIONS**
1011 First Ave.
New York, NY 10022
(212) 371-1000; Rev. Thomas A. Modugno, Director
Purpose: To provide financial support for the material
welfare of Catholic Indian Missions in the U.S. Established 1904.

**D'ARCY McNICKLE CENTER
FOR AMERICAN INDIAN HISTORY**
The Newberry Library
60 West Walton St.
Chicago, IL 60610
(312) 255-3564 Fax 255-3696
Brian Hosmer, Director
E-Mail: mcnickle@newberry.org
Website: www.newberry.org
Description: A research and education center on Indian history. Purpose: To improve the quality of teching
and scholarship about American Indian history and
culture through the use of the Newberry Library's prestigious collection of rare books, manuscripts, photographs, maps, and art. *Activities*: Offers numerous
fellowships, including the Power-Tanner Fellowship for
PhD candidates and postdoctoral scholars of American Indian heritage, the Frances C. Allen Fellowships
for women of Native American heritage, & Rockefeller
Foundation fellowships for community-centered research projects; coordinates the Committee on Institutional Cooperation's American Indian Studies Consortium, & alliance of the Big Ten universities, plus
the University of Chicago and University of Illinois at
Chicago; seminars & workshops. *Publications*: "Meeting Ground," bimonthly newsletter; publications list
available. The Newberry Library. Established 1972.

MIDWEST TREATY NETWORK
c/o South/Central Wisconsin Office
P.O. Box 14382 • Madison, WI 53714-4382
(608) 246-2256 (phone & fax)
Website: www.treatyland.com
E-mail: mtn@lgc.apc.org

MEIKLEJOHN CIVIL LIBERTIES INSTITUTE
Box 673 • Berkeley, CA 94701
(510) 848-0599 Fax 848-6008
Description: A center for peace, law, an information clearinghouse on social change, a publisher, a training center, a repository of history, and a provider of internships and work-study jobs. Provides reference and referrals for scholars, lawyers, students, researchers, and activists working on civil rights and peace law issues. *Publications*: Human Rights Organizations & Periodicals Directory (describes over 1,200 organizations and periodicals, many of special interest to Native Americans); The Peace Law Docket: 1945-1995 (describes over 1,000 cases).

MIGIZI COMMUNICATIONS, INC.
3123 E. Lake St. #200
Minneapolis, MN 55406
(612) 721-6631 Fax 721-3936
Jacqueline Fraedrich, Chair, Board of Directors
Laura Waterman Wittstock, President
E-mail: wittstock@migizi.org
Website: www.migizi.org
Purpose: To engage in the planning, development, implementation and evaluation of facilities and programs in the fields of communications and educational and literary activities and youth services in the areas of health and recreation to enhance the capacity of the American Indian community to meet the needs of its people. *Mission*: To educate elementary, secondary and adult students using the tools of communications; and to commit resources to addfress problems in partnership with the American Indian community. *Goals*: To improve the success rates of our students; increase organizational effectiveness through partnerships; and address problems through a greater use of communications. *Programs*: Two major programs: The American Indian community is our primary client group. They focus on the more than 2,100 American Indian families in Hennepin County, Minnesota. **Native Academy** - created in 1995 as a partner to schools with a primary focus on improving academic performance and to increase the number of American Indians moving into higher education, particularly in science or technology career fields. **Running Wolf Fitness Center** - provides family health and wellness assessments conducted pre-post by ceritifed personal trainers; personal wellness plans for dietary and fitness goals; fitness programming for diabetics; monthly health & wellness eucation seminars. **National Native Internet Communications (NNIC.COM)** - provides professional web services and acts as a provider of affordable web services for tribes, businesses, individuals, and community non-profit organizations. *Publication*: Communicator, organization newsletter; Aozanzanya, student newsletter. Established 1977.

MISS INDIAN WORLD
Gathering of Nations
3200 Coors NW #K235
Albuquerque, NM 87120
(505) 836-2810
Web site: www.atii.com.gathering.of.nations
Description: An annual contest to select Miss Indian World to serve as a goodwill ambassador for a year. Participants must be at least one-quarter Indian to qualify and have a good knowledge of tribal traditions. Takes place at the annual Gathering of Nations powwow, the fourth weekend of April, in Albuquerque.

MNI SOSE INTERTRIBAL WATER RIGHTS COALITION, INC.; INTERTRIBAL ENERGY NETWORK
P.O. Box 2890
Rapid City, SD 57709
(605) 343-6054 Fax 343-4722
E-mail: mnisose@qwest.net
Purpose: To address the coordinated development of tribal water and enery resources by Tribal Nations to exercise sovereignty and implement self-determination. *Activities*: Annual symposium, "Tribal Water & Energy: Essential for Self-Determination."

MORNING STAR INSTITUTE
403 10th St., SE • Washington, DC 20003
(202) 547-5531 Fax 546-6724
Susan Harjo, President & Executive Director
Website: www.morningstararts.com
Purpose: To secure statutory protections for Native peoples' sacred sites & religious freedom. *Activities*: Conducts programs for environmental and youth concerns promoting Native images and voices in popular culture; provides small grants to support cultural work of others. *Publications*: Bulletin, periodic. Established in 1984.

NATIONAL ADVISORY COUNCIL ON INDIAN EDUCATION (NACIE)
330 C St., SW, Room 4072
Washington, DC 20202
(202) 205-8353 Fax 205-8897
Robert K. Chiago, Executive Director
Purpose: To assist the Secretary of Education in carrying out responsibilities under Section 441(a) of the Indian Education Act (Title IV of P.L. 92-318), through advising Congress, the Secretary of Education, the Under Secretary of Education, and the Assistant Secretary of Elementary and Secondary Education with regard to education programs benefiting Indian children and adults. *Activities*: Full Council/Subcommittee meetings in the field on or near Indian reservations to receive public testimony regarding Title IV monies. *Publications*: Newsletters and annual reports. Library. Established in 1972.

NATIONAL AMERICAN INDIAN CATTLEMAN'S ASSOCIATION
1541 Foster Rd. • Toppenish, WA 98948
(509) 854-1329; Tim Foster, President
Description: Indian cattle producers. *Purpose*: To carry on all activities necessary for the betterment of the Indian cattle industry; & to serve as a clearinghouse for the accumulation & dissemination of information. *Publication*: Monthly newsletter; Yearbook. Established 1974.

NATIONAL AMERICAN INDIAN COURT JUDGES ASSOCIATION
3618 Reder St. • Rapid City, SD 57702
(605) 342-4804 Fax 719-9357
Website: www.naicja.org
Eugene White-Fish, President (715) 478-5805
Membership: 360. Indian court judges. *Purpose*: To improve the American Indian court system throughout the U.S. by furthering knowledge & understanding of it, & maintaining its integrity in providing equal protection to all persons. *Activities*: Offers periodic training sessions on criminal law & family law/child welfare; conducts research & continuing education programs; annual meeting. *Publication*: Indian Courts Newsletter, quarterly. Annual meeting. Established 1968.

NATIONAL AMERICAN INDIAN HOUSING COUNCIL
900 Second St., NE, #305
Washington, DC 20002 (800) 284-9165
(202) 789-1754 Fax 789-1758
Russell Sossamon, Chairperson
Gary L. Gordon, Executive Director
Website: www.naihc.indian.com
E-Mail: housing @naihc.net
Description: Nonprofit organization which promotes, upholds and supports Indian housing authorities in their efforts to provide decent, safe and sanitory housing for Native people in the U.S. *Activities*: Provides technical assistance and training programs for Indian housing authorities; conducts research on Indian housing issues; holds annual convention and legislative conferences. *Facilities*: Maintains Indian Housing Resource Center. *Publications*: Native American Housing News, Quarterly newsletter, "Pathway News"; NAIHC Annual Report. Established in 1974.

NATIONAL ASSOCIATION FOR NATIVE AMERICAN CHILDREN OF ALCOHOLICS (NANACA)
Seattle, WA 98188-2948
(800) 322-5601; (206) 467-7686 Fax 467-7689
Candace Fleming, PhD, President
E-Mail: nanacoa@aol.com
Membership: 1,450. *Purpose*: To provide communities with updated information and referrals on alcohol & drug abuse issues; to provide intensive training for communities; & to inform local & national policymakers about the needs of Native American children of alcoholics. *Activities*: Develops educational materials & support information for Native American communities; conducts programs to educate local and national policy makers. *Publication*: "Healing Our Hearts," quarterly newsletter. Annual conference. Established in 1988.

NATIONAL ASSOCIATION OF INDIAN LEGAL SERVICES
510 16th St., #301 • Oakland, CA 94612
(510) 835-0284
Michael Pfeffer, Executive Director
Mary Trimble Norris, Deputy Director

NATIONAL ASSOCIATION OF NATIVE AMERICAN DEAF
c/o Frank Bagley, 1130 S.W. 43rd St.
Oklahoma City, OK 73109

NATIONAL CENTER FOR AMERICAN INDIAN ENTERPRISE DEVELOPMENT (NCAIED) (Headquarters)
953 E. Juanita Ave. • Mesa, AZ 85204
(800) 462-2433; (480) 545-1298 Fax 545-4208
E-mail: ncaiedlah@aol.com
Website: www.ncaied.org
Ken Robbins, NCAIED President
E-mail: krobbins@ncaied.org
David Beaver, Executive Vice President
Michael Beeman, Southwest Regional Project Dir.
E-mail: ncaiedbeem@aol.com
Sharon Chambers, Pacific Regional Project Dir.
E-mail: schambers@ncaied.org
Mario Gonzalez, Northwest Regional Project Dir.
E-mail: ncaiedmg@aol.com
Evan Hong, CA/NV TTAP Director
E-mail: ehong@ncaied.org
Elaine Young, MPSP Dirctor
E-mail: ncaiedely@aol.com
Description: Business consulting firm which provides management services and technical assistance; sponsors Management Institute— training for Indian managers; workshops and seminars. *Purpose*: To promote business and economic development among American Indians and tribes, in cooperation with the U.S. Department of Commerce, Minority Business Development Agency. *Activities*: Provides management and technical assistance for Native Americans residing in California. Available for all stages of business from start-up to expansion. Operates three regional offices & a subsidiary: Southwest, Pacific, Northwest, and Eastern Office UIDA (subsidiary); as well as two programs: California/Nevada Tribal Technical Assistance Program (CA/NV TTAP), and Marketing & Procurement Services Program (MPSP). *Publication*: Reporter, quarterly voice of American Indian business; National American Indian Business Directory, annual. Annual Indian Progress in Business Conference; annual awards banquet and periodic Reservation Economic Summit. Established 1970. Formerly the United Indian Development Association.

NATIONAL CENTER FOR AMERICAN INDIAN MENTAL HEALTH RESEARCH
U. of South Dakota, Julian Hall, Rm. 341
Vermillion, SD 57069

NATIONAL CENTER FOR GREAT LAKES NATIVE AMERICAN CULTURE, INC.
5401 S. Cty. Rd. 900 E. • Lafayette, IN 47905
(765) 296-9943
Nicholas L. Clark, Sr., President
Gregory Ballew, Chairperson
Website: www.ncglnac.org
A not-for-profit membership organization. *Purpose*: To preserve & promote Great Lakes Native American art, history & tradition. Since 1987, NCGLNAC's leaders have worked with tribes, schools, corporations, individuals & other institutions throughout the Great Lakes Region to raise awareness as to the millenniums-long heritage of Great Lakes & Algonquian Tribes. *Activities*: Organizes Great Lakes Native American arts & crafts workshops, Native American history symposiums, Great Lakes Native American traditional pow wows, art & history exhibits for museums & galleries, educational programs & presentations for elementary & secondary schools as well as institutions of higher learning, & cooperative Great Lakes Native American cultural projects with government agencies. Also networks with Great Lakes Native American artists and

craftspeople to promote and sell their crafts and artwork. Established in 1987.

NATIONAL CONGRESS OF AMERICAN INDIANS
1301 Connecticut Ave. NW, #200
Washington, DC 20036
(202) 466-7767 Fax 466-7797
Website: www.ncai.org
Tex Hall, President (Mandan, Hidatsa & Arikara)
Jacqueline L. Johnson, Executive Director
Joe Garcia, First VP (San Juan Pueblo)
Alma Ransom, Treasurer (St. Regis Mohawk Tribe)
Membership: 2,600. Consists of individuals and more than 250 tribal governments representing over one million Native Americans. *Purpose*: To protect Native American traditional cultural and religious rights; to conserve and develop Indian natural and human resources; to serve legislative interests of Indian tribes; to improve the health, education, and economic conditions of Native-Americans. *Activities*: Through its committees, the NCAI involves Executive Council and delegates in formulating positions in a wide variety of issues; conducts research on Indian problems as service to Indian tribes; bestows congressional awards; administers NCAI fund for educational and charitable purposes; legal aid program; nuclear waste program; welfare reform program; maintains speakers bureau. *Members & positions*: John Dossett, General Counsel; Robert Holden, Nuclear Waste Program; R. Aura Kanegis, Deputy Director-Governmental Affairs; Sarah Hicks, Director-Welfare Reform Program. *Publications*: Sentinel, quarterly newsletter; bulletin, NCAI News; Tribal Government Textbook; annual conference report. Annual Congress. Established in 1944.

NATIONAL GEOGRAPHIC SOCIETY
1145 17th St., NW • Washington, DC 20036
(202) 857-7783 Fax 429-5731
Susan Fifer Canby, Director
Web site: www.national geographic.com
Membership: 10 million. *Activities*: Sponsors expeditions and research in geography, archaeology, and ethnology of American Indians; disseminates knowledge through its magazine, maps, books, films, filmstrips, and information services for press, radio and network programs; maintains Explorer's Hall; produces Audiovisual materials for schools; awards gold medals for outstanding achievement. *Publications*: National Geographic, monthly magazine; National Geographic World, monthly; National Geographic Research, quarterly; National Geographic Traveler, quarterly. Library. Established in 1888.

NATIONAL INDIAN ATHLETIC ASSOCIATION
P.O. Box 295 • Cass Lake, MN 56633
(218) 335-8289 Henry S. Harper, Contact

NATIONAL INDIAN BUSINESS ASSOCIATION
725 2nd St., NE • Washington, DC 20002
(202) 547-0580
Stuart Little, Director
Pete Homer, V.P. & CEO
Established in 1995.

NATIONAL INDIAN CHILD WELFARE ASSOCIATION, INC.
5100 SW Macadam Ave., Suite 300
Portland, OR 97201
(503) 222-4044 Fax 222-4007
E-mail: info@nicwa.org
Web site: www.nicwa.org
Gary W. Peterson, Board President
Eloise King, Vice President
Terry L. Cross, Executive Director
Staff: Iona Hansel, Administrative Assistant; Masha Azure, Training Coordinator; Evelyn Bolme, Development Coordinator; David Simmons, Program Specialist. *Purpose*: To preserve & protect Indian children by promoting safety, health, and a positive sense of Indian heritage. The Association claims to be "the only Native American organization focused specifically on issues of child abuse and neglect and tribal capacity to prevent and respond effectively to these problems." *Activities*: Maintains clearinghouse of more than 4,000 articles, books, and periodicals on Indian child welfare, mental health, and social work issues. Annual "Protecting Our Children" National American Indian Indian Conference on Child Abuse and Neglect. *Publications*: NICWA News, quarterly newsletter; Pathways Practice Digest, bimonthly newsletter; National Indian Child

Welfare Institute Directory (biennial); Heritage and Helping; Positive Indian Parenting; Cross Culture Skills; and Honoring the Children. Established in 1987.

NATIONAL INDIAN COUNCIL ON AGING
10501 Montgomery Blvd. NE #210
Albuquerque, NM 87111-3846
(505) 292-2001 Fax 292-1922
Website" www.nicoa.org
Dave Baldridge, Executive Director
Eva Gardipe, Executive Secretary
Frieda Clark, DOL/SCSEP Program Director
Laura Graham, SSI Project Director
Membership: 300. *Goal*: To bring about improved comprehensive services to American Indian and Alaskan Native elders. *Purpose*: To act as a focal point for the articulation of the needs of Indian elderly; to provide meaningful part-time employment experience in community services; and to enroll elders into the SSI entitlement program. *Activities*: disseminates information on Indian aging programs; provides technical assistance and training to tribal governments and organizations in the development of their programs; conducts research on needs of Indian elderly. *Publication*: Elder Voices, monthly newsletter. Biennial conference. Established in 1976.

NATIONAL INDIAN COUNSELORS ASSOCIATION
University of Nebraska, 223 Administration-M.C.A.
Lincoln, NE 68588 (402) 472-2027
Helen Long Soldier, Contact
Membership: 100. *Description*: Native American counselors concerned with improving the counseling of Native Americans. Promotes educational and counseling growth and leadership. *Activities*: Conducts networking among Native American counselors, and workshops related to counseling Native Americans. Maintains database. Established 1980.

NATIONAL INDIAN EDUCATION ASSOCIATION
700 N. Fairfax, Suite 210 • Alexandria, VA 22314
(703) 838-2870 Fax 838-1620
E-mail: niea@niea.org; Website: www.niea.org
Robin Butterfield, President-Board of Directors
John W. Cheek, Executive Director
Membership: 2,000. Advocates educational programs to improve the social and economic well-being of American Indians and Alaskan Native people. *Purpose*: To evaluate and improve the delivery of state and local educational services; and to intercede and establish liaison with state and federal agencies. *Activities*: Conducts an annual National Conference on American Indian Education and holds workshops in conjunction with the conferences; assesses and coordinates existing technical assistance sources. *Scholarship*: John Rouillard Scholarship. *Publications*: Indian Education Newsletter - quarterly; Contemporary Issues of the American Indian; and guides for establishing Indian libraries. Library. Established in 1969.

NATIONAL INDIAN FESTIVAL ASSOCIATION
P.O. Box 3492 • Albany, GA 31706
(912) 436-1625 Fax 883-7786
Marvin Banister, President
E-mail: marvinbb@surfsouth.com
Website: www.surfsouth.com/~nifa
Purpose: To broaden the public's knowledge of Native American culture & to educate them about the differences among these cultures. *Activities*: In the process of building a cultural center & a Native American village in Georgia; annual festival; dance/powwow competition, 3rd weekend in May; Ossahatchee Powwow, 3rd weekend in October.

NATIONAL INDIAN GAMING ASSOCIATION
224 Second St., SE • Washington, DC 20003
(202) 546-7711 Fax 546-1755
Mark Van Norman, Executive Director
Ernie Stevens, Jr. (Oneida), Chairperson
(920) 869-4413 Fax 869-4317
Gordon Adams, Jr. (Ojibwe), Vice Chairperson
Charlie Colombe (Rosebud Sioux), Treasurer
Carla J. Nicholas, Director of Public Relations
Shawn Johns, Research Director
E-mail: sjohns@indiangaming.org
Website: www.indiangaming.org
Description: Non-profit trade association comprised of 184 American Indian Nations and other non-voting associate members. Operates as a clearinghouse & educational, legislative & public policy resource for tribes,

policymakers and the public on Indian gaming issues and tribal community development. *Purpose*: To advance the lives of Indian people - economically, socially, and politically. *Activities*: Holds Indian Gaming Enterprise & Management Law Seminars; & Annual Convention & Trade Show. Professional training for tribal casino management, staff, and for tribal start up operations. *Publications*: Monthly newsletter; *books* - NIGA Indian Gaming Resource Directory; General Requirements & Parameters for Vendor Licensing; National Indian Gaming Minimum Internal Control Standards for Indian Casinos; The Indian Gaming Handbook. Maintains Library and Resource Center.

NATIONAL INDIAN GAMING COMMISSION
1441 L St., NW, #9100
Washington, DC 20005
(202) 632-7003 Fax 632-7066
Philip N. Hogan, Chairperson
Nelson W. Westrin, Vice Chairperson
Cloyce V. Choney, Commissioner
Purpose: To regulate gaming activities on Indian lands for the purpose of shielding Indian tribes from organized crime and other corrupting influences; to ensure that Indian tribes are the primary beneficiaries of gaming revenues; ; and to ensure that gaming is conducted fairly and honestly by both operators and players. *Five regional offices*: 620 SW Main St., Solomon Bldg., Suite 212, Portland, OR 97205 (503) 326-5095; 501 I St., Suite 12400, Sacramento, CA 95814 (916) 930-2230; 3636 N. Central Ave., One Columbus Plaza, Suite 880, Phoenix, AZ 85012 (602) 640-2951; 224 S. Boulder, Rm. 301, Tulsa, OK 74103 (918) 581-7924; 190 E. 5th St., Suite 170, St. Paul, MN 55101 (651) 290- 4004.

NATIONAL INDIAN GAMING & HOSPITALITY INSTITUTE
College of the Menominee Nation
P.O. Box 1179 • Keshena, WI 54135
(715) 799-5600 Fax 799-1308
Dr. Verna Fowler, Contact
Purpose: To explore and address economic, social and cultural issues related to the development of gaming enterprises on American Indian reservations; to provide certificate and associate degree education programs designed to expand the trained workforce with expertise in Indian gaming nationally; to establish a central clearinghouse and library; and a new gaming product development center.

NATIONAL INDIAN HEALTH BOARD
Office of Diversity, Campus Box AO49
4200 E. 9th Ave. • Denver, CO 80262
(303) 315-5598; Linda Yardley, Contact
Purpose: To elevate the health status of American Indians and Alaska Natives equal to that of the rest of the U.S. population; to secure maximum tribal and consumer participation in the delivery of health services to Indian people; and, to enhance and promote education of Indian health issues. *Activities*: Provides technical assistance to members and Indian organizations; bestows awards; and sponsors annual health conference. *Publications*: NIHB Health Reporter, newsletter; health conference report. Library. Annual conference. Established in 1972.

NATIONAL INDIAN HIGHER EDUCATION CONSORTIUM
121 Oronoco St. • Alexandria, VA 22314
(703) 838-0400 Fax 838-0388

NATIONAL INDIAN JUSTICE CENTER
5250 Aero Dr. • Santa Rosa, CA 95403-8069
(800) 966-0662; (707) 762-8113 Fax 762-7681
Joe Myers, Executive Director
E-mail: nijc@aol.com
Web site: www.nijc.indian.com

NATIONAL INDIAN POLICY CENTER
Washington, DC 20052
(202) 994-1446 Fax 994-4404
Dr. Ronald Trosper, Director
Orna Weinroth, Information Specialist
Description: Established by congressional initiative to provide information services on a wide range of policy issues to more than 500 U.S. American Indian tribes and Alaska Native villages. Operates under the direction of a planning committee comprised of tribal leaders, representatives of major Indian organizations and

Indian policy experts. The center has seven task forces conducting research projects. *Purpose*: To commission Native American research and policy analysis; to serve as an information clearinghouse for Native Americans; and to sponsor seminars and conferences on issues of concern to American Indians and Alaska Natives. *Activities*: Commissions reports and projects; conducts seminars & conferences; provides internships. Library, online clearinghouse. *Publication*: Bibliography of Demonstration Research & Policy Papers.

NATIONAL INDIAN SCHOOL BOARD ASSN.
P.O. Box 790 • Polson, MT 59860
(406) 883-3603 Fax 675-4801

NATIONAL INDIAN SOCIAL WORKERS ASSOCIATION, INC.
P.O. Box 45 • Valentine, AZ 86437-0045
Mary Kihega, Secretary-Treasurer
Membership: 200. *Purpose*: To develop, support, and promote social service programs which adequately meet the needs of American Indian people and that are consistent with the desires, customs, and lifestyle and traditions of Indians. *Activities*: Provides training and technical assistance to tribal and nontribal organizations; holds seminars on Indian child welfare; conducts survey research; sponsors competitions; maintains speakers' bureau. Annual conference; regional organizations. *Publication*: Quarterly newsletter. Established in1970.

NATIONAL INDIAN TRAINING & RESEARCH CENTER
1940 N. Rosemont • Mesa, AZ 85205-3203
(480) 967-9484 Fax 325-5288
Dr. C. Corbett, Executive Director
Purpose: To involve American Indians in leadership and professional roles in training and research projects for the social and economic betterment of Indian people; to orient and train professionals working with American Indians. *Activities*: Conduct training programs to educate; sponsors research and development to increase information and knowledge about American Indians. *Publication*: Introducing Public School Finance to Native Americans; Indian Education Update, newsletter. Library. Established in 1969.

NATIONAL INDIAN YOUTH COUNCIL
318 Elm St., SE • Albuquerque, NM 87102
(505) 247-2251 Fax 247-4251
Norman Ration, President-Board
Kenneth Tsosie, Executive Director
Jim Anaya, Staff Attorney
Membership: 45,000. *Purpose*: To provide young Indian people with a working knowledge of serving and understanding their tribal communities and to implement educational resources through research, training and planning on local, regional and national levels. *Activities*: Operates Indian health, education, and employment programs; annual meeting. *Publication*: Americans Before Columbus, bimonthly tabloid; Indian Voter Survey Reports, periodic describing political attitudes of Native Americans living on reservations. Annual meeting in June. Established in 1961.

NATIONAL LEGAL AID & DEFENDER ASSOCIATION
1625 K St., NW 8th Floor • Washington, DC 20006
(202) 452-0620 Clinton Lyons, Executive Director
Membership: 2,750. *Purpose*: To provide technical and management assistance to local organizations offering services to poor persons in civil or criminal cases. *Activities*: Clearinghouse for information; sponsors research & educational training programs; presents awards. *Committee*: Native American Committee. *Publications*: Cornerstone, 10/yr.; Directory of Legal Aid and Defender Offices in the U.S., semiannual. Established in 1911.

NATIONAL MARROW DONOR PROGRAM
7910 Woodmont Ave. • Bethesda, MD 20814
(800) 627-7693
Carol Field, Director-Native American Recruitment
Purpose: To interest Native American people in joining the National Registry of Marrow Donors so that Native American patients with Leukemia can locate a matching marrow donor for a life saving marrow transfusion. *Activities*: Offers simple, free blood test to Native people interested in joining the National Registry. Established 1987.

NATIONAL NATIVE AMERICAN AIDS PREVENTION CENTER
436 14th St., #1020
Oakland, CA 94609
(510) 444-2051 Fax 444-1593
Dana Ridling, President - Board of Directors
Michael Bird, MSW, MPH, Executive Director
Laura Oropeza, Deputy Director
Anno Elkhart-Nakai, Prevention Projects Manager
Larry Kairaiuak, Two Spirits Project Coordinator
E-mail: information@nnaapc.org
Website: www.nnaapc.org
Purpose: To stop the spread of HIV and related diseases among American Indians, Alaska Natives, and Native Hawaiians by improving their health status through empowerment and self determination. *Special programs*: Conduct outreach to Native organizations and communities; trains community-based HIV educators; and provides technical assistance in community organizing. *Activities*: Operates a national clearinghouse for Native-specific HIV/AIDS information; provides ongoing information services; and develops curricula for target populations. Division of Client Services, 205 West 8th St., Suite 103, Lawrence, KS 66044 (913) 865-4297 Fax 842-0145; National Indian AIDS Media Consortium (Native-owned newspapers, radio stations, and television programs), 1433 E. Franklin Ave., Suite 3A, Minneapolis, MN 55404 (612) 872-8860 Fax 872-8864; Ahalaya HIV Case Management Project, 1200 N. Walker, Suite 605, Oklahoma City, OK 73101 (405) 235-3701 Fax 235-1801. *Publications*: Seasons, quarterly magazine; Raven's Guide, resource guide; Policy Guidelines; Speaker's directory; books and videos. Library. Established in 1987.

NATIONAL NATIVE AMERICAN COOPERATIVE
P.O. Box 27626
Tucson, AZ 85726-7626
(520) 622-4900 Fax 622-3525
Fred Synder, Executive Officer
E-mail: info@usaindianinfo.org
Website: www.usaindianinfo.org
Description: Native American artists and craftsmen, cultural presenters, dance groups, and individuals interested in preserving American Indian crafts, culture, and traditional education. *Purpose*: To provide incentives to Native Americans to encourage the preservation of their culture. *Activities*: Provides educational programs; serves as a clearinghouse of information; offers assistance marketing American Indian crafts and locating material that is difficult to find; supplies referral information on public health, education, career counseling, scholarships and funding sources, marketing, models, and dance; sponsors crafts and cultural demonstrations; compiles statistics; operates speaker's bureau; maintains museum; annual meeting. *Published works*: Indian Information Packets; Native American Directory, quinquennial; Pow Wow on the Red Road, annual. Established 1969.

NATIONAL NATIVE AMERICAN LAW STUDENTS ASSOCIATION
American Indian Law Center, Box 4456, Sta. A
1117 Stanford, N.E. • Albuquerque, NM 87196
(505) 277-5462; Sally Hernandez

NATIONAL NATIVE AMERICAN PURCHASING ASSOCIATION
P.O. Box 309 • Willamina, OR 97396
(503) 876-3307 Fax 876-2123
Sharon Jacox, Executive Director

NATIONAL RELIEF CHARITIES
10029 SW Nimbus Ave., Suite 200
Beaverton, OR 97008
(800) 416-8102
(503) 641-5786 Fax 641-0495
Brian J. Brown, President
E-mail: nrcprogram@aol.com
Website: www.nrcprograms.org
Purpose/Goals: To help Native American people improve the quality of their lives by providing opportunities for them to bring about positive changes in their communities. *Activities/Programs*: A non-profit organization which develops self-help programs and emergency relief services for Native Americans across the country. National Relief Charities is the umbrella organization for American Indian Relief Council, Council of Indian Nations, American Indian Education Foundation, and Southwest Indian Relief Council. Services of member programs AIRC, CIN and SWIRC include: emergency food distributions, clothing and shoe distributions, winterization of homes, fuel assistance programs, school supplies, holiday dinners, gifts and stockings for children at Christmas and Easter, baby baskets for new mothers and incentive programs for seniors, adult volunteers and children. AIEF programs include: purchasing essential school supplies and curriculum materials, supporting student incentive programs, funding repair of structural deterioration in schools and awarding grants to American Indian students for tuition and living expenses. *Publication*: Quarterly newsletters are published for each program. Established in 1995.

NATIONAL SOCIETY FOR AMERICAN INDIAN ELDERLY (NSAIE)
2214 N. Central Ave., Suite 250
Phoenix, AZ 85004 (602) 307-1865
Website: www.nsaie.org
E-mail: info@nsaie.org
Description: Works to assist all Indian elderly service programs, both on-reservation and off, to improve quality of life for American Indian elders. Established in 1987.

NATIONAL TRIBAL CHAIRMAN'S ASSOCIATION
Washington, DC 20006
(202) 293-0031
Raymond Field, Executive Director
Membership: 190. *Description*: Consists of federally recognized tribes and their leaders. *Purpose*: To provide a united front for elected Indian leaders to consult with government officials; to assist Indian groups in obtaining full rights from federal agencies; to monitor federal programs that affect Indians. *Publication*: List of Tribes and Tribal Leaders, quarterly; Newsbrief, periodic. Established in 1971.

NATIONAL TRIBAL COURT CLERKS ASSOCIATION
Washington, DC 20036 (202) 296-0685
Janet Waupoose, President
Margaret Houten & Eliza Martinez, V.P.s
Tom Colosimo, Treasurer; Diana Muniz, Secretary
Membership: 300. *Description*: Consists of American Indian court clerks and administrators. *Purpose*: To improve the efficiency and provide for the upgrading of the American Indian court system; to provide support services for all court officers at a professional level; and to improve the integrity and capability of the court system; and to elevate the status of court clerks and administrators. *Programs*: Training and continuing education programs. *Publication*: Courtline, semiannual newsletter; reports, training materials for in-house programs. Established in 1980.

NATIONAL TRIBAL DEVELOPMENT ASSOCIATION (NTDA)
National FSA American Indian Credit Outreach Initiative
RR 1 Box 694 • Box Elder, MT 59521
(800) 963-0015; (406) 395-4095 Fax 395-4759
Alvin Windy Boy, Sr., Chairperson
John Sunchild, Chief Executive Officer
Billi Morsette, Program Administrator
Website: www.indiancreditoutreach.com
E-mail: info@indiancreditoutreach.comorg
Description: Works for the common interest in the development of tribal economies. *Programs*: Information services; electronic bulletin board. *Publication*: FSA Weekly Bulletin. Established in 1995.

NATIONAL TRIBAL ENVIRONMENTAL COUNCIL
2501 Rio Grande Blvd. NW, Suite A
Albuquerque, NM 87104
(505) 242-2175 Fax242-2654
David Conrad (Osage), Executive Director
Lisa Gover, Program Officer
E-mail: ntec@ntec.org; Website: www.ntec.org
Description: Native American tribes focusing on the environmental concerns of Native Americans. *Purpose*: Seeks to strengthen environmental management of lands by Native American tribes. *Activities*: Acts as a clearinghouse for environmental information; monitors legislation related to the environment; maintains speakers' bureau; holds annual conference. *Publication*: "Tribal Vision," quarterly newsletter. Library. Established in 1991.

NATIONAL TRIBAL ENVIRONMENTAL OFFICE
Eastern Band of Cherokee Indians
P.O. Box 455 • Cherokee, NC 28719
(800) 451-2764; (704) 497-3814 Fax 497-3615
Activities: Sponsors the National Tribal Conference on Environmental Management held in Cherokee, NC in May.

NATIONS MINISTRIES
P.O. Box 70 • Honobia, OK 74549
(918) 755-4570; Riley Donica, Director
Description: Consists of individuals and churches conducting evangelical Christian ministry on American Indian reservations in the U.S. *Activities*: Bestows awards; maintains speaker's bureau; Chaplains service - Indian Hospital, Talihina, OK; adult and youth camps; academic scholarships. *Publication*: The Nations News, bimonthly. Annual meeting. Established 1983.

NATIVE AMERICAN ALLIANCE FOUNDATION
5820 4th St. NW • Albuquerque, NM 87121
(800) 516-9340
Jenna Gourg-Galledous, Director
Website: www.native-alliance.org

NATIVE AMERICAN BANK, N.A. (NAB)
Headquarters: Website: www.nabna.com
165 S. Union Blvd., Suite 1000
Denver, CO 80228
(303) 988-2727 Fax 988-5533
John H. Beirise, President & CEO
(720) 963-5500
Lewis A. Anderson, Chairperson
Branch location: 125 N. Market Sq.
P.O. Box 730 • Browning, MT 59417
(800) 307-9199
(406) 338-7000 Fax 338-7008
Patty Gobert, Branch Manager
Branch location: Stone Child College
R.R. 1, Box 1082 • Box Elder, MT 59521
(406) 395-4355 Fax 395-4356
Theresa Hawley, Branch Manager
Description: A federally-chartered bank that is owned by Native American Bancorporation, a bank holding company that has been organized by a group of Tribal Nations and Alaska Native Corporations. Twenty tribal investors pooled their resources and established Native American Bank through the purchase of Blackfeet National Bank in Browning, Montana on October 29, 2001. *Mission Statement*: Pooling Indian economic resources to increase Indian economic independence; to be a powerful engine to Indian economic development, to establish a significant Indian presence in the financial marketplace, and to protect the growing economic power of tribes & Indian businesses onto the national scene. *Core Banking Function*: To provide Indian Country with a commercial bank that is expert in the unique aspects of doing business in Indian Country. It will be a business bank that focuses on large business and agricultural operations & community development loans and that endeavors to break down the barriers that have caused Indian Country to be vastly underserved by the banking community.

NATIVE AMERICAN BAR ASSOCIATION
Native American Legal Resource Center
Oklahoma City University Law School
2501 N. Blackwelder • Oklahoma City, OK 73106
(405) 521-5277
Lawrence R. Baca, President

NATIVE AMERICAN BUSINESS ALLIANCE (NABA)
30700 Telegraph Rd., Suite 1675
Bingham Farms, MI 48025
(248) 988-9344 Fax 988-9348
Lloyd W. Milby, Director
Website: www.native-american-bus.org/
E-mail: naba@native-american-bus.org
Description: Represents Native Americans to the private sector; facilitates business and cultural educational programs. *Activity*: Annual conference.

NATIVE AMERICAN CANCER RESEARCH (NACR)
3022 Nova Rd. • Pine, CO 80470-7830
(303) 838-9359 Fax 838-7629
Linda Burhansstipanov, President/Executive Dir.
Purpose: To reduce Native American cancer indcidence and mortality, and to increase survival from cancer among Native Americans. *Programs*: Imple-

ments cancer primary prevention, secondary prevention, risk reduction, screening, education, training, research, diagnosis, control, treatment, and support programs. *Meeting*: National Native American Cancer Survivors/Thrivers Conference & Workshop. *Publication*: Newsletter, 3x/year. Established in 1999.

NATIVE AMERICAN CENTER OF EXCELLENCE CONSORTIUM
College of Medicine, P.O. Box 26901
Oklahoma City, OK 73190 (405) 271-2316
Philip A. McHale, PhD
Purpose: To recruit and retain Native Americans to medical and dental school; recruit Native American faculty in medicine and dentistry; stimulate research on Native American health issues. *Activities*: MCAT Preparation; enrichment programs; faculty development programs; tutoring programs; extensive recruitment. Library. Established 1992.

NATIVE AMERICAN COMMUNITY BOARD
NATIVE AMERICAN WOMEN HEALTH EDUCATION RESOURCE CENTER
P.O. Box 572 • Lake Andes, SD 57356-0572
(605) 487-7072 Fax 487-7964
Charon Asetoyer, Director
Description: A non-membership organization that works toward the educational, social, and economic advancement of American Indians. *Purpose*: Concerned with treaty and environmental issues involving Native Americans. *Activities*: Women Health Education Resource Center provides self-help programs and workshops on issues such as fetal alcohol syndrome, AIDS awareness, family planning, child & domestic abuse. Conducts adult education classes, employment services; scholarship program; conducts charitable programs; offers children's services; maintains speaker's bureau and placement service. *Publication*: Wicozanni-Wowapi, quarterly newsletter; also publishes brochures and pamphlets. Established in 1984.

NATIVE AMERICAN CONSULTANTS
725 2nd St., NE • Washington, DC 20002
(202) 547-0576 Louis R. Bruce, President
Concerned with the growth and development of Native American-owned businesses in the Washington, DC area. With a grant from the Minority Business Development Center, Native American Consultants has been commissioned to manage an Indian consultant service program to states on the East Coast and most southern states.

NATIVE AMERICAN CONTRACTORS ASSOCIATION
888 17th St., NW, Suite 1100
Washington, DC 20006
(202) 775-8700 Fax 857-0200
Website: www.nativeamericancontractors.org
E-mail: info@nativeamericancontractors.org
Purpose: To establish, promote and defend policies, regulations and laws that foster a fair level of participation by Tribes, Alaska Native corporations, and Native Hawaiian organizations in the federal government marketplaces. Also seeks to serve as a vehicle for information sharing and partnership opportuities between and among its members.

NATIVE AMERICAN DANCE TROOPS
Chickahominy Red Men Dancers
P.O. Box 473 • Providence Forge, VA 23140
(804) 829-2152; Preston Adkins, Coordinator

NATIVE AMERICAN FILM FESTIVAL
Website: www.nativefilmfest.com

NATIVE AMERICAN FINANCE OFFICERS ASSOCIATION
P.O. Box • Green Bay, WI 54703
(920) 869-7172 Fax 869-1718
E-mail: nafoa2002@aol.com
Website: www.nafoa.org
Jeff Lamb, President (Gros Ventre)
(480) 704-1769 Fax 704-1780
E-mail: jlamb@millerschroeder.com
Edwin Kane, 1st V.P. (White Mountain Apache)
E-mail: ya125@yavapai-apache-nation.com
Membership: Over 100 tribal governments and organizations, as well as, private sector sponsors. *Purpose*: To provide a professional organization dedicated to

the improvement and quality of financial and business management of Native American governments and businesses which will strengthen tribal governments through sound financial management. *Activities*: To provide a clearinghouse network; to provide a forum for information, training and technical assistance to Native American organizations; to support legislative recommendations; to develop and maintain financial standards; to develop and support a scholarship training and internship program for Native American students and tribal employees from the financial and business areas. Established in 1982.

NATIVE AMERICAN FISH & WILDLIFE SOCIETY
750 Burbank St. • Broomfield, CO 80020
(303) 466-1725 Fax 466-5414
Ken Poynter, Executive Director
E-Mail: webmaster@nafws.org
Web site: www.nafws.org
Membership: 224 tribes. *Description:* Made up of Native professionals and technicians engaged in tribal natural resource management. *Purpose:* To facilitate and coordinate inter-tribal communications in regard to fish/wildlife issues; to promote the prudent use of Native natural resources; to educate Native youth toward professional management of tribal natural resources; and works to improve the welfare of tribal people. *Special program*: Summer Youth Practicum - to encourage Indian youth to pursue careers in the fish and wildlife fields. *Publication*: "Eagle's Nest", newsletter. Established in 1983.

NATIVE AMERICAN GRANT SCHOOL ADMINISTRATION
901 N. Kinlani Rd.
Flagstaff, AZ 86001 (520) 774-5279

NATIVE AMERICAN INDIAN MEDIA CORP.
P.O. Box 59 • Strawberry Plains, TN 37871
(615) 933-6246
Frank Eastes, Jr., Exec. Director
Purpose: To develop American Indian art and artists, and to develop Indian involvement in the media. *Programs*: Provides low-cost access to professional quality film and video equipment to independent filmmakers; provides equipment access grants; develops and sponsors Indian art projects. Maintains film, video and audio archives. Established in 1981.

NATIVE AMERICAN INTERNATIONAL CAUCUS
United Methodist Church
1503 Kimberly Rd. • New Bern, NC 28562-3307
(919) 424-0894; Dr. Sam Wynn, Exec. Director
Purpose: To provide a liaison between the Church and about 150 Native American congregations.

NATIVE AMERICAN JOURNALISTS ASSOCIATION
555 N. Dakota St. • Vermillion, SD 57069
(866) 694-4264 Fax (605) 677-5282
E-Mail: info@naja.com; Web site: www.naja.com
Patty Talahongva, President
E-mail: talahongva@naja.com
Ron Walters, Executive Director
E-mail: walters@naja.com
Purpose: To improve communications among Native people and between Native Americans and the general public; to serve and empower Native journalists through programs and actions designed to enrich journalism and promote Native cultures; to support and increase the involvement of Native Americans in the media. *Programs*: Provides educational and training for 500 plus Native communicators at its annual conference; recruits more Native Americans into the field of journalism through its summer high school workshops, college scholarships, career days and job referral service. Scholarships available for qualified American Indian journalist students. Board of directors: Mary Annette Pember, President; Patty Talahongva, Vice President; Lori Edmo-Suppah, Treasurer; Dennis McAuliffe, Secretary; George Benge, Dana Hedgpeth, Patty Loew, Monique Manatch, Andre Maurice Morriseau, Brian Wright-McLeod. *Publication*: NAJA News, quarterly newsletter. Established in 1984.

NATIVE AMERICAN LAW STUDENTS ASSOCIATION
American Indian Law Center
Box 4456, Sta. A, 1117 Stanford, NE
Albuquerque, NM 87196
(505) 277-5462

Ronald Eagleye Johnny, President
Indian Law Clinic, U. of Montana Law School
Missoula, MT 59806 (406) 243-6480
 Magel Bird, President
Membership: 160. American Indian and Native Alaskan law students. *Purpose*: To promote unity, communication and cooperation among Indian law students. *Programs*: Financial aid, and summer employment opportunities; research projects and curriculum development in Indian law; maintains speakers bureau of students in the field of Indian law. *Publication*: Newsletter. Annual meeting. Established in 1970.

NATIVE AMERICAN LEGAL RESOURCE CENTER
Oklahoma City University-School of Law
2501 Blackwelder • Oklahoma City, OK 73106
 (405) 521-5188 Kirke Kickingbird, Director

**NATIVE AMERICAN MANAGEMENT
& EDUCATIONAL SERVICES**
230 Louisiana Blvd. • Albuquerque, NM 87108
 (505) 265-8063
Purpose: To develop programs to help American Indian students.

NATIVE AMERICAN MINISTRIES
Presbyterian Church (USA)
100 Witherspoon St. • Louisville, KY 40202
 (502) 569-5000
Purpose: To make the church's resources available to Native Americans in the hopes of supporting their self-determination efforts.

**NATIVE AMERICAN MUSIC
AWARDS & ASSOCIATION**
511 Ave. of the Americas, Suite 371
New York, NY 10011 (212) 228-8300
 E-mail: nammys@aol.com
Purpose: Dedicated to the the archival and preservation of all Native American music and promotion of its artists. *Activities*: Annual Native American Blues Festival.

NATIVE AMERICAN NEWS SERVICE
1123 N. Pollock St. • Rosemead, CA 91770
 (818) 573-9023
Purpose: To disseminate news to Native American publications.

NATIVE AMERICAN POLICY NETWORK
Barry University, 11300 2nd Ave., N.E.
Miami, FL 33161 (305) 899-3473
 Michael E. Melody, Director
Membership: 400. Consists of social scientists, policy makers and Native American leaders. *Purpose*: To facilitate and to increase research in all areas of Native American policy as well as the policy-making process. Organizes panels and seminars at the annual conventions of the American Political Science Association and Western Social Science Association. *Publications*: Newsletter, 3/year; periodic Directory. Annual meeting. Established 1980.

**NATIVE AMERICAN PREVENTION
RESEARCH CENTER**
University of Oklahoma Health Sciences Center
800 N.E. 15th St., Rm. 532
Oklahoma City, OK 73104
 (405) 271-6285
 June E. Eichner, PhD, Co-director
 William E. Moore, Associate Director
 E-mail: naprc@ouhsc.edu
 Website: www.ouhsc.edu
Description: Works in partnership with American Indian tribes, communities and individuals to develop approaches to health promotion and disease prevention in Indian communities. *Program*: Tribal Health Planning & Education Program. Publications & presentations available.

**NATIVE AMERICAN PUBLIC
TELECOMMUNICATIONS**
1800 North 33rd St. • Lincoln, NE 68583
 (402) 472-3522 Fax 472-8675
 Faith Smith, Chairperson
 Jim May, Vice-Chairperson
 Frank Blythe, Executive Director
 E-mail: native@unl.edu
 Web site: www.nativetelecom.org
Purpose: To provide Native Americans and the gen-

eral public access, via telecommunications, to content and related interactive experiences that educate, inform, enlighten and entertain concerning the culture, history, achievements and concerns of the Native American peoples both on and outside the reservations. *Objective*: To carry out this mission as self-sufficiently as possible, and minimize dependence on outside sources for funds. *Activities*: Public Television Program Fund; provides training opportunities; new programs are screened and cataloged on a continuous basis from all available sources; bestows awards; sponsors workshops. Developed the Native American Public Radio Satellite Network in conjunction with the Indigenous Communications Association. Library of videotapes, films & radio programs. Established 1977.

**NATIVE AMERICAN RECREATION
& SPORT INSTITUTE**
c/o Judith G. Shepherd
116 W. Osage • Greenfield, IN 46140
 (317) 462-4245 (phone & fax)

**NATIVE AMERICAN RESEARCH
INFORMATION SERVICE (NARIS)**
American Indian Institute
555 Constitution Ave., Suite 237
Norman, OK 73072-7820
 (405) 325-4127 Fax 325-7757
 Anita Chisholm, Director
 E-Mail: aii@cce.occe.ou.edu
Descriptpion: A computerized database that systematically compiles a comprehensive catalog of published and unpublished research focusing on Native American human and economic development from 1969 to the present. Contains almost 14,000 entries and can be accessed to retrieve specific information of interest to tribal leaders and planners, Indian organizations, governmental agencies, IHS health facilities, private foundations, businesses, lawmakers, & researchers.

NATIVE AMERICAN RIGHTS FUND
1506 Broadway • Boulder, CO 80302
 (303) 447-8760 Fax 443-7776
 Website: www.narf.org
 E-mail: toya@narf.org
 Richard Hayward, Chairperson
 John E. Echohawk, Executive Director
Offices: 1712 N St., NW, Washington, DC 20036
(202) 785-4166; 310 K St., Suite 708, Anchorage,
Alaska 99501 (907) 276-0680. *Purpose*: The protection of Indian rights; the preservation of tribal existence; the protection of tribal natural resources; the promotion of human rights; the accountability of governments to Native-Americans; and the development of Indian law. *Activities*: Serves as National Indian Law Support Center; maintains the National Indian Law Library. *Publications*: NARF Legal Review, quarterly; Indian Law Support Center Reporter, monthly; monthly newsletter; National Indian Law Library Catalogue, supplemented quarterly; indexes to Indian Claims Commission Decisions; annual report. Semiannual board of directors' meeting in May and November. Established in 1970.

NATIVE AMERICAN SCHOLARSHIP FUND, INC.
8200 Mountain Rd. NE #203 • Albuquerque, NM 87110
 (505) 262-2351 Fax 262-0534
 Web site: www.nasf.com
 Dr. Dean Chavers, President
Purpose: To raise funds to provide Native American students with merit scholarships for university study at the undergraduate and graduate levels. *Activities*: Conducts educational programs. *Publication*: Brochures. Library. Established in 1987.

NATIVE AMERICAN SPORTS COUNCIL
P.O. Box 38249 • Colorado Springs, CO 80937
 (719) 527-8511

**NATIVE AMERICAN WOMEN'S HEALTH
EDUCATION RESOURCE CENTER**
P.O. Box 572 • Lake Andes, SD 57356
 (605) 487-7072 Fax 487-7964
 Website: www.nativeshop.org
 E-mail: nativewoman@igc.apc.org

NATIVE COFFEE, INC.
27 Union Square W. # 501
New York, NY 10003 (888) 628-4831
Description: Coffee organically grown in South and

Central America and roasted on sovereign Native American Indian territory. An American Indian product, owned-operated-financed 100% by Native Americans. *Goal*: To help the economic development of the indigenous peoples of North & South America.

NATIVE CULTURE & ECOLOGY FOUNDATION
c/o Mr. Alderson, R.R. 1, Box 3117
Havana, FL 32333-9801

NATIVE NATIONS INSTITUTE
Morris Udall Center - University of Arizona
Tucson, AZ 85721

NATIVE WHOLISTIC SPECIALISTS, INC.
P.O. Box 3297 • Window Rock, AZ 86515
 (928) 871-5726 Fax 871-4598
 Website: www.goodmedicine12.com
 Dr. kalvin White, CEO & Founder
Description: A Native-owned organization with the mission to promote positive mental health in Native communities throughout North America. The emphasis of treatment approach is to integrate Native American concepts with Western psychology. Provides assessment, consultation and counseling services to Native American people, organizations, and communities that serve Native American populations. *Activities*: "Warrior Spirit" an annual Indigenous Psychology Conference.

NATIVE WRITER'S CIRCLE OF THE AMERICAS
805 Dale Hall Tower, 455 Lindsey
Norman, OK 73019-0535
 (405) 325-2312 Fax 325-0842
 Geary Hobson, Project Director
 Website: www.ou.edu/cas/nas/writers.html
 E-mail: nas@ou.edu
Purpose: To maintain a Native American writer's address database/

NATIVE YOUTH ALLIANCE
1711 Kenyon St., NW • Washington, DC 20010-2616
 (202) 328-9060; Nathan Phillips, Executive Director
Purpose: To help Native children whose parents are in the prison system.

NAVAJO AREA SCHOOL BOARD ASSOCIATION
P.O. Box 3719 • Window Rock, AZ 86515-0578
 (520) 871-5226 Fax 871-5148
 Grace M. Boyne, Director
 E-mail: gmboyne@yahoo.com
Publication: Monthly newsletter.

NAVAJO ARTS & CRAFTS ENTERPRISES
P.O. Box 160 • Window Rock, AZ 86515
Purpose: The rehabilitation and better utilization of the resources of the Navajo and Hopi Tribes and reservations as (they) relate to the members of the Navajo Tribe. *Activities*: Maintains retail outlets; operates a mail order business and a wholesale business; crafts exhibit held at the Heard Museum. Established in 1941.

NAVAJO CODE TALKERS
P.O. Box 1182 • Window Rock, AZ 86515
 (520) 871-5468
 Dr. Samuel Billison, President
Description:: An organization of Indian marines that was responsible for developing the now highly-celebrated code. 420 Navajos operated a division of communications along the pacific front during World War II that incorporated more than 400 words, eventually making up the Code Talkers Dictionary. *Members*: Samuel Tso, Arthur Hubbard, Sr., Merril Sandoval, Alfred Peaches

NAVAJO NATION HEALTH FOUNDATION
Sage Memorial Hospital
P.O. Box 457 • Ganada, AZ 86505
 (520) 755-3411
Purpose: To provide health services to members of the Navajo Nation about 150,000 members.

NORTH AMERICA INDIAN MINISTRIES (NAIM)
P.O. Box 151 • Point Roberts, WA 98281
 (604) 946-1227 Fax 946-1465
 Ray Badgero, President
 E-mail: office@naim.ca
 Web site: www.naim.ca
Membership: 110. *Purpose*: To establish indigenous Native American fellowship gatherings in urban cen-

ters and on reservations. *Activities/Programs*: 8 week summer program for college students who live on reserve during the program; Wilderness Trails program, similar to Outward Bound; conducts economic, educational, social, & rehabilitation programs; offers alcohol treatment, sexual abuse & AIDS seminars, & cross-cultural communication seminars. *Publications*: Intercessor, bimonthly; NAIM News, semi-annual newsletter. Library. Annual meeting. Established 1949.

NORTH AMERICAN INDIAN ASSOCIATION
22720 Plymouth Rd. • Detroit, MI 48239
(313) 535-2966 Irene Lowry, Director
Membership: 300. At least one-quarter North American Indian blood. *Purpose*: To promote economic development and self-sufficiency for American Indian people through human services. *Activities*: Employment and educational services; senior center offers nutrition, social and educational services; Indian child welfare provides protective services for Indian children and families; Arts and Crafts Gallery business. Operates Native American Gallery; speaker's bureau. Russ Wright Scholarship Fund—assists students with the expense of educational supplies. *Publication*: Native Sun, monthly newsletter. Library. Annual meeting and powwow. Established 1940.

NORTH AMERICAN INDIAN WOMEN'S ASSOCIATION
P.O. Box 805 • Eagle Butte, SD 57625
(605) 964-2136 Marcella LeBau, President
Membership: Women 18 years old and over who are members of federally recognized tribes. *Purpose*: To promote inter-tribal communications, awareness of the Native American culture, betterment of family life, health and education. Brochure. Annual meeting. Established in 1970.

NORTH AMERICAN INDIGENOUS GAMES
Buffalo, NY (716) 852-2673; (866) 291-NAIG
E-mail: info@naig2005.org
Description: A celebration of Indigenous cultures from across the North American continent. The event, a combination of sport and culture, will feature performances by hosting competitions from a variety of sporting events. The next event will be held July 20-31, 2005.

NORTH AMERICAN NATIVE AMERICAN INDIAN INFORMATION & TRADE CENTER
P.O. Box 27626 • Tucson, AZ 85726-7626
(520) 622-4900; Fred Synder, Director-Consultant
Web site: www.usaindianinfo.org
Membership: 2,700+ American Indian artisans representing over 400 tribes. *Purpose*: To collect, organize, and disseminate current information on Native Americans of North America; to provide incentives for continuation of traditional and contemporary preservation of Indian culture, i.e., song, dance, crafts, education, health. *Activities*: American Indian Crafts Cooperative; 2,700+ artists from 410 different tribes and social needs; publish books; maintains museum of major crafts from contemporary artists, such as basketry, beadwork/quillwork; Indian doll collection; sponsors three major events each year: Native American Month Social Pow-wow &Craft Market (Thanksgiving weekend, Tucson); Indian America Competition Powwow & Indian Craft Market (New Year's weekend, Tucson); American Indian Exposition (first 15 days in Feb., Tucson); also maintain a research library containing over 5,000 books & research papers. *Scholarships*: Travel expenses to artists exhibiting at events, pow wows & celebrations. *Publications*: Native American Directory — Alaska, Canada, U.S.; Pow Wow on the Red Road; Pow Wow Calendar. Library. Established in 1990.

NORTHEAST NATIVE AMERICAN EDUCATION CENTER
23 Middle Grove Rd.
Greenfield Center, NY 12833
(518) 584-1018 Fax 583-9741
Joseph & James Bruchac, Owners/Managers
Description: A 70 acre native preserve with marked trails, Native American structures with exhibits, and a traditional garden. A learning environment for those who wish to learn more about the Northeast's rich Native American culture. *Activities*: School field trips; guided tours, book sales; lectures; teachers workshops; skills courses. Bookstore. Established 1987.

ORBIS ASSOCIATES
1411 K St., NW, #700
Washington, DC 20005
(202) 628-4444 Fax 628-2241
Gwen Shunatona, President
E-Mail: shunosoo@space link.msfc.nasa.gov
Description: An American Indian controlled and managed non-profit corporation. *Purpose*: To provide expertise in training and consulting for education, research, program administration and evaluation. *Activities*: Training and technical assistance in a variety of education, management, and evaluation related areas: classroom instructional strategies; youth development; holistic counseling; and primary prevention; culture-based curriculum development; research and data collection/analysis of community needs and services. Library - contains volumes on history, literature and research as well as culture-based curriculum materials for Grades K-12. Publications: Published a number of culture-based curriculum units for grades K-8. Established in 1982.

ORDER OF THE INDIAN WARS
P.O. Box 7401 • Little Rock, AR 72217
(501) 225-3996
Jerry L. Russell, Chairperson
E-mail: jlrussell@aristotle.net
Website: www.indianwars.com
Membership: 750. Professionals and informal historians interested in the study of the frontier conflicts between the Indians and the white man, and among Indian tribes during the early settlement of the U.S. *Purpose*: Seeks to protect and preserve historic sites related to those wars. *Activities*: Annual conferences and tours. *Publications*: Communique, monthly. Established in 1979.

ORGANIZATION OF NORTH AMERICAN INDIAN STUDENTS
Box 26, University Center
Northern Michigan U. • Marquette, MI 49855
(906) 227-2138; Ted DeVerney, Executive Officer
Membership: 45. University students of American Indian ancestry and other interested students. *Purpose*: To encourage pride and identity in Indian culture and tradition; to establish communications among the native communities; to promote scholarships among Indian students attending institutes of higher learning. *Activities*: Sponsors basket weaving seminars; annual Indian Awareness Week. Library. Established in 1971.

OYATE
2702 Mathews St. • Berkeley, CA 94702
(510) 848-6700 Fax 848-4815
Website: www.oyate.org
E-mail: oyate@oyate.org
Description: Promotes the history and culture, as well as respect, of the Native American Indian. *Programs*: Evaluates texts, resource materials and fiction by and about Native peoples; distributes books and materials, especially those written and illustrated by Native persons. *Activity*: Workshops for teachers. *Publications*: Catalog; online books and books foe sale.

PAN-AMERICAN INDIAN ASSOCIATION
8335 Sevigny Dr.
N. Fort Myers, FL 33917-1705
(941) 731-7029; 543-7727
Chief White Bear Barnard, President
Cindy "Spirit Catcher" Barnard, Executive Director
E-mail: panamia@msn.com
Description: A non-profit educational, religious and cultural organization helping individuals research Native Heritage, those who are of Native Heritage who are not enrolled, join PAIA or try for enrollment with their tribe. *Programs*: Ceremonies and lectures; "Quest of the Shield" program for teens/others; regularly scheduled Asi-Lodges. *Publication*: "Whirling Rainbow-Voice of the People," published quarterly. Established in 1984.

PHELPS-STOKES FUND
74 Trinity Place
New York, NY 10006
(212) 619-8100 Fax 619-5108
E-mail: phelps@admin.con2.com
Website: www.psfdc.com
Purpose: Works to promote the education of African & Native Americans by sponsoring research and education studies and fellowship programs.

QUALITY EDUCATION FOR MINORITIES NETWORK
1818 N St., NW, Suite 350
Washington, DC 20036
(202) 659-1818 Fax 659-5408
Shirley M. McBay, President
E-mail: gemnetwork@gem.org
Website: www.gemnetwork.gem.org
Publication: QEM Update, quarterly.

R.A.I.N. RIGHTS FOR ALL INDIGENOUS NATIONS, INC.
R.D. 1, Box 308A • Petersburg, NY 12138
(518) 658-3055; Hank Hazelton
Description: A non-profit educational and action organization dedicated to the survival of Indigenous Nations worldwide.

RESEARCH FOR BETTER SCHOOLS
Native Education Project
112 N. Broad St. • Philadelphia, PA 19102

SACRED RUN FOUNDATION, INC.
Dennis J. Banks, Director
Alice Lambert-Banks, Executive Director
Purpose: Dedicated to promoting Native American culture through spiritual running and special events. *Activities*: Local, national and international multi-cultural spiritual runs - sobriety New Years Eve Powwow; craft weekends; drum performances. *Publication*: Sacred Run Newsletter. Established in 1978; Incorporated in 1990.

SAVE THE CHILDREN FEDERATION
54 Wilton Rd. • Westport, CT 06880
(203) 226-7271; David L. Guyer, President
Purpose: To assist children, families and communities in the U.S. and abroad to achieve social and economic stability through community development and family self-help projects; and to aid victims of disaster. *Activities*: Conducts child sponsorship programs and community development projects, with emphasis on community self-help through grass roots organization as well as training and technical assistance; conducts programs on Indian reservations. *Scholarship*: Ruth Bronson Memorial Scholarship for American Indian Graduate Students. *Publications*: Lifeline Magazine, quarterly; annual reports, and papers on development issues. Library. Established 1932.

SEVENTH GENERATION FUND FOR INDIAN DEVELOPMENT
P.O. Box 4569 • Arcata, CA 95518
(707) 825-7640 Fax 825-7639
Chris Peters, Executive Director
E-mail: of7gen@pacbell.net
Website: www.7genfund.org
Description: Provides seed grants and technical assistance in order to increase self-relaince in Indian communities and decrease government dependency. The fund's title is drawn from the Hau de no sau nee (Six Nations) principle of considering the impact upon the seventh generation in the decision-making process. *Purpose/Goals*: To support and promote the spiritual, cultural, and physical well-being of the Native family. To reclaim and live on aboriginal lands; protect tribal lands and natural resources; redevelop self-sufficient communities through food production, appropriate technologies, and alternative energy yse; restore traditional indigenous forms of political organization or to modify existing governments along traditional lines. *Activities*: Reports on such subjects as Native American rights, Indian family life, and judicial issues and cases affecting American Indians. Maintains small library. *Publication*: Annual report.

S.H.A.R.E. (SACRED HOOP OF AMERICAN RESOURCE EXCHANGE)
114 Cat Rock Rd. • Cos Cob, CT 06807
(203) 622-6525; Tek Nickerson, National Director
Purpose/Goals: To build bridges of understanding and mutual support between the American Indian community & the North American community at large; to restore traditional values to Native youth; to help balance non-Native lives; to help balance Native communities. *Activities/Programs*: Cultural Camp; Sacred Sites Conservancy; Native Oral History Program; SHARE the Warmth Blanket Program; Native American awareness weeks & speaker's bureau; continual networking of employment opportunities; training staff

to manage SHARE programs and then spin them off for independent, wholly owned & operated Native operations. Established in 1984.

SMOKI PEOPLE
147 N. Arizona Ave., P.O. Box 10224
Prescott, AZ 86304 (928) 445-1230
　Michael E. Kennelly, Chief
　Ken Howell, Director
Membership: 1,600. Local business and professional people (non-Indian.) *Purpose*: To perpetuate by authentic artistic reproduction of the age-old ceremonials and dances of Indian tribes of North and South America. *Publication*: Smoki Ceremonials and Snake Dance, annual. Museum. Library. Annual meeting. Established in 1921.

SOCIETY FOR ADVANCEMENT OF CHICANOS & NATIVE AMERICANS IN SCIENCE (SACNAS)
P.O. Box 8526 • Santa Cruz, CA 95061
　(831) 459-0170 Fax 459-0194
　Judit Camacho, Executive Officer
　E-Mail: Info@sacnas.org
　Web site: www.sacnas.org
Membership: 2,000. *Membership*: College professors, science professionals, and students. *Purpose*: To encourage Chicano/Latino and Native American students to pursue graduate education in order to obtain the advanced degrees necessary for research careers and science teaching professions *Activities*: SACNAS Mathematical Science Summer Institute, SACNAS Conference; Graduate School Application Workshops; Conversations With Scientists Roundtable Discussions; K-12 Curriculum; Classroom Science Kits; Faculty Advising Program; Scholarship Fund; Scientific Symposia; Community Service Awards. *Publication*: SACNAS News, quarterly newsletter. Established in 1973.

SOCIETY FOR ETHNOMUSICOLOGY
Indiana University, Morrison Hall 005
Bloomington, IN 47405-2501
　(812) 855-6672 Fax 855-6673
　E-Mail: sem@indiana.edu
Membership: 2,000. Ethnomusicologists, anthropologists, musicologists, and laymen interested in music as an aspect of culture. *Purpose*: Seeks to integrate the study of manifold facets of non-Western music with Western folk and art music. *Awards*: Seeger Prize and Jaap Kunst Prize. *Publications*: Ethnomusicology, 3/yr.; Directory, biennial.; Newsletter, quarterly; publishes monographs, bibliographies and pamphlets. Annual Conference. Established in 1955.

SOCIETY FOR HISTORICAL ARCHAEOLOGY
P.O. Box 30446 • Tucson, AZ 85751
　(724) 886-8006 Fax 886-0182
　Leland G. Ferguson, President
　E-mail: sha@azstarnet.com
　Web site: www.sha.org
Membership: 2,000. *Purpose*: Concerned with the archaeology of the modern world (A.D. 1400-present), with the main focus the era since the beginning of European settlement and the effects on Native American peoples. *Activities*: Promotes scholarly research and the dissemination of knowledge concerning historical archaeology. *Publications*: Historical Archaeology, quarterly journal; quarterly newsletter; special publication series. Annual meeting. Established in 1967.

SOUTHWEST INDIAN RELIEF COUNCIL
P.O. Box 16777 • Mesa, AZ 85211
　(866) 228-0124 Fax (480) 281-0708
　Lisa Begay, Program Coordinator
　E-mail: info@swirc.org
　Website: www.swirc.org
Purpose: To help Native American people improve the quality of their lives by providing opportunities for them to bring about positive changes in their communities. *Activities/Programs*: A non-profit organization which develops self-help programs and emergency relief services for Native Americans on reservations in the Southwest. These services include: emergency food distribution, clothing and shoe distributions, winterization of homes, school supplies, holiday dinners, gifts and stockings for children at Christmas and Easter, baby baskets for new mothers and incentive programs for seniors, adult volunteers and children. *Publication*: Quarterly newsletter. Established in 2000.

SOUTHWESTERN ASSOCIATION FOR INDIAN ARTS, INC.
P.O. Box 969 • Santa Fe, NM 87504-0969
　(505) 983-5220 Fax 983-7647
　Jai Lakshman, Executive Director
　E-mail: info@swaia.org
　Web site: www.swaia.org
Purpose: To develop, sponsor and promote the Santa Fe Indian Market and other events that encourage cultural preservation, intercultural understanding and economic opportunity for American Indians through excellence in the arts. *Activities*: Santa Fe Indian Market - over 600 booths and more than 1,200 Indian artists - the third weekend in August each year. Provides educational programs which benefit the Native American artist. SWAI Fellowships (both youth & adult); lifetime achievement awards in the arts. *Publication*: Indian Market Magazine. Established 1922.

SURVIVAL INTERNATIONAL, U.S.A.
Washington, DC 20008 (202) 265-1077
　Mary George Hardman, Executive Director
Membership: 1,200. *Description*: Individuals concerned with the rights of tribal peoples. *Purpose*: To support tribal groups in their efforts towards self-determination. *Publication*: Survival International News, semiannual; pamphlets and documents. Established in 1979.

SURVIVAL OF AMERICAN INDIAN ASSOCIATIONS
7803-A Samurai Dr., SE • Olympia, WA 98503
　(206) 459-2679; Hank Adams, National Director
Membership: 500. *Activities*: Provides public education on Indian rights and tribal government reform action; supports independent Indian educational institutions; speakers bureau. *Publication*: The Renegade: A Strategy Journal of Indian Opinion, annual. Established 1964.

TEKAKWITHA CONFERENCE NATIONAL CENTER
P.O. Box 6768 • Great Falls, MT 59406
　(406) 727-0147 Fax 452-9845
　Sister Kateri Mitchell, SSA, Executive Director
　E-mail: tekconf@att.net; Website: www.tekconf.org
Membership: 1,800. Catholic missionaries among American Indians; Eskimo and American Indian deacons and lay persons involved in ministry. *Purpose*: To develop Catholic evangelization in the areas of Native American Ministry, catechesis, liturgy, family life, spirituality, and theology. It serves as the Voice, Presence, Identity of the American Indian and Eskimo Catholics by affirming our Faith under the protection of Blessed Kateri Tekakwitha, a Mohawk who lived from 1656 to 1680, and who is a candidate for Sainthood in the Roman Catholic Church. The Conference encourages development of Native American catechists for ministry among their own people. Provides a forum for the exchange of ideas among Catholic Native Americans, Eskimos, and missionaries. Encourages development of Native American ministry by Indian people. *Activities*: Sponsors an annual conference in various regions throughout the country; sponsors two summer ministry: Basic Directions in Native Ministry (nine days) and Native Ministry and Catechesis (five days). *Publications*: Cross and Feathers, five times annual newsletter; Sacramental Series of eight booklets. Library. Annual conference. Established in 1939.

THUNDERBIRD AMERICAN INDIAN DANCERS
c/o Louis Mofsie • McBurney YMCA
215 West 23rd St. • New York, NY 10011
　(201) 587-9633; Louis Mofsie, Director
Membership: 30. Indians and non-Indians who raise money for the Thunderbird Indian Scholarship Fund for Indian students. *Activities*: Offers cultural classes in crafts, singing, dancing, and language; sponsors Indian studies programs for Indian youth; monthly powwows in New York City—open to public. Established in 1956.

TIPI PRESS
St. Joseph's Indian School
P.O. Box 89 • Chamberlain, SD 57325
　(605) 734-6021; Rev. Tom Westhoven
Purpose: To promote better understanding of Siouan culture, and better understanding of Catholic/Christian evangelization among Plains Indian Tribes, and appreciation for Siouan art and artists through prints, calendars, and note cards.

UNITED INDIAN DEVELOPMENT ASSOCIATION
86 S. Cobb Dr. • Marietta, GA 30063
　(770) 494-0431 Fax 494-1236
　E-mail: uida1@uida.org; Website: www.uida.org
Purpose: To develop American Indian economic self-sufficiency through business ownership. *Program*: Business Services. *Activities*: Annual Conference & Trade Show in September.

UNITED INDIAN MISSIONS (UIM) INTERNATIONAL
P.O. Box 336010
Greeley, CO 80633-0601
　(970) 330-7788 Fax 392-2559
　Warren F. Cheek, General Director
　E-mail: uim@uim.org; Website: www.uim.org
Purpose: to establish indigenous churches among Native peoples of North America. *Publication*: UIM Magazine, brochures. Established in 1956.

UNITED NATIONAL INDIAN TRIBAL YOUTH, INC. (UNITY)
P.O. Box 800
Oklahoma City, OK 73101-0800
　(405) 424-3010 Fax 424-3018
　J.R. Cook, Executive Director
　E-Mail: unity@unityinc.org
Purpose: To empower American Indian and Alaska Native youth with the spiritual, mental, physical, and social qualities necessary to strengthen their lives and communities; to establish a National Leadership Training Center for American Indian/Alaska Native Youth through the development of a national UNITY council, annual national leadership development conferences, development of tribal, village, community youth councils, and motivational seminars. *Publications*: UNITY News, quarterly newsletter. Established in 1976.

UNITED NATIVE AMERICANS
2434 Faria Ave. • Pinole, CA 94564
　(415) 758-8160; Lehman L. Brightman, Director
Membership: 12,000. *Purpose*: To promote the general welfare of Native Americans; to establish educational scholarships; provide legal aid, housing and counseling for Indians. Maintains speakers' bureau. *Publication*: Warpath, monthly. Sells historical posters of Native American life. Annual meeting. Established 1968.

UNITED PEOPLES FOUNDATION
Meadowlark Communications
P.O. Box 7218 • Missoula, MT 59807
　(406) 728-2180 Fax 549-3090
　Chris Roberts, President
　E-mail: info@powwowcountry.com
　Web site: www.powwowcountry.com
Purpose: To promote ethnic and Native American arts, culture and dance. *Activities*: Provides scholarships adn educational programs; distribute visual materials on Native American culture....sell books and videos by catalog and on the web; annual Powwow and Cultural Rendezvous, 2nd week in August.

UNITED SOUTH & EASTERN TRIBES, INC. (USET)
711 Stewarts Ferry Pike, Suite 100
Nashville, TN 37214
　(615) 872-7900 Fax 872-7417
　James T. Martin, Executive Director
　E-mail: jtmartin@usetinc.org
　Website: www.oneida-nation.net/uset
Description: A non-profit inter-tribal organization of 24 federally recognized tribes: The Eastern Band of Cherokee (NC), Mississippi Band of Choctaws (MS), Seminole Tribe (FL); Miccosukee Tribe (FL); Chitimacha (LA), Coushatta Tribe (LA); Tunica Biloxi Tribe (LA); Jena Band of Choctaw (LA); Seneca Nation (NY); St. Regis Band of Mohawks (NY); Cayuga Nation (NY); Oneida Nation (NY); Passamaquoddy Pleasant Point (ME); Passamaquoddy Indian Township (ME); Houlton Band of Maliseets (ME), Penobscot Nation (ME); Aroostook Band of Micmac (ME); Mohegan Tribe (CT); Mashantucket Pequot (CT); Poarch Band of Creek (AL); Narragansett Indian Nation (RI); Wampanoag Tribe of Gay Head (Aquinnah) (MA); Alabama Coushatta Tribe (TX); Catawba Nation (SC). *Purpose*: Dedicated to enhancing the development of Indian Tribes; to improve the capabilities of Tribal governments; and assist the member tribes and their governments in dealing effectively with public policy issues; to provide a forum for the

exchange of information and ideas among the 24 USET Tribes; and, it provides a vehicle which allows these tribes to jointly receive contracts and grants from federal and state agencies, as well private sector. *Activities*: 10 USET comittees which deal with tribal justice, education, EMS & fire protection, health, housing, natural resources, social services, community and economic develoipment, culture & heritage, and taxation. provides four $500 scholarships each year to Indian students in the USET service area; administers a Health Information Office; and a Strategic Planning program; The Calumet Development Corp., a for-profit entity of USET, is involved in several financial ventures; the Annual Washington Impact Week in February. Annual Board meeting in December; Semiannual Board meeting in June. Established in 1969.

VIETNAM ERA VETERANS
INTER-TRIBAL ASSOCIATION
805 Rosa • Shawnee, OK 74801
(405) 382-3128
Randall Herrod, National Commander
Bill Haney, Assistant Commander
Membership: 1,000. American Indian veterans representing 200 tribes who served in Vietnam or who served in the armed forces during the Vietnam era. 1964-1975. *Purpose*: To promote a positive image of the Indian Vietnam veteran; to remember fellow servicemen who died in the ward and in the years following; to foster exchange of information on problems related to Vietnam. *Publications*: Redsmoke Indian News, quarterly newsletter; Souvenir Pow-Wow Program, annual; Membership List, periodic; Veteran Small Business Directory; papers. Annual National Pow-Wow. Established in 1981.

VIOLA WHITE WATER FOUNDATION
4225 Concord St.
Harrisburg, PA 17109
(717) 652-2040
Sandy Gutshall, President
Jimmy Little Turtle, Sec./Treas.
Description: Non-profit organization dedicated to helping Native Americans live and educate their children in the traditional ways. "Main goal now is Mohawk Valley settlement in Fonda, NY." *Activities*: Funding of Akwesasne Freedom School, and Mohawk Valley settlement in Fonda, NY. Grants are made to individuals, schools and colleges. *Publication*: quarterly newsletter. Established in 1978.

THE WALKER RESEARCH GROUP
P.O. Box 4147 • Boulder, CO 80306
(303) 492-6719 Fax 492-7970
Website: www.walkerresearchgroup.com
Candace J. Arroyo de Walker, President
Research Associates: Deward E. Walker, Jr., PhD; Sylvester (Bus) Lahren, PhD; Larry Pritchard, MA; David Stepehnson, JD, PhD; James Hester, PhD; Roderick Sprague, PhD. *Purpose*: To provide a wide range of applied social science services to Native Americans and other clients with specialized needs. "We have become familiar with the provisions and requirements of the Federal Heritage Legislation. Specifically, we have extensive experience with the Archaeological Resource Protection Act (ARPA), the National Historic Preservation Act as amended, Native American Graves Protection & Repatriation Act (NAGPRA), American Indian Religious Freedom Act (AIRFA), and Executive Orders including endangered species, sacred sites, and tribal consultation."

WASHINGTON CONSULTING &
MANAGEMENT ASSOCIATES, INC.
P.O. Box 5169 • Arlington, VA 22205
(703) 532-2210 Fax 532-0704
Ted Knight, President
Purpose: To provide quality training, technical assistance and consulting to the Native American community in the areas of: health programs, social services, economic development, elder care programs, housing, comprehensive parenting programs and tribal governance. *Activities*: On-site training programs and consultation. *Publications*: Starting Your Own Successful Indian Business; Preparing the Winning ANA Grant Application; Selected Private Foundations Supporting Native American Programs; Pursuing the Winning Grant; Infant Mortality Reduction Program Operations Guide; Planning for Colleges and Universities: The President's Guide. Established in 1979.

WESLEYAN NATIVE AMERICAN MINISTRIES
P.O. Box 7038 • Rapid City, SD 57709
(605) 343-9054 Fax 343-9219
Adrian Jacobs, Director
E-mail: wnam@wnam.org
Website: www.wnam.org
Publication: Native Reflections.

WHITE BISON
6145 Lehman Dr. #200
Colorado Springs, CO 80918
(719) 548-1000 Fax 548-9407
Website: www.whitebison.org
E-mail: info@whitebison.org

WINGS OF AMERICA
The Earth Circle Foundation, Inc.
1601 Cerrillos Rd. • Santa Fe, NM 87505
(505) 982-6761 Fax 989-8995
Edison Eskeets, Executive Director
Geoff Hollister, Chairperson
William E. Channing, Emeritus
E-mail: wingsamerica@aol.com
Website: www.wingsofamerica.org
Description: An American Indian youth development program. *Purpose*: To enhance the quality of life of American Indian youth. In partnership with Native communities, Wings uses running as a catalyst to empower American Indian & Alaskan Native youth to take pride in themselves and their cultural identity, leading to increased self esteem, health and wellness, leadership and hope, balance and harmony. *Programs*: The American Indian Running Coaches' Clinic; Wings Leadership/Camp Facilitator Training; Wings Running & Fitness Camps (for children 6-14 years old); Partnership & Outreach; Wind Messenger Foot races. Established 1988.

WOMEN OF ALL RED NATIONS
P.O. Box 2508 • Rapid City, SD 57709
Madonna Thunderhawk, Field Coordinator
Description: A grass roots organization of American Indian women seeking to advance the Native-American movement. *Activities*: Establish local chapters to work on issues like sterilization abuse and women's health, adoption and foster care abuse, community education, and problems caused by energy resource development; publishes reports on health problems of American Indian women. Established in 1978.

WORDCRAFT CIRCLE OF NATIVE
WRITERS & STORYTELLERS
4905 El Aguila Place, NW
Albuquerque, NM 87120-1009
(505) 352-9118
Lee Francis, National Director
E-mail: wordcraft@sockets.net
Website: www.wordcraftcircle.org
Description: Volunteer organization of 200 active members and 320 inactive members. *Activities*: Host/hold "Gatherings" throughout yhe U.S. Presents honors and awards annually to Native and non-Native individuals in a variety of areas: Writer of the Year in Poetry; Writer of the Year in Prose (fiction, non-fiction, autobiography, CD recording, newspaper writing/editing...etc.) These honors are "open to the world." Honors limited to Wordcraft Circle members only are Wordcrafter of the Year, Intern of the Year. We also present Honors for Storyteller of the Year (traditional, contemporary, readings, presentations, lectures) and Publisher of the Year (national, regional, small press, tribal, university, and outside the U.S.), Literary Agent of the Year, Sovereign Indigenous Native Nation of the Year. *Publication*: On-line juried journal: "Native Realities" - available to the general public. *Dues*: Regular, $40; Elder/Student, $25.

WORLD INDIGENOUS GAMES
34 Rolling Thunder Dr. • Jaspa, GA 30143
(770) 735-6275 (phone & fax)
Chipa Wolf, Executive Director
Purpose: To assure representation of the many skills, talents and athletics of Indigenous Peoples, while respectfully preserving the cultural significance of the former. Provides athletic competition featuring the traditional games played by Native Americans. Also, other sports and games played by native populations from other regions of the world, and displays of food, dance, costume, & art, all representing the cultures of indigenous people throughout the world. Established 1992.

NATIVE AMERICAN OWNED & OPERATED
FINANCIAL INSTITUTIONS

BANKS

BLACKFEET NATIONAL BANK
P.O. Box 730 • Browning, MT 59417
(406) 338-7000; Eloise Cobell, Contact
Merged to form the Native American Bank

FIRST OKLAHOMA BANK OF SHAWNEE
P.O. Box 68 • Shawnee, OK 74802
(405) 275-8830

FIRST STATE BANK OF OKLAHOMA
P.O. Box 459 • Hulbert, OK 74441
(918) 772-2572; J.D. Colbert, Contact

LUMBEE GUARANTEE BANK
P.O. Box 908 • Pembroke, NC 28372
(919) 521-9707

CREDIT UNIONS

FIRST AMERICAN CREDIT UNION
1001 N. Pinal Ave. • Casa Grande, AZ 85222
(602) 871-4767

SISSETON-WAHPETON FEDERAL CREDIT UNION
P.O. Box 627 • Agency Village, SD 57262
(605) 698-3462 Fax 698-3907
John R. Stewart, Director
Purpose: To provide consumer credit to members and employees of the Sisseton-Wahpeton Sioux Tribe.

FIRST AMERICAN COMPANIES;
EQUIPMENT LEASING & SECURITIES
527 Marquette Ave. #1600
Minneapolis, MN 55402-1302
(612) 305-1252 Fax 305-1064
John R. Herrera, MBA, J.D., President
Description: Full service equipment lessor and full service securities broker - dealer. Clients include Fortune 500 companies, non-profits, governmental units including Indian tribes. We are a certified Indian-owned company. Established in 1991.

RESERVATION-BASED LOAN FUNDS

THE LAKOTA FUND
P.O. Box 340 • Kyle, SD 57752
(605) 455-2500; Elsie Meeks, Executive Director
Purpose: Formed to help build a private sector economy on the Pine Ridge Reservation by providing loans, technical assistance & business training; and arts & crafts marketing assistance tribal members. *Activities*: Loans for small business & microenterprises. *Publication*: The Lakota Fund newsletter.

NEE-SHOCH-HA-CHEE
P.O. Box 748 • Winnebago, NE 68071
(402) 878-2972; John Vandell, Contact

SICANGU ENTERPRISE CENTER
P.O. Box 205, 516 West 2nd St.
Mission, SD 57555
(605) 856-2955 Fax 856-4671
Cheryl Crazy Bull, Executive Director
Mary Whiting, Assistant Director
Phyllis Halligan, Enterprise Development Specialist
Kathy Frederick, Mktg. & Development Specialist
Purpose: To promote and develop micro-enterprises (home-based businesses), affordable, culturally appropriate housing, community revitalization and cultural arts. *Activities*: Youth Enterprise Project. *Publications*: Poster and workbook series for youth that is based on culturally relevant economic knowledge. Established 1990.

THE TINAA CORPORATION
320 W. Willoughby, Suite 210
Juneau, AK 99801 (907) 463-7123
Dawn Dinwoodie, Contact

REGIONAL, STATE & LOCAL ORGANIZATIONS
(Includes Urban Indian Centers)

This section is an alpha-geographical listing of state and regional agencies and organizations concerned mainly with Native-American affairs in their particular state and/or region of the U.S.

ALABAMA

ALABAMA DEPARTMENT OF EDUCATION
Coordinator of Indian Education
Gordon Persons Bldg. • 50 N. Ripley St.
MONTGOMERY, AL 36130
(205) 242-8199 Fax 242-8024
Carolyn Carter, Contact
Serves as the liaison for the State Dept. of Education with the Indian Affairs Section of the U.S. Dept. of Education, the Indian Education Technical Assistance Center, the Alabama Commission on Indian Affairs, and local Indian education coordinators.

ALABAMA INDIAN AFFAIRS COMMISSION
MONTGOMERY, AL 36104
(800) 436-8261; (334) 242-2831 Fax 240-3408
Darla F. Graves, Executive Director
Purpose: To serve as a liaison agency between Alabama's seven state-recognized tribes (one of which is federally recognized), Indian individuals and the various levels of government and private sector entities. *Activities*: Sponsors an annual statewide pow-wow to raise money for the Alabama Indian Children's Scholarship Fund. Also does speaking engagements, presentations, workshops and seminars for schools, churches, military, governmental agencies, etc. regarding Alabama Indians. *Publications*: Annual Report; occasional newsletters. Established in 1984.

ALASKA

The Alaska Native Claims Settlement Act of December 18, 1971, established regional village corporations and associations, both profit and non-profit. Listings are arranged alphabetically.

ALASKA FEDERATION OF NATIVES
1577 C St. #300
ANCHORAGE, AK 99501-5133
(907) 276-7989; 258-6917
Julie E. Kitka, President
Membership: 77,000. Alaskan Natives (Aleut, Eskimo, and Indian); regional profit and non-profit corporations. *Purpose*: To act as lobbyist and advocate on behalf of statewide Native community and to provide technical assistance to these groups. *Activities*: Inuit Circumpolar Conference - An international organization of Inuit (Eskimo) from Alaska, Canada and Greenland holding non-governmental organizations status with the United Nations. The ICC is committed to upholding and advancing the cultural, economic, political, and civil rights of indigenous people across the Arctic rim countries and worldwide. *Publications*: Monthly newsletter; annual report. Maintains biographical archives and library of government reports and economic material. Annual meeting in October. Founded 1966.

ALASKA LEGAL SERVICES CORP.
1016 W. Sixth St., Suite 200
ANCHORAGE, AK 99501 (907) 272-6282
Purpose: To provide legal assistance to Alaskan Natives throughout the state.

ALASKA NATIVE COALITION
P.O. Box 200908
ANCHORAGE, AK 99520
(907) 258-6917
Purpose: Seeks to protect Native ancestral lands, strengthen tribal governments, and protect the subsistence way of life. It has also organized to monitor the 1991 legislative effort, in response to ANCSA provisions, which the Coalition believes threaten Native communities and their ancestral lands. Founded 1986.

ALASKA STATE COUNCIL ON THE ARTS
411 W. 4th Ave., Suite 1E
ANCHORAGE, AK 99501
(907) 297-1558 Fax 279-4330
Purpose: To provide grants to support Native Alaskan art and crafts.

ALASKAN ARTS
3503 Dobrandt
ANCHORAGE, AK 99503
(907) 563-7753
Purpose: To sponsor activites to support Native Alaskan arts.

ALEUTIAN PRIBILOFF ISLAND ASSOCIATION
201 E. 3rd Ave.
ANCHORAGE, AK 99501-2544
(907) 276-2700
Native non-profit association. Serves as a health clinic.

ANCHORAGE NATIVE ASSEMBLY
Box 201889 • ANCHORAGE, AK 99520
(907) 276-9509
Purpose: To represent the special concerns of Alaska's native peoples.

CHUGACH NATIVES, INCORPORATED
ANCHORAGE, AK 99503 (907) 276-1080
Native for-profit regional corporation.

COOK INLET NATIVE ASSOCIATION
ANCHORAGE, AK 99503 (907) 278-4641
Franklin L. Berry, Executive Director
Native non-profit association of approximately 1,500 Alaskan Natives and American Indians dedicated to nurturing pride in the heritage and traditions of Alaska Natives, and preserving the customs, folklore, and art of the people. Operates a health clinic, Alaska Native Community Center. *Publication*: Trail Blazer, quarterly newsletter.

COOK INLET REGION, INC.
P.O. Box 93330 • ANCHORAGE, AK 99509
(907) 274-8638 Fax 279-8836
E-Mail: jryan@ciri.com
Description: Native for-profit regional corporation representing about 7,000 Alaska Natives of southcentral Alaska. *Activities*: Educational, employment and human service programs. CIRI has been instrumental in the development of the Alaska Native Heritage Center, Inc., which is seeking to build an Alaska Native cultural and educational center in Anchorage; and Koahnic Broadcast Corp., parent organization fort he nation's first Native-owned urban public radio station. *Affiliations*: Cook Inlet Tribal Council; Alaska's People, Inc.; Cook Inlet Housing Authority; The CIRI Foundation; Southcentral Foundation.

KONIAG, INC.
4300 B St. • ANCHORAGE, AK 99503
(907) 561-2668
Sponsors a variety of economic activities for the benefit of its constituency.

NATIVE SPIRITUAL CULTURE COUNCILS, INC.
3212 W. 29th Ave. • ANCHORAGE, AK 99503
(907) 243-0135
Non-profit organization comprised of Alaskan Native Aleut, Eskimo, Indian and Native Americans formed for bringing about spiritual rebirth and reawakening of the native people.

ARCTIC VILLAGE TRADITIONAL COUNCIL
P.O. Box 22050
ARCTIC VILLAGE, AK 99722
(907) 587-5320 Trimble Gilbert, Chief
(907) 587-5226 Lincoln Tritt, 2nd Chief
Tribe: Gwitch'in Athapascan. *Elected officials*: Sarah James, Rose Lee, Louie John, Steve Lee, Jim Christian. Fairbanks Agency.

ARCTIC SLOPE NATIVE ASSOCIATION
P.O. Box 566 • BARROW, AK 99723
Native non-profit association.

ARCTIC SLOPE REGIONAL CORPORATION
P.O. Box 129 • BARROW, AK 99723
(907) 852-8633/8533
Native for-profit regional corporation.

ESKIMO, INC.
P.O. Box 536 • BARROW, AK 99723
(907) 852-3835

NORTH SLOPE BOROUGH HEALTH CORPORATION
P.O. Box 69 • BARROW, AK 99723
(907) 852-3999
Health Clinic.

ASSOCIATION OF VILLAGE COUNCIL PRESIDENTS, INC.
P.O. Box 219 • BETHEL, AK 99559
(907) 543-3521
Myron P. Naneng, President
Purpose: To provide human development, social services, and other culturally relevant programs for the people; to promote self-determination protection and enhancement of our culture and traditions through a working partnership with member villages of the Yukon-Kuskokwim Delta. *Activities*: Childcare Development services; economic development; education, employment & training; family justice; housing improvement; social services; tribal operations; financial aid-higher education scholarships; operates Yup'ik Cultural Center & Museum; Head Start Program. Founded 1964.

YUKON-KUSKOKWIM HEALTH CORPORATION
P.O. Box 528 • BETHEL, AK 99559
(907) 543-3321

COPPER RIVER HEALTH AUTHORITY
P.O. Drawer H
COPPER CENTER, AK 99573
(907) 822-3521
Health clinic of the Copper River Native Association.

COPPER RIVER NATIVE ASSOCIATION
P.O. Drawer G
COPPER RIVER, AK 99573
(907) 822-5241
Native non-profit association.

BRISTOL BAY AREA HEALTH CORPORATION
P.O. Box 10235 • DILLINGHAM, AK 99576
(907) 842-5266/7; 842-5201 (hospital)
Health clinic affiliated with Bristol Bay Native Association.

BRISTOL BAY NATIVE ASSOCIATION
P.O. Box 310 • DILLINGHAM, AK 99576
(907) 842-5257/5258
Native non-profit association. Head Start Program.

ALASKA NATIVE LANGUAGE CENTER
P.O. Box 757680 • FAIRBANKS, AK 99775
(907) 474-7874 Fax 474-6586
Purpose: To document the languages of Indians and Eskimos in Alaska.

DOYON LIMITED
201 1st Ave. • FAIRBANKS, AK 99701
(907) 452-4755
Native for-profit regional corporation.

FAIRBANKS NATIVE ASSOCIATION
310 1st Ave., 2nd Fl.
FAIRBANKS, AK 99701
(907) 452-1648
Samuel S. Demientieff, Executive Director
Purpose: To provide professional, quality human services to membership and Fairbanks community; to preserve Native culture and improve the quality of life for the community. *Programs*: Elders program; Public Assistance and Family Counseling; Employment, Education (small scholarships); Treatment Center for Alcohol and Drug Abuse; Substance Abuse Counselor Training; Head Start Program. *Publication*: Monthly newsletter. Library. Established in 1960.

INSTITUTE OF ALASKA NATIVE ARTS
FAIRBANKS, AK
(907) 456-7491 Fax 451-7268
Ron Manook, President
Susheila Khera, Exec. Director
Katherine Hunt, Program Director
Purpose: "To foster the continuation of Alaska Native traditions into contemporary expressions of the high-

est quality." *Activities*: Programs and services to enhance the artistic, professional and economic status
of Alaska Native artists and to heighten awareness of
Alaska Native aesthetics and traditions through exhibitions, workshops, scholarships, publications and
technical assistance. Operates Information Center
consisting of an artists registry of hard copy files and
slides; photographic files; and resource library with
over 600 titles and audio and video tapes. Offers scholarships for academic study. *Publication*: Journal of
Alaska Native Arts, quarterly; exhibit catalogs and resource materials on Alaska Native arts. Established
in 1976.

TANANA CHIEFS CONFERENCE, INC.
122 1st Ave. • FAIRBANKS, AK 99701
    (907) 452-8251; Sarah Kuenzil, Director
Regional non-profit corporation. Maintains
a health clinic. Head Start Program.

AHTNA, INC.
P.O. Box 649 • GLENNALLEN, AK 99588
    (907) 822-3476; Wilson Justin, President
A native for-profit regional corporation. *Activities*: Construction, real estate; student loans and scholarships,
and loans to shareholders for business ventures. *Publications*: Annual reports; Shareholder's Handbook. Library.

**ASSOCIATION OF ALASKA
HOUSING AUTHORITIES**
Copper River basin Regional Housing Authority
P.O. Box 89 • GLENNALLEN, AK 99588
    (907) 822-3633 FAX 822-3662
Jeff Doty, Executive Director

KLUKWAN HERITAGE FOUNDATION
P.O. Box 1389 • HAINES, AK 99827
Janice Hill, President

ATHABASCA CULTURAL JOURNEYS
P.O. Box 10, HUSLIA, AK 99746
(800) 423-0094 Fax (907) 452-8148.
Tourism project

**ALASKA DEPT. OF COMMUNITY
& REGIONAL AFFAIRS**
P.O. Box 112100 • JUNEAU, AK 99811
    (907) 465-4700
Edgae P. Blatchford, Commissioner

ALASKA DEPT. OF EDUCATION
Rural Native & Education Programs
P.O. Box F • JUNEAU, AK 99811
    (907) 465-8716 Fax 465-3396

ALASKA OFFICE OF THE GOVERNOR
P.O. Box A • JUNEAU, AK 99811
    (907) 465-3500
Mike Irwin, Special Staff Assistant

ASSISTANT FOR ALASKA NATIVE AFFAIRS
Office of the Governor
Pouch A • JUNEAU, AK 99811

**CENTRAL COUNCIL OF THE TLINGIT
& HAIDA INDIAN TRIBES OF ALASKA**
320 W. Willoughby Ave. #300
JUNEAU, AK 99801 (907) 585-1432
    Edward K. Thomas, President
Under jurisdiction of Southeast Agency
of the Bureau of Indian Affairs.

SEALASKA CORPORATION
1 Sealaska Plaza #400 • JUNEAU, AK 99801
    (907) 586-1512 Fax 586-1826
    Leo H. Barlow, President & CEO
    E-Mail: Vikki.mata@sealaska.com
    Web site: http://www.sealaska.com
Description: A regional Native for-profit corporation,
established by Congress under the Alaska Native
Claims Settlement Act of 1971. *Activities*: Sealaska
Timber Corp.; Forest Products Co.; Sealaska Heritage
Foundation. *Publications*: Sealaska Shareholder, bi-
monthly tabloid newspaper, also available on the
Internet; annual reports; Sealaska Heritage Founda-
tion publishes books and videos on cultural subjects.

SEALASKA HERITAGE FOUNDATION
1 Sealaska Plaza #201 • JUNEAU, AK 99801

(907) 463-4844
David G. Katzeek, Executive Director
Timothy Wilson, Development Director
Encourages and promotes the preservation of the arts
and culture of the Tlingit, Haida, and Tsimshian people
of Southeast Alaska through programs in language and
cultural studies, traditional celebrations, scholarship-
heritage studies, tribal archives, and Naa Kahidi theatre. *Publication*: Naa Kaani, a quarterly newsletter.

SOUTHEAST ALASKA REGIONAL HEALTH CORP.
3245 Hospital Dr. • JUNEAU, AK 99801
    (907) 463-4040 Fax 463-4012

TLINGIT/HAIDA CENTRAL COUNCIL
320 W. Willoughby Ave. #300
JUNEAU, AK 99801 (907) 585-1432
    Edward K. Thomas, President

**KENAITZE INDIAN TRIBE EXECUTIVE
COMMITTEE/TRIBAL COUNCIL**
P.O. Box 988 • KENAI, AK 99611
    (907) 283-3633
    Ms. Claire Swan, Chairperson
Serve more than 1,750 Alaska Natives on the Kenai
Peninsula. After three years of litigation, the Kenaitze
Tribe recently won a land-mark Federal Court deci-
sion restoring the Kenaitze Indian Tribal members the
right to enjoy their traditional and customary subsis-
tence fishing rights on the Kenai Peninsula. Those
rights had been denied for 40 years by the State of
Alaska.

KETCHIKAN INDIAN CORPORATION
429 Deermont Ave. • KETCHIKAN, AK 99901
    (907) 225-5158
A nonprofit Indian-controlled corporation.

KODIAK AREA NATIVE ASSOCIATION
3449 E. Rezanos Dr. • KODIAK, AK 99615
    (907) 486-5725; Gordon L. Pullar, President
Description: A native non-profit association promoting pride on the part of the natives of Alaska in their
heritage and traditions; promotes the physical, economic, and social well-being of the natives of Alaska.
Activities: Over 40 programs administered under the
Department of Health; education and family services;
community and economic development; health center. *Scholarships*: Higher education and adult vocational training scholarships funded by the Bureau of
Indian Affairs; education and social work scholarships
funded by the Department of Health and Human Services; Skip Eaton Scholarship, an independent local
award. Library.

MANIILAQ ASSOCIATION
P.O. Box 256 • KOTZEBUE, AK 99752
    (800) 478-3312; (907) 442-3311 Fax 442-2381
    Joseph A. Ballot, President
Description: A native non-profit association serving 12
Alaskan Eskimo villages ranging from 100 to 3,000 in
population. *Purpose*: Committed to individual
responsibilty for health and quality care through tribal
self-governance. *Activities*: Provide health, tribal and
social services in the Northwest Arctic Borough region
of Alaska. Established in 1966.

NANA REGIONAL CORPORATION
P.O. Box 49 • KOTZEBUE, AK 99752
    (907) 442-3301
A native for-profit regional corporation.

METLAKATLA INDIAN COMMUNITY COUNCIL
P.O. Box 8 • METLAKATLA, AK 99926
    (907) 886-4441 Fax 886-7997
    Casey Nelson, Mayor

BERING STRAITS ESKIMO VOCATION PROJECT
c/o University of Alaska at Nome
NOME, AK 97862 (907) 443-2201
Purpose: To prepare Native Americans
for employment.

BERING STRAITS NATIVE CORPORATION
P.O. Box 1008 • NOME, AK 99762
    (907) 443-5252
A native non-profit regional corporation sponsoring a
variety of economic and human service activities for
the benefit of its constituency, including an arts & crafts
cooperative.

KAWERAK, INC.
P.O. Box 948 • NOME, AK 99762
    (907) 443-5231
    Loretta Bullard, President
    Eileen Norbert, Vice President
    web site: www.kawerak.org
Description: A Native non-profit association organized
to promote the social and economic welfare of resi-
dents in 20 villages in the Bering Straits Region; pro-
vides services to three culturally distinct groups of
Eskimo people (Inupiaq, Yup'ik and Siberian Yupik).
Activities: Eskimo Heritage Program; Education, Em-
ployment & Training; Community services; Human &
Family Services Natural Resources. *Publication*:
"Kaniqsirugut News," joint newsletter with Norton
Sound Health Corp. Established 1973.

NORTON SOUND HEALTH CORPORATION
P.O. Box 966 • NOME, AK 99762
    (907) 443-3311
    Carolyn Michels, President
Description: A health care organization formed to improve the mental and physical health of the people of
the region to the highest possible levels through education, preventive programs and high quality health
care; and assist in creating a healthy and economically positive environment. *Publication*: Newsletter,
jointly with Kawerak, Inc. Medical Library. Established
in 1970.

SOVEREIGNTY NETWORK
HC04 Box 9880 • PALMER, AK 99645

**SOUTHEAST ALASKA INDIAN
CULTURAL CENTER**
106 Metlakatla St. • SITKA, AK 99835
    (907) 747-8061; Ellen Hays, Executive Director
Purpose: To displays native arts produced in the Center over the past 20 years, including wood carving,
silverwork, costumes, and robes. *Activities*: Audiovisual programs; provides demonstrations of traditional
native arts such as woodcarving, costume design, and
metalworking that are representative of the Tlingit
people and Southeast Alaska. Established in 1968.

ARIZONA

DINEH COOPERATIVES, INC.
P.O. Box 569 • CHINLE, AZ 86503
    (520) 674-3411
Purpose: To establish profit-making businesses and
creates jobs to improve the quality of life in the Navajo Nation.

FLAGSTAFF MISSION TO THE NAVAJOS, INC.
6 W. Cherry St. • FLAGSTAFF, AZ 86001
    (520) 774-2802
Purpose: To serve Navajos living in its area. Serves
as headquarters for the Mission's seven Navajo
churches on the Navajo Reservation.

INDIAN BIBLE INSTITUTE
2918 N. Aris • FLAGSTAFF, AZ 86001
    (520) 774-3890
Purpose: To provide bible study instruction to Native
Americans living in the greater Flagstaff area.

**NATIVE AMERICANS FOR
COMMUNITY ACTION, INC.**
Flagstaff Indian Center
2717 N. Steves Blvd. #11
FLAGSTAFF, AZ 86004
    (520) 526-2968 Fax 526-0708
    Rick Tewa, Jr., Executive Director
    Willard S. Gilbert, Board President
Purpose: A community based organization to meet the
needs of Native Americans residing off reservation in
Flagstaff. *Programs*: Family health center; substance
abuse counseling; child & family counseling; training
assistance & employment; adult education; social services; youth & elders programs; and economic development. Established in 1971.

APACHE CULTURE CENTER
P.O. Box 507 • FORT APACHE, AZ 85926
    (520) 338-4625
Purpose: To preserve and protect Apache culture.

INDIAN CHILDREN'S PROGRAM
Good Shepard Mission
FORT DEFIANCE, AZ 86504
(520) 729-5986 Fax 729-5856
Ela M. Yazzie-King, Coordinator
Purpose: To perform diagnostic services for children with special needs; to assist in health and education problems for Native American children in Arizona, Utah and New Mexico. *Activities*: Provides assessments in occupational, physical therapy, speech and language, psychological and vocational, and training for parents and agencies. Library. Established in 1991.

NATIVE AMERICAN FINANCE
OFFICERS ASSOCIATION
P.O. Box 170 • FORT DEFIANCE, AZ 86504
(520) 729-6218 Fax 729-2135
Marlene Lynch, President

NAVAJO NATION BUSINESS ASSOCIATION
P.O. Box 1217 • KAYENTA, AZ 86033
(520) 697-3534 Fax 697-3464
Richard Mike, President

ARIZONA NATIVE AMERICAN BUSINESS
DEVELOPMENT CENTER (AZNABDC)
953 E. Juanita Ave. • MESA, AZ 85204
(480) 545-1298 Fax 545-4208
Michael Beeman, Project Director
 E-mail: ncaiedbeem@aol.com
Elaine Young, MPSP Director
 E-mail: ncaiedely@aol.com
Project operated by the National Center for for American Indian Enterprise Development in cooperation with the U.S. Department of Commerce, Minority Business Development Agency. Provides management and technical assistance for Native Americans residing in Arizona. Available for all stages of business from start-up to expansion. Operates the Marketing & Procurement Services Program (MPSP)

ARIZONA COMMISSION OF INDIAN AFFAIRS
1400 W. Washington St. #300
PHOENIX, AZ 85007
(602) 542-3123 Fax 542-3223
Ron S. Lee, Executive Director
Purposes: To improve state/tribal relationships in Arizona; to identify state and/or Indian concerns, to research, analyze and evaluate information gathered and to disseminate that information. *Activities*: Commission's staff attends Indian-related meetings, confers with state, federal, local and tribal government officials. *Publication*: "Tribal Directory," directs Indians to the right organizations for their specific needs.

ARIZONA DEPARTMENT OF EDUCATION
Indian Education Unit
1535 W. Jefferson St. • PHOENIX, AZ 85007
(602) 542-4391 Fax 542-3099
Kathryn Stevens, Director

ARIZONA INDIAN AFFAIRS COMMISSION
1645 W. Jefferson, Rm. 127
PHOENIX, AZ 85007 (602) 542-3123

INDIAN COMMUNITY HEALTH SERVICE
3008 N. 3rd St. • PHOENIX, AZ 85012-3021
(602) 263-8094; Erma Mundy, Executive Director

NATIVE AMERICAN MINISTRY OF PRESENCE
1013 North 13th St. • PHOENIX, AZ 85013
(602) 254-7941

NATIVE AMERICAN PROGRAM
OF PARENTS ANONYMOUS OF AZ
2701 N. 16th St. #316 • PHOENIX, AZ 85006
(602) 248-0428
Purpose: To combat child abuse/neglect among Native American families in Maricopa County.

PHOENIX INDIAN CENTER, INC.
2601 North 3rd St. #100
PHOENIX, AZ 85004
(602) 264-6768 Fax 263-7822
Jo Lynn Gentry-Lewis, President of Board
Floyd Dallas, Vice President of Board
Faron Jack, Interim Executive Director
Website: www.phxindcenter.org
Purpose: To promote the social and economic self-sufficiency of the American Indian population in

Maricopa County. *Programs*: Employment & Training; Family & Children Services; Education. Established in 1947.

FOUR RIVERS INDIAN LEGAL SERVICES
P.O. Box 68 • SACATON, AZ 85247
(520) 562-3369
La Nita Plummer & Roger Sigal, Contacts

INDIAN LAW SECTION OF
ARIZONA BAR ASSOCIATION
P.O. Box 400 • SACATON, AZ 85247
(520) 562-3611; Rod Lewis, Chairperson

SOUTHWEST INDIAN HOUSING ASSOCIATION
Gila River Dept. of Community Housing
P.O. Box 528 • SACATON, AZ 85247
(520) 562-3904 Fax 562-3927
Joyce Eddie, Executive Director

APACHES FOR CULTURAL PRESERVATION
San Carlos Apache Reservation
P.O. Box 249 • SAN CARLOS, AZ 85550
(520) 475-2494
Wendsler Nosie, Sr., Co-Chairperson

APACHE SURVIVAL COALITION
P.O. Box 1237 • SAN CARLOS, AZ 85550
(520) 475-2543, or 294-1863
Ola Cassadore Davis, Chairperson

NATIVE AMERICAN COMMUNICATION
& CAREER DEVELOPMENT
P.O. Box 1281 • SCOTTSDALE, AZ 85252
(602) 483-8212
Purpose: To help Native American youth develop career and educational plans which take full advantage of their abilities.

HOPI CULTURAL CENTER
P.O. Box 67 • SECOND MESA, AZ 86043
(520) 734-2401
Purpose: To preserve Hopi traditions, customs and artifacts and to disseminate and display them.

DESERT INDIAN DANCERS
c/o Papgo Tribe • SELLS, AZ 85634
(520) 383-3250
A Native American performing organization.

TOHONO O'ODHAM KI:KI ASSOCIATION
P.O. Box 790 • SELLS, AZ 85634
(520) 383-3202 or 383-3571
Peter Soto, Executive Director
Description: A tribally designed housing entity.

TUBA CITY REGIONAL HEALTH CARE CORP.
167 N. Main St., P.O. Box 600
TUBA CITY, AZ 86045
(928) 283-2432 Fax 283-2901
Christine Begay, Contact
Website: www.tcrhcc.org
E-mail: cbegay@tcimc.ihs.gov

ARIZONA ARCHAEOLOGICAL
& HISTORICAL SOCIETY
Arizona State Museum
U. of Arizona • TUCSON, AZ 85721
(520) 621-4011; Ronald H. Towner, Director
Purpose: To encourage scholarly pursuits in areas of history and anthropology of the southwestern U.S. and Northern Mexico; to encourage the preservation of archaeological and historical sites; to publish the results of archaeological, historical, and ethnographic investigations; and to provide educational opportunities through lectures, field trips, and other activities. Provides scholarship, research and travel grants. *Publication*: Kiva: The Journal of Southwestern Anthropology and History. Established in 1916.

TRADITIONAL INDIAN ALLIANCE
2925 S. 12th Ave. • TUCSON, AZ 85713
(520) 882-0555 Fax 623-6529

TUCSON INDIAN CENTER
TUCSON, AZ 85702
(520) 884-7131 Fax 884-0240
William Quiroga, Executive Director
Purpose: To provide services to the urban Indian population of Pima County. *Activities/programs*: Employ-

ment & Training Services (vocational training); Housing Assistance for emergency shelter; also Counseling & Prevention activities to youth at risk for drug & gang involvement, crisis intervention; and referrals to other resources. Established in 1963.

DINEBEINNA NAHILNA BE AGADITAHE
P.O. Box 306 • WINDOW ROCK, AZ 86515
(520) 871-4151
Purpose: To provide legal assistance to Navajos and other Indians in Arizona, New Mexico, and Utah.

ARKANSAS

AMERICAN INDIAN CENTER OF ARKANSAS
235 N. Greenwood • FORT SMITH, AR 72901
(501) 785-5149 Fax 785-3510
Virginia Henry, Contact
Affiliate of Little Rock center. See listing below.

AMERICAN INDIAN CENTER OF ARKANSAS
1100 N. University #143
LITTLE ROCK, AR 72207-6344
(800) 441-4513; (501) 666-9032 Fax 666-5875
Paul S. Austin, Director
E-mail: aicpaul@aol.com
Purpose: To advance the social, cultural and economic well-being of Indian people residing in Arkansas through job training. *Program*: Indian Manpower Program offers employment assistance, training and counseling. *Publication*: "Lodge Tales," quarterly newsletter. Established in 1977.

ARKANSAS DEPARTMENT OF EDUCATION
Federal Programs, 34 Capitol Mall, Rm 205-B
LITTLE ROCK, AR 72201
(501) 682-4268; Clarence Lovell, Contact

CALIFORNIA

CALIFORNIA NATIONS INDIAN GAMING ASSN.
Website: www.cniga.com; (916) 448-8706
Anthony Miranda (Luiseno), Chairperson
Jacob L. Coin, (Hopi) Executive Director
E-mail: jlcoin@cniga.com

RESOURCES FOR INDIAN STUDENT EDUCATION
109 North St. • ALTURAS, CA 96101
(916) 233-2226; April Go Forth, Director

CENTER FOR INDIAN
COMMUNITY DEVELOPMENT
Humboldt State University
Brero House 93 • ARCATA, CA 95521
(707) 826-3711; Lois Risling, Director
Activities: Works with tribes, organizations and Indian communities to develop educational, economic and social programs to help gain self-determination.

UNITED INDIAN HEALTH SERVICES, INC.
1600 Weeot Way • ARCATA, CA 95521
(707) 825-5000
Jerome Simone, Director

AMERICAN INDIAN CENTER
OF CENTRAL CALIFORNIA
P.O. Box 607, 32980 Auberry Rd.
AUBERRY, CA 93602
(209) 855-2705 Fax 855-2695
David Works, Chairperson
Orie Medicinebull, Executive Director
Description: Educational entity seeking academic and social advancement for American Indian students. *Activities*: Pre-school to high school to college emphasis including: Indian education; California Indian Education Center; American Indian Women's Association; videotapes with handbook, produced and directed by Orie Medicinebull, "Colliding Worlds," "Visions of Youth," "Success for American Indian Children." Library. Established in 1989.

BIG PINE INDIAN EDUCATION CENTER
P.O. Box 684 • BIG PINE, CA 93513
(760) 938-2530 fax 938-2942
Nancy Madina, Director

CALIFORNIA INDIAN LEGAL SERVICES
787 N. Main St., Suite D • BISHOP, CA 93514
(800) 736-3582; (760) 873-3581 Fax 873-8788
Michael Pfeffer, Executive Director
See Oakland (main office) listing for description of services. *Counties served*: Alpine, Inyo, Kern, Mono, and Tuolumne.

INYO CHILD CARE SERVICES, INC.
Route 3, Box B-75 • BISHOP, CA 93514
(760) 872-3911
Head Start Program.

OWENS VALLEY INDIAN EDUCATION CENTER
P.O. Box 1648 • BISHOP, CA 93514
(760) 873-5740 Fax 873-4143
Peggy Vega, Director

PIT RIVER HEALTH SERVICES, INC.
P.O. Box 2720 • BURNEY, CA 96013
(916) 335-5090

FOUR WINDS OF INDIAN EDUCATION
CHICO, CA 95926
(916) 895-4212 Fax 895-6569
Caleen Sisk, Director
E-mail: csisk@csu.oa.vax.edu

INTERTRIBAL SOCIETY
P.O. Box 4052 • CHULA VISTA, CA 92011
(619) 422-6433
Sponsors cultural activities for local tribes.

CENTRAL VALLEY INDIAN HEALTH, INC.
20 N. Dewitt #8 • CLOVIS, CA 93612
(209) 299-2578
Purpose: To provide culturally sensitive medical and dental services to Indian people in the Central Valley. Includes Fresno, Madera, and Kings Counties.

LAKE COUNTY CITIZENS COMMITTEE
P.O. Box 90 • COBB, CA 95426
(707) 928-5591 Fax 928-6128
Bill Hecomovich, Director

SOUTHERN CALIFORNIA INDIAN CENTER
6055 E. Washington Blvd. #700
COMMERCE, CA 90040
(323) 728-8844 Fax 728-9834
E-Mail: indiancenter@earthlink.net
Web site: http://www.home.earthlink.net/
        Indiancenter/
Suzy Jensen, Acting Supervisor
Phil Hale, Education Component Director
Purpose: To promote social and economic self-sufficiency for American Indian people (Los Angeles & Orange counties) by establishing and maintaining educational, cultural, economic and recreational programs. *Goal*: To assist individuals in finding employment; other programs include: Tutorial Services, Cultural & Traditional Arts Education, Enrichment Trips and Activities, Advocacy, Career & Higher Education Guidance, Parent Development Workshops. Resource library.

ROUND VALLEY INDIAN HEALTH CENTER
P.O. Box 247 • COVELO, CA 95428
(707) 983-6181
Purpose: To provide medical, laboratory, and dental services to Indians and non-Indians in rural areas.

ROUND VALLEY INDIAN TRIBES EDUCATION CENTER
P.O. Box 448 • COVELO, CA 95428
(707) 983-1062 Fax 983-1073
James Russ, Director

FOOTHILL INDIAN EDUCATION ALLIANCE
P.O. Box 1418, EL DORADO, CA 95623
(916) 621-3096 Fax 621-3097
James Marquez, Director

CALIFORNIA NATIVE AMERICAN BUSINESS DEVELOPMENT CENTER (CANABDC)
11138 Valley Mall, Suite 200
EL MONTE, CA 91731
(626) 442-3701 Fax 442-7115
Sharon Chambers, Project Director
E-mail: schambers@ncaied.org
Website: www.ncaied.org
Project operated by the National Center for for American Indian Enterprise Development in cooperation with the U.S. Department of Commerce, Minority Business development Agency. Operates the California/Nevada Tribal Technical Assistance Program (CA/NV TTAP), providing management and technical assistance for Native Americans residing in California & Nevada. Available for all stages of business from start-up to expansion.

CALIFORNIA INDIAN LEGAL SERVICES
609 S. Escondido Blvd.
ESCONDIDO, CA 92025
(800) 743-8941; (760) 746-8941 Fax 746-1815
Michael Pfeffer, Executive Director
E-mail: cilsescondido@hotmail.com
Web site: www.calindian.org
See Oakland (main office) listing for description of services. *Counties served*: Imperial, Los Angeles, Orange, Riverside, San Bernardino, San Diego, Santa Barbara, and Ventura counties.

CALIFORNIA INDIAN LEGAL SERVICES
324 F St., Suite A • EUREKA, CA 95501
(707) 443-8397 Fax 443-8913
Michael Pfeffer, Executive Director
Marilyn Miles & Mary Risling, Staff Attorneys
See Oakland (main office) listing for description of services. *Counties served*: Del Norte, Humboldt, Lassen, Modoc, Shasta, Siskiyou, and Trinity.

NORTHERN CALIFORNIA INDIAN DEVELOPMENT CENTER
241 F St. • EUREKA, CA 95501
(707) 445-8451 Fax 445-8479
Terry Coltra, Executive Director
Website: www.ncidc.org
Description: A social service agency providing education and employment services through the Job Training and Partnership Act.

NATIVE AMERICAN WOLF CLAN
P.O. Box 1629 • FONTANA, CA 92334
(909) 823-8593
Description: An intertribal fraternal society of Native American people whose main precepts are charity and care for all Indian youth and elders. *Purpose*: To preserve all the tribes' histories, traditions & ways of life.

YA-KA-AMA INDIAN EDUCATION & DEVELOPMENT, INC.
6215 Eastside Rd.
FORESTVILLE, CA 95436
(707) 887-1541
Luwana Quitiquit, Executive Director
Purpose: Provide programs for five-county Native American population to advance their educational, economic, social and cultural opportunities necessary to the attainment of sovereignty and self-determination. *Special programs*: Vocational training in horticulture, business and merchandising. Operates Native plant nursery and organic produce; Native Arts Gallery and Native crafts store; Library. Publication: Quarterly newsletter. Established in 1972.

SOUTHERN CALIFORNIA INDIAN CENTER
10175 Slater Ave. #150
FOUNTAIN VALLEY, CA 92708
(714) 962-6673; Ms. Starr, Executive Director
Purpose: To promote social and economic self-sufficiency for American Indian people (Los Angeles & Orange counties) by establishing and maintaining educational, cultural, economic and recreational programs. *Special programs*: Senior citizens center, tutoring, annual pow-wow and job fair. *Publication*: SCIC News, monthly newsletter. Library. Established in 1968.

OSA/FRESNO-CLOVIS INDIAN EDUCATION CENTER
2236 N. Fine, Suite 103
FRESNO, CA 93727
(209) 252-8659 Fax 252-3824
Virginia Grieco, Director
Purpose: To create a better understanding of the history, culture, and contributions of California Indians; to stimulate and promote research and study of the early American Indian; to support the preservation of California's Native cultural heritage; and to encourage Indian parents to become involved in improving their children's education.

MENDOCINO COUNTY INDIAN CENTER
Native-American Education Center
P.O. Box 495, Hwy. 101 S.
HOPLAND, CA 95449 (707) 468-9269
Purpose: To educate, support, and motivate Native Americans in their social and professional lives through a variety of activites and events.

INDIAN FREE CLINIC
7300 South Santa Fe Ave.
HUNTINGTON PARK, CA 90225

LONE PINE INDIAN EDUCATION CENTER
1120 Goodwin St.
LONE PINE, CA 93545
(760) 876-5394 (phone & fax)
Ken Gilmore, Director
E-mail: lpmesa@telis.org

INDIAN ALCOHOLISM COMMISSION OF CALIF.
225 W. Eighth St.
LOS ANGELES, CA 90014
(213) 622-3424

LOS ANGELES AMERICAN INDIAN LIAISON TO THE MAYOR
200 N. Spring St.
LOS ANGELES, CA 90012
(213) 485-8881
Roxanne Burgess, Liaison

LOS ANGELES CITY/COUNTY NATIVE AMERICAN INDIAN COMMISSION
500 W. Temple St., Rm. 780
LOS ANGELES, CA 90012
(213) 974-7554 Fax 626-7034
Fr. Paul Ojibway, Commissioner
Glenda Ahhitty, Director
Purpose: To promote the general welfare, public interest, and well being of the Los Angeles Indian community, the largest urban Indian population in the U.S.

LOS ANGELES COUNTY DEPT. OF HEALTH SERVICES
313 N. Figueroa
LOS ANGELES, CA 90026-5027
(213) 974-7741
Colleen Colson, American Indian Community Liaison

UNITED AMERICAN INDIAN INVOLVEMENT, INC.
LOS ANGELES, CA 90013
(213) 625-2565
David L. Rambeau, Executive Director
Purpose: To provide assistance to the American Indian population within the Los Angeles County area suffering from the disease of alcoholism and other drugs. Emphasis targeted on skid row Los Angeles City. *Special programs*: Counseling; nutrition; personal hygiene; housing assistance; youth diversion programs, family activities; day sleep facilities; sober living; limited detox and other crisis assistance as needed. Established in 1974.

WOODFORDS INDIAN EDUCATION CENTER
96-B Washo Blvd.
MARKLEEVILLE, CA 96120
(916) 694-2964 Fax 694-2739
Kate Macartney, Director
E-mail: kmacartney@telis.org.

AMERICAN INDIAN CHILD RESOURCE CENTER
600 Grand Ave., Suite 400 • OAKLAND, CA 94612
(510) 208-1877 Fax 208-1886
Carol Wahpepah, Director

CALIFORNIA INDIAN LEGAL SERVICES
510 16th St., 4th Floor • OAKLAND, CA 94612
(510) 835-0284 Fax 835-1815
Michael S. Pfeffer, Executive Director
Description: A statewide nonprofit corporation organized to provide free legal services to qualifying individuals and organizations on a wide range of topics involving Indian law and legal issues unique to Native American people. CILS provides low-cost legal services to California Indian tribes that do not qualify for free services. Currently represents more than sixt California Indian tribes on a wide range of legal issues. This is the main office which houses the program administration and also serves as a field office. *Counties served*: Alameda, Amador, Butte, Calaveras,

Colusa, Contra Costa, El Dorado, Fresno, Glenn, Kings, Madera, Marin, Mariposa, Mendocino, Merced, Monterey, Napa, Nevada, Placer, Plumas, Sacramento, San Benito, San Francisco, San Joaquin, San Luis Obispo, San Mateo, Santa Clara, Santa Cruz, Sierra, Solano, Sonoma, Stanislaus, Sutter, Tehama, Tulare, Yolo, and Yuba. Services are provided by each office in the counties included within its service area. Each office has 2-3 attorneys and paralegals on staff. Other offices located in Bishop, Escondido, Eureka, Santa Rosa, CA; and Washington, DC. Indian Law Library. Established 1967.

CONSORTIUM OF UNITED INDIAN NATIONS
1404 Franklin St. #202 • OAKLAND, CA 94612
(415) 763-3410
Purpose: To provide job training and work experience for Native Americans in its area.

INTERTRIBAL FRIENDSHIP HOUSE
523 East 14th St. • OAKLAND, CA 94606
(510) 452-1235
Jim Lamenti, Executive Director
Loretta VanWinkle, Executive Secretary
Sharon Bennett, Social Worker
Susan Lobo, Community History Project Coord.
Purpose: To promote and maintain the well-being of American Indian life in the modern and traditional way. *Programs*: Cultural; social services; senior program; community history project. Gift Shop. Artifacts exhibit, visual arts and writing, tapes (video and music), historical records. Book currently being written. Established in 1955.

INTERTRIBAL TRADING POST
523 East 14th St. • OAKLAND, CA 94606
(510) 452-1235
A nonprofit organization selling Indian crafts.

NATIVE AMERICAN ALCOHOLISM & DRUG ABUSE PROGRAM
1815 39th Ave. No. A • OAKLAND, CA 94601

NATIVE AMERICAN HEALTH CENTER OF OAKLAND
3124 East 14th St. • OAKLAND, CA 94601
(510) 261-1962
Purpose: To provide health services for the Native American population in the Oakland area.

URBAN INDIAN CHILD RESOURCE CENTER
OAKLAND, CA 94610 (510) 832-2386
Carol Marquez-Balnes, MPH, Director
Serves the American Indian people residing in the San Francisco Bay area. *Programs*: Indian Child Welfare Act Advocacy; Mental Health Services; Foster Care Recruitment and Certification; Social Services; Cultural Awareness; Treatment Seminars; In-Service Training to public and private agencies; continuing education. Library.

CHRISTIAN HOPE INDIAN-ESKIMO FELLOWSHIP (CHIEF)
P.O. Box 2600 • ORANGE, CA 92669

UNITED CALIFORNIA INDIANS
2290 Elgin St. • OROVILLE, CA 95965

INDIAN HEALTH COUNCIL
P.O. Box 406 • PAUMA VALLEY, CA 92061
(619) 749-1410 x 286 Fax 749-3347
Dennis Magee, Executive Director
Regina Aguilera, Sr. Health Education Associate
Purpose: To create awareness and educate local Native American reservations on HIV/AIDS prevention. *Activities*: B.E.A.R. Program - Be Educated and Responsible, youth-adult program on HIV/AIDS awareness, prevention and incorporating wellness and healthy lifestyles.

TOWANITS INDIAN EDUCATION CENTER
P.O. Box 589 • PORTERVILLE, CA 93258
(209) 784-6135 Fax 784-1351
Linda Murr, Director

AMERICAN INDIAN TRAINING INSTITUTE
4221 Northgate Blvd. #2
SACRAMENTO, CA 95834
(916) 920-0731
Purpose: To prepare counselors and teachers to work

with Native Americans who have alcohol, drug, or other abuse problems.

CALIFORNIA DEPARTMENT OF EDUCATION
American Indian Education Office
P.O. Box 944272 • SACRAMENTO, CA 94244
(916) 657-3696 Fax 657-3859
Jane Holzmann, Consultant
Purpose: To provide statewide coordination and technical assistance. *Activity*: Has reissued, "The American Indian: Yesterday, Today and Tomorrow: A Handbook for Educators."

CALIFORNIA INDIAN NURSES ASSOCIATION
c/o State Health Dept., Indian Health Unit
714 P St. • SACRAMENTO, CA 95814
(916) 445-4171

CALIFORNIA HOUSING & COMMUNITY DEVELOPMENT
Indian Assistance Program
1800 3rd St. R. 365, P.O. Box 952054
SACRAMENTO, CA 94252-2054
(916) 445-4727

CALIFORNIA NATIVE AMERICAN HERITAGE COMMISSION
915 Capitol Mall, Rm. 364
SACRAMENTO, CA 95814
(916) 653-4082 - William Mungary, Chairperson
(916) 653-6251 - Carol Gaubatz, Program Analyst
Description: Composed of California tribal members.
Purpose: To protect historical remains uncovered through construction, and to ensure the return of remains to the appropriate tribe for reburial. Responsible for implementing California's strong state repatriation laws.

INTERTRIBAL COUNCIL OF CALIFORNIA, INC.
2021 P St. • SACRAMENTO, CA 95814
(916) 448-8687
Operates a Head Start Program.

SACRAMENTO INDIAN CENTER
Alcoholism Awareness Program
2729 P St. • SACRAMENTO, CA 95816

SACRAMENTO URBAN INDIAN HEALTH PROJECT
2020 J St. • SACRAMENTO, CA 95814
(916) 441-0918

AMERICAN INDIAN HEALTH CENTER
2630 First Ave., Suite 100
SAN DIEGO, CA 92103
(619) 234-2158 Fax 234-0206
3812 Ray St. • SAN DIEGO, CA 92104
(619) 298-9090 Fax 298-0677

INDIAN HUMAN RESOURCE CENTER
4040 30th St., Suite A • SAN DIEGO, CA 92104
(619) 281-5964 Fax 281-1466
E-mail: ihrc5@onp.wdsc.org
Juan Castellanos, Exec. Director
Joe Renteria, Chair (Cherokee)
Purpose: To serve Native Americans in San Diego County by providing job training. *Activities*: Developing San Diego's American Indiann Culture Center & Museum (AICCM) which is scheduled to open December 2002 (See AICCM listing in Museum's section).
Publication: Monthly newsletter.

NATIVE AMERICANS COUNCIL
P.O. Box 900089
SAN DIEGO, CA 92190
(619) 934-5387; Monica Kellar, Contact

AMERICAN INDIAN FILM FESTIVAL
333 Valencia St. #212
SAN FRANCISCO, CA 94103
(415) 554-0525

AMERICAN INDIAN FRIENDSHIP HOUSE
80 Julian Ave.
SAN FRANCISCO, CA 94103

NATIVE AMERICAN HEALTH CENTER
56 Julian Ave.
SAN FRANCISCO, CA 94103
(415) 621-8051
Martin Waukazoo, Executive Director

AHMIUM EDUCATION, INC.
701 Esplanade St., Suite H
SAN JACINTO, CA 92582
(909) 654-2781 Fax 654-3089
Ernie Salgado, Director
E-mail: ernie@ivic.net.

AMERICAN INDIAN ALLIANCE OF SANTA CLARA VALLEY
SAN JOSE, CA 95112
Laverne Morrissey, President
E-mail: aialliance@juno.com
Purpose: A coalition of organizations and individuals dedicated to preserving and perpetuating the heritage, values and traditions of American Indians. *Activities*: Monthly community meetings; the Annual Gathering Retreat; Pow wows. *Publications*: Indian Valley News (monthly newsletter); annual Bay Area American Indian Pow Wow Calendar.

URBAN INDIAN HEALTH PROJECT
610 Del Monte Ave.
SANTA BARBARA, CA 93101
(805) 965-0718

CALIFORNIA INDIAN LEGAL SERVICES
37 Old Courthouse Sq., Suite 209
SANTA ROSA, CA 95404
(866) 204-1831; (707) 573-8016 Fax 573-3925
Office location of CILS. See Oakland office for description. *Counties served*: Same counties as Oakland office.

LOCAL INDIANS FOR EDUCATION
P.O. Box 729 • SHASTA LAKE, CA 96019
(916) 275-1513 Fax 275-6260
Irma Davis, Director

HOWONQUET COMMUNITY ASSOCIATION
250 N. Indian Rd. • SMITH RIVER, CA 95567
(707) 487-4463

COUNCIL FOR THE AMERICAN INDIAN
P.O. Box 68 • STOCKTON, CA 95201
Local organization uniting the area's Native Americans.

NATIVE AMERICAN INDIAN CENTER
Stockton Unified School District
1425 S. Center • STOCKTON, CA 95206
(209) 953-4803 Fax 953-4261
Dale Fleming, Director
Purpose: To meet culturally related academic needs.

INDIAN ART CENTER OF CALIFORNIA
12666 Ventura Blvd.
STUDIO CITY, CA 91604
(818) 763-3430
Purpose: To support Indian artists and an appreciation of Native American culture.

ANTELOPE INDIAN CIRCLE RELIGIOUS CULTURE GROUP
P.O. Box 790
SUSANVILLE, CA 96130
(916) 257-2181 Ext. 1534
Ray Salsedo, Chairperson
Grant Purcell, Vice Chairperson
Donald Selsor, Native American Spiritual Leader
Description: An incarcerated men's prison Indian circle at the California Correctional Center. *Goal*: To rehabilitate the Indian inmate population through religious customs. *Special programs/activities*: Sweat Purification and Sacred Pipe Ceremony, Indian ancestral teachings and bead and leather-working. Established in 1974.

LASSEN COUNTY AMERICAN INDIAN ORGANIZATION
P.O. Box 1549, SUSANVILLE, CA 96130
(916) 257-2687 Fax 257-9071
Sandra Lowry, Director

CALIFORNIA INDIAN LEGAL SERVICES
Box 488, 200 W. Henry St.
UKIAH, CA 95482
(707) 462-3825 Fax 462-4235
Maureen Geary, Contact
See Oakland (main office) listing. *Counties served*: Butte, Colusa, Glenn, Lake, Mendocino, Napa, Nevada, Plumas, Sierra, Sonoma, Sutter, and Yuba.

AMERICAN INDIAN CULTURAL GROUP
P.O. Box 2000 • VACAVILLE, CA 95688

RINCON INDIAN EDUCATION CENTER
P.O. Box 1147 • VALLEY CENTER, CA 92082
(760) 749-1386 Fax 749-8838
Adela Kolb, Director
E-mail: mmmama2ps@aol.com

COLORADO

COLORADO INDIAN BAR ASSOCIATION
Native American Rights Fund
1506 Broadway • BOULDER, CO 80302
(303) 447-8760
Melody McCoy, President; L. Robert Muray, V.P.
Patrice Kunesh, Secretary/Treasurer

COLORADO COMMISSION ON INDIAN AFFAIRS
130 State Capitol
DENVER, CO 80203 (303) 866-3027
Karen D. Rogers, Executive Secretary
Purpose: To improve the government to government relationship of the Indian people of Colorado, primarily the two Ute tribes located in southwest Colorado.

COLORADO INDIAN EMPLOYMENT ASSISTANCE CENTER
Box 10134, University Park Station
DENVER, CO 80210 (303) 937-0401
Purpose: To provide research/job training and direct placement of Indians and Alaska Natives in job market. *Activities*: Various publications and research projects. Library (private).

DENVER INDIAN HEALTH BOARD
2035 East 18th St. # 8
DENVER, CO 80206 (303) 320-3974

DENVER NATIVE AMERICANS UNITED, INC.
Denver Indian Center, 4407 Morrison Rd.
DENVER, CO 80219 (303) 937-0401
Dorothy Brave Eaglej, Director
Program: *The Circle of Learning* program embodies a cultural approach to teaching in a preschool setting. Indian culture is interwoven into all classroom activities. Developed a multicultural preschool curriculum model called *The Circle Never Ends*.

EAGLE LODGE—AMERICAN INDIAN ALCOHOLISM REHABILITATION PROGRAM
1264 Race St. • DENVER, CO 80206
(303) 393-7773

SOUTHERN UTE CULTURAL CENTER
P.O. Box 737 • IGNACIO, CO 81137
(970) 563-9583 Fax 563-4641
Helen Hoskins, Director
E-mail: sumuseum@southern-ute.nso.us
Purpose: To educate about Southern Ute culture and preserve Southern Ute Indian artifacts. *Activities*: Workshops, tours. *Publications*: The Ute Legacy, education packet with Ute history books, videotape and study guide. Museum. Library. Established in 1972.

CONNECTICUT

CONNECTICUT INDIAN AFFAIRS COUNCIL
79 Elm St. • HARTFORD, CT 06106-5127
(860) 424-3066 Fax 424-4058
Paulette Crone-Morange, Chairpeson
Edward W. Sarabia,, Jr., Indian Affairs Coordinator
Purpose: To provide sevices and programs to the reservation communities; advises the DEP Commissioner about the general health, safety and well-being of people residing on reservations; and advises the Commissioner on care and management of reservation lands and buildings. Established in 1973.

AMERICAN INDIAN STUDIES INSTITUTE
Curtis Rd., Box 1260
WASHINGTON, CT 06793
(203) 868-0518; Susan F. Payne, Director
Purpose: To discover, preserve, and interpret information about the lifeways of the first peoples of the Northeast Woodlands area of the U.S., and to enhance appreciation for their cultures and achievements. *Activities*: Conducts archaeological surveys and excavations; provides indoor and outdoor exhibits; sponsors archaeological training sessions, teacher workshops, craft workshops, summer youth programs-educational programs to school groups. *Publication*: Artifacts, quarterly magazine; annual research report; bibliography and educational resource pamphlets. Annual conference, with symposium - always November, Lowell, MA. Museum. Library. Established in 1971.

DELAWARE

NANTICOKE INDIAN ASSOCIATION
Route 4, Box 107-A
MILLSBORO, DE 19966
(302) 945-7022 Kenneth Clark, Director

DELAWARE HUMAN RELATIONS DIVISION
820 N. French, 4th Fl.
WILMINGTON, DE 19801
(302) 571-3716 Andrew Turner, Jr., Director

DISTRICT OF COLUMBIA

AMERICAN INDIAN SOCIETY OF WASHINGTON, DC
P.O. Box 6431
FALLS CHURCH, VA 22040
(804) 448-3707 Jay Hill, President
See listing under Virginia.

INDIAN ARTS & CRAFTS BOARD
U.S. Dept. of the Interior
1849 C St., NW, MS: 2058, MIB
WASHINGTON 20240 (888) 278-3253
(202) 208-3773 Fax 208-5196
Meredith Z. Stanton, Director
Purpose: To promote the development of Indian and Alaskan Native arts and handicrafts. *Activities*: Provides business and personal professional advice, information, and promotion to artists and craftsmen and their organizations; operates the Museum of the Plains Indian, Browning, MT; Sioux Indian Museum, Rapid City, SD; and Southern Plains Indian Museum, Anadarko, OK. *Publication*: Source Director: Indian, Eskimo, Aleut Owned and Operated Arts and Crafts Businesses. Established 1935.

FLORIDA

SEMINOLE TRIBE OF FLORIDA HOUSING AUTHORITY
6300 Stirling Rd.
HOLLYWOOD, FL 33024
(800) 683-7800 Ext. 1703
Fax (954) 967-3496
Joel M. Frank, Sr., Director

AMERICAN INDIAN FEDERATION, INC.
3434 E. 7th St.
PANAMA CITY, FL 32401
(850) 763-1924 (phone & fax)
J.C. McCormick, President & CEO
Paul William Flaig (*White Bear*), Vice President
Purpose: To promote the interest and well being of all Native Americans in their improvement goals. to form a unity among Native American tribal governments. *Activities*: Artisans make handmade original Native American gemstone and silver necklaces of Cherokee design using diverse pendants with no synthetics.

FLORIDA GOVERNOR'S COUNCIL ON INDIAN AFFAIRS, INC.
1341 Cross Creek Cir.
TALLAHASSEE, FL 32301
(850) 488-0730 Fax 488-5875
Joe A. Quetone, Executive Director
Purpose: To create an awareness and serve the legal, social, and economic needs of the Native American citizens in the state of Florida

GEORGIA

AMERICAN CHEROKEE CONFEDERACY
Rt. 4, Box 120 • ALBANY, GA 31705
(912) 787-5722

COUNCIL ON AMERICAN INDIAN CONCERNS
205 Butler St., Suite 1352, East Tower
ATLANTA, GA 30334 (404) 656-2770
Website: www.ganet.org/indcouncil

OGLEWANAGI GALLERY & CENTER
ATLANTA 30306
Tom Perkins & Vickie Dunken, Co-directors
Purpose: To act as a networking facility for Indian concerns; to promote Indian arts & crafts *Activities*: Headquarters of Leonard Peltier Support Group-Atlanta; member, Indian Arts & Crafts Assocaition (IACA). *Publications*: Bi-annual newsletter; American Indian Trading Cards - "Pow Wow - A Living Tradition." Established in 1990.

GEORGIA CHEROKEE HERITAGE FOUNDATION
Rt. 3 Box 750
DAHLONEGA, GA 30533
(706) 864-6010; Mel Hawkins, Contact

CHEROKEE INDIANS OF GEORGIA
3291 Church St.
SCOTTSDALE, GA 30079
(404) 299-2940
Purpose: To aid Cherokees living in Georgia; seeks to perpetuate Cherokee tribal traditions; sponsors fund raising activities.

IDAHO

HUMAN RIGHTS COMMISSION
450 W. State St. • BOISE, ID 83720
(208) 334-2873; Marilyn Shuler, Director

IDAHO STATE INDIAN EDUCATION ADVISORY BOARD
Elementary Education & Indian Education
P.O. Box 83720 • BOISE, ID 83720-0027
(208) 332-6942 Fax 334-4664
Bob Sobotta, Sr., Director
Purpose: To meet the educational needs of all students of Indian heritage in the State of Idaho and to promote greater understanding among all students in regards to the diverse backgrounds and cultures of American people. Established in 1996.

INDIAN HERITAGE COUNCIL
P.O. Box 752 • McCALL, ID 83638
(423) 277-1103
Louis Hooban, CEO
Purpose: To promote Native American writers and literature, customs and beliefs. *Activities*: Conducts research and educational programs; cultural events; sponsors charitable events; operates speaker's bureau; and sponsors an annual National Powwow in October, in Townsend, Tennessee; monthly conference. *Award*: Native American Literary Award, annual. *Publications*: Quarterly newsletter; books - Crazy Horse's Philosophy of Riding Rainbows; Great American Indian Bible; Indian Drug Usage; Native American Play; Native American Poetry; Native American Poets' Anthology; Native American Prophecies; Native Letters to the People; Vision Quest. Library. Established 1988.

NORTHWEST INDIAN NEWS ASSOCIATION
Drawer C • PLUMMER, ID 83851
(208) 274-3101
Purpose: To develop and to improve communications among Indian people and between Indians and the non-Indian public by offering consultant services among members, workshops, and presenting job opportunities. Annual meeting and a news bureau. Publishes the "Sequoyah Sentinel," a monthly newsletter to keep members informed on the state of the art.

ILLINOIS

AMERICAN INDIAN CENTER
1630 West Wilson • CHICAGO, IL 60640
(312) 275-5871/561-8183
Samson Keahna, Director

AMERICAN INDIAN HEALTH SERVICE
838 West Irving Park Rd.
CHICAGO, IL 60613 (312) 883-9100

ILLINOIS BOARD OF EDUCATION
Adult and Ethnic Education
100 W. Randolph St. • CHICAGO, IL 60601
(312) 814-3606 Fax 814-2282
Joseph Frattaroli, Contact

MARCH, INC.
P.O. Box 2890 • CHICAGO, IL 60690
(312) 935-6188
A cultural organization concerned with
Native American presentations.

O-WAI-YA-WA SCHOOL
5120 N. Winthrop • CHICAGO, IL 60660
(312) 534-2518
An elementary and secondary school for
Native Americans.

ST. AUGUSTINE'S CENTER
4512 North Sheridan Rd.
CHICAGO, IL 60640 (312) 784-1050
Elmira McClure, Director

QUAD CITY LEAGUE OF NATIVE AMERICANS
418 19th St. • ROCK ISLAND, IL 61201
Regina M. Mahieu

INDIANA

AMERICAN INDIAN CENTER OF INDIANA, INC.
1026 S. Shelby St. • INDIANAPOLIS, IN 46203
(800) 745-5872; (317) 536-0225 Fax 536-0230
Mary Alexander, Executive Director

CIVIL RIGHTS COMMISSION ON INDIAN AFFAIRS
Indiana Government Center North
100 N. Senate Ave., Rm. N103
INDIANAPOLIS, IN 46204 (317) 232-2600

AMERICAN INDIAN CENTER OF INDIANA, INC.
406 N. Broadway • PERU, IN 46970
(800) 887-5872; (765) 473-3010 Fax 473-3018
James Cyr, Director

INDIAN AWARENESS CENTER
Fulton County Historical Society
37 E 375 N • ROCHESTER, IN 46975
(574) 223-4436
Chief WhiteEagle & Bobbie Bear, Co-presidents
Shirley Willard, Director
E-mail: fchs@rtcol.com
Website: www.icss.net/~fchs
Description: Organization of Potawatomi and Miami
Indians with roots in Indiana, and people interested in
Indians. Purpose: To make the public aware of and
appreciate American Indian history and culture, par-
ticularly Potowatomi. *Special projects:* Establishing
Trail of Death Regional Historic Trail with historical
markers from Indiana to Kansas, commemorating
forced removal in 1838 of Potawatomi from Northern
Indiana to Kansas. They completed marking the camp-
sites every 15 to 20 miles on the 660 mile Trail of Death
in 2003. There are now 74 historical markers on the
Trail of Death Regional Historic Trail, making this the
best marked American Indian historic trail; sponsors
Trail of Death Commemorative Caravan every five
years (next one planned for 2008); helps produce Trail
of Courage Living History Festival (3rd weekend in
September); sponsors Woodland Indian Village at
Festival, and Potawatomi Memorial Village; Indian craft
workshops; helps with Indian dances; meetings. Museum. Collection of genealogies of Potawatomi families. *Publication:* Semiannual newsletter; book:
Potwawtomi Trail of Death - Indiana to Kansas. Established in 1982.

IOWA

IOWA GOVERNOR'S LIAISON
1405 Truman Place, State Capitol
AMES, IA 50010 (515) 232-5320

IOWA DEPT. OF HUMAN SERVICES
Hoover State Office Bldg.
DES MOINES, IA 50319 (515) 281-5452
Charles M. Palmer, Director

IOWA CIVIL RIGHTS COMMISSION
c/o Grimes State Office Bldg.
211 E. Maple St., 2nd Floor
DES MOINES, IA 50319 (515) 281-4121

NATIVE FAMILY RESOURCE CENTER
809 W. 7th St. • SIOUX CITY, IA 51103
David Farley, Director
E-mail: info@nativefrc.org

**NATIVE AMERICAN ALCOHOLISM
TREATMENT PROGRAM**
P.O. Box 773 • Larpenteau Ave., Bldg. 544
SARGEANT BLUFF, IA 51054
(712) 277-9416 Fax 277-3144
Susan C. Barta, Executive Director
Purpose: To provide alcohol treatment services/reha-
bilitation to indigenous clients and peoples in the state
of Iowa and the Aberdeen Area Indian Health Service.
Established in 1976.

KANSAS

LAWRENCE INDIAN CENTER
1423 Haskell Ave. • LAWRENCE, KS 66044
(913) 841-7202; Charmain Billy, Exec. Director
Purpose: To provide community services, such as:
emergency food, utility and shelter assistance, housing, job board, craft workshops. Operates Tall Grass
Giftshop and Share/Care garden. *Personnel:* Dan
Spurgin and Nicole Jay. Library.

**KANSAS ASSOCIATION FOR
NATIVE AMERICAN EDUCATION**
Haskell Indian Nations University
P.O. Box H-1304 • LAWRENCE, KS 66044
(913) 749-8468 Marilyn Bread, Contact

MID-AMERICA ALL-INDIAN CENTER, INC.
650 N. Seneca • WICHITA, KS 67203
(316) 262-5221 Fax 262-4216
John A. Ortiz, Executive Director
Jerry Martin, Museum Director
E-Mail: wichita@esc.ttrc.dolteta.gov
Web site: http://www.2.southwind.net/~icm/
museum/museum.html
Purpose: To promote awareness of Native American
culture in the community; to offer emergency social
services for members of the Native American community and transients. *Programs/Activities:* Job Training Program Assistance; pow wows; kiva rental. Museum and Library. Established in 1969.

WICHITA INDIAN HEALTH CENTER
2318 East Central • WICHITA, KS 67214
(316) 262-2415

KENTUCKY

KENTUCKY INDIAN MANPOWER ORGANIZATION
933 Goss Ave. • LOUISVILLE, KY 40217
(502) 636-4214
Purpose: To provide job training, educational counseling, and placement to help Native Americans in its
area.

LOUISIANA

LOUISIANA DEPT. OF EDUCATION
Office of Migrant & Indian Education Programs
P.O. Box 44064 • BATON ROUGE, LA 70804
(504) 342-3517; Nedra Ourso Loftin, Contact

LOUISIANA INTERTRIBAL COUNCIL
BATON ROUGE, LA 70816 (504) 292-2474
Purpose: To develop communications among the five
member tribes: Jena Band of Choctaws; Chitimacha
Tribe of Louisiana; Coushatta Tribe of Louisiana;
United Houma Nation; and Tunica-Biloxi Tribe.

MAINE

MAINE INDIAN AFFAIRS COMMISSION
State House Sta., #38 • AUGUSTA, ME 04333
(207) 287-5800 Fax 287-5900
Leo Martin, Contact

MAINE INDIAN TRIBAL-STATE COMMISSION
P.O. Box 87 • HALLOWELL, ME 04347
(207) 622-4815; Diana C. Scully, Executive Director
An intergovernmental agency concerned with the re-
lationship between the state, the Passamaquoddy
Tribe and the Penobscot Indian Nation.

MAINE TRIBAL/STATE RELATIONS OFFICE
6 River Rd. • INDIAN HEAD, ME 04347
(202) 827-7776; Priscilla A. Attean, Contact

MAINE INDIAN BASKETMAKERS ALLIANCE
P.O. Box 3253 • OLD TOWN, ME 04468
A retail outlet for Maliseet, Micmac, Passamaquoddy
and Penobscot basketmakers

MARYLAND

BALTIMORE AMERICAN INDIAN CENTER
113 S. Broadway • BALTIMORE, MD 21231
(410) 675-3535
Barry Richardson, Executive Director
Purpose: To help American Indians with their cultural,
social, economic, housing and educational needs. *Programs:* BAIC Scholarship Fund; Rev. James Dial Memorial Fund; housing; business development; job
placement; community services; alcoholism; youth
program; Brantley Blue Awards; Annual Pow-Wow.
Publication: Smoke Signals, newsletter.

MARYLAND DEPARTMENT OF EDUCATION
Liaison to Indian Education
200 W. Baltimore St.
BALTIMORE, MD 21201
(410) 333-2234 Fax 333-2226
Jill S. Christianson

MARYLAND COMMISSION ON INDIAN AFFAIRS
100 Community Pl.
CROWNSVILLE, MD 21032
(410) 514-7616 Fax 987-4071
Suzanne C. Almalel Administrator
E-mail: almalel@dhcd.state.md.us
Consists of nine members appointed by the Governor
for three-year terms. *Purpose:* To support, initiate, coordinate and implement educational, social and economic projects which affect the diverse Indian communities in Maryland; and to increase public awareness and appreciation of the contributions that Indians have made to life in Maryland. Established in 1976.

**AMERICAN INDIAN INTERTRIBAL
CULTURAL ORGANIZATION**
P.O. Box 775 • ROCKVILLE, MD 20848
(301) 869-9381 Fax (703) 823-0609
Kathy Frick, President
E-mail: aiitco@webtv.net
Purpose: A membership group of Native Americans
and non-Indians interested and active in the preser-
vation and extension of knowledge of Native Ameri-
can cultures. *Activities:* annual pow wow in Frederick,
Maryland. *Publication:* Rattle & Drum (newsletter).

MASSACHUSETTS

**MASSACHUSETTS CENTER FOR
NATIVE AMERICAN AWARENESS, INC.**
P.O. Box 5885 • Boston, MA 02114
(617) 884-4227; Burne Stanley, Director

E-mail: mcnaa@aol.com; Website: www.mcnaa.org
Purpose: To serve the cultural, spiritual, and social needs of the Native American peoples residing in Massachusetts. Also, to promote and preserve the cultural and traditional ways of the Native Americans of the land. *Programs*: Chief Red Blanket Scholarship Program; Slow Turtle Youth Empowerment & Cultural Enrichment Program; Fuel Assistance Program. *Activities*: Adult lecture series (Spring & Fall); children's workshops (mid-Winter & Spring); monthly festivals/pow wows and socials. *Publication*: Turtletalk, quarterly newsletter. Established in 1989.

MASSACHUSETTS COMMISSION ON INDIAN AFFAIRS
1 Congress St., 10th Floor
BOSTON, MA 02114
(617) 727-6394 Fax 727-4938
Jim Peters, Executive Director
E-mail: jim.peters@state.ma.us
Website: www.state.ma.us/dhcd/
components/ind_affairs
Description: Consists of seven members of American Indian descent representing the major tribes of the Commonwealth of Massachusetts. *Purpose*: To assist Native American residents of Massachusetts with any problem common to them - social services, legal assistance, housing, employment, civil rights, treaty rights, etc. *Programs*: Reinterment Program; Scholarship Program. Established in 1976.

BOSTON INDIAN COUNCIL
105 S. Huntington
JAMAICA PLAIN, MA 02130
(617) 232-0343
Jimmy L. Sam, Executive Director
A multi-service social delivery system for the American Indian community of the Greater Boston area, and provides a mechanism for cultural activities. *Programs*: Employment and training; adult education; Head Start; day care; elderly; crafts; Indian Health Service; battered women; housing assistance; alcoholic treatment with halfway house; and speakers bureau. *Publication*: The Circle, monthly newsletter. Library.

GREATER LOWELL INDIAN CULTURAL ASSOCIATION
P.O. Box 1181 • LOWELL, MA 01853
(617) 957-4714

MASSACHUSETTS INDIAN ASSOCIATION
(508) 369-1235; Marjorie M. Findlay, Director
Purpose: To help Native Americans go to college. *Scholarship Fund*: Financial assistance to Native Americans who live in Massachusetts and are interested in pursuing postsecondary education. Stipends range up to $500 for undergraduates and $1,000 for graduate students

MICHIGAN

MICHIGAN INDIAN EMPLOYMENT & TRAINING SERVICES
1900 W. Stadium Blvd. C-1
ANN ARBOR, MI 48103 (313) 930-6860

MENTAL HEALTH INDIAN TASK FORCE
Rt. 1, Box 45 • BARAGA, MI 49908
(906) 353-6671
Purpose: To improve counseling and other services for Michigan's Native Americans.

SOUTH EASTERN MICHIGAN INDIANS, INC.
26641 Lawrence St. • CENTER LINE, MI 48090
(810) 956-1350 Fax 756-1352
Patrick Naganashe, President
Nancy Ragsdale, Director
Purpose: To provide services to the Native American Indian of the metro tri-county areas including: job placement, employment and training activities, classroom training, referrals for other services, emergency food and clothing, and the preservation of Indian culture. Activities: Senior programs & special summer youth programs; pow-wows, cultural activities; museum display area; arts & crafts store "The Crafts of Many Tribes"; in the process of setting up a library. *Publication*: Talking Peace Pipes, bimonthly newsletter. Founded 1975.

ABORIGINAL RESEARCH CLUB
c/o Jerry Atkinson, Dearborn Historical Museum
915 Brady Rd. • DEARBORN, MI 48124
(313) 565-3000; Jerry Atkinson, President
Membership: Professional and amateur archaeologists, historians and ethnologists interested in the archaeology of Michigan, Great Lakes region, and Indians of the area. Library. Bimonthly meeting. Founded 1940.

NORTH AMERICAN INDIAN ASSOCIATION OF DETROIT, INC.
22720 Plymouth Rd. • DETROIT, MI 48239
(313) 535-2966 Fax 535-8060
Euphemia 'Sue' Parrish, Executive Director
Website: www.naiadetroit.org
Membership: 450. *Purpose*: To promote self-sufficiency for Native Americans through education, assistance, employment training, and awareness of available human services; to foster and preserve Native American culture and heritage. *Programs*: WIA-DINAP, Native Literacy, Senior's Program, Youth Programs. Activities: Social, employment and educational services; Arts and Crafts Gallery business. *Publication*: Native Sun, bimonthly newsletter. Library. Annual meeting and powwow. Established 1940.

URBAN INDIAN AFFAIRS
1200 - 6th Ave., 8th Fl.
DETROIT, MI 48052
(313) 256-1633
Thelma Henry-Shipman, Contact

GENESSEE INDIAN CENTER
FLINT, MI 48503
Sam Fisher, Chairperson
Purpose: To provide social and economic development opportunities to the 6,000 Native-Americans living in the following Michigan Counties: Genesee, Lapeer, Shiawassee, Huron, Sanilac and Tuscola. *Programs*: Outreach services (housing, education, health, etc.); cultural and recreational activities; craft classes; Native-American art shows; Indian crafts store. *Publication*: GVIA Grapevine, monthly newsletter. Museum. Library.

MICHIGAN INDIAN PRESS
GRAND RAPIDS, MI 49504
J. Wagner Wheeler, Exec. Director
Purpose: To offer the unique perspective of Native Amerian peoples - striving for cultural accuracy in all publications. *Programs*: Publishes textbooks by and about Native Americans. *Publications*: People of the Three Fires, by James Clifton, George Cornell & James McClurken; Aobe NaBing, by M.T. Bussey, and Research & Writing Tribal Histories, by Dr. Duane Hale.

NATIVE AMERICAN ARTS & CRAFTS COUNCIL
P.O. Box 1049 • GRAYLING, MI 49788
(517) 348-3190

MICHIGAN COMMISSION ON INDIAN AFFAIRS
P.O. Box 30026 • LANSING, MI 48909
(517) 373-0654 Betty Klenitz, Director
Purpose: To represent the concerns of Indians in the state and works with them in liaison with private and public agencies including the federal government. Provides financial assistance to Native American high school graduates of Michigan who are interested in attending college in Michigan. Amount of awards vary. *Publication*: "The Michigan Indian."

MICHIGAN INDIAN EDUCATION OFFICE
Dept. of Education
P.O. Box 30008 • LANSING, MI 48909
(517) 373-6059
Pam Martell, Coordinator

LUCE COUNTY INTERTRIBAL COUNCIL
P.O. Box 155 • NEWBERRY, MI 49868
(906) 293-3491
Purpose: To coordinate activities of Native Americans residing in Luce County.

COMMITTEE FOR ACTION FOR RURAL INDIANS
401 Liberty St. • PETOSKEY, MI 49770
(616) 347-0059
Purpose: To work for programs and policies of special interest to Indians in isolated communities.

SAGINAW INTER-TRIBAL ASSOCIATION, INC.
3175 Christy Way • SAGINAW, MI 48603
(989) 792-4610
Victoria G. Miller, Executive Director
Purpose: To service the socio-economic needs of American Indians in the Saginaw-Bay area. *Programs*: Cultural enrichment and awareness classes; community health and health referrals; substance abuse referrals; genealogy referrals; information. *Publication*: Bear Talk, monthly newsletter.

INTER-TRIBAL COUNCIL OF MICHIGAN
2956 Ashmun St.
SAULT STE. MARIE, MI 49783
(906) 632-6896
Sharon L. Teeple, Executive Director
Purpose: To plan and carry out programs which will improve the economy, education and quality of life for Michigan Indian people. *Programs*: Families First Program; Commodity Food Program; Head Start and Parent Child Center Programs; Low Income Energy Assistance; Single Parent Program; Mental Health Program. Founded 1968.

MICHIGAN INDIAN CHILD WELFARE AGENCY
2956 Ashmun St.
SAULT STE. MARIE, MI 49783
(906) 635-9400
LeAnne E. Silvey, Executive Director
Purpose: To provide foster care and adoption/placement agency for Native American children, founded to facilitate P.L. 95-608 (The Indian Child Welfare Act) of 1978. Provides social services, foster care placement, foster home licensing, adoption placement and home studies. *Program*: Family Friend Program. *Publications*: Family Friend Training Manual; Model Tribal Adoption Code. Founded 1978.

NATIVE AMERICAN STUDIES CONFERENCE
c/o Native American Center
Lake Superior State University
SAULT STE. MARIE, MI 49783 (906) 635-2223

MINNESOTA

MINNESOTA STATE DEPT. OF EDUCATION
State Services Center
3801 Bemidji Ave. N, Suite 5
BEMIDJI, MN 56601 (218) 755-2926
Indian Scholarship Program: Financial assistance to Native American high school graduatess in Minnesota who are interested in pursuing postsecondary education. Scholarships range from $500 to $2,000. The average award is $1,200.

MINNESOTA INDIAN AFFAIRS COUNCIL
3801 Bemidji Ave. N, Suite 5
BEMIDJI, MN 56601 (218) 755-3825;
Roger Head, Executive Director

ANISHINABE LEGAL SERVICES, INC.
P.O. Box 157, 411 First St. N.W.
CASS LAKE, MN 56633
(218) 335-2223 Fax 335-7988
Margaret Seelye Treuer, Executive Director
Purpose: To provide legal assistance to low-income persons living within the boundaries of the Leech Lake, Red Lake, and White Earth Reservations in northern Minnesota. Limited law library for staff attorneys.

JUNIOR ACHIEVEMENT'S URBAN AMERICAN INDIAN PROGRAM
EDINA, MN 55435
Ron Cody, Contact
Purpose: To target the problems of urban Native American Youth. Programs: 20 Native American students 14-19 years old, who will develop and run their own business (developed with the American Indian Opportunities Industrialization Center); Native American Economic Initiative - provides Native American K-12 students at the Mille Lacs Reservation in-class economic education including work force readiness skills. Publication: Native Models for Business Success.

AMERICAN INDIAN SERVICES
73 Franklin Ave. E. • MINNEAPOLIS, MN 55404
(612) 871-2175
A halfway house for Native American men.

INDIAN NEIGHBORHOOD CLUB
1805 Portland Ave.
MINNEAPOLIS, MN 55404
(612) 871-7412

INDIAN FAMILY SERVICES, INC.
1305 E. 24th St.
MINNEAPOLIS, MN 55404
(612) 348-5788
Purpose: To provide services to Indian elderly and the disabled

INDIAN HEALTH BOARD OF MINNEAPOLIS
1315 East 24th St.
MINNEAPOLIS, MN 55404
(612) 721-7425
Noreen Smith, Director of Indian Family Services.

MINNEAPOLIS AMERICAN INDIAN CENTER
1530 E. Franklin Ave.
MINNEAPOLIS, MN 55404
(612) 871-4555
Frances Fairbanks, Executive Director
Goals: To foster the social and economic development of the Indian community of Minneapolis. Provides a variety of social, educational, cultural and economic programs and services, including: Indian Child Welfare; Chemical Dependency Counseling and Prevention Education; Adult Basic Education; JTPA Employment and Training; Youth Intervention; Recreation; and Senior Citizens. Operates Two Rivers Gallery art museum, First People's Gallery, and Circle Cafe. *Publication*: The Circle, monthly newspaper. Established 1974.

MINNEAPOLIS AMERICAN INDIAN SERVICES
735 Franklin St., NE
MINNEAPOLIS, MN55404
(612) 871-2175
A local service group which seeks to meet the needs of Native Americans living in the Twin City area.

MINNEAPOLIS INDIAN HEALTH BOARD
1315 East 24th St. • MINNEAPOLIS, MN 55404
(612) 721-9800
Purpose: To plan, carry out, and audit health services provided for the area's Indian community.

MINNESOTA DEPARTMENT OF INDIAN WORK
3045 Park Ave. • MINNEAPOLIS, MN 55407

MINNESOTA INDIAN EDUCATION ASSOCIATION
Metropolitan State University
730 Hennepin Ave.
MINNEAPOLIS, MN 56603
(612) 729-7397 Flo Wiger, Contact

MINNESOTA INDIAN WOMEN'S RESOURCE CENTER
2300 15th Ave. S.
MINNEAPOLIS, MN 55404
(612) 728-2000 Fax 728-2039
Margaret Peake Raymond, Executive Director
Purpose: To provide charitable services to American Indian women and their children in the following areas: housing, chemical dependency treatment, family reunification/crisis intervention, children's day care, and training. *Activities*: Staff training, community lectures and program technical assistance services; and parenting education training. Library. Established 1974.

UPPER MIDWEST AMERICAN INDIAN CENTER
1113 West Broadway
MINNEAPOLIS, MN 55411
(612) 522-4436
Dennis Morrison, Executive Director

LAKOTA CULTURAL EDUCATION SERVICE
806 S. Water St.
NORTH FIELD, MN 55057
(507) 663-1090

AMERICAN INDIAN CENTER
St. Cloud State University
720 4th Ave. S. • ST. CLOUD, MN 56301

IRA HAYES FRIENDSHIP HOUSE
1671 Summit Ave. • ST. PAUL, MN 55105

MINNESOTA DEPT. OF HUMAN SERVICES
Chemical Dependency Program Division
444 Lafayette Rd. • ST. PAUL, MN 55155

MINNESOTA HISTORICAL SOCIETY
690 Cedar St. • ST. PAUL, MN 55101

MINNESOTA INDIAN AFFAIRS COUNCIL
127 University Ave. • ST. PAUL, MN 55155
(612) 296-3611
JoAnne Stately, Acting Director
Purpose: The official liaison between state and tribal governments and advisor to the state on urban Indian issues and concerns: health, education, welfare and other public support, housing economic development, protection of the environment, and protection of tribal rights. The council is governed by the elected tribal chair of the 11 reservations throughout the state, and two at large members from other states. The council has an Urban Indian Advisory Committee. Minnesota has an American Indian population of about 52,000.

TWIN CITIES CHIPPEWA COUNCIL
1592 Hoyt Ave. East • ST. PAUL, MN 55105

SOUTH ST. PAUL INDIAN EDUCATION
125 Sixth Ave. N. • SO. ST. PAUL, MN 55075

MISSOURI

HEART OF AMERICA INDIAN CENTER
600 West 39th St. • KANSAS CITY, MO 64124
(816) 421-7608
Carolyn King, exec director
Gail Edmonds, Morning Star Program Coordinator
Activities: Blue Buffalo Trading Post

AMERICAN INDIAN CENTER
4115 Connecticut • ST. LOUIS, MO 63116
(314) 773-3316
Publication: Eyapaha, newsletter.

SOUTHWEST INDIAN CENTER
543 S. Scenic Ave. • SPRINGFIELD, MO 65802
(417) 869-9550; Mike Fields, Executive Director
Purpose: Established to alleviate the problems of low-income Native American Indians in the urban setting. To provide understanding between Indian people and the white dominated community. To provide cultural presentations to assist in the learning process. *Activities*: Social services, counseling, emergency services, referral, alcohol & drug abuse prevention program. *Publication*: "Rising Sun Newsletter, monthly newsletter.

MONTANA

INDIAN HEALTH BOARD OF BILLINGS
1127 Alderson Ave. • BILLINGS, MT 59102
(406) 245-7318 Fax 248-3043
Gloria Cohens, Director
Description: An urban Indian health program providing a walk-in clinic, outpatient substance abuse and mental health programs, health education, and community outreach services.

BLACKFEET CRAFTS ASSOCIATION
P.O. Box 51 • BROWNING, MT 59417
(406) 338-4075
Description: A craft organization marketing items made by members of the Blackfeet tribe.

MONTANA INTER-TRIBAL POLICY BOARD
c/o Roland Kennedy
P.O. Box 850 • BROWNING, MT 59417
(406) 652-3113
Purpose: To represent, develop, protect, and advance the economic, cultural, social, and political well-being of Indian people in the State of Montana. Provides training and technical assistance to seven Indian reservations in the areas of social services, economic development, law and order, natural resource development, and personnel management. *Publication*: Newsletter.

NORTHERN PLAINS INDIAN CRAFTS ASSOCIATION
P.O. Box E • BROWNING, MT 59417
(406) 338-5661
Description: An independent business owned by Native American craftsmen from the Northern Plains region. *Objectives*: To provide a sales outlet for the finest contemporary Native American arts and crafts products; and to help promote the careers of outstanding Native American artists and craftsmen. Products include paintings, Indian dance accessories, jewelry, dolls, Indian pipes, quill-work items, beadwork items, etc. Museum shop located in the Northern Plains Museum. Established 1942.

NORTH AMERICAN INDIAN ALLIANCE
P.O. Box 286 • BUTTE, MT 59701
(406) 723-4361
Purpose: To work for improved conditions for Native Americans in the Butte area; to sponsor cultural activities.

CROW AGENCY HISTORICAL & CULTURAL COMMISSION
Box 159 • CROW AGENCY, MT 59022
(406) 638-2328
Purpose: To collect and display items dealing with the Crow Nation and works for a more accurate presentation of its heritage.

NATIVE AMERICAN CENTER HEALTH PROGRAM
P.O. Box 2612 • GREAT FALLS, MT 59403

MONTANA INDIAN EDUCATION ASSOCIATION
P.O. Box 848 • HARLEM, MT 59526
(406) 353-2205; Carol Juneau, President
Activities: Sponsors an annual conference. *Publication*: The Buckskin Journal, bimonthly newsletter. Established in 1979.

GOVERNOR'S OFFICE OF INDIAN AFFAIRS
Rm. 202, State Capitol
Box 200801 • HELENA, MT 59620
(406) 444-3702
Kathleen M. Fleury, Coordinator
Purpose: To provide a greater understanding between Montana's Indian population and local, state and federal government agencies; to seek ways and means of communicating their opinions and needs to agencies of responsibility and actively assist them in organizing their efforts; and to act as representative for organized bodies of Indians.

HELENA INDIAN ALLIANCE
Leo Pocha Memorial Health Clinic
436 North Jackson
HELENA, MT 59601 (406) 442-9334
Purpose: To provide programs aimed toward the development of the Native American community

MONTANA COMMERCE DEPT.
Indian Affairs, 1424 9th Ave.
HELENA, MT 59260 (406) 444-3702
Kathleen Fleury, Coordinator

MONTANA STATE OFFICE OF PUBLIC INSTRUCTION
Indian Education Specialist
State Capitol - Rm. 106
HELENA, MT 59620
(406) 444-3031 Fax 444-3924
Robert Parsley, Contact
Purpose: To provide technical assistance and materials in the area of Indian education. *Activities*: Training for teaching Indian children is provided for parents, school boards and teachers.

NORTHERN CHEYENNE TRIBAL HOUSING AUTHORITY
P.O. Box 327
LAME DEER, MT 59043
John Walks Along, Executive Director
(406) 477-6419 ext. 107

INDIAN DEVELOPMENT & EDUCATION ALLIANCE
P.O. Box 726 • MILES CITY, MT 59301
(406) 232-6112

MISSOULA INDIAN CENTER
Native American Services Agency
MISSOULA, MT 59801
 (406) 329-3373 Fax 329-3398
 Bill Walls, Executive Director
 Debbie Tatsey, Health Coordinator
 Kitty Felix, Outreach Worker
 James Dempsey, Clinic Coordinator
 Jesse Collins, Mental Health Coordinator
Purpose: To provide for the general welfare of the
Missoula Urban Indian community through provision
of health and human services. *Special programs*: Youth
Indian Cultural Enrichment Programs; Health Interven-
tion & Prevention; AIDS/STD Awareness; Mental
Health Program; Chemical Dependence & Substance
Abuse Program; Child Welfare Act Program. *Publica-
tion*: Buffalo Grass Newsletter. Established 1970.

SALISH-KOOTENAI HOUSING AUTHORITY
P.O. Box 38 • PABLO, MT 89855
 (406) 675-4491 Fax 675-4495
 Robert Gauthier, Director

KICKING HORSE JOB CORPS CENTER
2000 Molman Pass Trail
RONAN, MT 59864 (800) 234-5705
Description: The first American Indian job corps center. It is operated by the Flathead Reservation and
complements job training activities with information on
the Native American cultural heritage.

NEBRASKA

AMERICAN INDIAN COUNCIL
128 S. Potash • ALLIANCE, NE 69301
 Mark Monroe

LINCOLN INDIAN CENTER
1100 Military Rd. • LINCOLN, NE 68508
 (402) 474-5231
 Lawrence SpottedBird, Executive Director
Publication: Lincoln Indian Journal.

**NEBRASKA STATE COMMISSION
ON INDIAN AFFAIRS**
State Capitol Bldg., 6th Floor
Box 94981 • LINCOLN, NE 68509-4981
 (402) 471-3475 Fax 471-3392
 Judi Morgan, Executive Director

OMAHA TRIBAL HOUSING AUTHORITY
P.O. Box 150 • MACY, NE 68039
 (402) 837-5728
 Erica Spears, Executive Director

AMERICAN NATIVE CORPORATION
2451 St. Mary's St. • OMAHA, NE 68102
 (402) 341-8471
 Violet M. Fickel, Executive Director

**NEBRASKA INDIAN INTER-TRIBAL
DEVELOPMENT CORPORATION**
Route 1, Box 66A • WINNEBAGO, NE 68071
 (402) 878-2242; Frank Dean La Mere, Director
Purpose: To aid in the social and economic develop-
ment of the Omaha, Winnebago and Santee Sioux
Tribes of Nebraska. *Programs*: Job Traiing Partner-
ship Act; Indian Food Distribution Program; Economic
& Community Development Programs; et al. Founded
1969.

NEVADA

NEVADA INDIAN COMMISSION
5366 Snyder Ave. • CARSON CITY, NV 89701
 (775) 687-8333 Fax 687-8330
 E-mail: nic@govmail.state.nv.us
 Leslie L. Blossom, Director
Purpose: To study matters affecting the social and economic welfare and well-being of American Indians residing in Nevada; to improve cooperation between
agencies & Indian groups; to enhance a general understanding of Indian law; and to assist tribes in acquiring or reacquiring federal land, identifying and researching problems to find solutions. *Publications*:

Directory; Supplement to directory; Guide to Nevada
Indian-Owned Businesses; and Population Profile. Established 1965.

NEVADA URBAN INDIANS
1802 N. Carson St.
CARSON CITY, NV 89701
 (702) 883-4439 Fax 883-6981
See Reno listing.

LAS VEGAS INDIAN CENTER
2300 W. Bonanza Rd.
LAS VEGAS, NV 89106
 (702) 647-5842
 Richard W. Arnold, Executive Director
 Anna Johnson, Associate Director
Promotes the social and economic self-sufficiency of
American Indians through the provision of education
and employment. *Special programs*: Social services,
adult education, career education, employment and
training assistance, cultural activities, alcoholics
anonymous, energy assistance, and special interest
workshops and seminars. Founded 1972.

NEVADA URBAN INDIANS
1190 Bible Way • RENO, NV 89502
 (775) 788-7600 Fax 788-7611
 Janet Reeves, Executive Director
Purpose: To provide quality health care to the area's
urban Indian population by providing a variety of social and health services using a blend of traditional &
modern medicine. *Activities*: Community health care,
health promotion and disease prevention, alcohol and
drug abuse prevention and treatment program, mental health services. *Publications*: Reno Talking Leaf,
quarterly newsletter; brochures on available services.
Established 1975.

**NEVADA-CALIFORNIA INDIAN
HOUSING ASSOCIATION**
Yerington Paiute Housing Authority
31 W. Loop Rd. • YERINGTON, NV 89447
 (775) 463-2225 Fax 463-2316
 Ralph Rogers, Executive Director

NEW HAMPSHIRE

**NEW ENGLAND ANTIQUITIES
RESEARCH ASSOCIATION**
305 Academy Rd. • PEMBROKE, NH 03275
 (603) 485-5655; Daniel J. Leary, President
Purpose: To explore the origins of enigmatic stone
structures throughout the Northeastern U.S.; to form
a better understanding of our historic and prehistoric
past. *Research activities*: Anthropology, archaeology;
Native American studies of stoneworks and related
structures in the northeastern U.S. Archaeology in
Maine and New Hampshire. *Publications*: NEARA
Journal, Semiannual; NEARA Transit Newsletter Semiannual. Library. Founded 1964.

NEW JERSEY

AMERICAN INDIAN COUNCIL OF NEW JERSEY
P.O. Box 553
BRIDGETON, NJ 08302
 (609) 455-6910

INTER-TRIBAL INDIANS OF NEW JERSEY
21 Village Rd.
MORGANVILLE, NJ 07751
 (732) 591-8335/390-1642
 Brenda Davis, President; Helen Rende, VP
Purpose: To support needs of members by providing
programs and projects which reflect the Native American Indian culture and heritage; to promote well-being and self-esteem of members through cultural activities; to collect information and serve as a resource
on American Indian cultures and services available to
Native Americans. *Council members*: Brenda & Marvin
Davis, Shirley Weiler, Monica Paul, Helen Rende, and
Rose Marie Terry and Dennis Keith. *Activities*: Language (Mohawk) and crafts classes; educational programs for self and community. Library. *Publication*:
Quarterly newsletter.

NEW JERSEY GOVERNOR'S OFFICE
Ethnic Advisory Council • State House CN001
125 W. State St. • TRENTON, NJ 08625
 (609) 292-6000; 261-4747
 Roy Crazy Horse, Chief
 Kathryn Schneberk-King, Attorney

NEW MEXICO

TEN SOUTHERN PUEBLOS COUNCIL
Pueblo of Acoma, P.O. Box 309
ACOMITA, NM 87034

**ALBUQUERQUE URBAN INDIAN
HEALTH-HUMAN SERVICES**
4100 Silver Ave., SE #B
ALBUQUERQUE, NM 87108

**ALL INDIAN BUSINESS
DEVELOPMENT CENTER**
P.O. Box 3256
ALBUQUERQUE, NM 87190
 (505) 889-9092
Purpose: To provide technical assistance and management consulting to Native American people and
other minorities in New Mexico who want to start a
business or who already own one. *Publication*: Directory of Indian-Owned Businesses for New Mexico.

ALL INDIAN PUEBLO COUNCIL
P.O. Box 400
 ALBUQUERQUE, NM 87190
 (505) 881-1992 Fax 883-7682
 Amadeo Shije, Chairperson
 Website: www.aipcinc.com
Membership: 19. *Purpose*: To serve as advocate on
behalf of 19 Pueblo Indian tribes on education, health,
social and economic issues. *Activities*: Operates
boarding school, Indian Pueblo Cultural Center Museum, and theatre in Albuquerque. Maintains business
development center, and library and archival collection. *Projects*: Indian Business Development Corporation; Social Economic Development Strategies. *Publication*: Governors 19 Indian Pueblos, annual directory; pamphlets and brochures. Library. Established
in 1598.

**AMERICAN INDIAN BILINGUAL
EDUCATION CENTER**
U. of New Mexico
ALBUQUERQUE, NM 87131
 (505) 277-3551
Purpose: To provide information about Title VII projects
in its area and helps to ensure better utilization of bi-
lingual education materials and techniques.

COMMISSION ON STATE TRIBAL RELATIONS
UNM - American Indian Law Center
Box 4456, Sta. A
ALBUQUERQUE, NM 87196
 (505) 277-5462
Purpose: To encourage and incite more favorable re-
lations between American Indian tribes among vari-
ous states.

**FARMINGTON INTERTRIBAL
INDIAN ORGANIZATION**
P.O. Box 2322
ALBUQUERQUE, NM 87401
 (505) 327-6296

FIRST NATIONS COMMUNITY HEALTH SERVICE
ALBUQUERQUE, NM 87108
 (505) 262-2481
 Charles J. Ederer, Executive Director
Purpose: To serve the Native American population of
Albuquerque with programs and services designed to
elevate the standard of health, socio-economic stand-
ing, and educational level. *Programs*: Primary Care
Clinic; WIC Nutrition; Alcohol and Substance Abuse;
Community Health and Health Education; Emergency
Assistance; Information and Referral. Established in
1985.

INDIAN ADVISORY COMMISSION
P.O. Box 1667 • ALBUQUERQUE, NM 87107

KIVA CLUB
U. of New Mexico, Mesa Vista Hall #1117-A
ALBUQUERQUE, NM 87131-2066
(505) 277-8259
Lucille Stillwell, Executive Director
Rick Cate, President; Shawn Secatero, V.P.
Felicia Begay, Secretary
Rosella Silversmith, Treasurer
Description: A social group that focuses on Native American cultures and heritage and retention among Native American students. *Special programs*: Counseling; career planning and placement; Anizhone Week in April that features Native American speakers, films, and contemporary singers, and ends with an on-campus pow-wow. Established in 1952.

SIPI ALCOHOLISM PROGRAM
P.O. Box 10146, 9169 Coors Rd., NW
ALBUQUERQUE, NM 87114

STATE TRIBAL RELATIONS COMMITTEE
P.O. Box 4456, Sta. A
ALBUQUERQUE, NM 87196
(505) 277-5462

WATER INFORMATION NETWORK
P.O. Box 4524
ALBUQUERQUE, NM 87106
(505) 255-4072 Fax 262-1864
Lila Bird, Contact

FIVE SANDOVAL INDIAN PUEBLOS, INC.
1043 Hwy. 313 • BERNALILLO, NM 87004
(505) 867-3351 Fax 867-3514
William F. Weahkee, Executive Director
Purpose: To serve pueblos (Sandia, Santa Ana, Jemez, Cochiti and Zia) as a consortium with various human services and needs. Programs: Health & Human Services; Employment & Training; Head Start, Women, Infant & Children's programs; Economic & Social Development program, etc. Small reference library. Established in 1966.

JICARILLA ART & CRAFTS
P.O. Box 507 • DULCE, NM 87528
(505) 759-3362

SOUTHWEST INDIAN FOUNDATION
P.O. Box 86 • GALLUP, NM 87305
(505) 863-9568 Fax 863-2760
William McCarthy, Contact
Purpose: To provide an outlet for local Native American handicrafts, including jewelry, clothing, mugs, books and toys. *Publication*: Catalog

**UNITED INDIAN PUEBLO
LAWYERS ASSOCIATION**
P.O. Box 402 • ISLETA PUEBLO, NM 87022
(505) 869-3421; Christine Zuni, Contact

EIGHT NORTHERN PUEBLOS, INC.
P.O. Box 969 • SAN JUAN PUEBLO, NM 87566
(505) 852-4265
Head Start Program.

**NEW MEXICO INDIAN
EDUCATION ASSOCIATION**
P.O. Box 16356 • SANTA FE, NM 87506
(505) 989-5569
Julia Nathanson/Catherine Coulter, Contacts
Purpose: To foster the self-sufficiency of Native Americans through the identification, development and dissemination of quality educational projects. *Publications*: The NMIEA Newsletter; three historical documents for teachers.

NEW MEXICO OFFICE ON INDIAN AFFAIRS
La Villa Rivera Bldg., 228 E. Palace Ave.
SANTA FE, NM 87501
(505) 827-6440 Fax 827-6445
Regis Pecos, Executive Director
Purpose: To serve as a coordinating agency for intergovernmental programs concerning tribal governments and the state of New Mexico; to recruit and place qualified Indians in jobs with state agencies.

**NEW MEXICO SENATE STANDING
COMMITTEE ON INDIAN AFFAIRS**
State Capitol • SANTA FE, NM 87503
(505) 986-4314; John Pinto, Contact

NEW MEXICO STATE DEPT. OF EDUCATION
Division of Indian Education, Education Bldg.
300 Don Gaspar • SANTA FE, NM 87501
(505) 827-6679 Fax 827-6696
Nancy Martine Alonzo, Contact
Purpose: Responsible for promoting quality education for Indian students in New Mexico. *Activities*: Assists schools in preparing curricula for Indian students; disseminates information, plans sessions with tribal entities, and developes workshops.

**SOUTHWESTERN ASSOCIATION
FOR INDIAN ARTS, INC.**
P.O. Box 969 • SANTA FE, NM 87504-0969
(505) 983-5220 Fax 983-7647
Jean F. Marquardt, Executive Director
E-mail: info@swaia.org
Web site: www.swaia.org
Purpose: To promote economic well being of Native American artists. Produces the Santa Fe Indian Market - over 600 booths and more than 1,200 Indian artists - the third weekend in August each year. Provides educational programs which benefit the Native American artist. Scholarship program. Established in 1922.

ST. BONAVENTURE NAVAJO MISSION
P.O. Box 610 • THOREAU, NM 87323
(505) 862-7847
A Roman Catholic social service mission working with impoverished Navajos. It offers school programs, health, food and other aid.

NEW YORK

TONAWANDA INDIAN COMMUNITY LIBRARY
P.O. Box 326, 372 Bloomingdale Rd.
AKRON, NY 14001 (716) 542-5618
Ramona Charles, Director

NY STATE EDUCATION DEPT.
Native Americans Program
543 Education Bldg. Annex
Washington Ave. • ALBANY, NY 12234
(518) 474-0537 Fax 486-2331
Minerva White, Coordinator

AMERICAN INDIAN INFORMATION CENTER
139-11 87th Ave. • BRIARWOOD, NY 11435
(718) 291-7732
Mifaunwy Shuntona Hines, Director

**NATIVE AMERICAN COMMUNITY SERVICES
OF ERIE & NIAGARA COUNTIES**
1047 Grant St. • BUFFALO, NY 14207
(716) 874-4990
Purpose: To offer education, job training, placement assistance, youth program, and family services.

NATIVE AMERICAN PEOPLE'S ALLIANCE
3435 Main St. • BUFFALO, NY 14214
(716) 836-1070
Description: A federation of Native Americans living in the Buffalo-Niagara Falls area.

**NEW YORK STATE OFFICE OF
CHILDREN & FAMILY SERVICES**
Native American Services.
General Donovan State Office Bldg.
125 Main St., Rm. 475 • BUFFALO, NY 14203
(716) 847-3123 Fax 847-3812
Kim M. Thomas, Native American Affairs Specialist
Purpose: To provide social services to Native Americans; to maintain liaison with Native American nations and other Native Americans organizations. *Activities*: provides consultative and information and referral services; searches and reviews historical files to assist Native Americans to research their ancestry. *Special programs*: provides special training programs to local departments; child welfare development services. *Publication*: A Proud Heritage - Native American Services in New York State.

**NORTHEASTERN NATIVE AMERICAN
ASSOCIATION, INC.**
P.O. Box 230266 • HOLLIS, NY 11423
(718) 978-7057 Fax 978-7200
E-Mail: rgibson230@aol.com
William "Wassaja" Gibson, President

Purpose: To honor, respect and keep alive the traditions and spirituality of our Native American ancestors. To acquaint our members with the current needs of our people. *Activities*: Oppose the desecration and commercialization of the graves and sacred places of all natives. *Publication*: Smoke Signals, quarterly newsletter. Established in 1990.

**ASSOCIATION OF EASTERN
INDIAN HOUSING AUTHORITIES**
P.O. Box 213 • IRVING, NY 14081
(716) 532-5000
Description: A federation of Native American housing authorities from a number of eastern tribes in the area.

AMERICAN INDIAN ARTISTS, INC. (AMERINDA)
c/o AFSC, 15 Rutherford Pl.
NEW YORK, NY 10003
(212) 598-0968 Fax 529-4603
Diane Fraher Thornton, Director
E-mail: amerinda@amerinda.org
Website: www.amerinda.org
Purpose: American Indian Artists works to empower Native Americans, break down barriers, and foster understanding and appreciation for Native culture. Through a variety of arts programs, productions and services to artists, AMERINDA supports Native artists who embody the traditional practices and values that define Indian culture. AMERINDA also promotes the indigenous perspective in the arts to a wide audience through mainstream art forms—visual, performing, literacy and media arts. *Publication*: "Talking Stick," Native arts quarterly. Established in 1987.

AMERICAN INDIAN COMMUNITY HOUSE
708 Broadway, 8th Floor
NEW YORK, NY 10003
(212) 598-0100 Fax 598-4909
Website: www.aich.org
Rosemary Richmond, Executive Director
Carrese P. Gullo, Communications Director
Anthony Hunter, Health Director
Cissy Elm, HIV/AIDS Project Director
LaTanya Hutchins, WIA Director
Jim Cyrus, Peforming Arts Director
Purpose: To further the status of American Indians and to educate the general public about American Indians, past and present. *Programs*: Job training and placement; higher education assistance, out-patient alcohol and substance abuse counseling and related services; health department; health education and referrals; social service advocacy; HIV/AIDS Project. education and case management; legal services; art gallery; The Circle, theater and rehearsal space. *PublicationS*: AICH Bulletin, quarterly newsletter; Elders' Morning Drum: Women's Wellness, Diabetes, and Youth Program Information, bimonthly newsletter; NALCHA News, HIV/AIDS project newsletter. Library. Gift Shop. Established in 1969.

AMERICAN INDIAN LAW ALLIANCE
708 Broadway, 8th Fl. • NEW YORK, NY 10003
(212) 598-0100 x 257
Tonya Gonnella Frichner, Esq., Director
Purpose: To advocate for the survival of Native cultures, individuals and nations with the emphasis of our advocacy in the law. *Activities/Programs*: Research and technical support for traditional original Native governments on national and international levels; legal services project for individuals in New York City with specific legal problems. Established in 1987.

NUYAGI KEETOOWAH SOCIETY
P.O. Box 429 • POMONA, NY 10970
David Michael Wolfe, Chairperson
Sam Beeler, Historian
Paula S. Washington, Treasurer
Christina Bryant, Scribe
Councilmembers: Diana Gubishay Ayala and Udanuhi Agehya Noquisi.

NATIVE AMERICAN CULTURAL CENTER, INC.
1344 University Ave., Suite 230
ROCHESTER, NY 14607
(716) 482-1100 Fax 482-1304
Martha Fahrer, Director
Description: Urban Indian center providing employement, education, health and human services to an 18-county service delivery area in upstate New York. Video library. Established in 1976.

ALLEGHENY INDIAN ARTS & CRAFTS COOP.
Haley Bldg. • SALAMANCA, NY 14779
(716) 945-1790
Purpose: To sell items made by the Allegheny Senecas, including beadwork, baskets, masks, and cornhusk dolls.

**SHINNECOCK NATIVE AMERICAN
CULTURAL COALITION**
P.O. Box 59 • SOUTHAMPTON, NY 11968
(516) 283-6143

AMERICAN INDIAN CENTER
740 N. Salina St. • SYRACUSE, NY 13208
(315) 475-6229; Theresa Steele, Director

NORTH AMERICAN INDIAN CLUB
P.O. Box 851 • SYRACUSE, NY 13201
(315) 476-7425; Carol Moses, Manager
Operates retail arts and crafts shop.

NORTH CAROLINA

**CHEROKEE BOYS CLUB, INC.
CHEROKEE CENTER FOR FAMILY SERVICES**
P.O. Box 507 • CHEROKEE, NC 28719
(704) 497-5001 Fax 497-5818
Joy Evans-Widenhouse, Editor
E-Mail: ccfs@dnet.net
The Club provides services and educational programs for Cherokee youth. The Center operates a children's home, emergency shelter, three child care centers, a substance abuse and crime prevention program for adolescents, two food pantries and clothes closets, parenting programs, transportation and utility assistance and a number of other social services. *Publications*: Club newsletter; Center newsletter, "Cherokee Voice." Established in 1965.

CHEROKEE HISTORICAL ASSOCIATION
P.O. Box 398 • CHEROKEE, NC 28719
(704) 497-2111
Dr. Ed Henson, Executive Director
Barry Hipps, General Manager
Purpose: To preserve and perpetuate history and culture of the Eastern Band of Cherokee Indians. *Exhibits*: Unto These Hills, an outdoor drama which portrays history of the Cherokee Indians from 1540 to their removal to Oklahoma in 1838 (Mid-June thru late August); the Oconaluftee Indian Village, a replica of a Cherokee community of the 1750 period (Mid-May thru late October). *Publication*: Annual souvenir booklet, $4. Established in 1948.

QUALLA INDIAN BOUNDARY
P.O. Box 1310 • CHEROKEE, NC 28719
(704) 497-9416
Head Start Program.

NATIVE AMERICAN HERITAGE
P.O. Box 3029 • DURHAM, NC 27715
Provides Native American Heritage cards.
Established in 1994.

**CUMBERLAND CO. ASSOCIATION
OF INDIAN PEOPLE**
FAYETTEVILLE, NC 28301
(910) 483-8442 Carol Gowan
Purpose: To assist American Indians in Cumberland County with their social services and economic, educational, and cultural needs. It offers job training, educational classes, cultural festivals, and other activity programs.

GUILFORD NATIVE AMERICAN ASSOCIATION
P.O. Box 5623 • GREENSBORO, NC 27403
(919) 273-8686
Financial assistance programs.

**NORTH CAROLINA ADVISORY
COUNCIL ON INDIAN EDUCATION**
c/o Hope County Schools
P.O. Box 468 • HALIFAX, NC 27839
(919) 583-5111; Ralph Evans, Chairperson

LUMBEE REGIONAL DEVELOPMENT ASSN
P.O. Box 68 • PEMBROKE, NC 28372
(910) 521-8602 Fax 521-8625

E-mail: aclark@lumbee.org
Website: www.lumbee.org
Dewey Locklear, Director
Purpose: To analyze and develop solutions for the health, education, economic, and general welfare of rural and urban Indians in its part of North Carolina. *Special programs*: Child services; Head Start, day care & infant mortality; employment - WIA. *Community services*: Food bank and clothes drives; housing; Lumbee homecoming; Lumbee powwow. *Publication*: Bimonthly The Lumbee News & Reporter. Begun 1968.

**NORTH CAROLINA ADVISORY
COUNCIL ON INDIAN EDUCATION**
NC Dept. of Public Instruction
c/o Pembroke State University
PEMBROKE, NC 28372
Gerald Maynor, Contact
Purpose: To advise the State Board of Education on ways to meet more effectively the education needs of Indian students.

**NORTH CAROLINA CONSORTIUM
ON INDIAN EDUCATION**
P.O. Box 666 • PEMBROKE, NC 28372
(919) 422-3467
Agnes H. Chavis, Director
Description: Statewide nonprofit organization chartered by the State of North Caolina. Consists of parents and guardians of Indian students who have served or currently serve on Title V. *Purpose*: To serve as an advocacy role on state and national issues related to Indian education and networks with more than 300 individuals, agencies, organizations, and projects involved in Indian education.

NORTH CAROLINA INDIAN CULTURAL CENTER
P.O. Box 20410 • PEMBROKE, NC 28372
(919) 833-1931
Purpose: To preserve and present the American Indian heritage.

**NORTH CAROLINA COMMISSION
OF INDIAN AFFAIRS**
North Carolina Dept. of Administration
325 N. Salisbury St. #579
RALEIGH, NC 27603 (919) 733-5998
A. Bruce Jones, Executive Director
North Carolina Amerian Indian Student Legislative Grant: Financial assistance to American Indians in North Carolina who are interested in postsecondary education in an approved North Carolina school. Up to $500 per year. Deadlines vary with each school.

**NORTH CAROLINA STATE
DEPT. OF PUBLIC INSTRUCTION**
Division of Indian Education
301 N. Wilmington St. • RALEIGH, NC 27601
(919) 715-1000; Betty Oxendine Mangum, Director

**STATE INDIAN SCHOLARSHIP
COMMISSION OF HIGHER EDUCATION**
State Capitol Bldg. • RALEIGH, NC 27611

TRIANGLE NATIVE AMERICAN SOCIETY
P.O. Box 26841 • RALEIGH, NC 27611
Mark Ulmer Native American Scholarship: Financial assistance to Native Americans in North Carolina who are interested in contiuing their college education. The stipend is $500 per year. *Deadline*: April.

NORTH DAKOTA

**NORTH DAKOTA INDIAN
EDUCATION ASSOCIATION**
c/o BIA • BELCOURT, ND 58316
(701) 477-3463
Description: A state association of Native American teachers and educators. *Activities*: Holds an annual meeting.

**NORTH DAKOTA DEPT.
OF PUBLIC INSTRUCTION**
Indian Education Office
600 E. Blvd., 9th Floor
BISMARCK, ND 58505-0440
(701) 328-2250 Fax 328-4770
Cheryl M. Kulas, Director

E-Mail: ckulas@ mail.dpi.state.nd.us
Web site: www.dpi.state.nd.us/indianeducation
Purpose: To increase the capacity of the state and school districts to more effectively develop and conduct educational programs for American Indian learners; to provide technical assistance in developing awareness and understanding of Indian learner needs. *Activities*: Maintains networking/liaison efforts in support of Indian education. Small library. *Publications*: Centennial Curriculum of North Dakota Native Americans; 1994 North Dakota Tribal Curriculum; Bibliography of Resource Materials for Educators. Research Library. Established 1952.

NORTH DAKOTA INDIAN AFFAIRS COMMISSION
600 E. Blvd., 1st Floor-State Capitol
BISMARCK, ND 58505 (701) 224-2428
Deborah A. Painte, Executive Director
Purpose: A liaison/referral agency established to facilitate tribal/state relations. *Programs*: Indian Youth Alcohol and Other Drug Prevention Programs. *Publications*: Update, quarterly newsletter; Directory of Statewide Indian Programs. Established 1947.

**NORTH DAKOTA/SOUTH DAKOTA NATIVE
AMERICAN BUSINESS DEVELOPMENT CENTER**
3315 University Dr. • BISMARCK, ND 58504
(701) 530-0608 Fax 530-0607
Brek Maxon, Project Director
E-mail: bmaxon@uttc.edu
Web site: www.ndsd-nabdc.com
Purpose: Provides assistance to Native American entrpreneurs in the Dakotas to foster economic development. A program of United Tribes Technical College, funded by the U.S. Dept. of Commerce's Minority Business Development Agency. Established in 1980.

**NORTH DAKOTA INDIAN
EDUCATION ASSOCIATION**
P.O. Box 199 • FORT TOTTEN, ND 58335
(701) 766-4161
Patricia Walking Eagle, Contact

DAKOTA WOMEN OF ALL RED NATIONS
P.O. Box 69 • FORT YATES, ND 58538
(701) 854-7592; Mabel Ann Phillips, Chairperson
Purpose: Advocacy for Native American treaty rights.
Program: Health Education Program. Newsletter.

NATIVE AMERICAN PROGRAMS
U. of North Dakota, Box 8274
GRAND FORKS, ND 58202 (701) 777-4291
Purpose: To provide tutoring services and educational and financial assistance for Native American students. Also seeks out and recruits talented Native American students and aids them in acquiring a post secondary education.

OHIO

**NORTH AMERICAN INDIAN
CULTURAL CENTERS**
655 N. Main St. • AKRON, OH 44310-3016
(216) 724-1280 Fax 724-9298
H. Clark Hosick, Executive Director
Purpose: To provide employment and exhibition/performance referrals for artists as well as education and training for Native Americans in non-arts fields.

AMERICAN INDIAN MOVEMENT (AIM)
5075 E. 86th St. • CLEVELAND, OH 44125
Bob Roche, Director

**NATIVE AMERICAN INDIAN
CENTER OF CENTRAL OHIO**
67 E. Innis Ave., P.O. Box 07705
COLUMBUS, OH 43207-0705
(614) 443-6120 Fax 443-2651
Carol L. Welsh, Executive Director
E-mail: naicco@aol.com; Web site: naicco.tripod.com
Purpose: To serve the social and cultural needs of the Native American Indian community of central Ohio. *Programs*: Employment referrals; health services; cultural programs; tutoring; drug and alcohol programs; food & clothing. *Activities*: Powwows (Memorial Day weekend & Labor Day weekend). *Publication*: Quarterly newsletter. Library. Established 1975.

OHIO CENTER FOR NATIVE AMERICAN AFFAIRS
7916 Braun Rd. • GROVEPORT, OH 43125
(614) 228-0460; Kenneth D. Irwin, Chairperson
Purpose: To provide a means through which issues of concern to the Native community may be forcefully considered; seeks to enhance and strengthen Native American cultures in Ohio and to inform all citizens of issues concerning the Native American community. *Activities*: Clearinghouse for Indian information; speaker's bureau; cultural programs, powwows and workshops. Library. Founded 1991.

**NATIVE AMERICAN INDIAN
& VETERANS CENTER, INC.**
P.O. Box 1319 • NORTON, OH 44203
(330) 825-7796
Jack (Little Eagle) Lyons, Founder
E-mail: naivc1@aol.com
Website: www.naivc.77th.com
Description: A human service agency made up of American Indians, veterans, and volunteers *Activities*: Provides social services, cultural recreational activities, and health education to low-income children, families, American Indians, and veterans at risk in Ohio.

**FRIENDS OF THE SERPENT MOUND
& THE OHIO BRUSH CREEK**
c/o Tom Johnson, 18240 SR 41
WEST UNION, OH 45693

OKLAHOMA

FIVE CIVILIZED TRIBES FOUNDATION
c/o Chickasaw Nation, P.O. Box 1548
ADA, OK 74820 (405) 436-2603
Overton James, Chairman
Comprised of the Cherokee, Choctaw, Chickasaw, Creek, and Seminole Nations of Oklahoma. *Purpose*: To provide coordination to tribal activities and programs including social programs, industrial development, and administrative activities; and provides representation for the tribes at the national level. Founded 1974.

**SOUTHERN PLAINS INDIAN
HOUSING ASSOCIATION**
Chickasaw Nation Division of Housing
P.O. Box 788 • ADA, OK 74821
(580) 421-8848 Fax 421-8879
Wayne Scribner, Housing Administrator

FOUR TRIBES CONSORTIUM OF OKLAHOMA
P.O. Box 1193 • ANADARKO, OK 73005
(405) 247-9711/2021
Jeff Foster, Executive Director
Purpose: To assist skilled men and women with employment and training; to educate Native American people of their civil rights, and assists in mediating discrimination toward the Native American. *Publication*: Program pamphlet. Founded 1987.

OKLAHOMA INDIAN ARTS & CRAFTS COOP.
P.O. Box 966 • ANADARKO, OK 73005
(888) 405-4963; (405) 247-3486
LaVerna Standing-Capes, Manager
Purpose: To promote the careers of contemporary Oklahoma Indian artists and craftsmen by providing a sales outlet for their works. Products include: beadwork, featherwork, jewelry, fashion accessories, leatherwork, dance costumes and accessories, dolls, musical instruments, as well as orginal paintings by Native American artists. Mail order price list available-send long S.A.S.E. Established 1955.

INTER-TRIBAL COUNCIL, INC.
P.O. Box 1308 • MIAMI, OK 74355
(918) 540-2508
Purpose: To serve eight tribes: Eastern Shawnee, Seneca-Cayuga, Wyandotte, Quapaw, Ottawa, Peoria, Miami, and Modoc.

MOORE INDIAN CENTER
1500 SE 4th St.
MOORE, OK 73160-8266

OKLAHOMA ANTHROPOLOGICAL SOCIETY
1000 Horn St. • MUSKOGEE, OK 74403
(405) 364-2279; Alicia Jones Hughes, President
Encourages scientific collection, preservation, classi-

fication and study of American Indian ethnological and archaeological materials. Newsletter; annual bulletin. Library (members only.)

OKLAHOMANS FOR INDIAN OPPORTUNITY
3001 S. Berry Rd. • NORMAN, OK 73069
(405) 329-3737; Iola Hayden, Executive Director
Purpose: To improve opportunities for Oklahoma Indians and draw them more fully into the Oklahoma economy and culture. *Programs*: Indian education; job opportunity and training; housing; health. *Publication*: OIO News - provides information on Indian business development and similar issues.

AMERICAN INDIAN CENTER
1608 N.W. 35th
OKLAHOMA CITY, OK 73117

OKLAHOMA CITY INDIAN HEALTH CLINIC
4913 W. Reno Ave.
OKLAHOMA CITY, OK 73127
(405) 948-4900 Fax 948-4932
Terry Hunter, Contact
Purpose: To provide outpatient primary medical care; general medical and dental services; mental health and substance abuse treatment; health education; seminars; prevention and outreach. Established 1974.

OKLAHOMA DEPT.OF INDIAN EDUCATION
Oklahoma Dept. of Education
2500 N. Lincoln Blvd. •
OKLAHOMA CITY, OK 73105
(405) 521-3311 Fax 521-6205
Mary Reid, Director

OKLAHOMA HISTORICAL SOCIETY
2100 N. Lincoln
OKLAHOMA CITY, OK 73105-4997
(405) 522-5248 Fax 522-5402
Website: www.ok-history.mus.ok.us
E-mail: dprovo@ok-history.mus.ok.us
Dan Provo, Director
Jeff Moore, Ethnology Curator
Dennis W. Zotigh, American Indian
  Research Historian
E-mail: dzotigh@ok-history.mus.ok.us
Purpose: The preservation microfilming of documents relating to the Indian tribes of Oklahoma. *Programs*: Maintains the Oklahoma Museum of History and an Archives and Manuscripts Division which acts as a repository of a large body of U.S. Government Indian records and papers of missionaries to the tribes of Oklahoma. *Publication*: Chronicles of Oklahoma, quarterly historical journal. Library and museum.

OKLAHOMA INDIAN AFFAIRS COMMISSION
4545 N. Lincoln Blvd., Suite 282
OKLAHOMA CITY, OK 73105
(405) 521-3828 Fax 522-4427
Barbara A. Warner, Executive Director
Purpose: To serve as the liaison between the Indian people of the state, Indian leaders of the state, tribal governments, private sector entities, the various federal and state agencies. *Special programs*: American Business Legislative Day; Sovereignty Symposium (co-sponsor); active participant in the Governors' Interstate Indian Council and various other activities. *Published works*: Legislative Handbook; Oklahoma Indian Nations Information Handbook for State Officials; Financial Aid Resource Guide; Liaison Quarterly Newsletter; Selected Oklahoma Statutes affecting Oklahoma Indians and Indian Nations. Established 1967.

OKLAHOMA INDIAN ART GALLERY
2335 SW 44th St.
OKLAHOMA CITY, OK 73119
(405) 685-6162
Purpose: To display works of art created by Native Americans in the Oklahoma City region.

OKLAHOMA INDIAN BAR ASSOCIATION
P.O. Box 1062
OKLAHOMA CITY, OK 73101
(405) 879-5924
Arvo Mikkanen, President; M. Allen Core, V.P.
Purpose: To provide a forum for Indian law practitioners to communicate with one another, exchange ideas on the issues involving the tribal sovereignty of Indian nations within the state.

OKLAHOMA INDIAN LEGAL SERVICES, INC.
OKLAHOMA CITY, OK 73112
(405) 840-5255 Fax 840-7060
Michael C. Snyder, Executive Director
Purpose: To provide legal services to low income Native Americans by direct representation on status related issues of significance; legal training. *Activities*: Sponsors and provides speakers to conference addressing Indian Child Welfare, Indian Housing, Tribal Sovereignty, Natural Resources, and Individual Rights; also sponsors Indian Law Legal Intern Program. Maintains Indian law library. *Publications*: Handbook on the Indian Child Welfare Act; brochures. Founded 1982.

RED EARTH INDIAN CENTER
2100 NE 52 St. • OKLAHOMA CITY, OK 73111
(405) 427-4228
Barbara Jobe, Executive Director
Christi Alcox, Festival Coordinator
Scott Tigert, Curator; Eric Oesch, PR Director
Dee Ann Lamebull, Exec. ass't
Micki Pratt, Special Projects
Purpose: To give tangible expression to American Indian cultures, and to increase appreciation of them through information exchange and cultural activities, such as the Red Earth Festival (second weekend in June) "world's largest Native American cultural festival; and annual Native American Fair (February); museum exhibits. Library. Founded 1976.

CREEK INDIAN MEMORIAL ASSOCIATION
Creek Council House Museum
Town Square • OKMULGEE, OK 74447
(918) 756-2324
James L. Milroy, President
Tommy A. Steinsiek, Curator
Membership: 115. *Purpose*: Established to collect and exhibit artifacts and documents pertaining to the Muscogee Creek Tribe. *Activities*: Operates Museum of Creek Indian Culture; sponsors annual Muscogee Creek Masters Exhibit every December; sponsors Oklahoma Indian Art Market every October. Publishes booklets and leaflets on Creek history and legend. Monthly meetings. Founded 1923.

CENTRAL TRIBES OF SHAWNEE
Route 5, Box 148-B • SHAWNEE, OK 74801
(405) 275-0663
Head Start Program.

INDIAN ACTION CENTER COUNCIL
2041 S. Gordon Cooper Dr.
SHAWNEE, OK 74801 (405) 275-5270
Purpose: To develop programs to aid Native Americans living in its area.

NATIVE AMERICANS IN BIOLOGICAL SCIENCES
306 Life Science East, OSU
STILLWATER, OK 74078
(405) 744-6802 Fax 744-6790
Myra Alexander, Manager-Counseling/Outreach
Bennett Arkeketa, Manager-Technical Programs
E-Mail: alex@osuunx.ucc.okstate.edu
  bark@vms.ucc.okstate.edu
Purpose: To improve recruitment and retention of American Indians into the biological sciences. *Activities*: Summer programs for Native American elementary, middle and senior high school students who are interested in further study in the bioloigcal sciences; pre-college bridge programs on OSU campus; science fairs. Undergraduate scholars program with $3,000 stipend. Small library. *Publications*: Video works in-progress; Video Magazine. Established 1992.

CHEROKEE NATION HEALTH CENTER
RR 2, Box 93 • STILWELL, OK 74960-9666

AMERICAN INDIAN RESOURCE CENTER
103 W. 2nd St. • TAHLEQUAH, OK 74464
(918) 456-5581
Purpose: To prepare Native Americans for teaching careers. It offers degrees at the master's and doctoral level.

CHEROKEE NATIONAL HISTORICAL SOCIETY
P.O. Box 515 • TAHLEQUAH, OK 74465
(918) 456-6007; Myrna Moss, Executive Director
Purpose: To preserve the history and traditions of the Cherokee Nation, and provide educational and social services to members of the Cherokee Indian tribe. *Ac-

tivities: Operates the Cherokee Heritage Center, which includes the Cherokee National Museum and Cherokee National Archives. Maintains a "living" Indian Village; sponsors annual Trail of Tears Indian art show; conducts a lecture series on Cherokee history and culture. Maintains Cherokee Hall of Fame. Also maintains the Ho-Chee-Nee Trail of Tears Memorial Chapel. *Publication*: The Columns, quarterly newsletter; Trail of Tears Drama Program, annual. Color prints of Indian art available. Founded 1963.

INDIAN HEALTH CARE RESOURCE CENTER
Box 184, 915 S. Cincinnati • TULSA, OK 74119
(918) 582-7225

NATIVE AMERICAN COALITION OF TULSA, INC.
1740 West 41st St.
TULSA, OK 74107 (918) 446-8432
Ben Shoemake, Chairperson
Ann Abbott, Executive Director
Purpose: To serve tribes and Native-Americans in the Tulsa area. *Programs*: Headstart school; clothing and food donations for families; referrals.

OREGON

MOTHER EARTH'S CHILDREN
COOS BAY, OR 97420
(541) 888-4584
Purpose: To promote positive Indian education, economic and social benefits through the development of innovative programs. *Activities*: An American Indian Repertory Theater, presents traditional Indian stories in a visual manner; The Anne C. Thornton Memorial Fund Scholarship, annual awards of $750 to four American Indian/Alaskan Native students who live in Oregon.

NANITCH SAHALLIE
Conferedated Tribes of the
Grand Ronde Tribal Council
9615 Grand Ronde Rd.
Grand Ronde, OR 97347
(503) 879-5211 Fax 879-5964
Description: A youth residential treatment program; a 44 bed facility for the treatment of Native American chemical dependent adolescents between the ages of 12 and 18 who reside in the Portland Area of the Indian Health Service.

ORGANIZATION OF THE
FORGOTTEN AMERICAN
P.O. Box 1257
KLAMATH FALLS, OR 97601
(503) 882-4441/2
Leonard Norris, Director
Purpose: To enhance the future of the Native American population. *Activities*: Administers the Job Training Partnership Act program for 22 counties; Employment and trainign services for eligible Native Americans. Branch offices in Astoria, Coos Bay, Medford, Pendleton, Roseburg, and The Dalles, Oregon.

AMERICAN INDIAN ASSN. OF PORTLAND
7831 S.E. Stark St. #101
PORTLAND, OR 97215
(503) 254-3091 Fax 254-3226

COLUMBIA RIVER INTER-TRIBAL
FISH COMMISSION (CRITFC)
729 NE Oregon St., Suite 200
PORTLAND, OR 97232
(503) 238-0667 Fax 235-4228
Olney Patt, Jr., Executive Director
Sue Seven, Executive Assistant to the Director
E-mail: sevs@critfc.org
Website: www.critfc.org
Purpose: To ensure a unified voice in the overall management of the fishery resources; to protect reserved treaty rights through exercise of inherent sovereign powers of the tribes: Yakima, Nez Perce, Umatilla and Warm Springs. *Publication*: Wana Chinook Tymoo (Columbia River Salmon Stories), quarterly magazine.

CONCERNED INDIAN COMMITTEE
6008 N. Syracuse • PORTLAND, OR 97203
(503) 285-4474

LEGAL AID SERVICE OF OREGON
Native American Porgram
812 SW Washington, Suite 700
PORTLAND, OR 97205
(503) 223-9483 Fax 294-1429
E-mail: napols@teleport.com
Purpose: To provide legal representation to Oregon's Indian community. Case load includes: economic development, protection of archaeological, sacred and burial sites, worship, Indian health services, Indian Child Welfare Act and protection of Tribal-Federal relationship, treaty rights, federal Indian law training tribal sovereignty. Founded 1979.

NATIVE AMERICAN ART COUNCIL
Portland Art Museum, 1219 SW Park Ave.
PORTLAND, OR 97205 (503) 226-2811
Description: An educational group organizaed to support the Portland Art Museum's collection of Native American art. *Activities*: Sponsors educational programs: guest speakers, films, demonstration and field trips. Founded 1985.

NATIVE AMERICAN BUSINESS ALLIANCE
8435 SE 17th Ave.
PORTLAND, OR 97202 (503) 233-4841
Description: Non-profit organiztion organizaed to promote economic development for all Indians through the formation of an alliance of profit-oriented Indian businesses. *Activities*: Conduct quarterly meetings in Oregon and Washington. *Publication*: Indian Business Review, quarterly.

NATIVE AMERICAN REHABILITATION
ASSOCIATION OF THE NORTHWEST
17645 NW St. Helens Hwy.
PORTLAND, OR 97231
(503) 621-1069 Fax 621-0200
Jackie Mercer, Director
Purpose: To Operate an outpatient clinic and two residential treatment centers, Totem Lodge—men and women and Women's Support Center—women and children, for the treatment of alcoholism and alcohol/drug abuse in the Native-American community with a specialist treatment approach which embodies Indian cultural awareness and the philosophy of Alcoholics Anonymous.

NORTHWEST NATIVE AMERICAN ARTS
1219 SW Park Ave.
PORTLAND, OR 97205 (503) 226-2811
Purpose: To stimulate interest and knowledge in Native American art. *Activities*: Monthly programs, lectures, field trips, and guest speakers.

NORTHWEST PORTLAND
AREA INDIAN HEALTH BOARD
527 SW Hall, Suite 300 • PORTLAND, OR 97201
(503) 228-4185 Fax 228-8182
Doni Wilder, Executive Director
Description: A federally-funded, non-profit advisory board which represents the 40 Federally recognized Tribes in Oregon, Washington, and Idaho on health related issues. The board is composed of delegates representing each tribe. *Purpose*: To serve as liaison between tribes and the Indian Health Service; to provide training for tribal reps and tribal staff on various health issues; to conduct research and evaluation projects; to serve as a regional center for statistics for Northwest Tribes. *Special programs*: Northwest Tribal Recruitment Project (recruit health professionals for the 40 different American Indian tribes located in Washington, Oregon, and Idaho).

OREGON INDIAN EDUCATION ASSOCIATION
2125 N. Flint • PORTLAND, OR 97227
(503) 275-9600
Purpose: To promote Indian education in schools and Indian communities, and to inform association members of state and federal laws affecting Indian education. *Activities*: Textbook review projects; to communicate concerns of Indian educators to the U.S. Office of Education; and administers AIDS Education and Prevention Program.

RESEARCH & DEVELOPMENT
PROGRAM FOR INDIAN EDUCATION
Northwest Regional Educational Laboratory
101 SW Main St., Suite 500
PORTLAND, OR 97204

(503) 275-9500 Fax 275-9489
Purpose: To provide in-service training on school improvement to schools serving Indian children in the Northwest. *Activities*: Annual, one week, "Institute of Excellence in American Indian Education. *Publications*: Effective Practices in Indian Education: Teacher Curriculum, Administrator Monographs, an Administrator's Guide; and Teachers Do Make A Difference: What Indian Graduates Say About Their School Experience.

INIPI O'YATE'KI - NATIVE AMERICAN CLUB
Oregon State Correctional Institution
3405 Deer Park Dr., SE
SALEM, OR 97301 (503) 373-0175
William Sonny Boyd, President
Description: A social organization within the walls of the correctional institution. *Purpose*: To teach and learn about different tribe traditions. To participate in Native Americannnn Sweat Lodge Ceremonies and to teach and learn how to drum, dance and sing. *Activities*: Bi-annual pow-wows focus on activities traditional to the Native American culture.

LAKOTA OYATE-KI - INDIAN CULTURE CLUB
Oregon State Penitentiary
2605 State St. • SALEM, OR 97310
(503) 378-2289
Description: Indian organization wiothin the walls of the penitentiary. Membership involved in cultural, traditional and religious activities.

NORTHWEST PAINT CLAN, INC.
585 Lorida Ave. S. • SALEM, OR 97302
(503) 399-8781
Purpose: To preserve American Indian heritage and provide cultural learning opportunities for members and the public.

OREGON INDIAN COALITION
ON POST SECONDARY EDUCATION
2708 Shelly Ann Way, NE
SALEM, OR 97305
Morrie Jimenez, Chairperson

OREGON COMMISSION ON INDIAN SERVICES
454 State Capitol • SALEM, OR 97310
(503) 986-1067 Fax 986-1071
Douglas W. Hutchinson, Director
Purpose: To develop and sponsor programs to make needs of Oregon Indians known to the public and private agencies which serve them; to recommend new or improved methods of meeting these needs; and to compile and disseminate information about services for Indians in Oregon. *Publication*: Oregon Directory of American Indian Resources.

OREGON DEPARTMENT OF EDUCATION
Indian Education and Race Equity
700 Pringle Parkway SE • SALEM, OR 97310
(503) 378-3606 Fax 373-7968
Robin A. Butterfield, Coordinator

SISTER'S OF THE FOUR WINDS-
OWCC INDIAN CLUB
Oregon Women's Correctional Center
2809 State St. • SALEM, OR 97310
(503) 378-2667
Purpose: To enhance the self-image of American Indian inmates and bring a better understanding of Indian ways to others.

TAHANA WHITECROW FOUNDATION
2350 Wallace Rd. NW • SALEM, OR 97304
(503) 585-0564 Fax 585-3302
E-mail: tahana@open.org
Web site: www.open.org/tahana
Melanie Smith, Director
Purpose: To promote and provide multi approaches to low income urban Indians and other special needs pops through education, direct services and advocacy. *Activities*: Outpatient substance abuse and mental health; Native AA/NA meetings, youth assistance, transitional housing for combat vets; dual diagnoses self-help, community referral and advocacy. *Publication*: "Circle of Reflections," (occasional) poetry anthology. Library. Established 1987.

ART MITCHELL SINGERS
P.O. Box 124 • WARM SPRINGS, OR 97761
(503) 553-1161

A Native American singing group who regularly provide drumming and singing for pow-wows, tribal celebrations and various cultural events on the Warm Springs Reservation. The group also performs for other reservations, communities, schools and universities, and coventions.

OREGON NATIVE AMERICAN BUSINESS & ENTREPRENEURIAL NETWORK
P.O. Box 1359 • WARM SPRINGS, OR 97761
Wes Patterson, President

PENNSYLVANIA

COUNCIL OF THREE RIVERS AMERICAN INDIAN CENTER, INC.
Rt. 2, Box 247-A • DORSEYVILLE, PA 15238
(412) 782-4457 Fax 767-4808
Russell Sims, Executive Director
Purpose: Addresses the needs and secures services for the Native-American community. *Programs*: Indian manpower employment and training; Native-American elders program; Native-American cultural programs; Native-American family and child services; Native-American Adoption Resource Exchange, and Indian Adoption Awareness Project (national); Singing Winds Head Start; Rainbow Project—adoption agency for western Pennsylvania. Financial assistance for education and training is provided through the Job Training Partnership Act Program. *Publication*: The Singing Winds Newsletter, monthly; Pow-Wow Booklet, annual. Library.

ERIE COUNTY COALITION FOR INDIAN AFFAIRS, INC.
2324 East 26th St. • ERIE, PA 16510
Edward Livingston, Contact

NATIVE AMERICAN INDIAN COMMUNITY
Rd. 2 Box 247A
KITTANNING, PA 16201
(412) 548-7335
Brandy Weeasayha Myers, Director
Purpose: To educate all people about American Indians. *Activities*: Support programs dealing with Native people; educational program for schools; and Prison Outreach (counseling for prison inmates). Twice a year family gathering - three days of Native activities. *Publications*: Spirit Walker Newsletter; educational material on Native people; cookbook.

NATIVE AMERICAN CULTURAL CENTER OF DELAWARE VALLEY
927 N. 6th St.
PHILADELPHIA, PA 19123
(215) 627-7304
Charles H. Juancito, Executive Director
Purpose: To provide programs in health, education and welfare for the Powhatan Renape Nation. Library. *Publication*: Catalog.

UNITED AMERICAN INDIANS OF THE DELAWARE VALLEY
225 Chestnut St.
PHILADELPHIA, PA 19106
(215) 574-9020/2/3/4
Susan Heide, Executive Director
Personnel: Yvonne Bernardino, Office Manager; John Albrecht, Vocational Counselor, Miriam Cathcart, Outreach Specialist; and Janice Ritt, Receptionist. *Purpose*: To be recognized and accepted as a community-based, social service organization assisting all American Indians residing within Philadelphia metropolitan area to enhance their standard of living and improve their social-economic self-sufficiency. *Special programs*: Trading Post & Exhibit; cultural, educational, employment, housing, and public relations. *Special activities*: Annual Pow-Wow, 1st weekend in August; annual Fall Festival, 2nd weekend in October. Trading Post.

RHODE ISLAND

RHODE ISLAND INDIAN COUNCIL
444 Friendship St. • PROVIDENCE, RI 02907

SOUTH CAROLINA

ASSISTANT TO THE GOVERNOR
P.O. Box 11450 • COLUMBIA, SC 29211

SOUTH CAROLINA COUNCIL ON NATIVE AMERICANS
P.O. Box 219221 • COLUMBIA, SC 29221

SOUTH CAROLINA STATE DEPT. OF EDUCATION
Multicultural/Equity Issues
1429 Senate St., 808 Rutledge Bldg.
COLUMBIA, SC 29201
(803) 734-8366 Fax 734-8624

FOUR HOLES INDIAN ORGANIZATION
1125 Ridge Rd. • RIDGEVILLE, SC 29472
(803) 871-2126

SOUTH DAKOTA

HAN-PA-O-YE
P.O. Box 624, Northern State College
ABERDEEN, SD 57401

DAKOTA INDIAN FOUNDATION
209 N. Main St., Box 340
CHAMBERLAIN, SD 57325-0340
(605) 734-5472
Purpose: To preserve the individual dignity, pride, hope, and self-determination of all Dakota Sioux people.

ST. JOSEPH'S LAKOTA DEVELOPMENT COUNCIL
St. Joseph's Indian School
CHAMBERLAIN, SD 57326 (605) 734-6021
A non-profit organization which sells products (kachina dolls, leatherwork, beadwork, quilts, etc.) through mail order and wholesale-retail.

UNITED NATIVE AMERICAN HOUSING ASSOCIATION
Cheyenne River Housing Authority
P.O. Box 480 • EAGLE BUTTE, SD 57625
(605) 964-4265 Fax 964-1070
Wayne Ducheanaux, Executive Director
A federation of Native American housing authorities serving a number of tribes in its area.

HARRY V. JOHNSON AMERICAN INDIAN CULTURAL CENTER
Cheyenne River Reservation, Box 857
EAGLE BUTTE, SD 57625 (605) 965-2542
The center is concerned with the history and culture of American Indians from its area.

THE LAKOTA FUND
P.O. Box 340 • KYLE, SD 57750
(605) 455-2500; Elsie Meeks, Executive Director
Purpose: To build a private sector economy on the Pine Ridge Indian Reservation by providing loans and technical assistance to Oglala Sioux tribal members. *Activities*: Small business loans; microenterprise loans; technical assistance & business training; and arts and crafts marketing assistance. *Publication*: The Lakota Fund newsletter. Established 1986.

NATIVE AMERICAN WOMEN'S HEALTH EDUCATION RESOURCE CENTER
Native American Community Board
P.O. Box 572 • LAKE ANDRES, SD 57356
(605) 487-7072 Fax 487-7964
Charon Asetoyer, Executive Director

DAKOTA PLAINS LEGAL SERVICES, INC.
P.O. Box 727 • MISSION, SD 57555
(605) 856-4444
A Native American legal assistance organization.

SOUTH DAKOTA STATE DEPT. OF EDUCATION & CULTURAL AFFAIRS
Indian Education Program
700 Governors Dr. • PIERRE, SD 57501
(605) 773-4670 Fax 773-6139
Don Schanadore, Contact

SOUTH DAKOTA HISTORICAL SOCIETY
900 Governors Dr.
PIERRE, SD 57501-2217
(605) 773-3458 Fax 773-6041
Mary B. Edelen, Director
E-Mail: mary.edelen@state.sd.us
Web site: www.state.sd.us/deca/cultural
Purpose: To preserve and exhibit the tangible reminders of South Dakota's history and heritage. Activities: Archaeological research, state archives, education programs, historic preservation, publications, historical markers, microfilming, museums. *Publications*: "South Dakota History," quarterly journal; "History Notes," newsletter; "Hoofprints," news for local history groups. Museums. Library. Established 1901.

SOUTH DAKOTA INDIAN AFFAIRS OFFICE
Public Safety Bldg., 118 W. Capitol, Rm. 300
PIERRE, SD 57501 (605) 773-3415
Francis WhiteBird, Coordinator

SOUTH DAKOTA INDIAN EDUCATION ASSN.
P.O. Box 2019
PINE RIDGE, SD 57770-2019
(605) 867-5633; Chris Bordeaux, President
Activity: Sponsors annual conference in October.

AMERICAN INDIAN RELIEF COUNCIL
P.O. Box 6200 • RAPID CITY, SD 57709
Brian J. Brown, President

MOTHER BUTLER INDIAN CENTER
230 Wright St. • RAPID CITY, SD 57709
(605) 342-2165
Description: A Native American service group which sponsors athletics and other activites for young people.

SIOUX SAN ALCOHOLISM PROGRAM
3200 Canyon Lake Dr.
RAPID CITY, SD 57701

BRULE SIOUX ARTS & CRAFTS CO-OP
P.O. Box 230
ST. FRANCIS, SD 57572
(605) 747-2099

KATERI INDIAN CENTER
300 N. Main St.
SIOUX FALLS, SD 57102
(605) 335-3321

MINNEHAHA INDIAN CLUB
1413 Thompson Dr.
SIOUX FALLS, SD 57105

LAKOTA AOMICIYE
Black Hills State College
SPEARFISH, SD 57783

TENNESSEE

TENNESSEE COMMISSION OF INDIAN AFFAIRS
112 Cynthia Ln., Apt. C • KNOXVILLE, TN 37922
John Martin, Chairperson

NATIVE AMERICAN INDIAN ASSOCIATION OF TENNESSEE
211 Union St., 932 Stahlman Bldg.
NASHVILLE, TN 37201-1505
(615) 726-0806 Fax 726-0810
Sally Wells, President
Ray Emanuel, Executive Director
Purpose: To improve the quality of life for Native Americans in Tennessee. *Programs*: Emergency Assistance, Scholarship, Case Management to the homeless, Job Search, Cultural Revitalization and Speaker Bureau. *Activities*: Annual Pow wow in October. Library. *Publication*: Newsletter. Established 1982.

TENNESSEE COMMISSION OF INDIAN AFFAIRS
NASHVILLE, TN 37243
Toye Heape, Executive Director
E-mail: theape@mail.state.tn.us
Web site: www.state.tn.us/environment/cia/index/hml
Purpose: To provide aid and technical assistance to Tennessee's Native American population and promote recognition of Native American cultural traditions. *Publication*: Annual report. Established in 1984.

TEXAS

TEXAS INDIAN COMMISSION
AUSTIN, TX 78768 (512) 458-1203
  Raymond D. Apodaca, Exec. Director
Purpose: To assist the Alabama-Coushatta Indian Tribe and the Tigua Tribe of Texas in the development of the human and economic resources of their respective Reservations; to assist the Texas Band of Kickapoo Indians in improving its health, educational, agricultural, business, and industrial capacities; to promote unity and understanding among the American Indian people of Texas, and promote and enhance increased understanding of American Indian and Texas Indian culture and history by the general public. Approximate Indian population is 65,000. *Publications*: Americans Indians in Texas, 1984; Texas Indian Commission Profile and History, 20 page report.

DALLAS INTER-TRIBAL CENTER
209 E. Jefferson • DALLAS, TX 75203
  (214) 941-1050 (Community/Health Services)
  (214) 941-6535 (Employment/Training Services)
  Richard Lucero, Executive Director
Purpose: To provide health care and other social services to Indian families residing in the Dallas/Fort Worth area. *Programs*: Community services such as: emergency food assistance, transportation, crisis intervention services, information and referral; Indian child welfare; medical-dental clinic; WIC Program; nutrition education services; health education; screening. *Publication*: DIC Smoke Signals, monthly newsletter.

UTAH

ALLEN CANYON UTE COUNCIL
P.O. Box 340 • BLANDING, UT 84511

UTAH NAVAJO DEVELOPMENT COUNCIL
P.O. Box 129 • BLUFF, UT 84512
  (801) 678-2285; Herbert Clah, Executive Director
Purpose: To help the Navajos on the Utah Portion of the Navajo Reservation provide services in health, education, natural resources, and housing. *Programs*: Operates clinics for medical services; adult education; vocational education; home rehabilitation; and construction. Scholarships. Artifacts exhibited.

THE MIXED BLOOD UINTAS OF UTAH
P.O. Box 465 • FT. DUCHESNE, UT 84026
  Oranna B. Felter (435) 722-3220
  Alvin R. Demver (435) 722-0230
Description: About 500 Uinta Band Utes who were terminated from their tribe after the Ute Partition Act was passed by the U.S. Congress in 1954.

UTE INDIAN HOUSING AUTHORITY
P.O. Box 447, 760 Shoshone Ave.
IGNACIO, CO 81137
  (970) 563-4575 Fax 563-4417

UTAH BOARD OF INDIAN AFFAIRS
144 N. Pinewood Cir. • LAYTON, UT 84041
  (801) 626-6818; Marcia Galli, Chairperson

MISS INDIAN SCHOLARSHIP PAGEANT
c/o Doreen Hendrickson
66 S. 980 W. • OREM, UT 84058
  (801) 225-2703
Description: Held each March for Indian women from Utah. The winner competes in the Miss Utah contest, and participants earn scholarship money for college study.

INDIAN ALCOHOLISM COUNSELING &RECOVERY HOUSE PROGRAM
P.O. Box 1500, 538 South West
SALT LAKE CITY, UT 84101

UTAH DIVISION OF INDIAN AFFAIRS
324 S. State St., Suite 500
SALT LAKE CITY, UT 84114
  (801) 538-8788 Fax 538-8803
  Forest S. Cuch, Executive Director

E-mail: fscuch@dced.state.ut.us
Purpose: To assist tribes and Native-American organizations in Utah in solving problems, and serve as a liaison between the State and all tribes and Indian organizations. *Activities*: Annual Conference in April.

UTAH STATE OFFICE OF EDUCATION
Special Assistant for Indian Education
250 E 500 S • SALT LAKE CITY, UT 84111
  (801) 538-7645 Shirley Weights, Contact

VERMONT

THE GOVERNOR'S ADVISORY COMMISSION ON NATIVE AMERICAN AFFAIRS
Pavilion Office Bldg, 109 State St.
MONTPELIER 05609 (802) 828-3333

ABENAKI SELF-HELP ASSOCIATION
P.O. Box 276 • SWANTON 05488
  (802) 868-2559

VIRGINIA

RISING WATERS DANCERS, FALLING WATER DRUM
Route 2, Box 107-B • BRUINGTON, VA 23023
  Nokomis Lemons, Coordinator

ARCHAEOLOGICAL SOCIETY OF VIRGINIA
P.O. Box 340 • COURTLAND, VA 23837
  Russell E. Darden, Contact
Activities: Traveling programs on Native American pre-history.

AMERICAN INDIAN SOCIETY OF WASHINGTON, DC
P.O. Box 6431 • FALLS CHURCH, VA 22040
  (703) 914-0548 • Jay Hill, President
  Bob Tenequer & Willie Chism, V.P.'s
  Karen Collins, Secretary; Barbara Davis, Treasurer
Purpose: To promote and preserve Indian tradition; provide scholarship assistance for young Indian people. *Special program*: American Indian Inaugural Ball. *Publications*: Monthly newsletter; American Indian Society Cookbook, $6.00. Established in 1966.

NATIVE AMERICAN PROGRAMS, FOREST SERVICE
500 W. Westmorland Rd.
FALLS CHURCH, VA 22046
  Robert Tippeconnie, Manager

AMERICAN INDIAN EDUCATIONAL OPPORTUNITY PROGRAM
Hampton University
HAMPTON, VA 23669 (757) 727-5981

MATTAPONI-PAMUNKEY-MONACAN JTPA CONSORTIUM
Rt 2, Box 360 • KING WILLIAM, VA 23086
  (804) 769-4767 • Warren Cook, Director
Educational and assistance services.

CHICKAHOMINY REDMAN DANCERS
8836 Sedberg Dr. • NEW KENT, VA 23124
  (804) 932-4406 • Wayne Adkins, Contact

VIRGINIA COUNCIL ON INDIANS
Virginia Health & Human Resources
P.O. Box 1475 • RICHMOND, VA 23219
  (804) 786-7765 • Gary Flowers, Director

VIRGINIA NATIVE AMERICAN CULTURE CENTER
P.O. Box 25959 • RICHMOND, VA 23260
  (804) 756-7035

RAPPAHANNOCK-MATTAPONI DANCERS
Route 1, Box 522 • TAPPAHANNOCK, VA 23023
  (804) 769-4205; Judy Fortune, Coordinator

WAHUNSUNACOCK DRUM GROUP
Mattaponi Reservation
Rt. 2, Box 325 • WEST POINT, VA 23181
  (804) 769-0165 • Lionel Custalow, Contact

PEPPER BIRD FOUNDATION
P.O. Box 1071
WILLIAMSBURG, VA 23187-1071
  (757) 220-5761 or 722-7485 Fax 220-6711
  Jean Tynan, Contact
Teacher Re-Certification.

WASHINGTON

NORTHWEST INTERTRIBAL COURT SYSTEM
EDMONDS, WA 98020
  (206) 774-5808 Fax 778-7704
  Elbridge Coochise, Administrator
Purpose: To provide judicial and prosecutorial services to its member tribes. *Programs*: Tribal Courts; Code Writing; Informal Dispute Resolution; Tribal Appellate Courts. *Publication*: "Appellate Opinions," codes for member tribes.

INDIGENOUS TRIBES ASSOCIATION
1030 S. 317th St.
FEDERAL WAY, WA 98003
  (206) 839-5635; Fred Tidewaters Raven, Contact

POINT NO POINT TREATY COUNCIL
7999 NE Salish Ln.
KINGSTON, WA 98346

TULALIP TRIBES ENTERTAINMENT CENTER
MARYSVILLE WA 98270
  (206) 653-5551

WASHINGTON STATE INDIAN EDUCATION ASSOCIATION
c/o Colville Conferedated Tribes
P.O. Box 150 • NESPELEM, WA 99155
  (509) 634-4711 Fax 634-8799
  Gloria Adkins, Contact
Activities: Sponsors annual conference and publishes newsletter, Washington State Indian Education Update.

GOVERNOR'S OFFICE OF INDIAN AFFAIRS
P.O. Box 40909, 1210 Eastside St., 1st Floor
OLYMPIA, WA 98504-0909
  (360) 753-2411 Fax 586-3653
  Kimberly Craven, Executive Director
  E-Mail: info@goia.wa.gov
  Website: www.goia.wa.gov
Purpose: To act as a liaison office between the State of Washington and the 27 federally recognized tribes, the 9 non-federally recognized tribes, and various Indian organizations; to educate; to work with Indian tribes; to establish a relationship involving tribal, local, state, and federal governments that will improve communications and joint problem-solving efforts. The office also seeks to enhance the government-to-government relationship between the state and tribes. *Programs*: Conducts "State-Tribal Relations Training," twice a month - this two-day class covers federal legislation and policy, tribal governments, cultural identity, spirituality, reservation economies. Small resource library. Established 1980.

NORTHWEST INDIAN FISHERIES COMMISSION
6730 Martin Way E. • OLYMPIA, WA 98506
  (360) 438-1180 Fax 754-8659
  Billy Frank, Jr., Chairperson
  Jim Anderson, Executive Director
  E-mail: janderson@nwifc.org
  Web site: www.nwifc.wa.gov
Purpose: To assist the tribes in conducting orderly and biologically sound fisheries and to provide member tribes with a single, unified voice on fisheries management and conservation issues. *Publication*: Quarterly newsletter. Established 1974.

WASHINGTON STATE DEPT. OF PUBLIC INSTRUCTION
Indian Education Office, Old Capitol Bldg.
P.O. Box 47200 • OLYMPIA, WA 98504
  (206) 753-3635 Fax 753-6754
  Patricia L. Martin, Supervisor
Purpose: To administer 20 Johnson O'Malley Indian education programs, funded by the Bureau of Indian Affairs. *Activities*:Provides technical assistance to schools, communities, organizations, etc. in matters pertaining to Indian education.

**AMERICAN INDIAN HERITAGE
SCHOOL & PROGRAM**
1330 North 90th St. • SEATTLE, WA 98103
 (206) 298-7895
Operates a secondary school program attuned to the
needs of Indian students. Conducts educational programs on Native American culture in schools in the
Seattle area.

**AMERICAN INDIAN WOMEN'S
SERVICE LEAGUE, INC.**
113 Cherry St. • SEATTLE, WA 98104
 (206) 621-0655
A social service organization.

**EVERGREEN LEGAL SERVICES
NATIVE AMERICAN PROJECT**
101 Yesler #301 • SEATTLE, WA 98104
 (216) 464-0838

NATIVE AMERICAN LAW CENTER
University of Washington
SEATTLE, WA 98195 (206) 685-2861
 Robert Anderson, Director

SEATTLE INDIAN ALCOHOLISM PROGRAM
1912 Minor Ave. • SEATTLE, WA 98101

SEATTLE INDIAN HEALTH BOARD
606 - 12th Ave. S. • SEATTLE, WA 98144-2008
 (206) 324-9360 ext. 1102 Fax 324-8910
 Ralph Forquera, Executive Director
 Rebecca Gonzales, Director of Operations
 E-Mail: ralph@compumedia.com
Purpose: To assist American Indians and Alaskan Natives improve their physical, mental, spiritual, & social
well being with respect for cultural traditions, and to
advocate for the needs of all Indian people, especially
the most vulnerable members of the community. *Activities*: Multi-service community health center for medical, dental, mental health, substance abuse, and community education services. Established in 1970.

UNITED INDIANS OF ALL TRIBES FOUNDATION
Discovery Park, P.O. Box 99100
SEATTLE, WA 98199
 (206) 285-4425 Fax 282-3640
 E-mail: info@unitedindians.com
 Website: www.unitedindians.com
Purpose: To establish an urban base for more than
25,000 Native Americans in the Seattle area. *Description*: Based at the Daybreak Star Cultural Center located on 20 acres in Seattle's Discovery Park. Over
25 years ago United Indians founder Berni Whitebear
and other Native Americans invaded this site, which
was orginally Indian land, to build a center that would
improve the spiritual, social, economic, educational
and cultural conditions of Native Americans. *Activities*:
Provides social and educational services, from early
child development and family counseling to housing
homeless youth and preparing meals for the elderly.
Programs: Education - Head Start & Early Childhood
Education & Assistance Program; Elders Services;
Employment; Family & Youth; Culture & Heritage - Arts
Program, Sacred Circle Art Gallery of American Indian Art; annual Seafair Indian Days PowWow.

EAST PLATEAU INDIAN CONFEDERATION
American Indian Community Center East
905 3rd Ave. • SPOKANE, WA 99202
 (509) 535-0886
Purpose: To develop and operate social and economic
development programs to aid Indian in Eastern Washington and North Idaho.

ALASKA NATIVE DANCE GROUP
5101 S. 9th St. • TACOMA, WA 98465
 (206) 566-9239
Purpose: To provide instruction in Native Aalskam
dances and presents performances.

NORTHWEST INDIAN HOUSING ASSOCIATION
P.O. Box 160 • TAHOLAH, WA 98587
 (206) 276-4320
Purpose: Seeks an improved standard of living for
Native Americans in the Northwestern states.

THE 13TH REGIONAL CORPORATION
13215-C8 Mill Plain, #393 • VANCOUVER, WA 98684
 (206) 254-0688 Fax 230-7703

**EAST CASCADE ASSOCIATION OF
INDIAN HOUSING AUTHORITIES**
611 S/ Camas Ave.
WAPATO, WA 98951 (509) 877-6171
A federation of Native American housing authorities.
It serves the housing authorities of nine tribes in East-
ern Washington, Oregon and Idaho.

NORTWEST INDIAN WOMEN'S CIRCLE
1013 Crystal Springs St. • YELM, WA 98597
 (360) 458-7610
Purpose: To strengthen the bonds within Indian families and to help Native Americans who are imprisoned.
Publication: Moccasin Line.

WEST VIRGINIA

**WEST VIRGINIA DIVISION
OF CULTURE & HISTORY**
The Cultural Center, Capitol Complex
CHARLESTON, WV 25305 (304) 348-0220

WISCONSIN

**WISCONSIN NATIVE AMERICAN
DOMESTIC ABUSE SHELTER**
Outreach advocates available in Bad River,
LCO, Mole Lake, and Red Cliff
 (800) 236-7660 - 24-hour confidential hotline
 Benase Equay Wakaigan, Contact

CITIZENS FOR TREATY RIGHTS
5013 Sundstein Rd. • EAGLE RIVER, WI 54521

AMERICAN INDIAN PROGRAM
2420 Nicolet Dr. • GREEN BAY, WI 54311
 (414) 465-2720
Purpose: To sponsor artistic programs on
Native American culture in the Green Bay area.

UNITED AMERINDIAN HEALTH CENTER
P.O. Box 2248 • GREEN BAY, WI 54306
 (414) 435-6773

WISCONSIN INDIAN EDUCATION ASSOCIATION
Menominee Indian Tribe
P.O. Box 910 • KESHENA, WI 54135
 (800) 362-4476; (715) 799-5110 Fax 799-1364
 Virginia Nuske, Director
 E-mail: vnuske@mitw.org
 Website: www.wiea.org
Purpose: To promote educational opportunities for In-
dian people of Wisconsin through a united effort of
Indian and non-Indian members interested in social
and economic advancement of Indian people. *Pro-
grams*: Educational scholarships, awards, and grants
for Indian students residing in Wisconsin. *Publication*:
Wisconsin Indian Education Resource Directory.

GREAT LAKES INTER-TRIBAL COUNCIL
P.O. Box 9 • LAC DU FLAMBEAU, WI 54538
 (715) 588-3324 Joseph N. Bresette, Exec. Director
Purpose: To link the more than 30,000 members of
ten federally recognized tribes in Wisconsin. Formed
in 1961. *Special program*: Elders Programs.

NORTHWEST INDIAN HOUSING ASSOCIATION
Swinomish Housing Authority
P.O. Box 677 • LaCONNER, WA 98257
 (360) 466-4081 Fax 466-7219
 John Petrich, Executive Director

**WISCONSIN DEPT. OF
HEALTH & SOCIAL SERVICES**
DCS/DES Tribal Programs, P.O. Box 7935
MADISON, WI 53707 (608) 266-5862
 Nancie Young, Director

WISCONSIN GOVERNOR'S INDIAN DESK
P.O. Box 7863 • MADISON, WI 53701

AMERICAN INDIAN CHAMBER OF COMMERCE
MILWAUKEE, WI 53201 (414) 221-9858
 Sharilynne Denning, Chairperson
 Craig Anderson, Director

MILWAUKEE INDIAN HEALTH CENTER
930 North 27th St. • MILWAUKEE, WI 53208
 (414) 931-8111 Sharilynne Denning, Director
Satelite: 1225 W. Mitchell, Milwaukee 53204 (383-9526

GREAT LAKES NATIVE DIABETES PROJECT
2318 W. Merrill St. • MILWAUKEE, WI 53204
 Laura Bearskin, Project Coordinator

MILWAUKEE UNITED INDIANS
1554 W. Bruce St. • MILWAUKEE, WI 53204
 (414) 384-8070
Description: An advocacy and service organization for
Indians in the Milwaukee area.

**GREAT LAKES INDIAN FISH
& WILDLIFE COMMISSION**
P.O. Box 9 • ODANAH, WI 54861
 (715) 682-6619 Fax 682-9294
 James H. Schlender, Executive Director
 E-Mail: pio.win.bright.net
11 Chippewa tribes concerned with wildlife conservation in the Great Lakes region. *Purpose*: To coordinate effective management of the resources and implement the exercise of treaty rights in an environmentally safe and meaningful manner. Promotes tribal self-
government, and encourages ecosystem protection.
Publications: Masinaigan, monthly newspaper;
Chippewa Treaty Rights; Moving Beyong Argument;
resource manuals; brochures; video tapes; and annual report. Established 1983.

WISCONSIN INDIAN LAWYERS LEAGUE
P.O. Box 365 • ONEIDA, WI 54155
 (414) 869-2345; Gerald L. Hill, Contact

WISCONSIN INDIAN VETERANS ASSOCIATION
P.O. Box 297 • ONEIDA, WI 54155

ONEIDA RIDERS ASSOCIATION
N6935 Hwy. 55 • SEYMOUR, WI 54165
 (414) 833-2323l Jacqueline Johnson, Exec. Director
Purpose: To educate members on the horse and its
role in Native American culture. *Activities*: Conducts
parades, trail rides, speakers, educational clinics, arts
& crafts; compiles information on how the horse was
used, stories and legends, regalia of horse and rider,
training, symbols, etc. Founded 1994.

WISCONSIN NATIVE AMERICAN ARTISTS
John Michael Kohler Arts Center
P.O. Box 489 • SHEBOYGAN, WI 53082

NATIVE AMERICAN CENTER
012 Old Main, UW-Stevens Point
STEVENS POINT, WI 54481
 (715) 346-2004
 Ben Raniirez-shlwegnaabi, Director

CENTRAL WISCONSIN INDIAN CENTER, INC.
1808 Grand Ave. • WAUSAU, WI 54401
 (715) 845-2613
Purpose: To serve Indians in Marathon County.

POTCH-CHEE-NUNK COOPERATIVE
Rt. 2, Box 247-A • WITENBERG, WI 54499
 (715) 253-2928
Description: An intertribal arts & crafts organization
of the Great Lakes tribes.

WYOMING

WYOMING INDIAN AFFAIRS COUNCIL
Community Services • CHEYENNE, WY 82002
 (307) 777-6779 Fax 777-6964
 Gary E. Maier, Commissioner
Purpose: To serve the needs of about 12,000 Native
Americans, primarily Northern Aarapaho and Eastern
Shoshone (although over 40 other tribs are repre-
sented at Wind River.) To act as liaison between the
tribes of Wyoming and the Wyoming state government.

WYOMING INDIAN EDUCATION ASSOCIATION
P.O. Box 248 • FORT WASHAKIE, WY 82514
 (307) 332-2681; Larry Murry, President
Purpose: To promote education of the Shoshone and
Arapaho youth on the Wind River Indian Reservation
and is supported by both tribes.

Indian children attend Federal, public, private and mission schools. There are about 250,000 Indian students, age 5 to 18 years inclusive, enrolled in these schools in the U.S. Education of Indian children residing in the states of California, Idaho, Michigan, Minnesota, Nebraska, Oregon, Texas, Washington, & Wisconsin is the responsibility of the state concerned.

Listed here are 66 elementary & secondary schools & three peripheral dormitories operated by the BIA. An additional 105 elementary & secondary schools & 11 peripheral dormitories are operated by Indian tribes and tribal organizations under contract/grant witht eh BIA. There are two post secondary institutions operated by the BIA & 26 tribally controlled community colleges/universities funded through the BIA. Listings are arranged by type of school (i.e., day & boarding schools), & by geographic location.

Listed first are Bureau of Indian Affairs' agencies and area offices with education program administrators, superintendents, and chairpersons; with telephone and telefax numbers.

OFFICE OF INDIAN EDUCATION PROGRAMS
Bureau of Indian Affairs
1849 C St., NW MS: 3512-MIB
WASHINGTON, DC 20240-0001
(202) 208-6123 Fax 208-3312
E-mail: cheryl_branum@ios.doi.gov
Joann Sebastian Morris, Director
William Mehojah, Deputy Director
Staff: Office of Field Director: Dr. Dennis Fox, Ass't Director (208-4542. *Branch of Administrative Services* (208-4555 Fax 208-3271): Rodney Young, Acting Chief, (208-4775); Cheryl Branum, Secretary; Dr. Joe Herrin (208-7658); Glenn Allison (208-3151); Jim Womack (208-7111). *Division of School Program Support-Southwest Team* (208-6020 Fax 208-3200): Charles Geboe, Chief (208-4040); Antoinette Fragua, Secretary (208-6364); Peter Camp (208) 4411); Bette haskins (208-4625); Loretta Draper (208-4871); Anita Tsinnajinnie (208-4110). School Support Team (273-2339): Dr. Sabdra Fox (273-2382); Gaye Leia King (273-7388); Donel Erickson (208-5026); Jennifer Davis (273-2339). *Branch of Exceptional Education* (208-6675): Dr. Angelita Felix, Chief (208-5037); Ken Whitehorn (208-4376). *Special Projects Team* (219-1127): Dr. Jim Martin, Acting Head (208-5810); Gail Veney (219-1128), Lana Shaughnessy (208-3601), Lucretia Herrin (208-3628), Garry Martin (208-3478). *Division of Planning* (208-3550): Dr. Jim Martin, Head (208-5810); Dalton Henry (208-5820), Keener Cobb (208-5962), Christine Brown (208-3559), Georgia Brown (208-3596).

OFFICE OF INDIAN EDUCATION PROGRAMS
B.I.A., 500 Gold Ave. SW, Rm. 7C
P.O. Box 769 • ALBUQUERQUE, NM 87103
(505) 248-6965 Fax 248-6997
Dr. Ken Ross, Special Assistant (346-6544)
Jimmy Baker, Special Assistant (346-6594)
Eileen Johnson, Acting Administrator (346-6801)
Robert Baracker, Area Director (346-7590)
Staff: Shawna Smith, Secretary; *Staffing Specialists:* Laurel Abrahamson, Mary Ann Begay, Amber Anne Deluca, Vivian Pacheco.

NAVAJO/OIEP PERSONNEL OFFICE
Gallup Area Office-BIA
301 W. Hill St., Box 1060
GALLUP, NM 87305
(505) 863-8216 Farx 863-8214
Jim Smith, Acting Supervisor (863-8462)
Staff specialists: Irene Benallie, Joann Davis, Fern Dennison

ABERDEEN AREA INSTRUCTIONAL COORDINATOR
Bureau of Indian Affairs
115 4th Ave., SE, Federal Bldg.
ABERDEEN, SD 57401
(605) 226-7431 Fax 226-7434
Cora Jones, Area Director
Sandra Carlsgaard, Special Education Coordinator

ANCHORAGE EDUCATION FIELD OFFICE
Bureau of Indian Affairs
3601 C St., Suite 1100 • ANCHORAGE, AK 99503
(907) 271-4115 Fax 271-3678
Robert Pringle, Education Administrator
The BIA no longer operates schools in Alaska based on Public Law 98-63, passed on July 30, 1983.

BILLINGS AREA OFFICE
Bureau of Indian Affairs
316 North 26th St. • BILLINGS, MT 59101
(406) 247-7953 Fax 247-7965
A. Levon French, Education Administrator
Responsible for the following schools: Blackfeet Dormitory; Busby School; St. Stephens Indian School.

CHEYENNE RIVER AGENCY
Bureau of Indian Affairs
100 N. Main, P.O. Box 2020
EAGLE BUTTE, SD 57625
(605) 964-8772 Fax 964-1155
Dr. Cherie Farlee, Education Administrator
Jane Azure, Special Education Coordinator
Responsible for the following schools: Takini School; Promise School; Swift Bird Day School; White Horse Day School; Cheyenne-Eagle Butte School; Pierre Indian Learning Center

CHINLE AGENCY
Bureau of Indian Affairs
Navajo Route 7, P.O. Box 6003
CHINLE, AZ 86503
(520) 674-5130/8 Fax 674-5134
Beverly Crawford, Education Administrator
Sandi Beeman, Special Education Coordinator
Responsible for the following schools: Cottonwood Day School; Low Mountain Boarding School; Lukachukai Boarding School; Nazlini Boarding School; Pinon Dormitory; Rock Point Community School; Rough Rock Demonstration School; Chinle Boarding School; Many Farms High School; Black Mesa Community School

CROW CREEK/LOWER BRULE AGENCY
Bureau of Indian Affairs
140 Education Ave., P.O. Box 139
FORT THOMPSON, SD 57339
(605) 245-2398; 473-5531 Fax 245-2399
Dan Schroyer, Education Administrator
Catherine Gallagher, Special Education Coordinator
Responsible for the following schools: Fort Thompson Elementary School; Crow Creek Reservation High School; Lower Brule Day School.

EASTERN NAVAJO AGENCY
Bureau of Indian Affairs
Main St. Bldg. 222, P.O. Box 328
CROWNPOINT, NM 87313
(505) 786-6150 Fax 786-6112
Larry D. Holman, Education Administrator
Kathy Spitz, Special Education Coordinator
Bertha Muskett, Handicap Program Coordinator
Responsible for the following schools: Baca Community School; Dibe Yazhi Habitiin Olta (Borrego Pass School); Bread Springs Day School; Chi-Ch'Il-Tah/Jones Ranch Community School; Huerfano Dormitory; Lake Valley Navajo School; Mariano Lake Community School; Ojo Encino Day School; Pueblo Pintado Community School; Standing Rock Community School; Dlo'ay Azhi Community School; Na'Neelzhiin Ji'Olta (Torreon); Wingate Elementary School; Wingate High School; Crownpoint Community School; Dzilth-Na-O-Dith-Hle Community School; To-Hajiilee-He (Canoncito); Alamo Navajo School

EASTERN & SOUTHERN STATES AGENCY
Bureau of Indian Affairs
3701 N. Fairfax Dr., Suite 260 Mailroom
ARLINGTON, VA 22203
(703) 235-3233 Fax 235-3351
LaVonna Weller, Education Administrator
Responsible for the following schools: Ahfachkee Day School; Beatrice Rafferty School; Boque Chitto Elementary School; Cherokee Central Elementary School & High School; Chitimacha Day School; Choctaw Central Middle School & High School; Indian Island School; Indian Township School; Indian Island School; Miccosukee Indian School; Pearl River Elementary School; Red Water Elementary School; Standing Pine Elementary School; Tucker Elementary School.

FORT DEFIANCE AGENCY
Bureau of Indian Affairs
P.O. Box 110 • FORT DEFIANCE, AZ 86504
(520) 729-7251 Fax 729-7286
Charles E. Johnson, Education Administrator
Angey Yazza, Special Education Coordinator
Responsible for the following schools: Chuska Community School; Crystal Boarding School; Dilcon Boarding School; Greasewood Springs Community School; Holbrook Dormitory; Hunters Point Boarding School; Kinlichee Boarding School; Pine Springs Boarding School; Seba Dalkai Boarding School; Wide Ruins Boarding School; Winslow Dormitory

HOPI AGENCY
Bureau of Indian Affairs
Hwy. 264, P.O. Box 568
KEAMS CANYON, AZ 86034
(520) 738-2262 Fax 738-5139
John D. Wahnee, Education Administrator
Beverly Wahnee, Special Education Coordinator
Responsible for the following schools: Hopi High School; Havasupai School; Hopi Day School; Hotevilla Bacavi Community School; Moencopi Day School; Keams Canyon Boarding School; Polacca Day School; Second Mesa Day School

IDAHO EDUCATION FIELD OFFICE
Bureau of Indian Affairs
P.O. Box 277 • LAPWAI, ID 83540
(202) 843-5025 FAX 843-7412
Barbra Murphey, Special Education Coordinator

MINNEAPOLIS AREA OFFICE
Bureau of Indian Affairs
331 South Second Ave.
MINNEAPOLIS, MN 55401
(612) 373-1000 x 1000 Fax 373-1065
Terry Portra, Education Administrator
Mary Hilfiker, Special Education Coordinator
Responsible for the following schools: Bahweting Anishnabe School; Bug-O-Nay-Ge Shig School; Circle of Life Survival School; Circle of Nations Wahpeton Indian Boarding School; Fond du Lac Ojibway School; Nay Ah Shing School; Lac Courte Oreeilles Ojibwa School; Oneida Tribal School; Menominee Tribal School; Hannahville Indian School; Flandreau Indian School; Sac & Fox Settlement School

NORTHERN PUEBLOS AGENCY
Bureau of Indian Affairs
P.O. Box 4269, Fairview Station
ESPANOLA, NM 87533
(505) 753-1465 Fax 753-1475
Kevin Skenandore, Education Administrator
Mary Ann Apodacca, Special Education Coordinator
Responsible for the following schools: San Ildefonso Day School; Ohkay Owingeh Community (San Juan) School; Santa Clara Day School; Taos Day School; Te Tsu Geh Oweenge (Tesuque) Day School; Santa Fe Indian School; Jicarilla Dormitory

OKLAHOMA EDUCATION OFFICE
Bureau of Indian Affairs
4149 Highline Blvd., Suite 380
Oklahoma City, OK 73180
(405) 945-6051/2/3/4 Fax 945-6057
Joy Martin, Education Administrator
Judy Littleman, Special Education Coordinator
Responsible for the following schools: Riverside Indian School; Carter Seminary; Kickapoo Nation School; Eufaula Dormitory; Sequoyah High School; Jones Academy

PAPAGO AGENCY
Bureau of Indian Affairs
P.O. Box 490 • SELLS, AZ 85634
(520) 383-3292/3/4 Fax 383-2399
Joe Frazier, Education Administrator
Luvette Russell, Special Education Coordinator
Responsible for the following schools: Santa Rosa Ranch School; Santa Rosa Boarding School; San Simon School; Tohono O'Odham High School.

PIMA AGENCY
Phoenix Area Office/BIA
400 N. 5th St., P.O. Box 10
PHOENIX, AZ 85001
(602) 379-3944, 963-6907 Fax 379-3946
Ray Interpreter, Acting Education Line Officer

David Dickman, Special Education Coordinator
Responsible for the following schools: Blackwater Community School; Casa Blanca Day School; Gila Crossing Day School; Salt River Day School

PINE RIDGE AGENCY
Bureau of Indian Affairs
101 Main St., P.O. Box 333
PINE RIDGE, SD 57770
(605) 867-1306 Fax 867-5610
Norma Tibbitts, Education Administrator
Julie Goings, Special Education Coordinator
Responsible for the following schools: American Horse School; Little Wound School; Wounded Knee District School; Loneman Day School; Pine Ridge School; Porcupine Day School; Crazy Horse School.

PORTLAND AREA OFFICE
Bureau of Indian Affairs
911 N.E. 11th Ave.
PORTLAND, OR 97232
(503) 872-2743 Fax 231-6219
John Reimer, Education Administrator
Responsible for the following schools: Chemawa Indian School; Paschal Sherman Indian School; Sho-Ban School District No. 512; Coeur D'Alene Tribal School; Quileute Tribal School; Wa He Lut Indian School; Lummi Tribal School System; Lummi High School; Chief Leschi (Puyallup) School; Muckleshoot Tribal School; Yakima Tribal School; Two Eagle River School

ROSEBUD AGENCY
Bureau of Indian Affairs
1001 Avenue D, P.O. Box 669
MISSION, SD 57555
(605) 856-4478 Fax 856-4487
Neva Sherwood, Education Administrator
Responsible for the following schools: St. Francis Indian School; Rosebud Dormitories; Marty Indian School.

SACRAMENTO AREA OFFICE
Bureau of Indian Affairs
2800 Cottage Way
SACRAMENTO, CA 95825
(916) 979-2560 Fax 979-3063
Fayetta Babby, Education Administrator
Responsible for the following schools: Sherman Indian High School; Pyramid Lake High School; Duckwater Shoshone Elementary School; Noli School.

SHIPROCK AGENCY
Bureau of Indian Affairs
Hwy. 666N, P.O. Box 3239
SHIPROCK, NM 87420
(505) 368-4427 Ext. 5 Fax 368-4427 Ext. 300
Lester Hudson, Education Administrator
Steve Gillenwater, Special Education Coordinator
Responsible for the following schools: Aneth Community School; Aztec Dormitory; Beclabito Day School; Cove Day School; Nenahnezad Community School; Red Rock Day School; Sanostee Day School; T'iis Nazbas (Teecnospos) Community School; Tohaali' (Toadlena) Community School; Shiprock Reservation Dormitory; Atsa' Biya' azh Community School (Shiprock Elementary); Shiprock Northwest High School; Navajo Prepatory School

SOUTHERN PUEBLOS AGENCY
Bureau of Indian Affairs
1000 Indian School Rd., NW,
P.O. Box 1667
ALBUQUERQUE, NM 87103
(505) 346-2431 Fax 346-2408
Dr. Benjamin Atencio, Education Administrator
Barbara Deloache, Special Education Coordinator
Responsible for the following schools: Sky City Community School; Isleta Elementary School; Jemez Day School; Laguna Elementary School; Laguna Middle School; San Felipe Pueblo Elementary School; Zia Day School; Pine Hill School; Mescalero Apache School

STANDING ROCK AGENCY
Bureau of Indian Affairs
Agency Ave., P.O. Box E
FORT YATES, ND 58538
(701) 854-3497 Fax 854-7280
Emmett White Temple, Education Administrator
Emma Jean Blue Earth, Special Ed. Coordinator

Responsible for the following schools: Rock Creek Day School; Littel Eagle Day School; Standing Rock Community School; Tate Topa Tribal School (Four Winds); Theodore Jamerson Elementary School.

TURTLE MOUNTAIN AGENCY
Bureau of Indian Affairs
School St., P.O. Box 30
BELCOURT, ND 58316
(701) 477-3463 Fax 477-5944
Dr. Loretta DeLong, Education Administrator
Galene Belgarde, Special Education Coordinator
Responsible for the following schools: Dunseith Day School; Ojibwa Indian School; Turtle Mountain Elementary School; Turtle Mountain Middle School; Turtle Mountain High School; Mandaree Day School; Trenton School; Twin Buttes Day School; White Shield School

WESTERN NAVAJO AGENCY
BIA, P.O. Box 746
TUBA CITY, AZ 86045
(520) 283-2221 Fax 283-2286
Serves the following schools: Chilchinbeto Community School; Tonalea (Red Lake) Day School; Dennehotso Boarding School; Kaibeto Boarding School; Kayenta Community School; Leupp Schools, Inc.; Naa Tsis' Aan Community School; Richfield Schools; Rocky Ridge Boarding School; Shonto Preparatory Schools; Residential Hall, Tuba City Boarding School; Greyhills High School; and Little Singer Community School.

ALABAMA

REEDS CHAPEL ELEMENTARY & CALCEDEAVER SCHOOLS
Choctaw Indian Reservation
1080 W. Red Fox Rd.
MT. VERNON, AL 36560
(205) 829-5500 Fax 829-5580

ALASKA

ARLICAQ SCHOOL
Yupiit School District
P.O. Box 227 • AKIAK, AK 99552
(907) 765-7212/5
Larry Ctibor, Principal
Day School; Grades K-12. *Enrollment*: 76. *Instructors*: Debbie Jackson, Elizabeth Lake, Ida Jasper, Lena Williams. *Special programs*: Bilingual Bicultural Education Program (Abbey Augustine, Coordinator); Yupiit Reading Project; Cultural Heritage Program. Library. Under jurisdiction of Anchorage Education Field Office.

CHEFORNAK IRA CONTRACT SCHOOL
CHEFORNAK, AK 99561
(907) 867-8707
Jerry Twitchell, Principal
Peter Panruk, Chair
Day School; Grades K-8. Under jurisdiction of Anchorage Education Field Office.

CHEVAK IRA CONTRACT SCHOOL
CHEVAK, AK 99563
(907) 858-7713
Alex Tatem, Principal
Xiver Atcherian, Chair
Day School; Grades K-12. Under jurisdiction of Anchorage Education Field Office.

KASIGLUK DAY SCHOOL
KASIGLUK, AK 99609
(907) 477-6714
Karen A. Rhoades, Principal
Yeako Slim, Chair
Day School; Grades K-8. Under jurisdiction of Anchorage Education Field Office.

KIPNUK DAY SCHOOL
KIPNUK, AK 99614
(907) 896-5513
Leslie Smith, Principal/Teacher

Peter J. Paul, Chair
Day School; Grades K-8. Under jurisdiction of Anchorage Education Field Office.

NEWTOK DAY SCHOOL
NEWTOK, AK 99559
(907) 237-2328
Rodney Sehorn, Principal
Joseph Tommy, Chair
Day School; Grades 1-8. Under jurisdiction of Anchorage Education Field Office.

NUNAPITCHUK DAY SCHOOL
NUNAPITCHUK, AK 99641
(907) 527-5711
Karen K. Waters, Principal
Jimmy Stevens, Chair
Day School; Grades K-8. Under jurisdiction of Anchorage Education Field Office.

MT. EDGECUMBE HIGH SCHOOL
1332 Seward • SITKA, AK 99835
(907) 966-2201
Bill Denkinger, Principal
Larrae Rocheleau, Supt.
Boarding School; Grades 9-12; *Enrollment*: 300.
Special courses: Pacific Rim Cultures; Alaska Native History.

TOKSOOK BAY DAY SCHOOL
TOKSOOK, AK 99637 (907) 543-2746
Wilma M. Moore, Principal
Joseph Henry, Chair
Day School; Grades 1-6. Under jurisdiction of Anchorage Education Field Office.

TULUKSAK IRA CONTRACT SCHOOL
TULUKSAK, AK 99679
(907) 695-6212
Howard Diamond, Principal
Andrew Alexie, Chair
Day School; Grades K-8. Under jurisdiction of Anchorage Education Field Office.

ARIZONA

CASA BLANCA DAY SCHOOL
P.O. Box 940 • BAPCHULE, AZ 85221
(520) 315-3489/10/11 Fax 315-1199
Jack Frost, Principal
Theresa Gibson, Chairperson
Day School; Grades K-4. Under jurisdiction of Pima Agency.

WIDE RUINS BOARDING SCHOOL
Hwy. 91, P.O. Box 309
CHAMBERS, AZ 86502
(520) 652-3251 Fax 652-3252
Albert Yazzie, Principal; Ronald Hale, Chairperson
Boarding School; Grades K-6. Under jurisdiction of Fort Defiance Agency.

COTTONWOOD DAY SCHOOL
Navajo Route 4
CHINLE, AZ 86503
(520) 725-3256/3235 Fax 725-3255
Theresa A. Kedelty, Supervisor
Ethelou Yazzie, Chairperson
Day School; Grades K-8. Under jurisdiction of Chinle Agency.

LOW MOUNTAIN BOARDING SCHOOL
Navajo Route 65 • CHINLE, AZ 86503
(520) 725-3308 Fax 725-3306
Dan Hundley, Principal
Venora Jimmy, Chairperson
Boarding School; Grades K-4.
Under jurisdiction of Chinle Agency.

ROUGH ROCK COMMUNITY SCHOOL
Hwy. 59, RRDS, Box 217
CHINLE, AZ 86503
(520) 728-3500 Fax 728-3502
Dr. Robert Roessel, Supervisor
Betty Dailey, Chairperson
Lorene Tohe-Van Pelt, FACE Coordinator
Day School; Grades K-12.
Under jurisdiction of Chinle Agency.

CIBECUE COMMUNITY SCHOOL
101 Main St., P.O. Box 80068
CIBECUE, AZ 85911
(520) 332-2480 Fax 332-3241
Isaiah Lee, Principal; Judy DeHose, Chairperson
Day School; Grades K-12; *Enrollment:* 350. *Special courses:* Bilingual (Apache). *Instructors:* Bonnie Luis, Bilingual; Joyce Kruger, Gifted; Fay Fernando, Chapter I Coordinator; Eric Carlson, Special Ed. Coordinator; Margaret Burnette, Indian Club. *Special programs:* American Indian Day Pageant, in Sept.; Arts and Crafts Fair/Pow-Wow, in May; Indian Club (children learn and perform Native American dances and music). Library Media Center with about 7,500 resources. *Publication:* Biweekly newsletter. Under jurisdiction of Fort Apache Agency.

BLACKWATER COMMUNITY SCHOOL
Route 1, Box 95 • COOLIDGE, AZ 85228
(520) 215-5859 Fax 215-5862
S. Jo Lewis, Principal
Cornelia Eschief, Chairperson
Jacquelyne Power, FACE Coordinator
Day School. Grades K-2.
Under jurisdiction of Pima Agency.

DENNEHOTSO BOARDING SCHOOL
P.O. Box LL • DENNEHOTSO, AZ 86535
(520) 658-3201/2 Fax 658-3221
Velma Eisenberger, Principal
Allen Gray, Chairperson
Boarding School; Grades K-8. Under jurisdiction of Western Navajo Agency.

FLAGSTAFF DORMITORY
FLAGSTAFF, AZ 86002
(520) 774-5270 (phone & fax)
James Kimery, Director
Chester Claw, Chairperson
Dormitory School; Grades 9-12. Under jurisdiction of Western Navajo Agency.

THEODORE ROOSEVELT SCHOOL
101 Thomas Rd., P.O. Box 567
FORT APACHE, AZ 85926
(520) 338-4464 Fax 338-1009
Michael Brock, Principal
Day School; Grades 6-8. Under jurisdiction of Fort Apache Agency.

GREASEWOOD SPRINGS COMMUNITY SCHOOL
HC 58, Box 60 • GANADO, AZ 86505
(520) 654-3331/2 Fax 654-3384
Ben Wade, Principal
Bertha Ben Chairperson
Boarding School; Grades K-8.
Under jurisdiction of Fort Defiance Agency.

KINLICHEE BOARDING SCHOOL
2 miles north of Hwy. 264 • GANADO, AZ 86505
(520) 755-3430/9 Fax 755-3448
Lena M. Draper, Principal; Calvin Kirk, Chairperson
Boarding School; Grades K-6. *Enrollment:* 110. *Instructors:* T. Piechewski, R. Venn, S. Litson, T. Cline, J. Lemler, H. Parkhurst. 95% of students are Navajo Indians. Library. Under jurisdiction of Fort Defiance Agency.

NAZLINI BOARDING SCHOOL
HC58 Box 35 • GANADO, AZ 86505
(520) 755-6125 Fax 755-3729
Benny Hale, Principal
Isabella Emberson, Chairperson
Boarding School; Grades K-6.
Under jurisdiction of Chinle Agency.

HOLBROOK DORMITORY
1100 W. Buffalo • HOLBROOK, AZ 86025
(520) 524-6222/3 Fax 524-2231
Jacqueline N. Wade, Principal
Maye Bigboy, Chairperson
Dormitory School; Grades 9-12.
Under jurisdiction of Fort Defiance Agency.

HOTEVILLA BACAVI COMMUNITY SCHOOL
Hwy. 264, P.O. Box 48
HOTEVILLA, AZ 86030
(520) 734-2462 Fax 734-2225
Adelbert Goldtooth, Administrator
Karen Shupla, Chairperson

Day School; Grades K-7. *Enrollment:* 125. *Special programs:* Bilingual computer program; special education. Community library. *Publication:* Tales in Hopi Language (published by students). Under jurisdiction of Hopi Agency.

PINE SPRINGS BOARDING SCHOOL
10021 Pine Springs Rd.
P.O. Box 4198 • HOUCK, AZ 86506
(520) 871-4311 Fax 871-4341/2
Bob G. Hooper, Principal
Annabelle Begay, Chairperson
Boarding School; Grades K-4. *Enrollment:* 62.
Under jurisdiction of Fort Defiance Agency.

KAIBETO BOARDING SCHOOL
East Hwy. 160 • KAIBETO, AZ 86053
(520) 673-3480 Fax 673-3489
Patrick Suriano Principal
Kelsey Begay, Chairperson
Boarding School; Grades K-8.
Under jurisdiction of Western Navajo Agency.

CHILCHINBETO DAY SCHOOL
P.O. Box 740 • KAYENTA, AZ 86033
(520) 697-3448 (phone & fax)
Stanley Kedelty, Principal
Instructors: Andee DeLaRosa, Jerrel Fields, Brian Pottorff, Prudy Wiseman, Alvin Watson, and Cecil Billie.
Day School; Grades K-8. *Enrollment:* 126. Under jurisdiction of Western Navajo Agency.

KAYENTA BOARDING SCHOOL
P.O. Box 188 • KAYENTA, AZ 86033
(520) 697-3439 Fax 697-3490
Jenny Jimenez, Principal
Daniel Peaches, Chairperson
Boarding School; Grades K-8.
Under jurisdiction of Western Navajo Agency.

HOPI MIDDLE/HIGH SCHOOL
Hwy. 264, P.O. Box 337
KEAMS CANYON, AZ 86034
(520) 738-5111 Fax 738-5266
E-Mail: Jdewilde@hjshs.k12.az.us
E-mail:: Bruin@hjshs.k12.az.us
Glenn Gilman, Principal
Joseph C. DeWilde, Librarian
Charter/Day School; Grades 7-12. 750 students, with about 80% Hopi and 20% Navajo. *Special project:* Hopilavayi Project - a Hopi tribal project to encourage the growth and acquisition of Hopi language and culture. Under jurisdiction of Hopi Agency.

KEAMS CANYON BOARDING SCHOOL
P.O. Box 397
KEAMS CANYON, AZ 86034
(520) 738-2385 Fax 738-2385
Albert T. Sinquah, Principal
Cheryl Mahle, Chairperson
Boarding School; Grades K-6.
Under jurisdiction of Hopi Agency.

HOPI DAY SCHOOL
HWY. 264, P.O. Box 42
KYKOTSMOVI, AZ 86039
(520) 734-2468 Fax 734-2470
Dr. John Thomas, Principal
Miona Kaping, Chairperson
Day School; Grades K-6.
Under jurisdiction of Hopi Agency.

ROCKY RIDGE BOARDING SCHOOL
P.O. Box 299
KYKOTSMOVI, AZ 86039
(602) 725-3415 (phone & fax)
Pam Emerson, Principal
Lorenzo Yazzie, Chairperson
Boarding School; Grades K-8.
Under jurisdiction of Western Navajo Agency.

GILA CROSSING DAY SCHOOL
P.O. Box 10
LAVEEN, AZ 85339
(520) 550-4834 Fax 550-4252
Bill Walters, Principal
Mike Zillioux, Chairperson
Day School; Grades K-6.
Under jurisdiction of Pima Agency.

LUKACHUKAI BOARDING SCHOOL
Navajo Route 12
LUKACHUKAI, AZ 86507
(520) 787-2301 Fax 787-2311
Rodney Bond, Principal
Samuel Tso, Chairperson
Boarding School; Grades K-8.
Under jurisdiction of Chinle Agency.

CHINLE BOARDING SCHOOL
P.O. Box 70 • MANY FARMS, AZ 86538
(520) 781-6221/2 Fax 781-6376
Dr. Frannie L. Spain, Supervisor
Calvin Tsosie, Chairperson
Boarding School; Grades K-8.
Under jurisdiction of Chinle Agency.

MANY FARMS HIGH SCHOOL
P.O. Box 307 • MANY FARMS, AZ 86532
(520) 781-6226/7 Fax 781-6355
Arthur K. Hobson, Principal
Samuel Tso, Chairperson
Boarding School; Grades 9-12.
Under jurisdiction of Chinle Agency.

PHOENIX INDIAN SCHOOL
P.O. Box 10 • PHOENIX, AZ 85001
(520) 241-2126
Fred Wilson, Principal
Boarding School; Grades 9-12.
Under jurisdiction of Phoenix Area Office.

BLACK MESA COMMUNITY SCHOOL
P.O. Box 97 • PINON, AZ 86510
(520) 674-3632 (phone & fax)
George Cukro, Supervisor
Jones Begay, Chairperson
Day School; Grades K-8.
Under jurisdiction of Chinle Agency.

PINON DORMITORY
P.O. Box 159 • PINON, AZ 86510
(520) 725-3250/3234 Fax 725-3232
Rose Mary Smith, Director
Preston McCabe, Chairperson
Boarding School; Grades K-12.
Under jurisdiction of Chinle Agency.

POLACCA DAY SCHOOL
P.O. Box 750 • POLACCA, AZ 86042
(520) 737-2581 Fax 737-2323
Bruce O. Steele, Principal
Katheryn Wright, Chairperson
Day School; Grades K-6.
Under jurisdiction of Hopi Agency.

COVE DAY SCHOOL
P.O. Box 2000
RED VALLEY, AZ 86544
(520) 653-4457 Fax 653-4457
Darryl Beaven, Principal
James Sorrelhorse, Chairperson
Day School; Grades K-6.
Under jurisdiction of Shiprock Agency.

RED ROCK DAY SCHOOL
P.O. Drawer 2007
RED VALLEY, AZ 86544
(520) 653-4456 Fax 653-5711
Mike Luther, Principal
Harry Tome, Chairperson
Day School; Grades K-8.
Under jurisdiction of Shiprock Agency.

ROCK POINT COMMUNITY SCHOOL
Hwy. 191 • ROCK POINT, AZ 86545
(520) 659-4221/4 Fax 659-4235
Jimmy C. Begay, Supervisor
Rex Lee Jim, Chairperson
Day School; Grades K-12.
Under jurisdiction of Chinle Agency.

HUNTERS POINT BOARDING SCHOOL
Rt. 12, P.O. Box 99
ST. MICHAELS, AZ 86511
(520) 871-4439 Fax 871-4435
Winifred C. Peters, Principal
Stanley Milford, Chairperson
Boarding School; Grades K-5.
Under jurisdiction of Fort Defiance Agency.

SALT RIVER DAY SCHOOL
10000 E. McDowell Rd. •
SCOTTSDALE, AZ 85256
  (602) 850-2900 Fax 850-2921
  Carolyn Tanner, Principal
  Leonard Rivers, Chairperson
Day School; Grades K-6.
Under jurisdiction of Pima Agency.

SECOND MESA DAY SCHOOL
Hwy. 264, P.O. Box 98
SECOND MESA, AZ 86043
  (520) 737-2571 Fax 737-2470
  Cindy Joe, Principal
  Tim Keevama, Chairperson
Day School; Grades K-6.
Under jurisdiction of Hopi Agency.

SAN SIMON SCHOOL
HC 01, Box 8292 • SELLS, AZ 85634
  (520) 362-2331 Fax 362-2405
  Elsie Flesher, Principal
  Fred Pablo, Chairperson
Boarding School; Grades K-8.
Under jurisdiction of Papago Agency.

SANTA ROSA BOARDING SCHOOL
HC 01, Box 8400 • SELLS, AZ 85634
  (520) 361-2331 Fax 361-2511
  George Sam, Chairperson
Boarding School; Grades K-8.
Under jurisdiction of Papago Agency.

SANTA ROSA RANCH SCHOOL
HC 02, Box 7570 • SELLS, AZ 85634
  (520) 383-2359 Fax 383-3960
  Patsy Delp, Principal
  Lorraine Venurz, Chairperson
Day School; Grades K-8. Under
jurisdiction of Papago Agency.

TOHONO O'ODHAM HIGH SCHOOL
HC01, Box 8513 • SELLS, AZ 85634
  (520) 362-2400 Fax 362-2256
  Karen Dawson, Principal
  Katherine Lopez, Chairperson
Day School; Grades 9-12.
Under jurisdiction of Papago Agency.

SHONTO BOARDING SCHOOL
P.O. Box 7900 • SHONTO, AZ 86054
  (520) 672-2652 Fax 672-2849
  Arthur Diamond, Principal
  Stanley Yazzie, Chairperson
Boarding School; Grades K-8. Under
jurisdiction of Western Navajo Agency.

HAVASUPAI SCHOOL
P.O. Box 40 • SUPAI, AZ 86435
  (520) 448-2901 Fax 448-2551
  Ronald Arias, Principal
  Lester Crooke, Chairperson
Day School; Grades K-8.
Under jurisdiction of Hopi Agency.

**T'IIS NAZBAS COMMUNITY
(TEECNOSPOS) SCHOOL**
P.O. Box 102 • TEECNOSPOS, AZ 86514
  (520) 656-3486 Fax 656-3252
  Ann Willyard, Principal
  Herman Farley, Chairperson
  Al Begay, FACE Coordinator
Boarding School; Grades K-8.
Under jurisdiction of Shiprock Agency.

NAVAJO MOUNTAIN BOARDING SCHOOL
P.O. Box 10010 • TONALEA, AZ 86044
  (520) 672-2851 Fax 672-2335
  Jamie Holgate, Chairperson
Boarding School; Grades K-8. Under
jurisdiction of Western Navajo Agency.

TONALEA (RED LAKE) DAY SCHOOL
P.O. Box 39 • TONALEA, AZ 86044
  (520) 283-6325 Fax 283-6326
  Glenn WhiteEagle, Principal
  Wilson Gray, Chairperson
Day School; Grades K-8. Under
jurisdiction of Western Navajo Agency.

MOENCOPI DAY SCHOOL
So. Hwy. 264, P.O. Box 185
TUBA CITY, AZ 86045
  (520) 283-5361 Fax 283-4662
  Noreen Sakiestewa, Principal
  Lenora Lewis, Chairperson
Day School; Grades K-6.
Under jurisdiction of Hopi Agency.

TUBA CITY BOARDING SCHOOL
P.O. Box 187
TUBA CITY, AZ 86045
  (520) 283-2330 Ext. 221 Fax 283-2265
  Jerry E. Diebel, Principal
  Mary Maloney, Chairperson
Boarding School; Grades K-8. Under
jurisdiction of Western Navajo Agency.

GREYHILLS HIGH SCHOOL
P.O. Box 160
TUBA CITY, AZ 86045
  (520) 283-6271 Fax 283-6604
  Lester Helton, Principal
  Kenneth Nez, Chairperson
Boarding School; Grades 9-12. *Enrollment*: 450. An
Academy High School with a uniquely Native Ameri-
can thrust in education. In partnership with Northern
Arizona University and Uiversity of Hawaii in develop-
ing a curriculum based on a Laboratory school ap-
proach. Library. Under jurisdiction of Western Navajo
Agency.

JOHN F. KENNEDY DAY SCHOOL
Hwy. 73, P.O. Box 130
WHITE RIVER, AZ 85941
  (520) 338-4593 Fax 338-4592
  Susan Higgins, Principal
  Jackie Altaha, Chairperson
Day School; Grades K-8. Under
jurisdiction of Fort Apache Agency.

DILCON BOARDING SCHOOL
HC63 Box G • WINSLOW, AZ 86047
  (520) 657-3211 Fax 657-3370
  Dr. Jenny D. Jimenez, Principal
  Thelma Barton, Chairperson
Boarding School; Grades K-8.
Under jurisdiction of Fort Defiance Agency.

LEUPP BOARDING SCHOOL
P.O. Box HC-61
WINSLOW, AZ 86047
  (520) 686-6211/6270 Fax 686-6216
  Donald Harvey, Director
  Jonathan R. Dover, Chairperson
Boarding School; Grades K-12. *Enrollment*: 375. *Spe-
cial course*: Entrepreneurship. *Instructor*: Jim Store.
Publication: Today at Leupp. Library. Under jurisdic-
tion of Western Navajo Agency.

LITTLE SINGER COMMUNITY SCHOOL
WINSLOW, AZ 86047
  (520) 526-6680 Fax 526-8994
  Lucinda Godinez, Principal
  Thomas Walker, Jr., Chairperson
Boarding School; Grades K-8. Under
jurisdiction of Western Navajo Agency.

SEBA DALKAI BOARDING SCHOOL
HC 63, Box H
WINSLOW, AZ 86047
  (520) 657-3208 Fax 657-3224
  Dr. Kyril Calsoyas, Principal
  Geraldine Clark, Chairperson
Boarding School; Grades K-6. *Enrollment*: 183. *Spe-
cial programs*: Special Education, Gifted and Talented;
Intensive Residential Guidance Program; and Sub-
stance Abuse. Bilingual Eduction.Under jurisdiction of
Fort Defiance Agency.

WINSLOW DORMITORY
600 N. Alfred Ave.
WINSLOW, AZ 86047
  (520) 829-4483/8 Fax 829-2821
  Helen C. Higdon, Principal
  Rose Bell Walker, Chairperson
Dormitory School; Grades 7-12.
Under jurisdiction of Fort Defiance Agency.

CALIFORNIA

SHERMAN INDIAN HIGH SCHOOL
9010 Magnolia Ave.
RIVERSIDE, CA 92503
  (888) 584-4004; (909) 276-6327 Fax 276-6336
  Jim Hastings, Principal
  Patricia Dixon, Chairperson
Boarding School; Grades 9-12.
Under jurisdiction of Sacramento Area Office.

NOLI SCHOOL
P.O. Box 487
SANTA JACINTO, CA 92581
  (909) 654-5596 Fax 654-4198
  Cathleen Salvis, Principal
  Lorraine Maseal, Chairperson
Day School; Grades 7-12. Under
jurisdiction of Sacramento Area Office.

FLORIDA

AHFACHKEE DAY SCHOOL
Star Route, Box 40
CLEWISTON, FL 33440
  (941) 983-6348 Fax 983-6535
  Dr. Patrick Gassney, Principal
  Chief James Billy, School Board President
Day School; Grades K-12. Under
jurisdiction of Eastern States Agency.

MICCOSUKEE INDIAN SCHOOL
Box 440021, Tamiami Station
MIAMI, FL 33144
  (305) 223-8380 ext. 323 Fax 223-1011
  America Novas, Principal
Day School; Grades K-12. Library.
Under jurisdiction of Eastern States Agency.

IDAHO

COEUR D'ALENE TRIBAL SCHOOL
Hwy. 95, P.O. Box 338
De SMET, ID 83824
  (208) 686-5808 Fax 686-5080
  Dave Peters, Supt.
Day School; Grades Pre K-8.
Under jurisdiction of Portland Area Office.

SHO'BAN SCHOOL DISTRICT #512
P.O. Box 790 • FORT HALL, ID 83203
  (208) 238-4300 Fax 238-2629
  Jim Philips, Principal
  Louis Headley, Supt.
Day School; Grades 7-12. Under
jurisdiction of Portland Area Office.

IOWA

SAC & FOX SETTLEMENT SCHOOL
1349 Meskwakie Rd.
TAMA, IA 52339
  (515) 484-4990 Fax 484-3265
  Paul Galer, Administrator
  Marjorie Mauskeno, Chairperson
Day School; Grades Pre-K-8. Under
jurisdiction of Minneapolis Area Office.

KANSAS

HASKELL INDIAN NATIONS UNIVERSITY
155 Indian Ave. #1305
LAWRENCE, KS 66046
  (913) 749-8404 Fax 749-8406
  Bob G. Martin, President
Grades: Freshman & Sophomore years. Administered
by the Bureau of Indian Affairs. Under jurisdiction of
the Horton Agency.

KICKAPOO NATION SCHOOL
P.O. Box 106 • POWHATTAN, KS 66527
(785) 474-3550 Fax 474-3498
Toby Melster, Principal
George "Pat" McAfee, Supt.
Debbie Whitebird, Chairperson
John Thomas, Tribal Representative
Day School; Grades Pre K-12. Special programs:
Gifted & talented program; special education; bilingual
progam for teaching Kickapoo language to students.
Under jurisdiction of Oklahoma Education Office.

LOUISIANA

CHITIMACHA DAY SCHOOL
3613 Chitimacha Trail
JEANERETTE, LA 70544
(318) 923-9960 Fax 923-7346
Dorothy Thompson, Principal
Jack Darden, Chairperson
Day School; Grades Pre K-8. Under jursidiction
of Eastern & Southern States Agency.

**CHOCTAW-APACHE OF
EBARB INDIAN SCHOOL**
P.O. Box 858 • ZWOLLE, LA 71486
(318) 645-2744
Day School. Grades: K-12. Enrollment: 285.
Only officially recognized "Indian School" in
the state of Louisiana.

MAINE

INDIAN ISLAND SCHOOL
1 River Rd. • OLD TOWN, ME 04468
(207) 827-4285 Fax 827-3599
Linda McLeod, Principal
E-Mail: lmcleod@iis.bia.edu
Web site: www.iis.bia.edu
Day School; Grades Pre K-8. Enrollment: 120. Spe-
cial courses & Instructors: Native American studies
(John Bear Mitchell); Penobscot Language (Carol
Dana). Under jurisdiction of Eastern & Southern States
Agency.

BEATRICE RAFFERTY SCHOOL
Pleasant Point Reservation
RR 1, Box 338 • PERRY, ME 04667
(207) 853-6085 Fax 853-6210
Dr. Veronica Magnam, Principal
Day School; Grades K-8. Under
jurisdiction of Eastern States Agency.

INDIAN TOWNSHIP SCHOOL
Peter Dana Point • HC 78, Box 1A
PRINCETON, ME 04668
(207) 796-2362 Fax 796-2726
Ralph Shannon, Principal
Day School; Grades Pre K-8; Enrollment: 100.
Special course: Passamaquoddy Language/Culture.
Instructor: Karen Sabbattus. Under jurisdiction of East-
ern & Southern States Agency.

MICHIGAN

HANNAHVILLE INDIAN SCHOOL
N14911 Hannahville B1 Rd.
WILSON, MI 49896
(906) 466-2952 Fax 466-2556
Tom Miller, Administrator
Robin Halfaday, Chairperson
Day School; Grades K-12. Under
jurisdiction of Minneapolis Area Office.

BAHWETING ANISHNABE SCHOOL
1301 Marquette Ave.
SAULT STE. MARIE, MI 49783
(906) 635-5055 FAX 635-3805
Nancy Hatch, Administrator
George Nolan, Chairperson
day School; Grades K-12. Under
jurisdiction of Minneapolis Area Office.

**GRAND TRAVERSE BAND TRIBAL
SCHOOL (WAABNO GIMAAK)**
2605 N. West Bay Shore Dr.
SUTTONS BAY, MI 49682
(231) 271-7505 Fax 271-7510
John Concannon, School Board Chairman
Day School; Grades K-8. Owned and operated by the
Grand Traverse Band of Ottawa & Chippewa Indians.

MINNESOTA

BUG-O-NAY-GE SHIG SCHOOL
Route 3, Box 1000
CASS LAKE, MN 56633
(800) 265-5576; (218) 335-3000 Fax 335-3024
Nncy Cooper, Administrator
Gerald White, Chairperson
Day School; Grades K-12. Under
jurisdiction of Minneapolis Area Office.

FOND DU LAC OJIBWAY SCHOOL
105 University Rd. • CLOQUET, MN 55720
(218) 878-4648 Fax 878-4687
Michael Rabideaux, School Administrator
Michael Himango, Chairperson
Day School; Grades: K-12. Enrollment: 270. Special
courses: Gifted & Talented; Ojibwe Language, Culture
& History. Publications: newsletter; newspaper. Library.
Under jurisdiction of Minneapolis Area Office.

NAY AH SHING SCHOOLS
Mille Lacs Band of Ojibwe
43651 Oodena Dr. • ONAMIA, MN 56359
(320) 532-4695 Fax 532-4675
Website: www.nas.k12.mn.us/
George Webbec, Administrator
Frances Davis, Chairperson
Day School; Abinoojiiyag School, grades K-4; Nay Ah
Shing Upper School, grades 5-12. Enrollment: 35.
Special courses: Native American Studies; Cultural
Crafts; Reservation History Curriculum; Native Ojibwe
Language Curriculum; basic core curriculum. Instruc-
tors: Millie Benjamin, Lynn Fischer, Kathy Morrow,
Natalie Weyaus, and Jade Racelo. Publications: Mille
Lacs Nay Ah Shing School Newsletter; Broken Win-
dows (book of poetry, 1980.) Under jurisdiction of Min-
neapolis Area Office.

MOUNDS PARK ALL-NATIONS MAGNET SCHOOL
1075 E. 3rd St. • SAINT PAUL, MN 55106
(612) 293-5938
Dr. Cornel Pewewardy, Principal
Day School; Grades K-8. Enrollment: 400.
Special program: Circle Time. Library.

CIRCLE OF LIFE SURVIVAL SCHOOL
P.O. Box 447 • WHITE EARTH, MN 56591
(218) 983-3285 ext. 269 Fax 983-3767
Ken Litzau, School Administrator
John Buckanaga, Chairperson
Day School; Grades K-12. Under
jurisdiction of Minneapolis Area Office.

MISSISSIPPI

RED WATER ELEMENTARY SCHOOL
555 Red Water Rd. • CARTHAGE, MS 39051
(601) 267-8500 Fax 267-5193
Sherry Tubby, Principal
Day School; Grades K-8. Under jurisdiction
of Eastern & Southern States Agency.

STANDING PINE ELEMENTARY SCHOOL
538 Hwy. 487 East • CATHAGE, MS 39051
(601) 267-9225 Fax 267-9129
Jackie Harpole, Principal
Day School; Grades K-6. Under jurisdiction
of Eastern & Southern States Agency.

CONEHATTA ELEMENTARYSCHOOL
851 Tushka Dr. • CONEHATTA, MS 39057
(601) 775-8254 Fax 775-9229
Calvin Isaac, Principal
Day School; Grades K-8. Under jurisdiction
of Eastern & Southern States Agency.

BOGUE CHITTO ELEMENTARY SCHOOL
Route 2, Box 274
PHILADELPHIA, MS 39350
(601) 656-8611 Fax 656-8648
Ken York, Principal
Day School; Grades K-8. Under jurisdiction
of Eastern & Southern States Agency.

CHOCTAW CENTRAL MIDDLE/HIGH SCHOOL
150 Recreation Rd.
PHILADELPHIA, MS 39350
(601) 656-8938 Fax 656-7077/7558
Randy Hodges, Principal (Day School; Grades 9-12).
Charles E. Hull, Principal (Day School; Grades 7-8)
Under jurisdiction of Eastern & Southern States
Agency.

PEARL RIVER ELEMENTARY SCHOOL
PHILADELPHIA, MS 39350
(601) 656-9051 Fax 656-3054
Robert McClelland, Principal
Day School; Grades K-6. Under jurisdiction
of Eastern & Southern States Agency.

TUCKER ELEMENTARY SCHOOL
126 E. Tucker Circle
PHILADELPHIA, MS 39350
(601) 656-8775 Fax 656-9341
Trina Cheathane, Principal
Day School; Grades K-8. Under jurisdiction
of Eastern & Southern States Agency.

MONTANA

LABRE INDIAN SCHOOL
P.O. Box 406 • ASHLAND, MT 59003
(406) 784-2347
William D. Walker, Superintendent
Day School; Grades K-12. Under
jurisdiction of Billings Area Office.

ROCKY BOY TRIBAL HIGH SCHOOL
Box 620, Rocky Boy Route
BOX ELDER, MT 59521
(406) 395-4291 Fax 395-4829
Sandra Murie, Acting Supt.
Day School; Grades 9-12. Under
jurisdiction of Billings Area Office.

BLACKFEET DORMITORY
Blackfeet Agency • P.O. Box 880
BROWNING, MT 59417-0880
(406) 338-7441 Fax 338-5725
Fred Guardipee, Chairperson
Wayne P. Bruno, Home Living Specialist
Dormitory School; Grades 1-12.
Under jurisdiction of Billings Area Office.

**NORTHERN CHEYENNE TRIBAL SCHOOL
(BUSBY SCHOOL)**
P.O. Box 150 • BUSBY, MT 59016
(406) 592-3646 Fax 592-3645
Dr. Harlan Krein Supt.; Alberta Fisher, Chairperson
Day School; Grades K-12. Under jurisdiction of Bill-
ings Area Office.

TWO EAGLE RIVER SCHOOL
P.O. Box 160 • PABLO, MT 59855
(406) 675-0292 Fax 674-0294
Clarice King, Supt.
E-mail: claudette@ronan.net
Website: www.twoeagleriver.com
Day School; Grades 7-12. Program: Culturally-relevant
curriculum. Under jurisdiction of Portland Area Office.

NEVADA

DUCKWATER SHOSHONE ELEMENTARY SCHOOL
P.O. Box 140038 • DUCKWATER, NV 89314
(702) 863-0242 Fax 863-0157
Linda Lawrence, Administrator
Michael Blackeye, Chairperson
Day School; Grades K-8. Under
jurisdiction of Sacramento Area Office.

PYRAMID LAKE HIGH SCHOOL
P.O. Box 256 • NIXON, NV 89424
(702) 574-1016 Fax 574-1037
Randy Melendez, Principal
Maurice Eben, Chairperson
Day School; Grades 7-12. Under
jurisdiction of Sacramento Area Office.

NEW MEXICO

SKY CITY COMMUNITY SCHOOL
P.O. Box 349 • ACOMA, NM 87304
(505) 552-6671 Fax 552-6672
Charlotte Garcia, Principal
William Estevan, Chairperson
Day School; Grades K-8. Enrollment: 250. *Special courses*: Gifted & Talented; Computer Laboratory. Library. Under jurisdiction of Southern Pueblos Agency.

**SOUTHWESTERN INDIAN
POLYTECHNIC INSTITUTE**
9169 Coors Rd., NW, Box 10146 • ALBUQUERQUE, NM 87184
(505) 897-5347 Fax 897-5343
Dr. Carolyn Elgin, President
Frederick Peso, Chairperson
Grades: Freshman & Sophomore years. Administered by the Bureau of Indian Affairs.

AZTEC DORMITORY
1600 Lydia Rippey Rd. • AZTEC, NM 87410
(801) 334-6565 Fax 334-8630
John C. Nolan, Home Living Specialist
Mae Rose Wolfe, Chairperson
Dormitory School; Grades 9-12.
Under jurisdiction of Shiprock Agency.

DZILTH-NA-0-DITH-HLE COMMUNITY SCHOOL
P.O. Box 5003 • BLOOMFIELD, NM 87413
(505) 632-1697 Fax 632-8563
D. Dwane Robinson, Principal
Angela Salazar, Ass't Principal
Evelyn Bekes, School Board Chairperson
Day School: K-8; Boarding School: Grades 1-12; Public School: 9-12. *Special Programs*: Annual Pow-wow in March; Annual Traditional Song & Dance Contest in November. Under jurisdiction of Eastern Navajo Agency.

HUERFANO DORMITORY
P.O. Box 639 • BLOOMFIELD, NM 87413
(505) 786-3411 Fax 327-3591
Darvin E. Homer, Principal
Pauline Platero, Chairperson
Dormitory School; Grades 1-12; K on day basis.
Under jurisdiction of Eastern Navajo Agency.

TO'HAJIILEE-HE (CANONCITO)
P.O. Box 438 • CANONCITO, NM 87026
(505) 831-6426 Fax 836-4914
Jim Byrnes, Principal
Margaret Platero, Chairperson
Colleen Alivado, FACE Coordinator
Boarding School; Grades K-12. Under
jurisdiction of Eastern Navajo Agency.

**T'IISTS'OOZI' BI'O'LTA (CROWNPOINT)
COMMUNITY SCHOOL**
P.O. Box 178 • CROWNPOINT, NM 87313
(505) 786-6159 Fax 786-6163
Virginia Jumbo, Principal
Cecilia J. Nez, Chairperson
Lorraine Yazzie, FACE Coordinator
Boarding School; Grades K-8. Under
jurisdiction of Eastern Navajo Agency.

DIBE YAZHI HABITIIN OLTA, INC.
Borrego Pass School
P.O. Box 679 • CROWNPOINT, NM 87313
(505) 786-5237 Fax 786-7078
Robbie Livingston, Principal
Thomas Barbone, Chairperson
Boarding School; Grades K-8. Under
jurisdiction of Eastern Navajo Agency.

LAKE VALLEY NAVAJO SCHOOL
CROWNPOINT, NM 87313
(505) 786-5392 Fax 786-5956

David J. Atanasoff, Principal
Wayne Dennison, Chairperson
Boarding School; Grades K-8. Under
jurisdiction of Eastern Navajo Agency.

MARIANO LAKE COMMUNITY SCHOOL
P.O. Box 787 • CROWNPOINT, NM 87313
(505) 786-5265 Fax 786-5203
Harry Jackson, Chairperson
Boarding School; Grades K-8. Under
jurisdiction of Eastern Navajo Agency.

**TSE'II'AHI' (STANDING ROCK)
COMMUNITY SCHOOL**
P.O. Box 828 • CROWNPOINT, NM 87313
(505) 786-5389 Fax 786-5635
Sherry Woodside, Principal
Chee Bobby Thompson, Chairperson
Boarding School; Grades K-4. Under
jurisdiction of Eastern Navajo Agency.

NA'NEELZHIIN JI' OLTA' (TORREON)
HCR 79, Box 9 • CUBA, NM 87013
(505) 731-2272 Fax 786-5203
Craig Brandow, Principal
Harry Jackson, Chairperson
David Acuba, FACE Coordinator
Boarding School; Grades K-8. Under
jurisdiction of Eastern Navajo Agency.

OJO ENCINO DAY SCHOOL
HCR 79, Box 7 • CUBA, NM 87013
(505) 731-2333 Fax 731-2361
William Poe, Principal; Jeanette Vice, Chairperson
Day School; Grades K-8. Under jurisdiction of Eastern Navajo Agency.

PUEBLO PINTADO COMMUNITY SCHOOL
HCR 79, Box 80 • CUBA, NM 87013
(505) 655-3341 Fax 655-3342
Clyde David Kannon, Principal
Robert Castillo, Chairperson
Boarding School; Grades K-8. Under
jurisdiction of Eastern Navajo Agency.

JICARILLA DORMITORY
P.O. Box 1009 • DULCE, NM 87528
(505) 759-3101 Fax 759-3338
Emilio Cordova, Principal
Bernard Inez, Chairperson
Dormitory School; Grades 1-12. Under
jurisdiction of Northern Pueblos Agency.

SANTA CLARA DAY SCHOOL
2 Kee St., P.O. Box 2183
ESPANOLA, NM 87532
(505) 753-4406 Fax 753-8866
Frank Nordstrum, Principal
Website: www.santaclara.bia.edu
Grades K-6. *Instructors*: Suzanne Uberauga, Elsie Casados, Arlene Romero, Patricia Madrid, Jackie Sanchez, Rose Naranjo, Frances Keevama, Carol Brewer, Phyllis Jenkins, Robin Rodar. Under jurisdiction of Northern Pueblos Agency.

NAVAJO PREPARATORY SCHOOL
1220 W. Apache • FARMINGTON, NM 87401
(505) 326-6571 Fax 326-2155
Web Site: www.cyberport.com/~navajoprep/
Betty O'jay, Director; Sam Sage, Chairperson
Boarding School; Grades 9-12. Program: College preparatory with emphasis on Navajo language and culture. Under jurisdiction of Shiprock Agency.

WINGATE ELEMENTARY SCHOOL
P.O. Box 1 • FORT WINGATE, NM 87316
(505) 488-6470 Fax 786-5635
Dianne T. Owens, Principal
Raphael Martin, Chairperson
Diane Owen, FACE Coordinator
Boarding School; Grades K-8. Enrollment: 400. Library.
Under jurisdiction of Eastern Navajo Agency.

WINGATE HIGH SCHOOL
P.O. Box 2 • FORT WINGATE, NM 87316
(505) 488-6400 Fax 488-6444
Adam Bull, Principal
Lawrence Morgan, Chairperson
Boarding School; Grades 9-12. Under
jurisdiction of Eastern Navajo Agency.

NENAHNEZAD COMMUNITY SCHOOL
P.O. Box 337 • FRUITLAND, NM 87416
(505) 598-6922 Fax 598-0970
Joe Collins, Principal
John E. Dodge, Chairperson
Boarding School; Grades K-6. *Enrollment*: 445. *Special courses*: Navajo Language and Culture; Writing Labs in Navajo and English. *Instructor*: Rosalyn Junes, Writing Lab. *Special program*: Navajo Language programs for all grades. Under jurisdiction of Shiprock Agency.

BREAD SPRINGS DAY SCHOOL
P.O. Box 1117 • GALLUP, NM 87305
(505) 778-5665 Fax 778-5692
Richard Toledo, Principal
Jimmie Yazzie, Chairperson
Day School; Grades K-3. *Enrollment*: 154.
Under jurisdiction of Eastern Navajo Agency.

ISLETA ELEMENTARY SCHOOL
P.O. Box 550 • ISLETA, NM 87022
(505) 869-2321 Fax 869-1625
Michael Romero, Principal
Christine Lucero, Chairperson
Day School; Grades K-8. *Enrollment*: 300.
Publication: Isleta Eagle Pride, newspaper.
Under jurisdiction of Southern Pueblos Agency.

JEMEZ DAY SCHOOL
P.O. Box 139
JEMEZ PUEBLO, NM 87024
(505) 834-7304 Fax 834-7081
Joseph V. Green, Principal
Roger Madalena, Chairperson
Day School; Grades K-6. Under
jurisdiction of Southern Pueblos Agency.

LAGUNA ELEMENTARY SCHOOL
P.O. Box 191 • LAGUNA, NM 87026
(505) 552-9200 Fax 552-7294
Gerald Kie, Principal
Josephine Cochran, Chairperson
Day School; Grades K-5. Under
jurisdiction of Southern Pueblos Agency.

LAGUNA MIDDLE SCHOOL
P.O. Box 268 • LAGUNA, NM 87026
(505) 552-9091 Fax 552-6466
Nicholas Cheromiah, Principal
Manuel Espindola, Chairperson
Day School; Grades 6-8. Under
jurisdiction of Southern Pueblos Agency.

ALAMO NAVAJO SCHOOL
P.O. Box 907
MAGDALENA, NM 87825
(505) 876-2769 Fax 854-2545
Ron Bateman, Principal
George Apachito, Chairperson
Gail Campbell, FACE Coordinator
Day School; Grades K-12. Under
jurisdiction of Eastern Navajo Agency.

MESCALERO APACHE SCHOOL
210 Central Mescalero Ave.
P.O. BOX 230 • MESCALERO, NM 88340
(505) 671-4431 Fax 671-4822
Gorman Swinney, Principal
Gerald Gray, Supt.
Day School; Grades K-12. Under
jurisdiction of Southern Pueblos Agency.

CRYSTAL BOARDING SCHOOL
Hwy. 134 • NAVAJO, NM 87328
(505) 777-2385 Fax 777-2648
M. Rosalie, Principal
Pauline Garnenez, Chairperson
Boarding School; Grades K-6. Under
jurisdiction of Fort Defiance Agency.

TOHAALI' (TOADLENA) COMMUNITY SCHOOL
P.O. Box 9857 • NEWCOMB, NM 87455
(505) 789-3201 Fax 789-3203
Rena H. Teller, Principal
Anna Peters, Chairperson
Kendall Conduff, FACE Coordinator
Boarding School; Grades Pre K-8. *Instructors*: Loretta Wheeler, Erma John, Elenora Curley, Etta Yazzie, Paul Yazzi. Under jurisdiction of Shiprock Agency.

PINE HILL SCHOOLS
P.O. Box 220 • PINE HILL, NM 87357
(505) 775-3243 Fax 775-3241
Dave Whitesell, High School Principal
Samuel Alonzo, Supt.
Yin May Li, FACE Coordinator
Boarding School; Grades K-12. Under
jurisdiction of Southern Pueblos Agency.

BACA COMMUNITY SCHOOL
P.O. Box 509 • PREWITT, NM 87045
(505) 876-2310
Beatrice L. Woodward, Principal
Rita Begay, Chairperson
Boarding School; Grades K-4. Under
jurisdiction of Eastern Navajo Agency.

SAN FELIPE PUEBLO ELEMENTARY SCHOOL
P.O. Box 4343
SAN FELIPE PUEBLO, NM 87001
(505) 867-3364 Fax 867-6253
Richard Ulibarri, Principal
Patrick Sandoval, Chairperson
Day School; Grades K-6. Under
jurisdiction of Southern Pueblos Agency.

**OHKAY OWINGEH COMMUNITY
(SAN JUAN) SCHOOL**
Hwy. 74, P.O. Box 1077
SAN JUAN PUEBLO, NM 87566
(505) 852-2154 FAX 852-4305
J.P. Lujan, Principal
Joe Garcia, Chairperson
Day School; Grades K-6. Under
jurisdiction of Northern Pueblos Agency.

ZIA DAY SCHOOL
350 Riverside Dr. • SAN YSIDRO, NM 87053
(505) 867-3553 Fax 867-5079
Dennis Gallegos, Principal
Celestino Gachupin, Chairperson
Day School; Grades K-6. Under
jurisdiction of Southern Pueblos Agency.

SANOSTEE DAY SCHOOL
P.O. Box 159 • SANOSTEE, NM 87461
(505) 723-2476 Fax 723-2425
Jeannie G. Haskie, Principal
James Bodie, Chairperson
Day School; Grades K-3. Under
jurisdiction of Shiprock Agency.

SAN ILDEFONSO DAY SCHOOL
Route 5, Box 308 • SANTA FE, NM 87501
(505) 455-2366 Fax 455-7351
Mary L. Naranjo, Principal/Teacher
Lorencita Naranjo, Chairperson
Day School; Grades K-6. Under
jurisdiction of Northern Pueblos Agency.

SANTA FE INDIAN SCHOOL
1501 Cerrillos Rd., P.O. Box 5340
SANTA FE, NM 87501
(505) 989-6300 Fax 989-6317
Joseph Abeyta, Jr., Supt.
Bernie Teba, Chairperson
Boarding School; Grades 7-12. Under
jurisdiction of Northern Pueblos Agency.

**TE TSU GEH OWEENGE
(TESUQUE) DAY SCHOOL**
Route 11, Box 2 • SANTA FE, NM 87501
(505) 982-1516 Fax 982-2331
Benny Gallegos, Principal
Charlie Dorame, Chairperson
Day School; Grades K-6. Under
jurisdiction of Northern Pueblos Agency.

BECLABITO DAY SCHOOL
SHIPROCK, NM 87420
(520) 653-4457 Fax 656-3555
Daniel Sosnowski, Principal
Wallace Begay, Chairperson
Day School; Grades K-4. Under
jurisdiction of Shiprock Agency.

ATSA' BI' YAAZH COMMUNITY SCHOOL
SHIPROCK ALTERNATIVE SCHOOLS
SHIPROCK, NM 87420
(505) 368-2084 Fax 368-5102

Hurley Hanley, Principal & FACE Coordinator
Day School; Grades K-8. Under jurisdiction of
Shiprock Agency.

SHIPROCK NORTHWEST HIGH SCHOOL
SHIPROCK ALTERNATIVE SCHOOLS
SHIPROCK, NM 87420
(505) 368-2070 Fax 368-5102
Frank Taylor, Principal
Faye Blue Eyes, Executive Director
Day School; Grades 9-12. Under
jurisdiction of Shiprock Agency.

SHIPROCK RESERVATION DORMITORY
SHIPROCK, NM 87420
(505) 368-2074 Fax 368-5012
Bobby Begay, Coordinator
Everett Howe, Chairperson
Dormitory School; Grades 9-12.
Under jurisdiction of Shiprock Agency.

TAOS DAY SCHOOL
P.O. Drawer X • TAOS, NM 87571
(505) 758-3652
Robert C. Martinez, Principal
Patrick Romero, Chairperson
Day School; Grades K-7. Under
jurisdiction of Northern Pueblos Agency.

DLO'AY AZHI COMMUNITY SCHOOL
P.O. Box 789 • THOREAU, NM 87323
(505) 862-7525 Fax 862-7910
Amy W. Mathis, Principal
David Henio, Chairperson
Boarding School; Grades K-6. Under
jurisdiction of Eastern Navajo Agency.

CHUSKA COMMUNITY SCHOOL
P.O. Box 321 • TOHATCHI, NM 87325
(505) 733-2280/2296 Fax 733-2222
Donald Creamer, Principal
Bobby Sandoval, Chairperson
Boarding School; Grades K-8. Under
jurisdiction of Fort Defiance Agency.

**CHI-CH'IL-TAH/JONES RANCH
COMMUNITY SCHOOL**
P.O. Box 278
VANDERWAGEN, NM 87326
(505) 778-5574 Fax 778-5575
Pauline Billie, Principal
Roselyn John, Chairperson
Barbar Hauke, FACE Coordinator
Day School; Grades K-8. Under
jurisdiction of Eastern Navajo Agency.

NEW YORK

ST. REGIS MOHAWK SCHOOL
Gowanda Central School District
Indian Education Program
HOGANSBURG, NY 13655
Irving Papineau, Principal

AHKWESAHSNE FREEDOM SCHOOL
Mohawk Nation via P.O. Box 290
ROOSEVELTOWN, NY 13683
(518) 358-2073 Fax 358-2081
E-mail: afs2@northnet.org
Elvera Sargent, Director
Day School; Grades Pre-K to 8. Description: A Mohawk
Immersion school with Mohawk taught in levels Pre-K
to 6. Levels 7 & 8 are the English transition classes.
All instructors are fluent speakers of the Mohawk Lan-
guage and come from the community of Ahkwesahsne.

NORTH CAROLINA

**CHEROKEE ELEMENTARY SCHOOL
& CENTRAL HIGH SCHOOL**
Acquioni Rd., P.O. Box 134
CHEROKEE 28719
(704) 497-9130 (K-6)
(704) 497-6370 (7-12) Fax (704) 497-4373
Joyce Dugan, Director
Jean Jones, Principal (K-6)

Doyce Cannon, Principal (7-12)
Cathy Wolf, Chairperson
Day School; Grades K-6 & 7-12. Enrollment: Approxi-
mately 1,500. Program: Cherokee Boys Club, Ray
Kinsland, Director. Under jurisdiction of Eastern Area
Office.

NORTH DAKOTA

OJIBWA INDIAN SCHOOL
P.O. Box 600 • BELCOURT, ND 58316
(701) 477-3108 Fax 477-6039
Dr. Wayne Trottier, Principal
Wanda Laducer, Chairperson
Boarding School; Grades K-8. Enrollment: 360.
Under jurisdiction of Turtle Mountain Agency.

TURTLE MOUNTAIN ELEMENTARY SCHOOL
P.O. Box 440 • BELCOURT, ND 58316
(701) 477-6471 Fax 477-6470
Roman Marcellais, Principal
Richard McCloud, Chairperson
Day School; Grades K-5. Under
jurisdiction of Turtle Mountain Agency.

TURTLE MOUNTAIN MIDDLE SCHOOL
P.O. Box 440 • BELCOURT, ND 58316
(701) 477-6471 Fax 477-6470
Louis Damphinais, Principal
Richard McCloud, Chairperson
Day School; Grades 6-8. Under
jurisdiction of Turtle Mountain Agency.

TURTLE MOUNTAIN HIGH SCHOOL
P.O. Box 440 • BELCOURT, ND 58316
(701) 477-6471 ext. 222 Fax 477-8821
Rosemary Jaros, Principal
Allen Malaterre, Chairperson
Day School; Grades 9-12. Enrollment: 405. Special
courses: Vocational (building, welding, health, distribu-
tive education); special education (speech and emo-
tionally disturbed.) Instructors: Verlin Allery, Robert
Marion, Marilyn Dionne, Frank Bercier, Tilmer Ruff,
Louise Fraser, Marie Hanson, Kristi Ammerman,
Sharon Rance, Mary Glover, and Tom Glover. Library.
Under jurisdiction of Turtle Mountain Agency.

THEODORE JAMERSON ELEMENTARY SCHOOL
3315 University Dr. • BISMARCK, ND 58504
(701) 255-3285 Ext. 305 Fax 766-4766
Francis Sam Azure, Principal
Boarding School; Grades K-8, plus pre school and
nursery. Enrollment: 95. Special courses: Math/Read-
ing; Special Education; Gifted & Talented. Instructors:
Judy Dasovick, Linda Heck, Terry Moericke, Marilyn
McClelland, Dorvin Froseth, among others. Media
Centrer-Library. Under jurisdiction of Standing Rock
Agency.

DUNSEITH DAY SCHOOL
P.O. Box 759 • DUNSEITH, ND 58371
(701) 263-4636 Fax 263-4200
Dennis DeCoteau, Principal
Gailord Peltier, Chairperson
Day School; Grades K-8. Under
jurisdiction of Turtle Mountain Agency.

TATE TOPA TRIBAL SCHOOL (FOUR WINDS)
P.O. Box 199
FORT TOTTEN, ND 58335
(701) 766-4161 Fax 766-4766
Pat Walking Eagle, Elementary Principal
Donna Johnson, High School Principal
Paul Yankton, Chairperson
Day School; Grades K-12. Under
jurisdiction of Standing Rock Agency.

STANDING ROCK COMMUNITY SCHOOL
P.O. Box 377
FORT YATES, ND 58538
(701) 854-3865 (K-6); 854-3461 (7-12)
Fax (701) 854-3461
Gayleen Yellow Fat, Elementary Principal
John Berry, Acting, High School Principal
Boarding School; Grades K-12. Enrollment: approxi-
mately 800. Under jurisdiction of Standing Rock
Agency.

TWIN BUTTES DAY SCHOOL
Route 1, Box 65 • HALLIDAY, ND 58636
(701) 938-4396 Fax 938-4398
Anna Rubia, Supt.
Lyndon Fredrick, Chairperson
Day School; Grades K-8. Under
jurisdiction of Turtle Mountain Agency.

MANDAREE DAY SCHOOL
P.O. Box 488 • MANDAREE, ND 58757
(701) 759-3311 Fax 759-3493
Ed Lone Fight, Supt.
Day School; Grades K-12. Enrollment: 250. Special
courses: Hidatsa Language; Tribal History & Govern-
ment; Special Education, Cultural. Special programs:
Indian Club and Rodeo Club; Alternative Education;
Gifted & Talented Programs. Under jurisdiction of Fort
Berthold Agency.

WHITE SHIELD SCHOOL
2 Second Ave. West • ROSEGLEN, ND 58775
(701) 743-4355 Fax 743-4501
Lloyd Fandrich, Supt.
Thomas Parsley, Chairperson
Day School; Grades K-12. Under
jurisdiction of Turtle Mountain Agency.

TRENTON SCHOOL
P.O. Box 239 • TRENTON, ND 58853
(701) 774-8221 Fax 774-8040
Lincoln Napton, Supt.; Janice Johnston, Chairperson
Day School; Grades K-12. Under jurisdiction of Turtle
Mountain Agency.

**CIRCLE OF NATIONS WAHPETON
INDIAN BOARDING SCHOOL**
832 8th St. North • WAHPETON, ND 58075
(701) 642-6631 Fax 642-5880
Joyce Burr, Administrator
Allen English, Chairperson
Boarding School; Grades 3-9. Enrollment: 280.
Special programs: Intense Residential Guidance
Program. Library (small museum included in library).
Under jurisdiction of Minneapolis Area Office.

OKLAHOMA

RIVERSIDE INDIAN SCHOOL
Route 1 • ANADARKO 73005
(405) 247-6670/9 Fax 247-5529
Don Sims, Supt.
Hank Kostzuta, Chairperson
Boarding School; Grades 4-12. Under
jurisdiction of Oklahoma Education Office.

CARTER SEMINARY
2400 Chickasaw Blvd.
ARDMORE 73401
(580) 223-8547 Fax 223-6325
Rebecca Kingsbery, Administrator
Becky Durringtron, Chairperson
Dormitory School; Grades 1-12. Under
jurisdiction of Oklahoma Education Office.

EUFAULA DORMITORY
Swadley Dr. • EUFAULA 74423
(918) 689-2522 Fax 689-2438
Greg Anderson, Administrator
Ramona Mason, Chairperson
Dormitory School; Grades 1-12. Under
jurisdiction of Oklahoma Education Office.

JONES ACADEMY
HCR 74, Box 102-5
HARTSHORNE, OK 74547
(918) 297-2518 Fax 297-2364
Brad Spears, Administrator
Alma Mason, Chairperson
Dormitory School; Grades 1-12. Under
jurisdiction of Oklahoma Education Office.

SEQUOYAH HIGH SCHOOL
P.O. Box 948 • TAHLEQUAH, OK 74464
(918) 456-0631 Fax 456-0634
Jim Quetone, Administrator
Amon Baker, Chairperson
Boarding School; Grades 9-12. Under
jurisdiction of Oklahoma Education Office.

OREGON

CHEMAWA INDIAN SCHOOL
3700 Chemawa Rd., NE • SALEM, OR 97305
(503) 399-5721 Fax 399-5870
Larry Byers, Principal
Louis King, School Supervisor
Boarding School; Grades 9-12.
Under jurisdiction of Portland Area Office.

SOUTH DAKOTA

TIOSPA ZINA TRIBAL SCHOOL
Crawfordsville Rd., P.O. Box 719
AGENCY VILLAGE, SD 57262
(605) 698-3953 Fax 698-7686
Gabe Kampeska, Elementary Principal
Dr. Roger Bordeaux, Supt
Susan Peters, Chairperson
Day School; Grades K-12. Under jurisdiction
of Crow Creek/Lower Brule Agency.

AMERICAN HORSE SCHOOL
P.O. Box 660 • ALLEN, SD 57714
(605) 455-2446 Fax 445-2249
Stan Curtis, Principal
Cornell Ruff, Chairperson
Day School; Grades K-8. Under
jurisdiction of Pine Ridge Agency.

ROCK CREEK DAY SCHOOL
P.O. Box 127 • BULLHEAD, SD 57621
(605) 823-4971 Fax 823-4350
Michael Kills Pretty Enemy, Principal
Lillian White Temple, Chairperson
Day School; Grades K-8. Under
jurisdiction of Standing Rock Agency.

CHERRY CREEK DAY SCHOOL
CHERRY CREEK, SD 57622
(605) 538-4238
Faye Longbrake, Principal
Day School; Grades K-6. Under
jurisdiction of Cheyenne River Agency.

CHEYENNE-EAGLE BUTTE SCHOOL
P.O. Box 672 • EAGLE BUTTE, SD 57625
(605) 964-8744/77 Fax 964-1155
Cynthia McCrea, Principal
Mike Rousseau, Chairperson
Boarding School; Grades K-12. Enrollment: 900.
Under jurisdiction of Cheyenne River Agency.

FLANDREAU INDIAN BOARDING SCHOOL
1000 N. Crescent • FLANDREAU, SD 57028
(605) 997-2724 Fax 997-2601
Jack Belkham, School Administrator
Cynthia Kipp, Chairperson
Boarding School; Grades 9-12. Enrollment: 750.
Under jurisdiction of Minneapolis Area Office.

**CROW CREEK SIOUX TRIBAL
ELEMENTARY SCHOOL**
Education Ave., P.O. Box 469
FORT THOMPSON, SD 57339
(605) 245-2373 Fax 245-2310
Robin Hawk, Principal; Harold Miller, Chairperson
Day School; Grades K-5. Enrollment: 200. Under
jurisdiction of Crow Creek/Lower Brule Agency.

TIOSPAYE TOPA SCHOOL
Hwy. 212 East • HOWES, SD 57652
(605) 733-2290 Fax 733-2299
Judy Bassett, Elementary Principal
Donald Farlee, High School Principal
Mike Bowker, Chairperson
Day School; Grades K-12. Under
jurisdiction of Cheyenne River Agency.

TAKINI SCHOOL
HC 77, Box 537 • HOWES, SD 57748
(605) 538-4399 Fax 538-4315
Charmayne Thompson, Elementary Principal
Charles Frederickson, High School Principal
Ted Knife, Chairperson
Marion Case, FACE Coordinator

Day School; Grades Pre K-12. Enrolment: 250+. In-
structors: Stephanie Charging Eagle, Culture Center;
Mike Jetty, Social Science Dept. Special courses:
Tribal Government, Lakota Drum and Singing Group.
Special programs: Annual Pow Wow and Wacipi in
Spring for fund raising and honoring people. Library.
Publications: Biweekly newsletter; yearbook. Under
jurisdiction of Cheyenne River Agency.

LITTLE WOUND DAY SCHOOL
P.O. Box 500 • KYLE, SD 57752
(605) 455-2461 Fax 455-2340
Linda Hunter, Supt. for Education
Everett Janis, Chairperson
Day School; Grades K-12. Enrollment: 500.
Under jurisdiction of Pine Ridge Agency.

LITTLE EAGLE DAY SCHOOL
P.O. Box 26 • LITTLE EAGLE, SD 57639
(605) 823-4235 Fax 823-2292
Gregory Sherwood, Principal
Magdelina Red Legs, Chairperson
Day School; Grades K-8. Enrollment: 100.
Under jurisdiction of Standing Rock Agency.

LOWER BRULE DAY SCHOOL
600 Crazy Horse St., P.O. Box 245
LOWER BRULE, SD 57546
(605) 473-5382(Elementary)
(605) 473-5510 (Secondary) Fax (605) 473-9217
Carol Miller, Elementary Principal
Neil Russell, Secondary Principal
Darrel Middletent, Chairperson
Day School; Grades K-12. Enrollment: 250.
Under jurisdiction of Crow Creek/Lower Brule Agency.

WOUNDED KNEE DISTRICT SCHOOL
100 Main St., P.O. Box 350
MANDERSON, SD 57756
(605) 867-5433 Fax 861-1219
Robin Renville, Principal
Hermis Earl Tal, Chairperson
Day School; Grades K-8. Enrollment: 225.
Under jurisdiction of Pine Ridge Agency.

MARTY INDIAN SCHOOL
P.O. Box 187 • MARTY, SD 57361
(605) 384-5431 Fax 384-5933
Robert Monson, Supt. for Education
Robert Cournoyer, Chairperson
Boarding School; Grades K-12.
Under jurisdiction of Rosebud Agency.

ROSEBUD DORMITORIES
P.O. Box 669 • MISSION, SD 57555
(605) 856-4486 Fax 856-4487
Patricia Brokenleg, Home Living Specialist
Sandy Murray Wilcox, Chairperson
Dormitory School; Grades 1-12. Enrollment: 250.
Under jurisdiction of Rosebud Agency.

LONEMAN DAY SCHOOL
P.O. Box 50 • OGLALA, SD 57764
(605) 867-5633 Fax 867-5109
Deborah Bordeaux, Principal
Leonard Little Finger, Cultural Resource Educator
Day School; Grades K-9. Under
jurisdiction of Pine Ridge Agency.

PIERRE INDIAN LEARNING CENTER
3001 E. Sully Ave.
PIERRE, SD 57501-4419
(605) 224-8661 Fax 224-8465
John Lakner, Principal
Gilbert Robertson, Chairperson
Boarding School; Grades 1-8. Enrollment: 100. Spe-
cial courses: Special education school for children with
learning disabilities or emotional problems. Contract
school serving 15 reservations in North and South
Dakota, and Nebraska. Under the jurisdiction of the
Cheyenne River Agency.

PINE RIDGE SCHOOL
101 Thorpe Ave., P.O. Box 1203
PINE RIDGE, SD 57770
(605) 867-5198 Fax 867-5482
Chuck Conroy, Principal
Tom Conroy, Chairperson
Boarding School; Grades K-12. Enrollment: 1,000.
Under jurisdiction of Pine Ridge Agency.

RED CLOUD INDIAN SCHOOL
Holy Rosary Mission
PINE RIDGE, SD 57770
(605) 867-5491
Rev. E.J. Kurth, S.J., Supt.
Boarding School; Grades K-12. *Special program*:
Montessori pre-school (ages 3 and up, including some
first graders.)

PORCUPINE DAY SCHOOL
P.O. Box 180 • PORCUPINE, SD 57772
(605) 867-5336 Fax 867-5480
Tally Plume, Principal
Ted Means, Chairperson
Day School; Grades K-8. Under
jurisdiction of Pine Ridge Agency.

ST. FRANCIS INDIAN SCHOOL
Sicangu Oyate Ho., Inc.
P.O. Box 379, HCR 59, Box 1A
ST. FRANCIS, SD 57572-0379
(605) 747-2299 Fax 747-2379
Web site: www.sfiskl2.org
Cheryl Crazy Bull, Chief Educational Officer
Carole Little Wounded, Secondary Administrator
Richard Bad Milk, Elementary Administrator
Grades K-12. Tribally controlled serving the Rosebud
Sioux Indian Reservation in south central South Da-
kota. Under jurisdiction of the Rosebud Agency, BIA.
Established in 1971.

CROW CREEK RESERVATION HIGH SCHOOL
Hwy. 34 & 47, Box 12 • STEPHAN, SD 57346
(605) 852-2455 Fax 852-2140
Elizabeth Samuel, Supt.; Harold Miller, Chairperson
Day School; Grades 6-12. *Enrollment*: 225. *Special
programs*: Special Education; Intensive Residential
Counseling; Career Counseling; Substance Abuse
Counseling. Under jurisdiction of Crow Creek/Lower
Brule Agency.

CRAZY HORSE SCHOOL
P.O. Box 260 • WANBLEE, SD 57577
(605) 462-6511 ext. 12 Fax 462-6510
Thomas Raymond, Elementary Principal
Bob Foufray, High School Principal
Mark Bordeaux, Supt.
Ron Randall, Chairperson
Day School; Grades K-12. Under
jurisdiction of Pine Ridge Agency.

ENEMY SWIM DAY SCHOOL
RR 1, Box 87 • WAUBAY, SD 57273
(605) 947-4605 Fax 947-4188
Cheryl Johnson, Education Director
Ellen M. Fisher, Chairperson
Day School; Grades K-3. Under jurisdiction
of Crow Creek/Lower Brule Agency.

UTAH

ANETH COMMUNITY SCHOOL
P.O. Box 600
MONTEZUMA CREEK UT 84534
(801) 651-3271 Fax 651-3272
Rena M. Yazzie, Principal
Julius Claw, Chairperson
Boarding School; Grades K-6.
Under jurisdiction of Shiprock Agency.

RICHFIELD DORMITORY
P.O. Box 638 • RICHFIELD, UT 84701
(801) 896-5101 Fax 896-6157
Boyd Keisel, Director
Stanley Yazzie, Chairperson
Dormitory School; Grades 9-12. Under
jurisdiction of Western Navajo Agency.

WASHINGTON

MUCKLESHOOT TRIBAL SCHOOL
39015 172nd Ave. SE • AUBURN, WA 98002
(253) 931-6709 Fax 939-2922
Dr. Carolyn Marsh, Director
Robert Guerrero, Education Coordinator
Charlotte Williams, Chairperson

Grades Pre K-10. *Enrollment*: 300. *Description of program*: Early childhood education, special education,
counseling program, multi-media curriculum for tribal
language and culture, using computers, video and
books, crossing all curriculum areas. Head Start. Under jurisdiction of Portland Area Office.

LUMMI HIGH SCHOOL
2530 Kwina Rd. • BELLINGHAM, WA 98266
(360) 384-2330 Fax 380-1464
Bob Brown, Administrator
Day School; Grades 9-12. Under
jurisdiction of Portland Area Office.

LUMMI TRIBAL SCHOOL SYSTEM
2530 Kwina Rd. • BELLINGHAM , WA 98226
(360) 384-2292 Fax 384-2334
Owen Carter, Principal
Bob Brown, Supt.
Day School; Grades K-8. *Enrollment*: 125. Library.
Under jurisdiction of Portland Area Office.

QUILEUTE TRIBAL SCHOOL
P.O. Box 39 • LA PUSH, WA 98350
(360) 374-2061 Fax 374-9608
Franklin S. Hanson, Supt.
Day School; Grades K-12. Under
jurisdiction of Portland Area Office.

WA HE LUT INDIAN SCHOOL
11110 Connie Ave., SE
OLYMPIA, WA 98513
(360) 456-1311 Fax 456-1319
Tiffany Johnson, Principal
Mike Reichert, Supt.
Day School; Grades Pre K-9. *Enrollment*: 50. Course
emphasis on Native American culture. Instructors:
Teresa Shattuck, Marilyn Clements, Sue Schumacher,
Linda Dittmar, Rob Brainerd. *Special program*: Spe-
cial Education (Marylynn Twohy); Chapter One (Annie
Schlipphacke); Talented/Gifted (Judy Fitzpatrick); Art
(Vivian Kendall); Speech (Sherri Nemec); and
Ocuupational Therapy (Jan Harrison). Library. Under
jurisdiction of Portland Area Office.

PASCHAL SHERMAN INDIAN SCHOOL
Omak Lake Rd. • OMAK, WA 98841
(509) 826-2097 Fax 826-3855
Dorothy Marchand, Principal
Van A. Peters, Chairperson
Boarding School; Grades Pre K-9.
Under jurisdiction of Portland Area Office.

AMERICAN INDIAN HERITAGE SCHOOL
9600 College Way N.
SEATTLE, WA 98103
(206) 298-7895
Robert Eaglestaff, Principal
Day School; Grades 6-12. *Enrollment*: 120.All academic classes are taught with an enrichment from the
Indian culture. Cultural classes in art, sewing, singing, dancing, drama, and computers. *Instructors*: Mary
Lee Colby, R. Marina Sabbas, Courage Benally, Turk
Markishtum, Marc Strash, and Bonnie Harding. *Special courses*: Native American Literature, History and
Government. *Special programs*: American Indian Heritage Pupil Services Program - enrollment of 1,436 -
provides, on a referral basis district wide, Indian cultural enrichment and awareness activities in various
subjects and levels; Culture Night every Wednesday;
2 major Pow Wows. Library. *Publication*: Pathways,
monthly newspaper.

CHIEF LESCHI (PUYALLUP) SCHOOL SYSTEM
5625 52nd St. East
PUYALLUP, WA 98371
(253) 445-6000 EXT. 3000 Fax 445-2350
Verna M. Houle, Acting Supt.
Daryl Summers, FACE Coordinator
Day School; Grades Pre K-12. *Enrollment*: 350+.
Library. Under jurisdiction of Portland Area Office.

YAKAMA TRIBAL SCHOOL
601 Linden St., P.O. Box 151
TOPPENISH, WA 98948
(509) 865-5121 Fax 865-6092
Jim Craig, Principal; Anita L. Swan, Supt.
Day School; Pre-K and Grades 7-12. *Enrollment*: 105.
Special course: Yakama Language. Under jurisdiction
of Portland Area Office.

WISCONSIN

LAC COURTE OREILLES OJIBWA SCHOOL
8575 N. Round Lake School Rd.
Route 2, Box 2800 • HAYWARD, WI 54843
(715) 634-1442 Fax 634-6058
Terry "Hawk" Mayer, School Administrator
Gaiashkibos, Chairperson
Trixie Duffy, FACE Coordinator
Day School; Grades K-12. Under
jurisdiction of Minneapolis Area Office.

INDIAN COMMUNITY SCHOOL
3126 W. Kilbourn Ave.
MILWAUKEE, WI 53208

MENOMINEE TRIBAL SCHOOL
P.O. Box 39 • NEOPIT, WI 54150
(715) 756-2354 Fax 756-2364
Bonita Klein, School Administrator
Eugene Caldwell, Chairperson
Day School; Grades K-8. *Enrollment*: 250.
Special courses: Menominee Cultural Couses. Library.
Under jurisdiction of Minneapolis Area Office.

ONEIDA TURTLE SCHOOL
P.O. Box 365 • ONEIDA, WI 54155
(920) 869-4364 Fax 869-4440
Mary Peterson, Administrator
Deborah Danforth, Chairperson
Day School; Grades K-10. Under
jurisdiction of Minneapolis Area Office.

WYOMING

ST. STEPHENS INDIAN SCHOOL
128 Mission Rd., P.O. Box 345
ST. STEPHENS, WY 82524
(307) 856-4147 Fax 856-3742
Margaret J. Puebla, Supt.
Eugene Monroe, Chairperson
Boarding School; Grades Pre K-12.
Under jurisdiction of Billings Area Office.

INDIAN EDUCATION TECHNICAL ASSISTANCE CENTERS (IETAC)

Listed here are six regional Indian Education Technical Assistance Centers (IETACs) funded by the U.S.
Department of Education, Office of Indian Education
to serve educators of Native students within specific
geographical regions.

U.S. DEPT. OF EDUCATION
Office of Indian Education
Rm. 2177, 400 Maryland Ave., SW
WASHINGTON, DC 20202-6335
(202) 401-1887
Elizabeth Whitehorn
Disseminates information, provide training and tech-
nical assistance to grantees and prospective grant-
ees in program planning, developing, management and
evaluation.

INDIAN EDUCATION PROGRAMS

Listed, are Indian Education Programs in public
schools throughout the U.S. Arranged alpha-geographically. First listed are the five regional Technical
Assistance Centers.

IETAC II - UNITED TRIBES TECHNICAL COLLEGE
3315 University Dr. • Bismarck, ND 58504
(800) 437-8054; (701) 258-0437 Fax 258-0454
Phil Baird, Contact
Serves schools in the following states:
IA, KS, MN, NE, ND, SD, WI.

IETAC III - GONZAGA UNIVERSITY
School of Education
302 E. Sharp • Spokane, WA 99258
(800) 533-2554
(509) 328-4220 ext. 2812 Fax 484-6965
Raymond Reyes, Contact
Serves schools in the following states:
CO, ID,MT,OR,UT,WA,WY.

**IETAC IV - NATIONAL INDIAN
TRAINING & RESEARCH CENTER**
2121 S. Mill Ave., Suite 216
Tempe, AZ 85282
  (800) 528-6425
  (602) 967-9428 Fax 921-1015
  Shirley Hendricks, Contact
Serves schools in the following states:
AZ, CA, HI, NM, NV.

**IETAC V - INDIAN EDUCATION
TECHNICAL ASSISTANCE CENTER**
Norman, OK (800) 422-0966 (in OK)
  (800) 451-2191 (National)
  (405) 360-1163 Fax 364-5464
  Mary Ann Brittan, Contact
Serves schools in the following states: OK, TX. *Activities*: Sponsors an annual conference in September; co-sponsors Oklahoma Exposition in April. *Publication*: OCIE Newsletter

IETAC VI - COOK INLET TRIBAL COUNCIL
670 Fireweed Ln. • Anchorage, AK 99503
  (800) 478-0014; (907) 272-7529 Fax 277-9071
  Ramona Suetopka-Duerre, Contact
Serves schools in Alaska Native villages and Native organizations, institutions, and parent committees involved in the education of Alaska Native and Native American students.

REGIONAL EDUCATIONAL
LABORATORIES

Funded by the U.S. Department of Education, these ten Regional Educational Laboratories each serve a designated geographical region. Their purpose is to link the communities of research and practice. Thus they offer training, technical assistance, and publications based on research that address the practical concerns of educators and policymakers. The laboratories have joined together to form the Native Education Initiative - the purpose is to improve the access of educators serving Native students to the many resources available through the various laboratories.

**ERIC CLEARINGHOUSE ON RURAL
EDUCATION & SMALL SCHOOLS
APPALACHIA EDUCATIONAL
LABORATORY, INC. (AEL)**
P.O. Box 1348, 1031 Quarrier St., #610 (25301)
Charleston, WV 25325-1348
  (800) 624-9120; Fax (304) 347-0467
  Patricia Cahape Hammer, Director
  E-mail: hammerp@ael.org
  Website: www.ael.org/eric;
     www.indianeduresearch.net
Provides information services and publications related to the education of American Indians and Alaska Natives.

**FAR WEST LABORATORY FOR EDUCATIONAL
RESEARCH & DEVELOPMENT (FWL)**
Rural Schools Assistance Program
730 Harrison St.
San Francisco, CA 94107-1242
  (415) 565-3040 Fax 565-3012
  Elsie Trumbull Estrin, Contact
Serves Native students, state, tribal and local agencies and K-12 schools in the following states: AZ, CA, NV, UT.

**MID-CONTINENT REGIONAL
EDUCATIONAL LABORATORY (McREL)**
2550 S. Parker Rd., Suite 500
Aurora, CO 80014
  (303) 337-0990 ext. 3012 Fax 337-3005
  Joann Sebastian Morris, Contact
Serves Native students, state, tribal and local agencies and K-12 schools in the following states: CO, KS, MO, NE, ND, SD, WY.

**NORTH CENTRAL REGIONAL
EDUCATIONAL LABORATORY (NCREL)**
1120 E. Diehl Rd. #200
Naperville, IL 60563-1460
  (630) 649-6500; Beverly J. Walker, Contact
Serves Native students, state, tribal and local agencies and K-12 schools in the following states: IL, IN, IA, OH, MI, MN, WI.

**NORTHWEST REGIONAL EDUCATIONAL
LABORATORY (NWREL)**
Research & Development for Indian Education
101 SW Main St., #500 • Portland, OR 97204
  (503) 275-9500 Fax 275-9489
  Anita Tsinnajinnie, Contact
Serves Native students, state, tribal and local agencies and K-12 schools in the following states: AK, ID, MT, OR, WA. Act*ivities*: Conducts studies of issues and qualities of Indian education. *Publications*: Effective Practices in Indian Education, teacher's curriculum monograph; newsletter, Northwest Report.

**REGIONAL LABORATORY FOR EDUCATIONAL
IMPROVEMENT OF THE NORTHEAST &
VIRGIN ISLANDS/THE NETWORK, INC.**
Andover, MA (800) 347-4200
  (508) 470-0098 ext. 246 Fax 475-9220
  Cinnamon Noley, Contact
Serves Native students, state, tribal and local agencies and K-12 schools in the following states: CT, ME, MA, NH, NY, ,PR, RI, VT, VI (Virgin Islands).

RESEARCH FOR BETTER SCHOOLS, INC. (RBS)
Native Education Project
444 N. 3rd St. • Philadelphia, PA 19123
  (215) 574-9300 ext. 230 Fax 574-0133
  Margaret Lion, Contact
Serves Native students, state, tribal and local agencies and K-12 schools in the following states: DE, DC, MD, NJ, PA.

**SOUTH EASTERN REGIONAL
VISION FOR EDUCATION (SERVE)**
1203 Governors Square Blvd., Suite 400
Tallahassee, FL 32301
  (800) 352-6001; (904) 922-2300 Fax 352-6001
  Jack Sanders, Director
Serves Native students, state, tribal and local agencies and K-12 schools in the following states: AL, FL, GA, MS, NC, SC. *Activities*: Provides outreach, information and assistance to Native American communities in the Southeast regarding early childhood education, parent involvement and education, and substance abuse prevention.

**SOUTHWEST EDUCATIONAL DEVELOPMENT
LABORATORY (SEDL)**
211 E. 7th St. • Austin, TX 78701
  (512) 476-6861 Fax 476-2286
  Nancy Fuentes, Contact
Serves Native students, state, tribal and local agencies and K-12 schools in the following states: AR, LA, NM, OK, TX.

This section lists Indian Education programs inthe public school systems throughout the U.S.

ALABAMA

Escambia County Middle School
Indian Education Program
P.O. Drawer 1236 • Atmore, AL 36504
(205) 368-9105 Fax 368-0674
David Nolin, Director
Grades K-8. *Description*: Provides tutoring services and cultural enrichment programs. *Instructors*: Hazel Rolin, Mary Boytte, Joyce Pilyaw.

Poarch Band of Creeks
Indian Education Program
HCR69A, Box 85-B • Atmore, AL 36502
Gloria Fowler, Contact

Washington County Schools
Indian Education Program
P.O. Drawer L • Chatom, AL 36518
Vivian Dearman, Contact

Coffee County School System
Indian Education Program
400 Reddoch Hill Rd. • Elba, AL 36323
(205) 897-5016 Fax 897-6207
Laura June Brown, Director
Grades K-12. *Description*: Provides culturally related academic activities and computer instruction for Indian students enrolled in the Coffee County School System. *Instructors*: Vicki Chamblee, Pam Flowers, Bonnie Campbell.

DeKalb County Schools
Indian Education Program
Box 777, 209 Grand Ave. S.
Fort Payne, AL 35967
Maurice McGee, Contact

Fort Payne City Schools
Indian Education Program
P.O. Box 1029 • Fort Payne, AL 35967
Bill Rupil, Contact

Madison County Schools
Indian Education Program
P.O. Box 226 • Huntsville, AL 35804
(205) 852-7073 Fax 852-6708
Melvina Phillips, Director
Grades K-12. *Description*: Designed to meet the academic and cultural needs of Indian students; works with high school students to get scholarships, participation in academic camps, etc. *Instructor*: Linda Williams. *Special project*: Develop cultural software

Washington County Schools
Indian Education Program
P.O. Box 209 • McIntosh, AL 36553
Gallasnead Weaver, Contact

Mobile County Schools
Indian Education Program
P.O. Box 1327 • Mobile, AL 36633
Henrietta Powell, Contact

Monroe County Schools
Indian Education Program
P.O. Box 967 • Monroeville, AL 36461
Dr. Brooks Steele, Contact

Lawrence County Schools
Indian Education Program
Oakville Indian Mounds Park & Museum
1219 County Rd. 187 • Danville, AL 35619
(205) 905-2494 Fax 905-2428
E-mail: Indian@lawrenceal.org
Rickey Butch Walker, Director
Dexter Rutherford, Superintendent
Grades K-12. *Description*: Provides a cultural heritage and enrichment program; sponsors a local Indian museum and annual Indian Festival in May. *Instructors*: Dustin Kirby, Kelly Dutton, Lisa Terry, Dawn Little, Larry Black, Anita Sims, Pamela Jones, Tanaya Malcom, Shannon Reed, Marshela Segars, Gina McCarley, Brandi Rose, Chad Little, Brandy Sutton.

Mobile County Schools
Indian Education Program
20185 Richard Weaver Rd.
Mt. Vernon, AL 36560
Johnny Weaver, Jr., Contact

Scottsboro City Schools
Indian Education Program
906 S. Scott St. • Scottsboro, AL 35971
Sue DeWitt, Contact

ARKANSAS

Cedarville School District
Indian Education Program
P.O. Box 97 • Cedarville, AR 72932
Dr. Melvin Landers

Fort Smith School District
Title IX Indian Education Program
P.O. Box 1948 • Fort Smith, AR 72902
(501) 783-1202 Fax 784-8132
E-mail: jstory@rogers.fssc.k12.ar.us
Judy Bivens Story, Director
Grades K-12. Program: There are paraeducators who work with Indian students in need of academic assistance in 12 targeted elementary school.

Gravette Public Schools
Indian Education Program
P.O. Box 480 • Gravette, AR 72736
Larry Ben, Contact

ARIZONA

Ajo Unified School District
Indian Education Program
P.O. Box 68 • Ajo, AZ 85321
Siana Chalrey, Contact

Casa Blanca Day School
Indian Education Program
P.O. Box 940 • Bapchule, AZ 85221
Betty Sanchez, Contact

Colorado River Unified HS Dist.
Indian Education Program
2251 Highway 95 • Bullhead City, AZ 86442
Nancy Doss, Contact

Casa Grande Schools
Indian Education Program
1460 N. Pinal Ave. • Casa Grande, AZ 85222
Gene Moffett, Contact

Wide Ruins Boarding School
Indian Education Program
P.O. Box 309 • Chambers, AZ 86502
Ernestine Reeder, Contact

Chandler Unified School District
Indian Education Program
500 W. Galveston St. • Chandler, AZ 85224
Lucinda Williams, Contact

Black Mesa Community School
Indian Education Program
Star Rt. 1, Box 215-RRDS
Chinle, AZ 86503
George Cukro, Contact

Chinle Unified School District
Indian Education Program
P.O. Box 587 • Chinle, AZ 86503
Dinah Todacheeny, Contact

Cottonwood Day School
Indian Education Program
Chinle, AZ 86503
Carol Greene, Contact

Low Mountain Boarding School
Indian Education Program
Chinle, AZ 86503
Joe Hardy, Contact

Rock Point Commuity School
Indian Education Program
General Delivery • Chinle, AZ 86503
Jimmie C. Begay, Contact

Rough Rock Demonstration School
Indian Education Program
RRDS-P.O. Box 217 • Chinle, AZ 86503
Mary Benally, Contact

Cibecue Community School
Indian Education Program
Cibecue, AZ 85911
Raymond Bierner, Contact

Blackwater Community School
Indian Education Program
Route 1, Box 95 • Coolidge, AZ 85228
S. Jo Lewis, Contact

Coolidge Unified School District
Indian Education Program
Coolidge, AZ 85228
Pam Thompson, Contact

Dennehotso Boarding School
Indian Education Program
P.O. Box LL • Dennehotso, AZ 86535
Velma Eisenberger

Flagstaff Unified School District
Indian Education Program
3285 E. Sparrow Ave. • Flagstaff, AZ 86004
Jane Wilson, Contact

Window Rock Unified School District
Indian Education Program
P.O. Box 559 • Fort Defiance, AZ 86504
Tim Clashin, Contact

Ft. Thomas Unified School District
Indian Education Program
P.O. Box 28 • Fort Thomas, AZ 85536
Eldon Woodall, Contact

Fountain Hills Unified School District
Indian Education Program
14605 North Del Cambre
Fountain Hills, AZ 85268
Walter Dunne, Contact

Fredonia-Moccasin Unified School District
Indian Education Program
P.O. Box 247 • Fredonia, AZ 86022
Charles Eberhard, Contact

Ganado Unified School District
Indian Education Program
P.O. Box 1757 • Ganado, AZ 86505
Evelyn Begay, Contact

Greasewood/Toyei School
Indian Education Program
Ganado, AZ 86505
Janet Lope, Contact

Kinlichee Boarding School
Indian Education Program
Ganado, AZ 86505
Patricia Rigby, Contact

Nazlini Boarding School
Indian Education Program
Ganado, AZ 86505
William H. Draper, Contact

Gila Bend Unified School Dist. #24
Indian Education Program
P.O. Box V • Gila Bend, AZ 85337
Dr. Charles Landis, Contact

Glendale Unified School District
Indian Education Program
4508 W. Northern Ave. • Glendale, AZ 85302
Toni Munoz, Contact

Globe Unified School District
Indian Education Program
501 Ash St. • Globe, AZ 85501
Dr. James Hazzard, Contact

Grand Canyon Unified School District
Indian Education Program
P.O. Box 519 • Grand Canyon, AZ 86023
Shana Henry, Contact

Holbrook Unified School District
Indian Education Program
P.O. Box 640 • Holbrook, AZ 86025
Esther Stant, Contact

Hotevilla Bocavi Community School
Indian Education Program
P.O. Box 48 • Hotevilla, AZ 86030
Jeanette Cole, Contact

Pine Springs Boarding School
Indian Education Program
P.O. Box 198 • Houck, AZ 86506
Charles Riley, Contact

Kaibeto Boarding School
Indian Education Program
Kaibeto, AZ 86053
Charlotte Webb, Contact

Chilchinbeto Day School
Indian Education Program
P.O. Box 547 • Kayenta, AZ 86033
Gerald Fields, Contact

Kayenta Boarding School
Indian Education Program
P.O. Box 188 • Kayenta, AZ 86033
Charlene Nez, Contact

Kayenta Unified School District
Indian Education Program
P.O. Box 337 • Kayenta, AZ 86033
Dan McLaughlin, Contact

Cedar Unified School District #25
Indian Education Program
P.O. Box 367 • Keams Canyon, AZ 86034
Bob Breton, Contact

Hopi Jr./Sr. High School
Indian Education Program
P.O. Box 337 • Keams Canyon, AZ 86034
Bruce Steele, Contact

Keams Canyon Boarding School
Indian Education Program
P.O. Box 397 • Keams Canyon, AZ 86034
Sam Billison, Contact

Hopi Day School
Indian Education Program
P.O. Box 42 • Kykotsmovi, AZ 86039
Ed Vermillion, Contact

Rocky Ridge Boarding School
Indian Education Program
P.O. Box 299 • Kykotsmovi, AZ 86039
Fred M. Johnson, Contact

Gila Crossing Day School
Indian Education Program
P.O. Box 10 • Laveen, AZ 85339
Mary Jo Walter, Contact

Laveen Elementary School District
Indian Education Program
P.O. Box 29 • Laveen, AZ 85339
Donna Boe, Contact

Lukachukai Boarding School
Indian Education Program
Lukachukai, AZ 86507
Leo Gishie, Contact

Chinle Boarding School
Indian Education Program
P.O. Box 70 • Many Farms, AZ 86538
Dr. F. Anderson, Contact

Many Farms High School
Indian Education Program
P.O. Box 307 • Many Farms, AZ 86538
S. Norman Rodgers, Contact

Marana Unified School Dist. #6
Indian Education Program
11279 W. Grier Rd. • Marana, AZ 85653
Fredrica Powell, Contact

Maricopa Unified School District #20
Indian Education Program
45012 W. Honeycutt Ave.
Maricopa, AZ 85239

McNary Elementary School District
Indian Education Program
P.O. Box 598 • McNary, AZ 85930
Lizzie Shumate, Contact

Mesa Unified School District
Indian Education Program
1025 N. Country Club • Mesa, AZ 85201
Theresa Price, Contact

Mohave Valley Elem. School Dist.
Indian Education Program
P.O. Box 5070 • Mohave Valley, AZ 86440
Lee Robinson, Contact

Page Unified School District
Indian Education Program
500 S. Navajo, Box 1927
Page, AZ 86040
Kathy Hannemann, Contact

Parker Unified School District
Indian Education Program
P.O. Box 1089 • Parker, AZ 85344
Judy Holmes, Contact

Peach Springs Elem. USD
Indian Education Program
P.O. Box 360 • Peach Springs, AZ 86434
Lucille Watahomigie, Contact

Alhambra Elementary School District #68
Indian Education Program
4510 N. 37th Ave.
Phoenix, AZ 85019-3206
(602) 336-2944 Fax 336-2271
Mary Beyda, Coordinator
Grades K-8. *Description:* Provides tutoring services
and promotes parental involvement through communications, parent workshops, meetings, fundraisers,
and family activities. 550 Native American students,
representing more than 20 tribes, have been identified and attend schools in Alhambra District. *Instructors:* Shirley Maves, Lois Lindsay.

Balsz School District
Indian Education Program
4309 E. Bellview • Phoenix, AZ 85008
Janet Glass, Contact

Creighton School District #14
Indian Education Program
2702 E. Flower St. • Phoenix, AZ 85016
Pamela Burkhart, Contact

Isaac School District
Indian Education Program
3801 W. Roanoke • Phoenix, AZ 85009
Patti Cobos, Contact

Madison Elementary School Dist. #38
Indian Education Program
5601 N. 16th St. • Phoenix, AZ 85016
Mike Melton, Contact

Murphy Elementary School District
Indian Education Program
2615 W. Buckeye Rd. • Phoenix, AZ 85009
Rosemary Ruiz, Contact

Osborn School District #8
Indian Education Program
1226 W. Osborn Rd. • Phoenix, AZ 85013
Alice Zimmerman, Contact

Paradise Valley Unified School District
Indian Education Program
15002 North 32nd St. • Phoenix, AZ 85032
Don Skowski, Contact

Phoenix Elem. School District #1
Indian Education Program
1817 North 7th St. • Phoenix, AZ 85006
Alvis Robertson, Contact

Phoenix Union High School District
Native American Education Program
4502 N. Central Ave. • Phoenix, AZ 85012
(602) 271-3514 Fax 271-3204
Ted Hibbeler, Director
E-mail: ted.hibbeler@qm.phxhs.k12.az.us
Grades 9-12. *Description:* Program focuses on the
wellness of our Native American students. Creates
activities that will insure the academic success, career development, cultural awareness, environmental
preservation and healthy lifestyles of our Native American students in the Phoenix Union High School District. *Advisors:* Deanna Talayumptewa, Sam Hogue and
Bernice Begay

Scottsdale Unified School District #48
Indian Education Program
3811 N. 44th St. • Phoenix, AZ 85018
Rosa Muna, Contact

Washington Elementary School District
Indian Education Program
8610 N. 19th Ave. • Phoenix, AZ 85201
Jesus Escarcego, Contact

Pinon Community School
Indian Education Program
P.O. Box 159 • Pinon, AZ 86510
Phyllis Badoni, Contact

Pinon Unified School District #4
Indian Education Program
P.O. Box 839 • Pinon, AZ 86510
Margaret Etsitty, Contact

Polacca Day School
Indian Education Program
P.O. Box 750 • Polacca, AZ 86042
Glenn White Eagle, Contact

Prescott Unified School District
Indian Education Program
146 S. Granite St. • Prescott, AZ 86303
Gordon Meredith, Contact

Red Rock Day School
Indian Education Program
P.O. Drawer 10 • Red Valley, AZ 86544
Hazel Dayish, Contact

Sacaton Public Schools #18
Indian Education Program
P.O. Box 98 • Sacaton, AZ 85247
Scott Goodson, Contact

Hunter's Point Boarding School
Indian Education Program
P.O. Box 99 • St. Michaels, AZ 86511
Winnifred Peters, Contact

Small Fires Hawk
Indian Education Program
P.O. Box 280 • Salome, AZ 85348-0280

San Carlos School District
Indian Education Program
P.O. Box 207
San Carlos, AZ 85550
Catherine Steele, Contact

Sanders Unified School District
Indian Education Program
P.O. Box 250 • Sanders, AZ 86515
Doug McIntyre, Contact

Second Mesa Day School
Indian Education Program
P.O. Box 98 • Second Mesa, AZ 86043
Allen Doering, Contact

Indian Oasis Baboquivari USD #40
Indian Education Program
P.O. Box 248 • Sells, AZ 85634
Mike Ryan, Contact

San Simon School
Indian Education Program
Star Route 1, Box 92 • Sells, AZ 85634
Della R. Williams, Contact

Santa Rosa Boarding School
Indian Education Program
Sells, AZ 85634
John Leffue, Contact

Theodore Roosevelt Boarding School
Indian Education Program
P.O. Box 513 • Sells, AZ 85634
Mark Wilkerson, Contact

Tohono O'Odham High School
Indian Education Program
Sells, AZ 85634
Karen Dawson, Contact

Shonto Boarding School
Indian Education Program
Shonto, AZ 86054
Arnold Studebaker, Contact

Snowflake Unified School District
Indian Education Program
Snowflake, AZ 85937
Pearl Evans, Contact

Stanfield Elem. School District
Indian Education Program
P.O. Box 578 • Stanfield, AZ 85272
Bryant Ridgeway, Contact

Havasupai Elementary School
Indian Education Program
P.O. Box 40 • Supai, AZ 86435
Harry Doten, Contact

Red Mesa Unified School District
Indian Education Program
HCR 6100, Box 40
Teec Nos Pos, AZ 86514
Sarah Begay, Contact

Teec Nos Pos Boarding School
Indian Education Program
P.O. Box 102 • Teec Nos Pos, AZ 86514
K. Holiday, Contact

Kyrene Elementary School Dist. #28
Indian Education Program
8700 S. Kyrene Rd. • Tempe, AZ 85284
Rita Van Loenen, Contact

Tempe Elementary School District
Indian Education Program
P.O. Box 27708 • Tempe, AZ 85282
Michael Walsh, Contact

Tempe Union High School District
Indian Education Program
500 W. Guadalupe Rd. • Tempe, AZ 85283
Jean Paisley, Contact

Union Elementary School District
Indian Education Program
3834 S. 91st Ave. • Tolleson, AZ 85353
Lee Kemper, Contact

Tolleson Union High School District
Indian Education Program
9419 W. Van Buren • Tolleson, AZ 85353
Gene Hernandez, Contact

Navajo Mountain Boarding School
Indian Education Program
P.O. Box 10010 • Tonalea, AZ 86044
Julie Richardson, Contact

Red Lake Day School
Indian Education Program
P.O. Box 39 • Tonalea, AZ 86044
Perrell Whitey, Contact

Moencopi Day School
Indian Education Program
P.O. Box 185 • Tuba City, AZ 86045
John Thomas, Contact

Tuba City Boarding School
Indian Education Program
P.O. Box 187 • Tuba City, AZ 86045
Roxanne Brown, Contact

Tuba City High School Board
Indian Education Program
Box 160 • Tuba City, AZ 86045
Kyril Calsoyas, Contact

Amphitheater School District
Indian Education Program
701 West Wetmore • Tucson, AZ 85705
Anna Chana, Contact

Santa Rosa Ranch School
Indian Education Program
HCO4 #7570 • Tucson, AZ 85735
Louis Barajas, Contact

Sunnyside Unified School District
Indian Education Program
2238 E. Ginter Rd. • Tucson, AZ 85706
(520) 741-2500 ext. 573 Fax 573-0969
Sandy Lucas Tevis, Director
Grades K-12. *Description*: Provides mentoring, tutoring, service learning, cultural awareness, counseling.

Tucson Unified School District
Indian Education Program
P.O. Box 40400 • Tucson, AZ 85717
Alberta Plannery, Contact

Tuba City Unified School District
Indian Education Program
P.O. Box 67 • Tuba City, AZ 86045
Chee Benally, Contact

John F. Kennedy Day School
Indian Education Program
P.O Box 130 • White River, AZ 85941
Patricia Allen, Contact

Whiteriver Unified School Dist. #20
Indian Education Program
P.O. Box 190 • Whiteriver, AZ 85941
Brian Patrick, Contact

Dilcon Boarding School
Indian Education Program
Star Route • Winslow, AZ 86047
Steve Summers, Contact

Leupp Boarding School
Indian Education Program
HC61 • Winslow, AZ 86047
Victoria Sorrell, Contact

Little Singer Community School
Indian Education Program
P.O. Box 310 • Winslow, AZ 86047
Mark Sorenson, Contact

Seba Dalkai Boarding School
Indian Education Program
Winslow, AZ 86047
Deborah Kent, Contact

Winslow Unified School District
Indian Education Program
P.O. Box 580 • Winslow, AZ 86047
Sr. Michael Wilson, Contact

CALIFORNIA

Alpine Union School District
Indian Education Program
1323 Administration Way • Alpine, CA 92001
Barbara Miller, Contact

Viejas Indian School
P.O. Box 1389 • Alpine, CA 91903
(619) 445-4938 Fax 445-8912
Robert Brown, Director

Modoc Joint Unified School District
Indian Education Program
906 West 4th St. • Alturas, CA 96101

Anderson Union High School
Indian Education Program
1471 Perry St. • Anderson, CA 96007
Vickie McMasters, Contact

Cascade Union Elementary District
Indian Education Program
1645 W. Mill St. • Anderson, CA 96007
Tom Worthen, Contact

Happy Valley Union School District
Indian Education Program
7480 Palm Ave. • Anderson, CA 96007
Robert Ferrera, Contact

Auberry Union Elem. School District
Indian Education Program
33367 N. Auberry Rd. • Auberry, CA 93602
Madeline Elliott, Contact

Golden Hills School District
Indian Education Program
33367 N. Auberry • Auberry, CA 93602
Joyce Harper, Contact

Placer Union High School District
Indian Education Program
P.O. Box 5048 • Auburn, CA 95603
Patti Stone, Contact

Banning Unified School District
Indian Education Program
161 W. Williams • Banning, CA 92220
Olivia Hershey, Contact

Barstow Unified School District
Indian Education Program
551 S. Avenue H • Barstow, CA 92311
Dennis Wilson, Contact

Big Pine Unified School District
Indian Education Program
500 S. Main St. • Big Pine, CA 93513
Dave Manship, Contact

Bishop Union High School District
Indian Education Program
301 N. Fowler St. • Bishop, CA 93514
Dollie Manuelito, Contact

Bonsall Union School District
Indian Education Program
P.O. Box 3 • Bonsall, CA 92003
Barbara Rohrer, Contact

San Juan Unified School District
Indian Education Program
3738 Walnut Ave. • Carmichael, CA 95608
(916) 971-5206; Isabel Johnson, Contact
Grades K-12. Indian cultural curriculum.

Surprise Valley Joint USD
Indian Education Program
P.O. Box 28-F • Cedarville, CA 96104
Richard Cunnison, Contact

Shasta Lake Union Elem. School Dist.
Indian Education Program
P.O. Box 818 • Central Valley, CA 96019
Robert Stathem, Contact

Ceres Unified School District
Indian Education Program
P.O. Box 307 • Ceres, CA 95307
Lillie Fiskin, Contact

ABC Unified School District
Indian Education Program
16700 Norwalk Blvd. • Cerritos, CA 90701
Mary Sieu Anderson, Contact

Konocti School District
Indian Education Program
P.O. Box 577 • Clearlake Oaks, CA 95422
Nancy Todd, Contact

Colfax Elementary School
Indian Education Program
24825 Ben Taylor Rd. • Colfax, CA 95713
Tamara Randi, Contact

Grades K-8. *Description*: Provides tutoring services, cultural activities and education of Indian customs and heritage.

Colusa County School Districts
Native American Education Program
345-5th St., Suite C • Colusa, CA 95932
(916) 458-0305 Fax 458-2376
Joan Saltzen, Director
Grades K-12. *Description*: Promotes cultural awareness activities, and parental involvement; monitors Native American students grades and attendance; and acts as a resource center for the general public. *Instructor*: Serena Morrow, Resource Specialist.

Round Valley USD
Indian Education Program
P.O. Box 276 • Covelo, CA 95428
Howard Chavez, Contact

Del Norte Co. Unified School Dist.
Indian Education Program
301 W. Washington Blvd.
Crescent City, CA 95531
Robert Appel, Contact

Butte Co. Office of Education
Indian Education Program
5 A County Center Dr. • Croville, CA 95965
Terri Tozier, Contact

Jefferson School District
Indian Education Program
101 Lincoln Way • Daly City, CA 94015
James Cannon, Contact

Capistrano Unified School District
Indian Education Program
24242 La Cresta Dr. • Dana Point, CA 92629
(714) 248-7037 Fax 248-5507
Lois Madson, Coordinator
E-Mail: indianed@deltanet.com
Web site: http://www.capousd.K12.ca.us/indian_ed
Grades K-12. *Description*: Over 600 American Indian students are enrolled. Provides tutoring services, cultural activities and education of Indian customs and heritage. Lobo Lodge: a hands-on, multimedia exhibit about the American Indian experience, with presentations for all grade levels. *Instructor*: Martyne Van Hofwegen.

Escondido Union High School Dist.
Indian Education Program
240 S. Maple St. • Escondido, CA 92025
Marsha Mooradian, Contact

Eureka City Schools
Indian Education Program
3200 Walford Ave. • Eureka, CA 95501
(707) 441-2454 Fax 445-1956
Sandra Burton, Director
Grades K-12. *Description*: Provides tutoring services and cultural enrichment programs.

Fallbrook Union High School Dist.
Indian Education Program
P.O. Box 368 • Fallbrook, CA 92028
Ken Brower, Contact

Farmersville Elem. School District
Indian Education Program
281 S. Farmersville Blvd. • Farmersville, CA 93223
Ronald Garcia, Contact

Fontana Unified School District
Indian Education Program
9453 Citrus Ave. • Fontana, CA 92335
Linda Donaldson, Contact

Fortuna Union High School District
Indian Education Program
379 12th St. • Fortuna, CA 95540
Sheri Johnson, Contact

Fresno Unified School District
Indian Education Program-Title VII
2348 Mariposa St. • Fresno, CA 93726
(559) 457-3634 Fax 457-3641
Margarita Villareal, Program Manager
Frolyn Ramirez, Program Director

Grades Pre-school to 12th grade. *Description of Program*: To assist American Indian students by referrals to appropriate assistance programs; cultural enrichment classes; cultural awareness - classroom presentations; activities to meet the culturally related academic needs of Native American children. *Instructors*: Cecelia DeAnda (school/community liaison (559) 457-3949; E-mail: cxdeand@fresno.k12.ca.us). Louise Appodaca (school/community liaison (559) 457-3948; E-mail: leappod@fresno.k12.ca.us).

Southern Humboldt USD
Indian Education Program
P.O. Box 129 • Garberville, CA 95542
Cynthia Grover, Contact

Garden Grove Unified School District
Indian Education Program
10331 Stanford Ave. • Garden Grove, CA 92640
Eileen Dibb, Contact

Siskiyou Union H.S. District
Indian Education Program
P.O. Box 437 • Happy Camp, CA 96039
Jay Clark, Contact

Hemet Unified School District
Indian Education Program
2350 W. Latham Ave. • Hemet, CA 92343
Sid Cottrell, Contact

Klamath-Trinity Joint USD
Indian Education Program
P.O. Box 1308 • Hoopa, CA 95546
(916) 625-4412 (Phone & Fax)
Sarah Supahan, Director
E-mail: ssupahan@humboldt.k12.ca.us
Grades K-12. *Description*: Develops locally produced curriculum integrating Indian culture into all academic areas; tutoring. *Instructors*: EllieColeman, Erma Marshall, Sherlee Preston, Irene Treesong, Socorro Valdez. *Videos produced*: The Theft of Fire; How Panther Got Tear Marks; Karuk Basketmakers-A Way of Life; Why Coyote Has the Best Eyes; Tribal Law.

Huntington Beach Union H.S. District
Indian Education Program
10251 Yorktown Ave.
Huntington Beach, CA 92646
Alma Rail, Contact

Lake Co. Office of Ed.
Indian Education Program
1152 S. Main St. • Lakeport, CA 95453
Richard Gage, Contact

Lakeside Union School District
Indian Education Program
P.O. Box 578 • Lakeside, CA 92040
Dan Nasman, Contact

Laytonville Unified School District
Indian Education Program
P.O. Box 868 • Laytonville, CA 95454
Mark Iacuaniello, Contact

Lemoore Union H.S. District
Indian Education Program
101 E. Bush St. • Lemoore, CA 93245
David Ross, Contact

Livermore Valley Joint Union School Dist.
Indian Education Program
685 E. Jack London Blvd. • Livermore, CA 94550
Mary Puthoff, Contact

Long Beach Uified School District
Indian Education Program
1515 Hughes Way • Long Beach, CA 90810
Eva Northrup, Contact

Los Angeles Unified School District
Indian Education Program
P.O. Box 513307 • Los Angeles, CA 90051
(213) 229-2043 Fax 687-7482
Tim Faulkner, Director
E-mail: tfaulkne@lausd.k12.ca.us
Grades K-12. *Description*: Provides cultural & academic enrichment programs for American Indian and Native Alaskan students.

Lone Pine Unified School District
Indian Education Program
P.O. Box 159 • Lone Pine, CA 93545
William Schmidt, Contact

Mariposa Co. Unified School District
Indian Education Program
P.O. Box 127 • Mariposa, CA 95338
Lynette Carpenter, Contact

Marysville Joint Unified School District
Indian Education Program
1919 B St. • Marysville, CA 95901
Jim Graham, Contact

McKinleyville High School
Indian Education Program
1300 Murray Rd. • McKinleyville, CA 95521
Kenny Richard, Contact

Placer Hills Union School District
Indian Education Program
P.O. Box 68 • Meadow Vista, CA 95722
April Moore, Contact

Milpitas/Berryessa/Oak Grove School Districts
Indian Education Program
1331 E. Calaveras Blvd.
Milpitas, CA 95035 (408) 945-2387
Nicholas V. Comella, Contact
Grades K-12. *Programs*: Provides referral services, tutorial services, cultural classes, student advocacy, and parent training.

Mountain Union School District
Indian Education Program
Box 368 • Montgomery Creek, CA 96065
Stan Caspary, Contact

Napa Valley Unified School District
Indian Education Program
2425 Jefferson St. • Napa, CA 94558
Evelyn Agnew, Contact

Needles Unified School District
Indian Education Program
1900 Erin Dr. • Needles, CA 92363
Terry Brace, Contact

Newcastle Elementary School District
Indian Education Program
Valley View Dr. • Newscastle, CA 95658
Dr. Edward F. Gilligan, Contact

Twin Ridges Elem. School District
Indian Education Program
P.O. Box 529 • North San Juan, CA 95960
Donna Hajuk, Contact

Bass lake School District
Indian Education Program
P.O. Box 395 • Oakhurst, CA 93644

Oakland Unified School District
Indian Education Program
1025 Second Ave. • Oakland, CA 94606
Evelyn Lamenti, Contact

Orange Unified School District
Indian Education Program
370 North Glassell • Orange, CA 92666
Thomas Saenz, Contact

Oroville Union High School District
Indian Education Program
2211 Washington Ave. • Oroville, CA 95966
Judith Wilmarth, Contact

Vivian Banks Charter School
Pala Band of Mission Indians
P.O. Box 80 • Pala, CA 92059
(760) 742-3300 Fax 742-3102
Barbara Rohrer, Principal
E-mail: vbpala@juno.com
Grades K-12.

Palermo Union Elem. School District
Indian Education Program
7350 Bulldog Way • Palermo, CA 95968
Bill Linebarger, Contact

Palm Springs Unifie School Dist.
Indian Education Program
980 E. Tahquitz Canyon Way
Palm Springs, CA 92262
  Sandia Williams, Contact

Pauma Valley USD
Indian Education Program
P.O. Box 409 • Pauma Valley, CA 92016
  Suzan Cooke, Contact

Penryn Elem. School District
Indian Education Program
P.O. Box 349 • Penryn, CA 95663
  Mary L. Roche, Contact

Pittsburg Unified School District
Indian Education Program
2000 Railroad Ave. • Pittsburg, CA 94565
  Wayne Miller, Contact

El Dorado Co. Office of Education
Indian Education Program
6767 Green Valley Rd.
Placerville, CA 95667
  James Marquez, Contact

Porterville Public Schools
Indian Education Program
589 W. Vine • Porterville, CA 93257
  Jim Edwards, Contact

Plumas Unified School District
Indian Education Program
xPortola, CA 96122
  Donna Waller, Contact

Ramona Unified School District
Indian Education Program
415 8th St. • Ramona, CA 92065
  (619) 788-5010; Pauline Parker, Director
Grades K-12. Provides tutorial, career guidance, financial aid information, and cultural awareness programs.

Kings Canyon USD
Indian Education Program
P.O. Box 552 • Reedly, CA 93654
  Dr. Marvin L. Sohns, Contact

Richmond Unified School District
Indian Education Program
P.O. Box 4014 • Richmond, CA 94802
  Pat Lasarte, Contact

Sherman Indian High School
Indian Education Program
9010 Magnolia Ave. • Riverside, CA 92503

Sacramento City USD
Indian Education Program
4701 Joaquin Way
Sacramento, CA 95822
  Paulette Kelly, Contact

San Bernardino City USD
Indian Education Program
777 North F St. • San Bernardino, CA 92410
  Betsy Manzano, Contact

San Diego Unified School District
Indian Education Program
6880 Mohawk St., Rm. 3
San Diego, CA 92115

San Francisco USD
Indian Education Program
1950 Mission St., Rm. 12
San Francisco, CA 94103
  Carolyn Silverman, Contact

Alum Rock Union Elem. School District
Indian Education Program
2930 Gay Ave. • San Jose, CA 95127
  Gloria Lundine, Contact

East Side Union High School District
Indian Education Program
830 N. Capital Ave. • San Jose, CA 95133
  John Amon, Contact

Oak Grove Elem. School District
Indian Education Program
6578 Santa Teresa Blvd.
San Jose, CA 95119
  Charles Loyd, Contact

San Lorenzo USD
Indian Education Program
15510 Usher St. • San Lorenzo, CA 94580
  Deanna Espina, Contact

San Marcos Jr. High School
Indian Education Program
650 W. Mission Rd.
San Marcos, CA 92069

Santa Clara USD
Indian Education Program
P.O. Box 397 • Santa Clara, CA 95052
  Gwen Stierer, Contact

Mark West Union School District
Indian Education Program
5187 Old Redwood Hwy.
Santa Rosa, CA 95401
  Ida Victorson, Contact

Roseland School District
Indian Education Program
950 Sebastopol Rd.
Santa Rosa, CA 95407
  Jane Clayton, Contact

Santa Rosa City Schools
Indian Education Program
211 Ridgway Ave.
Santa Rosa, CA 95401-4386
  Marcie Becerra, Contact

Sebastopol Union Schools
Indian Education Program
7611 Huntley St. • Sebastopol, CA 95472
  James Pascoe, Contact

Sonora Union High School
Indian Education Program
251 S. Baretta St. • Sonora, CA 95370
  Edmund B. Duggan, Jr., Contact

San Mateo Co. Office of Education
Indian Education Program
227 Arroyo Dr. • S. San Francisco, CA 94080
  Lonni Sopko, Contact

Stockton Unified School District
Native American Indian Center
1425 S. Center • Stockton, CA 95206
  (209) 953-4803 Fax 953-4261
  Dale Fleming, Director
  E-Mail: dfleming@telis.org
Grades K-12. *Description:* Provides tutoring, counseling, and cultural heritage programs; Native American science program. *Instructors:* Terri Johnson, Alberta Snyder, Rosalinda Fleming, Caroline Wilson.

Fremont Union High School District
Indian Education Program
P.O. Box F • Sunnyvale, CA 94087
  Mary Stone, Contact

Lassen Union H.S. District
Indian Education Program
1110 Main St. • Susanville, CA 96130
  Nancy Ash, Contact

Susanville Elem. School District
Indian Education Program
2005 4th St. • Susanville, CA 96130
  David Burriel, Contact

Coachella Valley Unified School District
Indian Education Program
P.O. Box 847 • Thermal, CA 92274
  Joe Gallegos, Contact

Sierra Joint Union H.S. District
Indian Education Program
33326 N. Lodge Rd. • Tollhouse, CA 93667
  John Ginet, Contact

Tracy Public Schools
Indian Education Program
315 E. 11th St. • Tracy, CA 95376
  Alda Brothers, Contact

Summerville Elementary School District
Indian Education Program
18451 Carter St. • Tuolumne, CA 95379
  Karen Bretz, Contact

Summerville Union H.S.
Indian Education Program
17555 Tuolumne Rd.
Tuolumne, CA 95379
  Richard Thorsted, Contact

Ukiah Unified School District
Indian Education Program
925 N. State St. • Ukiah, CA 95482
  Damon Dickenson, Contact

Vacaville Unified School District
Indian Education Program
751 School St. • Vacaville, CA 95688
  Judith Cook, Contact

Ventura Unified School District
Indian Education Program
120 E. Santa Clara St.
Ventura, CA 93001
  Floyd O. Beller, Contact

Visalia Unified School District
Indian Education Program
315 E. Acequia St. • Visalia, CA 93291
  Juan Lopez, Contact

Warner School District
Indian Education Program
P.O. Box 8 • Warner Springs, CA 92086
  Wayne Taylor, Contact

Washington Unified School District
Indian Education Program
930 West Acres Rd., Room 17
West Sacramento, CA 95691
  (916) 371-9300 ext. 70 Fax 371-8319
  Sarah Taylor, Director
Grades 5-9. *Description:* Provides academic, cultural and advisory services for approximately 150 Indian students enrolled in the program. *Instructor:* Lori L. Rigney.

Westminster School District
Indian Education Program
14121 Cedarwood Ave.
Westminster, CA 92683
  Marilyn Moniz, Contact

Windsor Union School District
Indian Education Program
7650 Bell Rd. • Windsor, CA 95492
  Linda Chase, Contact

San Pasqual Valley USD
Indian Education Program
Rte. 1, 676 Baseline Rd.
Winterhaven, CA 92283
  Herbert Jagow, Contact

Yreka Union School District
Indian Education Program
405 Jackson St. • Yreka, CA 96097
  Pat Spillers, Contact

COLORADO

Adams-Arapahoe School District
Indian Education Program
15700 East 1st Ave. • Aurora, CO 80011
  (303) 340-0510 ext. 302 Fax 343-7064
  Dr. D Woods, Director
  Joyce Vigil, Coordinator
Grades K-12. *Description:* Provides academic enrichment, counseling and tutoring services for American Indian children in the Aurora schools. *Instructors:* American Indian artists, elders and scholars.

MCREL
Indian Education Program
2550 S. Parker Rd., Suite 500
Aurora, CO 80014
J. Morris, Contact

Boulder Valley School District
Indian Education Program
P.O. Box 9011 • Boulder, CO 80301
Teressa Halsey, Contact

Montezuma Cortez District RE-1
Indian Education Program
P.O. Drawer R • Cortez, CO 81321
George Schumpelt, Contact

Colorado Dept. of Education
Indian Education Program
201 E. Colfax Ave. • Denver, CO 80203
Vicente Z. Serrano, Contact

Denver Public School District
Indian Education Program
900 Grant St., Rm 604 • Denver, CO 80203
D. Echohawk, Contact

Mapleton Public Schools
Indian Education Program
501 E. 80th Ave. • Denver, CO 80229
Frieda Diaz, Contact

Cherry Creek School District
Indian Education Program
4700 S. Yosemite St. • Englewood, CO 80111
A. Clyburn, Contact

Jefferson Co. P.S., Div. of Hum.
Indian Education Program
1829 Denver West Dr., Bldg. 27
Golden, CO 80401
Dr. Patsy James, Contact

Ignacio United School District
Indian Education Program
P.O. Box 460 • Ignacio, CO 81137
Bryce Fauble, B. Chevarillo, Contacts

St. Vrain Valley School District
Indian Education Program
395 S. Pratt Pkwy. • Longmont, CO 80501
Lu Munoz, Elaine Worrell, Contacts

CONNECTICUT

Bridgeport Board of Education
Indian Education Program
45 Lyon Ter., Rm. 318 • Bridgeport, CT 06604
Michael Kelly, Contact

FLORIDA

Hendry Co. School District
Indian Education Program
475 E. Osceola St. • Clewiston, FL 33440
Sylvester Humphrey, Contact

Seminole Tribe of Florida
Ahfachkee School
Star Route, Box 40 • Clewiston, FL 33440
Martin Coyle, Principal

Broward Co. School District
Indian Education Program
701 N. 31st Ave. • Ft. Lauderdale, FL 33311
Tina Van Vleet, Contact

Seminole Tribe of Florida
Indian Education Program
6075 Stirling Rd. • Hollywood, FL 33024
Pat Jagiel, Contact

Miccosukee Corp.
Indian Education Program
Tamiami Station, Box 440021
Miami, FL 33144
Delores Billie, Contact

Collier Co. Public Schools
Indian Education Program
3710 Estey Ave. • Naples, FL 33942
Dr. John Visosky, Contact

Okeechobee Co. School District
Brighton Reservation
700 SW 2nd Ave. • Okeechobee, FL 34974
Nancy Billy, Zella Kirk, Contact

IDAHO

American Falls School District #381
Indian Education Program
827 Fort Hall Ave.
American Falls, ID 83211
J. Brulotte, Contact

Blackfoot School District #55
Indian Education Program
270 E. Bridge • Blackfoot, ID 83221
S. Norton, Contact

Idaho Dept. of Education
Indian Education Program
650 W. State St. • Boise, ID 83720
Shirley Spencer, Contact

Boundary Co. School District #101
Indian Education Program
P.O. Box 899 • Bonners Ferry, ID 83805
R. Singleton, Contact

Coeur d'Alene Tribal School
Indian Education Program
P.O. Box 338 • Desmet, ID 83824
D. Beach, Contact

Shoshone-Bannock Jr./Sr. High School
P.O. Box 790 • Fort Hall, ID 83203
(208) 238-4300 Fax 238-2628
Jim Philips, Principal
E-mail: jphilips@shoban.com
Web site: www.shoban.com
Grades 7-12. State accredited Jr./Sr. high school. *Instructors*: Kris Hansen, Ed Galindo, Tim Norton, Ramon Murillo, Roseanne Abrahamson, Barbara Hakiel, Frank Pebeahsy, Anna Ridley, June Ward, Don Pine, Adele Stacey, Ben Bloom, William Burns, Danielle Gunn, Pam Davis, Amy Snow.

Tribal High School
Indian Education Program
P.O. Box 306 • Fort Hall, ID 83203
Leona Jim, Contact

Kamiah School District #304
Indian Education Program
P.O. Box 877 • Kamiah, ID 83536
H. Yates, Contact

Lapwai School District #341
Indian Education Program
P.O. Box 247 • Lapwai, ID 83540
R. Sobotta, Doug Wells, Contacts

Lewiston Independent School District #1
Indian Education Program
3317 12th St., T-12 South
Lewiston, ID 83501
(208) 748-3000 Fax 748-3059
Dawn Leighton, Coordinator, Indian Education
C.Mont. Hibbard, Director of Special Services
E-mail: dleighton@mail.lewiston.k12.id.us
Website: www.lewiston.k12.id.us
Description: Cultural enrichment activities K-12, tutoring K-6, career awareness and higher educational counseling, 7-12.

W. Benawah School District #42
Indian Education Program
P.O. Box 130 • Plummer, ID 83851
K. Browning, Contact

Bannock Co. School District #25
Indian Education Program
P.O. Box 1390 • Pocatello, ID 83204
G. Von Houten, Contact

Idaho State University
Indian Education Program
Campus Box 8054 • Pocatello, ID 83209
Donna Ellsworth, Contact

Worley School District #275
Indian Education Program
P.O. Box 98 • Worley, ID 83876
J. Brock, Contact

ILLINOIS

Audubon Elementary School
Title IX Indian Education Program
3500 N. Hoyne • Chicago, IL 60618
(773) 534-5709 Fax 534-5785
Cynthia Soto, Director
Renee de la Cruz, Instructor
Grades Pre K - 6. Offers services to all Native American students within the Chicago Public Schools; and a Native American studies class at Audubon Elementary School.

Chicago Public Schools
Indian Education Program
1819 W. Pershing Rd. • Chicago, IL 60609
Fernando Martinez, Dr. James Somday, Contacts

INDIANA

South Bend Community Schools
Indian Education Program
635 S. Main St. • South Bend, IN 46635
Edward Myers, Contact

IOWA

Davenport Community School District
Federal Program Coordinator
1002 W. Kimberly Rd. • Davenport, IA 52806
(319) 386-0404
Denise Jensen, Title V Liaison

Sioux City Commuity Schools
Indian Education Program
1221 Pierce St. • Sioux City, IA 51105
Lynn Huenemann

Sac & Fox Settlement School
Title V Director
RR #2, Box 56C
Tama, IA 52339
Wayne Pushetonequa, Contact

South Tama Co. Community Schools
Title V Director
1702 Harding St. • Tama, IA 52339
Billie Jean Snyder, Contact

KANSAS

Arkansas City Schools - USD #470
Indian Education Program
420 South 5th • Arkansas City, KS 67005
(316) 441-2000 Fax 441-2009
Glenn Clarkson, Director
Grades K-12. Provides school-home liaison.

Coffeyville Public School
Indian Education Program
7th and Ellis • Coffeyville, KS 67337
Larry Thomas, Contact

South Brown County, USD #430
Indian Education Program
522 Central • Horton, KS 66439
(785) 486-2611 Fax 486-2496
Dr. Steven J. Davies, Superintendent
E-mail: beckerj@usd430.k-12.ks.us
Grades K-12. *Instructor*: Viki Stone.
Program: Tutorial program.

Lawrence Public Schools
Indian Education Program
1919 Delware St. • Lawrence, KS 66046
Theresa Rogers, Contact

Royal Valley U.S.D. #337
Indian Education Program
P.O. Box 155 • Mayetta, KS 66509
(913) 966-2251 or 986-6251
Fax (913) 966-2253 or 986-6479
Anita Evans, Director
Grades K-12. *Description*: Provides tutoring services,
cultural enrichment programs, and guidance counsel-
ing. *Instructors*: Anita Evans, Connie Peters

U.S.D. #321 Kaw Valley Special Services
P.O. Box 578 - 303 E. Hwy. 24
Rossville, KS 66533
(913) 584-6731 Fax 584-6720
Dorothy Rockefeller, PhD, Director
Grades K-12. *Description*: Provides tutoring in academic areas, cultural enrichment with related activities, and developing a plan for employment or education after graduation. Approximately 30 identified Native Americans in the district enrollment.

Kaw Valley USD
P.O. Box 160 • St. Mary's, KS 66536
George Brown, Contact

Topeka Public Schools
624 West 24th St. • Topeka, KS 66611
Phyllis Chase, Contact

Wichita Public School
Indian Studies
217 N. Water • Wichita, KS 67202
Dr. Tulio Tablada, Contact

LOUISIANA

Rapides Parish School District
Indian Education Program
P.O. Box 1230 • Alexandria, LA 71309
Karyn Richardson, Contact

Chitimacha Tribe of LA
Indian Education Program
P.O. Box 661 • Charenton, LA 70523
Alton LeBlanc, Jr., Contact

Lafourche Parish School District
Indian Education Program
2617 Alcide St.
Golden Meadow, LA 70357
Brenda Pitre, Contact

Jefferson Parish School District
Indian Education Program
501 Manhattan Blvd. • Harvey, LA 70058
John Alexander, Contact

Terrebonne Parish School District
Indian Education Program
301 Academy St. • Houma, LA 70360
(504) 851-1553 Fax 868-6278
Gerald Picou, Director
Kirby Verret, Coordinator
Grades: K-12. Description:Provides tutoring, and improve attendance, academic achievement, and cultural
knowledge of Indian students.

Chitimacha Day School
Indian Education Program
Rt. 2, Box 222 • Jeanerette, LA 70544
Leonard Sudduth

LaSalle Parish School District
Indian Education Program
P.O. Drawer 90 • Jena, LA 71342
Lee A. McDowell, Contact

Sabine Parish School District
Indian Education Program
P.O. Box 1079 • Many, LA 71449
Lambert Peterson, Contact

Allen Parish School District
Indian Education Program
P.O. Drawer C • Oberlin, LA 70655
Linda Sylestine, Contact

Terrebonne Parish School
Indian Education Program
2247 Brady Rd. • Theriot, LA 70397
Janie Luster, Contact

Lafourche Parish School Board
Indian Education Program
P.O. Box 879 • Thibodeaux, LA 70302
Lorene Watkins, Contact

MAINE

Indian Township School
Indian Education Program
River Rd., Box 412 • Calais, ME 04619
Linda Leotsakos, Principal

Maine Indian Education
P.O. Box 412 • Calais, ME 04619
Brian Smith, Supt.

Maine School Admin. Dist. 29
Indian Education Program
P.O. Box 190 • Houlton, ME 04730
William E. McDonnell, Contact

Indian Island School
Indian Education Program
1 River Rd. • Old Town, ME 04468
(207) 827-4285 Fax 827-3599
Linda McLeod, Principal
E-mail: lmcleod@iis.bia.edu
Website: www.iis.bia.edu

Beatrice Rafferty School
Indian Education Program
Box 412, River Rd. • Perry, ME 04667
Sr. Maureen Wallace, Contact

MARYLAND

Baltimore City Schools
Hampstead Hill Middle School
101 S. Ellwood Ave.
Baltimore, MD 21224
Jeanette Walker, Contact

Baltimore City Public Schools
Indian Education Program
200 E. North Ave.
Baltimore, MD 21202
Art Pierce, Contact

Baltimore City Schools
Office of Adult & Alt. Ed.
200 E. North Ave., Rm. 105-M2
Baltimore, MD 21202
Irene Williams, Contact

Charles Co. Board of Ed.
Indian Education Program
Box D • LaPlata, MD 20646
Mervin Savoy, Contact

P.G. Co. Public Schools
Oxon Hill Staff Dev. Center
7711 Livingstone • Oxon Hill, MD 20745
Betty C. Proctor, Contact

Montgomery Co. Public Schools
Indian Education Program
850 Hungerford Dr., Rm. 232
Rockville, MD 20850
Mary Gabarde, Contact

Montgomery Co. Public Schools
Indian Education Program
4910 Macon Rd. • Rockville, MD 20852
Madeline McElveen, Contact

P.G. Co. Public Schools
Indian Education Program
14201 School Lane, Sasser Bldg.
Upper Marlboro, MD 20772
Robert T. Coombs, Contact

MASSACHUSETTS

Boston Public Schools
Indian Education Program
26 Court St. • Boston, MA 02108
Josephine Brooks, Contact

Martha's Vineyard Schools
Indian Education Program
RR 1, Box 161B • Gayhead, MA 02535
Adriana Ignacio, Contact

Mashpee School District
Indian Education Program
150 Old Barnstable Rd.
Mashpee, MA 02649
Joan Tavares, Contact

Martha's Vineyard Schools
Indian Education Program
Regional HS, Edgartown Rd.
Oak Bluffs, MA 02557
Gregory Scotten, Contact

MICHIGAN

Avondale School District
Indian Education Program
2950 Waukegan • Auburn Hills, MI 48326
Eva Young, Contact

Bay City Public School District
Indian Education Program
1201 4th St. • Bay City, MI 48708
Dr. Jose Valderes

Brighton Area Schools
Indian Education Program
4740 Bauer Rd. • Brighton, MI 48116
Dr. Sally Bell, Contact

Brighton Area Schools
Indian Education Program
125 S. Church St. • Brighton, MI 48116
Teresa Lysz, Contact

Brimley Area Schools
Indian Education Program
P.O. Box 156 • Brimley, MI 49715
Kaye A. Clarke, Contact

Les Cheneaux Community Schools
Indian Education Program
P.O. Box 366 • Cedarville, MI 49719
John Causley, Jr., Contact

Big Bay de Noc School
Indian Education Program
HC 01, Box 62• Cooks, MI 49817
(906) 644-2773 ext. 120 Fax 644-2615
Colleen Weinert, Coordinator
Grades K-12. *Description*: Provides tutoring services,
cultural activities and education of Native American
customs and heritage.

Davison School District
Indian Education Program
1250 N. Oak St. • Davison, MI 48423
(810) 591-3531 ext. 300 Fax 591-0918
Linda DeCamp, Coordinator
E-mail: ldecamp@mail.davison.k12.mi.us
Grades K-12. *Description*: Title VII Indian Education
Program providing academic anbd cultural classes to
Native American students.

Detroit School District
Pelham Middle School, Rm. 105
2001 Martin Luther King • Detroit, MI 48208
Judith Mays, Contact

Detroit Public Schools
Indian Education Program
5057 Woodward Ave.
Detroit, MI 48202
  Barbara Shorts, Contact

East Jordan Public Schools
Indian Education Program
P.O. Box 399 • East Jordan, MI 49727
  Lori Gee, Contact

Mason Consolidated School Dist.
Indian Education Program
2400 Lakeside Rd. • Erie, MI 48133
  Mary Weglian, Contact

Escanaba Area Public Schools
Indian Education Program
1919 14th Ave. N. • Escanaba, MI 49829
  (906) 786-8615 Phone & Fax
  Robin Menard, Coordinator
  E-Mail:escindianed@bresnanlink.net
Grades K-12. *Instructors*: Robin Menard
and Peggy Derwin.

Escanaba P.S.-Kennedy School
Indian Education Program
1919 14th Ave., North • Escanaba, MI 49829
  Phyllis Eastman, Contact

Algonac Community Schools
Indian Education Program
A361 Broad Bridge, FH Elem. School
Fair Haven, MI 48023
  John Clyne, Contact

Hazel Park Schools
Indian Education Program
1700 Shevlin, Edison School
Ferndale, MI 48220
  Cathy Pappas, Contact

Carman-Ainsworth/Westwood Heights
Native American Education Program
Carman-Ainsworth Support Services Center
5089 Pilgrim Rd. • Flint, MI 48507
  (810) 768-4970 Fax 768-4972
  Jean Keen, Specialist

Beecher Commuity School District
Indian Education Program
1020 W. Coldwater Rd. • Flint, MI 48505
  Burnestyne Allen, Contact

Flint City School District
Indian Education Program
2421 Corunna Rd. • Flint, MI 48503
  (810) 760-1562 Fax 760-1898
  Veda D. Balla, Director

Fowlerville Community Schools
Indian Education Program
P.O. Box 769 • Fowlerville, MI 48836
  David Peden, Diana Woods, ContactS

Gladstone School District
Indian Education Program
400 S. 10th St. • Gladstone, MI 49837
  Jessie Sargent, Contact

Grand Haven School District
Indian Education Program
1415 Beech Tree St.
Grand Haven, MI, 49417
  Christine Baker, Contact

Grand Rapids Public Schools
Indian Education Program
143 Bostwick, NE • Grand Rapids, MI 49503
  Jose Florez, Contact

Grand Rapids Public Schools
Indian Education Program
615 Turner NW • Grand Rapids, MI 49504
  Sherri Mamagona, Contact

Harbor Springs Schools
Indian Education Program
327 E. Bluff Dr. • Harbor Springs, MI 49740
  Michael Breen, Contact

Bark River-Harris School District
Indian Education Program
P.O. Box 350 • Harris, MI 49845
  (906) 466-9981 Fax 466-2925
  William W. Lake, Jr., Director
  E-mail: blake@dsisd.k12.mi.us
  Website: www.dsisd.k12.mi.us/barkriver
Grades K-12. *Description*: Provides tutoring services
and cultural activities. *Instructor*: Sherry DeBen.

Hart Public Schools
Indian Education Program
300 Johnson St. • Hart, MI 49420
  Jane Thocher, Contact

Hazel Park City School Dist.
Indian Education Program
23136 Hughes • Hazel Park, MI 48030
  Ann Bachynski, Contact

Huron Valley Public Schools
Indian Education Program
5061 Duck Lake Rd. • Highland, MI 48356
  Charlotte McKeough, Contact

Howell Public Schools
Indian Education Program
511 N. Highlander Way • Howell, MI 48843
  Audrey Dunlap, Contact

Wilson School
Indian Education Program
100 Helen St. • Inkster, MI 48141
  Barbara Skone, Contact

Kalamazoo City Schools
Indian Education Program
403 Portage St. • Kalamazoo, MI 49007
  Dianne Spencer, Contact

Kalamazoo City Schools
Indian Education Program
604 W. Vine St. • Kalamazoo, MI 49008
  Jodie Palmer, Contact

L'Anse Township Schools
Indian Education Program
201 N. Fourth • L'Anse, MI 49946
  Lynn Ketola, Contact

Lansing School District
Indian Education Program
519 W. Kalamazoo • Lansing, MI 48933
  Linda Kent, Contact

Mackinac Island Schools
Indian Education Program
Box 340, Lake Shore Dr.
Mackinac Island, MI 49757
  Dan Seeley, Contact

Manistique Area Schools
Indian Education Program
100 N. Cedar St. • Manistique, MI 49854
  (906) 341-2195 ext. 142
  Janet Krueger, Coordinator
Grades K-12. *Description*: Provides
tutoring and cultural awareness program.

Marquette Public Schools
Indian Education Program
1201 W. Fair Ave. • Marquette, MI 49855
  Char Shelafoe & Pat Bawden, Contacts

Clintondale School District
Indian Education Program
35300 Little Mack • Mt. Clemens, MI 48043
  Regina Zapinski, Contact

Mt. Morris Central Schools
Indian Education Program
1000 Genesee St. • Mt. Morris, MI 48458
  (810) 591-5740 Fax 687-8052
  Stephanie Lee, Coordinator
Grades K-12. Description: Academic tutoring and cul-
tural awareness. Instructors: Mary Iverson, Sr. High;
Linda DeGuise, Jr. High; Sherry Ross, Moore Elemen-
tary; Melissa Iverson, Montague Elementary; Kimberly
Galbreath, Pinehurst Elementary; Tiffany Schultz,
Central Elementary.

Mt. Morris Cons. Schools
Indian Education Program
12356 Walter St. • Mt. Morris, MI 48458
  Burton Jones, Contact

Mt. Pleasant Public Schools
Indian Education Program
7070 E. Broadway • Mt. Pleasant, MI 48858
  Bonnie Eckdahl, Contact

Mt. Pleasant Public Schools
Indian Education Program
201 S. University • Mt. Pleasant, MI 48858
  Judith Schaftenaar, Contact

Mt. Pleasant Public Schools
Saginaw Chippewa Education Dept.
7070 E. Broadway • Mt. Pleasant, MI 48858
  (517) 775-3672 Fax 772-0672
  Carla Sineway, Director
Grades K-12 & Community College. *Description*: Provides tutoring services, cultural activities and education of Indian customs and heritage; Ojibway language;
community education.

Munising Public Schools
Indian Education Program
411 Elm Ave. • Munising, MI 49862
  (906) 387-3861 Fax 387-5311
  E-mail: swanbergk@mps-up.com
  Kim Swanberg, Director
Grades K-12. *Programs*: Cultural instruction, tutoring,
college preparation, job training & placement. *Instructors*: Kim Swanberg and Marnie Kate Sanders.

Muskegon Hts. School District
Indian Education Program
2603 Leahy St. • Muskegon, MI 49444
  Malcom Stevens, Contact

Muskegon Public Schools
Indian Education Program
1580 Park St. • Muskegon, MI 49440
  Carol Wimpee, Contact

Anchor Bay School District
Indian Education Program
33700 Hooker Rd. • New Baltimore, MI 48047
  Karen Gorman, Contact

Tahquamenon Area Schools
Indian Education Program
700 Newberry Ave. • Newberry, MI 49868
  William Peltier

Northport Public Schools
Indian Education Program
P.O. Box 188 • Northport, MI 49670
  Sheri Hough, Contact

Pellston Public Schools
Indian Education Program
4644 Tower Rd. • Pellston, MI 49769
  Sally Scheier, Contact

Charlevoix/Petoskey Public Schools
Indian Education Program
1500 Hill St. • Petoskey, MI 49770
  (231) 348-2169 Fax 348-2214
  Connie Marshall, Coordinator
  E-mail: marshall.cf.u@petoskeyschools.org
Grades K-12. *Description*: Provides support services
to Native American students K-12. Our major empha-
sis is academic but we provide referrals to appropri-
ate agencies for social needs. *Instructors*: Connie
Marshall, Diann Gaylord, Evelyn Charerat, and Julie
Weaver. *Tutors*: Karen Dickson & Karen Rockafellow.

Pontiac City School District
Indian Education Program
350 E. Wide Track Dr. • Pontiac, MI 48058
  Maria Y. Etienne, Contact

Port Huron Area School District
Indian Education Program
1320 Washington St. • Port Huron, MI 48061
  (810) 989-2727 Fax 984-6624
  Sharon L. Kota, Director
Grades K-12. *Description*: Provides academic, cultural
enrichment and tutoring services for American Indian

children residing in the district. *Instructors*: American Indian artists, elders and scholars.

Rapid River Schools/Tri-Township Campus
Indian Education Program
P.O. Box 68 • Rapid River, MI 49878
(906) 474-6411 Fax 474-9883
E-mail: leskofski@rapidriver.k12.mi.us
Marlene M. Lollie Eskofski, Coordinator of Indian Ed.
Grades K-12. *Description*: Tutorial with craft classes; field trips, fun family activities; Native American presentations; fry bread/blanket dog sales; sponsors dances; promote Native American Summer Youth Camps. *Instructors*: Lynn D. Hill and M. Lollie Eskofski.

Chippewa Hill Schools
Indian Education Program
3226 Arthur Rd., Rt. 2 • Remus, MI 49340
Marvin Lett, Contact

Rudyard Public Schools
Indian Education Program
Second & Williams • Rudyard, MI 49780
Debra Crozier, Contact

Sault Ste. Marie Area Public Schools
Indian Education Program
460 W. Spruce St. • Sault Ste. Marie, MI 49783
(906) 635-6620 Fax 635-6642
Adel Easterday, Director
Grades K-12. *Description*: Provides tutoring services, cultural activities and education of Indian customs and heritage. *Instructors*: Mary Kessinger, Patti O'shelski.

St. Ignace Area Schools
Indian Education Program
840 Portage Rd. • St. Ignace, MI 49781
Don Gustafson, Contact

Airport Community Schools
Indian Education Program
5650 Carleton Rockwood
S. Rockwood, MI 48179
Louanna Czaikolski, Contact

Grand Traverse Band Tribal School
2605 N. West Bay Shore Dr.
Suttons Bay, MI 49682
(231) 271-7505 Fax 271-7510
Joyce Wilson, Education Director
Day School. Grades K-8. *Programs*: Scholarships are available to GTB tribal members who attend a public university or college in the state of Michigan full time and maintain a GPA of at least 2.0.

Suttons Bay Public Schools
Indian Education Program
P.O. Box 367 • Suttons Bay, MI 49682
Fred Elmore, Contact

Swartz Creek Community Schools
Indian Education Program
8354 Cappy Lane • Swartz Creek, MI 48473
(810) 591-2312 ext. 252
Cheryl Spaniola, Director
Grades K-12. *Description*: Basic skills reinforcement with culture and Great Lakes area Native language. Provides academic, cultural enrichment and tutoring services for American Indian children residing in the district. *Instructor*: Cheryl Spaniola.

Taylor School District
Indian Education Program
11010 Janet • Taylor, MI 48180
Vicky Horth, Contact

Taylor School District
Indian Education Program
9601 Westlake • Taylor, MI 48180
Dr. Gary Ford, Contact

Traverse City Public Schools
Indian Education Program
P.O. Box 32 • Traverse, MI 49685
Cherie Domine, Contact

Walled Lake Cons. Schools
Indian Education Program
615 N. Pontiac Trail • Walled Lake, MI 48390
Sally Banks, Contact

Warren Consolidated Schools
Indian Education Program
29500 Cosgrove • Warren, MI 48089
Alfred Snider, Contact

Warren Consolidated Schools
Indian Education Program
2460 Arden • Warren, MI 48092
Shirley Zapinski, Contact

Watersmeet Township School District
Indian Education Program
C Ave., Box 217 • Watersmeet, MI 49969
J.E. Vesitch, Contact

Wayne-Westland Community Schools
Indian Education Program
1225 S. Wildwood • Westland, MI 48185
Dorothy Tufnell, Contact

Hannahville Indian School (Nah Tah Wahsh)
Indian Education Program
N14911 Hannahville B-1 Rd.
Wilson, MI 49896 (906) 466-2952
Tom Miller, Director
Grades K-12. *Description*: Culture program revolves around Ojibwa language instruction. *Instructors*: Larry Matrious, Vicki Dowd.

Hannahville Indian School
Indian Education Program
Route 1 • Wilson, MI 49896
Bill Boda, Contact

MINNESOTA

Bemidji ISD
Title IX Director
201-l5th St., NW
Bemidji, MN 56601
Vince Beyl, Contact

Bloomfield Municipal Schools
Indian Education Program
325 N. Bergin Lane
Bloomfield, MN 87413
Irma Arrellano, Contact

Browns Valley Public School
Indian Education Program
P.O. Box N • Browns Valley, MN 56219
Todd Cameron, Contact

Carlton ISD #93
Indian Education Program
Box 310 • Carlton, MN 55718
Sandra Shabiash, Contact

Cass Lake-Bena Public Schools
Indian Education Program
Rt 3, Box 4 • Cass Lake, MN 56633
Judy Hanks, Contact

Chief Bug O Nay Ge Shig School
Rt. 3, Box 100 • Cass Lake, MN 56633
Patt Cornelius, Contact

Chisholm ISD
Indian Education Program
300 SW 3rd Ave. • Chisholm, MN 55719
Barbara Paradis, Contact

Centennial School District
Indian Education Program
4707 North Rd. • Circle Pines, MN 55014
Clifford Holman, Contact

Cloquet ISD #94
509 Carlton Ave. • Cloquet, MN 55720
Mary Bassett, Contact

Fond du Lac Ojibwe School
Indian Education Program
105 University Rd. • Cloquet, MN 55720
(218) 879-4593/0241 Fax 879-0007
Michael Rabideaux, Director
Early Childhood-Grade 12. *Mission Statement*: "In order to survive both as a people and a culture, we must

return full circle to our traditional manner of education. Traditional Anishinabe society was outcome based and results oriented. Our society was community focused; it was so in order to survive." *Returning Full Circle*: "A conceptual model for implementing a results oriented tribal-operated community learning center which focuses upon life long learning."

Greenway Schools ISD #316/319
Coleraine/Mashwauk
Office of Indian Education
P.O. Box 520 • Coleraine, MN 55722
(218) 295-1287 ext. 26 Fax 245-2019
Jean E. Tyz, Director
Grades K-12. *Description*: Provides academic, cultural enrichment and tutoring services for American Indian children residing in the district. Also post secondary opportunities. *Instructors*: Jean E. Tyz, Laurie J. Eide.

Anoka-Hennepin ISD
Indian Education
11299 Hanson Blvd. NW
Coon Rapids, MN 55433
Jerry Staples, Contact

Deer River ISD #317
Indian Education Program
P.O. Box 307 • Deer River, MN 56636
Warren Goggleye, Contact

Detroit Lakes ISD #22
Indian Education Program
702 Lake Ave.
Detroit Lakes, MN 56501
James Kjelstrup, Contact

Duluth Public Schools
Indian Education Program
215 N. 1st Ave. East • Duluth, MN 55802
(218) 723-4150 Fax 723-4194
Geraldine Kozlowski, Director
Grades: Pre-K-12. *Description*: Provides tutorial afterschool programs, bicultural pre-school, post-secondary preparation program, parental costs, advocacy. Instructors: Phyllis Stott, pre-school teacher; Gayle Daniel, elementary teacher.

Ely ISD #696
Indian Education Program
600 E. Harvey St. • Ely, MN 55731
(218) 365-6196
Dawn Gerzin, Director
Grades K-12. *Description*: Provides cultural activities and tutoring.

Eveleth ISD #697
Indian Education Program
801 Jones St. • Eveleth, MN 55734
Sue Emery, Contact

Fosston ISD #601
Indian Education Program
301 E. First St.
Fosston, MN 56592
(218) 435-1909 Fax 435-6340
Dianne Sonstelie, Title IX Director

Frazee/Vergas Public Schools
Indian Education Program
P.O. Box 186 • Frazee, MN 56544
Renee Christofferson, Contact

Cook Co. ISD #166
Indian Education Program
P.O. Box 1030
Grand Marais, MN 55604
Sue Smith, Contact

Grand Rapids ISD #318
Indian Education Program
820 N. Pokegama Ave.
Grand Rapids, MN 55744-2651
(218) 326-1409 Fax 327-2269
Caroline Stangel, Cordinator
Grades K-12. *Description*: Provides academic, special education, language & cultural enrichment, career counseling, placement services, and tutoring services for American Indian children residing in the district. Also post secondary opportunities. *Instructors*: Kay Kirt, Carol Solberg, Patty Jo Erven.

Granite Falls Public School
Indian Education Program
450 Ninth Ave. • Granite Falls, MN 56241
Patricia Kubly, Contact

Hibbing ISD #701
Indian Education Program
8th Ave. E. & 21st St. • Hibbing, MN 55746
Jean Tye, Contact

Hinckley/Finlayson Public Schools
P.O. Box 308 • Hinkley, MN 55037
O.W Pat Ostrand, Contact

International Falls Public School
Indian Education Program
900 5th St. • International Falls, MN 56649
Beth Parmeter, Contact

Isle School District ISD #473
Indian Education Program
Box 25 • Isle, MN 56342
Sarah Gravel, Contact

Kelliher School District #36
Indian Education Program
P.O. Box 259 • Kelliher, MN 56650
James Gednalske, Contact

Mahnomen ISD #432
Indian Education Program
P.O. Box 319 • Mahnomen, MN 56557
Brent Gish, Contact

Osseo ISD #279
Indian Education Program
11200 93rd Ave. N.
Maple Grove, MN 55369
Jerry Buckanaga, Contact

McGregor ISD #4
Indian Education Program
P.O. Box 160 • McGregor, MN 55760
Antoinette F. Johns, Contact

Four Winds School
Indian Education Program
2300 Chicago Ave. S.
Minneapolis, MN 55404
Dale Weston, Contact

Minneapolis Public Schools
Indian Education Program
807 NE Broadway • Minneapolis, MN 55413
Dr. Robert Ferrera, Jan Witthuhn, Contacts

Robbinsdale ISD #281
Multicultural Coordinator
4148 Winnetka Ave. North
Minneapolis, MN 55427
Jacqueline Fraedrich, Contact

South West High School
3419 W. 47th St. • Minneapolis, MN 55410
Michelle Thompson Tuttle, Contact

Moorhead Public School
1330 8th Ave. N. • Moorhead, MN 56560
Mary Jo Schmid, Contact

Mt. Iron/Buhl High School
Indian Education Program
5720 Mineral Ave. • Mt. Iron, MN 55768
(218) 735-8216
Renee M. Koski, Title IX Director
Grades K-12. *Description*: Offers services to Native American children. These services include resources of books, films, literature, as well as counseling, and tutorial services; cultural activities and education of Indian customs and heritage. *Instructor*: Sue Arko.

Nett Lake ISD #707
13090 Westley Dr. • Nett Lake, MN 55772
Ray Toutloff, Contact

Onamia ISD #480
Indian Education Program
35465 - 125th Ave. • Onamia, MN 56359
(320) 532-4174 ext. 208 Fax 532-4658
Donna J. Burr, Instructor

Grades K-12. *Description*: Facilitate leadership opportunities for Indian students; tutor; language and cultural instructions; conduct monthly parent advisory committee meetings.

May Ah Shing/Mille Lacs School
Indian Education Program
HC 67, Box 242 • Onamia, MN 56359
George Weber, Contact

Park Rapids ISD #309
Indian Education Dept.
P.O. Box 591 • Park Rapids, MN 56470
Sharon Fisher, Contact

Pine City Public School
Indian Education Program
1400 S. 6th St. • Pine City, MN 55063
Emmaline Dunkley, Contact

Pine Poit SD #25
Indian Education Program
P.O. Box 61 • Ponsford, MN 56575
Dr. James Noonan, Contact

Red Lake ISD #38
Indian Education Program
Red Lake Indian Reservation
Red Lake, MN 56671
E.D. Kroenke, Contact

Red Lake ISD #38
Indian Education Program
P.O. Box 280 • Red Lake, MN 56671
Delores Cloud, Contact

Red Wing ISD #256
Indian Education Program
444 6th St. • Red Wing, MN 55066
Stanley Nerhaugen, Contact

Morton Public School District #652
Indian Education Program
100 George Ramseth Dr.
Redwood Falls, MN 56283-1939
Jan Dallenback, Contact

Remer ISD #118
Indian Education Program
Rt. 1, Box A • Remer, MN 56672
Cecelia McKeig, Contact

Rochester ISD #535
Indian Education Program
615 SW 7th St. • Rochester, MN 55902
Patricia Mohn, Contact

St. Louis Co. School ISD #706
Indian Education Program
P.O. Box 128 • Saginaw, MN 55779
Robert Malander, Contact

Virginia ISD #706
Indian Education Program
Tech Bldg./5th Ave. South
St. Louis, MN 55792
Darlene Johnson, Contact

Mounds View School Dist. #621
Indian Education Program
2959 Hamline Ave.
St. Paul, MN 55113
Leanne Peterson, Contact

St. Paul Public Schools
Indian Education Program
St. Paul, MN 55103
Loretta Gagnon, Contact

Sandstone Public Schools
Indian Education Program
Court Ave. at 5th St.
Sandstone, MN 55072
Harold Berg, Contact

Shakopee ISD #720
Indian Education Program
505 S. Holmes St.
Shakopee, MN 55379
Ronald Ward, Contact

Victoria St. Center
4665 N. Victoria St.
Shoreview, MN 55126
Leanne Peterson-Burnette, Contact

Stillwater ISD #834
Indian Education Program
1875 S. Greeley St.
Stillwater, MN 55082
David Wettergren, Contact

Stilwater ISD #834
Coord. Gifted/Talented
1875 S. Greeley St.
Stillwater, MN 55082
Nancy Hof, Contact

Thief River Falls ID #564
Indian Education Program
808 S. Crocker
Thief River Falls, MN 56701
Julie Rambeck, Contact

Tower ISD #708
Indian Education Program
P.O. Box 469 • Tower, MN 55790
Barbara Babcock, Contact

Walker-Hackensack-Akeley ISD #113
Indian Education Program
P.O. Box 4000 • Walker, MN 56484
Sharon Simpson, Contact

Warroad Public Schools - ISD #690
Indian Education Dept.
510 Cedar Ave.
Warroad, MN 56763
(218) 386-1820 Fax 386-1909
Shirley Flick, Coordinator
E-mail: shirley_flick@warroad.k12.mn.us
Grades K-12. *Description*: Provides tutorial assistance, information and referral services, post-secondary financial aid information, home/school liaison services, cultural awareness, and traditional teaching. *Instructors*: Karen Pearson - Middle School; Brenda Price - Elementary.

Waubun-Ogema ISD #435
Indian Education Program
Box 98 • Waubun, MN 56589
John Clark, Contact

Circle of Life School
P.O. Box 447
White Earth, MN 56591
William Wessels, Contact

MISSOURI

Independence School District
Indian Education Program
1231 S. Windsor
Independence, MO 64055
Marcia Haskin, Contact

N. Kansas City School District
Indian Education Program
2000 N.E. 46th St.
Kansas City, MO 64116
Larry Keisker, Contact

Neosho R-5 School District
Indian Education Program
511 Neosho Blvd.
Neosho, MO 64850
Roy B. Shaver, Contact

Seneca R7 School District
Indian Education Program
P.O. Box 469
Seneca, MO 64865
Mary Rule, Contact

School District of Springfield
Indian Education Program
940 N. Jefferson St.
Springfield, MO 65802
Dr. Paul Hagerty, Contact

MISSISSIPPI

Newton Co. School District
Indian Education Program
P.O. Box 97 • Decatur, MS 39327
Dr. Ken Evans, Contact

Louisville Municipal School Dist.
Indian Education Program
200 Ivy Ave. • Louisville, MS 39339
Gladys Taylor, Contact

Mississippi Band of Choctaws
Indian Education Program
P.O. Box 6010 • Philadelphia, MS 39350
Douglas Weaver

Jones Co. School District
Indian Education Program
P.O. Drawer E • Sandersville, MS 39477
Mary Ann Stevens, Contact

MONTANA

Arlee Elem. & H.S. District 8J
Indian Education Program
P.O. Box 37 • Arlee, MT 59821
L. LaCounte, Contact

Billings Public Schools
Indian Education Program
415 North 30th St. • Billings, MT 59102
N. Laird, Contact

Eastern Montana College
Indian Education Program
1500 North 30th St. • Billings, MT 59101
J. Reyhner, Contact

Title V Parent Committee
Indian Education Program
2240 Dallas Dr. • Billings, MT 59102
M.E. Matt, Contact

Charlo School District #7
Indian Education Program
P.O. Box 5 • Charlo, MT 59824
Steve Gaub, Contact

Box Elder Public Schools
Indian Education Program
P.O. Box 205 • Box Elder, MT 59521
R. Hughes, Contact

Rocky Boy Elem. S.D. #87-J
Indian Education Program
P.O. Box 620 • Box Elder, MT 59521
S. Murie, Contact

Brockton Public S.D. #55-55F
Indian Education Program
P.O. Box 198 • Brockton, MT 59213
Dr. James Hall, Contact

Browning Elem./HS Dist. #9
Indian Education Program
P.O. Box 610 • Browning, MT 59417
Ivan Small, Contact

Busby School
Indian Education Program
P.O. Box 38 • Busby, MT 59016

Butte School District #1
Indian Education Program
111 N. Montana St. • Butte, MT 59701
Daniel Ferriter, Contact

Culbertson Public School 17J/C
Indian Education Program
P.O. Box 615 • Culbertson, MT 59218
R. Stuber, Contact

Cut Bank Public Schools
Indian Education Program, Title IX
101 Third Ave. S.E. • Cut Bank, MT 59427
(406) 873-4421 Fax 873-4691

Doug Freeman, Coordinator
E-mail: cbmsdf@montanavision.net
Grades K-12. *Description*: Offers culture club opportunities for all students and Native American studies at both the middle school and the high school level.
Instructors: Angela Orr, Mary Lou deRoulhac, Ray Maier, Laurine Running Crane, Carol Flammond.

Dixon Elem. School District #9
Indian Education Program
P.O. Box 10 • Dixon, MT 59831
Keith Cable, Contact

Dodson Elem. School District 2A
Indian Education Program
P.O. Box 278 • Dodson, MT 59524
N. Sherman, Contact

Frazer School District 2-2B
Indian Education Program
P.O. Box 488 • Frazer, MT 59225
J. Marlett, Contact

Great Falls Public School
Indian Education Program
P.O. Box 2429 • Great Falls, MT 59403
Deeanna Leader, Director
(406) 268-7340
E-mail: deeanna_leader@gfps.k12.nt.us

Harlem P.S. District #12
Indian Education Program
P.O. Box 339 • Harlem, MT 59526
D. Wetzel, L. Brockie, Contacts

Havre Public School
Indian Education Program
P.O. Box 7791 • Havre, MT 59501
J. Erickson, L. Larson, Contacts

Hays/Lodge Pole Schools
Indian Education Program
P.O. Box 110 • Hays, MT 59527
R. Dahl, Contact

Hays/Lodge Pole Public S.D. #150
Indian Education Program
P.O. Box 880 • Hays, MT 59527
M. Allen, Contact

Heart Butte School District #1
Indian Education Program
P.O. Box 259 • Heart Butte, MT 59448
Jack Edmo, Dale Shupe, Contacts

Helena School District #1
Indian Education Program
55 S. Rodney St. • Helena, MT 59601-5763
Ervin Winslow, Aaron Stansberry, Contacts

State Office of Public Instruction
Indian Education Program
State Capitol, Rm. 106 • Helena, MT 59620
R. Parsley, Contact

Lame Deer School
Indian Education Program
P.O. Box 96 • Lame Deer, MT 59043
C. Baker, B. Charette, Contacts

Northern Cheyenne Tribal Ed. Dept.
Indian Education Program
P.O. Box 307 • Lame Deer, MT 59043
Norma Bixby, Contact

Lodge Grass School District 2 & 27
Indian Education Program
Drawer AF • Lodge Grass, MT 59050
R. Heppner, Contact

Missoula School District #1
Indian Education Program
215 S. 6th West • Missoula, MT 59801
J. Block, Contact

Two Eagle River School
Flathead Indian Reservation
P.O. Box 160 • Pablo, MT 59855
(406) 675-0292 (phone & fax)
Clarice King, Supt.

Grades 9-12. *Description*: Alternative school, tribally operated, serving 100 students focusing on academic improvement, cultural integration & parent involvement.

Polson School District #23
Indian Education Program
111 4th Ave. E • Polson, MT 59860
A. Vies, Contact

Poplar Public School
Indian Education Program
P.O. Box 458 • Poplar, MT 59255
D. Sullivan, Contact

Pryor Public S.D. 2 & 3
Indian Education Program
P.O. Box 229 • Pryor, MT 59066
J. Tietema, Contact

Ronan School District #30
Indian Education Program
P.O. Box R • Ronan, MT 59864
B. Halgren, Contact

St. Ignatius School District #28
Indian Education Program
P.O. Box 400 • St. Ignatius, MT 59865
S. Pasquale, Contact

Valier High/Elem. School
Indian Education Program
P.O. Box 528 • Valier, MT 59486
J. Brott, Contact

Wolf Point Public S.D. #45-45A
Indian Education Program/Title IX
220 4th Ave. S. • Wolf Point, MT 59201
(406) 653-2361 Fax 653-1881
Lisa Horsmon, Special Projects Coordinator
Grades K-12. *Description*: Provides tutoring services, cultural activities and education of Indian customs and heritage.

Wyola School District #29
Indian Education Program
P.O. Box 66 • Wyola, MT 59089
TurnPlenty, Contact

NEBRASKA

Alliance Public Schools
Indian Education Program
1604 Sweetwater • Alliance, NE 69301
(308) 762-1580 Fax 762-8249
Lonnie Sherlock, Coordinator
E-Mail: sherlock@aps.k12.ne.us
Grades K-12. *Description*: Provides for a variety of educational needs in an attempt to improve the attendance and academic standings of Native American students. Includes tutoring services, cultural activities and financial aid.

Alliance Middle School
Indian Education Program
1115 Laramie St. • Alliance, NE 69301
Jim Bovee, Contact

Chadron Public Schools
Indian Education Program
Brooks Hall, 245 E. 10th
Chadron, NE 69337
Stephen Sexton, Contact

Lincoln Public Schools
Indian Education Program
P.O. Box 82889 • Lincoln, NE 68501
James Lapointe, Contact

Lincoln Public Schools
Indian Education Program
P.O. Box 82889 • Lincoln, NE 68501
Dr. Deila Stiener, Contact

Macy Public School
Indian Education Program
P.O. Box 280 • Macy, NE 68039
Mitchell Sheridan, Contact

Omaha Public Schools
Indian Education Program
3215 Cuming St. • Omaha, NE 68131
Sandra Mehojah, Contact

Rushville Public Schools
Indian Education Program
P.O. Box 590 • Rushville, NE 69360
Dr. John Cruzeiro, Contact

Santee Public School
Indian Education Program
Route 2, Box 207 • Santee, NE 68760
Jim Berryman, Contact

Scottsbluff/Gering Public Schools
Indian Ed. Program
2601 Broadway • Scottsbluff, NE 69361
Ronald Sylvester, Contact

Winnebago Public School
Indian Education Program
P.O. Box KK • Winnebago, NE 68071
Jeff Pope, Contact

Walthill Public School
Indian Education Program
Little & Main St., Box 3C
Walthill, NE 68067
Diane Bockman, Contact

Gordon Public Schools
Indian Education Program
P.O. Box 530 • Gordon, NE 69343
Catherine Cole, Contact

NEVADA

Lander County School District
Indian Education Program
P.O. Box 1300 • Battle Mountain, NV 89820
Steve Larsgaard, Contact

Carsen City School District
Indian Education Program
P.O. Box 603 • Carson City, NV 89702
James Parry, Contact

Duckwater Shoshone Elementary School
P.O. Box 140038 • Duckwater, NV 89314
(702) 863-0242 Fax 863-0301
Laurel Weaver, Education Administrator
Grades K-8. Duckwater Shoshone tribal school. Instructors: Keith Honaker, grades 5-8; Lynn Lawrence, grades K-3. Shelly Lupe

Elko County School District
Indian Education Program
Box 1012 • Elko, NV 89801
Gretchen Greiner, Contact

Churchill County School District
Indian Education Program
545 E. Richards St. • Fallon, NV 89406
Dr. Bonnie Carter, Contact

Douglas County School District
Indian Education Program
Gardnerville, NV 89410
Sherry Smokey, Contact

Mineral County School District
Indian Education Program
P.O. Box 1540 • Hawthorne, NV 89415
Ihsan Qureshi, Contact

Pyramid Lake High School
Title IX - Indian Education Program
P.O. Box 256 • Nixon, NV 89424
Hal Saylor, Contact

Washoe County School District
Title VII - Indian Education Program
P.O. Box 30425 • Reno, NV 89520-3425
(775) 850-8017 Fax 851-5649
Sheryl Hicks, Director
E-mail: shicks@washoe.k12.nv.us
Website: www.washoe.k12.nv.us/indianed

Graduation Specialists: Anthony Abbie, Bernadette DeLucchi, Rebecca Morrison. Grades 7-12. *Description*: Provides supplemental services and/or programs to enhance the learning opportunities for our Native American/Alaska Native students. These include our student liaisons, graduation specialists; dropout prevention activities; college, career & personal advisement; tutoring, cultural enrichment & supplemental credit fee waivers. *Student Liaisons*: Bernadette Harry & Rebecca Cook. Services offered include tutoring, cultural enrichment & summer school tuition waivers.

Humboldt County School District
Indian Education Program
310 E. 4th St. • Winnemucca, NV 89445
Gerald H. Lugert, Contact

Lyon County School District
Indian Education Program
25 E. Goldfield Ave. • Yerington, NV 89447
Dr. J. Higginbotham, Contact

NEW JERSEY

Fairfield Twp. Board of Education
Indian Education Program
RD #4, Ramah Rd., Box 337
Bridgeton, NJ 08302
Vivian Noblett, Contact

Mahwah Twp. Public Schools
Indian Education Program
Admin. Center, Ridge Rd. • Mahwah, NJ 07430
Barrent M. Henry, Marcella Perrano, Contacts

Ringwood Borough Schools
Indian Education Program
121 Carletondale Rd. • Ringwood, NJ 07456
Carla M. Alexander-Juarez, Director

Ringwood Borough Schools
Indian Education Program
EG Hewitt School, Sloatsburg Rd.
Ringwood, NJ 07456
Frank Van Dunk, Contact

NEW MEXICO

Sky City Community School
Indian Education Program
P.O. Box 349 • Acoma, NM 87034
Fred Vallo, Contact

Albuquerque Public Schools
Indian Education Program
3315 Louisiana Blvd. NE
Albuquerque, NM 87110
Gus Keene, Contact

Bernalillo Public Schools
Indian Education Program
Bernalillo, NM 87004
Barbara Jiron-Sanchez, Contact

Dzilth-Na-O-Dith Hle Community School
Indian Education Program
35 Rd. 7585, Box 5003
Bloomfield, NM 87413
(505) 632-1697 Fax 632-8563
D. Dwane Robinson, Principal

Borrego Pass School
Indian Education Program
P.O. Drawer A • Crownpoint, NM 87313
William Poe, Contact

Crownpoint Community School
Indian Education Program
PO. Box 178 • Crownpoint, NM 87313
Laura Garcia, Contact

Lake Valley Navajo School
Indian Education Program
P.O. Drawer E • Crownpoint, NM 87313
Frances Vitali, Contact

Mariano Lake Community School
Indian Education Program
P.O. Box 498 • Crownpoint, NM 87313
Stanton D. Curtis, Contact

Tse' ii'ahi Community School
Indian Education Program
P.O. Box 828
Crownpoint, NM 87313
(505) 786-5389
Sherry A. Woodside, Principal
Grades K-14. *Description*: Provides academic, cultural enrichment and tutoring services for American Indian children, including instruction in Navajo language and culture. *Instructors*: Barbara White hair, Kimberly Eubanks, Janice Hayden, Tammy Lankford, Patricia Quirk, Diane Griego, Tara Curtis, Richard Kiefer.

Cuba Independent Schools
Indian Education Program
P.O. Box 70 • Cuba, NM 87013
Anita Tsinnijinnie, Contact

Torreon Day School
Indian Education Program
Star Route • Cuba, NM 87013
Johnny Abeyta, Contact

Ojo Encino Day School
Indian Education Program
Cuba, NM 87013
Olsen Juan, Contact

Pueblo Pintado Community School
Indian Education Program
HCR 79, Box 80 • Cuba, NM 87013
Mike Craig, Contact

Dulce Independent Schools
Indian Education Program
P.O. Box 547 • Dulce, NM 87528
Gloria Bissmeyer, Contact

Espanola Municipal Schools
Indian Education Program
P.O. Box 249 • Espanola, NM 87532
Ursula Bowie, Contact

Santa Clara Day School
Indian Education Program
Espanola, NM 87532
Solomon Padilla, Contact

Farmington Municipal School #5
Indian Education Program
P.O. Box 5850
Farmington, NM 87499
Arlene Kirstine, Contact

Navajo Preparatory School
Indian Education Program
1200 W. Apache St.
Farmington, NM 87401
Dr. Henry Schmitt, Contact

Wingate Elementary School
Indian Education Program
P.O. Box 1 • Fort Wingate, NM 87316
Diane Owens, Contact

Wingate Board of Education
Indian Education Program
P.O. Box 2 • Fort Wingate, NM 87316
Frank A. Shepard, Contact

Nenahnezad Boarding School
Indian Education Program
P.O. Box 337 • Fruitland, NM 87416
Rena Teller, Contact

Jemez Mountain School District 53
Indian Education Program
Box 121 • Gallina, NM 87017
Mary Robinson, Contact

Gallup-McKinley County Schools
Indian Education Program
P.O. Box 1318 • Gallup, NM 87301
Boyd Hogner, Contact

Grants-Cibola County Schools
Indian Education Program
P.O. Box 8 • Grants, NM 87020
Wilfred Toya, Contact

Bread Springs Day School
Indian Education Program
P.O. Box 1117 • Gallup, NM 87313
Richard Toledo, Contact

Isleta Elementary School
Indian Education Program
PO. Box 550 • Isleta, NM 87022
Joseph Green, Contact

Jemez Day School
Indian Education Program
P.O. Box 139 • Jemez Pueblo, NM 87024
Jonnito Complo, Contact

Jemez Valley Public Schools
Indian Education Program
Canyon Rt. Box 4A
Jemez Pueblo, NM 87024
Paul Tosa, Contact

Canoncito Community School
Indian Education Program
P.O. Box 438 • Laguna, NM 87026
Jim Byrnes

Laguna Elementary School
Indian Education Program
P.O. Box 191 • Laguna, NM 87026
Dale Hunt, Contact

Los Lunas Schools
Indian Education Program
Drawer 1300 • Los Lunas, NM 87031
Rebecca Garcia Lutz, Contact

Alamo Navajo School Board
Indian Education Program
P.O. Box 907 • Magdalena, NM 87825
Herman James, Contact

Magdalena Municipal School
Indian Education Program
P.O. Box 24 • Magdalena, NM 87825
Peggy Summers, Contact

Mescalero Apache Elementary School
Indian Education Program
P.O. Box 230 • Mescalero, NM 88340
Bill Butler, Contact

Crystal Boarding School
Indian Education Program
Navajo, NM 87328
Lena R. Wilson, Contact

Penasco Independent School
Indian Education Program
P.O. Box 520 • Penasco, NM 87553
Michael Garcia, Contact

Ramah Navajo School Board
Indian Education Program
CPO Drawer H • Pine Hill, NM 87321
Mary Cohoe, Contact

Baca Community School
Indian Education Program
P.O. Box 509 • Prewitt, NM 87045
Beatrice Woodward, Contact

Ruidoso Municipal Schools
Indian Education Program
200 Horton Cr. • Ruidoso, NM 88345
Paul Wirth, Contact

San Felipe School
Indian Education Program
P.O. Box 4339 • San Felipe Pueblo, NM 87001
Edward Doler, Contact

San Juan Day School
Indian Education Program
P.O. Box 1077 • San Juan Pueblo, NM 87566
Mary Shoemaker, Contact

Zia Day School
Indian Education Program
San Ysidro, NM 87053
Gilbert Lucero, Contact

Sanostee Day School
Indian Education Program
P.O. Box 159 • Sanostee, NM 87461
Jeanne Haskie, Contact

Pojoaque Valley School
Indian Education Program
P.O. Box 3468 • Santa Fe, NM 87501
Arthur Blea, Contact

San Ildefonso Day School
Indian Education Program
Route 5, Box 308 • Santa Fe, NM 87501
Mary Naranjo, Contact

Santa Fe Public Schools
Indian Education Program
610 Alta Vista St. • Santa Fe, NM 87501
Wilson Romero, Contact

Tesuque Day School
Indian Education Program
Route 11, Box 2 • Santa Fe, NM 87501
Dolly Smith, Contact

Beclabito Day School
Indian Education Program
P.O. Box 1146 • Shiprock, NM 87420
Daniel Sosnowski, Contact

Shiprock Alt. High School
Indian Education Program
P.O. Box 1799 • Shiprock, NM 87420
Karen Bates, Contact

Taos Day School
Indian Education Program
P.O. Drawer X • Taos, NM 87571
Robert Martinez, Contact

Taos Municipal School District
Indian Education Program
213 Paseo del Canon • Taos, NM 87571
(505) 758-3884 ext. 49 Fax 758-5298
John Romero, Jr., Contact
Grades 10-12. *Program*: Only public school in New Mexico that has made Native American history as part of the core curriculum. Focus is on Taos Pueblo history, and contributions made by Native Americans in the development of this nation. *Instructors*: Marge Neddo, John Romero.

Dlo Ay Azhi Community School
Indian Education Program
P.O. Box 789 • Thoreau, NM 87323
David Braswell, Contact

Toadlena Boarding School
Indian Education Program
P.O. Box 857
Toadlena, NM 87324
Evangeline Yazzie, Contact

Chuska Boarding School
Indian Education Program
P.O. Box 321
Tohatchi, NM 87325
Bruce Fredericks, Contact

Tularosa Municipal Schools
Indian Education Program
504 First St. • Tularosa, NM 88352
Michael Dorame, Contact

Chichiltah-Jones Ranch School
Indian Education Program
P.O. Box 365
Vanderwagon, NM 87236
John Lewis Taylor, Contact

Zuni Public School District
Indian Education Program
P.O. Drawer A • Zuni, NM 87327
Hayes Lewis, Contact

NEW YORK

Akron Central Schools
Indian Education Program
47 Bloomingdale Ave. • Akron, NY 14001
Linda LaPress, Contact

Buffalo School District - School #19
Indian Education Program
97 W. Delavan • Buffalo, NY 14213
Dr. Lloyd Elm, Contact

Center Moriches USD
Indian Education Program
511 Main St. • Center Moriches, NY 11934
Arlene Crandall, Contact

N. Syracuse School District
Indian Education Program
CNS High Norstar Dr., Rt. 3
Cicero, NY 13039
Ellie M. Peavey, Contact

E. Bloomfield Central School
Indian Education Program
Oakmount Ave. • East Bloomfield, NY 14443
Pat Cowley, Contact

Salmon River Central Schools
Indian Education Program
Akwesasne Mohawk Project
Fort Covington, NY 12937
William Perkins, Principal
Ann Marie FitzRandolph, Director

St. Regis Mohawk School
Indian Education Program
Hogansburg, NY 13655
Irving Papineau, Principal

Rush-Henrietta Central School District
Indian Education Project
2034 Lehigh Station Rd. • Henrietta, NY 14467
(716) 359-5047; Jeanette Miller, Director
Grades K-12. *Description*: Teaches culture, history, arts & crafts; provides field trips for children; brings in speakers; teaches traditional dancing, singing, modified Mohawk language; provides workshops for teachers, and presentations on Native American culture.

Gowanda Central School District
Indian Education Program
Prospect St. • Irving, NY 14070
William Berg, Contact

New York City Public Schools
Indian Education Program
234 W. 109th St., Rm. 507
New York, NY 10025
Wanda Hunter, Contact

Niagara Falls City Schools
Indian Education Program
P.O. Box 399, 561 Portage Rd.
Niagara Falls, NY 14302
C. Bianco/Loretta Hill, Contacts

Rochester City School District
Native American Resource Center
200 University Ave.
Rochester, NY 14605
(716) 262-8970 Fax 262-8963
Barbara Smoke, Director
Grades K-6. *Description*: Designed to meet the educational and cultural-related academic needs of Native American students in the District; teach students their cultural heritage through traditional arts & crafts and history. *Instructor*: Gloria Gearhart.

Salamanca City Schools
Indian Education Program
50 Iroquois Dr. • Salamanca, NY 14779
Brian Mohr, Contact

Silver Creek Central School
Indian Education Program
Box 270, Dickinson St.
Silver Creek, NY 14136
Audrey Thompson, Contact

Southampton Schools
Indian Education Program
P.O. Box 59, 70 Leland Lane
Southampton, NY 11968
  Sherry Smith, Contact

Syracuse City Schools
c/o Blodgett School-Indian Education Program
725 Harrison St. • Syracuse, NY 13210
  (315) 435-4288 Fax 435-6553
  Bonnie White, Director
  E-mail: blwhite315@aol.com
Grades K-12. *Description*: Culturally-based, community-building activities; tutoring, student advocacy; peer leadership training. *Instructors*: Eva Cook, Russell Smith, Kathleen Thomas.

North Syracuse Central Schools
Native American Education Program
5355 W. Taft Rd. • No. Syracuse, NY 13212
  (315) 452-3189 Fax 452-3055
  Theresa E. Schneider, Coordinator
Grades K-12. *Description*: Provides tutoring, cultural activities and a Spring cultural event. *Instructors*: Diane Fini, LEA; Kim Ostrander, Gail Henderson.

NORTH CAROLINA

Swain County Schools
Indian Education Program
Whittier School, P.O. Box U
Bryson City, NC 28713
  Sue Carpenter, Contact

Charlotte/Mecklenburg Schools
Indian Education Program
Euclid Center, 1501 Euclid Ave.
Charlotte, NC 28203
  Rosa Winfree, Contact

Cherokee Central School System
Indian Education Program
P.O. Box 134 • Cherokee, NC 28719
  (704) 497-6370; Joyce Dugan, Director
Grades K-12. *Description*: Offers "state of the art" curriculum with modern computer labs; alternative approach classrooms with integrated subjects.

Clinton City Schools
Indian Education Program
P.O. Box 646 • Clinton, NC 28328
  Farrell Carter, Contact

Cabarrus County Schools
Indian Education Program
Box 388, 505 Hwy. 495 • Concord, NC 28025
  Robin R. Odell, Contact

Halifax County Schools
Indian Education Program
Box 143-A, Rt. 2 • Enfield, NC 27823
  Angela Richardson, Contact

Cumberland County Schools
Indian Education Program
P.O. Box 2357 • Fayetteville, NC 28302
  Trudy Locklear, Contact

Greensboro City Schools
Indian Education Program
712 N. Eugene, Drawer V
Greensboro, NC 27401
  Derek Lowry, Contact

Halifax County Schools
Indian Education Program
P.O. Box 468 • Halifax, NC 27839
  Joseph Ray, Contact

Richmond County Schools
Indian Education Program
P.O. Box 1259 • Hamlet, NC 28345
  Trent Strickland, Contact

Scotland County Schools
Indian Education Program
233 E. Church St. • Laurinburg, NC 28352
  Vicki Jones/Rose McNeil, Contacts

Harnett County Schools
Indian Education Program
P.O. Box 1029 • Lillington, NC 27546
  Dr. Sue Arnold, Contact

Robeson County School District
Indian Education Program
P.O. Box 2909
Lumberton, NC 28359
  Maybelle Elk, Contact

Hoke County School System
Indian Education Program
P.O. Box 370 • Raeford, NC 28376
  Jerry Oxendine, Contact

Graham County Schools
Indian Education Program
P.O. Box 605 • Robbinsville, NC 28771
  Chip Carringer, Contact

Person County Schools
Indian Education Program
P.O. Drawer 1078 • Roxboro, NC 27573
  Leon Hanlin, Contact

Smokey Mountain High School
Indian Education Program
505 E. Main St. • Sylva, NC 28779
  (704) 586-2311 Fax 586-5450
  Nancy Sherrill, Coordinator
Grades 9-12. *Description*: Works directly with Indian students on attendance, academics, and special programs; parental involvement on health issues, rules and regulations, scholarships and special programs. *Social worker*: Vangie Stephens.

Warren County School District
Indian Education Program
P.O. Box 110 • Warrenton, NC 27589
  Ogletree Richardson, Contact

Columbus County Schools
Indian Education Program
P.O. Box 279 • Whiteville, NC 28472
  Kenwood Royal, Contact

Smokey Mountain Elementary School
Indian Education Program
Rte. 1, Box 242 • Whittier, NC 28789
  (704) 586-2334 Fax 586-5450
  Clarence Hubbell, Director
Grades K-8. *Description*: Provides tutoring services, and cultural enrichment programs. *Instructors*: Rose Long & Barbara Gilbert.

Hertford Co. Board of Ed.
Indian Education Program
P.O. Box 158 • Winton, NC 27986
  Arthur Brown, Contact

NORTH DAKOTA

Belcourt School District
Indian Education Program
P.O. Box 440 • Belcourt, ND 58316
  Mike Vann, Contact

Ojibwa Indian School
Indian Education Program
P.O. Box 600 • Belcourt, ND 58316
  Cathie Lafountaine, Contact

Bismarck Public School District
Indian Education Program
Bismarck, ND 58501
  Sue Kramer, Contact

Theodore Jamerson Elementary School
Indian Education Program
3315 University Dr. • Bismarck, ND 58504
  Sam Azure, Contact

Devils Lake Public School
Indian Education Program
325 7th St. • Devils Lake, ND 58301
  Robert Gibson, Contact

Dunseith Indian Day School
P.O. Box 759 • Dunseith, ND 58329
  Karen Gillis, Contact

Dunseith Public School District
Indian Education Program
P.O. Box 789 • Dunseith, ND 58329
  Myron Haugse, Contact

Fargo Public Schools
Indian Education Program
415 4th St. N. • Fargo, ND 58102-4514
  Renee Perala, Contact

Fort Totten Public School
Indian Education Program
P.O. Box 239 • Fort Totten, ND 58335
  Adelaine Trottier, Contact

Tate Topa Tribal School
Indian Education Program
P.O. Box 199 • Fort Totten, ND 58335
  Evelyn Cavenvagh, Contact

Fort Yates Public School
Indian Education Program
P.O. Box 428 • Fort Yates, ND 58538
  Della No Heart, Contact

Standing Rock Community School
Indian Education Program
P.O. Box 377 • Fort Yates, ND 58538
  Sherman Laubach, Contact

Garrison Public School District
Indian Education Program
Box 249 • Garrison, ND 58540
  Hy Schlieve, Contact

Grand Forks Public Schools
Indian Education Program
P.O. Box 6000 • Grand Forks, ND 58201
  Glenn Gilbraigh, Contact

Lake Agassiz Elem. School
Indian Education Program
605 Stanford Rd.
Grand Forks, ND 58203
  Sheri Baker, Contact

Twin Buttes Public School
Indian Education Program
RR 1, Box 65 • Halliday, ND 58636
  Eugene Holen, Contact

Hazen Public School
Indian Education Program
Hazen, ND 58545
  Jerry Enget, Contact

Mandaree Public School
P.O. Box 488 • Mandaree, ND 58757
  (701) 759-3311 Fax 759-3493
  Ed Lone Fight, Supt.
Grades K-12. *Enrollment*: 250. *Description*: Special courses: Hidatsa Language; Tribal History & Government; Special Education; Culture. *Special programs*: Indian Club; Rodeo Club; Alternative Education; Gifted & Talented.

New Town Public School District
Indian Education Program
P.O. Box 700 • New Town, ND 58767
  Marc Bluestone, Contact

Parshall School District
Indian Education Program
P.O. Box 158 • Parshall, ND 58770
  Henry Friedt, Contact

Rolette Public School District
Indian Education Program
P.O. Box 97 • Rolette, ND 58366
  Merrill Krueger, Contact

Mt. Pleasant School District
Indian Education Program
RR 1, Box 93 • Rolla, ND 58367
  Norman Baumgarn

White Shield School District
Indian Education Program
HC 1, Box 45 • Roseglen, ND 58775
Clyde Bearstail, Contact

St. John School District
Indian Education Program
P.O. Box 200 • St. John, ND 58369
Donald Davis, Contact

Selfridge School District
Indian Education Program
P.O. Box 45 • Selfridge, ND 58568
Charles Fields, Contact

Sheyenne Public School
Indian Education Program
P.O. Box 67 • Sheyenne, ND 58374
Myron Jury, Contact

Solen School District
Indian Education Program
P.O. Box 128 • Solen, ND 58570
Bruce Houck, Contact

Eight Mile School District
Indian Education Program
P.O. Box 239 • Trenton, ND 58853
Lincoln Napton, Contact

Wahpeton Indian School
Indian Education Program
832 8th St. N. • Wahpeton, ND 58075
Bob Hall, Contact

Warwick Public School District
Indian Education Program
P.O. Box 7 • Warwick, ND 58381
Rocklyn Cofer, Contact

Williston Public School
Indian Education Program
P.O. Box 1407 • Williston, ND 58801
Valli Helstad, Contact

Warwick Public School District
Indian Education Program
P.O. Box 7 • Warwick, ND 58381
Kelly Gannon, Contact

OHIO

Columbus Public Schools
Indian Education Program
873 Walcutt Ave. • Columbus, OH 43219
Richard Snide, Contact

OKLAHOMA

Achille Public Schools
Indian Education Program
P.O. Box 820 • Achille, OK 74720

Vanoss Public School
Indian Education/Title V
Rt. 5, Box 119 • Ada, OK 74820

Ada City Schools, I.S.D. #19
Indian Education Program
P.O. Box 1359 • Ada, OK 74820

Byng School I-16
Indian Education Program
Rt. 3 • Ada, OK 74820

Latta Public School
Indian Education Program
Rt. 8, Box 811 • Ada, OK 74820

Pickett-Center School
Indian Education Program
P.O. Box 1363 • Ada, OK 74820

Adair Public Schools
Indian Education Program
P.O. Box 197 • Adair, OK 74330

Afton Public School
Indian Education Program
P.O. Box 100 • Afton, OK 74331

Agra Public School I-134
Indian Education Program
P.O. Box 279 • Agra, OK 74824

Albion Grade School
Indian Education Program
P.O. Box 189 • Albion, OK 74521

Alex Public Schools
Indian Education Program
P.O. Box 188 • Alex, OK 73002

Allen Public Schools
Indian Education Program
P.O. Box 430 • Allen, OK 74825
(405) 857-2419 Fax 857-2636
Gayla Hudson, Director
Grades K-12. *Description*: Provides academic, cultural
enrichment and tutoring services for American Indian
children residing in the district. *Instructor*: Diane
Nemecek.

Anadarko School District
Indian Education Program
1400 S. Mission • Anadarko, OK 73005

Riverside Indian School
Indian Education Program
Route 1 • Anadarko, OK 73005

Antlers Public Schools
Indian Education Program
P.O Drawer 627 • Antlers, OK 74523

Boone/Apache Public Schools
Indian Education Program
Rt. 2, Box 177 • Apache, OK 73006

Ardmore City Schools
Indian Education Program
P.O. Box 1709 • Ardmore, OK 73402

Dickson ISD #77
Indian Education Program
Rt. 4, Box 122 • Ardmore, OK 73401

Plainview Public Schools
Indian Education Program
1140 S. Plainview Rd.
Ardmore, OK 73401

Arkoma Public School
Indian Education Program
P.O. Box 349 • Arkoma, OK 74901

Tushka Public Schools
Indian Education Program
Rt. 4, Box T 2630 • Atoka, OK 74525

Atoka Public Schools
Indian Education Program
P.O. Box 720 • Atoka, OK 74525

Harmony School
Indian Education/Title V
Rt. 2, Box 2215 • Atoka, OK 74525

Barnsdale Public School District I-29
Indian Education Program
P.O. Box 629 • Barnsdale, OK 74002

Bartlesville School District I-30
Indian Education Program
P.O. Box 1357 • Bartlesville, OK 74005

Tri-County Area Voc-Tech
Indian Education Program
6101 Nowata Rd. • Bartlesville, OK 74006

Battiest Public School I-71
Indian Education Program
P.O. Box 199 • Battiest, OK 74722

Bennington ISD
Indian Education Program
P.O. Box 10 • Bennington, OK 74723

Binger/Olney ISD #15
Indian Education Program
P.O. Box 280 • Binger, OK 73009

Blackwell Public Schools I-45
Indian Education Program
934 South First • Blackwell, OK 74631

Blanchard Public Schools
Indian Education Program
P.O. Box 2620 • Blanchard, OK 73010

Rock Creek I.S.D.
Indian Education Program
P.O. Box 208 • Bokchito, OK 74849

Bokoshe Public Schools I-26
Indian Education Program
P.O. Box 158 • Bokoshe, OK 74930

Boswell School I-1
Indian Education Program
Box 839 • Boswell, OK 74727

Bowlegs Public School
Indian Education Program
P.O. Box 88 • Bowlegs, OK 74830

Boynton Public School
Indian Education Program
P.O. Box 97 • Boynton, OK 74422

Braggs Public Schools
Indian Education Program
P.O. Box 59 • Braggs, OK 74423

Braman School
Indian Education Program
P.O. Box 130 • Braman, OK 74632

Bristow Schools
Indian Education/Title V
134 West 9th • Bristow, OK 74010

Broken Bow ISD #74
Indian Education Program
108 W. Fifth St.
Broken Bow, OK 74728

Lukfata School District #9
Indian Education Program
P.O. Box 940
Broken Bow, OK 74728

Cache Public School
Indian Education Program
P.O. Box 418 • Cache, OK 73527

Caddo Public School
Indian Education Program
P.O. Box 128 • Caddo, OK 74729

Calera Public School
Indian Education Program
P.O. Box 386 • Calera, OK 74730

Calumet School
Indian Education Program
P.O. Box 10 • Calumet, OK 73014

Calvin Public School ISD #48
Indian Education Program
P.O. Box 127 • Calvin, OK 74531

Cameron School Grades 1-12
Indian Education Program
P.O. Box 190 • Cameron, OK 74932

Caney Public School
Indian Education Program
P.O. Box 368 • Caney, OK 74533

Canton/Longdale Public School I-105
Indian Education Program
P.O. Box 639 • Canton, OK 73724

Carnegie ISD 33
Indian Education Program
P.O. Box 159 • Carnegie, OK 73015

Catoosa ISD #2
Indian Education Program
2000 S. Cherokee • Catoosa, OK 74015

Checotah ISD 19
Indian Education Program
310 Southwest Second
Checotah, OK 74426

Chelsea Public Schools
Indian Education Program
508 Vine • Chelsea, OK 74016
   (918) 789-2528 Fax 789-3271
   Nicky Harris, Coordinator
Grades PK-12. *Description*: Provides tutoring and
counselingservices, cultural activities and education
of Indian customs and heritage.

Choctaw/Nicoma Park P.S.
Indian Education Program
12880 N.E. 10th • Choctaw, OK 73020

Tiawah School
Indian Education Program
Rt. 7, Box 257 • Claremore, OK 74017

Verdigris School I-8
Indian Education Program
6101 S.W. Verdigris Rd.
Claremore, OK 74017

Claremore Public Schools
Indian Education Program
Claremore, OK 74018
   (918) 341-5270 Fax 341-8447
   Pam Leuthen, Counselor
Grades 1-12. Provides tutorial program, and counsel-
ing for grades 9-12.

Justus Public School District 0
Indian Education Program
P.O. Box 864 • Claremore, OK 74018

Clayton Public School District I-10
Indian Education Program
P.O. Box 190 • Clayton, OK 74536

Clinton Public Schools
Indian Education Program
P.O. Box 729 • Clinton, OK 73601

Coalgate Public Schools I-1
Indian Education Program
P.O Box 1368 • Coalgate, OK 74538

Cottonwood School
Indian Education Program
P.O. Box 347 • Coalgate, OK 74538

Colbert Public Schools
Indian Education Program
P.O. Box 310 • Colbert, OK 74733-0310

Colcord Public Schools
Indian Education Program
P.O. Box 188 • Colcord, OK 74338

Mosseley Public School
Indian Education Program
Rt. 4, Box 88 • Colcord, OK 74338

Commerce Public School District I-18
Indian Education Program
420 D St. • Commerce, OK 74339

Collinsville Public School I-6
Indian Education Program
2400 W. Broadway • Collinsville, OK 74021

Coweta Public School I-17
Indian Education Program
P.O. Box 550 • Coweta, OK 74429

Butner Schools
Indian Education Program
P.O. Box 157 • Cromwell, OK 74837

Crowder Public Schools
Indian Education Program
P.O. Box B • Crowder, OK 74430

Cushing Public Schools
Indian Education Program
P.O Drawer 1609 • Cushing, OK 74023

Custer Public School
Indian Education Program
P.O. Box 200 • Custer City, OK 73639

Davis Public School
Indian Education Program
400 East Atlanta • Davis, OK 73030

Delaware Public School I-30
Indian Education Program
Delaware, OK 74027

Leach School District 14
Indian Education Program
P.O. Box 211 • Delaware, OK 74368

Depew School District
Indian Education Program
P.O. Box 257 • Depew, OK 74028

Gypsy School D-12
Indian Education Program
Rt. 1, Box 400 • Depew, OK 74028

Dewar Public Schools
Indian Education Program
P.O. Box 790 • Dewar, OK 74431

Dibble Public Schools I-002
Indian Education Program
P.O. Box 9 • Dibble, OK 73031

Olive Independent S.D. I-17
Indian Education Program
Rt. 1, Box 337 • Drumright, OK 74030

Durant Public Schools I-72
Indian Education Program
118 North 7th • Durant, OK 74701

Silo School
Indian Education Program
HC-62, Box 227 • Durant, OK 74701
   (405) 924-7000 Fax 924-7045
   Sue Hopkins, Director
Grades K-12. *Description*: Provides tutorial services,
arts & crafts and music programs. *Instructors*: Thelma
Andrew, Michael Payne, Dolores Whiye, Sue Hopkins.

Dustin Public Schools
Indian Education Program
P.O. Box 660 • Dustin, OK 74893

Edmond Public School District I-12
Indian Education Program
215 North Blvd. • Edmond, OK 73034

Elgin Public Schools I-16
Indian Education Program
P.O. Box 369 • Elgin, OK 73583

Stony Point School #124
Indian Education Program
Rt. 1, Box 2200 • Elgin, OK 73538

Elmore City Public Schools
Indian Education Program
P.O. Box 99 • Elmore City, OK 73035

Darlington School
Indian Education Program
Box 145-A Rt. 3 • El Reno, OK 73036

El Reno ISD #34
Indian Education Program
P.O. Box 580 • El Reno, OK 73036

Enid Public Schools
Indian Education Program/Title IX
2102 Beverly Dr. • Enid, OK 73703
   (580) 242-7185 Fax 242-6177
   Margie E. Marney, Director
   E-Mail: mmarney@ionet.net
Grades 1-12. *Description*: Provides tutoring services,
cultural activities and education of Indian customs and
heritage. *Instructors*: Marsha Booth, Veryl Mills, Mary

Chaplin, Susan Meyer, Gary Dowers,
Robin Hatfield, Cindy Humphrey, Chris Smith.

Eufaula Public Schools I-1
Indian Education Program
P.O. Box 609 • Eufaula, OK 74432

Woodland Public Schools
Indian Education Program
P.O. Box 487 • Fairfax, OK 74637

Fairland Public Schools I-31
Indian Education/Title V
P.O. Box 689 • Fairland, OK 74343

Fanshawe School District #39
Indian Education/Title V
P.O. Box 55 • Fanshawe, OK 74935

McLish Public Schools
Indian Education/Title V
I-22, Box 29 • Fittstown, OK 74842

Ft. Cobb/Broxton Public S.D. I-17
Indian Education/Title V
P.O. Box 130 • Ft. Cobb, OK 73038

Fort Gibson Public Schools
Indian Education/Title V
P.O. Box 280 • Fort Gibson, OK 74434

Ft. Towson Schools
Indian Education Program
P.O. Box 39 • Ft. Towson, OK 74735
   (405) 873-2712; James Gibbs, Supt.
Grades K-12. *Description*: Home liaison/curriculum
aide to improve knowledge of Indian history and culture and home/school communications.

Foyil Public Schools
Indian Education Program
P.O. Box 49 • Foyil, OK 74031

Fox Public Schools
Indian Education Program
P.O. Box 248 • Fox, OK 73435

Frederick Public Schools
Indian Education Program
P.O. Box 370 • Frederick, OK 73542

Gans Public School
Indian Education Program
P.O. Box 52 • Gans, OK 74936

Geary School District I-80
Indian Education Program
P.O. Box 188 • Geary, OK 73040

Glenpool Public Schools
Indian Education/Title V
P.O. Box 1149 • Glenpool, OK 74033

Gore Public School
Indian Education Program
P.O. Box 580 • Gore, OK 74435

Gum Springs School D-69
Indian Education Program
Rt. 1, Box 129-T • Gore, OK 74435

Grandfield Public Schools
Indian Education Program
Box 639 • Grandfield, OK 73546

Grove Public Schools
Indian Education Program
P.O. Box 789 • Grove, OK 74344

Guthrie Public School
Indian Education Program
802 East Vilas • Guthrie, OK 73044

Haileyville Public Schools
Indian Education Program
P.O. Box 29 • Haileyville, OK 74546

Hammon Public School I-66
Indian Education Program
P.O. Box 279 • Hammon, OK 73650

Hanna Public Schools
Indian Education Program
P.O. Box "H" • Hanna, OK 74845

Harrah Public School District ISD-1007
Indian Education Program
20670 Walker St. • Harrah, OK 73045
(405) 454-6244 Fax 454-6844
Vernon L. Pierce, Assistant Supt.
Grades K-12. *Description*: Provides tutorial services, classroom/activity supplies, and a Native American Heritage Program. *Instructors*: Connie Norris, Cecillia Ann Fujii, Frances Benson, Laura Roberts.

Hartshorne Public School Dist. I-1
Indian Education Program
520 S. Fifth St. • Hartshorne, OK 74547

Healdton Public School
Indian Education Program
432 West Texas • Healdton, OK 73438

Haskell ISD #2
Indian Education Program
P.O. Box 278 • Haskell, OK 74436

Haworth Public School
Indian Education Program
P.O. Box 99 • Haworth, OK 74740

Heavener Public School
Indian Education Program
P.O. Box 698 • Heavener, OK 74937

Wilson School I-7
Indian Education Program
Rt. 1, Box 274 • Henryetta, OK 74437

Henryetta Public Schools
Indian Education Program
618 W. Main • Henryetta, OK 74437

Ryal School
Indian Education Program
Route 2 • Henryetta, OK 74437

Hodgen Public School
Indian Education Program
P.O. Box 69 • Hodgen, OK 74939

Holdenville Schools
Indian Education Program
210 Grimes St. • Holdenville, OK 74848-4036

Moss Public School I-01
Indian Education Program
Rt. 2, Box 57 • Holdenville, OK 74848

Hominy ISD #38
Indian Education Program
P.O. Box 400 • Hominy, OK 74035

Howe Public Schools
Indian Education Program
P.O. Box 259 • Howe, OK 74940

Hugo City Public Schools
Indian Education Program
208 N. 2nd St. • Hugo, OK 74743

Hulbert Public School ISD #16
Indian Education Program
P.O. Box 125 • Hulbert, OK 74441

Lost City Public School
Indian Education Program
Route 3 • Hulbert, OK 74441

Norwood School
Indian Education Program
Rt. 1, Box 537 • Hulbert OK 74441

Shady Grove School
Indian Education Program
Rt. 2, Box 438 • Hulbert, OK 74441

McCurtain Co. School District
Indian Education Program
Court Plaza Bldg. • Idabel, OK 74745

Indiahoma Public School
Indian Education Program
P.O. Box 8 • Indiahoma, OK 73552

Inola Public School
Indian Education Program
P.O. Box 1149 • Inola, OK 74036

Jay Public Schools ISD #1
Indian Education Program
P.O. Box C-1 • Jay, OK 74346

Jenks Public Schools
Indian Education Program
205 East "B" St. • Jenks, OK 74037
(918) 299-4411 ext. 213 Fax 299-9197
Sharon Pyeatte, Director
Grades K-12. *Description*: Provides academic enhancement and advancement through tutoring, evening and/or summer school programs. Cultural enrichment through community and school assemblies, classes, and activities.

Jennings Public School
Indian Education Program
Drawer 439 • Jennings, OK 74038

Jones Public Schools
Indian Education Program/Title IX
13145 Hiwassee • Jones, OK 73049
(405) 399-9118; Tracy L. Palmer, Director
Grades K-12. *Description*: Provides tutoring services, counseling and cultural activities; education of Indian customs and heritage.

Kansas Public School
Indian Education Program
P.O. Box 196 • Kansas, OK 74347

Kellyville Public Schools
Indian Education Program
P.O. Box 99 • Kellyville, OK 74039

Keota Public Schools
Indian Education Program
P.O. Box 160 • Keota, OK 74941

Ketchum Public Schools
Indian Education Program
P.O. Box 720 • Ketchum, OK 74349

Kingston Public School
Indian Education Program
P.O. Box 370 • Kingston, OK 73439

Kinta Public Schools
Indian Education Program
Box 219 • Kinta, OK 74552

Kiowa Public Schools
Indian Education Program
P.O. Box 6 • Kiowa, OK 74553

Konawa Public Schools
Indian Education Program
Rt. 1, Box 3 • Konawa, OK 74849

Lane School
Indian Education Program
P.O. Box 39 • Lane, OK 74555

Lawton Public Schools
Indian Education Program
753 Fort Sill Blvd. • Lawton, OK 73502
(580) 357-6900 ext. 279 Fax 585-6473
Dr. Anquanita Kaigler, Executive Director
Barry Beauchamp, Superintendent
E-mail: akaigler@lawtonps.org
Website: www.lawtonps.org/lps/index.asp
Grades Pre-K-12. *Instructors*: Six elementary tutors; 3 secondary liaisons; 3 secondary tutors. *Description*: A Federally funded program designed to meet the needs of Native American students. The goals and objectives are to enhance positive school performance, academic achievement, good attendance, and to promote cultural awareness. These objectives are carried out through the elementary tutoring program, cultural enrichment program, and secondary education program.

Leflore School Board
Indian Education Program
P.O. Box 147 • Leflore, OK 74942

Lexington Public Schools
Indian Education Program
420 NE 4th • Lexington, OK 73051

Locust Grove Public S.D. #17
Indian Education Program
P.O. Box 399 • Locust Grove, OK 74352

Lone Grove School
Indian Education Program
Box 1330 • Lone Grove, OK 73443

Lookeba-Sickley Public School
Indian Education Program
P.O. Box 34 • Lookeba, OK 73053

Macomb Public School
Indian Education Program
P.O. Box 10 • Macomb, OK 74852

Madill ISD #2
Indian Education Program
601 W. McArthur • Madill, OK 73446

Mannford Public Schools
Indian Education Program
P.O. Box 100 • Mannford, OK 74044

Marble City School District 35
Indian Education Program
P.O. Box 1 • Marble City, OK 74945

Marietta School District I-016
Indian Education Program
P.O. Box 289 • Marietta, OK 73448

Mason School District I-2
Indian Education Program
Rt. 1, Box 143B • Mason, OK 74859

Maud ISD #117
Indian Education Program
Box 130 • Maud, OK 74854

Maysville Public Schools I-7
Indian Education Program
Box 780 • Maysville, OK 73057

McAlester Public Schools
Indian Education Program
P.O. Box 1027 • McAlester, OK 74502

McLoud Public Schools
Indian Education Program
P.O. Box 40 • McLoud, OK 74851

Meeker Public School
Indian Education Program
P.O. Box 68 • Meeker, OK 74855

Sparks Schools
Indian Education Program
P.O. Box 68 • Meeker, OK 74855

Milburn Public School
Indian Education Program
P.O. Box 429 • Milburn, OK 73450
(405) 443-5522 Fax 443-5303
Richard McKee, Supt.
Instructor: Debbie Speers.

Mill Creek Public Schools
Indian Education Program
Box 105 • Mill Creek, OK 74856

Moffett Elementary School
Indian Education Program
P.O. Box 180 • Moffett, OK 74946

Monroe Elementary School
Indian Education Program
P.O. Box 10 • Monroe, OK 74947

Moore Indian Center
Indian Education Program
1500 SE 4th St. • Moore, OK 73160-8266

Morris Public Schools
Indian Education Program
P.O. Box 80 • Morris, OK 74445

Liberty Public Schools I-14
Indian Education Program
Rt. 1, Box 354 • Mounds, OK 74047

Mounds Public Schools
Indian Education Program
P.O. Box 189 • Mounds, OK 74047
(918) 827-6758 Fax 827-3704
Yvette Britt, Director
Grades K-12. *Description*: Provides tutorial services,
Indian cultural awareness programs, and career coun-
seling to Indian students in the Mounds Public Schools.

Mountain View/Gotebo Public School
Indian Education Program
P.O. Box B • Mountain View, OK 73062

Moyers Public School
Indian Education Program
P.O. Box 88 • Moyer, OK 74557

Belfonte School District 50
Indian Education Program
Rt. 3, Box 282 • Muldrow, OK 74948

Muldrow Public Schools
Indian Education Program
P.O. Box 660 • Muldrow, OK 74948

Hilldale Public Schools, I-29
Indian Education Program
Rt. 8, Box 141 • Muskogee, OK 74401

Muskogee City Schools
Indian Education Program
202 W. Broadway • Muskogee, OK 74401

Nashoba Public Schools
Indian Education Program
P.O. Box 17 • Nashoba, OK 74558

Newcastle Public Schools I-1
Indian Education Program
101 N. Main St. • Newcastle, OK 73065
(405) 387-4304 Fax 387-2891
Sharon Giles, Director
Grades K-12. *Description*: Provides academic tutor-
ing and cultural heritage programs. *Instructors*: Deana
Sykes, Georgia Small, Julie Wickersham.

Noble Public School I-40
Indian Education Program
P.O. Box 499 • Noble, OK 73068

Norman Public Schools
Indian Education Program
1133 W. Main • Norman, OK 73069

Little Axe Schools
Indian Education Program
Rt. 2, Box 266 • Norman, OK 73071

Nowata Public School
Indian Education Program
707 West Osage • Nowata, OK 74048

Oaks Mission Public Schools
Indian Education Program
P.O. Box 160 • Oaks, OK 74359

Okay Public School
Indian Education Program
P.O. Box 188 • Okay, OK 74446

Okemah Public Schools
Indian Education Program
Second & Date Sts. • Okemah, OK 74859

Oklahoma City Public Schools
Indian Education Program
P.O. Box 25428 • Oklahoma City, OK 73125

Putman City Independent School
Indian Education Program
5700 NW 40th • Oklahoma City, OK 73122

Western Heights P.S. I-51
Indian Education Program
8401 SW 44th St. • Oklahoma City, OK 73179

Okmulgee Public Schools District I-1
Indian Education Program
P.O. Box 1346 • Okmulgee, OK 74447

Oktaha Public Schools
Indian Education Program
P.O. Box 9 • Oktaha, OK 74437

Oologah-Talala Public School
Indian Education Program
P.O. Box 189 • Oologah, OK 74053

Paden Schools
Indian Education Program
Box 370 • Paden, OK 74860

Panama Public Schools
Indian Education Program
P.O. Box 550 • Panama, OK 74951

Keys Elementary School
Indian Education Program
HC 69, Box 151 • Park Hill, OK 74451
(918) 456-4501 Fax 456-7559
Charles A. Gourd, PhD, Director
Grades K-6. *Description*: Provides transitional bi-lin-
gual education. *Instructors*: Norma Fourkiller, Kelly
Porter, Kathy Roark.

Pauls Valley School I-18
Indian Education Program
P.O. Box 780 • Pauls Valley, OK 73075

Whitebread School
Indian Education Program
Rt. 3, Box 214 • Pauls Valley, OK 73975

Pawhuska School District I-2
Indian Education Program
1505 N. Lynn Ave.
Pawhuska, OK 74056

Pawnee Public Schools
Indian Education Program
P.O. Box 615 • Pawnee, OK 74059

Peggs School
Indian Education Program
P.O. Box 49 • Peggs, OK 74452

Pittsburg Public School
Indian Education Program
P.O. Box 200 • Pittsburg, OK 74560

Pocola Public Schools
Indian Education Program
P.O. Box 640 • Pocola, OK 74902

Ponca City Public S.D. I-71
Indian Education Program
111 W. Grand Ave. • Ponca City, OK 74602

Porter Consolidated District I-365
Indian Education Program
P.O. Box 120 • Porter, OK 74454

Porum Public Schools
Indian Education Program
P.O. Box 189 • Porum, OK 74455

Poteau Public S.D. I-29
Indian Education Program
307 Mockingbird Lane
Poteau, OK 74953

Prue Public Schools
Indian Education Program
P.O. Box 130 • Prue, OK 74060

Quapaw Public Schools
Indian Education Program
P.O. Box 130 • Prue, OK 74060

Osage Elementary
Indian Education Program
P.O. Box 579 • Pryor, OK 74362

Purcell Public School K-12
Indian Education Program
919 N. Ninth St. • Purcell, OK 73080

Quinton Public S.D. I-17
Indian Education Program
P.O.Box 670 • Quinton, OK 74561

Rattan Public School
Indian Education Program
P.O. Box 44 • Rattan, OK 74562

Red Oak Public Schools
Indian Education/Title IX
P.O. Box 310 • Red Oak, OK 74563
(918) 754-2647; Eva Coleman, Director
Grades K-12. *Description*: Provides academic tutoring and cultural heritage programs; 90 students enrolled in program. *Instructor*: Eva Coleman.

Frontier Public Schools I-4
Indian Education Program
P.O. Box 130 • Red Rock, OK 73651

Ringling Public Schools
Indian Education Program
P.O. Box 1010 • Ringling, OK 73456

Ripley Public School Dist. I-3
Indian Education Program
P.O. Box 97 • Ripley, OK 74062

Liberty School
Indian Education Program
P.O. Box 70 • Roland, OK 74954-0070

Kenwood School
Indian Education Program
Rt. 1, Box 179 • Salina, OK 74365

Salina Public S.D. I-16
Indian Education Program
PO. Box 98 • Salina, OK 74365

Wickliffe Public School
Indian Education Program
Rt. 1, Box 130 • Salina, OK 74365

Brushy School District D-36
Indian Education Program
P.O. Box 507 • Sallisaw, OK 74955

Central Public Schools
Indian Education Program
Rt. 1, Box 36 • Sallisaw, OK 74955

Sallisaw Public School I-1
Indian Education Program
604 E. Cherokee • Sallisaw, OK 74955

Anderson Elementary School
Indian Education Program
Rt. 5, Box 161 • Sand Springs, OK 74063

Sand Springs Public Schools
Indian Education Program
P.O. Box 970 • Sand Springs, OK 74063
(918) 245-1088; Jerre Brokaw, Coordinator
Grades K-12. *Description*: Provides tutoring, cultural
programs, and college/vocational information. Staff is
of Indian descent.

Sapulpa Public Schools
Indian Education Program
3 So. Mission • Sapulpa, OK 74066
(918) 224-9322 Fax 224-0174
Laura I. Hurd, Director; Flora Davis, Secretary
Grades K-12. *Description*: Covers academic needs and
cultural heritage. High school offers Muscogee (Creek)
& Cherokee language courses. *Instructors*: Linda
Harjo, Beatrice Harrell, Dorothea Bemo, Sherry
Garrett, Naomi Pickering, Wanda Weaver.

Lone Star School
Indian Education Program
P.O. Box 1170 • Sapulpa, OK 74067

Sasakwa I.S.D. I-10
Indian Education Program
PO. Box 323 • Sasakwa, OK 74867

Savanna Public Schools
Indian Education Program
P.O. Box 266 • Savanna, OK 74565

Schulter Public Schools
Indian Education Program
P.O. Box 203 • Schulter, OK 74460

Seiling Public School
Indian Education Program
P.O. Box 780 • Seiling, OK 73668

Pleasant Grove S.D. I-5
Indian Education Program
Rt. 1, Box 247 • Seminole, OK 74868

Seminole I.S.D. #1
Indian Education Program
P.O. Box 1031 • Seminole, OK 74868

Strother Public School
Indian Education Program
Rt. 3, Box 265 • Seminole, OK 74868

Varnum School
Indian Education Program
Rt. 4, Box 148 • Seminole. OK 74868

Shady Point Elementary
Indian Education Program
P.O. Drawer C • Shady Point, OK 74956

Bethel Public School ISD #3
Indian Education Program
36000 Clear Pond Dr.
Shawnee, OK 74801

North Rock Creek S.D. 10
Indian Education Program
42400 Garretts Lake Rd.
Shawnee, OK 74801

Pleasant Grove School
Indian Education Program
1927 E. Walnut • Shawnee, OK 74801

Shawnee Public School I-93
Indian Education Program
326 N. Union St. • Shawnee, OK 74801

Skiatook Public Schools
Indian Education Program
710 S. Osage • Skiatook, OK 74070

Smithville Public School I-14
Indian Education Program
P.O. Box 8 • Smithville, OK 74957

Soper Public School
Indian Education Program
P.O. Box 149 • Soper, OK 74759

Spavinaw School
Indian Education Program
Box 108 • Spavinaw, OK 74336

Sperry Public Schools
Indian Education Program
P.O. Box 610 • Sperry, OK 74073

Spiro Schools
Indian Education Program
600 W. Broadway • Spiro, OK 74959

Springer Public Schools
Indian Education Program
P.O Box 249 • Springer, OK 73458

Sterling Public Schools
Indian Education Program
P.O. Box 158 • Sterling, OK 73567

Stidham Public School D-16
Indian Education Program
General Delivery • Stidham, OK 74461

Stigler Public Schools
Indian Education Program
302 N.W. E St. • Stigler, OK 74462

Stillwater Independent School
Indian Education Program
314 S. Lewis • Stillwater, OK 74074

Bell Elementary School
Indian Education Program
P.O. Box 346 • Stilwell, OK 74960

Dahlonegah Elem. School District #29
Indian Education Program
Rt. 1, Box 351 • Stilwell, OK 74960

Greasy Public School
Indian Education Program
P.O. Box 467 • Stilwell, OK 74960

Maryetta Public School District 22
Indian Education Program
Rt. 4, Box 413 • Stilwell, OK 74960

Peavine S.D. #19
Indian Education Program
P.O. Box 389 • Stilwell, OK 74960

Rocky Mountain S.D. 24
Indian Education Program
Rt. 1, Box 665 • Stilwell, OK 74960

Stilwell Public School
Indian Education Program
1801 W. Locust • Stilwell, OK 74960

Zion School
Indian Education Program
P.O. Box 347 • Stilwell, OK 74960

Stonewall Schools
Indian Education Program
Rt. 2, Box 1-A • Stonewall, OK 74871

Stratford Public S.D. I-2
Indian Education Program
241 N. Oak St., Box 589
Stratford, OK 74872

Stringtown ISD #7
Indian Education Program
P.O. Box 130 • Stringtown, OK 74569

Stroud Independent S.D. 54
Indian Education Program
212 W. 7th, Box 410 • Stroud, OK 74079

Sulphur Public Schools
Indian Education Program
1021 West 9th St. • Sulphur, OK 73086

Swink Elementary School
Indian Education Program
P.O. Box 73 • Swink, OK 74761

Woodall School
Indian Education/Title V
Rt. 5, Box 226 • Tahlequah, OK 74464

Briggs Elementary School
Indian Education Program
Rt. 3, Box 656 • Tahlequah, OK 74464
  (18) 456-4221 Fax 456-4049
  Mrs. Jessie Craig, Director
Grades K-8. *Description:* Organizes cultural trips and programs; Sponsors Indian Club; teaches Cherokee language.

Grand View School
Indian Education Program
Rt. 4, Box 195 • Tahlequah, OK 74464

Lowrey School D-10
Indian Education Program
HC-11, Box 190-1 • Tahlequah, OK 74464

Tahlequah Public School District I-35
Indian Education Program
P.O. Box 517 • Tahlequah, OK 74465
  (918) 458-4162 Fax 458-4103
  Georgia Dick, Director
Grades K-12. *Description:* Provides tutoring services, cultural activities and education of Indian customs and

heritage; arts & crafts. Sponsors Indian Heritage Club activities for middle school and high school; also a youth group called Native Reflections in which students perform service-learning projects in the community. *Instructor:* Mike Daniel

Sequoyah High School
Indian Education Program
P.O. Box 948 • Tahlequah, OK 74465

Buffalo Valley Public School I-3
Indian Education Program
Rt. 2, Box 3505 • Talihina, OK 74571

Talihina Public School
Indian Education Program
P.O. Box 38 • Talihina, OK 74571

Tecumseh Public Schools
Indian Education Program
302 S. 9th • Tecumseh, OK 74873

Temple Public Schools
Indian Education Program
206 School Rd. • Temple, OK 73568

Thomas I-6 Public School
Indian Education Program
P.O. Box 190 • Thomas, OK 73669

Tuskahoma Public School
Indian Education Program
P.O. Box 97 • Tiskahoma, OK 74574

Tonkawa Public Schools
Indian Education Program
P.O Box 10 • Tonkawa, OK 74653

Berryhill Public School I-10
Indian Education Program
3128 South 63 West Ave. • Tulsa, OK 74107

Tulsa Independent S.D. #1
Indian Education Program
3909 E. 5th Place • Tulsa, OK 74112

Tupelo Public Schools
Indian Education Program
P.O. Box 310 • Tupelo, OK 74572

Valliant Public Schools
Indian Education Program
P.O. Box 777 • Valliant, OK 74764

Vian Public School I-2
Indian Education Program
P.O. Box 434 • Vian, OK 74962

Vinita Public Schools I-65
Indian Education Program
P.O. Box 408 • Vinita, OK 74301

Wagoner Public School Dist. I-19
Indian Education Program
204 Casaver • Wagoner, OK 74467

Walter Independent S.D. I-00
Indian Education Program
418 S. Broadway • Walter, OK 73572

Wanette Public School
Indian Education Program
P.O. Box 161 • Wanette, OK 74878

Wapanucka Public School
Indian Education Program
P.O. Box 88 • Wapanucka, OK 73461

Warner Public School
Indian Education Program
Rt. 1, Box 1240 • Warner, OK 74469

Washington Public School
Indian Education Program
P.O. Box 98 • Washington, OK 73093

Watonga Public School Dist. I-42
Indian Education Program
P.O. Box 310 • Watonga, OK 73772

Watts Public School Dist. I-4
Indian Education Program
P.O. Box 10 • Watts, OK 74964

Skelly School District I
Indian Education Program
Rt. 1, Box 918 • Watts, OK 74964

Wayne Public School
Indian Education Program
P.O. Box 40 • Wayne, OK 73095

Weatherford Public Schools
Indian Education Program
516 N. Broadway • Weatherford, OK 73096

Webbers Falls Public Schools
Indian Education Program
P.O. Box 300 • Webber Falls, OK 74470

Welch School District I-17
Indian Education Program
P.O. Box 189 • Welch, OK 74369

Weleetka Public Schools I-31
Indian Education Program
P.O. Box 278 • Weleetka, OK 74880

Graham Public School
Indian Education Program
Route 1 • Weleetka, OK 74880

Tenkiller Public Schools
Indian Education Program
Rt. 1, Box 750 • Welling, OK 74653

Westville Public Schools
Indian Education Program
P.O. Box 410 • Westville, OK 74965

Justice School District 54
Indian Education Program
Rt. 1, Box 246 • Wewoka, OK 74884

Wewoka Public Schools
Indian Education Program
P.O. Box 870 • Wewoka, OK 74884

New Lima ISD 6
Indian Education Program
Rt. 1, Box 96 • Wewoka, OK 74884

Whitefield Elementary School
Indian Education Program
P.O. Box 188 • Whitefield, OK 74472

Whitesboro Public Schools I-65
Indian Education Program
P.O. Box 150 • Whitesboro, OK 74577

Wilburton Public S.D. I-1
Indian Education Program
1201 W. Blair St. • Wilburton, OK 74578

Wilson Public School
Indian Education Program
P.O. Drawer 730 • Wilson, OK 73463

Wister Public School
Indian Education Program
P.O. Box 489 • Wister, OK 74966

Wright City Public Schools
Indian Education Program
P.O. Box 329 • Wright, OK 74766

Wyandotte P.S. Dist. I-1
Indian Education Program
P.O. Box 360 • Wyandotte, OK 74370

Joy Public School
Indian Education Program
Rt. 1, Box 57 • Wynnewood, OK 73098

Wynona Public School
Indian Education Program
P.O. Box 700 • Wynona, OK 74084
  (918) 846-2467 Fax 846-2883
  Richard Nissen, Instructor
Grades: 9-12. *Program*: Indian history.

OREGON

Bandon School District #54
Indian Education Program
455 Ninth St., SW • Bandon, OR 97411
  Jackie Beacher, Contact

Brookings Harbor S.D. 17C
Indian Education Program
564 Ferm St. • Brookings Harbor, OR 97415
  Linda Timeus, Contact

Burns Paiute Reservation
Indian Education Program
HC-71, 100 PaSiGo St. • Burns, OR 97720
  J. Holbrook, Contact

Harney Co. School District
Indian Education Program
458 E. Washington St. • Burns, OR 97720
  N. Eddy, Contact

Coos Bay School District #9
Indian Education Program
P.O. Box 509 • Coos Bay, OR 97420
  Jim Thornton, Gloria Reeves, Contacts

Coquille School District #8
Indian Education Program
201 N. Gould St. • Coquille, OR 97423
  C. Crawford, Contact

London School
Indian Education Program
73288 London Rd. • Cottage Grove, OR 97424

  Mary Nisewander, Contact

Eugene School District 4-J
Indian Education Program
Eugene, OR 97405
  Twila Souers, Contact

Grand Ronde Grade School
Indian Education Program
P.O. Box 7 • Grand Ronde, OR 97347
  M. Kimsey, Contact

Klamath Co. School District
Indian Education Program
10501 Washburn Way
Klamath Falls, OR 97603
  Lynn Corwin, Contact

Klamath Falls Dist. #1
Indian Education Program
475 S. Alameda Ave.
Klamath Falls, OR 97603
  C. Fries, Contact

K.U.H.S.
Indian Education Program
Mon Claire St. • Klamath Falls, OR 97601
  H. Smith, Contact

Jefferson Co. School District 509-J
Indian Education Program
1355 Buff St. • Madras, OR 97741
  P. Riley, Contact

South Umpqua School District
Indian Education Program/Title IX
558 Chadwick Ln.
Myrtle Creek, OR 97457
  (503) 863-3118; Bill Burnett, Director
Grades K-12. *Description*: Provides academic, cultural
enrichment and tutoring services for American Indian
children residing in the district.

Myrtle Point School District #41
Indian Education Program
212 Spruce St. • Myrtle Point, OR 97458
  C. Leibelt, Contact

Lincoln Co. School District
Indian Education Program
P.O. Box 1110 • Newport, OR 97365
  M. Darcy, Contact

North Bend School District #13
Indian Education Program
1313 Airport Ln. • North Bend, OR 97459
  D. Caldwell, Contact

Oregon City School District
Indian Education Program
P.O. Box 591 • Oregon City, OR 97045
  Ruth Jensen, Contact

Umatilla School District
Indian Education Program
2001 SW Rye • Pendleton, OR 97801
  V. Lyles, Contact

Indian Education Program
3558 SE Harold Ct. • Portland, OR 97202
  Norine S. Smith, Contact

Northwest Reg. Ed. Lab
Indian Education Program
101 SW Main St., Suite 500
Portland, OR 97204
  Joe Coburn, Contact

Portland School District #1
Indian Education Program
P.O. Box 3107 • Portland, OR 97208
  M. Caba, Contact

Portland Schools
Indian Education Program
8020 N.E. Tillamook • Portland, OR 97213
  Robie Clark, Contact

Powers School District #1
Indian Education Program
P.O. Box 479 • Portland, OR 97266
  S. Stallard, Contact

Chemawa Indian School
Indian Education Program
3700 Chemawa Rd. NE • Salem, OR 97305
  G. Gray, Contact

Salem-Keizer Schools
Indian Education Program
P.O. Box 12024 • Salem, OR 97302
  G. Hammond, Contact

State Dept. of Education
Indian Education Program
700 Pringle Park S.E. • Salem, OR 97310
  Robin Butterfield, Contact

Springfield Public Schools
Indian Education Program
525 Mill St. • Springfield, OR 97477
  (503) 726-3430 Fax 726-9555
  Laurie Brown-Godfrey, Director
Grades K-12. *Description*: Provides educational and
cultural services to students enrolled in the program.

Indian Education Program
P.O. Box 849 • Warm Springs, OR 97761
  R. Danzuha, Contact

Columbia School District 5-J
Indian Education Program
Westport, OR 97016
  R. Theis, Contact

Willamina School District 30-J
Indian Education Program
324 SE Adams • Willamina, OR 97396
  K. Shelly, Contact

RHODE ISLAND

Narragansett Indian Tribe
Indian Education Program
P.O. Box 268 • Charleston, RI 02813

Charijo School District
Indian Education Program
Switch Rd. • Wood River Junction, RI 02894
  Robert Andreotti, Contact

SOUTH DAKOTA

Aberdeen Public Schools
Indian Education Program
203 Third Ave., SE • Aberdeen, SD 57401
Georgine Tyon-Pourier, Contact

Tiospa Zina Tribal School
P.O. Box 719 • Agency Village, SD 57262
Dr. Roger Bordeaux, Contact

Tiospa Zina Tribal School
P.O. Box 719 • Agency Village, SD 57262
Dick Thompson, Contact

American Horse School Principal
P.O. Box 660 • Allen, SD 57714
Donald Standing Elk, Contact

Shannon Co. School District
Indian Education Program
P.O. Box 109 • Batesland, SD 57716
Maurice Twiss, Contact

Bonesteel-Fairfax School District
P.O. Box 410 • Bonesteel, SD 57317
Richard W. Parry, Contact

Rock Creek Day School
P.O. Box 127 • Bullhead, SD 57621
Emmett White Temple, Contact

Dupree School District
P.O. Box 10 • Dupree, SD 57623
Bruce Carrier, Contact

Eagle Butte School District
Indian Education Program
P.O. Box 260 • Eagle Butte, SD 57625
Jean Bowman, Contact

Flandreau Indian School
Indian Education Program
1000 N. Crescent • Flandreau, SD 57028
Bernie Wells, Jack Belkham, Contacts

Flandreau Public School
600 1st Ave. West • Flandreau, SD 57028
Troy Garrett/Cindy Jones, Contacts

Fort Thompson Elem. School
P.O. Box 139 • Fort Thompson, SD 57339
Douglas Daughters, Contact

Swift Bird Day School
HCR #3, Box 121 • Gettysburg, SD 57442
Principal, Contact

Hot Springs Public Schools
Indian Education Program
1609 University Ave. • Hot Springs, SD 57747

(605) 745-4145 Fax 745-4178
Ronald J. Bergen, Director
Grades K-12. *Description*: Provides tutoring services and career education. *Instructors*: Barbara Blosser, Arlene Chavez.

Takini School
Indian Education Program
P.O. Box 168 • Howes, SD 57748
Dr. Loretta Engelhardt, Contact

Isabel School District 20-2
P.O. Box 267 • Isabel, SD 57633-0267
Charles Begeman, Contact

Little Wound School
P.O. Box 500 • Kyle, SD 57752
Dr. Lynda Earring, Gerald Bettelyoun, Contacts

Andes Central School
P.O. Box 40 • Lake Andes, SD 57356
Clifford Bernie, Janet Varejcka, Contacts

Little Eagle Day School
P.O. Box 26 • Little Eagle, SD 57639
Adele Little Dog, Contact

Lower Brule School
Indian Education Program
P.O. Box 245 • Lower Brule, SD 57548
Cody Russell, Contact

Wounded Knee School District
P.O. Box 350 • Manderson, SD 57756
Shirley Garnette, Contact

Bennett Co. School District
P.O. Box 580 • Martin, SD 57551
Wade R. Olson, Contact

Marty Indian School
P.O. Box 187 • Marty , SD 57361
Vince Two Eagle, Contact

McIntosh School District
Box 80 • McIntosh, SD 57641
Olaus Njas, Contact

McLaughlin School District
P.O. Box 880 • McLaughlin, SD 57642
Harlan Krein, Contact

Todd Co. School District
Indian Education Program
P.O. Box 87 • Mission, SD 57555
(605) 856-4869 Fax 856-2449
Richard Bordeaux, Supt.
Dennis Gaspar, Director-Title IX
Grades Pre K-12. *Description*: Serves over 2,100 Native American students, mostly enrolled members of the Rosebud Sioux Tribe. Provides academic, cultural enrichment and tutoring services for American Indian children residing in the district.

Mitchell School District
Native Am. H/S Coord.
P.O. Box 7760 • Mitchell, SD 57301
Bette Masheck, Contact

Mobridge District Schools
114 East 10th • Mobridge, SD 57601
Dixie Silva, Contact

Loneman School
P.O. Box 50 • Oglala, SD 57764
Saunie Wilson, Goldie Starr, Contacts

Pierre Indian Learning Center
HC 31, Box 148 • Pierre, SD 57501
Darrell Jeanotte, Contact

Pierre Jr. High School
Indian Education Program
120 S. Highland • Pierre, SD 57501
Joanne Beare, Contact

Pierre School District
Indian Education Program
302 E. Dakota • Pierre, SD 57501
Thomas W. Sogaard, Contact

Pine Ridge School
P.O. Box 1202
Pine Ridge, SD 57770
Imogene Horse, Basil Brave Heart, Contacts

Rapid City School District
Title VII Indian Education Program
300 Sixth St. • Rapid City, SD 57701
(605) 394-4071 Fax 394-4085
Dr. Arthur W. Zimiga, Director
E-mail: arthur.zumiga@csac.rcas.org
Grades K-12. *Description*: Provides instructional assistance, and supplemental special educational and culturally related needs to Native American Indian students.

St. Francis Indian School
Sicangu Oyate Ho., Inc.
P.O. Box 379, HCR 59, Box 1A
St. Francis, SD 57572-0379
(605) 747-2299 Fax 747-2379
Web site: www.sfiskl2.org
Cheryl Crazy Bull, Chief Educational Officer
Carole Little Wounded, Secondary Administrator
Richard Bad Milk, Elementary Administrator
Grades K-12. Tribally controlled serving the Rosebud

Sioux Indian Reservation in south central South Dakota. Under jurisdiction of the Rosebud Agency, BIA. Established in 1971.

Sioux Falls School District
Indian Education Program
201 East 38th St.
Sioux Falls, SD 57117
Marilyn Charging, Contact

Sisseton Public School District
Indian Education Program
302 E. Maple St. • Sisseton, SD 57262
Delphine Wanna, Contact

Crow Creek High School
P.O. Box 12 • Stephan, SD 57346
Gary Spawn, Contact

Timber Lake School District
P.O. Box 1000
Timber Lake, SD 57656
Frank Seiler, Contact

Vermillion School District
Indian Education Program
17 Prospect St.
Vermillion, SD 57069
Kathy Prasek, Contact

Wagner Community Schools
Indian Education Program
P.O. Box 310 • Wagner, SD 57380
Dana Sanderson, Contact

Smee School District
P.O. Box 8 • Wakpala, SD 57658
Greg East, Contact

Crazy Horse School
Indian Education Program
P.O. Box 260 • Wanblee, SD 57577
Lamoine Pulliam

Enemy Swim Day School
RR 1, Box 87 • Waubay, SD 57273
Edna Greenhagen, Contact

Waubay School District
RR 1, Box 11 • Waubay, SD 57273
Dennis Nelson, Contact

White Horse School District
P.O. Box 7 • White Horse, SD 57661
Barbara Longcrow, Contact

White River School District
P.O. Box 273
White River, SD 57579
Dr. Don Barnhart, Contact

Wilmot School District 54-7
Indian Education Program
P.O. Box 100, 800 Ordway St.
Wilmot, SD 57279
(605) 938-4647 Fax 938-4185
Tim Graf, Director
E-mail: tim.graf@K12.sd.us
Grades PS-12. *Description*: Provides tutoring services and cultural enrichment programs. *Instructor*: Donna Hansen.

Winner School District
P.O. Box 231 • Winner, SD 57580
Keith Gebhart, Contact

Yankton School District
Indian Education Program
1900 Ferdig Ave. • Yankton, SD 57078
Joyce Wentworth, Contact

TENNESSEE

Lauderdale Board of Education
Indian Education Program
402 S. Washington • Ripley, TN 38063
Robert Webb, Contact

TEXAS

Dallas I.S.D.
Indian Education Program
3700 Ross Ave. • Dallas, TX 75204

Ysleta I.S.D.
Indian Education Program
9600 Sims • El Paso, TX 79925

Grand Prairie I.S.D.
Indian Education Program
202 West College • Grand Prairie, TX 75050

UTAH

Neola Elementary School
Indian Education Program
P.O. Box 446 • Duchesne, UT 84021
Coordinator

Davis Co. School District
Indian Education Program
45 E. State St. • Farmington, UT 84025
Susan Ross, Contact

Ute Tribe Adult Education
Indian Education Program
P.O. Box 146 • Ft. Duchesne, UT 84026
Jean Noble, Contact

Aneth Commuity School
Indian Education Program
P.O. Box 600 • Montezuma Creek, UT 84534
Eva Benally, Contact

Division of Indian Affairs
Indian Education Program
324 S. State St., Suite 103
Salt Lake City, UT 84111
Wil Numkena, Contact

Granite S.D. Multicultural Ctr.
Indian Education Program
340 E. 3545 South • Salt Lake City, UT 84115

State Office of Education
Indian Education Program
250 East 500 South • Salt Lake City, UT 84111
Jay Taggart, Contact

Jordan School District
Indian Education Program
9361 South 300 East • Sandy, UT 84070

VERMONT

Franklin NW Supv. USD
Indian Education Program
17 Grand Ave. • Swanton, VT 05488
Jeff Benay, Contact

VIRGINIA

Charles City Co. Public Schools
Indian Education Program
10910 Court House Rd.
Charles City, VA 22030
Melvin Robertson, Contact

King William Co. School Board
Indian Education Program
P.O. Box 185 • King William, VA 23086
Miles A. Reid, Contact

WASHINGTON

Aberdeen School District #5
Indian Education Program
216 No. G St. • Aberdeen, WA 98520

Arlington School District
Indian Education Program
600 E. First St. • Arlington, WA 98223

Auburn School District
Indian Education Program
915 Fourth St. NE • Auburn, WA 98002

Muckleshoot Tribal School
Indian Education Program
39015 172nd Ave. SE • Auburn, WA 98092
(253) 931-6709 Fax 939-2922
Dr. Carolyn Marsh, Director

Bellingham High School
Indian Education Program
2020 Cornwall Ave.
Bellingham, WA 98225
Janice Smith, Contact

Bellingham School District #501
Indian Education Program
P.O Box 878 • Bellingham, WA 98227
M. Montague, Contact

Lummi Tribal School
Indian Education Program
2530 Kwina Rd. • Bellingham, WA 98226
(360) 384-2330 Fax 380-1464
C. Wilson, Contact

Puget Sound Educational Service District
Indian Education Program
400 S.W. 152nd St. • Burien, WA 98166
(360) 439-3636 Fax 439-3961
Carol DittBenner, Director
Grades K-12. *Description*: Provides personalized services to Native American students attending public schools in the district. Services include tutoring, and career/vocational counseling. *Instructors*: David Norman, Myrna Gonzalez, Alice Thoreson, Phyllis Covington, Galen Williams.

Grand Coulee Dam School District
Indian Education Program
Stevens and Grant
Coulee Dam, WA 99116
E. Moses, Contact

Cusick School District #59
Indian Education Program
305 Monumental Way, Box 270
Cusick, WA 99119
C. Crickman, Contact

Darrington School District #330
Indian Education Program
P.O. Box 27 • Darrington, WA 98241
B. Mmauldin, Contact

Nooksack Parent Ed. Comm.
Indian Education Program
P.O. Box 34 • Deming, WA 98244
Sandra Joseph, Contact

Mt. Baker School District
Indian Education Program
P.O. Box 45 • Deming, WA 98244
(360) 383-2015 ext. 4511 Fax 383-2029
Juan Ortiz, Director
Grades: 7-12. *Description*: Services include tutoring, grade improvement; class in Native culture, leadership ab=nd self-esteem.

Nooksack Indian Tribe
Indian Education Program
5048 Mt. Baker Hwy.
Deming, WA 98244
E. Tom, Contact

Elma School District
Indian Education Program
30 Elma Monte Rd. • Elma, WA 98541
L. Burbridge, Contact

Federal Way School District #210
Indian Education Program
31405 18th Ave. S.
Federal Way, WA 98003
D. Salyers, Contact

Ferndale School District #502
Indian Education Program
P.O. Box 428 • Ferndale, WA 98248
Tracy Parker, L. Lane-Oreiro, Contacts

Queets-Clearwater S.D. #20
Indian Education Program
146000 Hwy. 101 • Forks, WA 98331
F. Hansen, Contact

Quillayute Valley S.D. #402
Indian Education Program
P.O. Box 60 • Forks, WA 98331
R. Harmon, Contact

Glenwood School District #401
Indian Education Program
P.O. Box 12, 320 Bunnell St.
Glenwood, WA 98619
(509) 364-3438 Fax 364-3689
Chris Anderson, Director
Grades K-12. *Description*: Provides support for students to attend youth conference; cultural activities and awareness education; and summer school, athletic and academic camps. *Instructor*: Emma Jane LaVallie.

Granger School District #204
Indian Education Program
P.O. Box 400 • Granger, WA 98932
K. Heggens, Contact

Central Valley S.D. #356
Indian Education Program
E. 19307 Cataldo
Greenacres, WA 99016
Dan Iyall, Contact

Hoquiam School District
Indian Education Program
312 Simpson • Hoquiam, WA 98550
E. Rusi, Contact

Columbia School District #206
Indian Education Program
P.O. Box 7 • Hunters, WA 99137
K. Anderson, Contact

Ocean Beach School District #101
Indian Education Program
P.O. Box 860 • Ilwaco, WA 98624
T. Akerlund, Contact

Inchelium School District #70
Indian Education Program
P.O. Box 285 • Inchelium, WA 99138
N. Kirby, Jim Perkins, Contacts

WA State Indian Education
Indian Education Program
P.O. Box 259 • Indianola, WA 98342
M. Boushie, Contact

Crescent School District #313
Indian Education Program
P.O. Box 2 • Joyce, WA 98343
R. Wilson, Contact

Kelso School District #453
Indian Education Program
404 Long Ave. • Kelso, WA 98626
D. Taylor, Contact

Kent School District
Indian Education Program
12033 SE 256th St. • Kent, WA 98031
J. Brownell, Contact

La Conner School District
Indian Education Program
P.O. Box D • La Conner, WA 98257
N. Hoffman, Contact

Indian Education Program
P.O. Box 33 • La Push, WA 98350
Roger Jackson, Contact

Quileute Tribal School
Indian Education Program
P.O. Box 39 • La Push, WA 98350
T. Tavenner, Contact

North Thurston School District
Indian Education Program
305 College St., NE • Lacey, WA 98506

Longview School District #122
Title IX, Indian Education Program
1410 8th Ave. • Longview, WA 98632
(360) 575-7437 Fax 575-7456
E-mail: jduff@longview.kl2.wa.us
Ann Cavanaugh, Director
Judy Duff, Coordinator
Grades K-12. *Instructors*: Raquel Johnston, Tina Thompson, Benita Revis, Jodi Traub, Tanya Beltz. *Programs*: Provides culture classes and tutoring; classroom & community presentations; newsletter and annual pow-wow.

Lyle School District #406
Indian Education Program
P.O. Box 368 • Lyle, WA 98635
D. Oldenberg, Contact

Edmonds School District #15
Indian Education Program
20420 68th Ave. W
Lynwood, WA 98036
S. Fink, Contact

Marysville School District
Indian Education Program
4220 80th NE • Marysville, WA 98270
Roberta Basch, Contact

Indian Education Program
P.O. Box 127 • Nespelem, WA 99155
Valorie Smith, Contact

Indian Heritage Association
Makah Cultural Center
P.O. Box 160 • Neah Bay, WA 98357
A. Renker, Contact

Nespelem School District #014
Indian Education Program
P.O. Box 291 • Nespelem, WA 99155
E. Hyde, Contact

Nooksack Valley School District
Indian Education Program
P.O. Box 307 • Nooksack, WA 98276
D. Newell, Contact

North Kitsap School District
Indian Education Program
18360 Caldart NE
North Kitsap, WA 98370

Oakville School District #400
Indian Education Program
P.O. Box H • Oakville, WA 98568
L. Eliason, Contact

Okanogan School District #105
Indian Education Program
P.O. Box 592 • Okanogan, WA 98840
(509) 422-3770; Dorothy Hamner, Director
Grades K-12. *Description*: Serves the special and unique needs of Native American studnets. J.O.M./Title IX Programs.

Nisqually Indian Tribe
Indian Education Program
4820 She-Nah-Num Dr. SE
Olympia, WA 98503
Y. Scott/A. Frazier, Contact

Olympia School District #111
Indian Education Program
1113 E. Legion Way • Olympia, WA 98501
E. Allen, Contact

Wa He Lut Indian Day
Indian Education Program
1111 Conine Ave. SE • Olympia, WA 98503
B. Przusnyski, Contact

North Beach School District #64
Indian Education Program
P.O. Box 159 • Ocean Shores, WA 98569
R. Torrens, Contact

Indian Education Office
Indian Education Program
State Dept. of Public Instruction
Olympia, WA 98504
Patsy Martin, Contact

Omak School District #19
Indian Education Program
P.O. Box 833 • Omak, WA 98841
M.V. Power, Contact

Port Angeles School District #121
Indian Education Program
216 E. Fourth St.
Port Angeles, WA 98362
R. Carr, Contact

South Kitsap School District #402
Indian Education Program
1962 Hoover SE
Port Orchard, WA 98366
S. Blanchard, Contact

North Kitsap School District
Indian Education Program
18360 Caldart NE • Poulsbo, WA 98370
J. Schiersch, Contact

Parent Committee
Indian Education Program
7415 56th St. E • Puyallup, WA 98371
Helen Gray-Teo, Contact

Puyallup School District
Indian Education Program
214 W. Main St. • Puyallup, WA 98371
N. Polich, Contact

Lake Washington School District #414
Indian Education Program
P.O. Box 97039 • Redmond, WA 98073
R. Watt, Contact

Renton School District #403
Indian Education Program
435 Main Ave. S • Renton, WA 98056
C. Rekdal, Contact

ACE Project
Indian Education Program
9010 13th Ave. NW • Seattle, WA 98117
N. George, Contact

American Indian Heritage Program
Seattle Public School District
Middle College High School
Seattle, WA 98103 (206) 527-3733
Robert Eaglestaff, Principal
Grades: 6-12.

Huchoosedah Indian Education Program
1330 N. 90th St. • Seattle, WA 98103
(206) 298-7945 Fax 298-7946
E-mail: mtulee@is.ssd.kiz.wa.us
Mike Tulee, Program Manager
Grades K-12. *Description*: Conducts various social service activities which are designed to assist Native American students acclimate to the urban public school system.

Highline Public S.D. #401
Indian Education Program
15675 Ambaum Blvd. SW
Seattle, WA 98166
J. Hopkins, Contact

Indian Center Education Clinic
Indian Education Program
611 12th Ave. S, Suite 300
Seattle, WA 98144
B. Gutierrez, Contact

Indian Education Program
9600 College Way N. • Seattle, WA 98103
Willard Bill, Contact

Seattle Indian Center
Indian Education Program
611 12th Ave. S. • Seattle, WA 98144
J. Shelton, Contact

Seattle Public School District 1
Indian Education Program
815 Fourth Ave. • Seattle, WA 98109
J. Iman, Contact

Title V Parent Committee
Indian Education Program
6702 Earl St. • Seattle, WA 98117
Cissy Leask, Contact

United Indians of All Tribes
Indian Education Program
P.O. Box 99100 • Seattle, WA 98199
G. Boots, Contact

University of Washington
Indian Education Program
375 Schmitz Hall, PC45
Seattle, WA 98195
R. Haines, Contact

Sedro-Woolley S.D. #101
Indian Education Program
Sedro-Woolley, WA 98284
D. Handy, Contact

Upper Skagit Indian Tribe
Indian Education Program
25944 Community Plaza
Sedro Woolley, WA 98284
(360) 856-5501 Fax 856-3175
Archy Cavanaugh, Contact

Cape Flattery S.D. #401
Indian Education Program
P.O. Box 109 • Sekiu, WA, 98381
D. Hunter, Contact

Hood Canal S.D. #404
Indian Education Program
N. 111 Hwy. 106 • Shelton, WA 98584
Dr. R. Weir, Contact

Skokomish Indian Tribe
Indian Education Program
N. 80 Tribal Center Rd. • Shelton, WA 98584
Roberta Peterson, Contact

South Bend Schools
Indian Education Program
P.O. Box 437 • South Bend, WA 98586
(360) 875-5707; Gary C. Johnson, Director
Grades K-12. *Description*: Serves 70 students in Chinook Indian Country; students learn about Chinook culture; provides counseling and educational guidance.

Native Project
Indian Education Program
W 1803 Maxwell • Spokane, WA 99201
F. Spotted Eagle, Contact

Spokane Public School District
Indian Education Program
Ad Bldg. N. 200 Bernard St.
Spokane, WA 99201
Don Barlow, Contact

Mary Walker School District #207
Indian Education Program
P.O. Box 159 • Springdale, WA 99173
F. Jones, Contact

Clover Park School District #400
Indian Education Program
10903 Gravelly Lake Dr. SW
Tacoma, WA 98499
K. Lemmer, Contact

Indian Education Program
1329 E. 55th St. • Tacoma, WA 98404
Virginia Bill, Contact

Indian Education Program
6316 South C St. • Tacoma, WA 98408
Jack Shepard, Contact

Puyallup Tribal School
Indian Education Program
2002 E. 28th • Tacoma, WA 98404
N. Dorpat, Contact

Tacoma School District #10
Indian Education Program
601 So. 8th St., P.O. Box 1357
Tacoma, WA 98401
 (253) 571-1139 Fax 571-2637
Ethelda Burke, Ass't Supt.
Ruby K. Russonielllo-Damaskos, Facilitator
E-mail: rdamask@tacoma.k12.wa.us
Website: www.tacoma.k12.wa.us
Grades: K-12. Description: Two goals - career development for grades 9-12 and student advisement for grades K-12. Works cooperatively with Special Education; Learning Assistant Program (LAP); Title One; English as a Second Language, general education, career services and counseling to meet the needs of Indian students.

Taholah School District #77
Indian Education Program
P.O. Box 249 • Taholah, WA 98587
 R. Anthony, Contact

Toppenish School District #202
Indian Education Program
Toppenish, WA 98948
 Irene Sumner, J. Torres, Contacts

Yakima Tribal Ed. Center
Indian Education Program
P.O. Box 151 • Toppenish, WA 98948
 Alvin Schuster, Contact

Yakima School District
Indian Education Program
P.O. Box 151 • Toppenish, WA 98948
 P. Martin, H. Umtuck, Contacts

Vancouver School District #37
Indian Education Program
Vancouver, WA 98668
 J. Tangeman, Contact

Weelpinit School District #49
Indian Education Program
P.O. Box 390 • Wellpinit, WA 99040
 J. Cruzen, Contact

Wapato School District #207
Indian Education Program
P.O. Box 38 • Wapato, WA 98951
 R. Foss, Contact

Indian Education Program
P.O. Box 324 • Wellpinit, WA 99040
 Teresa Payne, Contact

Mt. Adams School District #209
Indian Education Program
P.O. Box 578 • White Swan, WA 98952
 R.J. Hoptowit, Contact

Educational Service District #105
Indian Education Program
33 S. Second Ave. • Yakima, WA 98902
 Marsha Pastrana, Contact

Yakama School District
Indian Education Program
104 N. Fourth Ave. • Yakama, WA 98902
 N. Le Cuyer, Contact

Yelm School District
Indian Education Program
P.O. Box 476 • Yelm, WA 98597
 M. Zodrow, Contact

WISCONSIN

Appleton Area School District
Indian Education Program
P.O. Box 2019 • Appleton, WI 54913
 Debra Torbeck, Contact

Houdini Elementary School
Indian Education Program
2305 W. Capitol Rd. • Appleton, WI 54915
 Alan Schroeder, Contact

Ashland School District
Indian Education Program
1900 Beaser Ave. • Ashland, WI 54806
 Timothy Foley, Contact

Unity School
Home-School Coord.
P.O. Box 307 • Balsam Lake, WI 54810
 Jeanie Buck, Contact

Baraboo School District
Indian Education Program
101 Second St. • Baraboo, WI 53913
 Anthony Kujawa, Contact

Fairfield Center
Indian Education Program
E-12654 County Hiway T
Baraboo, WI 53913
 Dianne Littlegeorge, Contact

Bayfield School District-Supt.
Indian Education Program
P.O. Box 5001 • Bayfield, WI 54814
 Guy Habeck, Contact

Black River Falls School
Indian Education Program
301 N. 4th St.
Black River Falls, WI 54615
 Ted Kozlowski, Contact

Bowler Public Schools
500 S. Almon Rd.
P.O. Box 8 • Bowler, WI 54416
 (715) 793-4101 Fax 793-1302
 E-mail: millerd@bowler.k12.wi.us
 Donna Miller, Title IX Program Director
Grades Pre K-12. Description: Provides tutorial assistance, cultural activities & opportunities, and resources for both staff and students.

Crandon School District
Indian Education Program
P.O. Box 310 • Crandon, WI 54520
 Tim Laabs, Contact

Cumberland School District
P.O. Box 67 • Cumberland, WI 54829
 Merwin Moen, Contact

West De Pere School District
1155 Westwood St. • De Pere, WI 54115
 James Lamal, Contact

Eau Claire School District
Indian Education Program
500 Main St. • Eau Claire, WI 54701
 (715) 833-3491; Julie Harris, Title IX Director
Grades K-12. Description: Designed to meet the special educational needs of American Indian children in the Eau Claire School District.

Freedom Area School District
Indian Education Program
P.O. Box 1008 • Freedom, WI 54131
 Tonie Anderson, Contact

Green Bay Area Public School Dist.
Indian Education Program
P.O. Box 23387 • Green Bay, WI 54305
 Adam Webster, Contact

Howard-Suamico School District
Indian Education Program
1935 Cardinal Lane
Green Bay, WI 54313
 (920) 662-7886 Fax 662-7900
 Brian Stevens, Director
 E-mail: briastev@hssd.k12.wi.us
Grades K-12. Program: Title VII Indian education program provides classroom teachers activities that are culture based and relevant to those students who are affiliated with tribes here in Wisconsin. Activities: Workshops that address Chapter 31, preparing sovereign rights of American Indians. Families are stregthened via Native staff whose responsibility includes providing support to both students and parents. Instructor: Brian Stevens.

Hayward Community Schools
P.O. Box 860 • Hayward, WI 54843
 (715) 634-2619 Fax 634-3560
 William Trautt, District Administrator
Grades: K-12. Program: Teaches the Ojibwa language & culture. Instructors: Donna Johnson, Darlene Stockinger.

Lac Courte Oreilles Ojibwe School
Route 2, Box 2800 • Hayward, WI 54843
 School Administrator

Menominee Indian School District
Indian Education Program
P.O. Box 399 • Keshena, WI 54135
 Mark Smits, Contact

Madison Metro. School District
Indian Education Program
545 W. Dayton St. • Madison, WI 53703
 Kenneth White Horse, Contact

Menominee Indian School District
Indian Education Program
P.O. Box 399 • Keshena, WI 54135
 Joseph Vigil, Contact

Menominee Tribal School
Indian Education Program
P.O. Box 910 • Keshena, WI 54135
 Kenneth Lehman, Contact

La Crosse School District
Indian Education Program
807 East Ave. South • La Crosse, WI 54601
 Karen Murray, Contact

Lac du Flambeau Public School
510 Old Abe Rd.
Lac du Flambeau, WI 54538
 Dr. Lauren Villagomez, Contact

Milwaukee Public Schools
Indian Education Program
P.O. Drawer 10-K • Milwaukee, WI 53201
 John Clifford, Contact

Lakeland Union High School
Indian Education Program
8669 Old Hwy. 70 West
Minocqua, WI 54548
 Renee Tennant, Contact

Nekoosa Public Schools
310 1st St. • Nekoosa, WI 54457
 Peter Pavioski, Contact

Oneida Tribal School
Indian Education Program
P.O. Box 365 • Oneida, WI 54155
 Grace Wills, Sharon Mousseau, Contacts

Osseo-Fairchild School District-Supt.
P.O. Box 130 • Osseo, WI 54758
 Gerald Nelson, Contact

Pulaski Community School
Indian Education Program
P.O. Box 36 • Pulaski, WI 54162
 Judy Kasper, Contact

Seymour Community School District
Indian Education Program
10 Circle Dr. • Seymour, WI 54165
 Thomas Hughes, Contact

Shawano-Gresham School District
Indian Education Program
210 S. Franklin • Shawano, WI 54166
 William Matthias, Contact

Siren School District
Indian Education Program
P.O. Box 29 • Siren, WI 54872
 Francis Decorah, Contact

Stevens Point Public School
Indian Education Program
1900 Polk St. • Stevens Point, WI 54481
 Mike Bubla, Contact

Superior School District
Indian Education Program
3025 Tower Ave. • Superior, WI 54880
Carol Stevens, Contact

Tomah Area School District
Indian Education Program
901 Lincoln Ave. • Tomah, WI 54660
Pamela Knorr, Contact

Wabeno School District
Indian Education Program
4343 Mill Lane • Wabeno, WI 54566
Debra Tucker Kruger, Contact

Washburn School District
Indian Education Program
305 W. 4th St. • Washburn, WI 54891
Clyde Sukanen

Wausau School District
Indian Education Program
415 Seymour St. • Wausau, WI 54401
Berland Meyer, Contact

Webster School District
Indian Education Program
26428 Lakeland Ave. • Webster, WI 54893
Jery Olson, Contact

Winter Community Schools
Indian Education Program
P.O. Box 7 • Winter, WI 54896
Richard C. Olson, Contact

Wisconsin Dells School District
Director of Curriculum
300 Vine St. • Wisconsin Dells, WI 53965
Scott Herrmann, Contact

Wisconsin Rapids Public Schools
Native American Coordinator
510 Peach St. • Wisconsin Rapids, WI 54494
Bonnie Smith, Contact

Wittenberg-Birnamwood School
Indian Education Program
P.O. Box 269 • Wittenberg, WI 54499
Richard Roth, Contact

WYOMING

Arapahoe School
Fremont County School District #38
P.O. Box 9211
Arapahoe, WY 82510
(307) 856-9333
Marilyn Clausen, Contact
E-mail: mclausen@fremont38.k12.wy.us
Grades K-18. 270 students. Located on the
Wind River Indian Reservation

Ft. Washakie School District #21
Indian Education Program
Box 110 Ethete Rd.
Fort Washakie, WY 82512
George Zerga, Contact

Wyoming Indian Education Office
Indian Education Program
Fort Washakie, WY 82514
Nola McLeod, Contact

Fremont Co. School District #1
Indian Education Program
Baldwin Creek Rd.
Lander, WY 82520
Jim Robeson, Contact

Riverton High School/S.D.#25
Indian Education Program
2001 West Sunset
Riverton, WY 82501
(307) 856-9491 ext. 13 Fax 856-2333
June Shakespeare, Director
Grades K-12. *Description*: Provides academic, cultural
enrichment and tutoring services for American Indian
children residing in the district; also service referrals,
Indian clubs.

St. Stephans Indian School
Indian Education Program
P.O. Box 345
St. Stephans, WY 82524
George Moss, Contact

This section, alpha-geographically arranged, lists departments and personnel of various institutions of higher learning which offer courses on the American Indian. Includes both Indian colleges, and universities with Native Studies Departments, departments of anthropology, and other departments offering related courses.

ALABAMA

AUBURN UNIVERSITY
Department of Sociology & Anthropology
6090 Haley Center • AUBURN, AL 36849
  (334) 844-5049
Instructors: John Cottier, PhD, Craig T. Sheldon, Jr., PhD. *Facilities*: Library-study collections. *Publications*: Archaeological monograph series.

UNIVERSITY OF ALABAMA
Dept. of Anthropology, 19 Ten Hoor Hall
Box 870210 • TUSCALOOSA, AL 35487
  (205) 348-5947 Web site: www.as.ua.edu/ant/
Graduate program emphasizes the anthropology of health & complex societies of Native Americans.

ALASKA

UNIVERSITY OF ALASKA
Dept. of Anthropology, 3211 Providence Dr.
ANCHORAGE, AK 99508
  (907) 786-6840 Fax 786-6850
  William B. Workman, PhD, Chairperson
Instructors: William B. Workman, PhD, Douglas W. Veltre, PhD, Alan Boraas, PhD, Robert A. Mack, Charles E. Holmes, PhD (Northern Athabascan ethnoarchaeology). Institute of Social and Economic Research. *Special program*: Summer school in Alaskan archaeology.

UNIVERSITY OF ALASKA
Department of Alaskan Native Studies
Department of Anthropology, Box 757720
310 Eielson Bldg. • FAIRBANKS, AK 99775
  (907) 474-7288; 474-7453
  Phyllis Morrow, PhD, Dept. Head
Courses: Native Cultures of North America, South America, and Alaska; Arctic and New World Prehistory; Biology of Arctic Peoples; seminars on specialized aspects of Eskimo, Aleut, and Athapaskan groups. Regular instruction in Inupiaq, Yup'ik, and Athabaskan offered by the Alaska Native Language Center. *Instructors*: David C. Koester, PhD, Molly Lee, PhD, Phyllis Fast, PhD, Maribeth Murray, PhD, Peter Schweitzer, PhD, David M. Smith, PhD, Lydia T. Black, PhD, Phyllis Morrow, PhD, W. Rogers Powers, PhD, G. Richard Scott, PhD William S. Schneider, PhD. *Programs*: Graduate and faculty research is primarily directed to the study of Eskimo-Aleuts and North American Indians (their prehistory, cultural variability, and human biology); teaching assistantships to graduate students. *Affiliated facilities*: University of Alaska Museum; Alaska Native Language Center. *Publications*: Anthropological Papers of the University of Alaska.

UNIVERSITY OF ALASKA
Northwest College Campus
Pouch 400 • NOME, AK 99762
  (907) 443-2201 Barbara Oleson, Contact
A rural site of the Rural College of the University of Alaska, Fairbanks providing post-secondary education to the Seward Peninsula region.

SHELDON JACKSON COLLEGE
SITKA 99835
Native Studies Program.

ARIZONA

NORTHERN ARIZONA UNIVERSITY
Graduate College-Consortium for
Graduate Opportunities for American Indians

P.O. Box 4085 • FLAGSTAFF 86011
Description: A consortium of institutions cooperating in the recruitment of American Indian students to academic graduate programs. *Activities*: Identifies a pool of qualified Indian undergraduate students at participating institutions; organizes faculty networks; provides inforamtion on financial aid. *Publication*: Newsletter.

NORTHERN ARIZONA UNIVERSITY
Department of Anthropology, Box 15200
FLAGSTAFF, AZ 86011 (520) 523-3180
  Francis E. Smiley, Chairperson
Special Program: Native American Indian Studies. *Courses*: Native American Indian History; Contemporary U.S. Indians; Southwest Ethnology: Pueblo and non-Pueblo; Tribal Law and Government; Financing Tribal Government and Administration; Tribal Planning and Management; Current Issues in Tribal Administration. *Instructors*: Reed D. Riner, PhD (Advisor to Program); Joanne W. Keallinohomoku, PhD, Kurt E. Dongoske, MA, Anthony L. Klesert, PhD, Diane M. Notarianni, PhD, Zdenek Salzmann, PhD, Robert M. Schacht, PhD, , David R. Wilcox, PhD (Curator, Museum of Northern Arizona), Michael Yeatts, MA, Phyllis Hogan (Arizona Indian herbology). *Special program*: Native American United Club. *Affiliated facilities*: Department participates in the Museum of Northern Arizona Joint Scholar in Residence Program; a cooperative program with the Navajo Nation Archaeology Dept. and the Hopi Nation; and has cooperative agreements with Grand Canyon National Park, Glen Canyon National Recreation Area, and Wupatki National Monument; Native Americans for Community Action, Flagstaff. *Publications*: Anthropological Papers; Technical Report Series.

NORTHERN ARIZONA UNIVERSITY
Native American Forestry Program
School of Forestry • FLAGSTAFF 86011
  (520) 523-6653 Fax 523-6143
  Ronald L. Trosper, Contact
Purpose: To develop educational and research activities that support Native American tribes in achieving self-determination in the management of their natural resources. *Goal*: To increase the retention and graduation of Native Americans at the School of Forestry.

NORTHERN ARIZONA UNIVERSITY
Navajo Nation Archaeology Dept.
P.O. Box 6013 • FLAGSTAFF, AZ 86011
  (520) 523-7428
  Anthony L. Klesert, PhD, Director
Established to enable Navajos who are interested in a career in anthropology and gaining practical experience and training in cultural resource management.

SCOTTSDALE COMMUNITY COLLEGE
Native American Studies Program
9000 E. Chaparral St. • SCOTTSDALE, AZ 85256
  (602) 423-6139
  John Silvester, Contact

*TOHONO O'ODHAM COMMUNITY COLLEGE
P.O. Box 3129 • SELLS, AZ 85634
  Dr. Robert G. Martin, President

ARIZONA STATE UNIVERSITY
Department of Anthropology
Box 872402 • TEMPE, AZ 85287
  (480) 965-6213 Fax 965-7671
Division: Indian Education; American Indian Linguistics; and Center for Indian Affairs. *Instructors (partial)*: Elizabeth A. Brandt, PhD (North American Indian languages); Scott C. Russell, PhD (Native American Studies); Peter Welsh, PhD; Tressa L. Berman, PhD (sociocultural anthropology); Kathleen M. Sands, PhD (American Indian literature, Dept. of English). *Facilities*: Heard Museum; Pueblo Grande Museum; A.A. Dahlberg Memorial Collection of 9,000 Pima Indian dental casts and genealogies.

ARIZONA STATE UNIVERSITY
Center for Indian Education
College of Education • TEMPE, AZ 85287
  (480) 965-6292

ARIZONA STATE UNIVERSITY
College of Law-Indian Legal Program
Box 877906 • TEMPE, AZ 85287

  (480) 965-6204
  Siera Russell, Director
ARIZONA STATE UNIVERSITY
Labriola National American Indian Data Center
Box 871006 • TEMPE, AZ 85287-1006
  (480) 965-3417 Fax 965-9169
  Patricia A. Etta, Curator
Website: www.asu.edu/libarchives/labriola.htm
Supports the American Indian Studies Program and provides a facility where students can research and study. Collection contains information on all North American tribes including Alaskan Natives. Provides access to the information through the use of computer databnases, the Internet, and CD-ROM. Newsletter.

COOK COLLEGE & THEOLOGICAL SCHOOL
Academic Affairs Dept.
708 S. Lindon Lane • TEMPE, AZ 85281
  (480) 968-9354 Fax 968-9357
  Susan Rockwell, PhD, Dean
  E-mail: srockwell@cookcollege.org
Website: www.cookcollege.org
Instructor: Larry Norris, PhD, Susan Rockwell, PhD, Dona Avery, Dale Randefeld, Ron Patnaude, Mark Thomas, Spencer Hoff, Phil Keller, Judy Hunnicutt, Kenny Kim. *Programs*: AA Programs: Christian Ministry, American Indian Studies, Liberal Studies; College Bridge Program to help students learn the skills and develop the attitudes for college success using culturally relevant materials and practices; Residency Program offers foundational studies and an AA Degree in Pastoral Studies. Member of the Native American Theological Education Consortium in the U.S. Theological Library Cooperative of Arizona.

*DINE COLLEGE
P.O. Box 126 • TSAILE, AZ 86556
  (520) 724-6671 Fax 724-3327
  Ferlin Clark, Interim President
  James K. McNeley, Ph.D., Vice-President
  Web site: www.crystal.ncc.cc.nm.us/
Fully accredited and chartered by the Navajo Nation Council. Enrolls an average of 1,800 students. *Degrees*: Associate of Arts, Associate of Applied Science; Preprofessional programs; Certification programs. Navajo history, language and culture are integrated into the traditional academic subjects of all College curriculum to enhance students' respect for the Navajo heritage. *Navajo and Indian Studies Program*: Offers many courses in the broad area of Navajo studies; some are directly related to the Navajo, and others are related to Indians in general. *Courses (partial)*: Navajo History and Culture; Navajo Language; American Indian Economic Development; The Urban Indians; Navajo Crafts courses. *Center for Dine Studies Faculty*: Wilson Aronilth, Jr., Avery Denny, Donald Denetdeal, Martha Jackson, and Thomas Littlebren, Jr. *Community Campus Faculty*: Edna Braxton and Lorene Legah. DC West Community Campus Staff: Chinle Campus: Carletta Nez, Director, Susie Salt, Academic Advisor; Ganado Campus: Paul Willeto, Director/Academic Advisor; Kaytenta Office: Lawrence Issac, Jr., Coordinator; Tuba City Campus: Harold Joseph, Director, Phyllis T. Begay, Academic Advisor; Window Rock Campus: Edith Begaye, Director/Academic Advisor; Continuing Education-Tuba City: Lena Fowler, Director. *Programs*: Special Services Program for academically unprepared students; Learning Center provides tutorial services for students. *Scholarships*: For information, contact the Financial Aide Office, ext. 223/224. *Facility*: College Library houses the Moses Donner Indian Collection; Hatathli Gallery - products include jewelry, paintings, rugs, sand paintings and other art items. *Branches*: see Dine College East-Shiprock Branch.

UNIVERSITY OF ARIZONA
Dept. of Anthropology
Emil Haury Anthropology Bldg., Rm. 221A
1009 E. South Campus Dr., Bldg. #30
TUCSON, AZ 85721
  (520) 621-2585 Fax 621-2088
  John W. Olsen, PhD, Chairperson
  E-mail: anthro@u.arizona.edu
Website: www.w3.arizona.edu/~anthro/
Faculty: Jane E. Hill, PhD (Native American languages); Bruce Hilpert, MA (American Indians of the Southwest); E. Charles Adams, PhD (director of Homolovi Research Program; Pueblo groups); Diane

Austin, PhD (Native American Environmental policy); Thomas R. McGuire, PhD (Native American economic development); Nancy J. Parezo, PhD (Native American art and material culture); Emory Sekaquaptewa, JD (Hopi language and culture); Richard W. Stoffle, PhD (Native peoples of the Southwest); M. Nieves Zedeno, PhD (American Indian cultural resource preservation).

UNIVERSITY OF ARIZONA
American Indian Professional Training Program
in Speech-Language Pathology & Audiology
Dept. of Speech & Hearing Sciences
TUCSON, AZ 85721 (520) 621-1969
Dr. Ted Glatke, Director
Betty Nunnery, Program Coordinator
Objectives: To recruit, retain, and provide education to American Indian men and women in the fields of speech-language pathology or audiology. *Goals*: To qualify students for a Master's degree in speech-language pathology or audiology; to integrate the study of Indian languages and cultures into the training program; to develop therapy programs sensitive to Indian cultural needs; to establish a professional work force to serve American Indians who have communication disorders both on and off reservations. *Activities/Programs*: Speech & hearing clinics operated on two reservation sites. Scholarship recipients receive a tuition waiver and a stipend. Library. *Publications*: Directory of Native Americans in Speech-Language Pathology & Audiology; newsletter, Desert Connections, a network publication for Native American speech-language pathologists & audiologists.

UNIVERSITY OF ARIZONA
American Indian Studies Programs
The Harvill Bldg, Room 430
P.O. Box 210076 • TUCSON, AZ 85721
(520) 621-7108 Fax 621-7952
Shelly Lowe (Navajo), Graduate Education
Program Facilitator
Hamp Merrill, Special Assistant to the
Director of American Indian Studies
Sheilah Nicholas (Hopi), Program
Coordinator for (AILDI)
Sylvia Polacca (Tewa), Program Facilitator
for Community Development
E-mail: aisp@email.arizona.edu
Website: http://w3.arizona.edu/~aisp/index.html
The University of Arizona was the first educational institution in the country to offer a PhD program in American Indian Studies. The Inter-Tribal Graduate Interdisciplinary Program in American Indian Studies (AISP) provides graduate programs offering opportunities for advanced study in American Indian Law and Policy, Literatures, Societies and Culture, and American Indian Education. *Outreach & Service Opportunities*: The AISP Office of Community Development; Red Ink, a biannual publication providing opportunities for students to work on a nationall distributed publication of poetry, short stories, creative non-fiction, original artwork, book and film reviews; The American Indian Language Development Institute (AILDI); Tribal Law & Policy Program. *Faculty*: Barbara Babcock, PhD (Southwest Indian cultures, especially Pueblo); Manley Begay, (Navajo) EdD (tribal economic development); Stephen Cornell, PhD (American Indian policy); Larry Evers, PhD (American Indian literature); Mary Jo Tippeconnic Fox, (Comanche/Cherokee) PhD (American Indian higher education; American Indian women's issues); Robert Alan Hershey, J.D. (Indian law); Joe Hiller (Lakota), PhD (agriculture and natural resources technical & policy issues, especially water); Tom Helm (Creek/Cherokee), PhD (Federal Indian policy); Jennie Joe (Navajo), PhD (American Indian health issues); Hartman M. Lomawaima (Hopi), EdM (museology & ethnology); K. Tsianina Lomawaima (Creek), PhD (history of American Indian education, ethnohistory); Eileen Luna (Choctaw/Cherokee), J.D. (Tribal governments, law enforcement on reservations, Federal Indian policy); Teresa L. McCarty, PhD (bilingual/bicultural education); N. Scott Momaday (Kiowa), PhD (Oral traditions); Nancy J. Parezo, PhD (ethnohistory, especially Navajo); Alice Paul (Tohono O'odham), PhD (Emeritus); Emory Sekaquaptewa (Hopi), J.D. (Hopi language & culture); Jay Stauss (Jamestown Band S'Klallam), PhD (Pacific Northwest tribes); Richard Stoffle, PhD (American Indian social impact assessment, natural resource policy); Luci Tapahonso (Na-

vajo), MA (contemporary poetry in American Indian literature); Robert Williams, Jr. (Lumbee) J.D. (Indian law and policy); Mary Ann Willie (Navajo) PhD (Navajo syntax, Athabaskan linguistics); Melanie Yazzie (Navajo) MFA (contemporary indigenous artists); Ofelia Zepeda (Tohono O'odham) PhD (structure of Tohono O'odham language). *Special Programs*: Archaeological Field School; Native American Research and Training Center (602) 621-5075; Native American Speech and Hearing Program (602) 621-1969. *Financial Aid*: Graduate Student support. *Facilities*: American Indian Language Development Institute (AILDI); Native American Resource Center (602) 621-3835; Western Archaeological Center; Arizona State Museum. *Publication*: Anthropological Papers of the University of Arizona.

UNIVERSITY OF ARIZONA
American Indian Graduate Student Center
Office of Indian Programs • TUCSON, AZ 85721
(520) 621-2794; Glenn Johnson, Director
Responsible for providing financial support, publication opportunities, academic counseling and cultural support to the 80 Native American graduate students at the University. It is the only graduate center of its kind in the nation.

UNIVERSITY OF ARIZONA
Native American Research and Training Center
TUCSON, AZ 85721
Carol Locust, Contact
Project: American Indian Disability Legislation: Toward the Development of a Process that Respects Soveriegnty and Cultural Diversity.

ARKANSAS

UNIVERSITY OF ARKANSAS
Department of Anthropology
Old Main 330 • FAYETTEVILLE, AR 72701
(501) 575-2508 Fax 575-6595
Instructors: Michael P. Hoffman, PhD; Marvin Kay, PhD; and Allen McCartney, PhD. *Special Programs*: Summer Archaeological Field School. *Scholarships*: Arkansas residency for tuition purposes to tribes which once lived in the State (Caddo, Cherokee, Choctaw, Creek, Kickapoo, Osage, Quapaw, Shawnee and Tunica). S.C. Dellinger Award for promising anthropology students; minority graduate fellowships. *Facility*: University of Arkansas Museum. *Publications*: Plains Anthropologist; Arctic Anthropology; publications of the Arkansas Archaeological Survey.

CALIFORNIA

HUMBOLDT STATE UNIVERSITY
The Center for Indian Community Development
ARCATA, CA 95521 (707) 826-3711
Lois J. Risling, Director
American Indian Languages and Literature Program: The program first adapted an internationally acknowledged, easy-to-learn, uniphonetic alphabet to write Indian languages precisely, and then schooled fluent local speakers in its use and dissemination. The program has enabled four northwestern California tribes to salvage their venerable literatures; publish them in tribally compiled textbooks; document their (pre-) history; and, record and compile their traditional music. The Program has produced five internationally acclaimed documentary films explicating this complex cultural regenerative process; and organize these elements into curricula for use in preschool, elementary and secondary schools, and in college and unverstiy classrooms. A scholarly curriculum was created in an intertribal network of American Indian community development projects. The California Department of Education recognized the program, and the most eminent (generally elderly) Indian graduates were given credentials to teach in the public schools and colleges. *Special program*: Special project/lectureship stipends and bilingual teacher training internships. *Publications*. Library (primarily own publications, such as Indian language and literature texts, and American Indian bilingual teacher training instructional materials.)

HUMBOLDT STATE UNIVERSITY
Dept. of Sociology, Anthropology & Social Work
ARCATA, CA 95521
(707) 826-3139
Instructors: Llyn Smith, PhC (Religion), Pat Wenger, PhD (Linguistics), Allan Bramlette (Native American Studies), Victor Golla, PhD (Native American Studies; Director, Center for Community Development).

HUMBOLDT STATE UNIVERSITY
Indian Natural Resource, Science
& Engineering Program
McMahan House 80 • ARCATA, CA 95521
(707) 826-4994
Russell Boham, Director
Description: Support program for Native American students pursuing a degree in Natural Resources, Science, or Engineering. Courtses pertinent to Native American natural resources (e.g. Native American water law, tribal government, abd tribal perspectives toward natural resources.

HUMBOLDT STATE UNIVERSITY
Indian Teacher & Educational
Personnel Program (ITEPP)
1 Harpst St., Spidell House #85
ARCATA, CA 95521
(707) 826-3672 Fax 826-3675
Suzanne M. Burcell, Director
E-Mail: smb7001@humboldt.edu
Web site: www.humboldt.edu/~hsuitepp
Description: A support program (the oldest in the nation) which recruits and trains American Indians to become educators and ancillary education personnel. Offers courses and field work. *Instructors*: Carolyn Anderson, PhD; Susan Cameron, PhD; Suzanne Burcell. *Special program*: American Indian Education Summer Institutes. *Facility*: ITEPP's Curriculum Resource Center houses a collection of books, videos, microfilm, and curricula materials all relating to Native American issues and topics. Library

UNIVERSITY OF CALIFORNIA
Native American Studies Department
Dwinelle Hall, Suite 3415
BERKELEY, CA 94720
(510) 642-6717
Instructors (partial): Robert A. Black, PhD; Terry P. Wilson, PhD; Jean Molesky, MA, Gerald Vizenor, MA, Clara Sue Kidwell, PhD, Karen Biestman, LLD, and Louana Ross, PhD.

UNIVERSITY OF CALIFORNIA
American Indian Graduate Program
316 Sproul Hall #5900
BERKELEY, CA 94720-5900
(510) 642-3228 Fax 643-8909
Carmen A. Foghorn, Coordinator
E-Mail: aigp@berkeley.edu
Website: www.grad.berkeley.edu/aigp
Description: Provides outreach, recruitment, and student services to counteract the barriers that prevent the full participation of American Indian and Alaska Native students in graduate education.

FOOTHILL-DE ANZA COMMUNITY COLLEGE
12345 El Monte Rd.
LOS ALTOS HILLS, CA 94022
(650) 949-6217

***DEGANAWIDA QUETZECOATL
D-Q UNIVERSITY**
Native American Studies Program
P.O. Box 409 • DAVIS, CA 95617
(530) 758-0470 Fax 758-4891
Dr. Morgan G. Otis, President
Description: A two-year community college, tribally owned and controlled, dedicated to the progress of the Native-American and Chicano people. The student body is 70% Native American (with an upward of 60 tribal affiliations from across the country represented). *Purpose*: To educate indigenous people, while offering the traditional programs as well as specialized majors in indigenous studies. *Programs*: Provides educational and community services to Indian tribes and their people. The curriculum leads to an A.A. or A.S. degree in 9 academic majors. Financial aid available. Library.

UNIVERSITY OF CALIFORNIA
College of Letters and Science
Native American Studies Dept.
2401 Hart Hall • DAVIS, CA 95616
(916) 752-3237 Fax 752-7097
  Jack D. Forbes, PhD, Dept. Head
Description: Interdisciplinary in its approach, the department focuses upon the indigenous people of the Americas - the peoples, nations, and tribes who have lived in North, Central, and South America for thousands of years. Offers undergraduate and graduate degrees in Native American Studies *Instructors*: Jack D. Forbes, PhD; Steven Crum, PhD; Ines Hernandez-Avila, PhD; Sarah Hutchison, MA, Emeritus; George C. Longfish, PhD; Martha Macri, PhD; Annette Reed-Crum, MA; David Risling, Jr., MA, Emeritus; Stefano Varese, PhD; Wilbor Wilson, PhD. *Services/Programs*: Native American Organized Research Program (Director, Dr. Stefano Varese); EOP Outreach Services; Counseling; workshops, educational programs, lectures, and conferences. *Financial Aid*:Various awards; Mentorships & Internships. *Facilities*: The C.N. Gorman Museum and Art Gallery - maintains a permanent collection and shows works by Indian and Chicano artists as well as staff and students. *Publications*: American Words...Native Words Used in English; A Model of Grassroots Community Development: The DQU Native American Language Project; History of Tecumseh Center; Racism, Scholarship & Pluralism in Higher Education; Religious Freedom & the Protection of Native American Places of Worship; The Papago-Apache Treaty of 1853: Property Rights & Religious Liberties.

KUMEYAAY COMMUNITY COLLEGE
Sycuan Band of Kumeyaay Nation Reservation
5459 Dehesa Rd. • EL CAJON, CA 92021
(619) 445-2613 Fax 445-1927

COLLEGE OF THE REDWOODS
Native American Studies Progam
EUREKA, CA 95501
(800) 458-5300; (707) 445-6761
  Jim Harrington, Dean of Student Services

CALIFORNIA STATE UNIVERSITY
Dept. of Anthropology
HAYWARD, CA 94542
(415) 881-3168
  Instructor: Lowell J. Bean, Ph.D. (Director, Smith Museum of Anthropology). *Special Facility*: Clarence E. Smith Museum of Anthropology.

CALIFORNIA STATE UNIVERSITY
Dept. of Ethnic Studies
HAYWARD, CA 94542
(415) 881-3181
  Michael Clark, Chairperson
Instructor: Roxanne Dubar Ortiz, Native American Studies.

UNIVERSITY OF CALIFORNIA, IRVINE
School of Social Sciences
3151 Social Science Plaza
IRVINE, CA 92697-5100
(714) 824-5894
  E-Mail: jjorgens@orion.oac.eci.edu
Courses pertaining to the Indians, Aleuts, and Eskimos of North America (Past and Present). *Instructors*: Joseph G. Jorgensen, PhD; Stephanie Reynolds, PhD.

UNIVERSITY OF CALIFORNIA, IRVINE
Native American Preparatory School
School of Social Ecology
IRVINE, CA 92717
(714) 856-7698
  Randal Ray, Admissions
Summer program - a five-week residential learning experience open too gifted and talented Native American students entering 8th or 9th grade.

CALIFORNIA STATE UNIVERSITY
Dept. of Anthropology, 1250 Bellflower Blvd.
LONG BEACH, CA 90840 (213) 498-5171
  Pamela A. Bunte, Chair
Special program: Certificates in American Indian Studies. *Instructors* (partial): Pamela A. Bunte, PhD, and Keith Dixon, PhD.

UNIVERSITY OF CALIFORNIA, LOS ANGELES
American Indian Studies Center & Library
3220 Campbell Hall, Box 951548
LOS ANGELES, CA 90095-1548
(310) 825-7315 Fax 206-7060
  Duane Champagne, Director
  Paul V. Kroskrity, Chair (IDP Program)
Description: The Center ranks among the top research centers of its kind in the country serving the educational and cultural needs of the American Indian community. *Activities*: Sponsors research and administers competetive grants; offers a minor, masters and a concurrent law program; publishes books; encourages the development of new courses, addresses recruitment of American Indian students and faculty; offers a forum for scholarly exchange for American Indian students, the community and alumni; and sponsors an annual Pow Wow in the Spring quarter. *Program*: Administers an Interdepartmental Master's Program in American Indian Studies. *Fellowships*: Postdoctoral Fellowships in American Indian Studies. *Facilities*: The Museum of Cultural History; Library; the publications unit produces numerous books, bibliographies, monographs. *Publication*: "American Indian Culture and Research Journal."

UNIVERSITY OF CALIFORNIA, LOS ANGELES
Dept. of Anthropology, 3207 Hershey Hall
Box 951553 • LOS ANGELES, CA 90024
(310) 825-2055 Fax 206-7833
  Joan B. Silk, Chairperson
Faculty: Gail E. Kennedy, PhD; Linda Garro, PhD; Russell Thronton, PhD; Paul V. Kroskrity, PhD (American Indian languages).

CALIFORNIA STATE UNIVERSITY
Dept. of Anthropology, 18111 Nordhoff St.
NORTHRIDGE, CA 91330 (818) 885-3331
Program: American Indian Studies Program.
Instructors: Beatrice Medicine, PhD; Charles Muzny, PhD.

UNIVERSITY OF CALIFORNIA, RIVERSIDE
Dept. of History • RIVERSIDE, CA 92521
(909) 787-5401 ext. 11974 Fax 787-5299
  Sharon Salinger, Chairperson
  Clifford Trafzer & Monte Kugel, Professors
  E-mail: cetrafzer@aol.com
Program: American Indian Studies. *Instructors*: Clifford Trafzer (History, Literature, Religion), Rebecca "Monte" Kugel, Michelle Raheja, Robert Perez, Jacqueline Shea-Murphy; Victoria Bomberry. *Special programs*: MA and PhD in American Indian History; California Indians and the Southwest; Oral History; American Indians and Public History; Sherman Indian School Museum *Publications*: Native American Studies: University of California, Riverside, by Clifford Trafzer, 1991; Dear Christopher, Letters by Contemporary Native Americans to Christopher Columbus, by Darryl Wilson and Barry Joyce, 1992.

SONOMA STATE UNIVERSITY
Native American Studies Program
ROHNERT PARK, CA 94928
(707) 664-2450
  Edward D. Castillo, PhD, Director
Provides a minor featuring a multi-disciplinary approach to Indian ethnography, history, sociology, and humanities. Courses: Indians of California, North America, and Southwest; Native American Philosophic Systems; Archaeology of California; Seminar of California Indian Communities. *Instructors*: Priscilla Rios, David A. Frederickson, PhD, Shirley K. Silver, PhD, Albert L. Wahrhaftig, PhD, and David W. Peri. *Special activity*: Spring Indian Fair. *Scholarships*: E.O.P. Scholarships; Sonoma State University Native American Student Scholarship. *Facilities*: Archaeology and ethnography labs and archives. *Publications*: Occasional Papers of Native American Studies.

CALIFORNIA STATE UNIVERSITY
Department of Anthropology
6000 Jay St.
SACRAMENTO, CA 95819
(916) 278-6452
Special program: California Indian Studies. *Instructors*: Troy Armstrong, PhD; Michael G. Delacorte, PhD; Dorothea J. Theodoratus, PhD, & Valerie Wheeler, PhD

CALIFORNIA STATE UNIVERSITY
Native American Studies Program
6000 Jay St. • SACRAMENTO, CA 95819
(916) 278-3901
  Larry Glasmire, Contact

SAN DIEGO STATE UNIVERSITY
American Indian Studies Department
College Ave. • SAN DIEGO, CA 92182-0387
(619) 594-6991
  Dr. Clifford E. Trafzer, Professor & Chair
Description: Offers a minor in American Indian studies offering courses on a variety of subjects from Indian heritage to contemporary society, literature, music, and history. *Instructors*: Linda S. Parker, Jay Stauss, Alan Kilpatrick, David Whitehorse, Ralph Forquera, Patricia Dixon, Richard Carrico. *Special programs*: American Indian Storytellings; annual American Indian Pow Wow. Student Organization: The North American Indian Student Alliance. American Indian Culture Week each spring. Library: Golsh Collection - consists of rare documents and books. *Publications*: Publications in American Indian Studies; American Indian Identity, edited by C.E. Trafzer; Strangers in a Stolen Land, by Carrico; The Quechens; Gods Among Us, by Coates.

SAN DIEGO STATE UNIVERSITY
Department of Anthropology
5500 Campanile Dr. • SAN DIEGO, CA 92182
(619) 594-5527 Fax 594-1150
Special facilities: The linguistics laboratory offers facilities for experience with local Indian dialects; Athabaskan. *Instructor*: Philip J. Greenfield, PhD (Linguistics); Michael G. Baksh, PhD (culture change); Alan Kilpatrick, PhD (witchcraft & shamanism).

SAN FRANCISCO STATE UNIVERSITY
American Indian Studies Department
1600 Holloway Ave.
SAN FRANCISCO, CA 94132
(415) 338-1934 E-mail: luiseno@sfsu.edu
Instructors: Joely De La Torre, Jow Meyers, Betty Parent. *Programs*: American Indian Studies Review Journal; Annual Pow Wow. *Financial Aid*: Jacques Johnet Scholarship for American Indians. Library. *Facility*: The Adan E. Treganza Anthropology Museum.

CALIFORNIA POLYTECHNIC UNIVERSITY
Ethnic Studies Program
SAN LUIS OBISPO, CA 93401
(805) 756-1707
  Robert F. Gish, Chairperson
  E-Mail: rgish@calpoly.edu
  Web site: http://www.calpoly.edu/~es
Program offers a minor in Ethnic Studies with concentration in American Indian Studies. *Instructor*: Robert Gish. *Course*: American Cultural Images: American Indians Ethnicity and the Land. *Publication*: SIYO; A Journal of New Writers. Library.

PALOMAR COMMUNITY COLLEGE
American Indian Studies Program
1140 W. Mission Rd.
SAN MARCOS, CA 92069
(619) 744-1150 Fax 744-8123
  Patricia Dixon, Chairperson
Programs: Certification Program in American Indian Studies/American Indian Education Center at Pauma Reservation. *Courses*: History of Native American Arts; California Indian Arts, American Indian Literature; American Indian Philosophy & Religion; American Indian Women; History of the Plains and Southwest Indians; American Indian Education; among others. *Faculty*: Steven Crouthamel, Patricia Dixon, Linda Locklear. *Instructors*: Flora Howe, Larry Lewis, Victoria Featherstone, John Grider, Kathryn Clenney, James Barker, Christopher Sullivan, Juana Majel Dixon. Naida Garcia, Education Center Assistant at Pauma Reservation. *Activities*: American Indian Organization - established in 1969 by Indian students at Palomar to encourage Indian participation & organization in education, & promotes cultural activities. Financial aid.

SANTA BARBARA CITY COLLEGE
Native American Studies Program
SANTA BARBARA, CA 93109
(805) 965-0581; Jane G. Craven

STANFORD UNIVERSITY
American Indian & Alaska Native Program
Old Union Clubhouse #12
STANFORD, CA 94305
(415) 725-6944 Fax 725-6900
Denni Diane Woodward, Administrator
E-Mail: denni.woodward@forsyth.stanford.edu
Web site: http://www.stanford.edu
Description: A division of Student Affairs, the American Indian & Alaska Native Program and its Native American Cultural Center provide resources and nurturing environments for Stanford's Native community. AIANP/NACC is the site of events, a headquarters for student organizations, the publisher of "ComingVoice," and liaison between local and national Native American groups, including Native Hawaiians.

COLORADO

UNIVERSITY OF COLORADO
Dept. of Anthropology
American Indian Studies Program
CB 233 • BOULDER, CO 80309
(303) 492-7947; Fax 492-1871
Web site: www.colorado.edu/anthropology
Special program: American Indian Studies Program.
Instructors: Frank W. Eddy, PhD; Deward E. Walker, Jr., PhD; Dorothea V. Kaschube, PhD; Jack Kelso, PhD.

UNIVERSITY OF COLORADO
SCHOOL OF LAW
American Indian Law Program
404 UCB - Fleming Law Bldg., Rm. 080
BOULDER, CO 80309-0404
(303) 492-0966 Fax 492-4587
Jill E. Tompkins, Director, Indian Law Clinic
E-mail: jill.tompkins@colorado.edu
Website: www.colorado.edu/law
Faculty: David Getches, Dean & Professor of Law; Prof. Charles Wilkinson; Assoc. Prof. Sarah Krakoff; Jill Tompkins, Clinic Director. *Description*: - The American Indian Law Clinic gives students hand-on experience in the practice of federal and tribal Indian law while providing low-income persons with quality legal representation. Under the supervision of the Clinic's director, student attorneys are involved in a wide spectrum of Indian law work including representing tribes or Indian parents in Indian Child Welfare Act cases, assisting individuals with tribal enrollment, advocating for protection of Indian religious practices and sacred lands and addressing racial discrimination. Students have the opportunity t work directly with Indian tribes on tribal constitution and code development. *Special programs*: Externships with NARF, Native American Rights Fund, the Tribal Program of the U.S. Environmental Protection Agent (EPA), the Intertribal Council on Utility Policy, and the Southern Ute Tribal Court; Indian law career opportunities; scholarships & fellowships; Native American Law Students Association (NALSA). Library.

UNIVERSITY OF COLORADO
Dept.of Ethnic Studies
Ketchum 30, CB 339
BOULDER, CO 80309
(303) 492-8852
Dr. Evelyn Hu-DeHart, Chair
Research activities: Comparative race and ethnicity and specific ethnic groups, including Native Americans.

UNIVERSITY OF COLORADO
Dept. of Linguistics, Center for the Study of Native Languages of the Plains & Southwest
CB 295 • BOULDER, CO 80309
(303) 492-2748
Dr. Allen R. Taylor, Director
Research activities: Collects data and conducts research on Native American languages of the Great Plains and Southwest, including the Siouan languages, Gros Ventre, Kiowa, and Wichita. Also includes the Lakota Project, which offers instructional materials to aid in learning Dakota Sioux language.

COLORADO COLLEGE
Dept. of Anthropology
14 E. Cache la Poudre
COLORADO SPRINGS, CO 80903
(719) 389-6360 Fax 389-6258
Instructors: Paul Kutsche, PhD (Cherokee); Marianne L. Stoller, PhD (Social Anthropology); Laurel J. Watkins, PhD (Linguistics); Victoria L. Levine, PhD (Music). *Facility*: Alice Bemis Taylor Museum.

UNIVERSITY OF DENVER
University College, Liberal Studies Dept.
American Indian Studies Program
2211 S. Josephine St. • DENVER, CO 80208
(303) 871-3381 or 871-2306 Fax 871-4877
Jan Steinhauser, Dept. Director
Farrell Howell, Program Director
E-Mail: jsteinha@dv.edu; fhowell@du.edu
Program: Developed to be reflective of Indian perspectives and the Indian faculty presents an interdisciplinary approach to the variety of beliefs and practices within American Indian communities and focuses on the current vitality and continuous development of the Indian people. *Courses*: Courses leading to a Certificate of Advanced Study in American Indian History and Cultures, as well as a Master of Liberal Arts with a concentration in American Indian Studies. *Instructors*: Rick Williams; John Compton; George Tinker, PhD; Jeanne Whiteing, JD; Suzanne Benally; Jan Jacobs; Mark Guthrie; Richard Conn; James Jordan, PhD; Lisa Harjo. *Special programs*: On campus lectures by visiting Indian writers and scholars presented as free events to the community; Native American Student Alliance on campus. Financial aid available. *Facility*: Penrose Library.

FORT LEWIS COLLEGE
Department of Anthropology
FORT LEWIS, CO 81301
(970) 247-7500 Fax 247-7205
Susan Riches, Chairperson
Special programs: Southern Ute archaeological field school, cooperative training and education program conducted with the Navajo Nation Archaeology Department (NNAD). *Instructors*: David L. Kozak, PhD; Anthony L. Klesert, PhD (Director of NNAD).

FORT LEWIS COLLEGE
Dept. of Southwest Studies
120 Miller Student Center
100 Rim Dr. • DURANGO, CO 81301
(970) 247-7590 Fax 247-7686
Richard N. Ellis, PhD, Chair
E-Mail: ellis_r@fortlewis.edu
Courses: Native American & Southwest Studies; other Indian content courses offered through other departments. *Faculty*: Robert Bunting, Richard Ellis, Andrew Gulliford, Mary Jean Moseley, Duane Smith, Richard Wheelock. *Special programs*: Minor in Native American Studies; Minor in Heritage Preservation. *Activities*: Hozhoni Days—a celebration sponsored by the Indian Club for sharing Native-American culture with students and faculty on campus. *Scholarships*: Tuition waiver for Native-American students certified by their respective tribes. *Facility*: The Center for Southwest Studies—a research oriented center holding collections of documents focused on various regional topics including the American Indian; The Native American Center - an academic and social support center for Native American students enrolled at Fort Lewis College. Library. *Publication*: Intertribal Newsletter.

COLORADO STATE UNIVERSITY
Native American Student Services
312 Student Services Bldg.
FORT COLLINS, CO 80523
(303) 491-1332
Carolyn K. Fiscus, Director
Purpose: Provides support services for Native-American students of Colorado State University; to educate the university and Fort Collins communities about Native American culture and history. *Programs*: Recruiting; orientation; skill development workshops; tutorial assistance; employment opportunity advisement; financial aid assistance; peer counseling; social and cultural activities.

CONNECTICUT

WESLEYAN UNIVERSITY
Dept. of Anthropology
MIDDLETOWN, CT 06459
(860) 685-2050 Fax 685-2051
Courses: Ethnography of Southeastern, Southwestern and Northeastern U.S.; Native American Music.
Instructor: Willard Walker, PhD.

UNIVERSITY OF CONNECTICUT
Dept. of Anthropology
Box U-158 • STORRS, CT 06269
(860) 486-4512 Fax 486-1719
Program: Developing a program for undergraduate and graduate students offering course work in Native cultures, histories, and contemporary political issues, as well as courses that would directly serve the particular economic needs and concerns of Native communities in New England and surrounding areas.

DISTRICT OF COLUMBIA

THE AMERICAN UNIVERSITY
Department of Anthropology
4400 Massachusetts Ave., NW
WASHINGTON, DC 20016 (202) 885-1830
Courses: North American Indians; Bilingual Eduction (heavy Indian emphasis); American Indian Languages. A graduate (MA) degree in applied anthropology, emphasizing language and education, cultural resource management, and the process of rural community development is available throughout the department. Doctoral students often concentrate on American Indian related cultural and/or linguistic questions. *Instructors*: John J. Bodine, PhD, William L. Leap, PhD, and Lynne S. Robins, PhD. *Special program*: Summer training program operated on Northern Ute reservation providing instruction in language analysis, language awareness, curriculum development, and language instruction techniques to teachers of Uto-Aztecan languages and cultures in public and tribally controlled schools. *Financial assistance*: Students of American Indian background are eligible for special opportunity funds from several sources. *Facilities*: Library of Congress and Smithsonian Institution (among others.)

AMERICAN UNIVERSITY
Native American National Intern Program
4400 Massachusetts Ave., NW
WASHINGTON, DC 20016
(202) 885-5951
David Harrison, Director
Description: University plays host to 50 Native American and Alaska Native college students from June 4 to August 15. Designed to give the students a Washington based education, experience, and training that they can use to help their tribal communities. Program consists of three phases. The first year - a ten week internship at the White House, U.S. Congress, Dept. of HH, or other government agency & studying government at American University; the second year - an inter-tribal work-study program; and the third phase - for Native American graduate students to work & study on a reservation while writing their graduate thesis.

HAWAII

UNIVERSITY OF HAWAII
American Indian & Alaska Native Program
1890 East West Rd., Moore Hall 405
School of Public Health
HONOLULU, HI 96822
(800) 927-3297 Fax (808) 956-6230
Rick Haverkate, MPH, Director
Special program: Educational Opportunities Program recruits Native Americans into the School as part IHS emphasis to increase numbers of Native Americans with Master's Degrees. *Instructors*: Gigliola Baruffi, MD, MPH; Kathryn L. Braun, MPH, DrPH; John Casken, RN, MPH, PhD; Alan R. Katz, MD, MPH; Walter K. Partick, MPH; and Barbara Z. Siegel, PhD.

IDAHO

IDAHO STATE UNIVERSITY
Dept. of Sociology, Anthropology, Social Work
Indian Studies Program
P.O. Box 8005 • POCATELLO, ID 83209
(208) 236-2629
Web site: www.isu.edu/departments/anthro/
Teri R. Hall, Chairperson
Instructors: Christopher Loether, PhD, Director (Linguistics, Language; Indians of California); Wesley K. Thomas, PhD (Navajo Indians); Jeanette Wolfley, JD (Federal Indian law; Shoshone-Bannock/Navajo); Earnest Lohse, PhD (Native American Material Culture).

ILLINOIS

NAES COLLEGE (NATIVE AMERICAN EDUCATIONAL SERVICES)
Tribal Research Center
2838 W. Peterson Ave. • CHICAGO, IL 60659
(773) 761-5000 Fax 761-3808
Web site: www.naes.indian.com
Faith Smith, President (NAES)
Roger Buffalohead, Center Director
Description: An educational program accredited by the Commission on Institutions of Higher Education of the North Central Association of Colleges & Schools. Offers a B.A. degree in community studies for persons employed in American Indian programs in four communities: Chicago, Minneapolis-St. Paul; Fort Peck Reservation, MT; and Menominee Reservation, WI. *Courses & Instructors*: Public Policy (Roger Buffalohead); History, Government & Law (David Beck); Education (Joel Beck); Menominee Language (Karen Washinawatok). *Special programs*: Youth & Women's Leadership; Institute for Self-Determination. The Tribal Research Center runs the Advanced Studies program offering courses in issues germane to tribal communities. Week-long seminar courses in Tribal Language, History, Child & Family Issues, & research courses such as Indian Archival Research in Washington, DC and in Chicago. Students may earn an Advanced Studies Certificate in Tribal Research. In addition, the Tribal Research Center creates & disseminates bibliographies in areas relevant to the college curriculum, and provides research services to Indian communities by contract. *Facilities*: Library & Resource Center; Archives. Archival Papers include LaDonna Harris, David Beaulieu, Sol Tax, Robert Rietz, Robert Dumont, Jr., Michael Chapman; Chicago Urban Indian Records Collection. *Publications*: College catalog directory (biennial); Indians of the Chicago Area. Monthly newsletter, TRC News; "Public Policy Issues for American Indian Families & Children"; "Demographic Study of Children and Families in Chicago American Indian Community." Financial aid is available through the NAES College Financial Aid Office. Library.

SOUTHERN ILLINOIS UNIVERSITY
Dept. of Anthropology, P.O. Box 1451
EDWARDSVILLE, IL 62026
618) 692-2744
Instructors: Charlotte J. Frisbie, PhD, Theodore R. Frisbie, PhD, Ernest L. Schusky, PhD, Fred W. Voget, PhD (Prof. Emeritus), Margaret K. Brown, PhD (Site Director, Cahokia Mounds Interpretive Center, Collinsville, IL).

INDIANA

INDIANA UNIVERSITY
Dept. of Anthropology, Student Bldg. 130
BLOOMINGTON, IN 47405
(812) 855-1041 Fax 855-4358
Richard Wilk, Chairperson
Web site: www.indiana.edu/~anthro/home.html
Instructors: Raymond DeMallie, PhD; Douglas R. Parks, PhD (linguistics); Phil LeSourd, PhD (Native American languages); Wesley Thomas, PhD (Navajo culture and language; Native American art, religions, gender & sexuality); William Adams (American Indian subsistance). *Special Resources & Facilities*: Ameri-

can Indian Studies Research Institute focuses on Native North American cultures, languages and ethnohistory; American Indian Students Association; First Nations at Indiana University (www.indiana.edu/~fniu/. Financial Aid available.

INDIANA UNIVERSITY-PURDUE UNIVERSITY
Dept. of Sociology & Anthropology
2101 Coliseum Blvd. E.
FORT WAYNE, IN 46805
(219) 481-6842 Fax 481-6985
Lawrence A. Kuznar, Coordinator
Special program: Certificate in Native American Studies. *Instructors*: Lawrence Kuznar, PhD (Navajo); Alan Sandstrom, PhD (Indians of Middle America); Chad Thompson, PhD (linguistics & languages).

GOSHEN COLLEGE
1700 S. Main St. • GOSHEN, IN 46526
(219) 535-7400 Fax 535-7234
Ronald L. Stutzman, PhD, Chair
Special program: Jacob L. Lind Collection of Native American and Alaskan artifacts for teaching and study.

BALL STATE UNIVERSITY
Dept. of Anthropology
Native American Studies Program
MUNCIE, IN 47306
(765) 285-1575 Fax 285-2163
Paul Wohlt, Chairperson
Web site: www.bsu.edu/csh/anthro/index.html
Native American Studies Minor. *Instructors*: Luke E. Lassiter, PhD; Gerald E. Waite, MA; William R. Wepler, MA; James L. Coffin, PhD. *Facility*: Archaeology Laboratory.

PURDUE UNIVERSITY
Dept. of Sociology & Anthropology
WEST LAFAYETTE, IN 47907
(317) 494-4672
Courses: Indians of North America; Indians of the Greater Southwest and Great Basin; Archaeology of North America; Native American Religions and World Views; Peoples of Middle America. *Instructors*: Richard E. Blanton, PhD, and Jack O. Waddell, PhD.

IOWA

IOWA STATE UNIVERSITY
American Indian Studies Program
351 Catt Hall • AMES, IA 50011
(515) 294-7139 Fax 294-1708
Zora Zimmerman, Interim Director
Instructors: Jill Maria Wagner, PhD; Larry Gross, PhD; Devery Fairbanks, MA. *Special Program*: American Indian Symposium held each Spring.

UNIVERSITY OF IOWA
American Indian & Native Studies Program
404 Jefferson Bldg. • IOWA CITY, IA 52242
(319) 335-1980 Fax 335-3884
Larry J. Zimmerman, Director
Web site: www.uiowa.edu/~ainsp
A number of courses from the departments of American Studies, Anthropology, Art History, English, History, and Law are approved courses leading to a certificate or minor in the undergraduate program. *Instructors*: Donaldson, Whelan, Coulter, Zimmerman, Bolton, Goldstein, Clinton, Helm, Lensink, Dewey. *Special programs*: American Indian Science and Engineering Society; annual pow wow, student conference. *Financial aid*: Iowa First Nations offers resident tuition to members of tribes historically connected to Iowa.

UNIVERSITY OF IOWA
College of Law, 276 Boyd Law Bldg.
IOWA CITY, IA 52242 (319) 335-9071
James Thomas & John Gates, Contacts
Offers one of the strongest Native American law programs in the country. *Faculty*: Indian law specialists - Profs. Robert Clinton & S. James Anaya. *Activities*: The Native American Law Student Association and the University of Iowa College of Law have established the Iowa Indian Defense Network, a computer bulletin board dedicated to the exchange of information, views, assistance, and rights, to Indian policy, tribal government, tribal news, and other Indian affairs questions.

MORNINGSIDE COLLEGE
History-Indian Studies-Political Science Dept.
1503 Morningside Ave.
SIOUX CITY, IA 51106
(712) 274-5105 Fax 274-5101
Denny J. Smith, Dept. Head
E-Mail: djs001@alpha.morningside.edu
Courses: Dakota Languages; The Indian in American History; Indian History; American Indian Literature, North American Tribal Cultures; Indian Education; Contemporary American Indian Political Issues; American Indian Law; American Indian Religions. *Instructors*: Denny Smith, Jerome Kills Small (adjunct). *Programs*: Major & Minor in Indian Studies. *Activities*: Annual Indian Awareness Days program & pow-wow. *Facility*: College Library with special Indian studies collection.

KANSAS

*HASKELL INDIAN NATIONS UNIVERSITY
155 Indian Ave. #1305
LAWRENCE, KS 66046
(875) 749-8404 Fax 749-8406
Dr. Karen Gayton Swisher, President
Marvin Buzzard, Administrative Officer
Deborah Wetsit, Ed.D, Dean of Instruction
E-Mail: dwetsit@rossl.cc.haskell.edu
Haskell offers three associate degrees and a bachelor of science degree in elementary education, which is accredited for teacher certification by the State of Kansas. The instructional division of the college is committed to fostering the intellectual and personal growth of each student and to enable students to pursue constructive and responsible personal and professional lives grounded in Native American cultural values and an ethical concern for life. The program consists of college preparatory instruction in language arts and mathematics. Specific courses explore the history, institutions, values and contemporary issues of American Indians/Alaska Natives. *Programs*: Natural and Social Sciences, Humanities, Health and Physical Education, Business, Teacher Education. Haskell also provides a program of study that addresses issues, research, and law currently affecting tribal governments nationwide. The Tribal Management Program offers a unique approach in the study of the evolution of tribal government into the complexities of the 21st century. *Instructional Administration*: Susan Arkeketa, Chair, Humanities; Don Bread, Chair, Business; George Godfrey, Chair, Natural & Social Sciences; Karen Highfill, Interim Director, Academic Support Center; Ricky A. Robinson, Chair, Teacher Education; Gerald Tuckwin, Chair, Health/Physical Education. Operated by the Bureau of Indian Affairs.

UNIVERSITY OF KANSAS
Department of Anthropology
622 Fraser Hall • LAWRENCE, KS 66045
(785) 864-4103 Fax 864-5224
E-mail: kuanthro@ukans.edu
Web site: www.cc.ukans.edu/~kuanth
Courses: Northern American Indians; Contemporary North American Indians; North American Archaeology; Archaeology of the Great Plains; Ancient American Civilizations; Indians of South America; Physical Anthropology of American Indians; North American Indian Languages. *Instructors*: Jack L. Hofman, PhD, Alfred E. Johnson, PhD, Donald D. Stull, PhD, Robert J. Squier, PhD, Michael J. Crawford, PhD, Akira Y. Yamamoto, PhD, Robert J. Smith, PhD, and Jerry A. Schultz, PhD. *Special programs*: Dr. Yamamoto works closely with the Hualapai; Dr. Stull works closely with the Kansas Kickapoo. Research, technical assistance, and employment opportunities are available in the areas of applied linguistics, applied anthropology, planning and development, tribal studies, and curriculum development. *Scholarships*: Graduate fellowships and teaching and research assistantships. *Facility*: Museum of Anthropology.

KANSAS STATE UNIVERSITY
Dept. of Sociology, Anthropology, and Social Work
204 Waters Hall • MANHATTAN, KS 66506
(913) 532-6865 Fax 532-7004
Dr. Martin Ottenheimer, Dept. Head
Instructors: Harald Prins, PhD (Indigenous Peoples

and Cultures, Native Rights Issues, Indians of Kansas); Patricia J. O'Brien, PhD (American Indian Archaeology, pre-Columbian Civilizations); Harriet Ottenheimer, PhD, Director, American Ethnic Studies Program. *Special program*: Kansas Archaeological Field School during summer with the University of Kansas. *Financial Aid*: Educational Opportunity Fund; Minority Leadership Scholarship. *Publication*: Plains Anthropologist.

KENTUCKY

NORTHERN KENTUCKY UNIVERSITY
Department of Anthropology
Nunn Drive
HIGHLAND HEIGHTS, KY 41099
(606) 572-5259 Fax 572-5566
Sharlotte Neely, Anthropology Coordinator
Web site: www.nku.edu/~nas
Program: Minor in Native American Studies. *Courses*: North American Indians; Modern American Indians; Indians of Mexico and Guatemala; North American Archaeology; Mesoamerican Archaeology. *Instructors*: James F. Hopgood, PhD, Timothy D. Murphy, PhD, Sharlotte Neely, PhD, Barbara Thiel, PhD, and Rebecca Hawkins, MA. *Facility*: Museum of Anthropology.

MASSACHUSETTS

HAMPSHIRE COLLEGE
Native American Studies Program
AMHERST, MA 01002
(413) 549-4600
Olga Euben, Contact

UNIVERSITY OF MASSACHUSETTS
American Indian Studies Program
Native American Resource Center
100 Morrissey Blvd.
BOSTON, MA 02125
(617) 287-6844 Fax 287-6857
Thomas Buckley, Academic Director
E-mail: tbuckley@umbsky.cc.umb.edu
Instructors: Thomas Buckley, PhD, Barbara E. Luedtke, PhD, Lucy Kaplan, MA, David Landy, PhD, Elaine S. Morse, PhD. *Special programs*: Native American Studies Concentration, Native American Resource Center; Field seminar in archaeology; Independent Research in Native-American Cultures and History; programs in urban anthropology and in contemporary ethnicity in the U.S.; Native American Support Group (student organization.) *Financial aid*: Massachusetts scholarships available for Native American students. *Facilities*: Boston Library Consortium. Library in Native American Resource Center (forthcoming).

HARVARD UNIVERSITY
Native American Program
Read House, Appian Way
CAMBRIDGE, MA 02138
(617) 495-4923 Fax 496-3312
Eileen Egan, Program Coordinator
E-Mail: nap@hugse1.harvard.edu
Web site: http://hugse1.harvard.edu/~nap/
Purpose: To bring together Native American students and interested individuals from the Harvard community for the purpose of advancing the well-being of indigenous peoples through self-determination, academic achievement, and community service. Native Americans are recruited to the University and provided with the community support and academic resources necessary to succeed at Harvard and beyond. An important goal of the program is to foster a sense of community among students from reservation, rural, and urban backgrounds with diverse academic and research interests. *Activities*: Supports student and faculty research; plans educational forums and conferences; works with Native communities throughout North America, including the North American Indian Center of Boston; hosts monthly potlucks for students and their families; and organizes the annual Harvard University powwow.

MICHIGAN

*KEWEENAW BAY OJIBWA
COMMUNITY COLLEGE
325 Superior Ave. • BARAGA, MI 49908

*BAY MILLS COMMUNITY COLLEGE
12214 W. Lakeshore Dr. • BRIMLEY, MI 49715
(906) 248-3354 Fax 248-3351
Martha A. McLeod, President
Description: A 2-year college providing career-oriented degree programs promoting the preservation of the customs and beliefs of Native Americans. Offers extension classes on every reservation in Michigan and many neighboring communities. *Degree programs*: Associate of Arts in Great Lakes Native American studies-Ojibway language and tribal history and literature; Associate of Applied Science in computer infomation systems, office technology and tribal administration; and Certificate programs in general business, and retailing. *Instructors*: Donald Abel (Ojibwe Language), Richard Jacobson, Susan Johnson-Cox, Mary McGarvey, Christine Miller, Barbara Ogston, Steven Pietrangelo, Patricia Ewing, Shirley Smart, Judy Webb, and David Williams. *Special program*: Inter-Active Television Program. *Facility*: James Keene Cultural Heritage Center. Financial aid available.

CENTRAL MICHIGAN UNIVERSITY
Dept. of Sociology, Anthropology & Social Work
MT. PLEASANT, MI 48859
(517) 774-3160 Fax 774-7106
American Indian Studies minor.

*SAGINAW CHIPPEWA TRIBAL COLLEGE
2274 Enterprise Dr.
MT. PLEASANT, MI 48858
Dr. Jeffrey Hamley, President

LAKE SUPERIOR STATE UNIVERSITY
Native American Center, 1000 College Dr.
SAULT STE. MARIE, MI 49783
(906) 635-2223/2195
John F. Kibble, Director

MINNESOTA

BEMIDJI STATE UNIVERSITY
1500 Birchmont Dr. NE
BEMIDJI, MN 56601-2699 (218) 755 + ext.
Kent Smith, Director-Indian Studies Program (3977)
Don Day, Director-Indian Student Services Program (2032)
Ranae Bohan, Coordinator-Native Americans Into Medicine Program (4009)
Louis Churack, Director-Educational Development Center (2614)
Situated in the center of three reservations: White Earth, Red Lake and Leech Lake. Its location offers easy access to reservation culture life. Resource people from the from the reservations are used as teachers and demonstrators. Bemidji State University offers an interdivisional program in Indian Studies which includes lectures in the Division of Behavioral Science and Humanities, and Fine Arts and various student and service projects. The program is designed to provide Ojibwe and other Indian students with a viable academic area of study relevant to their cultural heritage and diversity and to enable all students to develop a better understanding and appreciation of Indian history, language and culture. The Dept. of Modern Languages offers a minor in Ojibwe Language. The Council of Indian Students' activities include: Indian Week (first week in May), pow-wows, Ojibwe Art Expo, Native American culture classes.

*LEECH LAKE TRIBAL COLLEGE
P.O. Box 180, 113 Balsam Ave.
CASS LAKE, MN 56633
(218) 335-4220 Fax 335-4209
Larry P. Aitken, President
Penny DeVault, Dean of Student Services
E-mail: penny@lltc.org
Faculty: Yvonne Armstrong (Leech Lake Ojibwe); Virginia Carney (Eastern Cherokee); Valerie Cloud (Leech Lake Ojibwe); Richard Cutbank (Leech Lake Ojibwe); Darlene Enno (Turtle Mountain Chippewa); Elaine Fleming (Leech Lake Ojibwe); Henry Flocken (White Earth Ojibwe); Duane Goodwin (White Earth Ojibwe); Joseph Jourdain (Couchiching First Nations); Wayne Lee (Bois Forte Ojibwe); Adrian Liberty (Leech Lake Ojibwe); Scott Lyons (Leech Lake Ojibwe); Renee Martin (Turtle Mountain Chippewa); Louis Northbird (Leech Lake Ojibwe); among others. Library. Bookstore.

*FOND DU LAC TRIBAL
& COMMUNITY COLLEGE
2101 14th St. • CLOQUET, MN 55720
(218) 879-0804 Fax 879-0814
Dr. Don Day, President
Description: Tribal/state co-governed 1994 land grant 2-year liberal arts college offering more than 30 associate and certificate degree programs, including Anishinaabe language and culture, human services, law enforcement, nursing, business/finance, computer science, and environmental studies. FDLTCC is a designated Center of Excellence in partnership with the U.S. Dept. of Agriculture-National Resources Conservation Service focusing on soil science and conservation in application with Geographic Information Systems (GIS). Ruth A. Myers Library, special collection of regional Native American publications.

ANOKA RAMSEY COMMUNITY COLLEGE
American Indian Student Services
11200 Mississippi Blvd., NW
COON RAPIDS, MN 55433
(612) 422-3470 Fax 422-3341
Sharon Romano, Director

COLLEGE OF ST. SCHOLASTICA
Native American Studies Dept.
DULUTH, MN 55811 (218) 723-6046
Nancy J. Ferreira, Contact

UNIVERSITY OF MINNESOTA, DULUTH
American Indian Learning Resource Center
114 Cina Hall, 10 University Dr.
DULUTH, MN 55812
(218) 726-6379 Fax 726-6331
Rick J. Smith, Director
Provides campus-wide student support services to American Indian students. The goals are the recruitment and retention of American Indians, and the enhancement of their educational experience. Services: Academic, personal and financial aid counseling; recruitment; tutorial services; culturally oriented library; computer access; also consulting services to tribal governments and organizations; coordinates forums, seminars, and speakers.

UNIVERSITY OF MINNESOTA, DULUTH
American Indian Studies Program
American Indian Teacher Training Program
114 Cina Hall, 10 University Dr.
DULUTH, MN 55812 (218) 726-1339
Works to prepare American Indian students for careers in professional fields including teaching, medicine, social work, and business administration. *Special program*: Master of Social Work program with a special focus on American Indian communities. *Facilities*: American Indian Learning Resource Center; Center of American Indian and Minority Health; Center of Excellence for American Indian Medical Education.

*WHITE EARTH TRIBAL
& COMMUNITY COLLEGE
210 Main St. South, P.O. Box 478
MAHNOMEN, MN 56557

SOUTHWEST STATE UNIVERSITY
1501 State St. • MARSHALL, MN 56258
(507) 537-6169
Bruce Carter, Contact
Provides courses in Native American history, anthropology and language.

AUGSBURG COLLEGE
American Indian Support Program
MINNEAPOLIS, MN 55455
(612) 330-1138
Bonnie Wallace, Director
Cindy Peterson, Education Assistant

Programs: Direct assistance; counseling; advocacy. An American Indian Studies minor is being proposed. The Program is connected to many community and tribal agencies. We interface with the Minneapolis American Indian Center, the Indian Health Board, the Minnesota Indian Women's Resource Center, the Division of Indian Work, as well as Indian support programs in other institutions of higher education throughout the State. Also, works closely with tribal education offices and departments of Indian education for Minneapolis, St. Paul and the State of Minnesota. Founded 1978.

MINNESOTA COMMUNITY COLLEGE
Dept. of Social Sciences/American Indian Studies
1501 Hennepin Ave. • MINNEAPOLIS, MN 55403

UNIVERSITY OF MINNESOTA
American Indian Studies Dept.
102 Scott Hall, 72 Pleasant St. SE
MINNEAPOLIS, MN 55455
 (612) 624-1338; 624-3858
Thomas King, Chairperson
Leo D. Abbott, Director of Administration
Courses: Ojibwe and Dakota language, literature, philosophies, art, history, and other various topics covered. Offers a committment to the education of American Indian students through the following resources: American Indian Learning Resource Center, American Indian Student Cultural Center, OMSSA Summer Institute, five American Indian student organizations, and 300 American Indian students. Financial aid available.

MOORHEAD STATE UNIVERSITY
Department of Indian Studies
11th St. South • MOORHEAD, MN 56560

ST. CLOUD STATE UNIVERSITY
720 4th Ave. S. • ST. CLOUD, MN 56301

**MESABI RANGE COMMUNITY
& TECHNICAL COLLEGE**
Indian/Minority Services Dept.
1001 Chestnut St. W. • VIRGINIA, MN 55792
 (218) 749-7727 Fax 749-0318
 E-mail: m.king-tanttu@mailmr.mnscu.edu
Margaret King-Tanttu, Director
Instructor: Donald Chosa. *Courses*: Native American history, philosophy & art; Ojibwe language & culture.

MISSOURI

UNIVERSITY OF MISSOURI
Department of Anthropology
210 Switzler Hall • COLUMBIA, MO 65211
 (314) 882-4731
Courses: Cultures of Native America; Ancient American Civilization; North American Archaeology; North American Indian Culture. *Instructors*: Louanna Furbee, PhD, H. Clyde Wilson, PhD, W. Raymond Wood, PhD, and Robert F.G. Spier, PhD, and Harold W. Marshall, Director-Missouri Cultural Heritage Center—provides research opportunities in historical archaeology, history & ethnography of Missouri and surrounding states.

WASHINGTON UNIVERSITY
Center for American Indian Studies in Social Services
Campus Box 1196 • ST. LOUIS, MO 63130
 (314) 889-6288
Dana Wilson Kar, MSW, JD, Director
Established to promote the higher education of Native Americans and prepare educational and social work practitioner leaders to serve American Indians. A scholarship is offered to Native American students intending to teach or practice social work with Indian people.

MONTANA

MONTANA STATE UNIVERSITY
Dept. of Native American Studies
1500 North 30th St. • BILLINGS, MT 59101
 (406) 657-2311 Fax 657-2187
Dr. Jeffrey Sanders, Director
E-mail: soc_jscvixen@emcmt.edu

Web site: www.msubillings.edu
Offers a complete array of Native American Studies courses from introductory courses to upper division couses specializing in Indian law, art, literature, federal policy, and environmental issues. *Instructors*: Dr. Jeffrey Sanders and Dr. C. Adrian Heidenreich.

*STONE CHILD COMMUNITY COLLEGE
RR 1, Box 1082 • BOX ELDER, MT 59521
 (406) 395-4313 Fax 395-4836
Steve Galbavy, President
A tribally-controlled (2-year) college of the Chippewa-Cree Tribe.

MONTANA STATE UNIVERSITY
Native American Studies Dept.
2-179 Wilson Hall, P.O. Box 172340
BOZEMAN, MT 59717-2340
 (406) 994-3881 Fax 994-6879
Dr. Walter C. Fleming, Chairperson
E-mail: gburmeister@montana.edu
Website: www.montana.edu/wwwnas/
Instructors: Lisa Aldred, J.D., PhD (Native American Women, Federal Indian Policy and Law); Walter C. Fleming, PhD (Native American Literature, Montana Indians); Dr. Henrietta Mann (American Indian Religion); Alexandra New Holy , PhD (Federal Indian Policy and Law, Native Americans and the Cinema); James C. Burns, B.S. (Native American Education), Student Advisor, Advocate, Counselor; Wayne J. Stein, EdD (Contemporary Issues); Saralyn Sebern, Office of Tribal Service, MA Program. *Special programs:* Non-Teaching Minor in Native American Studies; Masters of Arts in Native American Studies.

*BLACKFEET COMMUNITY COLLEGE
P.O. Box 819 • BROWNING, MT 59417
 (406) 338-7755 Fax 338-3272
Terrance Whitright, President

*LITTLE BIG HORN COLLEGE
P.O. Box 370
CROW AGENCY, MT 59022
 (406) 638-7211 Fax 638-2229
Dr. David Yarlott, Jr., President

*FORT BELKNAP COLLEGE
P.O. Box 159 • HARLEM, MT 59526-0159
 (406) 353-2607 Fax 353-2898
Carole Falcon-Chandler, President
Tribally controlled community college providing quality post-secondary educational opportunities for Indian residents (Assiniboine and Gros Ventre Tribes) of the Fort Belknap communities. About 500 full-time and part-time students attend. *Programs*: Vocational education, cooperative education, academic, cultural, community interest programs, courses and activities. *Services*: Assistance to tribal institutions, departments in staff preparation, planning research and evaluation services. Library. Financial aid available. Established 1984.

FLATHEAD VALLEY COMMUNITY COLLEGE
Native American/Multicultural Affairs
777 Grandview Dr. • KALISPEL, MT 59901
 (406) 756-3945 Fax 756-3815
Sharon Moses, Coordinator
Courses: Gender: Native vs. Non-Native Perspectives; ART/NAS: Native Beadwork & Adornments; Diversity in America. *Programs*: Native Arts/Crafts; Mutlicultural Arts/Crafts for Children. *Financial Aid*: Native American Tuition Waiver - to Indian students with financial need, from any North American tribe and a resident of Montana, and holding a 2.0 or better GPA.

*CHIEF DULL KNIFE COLLEGE
P.O. Box 98 • LAME DEER, MT 59043
 (406) 477-6215 Fax 477-6219
Dr. Alonzo Spang, President
Special program: Native American Studies Program - Dr. Richard Littlebear, Coordinator. *Financial aid*: BIA - Higher Education Grants; Federal Pell Grant; scholarships; cooperative education. Dr. John Woodenlegs Memorial Library.

UNIVERSITY OF MONTANA
Dept. of Anthropology
32 Campus Dr. #5112
MISSOULA, MT 59812-1001

 (406) 243-4245 Fax 243-4918
Gregory R. Campbell, Chairperson
Undergraduate emphasis in archaeology, linguistics, ethnic and cultural diversified studies, and forensic anthropology; graduate program offering a M.A. in Cultural Heritage Studies and forensic anthropology. *Programs*: Native American Studies; Ethnological and archaeological field courses. *Instructors*: Carling I. Malouf, PhD; Anthony Mattina, PhD; Charlene G. Smith, PhD; Gregory R. Campbell, PhD; Stephen Greymorning, PhD; John E. Douglas, PhD; Thomas A. Foor, PhD; Richmond L. Clow, PhD; William C. Prentiss, PhD. *Special resources*: Extensive study collections of northwest plains ethnological and archaeological materials; Northern Plains Ethnohistory Project; Linguistics Laboratory and Reading Room maintains a strong collection of material on Native American linguistics. *Financial Aid*: Undergraduate - Several competetive scholarships open to majors; Graduate - Teaching Assistants. *Publications*: Occasional Papers in anthropological linguistics.

UNIVERSITY OF MONTANA SCHOOL OF LAW
Indian Law Clinic
MISSOULA, MT 59812
 (406) 243-4311

*SALISH KOOTENAI COLLEGE
P.O. Box 117 • PABLO, MT 59855
 (406) 675-4800 Fax 675-4801
Dr. Joseph McDonald, President
Established in 1977 by the Salish & Kootenai Tribal Council and is designed to serve the postsecondary needs of the Flathead Reservation as well as other Native Americans. *Degrees*: Offers a four-year Bachelor Degree in Human Services and several Associate Degrees and Certificates. Provides instruction in a wide variety of Native American culture programs.

*FORT PECK COMMUNITY COLLEGE
P.O. Box 398 • POPLAR, MT 59255
 (406) 768-5551 ext. 22 Fax 768-5552
Dr. James Shanley, President
Ronald Craig, Chair-Native American Studies
Anita Scheetz, Director-Library
Fully accredited two-year associates degree program. *Programs*: Native American Studies Program; and General Studies Program (business, computers, electronics, etc.); Workshop Programs. *Instructors*: Ronald Craig, Robert Four Star. *Financial aid*: Pell Grant; scholarships. Tribal Library.

NEBRASKA

UNIVERSITY OF NEBRASKA
Department of Anthropology & Geography
Bessey Hall 126 • LINCOLN, NE 68588
 (402) 472-2411 Fax 472-9642
Patricia Draper, PhD, Chairperson
Website: www.unl.edu/anthro
Program: Native American Studies component; Native languages. *Faculty*: Mark Awakuni-Swetland, PhD, Martha McCollough, PhD, Mary Willis, PhD, William T. Waters, PhD.

**AMERICAN INDIAN SATELLITE
COMMUNITY COLLEGE**
801 E. Benjamin Ave. •
NORFOLK, NE 68701
Established 1973.

NEBRASKA INDIAN COMMUNITY COLLEGE
P.O. Box 428 • MACY, NE 68039
 (402) 837-5078 Fax 837-4183
David Beaver, Dev. Officer
Description: A co-educational liberal arts and vocational education institution chartered by the Omaha, Santee Sioux and Winnebago Tribes of Nebraska. *Program*: Native American Studies.

LITTLE PRIEST TRIBAL COLLEGE
P.O. Box 270 • WINNEBAGO, NE 68071
 (402) 878-2380 Fax 878-2355
John Blackhawk, President

NEVADA

UNIVERSITY OF NEVADA, LAS VEGAS
Dept. of Anthropology & Ethnic Studies
4505 Maryland Pkwy.
LAS VEGAS, NV 89154
(702) 895-3590 Fax 895-4823
Courses: Indians of the Southwest (Benyshek); Peoples & Cultures of Native North America; Contemporary Native Americans; Indians of Nevada & Utah; Native Americans & the Law (Martha C. Knack); American Indian Myth & Religion (Palmer). *Publication*: University of Nevada Papers in Anthropology, annual.

NEW HAMPSHIRE

DARTMOUTH COLLEGE
Native American Studies Center
Sherman House, 37 N. Main St.
HANOVER, NH 03755
(603) 646-3530 Fax 646-0333
Colin Calloway, PhD, Samson Occom Chair
Linda M.F. Welch, Program Administrator
E-Mail: LindaWelch@Dartmouth.edu
Web site: www.dartmouth.edu/~nas/
Instructors: Colin G. Calloway, PhD & Chair (American Indian History); Dale A. Turner, Teme-Augama Anishnabai, northern Ontario, PhD, Government (Tribal Sovereignty, Contemporary Issues); Sergei Kan, PhD - Anthropology (Peoples and Cultures of Native North America); Deborah Nichols, PhD - Archaeology (Ancient Native Americans); Vera B. Palmer (Tuscarora, Native American Literature); Dennis "Dan" Runnels, San Poil Salish (American Indian Languages and Literature) N. Bruce Duthu, JD , Houma of Louisiana (American Indian Law & Policy); Darren Ranco, Penobscot (Environmental Studies and Justice Issues). *Affiliated College Officials*: Jim Larimore, Comanche (Dean of the College); Colleen Larimore, Comanche (Support Services in First Year Office); Michael Hanitchak, Choctaw (Director of the Native American Program); The Native American House (a residential house for 16 upper class Native American studnets, and a central meeting/cultural/activities center for students); Lori Alvord Arviso, Navajo (Assistant Director of Admissions, Dartmouth Medical School, surgeon, Dartmouth-Hitchcock Medical Center). *Special programs*: Native American Program (see below); Angela K. Parker, Mandan-Hidatsa (Admissions Recruiter for Native American students); Horizons Program and Native American Fly-In (Native American high school seniors come to Dartmouth in a group for a visit, all travel expenses paid for by the College, submit application to admissions office); Charles Eastman, PhD Fellowship (annual residential fellowship for Native scholars writing PhD dissertations, $25,000 salary, office support, $2,500 expense account; Class of 1943 Tribal Research Fellowship, up to $8,000). *Activities*: Conferences and symposia addressing current issues in Indian country, historical perspectives, religious traditions, education, material culture, language, sovereignty; Internship program, seniors majoring in NAS go on term-long internships in Indian country or Washington, DC; Honors Program: Students may become honors majors in NAS upon application and a GPA of 3.00 or higher. *Facilities*: Native American Studies Center includes a research library (over 5,000 books, many newspapers, periodicals, tribal publications, language research project archives); Baker Library, main college library has excellent and broad collections on American Indian ethnography, history and contemporary life, art, material culture; Hood Museum of Art (collections of American Indian art, artifacts, and cultural objects).

DARTMOUTH COLLEGE
Native American Studies Program
201 Collis Center, HB 6037
HANOVER, NH 03755
(603) 646-2110 Fax 646-0333
Michael S. Hanitchak (Choctaw), Director
Julie Ratico, Academic Assistant
E-Mail: native.american.program@dartmouth.edu
Structure and Responsibilities: The Native American Program provides Native American student support services; works with students, administrators, campus-wide faculty and programs to insure the success of Native American students to insure their four-year residency on campus; strives to provide spiritual, emotional, personal support, and tutorial help — often times on an individual basis — to insure the success of all Native students. NAP works to increase understanding of native issues both on campus and beyond. In 1992 a record high of 142 Native American students from 30 states and 55 different tribes were enrolled at the College. Student graduation rates have grown significantly since the inception of the Native American Program in 1970. During the first decade of the program's existence, the Native student graduation rate averaged 50%; since that time, the rate has risen to an average of 72%, nearly ten times the average graduation rate for Native Americans attending college nationwide. Currently, 117 Native American students are enrolled. *Activities*: Annual Dartmouth College Pow-Wow (usually held the Saturday before Mother's Day each Spring); annual guests, lectures, Talking Circle, cultural events to promote understanding. Affiliates: Native American Council (NAC), meets four times each term; Native American Visiting Committee (NAVC) alumni review committee, annual meetings and report; Native Americans at Dartmouth (NAD), student organization, sharing affinity and student life; Native American House (affinity residence house for Native American students and non-Native students interested in sharing cultural life); NAAA (Native American Alumni Association); alumni group at Dartmouth College with over 500 members.

NEW JERSEY

RAMAPO COLLEGE
School of Intercultural Studies
Anthropology Program
P.O. Box 542 • MAHWAH, NJ 07430

RUTGERS UNIVERSITY
Department of Anthropology
Douglass College, Box 270
NEW BRUNSWICK, NJ 08903
(908) 932-9886
Special program: Native American Indian studies. Faculty: Anne-Marie Cantwell, PhD, Marla N. Powers, PhD, William K. Powers, PhD.

SETON HALL UNIVERSITY
Department of Sociology & Anthropology
Fahy Hall
SOUTH ORANGE, NJ 07070
(201) 761-9170
Faculty: Herbert Kraft, DHL, and Maria Powers, PhD. *Special program*: Summer Lakota Field School at the Pine Ridge Reservation, Pine Ridge, South Dakota. *Special resources*: University Museum & Archaeological Research Center maintains extensive collections of material culture of New Jersey Indian; and archaeological and ethnographical materials.

NEW MEXICO

SOUTHWESTERN INDIAN POLYTECHNIC INSTITUTE
9169 Coors Rd., NW
ALBUQUERQUE, MT 87184
(505) 346-2347 Fax 346-2343
Dr. Carolyn Elgin, President
Duane Yazzie, Chairperson
Administered by the Bureau of Indian Affairs, under the jurisdiction of Albuquerque Area Office. SIPI is dedicated to training American Indian adults for jobs in the technical-vocational fields. *Special Student Services*: Program offers special assistance and support services to students and staff in the understanding and treatment of alcohol and drug abuse. Sponsors health promotion education class, support groups, sweatlodge, peer counseling training, and substance abuse education classes. Library. Publishes numerous pamphlets related to substance abuse. Established in 1974.

UNIVERSITY OF NEW MEXICO
American Indian Graduate Center
4520 Montgomery Blvd. NE, Suite 1-B
ALBUQUERQUE, NM 87131
(505) 881-4584
Provides fellowship grants to Indian graduate students. Assists about 600 students from 130 tribes at over 200 colleges throughout the U.S.

UNIVERSITY OIF NEW MEXICO SCHOOL OF LAW
American Indian Law Center
1117 Stanford Dr. NE
ALBUQUERQUE, NM 87131

UNIVERSITY OF NEW MEXICO
Dept. of Anthropology
ALBUQUERQUE, NM 87131
(505) 277-4524 Fax 277-0874
Instructors: David W. Dinwoodie, PhD, Louise A. Lamphere, PhD, Keith H. Basso, PhD, Frank C. Hibben, PhD, Bruce B. Huckell, PhD, Chris Musello, PhD, Willow R. Powers, PhD. *Facility*: Maxwell Museum of Anthropology. *Publication*: Journal of Anthropological Research. Library.

UNIVERSITY OF NEW MEXICO
Native American Studies Dept.
Mesa Vista 3080
ALBUQUERQUE, NM 87131
(505) 277-3917 Fax 277-1818
Jimmy Shendo, Student Resource Specialist
Description: Develops and promotes regional studies of Native Americans, their concerns and their communities. *Special programs*: Native American Inervention and Retention Project; Information and Materials Resource Collection. *Activities*: Sponsors lecture series, specialized seminars and conferences; regular course offerings. Library. *Facilities*: Institute for Native American Development. *Financial aid*: Various scholarships available. *Publications*: NAS Newsline, monthly newsletter; Pathways Off the Rez, a student handbook.

CROWNPOINT INSTITUTE OF TECHNOLOGY
P.O. Box 849 • CROWNPOINT, NM 87313
(505) 786-5851 Fax 786-5644
Robert M. Dorak, President
Description: Tribally owned and controlled education institution chartered by the Navajo Nation. *Programs*: Training; adult basic education; academic remediation; income tax preparation; and young entrpreneurship training.

NEW MEXICO STATE UNIVERSITY
Department of Sociology & Anthropology.
Box 30001, Dept. 3BV • LAS CRUCES, NM 88003
(505) 646-3822 Fax 646-3725
Scott Rushforth, PhD, Chairperson
Program: American Indian Studies. *Instructors*: E. Scott Rushforth, PhD (People of the Southwest); Andrew Wiggett (American Indian Literature); Darlis Miller (American Indian History); Elizabeth Zarur (Native American Art & Culture). *Special programs*: American Indian Program (Student Services); Cultural Resources Management Division—specializing in New Mexico; summer field school in archaeology (Mogollon), Southwest studies; Indian Resource Development (see below). *Facilities*: University Museum; laboratories for research.

NEW MEXICO UNIVERSITY
Indian Resource Development
Box 30001, Dept. MSC
LAS CRUCES, NM 88003
(505) 646-1347 Fax 646-5975
Lance Lujan, Director
Purpose: To encourage American Indian students to attend the university of their choice and major in natural resouce related fields. *Publications*: Indian Country Student News; Sources of Financial Aid Available to American Indian Students (booklet). Established in 1977.

NEW MEXICO HIGHLANDS UNIVERSITY
Behavioral Sciences Dept.
National Ave. • LAS VEGAS, NM 87701
(505) 454-3343 Fax 454-3331
Tom Ward, Chairperson

E-Mail: tsward@nmhu.edu
Native American Studies Program. Description: Provides an opportunity for Indians and non-Indians to study Indian cultures and their significant contributions to contemporary U.S. culture. It is a component of the Behavioral Sciences Department and has the concentration of study in sociology/anthropology; provided in combination with courses containing Indian content offered in other University departments. *Instructors*: Mario Gonzales, PhD (Anthropology), Orit Tamir, PhD (history), Robert Mishler, MA (Anthropology); James Leger, MA (ethnomusicology). Special program: Native American Club; American Indian in Science & Engineering (AISES). Scholarships available - write to Financial Aid Services.

EASTERN NEW MEXICO UNIVERSITY
Dept. of Social & Behavioral Sciences
PORTALES, NM 88130 (505) 562-2583
Dr. Phillip H. Shelley, Dept. Head
Instructors: George Agogino, PhD, William Hawk, PhD, Phillip Shelley, PhD, Joanne Dickenson, MA, and John L. Montgomery, PhD. Financial Aid: Graduate Assistantships, work study, Blackwater Draw Undergraduate Museum Fellowships. *Special facilities*: Paleo-Indian Institute and Museum; ceramic and lithic anaylsis laboratories; University Library.

INSTITUTE OF AMERICAN INDIAN ARTS
83 Avan Nu Po Rd. • SANTA FE, NM 87508
(505) 988-6463 Fax 988-6446
Della Warrior, President
Robert H. Ames Piestewa (Hopi)
Wiley T. Buchanan III, David Lester (Creek), and William S. Johnson, Board of Trustees
Description: Federally chartered private institution. The only accredited fine arts college devoted solely to the study of American Indian and Alaska Native art. Offers learning opportunities in the arts and crafts to Native American youth (Indian, Eskimo and Aleut.) Emphasis is placed upon Indian traditions as the basis for creative expression in the fine arts. *Activities*: Maintains the Center for Research and Cultural Exchanges, Reuben A. Snake, Dean. Sponsors Indian arts-oriented Junior College offering Associate of Fine Arts degrees in various fields as well as seminars, and exhibition program, and traveling exhibits; maintains extensive library, museum, and biographical archives. *Publications*: Coyote on the Turtle's Back, annual; Faculty & Student Handbooks and School Catalog, annual; Spawning the Medicine River, annual. established in 1962.

SCHOOL OF AMERICAN RESEARCH
Indian Arts Research Center
P.O. Box 2188 • SANTA FE, NM 87504
(505) 954-7205 Fax 954-7207
E-mail: iarc@sarsf.org
Website: www.sarweb.org
Kathy Whitaker, PhD, Director
Shannon Parker, Collections Manager
Deborah Winton, Registrar
Rita Iringan, Native American Heritage Prog. Coord.
Native American Artist Fellowships: The Eric & Barbara Dobkin, Ronald & Susan Dubin, and Rollin & Mary Ella King fellowships; lectures and exhibitions; annual Native American Internship. *Special resources*: collection of 9,000+ objects of Southwestern American Indian art and anthropology; archaeology laboratory. *Fellowships*: Katrin H. Lamon Resident Scholar and Artist Fellowships for Native Americans. *Publications*: Books pertaining to the Southwest and native american arts and culture. Library.

*DINE COLLEGE EAST
Navajo Community College
P.O. Box 580 • SHIPROCK, NM 87420
(520) 368-3501 Fax 368-3519
Irene Charles-Lutz, Director/Academic Advisor
Eleanor K. Kuhl, Librarian
Web site: www.shiprock.ncc.cc.nm.us/
See Dine College West for description. *Center for Dine Studies Faculty*: Martha Austin-Garrison, Herbert Benally, Bernice Casaus, and Anthony Goldtooth, Sr.

NAVAJO COMMUNITY COLLEGE
P.O. Box 580 • SHIPROCK, NM 87420
(505) 368-5291
See Navajo Community College (Tsaile, Arizona)

ZUNI ARCHAEOLOGY PROGRAM
Pueblo of Zuni, P.O. Box 339
ZUNI, NM 87327 (505) 782-4814
Roger Anyon, Director
Staff: Roger Anyon, Ramona Avallone, Craig Birrell, Carol Brandt, Edward Kotyk, Kaer Morris, Jeanette Quintero, Patricia Ruppe, Mark Sant, Elizabeth Skinner, Jeffrey Waseta, Robert Waterworth, Rose Wyaco, Jerome Zunie. *Research Facilities*: Collections; large amounts of unpublished data & historical photos for Zuni Indian Reservation. Library. *Publications*: Report Series.

NEW YORK

STATE UNIVERSITY OF NEW YORK AT ALBANY
Department of Anthropology
1400 Washington Ave. • ALBANY, NY 12222
(518) 442-4700 Fax 442-5710
Robert W. Jarvenpa, Chairperson
Web site: www.albany.edu/anthro/
Faculty: Richard Wilkinson, PhD; Liliana R. Goldin, PhD; Gary H. Gossen, PhD; Robert W. Jarvenpa, PhD; Gail H. Landsman, PhD; Lawrence M. Schell, PhD; Gary A. Wright, PhD; G. Aaron Broadwell, PhD; Hetty Jo Brumbach, PhD; Louise Burkhart, PhD; James Collins, PhD; John Justeson, PhD; Michael Smith, PhD; Dean Snow, PhD. *Special programs/facilities*: Teaching laboratories in archaeology and physical anthropology; field schools in archaeology and ethnology, U.S. and Mesoamerica. Financial aid available. *Publications*: Northeast Anthropology; Institute for Mesoamerican Studies publications; Institute for Archaeological Studies publications; Departmental Guide for Graduate Studies.

STATE UNIVERSITY OF NEW YORK, BUFFALO
Dept. of Anthropology, 380 MFAC/Ellicott
AMHERST, NY 14261 (716) 645-2414 Fax 645-3808
Programs: Linguistics; American Studies. *Instructors*: Frederick Gearing, PhD, Ann P. McElroy, PhD, Edward R. Starr, PhD, Ezra B. W. Zubrow, PhD, William Engelbrecht, PhD, Sara M. Elder, MA, Dennis Tedlock, PhD. *Special program*: Contemporary North American Indians and Eskimos; Northeast U.S. prehistory. Museum. Library.

BUFFALO STATE COLLEGE
Native American Student Services
1300 Elmwood Ave. • BUFFALO, NY 14222
(716) 878-4631 Fax 878-6600

STATE UNIVERSITY OF NEW YORK, BUFFALO
Native American Studies Programs
Hayes Annex A, Main St. Campus
BUFFALO, NY 14214 (716) 831-2111

STATE UNIVERSITY OF NEW YORK, GENESEO
Dept. of Anthropology • GENESEO, NY 14454
(716) 245-5277
Instructors: Russell Judkins, PhD (Iroquois, Catawba); Sue N. Roark-Calnek, PhD (Native American ethnicity, Algonquin and Woodlands ethnology).

COLGATE UNIVERSITY
Department of Sociology & Anthropology
HAMILTON, NY 13346
(315) 228-7543 Fax 228-7974
Instructors: Gary Urton, PhD and Anthony F. Aveni, PhD. *Special program*: Interdisciplinary topical concentration in Amerindian Studies, embracing the fields of Native-American religion, astronomy, art, and archaeology. *Special facility*: Longyear Museum of Anthropology and laboratory—features large collections of local Oneida Iroquois and Mesoamerican archaeological materials.

CORNELL UNIVERSITY
American Indian Program
450 Caldwell Hall • ITHACA, NY 14853
(607) 255-8402 Fax 255-6246
E-mail: AIPoffice@cornell.edu
Web site: www.aip.cornell.edu
Daniel H. Usner, Jr., Director
Reann Skenandore, Associate Director-Student Services & Operations

Kathy Halbig, Acct. Rep. III
The American Indian Program is a multidisciplinary, academic program which serves students with diverse interests and goals; student support providing academic, financial and personal counseling; and community outreach which connects University resources with problems and concerns of Native communities. *Faculty*: B. Baker, B. Lambert, C. Carrick, A. Gonzales, Jane Mt. Pleasant, and Robert Venables. *Publication*: Akwe:kon Press publishes "Native Americas"© a journal of indigenous issues.

STATE UNIVERSITY OF NEW YORK
Department of Anthropology
Anthropology House • NEW PALTZ, NY 12561
(914) 257-2990 Fax 257-3009
B.E. Pierce, PhD, Chairperson
Programs: Native American Studies Minor. *Instructors*: Karin Andriolo, PhD (Ancient MesoAmerica); Joseph Diamond, PhD (Archaeology); Giselle Hendel-Sebastyen, PhD (Indians of North America). *Special programs*: Archeology Field School (summers); excavations in the Hudson Valley.

JOHN JAY COLLEGE OF CRIMINAL JUSTICE
CUNY - Dept. of Anthropology
445 W. 59th St. • NEW YORK, NY 10019
(212) 237-8286
Instructors: Kirk Dombrowski, PhD, Anne Buddenhagen, MA.

STATE UNIVERSITY OF NEW YORK
Dept. of Anthropology • ONEONTA, NY 13820
(607) 431-3345
Instructor: William A. Starna, PhD. Eastern Woodlands, Iroquoians, Algonquians.

STATE UNIVERSITY OF NEW YORK
Dept. of Anthropology & Sociology
OSWEGO, NY 13126 (315) 341-4190
Program: Native American Studies.
Instructor: Stephen C. Saraydar, PhD.

STATE UNIVERSITY OF NEW YORK COLLEGE, POTSDAM
Department of Anthropology
119A MacVicar, 44 Pierrepont Ave.
POTSDAM, NY 13676-2294
(315) 267-2053 Fax 267-3176
E-Mail: stebbisa@pottsdam.edu
Program: Native American Studies minor - The study of indigenous peoples of the Americas - their prehistory, history and cultures - is the focus of courses taught. The minor in Native American Studies is a vehicle enabling students interested in the serious and intensive study of Native Americans to benefit from its diverse offerings. *Special program*: Mohawk language. *Instructor*: Susan Stebbins, PhD. Financial aid available.

SYRACUSE UNIVERSITY COLLEGE OF LAW
Center for Indigenous Law, Governance & Citizenship
E.I. White Hall • SURACUSE, NY 13244
(315) 443-1712
E-mail: ndnlaw@law.syr.edu
Website: www.law.syr.edu/indigenous

NORTH CAROLINA

WESTERN CAROLINA UNIVERSITY
Dept. of Anthropology & Sociology
CULLOWHEE, NC 28723-9047
(828) 227-7268 Fax 227-7647
Anne F. Rogers, Dept. Head
Special program: Minor in Cherokee studies. *Instructors*: Anne F. Rogers, PhD, Jane L. Brown, MA, Laura Hill Pinnix, MA. *Special facility*: Archaeology Laboratory, Human Relations Area Files and collection of documents related to Cherokees available in library.

UNIVERSITY OF NORTH CAROLINA AT PEMBROKE
American Indian Studies Department
P.O. Box 1510 • PEMBROKE, NC 28372
(910) 521-6266
Linda Oxendine, PhD, Chairperson

E-Mail: linda@papa.uncp.edu
Courses: Contemporary Issues of American Indians; American Indian Culture; American Indian Education; Americn Indian Literature; History of the American Indian; Indians of the Southeast; Federal Policy and the American Indian; American Indian Religious Traditions; American Indian Health. *Instructors*: John Bowman, PhD; Manuel Conley; David Eliades, PhD; Stanley Knick, PhD; Robert Reising, PhD; Ralph Steeds.

NORTH DAKOTA

*TURTLE MOUNTAIN COMMUNITY COLLEGE
P.O. Box 340 • BELCOURT, ND 58316
(701) 477-5605 Fax 477-5028
Dr. Gerald "Carty" Monette, President
Carol Davis, Vice-President
Dr. William Gourneau, Academic Dean
Wanda Laducer, Financial Aid Director
E-Mail: cdavis@giizis.turtle-mountain.cc.nd.us
Web site: http://www.giizis.turtle-mountain.cc.nd.us
Description: Functions as an autonomous Indian controlled college on the Turtle Mountain Band of Chippewa Indian Reservation focusing on general studies and vocational education programs. Seeks to establish an administration, faculty and student body involved in community affairs. *Courses and Faculty*: Social Sciences (Rollin Kekahbah, Leslie Peltier); Business (Julie Desjarlais, Tracey Azure, Rhonda Gustafson); Humanities (Andrew Johnson, Margaret Johnson, Ina Mikkelson); Life Sciences (Scott Hanson, Charmane Disrud); Building Trades (Ronald Parisien); Art (Cynthia Jeelleberg); Computer (Chad Davis); Music (Cheryl Haagensen); Elementary Education (Linda Marsh & Zelma Peltier); Math (Miles Pfahl & Luther Olson); Early Childhood Education (Carol Parisien); among others. *Special program*: Vocational Education (Sheila Trottier, Director); Indian Entrepreneurship Program. Financial aid available. *Publications*: The Mitchif Dictionary (local native language); Chippewa/Cree Language; The Cree Dictionary; Course Catalog & Bulletin. Library.

*UNITED TRIBES TECHNICAL COLLEGE
3315 University Dr. • BISMARCK, ND 58504
(701) 255-3285 Fax 255-1844
Dr. David M. Gipp, President
Vince Schanandore, Contact
UTTC is committed to the needs of the American Indians in the cultural preservation of their heritage. The Four Winds Cultural Center works to cultivate, preserve, and transmit traditional skills and knowledge by teaching American Indian arts and crafts, music, dance, and history of Indian people. *Special programs*: Certificate Programs, and Associate of Applied Science Degrees. *Annual events*: Native American Livesavers Conference "Implementing Effective Interventions for Injury Prevention in Indian Country," held in mid-July; The United Tribes Annual International Powwow held the first Thursday through Sunday after Labor Day; The United Tribes Indian Art Expo & Market is held in May. *Publications*: Arrow Graphics Printing Dept. publishes the 'Indian Recipe Book,' $5.00; 'Powwow Questions & Answers,' $3; the American Indian Curriculum Development Program offers a series of curriculum manuals set up for students that incorporate Native American folklore, customs, and themes, available K-12 and adult skills.

*CANKDESKA CIKANA COMMUNITY COLLEGE
P.O. Box 269
FORT TOTTEN, ND 58335
(701) 766-4415 Fax 766-4077
Erich Longie, President
Head Start Program.

*SITTING BULL (STANDING ROCK) COLLEGE
1341 92nd St.
FORT YATES, ND 58538
(701) 854-3861 Fax 854-3403
Dr. Ron "His Horse is Thunder" McNeil, President
Offers A.A., A.A.S. & A.S. two year degrees. *Special programs*: B.A. degree through Minot State University; offer Irrigation Farm Management program. Scholarships. *Affiliation*: American Indian Higher Education Consortium.

UNIVERSITY OF NORTH DAKOTA
Indian Studies Dept., Campus Box 7103
GRAND FORKS, ND 58202
(701) 777-4314 Fax 777-4145
Mary Jane Schneider, PhD, Chairperson
Website: www.und.nodak.edu/
dept/indian/index~1.htm
Offers a major and minor in Indian Studies leading to a B.A. degree. *Instructors*: Chester Fritz, PhD, Distinguished Professor; Mary Jane Schneider, PhD, traditional & contemporary Plains Indian culture, Native American child development, and survey of Native American art; Birgit Hans, PhD, oral & contemporary literature, research & writing in Indian Studies, contemporary Indian women, American Indian philosophical thought; Greg Gagnon, PhD, history of North American Indians, federal Indian law & policy, reservation economic development

UNIVERSITY OF NORTH DAKOTA
School of Medicine
Indians Into Medicine Program
501 N. Columbia Rd., Box 9001
GRAND FORKS, ND 58203
(701) 777-3037 Gary Farris, Director
Program: Offers assistance to students who are preparing to study or are currently studying to become physicians, nurses and other health professionals. *Publication*: Serpent, Staff and Drum, a quarterly newsletter.

UNIVERSITY OF NORTH DAKOTA
College of Nursing
P.O. Box 9025 • GRAND FORKS, ND 58203
(701) 777-3224 Fax 777-4558
Elizabeth G. Nichols, RN, DNS, FAAN, Director
Deb Wilson, MS, Coordinator
E-mail: deb_wilson@mail.und.nodak.edu
Website: www.und.edu/dept/nursing/rain.html
Program: Quentin N. Burdick Indians Into Nursing (RAIN Program - The Recruitment/Retention of American Indians Into Nursing (RAIN) Project is a support program for American Indians pursuing their bachelors or master's degrees in nursing at the University of North Dakota. *Financial aid*: Scholarships are based on availability of funds. *Publication*: RAIN Notes, newsletter.

MINOT STATE UNIVERSITY
Native American Cultural Center
500 University Ave. West
MINOT, ND 58707 (701) 858-3112
Wylie Hammond, Director

*FORT BERTHOLD COMMUNITY COLLEGE
220 8th Ave. N.
P.O. Box 490 • NEW TOWN, ND 58763
(701) 627-4738 Fax 627-3609
Website: www.fbcc.bia.edu
Bernadine Young Bird, President
Frederick Baker, Vice President
Description: Located near the scenic Lake Sakakawea area of Fort Berthold Reservation. Tribally owned and controlled. The curriculum is founded in liberal arts, which integrates successfully with most professional and paraprofessional career pursuits.

OKLAHOMA

UNIVERSITY OF SCIENCE & ARTS OF OKLAHOMA
Dept. of American Indian Studies
17th & Grand • CHICKASHA, OK 73018
(405) 574-1289 Fax 521-1220
E-mail: fachester1@usao.edu
Web site: www.usao.edu
Dr. Lee Hester, Chairperson
Courses: Cross-Cultural Communication; Oklahoma Indian Tradition & History; Contemporary American Indian Issues; American Indian Literature, Education, Economics, History and Arts; Tribal Government & Law. *Faculty*: Alicia Gonzales, David Padellety, Juanita Pahdopony. *Special program*: Internships with regional tribes and organizations. Financial aid available. Nash Library.

ROGERS STATE COLLEGE
Native American Studies Program
CLAREMORE, OK 74017
(918) 341-7510 Betty F. Scott, Contact

COMANCHE NATION COLLEGE
1608 S.W. 9th St. • LAWTON, OK 73501
Chartered in 2002 by the Comanche Nation'

ROSE STATE COLLEGE
Native American Studies Program
MIDWEST CITY, OK 73110
(405) 733-7308 Joe Johnson, Contact

BACONE COLLEGE
2299 Old Bacone Rd.
MUSKOGEE, OK 74403 (918) 683-4581
Louie Jackson, Counselor; David Cornsilk, Contact
Description: 115 year-old, one-room schoolhouse at Cherokee Baptist Mission in Tahlequah (Indian Territory), Oklahoma's oldest continuing center of higher education, and the only church-related college in the country with an educational mission to American Indians. *Progams*: Offers Associate degrees in the arts and sciences, and various certificate programs.

UNIVERSITY OF OKLAHOMA
Native American Studies
455 W. Lindsey, Rm. 805
NORMAN, OK 73019
(405) 325-2312 Fax 325-0842
Special program: The Native American Studies offers interdisciplinary bachjelor's and master's degree programs designed to provide an academic context that will broaden an understanding of cultural diversity by focusing on Native American cultures and issues. These interdisciplinary degree programs include courses offered by several departments, including anthropology, English, history, music, art history, communication, and geography; Native American Language Program offers instruction by Native speakers in Cherokee, Choctaw, Creek/Seminole, and Kiowa; The Internship Program provides opportunities for students to have the experience of working in a tribal community. Internships will be available with tribal governments, cultural organizations, schools, and federal agencies that serve Indian people. *Faculty*: Barbara Hobson, PhD (Native American Studies); Margaret Mauldin (Native Language Program-Creek); Durbin Feeling (Native Language Program-Cherokee); Leroy Sealy (Native American Language Program-Choctaw); Gus Palmer, Jr., PhD (Anthropology & Native Language Program-Kiowa); Gary C. Anderson, PhD; Jerry Bread, Paula Conlon, PhD; Edgar Heap of Birds, MFA; Craig Womack, PhD; Clara Sue Kidwell, PhD; Alan Velie, PhD; Robert Warrior, PhD; Circe Sturm, PhD; Warren Metcalf, PhD; Joshua Piker, PhD; Morris Foster, PhD; Geary Hobson, PhD; Mary Jo Watson, PhD; Loretta Fowler, PhD; Marcia Haag, PhD; Robert Fields, PhD; . Financial aid: Graduate Teaching Assistantships. Facilities: Western History Collection; Oklahoma Museum of Natural History; within easy access to representatives of more than 60 Indian tribes; the presence of an active Salvage archaeology program for the State of Oklahoma; the resources of the Stovall Museum, and an extensive library collection on the American Indian offer special opportunities for the study of the archaeology, linguistics, ethnohistory and ethnology of the American Indian.

UNIVERSITY OF OKLAHOMA COLLEGE OF LAW
Center for the Study of American Indian Law & Policy
300 W. Timberdell Rd.
NORMAN, OK 73019
(405) 325-4699
Prof. Rennard Strickland, Director

UNIVERSITY OF OKLAHOMA HEALTH SCIENCES CENTER
College of Public Health, Native Amrican Programs
801 N.E. 13th St., P.O. Box 26901
OKLAHOMA CITY, OK 73190 (877) 805-6901
(405) 271-2232 Fax 271-3039
Dolores Subia Bigfoot, Director (405) 271-8858
E-mail: dee-bigfoot@ouhsc.edu
E-mail: coph@ouhsc.edu
Website: www.ouhsc.edu

Center for American Indian Health Research; Headlands Indian Health Careers. Financial aid: Grants to Native American students who are interested in preparing for careers as health professionals.

UNIVERSITY OF OKLAHOMA
COLLEGE OF MEDICINE
Native American Center of Excellence Consortium
P.O. Box 26901
OKLAHOMA CITY, OK 73190
(405) 271-2316
Philip A. McHale, Contact
A federally-funded collaborative program whose ultimate goal is to increase the number of Native American physicians practicing medicine in the U.S. Jointly sponsored by the Center for Tribal Studies, Northeastern State University (Tahlequah, OK) and the University of Oklahoma College of Medicine.

NORTHEASTERN STATE UNIVERSITY
Native American Center of Excellence
Center for Tribal Studies
TAHLEQUAH, OK 74464
(918) 456-5511 ext. 3690 Fax 458-2193
Dr. Neil Morton, Director
Description: A federally-funded collaborative program whose ultimate aim is to increase the number of Native American physicians practicing medicine in the U.S. It is jointly sponsored by the Center for Tribal Studies at Northeastern State University and The University of Oklahoma College of Medicine.

UNIVERSITY OF TULSA
Dept. of Anthropology • TULSA, OK 74104
(918) 631-2348 Fax 631-2540
Instructors: Richard A. Grounds, PhD, Jason Baird Jackson, PhD. *Special facility*: The McFarlin Library; Gilcrease Museum.

UNIVERSITY OF TULSA COLLEGE OF LAW
Native American Law Certificate Program
3120 E. 4th Place • TULSA, OK 74104
(918) 631-3139 Fax 631-2194
Judith Royster, William Rice, Co-directors
E-mail: judith-royster@utulsa.edu
Prepares students for legal work on critical issues that concern American Indians and Native Alaskans. Studies include course work, research, and practical experience in externships and tribal entities. Students completing the program receive the J.D. degree and certification in the Indian law specialty. *Courses*: Federal Indian Law; Native American Natural Resources Law; American Indian Law Seminar; Tribal Government. *Instructors*: Judith Royster and Bill Rice. *Activities*: The American Indian Law Student Organization at the University of Tulsa College of Law is devoted to meeting the social, cultural and educational needs of its membership.

OREGON

OREGON STATE UNIVERSITY
Department of Anthropology
Waldo Hall 238 • CORVALLIS, OR 97331
(503) 737-4515
Special programs: Devotes special emphasis and coordination to programs in cultural resources, applied anthropology, cooperative studies with American Indians, historical archaeology, and ethnohistory; also a summer field school in Oregon archaeolgy. *Instructors*: David R. Brauner, PhD, Robson Bonnichsen, PhD, Director of the Center for the Study of the First Americans.

UNIVERSITY OF OREGON
Dept. of Anthropology • EUGENE, OR 97403
(541) 346-5102 Fax 346-0668
Instructors: C. Melvin Aikens, PhD, Madonna L. Moss, PhD, Ann Gibson Simonds, PhD; Theresa D. O'Nell, PhD, and Thomas J. Connolly (Archaeology-Museum of Anthropology).

EASTERN OREGON UNIVERSITY
Native American Program
1410 "L" Ave. • LA GRANDE, OR 97850
(541) 962-3741 FAX 962-3849

Jackie Leno-Grant, Chair
E-mail: jgrant@eou.edu
Web site: www.eou.edu/~native
Goal: To assist in the development of student potential so that they may achieve educational and personal goals. Assists American Indian and Alaskan Native students in financial aid planning, academic and career counseling and personal guidance. *Activities*: Speel-Ya Indian Student Organization - a cultural and social support group on campus working to educate the campus and community of La Grande on traditional and contemporary Native American life.

LINFIELD COLLEGE
Dept.of Sociology/Anthropology
McMINNVILLE, OR 97128
(503) 434-2286 Fax 434-2566
Special resources: John Dulin Native American art collection.

WESTERN OREGON UNIVERSITY
Department of Anthropology
MONMOUTH, OR 97361
(503) 838-8000
Robin L. Smith, PhD, Chairperson
E-mail: rsmithr@wou.edu
Instructors: Kenneth D. Jensen, PhD, Robin L. Smith, PhD, Paul W. Baxter, PhD, Mariana L. Mace, MA, Curator of Paul Jensen Arctic Museum.

BLUE MOUNTAIN COMMUNITY COLLEGE
Indian Education Coordinator
P.O. Box 100, 2411 NW Carden
PENDLETON, OR 97801
(503) 276-1260 ext. 289
Special program: Provides assistance for Native American students in securing financial aid, academic and social counseling and general assistance.

PORTLAND STATE UIVERSITY
Department of Anthropology
P.O. Box 751 • PORTLAND, OR 97207
(503) 725-3914
Instructors: Thomas Biolsi, PhD, Joe E. Pierce (Professor Emeritus), Fred W. Voget, PhD (Adjunct Professor).

WILLAMETTE UNIVERSITY
Department of Anthropology
900 State St. • SALEM, OR 97301
(503) 370-6060 Fax 375-5398
Instructor: Rebecca J. Dobkins, PhD. *Special resources & facilities*: Byrd & Polleski Collection of Native North American ethnographic and archaeological materials; Native American Gallery of the Ford Museum of Art.

PENNSYLVANIA

GETTYSBURG COLLEGE
Dept. of Sociology & Anthropology
P.O. Box 412 • GETTYSBURG, PA 17325
(717) 337-6191
Instructors: Franklin Loveland, PhD; Frank W. Porter, III, Amelia M. Trevelyan, PhD (Native American art, symbolic anthropology). *Special Resources*: Harcourt Library holdings on Native Americans; The Herman Finkelstein Primitive Mask Collection.

PENNSYLVANIA STATE UNIVERSITY
American Indian Leadership Program (AILP)
320 Rackley Bldg.
UNIVERSITY PARK, PA 16802
(814) 865-1489
Linda Warner, PhD, Director
Description: "AILP is the oldest on-going graduate program for Native Americans in the country. The training of qualified leaders for service to Indian nations is the central aim of the program." Provides advanced degrees offered are MBA, MEd, MS, DEd, and PhD. *Activities*: American Indian Seminar; Native American Indian Student Association; Research Projects; National Conferences; Field Trips. Fianncial aid available in the form of fellowships and graduate asistantships. Publications. Library. Established 1970.

PENNSYLVANIA STATE UNIVERSITY
American Indian Special Education
Teacher Training Program
226B Moore Bldg.
UNIVERSITY PARK, PA 16802
(814) 863-2284
Dr. Anna H. Gajar, Director
Description: Designed to prepare highly trained professionals for careers in the field. The program integrates a behavioral approach to special educatin in the areas of autism, mental retardation, severe emotional disorders, mild learning and behavioral disabilities, and early childhood disabilities. Issues in American Indian special and regular education are emphasized in seminars and coursework. Graduates receive a master's or a doctoral degree in special education. Financial aid available. Established 1983.

SOUTH DAKOTA

*SI TANKA UNIVERSITY
P.O. Box 220 • EAGLE BUTTE, SD 57625
(605) 964-8635 Fax 964-1144
Francine Hall, President
Description: Located on the Cheyenne River Sioux Reservation serving the higher education needs of over 10,000 area residents and and approximately 5,500 enrolled tribal members.

*OGLALA LAKOTA COLLEGE
P.O. Box 490 • KYLE, SD 57752
(605) 455-2321 Fax 455-2787
Thomas Shortbull, President
Stephanie Charging Eagle, Graduate Dept. Director
Programs: Native American Studies Program; Native American Studies Graduate Program.

*SINTE GLESKA UNIVERSITY
Lakota Studies/Creative Writing Program
P.O. Box 107 • MISSION, SD 57555
(605) 856-2355 Fax 856-2011
Victor Douville, Dept. Head
Web site: http://sinte.hills.net/
Instructors: Charlene Lowry, Doris Leader Charge, Simon J. Ortiz. *Special activities*: Annual creative writing and storytelling festival; poetry reading series and residences, and performances and lectures by writers, scholars, and oral tradition masters; awards for creative writing (fiction and poetry). *Publication*: Wanbli Ho Journal, by creative writing program. Library.

DAKOTA WESLEYAN UNIVERSITY
Native American Studies Program
MITCHELL, SD 57301 (605) 995-2650

*SINTE GLESKA UNIVERSITY
P.O. Box 490 • ROSEBUD, SD 57570
(605) 747-2263 Fax 747-2098
Dr. Lionel Bordeaux, President
Leland Bordeaux, V.P.
Lavina Mile, East Reservation Branch Coordinator
The only reservation-based tribal university in the U.S. Established to provide postsecondary education on the Rosebud Sioux Reservation. Offers over 30 certificates, associates or bachelors degree programs. The only Master's in Education for Elementary Teachers located on an Indian Reservation. *Departments & Faculty*: General Studies: Godfrey Loudner & Janice Miller (Co-Chair); Curt Yehnert and Don Krug; Lakota Studies: Victor Douville (Chair), Duane Hollow Horn Bear, Doris Leader Charge, Leland Little Dog, Stanley Red Bird, and Albert White Hat; Education: Archie Beauvais & Cheryl Medearis (Co-Chair) and Trudy Knowles; Secondary Education: Leland Bordeaux (Director), Joe Gill, Mark Ward and David Wiesser; Applied Science (Vocational Education): James Poignee (Director/ Chair), Arlene Brandis, Rod Bordeaux, Vernon Kuper, Trent Teegerstrom, and Benjamin Whiting; Human Services: Sheryl Klein (Chair), Bill Akard, Burdette Clifford and Rodger Hornby; Student Support Services: Fred Leader Charge (Chair), Irene Garrett, Scot Harrison, Jerry Lester and Dwayne Stenstrom; Special Education: Wendy Murray; Art Institute: Margaret MacKichan and Paul Koehler; Business Administration & Management: Nora Antoine (Chair), Craig Anderson and Ron Hutchinson. *Special program*: A Health

Careers Opportunity Program (Oyate Kin Zanipi Ktelo-Health for the People) designed to increase the number of American Indians entering health professions—health careers financial aid information is available directly from the Health Careers Program. *Financial Aid*: Available through the College's Financial Aid Office. *Special facility*: Lakota Archives and Historical Center.

SIOUX FALLS COLLEGE
Dpartment of Native American Studies
1501 South Prairie Ave.
SIOUX FALLS, SD 57101

*SISSETON-WAHPETON
COMMUNITY COLLEGE
P.O. Box 689, Agency Village
SISSETON, SD 57262
 (605) 698-3966 Fax 698-3132
 Elden Lawrence, President
A 2-year tribal college offering Associate of Arts degrees. Special p*rograms*: Community education; Dakota Studies Department. Scholarship: $500 for graduating high school senior that attend SWCC. *Facilities*: Tribal Archives Development. *Publication*: Dakota Language Text (3 texts for learning the Dakota Language). Founded 1974.

BLACK HILLS STATE UNIVERSITY
Native American Studies Program
SPEARFISH, SD 57783
 (605) 642-6343

UNIVERSITY OF SOUTH DAKOTA
Institute of American Indian Studies
414 East Clark St.
VERMILLION, SD 57069-2390
 (605) 677-5209 Fax 677-6525
 Leonard R. Bruguier, Director
 E-Mail: iais@usd.edu
 Web site: www.usd.edu/iais
Serves as the focal point for American Indian related projects, activities, and programs involving the University of South Dakota. Maintains the South Dakota Oral History Center - an active archive of 5,000+ oral history interviews by Indian and non-Indian peoples. *Programs*: Indian Studies major; Indian Studies minor, Masters of Interdisciplinary Studies. *Activities*: Organizes campus programs to promote education and awareness of American Indian culture, issues, and problems; assisting University efforts to recruit and retain American Indian students and faculty; encouraging increased levels of research on American Indian life; and strengthening relations with tribes, tribal colleges, and other appropriate American Indian organizations in the state and region. University sponsored graduate/research assistantship for school year. Library.

TEXAS

UNIVERSITY OF TEXAS
Dept. of Anthropology
AUSTIN, TX 78712 (512) 471-4206
Instructors: Thomas N. Campbell, PhD, E. Mott Davis, PhD, James A. Neely, PhD, Joel Sherzer, PhD, Brian M. Stross, PhD, Greg P. Urban, PhD, Darrell G. Creel, PhD, Anthony C. Woodbury (Linguistics Dept.) *Special programs*: MA and PhD in Folklore. *Special facility*: Texas Archaeological Research Laboratory; Texas Memorial Museum; Linguistic Research Center; A.A. Hill Linguistics Library.

INCARNATE WORD COLLEGE
Department of Anthropology
SAN ANTONIO, TX 78209
 (210) 829-3855 Eloise Stoker, Chairperson
Special program: Native American Studies Program - Interdisciplinary program includes study of land and native plants and animals. *Instructors*: Gilberto Hinojosa, PhD (history); Sara Kerr, PhD (biology); Christy Mackinnon, PhD (biology); Hugh Robichaux, PhD (anthropology); Matthias Schubnell, PhD (Native American Literature); and Eloise Stoker. Library.

UTAH

UTAH STATE UNIVERSITY
Native American Studies Program
LOGAN, UT 84322
 (801) 750-1106

BRIGHAM YOUNG UNIVERSITY
Indian Education Program
Dept. of Anthropology • PROVO, UT 84602
 (801) 378-3058 Fax 378-9368
 E-mail: anthro@byu.edu
 Web site: www.fhss.byu.edu/anthro/
Instructors: Willis M. Banks, Owen C. Bennion, Hall L. Black, Janice White Clemmer, Arturo DeHoyos, William Fox, Frederick R. Gowans, Rondo S. Harmon, Kenneth Rush Sumpter, Victor R. Westover, Darlene Herndon, Charlotte D. Lofgreen, John R. Maestas, Vergus C. Osborn, and W. Dean Rigby. *Anthropology Instructors*: Dale L. Berge, PhD, Donald W. Forsyth, PhD, Ray T. Matheny, PhD, Joel C. Janetski, PhD, James D. Wilde, PhD (Museum of Peoples and Cultures). *Special programs*: Field Schools, historic and prehistoric site, Utah; Nancy Patterson Village Project, southeastern Utah. *Special facilities*: Museum of Peoples and Cultures; archaeological laboratories; Gates Collection on Middle American Languages. Library.

UNIVERSITY OF UTAH
The American West Cernter
1901 E. South Campus Dr., Rm. 1023
SALT LAKE CITY, UT 84112-8922
 (801) 581-7611 Fax 581-7612
 Daniel McCool, PhD, Director
Description: Research unit of the University of Utah, affiliated with the College of Social and Behavioral Sciences. The center consults, researches, publishes, provides educational and curricular support to Indian tribes, school districts, other organizations, and the general public. *Activities*: Works with tribes to develop historical and ethnographical documentation to support legal claims. It has assisted 15 tribes to develop tribal archives relevant to their land, water, and culture. e.g. Ute Mountain Ute Tribal Archive; The Rivers and Fisheries of the Shoshone-Bannock Peoples; The Tohono O'odham Tribal Archive. It provided 1,500 interviews of Native Americans to the Doris Duke Indian Oral History Project.

VIRGINIA

LONGWOOD COLLEGE
Dept. of Sociology & Anthropology
FARMVILLE, VA 23909
 (804) 395-2241 Fax 395-2142
 E-mail: ddalton@longwood.lwc.edu
Special program: The Archaeology Field School is engaged in a long-term project at the site of a Late Woodland prehistoric village located at Staunton River Battlefield State Park in Clover, VA. Library holds the O'Brien Collection of over 5,000 prehistoric Virginia Indian artifacts.

HAMPTON UNIVERSITY
American Indian Educational Opportunities Program
HAMPTON, VA 23668
 (757) 727-5000 Fax 727-5170
 Web site: www.hamptonu.edu
The American Indian Educational Opportunities Program provides scholarship support and other services to eligible students accepted for admission at Hampton University. The program, which is located in the campus museum, has hosted visiting researchers, speakers, conferences, and descendants of early students. It has also contributed short-term support to Native Americans to conduct research on aspects of Hampton's historic American Indian education program. Additional work includes initiating a photographic preservation project centering around the preservation of historic documents, such as those reproduced in "To Lead and To Serve: American Indian Education at Hampton Institute, 1878-1923." The program has sponsored a variety of events, including a regional conference of the American Indian Science & Engi-

neering Society (AISES). In connection with AISES efforts, the program established the first campus chapter of the organization in the state of Virginia and the first at a historically black college and university.

RADFORD UNIVERSITY
Dept. of Sociology & Anthropology
RADFORD, VA 24142
 (540) 831-5253
 Cheryl R. Tieman, Chairperson
Special program: Native American Heritage Association. *Instructors*: Mary Burkheimer La Lone, PhD, Melinda Bollar Wagner, PhD.

WASHINGTON

*NORTHWEST INDIAN COLLEGE
2522 Kwina Rd. • BELLINGHAM, WA 98226
 (360) 676-2772 Fax 738-0136
 Dr. Robert J. Lorence, President
Purpose: To provide postsecondary opportunities for Indian people. Includes academic and vocational education. Provides in-service training, planning, research, and evaluation services to tribal institutions and departments. A tribally-controlled insitution chartered by the Lummi Indian Business Council.

WESTERN WASHINGTON UNIVERSITY
Department of Anthropology, MS-9083
516 High St. AH315
BELLINGHAM, WA 98225
 (360) 650-3620 Fax 650-7668
 Robert C. Marshall, Chairperson
 E-mail: barnes@cc.wwu.edu
 Web site: www.edu/anthro
Courses: Native Peoples of North America, Indians of the Northwest Coast; Ethnohistory, Prehistory of North America, Archaeology of North America. *Instructors*: Daniel L. Boxberger, PhD, Sarah Campbell, PhD, and James Loucky, PhD; Todd Koetje, PhD and adjunct faculty: Lynn A. Robbins, PhD & Leslie Conton, PhD. *Special program*: Archaeological and Ethnohistory Field Schools. *Special facilities*: Archaeological laboratory; The Department of American Cultural Studies offers: The Native American Experience.

EASTERN WASHINGTON UNIVERSITY
Native American Studies Dept.
706 5th St. • CHENEY, WA 99004
 (509) 359-2433

EVERGREEN STATE COLLEGE
Native American Studies Program
OLYMPIA, WA 98505 (206) 866-6000

WASHINGTON STATE UNIVERSITY
Dept. of Anthropology • PULLMAN, WA 99164
 (509) 335-3441 Fax 335-3999
 Tim A. Kohler, PhD, Chairperson
 E-mail: tak@wsu.edu
 Web site: www.edu/lanthro/
Special program: Comparative American Studies; Archaeology and ethnography of the western U.S., with emphasis on American Indian, Pacific and Asian cultural, anthropology, linguistics and archaeology. *Instructors*: Robert E. Ackerman, PhD, John H. Bodley, PhD, Timothy A. Kohler, PhD, William D. Lipe, PhD, Peter J. Mehringer, Jr., PhD, Allan H. Smith, PhD (Prof. Emeritus), Lillian A. Ackerman, PhD (Researcher), Teresa M. Schenck, PhD, and William Willard, PhD (Comparative American Studies.)*Special facilities*: Research laboratories; Museum; extensive research and reference collections in western U.S. archaeology, botany, and ethnographic basketry.

UNIVERSITY OF WASHINGTON
American Indian Studies Center
Department of Anthropology
Box 353100 • SEATTLE, WA 98195
 (206) 543-5240 Fax 543-3285
Special program: The principal areal interests represented by the faculty include Native North America; the American Indian Studies Center, which offers some instruction in North American Indian languages, is an integral part of the Department. *Full-time Faculty*: Donald K. Grayson, PhD, Eugene S. Hunn, PhD, Eric

Alden Smith, PhD, Julie K. Stein, PhD, Gary J. Witherspoon, PhD; *Part-time Faculty*: James D. Nason, PhD and Gail Thompson, PhD. *Special facilities*: Specialized library collection on the American Indian; Thomas Burke Memorial Museum (extensive collections of Northwest Coast Indians and Eskimos artifacts.)

UNIVERSITY OF WASHINGTON
Native American Law Center
SEATTLE, WA 98195 (206) 685-2861
    Robert Anderson, Director

*MEDICINE CREEK TRIBAL COLLEGE
TACOMA, WA 98404
    (253) 593-7950 Fax 593-7895
    Kay Rhoads, President

WISCONSIN

NORTHLAND COLLEGE
Native American Studies Program
P.O. Box 165 • ASHLAND, WI 54806
    (715) 682-1240

UNIVERSITY OF WISCONSIN-EAU CLAIRE
American Ethnic Coordinating Office
105 Garfield Ave., 225 Schofield Hall
EAU CLAIRE, WI 54701
    (715) 836-5989 Fax 836-3499
    Marge Hebbring, Director
    Mary Kuzma, Teacher
    E-mail: hebbrima@uwec.edu
    Marge Hebbring, American Indian
    Student & Services Coordinator
American Indian Studies *Program*: Eau Claire Gear Up Program: A federal grant designed to raise awareness and readiness for undergraduate programs.

*LAC COURTE OREILLES
OJIBWA COMMUNITY COLLEGE
13466 W. Trepania Rd. • HAYWARD, WI 54843
    (715) 634-4790 Fax 634-5049
    Dr. Schuyler Houser, President

*COLLEGE OF MENOMINEE NATION
P.O. Box 1179 • KESHENA, WI 54135
    (715) 799-4921 Fax 799-1308
    Dr. Verna Fowler, President
Offers Associate of Arts and Associate of Science degrees in College Academics, Natural Resources, Health/Nursing, Early Childhood Education, and one in Hospitality Industry and Gaming Management from the National Indian Gaming and Hospitality Institute at the College. Credits are transferable to University of Wisconsin colleges and technical colleges.

MADISON AREA TECHNICAL COLLEGE
3550 Anderson St., Rm. 171
MADISON, WI 53704 (608) 246-6109
    Larry J. White Feather, Counselor
Two year degree programs.

UNIVERSITY OF WISCONSIN
American Indian Studies Program
1188 Educational Sciences
1025 W. Johnson St. • MADISON, WI 53706
    (608) 263-5501 Fax 263-6448
    C. Matthew Snipp, Director
    Beth Ketterer, Program Assistant
    Jeanne Lacourt & Darlene St. Clair,
    Graduate Project Assistant
Description: Recruits Indian faculty and develop courses that deal in depth with American Indians. Assists and encourages Indian students to pursue advanced and professional degrees. Provides information and assistance to individuals and groups interested in American Indians. *Faculty*: Ada E. Deer (senior lecturer-on leave-now serving as Secretary of Interior for Indian Affairs in Washington, DC); Teresa D. LaFromboise (Counseling Psychology & Education); Richard A. Monette (Law); Peter Nabokov and James B. Stoltman (Anthropology); Catherine Price (History); Gary D. Sandefur (Sociology); C. Matthews Snipp, Thomas A. Heberlein, and Gene Summers (Rural Sociology); Jeffrey Steele and Roberta Hill Whiteman (English). *Special programs*: Brown Bag Lecture Series; Resource Center; Student Organization, "Wunk

Sheek"; Indigenous Law Student Association; Council of American Indian Graduate and Professional Students; branch of American Indian Science & Engineering Society. *Publication*: Newsletter.

UNIVERSITY OF WISCONSIN
Native American Studies Program
College of Letters & Sciences
P.O. Box 413 • MILWAUKEE, WI 53201
    John Boatman, PhD, Coordinator
Courses: Great Lakes American Indian ethnobotany; anthropology (courses on American Indians of Northeast, Wisconsin, general American Indian societies and cultures, religions, and the southwest); ethnic studies (western Great Lakes American Indian community life of the past); history (courses on American Indian history); philosophy (Great Lakes American Indian philosophy); dreams and visions in American Indian metaphysics. *Instructors*: John Boatman, PhD; Jo Allyn Archambault, PhD; Keewaydinoquay, and Fixico. Special programs: American Indian Art Festival; Wisconsin Woodland American Indian Summer Field Institute. *Financial aid*: Minority Achievement Scholarship for high school seniors; Undergraduate Minority Retention Grant for 2nd, 3rd and 4th year college students; Bureau of Indian Affairs and Wisconsin Indian grants. *Special facility*: Milwaukee Public Museum.

UNIVERSITY OF WISCONSIN-OSHKOSH
Dept. of Anthropology • OSHKOSH, WI 54901
    (414) 424-4406
Special program: Minority Studies Program.
Instructor: Jack Steinbring, PhD.

UNIVERSITY OF WISCONSIN-STEVENS POINT
Weekend College Program for Native Americans
122 Collins Classroom Center
STEVENS POINT, WI 54481
    (715) 346-2044
    Beth Rose Hanson, Coordinator
Associates Degree program for Native Americans designed to accomodate the employment and family obligations of the individual.

WYOMING

WIND RIVER TRIBAL COLLEGE
ETHETE, WY
Bilingual Education program
    Eugene Ridgely, Jr., Director
Arapaho language revitalization effort.

UNIVERSITY OF WYOMING
American Indian Studies Program
Room 109A, Anthropology Bldg.
P.O. Box 3431 • LARAMIE, WY 82071
    (307) 766-6521 Fax 766-2473
    Judith Antell, Director
    E-mail: antell@uwyo.edu
    Website: www.uwadmnweb.uwyo.edu/aist/
Faculty members: Judith Antell; Adrian Bantjes; Silvester Brito, PhD; William Gribb, PhD; Michael Harkin, PhD; Jeanne Holland, PhD; Brian Hosmer, PhD; Pamela Innes; Mary Lou Larson, PhD. *Description*: Offers an 18 credit hour academic minor. Examines Native North American culture and social life from both historical and contemporary perspectives. Offers support services designed for the intellectual, social, and cultural needs and interests of Native students. Outreach efforts; American Indian Alumni Association; Honoring of American Indian Graduates. *Events*: Fall Forum each November brings renowned American Indian scholars, writers, and artists to the campus; and American Indian Week in March. *Financial Aid*: The Frank and Cynthia McCarthy Scholarship; John and Ada Thorpe Scholarship; Robert W. Winner Memorial Scholarship; deadline Feb. 15th. Library (books mainly about Wind River Reservation, Eastern Shoshone and Northern Arapahoe people.

UNIVERSITY OF WYOMING
College of Arts and Sciences
Indian Education Office, P.O. Box 3254
LARAMIE, WY 82071
    (307) 766-6520
Provides support services to American Indian students who attend the University of Wyoming.

AMERICAN INDIAN COLLEGE FUND MEMBER COLLEGES

Bay Mills Community College, Brimley, MI
Blackfeet Community College, Browning, MT
Cankdeska Cikana Community College,
    Fort Totten, ND
Chief Dull Knife College, Lame Deer, MT
College of Menominee Nation, Keshena, WI
Crownpoint Institute of Technology, Crownpoint, NM
D-Q University, Davis, CA
Dine College, Tsaile, AZ
Fond du Lac Community College, Cloquet, MN
Fort Belknap Community College, Harlem, MT
Fort Berthold Community College, New Town, ND
Fort Peck Community College, Poplar, MT
Haskell Indian Nations University, Lawrence, KS
Institute of American Indian Arts, Santa Fe, NM
Keweenaw Bay Ojibwa Community College,
    Baraga, MI
Lac Courte Oreilles Ojibwa Community College,
    Hayward, WI
Leech Lake Tribal College, Cass Lake, MN
Little Big Horn College, Crow Agency, MT
Little Priest Tribal College, Winnebago, NE
Nebraska Indian Community College, Macy, NE
Northwest Indian College, Bellingham, WA
Oglala Lakota College, Kyle, SD
Saginaw Chippewa Tribal College, Mt. Pleasant, MI
Salish Kootenai College, Pablo, MT
Si Tanka University, Eagle Butte, SD
Sinte Gleska University, Rosebud, SD
Sisseton Wahpeton Community College, Sisseton, SD
Sitting Bull (Standing Rock) College, Fort Yates, ND
Southwest Indian Polytechnic Institute,
    Albuquerque, NM
Stone Child Community College, Box Elder, MT
Tohono O'odham Community College,
Turtle Mountain Community College, Belcourt, ND
United Tribes Technical College, Bismarck, ND
White Earth Tribal & Community College,
    Mahnomen, MN
Wind River Tribal College, Ethete, WY

DIRECTORIES & REFERENCE BOOKS

CHURCH PHILANTHROPY FOR NATIVE AMERICANS & OTHER MINORITIES
Phyllis A. Meiners, Editor
Profiles over 65 grant programs & about 35 loan programs from church & religious institutions for Native American, Hispanic, and other minority groups. Eleven denominations are included. with contact persons, special interests, sample grants, application deadlines & procedures, etc. 280 pp. CRC Publishing. $118.95.

THE CORPORATE & FOUNDATION FUNDRAISING MANUAL FOR NATIVE AMERICANS
A step-by-step guide to securing private sector grants, outlining basic fundraising and research procedures. Helps Native American planners diversify their funding base with private sector dollars. 3rd Edition. 288 pp. CRC Publishing. $129.95.

EDUCATION ASSISTANCE FOR AMERICAN INDIANS & ALASKA NATIVES
Master of Public Health Program for American Indians
School of Public Health, 1994. No charge.

FEDERAL PROGRAMS OF ASSISTANCE TO AMERICAN INDIANS: A REPORT PREPARED FOR THE SENATE SELECT COMMITTEE ON INDIAN AFFAIRS OF THE U.S. SENATE
Roger Walke, Editor
335 pp. U.S. Government Printing Office. No charge.

FINANCIAL AID FOR NATIVE AMERICANS
Gaill A. Schlachter & R. David Weber
Describes 1,500 grants, scholarships, fellowships, loans, awards, prizes, and internships open specifically to Native Americans. Includes sponsor, title, residency requirements, where the money can be spent, type of funding, and deadline date; Also, purpose, financial data, eligibility, duration, special features, limitations, number awarded, and deadline date. Includes contact information, fax numbers, toll-free numbers, e-mail addresses, and web site. 500 pp. Reference Service Press, El Dorado Hills Business park, 5000 Windplay Dr., Suite 4, El Dorado Hills, CA 95762 (916) 939-9620 Fax 939-9626. E-mail: findaid@aol.com Web site: www.rspfunding.com

NATIONAL DIRECTORY OF CORPORATE PHILANTHROPY FOR NATIVE AMERICANS
Contains some 40 corporate giving programs and corporate foundations each of whom have made multiple grants to Native American tribes and organizations in the last few years. 240 pp. CRC Publishing. $98.95.

NATIONAL DIRECTORY OF FOUNDATION GRANTS FOR NATIVE AMERICANS
Documents the philanthropy of 56 private Foundations considered to be the prominent funders of Native American programs. Mainstream foundations who target American Indian communities and those who earmark Native American studies and education programs are featured. 205 pp. CRC Publishing. $9w9.95

NATIONAL DIRECTORY OF PHILANTHROPY FOR NATIVE AMERICANS
Phyllis A. Meiners, Editor
Profiles 39 private sector grant makers (24 foundations, 12 corporations, and 3 religious institutions), prominent funders of Native American programs. 160 pp. CRC Publishing. $69.95.

NATIONAL DIRECTORY OF SEED MONEY GRANTS FOR AMERICAN INDIAN PROJECTS
Lists private sector seed money grants for start-up and innovative programs managed by Native Americans. Small "alternative" foundation grantmakers who focus on projects of self determination and social change are featured. A section devoted to American Indian foudnations (grants from American Indians to American Indians) is included. 220 pp. CRC Publishing, $109.95.

SOURCES OF FINANCIAL AID AVAILABLE TO AMERICAN INDIAN STUDENTS
Leslie A. Kedelty, Editor
Major sources of financial aid for Native American students; and admissions & financial aid information. Includes program reps, BIA area offices, and job opportunities. 78 pp. Annual. Paper. Indian Resource Development (IRD), $5.

FOUNDATION GRANT MAKERS

ACADEMY OF APPLIED SCIENCES
1 Maple St. • Concord, NH 03301
(603) 225-2072
Research and Engineering Apprenticeship Program (REAP) for High School Students. $1,250 stipend. *Deadline*: February.

ALASKA STATE COUNCIL ON THE ARTS
411 W. Fourth St. #1E • Anchorage, AK 99501
(888) 278-7424; (907) 269-6610 Fax 269-6601
Traditional Native Arts Apprenticeships: Grants of $2,000 each for the maintenance and development of the traditional arts of Alaska's native people. *Deadline*: April for Fall and September for Spring.

AMERICAN ASSOCIATION OF UNIVERSITY WOMEN EDUCATIONAL FOUNDATION
1111 16th St., NW • Washington, DC 20036
(202) 728-7603
Focus Professions Fellowships: Financial assistance to underrepresented minority women who are interested in entering designated fields with traditionally low female participation. The stipends range from $5,000 to $9,500 for full-time study. *Deadline*: December. *Harris Fellowship*: To minority women postdoctorates who have achieved distinction or promise of distinction. The stipend is $20,000. *Deadline*: November. *Postdoctoral Fellowships*: The stipend ranges from $20,000 to $25,000. *Deadline*: November.

AMERICAN BAPTIST CHURCHES USA
P.O. Box 851 • Valley Forge, PA 19482
(800) ABC-3USA, ext. 2067
Fax (610) 768-2056
Web site: www.abc-em.org
ABC Native American Grants: To provide financial assistance in preparing for a ministerial career. Open to Native Americans who are American Baptists and are interetsed in preparing for ministerial service.

AMERICAN BAR FOUNDATION
750 N. Lake Shore Dr. • Chicago, IL 60611
(312) 988-600
Law and Social Science Summer Research Fellowships for Minorities: To provide work experience to underrepresented minority undergraduates who might be considering a legal career. Participants receive $300 per week for ten weeks during the summer. *Deadline*: May.

AMERICAN CHEMICAL SOCIETY
1155 16th St., NW • Washington, DC 20036
Dept. of Minority Affairs (800) 227-5558 x 6250
(202) 872-6250 Fax 776-8003
E-mail: r_hughes@acs.org
Web site: www.acs.org
Scholars Program: For underrepsented minority students with a strong interest in chemistry and a desire to pursue a career in a chemically-related science. Up to $2,500 per year for up to two years. *PPG Scholarship Plus Awards*: To provide financial assistance and work experience to underrepresented minority students. Up to $2,500 for up to four years. *Deadlines*: February of each year.

AMERICAN FUND FOR DENTAL HEALTH
ADA Endowment & Assistance Fund, Inc.
211 East Chicago Ave., Suite 820
Chicago, IL 60611
(312) 440-2567 Fax 440-2822
Marsha Mountz, Contact
Dental Scholarships for Minority Students: To recruit more minority Americans into the field of dentistry. $2,000 per year. *Deadline*: July 1. *Dental Laboratory Technology Scholarship*. $1,000 per year. Deadline: August 15. *Requirements*: Must be a member of a minority group, including Native Americans; must have at least a 2.5 GPA.

AMERICAN GEOLOGICAL INSTITUTE
4220 King St. • Alexandria, VA 22302
(703) 379-2480 Fax 379-7563
Web site: www.agiweb.org
AGI Minority Geoscience Scholarships: To minority undergraduate or graduate students interestd in pursuing degrees in the geosciences. Up to $10,000 per year. *AGI Fellowships for Ethnic Minorities*:   Up to $4,000 per year. *Deadline*: January.

AMERICAN INDIAN GRADUATE CENTER
4520 Montgomery Blvd. NE, Suite 1-B
Albuquerque, NM 87109
(505) 881-4584 Fax 883-6694
Graduate Fellowships for American Indian & Alaskan Native Students: Provides fellowship grants to American Indian and Alaska Native graduate students. In 1994 the Center assisted over 600 students from 130 tribes who were working on graduate degrees at over 200 colleges throughout the U.S. *Deadline*: May.

AMERICAN INDIAN HERITAGE FOUNDATION
6051 Arlington Blvd. • Falls Church, VA 22044
(202) INDIANS Fax (703) 532-1921
E-mail: aihf@dgsys.com
Web site: www.indians.org/aihf
Scholarship: To Native American youth interested in pursuing postsecondary education. Up to $1,000. *Miss Indian USA Scholarship Program*: To recognize and reward the most beautiful and talented Native American women. An academic scholarship to a college or university of up to $4,000 plus a cash grant of $6,500, a wardrobe allowance of $2,000, appearance fees of $3,000, gifts worth more than $4,000. A total of over $26,000. Deadline: October.. *Outstanding Indian Youth Program*: Financial assistance to Native American youth interested in pursuing postsecondary education.

AMERICAN INDIAN LAW CENTER
1117 Stanford, NE, P.O. Box 4456, Sta. A
Albuquerque, NM 87196
(505) 277-5462 Fax 277-1035
Prelaw Summer Institutes for American Indians and Alaska Natives: To prepare Native Amerians to be successful law students and lawyers. Students receive funding to cover tuition, textbooks, personal expenses, and some travel. $1,500. *Deadline*: March.

AMERICAN INDIAN LAW REVIEW
300 Timberdell Rd. • Norman, OK 73019
(405) 325-2840 Fax 325-6282
E-mail: lockarjh@wilkinson.law.ou.edu
Web site: www.law.ou.edu
American Indian Law Writing Competition: To reward outstanding unpublished papers written by law students on American Indian law. First prize, $1,000 and publication of paper in Law Review. Second prize, $500; Third prize, $250. *Deadline*: January.

AMERICAN INDIAN MENTAL HEALTH RESEARCH & DEVELOPMENT CENTER
Minority Research Resources Branch
National Institute of Mental Health
Parklawn Bldg., Rm. 1895
5600 Fishers Lane • Rockville, MD 20857
(301) 443-3724
Grants: To provide funding for American Indian mental health research and development centers. The amount varies, depending upon the nature of the proposed program. Recipient organizations must agree to serve as a resource for the training of both new and established American Indian mental health researchers. *Deadline*: dates vary each year. Check the Federal Register for current schedule.

AMERICAN INDIAN SCHOLARSHIP FUND/TRY, INC.
c/o American Indian Studies Center
University of California, Los Angeles
405 Hilgard Ave. • Los Angeles, CA 90024
(213) 825-0893 Earl Dean Sisto, Contact
American Indian Loan Program: To Native American college students on an emergency basis. Up to $500 per application. No deadlines.

AMERICAN INDIAN SCHOLARSHIPS, INC.
4520 Montgomery Blvd., N.E., Suite 1-B
Albuquerque, NM 87109; (505) 881-4584

Graduate Fellowships for American Indians: Financial assistance to Native American students who wish to pursue graduate education. From $250 to $10,000 per year based on need. *Deadline*: April for summer session; May for fall session.

AMERICAN INDIAN SCIENCE & ENGINEERING SOCIETY
P.O. Box 9828 • Albuquerque, NM 87119-9828
(505) 765-1052 Fax 765-5608
Norbert S. Hill, Jr., Executive Director
A.T. Anderson Memorial Scholarship Program: To aid Native American (at least 25% descent) science and engineering students. Must attend an accredited college, be a member of the Society, and major in science, engineering, or a related discipline. Average scholarship is $1,000 per year, renewable. *Deadline*: June 30th - August 1st. *Al Qoyawayma Award for Excellence in Arts & Science*: To artistically-talented students who are members of the society. Applicants must have applied for Anderson Memorial Scholarship. $1,500 for one year. *Deadline*: June. *Circle of Life Essay Scholarship Prizes*: To recognize and reward American Indian high school students who write an essay on their spiritual values. $1,000 scholarship and a $200 personal cash award. *Deadline*: March. *Conference Grants*: Financial assistance for members of the society who wish to attend the society's annual conference. Pays conference fees, room and board. 200 awarded each year. *EPA Tribal Lands Environmental Science Scholarship*: For outstanding college students interested in studying environmental or related sciences. $4,000 per year; one year, renewable upon reapplication. *Deadline*: June. *Santa Fe Pacific Foundation Grant*: Financial assistance to outstanding Native American high school seniors interested in pursuing postsecondary education. Amount ranges from $1,000 to $2,500 per year. *Deadline*: March. *Polingaysi Qoyawayma Scholarship*: Continued teacher education in science and math. Graduate study. $1,000. *Deadline*: June. *Norbert S. Hill, Jr. Leadership Award*: Financial assistance to members for college. $1,500. *Deadline*: June. *Robert W. Brocksbank Scholarship*: For members who wish to pursue undergraduate or graduate school education. $1,500. *Deadline*: June. *Schuyler M. Meyer, Jr. Scholarship Fund*: Financial assistance to members who are single parents. $1,000. *Deadline*: June.

AMERICAN INDIAN STUDIES CENTER
University of California, Los Angeles
Attn: Fellowship Coordinator
3220 Campbell Hall, Box 951548
Los Angeles, CA 90024 (310) 825-7315
Web site: www.gdnet.ucla.edu/iacweb/iachome.htm
American Indian Studies Postdoctoral & Visiting Scholars Fellowship Program: Financial assistance to Native Americans who wish to pursue their research at UCLA's American Indian Studies Center. Postdoctoral fellows receive from $23,000 to 28,000 per year. *Deadline*: December.

AMERICAN INDIAN TEACHER TRAINING PROGRAM
2424 Springer Dr., Suite 200
Norman, OK 73069 (405) 364-0656
Stuart A. Tonemah, Contact
Requirements: Must be an American Indian or Alaska Native; undergraduate degree with 3.0 GPA; must be an American Indian teacher or teacher of American Indian/Alaska Natives. Selected participants will study for a Masters of Education degree at Oklahoma City University. *Amount*: Full tuition, living stipend, and dependence allowance.

AMERICAN LEGION AUXILIARY
1718 Statz St. • N. Las Vegas, NV 89030
Silver Eagle Indian Scholarship: Financial assistance for postsecondary education to the dependents of American Indian veterans. The stipend is $200.

AMERICAN PHILOSOPHICAL SOCIETY
Attn: Library, 105 S. Fifth St.
Philadelphia, PA 19106
(215) 440-3400 Fax 440-3436
Dr. Edward C. Carter, Librarian
Phillips Fund Grants for Research in American Indian Linguistics and Ethnohistory. Prefers supporting the

work of younger scholars, including graduate students. From $1,200 to 1,500 per year. *Deadline*: February.

AMERICAN PHYSICAL SOCIETY
Minorities Scholarship Program
1 Physics Ellipse • College Park, MD 20740
(301) 209-3200 Fax 209-0865
Web site: www.aps.org
Corporate Sponsored Scholarships for Minority Undergraduate Students in Physics. $2,000 awarded to the student for tuition, room and board, and $500 awarded to the host department. *Deadline*: Feb. 14th of each year.

AMERICAN PLANNING ASSOCIATION
1776 Massachusetts Ave., N.W.
Washington, DC 20036
(202) 872-0611 Fax 872-0643
C. Vlaskamp, Contact
Planning Fellowships: For minority students enroled in a master's degree program at recognized planning schools. From $2,000 to $5,000 per year. *Deadline*: May. *The Planning and the Black Commuity Division - Undergraduate Minority Scholarship Program*: Available to minority students seeking an undergraduate planning degree. *Deadline*: May 15th.

AMERICAN SOCIETY FOR MICROBIOLOGY
1325 Massachusetts Ave., NW
Washington, DC 20005
(202) 737-3600 Ext. 295
Predoctoral Minority Fellowship Program: Financial assistance to minority predoctoral graduate students in microbiology. A stipend of up to $5,000 and an additional amount of up to $4,250 to cover tuition and fees. Funded by the Proctor & Gamble Co. and the Foundation for Microbiology. *Deadline*: April.

ARIZONA BOARD OF REGENTS
2020 N. Central Ave. #230
Phoenix, AZ 85004-4503
(602) 255-4082
Arizona Indian Tuition Remission: To Native Americns in Arizona who wish to pursue postsecondary education. *Deadline*: Applications are to be submitted to the student aid offices at the campuses where the students are accepted.

ARROW, INC.
1000 Connecticut Ave., NW #1204
Washington, DC 20036 (888) ARROW10
(202) 296-0685 Fax 659-4377
E-mail: arrow1949@aol.com
Graduate Scholarship Program: Financial assistance to Native American graduate students in nursing and other fields. Administered by the American Indian Graduate Center.

ASSOCIATION OF AMERICAN INDIAN PHYSICIANS
1235 Sovereign Row, Suite C-7
Oklahoma City, OK 73108
(405) 946-7072 Fax 946-7651
Matthew Kauley, Executive Director
Pew Memorial Trust Scholarship: Financial assistance for Native American students interested in the medical sciences. Amount varies. *Deadline*: July. *Whitecloud Scholarship Fund*: Financial aid to Native American medical students in need of emergency assistance. Up to $250.

ASSOCIATION ON AMERICAN INDIAN AFFAIRS
Attn: Scholarship Coordinator
966 Hungerford Dr., Suite 12-B
Rockville, MD 20850
(240) 314-7155 Fax 314-7159
Jack F. Trope, Executive Director
Web site: www.bluecloud.org/aaia
AAIA Displaced Homemaker Scholarships: To provide financial assistance to Native American mid-life homemakers, both men and women, who are trying to complete their college education;of degree of Indian *Deadline*: August. *Adolph Van Pelt Scholarships*: To provide financial assistance to Native American students interested in postsecondary education. $500-800 per year. *Deadline*: July. *Sequoyah Graduate Fellowships*: To Native Americans interested in pursuing graduate education. $1,500 per year. *Deadline*: September.

BACONE COLLEGE
2299 Old Bacone Rd.
Muskogee, OK 74403
(918) 683-4581
Sarah Morgan, Contact
Miss Louie LeFlore Scholarship and Mr. Grant Foreman Centennial Award. Must be a member of one of the Five Civilized Tribes of Oklahoma and be at least 1/4 Indian blood. Preference is given to students in nursing or health related fields. From $100 to $300. *Deadline*: July 1.

BAY AREA URBAN LEAGUE
Attn: Education Committee
344 20th St., Suite 211
Oakland, CA 94612 (510) 839-8011
Scholarhip Awards: Financial assistance to Native Americans who live in northern California and who are interested in pursuing postsecondary education. Minimum 3.0 grade point average. The stipends are $1,000 each. *Deadline*: May.

BERGER MEMORIAL SCHOLARSHIP
Center for Native American Studies
2-152 Wilson Hall - Montana State University
Bozeman, MT 59717 (406) 994-3881
Requirements: Must be a Native American attending MSU and maintain the required GPA. Amount: $1,000 per year per student. *Deadline*: March1.

BHP-MINERALS SCHOLARSHIP
Attn: Human Resources
P.O Box 155 • Fruitland, NM 87416
(505) 598-5861
Raymond O. Tsosie, Contact
Scholarship for enrolled member of Navajo or Ute Mountain Ute Indian. One year, renewable contingent on eligibility until attainment of Bachelor's Degree. Minimum 3.0 grade point average. Minimum individual awards of $500. *Deadline*. August 1.

BREMER (OTTO) FOUNDATION
445 Minnesota St., #2000
St. Paul, MN 55101
(612) 227-8036 Fax 227-2522
Charlotte S. Johnson, Contact
Grants awarded to promote cooperation that makes people self-reliant. Programs which focus on racism and rural poverty are of high priority. Also specific priorities include: community affairs, education, health, human services, and religion. *Geographic Interest*: Minnesota, North Dakota, and Wisconsin.

BROWN UNIVERSITY
John Carter Brown Library
P.O. Box 1894 • Providence, RI 02912
(401) 863-2725
John Carter Brown Library Long-Term & Short-Term Research Fellowships: To support scholars interested i conducting reseach at the library, renowned for its collection of historical sources pertaining to the exploration, settlement, and development of the New World (especially those relating to Native American populations and development.) Long-Term - stipends for 6-month fellowships are $13,750; stipends for 12-month fellowships are $27,500; Short-Term - $800 per month. *Deadline*: January.

BUDER SCHOLARSHIP FOR AMERICAN INDIAN LAW STUDENTS
Washington University School of Law
C.B. 1120 • St. Louis, MO 63130
(314) 935-4525; Kip Darcy, Contact
Requirements: Must be enrolled in a federally recognized Indian tribe or possessing one-eighth degree of Indian blood; appllicant must be accepted into any School of Law. *Amount*: Full tuition or partial tuition for three years. *Deadline*: March 1.

BUSH FOUNDATION
E-900 First National Bank Bldg.
332 Minnesota • St. Paul, MN 55101
(612) 227-0891
Humphrey Doermann, President
170 grants awarded in the following special interest areas: education, culture, arts, social services, health, scholarships, minorities, women, historic preservation, medicine

**BUSINESS & PROFESSIONAL
WOMEN'S FOUNDATION**
2012 Massachusetts Ave., N.W.
Washington, D.C. 20036 (202) 293-1200
  Linda Sayer & Jean Findeis, Contacts

JOHN CARTER BROWN LIBRARY
Brown University • P.O. Box 1894
Providence, RI 02912 (401) 863-2725
Long-Term and Short-Term Research Fellowships: For scholars interested in doing research at the Library. Applicant must hold a doctorate. Long-Term - $13,750 (6 months) and $27,500 (one year.); Short-Term -$800 per month (1-4 months). *Deadline*: February.

CALIFORNIA DEPARTMENT OF EDUCATION
c/o American Indian Education Office
P.O. Box 944272 • Sacramento, CA 94244
  (916) 322-9744
Maple Creek Willie Scholarship Fund: For educational purposes to high school graduate California Indians. Up to $1,250 per year.

CARMINE FELICA D'ONOFRIO SCHOLARSHIP
Georgia Tech University • Atlanta, GA 30332
  (404) 894-3354 Dr. Lytia Howard
Scholarship open to any Native American who will attend Georgia Institute of Technology in the disciplines of engineering or computer science. Must be a member of a Federal or State recognized tribe. $3,000 per year. Deadline: flexible.

CARNEGIE CORPORATION OF NEW YORK
437 Madison Ave. • New York, NY 10022
  (212) 371-3200 David A. Hamburg, President
Special interests include: public affairs, education, health, children, youth, minorities, world peace, drug abuse, nonprofit management, scholarships. Grants to schools, colleges, universities, and organizations.

**CITIZEN'S SCHOLARSHIP
FOUNDATION OF AMERICA, INC.**
P.O. Box 297 • St. Peter, MN 56082
  (507) 931-1682
Fluor Daniel Engineering Scholarship Program for Minorities and Women. Applicants are limited to a small number of major universities. Amount awarded varies but is generally at least $1,000 each year. *Deadline*: February of each year.

CLARK (EDNA McCONNELL) FOUNDATION
250 Park Ave., Rm. 900 • New York, NY 10177
  (212) 986-7050; Peter D. Bell, President
Special interests" children, disadvantaged, youth, homelessness, families, justice, research, education. The foundation's mission is to improve conditions of people who are poorly served by existing social institutions. The foundation has in recent years made several grants to American Indian projects.

**COLLEGE SCHOLARSHIP SERVICE
OF THE COLLEGE BOARD**
45 Columbus Ave. • New York, NY 10019
  (212) 713-8000
Business Administration & Engineering Scholarship Programs for Minority Community College Graduates. Sponsored by the General Electric Foundation. Amounts awarded depends upon financial needs. *Deadline*: December of each year.

**CONSORTIUM FOR GRADUATE
STUDY IN MANAGEMENT**
Box 1132, One Brookings Dr.
St. Louis, MO 63130 (314) 889-6353
  Dr. Wallace L. Jones, Executive Director
Graduate Fellowships in Business Administration for Minorities: Tuition and $3,000 stipend (first year) and $2,000 (second year). *Deadline*: January.

**CONTINENTAL SOCIETY,
DAUGHTERS OF INDIAN WARS**
2876 Faraday Court • Decatur, GA 30033
  Denise G. Rice, Contact
Scholarship to a certified tribal member of a Federally recognized tribe who plan to work in the field of education or social services on a reservation. *Amount*: $500. One year renewable. *Deadline*: March.

CORNELL UNIVERSITY
Mathematical & Theoretical Biology Institute
Attn: Biometrics Unit
435 Warren Hall • Ithaca, NY 14853
  (607) 255-8103 Fax 255-4698
  E-mail: mtbi@cornell.edu
  Web site: www.biom.cornell.edu/MTB/index.html
Cornell-Sacnas Summer Program for Latinos & Native Americans: To enable Chicano, Latino and Native American students to participate in a summer institute on mathematical biology at Cornell University. $2,000 & transportation, room and board. *Deadline*: February.

**COUNCIL OF ENERGY
RESOURCE TRIBES (CERT)**
1999 Broadway #2600 • Denver, CO 80202
  (303) 297-2378 Fax 296-5690
  Attn: Education Program Director
CERT Scholarships: To Native American college students who are interested in pursuing postsecondary education in the areas of engineering, sciences, or business, and have at least a 2.5 GPA. $1,000 per year. *Deadline*: July of each year. *CERT Tribal Internship Program*: To offer work opportunities to American Indian college students who are interested in the scientific, technical, or policy areas. *Deadline*: March. *CERT Year-Long Internship*: To provide work experience to Indian undergraduate and graduate students at the offices of CERT. $10 per hour for 30 hours a week.

CROWE MEMORIAL SCHOLARSHIP FUND
P.O. Box 892 • Cherokee, NC 28719
  Amy Walker, President; Doris Hipps, V.P.

DANFORTH FOUNDATION
231 S. Bemiston Ave.
St. Louis, MO 63105
  (314) 862-6200
Dorothy Danforth Compton Minority Fellowships: To minority graduate students who wish to be college teachers and who attend one of 10 universities supported by Danforth Foundation grants: Brown, Chicago, Columbia, Howard, Stanford, Texas at Austin, UCLA, Vanderbilt, Washington and Yale. Contact universities for application and information.

**D'ARCY McNICKLE CENTER FOR THE
HISTORY OF THE AMERICAN INDIAN**
Newberry Library, 60 W. Walton St.
Chicago, IL 60610 (312) 943-9090
  Margaret Curtis, Contact
Predoctoral Fellowships: To support doctoral research in residence at the Newberry Library's D'Arcy McNickel Center. $9,000 per year. *Deadline*: January. *Memorial Fellowships*: Short-term fellowships for Native Americans interested in writing their tribal histories, or graduate research. $300 per each week of residency. *Deadline*: January & July. *Frances C. Allen Fellowships*: To promote Native American women college graduates. Amount varies. *Dealine*: January & July. *Rockefeller Foundation Junior & Senior Postdoctoral Fellowships for Indian History*: To support research in residence at the Center for scholars interested in Indian-white relations and Western Americana. Junior - $17,000 per year; Senior - $27,500 per year. *Deadline*: January. *Summer Institute in American Indian History Fellowships*: Financial assistance to secondary school teachers and administrators interested in attending the Summer Institute at the Newberry Library. $2,200 per year. *Deadline*: March. *Documentary Fellowships*: To college and university faculty who have participated in the center's Documentary Workshop. $800 per month. *Deadline*: February or July.

DARTMOUTH COLLEGE
Attn: Asst. Dean of Graduate Studies
6062 Wentworth, Rm. 305
Hanover, NH 03755 (603) 646-2107
Charles A. Eastman Dissertation Fellowship for Native American Scholars: To Native American doctoral students who are interested in working ontheir dissertation at Dartmouth College. $25,000. *Deadline*: March.

DAUGHTERS OF THE AMERICAN REVOLUTION
American Indians Committee
1776 D St., NW • Washington, DC 20006

  (202) 628-1776
American Indian Scholarships: Financial assistance for Native American students who wish to pursue postsecondary education. $500 per year; one time award. *Deadlines*: October for Spring, June for Fall.

THE EDUCATIONAL FOUNDATION OF AMERICA
23161 Ventura Blvd., Suite 201
Woodland Hills, CA 91364
  (818) 999-0921
  Richard W. Hansen, Executive Director
Ettinger Scholarships provides educational grants—aid for Native Americans. Has supported a variety of projects for American Indian educational institutions.

FALMOUTH INSTITUTE SCHOLARSHIP
Attn: Scholarship Program
3702 Pender Dr., Suite 300
Fairfax, VA 22030 (800) 992-4489
  (703) 352-2250 Fax 352-2323
  Web site: www.falmouthinst.com
Purpose: To provide financial assistance for postsecondary education to American Indian high school seniors. $1,000 per year. *Deadline*: April.

FLORIDA DEPARTMENT OF EDUCATION
Attn: Office of Student Financial Assistance
255 Collins Bldg., 325 W. Gaines St.
Tallahassee, FL 32399 (888) 827-2004
  (850) 488-4095 Fax 488-3612
Seminole - Miccosukee Indian Scholarship Program: For Florida's Seminole and Miccosukee Indian students who wish to pursue postsecondary education in a Florida college or university. Up to $2,000 per year. *Deadline*: August.

FORD FOUNDATION
National Research Council
Attn: Fellowship Office
2101 Constitution Ave., NW
Washington, DC 20418
  (202) 334-2860 Fax 334-3419
  E-mail: infofell@nas.edu
  Web site: fellowships.nas.edu
Predoctoral & Postdoctoral Fellowhsip Programs for Minorities: To provide financial assistance to minority students. See listing under National Research Council.

FUND OF THE SACRED CIRCLE
122 W. Franklin Ave. # 518
Minneapolis, MN 55404
  (612) 879-0602 Fax 879-0613
  Steven Newcom, Executive Director
  Lucy Rogers, Development Director
  Jim Sauder, Operations Director
  Joy Palmer, Program Director
  E-mail: joy@headwatersfund.org
  Website: www.headwatersfund.org
A cooperative program of The Headwaters Fund and the Wisconsin Community Fund, directed by The Headwaters Fund, and a catalyst for social change which supports grassroots communities working to create social, economic, racial, and cultural justice in Minnesota. This new fund is designed to grant funds for American Indian organziations affecting social change in Minnesota and Wisconsin. *Committee*: Omie Baldwin, Navajo Nation; Rev. marlene Helgemo, HoChunk Nation; Norbert S. Hill, Jr., Oneida Tribe of Wisconsin; Winona LaDuke, Mississippi Band Anishanaabe; Ron McKinley, Mescalero Apache; Elaine Salinas, Minnesota Chippewa: White Earth; Jo-Anne Stately, Minnesota Chippewa: White Earth; Chaz Wheelock, Oneida Nation; Medora Woods. *Deadlines*: General proposals are due August 1; proposals for smaller, Special Opportunity Grants, will be accepted each month.

GAY INDIAN STUDIES ASSOCIATION
13730 Loumont St. • Whittier, CA 90601
Berdach Research Grants: Financial assistance to American Indian graduate students interested in conducting research (for a master's degree thesis or a doctoral dissertation) on the phenomenon of berdaches (male Indians who lived as women) in the southwestern U.S. The stipend is $10,000. *Deadline*: December.

GENERAL SERVICE FOUNDATION
P.O. Box 4659 • Boulder, CO 80306
(303) 447-9541 Fax 447-0593
Robert W. Musser, President/Director
More than 50 grants are given in special interests of: natural resources, environment, health, economic development, human rights, nonprofit management. Emphasis is placed on improving the management and quality f water, particularly west of the Mississippi.

GOLDEN STATE MINORITY FOUNDATION
1999 W. Adams Blvd.
Los Angeles, CA 90018
(213) 731-7771
Ivan A. Houston, Contact
Scholarship of $2,000 per year for ethnic minority with at least a 3.0 GPA and attending any accredited 4-year college of university in California, Michigan, or Houston, Texas in business administration, economics, or related field.

GOUGH (HELEN) SCHOLARSHIP FOUNDATION
P.O. Box 156 • Stanley, ND 58784
(701) 628-2955 Fax 628-3706
Karen Colbenson, Chairperson
Financial assistance for educational purposes to members of the Three Affiliated Tribes of the Fort Berthold Reservation in North Dakota. Up to $500 per year, renewable. *Deadline*: June 1.

GOULD (CHARLES P.) AWARD
Financial Aid Office, UC, Davis
Davis, CA 95616 (916) 752-2390
Felicia Miller, Contact
Awards to UCD American Indian students only, with students from Arizona tribes receiving first priority. *Amount*: $200-$3,000 as determined by financial need.

GOULD (EDWIN) FOUNDATION FOR CHILDREN
23 Gramacy Park S. • New York, NY 10003
Helen Alessi, Contact
Student mentor scholarship program for needy children, including those in the foster care system.

GRINNELL (GEORGE BIRD) AMERICAN INDIAN CHILDREN'S EDUCATION FOUNDATION
Box 47H, Rd. #1 • Dover Plains, NY 12522
(914) 877-6425
Schuyler M. Meyer, Jr., Secretary/Treasurer
The Al Qoyawayma Award for Excellence in Science, Engineering, and the Arts. $2,000, annually to a Native American undergraduate college student majoring either in science or engineering, and who has a documented knowledge of American Indian culture and religion.

GROTTO FOUNDATION, INC.
West - 2090 First National Bank Bldg.
St. Paul, MN 55101; (612) 224-9431
A.A. Heckman, Executive Director
Provides grants for special projects relating to American Indians.

GUILFORD NATIVE AMERICAN ASSOCIATION
P.O. Box 5623 • Greensboro, NC 27403
(919) 273-8686
Scholarship: To native-Americans who are planning to attend college. Native-American high school seniors in the Guilford, Alamance, Forsyth and other adjacent counties in North Carolina. Stipends range from $250 to $1,000 per year. *Deadline*: February.

HAHN (PHILIP Y.) FOUNDATION
c/o California First Bank, P.O. Box B
Rancho Santa Fe, CA 92067 (714) 294-4592
c/o Gilbert L. Brown, Jr., Manager
Alcala Park, San Diego, CA 92110
Provides financial aid for needy American Indian children in the Southwest.

HARVARD GRADUATE PRIZE FELLOWSHIP
Harvard - GSAS, 8 Garden St.
Cambridge, MA 02138
Requirement: Must be a member of a minority group, including Native Americans; must enroll at Harvard GSAS. Any Native American who is admitted to the GSAS will receive this fellowship. *Amount*: Tuition + $10,500 stipend. *Deadline*. January 2md.

HEADLANDS INDIAN HEALTH CAREERS
P.O. Box 26901
Oklahoma City, OK 73190
(405) 271-2250
Grants: For Native American students who are interested in preparing for careers as health professionals. The Headlands program is held at the Headlands Conference Center near Mackinaw City, Michigan. The program is sponsored by the University of Oklahoma's Health Sciences Center. *Deadline*: March.

HEARST FOUNDATION
90 New Montgomery St., Suite 1212
San Francisco, CA 94105
(415) 543-0400
Thomas Eastham, V.P.
Awards more than 270 grants in educationm arts, culture, social services, children, youth, mental health, religion, and historic preservation. Support for Indian organizations tend to fall under the category of education.

HOWARD SIMONS FUND FOR AMERICAN INDIAN JOURNALISTS
403 Tenth St., SE • Washington, DC 20003
(202) 547-5531 Fax 546-6724
Suzan Harjo or Margaret Engel (301) 986-5342
Short-term fellowships for Native American journalists.

INDIANA UNIVERSITY
Kirkwood Hall 114 • Bloomington, IN 47405
(800) 457-4420 in IN (812) 855-0822
CIC Minorities Fellowships Program : To increase the number of undrepresented minority group members among Ph.D. degree recipients in the humanities, social sciences, sciences, mathematics and engineering. Full tuition plus a stipend of at least $9,000 for graduate study at a CIC-affiliated university. *Deadline*: January. Minority Faculty Recruitment Fellowship Program: Includes a salary equivalent to that ordinarily paid to an Indiana University faculty, plus a $3,000 stipend for research and living expenses. *Deadline*: September.

INDUSTRIAL RELATIONS COUNCIL ON GOALS
P.O. Box 44218 • Eden Prairie, MN 55344
(612) 833-1691 Fax 833-1692
Graduate Fellowship Program for Minorities in Labor and Industrial Relations: To provide funding for minority students who are interested in obtaining a master's degree in human resource management/industrial relations. Pays tuition, fees, and a stipend of $7,800 per academic year.

INROADS, INC.
1221 Locust • St. Louis, MO 63108
(314) 241-7488
INROADS/College Internship: Places minority youth interns in local companies in various cities. *Deadline*: January.

INSTITUTE FOR THE STUDY OF WORLD POLITICS
1775 Massachusetts Ave., NW, # 500
Washington, DC 20036 (202) 797-0882
Dorothy Danforth Compton Fellowships for Minority-Group Students on World Affairs: Amount of award varies. *Deadline*: February.

INSTITUTE OF ALASKA NATIVE ARTS
P.O. Box 70769, 455 Third Ave. #117
FAIRBANKS, AK 99707 (907) 456-7491
Susie Bevins-Ericsen, President
Patricia Petrivelli, Executive Director
Scholarships for academic study, up to $2,000; and for short-term study, $500.

INTER-TRIBAL COUNCIL OF THE FIVE CIVILIZED TRIBES
c/o Financial Aid Office, Bacone College
Muskogee, OK 74403; (918) 683-4581
Grant Foreman Scholarships: Assistance to male Native American high school graduates who are interested in postsecondary education. *Louie Leflore Scholarship*: Financial assistance to female Native American high school graduates. $100 to $300 per year. Applicants must be members of one of the Five Civilized Tribes of Oklahoma. Deadline: June.

INTER-TRIBAL INDIAN CEREMONIAL ASSOCIATION
P.O. Box 1 • Church Rock, NM 87311
(505) 863-3896
Laurence D. Linford, Executive Director
Indian art scholarships to accredited colleges and universities.

INTERTRIBAL TIMBER COUNCIL
Attn: Education Committee
4370 N.E. Halsey St. • Portland, OR 97213
(503) 282-4296
Truman D. Picard Scholarship Program: Financial assistance to American Indians or Alaskan Natives who are interested in studying natural resources in college. $1,500. *Deadline*: February.

INTERNATIONAL ORDER OF THE KING'S DAUGHTERS & SONS
North American Indian Scholarship Program
P.O. Box 1017 • Chautauqua, NY 14722
(716) 357-1951
Indian Scholarship Program: To provide supplemental aid to Native American students interested in pursuing secondary and postsecondary education in the health fields or Christian studies. Up to $500 per year. *Deadline*: April in even-numbered years, June in odd-numbered years.

JOHNSON (ROBERT WOOD) FOUNDATION
P.O. Box 2316 • Princeton, NJ 08543
(609) 452-8701
Edward H. Robbins, Proposal Manager
Serving populations where services are not available is a traditional foundation focus. Improving the health of Native Americans is a priority. *Minority Medical Faculty Development Program*: For minority physicians who are interested in academic medicine. Stipend is $50,000 per year, plus a $25,000 annual research allowance. *Deadline*: April.

JOYCE FOUNDATION
135 S. LaSalle St. #4010
Chicago, IL 60603
(312) 782-2464 Fax 782-4160
Joel D. Gretzendanner, V.P. Programs
Special interests: economic development, disadvantaged, conservation, environment, education, arts, culture, public affairs. Focuses on "the Strength of Diversity."

KELLOGG (W.K.) FOUNDATION
400 North Ave. • Battle Creek, MI 49016
(616) 968-1611; Norman A. Brown, President
Specific priorities: youth, leadership, community-based, problem-focused health services, higher education, and food systems. Supports educational and service projects with an emphasis on the application of new knowledge to human needs. *Geographic interest*: national, especially Michigan.

KEMPER (JAMES S.) FOUNDATION
Long Grove, IL 60049
Kemper Grantee Program Scholarships. $1,000-3,500 per year. *Deadline*: Varies at each participating institution.

LILLY ENDOWMENT, INC.
2801 N. Meridian, Box 88068
Indianapolis, IN 46208
(317) 924-5471 Fax 926-4431
John M. Mutz, President
Special interests: religion, education, community development, children/youth, and nonprofit management. *Geographic interest*: national, especially Indiana.

MAINE INDIAN SCHOLARSHIPS
Finance Authority of Maine
Attn: Maine Education Assistance Division
One Weston Court, State House Sta. 119
Augusta, ME 04333 (800) 228-3734
(207) 626-8200 Fax 626-8208
E-mail: info@famemaine.com
Web site: www.famemaine.com
Scholarships: To provide financial assistance for postsecondary education to members of the Passamaquoddy, Penobscot, Micmac & Maliseet tribes.

MALKI MUSEUM SCHOLARSHIPS
Morongo Indian Reservation
P.O. Box 578 • Banning, CA 92220
 (909) 849-7289
Scholarships: For enrolled members of southern California Indian reservations as members of their tribe interested in pursuing postsecondary education in California. $300 per quarter or semester.

MASSACHUSETTS INDIAN ASSOCIATION
c/o Marjorie Findlay
245 Rockland Rd. • Carlisle, MA 01741
Scholarship Fund: For Massachusetts Indians who are interested in pursuing postsecondary education. Up to $500 per year for undergraduates; up to $1,000 for graduate students. *Deadlines*: January for Fall and September for Spring semester.

MASSACHUSETTS NATIVE AMERICAN TUITION WAIVER PROGRAM
Board of Higher Education
McCormack Bldg., One Ashburton Pl., #1401
Boston, MA 02108
 (617) 727-7785 Fax 727-6397
 E-mail: bhe@bhe.mass.edu
 Web site: www.mass.edu
Purpose: Financial assistance for postsecondary education of Massachusetts residents who are Native Ameican.

McCARTHUR (JOHN D. & CATHERINE T.) FOUNDATION
140 S. Dearborn St.
Chicago, IL 60603
 (312) 726-8000; Adele Simmons, President
The foundation has demonstrated an interest in native rights and the self determination of Native peoples. *Special interests*: education, resources, economic development, health, and the environment. *Geographic interest*: national, especially Florida.

McKNIGHT FOUNDATION
TCF Tower, 121 S. 8th St. #600
Minneapolis, MN 55402 (612) 333-4220
 Cynthia Binger Boynton, President
Special interests: human services, economic development, health, education, and environment. *Geographic interest*: national, especially Minnesota.

METROLINA NATIVE AMERICAN ASSOCIATION
2601-A East Seventh St.
Charlotte, NC 28204
 (704) 331-4818 Fax 331-9501
Johnny Strickland Memorial College Scholarship Fund: Financial assistance to children of members of the Association who are interested in continuing their college education. $500 per year. *Deadline*: April; *Employment & Training Program*: Financial assistance to needy Native Americans in North Carolina who are interested inobtaining additional education or training.

MEYER MEMORIAL TRUST
1515 W. Fifth Ave., Suite 500
Portland, OR 97201
 (503) 228-5512
 Charles S. Rooks, Executive Director
Special interests: children/youth, arts & humanities, health, education, social welfare. *Geographic interest*: national groups; Alaska, Idaho, Montana; Oregon (especially Portland), Washington.

MICHIGAN COMMISSION ON INDIAN AFFAIRS
Dept. of Management & Budget
P.O. Box 30026 • Lansing, MI 48909
 (517) 373-0654
Michigan Indian Awards: To Native American high school graduates who are interested in attending college in Michigan. Applicant must be a legal resident of Michiga for at least one year. Free tuition at any Michigan public 2-4 college or university.

MINNESOTA STATE DEPT. OF EDUCATION
Attn: Indian Education
1819 Bemidji Ave. • Bemidji, MN 5601
 (218) 755-2926 Fax 755-2008
Minnesota Indian Scholarship Program: For Native American high school graduates in Minnesota who wish to pursue postsecondary education. From $500 to $3,000. The average award is $1,500.

MONTANA GUARANTEED STDUENT LOAN PROGRAM
2500 Broadway, P.O. Box 203101
Helena, MT 59620 (800) 537-7508
 (406) 444-6570 Fax 444-1869
 E-mail: custserve@mgsip.state.mt.us
 Web site: www.mgslp.mt.us
Montana Indian Student Fee-Waiver Program: Financial assistance for Montana Indian students interested in pursuing postsecondary education. Tuition is waved for recipients at a select number of Montana schools.

MOTT (CHARLES STEWART) FOUNDATION
500 Mott Bldg. • Flint, MI 48502
 (313) 238-5651
 Jim L. Krause, Director
Special interests: education, environment, community & economic development, arts, health. *Geographical interest*: national groups, especially Michigan.

MR. COGITO
c/o John M. Gogol, Editor
P.O. Box 66124 • Portland, OR 97266
 American Indian Poetry Prize: To recognize and reward outstanding poetry on the topic of the American Indian. $50 and publication in Mr. Cogito magazine. *Deadline*: May.

MURDOCK (M.J.) CHARITABLE TRUST
P.O. Box 1618 • Vancouver, WA 98668
 (206) 694-8415 Fax (503) 285-4086
 Ford A. Anderson, Executive Director
Special interests: education, community & economic development, health, arts & culture, social services, religion. *Geographic interest*: national groups; Alaska, Idaho, Montana, Oregon, Washington (especially Greater Vancouver.)

MUSKOGEE TRIBE
Old Federal Bldg.
Muskogee, OK 74401
 (918) 687-2306
Tribal Scholarship Grant: Financial assistance for postsecondary education to undergraduates and graduate students who belong to the Muskogee Tribe. Up to $2,000 per year.

NATIONAL ACTION COUNCIL FOR MINORITIES IN ENGINEERING
350 Fifth Ave. #2212 • New York, NY 10118
 (212) 279-2626 Fax 629-5178
Incentive Grant Program: financial support to minority students in engineering. Colleges and universities with engineering curricula may submit requests for scholarship funds. Grants to participating schools range from $5,000 to $40,000. *Summer Engineering Employment Project (SEEP)*: Internships in NACME donor corporations for minority engineering students. $3,600 for the summer. For scholarships please contact the financial aid office at your school. *Techforce Preengineering Prize*: Financial assistance to outstanding underrepresented minority hgih school seniors who are planning to pursue a career in engineering. *Deadline*: January.

NATIONAL ASSOCIATION FOR BILINGUAL EDUCATION
Maricopa Community College
3910 E. Washington St.
Phoenix, AZ 85034 (602) 392-2233
Outstanding Dissertations Competition: To recognize and reward dissertations in bilingual education field. Semifinalists receive certificates of recognition and finalists receive travel & lodging expenses to the annual convention. *Deadline*: November.

NATIONAL ASSOCIATION FOR THE ADVANCEMENT OF COLORED PEOPLE
4805 Mt. Hope Dr. • Baltimore, MD 21215
 (301) 358-8900
NAACP Honeywell Engineering Scholarship: Financial assistance to underrepresented minority students interested in majoring in engineering in college. Up to $4,000 per year and opportunity to work summers prior to graduation at a Honeywell division. *Deadline*: April.

NATIONAL CENTER FOR GRADUATE EDUCATION FOR MINORITIES (GEM)
National Consortium for Graduate Degrees for Minori-

ties in Engineering & Science
P.O. Box 537 • Notre Dame, IN 46556
 (219) 631-7778 Fax 287-1486
 E-mail: GEM.1@nd.edu
 Web site: www.nd.edu/~gem
Master's Fellowship Program: For minority students entering graduate engineering studies. Tuition, fees, and a stipend of $6,000 for one year and a summer internship; *Ph.D. Engineering & Science Fellowship Program*: To provide opportunities for minority students to obtain a Ph.D. in engineering and the natural sciences. Tuition, fees and a stipend of $12,000 per year. Recipients must participate in the GEM summer internship. *Deadline*: November.

NATIONAL FEDERATION OF STATE POETRY SOCIETIES
c/o Pat Stodghill, 1424 Highland Rd.
Dallas, TX 75218
Our American Indian Heritage Poetry Contest: To recognize and reward outstanding poems written about American Indians. $25 first place, $15 second place, $10 third place. *Deadline*: March.

NATIONAL GALLERY OF ART
Attn: Academic Programs
Washington, DC 20565 (202) 842-6182
Minority Internships: To provide work experience to underrepresented minority undergraduates who might be considering a museum career. The stipend is $14,000. *Deadline*: March.

NATIONAL INDIAN CHILD CONFERENCE
129 Jackson, NE • Albuquerque, NM 87108
Ruth Muskrat Bronson Memorial Scholarship: To assist American Indian and Alaskan Native graduate students in meeting the costs of a graduate education. Amount awarded varies. *Deadline*: November and March.

NATIONAL MEDICAL FELLOWSHIPS, INC.
254 W.31st St., 7th Fl. • New York, NY 10001
 (212) 714-0933 Fax 239-9718
Franklin C. McLean Award: For senior medical school minority students. $3,000. *Deadline*: June. *Hugh H. Anderson Memorial Scholarships*: For minority students attending Minnesota medical schools. $2,500 to $4,000 per year. *Deadline*: August. *Irving Graef Memorial Scholarship*: Third-year minority medical school students' achievements. $2,000. *Deadline*: July. *William and Charlotte Cadbury Award*: Minority school students' achievements. $2,000. *Deadline*: June. *Henry J. Kaiser Family Foundation Merit Awards Programs*: For contributions to medicine on the part of graduating medical students. $3,000, average award. *Baxter Foundation Scholarship*: Open to second-year minority medical students who received NMF financial assistance during their first year. $2,500. *Deadline*: July. *The Commonwealth Fund Medical Fellowship*: To minority students attending accredited U.S. medical schools. Preference is given to third-year students. $5,000. *Deadline*: October. Glaxo, Inc. *Fellowship Program in Aids Research*: To second and third-year minority students for research into academic medicine or health education and policy. The stipend is $5,000. Nominations requested in August. *William T. Grant Behavior Development Research Fellowships*: For minority students who show promise for careers in child psychiatry, behavior development research or mental health policy. $3,500. *Deadline*: September. *AT&T Foundation Fellowship Program in Aids Education and Public Policy*. The stipend is $5,000. Nominations requested in August. *Metropolitan Life Foundation Awards for Academic Excellence in Medicine*: $2,500 per year. *Deadline*: August. *W.K. Kellogg Foundation Fellowship Program in Community Medicine*: To underepresented minority medical students who wish to work in community-based health centers. The stipend is $5,000. *Deadline*: October. Syntex Corporation Award for Postgraduate Medical Research and Training. $2,000.

NATIONAL MUSEUM OF THE AMERICAN INDIAN
Attn: Intern Coordinator
470 L'Enfant Plaza, Suite 7103
Washington, DC 20560
 (202) 287-2020
 E-mail: interns@ic.si.edu

Web site: www.si.edu/nmai

NMAI Internship Program: To provide work and/or research opportunities for native American students in the area of museum practice and related programming at the Smithsonian Institution's National Museum of the American Indian. $3,000. *Deadline*: February.

NATIONAL MUSEUM OF NATURAL HISTORY
Attn: Dept. of Anthropology
10th St. & Constitution Ave., NW
Washington, DC 20560
(202) 357-4760 Fax 357-2208
E-mail: archambj@nmnh.si.edu
American Indian Program: Grants to provide assistance for research, exhibitions, and public programming by and about Indian people.

NATIONAL NATIVE AMERICAN COOPERATIVE
P.O. Box 1000 • San Carlos, AZ 85550
(602) 230-3399
Purpose: To assist in the continuation of traditional or contemporary American Indian culture. Applicant must be a Native American artist. Raw craft materials are presented to the artist.

NATIONAL RESEARCH COUNCIL
The Fellowship Office
2101 Constitution Ave.
Washington, DC 20418
(202) 334-2860 Fax 334-3419
E-mail: infofell@nas.edu
Web site: fellowships.nas.edu
To increase minority presence in the arts and sciences on college and university faculties. Financial assistance for master's and doctoral degree minority students. Awards will be made in the behavioral and social sciences, humanities, engineering, math, physical sciences, and biological sciences. *NSF Incentives for Excellence Scholarship Prizes*: For outstanding minority undergraduate students who are preparing for careers in engineering or science. Up to $1,000. Awards each Spring. *Ford Foundation Dissertation Fellowship Program for Minorities*: $18,000 per year. *Deadline*: November. *Ford Foundation Predoctoral Fellowship Program for Minorities*: $11,000 per year. *Deadline*: November. *Ford Foundation Postdoctoral Fellowships for Minorities*: $25,000 per year. *Deadline*: January. *National Science Foundation Graduate Fellowships & Minority Graduate Fellowships*: $12,900 per year each. *Deadline*: October. *Minority Women in Engineering*: Fellows receive about $13,000 and a $1,000 research travel allowance. Fellowship institutions, on behalf of each fellow, a cost-of-education allowance of $6,000 to cover all tuition costs and fees. *Deadline*: November.

NATIONAL SCIENCE FOUNDATION
1800 G St., Rm. 321 • Washington, DC 20550
(202) 357-7474
Comprehensive Regional Centers for Minorities Projects:Financial assistance to centers designed to increase minority presence in science and engineering. *Deadline*: December. *Directorate for Engineering Supplemental Funding for Support of Women, Minority, and Handicapped Engineering Research Assistants*. *Minority Research Initiation Planning Grants*. Up to $10,000. *Deadline*: February & June. *Minority Research Initiation Program Grants*. From $25,000 to $90,000 per year. *Research Improvement in Minority Institutions*: To foster research activities of predominantly minority colleges and universities in the U.S. by supporting research. Up to $300,000. *Deadline*: November. *BBS/DCB Minority Postdoctoral Fellowships*: To prepare minority scientists for positions of scientific research in the disciplines covered by the Biological, Behavioral and Social Sciences Directorate (BBS) of the NSF at U.S. research institutes. Fellows receive $28,000 per year, plus $4,600 for research-related costs or health insurance and $24,000 per year for an institutional allowance. Also, up to $3,000 for travel expense. *Deadline*: October.

**NATIONAL SCIENCE FOUNDATION -
MINORITY GRADUATE FELLOWSHIPS**
Oak Ridge Associated Universities
P.O. Box 3010 • Oak Ridge, TN 37831
(615) 483-3344
Requirements: U.S. citizen and member of minority group, including American Indian and Native Alaskan-

Eskimo or Aleut. Awarded for study and research leading to master's or doctoral degrees in the mathematical, physical, biological, engineering, behavioral and social sciences. *Amount*: stipend of $14,000 per year and$7,500 cost-of-education allowance.

**NATIONAL SOCIETY OF THE
COLONIAL DAMES OF AMERICA**
c/o Mrs. H. Eugene Trotter
3064 Luvan Blvd. deBordieu Colony
Georgetown, SC 29440 (803) 527-3140
Indian Nurse Scholarship Awards: Financial assistance to American Indians interested in preparing for a career innursing. Up to $1,000 per year.

**NATIONAL SOCIETY OF THE DAUGHTERS
OF THE AMERICAN REVOLUTION**
American Indian Scholarship Committee
11001 Elon Dr. • Mitchellville, MD 20720
(301) 262-6654
Suzanne W. O'Malley, Contact
Requirements: Must be Native American undergraduate student with at least a 2.75 GPA and show financial need. Amount: $500 renewable. *Deadlines*: December 1 and August 1.

**NATIONAL SOCIETY OF PROFESSIONAL
ENGINEERS EDUCATIONAL FOUNDATION**
1420 King St. • Alexandria, VA 22314
(703) 684-2800
NSPE Minority Scholarships: Financial assistance to high school seniors from underrepresented minority groups who have a genuine interest in a career in engineering. $1,000 per year. *Deadline*: December.

NATIONAL WILDLIFE FEDERATION
1412 Sixteenth St.
Washington, D.C. 20036
(703) 790-4267; Maurice N. LeFranc, Jr., Contact
Environmental Conservation Fellowship Program: For graduate research in environmental studies, natural resources, etc. Up to $10,000 per year. *Deadline*: July 15 for upcoming academic year.

NATIONS MINISTRIES
P.O. Box 70 • Honobia, OK 74549
(918) 755-4570 • Riley Donica, Editor
Academic scholarships.

NATIVE AMERICAN JOURNALISTS ASSOCIATION
Attn: College Scholarships
555 N. Dakota St.
Vermillion, SD 57069
(866) 694-4264 Fax (605) 677-5282
E-Mail: info@naja.com; Web site: www.naja.com
Scholarships: Financial assistance to Native American students who are majoring in journalism in college. $2,500. *Deadline*: April. *Internships*: To provide work experience to Native American undergraduates who are interested in majoring in journalism in college. Placements are made in Native and mainstream media organizations.

**NATIVE AMERICAN PUBLIC
BROADCASTING CONSORTIUM**
P.O. Box 83111 • Lincoln, NE 68501
(402) 472-3522 Fax 472-8675
E-mail: native@unlinfo.unl.edu
Web site: www.nativetelecom.org
National Indian Communications Scholarships: Travel expenses to Native American college students who wish to attend the annual National Indian Communications conference. Public Television Program Fund. *Deadline*: September.

NATIVE AMERICAN MINISTRIES
The Presbyterian Center
100 Whitherspoon St. • Louisville, KY 40202
Native American Education Grants: For needy Native American students to continue their college education. From $200 to $1,500. *Deadline*: June 1. *Native American Seminary Scholarships*: For students interested in preparing for church occupations. Amount varies.

NATIVE AMERICAN RIGHTS FUND
1506 Broadway • Boulder, CO 80302
(303) 447-8760 Fax 443-7776
Summer Clerkship: To provide work experience to law students with an interest in Native American law. Po-

sitions available at Native Americn Rights Fund offices. *Deadline*: November.

NATIVE AMERICAN SCHOLARSHIP FUND, INC.
8200 Mountain Rd. NE #203
Albuquerque, NM 87110
(505) 262-2351 Fax 262-0534
Website: www.nasf.com
MESBEC Program: Financial assistance to Native American students interested in pursuing postsecondary education. Amount varies but is generally about $500 per year. Deadline: April for Fall, September for Spring, and March for Summer. *Native American Leadership in Education (NALE)*: Financial assistance to American Indian paraprofessionals in the education field who wish to return to school. From $500 and up.

NATIVE AMERICAN SCHOLARSHIP PROGRAM
Santa Fe Pacific Foundation
1700 E. Golf Rd. • Schaumburg, IL 60173
Requirements: Open to high school seniors who are at least 1/4 Native American. *Amount*: Up to $2,500 per year, 4-year renewable, depending on need. *Deadline*: March.

NATIVE WRITERS CIRCLE OF THE AMERICAS
c/o University of Oklahoma
Dept. of English • Norman, OK 73019
(405) 325-6231
Diane Decorah Memorial Award: To recognize and reward outstanding new Native American poets. $500. *Deadline*: February.

NAVAJO CODE TALKERS ASSOCIATION
Attn: President, Box 1182
Window Rock, AZ 86515 (520) 871-5573
Scholarships: Financial assistance to children and grandchildren of navajo "code talkers" who served during World War II. $500.

NAVAJO GENERATING STATION
Salt River Project, P.O. Box 850
Page, AZ 86040 (520) 645-6539
E-mail: ljdawave@srp.gov
Scholarship: Financial assistance to members of the Navajo Nation who have completed at least 2 years of college and majoring in a field of study refcognized as significant to the Navajo Nation, Salt River Project, or Navajo Generating Station.

NEEDMOR FUND
1730 15th St. • Boulder, CO 80302
(303) 449-5801
Special interests: community & economic development, family, disadvantaged. Geographic interest: national, especially Ohio (Toledo).

NEVADA INTER-TRIBAL COUNCIL
806 Holman Way • Sparks, NV 89431
(702) 355-0600
Health Occupations Indian Scholarship Program: To Indian students in Nevada interested in careers in the health fields. *John H. Dressler Memorial Scholarship*: Emergency financial assistance to Native American college students who are residents of Nevada. $200. *Deadline*: August.

**NEW MEXICO EDUCATIONAL
ASSISTANCE FOUNDATION**
3900 Osuna Rd., NE, P.O. Box 27020
Albuquerque, NM 87125-7020
(505) 345-3371 ext. 315 Fax (505) 345-3371 ext. 400
New Mexico Minority Doctoral Fellowship/Loan Program: Minority students graduating from a school in New Mexico and who wish to pursue a doctoral degree in mathematics, engineering, or the physical or life sciences in the state. The stipend is $25,000 per year. *Deadline*: January.

NEW YORK STATE EDUCATION DEPARTMENT
State and Federal Scholarship and Fellowship Unit
Cultural Education Center, Room 5C64
Albany, NY 12230 (518) 474-3852
E-mail: heop1@mail.nysed.gov
Web site: www.nysed.gov
Regents Professional Opportunity Scholarships:From $1,000 to $5,000 per year for Native Americans and other minority students interested in pursuing profes-

sional careers. Recipients must enroll in approved programs in New York state. *Deadline*: April. *Regents Health Care Scholarships*: Financial assistance to minority students enrolled in an approved program in medicine or dentistry. From $1,000 to $5,000 per year. *Deadline*: April.

NEW YORK STATE EDUCATION DEPARTMENT
Native American Indian Education Unit
543 Education Bldg. Annex
Albany, NY 12234 (518) 474-0537
  Deborah H. Cunningham, Contact
State Aid for Native Americans at Postsecondary Institutions in the State of New York. Applicants must be residents of New York state and be accepted by an approved accredited postsecondary institution. $1,550 per year for full-time study. *Deadline*: May for Summer term, July for Fall term, and December for Spring term.

NEW YORK UNIVERSITY
Institute of Afro-American Affairs
269 Mercer St., Rm. 601
New York, NY 10003 (212) 598-7095
AEJ/NYU Summer Internship Program for Minorities in Journalism: To provide work experience in the communications industry for minority group members who are interested in journalism. $200 per week and housing accommodations at NYU. *Deadline*: December.

**NORTH AMERICAN INDIAN
SCHOLARSHIP PROGRAM**
The International Order of the King's,
Daughters & Sons, Inc.
1916 Rosedale Dr. • Indianapolis, IN 46227
  (317) 784-5163 Mrs. Vernon Parish
Requirement: Must be a Native American undergraduate student with proof of Indian blood. Scholarships are awarded for vocational, technical & college training.

**NORTH CAROLINA COMMISSION
OF INDIAN AFFAIRS**
North Carolina Dept. of Administration
217 W. Jones St. • Raleigh, NC 27603
(919) 733-5998 Fax 733-1207
Scholarship & Grant Program - Merit-Based & Need-Based Scholarships: Financial assistance to Native Americans in North Carolina who are interested in continuing their college education. $3,000 & $5,000 respectively. *Deadline*: March. *American Indian Student Legislative Grant*: To needy North Carolina Indian students who are interested in pursuing postsecondary education. Applicants must be admitted to or attending to enroll in one of the constituent institutions of the University of North Carolina. $700 per year. *American Indian Doctoral Fellowship*: Financial assistance to American Indians who wish to pursue doctoral degrees in one of four institutions of the University of North Carolina system. $5,000 per year.

NORTH DAKOTA INDIAN AFFAIRS COMMISSION
State Capitol Bldg., 10th Floor
600 East Blvd. Ave. • Bismarck, ND 58505
  (701) 328-2166; Jillian D. Nodland, Contact
Scholarship Program: To provide financial assistance to undergraduate and graduate Native American students in North Dakota colleges and universities. From $600 to $2,000 per year. *Deadline*: July.

NORTHWEST AREA FOUNDATION
West 975 National Bank Bldg.
332 Minnesota • St. Paul, MN 55101
  (612) 224-9635; Terry T. Saario, President
Special interests: economic development, health, natural resources, social & legal services. *Geographic interests*: national groups; Idaho, Iowa, Minnesota, North & South Dakota, Oregon, and Washington.

OAK RIDGE ASSOCIATED UNIVERSITIES
P.O. Box 117 • Oak Ridge, TN 37831
(615) 576-1090
Minority Institution Research Travel Program: Financial assistance for energy-related research at minority academic institutions. All approved travel expenses are covered. Applications must be received at least 30 days prior to the planned departure date from home campus.

OREGON STATE SCHOLARSHIP COMMISSION
Attn: Private Awards Grant Dept.
1500 Valley River Dr., Suite 100
Eugene, OR 97401 (800) 452-8807
  (541) 687-7400 Fax 687-7419
  Web site: www.ossc.state.or.us
Howard Vollum American Indian Scholarships: Financial assistance for college to American Indians who reside in the Portalnd, Oregon area. Amounts depend upon need. *Deadline*: February.

PEW CHARITABLE TRUSTS
One Commerce Square
2005 Market St., Suite 1700
Philadelphia, PA 19103
  (215) 575-4700 Fax 575-4939
  Thomas W. Langfitt, M.D., President
Specific priorities: religion, health & human services, health care, education, culture, and environment.

PUBLIC LIBRARY ASSOCIATION
American Library Association
50 E. Huron St. • Chicago, IL 60611
  (800) 545-2433 (312) 944-6780
  Fax (312) 440-9374
Leonard Wertheimer Multilingual Award: To recognize and reward work that enhances and promotes multilingual public library service. $1,000 and a certificate. *Deadline*: November.

PUBLIC WELFARE FOUNDATION
2600 Virginia Ave., NW, Suite 505
Washington, DC 20037 (202) 965-1800
  Veronica Keating, Director
Special interests: disadvantaged, environment, community development, education, health, social services.

RED CLOUD INDIAN ART SHOW
Heritage Center, Inc.
Box 100 • Pine Ridge, SD 57770
Thunderbird Foundation Scholarship: Financial assistance for the education of Native American artists. Native American tribal members (18 years of age or older) who submit artistic works to the Indian Art Show are considered for this award. $5,000 in art scholarships is awarded. *Deadline*: May. *Edward S. Curtis Purchase Awards*: To recognize and reward young Native American artists at the show. $2,000. *Red Cloud Indian Art Show Awards*: To recognize and reward Native American artists who submit works to the Show. $300 each. Also, *Allan & Joyce Niederman Award & Aplan Award*: To recognize and reward the best traditional art work submitted at the art show. $100 each. *Bonnie Erickson Award*: To recognize and reward the best art work representing children. $100. *M.L. Woodard Award, Tony Begay Memorial Award & Pepion Family Award*: $50 each. *Powers Award*: To recognize and reward artists whose works at the Show depict Indian women. $100. *Bill and Sue Hensler Award*: To recognize and reward Native American sculptors. $50. Awards presented annually in May. *Barkley Art Center Award*: To recognize and reward the most innovative art work at the show. $100. *Rich Decker Award*: For the best artistic representation of American Indian heritage submitted to show. $200.

ROCK (HOWARD) FOUNDATION
1577 C St., Suite 304 • Anchorage, AK 99501
  (907) 274-5400; (800) 478-2332 (within Alaska)
  Irmtraud Wieghel, Contact
Graduate Scholarships: To Native Alaskans interested in pursuing a graduate degree. *Requirements*: Must be a member of a Community Enterprise Development Corporation of Alaska membership organization; must be majoring in fields of study that promote the economic well-being of life for residents of rural Alaska; must be a full-time student and must be able to prove financial need. *Amount*: $2,500 (undergraduate); and $5,000 (graduate).

SCHOOL OF AMERICAN RESEARCH
Attn: Indian Arts Research Center
P.O. Box 2188 • Santa Fe, NM 87504
  (505) 954-7205 Fax 989-9809
  E-mail: iarc@sarsf.org
  Web site: www.sarweb.org/iarc/iarc.htm
Katrin H. Lamon Resident Scholar Program for Native

Americans: Funding for Native American scholars who would benefit from a residency at the School. Scholars in the areas of anthropology, the humanities, the social sciences, or the arts. Participants receive room, board, medical insurance, and a stipend of up to $28,000. *Deadline*: November. *Harvey W. Branigar, Jr. Native American Fellowship*: Financial assistance to Native American college graduates interested in preparing for a career related to Native American arts.

SEALASKA HERITAGE FOUNDATION
One Sealaska Plaza #201 • Juneau, AK 99801
  (907) 463-4844 Fax 586-1807
Come-Back Scholarships: To older Native Alaskans who are interested in returning to college to work on a degree. Up to $2,500 per year depending upon the recipient's need. *Deadline*: March. *Part-Time Scholarships*: To older Native Alaskans who are interested in returning to college part-time to work on a degree. *Specific Field Scholarships*: To native Alaskans interested in working on a degree in natural resources or business-related fields. Up to $5,000, depending upon the recipient's need. *Deadline*: February.

SEVENTH GENERATION FUND
P.O. Box 10 • Forestville, CA 95436
  (707) 887-7256
Seed Grants:To support Native American efforts to restore their culture and promote their well-being. Average of $3,000 per year. Applications may be submitted at any time.

SIMPLOT (J.R.) COMPANY
Minerals and Chemcials Division
P.O. Box 912 • Pocatello, ID 83204
  (208) 232-6620
Simplot Company Indian Scholarships: Financial assistance for educational purposes to members of the Shoshone-Bannock Tribes who live on the Fort Hall Indian Reservation. Amount varies. *Tommy Hugues Scholarship Award*: To Shoshone Indians who are interested in majoring in business or science in college. $1,000 per year.

SKAGGS (L.J. & MARY C.) FOUNDATION
1221 Broadway, 21st Fl. • Oakland, CA 94612
  (510) 451-3300 Fax 451-1527
  David Knight, Program Director
Special interests: arts, culture, historic preservation, environment, education, medicine. *Geographic interest*: national groups, especially California (Oakland).

SMITHSONIAN INSTITUTION
Attn: Center for Museum Studies
Arts & Industries Bldg., Suite 2235
Washington, DC 20560
  (202) 357-3101 Fax 357-3346
Native American Community Scholar Fellowship: Subsistence and travel expenses to Native Americans to pursue projects related to Native American topics at the Smithsonian. *American Indian Museum Studies Program*: To provide educational training opportunities to staff who work in museums and cultural centers that house Native American collections. *Deadline*: February, June & October. *Native American Student Internship Program*: Financial assistance for Native Americans to pursue projects related to Native American topics at the Smithsonian. $300 per week for graduates, and $250 per week for undergraduates. *Deadline*: April, May & September.

SMITHSONIAN INSTITUTION
Attn: Office of Fellowships & Grants
955 L'Enfant Plaza, Suite 7000
Washington, DC 20560
  (202) 287-3271 Fax 287-3691
  E-mail: siofg@ofg.si.edu
  Web site: www.si.edu/research+study
Native American Visiting Student Awards: To provide opportunities for Native American graduate students to pursue projects related to Native American topics at the Smithsonian Institution. $75 per day for short term and $300 per week for long term. *Deadline*: June for Fall, October for Spring, and February for Summer. *Minority Student Internship*: To provide minority students the opportunity to work on research or museum procedure at the Smithsonian. $300 per week for 10 weeks. *Deadline*: February. *Smithsonian Na-*

tive American Student Internship Awards: To support Native Ameriacn students interested in pursuing projects related to native American topics at the Smithsonian. $300 per week for up to 12 weeks. *Deadline*: February for Summer, June for Fall, and October for Spring.

SOCIAL SCIENCE RESEARCH COUNCIL
810 Seventh Ave. • New York, NY 10019
(212) 377-2700 Fax 377-2727
Web site: www.ssrc.org
Mellon Minority Fellowship Program: Financial assistance for graduate research and study to underrepresented minorities. $5,000. *Undergraduate Research Assistantships*: To provide funding to faculty members for the support and training of talented undergraduate students (at least one half of whom must be minorities) while contributing to an understanding. Up to $4,000 per year. *Deadline*: January. *Urban Underclass Dissertation Fellowships*: To minority graduate students working on a dissertation dealing with the urban underclass. The stipend is $1,000 per month. In addition, there is a $4,000 allowance to cover research expenses incurred during the fellowship period. *Deadline*: January.

SOCIETY FOR ADVANCEMENT OF CHICANOS & NATIVE AMERICANS IN SCIENCE
P.O. Box 8526 • Santa Cruz, CA 95061
(408) 459-0170
E-mail: info@sacnas.org
Web site: www.sacnas.org
Eli Lilly Graduate Scholarships: Financial assistance for graduate study in biology or organic chemistry to Chicano or Native American students. $1,250. *SACNAS Conference Grants*: Funds for conference attendance costs of Chicano and Native American students and faculty who are eligible. *Vigil Awards*: To recognize and reward outstanding undergraduate research posters presented at the annual conference of the Society. $500.

SOUTH DAKOTA BOARD OF REGENTS
207 E. Capitol Ave. • Pierre, SD 57501
(605) 773-3455 Fax 773-5320
Ardell Bjugstad Memorial Scholarship: Undergraduate scholarship for a North or South Dakota resident and member of a federally recognized tribe whose reservation is located in the Dakotas. For a freshman with a agricutlural major. $500.

SOUTHWESTERN ASSOCIATION ON INDIAN ART (SAIA)
P.O. Box 969 • Santa Fe, NM 87504-0969
(505) 983-5220 Fax 983-7647
Jai Lakshman, Executive Director
E-mail: info@swaia.org
Web site: www.swaia.org
Scholarship Program: Financial assistance to American Indian students who wish to pursue a college education. Amount varies. Indian Craftsmen Fellowships: To contribute to the growth and development of Native American art. From $1,000 to $2,500. *Deadline*: April. *Annual Indian Market and Competition*: To recognize and reward outstanding Indian fiber-textile and basketry work submitted at the Indian Market each August. $1,000 Best of Show award. Up to $300 in special awards; and up to $500 in prizes.

STANFORD U. HUMANITIES CENTER
Mariposa House, 546 Salvatierra Walk
Stanford, CA 94305-8630
(650) 723-3052 Fax 723-1895
Stanford External Faculty Fellowships: For minority scholars interested in conducting research and teach at Stanford University. $25,000 for junior fellows and up to $40,000 for senior fellows; and housing/travel subsidy of $12,500. *Deadline*: November.

TRIANGLE NATIVE AMERICAN SOCIETY
P.O. Box 26841 • Raleigh, NC 27611
Mark Ulmer Native American Scholarship: Financial assistance to Native Americans in North Carolina who are interested in continuing their college education. The stipend is $500 per year. *Deadline*: April.

MORRIS K. UDALL SCHOLARSHIP & EXCELLENCE IN NATIONAL ENVIRONMENTAL POLICY FOUNDATION
803 E. First St. • Tucson, AZ 85719
(520) 670-5529 Fax 670-5530
Web site: udallfoundation.org
Morris K. Udall Scholarships: Financial assistance to Native American & Alaska Native students who intend to pursue careers in health care or tribal public policy. Up to $5,000 per year. *Deadline*: March.

UNITED NATIONAL INDIAN TRIBAL YOUTH, INC.
P.O. Box 25042 • Oklahoma City, OK 73125
(405) 236-2800 Fax 971-1071
Kody Tracey Memorial Scholarships: Financial assistance for college to students who have been active in organization (UNITY). $1,000 per year.

UNITED SOUTH & EASTERN TRIBES
711 Stewarts Ferry Pike #100
Nashville, TN 37214
(615) 872-7900 Fax 872-7417
Christine Garduno, Contact
Scholarship Fund: To provide financial assistance to Native Americans in the United South and Eastern Tribes service area who wish to pursue postsecondary education. $500 per year. *Deadline*: April.

UNIVERSITY OF CALIFORNIA
American Indian Graduate Program
140 Earl Warren Program
Berkeley, CA 94720
(510) 642-3228 Fax 642-3583
Dr. Felicia Hodge, Contact
E-Mail: aigp@uclink.berkeley.edu
Fellowship/Graduate Minority Scholarship: For graduate study at the University of California, Berkeley. Tuition and fees plus stipend. *Deadline*: January 5.

UNIVERSITY OF ILLINOIS, URBANA-CHAMPAIGN
Attn: Associate Dean, Graduate College
202 Coble Hall, 801 S. Wright St.
Champaign, IL 61820 (217) 333-4860
Illinois Minority Graduate Incentive Program: To increase the number of underrepresented minority students pursuing doctoral degrees in the natural sciences at graduate schools in Illinois. Full tuition and fees and an annual stipend of $12,500 and annual allowance for books, travel, etc. of $1,500. *Deadline*: February.

UNIVERSITY OF ILLINOIS AT URBANA-CHAMPAIGN
Associate Vice Chancellor for Academic Affairs
Swanlund Administration Bldg.
601 East John St. • Champaign, IL 61802
(217) 333-0885
Chancellor's Minority Fellow Program: To assist underrepresented faculty interested in research careers. The stipends range from $25,000 to $30,000 per year. Health coverage and funds for research-related expenses (up to $1,800 per year.) *Deadline*: November.

UNIVERSITY OF NEBRASKA PRESS
P.O. Box 880484 • Lincoln, NE 68588
(402) 472-3581 Fax 472-0308
North American Indian Prose Award: To recognize and reward outstanding book-length nonfiction manuscripts written by authors of American Indian descent. $1,000 and publication of the their manuscript. *Deadline*: June.

UNIVERSITY OF NEW MEXICO
American Indian Graduate Center
4520 Montgomery Blvd. NE, Suite 1-B
Albuquerque, NM 87131 (505) 881-4584
Provides fellowship grants to Indian graduate students. Assists about 600 students from 130 tribes at over 200 colleges throughout the U.S. *Deadline*: April 30th.

UNIVERSITY OF NEW MEXICO
College of Engineering, Student Programs Office
Farris Engineering Center, Rm. 157
Albuquerque, NM 87131 (505) 277-4354
Freshman Scholarship Program. *Requirements*: Must be a Native American (or another minority), and attend UNM full time in enginnering or computer science. *Deadline*: April 1.

UNIVERSITY OF OKLAHOMA HEALTH SCIENCES CENTER
Basic Sciences Education Bldg., Rm. 200
P.O. Box 26901 • Oklahoma City, OK 73190
(405) 271-2250 Fax 271-2254
Purpose: To aid Native American students who are interested in preparing for careers as health professionalsEach participant is provided with free room and board, and tuition as well as round-trip airfare and a stipend of $500. Duration: 8 weeks during the summer. *Deadline*: March.

UNIVERSITY OF WYOMING
American Indian Studies Program
Rm. 109, Anthropology Bldg.
Laramie, WY 82071 (307) 766-6521
Dr. Judith A. Antell, Director
The Frank & Cynthia McCarthy Scholarship: Each year four American Indian students can receive a McCarthy Scholarship in the amount of $500 each. Selection is based on academic achievement and record of university service.

UNTO THESE HILLS EDUCATIONAL FUND, INC.
P.O. Box 398 • Cherokee, NC 28719
(704) 497-2111
Scholarship: Financial assistance to Eastern Band of Cherokee Indians who wish to pursue postsecondary education at the undergraduate level. $500 per year. *Deadline*: April.

VANGUARD PUBLIC FOUNDATION
14 Precita Ave. • San Francisco, CA 94110
(415) 285-2005
Grants to support grassroots, social change-organizing projects in the San Francisco Bay area with priotiy given to proposals submitted by groups working for the rights of Native Americans. Up to $10,000 per grant. Average grant is $5,000. Emergency grants up to $500 are also available. *Deadlines*: March, June, September & December.

VIRGINIA CENTER FOR THE HUMANITIES
Virginia Foundation for the Humanities
1939 Ivy Rd. • Charlottesville, VA 22903
(804) 924-3296
Residencies Fellowships: To offer funding for research, writing, or programming at the Center. The stipend varies, up to $3,000 per month. *Deadline*: March or October.

WASHINGTON CENTER SCHOLARSHIPS
The Washington Center for Internships
& Academic Seminars
750 First St., NE, Suite 650
Washington, DC 20002 (202) 336-1593
Arleen R. Borysiewicz, Contact
Minority scholarship available.

WASHINGTON HIGHER EDUCATION COORDINATING BOARD
917 Lakeridge Way, P.O. Box 43430
Olympia, WA 98504
(360) 753-7843 Fax 753-7808
Washington State American Indian Endowed Scholarship Program: Financial assistance to American Indian students in Washington. *Deadline*: May.

WENNER-GREN FOUNDATION
220 Fifth Ave., 16th Floor
New York, NY 10001 (212) 683-5000
Dr. Sydel Silverman, President
Activities: Provides grants-in-aid to scholars for research and preparation of publications in all branches of anthropology and in related disciplines. *Activities*: Awards up to $12,000 to qualified scholars to aid basic research, doctoral dissertation research, and write-up of research results for publications. Conference grants up to $10,000. Includes a limited number of Richard Carley Hunt Postdoctoral Fellowships. *Publications*: Current Anthropology, bimonthly journal; Annual Report; issues Viking Fund Publications in Anthropology. Periodic conferences. Founded 1941.

WHATCOM MUSEUM
Jacobs Research Funds
121 Prospect St. • Bellingham, WA 98225
(206) 676-6981

Gladys Fullford, Contact
Kathrine S. French, Ph.D., Chairperson,
Provides small grants (maximum $1,200) for research in the field of social and cultural anthropology among living North American native peoples: Indians, Eskimos, Inuits, and Aleuts. Preference is given to the Pacific Northwest as an area of study, but other regions of North America are considered. Cultural expressive systems - music, language, dance, mythology, world view, plastic and graphic arts, intellectual life, religion - are appropriate topics. *Deadline:* February 15th.

WISCONSIN HIGHER EDUCATIONAL AIDS BOARD
P.O. Box 7885 • Madison, WI 53707
(608) 267-2206 Fax 267-2808
E-mail: thomas2@mail.state.wi.us
Wisconsin Native American Grants: Financial aid for higher education to Native Americans in Wisconsin. From $250 to $1,100 per year up to five years. Additional funds are available on a matching basis from the Bureau of Indian Affairs.

**WOODROW WILSON NATIONAL
FELLOWSHIP FOUNDATION**
P.O. Box 642 • Princeton, NJ 08540
(609) 924-4758
Minority Advancement Program (MAP): Financial assistance to underpresented minority students who are interested in careers in public service and international affairs. Junior & Senior year summer institute undergraduate students receive room, board, and a living allowance. Fellowships given to graduate students cover tuition, fees, and living expenses. *Deadline:* March. Administrative Fellows Program in Higher Education Administration. Relocation expenses and partial salary subsidy of from $22,000 to $32,000 per year to interns who qualify. *Deadline:* January.

ZONTA INTERNATIONAL FOUNDATION
557 W. Randolph St. • Chicago, IL 60606
(312) 930-5848 Lorelei Marshall, Contact
Zonta Amelia Earhart Fellowship: For women pursuing graduate study in aerosapce science or engineering. $6,000 per year. *Deadline:* December 1.

U.S. GOVERNMENT FINANCIAL AID

BUREAU OF INDIAN AFFAIRS
Deputy to the Assistant Secretary of Indian Affairs
Office of Trust & Economic Development
18th & C Sts., NW • Washington, DC 20245
(202) 208-5831
Indian Loans - Claims Assistance: To Indian tribes or groups of Indians without available funds to obtain assistance in preparing and processing claims pending before the U.S. Court of Claims. From $500 to $250,000. *Economic Development (Indian Business Development Program):* To Indians, tribes and organizations to help promote the economic development of reservations. From $20,000 to $250,000.

BUREAU OF INDIAN AFFAIRS
Office of Indian Education Programs
1849 C St., NW • MS 3512-MIB
Washington, DC 20240 (202) 219-1127
Web site: www.doe.gov/bureau-indian-affairs.html
B.I.A. Higher Education Grant Program: Must be a member of an Indian tribe recognized by the Bureau. There are three funding programs available: Educational scholarships - administered by the following B.I.A. area offices:

Billings Area Office, 316 North 26th St., Billings, MT 59101 (406) 247-7943; **Eastern Area Office**, 3701 N. Fairfax Dr., MS #260, Arlington, VA 22203 (703) 235-2571; **Juneau Area Office**, P.O. Box 25520, Juneau, AK 99802 (907) 586-7183; **Minneapolis Area Office**, 331 South 2nd Ave., Minneapolis, MN 55401 (612) 373-1090; **Navajo Area Office**, Higher Education Office, P.O. Box 1060, Gallup, NM 87301 (800) 223-7133 (in AZ); (800) 243-2956 (in NM, UT & CO); **Portland Area Office**, 911 NE 11th Ave., Portland, OR 97232 (503) 231-6702; **Sacramento Area Office**, Office of Indian Education, 2800 Cottage Way, Sacramento, CA 95825 (916) 978-4680.

Fellowhsips are available from Bureau's contractor, American Indian Scholarships, 4520 Montgomery Blvd., NE, Albuquerque, NM 87109; and educational loans are administered from the Revolving Loan Fund. Applications for these loans must be made through either the Tribal Credit Association or the bureau's agency offices. Amount awarded varies depending upon the program's funding and the recipient's needs. *Deadlines:* March for Fall, April for Summer, and October for Winter semesters.

Indian Education-Colleges and Universities: Financial aid to eligible Indian students (recognized by the Bureau as members of an Indian tribe, and have at least 25% Indian blood. Amount depends upon financial need. Awards range from $300 to $5,000 per year. *Deadline:* April, June & October.

BUREAU OF INDIAN AFFAIRS
Division of Social Services
Office of Indian Services
1951 Constitution Ave., NW, Rm. 310-S
Washington, DC 20245 (202) 343-6434
Indian Housing Assistance: Grants for repairs, temporary and emergency housing, down payments, and new housing. Child Welfare Assistance; For foster home care and other institutional care for Indian children residing on or near reservations. From $100 to $1,000 monthly. *Indian Child Welfare Act - Title II Grants:* Financial assistance for child-related facilities-day care centers, after-school care programs, foster care, family assistance centers. From $15,000 to $300,000. *General Assistance:* Financial assistance to needy Indians living on or near reservations. *Deadline:* Generally applications are due in February.

BUREAU OF INDIAN AFFAIRS
Division of Self-Determination Services
Office of Indian Services
1951 Constitution Ave., NW
Washington, DC 20240 (202) 343-4045
Self Determination Grants-Indian Tribal Governments: Funds for improving governing capabilities of the tribes. *Training and Technical Assistance-Indian Tribal Governments:* Funds to tribal governments to develop skills needed to improve capabilities of tribal management. Amount varies.

BUREAU OF INDIAN AFFAIRS
Division of Financial Assistance
1849 C St., NW • Washington, DC 20240
(202) 343-8427
Indian Loan Guaranty Fund: To finance Indian-owned, commercial, industrial, agricultural, or business activity organized for profit, provided that eligible Indian ownership constitutes not less than 51 percent of the business. No limits on the amount available for tribes or organizations, but there is a $500,000 limitation on guaranteed loans to individuals. Up to 30-year loans available. Requested must benefit the economy of an Indian reservation. *Indian Revolving Loan Fund:* Direct loans to Indian tribes, organizations and individuals for financing of economic enterprises that will contribute to the economy of an Indian reservation. *Indian Business Development Grants:* Matching grants to Native American individuals and public and private entities for the development, construction, improvement, and operation of business enterprises that will improve economies on Indian reservations or in Alaskan native villages. Up to $100,000 for individuals, and $250,000 for tribes and villages.

BUREAU OF INDIAN AFFAIRS
Division of Housing Assistance
Office of Tribal Services
18th & C Sts., NW, Rm. 316S
Washington, DC 20245
(202) 343-8427
Indian Housing Assistance: Grants for home improvements, for housing construction in isolated areas, and for technical assistance in establishing housing plans and in obtaining other federal funds. Grants include a maximum of $20,000 per recipient for repairs; $2,500 for temporary and emergency housing; $5,000 for a down payment to obtain a housing loan; and $45,000 for new standard housing ($55,000 in Alaska only.)

BUREAU OF INDIAN AFFAIRS
Division of Job Placement & Training
Office of Tribal Services
18th & C Sts., NW, Rm. 2061 MIB
Washington, DC 20245 (202) 208-2671
Employment Assistance for Adult Indians: To provide vocational training and job placement for Native Americans. Grants to individuals range from $200 to $10,000 per year and average about $5,000. Grants to tribal governments range from $7,000 to $350,000 and average about $50,000.

BUREAU OF INDIAN AFFAIRS
General Manager, Indian Arts & Crafts Board
18th & C Sts., NW, Rm 4004M
Washington, DC 20245 (202) 343-2773
Program planning assistance toward the encouragement and promotion of the development of American Indian arts & crafts.

**INDIAN HEALTH EMPLOYEES
SCHOLARSHIP FUND, INC.**
Federal Bldg., Rm 215, 115 Fourth Ave. SE
Aberdeen, SD 57401 (605) 226-7451
Scholarship: Postsecondary education, particularly in health fields. Stipends are usually in the $200 to $300 range. *Deadlines:* May, September, and December.

INDIAN HEALTH SERVICE
Attn: Scholarship Program
Twinbrook Metro Plaza, Suite 100
12300 Twinbrook Pkwy. • Rockville, MD 20852
(301) 443-6197 Fax 443-6048
Three Scholarship Programs: Health Professions Preparatory; Health Professionals Pregraduate; and *Health Professions.* Applicants must be American Indian or Alaska Native, high school graduate or equivalent with at least a 2.5 GPA, and intend to serve Indian people upon completion of program. Up to 4 years support available. $18,000 per year. *Deadline:* April. *IHS Loan Repayment Program:* To repay health professions educational loans of Native American or other health professionals who are willing to work for 2 years serving the health needs of American Indians. Up to $30,000 each year of service.

U.S. DEPT. OF AGRICULTURE
Farmers Home Administration
South Agricultural Bldg., Rm. 6304
Washington, DC 20250 (202) 720-3805
Indian Tribal Land Acquisition Loans: To enable tribes and tribal corporations to mortgage lands as secutiry for loans from the Farmers Home Administration to buy additional land within the reservation. Amount varies depending upon project costs. Each loan must be adequately secured.

U.S. DEPT. OF COMMERCE
Office of Program Development
Minority Business Agency-American Indian Program
14th & Constitution Ave., NW, Rm. 5096
Washington, DC 20230 (202) 377-5770
Competetive grant awards to six Indian Business Development Centers and one American Indian Business Consultant, to provide management and technical assistance of all types to new or existing American Indian businesses. *Amount:* From $165,000 to $300,000.

U.S. DEPT. OF EDUCATION
Division of Innovation & Development
400 Maryland Ave., SW • Washington, DC 20202
(202) 732-2379/80
Vocational Education-Indian and Hawaiian Natives Grants and Contracts. Amount: From $50,000 to $2+ million.

U.S. DEPT. OF EDUCATION
Office of Bilingual Education
& Minority Languages Affairs
400 Maryland Ave., SW
Washington, DC 20202
(202) 245-2595, 732-1840 & 732-2369
Fellowships Grants: Financial assistance to bilingual education programs and activities that meet special bilingual needs of children 3 to 18 years of age who have limited English language ability and who come from families where primary language is not English. From $25,000 to $1.5 million. *Deadline:* July. *Devel-

opment of *Instructional Materials in Bilingual Education Grants*. Up to $250,000 per year. *Deadline*: June. *Educational Personnel Training Program Grants*. $4 million per year is available for distribution. *Deadline*: June. *Special Populations Program Grants*: Financial support for bilingual education programs designed for special education for preschool children. Up to $2.5 million is available for distribution each year. *Deadline*: June. *Bilingual Vocational Instructional Materials, Methods, and Techniques Grants and Contracts*. Average $250,000. *Bilingual Vocational Instructor Training Grants*. From $125,000 to $225,000. *Deadline*: January. *Bilingual Vocational Training Grants*. From $100,000 to $350,000. *Family English Literacy Program Grants*. $250,000. *Deadline*: June. *Transitional Bilingual Education Grants*. To support structured English-language instruction and native language instruction. *Deadline*: June.

U.S. DEPT. OF EDUCATION
Office of Indian Education
400 Maryland Ave., SW, Rm. 2177
M.S. 6335 • Washington, DC 20202
(202) 401-1902/1916
Bruce Stacey, Contact
Indian Fellowship Program: financial assistance to graduate students and selected undergraduate students who are Native Americans interested in preparing for various professional careers. Awards range from $2,500 to $13,000 per year; $6,000 average. *Deadline*: January 21. *Adult Indian Education Grants*: support of programs for adult Indian education. From $30,000 to $250,000. *Deadline*: December. *Johnson-O'Malley Educational Assistance Program*: assistance to schools - reimburse schools that provide supplementary educational programs to eligible Indian students. *Formula Grants to Local Educational Agencies and Tribal Schools*: financial assistance to agencies or tribal schools for programs designed to meet the special and culturally-related educational needs of Indian children. From $2,000 to over $1 million. *Deadline*: January. *Grants to Indian Controlled Schools*. From $37,000 to $300,000. *Deadline*: December. *Special Programs and Projects Grants*: To provide financial assistance in improving educational opportunities for Indian children. From $20,000 to $300,000. *Deadline*: December.

U.S. DEPT. OF ENERGY
National Advisory Council on Indian Education
330 C St., SW, Rm. 4072 • Washington, DC 20202
(202) 205-8353 Fax 205-8897
Robert K. Chiago, Executive Director
Native American Scholarship Program: Intended to encourage Native Americans to pursue math and science degrees within the Nation's community college system. Focused primarily towards students enrolled at two-year community colleges.

U.S. DEPT. OF HEALTH & HUMAN SERVICES
Administration for Native Americans
Director, Planning & Support Division
200 Independence Ave., SW, Rm. 344F
Washington, DC 20201 (202) 245- 7776
Financial Assistance Grants. to promote self-sufficiency among Native Americans; for business starts for Indian-owned companies, improved Indian housing management, development of tribal health care systems, and local control of social services. From $40,000 to $2 Million; awards average $125,000 for tribal grants and $100,000 for urban grants. *Deadline*: June. *Research, Demonstration, and Evaluation Grants*: financial assistance for new methods of promoting social and economic self-sufficiency. From $46,000 to $250,000; awards average $130,000. *Training and Technical Assistance Grants*: for the planning and management of community-based social and economic programs. From $8,000 to $80,000; awards average $15,000.

U.S. DEPT. OF HEALTH & HUMAN SERVICES
Office for American Indian & Alaskan Natives
330 Independence Ave., SW, Rm. 4752
Washington, DC 20201 (202) 245- 2957
Grants to Native Americans for Aging Services: Financial assistance to Indian tribes to provide nutritional and supportive services to older Native Americans. The average grant is $50,000. Check Federal Register for schedule of deadline dates.

U.S. DEPT. OF HEALTH & HUMAN SERVICES
Division of Research & Demonstrations
Office of Policy Development
200 Independence Ave., SW
Washington, DC 20201 (202) 245-6233
Social Services Research & Demonstration: Funds for new social service concepts. From $100,000 to $250,000.

U.S. DEPT. OF HEALTH & HUMAN SERVICES
Indian Health Service
5600 Fishers Lane, Rm. 6A05
Rockville, MD 20857 (301) 443-1104
Larry Thomas, Branch Chief
Health Professional Pregraduate Scholarship Program: To American Indian or Alaska Native students interested in pursuing postsecondary education in the health professions; *Health Professions Preparatory Scholarship Program for Indians*: To students who need compensatory preprofessional education to qualify for enrollemnt or reenrollment in a health professions school. From $5,000 to $12,000 per year; *Health Professions Program*: Financial assistance to Native Americans who are interested in completing health professional degrees. From $7,000 to $12,000 per year. *Deadline*: April. *Management Development Program*: For projects that help encourage Indians to pursue a career in the health professions. From $40,000 to over $250,000 per year. *Indian Health Care Improvement Grants*. Average $80,000 per grant.

U.S. DEPT. OF HEALTH & HUMAN SERVICES
Indian Health Service, Manpower Support Branch
12300 Twinbrook Pkwy., Suite 100
Rockville, MD 20852 (301) 443-4242
IHS Loan Repayment Program: Provides financial assistance to Native Americans who are studying a health-related curriculum in graduate school and would be willing to work at an Indian Health Service (IHS) facility upon graduation. From $3,000 to $75,000.

U.S. DEPT. OF HOUSING & URBAN DEVELOPMENT
Community Planning & Development
451 7th St., SW • Washington, DC 20410
(202) 755-6092
Indian Community Development Block Grant Program: From $10,000 to $600,000 to improve housing, community facilities, and expand job opportunities for Indian tribes and Alaskan Native villages. The average award is about $300,000. Deadlines may be found in the Federal Register.

U.S. DEPT. OF LABOR
Division of Indian & Native American Programs
Employment & Training Administration
601 D St., NW • Washington, DC 20213
(202) 376-6102
Employment & Training Grants: To reduce the economic disadvantages and advance the economic and social development of Indians and others of Native American descent. From $50,000 to over $7 million per year. Notice of intent to apply due by March of each year.

U.S. DEPT OF TRANSPORTATION
Federal Highway Administration
Attn: National Highway Institute
4600 N. Fairfax Dr., Suite 800
Arlington, VA 22203
(703) 235-0538 Fax 235-0593
Web site: www.nhi.fhwa.dot.gov/fellowships.html
Eisenhower Tribal Colleges Initiatives: To provide financial assistance for Native American students and faculty in transportation-related fields at tribal colleges. Fellows receive the full cost of education, including tuition and fees. *Deadline*: February.

U.S. DEPT. OF VETERANS AFFAIRS
810 Vermont Ave., NW • Washington, DC 20420
(800) 827-1000; (202) 418-4343
Web site: www.va.gov
VA Home Loans for Native Americans. Up to $80,000.

U.S. FISH & WILDLIFE SERVICE
Cooperative Research Units Center
Dept. of the Interior • Washington, DC 20240
Cooperative Education Agreement: Tuition and up to $11,000 per year for part-time employment in turn for graduate education and work assignments at the ser-

vice facilities. Contact your local Cooperative and Wildlife Research Unit. No deadline.

U.S. JUSTICE DEPT.
Main Justice Bldg., 10th St. & Constitution Ave.
Washington, DC 20530 (202) 633-2007
Aleut Reparations: To compensate Aleuts taken to internment camps during World War II. Each eligible Aleut receives $12,000. Of th original 881 Aleuts taken to the camps and the children born there, about 400 are still alive and eligible for this payment.

U.S. NATIONAL INSTITUTES OF HEALTH
Division of Research Grants
Westwood Bldg., Rm. A27
Bethesda, MD 20892 (301) 496-7221
Short-Term Training Students in Health Professional Schools Grants: Financial assistance to attract qualified minority professional students into biomedical and behavioral research careers. The current stipend is about $550 per month with up to $125 per month to defray other costs. *Deadline*: January.

TRIBAL SCHOLARSHIPS

ALL INDIAN PUEBLO COUNCIL, INC.
3939 San Pedro NE, Suite #D
P.O. Box 3256 • Albuquerque, NM 87190
(505) 884-3820 Fax 883-7682
Ray H. Trujillo, Contact
Scholarship Grant Program: Financial assistance for postsecondary education to Pueblo Indians. Amount awarded varies. *Deadline*: Februrary for Summer or Fall terms, and October for Spring term. *Jobs Training Partnership Program*: To provide employment and training to selected Pueblo Indians. Enrolled and verified members of the Isleta and San Felipe Pueblos are eleigible. Grants for eligible unergraduate students from Cochiti, Sandia, and Santa Ana Pueblos. *Deadlines*: March & November. *Summer Youth Employment Program*: To provide summer employment to Pueblo Indian youth.

BLACKFEET TRIBAL EDUCATION DEPARTMENT
Blackfeet Nation Higher Education Program
P.O. Box 850 • Browning, MT 59417
(406) 338-7539 Fax 338-7530
E-mail: bhep@3rivers.net
Graduation Grant: To recognize and reward Blackfeet Indians who complete their high school requirements. The award is $50. *Education Grant*. For undergraduate or graduate education to members of the Blackfeet Tribe. The amount awarded varies depending upon the recipient's educational requirements and financial needs. *Deadlines*: February for Spring; June for Fall; and November for Winter. *Adult Vocational Training Grants*: Fopr vocational training to members of the Blackfeet Tribe. $2,800 to $3,500 per year. Up to 24 months. *Deadline*: February of each year; March for summer term.

CHEROKEE NATION OF OKLAHOMA
Higher Education Program
P.O. Box 948 • Tahlequah, OK 74465
(800) 256-0671; (918) 456-0671
Higher Education Undergraduate Grant Program: To members of the tribe for postsecondary education. Amount awarded varies. *Deadline*: March for Summer & Fall terms, and November for Spring term. *Trail of Tears Scholarship*: Must be a Cherokee college junior or senior with a 3.0 GPA. *Deadline*: April 1. *Graduate Scholarship Award*: Financial assistance to college graduates who belong to the Cherokee Nation of Oklahoma who wish to pursue a graduate education. Amount awarded varies depending upon the educational requirements and the financial needs of the recipient. *Deadline*: June for Fall term, and October for Spring term. *Louie Leflore/Grant Foreman Scholarships*: Financial assistance to Native American high school graduates who are interested in pursuing nursing or other health-related education. $650 per year. *Deadline*: June.

CHEYENNE & ARAPAHO TRIBES OF OKLAHOMA
Department of Education
P.O. Box 38 • Concho, OK 73022

(800) 247-4612; (405) 262-0345 Fax 262-0745
Higher Education Grants: To tribal members who are interested in pursuing postsecondary education. $75-250. *Deadline*: March for Summer, May for Fall, and October for Spring.

CHICKASAW NATION
EDUCATION FOUNDATION
Department of Education
P.O. Box 1548 • Ada, OK 74820
(405) 436-2603 Fax 436-4287
Roland Barrick, Director
Scholarship grant of $200-$350 per semester. Applicants must have proof of Chickasaw ancestry, and at least a 2.5 GPA. *Deadline*: May 1.

CHOCTAW NATION
Higher Education Department
P.O. Drawer 1210 • Durant, OK 74702
(800) 522-6170 (in OK); (580) 924-8280
Higher Education Program: Financial assistance to Choctaw Indians who are interested in pursuing postsecondary education. Applicants must be at least 25% Choctaw/Indian blood. Up to $1,600 per year for single students and $2,000 for married students. *Deadline*: March of each year.

CREEK NATION
Higher Education Program
P.O. Box 580 • Okmulgee, OK 74447
(918) 756-8700
Undergraduate Grant Program: Provides educational grants to aid Creek undergraduate or graduate students who are interested in pursuing postsecondary studies. Up to $2,000 per year. *Deadline*: May for Fall semester; October for Spring. *Tribal Funds Grant*: Grants to aid enrolled citizens of the Muskogee (Creek) Nation attending an accredited college or university. $400 per year to full-time students, $200 per year to part-time students. *Tribal Incentive Grant Program*: Financial assistance to enrolled citizens of the Muskogee (Creek) Nation attending an accredited college or university. $300 per semester for full-time students; $150 per semester for part-time students. *Deadline*: June for Fall semester, November for Spring semester.

EIGHT NORTHERN INDIAN
PUEBLOS COUNCIL, INC.
P.O. Box 969 • San Juan Pueblo, NM 87566
(800) 750-1808; (505) 753-1808 Fax 735-8988
Francis Tafoya, Director
Scholarship Program: Financial assistance for postsecondary education. Must be an enrolled member of one of the Eight Northern Pueblos. Up to $5,000, depending upon recipient's need. *Deadlines*: February for Fall semester & October for Spring semester.

FOND DU LAC RESERVATION
Attn: Scholarship Director
1720 Big Lake Rd. • Cloquet, MN 55720
(218) 879-4593 Fax 878-2687
Scholarship Program: For Lake Superior Chippewa students who are interested in pursuing postsecondary education. *Critical Professions Program*: To provide financial assistance to Indian students who wish to pursue a course of study leading to an undergraduate degree in business administration, natural resources or forestry, computer programming, urban or rural planning or elementary or secondary education. $450-650 per month. No deadline.

GRAND PORTAGE CHIPPEWA TRIBE
Attn: Education Director
P.O. Box 428 • Grand Portage, MN 55605
(218) 475-0121 Fax 475-2455
Scholarship Program: For Minnesota Chippewa Tribe members who are interested in pursuing postsecondary education. Amount of award is based on need. *Deadline*: At least 8 weeks before school starts.

HOPI TRIBE
c/o Grants & Scholarship Program
P.O. Box 123 • Kykotsmovi, AZ 86039
(800) 762-9630; (520) 734-3533 Fax 762-9630
Tribal Grants & Scholarship Program: To provide financial assistance to Hopi Indians who are interested in attending college at all levels. $1,000 per semester.

Deadline: July. *Supplemental Grant*: Up to $4,000 per semester and $2,750 for summer. *Priority Scholarship*: To encourage Hopi students to get a degree in an area of interest to the Hopi Tribe. *Tuition/Book Scholarship*: To Hopi students for their books and tuition fees. Deadline: July for Fall, November for Spring, and April for Summer.

HUALAPAI TRIBAL COUNCIL
Attn: Education Specialist
P.O. Box 179 • Peach Springs, AZ 86434
(520) 769-2200 Fax 769-2250
Higher Education Grants: Financial assistance for members of the Hualapai Tribe who are interested in pursuing undergraduate education. Up to $5,000 per year. *Graduate Student Grants*: For Hualapai Tribal member interested in pursuing graduate education. Up t $13,000 per year. *Deadline*: June for Fall, November for Spring. *Employment Assistance Program*: For tribal members who have graduated high school or earned the GED. Amount varies. Applications must be submitted at least 2 weeks before each term begins.

JEMEZ PUEBLO SCHOLARSHIP PROGRAM
P.O. Box 9 • Jemez Pueblo, NM 87024
(505) 834-9171 Fax 834-7331
Dr. Nilla Vallo, Education Director
Tribal Scholarships. *Deadlines*: June 30 & October 30.

JICARILLA APACHE TRIBE
Attn: Higher Education Program
P.O. Box 1099 • Dulce, NM 87528
(505) 759-3316
Josephine Lefthand, Director
Norman Tecube, Sr. Higher Education Fund: Financial assistance for undergraduate or graduate education to members of the Jicarilla Apache tribe. Up to $1,800 per year. *Deadlines*: February & September. :

LAGUNA PUEBLO SCHOLARSHIP PROGRAM
P.O. Box 194 • Old Laguna, NM 87026
(505) 552-6654 Ext. 33/66
Vivian Brewster, Director
Tribal scholarships. *Deadlines*: May 1 for Fall semester; October 1 for Spring semester; and April 15 for Summer semester.

LEECH LAKE TRIBE
Attn: Education Division
Rt. 3, Box 100 • Cass Lake, MN 56633
(218) 711-0443 Fax (218) 335-8339
Scholarship Program: Financial assistance to Minnesota Chippewa Tribe high school graduates who are interested in postsecondary education. Up to $3,000 per year, depending on need. *Deadline*: At least 8 weeks befire school starts.

MENOMINEE INDIAN TRIBE OF WISCONSIN
P.O. Box 910 • Keshena, WI 54135
(715) 799-5110
Higher Education Program: For Menominee Indians who are interested in pursuing postsecondary studies. Up to $2,200 per year. Deadline: February. *Adult Vocational Training Program*: Financial assistance to Menominee Indians who are interested in obtaining a diploma or certificate or associates of arts at a vocational/technical/junior college. Up to $2,200 per year; *Adult Education Program*: For Menominee Indians who are interested in pursuing additional employment-related training. *Deadlines*: February.

MESCALERO APACHE TRIBE
Attn: Tribal Education Dept.
P.O. Box 226 • Mescalero, NM 88340
(505) 671-4494 Fax 671-4454
Tribal scholarships: Financial assistance for undergraduate or graduate education to members of the tribe. *Amount*: maximum of $6,000 per year. *Deadline*: July for Fall & November for Spring.

MILLE LACS BAND OF CHIPPEWA
Attn: Education Division
HCR 67, Box 242 • Onamia, MN 56359
(320) 532-3451 Fax 532-4675
Scholarship Program: Financial assistance to members of the Band who are interested in postsecondary education. Up to $2,500 per year. *Deadline*: June.

MINNESOTA CHIPPEWA TRIBE
SCHOLARSHIP PROGRAM
P.O. Box 217 • Cass Lake, MN 56633
(218) 335-8584
Critical Professions Program: For Minnesota Chippewa Indian students with at least a 2.0 GPA, who wish to pursue an undergraduate or graduate degree in critical professions (business, natural resources-forestry, computer programming, urban and rural planning, or teaching.) Award varies; graduate students receive $650 per month and undergraduate students receive $450 per month (plus $90 per dependent) . *Scholarship Program*: For Tribal high school graduates who wish to pursue postsecondary education. From $500 to $3,000 per year, based on need. *Deadline*: June.

NAVAJO NATION
Division of Dine Education
Office of Navajo Nation Scholarship
& Financial Assistance Program
P.O. Box 1870 • Window Rock, AZ 86515
(800) 243-2956; (520) 871-7640
Chief Manuelito Scholarship Program: For members of the Navajo Nation who are interested in pursuing undergraduate education. $5,000 per year. *Deadline*: April. *Miss Navajo Nation Grant*: to recognize and reward outstanding young Navajo women. The winner is selected at the annual Navajo Tribal Fair. Tribal position - $15,000 per year. *College Developmental Studies Program*: Financial assistance to members who require remedial education at the college level. *Deadline*: April. *Financial Need-Based Assistance Program*: To members who are interested in pursuing undergraduate or graduate education. *Deadline*: April. *Trust Fund for Vocational Education*: To members who wish to study vocational education. *Deadline*: April. *Trust Fund & Fellowship*: To Navajo Nation members who wish to pursue graduate or postgraduate study. $10,000-15,000 per year. *Deadline*: April. *Teacher Education Program*: Navajo Nation members who wish to pursue a career as a teacher.

NAVAJO VETERAN AFFAIRS OFFICE
P.O. Box 430 • Window Rock, AZ 86515
(520) 871-6413 Fax 871-7288
Navajo Nation Veterans Fund: Emergency aid (From $200 to $3,000 - interest rate is 9%) to Navajo veterans waiting for assistance from the Veterans Administration.

NETT LAKE/BOIS FORTE CHIPPEWA TRIBE
P.O. Box 16 • Nett lake, MN 55772
(800) 221-8129; (218) 757-3261 Fax 757-3312
Scholarship Program: To Minnesota Chippewa Tribe high school graduates who are interested in postsecondary education. Up to $3,000 per year. *Deadline*: 8 weeks before school starts.

NORTHERN ARAPAHOE TRIBE
Sky People Higher Education
P.O. Box 8480 • Ethete, WY 82520
(307) 332-5286 Fax 332-9104
Tribal Scholarship: Financial assistance to members of the Northern Arapahoe Tribe who are high school graduates or seniors about to graduate and are interested in postsecondary education. Up to $2,000 per year. *Deadline*: May.

NORTHERN CHEYENNE TRIBE
Attn: Tribal Education Dept.
P.O. Box 307 • Lame Deer, MT 59043
(406) 477-6567
Northern Cheyenne Adult Vocational Training Program: Financial assistance to tribal members who are interested in pursuing voctional training. *Career Development Scholarships*: Financial assistance to members of the Northern Cheyenne Tribe who are high school graduates or seniors about to graduate and are interested in postsecondary education in the state of Montana. *Deadline*: February. *Higher Education Program*: Financial assistance to tribal high scholl graduates who are interested in pursuing postsecondary education. *Deadline*: February.

MAE LASLEY/OSAGE SCHOLARSHIP FUND
P.O. Box 2009 • Tulsa, OK 74101
(918) 587-3115 Marilyn Connor
Tribal Scholarship Grant: Financial assistance to eli-

gible tribal members for postsecondary education. Requirements: Proof of Osage Indian descent, and must show financial need. Amount: $1,000 per year, renewable. *Deadline*: June 15.

MARY TINKER SCHOLARSHIP
Osage Agency • Pawhuska, OK 74056
  (918) 287-1032 Marion Cass, Contact
Scholarships are awarded for college/university training. Must have at least a 2.0 GPA. Amount: $20-$50 per semester; up to eight semesters.

ONEIDA NATION OF WISCONSIN
Attn: Higher Education Office
P.O. Box 365 • Oneida, WI 54155
  (800) 236-2214 ext. 4333
  (920) 869-4333 Fax 869-4039
High Education Program: Financial assistance to tribal members who are pursuing undergraduate or graduate study. Up to $20,000 per year. *Adult Vocational Training Program*: Financial assistance to tribal members who are interested in earning a vocational, technical, or junior college degree. Up to $3,000 per year. *Deadlines*: April for Fall & September for Spring. *Purcell Powless Scholarship Fund*: Financial assistance for graduate education. *Deadline*: August for Fall and November for Spring.

OSAGE TRIBAL EDUCATION
COMMITTEE SCHOLARSHIP
c/o Oklahoma Area Indian Education Office
4149 Highline #380 • Oklahoma City, OK 73108
  (405) 945-6051 Fax 945-6057
Requirements: Proof of Osage Indian descent; verification of school enrollment. Must have at least a 2.0 GPA. Scholarships are awarded for vocational, technical and college/university training. *Amount*: $200-$500 per semester. *Deadlines*: June for Fall, and December for Spring, and April for Summer.

PUEBLO OF ACOMA
Higher Education Coordinator
P.O. Box 307 • Pueblo of Acoma, NM 87034
  (505) 552-6621/2 Lloyd Tortalita, Director
  Carleen Salvador, Higher Education Coordinator
Higher Education Grant Program: To Pueblo of Acoma high school graduates who are interested in postsecondary education. $1,000 to $1,800 per year. *Deadlines*: February for Fall & August for Spring.

PUEBLO OF LAGUNA
Attn: Dept. of Education
P.O. Box 207 • Laguna, NM 87026
  (505) 552-7182 Fax 552-7235
Adult Vocational Training Grant: For vocational training to regular members of the Laguna Pueblo. $300-500 per month. *Scholarship Program*: Fianancial assistance for college.

RED LAKE TRIBAL SCHOLARSHIPS
Red Lake Band of Chippewa
Red Lake Agency, BIA • Red Lake, MN 56671
  (218) 679-3371
  Peggy Whitefeather, Scholarship Officer

SANTO DOMINGO SCHOLARSHIP PROGRAM
P.O. Box 99 • Santo Domingo Pueblo, NM 87052
  (505) 465-2214 ext. 25
  Guadalupe Mina Sr., Director
Tribal scholarships. *Deadlines*: March & November.

SENECA NATION OF INDIANS
Attn: Higher Education Program
P.O. Box 231, 8183 Center Rd.
Salamanca, NY 14779 (716) 945-1790
Scholarship Fund: Financial assistance to Seneca Nation members who are interested in pursuing postsecondary education. Up to $8,000 per year.

SHOSHONE TRIBE
Community Development Office
Wind River Indian Agency
Fort Washakie, WY 82514
Tribal Scholarships: Financial assistance to members of the Wind River Shoshone Tribe who are high school graduates or seniors about to graduate and are interested in postsecondary education. Up to $2,000 per year. *Deadline*: June.

WHITE EARTH CHIPPEWA TRIBE
Attn: Dana Chaffey • P.O. Box 70
Naytahwaush, MN 56566 (800) 950-3248
  (218) 935-5554 Fax 935-2593
Critical Professions Program: Financial assistance to Indian students who wish to pursue a course of study leading to an undergraduate or graduate degree in business administration, natural resources, forestry, computer programming, urban or rural planning, or elementary or secondary school teaching. Up to $650 per month. *Scholarship Program*: Financial assistance to Minnesota Chippewa Tribe high school graduates interested in postsecondary education. Up to $3,000 per year. *Deadline*: June.

WIND RIVER INDIAN AGENCY
Community Development Office
Fort Washakie, WY 82514
Northern Arapahoe Tribal Scholarship: For enrolled members of the tribe who are interested in postsecondary education (any public institution in Wyoming.) Up to $2,00 per year. *Shoshone Tribal Scholarship*: For Wind River Shoshone Indian students who are interested in pursuing postsecondary education. Up to $2,00 per year.

WISCONSIN HIGHER
EDUCATIONAL AIDS BOARD
P.O. Box 7885 • Madison, WI 53707
  (608) 266-0888 Fax 267-2808
  E-mail: thomas2@mail.state.wi.us
Wisconsin Indian Student Grants: Financial assistance for higher education to Native Americans in Wisconsin. From $250 to $1,100 per year.

YAKIMA INDIAN NATION
Higher Education Programs
Dept. of Human Services, P.O. Box 151
Toppenish, WA 98948; (800) 543-2802
  (509) 865-5121 Fax 865-6994
Tribal Scholarship: Financial assistance to Yakima tribal members who wish to pursue postsecondary education. $1,500 per year for undergraduate students; $3,000 per year for graduate students. *Deadline*: January, April, June & October. *Yakima College Student Assistance Program*: For Yakima Indians who wish to pursue postsecondary education. Amount varies according to need. *Deadline*: January, April, June and October. *Yakima Incentive Awards Program*: To recognize and reward outstanding academic achievement of Yakima Indians. *Vocational Training for Adults Program*: To Yakima Indians who are interested in acquiring technical training by attending an accredited vocational school, college, or trade institute. *Direct Employment Assistance for Adults*: To eligible Yakima Indians who are searching for a permanent job.

ZUNI TRIBE
Attn: Dept. of Higher Education
P.O. Box 339 • Zuni, NM 87327
  (505) 782-4481 Ext. 482 Fax 782-2921
  E-mail: zunihe@unm.edu
Tribal scholarships: Fianancial assistance for postsecondary education to members of the Zuni tribe. Up to $5,000 per year, depending upon the recipient's need. *Deadlines*: May for Fall, September for Spring, and March for Summer semester. *Zuni Employment Assistance Program*: Fianancial assistance for vocational education to members of the Zuni tribe. Amount awarded depends on recipient's need.

CORPORATE GRANT MAKERS

ALCOA FOUNDATION
1501 Alcoa Bldg. • Pittsburgh, PA 15219
  (412) 553-4694 F. Worth Hobbs, Director
Places a high priority on serving populations in areas where the company has facilities. *Special interests*: education, health & welfare, cultural, covic & community, youth.

AMOCO FOUNDATION
200 E. Randolph Dr. • Chicago, IL 60601
  (312) 856-6306 Pamela J. Barbara, Director
Special interests: education, community service, environment, culture & art, neighborhood economies.

ARCO FOUNDATION
515 S. Flower St.
Los Angeles, CA 90071
  (213) 486-3342
  Eugene R. Wilson, Director
Special interests: education, arts & humanities, community development, environment, and public information (media).

AT&T BELL LABORATORIES
Special Programs Administrator
Crawfords Corner Rd., Room 1E-219
Holmdel, NJ 07733
  (908) 949-4301
Dual Degree Scholarship Program; Engineering Scholarship Program; Summer Employment Programs; and AT&T Graduate Research Fellowship Program for Women: To develop scientists and engineers among minority group members, and to provide work experience at AT&T Bell Labs. Annual award of $1,500. *Deadline*: January 15th.

DAYTON HUDSON FOUNDATION
Dayton Hudson Corp.
777 Nicollet Mall • Minneapolis, MN 55402
  (612) 370-6553
  Vivian K. Stuck, Administrative Officer
Special interests: community & economic development, social services, arts & cultural. Twins Cities Program and National Program.

EXXON EDUCATION FOUNDATION
225 E. John W. Carpenter Freeway
Irving, TX 75062
  (214) 444-1104
  Edward F. Ahnert, Executive Director
Special interests: education, community & economic development, health, arts.

GENERAL MILLS FOUNDATION
9200 Wayzata Blvd., Box 1113
Minneapolis, MN 55440
  (612) 540-4662 Fax 540-4925
  Dr. Reatha Clark King, Executive Director
Special interests: education, social services, health, arts & culture, civic affairs.

HUGHES AIRCRAFT COMPANY
Corporate Fellowship & Rotation Programs
Technical Education Center
P.O. Box 80028
Los Angeles, CA 90080
  (310) 568-6736
  Peggy Heathscote, Contact
Master of Science Fellowship, Howard Hughes Doctoral Fellowship and Engineer Degree Fellowship are awarded on a competetive basis to qualified individuals in engineering, computer sciences, physics and mathematics. *Amount*: Tuition, books, stipend ($25,000-$50,000).

IBM CORPORATION
Manager, University & Scientific Relations
Thomas J. Watson Research Center
P.O. Box 218 • Yorktown Hts., NY 10598
IBM Miority/Women's Fellowship Program: For graduate research in engineering and the sciences. $10,000 stipend and tuition. *Deadline*: February 15.

MICROSOFT CORPORATION
One Microsoft Way • Redmond, WA 98025
  (425) 882-8080 Fax 892-9811
  Web site: www.microsoft.com/
    college/scholarship.htm
National Minority Technical Scholarship: To encourage undergraduate students of color to pursue careers in computer science and other related technical fields. $1,000 a year. Deadline: February.

PACIFIC GAS & ELECTRIC CO.
c/o Citizens' Scholarship Foundation of America
P.O. Box 297 • St. Peter, MN 56082
  (800) 537-4180
Scholarship Program: Financial assistance for high school seniors, who live or attend schools in PG&E's service area, for postsecondary education to Black, Hispanic and Native American students in California. $2,000. *Deadline*: January.

RELIGIOUS INSTITUTION GRANT MAKERS

AMERICAN BAPTIST CHURCHES USA
Attn: Educational Ministries
P.O. Box 851 • Valley Forge, PA 19482
  (800) ABC-3USA ext. 2067 Fax (610) 768-2056
  Web site: www.abc-em.org
ABC Native American Grants: To provide financial assistance to Native American students interested in preparing for a ministerial career.

EPISCOPAL CHURCH CENTER
Attn: Episcopal Council of Indian Ministries
815 Second Ave. • New York, NY 10017
  (800) 334-7626 Fax (212) 867-0395
ECIM Scholarships: Financial assistance to Native Americans and Alaskan Natives interested in theological education within the Episcopal Church in the U.S. *Deadline*: May. *Continuing Education & Fellowships*: To Native Americans seeking ordination and serving in a ministry involving Native Americans in the Episcopal Church. Up to $4,000 per semester for seminary study and $2,500 per semester for diocesan theological study programs. *Deadline*: April.

NORTH SHORE UNITARIAN
UNIVERSALIST VEATCH PROGRAM
Plandome Rd. • Plandome, NY 11030
  (516) 627-6576
  Barbara Dudley, Exec. Director
Special interests: social & economic justice, civil & constitutional rights, religion, environmental.

PRESBYTERIAN CHURCH U.A.S.
Office of Financial Aid for Studies
100 Witherspoon St. • Louisville, KY 40202
  (502) 569-5760 fax 569-8766
  Maria Alvarez, Contact
  E-mail: maria_alvarez@pcusa.org
  Web site: www.pcusa.org

Special interests: Disadvantaged, social services, human rights, religion, community & economic development. *Native American Education Grants*: To provide Indian, Eskimo and Aleut students financial assistance to continue their college education. *Requirements*: Preference is given to Presbyterian students at an undergraduate level who can confirm at least a 1/4 Native American ancestry. Stipends range from $200 to $1,500 per year, renewable. *Deadline*: June. *Native American Seminary Scholarships*: Financial assistance to Native American students interested in preparing for church occupations. From $1,000 to $3,000 per year. *Scholarships for Ethnic Minority Groups*: Financial assistance for educational purposes to members of racial/ethnic minoirty who are Presbyterians. $100 to $1,400 per year. *Deadline*: March.

UNITED METHODIST CHURCH
General Commission on Religion & Race
36 Madison Ave., P.O. Box 127
Madison, NJ 07940
  (973) 408-3189 Fax 408-3909
  E-mail: dpatterson@gcah.org
  Web site: www.gcah.org
Native American United Methodist History Research Awards: Support for research on the history of ethnic groups in the United Methodist Church or its antecedents. $1,500 or $3,000. *Deadline*: December.

UNITED METHODIST CHURCH
Board of Higher Education & Ministry
P.O. Box 871 • Nashville, TN 37202-0871
  (615) 340-7344
  Diane DeForest, Contact
HANA Scholars Program: Financial assistance to outstanding United Methodist Native American undergraduate and graduate full-time college students. Applicants must be a member of the Church for at least one year. Stipend is $1,000 for undergraduates and $3,000 for graduate students. *Deadline*: April 1. *Ethnic Minority Scholarships*: Must be an active member of the Church. From $100 to $1,000. *Deadline*: May 1.

Since 1955, the U.S. Public Health Service (PHS), through its Indian Health Service (IHS), an agency of the Department of Health and Human Services, is responsible for providing federal health services to American Indians and Alaska Natives. The provision of health services to federally recognized Indians grew out of a special relationship between the federal government and Indian tribes. This government-to-government relationship has been given form and substance by numerous treaties, laws, Supreme Court decisions, and Executive Orders. The IHS is the principal federal health care provider and health advocate for Indian people. The IHS provides health services to approximately 1.4 million American Indians and Alaska Natives who belong to more than 550 federally recognized tribes in 35 states. The goal is to raise their health status to the highest possible level; to ensure the equity, availability and accessibility of a comprehensive high quality health care delivery system providing maximum involvement of American Indians and Alaska Natives in defining their health needs, setting priorities for their local areas, and managing and controlling their health program. The IHS budget for fiscal year 1997 is just over $2 billion. This section lists hospitals, medical and health centers under the jurisdiction of the Indian Health Service. Listings are arranged alpha-geographically.

DHHS HOTLINE NUMBER: (800) 447-8477
Office of the Inspector General (OIG) Hotline
P.O. Box 23489, Washington, DC 20007
Fax (800) 223-8164
E-Mail: hhstips@hotline.oig

(OUTBOUND BUILDING ADDRESS)
Indian Health Service (TMP)
12300 Twinbrook Metro Plaza
Rockville, MD 20852

(HEADQUARTERS)
Indian Health Service
801 Thompson Ave., Suite 400
The Reyes Bldg. • Rockville, MD 20852
(301) 443-1083 Fax 443-4794
IHS Hotline Number (301)443-0658
Website: www.ihs.gov

Office of the Director:
Rm. 6-05 (301) 443-1083
Charles W. Grim, DDS, MHSA, Director
Robert H. Harry, DDS, Executive Assistant Director
Michel E. Lincoln, Deputy Director
Paula K. Williams, Director-Tribal Self-Governance
Rm. 5A-55 (443-7821)
Douglas P. Black, Director of Tribal Programs
Rm. 6A-05 (443-1104)
Michael Mahsetky, JD, Director of Legislative Affairs
Rm. 6-22 (443-7261)
Ray J. Snyder, Director of Urban Programs
Rm. 6-12 (443-4680)
Tony Kendrick, MA, Director of Public Affairs
Rm. 6-35 (443-3593)
Cecilia Heftel, Director of EEO and Civil Rights
Rm. 6A-14 (443-1108)

Office of General Counsel:
Rm. 4A-37 (301) 443-8220
Gary J. Hartz, P.E, Chief, IHS Branch, Public Health

Office of Public Health:
Rm. 6A-55 (301) 443-3024
Gary J. Hartz, P.E., Acting Director

Office of Management Support:
Room 6-49 (301) 443-6290
Robert G. McSwain, Director

Clinical Support Center, IHS
1616 E. Indian School Rd.
Aztec Square, Suite 375
Phoenix, AZ 85016 (602) 640-2140
Wesley J. Picciotti, Director

IHS-Seattle Office of Engineering Services
2201 6th Ave., RX-24
Seattle, WA 98121-2500
(206) 615-2452 Fax 615-2466
Kenneth Harper, Director

IHS-Dallas Office of Engineering Services
PHS-6, 1200 Main St., Rm. 1900
Dallas, TX 75202
(214) 767-3492 Fax 767-5194
Thomas Gallegos, Director

National Council of Nursing, IHS
5600 Fishers Lane, Rockville, MD 20857
(301) 443-1840
LaVerne V. Parker, RN, Chairperson

Personnel Field Support Officers
Federal Office Bldg., Rm. 144
50 UN Plaza, San Francisco, CA 94102
(415) 437-7619
Barbara Davis, Personal Management Specialist
Judith Scherr, Labor Relations Specialist

(HEADQUARTERS WEST)
5300 Homestead Rd., NE
Albuquerque, NM 87110
(505) 248-4102 Fax 248-4115

Office of the Director
Bernie Dailleboust, Director -
Management Program Analyst (505) 248-4137
Leonore Garcia, Office Services Coordinator
(248-4131)
Cheryl Wilson, Coordinator - Headstart Project
(248-4231)

Dental Field Support & Program Development
(505) 248-4175 Fax 248-4181
Scott Bingham, Director - Dental Staff Development

Office of Information Resource Management
(505) 248-4189 Fax 248-4199
George Huggins, Director - Systems
Development Div.

Nutrition & Dietetics Training Branch
P.O. Box 5558, Santa Fe, NM 87502
(505) 988-6518
Jean Charles-Azure, Chief

IHS OWNED/OPERATED WAREHOUSE

Navajo Area Supply Service Center
P.O. Box 9020 • Window Rock, AZ 86515
(505) 722-1578 Bob Stopp, Director

Oklahoma Area Regional Supply Service Center
1005 N. Country Club Rd. • Ada, OK 74820
(405) 436-5000 Wyman Ford, Director

Portland Area Supply Service Center
11824 N.E. Ainsworth Circle, Suite B
Portland, OR 97220 (503) 231-2115
Ed Wermy, Supervisor

IHS AREA OFFICES
(Alphabetically Arranged)

ABERDEEN IHS AREA OFFICE
Federal Bldg., 115 Fourth Ave., SE
Aberdeen, SD 57401
(605) 226-7581; Fax 226-7321
Douglas Peter, M.D., Area Director (7581)
Tony Peterson, Executive Officer (7581)
Sara Dye, MD, Chief Medical Officer (7501)
Daryl Russell, Deputy Director & Public
Relation Officer (7581)
Tribal Projects Specialists: Dennis Renvilles (Bismarck) (701) 222-3540; Priscilla Lee (Pierre) (605) 224-8544 Roger Condon (Aberdeen) (605) 226-7584; and Pat Giroux Rapid City) (605) 348-1900. *States served:* North & South Dakota & Iowa. *Has jurisdiction over the following Indian hospitals:* Eagle Butte (SD); Winnebago (NE) ; Pine Ridge (SD); Rapid City (SD); Rosebud (SD); Sisseton (SD); Fort Yates (ND); Belcourt (ND); Wagner (SD); and the following health centers: Fort Berthold (New Town, ND); Fort Totten

(ND); Carl T. Curtis Health Center (Macy, NE); Sac & Fox Tribe of the Mississippi in Iowa (Tama, IA); Fort Thompson (SD); Lower Brule (SD); Kyle (SD); Wanblee (SD); McLaughlin (SD); Trenton-Williston (ND); and Youth Regional Treatment Center (SD).

ALASKA AREA INDIAN HEALTH SERVICES
4141 Ambassador Dr.
Anchorage, AK 99508-5928
(907) 729-3686 Fax 729-3689
Christopher Mandregan, Jr., Area Director
David J. Schraer, MD, Deputy Director/
Chief Medical Officer 3925 Tudor Centre Dr.,
Anchorage, AK 99508 (907) 729-3600
State served: Alaska. Has jurisdiction over the following Indian hospitals in Alaska: Anchorage; Barrow; Bethel (Yukon-Kuskokwim Delta); Bristol Bay Area (Dillingham); Kotzebue; Mt. Edgecumbe (Sitka); Norton Sound (Nome); & the following health centers: Metlakatla; Fairbanks; Juneau; and Ketchikan.

ALBUQUERQUE AREA IHS
5338 Montgomery Blvd., NE
Albuquerque, NM 87109
(505) 248-4500 Fax 248-4624
James L. Toya, Area Director (4500)
Judith A. Kitzes, MD, Chief Medical Officer (4500)
Sandra Winfrey, Executive Officer (4500)
States served: New Mexico & Colorado. *Has jurisdiction over the following Indian hospitals:* Acomita-Canoncita-Laguna (San Fidel); Albuquerque; Mescalero; Santa Fe; and Zuni (all in NM); and the following health centers: Alamo Navajo (Magdalena); Jicarilla (Dulce); New Sunrise (San Fidel); Santa Clara (Espanola); Taos; Ramah; Pine Hill; in CO: Southern Colorado Ute, Ignacio and Towaoc; in TX: Ysleta Del Sur (El Paso); and Southwestern Indian Polytechnic Institute Dental Center (Albuquerque).

BEMIDJI AREA IHS
522 Minnesota Ave., NW
Bemidji, MN 56601 (800) 892-3079
(218) 444-0458 ; Fax 444-0461
Kathleen Annette, MD, Area Director
Charlene RedThunder, Executive Officer

Field Offices

Rhinelander Field Office
P.O. Box 537 • Rhinelander, WI 54501
(715) 362-5145

Ashland OEH Field Office
2800 Lake Shore Dr. E. • Ashland, WI 54806

Field Health Office/MITC
3601 Mackinaw Trail
Sault Ste. Marie, MI 49788
(906) 635-4208 Fax 635-4212
Char Hewitt, Director
States served: Minnesota, Michigan & Wisconsin. *Has jurisdiction over the following Indian hospitals:* Cass Lake and Red Lake (in MN); and the following Indian health centers : Min-No-Aya-Win Clinic (Cloquet, MN); White Earth (MN); Nimkee Memorial Wellness Center (Mt. Pleasant, MI); Stockbridge-Munsee Health Center (Bowler, WI); Ho Chunk Nation Health Dept. (Black River Falls, WI); Lac Courte Oreilles (Hayward, WI); Menominee Tribal Clinic (Keshena, WI); Chippewa Health Center (Lac du Flambeau, WI); Oneida Community Health Center (Oneida, WI); White Earth, MN.

BILLINGS AREA IHS
P.O. Box 2143, 2900 4th Ave. N.
Billings, MT 59103, 59101
(406) 247 + 7107; Fax 247-7230
C. Pete Conway, Area Director
States served: Montana & Wyoming. *Has jurisdiction over the following Indian hospitals:* Browning; Crow Agency; and Harlem; and the following Indian health centers: Lodge Grass; Poplar; Wolf Point; Lame Deer; Box Elder; and Fort Washakie and Arapaho (in WY); and the tribally operated programs at St. Ignatius and Box Elder.

CALIFORNIA AREA IHS
650 Capital Mall • Sacramento, CA 95825
(916) 930-3981

Margo D. Kerrigan, Area Director (Ext. 306)
J. Paul Redeagle, Deputy Area Director (Ext. 307)
Stephen Mader, MD, Chief Medical Officer (Ext. 308)

Field Offices

Arcata Field Office
1125 16th St. #100 • Arcata, CA 95521
(707) 822-1688 Fax 822-1692
Paul Robinson, Contact

Fresno Field Office
2130 Monterey St. • Fresno, CA 93721
(559) 487-5609 Fax 487-5913
Matt Williams, Contact

Ukiah Field Office
169 Mason St. #400 • Ukiah, CA 95482
(707) 462-531'4 Fax 462-6907
Andrew Sallach, Contact

Redding District Office
P.O. Box 492050 • Redding, CA 96049
(530) 246-5339 Fax 246-5210
James Ludington, Contact

Escondido District Office
1320 W. Valley Pkwy. • Escondido, CA 92029
(760) 735-6885 Fax 735-6893
Ray Suarez, Contact

State served: California. *Contracted and Suncontracted Programs served:* American Indian Council of Central California (Bakersfield); American Indian Health & Services (Santa Barbara); Berry Creek/Mooretown Tribal Health Organization (Oroville); California Rural Indian Health Board (Sacramento); Chapa-De Indian Health Progam (Auburn); Central Valley Indian Health Project (Clovis); Consolidated Tribal Health Project (Ukiah); Hoopa Health Association (Hoopa); Fresno Indian Health Association (Fresno); Greenville Rancheria Tribal Health Program (Greenville); Indian Health Center of Santa Clara Valley (San Jose); Indian Health Council (Pauma Valley); Lake County Tribal Health Consortium (Lakeport); Lassen Indian Health Program (Susanville) Modoc Indian Health Project (Alturas); Northern Valley Indian Health (Willows); Pit River Health Services (Burney); Redding Rancheria Indian Health Services; Riverside/San Bernardino County Indian Health (Banning); Round Valley Indian Health Program (Covelo); Sacramento Urban Indian Health Project (Sacramento); San Diego American Indian Health Center (San Diego); Santa Ynez Tribal Health Program (Santa Ynez); Sonoma County Indian Health Program (Santa Rosa); Southern Indian Health Council (Al Pine); Shingle Springs Rancheria Tribal Health Program (Shingle Springs); Sycuan Medical/Dental Center (El Cajon); Toiyabe Indian Health Program (Bishop); Tule River Indian Health Center (Porterville); Tuolumne Rural Indian Health Program (Tuolumne); United Indian Health Services (Trinidad); Urban Indian Health Board (Oakland); Warner Mountain Indian Health Project (Ft. Bidwell);

NASHVILLE AREA IHS
711 Stewarts Ferry Pike • Nashville, TN 37214
(615) 467-1500; Fax 467-1580
Michael D. Tiger, Area Director (1505)
Roy S. Kennon, MD, Director,
Office of Public Health (1531)
Gladys Bratcher, Director,
Office of Tribal Activities (1509)

States served: Eastern states. Has jurisdiction over Cherokee Indian Hospital (Cherokee, NC); and Choctaw Health Center (Philadelphia, MS).

NAVAJO AREA IHS
P.O. Box 9020 • Window Rock, AZ 86515
(520) 871-5811 Fax 871-5896
John Hubbard, Jr., Area Director (5811)
Pete Hoskie, Tribal Affairs (5811)
Douglas G. Peter, MD, Chief Medical Officer (5813)
Ron C. Wood, Executive Officer (5812)
Taylor McKenzie, MD, Administrator,
Navajo Nation Div. of Health (6350)

States served: Northeast Arizona, Northwest New Mexico, Southern Utah. Has jurisdiction over the fol-lowing Indian hospitals: Chinle; Fort Defiance (AZ); Tuba City (AZ); Crownpoint (NM); Gallup (NM); Shiprock (NM); and the following Indian health cen-ters: Chinle (AZ), Tsaile (AZ), Tohatchi (NM); Kayenta (AZ); Inscription House (Tonalea, AZ); Winslow; and Dzilth-Na-O-Dith-Hle (Bloomfield, NM).

OKLAHOMA CITY AREA IHS
5 Corporate Plaza, 3625 NW 56th St.
Oklahoma City, OK 73112
(405) 951-3768 Fax 951-3780
Franklin Dale Keel, Area Director (3768)
Randy Grinnell, Deputy Area Director (3768)
Bernadine Tolbert, MD, Chief Medical Officer (3837)
Luke McIntosh, Office of Administration
& Management (3717)
Max Tahsuda, Office of Tribal Development (3761)

This is the largest IHS service population in the U.S. extending health care to over 281,000 American Indians. Maintains 7 Indian hospitals and 40 outpatient health centers located throughout Oklahoma, northeastern Kansas, and Eagle Pass, Texas. Additional services are provided through two urban programs located in Wichita, Kansas and Dallas, Texas.

States served: Oklahoma & Kansas. Has jurisdiction over the following Indian hospitals: Carl Albert (Ada, OK); Claremore; Creek Nation (Okemah); Clinton; Lawton; W.W. Hastings (Tahlequah); and the follow-ing Indian health centers in OKlahoma: Anadarko, Ardmore, Broken Bow, Carnegie, Durant,El Reno, Eufaula, Hugo, McLoud, Miami, Muskogee, Norman, Nowata, Okemah, Oklahoma City, Okmulgee, Pawnee, Pawhuska, Ponca City, Salina, Salisaw, Sam Hider Jay, Shawnee, Stilwell, Tahlequah, Talihina, Tishomingo, Tulsa, Watonga, Wewoka, White Eagle (Ponca City), Wyandotte; in Kansas: Lawrence, Horton, Holton, and Wichita; and in Texas: Dallas and Eagle Pass.

PHOENIX AREA IHS
40 N. Cental Ave. Two Renaissance Sq.
Phoenix, AZ 85004
(602) 364-5039 Fax 640-2557
Don J. Davis, Area Director (5039)
Mary Lou Stanton, Deputy Director (5039)
Richard Olson, MD, Chief Medical Officer (5039)
Theodore J. Redding, Chief Health Advisor (5039)
Gary P. Breshears, Executive Officer (5039)

Center for Native American Health
P.O. Box 245037, Tucson, AZ 85724
(520) 626-7909 Fax 626-8080
James M. Galloway, MD, Director

ORYX Program
5300 Homestead Rd.
Albuquerque, NM 87110
(505) 248-4152 Fax 248-4172
Michael Gomez, Director

Desert Visions Youth Wellness Center/RTC
P.O. Box 458, 198 S. Skill Center Rd.
Sacaton, AZ 85247
(520) 562-3801 Fax 562-3415
Theda Starr, Director

Southwest Native American Cardiology Program
3601 S. Sixth Ave. • Tucson, AZ 85723
Dr. James M. Galloway (520) 629-1899

**Phoenix/Tucson Area Adolescent
Regional Treatment Center**
P.O. Box 458, 198 S. Skill Center Rd.
Sacaton, AZ 85247 (520) 562-3801
Theta Star, Director

Has jurisdiction over the following Indian hospitals: Parker; Fort Yuma; Keams Canyon; Phoenix Indian Medical Center; San Carlos; Whiteriver; and Owyhee Tribal Hospital (in NV); and the following Indian health centers: in AZ: Peach Springs; Havasupai; Second Mesa; Cibicue; Scottsdale Salt River Clinic; in NV: Elko (NV); McDermitt (NV); Pyramid Lake (Nixon, NV); Washoe Tribal Health center, Yerington Health dept., Las Vegas Tribal Health Clinic, Schurz Indian health Center, Reno Tribal Health Station, Reno Spark Health Center, Fallon Clinic; and in UT: Fort Duchesne (Roosevelt, UT).

Consists of one medical center, eight hospitals, four health centers, and two school health clinics. *States served*: Arizona, Nevada & Utah. *Tribes served*: (47 separate tribes-Papago, Apache, Pima, Maricopa, Hopi, Paiute, Navajo, Ute, Goshute, Shoshone, Washoe, Hualapai, Havasupai, Mojave, Cocopah, Quechan, and urban tribes in the metropolitan area.) *Number of professionals on staff*: 772. *Number of beds*: 424. *Numbers served annually*: In-patient, 15,000; Out-patient, 450,000. *Services*: All primary medical services are provided. Programs: Accredited residency programs in obstetrics, pediatrics, family practice, dental, general practice, and public health nursing; continuing education; research (sponsored by the National Institutes of Health) at several facilities; Health Education Program—comprised of 15 professional staff who provide a coordinated program of health education throughout the Phoenix area; Indian Health Service Training Committee; instrumental in implementing the Health Emphasis Campaign, a seven year program to develop disease prevention and health promotion practices among Indian community residents. Scholarships: Participates in the National Health Service Corps and the Indian Health Care Improvement Scholarship Programs. Library.

PORTLAND AREA IHS
1220 S.W. Third Ave. #476
Portland, OR 97204
(503) 326 + Ext.; Fax 326-7280
Doni Budlong Wilder, Area Director (2020)
Clark T. Marquart, MD, Chief Medical Officer (3900)
Frank H. Williams, Executive Officer (3288)
J. Michael Wood, Self-Governance Coord. (2009)
Joyce M. Reyes, Office of Tribal Operations (7270)
Richard R. Truitt, Director of Office of Environmental
Health & Engineering (2001)
Cheryl A. Bittle, PhD, Director of
Health Programs (3288)

Provides access to health care for an estimated 160,000 Indian residents of 42 Tribes located in Idaho, Oregon and Washington. There are 15 health centers, 8 tribally operated and 7 federally operated. Health stations total 23, 22 are tribally operated amd 1 federally operated. Ten tribally operated preventive programs, and 3 tribally operated urban programs.

States served: Idaho, Oregon, Washington. *Has juris-diction over the following Indian health centers*: Yellowhawk (Pendleton, OR); Warm Springs (OR); Chemawa Indian Health Centers (Salem, OR); Kla-math Service Unit (Chiloquin, OR); Colville (Nespelem, WA); Neah Bay (WA); Northwest Washington (Bellingham, WA); Puget Sound (Seattle, WA); Taholah (WA); Wellpinit (WA); Yakima (Toppenish, WA); Fort Hall (ID); and Northern Idaho (Lapwai, ID).

TUCSON AREA IHS
7900 S. "J" Stock Rd. • Tucson, AZ 85746
(520) 295-2405 Fax 295-2602
Taylor Jones Satala, Area Director (2405)
State served: Arizona. Has jurisdiction over the fol-lowing Indian hospital and health centers: Sells Indian Hospital, Sells, AZ; Santa Rosa Indian Health Center, Sells, AZ; and San Xavier Indian Health Center, Tucson, AZ.

IHS SERVICE UNITS

ALASKA

AKIACHAK NATIVE COMMUNITY
P.O. Box 70 • AKIACHAK, AK 99551
(907) 825-4626 FAX 825-4029
George Peter, President
Affiliated with Alaska Area Native Health Service.
Tribally operated.

ALASKA NATIVE MEDICAL CENTER
4315 Diplomacy Dr. • ANCHORAGE, AK 99508
(907) 279-1994; Fax 729-1984
Richard Mandsager, MD, Director
Frank Williams, Executive Officer
Michael Westley, MD, Medical Director
Number of Beds: 170. Affiliated with Alaska Area Native Health Service.

ALEUTIAN/PRIBILOF ISLANDS ASSOCIATION
401 E. Fireweed Lane, Suite 201
ANCHORAGE, AK 99503
   (907) 276-2700; Fax 279-4351
   Demitri Philemonof, Health Director
Affiliated with Alaska Area Native Health Service.
Tribally operated.

CHITINA TRADITIONAL VILLAGE COUNCIL
3701 Eureka, #16A
ANCHORAGE, AK 99503
   (907) 563-6643 (phone & fax)
   Harry Billum, President
Affiliated with Alaska Area Native Health Service.
Tribally operated.

CHUGACHMIUT
4201 Tudor Centre, Suite 210
ANCHORAGE, AK 99508
   (907) 562-4155; Fax 563-2891
   Anne M. Walker, Executive Director
   Joan Domnick, Clinical Director
Affiliated with Alaska Area Native Health Service.
Tribally operated.

EASTERN ALEUTIAN TRIBES
721 Sesame St., Suite 2C
ANCHORAGE, AK 99503
   (907) 563-1414 FAX 563-1428
   Steve Levinson, Executive Administrator
Affiliated with Alaska Area Native Health Service.
Tribally operated.

SOUTHCENTRAL FOUNDATION
4501 Diplomacy Dr., Suite 200
ANCHORAGE, AK 99508
   (907) 265-4900; Fax 265-5925
   Katherine Grosdidier, President/CEO
   Ted Mala, MD, Executive Planner
Affiliated with Alaska Area Native Health Service.
Tribally operated.

UKPEAGVIK INUPIAT CORPORATION
5300 "A" St. • ANCHORAGE, AK 99518
   (907) 762-0111 Fax 762-0103
   Lewis Schnaper, Special Project Manager
Affiliated with Alaska Area Native Health Service.
Tribally operated.

ARCTIC SLOPE NATIVE ASSOCIATION
P.O. Box 1232 • BARROW, AK 99723
   (907) 852-2762 Fax 852-1763
   Eben Hopson, Executive Director
Affiliated with Alaska Area Native Health Service.
Tribally operated.

SAMUEL SIMMONDS MEMORIAL HOSPITAL
P.O. Box 29 • BARROW, AK 99723
   (907) 852-4611; Fax 852-6408
   Mike Herring, Administrator
Number of Beds: 14. Affiliated with Alaska Area
Native Health Service.

**NORTH SLOPE BOROUGH DEPT.
OF HEALTH & SOCIAL SERVICES**
P.O. Box 69 • BARROW, AK 99723
   (907) 852-0260; Fax 852-0268
   Doreen Knodel, Health Director
Affiliated with Alaska Area Native Health Service.
Tribally operated.

YUKON-KUSKOKWIM HEALTH CORP.
P.O. Box 528 • BETHEL, AK 99559
   (907) 543-6000; Fax 543-5277
   Gene Peltola, President/CEO
   Orie Williams, Executive VP
   Donald Kruse, MD, Medical Director
Affiliated with Alaska Area Native Health Service.
Tribally operated.

**YUKON-KUSKOKWIM DELTA
REGIONAL HOSPITAL**
Pouch 3000 • BETHEL, AK 99559
   (907) 543-6300; Fax 543-5295
   Ed Hansen, VP Hospital Operations
   Shawn Stitham, MD, Clinical Director
Number of Beds: 50. Affiliated with Alaska Area
Native Health Service.

CHICKALOON NATIVE VILLAGE
P.O. Box 1105 • CHICKALOON, AK 99674
   (907) 745-7184 FAX 745-7154
   Gary Harrison, Chief & Chairperson
Affiliated with Alaska Area Native Health Service.
Tribally operated.

NATIVE VILLAGE OF EKLUTNA
26339 Eklutna Village Rd.
CHUGIAK, AK 99567
   (907) 688-6020 Fax 688-6021
   Dorothy Cook, President
Affiliated with Alaska Area Native Health Service.
Tribally operated.

COPPER RIVER NATIVE ASSOCIATION
Health & Human Services, Drawer H
COPPER CENTER, AK 99573
   (907) 822-5241; Fax 822-5247
   Ken Johns, Executive Director
   Mark Wuitschick, Health Director
Affiliated with Alaska Area Native Health Service.
Tribally operated.

BRISTOL BAY AREA HEALTH CORP.
P.O. Box 130 • DILLINGHAM, AK 99576
   (800) 478-5201; (907) 842-5201; Fax 842-9354
   Robert J. Clark, CEO; Darrel Richardson, COO
Area served: 32 villages in Bristol Bay region. Population served: 7,500. *Number of Beds*: 16. Primary medical services: Medical, dental, optometry, audiology,
health, alcohol/drug rehabilitation, obstetrical; emergency services. Special programs: Laboratory; medical imaging; pharmacy; home health care; WIC; infant
learning; medical supplies; environmental health; injury prevention; health education; dietary counseling.
Medical Library. Affiliated with Alaska Area Native
Health Service. Tribally operated.

DIOMEDE NATIVE VILLAGE HEALTH CENTER
P.O. Box 7079 • DIOMEDE, AK 99762
   (907) 686-2175 Fax 686-2203
   Patrick F. Omiak, Sr., President
Affiliated with Alaska Area Native Health Service.
Tribally operated.

CHIEF ANDREW ISAAC HEALTH CENTER
1638 Cowles St. • FAIRBANKS, AK 99701
   (907) 451-6682; Fax 459-3811
   Marilyn Harasick, Director
Affiliated with Alaska Area Native Health Service.
Tribally operated.

**FAIRBANKS NATIVE ASSOCIATION
HEALTH CENTER**
201 First Ave., #200 • FAIRBANKS, AK 99701
   (907) 452-1648 Fax 456-4849
   John Regitano, Executive Director
Affiliated with Alaska Area Native Health Service.
Tribally operated.

**TANANA CHIEFS CONFERENCE, INC.
HEALTH CENTER**
122 First Ave. #600 • FAIRBANKS, AK 99701
   (907) 452-8251; Fax 459-3850
   Will Mayo, President
   Eileen Kozevnikoff, Health Service Director
Affiliated with Alaska Area Native Health Service.
Tribally operated.

**COUNCIL OF ATHABASCAN
GOVERNMENT HEALTH CENTER**
P.O. Box 33 • FORT YUKON, AK 99740
   (907) 662-2587 Fax 662-3333
   Patricia Stanley, Executive Director
Affiliated with Alaska Area Native Health Service.
Tribally operated.

**MT. SANFORD TRIBAL CONSORTIUM
HEALTH CENTER**
P.O. Box 357 • GAKONA, AK 99586
   (907) 822-5399 Fax 822-5810
   Evelyn Beeter, President
Affiliated with Alaska Area Native Health Service.
Tribally operated.

HOONAH INDIAN CORP. HEALTH CENTER
P.O. Box 602 • HOONAH, AK 99829
   (907) 945-3545 FAX 945-3703

   Kennet J. Grant, President
Affiliated with Alaska Area Native Health Service.
Tribally operated.

SEARHC JUNEAU MEDICAL CENTER
3245 Hospital Dr. • JUNEAU, AK 99801
   (907) 463-4052; Fax 463-4075
   Ethel Lund, President
   Joe Cladouhos, Clinic Administrator
   Mark Peterson, MD, Clinical Director
Serves 19 communities and villages in Southeast
Alaska. Affiliated with Alaska Area Native Health Ser-
vice. Tribally operated.

KARLUK TRIBAL HEALTH CENTER
P.O. Box 22 • KARLUK, AK 99608
   (907) 241-2218 Fax 241-2208
   Alicia Lynn Reft, President
Affiliated with Alaska Area Native Health Service.
Tribally operated.

KENAITZE INDIAN TRIBE HEALTH CENTER
P.O. Box 988 • KENAI, AK 99611
   (907) 283-3633; Fax 283-3052
   Rita Smagge, Executive Director
   Barry Campbell, MD, Administrator
Affiliated with Alaska Area Native Health Service.
Tribally operated.

SEARHC HEALTH CENTER
201 Deermount St. • KETCHIKAN, AK 99901
   (907) 225-4156; Fax 247-6174
   David Garrison, Director
   Carol Alley, MD, Clinical Director
Affiliated with Alaska Area Native Health Service.

KODIAK AREA NATIVE ASSN. HEALTH CENTER
3449 E. Rezanof • KODIAK, AK 99615
   (907) 486-9800 Fax 486-9898
   Rita Stevens, Interim President
Affiliated with Alaska Area Native Health Service.
Tribally operated.

MANIILAQ ASSOCIATION MEDICAL CENTER
P.O. Box 43 • KOTZEBUE, AK 99752
   (907) 442-3321; Fax 442-7250
   Dennis Tiepleman, President
Affiliated with Alaska Area Native Health Service.
Tribally operated.

ANNETTE ISLAND SERVICE UNIT
Metlakatla Indian Community
P.O. Box 439 • METLAKATLA, AK 99926
   (907) 886-4441; Fax 886-4470
   Harris Atkinson, Mayor
   Terry Baines, Service Unit Director
   Jamie McAllister, Clinical Director
Affiliated with Alaska Area Native Health Service.

**NINILCHIK TRADITIONAL
COUNCIL HEALTH CLINIC**
P.O. Box 39070 • NINILCHIK, AK 99639
   (907) 567-3313; Fax 567-3308
   Debra L. Oskolkoff, Executive Director
   Pat Oskolkoff, Health Director
Affiliated with Alaska Area Native Health Service.
Tribally operated.

NORTON SOUND HEALTH CORP.
P.O. Box 966 • NOME, AK 99762
   (907) 443-3311 Fax 443-2113
   Carolyn J. Crowder, President/CEO
   David Head, MD, Clinical Director;
Tribes served: 20 Federally recognized tribes in Bering
Straits Region. *Professionals on staff*: 7 physicians.
Services: Inpatient, Outpatient, Emergency, Mental
Health and Substance Abuse. *Programs*: Staff Edu-
cation; Community Health Education. Scholarships
provided to Natives of region who are interested in
pursuing health careers. Library. Affiliated with Alaska
Native Health Service. Tribally owned & operated.

ST. GEORGE TRADITIONAL COUNCIL
P.O. Box 940
ST. GEORGE ISLAND, AK 99591
   (907) 859-2205 Fax 859-2242
   Boris R. Merculief, President
Affiliated with Alaska Area Native Health Service.
Tribally operated.

SELDOVIA VILLAGE TRIBE HEALTH CENTER
Drawer L • SELDOVA, AK 99663
(907) 234-7625 Fax 234-7637
Crystal Collier, Director
Affiliated with Alaska Area Native Health Service.
Tribally operated.

SEARHC MT. EDGECUMBE HOSPITAL
222 Tongass Dr. • SITKA, AK 99835
(907) 966-8310; Fax 966-8656
Frank L. Sutton, VP Hospital Services
E-mail: frank.sutton@searhc.org
Website: www.searhc.org
Number of Beds: 60. Serves 18 tribes in Southeast Alaska. Affiliated with Alaska Area Native Health Service. Tribally operated.

TANANA IRA NATIVE COUNCIL HEALTH CENTER
P.O. Box 130 • TANANA, AK 99777
(907) 366-7160 Fax 366-7195
Carla K. Bonney, Director
Affiliated with Alaska Area Native Health Service.
Tribally operated.

TYONEK NATIVE VILLAGE HEALTH CENTER
P.O. Box 39070 • TYONEK, AK 99682
(907) 583-2201 Fax 583-2442
Peter Merryman, President
Affiliated with Alaska Area Native Health Service.
Tribally operated.

VALDEZ NATIVE TRIBE HEALTH CENTER
P.O. Box 1108 • VALDEZ, AK 99686
(907) 835-4951 Fax 835-5589
Benna Hughey, President
Affiliated with Alaska Area Native Health Service.
Tribally operated.

YAKUTAT TLINGIT TRIBAL HEALTH CENTER
P.O. Box 418 • YAKUTAT, AK 99689
(907) 784-3238 Fax 784-3595
Bert Adams, President
Affiliated with Alaska Area Native Health Service.
Tribally operated.

ARIZONA

**CHINLE COMPREHENSIVE
HEALTH CARE FACILITY**
P.O. Drawer PH • CHINLE, AZ 86503
(520) 674-7001 Fax 674-7008
Ronald Tso, Director
Number of Beds: 52. *Affiliated with Navajo Area Indian Health Service.*

CIBECUE PHS INDIAN HEALTH CENTER
P.O. Box 80037 • CIBECUE, AZ 85941
(520) 332-2560 Fax 332-2418
Charlene Hamilton, Director
E-mail: charlenemhamilton@wr.2phx@ihs
Tribes served: White Mountain Apache, Fort Apache Agency. *Total population served*: 1,500. *Number of beds*: 2. *Primary medical services*: Ambulatory care. Library. Affiliated with Phoenix Area Indian Health Service.

FT. DEFIANCE PHS INDIAN HOSPITAL
P.O. Box 649 • FT. DEFIANCE, AZ 86504
(520) 729-5741 Fax 729-3222
Franklin Freeland, EdD, Director
Number of Beds: 68. Affiliated with Navajo Area Indian Health Service.

KAYENTA PHS INDIAN HEALTH CENTER
P.O. Box 368 • KAYENTA, AZ 86033
(520) 697-4000 Fax 697-3264
Linda L. White, R.P., Director
Lori Lo Schert, MD, Clinical Director
Affiliated with Navajo Area Indian Health Service.

**KEAMS CANYON PHS INDIAN HOSPITAL
SECOND MESA PHS INDIAN HEALTH CENTER**
P.O. Box 98 • KEAMS CANYON, AZ 86034
(520) 738-2211 (hospital)
(520) 738-2297 Fax 738-5442 (health center)
Taylor Satala, Director

Tribes served: Hopi, Kaibab-Paiute, Navajo. Number of professionals on staff: 71. *Number of Beds*: 24. *Numbers served annually*: 950; outpatient: 33,000. *Community health education programs*: Substance abuse, health education, et al. Affiliated with Phoenix Area Indian Health Service.

PARKER PHS INDIAN HOSPITAL
Rt. 1, Box 12 • PARKER, AZ 85344
(520) 669-2137
Gary D. Davis, Director
Robert O'Reilly, Administrative Officer
Claire Helminiak, MD, Acting Clinical Director
Number of Beds: 20. Affiliated with
Phoenix Area Indian Health Service.

PEACH SPRINGS PHS INDIAN HEALTH CENTER
P.O. Box 190 • PEACH SPRINGS, AZ 86434
(520) 769-2204
Angelita Orton, Director
Tribes served: Hualapai, Havasupai. *Professionals on staff*: 6. *Services*: General outpatient medical care; dental. *Program*: Community Health Education. Affiliated with Phoenix Area Indian Health Service.

PHOENIX INDIAN MEDICAL CENTER
4212 North 16th St. • PHOENIX, AZ 85016
(602) 263-1200 Fax 379-4281
Anna Albert, Service Unit Director
Vincent Berkley, D.O., Clinical Services
Tribes served: Navajo, Hopi, Apache, Hualapai, Pima, Papago, Mohave, Yavapai, Havasupai, Cocopah, Paiute, and Pascua-Yaqui. *Professionals on staff*: 70 physicians, 400 nurses. *Number of Beds*: 150. *Services*: Primary Care/Family Practice, Pediatrics, Dental, OB-GYN, Surgery, Emergency Medicine, Mental Health, Ophthalmology, Pharmacy, Physical Therapy, Podiatry, Radiology. *Programs*: Staff Education, Training and Research; Community Health Education. Library. *Publication*: The IHS Primary Care Provider. Affiliated with Phoenix Area Indian Health Service.

**HUHUKAM MEMORIAL HOSPITAL
GILA RIVER HEALTHCARE CORP.**
P.O. Box 38 • SACATON, AZ 85247
(520) 562-3321; Viola Johnson, CEO
David Rogers, Director of Business Operations
Joell Brill, MD, Chief of Staff
Affiliated with Phoenix Area Indian Health Service.
Tribally operated.

BYLAS HEALTH CENTER
P.O. Box 208 • SAN CARLOS, AZ 85550
(520) 485-2686 Fax 485-9683
Arlie Beeson, Director
Affiliated with Phoenix Area Indian Health Service.

SAN CARLOS PHS INDIAN HOSPITAL
P.O. Box 208 • SAN CARLOS, AZ 85550
(520) 475-2371 Fax 475-2284
Nella Ben, Unit Director
Shirley Boni, Administrative Officer
Number of Beds: 28. Affiliated with
Phoenix Area Indian Health Service.

SCOTTSDALE SALT RIVER CLINIC
Rt. 1, Box 215 • SCOTTSDALE, AZ 85256
(602) 379-4281
Affiliated with Phoenix Area Indian Health Service.

SANTA ROSA PHS INDIAN HEALTH CENTER
Star Route, Box 71 • SELLS, AZ 85634
(520) 383-2261
Francis Stout, RN, Director
Affiliated with Tucson Office of Health
Programs Research and Development.

SELLS PHS INDIAN HOSPITAL
P.O. Box 548 • SELLS, AZ 85634
(520) 383-7251
Darrel Rumley, Director
Theresa Cullen, MD, Clinical Director
Number of Beds: 40. Affiliated with Tucson Office of Health Programs Research and Development.

HAVASUPAI INDIAN HEALTH STATION
SUPAI, AZ 86435 (520) 448-2641
Tribe served: Havasupai. *Staff*: 1. *Primary medical ser-*

vices: Provides 7 days a week 24 hours a day outpatient medical services to 4,200 patients, annually, at isolated site at bottom of the Grand Canyon. Affiliated with Phoenix Area Indian Health Service. *Special programs*: Prenatal education, diabetic education, substance abuse program, weight reduction/exercise programs.

INSCRIPTION HOUSE HEALTH CENTER
P.O. Box 7397 • TONALEA, AZ 86044
(520) 672-2611 Fax 672-2611
Darlene Walker, Director
Deena Neff, MD, Clinical Director
Affiliated with Navajo Area Indian Health Service.

TSAILE PHS INDIAN HEALTH CENTER
P.O. Box 467 • TSAILE, AZ 86556
(520) 724-3391 Fax 724-6100
Lillie M. Haskie, Health Administrator
Beulah Allen, MD, Medical Director
Tribe served: Navajo, mainly. *Professional on staff*: 17. *Services*: Family Medicine, Ambulatory Care. *Program*: Community Health Education. Affiliated with Navajo Area Indian Health Service.

TUBA CITY INDIAN MEDICAL CENTER
P.O. Box 600 • TUBA CITY, AZ 86045
(520) 283-2501 Fax 283-2516
Susie John, MD, Director
Carenda Little, Administrative Officer
Dudley Beck MD, Clinical Director
Number of Beds: 101. Affiliated with
Navajo Area Indian Health Service.

SAN XAVIER PHS INDIAN HEALTH CENTER
7900 S.J. Stock Rd. • TUCSON, AZ 85746
(520) 295-2480 Bernard DeAsis, Director
Affiliated with Tucson Office of Health
Programs Research and Development.

WHITERIVER PHS INDIAN HOSPITAL
P.O. Box 860 • WHITERIVER, AZ 85941
(520) 338-4911 Fax 338-1122
Carla Alchesay-Nachu, Director
Morland McCurtain, Administrative Officer
David Yost, MD, Clinical Director
Number of Beds: 44. Affiliated with
Phoenix Area Indian Health Service.

WINSLOW PHS INDIAN HEALTH CENTER
P.O. Drawer 40 • WINSLOW, AZ 86047
(520) 289-4646 Fax 289-5264
Vida Khow, Director
Frank Armao, MD, Clinical Director
Affiliated with Navajo Area Indian Health Service.

FORT YUMA PHS INDIAN HOSPITAL
P.O. Box 1368 • YUMA, AZ 85364
(520) 572-0217
Hortense Miguel, Director
James Battese, Administrative Officer
Raouf Hanna, MD, Clinical Director
Number of Beds: 17. Affiliated with
Phoenix Area Indian Health Service.

CALIFORNIA

SOUTHERN INDIAN HEALTH COUNCIL
P.O. Box 2128 • ALPINE, CA 91903
(619) 445-1188 Fax 445-4131
Joseph E. Bulfer, Director
Reservations served: Barona, Campo, Ewiiaapaayp, Jamul, La Posta, Manzanita, Viejas. *Total population served*: 8,000. *Medical services*: Outpatient primary care. Family practice, internal medicine, pediatrics, podiatry & GYN clinic. *Programs*: Dental, community health, social services, mental health, and La Posta Substance Abuse Center. Affiliated with California Program Office. Tribally operated.

MODOC COUNTY INDIAN HEALTH
P.O. Box 251 • ALTURAS, CA 96101
(530) 233-4591 Fax 233-3055
Erin Forrest, Director
Affiliated with California Program Office.
Tribally operated.

UNITED INDIAN HEALTH SERVICES
1600 Weeot Way • ARCATA, CA 95521
 (707) 825-5000
 Jerome J. Simone, Director
Tribes served: All American Indians with verification.
Professionals on staff: 8. *Population served*: 20,000
patients served annually. *Primary Medical Services*:
Complete family practice including obstetrics. Awards
to local American Indians who are pursuing health careers. Medical and dental libraries. Affiliated with California Program Office. Tribally operated.

CHAPA-DE INDIAN HEALTH
11670 Atwood Rd. • AUBURN, CA 95603
 (530) 887-2800 Fax 887-2819
 Carol Ervin, Director
Affiliated with California Program Office.
Tribally operated.

**BAKERSFIELD EDUCATION
CENTER FOR NATIVE AMERICANS**
1830 Truxton Ave., Suite 100
BAKERSFIELD, CA 93301 (661) 859-2940
 Annie Langdeaux, Director
Affiliated with California Program Office.
Tribally operated.

RIVERSIDE/SAN BERNADINO INDIAN HEALTH
11555 1/2 Potrero Rd. • BANNING, CA 92220
 (909) 849-4761 Fax 849-5612
 Lin Killam, Acting Director
Affiliated with California Program Office.
Tribally operated.

LOS ANGELES NATIVE AMERICAN CENTER
9500 E. Artesia Blvd. • BELLFLOWER, CA 90708
 (310) 920-7272 Fax 920-5677
 William Beckley, DHSc, MPH, President/CEO
Total population served: 80,000. Medical services:
General health care; dental care; prenatal and perinatal
care; immunizations; W.I.C. program. *Special programs*: Residential recovery program; family shelter
program; provide a variety of culturally-based activities. Established 1996.

TOIYABE INDIAN HEALTH COUNCIL
52 Tu Su Lane • BISHOP, CA 93515
 (760) 873-8464 Fax 873-3935
 Andrea Durocher-Cortez, Acting Director
Affiliated with California Program Office.
Tribally operated.

PIT RIVER INDIAN HEALTH ENTER
P.O. Box 2720 • BURNEY, CA 96013
 (530) 335-5091 Fax 335-5241
 Roberto Dansie, Director
Affiliated with California Program Office.
Tribally operated.

CONSOLIDATED TRIBAL HEALTH
P.O. Box 319 • CALPELLA, CA 95418
 (707) 485-5115 Fax 485-5199
 Maria Anaya, Director
Affiliated with California Program Office.
Tribally operated.

CENTRAL VALLEY INDIAN HEALTH PROGRAM
20 N. Dewitt • CLOVIS, CA 93612
 (209) 299-2578 Fax 299-0245
 Chuck Fowler, Director
Affiliated with California Program Office.
Tribally operated.

ROUND VALLEY INDIAN HEALTH PROGRAM
P.O. Box 247 • COVELO, CA 95428
 (707) 983-6181 Fax 983-6842
 Peter Masten, Jr., Director
Affiliated with California Program Office.
Tribally operated.

SYCUAN MEDICAL/DENTAL CENTER
5442 Dehesa Rd. • EL CAJON, CA 92019
 (619) 445-0707 Fax 445-0988
 Ben Cordova, Director
Affiliated with California Program Office.

WARNER MOUNTAIN INDIAN HEALTH
P.O. Box 126 • FORT BIDWELL, CA 96112

 (530) 279-6194 Fax 279-2233
 Barbara Rutherford, Clinic Director
Affiliated with California Program Office.

FRESNO INDIAN HEALTH ASSOCIATION
4991 E. McKinley #118 • FRESNO, CA 93727
 (209) 255-0261 Fax 255-2149
 Dr. Eric Don-Pedro, Executive Director
Tribes served: Urban Natve Americans residing in metropolitan Fresno. *Total population served*: 6,000. *Medical services*: Outpatient primary care; mental health.
Programs: Free TB and Flue vaccine. Affiliated with
California Program Office.

GREENVILLE RANCHERIA TRIBAL HEALTH
P.O. Box 279 • GREENVILLE, CA 95947
 (916) 284-6135 Fax 284-7135
 Susanne Weston, Director
Affiliated with California Program Office.

KARUK TRIBAL HEALTH PROGRAM
P.O. Box 1016 • HAPPY CAMP, CA 96039
 (530) 493-5305 Fax 493-5322
 Greg Gehr, Chief of Staff
Affiliated with California Program Office.
Tribally operated.

HOOPA HEALTH ASSOCIATION
P.O. Box 1288 • HOOPA, CA 95546
 (530) 625-4261 Fax 625-4781
 Emmett Chase, MD, Director
Affiliated with California Program Office.
Tribally operated.

LAKE COUNTY TRIBAL HEALTH
5116 Hill Rd. E. • LAKEPORT, CA 95453
 (707) 263-8322 Fax 263-0329
 Lydia Hubbard Pouier, Director, Director
Tribe served: Pomo. *Services*: Outpatient. Affiliated
with California Program Office. Tribally operated.

LOS ANGELES AMERICAN INDIAN PROJECT
1125 West 6th St., Suite 400
LOS ANGELES, CA 90017 (213) 202-3970
 Dave Rambeau, Director
Affiliated with California Program Office.
Tribally operated.

URBAN INDIAN HEALTH BOARD
3124 E. 14th St. • OAKLAND, CA 94601
 (510) 261-0524 Fax 261-6438
 Martin Waukazoo, Director
Affiliated with California Program Office.
Tribally operated.

FEATHER RIVER INDIAN HEALTH
2167 Montgomery St. • OROVILLE, CA 95965
 (530) 534-3793 Fax 534-3820
 William Holman, Director
Affiliated with California Program Office.

INDIAN HEALTH COUNCIL, INC.
P.O. Box 406 • PAUMA VALLEY, CA 92061
 (760) 749-1410 Fax 749-1564
 Dennis Magee, Director
Tribes served: Luiseno, Digueno, Cahuilla and
Cupeno, Bands of California Mission Indians in San
Diego County. *Professionals on staff*: 12. *Population
served*: 7,500, annually. *Services*: Medical and dental
outpatient care including social services, public health
nursing, counseling, etc. Affiliated with California Program Office. Tribally operated.

TULE RIVER INDIAN HEALTH PROGRAM
P.O. Box 768 • PORTERVILLE, CA 93258
 (209) 784-2316 Fax 781-6514
 Sajjan Bajwa, Director
Affiliated with California Program Office.
Tribally operated.

GREENVILLE RANCHERIA TRIBAL HEALTH
645 Antelope Blvd., Suite 17
RED BLUFF, CA 96030
 (530) 528-8600 Fax 528-8612
 Susanne Weston, Director

REDDING RANCHERIA HEALTH CENTER
3184 Chum Creek Rd. • REDDING, CA 96002

 (530) 224-2700 Fax 224-2738
 Carla Maslin, Director
Affiliated with California Program Office.
Tribally operated.

SACRAMENTO URBAN INDIAN HEALTH
2020 "J" St. • SACRAMENTO, CA 95814
 (916) 441-0918 Fax 441-1261
 Daniel Tatum, Director, Director
Affiliated with California Program Office.
Tribally operated.

SAN DIEGO AMERICAN INDIAN HEALTH
2561 First Ave. • SAN DIEGO, CA 92103
 (619) 234-2158 Fax 234-0206
 Ron Morton, Director
Affiliated with California Program Office.

NATIVE AMERICAN HEALTH CLINIC
56 Julian Ave. • SAN FRANCISCO, CA 94103
 (415) 621-8051 Fax 621-3985
 Martin Waukazoo, Director
Affiliated with California Program Office.

**INDIAN HEALTH CENTER
OF SANTA CLARA VALLEY**
1333 Meridian Ave. • SAN JOSE, CA 95125
 (408) 445-3400 Fax 269-9273
 Peter V. Long, Director
 Indianbls@aol.com
Tribes served: Many Indian tribes served. *Professionals on staff*: 10. *Population served*: 500-600 outpatients per month. *Primary medical services*: Medical,
dental, counseling. *Programs*: General medicine; prenatal; diabetes; weight management; alchohol and
drug abuse counseling; nutrition; mental health outreach & referral; AIDS/HIV testing & counseling; dental; and community health education programs. Library.
Affiliated with California Program Office.

AMERICAN INDIAN HEALTH SERVICES
4141 State St., B-6 •
SANTA BARBARA, CA 93110
 (805) 681-7356
 Seh Welch, Director
Affiliated with California Program Office.
Tribally operated.

SONOMA COUNTY INDIAN HEALTH
P.O. Box 7308 • SANTA ROSA, CA 95407
 (707) 544-4056 Fax 526-1015
 Molin Malicay, Director
Affiliated with California Program Office.
Tribally operated.

SANTA YNEZ INDIAN HEALTH
P.O. Box 539 • SANTA YNEZ, CA 93460
 (805) 688-4886 Fax 688-2060
 Rosa Pace, Administrator
Affiliated with California Program Office.
Tribally operated.

LASSEN INDIAN HEALTH CENTER
795 Joaquin St. • SUSANVILLE, CA 96130
 (530) 257-2542 Fax 257-6983
 Leah Exendine, Director
Affiliated with California Program Office.

TUOLUMNE INDIAN HEALTH
P.O. Box 577 • TUOLUMNE, CA 95379
 (209) 928-4277 Fax 928-1295
 John Highsmith, Director
Affiliated with California Program Office.
Tribally operated.

CONSOLIDATED TRIBAL HEALTH PROJECT
564 S. Dora St. #D • UKIAH, CA 95482
 (707) 468-5341 Fax 468-8610
 Maria Anaya, MPH, Director
Tribe served: Pomo Tribes - Coyote Valley, Hopland
Band, Guidiville Reservation, Laytonville Vahto Tribe,
Pinoleville Indian Community, Potter Valley Rancheria,
Redwood Valley Rancheria, Sherwood Valley
Rancheria. *Professionals on staff*: 30-35. *Services*:
Outpatient; Family Practice-Perinatal Program; Den-
tal. *Programs*: Staff Education, Training and Research;
Community Health Education. Affiliated with Califor-
nia Program Office. Tribally operated.

NORTHERN VALLEY INDIAN HEALTH
207 N. Butte St. • WILLOWS, CA 95988
(530) 934-9293 Fax 534-6140
  Carol Ervin, Director
Affiliated with California Program Office.
Tribally operated.

COLORADO

SOUTHERN COLORADO UTE SERVICE UNIT
P.O. Box 778 • IGNACIO, CO 81137
(970) 563-9447 (phone & fax)
  Nina Desbien, Director
  George H. Maxted, MD, Clinical Director
Affiliated with Albuquerque Area Indian Health Service.
Tribally operated

IGNACIO PHS INDIAN HEALTH CENTER
P.O. Box 889 • IGNACIO, CO 81137
(970) 563-4581
  Michael N. Mericle, Director
  George H. Maxted, MD, Clinical Director
Affiliated with Albuquerque Area Indian Health Service.

TOWAOC PHS INDIAN HEALTH CENTER
General Delivery • TOWAOC, CO 81334
(970) 565-4441 Fax 565-4945
  Ronald D. Thomas, Director
  George H. Maxted, MD, Clinical Director
Affiliated with Albuquerque Area Indian Health Service.

IDAHO

NOT-TSOO GAH-NEE INDIAN HEALTH CENTER
P.O. Box 717 • FORT HALL, ID 83203
(208) 238-2400
  Curtis W. Smith, Director
  Bernadine R. Ricker, Administrative Officer
  Craig Nicholson, MD, Clinical Director
Affiliated with Portland Area Indian Health Service.

**NORTHERN IDAHO INDIAN
HEALTH SERVICE UNIT**
P.O. Drawer 367 • LAPWAI, ID 83540
(208) 843-2271 Fax 843-2102
  Joseph Moquino, Unit Director
  Tina Orton, Administrative Officer
  Helen Wootton, MD, Clinical Director
Reservation served: Nez Perce. *Total population served*: 3,110. *Medical services*: Clinic - outpatient primary care; community health/preventive; mental health; health education. *Programs*: Diabetes; safety; holistic health; tribal environmental restoration waste management; tribal well-child care. Library. Affiliated with Portland Area Indian Health Service.

IOWA

**SAC & FOX TRIBE OF THE MISSISSIPPI IN
IOWA INDIAN HEALTH CENTER**
TAMA, IA 52339
(515) 484-4094
Affiliated with Aberdeen Area Indian Health Service.
Tribally operated.

KANSAS

PHS INDIAN HEALTH CENTER
100 West 6th St.
HOLTON, KS 66436
(785) 364-2177 Fax 364-3691
  Arlene Wahwasuck, Acting Administrative Officer
  Greg Abbott, DO, Clinical Director
Tribes served: Kickapoo of Kansas, Potawatomi, Sac & Fox of Kansas & Nebraska, and Iowa Tribe. *Profesionals on staff*: 8. *Services*: General outpatient medical care, with laboratory & pharmacy. Library. Affiliated with Oklahoma City Area Indian Health Service.

KICKAPOO HEALTH CENTER
Kickapoo Tribe of Kansas
Rt. 1, Box 221C • HORTON, KS 66439
(785) 486-2154
  Debbie Whitebird, Acting Facility Director
Affiliated with Oklahoma City Area
Indian Health Service. Tribally operated.

HASKELL PHS INDIAN HEALTH CENTER
2415 Massachusetts Ave.
LAWRENCE, KS 66044
(785) 843-3750 Fax 843-8815
  Randy Barnoskie, Director
  Bonnie Abram, Administrative Officer
  Rick Caldwell, MD, Clinical Director
Tribes served: Students attending Haskell Indian Junior College - representing over 135 different tribes; Indians residing in Northeast Kansas. *Professionals on staff*: 20. *Numbers served*: 15,600 outpatients served annually. *Primary Medical Services*: Family practice, alcohol/drug abuse, dental. *Programs*: Staff education; community health education. Library. Affiliated with Oklahoma City Area Indian Health Service.

HUNTER HEALTH CENTER
2318 E. Central • WICHITA, KS 67214
(316) 262-2415 Fax 262-0741
  Hoover Harlan, Executive Director
Affiliated with Oklahoma City Area
Indian Health Service.

MICHIGAN

**KEWEENAW BAY INDIAN
COMMUNITY HEALTH CLINIC**
Route 1 • BARAGA, MI 49908
(906) 353-8666 Ext. 25 Fax 353-8799
  John Seppanen, Director
  Geoffrey Coleman, MD, Clinical Director
Affiliated with Bemidji Area Office. Tribally operated.

BAY MILLS INDIAN COMMUNITY HEALTH CLINIC
Route 1, Box 313 • BRIMLEY, MI 49715
(906) 248-3204 Fax 248-5765
  Laurel Keenan, Director
  Vicki Newland, Clinical Director
Affiliated with Bemidji Area Office. Tribally operated.

MIN-NO-AYA-WIN CLINIC
927 Trettel Ln. • CLOQUET, MI 55720
(218) 879-1227 Fax 879-8379
  Phil Norrgard, Director
  Harlen Whitling, RN, Clinical Director
Affiliated with Bemidji Area Office. Tribally operated.

**POKAGON BAND OF POTAWATOMI
HEALTH CENTER**
104 Riverside Dr. • DOWAGIAC, MI 49047
(616) 723-8288
  Christine Daugherty, Health Director
Affiliated with Bemidji Area Office. Tribally operated.

HURON POTAWATOMI BAND HEALTH CLINIC
2221 1-1/2 Mile Rd. • FULTON, MI 49052
(616) 729-5151
  Paul Mackety, Health Director
Affiliated with Bemidji Area Office. Tribally operated.

LITTLE RIVER BAND OF OTTAWA HEALTH CLINIC
P.O. Box 314 • MANISTEE, MI 49660-0314
(616) 723-8288
  Steve Bronson, Health Director
Affiliated with Bemidji Area Office. Tribally operated.

NIMKEE MEMORIAL WELLNESS CENTER
2591 S. Leaton Rd. • MT. PLEASANT, MI 48858
(517) 773-9887 Fax 773-2028
  Gail George, Health Director
Tribes served: Saginaw Chippewa Indian Tribe of Michigan, and other federally recognized tribes. *Professionals on staff*: 25. *Services*: Primary pateint care; dental, nursing, psychological, substance abuse counseling, and health education and fitness. *Programs*: Staff Education, Training and Research; Community Health Education. Scholarships. Affiliated with Bemidji Area Office. Tribally operated.

**LITTLE TRAVERSE BAND
OF ODAWA HEALTH CLINIC**
P.O. Box 246
PETOSKEY, MI 49770-0246
(616) 782-4141
  Arlene Naganashe, Health Director
Affiliated with Bemidji Area Office. Tribally operated.

**SAULT STE. MARIE HEALTH
& HUMAN SERVICES CENTER**
2684 Ashmun St.
SAULT STE. MARIE, MI 49783
(906) 632-5200 Fax 632-5276
  Russell J. Vizina, Director
  David Vogt, D.O., Clinical Director
Tribe served: Sault Ste. Marie Tribe of Chippewa Indians. *Total population served*: 15,500. *Medical services*: Family practice. *Programs*: Dental, lab, radiology, mental health and substance abuse counseling, HIV prevention and treatment; optical; podiatry; audiology; pharmacy; community health. Library. Affiliated with Bemidji Area Office. Tribally operated.

**GRAND TRAVERSE OTTAWA/
CHIPPEWA HEALTH CLINIC**
2605 NW Bayshore Dr.
SUTTONS BAY, MI 49682
(616) 271-5256 Fax 271-5952
  Ruth Bussey, Director
Affiliated with Bemidji Area Office. Tribally operated.

LAC VIEUX DESERT BAND HEALTH CLINIC
P.O. Box 249 • WATERSMEET, MI 49969
(906) 358-4457 Fax 358-4118
  Beatrice Kelley, Health Administrator
Affiliated with Bemidji Area Office. Tribally operated.

**HANNAHVILLE INDIAN
COMMUNITY HEALTH CLINIC**
N14911 Hannahville B1 Rd.
WILSON, MI 49896
(906) 466-2782 Fax 466-7454
  Jeff Pecotte, Director
  Cynthia Lack, MD, Clinical Director
Affiliated with Bemidji Area Office. Tribally operated.

MINNESOTA

LEECH LAKE BAND HEALTH CLINIC
Route 3 - Box 100 • CASS LAKE, MN 56633
(218) 335-8851 Fax 335-8219
  Doris Jones, Health Director
Affiliated with Bemidji Area Office.

LEECH LAKE PHS INDIAN HOSPITAL
RR 3, Box 211 • CASS LAKE, MN 56633
(218) 335-2293 Fax 335-2601
  Luella Brown, RN, Director
  Mark Becker, MD, Clinical Director
Number of Beds: 22. Affiliated with
Bemidji Area Office.

MIN NO AYA WIN HUMAN SERVICES CENTER
927 Trettel Lane • CLOQUET, MN 55720
(218) 879-1227
  Phil Norrgard, Director
  Harlen Whitling, R.N., Medical Coordinator
  Charles Vergona, MD, Medical Staff
Tribe served: Fond du Lac Reservation. 17 professionals on staff. 3,700 outpatients and 400 inpatients annually. *Primary services*: Outpatient medical and dental services; public health nursing; social services Professional staff education, training and research programs. Community health education programs. Library. Affiliated with Bemidji Area Office. Tribally operated.

GRAND PORTAGE BAND HEALTH CLINIC
P.O. Box 428 • GRAND PORTAGE, MN 55605
(218) 475-2235 Fax 475-2261
  Lorna Turner, Health Director
Affiliated with Bemidji Area Office. Tribally operated.

UPPER SIOUX BOARD OF TRUSTEES
P.O. Box 147 • GRANITE FALLS, MN 56241
(320) 564-2360 Fax 564-3264
  Sharon Brockman, Administrator

Tribes served: Upper Sioux Community - two counties, Yellow Medicine County and Chippewa County. *Medical Services*: Contract Health, Mental Health, Chemical Dependency; Indian Child Welfare; Community Health. Affiliated with Bemidji Area Office. Tribally operated.

LOWER SIOUX COMMUNITY COUNCIL
P.O. Box 308, Rt. 1 • MORTON, MN 56270
(507) 697-6185 Fax 637-4380
Teri Schemmel, Health Director
Affiliated with Bemidji Area Office. Tribally operated.

BOIS FORT TRIBAL CLINIC
P.O. Box 16 • NETT LAKE, MN 55772
(218) 757-3295 Fax 757-3636
Jeneal Goggleye, Health Director
Ray Hawk, Clinical Director
Affiliated with Bemidji Area Office. Tribally operated.

NE-IA-SHING CLINIC
Mille Lacs Band Dept. of HHS
HCR 67, Box 241 • ONAMIA, MN 56359
(320) 532-4163 Fax 532-4354
Sharon Gislason, Executive Director
Tribe served: Mille Lacs Band of Ojibwe. Total population served: 3,000. *Medical services*: Family Medicine; Internal Medicine; Medical Laboratory; Radiology; Pharmacy. *Special programs*: Dental & oral surgery; optometry & optical, audiology, home care, social nutrition, emergency assistance; Migizi elder services; public health; WIC; psychology; chemical dependency; social services. Believed to be the first clinic in the nation built with casino profits. Affiliated with Bemidji Area Office. Tribally operated.

SHAKOPEE MDEWAKANTON BUSINESS COUNCIL
2320 Sioux Trail, NW • PRIOR LAKE, MN 55372
(612) 445-8900 Fax 445-8906
Susan Blomker, Health Director
Affiliated with Bemidji Area Office. Tribally operated.

RED LAKE COMPREHENSIVE HEALTH SERVICE
RED LAKE, MN 56671
(218) 679-3316 Fax 679-3390
Oran Beaulieu, Health Director
Affiliated with Bemidji Area Office.

PHS INDIAN HOSPITAL
RED LAKE, MN 56671
(218) 679-3912 Fax 679-2853
Essimae Stevens, Director
John Robinson, MD, Clinical Director
Number of Beds: 23. Affiliated with Bemidji Area Office.

PRAIRIE ISLAND COMMUNITY HEALTH CLINIC
5636 Stargeon Lake Rd. • WELCH, MN 55089
(612) 385-2554 Fax 385-4110
Christina Sellers, Health Director
Mike Anderson, MD, Medical Director
Affiliated with Bemidji Area Office. Tribally operated.

WHITE EARTH BAND CLINIC
P.O. Box 418 • WHITE EARTH, MN 56591
(218) 983-3285 Fax 983-3641
JoEllen Anywaush, Health Director
Affiliated with Bemidji Area Office.

PHS INDIAN HEALTH CENTER
WHITE EARTH, MN 56591
(218) 983-4300 Fax 983-6217
Jon McArthur, Director
Howard Hayes, MD, Clinical Director
Affiliated with Bemidji Area Office.

MISSISSIPPI

CHOCTAW HEALTH CENTER
Route 7, Box R-50 • PHILADELPHIA, MS 39350
(601) 656-2211
Marianna Hane, Director
Nolan Fulton, M.D., Chief of Staff
Hospital. *Number of Beds*: 40. Affiliated with Nashville Area Office. Tribally operated.

MONTANA

ROCKY BOY/CHIPPEWA CREE HEALTH CENTER
RR 1 Box 664 • BOX ELDER, MT 59521
(406) 395-4064
Sybil Sangrey, Planning Director
Edward Parisian, Health Board Director
Alvin Windy Boy, Sr., Health Board Chairperson
Tribes served: Chippewa/Cree; any enrolled member of a federally-recognized tribe. *Total population served*: 13,000. *Professionals on staff*: 20. *Services*: Primary patient care; emergency medical services; community health. *Programs*: HIV/AIDS Prevention Program; Tobacco Cessation. Affiliated with Billings Area Indian Health Service.

BROWNING PHS INDIAN HOSPITAL
BROWNING, MT 59417
(406) 338-6154 (Admin.); 338-6200 (Clinic)
Reis Fisher, Director
Lis Wells, Administrative Officer
Dana Damron, MD, Clinical Director
Number of Beds: 34. Affiliated with Billings Area Indian Health Service.

CROW/NORTHERN CHEYENNE PHS INDIAN HOSPITAL
P.O. BOX 9 • CROW AGENCY, MT 59022
(406) 638-3461 (Admin.); 638-3500 (Clinic)
Tenneyson Doney, Director
Leonard Bends, Administrative Officer
Robert Byron, MD, Clinical Director
Number of Beds: 34. Affiliated with Billings Area Indian Health Service.

HARLEM PHS INDIAN HOSPITAL
RR1 Box 67 • HARLEM, MT 59526-9705
(406) 353-2651
Charles J. Plumage, Director
Marjorie Archambault, Administrative Officer
Ethel Moore, MD, Clinical Director
Number of Beds: 18. Affiliated with Billings Area Indian Health Service.

LAME DEER PHS INDIAN HEALTH CENTER
P.O. Box 70 • LAME DEER, MT 59043
(406) 477-6700
Bernard Long, Acting Director
Debbie Bends, Administrative Officer
Mary Ann Nieson, PharmD, Clinical Director
Affiliated with Billings Area Indian Health Service.

LODGE GRASS PHS INDIAN HEALTH CENTER
LODGE GRASS, MT 59050 (406) 639-2317
Dan Gun Shows, Administrative Officer
Charles Lambiotte, MD, Medical Officer
Affiliated with Billings Area Indian Health Service.

POPLAR PHS INDIAN HEALTH CENTER
POPLAR, MT 59255 (406) 768-3491
Kenneth Smoker, Jr., Director
Edna Wetsit, Administrative Officer
Julie Bemer, DPHN, Clinical Director
Affiliated with Billings Area Indian Health Service.

FLATHEAD PHS INDIAN HEALTH CENTER
P.O. Box 880
ST. IGNATIUS, MT 59865
(406) 745-2411/3525
Joe Dupuis, Acting Director
Jim Paro, Administrator
Yvonne Grenier, Community Health Planner
Tribes served: Confederated Salish & Kootenai Tribes-Flathead Reservation. 10 professionals on staff. Outpatient clinics with main focus on Women's Clinics. *Special Program*: Narcotic Treatment Program, Sherry Saddler, Director. Community health education programs. Affiliated with Billings Area Indian Health Service.

WOLF POINT PHS INDIAN HEALTH CENTER
WOLF POINT, MT 59201
(406) 653-1641
Charles Headdress, Health Systems Specialist
Aziza Keval, MD, Medical Officer
Affiliated with Billings Area Indian Health Service.

NEBRASKA

CARL T. CURTIS HEALTH CENTER
MACY, NE 68039
(402) 837-5381 Fax 837-5303
Hoover Harlan, Health Director
Tribes served: Omaha & Winnebago or any other Native American on the reservation needing medical care. *Professionals on staff*: 2. *Services*: Ambulatory Care, Family Practice, OB/GYN, Well Child, WIC, and Community Health. *Programs*: Staff Education, Training & Research; Community Health Education. Library. Affiliated with Aberdeen Area Indian Health Service. Tribally operated.

WINNEBAGO PHS INDIAN HOSPITAL
WINNEBAGO, NE 68071
(402) 878-2231 Fax 878-2535
Don Lee, Director
Gina Scott, Administrative Officer
J. Eddie Nicholas, MD, Clinical Director
Tribes served: Omaha & Winnebago. *Number of Beds*: 38. Affiliated with Aberdeen Area Indian Health Service.

NEVADA

SOUTHERN BANDS CLINIC
515 Shoshone Cir. • ELKO, NV 89801
(702) 738-2252 Fax 738-4219
Norman Cavanaugh, Unit Director
Antonio Rivera, MD, Clinical Director
Affiliated with Phoenix Area Indian Health Service. Tribally operated.

FALLON COMMUNITY CLINIC
P.O. Box 1980 • FALLON, NV 89407
(702) 423-3634 Fax 423-1453
Kathy Bowen-Curley, Tribal Health Director
Affiliated with Phoenix Area Indian Health Service. Tribally operated.

WASHOE TRIBAL HEALTH CENTER
950 Hwy. 395 S.
GARDNERVILLE, NV 89410
(702) 265-4215 Fax 265-3429
John Ketcher, Tribal Health Director
Affiliated with Phoenix Area Indian Health Service. Tribally operated.

LAS VEGAS PAIUTE TRIBAL CLINIC
6 Paiute Dr. • LAS VEGAS, NV 89106
Richard Skelskey, MD, Health Director
Affiliated with Phoenix Area Indian Health Service. Tribally operated.

McDERMITT TRIBAL HEALTH CENTER
P.O. Box 315 • McDERMITT, NV 89421
(702) 532-8259 Fax 532-8903
Helen Snapp, Tribal Health Director
Tribes served: Paiute/Shoshone. *Number of professionals on staff*: 6. General medical services provided. Affiliated with Phoenix Area Indian Health Service. Tribally operated.

PYRAMID LAKE HEALTH DEPT.
P.O Box 227 • NIXON, NV 89424
(702) 574-1018 (phone & fax)
William Elliot, Tribal Health Director
Tribe served: Pyramid Lake Paiute. *Professionals on staff*: 4. *Services*: General outpatient medical care. *Program*: Community Health Education. Affiliated with Phoenix Area Indian Health Service. Tribally operated.

OWYHEE PHS INDIAN HOSPITAL
P.O. Box 130
OWYHEE, NV 89832
(702) 757-2415 Fax 757-2351
Walden Townsend, Tribal Health Director
Tribes served: Northeastern Nevada Tribes of Western Shoshone. 57 professionals on staff. Number of Beds: 15. Outpatient medical services. Community health education programs. Affiliated with Phoenix Area Indian Health Service.

RENO-SPARKS TRIBAL HEALTH STATION
34 Reservation Rd. • RENO, NV 89502
(702) 329-5162 Fax 329-4129
Jim Bednark, Director
Affiliated with Phoenix Area Indian Health Service.
Tribally operated.

SCHURZ INDIAN HEALTH CENTER
P.O. Drawer A • SCHURZ, NV 89427
(702) 773-2345 Fax 773-2425
Elvin Willie, Jr., Director
Karen Miller, Administrative Officer
John Friedrich, MD, Clinical Director
Number of Beds: 14. Affiliated with
Phoenix Area Indian Health Service.

**WALKER RIVER PAIUTE
TRIBAL HEALTH CENTER**
P.O. Drawer "C" • SCHURZ, NV 89427
(702) 773-2005 Fax 773-2576
Kenneth Richardson, Tribal Health Director
Affiliated with Phoenix Area Indian Health Service.

YERINGTON HEALTH DEPT.
171 Campbell Lane • YERINGTON, NV 89447
(702) 463-3301 Fax 463-3390
Linda Sheldon, Tribal Health Director
Affiliated with Phoenix Area Indian Health Service.

NEW MEXICO

ALBUQUERQUE PHS INDIAN HOSPITAL
801 Vassar Dr., NE
ALBUQUERQUE, NM 87106
(505) 248-4000 Fax 248-4093
Cheri Lyon, Director
Charlotte Little, Administrative Officer
Charles North, MD, Clinical Director
Number of Beds: 54. Affiliated with Albuquerque Area
Indian Health Service.

**SOUTHWESTERN INDIAN POLYTECHNIC
INSTITUTE DENTAL CENTER**
9169 Coors Rd. NW • P.O. Box 67830
ALBUQUERQUE, NM 87193
(505) 897-5306 Fax 897-5311
Darlene Sorrell, DMD, Chief of Dental Program
Tribes served: Albuquerque Urban Indians, Zia,
Sandia, Santa Ana, Alamo Navajo, Jemez, and Isleta.
Total population served: 27,000. *Program*: Dental, Includes periodontics, orthodontics, prosthodontics; and
pediatric dentistry. Research Library. Affiliated with Albuquerque Area Indian Health Service.

**DZILTH-NA-O-DITH-HLE
PHS INDIAN HEALTH CENTER**
6 Road 7586 • BLOOMFIELD, NM 87413
(505) 632-1801 Fax 632-0542
Jim Couch, MD, Medical Director
Tribe served: 85% Navajo. *Professionals on staff*: 7.
Population served: 26,000 people per year. *Services*:
Complete diagnostic medical treatment services are
provided: medical outpatient clinic, dental service,
counseling service, community health nursing service.
Affiliated with Navajo Area Indian Health Service.

CROWNPOINT HEALTHCARE FACILITY
P.O. Box 358 • CROWNPOINT, NM 87313
(505) 786-5291 Fax 786-5840
Anita Muneta, Chief Executive Officer
Ronald C. Begay, Administrative Officer
Naville Davis, MD, Clinical Director
Reservation served: Eastern agency of the navajo Indian Reservation. *Total population served*: 19,500.
Number of Beds: 34. *Primary medical services*: OB/
GYN;Emergency Room; ACC; Medical Pediatrics;
Physical Therapy; Optometry. *Special programs*: Inpatient. Library. Affiliated with Navajo Area Indian
Health Service.

JICARILLA PHS INDIAN HEALTH CENTER
P.O. Box 187 • DULCE, NM 87528
(505) 759-3291 Fax 759-3532
Pete DeMonte, Director
Affiliated with Albuquerque Area Indian Health Service.

SANTA CLARA PHS INDIAN HEALTH CENTER
RR 5, Box 446 • ESPANOLA, NM 87532
(505) 753-9421 Fax 753-5039
Robert Palmer, Acting Director
Affiliated with Albuquerque Area Indian Health Service.

GALLUP INDIAN MEDICAL CENTER
P.O. Box 1337 • GALLUP, NM 87305
(505) 722-1000 Fax 722-1554
Timothy Flemming, MD, Director
Bennie Yazzie, Administrative Officer
Gary Escudero, MD, Clinical Director
Number of Beds: 116. Affiliated with
Navajo Area Indian Health Service.

ALAMO NAVAJO HEALTH STATION
P.O. Box 907 • MAGDALENA, NM 87825
(505) 854-2626 Fax 854-2545
Mary Helen Creamer, Director
Affiliated with Albuquerque Area Indian Health Service.
Tribally operated.

MESCALERO PHS INDIAN HOSPITAL
P.O. Box 210 • MESCALERO, NM 88340
(505) 671-4441 Fax 671-4422
Greg Powers, Acting Administrative Officer
Gabriel Fernandez, MD, Acting Clinical Director
Affiliated with Albuquerque Area Native
Health Service. Tribally operated.

PINE HILL PHS INDIAN HEALTH CENTER
P.O. Box 310 • PINE HILL, NM 87357
(505) 775-3271 Fax 775-3240
Ken Whitehair, Director
Carolyn E. Finster, Clinic Administrator
Steven J. Drilling, MD, Clinical Director
Affiliated with Albuquerque Area Indian Health Service.
Tribally operated.

**ACOMA-CANONCITO
LAGUNA PHS INDIAN HOSPITAL**
P.O. Box 130 • SAN FIDEL, NM 87049
(505) 552-6634 Fax 552-7363
Richard Zephier, PhD, Director
Barbara Felipe, Administrative Officer
Judith Thierry, MD, Clinical Director
Affiliated with Albuquerque Area Indian Health Service.

NEW SUNRISE REGIONAL TREATMENT CENTER
P.O. Box 219 • SAN FIDEL, NM 87049
(505) 552-6091 Fax 552-6527
Melissa Ring, PhD, Acting Program Director
Affiliated with Albuquerque Area Indian Health Service.

SANTA FE PHS INDIAN HOSPITAL
1700 Cerrillos Rd. • SANTA FE, NM 87501
(505) 988-9821 Fax 983-6243
Joseph L. Montoya, Administrative Officer
Robert Wirth, MD, Clinical Director
Number of Beds: 55. Affiliated with Albuquerque Area
Indian Health Service.

NORTHERN NAVAJO MEDICAL CENTER
P.O. Box 160 • SHIPROCK, NM 87420
(505) 368-6001 Fax 368-6260
Daalbaaleh Hutchison, Director
Fanessa Comer, Administrative Officer
George Baacke, MD, Clinical Director
Affiliated with Navajo Area Indian Health Service.

TAOS PHS INDIAN HEALTH CENTER
P.O. Box 1956 • TAOS, NM 87571
(505) 758-4224 Fax 758-1822
Kay Tsouhlarakis, Director
Affiliated with Albuquerque Area Indian Health Service.

PHS INDIAN HEALTH CENTER
P.O. Box 142 • TOHATCHI, NM 87325
(505) 733-8100 Fax 733-2239
Valerie Leslie, Facility Director
Affiliated with Navajo Area Indian Health Service.

ZUNI PHS INDIAN HOSPITAL
P.O. Box 467 • ZUNI, NM 87327
(505) 775-4431 Fax 782-5723
Jean Othole, Director
Clyde Yatsattie, Administrative Officer
David Kessler, MD, Clinical Director

Number of Beds: 45. Affiliated with
Albuquerque Area Indian Health Service.

NORTH CAROLINA

CHEROKEE PHS INDIAN HOSPITAL
CHEROKEE, NC 28719
(828) 497-9163 Fax 497-5343
Janet Belcourt, Health Systems Administrator
James Eller, Administrative Officer
Salvatore D'Angio, MD, Acting Clinical Director
Number of Beds: 35. Affiliated with
Nashville Area Indian Health Service.

CHEROKEE TECHNICAL SUPPORT CENTER
P.O. Box 429, Butler Bldg.
Rt. 1, Sequoyah Trail
CHEROKEE, NC 28719
(828) 497-5030 Fax 497-5104
Mary G. Wachacha, Health Education Coordinator
Affiliated with Nashville Area Indian Health Service.

**UNITY REGIONAL YOUTH
TREATMENT CENTER**
P.O. Box C-201, 441 N. Sequoyah Trail Dr.
CHEROKEE, NC 28719
(828) 497-3958 Fax 497-6826
Margaret Jenks, Director
Affiliated with Nashville Area Indian Health Service.

NORTH DAKOTA

BELCOURT PHS INDIAN HOSPITAL
P.O. Box 160 • BELCOURT, ND 58316
(701) 477-6112 Fax 477-8410
Raymond Grandbois, Director
Lynn Davis, Administrative Officer
Paula Bercier, MD, Clinical Director
Tribe served: Turtle Mountain Sioux.
Number of Beds: 46. Affiliated with
Aberdeen Area Indian Health Service.

**TURTLE MOUNTAIN COMPREHENSIVE
HEALTHCARE CENTER**
P.O. Box 130 • BECLOURT, ND 58316
(701) 477-6111 Fax 477-8410

FORT TOTTEN PHS INDIAN HEALTH CENTER
P.O. Box 200
FORT TOTTEN, ND 58335
(701) 766-4291 Fax 766-4295
John Gobert, Director
Lillie Owl boy, Administrative Officer
Necito Mentaniel, MD, Clinical Director
Tribe served: Devils Lake Sioux Tribe. *Professionals
on staff*: 11. *Services*: Family Practice. *Programs*: Staff
Education, Training and Research; Community Health
Education. Medical Library. Affiliated with Aberdeen
Area Indian Health Service.

FORT YATES PHS INDIAN HOSPITAL
P.o. Box J • FORT YATES, ND 58538
(701) 854-3831 Fax 854-7399
Terry Pouier, Director
Sonja Keener, Administrative Officer
Eduardo Lago, MD, Clinical Director
Number of Beds: 32. Affiliated with
Aberdeen Area Indian Health Service.

**FORT BERTHOLD PHS
INDIAN HEALTH CENTER**
P.O. Box 400 • NEW TOWN, ND 58763
(701) 627-4701 Fax 627-4318
Fred Baker, Director
Affiliated with Aberdeen Area Indian Health Service.

TRENTON-WILLISTON INDIAN SERVICE AREA
P.O. Box 210 • TRENTON, ND 58853
(701) 774-0461 Fax 774-8003
Ron Falcon, Tribal Health Director
Bhanat K. Patel, MD, Medical Officer
Affiliated with Aberdeen Area Indian Health Service.
Tribally operated.

OKLAHOMA

CARL ALBERT INDIAN HOSPITAL
1001 N. Country Club Dr. • ADA, OK 74820
(580) 436-3980 Fax 332-1421
Kenneth R. Ross, Administrative Officer
Joanne Chinnici, D.O., Clinical Director
Professionals on staff: 4. *Number of Beds*: 53. *Services*: Offers general out-patient medical services; workshops and in-service training. Affiliated with Oklahoma City Area Indian Health Service. Tribally operated.

PHS INDIAN HEALTH CENTER
P.O. Box 828 • ANADARKO, OK 73005
(405) 247-2458 Fax 247-7052
Gary Cody, Director
Affiliated with Oklahoma City Area
Indian Health Service.

ARDMORE CHICKASAW HEALTH CLINIC
2510 Chickasaw Blvd.
ARDMORE, OK 73401
(580) 226-8181
Loretta Anatubby, Director
Tribe served: Chickasaw. *Professionals on staff*: 7. *Numbers served*: 5,400 annually. *Services*: Offers general out-patient medical services; workshops and in-service training. Library. Affiliated with Oklahoma City Area Indian Health Service. Tribally operated.

CHOCTAW NATION HEALTH CLINIC
205 E. 3rd St. • BROKEN BOW, OK 74728
(580) 584-2740 Fax 584-2073
Jill Mayes, Director
Affiliated with Oklahoma City Area Indian Health Service. Tribally operated.

CARNEGIE PHS INDIAN HEALTH CENTER
P.O. Box 1120 • CARNEGIE, OK 73105
(580) 654-1100 Fax 654-2533
Bill Singleton, Acting Director
Affiliated with Oklahoma City Area
ndian Health Service.

CLAREMORE INDIAN HOSPITAL
101 S. Moore Ave. • CLAREMORE, OK 74017
(918) 342-6200 Fax 342-6585
John Daugherty, Service Unit Director
Vicki Snell, Administrative Officer
Paul Mobley, D.O., Clinical Director
E-mail: health@cherokee.org
Number of Beds: 50. *Description*: A general medical and surgical facility, also offering optometry, dental, audiology, mental health, social services, nutrition and community health, and nursing services. Specialty clinics are also offered in OB-GYN, pediatrics, internal medicine and emergency medicine. *Total population served*: 80,000; 160,000 outpatient visits per year. The staff consists of 375 employees in various professional, paraprofessional & technical positions. Affiliated with Oklahoma City Area Indian Health Service. Operated by the Cherokee Indian Nation.

CLINTON PHS INDIAN HOSPITAL
Route 1, Box 3060 • CLINTON, OK 73601
(580) 323-2884 Fax 323-2884 Ext. 211
Thedis Mitchell, Director
Fred Koebrick, Administrative Officer
Dolly Garcia, MD, Clinical Director
Number of Beds: 14. Affiliated with Oklahoma City Area Indian Health Service.

CHICKASAW/DURANT HEALTH CENTER
1702 W. Elm • DURANT, OK 74701
(580) 920-2100 Fax 920-1191
Madeline Johnson, Facility Director
Affiliated with Oklahoma City Area
Indian Health Service.

PHS INDIAN HEALTH CLINIC
1631A E. Hwy. 66 • EL RENO, OK 73036
(405) 262-7631 Fax 262-8099
Imelda Buendia, MD, Acting Director
Affiliated with Oklahoma City Area
Indian Health Service.

EUFAULA INDIAN HEALTH CLINIC
800 Forrest Ave. • EUFAULA, OK 74432
(918) 689-2547
Linda Lowe, Administrator
Tribes served: Mostly Creek, but all tribes within area. *Professionals on staff*: 21. *Services*: General outpatient medical care; dental, laboratory, counseling, nursing. *Program*: Community Health Education. Affiliated with Oklahoma City Area Indian Health Service. Tribally operated.

HUGO HEALTH CENTER
P.O. Box 340 • HUGO, OK 74743
(580) 326-7561
Randy Hammons, Director
Affiliated with Oklahoma City Area
Indian Health Service. Tribally operated.

SAM HIDER JAY COMMUNITY CLINIC
1015 Washburn, P.O. Box 350
JAY, OK 74346 (877) 293-4271
(918) 253-4271 Fax 434-5397
Ron Little, Director
E-mail: health@cherokee.org
Services: 25,000 outpatient visits per year. Provides outpatient medical services, public health nursing, laboratory, pharmacy, dental, WIC, radiology, mammography, community nutrition and contract care. Affiliated with Oklahoma City Area Indian Health Service. Operated by the Cherokee Nation.

LAWTON PHS INDIAN CENTER
1515 Lawrie Tatum Rd.
LAWTON, OK 73501
(580) 353-0350 Fax 353-0350 Ext. 206
George Howell, Director
Nadine Kauley, Administrative Officer
Edwin Chappabitty, MD, Clinical Director
Number of Beds: 52. Affiliated with Oklahoma City Area Indian Health Service.

CHOCTAW NATION INDIAN HEALTH CENTER
903 E. Monroe
McALESTER, OK 74501
(918) 423-8440 Fax 423-6781
Donald Ratliff, Director
Tribes served: All tribes in this area, predominantly Choctaw. *Total population served*: 15,000 annually. *Medical services*: Family practice; Dental Clinic. *Programs*: Diabetic and pre-natal classes; hypertension; well-child clinics; immunization program; home health care; service services; audiology; dietition. Affiliated with Oklahoma City Area Indian Health Service. Tribally operated.

KICKAPOO HEALTH CENTER
P.O. Box 1059 • McCLOUD, OK 74851
(405) 964-2081 Fax 964-2722
Ronald Fried, DO, Director
Affiliated with Oklahoma City Area
Indian Health Service.

MIAMI PHS INDIAN HEALTH CENTER
P.O. Box 1498 • MIAMI, OK 74355
(918) 542-1655 Fax 540-1685
Marion Ted Bearden, Director
Tribes served: Seneca-Cayuga, Eastern Shawnee, Miami, Modoc, Ottawa, Quapaw, Peoria, Wyandott and Cherokee. *Professionals on staff*: 15; *Numbers served*: Out-patients, 35,000 annually. *Medical services*: Medical, pharmacy, dental, optometry, mental health, public health nursing and laboratory. *Community programs*: Educational activities in the schools and tribal communities. Small medical library.

MUSKOGEE INDIAN HEALTH CENTER
212 South 38th St.
MUSKOGEE, OK 74401
(918) 687-0201 Fax 687-0665
Robert Park, Clinic Administrator
E-mail: health@cherokee.org
Services: 17,000 outpatient visits per year. Serves eligible members of both the Creek and Cherokee Nations. Offers outpatient medical services; WIC; laboratory; pharmacy; and behavioral health services. Affiliated with Oklahoma City Area Indian Health Service. Operated by the Cherokee Nation.

LITTLE AXE HEALTH CENTER
15702 E. Hwy. 9 • NORMAN, OK 73071
(405) 447-0300
Ruby Withrow, Clinical Director
Affiliated with Oklahoma City Area
Indian Health Service.

NOWATA INDIAN HEALTH CLINIC
Cherokee Nation of Oklahoma
202 E. Gator • NOWATA, OK 74048
(918) 273-0192; (877) 373-0192
Chris Walker, Clinic Administrator
E-mail: health@cherokee.org
Services: 14,500 outpatient visits per year. Offers outpatient medical services; public health nursing, laboratory, pharmacy, WIC, community health representatives, and contract care. Affiliated with Oklahoma City Area Indian Health Service. Operated by the Cherokee Nation operated.

CREEK NATION COMMUNITY HOSPITAL
Creek Nation of Oklahoma
P.O. Box 228 • OKEMAH, OK 74859
(918) 623-1424
Phillip Barnoski, Health Service Administrator
Affiliated with Oklahoma City Area
Indian Health Service. Tribally operated.

OKEMAH INDIAN HEALTH CENTER
P.O. Box 429 • OKEMAH, OK 74859
(918) 623-0555 Fax 623-1424
William Galvin, Health Systems Administrator
Affiliated with Oklahoma City Area Indian Health Service. Tribally operated.

OKLAHOMA CITY INDIAN CLINIC
Central Oklahoma American Indian Health Council
4913 W. Reno Ave.
OKLAHOMA CITY, OK 73127
(405) 948-4900 Fax 948-4932
Terry Hunter, Contact
Purpose: To provide outpatient primary medical care, general medical and dental services, mental health and substance abuse treatment, health education; seminars, prevention and outreach. Established 1974.

CREEK NATION DENTAL CLINIC
700 N. Mission, Box 10
OKMULGEE, OK 74447
(918) 756-2800
Doug White, Dental Officer
Tribally operated.

OKMULGEE HEALTH CENTER
1313 East 20th • OKMULGEE, OK 74447
(918) 756-2717
Jimmy (Bunny) Hill, Administrator
Affiliated with Oklahoma City Area
Indian Health Service.

PAWHUSKA PHS INDIAN HEALTH CENTER
715 Grandview • PAWHUSKA, OK 74056
(918) 287-4491 Fax 287-4491
John W. Williams, Director
Affiliated with Oklahoma City Area IHS

PAWNEE PHS INDIAN HEALTH CENTER
RR 2, Box 1 • PAWNEE, OK 74058
(918) 762-2517 Fax 762-2517 Ext. 200
James Norris, Director
Anita Ahhaitty, Administrative Officer
Steve Sanders, D.O., Clinical Director
Affiliated with Oklahoma City Area
Indian Health Service.

WHITE EAGLE PHS INDIAN HEALTH CENTER
P.O. Box 2071 • PONCA CITY, OK 74601
(580) 765-2501 Fax 765-6348
Gwen Pickering, Director
Affiliated with Oklahoma City Area
Indian Health Service.

CHOCTAW/REUBEN WHITE HEALTH CLINIC
109 Kerr Ave. • POTEAU, OK 74953
(918) 649-1100 Fax 649-1199
Jo Graves, Facility Director
Affiliated with Oklahoma City Area IHS

SALINA A-MO COMMUNITY CLINIC
900 N. Owen Walter Blvd.
P.O. Box 936 • SALINA, OK 74365
(877) 434-8500; (918) 434-8500
Shawn Terry, Clinic Administrator
E-mail: health@cherokee.org
Services: 22,500 outpatient visits per year. Offers outpatient medical services; public health nursing, laboratory, pharmacy, WIC, community nutrition, optometry, and radiology. Affiliated with Oklahoma City Area Indian Health Service. Operated by the Cherokee Nation.

REDBIRD SMITH HEALTH CENTER
301 S. JT Stities Ave. • SALLISAW, OK 74955
(888) 775-9159; (918) 775-9159 Fax 775-4778
Robert Park, Clinic Administrator
E-mail: health@cherokee.org
Services: 38,500 outpatient visits per year. Offers outpatient medical services; public health nursing, dental, optometry, laboratory, pharmacy, WIC, radiology, behavioral health, community nutrition, and contract care. Affiliated with Oklahoma City Area Indian Health Service. Operated by the Cherokee Nation.

SAPULPA HEALTH CENTER
Creek Nation of Oklahoma
1125 E. Cleveland • SAPULPA, OK 74066
(918) 224-9310 Judy Aaron, Director
Affiliated with Oklahoma City Area Indian Health Service. Tribally operated.

SHAWNEE PHS INDIAN HEALTH CENTER
2001 S. Gordon Cooper Dr. • SHAWNEE, OK 74801
(405) 275-4270 Fax 275-4270 Ext. 268
James Cussen, Director
Ronald Fried, DO, Clinical Director
Serves patients from various tribes. *Professionals on staff*: 30. *Numbers served*: 45,000 outpatients, annually. *Primary service*: Family practice. *Programs*: Staff education and training; community health education. Scholarships available. Library. Affiliated with Oklahoma City Area Indian Health Service.

WILMA P. MANKILLER HEALTH CENTER
Rt. 2, Box 93 • STILWELL, OK 74960
(877) 747-8800; (918) 696-8800
Gordon Watkins, Clinic Administrator
E-mail: health@cherokee.org
Services: 41,500 outpatient visits per year. Offers outpatient medical services; public health nursing, dental, optometry, laboratory, pharmacy, WIC, radiology, behavioral health, community nutrition, and contract care. Affiliated with Oklahoma City Area Indian Health Service. Operated by the Cherokee Nation.

BLACK HAWK HEALTH CENTER
Sac & Fox Nation of Oklahoma
Rt. 2, Box 246 • STROUD, OK 73079
(918) 968-9531 Cindy Schoenecke, Director
Affiliated with Oklahoma City Area IHS.
Tribally operated.

W.W. HASTINGS HOSPITAL
100 S. Bliss Ave. • TAHLEQUAH, OK 74464
(918) 458-3100 Fax 458-3262
Hickory Starr, Jr., Service Unit Director
Keith Barrick, Administrative Officer
John Farris, MD, Clinical Director
E-mail: health@cherokee.org
Number of Beds: 65. *Description*: A general medical and surgical facility, also offering optometry, dental, audiology, mental health, social services, nutrition and community health, and nursing services. Specialty clinics are also offered in OB-GYN, pediatrics, internal medicine and emergency medicine. *Total population served*: 80,000 eligible Indians; 150,000 outpatient visits per year. The staff consists of 300 employees in various professional, paraprofessional and technical positions. Affiliated with Oklahoma City Area Indian Health Service. Operated by the Cherokee Nation.

CHOCTAW NATION HEALTHCARE CENTER
One Choctaw Way • TALIHINA, OK 74571
(800) 349-7026; (918) 567-7000
Rosemary Hooser, Administrator
Debbie Smith, Administrative Officer
Jean Olivia Grant, MD, Chief of Staff

Tribes served: Choctaw and all nationally recognized tribes. *Professionals on staff*: 77. *Number of Beds*: 37. *Numbers served*: 1,300 inpatients and 32,000 outpatients, annually. *Primary medical services*: Audiology; behavioral health; dental; diabetes treatment; dietition services; emergency room - OB/GYN - lab services; optometry; pediatrics; pharmacy; physical therapy; radiology; respiratory therapy; surgery. *Programs*: WIC Program; social services; contract health; substance abuse recovery; community health reps; public health nursing. Medical Library. Affiliated with Oklahoma City Area Indian Health Service. Tribally operated.

TISHOMINGO CHICKASAW HEALTH CENTER
815 E. 6th St. • TISHOMINGO, OK 73460
(580) 371-2392 Fax 371-9323
William Shepard, Director
Tribe served: Chickasaw. *Professionals on staff*: 8.
Numbers served: 8,000 annually. Library. Affiliated with Oklahoma City Area Indian Health Service. Tribally operated.

INDIAN HEALTH CARE
RESOURCE CENTER OF TULSA
550 S. Peoria Ave. • TULSA, OK 74120
(918) 382-1201 Fax 582-6405
Carmelita Skeeter, Executive Director
E-mail: cskeeter@ihcrc.org
Website: www.administration.ihcrc.org
Tribes served: All. Population served: 26,000. *Medical services*: Pediatrician, OB/Gyn, Adult Acute and Chronic Medicine, Dental, Optometry, Mental Health and Substance Abuse Counseling-Adult & Children. *Special programs*: Diabetes, HIV/AID'S, WIC, REACH, Well baby classes, Outreach, Public Health Nursing, Transportation, Pharmacy. Library.

WATONGA PHS INDIAN HEALTH CENTER
Rt. 1, Box 34-A • WATONGA, OK 73772
(580) 623-4991 Fax 623-5490
Larry Scott, Director
Tribes served: Primarily Cheyenne and Arapaho; members of all local tribes. *Professionals on staff*: 10. *Numbers served annually*: Out-patient, 1,200 plus. *Medical services*: General out-patient medical and dental services. *Community programs*: Weekly diabetic and prenatal clinics; headstart dental prevention and nursing bottle caries prevention. Small medical library. Affiliated with Oklahoma City Area Indian Health Service.

WEWOKA PHS INDIAN HEALTH CENTER
P.O. Box 1475 • WEWOKA, OK 74884
(405) 257-6281 Fax 257-2696
Travis Jackson, Director
Mildred Blackmon, Administrative Officer
Ahja Chon, MD, Clinical Director
Affiliated with Oklahoma City Area
Indian Health Service.

BEARSKIN HEALTH CENTER
P.O. Box 30 • WYANDOTTE, OK 74370
(918) 678-2297 Fax 678-2759
Dennis Fitzgerald, Facility Director
Affiliated with Oklahoma City Area IHS

OREGON

YELLOWHAWK PHS INDIAN HEALTH CENTER
P.O. Box 160 • PENDLETON, OR 97801
(503) 278-3870
Doris W. Thompson, Director
Allan Jio, Pharm., Clinical Director
Services provided: Contract health, dental care, environmental health, health education, Lab/X-ray, mental health, outpatient clinic, pharmacy, public health nursing, and wellness programs. Affiliated with Portland Area Indian Health Service.

CHEMAWA INDIAN HEALTH CENTER
3750 Chemawa Rd., NE • SALEM, OR 97305
(503) 399-5937
James E. Edge, MPH, Director
Lorraine A. Hesketh, Administrative Officer
Mark J. Nurre, MD, Clinical Director
Tribes served: Confederated Tribes of Siletz; Confed-

erated Tribes of Grand Ronde; Cow Creek Band of Umpqua Tribe; Confederated Tribes of Coos, Lower Umpqua, Siuslaw; Coquille Tribe. *Number of professionals on staff*: 30. *Numbers served*: 15,000, Outpatient. *Services provided*: Outpatient medical, dental, mental health, nutrition, public health nursing. Affiliated with Portland Area Indian Health Service.

CONFEDERATED TRIBES OF
SILETZ COMMUNITY HEALTH CLINIC
P.O. Box 320 • SILETZ, OR 97380
(800) 648-0449; Fax (503) 444-1278
Provides comprehensive health care to federally recognized American Indians.

WARM SPRINGS PHS INDIAN HEALTH CENTER
P.O. Box 1209 • WARM SPRINGS, OR 97761
(541) 553-1196
Russ Alger, Director
Roberta Queahpama, Administrative Officer
Thomas J. Creelman, MD, Clinical Director
Services provided: Out-patient clinical; dental care; contract health; nutrition; and public health nursing. Affiliated with Portland Area Indian Health Service.

SOUTH DAKOTA

EAGLE BUTTE PHS INDIAN HOSPITAL
P.O. Box 1012 • EAGLE BUTTE, SD 57625
(605) 964-3001 FAX 964-1169
Orville Night Pipe, Director
Don Annis, Administrative Officer
Margaret Upell, MD, Clinical Director
Tribe served: Cheyenne River Sioux. *Professionals on staff*: 6. *Number of Beds*: 26. 680 inpatients anmd 3,600 outpatients, annually. *Primary services*: Acute medicine; OB/GYN' Pediatrics. Community Health Education Programs. Affiliated with Aberdeen Area IHS

FORT THOMPSON PHS INDIAN HEALTH CENTER
P.O. Box 200 • FORT THOMPSON, SD 57339
(605) 245-2285 Fax 245-2384
Nancy Miller, Director
Rhoda Kerwin, Administrative Officer
Richard Harris, DO, Clinical Director
Affiliated with Aberdeen Area Indian Health Service.

KYLE PHS HEALTH CENTER
P.O. Box 540 • KYLE, SD 57752
(605) 455-2451 Fax 455-2808
Georgia Amiotte, Administrative Officer
Affiliated with Aberdeen Area Indian Health Service.

LOWER BRULE PHS INDIAN HEALTH CENTER
P.O. Box 248 • LOWER BRULE, SD 57548
(605) 473-5544 Fax 473-5677
Clarenda Menzie, Administrative Officer
Peter Magnus, MD, Clinical Director
Affiliated with Aberdeen Area Indian Health Service.

McLAUGHLIN PHS INDIAN HEALTH CENTER
P.O. Box 879 • MCLAUGHLIN, SD 57642
(605) 823-4458 Fax 823-4181
James Foote, Director
Daisy LeCompte, Administrative Assistant
Tribes served: Standing Rock Sioux, Cheyenne River Sioux, Rosebud Sioux, Fort Totten Sioux, Fort Thompson Crow Creek Sioux, and Yankton Sioux. *Professionals on staff*: 8. 9,500 outpatients, annually. *Primary services*: Outpatient and dental services. Library. Affiliated with Aberdeen Area Indian Health Service.

YOUTH REGIONAL TREATMENT CENTER
P.O. Box 68 • MOBRIDGE, SD 57401
(605) 845-7181 Fax 845-5072
Tom Eagle Staff, Director
Affiliated with Aberdeen Area Indian Health Service. Tribally operated.

PINE RIDGE PHS INDIAN HOSPITAL
PINE RIDGE, SD 57770
(605) 867-5131 Fax 867-3271
Vern Donnell, Director
Bill Pourier, Administrative Officer
Julie Dixon, DO, Clinical Director
Number of Beds: 58. Affiliated with Aberdeen Area IHS

RAPID CITY PHS INDIAN HEALTH HOSPITAL
3200 Canyon Lake Dr. • RAPID CITY, SD 57702
(605) 355-2500 Fax 355-2504
Midge Breen, Administrative Officer
Rodney Larson, MD, Clinical Director
Number of Beds: 39. Affiliated with Aberdeen Area IHS

ROSEBUD PHS INDIAN HOSPITAL
ROSEBUD, SD 57570
(605) 747-2231 Fax 747-2216
Gayla Twiss, Director
Michelle Leach, Deputy SUD
Timothy Ryschon, MD, Clinical Director
Number of Beds: 29. Affiliated with Aberdeen Area IHS

SISSETON PHS INDIAN HOSPITAL
P.O. Box 189 • SISSETON, SD 57262
(605) 698-7606 Fax 698-4270
Richard Huff, Director
Ramona Saul, Administrative Officer
Fernando Zambrana, MD, Clinical Director
Number of Beds: 20. Affiliated with Aberdeen Area IHS

WAGNER PHS INDIAN HOSPITAL
110 Washington St. • WAGNER, SD 57380
(605) 384-3621 Fax 384-5229
Priscilla Lee, Director
Darlene Williamson, Administrative Officer
Victor L. Dominguez, MD, Clinical Director
Tribes served: Yankton Sioux and Santee Sioux. *Professionals on staff*: 30; *Number of Beds*: 26. *Medical services*: In-patient; medical and surgical. Library. Affiliated with Aberdeen Area Indian Health Service.

WANBLEE PHS HEALTH CENTER
WANBLEE, SD 57577
(605) 462-6155 Fax 462-6551
Patrick Giroux, Director
Affiliated with Aberdeen Area Indian Health Service.

TEXAS

**DALLAS INTER-TRIBAL COUNCIL
HEALTH CENTER**
209 E. Jefferson • DALLAS, TX 75203
(214) 941-1050 Fax 941-6537
Dean Bridges, Executive Director
Affiliated with Oklahoma City Area IHS

EAGLE PASS HEALTH CENTER
P.O. Box 972 • EAGLE PASS, TX 78853
(210) 757-0322 Fax 757-0496
Francis Rodriguez, Facility Director
Affiliated with Oklahoma City Area IHS

YSLETA DEL SUR SERVICE UNIT
119 S. Old Pueblo Rd.
P.O. Box 17579 • EL PASO, TX 79907
(915) 859-7913 Fax 859-2988
Irene Agurrie, Director
Affiliated with Albuquerque Area Service Unit.

UTAH

PHS INDIAN HEALTH CENTER
P.O. Box 160 • Ft. Duchesne, UT 84026
(435) 722-5122 Fax 722-9137
Tom Gann, Director
Dinah Peltier, Administrative Officer
Paul Ebbert, MD, Clinical Director
Tribes served: Northern Ute; Paiute Tribe of Utah; and Skull Valley Goshute. *Professionals on staff*: 47. Community health education. Affiliated with Phoenix Area Indian Health Service.

WASHINGTON

LUMMI PHS INDIAN HEALTH CENTER
2592 Kwina Rd. • BELLINGHAM, WA 98226
(206) 676-8373
Marilyn M. Scott, Director
Affiliated with Portland Area Indian Health Service.

SOPHIE TRETTEVICK INDIAN HEALTH CENTER
P.O. Box 410 • NEAH BAY, WA 98357
(360) 645-2233
A. Thomas Birdinground, Director
Shirley M. Johnson, Administrative Officer
David A. Knowlton, MD, Clinical Director
Affiliated with Portland Area Indian Health Service.

COLVILLE PHS INDIAN HEALTH CENTER
P.O. Box 71, Agency Campus
NESPELEM, WA 99155
(509) 634-4771
Mel C. Tonasket, Director
Janice Matt, Administrative Officer
Aloe Marie, Clinical Director
Affiliated with Portland Area Indian Health Service.

PUGET SOUND PHS INDIAN HEALTH STATION
2201 Sixth Ave., Rm. 300
SEATTLE, WA 98121 (206) 615-2781
Ernest H. Kimball, Director
Affiliated with Portland Area Indian Health Service.

SEATTLE INDIAN HEALTH BOARD
606 - 12th Ave. South
SEATTLE, WA 98144-2008
(206) 324-9360 ext. 1102 Fax 324-8910
Ralph Forquera, Executive Director
Rebecca Gonzales, Director of Operations
E-Mail: ralph@compumedia.com
Population served: A multi—service community health center serving the Indian population of Seattle. *Medical services*: Full-service outpatient primary medical clinic providing preventive, acute, and chronic care, dental, mental health, substance abuse and treatment, outreach and case management, and community education services. Established 1970.

TAHOLAH PHS INDIAN HEALTH CENTER
P.O. Box 219 • TAHOLAH, WA 98587
(206) 276-4405
Dorothy L. DeLaCruz, Director
Carl Schilling, Clinical Director
Affiliated with Portland Area Indian Health Service.

YAKIMA PHS INDIAN HEALTH CENTER
401 Buster Rd.
TOPPENISH, WA 98948
(509) 865-2102
Colleen R. Reimer, Director
Frances M. Spencer, Administrative Officer
John K. Moran, MD, Clinical Director
Affiliated with Portland Area Indian Health Service.

DAVID C. WYNECOOP MEMORIAL CLINIC
P.O. Box 357 • WELLPINIT, WA 99040
(509) 258-4517
Virgil L. Gunn, Director
Janice K. Moyer, Administrative Officer
Paul A. Willard, MD, Clinical Director
Affiliated with Portland Area Indian Health Service.

WISCONSIN

RED CLIFF HEALTH SERVICES
P.O. Box 529 • BAYFIELD, WI 54814
(715) 779-3707 Fax 779-3777
Patricia Deragon, Director
Affiliated with Bemidji Area Office. Tribally operated.

HO CHUNK NATION HEALTH DEPT.
P.O. Box 636
BLACK RIVER FALLS, WI 54615
(715) 284-7548/7830 Fax 284-9592
Roberta Hall, Health Director
Ben Boardman, MD, Clinical Director
Affiliated with Bemidji Area Office. Tribally operated.

STOCKBRIDGE-MUNSEE HEALTH CENTER
P.O. Box 86-N8705 Moh He Con Nuk Rd.
BOWLER, WI 54416
(715) 793-5904
Leone Onestie, Director
Richard Dalve, MD, Clinical Director
Affiliated with Bemidji Area Office. Tribally operated.

FOREST CO. POTAWATOMI COMMUNITY CLINIC
P.O. Box 396 • CRANDON, WI 54520
(715) 478-7800 Fax 478-7316
Dori Shewano, Health Administrator
Affiliated with Bemidji Area Office. Tribally operated.

SOKAOGAN CHIPPEWA COMMUNITY CLINIC
P.O. Box 616 • CRANDON, WI 54520
(715) 478-5180 Fax 478-5904
Judy Anaya, Health Administrator
Affiliated with Bemidji Area Office. Tribally operated.

LAC COURTE OREILLES TRIBAL CLINIC
Route #2, Box 2750
HAYWARD, WI 54843
(715) 634-4153/4795 Fax 634-6107
Don Smith, Director
Modesto Ferrar, MD, Clinical Director
Affiliated with Bemidji Area Office.Tribally operated.

ST. CROIX HEALTH SERVICES
P.O. Box 287 • HERTEL, WI 54845
(715) 349-2195 Fax 349-2559
Phyllis Lowe, Director
Bill Marx, Clinical Director
Affiliated with Bemidji Area Office. Tribally operated.

MENOMINEE TRIBAL CLINIC
P.O. Box 970 • KESHENA, WI 54135
(715) 799-5482 Fax 799-3099
Jerry L. Waukau, Health Director
Kevin Culhane, MD, Clinical Director
Tribe served: Menominee. *Professionals on staff*: 80. Consists of four full-time physicians with staff privileges at the Shawano Community Hospital. *Services*: The Community Health Nursing Service consists of a staff of eight that provides a number of outreach services to the community; the Human Resource Center provides outpatient mental health services; Emergency Medical Services. *Programs*: Staff education, training and research; community health education; environmental health program. Library. Affiliated with Bemidji Area Office. Tribally operated.

PETER CHRISTENSEN HEALTH CENTER
450 Old Abe Rd.
LAC DU FLAMBEAU, WI 54538
(715) 588-3371 Fax 588-7884
Robin Carufel & Leon Valliere, Health Administrators
Affiliated with Bemidji Area Office. Tribally operated.

BAD RIVER HEALTH SERVICES
P.O Box 39 • ODANAH, WI 54861
(715) 682-7137 Fax 682-7883
Mary Bigboy, Health Director
Affiliated with Bemidji Area Office. Tribally operated.

ONEIDA COMMUNITY HEALTH CENTER
P.O. Box 365 • ONEIDA, WI 54155
(414) 869-2711 Fax 869-1780
Deanna Bauman, Director
Tammy Fox, PA, Clinical Director
Affiliated with Bemidji Area Office. Tribally operated.

WYOMING

ARAPAHO PHS INDIAN HEALTH CENTER
ARAPAHO, WY 82510
(307) 856-9281
Margaret Cooper, Clinical Director
Affiliated with Billings Area Indian Health Service.

WIND RIVER PHS INDIAN HEALTH CENTER
P.O. Box 128
FORT WASHAKIE, WY 82514
(307) 332-9416 Fax 332-9418
Catherine Keene, Director
Richard Brannon, Administrative Officer
Robert McKnight, MD, Clinical Director
Reservation served: Wind River Indian Reservation. *Tribe served*: Eastern Shoshone and Northern Arapaho. Total population served: 10,000. *Medical services*: Outpatient clinic. Library. Affiliated with Billings Area Indian Health Service.

This section is an alpha-geographical listing of museums, monuments and parks maintaining permanent exhibits or collections related to the Native-American. Where no annotation follows a listing, the museum failed to answer our questionnaire, but is known, from other sources, to display Indian artifacts.

SMITHSONIAN INSTITUTION
NATIONAL MUSEUM OF THE AMERICAN INDIAN
Fourth St. & Independence Ave., S.W.
Washington, DC 20560 (202) 633-1000
Richard West, Executive Director
Website: www.nmai.si.edu
E-mail: nin@ic.si.edu
E-mail: nmaicollections@si.edi
The new National Museum of the American Indian on The National Mall in Washington, D.C., was opened September 21, 2004. It's a living memorial dedicated to the collection, preservation, study and exhibition of American Indian languages, literature, history, art and culture. The centerpiece of the new museum is the priceless collection of almost 1 million objects, once stored in the Museum of the American Indian, Heye Foundation in New York City, representing 10,000 years of history from more than 1,000 indigenous cultures. This collection which includes a library, photo archives and other resource materials has been transferred to this new National Museum in Washington, DC. Also a Resource Center. All three resource centers will be digitally connected, and information will flow between all facilities. Visitors to NMAI on The National Mall will be able to access information and materials from either of the other NMAI Resource Center locations, and vice versa. The Mall Resource Center will contain 18 public access computers in the Interactive Learning Center, a work-study area, book stacks, workrooms and a classroom.

NATIONAL MUSEUM OF THE AMERICAN INDIAN
CULTURAL RESOURCES CENTER
4220 Silver Hill Rd. •˝Suitland, MD 20746
(301) 238-6624
Caleb Strickland, Director, Community Services
Thomas Sweeney, Director of Public Affairs
Ext. 6404
Marti Kriepe De Montano, Director, Resource Dept.
Ext. 6404
Stephanie Makseyn-Kelley, Repatriation Office
Ext. 6393
1of 3 resource centers of the National Museum of the American Indian, providing storage facilities, & containing research, conservation & repatriation offices.

NATIONAL MUSEUM OF THE AMERICAN INDIAN
THE GEORGE GUSTAV HEYE CENTER
U.S. Custom House, One Bowling Green
New York, NY 10004
(212) 514-3700 Fax 514-3800
John Haworth, Director
Karen Savage, Assistant Director
Gaetana DeGennaro, Resource Center Manager
One of three Resource Centers of the National Museum of the American Indian exhibiting artifacts of the North & South American Indians.

ALABAMA

POARCH CREEK INDIAN HERITAGE CENTER
HCR 69A, Box 85B • ATMORE, AL 36502
(205) 368-9136
Patricia L. Brewer, Executive Director
Sandra L. Ridley, Curator
Collections pertain to Creek Indians of the Southeast.
Library. Opened 1990.

RUSSELL CAVE NATIONAL MONUMENT
3729 County Road 98
BRIDGEPORT, AL 35740
(256) 495-2672 Fax 495-9220
William Springer, Supt.; Larry N. Beane, Curator
Stephen McGee, Park Ranger
E-mail: ruca_ranger_activities@nps.gov
Website: www.nps.gov/ruca
Description: An excavated, 310-acre archaeological site which shows the life of the people Russell Cave

sheltered for 8,000 years. From archaic man to Indians—Woodlands and Cherokee. Museum contains artifacts from the Archaic, Woodland, and Mississippian periods. *Special program*: Indian Day - April, includes demonstrations of prehistoric techniques, arts and crafts. *Publications*: Investigations in Russell Cave. Library. Opened in 1961.

OAKVILLE INDIAN MOUNDS PARK & MUSEUM
1219 County Road 187 • DANVILLE, AL 35619
(205) 905-2494 Fax 905-2428
E-mail: indian@lawrenceal.org
Rickey Butch Walker, Director
Description: The pre-Columbian Indian mound is one of the largest domiciliary Indian mounds in the Tennessee Valley. The museum contains Indian artifacts.

ALABAMA STATE ARCHIVES & HISTORY MUSEUM
624 Washington Ave.
MONTGOMERY, AL 36130
(205) 242-4363
Descritpion: Collections include artifacts that trace the culture of five American Indian tribes that lived in Alabama.

MOUNDVILLE ARCHAEOLOGICAL PARK
Jones Archaeological Museum
P.O. Box 66 • MOUNDVILLE, AL 35474
(205) 371-2572 Fax 371-4180
Web site: http://moundville.ua.edu
Bill Bomar, Director; Eugene Futato, Curator
Description: A park and museum located on the Black Warrior River, preserves 325 acres of what was once a large and powerful Southeastern Indian community of about 3,000 @ 1300 A.D. The site is internationally known for its 20 preserved mounds and the building of the wooden palisade that once defended the site. An Archaeological Museum holds one of the largest and most important collections of Native American artifacts and related materials for scientific research anywhere in the Southeast. *Activities*: Moundville Native American Festival featuring Southeastern Native American crafts, food, storytelling, musicians and dancers; other special programs with Native Americans from Choctaw, Creek, Cherokee, and Seminole tribes. Opened in 1939.

FORT TOULOUSE-JACKSON PARK
2521 W. Ft. Toulouse Rd. • WETUMPKA, AL 36093
(205) 567-3002 Ned Jenkins, Site Manager
Description: A 165 acre National Historic Landmark situated at the junction of the Coos and Tallapoosa Rivers where they form the Alabama River. Occupied by the moundbuilder Alabama Indians, who were part of the Creek Confederacy. Like the other mound-builders in the area, these Indians were the first farmers-corn, beans and squash. When DeSoto passed through in 1540 this area was probably a part of the chiefdom of Talise.

ALASKA

AKUTAN ALEUT HERITAGE MUSEUM
P.O. Box 89 • AKUTAN, AK 99553
(907) 689-2300 FAX 689-2301
Jacob Stepetin, Director
Opened in 1995.

SIMON PANEAK MEMORIAL MUSEUM
P.O. Box 21085, 341 Mekiana Rd.
ANAKTUVUK PASS 99721
(907) 661-3413 Fax 661-3414
Grant Spearman, Curator
E-mail: gspearman@co.north-slope.ak.us
Description: Local history and culture museum pertaining to the "Nunamiut" or inland Eskimos of Alaska's Central Brooks Range. Collections represent a combination of archaeological and ethnographic objects as well as extensive oral history, photographic and archival materials. *Special Education Program*: Work in conjunction with the North Slope Borough School District and the Borough's Inupiaq History, Language and Culture Commission to research and produce educational materials based on oral history research with Nunamiut elders about traditional tools, implements, practices and values. Library. Gift Shop. Opened in 1986.

ALASKA NATIVE HERITAGE CENTER
ANCHORAGE, AK 99503
(907) 263-5170 Fax 263-5575
Roy Huhndorf, Director
Description: A statewide culture center dedicated to the perpetuation of Alaska Native culture, language, arts, and customs and will serve as a learning center, a gathering place, and a clearinghouse. Includes a theater and outside traditional village exhibits representing the five major cultural groups. Opened in 1999.

ANCHORAGE MUSEUM OF HISTORY & ART
121 W. 7th Ave. • ANCHORAGE, AK 99501
(907) 343-4326 Fax 343-6149
Patricia B. Wolf, Director
Web site: www.ci.anchorage.us
Description: Permanent exhibits on Alaskan art and artifacts of all periods. Eskimo, Aleut, Tlingit and Athapaskan crafts. 8,000 ethnographic pieces. *Special programs*: Annual Native Heritage Festival (March) which features 10-20 contemporary Alaskan Native craftsmen and artists; Summer Native dance series provided by Cook Inlet Tribal Council. *Publications*: An Introduction to the Native Art of Alaska; monthly newsletter. Library. Museum shop. Opened in 1968.

ILISAGVIK COLLEGE CULTURAL CENTER
P.O. Box 749 • BARROW, AK 99723
(907) 852-0165 Fax 852-1752
Leona Okakok, Director
Opened in 1998.

YUPIIT PICIRYARAIT CULTURAL
CENTER & MUSEUM
Association of Village Council Presidents
P.O. Box 219 • BETHEL, AK 99559
(907) 543-1819 Fax 543-1885
Mary Stachelrodt, Director
Description: Exhibits Yup'ik Eskimo artifacts of southwest Alaska, such as baskets, clothing, utensils, ceremonial regalia, masks, and other items of historical value. *Programs*: Elder Mentor Program; Community Educational Programming Outreach; Interactive Exhibitions & Seasonal Yup'ik Ceremonies & Festivals. Opened in 1994.

NAY'DINI'AA NA TRIBAL CULTURAL CENTER
P.O. Box 1105 • CHICKALOON, AK 99674
(907) 745-0707 Fax 745-7154
Jennifer Dahle Harrison, Director
Description: Exhibits describing the Athabascan people of Chickaloon Village from the 1800's to the present. *Activities*: Assists Elders in teaching the tribe's traditions to children attending the first tribal school in Alaska, the Ya Ne Dah Ah School. Opened in 2000.

SAMUEL K. FOX MUSEUM
Dillngham Public Library Bldg.
Seward & D Sts. • DILLINGHAM, AK 99576
(907) 842-2322 Fax 842-5691
Lynn M. Fox, Director/Curator
Phil Pryse, Curator
Description: Located in the Dillingham Public Library Building, the museum houses southwest Yup'ik Eskimo arts and crafts, and Siberian Yup'ik and Inupiak Eskimo artifacts. Also, a collection of art from the late Eskimo artist Sam Fox.

DILLINGHAM HERITAGE MUSEUM
DILLINGHAM, AK 99576
(907) 842-5601/5221
Irma O'Brien, Coordinator
Norma Adkison, Chairwoman
Description: Alaskan Indian museum with southwest Yup'ik Eskimo arts and crafts, and Siberian Yup'ik and Inupiak Eskimo artifacts.

UNIVERSITY OF ALASKA MUSEUM
907 Yukon Dr. • FAIRBANKS, AK 99775
(907) 474-7505 Fax 474-5469
Aldona Jonaitis, PhD, Director
E-Mail: ffaj@aurora.alaska.edu
Web site: http://www.uaf.alaska.edu/
sradnet/index.html
Description: Large collection of Alaskan arctic archaeology, Tlingit, Athapascan, Aleut, Alutiiq, Inupiat, Yupik, Siberian Yupik ethnology, contemporary artwork by Alaskan Natives. *Programs*: "Northern Inua" 50-minute summer program of Alaskan Native athletics and

dance; "Gatherings North" winter celebration of Alaskan Native Culture. *Publications*: Museum Guide; "Reflections" annual newsletter. Opened in 1922.

ALASKA INDIAN ARTS, INC.
P.O. Box 271, 23 Fort Seward Dr.
HAINES, AK 99827 (907) 766-2160
  Carl W. Heinmiller, Executive Director
Description: Indian Living Village Museum, collection of Tlingit Indian costumes and art; Chilkat Indian dancing. Small reference library.

SHELDON MUSEUM & CULTURAL CENTER
P.O. Box 269 • HAINES, AK 99827
  (907) 766-2366 Fax 766-2368
  Cynthia L. Jones, Director/Curator
  Elisabeth S. Hakkinen, Historian
  E-Mail: curator@sheldonmuseum.org
  Website: www.sheldonmuseum.org
Description: Historical and Tlingit art museum, depicting the Tlingit Indian culture and history of the Upper Lynn Canal (northern part of Southeast Alaska). Tlingit artifacts, including blankets, baskets, costumes, and implements. *Special programs*: Movies/slide shows; Haines Mission (Indian school/orphanage); travelling & special exhibits-often including native artists; school programs; Tlingit Awareness Week; Tlingit Language classes. *Publications*: A Personal Look at the Sheldon Museum; Haines: The First Century; The Tlingit Indian: Journey to the Tlingits; historical monographs about local history and Tlingit culture. Library. Opened in1925 (private), 1975 (public).

ALASKA STATE MUSEUM
395 Whittier St. • JUNEAU, AK 99801-1718
  (907) 465-2901 Fax 465-2976
  E-mail: bruce_kato@eed.state.ak.us
  Web site: www.museums.state.ak.us
Description: *Maint*ains a collection of more than 10,000 objects relating to the Eskimo, Tlingit, Northwest Coast, Athabascan, Aleut, and Haida. Resource Library. *Publications*: Bulletin, Review, Concepts, Occasional exhibit catalogs; traveling exhibitions. Established 1900.

SEALASKA GALLERY CULTURAL MUSEUM
Sealaska Plaza Bldg. • JUNEAU, AK 99801

KENAITZE INTERPRETIVE SITE
Chugach National Forest
c/o Kenaitze Indian Tribe IRA
P.O. Box 988 • KENAI, AK 99611
  (907) 283-4321 Fax 283-4437
  Rita Smagge, Director
Opened in 1994.

KETCHIKAN INDIAN MUSEUM
P.O. Box 5454 • KETCHIKAN, AK 99901

**TOTEM HERITAGE CENTER
TONGASS HISTORICAL MUSEUM**
629 Dock St. • KETCHIKAN, AK 99901
  (907) 225-5600 Fax 225-5602
  E-mail: museumdir@city.ketchikan.ak.us
  Michael Naab, Director
Description: City of Ketchikan's museum department and archives holdings include photographs on all Alaska villages with totem poles; index to all Alaska totem poles; vertical file on Northwest Coast Indian art and culture. Covers Tlingit, Haida and Tsimshian tribes - art, anthropology, totem poles. Displays the world's finest collection of 19th century totem poles, retrieved from old village sites. *Programs*: Native Arts Studies Program offers an annual series of workshops, seminars, and classes in Tlingit, Haida, and Tsimshian arts and culture, with college credit available. The program is designed for all levels. Art and crafts slides available for use; lecture series on traditional Alaska Native arts and culture. Museum shop offers a selection of Alaska Native crafts, books, clothing and momentos. Library. *Publication*: Quarterly newsletter. Opened in1961.

**ALUTIIQ MUSEUM & ARCHAEOLOGICAL
REPOSITORY**
215 Mission Rd., Suite 101
KODIAK, AK 99615
  (907) 486-7004 Fax 486-7048
  Sven Haakanson, Jr., Director
  E-mail: alutiiq2@ptialaska.net

Website: www.alutiiqmuseum.com
Description: An educational facility, research center, and repository. Exhibits archaeological, ethnographic and archival materials from Alutiiq sites dating between 100 and 7500 years ago. *Special programs*: Hosts annual traveling exhibit on Native American Alaskan culture; provides educational outreach programs; and conducts archaeological excavations. Library. Opened in 1995.

BARANOV MUSEUM/ERSKINE HOUSE
101 Marine Way • KODIAK, AK 99615
  (907) 486-5920 Fax 486-3166
  Ann Stone, President; Marian Johnson, Director
Description: The Kodiak Historical Society operates the Baranov Museum in the old Rissian warehouse, the Erskine House, in downtown Kodiak. The collection consists of Aleut, Koniag, Russian and American objects from the area prehistoric to present. Research Center for Kodiak and the Aleutians with photos, rare books, papers and maps. *Publications*: Educational papers. Museum store.

KOTZEBUE MUSEUM, INC.
P.O. Box 46 • KOTZEBUE, AK 99752
  (907) 442-3401 Fax 442-3742
  Gene Moore, Manager
Description: Contains Eskimo artifacts, arts and crafts, costumes, and Indian artifacts.

NANA MUSEUM OF THE ARCTIC
P.O. Box 49 • KOTZEBUE, AK 99752
  (907) 442-3301 Fax 442-2866
  Gia Hanna, Director
Description: Inupiat Museum of the Arctic houses land and sea mammal exhibits, arts & crafts, technical diorama & slide presentations. *Activities*: Eskimo dancers and a traditional Eskimo Blanket Toss. *Program*: Maintains a multi-media interpretive program explaining traditional Inupiat skills and culture. Opened in 1976.

DUNCAN COTTAGE MUSEUM
P.O. Box 282, Duncan St.
Annette Island Reserve
METLAKATLA, AK 99926
  LaVerne Welcome, Director/Curator
Description: Historic House, 1894—home of Father William Duncan, missionary teacher of the Tsimshian Indian people of Metlakatla.

KUZHGIE CULTURAL CENTER MUSEUM
P.O. Box 949 • NOME, AK 99762

CARRIE McLAIN MUSEUM
P.O. Box 53 • NOME, AK 99762
  (907) 443-2566 Marlene Carpenter, Director
Description: Old Eskimo artifacts. Library.

CLAUSEN MEMORIAL MUSEUM
203 Fram St., Box 708
PETERSBURG, AK 99833
  (907) 772-3598 Michale Edgington, Director
Description: Collections contain material on Tlingit Indians, including canoes and tools.

SELDOVIA NATIVE ASSOCIATION
Fine Arts and Cultural Center Museum
P.O. Box 201 • SELDOVIA, AK 99663

SHELDON JACKSON MUSEUM
104 College Dr. • SITKA, AK 99835
  (907) 747-8981 Fax 747-3004
  Website: www.museums.state.ak.us
  Rosemary Carlton, Curator of Collections
  Web site: www.educ.state.ak.us/lam/museum/home.html
Description: Museum is the oldest museum in the state of Alaska and is housed in the first concrete building erected in Alaska. Present collections are representative of the four major Native groups in Alaska. Features Alaskan Eskimo, Aleut, Athapascan, Tlingit, Haida and Tsimshian artifacts (period 1888-1930). *Special collections*: Argillite carvings; 400 Eskimo dance masks. Programs: Interpretation & education for groups; artist demonstrator program in summer. *Publications*: Tlingit Women's Root Basket; Tlingit Legends. Library/Archives. Museum Shop. Opened in 1887.

**SOUTHEAST ALASKA
INDIAN CULTURAL CENTER**
106 Metlakatla St. • SITKA, AK 99835
  (907) 747-8061 Fax 747-5938
  Kathie Wasserman, Director
  E-mail: seaicc@ptialaska.net
Description: Displays Native arts produced in the Center over the past 30 years, including wood carving, silverwork, costumes, and robes. *Activities*: Audiovisual programs and workshops; Provides demonstrations of traditional Tlingit art such as woodcarving, costume design, and metalworking that are representative of the Tlingit people and Southeast Alaska. Opened in 1967.

SITKA NATIONAL HISTORICAL PARK
103 Monastery St. • SITKA, AK 99835
  (907) 747-6281
  Michele M. Hellickson, Supt.
  Sue Thorsen, Curator
Description: A collection of more than 4,000 artifacts; totem poles and Chilkat Robes; traditional native arts such as woodcarving, costume design, and metalworking. *Publication*: Carved History: A Guide to the Totem Poles of Sitka National Historical Park. Library.

TATITLEK MUSEUM & CULTURAL CENTER
P.O. Box 171 • TATITLEK, AK 99677
  (907) 325-2311 Fax 325-2298
Opened in 1983.

TRIBAL HOUSE OF THE BEAR
P.O. Box 868 • WRANGELL, AK 99929
  (907) 847-3841 Fax 847-2982
  Nora Black-Rinehart, Director
  Margaret Sturtevant, Curator
Description: Located on Shakes Island, this Indian Museum is housed in Tribal House with exhibits of costumes, Tlingit totem poles, ancient wood carving. *Publication*: Guide to Shakes Island. Opened in1938.

WRANGELL MUSEUM
Box 1050 • WRANGELL, AK 99929
  (907) 874-3770
  Pat Green, Director/Curator
Description: Displays Tlingit totem poles and artifacts; photo collection. *Publication*: The History of Chief Shakes and His Clan; newsletter.

ARIZONA

MONTEZUMA CASTLE NATIONAL MONUMENT
P.O. Box 219 • CAMP VERDE, AZ 86322
  (520) 567-3322
  Glen E. Henderson, Supt.
Description: Prehistoric Pueblo Indian ruins. *Museum*: Indian artifacts obtained from the Monument excavations. Library.

YAVAPAI-APACHE VISITOR ACTIVITY CENTER
P.O. Box 219 • CAMP VERDE, AZ 86322
  (520) 567-5276
Description: Exhibits depict historic and contemporary Indian lifestyles. *Programs*: A slide presentation of area's prhistoric Indian cultures and a film on the Yavapai-Apache tribe.

CANYON DE CHELLY NATIONAL MONUMENT
P.O. Box 588 • CHINLE, AZ 86503
  (520) 674-5518 Fax 674-5507
  Anna Marie Fender, Supt.
  Tara Travis, Historian/Curator
  E-Mail: tara_travis@nps.gov
  Web site: http://www.nps.cach
Description: One of the largest archaeological preserves in North America (A National Historic Landmark) with over 2,500 sites within the 83,00 acres. The area is still inhabited by members of the Navajo Nation. Exhibits concentrates on the occupational sequence of American Indians at Canyon de Chelly National Monument: Archaic, Basketmaker, Anasazi, Puebloan, and Navajo culture. Displays Anasazi and Navajo Indian artifacts from the area. *Programs*: Navajo Guides are available to provide tours for school and tour groups. Publication: Park brochure available. Library. Bookstore. Opened in 1931.

TUZIGOOT NATIONAL MONUMENT
P.O. Box 68 • CLARKDALE, AZ 86324
(520) 634-5564 Glen E. Henderson, Supt.
Description: Remnants of prehistoric town built by the Sinagua Indians who farmed Arizona's Verde Valley between 1125-1400 A.D. Museum: Exhibits artifacts found during excavations. Library.

CASA GRANDE RUINS NATIONAL MONUMENT
1100 N. Ruins Dr. • COOLIDGE, AZ 85228
(520) 723-3172 Fax 723-7209
Sam R. Henderson, Supt.
Museum: Located on the Hohokam village site of 500-1450 A.D.; contains pre-Columbian Pueblo and Hohokam Indian artifacts; ethnological material of the Pima and Papago Indians—basketry and pottery. A National Historic Landmark. Library.

THE AMERIND FOUNDATION, INC.
P.O. Box 400 • DRAGOON 85609
(520) 586-3666 Fax 586-4679
E-mail: amerind@amerind.org
Web site: www.amerind.org
Dr. John A. Ware, Director
Archaeology and Ethnology Museum: Maintains collections of North American and some Central and South American ethnological and archaeological materials; slides and photos; manusacripts; field notes. *Special programs*: Advanced seminars, visiting scholars. Museum shop. Art Gallery. Library. *Publications*: Archaeology & New World Studies Series. Opened in 1937.

MUSEUM OF NORTHERN ARIZONA
3101 N. Fort Valley Rd. • FLAGSTAFF 86001
(520) 774-5211 Fax 779-1527
Michael J. Fox, President
David R. Wilcox, Curator
Description: Exhibits the arts and artifacts of the Indians of Northern Arizona, with specific reference to the Hopi and Navajo. Annual art show. Book store. *Publication*: Plateau, quarterly journal; bimonthly newsletter; Archaeological Research Papers; bulletins. Library.

WALNUT CANYON NATIONAL MONUMENT
Walnut Canyon Rd. • FLAGSTAFF 86004
(520) 526-3367 Sam Henderson, Supt.
Description: Located on the site of approximately 400 prehistoric Indian ruins of the Sinagua Indians dating back to 1100-1270 A.D. Displays artifacts excavated from the site. Library.

**WUPATKI & SUNSET CRATER
NATIONAL MONUMENT**
HC 33, Box 444A • FLAGSTAFF, AZ 86001
(520) 527-7152 Fax 556-7154
Henry L. Jones, Supt.; Anna Fender, Chief Ranger
Description: Exhibits four sets of ruins: Lomaki, Nalakihu-Citadel, Wuwoki, and Wupatki. Displays artifacts excavated from the ruins. Library.

**WHITE MOUNTAIN APACHE CULTURAL CENTER
& MUSEUM**
P.O. Box 507 • FORT APACHE, AZ 85926
(928) 338-4625 Fax 338-1716
Karl A. Hoerig, PHD, Director
E-mail: fortapachemuseum@hotmail.com
Website: www.wmat.nsn.us
Description: Art, archives, and material culture of the White Mountain Apache Tribe and Fort Apache Historic Park. *Programs*: Arts & crafts demonstrations; guided tours, Fort Apache Heritage Reunion each May. Library. Originally opened in 1969...new facility opened in June 1997.

**FORT McDOWELL MOHAVE-APACHE
CULTURAL CENTER**
Fort McDowell Indian Community
P.O. Box 1779 • FOUNTAIN HILLS, AZ 85269
(602) 837-5121 Fax 837-4896
Louis Hood, Director
Opened in 1998.

**HUBBELL TRADING POST
NATIONAL HISTORIC SITE**
P.O. Box 150 • GANADO, AZ 86505
(520) 755-3475
Charles D. Wyatt, Supt.; Shirley Harding, Curator
Description: The oldest continually operating Indian trading post (1878) maintains artifacts related to Lorenzo Hubbell - his historic 1902 home and furnishings are part of the collection. Extensive collections of Native American and Southwest art on display. *Special programs*: Navajo rug weaving and silversmithing demonstrations; tours; buying and selling Navajo, Hopi, Pueblo, Zuni and other tribal crafts. Library. Opened in 1967.

GILA COUNTY HISTORICAL MUSEUM
Box 2891, 1330 N. Broad St.
GLOBE, AZ 85502 (520) 425-7385
Wilbur A. Haak, Director
Description: Maintains prehistoric Indian artifacts, Apache basket collection and photographs (1125-1400 A.D.) Library. Opened in 1972.

TUSAYAN RUIN & MUSEUM
Grand Canyon National Park
P.O. Box 129
GRAND CANYON, AZ 86023
(520) 638-2305
Robert S. Chandler, Supt.
Carolyn Richard, Curator
Description: Exhibits artifacts from the Tusayan prehistoric ruins; from Grand Canyon area Native American cultures...over 200,000 objects in six areas: archaeology, history, geology, ethnography, biology and paleontology. *Programs*: Guided tours. Library. A National Historic Landmark. Established 1919. Museum erected 1931.

MOHAVE MUSEUM OF HISTORY & ARTS
400 W. Beale St. • KINGMAN, AZ 86401
(520) 753-3195 Robert R. Yost, Director
Karin Goudy, Photographs
Mona Cochran, Library & Archives
Description: The Walapai Room: Houses a life size Indian wickieup and figures, Hopi kachinas; also Hualapai, Mohave basketry and pottery. Mohave Miniature: A miniature rendition of a typical Mohave Indian Village. *Publication*: The History of Mohave County to 1912; monthly newsletter, Mohave Epic. Research Library. Opened in 1960.

AK CHIN INDIAN HIM-DAK MUSEUM/ARCHIVES
42507 W. Peters & Nall Rd.
MARICOPA, AZ 85239
(520) 568-9480 Fax 568-9557
Elaine F. Peters, Director
Description: Maintains 8,000 square feet of Ak-Chin artifacts - over 700 boxes of artifacts on exhibit and storage. *Archives*: Ak-Chin Tribal Records from early 1900's to present. *Special program*: Language programs. *Publication*: Tribal newsletter. Library. Opened in 1991.

COLORADO RIVER INDIAN TRIBES MUSEUM
Route 1, Box 23-B • PARKER, AZ 85344
(520) 669-1335 Fax 669-5675
Betty L. Cornelius, Executive Director
Description: Indian Museum displaying Mohave, Chemehuevi, Navajo and Hopi artifacts, including pottery, baskets, silver, wool rugs, fine arts, Kachinas, beadwork; also prehistoric Mogollon, Anasazi, Hohokam and Patayan collections. *Special collections/ exhibits*: Chemehuevi Basket Collection; Mohave Pottery; historical information; Old Presbyterian Indian Church; Mohave and Chemehuevi Archives. Library. Opened in 1966.

HUALAPAI TRIBAL MUSEUM
P.O. Box 179
PEACH SPRINGS, AZ 86434

SAN CARLOS APACHE CULTURAL CENTER
P.O. Box 760 • PERIDOT, AZ 85542
(520) 475-2894 (Phone & Fax)
Herb Stevens, Director
Opened in 1995.

THE HEARD MUSEUM
2301 N. Central Ave. • PHOENIX 85004
(602) 252-8840 Fax 252-9757
Richard Silverman, President
Frank H. Goodyear, Jr., Director
Diana Pardue, Curator of Collections
Joe Baker, Curator of Fine Arts
Gloria Lomahaftewa, Assistant to the Director
for Native American Relations
Mario Nick Klimiades, Library & Archives Director
Website: www.heard.org
Description: Living museum dedicated to Native art and cultures exhibiting works by American Indians. Paintings, prints, sculpture, and the finest in contemporary craft arts are regularly on exhibit, as well as an extensive exhibit of historic materials from the Southwest. Southwestern archaeological and ethnological collection of more than 32,000 works of traditional and contemporary Native arts and crafts. Includes artifacts from North American Indian tribes, as well as native cultures of South America, Asia, and Africa. The Museum staff has developed social studies instructional materials. *Special collections*: Hopi Kachina dolls, and Navajo rugs and blankets. *Special programs*: Guided tours; lectures; workshops; annual Indian Fair and Market; Speakers Bureau; films; traveling exhibitions. Publication: EarthSong, Heard Museum Journal; Museum membership newsletter; variety of catalogues accompanying exhibitions. Library & Archives. Opened in 1929.

**PUEBLO GRANDE MUSEUM
& ARCHAELOGICAL PARK**
4619 E. Washington St.
PHOENIX, AZ 85034
(602) 495-0901 Fax 495-5645
Roger W. Lidman, Director
Glena Cain & Holly Young, Curators
E-mail: prlpgstf@phoenix.gov
Web site: www.pueblogrande.com
Description: Archaeological site museum containing exhibits of prehistoric Hohokam cultural material, circa A.D. 500 to A.D. 1450. Ethnographic material from the Indians of the Greater Southwest. *Special programs*: Annual Indian market in early December; how-to workshops taught by Native-Americans. *Publications*: Pueblo Grande Museum Anthropology Papers; museum brochures and catalogs. Library. Opened in 1929.

SMOKI MUSEUM, INC.
147 N. Arizona Ave.
P.O. Box 10224 • PRESCOTT, AZ 86304
(928) 445-1230
John Tannous, Director
E-mail: info@smokimuseum.org
Website: www.smokimuseum.org
Description: Indian Museum featuring archaeological and ethnological artifacts of Southwest and Plains Indians; Kate T. Cory paintings and photographs; Edward S. Curtis prints; artifacts of the Tuzigoot, King and Fitzmaurice ruins. Library. Gift Shop. Opened in 1935 and Incorporated in 1991.

TONTO NATIONAL MONUMENT
HC 02 Box 4602 • ROOSEVELT, AZ 85545
(520) 467-2241 Fax 467-2225
Brad Traver, Superintendent
Description: Prehistoric Salado Cliff Dwellings in Sonoran Desert setting. *Museum*: Collection of prehistoric Salado artifacts—pottery, cloth, tools, etc. *Special programs*: Upper Cliff Dwelling tours on weekends from November thru April. Library.

GILA RIVER INDIAN CENTER & MUSEUM
P.O. Box 457 • SACATON, AZ 85247
(602) 963-3981 Fax (520) 315-3968
Jon Long, Director
Description: Contains a park with reconstructed Indian villages that depict more than 2,000 years of Native American life in the Gila River Basin. The Hohokum, Papago, and Apache cultures are represented. A museum and craft center adjoin the park. Opened in 1970.

HOO-HOOGAM KI MUSEUM
Salt River Pima-Maricopa Cultural Center
10005 E. Osborn
SCOTTSDALE, AZ 85256
(602) 850-8190 Fax 850-8961
Opened in 1987.

HOPI CULTURAL CENTER MUSEUM
P.O. Box 7 • SECOND MESA, AZ 86043
(520) 734-6650 Anna Siles, Director
Description: Dedicated to the maintenance and preservation of Hopi traditions and to the presentation of aspects of these traditions to our non-Hopi visitors.

COCOPAH MUSEUM
County Rd. 15 & G Ave.
SOMERTON, AZ 85350
 (520) 627-1992 Fax 627-2280
 Lisa Wanstall, Director
Opened in 1994.

HAVASUPAI TRIBAL MUSEUM
P.O. Box 10 • SUPAI, AZ 86435
 (520) 448-2731 EXT. 520
 Matthew Putesoy, Director
Opened in 1971.

**EASTERN ARIZONA COLLEGE
MUSEUM OF ANTHROPOLOGY**
626 Church St. • THATCHER, AZ 85552
 (520) 428-1133 Betty Graham Lee, Director
Description: Displays artifacts from Mogollon, Anasazi
and Hohokam material culture; ethnographics in
Apache, Navajo and Hopi. Library.

NAVAJO NATIONAL MONUMENT
HC 71 Box 3 • TONALEA , AZ 86044-9704
 (520) 672-2366 Fax 672-2345
 Russ Bodnar, Supt.
Description: Exhibits materials of the Kayenta, Anasazi
and Navajo cultures. On the site of three prehistoric
Cliff Villages. Library. Arts and crafts for sale.

THE NED A. HATATCHLI CENTER MUSEUM
Dine College
P.O. Box 37 • TSAILE, AZ 86556
 (520) 724-3311 Fax 724-3349
 Harry Walters, Director
Opened in 1976.

THE ARIZONA STATE MUSEUM
Box 210026, University of Arizona
TUCSON, AZ 85721-0026
 (520) 621-6281 Fax 626-6761
 Hartman H. Lomawaima, Director
 E-mail: lomawaima@email.arizona.edu
 Web site: www.statemuseum.arizona.edu
Description: Collections include artifacts related to the
cultural history of the Greater Southwest. Prehistoric
materials include Hohokam and Mogollon decorated
ceramic bowls, human figurines of clay and stone,
carved shell jewelry, and turquoise beads. Also has
extensive collections of objects from contemporary
Indian cultures of Arizona and Mexico. Historic tools,
clothing, and other utensils help Indian and non-Indian scholars understand past lifestyles. *Programs*:
"Documentary Relations of the Southwest," archival
research project focusing on the history of Spanish
contact with Native peoples of the Greater Southwest;
annual Southwest Indian Art Fair in late February.
Publications: Paths of Life," a companion piece to a
new permanent exhibit and presents the origins, histories and contemporary lives of Native people of the
Southwest; Archaeological series reports distributed
by University of Arizona Press. Library. Opened in
1893.

MISSION SAN XAVIER DEL BAC
1950 W. San Xavier Rd. • TUCSON, AZ 85746
 (520) 294-2624 • Father Michael Dallmeier, Rector
Description: Historic building and site of the Spanish-
Colonial Indian Mission of 1783. Library.

COCHISE VISITOR CENTER & MUSEUM
c/o Willcox Chamber of Commerce
1500 N. Circle I Rd. • WILLCOX, AZ 85643
 (520) 384-2272
Description: Collections include Apache
Indian artifacts.

NAVAJO NATION MUSEUM
P.O. Box 9000
WINDOW ROCK, AZ 86515
 (520) 871-6673 Fax 871-7886
 Russell P. Hartman, Director/Curator
Description: Exhibits approximately 4,500 objects relating to the history and culture of the Navajo Indians
and the prehistory and natural history of the Four-Cor-
ners area. Photo archive of about 35,000 negatives
and prints, mostly from 1930-1960, relating to the
Navajos. *Special programs*: Art exhibits/sales; Navajo
information service; school and group tours. Publications. Opened in 1961.

QUECHAN TRIBAL MUSEUM
P.O. Box 1899
YUMA, AZ 85366
 (760) 572-0661 Fax 572-2102
 Pauline P. Jose, Director
Description: Houses the Spanish Era, the Military, and
the Quechan history. Artifacts among others. *Special
activities*: Celebrates the yearly Yuma Crossing day
commemorating the first crossing of the Colorado River
from Arizona side to California. Opened in 1969.

ARKANSAS

THE UNIVERSITY MUSEUM
University of Arkansas
Biomass Research Center 125
FAYETTEVILLE, AR 72701
 (479) 575-3456 Fax 575-7464
 Mary Suter, Curator of Collections
Description: Native Arkansas archaeology collections;
exhibits Mimbres pottery, Plains Indian artifacts, eth-
nographic artifacts, and South American artifacts. Es-
tablished in 1873.

HOT SPRINGS NATIONAL PARK
P.O. Box 1860
HOT SPRINGS, AR 71901
Description: Interpretive programs about the life of the
Caddo Indians and their predecessors and explains
the use of the thermal springs by the Indians. *Museum*:
Exhibits Indian artifacts. *Publications*: Indians of
Tonico; The Valley of the Vapors.

MUSEUM OF SCIENCE AND HISTORY
MacArthur Park
LITTLE ROCK, AR 72202
Description: Exhibits include material relating to Ar-
kansas Mound Builders, American Plains Indians, and
Southwestern Indians. Library.

KA-DO—HA INDIAN VILLAGE
P.O. Box 669
MURFREESBORO, AR 71958
 (870) 285-3736
 Sam Johnson, Director
 E-mail: caddotc@alltel.net;
 Website: www.caddotc.com
Description: Prehistoric Caddo Indian (Mound Build-
ers) grounds with museum housing artifacts from the
excavation with the site. Publications for sale. Library.

**TOLTEC MOUNDS
ARCHAEOLOGICAL STATE PARK**
490 Toltec Mounds Rd.
SCOTT, AR 72142
 (501) 961-9442 Fax 961-9221
 E-mail: toltecmounds@arkansas.com
 Randall Watts, Supt.
 Robin Gabe, Susan Nichols, Park Interpreters
Description: Situated in the modern farmlands of the
Arkansas River Valley, 16 miles southeast of North
Little Rock, off US Hwy. 165, are the remains of a large
group of ancient Indian earthworks known as Toltec
Mounds. Maintains a museum which displays a col-
lection of prehistoric artifacts of the Plum Bayou In-
dian culture. Designated a National Historic Landmark
in 1978, Toltec contained 16 mounds a century ago.
Today, several mounds and a remnant of the embank-
ment are visible. *Activities*: Archaeological research
and interpretive programs; tours; workshops. *Publication*: "Toltec Mounds and Plum Bayou Culture: Mound
D Excavations," Surveyors of the Ancient Mississippi
Valley. Opened in 1975.

ARKANSAS STATE UNIVERSITY MUSEUM
P.O. Box 490
STATE UNIVERSITY, AR 72467
 (501) 972-2074 Fax 972-2793
 Charlott A. Jones, PhD, Director
 E-Mail: squalls@choctaw.astate.edu
Description: Displays Native-American artifacts includ-
ing Arkansas—Quapaw, Caddo, Osage, Cherokee,
Choctaw and Chickasaw; Southwestern— Navajo,
Hopi, Pueblo and Apache; and an exhibit of Indian
baskets and Indian dolls. Newsletter. Library.

CALIFORNIA

MALKI MUSEUM, INC.
11-795 Fields Rd., Morongo Indian Reservation
P.O. Box 578 • BANNING, CA 92220
 (909) 849-7289
 Katherine Siva Saubel, President
 Matt Pablo, Director/Curator
Description: Adobe museum building housing Southern California Indian artifacts of the Cahuilla, Serrano,
Luiseno, and other tribal groups; large collection of
Indian basketry. *Programs*: College scholarship program for Southern California Indian students; research
on California Indians; Annual Malki Museum fiesta on
Sunday of Labor Day weekend. *Publications*: Journal
of California & Great Basin Anthropology, twice annually; brochures on the Cahuilla, Serrano, Chemehuevi
and Chumash; Malki Museum Press publishes books
on the California Indians. Library. Opened in 1964.

PHOEBE HEARST MUSEUM OF ANTHROPOLOGY
103 Kroeber Hall, University of California
BERKELEY, CA 94720
 (510) 642-3682 FAX 642-6271
 E-mail: pahmu@montu.berkeley.edu
 Web site: www.qal.berkeley.edu/~hearst
 James J. Deetz, Curator
Description: Research and study collections include
California archaeological and ethnographical items,
majority of which are basketry items representing prac-
tically every tribe in California; also Eskimo and Aleut
material, and Plains Indian artifacts; large collections
of baskets and carvings from Northwest Coast tribes,
especially Haida, Tlingit and Tsimshean. Also an extensive collection of recorded materials. *Special programs*: Montly lectures, demonstrations, and panel
discussions. Library. Publications.

**OWENS VALLEY PAIUTE-SHOSHONE
INDIAN CULTURAL CENTER MUSEUM**
P.O. Box 1281 • BISHOP, CA 93514
 (619) 873-4478
 Dorothy Stewart & Pat Howard, Directors
Opened in 1986.

CARL NELSON GORMAN MUSEUM
2401 Hart Hall, Native American Studies
University of California • DAVIS, CA 95616
 (916) 752-6567
 George Longfish, Director; Theresa Horlan, Curator
Description: Maintains a permanent collection of California basketry, Navajo weavings, and contemporary
American Indian art, and shows works by Indian and
Chicano artists as well as staff and students. *Special
program*: Changing exhibitions program - 4 each year
with speciific focus on American Indian issues. *Publications*: Artist monographs for each exhibition with interviews with the artists.

**CABOT'S OLD INDIAN PUEBLO MUSEUM
CALIFORNIA INDIAN MONUMENT**
67-616 E. Desert View Ave.
DESERT HOT SPRINGS, CA 92240
 (619) 329-7610 Fax 329-1956
 Colbert H. Eyraud, President & Chief Curator
Description: A four story Hopi Indian style Pueblo built
by Cabot Yerxa as a tribute to the Indian cultures; Peter
Toth sculpture—monument 43' high, 20 tons from a
Sequoia redwood; Pueblo Art Gallery. *Exhibits*: Inuit
collection; and Sioux collection from the Battle of the
Little Big Horn; Chumash and Pueblo culture collections. *Special programs*: Slide and lecture presentations to schools and organizations; sculpting for the
handicapped; single artist exhibitions; arts interview
radio show. *Publication*: Musings From the Pueblo.
Trading Post. Library. Opened in 1968.

HOOPA TRIBAL MUSEUM
P.O. Box 1348 • HOOPA, CA 95546
 (916) 625-4110
 David E. Hostler, Curator
Description: A living museum which maintains a collection of baskets from the Hupa, Yurok and Karuk
tribes; also jewelry, artifacts, and Indian dance regalia
with feathers used in the dances. Special programs:
Ceremonial displays; cultural shows and village tours.
Publications: Museum brochures; Hoopa history books
and pamphlets. Opened in 1974.

EASTERN CALIFORNIA MUSEUM
155 N. Grant St., Box 206
INDEPENDENCE, CA 93526
(760) 878-0258; William H. Michael, Director
E-mail: ecmuseum@qnet.com
Description: Collections of Inyo County Paiute, Shoshone, Washoe and Yokut Indian artifacts, including basketry, beadwork and lithics. *Publication*: Quarterly newsletter; book - Mountains to Desert: Selected Inyo Readings. Library. Opened in 1928.

CABAZON CULTURAL MUSEUM
Cabazon Band of Mission Indians
84-245 Indio Springs Dr. • INDIO, CA 92203
(619) 342-2593 Fax 347-7880
John James, Tribal Chairperson
Judy Stapp, Cultural Programs Manager
Description: Collections of historical and local exhibits; memorial to the genocide of Indian people in North and South America. Future exhibits will depict economic development of local tribes. *Programs*: Two annual pow-wows, Thanksgiving weekend and the last weekend in March. *Publication*: "The Cabazon Circle" tribal newsletter. Opened in 1993.

END OF THE TRAIL MUSEUM/TREES OF MYSTERY
15500 Hwy. 101 N. • KLAMATH, CA 95548
(707) 482-2251 Fax 482-2005
Website: www.treesofmystery.net
John Thompson, General Manager
(Trees of Mystery)
Marylee Smith, Curator
Description: Private museum permanently exhibiting the collection of Marylee Smith (over 2,000 objects.) Five rooms of continent-wide Indian baskets, clothing, tools, kachinas, Navajo rugs, Northwest Coast carvings, pottery, masks. *Special collection*: extensive collection of baby baskets and cradles from entire North American Continent; extensive collection of original Edward Curtis photographs. Research library. Opened in 1983.

BARONA CULTURAL CENTER & MUSEUM
1095 Barona Rd. • LAKESIDE, CA 92040
(619) 443-7003 ext. 2 Fax 443-0173
Cheryl M. Hinton, Director/Curator
E-mail: chinton@barona.org
Website: www.baronatribe.com/history.html
Description: Maintains artifacts of southern California Indian tribes focusing on 'Ipay/Kumayaay prehistory; pottery, baskets, bone, shell and historic artifacts; current Indian art. *Special programs*: Barona senior events; NMAI workshops; Ancient Spirits Speak classes; Southern California Indian Seminar for Educators; Outreach programs. Library. *Publications*: Quarterly newsletter; museum publication series. Opened in 2001.

THE LOMPOC MUSEUM
200 South H St. • LOMPOC, CA 93436
(805) 736-3888
Lisa A. Renken, PhD, Director, Curator of Anthropology
Angie Pasquini, Administrative Assistant
Description: Holds a large collection of archaeological and ethnographic specimens, mostly from northern Santa Barbara County. Other areas include northern California and Oregon. *Special Collection*: Clarence Ruth Collection: Chumash and western Alaskan Indian artifacts. *Publication*: Galleries, bi-monthly newsletter. Library. Opened in 1969.

AUTRY NATIONAL CENTER
MUSEUM OF THE AMERICAN WEST
4700 Western Heritage Way
LOS ANGELES 90027
(213) 667-2000 Fax 660-5721
Alicia Gonzalez, Director
E-Mail: agonzalez@autrynationalcenter.org
Description: Art, artifact and research collections relating to trans-Mississippi Western history and culture. *Programs*: Educational (children's workshops); docent tours, lectures, symposia. Research Center. *Publication*: "Spur" membership newsletter. Opened in 1988.

NATURAL HISTORY MUSEUM OF LOS ANGELES
900 Exposition Blvd.
LOS ANGELES, CA 90007
(213) 744-3414

AUTRY NATIONAL CENTER
SOUTHWEST MUSEUM
OF THE AMERICAN INDIAN
234 Museum Dr. • LOS ANGELES, CA 90065
(323) 221-2164 Fax 224-8223
E-mail: dking@annex.com
Web site: www.southwestmuseum.org
E-mail: dking@autrynationalcenter.org
Dr. Duane H. King, Executive Director
Dr. Kathleen Whitaker, Chief Curator
Description: Collections focus on Native peoples of the Americas, mostly North America west of the Mississippi, including 13,400 baskets, 11,000 ceramics, 2,000 textiles, 700 kachinas, 800 pieces of Southwest jewelry; archaeological items, pertaining to the American Indian, Eskimo, and Aleut from prehistoric, historic and modern times; 150,000 photographs; archival materials; paintings, and prints. *Special collections*: Plains, California, Southwest, and Northwest Indians. *Special program*: Intertribal Marketplace (over 120 artisans) first weekend in November; Mercado! (Mexican and Central American marketplace) each Spring. *Publications*: The Masterkey, quarterly journal; "Common Threads: Navajo and Pueblo Textiles in the Southwest Museum" and "Southwest Textiles: Weavings of the Navajo and Pueblo." Braun Research Library. Museum shop. Opened in 1907.

MARIPOSA MUSEUM & HISTORY CENTER, INC.
P.O. Box 606 • MARIPOSA, CA 95338
(209) 966-2924 Muriel Powers, Curator
Description: Located on the museum grounds is an Indian Village and its bark houses and sweat house, constructed by local Indians. *Publication*: Quarterly newsletter. Library.

MONTEREY STATE HISTORICAL PARK
20 Custom House Plaza
MONTEREY, CA 93940
(408) 649-2836
Mary Wright, Director; Kris Quist, Curator
Description: Holman Exhibit of American Indian Artifacts. Primarily California and Western North America basketry and weavings.

SIERRA MONO MUSEUM
P.O. Box 275 • NORTH FORK 93643
(209) 877-2115 Anna Dandy, Director
Description: Maintains a collection of baskets and art work by the Mono Indian People. Other tribes are also represented with their baskets and beadwork.

MARIN MIWOK MUSEUM
P.O. Box 864, 2200 Novato Blvd.
NOVATO, CA 94947 (415) 897-4064
Mary Hilderman Smith, Executive Director
Dawn Carlson, Chairperson
Description: Collections oriented to Native-American cultures of western North America, with particular emphasis on Indian cultures of California, especially local Coast Miwok people of Marin and southern Sonoma Counties. The Kettenhofen Collection of Edward Curtis Photogravures. Includes archival materials from Alaska. *Special program*: Educational classes, lectures, and instruction. *Publication*: Surface Scatter, quarterly newsletter. Library. Opened in 1973.

THE OAKLAND MUSEUM
1000 Oak St. • OAKLAND, CA 94607
(510) 834-2413
Description: Exhibits present native Californians in pre-contact times.

WILL ROGERS STATE HISTORIC PARK
1501 Will Rogers State Park Rd.
PACIFIC PALISADES, CA 90272
(310) 454-8212 Fax 459-2031
Nancy Mendez, Museum Curator
Description: Ranch belonged to the American humorist, Will Rogers (of Cherokee Indian descent), containing original buildings and furnishings; Indian artifacts, rugs and blankets. *Publication*: Monthly newsletter. Library. Opened in 1944.

CUPA CULTURAL CENTER
P.O. Box 445 • PALA, CA 92059
(760) 742-1590 Fax 742-4543
Leroy Miranda, Director
Description: Located on the Pala Indian Reservation

in San Diego County, the Cultural Center maintains a museum exhibitng Cupeno artifacts and historic pictures; also other Native American artifacts; historical information about the removal of Cupa Indians. Special programs: Teaching of traditional dancing, songs and Cupeno language; annual event, "Cupa Days" in remembrance of the removal of Cupenos from Warners Hot Springs in 1903, is held the first weekend in May.

MUSEUM OF MISSION SAN ANTONIO DE PALA
P.O. Box 70 • PALA, CA 92059
(619) 742-3317
Description: Historic Mission Building (Pala Indians.) Exhibits Indian artifacts—basketry, stone carvings, pottery and jewelry. *Activities*: Dance festivals.

AGUA CALIENTE CULTURAL MUSEUM
219 S. Palm Canyon Dr.
PALM SPRINGS, CA 92262
(760) 323-0151 Fax 320-0350
Dr. Michael Hammond, Executive Director
Ginger Ridgway, Curator/Director
Website: www.accmuseum.org
E-mail: gridgway@accmuseum.org
Description: 50-acre museum complex adjacent to the Indian Canyons includes a 98,000 sq. ft. museum building which includes galleries and cultural facilties for artifacts and archives, classrooms and meeting rooms; research library and 150-seat theatre. *Programs*: Graves Protection & Repatriation (www.cahuilla repatriation.org). *Activities*: Camelot Theaters (760) 325-6565 - Annual Palm Springs Native American Film Festival (www.nativefilmfest.org), part of the annual cultural weekend in March. Reference Library. Opened 1991.

PALM SPRINGS DESERT MUSEUM
101 Museum Dr. • PALM SPRINGS, CA 92262
(760) 325-7168 Fax 327-5069
Dr. Janice Lyle, Director
E-Mail: psmuseum@aol.com
Description: Western American and Native American Art - These galleries will include selections from the Museum's permanent collection of traditional and contemporary artworks depicting the American West. A combination of paintings, sculpture and Native American objects will show the diversity of Western American art over the past 100 years. Opened in 1938.

CHAW SE REGIONAL MUSEUM
P.O. Box 1458 • PINE GROVE, CA 95665
(209) 296-7488
Located at 144881 Pine Grove Volcano Rd.
Opened in 1978.

SAN BERNARDINO COUNTY MUSEUM
2024 Orange Tree Lane • REDLANDS, CA 92374
(714) 798-8570 Dr. Allan Griesemer, Director
Carol Rector, Curator of Anthropology
Description: Displays various artifacts and lithic tools of Indian occupation of San Bernardino County; history and artifacts of local bands—Serrano, Cahuilla, Mojave, Chemehuevi, and others are being preserved. *Publication*: Bi-monthly newsletter; quarterly journal. Library. Opened in 1956.

SHERMAN INDIAN MUSEUM
9010 Magnolia Ave. • RIVERSIDE, CA 92503
(909) 275-6719 Fax 276-6332
Lorene Sisquoc, Director
Opened in 1970.

CALIFORNIA STATE INDIAN MUSEUM
2618 K St. • SACRAMENTO, CA 95816
(916) 324-0971 Fax 322-5231
Joann Helmich, Lead Ranger
Website: www.gov.state.parks
Description: Collections pertain to the cultures of the Indians of California. Pomo feather baskets; artifacts from Ishi; north coast redwood dugout. Emphasis is on lifestyle, spiritual and the continuing culture. *Special programs*: Summer programs for the 4th-6th grades; sell books pertaining to California Indians and Indian handcrafted items. Opened in 1940.

ANTHROPOLOGY MUSEUM
University of San Diego
5998 Alcala Park • SAN DIEGO, CA 92110
(619) 260-4525 Fax 260-2260

Description: David W. May Indian Artifacts Collection consists primarily of about 1,650 prehistoric and contemporary objects from the American Southwest.

AMERICAN INDIAN CULTURE CENTER & MUSEUM
Inspiration Point, Balboa Park
2135 Park Blvd. • SAN DIEGO, CA 92101
  (619) 281-5964 Fax 281-1466
  Richard Bugbee, Associate Director
  E-mail: hunwut@aol.com; aiccm@aol.com
Purpose: To interpret the history and culture of American Indian people from ancient times to the present in order to foster public appreciation and understanding, to enhance the preservation, perpetuation, and study of American Inian history and culture, to develop and provide educational resources locally and nationally, and to encourage American Indian participation. *Description*: Features an Inter-tribal exhibit hall, the San Diego County Indians exhibit (Kanap Kwahan) that will focus on the maritime traditions of the Indians of San Diego County; a RezTV station that will be connected to the Tribal Digital Village; advocated for Indigenous California Language workstations; an Art Studio/Gallery where talented Native artists can develop, exhibit, and sell their art work; the Performance Arts Center, a 100-seat community performance, audio-vidual, lecture, and presentation space; a Gift Shop; and Research Library. Opened in 2002.

AMERICAN INDIAN HISTORICAL SOCIETY
1451 Masonic Ave.
SAN FRANCISCO, CA 94117
  Jeanette Henry Costo, Director
Description: Maintains a library and museum of Indian Arts. In the process of establishing the Rupert Costo Hall of American Indians at the University of California.

**SANTA BARBARA MUSEUM
OF NATURAL HISTORY**
2559 Puesta del Sol
SANTA BARBARA, CA 93105
  (805) 682-4711 Fax 569-3170
  John R. Johnson, Curator
Description: 60,000 archaeological specimens from Santa Barabra Channel region of California and 2,500 ethnographic objects from western North America. Includes Chumash linguistic records, Cahuilla Basketry, rock art drawings. Library with special emphasis on the Chumash Indians.

JESSE PETER MUSEUM
1501 Mendocino Ave.
SANTA ROSA, CA 95401
  (707) 527-4479 Fax 524-1861
  Benjamin F. Benson, Director/Curator
  Christine Vasquez, Exhibit Specialist
  E-mail: museum@santarosa.edu
  Website: www.santarosa.edu/museum
Description: Collections of traditional Native-American art, including California basketry, Southwest pottery and basketry; Navajo textiles and jewelry; Plains, Plateau and Great Lakes beadwork; Eskimo and Arctic stone carvings and regalia; Living wall - photographic essay of Native Americans of today from several cultures; Pomo Roundhouse and baskets. Special program: Self-guided tours for elementary, secondary and college classes. *Publications*: Hopitu — A Collection of Kachina Dolls of the Hopi Indians; Straw Into Gold (North American Basketry) by Foley Benson. Small reference library. Opened in 1932.

STANFORD UNIVERSITY MUSEUM OF ART
Lomita Dr. • STANFORD, CA 94305
  (415) 725-0462
  Thomas K. Seligman, Director
  Ruth W. Franklin, Curator
Description: Collection of Native American works, especially basketry of the Yurok, Karuk, and Hupa tribes of California; and a group of Haida argilites. *Publication*: Museum Journal, biennial. The main museum building is closed for repairs due to earthquake damage. Reopened in 1997.

THE HAGGIN MUSEUM
1201 N. Pershing Ave. • STOCKTON, CA 95203
  (209) 462-4116
  Tod Ruhstaller, Director
  Barry J. Ward, Archivist

Description: Fine art and regional history collections, including significant displays on Native Americans of the area. Library. Publications. Opened in 1931.

LAVA BEDS NATIONAL MONUMENT
P.O. Box 867 • TULELAKE, CA 96134
  (916) 667-2282 Gary Hathaway, Curator
Description: Site of the Modoc Indian War (November 1872 to June 1873.) *Museum*: Modoc Indian artifacts; Indian rock art and pictographs on walls of caves.

RINCON TRIBAL EDUCATION CENTER
P.O. Box 1147
VALLEY CENTER, CA 92082

YOSEMITE MUSEUM
P.O. Box 577
YOSEMITE NATIONAL PARK, CA 95389
  (209) 372-0282 David M. Forgang, Curator
  Craig D. Bates, Curator of Ethnography
Description: Collection of over 4,000 Sierra Miwok, Mono Lake Paiute and other ethnographic materials; over 20,000 archaeological specimens. A reconstructed Miwok/Paiute village and museum exhibits depicts the traditional culture of the Miwok and Paiute people of the Yosemite region, from pre-contact times through present day. *Special Programs*: Conducts walks and lectures, classes; demonstrations of native crafts. *Publications*: Various, including "Tradition and Innovation: A Basket History of the Indians of the Yosemite - Mono Lake Area." Library. Opened in 1915.

SISKIYOU COUNTY MUSEUM
910 S. Main St. • YREKA, CA 96097
  (916) 842-3836 Fax 842-3166
  E-mail: hismus@inreach.com
  Michael Hendryx, Director
Description: Contains displays on Indians of Siskiyou County—, Karuk, Shasta, and Modoc. Maintains an extensive basket collection of the Karuk and Shasta tribes. *Special programs*: School program for 3rd graders; interpretive programs; field trips. Library. *Publications*: The Siskiyou Pioneer, 1947-1999; occasional paper series; technical leaflets - "Walking the Medicine Path," and "Plants & the People - Ethnobotany of the Karuk Tribe. Opened 1950.

COLORADO

LUTHER E. BEAN MUSEUM
Adams State College, Richardson Hall
ALAMOSA, CO 81102
  (719) 589-7121 Fax 589-7522
  Rosalie Martinez, Curator
Description: Exhibits Pueblo Indian cultural artifacts, primarily pottery; Navajo weavings. *Programs*: Monthly art shows showcasing local (San Luis Valley) artists - ranging from paintings, pottery and bronze sculptures. Opened in 1984.

SAND CREEK MASSACRE MONUMENT
Hwy. 96 • CHIVINGTON, CO 81031
Description: A monument to the over 500 Cheyenne Indians who were massacred in November 1864 by the U.S. Army led by Major John Chivington.

**THE TAYLOR MUSEUM FOR
SOUTHWESTERN STUDIES**
Colorado Springs Fine Arts Center
30 West Dale St.
COLORADO SPRINGS, CO 80903
  (719) 634-5581 Fax 634-0570
  Cathy L. Wright, Curator & Director
Description: Collections of Native-American arts of the Southwest, Great Plains, Great Basin, and California, including: Navajo textiles and jewelry; Pueblo textiles, baskets and pottery, kachinas, and jewelry. *Special collection*: John Frederick Huckel Collection of Navajo sandpainting reproductions. *Special exhibition*: "Mountain—Family—Spirit: The Arts and Culture of the Ute Indians," the first national exhibition featuring the arts and rich traditions of the Nuche - the Ute people of Colorado and eastern Utah, also identified as the Eastern Ute. The exhibition and accompanying catalog provide an overview of Ute history, culture and art from the prehistoric period through the historic period to the present day. With 140 historical artifacts and over 40

contemporary works including many rare examples of art from major museum and private collections, as well as numerous photographs, the exhibition interprets daily and spiritual aspets of Ute life. *Publications*: Navajo Sandpainting: The Huckel Collection; Arroyo Hondo: The Folk Art of a New Mexican Village; Pottery of the Pueblos of New Mexico, 1700-1940. Library.

**CROW CANYON CENTER FOR
SOUTHWESTERN ARCHAEOLOGY**
23390 County Rd. K
CORTEZ, CO 81321
  (303) 565-8975
  Ian Thompson, Director
Research activities: Archaeological investigation, including excavation and cataloging of artifacts. Specializes in Anasazi Indian culture, excavates sites in the Four Corners area of the southwest U.S. Research expeditions open to the public.

COLORADO HISTORY MUSEUM
Colorado Historical Society
1300 Broadway • DENVER, CO 80203
  (303) 866-3682 Fax 866-5739
  James E. Hartmann, President
Description: Extensive ethnological and photographic collections of Plains and Southwest Indians; source materials on the Indian Wars; materials from the Rosebud Indian Agency, 1885 to 1890; earliest known Cheyenne Dog Soldier ledgerbook. *Publications*: "The Colorado History Journal"; "Colorado Heritage" magazine. Library. Opened in 1879.

DENVER ART MUSEUM
100 W. 14th Ave. Pkwy.
DENVER, CO 80204
  (720) 865-5000 Fax 865-5028
  Website: www.denverartmuseum.org
  Nancy Blomberg, Dept. Head/Curator of Native Arts
  E-mail: nblomberg@denverartmuseum.org
  Roger C. Echo-Hawk, Repatriation Coordinator
Description: Encyclopedic collection of American Indian art from all tribes across the U.S. and Canada from prehistoric times to the present; also, an ethnographic collection of Indian women's costumes, Navajo and Pueblo pottery, Hopi kachina dolls, Blackfoot ceremonial equipment, and wood carvings of the Northwest Coast. *Special programs*: Lectures; programs for childrem; annual Pow-wow; and classes. *Publications*: Membership newsletter; exhibition and collection catalogues. Library. Founded 1893.

DENVER MUSEUM OF NATURAL HISTORY
2001 Colorado Blvd. • DENVER, CO 80205
  (303) 370-6388 Fax 370-6313
  Dr. Robert B. Pickering, Chair/
    Curator of Anthropology
  Joyce I. Herold, Curator of Ethnology
  Ryntha Johnson, Collections Manager
Description: Hall of Prehistoric People of the Americas: Exhibits on early man, and collections of Paleo-Indian specimens. Emphasis includes North American Indian archaeological and ethnographic material. Basketry from around the world. *Special collection*: Crane Collection of American Indian Materials. *Publications*: Proceedings of DMNH (scientific publications); exhibit catalogs; symposia volumes; children's books on natural history subjects. Library. Opened in 1900.

ANASAZI HERITAGE CENTER
27501 Hwy. 184
DOLORES, CO 81323
  (970) 882-4811 Fax 882-7035
  LouAnn Jacobson, Director
Description: Preserved sites of two late Anasazi communities. Museum exhibits of Northern San Juan prehistory; 2.5 million artifacts and archives. Includes Anasazi farming, food preparation, crafts, and trade. Activities: "Hands-on activities: weaving, microscopes, computers. Videos. Traveling exhibits. Library. Opened in 1988.

**HISTORICAL MUSEUM & INSTITUTE
OF WESTERN COLORADO**
4th and Ute
GRAND JUNCTION, CO 81501
Special collections: Ute Indian Collection and Teller Indian School Collection: Basketry, artifacts, manuscripts and photographs of the Ute Indians. Library.

SOUTHERN UTE INDIAN
CULTURAL CENTER & MUSEUM
P.O. Box 737 • IGNACIO, CO 81137
(970) 563-9583 Fax 563-4641
E-mail: sum@frontier.net
Lynn Brittner, Director
Description: Located on the Southern Ute Indian Reservation, 1/4 mile north of Sky Ute Casino on Highway 172. Maintains photo and artifact collections pertaining to Ute and neighboring tribes, historical to contemporary. *Activities*: It sponsors art festivals, Native American dance recitals, hobby workshops, and lectures. Gift Shop. Opened 1972.

KOSHARE INDIAN MUSEUM
P.O. Box 580, 115 W. 18th St.
LA JUNTA, CO 81050
(719) 384-4411 Fax 384-8836
Joe Clay, Director of Programs
Description: Maintains a collection of Native American art and artifacts emphasizing the Plains and Pueblo tribes. Artists range from Taos founders (Denton, Phillips, Couse, Sharp and others) to notables such as Woody Crumbo, T.E. Mails, Joseph Imhof, Bettina Steinke, and Ernesto Zepeda. Pottery by the Martinez and Nampeyo families are featured, as is baskets, beadwork and quillwork. Special programs: Koshare Indian Dncers present a variety of Plains & Pueblo dances biannually. Winter Ceremonials are held in December; Summer shows are held June thru August. *Publication*: Koshare News. Library. Indian arts and crafts for sale.

MANITOU CLIFF DWELLINGS MUSEUM
U.S. Hwy 24, Box 272
MANITOU, CO 80829
(719) 685-5242
Description: De[icts the lives and architectural achievements of the Indians of the Southwest during the Great Pueblo Period, 1100-1300 A.D.

MESA VERDE NATIONAL PARK MUSEUM
MESA VERDE, CO 81330
(303) 529-4475 Fax 529-4465
Donald C. Fiero, Chief of Interpretation
Description: A prehistoric Pueblo Indian community — pithouses, cliff dwellings, etc. Museum preserves Anasazi archaeological remains dating from 500-1330 A.D. Library.

UTE INDIAN MUSEUM
OURAY MEMORIAL PARK
17253 Chipeta Dr.
MONTROSE, CO 81402
(970) 249-3098 Fax 252-8741
C.J. Brafford, Director
E-mail: cj.brafford@state.co.us
Description: Indian History Museum located on the site of Chief Ouray's 400 acre farm. Depicts the history of the Utes through use of dioramas and objects which the Utes made and used; photographs and maps; portraits of some Ute leaders. *Activities*: Exhibits artifacts; maintains botanical gardens of plants used by the Native American Culture; hanging exhibit gallery; lectures; and American Indian Heritage Day, a cultural fair in November. *Publication*: Colorado History News. Opened in 1956.

UTE MOUNTAIN TRIBAL PARK & MUSEUM
P.O. Box 109 • TOWAOC, CO 81334
(970) 565-9653 Fax 564-5317
Veronica Cuthair, Director
E-mail: utepark@fone.net
Description: Collection contains Anasazi artifacts and rare Ute photographs. *Special program*: Tours of the Tribal Park. *Publication*: The Other Mesa Verde, by Gene Atkins, about the Tribal Park. Opened in 1972.

CONNECTICUT

CONNECTICUT HISTORICAL SOCIETY MUSEUM
1 Elizabeth St. • HARTFORD, CT 06105
(203) 236-5621
Christopher P. Bickford, Exec. Director
Elizabeth Pratt Fox, Curator
Description: Collections of more than 100,000 artifacts, including Native American baskets, tools, and lithic materials. *Special collection*: Bates Collection of Native American baskets, tools, and implements. Library. *Publications*: Notes & News, newsletter; Bulletin, quarterly scholarly journal; numerous books relating to Connecticut. Opened in 1825.

MUSEUM OF CONNECTICUT HISTORY
Connecticut State Library
231 Capitol Ave.
HARTFORD, CT 06115
Special collection: George Mitchelson Collection: Contains pottery, tools, arrowheads, and other artifacts of Native-American culture of Connecticut. Library.

MASHANTUCKET PEQUOT MUSEUM
& CULTURAL RESEARCH CENTER
110 Pequot Trail, P.O. Box 3180
MASHANTUCKET, CT 06338-3180
(800) 411-9671
(860) 396-6800 Fax 396-7005
E-mail: reference@mptn.org
Web site: www.pequotmuseum.org
Theresa Bell, Executive Director
Description: A 308,000 square-foot building located within the 350-year-old Pequot Village. It is open to the general public, but it also serves people conducting scholarly research on American Indians, particularly natives of the Eastern Woodlands. There are three main exhibits: the era up to European contact; the era of increasing aggression by the English, leading up to the Pequot Massacre of 1637; and what life at Mashantucket has been like in the 350 years since. *Exhibits*: Dioramas of paleo or prehistoric era up to European contact; Clash of Cultures; The Mashantucket Pequots Today; photos, sculptures and craft work, diaries and other documents, and tribal voices all will be used to personalize the museum. *Facilities*: Maintains a recreated Pequot village of 350 years ago; the Cultural Research Center contains a research library, a circular theater which seats 100 people; research laboratories; and herbarium; photo/technical rooms; a 300-seat auditorium; gift shops; and cafe-style restaurant with full banquet and varied meeting facilities/.

EELS-STOW HOUSE
Milford Historical Society
34 High St., Box 337
MILFORD, CT 06460
(203) 874-2664
Virginia Hoagland, President
Special collection: Claude C. Coffin Indian Collection: Indian relics and artifacts primarily from the Milford-Stratford area of southern Connecticut. Library.

MOHEGAN MUSEUM
Mohegan Church
UNCASVILLE, CT 06382
(800) MOHEGAN ext. 6144
E-mail: museum@moheganmail.com
Melissa Tantaquidgeon, Tribal Historian
Description: Mohegan Chief Occum (Lemuel Fielding), who led the Tribe from 1903 to 1928. His regalia is displayed along with significant artifacts relating to the church, which for 172 years has stood as a symbol of the Mohegan Tribe's survival.

TANTAQUIDGEON INDIAN MUSEUM
Rte. 32, 1819 Norwich-New London Rd.
UNCASVILLE, CT 06382 (860) 848-9145
Gladys Tantaquidgeon, Owner/Curator
Description: Built in 1931 by the late John Tantaquidgeon and his son, Harold, direct descendants of Uncas, Chief of the once powerful Mohegan Nation. To preserve and perpetuate the history and traditions of the Mohegan and other Indian tribes. Displays objects of stone, bone, and wood made by Mohegan and other New England Indian artists and craftsmen, past and present. Opened in 1931.

INSTITUTE FOR AMERICAN INDIAN STUDIES
38 Curtis Rd., P.O. Box 1260
WASHINGTON, CT 06793-0260
(203) 868-0518 Fax 868-1649
Alberto C. Meloni, Director
Lynne Williamson, Curator
Description: A research and education museum dedicated to discovering and interpreting our 10,000 year-old American Indian heritage—the history of Native-American people of the Northeast Woodlands. Algonkian Village-3 wigwams, a longhouse, a rock shelter and a garden. Exhibits Plains Indian artifacts from Senator Orville Platt including more than 100 baskets from many western tribes. *Special Programs*: Educational services - Field Trips/Assemblies; craft workshops; lectures; training sessions; exhibitions. *Publications*: Artifacts, magazine; research reports; books: A Key Into the Language of Woodsplint Baskets; Native Harvests; and exhibition pamphlets. Library. Formerly The American Indian Archaeological Institute. Opened in 1975.

DELAWARE

NANTICOKE INDIAN MUSEUM
Rt. 13, Box 170A
MILLSBORO, DE 19966
(302) 945-7022
Pat Harmon, Joan Ridolfi, Docent
Description: Collection contains Native American artifacts - clothing, baskets, pottery, etc. Special programs for school groups. Annual Nanticoke Pow-wow. Library. Opened in 1984.

DISTRICT OF COLUMBIA

NATIONAL MUSEUM OF NATURAL HISTORY
Departrment of Anthropology
National Museum of Man
MRC 112, Smithsonian Institution
WASHINGTON, DC 20560
(202) 357-4760
JoAllyn Archambault, Director-
American Indian Program
R.H. Ives Goddard, III, Curator-Linguistics
William C. Sturtevant, Curator-Ethnology
Description: Established in 1986 to serve as an outreach program to Native American reservations and communities; to make the Smithsonian more accessible to Indian people; and to encourage collection, research, exhibitions, and public programming by and about Indian peoples. Collection includes about 62,000 ethnological objects representing historic Indian groups from all parts of North America, and 250,000 archaeological specimens; film and video materials of Native Americans are part of the museum's Human Studies Film Archives and include historic film from the early 20th century, as well as more recent ethnographic footage. In the Department of Anthropology are eight curators with research specialties in North American Indian/Inuit ethnology, archaeology, linguistics, and ethnohistory. Supervised internships and research fellowships are available through the Native American Awards Program. *Special activities*: Provides outreach and training to Native tribes, communities and individuals; Repatriation Office. *Publication*: Handbook of North American Indians, William C. Sturtevant, General Editor. Library of over 75,000 volumes.

SMITHSONIAN INSTITUTION
American Indian Museums Studies Program
Center for Museum Studies MRC 427
Arts & Industries Bldg., Room 2235
WASHINGTON, DC 20560
(202) 357-3101
Karen Cooper, Curriculum Program Manager
Description: Provides information services, educational opportunities, and access to resources to Native Americans working in museums.

U.S. DEPT. OF THE INTERIOR MUSEUM
1849 C St., NW, MS 1221-MIB
WASHINGTON, DC 20240
(202) 208-4743 Fax 208-6950
Debra Berke, Director
John Sherrod, Project Mgr.
E-Mail: dberke@ios.gov
Description: Exhibits include dioramas, scientific specimens, and paintings. A collection of Native American pottery, baskets, carvings, beadwork and other artifacts such as kachinas and weavings. *Special program*: Interview with an Interior staff person who is an American Indian and grew up on or near a reservation. Opened in 1938.

FLORIDA

AH-THA-THI-KI MUSEUM
Big Cypress Seminole Reservation
HC 61, Box 21-A • CLEWISTON, FL 33440
(863) 902-1113 Fax 902-1117
Billy L. Cypress, Executive Director
Peggy Davis Osceola, Development Specialist
Tom Gallaher, Development Coordinator
E-mail: museum@semtribe.com
Website: www.seminoletribe.com/museum
Description: Ethnographic and historic (Seminole specific) collections. *Special programs*: Historical Reinactment, 1st weekend in February; Seminole Arts School, in October; Native Arts Celebration, in November. Library. *Publications*: Museum News, quarterly newsletter. Opened in 1997.

LOWE ART MUSEUM
University of Miami, 1301 Stanford Dr.
CORAL GABLES, FL 33124-6310
(305) 284-3535 Fax 284-2024
Website: www.lowemuseum.org
Description: The Native American Collection consists of more than 3,000 objects: the Alfred I. Barton native American Collection includes blankets, Pueblo pottery, Plains Indian baskets, kachina dolls, jewelry, costumes and ceramics, largely of Southwestern origin. the Samuel K. Lothrop Guatemalan Textile Collection; and one of the largest collections of the art of ancient Mexico, Mesoamerica, and the Andes; in the Southeast U.S. of ceramic, stone, bone, metal, wood, and textile examples. *Special programs*: Group tours, art classes; annual outdoor arts festival is held on the grounds of Lowe each January. Publications. Library.

ST. LUCIE COUNTY HISTORICAL MUSEUM
414 Seaway Dr. • FORT PIERCE, FL 33450
Description: Features Seminole Indian pictures, artifacts and records from the Brighton Seminole Indian Reservation. Indian-made handicrafts are sold.

INDIAN TEMPLE MOUND MUSEUM
P.O. Box 4009, 139 Miracle Strip Pkwy.
FT. WALTON BEACH, FL 32549
(850) 833-9595 Anna Peele, Director
Description: Exhibits prehistoric Indian artifacts found within a 40 mile radius of the museum are displayed interpreting 10,000 years of Gulf Coast living. The Temple Mound, a National Historic Landmark, is the largest Mississippian Temple Mound on the Gulf Coast. *Special programs*: Educational programs; guided tours. *Publications*: Indians of the Florida Panhandle; Pottery of the Fort Walton Period; The Buck Burial Mound. Library. Museum Shop.

JACKSONVILLE CHILDREN'S MUSEUM
1025 Gulf Life Dr. • JACKSONVILLE, FL 32207
Description: Displays artifacts of the Florida Indians of the past and present, including the Seminole and Micosukee tribes. Research library.

HISTORICAL MUSEUM OF SOUTHERN FLORIDA
101 W. Flagler St. • MIAMI, FL 33130
(305) 375-1492
Randy Nimnicht, Exec. Director
Description: A depository of maps, manuscripts, and published materials of Southern Florida and the Caribbean. Permanent and temporary exhibitions, 28,600 artifacts, including Seminole/Miccosukee objects. *Programs*: Folklife programs, research, off-site programs for all ages; annual Harvest Festival. Publications. Library. Opened in 1940.

MICCOSUKEE CULTURAL CENTER
P.O. Box 40021, Tamiami Sta.
MIAMI, FL 33144
(305) 223-8388 Fax 223-1011
Steven Tiger, Director

SAN LUIS ARCHAEOLOGICAL & HISTORIC SITE
2020 W. Mission Rd.
TALAHASSEE, FL 32399
(904) 487-3711/3655
Bonnie G. McEwan, Director
Description: An active dig that was on the site of a 17th century Apalachee Indian village and a Spanish mission. Maintains trails with interpretive displays describing the excavations and history of the site. The 50-acre outdoor museum offers exhibits across the site, a visitor center and a history shop. Collection consists primarily of archaeological remains from the Apalachee and Spanish residents of the mission community. *Publications*: Apalachee: The Land Between the Rivers, by John Hann; and The Spanish Missions of La Florida, edited by Bonnie McEwan (University Press of Florida). Opened in 1983.

SOUTHEAST ARCHAEOLOGICAL CENTER
P.O. Box 2416 • TALLAHASSEE, FL 32316
(904) 222-1167
Richard D. Faust, Chief

TALLAHASSEE JUNIOR MUSEUM, INC.
3945 Museum Dr.
TALLAHASSEE, FL 32304
Special collection: Gundrum Collection: Displays reproductions of pre-Columbian Florida Indian pottery and weapons; Apalachee Indian Farm (Reconstructed.) *Publication*: Apalachee Indian Farm Guide.

GEORGIA

KOLOMOKI MOUNDS STATE HISTORIC PARK
Route 1, Box 114 • BLAKELY, GA 31723
(229) 724-2150 Fax 724-2152
Eric T. Bentley, Park Manager
E-mail: kolomoki@alltel.net
Website: www.geocities.com/kolomokistatepark
Description: Historic site—13th-century Indian burial mound and village—artifacts from the excavations are on display. About 1,300 acres located six mile north of Blakely off Hwy. 27. Museum - exhibits artifacts and interprets the seven Indian mounds and Indian culture. Museum is built on top of an Indian mound. Special program: Kolomoki Festival, 2nd Sat. in October. *Publication*: Report of the Excavations at Kolomoki. Opened in 1938.

NEW ECHOTA HISTORIC SITE
1211 Chatsworth Hwy. N.E.
CALHOUN, GA 30701
(706) 624-1321 Fax 624-1323
David Gomez, Director; E-mail: n_echota@innerx.net
Description: A Preservation Project — 1825 Capitol town of the Cherokee Nation. Museum and several historical buildings housing archaeological materials used by the Cherokees in the early 1800's. *Research*: Cherokee genealogy; Trail of Tears. Library. Opened in 1961.

ETOWAH INDIAN MOUNDS HISTORIC SITE
813 Indian Mounds Rd., S.W.
CARTERSVILLE, GA 30120
(404) 387-3747
Libby Forehand Bell, Manager
Description: A National Historic Landmark. Large Indian site with seven mounds surrounded by a moat partially filled. Materials recovered from the excavations are on display. The Etowah Indians occupied the Valley between A.D. 700 and 1650. Several thousand Indians lived in this fortified town. Opened in 1953.

INDIAN SPRINGS STATE PARK MUSEUM
678 Lake Clark Rd. • FLOVILLA, GA 30216
(770) 504-2277 Fax 504-2178
Don Coleman, Park Manager
Description: Traces the history of Indian Springs including items that reflect stages of Indian civilizations, treaties signed, Chief McIntosh's Assassination, Resort Era, and Civilian Conservation Corps; and exhibits Creek Indian artifacts. *Research*: Creek Indians in Georgia. *Special programs*: Assorted Native American arts & crafts; Primitive Skills: hunting techniques, pottery, basket making, pictographic writing, etc. Opened in 1825.

OCMULGEE NATIONAL MONUMENT
1207 Emery Highway • MACON, GA 31201
(912) 752-8257
Mark Corey, Supt.
Sylvia Flowers, Cultural Resource Specialist
Sam Lawson, Park Ranger/Interpretive Specialist
Description: Site of seven mounds constructed by a group of farming Indians one thousand years ago. Located on the eastern edge of Macon, GA, along U.S. 80. An estimated 2,000 people lived here at one time. Archaeology Museum: Collections explain the culture of the Indians who constructed the area mounds, and of five other Indian groups that have inhabited the area since. Publications. Creek Indian Trading Post. Library. A National Historic Landmark. Opened in 1936.

CHIEFTAINS MUSEUM
501 Riverside Pkwy.
ROME, GA 30162
(404) 291-9494
Josephine Ransom, Director
Description: History museum housed in a 1794 log cabin, and an 1820 plantation house belonging to Cherokee leader Major Ridge. Contains items from archaic Indian occupation to the present. Artifacts reflect life style of a rapidly changing Indian society; story of removal to the west. Maintains rotating art and history exhibits, local history. *Special programs*: Lecture series; educational programs. *Publication*: Quarterly membership newsletter. Library. Opened in 1970.

THE CHIEF JOHN ROSS HOUSE
P.O. Box 863 • ROSSVILLE, GA 30741
(706) 861-3954
Frances Jackson, President
Description: Historic house of 1797 with displays of artifacts; Cherokee alphabet.

TAMA MUSEUM
Tama Tribal Town, 107 Long Pine Dr.
WHIGHAM, GA 31797
(912) 762-3165 FAX 762-3165

IDAHO

IDAHO STATE HISTORICAL MUSEUM
610 N. Julia Davis Dr. • BOISE, ID 83702
(208) 334-2120
Linda Morton-Keithley, Administrator
Website: www.idahohistory.net
Description: A collection of prehistoric and historic artifacts of the Shoshone, Nez Perce, Northern Paiute, with general Plains Indian material represented; a large collection of Northwest Coast and Alaskan material collected in the early 1900's. *Publications*: Idaho Yesterdays, quarterly magazine; newsletter. Library.

SHOSHONE-BANNOCK TRIBAL MUSEUM
P.O. Box 793 • FORT HALL, ID 83203
(208) 237-9791
Rosemary DaVinney, Director
Description: Views prehistoric and contemporary lifestyles of the Shoshone-Bannock Tribes. Several exhibits display artifacts, photographs and contemporary fine art of tribal members. *Special programs*: Hosts a Spring and Fall Art Show for local artists; special tours to view tribes buffalo herd and a monument marking the original Fort Hall site in the "Bottoms" area (an important fish and wildlife habitat on the Snake River) of the Reservation. Library. *Publication*: Sho-Ban News, weekly newspaper. Opened in 1985.

INDIAN HERITAGE COUNCIL LIBRARY
Oakwood Dr., P.O. Box 752
McCALLI • ID 83638
(423) 277-1103
Homer Hooban, Librarian
Description: Maintains a collection of Native American books, pamphlets and letters on Indian religion and history. Includes the Great American Indian Bible, The Scorched Earth, Indian Nation, The Native American Anthology of Poetry, and other books. *Special activities*: Publishes Indian books approved by the Board and that are deemed worthy. Open to the public by appointment. Established 1988.

NEZ PERCE NATIONAL HISTORICAL PARK & MUSEUM
P.O. Box 93, Hwy. 95 • SPALDING, ID 83551
(208) 843-2261
Franklin C. Walker, Supt.
Susan J. Buchel, Curator
Description: 24 sites which illustrate the history and

culture of the Nez Perce Indians, and historic events which affected them. Museum houses exhibits of Nez Perce ethnological material; 4,000 photos of Nez Perce Indians. *Research*: Nez Perce Indians. *Publications*: Sapat'gayn: 20th-Century Nez Perce Artists, 72 page book; Nez Perce Country - 220 page book. Library.

HERRETT CENTER FOR ARTS & SCIENCE
College of Southern Idaho
315 Falls Ave., P.O. Box 1238
TWIN FALLS, ID 83303
(208) 732-6655 Fax 736-4712
James C. Woods, Director
Website: www.csi.edu/herrett
E-mail: herrett@csi.edu
Description: Maintains collections on American Indians, archaeology, and ethnology.

IDAHO HERITAGE MUSEUM
2390 Hwy. 93 S. • TWIN FALLS, ID 83303
(208) 655-4444
Description: Maintains collections of Indian artifacts.

ILLINOIS

**SCHINGOETHE CENTER FOR
NATIVE AMERICAN CULTURES**
347 S. Gladstone, Dunham Hall
Aurora University • AURORA, IL 60506
(630) 844-5402 Fax 844-8884
Dr. Michael Sawdey, Director
E-Mail: msawdey@admin.aurora.edu
Description: Contemporary Native American art and ethnographic materials, including beadwork, pottery, clothing, textiles, basketry, some prehistoric stone tools. *Special collections*: Southwestern pottery and kachinas. *Special program*: Annual Native American Festival and Pow-Wow in May. *Publication*: Spreading Wings, member newsletter. Library. Opened in 1990.

FIELD MUSEUM OF NATURAL HISTORY
Roosevelt Rd. at Lake Shore Dr.
CHICAGO, IL 60605
(312) 922-9410
Dr. William Boyd, President
Dr. Bennett Bronson, Chairman-Anthropology
Description: Seven exhibit halls devoted to the American Indian. Collections cover prehistoric and living Indians and Eskimos from Alaska to Cape Horn. *Publications*: Field Museum Bulletin; catalogs, handbooks, leaflets. Library. Opened in 1893.

**CAHOKIA MOUNDS STATE HISTORIC SITE
INTERPRETIVE CENTER MUSEUM**
30 Ramey St. • COLLINSVILLE, IL 62234
(618) 346-5160 Fax 346-5162
Dr. Mark Esarey, Site Manager
E-mail: cahokiamounds@ezl.com
Website: www.cahokiamounds.com
Description: Contains over 30 exhibits, including life size village diorama, 7 exhibit islands with graphics, artifacts, dioramas & videos which interpret the archaeology and the Mississippian culture and their accomplishments at Cahokia, the largest prehistoric site north of Mexico with over 100 mounds. Woodhenge reconstruction. *Special programs*: Orientation show; Rediscover Cahokia festival; storytelling; slide/tape presentations; guided tours; Native-American craft classes; lecture series. *Publications*: Cahokia: City of the Sun; Journey to Cahokia; Cahokian, newsletter. *Video*: "Cahokia Mounds: Ancient Metropolis". Museum shop. Library. A National Historic Landmark. Opened in 1989.

MADISON COUNTY HISTORICAL MUSEUM
715 N. Main St.
EDWARDSVILLE, IL 62025
(618) 656-7562 Anna Symanski, Director
Special collection: John R. Sutter and Raymond P. Smith Collections—Contains more than 3,000 American Indian artifacts of local and south central Illinois, as well as some from Southwest tribes. Library. *Publication*: Museum newsletter.

SCHOOL OF NATIONS MUSEUM
Principia College • ELSAH, IL 62028
(618) 374-2131 ext. 5236

E-mail: drh@prin.edu
Dan Hanna, Director
Description: Maintains a collection of American Indian crafts—baskets, clothing, dolls, pottery, textiles, etc. Library.

MITCHELL MUSEUM OF THE AMERICAN INDIAN
2600 Central Park Ave.
EVANSTON, IL 60201
(847) 475-1030 Fax 475-0911
Janice Klein, Director
E-mail: mitchellmuseum@mindspring.com
Website: www.mitchellmuseum.org
Description: Collection of about 10,000 objects representing the art, history and culture of Native peoples of North America, including Woodland, Plains, Southwest, Northwest Coast and Arctic. Library. Opened 1977.

DICKSON MOUNDS MUSEUM
LEWISTON, IL 61542
(309) 547-3721 Fax 547-3189
Judith A. Franke, Director
Description: Exhibits archaeological material from west central Illinois, Mississippian and Middle Woodland sites on grounds—Paleo-Indian to Mississippian cultures.

HAUBERG INDIAN MUSEUM
Black Hawk State Park
1510 46th Ave. • ROCK ISLAND, IL 61201
(309) 788-9536
Elizabeth A. Carvey, Director
Neil Rangen, Supt.
Description: Located on the site of the main villages of the Sauk and Fox Indian Nations. Artifacts on permanent display are of Sauk and Mesquakie origin; also other Eastern Woodland artifacts; includes many articles of Plains origin; large basket collection of the Northwest, West and Southwest; four dioramas depicting the daily life of the Sauk and Mesquakie about 1800. *Publication*: Two Nations, One Land: A Cultural Summation of the Sauk and Mesquakie in Illinois.

ILLINOIS STATE MUSEUM
Corner of Spring & Edwards Sts.
SPRINGFIELD, IL 62706
(217) 785-0037 Fax 785-2857
Dr. R. Bruce McMillan, Director
E-Mail: anthro@museum.state.il.us
Web site: http://www.museum.state.il.us
Description: Collections of Midwestern archaeology; prehistory and history; North American ethnographic materials especially western basketry, southwestern pottery and textiles. *Special programs*: Dickson Mounds Museum, Lewiston, IL skeletal collection; field trips, archaeology lecture series. *Publications*: Reports of Investigations; Scientific Papers; Research Series; Dickson Mounds Anthropological Studies; The Living Museum. Library. Opened in 1877.

MUSEUM OF NATURAL HISTORY
University of Illinois • URBANA, IL 61801
Description: Maintains prehistoric and historic exhibits of Indians of North America, with emphasis on the prehistory of Illinois, the Navajo and Pueblo Indians, and the Eskimo of Greenland.

STARVED ROCK STATE PARK
P.O. Box 509 • UTICA, IL 61373
(815) 667-4726 Fax 667-5353
Jon Blume, Complex Supt.
Description: Located on the site of former Indian village of Illinois Indians, later occupied by Ottawa and Potawatomi Indians, 1673-1760.

INDIANA

INDIANA UNIVERSITY MUSEUM
Student Bldg. • BLOOMINGTON, IN 47401
Description: Exhibits approximately 100,000 archaeological and ethnological specimens on American Indians from many areas of the New World. *Special collection*: Wanamaker Collection of American Indian Photographs, taken by Joseph Dixon—includes about 15,000 items. Library.

MATHERS MUSEUM OF WORLD CULTURES
601 East Eighth St.
BLOOMINGTON, IN 47408-3812
(812) 855-6873 Fax 855-0205
Geoffrey W. Conrad, Director
E-mail: mathers@indiana.edu
Website: www.indiana.edu/~mathers
Description: Contains more than 24,000 ethnographic artifacts from all over the world, including over 3,000 from indigenous cultures of North, Central and South America. *Special Collection*: Wanamaker Collection of American Indian Photographs - features over 7,500 images (primarily portraits) of American Indians taken between 1908 and 1922 under the direction of photographer, Dr. Joseph Dixon, including about 400 images of American Indians veterans of World War I. Opened 1963.

ANGEL MOUNDS STATE HISTORIC SITE
8215 Pollack Ave. • EVANSVILLE, IN 47715
(812) 853-3956
Rebecca Means Harris, Director
Kate Jones, Curator
Description: A 103 acre prehistoric Mississippian Indian archaeological site. Ten mounds, 1250-1450, inhabiting 1000 people; reconstructed structures: portion of a stockade house, and the temple. *Special programs*: Monthly lecture series on archaeology and nature; Native American Days Festival, annual in August. *Publication*: Smoke Signals, quarterly newsletter; Ancient Treasure of the Americas: A Pre-Columbian Exhibition, exhibit catalogue. Library. Opened in 1939.

THE POTAWATOMI MUSEUM
P.O. Box 631 • FREMONT, IN 46737
Description: Exhibits over 5,000 material cultural items of prehistoric and historic periods. Library.

CHILDREN'S MUSEUM OF INDIANAPOLIS
3010 N. Meridian St. • INDIANAPOLIS, IN 46208
Description: Collections consist of over 2,000 objects representing the tribes of Woodlands, Southeast, Plains, Plateau, Southwest, Northwest Coast, California and Canadian Indians. Publication: Newsletter. Library.

**EITELJORG MUSEUM OF AMERICAN
INDIANS & WESTERN ART**
500 W. Washington St.
INDIANAPOLIS, IN 46204
(317) 636-9378 Fax 264-1724
John Vanausdall, Director
Cindy Dashnaw, Director of Communications
James Nottage, Jennifer Complo McNutt
& Ray Gonyea, Curators
E-mail: cdashnaw@eiteljorg.com
Website: www.eiteljorg.com
Description: The American Western collection spans the early 19th century to the present and includes paintings, drawings, graphics, and sculpture - works by members of the original Taos art colony, such as Joseph Henry Sharp, E.I. Couse, Ernest Blumenschein, and Victor Higgins, as well as Western American artists, including Albert Bierstadt, Frederic Remington, Charles Russell, and Georgia O'Keeffe; the Native American collection consists of art and artifacts from throughout North America, and includes pottery, basketry, woodcarvings, and clothing. *Special programs*: Conducts research on Native American culture; lectures, film series, workshops, and craft demonstrations; special programs for school children; Annual Indian Market (August); Artists-in-Residence; Buckaroo Bash (October). Small library. *Publication*: Eiteljorg Museum Newsletter, quarterly; exhibition catalogues. Museum Shop. Opened in 1989.

FULTON COUNTY HISTORICAL SOCIETY MUSEUM
37 E. 375 N. • ROCHESTER, IN 46975
(574) 223-4436
E-mail: fchs@rtcol.com
Web site: icss.net/~fchs
Indian Awareness Center. Potawatomi Trail of Death, Chief White Eagle and Ervin Stuntz Indian artifact collections. Historic Encampments at Trail of Courage Living History Festival: French & Indian War, Plains Indians, Woodland Indians - Miami & Potawatomi life ways; Chippeway Village - 3rd weekend of September. Reference library. *Admission*: Adults, $5; ages 6-12, $2.

**NORTHERN INDIANA HISTORICAL
SOCIETY MUSEUM**
808 W. Washington St.
SOUTH BEND, IN 46601
Description: Exhibits on prehistoric Indians, the Mound
Builders in Indiana; an historic Indian exhibit on the
lifestyle of the Potawatomis and Miamis of northern
Indiana. *Publication*: The Old Courthouse News, quar-
terly magazine.

**SONOTABAC PREHISTORIC
INDIAN MOUND & MUSEUM**
P.O. Box 941 • VINCENNES, IN 47591
(812) 885-4330/7679
John A. Ward, President
Description: Indian Museum and Historic Site located
at the foot of the largest Ceremonial Mound in Indiana, containing exhibits covering 10,000 B.C. to the
present. *Publication*: Monthly newsletter.

IOWA

UNIVERSITY OF NORTHERN IOWA MUSEUM
31st and Hudson Rd.
CEDAR FALLS, IA 50613
Description: Maintains a collection of
approximately 8,000 Indian artifacts.

**PUTNAM MUSEUM OF HISTORY
& NATURAL SCIENCE**
1717 W. 12th St. • DAVENPORT, IA 52804
(563) 324-1054 Fax 324-6638
Christopher J. Reich, Director/CEO
E-mail: museum@putnam.org
Website: www.putnam.org
Description: Maintains collections of prehistoric Indian
artifacts from Mounds in central Mississippi River Valley; Southwestern basketry and pottery; and ethnological items from various tribes, primarily from the
upper Great Lakes region and Plains. Special programs: Presents a variety of programs for schools and
the general public based on its collections and exhibits. Library. Opened in 1867.

STATE HISTORICAL SOCIETY OF IOWA MUSEUM
600 E. Locust • DES MOINES, IA 50319
(515) 281-4221 Fax 242-6498
Jerome Thompson, Museum Bureau Chief
E-mail: jerome.thompson@dca.state.ia.us
Website: www.iowahistory.org
Description: Displays Indian beadwork; historic and
prehistoric artifacts, photos, and relative written material. *Publications*: The Annals of Iowa, quarterly scholarly journal; Iowa Heritage Illustrated. Library. Opened
in 1892.

MISSISSIPPI RIVER MUSEUM
400 E. 3rd St., Box 266
DUBUQUE, IA 52004
(319) 557-9545
Jerome A. Enzler, Director
Description: History of the Mississippi River from prehistoric times to present. Collections include Indian-
made circa 1860 dugout canoe, two birchbarks made
in Chippewa tradition, several prehistoric stone artifacts from the Upper Mississippi, and historic trade
material from EuroAmerican contact period -
Winnebago, Mesquakie, Crow, and Cheyenne. The
museum houses a small collection of baskets and pottery (Zuni and Navajo). Publications: Museum monographs. Library. Opened in 1964.

EFFIGY MOUNDS NATIONAL MONUMENT
151 Hwy. 76
HARPERS FERRY, IA 52146
(563) 873-3491 Fax 873-3743
Phyllis Ewing, Supt.
E-mail: efmo_superintendent@nps.gov
Website: www.nps.gov/efmo
Description: A 2,500 acre park with visitor center, the
collection contains archaeological and archival material from 500 BC to the present. Preserves 206 prehistoric Woodland Indian burial mounds with an archaeological museum exhibiting artifacts excavated
from the mounds area. *Special programs*: Bird walks,
moonlight hikes, American Indian Heritage celebration,
Chautauquas, hawk watch. Library. Opened in 1949.

SIOUX CITY PUBLIC MUSEUM
2901 Jackson St. • SIOUX CITY, IA 51104
Description: Exhibits artifacts of the Plains and Eastern Woodlands Indians. Library.

KANSAS

KAW INDIAN MISSION
500 North Mission
COUNCIL GROVE, KS 66846
(316) 767-5410
Ron Parks, Director
Description: Mission school opened by the Methodist
Episcopal Church in 1851 for the Kaw (Kansa) Indians. An historic house and museum featuring Kaw Indian relics. *Special program*: Wah Shun Gah Days,
summer.

IOWA, SAC & FOX PRESBYTERIAN MISSION
1737 Elgin Rd. • HIGHLAND, KS 66035
(913) 442-3304; Mark A. Hunt, Director
Andrew Clements, Curator
Description: A three story stone house serving as a
mission to the Iowa, and Sac and Fox Indians. Displays Iowa, and Sac and Fox Indian artifacts.

MUSEUM OF ANTHROPOLOGY
University of Kansas • LAWRENCE,KS 66045
(913) 864-4245
Alfred E. Johnson, Ph.D., Director
Anta Montet-White, Doct., Director
Robert J. Smith, Ph.D., Curator
Description: Maintains a collection of over 100,000
prehistoric American Indian artifacts, mainly from the
Midwestern U.S.; about 4,000 North American Indian
ethnographic items from the Plains, Southwest, and
Northwest Coast; and an extensive skeletal collection.
Special collection: Contemporary American Indian art
displayed in the Lawrence, Kansas Indian Art Show.
Publication: Quarterly newsletter. Library. Opened in
1979.

CORONADO-QUIVIRA MUSEUM
221 E Ave. South • LYONS, KS 67554
(316) 257-3941 Clyde Ernst, Director/Curator
Description: Exhibits Coronado and Quivira Indian artifacts, and Papago Indian baskets, pre-1934.

RILEY COUNTY HISTORICAL SOCIETY & MUSEUM
2309 Claflin Rd. • MANHATTAN, KS 66502
(913) 565-6490 D. Cheryl Collins, Director
Special collection: The Walter Collection—900+ Indian
relics and artifacts of northeast Kansas and southwest
Nebraska, especially arrowheads and stone tools.
Publication: Newsletter. Library. Opened in 1914.

LAST INDIAN RAID MUSEUM
258 S. Penn Ave. • OBERLIN, KS 67749
(913) 475-2712 Fonda Farr, Director
Description: Historical museum located near the sites
of the 1878 Last Indian Raid on Kansas soil with the
Northern Cheyenne Indians. One room dedicated to
the Native American artifacts and the story of the Last
Indian Raid. *Publication*: Quarterly newsletter. Opened
in 1958.

OLD DEPOT MUSEUM
135 W. Tecumseh
OTTAWA, KS 66067
(913) 242-1232
Deborah Barker, Director
Special collection: Indians of Franklin County, and
Early Indian Clothing. Displays scrolls of membership
in the Chippewa Tribe, and maps locating tribal lands.
Maintains an archives that contain over 10,000 photographs, verticle files and original documents from city,
county and various institutions. Opened in 1963.

**PAWNEE INDIAN VILLAGE
STATE HISTORIC SITE MUSEUM**
480 Pawnee Trail • REPUBLIC, KS 66964
(785) 361-2255 (phone & fax)
Richard Gould, Director
E-mail: piv@kshs.org
Website: www.kshs.org
Description: Archaeology museum located on the best
preserved Pawnee earth lodge site on the Plains. Dis-

plays describe Pawnee life on the Great Plains. *Special program*: Lectures, video series, and living history programming; Pawnee Indian dancers and singers. Brochure. Library. Opened in 1901.

THE SAC & FOX TRIBAL MUSEUM
Sac & Fox Nation of Missouri
Rt. 1, Box 60 • RESERVE, KS 66434
(913) 742-7471 Fax 742-3785
Opened April 1996.

EL QUARTELEJO KIVA INDIAN MUSEUM
c/o News Chronicle Printing Co., Inc.
P.O. Box 218 • SCOTT CITY, KS 67871
Description: Displays Cheyenne and Pueblo artifacts,
especially Taos; Indian War material.

SHAWNEE METHODIST MISSION
3403 W. 53rd
SHAWNEE MISSION, KS 66205
(913) 262-0867
Mark A. Hunt, Director; Lee Wright, Curator
Description: Re-creation of Indian Manual Labor
School, operated 1830-1862, for Shawnee children
and other emigrant tribes. *Special program*: Slide show
of the history of the Mission.

KANSAS MUSEUM OF HISTORY
Kansas State Historical Society
6425 SW 6th St. • TOPEKA, KS 66615-1099
Mark A. Hunt, Director; Diane Good, Curator
Description: Collection features Indian relics—tools,
utensils and clothing of Kansas Indian tribes. Library.
Opened in 1876.

MID-AMERICA ALL-INDIAN CENTER MUSEUM
650 N. Seneca • WICHITA, KS 67203
(316) 262-5221 Fax 262-4216
E-mail: icm@southwind.net
John Ortiz, Executive Director
Jerry Martin, Museum Director
Description: Located on the site of old Indian Council
grounds. Maintains collections of Native American art
and artifacts. *Research*: Native-American life, art, and
religion. *Publication*: Gallery Notes, quarterly newsletter. Library. Opened in 1975.

KENTUCKY

MUSEUM OF ANTHROPOLOGY
Northern Kentucky University
200 Landrum Academic Center
HIGHLAND HEIGHTS, KY 41099
(606) 572-5259 James F. Hopgood, Director
Description: Collections focus on contemporary Na-
tive American arts of the Southeast and Southwest
U.S. Library.

**WILLIAM S. WEBB MUSEUM
OF ANTHROPOLOGY**
University of Kentucky, 211 Lafferty Hall
LEXINGTON, KY 40506-0024
(859) 257-8208 Fax 323-1968
Dr. George M. Crothers, Director
E-Mail: gmcrot2@uky.edu
Website: www.uky.edu/as/anthropology.museum/
museum.htm
Description: Exhibits document 12,000 years of human history in Kentucky including Native American,
African American, and European American archaeological material as well as cultural and biological anthropology. *Special program*: Tours for groups. Research library maintains archaeological reports and
records of projects conducted in the state. Opened in
1931.

J.B. SPEED ART MUSEUM
2035 S. Third St.
LOUISVILLE, KY 40208
(502) 636-2893 Fax 636-2899
Peter Morrin, Director; Ruth Cloudman, Curator
Description: Maintains ethnological and archaeological exhibits illustrating Indian life of 19th and early 20th
century Plains groups. *Special collection*: The Charles
and Charlotte Price Gallery for Native Amerian Art
consists primarily of works from the Plains region.
Objects from many tribes including Dakota or Sioux,

the Cheyenne, the Arapaho, the Kiowa, and the Crow are represented. Frederick Weygold Collection—Work in flint, stone and bone from prehistoric Kentucky and southern Indiana. *Publication*: Quarterly Program Guide; J.B. Speed Art Museum Handbook. Library. Opened in 1927.

WICKLIFFE MOUNDS RESEARCH CENTER
P.O. Box 155, 94 Green St., Hwy. 60
WICKLIFFE, KY 42087 (270) 335-3681
Kit W. Wesler, Director
Carla Hildebrand, Assistant Director
E-mail: wmounds@brtc.net
Website: http://campus.murraystate.edu/
org/wmrc/wmrc.htm
Description: Program of Murray State University, the center is based on archaeological site of the Mississippi period, dated ca. A.D. 1100-1350. The museum displays artifacts from the excavations of the Mound Builders. *Special programs*: Educational; special events. *Publication*: Wickliffe Mounds Research Center Reports Series. Research library. Opened in 1983.

LOUISIANA

LOUISIANA ARTS & SCIENCE CENTER
100 S. River Rd. • BATON ROUGE, LA 70801
Description: Exhibits Eskimo soapstone carvings, artifacts and lithographs; North American Indian crafts, contemporary pottery and weaving.

LAFAYETTE NATURAL HISTORY MUSEUM
637 Girard Park Dr. • LAFAYETTE, LA 70503
Special collection: Contemporary Baskets of Chitimacha and Koasati Indians of Louisiana—Baskets and weaving of the Acadian culture and Louisiana Indian cultures. Publications. Library.

TUNICA-BILOXI REGIONAL INDIAN CENTER & MUSEUM
P.O. Box 331 • MARKSVILLE, LA 71351
(318) 253-8174 Fax 253-7711
Bill Day, Director;
E-mail: bill_day@tunica.org
Opened in 1989.

MAINE

ABBE MUSEUM
P.O. Box 286, 26 Mt. Desert St.
BAR HARBOR, ME 04609
(207) 288-3519 Fax 288-8979
E-mail: abbe@midmaine.com
Website: www.abbemuseum.org
Diane R. Kopec, Director
Rebecca Cole-Will, Curator
Description: Displays archaeological, ethnographic and contemporary art collections; Native-American prehistoric and ethnographic materials with emphasis on Maine and the Maritime provinces. Includes baskets, woodcarvings, and artifacts. Also, quillwork, and birchbark of Passamaquoddy Penobscot, Micmac and Malicite artists ca. 1800 - contemporary. *Special collection*: Mary C. Wheelwright Collections of ethnographic northeastern baskets of ash, birchbark and quill; archival photos and documents. *Special programs*: Workshops, demonstrations, and children's programs throughout the summer. School programs year around. Lecture series for specific exhibits. *Publications*: Bulletin series on Native American arts and crafts and archaeological research. Library. Open mid-May to mid-October. Established 1923.

THE PEARY-MacMILLAN ARCTIC MUSEUM
Bowdoin College, 9500 College Station
BRUNSWICK, ME 04011 (207) 725-3416
Dr. Susan A. Kaplan, Director
Dr. Genevieve LeMoine, Curator
Description: An exhibition of Peary and MacMillan Arctic explorations — Labrador, Baffin and Greenland Inuit & Indian cultures; photographic archives. Collections include historic artifacts, photographs & Inuit art, clothing & equipment. *Special programs*: Lecture series; tours. *Publication*: Occasional exhibit catalogs; posters. Library.

WILSON MUSEUM
P.O. Box 196 • CASTINE, ME 04421
(207) 326-8753
E.W. Doudiet, Director
Patricia L. Hutchins, Curator
Description: North American and some South American Indian stone artifacts, pottery and baskets, most obtained between 1880 and 1920. *Publications*: Triannual newsletter; pamphlets and book on local history. Open May 27th thru September 30th, 2-5 PM, except Monday. Established 1921.

NOWETAH'S AMERICAN INDIAN MUSEUM
2 Colegrove Rd. (Route 27)
NEW PORTLAND, ME 04961-3821
(207) 628-4981
Nowetah Wirick, Owner/Curator
Website: www.mainemuseums.org
Description: Displays American Indian art and crafts focusing on the Abenaki of Maine, including over 400 old Maine Indian baskets and bark containers. *Special program*: Educational programs, visits and classes available for schools and scout groups. Library. *Publications*: Illustrated booklets on past Indian life including, "The History of Indian Wampum," "Brain Tanning Hides," "How to Weave an Indian Rug," "The Abenaki Indian 1724 Massacre at Narrantsauak (Maine)," "Indian Legends, Recipes, & Names," "The Ancient Wisdom & Knowledge of the Abenaki Indians." Gift Store. Opened 1969.

PENOBSCOT NATION MUSEUM
6 River Rd., Indian Island
OLD TOWN, ME 04468 (207) 827-4153
James E. Neptune, Director

WAPONAHKI MUSEUM & RESOURCE CENTER
Pleasant Point Passamaquoddy Tribe
P.O. Box 295 • PERRY, ME 04667
(207) 853-4001 Fax 853-6039
Joseph A. Nicholas, Director
Description: A collection of artifacts of the Passamaquoddy Indians. Opened in 1987.

MAINE TRIBAL UNITY MUSEUM
Quaker Hill Rd. • UNITY, ME 04988
(207) 948-3131; Christopher Marshall, Director
Description: Indian Museum housed in 1880 Old Unity Town House, maintaining a collection of Northeast Indian basketry and artifacts. *Research*: Basket-making techniques. Library.

MARYLAND

NATIONAL COLONIAL FARM OF THE ACCOKEEK FOUNDATION
3400 Bryan Point Rd. • ACCOKEEK, MD 20607
(301) 283-2113 Fax 283-2049
Robert Ware Staus, President
Description: Collections include Indian artifacts.

PISCATAWAY INDIAN MUSEUM
16816 Country Ln. • WALDORF, MD 20616
(301) 372-1932
Opened in 1993.

MASSACHUSETTS

ROBERT S. PEABODY MUSEUM OF ARCHAEOLOGY
Phillips Academy • ANDOVER, MA 01810
(978) 749-4490 Fax 749-4495
Malinda S. Blustain, Director
E-Mail: rspeabody@andover.edu
Web site: http://www.andover.edu/~rspeabody/
Description: One of the nation's *major* repositories of Native American archaeological collections, representing nearly every culture area in North America. Collections are especially strong in the Northeast, Southeast, Midwest, Southwest, Mexico, and the Arctic, in many areas from Paleo-Indian (11,500 years ago) to European contact. Material includes stone and bone tools, pottery, and carved shell and copper artifacts. Ethnographic collection, from the last 150 years, in-

cludes baskets, textiles, and other objects. *Special collections*: Kidder collection from Pecos Pueblo; pre-contact Southeastern ceramics; West Coast baskets (19th century); Tehuacan Valley collection; artifacts of the Northeast. *Special programs*: Outreach; hosts meetings, special classes, and visiting speakers. Research library - 5,000 volumes and a large collection of historical photographs. Publications. Established in 1901.

TRUSTEES OF RESERVATIONS
572 Essex St. • BEVERLY, MA 01915
(508) 921-1944 Fax 921-1948
Herbert W. Vaughan, Chairperson
Description: An open space and historic preservation project maintaining and protecting about 75 properties in Massachusetts.

CHILDREN'S MUSEUM
Museum Wharf, 300 Congress St.
BOSTON, MA 02210 (617) 426-6500
Lou Casagrande, Director
Joan Lester, Native American Collection Consultant
Description: Collection includes Penobscot, Passamaquoddy, Iroquois, Chippewa, Wampanoag and Narragansett materials from both past and present traditions. *Special exhibit*: We're Still Here—American Indians in New England Long Ago and Today. *Programs*: Workshops/courses. Museum Shop. Library. Museum open daily 10 am - 5 pm.

PEABODY MUSEUM OF ARCHAEOLOGY & ETHNOLOGY
Harvard University, 11 Divinity Ave.
CAMBRIDGE, MA 02138
(617) 496-1027 Fax 495-7535
William L. Fash, Director
Web site: www.peabody.harvard.edu
Description: Contains large collections of archaeological and ethnographic materials of global scope, but primarily North America and Central America. Also, substantial ethnographic and archaeological photo archives. *Special exhibits*: "Change and Continuity," considers how native peoples across the continent responded to the arrival of Europeans. "Encounters with the Americas," explores native cultures of Mesoamerica before and after Spanish contact. "Painted by a Distant Hand: Mimbres Pottery of the American Southwest" examines the development and artistry of the Peabody's extensive and rare collection of prehistoric painted pottery. "From Nation to Nation Examining Lewis and Clark's Indian Collection" illustrates the role of Native Americans in Lewis and Clark's journey and displays the only surviving Native American objects brought back by Lewis and Clark. *Publication*: "Symbols," newsletter; scientific papers and memoirs. Library. Established 1866.

INDIAN HOUSE MEMORIAL
Box 121, Main St. • DEERFIELD, MA 01342
(413) 772-0845 John Abercrombie, President
Description: Collections include Native American artifacts, decorative arts, pottery, weaving, and looms.

LONGHOUSE MUSEUM
Hassanamisco Reservation
GRAFTON, MA 01519
Description: Memorial to the Eastern Native-American: Artifacts of the Nipmuc Tribe (central Massachusetts); beadwork, utensils, baskets, paintings, and rugs. Publications. Library.

FRUITLANDS MUSEUMS
102 Prospect Hill Rd. • HARVARD, MA 01451
(978) 456-3924 Fax 456-8078
Michael Volmar, Curator
Description: Indian museum collection focus on New England and Plains ethnographic materials, Southwestern pottery and basketry, California and Northwest Coast baskets and Eastern Woodlands. *Exhibits*: Dioramas of local Indian scenes and specimens of historic Indian arts and industries. *Special programs*: Educational programs; tours for school groups. Library. Opened 1928.

WISTARIAHURST MUSEUM
238 Cabot St. • HOLYOKE, MA 01040
(413) 534-2216 Fax 534-2344
Sandra Christofordis, Director

Description: Maintains a collection of Native American art and artifacts, including Iroquois masks and rattles; pottery of the Southeast and Southwest; basketry of the Southwest, Plains and Northwest Coast; Iroquois and Plains Indian beadwork. Programs: Craft workshops for children. Library.

PLIMOTH PLANTATION
Wampanoag Indian Program
P.O. Box 1620 • PLYMOUTH, MA 02360
(508) 746-1622 ext. 8385 Fax 830-6026
Nancy Brennan, Executive Director
Linda Coombs, Associate Director, Indian Program
E-mail: lcoombs@plimoth.org
Website: www.plimoth.org
Description: An outdoor living history museum which displays Native American artifacts from the colonial period, and recreates the life and times of a Wampanoag family which lived at Plymouth in the 1620's. Researches and depicts oriiginal 17th-century indigenous Wampanoag history and culture. Activities: "Strawberry Thanksgiving" special event 4th Saturday in June; staff demonstrations and discussions. *Publication*: "Almanack" membership newsletter. "Visible Images - Invisible People: Four Centuries of Wampanoag History" - conference series-proceedings. Library. Established 1947; Wampanoag Indian Program established in 1972.

MICHIGAN

MUSEUM OF ANTHROPOLOGY
University of Michigan
ANN ARBOR, MI 48109-1079
(734) 764-0485 Fax 763-7783
Dr. Robert Whallon, Director
Description: Contains extensive holdings in North American archaeology and ethnography. *Special collections*: Hinsdale Collection—Great Lakes Basketry; Greenland Eskimo Collection; Seri and Tarahumara Indian Collection. *Publications*: Papers, memoirs, and technical reports. Library.

CRANBROOK INSTITUTE OF SCIENCE
1221 N. Woodward, P.O. Box 801
BLOOMFIELD HILLS, MI 48303-0801
(810) 645-3200 Fax 645-3034
Gretchen Young-Weiner, Director
Description: Exhibits cover all major culture areas of North America, especially Woodlands and Plains. *Activities*: School group program. *Publications*: Bimonthly newsletter and brochure; bulletin series; annual report. Selective government depository. Library. Opened in 1930.

CULTURAL HERITAGE CENTER
Bay Mills Community College
12214 W. Lakeshore Dr. • BRIMLEY, MI 497715
(906) 248-5645 Fax 248-3351
Roger J. Pilon, Director
Opened in 1989.

CHILDREN'S MUSEUM
Detroit Public Schools
67 East Kirby • DETROIT, MI 48202
Special collection: American Indian Collection—basketry, costumes, crafts, dolls, textiles, musical instruments, tools and weapons for various cultural areas of American Indians. Reference Library.

DETROIT INSTITUTE OF THE ARTS
5200 Woodward Ave. • DETROIT, MI 48221
(313) 833-7900 Fax 883-3756
Dr. David Penney, Contact
Special collection: The Chandler-Pohrt Collection - 19th-century Native American objects from tribes of the North American woodlands, prairies, and plains. It is notable for being focused on the artistic quality of Indian material at a time when it was not considered art. It includes clothing, pipes, drums, shields, drawings, etc. *Publications*: Monthly DIA magazine; exhibition and permanent collection catalogues. Library. Opened in 1885.

MUSEUM OF ANTHROPOLOGY
Wayne State University
6001 Cass Ave. • DETROIT, MI 48202

(313) 577-2598/3056
Tamara Bray, PhD, Director
Description: Maintains a collection of American Indian artifacts. Research Library.

MICHIGAN STATE UNIVERSITY MUSEUM
Div. of Anthropology • EAST LANSING, MI 48824
(517) 355-2370 Fax 432-2846
E-mail: lovis@pilot.msu.edu
William A. Lovis, Curator of Anthropology
Charles E. Cleland, PhD, Curator-
Great Lakes Arch. & Ethnology
Special collection: Indians of the Great Lakes—Contains 30 displays relating to the history, technology, religion, and social organization of the Indians of the Great Lakes area.

PUBLIC MUSEUM OF GRAND RAPIDS
272 Pearl NW • GRAND RAPIDS, MI 49504
(616) 456-3977 Fax 456-3873
Tim Chester, Director
E-Mail: staff@grmuseum.org
Description: Exhibits Hopewell archaeological material; artifacts from the Historic Site—Norton Indian Mounds (Hopewell.) *Special collection*: Large permanent exhibit on Native people of West Michigan. *Publication*: Beads: Their Use by Upper Great Lakes Indians (1977); newsletter & magazine.

FORT DE BUADE MUSEUM, INC.
5123 W. St. Joseph Hwy. #104
LANSING, MI 48917-4028
(906) 643-8686
Donald E. Benson, Director
Description: Indian Museum located on the site of 1681, Fort de Buade, built by the French. Displays artifacts, beadwork, photos, lithos, and oils of Woodland Indians.

MICHIGAN HISTORICAL MUSEUM
Michigan History Div.-Dept. of State
505 N. Washington Ave. • LANSING, MI 48918
Description: Maintains Indian exhibits related to the history of Michigan and the old Northwest Territory.

MACKINAC ISLAND STATE PARK MUSEUM
P.O. Box 370
MACKINAC ISLAND, MI 49757
Description: Features Indian material from the upper Great Lakes; Chippewa Indian costumes. Publications. Library.

TEYSEN'S WOODLAND INDIAN MUSEUM
P.O. Box 399, 415 W. Huron Ave.
MACKINAW CITY,MI 49701
(616) 436-7011
Kenneth Teysen, CEO
Description: Collections include Indian artifacts from the Great Lakes area, including tools, weapons, clothing, food, and trade items.

**MARQUETTE COUNTY
HISTORICAL SOCIETY MUSEUM**
213 N. Front St. • MARQUETTE, MI 49855
(906) 226-3571
Frances Porter, Executive Director
Description: Displays Indian archaeological and historical material of the upper peninsula of Michigan, with main focus on the Chippewa. Dioramas depicting a Chippewa family group. Includes baskets, beadwork, medicine bags, calumets, moccasins, canoes. *Publications*: Indians of Gitche Gumee; Harlow's Wooden Man, quarterly magazine; books for sale. Library.Established 1918.

FORT ST. JOSEPH MUSEUM
508 East Main St. • NILES, MI 49120
(269) 683-4702
Carol Bainbridge, Director
E-mail: cbainbridge@qtm.net
Website: www.ci.niles.mi.us
Special collections: Collection of Lakota Indian artifacts; 12 drawings by Sitting Bull; large pictograph tapestry by Rain-in-the-Face; Potawatomi and early Native American objects (projectile points, stone tools). Established 1932.

CROOKED TREE ARTS COUNCIL
461 E. Mitchell St. • PETOSKEY, MI 49770

(616) 347-4337 Fax 347-3429
Sean Ley, Director
Description: Maintains a fine arts collection with emphasis on Indians of the Great Lakes area. Research: Art of Ojibway, Odawa, and Nishnawbe Indians.

**FATHER MARQUETTE NATIONAL
MEMORIAL & MUSEUM**
Father Marquette State Park, 720 Church St.
SAINT IGNACE, MI 49781 (906) 643-8620
Description: Displays artifacts, including an Indian longhouse and canoe, and maintains exhibits of early French and Indian cultures.

MUSEUM OF OJIBWA CULTURE
500-566 N. State St. • ST. IGNACE, MI 49781
(906) 643-9161 Fax 643-9380
Molly M. Perry, Director
E-mail: mmperry@up.net
Description: Displays artifacts and reproductions relating to Ojibwa culture. Portrays a vivid picture of Straits of mackinac life over 300 years ago when Ojibwa, Huron, Odawa, and French lifestyles met at this protected bay. *Special programs*: Native American Art Festival, 3rd weekend in August; Pow-Wow on Labor Day weekend; traditional arts & crafts workshops; educational programs, and archaeological digs. Opened in 1987.

LUCKHARD'S MUSEUM-THE INDIAN MISSION
612 E. Bay St. • SEBEWAING, MI 48759
Description: Using 17th century archaeological items, the museum interprets the Ojibwa who lived in the area prior to contact, and the Huron and Ojibwa refugees who came. The French fur trader and Jesuits and their impact on Native culture. Exhibits Indian artifacts and pioneer relics of the 19th-century, housed in original Indian mission of the Chippewa Indians (1845). *Special program*: A video presentation on the Ojibwa family - the importance of every member, the interdependence. *Publications*: "The Story of Wafted Across," and "Southern Feather's Story," by Margaret Peacock, short stories about an Ojibwa family (fiction).

SEBEWAING INDIAN MUSEUM
612 E. Bay St. • SEBEWAING, MI 48759
(517) 883-3730 Jim Bunke, CEO
Description: An 1849 mission home, with collections of Native American canoes, arrowheads, and headress.

INDIAN DRUM LODGE MUSEUM
Mail: 2308 North U.S. 31, Camp Greilick
4754 Scout Camp Rd.
TRAVERSE CITY, MI 49684
Martin A. Melkild, Curator
Description: Indian Museum housed in 1850, Chief Peter Ringnose's log cabin, maintaining ceremonial artifacts, clothing, and wood crafts.

MINNESOTA

GRAND MOUND HISTORY CENTER
6749 Hwy. 11 •
INTERNATIONAL FALLS, MN 56649
(218) 279-3332
Michael K. Budak, Director
Description: A prehistoric Native American mounds and habitation area exhibiting ceramics, lithics, and bone tools from the site. Programs: Monthly programs Jan.-Aug. on regional American Indian history and culture, archaeology, and natural environment. *Publication*: "Grand Mound". Library. Established 1976.

TWO RIVERS GALLERY
Minneapolis American Indian Center
1530 E. Franklin Ave.
MINNEAPOLIS, MN 55404
(612) 879-1780 Fax 879-1795
J. Espinoa, Director
Website: www.maicnet.org
E-mail: jespinosa@maicnet.org
Description: More than 100 oil paintings by various American Indian artists. Ongoing visual arts exhibitions of both contemporary and more traditional artforms. *Programs*: School tours; special lectures. *Publication*: The Dragonfly, biannual newsletter.

THE ROURKE ART MUSEUM
521 Main Ave. • MOOREHEAD, MN 56560
(218) 236-8861 James O'Rourke, Director
Description: Permanent collections include both historic and contemporary Native American art as well as Inuit and Pre-Columbian art of Mexico. Temporary exhibitions of Native American art and Eskimo sculpture. *Publications*: Catalogs for special exhibitors. Museum Shop. Established 1960.

LOWER SIOUX AGENCY HISTORIC SITE
32469 County Hwy. 2 • MORTON, MN 56270
(507) 697-6321
Mary C. Talbot, Acting Site Manager
Description: 260 acre site of beginning of U.S.-Dakota War of 1862. Site includes History Center and new exhibits and interactive activities telling the story of the Eastern Dakota people from white contact to just after the U.S.-Dakota war. *Special programs*: Focus on various aspects of Native and Euro-American history and culture, during the summer season. Also, new walking trails with interpretive signage. *Publications*: Minnesota Historical Society publications and others pertaining to Dakota and Plains Indians history; also books and sales items of Indian culture. Library. Museum Store. Established 1972.

MILLE LACS INDIAN MUSEUM
Mille Lacs Indian Reservation
ONAMIA, MN 56359
(320) 532-3632 Fax 532-4625
Joyce Shingobe-Wedll, Director
Description: This trading post and museum portrays Ojibwe culture. Exhibits include life-size dioramas showing typical scenes of Ojibwe life for each season; elders talk about the Anishinabeg's past, and demonstrations of traditional activities. Operated by the Minnesota Historical Society. Opened in 1964.

PIPESTONE COUNTY MUSEUM
113 S. Hiawatha • PIPESTONE, MN 56164
(507) 825-2563
Dave Rambow, Director
Joe Ager, Curator
E-Mail: pipctymu@rconnect.com
Web site: http://www.pipestone.mn.us/
museum/homepa~1.htm
Description: Contains artifacts from the Dakota and Ojibwa Tribes—Plains Indian saddle, and ceremonial pipes. Library. *Publication*: Quarterly journal. Established 1880.

PIPESTONE NATIONAL MONUMENT
UPPER MIDWEST INDIAN CULTURE CENTER
Pipestone National Monument
P.O. Box 727 • PIPESTONE 56164
(507) 825-5463 Maddie Redwing, Director
(507) 825-5464 Vincent J. Halvorson, Supt.
(888) 209-0418 Fax (507) 825-2903
E-Mail: info@authenticpipestone.com
Website: www.authenticpipestone.com
Description: Original pipestone (catlinite, named for noted painter of Indians, George Catlin) quarry from which the Dakota Sioux fashioned their ceremonial pipes. *Local History Museum* exhibits Indian ceremonial pipes and pipestone objects; pipestone quarries. *Special program*: Cultural demonstration programs-April thru October-pipecarving, beadwork, quillwork, etc. *Publications*: Pipes on the Plains, Pipestone: A History; and Circle Trail booklet. Library. Opened in 1955.

MINNESOTA HISTORICAL SOCIETY MUSEUM
345 Kellogg Blvd. W. • ST. PAUL, MN 55102
(612) 297-7913 Fax 296-1004
Timothy C. Glines, Administrative Officer
Description: Exhibits depicting prehistoric and contemporary Indian life in Minnesota. Major collecting areas include Dakota and Ojibwa material; photo collection. Maintains Grand Mound History Center. *Publication*: Minnesota History, quarterly magazine; Historic Sites Travel Guide brochure; publications from the Minnesota Historical Society Press. Library.

MINNESOTA MUSEUM OF ART
75 W. Fifth St. • ST. PAUL, MN 55102
(612) 292-4355 Katherine Van Tassell, Curator
Description: American art 1850 to the present. Small collection of Native American artifacts (half Southwestern, half Northwest Coast). *Special programs*: Occasional shows of Native American artists. Publications: Newsletter; occasional catalogs. Established 1927.

SCIENCE MUSEUM OF MINNESOTA
120 W. Kellogg St. • ST. PAUL, MN 5102
(651) 221-9424 Fax 221-4525
E-mail: oshane@smm.org
Web site: www.smm.org
Orrin C. Shane, III, Curator
Faith G. Bad Bear, Asst. Curator
Description: Large collection on the North American Indian. Library.

WALKER WILDLIFE & INDIAN ARTIFACTS MUSEUM
St. Hwy. 200, Box 336 • WALKER, MN 56484
(218) 547-1257
Renee Geving, Manager
Description: Collections include Ojibway and Chippewa Indian handicraft and artifacts from 1892-1962.

WINNEBAGO AREA MUSEUM
WINNEBAGO, MN 56098
(506) 893-3692 Marion Muir, President
Description: An archaeological museum exhibiting Oneonta (900-1500 A.D.) artifacts, Woodland (1000-8000 B.C.) artifacts; beadwork of the Chippewa and Sioux. Library.

MISSISSIPPI

WINTERVILLE INDIAN MOUNDS STATE PARK
Rt. 3, Box 600 • GREENVILLE, MS 38701
Description: Maintains museum with a collection of Indian artifacts, excavated from the Mounds area. Library.

COBB INSTITUTE OF ARCHAEOLOGY
Drawer AR •
MISSISSIPPI STATE UNIVERSITY, MS 39762
(601) 325-3826 E.J. Vardaman, Director
Description: Exhibits Indian materials of Mississippi culture. *Publication*: Indians of Mississippi. Library.

GRAND VILLAGE OF THE NATCHEZ INDIANS
400 Jefferson Davis Blvd. • NATCHEZ, MS 39120
(601) 446-6502 Fax 359-6905
James F. Barnett, Jr., Director
Description: A 128 acre National Historic Landmark site is the location of the ceremonial mound center for the Natchez tribe during the French colonization of the area (ca. 1682-1730.) *Museum*: Contains Indian and European artifacts gathered from the excavations and interpreted exhibits on the Natchez and Southeastern Indians. *Special programs*: Educational programs; slide lectures and guided tours. Library.

OLD SPANISH FORT AND MUSEUM
4602 Fort St. • PASCAGOULA, MS 39567
Description: Features Indian artifacts, tools and implements; and maps showing Indian settlements prior to 1700. Library.

CHOCTAW MUSEUM OF THE SOUTHERN INDIAN
Mississippi Band of Choctaw Indians
P.O. Box 6010 • PHILADELPHIA, MS 39350
(601) 650-1685 Fax 656-6696
Bob Ferguson, Director
E-mail: choctaw@cybertron.com
Description: Houses many permanent exhibits and occasionally offers traveling exhibits. Promotes continuation of Choctaw crafts and culture. Opened in 1981.

MISSOURI

MUSEUM OF ANTHROPOLOGY
University of Missouri, 104 Swallow Hall
COLUMBIA, MO 65211
(573) 882-3764 Fax 884-5450
Dr. Michael J. O'Brien, Director
Molly K. O'Donnell, Associate Curator
Description: Displays of Native American material, Missouri archaeology, and Missouri history. Maintains

collections of ethnographic material from the around the world. *Special collection*: The Grayson Collection of archery and archery-related material; Museum Curation Center. *Special programs*: Tours; Outreach. Gift Shop. Established in 1939.

TOWOSAHGY STATE HISTORIC SITE
Big Oak Tree State Park, 13640 S. Hwy. 102
EAST PRAIRIE, MO 63845
(573) 649-3149
Ruben Templeton, Park Supt.
Description: This 64-acre state historic site preserves the remains of a once-fortified Indian village, which was an important ceremonial center. Indians of the Mississippian Culture inhabited the site between 1000 A.D. and 1400 A.D. Archaeologists periodically excavate at the site. Collections are currently curated off-site and are not on public display. *Programs*: Interpretive shelter and trail focusing on stockaded, multi-Mound Mississippian Culture prhistoric civic-ceremonial center AD 100-1400. *Publications*: Site brochure; information guides beng developed. Established 1967.

MISSOURI STATE MUSEUM
State Capitol
JEFFERSON CITY, MO 65101
Description: Collections include Musquakie ceremonial material, Missouri pottery, Kema Cave artifacts, Indian burial mound material, stone artifacts and archaic Indian artifacts.

OSAGE VILLAGE HISTORIC SITE
P.O. Box 176 • JEFFERSON CITY, MO 65102
(314) 751-8363 Fax 751-8656
Larry Grantham, Contact
Description: Houses collections of excavated materials and conducts research on Osage Indians.

KANSAS CITY MUSEUM
3218 Gladstone Blvd.
KANSAS CITY, MO 64123
(816) 483-8300
Dr. David Ucko, President
Denise Morrison, Archivist
Description: The American Indian collections number about 2,500 pieces, most of which were collected by Col. Daniel Dyer and Ida Dyer during his tenure as Indian Agent at Fort Reno, Oklahoma in 1884-85, includes clothing and textiles, rocks and minerals, tools and technology, and archival documents. Also, other collections include artifacts from Southern and Central Plains, Eastern Woodlands, the Southwest and Northwest Coast Indian cultures. Two notable objects in the collection are the First Greenville Treaty Peace Medal and the Second Greenville Treaty Peace Pipe. The Peace Medal dates to 1795, when it was presented by a representative of George Washington to Chief White Swan of the Wea tribe. The Pipe is one of three presented to Wyandotte, Delaware and Shawnee Tribes by a representative of President James Madison at the Second Treaty of Greenville, Ohio in 1814. *Publication*: Quarterly newsletter. Reference Library. Established1939.

WILLIAM ROCKHILL NELSON GALLERY & ATKINS MUSEUM OF FINE ARTS
4525 Oak St. • KANSAS CITY, MO 64111
Description: Exhibits Native arts of the Americas, with emphasis on the Southwest, Mesoamerica, and South America. Publications. Library.

THE ST. LOUIS ART MUSEUM
Forest Park • ST. LOUIS, MO 63110
(314) 721-0067 James Burke, Supt.
John W. Nunley & Jackie Lewis Harris, Curators
Description: Maintains a collection of artifacts, pottery, carvings, basketry and clothing of the Pueblo, Pueblo Mimbres, Plains, West Coast, and Mound Builder Indians. Bulletin. Library. Established 1904.

MONTANA

CHEYENNE INDIAN MUSEUM
P.O. Box 216 • ASHLAND, MT 59003
(406) 784-2741 Fax 784-6161
Dewanda Little Coyote-Backbone
Opened in 1971.

MUSEUM OF THE ROCKIES
Montana State University
BOZEMAN, MT 59717 (406) 994-2251
  Arthur H. Wolf, Director
  Leslie B. Davis, PhD, Curator
  Christopher Hill, PhD, Associate Curator
Special collections: "Enduring Peoples" - 1,500-piece
Ethnology Collection, primarily an exhibit collection,
represents Native Americans of the Plains, Northern
Rockies and Plateau culture areas; and The Prehis-
toric Archaeology Collection - 100,000 artifacts of stone,
bone and antler.

MUSEUM OF THE PLAINS INDIAN
P.O. Box 410 • BROWNING, MT 59417
  (406) 338-2230 Fax 338-7404
  Loretta F. Pepion, Curator
  E-mail: mpl@3rivers.net
Description: Administered by the Indian Arts and Crafts
Board. Presents historic arts created by the tribal
peoples of the Northern Plains, including the Blackfeet,
Crow, Northern Cheyenne, Sioux, Assiniboine,
Arapaho, Shoshone, Nez Perce, Flathead, Chippewa,
& Cree. Displays the varied traditional costumes of
Northern Plains men, women and children in complete
detail on life-size figures. *Special programs*: North
American Indian Days - annual public event presented
in the second week of July on the Blackfeet Tribal
Fairgrounds, adjacent to the museum. A four-day program of Indian dancing, games & sports events, and
parades; slide presentation, "Winds of Change"—about
the evolution of Indian cultures on the Northern Plains,
narrated by Vincent Price; series of one-person exhibitions; painted tipis on the grounds during summer;
demonstrations of Native American arts & crafts techniques; tours. Publ*ications*: Illustrated catalogs and
brochures. Opened in 1941.

LITTLE BIGHORN BATTLEFIELD
NATIONAL MONUMENT
P.O. Box 39 • CROW AGENCY, MT 59022
  (406) 638-2621 Fax 638-2623
  Neil C. Mangum, Supt.
  Kitty Belle Deernose, Curator
  E-mail: neil-mangum@nps.gov
  E-mail: kitty_deernose@nps.gov
  Web site: www.nps.gov/libi/
Description: Historic site of the Battle of the Little Big
Horn, June 25-26, 1876. Arapaho, Sioux, and Chey-
enne Indians fought and defeated Lt. Col. George
Armstrong Custer and his troops of the 7th U.S.
CavalryArikara and Crow Indians scouted for military.
Museum: Educational and interpretive exhibits and a
permanent museum collection of 24,000 objects, in-
cludes historical documents authored by or associated
with George A. Custer, the Battle of the Little Big Horn,
and other events and persons associated with the Indian Wars on the Northern Plains (1865-1891.) Military and ethnographic specimens relating to the conflict, including items associated with the Sioux, Crow,
and Northern Cheyenne Tribes. *Special programs*:
Talks on the Battle; 30 minute documentary film, "Last
Stand at Little Bighorn" available on request to schools
and organizations; tours. Publications available from
Southwest Parks & Monuments Association (SPMA).
White Swan Memorial Library: 2,050 volumes. Established in 1952.

CROW TRIBE HISTORICAL
& CULTURAL COMMISSION
P.O. Box 173 • CROW AGENCY, MT 59022
  (406) 638-2328

H. EARLE CLACK MUSEUM
P.O. Box 1675 • HAVRE, MT 59501
  (406) 265-9641 Duane Nabor, Director
  Mrs. Louis Clack, Curator
Exhibit includes historic artifacts from the Chippewa
and Cree Indians, excavated from site area; dioramas.

MONTANA HISTORICAL SOCIETY MUSEUM
225 No. Roberts • HELENA, MT 59620
  (406) 444-2394 Lawrence Sommer, Director
  Susan R. Near, Curator
Description: Collection contains approximately 3,500
pieces of ethnographic artifacts primarily of tribes of
the region, mostly Blackfeet and Sioux. The Photographic Archives contains over 2,000 photo prints and
negatives that depict Indians, primarily of the Blackfeet,

Sioux, Crow and Flathead. *Special collection*: Towe
Ford Collection—Features the chronological story of
Montana's frontier through dioramas and other displays. C.M. Russell Gallery of Western Art. Publication: Montana: The Magazine of Western History, quarterly. Library. Founded 1865.

NORTHERN CHEYENNE TRIBAL MUSEUM
P.O. Box 128 • LAME DEER, MT 59043

CENTRAL MONTANA MUSEUM
P.O. Box 818, 408 NE Main St.
LEWISTON, MT 59457 (406) 538-5436
  Frank Machler, Curator
Description: A collection of Native American artifacts.

MONTANA STATE UNIVERSITY MUSEUM
Fine Arts Bldg. • MISSOULA, MT 59801
Description: Displays Indian art and artifacts of Mon-
tana.

SQELIX / AQ SMAKNI•K CENTER MUSEUM
The Peoples Center
Confederated Salish & Kootenai Tribes
Flathead Indian Reservation
P.O. Box 278 • PABLO, MT 59855
  (800) 883-5344; (406) 675-0160 Fax 675-0260
  Vicki Munson, Director
  E-mail: tours@peoplescenter.org
  Website: www.peoplescenter.org.
Opened 1994.

FORT PECK TRIBAL MUSEUM
P.O. Box 115 • POPLAR, MT 59255
  (406) 768-5155 Fax 768-5478
  Curley Youpee, Director
Opened in 1978.

CHIEF PLENTY COUPS
STATE PARK & MUSEUM
P.O. Box 100 • PRYOR, MT 59066
  (406) 252-1289 Fax 252-6668
  Rich Furber, Park Manager
  E-mail: plentycoups@plentycoups.org
  Website: www.plentycoups.org
Description: Memorial museum to Chief Plenty Coups
- last chief of the Crow - includes personal collection
of medicine bundles, clothing, weapons, pictures,
documents; Crow Indian artifacts; ethnographic ma-
terial of the Crow people; paintings, drawings; prehis-
toric artifacts. *Special program*: Crow Life ways programs (cultural demonstrations) on Saturdays during
July and August; Chief Plenty Coups "Day of Honor."
Research Library. Opened in 1932.

FLATHEAD INDIAN MUSEUM
Flathead Indian Reservation
#1 Museum Lane • ST. IGNATIUS, MT 59865
  (406) 745-2951 Jeanine Allard, Director
  Col. Doug Allard, Curator
Description: Indian artifacts from the Flathead Tribe
and other Western tribes. Special collection: Flathead
Photo Collection. Established in 1975.

BIG HOLE NATIONAL BATTLEFIELD
P.O. Box 237 • WISDOM, MT 59761
  (406) 689-3155 Fax 689-3151
  John James, Supt.; Bob Chenoweth, Curator
Description: A 655 acre battlefield which preserves the
scene of a battle between Nez Perce Indians and the
Seventh U.S. Infantry, fought on August 9 and 10,
1877. The Heritage Center is located in the historic
old school building constructed in 1888 by Jesuit
priests. *Museum*: Exhibits detailing Nez Perce culture
and soldier life of the 1870's; Native American art, including paintings, graphics, and sculptures; artifacts
from battle participants, including beadwork. *Special
programs*: Audiovisual program; self guiding trails; presentations by rangers. Library. Gift Shop. Publications;
Information packets; brochure.

NEBRASKA

MUSEUM OF THE FUR TRADE
HC 74, Box 18, 6321 Hwy. 20
CHADRON, NE 69337 (308) 432-3843
  Charles E. Hanson, Jr., Director

  Brenda Olsen, Curator
Description: Maintains a collection of material illustrating the cultures of North American Indians, and the
influence of the fur trade on those cultures. Restored
and outfitted 1833 Indian trading post and warehouse.
Indian garden for crops obtained from Mandan, Dakota, Assiniboine, Arikara, Hidatsa and Omaha Indians. *Publication*: Quarterly magazine. Library. Established in 1955.

FORT ROBINSON MUSEUM
Nebraska State Historical Society
P.O. Box 304 • CRAWFORD, NE 69339
  (308) 665-2919 Fax 665-2917
  Thomas R. Buecker, Curator
Description: Interpretive exhibits housed in 1905 Post
Headquarters with displays of artifacts from Fort
Robinson (1874 to 1948.) Crazy Horse, the great
Oglala warrior, met his death there in 1877. Microfilm
records of Red Cloud and Spotted Tail Indian Agen-
cies. Guided tours.

HASTINGS MUSEUM
P.O. Box 1286 • HASTINGS, NE 68902
Description: A collection of Indian artifacts;
Sioux Indian habitat group. Indian film. Publications.

FORT KEARNEY MUSEUM
311 South Central Ave.
KEARNEY, NE 68847
Description: Displays Indian art from the
Rosebud Indian Reservation.

INDIAN CENTER, INC.
1100 Military Rd. • LINCOLN, NE 68508
  (402) 438-5231 Fax 438-5236
  Jackie Jackson, Director
  E-mail: indianctr@navix.net

MUSEUM OF NEBRASKA HISTORY
Nebraska State Historical Society
P.O. Box 82554 • LINCOLN, NE 68501
  (402) 471-4754 Fax 471-3314
  Brent Carmack, Director
  Deb Arenz, Curator
  E-mail: carmack@nshs.state.ne.us
  Website: www.nebraskahistory.org
Description: A 5,000 square foot exhibit "The First
Nebraskans," Plains Indian archaeology, and historic
artifacts primarily from the 19th & 20th centuries. Pe-
riod settings include a Pawnee earthlodge, and a
Winnebago Reservation house. *Special collection*:
Photo collection - Indians of Nebraska and the Great
Plains. *Publications*: Nebraska History, quarterly; His-
torical Newsletter; monographs on Nebraska history
and anthropology; educational materials. Library/Ar-
chives. Museum Shop. Established in 1878.

UNIVERSITY OF NEBRASKA STATE MUSEUM
Morrill Hall • LINCOLN, NE 68508
  (402) 472-5044 Fax 472-8949
  Priscilla Grew, Director
  Thomas Myers, Curator
  E-Mail: pgrew@ccmail.unl.edu
  Web site: www.museum.unl.edu
Description: Features more than 2,500 Native Ameri-
can ethnographic artifacts with emphasis on Plains and
Southwest. Includes costumes and artifacts of Indi-
ans of Nebraska. *Special exhibit*: "Nomads of the
Plains" Gallery. *Publication*: "Magic in Clay," and Birth
and Rebirth of the Omaha." Established 1879.

HERITAGE HOUSE MUSEUM
107 Clinton • WEEPING WATER, NE 68463
  (402) 267-4765 Deborah Freeman, President
Description: Maintains a prehistoric Indian artifact collection with items that date back 20,000 years.

NEVADA

NEVADA STATE MUSEUM
600 N. Carson St. • CARSON CITY, NV 89701
  (775) 687-4810 Fax 687-4168
  Website: www.nevadaculture.org
  James Barmore, Director
  Eugene Hattori, Curator of Anthropology
Description: Maintains extensive archaeological col-

lections from Nevada; Great Basin and California basketry and other ethnographic materials collections. *Special programs*: Under One Sky: Nevada's Native American Heritage - chronicles Native American history & prehistory in Nevada; Behind the Scenes tours, last Friday of the month; annual Native American art exhibition. Publications. Library. Established in 1939.

NORTHEASTERN NEVADA MUSEUM
1515 Idaho St. • ELKO, NV 89801
(702) 738-3418
Howard Hickson, Exec. Director
Shawn Hall, Assistant Director
Description: Contains ten local Shoshone Indian exhibits. *Special programs*: Talks on Native American culture and customs; contiuous art exhibit featuring 2 different artists each month. *Publication*: Quarterly historical journal. Library. Established 1969.

NEVADA STATE LOST CITY MUSEUM OF ARCHAEOLOGY
721 S. Moapa Valley Blvd.
P.O. Box 753 • OVERTON, NV 89040
(702) 397-2193
Kathryn Olson, Curator
Description: Collections include prehistoric, protohistoric, and historic Native American material culture, including: lithics, basketry, fiber arts, articles of adornment, historic photos, etc. Housed in Adobe facility constructed in 1935. Puebloan artifacts excavated from Pueblo Grande de Nevada, Lost City, Paiute Indian artifacts, and southwestern Indian crafts. *Special collection*: Photographs of 1920-30 Lost City Excavations and local history. Library.

PYRAMID LAKE MARINA MUSEUM
2500 Lake View Dr. • SUTCLIFFE, NV 89510
(702) 476-1156 Marsha Livingston, Director
Opened 1995.

NEW JERSEY

WOODRUFF MUSEUM OF INDIAN ARTIFACTS
Bridgeton Public Library
150 E. Commerce St. BRIDGETON, NJ 08302
(856) 451-2620
Gail S. Robinson, Director
Website: www.clueslib.org.
Description: Located within the Bridgeton Public Library, the museum includes approximately 20,000 Indian artifacts collected within a 30-mile radius of the library. The library has a collection of 2,000 volumes on Cumberland County history, local genealogy, and Woodland Indians. Open to the public. Opened in 1976.

THE MONTCLAIR ART MUSEUM
3 S. Mountain Ave. • MONTCLAIR, NJ 07042
(973) 746-5555 Fax 746-9118
Patterson Sims, Director
Twig Johnson, Curator of Native American Art
E-mail: tjohnson@montclairartmuseum.org
Website: www.montclairartmuseum.org
Description: Exhibits feature over 4,000 objects representing all the major culture areas: Southwest, Northwest Coast, Plains, Woodland, California, Southeast Tribes and Arctic. Exhibits of Native American art and artifacts. *Special programs*: Monthly Native American programs; teacher training workshops. Includes costumes, jewelry, and archaeological and ethnological artifacts. *Publications*: Collection and exhibition catalogs. Library. Opened in 1914.

MORRIS MUSEUM
6 Normandy Heights Rd.
MORRISTOWN, NJ 07960
(973) 971-3700 Fax 538-1842
Steven H. Miller, Executive Director
E-mail: info@morrismuseum.org
Website: www.morrismuseum.org
Description: Woodland Indians Gallery: Shows the development of Woodland culture from the Paleo-Indian through Archaic to Woodland and historic periods. North American Indian Gallery: Exhibits on the Northwest Coast, the Southwest, and the Plains Indians. *Special programs*: Educational programs for children and adults. *Publications*: Exhibition catalogs. Museum shop. Opened in 1913.

THE NEWARK MUSEUM
49 Washington St.
P.O. Box 540 • NEWARK, NJ 07101
(201) 596-6550
Mary Sue Sweeney Price, Director
Anne M. Spencer, Curator of Ethnology
Description: Maintains a permanent Native American Gallery with Indian art and artifacts representative of major culture areas of the U.S., and some from Canada. Includes pottery and textiles of the Southwest, extensive basket collection, bead and quillwork. Publications. Library. Opened in 1909.

PRINCETON UNIVERSITY- MUSEUM OF NATURAL HISTORY
Guyot Hall • PRINCETON, NJ 08540
Description: Exhibits Northwest Coast Indian art; also, artifacts, mainly Tlingit, of Yukatat and Sitka areas, Alaska, period 1876-1886. Publications. Library.

POWHATAN RENAPE NATION INDIAN HERITAGE MUSEUM
P.O. Box 225 • RANCOCAS, NJ 08073
(609) 261-4747 Fax 261-7313
Roy Crazy Horse, Director
Description: Shows the Life of the Creation; an Ancestral Village; and exhibits crafts and artifacts of the Powhatan Renape Nation. Art Gallery; Gift shop. Opened 1992.

SETON HALL UNIVERSITY MUSEUM
South Orange Ave. - Fahy Hall
SOUTH ORANGE, NJ 07079
(201) 761-9543
Dr. Herbert C. Kraft, Director
Description: An archaeology and Indian museum featuring Eastern Woodlands Indian artifacts, with emphasis on New Jersey prehistory - Paleo-Indian to European contact. Includes petroglyphs, effigies, ceramics. *Publications*: Occasional publications concerning the Lenape/Delaware Indians, prehistoric archaeology; report of excavations, etc. Library. Established 1960.

LENAPE INDIAN VILLAGE AT THE HISTORIC VILLAGE OF WATERLOO
525 Waterloo Rd. • STANHOPE, NJ 07874
(973) 347-0900 Fax 347-3573
John T. Kraft, Curator
E-mail: info@waterloovillage.org
Web site: www.waterloovillage.org
Recreated late Woodland Lenape (Delaware) Village - longhouses, ceremonial areas, simulated archaelogical site, bark wikwams, etc. Established 1985.

NEW JERSEY STATE MUSEUM
205 West State St. • TRENTON, NJ 08625
Description: Maintains a collection of ethnographic artifacts of the Lenni Lenape; also, Plains Indian beadwork, and material from Southwest, Eskimo and Northeast Indians. Library.

NEW MEXICO

ACOMA MUSEUM
Sky City Cultural Center
P.O. Box 309, Pueblo of Acoma
ACOMITA, NM 87034
(800) 747-0181
(505) 469-1052 Fax 552-7204
Brian D. Vallo, Director
Website: www.skycitytourism.com
Description: Indian history and culture museum with exhibits, photo archives and documents relating to the history of Acoma. *Special activities*: Annual Feast Day, Sept. 2nd; Christmas Celebration, Dec. 24-28; open to the public. Daily walking guided tours of "Sky City." Gift shop. Library. *Publication*: One Thousand Years of Clay, catalog. Library. Opened in 1977.

M. TULAROSA BASIN HISTORICAL SOCIETY
P.O. Box 518, 1301 White Sands Blvd.
ALAMOGORDO, NM 88310
(505) 437-4760
Terry Benson, Director
Description: Maintains a collection of Indian artifacts from the area. Opened in 1978.

INDIAN PUEBLO CULTURAL CENTER
2401 12th St., NW
ALBUQUERQUE, NM 87104
(800) 766-4405 (outside NM)
(505) 843-7270 Fax 842-6959
Rafael Gutierrez, President; Pat Reck, Curator
Description: The Main Museum consists of prehistoric to contemporary arts and crafts. A vast collection that traces the development of the Pueblo culture. Pueblo House Children's Museum offers a unique "hands on" experience for children. *Special programs*: Arts and craft demonstration program each weekend. Library/Archives. Gift Shop. Opened in 1976.

MAXWELL MUSEUM OF ANTHROPOLOGY
University & Ash, NE
ALBUQUERQUE, NM 87131
(505) 277-4404
Garth Bawden Director
E-mail: gbawden@unm.edu
Description: Exhibits relating to cultures around the world, with a special emphasis on the cultural heritage of the Southwest. Permanent exhibit: "People of the Southwest." Rotating exhibits periodically feature Native American items, including Navajo weaving, Mimbres and Pueblo pottery, Hopi Kachinas, North American Indian basketry. *Publications*: Seven Families in Pueblo Pottery; Anasazi Pottery, et al. Library. Navajo and Pueblo silver jewelry for sale.

AZTEC MUSEUM & PIONEER VILLAGE
125 N. Main Ave. • AZTEC, NM 87410
(505) 334-9829 Deah Folk, Director
Description: Historical archives, buildings and artifacts from the late 1800's. Opened in 1974.

AZTEC RUINS NATIONAL MONUMENT
84 Road 2900 • AZTEC, NM 87410
(505) 334-6174 Fax 334-6372
Charles B. Cooper, Supt.
Dana Howlett, Curator
Description: Prehistoric Pueblo Indian ruin. Two-(cultural) phase inhabitation, Chaco Canyon and Mesa Verde. *Archaeology Museum*: Anasazi artifacts gathered from excavations of area sites, and from sites in the Lower San Juan Basin. Library. Open June-August. A National Historic Landmark. Opened in 1923.

CORONADO STATE MONUMENT
P.O. Box 95 • BERNALILLO, NM 87004
(505) 867-5351
Nathan Stone, Manager
Description: Site of a partially reconstructed Pueblo Indian village ruin occupied circa 1300-1600. Includes a completely reconstructed underground ceremonial kiva, which was the first to be discovered bearing ceremonial murals. Exhibits material from the excavations and Pueblo Indian culture.

RED ROCK MUSEUM
Box 10 • CHURCH ROCK, NM 87311
(505) 863-1337 Fax 863-1297
E-mail: rrsp@ci.gallup.nm.us
Web site: www.ci.gallup.nm.us
John R. Vidal, Curator
Description: Collections consists of ethnographic and archaeological objects of the four corners cultures; fine arts and crafts of southwest Native American cultures; and photographs and archives of the history of the Gallup area. Material of prehistoric Anasazi and Navajo, Hopi, Zuni, Rio Grande Pueblos, Apache and Plains Indians. *Special collection*: Zuni kachina dolls. Special programs: Monthly art shows and traveling exhibits; artist presentations. Library. Established 1951.

DEMING LUNA MIMBRES MUSEUM
301 S. Silver St. • DEMING, NM 88030
(505) 546-2382
Treva L. Mester, Coordinator
Description: Exhibits Mimbrano Indian artifacts, and pottery.

JICARILLA ARTS & CRAFTS & MUSEUM
P.O. Box 507 • DULCE, NM 87528
(505) 759-4274
Brenda Julian, Director
Description: Collections of Jicarilla Apache baskets, paintings, pottery and beadwork. Opened in 1965.

SAN JUAN COUNTY ARCHAEOLOGICAL RESEARCH CENTER
FARMINGTON, NM 87401
(505) 632-2013 Fax 632-1707
Larry L. Baker, Executive Director
Description: Contains exhibits of artifacts taken from the Anasazi-Salmon Ruin: 1.5 million prehistoric Pueblo artifacts, replicated domiciles and exhibits representing Navajo, Ute, Jicarilla and Hispanic cultures; slides of rock art; oral history tapes; maps. *Special programs*: Educational programs and guided tours to Chaco Canyon and remote Navajo pueblos. *Publications*: Division of Conservation Archaeology Report Series; Cultural Resource Management Reports; 4,000+ archaeological reports; and historical publications. Research library. Opened in 1973.

WALATOWA VISITOR CENTER
P.O. Box 100 • JEMEZ PUEBLO, NM 87024
(505) 834-7235 Fax 834-7331
Christine Waquie, Director
Description: Maintains a replica ancestral field house; photo exhibit; nature walk. Offers visitor information and a gift shop featuring Jemez pottery and souvenirs. *Activities*: Three annual arts & crafts shows. Opened in 1993.

BANDELIER NATIONAL MONUMENT
HCR 1 Box 1, Rte. 4, Suite 15
LOS ALAMOS, NM 87544
(505) 672-3861
John D. Hunter, Supt.
Description: Approximately 29,000 acres of ruins of the Pueblo (Anasazi) culture, dating from about 1200-1600 A.D. Publications. Library. A National Historic Landmark.

MESCALERO APACHE CULTURAL CENTER MUSEUM
P.O. Box 227 • MESCALERO, NM 88340
(505) 671-4944 Fax 671-9191
Ellyn Big Rope, Director
Opened in 1972.

GADSEN MUSEUM
Barker Rd. and Hwy. 28
P.O. Box 147 • MESILLA, NM 88046
(505) 526-6293
Mary Veitch Alexander, Curator/Owner
Description: Collections include Indian artifacts from the Southwest.

SALINAS NATIONAL MONUMENT
Route 1, Box 496 • MOUNTAINAIR, NM 87036
(505) 847-2585 Thomas B. Carroll, Supt.
Description: Located on the site of prehistoric pithouses, 800 A.D.; prehistoric Indian ruins 1100-1670 A.D.; four Spanish Mission ruins, 1627-1672. An archaeology museum maintains a collection of artifacts from the ruins. Library.

CHACO CULTURE NATIONAL HISTORIC PARK
P.O. Box 220 • NAGEEZI, NM 87037-0220
(505) 786-7014
C.T. Wilson, Supt.; Philip LoPiccolo, Curator
Description: A National Historic Landmark - 13 major prehistoric Anasazi sites, and over 400 smaller village sites. *Museum*: Features 26 exhibits on Anasazi and Navajo cultures. *Special collections*: Large archaeological collection of two million artifacts and samples; Associated Documentation mostly Chaco Project including: 2,000 maps, Field Notes and Archives, 35,000 photographs and negatives, and over 5,000 color slides. Library. *Publications*: 1,500 published and unpublished manuscripts housed in Albuquerque, NM.

PECOS NATIONAL HISTORICAL PARK
P.O. Drawer 418 • PECOS, NM 87552
(505) 757-6414 • Duane L. Alire Supt.
Judy Reed, Cultural Resources Manager
Description: Pecos preserves the ruins of the great Pecos Pueblo (1400-1838) and two associated Spanish colonial missions, 17th & 18th centuries; visitor center displays over 100 artifacts, historical timeline and ten minute introductory film. Special collection: Kidder Collection - 15,000 artifacts excavated from Pecos Pueblo from 1915-1929. *Publication*: Pecos: Gateway to Pueblo and Plains: The Anthology. Library. Opened in 1965.

PICURIS PUEBLO MUSEUM
P.O. Box 487 • PENASCO, NM 87553
(505) 587-2957 Sheila Miller, Director
Opened in 1969.

BLACKWATER DRAW SITE & MUSEUM
Eastern New Mexico University, Station 3
PORTALES, NM 88130
(505) 562-2202 Fax 562-2291
Matthew J. Hillsman, Curator
Description: Maintains collection of Paleo-Indian archaeology and anthropology. Archaeological site "Clovis." *Programs*: Films, tours and lectures. *Publications*: ENMU Contributions in Anthropology. Opened in 1969.

PALEO-INDIAN INSTITUTE
Eastern New Mexico University
P.O. Box 2154 • PORTALES, NM 88130
Dr. George Agogino, Director
Description: Maintains exhibits illustrating the life of the paleo-archaic and modern Indian. Library.

EL MORRO NATIONAL MONUMENT
RAMAH, NM 87321 (505) 783-5132
Douglas Eury, Supt.
Description: Archaeological site of Inscription Rock, prehistoric Pueblo ruins. Library.

STRADLING MUSEUM OF THE HORSE
P.O. Box 40 • RUIDOSO DOWNS 88346-0040
Anne C. Stradling, Director
Description: Equine and Indian Museum. Library.

INDIAN ARTS RESEARCH CENTER
School of American Research
P.O. Box 2188 • SANTA FE, NM 87504
(505) 954-7205 Fax 954-7207
E-mail: iarc@sarsf.org
Website: www.sarweb.org
Kathy Whitaker, PhD, Director
Shannon Parker, Collections Manager
Description: Collection of 11,000+ objects of Southwestern American Indian art and anthropology; archaeology laboratory. Includes ceramics, textiles, jewelry, silverwork, paintings, basketry, katsinam, and miscellaneous objects (clothing, cradleboards, musical instruments, etc.) *Native American Artist Fellowships*: The Eric & Barbara Dobkin, Ronald & Susan Dubin, and Rollin & Mary Ella King fellowships; lectures and exhibitions; annual Native American Internship. *Fellowships*: Katrin H. Lamon Resident Scholar and Artist Fellowships for Native Americans. *Publications*: Books pertaining to the Southwest and Native American arts and culture. Library.

INSTITUTE OF AMERICAN INDIAN ARTS MUSEUM
108 Cathedral Place • SANTA FE, NM 87501
(505) 983-8900; Marguerite L. Wood, Manager
Website: www.iaiancad.org
Special collection: Student Honors Collection—Contains approximately 8,000 items—paintings, graphics, sculpture, ceramics, textiles, costumes, jewelry, and ethnological material of Native American students' work. Also, more than 1,000 items of non-student work done by Indian artists throughout the U.S. *Museum staff*: Thomas Atencio, Jary Earl, Maria Favela, Magdalene Ohnesorgen, Alison Ryan, Tatiana Slock. *Special programs*: Art festival, lectures, workshops; arts and crafts for sale. *Publication*: Spawning the Medicine River, quarterly. Native American Videotape Archives. Library & Museum shop.

MORNING STAR GALLERY
513 Canyon Rd. • SANTA FE, NM 87501
(505) 982-8187 Fax 984-2368
Joe Rivera, President
E-Mail: indian@morningstargallery.com
Website: www.morningstargallery.com
Description: Antique American Indian art.

MUSEUM OF INDIAN ARTS & CULTURE
Laboratory of Anthropology-Museum of New Mexico
708-710 Camino Lejo
P.O. Box 2087 • SANTA FE, NM 87504
(505) 476-1269 Fax 476-1330
Website: www.miaclab,org
Duane Anderson, Director
E-mail: danderson@miaclab.org

Diane Bird, Archivist
Joyce Begay-Foss, Director of Education
Valerie Verzuh, Collections Manager
Chris Baca, Information Systems
John Torres, Curator of Archaeology
Description: Consists of over 15,000 ethnographic objects and more than 26,000 archaeological objects, with emphasis on artifacts from the prehistoric, ethnographic, and present-day Indian Southwest. Features permanent exhibitions of Southwestern Indian culture. *Publications*: Papers in Anthropology; Research Records; Lab Notes; and Archaeological Surveys. Library. Laboratory established in 1930. Museum opened in 1987.

MUSEUM OF NEW MEXICO MUSEUM OF FINE ARTS
107 West Palace Ave.
P.O. Box 2087 • SANTA FE, NM 87501
(505) 476- 5072 Fax 476-5076
Website: www.mnm.state.nm.us
Marsha Bol, Director
E-mail: mbol@mnm.state.nm.us
Carla Ortiz, Administrative Assistant
Dorothy Montano, Administrative Assistant
Special collection: Indian Arts Fund Collection-Contains pottery, jewelry, and costumes; art of the Southwest. Mueum shop. Library.

MUSEUM OF NEW MEXICO
Palace of the Governors
105 West Palace Ave.
P.O. Box 2087 • SANTA FE, NM 87501
(505) 476-5100 Fax 476-5104
Website: www.mnm.state.nm.us
Fran Levine, Director
E-mail: flevine@mnm.state.nm.us
Carolotta Boettcher, Portal Program Manager
E-mail: cboettcher@mnm.state.nm.us
Tomas Jaehn, Photo Archives Curator
E-mail: tjaehn@mnm.state.nm.us
Special programs: Museum of Fine Arts; Museum of Indian Arts & Culture; Native American Vendors Portal Program (505) 827-6474 Fax 827-6521 - Includes traditional crafts of the 22 recognized New Mexico tribes and pueblos, with more than 775 Native American artists and craftspeople displaying and selling their work beneath the portal, or front porch of the museum; History Library/Photo Archives (505) 476-5090; Museum of New Mexico Press (800) 622-8667

POEH CULTURAL CENTER
Pueblo of Pojoaque
Rt. 11, Box 27-E • SANTA FE, NM 87501
(505) 455-2489 Fax 455-0174
George Rivera, Director
Opened in 1990.

SAN ILDEFONSO PUEBLO MUSEUM
Route 5, Box 315-A • SANTA FE, NM 87501
(505) 455-2424 Fax 455-7351
Opened in 1982.

WHEELWRIGHT MUSEUM OF THE AMERICAN INDIAN
P.O. Box 5153, 704 Camino Lejo
SANTA FE, NM 87502
(505) 982-4636 Fax 989-7386
Jonathan Batkin, Director
Cheri Falkenstein-Doyle, Curator
Web site: www.wheelwright.org
Description: Collections of Southwest ethnology—Navajo textiles and silver; Navajo, Apache, and Hopi basketry; Pueblo pottery; Navajo, Apache, and Pueblo cradleboards; Navajo sandpainting reproductions. *Special programs*: Lecture series; textile and basket-weaving workshops; craft demonstrations; Indian arts and crafts and books for sale. Note: Library, archives and collections not available until 2001 due to construction of new building. *Publication*: Catalogs of exhibitions; bimonthly newsletter; annual magazine. Library.

WESTERN NEW MEXICO UNIVERSITY MUSEUM
1000 W. College Ave. • SILVER CITY, NM 88061
(505) 538-6386 Fax 538-6178
Web site: www.wnmu.edu/univ/museum.htm
Dr. Cynthia Ann Bettison, Director & Archaeologist
Special collection: Eisele Collection of Southwest Pot-

tery and Artifacts; the largest permanent display of Mimbres pottery & culture in the world; Casas Grandes pottery, mining displays, traveling exhibits. *Publication*: Newsletter. Opened in 1974.

KIT CARSON HISTORIC MUSEUMS
P.O. Drawer CCC • TAOS, NM 87571
(505) 758-0505; 758-0062 (Archives) Fax 758-0330
Karen Young, Director; Skip Miller, Supt.
E-mail: skipper@laplaza.org
Web site: www.taosmuseums.org
Description: Kit Carson's 21 room Spanish colonial fortified hacienda and museum - Historic Landmark. Displays artifacts of prehistoric Indian culture of Taos and the Southwest. Southwest Research Center of Northern New Mexico, Publications: Taos Lightnin' - Kit Carson Historic Museums newsletter.

MILLICENT ROGERS MUSEUM
OF NORTHERN NEW MEXICO
P.O. Box A • TAOS, NM 87571
(505) 758-2462 Fax 758-5751
E-mail: mrm@newmex.com
Web site: www.millicentrogers.org
Dr. Shelby Tisdale, Executive Director
Description: Permanant collections feature prehistoric to contemporary works in pottery, jewelry, textiles by Native American artists & designers of the Southwest and the Plains. *Educational programs*: Lectures, workshops, guided tours. Research library. *Publications*: Membership announcements, catalogues. Opened 1956.

A:SHIWI AWAN MUSEUM & HERITAGE CENTER
P.O. Box 1009 • ZUNI, NM 87327
(505) 782-4403 FAX 782-2700
Tom Kennedy, Director
Opened in 1990.

ZUNI CULTURAL RESOURCE ENTERPRISE
Pueblo of Zuni
P.O. Box 1149 • ZUNI, NM 87327
(505) 782-4814 Fax 782-2393
Jonathan Damp, Principal Investigator
E-mail: zcre@nm.net
Description: Archaeological site record files are maintained as are a comprehensive map file and air photo file of the Reservation and surrounding areas. Unpublished manuscripts on Zuni history and archaeology are maintained. Historic photographs. *Publications*: Report Series; Research Series. Library. Opened in 1975.

NEW YORK

NEW YORK STATE MUSEUM
Cultural Education Center, Rm. 3122
Empire State Plaza • ALBANY, NY 12224
(518) 474-5813 Web site: www.nysm.nysed.gov
Toni Benedict, Specialist in Indian Culture
Special collections: Morgan Collection—Mid 19th century Seneca ethnographic material; The Beauchamp Collection—Onondaga ethnographic material; The Parker Collection—Late 19th and 20th century Iroquois ethnological and general New York archaeological materials. Publications. Library.

CAYUGA MUSEUM IROQUOIS CENTER
Rt. 38A Emerson Park, 203 Genesee St.
AUBURN, NY 13021
(315) 253-8051 Fax 253-9829
E-mail: cayugamuseum@cayuganet.org
Web site: www.cayuganet.org/cayugamuseum
Eileen McHugh, Director
Description: A collection of Iroquois and Owasco Native American artifacts including baskets, pottery, a model longhouse, French missionary rings, crosses, etc. Ely Parker, Redjacket items, and John S. Clark maps. *Special programs*: Craft classes for children in bead work, Iroquois food, games and myths. Crafts for sale. *Publication*: Quarterly museum newsletter. Library.

KATERI GALLERIES
National Shrine of North American Martyrs
AURIESVILLE, NY 12016 (518) 853-3033
Rec. Robert J. Boyle, S.J., Director

Rev. John M. Dovlan, S.J., Curator
Description: Located on the site of the martyrdom of Father Isaac Jogues, French Jesuit priest, and his companions who were killed by the Mohawk Indians in 1642. Also, the 1656 Birthplace of Kateri Tekakwitha. *Special collection*: Mohawk Indian Culture Collection—Indian artifacts and handicrafts; Indian longhouse dioramas. *Publication*: Pilgrim, quarterly magazine. Library.

TONAWANDA-SENECA MUSEUM
Tonawanda-Seneca Reservation
BASOM, NY 14013

THE BROOKLYN CHILDREN'S MUSEUM
145 Brooklyn Ave. • BROOKLYN, NY 11213
Description: Exhibits Plains Indian material; also, Southwestern, Eastern Woodlands and Northwest Indian artifacts. Library.

BUFFALO & ERIE COUNTY
HISTORICAL SOCIETY MUSEUM
Humboldt Park • BUFFALO, NY 14211
Description: Maintains a collection of Niagara frontier Indian artifacts, including clothing, masks, and tools, mostly of Iroquois village life. Publications. Library.

CULTURAL CENTER OF THE
TAINO NATION OF THE ANTILLES, INC.
58 Brightside Ave. • CENTRAL ISLIP, NY 11722
(516) 348-0786 Fax 348-1981
Miguel Angel Macano Alvarez, Chair
Purpose: To promote the history and culture of the Taino peoples located on various islands in the Caribbean; and to reclaim, restore and preserve the Taino peoples' heritage and natural language. *Programs*: Educational & tutorial programs. Another center is also located in Santa Isabel, Puerto Rico

ROCKWELL MUSEUM OF WESTERN ART
111 Cedar St. • CORNING, NY 14830
(607) 937-5386 Fax 974-4536
Kristin Swain, Executive Director
E-mail: info@rockwellmuseum.org
Web site: www.rockwellmuseum.org
Description: Houses a collection of American western and Native American art in the Eastern U.S. The collection contains masterworks by 19th & early 20th century painters and sculptors like Remington, Russell, Bierstadt, Sharp, Dallin, Moran, as well as recent works by Native American and emerging western artists like Butterfield, Quick-to-See Smith, Warhol, WalkingStick, and McHorse. *Special programs*: Tours on Native American art for all ages; hands-on collections; teacher training and outreach programs on the Iroquois. Library. Trading Post. Opened in 1976.

MUSEUM OF THE HUDSON HIGHLANDS
The Boulevard, P.O. Box 181
CORNWALL-ON-HUDSON, NY 12520
(914) 534-7781 Charles I. Keene, Director
Special collection: Eastern Woodlands Indians—Exhibits more than 80 stone artifacts; 40 modern reproductions made by a group of Iroquois. *Special program*: Native American educational aides for programs and presentations to school groups, kindergarten to fourth grades. An Indian Loan Kit comprised of an Iroquois pack basket filled with artifacts and reproductions is designed for teachers to use to complement the NYS fourth grade history curriculum. Library. Opened in 1962.

BLACK BEAR MUSEUM
P.O. Box 47 • ESOPUS, NY 12429
Roy Black Bear, Owner

TEKAKWITHA SHRINE
NATIVE AMERICAN EXHIBIT
THE MOHAWK-CAUGHNAWAGA MUSEUM
Route 5, Box 627 • FONDA, NY 12068
(518) 853-3646 Fax 853-3371
Rev. Kevin Kenny, Director
E-Mail: kkenny@klink.net
Description: Religious Shrine and Historic Archaeological Site, 1666-1693. Located on the site of the 1666-1693 excavated Caughnawaga Indian Village; Mohawk Indian Castle: residence of Kateri Tekakwitha. Displays North, South and Central American Indian artifacts, with emphasis on the Iroquois of central New

York State. Comprehensive collection of Native American artifacts, mostly Iroquois. *Publication*: Tekakwitha Nesletter, published 3 times annually. Library. Opened in 1935.

LONGYEAR MUSEUM OF ANTHROPOLOGY
Colgate University • HAMILTON, NY 13346
(315) 824-7543
Description: Features large collections of local Oneida Iroquois and Mesoamerican archaeological materials.

AKWESASNE MUSEUM
Akwesasne Cultural Center
St. Regis Mohawk Nation
RR 1, Box 14C Route 37
HOGANSBURG, NY 13655
Carol White, Director
(518) 358-2240 Fax 358-2649
Description: Showcases Mohawk culture by exhibiting contemporary Iroquoian art and mor than 3,000 historic artifacts. *Special programs*: Changing art exhibit; contemporary baskets by master basketmakers of Akwesasne; slide-tape shows on Iroquoian art; Native arts and basketmaking classes; produces movies, slide shows, and video; sells original handicrafts through Sweetgrass Gift Shop. *Publication*: Teionkwahontasen; Sweetgrass Is Around Us-Basketmakers of Akwesasne; Library. Opened in 1972.

IROQUOIS INDIAN MUSEUM
P.O. Box 7, 324 Caverns Rd.
HOWES CAVE, NY 12092
(518) 296-8949 Fax 296-8955
Erynne Ansel, Director
Stephanie Shuttes, Curator
Mike Tarbell, Museum Educator
Website: www.iroquoismuseum.org
Description: A 45-acre nature park with educational trails explaining the ethnobotany of Iroquois culture. Maintains an extensive collection of contemporary Iroquois fine art and craftwork for all six Iroquois nations; archaeological collections from the local area; photographic collections of contemporary Iroquois arts, ethnographic objects, events and people. Special programs: Children's museum - a restatement of the adult museum designed to break down stereotypes and to introduce to children the Iroquois people of today; educational programs; two Annual Iroquois Indian Festivals (Memorial Day weekend, and Labor Day weekend). Publications: Museum Notes, quarterly newsletter; Directory of Iroquois Artists & Crafts People; "Joe Jacobs, Iroquois Art," "Pete Jones: Iroquois Art," and Visual Voices of the Iroquois," and other recent exhibition catalogs. Library. Opened in 1980.

STE. MARIE AMONG THE IROQUOIS
P.O. Box 146, Onondaga Lake Park
LIVERPOOL, NY 13088
(315) 457-2990
Robert Geaci, Director; Valerie Bell, Curator
Description: A reconstruction of a 1656 French settlement among the Onondaga Iroquois. Maintains archaeological material from area sites—Onondaga cultural material. *Special programs*: Living History Program—interpretation of Onondaga Indian culture; lectures. *Publication*: Onondaga Portrait of a Native People. Library.

AMERICAN INDIAN GALLERY & GIFT SHOP
American Indian Community House
708 Broadway, 2nd Fl. • NEW YORK, NY 10003
(212) 598-0100 ext. 241 Fax 598-4909
Website: www.aich.org/gallery/gal.htm
Kathleen Ash-Milby, Curator
Monica Green, Gift Shop Manager
Description: Displays Native-American art work. Opened in 1978.

AMERICAN MUSEUM OF NATURAL HISTORY
79th St. & C.P.W. • NEW YORK, NY 10024
(212) 769-5375 Ian Tattersall, PhD, Chairman
Stanley A. Freed, PhD, Curator
Special collections: Eskimo Exhibit, and Indians of the Northwest Coast—Artifacts of the Coast Salish, Nootka, Haida, Tsimpshean, Thompson, Bella Coola, Tlingit, and Kwakiutl; also, shamanistic regalia and ceremonial objects. *Publications*: Natural History; Curator; Bulletin; Anthropological Papers. Library and Reading Room.

GEORGE GUSTAV HEYE CENTER
NATIONAL MUSEUM OF THE AMERICAN INDIAN
Smithsonian Institution
1 Bowling Green • NEW YORK, NY 10004
(212) 283-2420 Fax 491-9302
Dr. Duane King, Director
Vine Deloria, Jr., Vice-Chairperson, Trustees
Mary Jane , Curator of North American Ethnology
Peter Scott Brill, Curator of Exhibits
Lee A. Callander, Registrar
Carmen Sanchez, Public Affairs Specialist
Judith A. Brundin, Head Educator
Elizabeth Weatherford, Curator/Film & Video Center
Barbara J. Christ, Manager, Museum Store
Ellen Jamieson, Publications Manager
Description: Acknowledged to be one of the largest and finest assemblage of artifacts representing the native cultures of North, Central & South America, the Museum (founded 1916) is a national treasury unsurpassed for its potential for education and research. Its areal and temporal scope is vast, ranging from Alaska to Chile and from the Paleo-Indian period to the present, encompassing societies as diverse as the 20th century hunting band societies of the Arctic and subarctic and the ancient agricultural civilizations of the Aztec and Inca. The artifacts in the collections range from precious ornaments to commonplace tools, from projectile points to abstract paintings by contemporary Indian artists. The Central & South American and the Caribbean collections include ancient ornaments of Mexican jade and turquoise, ancient gold, silver, basketry, fabrics, and pottery, stone, and shell sculptures from the Antilles. The North American collections include silver and turquoise jewelry, weavings, and pottery from the Southwest; painted wooden sculptures from the Northwest Coast; ancient carved shell artifacts from the Southeast; and carved ivory and stone from the Arctic. *Special programs*: Education Department offers guided tours, visiting Native American artists and artisans, and a lecture series; The Film and Video Center researches and exhibits film and video productions concerned with Inuit & Indian peoples of the Americas; The Indian Information Center makes available to the public a wide variety of information concerning the native peoples of the Americas; The Museum Store offers a wide variety of contemporary Indian crafts from many tribes, and books, slides, etc. *Publications*: Indian Notes; quarterly newsletter; Museum schedule of exhibits & public programs; exhibition catalogs, archaeological reports, ethnological studies, bibliographies & biographies published by the Museum for sale; Native American Film & Video Catalog. *Photographic Archives*: Contains approximately 70,000 photographs documenting Native American life in the Western Hemisphere. Slides & prints are available for purchase. Library.

SIX NATIONS INDIAN MUSEUM
HCR 1, Box 10 • ONCHIOTA, NY 12989
(518) 891-2299
John Fadden, Director
E-mail: redmaple@northnet.org
Website: www.thebeadsite.com/mus-f4.htm
Description: Located in the northeastern Adirondack Mountains. Dedicated to preserving the culture of the Iroquois Confederacy (Mohawks, Senecas, Onondagas, Oneidas, Cayugas and Tuscaroras), the Museum exhibits pre-Columbian, historic, as well as contemporary items of Iroquois culture—clothing, tools, crafts, baskets, and objects of art; a collection of charts, posters, and written material; miniature Abenaki, Lakota, Delaware and Mohegan villages. Provides the viewing of 3,000+ artifacts with an emphasis on the Six Nations of the Iroquois Confederacy. *Special programs*: Lectures on Native-American history and culture, story telling, lectures; Gift shop carries Mohawk baskets, beadwork, soapstone carving, wooden jewelry, and acrylic paintings reflecting Six Nations Iroquois culture. Open July-August; open by appointment to groups from mid-May through June 30, and September. Closed on Mondays. Admission. Brochure with S.A.S.E. Opened in 1954.

SHAKO:WI CULTURAL CENTER
5 Territory Rd. • ONEIDA, NY 13421-9304
(315) 363-1424 FAX 363-1843
David Drucker, Director
E-mail: drucker@oneida-nation.org
Website: www.one-web.org/oneida/

Description: Contains historic and contemporary exhibits. Activities: Tours, craft and dance workshops, lectures, language and literature classes. Opened in 1993.

MUSEUMS AT HARTWICK
Hartwick College • ONEONTA, NY 13820-9989
(607) 431-4480
George H.J. Abrams, Director
Dr. David Anthony, Curator of Collection
Yager Museum: A collection of upper Susquehanna Indian artifacts, and Southwest basketry and pottery. Library. Opened in 1928.

ROCHESTER MUSEUM & SCIENCE CENTER
657 East Ave. • ROCHESTER, NY 14607
(716) 271-4320 Fax 271-0492
Kate Bennett, President
Dr. George McIntosh, Director of Collections
E-mail: george-mcintosh@rmsc.org
Web site: www.rmsc.org
Description: Exhibits and collections of natural science, regional history, and anthropology. Exhibits and collections in archaeology, from 12,000 B.C. through the 19th century, and in ethnology, from the 18th through the 20th centuries, relating to non-Indians and to American Indians with emphasis on New York State Haudenosaunee people, especially Senecas. *Special archaeological and ethnological collections*: Lewis Henry Morgan mid-19th Century collection of Woodlands, Plains, and Southwestern Indian material; Indian Arts Project collection produced by Haudenosaunee arts and crafts workers in the 1930's and 40's. "At the Western Door," permanent exhibit detailing story of contact between Senecas, Europeans and Americans in western New York, A.D. 1550 to the present. *Publications*: Members' newsletter; Research Records series, and exhibit catalogs. Research library. Opened in 1912.

SENECA-IROQUOIS NATIONAL MUSEUM
Allegany Indian Reservation
794-814 Broad St. • SALAMANCA, NY 14779
(716) 945-1738/3895 Fax 945-1760
Michele Dean Stock, Director
E-mail: seniroqm@localnet.com
Description: Devoted to the presentation of the prehistory, history, and contemporary heritage of the Seneca Nation of Indians, and, in a wider sense, the Iroquois culture. Collection includes an extensive array of prehistoric Iroquois artifacts, post-contact trade beads, material culture items, and contemporary Iroquois art, as well as photos and papers. Special programs: Special exhibits on a regular basis, which have included Iroquois basketry, Iroquois Veterans in Two Worlds, and the Death & Rebirth of Iroquois Pottery. Also limited off-site cultural presentations. *Publication*: 1981 Collections of the Seneca-Iroquois National Museum. Library. Museum shop. Opened in 1977.

SHINNECOCK NATION
CULTURAL CENTER & MUSEUM
Shinnecock Indian Reservation
P.O. Box 5059
SOUTHAMPTON, NY 11969-5059
(631) 287-4923 Fax 287-7153
Website: www: shinnecock-museum@yahoo.org
David Bunn Martine, Director
Description: Collections span the six cultural phases of history from palelithic to historic, consisting of baskets, arrowheads, painted murals, wood carvings, photographs, whalebone, stuffer animals. Programs: Education, art festivals, oral history. *Activities*: Monthly cable show "Voices of Native America," Channel 25 cable vision. Archives - documents, books, photos. Opened 1994.

SOUTHOLD INDIAN MUSEUM
The Incorporated Long Island Chapter
New York State Archaeological Assn.
1080 Main Bayview Rd., P.O. Box 268
SOUTHOLD, NY 11971 (631) 965-5577
E-mail: indianmuseum@aol.com
Ellen Barcel, President
Description: Collections include artifacts of Long Island Indians including wood, stone and bone tools. Colorful murals list the subdivisions of Algonquins that inhabited Eastern Long Island and illustrate their mode

of life. Also a large collection of Algonquin ceramic pottery, pots and bowls carved out of soapstone and a collection of projectile points (arrow heads). *Special programs*: Educational for students in grades K-5; Summer programs for students in grades 3-6. *Activities*: Guided tours of the Algonquin Flint Mines at Coxsackie, New York. *Publications*: Southold Indian Museum News (quarterly newsletter); teachers kits, informational leaflets, museum guide, and other educational materials. Library. Gift shop. Established 1962.

GANONDAGAN STATE HISTORIC SITE
P.O. Box 239, 1488 State Route 444
VICTOR, NY 14564
(585) 924-5848 Fax 742-2353
G. Peter Jemison, Historic Site Manager
Website: www.ganondagan.org
Description: Located at the late 17th century Seneca Indian settlement. Maintains collections of site related artifacts. Seneca artifacts and other Haudenosaunee (Iroquois) artifacts. Also, contemporary Iroquois arts and crafts. *Special programs*: Lectures, workshops, demonstrations and festivals, i.e. Native American Dance and Music Festival, last weekend in July. Small reference library. *Publications*: Si Wong Geh, newsletter; Art from Ganondagan; War Against the Seneca by John Mohawk. *Hours*: 9-5 Tues.-Sun., mid-May to end of October. Opened in 1987.

NORTH CAROLINA

RESEARCH LABORATORIES OF ARCHAEOLOGY
University of North Carolina
CB #3120 Alumni Bldg.
CHAPEL HILL, NC 27599
(919) 962-6574
Vincas Steponaitis, Director
Description: Large collection of Southeastern archaeological materials, including over 5 million specimens, extensive photographic collection dating from the 1930s. *Publication*: "North Carolina Archaeology," published jointly with the North Carolina Archaeological Society. Library.

MUSEUM OF THE CHEROKEE INDIAN
U.S. Hwy. 441 North, Box 770-A
CHEROKEE, NC 28719
(704-497-3481 Fax 497-4985
E-mail: cherokeeinfo@cherokee-nc.com
Website: www.cherokee-nc.com/cultural.htm
Juanita Hughes, Curator
Ken Blankenship, Director
Maxine Hill, General Manager
Description: Exhibits Cherokee Indian artifacts, relics and documents. *Publication*: Journal of Cherokee Studies, semiannual. Library. Opened in 1948.

SCHIELE MUSEUM REFERENCE LIBRARY
& CENTER FOR SOUTHEASTERN
NATIVE AMERICAN STUDIES
1500 E. Garrison Blvd. • GASTONIA, NC 28054
(704) 865-6131 Alan May, Archaeologist
Steve Watts & Melissa Turney, Native American Ed.
Ms. M. Turner, Registrar & Librarian
Description: Maintains extensive holdings of Native-American artifacts, clothing, utensils, rugs, pottery, jewelry, costumes, arts and crafts, etc. spanning known history; collections of 12 major cultural areas throughout the U.S. and Canada; specialized collections on Southeast Indians, especially pottery; also, lithic material from the Southeast with special sections relating to local areas of North Carolina. The Catawba Village: A replicated Southeastern Indian village, circa 1550, representing Catawba and Southeastern Indian architecture and lifestyles from the 16th through 19th centuries. *Special programs*: Catawba Village Study-Tour Program designed for grades 4 and up, where students explore the ways and means of aboriginal life; contract courses; workshops; The Southeastern Indian Culture Study Group; annual Native-American Fall Festival in September. Library.

INDIAN MUSEUM OF THE CAROLINAS
607 Turnpike Rd. • LAURINBURG, NC 28352
(910) 276-5880
Dr. Margaret Houston, Director
Description: Exhibits Indian archaeological material

and modern Native American art and artifacts of North and South Carolina, and the Southeast U.S. Comparative displays show artifacts from other geographic areas. *Special programs*: Evening speakers program; guided tours. Library.

TOWN CREEK INDIAN MOUND
STATE HISTORIC SITE
509 Town Creek Mound Rd.
MT. GILEAD, NC 27306
(910) 439-6802 Fax 439-6441
Archie C. Smith, Jr., Site Manager
Description: A reconstructed 14th century Indian ceremonial center, based on archaeological data and early documents, includes major temple on an earthen mound, minor temple, priest house, mortuary, game pole, and stockade surrounding the ceremonial area. *Museum*: Exhibits area interpreting way of life of the Indians at Town Creek, includes artifacts discovered during excavation of the site.*Special program*: 18-minute slide presentation on way of life of the Indians at Town Creek; guided tours; Festival and Pow-Wow in November. Opened in 1937.

NATIVE AMERICAN RESOURCE CENTER
University of North Carolina at Pembroke
P.O. Box 1510 • PEMBROKE, NC 28372
(910) 521-6282
Dr. Stanley Knick, Director/Curator
E-Mail: knick@nat.uncp.edu
Web site: www.uncp.edu/native museum
Description: Museum housing various collections of archaeological and ethnographic artifacts from Native Americans in North and South America, with emphasis on Eastern Woodlands. *Publications*: "Spirit!", quarterly newsletter; Along the Trail: A Reader About Native Americans; Robeson Trails Archaeological Survey. Library. Opened in 1979.

MUSEUM OF ANTHROPOLOGY
Wake Forest University, Box 7267
WINSTON-SALEM, NC 27109
(919) 759-5282 Fax 759-5116
Dr. Mary Jane Berman, Director/Curator
E-Mail: berman@wfu.edu
Web site: http://www.wfu.edu/museum.html
Description: An anthropology museum exhibiting North and South American Indian cultures. *Special programs*: School tours and lectures, kindergarten to 8th grade; college classes, adult education; traveling exhibitions. Library.*Publication*: Newsletter; gallery guides. Opened in 1963.

NORTH DAKOTA

TURTLE MOUNTAIN CHIPPEWA
HERITAGE CENTER
Hwy. 5, P.O. Box 257
BELCOURT, ND 58316
(701) 477-6140
Denise Lajimodierre, CEO & Chair
Juanita Bennett, Director
Description: Maintains collections of CVhippewa Indian artifacts and contemporary art. Opened in 1981.

STATE HISTORICAL SOCIETY OF NORTH DAKOTA
North Dakota Heritage Center
Capitol Grounds • BISMARCK, ND 58505
(701) 224-2666
James E. Sperry, Supt.
Description: Collections include ethnological, ethnographical, and prehistory materials of all types dating throughout the eras of known occupation of the northern Great Plains by human beings (circa 10,000 B.C. to present.) *Publications*: North Dakota History: Journal of the Northern Great Plains; Plains Talk, Newsletter. Archives and Library.

BUFFALO TRAILS MUSEUM
Box 22, Main St. • EPPING, ND 58801
(701) 859-4082
John Hanson, President
Description: Depicts Indian culture native to the region (Upper Missouri area.) Exhibits Plains Indian artifacts; Diorama of Assiniboin Indian Village; Diorama of Fortified Hidatsa Village. *Publication*: Museum brochure. Library. Opened in 1966.

STANDING ROCK RESERVATION MUSEUM
FORT YATES, ND 58538

NORTH DAKOTA MUSEUM OF ART
P.O. Box 7305, University Station
GRAND FORKS, ND 58202
(701) 777-4195
Laurel J. Reuter, Director
Displays American Indian art.

MUSEUM OF THE BADLANDS
P.O. Box 198 • MEDORA, ND 58645
(701) 623-4444
Description: Exhibits attire & crafts
of North American Indian tribes.

FORT ABRAHAM LINCOLN STATE PARK
4480 Fort Lincoln Rd. • MANDAN, ND 58554
(701) 667-6340 Fax 667-6349
E-mail: falsp@state.nd.us
Web site: www.state.nd.us/ndparks
Dan Schelske, Director
Dale Carlson, Curator
Description: Museum houses artifacts from Great Plains tribes including the Mandan. There is also a reconstructed Mandan Indian Village within walking distance. *Special program*: Cultural Indian Celebration (Nu'Eta Corn & Buffalo Festival) held first weekendeach August. Library. Established 1907.

THREE AFFILIATED TRIBES MUSEUM
P.O. Box 147 • NEW TOWN, ND 58763
(701) 627-4477 Fax 627-3805
Marilyn Hudson, Administrator
Description: History and cultural artifacts, including exhibits and photos relating to the Mandan, Hidatsa and Arikara tribes of the Fort Berthold Reservation from the early 1800's to the present time. Library. Opened in 1964.

KNIFE RIVER INDIAN VILLAGES
NATIONAL HISTORIC SITE
P.O. Box 9 • STANTON, ND 58571
(701) 745-3300 Fax 745-3708
Lisa Eckert, Supt.; E-mail: knri_info@nps.gov
Website: www.nps.gov/knri
Description: Established as a National Historic Site in 1974 to preserve remnants of the culture and agricultural lifeways of the Northern Plains Indians. Exhibits, an orientation film, and a full-sized earthlodge show the day-to-day life and customs of the Northern Plains Indians; includes Hidatsa/Mandan cultural artifacts. *Programs*: Weekend activities and special events may include demonstrations on gardening, hide tanning, tool making, clothing decorating, or native American dancing; laboratory provides for continuing archaeological research. The Northern Plains Indian Culture Fest is in the 4h weekend of July. *Publication*: Brochure. Library. Opened in 1974.

OHIO

MOUND CITY GROUP NATIONAL MONUMENT
16062 State Rt. 104 • CHILLICOTHE, OH 45601
(614) 774-1125 William Gibson, Supt.
Robert Petersen, Park Ranger
Description: A 240 acre park preserving 23 burial mounds and two Hopewell earthen enclosures. Collections illustrate the wide spread Hopewell trade network between B.C. 200 and 500 A.D. *Museum*: Exhibits of Hopewell artifacts. Library. Opened in 1923.

CINCINNATI ART MUSEUM
Eden Park • CINCINNATI, OH 45202
(513) 721-5204 Fax 721-0129
Barbara K. Gibbs, Director; Bill Mercer, Curator
Description: Displays archaeological and ethnographic objects. Archaeological—principally Mound Builder, also Adena, Hopewell, Fort Ancient cultures from Ohio; stone, bone, metal, shell, and pottery from Tennessee and Arkansas; Casas Grandes pottery. Ethnographic collections primarily Northwest Coast, Plains and Pueblo pottery. Some prehistoric and historic Woodlands material in collection. *Special collection*: A permanent exhibition gallery for Native American art; periodic speial temporaryt exhibitions and programming (speakers and art demonstrations) related to Native

American art. *Publication*: "Art of the First Americans" and "Singing the Clay: Pueblo Pottery of the Southwest Yesterday and Today" exhibition catalogs. Library. Opened in 1881.

JOHNSON-HUMRICKHOUSE MUSEUM
300 N. Whitewoman St., Roscoe Village
COSHOCTON, OH 43812
(740) 622-8710 Fax 622-8710 *51
Patti Malenke & Terry Reddick, Co-directors
E-mail: jhmuseum@clover.net
Website: www.jhm.lib.oh.us
Description: Native American Gallery exhibits paleo to modern North American Indian and Inuit arts, crafts, basketry, beadwork, blankets and jewelry. Chronologically arranged prehistoric artifacts date back thousands of years and include projectile points, primitive tools and pottery made by Ohio's aboriginal people. *Special collection*: Indian-made baskets are displayed geographically, depicting various designs and styles from tribes coast to coast. *Special programs*: Educational programs. *Publication*: Quarterly newsletter; "American Indian Basketry," a catalog featuring baskets in the museum's collection. Reference library. Opened in 1931.

RUTHERFORD B. HAYES PRESIDENTIAL CENTER
Spiegel Grove • FREMONT, OH 43420
(800) 998-7737 Fax (419) 332-4952
Dr. Murney Gerlach, Director
E-mail: mgerlach@rbhayes.org
Web site: www.rbhayes.org
Description: A collection of artifacts, largely of the Plains Indians, the Sioux, and some Pueblo; prehistoric Ohio Indian artifacts. *Publications*: The Statesman, newsletter. Library. Opened 1916.

FLINT RIDGE STATE MEMORIAL
The Ohio Historical Society
7091 Brownsville Rd. SE
GLENFORD, OH 43739
(614) 787-2476
James Kingery, Site Manager
Andy Hite, Educational Specialist
Description: The museum is built around an original Hopewell Flint Quarry site and emphasizes the uses of flint by prehistoric Native Americans. Collections include art objects and other media representing achievements of the Adeba and Hopewell cultures 1000 B.C. to 700 A.D. *Special collection*: Display objects made of flint; depict Native Americans quarrying and chipping the mineral. Programs are scheduled for the general public.

FORT ANCIENT MUSEUM
LEBANON, OH 45036
(513) 932-4421
Description: Located 7 miles southeast of Lebanon, 240 feet above the Little Miami River, the prehistoric Hopewell Indians (ca. 100 B.C. - A.D. 500) constructed earth and stone walls 4-23 feet high. Around A.D. 1200, groups of Fort Ancient Indians established themselves in villages. Exhibits models and life study groups of the Hopewell and Fort Ancient people who occupied the site. A National Historic Landmark.

SCHOENBRUNN VILLAGE STATE MEMORIAL
P.O. Box 129, East High Ave.
NEW PHILADELPHIA, OH 44663-0129
(216) 339-3636
Susan Goehring, Site Mgr.
Description: Founded by David Zeisberger in 1772 as a Moravian mission to the Delaware Indians. Restored to appear as it did over 200 years ago. *Museum*: Tells the story of the Christian Delawares and the Moravian missionaries at Schoenbrunn. Special program: Volunteer interpreters conduct daily life demonstrations in period costume. *Publication*: Schoenbrunn and the Moravian Missions in Ohio. Opened in 1923.

MOUNDBUILDERS STATE MEMORIAL
THE OHIO INDIAN ART MUSEUM
99 Cooper Ave. • NEWARK, OH 43055
(614) 344-1920
James Kingery, Site Manager
Andy Hite, Education Specialist
Description: Prehistoric Indian Art Museum and Historic Site depicting The Great Circle Earthworks—ceremonial grounds of prehistoric Hopewell Indians, circa

1000 B.C. - 700 A.D. Exhibits art objects and other relics representing Adena and Hopewell cultures. The art museum is the nation's first museum devoted to prehistoric Native American art. It is centered around a prehistoric timeline. Exhibits follow this timeline from paleo to Fort Ancient peoples. Programs are scheduled for the general public.

INDIAN MUSEUM OF LAKE COUNTY
391 W. Washington • PAINESVILLE, OH 44077
(440) 352-1911; Ann L. Dewald, Director
Description: Houses pre-contact artifacts: crafts and art of Native North American cultures from 1800 to the present. Library. Opened 1980.

SERPENT MOUND MUSEUM
State Rt. 73, Box 234
PEEBLES, OH 45660
(937) 587-2796
Website: www.ohiohistory.org
Keith A. Bengtson, Site Manager
Description: One of 63 sites maintained by the Ohio Historical Society. The museum has displays on the prehistoric cultures that occupied the area. *Special programs:* Archaeolgy days festival; 4th grade educational programs.

PIQUA HISTORICAL AREA STATE MEMORIAL WOODLAND INDIAN MUSEUM
9845 N. Hardin Rd. • PIQUA, OH 45356-9707
(800) 752-2619; (937) 773-2522 Fax 773-4311
Andy Hite, Site Manager
E-mail: johnstonfarm@mail2.wesnet.com
Website: www.ohiohistory.org
Description: Restored 1829 home and outbuildings of federal Indian agent John Johnston. He was well respected by the Indians of Ohio and handled many of the important treaties of his era. The site has been recently renovated to include exhibits telling the story of the Woodland peoples of Ohio from the time of Euro-American contact to 1843. The impact of trade between these people is a major focus, as is the story of the Pickawillany village site, also a part of this 250-acre State Memorial. The story is told through objects of the time period, many from the site itself, and a life-size diorama featuring a trade scene between the Indians and an English trader. There are several interactive exhibits containing artifacts of Native American tools, art, canoes, costumes, etc. A collection of McKenney-Hall prints as well as Catlin prints are displayed. Museum shop. Opened in 1972.

OKLAHOMA

CHICKASAW CULTURAL CENTER
520 E. Arlington St. • ADA, OK 74820
(405) 436-2603 Fax 436-7226
Glenda A. Galvan, Director
E-mail: cnation@chickasaw.com
Description: Preservews artifacts, pictures and items used by Chickasaws. *Activities:* Oral history videos, public speaking, demonstrations, storytelling, tours, traveling exhibits; Chickasaw language ad genealogy research. Opened in 1986.

APACHE TRIBAL MUSEUM
P.O. Box 1220 • ANADARKO, OK 73005
(405) 247-9493

DELAWARE TRIBAL MUSEUM
c/o Delaware Executive Board
P.O. Box 825 • ANADARKO, OK 73005

INDIAN CITY, USA, INC.
P.O. Box 695 • ANADARKO, OK 73005
(800) 433-5661; (405) 247-5661 Fax 247-2467
George F. Moran, Director
E-mail: info@indiancityusa.com
Website: www.indiancityusa.com
Description: Features reconstructed Plains Indian dwellings; also, Indian history museum located on site of 1887, Tonkawa Massacre. Exhibits Indian artifacts, including pottery, paintings, weapons, traditional clothing, dance costumes, and dolls. *Activities:* Guided tours through reconstructed Indian dwellings year 'round; traditional dance performances during summer months. Opened in 1955.

NATIONAL HALL OF FAME FOR FAMOUS AMERICAN INDIANS
Highway 62, Box 808 • ANADARKO, OK 73005
(405) 247-5795
Allie Reynolds, President
Paul T. Stonum, Executive V.P.
Description: An outdoor museum containing sculptured bronze portraits of famous American Indians in a landscaped area. Includes portraits of Will Rogers, Jim Thorpe, Pocahontas, Chief Joseph, Sacajawea, Chief Quanah Parker, Charles Curtis, Osceola, Sequoyah, Pontiac, Hiawatha, et al. Special programs: Annual dedication ceremonies in August, when an honoree is inducted; educational seminars regarding inductee's history and contribution to the American way of life.

SOUTHERN PLAINS INDIAN MUSEUM
715 E. Central Blvd.
P.O. Box 749 ANADARKO, OK 73005
(405) 247-6221 Fax 247-7593
Rosemary Ellison, Curator
E-mail: iacb@os.doi.gov
Website: www.iacb.doi.gov
Description: Presents the richness and diversity of historic arts created by the tribal peoples of western Oklahoma, including the Kiowa, Comanche, Kiowa-Apache, Southern Cheyenne, Southern Arapaho, Wichita, Caddo, Delaware, and Fort Sill Apache. Exhibits the creative achievements of Native American artists and craftspeople of the U.S. Highlighting the exhibit is a display of the varied traditional costumes of Southern Plains men, women and children, presented in complete detail on life-size figures; four dioramas and a mural illustrating historic Indian cultural subjects, created by artist and sculptor, Allan Houser, a Fort Sill Apache and native Oklahoman. *Special programs:* Annual series of one-person exhibitions; demonstrations of Native American arts and crafts techniques; hosts events honoring Native-Americans; The American Indian Exposition, in August, features a week-long event of dance contests, arts and crafts; tours and Gallery discussions. *Publications:* Illustrated catalogs and brochures. Craft shop. Administered by the Indian Arts and Crafts Board. Opened in 1947.

WICHITA & AFFILIATED TRIBES MUSEUM
P.O. Box 729 • ANADARKO, OK 73005
(405) 247-2425 Fax 247-2430
Description: General collection consists of very small displays depicting traditional homes, clothing, food, and/or household items; cultural artifacts of religious significance; pictures of tribal members and places of importance with explanations of mythology, religious occasions or ceremonials. Also traditional construction of dwellings with a display of a grass lodge diorama; and displays of various items found by archaeologists at several digging sites. *Publications:* Wichita Tribal Newsletter, quarterly; book - "The Wichita People," by W.W. Newcomb, Jr.; two pamphlets: "Wichita Memories" and "Southern Plains Lifeways," Apache and Wichita. Opened in 1978.

FORT SILL APACHE TRIBAL MUSEUM
Rt. 2, Box 121 • APACHE, OK 73006
(405) 588-2298 FAX 588-3133
Ruey Barrow, Director

WOOLAROC MUSEUM
RR 3, Box 2100
BARTLESVILLE, OK 74003
(918) 336-0307 Fax 336-0084
E-mail: woolaroc1@aol.com
Website: www.woolaroc.org
Kenneth Meek, Interim Director
Description: Exhibits art and artifacts of the Plains and Southwest Indian tribes, as well as archaeological material from Oklahoma excavations and elsewhere. *Special program:* Docent-led tours. Publications. Library. Opened 1929.

CADDO CULTURAL CENTER
P.O. Box 487 • BINGER, OK 73009
(405) 656-2344 Fax 656-2892
Stacey Halfmoon, Director

MEMORIAL INDIAN MUSEUM
P.O. Box 483, Second & Allen Sts.
BROKEN BOW, OK 74728
(405) 584-6531 LaMarr Smith, Director

Description: A collection of prehistoric Indian artifacts, early beadwork; displays modern textiles and basketry. *Research:* Prehistoric Caddo Indians and their pottery. Library.

KIOWA TRIBAL MUSEUM
P.O. Box 369 • CARNEGIE, OK 73015
(405) 654-2300 Fax 654-2188
Juanita Ahtone, Director
Exhibit: "The View From Rainy Mountain." The New Kiowa Murals by Parker Boyiddle, Mirac Creepingbear, and Sherman Chaddleson. Each artist produced three 6'x8' paintings depicting periods of Kiowa existence. Listening to their elders, they selected highlights from the creation stories, pre-history, and historic periods. A tenth mural, a collaborative painting, represents Kiowa reality today and its journey into tomorrow.

WILL ROGERS MEMORIAL & BIRTHPLACE
P.O. Box 157 • CLAREMORE, OK 74018
(918) 341-0719 Joseph H. Carter, Director
Web site: www.willrogers.org
Description: Consists of eight main galleries displaying the personal effects and memorabilia belonging to Will Rogers. The family tomb adjoins the Memorial building. *Special collection:* The original manuscripts and papers belonging to Will Rogers. *Activity:* An annual Will Rogers Day celebration is held on November 4th to commemorate his birthday. Library.

CHEYENNE CULTURAL CENTER
RR 1 Box 3130 • CLINTON, OK 73601
(405) 323-6224
Lawrence H. Hart, Director

NO MAN'S LAND HISTORICAL MUSEUM
P.O. Box 278, Sewell St.
GOODWELL, OK 73939
(405) 349-2670 (phone & fax)
Dr. Kenneth R. Turner, Director
Special collections: William E. Baker Archaeology Collection, W. Guy Clark Collection, and Duckett alabaster carvings. Contains artifacts of the Plains Indians collected by local residents of the Oklahoma Panhandle on their land to preserve the Indian cultures that preceded them on the land. Library. Opened in 1932.

CHEROKEE COURTHOUSE
Rte. 2 Box 37-1 • GORE, OK 74435
(918) 489-5663
John Pruitt, Curator
Description: Displays and exhibits on the history of the Cherokee Indians

MUSEUM OF THE RED RIVER
812 E. Lincoln Rd. • IDABEL, OK 74745
(580) 286-3616
Henry Moy, Director
E-mail: motrr@hotmail.com
Website: www.museumoftheredriver.org
Description: Collections include art and artifacts of historic, prehistoric and contemporary Native peoples of North and South America. Emphasis on local Caddoan prehistory and early Oklahoma Choctaws. Regularly changing exhibits interpret other Native American arts and cultures. Library. *Publications:* Leaflets supplement exhibits. Opened 1975.

KANZA MUSEUM
Drawer 50, 698 Grandview Dr.
KAW CITY, OK 74641
(405) 269-2552 Fax 269-2301
James Pepper Henry, Director
E-mail: kanza@southwind.net
Website: www.southwind.net/kanza
Opened in 1996.

COMANCHE CULTURAL CENTER
P.O. Box 908 • LAWTON, OK 73502
(405) 429-1990

MUSEUM OF THE GREAT PLAINS
P.O. Box 68 • LAWTON, OK 73502
Steve Wilson, Director; Dan Provo, Curator
Description: Maintains exhibits and artifacts representing the Plains Indian material culture from prehistoric times to present. *Publications:* Great Plains Journal; Newsletter; books for sale. Library.

ATALOA LODGE MUSEUM
Bacone College, 2299 Old Bacone Rd.
MUSKOGEE, OK 74403
(918) 683-4581 ext. 283 Fax 687-5913
Dr. Dennis Tanner, President
Thomas R. McKinney, Director
Description: Historic site. Displays Native American artifacts: rugs, beadwork, blankets, basketry, pottery and quillwork. *Special collections*: Large collection of San Ildenfonso pottery; items that were personal property of Native American chiefs; signed documents by President Abraham Lincoln and Chief John Ross of the Cherokee Nation. Library. *Publications*: Baconian and Smoke Signals, booklets; brochures on the museum. Opened in 1967.

FIVE CIVILIZED TRIBES MUSEUM
Agency Hill on Honor Heights Dr.
MUSKOGEE, OK 74401
(918) 683-1701 Fax 683-3070
Lynn Hart Thornley, Director
Description: Exhibits art, artifacts, books, documents, and letters pertaining to the history and culture of the Cherokees, Choctaws, Creeks, Chickasaws, and Seminoles. Housed in the Indian Agency Building built in 1875. Depicts "Trail of Tears" travel and artifacts. Art Gallery of Traditional Indian Art, only by artists of Five Tribes heritage. Maintains an extensive art and sculpture collection, Jerome Tiger Originals; original carvings and sculptures of Willard Stone. *Special program*: Sponsors four competitive art shows annually - crafts, sculpture, paintings. *Publications*: Quarterly newsletter; Pow Wow Chow Cookbook; The Cherokees; The Muskogee Book; Limited edition artist signed art prints. Gift Shop. Library. Opened in 1966.

FRED JONES, JR. MUSEUM OF ART
University of Oklahoma
410 W. Boyd St. • NORMAN, OK 73019
(405) 325-3272 Fax 325-7696
Eric M. Lee, Director/ Chief Curator
Web site: http://ou.edu/fjjma
Description: Traditional and contemporary Native American art including painting, sculpture, ceramics, baskets, and textiles. *Publications*: Exhibition catalogs. Library. Opened in 1936.

OKLAHOMA MUSEUM OF NATURAL HISTORY
University of Oklahoma
1335 Asp Ave. • NORMAN, OK 73019
(405) 325-4711
Dr. Michael A. Mares, Director
Description: Maintains a permanent exhibit on Oklahoma prehistoric and historic Indian tribes; North American archaeological and ethnological specimens, depicting the development of Southern Plains, Southwest and Northwest Coast Indian cultures; also, material from the Spiro Mounds. *Special programs*: Educational; slide/tape programs: Wichita Memories, The Plains Apache, Native American Games, and Spiro Mounds. *Publications*: Newsletter; "Heritage at Risk"; Oklahoma Indian Artifacts. Opened in 1899.

OKLAHOMA MUSEUM OF HISTORY
Oklahoma Historical Society
2100 N. Lincoln Blvd.
OKLAHOMA CITY, OK 73105
(405) 522-5248 Fax 522-5402
Dan Provo, Director
Jeff Moore, Ethnology Curator
E-mail: dprovo@ok-history.mus.ok.us
E-mail: jeffmoore@ok-history.mus.ok.us
Dennis W. Zotigh, Indian Research Historian
E-mail: dzotigh@ok-history.mus.ok.us
Website: www.ok-history.mus.ok.us
Description: Maintains Indian and Regional History Museum exhibiting approximately 3,000 prehistoric and 3,000 historic Indian artifacts; houses over a quarter of a million related photographs, 60,000 of which are of recent intertribal activities. Photos are from 1843 to the present, starting with the Cherokee Indian School. Collection includes 1,200 Indian music recordings and 600 oral interviews, 20% are on videotape and 600 recorded events including Indian conferences, powwows, meetings, dedications, etc. *Research*: OHS is one of several national locations serving as satellites of the National Archives and one of two Smithsonian Affiliates in the state of Oklahoma. The OHS Indian Archive includes more than 3.5 million

documents and abut 8,000 manuscripts, the majority of which are on microfilm. Included are the Indian Pioneer History Manuscripts from the 1937 Federal Writer's Project which includes over 400 subjects ranging from two-page documents to 100's of boxes. *Special programs*: The Oklahoma Museum is partnering with the National Museum of the American Indian (NMAI) to provide a database of original images of the NMAI collections relating to Oklahoma tribes. This database will be housed in the new Oklahoma Museum of History scheduled to open in November of 2005. The OHS has hired an American Indian to do specific tribal outreach for the new museum. His duties include meeting with Oklahoma's 39 tribal governments to collaborate appropriate content that will be included in the new museum. Included in this effort are interviews with Indian elders, ceremonial leaders and elected leaders. Currently, there are lectures and tours of the Indian Gallery available. A special traveling beading exhibit is also available. Library. Opened in 1893.

RED EARTH INDIAN CENTER MUSEUM
2100 NE 52 St. • OKLAHOMA CITY, OK 73111
(405) 427-4228 Scott Tigert, Curator
Exhibits ethnographic items, late 1700s
to present; paintings.

CREEK COUNCIL HOUSE MUSEUM
106 W. 6th • OKMULGEE, OK 74447
(918) 756-2324 Fax 756-3671
Debbie Martin, Director
Terry Bemis, President
E-mail: creekmuseum@prodigy.net
Description: Displays arts and artifacts of the Muscogee (Creek) Nation. *Publications*: History and Legends of the Creek; Indians of Oklahoma; Creek Nation Capitol. Library. Red Stick Gallery Gift Shop has books on Muscogee history, culture and language. Opened in 1923.

OSAGE TRIBAL MUSEUM
P.O. Box 779, 819 Grandview
PAWHUSKA, OK 74056
(918) 287-4622 Fax 287-4623
Description: Exhibits Osage artifacts, donations, books, clothing of the past; paintings, and pictures. *Special programs*: Culture classes - language (Osage); fingerweaving, ribbon work, beading on broadcloth, roach making; tribal history, Osage religion and family ties; workshops. Opened in 1938.

PONCA CITY CULTURAL CENTER & MUSEUM
1000 E. Grand • PONCA CITY, OK 74601
(405) 767-0427; La Wanda French, Director
Description: Collections feature clothing, utensils, photographs, weapons, art, musical instruments, and ceremonial materials of the tribes of the Ponca City area: the Osage, Kaw, Ponca, and Otoe; also, Hopi pottery and kachinas; relics from the early French-Indian trading post in Oklahoma; Northwest Coast material, and Quileute and other northern tribes' material. Library.

SEQUOYAH'S HOME SITE
Rt. 1, Box 141 • SALLISAW, OK 74955
(918) 775-2413 Stephen Foster, Manager
Description: 1829 log cabin of Sequoyah, inventor of Cherokee Syllibary. Located 11 miles northeast of Sallisaw on State Hwy. 101. Includes personal furnishings and artifacts of the life of Sequoyah and western Cherokees. *Special program*: Computer printout of visitors name in Cherokee to help teach Cherokee language on site. Living history of early Cherokee life to large groups and schools. Library. Opened in 1936.

CITIZEN POTAWATOMI NATION TRIBAL MUSEUM
1901 S. Gordon Cooper • SHAWNEE, OK 74801
(405) 275-3119 Fax 275-0198
Leslie Deer, Director
Website: www.potawatomi.org
Description: Clothing and artifacts relevant to Citizen Potawatomi culture. Opened in 1976.

SHAWNEE INDIAN MISSION
SHAWNEE, OK 74801

DISTRICT CHOCTAW CHIEF'S HOUSE
P.O. Box 165 • SWINK, OK 74761
(405) 873-2301; Randle Swink, President

Gale Carter, Site Attendant
Description: An Historic 1832 Old Chief's House with furniture and furnishings of the 1800's. LeFlore family memorabilia - farm & ranch impliments. Program: Choctaw Trail of Tears tour. Opened in 1994.

CHEROKEE NATIONAL MUSEUM (TSA-LA-GI)
Cherokee Heritage Center
P.O. Box 515 • TAHLEQUAH, OK 74464
(888) 999-6007; (918) 456-6007 Fax 456-6165
Mac R. Harris, Director; E-mail: macrh@juno.com
Website: www.netsites.net/cnhs/
Description: Located on the site of the original 1851 Cherokee Female Seminary and Ancient Village. The grounds contain a museum, Adams Corner (a typical Cherokee town in the 1800's), the Ancient Village (a typical Cherokee town in the 1600's), and an amphitheater for the outdoor "Trail of Tears: Nation" drama. Museum exhibits materials on Cherokee history, heritage and culture. *Activity*: The annual Trail of Tears Art Show is held in the Fall. *Publication*: Columns Newsletter. Library.

CHICKASAW COUNCIL HOUSE MUSEUM
205 N. Fisher St. • TISHOMINGO 73460
(405) 371-3351
Faye Orr, Director; Vickie Luster, Genealogist
Description: Indian museum exhibiting items pertaining to the history and culture—government, education, religious and social life—of the Chickasaw Indians. Emphasis is placed on the Chickasaw Governors, their families and administrations, from 1855 to the present day. Library. Opened in 1971.

TONKAWA TRIBAL MUSEUM
RR 1 Box 436 • TONKAWA, OK 74653
(405) 628-5301 Fax 628-3378
Dawn Patterson, Director
Anna Beard & Cynthia Gould, Curators
Description: Tonkawa artifacts located in Tribal Housing Building. Opened in 1970.

PHILBROOK MUSEUM OF ART
P.O. Box 52510, 2727 S. Rockford Rd.
TULSA, OK 74152
(918) 749-7941 Fax 743-4230
Brian Ferriso, Executive Director
Website: www.philbrook.org
Special collections: Clark Field Collection—American Indian Basketry and Pueblo Pottery; Roberta Campbell Lawson Collection of American Indian Costumes and Artifacts; Philbrook Collection of American Indian Paintings; The Bright Roddy & Ellis Soper Collections of American Indian Artifacts; Artist Biographies. *Special programs*: Friends of Native American Art; Internnships. *Publications*: Visions & Voices: Native American Painting From the Philbrook Museum of Art (1996); Woven Worlds: Basketry From the Clark Field Collection (2001). Library. Opened in 1939.

GILCREASE MUSEUM
1400 Gilcrease Museum Rd.
TULSA , OK74127 (918) 596-2700
(918) 596-2700 Fax 596-2770
E-mail: gilcreas@ionet.net
Web site: www.gilcrease.org
Daniel C. Swan, Senior Curator
Jason Baird Jackson, Curator of Anthropology
Sarah Erwin, Curator of Archival Collections
Description: The world's largest collection of art of the American West. The story of many cultures of North America is told through art, documents and artifacts from the pre-Columbian era through the 20th century. Exhibits artifacts relating to the culture of the Five Civilized Tribes. *Internships*: Charles Banks Wilson Internship for Native American Studies. *Publications*: Gilcrease Journal, Biannual; Catlin Catalogue. Library.

YELLOW BULL MUSEUM
Northern Oklahoma College
P.O. Box 310 • TONKAWA, OK 74653

CHOCTAW NATION MUSEUM
HC 64, Box 3270 • TUSKAHOMA, OK 74574
(918) 569-4465 (phone & fax)
Mike Bailey, Director; Donna Jo Heflin, Curator
Description: The Choctaw Capitol building, a three-story red brick and sandstone structure was completed in 1884 and houses the courtroom which seats three

tribal judges appointed by the present Choctaw Chief. Exhibits artifacts such as bone spoons, clay pots, and arrowheads; also items moved over the Trail of Tears are displayed; a spinning wheel and iron pots; vintage clothing, old documents and Choctaw pottery. Guided tours available. Opened in 1975.

SEMINOLE NATION MUSEUM
524 S. Wewoka Ave., P.O. Box 1532
WEWOKA, OK 74884 (405) 257-5580
 Leta Smith, Administrator
 Margaret Jane Norman, Curator
Description: Maintains exhibits and artifacts relating to the history of the Oklahoma Seminoles, the Freedmen, early pioneers and oil boom history of the area. *Special exhibits*: Dioramas depicting the Indian Stick Ball Game, The Seminole Whipping Tree, a life-size replica of the Florida Seminole home (Chickee), and exhibits depicting the Florida Seminoles, The Seminole Hunter Warrior, Law-Man (Lighthorseman), and Medicine Man. *Special programs*: Heritage Day - May 22; Sorghum Day - 4th Saturday of October; Annual Bazaar - Friday before Thanksgiving. *Publication*: Annual newsletter; Este Cate, a history of the Seminoles written by Museum Director, Tuskahoma B. Miller. Gift shop. Library. Opened in 1974.

PLAINS INDIANS & PIONEERS MUSEUM
2009 Williams Ave. • WOODWARD, OK 73801
 (580) 256-6136 Fax 256-2577
 Louise B. James, Director
 E-mail: plains@pldi.net
Description: Collection consists of archival materials, agricultural equipment, items from early settlers, and local Plains Indian items, including beadwork, tools and clothing. *Special programs*: Lectures. Library. *Publication*: "Below Devil's Gap", a history of Woodward County. Opened in 1966.

JIM THORPE'S HOME
YALE, OK 74085

OREGON

**UNIVERSITY OF OREGON MUSEUM
OF NATURAL HISTORY**
1680 E. 15th Ave. • EUGENE, OR 97403
 (541) 346-3024 Fax 346-5334
 C. Melvin Aikens, Director
 E-Mail: mnh@oregon.uoregon.edu
 Web site: www.natural-history.uoregon.edu
Description: Holdings include archaeological collections, primarily from Oregon and Alaska, and ethnographic collections from around the world. *Programs*: Occasional lectures and workshops on Native American topics. Small reference library. *Publications*: Fieldnotes, quarterly newsletter; museum bulletin series. Opened in 1936.

COLLIER STATE PARK LOGGING MUSEUM
P.O. Box 428 • KLAMATH FALLS, OR 97601
Description: Located on the Klamath Indian Reservation, the museum exhibits Indian stone utensils and unexcavated pit houses. Library.

FAVELL MUSEUM OF WESTERN ART & INDIAN ARTIFACTS
125 W. Main • KLAMATH FALLS, OR 97601
 (541) 882-9996 Fax 850-0125
 Gene H. Favell, Director
 E-mail: favmuseum@internetcds.com
Description: Exhibits of contemporary Western and wildlife art; 60,000 arrowheads; pictographs, baskets, pottery, and mortors. *Publication*: The Favell Museum: A Treasury of Our Western Heritage. Opened in 1972.

LINFIELD ANTHROPOLOGY MUSEUM
Linfield College • McMINNVILLE, OR 97128
 (503) 472-4121
Special collection: John Dulin Native American Art Collection.

TAMASTSLIKT CULTURAL INSTITUTE
72789 Highway 331 • PENDLETON, OR 97801
 (541) 966-9748 Fax 966-9927
 Roberta Conner, Director
 Marjorie Waheneka, Exhibits Manager

Website: www.tomastslikt.com
 E-mail: tci.visitor@tomastslikt.org
Description: Exhibits which displays the history and culture of the Cayuse, Walla Walla, and Umatilla Tribes. Exhibits chronicle thousands of years on the Columbia Plateau before, during and after contact with Europeans. Research library. Museum store. Opened in 1998.

PORTLAND ART MUSEUM
1219 S.W. Park • PORTLAND, OR 97205
 (503) 226-2811 Ext. 231
 Dan Monroe, President
 Paul Faulstick, Curator-Native American Art
Special collections: Axel Rasmussen Collection of Northwest Indian Art—Contains approximately 500 objects—items of dress, tools and equipment used in hunting and fishing; also, Eskimo pieces; Pueblo Indian ceramic pieces and prehistoric stone sculpture from the Columbia River basin. also, the Butler Collection-includes about 1,800 pieces dating from the 18th century to the 20th century from virtually every tribe and geographic region in the U.S. *Publication*: Art in the Life of the Northwest Coast Indian. Library.

MUSEUM AT WARM SPRINGS
P.O. Box C • WARM SPRINGS, OR 97761
 (541) 553-3331 Fax 553-3338
 Michael Hammond, Director
 E-mail: museum@justicenet.net
 Website: www.tmaws.org
Description: Contains more than 2,500 artifacts and interprets the culture and heritage of the Warm Springs, Wasco, and Paiute tribes in a 25,000 square foot building. In addition to its permanent exhibit, there are four shows a year in its changing exhibits gallery. Opened in 1993.

PENNSYLVANIA

**LENNI LENAPE HISTORICAL SOCIETY
MUSEUM OF INDIAN CULTURE**
2825 Fish Hatchery Rd. • ALLENTOWN, PA 18103
 (610) 794-2121 Fax 797-2801
 James Albany, President
 Nome Alexander, Curator
 E-Mail: lenape@comcat.com
 Web site: www.lenape.org
Description: The heritage of the Lenni Lenape (Delaware Indians), the earliest known inhabitants of the Lehigh Valley. The museum exhibits inter-tribal artifacts and a traditional village and gardens. *Special programs*: Pre-school, school, youth groups, special interest groups, and programs, as well as public workshops; Life Ways Demonstrations; Spring Corn Festival in May; Roasting Ears of Corn Ceremony, in August; and A Time of Thanksgiving, in October; slide/lectures, and arts and crafts workshops; speaker's bureau. *Publications*: The Time of the Autumn Moon; Native American Cookbook; Quarterly newsletter. Library. Gift Shop. Opened in 1981.

**CUMBERLAND COUNTY
HISTORICAL SOCIETY MUSEUM**
21 North Pitt St. • CARLISLE, PA 17013
Special collection: Carlisle Indian School Collection—Contains photographs, publications, and memorabilia. *Publications*: An Account of Illustrated Talks to Indian Chiefs, by Charles F. Himes; and The Indian Industrial School at Carlisle: Its Origin, Purpose, Progress and Difficulties, by Richard H. Pratt. Library.

BUSHY RUN BATTLEFIELD PARK
P.O. Box 468 • HARRISON CITY, PA 15636
Description: Located on the site of Chief Pontiac's rebellion of 1763. Museum: Contains copies of maps and letters relating to the Campaign of 1763, Pontiac's War; exhibits Indian artifacts.

HERSHEY MUSEUM
170 W. Hersheypark Dr.
HERSHEY, PA 17033
 (717) 534-3439
 David L. Park, Jr., Director
 James D. McMahon, Jr., Curator
Description: The Hershey Museum began as the Hershey Indian Museum in 1933 and showcased the

collection of Col. John Worth. He put together his extensive collection at the end of the 19th century. The museum has artifacts from the Eastern Woodland tribes, including archaeological objects from the Susquehannocks, as well as items representing Southwest, Plains, and Northwest Coast tribes. The museum also has an Eskimo collection.

THE AMERICAN INDIAN TRADING POST & EXHIBIT
United Indians of Delaware Valley
225 Chestnut St. • PHILADELPHIA, PA 19106
 (215) 574-0902 Fax 574-9024
 Michelle Leonard, Director

CARNEGIE MUSEUM OF NATURAL HISTORY
Division of Anthropology, O'Neil Research Center
5800 Baum Blvd. • PITTSBURGH, PA 15206
 (412) 665-2600
 Dr. Marsha C. Bol, Curator
Description: Developing an American Indian Hall which is to open in 1997.

READING PUBLIC MUSEUM
500 Museum Rd. • READING, PA 19611
 (215) 371-5850
 Ronald C. Roth, Director & CEO
 E-mail: museum@ptd.net
 Website: www.readingpublicmuseum.org
Description: Exhibit includes examples of cultural materials, pottery, clothing, tools, toys, ceremonial objects of the following cultural areas: Woodland, Plains, Southwest Desert, California, Northwest Coast, and Inuit. *Special collections*: Study collection of southeastern Pennsylvania lithic objects, approximately 10,000 pieces; study collection of mound pottery; Speck Collection—Delaware material collected during Speck's research of Oklahoma and Canadian dwellings of Delaware peoples. *Special program*: A Museum-School Native-American Studies Project—Elementary education programs for local schools using exhibit areas and Museum classroom lessons. Publications. Library. Opened in 1904.

**EVERHART MUSEUM OF NATURAL HISTORY,
SCIENCE & ART**
Nay Aug Park • SCRANTON, PA 18510
Description: Maintains American Indian Gallery with exhibits of American Indian art covering five major regions of the U.S. Library.

RHODE ISLAND

HAFFENREFFER MUSEUM OF ANTHROPOLOGY
Brown University, Mt. Hope Grant
300 Tower St. • BRISTOL, RI 02809
 (401) 253-8388 Fax 253-1198
 E-mail: kathleen_luke@brown.edu
 Shepard Krech, III, Director
 Kevin P. Smith, Deputy Director & Chief Curator
Description: Located on the lands significant to the Wampanoag peoples, the museum houses artifacts from the native peoples of the Americas and indigenous cultures from around the world. Collections of over 15,000 ethnographic objects and over 70,000 archaeological specimens. Extensive prehistoric Arctic collections. Special programs: Education programs for school children; lectures and seminars. *Publications*: Burris Hill: A 17th Century Wampanoag Burial Ground in Warren, RI; Hau, Kola! The Plains Indian Collection of the Haffenreffer Museum of Anthropology; Out of the North: The Subarctic Collection of the Haffenreffer Museum of Anthropology; Passionate Hobby: Rudolf Haffenreffer and the King Philip Museum; Gifts of Pride and Love: Kiowa and Comanche Cradles. Library. Opened in 1956.

TOMAQUAG INDIAN MEMORIAL MUSEUM
Dovecrest Indian Cultural Center
390-B Summit Rd., Arcadia Village
EXETER, RI 02822
 (401) 539-7213
 Dawn Dove, Director
Description: Archaeology, ethnology, and natural history exhibits related to southern New England Indian cultures; basketry of the Northeast. *Special programs*: Native American educational programs - dance, history, customs & culture, song and ceremony;

storytelling; Thanksgiving program *Publications*: Indians of Southern New England, by Princess Red Wing; Musical Expressions of Early Indians of Rhode Island; Indian Communications. Gift shop. Library. Opened in 1954.

MUSEUM OF PRIMITIVE ART & CULTURE
1058 Kingstown Rd., P.O. Drawer A
PEACE DALE, RI 02883
(401) 783-5711
  Sarah Peabody Turnbaugh, Director
Description: An archaeological and ethnology museum exhibiting artifacts from around the world, with an emphasis on North America and especially the Northeast. *Special programs*: Community-oriented multicultural programming; evening lecture series; public education program; gift shop. *Publication*: "The Nineteenth-Century American Collector: A Rhode Island Perspective" (centennial catalog), 1992. Opened 1892.

RHODE ISLAND HISTORICAL SOCIETY MUSEUM
52 Power St. • PROVIDENCE, RI 02906
(401) 331-8575
  Nina Zannieri, Curator
Description: Maintains a collection of 11,000 objects and artifacts pertaining to Rhode Island history; displays Narragansett and Wampanoag Tribes' artifacts—stone bowls, baskets, metal combs, jewelry, hair ornaments. *Publication*: Rhode Island History, journal. Library.

MUSEUM OF NATURAL HISTORY
Roger Williams Park • PROVIDENCE, RI 02906
(401) 785-9450 Ext. 225
  Elizabeth R.T. Fradin, Director
  Marilyn Massaro, Curator
Description: Archaeological and ethnological collections from North America. *Special program*: An educational kit - Native Americans in the Northeast: An Archaeological Perspective. Exhibits feature Woodland Indian culture—model village; canoe; model Pueblo; Plains and Northwest Coast Indian artifacts; Eskimo material; American Indian plants; and maps. *Publication*: The Explorer Newsletter. Library. Opened in 1896.

SOUTH CAROLINA

McKISSICK MUSEUM
University of South Carolina
COLUMBIA, SC 29208 (803) 777-7251
  George D. Terry, Director
  Catherine W. Horne, Curator
Description: Exhibits more than 200 Catawba Indian pottery and baskets from the 19th and 20th centuries; Folk Art Resource Center with primary and secondary sources on South Carolina Indians.

FLORENCE MUSEUM
558 Spruce St. • FLORENCE, SC 29501
(843) 662-3351
  E-mail: flomus@bell.south.net
  Betsy Olsen, Director
Description: Collection includes Southwestern Pueblo pottery. *Special program*: Children's program available by appointment. Opened 1924.

CATAWBA CULTURAL CENTER
ROCK HILL, SC 29730
(803) 328-2427 Fax 328-5791
  Wenonah G. Haire, Director
Description: Houses departments of archaeology, language, archives, and exhibits and offers classes in Native arts on a weekly basis. The Center teaches Catawba history to the tri-county school district, area tour groups, and other local organizations. *Activities*: The Yap Ye Iswa festival is held the Saturday after Thanksgiving. Opened in 1989.

SOUTH DAKOTA

DACOTAH PRAIRIE MUSEUM
21 S. Main St. • ABERDEEN, SD 57401
(605) 626-7117 Fax 626-4026
  E-mail: dpm@brown.sd.us

Website: www.brown.sd.us/museum
  Sue Gates, Curator
Description: Exhibits Sioux (Lakota) artifacts—beadwork, quillwork, decorated ceremonial and functional leather items, tools, pictographs, and photographs. *Special program*: Lectures. Sales Shop features contemporary Sioux handicrafts. Opened 1969.

AGRICULTURAL HERITAGE MUSEUM
South Dakota State University
BROOKINGS, SD 57007
Special collection: Indian Agricultural Heritage Collection of South Dakota. Reference Library.

AKTA LAKOTA MUSEUM & CULTURAL CENTER
St. Joseph Indian School
P.O. Box 89 • CHAMBERLAIN, SD 57325
(605) 734-3455 Fax 734-3388
  Jim O'Donnell, Director
Description: The Akta Lakota Museum is a tribute to the Sioux Nation striving to preserve and promote Sioux heritage and culture. Displays Native American art and artifacts; a collection of first class beadwork and quillwork. *Programs*: Visiting artists present lectures and shows; school tours; Native American history research. Library. Established 1991.

CRAZY HORSE MEMORIAL & INDIAN MUSEUM OF NORTH AMERICA
Avenue of the Chiefs
CRAZY HORSE, SD 57730
(605) 673-4681 Fax 673-2185
  Website: www.crazyhorsememorial.org
  E-mail: memorial@crazyhorse.org
  Ruth Ziolkowski, Director
Description: Maintains a collection of art and artifacts reflecting the diverse histories and cultures of the American Indian people. The Museum, designed to complement the story being told in stone on the mountain, speaks eloquently to present and future generations about American Indian life. *Special collections*: Sculpture, furniture and art work of of Korczak Ziolkowski, creator of Crazy Horse Memorial. *Special programs*: Scholarship program for Native American students attending institutions of higher education in South Dakota; college classes offered on site in cooperation with Black Hills State University; Summer Lecture and Performance Series, and educational activities for students visiting the Indian Museum of North America. *Publications*: Books - Crazy Horse and Korczak; The Saga of Sitting Bull's Bones; 50th Anniversary of Crazy Horse Memorial; Indian Museum of North America; and Crazy Horse coloring books. Serial publication, Crazy Horse Progress, 3/yr. Library. Established in 1948 and opened in 1974.

HARVEY V. JOHNSON LAKOTA CULTURAL CENTER MUSEUM
Cheyenne River Sioux Reservation
P.O. Box 590 • EAGLE BUTTE, SD 57625
(605) 964-2542 Fax 964-4151
  James Picotte, Director
  E-mail: lakotaculture@sioux.sodak.net
  Website: www.sodak.net/~lakotaculture
Description: Maintains a small exhibit of locally beaded artifacts dating back to the early 1800s, six large murals that decorate the rotunda, & photographs of the early years on the reservation. Gift shop. Opened 1973.

OGLALA SIOUX COMMUNITY COLLEGE RESOURCE CENTER
P.O. Box 310 • KYLE, SD 57752
(605) 455-2321 Fax 455-2787
  John Haas, Director
Opened in 1996.

OSCAR HOWE CULTURAL CENTER
119 West Third • MITCHELL, SD 57301
Description: A collection of twelve paintings by Oscar Howe, Sioux artist.

ROBINSON MUSEUM
500 E. Capitol, Memorial Bldg.
PIERRE, SD 57501 (605) 773-3797
  David B. Hartley, Director
Special collection: Plains Indian Collection—Contains primarily Sioux Indian artifacts. *Publication*: South Dakota History, quarterly. Library.

SOUTH DAKOTA STATE HISTORICAL SOCIETY
Cultural Heritage Center
PIERRE, SD 57501-2217
(605) 773-3458
  David B. Hartley, Museum Director
  Sarah Ackermann, Curator of Exhibits
  Claudia J. Nicholson, Curator of Collections
Description: Exhibits Sioux items collected by Delorme W. Robinson prior to 1910 and the Mary C. Collins collection of Lakota items. Lakota game pieces collected by J. Walker, paintings by Oscar Howe. Lifesize buffalo & tipi. Opened in 1901.

THE HERITAGE CENTER
Red Cloud Indian School
100 Mission Dr. • PINE RIDGE, SD 57770
(605) 867-5491 Fax 867-1291
  Brother C.M. Simon, S.J., Director/Curator
Description: Maintains Indian Art Museum which is housed in 1888 Holy Rosary Mission, scene of Battle day after the Wounded Knee Massacre; maintains a collection of paintings by Native American artists from many different tribes; also, starquilt collection; Oglala Sioux beadwork and quillwork collection; and small pottery collection; graphics, Inuit prints, and Northwest Coast prints. *Special program*: Traveling shows; Red Cloud Indian Art Show held every summer. *Publications*: Standing Soldier: A Retrospective; Five Families: An Art Exhibition. Library. Opened in 1982.

WHITE RIVER VISITOR CENTER
Rocky Fort RR • PORCUPINE, SD 57772
(605) 455-2878; (608) 698-7058
  Fr. Norman Volk, Director
Description: Maintains Indian cultural exhibits and an audiovisual program.

SIOUX INDIAN MUSEUM
222 New York St., P.O. Box 1504
RAPID CITY, SD 57701
(605) 394-2381 Fax 348-6182
  E-mail: journey@journeymuseum.org
  Web site: www.journeymuseum.org
Description: Administered by the Indian Arts and Crafts Board of the U.S. Dept. of the Interior. Exhibits historic Sioux arts and other Native American arts and crafts of the U.S.; a permanent exhibit presents the rich diversity of historic Sioux arts and a special exhibition gallery is devoted to changing presentations promoting the creative works of outstandingly talented contemporary Native artists and craftsmen. *Special program*: One-person exhibition series with demonstrations of contemporary Native American arts and crafts techniques in a variety of media; tours. Brochures. Opened 1939.

BUECHEL MEMORIAL LAKOTA MUSEUM
350 S. Oak St., P.O. Box 499
ST. FRANCIS, SD 57572
(605) 747-2745 Fax 747-5057
  Mike Marshall, Director
  Website: www.littlesioux.org
Description: Sioux Indian Museum exhibits ethnographic material (over 3,000 artifacts, and 2,100 photos) of the reservation period of the Rosebud and Pine Ridge Sioux. Church artifacts. *Special collections*: "Crying for a Vision" - photo exhibit; Rosebud Sioux quilts. *Publications*: A Grammar of Lakota; Everyday Lakota; Dictionary; Bible History in Lakota; Lakota Prayer Book; Lakota Names and Traditional Uses of Native Plants by Sigangu People; Crying for a Vision; A Rosebud Sioux Trilogy; Bettelyoun Manuscripts; Walker Papers; Buechel's Diary; and documents relating to Sioux culture. Indian arts and crafts for sale. Resource Library. Opened in 1947.

CENTER FOR WESTERN STUDIES
Augustana College, P.O. Box 727
SIOUX FALLS, SD 57197 (605) 274-4007
  Harry F. Thompson, Director of Research
   Collections & Publications
Description: An Historical Research and Archival Agency which maintains a collection of Native American (mostly Sioux) art work and artifacts. *Research*: Native Americans. *Publications*: Sundancing at Rosebud and Pine Ridge; Yanktmai Sioux Water Colors; The Last Contrary; Tomahawk and Cross. Library, Archives.

SIOUXLAND HERITAGE MUSEUM
THE PETTIGREW MUSEUM
131 N. Duluth • SIOUX FALLS, SD 57104
Special collections: The Pettigrew-Drady Indian Collection: Chief emphasis is on Dakota (Sioux) Indian artifacts, circa 1870-1920, including: clothing, tools, pipes, weapons, tepee, Ghost Dance shirt; and a Photograph Collection covering 1870-1900. Library.

TEKAKWITHA FINE ARTS CENTER
120 Chestnut St. E. • SISSETON, SD 57262
(608) 698-7058; Fr. Norman Volk, Director
Description: Maintains a collection of two dimensional art of the Lake Traverse Dakotah Sioux Reservation. *Activities*: Sponsors art festivals, concerts, workshops, and the annual Coteau Heritage Festival.

BEAR BUTTE STATE PARK
STURGIS, SD 57785
(605) 347-3176
William A. Gullet, Park Manager
Description: Located on a Native-American traditional religious site. *Museum*: Exhibits archaeological site materials; Native-American clothing and religious artifacts. *Research*: Native-American Indian religion, anthropology, archaeology and geography.

W.H. OVER MUSEUM
414 East Clark
VERMILLION, SD 57069-2390
(605) 677-5228
Web site: http://www.usd.edu/whom/
Displays Sioux artifacts from the late 19th century to the present. Lakota Family Tipi Exhibit. *Special collections*: Clark Memorial Collection of Lakota Artifacts; and Stanley J. Morrow Historical Photographs, 1869-1883. Programs: Tours, school loan kits. Library. Opened in 1883.

WOUNDED KNEE MUSEUM
Located off Exit 110 on I-90 • WALL, SD
(605) 279-2573
Website: www.woundedkneemuseum.org

DAKOTA TERRITORIAL MUSEUM
P.O. Box 1033 • YANKTON, SD 57078
Description: Exhibits Indian artifacts from the Dakota Territory, and the history of Yankton.

TENNESSEE

RED CLAY STATE HISTORICAL PARK
1140 Red Clay Park Rd., S.W.
CLEVELAND, TN 37311
(423) 478-0339 Fax 614-7251
Lois I. Osborne, Park Manager
Website: www.tnstateparks.com
Description: The 1832-1838 seat of the Cherokee Government, and site of 11 General Councils on national affairs. *Collection*: Paleo, Archaic, Mississippian, Woodland, and historical period artifacts. Trail of Tears exhibit. *Research*: Cherokee Removal Story, 1832-1838. Small research library of Cherokee history.

OLD STONE FORT ARCHAEOLOGICAL AREA
Rt. 7, Box 7400 • MANCHESTER, TN 37355
(423) 723-5073; Ward Weems, Site manager
Description: The Old Stone Fort is a 2,000-year-old American Indian ceremonial site. It consists of mounds and walls which combine with cliffs and rivers to form an enclosure measuring 1-1/4 mile around. *Special programs*: educational and entertaining programs. An exhibit hall complex includes exhibits relating to the history, archaeology, and legends surrounding the Old Stone Fort and its builders.

C.G. NASH MUSEUM - CHUCALISSA ARCHAEOLOGICAL MUSEUM
1987 Indian Village Dr. • MEMPHIS, TN 38109
(901) 785-3160 Fax 785-0519
M.L. Moore, Assistant Director
E-Mail: mlmoore@cc.memphis.edu
Web site: http://msux2.memphis.edu/~ anthropology/chuc.html
Description: Preserves the site of a 15th-century Mississippian-period village (in western Tennessee) partially reconstructed with life-size dioramas. The exhibit hall displays Southeast Indian culture, a collection of Indian artifacts from the site and adjacent areas. *Special programs*: group tours; demonstrations of hunting technologies; lecture series; Native American Days (end of October); Pow Wows; Changing exhibits; Choctaw Indian Heritage Festival; Educational programs: School visits, field trips, educational kits; demonstrations of art and traditional techniques; Tennessee Archaeology Awareness Week. *Publication*: Chucalissa Revisited; occassional papers. Library. Opened in 1955.

CUMBERLAND MUSEUM & SCIENCE CENTER
800 Ridley Blvd. • NASHVILLE, TN 37203
(615) 259-6099
Bill Bradshaw, Director
Description: Maintains approximately 4,000 objects on Native-Americans; small exhibit on Native-Americans in their environment. Special program: School programs on Native-Americans and archaeology. *Publication*: Museum Notes, monthly newsletter.

TENNESSEE STATE MUSEUM
James K. Polk Cultural Center
505 Deaderick St. • NASHVILLE, TN 37243
(615) 741-2692 Fax 741-7231
Lois Riggins Ezzell, Executive Director
Dan Pomeroy , Director of Collections
Description: A collection of over 10,000 artifacts of prehistoric and historic Indian cultures in Tennessee, including stone implements, ceremonial objects and ornaments, and pottery. *Publication*: "Art and Artisans of Prehistoric Middle Tennessee," by Stephen D. Cox. Library. Opened in 1937.

PINSON MOUNDS STATE ARCHAEOLOGICAL AREA
Ozier Rd., Route 1, Box 316
PINSON, TN 38366 (901) 988-5614
Mary L. Kwas, Area Supervisor
Description: A Middle Woodland Period ceremonial site with mounds and earthworks. *Collection*: Historic and prehistoric material from throughout Tennessee and on-site fieldwork. *Special program*: Indian Culture Festival. Library.

SEQUOYAH BIRTHPLACE MUSEUM
P.O. Box 69 • VONORE, TN 37885
(423) 884-6246 Fax 884-6469
Robert Haynes, Director

TEXAS

CADDOAN MOUNDS STATE HISTORIC PARK
Route 2, Box 85-C • ALTO, TX 75925
(409) 858-3218 David D. Turner, Supt.
Description: An archaeological site of prehistoric Caddoan village and ceremonial center, with three earthen mounds occupied 750-1300 A.D. *Collection*: Dioramas and prehistoric artifacts of early Caddoan culture excavated at the site—ceramic vessels, stone tools, etc.; replicated Caddo house on the site. *Activities*: School tours, techer packet; outreach-off site presentations. *Publication*: Caddoan Mounds, Temples and Tombs of an Ancient People. Reference library. Opened in 1979.

TEXAS MEMORIAL MUSEUM
University of Texas, 2400 Trinity St.
AUSTIN, TX 78705 (512) 471-1604
Dr. William Reeder, Director
P. Lynn Denton, Curator
Description: Collections include artifacts from Native Americans throughout the U.S.; and a series of exhibits highlighting the major native North American cultural groups which includes: costumes and artifacts of Indians of the Plains, Woodlands, Southwest, Northwest Coast, and Eskimo populations. *Publications*: Newsletter; monographs; bulletin series. Library. Opened in 1936.

PANHANDLE-PLAINS HISTORICAL MUSEUM
WTAMU Box 967 • CANYON, TX 79016
(806) 656-2244
Walter R. Davis, II, Director
Description: Hall of the Southern Plains: Exhibit of over 5,000 items from 70 groups, the majority from Southern Plains tribes—Comanche, Kiowa, Cheyenne, Arapaho, Apache and includes important collections of basketry, pottery, and beadwork; Nanvjo weavings; material on the Indian wars; trade goods. *Special programs*: Educational programs include Interpretive overviews and special-focus tours for students (grades K-12) and adults; Outreach programs - Native American Dance and Traditional Clothing; Life of the Southern Plains Indian. *Publication*: Panhandle Plains Historical Review, newsletter. Research Center houses archival material - more than 17,000 books (a 1,200 volume art library) and more than 250,000 historical photographs. Museum Store. Opened in 1933

NATIVE AMERICAN CULTURAL HERITAGE CENTER
Dallas Independent School District
DALLAS, TX 75204

TIGUA INDIAN CULTURAL CENTER MUSEUM
Tigua Indian Reservation
305 Yaya Lane • EL PASO, TX 79907
(915) 859-5287 Fax 859-8972
Corina Munoz, Director

YSLETA DEL SUR PUEBLO MUSEUM
P.O. Box 17579, 119 S. Old Pueblo Rd.
Tigua Indian Reservation
EL PASO, TX 79917
(915) 859-7913/3916
Johnny R. Hisa, Tribal Governor
Raymond Ramiriz, Superintendent
Description: Historic House, 1700-1850 Alderite/ Candelaria House; on grounds of 1680 Ysleta and Sur Pueblos and Mission Church. Maintains a collection of art of the Pueblos.

ALABAMA-COUSHATTA INDIAN MUSEUM
571 State Park Rd. 56
LIVINGSTON, TX 77351
(713) 563-4391; (800) 444-3507
Tony Byars, Superintendent
Jo Ann Battise, Tribal Administrator
Description: Located on the Alabama-Coushatta Indian Reservation, the museum contains a dioramic historical display of tribes, and a Living Indian Village. Indian arts and crafts for sale.

AMERICAN INDIAN HORSE MUSEUM
American Indian Horse Registry
9028 State Park Rd.
LOCKHART, TX 78644
(512) 398-6642
Nanci Falley, President & Curator
*Description: Museu*m: A collection of horse tack, art and books representing 19th century Southwest U.S. Library. *Publication*: American Indian Horse News. By appointment only. Library. Opened in 1979.

CADDO INDIAN MUSEUM
LONGVIEW, TX 75604
Mrs. James L. Jones, Director
Description: Collection includes approximately 30,000 artifacts pertaining to the prehistoric and historic Indian cultures who inhabited east Texas, primarily tribes of the Kad had acho, Hasinai, and Natchitoches confederacies of the Caddo Indians; extensive ceramic and stone pre-Columbian burial artifacts belonging to the prehistoric Indians of east Texas.

THE MUSEUM OF TEXAS TECH UNIVERSITY
P.O. Box 4499
LUBBOCK, TX 79409
Description: Exhibits Yaqui, Comanche and other Indian artifacts. Publications. Library.

SFASU ANTHROPOLOGY LAB
NACOGDOCHES, TX 75962
Special collection: Caddo Indian Artifacts Collection— beads, pottery, arrow points, pipes, etc. from the site of new Lake Nacogdoches, as well as from various Indian sites across the County.

CROCKETT COUNTY MUSEUM
404 11th St., Box 667 • OZONA, TX 76943
Special collection: Frank Mills Indian Collection—ornaments, jewelry, pottery, weapons, utensils, implements and ceremonial costumes. Cave exhibits. Library.

THE WITTE MUSEUM
3801 Broadway • SAN ANTONIO, TX 78209
(210) 357-1900 Fax 357-1882
E-mail: witte@wittemuseum.org
Web site: www.wittemuseum.org
Elisa Phelps, Director of Collections
Description: Periodic displays of artifacts of the Plains Indian (Lakota, Kiowa, Comanche, Apache, Navajo), Great Basin (Paiute), California, Eastern Woodlands, Northwest Coast, and Alaskan Native Peoples including basketry, pottery, weavings and clothing; Casas Grandes pottery; permanent exhibit of archaic archaeological materials from the Lower Pecos area of Texas and Northern Mexico. Library. Opened in 1926.

SUNSET TRADING POST OLD WEST MUSEUM
Rt. 1, Box 365C • SUNSET, TX 76270
(817) 872-2027; Jack N. Glover, Owner/Curator
Description: Exhibits Indian artifacts. *Publication*: Sex Life of American Indians. Library.

UTAH

EDGE OF THE CEDARS STATE
HISTORICAL MONUMENT & MUSEUM
660 West 400 North • BLANDING, UT 84511
(435) 678-2238
Michael M. Nelson, Museum/Park Manager
Debbie Westfall, Curator
Description: Located on the Anasazi Ruin dating from 700-1200 A.D., ancient dwellings of the Anasazi Indian culture. Maintains artifacts of prehistoric Anasazi Indian Tribe; Anasazi pottery; also, Navajo, Ute and Paiute Indian artifacts. *Special collection*: Rock Art Exhibit. Indian arts and crafts for sale. Reference Library. Publication: Spirit Windows—Native American Rock Art of Southeastern Utah. Opened in 1978.

ANASAZI STATE PARK
P.O. Box 1329 • BOULDER, UT 84716
(801) 335-7308
Larry Davis, Park Manager
William R. Latady, Curator
Description: Located on a 1050-1200 A.D. excavated Anasazi village site. *Museum*: Maintains and exhibits a collection of artifacts representative of the Kayenta Anasazi culture; diorama of Anasazi village (Coombs site). *Special programs*: Priitive techology demonstrations; guided tours of ruins; 14 video presentations. Small library. Opened in 1970.

UTE TRIBAL MUSEUM
P.O. Box 190, Highway 40
FORT DUCHESNE, UT 84026
(801) 722- 4992; Clifford Duncan, Director
Description: Located on the site of U.S. Cavalry and Old Fort Duchesne. Maintains Indian produced artwork in various media artifacts. *Research*: Ute history archives; personal interviews with elderly to document verbal Indian history. *Publication*: A History of Northern Ute People. Library.

COLLEGE OF EASTERN UTAH
PREHISTORIC MUSEUM
451 E. 400 North (mailing) 155 E. Main (physical)
PRICE, UT 84501 (800) 817-9949
(435) 613-5111 Fax 637-2514
Don Burge, Director; Pam Miller, Curator
E-Mail: pmiller@ceu.edu; Website: www.ceu.edu
Description: Utah archaeological exhibits, including 9th century Indian material of the Fremont culture. Emphasis on Nine Mile Canyon cultural and rock art area, Anasazi artifacts, lifesize Ute Indian diorama, Ute lifeways. *Special collections*: Pillings Figurines - set of 10 Fremont Indian clay figurines; two protohistoric painted hides and one Shoshone painted robe by Charlie Washakie. *Special programs*: Utah Prehistory and Heritage Week Celebration; lectures, children's programs; tours to archaeological sites. *Publication*: "Al's Archives" a quarterly newsletter. Library. Opened in 1960.

MUSEUM OF PEOPLES & CULTURES
Brigham Young University
100 E 700 N, 105 Allen Hall
PROVO, UT 84602
(801) 422-0020 Fax 422-0026

Dr. Marti L. Allen, Curator/Director
E-mail: mpc@byu.edu
Website: www.fhss.byu.edu/anthro/mopc/main.html
Description: An archaeology and ethnology museum exhibiting artifacts of prehistoric and historic native cultures. *Collections*: Changing exhibitions highlighting the Great Basin, Southwest, Mesoamerica, Polynesia. Special programs: Certificate in Museum Practices, graduate level program in conjunction with a masters degree in another discipline. *Activities*: Guided tours; teaching kits; scout patch program; training in museum practices and archaeological field techniques. *Publications*: Papers; technical series. Library. Opened in 1946.

UTAH FIELD HOUSE OF
NATURAL HISTORY STATE PARK
235 E. Main St. • VERNAL 84078
(801) 789-3799 Alden H. Hamblin, Supt.
Sue Ann Bilbey, Curator
Description: Ute Indian Hall: Exhibits Ute Indian artifacts. Library. Opened in 1948.

VERMONT

ABENAKI CULTURAL CENTER
17 Spring St. • SWANTON, VA 05488
(802) 868-3808
Fred Wiseman, Director
Opened in 1996.

VIRGINIA

MONACAN ANCESTRAL MUSEUM
2009 Kenmore Rd. • AMHERST, VA 24521
(804) 946-5391 Phyllis Hicks, Director
Opened in 1999.

SOUTHWEST VIRGINIA MUSEUM
Box 742, 10 W. First St.
BIG STONE GAP, VA 24219
(703) 523-1322 Janet H. Blevins, Park Manager
Description: Maintains artifacts representing the culture of the southern Appalachians, including artifacts of the Cherokee and Shawnee Nations. Developing a children's program on Native Americans. Library. Opened in 1948.

AMERICAN INDIAN HERITAGE
FOUNDATION MUSEUM
6051 Arlington Blvd.
FALLS CHURCH, VA 22044
(703) 237-7500

LANCASTER LIBRARY
Longwood College • FARMVILLE, VA 23909
(804) 395-2241
Special collection: O'Brien Collection of over 5,000 prehistoric Virginia Indian artifacts.

HAMPTON UNIVERSITY MUSEUM
American Indian Educational Opportunities Program
HAMPTON, VA 23668
(757) 727-5981 Fax 727-5084
Dr. Paulette F. Molin, Director
Description: Maintains a permanent gallery devoted to the school's historic American Indian education program. It also sponsors changing exhibitions of American Indian art and other programs.

SYMS-EATON MUSEUM
418 W. Mercury Blvd. • HAMPTON, VA 23666
(804) 727-6248 Charles E. Smith, Manager
Description: Historic Kecoughtan Indian Village; exhibits artifacts from Village area. *Publication*: Indian Recipe.

PAMUNKEY INDIAN VILLAGE
& CULTURAL MUSEUM
Pamunkey Indian Reservation
Rt. 1, Box 2011 • KING WILLIAM, VA 23086
(804) 843-4792
Warren Cook, Director
Description: A collection of Pamunkey Indian crafts and artifacts from the area. Videos available. Opened in

1979.

HISTORIC CRAB ORCHARD MUSEUM
P.O. Box 194 • TAZEWELL, VA 24651
(703) 988-6755
Nellie White Bundy, Director
Description: Located on Big Crab Orchard Archaeological and Historic Site, exhibiting prehistoric Woodlands Indian artifacts. *Publication*: Quarterly newsletter. Library.

MATTAPONI INDIAN MUSEUM & TRADING POST
Mattaponi Indian Reservation
Rt. 2 Box 255 • WEST POINT, VA 23181
(804) 769-2194
Minnie-Ha-Ha Gertrude Custalow, Director
Description: Tells the history of the people of Powhatan and Pocahontas and has artifacts dating back over 5,000 years. The museum is located on the Mattaponi reservation and is operated by the Custalow family. *Activities*: Develops specialized program presentations when requested.

JAMESTOWN SETTLEMENT
P.O. Box 1607 • WILLIAMSBURG, VA 23187
(888) 593-4682; (757) 253-4838 Fax 253-5299
Website: www.historyisfun.org
Joseph A. Gutierrez, Jr., Sr. Director
of Museum Operations & Education
Dr. Thomas E. Davidson, Sr. Curators
Description: Museum of Virginia history focusing on 17th century English colonization, and the Powhatan Indians. Exhibits prehistoric artifacts of the Virginia coastal plain. Also, other Indian artifacts and European and African items of the 17th century; recreated Powhatan Indian village. *Publication*: Jamestown-Yorktown Foundation Dispatch, periodical newsletter; Jamestown Settlement Guidebook. Library. Opened in 1957.

WASHINGTON

LELOOSKA FAMILY MUSEUM
5618 Lewis River Rd. • ARIEL, WA 98603

WHATCOM MUSEUM OF HISTORY & ART
121 Prospect St. • BELLINGHAM, WA 98225
(206) 676-6981

CHELAN COUNTY HISTORICAL
MUSEUM & PIONEER VILLAGE
600 Cottage Ave., Box 22 •
CASHMERE, WA 98815
(509) 782-3230
Description: Recreates the history of the Columbia River Indians before the arrival of the first pioneers and maintains an extensive collection of artifacts.

LEWIS COUNTY HISTORICAL MUSEUM
599 N.W. Front St. • CHEHALIS, WA 98532
(206) 748-0831; James Buckman, President
Description: Maintains a collection of Chehalis Indian artifacts. Indian archive collection in library.

ALPOWAI INTERPRETIVE CENTER
Highway 12 • CLARKSTON, WA 99403
(509) 758-9580
Description: An ethnology and Indian museum exhibiting Nez Perce Indian artifacts from 1880-1920; Nez Perce canoe. *Research*: Nez Perce Indians.

COLVILLE CONFEDERATED TRIBES MUSEUM
P.O. Box 233 • COULEE DAM, WA 99116
(509) 633-0751 Fax 633-2320
Cheryl Grunlose, Director
Andrew C. Joseph, Director/Curator
Description: Museum exhibits include an 1801 Thomas Jefferson Peace Medal, given to Nez Perce on the Snake River in 1805. There is an authentic Indian Village Sweatlodge and Tulle Mat Tipi, a fishing scene (12,000 - 100 years ago), and a cedar and bear grass basketmaking display and video. The collection includes arrowheads and spearpoints, pestles and other tools. *Special collection*: Tribal membership photos from 1855 to 1950. *Publication*: "Salish" Okanagan/Colville Indian language cassette tapes with dictionary ($24.95), by staff. Gift Shop. Opened in 1990.

WANAPUM DAM HERITAGE CENTER
P.O. Box 878 • EPHRATA, WA 98823
  (509) 754-3541 ext. 2571 Fax 754-5074
  Kathy Kiefer, Director
Opened in 1962.

MAKAH CULTURAL & RESEARCH CENTER
P.O. Box 160 • NEAH BAY, WA 98357
  (360) 645-2711 FAX 645-2656
  Janine Bowechop, Director
Opened in 1979.

COLVILLE CONFEDERATED TRIBES MUSEUM
P.O. Box 150 • NESPELEM, WA 99155
  (509) 634-4711
  Arnold N. Marchand, Director
Description: Contributes culturally as well as educationally to the communities of the five counties touched by the Colville Tribes. Maintains a gallery and gift shop.

SACAJAWEA INTERPRETIVE CENTER
Sacajawea State Park
2503 Sacajawea Park Rd.
PASCO, WA 99301
  (509) 545-2361
Description: Interpretive Center focus is Indians of the Columbia Basin Plateau (stone, bone tools, tool making, physical culture) and the Lewis and Clark Expedition, including the park's namesake, Sacajawea; photoessay of culture and lifestyle. *Special programs*: Photoessay and slide show of Lewis and Clark Expedition; summer interpretive programs related to area Indians and the Lewis and Clark Expedition. *Publications*: Pacific Northwest Resources (resource book for area teachers). Library. Open from mid April-mid September. Opened in 1940.

FORT OKANOGAN INTERPRETIVE CENTER
c/o Alta Lake State Park
HCR 88, Box 40 • PATEROS, WA 98846
  (509) 923-2400; Mike Nickerson, Supt.
  Steve Wang, Chief-Interpretive Services
Description: Exhibits fur trade items, and Indian and pioneer artifacts—basketry, weapons, etc. *Special program*: Verbal presentation of the history of Fort Okanogan area.

THE BURKE MUSEUM
Box 353010 - UW • SEATTLE, WA 98195
  (206) 543-7907 Fax 685-3039
  Dr. Karl Hutterer, Director
  Dr. Robin Wright, Chair-Anthropology Division
    & Curator-Native American Art
  Marvin Oliver, Curator-Contemporary Native Am. Art
  Dr. James D. Nason, Curator-Indian Ethnology
  E-Mail: recept@u.washington.edu
  Web site: www.washington.edu/burkemuseum
Description: Exhibits the largest USA collection of Northwest Coast Native art west of the Mississippi; maintains ethnological and archaeological collections of the Pacific Rim and Islands. *Special programs*: Exhibits, workshops, lectures. Library. Publications. E-mail: museumdir@city.ketchikan.ak.us

SACRED CIRCLE GALLERY
OF AMERICAN INDIAN ART
Discovery Park, P.O. Box 99100
Daybreak Star Arts Center
SEATTLE, WA 98199
  (206) 285-4425 Fax 285-3640
  Merlee Markishtum, Director
  E-mail: info@unitedindians.com
Description: Maintains collections of original art by contemporary Native American artists. *Activities*: Presents contemporary Native artist exhibitions throughout the year.

SKOKOMISH TRIBAL CENTER & MUSEUM
N.80 Tribal Center • SHELTON, WA 98584
  (360) 426-4232 Fax 877-5943
Opened in 1989.

CHENEY COWLES MUSEUM
Eastern Washington State Historical Society
2316 West 1st Ave. • SPOKANE, WA 99204
  (509) 456-3931 Fax 456-7690
  Jane A. Johnson, CEO
  Karen DeSeve, Archivist
  Lynn Pankonin, Curator of American Indian Collec-
tions
  Web site: www.cheneycowles.org
Description: American Indian collections consist of over 35,000 items representing all cultural groups of the Americas, with special emphasis on the Plateau tribes. In 1992, the Museum of Native American Cultures turned over its holdings to make the combined collections one of the largest and most extensive in the Northwest. *Major collections*: Plateau baskets, beadwork, cornhusk bags, regalia and other examples of material culture; Photograph collection of approximately 20,000 images; Manuscript Collection: Clifford Drury, Estelle Reel, Sr. Providencia. Special programs: Exhibits; Friendship Dance; Plateau Indian market *Publications*: Exhibit catalogs, "Beadwork of the Native American;" "Patriotic Symbols," "The Chap C. Dunning Collection;" and "From Earth & Sky." Book - Cornhusk Bags of the Plateau Indian; Text/fiche of 170 cornhusk bags (both sides illustrated.) Exhibition poster on sale, Native American Collection. Library. Opened in 1916.

STEILACOOM CULTURAL CENTER & MUSEUM
1515 Lafayette St., P.O. Box 88419
STEILACOOM, WA 98388
  (253) 584-6308 Fax 584-0224
  Joan K. Ortez, Director
Description: Promotes cultural and educational exhibits to insure the preservation of the history and culture of the Steilacoom tribe. *Special exhibits*: Gallery I - changing gallery with a new exhibit on a Native American theme about every six months; Gallery II - a permanent exhibit on the history and contemporary lifestyles of the Steilacoom Tribe, beginning with first European contact in 1792; Gallery III - "Visions of the Past...Legacy to the Steilacoom Tribe" - prehistory of traditional homeland of Steilacoom Tribe. *Special programs*: Education programs - tours in education about Coast Salish culture; lectures, conferences, and cultural demonstrations. Gift Shop. Library. Opened in 1988.

SUQUAMISH MUSEUM
15838 Sandy Hook NE
P.O. Box 498 • SUQUAMISH, WA 98392
  (206) 598-3311
  Leonard Forsman, Superintendent
  Marilyn Jones, Director; Charles Sigo, Curator
Description: The Museum is dedicated to preservation of Suquamish and other Puget Sound Indian culture and history. Exhibit: The Eyes of Chief Seattle - The history and culture of the Puget Sound Indians; Old Man House - The people and their way of life at D'Suq'Wub' and it tells the history of a 600 foot traditional longhouse located on what is now known as the Port Madison Indian Reservation, home to the Suquamish Indian Tribe of 750 members. *Publications*: Suquamish Museum Newsletter; "Eyes of Chief Seattle" Exhibit Catalogue. Library - Suquamish Tribal Archives. Opened in 1983.

PUYALLUP TRIBAL MUSEUM
1850 E. Alexander Ave.
TACOMA, WA 98421-4105
  (253) 597-6200 Fax 593-0197
  Mary Frank, Director
Opened in 1981.

WASHINGTON STATE HISTORY MUSEUM
1911 Pacific Ave. • TACOMA, WA 98402
  (253) 272-3500 Fax 272-9518
  David Nicandri, Director
  Lynn D. Anderson, Head of Museum Collections
  Website: www.washingtonhistory.org
Description: Exhibits and collections focus on the history of the people and forces that shaped the history of Washington State. Collection contains about 6,500 objects focusing on tribes of the Pacific Northwest, including basketry, tools, carvings, clothing, and personal artifacts. *Publications*: Columbia Magazine, quarterly journal of popular history. Opened 1891.

TOPPENISH MUSEUM
1 South Elm • TOPPENISH, WA 98945
  (509) 865-4510 Tish Cooper, Director
Description: Historic Museum housed in 1923 first Agency Building for the Yakima Indian Nation. Exhibits artifacts and Indian baskets. Library.

YAKAMA NATION MUSEUM
Yakama Nation Cultural Center
P.O. Box 151 • TOPPENISH, WA 98948
  (509) 865-2800 Fax 685-6101
  Marilyn Malatare, Director
  Brycene Neaman, Curator
Description: Collection reflects traditional crafts of the Yakima people, including utility and ceremonial items; also, items from Southwest and Plains tribes, but mainly items important to Yakama (or Columbia Basin Plateau area) tribes and bands culture and history. Includes baskets, parfleches, beaded clothing, stones, pipes; Navajo blankets, kachinas, clothing and jewelry; several large oil paintings of Columbia Plateau family elders. *Publications*: Time Ball; Mother Nature Is Our Teacher. Library. Opened in 1980.

WEST VIRGINIA\

WEST VIRGINIA STATE GOVERNMENT ARCHIVES AND HISTORY MUSEUM
Capitol Complex-Science and Cultural Center
Dept. of Archives & History
CHARLESTON, WV 25305

MOUND MUSEUM
Tenth St. and Tomlinson Ave.
MOUNDSVILLE, WV 26041

WISCONSIN

RED CLIFF TRIBAL MUSEUM
Arts and Crafts Cultural Center
P.O. Box 529 • BAYFIELD, WI 54814
  (715) 779-5609/5805
  Francis Montano, Director

LOGAN MUSEUM OF ANTHROPOLOGY
Beloit College, 700 College St.
BELOIT, WI 53511-5595
  (608) 363-2677
  Website: www.beloit.edu/~museum/logan
  William Green, Director
Description: Exhibits material (over 200,000 artifacts) of North American Indian ethnology (Great Lakes, Plains, and Southwest), Arikara-Mandan archaeology, Archaic and Woodland archaeology, and northern Wisconsin. *Special collection*: The Albert Green Heath Collection of Native American artifacts. Library. Publications: Bulletin; exhibit catalogs; occasional papers. Opened in 1893.

CHIPPEWA VALLEY MUSEUM
P.O. Box 1204 • EAU CLAIRE, WI 54702
  (715) 834-7871 Fax 834-6624
  Susan McLeod, Director
  E-mail: info@cvmuseum.com
Description: Maintains a collection of artifacts and historical photographs of the Ojibwe and Winnebago Indians. *Publications*: Guide to Archives and Manuscripts in the Chippewa Valley Museum; Paths of the People: The Ojibwe in the Chippewa Valley. Library. Opened in 1964.

CHIEF OSHKOSH MUSEUM
7631 Egg Harbor Rd.
EGG HARBOR, WI 54209
  (414) 868-3240
  Jeanette L. Hutchins, Director/Curator
Description: Indian Museum exhibiting Indian artifacts, craftwork and possessions belonging to the late Chief Oshkosh, last Chief of the Menominees. Open May-October. Opened in 1975.

MENOMINEE LOGGING CAMP MUSEUM
Menominee Indian Tribe of Wisconsin
Historic Preservation Dept.
P.O. Box 910 • KESHENA, WI 54135
  (715) 599-5258 FAX 799-4524

GEORGE W. BROWN, JR. OJIBWE
MUSEUM & CULTURAL CENTER
P.O. Box 804 • LAC DU FLAMBEAU, WI 54538
  (715) 588-3333 Fax 588-9408

Gregg Guthrie, Director
Description: Displays collections of artifacts from the Lac du Flambeau Chippewa Indian Reservation. Maintains a four seasons diorama and other exhibits including a 24-foot dugout canoe, smaller birchbark canoes, Ojibwe arts & crafts, traditional clothing, a French fur trading post. *Activities*: Year-round programs, classes, special events. Opened in 1989.

MUSEUM OF THE STATE HISTORICAL SOCIETY OF WISCONSIN
30 N. Carroll St. (exhibits)
816 State St. (collections)
MADISON, WI 53703/6 (608) 264-6555
William C. Crowley, Director of Museum
Joan E. Freeman, Curator of Anthropology
Description: Historic Wisconsin and Plains Indian artifacts and prehistoric archaeological artifacts from Wisconsin. *Special collections*: H.P. Hamilton Collection—Contains old copper implements from Wisconsin. Ethnological collections are from all Wisconsin tribes, Plains Indians, Northwest Coast, and Eskimo. *Special programs*: Classroom lessons on Wisconsin Indian life; photograph, manuscript and tape collections. *Publications*: Magazine of History; six volumes on History of Wisconsin. Library. Opened in 1846.

RAHR-WEST ART MUSEUM
610 North 8th St. • MANITOWOC, WI 54220
(414) 683-4501 Richard Quick, Director
Special collection: Exhibits stone, copper, and bead artifacts from a personal collection obtained in the Manitowoc County area. Library. Established 1941.

MILWAUKEE PUBLIC MUSEUM
800 W. Wells St. • MILWAUKEE, WI 53233
(414) 278-2700 Fax 278-6100
Michael Stafford, PhD, President/CEO
Alex W. Barker, PhD, Head, Anthropology Section
Dawn Scher Thomae, Anthropology Collections Mgr.
E-Mail: barker@mpm.edu; Website: www.mpm.edu
Description: Maintains a collection of approximately 23,000 North American ethnographic Indian items representing more than 180 Native American groups and tribes, including Inuit; Also holds significant North American archaeological collections (some 47,000 objects or lots), with strengths in Midwestern prehistory. *Special collections*: James Howard collection of 20th-century powwow outfits and artifacts. Dioramas, including "A Tribute to Survival" and the Crow Bison Hunt; Indian photograph collection (ca. 10,000 prints and 10,000 negatives). *Special programs*: Study collections; tours of American Indian areas from schools and other groups. *Publications*: Lore, quarterly member magazine; North American Indian Lives; Building a Chippewa Indian Birchbark Canoe; Prehistoric Indians of Wisconsin, etc.; Wisconsin Indian Resource Pages (WIRP), at www.mpm.edu/wirp. Reference Library. Opened in 1882.

ONEIDA NATION MUSEUM
P.O. Box 365 • ONEIDA, WI 54155
(920) 869-2768 Fax 869-2959
Karen S. Brockman, Director
Description: Exhibits approximately 1,000 artifacts and photographs; primarily ethnographic objects including dolls, baskets, clothing, wooden objects, beadwork, pottery relating to the history, culture and art of the Oneida and Iroquois people. Small reference library. Opened in 1979.

OSHKOSH PUBLIC MUSEUM
1331 Algoma Blvd. • OSHKOSH, WI 54901
(414) 424-0452
Robert Hruska, Director/Curator
Description: Maintains a collection of Wisconsin Indian archaeological & ethnographical artifacts. Library.

WAUKESHA COUNTY HISTORICAL SOCIETY & MUSEUM
101 W. Main St. • WAUKESHA, WI 53186
(262) 521-2859 Fax 521-2865
Susan K. Baker, Executive Director
Description: Collections focus on Waukesha County from Native American settlement to the present, exhibiting Native American artifacts from the area. Research Center Library contains historic documents, photographs, maps. *Publication*: Landmark, quarterly; book - "From Farmland to Freeways: A History of Waukesha County," includes a chapter on Americans Indians including some mound maps. Opened 1914.

WINNEBAGO INDIAN MUSEUM
3889 N. River
WISCONSIN DELLS, WI 53965
(608) 254-2268
Roxanne Tallmadge Johnson, Manager
Bernadine Tallmadge, Curator
Description: An extensive collection of stone artifacts, clothing, methods of ornamentation (i.e., beadwork, quillwork, metal) as well as oil paintings. *Special programs*: On-site lectures describing current and traditional issues; festival. Opened in 1953.

WYOMING

BRADFORD BRINTON MEMORIAL MUSEUM
P.O. Box 460, 239 Brinton Rd.
BIG HORN, WY 82833
(307) 672-3173
Kenneth L. Schuster, Director
Description: Exhibits Native American objects of art - costumes, bead and quill work, tools, baskets, blankets, weapons, and interpretive materials; mostly Plains tribes, but also some from the Southwest and Northwest Coast. Library. Opened in 1961.

WYOMING STATE MUSEUM
Barrett Bldg., 2301 Central Ave.
CHEYENNE, WY 82002
(307) 777-7022 Fax 777-5375
E-mail: wsm@missc.state.wy.us
Web site: www.commerce.state.wy.
us/cr/wsm/index.htm
Marie Wilson-McKee, Director
Ellen E. Atkinson, Curator of Interpretation
Description: Collection contains over 100,000 artifacts related to Wyoming's heritage. Strengths include textiles, firearms, household artifacts, military artifacts, and Native American artifacts from the Lakota, Arapaho, Crow, Shoshone, and Flathead tribes among other. Library. Exhibition brochures and handouts. Opened in 1895.

BUFFALO BILL HISTORICAL CENTER
720 Sheridan Ave. • Cody, WY 82414
(307) 587-4771
Purpose: The preservation and exhibition of Western Americana pertaining to Rocky Mountain and North-

ern Plains region. *Activities*: Operates the Buffalo Bill Museum, Whitney Gallery of Western Art, Cody Firearms Museum, Plains Indian Museum, Draper Museum of natural History, and the McCracken Research Library. *Publication*: Points West, quarterly magazine. Library. Established 1917.

PLAINS INDIAN MUSEUM
Buffalo Bill Historical Center
720 Sheridan Ave. • CODY, WY 82414
(307) 578-4052 Fax 578-5714
Emma Hansen, Curator
E-mail: thomh@bbhc.org
Web site: www.bbhc.org
Description: Contains over 5,000 ethnographic items representing the Northern, Central, and Southern Plains people- Sioux, Cheyenne, Shoshone, Crow, Arapaho, Blackfeet, Gros Ventre. Exhibits provide an introduction to economic, religious and social lives of Plains Indians, and include a re-creation of an 1890 Sioux camp as well as a gallery of contemporary art. *Programs*: Annual Northern Plains pow wow in June at the Robbie Pow Wow Grounds; the Plains Indian Art Seminar, a symposium relating to Plains cultures each Fall; and a variety of temporary exhibitions which explore elements of the Plains Indian culture. Buffalo Bill Museum. Whitney Gallery of Western Art. The McCracken Research Library. *Publications*: Catalogues of exhibitions; papers and proceedings from Plains Indian Seminar. Opened in 1979.

SHOSHONE TRIBAL CULTURAL CENTER
P.O. Box 1008
FORT WASHAKIE, WY 82514
(307) 332-9106 Fax 332-3055
Joyce Posey, Director
Opened in 1988.

UNIVERSITY OF WYOMING ANTHROPOLOGY MUSEUM
Anthropology Bldg.
LARAMIE, WY 82071
(307) 766-5136
George W. Gill, Curator
Description: Maintains a collection of American Indian artifacts.

COLTER BAY INDIAN ART MUSEUM
Grand Teton National Park
P.O. Drawer 170 • MOOSE, WY 83012
(307) 739-3591 Fax 739-3504
Description: Displays approximately 1,500 items of American Indian art (collected by David T. Vernon) from most culture areas and the Reservation Period, 1850-1920, with emphasis on the high plains. *Special programs*: Cultural films during the summer, museum tours, guest artists, and Native-American crafts demonstrations. Programs conducted during summer months. Opened in 1972.

RIVERTON MUSEUM
700 E. Park Ave. • RIVERTON, WY 82501
(307) 856-2665
Description: Collections include Shoshone and Arapaho costumes and artifacts.

These alpha-geographically arranged listings, like those in the Museums section, include libraries with both large and small holdings, pertaining, in whole or part, to the subject of the North American Indian.

ALABAMA

**POARCH CREEK INDIAN
HERITAGE CENTER LIBRARY**
HCR 69A, Box 85B • ATMORE, AL 36502
(205) 368-9136
Sandra Ridley, Director
Description: Maintains a major collection on Southeastern Creek Indians; & minor for Five Civilized Tribes.

ALASKA

**ANCHORAGE MUSEUM
OF HISTORY & ART LIBRARY**
121 West Seventh Ave.
ANCHORAGE, AK 99501
(907) 343-4326 Fax 343-6149
M. Diane Brenner, Museum Archivist
Web site: http://www.ci.anchorage.us
Description: Collection includes more than 1,000 volumes on the Tlingit, Haida, Northwest Coast, Athapaskan, Aleut and Eskimo cultures with an emphasis on material culture; 1890-1960 photograph collection. Interlibrary loans. Open to the public.

**ARCTIC ENVIRONMENTAL
INFORMATION & DATA CENTER**
University of Alaska, Anchorage
707 A St. • ANCHORAGE, AK 99501
(907) 257-2733
Research activities: Conducts field studies and provides assistance on resource management issues in Alaska, including Native land selection under the Alaska Native Claims Settlement Act.

INSTITUTE OF SOCIAL & ECONOMIC RESEARCH
University of Alaska, Anchorage
3211 Providence Dr. • ANCHORAGE, AK 99508
(907) 786-7710
Edward L. Gorsuch, Director
Research activities: Conducts Alaska Native studies, federal-state relations, economic development, natural resources management, social and economic impact studies, etc. *Publication*: Alaska Review of Social and Economic Conditions.

**HANS VAN DER LAAN MEMORIAL
BROOKS RANGE LIBRARY**
Simon Paneak Memorial Museum
P.O. Box 21085, 341 Mekiana Rd.
ANAKTUVUK PASS, AK 99721
(907) 661-3413 Fax 661-3414
Grant Spearman, Curator
E-mail: gspearman@co.north-slope.ak.us
Description: 1,000 volumes concerning the natural and cultural history of the Arctic with special emphasis on the Brooks Range of Alaska. Opened in 1986.

**ALASKA'S MOTION PICTURE
FILM ARCHIVE CENTER**
P.O. Box 95203, University of Alaska
FAIRBANKS 99701
(907) 479-7296
Reg Emmert, Director
Description: A repository of Alaskan archival film. Catalog of available films is available.

ALASKA NATIVE KNOWLEDGE NETWORK
Center for Cross-Cultural Studies
University of Alaska
FAIRBANKS, AK 99775
(907) 474-5086 Fax 474-5208
Dr. Ray Barnhardt, Director
E-Mail: ftlma@aurora.alaska.edu
Web site: http://www.zorba.uafadm.alaska/ankn
Research activities: Resource materials related to Alaska Native people and Alaska Native education. Open to the public. Established 1995.

**ALASKA NATIVE LANGUAGE
CENTER RESEARCH LIBRARY**
University of Alaska, Fairbanks
Brooks Bldg., 4th Floor, P.O. Box 757680
FAIRBANKS, AK 99775-7680
(907) 474-7874 Fax 474-6586
Dr. Lawrence Kaplan, Director
E-Mail: fryanlp@aurora.alaska.edu
Description: Collection contains more than 10,000 items: books, journals, papers, and archival material in or on 20 Alaska Native languages and languages connected to Alaskan languages. *Special activities*: Publish books in and on Alaska Native languages. Open to scholars.

**INSTITUTE OF ALASKA NATIVE ARTS
INFORMATION CENTER**
455 Third Ave. #117 • FAIRBANKS, AK 99707
(907) 456-7491; Susheila Khora, Executive Director
Resource library with over 600 titles; audio & video tapes, and magazines/periodicals. Also consists of an artists registry of hard copy files and slides, and photographic files.

ELMER E. RASMUSON LIBRARY
University of Alaska • FAIRBANKS 99701
Special collections: Skinner Collection—Contains material regarding Alaska and the Polar regions (Arctic and Antarctic); more than 4,000 volumes on the Athapaskan, Haida, Tlingit, Tsimshean and Eskimo. University Archives and Manuscript Collections (Alaskana only)—Consists of journals, records, historic photos, tape recordings (Alaska Native Stories); 4,000 historic photos of Alaska natives.

AHTNA, INC. LIBRARY
P.O. Box 649 • GLENNALLEN, AK 99588
(907) 822-3476
Description: Contains mostly publications dealing with land and resources in interior Alaska, with some on native culture (Athabascan.)

**CHILKAT VALLEY HISTORICAL SOCIETY
SHELDON MUSEUM & CULTURAL CENTER
LIBRARY**
P.O. Box 269 • HAINES, AK 99827
(907) 766-2366 Fax 766-2368
Cynthia L. Jones, Director
E-Mail: curator@sheldonmuseum.org
Website: www.sheldonmuseum.org
Description: Material on Tlingit and other Indian art and culture; local history; Alaska history. Also, archives with unpublished local documents (diaries, city records, school records, etc.) Open to the public. Opened in 1975

**ALASKA STATE DIVISION OF STATE
LIBRARIES HISTORICAL LIBRARY**
Pouch G • JUNEAU, AK 99801

TONGASS HISTORICAL MUSEUM LIBRARY
629 Dock St. • KETCHIKAN, AK 99901
(907) 225-5600 Fax 225-5602
E-mail: museumdir@city.ketchikan.ak.us
Description: Vast collection on Alaskana and books relating to Tlingit, Tsimshian and Haida culture & heritage and Northwest Coast Native art.

TOTEM HERITAGE CENTER LIBRARY
629 Dock St. • KETCHIKAN, AK 99901
(907) 225-5900 Fax 225-5602
E-mail: museumdir@city.ketchikan.ak.us
Description: City of Ketchikan's museum department and archives holdings include photographs on all Alaska villages with totem poles; index to all Alaska totem poles; vertical file on Northwest Coast Indian art and culture. Covers Tlingit, Haida and Tsimshian tribes - art, anthropology, totem poles. *Programs*: Art and crafts slides available for use; lecture series on traditional Alaska Native arts and culture.

BARANOV MUSEUM LIBRARY
Erskine House, 101 Marine Way
KODIAK, AK 99615
(907) 486-5920 Fax 486-3166
Ann Stone, President
Marian Johnson, Director
Description: The Kodiak Historical Society operates the Baranov Museum in the old Rissian warehouse,

the Erskine House, in downtown Kodiak. Research Center with over 5,000 photos, 300 rare books covering Kodiak and the Aleutians with some emphasis on major Alaskan events. Also 30 educational albums from the archives covering Kodiak events.

KODIAK AREA NATIVE ASSN. LIBRARY
3449 E. Rezanof Dr.
KODIAK, AK 99615-6928
(907) 486-5725
Maintains a general book collection. Museum/Cultural Center and Research Library in planning stages.

**NOME LIBRARY/KEGOAYAH KOZGA
PUBLIC LIBRARY**
Front St., Box 1168 • NOME, AK 99762
(907) 443-5133
Dee J. McKenna, Librarian
Description: Collection contains about 15,000 books, 3,000 cassette tapes, 1,200 AV programs, photographs, and bilingual and oral history materials on Alaska, Eskimos, and Gold Rush artifacts.

SITKA NATIONAL HISTORICAL PARK LIBRARY
103 Monastery St. • SITKA, AK 99835
(907) 747-6281 Fax 747-5938
Carol Burkhart, Director
E-Mail: carol_burkhart@nps.gov
Description: Contains about 1,400 books; 150 tapes, 150 films and special papers on Tlingit Indians, Northwest Coast Indian arts and culture. Substantial research materials on Russian American history. Research library for park staff. Established 1966.

ARIZONA

**CANYON DE CHELLY
NATIONAL MONUMENT LIBRARY**
P.O. Box 588 • CHINLE, AZ 86503
(520) 674-5518 Fax 674-5507
Tara Travis, Historian/Curator
E-Mail: tara_travis@nps.gov
Web site: http://www.nps.cach
Description: Collection consists of library materials pertinent to the research and management of the park's resources. Archival materials consist of maps, photographs, documents and reports on Canyon de Chelly National Monument. *Special programs*: Ranger Talks. Open to the public by appointment only. Established 1931.

TUZIGOOT NATIONAL MONUMENT LIBRARY
P.O. Box 68 • CLARKDALE, AZ 86324
(520) 634-5564

**CASA GRANDE RUINS
NATIONAL MONUMENT LIBRARY**
1100 N. Ruins Dr. • COOLIDGE, AZ 85228
(602) 723-3172
Description: Contains a collection of 1,500 volumes on Hohokam archaeology and culture; Indians of area.

**AMERIND FOUNDATION
FULTON-HAYDEN MEMORIAL LIBRARY**
P.O. Box 400 • DRAGOON, AZ 85609
(520) 586-3666 Fax 586-4679
E-mail: amerind@amerind.org
Web site: www.amerind.org
Celia Skeeles, Librarian
Description: Reference materials focusing on archaeology, anthropology, ethnology, Greater American Southwest; ethnology, history and art; Parral Archives on microfilm; 28,000 books, 2,260 pamphlets and reprints, 550 manuscripts, 250 maps, 12,000 slides and photos, 150 journals and other serial subscriptions. Open to research scholars by appointment only and with written statement of intent. Established 1962.

CLINE LIBRARY
Northern Arizona University
P.O. Box 6022 • FLAGSTAFF, AZ 86011
(928) 523-5551 Fax 523-3770
Karen J. Underhill, Archivist
Website: www.nau.edu/library/speccoll
Special Collections & Archives Department: Subjects include Navajo and Hopi Indians, and Southwestern U.S. *Special collections*: Alexander and Dorothea

Lieghton Collection; Apachean Language Collection, including Chiricahua dialects-320 cassettes; A.F. Whiting, Leo Crane, Jo Mora, and Phillip Johnston. Opened in 1968.

HAROLD S. COLTON MEMORIAL LIBRARY
Museum of Northern Arizona
3101 N. Fort Valley Rd. • FLAGSTAFF 86001
(520) 774-5211 Fax 779-1527
Dorothy A. House, Librarian
Description: Special collections on Hopi and Navajo Indians, and archaeology of the Southwestern U.S. A major repository of documentation on Native American art.

WUPATKI NATIONAL MONUMENT LIBRARY
HC 33, Box 444A • FLAGSTAFF, AZ 86001
(520) 527-7152

THE WHITE MOUNTAIN APACHE
CULTURAL CENTER & MUSEUM LIBRARY
P.O. Box 507 • FORT APACHE, AZ 85926
(928) 338-4625 Fax 338-1716
Karl A. Hoerig, PHD, Director
E-mail: fortapachemuseum@hotmail.com
Website: www.wmat.nsn.us
Description: Non-circulating library of materials relevant to Apache culture and history, Fort Apache, and Fort Apache Indian Reservation. Opened in 1969...new facility opened in June 1997.

HUBBELL TRADING POST LIBRARY
P.O. Box 150 • GANADO, AZ 86505
(520) 755-3475
Description: Contains materials relevant to Native American and Southwest history; Navajo culture, Indian arts and crafts, oral interviews, and trading posts and Indian traders; and NPS planning documents, standards and policies.

AK CHIN HIM-DAK LIBRARY
42507 W. Peters & Nall Rd.
MARICOPA, AZ 85239
(520) 568-2227 Fax 568-4566
Elaine F. Peters, Director
Description: Collection of Native American publications, videos and audios, oral histories; Archives of tribal records.

COLORADO RIVER INDIAN TRIBES
PUBLIC LIBRARY/ARCHIVES
Tribal Administration Center
Route 1, Box 23-B • PARKER, AZ 85344
(520) 669-9211 x 285 Fax 669-5675
Amelia Flores, Library Director
Description: Holdings include 12,000 volumes in the general sections. Extensive collection on the Native American. Archives includes over 1,000 documents, videotape and oral history tapes, personal correspondence, and works of historians, ethnologists and anthropologists; also microfilm relating to the history and culture of the four tribes of the Colorado River Indian Reservation - the Mohave, Chemehuevi, Navajo and Hopi. Also includes a Photograph Collection. Interlibrary loans. Established in 1958

ARIZONA DEPARTMENT OF LIBRARY,
ARCHIVES & PUBLIC RECORDS
History & Archives Division
State Capitol, 1700 W. Washington
PHOENIX, AZ 85007
(602) 542-4159 Fax 542-4402
Don Langlois, Arizona History Librarian
E-mail: archive@lib.az.us
Website: www.lib.az.us/archives/index.html
Description: Contains over 105,000 volumes on Arizona and the Southwest, including material on Southwestern Indians. Open to the public.

BROWN & BAIN, P.A. LIBRARY
2901 N. Central • PHOENIX, AZ 85012
(520) 351-8039 Fax 351-8516
Ellen Hepner, Librarian
Description: A special collection on American Indian law.

DOROTHY CUMMINGS MEMORIAL LIBRARY
American Indian Bible College
10020 N. 15th Ave. • PHOENIX, AZ 85021

(602) 944-3335; John S. Rose, Director
Description: Maintains a special Native American collection of books, audiocassettes, and microfiche.

BILLIE JANE BAGULEY LIBRARY & ARCHIVES
Heard Museum, 2301 N. Central Ave.
PHOENIX, AZ 85004-1480
(602) 252-8840 Fax 252-9757
Mario Nick Klimiades, Library & Archives Director
Web site: www.heard.org
Description: Maintains a collection of approximately 30,000 volumes in the areas of Native American art and culture with an emphasis on the Greater Southwest, contemporary Native American fine arts, Native American writings, ethnoarts, anthropology and museum studies; 240 current periodical subscriptions-journals and newsletters; pamphlet file; archives of manuscripts, posters and library prints, photographs and negatives, and museum papers; sound recordings include audiocassettes and record albums of primarily native Southwestern music, taped lectures, and interviews; 500 films and videos ; and thousands of slides. *Special program*: Native American Artists Resource Collection - includes files on about 22,000 traditional to contemporary artists working in all media. Artists, collectors, students, and art enthusiasts can contribute information to the collection. Open to the public for reference only - appointments are necessary for archives and videos and sound recordings. Opened in 1929.

MARICOPA COUNTY LAW LIBRARY
East Court Bldg., 2nd Floor
101 W. Jefferson St. • PHOENIX, AZ 85003
(602) 262-3461 Fax 262-3677
Elizabeth Kelley Schneider, Director
Description: A special collection on Native American law.

PHOENIX INDIAN MEDICAL CENTER
HEALTH SCIENCES LIBRARY
4212 North 16th St. • PHOENIX, AZ 85016
(602) 263-1200 Fax 263-1669
Jean Crosier, Administrative Librarian
Description: Basic professional and medical collection with small Native American collection includes medical, cultural, fiction and non-fiction titles about and written by Native Americans; also focus is on Southwestern tribes (approx. 200 books and documents). Open to the public.

PHOENIX PUBLIC LIBRARY
Arizona Room • 1221 N. Central
PHOENIX, AZ 85004
(602) 262-4636
Description: Subjects cover Southwestern Indians. *Special collection*: James Harvey McClintock papers, 1864-1934.

PUEBLO GRANDE MUSEUM LIBRARY
4619 E. Washington St.
PHOENIX, AZ 85034
(602) 495-4901 Fax 495-5645
E-mail: prlpgstf@phoenix.gov
Web site: www.pueblogrande.com
Description: Collection primarily on Southwest archaeology with volumes pertaining to the American Indian. Open to scholars on appointment basis only.

SHARLOT HALL MUSEUM ARCHIVES & LIBRARY
415 W. Gurley St. • PRESCOTT, AZ 86301
(520) 445-3122 Fax 776-9053
E-mail: research@sharlot.org
Web site: www.sharlot.org/archives
Michael Wurtz, Archivist
Description: History of Yavapai County and Central Mountain Region of Arizona. Collections include information on the area's archaeology and anthropology, and the history/prehistory of the Yavapai Indians. *Special activities*: Prescott Indian Arts Market each July. Established 1928.

SMOKI MUSEUM LIBRARY
147 N. Arizona Ave., P.O. Box 10224
PRESCOTT, AZ 86304
(928) 445-1230
John Tannous, Director
E-mail: info@smokimuseum.org
Website: www.smokimuseum.org

Description: All books are cataloged (Dewey) and entered on Yavapai Library Network. Periodicals are recorded in Prscott Union List, published annually. Free by appt. Opened in 1935 and Incorporated in 1991.

YAVAPAI-PRESCOTT TRIBAL LIBRARY
530 E. Merritt • PRESCOTT, AZ 86301
(928) 445-8790 Fax 778-9445
Barbara Royer, Director
Description: Maintains a collection (non-circulating) of approximately 5,000 volumes with special emphasis on the education, history and culture of Native Americans. *Special programs*: Public access computers for Tribal members and Tribal community members provided by Bill & Melinda Gates Foundation. Weekly story times provided for Tribal pre-school and after school programs. Open to Tribal members and Tribal community members.

SAFFORD-THATCHER STAKES
FAMILY HISTORY CENTER
Church of Jesus Christ of Latter-Day Saints
1803 S. 8th Ave. • SAFFORD, AZ 85546
(520) 428-3194
Lorin W. Moffett, Director
Description: A special collection on Indian tribes. Genealoical Society Series; microfiche; films.

THE ARIZONA COLLECTION
Dept. of Archives & Manuscripts
University Libraries, Arizona State University
Box 871006 • TEMPE, AZ 85287
(480) 965-0270 Fax 965-0776
Patricia A. Etter, Archivist for Information Services
E-Mail: patricia.etter@asu.edu
Website: www.asu.edu/lib/archives
Description: A research repository containing over 30,000 volumes in addition to primary source materials covering prehistoric Arizona to the present. There are ephemeral materials and photographs. Contains information on prehistoric, historic, and current tribes in Arizona and New Mexico. *Special collections*: Manuscript material includes papers of Carlos Montezuma, the Odd Halseth Papers and the Thomas H. Dodge Collection. Open daily to the public.

CENTER FOR INDIAN EDUCATION
Arizona State University, College of Education
Farmer Education Bldg., Rm. 415
TEMPE, AZ 85287 (480) 965-6292
Karen Swisher, Director
Description: Covers all phases of American Indian education and related interdisciplinary issues. *Publication*: Journal of American Indian Education.

COOK COLLEGE & THEOLOGICAL SCHOOL
708 S. Lindon Lane • TEMPE, AZ 85281
(480) 968-9354 Fax 968-9357
Dr. Berta Parrish, Contact
Description: 13,000 volumes, 1,500 of which are Native American works. Major areas emphasis of the collection includes religious & Native American studies.

LABRIOLA NATIONAL AMERICAN
INDIAN DATA CENTER
Dept. of Archives & Manuscripts
University Libraries, A.S.U.
Box 871006 • TEMPE, AZ 85287
(480) 965-0270 Fax 965-0776
E-Mail: patricia.etter@asu.edu
Web site: www.asu.edu/lib/archives/labriola.htm
Patricia A. Etter, Curator
Description: Serves as a national repository of research materials on North American Indians and First Nations people. It provides access to this information through the use of computer databases, the Internet, and CD-ROM. The collection is international in scope and brings together current & historic information on government, education, culture, religion & world view, social life & customs, tribal history, & biography. The online, "American Indian Index" gives access to thousands of photographs, pamphlets, newsletters, & articles dealing with Native Americans. Contains 3,000 books, films, slides, cassette tapes, & video in addition to CD-ROM indexes. Holds manuscript collections, including the papers of Peterson Zah, former President of the Navajo Nation, & Wayne T. Pratt, Ass't Chief of the Branch of Education, Bureau of Indian Affairs. Open Mon-Fri. from 10 am to 5 pm Opened in 1993.

MARY MILDRED McCARTHY LIBRARY
Cook College & Theological School
708 S. Lindon Lane • TEMPE, AZ 85281
(602) 968-9354 Fax 968-9357
Mark Thomas, Librarian
Description: A special collection of about 1,500 books on Native American history and culture. Interlibrary loans. Established 1911.

NAVAJO NATIONAL MONUMENT LIBRARY
HC 71 Box 3 • TONALEA, AZ 86044-9704
(520) 672-2366 Fax 672-2345
Russ Bodnar, Supt.
Description: A collection of approximately 600 volumes on Southwest archaeology, history of Hopi and Navajo culture. Open to the public by appointment only.

NAVAJO COMMUNITY COLLEGE LIBRARY
TSAILE, AZ 86556
(520) 724-3311
Special collection: Collection of over 45,000 volumes and an extensive pamphlet file on more than 100 Indain-related topics. Central to the collection is the Moses Donner Indian Collection—An extensive collection of publications on Indians.

**ARIZONA HISTORICAL SOCIETY
RESEARCH LIBRARY**
949 East Second St.
TUCSON, AZ 85719
(520) 628-5774 Fax 628-5695
E-mail: azhist@azstarnet.com
Web site: www.ahs.state.az.us
Deborah Shelton, Library Head
Description: Holdings include 50,000 books, 750,000 photographs, 5,000 maps, 1,000 manuscript collections, 1,000 oral histories, and periodicals and ephemera related to Arizona, the Southwest and northern Mexico, 1540 to the present. Special programs and exhibits. Established 1884.

ARIZONA STATE MUSEUM LIBRARY
Box 210026, University of Arizona
TUCSON, AZ 85721-0026
(520) 621-4695 Fax 621-2976
Mary Graham, Librarian
E-Mail: megraham@email.arizona.edu
Website: www.statemuseum.arizona.edu
Description: A major U.S. repository of documentation on Native American art. Contains approximately 43,000 volumes of published materials as well as archives of unpublished documents, field notes, diaries, with emphasis on prehistory and ethnology of Greater Southwest and Northern Mexico, and cultures of Arizona and New Mexico; many of which are on the subject of Native Americans; extensive microfilm collection. Interlibrary loans (limited). Open to the public.

COLLEGE OF LAW LIBRARY
University of Arizona • TUCSON, AZ 85721
(520) 621-5455
Ronald L. Cherry, Librarian
Description: Maintains a special collection on law relating to the American Indian. Subjects includes Federal laws, Indian constitutions, laws and codes, tribal court reports, U.S. Congressional hearings and reports, periodicals, treatises, and treaties. Interlibrary loans. Open to the public.

**NATIVE AMERICAN RESEARCH
& TRAINING CENTER**
University of Arizona
1642 E. Helen • TUCSON, AZ 85719
(520) 621-5075
Jennie R. Joe, Ph.D., Director
Research activities: Health and rehabilitation of disabled and chronically ill Native Americans. Studies the impact of government policy on the delivery of health care. Serves as a national resource for all North American tribes and Alaska natives.

MISSION SAN XAVIER DEL BAC LIBRARY
1950 W. San Xavier Rd.
TUCSON, AZ 85746
(520) 294-2624
Father Michael Dallmeier, Rector
Description: A collection of about 5,000 volumes pertaining to Aztec and Native-American ethnography and anthropology.

SOUTHWEST FOLKLORE CENTER
University of Arizona • TUCSON, AZ 85706
(520) 626-3392
Description: Contains four videotaped conversations: Navajo singer Andrew Natonabah, writers Leslie Marmon Silko and N. Scott Momaday, and Papago storyteller Ted Rios. Available on 2 videotape.

NAVAJO NATION BOOK PROJECT
P.O. Box 9040
WINDOW ROCK, AZ 86515
(520) 871-6376/7303 Fax 871-7304
Purpose: To distribute free book materials, non-book materials, and equipment to elegible organizations and individuals. See listing under Window Rock, AZ for more information.

NAVAJO NATION LIBRARY SYSTEM
Window Rock Public Library
P.O. Box 9040
WINDOW ROCK, AZ 86515
Irving Nelson, Manager
(520) 871-6376/7303 Fax 871-7304
Purpose: To plan, develop, and implement a library and information system which will serve the residents of the Navajo Nation. To be the primary source of information for all who are interested in the Navajo people, their land and culture. *Special collections*: General Reference Collection: 2,500 books and documents; Environmental Assessment Collection: 200 folders; Navajo Nation Government Documents Collection: 1,000 documents & publications; Navajo Times Today Collection: 120 boxes of hard copy and microfilm copies; Vertical File Collection: 930 folders of articles; Correll Collection: 30 filing cabinets of historical documents; Native American Music Collection: 350 cassettes; Oral History Collection: 200 cassettes; Native American Research Library Collection: 2,000 books. Subjects covered are Navajo Indians; Southwest archaeology, Indians of America, & Arizona history. Bookmobile services: 2 bookmobiles provide services to 90 communities across the reservation within Arizona, New Mexico & Utah. Audio Visual Services. Computer Software Service: Uses hypercard application on a MacIntosh Computer to create interactive computer software, "Information on the Navajo Nation."

ARKANSAS

**ARKANSAS STATE UNIVERSITY
MUSEUM LIBRARY & ARCHIVES**
P.O. Box 490
STATE UNIVERSITY, AR 72467
(501) 972-2074 Fax 972-2793
Charlott A. Jones, PhD, Director
E-Mail: squalls@choctaw.astate.edu
Description: Contains over 1,200 books and reference material on Indian history and culture with focus on Southeast, Southwest and Plains groups related to Arkansas native tribal groups; ethnology and archaeology exhibits. Interlibrary loans via Dean B. Ellis Library. Open to the public.

**AMERICAN INDIAN & ALASKA NATIVE
PERIODICALS RESEARCH CLEARINGHOUSE**
Stabler Hall 502, University of Arkansas
33rd & University Ave.
LITTLE ROCK, AR 72204

SOUTHWEST ARKANSAS REGIONAL ARCHIVES
P.O. Box 134 • WASHINGTON, AR 71862
(501) 983-2633
Mary Medearis, Director
Description: Subjects cover the history of Southwest Arkansas, Caddo Indians

CALIFORNIA

**CENTER FOR INDIAN COMMUNITY
DEVELOPMENT LIBRARY**
Humbodt State University
Brero House 93 • ARCATA, CA 95521
(707) 826-3711
Lois J. Risling, Director

Description: Collection covers community economic and organizational development, assessment of local needs for archaeological research, regeneration of American Indian languages and literatures and the application of computer systems to publication of Indian languages. Publishes textbooks and instructional material in and about Hupa, Karuk, Tolowa, Yurok, and other Indian languages.

ITEPP - CURRICULUM RESOURCE CENTER (CRC)
Indian Teacher & Educational Personnel Program
Humboldt State University, #1 Harpst St.
Spidell House #83 • ARCATA , CA 95521
(707) 826-5199 Fax 826-3675
E-Mail: mmj5@humboldt.edu
Web site: www.humboldt.edu/~hsuitepp/crc
Marlette Grant-Jackson, CRC Coordinator
Suzanne M. Burcell, Director
Web site: http://www.humboldt.edu/~hsuitepp/
Description: Houses a collection of over 3,500 books, videos, audiocassettes, periodicals, CD-ROM's, posters, and 100+ microfilm rolls dating back to the 1850's. Curricula materials are all related to Native American issues and topics.

MALKI MUSEUM LIBRARY
11-795 Fields Rd.
Morongo Indian Reservation
BANNING, CA 92220
(714) 849-7289
Description: Collection consists of 500 volumes on southern California Indians.

**BANCROFT LIBRARY & THE HEARST
MUSEUM OF ANTHROPOLOGY LIBRARY**
University of California - 103 Kroeber Hall
BERKELEY, CA 94720
(510) 642-3781 (Bancroft)
(510) 642-3682 (Heart Museum Library)
Description: Major U.S. repositories of documentation on Native American art.

ETHNIC STUDIES LIBRARY
Native American Studies-Library Collection
30 Stephens Hall, #2360
University of California, Berkeley
BERKELEY, CA 94720
(510) 643-1234 Fax 643-8433
John D. Berry, Native American Studies-
Comparative Ethnic Studies Librarian
(510) 642-0941 (office)
E-mail: jberry@library.berkeley.edu
Website: www.eslibrary.berkeley.edu
Description: The collection is focused on Native Americans, First Nations peoples of Canada, and some representation of Native peoples in Central and South America in all topical areas. *Estimated holdings*: 15,000 monographs; 1,000 serial titles (200 current); 400 sound recordings in varied formats; 300 videotapes; 1,000 35mm slides; 1,000 photos. NAS Bibliographic Database - 30,000 records. *Special collections*: American Indian Correspondence: The Presbyterian Historical Society Collection of Missionary Letters, 1833-1893; Annual Reports of the Commissioner of Indian Affairs, 1849-1949; John Collier papers, 1922-1968; Survey of the Conditions of the Indians of the U.S., 1929-1944; Records of the Bureau of Indian Affairs; Indian Census, 1885-1941; Harvard University Peabody Museum papers and memoirs, 1896-1957; Indian Rights Association papers, 1864-1973; Papewrs of the Society of Ameriucan Indians; Indian Claims Commission Reports; California Indian Library Collection (CILC); U.S. Congressional and Senate Reports; Dissertations on microfilm; 72 feet of vertical files and ephemera. *Special programs*: Readings by Native Authors and indigenous Story Telling. Opened in 1969 to the public for reference use only. Interlibrary loan via main UC Berkeley campus library.

**CABOT'S OLD INDIAN PUEBLO
MUSEUM LIBRARY**
67-616 East Desert View Ave.
DESERT HOT SPRINGS, CA 92240
(619) 329-7610 Fax 329-1956
Colbert H. Eyraud, Director
Description: Contains ten 4-drawer file cabinets of Desert Hot Springs newspapers; a collection of historical papers on microfilm, dated 1940-1980 at public library; City Government meetings, dated 1976-1990.

FRESNO COUNTY FREE LIBRARY
2420 Mariposa St. • FRESNO, CA 93721
(559) 488-3184 Fax 488-1971
Website: www.fresnolibrary.org
Karen Bosch-Cobb, Interim Librarian
Description: Covers American Indians of Fresno County, including Mono, Miwok, and Yokut tribes. *Special collection*: Ta-Kwa-Teu-Nee-Ya-Y Collection of about 200 books.

AMERICAN INDIAN RESOURCE CENTER (AIRC)
Los Angeles County Public Library
6518 Miles Ave. • HUNTINGTON PARK, CA 90255
(323) 583-2794 Fax 587-2061
Michael McLaughlin, Librarian
E-mail: airc@colapl.org
Website: www.colapublib.org/libs/huntington
park/indian.html
Description: Serves as an information referral center for and about American Indians. Maintains a collection of approximately 20,000 titles (Southwest, Plains, Woodlands); including books, magazines, scholarly journals, newspapers, theses, and dissertations. The collection covers the full spectrum of American Indian experience inthe continental U.S. and Alaska - from pre-Columbian times to the present. Non-book items include films, photographs, audiocassetes, videocassettes, and compact discs. 130 periodical titles; 100 16mm films; 250 videocassettes; 500 audiocassettes; 300 phonorecords; current events clipping file (8 drawers, 350 subject headings). AIRC has a large microfilm collection that includes monographs, oral histories, federal government publications, tribal government publications, and tribal newspapers and newsletters. Federal Government publications include complete sets of Indian Census Rolls, 702 microfilm reels and Records of the Indian Claims Commission, 6,128 microfiche; copies of the Code of Federal Regulations (CFR) 25 Indians, treaties, and other government reports. Tribal government publications include tribal codes, tribal bylaws, and other specialized publications. The Vertical Files (VF) consist of about 800 alphabetically arranged files by subject headings with unique significance to American Indians - notable individuals, organizations, Indian specific issues, and events - historic and contemporary. Also, maintains directories of the B.I.A. offices and tribal government offices throughout the U.S. and Alaska. *Special programs*: Information and referral services; outreach program; meeting room (free for Indian groups). Interlibrary loans. Open to public. Affiliated with Los Angeles County Public Library. Opened in 1979.

CABAZON TRIBAL REFERENCE LIBRARY
Cabazon Band of Mission Indians
84-245 Indio Springs Dr. • INDIO, CA 92203

LAKE COUNTY HISTORICAL SOCIETY LIBRARY
P.O. Box 1011 • LAKEPORT, CA 95453
(707) 279-4466
Norma Wright, President
Description: Covers Pomo Indian history and culture. Includes photographs, manuscripts, oral history tapes, and genealogical data.

BARONA CULTURAL CENTER LIBRARY
1095 Barona Rd. • LAKESIDE, CA 92040
(619) 443-7003 ext. 2 Fax 443-0173
Cheryl M. Hinton, Curator
E-mail: chinton@barona.org
Website: www.baronatribe.com/history.html
Description: Research primarily on southern California Indians with a focus on Barona 'Ipay/Kumayaay. Opened in 2001.

LOMPOC MUSEUM LIBRARY
200 South H St. • LOMPOC, CA 93436
(805) 736-3888
Description: Contains over 1,000 volumes on Chumash Indians, Indians of southern California, and Lompoc history and archaeology.

AMERICAN INDIAN STUDIES CENTER & LIBRARY
UCLA, 3220 Campbell Hall, Box 951548
LOS ANGELES, CA 90095-1548
(310) 206-7510 Fax 206-7060
Ken Wade, Librarian
Web site: www.sscnet.ucla.edu/indian
Description: Coordinates educational, research, and action-oriented programs designed to meet the needs of American Indian students at UCLA and the American Indian communities in general. *Activities*: Encourages the development of new courses; promotes hiring of Native American faculty; sponsors research on American Indians; publishes journals, books, monographs, and other media reflecting contemporary Indian research and issues. *Library*: Approximately 8,000 volumes comprise the Library's core collection, covering the subject of the Indians of North America, with a strong emphasis on California and the Southwest. The primary focus is on American Indian cultures in both historical and contemporary perspectives. Augmenting the circulating and reference collections are serials/periodicals, and a vertical file. *Publication*: American Indian Culture and Research Journal.

AUTRY NATIONAL CENTER LIBRARY
Museum of the American West
4700 Western Heritage Way
LOS ANGELES, CA 90027
(213) 667-2000 Fax 660-5721
Alicia Gonzalez, Director
E-Mail: agonzalez@autrynationalcenter.org
Description: Contains over 25,000 book and serial tites; 2,000 linear feet of non-book materials, including manuscripts, photographs, maps, sound recordings, music scores, films, etc. that document the history of the American West. *Special collections*: Fred Rosenstock collection, which contains more than 15,000 rare titles of Western Americana; the Foundation for American Indian Tribal History collection. Opened in 1988.

BRAUN RESEARCH LIBRARY
Southwest Museum, Autry National Center
Institute for the Study of the American West
234 Museum Dr. • LOS ANGELES, CA 90065
(323) 221-2164 Fax 224-8223
Kim Walters, Librarian
E-mail: kwalters@autrynationalcenters.org
Website: www.southwestmuseum.org
Description: Collection consists of 50,000 volumes of books and serials; includes 700 manuscript collections,1,300 sound recordings, and over 147,000 photographs. The Photo Archive is strongest on Indians of the Southwest, with many pictures of Native Americans of Alaska, the Northwest Coast, California, and the Plains. *Special collections*: The Papers of Frederick Webb Hodge, Frank Hamilton Cushing, George Bird Grinnell, Charle F. Lummis, and George Wharton James. *Special programs*: Lecture series (quarterly). Opened in 1907.

LOS ANGELES PUBLIC LIBRARY
History/Genealogy Department
630 W. Fifth St. • LOS ANGELES, CA 90071
(213) 228-7400 Fax 228-7419
Jane Nowak, Dept. Manager
E-Mail: hiscen@lapl.org
Web site: www.lapl.com
Description: Maintains a special collection on the American Indian; 8,000 volumes on the Indians of the Americas with an emphasis on the Southwestern U.S. Monographs, periodicals, pamphlet material, and specialized newsletters and newspapers are accessed through the general catalog and through the Indian File, a detailed computer based index. Interlibrary loans. Open to the public.

UCLA LIBRARY - SPECIAL COLLECTIONS
405 Hilgard Ave. • LOS ANGELES, CA 90095
(310) 825-1201
Description: A major U.S. repository of documentation on Native American art.

FORT MOJAVE TRIBAL LIBRARY
500 Merriman Ave. • NEEDLES, CA 92363
(760) 629-4591 Fax 629-5767
Debbie Jackson, Contact

MARIN MUSEUM OF THE AMERICAN INDIAN LIBRARY
P.O. Box 864, 2200 Novato Blvd.
NOVATO, CA 94948 (415) 897-4064
Katharine J. Volz, Executive Director
Description: A reference library of approximately 1,000 volumes/periodicals oriented heavily to California Indians, especially Coast Miwok.

OAKLAND PUBLIC LIBRARY
American Indian Library Project
Dimond Branch Library
3565 Fruitvale Ave. • OAKLAND, CA 94602
(510) 482-7844 Fax 482-7824
Description: Collection contains 1,500+ volumes on Native American literature, culture, and history.

NATIONAL ARCHIVES & RECORDS ADMINISTRATION - PACIFIC REGION
1000 Commodore Dr. • SAN BRUNO, CA 94066
(650) 238-3501 Fax 238-3510
Daniel Nealand, Director
E-Mail: sanbruno.archives@nara.gov
Web site: www.nara.gov
Description: Archival records of the Federal Government in Nevada (except Clark County), Northern California, Hawaii, and the Pacific Trust territories. Holdings include over 52,000 cubic feet of original records ocreated by various federal agency field offices from 1850 to 1970, a large collection of National Archives microfilm, and over 2900 cubic feet of records of Bureau of Indian Affairs offices in California and Nevada. Spec*ial programs*: Genealogy and other historical records workshops; internships and volunteer programs. Open to the public since 1969.

AMERICAN INDIAN STUDIES LIBRARY
Dept. of American Indian Studies
San Diego State University
SAN DIEGO, CA 92182 (619) 594-6991
Description: The Golsh Collection: Consists of rare documents and books.

PALOMAR COMMUNITY COLLEGE LIBRARY
1140 W. Mission Rd. • SAN MARCOS, CA 92069
(619) 744-1150
Judy J. Carter, Director
Description: A collection of 3,500 volumes pertaining to American Indian culture, history, arts and crafts, and social problems; Bureau of Ethnology Reports.

THE HUNTINGTON LIBRARY
1151 Oxford Rd. • SAN MARINO, CA 91108
(626) 405-2100 Fax 449-5720
David S. Zeidberg, Director
Website: www.huntington.org
Description: A major U.S. repository of documentation on Native American art. Includes scores of manuscript collections that document political, military, religious or educational contacts between various American Indians and Euro-Americans, particularly in the 19th & 20th centuries. Researchers interested in more details about the Huntington's manuscript holdings should consult its Guide to American Historical Manuscripts in the Huntington Library (San Marino, CA, 1979). Not open to the public.

MESA GRANDE RESERVATION LIBRARY
P.O. Box 270 • SANTA YSABEL, CA 92070
(619) 782-3835

HELD-POAGE RESEARCH LIBRARY
603 W. Perkins St. • UKIAH, CA 95482
(707) 462-6969
Lila J. Lee, Director
Description: Local history and ethnography collection of over 6,000 volumes; many on American Indians. *Special collections*: Estle Beard Collection-research material for Genocide & Vendetta: The Round Valley Wars of Northern California; the Edith Van Allen Collection for Indian Uses of native plants; California and western states anthropology and archaeology; and Photographic Negative Collection; artifacts, maps.

UNIVERSAL CITY STUDIOS RESEARCH DEPARTMENT LIBRARY
UNIVERSAL CITY, CA 91608
Special collection: 7,500 books dealing with Western Americana and the American Indian.

YOSEMITE MUSEUM LIBRARY
P.O. Box 577
YOSEMITE NATIONAL PARK, CA 95389
(209) 372-0282
Linda Eade, Librarian
Description: Contains approximately 20,000 volumes and a large archival and photographic collection relating to Yosemite and Central California Indian people.

COLORADO

UNIVERSITY OF COLORADO LIBRARY
Center for the Study of Native Languages
of the Plains & Southwest
BOULDER, CO 80309 (303) 492-2748
Dr. Allen R. Taylor, Director
Research activities: Collects data and conducts re-
search on Native American languages of the Great
Plains and Southwest, including the Siouan languages,
Gros Ventre, Kiowa, and Wichita. Also includes the
Lakota Project, which offers instructional materials to
aid in learning Dakota Sioux language.

NATIONAL INDIAN LAW LIBRARY
Native American Rights Fund
1522 Broadway • BOULDER, CO 80302
(303) 447-8760 Fax 443-7776
David Selden, Director
E-mail: dselden@narf.org
Website: www.narf.org/nillindex.html
Description: American Indian law and tribal law collection, including tribal codes, constitutions, intergovernmental agreements, legal pleadings from major
Indian law cases, law review articles, handbooks,
manuals and books related to Federal Indian law and
tribal law; government documents. Special program:
Indian Law current awareness bulletin service. *Publications*: Landmark Indian Law cases. Provides reference and research, assistance and document delivery for the public. Opened in 1972.

COLORADO SPRINGS
FINE ARTS CENTER LIBRARY
30 W. Dale St. • COLORADO SPRINGS, CO 80903
(719) 634-5581
Roderick Dew, Director
Description: A collection of approximately 9,000 volumes on Indians of the Southwest, Mexico and Guatemala, with emphasis on art, textiles and pottery.
Contains a large collection of periodicals, some from
the late 19th century. Open to the public.

COLORADO HISTORICAL SOCIETY
STEPHEN H. HART LIBRARY
1300 Broadway • DENVER, CO 80203
(303) 866-2305 Fax 866-5739
Katherine Kane, Director
Description: Walker Colection (Sioux); W.H. Jackson
photos (Southwestern tribes); many other photos -
emphasis on the Ute, Cheyenne, Arapaho, Navajo,
Hopi, Zuni; extensive ethnological collections on Plains
and Southwest Indians; Mesa Verde Plains and Mountain Indian materials; source materials on the history
of the Indian wars; materials from the Rosebud Indian
Agency, 1885-1890; and photograph collection. Open
to the public.

FOURTH WORLD CENTER FOR THE
STUDY OF INDIGENOUS LAW & POLITICS
University of Colorado at Denver
Campus Box 190, P.O. Box 173364
DENVER, CO 80217 (303) 556-2850
Glenn T. Morris, Prof.

DENVER ART MUSEUM LIBRARY
100 West 14th Ave. Pkwy.
DENVER, CO 80204
(720) 865-5000 Fax 865-5028
Nancy Simon, Director
Description: Holdings include more than 25,000 vol-
umes; 50 journals; and a special collection on the
American Indians.

CENTER OF SOUTHWEST STUDIES
Fort Lewis College, 1000 Rim Dr.
DURANGO, CO 81301-3999
(970) 247-7126 Fax 247-7422
Duane Smith & Philip Duke, Directors
E-Mail: duke_p@fortlewis.edu
Web site: http://www.fortlewis.edu
Description: Includes significant historical and ethnographic collections pertaining to American Indians:
books, periodicals, microfilm, printed materials, archives, photographs, maps and artifacts. *Special programs*: Courses on archival management and oral history; train Indian students in the interpretation of cultural resources. Established 1964.

REED LIBRARY
Fort Lewis College
1000 Rim Dr. • DURANGO, CO 81301-3999
(970) 247-7662 Fax 247-7422
Margaret C. Landrum, Director
Elayne S. Walstedter, Librarian
Description: Collection includes hundreds of volumes
on the North American Indian, Fort Lewis College began as an Indian school in the late 1800's.

GRAND CANYON NATIONAL PARK LIBRARY
P.O. Box 129 • GRAND CANYON, CO 86023
(928) 638-7768 Fax 638-7776
Susan Eubank, Librarian
E-mail: susan_eubank@nps.gov
Website: www.library.nps.gov
Description: Maintains a collection of approximately
10,000 volumes. Material on the Grand Canyon, natu-
ral history, archaeology, etc. Interlibrary loans. Opened
in 1940.

MUSEUM OF WESTERN COLORADO ARCHIVES
248 S. 4th St.
GRAND JUNCTION, CO 81501
(303) 242-0971
Judy Prosser-Armstrong, Archivist
Description: Covers the history of western Colorado;
anthropology of southwestern Indians.

KOSHARE INDIAN MUSEUM LIBRARY
P.O. Box 580 • LA JUNTA, CO 81050
(719) 384-4411 Fax 384-8836
Joe Clay, Director of Programs
Description: Collection contains 2,000 volumes on In-
dian history, religion, legends, art, handicrafts, etc.
Reference use only.

MESA VERDE RESEARCH LIBRARY
P.O. Box 38
MESA VERDE NATIONAL PARK, CO 81330
(303) 529-4475 Fax 529-4498
Beverly J. Cunningham, Librarian
Description: Maintains more than 6,500 volumes on
archaeology and ethnography, with many on the Indians of the Mesa Verde area, and North America. Interlibrary loans.

CONNECTICUT

CONNECTICUT HISTORICAL SOCIETY LIBRARY
1 Elizabeth St. • HARTFORD, CT 06105
(203) 236-5621
Christopher P. Bickford, Executive Director
Description: Collection contains 70,000 volumes and
two million manuscripts relating to Connecticut and
New England history and genealogy.

CONNECTICUT STATE LIBRARY
231 Capitol Ave. • HARTFORD, CT 06115
Description: Maintains an American Indian collection
emphasizing languages and history; its core deriving
from the library of J. Hammond Trumball.

MASHANTUCKET PEQUOT RESEARCH LIBRARY
ARCHIVES & SPECIAL COLLECTIONS
CHILDREN'S RESEARCH LIBRARY
110 Pequot Trail, P.O. Box 3180
MASHANTUCKET, CT 06338-3180
(860) 396-6897 Fax 396-7005 (Reference)
(860) 396-7001 (Archives) 396-6899 (Children's)
Cheryl A. Metoyer, PhD, Director
E-mail: reference@mptn.org
Web site: www.mashantucket.com
Description: The Information Resources Dept. is comprised of a Research Library, a Children's Research
Library, and an Archives & Special Collections. The
Research Library's collection contains over 35,000
titles of current and historical works on the histories
and cultures of indigenous peoples north of Mexico,
including Canada, Alaska and Hawaii, with an emphasis on 20th century materials. Print formats include
books, serials, maps, pamphlets and brochures. The
collection includes visual and audio recordings and
electronic media. The serials collection of more than
800 titles include journals, magazines, newspapers,
newsletters and auction catalogs supporting the
Library's mission. It includes a large collection of tribal

publications. Archives & Special Collections is comprised of two interconnected collecting areas. The *Archives* is a repository for the historical materials and
non-current records of the Mashantucket Pequot Tribal
Nation. It also holds the family papers of tribal members. *The Special Collections* contains a variety of materials that document the histories and cultures of
Native America, including letters and other manuscripts, maps, pamphlets, ephemera, rare books, and
photographs. The *Children's Library* introduces students to the Mashantucket Pequot Tribal Nation and
other North American indigenous peoples through programs and through its collections. The Children's Library serves students through 8th grade, adults who
work with children, and researchers of children's literature. The collection contains current and historical
materials by and about Native Americans, and includes
fiction and non-fiction books, serials, reference works,
and multimedia. The *Education Collection* supports the
educational aims of the museum and includes materials on educational theory and curriculum development
relating to Native American studies. *Special programs*:
Visiting Scholars Program; Budding Scholars Program;
Bibliographic Instruction Courses; educational workshops; lectures and orientations. Established 1998.

YALE UNIVERSITY LIBRARY
120 High St. • NEW HAVEN, CT 06520
(203) 432-2798 Fax 432-7231
Scott Bennett, PhD, Director
Web site: http://www.library.yale.edu/
Description: A major U.S. repository of documentation
on Native American art. Interlibrary loans.

EVA BUTLER LIBRARY
INDIAN & COLONIAL RESEARCH CENTER
Main St., Rte. 27, P.O. Box 525
OLD MYSTIC, CT 06372
(860) 536-9771
Website: www.theicrc.org
Joan Cohn, President/Director
Description: Subjects cover Native American geneal-
ogy, culture, history, and colonial history and local fam-
ily genealogy. *Special programs*: School progams
available for a fee; speaker at annual meeting in No-
vember each year. Open to the public. Opened in 1965.

THE INSTITUTE FOR AMERICAN INDIAN
STUDIES & RESEARCH LIBRARY
38 Curtis Rd., Box 1260
WASHINGTON GREEN, CT 06793
(203) 868-0518 Fax 868-1649
Alberto C. Meloni, Director
Purpose: The discovery, preservation, and interpretation of Native American cultures of the Northeastern
Woodlands rgion of the U.S. *Activities*: Conducts surveys for prehistoric and historic evidence of human
occupation; excavations of historic sites. *Research Library*: Collection of 2,000 volumes, periodicals, archival documents, and maps. For use by members, scholars and students with letters from professors. By appointment only.

DELAWARE

NANTICOKE INDIAN MUSEUM LIBRARY
Rt. 13, Box 107A • MILLSBORO, DE 19966
(302) 945-7022
Pat Harmon, Joan Ridolfi, Docent
Description: A collection of about 500 books
on the Nanticoke and other tribes.

DISTRICT OF COLUMBIA

AMERICAN HISTORICAL ASSOCIATION LIBRARY
400 A St., S.E. • WASHINGTON, DC 20003
(202) 544-2422

DAUGHTERS OF THE AMERICAN REVOLUTION
NATIONAL SOCIETY LIBRARY
1776 D St., NW • WASHINGTON, DC 20006
(202) 879-3229 Fax 879-3252
Eric G. Grundset, Library Director
Description: Subjects cover American Indian
history, genealogy and culture.

LIBRARY OF CONGRESS
101 Independence Ave., SE
WASHINGTON, DC 20540 (202) 707-5522
James H. Billington, Librarian
GENERAL REFERENCE AND BIBLIOGRAPHY DIVISION: A collection of approximately 16,000 volumes covering virtually all subjects relating to North American tribes. Includes various bibliographies, catalogs, and guides to other collections containing material on Indians, such as Dictionary Catalog of the Edward E. Ayer Collection of Americana and American Indians, the Dictionary Catalog of the American Indian Collection, Huntington Free Library and Reading Room, New York, and the Biographical and Historical Index of American Indians and Persons Involved in Indian Affairs. *MICROFORM READING ROOM*: Contains much Indian-related material from a variety of print and nonprint sources. For example: North American Indians: Photographs from the National Anthropological Archives, Smithsonian Institution, compiled by Herman Viola—contains approximately 4,700 photographs on microfiche of Indians and Indian artifacts; individual and group portraits; Doctoral Dissertation Series. University Microfilms has published North American Indians: Dissertation Index, written between 1904-1976 at North American universities; Early State Records—The study of colonial relations with Indians; also includes public and private collections noted for Indian-related material, such as: The Connecticut Archives Indian Volumes, 1647-1820; The Henry O'Reilly Papers, 1744-1825—Relating to the Six Nations and Indians of the Old Northwest; Records of the Five Civilized Tribes, 1840-1905; The Penn Manuscripts, 1687-1801; and, The Timothy Horsfield Papers, 1733-1771—The last two collections involving Indians in Pennsylvania and surrounding areas; Pamphlets in American History—Microfiche collection of rare pamphlets includes many dealings with American Indians; British Manuscripts Project—contains abundant source material on Indians especially for the period of the French and Indian War. *MANUSCRIPT DIVISION*: The Papers of the President, military officers, agents in Indian affairs, and other public and private individuals who dealt with Indians at various periods, such as those of Thomas A. Jesup, Henry L. Dawes, Edward S. Godfrey, Henry Rowe Schoolcraft, Philip Sheridan, Samuel P. Heintzelman, and John M. Schofield. Important collections available on microfilm include the papers of the American Missionary Society, the American Indian Correspondence Collection, and the Moravian Archives, as well as the papers of Timothy Pickering, Henry Knox, and Lyman C. Draper. Transcripts and photocopies of collections in foreign archives and libraries, such as the Indian records in the Public Archives of Canada. *SERIAL AND GOVERNMENT PUBLICATIONS DIVISION*: The Senate Confidential Executive Documents and Reports: Dating from the 17th Congress (1821)—comprised of formerly confidential documents which relate primarily to treaties. Patrons who wish to use this material should write to the Chief of this Division of the Library of Congress, or phone (202) 707-5647. *PRINTS AND PHOTOGRAPHS DIVISION*: Maintains holdings of nearly 4,000 prints, photographs, and engravings. The Edward S. Curtis Collection—Contains more than 1,600 photographs of Indians of the Plains, the Central Plateau, the Northwest Coast, the Southwest, and California; The Heyn-Matzen Collection—Contains approximately 550 photographs, mostly of Sioux, Crow and other Plains tribes; The John Grabill Collection—Consists mainly of photographs of Western frontier life, but includes many of Indians; More than 200 stereo views of Indians, and a miscellaneous collection of uncataloged and unsorted prints and photographs. Copies of the division's material not covered by copyright may be purchased from the Library's Photoduplication Service. *ARCHIVE OF FOLK CULTURE*: Joseph C. Hickerson, Head. The Smithsonian-Densmore Collection—Contains more than 3,500 cylinder recordings of songs of 35 tribal groups, compiled from 1907-1932; Peabody Museum Collection—Compiled in the 1890's by anthropologist Jesse Walter Fewkes, this collection contains more than 50 recordings reproducing the music and language of tribes like the Passamaquoddy, Hopi and Zuni; The Willard Rhodes Collection—Contains the music of 50 Indian tribes, recorded on disc and tape from 1940-1952, when Rhodes worked for the B.I.A. 20 long-playing records of selections from these and other collections are avail-

able for purchase. The Federal Cylinder Project- Judith A. Gray, Ethnomusicologist - began in 1979 to organize, catalog, duplicate for preservation, and disseminate wax cylinder recordings, most of which document the music and lore of American Indian cultures. Includes recordings of 15 Native American groups initially resident in the Northeastern and Southeastern woodlands-Passamaquoddy, Chippewa, Menominee, Seminole, and Winnebago recordings. Also recordings from the Great Basin/Plateau regions and 20 collections from the Pacific Northwest and Arctic areas. Maintains a file of bibliographies and related lists. For information and descriptive literature write the Archive, or phone (202) 707-5510. *MOTION PICTURE, BROADCASTING AND RECORDED SOUND DIVISION*: Contains films of ceremonial dances and of everyday Indian life; maintains several filmographies and guides to titles of films about Indians. For information regarding viewing films and video tapes write Division.

NATIONAL ANTHROPOLOGICAL ARCHIVES
National Museum of Natural History
Smithsonian Institution • Museum Support Center
4210 Silver Hill Rd. • SUITLAND, MD 20746
(301) 238-2872 Fax 238-2883
E-mail: naa@nmnh.si.edu
Web site: www.nmnh.si.edu/naa
John P. Hormiak, Director
Description: The nation's only repository dedicated exclusively to preserving the ethnographic, archaeological and linguistic fieldnotes, physical anthropological data, photographs, and recordings of American anthropologists and the records of anthropological organizations. It holds the records of the National Congress of American Indians and the National Tribal Chairman's Association, and includes the largest collection of Plains Indian ledger art. *Fellowship*: Native American Community Scholar Awards for research on Smithsonian collections.

NATIONAL ARCHIVES & RECORDS ADMINISTRATION (NARA)
8th & Pennsylvania Ave., NW •
WASHINGTON, DC 20408
(202) 501-5395 Fax 501-7170
Fax inquiries relating to the BIA (202) 219-6273
Cynthia G. Fox, Branch Chief
Aloha P. Smith, Assistant Chief
Description: The textual records of the Bureau of Indian Affairs (BIA) are in the custody of the Archives I Reference Branch, NARA, 8th & Penn Ave. NW, Washington, DC 20480. Motion pictures accessioned from the BIA are in the custody of the Motion Picture, Sound and Video Branch; Photographs showing activities of BIA are in custody of the Still Picture Branch; and Maps created by the BIA and accessioned by the National Archives are in the custody of the Cartographic and Architectural Branch of NARA all located at 8601 Adelphi Rd., College Park, MD 20740-6001 - (301) 713-7200 Fax 713-7205. Information abourt NARA holdings is available online. Publications: The NARA Archival Information Locator (NAIL) includes information about NARA holdings of the BIA, with some item lists; The "Guide to Federal Records in the National Archives of the U.S.;" "Information About the National Archives for Researchers," pamphlet.

NATIONAL GEOGRAPHIC SOCIETY LIBRARIES
1145 17th St., NW
WASHINGTON, DC 20036
(202) 857-7783 Fax 429-5731
Susan Fifer Canby, Director
Web site: www.national geographic.com
Description: Contains over 50,000 books, 400 periodicals on discovery & exploration, geography and natural sciences. Interlibrary loans. Open to the public by appointment.

NATURAL RESOURCES LIBRARY
U.S. Department of the Interior
1849 C St., NW
WASHINGTON, DC 20240
(202) 208-5815
Victoria Nozero, Project Director
Description: Holdings include all publications issued by the Bureau of Indian Affairs: Native American treaties, history, policy; and Native American education. Open to the public.

U.S. DEPARTMENT OF THE INTERIOR LIBRARY
1849 C St., NW, MS 5412-MIB
WASHINGTON, DC 20240
(202) 208-5815
John Sherrod, Project Manager
Description: Maintains a large collection of Indian reference material.

U.S. DEPARTMENT OF JUSTICE ENVIRONMENT LIBRARY
10th & Pennsylvania Ave., NW, Rm. 2333
WASHINGTON, DC 20530
(202) 514-2768 Fax 371-0570
Lee Decker, Branch Librarian
Description: Serves the Environment & Natural Resources Division at the Dept. of Justice, including the Indian Resources section; holdings of 18,000 volumes, many of which are on Indian claims and natural resources as related to Indian lands.

FLORIDA

WILLIE FRANK MEMORIAL LIBRARY
HC 61 Box 46A • CLEWISTON, FL 33440
(863) 983-6724 Fax 983-3539
E-mail: libbc@semtribe.com
Claudia Doctor, Library Aide
Description: Collection includes books, manuscripts, periodicals, photographs on the history and culture of the Seminole Tribe of Florida. *Special programs*: Summer program for children; story hours. Opened in 1976.

INDIAN TEMPLE MOUND MUSEUM LIBRARY
P.O. Box 4009, 139 Miraclestrip Pkwy SE
FORT WALTON BEACH, FL 32549
(850) 833-9595
Anna Peele, Museum Director
Description: Collection consists of 1,500 volumes on the archaeology of the site and related sites, and Indians of the region; slides and photographs. Open to the public. Opened in 1970.

DOROTHY SCOTT OSCEOLA MEMORIAL LIBRARY
3100 N.W. 63rd Ave. • HOLLYWOOD, FL 33024
(954) 989-6840 Fax 967-2395
E-mail: libho@semtribe.com
Diane Diaz, Librarian
Description: Collection includes books, manuscripts, periodicals, photographs on the history and culture of the Seminole Tribe of Florida. *Special programs*: Summer program for children; story hours weekly. Opened in 1981.

IMMOKALEE RESERVATION LIBRARY
303 Lena Frank Dr. #3 • IMMOKALEE, FL 33934
(941) 657-3400 Fax 657-9547
E-mail: libim@semtribe.com
Gale Boone, Library Aide
Description: Small collection includes books, manuscripts, and periodicals of the Seminole Tribe of Florida. *Special programs*: Summer library program; tutoring. Opened in 1992.

FLORIDA HISTORICAL SOCIETY LIBRARY
1320 Highland Ave. • MELBOURNE, FL 32935
Description: Holdings are mainly of Seminole Indian material.

BILLY OSCEOLA MEMORIAL LIBRARY
Rt. 6 Box 668 • OKEECHOBEE, FL 34974
(941) 763-4236 Fax 763-0679
E-mail: libbrsem@okeechobee.com
Norman H. Tribbett, Librarian/Director
Description: Contains books, manuscripts, periodicals, photographs, microfilm and rare books on the history and culture of the Seminole Indian Tribe of Florida. *Special programs*: Summer children's program; story hours. Opened in 1976.

JOHN C. PACE LIBRARY
Special Collections Department
The University of West Florida
11000 University Parkway
PENSACOLA, FL 32514-5750
(904) 474-2213
Dean DeBolt, Librarian
Description: Collection of manuscripts, archival

records, microfilms, and research materials include the history of the Creek Indians of the Southeast from earliest contact with white man, up to the present-day attempts to gain recognition as tribal groups.

GEORGIA

NEW ECHOTA HISTORIC SITE LIBRARY
1211 Chatsworth Hwy. N.E.
CALHOUN, GA 30701
  (706) 624-1321 Fax 624-1323
  David Gomez, Director; E-mail: n_echota@innerx.net
Description: General works on the Cherokee Indians and microfilm of the 1828-1834 Cherokee Phoenix newspaper, and the 1836-37 property evaluations of the Cherokee Nation and Cherokee genealogy.

OCMULGEE NATIONAL MONUMENT LIBRARY
1207 Emery Hwy.
MACON, GA 31201
  (912) 742-0447
Description: A collection of over 1,000 volumes on anthropology, archaeology, and prehistoric and historic Indians of the area; history of the Southeast U.S.

CHIEFTAINS MUSEUM LIBRARY
501 Riverside Pkwy. • ROME, GA 30162
  (404) 291-9494
  Josephine Ransom, Director
Description: Holdings include books and magazines dealing with Cherokee history, local history; videocasettes. Hours: Tue-Fri 11-4PM; Sunday 2-5PM; $1/adults.

IDAHO

IDAHO STATE HISTORICAL SOCIETY LIBRARY & ARCHIVES
450 N. 4th St.
BOISE, ID 83702
  (208) 334-3356 Fax 334-3198
  Linda Morton-Keithley, Administrator
  Website: www.idahohistory.net
Description: Collections include more than 200 volumes of Lapwai Agency records of 1871-1883; diaries and private papers. The Alice Fletcher-Jane Gay Nez Perce Allotment Photograph Collection, 1882-1892; Idaho Superintendency and other Indian records (National Archives microfilm); Indian files in the territorial section of State Archives; Nez Perce and Shoshone literature. Interlibrary loans. Open to the public.

PACIFIC NORTHWEST ANTHROPOLOGICAL ARCHIVES
Laboratory of Anthropology
University of Idaho
MOSCOW, ID 83844
  (208) 885-6123 Fax 885-5878
  Roderick Sprague, Director
Description: Originals or copies of virtually all sources of material pertaining to Pacific Northwest ethnography, archaeology, physical anthropology, and anthopological linguistics. Also personal papers of Don Crabtree, Alfred W. Bowers, and Frank C. Leonhardy. Also includes the Don Crabtree Lithic Technology collection of publications, reprints, correspondence, and specimens. Holdings number ca. 5,000. Area most strongly covered is the Plateau, secondly the Northwest. Open to the public.

NEZ PERCE NATIONAL HISTORICAL PARK LIBRARY
P.O. Box 93
SPALDING, ID 83551
  (208) 843-2261 x 41/42 Fax 843-2001
  Susan Buchel, Curator
Description: Collection consists of about 1,700 volumes on Nez Perce Indian history and culture, and culture and history of other Columbia Plateau and Pacific Northwest tribes. Special collection: 5,000 historical photographs.Open to the public by special arrangements (2-3 weeks advance notice needed.)

ILLINOIS

FIELD MUSEUM OF NATURAL HISTORY LIBRARY
Roosevelt Rd. at Lake Shore Dr.
CHICAGO, IL 60605
  (312) 922-9410
Description: A major U.S. repository of documentation on Native American art.

LIBRARY MEDIA PROJECT
1807 W. Sunnyside #1D
CHICAGO, IL 60640
  (800) 847-3671; (773) 275-0133 Fax 878-8404
  Mary M. Kirby, Director
  E-mail: info@librarymedia.org
  Website: www.librarymedia.org
Description: A non-profit organization providing public librarians, Native American organizations, and tribal libraries with a listing of Native American videos suggested by a panel of Native Americans. Many of these works are independent films normally not seen on TV or in collections by major distributors. *Publications*: Videoforum (1993), first issue includes Native American videos.

THE NEWBERRY LIBRARY
D'Arcy McNickle Center for American Indian History
60 W. Walton • CHICAGO, IL 60610
  (312) 255-3564 Fax 255-3696
  Brian Hosmer, Director
  E-Mail: mcnickle@newberry.org
  Website: www.newberry.org
Goals: To encourage the use of the Newberry collections on American Indian history; improve the quality of what is written about American Indians, educate teachers about American Indian culture, history, and literature; assist American Indian tribal historians in their research; and provide a meeting ground where scholars, teachers, tribal historians, and others interested in American Indian studies can discuss their work with each other. *Description*: The Edward E. Ayer and Everett O. Graff collections contain over 150,000 volumes on American Indians, and includes manuscripts, art, maps, and photographs devoted to American Indian peoples from Indian-White contact to the middle of the 20th century, Also houses a curriculum library of its own that includes books, tribal newspapers, and reference works. *Activities*: Offers numerous fellowships, including the Power-Tanner Fellowship for PhD candidates and postdoctoral scholars of American Indian heritage, the Frances C. Allen Fellowships for women of Native American heritage, and Rockefeller Foundation fellowships for community-centered research projects; coordinates the Committee on Institutional Cooperation's American Indian Studies Consortium, and alliance of the Big Ten universities, plus the University of Chicago and University of Illinois at Chicago. *Publication*: "Meeting Ground," a national bimonthly newsletter. Opened in 1887.

CAHOKIA MOUNDS STATE HISTORIC SITE LIBRARY
30 Ramey St.
COLLINSVILLE, IL 62234
  (618) 346-5160 Fax 346-5162
  Dr. Mark Esarey, Site Manager
  E-mail: cahokiamounds@ezl.com
  Website: www.cahokiamounds.com
Description: Contains books, periodicals, and papers that focus on the archaeology of Cahokia Mounds and surrounding region; the Mississippian culture; Illinois archaeology; general North American & Eastern U.S. archaeology; Native American cultures, crafts, and technology. Open to the public by appointment only. Opened in 1989.

THE STANLEY GOLDER LIBRARY
Mitchell Museum of the American Indian
2600 Central Park Ave.
EVANSTON, IL 60201
  (847) 475-1030 Fax 475-0911
  E-mail: mitchellmuseum@mindspring.com
  Website: www.mitchellmuseum.org
  Janice Klein, Director
Description: Contains about 5,000 books and journals relating to Native American history and culture. Interlibrary loans. Opened in 1977.

INDIANA

THE ARCHIVES OF TRADITIONAL MUSIC
Indiana University, Morrison Hall 117
BLOOMINGTON, IN 47405
  (812) 855-4679 Fax 855-6672
  Daniel Reed, Director; E-mail: atmusic@indiana.edu
Description: A library of sound recordings of world music, including a significant number of recordings of Native American music and language, and other oral data made from the late 1890s to the present. *Special collection*: Edward S. Curtis Collection of American Indian Music. *Special program*: Outreach program that helps Native American communities obtain copies of recordings of their own music and enhances the existing documentation of these materials. *Publication*: Resound, quarterly. Opened in 1954.

INDIANA UNIVERSITY MUSEUM LIBRARY
Student Bldg. 107
BLOOMINGTON, IN 47401
Description: A collection of 2,000 volumes on the American Indian.

AMERICAN INDIAN STUDIES RESEARCH INSTITUTE
Indiana University
422 N. Indiana Ave.
BLOOMINGTON, IN 47408
  (812) 855-4086
  Douglas R. Parks

THE POTAWATOMI MUSEUM LIBRARY
P.O. Box 631 • FREMONT, IN 46737
Description: Holdings include 1,000 reference books on the American Indian. By appointment only.

MUSEUM OF INDIAN HERITAGE REFERENCE LIBRARY
500 W. Washington St.
INDIANAPOLIS, IN 46204
  (317) 636-9378 Fax 264-1724
  John Vanausdall, Director
Description: Collections consist of approximately 2,000 volumes on Native American ethnology, archaeology, art, and language; also, periodicals; Bureau of American Ethnology annual reports; historical accounts of early contact; treaties; and literature. Tribal works emphasize Northwest Coast, Eskimo, Southwest, California, Great Plains, Eastern Woodlands, and works on Central and South American tribes.

IOWA

IOWA STATE HISTORICAL MUSEUM LIBRARY
East 12th & Grand Ave.
DES MOINES, IA 50319
  (515) 281-5111

STATE HISTORICAL SOCIETY OF IOWA LIBRARY
402 Iowa Ave. • IOWA CITY, IA 52240-1806
  (319) 335-3916 Fax 335-3935
  Shaner Magalhaes, Director
  Web site: www.iowahistory.org
Description: A collection of 150,000 books and bound periodicals, microforms, newspapers, maps, etc. of which there is a small collection of books relating to tribes that lived in Iowa, census data, public records, documents from Indian Claims Commission court cases, theses, manuscripts, maps, paintings and drawings, and several hundred Mesquakie Indian photographs.

EFFIGY MOUNDS NATIONAL MONUMENT LIBRARY
151 Hwy. 76 • HARPERS FERRY, IA 52146
  (563) 873-3491 Fax 873-3743
  Phyllis Ewing, Supt.
  E-mail: efmo_superintendent@nps.gov
  Website: www.nps.gov/efmo
Description: Books and periodicals relating to prehistoric Indians, archaeology, history of Iowa, Wisconsin, Mississippi River, natural resources, and specifically on the archaeology and ethnography of Effigy Mounds region. Opened 1949.

MORNINGSIDE COLLEGE LIBRARY
SIOUX CITY 51106
Description: Contains a special collection
on the American Indian.

KANSAS

MENNONITE LIBRARY & ARCHIVES
Bethel College, 300 E. 27th
NORTH NEWTON 67117
(316) 284-5304 Fax 284-5843
John D. Thiesen, Director
E-mail: mla@bethelks.edu
Website: www.bethelks.edu/services/mla
Special collection: Includes the H.R. Voth Manuscript
and Photograph Collection on Hopi Indians; and
Rodolphe Petter Manuscript Collection on Cheyenne
Indians. Also includes microfilm, audiotapes, and
maps. Interlibrary loans.

PAWNEE INDIAN VILLAGE
STATE HISTORIC SITE LIBRARY
480 Pawnee Trail • REPUBLIC, KS 66964
(785) 361-2255 (phone & fax)
Richard Gould, Director
E-mail: piv@kshs.org
Website: www.kshs.org
Description: A resource/research center with books,
articles, photographs and materials; specializes on the
Pawnee Nation. Open to the public. Opened in 1968.

MID-AMERICA ALL INDIAN CENTER LIBRARY
650 North Seneca • WICHITA, KS 67203
(316) 262-5221
Description: Contains a collection of over 1,200 books
on the American Indian. Open to the public.

KENTUCKY

J.B. SPEED ART MUSEUM LIBRARY
2035 S. Third St., P.O. Box 2600
LOUISVILLE, KY 40201
(502) 636-2893 Fax 636-2899
Ruth Cloudman, Curator
Description: Collection includes over 14,300 books,
72 periodical subscriptions; artists pamphlet files: 54
drawers. *Special collection*: Frederick Weygold's books
on American Indians.

LOUISIANA

GRINDSTONE BLUFF MUSEUM LIBRARY
501 Jenkins Rd. • SHREVEPORT, LA 71107
Description: Collection consists of approximately 3,600
volumes, with emphasis on Caddo and other area Indians.

MAINE

ABBE MUSEUM LIBRARY
P.O. Box 286 • BAR HARBOR, ME 04609
(207) 288-3519
Rebecca Cole-Will, Curator
Description: Includes over 5,000 volumes on Native
Americans, archaeology, Maine prehistory and Maine
Native peoples. Open to members and scholars by
appointment only.

WAPONAHKI MUSEUM & RESOURCE CENTER
Pleasant Point Passamaquoddy Tribe
P.O. Box 343 • PERRY, ME 04667
(207) 853-2600 Fax 853-6039

MAINE TRIBAL UNITY MUSEUM LIBRARY
Quaker Hill Rd. • UNITY, ME 04988
(207) 948-3131
Description: A collection of more than 500 volumes on
the Indians of Maine and American Indians in general.

MASSACHUSETTS

ROBERT S. PEABODY MUSEUM
OF ARCHAEOLOGY LIBRARY
Phillips Academy
ANDOVER, MA 01810
(978) 749-4490 Fax 749-4495
Malinda S. Blustain, Director
Description: 5,000 archaeological, anthropological
and ethnological sources; rare book, journals; and his-
torical photographs.

CHILDREN'S MUSEUM RESOURCE CENTER
300 Congress St.
BOSTON, MA 02210
(617) 426-6500
Lou Casagrande, Director
Joan Lester, Native American Collection Consultant
Description: Holdings include 10,000 cultural materi-
als relating to the American Indian. Open Sept. - May:
Tues, Thurs. & Saturday, 10 am - 5 pm; and June -
August: Monday-Friday, 10 am - 5 pm.

TOZZER LIBRARY
Harvard University, 21 Divinity Ave.
CAMBRIDGE, MA 02138
(617) 495-2248
Lynne M. Schmelz-Keil, Librarian
Description: A major U.S. repository of documentation
on Native American art. Collection consists of over
175,000 volumes relating to the major subfields of
anthropology, including archaeology, biological anthropology; cultural anthropology, and linguistics; strong
collection on Mayan archaeology and ethnology. *Publications*: Author and Title Catalogues of the Tozzer
Library (microfiche); Bibliographic Guide to Anthropology and Archaeology, annual; Anthropological Literature: An Index to Periodical Articles and Essays, quarterly. Interlibrary loans. Open to public.

BOSTON INDIAN COUNCIL LIBRARY
105 S. Huntington
JAMAICA PLAIN, MA 02130
(617) 232-0343
Description: A collection of various materials
related to Indian programs, history and culture.

PLIMOTH PLANTATION LIBRARY
P.O. Box 1620 • PLYMOUTH, MA 02362
(508) 746-1622 ext. 8385 Fax 830-6026
Carolyn Freeman Travers, Director
Website: www.plimoth.org
Description: In addition to Pilgrim related topics, there
is a growing body of southern New England Native
literature. Not opened to the public.

PHILLIPS LIBRARY
Peabody Essex Museum
East Indian Square
SALEM, MA 01970
(508) 745-1876
Description: Collection contains 1,000 books, plus
periodicals and pamphlets on the history and culture
of North American Indians, with emphasis on the Northeastern section of the U.S. Special collections: Papers of Native American researchers Frank Speck and
E. Tappan Adney. Interlibrary loans. Open to public.

CHAPIN LIBRARY OF RARE BOOKS
Williams College
WILLIAMSTOWN, MA 01267
(413) 597-2462 Fax 597-2929
Robert L. Volz, Custodian
E-Mail: chapin.library@williams.edu
Website: www.williams.edu/resources/chapin
Description: Collection of 15th to 20th-century books
relating to Indians of North and South America. Open
to the public. Opened in 1923.

AMERICAN ANTIQUARIAN SOCIETY LIBRARY
185 Salisbury St.
WORCESTER, MA 01609
(617) 755-5221
Description: A collection of five million books, prints,
maps, and periodicals on American history, archaeology, and life through 1876.

MICHIGAN

UNIVERSITY OF MICHIGAN -
WILLIAM L. CLEMENTS LIBRARY
909 S. University St.
ANN ARBOR, MI 48104-1190
(313) 764-2347 Fax 647-0716
Dr. John C. Dann, Director
E-Mail: clements.library@umich.edu
Web site: www.clements.umich.edu
Description: Collection consists of over 75,000 books
and bound periodicals, 600,000 manuscript items and
other materials relating to the Americas to 1930, including Indian relations..especially in later 18th century. Open to the public. Established 1922.

CRANBROOK INSTITUTE OF SCIENCE LIBRARY
1221 N. Woodward, P.O. Box 801
BLOOMFIELD HILLS, MI 48303-0801
(810) 645-3200 Fax 645-3034
Gretchen Young-Weiner, Director
Description: Collection includes over 18,000 volumes
on various topics including anthropology and ethnology; also, about 200 journal subscriptions. Interlibrary
loan. Open to the public by appointment only.

BISHOP BARAGA ASSOCIATION ARCHIVES
347 Rock St., P.O. Box 550
MARQUETTE, MI 49855
(906) 227-9117 Fax 228-2469
Elizabeth Delene, Archivist
E-mail: edelene@dioceseofmarquette.org
Description: Collection contains papers of Bishop
Frederic Baraga, the first bishop of the Upper Peninsula of Michigan and missionary to the Indians (1830-
1868). Includes Native American records from the early
1800's. Baraga published a dictionary of the Ojibway
language in 1853 and several other Ojibway books
for which they also have records. Records also include
Office of Indian Affairs, Fur Company Papers and
material pertaining to the Great Lakes region. *Special
activities*: Bishop Baraga Days, annual; Mass in Crypt
of Bishop Baraga, monthly *Publications*: The Baraga
Bulletin (quarterly, membership is $10 per year); His
Diary & Shephard of the Wilderness, which deal with
Frederic Baraga's encounters with the Ojibway and
Ottawa. Available to the public by appointment for research only. Opened 1930.

LAKE SUPERIOR STATE COLLEGE -
MICHIGAN COLLECTION
SAULT STE. MARIE, MI 49783
Description: Collection of 1,000 volumes on the his-
tory of Michigan's Upper Peninsula, including Indians
and local history.

GTB HERITAGE LIBRARY
Grand Traverse Band of Ottawa & Chippewa Indians
2605 NW Bay Shore Dr.
SUTTONS BAY, MI 49682
(231) 271-3538 Fax 271-4861
Description: Maintains many books, publications, periodicals, videos, and CD ROMs on Native American
events, history, culture, etc.

MINNESOTA

RUTH A. MYERS LIBRARY
Fond du Lac Tribal & Community College
2101 14th St. • CLOQUET, MN 55720
(218) 879-0804 Fax 879-0814
Description: Special collection of regional
Native American publications.

BECKER COUNTY HISTORICAL
SOCIETY LIBRARY
P.O. Box 622
DETROIT LAKES, MN 56502
Dean Sather, Director
Description: Holdings include 1,500 volumes pertain-
ing to the White Earth Indian Reservation, covering
twelve townships of Becker County, Minnesota.

**MINNEAPOLIS COLLEGE OF ART &
DESIGN—LEARNING RESOURCE CENTER**
200 East 25th St. • MINNEAPOLIS, MN 55404
Special collection: The American Indian Book Collection.

MINNEAPOLIS ATHENAEUM
300 Nicollet Mall
MINNEAPOLIS, MN 55401-1992
(612) 630-6351 Fax 630-6210
Edward R. Kukla, Director
E-mail: ekukla@mplib.org
Website: www.mplib.org/athenaeum.asp
Description: Holdings include approximately 500 volumes dealing with Indian affairs and activities on 18th and 19th century travel books. Specializing in the following tribes: Dakota (Sioux); Mandan; Ojibwa (Chippewa). Open to the public. Opened in 1859.

**UPPER MIDWEST INDIAN
CULTURE CENTER LIBRARY**
Pipestone National Monument
P.O. Box 727 • PIPESTONE, MN 56164
(507) 825-5463
Maddie Redwing, Director
Description: Collection of 500 volumes on Indian history of the northern Plains. Opened in 1955

RED LAKE NATION TRIBAL ARCHIVES & LIBRARY
P.O. Box 297 • RED LAKE, MN 56671
(218) 679-2324 Fax 679-3378
Kathryn "Jodie" Beaulieu, Director
Purpose: To collect, preserve, and make available the history of the Red Lake Band of Chippewa Indians.
Description: Exhibits are changed seasonally and oral history presentations are provided. Opened in 1989.

**MINNESOTA HISTORICAL SOCIETY
RESEARCH CENTER**
345 Kellogg Blvd. W.
ST. PAUL, MN 55102-1906
(612) 296-2143 Fax 297-7436
Denise E. Carlson, Head of Reference
Description: A major U.S. repository of documentation on Native American art. Maintains a collection of material on the Ojibwe and Dakota tribes, plus a small amount on Winnebago; includes information on Indian education, state census schedules with listings of Indian people, and correspondence on Indian matters in the Governor's papers. Collections include books, photos, newspapers, periodicals, oral histories, sound and visual recordings, and artworks. Also, Dakota and Ojibwe dictionaries, histories of Native peoples in Minnesota, and material on the U.S.-Dakota conflicts of 1862. *Activities*: Mini-classes on genealogy resources, house history research, etc. Interlibrary loans. Open to the public.

MISSISSIPPI

**THE GRAND VILLAGE OF THE
NATCHEZ INDIANS—LIBRARY**
400 Jefferson Davis Blvd.
NATCHEZ, MS 39120
(601) 446-6502
James F. Barnett, Jr., Director
Description: A collection of 300 volumes on archaeology and Southeastern Indians. Special programs: Seminars, workshops, and educational programs. Open to public for reference only.

NATCHEZ TRACE PARKWAY LIBRARY
2680 Natchez Trace Parkway
TUPELO, MS 38804
Description: Maintains a special collection of 200 items of papers and letters relating to Choctaw and Chickasaw Indians.

MISSOURI

**SOUTHEAST MISSOURI STATE
UNIVERSITY LIBRARY**
CAPE GIRARDEAU, MO 63701
Description: Extensive collection on North American archaeology and Indians.

KANSAS CITY MUSEUM LIBRARY
3218 Gladstone Blvd.
KANSAS CITY, MO 64123
(816) 483-8300
David Ucko, President
Description: Maintains a general reference library with about 4,000 volumes covering primarily local and regional history, Native American art and history, natural sciences, material culture, and museum-related publications.

**NATIONAL ARCHIVES-
CENTRAL PLAINS REGION**
2312 East Bannister Rd.
KANSAS CITY, MO 64131
(816) 268-8000 Fax 268-8038
Diana Duff, Director
E-mail: kansascity.archives@nara.gov
Website: www.archives.gov
Description: Collection consists of Federal Indian records created on Indian reservations and schools in North and South Dakota, Minnesota, Kansas and Nebraska. The tribes included on these reservations include the Chippewa and the various tribes of the Sioux Confederation, as well as the Iowa, Kickapoo, Omaha, Potawatomi, Ponca, Sac and Fox, Winnebago and Munsee; also, records of the Bismarck, Flandreau, Haskell, Pierre, Pipestone, Rapid City, and Wahpeton Indian schools; some records relate to tribes and reservations in Wisconsin, primarily the Menominee. Information contained are: censuses, tribal enrollment rosters, annuity payrolls, individual Indian bank account ledgers, land allotment rolls, employee payrolls and student case files; also extensive series of superintendent's (agent's) correspondence files. *Activities*: Monthly Indian study group.

**UNIVERSITY OF MISSOURI,
K.C. GENERAL LIBRARY**
5100 Rockhill Rd.
KANSAS CITY, MO 64110
Special collection: Snyder Collection of Americana—25,000 volumes—historical and Indian-related works.

MISSOURI HISTORICAL SOCIETY LIBRARY
P.O. Box 11940 • ST. LOUIS, MO 63112-0040
(314) 746-4500 Fax 746-4548
Emily Jaycox, Librarian
E-mail: library@mohistory.org
Web site: www.mohistory.org
Description: Holdings include more than 2,000 volumes on the American Indian. Strongest on the fur trade in the Trans-Mississippi West. Open to the public. Established 1866.

MONTANA

CENTER FOR NATIVE AMERICAN STUDIES
Univerity of Montana • BOZEMAN, MT 59717
(406) 994-3881
Dr. Wayne J. Stein, Director
Research activities: American Indian studies, including research on Montana tribal histories and culture and Indian-white relations.

WHITE SWAN MEMORIAL LIBRARY
Little Bighorn Battlefield National Monument
P.O. Box 39 • CROW AGENCY, MT 59022
(406) 638-2621 ext. 131 Fax 638-2623
John Doerner, Historian/Librarian
E-mail: johndoernere@nps.gov
Web site: www.nps.gov/libi
Elizabeth & George Custer Collection - correspondence with statesmen and military personnel of the period; 2,000 photographs, including military personnel, the Custer family; Native Americans (Crow, Sioux, Cheyenne). Research by appointment.

CROW INDIAN HOSPITAL
MEDICAL LIBRARY
U.S. Public Health Service
CROW AGENCY, MT 59022

MILES ROMNEY MEMORIAL LIBRARY
Bitter Root Valley Historical Society
205 Bedford Ave. • HAMILTON, MT 59840
(406) 363-3338 (phone & fax)

Helen Ann Bibler, Director
E-mail: rcmuseum@cybernet1.com
Web site: www.cybernet1.com/rcmuseum/
Description: Subjects include Indian history, pioneer and the Lewsi & Clark expedition. *Special programs*: Sunday Series Program; Bitter Root Days; MacIntosh Apple Day.

**HISTORICAL SOCIETY OF
MONTANA LIBRARY & ARCHIVES**
225 North Roberts • HELENA, MT 59601
Description: Holdings include 50,000 volumes on Montana history, frontier life, Indians & Indian affairs, Lewis and Clark Expedition, and other related subjects.

DR. JOHN WOODENLEGS MEMORIAL LIBRARY
Dull Knife Memorial College
P.O. Box 98, 1 College Dr.
LAME DEER, MT 59043
(406) 477-6215 Fax 477-6219
Description: Contains over 14,000 circulated items; Special Cheyenne Collection; more than 100 periodical titles and newspapers.

**UNIVERSITY OF MONTANA-
SCHOOL OF LAW LIBRARY**
MISSOULA, MT 59801
Description: Maintains a special collection on Indian law; 120 treaties.

**BIG HOLE NATIONAL BATTLEFIELD
RESEARCH LIBRARY**
P.O. Box 237 • WISDOM, MT 59761
(406) 689-3155 Fax 689-3151
Jon James, Supt.
Description: Collection contains over 400 volumes on Nez Perce history, culture; military history of the 1870s, Nez Perce War related materials, and frontier army. *Special program*: Interpretive program/guided walks of the historic site in summer. Open to the public by appointment for reference only.

NEBRASKA

CENTER FOR GREAT PLAINS STUDIES
University of Nebraska-Lincoln
1155 Q St., P.O. Box 880250
LINCOLN, NE 68588-0250
(402) 472-0599 Fax 472-0463
Reece Summers, Director
E-mail: asummers@unl.edu
Web site: www.unl.edu/plains
Description: A collection of Western art and fiction with emphasis on American Indian art. Also a large collection of reference books on Canada. A complete set of photos of American Indians by Edward S. Curtis from his, The North American Indian (1907-1930). Six art exhibitions displayed each year with accompanying opening talk. Established 1980.

UNIVERSITY OF NEBRASKA STATE MUSEUM
Nebraska Hall • LINCOLN, NE 68588
(402) 472-6365
Hugh H. Genoways, Director
Research activities: Studies include the culture and history of the Plains Apache. *Publication*: Bulletin of the University of Nebraska State Museum

**NATIVE AMERICAN PUBLIC BROADCASTING
CONSORTIUM LIBRARY**
P.O. Box 83111 • LINCOLN, NE 68501
(402) 472-3522
Description: A collection of videotapes and films include Native-American programs which have been screened and evaluated by the Consortium for technical quality and accuracy of portrayal and content. Topics include: history, culture, education, economic development, current events and the arts.

**NEBRASKA STATE HISTORICAL
SOCIETY LIBRARY/ARCHIVES**
P.O. Box 82554, 1500 R St.
LINCOLN, NE 68501
(402) 471-4751 Fax 471-8922
Andrea Faling, Archivist
E-mail: lanshs@nebraskahistory.org
Website: www.nebraskahistory.org

Description: Holdings include more than 70,000 volumes on Nebraska history, Indians of the Great Plains, genealogy; 465 photographs in the John A. Anderson Photograph Collection of Brule Sioux. A collection of videotapes on several Nebraska tribes including storytelling, history, and elders' reminiscences by members of the Lakota, Brule Sioux, Santee Sioux, Omaha, Pawnee and Winnebago tribes.

NEVADA

COLLEGE CAREER & VOCATIONAL RESOURCE LIBRARY
Nevada Urban Indians
1190 Bible Way • RENO, NV 89502
(775) 788-7600 Fax 788-7611
Belvin Hill, Director
Description: Provides information on all major colleges with Native American Studies Programs from across the nation. Includes brochures and applications, scholarships, grants and vocational schools.

NEW JERSEY

BRIDGETON PUBLIC LIBRARY
Woodruff Museum of Indian Artifacts
150 E. Commerce St.
BRIDGETON, NJ 08302
(856) 451-2620
Gail S. Robinson, Director
Website: www.clueslib.org.
Description: 2,000 volumes on Cumberland County history, local genealogy, and Woodland Indians. Holdings include 20,000 Indian artifacts collected within a 30-mile radius of library. Interlibrary loans. Open to the public. Opened in 1976.

THE MONTCLAIR ART MUSEUM LIBRARY
3 S. Mountain Ave.
MONTCLAIR, NJ 07042
(973) 746-5555 Fax 746-9118
Patterson Sims, Director
E-mail: tjohnson@montclairartmuseum.org
Website: www.montclairartmuseum.org
Description: Maintains a collection of 13,000 volumes. Includes 7,000 exhibit catalogs; 20,000 slides, 7,000 bookplares; clipping files on American and Native American art. Opened in 1914.

NEWARK MUSEUM LIBRARY
43-49 Washington St.
NEWARK, NJ 07101
(201) 596-6625 Fax 642-0459
William A. Peniston, Librarian
Description: Collection covers American Indian art, crafts, life, ethnology, etc. Interlibrary loans. Open to the public by appointment only. Opened in 1909.

PRINCETON UNIVERSITY LIBRARIES
PRINCETON, NJ 08540
(609) 452-3180
Description: A major U.S. repository of documentation on Native American art.

SETON HALL UNIVERSITY MUSEUM LIBRARY
S. Orange Ave.
SOUTH ORANGE, NJ 07079
(201) 761-9543
Description: Contains a collection of 1,000 volumes on prehistoric Indians of New Jersey.

NEW MEXICO

ACOMA MUSEUM LIBRARY & ARCHIVES
Sky City Cultural Center
P.O. Box 309, Pueblo of Acoma
ACOMITA, NM 87034
(800) 747-0181
(505) 469-1052 Fax 552-7204
Brian D. Vallo, Director
Description: Contains photographs and documents relating to the history of Acoma Pueblo. Opened 1977.

AMERICAN INDIAN LAW CENTER LIBRARY
University of New Mexico-School of Law
P.O. Box 4456, Station A, 1117 Stanford N.E.
ALBUQUERQUE, NM 87196
(505) 277-5462
Description: Maintains a special collection on American Indian law.

CLARK FIELD ARCHIVE & LIBRARY
Maxwell Museum of Anthropology
University of New Mexico, MSC01 1050
ALBUQUERQUE, NM 87131
(505) 277-8675
Alan M. Shalette, Director
E-mail: alshal@unm.edu
Website: unm.edu/~maxwell/clark_field.htm
Description: Collection of 12,000 volumes plus 200 journals on world anthropology and archaeology, with special emphasis on the American Southwest. Collections are cataloged online at www.libros.unm.edu. Activities: Annual Albuquerque Antiquarian Book Fair Fundraiser, 1st weekend in April.

NATIVE AMERICAN STUDIES - INFORMATION & MATERIALS RESOURCE COLLECTION
U. of New Mexico, 1812 Las Lomas Dr. NE
ALBUQUERQUE, NM 87131
(505) 277-3917 Fax 277-1818
Alison Freese, PhD, Information Specialist
Description: A resource/research center with books, journals, Native newspapers, videos, and newsclippings on Native issues, specializing in stereotyping, Native American economic development, Southwestern history, Native American literature, Native perspectives of American history, and a Quincentennial archive. *Special programs:* Speakers series; computer networking with tribal offices, schools, and libraries. *Publication:* Monthly newsletter. Open to the public.

PUEBLO ARCHIVES & RESEARCH LIBRARY
Institute for Pueblo Indian Studies
Indian Pueblo Cultural Center
2401 12th St., NW
ALBUQUERQUE, NM 87104
(505) 843-7270 ext. 329 Fax 842-6959
Ted Sturm, Associate Director
Description: Collection consists of books and monographs; periodicals; newspapers; Newspaper Clipping File, Government documents; microfilmed documents; maps, photographs and postcards, slides; audio, visual tapes & recordings; special collections concerning Pueblo Indians. *Special programs:* Sponsors education programs; seminars and symposia; research projects dealing with Pueblo Indians and issues affecting them. Open to the public. Opened in 1976.

AZTEC RUINS NATIONAL MONUMENT LIBRARY
84 Road 2900 • AZTEC, NM 87410
(505) 334-6174
Description: A collection of 300 volumes on the ethnography and archaeology of Southwestern Indians and prehistoric Pueblo Indians.

SAN JUAN COUNTY ARCHAEOLOGICAL RESEARCH CENTER LIBRARY
FARMINGTON, NM 87401
(505) 632-2013 Fax 632-1707
Kurt Mantonya, Librarian
Description: Research library focusing upon archaeology and history of the Four Corners area, including archaeological reports, historical documents, slides of Navajo rock art; 4,000 books, 1,200 pamphlets, 35 oral history tapes, photographs and color slides, transcriptions, and maps; and an on-loan collection of Navajo material. Open to the public. Opened in 1973.

GALLUP INDIAN MEDICAL CENTER LIBRARY
PHS — Indian Health Service
P.O. Box 1337 • GALLUP, NM 87301
Description: Maintains a special collection on the Navajo Indians.

GALLUP PUBLIC LIBRARY
115 West Hill • GALLUP, NM 87301
Description: A collection of rare, out-of-print and contemporary titles on Southwestern tribes: Navajo, Hopi and Zuni.

BANDELIER NATIONAL MONUMENT LIBRARY
LOS ALAMOS, NM 87544 (505) 672-3861
Description: Contains a collection of 2,000 volumes on the archaeology of the area, and Pueblo Indians.

CHACO CULTURE NATIONAL HISTORICAL PARK LIBRARY
P.O. Box 220 • NAGEEZI, NM 87037
(505) 786-5384
Description: Study library housing hundreds of volumes on prehistory and history of Chaco area, Southwestern archaeology, ethnology, including journals, photographs, and records of historic period.

NAVAJO NATION LIBRARY SYSTEM
Navajo Community Library
NAVAJO, NM 87328
See listing under Window Rock, AZ.

PALEO-INDIAN INSTITUTE LIBRARY
Eastern New Mexico University
Campus Box 2154
PORTALES, NM 88130

EL MORRO NATIONAL MONUMENT LIBRARY
RAMAH, NM 87321
(505) 783-5132
Description: A collection of 400 volumes on the archaeology of the prehistoric site and historic Pueblos.

FORT BURGWIN RESEARCH CENTER
Southern Methodist University
P.O. Box 300
RANCHOS DE TAOS, NM 87557
(505) 758-8322
Dr, William B., Stallcup, Jr. Research Director
Research activities: Includes field studies in prehistoric pithouses and Pueblo settlements. Performs archaeological site preservation technology.

STRADLING MUSEUM OF THE HORSE LIBRARY
RUIDOSO, NM 88345
Description: Maintains a collection of 1,000 volumes on Indian history; Indian rugs.

ANTHROPOLOGY FILM CENTER FOUNDATION LIBRARY
P.O. Box 493 • SANTA FE, NM 87594-0493
(505) 983-4127
Description: A study collection of films, especially those produced by graduates of the Film Center training program.

HISTORY LIBRARY/PHOTO ARCHIVES
Palace of the Governors-Museum of New Mexico
110 Washington Ave. • SANTA FE, NM 87501
(505) 476-5090/5092 Fax 476-5104
Website: www.mnm.state.nm.us
Tomas Jaehn, Curator
E-mail: tjaehn@mnm.state.nm.us
Art Olivas, Photo Archivist
E-mail: aolivas@mnm.state.nm.us
Dick Rudisill, Photo Archivist
E-mail: drudisill@mnm.state.nm.us

INSTITUTE OF AMERICAN INDIAN ARTS LIBRARY
83 Avan Nu Po Rd. • SANTA FE, NM 87508
(505) 424-2398/9
Grace Nuvayestewa & Jennifer James, Librarians
E-mail: gnuva@iaiancad.org
E-mail: jjames@iaiancad.org
Web site: www.iaiancad.org
Description: Collection consists of about 20,000 volumes on North American Indian art, history and culture; 800 videotapes, recording tribal and reservation history, tribal projects and activities, such as the reservation medical center or tribal government—30,000 Smithsonian photographs of Native American culture; more than 900 recordings of Native American music; 9,000 slides of art of all types and Native American art objects. Open to the public for research only. Opened in 1962.

LABORATORY OF ANTHROPOLOGY LIBRARY
Museum of Indian Arts & Culture
Museum of New Mexico
P.O. Box 2087, 708 Camino Lejo
SANTA FE, NM 87504
(505) 476-1263/4 Fax 476-1330

Website: www.miaclab.org
Mara Yarbrough, Librarian
E-mail: myarbrough@miaclab.org
Description: A major U.S. repository of documentation on Native American art. Focuses on Native American cultures of the Southwest from prehistory to contemporary times. Southwest anthropology research library of approximately 5,000 volumes with holdings in 1,000 journal titles; as well as the personal library of Sylvanus G. Morley with rare Mesoamerican titles.

NEW MEXICO STATE LIBRARY
325 Don Gaspar • SANTA FE, NM 87503
(505) 827-3800 Fax 827-3820
Karen Watkins, Acting Director
Description: Contains 11,000 books on Southwest history; New Mexico newspapers. Interlibrary loans. Open to the public.

WHEELWRIGHT MUSEUM OF THE AMERICAN INDIAN - MARY CABOT WHEELWRIGHT RESEARCH LIBRARY
P.O. Box 5153, 704 Camino Lejo
SANTA FE, NM 87501
(505) 982-4636
Steve Rogers, Curator
Description: Maintains about 10,000 volumes on the art, history, and religions of the Navajo and other tribes; archives contain 1,000 examples of Navajo ceremonial art, 3,000 Navajo ceremonial music recordings, 100 Navajo myth texts, 1,000 Navajo sandpaintings on slides, and 100 music and prayer tapes. Open to public by appointment. Library closed until 2001 because of construction of a new building.

DINE COLLEGE LIBRARY
P.O. Box 580, 1228 Yucca St.
SHIPROCK, NM 87420-0580
(505) 368-3542 Fax 368-3539
Annie Lewis, Acting Director
E-mail: amlewis@shiprock.ncc.cc
Website: www.crystal.ncc.cc..nm.us
Description: Collection of books, periodicals, video tapes, pamphlets, and maps. *Special collections*: Native American Special collection, and the Caswell and Betty Silver Southwest Geoscience Collection. Interlibrary loans. Opened in 1969.

GILA CLIFF DWELLINGS NATIONAL MONUMENT—VISITOR CENTER LIBRARY
Route 11, Box 100
SILVER CITY, NM 88061
Description: A collection of books on prehistoric Mogollon Indians, archaeology and natural history.

SOUTHWEST RESEARCH CENTER OF NORTHERN NEW MEXICO
P.O. Drawer CCC, 238 Ledoux St.
TAOS, NM 87571
(505) 758-5440 Fax 758-0330
Nita Murphy, Librarian
E-mail: nitkit@laplaza.org
Description: Combined Kit Carson Museum & Harwood Museum libraries. Contains a collection of 6,500 volumes on the prehistoric Indian culture of Taos and the Southwest from the Kit Carson Museum library and the Harwood collection with an emphasis on art. Open to the public. Opened in 1999.

MILLICENT ROGERS MUSEUM OF NORTHERN NEW MEXICO LIBRARY
P.O. Box A • TAOS, NM 87571
(505) 758-2462 Fax 758-5751
Dr. Shelby Tisdale, Executive Director
Description: Research library related to collections.

ZUNI HERITAGE & HISTORIC PRESERVATION OFFICE - LIBRARY
P.O. Box 339 • ZUNI, NM 87327
(505) 782-4113 Fax 782-4119
Elaine Kallestewa, Librarian
Joseph Dishta, Director
Description: Comprehensive holdings concerning Zuni prehistory, archaeology, history, and land use. 3,000 books, 300 bound periodical volumes, 3,250 reports, journals and other serials. Unpublished field notes, ethnographic interviews, papers, and published works are on file. Opened in 1978.

NEW YORK

TONAWANDA INDIAN COMMUNITY LIBRARY
P.O. Box 326, 372 Bloomingdale Rd.
AKRON, NY 14001-0326
(716) 542-5618
Ramona Charles, Director

INSTITUTE FOR ARCHAEOLOGICAL STUDIES
SUNY at Albany-Social Science, Rm. 263
1400 Washington Ave. • ALBANY, NY 12222
(518) 442-4700
Prof. Dean R. Snow, Director
Description: Northeastern archaeology, ethnology and linguistics. Supports research activities on Native Northeasten peoples, primarily Algonquian and Iroquois tribes. *Publication*: Man in the Northeast.

CAYUGA MUSEUM LIBRARY & ARCHIVES
203 Genesee St. • AUBURN, NY 13021
(315) 253-8051 Fax 253-9829
Description: Includes manuscripts, books, and periodicals relating to the history of the Iroquois in central New York State.

NATIONAL KATERI CENTER LIBRARY
The National Shrine of N.A. Martyrs
AURIESVILLE, NY 12016
(518) 853-3033
Rec. Robert J. Boyle, S.J., Director

HUNTINGTON FREE LIBRARY
9 Westchester Square • BRONX, NY 10461
(718) 829-7770 Fax 829-4875
Catherine McChesney, Library Director
Website: www.binc.org/hfl
Description: A major U.S. repository of documentation on Native American studies. One of the leading research sources on Indians of the Western Hemisphere, this non-circulating collection contains more than 40,000 volumes on the archaeology, art, ethnology, and history of the Native peoples of the Americas, as well as exceptional selections in Indian languages, codices, current Native American affairs, and Indian biography and related ephemera; maintains a large collection of Indian newspapers, manuscripts and field notes, and microform and audio-visual material. Special programs: Lectures on Native American subjects; storytelling, dance and music programs. Interlibrary loans (photocopies only). Open to the public by appointment.

BROOKLYN MUSEUM OF ART
LIBRARY & ARCHIVES
200 Eastern Pkwy.
BROOKLYN, NY 11238
(718) 501-6308 Fax 501-6125
Dierdre Lawrence, Librarian & Coordinator
  of Research Services
E-mail: deirdre.lawrence@brooklynmuseum.org
Website: www.brooklynmuseum.org
Description: A major U.S. repository of documentation on Native American art. Holds extensive research documents on Native North and South American art and culture. Has many published textual and visual resources which document objects, people and places. The Archives, in addition to institutional records, hold the Stewart Culin Archives which represents the documentation assembled by the Museum's First Curator of Ethnology (1903-1929).

BUFFALO & ERIE COUNTY
HISTORICAL SOCIETY LIBRARY
5 Nottingham Court • BUFFALO, NY 14216
Description: Holdings include books and manuscripts related to the Seneca Indians and other Indians of the Niagara frontier.

THE MOHAWK-CAUGHNAWAGA
MUSEUM LIBRARY
Route 5, Box 627, RD 1
FONDA, NY 12068
(518) 853-3646
Rev. Nicholas Weiss, Director
Description: A collection of 4,500 volumes on American Indians and American history.

AKWESASNE LIBRARY
Akwesasne Cultural Center
St. Regis Mohawk Reservation
RR 1, Box 14C • HOGANSBURG, NY 13655
(518) 358-2240 Fax 358-2649
Carol White, Director
Description: Public library with holdings of 27,000 volumes; with special collection on the North American Indian. *Publication*: Ka-ri-wen-hawi, monthly newsletter. Interlibrary loans. Open to the public.

IROQUOIS INDIAN MUSEUM LIBRARY
P.O. Box 7, Caverns Rd.
HOWES CAVE, NY 12092
(518) 296-8949
Thomas M. Elliott, Director
Description: A collection of books, periodicals, pamphlets and files relating to the Iroquois.

THE SENECA NATION LIBRARY
The Cattaraugus Reservation Branch
1490 Rte. 438 • IRVING, NY 14081
(716) 532-9449 Fax 532-6115
Ethel E. Bray, Library Director
Ann John, Branch Supervisor
E-mail: snilibc2@localnet.com
Description: A collection of books and periodicals, with a special collectionon the history of the Iroquois Indians on microfilm; videotapes, books on tape, periodicals, large print books, and college and career catalogs. *Special programs*: Native American Art Show; speakers and displays; classes, exhibits and cultural presentations; Summer Reading program; Lupus Resource Center; Native American film programs. *Publication*: Seneca Nation Arts & Crafts Directory. Allegany Reservation Branch in Salamanca, NY. Interlibrary loans. Open to the public.

AMERICAN INDIAN COMMUNITY HOUSE LIBRARY
708 Broadway, 8th Floor
NEW YORK, NY 10003
(212) 598-0100 Fax 598-4909
Rosemary Richmond, Executive Director
Description: Indian books, periodicals, newspapers and subject files. Access by appointment to educators, students and community members.

AMERICAN MUSEUM OF NATURAL HISTORY
DEPARTMENT OF LIBRARY SERVICES
Central Park West at 79th St.
NEW YORK, NY 10024
(212) 769-5406
Nina J. Root, Dept. Chairperson
Description: A major U.S. repository of documentation on Native American art. Out of a collection of 410,000 volumes, approximately 50,000 volumes on the anthropology of North American Indian tribes (ethnology and archaeology - especially strong holdings on Northwest Coast cultures) along with accounts and descriptions of explorers; 125,000 photographs, primarily black-and-white of the early 20th century and some recent color photographs of artifacts. Maintains a special film collection with a limited number of films on Indians. Interlibrary loans. Open to the public.

THE NEW YORK PUBLIC LIBRARY
42nd St. & Fifth Ave.
NEW YORK, NY 10018
(212) 930-0826
Timothy Troy, Bib. of American Indian Material
Description: A major U.S. repository of documentation on Native American art. Maintains one of the largest collections of Indian bibliographical material in the world. Includes material from all cultural areas and time periods, from pre-Columbian eras to the present. The collections range through the disciplines of anthropology, archaeology, history, linguistics, and literature. Contains writings by Indians, runs of related periodicals and serials, pictures (photographs and engravings), works on Indian place names, and a collection of Indian captivity journals. Collects contemporary Native-American literature (in English or Indian languages.) The Library has materials in all written Indian languages from throughout the Western Hemisphere. Many items concerning the Indians of the Americas, particularly 16th & 17th century material in Spanish and English, are located in various special collections.

YAGER LIBRARY
Hartwick College
ONEONTA, NY 13820
(607) 432-4200
Description: A collection of over 1,000 volumes
on North American Indian history and culture.

ROCHESTER MUSEUM & SCIENCE CENTER
Department of Collections and Research
Library and Information Services Program
657 East Ave. • ROCHESTER, NY 14607
(716) 271-4320 Fax 271-2119
Leatrice M. Kemp, Librarian
E-mail: lea_kemp@rmsc.org
Web site: www.rmsc.org/
Description: Field and laboratory work in anthropology, natural science, and regional history (especially American Indians and Genesee Valley region during 16th-20th centuries). *Library*: Contains more than 30,000 books, 50,000 photographic slides, and numerous manuscripts and photographs on the history, technology and anthropology of the Genesee Valley region, with emphasis on archaeology and ethnography of New York Haudenosaunee (Iroquois) peoples, especially Senecas.

SENECA-IROQUOIS NATIONAL MUSEUM LIBRARY
Allegany Indian Reservation
794-814 Broad St.
SALAMANCA , NY14779-1331
(716) 945-1738

THE SENECA NATION LIBRARY
The Allegany Reservation Branch
P.O. Box 231 • SALAMANCA, NY 14779
(716) 945-3157
Ethel E. Bray, Library Director
Dorsie Familo, Branch Supervisor
Description: A collection of books and periodicals, with a special collectionon the history of the Iroquois Indians on microfilm; videotapes, and college and career catalogs. *Special programs*: Native American Art Show; speakers and displays; exhibts and cultural presentations; Native American film programs. *Publication*: Seneca Nation Arts & Crafts Director. Cattaraugus Reservation Branch in Irving, NY. Interlibrary loans.

NORTH CAROLINA

MUSEUM OF THE CHEROKEE INDIAN LIBRARY
P.O. Box 770-A, U.S. Hwy. 441 North
CHEROKEE, NC 28719 (704) 497-3481
Description: Collection contains more than 3,000 volumes on Cherokee Indian history and culture. Reference use only.

SCHIELE MUSEUM REFERENCE LIBRARY
Center for Southeastern Native American Studies
1500 East Garrison Blvd.
GASTONIA, NC 28054
(704) 866-6900 Fax 866-6041
Melissa Turney, Registrar/Librarian
Description: Contains a collection of more than 6,000 volumes serving the Reference Centers for the Library of Congress. 20 of holdings, including subject index files, graduate papers, monographs, as well as bound volumes, are on broad areas of Native-American topics representing all major Indian groups in U.S. and Canada with special emphasis on Indians of the Southeast. *Special collections*: Lilly Hobbs Schiele Collection; W.M. Modisette Collection; The Red Dawn Collection; and, The McCuen Collection. Open to the public by appointment only.

INDIAN MUSEUM OF THE CAROLINAS LIBRARY
607 Turnpike Rd.
LAURINBURG, NC 28352
(910) 276-5880
Dr. Margaret Houston, Director
Description: Maintains a collection of 500 volumes on Indian literature, archaeology, and history. Reference.

NATIVE AMERICAN LIBRARY
Lumbee Indian Education
Lumbee Regional Development Association
P.O. Box 637 • PEMBROKE, NC 28372

NATIVE AMERICAN RESOURCE CENTER & LIBRARY
Pembroke State University
College Rd. • PEMBROKE, NC 28372
(919) 521-4214
Dr. Robert C. Hersch, Librarian
Description: Research into Lumbee Indians, American Indian tribal histories and culture. Conducted in conjunction with tribal organizations. *Library*: A collection of 500 volumes with emphasis on Lumbee Indians of North Carolina; audio-visual material; archival documents. *Publications*: SPIRIT! (quarterly newsletter); Robeson Trails Archaeological Survey.

NORTH DAKOTA

TURTLE MOUNTAIN COMMUNITY COLLEGE LIBRARY
P.O. Box 340 • BELCOURT, ND 58316
(701) 477-5605 Fax 477-5028
Dr. Gerald "Carty" Monette, President
E-Mail: cdavis@giizis.turtle-mountain.cc.nd.us
Web site: http://www.giizis.turtle-mountain.cc.nd.us
Description: Has 27,500 cataloged items including three special collections: 5,400 Native American items (books, videos, audiocassettes, software), 283 elementary education books, and 25 items in the Louise Erdrich collection.

STATE HISTORICAL SOCIETY OF NORTH DAKOTA LIBRARY
North Dakota Heritage Center
Capitol Grounds • BISMARCK, ND 58505
(701) 224-2666
Description: Holdings include 20,000 volumes on North Dakota history and the history of the American Indian; extensive photographs archive; government documents; genealogical collections; sound and visual recordings, including Native-American music.

CENTER FOR RURAL HEALTH
University of North Dakota
501 Columbia Rd.
GRAND FORKS, ND 58203
(701) 777-3848
Jack M. Geller, Ph.D., Director
Description: Research into rural health care delivery, including Native American health care. *Publication*: Focus on Rural Health (semiannual).

GORDON B. OLSON LIBRARY
Minot State University
500 University Ave. W. • MINOT, ND 58707
(701) 858-3200 Fax 858-3581
Larry Greenwood, Director
E-mail: reference@minotstateu.edu
Web site: www.misu.nodak.edu/library/index1.htm
Description: Maintains a 1,500 volume collection focusing on Indians of the North Central U.S. and South Central Canada. Open to the public. Interlibrary loan.

FORT BERTHOLD RESERVATION PUBLIC LIBRARY
P.O. Box 788 • NEW TOWN, ND 58763
(701) 627-4738
Quincee Baker, Director
Description: A collection of 10,000 books, videos, and microfiche serving the Three Affiliated Tribes: Arikara, Hidatsa, and Mandan, and the Fort Berthold Community College. An Indian studies collection reflect the cultural interests of tribal residents. Emphasis recently has been placed on children's programming and services. Established in 1985.

OHIO

MOUND CITY GROUP NATIONAL MONUMENT LIBRARY
16062 State Rte. 104
CHILLICOTHE, OH 45601
(614) 774-1125
Description: A collection of 1,500 volumes on Hopewell and Adena Indian culture, and other Indian culture of Ohio; archaeological research on Hopewell and Adena cultures is conducted at Monument.

RUTHERFORD B. HAYES PRESIDENTIAL CENTER LIBRARY
Spiegel Grove • FREMONT, OH 43420
(800) 998-7737 Fax (419) 332-4952
Nan J. Card, Curator of Manuscripts
E-mail: ncard@rbhayes.org
Web site: www.rbhayes.org
Description: Contains a collection of 1,000 books and pamphlets on Plains tribes and Wyandot. Also microfilm sets of the record of the Michigan Supt. of Indian Affairs, 1814-1851; General George Crook Papers; correspondence of Rev. James B. Finley, minister to the Wyandot Indians; diary of John G. Bourke, ethnologist, 1872-1895; photos and stereoviews of students at Carlisle Indian Industrial School; Western Expedition Photos, 1873; Ledger Art, 63 pictographs by five artists, 3 identified Arapaho, Cheyenne and Sioux. Interlibrary loans. Open to the public in 1916.

OKLAHOMA

WOOLAROC MUSEUM LIBRARY
RR 3, Box 2100
BARTLESVILLE, OK 74003
(918) 336-0307 Fax 336-0084
E-mail: woolaroc1@aol.com
Website: www.woolaroc.org
Kenneth Meek, Interim Director
Description: A collection of 1,000 volumes on American Indians and Oklahoma history.

MEMORIAL INDIAN MUSEUM LIBRARY
P.O. Box 483, Second & Allen Sts.
BROKEN BOW, OK 74728
(405) 584-6531
Description: Maintains a collection of 3,000 volumes on American Indian history and culture.

KIOWA TRIBAL LIBRARY
P.O. Box 369 • CARNEGIE, OK 73015
(405) 654-2300; Grace Bointy, Librarian
Description: Maintains a collection of books and documents on Kiowa Indian tribal history and culture.

NASH LIBRARY
University of Science & Arts of Oklahoma
17th & Grand • CHICKASHA, OK 73018
(405) 574-1343 Fax 574-1220
Kelly Brown, Librarian
Website: www.usao.edu/library
Description: Large collection of Native American studies, including collections of Indian treaties, tribal constitutions, Indian law and art. Opened 1908.

WILL ROGERS MEMORIAL LIBRARY
P.O. Box 157 • CLAREMORE, OK 74018
(918) 341-0719
Patricia Lowe, Librarian
Description: Contains the original papers of Will Rogers; also, 2,500 volumes concerning Will Rogers and his times; 6,000 photos of Roger's family and others; and Will Rogers memoirs.

MUSEUM OF THE RED RIVER LIBRARY
812 E. Lincoln Rd. • IDABEL, OK 74745
(405) 286-3616
Maintains a collection of approximately 2,500 books relating to American Indians, with emphasis on Choctaw Indians.

MUSEUM OF THE GREAT PLAINS RESEARCH LIBRARY
P.O. Box 68 • LAWTON, OK 73502
(405) 581-3460 Fax 581-3458
Deborah Ann Baroff, Librarian
Description: Collection consists of a special collection of over 25,000 volumes on Plains Indian history and prehistory; documents and photos. *Special programs*: Living History Reenactments (2 times per year). Opened in 1962.

MIAMI TRIBE OF OKLAHOMA LIBRARY
P.O. Box 1326 • MIAMI, OK 74355
(918) 542-4505 Fax 542-7260
Karen Alexander, Librarian
Description: A collection of 16,000 volumes serving all Native Americans of all tribes, emphasizing the

Northeast Eight Tribes of Oklahoma. *Special programs*: Roots and Wings, Storyteller, CHARLIE Library Network; partnerships with Miami University, Oxford, Ohio; Integris Health Systems in Oklahoma City, OK. Affiliated with the Miami Tribes of Oklahoma. Open to the public. Opened in 1987.

BACONE COLLEGE LIBRARY
2299 Old Bacone Rd.
MUSKOGEE, OK 74403
  (918) 683-4581 ext. 263
  Frances A. Donelson, Librarian
Description: Maintains a rare book collection of over 10,000 books on Native American culture, including some of the original Dawes Commission papers. Open to the public.

OKLAHOMA ANTHROPOLOGICAL SOCIETY LIBRARY
1000 Horn St.
MUSKOGEE, OK 74403
  (405) 364-2279
Description: Holdings of more than 35,000 volumes; archives contain over three million documents of the Five Civilized Tribes; newspaper library of thirty million pages.

AMERICAN INDIAN INSTITUTE LIBRARY
555 Constitution St., Suite 237
NORMAN, OK 73072-7820
  (405) 325-4127 Fax 325-7757
  Anita Chisholm, Director
Description: Resource library containing over 3,000 books, periodicals, and newspapers on art, economics, education, government, head start, health, history, language, social & human services, and substance abuse.

UNIVERSITY OF OKLAHOMA LAW LIBRARY
300 Timberdell Rd. • NORMAN, OK 73019
  (405) 325-4311 Fax 325-6282
  Nina Miley, Interim Director
Description: Maintains a collection on American Indian law and law relating to Native Americans, including mineral rights, water issues, land titles, jurisdiction, and the like, with emphasis on Oklahoma tribes. Special collection: Native Peoples Collection - 2,300 titles on indigenous peoples, mostly Native American. Interlibrary loans. Open to the public.

WESTERN HISTORY COLLECTION-DIVISION OF MANUSCRIPTS & LIBRARY
U. of Oklahoma
630 Parrington Oval, Rm. 452
NORMAN, OK 73019
  (405) 325-3641 Fax 325-6069
  Web site: www-lib.ou.edu/depts/west/index.htm
  Donald L. DeWitt, Curator
Description: A major collection of Indian-related books, serials, photographs, manuscripts, and sound recordings. The collection includes 40,000 books and microforms; 200,000 historic photos; 275 manuscript collections; and 21 sound recording collections. *Publication*: "American Indian Resource Materials in the Western History Collections, University of Oklahoma, Norman" (University of Oklahoma Press, 1990). Opened in 1927.

COOKSON INSTITUTE LIBRARY
623 Culbertson Dr., Suite A
OKLAHOMA CITY, OK 73105
Description: A collection of 1,000 volumes on American Indian thought with emphasis on Cherokee, Arawak, Maya, and Caddo Indians. Available to research scholars associated with the Institute.

OKLAHOMA CITY UNIVERSITY-SCHOOL OF LAW LIBRARY
2501 N. Blackwelder
OKLAHOMA CITY, OK 73106
  (405) 521-5062 Fax 521-5172
  Judy Morgan, Librarian
  E-Mail: jmorgan@lec.okca.edu
Description: An extension collection of Indian-law materials with special emphasis on Federal and Tribal Law (including tribal casework). Special attention is also given to historical materials and books about Plains tribes and tribes now residing in Oklahoma. Open to the public. Opened in 1987.

OKLAHOMA HISTORICAL SOCIETY INDIAN ARCHIVES DIVISION
2100 N. Lincoln Blvd.
OKLAHOMA CITY, OK 73105
  (405) 522-5248 Fax 522-5402
  Jack Wettengel, Public Information Director
  Dennis W. Zotigh, Indian Research Historian
Description: Holdings include thousands of books about Oklahoma's history and more than 6,000 books covering the subject areas of the Creek Nation, and Indian and pioneer history; 3.5 million documents and 8,000 manuscripts, the majority of them on microfilm, recordings, photographs, and newspapers of Indian Territory. many rare books are available for research.

RED EARTH INDIAN CENTER MUSEUM
2100 NE 52 St. • OKLAHOMA CITY, OK 73111
  (405) 427-4228; Barbara Jobe, Executive Director
Collection of approximately 300 books and periodicals.

CREEK COUNCIL HOUSE MUSEUM RESEARCH LIBRARY
106 W. 6th • OKMULGEE, OK 74447
  (918) 756-2324 Fax 756-3671
  Debbie Martin, Director
Description: Contains a collection of over 500 volumes on Muscogee (Creek) culture and history; records of early day Creek Government; diaries and journals of past principal chiefs; also, Indian readers, dictionaries, documents and newspapers on Oklahoma and Indian history.

OKLAHOMA STATE UNIVERSITY LIBRARY
Curriculum Materials Laboratory
STILLWATER, OK 74074
Description: Maintains a children's collection of books on the Indians of North America.

SAC AND FOX NATIONAL PUBLIC LIBRARY
Sac and Fox Nation of Oklahoma
Route 2, Box 246 • STROUD, OK 74079
  (918) 968-3526 Fax 968-4837
  Debra M. Bailey, Librarian
  E-mail: sfnpl@brightok.net
Description: Maintains a 4,000 volume collection of general interest, including a large collection of books on Native Americans, especially Oklahoma tribes. The archives contain Sac and Fox history, photographs, tribal newspapers, allotment rolls, government documents and genealogies. Special programs: Photo and art exhibits; seminars on tribal archives; arts and crafts shop; book sales; Sac & Fox language classes.

CHEROKEE HERITAGE CENTER LIBRARY
P.O. Box 515, TSA-LA-GI
TAHLEQUAH, OK 74464
Description: A collection of 2,500 volumes on Cherokee heritage, including manuscripts and photographs.

JOHN VAUGHAN LIBRARY
Northeastern State University
TAHLEQUAH, OK 74464
  (918) 456-5511 ext. 3252 Fax 458-2197
  Delores T. Sumner, Special Collections Librarian
  E-mail: sumner@cherokee.nsuok.edu
Special collections: Approximately 12,600 books on Cherokee history; tribes of Oklahoma; American Indian mythology and religion; Oklahoma history; Indian Territory history; American Indian history, culture, social structures, and conditions; local towns, counties, city histories; Tribal language materials (majority Oklahoma tribes); Oklahoma tribal rolls; houses microfilm copies of important regional historical newspapers of the late 1800's and early 1900's such as the Cherokee Advocate, Indian Chieftain, and Tahlequah Arrow; U.S. Office of Indian Affairs, and the Historical Information Relating to Military Posts and Other Installations. Also with the Indian Affairs microfilms are records from the U.S. Army and the U.S. Department of War (1800-1823). Contains microfilm of American Indian and Oklahoma-related subjects; John Ross Letters; Indian Affairs Miscellaneous Letters; Ballenger Miscellaneous Letters; Ballenger Manuscripts Relating to Cherokee History; Andrew Nave Collections (Business Accounts and Letters); Letters To and From Stand Watie. All bound volumes typed from the originals. Originals are housed in Archives. *Special program*: Symposium on the American Indian held annually at NSU. Open to the public.

CHICKASAW COUNCIL HOUSE LIBRARY
205 N. Fisher St. • TISHOMINGO, OK 73460
  (405) 371-3351; Faye Orr, Director
Description: Contains about 150 volumes on Chickasaw Indian history, geography and genealogy.

H.A. & MARY K. CHAPMAN LIBRARY
Philbrook Museum of Art
P.O. Box 52510, 2727 S. Rockford Rd.
TULSA, OK 74114-4104
  (918) 748-5306 Fax 748-5303
  Thomas E. Young, Librarian
  E-mail: tyoung@philbrook.org
Description: Visual arts and art histor reference library with one area of specialization relates to Native American art. Also includes special collections, including the Roberta Campbell Lawson Indian Library with about 1,000 volumes on North America & Native American art & history. A major U.S. repository of documentation on Native American art. A collection of approximately 2,000 volumes on Indian art and history. Reference only. Open to the public by appointment.

THOMAS GILCREASE INSTITUTE OF AMERICAN HISTORY & ART LIBRARY
1400 Gilcrease Museum Rd.
TULSA, OK 74127
  (918) 596-2700 Fax 596-2770
  Sarah Erwin, Curator of Archival Collections
Description: A major U.S. repository of documentation on Native American art. Contains a collection of about 7,500 volumes relating to most American Indian tribes with emphasis on the Five Civilized Tribes. Includes 40,000 manuscript items, 10,000 imprints, and 10,000 photographs. *Special collections*: John Ross Papers (Cherokee); Peter Pitchlynn Papers (Choctaw); John Drew Papers (Cherokee); Cherokee Papers; Chickasaw Papers; Choctaw Papers; Creek Papers; and Seminole Papers. Open to the public by appointment only.

THE McFARLIN LIBRARY
University of Tulsa • TULSA, OK 74104
  (918) 592-6000
Description: The repository for many unique primary documents and published works pertinent to Native-Americans and governmental relations of the historic period in eastern Oklahoma and adjacent areas.

UNIVERSITY OF TULSA COLLEGE OF LAW LIBRARY
3120 E. Fourth Pl. • TULSA, OK 74104
  (918) 592-6000
Description: A collection of 750 volumes on Indian law.

SEMINOLE NATION MUSEUM - LIBRARY
P.O. Box 1532, 524 S. Wewoka
WEWOKA, OK 74884 (405) 257-5580
  Leta Smith, Administrator
Description: Contains books, and documents on the history of the Seminoles, the history of Wewoka, and the history of oil in Oklahoma. *Special exhibit*: Cultural Continuities in Seminole County, Oklahoma—provides detailed information on the clans, bands, churches, and homes of the Seminoles; and the Dawes rolls for reference into Seminole genealogy. Open to the public. Opened in 1974.

OREGON

NATIONAL INDIAN CHILD WELFARE ASSOCIATION LIBRARY
5100 SW Macadam Ave., Suite 300
PORTLAND, OR 97239
  (503) 222-4044 ext. 138 Fax 222-4007
  Lois C. Chilcott, Library Assistant
  E-mail: info@nicwa.org
  Website: www.nicwa.org

A clearinghouse of over 3,000 articles, books, periodicals on Indian child welfare, mental health, and social work issues.

THE REX ARRAGON LIBRARY
1219 SW Park Ave.• PORTLAND, OR 97205
  (503) 226-2811 Fax 226-4842
  Dan Lucas, Director

E-Mail: library@pam.org
Web site: http://www.pam.org
Library of the Portland Art Museum and Pacific Northwest College of Art. Consists of over 25,000 volumes on art and art history. Special collection: American Indian art books, particularly Pacific Northwest Coast Indians. Interlibrary loans. Open to the public.

PENNSYLVANIA

LENNI LENAPE HISTORICAL SOCIETY
MUSEUM OF INDIAN CULTURE LIBRARY
2825 Fish Hatchery Rd. • ALLENTOWN, PA 18103
(610) 797-2121 Fax 797-2801
Carla J.S. Messinger, Executive Director
E-Mail: lenape@lenape.org
Web site: www.lenape.org
Description: A resource library which maintains over 300 video tapes, audiotapes, CDRoms and more than 3,000 books concerning Lenni Lenape and other Native peoples.

CUMBERLAND COUNTY HISTORICAL SOCIETY —
HAMILTON LIBRARY
21 North Pitt St. • CARLISLE, PA 17013
Description: Maintains a special collection of magazines and journals published by the Carlisle Indian School.

HARCOURT LIBRARY
American Indian Research & Resource Institute
Gettysburg College
GETTYSBURG, PA 17325
(717) 337-6265
Dr. Frank W. Porter, III, Director
Description: Harcourt Library maintains a special collection on Native Americans; also the Herman Finkelstein Primitive Mask Collection. Established in 1983.

AMERICAN PHILOSOPHICAL SOCIETY LIBRARY
105 South 5th St.
PHILADELPHIA, PA 19106
(215) 440-3400 Fax 440-34232
Web site: www.amphilsoc.org
Dr, Edward C. Carter, III, Librarian
Description: A major U.S. repository of documentation on Native American art. *Special collection*: American Indian linguistics; Franz Boas collection of 18th and 19th century Indian vocabularies. Open to the public by appointment only. Established 1743.

FREE LIBRARY OF PHILADELPHIA
Social Science & History Department
Logan Square
PHILADELPHIA, PA 19103
Special collection: The Wilberforce Eames Collection on American Indians.

HISTORICAL SOCIETY OF
PENNSYLVANIA LIBRARY
1300 Locust St.
PHILADELPHIA , PA 19107
(215) 732-6200 Fax 732-2680
Lee Arnold, Director of Library
E-Mail: hsppr@hsp.org; Web site: www.hsp.org
Description: Maintains library and archives of the Indian Rights Association Papers, Indians of North American Collection; Colonial & Early American History; Civil War; family history and genealogy; local history. *Activities*: Publications; tours. Open to the public, $5 per day. Opened in 1824.

UNIVERSITY OF PENNSYLVANIA
MUSEUM LIBRARY
3260 South St.
PHILADELPHIA, PA 19104-6324
(215) 898-7840 Fax 573-2008
E-Mail: muselib@pobox.upenn.edu
Web site: library.upenn.edu/museum/museum.html
Description: A major U.S. repository of documentation on Native American art. Collection consists of 150,000 volumes on world archaeology, anthropology and ethnology. *Special collection*: Brinton Collection—Aboriginal American linguistics and ethnology. Interlibrary loans. Open to the public.

COUNCIL OF THREE RIVERS
AMERICAN INDIAN CENTER LIBRARY
200 Charles St. • PITTSBURGH, PA 15238
(412) 782-4457
Description: Cultural library on Indian tribes, cultures, customs and traditions. Maintains the Indian Child Welfare Resource Library.

AMERICAN INDIAN EDUCATION
POLICY CENTER LIBRARY
Penn State University, 320 Rackley Bldg.
UNIVERSITY PARK, PA 16803
(814) 865-1489
Dr. L.A. Napier, Director
Description: Maintains a collection of 1,000 volumes on American Indian education.

RHODE ISLAND

HAFFENREFFER MUSEUM
OF ANTHROPOLOGY LIBRARY
Brown University, Mt. Hope Grant
300 Tower St. • BRISTOL, RI 02809
(401) 253-8388 Fax 253-1198
Kevin P. Smith, Deputy Director & Chief Curator
Description: A major U.S. repository of documentation on Native American art. Contains a collection of about 5,000 volumes in the field of anthropology, with material on American Indian culture and history.

TOMAQUAG INDIAN MEMORIAL
MUSEUM LIBRARY
390B Summit Rd. • EXETER, RI 02822
(401) 539-7795

CENTER FOR THE STUDY OF
RACE & ETHNICITY IN AMERICA
Brown University, Box 1886
PROVIDENCE, RI 02912
(401) 863-3080
Rhett S. Jones, Director

JOHN CARTER BROWN LIBRARY
Brown University, Box 1894
PROVIDENCE, RI 02912
(401) 863-2725 Fax 863-3477
Norman Fiering, Librarian
Description: A collection of historical sources pertaining to the discovery, exploration, colonization, settlement, and development of the New World (especially those relating to Native American populations and development.) Includes native language materials published in colonial era. *Activities*: Exhibitions, lectures, conferences, publications for sale. Research fellowships awarded.

SOUTH CAROLINA

SOUTH CAROLINA ARCHIVES
& HISTORY CENTER
8301 Parklane Rd.
COLUMBIA , SC29223-4905
(803) 896-6100 Fax 896-6167
Website: www.state.sc/scdah
Alexis J. Helsley, Director-Education
Special collections: Cherokee Indian Treaties, 1759-77; Journals of the Commissioners of Indian Trade, 1710-18; Documents Relating to Indian Affairs, 1750-65; Evidence of Leasehold and Taxes Paid, Catawba Indian Lands, 1791-1856; Supt. of the Catawba Nation Record Book of Plots and Leases, 1810-25, and Accounts of Rents, 1810-1831; Records of the Commissioner to Carry into Effect the Treaty of Nation Ford 1840: and Journal of a Journey to the Catawba Nation, 1727-28.

SOUTH DAKOTA

CRAZY HORSE MEMORIAL LIBRARY
Ave. of the Chiefs • CRAZY HORSE, SD 57730
(605) 673-4681 Fax 673-2185
Ruth Ziolkowski, Director

Website: www.crazyhorsememorial.org
E-mail: memorial@crazyhorsememorial.org
Description: A research library with a collection of 22,000 plus volumes on American Indian art, culture and history. Emphasis on Native American literature. Opened in 1974.

BADLANDS NATIONAL MONUMENT LIBRARY
P.O. Box 72 • INTERIOR, SD 57750
Description: Maintains a collection of 1,000 books and 500 bound periodicals on the Badlands and Indians of South Dakota.

THE OGLALA LAKOTA
HISTORICAL CENTER LIBRARY
Oglala Lakota College
P.O. Box 490 • KYLE, SD 57752
(605) 455-2321
Description: Holdings include tribal college and government records; personal papers of Dr. Valentine T. McGillycuddy; photographs and oral histories, and other historical material.

AMERICAN INDIAN CULTURE
RESEARCH CENTER
Blue Cloud Abbey
P.O. Box 98 • MARVIN, SD 57251
(605) 398-9200 Fax 398-9201
Rev. Stanislaus Maudlin, Director
Description: Collection of more than 3,000 books on Native American culture. *Purpose*: To support Indian leaders, and educators in their ambitions for rebuilding the Indian community; aids in teaching the non-Indian public of the culture and philosophy of the Indian. *Programs*: Compiled oral history and photographic collection; distributes films, records and tapes; conducts workshops and seminars; maintains speakers bureau. *Publication*: Blue Cloud Quarterly. Distributes films, books, records and tapes. Opened in 1967.

SOUTH DAKOTA STATE ARCHIVES
900 Governors Dr. • PIERRE, SD 57501
(605) 773-3804 Fax 773-6041
LaVera Rose, Librarian
Richard Popp, Director
E-mail: archref@state.sd.us
Web site: www.state.sd.us/deca/cultural/archives.htm
Description: Contains books, manuscripts, government records, photos, and maps relating to Indian tribes and reservations in South Dakota and northern Great Plains region. Opened in 1975.

THE HERITAGE CENTER LIBRARY
Red Cloud Indian School, Hwy. 18 W.
PINE RIDGE, SD 57770
(605) 867-5491
Brother C.M. Simon, S.J., Director
Description: Collection of 1,000 volumes on Lakota history and culture; Native American art.

LAKOTA ARCHIVES & HISTORICAL
RESEARCH CENTER
Sinte Gleska University
P.O. Box 490 • ROSEBUD, SD 57570
(605) 747-2263 Fax 747-2098
Marcella Cash, Director
Description: Archival reporsitory for the records of the Rosebud Sioux Tribe and Sinte Gleska College; Native American Periodicals and Oral History collections; and manuscript material related to the Rosebud Sioux Reservation, including records of the Episcopal Mission which date back to the 1870's. Open to public.

THE CENTER FOR WESTERN STUDIES LIBRARY
Augustana College, Box 727
SIOUX FALLS, SD 57197
(605) 274-4007 Fax 274-4999
Harry F. Thompson, Director of Research Collections
Description: The collections focus is Northern Plains history and cultures, including native (mostly Sioux) and immigrant peoples. A reference library of 30,000 volumes on the American West with emphasis on South Dakota and the Northern Plains plus 4,000 linear feet of archives and manuscripts. Includes the Papers of the Riggs family of missionaries to the Sioux. *Activities*: Annual Dakota Conference in the spring; annual art show; book publications on the Northern Plains with special emphasis on Sioux life and art. Interlibrary loans. Open to the public.

**ASSOCIATION ON AMERICAN
INDIAN AFFAIRS, INC. LIBRARY**
966 Hungerford Dr., Suite 12-B
ROCKVILLE, MD 20850
  (240) 314-7155 Fax 314-7159
  Jack Trope, Director
Description: Over 400 books relating to American
Indians. Available to general public.

E.Y. BERRY LIBRARY-LEARNING CENTER
Black Hills State University
1200 University • SPEARFISH, SD 57799
  (605) 642-6833 Fax 642-6298
  Dora Ann Jones, Special Collections Librarian
Description: Subjects deal with Dakota Indians
and North American Indians.

**BUECHEL MEMORIAL LAKOTA
MUSEUM ARCHIVES**
350 S. Oak St., P.O. Box 499
ST. FRANCIS, SD 57572
  (605) 747-2745 Fax 747-5057
  Mike Marshall, Director; Website: www.littlesioux.org
Description: Archives house photographs and documents of post-reservation era. Native American subjects, church subjects, diaries and documents related
to Sicango (Rosebud Sioux) history. Opened in 1954.
Open to the public Memorial Day to Labor Day.

**INSTITUTE OF AMERICAN INDIAN
STUDIES LIBRARY**
University of South Dakota
Dakota Hall, 414 E. Clark St.
VERMILLION, SD 57069
  (605) 677-5209
  Dr. Herbert Hoover, Director
Description: American Indian Research Project: Maintains a collection of 1,500 oral interview tapes with
emphasis on tribes of the northern plains; subject
matter is widely varied; also a collection of about 1,000
books on ethnology and contemporary affairs of the
northwest Plains Indians. Open to public by appointment.

SOCIAL SCIENCE RESEARCH INSTITUTE
U. of South Dakota • VERMILLION, SD 57069
  (605) 677-5401
  Prof. Thomas E. Allen, Jr., Director
Description: Research includes studies in medical and
educational problems on American Indian reservations.
Conducts anthropological studies. Recent studies on
impact of Indian law and communities.

W.H. OVER MUSEUM LIBRARY
414 E. Clark St. • VERMILLION, SD 57069
  (605) 677-5228
  Web site: http://www.usd.edu/whom/
Description: Collection on local histroy, Indian history,
and northern Plains ethnography and history. Open to
the public for reference use only.

TENNESSEE

**CHUCALISSA ARCHAEOLOGICAL
MUSEUM—LIBRARY**
1987 Indian Village Dr. • MEMPHIS, TN 38109
  (901) 785-3160
  Gerald P. Smith, Director
  Mary L. Kwas, Curator of Education
Description: Contains a collection of 2,000 volumes
on Indian history, culture and archaeology. Material
available to public upon request.

TENNESSEE STATE LIBRARY & ARCHIVES
403 Seventh Ave. North
NASHVILLE, TN 37243-0312
  (615) 741-2764 Fax (615) 532-2472
  Dr. Edwin S. Gleaves, State Librarian & Archivist
  E-Mail: reference@mail.state.tn.us
  Web site: state.tn.us/sos/statelib/tslahome.htm
Description: Reference works deal mainly with Tennessee history and items of material culture; Indian-
related works deal with tribes of the Southeastern U.S.,
and are concerned mostly with genealogical research;
photographic archives. *Special programs*: Conducts
occasional workshops and seminars dealing with Indian genealogical research; exhibit of Indian materi-

als constructed during the Year of the American Indian. *Publication*: Native American (Cherokee) Research at the Tennessee State Library & Archives. Interlibrary loans. Open to the public.

**PINSON MOUNDS STATE
ARCHAEOLOGICAL AREA LIBRARY**
Rt. 1, Box 316, Ozier Rd.
PINSON, TN 38366 (901) 988-5614
Description: Consists of 400 volumes on the
archaeology of Pinson Mounds area.

TEXAS

**AMARILLO PUBLIC LIBRARY-
LOCAL HISTORY COLLECTION**
413 E. 4th, Box 2171 • AMARILLO, TX 79189
  (806) 378-3054 Fax 378-4245
  Mary Kay Snell, Director of Services

**PANHANDLE-PLAINS HISTORICAL MUSEUM—
LIBRARY & ARCHIVES**
P.O. Box 967, W.T. Sta. • CANYON, TX 79016
  (806) 656-2261 Fax 656-2250
  Lisa Lambert, Librarian
Description: Contains a collection of about 400 titles
on the Indians of the SouthernPlains, such as
Comanche, Apache, Kiowa, Navaho, Cheyenne, and
Indians of Oklahoma; & archaeology of the Texas Pan-
handle. Also photographs of individual tribe members,
maps, brochures, periodicals, etc. Open to public.

**AMON CARTER MUSEUM
PHOTOGRAPHY COLLECTION**
3501 Camp Bowie Blvd.
FORT WORTH, TX 76107
  (817) 738-1933 Fax 738-4066
  John Rohrbach, Curator of Photographic Collections
  Barbara McCandless, Curator of Photographs
  E-Mail: barbara.mccandless@cartermuseum.org
  E-Mail: john.rohrbach@cartermuseum.org
Description: E.A. Brininstool Collection: 3,500 items
(2,680 prints, 550 negatives) - b/w images of natives
1868-1937, sometimes staged environments as well
as natural landscapes; photographs of geographic locations, monuments, battlefields of the Plains and Indian wars. Helen M. Post Collection: 11,000 pieces
(6,000 prints, 4,000 negatives) - B/W documentation
from 1936-41 of Indian reservation life, primarily Sioux,
Navajo and Crow on a personal and intimate level;
Laura Gilpin Collection: 25,000 prints, 27,000 negatives & transparencies, b/w & color documentation of
Navajo life, 1930s-70s.

**ALABAMA-COUSHATTA TRIBE
OF TEXAS TRIBAL LIBRARY**
571 State Park Rd. 56 • LIVINGSTON, TX 77351
  (936) 563-1316
  Delores Poncho, Librarian
  E-mail: library@actribe.org
Description: Small one-room library containing Native
American books and reference materials and assorted
software for computers to serve K-12, service to
Headstart program and special resource for continuing education. Includes a computer room with internet
access. Moderately supplied video library and a special Tony Hillerman collection.

INCARNATE WORD COLLEGE LIBRARY
4301 Broadway • SAN ANTONIO, TX 78209
  (210) 829-3855
Titles in all areas of Native America studies.
Native American art history particularly strong.

**SUNSET TRADING POST
OLD WEST MUSEUM—LIBRARY**
Route 1 • SUNSET, TX 76270
  (817) 872-2027
Description: A collection of 500 volumes on
American Indians, and the frontier.

UTAH

**EDGE OF THE CEDARS STATE
HISTORICAL MONUMENT & MUSEUM LIBRARY**
660 West 400 North • BLANDING, UT 84511

  (435) 678-2238
  Michael M. Nelson, Museum/Park Manager
Description: Materials related directly to archaeology,
and Native American cultures of the American Southwest, particularly the Four Corners area.

UTE TRIBAL MUSEUM LIBRARY
Ute Tribe, P.O. Box 190, Highway 40
FORT DUCHESNE, UT 84026
  (801) 722-4992
Description: Maintains a collection of books on the Ute
Indians; American Indian history and culture; and early
Western American history.

AMERICAN WEST CENTER
The University of Utah
1901 E. South Campus Dr., Rm. 1023
SALT LAKE CITY, UT 84112-9152
  (801) 581-7611 Fax 581-7612
  Dr. Daniel C. McCool, Director
  E-mail: dan.mccool@poli-sci.utah.edu
Description: Research includes American Indian his-
tory and traditions; hunting, fishing, water rights, and
voting rights.

UTAH STATE HISTORICAL SOCIETY LIBRARY
300 Rio Grande • SALT LAKE CITY, UT 84101
  (801) 533-5755; Melvin T. Smith, Director
Description: A collection of books and periodicals on
the history of Utah, Mormons, Indians, and the West.

VIRGINIA

LONGWOOD COLLEGE LIBRARY
FARMVILLE, VA 23909
  (804) 395-2241 Fax 395-2142
Description: Contains the O'Brien Collection of
over 5,000 prehistoric Virginia Indian artifacts.

HAMPTON UNIVERSITY LIBRARY
American Indian Educational Opportunities Program
HAMPTON, VA 23668
  (757) 727-5981 Fax 727-5084
  Dr. Paulette F. Molin, Director
Description: Maintains archival, photographic
and art collections

WASHINGTON

CENTER FOR PACIFIC NORTHWEST STUDIES
Western Washington University
High St. • BELLINGHAM, WA 98225
  (206) 676-3284/3125
  Dr. James W. Scott
Purpose: To collect materials of every sort—manuscripts, business records, maps, photographs, tapes,
etc.—of the people and activities of the Pacific Northwest, past and present. *Publications*: Publishes two
series: Occasional Papers (21 to-date) and Informational Papers (5 to-date.) Archive-Library. Opened in
1971.

LEWIS COUNTY HISTORICAL LIBRARY
599 N.W. Front St. • CHEHALIS, WA 98532
  (206) 748-0831
Description: Holdings of about 1,600 volumes
in the Indian archive collection.

MAKAH CULTURAL & RESEARCH CENTER
P.O. Box 160 • NEAH BAY, WA 98357
  (206) 645-2711
Description: Studies Makah language, culture, and
ethnohistory; comparative Wakashan linguistics and
Nootkin studies. *Publication*: Portraits In Time.

WEUSSO: NISQUALLY TRIBAL LIBRARY
4814 She-Nah-Num Dr. SE
OLYMPIA, WA 98513
  (360) 456-5221 Fax 438-8618
  Faith Hagenhofer, Librarian
  E-Mail: nisqlibr@orcalink.com
Description: Maintains a collection of over 5,000 books,
Native American periodicals, and 750+ videos. Em-
phasis is on Native American and children's materi-
als. Serves the community's members, both tribal and

nontribal. *Programs*: Vocational education computer training. Interlibrary loans. Open to the public. Established 1987.

**NORTH AMERICAN INDIAN MISSION
(NAIM) MINISTRIES LIBRARY**
P.O. Box 151 • POINT ROBERTS, WA 98281
(604) 946-1227 Fax 946-1465
Ray Badgero, President
E-mail: badgero@naim.ca; Website: www.naim.ca
Description: Collection contains 600 volumes including audio and video tapes.

AMERICAN INDIAN HERITAGE SCHOOL LIBRARY
1330 N. 90th St. • SEATTLE, WA 98103
(206) 298-7895
Description: Large Native American collection - both print and audio-video.

UNIVERSITY OF WASHINGTON LIBRARIES
Special Collections, Manuscripts & University Archives
Allen Library, Box 352900
SEATTLE, WA 98195-2900
(206) 543-1929 Fax 543-1931
Carla Rickerson, Acting Head
E-Mail: speccoll@u.washington.edu
Web site: www.lib.washington.edu/specialcoll/
Description: A major U.S. repository of documentation on Native American art. Extensive holdings of published and photographic material on native Americans of the northwest coast of North America, Alaska, and Pacific Northwest plateau area. *Special collection*: Native Americans of the Pacific Northwest: A Photographic Record: Over 4,000 photographs plus a 17,000 entry index - microfiche (112 sheets), $115 per set; Viola E. Garfield Albums on Totem Art: 1,749 photographs - microfiche (60 sheets), $60 per set. Open to the public.

EASTERN WASHINGTON HISTORICAL SOCIETY
Northwest Museum of Arts & Culture
2316 W. First Ave. • SPOKANE, WA 99204
(509) 363-5313 Fax 363-5303
Rayette Wilder, Archivist
E-mail: rayettew@ztc.net
Website: www.northwestmuseum.org
Description: The American Indian portion of the collection contains approximately 8,000 books on the American Indian; manuscript collections, 20,000 photographs, ephemera; newspaper clippings; and oral history tapes. Opened in 1916. By appointment only.

JESUIT OREGON PROVINCE ARCHIVES
Foley Library, Gonzaga University
SPOKANE, WA 99258-0001
(509) 323-3814 Fax 324-5904
David Kingma, Archivist
E-Mail: jopa@its.gonzaga.edu
Web site: www.gonzaga.edu/foley/jopa.html
Special collections: Jesuit Missions Collections of the Pacific Northwest & Alaska—150 volumes of Jesuit missionaries among Indians of Northwest—Blackfeet, Coeur d' Alenes, Yakimas, Cheyennes. Northwest Mission Papers—500 boxes, 45,000 items—correspondence, diaries, photos, microfilm, relating to Jesuit Missionary activity in Alaska, and the Northwest States, including the Athapaskans and Eskimos to the previous tribes mentioned. The Indian Language Collection—50,600 pages—manuscript dictionaries, grammars, catechisms, gospels, prayer books, sermons in the Indian languages of the Rocky Mountains, and the Eskimo languages of Alaska. Among the languages are: Assiniboine, Blackfoot, Crow, Chinook, Columbia, Colville, Gros Ventre, Inuit, Kalispel, Nez Perce, Okanagan, Sioux, Tlingit, and Yakima. Most are contained on microfilm-125 reels. Open to the public. Opened in 1925.

**STEILACOOM TRIBAL
CULTURAL CENTER LIBRARY**
1515 Lafayette St., P.O. Box 88419
STEILACOOM, WA 98388 (206) 584-6308
Joan K. Ortez, Director
Description: Research material - books, articles, videotapes and other materials, all on Native Americans.

SUQUAMISH MUSEUM LIBRARY
15838 Sandy Hook NE, Box 498
SUQUAMISH, WA 98392 (206) 598-3311

Description: The Suquamish Tribal Archives has a large collection of written documents, oral history tapes and transcripts, historical photographs, maps, and historical and cultural texts, relating to the Suquamish and other Puget Sound tribes.

**WASHINGTON STATE HISTORICAL
SOCIETY SPECIAL COLLECTIONS**
1911 Pacific Ave. • TACOMA, WA 98402
(253) 272-3500 Fax 597-9518
Edward W. Nolan, Head of Special Collections
Website: www.washingtonhistory.org
Description: A collection of books, pamphlets, manuscripts and photographs that include Pacific Northwest Indians in general and Washington tribes in particular. Complete set of Edward Curtis with folios; papers of Louis Mann (Indian activist), 1914-36; Judge George Boldt (Indian fishing rights decision); Records of Indian Shaker Church of WA; papers of George R. Chute (historian of Native North Pacific halibut fishery, 1925-50); R.B. Milroy papers (Indian agent in Washington Territory, 1880-90), fragmentary; Yakima Indian Agency Records, 1880-1900, fragmentary; photo collections include 600 negatives of Makah tribe taken by Morse; and a file of newspaper clippings. Open to the public by appointment.

TOPPENISH MUSEUM LIBRARY
1 South Elm • TOPPENISH, WA 98945
(509) 865-4510
Description: Maintains a collection of 18,500 volumes including many on the Indians of the Northwest, and Native-American history and culture.

YAKAMA NATION LIBRARY
Yakama Nation Cultural Heritage Center
P.O. Box 151, 101 Speil-Yi-Loop
TOPPENISH, WA 98948
(509) 865-2800
Vivian M. Adams, Librarian
Jolena M. Umtuch, Asst. Librarian
Katrina Walsey, Library Technician II
Description: Special collections include the Nipo Strongheart, Bob Pace, Dr. Helen Schuster, and Special reference books and videos. Regular collections are historical reference books, contemporary native-related books, periodicals, magazines, and tribal newspapers.

WEST VIRGINIA

**ERIC CLEARINGHOUSE ON RURAL
EDUCATION & SMALL SCHOOLS**
Appalachia Educational Laboratory
P.O. Box 1348 • CHARLESTON, WV 25325
(800) 624-9120; (304) 347-0400 Fax 347-0487
Craig Howley, Co-director
Description: Holdings include 300,000 (education-related professional literature in English) documents on microfiche, including many on American Indians (North & South America) and Alaskan Natives. *Special programs*: Workshops on how to use ERIC database; free searches of ERIC database; free Digests on topics of current interest. Publications: Newsletter; book for sale. Open to the public.

WISCONSIN

ARVID E. MILLER MEMORIAL LIBRARY-MUSEUM
Mohican Nation Stockbridge-Munsee Band
N8510 Moh He Con Nuck Rd.
BOWLER, WI 54416
(715) 793-4240 Fax 793-4836
Arletta Davids, Director
E-mail: arlee_davids@yahoo.com
Website: www.mohican.com
Description: Holds the largest collection of material, rare books, missionary journals, maps, microfilm, historical papers on Mohican Indians; also called Stockbridge-Munsee; includes artifacts such as baskets made of splints and birch bark, arrow heads, projectile points, tobacco pipes, stone axes; fur trade era & missionary era. *Activities*: Winter Ceremony; annual pow-wow; Mohican History Conference. Publications for sale. Opened in 1974.

HOARD HISTORICAL MUSEUM LIBRARY
407 Merchant Ave.
FORT ATKINSON, WI 53538
Description: Maintains a special collection of rare books on the Black Hawk War, 1800-1840.

**STATE HISTORICAL SOCIETY OF WISCONSIN
LIBRARY/ARCHIVES DIVISION**
816 State St. • MADISON, WI 53706
(608) 264-6535 Fax 264-6404
Peter Gottlieb, Director
Web site: www.wisconhistory.org
Description: A major U.S. repository of documentation on Native American history. *Special collection*: "Largest library in the nation devoted to North American history." Extensive holdings on North American Indians; Native American newspapers and periodicals; manuscripts and photographs. Interlibrary loans. Open to the public. Established 1846.

MARQUETTE UNIVERSITY LIBRARY
Special Archives • MILWAUKEE, WI 53201
(414)288-6838 Fax 288-3755
Mark G. Thiel, Archivist
Website: www.marquette.edu/library/
collections/archives/index.html
Description: Collections primarily document Native American socio-culture change, education, legal issues, and Catholic Church relationships, 1870-present in U.S. and Canada. Also includes special website on K-12 curricula about Native Americans (funded by the National Endowment for the Humanities. Website: www.marquette.edu/library/neh/general/index.htm. Interlibrary loans. Open to the public.

MILWAUKEE PUBLIC MUSEUM LIBRARY
800 W. Wells St.
MILWAUKEE, WI 53233
(414) 278-2736 Fax 278-6100
Judith Turner, Librarian
E-Mail: jat@mpm1.mpm.edu
Web site: http://www.mpm.edu
Description: Maintains a collection of 125,000 volumes of monographs and periodicals in the subject areas of natural and human history; literature on the archaeology, ethnology, ethnohistory and material culture of American Indians is well-represented; 300,000 item Photographic Collection is especially strong in photographs depicting Native American culture and objects. Interlibrary loans. Open to the public.

WYOMING

WYOMING STATE ARCHIVES
2301 Central Ave., Barrett Bldg.
CHEYENNE, WY 82002
(307) 777-7826 Fax 777-7044
Tony Adams, Director
Description: Collections contain the records of the State of Wyoming and political subdivisions. Non-government collections focus on the history of Wyoming and the American West. Includes periodicals, maps, photographs, oral history, military and census records; primary sources for Native American history, especially Wyoming tribes. Open to the public. Opened in 1895.

McCRACKEN RESEARCH LIBRARY
Buffalo Bill Historical Center
720 Sheridan Ave. • CODY, WY 82414
(307) 578-4059 Fax 527-6042
Nathan E. Bender, Curator
Frances B. Clymer, Librarian
E-Mail: hmrl@bbhc.org
Website: www.bbhc.org
Description: Research collection focusing on the Great Plains and Northern Rockies culture and history, including much on Plains Indians specifically and native American studies in general. Library collection has 25,000 volumes with 3,000 linear feet of archival collections. Photograph holdings are particularly strong for the Crow, Cheyenne. and other Plains Indian peoples, with collections from photographers D.F. Barry, Thomas Marquis, W.A. Petzoldt, J.H. Sharp, L.A. Huffman, George Bird Grinnell and others;Bureau of American Ethnology Annual Reports, 1880's to 1940's. Interlibrary loans. Opened to the public in 1980.

ORGANIZATIONS

**ABLEZA - A NATIVE AMERICAN
ARTS & FILM INSTITUTE**
1279 Mildred Ave. • San Jose, CA 95125
(408) 267-4609 Fax 267-9609
E-mail: ableza@ableza.org
Web site: www.ableza.org

AMERICAN INDIAN FILM & VIDEO COMPETITION
Red Earth, Inc., 2100 NE 52nd St.
Oklahoma City, OK 73111
(918) 747-8276
Annual event open to both Indian and non-Indian
filmmakers.

AMERICAN INDIAN FILM INSTITUTE
333 Valencia St., Suite 322
San Francisco, CA 94103
(415) 554-0525 Fax 554-0542
International film exposition dedicated to the preservation of Native Americans in the cinema. Film festival the second weekend in November at the Palace of
Fine Arts in San Francisco.

AMERIND ENTERTAINMENT
65 N. Allen Ave., Suite 105
Pasadena, CA 91106
(818) 384-0344 (phone & fax)
Film production company formed by former actor
Sonny Sky Hawk to make films by Indians for Indians.

B.V., LTD.
4550 S. Quincy Ave. • Milwaukee, WI 53007
(414) 769-0777; Maria Boyer-Jensen, Principal
Distributors of filmscreen products and audiovisual
equipment.

BEAR TRIBE VIDEOS
P.O. Box 959 • Canandaigua, NY 14424
(716) 554-4906 (phone & fax)
Distributes videos.

BROWN EYES PRODUCTIONS
933 E. 12th #3 • Anchorage, AK 99501
(907) 257-1110 Fax 257-1835
Tony Brown, Principal
Media productions.

CHARIOT DISTRIBUTION
1274 Lambert Cir. • Lafayette, CO 80026
(800) 477-5128
Native American videos for grades 4-adult.

CHEROKEE LANGUAGE & CULTURE
4158 E. 48th Pl. • Tulsa, OK 74135
(918) 749-3082
Prentice Robinson, Principal
Cherokee language and culture on video.

CHEROKEE TRIBAL TELECOMMUNICATIONS CO.
Cherokee, NC 28719 (704) 497-7380

CORPORATION FOR PUBLIC BROADCASTING
901 E St., NW • Washington, DC 20004
(202) 879-9742 Fax 783-1019
Multi-cultural programs.

DESCENDING EAGLE
2017 Mission St. #303
San Francisco, CA 94110
(415) 750-9036
Media training program.

FIRST AMERICAN AWARDS
First Americans in the Arts
P.O. Box 17780
Beverly Hills, CA 90209
(310) 278-3848 Fax (818) 772-9772
Annual event for Native performing artists
in February.

FIRST NATIONS FILM & VIDEO FESTIVAL
Institute for Native American Development
Truman College, 1145 W. Wilson Ave.
Chicago, IL 60640
(312) 907-4665 Fax 907-4464
Usually held late November, early December.

FULL CIRCLE VIDEOS
1131 S. College Ave. • Tulsa, OK 74104
(800) 940-8849 Fax (918) 585-3911
E-mail: fullcir@aol.com
Videos on Native American arts, music, and culture.

INDIGENOUS COMMUNICATIONS ASSOCIATION
P.O. Box 932 • Hoopa, CA 95546
(916) 625-5033 Fax 625-5231
E-mail: kroica@aol.com
Provides technical assistance to Native American
communities who want to own their own stations.

NATIVE AMERICA CALLING
P.O. Box 40164 • Albuquerque, NM 87196
(800) 99-NATIVE; (505) 277-8009 Fax 277-4286
E-mail: chato@unm.edu
Web site: indiannet.indian.com/NAC/html

NATIVE AMERICAN BROADCASTING
Web site: www.jlc.net/~jcatlin/interworld/nab.htm

NATIVE AMERICAN INDIANS IN FILM
65 N. Allen Ave., Suite 105
Pasadena, CA 91106
(818) 578-0344 Fax 578-0344

NATIVE AMERICAN MEDIA ENTERPRISES
1750 N. Wilcox #223 • Los Angeles, CA 90028
(213) 463-8535
Hanay Geiogamah, CEO

**NATIVE AMERICAN PUBLIC
TELECOMMUNICATIONS, INC.
VISION MAKER VIDEO**
P.O.Box 83111 • Lincoln, NE 68501
(800) 835-7087; (402) 472-3522 Fax 472-8675
Frank Blythe, Executive Director
E-mail: fblythe@unlinfo.unl.edu
Web site: http://www.indian.monterey.edu

NATIVE YOUTH MEDIA INSTITUTE
Native Media Center
UND School of Communication
P.O. Box 7169 • Grand Forks, ND 58202
(701) 777-2478
Robin Powell, Director

NATIVERADIO.COM
1212 Bath Ave., 1st Floor Suite 2
Ashland, KY 41101 (606) 326-1917
Website: www.nativeradio.com

PATH OF THE SUN IMAGES
3020 Lowell Blvd. • Denver, CO 80211
(303) 477-8442
Susan Aikman, Principal
Radio and television productions.

RED EAGLE PRODUCTIONS
1704 Elaine St. • Billings, MT 59105
(406) 254-2396; Ron Holt, Principal

RED EARTH, INC.
2100 NE 52nd St.
Oklahoma City, OK 73111
(405) 427-5228
Sponsors the annual American Film & Video
Competition open to both Indian and non-Indian
filmmakers.

SERENE FX HEDIN PRODUCTIONS
12089 W. Dakota Dr.
Lakewood, CO 80228-2935
(303) 980-8582
Serene Hedin, Principal
Film/video productions

SHENANDOAH FILM PRODUCTIONS
538 G St. • Arcada, CA 95521 (707) 822-1030

SPOTTED EAGLE PRODUCTIONS
2524 Hennepin Ave. #6
Minneapolis, MN 55405
(612) 377-4212 Fax 377-7020
Chris Spotted Eagle, Principal
E-mail: cseagle@maroon.tc.umn.edu
Film production company.

TWO RIVERS NATIVE FILM & VIDEO FESTIVAL
Native Arts Circle • 3121 Elliot Ave.
Minneapolis, MN 55407-1507
(612) 870-7173 Fax 870-0327
Usually held in mid-October.

**UNITED NATIVE AMERICAN
TELEVISION PROJECT**
Web site: www.jlc.net/~jcatlin/interworld/main1.ht

VISION QUEST FILM & VIDEO PRODUCTIONS, INC.
7 Milburn Lane • Huntington, NY 11743
(516) 385-7459
Kathy Paschal, Principal
Film and video festivals.

WRITTEN HERITAGE VIDEOS
P.O. Box 1390 • Folsom, LA 70437
(504) 796-5433 Fax 796-9236

**The following is a list of radio and
television stations, programs, and
projects throughout the U.S. arranged
alpha-geographically.**

**AIROS (American Indian Radio on Satellite)
(402) 472-3287
E-mail: airos@unl.edu
Website: www.airos.org**

ALABAMA

WASG - 550 AM & WYDH - FM
Alabama Native American Broadcasting Co.
1210 S. Main St. • ATMORE, AL 36502
(205) 368-2511 Fax 368-4227
Dale Gehman, General Manager
Jerry Gehman, News Director
David Gehman, Operations Manager
Commercial station. "Our company is comprised of
partners who are members of the Poarch Band of
Creek Indians, a federally recognized tribe, located
adjacent to Atmore, Alabama. WASG airs and produces many programs aimed at and for members of
the tribe and airs other American Indian programs produced by other Indian media." Begun 1981.

ALASKA

KNBA 90.3 FM
ANCHORAGE, AK

BROWN EYES PRODUCTIONS
933 E. 12th #3 • ANCHORAGE, AK 99501
(907) 257-1110 Fax 257-1835
Tony Brown, Principal
Media productions.

INDIGENOUS BROADCAST CENTER
Alaska Public Radio Network
810 E. 9th Ave. • ANCHORAGE, AK 99501
(907) 263-7427 Fax 263-7450
Diane Kaplan, President & CEO
D'Anne Hamilton, Host & Producer
(National Native News)
The Indigenous Broadcast Center, a project of the
Alaska Public Radio Network, is designed to provide
public broadcast training at all skill levels for Native
Americans. The Center will provide culturally-sensi-
tive training that is currently non-existent in the areas
of management, development, engineering, operations, production and news. The Center is also designed to introduce more Native Americans to public
broadasting. National Native News is the country's
only daily Native news service which is carried by over
175 stations in live five-minute headline weekday
newscasts across the country.

KOAHNIC BROADCAST CORP.
818 E. 9th Ave. • ANCHORAGE, AK 99501
(907) 263-7498 Fax 263-7454

ONE SKY PRODUCTIONS, LTD.
2611 Fairbanks St. #D • ANCHORAGE, AK 99503
    (907) 272-8111 Fax 272 7007
    Jeanie Greene, Host/Director/Producer
    John Tepton & Gary Fife, Moderators (One Sky)
Programs: "Heartbeat Alaska" and "One Sky." "Heartbeat Alaska," a 30-minute news program hosted by Ms. Greene, is seen on Channel 13, Channel 7, and RATNET, and focuses on the life and times of rural Alaska residents. It airs over networks in Anchorage, Fairbanks and Juneau and is beamed 20 247 Alaska communities via the Rural Alaska Television Network (RATNET); "One Sky," which airs immediately after "Heartbeat Alaska," is a discussion style forum for rural issues.

ASRC COMMUNICATIONS, INC.
P.O. Box 129 • BARROW, AK 99723
    (907) 852-8633
    Barrow Cable TV.

KBRW - 680 AM
Silakkuagvik Communications, Inc.
P.O. Box 109 • BARROW, AK 99723
    (907) 852-6811/6300 Fax 852-2274
    Don Rinker, Manager
    Inuit station. Non-commercial station.

KYUK - 640 AM/TV
Bethel Broadcasting, Inc.
Pouch 468, 640 Radio St.
BETHEL, AK 99559
    (907) 543-3131 Fax 543-3130
    Ron Daugherty, General Manager
    Mike Martz, Sr. Video Producer (TV)
    E-mail: gm@kyuk.org; Website: www.@kyuk..org.
Yup'ik Eskimo station focusing on Yup'ik kifestyle, culture, history and current social issues. Library. Begun 1971.

KCUK - 88.1 FM
Kashunaniut School District
CHEVAK, AK 99563
    (907) 858-7014 Fax 858-7114
    Peter Tuluk, Manager
    Yupik Eskimo. Repeats KYUK.
    Noncommercial station.

KDLG - 670 AM
P.O. Box 670 • DILLINGHAM, AK 99576
    (907) 842-5281 Fax 842-5645
    Casey Jackson, Manager
    Aleut news. Noncommercial station. Begun 1975.

KZPA - 900 AM
P.O. Box 126 • FORT YUKON, AK 99740
    (907) 662-2587 Fax 662-2222
    Marilyn Savage, Manager
    Athabascan. Noncommercial station.

KBBI 890 AM
HOMER, AK

KTOO - FM
360 Egan Dr. • JUNEAU, AK 99801
    (907) 586-1670 Fax 586-3612
    Jeff Brown, Director; Kathy Ruddy, Producer
Program: Southeast Native Radio. A program about native issues for natives and non-natives. Monday night, 6:30-7 pm. *Hosts*: Cy Peck, Jr. & Kim Metcalfe-Helmar

KDLL - 91.9 FM
KENIA, AK

KRBD - 105.9 FM
KETCHIKAN, AK

KOTZ - 720 AM
Kotzebue Broadcasting, Inc.
P.O. Box 78 • KOTZEBUE, AK 99752
    (907) 442-3434 Fax 442-2292
    E-mail: kotzengr@eagle.ptialaska.net
Programming is directed to our Native Inupiaq Eskimo audience which is 85% of the local population. This is a native-owned and operated station. established 1973.

KSKO 870 AM
P.O. Box 195 • McGRATH, AK 99627
    (907) 524-3001 Fax 524-3436
    Betsy McGuire, Manager
    Athabascan. Noncommercial station.

METLAKATLA INDIAN COMMUNITY CABLE TV
P.O. Box 8 • METLAKATLA, AK 99926
    Bonnie Scudero, Contact

KSDP 830 AM
SAND POINT, AK

KUHB - 91.9 FM
Pribiloff School District
ST. PAUL, AK 99660
    (907) 546-2254 Fax 546-2327
    Alicia Misikin, Manager
    Aleut. Noncommercial station.

KNSA - 930 AM
P.O. Box 178 • UNALAKLEET, AK 99684
    (907) 624-3101 Fax 624-3130
    Henry Ivanoff, Manager
    Inupiaq Eskimo. Noncommercial station.

ARIZONA

KUYI 88.1 FM
HOTEVILLA, AZ

CHANNEL 3
P.O. Box 5968 • PHOENIX , AZ 85010
    Mary Kim Titla, Contact

APACHE CABLEVISION
12 San Carlos Ave. • SAN CARLOS, AZ 85550
    (520) 475-2550

KNCC - FM
Navajo Community College
TSAILE, AZ 85445 (602) 724-3311

KGHR - 91.5 FM
Navajo/Greyhills High School
P.O. Box 160 • TUBA CITY, AZ 86045
    (520) 283-6271 Fax 283-6604
    Stu Schader, Acting Manager
Noncommercial station.

KUAT - AM
University of Arizona
TUCSON, AZ 85721
Program: Desert Visions. Native American Radio Program.

KNNB - 88.1 FM
White Mountain Apache Tribe
P.O. Box 310 • WHITERIVER, AZ 85941
    (520) 338-5211 Fax 338-1744
    Phoebe Nez, Manager
Native American Radio Program.
Noncommercial station.

KTNN - 660 AM
Navajo Nation, P.O. Box 2569
WINDOW ROCK, AZ 86515
    (520) 871-2582 Fax 871-3479
    Roy Hubbell, Manager
Commercial station.

NAVAJO NATION BROADCAST SERVICES & FILM OFFICE
P.O. Box 2310 • WINDOW ROCK, AZ 86515
    (520) 871-6656 Fax 7355

CALIFORNIA

KTQX 90.5 FM
BAKERSFIELD, CA

AMERICAN INDIAN CABLE TV
9500 Artesia Blvd. • BELLFLOWER, CA 90706
    (310) 920-7227 ext. 22

KPFA, KPFB, KFCF 94.1 FM
BERKELEY, CA

KZFR - 90.1 FM
CHICO, CA 95929
    Mark Franco, Host & Producer
    Rick Wilson, Co-producer
Pow Wow Highway.

KIDE - 91.3 FM
Hoopa Tribal Broadcasting Co.
P.O. Box 1220 • HOOPA, CA 95546
    (916) 625-4245 Fax 625-4594
    Frank Starkey, Acting Manager
The first and only Native owned and operated radio station in California. Owned by Hoopa Valley Tribe. Noncommercial station.

THE AMERICAN INDIAN HOUR
American Indian Liberation Crusade
4009 S. Halldale Ave. • LOS ANGELES, CA 90062
    (213) 299-1810; Dr. Henry E. Hedrick, President
The radio voice of the American Indian Liberation Crusade (see National Associations section.) Broadcasts on 17 radio stations across the country.

NATIVE AMERICAN MEDIA
1015 Gayle Ave., Suite 1024
LOS ANGELES, CA 90024
    (310) 475-6845
    Mike Roberts

KPFA - 94.1 FM
International Indian Treaty Council
2390 Mission St., Suite 301
SAN FRANCISCO, CA 94117-1836
    (415) 566-0251 Fax 566-0442
Living on Indian Time. Weekly news show.

KPOO - 89.5 FM
P.O. Box 11008 • SAN FRANCISCO, CA 94101
    (415) 346-5373
Red Voices of Native Nations. Tuesday, 7:00 PM.

COLORADO

KRZA - 88.7 FM
ALAMOSA, CO

KGNU - 88.5 FM PUBLIC RADIO
P.O. Box 885 • BOULDER, CO 80306
    (303) 449-4885 Fax 447-9955
    Theresa Halsey, Host & Producer
    Sam Fuqua, News & Public Affairs Director
    E-mail: halsey@bvsd.k12.co.us
    Web site: kgnu.org/indianvoices
Program: "Indian Voices" airs weekly from 3-4pm on Sundays dealing with local and national American Indian news, interviews, along with traditional and contemporary music, reaching Denver, Boulder, Fort Collins, and Ward, Colorado. Maintains a music library of American Indian music. Program started 1983.

KSJD - 91.5 FM
CORTEZ, CO

KUVO 89.3 FM
alter • NATIVE VOICES
Path of the Sun Images
P.O. Box 11443 • DENVER, CO 80211
    (303) 477-8442 Fax 291-0757
    Z. Susanne Aikman, Host/Producer
    E-mail: producer@alternativevoices
Program: alter • NATIVE VOICES on American Indian Radio on Satellite network. Live every Sunday mornings from 7-8 a.m. on Denver's Public Radio, KUVO.FM 89.3. American Indian woman-owned independent design and production company. Features traditional and contemporary American Indian music, live interviews, news briefs, health reports and legislative updates as well as announcing local events and events of interest all across the country. Begun 1992.

KSUT - 91.3 FM
Southern Ute Tribe
P.O. Box 737 • IGNACIO, CO 81137

(303) 563-0255 Fax 563-0396
Carlos Sena, Manager
Noncommercial station.

IDAHO

KISU - 91.1 FM
POCATELLO, ID

ILLINOIS

WLUW - 88.7 FM
CHICAGO, IL

MAINE

WQDY - AM/FM
281 Main St.
CALAIS, ME 04619

WRKD - AM
415 Main St.
ROCKLAND, ME 04841

MICHIGAN

WLNZ - 89.7 FM
LANSING, MI

MINNESOTA

KAXE - 91.7 FM
GRAND RAPIDS, MN

FIRST AMERICAN TELEVISION, INC.
MINNEAPOLIS , MN 55408
 (612) 825-9525
 Lynne C. Gray, President
Produces weekly television programs: "First Americans
Journal," "Indian News Network," "Sovereignty On Our
Own Terms," "Native American Forum."

FIRST PERSON RADIO
Migizi Communications
3123 E. Lake St., Suite 200
MINNEAPOLIS, MN 55406
 (612) 721-6631

WUSA - TV
1113 W. Broadway
MINNEAPOLIS, MN 55411
 Mark Houle, Contact

**RED LAKE CHIPPEWA TRIBAL
COUNCIL RADIO PROJECT**
RED LAKE, MN 56671
 (218) 679-3331
 Francis Downwind, Contact
Native American Radio Project.

KTCA-TV Channel 2
172 E. 4th St. • ST. PAUL, MN 55101
 (612) 646-4611
 Susan Robeson, Director
Native American TV Program. Tom Beaver, Host.

MISSISSIPPI

WHTV (CABLE TV)
Mississippi Band of Choctaw Indians
P.O. Box 6010
PHILADELPHIA, MS 39350
 (601) 656-5251

MONTANA

KGVA - 88.1 FM
Fort Belknap Reservation
RR 1, Box 66 • Harlem, MT 59526
 Will Gray, Jr., Station Manager
 Brian Hammett, Radio announcer

KHMT - Channel 4
445 S. 24th St. W., Suite 404
BILLING, MT 59102
 (406) 652-7366 Fax 652-6963
 Ronald S. Holt & Muriel One Bear-Holt, Principals
American Indian-owned TV station seving the Crow
and Cheyenne Reservations.

NATIVE VOICES PUBLIC TELEVISION
VCB Rm. 222, Montana State University
BOZEMAN, MT 59717
 (406) 994-6218 Fax 994-6545
E-mail: hart@sesame.kusm.montana.edu
Web site: www.kusm.montana.edu/nativevoices/

BLACKFEET MEDIA
Blackfeet Tribe, P.O. Box 850
BROWNING, MT 59417
Native-American Radio Project.

KBFT - FM
P.O. Box 819 • BROWNING, MT 59417

KFBB - TV Channel 5
P.O. Box 1139 • GREAT FALLS, MT 59401
 (406) 453-4377
 Darnell Doore, Contact
Program: Native-American TV Program.
On the Air 4th Sunday of each month at 11:30 AM.

1230-AM RADIO
HARDIN, MT 59034
 Sterling Watan, Owner
Recently bought former KKUL-AM radio station. Broad-
casting at 1230 on the AM dial, under new call letters,
will serve Big Horn and Rosebud counties.

KOBL - TV
Dull Knife Memorial College
P.O. Box 98 • LAME DEER, MT 59043
 Ron Holt, Director

KZIN - FM; KSEN 1150 AM
830 Oilfield Ave. • SHELBY, MT 59474
On the Air Monday, Wednesday, and
Friday at 9:10 AM.

NEBRASKA

KCSR - AM
CHADRON, NE 69337
 (308) 432-5545

KZUM - 89.3 FM
AIROS (American Indian Radio on Satellite)
University Television/NAPT
P.O. Box 83111 • LINCOLN, NE 68501
 (800) 571-6885; (402) 472-9333 Fax 472-8675
 John Belindo, Network Manager
Satellite network that serves 25 Native radio stations
and the public radio system in the lower 48 states and
Alaska.

OMAHA CABLE TV SERVICE
Omaha Indian Reservation
P.O. Box 368 • MACY, NE 68039

NEW MEXICO

KABR - 1500 AM
P.O. Box 907 • ALAMO, NM 87825
 (505) 854-2543; Trowen Hulett, Owner
Navajo language.

KNME - TV
1130 University Blvd., NE
ALBUQUERQUE, NM 87102
 Jeffrey Harjo, Contact

KOAT - TV
P.O. Box 25982
ALBUQUERQUE, NM 87125
 Duane Boyd, Contact

KUNM - 89.9 FM
ALBUQUERQUE, NM

CROWNPOINT CABLE TV
CROWNPOINT, NM87313
 (505) 786-5541
Serves the Navajo Nation.

KCIE - 90.5 FM
Jicarilla Apache Tribe
P.O. Box 603 • DULCE, NM 87528
 (505) 759-3681 Fax 759-3005
 Lee Martinez, Jr., Manager
Noncommercial station.

KGLP - 91.7 FM
GALLUP, NM

KABR - 1500 AM
Alamo Navajo School Board
P.O. Box 907 • MAGDALENA, NM 87825
 (505) 854-2632 Fax 854-2641
 Patsy Apachito, Manager
Noncommercial station.

KTDB - 89.7 FM
Ramah Navajo School Board
P.O. Box 40 • PINEHILL, NM 87357
 (505) 775-3215 Fax 775-3551
 Bernie Bustos, Manager
Public radio; talk; ethnic (Indian cultural affairs) news.
Begun 1972.

KSHI - 90.0 FM
P.O. Box 339 • ZUNI, NM 87327
 (505) 782-4811 Fax 782-2700
 Arden Kucate, Manager
Pueblo of Zuni noncommercial station.

NEW YORK

WBAI - FM
505 Eighth Ave.
NEW YORK, NY 10018
 (212) 279-0707
 Jim Buck, Host/Producer
Program: Circle of Red Nations. Weekly one hour
Native American news program. Airs Mondays at 9:00
PM.

CKON - 97.3 FM
Akwesasne Communication Society
P.O. Box 140
ROOSEVELTOWN, NY 13683
 (518) 358-3426 Fax (613) 575-2935
 Kallen M. Martin, General Manager
Mohawk. *Program*: National Native News,
12 noon, 4pm, 8pm daily.

CHANNEL 25 CABLE VISION
Shinnecock Indian Tribe
Box 59, Rte. 27A, Montauk Hwy.
SOUTHAMPTON, NY 11968
 (516) 283-1643
 David Martine, Director
Program: Voices of Native America. Monthly .

NORTH CAROLINA

EASTERN BAND OF CHEROKEE
Indian Cable TV Service
P.O. Box 455 • CHEROKEE, NC 28719

WPSU - TV
Pembroke State University
PEMBROKE, NC 28372

WYRU - 1160 AM
P.O. Box 0711 • RED SPRINGS, NC 28377
(919) 843-5946 Fax 521-8694
Gene Hanrahan, Manager
Lumbee Tribal commercial station.
Religious format. Begun 1970.

NORTH DAKOTA

KEYA - 88.5 FM
Turtle Mountain Chippewa Tribe
P.O. Box 190 • BELCOURT, ND 58316
(701) 477-5686 Fax 477-3252
Michael V. Vann, President
Betty Hanley, Manager
Noncommercial station.

KABU - 90.7 FM
FORT TOTTEN, ND

STANDING ROCK CABLE TV SERVICE
P.O. Box 470 • FORT YATES, ND 58538
(701) 854-3895
Victor & Helen Brave Thunder, Principals

KAEN - 89.5 FM
Standing Rock Sioux Radio Project
P.O. Box D • FORT YATES, ND 58538
(701) 854-7226
Alex Looking Elk, Contact

KMHA - 91.3 FM
Fort Berthold Communications Enterprise
HCR 3, Box 1 • NEW TOWN, ND 58763
(701) 627-3333 Fax 627-4212
Pete Coffey, Jr., Producer
Mandan-Hidatsa-Arikara Native-American
Radio Project.

OHIO

WYSO - 91.3 FM
YELLOW SPRINGS/DAYTON, OH

OKLAHOMA

KIOWA TRIBAL RADIO STATION
P.O. Box 361 • CARNEGIE, OK 73015
(405) 654-2300

KGOU - 106.3 FM
NORMAN/OKLAHOMA CITY, OK

KROU - 105.7 FM
SPENCER/OKLAHOMA CITY, OK

KOTV - TV
302 S. Frankfort • TULSA, OK 74107
George Tiger, Contact

OREGON

KBOO - FM
20 SE 8th Ave.
PORTLAND, OR 97214
(503) 231-8032
Indian World - A radio program which airs Native American music, social events, interviews, poetry, legends, and news which relates to all Indians in North and South America. Airs on Mondays from 8-9 p.m.

**CONFEDERATED TRIBES
TELECOMMUNICATION PROJECT**
P.O. Box 584 • WARM SPRINGS, OR 97761
Native-American Radio Project.
KWSO - 91.9 FM
Warm Springs Confederated Tribes
P.O. Box 489 • WARM SPRINGS, OR 97761
(503) 553-1968 Fax 553-3348
Mike Villalobos, Manager
Warm Springs Confederated Tribes

SOUTH DAKOTA

KLND - 89.5 FM
LITTLE EAGLE, SD

YANKTON SIOUX TRIBE RADIO PROJECT
KONA, Inc. - Marty School
P.O. Box 222 • MARTY, SD 57361
(605) 384-5431
Vince Two Eagles, Coordinator

PINE RIDGE CABLE TV
PINE RIDGE, SD 57770
(605) 867-1166
Non-Native owned but serves the
Pine Ridge Reservation.

KILI - 90.1 FM
Lakota Communications
P.O. Box 150 • PORCUPINE, SD 57772
(605) 867-5002 Fax 867-5634
Melanie Janis, Station Manager
Larry Swalley, Program Director
Wilson Two Lance, Production Coordinator
Native-American Radio Project, noncommercial station, with programming dedicated to providing education, traditions, culture, and entertainment for the people of the Lakota (Sioux) Nation. Focuses on contemporary issues which affect the people such as treaty rights, healthcare, education, attitutdes of sovereignty, environmental issues, among others.

KINI - 96.1 FM
P.O. Box 419 • ST. FRANCIS, SD 57572
(605) 747-2291 Fax 747-5057
Bernard Whiting, Manager
Rosebud Lakota Sioux noncommercial station.

KSWS - 89.3 FM
Dakota Nation Broadcasting Corporation
P.O. Box 142 • SISSETON, SD 57262
(605) 698-7972 Fax 698-7897
Michael James LaBelle, Manager

KUSD - TV
414 E. Clark St.
VERMILLION, SD 57069

SOUTH DAKOTA PUBLIC BROADCASTING
South Dakota Public Radio Network
P.O. Box 5000 • VERMILLION, SD 57069
(605) 677-5861 Fax 677-5010
Tom Sorensen, News Director & Host
Leonard Bruguier, Voices of the Plains' Host
Ross King, Program Director
Programs: South Dakota Forum & Voices of the Plains - A ten-station network producing a variety of news programs, features and call-in talk shows dealing with Native issues. Suggestions for topics are welcome.

TEXAS

KETR FM
P.O. Box 4504 • Commerce, TX 75429
(903) 886-5848 Fax 886-5850
Radio program: Indian Country with Gregg Howard and Noble Hughes. Sunday at 6:30 pm.

UTAH

AMERICAN INDIAN TV SERVICES
Rm 234 - HRCB, BYU • PROVO, UT 84602
Howard Rainer, Contact

KRCL COMMUNITY RADIO STATION 91 FM
208 West 800 South
SALT LAKE CITY, UT84101
(801) 363-1818
Indian programming on Sundays, 7-10 am.

WASHINGTON

TULALIP CABLEVISION
MARYSVILLE, WA 98270
(360) 653-0235

OLYMPIC TV CABLE
P.O. Box 88
PORT ORCHARD, WA 98366

KSFC - 89.3 FM
SPOKANE, WA

QUINAULT TRIBE RADIO PROJECT
P.O. Box 332 • TAHOLAH, WA 98587
(206) 276-4353
Gilbert Thunder Corwin, Coordinator
Commercial station.

KOTY - 1490 AM
TOPPENISH, WA

WISCONSIN

WOJB - 88.9 FM
Lac Court Oreilles Ojibwe Broadcasting Corp.
Rt. 2, Box 2788 • HAYWARD, WI 54843
(715) 634-2100 Fax 634-3906
Camille Lacapa-Morrison, Manager
David Kellar, Program Director
Joan Kozak, Asst. Program Director
Dave Collins, Sherrole Benton, Eric Schubring,
Jeff St. Germaine, Producers
Provides public radio service with 100,000 watt audio production and radio services. *Publication*: Monthly program guide ($10 per year).

WYMS - 88.9 FM
MILWAUKEE, WI

WIRC - FM
University of Wisconsin
216 College of Professional Studies
STEVENS POINT, WI 54481
(715) 346-2746

WYOMING

KIEA - FM
Wind River Indian Education Association
Wyoming Indian High School
ETHETE, WY 82520
(307) 332-2793
Native American Radio Project.

Arranged alphabetically by publication title, this section lists those periodicals which deal directly or indirectly with the history, culture, and contemporary issues of the North American Indian and Eskimo.

ABSARAKA
Crow Indian Tribe • Crow Agency, MT 59022

ABSENTEE SHAWNEE NEWS
2025 S. Gordon Cooper • Shawnee, OK 74801

ACTION NEWS
P.O. Box 607 • New Town, ND 58763

AGUA COUNCIL LETTER
960 E. Tahquitz Wat, Suite 106
Palm Springs, CA 92262

AH-WAH-KO-WA
Yavapai Prescott Indian Tribe
530 E. Merritt • Prescott, AZ 86301
  (520) 445-8790

AHTNA KANAS
Ahtna, Inc., P.O. Box 649
Glennallen, AK 99588
  (907) 822-3476
Bimonthly shareholder newsletter of Ahtna, Inc., the Copper River Native Association.

AICH NEWSLETTER
American Indian Community House
708 Broadway, 8th Floor
New York, NY 10003
  (212) 598-0100
Reports on activities of the organization, which serves the needs of Native Americans residing in the New York metropolitan area. News and reviews of interest to American Indians. 5x/yr. Donations requested. Begun 1969.

AISES EDUCATION NEWSLETTER
American Indian Science & Engineering Society
P.O. Box 9828 • Albuquerque, NM 87119-9828
  (505) 765-1052 Fax 765-5608
Quarterly.

AK-CHIN O'ODHAM RUNNER NEWS
Ak Chin Indian Reservation
42507 Peters & Nall Rd. • Maricopa, AZ 85239
  (602) 568-2095 Cyndee Justus, Editor
Monthly newspaper includes articles, photos, puzzles and recipes provided by Ak-Chin members. Articles deal with events that pertain to the people of Ak-Chin Indian community. Advertising accepted. No charge. Begun 1986.

AKWE:KON PRESS
American Indian Program
Cornell University, 400 Caldwell Hall
Ithaca, NY 14853
  (607) 255-4308 Fax 255-0185

AKWESASNE NOTES
Mohawk Nation, P.O. Box 868
Hogansburg, NY 13655
  (518) 358-3326 Fax 358-3488
Web site: www.slic.com/~mohawkna/mnnotes.htm
Teresa David, Publisher
Douglas M. George - Kanentiio, Editor
Covers news by and about indigenous people in the Americas: poetry, cultural essays, book reviews, current event lists, pow-wows, conferences, and letters. Bimonthly tabloid. 12,000 cir. $15/year. Complimentary copies, exchanges. Microfilm/fiche available. Begun 1968.

ALAMO NEWSLETTER
Alamo Navajo High School
P.O. Box 907 • Magdalena, NM 87825

ALASKA FEDERATION OF NATIVES (AFN) NEWS
1577 C St. #100 • Anchorage, AK 99501
  (905) 274-3611
Julia E. Kitka, Editor
Monthly newsletter.

ALASKA GEOGRAPHIC
The Alaska Geographic Society
P.O. Box 93370 • Anchorage, AK 99509-3370
  (907) 562-0164 Fax 562-0479
Penny Rennick, Editor
Pattey Mancini, Contact
E-Mail: akgeo@anc.ak.net
Deals with the culture, history or region of Alaska or northwestern Canada including extensive coverage of Alaska's native peoples. Quarterly magazine. 8,000 cir. $49/year; prices of individual issues vary. Free catalog available.Begun 1968.

ALASKA STATE MUSEUM NEWSLETTER
Pouch FM • Juneau, AK 99811
  (907) 465-2901

ALEXIC ISAAC
K Y U K - TV
P.O. Box 468 • Bethel, AK 99559

ALLIGATOR TIMES
Seminole Tribe
6073 Stirling Rd. • Hollywood, FL 33024
Monthly Seminole news.

ALMANACK
Plimoth Plantation
Wampanoag Indian Program
P.O. Box 1620 • Plymouth, MA 02362
  (508) 746-1622 FAX 830-6026
Nanepashemet, Editor
Membership newsletter.

AMERICA'S EAGLE
Electronic periodical
Web site: www.alphacdc.com/eagle/

AMERICAN ANTHROPOLOGICAL ASSOCIATION NEWSLETTER
4350 N. Fairfax Dr. #640 • Arlington, VA 22203
  (703) 528-1902
Published ten times per year.

AMERICAN ANTHROPOLOGIST
American Anthropological Association
4350 N. Fairfax Dr. #640
Arlington, VA 22203
  (703) 528-1902
Janet Dixon Keller, Editor
Devoted to cross-field and theoretical articles; book reviews. Quarterly journal. 9,000 cir. $85/year. Advertising. Began 1889.

AMERICAN ANTIQUARIAN SOCIETY NEWSLETTER
185 Salisbury • Worcester, MA 01609
  (617) 755-5221

AMERICAN CHEROKEE CONFEDERACY NEWSLETTER
619 Pine Cone Rd.
Albany, GA 31705-6906
  (229) 787-5722
Prin. Chief William "Rattlesnake" Jackson, Editor
Covers tribal events. Quarterly , 4-page newsletter . Advertising accepted. Began 1976.

AMERICAN ETHNOLOGIST
American Anthropological Association
4350 N. Fairfax Dr. #640
Arlington, VA 22203
  (703) 528-1902
Don Brenneis, Editor
Concerned with 'ethnology' in the broadest sense; book reviews. Quarterly journal. 3,000 cir. $50/year. Advertising. Began 1974.

THE AMERICAN HISTORICAL REVIEW
American Historical Association
400 A St., SE • Washington, DC 20003
  (202) 544-2422
Published five times per year.

AMERICAN INDIAN
Telecommunications Corporation
P.O. Box 333 • Lapwai, ID 83540

AMERICAN INDIAN & ALASKA NATIVE MENTAL HEALTH RESEARCH JOURNAL
American Indian & Alaska Native Programs
University of Colorado Health Sciences Center
Dept. of Psychiatry
Nighthorse Campbell Native Health Bldg.
P.O. Box 6508, Mail Stop F800
Aurora, CO 80045-0508
  (303) 724-1414 Fax 724-1474
Spero M. Manson, PhD, Editor
Web site: www.uchsc.edu/sm/ncaianmhr
Provides better understanding of current mental health issues and concerns of Native Americans and Alaska Natives. Began 1987.

AMERICAN INDIAN/ALASKA NATIVE TRADERS DIRECTORY
Arrowstar Publishing, P.O. Box 427
Englewood, CO 80151 (303) 231-6599
Published annually. Began 1985.

AMERICAN INDIAN ART MAGAZINE
7314 East Osborn Dr., Suite B
Scottsdale, AZ 85251
  (602) 994-5445
Mary G. Hamilton, Publisher
Roanne P. Goldfein, Editor
Mary B. O'Halloran, Editorial
Quarterly art journal devoted exclusively to the art forms of the American Indian. Art forms are presented by full-color photographs and articles written by leading scholars in the field. Also includes book and exhibition reviews, legal news, auction listings, and listings of major museum and gallery exhibitions. 30,000 circulation. $6/copy. $20/year; $24/year, foreign. Advertising. Began 1975.

AMERICAN INDIAN ART REGISTRY NEWSLETTER
1717 N. Highland Ave. #614
Los Angeles, CA 90028-4497

AMERICAN INDIAN BASKETRY MAGAZINE
P.O. Box 66124 • Portland, OR 97266
  (503) 233-8131
John M. Gogol, Ed. & Publisher
Quarterly. Contains articles, book reviews, and lists of new exhibits; sponsors research and communications in the study of American Indian basketry. 5,000 cir. $7/copy; $30/year. Advertising. Began 1979.

AMERICAN INDIAN COMMUNITY SERVICES — DIRECTORY
NAES College Press
2838 W. Peterson • Chicago, IL 60659

AMERICAN INDIAN COURTLINE
NAICCA/Arrow, Inc.
1000 Connecticut Ave., NW #1206
Washington, DC 20036

AMERICAN INDIAN CULTURAL RESOURCES: A PRESERVATION HANDBOOK
Oregon Commission on Indian Affairs
454 State Capitol • Salem, OR 97310
  (503) 378-5481

AMERICAN INDIAN CULTURE & RESEARCH JOURNAL
University of California, Los Angeles
American Indian Studies Center
3220 Campbell Hall, Box 951548
Los Angeles, CA 90095-1548
  (310) 206-7508 Fax 206-7060
Duane Champagne, Editor
E-mail: aiscpubs@ucla.edu
Web site: www.sscnet.ucla.edu/esplaiscl/index.html
An interdisciplinary research forum for scholars and innovators in the areas of historical and contemporary American Indian life and culture. Book reviews; essays, poems, and monographs. Quarterly. $25/individuals; $60/institutions; foreign, add $10. Advertising accepted. Began 1971.

AMERICAN INDIAN GRADUATE RECORD
4520 Montgomery Blvd., NE, Suite 1-B
Albuquerque, NM 87109
  (505) 881-4584
Oran LaPointe & Lorraine Edmo, Editors

This newsletter describes graduate opportunities for American Indians and Alaska Natives. No subscription price since it is usually circulated to students, Indian higher education programs and those who are interested in contributing to the organization. Published once or twice per year. Began 1972.

AMERICAN INDIAN HORSE NEWS
American Indian Horse Registry
Route 3, Box 64 • Lockhart, TX 78644
(512) 398-6642 Nanci Falley, Editor
Quarterly breed publication of the AIHR.

AMERICAN INDIAN JOURNAL
Institute for the Development of Indian Law
2600 Summit Dr. • Edmond, OK 73034-5984
Lynn Kickingbird, Editor
Contains scholarly articles on American Indian history and law, as well as articles of current interest in Indian affairs. Book reviews. Quarterly. 350 cir. $13/copy; $50/year. Advertising. Began 1971.

AMERICAN INDIAN LAW REVIEW
University of Oklahoma Law Center
300 Timberdell Rd. • Norman, OK 73019
(405) 325-2840 Fax 325-6282
Tina Fowler & Jamelle King, Editorial Advisors
This semiannual journal documents and analyzes legal, cultural, and historical issues of interest to Native American communities. Includes articles by legal professionals and scholars, notes written by students, and recent developments in the federal courts on American Indian issues. Book reviews. Advertising. *Contest*: The American Indian Law Writing Competition. $20/year. Back copies available from William S. Hein & Co. by calling toll-free (800) 828-7571.

AMERICAN INDIAN LAW NEWSLETTER
American Indian Law Center
University of New Mexico-School of Law
1117 Stanford Dr., NE, P.O. Box 4456
Albuquerque, NM 87196 (505) 277-5462
Published irregularly.

AMERICAN INDIAN LAWYER
TRAINING PROGRAM NEWSLETTER
American Indian Resource Institute
319 MacArthur Blvd. • Oakland, CA 94610
(510) 834-9333 Fax 834-3836

AMERICAN INDIAN LIBRARIES NEWSLETTER
American Indian Library Association
School of Library and Information Studies
University of Oklahoma, 401 W. Brooks
Norman, OK 73019
(405) 325-3921 Fax 325-7648
Rhonda Taylor, Editor
Contains information of interest to those interested in library services to Native Americans in the U.S. and Canada. Includes news, items of interest, reviews, advertisements, and Association information. Quarterly newsletter. 1,500 Cir. $10 membership in Association for individuals, $5, students, $25, institutions. Send subscriptions to: Joan Howland, Law Library, University of Minnesota, 229 19th Ave. S., Minneapolis, MN 55455. Began 1976.

AMERICAN INDIAN NEWS
Office of Native American Programs
P.O. Box 217 • Fort Washakie, WY 82514

AMERICAN INDIAN QUARTERLY
orders to: University of Nebraska Press
233 North 8th St. • Lincoln, NE 68588
(800) 755-1105 Fax (800) 526-2617
(402) 472-3584 (outside U.S.)
Submissions to: Devon A. Mihesuah, Editor
Dept. of Applied Indigenous Studies
Northern Arizona University
P.O. Box 15020 • Flagstaff, AZ 86011
E-mail: aiquarterly@nau.edu
Website: www.jan.ucc.nau.edu/~mihesuah
A quarterly interdisciplinary journal of Native American Studies including the history, anthropology, literature, and the arts of Native North America. Book reviews. Published quarterly. AIQ is a peer-reviewed academic journal with a circulation of 1,200. $30/year, individuals; $75/year, institutions; single issue, $18. Advertising. Begun 1979.

AMERICAN INDIAN REHABILITATION
American Indian Rehabilitation
Research & Training Center
Institute for Human Development
Northern Arizona University
CU Box 5630 • Flagstaff, AZ 86011
(520) 523-4791 Fax 523-9127
Dr. Timothy Thomason, Editor
Web site: http://www.nav.edu/~ihd
Quarterly newsletter covering the activities of the Center, which aims to improve the lives of American Indians with disabilities. Contains articles on rehabilitation. No charge. Begun 1983.

AMERICAN INDIAN REPORT
The Falmouth Institute, Inc.
3702 Pender Dr. #300 • Fairfax, VA 22030
(800) 992-4489; (703) 352-2250 Fax 352-2323
Marguerite Carroll, Editor
E-mail: mcarroll@falmouthinst.com
Web site: www.falmouthinst.com
A monthly magazine focusing on national issues, financial news, law, environmental news, education, health, news and isues affecting American Indians and Alaska natives. $49.95, annual subscription. A complimentary issue is available upon request. Begun 1985.

AMERICAN INDIAN RESOURCE
CENTER NEWSLETTER
Los Angeles County Public Library
6518 Miles Ave. • Huntington Park, CA 90255

AMERICAN INDIAN REVIEW
Twin Light Trail, 11 The Mews
79-81 Turnpike Ln.
London N8 OED England
011 44 181 340-3618

AMERICAN INDIAN SERVICES DIRECTORY
NAES College Press
2838 W. Peterson • Chicago, IL 60659-3813
(312) 761-5000 Ronald Bowan, Editor
Florence Dunham, Publisher

AMERICAN INDIAN SOCIETY NEWSLETTER
American Indian Society of Washington, DC
P.O. Box 6431 • Falls Church, VA 22040
(703) 914-0548
Jay Hill, Editor
Web site: www.tuscaroras.com/ais/
Community newsletter which reports on Indian life in Washington, DC metro area. It features a calendar of coming events of interest to local Indians. Monthly. 650 cir. $8/year. Limited advertising. Accepts material for review. Begun 1966.

AMERICAN INDIAN STUDIES NEWSLETTER
University of Minnesota
Dept. of American Indian Studies
102 Scott Hall, 72 Pleasant St. SE
Minneapolis, MN 55455

AMERICAN JOURNAL OF ARCHAEOLOGY
Archaeological Institute of America
675 Commonwealth Ave.
Boston, MA 02215 (617) 353-9361
Quarterly. Professional archaeological journal with book reviews on New World archaeology.

AMERICAN NATIVE PRESS
American Indian & Alaska Native
Newspapers & Periodicals Resources
2801 S. University • Little Rock, AR 72204
(501) 569-3160
Dan Littlefield, Editor
Native American book reviews. Quarterly newsletter. 1,100 cir. Began 1983.

AMERICAN QUARTERLY
American Studies Association
307 College Hall, University of Pennsylvania
Philadelphia, PA 19104-6303
(215) 898-6252 Janice Radway, Editor
Contains scholarly articles on various aspects of American culture. Advertising. Published six times per year; last issue of year contains book reviews. Subscription: $30/year (libraries).

AMERICAN WEST
Buffalo Bill Memorial Association
Buffalo Bill Historical Center
P.O. Box 1000 • Cody, WY 82414
(307) 587-4771
Published six times per year.

AMERICANS BEFORE COLUMBUS
National Indian Youth Council
318 Elm St., SE • Albuquerque, NM 87102
(505) 247-2251 Fax 247-4251
Sherry Robinson
Covers tribal rights and values through education and litigation. Bimonthly newsletter. Free to members; $20/year to non-members.

AN-CHI-MO-WIN
Rocky Boys Reservation
Chippewa Cree Tribe • Box Elder, MT 59521

ANICA NEWS HIGHLIGHTS
Alaska Native Industries
4634 E. Marginal Way South
Seattle, WA 98101

ANISHINAABE NEWS
Native American Studies Program
UW-College of Letters & Sciences
P.O. Box 413 • Milwaukee, WI 53201

ANISHINAABEG TODAY
White Earth Reservation Tribal Council
P.O. Box 418 • White Earth, MN 56591
(218) 983-3285 Norma L. Felty, Editor
Website: www.whiteearth.com

ANTHROPOLOGICAL LINGUISTICS JOURNAL
Indiana UniversitY
Dept. of Anthropology-Student Bldg. 130
Bloomington, IN 47405
(812) 855-1203
Douglas R. Parks, Editor
Published jointly with the American Indian Studies Research Institute.

ANTHROPOLOGICAL LITERATURE: AN INDEX
TO PERIODICAL ARTICLES & ESSAYS
Tozzer Library-Harvard University
Cambridge, MA 02138
Quarterly index that provides access to scholarly articles on Native Americans.

ANTHROPOLOGICAL PAPERS
OF THE UNIVERSITY OF ALASKA
Dept. of Anthropology
University of Alaska, 310 Eielson
Fairbanks, AK 99775
(907) 474-7288 Fax 474-7720
Linda J. Ellana, Ph.D., Editor
Articles dealing with northern socio-cultural anthropology and archaeology. Semiannually. $8/issue. Begun 1956.

ANTHROPOLOGICAL PAPERS OF THE
AMERICAN MUSEUM OF NATURAL HISTORY
Central Park West at 79th St.
New York, NY 10024
Contains the current reports of the Museum's Department of Anthropology.

THE APACHE SCOUT
Mescalero Apache Tribe
P.O. Box 227 • Mescalero, NM 88340

ARCHAEOLOGICAL CONSERVANCY
NEWSLETTER
415 Orchard Dr. • Santa Fe, NM 87501
(505) 982-3278
Published quarterly.

ARCHAEOLOGY MAGAZINE
135 William St. • New York, NY 10038
(212) 732-5154
Peter A. Young, Editor
Provides consistent treatment of the archaeology of North and South American Indians; book reviews on the art and archaeology of the Americas. Bimonthly by the Archaeological Institute of America. Subscrip-

tion, $20 per year; $26, foreign; $3.95 each issue. All subscriptions to Box 50260, Boulder, CO 80321. Advertising.

ARIZONA TRIBAL DIRECTORY
Arizona Commission on Indian Affairs
1400 W. Washington St. #300
Phoenix, AZ 85007
(602) 542-3123 Fax 542-3223
Eleanor Descheeny-Joe, Executive Director
Diane C. Dankerl, Editor
Indian tribes and associations, government agencies and other organizations concerned with Indian affairs in Arizona. Annual.

ARROW
Labre Indian School
P.O. Box 406 • Ashland, MT 59003
(406) 784-2347

ARROW NEWS
Mandaree Day School
P.O. Box 488 • Mandaree, ND 58757
(701) 759-3311

ARTIFACTS
The Institute for American Indian Studies
38 Curtis Rd., P.O.Box 1260
Washington Green, CT 06793
(203) 868-0518 Alberto C. Meloni, Director
Quarterly membership magazine.

ARTS & CULTURE OF THE NORTH
Box 1333, Gracie Square Station
New York, NY 10028 (212) 879-9019
Newsletter devoted to Eskimo art and culture. Back issues available. Publication ceased end of 1984.

ARTWINDS
Institute of American Indian Arts
83 Avan Nu Po Rd. • Santa Fe, NM 87508
(505) 988-6440 Fax 988-6448
Quarterly.

ASSOCIATION OF AMERICAN INDIAN PHYSICIANS—NEWSLETTER
1235 Sovereign Row #C-7
Oklahoma City, OK 73108 (405) 946-7072
Quarterly.

ASSOCIATION OF CONTRACT TRIBAL SCHOOLS - (ACTS) NEWSLETTER
c/o St. Francis Indian School
P.O. Box 379 • St. Francis, SD 57572
(605) 747-2296
Monthly.

ATOKA INDIAN CITIZEN
P.O. Box 160 • Atoka, OK 74525

ATTAN-AKAMIK
Rankikus Rd., Box 225
Rankokous, NJ 08073

AU-AUTHM ACTION NEWS
Salt River Tribal Office
10005 E. Osborn • Scottsdale, AZ 85256
(602) 941-7333

AWARENESS INFORMATION
Nez Perce Nuclear Waste Program
P.O. Box 305 • Lapwai, ID 83540

B

BAH-KHO-JE JOURNAL
P.O. Box 190 • Perkins, OK 74059

THE BEAVERTAIL TIMES
P.O. Box 721 • Cass Lake, MN 56633
(218) 335-2538 Anne Dunn, Contact
Monthly.

BEAVER TRAILS
Coos, Lower Umpqua & Siuslaw Tribe
533 Buchanan • Coos Bay, OR 97420

BERING STRAITS AGLUKTUK
Bering Straits Native Corporation
P.O. Box 1008 • Nome, AK 99762

BILLINGS INDIAN NEWSLETTER
Billings American Indian Council
208 N. 29th St. #228 • Billings, MT 59101
(406) 248-3343

BISHINIK
Choctaw Nation of Oklahoma
P.O. Drawer 1210 • Durant, OK 74702
(405) 924-8280 Fax 924-1150
Judy Allen, Editor
Monthly tribal newspaper.

BIZHII
Cibecue Community School
101 Main St., P.O. Box 80068
Cibecue, AZ 85911 (520) 332-2480
Student magazine. Published four times per year.

BLACKFEET TRIBAL NEWS
Blackfeet Media
P.O. Box 850 • Browning, MT 59417

BOIS FORTE NEWS
P.O. Box 16 • Nett Lake, MN 55772

BOOKS INTERNATIONAL
3739 Canyon Dr. • Rapid City, SD 57702
(605) 343-6064 (phone & fax)
Ray Gowan, Editor & Publisher
A newspaper format catalog featuring over 800 Indian books. Semiannual. $2.00. Begun 1989.

BOSTON INDIAN CENTER NEWSLETTER
105 S. Huntington Ave. • Jamaica Plain, MA 02130
(617) 232-0343

BTIR TRIBAL NEWSLETTER
Burns Paiute Reservation
HC 71, 100 Pa Si Go St. • Burns, OR 97720

BUFFALO TRACKS
Intertribal Bison Coop
P.O. Box 8105 • Rapid City, SD 57709

BULLHEAD
2205 Moore St. • Ashland, KY 41101
Joe Napora, Editor
Poetry, prose and graphics, focusing on the Serpent Mounds of Ohio. 52 pp.

BUREAU OF CATHOLIC INDIAN MISSIONS NEWSLETTER
2021 H St., NW • Washington, DC 20006
(202) 331-8542 Fax 331-8544
Covers news and concerns of the Bureau, especially those issues pertaining to the Catholic Church and the Indian community. Updates on legislation affecting the Indian community. 10x/yr. No charge. Begun 1977.

BUREAU OF INDIAN AFFAIRS RESEARCH BULLETIN
Indian Education Center
615 1st St., Box 26567
Albuquerque, NM 87125-6567

BUREAU OF INDIAN AFFAIRS TRIBAL NEWSLETTER
Phoenix Area Office
Box 10, 1 N. 1st St. • Phoenix, AZ 85001

BUYERS GUIDE TO PRODUCTS MANUFACTURED ON AMERICAN INDIAN RESERVATIONS
U.S. GPO • Washington, DC 20402
(202) 275-3314

C

THE CABAZON CIRCLE
Cabazon Band of Mission Indians
84-245 Indio Springs Dr. • Indio, CA 92203
(619) 342-2593 Fax 347-7880
Tribal newsletter.

CAHOKIAN
Cahokia Mounds Museum Society, Publisher
30 Ramey St. • Collinsville, IL 62234
(618) 344-7316
Chris Pallozola, Editor
Newsletter.

CALIFORNIA INDIAN BASKETWEAVERS ASSOCIATION NEWSLETTER
16894 China Flats Rd. • Nevada City, CA 95959
(916) 292-0141
E-mail: ciba@oro.net
Quarterly.

CALIFORNIA NATIONS INDIAN GAMING INTERNET NEWSLETTER
Website: www.pechanga.net

CALISTEM ERINI
Calista Corporation
601 W. 5th St. #200 • Anchorage, AK 99501

THE CALUMET
United Southern & Eastern Tribes
711 Stewarts Ferry Pike, #100
Nashville, TN 37214
(615) 872-7900 Fax 872-7417
James T. Martin, Executive Director
Bimonthly newsletter.

CAMP CRIER
Fort Belknap Agency
RR 1, Box 66 • Halem, MT 59526

CAREER DEVELOPMENT OPPORTUNITIES FOR NATIVE AMERICANS
B.I.A-Bureau of Higher Education
P.O. Box 26567 • Albuquerque, NM 87125
(505) 766-3131
Mary F. Asbill, Editor

CAREER PATH
P.O. Box 9505 • Moscow, ID 83843
(208) 882-4726 E-mail: careers@moscow.com
Tribal employment newsletter

CAROLINA INDIAN VOICE
P.O. Box 1075, College Plaza
Pembroke, NC 28372
(919) 521-2826
Connie Brayboy, Editor
Community newspaper to give Indians in North Carolina (and other minorities) a united voice to be heard from coast to coast. Weekly. $12/year in NC; $15/year, elsewhere. Advertising accepted. Begun 1973.

CASINO CRIME DIGEST
The Falmouth Institute, Inc.
3702 Pender Dr., Suite 300
Fairfax, VA 22030
(800) 992-4489; (703) 352-2250 Fax 352-2323
Linda Clark, Editor
E-mail: lclark@falmouthinst.com
Web site: www.falmouthinst.com
Monthly newsletter summarizing news relevant to the casino industry. Contains reports from casinos of the latest cheats, scams, security breaches and legal issues that impact casinos. $129 per year.

CATCHING THE DREAM NEWSLETTER
8200 Mountain Rd. NE Suite 203
Albuquerque, NM 87110
(505) 262-2351
Dr. Dean Chavers, Editor
Triannual newsletter includes updates on federal legislation and association activities. Price- included in membership dues. Advertising accepted. Begun 1988.

CENTER FOR INDIAN EDUCATION NEWSLETTER
302 Farmer Education Bldg., Rm. 302
Arizona State University
Tempe, AZ 85287

CENTER FOR THE STUDY OF EARLY MAN — CURRENT RESEARCH
University of Maine
495 College Ave.
Orono, ME 04473

**THE CENTER FOR WESTERN
STUDIES NEWSLETTER**
Box 727, Augustana College
Sioux Falls, SD 57197
(605) 336-4007 Fax 336-5447
Arthur R. Huseboe, Executive Director
Contains articles describing the programs of the Center, which often focus on Native Americans, specifically Sioux culture. Announces research projects, exhibits, and publications by or about Sioux Indians. Published 3x/year. Membership, $40.

CHAR-KOOSTA
Confederated Salish and Kootenai Tribes
P.O. Box 278 • Pablo, MT 59855-0278
(406) 675-3000 Fax 675-2806
Ron Bick, Editor
Weekly newspaper featuring news of interest to Native Americans focusing on memerbs of the Confederated Salish and Kootenai Tribes, Montana and reservation reisdents. Book reviews. 3,900 circ. $18/year, local; $20/year, in state; $25/year, out-of-state; $45/year, foreign. Advertising. Begun 1957.

CHEHALIS NEWSLETTER
P.O. Box 536 • Oakvilke, WA 98568

CHEMAWA AMERICAN
Chemawa Indian School
5495 Chugach St., NE
Chemawa, OR 97303

CHEMAWA CHATTER
Indian Health Service
Chemawa Indian Health Center
3750 Chemawa Rd. NE • Salem, OR 97305
(503) 399-5931

CHEROKEE ADVOCATE
Cherokee Nation Communications Dept.
P.O. Box 948 • Tahlequah, OK 74465-0948
(918) 456-0671 Fax 456-6136
Lynn Adair, News Bureau Manager & Editor
E-mail: lyadalr@cherokee.org
Web site: www.cherokee.org
Tribal newspaper contains information on programs, services, etc. regarding and tribal government of the Cherokee Nation. Book reviews. Monthly newspaper. 90,000 circ. $12.50/year in-state, and $15/year out-of-state. Advertising. Begun 1977.

CHEROKEE BOYS CLUB NEWSLETTER
P.O. Box 507 • Cherokee, NC 28719
(704) 497-5001 Fax 497-5818
Joy Evans-Widenhouse, Editor
E-Mail: ccfs@dnet.net
Quarterly newsletter containing general information about the services and educational programs of the Club, as well as certain community information about the Qualla Boundary of the Eastern Band of Cherokee Indians. 2,500 circ. Begun 1965.

CHEROKEE MESSENGER
The Cherokee Cultural Society of Houston
P.O. Box 1506 • Houston, TX 77402
(713) 668-9998 Fax 668-0153
E-mail: dpscott@neosoft.com

CHEROKEE ONE FEATHER
Eastern Band of Cherokee Indians
P.O. Box 501 • Cherokee, NC 28719-0501
(704) 497-5513
Richard Welch, Editor
Pat Taylor, Circulation Manager
Provides information on tribal policies and news. Book reviews. Weekly tabloid. 2,000 circ. $20/yr. Advertising. Begun 1966.

CHEROKEE VOICE
Cherokee Boys Club, Inc.
P.O. Box 507 • Cherokee, NC 28719
(704) 497-5001 Fax 497-5818
Joy Evans-Widenhouse, Editor
E-Mail: ccfs@dnet.net
A newsletter providing information about the human services programs of the Cherokee Center for Family Services which is a department of the Club.

CHEYENNE AND ARAPAHO BULLETIN
Cheyenne and Arapaho Tribes
P.O. Box 38 • Concho, OK 73022
(800) 247-4612; (405) 262-0345 Fax 262-0745
Monthly tribal newsletter.

CHEYENNE RIVER AGENCY NEWS BULLETIN
Eagle Butte, SD 57625

**CHICAGO'S NATIVE AMERICAN
URBAN INDIAN RETREAT**
1819 W. Wilson Ave. • Chicago, IL 60640
(773) 561-1336 Fax 561-1331
Joseph Peralez, Chairperson
Quarterly newsletter of the organization.

CHICKASAW TIMES
Chickasaw Nation Tribal Government
P.O. Box 1548 • Ada, OK 74821-1548
(405) 436-2603
Emil Farve, Pub./Editor
Contains information on tribal goals, operations, procedures, services, accomplishments, or opinions of Chickasaw citizens. Book reviews. Monthly newspaper. 8,500 cir. Begun 1970.

CHIEF YAHWEH NEWSLETTER
Box 351 • Zeigler, IL 62999
Jim Bauer, Publisher
Begun 1999.

CHIEFS GAZETTE
Box 145, Lander Rt. • Ethete, WY 82520

CHOCTAW COMMUNITY NEWS
Mississippi Band of Choctaw Indians
Box 6010-Choctaw Branch
Philadelphia, MS 39350
(601) 656-5251 Julie Kelsey, Editor
Monthly tribal newspaper containing articles; primarily concerned with local events which involve Mississippi Choctaws. Book reviews. 5,000 cir. Limited advertising. Free subscription by request, donations accepted. Begun 1970.

**CHOCTAW PRODUCTIONS
& CABLE PROGRAMMING**
Mississippi Band of Choctaw Indians
Rt. 7, Box 21
Philadelphia, MS 39350-9807
(601) 656-5251

THE CIRCLE
Boston Indian Council
105 S. Huntington Ave.
Jamaica Plain, MA 02130-4799
(617) 232-0343
Helen Blue, Editor
Monthly newspaper containing information on urban Indians, particularly in the Boston area, as well as significant events involving Native peoples in New England and throughout the U.S. and Canada. Book reviews. 5,000 circ. $10/yr. Advertising. Begun 1976.

THE CIRCLE
The Circle Corp.
P.O. Box 6026 • Minneapolis, MN 55406
(612) 722-3686 Fax 722-3773
Catherine Whipple, Managing Editor
E-mail: circlempls@aol.com
Website: www.thecirclenews.org
Monthly tabloid size newspaper covering the news and events of the Native Americans in Minnesota. Includes reviews of books, movies, arts, etc. 15,000 circ. Advertising accepted. Begun 1979.

COCOPAH NEWSLETTER
P.O. Box G • Somerton, AZ 85350
(520) 627-2102

COEUR D'ALENE COUNCIL FIRES
Coeur D'Alene Tribal Council
Plummer, ID 83851

COKTV TVLEME
Seminole Nation of Oklahoma
P.O. Box 1498 • Wewoka, OK 74884

COLORADO HISTORY NEWS
Ute Indian Museum, Ouray Memorial Park
P.O. Box 1736 • Montrose, CO 81402
Glen Gross, Editor

THE COLUMNS
Cherokee National Historical Society
P.O. Box 515 • Tahlequah, OK 74465
(918) 456-6007 Fax 456-6165
Tom Mooney, Editor
Website: http://powersource.com/
powersource/heritage
Quarterly newsletter.

COMANCHE
Comanche Tribe of Oklahoma
P.O. Box 908 • Lawton, OK 73502
Tribal newspaper.

THE COMMUNICATOR
Migizi Communications, Inc.
3123 E. Lake St., Suite 200
Minneapolis, MN 55406
(612) 721-6631 Fax 721-3936
Laura Wittstock, Director

COMMUNIQUE
Order of the Indian Wars
P.O. Box 7401 • Little Rock, AR 72217
(501) 225-3996
Jerry L. Russell, Editor
Monthly newsletter.

COMMUNITY BULLETIN
American Indian Community House
708 Broadway, 8th Floor
NEW YORK, NY 10003
(212) 598-0100 Fax 598-4909
Website: www.aich.org
Rosemary Richmond & Carrese P. Gullo, Editors
Quarterly newsletter. Reports on activities of the organization, which serves the need of Native Americans residing in the New York metropolitan area. News and reviews of interest to Native Americans. Circulation: 12,000+. *Price*: Donations accepted.

CONFEDERATED INDIAN TRIBES
Washington State Penitentiary
P.O. Box 520 • Walla Walla, WA 99362

**CONFEDERATED TRIBES OF COOS,
LOWER UMPQUA & SIUSLAW INDIANS -
TRIBAL NEWSLETTER**
338 Wallace Ave. • Coos Bay, OR 97420
(503) 267-5454
Monthly.

**CONFEDERATED TRIBES OF SILETZ-
SPRINGFIELD AREA OFFICE NEWS**
188 West B St., Bldg. P
Springfield, OR 97477
(503) 746-9658

CONFEDERATED UMATILLA JOURNAL
P.O. Box 638 • Pendleton, OR 97801

CONTEMPORARY INDIAN AFFAIRS
Navajo Community College
Tsaile, AZ 86556

THE CORNPLANTER
Rhode Island Indian Council
444 Friendship St. • Providence, RI 02907

THE COUNCIL
Tanana Chiefs Conference
122 1st Ave. • Fairbanks, AK 99701

COUNCIL DRUM NEWS
Grand Valley American Indian Lodge
2512 Union Ave. NE
Grand Rapids, MI 49505
(616) 361-5380
Monthly newsletter.

COUNCIL FIRES
Coeur D'Alene Tribal Council
Plummer, ID 83851

COUNCIL FOR AMERICAN INDIAN MINISTRY
122 W. Franklin • Minneapolis, MN 55404

COUNCIL FOR MINORITY EDUCATION NEWS
470 Oregon Hall, University of Oregon
Eugene, OR 97403

COUNCIL OF ENERGY RESOURCE TRIBES (CERT) REPORT
695 S. Colorado Blvd., Suite 10
Denver, CO 80246
　(303) 282-7576 Fax 282-7584
　A. David Lester, President

COUNCIL SIGNALS
Montana Dept. of Indian Affairs
1218 E. 6th Ave. • Helena, MT 59620

COYOTE ON THE TURTLE'S BACK
Institute of American Indian Arts
College of Santa Fe Campus
83 Avan Nu Po Rd. • Santa Fe, NM 87503
　(505) 988-6463
Published annually.

CRAFTS: AMERICAN INDIAN PAST & PRESENT
Written Heritage
P.O. Box 1390 • Folsom, LA 70437
　(800) 301-8009; (504) 796-5433 Fax 796-9236
　Jack Heriard, Editor
　E-Mail: whiswind@i-55.com
Annual journal covering American Indian crafts and material culture. 7,000 cir. $7/copy. Begun 1988.

CRAZY HORSE PROGRESS
Crazy Horse Memorial Foundation
Avenue of the Chiefs—The Black Hills
Crazy Horse, SD 57730-9506
　(605) 673-4681
　Robb DeWall, Editor
Published 3x/year. No charge.

CREEK NATION NEWS
Creek Nation of Oklahoma
P.O. Box 580 • Okmulgee, OK 74447

CRIT NEWSLETTER
Colorado River Indian Tribes
Rte. 1, Box 23-B • Parker, AZ 85344
　(602) 669-9211 Fax 669-5675
Quarterly tribal newsletter.

CRITFC NEWS
729 NE Oregon St.
Portland, OR 97232
　(503) 238-0667

CROSS & FEATHERS
Tekakwitha Conference National Center
P.O. Box 6768 • Great Falls, MT 59406
　(406) 727-0147 Fax 452-9845
　Website: www.tekconf.org
　E-mail: tekconf@att.net
　Sister Kateri Mitchell, S.S.A., Executive Director
Staff: Wilson Boni, Billie Jo Moore, Terri Jarvey, and Christine Collins. Description: Five times annual newsletter containing articles addressing religious, social, and legislative issues concerning Native American Catholics or people involved with the blessed Kateri Tekakwitha (a Mohawk who lived from 1656 to 1680, and who is now a candidate for Sainthood in the Roman Catholic Church.) Also includes reports on workshops, conferences, and meetings. $10, membership. Begun 1979.

CROW NEWS
Crow Tribal Government
P.O. Box 400 • Crow Agency, MT 59022

CROWNDANCER
San Carlos Apache Tribe
P.O. Box 0 • San Carlos, AZ 85550

CULTURAL NOTES
Indian Arts & Crafts Board,
Rm. 4004, U.S. Dept. of the Interior
Washington, DC 20240 (202) 208-3773

CULTURAL SURVIVAL QUARTERLY
96 Mt. Auburn St. • Cambridge, MA 02138
　(617) 441-5400 Fax 441-5417
　Maria Tocco, Managing Director
International advocate for the human rights of indigenous peoples. Includes news, resources, and general-interest articles. $5/issue.

CURRENT ANTHROPOLOGY
Wenner-Gren Foundation
220 Fifth Ave. • New York, NY 10001
　(212) 683-5000
Bimonthly journal.

CURTIS (CARL T.) HEALTH CENTER NEWS
Omaha Indian Reservation
P.O. Box 368 • Macy, NE 68039

CUSTER BATTLEFIELD NATIONAL MONUMENT NEWSLETTER
P.O. Box 39 • Crow Agency, MT 59022
　(406) 638-2622
Published quarterly.

D

DAKOTA WOWAPIPHI
P.O. Box 157 • Marty, SD 57361

DARTMOUTH NATIVE ALUMNI NEWS
P.O. Box A-162 • Hanover, NH 03755

DAYBREAK STAR INDIAN READER
P.O. Box 99100 • Seattle, WA 98199
　(206) 285-4425 Fax 282-3640
　Kathryn Onetta, Director
A 24-page, monthly (October through May) children's learning resource featuring culturally focused articles of interest to students in grades 4-6. Includes creative writing exercises, games and puzzles, legends, math and science activities, book and movie reviews. See publisher for multiple copy rates.

DE-BAH-JI-MON
P.O. Box 308 • Cass Lake, MN 56633

DEER TRACKS
Deer Clan of Louisiana
3303 E. 133th Ter. #B
Kansas City, MO 64137
　(816) 761-3801
　Tall Oka, Editor

DELAWARE NEWSLETTER
P.O. Box 825 • Anadarko, OK 73005

DENVER NATIVE AMERICANS UNITED NEWSLETTER
4407 Morrison Rd. • Denver, CO 80219
　(303) 937-0401

DESERT CONNECTIONS
American Indian Professional Training Program in Speech-Language Pathology & Audiology
Dept. of Speech & Hearing Sciences
University of Arizona • Tucson, AZ 85721
　(602) 621-1969/1644
　Betty Nunnery, Program Coordinator
A network publication for Native American speech-language pathologists and audiologists.

DINE BI KEYAH MAGAZINE
P.O. Box 580 • Window Rock, AZ 86515

DIRECTORY OF AMERICAN INDIAN BUSINESSES
National Center for American Indian Enterprise Development
953 E. Juanita Ave. • Mesa, AZ 85204
　(800) 462-2433; Fax (602) 545-4208
　Ken Robbins, Editor
Annual.

DIRECTORY OF NATIVE AMERICANS IN SPEECH-LANGUAGE PATHOLOGY & AUDIOLOGY
American Indian Professional Training Program in Speech-Language Pathology & Audiology, Dept. of Speech & Hearing Sciences
University of Arizona • Tucson, AZ 85721
　(602) 621-1969/1644
　Betty Nunnery, Program Coordinator

DOMESTIC ABUSE IS NOT AN INDIAN TRADITION
Ne-Naiah-Kaha-Kok
P.O. Box 82 • Keshena, WI 54135
　(715) 799-4398

THE DRAGONFLY
Two Rivers Gallery
Minneapolis American Indian Center
1530 E. Franklin Ave.
Minneapolis, MN 55404
　Sammy Watso & Mason Riddle, Directors
A cultural arts department newsletter.

THE DREAM CATCHER
Northern Plains Healthy Start
Berkshire Plaza, Suite 205
Aberdeen, SD 57401
　(605) 229-3846 Fax 229-6893
Quarterly newsletter.

DREAM CATCHER QUARTERLY
HUD Northwest Office of Native American Programs
909-1st Ave., Suite 300 • Seattle, WA 98104
　(206) 220-5273 E-mail: jan_engle@hud.gov
　Web site: www.codetalk.fed.us/dremcach.html

THE DREAM WEAVER
Tribal American Network (TAN)
P.O. Box 542231 • Dallas, TX 75354
　(214) 296-9431

THE DRUMBEAT
Confederated Tribes of Siletz-Salem Area Office
3789 River Rd. N. Suite D
Keizer, OR 97303
　(503) 390-9494
Monthly newsletter.

DSUQ' WUB' SIATSUB
Suquamish Tribe
P.O. Box 498
Suquamish, WA 98392

DUCK VALLEY ROUNDUP
P.O. Box 219 • Owynee, NV 89832

DUWAMISH TRIBAL NEWSLETTER
Duwamish Tribe
140 Rainier Ave. S., #7
Renton, WA 98055-2000
　(206) 226-5185 Fax 226-5240

DWOQ'WUB'STATSUB
Suquamish Tribe, P.O. Box 498
Suquamish, WA 98392-0498

DXWHIIDA
National Coalition to Support Indian Treaties
814 N.E. 40th St. • Seattle, WA 98105

E

E'YANAPAHA
Devil's Lake Sioux Tribe
Public Information Office
Fort Totten, ND 58335

THE EAGLE
P.O. Box 2372
Marysville, CA 95901
　(916) 633-4038
Bimonthly. Published by the Cherokees of California.

EAGLE BUTTE NEWS
P.O. Box 210 • Eagle Butte, SD 57625

EAGLE FREE PRESS
Phoenix Indian Center, Inc.
333 W. Indian School Rd.
Phoenix, AZ 85013-3215
　(602) 256-2000

THE EAGLE WHISTLE
North American Indian Center of Boston
105 S. Huntington Ave. • Jamaica Plain, MA 02130
(617) 232-0343 Fax 232-3863
Bi-monthly newsletter containing information relevant both to Native Americans living in the New England area and throughout the U.S. and Canada. Pow-wow listings.

EAGLE'S EYE
Brigham Young University
Multicultural Student Services
1320 WSC • Provo, UT 84602
(801) 378-5877 Fax 378-2630
Harold D. Nez, Editor
E-mail: eagleseye@byu.edu
Web site: www.byu.edu/stlife/campus-life/
multi/eagle.html
Magazine published each semester for Native American and other mutlicultural students at BYU. Book reviews. 3,500 circ. Free upon request. Begun 1967.

EAGLE'S NEST
Native American Fish & Wildlife Society
750 Burbank St. • Broomfield, CO 80020
(303) 466-1725 Fax 466-5414
Ken Poynter, Executive Director
E-Mail: nafws@usa.net
Newsletter.

EAGLE'S VOICE
Sinte Gleska College
Box 8 • Mission, SD 57555
(605) 856-2321
Contains literature on Native American experiences on the High Plains. Text also in Lakota. Begun 1975.

EARLY SITES RESEARCH SOCIETY NEWSLETTER
c/o James Whittall, Archaeology Director
Long Hill • Rowley, MA 01969
(617) 948-2410
Published bimonthly.

EARTH WALK
Council for Native American Indian Progress
280 Broadway, #316 • New York, NY 10007
(212) 732-0485
Newsletter.

EARTHSONG
The Heard Museum
2301 N. Central Ave. • Phoenix, AZ 85004
(602) 252-8840 Fax 252-9757
Rebecca Murray, Editor
Web site: www.heard.org
Newsletter targeted at Museum members. Content includes articles on upcoming exhibitions and events, as well as behind-the-scenes features on museum happenings. Published five times a year.

ECH-KA-NAV-CHA NEWSLETTER
Fort Mojave Indian Tribe
500 Merriman Ave. • Needles, CA 92363
(619) 326-4810

ECHO—TOWAOC COMMUNITY NEWSPAPER
Ute Mountain Ute Tribe
Towaoc, CO 81334
(970) 565-3751

EL PALACIO
Museum of New Mexico
Box 2087 • Santa Fe, NM 87504-2087
(505) 827-6794
Karen Meadows, Editor
Articles on anthropology, archaeology, fine arts, folk arts, Southwest history and geography. Book reivews. Triannual magazine. 3,000 cir. $6/copy; $18/year. Begun 1913.

ELDER VOICES
National Indian Council on Aging
10501 Montgomery Blvd. NE #210
Albuquerque, NM 87111-3846
(505) 888-3302 Fax 888-3276
Larry Curley, Editor
Covers issues affecting Native American elders, including services and related legislative issues. Published periodically. Begun 1977.

ELKO COMMUNITY NEWS
Nevada Intertribal Council
806 Holman Way • Sparks, NV 89431
(702) 355-0600

ENTERPRISE EYAPAHA
P.O. Box 363
Manderson, SD 57756

ETHNIC REPORTER
National Association for Ethnic Studies
Dept. of English, Arizona State University
Tempe, AZ 85287-0001
(602) 965-3391 Fax 965-1093
Gretchen Bataille, Editor
Covers NAES activities. Semiannual newsletter. $35/year, individuals; $45/year, institutions; $5/copy. Advertising. Begun 1975.

ETHNOHISTORY
American Society for Ethnohistory
Published by Duke University Press
Durham, NC 27708
(919) 688-5134 Fax 688-5474
Website: www.duke.edu/web/dupress/
Shepard Krech, III, Editor
Studies of native peoples in the Americas and throughout the world. Quarterly journal. 1,200 cir. $34/year, institutions; $21, individuals. Begun 1953.

EYAPAHA
American Indian Center Newsletter
4115 Connecticut • St. Louis, MO 63116
(314) 773-3316

EYAPIOAYE
Assiniboine and Sioux Tribes
P.O. BOX 1027 • Poplar, MT 59255

F

FAIRBANKS NATIVE ASSOCIATION NEWSLETTER
201 First Ave. • Fairbanks, AK 99701
(907) 452-1648
Monthly newsletter.

FAMILY SERVICES NEWSLETTER
Family Services Program
Toiyabe Indian Health Project
P.O. Box 1296 • Bishop, CA 93515
(619) 873-6394 Fax 873-3935
Focuses on concerns of Indian families, such as drugs and alcohol, child abuse and neglect, and women's concerns. Quarterly. No charge. Begun 1980.

FEATHER REVIEW
P.O. Box 149
Mountain View, OK 73062
(405) 347-2875
Deborah Ahtone, Editor/Publisher
Monthly state wide Indian and government agencies newspaper. $15/year.

FIREWEED
Many Walks Medicine Council Band
of Free Cherokees
P.O. Box 54 • Stony Creek, NY 12878
(518) 693-3180

FIRST NATIONS BUSINESS ALERT
First Nations Development Institute
The Stores Bldg., 11917 Main St.
Fredericksburg, VA 22408
(540) 371-5615 Fax 371-3505
Quarterly newsletter providing business news about and of interest to tribes. No charge to tribes; $12/year, others. Advertising.

FIVE CIVILIZED TRIBES MUSEUM NEWSLETTER
Agency Hill on Honor Heights
Muskogee, OK 74401
(918) 683-1701

FIVE FEATHERS NEWS
Tribe of Five Feathers
P.O. Box W • Lompoc, CA 93436

FIVE TRIBES JOURNAL
Five Civilized Tribes Foundation
c/o Chickasaw Nation
P.O. Box 1548 • Ada, OK 74820

FLAGSTAFF INDIAN CENTER NEWSLETTER
2717 N. Steves Blvd. #11
Flagstaff, AZ 86004

FLANDREAU SPIRIT
Flandreau Indian High School
Flandreau, SD 57028

THE FLOWERING TREE NEWSLETTER
Good Medicine Band (Free Cherokees)
HC 62 Box 378 • Old Joe, AR 72658
(501) 499-8083
Grandmother Alloday, Contact
Quarterly.

FOCUS: INDIAN EDUCATION
Minnesota Department of Education
Capitol Square Bldg. • St. Paul, MN 55101

FOLKLIFE CENTER NEWS
American Folklife Center
The Library of Congress
Washington, DC 20540
(202) 707-6590
Provides information about current projects; and lists current publications. Quarterly newsletter.

FOND DU LAC NEWS
105 University Dr.
Cloquet, MN 55720

FORT APACHE SCOUT
White Mountain Apache Tribe
P.O. Box 890 • Whiteriver, AZ 85941
(520) 338-4813 Fax 338-1894
Kathy Antonio, Office Manager
Biweekly newspaper covering news of the tribe and its people. 2,800 cir. $10/year to Reservation residents; $12 in Arizona offf Reservation; $18, outside Arizona. Advertising. Begun 1962.

FORT BERTHOLD COMMUNITY ENTERPRISE
P.O. Box 699 • New Town, ND 58763

FORT McDOWELL NEWSLETTER
Southwestern Marketing
P.O. Box 18244 • Fountain Hills, AZ 85269
(602) 837-4282 Fax 837-7750
E-mail: swmarke@aol.com

FOUNDATION FOR INDIAN
LEADERSHIP NEWSLETTER
P.O. Box 5335 • Santa Fe, NM 87502
(505) 988-6291

FOUR DIRECTIONS
3315 University Dr.
Bismarck, ND 58763
(701) 255-3285

THE FOUR DIRECTIONS:
AMERICAN INDIAN LITERARY MAGAZINE
Snowbird Publishing Co.
P.O. Box 729 • Tellico Plains, TN 37385
(423) 253-3680
Joanna & William Meyer, Editors
Contains all-Native American authored poetry, short stories, essays and articles. Reviews. Published irregularly. $6/issue. Begun 1992.

FOUR DIRECTIONS FOR
PEACE & MEDICINE LODGE
Council for Native American Indian Progress
280 Broadway #316 • New York, NY 10007
(212) 732-0485
Newsletter.

FOUR WINDS
Hundred Arrows Press
P.O. Box 156 • Austin, TX 78767
(512) 472-8877/956-7048
Quarterly magazine focusing on Native American art, literature and history. $22/year.

FOUR WINDS NEWSLETTER
Confederated Indian Tribes
Washington State Penitentiary
P.O. Box 520 • Walla Walla, WA 99362

THE FREE CHEROKEE NEWSLETTER
Wild Potato Band of Free Cherokees of Mass.
P.O. Box 385 • Feeding Hill, MA 01030
(413) 785-5912
Chief Rainbow Newmoon Shootingstar

FROM THE EAGLE'S NEST
750 Burbank St. • Broomfield, CO 80020
(303) 466-1725

G

GALLERY NOTES
The Indian Museum
Mid-America All Indian Center
650 North Seneca • Wichita, KS 67203
Quarterly newsletter.

GAMYU
Hualapai Tribe
P.O. Box 179 • Peach Springs, AZ 86434
(520) 769-2216

GILA RIVER INDIAN NEWS
P.O. Box 459 • Sacaton, AZ 85247
(520) 562-3311

GILCREASE JOURNAL
Thomas Gilcrease Museum Association
1400 Gilcrease Museum Rd.
Tulsa, OK 74127-2100
(918) 596-2700 Fax 596-2770
Carol Haralson, Editor
E-mail: gilcreas@ionet.net
Web site: www.gilcrease.org
Features stories concerning the art, artifacts, and archival materials of the Gilcrease Museum. Includes
photographic and artistic reproductions from the collections. The collections emphasize the Old West and
the American Indian. Semiannual. 4,500 cir. $50/year
membership; $18/copy; $35/year for libraries. Begun
1958.

GREAT PLAINS JOURNAL
Institute of the Great Plains
Museum of the Great Plains
P.O. Box 68 • Lawton, OK 73502
Contains articles concerning the history, archaeology,
ecology or natural history of the ten-state Great Plains
region. Published annually.

GREAT PLAINS QUARTERLY
Center for Great Plains Studies
Univ. of Nebraska, 1214 Oldfather Hall
P.O. Box 880313 • Lincoln, NE 68588-0313
(402) 472-6058 Fax 472-0463
Charlene Porsild, Editor
E-Mail: gpq@unlinfo.unl.edu
Web site: www.unl.edu/plains/gpq.htm
A scholarly, interdisciplinary journal that publishes refereed articles in the geography, history, literature, anthropology, ethnology, folklore, fine arts, sociology, and
political science of the Great Plains region of the U.S.
and Canada. Book reviews. Advertising accepted. Subscription: Individuals: U.S. - $25/year, $48/2 years;
Canada - $34/year; $60/2 years; Overseas - $38/year,
$72/2 years. Institutions: U.S. $50/year, $90/2 years;
Canada - $60/year, $110/2 years; Overseas - $70/year,
$130/2 years. $5 (single issue). Complimentary copies available. Begun 1981.

GREAT PLAINS RESEARCH
Center for Great Plains Studies
University of Nebraska, 1215 Oldfather Hall
Lincoln, NE 68588-0317
(402) 472-6970 Fax 472-0463
Svata M. Louda, Editor
E-Mail: gpr@unlinfo.unl.edu
Web site: www.unl.edu/plains/gpr.htm
A biannual multidisicplinary journal, publishes creative
syntheses and original scholarly papers in the natural

and social sciences dealing with issues of regional concern. It includes reports on symposia and conferences
and reviews of books. U.S. - $25/year, individuals; $50,
institutional; Canada - $30/year, individuals, $55, institutional; other foreign - $35/year, individuals, $60,
institutional. Complimentary copies available.

GREAT PROMISE MAGAZINE
1103 Hatteras • Austin, TX 78753
A magazine for Indian children, grades 5-8.

**GREATER LOWELL INDIAN CULTURAL
ASSOCIATION—NEWSLETTER**
551 Textile Ave. • Dracut, MA 01826

GTB NEWS
Grand Traverse Band of Ottawa & Chippewa Indians
2605 NW Bay Shore Dr. • Suttons Bay, MI 49682
(616) 271-3538 Fax 271-4861
Monthly tribal newsletter. Free to member households
in the tribe's service area; available $12/one year sub-
scription to members out of service area.

H

HARVARD INDIAN NEWSLETTER
Native American Program
Graduate School of Education
Harvard University • Cambridge, MA 02138

**HASKELL INDIAN JUNIOR COLLEGE
LEARNING RESOURCE CENTER NEWSLETTER**
P.O. Box H1305 • Lawrence, KS 66044

HEALING OUR HEARTS
National Association for Native American
Children of Alcoholics
Seattle, WA 98101
(206) 467-7686 Fax 467-7689
Anna M. Latimer, Editor
Quarterly newsletter. 5,000 cir.
No charge for members.

HEALTH NOTES
St. Croix Chippewas of Wisconsin
St. Croix Tribal Center
P.O. Box 287 • Hertel, WI 54845

**HEART OF AMERICA INDIAN
CENTER NEWSLETTER**
1340 E. Admiral Blvd. • Kansas City, MO 64124
(816) 421-7608

HELLO CHOCTAW
P.O. Box 59 • Durant, OK 74701

HISTORICAL ARCHAEOLOGY
Society for Historical Archaeology
P.O. Box 30446 • Tucson, AZ 85751
(724) 438-7789 Fax 438-9348
E-Mail: sha-editor@cup.edu
Web Site: www.sha.org
Ronald L. Michael, Editor
Quarterly journal containing articles on theoretical perspectives, comparative studies, artifact and site analyses, as well as book reviews. The main focus is on
the era since the beginning of European exploration.
$40/students; $75/individuals; $105/institutions, annual
membership dues. Begun 1967.

HO CHUNK WO-LDUK
Wisconsin Winnebago Business Committee
133 Main St. • Black River Falls, WI 54615
(715) 284-2388 Fax 284-7852

HOPI TU-TU-VEH-NI
P.O. Box 123 • Kykotsmovi, AZ 86039
(520) 734-2441 ext. 190 Fax 734-6648

HOW NI KAN
Citizen Band Potawatomi Tribe
1901 S. Gordon Cooper
Shawnee, OK 74801
(405) 275-3121
Patricia Sulcer, Editor
Monthly tribal newsletter. Subscription:. $6/year.

I

ICE (INDIAN CINEMA ENTERTAINMENT)
American Indian Film Institute
333 Valencia St., Suite 322
San Francisco, CA 94103
(415) 554-0525 Fax 554-0542
Quarterly. $25 per year.

IKHANA
Office of Native American Ministries
The Episcopal Church Center
815 Second Ave.
New York, NY 10017
(800) 334-7626
Warren Anderson, Contact
The newsletter of American Indian/Alaska Native Ministry of the Episcopal Chuech. Focuses on American
Indian affairs. Informs readers of programs and
projects of the Committee and other groups affiliated
with the Episcopal Church. Quarterly. No charge. Begun 1979.

IMPACT
Public Information Division of Save the Children
54 Wilton Rd.
Westport, CT 06881
(203) 221-4000
Lee Mullane, Editor
Published quarterly.

IN HARMONY
Institute for the Study of Natural Systems
P.O. Box 637
Mill Valley, CA 94942
(415) 383-5064
Semiannual newsletter including articles on the pres-
ervation of Native American sacred sites. 8,000 cir.
$15/year. Begun 1987.

INDEPENDENT AMERICAN INDIAN REVIEW
4801 S. Lakeshore Dr. #200
Tempe, AZ 85282
(602) 839-8355 Fax 839-8223
Quarterly magazine.

**INDEX TO REPRODUCTIONS
IN ART PERIODICALS**
Data Arts, P.O. Box 30789
Seattle, WA 98103-0789
Quarterly index to reproductions in in art periodicals
for American Indian arts, African arts, arts of Asia, and
art in America. $44/year. Begun 1987.

INDIAN AFFAIRS
Association on American Indian Affairs
966 Hungerford Dr., Suite 12-B
Rockville, MD 20850
(240) 314-7155 Fax 314-7159
Jack F. Trope, Executive Director
E-mail: aaia@tnics.com
Web site: www.indian-affairs.org
Covers current news about and of interest to Ameri-
can Indians and to those interested in Indian affairs.
Published three times a year with occasional special
issues. 45,000 cir. $25/year. Begun 1949.

INDIAN AFFAIRS NEWSLETTER
Bureau of Indian Affairs
1951 Constitution Ave., NW
Washington, DC 20245

INDIAN ARIZONA TODAY
IDDA, 4560 N. 19th Ave. #200
Phoenix, AZ 85015-4113

INDIAN ARTIFACT MAGAZINE
Indian Artifact Magazine, Inc.
RD #1, Box 240
Turbotville, PA 17772
(717) 437-3698
Gary L. Fogelman, Editor
Concentrates on American Indain pre-history: artifacts,
tools, lifestyles, customs, archaeology, tribes, etc. Book
reviews included. Published quarterly. Advertising ac-
cepted. $17/year. Sample, $5. Begun 1982.

IACA NEWSLETTER
Indian Arts & Crafts Association
4010 Carlisle NE, Suite C
Albuquerque, NM 87108
(505) 265-9149 Fax 265-8251
Helen Skredergard, Editor
Contains information on markets, meetings, new members, applications, and other news of interest to those in the industry; helps in the education of consumers. Advertising accepted from members only. Published monthly for IACA members and a limited press list. Begun 1974.

INDIAN AWARENESS CENTER NEWSLETTER
Fulton County Historical Society
37 E 375 N • Rochester, IN 46975
(574) 223-4436
Shirley Willard, Editor
Covers projects and activities of the Center which encourages the awareness, appreciation, and preservation of Native American culture and traditions, especially that of the Potawatomi and Miami Indians of northern Indiana. Had Potawatomi Trail of Death" declared a Regional Historic Trail by the state legislatures of Indiana, Illinois, Missouri and Kansas (see Association listing). Quarterly. $10 per year. Begun 1984.

INDIAN BUSINESS & MANAGEMENT MAGAZINE
National Center for American Indian
Enterprise Development
953 E. Juanita • Mesa, AZ 85204
(602) 831-7524 Fax 491-1332
Quarterly.

INDIAN BUSINESS REVIEW
Native American Business Alliance
8435 SE 17th Ave. • Portland, OR 97202
(503) 233-4841
Covers programs and projects of the Alliance and its efforts to promote economic development for all Indians. Quarterly. $10/year; free to members.

INDIAN COMMUNICATIONS
Dovecrest Indian Cultural Center
390 Summit Rd. • Exeter, RI 02822
Monthly newsletter.

INDIAN COUNTRY TODAY
Four Directions Media, Inc.
Corporate & Editorial Headquarters:
3059 Seneca Turnpike • Canastota, NY 13032
(888) 327-1013; (315) 829-8355 Fax 829-8028
Editorial Fax (315) 829-8393
Ray Halbritter, Presdient & CEO
Peter Golia, COO
Tim Johnson, Executive Editor
Jose Barreiro, Senior Editor
Kerri Lis, Managing Editor
E-Mail: editor@indiancountry.com
Web site: www.indiancountry.com
Washington DC Bureau:
400 N. Capitol St., NW, Suite 585
Washington, DC 20001
(202) 783-0212 Fax 393-5218
Description: A weekly newspaper serving 21 Indian reservations in North and South Dakota, Nebraska and Montana. With the addition in 1991 of a Washington, DC bureau, it also covers the U.S. Capitol from an Indian perspective. 25,000 cir. (the largest independent Indian-owned weekly). $48/year, local; $83/year, Canada & Mexico; $227/year, Overseas. Advertising. Began 1980.

INDIAN COUNTRY TODAY
Southwest Branch
1625 Rio Bravo Blvd., Suite 16
Albuquerque, NM 87105
(505) 877-0001 Fax 877-0075

INDIAN COUNTRY TODAY
Northwest Branch
1905 E. Montgomery Ave., Suite 3
Spokane, WA 99206 (509) 921-0512

INDIAN COURTS
National American Indian Court Judges
1000 Connecticut Ave., NW, Suite 1206
Washington, DC 20036 (202) 296-0685
Quarterly newsletter.

INDIAN CRUSADER
American Indian Liberation Crusade, Inc.
4009 S. Halldale Ave. • Los Angeles, CA 90062
(323) 299-1810 Basil M. Gaynor, Editors
Reports on programs to aid Indian reservations. Quarterly. No charge (tax deductible donations accepted.) Begun 1954.

INDIAN EDUCATION
National Indian Education Association
700 N. Fairfax, Suite 210 • Alexandria, VA 22314
(703) 838-2870 Fax 838-1620
John W. Cheek, Executive Director
Robin Butterfield, President

INDIAN EDUCATION NEWS
Coos County Indian Education Coordination Program
9140 Cape Arago Hwy. • Coos Bay, OR 97420
(503) 888-4584

INDIAN EDUCATION NEWSLETTER
United Sioux Tribes of South Dakota
P.O. Box 1193 • Pierre, SD 57501

INDIAN EDUCATION UPDATE
National Indian Training & Research Center
2121 S. Mill Ave. #216 • Tempe, AZ 85282
(602) 967-9484
Quarterly newsletter.

INDIAN, ESKIMO, ALEUT OWNED & OPERATED ARTS BUSINESS SOURCE DIRECTORY
Indian Arts & Crafts Board
Rm. 4004, U.S. Dept. of the Interior
Washington, DC 20240
(202) 208-3773
Published annually.

INDIAN EXTENSION NEWS
New Mexico State University
Box 3AP • Las Cruces, NM 88003

INDIAN FORERUNNER
Eight Northern Pueblos
P.O. Box 927
San Juan Pueblo, NM 87566

INDIAN GAMING MAGAZINE
ArrowPoint Media, Inc.
14205 SE 36th St., Suite 100
Bellevue, WA 98006
(425) 519-3710 Fax 883-7209
Steve Burke, Publisher (425) 885-6997
Website: www.igmagazine.com
E-mail: steveigm@aol.com
Monthly magazine for the industry.

INDIAN HEALTH COMMUNICATOR
5600 Fishers lane, Rm. 6-35
Rockville, MD 20857

THE INDIAN HISTORIAN
American Indian Historical Society
1451 Masonic Ave.
San Francisco, CA 94117
(415) 626-5235
Jeanette Henry, Editor
Back issues of magazines covering American Indian culture and history.

INDIAN HUMAN RESOURCE CENTER, INC. COMMUNITY NEWSLETTER
4040 30th St., Suite A • San Diego, CA 92104
(619) 281-5964 Fax 281-1466
E-mail: ihrc5@onp.wdsc.org
Monthly newsletter which serves the San Diego County American Indian community. Subscriptions: $5/yr., $8/two yrs. Advertising accepted. Begun 1987.

INDIAN LAW REPORTER
American Indian Lawyer Training Program
319 MacArthur Blvd. • Oakland, CA 94610
(510) 834-9333 Fax 834-3836
Patricia Zell, Editor
Christine Miklas, Managing Editor
Legal reporting service reporting current developments in Indian law. Monthly journal. 650 cir. $396/year. Begun 1973.

INDIAN LAW SUPPORT CENTER REPORTER
Native American Rights Fund
1506 Broadway
Boulder, Colorado 80302
(303) 447-8760 Fax 443-7776
Monthly newsletter providing local legal services attorneys with information on developments in the area of Indian law. Includes summaries of recent court decisions in Indian country; Federal Register highlights, and new publications and materials. $36/year.

THE INDIAN LEADER
Haskell Indian Nations University
155 Indian Ave. • Ross Hall, Rm. 122
Lawrence, KS 66046
(785) 749-8477 Fax 749-8408
Theresa Milk, Editor
Glen Gary, Assoc. Editor
E-mail: idnldr@ross1.cc.haskell.edu
Bimonthly publication produced by the students of Haskell Indian Nations University. $15 per year.

INDIAN LIFE NEWSPAPER
Indian Life Ministries
P.O. Box 3765 RPO Redwood Centre
Winnipeg, Manitoba R2W 3R6 Canada
(204) 661-9333 Fax 661-3982
E-Mail: 103100.2735@compuserve.com
Web site: http://www.indianlife.org
James Uttley, Editor
Bimonthly covering culturally relevant material to Native North Americans, evangelistic outreach in content. $7/six issues. 23,000 circ. Begun 1979.

INDIAN MARKET MAGAZINE
Southwestern Association for Indian Arts (SWAIA)
P.O. Box 969 • Santa Fe, NM 87504
(505) 983-5220 Fax 983-7647
E-mail: info@swaia.org
Website: www.swaia.org
Quarterly magazine on the Santa Fe Indian market and other events.

INDIAN NATION NEWS
American Indian Nations Ministries
P.O. Box 70 • Honobia, OK 74579-0070
(918) 755-4570 Fax 755-4577

INDIAN NEWS NOTES
Public Information Office, BIA
1849 C St., NW MS: 1340 MIB
Washington, DC 20240
(202) 208-3710 Fax 501-1516
Biweekly publication of the Bureauof Indian Affairs.

INDIAN NOTES
Museum of the American Indian
Smithsonian Institution
1 Bowling Green • New York 10004
(212) 283-2420 Fax 491-9302
Quarterly newsletter

INDIAN PROGRESS
Associated Committee of Friends on Indian Affairs
P.O. Box 2326 • Richmond, IN 47375-2326
Website: www.acfiaquaker.org
H. Keith Kendall, Executive Secretary
Deboral Lilly, Editor
Quarterly newsletter about the activities of the Committee in Oklahoma, Alabama, and Iowa. Published for those persons interested in Indian affairs and those persons contributing to the Committee. Complimentary copies sent upon written request. Begun 1869.

THE INDIAN RELIC TRADER
P.O. Box 88 • Sunbury, OH 43074
Janie Jinks-Weidner, Editor
Features articles on prehistoric relics, current archaeological findings and research; calendar of events and meetings; sources for books and supplies. Advertising. Subscription: $8/year; sample copies available, $1.00 each.

INDIAN RECORD
Bureau of Indian Affairs
1951 Constitution Ave., NW
Washington, DC 20245

INDIAN REPORT

Friends Committee on National Legislation
245 Second St., NE • Washington, DC 20002
(202) 547-6000 Fax 547-6019
E-mail: fcnl@fcnl.org
Web site: www.fcnl.org
Aura Kanegis, Editor
Quarterly newsletter containing articles focusing on issues and national legislation of interest to American Indians and Alaskan natives. Complimentary copies available upon request. Begun 1977. Native American Legislative Updates (NALU) provides up-to-date information and action suggestions on legislation affecting Native Americans. Distributed bi-weekly when Congress is in session. Available by e-mail, fax, or via FCNL's web page. Hard copy versions are available by mail. These updates supplement the quarterly FCNL Indian Report.

INDIAN TIME

Akwesasne Notes
P.O. Box 868, Mohawk Nation
Hogansburg, NY 13655-0868
(518) 358-9535/9531
Promotes unity for all Mohawk groups through communicating information on the environment, health, women, youth and Iroquois history; also Native American and Canadian news. An eight page weekly newspaper of the St. Regis Mohawk Reservation (New York-Quebec-Ontario.) Advertising. Subscription: $33/year, U.S.; $40/year, Canada. Sample copies, $1.00 each. Begun 1983.

INDIAN TRADER

Indian Trader, Inc.
P.O. Box 1421 • Gallup, NM 87305
(505) 722-6694
Martin Link, Publisher
William Donovan, Editor
E-Mail: trader@cia-g.com
Covers American Indian arts and crafts, cultures and history, contemporary Indian news items, and western Americana. Book reviews. Monthly newspaper. 4,000 cir. $2/copy; $20/year; $32/year, foreign. Advertising. Begun 1969.

INDIAN VOICE

Southwest Indian Polytechnic Institute
P.O. Box 10146 • Albuquerque, NM 87184

INDIAN VOICE, STOWW

P.O. Box 578 • Sumner, WA 98390

INDIAN VOICES

618 E. Carson St., Suite 305
Las Vegas, NV 89101
(702) 382-0808
Rose Davis, Editor/Publisher
E-mail: rdavis4973@aol.com

INDIAN WORLD

3110 State Office Annex
117 University Ave. • St. Paul, MN 55101

INDIGENOUS EYE:
AN INTERNATIONAL QUARTERLY

P.O. Box 612 • Tahlequah, OK 74465
(918) 696-3335

INI-MI-KWA-ZOO-MIN

Minnesota Chippewa Tribe
P.O. Box 217 • Cass Lake, MN 56633
Betty Blue, Editor

INTER-COM NEWSLETTER

Native American Educational Service
2838 W. Peterson Ave. • Chicago, IL 60659
(312) 761-5000
Faith Smith, Editor
Monthly newsletter.

INTER-TRIBAL TIMBER COUNCIL NEWSLETTER

Intertribal Timber Council
4370 NE Halsey St. • Portland, OR 97213

INTER-TRIBAL TIMES NEWSPAPER

Inter-Tribal Council, Inc.
P.O. Box 1308 • Miami, OK 74355

(918) 542-4486 Fax 540-2500
Liz Gaines, Editor
Newakis Burkybile, Advertising
Involves at least seven Northeastern Oklahoma area tribal newsletters, each using a full page to announce their monthly news. Also included is a national, state, and local news that holds intyerest for local tribal members. Monthly. 10,000 circulation in northeastern Oklahoma, Arkansas, Missouri and Kansas. Advertising. Begun 1994.

INTERTRIBAL NATIVE NEWS

219 Manchester St. W.
Battle Creek, MI 49017
Web site: www.mia.org/inn/
News and pow-wow list.

INTERTRIBAL NEWS

Native American Center
Fort Lewis College, College Hts.
Durango, CO 81137
(303) 247-7221 Fax 247-7108
Rick Wheelock, Faculty Sponsor
Indian student tabloid-size newspaper. Published biweekly - Fall & Winter trimesters only. 1,000 cir (approx. 450 Indian students). No charge. Advertising accepted. Limited number of complimentary copies available. Begun 1981.

ISLETA EAGLE PRIDE

Isleta Elementary School
P.O. Box 312 • Isleta, NM 87022
(505) 869-2321
School newspaper.

J

JICARILLA CHIEFTAIN

Jicarilla Apache Tribe
P.O. Box 507 • Dulce, NM 87528-0507
(505) 759-3242 Ext. 224 Fax 759-3005
Mary F. Polanco, Editor; Lori M. Vicenti, Co-Editor
Shane S. Valdez, Computer Specialist
Biweekly newsletter containing information of general importance to tribal members, as well as national and state news pertaining to other tribes and Indian affairs. Book reviews. 1,200 cir. $12/year, local; $24/year, foreign. Advertising. Begun 1960.

JOURNAL OF ALASKA NATIVE ARTS

Institute of Alaska Native Arts
P.O. Box 70769 • Fairbanks, AK 99707
(907) 456-7491 Fax 451-7268
Susheila Khera, Editor
A 10-page quarterly journal containing interviews with Alaska Native artists; news of opportunities of interest to artists; and photographs, poetry and issues affecting Alaska Native artists. 1,400 circ. $25/year.

JOURNAL OF AMERICAN INDIAN EDUCATION

Center for Indian Education
Arizona State University, Box 871311
Tempe, AZ 85287-1311
(602) 965-6292 Fax 965-8115
Dr. Karen Swisher, Editor
Laura Williams & Rick Noguchi, Staff
Publishes papers directly related to the education of North American Indians and Alaskan Natives. Emphasis is on research - basic and applied. Published three times per year (October, January, and May.) Submits five complimentary copies of the Journal to authors of accepted manuscripts. 700 cir. $16/year, U.S.; $18.50/year, Canada & foreign. Available on microfilm from Xerox University Microfilms, 300 North Zeeb Rd., Ann Arbor, Michigan 48106. Begun 1961.

JOURNAL OF ARIZONA HISTORY

Arizona Historical Society
949 E. Second St. • Tucson, AZ 85719
(520) 628-5774 Fax 628-5695
Bruce J. Dinges, Editor
A quarterly history journal containing articles, critical essays, and book reviews on the history of Arizona and the Southwest, and northern Mexico when appropriate. Articles often include appraisals of American Indian life and lore, the Indian wars and Anglo-Indian

relations. 2,400 circulation. Subscription: $40/year. Begun 1960.

JOURNAL OF CALIFORNIA &
GREAT BASIN ANTHROPOLOGY

Dept. of Anthropology, University of California
Riverside, CA 92521-0001
(714) 787-7317
Philip J. Wilke, Editor
Publishes original manuscripts on the ethnography, languages, arts, archaeology, and prehistory of ther Native peoples of California, the Great Basin, and Baja California. Book reviews. Semiannual. $18/year. Advertising. Begun 1974. Back issues may be obtained from Coyote Press, P.O. Box 3377, Salinas, California 93912.

JOURNAL OF CHEROKEE STUDIES

Museum of the Cherokee Indian
P.O. Box 770-A • Cherokee, NC 28719
(704) 497-3481
Duane King, Editor
Published semiannually.

JOURNAL OF THE WEST

Box 1009, 1531 Yuma
Manhattan, KS 66502-4228
(913) 539-1888
Robin Higham, Editor
Covers western history and culture containing articles, book reviews, pieces about the West. A Quarterly. Advertising accepted. $30/year, individuals; $40/year, institutions. Begun 1962.

K

KALIHWISAKS

Oneida Communications
Nobert Hill Center
P.O. Box 365 • Oneida, WI 54415
(414) 490-2452 Fax 490-2453

KANZA NEWS

Drawer 50 • Kaw City, OK 74641

KARIWENHAWI NEWSLETTER

St. Regis Mohawk Reservation
RR 1, Box 8A • Hogansburg, NY 13655
(518) 358-2240
Carol White, Editor
Covers news of the Reservation community and the Akwesasne Cultural Center. Monthly. 1,100 cir. No charge. Began 1970.

KEE-YOKS

Swinomish Tribal Community
P.O. Box 388 • La Conner, WA 98257

KEYAPI NEWS

P.O. Box 200
Ft. Thompson, SD 57339

KIOWA INDIAN NEWS

Kiowa Tribe, P.O. Box 397
Carnegie, OK 73015
(405) 347-2875
Deborah Ahtone, Editor
Monthly tribal newspaper.
No charge to tribal members.

KIOWA VIDEO

Kiowa Nation of Oklahoma
P.O. Box 369 • Carnegie, OK 73015

KIVA: THE JOURNAL OF SOUTHWESTERN
ANTHROPOLOGY & HISTORY

Arizona Archaeological & Historical Society
Arizona State Museum
University of Arizona
Tucson, AZ 85721
(602) 621-4011
Gayle Harrison Hartmann, Editor
Covers original research relating to the prehistoric and historic archaeology and ethnology of the southwestern U.S. and northwestern Mexico. Quarterly. 1,100 cir. $25/year.

KLAH'CHE'MIN
Squaxin Tribal Center
SE 70 Squaxin Lane
Shelton, WA 98584

KLALLAM NEWSLETTER
Port Gamble-Klallam Nation Tribal Council
P.O. Box 280 • Kingston, WA 98346

KLAMATH TRIBUNE
Klamath Tribe, P.O. Box 436
Chiloquin, OR 97624
(541) 783-2219
Monthly tribal newsletter

KO-BUN-DA
Potawatomi Indian Nation (Pokagon Band)
43237 Town Hall Rd. • Dowagiac, MI 49047
(616) 782-6323 Fax 782-9625

KOOTAH
P.O. Box 157
Crow Agency, MT 59022

KROEBER ANTHROPOLOGY SOCIETY PAPERS
Dept. of Anthropology, University of California
Berkeley, CA 94720-0001
(415) 642-6932
Contains original research in all aspects of anthropology and related disciplines; also bibliographies and texts. Biannual journal. 450 cir. $15/copy. Begun 1949.

KUMTUX
Native American Network
419 Occidental South • Seattle, WA 98104
(206) 528-9585 Fax 625-9791
Helen Night Raven, Editor
Monthly calendar of events in Washington State's Indian country. $18/yr. Began 1991.

L

LAC COURTE OREILLES JOURNAL
LCO Graphic Arts
Rt. 2 • Hayward, WI 54843 (715) 634-8934

LAC DU FLAMBEAU UPDATE
LDF Tribal Office, P.O. Box 67
Lac du Flambeau, WI 54538

LAGH'-WEGH A-MOO-E'SHA
Confederated Tribes of the Umatilla
P.O. Box 638 • Pendleton, OR 97801

THE LAKOTA FUND NEWSLETTER
P.O. Box 340 • Kyle, SD 57750
(605) 455-2500
Elsie Meeks, Exec. Director
A fund formed to help build a private sector economy on the Reservation by providing loans and technical assistance & business training; and arts & crafts marketing assistance tribal members.

THE LAKOTA NATION JOURNAL
P.O. Box 3080, Maple Ave. Plaza
105 E. Omaha • Rapid City, SD 57709
(605) 399-1999 Fax 399-1998
Helen Felix-Baca, Sales Rep.
E-mail: sales@lakotanationjournal.com

LAKOTA OYATE-KI
Oregon State Penitentiary
2605 State St. • Salem, OR 97310

LESCHI TRIBUNE
2002 E. 28th St. • Tacoma, WA 98404

LINCOLN INDIAN JOURNAL
Lincoln Indian Center
1100 Military Rd. • Lincoln, NE 68508
(402) 474-5231

LITTLE HOOP COMMUNITY COLLEGE BULLETIN
P.O. Box 269 • Fort Totten, ND 58335
(701) 766-4415 Fax 766-4077

LODGE TALES
American Indian Center of Arkansas
1100 N. University, Suite 133
Little Rock, AR 72207-6344
(501) 666-9032 Fax 666-5875
Paul S. Austin, Director
Quarterly newsletter.

LORE
Friends of the Museum, Inc.
Milwaukee Public Museum
800 West Wells St. • Milwaukee, WI 53233
(414) 278-2752
Published quarterly.

LUMBEE OUTREACH
Lumbee Regional Development Association
P.O. Box 68 • Pembroke, NC 28372
(919) 521-8602 Fax 521-8625

LUMMI INDIAN NEWS
2616 Kwina Rd. • Bellingham, WA 98226
(206) 734-8180
A bi-weekly community newsletter.

M

MAINE INDIAN NEWSLETTER
Maine Indian Affairs Commission
State Health Station No. 38
Augusta, ME 04333

MAKAH DAKAH
P.O. Box 547 • Neah Bay, WA 98357

MAKAH VIEWERS
P.O. Box 115 • Neah Bay, WA 98357

MANASSEH-JOURNAL OF THE TRIBES
Eagle Communications
29 Brimmer St. • Brewer, ME 04412
Reginald Roberts, Jr., Publisher
Quarterly. $24/year.

MANATABA MESSENGER
P.O. Box 810 • Parker, AZ 85344

MANDAN, HIDATSA & ARIKARA TIMES
Three Affiliated Tribes Tribal Council
HC 3, Box 2, Administration Bldg.
New Town, ND 58763
(701) 627-4781 Fax 627-3626

MANIILAQ DIRECTORY
Maniilaq Association
P.O. Box 256 • Kotzebue AK 99752
(907) 442-3311
Marie N. Greene, President
Annual directory of members.

MANUAL OF INDIAN GAMING LAW
The Falmouth Institute, Inc.
3702 Pender Dr., Suite 300
Fairfax, VA 22030
(800) 992-4489; (703) 352-2250 Fax 352-2323
James Casey, Esq., Editor
Web site: www.falmouthinst.com
Addresses virtually every legal, regulatory, administrative and policy issue affecting Indian gaming. Fully indexed and annotated. 2-volume set with 3 updates per year. $484; renewal, $329.

MANY SMOKES METIS/EARTH
Awareness Magazine
Bear Tribe Medicine Society
P.O. Box 9167 • Spokane, WA 99206

MARIN MUSEUM OF THE AMERICAN INDIAN—MUSEUM QUARTERLY
P.O. Box 864, 2200 Novato Blvd.
Novato, CA 94948 (415) 897-4064

MARYLAND AMERICAN INDIAN DIRECTORY
Maryland Commission on Indian Affairs
100 Community Place • Crownsville, MD 21032
(410) 514-7651

MASINAIGAN
Great Lakes Indian Fish & Wildlife Commission
P.O. Box 9 • Odanah, WI 54861
(715) 682-6619
Monthly newspaper.

THE MASTERKEY
Southwest Museum
P.O. Box 41558 • Los Angeles, CA 90041
(213) 221-2164 Fax 224-8223
Steven Le Blanc, Editor
Devoted to the anthropology and archaeology of the Americas; contains articles, book reviews, and a conservation column. Book reviews. Quarterly journal. 5,500 cir. $15/year. Begun 1927.

MAWIW-KILUN
Tribal Governors, Inc.
Indian Township • Princeton, ME 04668
Contains community news, tribal activities, health and social service articles. Published bimonthly.

MAZEENA-IGAN
1305 E. 24th St. So. • Minneapolis, MN 55404
(612) 721-1909
Inter-tribal newspaper.

McKINLEY MISSION NEWSLETTER
American Indian Evangelical Society
P.O. Box 231 • Toppenish, WA 98848

A MEASURE OF EXCELLENCE
Inter-Tribal Indian Ceremonial Association
226 W. Coal Ave. • Gallup, NM 87301
(505) 863-3896
Laurence D. Linford, Editor
A full-color annual publication focusing on each year's top art award-winners at the Ceremonial.

MEADOWLARK COMMUNICATIONS
P.O.Box 7218 • Missoula, MT 59807
(888) 728-2180
Web site: www.powwowcountry.com
Mail order catalog of books and videos.

MEDICINE BAG
Salt LakeCity Indian Health Center
508 East South Temple, No. 219
Salt Lake City, UT 84102 (801) 532-2034

MEDIUM RARE
Native American Journalist Association
1433 E. Franklin, Suite 11
Minneapolis, MN 55404
(612) 874-8833 Fax 874-9007
E-mail: najanut@aol.com

MEETING GROUND
D'Arcy McNickle Center for American Indian History
60 W. Walton St. • Chicago, IL 60610
(312) 255-3564
Harvey Markowitz, Editor
E-Mail: mcnickle@newberry.org
A national biannual newsletter containing information on the Center's activities, research, and teaching materials. 1,000 circ. Begun 1972.

MENOMINEE NATION NEWS
Menominee Indian Tribe
P.O. Box 910 • Keshena, WI 54135
(715) 799-5167/8 Fax 799-5250
Yvonne M. Kaquatosh-Aragon, Editor
Michael Wilber & Llona May, Reporters
E-mail: mnn@mail.wiscnet.net
Web site: www.menominee.com/mnn/home.html
Biweekly tribal newspaper. 1,400 cir. 50¢/copy.
Advertising. Begun 1976.

MICCOSUKEE EVERGLADES NEWS
Miccosukee Tribe of Florida
Box 440021, Tamiami Station
Miami, FL 33144

THE MICHIGAN INDIAN
Michigan Commission on Indian Affairs
P.O. Box 30026 • Lansing, MI 48909
(517) 373-0654 Fax 335-1642
Quarterly newsletter.

MID-AMERICA ALL INDIAN CENTER NEWSLETTER
650 N. Seneca • Wichita, KS 67203
(316) 262-5221 Fax 262-4216
John A. Ortiz, Executive Director
E-Mail: wichita@esc.ttrc.dolteta.gov

MILLE LACS PROGRESS
Goff & Howard, Inc.
255 E. Kellogg Blvd. #102
St. Paul, MN 55101
(612) 292-8062 Fax 292-8091
Bi-annual newspaper for Mille Lacs Band Ojibwe members abd tribal government employees reporting on the Band's successes.

MINNESOTA HISTORY
Minnesota Historical Society
690 Cedar St. • St. Paul, MN 55101
Deals with events, places, and personalities in Minnesota history, often touching upon events related to Minnesota's Indian tribes. Quarterly.

MINO-BIMADIZIWIN
White Earth Land Recovery Project
P.O. Box 327 • White Earth, MN 56591
(218) 573-3448 Fax 573-3444
Quarterly newsletter.

THE MOCCASIN
San Carlos Apache Tribe
P.O. Box 1711 • San Carlos, AZ 85550
(520) 475-2361 Fax 475-2567
Tribal newspaper featuring news about the San Carlos Apache people and its tribal government.

MOCCASIN TELEGRAPH
9 E. Burnam Rd. • Columbia, MO 65203
(573) 817-3301 Fax 817-3244
E-mail: wordcraft@sockets.net
Lee Francis, III, PhD, Editor
Joseph Bruchac, III, Co-Editor
D.L. "Don" Birchfield, Contributing Editor
A monthly news journal for Native writers and storytellers particularly members of Wordcraft Circle of Native Writers and Storytellers. Includes original poetry, fiction, and essays by Native writers. Also reports on writer's conferences and workshops, and profiles of Native authors. $24/yr. $2 for sample copy.

MOHICAN NEWS
Stockbridge-Munsee Tribe
N 8476 Moheconnuck Rd.
Bowler, WI 54416
(715) 793-4111 Fax 793-1307
Tribal news. Biweekly.

MOLE LAKE ENVIRONMENTAL NEWSLETTER
Sokaogon Chippewa Community
Rt. 1, Box 625 • Crandon, WI 54520
(715) 478-7616 Fax 478-7618

MONTANA INTER-TRIBAL POLICY BOARD NEWSLETTER
c/o Roland Kennedy, P.O. Box 850
Browning, MT 59417 (406) 652-3113
Merle R. Lucas, Executive Director

MONTANA, THE MAGAZINE OF WESTERN HISTORY
Montana Historical Society
Roberts & Sixth Ave. • Helena, MT 59601
Deals with Western history, often touching upon the Indian's involvement. Quarterly.

MOUNTAIN LIGHT NEWS & VIEWS FROM THE SOUTHWEST
Southwest learning Centers of Santa Fe
P.O. Box 8627 • Santa Fe, NM 87504
Semiannual.

MUKLUKS HEMCUNGA
Organization of the Forgotten American
P.O. Box 1257 • Klamath Falls, OR 97601

MULTICULTURAL EDUCATION
Caddo Gap Press, 317 S. Division St. #2
Ann Arbor, MI 48104 (313) 662-0886
Quarterly journal of the National Association for Multicultural Education (NAME). Features articles, interviews, practical advice, reviews, and resources for multicultural educators. 40 pp. $40/year.

THE MULTICULTURAL LINK
Margaret Moran, 1 Lake St.
Upper Saddle River, NJ 07458-9958
(201) 236-5586 Fax 236-5405
Nicole Millman-Falk, Editor
E-Mail: millmanfal@aol.com
Published 5 times a year, The Multicultural Link is designed for a growing network of educators interested in furthering multiculturally aware and sensitive education. Features exemplary programs, funding, ESL/bilingual education, gender issues, plus 8 pages of practical lesson plans and reproducible activities for classroom. Subscription: $25/year; $40/2 years.

MULTICULTURAL REVIEW
Greenwood Publishing Group
88 Post Rd. W. • Westport, CT 06861
(203) 226-3571 Fax 226-6009
Lyn Miller-Lachmann, Editor
E-Mail: mcreview@aol.com
Quarterly journal for librarians and educators that reviews multicultural materials and includes feature articles on cultural diversity. $59/year. Advertising. Begun 1992.

MUSEUM NOTES
Iroquois Indian Museum
P.O. Box 7, Caverns Rd.
Howes Cave, NY 12092 (518) 296-8949
A newsletter reporting on the museum's activities; scholarly articles on the Iroquois. Sunscription: $10 per year.

THE MUSCOGEE NATION NEWS
The Muscogee (Creek) Nation
P.O. Box 580 • Okmulgee, OK 74447
(918) 756-8700 Fax 758-0824
Jim Wolfe, Editor
Stephanie Berryhill, Associate Editor
Monthly tribal news tabloid of the Muscogee (Creek) Nation. No charge to tribal members. 8,100 cir. $12/year to non-tribal members. Begun 1971.

MUSEUM OF THE GREAT PLAINS NEWSLETTER
P.O. Box 68 • Lawton, OK 73502
(405) 353-5675

MUSEUM OF INDIAN HERITAGE NEWSLETTER
500 W. Washington St.
Indianapolis, IN 46204 (317) 293-4488
Quarterly.

N

NA TINI XWE
Hoopa Valley Business Council
P.O. Box 1438 • Hoopa, CA 95546

NACIE NEWSLETTER
National Advisory Council on Indian Education
Switzer Bldg., 330 C St., SW #4072
Washington, DC 20202
(202) 205-8353 Fax 205-8897
Robert K. Chiago, Executive Director

NAICCO
Native American Indian Center of Central Ohio
P.O. Box 07705, 67 E. Innis Ave.
Columbus, OH 43207
(614) 443-6120 Fax 443-2651
Carol Welsh, Executive Director
E-mail: naicco@aol.com
Website: www.naicco.tripod.com
Bimonthly newsletter.

NAJA NEWS
Native American Journalists Association
555 N. Dakota St. • Vermillion, SD 57069
(866) 694-4264 Fax (605) 677-5282
E-Mail: info@naja.com
Web site: www.naja.com
Patty Talahongva, President
E-mail: talahongva@naja.com
Ron Walters, Executive Director
E-mail: walters@naja.com
Quarterly newsletter distributed to members of the association. The only publication by, for and about Native American communicators. 2,000 circ. Begun 1984.

NAPA NEWS
Native American Preservation Association of Georgia
P.O. Box 565 • Rome, GA 30162
(706) 295-0012
E-mail: napanewsletter@cs.com
Carlton & Brenda Yancey, Editors
Monthly newsletter.

NARF LEGAL REVIEW
Native American Rights Fund
1506 Broadway • Boulder, CO 80302
(303) 447-8760 Fax 443-7776
Ray Ramirez, Editor
E-Mail: ramirezr@stripe.colorado.edu
Web site: http://www.narf.org
A biannual newsletter covering NARF's involvement in Indian legal issues and updates NARF's cases. Discusses current Indian law issues, legislation and court decisions. Announcements of NARF's services and publications through the National Indian Law Library. No charge. Donations accepted. Begun 1973.

NARRAGANSETT INDIAN TRIBE NEWSLETTER
P.O. Box 268 • Charleston, RI 02813

NASBA NEWS
Navajo Area School Board Association
P.O. Box 578 • Window Rock, AZ 86515
Monthly.

NASHAUONK MITTARK
Mashpee Wampanoag Indian Tribal Council
89 Shellback Way #N • Mashpee, MA 02649
(617) 477-1825
Quarterly.

NASP NEWS
Native American Student Program
University of California-233 Library South
Riverside, CA 92521 (714) 787-3821

NATION NOTES
Penobscot Nation Newsletter
Community Bldg., 6 River Rd.
Indian Island • Old Town, ME 04468

NATIONAL ADVISORY COUNCIL ON INDIAN EDUCATION NEWSLETTER
Switzer Bldg., 330 C St., SW, Rm. 4072
Washington, DC 20202-7556
(202) 205-8353 Fax 205-9446

NATIONAL AMERICAN INDIAN CATTLEMAN'S ASSOCIATION NEWSLETTER & YEARBOOK
c/o Tim Foster, President
1541 Foster Rd. • Toppenish, WA 98948
(509) 854-1329
Monthly newsletter.

NATIONAL ASSOCIATION OF BLACKFEET INDIANS BULLETIN
P.O. Box 340 • Browning, MT 59417

NATIONAL CENTER FOR AMERIAN INDIAN ENTERPRISE DEVELOPMENT REPORTER & REVIEW
953 E. Juanita Ave. • Mesa. AZ 85204
(800) 462-2433; Fax (602) 545-4208
Ken Robbins, President
The voice of American Indian business.
Quarterly journals.

NATIONAL COALITION TO SUPPORT INDIAN TREATIES NEWSLETTER
814 N.E. 40th St. • Seattle, WA 98105

NATIONAL CONGRESS OF AMERICAN INDIANS NEWS
1301 Connecticut Ave., NW #200
Washington, DC 20036
(202) 466-7767 Fax 466-7797

**NATIONAL INDIAN HEALTH BOARD
(NIHB) HEALTH REPORTER**
Office of Diversity, Campus Box AO49
4200 E. 9th Ave. • Denver, CO 80262
  (303) 315-5598 Linda Yardley, Contact
Bimonthly newsletter, No charge.

**NATIONAL INDIAN SOCIAL WORKERS
ASSOCIATION - THE ASSOCIATION**
P.O. Box 45 • Valentine, AZ 86437-0045
  Mary Kihega, Sec.-Treas.
Quarterly newsletter containing a calendar of events,
news of members, research, and awards. Price in-
cluded in membership dues.

NMAI RUNNER
National Museum of the American Indian (NMAI)
Office of Public Affairs
470 L'Enfant Plaza, SW #7103
Washington, DC 20560
  (202) 287-2525 Fax 287-2033
  Liz Hill, Editor
  E-Mail: lizh@ic.si.edu
  Web site: http://www.si.edu/nmai
An 8-page bimonthly newsletter from the National Mu-
seum of the American Indian. 36,000 circulation. Be-
gun 1990.n

THE NATIONS NEWS
Nations Ministries
P.O. Box 70 • Honobia, OK 74549
  (918) 755-4570
  Riley Donica, Editor
Quarterly newsletter.

NATIVE AMERICAN CONNECTIONS
Gloria J. Davis, Publisher
P.O. Box 579 • Winchester, CA 92596
  (909) 926-2119
  Dayne E. Lopez & Robert Kendall, Editors
  E-mail: ponchefoo@com
  Website: www.hispanictimescarees.com
A yearbook/directory, published annually in July for
Native Americans and businesses. $28 plus postage
per year.Begun 1993.

NATIVE AMERICAN COUNCIL NEWS
204 Hagested Student Center
University of Wisconsin • River Falls, WI 54022

**NATIVE AMERICAN CULTURAL
CENTER NEWSLETTER**
2115 E. Main St.
Rochester, NY 14609

NATIVE AMERICAN DIRECTORY
National Native American Co-op
P.O. Box 1000 • San Carlos, AZ 85550
  (602) 622-4900
  Fred Synder, Editor
Provides information about American Indian events,
organizations, and crafts. Includes pow-wows and celebrations, Indian rodeos, conventions, arts and crafts
shows; also, Indian crafts guilds and cooperatives and
Indian performing artists, dancers and exhibitors. Published periodically.

**NATIVE AMERICAN EDUCATIONAL
SERVICE RULE**
2838 W. Peterson Ave. • Chicago, IL 60659
  (312) 761-5000
  Faith Smith, Editor
Quarterly journal.

NATIVE AMERICAN HOUSING NEWS
900 Second St., NE, Suite 305
Washington, DC 20002
  (800) 284-9165; (202) 789-1754 Fax 789-1758
Quarterly newsletter.

NATIVE AMERICAN LAW DIGEST
The Falmouth Institute, Inc.
3702 Pender Dr., Suite 300
Fairfax, VA 22030 (800) 992-4489
  (703) 352-2250 Fax 352-2323
  Gregory Smith, Esq., Editor
  Web site: www.falmouthinstitute.com
  E-mail: information@falmouthinstitute.com

A monthly summary of all legal decisions significant
to the Indian community. This comprehensive law digest covers all issues affecting tribes and tribal organizations. In addition to summarized cases, the digest
publishes numerous law review articles covering topics such as Indian gaming, Indian taxation, sovereign
immunity and tribal self-governance. $299 per year.

**NATIVE AMERICAN POLICY
NETWORK NEWSLETTER**
Barry University, 11300 NE 2nd Ave.
Miami Shores, FL 33161
  (305) 899-3000 Fax 899-3279
  Prof. Michael E. Melody, Editor
An offset newsletter for 425 policy makers, political
scientists and Native American leaders, issued three
times per year. Articles and news relevant to Native
American policy issues. Book reviews. 1,500 cir. $5/
year. Begun 1980.

NATIVE AMERICAN PROGRAMS NEWSLETTER
University of North Dakota
P.O. Box 1874 • Grand Forks, ND 58202
  (701) 777-4291 Fax 777-3292

NATIVE AMERICAN LAW REPORT
Business Publishers, Inc.
8737 Colesville Rd., Suite 1100
Silver Spring, MD 20910
  (800) 274-6737 or (301) 589-5103
  Fax (301) 589-8493 or 587-4530
  Charlotte Wright, Editorial Director
  Susan Hsu, Editor
  E-mail: custserv@bpinews.com
  Website: www.bpinews.com
The independent, authorative source on tribal sov-
ereignty and juridictional issues. 8-page monthly news-
letter covering news of tribal courts, Indian law, U.S.
Government - Congress & BIA of Native American
interest. *Publication*: Under Seige: Tribal Sovereignty
& Native American Jurisdiction. Published biweekly.
Price: $271 per year.

NATIVE AMERICAN SCHOLAR
Bureau of Indian Affairs, Higher Ed. Program
P.O. Box 26567 • Albuquerque, NM 87125
  (505) 766-3170

NATIVE AMERICAN STUDIES
Edwin Mellon Press
240 Portage Rd., Box 450
Lewiston, NY 14092
  (716) 754-8566 Fax 754-4335

NATIVE AMERICAN TIMES
Oklahoma Indian Times, Inc.
P.O. Box 6920050 • Tulsa, OK 74169
  (918) 438-6548 Fax 438-6545
  Jim Gray & Elizabeth Gaines-Gray, Publishers
  E-mail: editor@okit.com; liz@okit.com
  Website: nativetimes.com
Monthly national Indian newspaper.
Circulation: 36,000.

NATIVE AMERICAS JOURNAL
Akwe:kon Press, American Indian Program
450 Caldwell Hall, Cornell University
Ithaca, NY 14853 (800) 9—NATIVE
  (607) 255-0421 Fax 255-0185
  Jose Barreiro, Editor-in-Chief
  Leslie Logan, Managing Editor
  E-mail: nativeamericas@cornell.edu
  Web site: www.nativeamericas.com
A quarterly publication that reports on issues and
events that impact indigenous nations in the Western
Hemisphers. *Price*: $20/year (individuals); $35/year
(Institutions); $25/year, (Canada); $30/year (foreign).

NATIVE ARTISTS MAGAZINE
Media Concepts Group, Inc.
5333 N. 7th St. #224C • Phoenix, AZ 85014
  (602) 265-4855 Fax 265-3113
  Gary Avey, Publisher
  Michael Hice, Editor
  E-mail: editorial@nativepeoples.com
  Web site: www.nativeartists.com
Features full-color articles on contemporary Native fine
art and artists in all media throughout the U.S. and

Canada. The quarterly magazine highlights contemporary forms with traditional foundations including
pottery, jewelry, weaving & basket making. It also features dynamic new works of Native music, film, dance,
poetry and fashion. Single copies, $5.95; one year,
$17.95; Editorial department is based in Santa Fe, NM.

NATIVE ARTS JOURNAL
ATLATL • P.O. Box 34090
Phoenix, AZ 85067-4090
  (602) 277-3711 Fax 277-3690
  Linda R. Martin, Editor
  E-Mail: atlatl@atlatl.org
  Web site: www.atlatl.org
Quarterly newsletter promoting contemporary Native
American artists and cultural organizations. Includes
issues, regional highlights, interviews, exhibition list-
ings, opportunities, & book reviews. 2,000 cir. $25/year.

**NATIVE CULTURAL ORGANIZATIONS SURVEY
RESULTS & TECHNICAL ASSISTANCE NEEDS
ASSESSMENT**
ATLATL, INC. • P.O. Box 34090
Phoenix, AZ 85067-4090
  (602) 277-3711 Fax 277-3690
  E-Mail: atlatl@atlatl.org
  Web site: www.atlatl.org
A 70-page publication profiling Native-controlled or-
ganizations and the technical needs of Native artists
and cultural workers. $30.

NATIVE DRUMS
LOST/League of Separated Tribes
P.O. Box 68 • Saltsburg, PA 15681
  Pat Selinger, Editor

THE NATIVE EXPERIENCE NEWS
7406 Waldran Ave. • Temple Hills, MD 20748
  (301) 449-6730 (phone & fax)
Bimonthly newsletter. $25 per year.

NATIVE HORIZONS
American Indian Head Start
Quality Improvement Center
American Indian Institute-
College of Continuing Education
The University of Oklahoma
555 Constitution St., Suite 228
Norman, OK 73072-7820 (800) 379-3869
  (405) 325-4129 Fax 325-7319
  Geneva Strech, Editor
  E-mail: strech@ou.edu
  Website: www.aihsqic.ou.edu
Quarterly newsletter which serves as a source of
shared ideas, informational resources and Indian Head
Start community happenings.

NATIVE LIFE & TIMES
2003 S. Muskogee Ave., Suite 115
Tahlequah, OK 74464
  (918) 456-1876

THE NATIVE NEVADAN
Reno-Sparks Indian Colony
98 Colony Rd. • Sparks, NV 89502-1288
  (702) 359-9449
  Becky Lemon, Editor
Covers all facets of Native American life, primarily in
Nevada and California. Book reviews. Monthly newspaper. 2,200 cir. $15/year; $2/copy. Advertising. Begun 1964.

NATIVE NEWS
Indian Education - Title VII Program
2295 Four Oaks Grange Rd.
Eugene, OR 97405
  (541) 687-3489 Fax 687-3892
  Brenda Brainard, Editor
  E-mail: brainard@4j.lane.edu
Monthly newsletter for families and Native American
students enrolled in Eugene, Bethel, Fern Ridge,
Creswell, Lowell, Junction City, Crow-Applegate-
Lorane, South Lane and Pleasant Hill School Districts;
and for Native American community members. Includes overview of student activities plus a monthly
educational theme, complete with reading lists, visual
material references, website information and a recipe
page. Free upon request.

NATIVE NEWS & B.I.A. BULLETIN
Bureau of Indian Affairs
P.O. Box 3-8000 • Juneau, AK 99801

NATIVE PEOPLES MAGAZINE
5333 N. 7th St. #224 • Phoenix, AZ 85012
(602) 265-4855 Fax 265-3113
Gary Avey, Publisher
Ben Winton, Editor
Website: www.nativepeoples,com
E-mail: editorial@nativepeoples.com
A full-color, bimonthly magazine portraying the history, arts and lifeways of Native peoples of the Americas. Includes book and audio/video reviews, Native American foods, collectors corner, guest essays, and in the news section on Native American role models. Affiliated with ten organizations including the National Museum of the American Indian/Smithsonian Institution. $4.95/copy; $17.95/year, 6 issues; $29/2-year, 12 issues, foreign. Advertising. Begun 1987.

NATIVE PLAYWRIGHTS' NEWSLETTER
P.O. Box 664 • Cocoa, FL 32923
Published three times epr year. $15/year.

NATIVE PRESS RESEARCH JOURNAL
University of Arkansas, Little Rock
Stabler Hall 502, 2801 S. University
Little Rock, AR 72204
Daniel F. Littlefield, Jr., Editor
Suspended publication. Back issues available.

NATIVE REFLECTIONS
Wesleyan Native American Ministries
P.O. Box 7038 • Rapid City, SD 57709
(605) 343-9054
E-mail: wnam2000@aol.com
Quarterly. $15.

NATIVE SELF-SUFFICIENCY
The Seventh Generation Fund
P.O. Box 4569 • Arcata, CA 95521
(707) 825-7640 Fax 825-7639

NATIVE SUN
North American Indian Association of Detroit
22720 Plymouth Rd. • Detroit, MI 48239
(313) 535-2966 Fax (810) 533-1080
Andrew Butterfly, Editor
Reports on news and activities of the center; and issues of importance to American Indians of Wayne County, Michigan. Monthly newsletter. 200 cir. $1/copy; $8/year. Begun 1975.

THE NATIVE VOICE
601 12th St., Suite 3
Rapid City, SD 57701
(800) 449-8176
(605) 718-9141 Fax 718-9143
Frank J. King, III, Publisher & Editor-in-Chief
Lise King, Co-editor
E-Mail: info@native-voice.com
Website: www.native-voice.com
Biweekly. 50,000 Cir.

NATIVE VOICES
The Mail Order Catalog
P.O. Box 180 • Summertown, TN 38483
(800) 695-2241
Source for books on Native history, culture, crafts, etc. Also children's books and Native music and video. Semiannually. No charge

NATIVE WIND
P.O. Box 205 • Plummer, ID 83851
(800) 524-1588
(208) 686-1176 Fax 686-1817
Web site: www.gospelcom.net/ibs/native-wind
Monthly. Christian.

NATIVE WRITERS INK
Institute of Alaska Native Arts
P.O. Box 80583, 524 Third Ave.
Fairbanks, AK 99708 (907) 456-7491/7406

NATIVE YOUTH MEDIA INSTITUTE
Native Media Center-UND School of Communications
P.O. Box 7169 • Grand Forks, ND 58202
(701) 777-2478

NATIVENET
43 Jackson Rd. • Somerville, MA 02145
Gary Trujillo, Contact
(617) 776-0121
Computer online service.

NAVAHO-A MAGAZINE FOR THE DINEH
Maazo Publishing, P.O. Box 1245
Window Rock, AZ 86515
(602) 729-2233
Covers Navajo Indian culture. Quarterly.
$12/year; $28/year, foreign.

NAVAJO AREA NEWSLETTER
Bureau of Indian Affairs
P.O. Box 1060 • Gallup, NM 87301
(505) 863-8314 Fax 863-8324
Frank Hardwick, Editor
Contains information of interest to Navajo Area, B.I.A.'s employees on education, personnel actions, Bureau policy, etc. Monthly. 4,000 cir. No charge.

NAVAJO COMMUNITY COLLEGE NEWSLETTER
Publications Dept. • Tsaile, AZ 86556

NAVAJO EDUCATION NEWSLETTER
Navajo Area Office, Bureau of Indian Affairs
Window Rock, AZ 86515

NAVAJO-HOPI OBSERVER
2608 N. Steves Blvd. • Flagstaff, AZ 86004
(520) 526-3881 Fax 527-0217

NAVAJO NATION ENQUIRY
P.O. Box 490 • Window Rock, AZ 86515

NAVAJO SOUTHWEST SCENE
P.O. Box 580 • Window Rock, AZ 86515
(505) 371-5392

THE NAVAJO TIMES
The Navajo Nation
P.O. Box 310 • Window Rock, AZ 86515
(520) 871-6641 Fax 871-6409
Mark Trahant, Editor & Publisher
Angie Damon, Circulation Manager
Michael Kellogg, Advertising Director
Paul Natonabah, Art Director
Only American Indian daily newspaper reporting Navajo, national and regional news. Book reviews. 4,500 cir. $90/year. Advertising. Begun 1959.

NAVAJOLAND PUBLICATIONS
Navajo Tribal Museum
Window Rock, AZ 86515

NETT LAKE NEWS
Nett Lake, MN 55772

NETWORK NEWS
Devils Lake Sioux Tribe
P.O. Box 400 • Fort Totten, ND 58335
(701) 766-4211 Fax 766-4618

NEW MEXICO HISTORICAL REVIEW
1013 Mesa Vista Hall • U. of New Mexico
Albuquerque, NM 87131
(505) 277-5839 Fax 277-0992
E-mail: nmhr@unm.edu
Website: www.unm.edu/~nmhr
Dr. Durwood Ball, Editor
Covers New Mexico and Southwest history, its people and their cultures. Includes articles, book reviews, essays and notes, and history news notes dealing with American Indian topics. Quarterly journal. $48/year, institutions; $28/year, individuals; single copies, $10. Advertising accepted. Begun 1926.

NEW MEXICO INDIAN AFFAIRS SOURCE
LaVilla Revera Bldg., 224 E. Palace Ave.
Santa Fe, NM 87501

THE NEW PHOENIX
The Free Cherokees
P.O. Box 414 • Chaptico, MD 20653
(301) 884-0143
Official newsletter of the Free Cherokees, an independent tribe dedicated to the preservation of authentic Native American teachings. $16/year.

NEWS FROM INDIAN COUNTRY
Indian Country Communications, Inc.
7831N Grindstone Ave.
Hayward, WI 54843-2052
(715) 634-5226 Fax 634-3243
Advertising (715) 634-1429
E-mail: nficad@cheqnet.com
Web site: www.indiancountrynews.com
Paul DeMain, Editor; Pat Calliotte, Associate Editor
Staff: Kim Hall, Advertising; Willard Gourge, Subscriptions. *Description:* National bi-monthly newspaper (24 issues annually) with circulation in Canada and 21 other countries. Covers news and community events of the American Indian, business activities, and cultural events. Special features on treaty rights, legislation; year-round pow-wow locations, etc. $35/year - 3rd Class, $52/year - 1st Class. Advertising accepted; EEO/AA Job Search. Begun 1977. *Supplement:* "Explore Indian Country," Kim Hall, Editor. Published monthly for tourist and casino patrons, including articles and letters related to gaming, entertainment, music, historical information, museums, hotels. Also, casino and bingo information located in Indian country. Advertising accepted.

NEWS FROM NATIVE CALIFORNIA
Heyday Books, P.O. Box 9145
Berkeley, CA 94709
(510) 549-3564 Fax 549-1889
E-mail: nnc@heydaybooks.com
Malcolm Margolin, Publisher
Jeannine Gendar, Editor
Written for major figures and organizations in the California Indian community, from individuals on reservations to government officials. Quarterly magazine. 3,300 circ.$19 per year; $4.50 per single copy; $34 per year, foreign. Begun 1987.

NEWS & NOTES
American Indian Ritual Object/
Repatriation Foundation
463 E. 57th St. • New York, NY 10022
(212) 980-9441 Fax 421-2746
Published twice yearly.

NEWSLETTER FROM THE NATION OF WOBAN AKI
Abenaki Self Help Association
P.O. Box 276 • Swanton, VT 05488
(802) 868-2559 Fax 868-5118

NEZ PERCE TRIBAL NEWSPAPER
P.O. Box 305 • Lapwai, ID 85341

NI-MI-KWA-ZOO-MIN
Minnesota Chippewa Tribe
P.O. Box 217 • Cass Lake, MN 56633

NI YA YO
Mohegan Tribe
5 Crow Hill Rd.
Uncasville, CT 06382
(800) MOHEGAN; Fax (860) 862-6115
Jonathan S. Hamilton, Editor
Nancy Trimble, Managing Editor
Web site: www.mohegan.nsn.us
Mohegan Tribal newspaper.

NISHNAWBE NEWS
Organization of North American Indian Students
Northern Michigan University
140 University Center • Marquette, MI 49855
Mike Wright, Editor
Monthly magazine. 8,500 cir. $5/year. Begun 1971.

NMIEA NEWSLETTER
New Mexico Indian Education Association (NMIEA)
P.O. Box 16356 • Santa Fe, NM 87506
(505) 989-5569

NOOKSACK NEWSLETTER
P.O. Box 157 • Deming, WA 98244

NORTH AMERICAN INDIAN MUSEUMS ASSOCIATION NEWSLETTER
c/o Seneca Iroquois National Museum
Allegany Indian Reservation
P.O. Box 442 • Salamanca, NY 14779
(716) 945-1738

NORTH AMERICAN NATIVE AUTHORS CATALOG
The Greenfield Review Press
P.O. Box 308 • Greenfield Center, NY 12833
(518) 583-1440 Fax 583-9741
James Bruchac, Editor
E-Mail: asban@aol.com
Web site: http://www.nativeauthors.com
A catalog of publications by Native American authors, including more than 600 titles from over 90 different publishers; mostly books, but including current & back issues of Native periodicals. Catalog, $2. Begun 1980.

NORTH AMERICAN POW-WOW MAGAZINE
JTH Industries, 8129 N. 35th Ave. #2-305
Phoenix, AZ 85051-5892
Jessie Two Hawks, Editor/Publisher

NORTH CAROLINA HISTORICAL REVIEW
North Carolina Division of Archaeology and History
109 East Jones St. • Raleigh, NC 27601

NORTH DAKOTA HISTORY:
JOURNAL OF THE NORTHERN PLAINS
State Historical Society of North Dakota
612 E. Boulevard Ave. • Bismarck, ND 58505
(701) 328-2799 Fax 328-3710
Janet Daley, Editor/Historian
Kathy Davison, Publications Assistant
E-Mail: jdaley@state.nd.us
Web site: www.state.nd.us/hist/
A quarterly scholarly journal that focuses on the history and culture of the northern Great Plains. Each issue contans two to three articles which are refereed. 1,800 circ. $4/issue; $30/year for individuals. All subscribers are members of the State Historical Society of North Dakota Foundation.

NORTH DAKOTA QUARTERLY
University of North Dakota
P.O. Box 7209 • Grand Forks, ND 58202
(701) 777-3322 Fax 777-3650
Robert W. Lewis, Editor
E-Mail: rolewis@badlands.nodak.edu
Quarterly university journal in the humanities, arts, and social sciences, with a special interest in Native American writing and writing about it. $25/year; $8 per single issue. Begun 1910.

NORTHERN CHEYENNE NEWS
P.O. Box 401 • Lame Deer, MT 59043

NORTHERN PUEBLOS AGENCY NEWS DIGEST
P.O. Box C-22 • Santa Fe, NM 87501

NORTHLAND NATIVE AMERICAN NEWS
Northland College • Ashland, WI 54806

NORTHWEST ARCTIC NUNA
Maniilaq Association
P.O. Box 256 • Kotzebue, AK 99752
(907) 442-3311
Monthly newsletter includes local news and program information. No charge. Advertising.

NORTHWEST ETHNIC NEWS
Ethnic Heritage Council
305 Harrison St. #326 • Seattle, WA 98109
(206) 443-1410 Fax 443-1408
Sarah Sarai, Editor
Monthly newspaper covering arts and issues relevant to ethnic communities of the Pacific Northwest. 13,000 cir. $12/year. Begun 1984.

NORTHWEST INDIAN FISHERIES
COMMISSION NEWS
6730 Marti Way E. • Olympia, WA 98506
Monthly

NPAIHB HEALTH NEWS & NOTES
Northwest Portland Area Indian Health Board
520 SW Harrison #440 • Portland, OR 97201
(503) 228-4185
Quarterly.

NU QWAH NEUM
North Fork Rancheria
P.O. Box 929 • North Fork, CA 93643
(559) 877-2461 Fax 877-2467
Quarterly tribal newsletter

NUGGUAM
Quinault Tribal Affairs
P.O. Box 1118 • Taholah, WA 98587

NUHMUH NEWS
Fallon Paiute Shoshone Tribe
8955 Mission Rd. • Fallon, NV 89406
(775) 423-6075 Fax 423-5202
Tribal newsletter.

O

O-HE-YOY NOH
Seneca Nation of Indians
Plummer Bldg., Box 231
Salamanca, NY14779
Eldena Halftown, Editor
Monthly newsletter devoted to the Seneca Nation of Indians. 500 cir. Begun 1970.

ODAWA TRAILS NEWSLETTER
Grand Traverse Band of Ottawa & Chippewa Indians
2605 NW Bayshore Dr. • Suttons Bay, MI 49682
(616) 271-3538 Fax 271-4861

OGLALA WICAHPI
Journalism Department
Oglala Lakota College
P.O. Box 490 • Kyle, SD 57752

OJIBWE AKIING (OJIBWE TURF)
Indian Country Communications, Inc.
7831N Grindstone Ave.
Hayward, WI 54843-2052
(715) 634-5226 Fax 634-3243
Advertising (715) 634-1429
E-mail: nficad@cheqnet.com
Web site: www.indiancountrynews.com
Terri Morrow, Editor; Sara Begay, Advertising
Monthly Great Lakes publication devoted to the Ojibwe/Chippewa communities of Wisconsin, Michigan and Minnesota. Includes Canadian First nations. Special features, local and regional news, health, letters, Ojibwe language. $16/year, 3rd class mail; $22/year, 1st class. Advertising accepted. Begun 1996.

OJIBWE INAAJIMOWIN
Mille Lacs Band of Ojibwe
HCR 67, Box 194 • Onamia, MN 56359
(320) 532-4181 ext. 7486 Fax 532-5800
A monthly internal newspaper for Band members and tribal government employees.

NATIVE AMERICAN PRESS/OJIBWE NEWS
500 N. Robert St., Suite 205
St. Paul, MN 55101
(651) 224-6656 Fax 224-6304
Bill Lawrence, Publisher
Julie Shortridge, Editor
The only independent self-supporting Indian news weekly in the nation. Covers national news with an emphasis on Minnesota. 10,000 cir. Subsc. $58 per year. Advertising accepted. Established 1988.

OKLAHOMA ANTHROPOLOGICAL
SOCIETY NEWSLETTER
Oklahoma Anthropological Society
Route 1, Box 62B
Cheyenne, OK 73628
(918) 682-5091
Frieda Odell, Editor & Publisher
Information on statewide archaeological investigations.; articles of Oklahoma history and prehistory. Book reviews. Monthly newsletter (September-May). 600 cir. Subscription: $12/year. individuals; $17/year, institutions; $20/year, foreign. Begun 1952.

OKLAHOMANS FOR INDIAN
OPPORTUNITY NEWSLETTER
555 Constitution • Norman, OK 73069

OLD NORTHWEST CORPORATION NEWSLETTER
Sonotabac Prehistoric Indian Mounds and Museum
P.O. Box 941 • Vincennes, IN 47591
(812) 885-4330/7679
Published monthly.

ON EAGLE'S WINGS
P.O. Box 8264 • Cranston, RI 02920
Newsletter of Native New England.

ON INDIAN LAND
Support for Native Soverignty
P.O. Box 2104 • Seattle, WA 98111

ON THE WAY UP
American Indian Science & Engineering Society
P.O. Box 9828
Albuquerque, NM 87119-9828
(505) 765-1052 Fax 765-5608
Published three times per year.

ONEIDA NATION NEWSLETTER
Oneida Indian Nation
223 Genesee St. • Oneida, NY 13421
(315) 697-8251 Fax 697-7581
Ray Halbritter, Representative
Provides tribal and reservation news.

OREGON DIRECTORY OF
AMERICAN INDIAN RESOURCES
Commission on Indian Services
167 State Capitol • Salem, OR 97310
(503) 986-1067 Fax 986-1071
Gladine G. Ritter, Editor
E-Mail: gladine.g.ritter@state.or.us
Web site: http://www.leg.state.or.us
1997-99. Published biennially.

OREGON INDIAN EDUCATION NEWSLETTER
Oregon Indian Educaion Association
2125 N. Flint • Portland, OR 97227
(503) 275-9600

OREGON INDIANS: CULTURE,
HISTORY & CURRENT AFFAIRS
The Oregon Historical Society Press
1230 SW Park Ave. • Portland, OR 97205

ORIC NEWS
Orange County Indian Center
P.O. Box 250 • Garden Grove, CA 92642

OSAGE NATION NEWS
Osage Tribal Council
P.O. Box 178 • Pawhuska, OK 74056

OSHKAABEWIS NATIVE JOURNAL
Indian Studies Program, Bemidji State U.
1500 Birchmont Dr. NE
Staford Hall, Box 19 • Bemidji, MN 56601

OURSELVES
Minnesota Chippewa Tribe
P.O. Box 217 • Cass Lake, MN 56633

OWENS VALLEY INDIAN
EDUCATION CENTER NEWSLETTER
P.O. Box 1648 • Bishop, CA 93514

OYATE-ANISHNANABE NEWS
American Indian Student Cultural Center
104 Jone Hall, 27 Pleasant SE
Minneapolis, MN 55404

OYATE NAT E NATA YAZADI PHEZUTA
University of Colorado
CB 135 • Boulder, CO 80309

OYATE-VISION
P.O. Box 393 • Pine Ridge, SD 57770

OYATE WO'WAPI
Tahana Whitecrow Foundation
P.O. Box 18181 • Salem, OR 97305
(503) 585-0564
Quarterly.

P

PAN-AMERICAN INDIAN ASSOCIATION NEWS
8335 Sevigny Dr. • N. Fort Myers, FL 33917-1705
(941) 731-7029 or 543-7727

Cindy "Spirit Catcher" Barnard, Editor
Heritage revival for native Americans and other tribal peoples. Help in genealogy; networking of groups and resources. Book reviews. Irregular. 16-page tabloid. 5,000 cir. $5/year; $10/year, foreign. Advertising. Begun 1984.

PANA PANA NEWSLETTER
National Indian Youth Council
318 Elm, SE • Albuquerque, NM 87102
(505) 247-2251 Fax 247-4251

PANHANDLE-PLAINS HISTORICAL REVIEW
Panhandle-Plains Historical Museum
P.O. Box 967, W.T. Station
2401 Fourth Ave. • Canyon, TX 79016
(806) 655-7194

PAPAGO BULLETIN
P.O. Box 364 • Sells, AZ 85634

PASCUA PUEBLO NEWS
4821 W. Calle Vicam • Tucson, AZ 85706

PATHFINDER COMMUNICATIONS
817 East Dr. • Oklahoma City, OK 73105

PATHFINDER NEWSLETTER
American Indian Heritage Foundation
6051 Arlington Blvd. • Falls Church, VA 22044
(703) 237-7500 fax 532-1921
Informs Indians and non-Indians about the culture and heritage of Native Americans. Addresses the spiritual and physical needs of American Indians and aims to encourage Indian youth. Quarterly. Membership, $20/ yr. Begun 1982.

PATHWAY NEWS
National American Indian Housing Council
900 2nd St., NE # 007 • Washington, DC 20002
(202) 789-1754 Fax 789-1758
Quarterly newsletter

THE PEOPLE BEFORE COLUMBUS
Southwest Indian Student Coalition
1812 Los Lomas • Albuquerque, NM 87131
(503) 277-6065
Annual journal.

THE PEOPLE'S VOICE
Kanienkehaka Teritory
P.O. Box 216 • Hogansburg, NY 13655
(518) 358-3022
Cindy Terrance, Editor
Weekly newspaper for the St. Regis Mohawk Reservation (both U.S. and Canadian portions); also serves Mohawk people in Kahnawake Quebec (near Montreal) and California. Begun 1987.

PEQUOT TIMES
Mashantucket Pequot Tribal Nation
P.O. Box 3130, 4 Ann Wampey Dr.
Mashantucket, CT 06338
(860) 396-6572 Fax 396-6570
Trace DeMeyer, Editor
E-mail: pequot-times@mptn-nsn.gov
Monthly tribal newspaper. Free subscription; circ: 30,000. Begun 1992.

PHOENIX INDIAN CENTER NEWSLETTER
333 W. Indian School Rd.
Phoenix, AZ 85013-3215
(602) 256-2000

PIERRE CHIEFTAIN
Pierre Indian School
Pierre, SD 57501

PIERRE INDIAN LEARNING CENTER (PILC) NEWS
Star Route 3 • Pierre, SD 57501

PILGRIM
Shrine of Our Lady of Martyrs
Noeltner Rd. • Auriesville, NY 12016
(518) 853-3033 Fax 853-3051
John J. Paret.S.J., Editor
Newsletter for persons interested in the three martyrs venerated here: Sts. Isaac Joques, Rene Goupil, and John Lalande - and in the Shrine itself, and in Blessed Kateri Tekakwitha, the young Mohawk-Algonquin woman who was born here.

PIMA-MARICOPA ECHO
Gila River Indian Community
P.O. Box 97 • Sacaton, AZ 85247

THE PINE KNOT
1418 Hwy. 33S. at Cloquet
Carlton County, MN 55720

PLAINS ANTHROPOLOGIST
Plains Anthropological Society
Univ. of Wisconsin-Milwaukee
Dept. of Anthropology • Milwaukee, WI 53201
(414) 229-4720 Fax 229-5848
Linea Sundstrom, Editor
E-mail: plains-anthro@uwm.edu
Web site: www.uiowa.edu/~osa/plainsanth/
A quarterly journal containing articles on all aspects of anthropology in the Plains area of the U.S. Book reviews. 1,500 cir. $25/year, individuals; $20/year, students; $45/year, institutions. Began 1954.

PLAINS TALK
State Historical Society of North Dakota
612 E. Boulevard Ave. • Bismarck, ND 58505
(701) 328-2799 Fax 328-3710
Janet Daley, Editor
E-Mail: jdaley@state.nd.us
Web site: www.state.nd.us/hist/
Quarterly newsletter about the activities of the State Historical Society of North Dakota . No charge to members.

POARCH CREEK NEWS
Poarch Band of Creek Indians
Route 3, Box 243-A • Atmore, AL 36502

POCAHONTAS TRAILS - QUARTERLY
Pocahontas Trails Genealogical Society
6015 Robin Hill Dr. • Lakeport, CA 95453
Focuses on the pursuit and study of the genealogy of Pocahontas and Powhatan. Membership dues. Begun 1983.

POINT HOPE NEWS
Point Hope Village
Point Hope, AK 99766

POINT NO POINT TREATY COUNCIL NEWSLETTER
7999 NE Salish Lane
Kingston, WA 98346

PONCA CITY NEWS
Ponca Tribe • Ponca City, OK 74601

PORTLAND PUBLIC SCHOOLS INDIAN EDUCATION ACT PROJECT NEWSLETTER
Portland Public Schools
8020 N.E. Tillamook • Portland, OR 97213
(503) 280-6474

POTTERY SOUTHWEST
Albuquerque Archaeological Society
6207 Mossman Place NE
Albuquerque, NM 87110
(505) 881-1675
Carries news and queries on prehistoric pottery of the Indians of New Mexico, Arizona, Utah, Colorado, and parts of Texas and Mexico. Quarterly. $3/yr. Begun 1974.

POW WOW CALENDAR
Native American Cooperative
P.O. Box 27626 • Tucson, AZ 85726
(520) 622-4900
Quarterly schedule of events.
Free with priority mail SASE.

POW WOW TRAIL NEWS
P.O. Box 1132 • Fairbanks, AK 99707

PREHISTORIC ARTIFACTS
Genuine Indian Relic Society
3335 Junaluska • Columbus, GA 31907

PREVENTION QUARTERLY
Falmouth Institute
3702 Pender Dr., Suite 300
Fairfax, VA 22030
(800) 992-4489; (703) 352-2250 Fax 352-2323
Bonnie Paquin, Contact
Covers news, programs, and issues in the area of Indian alcohol and substance abuse prevention and treatment.

THE PROMISE NEWSLETTER
P.O. Box 113 • Great Bend, PA 18821
(814) 663-2161

PUEBLO HORIZON
Indian Pueblo Cultural Center, Inc.
2401 12th St. NW
Albuquerque, NM 87102

PUEBLO COUNCIL NEWS
P.O. Box 3256 • Albuquerque, NM 87190

PUEBLO TIMES
Pueblo Times Publishing Co.
1860 Don Pasqual Rd.
Los Lunas, NM 87031
(505) 865-4508
George E. Gorospe, Owner/Publisher
Weekly (Wednesday) newspaper for the 19 Indian Pueblos of northern New Mexico. Distribution includes part of the Navajo Nation. Circulation about 10,000. Begun 1985.

PUYALLUP TRIBAL NEWS
2002 E. 28th St. • Tacoma, WA 98404

PYRAMID LAKE INDIAN RESERVATION NEWSLETTER
P.O. Box 256 • Nixon, NV 89424

Q

QUALLA RESERVATION NEWS
Cherokee Agency
Cherokee, NC 28719

QUECHAN NEWS
Fort Yuma Indian Reservation
P.O. Box 1352 • Yuma, AZ 85364
(619) 572-0213 Fax 572-2102

QUILEUTE INDIAN NEWS
Quileute Tribal Council
P.O. Box 279 • La Push, WA 98350
(206) 374-6163 Fax 374-6311
Anne Cooper, Editor
Monthly.

QUIN-A-MONTH-A'
Stockbridge Historical Museum
Route 1, Box 300 • Bowler, WI 54416

QUINAULT NATURAL RESOURCES
Quinault Department of Natural Resources and Economic Development
P.O. Box 189 • Tahola, WA 98587
Jacqueline Storm

R

RAIN NOTES
Recruitment and Retention of American Indians in Nursing (RAIN)
UND College of Nursing
P.O. Box 9025
Grand Forks, ND 58202
(701) 777-4519 Fax 777-4558
Published twice yearly.

THE RAVEN CHRONICLES
P.O. Box 95918 • Seattle, WA 98145
Multi-cultural journal of the arts and literature, including native American literature. $12/yr. $3 sample issue.

THE RAWHIDE PRESS
Spokane Tribal Business Council
P.O. Box 359 • Wellpinit, WA 99040-0359
(509) 258-7320
Bertha Seyler, Editor
Monthly newspaper covering news regarding Indian affairs including historical features, biographies, etc. on Indian culture. Book reviews. 800 cir. $12/year. Advertising. Begun 1972.

RED ALERT
Americans for Indian Opportunity
681 Juniper Hill Rd. • Bernalillo, NM 87004
(505) 867-0278 Fax 867-0441

RED CLIFF TRIBAL NEWS
P.O. Box 529 • Bayfield, WI 54814

RED CLOUD COUNTRY
Red Cloud Indian School
Holy Rosary Mission • Pine Ridge, SD 57770
(605) 867-5491
Fr. Roger, S.V., Editor
Contains information about Red Cloud School. Sent to donors, friends and benefactors of the school. Quarterly newsletter. $10/year.

REDEARTH MAGAZINE
Council Publications
Council of Energy Resource (CERT)
695 S. Colorado Blvd., Suite 10
Denver, CO 80246
(303) 282-7576 Fax 282-7584
Website: www.certredearth
A. David Lester, Executive Director & Co-Publisher
National Center for American Indian Enterprise Development (NCAIED)
953 E. Juanita Ave. • Mesa, AZ 85204
(480) 545-1298 Fax 545-4208
Website: www.ncaied.org
Kenneth Robbins, CEO/President & Co-Publisher
A journal of contemporary American Indian development, co-published by CERT & NCAIED. RedEarth Magazine is the recipient of the "2001 National Communicator Award of Excellence."

RED HILLS NEWSLETTER
Kaibab Tribal Council, Tribal Affairs Bldg.
Fredonia, AZ 86022

RED INK: A NATIVE AMERICAN STUDENT PUBLICATION
American Indian Studies Program
University of Arizona, Harvill Bldg. Rm. 430
P.O. Box 210076 • Tucson, AZ 85721
(520) 622-3504 Fax 791-3735
Ian Record & Christina Castro, Editors
E-mail: redink@ccit.arizona.edu
Web site: www.w3.arizona.edu/~aisp.redink.htm
A semi-annual student-run publication (magazine) that solicits creative writing and artistic submissions from indigenous peoples of the Western Hempisphere, including: poetry, short stories, original artwork, book and film reviews. Red Ink also publishes scholarly articles dealing with contemporary indigenous issues. One-year individual subscription is $15; institutional subscriptions is $25. Begun 1990.

RED LAKE NEWSLETTER
Red Lake Reservation
Red Lake, MN 56671

REDSKIN
Phoenix Indian High School
37 E. Indian School Rd.
Phoenix, AZ 85012

RED VOICES
American Indian Training Institute, Inc.
4153 Northgate Blvd.
Sacramento, CA 95834
(916) 920-0731

REDSMOKE INDIAN NEWS
Vietnam Era Veterans Inter-Tribal Association
805 Rosa • Shawnee, OK 74801
(405) 382-3128
Provides news of interest on American Indians who served in the Vietnam War. Quarterly.

THE RENEGADE: A STRATEGY JOURNAL OF INDIAN OPINION
Survival of American Indian Associations
7803-A Samurai Dr., SE • Olympia, WA 98503
(206) 459-2679
Published annually.

THE RENEGADER
Florida Indian Re-Enactment Society
1509 Wilbar Cir. • Winter Park, FL 32789

THE RENO TALKING LEAF
Nevada Urban Indians, Inc.
917 E. 6th St. • Reno, NV 89512
(702) 329-2573/4
Contains community events, atcivities, services and resources, and educational articles. Monthly newsletter.

REPORT TO INDIAN COUNTRY
Senate Committee on Indian Affairs
838 Hart Senate Office Bldg.
Washington, DC 20510
(202) 224-2251 Fax 224-2309

RESERVATION TIMES
Seneca Nation Education Department
1500 Route 438 • Irving, NY 14081

REZNET NEWS
University of Montana
School of Journalism
Missoula, MT 59812
(406) 243-2191
Website: www.reznetnews.org
E-mail: dmcauliffe@reznetnews.org
Denny McAuliffe, Founder & Project Director
Steven Chin, Managing Editor
Online newspaper by Native American college students. Project of the University of Montana School of Journalism and the Robert C. Maynard Institute for Journalism Education. Winner of the Native American Journalists Association's 2003 Native Media Award for Best Internet News Site, each year, Reznet hires 20 Native American college students from around the country as reporters and photographers to cover their tribal communities or colleges. The purpose is to produce more Native Americans who will enter professional journalism.

RIDGE NOTES
Chieftains Museum
501 Riverside Pkwy., Box 373
Rome, GA 30162 (706) 291-9494
Janine E. Joslin, Editor
Quarterly membership newsletter focusing on museum activities and historical articles on the region's history.

ROCKY BOY'S NEWS
Rocky Boy's Rte. • Box Elder, MT 59521

WILL ROGERS TIMES
Will Rogers Memorial
P.O. Box 157 • Claremore, OK 74018
(918) 341-0719

ROSEBUD SIOUX HERALD
P.O. Box 430 • Rosebud, SD 57570

ROUGH ROCK NEWS
Dine'Biolta'Daahani
Rough Rock Demonstration School
P.O. Box 217 • Chinle, AZ 86503
Provides a view of the life-style and attitudes of a desert community that is determined to control its own destiny. Published monthly during academic year.

S

SAC & FOX NEWS
Rt. 2, Box 246 • Stroud, OK 74079

SACRED DIRECTIONS
P.O. Box 293688
Lewisville, TX 75029
(214) 436-7727 (phone & fax)

SAIIC NEWSLETTER
South and Meso American Indian Information Center
P.O. Box 28703 • Oakland, CA 94604
(510) 834-4263 Fax 834-4264
Contains articles about issues of importance to indigenous people in Central and South America.

SAIL: STUDIES IN AMERICAN INDIAN LITERATURES
The Association for the Study of American Indian Literatures
Michigan State University, 235 Bessey Hall
Dept. of American Thought & Language
East Lansing, MI 48824—1033
(517) 355-5256 Fax 353-5250
Malea Powell, General Editor
E-mail: sail2@msu.edu
Advertising & Subscription:
Box 112, 28 Westhampton Way
University of Richmond
Richmond, VA 23173 (804) 289-8313 (Fax)
Robert M. Nelson, Contact
E-mail: rnelson@richmond.edu
Website: www.oncampus.richmond.edu/faculty/asail/sail-hp.html
Quarterly scholarly journal which focuses exclusively on American Indian literatures, including all written, spoken and visual texts created by Native peoples. Subscriptionnn rate: $25 (indiviiduals) and $35 (institutions) per year. Back issues are available.

SAN CARLOS MOCCASIN
P.O. Box 0 • San Carlos, AZ 85550
(520) 475-2361

SAN JUAN COUNTY ARCHAEOLOGICAL RESEARCH CENTER NEWSLETTER
San Juan County Museum Association
6131 U.S. Hwy. 64 • Farmington, NM 87401
(505) 632-2013 Fax 632-1707
Kurt T. Mantonya, Editor
Larry L. Baker, Executive Director
Web site: http://205.218.41.126.80/salmon/
Quarterly newsletter focusing on the activities, exhibits, and programs of the Center. Begun 1964.

SANDPAINTER
P.O. Box 791
Chinle, AZ 86503

SAPONI
102 Indian Dr.
Fayetteville, NC 28306

SATWIWA NEWS
Friends of Satwiwa
4126 Potrero Rd.
Newbury Park, CA 91320
(805) 499-2837 (phone & fax)

SCAN
P.O. Box 38
Concho, OK 73022

SCHOHARIE MUSEUM OF THE IROQUOIS INDIAN-MUSEUM NOTES
P.O. Box 158 • Schoharie, NY 12157
(518) 295-8553/234-2276
Dr. John P. Ferguson, Editor
A newsletter reporting on the Museum's activities; scholarly articles on the Iroquois. Subscription: $10/year. Complimentary copies available upon request.

THE SCOUT
Fort Berthold Community College
P.O. Box 490 • New Town, ND 58763
(701) 627-3274 Fax 627-3609

SCREAMING EAGLE
2400 Southeast Circle Dr.
Bartlesville, OK 74006

SEALASKA SHAREHOLDER
Sealaska Corporation
One Sealaska Plaza, 400
Juneau, AK 99801
Ross Soboleff, Editor

SEASONS
The National Native American
AIDS Prevention Center
436 14th St., Suite 1020
Oakland, CA 94609
  (510) 444-2051 Fax 444-1593
  Ronald Rowell, MPH, Director
  Andrea Green Rush, Editor
A quarterly newsletter featuring articles by Native
Americans with HIV and Native American health edu-
cators, and health care providers. 3,000 cir. No charge.

SECCI NEWSLETTER
Southeastern Cherokee Confederacy
120 Will Hatcher Rd.
Albany, GA 31705
  White Wolf Crider & Elk Dreamer Crider, Editors
Monthly newsletter of the Southeastern Cherokee Con-
federacy.

SEMINOLE TRIBUNE
Seminole Tribe of Florida
6300 Stirling Rd. • Hollywood, FL 33024
  (954) 967-3416 Fax 967-3482
  Website: www.semtribe.com/tribune
  E-mail: tribune@semtribe.com
  Betty Mae Jumper, Director of Communications
  Virginia Mitchell, Editor
Biweekly newspaper providing news about the Semi-
nole Tribe from five reservations in Florida; also, news
about other tribes across the country. Book reviews.
$20/year. 6,000 cir. Advertising. Begun 1973.

SENECA TRIBAL NEWSLETTER
Cattaraugus Indian Reservation
1490 Route 438 • Irving, NY 14081
  Debbie Hoag, Editor

SENTINEL
White Shield School
HC 1-Box 45 • Roseglen, ND 58775
  (701) 743-4350

THE SENTINEL
National Congress of American Indians
1301 Connecticut Ave., NW #200
Washington, DC 20036
  (202) 466-7767 Fax 466-7797
  Emily Segar, Editor
Focuses on national issues affecting Native Americans.
Examines federal legislation and governmental policy
developments that affect Indians. Book reviews.
Monthly magazine. 3,000 cir. $25/year, individuals;
$50/year, institutions. Advertising. Begun 1944.

SEQUOYAH SENTINEL
Northwest Indian News Association
Drawer C • Plummer, ID 83851
  (208) 274-3101
Monthly newsletter of the association.

SHAMAN'S DRUM
Cross-Cultural Shaman's Network
Box 270 • Williams, OR 97544
  (541) 846-1313 Fax 846-1204
  Timothy White, Editor
Covers experiential international shamanism, native
medicine ways and spirituality. Book reviews. Quarterly magazine. 14,000 cir.$6/copy; $18/year, individuals; $35/year, institutions; $24/year, foreign. Advertising. Begun 1985.

SHENANDOAH NEWSLETTER
736 W. Oklahoma St.
Appleton, WI 54914
  (414) 832-9525
  Paul A. Skenandore (Scan doa), Publisher/Editor
Discusses the history and legal rights of the native
peoples of Great Turtle Island. Reports news of treaty
and discrimination disputes. Monthly. 1,000 circulation.
$17.50/year, individuals; $22.50/year, institutions; $30/
year, foreign. Begun 1973.

SHO-BAN NEWS
Fort Hall Business Council
P.O. Box 900 • Fort Hall, ID 83203
  (208) 478-3701 Fax 478-3702
  E-mail: shobnews@cyberhighway.net

Weekly tribal newspaper covering local, regional and
national news of interest to American Indians. Advertising accepted. *Subscription:* $30/year, Shoshone-
Bannock tribal members; $35/year, non-members; 75¢
each. Begun 1970.

SHOOTING STAR
Eastern Shawnee Tribe of Oklahoma
P.O. Box 350 • Seneca, MO 64865
  (918) 666-2435 Fax 666-3325
Tribal newsletter.

SICANGU SUN TIMES
116 Fairgrounds • Rosebud, SD 57570
  (605) 747-2058

SILETZ NEWSLETTER
Confederated Tribes of Siletz
P.O. Box 549 • Siletz, OR 97380
  (503) 444-2532 ext. 134
Monthly.

THE SINGING SANDS
Ramah Navajo High School
Ramah, NM 87351

THE SINGING WINDS NEWSLETTER
Council of Three Rivers American Indian Center, Inc.
Rt. 2, Box 247-A • Dorseyville, PA 15238
  (412) 782-4457 Fax 767-4808
  Russell Simms, Editor
Monthly newsletter focusing on the activities
of the Center.

SINTE GLESKA COLLEGE NEWS
Library-Media Center
Box 107, Rosebud Reservation
Mission, SD 57555

SIOUX JOURNAL
Cheyenne River Sioux Tribal Council
P.O. Box 590 • Eagle Butte, SD 57625

SIOUX MESSENGER
Yankton Sioux Tribe
Route 248 • Marty, SD 57361

SIOUX SAN SUN
PHS Indian Hospital
Rapid City, SD 57701

SISSETON AGENCY NEWS
BIA • Sisseton, SD 57262

SMITHSONIAN RUNNER
Smithsonian Institution
Office of Public Affairs
Arts & Industry, 2410 MRC 421
Washington, DC 20560
  (202) 357-2627

SMOKE & FIRE NEWS
P.O. Box 166
Grand Rapids, OH 43522
  (419) 878-8564 Fax 878-3653
  Donlyn Meyers & David Weir, Editors/Publishers
Monthly newspaper that covers all living history periods on a regular schedule supplying Living History Participants with event dates, articles, recipes, updates,
information resources, cartoons, etc. $18 per year.

SMOKE SIGNALS
Bacone College
2299 Old Bacone Rd. • Muskogee, OK 74403

SMOKE SIGNALS
Baltimore American Indian Center
113 S. Broadway
Baltimore, MD 21231
  (410) 675-3535
  Archie Lynch, Editor
Contains news and events concerning the Native
American community of the Baltimore metropolitan
area. No charge; donations accepted.

SMOKE SIGNALS
Colorado River Indian Tribes
Route 1, Box 23-B • Parker, AZ 85344

SMOKE SIGNALS
Northeastern Native American Association, Inc.
P.O. Box 230266 • Hollis, NY 11423
  (718) 978-7057 Fax 978-7200
  E-Mail: rgibson230@aol.com
  William "Wassaja" Gibson, President
Quarterly newsletter.

SMOKE SIGNALS
Confederated Tribes of the
Grand Ronde Community of Oregon
9615 Grand Ronde Rd.
Grand Ronde, OR 97347
  (800) 422-0232
  (503) 879-2254 Fax 879-2173
  Tracy Dugan, Newsletter Director
  E-mail: tracy.dugan@grandronde.org
Twice monthly tribal newspaper, 5,500 cir. Covers
Grand Ronde tribal news, local and regional tribes.
Award winner - Best Layout and Design for twice-
monthly Native paper given by the Native American
Journalists Association. No charge. Began 1980.

SMOKE SIGNALS
Dallas Inter-Tribal Center
209 E. Jefferson Blvd. • Dallas, TX 75203
  (214) 941-1050 Fax 941-6537
  Cindy McKnight, Editor
Covers the news and events of the Native American
community in the Dallas area. Quarterly newsletter.
1,200 cir. (nationwide distribution). No charge.

SMOKE SIGNALS: BUSINESS DIRECTORY
Arrowstar Publishing
P.O. Box 100134 • Denver, CO 80250
  (303) 715-9292
  J. Bell, Editor
Lists over 3,500 American Indian/Alaska Native owned
and operated businesses. $24.95, plus $2.50 shipping
and handling.

SMOKE TALK
Brotherhood of American Indians
P.O. Box 500 • Steilacoom, WA 98388

SMOKI CEREMONIALS & SNAKE DANCE
Smoki People, P.O.Box 123
Prescott, AZ 86302
  (602) 778-5228
Published annually.

SNEE-NEE-CHUM
Nooksack Indian Tribe
P.O. Box 157 • Deming, WA 98925
  (360) 592-5176

**SOCIETY FOR HISTORICAL
ARCHAEOLOGY NEWSLETTER**
P.O. Box 30446 • Tucson, AZ 85751
  (520) 886-8006 Fax 886-0182
  Norman F. Barka, Editor
  E-Mail: sha@azstarnet.com
  Web Site: http://www.sha.org
Presents information on current research and recent
publications, forums on archaeological conservation
and urban archaeology, and information on Society
activities. Quarterly newsletter. Annual membership
dues - $35/students; $55, individuals; $70/institutions.
Begun 1968.

SOTA-EYE-YE-YAPI
P.O. Box 509 • Agency Village, SD 57262

THE SOURCE
New Mexico Office of Indian Affairs
O1A, Villa Rivera Bldg.
224 E. Palace Ave. • Santa Fe, NM 87501
  (505) 827-6440 Fax 827-7308
Provides information on intergovernmental relations,
commissioner activities, culture, arts, and educational
issues of the American Indians. Triannually. Begun
1985.

SOUTH DAKOTA HISTORY
South Dakota State Historical Society
900 Governors Dr. • Pierre, SD 57501-2217
  (605) 773-3458 Fax 773-6041
  Nancy Tystad Koupal, Editor

Web site: www.state.sd.us/deca/cultural
A quarterly scholarly, refereed journal designed for professional historians and lay readers interested in western and Great Plains history. Includes scholarly articles, edited documents, and other annotated, unpublished primary materials that contribute to the knowledge of the history of South Dakota and the surrounding region. 1,600 circ. $30/yr.; $50, foreign. Begun 1972.

SOUTH FLORIDA HISTORY MAGAZINE
Historical Association of Southern Florida
101 West Flagler St. • Miami, FL 33130
(305) 375-1492 Fax 375-1609
Stuart McIver & Rebecca Eads, Editors
E-Mail: hasf@ix.netcom.com
Web site: http://www.historical-museum.org
A quarterly popular history magazine that focuses on the history and folklife of southern Florida and the Caribbean. $35/yr. 5,000 circ. Begun 1973.

**SOUTHERN CALIFORNIA
INDIAN CENTER, INC. - NEWS**
10175 Slater Ave. #150
FOUNTAIN VALLEY, CA 92708
(714) 962-6673
Ms. Starr, Executive Director
Cathi Garfield, Editor
Monthly newsletter. Community articles, news on local pow wow; promotes in-house programs. Complimentary copies are available upon request. Begun 1985.

**SOUTHERN CHEYENNE
& ARAPAHO NATION NEWS**
P.O. Box 91 • Concho, OK 73002

SOUTHERN PUEBLOS AGENCY BULLETIN
BIA, 1000 Indian School Rd., NW
Albuquerque, NM 87103

SOUTHERN UTE DRUM
P.O. Box 737 • Ignacio, CO 81137
(970) 563-0118

SOUTHOLD INDIAN MUSEUM NEWS
1080 Main Bayview Rd.
P.O. Box 268 • Southold, NY 11971
(631) 965-5577
E-mail: indianmuseum@aol.com
Ellen Barcel, President
Quarterly newsletter.

**SOUTHWEST ASSOCIATION ON
INDIAN AFFAIRS NEWSLETTER**
P.O. Box 1964 • Santa Fe, NM 87501

SOUTHWEST MUSEUM NEWS
P.O. Box 41558 • Los Angeles, CA 90041
(213) 261-2164 ext. 233

**SOUTHWEST RESOURCE &
EVALUATION NEWSLETTER**
National Indian Training Research Center
2121 S. Mill Ave. #218 • Tempe, AZ 85282

**SOUTHWESTERN ASSOCIATION OF
INDIAN AFFAIRS, INC. QUARTERLY**
Roswell Printing Co., 110 N. Pennsylvania
Roswell, NM 88201-4620
(505) 983-5220
John Bott, Editor
Quarterly journal covering Indian arts, crafts and writing. 1,000 cir. $15/Year. Begun 1964.

SOUTHWIND
American Indian Association
Southwind, Inc., P.O. Box 59
Charleton, MI 48117 (313) 379-2056

SOVEREIGN NATIONS
Tribal Self-Governance Demonstration Project
Alumni Indian Business Council
2616 Kwina Rd. • Bellingham, WA 98226

SPAWING THE MEDICINE RIVER
Institute of American Indian Arts Museum
P.O. Box 20007 • Santa Fe, NM 87504
(505) 988-6463 Fax 988-6446

Charles A. Dailey, Director
Philip Foss, Jr., Editor
Published quarterly.

SPEAKING LEAVES
American Indian Cultural Group
P.O. Box 2000 • Vacaville, CA 95688

**SPEAKING OF OURSELVES
NI-MI-KWA-ZOO-MIN**
Minnesota Chippewa Tribe
P.O. Box 217 • Cass Lake, MN 56633

THE SPIKE
P.O.Box 368 • Milltown, NJ 08850
(908) 656-0074
Web site: http://typn.com/thespike
Monthly newsletter on Native East Coast events.

SPILYAY TYMOO
Confederated Tribes of Warm Springs
P.O. Box 870 • Warm Springs, OR 97761
(541) 553-3274 Fax 553-3539
Bi-weekly newsletter.

SPIPA INTERTRIBAL NEWS
SE 2750 Old Olympic Hwy.
Shelton, WA 98584

SPIRIT!
Native American Resource Center
Pembroke State University
Pembroke, NC 28372
(919) 521-4214
Contains news of projects and events of the Center. Quarterly. No charge. Begun 1987.

SPIRIT OF CRAZY HORSE
Leonard Peltier Defense Committee
P.O. Box 583 • Lawrence, KS 66044
(785) 842-5774 Fax 842-5796
Pat Benabe, Editor
E-Mail: lpdc@idir.net
Web site: http://members.xoom.com/
freepeltier/index.html.
Bimonthly newspaper dealing with the current campaign to free Leonard Peltier, as well as Indigenous, environmental, social and political issues. Statements from Leonard Peltier appear in each publication. $15/year; $22, international; $7, senior; no charge to prisoners.

SPIRIT TALK
The Blackfoot Nation
P.O. Box 430 • Browning, MT 59417
(800) 350-2882; (406) 338-2882 Fax 338-5120
Long Standing Bear Chief, Editor
A quarterly magazine in celebration of Indian culture. Topics include: respect for the earth, the sacredness of the family, stories and legends, profiles of significant people, Indian music and dance, Indian art and artisans, history, Indian foods, uses of plants; books, movie and video reviews; cultural seminars; places to visit in Indian Country; and events in Indian Country: celebrations, rodeos and fairs. 50,000 cir. $4.75, single copies; $18/year. Advertising. Begun 1994.

SPIRIT WALKER
Native American Indian Community
Rd. 2 Box 247A • Kittanning, PA 16201
(412) 548-7335
Newsletter.

SPIRIT WIND
United Native American Educational Council
P.O. Box 17052 • Spartanburg, SC 29301
(803) 574-8633

SPRING CREEK PACKET
3925 Bissell Rd. • Springfield, IL 62707
(217) 525-2698
Lists pow-wows; other Native news items.
Monthly. $15/year.

SPRINGFIELD AREA OFFICE NEWS
Confederated Tribes of Siletz
188 W. B St., Bldg. P • Springfield, OR 97477
(541) 746-9658

THE SQUAW'S MESSAGE
Sisterhood of American Indians
P.O. Box 17 • Big Harbor, WA 98335

SQUOL - QUOL
Lummi Nation Tribal Office
2616 Kwina Rd.
Bellingham, WA 98255
(360) 384-1489

STANDING ROCK SIOUX TRIBAL NEWSLETTER
P.O. Box D • Fort Yates, ND 58538

STAR HORSE NEWS
3200 Coors NW, Suite K #231
Albuquerque, NM 87120
Quarterly newsletter with news of the pow-wow world.

STEALING OF CALIFORNIA
Native American Training Association Institute
P.O. Box 1505
Sacramento, CA 95807

STOCKBRIDGE MUNSEE TRIBAL NEWSLETTER
RR 1 • Bowler, WI 54416

STOWW INDIAN VOICE
P.O. Box 578 • Sumner, WA 98390

STUDIES IN AMERICAN INDIAN LITERATURES
orders to: University of Nebraska Press
233 North 8th St. • Lincoln, NE 68588
(800) 755-1105 Fax (800) 526-2617
(402) 472-3584 (outside U.S.)
Submissions to: Malea Powell, Editor
c/o Studies in American Indian Literatures
Michigan State University, 273 Bessey Hall
East Lansing, MI 48824-1033
E-mail: sail2@msu.edu
Quarterly scholarly journal focusing exclusively on American Indian literature, primarily academic, and those involved one way or another with the study of or creation of Native American literatures (oral as well as print, old time as well as contemporary); also includes reviews, interviews, bibliographies, scholarly and theoretical articles. 400 cir. $28/yr., individuals; $56/yr., institutions; $20, single issues.

SUISA NEWS
Survival International USA
2121 Decatur Place, NW
Washington, DC 20008

SUNDEVIL ROUNDUP
Rough Rock Community High School
Star Route 1 • Rough Rock, AZ 85021

SUNLODGE BUFFALO TALES
c/o Gene Barbee, P.O. Box 262
Spencer, NC 28159-0262
Gene Barbee, Editor
Quarterly magazine. $12/year.

SUQUAMISH NEWS
Suquamish Tribe, P.O. Box 498
Suquamish, WA 98392
(360) 598-3311
Leonard Forsman, Editor

**SUSQUEHANNA VALLEY
NATIVE AMERICAN EAGLE**
P.O. Box 99 • Loganville, PA 17342-0099 ·
(717) 428-1440
Gerald Dietz, Editor
Bi-monthly newsletter for Native and non-Native people interested in current events, powwows, festivals, and historic articles on native people of the mid-Atlantic region. Also includes recipes, poetry, etc. $6/year.

SURFACE SCATTER
Marin Museum of the American Indian
P.O. Box 864, 2200 Novato Blvd.
Novato, CA 94947 (415) 897-4064
Quarterly newsletter.

SWAIA INDIAN MARKET
Southwestern American Indian Arts
320 Galisteo, Suite 600 • Gallup, NM 87501

T

TA NEWSLETTER OF UIATF
Daybreak Star Press • Box 99253
Seattle, WA 98199

TALKING LEAVES
American Indianist Society
15 Mattson Ave. • Worcester, MA 01606
(508) 852-6271

TALKING PEACEPIPE
Southeast Michigan Indians, Inc.
P.O. Box 861 • Warren, MI 48090
(313) 756-1350
Monthly newsletter. Advertising. $3/year.

TALKING STICK
American Indian Artists (AMERINDA), INC.
c/o AFSC, 15 Rutherford Pl. • New York, NY 10003
(212) 598-0968 Fax 529-4603
Diane Fraher Thornton, Artistic Director
E-mail: amerinda@amerinda.org
Website: www.amerinda.org
Native arts quarterly.

TEKAKWITHA CONFERENCE NEWSLETTER
Tekakwitha Conference National Center
1800 9th Ave. S., Box 6759
Great Falls, MT 59406-6759
(406) 727-0147 Gilbert Hemauer
Quarterly. 15,000 cir. Begun 1979.

TEQUESTA
Historical Association of Southern Florida
101 West Flagler St. • Miami, FL 33130
(305) 375-1492 Fax 375-1609
Paul S. George, PhD, Editor
E-Mail: hasf@ix.netcom.com
Web site: http://www.historical-museum.org
Annual scholarly journal focusing on southern Florida
and the Caribbean. 3,500 cir. $35/annual dues. Begun 1941.

THEATA
Cross Cultural Communications Department
University of Alaska, Alaskan Native Program
Fairbanks, AK 99708
(907) 474-7181
Pat Kwachka, Editor
Alaskan Native college students writing on traditional
and contemporary topics. Annual journal. 4,000 cir.
$5/year. Begun 1973.

THUNDERCHILD NEWS
Thunderchild Treatment Center
1000 Decca Rd. • Sheridan, WY 82801
(307) 750-2255 Fax 750-2260
Published three times per year.

THE THUNDERER
American Indian Bible Institute
100020 N. 15th Ave. • Phoenix, AZ 85021

TI SWANNI ITST
Skokomish Indian Tribal Center
Rt. 5, Box 432 • Shelton, WA 98584

TLIN TSIM HAI
Ketchikan Indian Corporation
429 Deermount • Ketchikan, AK 99901

TLINGIT/HAIDA TRIBAL NEWS
Tlingit/Haida Central Council
One Sealaska Plaza, Suite 300
Juneau, AK 99801 (312) 784-1050

TODAY'S MINORITIES: THE
VOICE OF AMERICA'S FUTURE
3220 N St., NW • Washington, DC 20007
(800) 398-2201; (800) 735-5397
Charles Bivonia, Jr., Editor
Quarterly newspaper. $15/yr.; $18/2 yrs.

TOMAHAWK
Oregon State University
P.O. Box 428 • Warm Springs, OR 97761

TONAWANDA INDIAN NEWS
P.O. Box 64 • Akron, NY 14001

TOSAN
P.O. Box 162 • Dayton, OH 45401

TRAILBLAZER
Cook Inlet Native Association
Anchorage, Alaska 99503
(907) 278-4641

TRC NEWS
Tribal Research Center-NAES College
2838 W. Peterson Ave. • Chicago, IL 60659
(312) 761-5000
Reports on the activities of the center.
Monthly newsletter. Begun 1987.

TREATY COUNCIL NEWS
International Indian Treaty Council
2390 Mission St., Suite 301
San Francisco, CA 94110
(415) 641-4482 Fax 641-1298
Andrea Carmen, Executive Director
$10/year, individuals; $15/year, institutions.

TRENDS IN INDIAN HEALTH
Indian Health Service
5600 Fisher's Ln. • Rockville, MD 20857
(301) 443-1083
Annual publication.

TRIBAL ADVOCATE
Piliero Mazza and Pargament, PLCC
888 17th St., NW, Suite 1100
Washington, DC 20006
(202) 857-1000 Fax 857-0200
Pamela J. Mazza, Editor
E-mail: pmazza@pmplawfirm.com
Website: www.pmplawfirm.com
Subscription newsletter, published ten times per year,
devoted exclusively to legal and business issues affecting tribes, Alaska Native corporations and their
businesses. Also, conducts interviews with various
business and government officials.

TRIBAL COLLEGE JOURNAL
American Indian Higher Education Consortium
P.O. Box 720 • Mancos, CO 81328
(970) 533-9170 Fax 533-9145
Marjane Ambler, Editor
E-mail: info@tribalcollegejournal.org
Web site: www.tribalcollegejournal.org
The official journal of the Consortium, focusing on postsecondary education of Native Americans. 4x/yr. $34/
yr. Begun 1989.

TRIBAL DIRECTORY
Arizona Commission on Indian Affairs
1400 W. Washington St. #300
Phoenix, AZ 85007
(602) 542-3123 Fax 542-3223
Eleanor Descheeny-Joe, Editor

TRIBAL NEWSLETTER
Confederated Tribes of Coos
Lower Umpqua & Suislaw Indians
338 Wallace Ave. • Coos Bay, OR 97420
(541) 267-5454 Fax 269-1647

TRIBAL TRIBUNE
Colville Confederated Tribes
P.O. Box 150 • Nespelem, WA 99155
(509) 634-8835 Fax 634-4617
Sheila Whitelaw, Editor
Monthly newspaper of the Confederated Tribes of the
Colville Reservation. 4,500 cir. $15/year in Washington; $20/year outside Washington.

TRIBAL VISION
National Tribal Environmental Council
2221 Rio Grande NW
Albuquerque, NM 87104
(505) 242-2175
Jerry Pardilla, Executive Director
E-mail: ntec@ntec.org; Website: www.ntec.org
Quarterly newsletter focusing on the environmental
concerns of Native Americans. Begun in 1991.

TRIBE OF FIVE FEATHERS NEWS
P.O. Box W • Lompoc, CA 93436

TSISTSISTAS PRESS
P.O. Box 693 • Lame Deer, MT 59043

TU'KWA HONE' NEWSLETTER
Burns Paiute Tribe
HC-71, 100 Pa'Si'Go' St.
Burns, OR 97720 (503) 573-2088
Weekly tribal newsletter.

TURTLE MOUNTAIN TIMES
Turtle Mountain Tribe
P.O. Box 1270 • Belcourt, ND 58316
(701) 477-6451 Fax 477-6836
Brenda Greenwood & Orie Richard, Co-editors
Bryant LaVallie, Manager
Weekly tribal newspaper.

THE TURTLE TIMES
The Free Cherokees-Turtle Clan
3200 Lenox Rd. NE #A-107
Atlanta, GA 30324 (404) 381-0628
Satinka Browne, Editor

TURTLETALK
Massachusetts Center for Native American Awareness
P.O. Box 5885 • Boston, MA 02114
(617) 884-4227
Burne Stanley, Editor
E-mail: mcnaa@aol.com
Website: www.mcnaa.org
Quarterly newsletter.

U

UMATILLA AGENCY NEWSLETTER
Bureau of Indian Affairs
P.O. Box 520 • Pendleton, OR 97801

UNITED INDIANS OF ALL TRIBES
FOUNDATION—TA NEWSLETTER
United Indians of All Tribes
P.O. Box 99100
Seattle, WA 98199

UNITED LENAPE NATION NEWSLETTER
P.O. Box 1198 • Fredonia, AZ 86022

UNITED LUMBEE NATION TIMES
United Lumbee Nation of N.C. and America
P.O. Box 512
Fall River Mills, CA 96028-0512
(916) 336-6701
Silver Star Reed, Editor
Tribal newspaper containing articles and information
concerning members of the Lumbee Nation of Indians. Published 3-4 times per year. 1,500 cir. $2 per
copy. Complimentary copies available upon request.
Advertising. Begun 1979.

UNITED TRIBES NEWS
3315 University Dr. • Bismarck, ND 58504
(701) 255-3285 Fax 255-1844

UNITY NEWS
United National Indian Tribal Youth (UNITY)
P.O. Box 800
Oklahoma City, OK 73101-0800
(405) 424-3010 Fax 424-3018
J.R. Cook, Executive Director
Sherry Kast, Communications Director
E-Mail: unity@unityinc.org
Quarterly newspaper for Native American youth, youth
advisors and coordinators, and others interested in
American Indian and Alaskan Native youth. Contents
promotes the activities, training sessions and conferences of UNITY, and promotes the positive actions and
leadership ability of outstanding Native youth ages 15-
24. Advertising accepted. No charge.

THE USET CALUMET
711 Stewarts Ferry Pike, #100
Nashville, TN 37214
(615) 872-7900 Fax 872-7417

UTE BULLETIN
Uintah & Ouray Tribe
P.O. Box 190
Fort Duchesne, UT 84026
(801) 722-5141 Fax 722-2374
Carleen Kurip, Editor
Monthly newspaper covering American Indian interests. Book reviews. 1,500 cir. $1/copy; $6/year. Advertising. Begun 1974.

V

VALLEY ROUND UP
Shoshone-Paiute Business Council
P.O. Box 219
Owyhee, Nevada 89832

VALLEY SPIRIT NEWS
P.O. Box 3122
Scottsdale, AZ 85271

VIDEOFORUM
MacArthur Foundation Library Video Project
P.O. Box 409113 • Chicago, IL 60640
(800) 847-3671
Mary M. Kirby, Director
First issue is on Native American videos.

VIRGINIA HERITAGE
P.O. Box 3695
Fredericksburg, VA 22401
(540) 371-2339
Tina M. Sears, Publisher
E-mail: virginiaheritage@cox.net
Website: www.virginiaheritage.net
Bimonthly magazine. Virginia history, tribes, issues.

THE VISION MAKER
Native American Public Telecommunications
1800 North 33rd St.
Lincoln, NE 68501
(402) 472-3522 Fax 472-8675
Justin Grotelueschen, Editor
E-mail: native@unl.edu
Website: www.nativetelecom.org
A seasonal newsletter.

VISIONS
Communications Publishing Group, Inc.
3100 Broadway, #225
Kansas City, MO 64111
(816) 756-3039
Georgia Lee Clark, President & Editor
A resource guide for Native-American students containing individual profiles, scholarships and financial aid information, calendar of events, etc. Semiannually in March and September. $1.50 each.

THE VOICE
Denver Indian Center
4407 Morrison Rd.
Denver, CO 80219
(303) 937-0401
Lisa Harjo, Editor
Monthly newsletter reporting on local programs, activities, issues. $10/yr.

THE VOICE OF BROTHERHOOD
423 Seward St.
Juneau, Alaska 99801

VOICE OF THE CROOKED TREE
Route 1, Box 135
Suttons Bay, MI 49632

VOICE OF THUNDER
Amerine Enterprises
P.O. Box 238 • Carlin, NV 89822

VOICE OF THE TURTLE
Tolba, Inc., P.O. Box 8113
North Brattleboro, VT 05304
(802) 254-8790
Quarterly.

W

WAAYP 'ESTIK BARONA NEWS
Barona Band of Mission Indians
1095 Barona Rd. • Lakeside, CA 92040
(619) 443-6612
Laura White Cloud, Editor
E-mail: lwhitecloud@barona.org
Tribal newsletter.

WAHPETON HIGHLIGHTS
Wahpeton Indian School
Wahpeton, ND 58075

WALKER RIVER PAIUTE TRIBAL NEWS NOTES
Walker River Paiute Tribe
P.O. Box 220, Schurz, NV 89427
(702) 773-2306 Fax 773-2585

WAMIDIOTA NEWSLETTER
Fort Lewis College, Div. of Intercultural Studies
120 Miller Student Ctr.
Durango, CO 81301

WANA CHINOOK TYMOO
Columbia River Inter-Tribal Fish Commission
729 N.E. Oregon, #200
Portland, OR 97232
(503) 238-0667 Fax 235-4228
Laura Berg, Editor
Carol Craig & Dan Kane, Staff
Columbia River salmon stories.
Quarterly magazine. 6,000 cir.

WANBLI HO: A LITERARY ARTS JOURNAL
Lakota Studies/Creative Writing Program
Sinte Gleska College
P.O. Box 8 • Mission, SD 57555
Victor Douville, Editor
Features short fiction, poetry, literary articles, oral tradition texts, and artwork. Focuses on contemporary and traditional Native-American literature and art. Published twice a year. Subscription: $7.50/year; $4.50 each issue.

WARM SPRINGS TRIBAL NEWSLETTER
P.O. Box C, Warm Springs, OR 97761
(541) 553-1161 Fax 553-1924

WARPATH
United Native Americans
2434 Faria Ave. • Pinole, CA 94564
(415) 758-8160
Lehman L. Brightman, Editor
Monthly newsletter.

THE WARRIOR
American Indian Center
1630 W. Wilson • Chicago, IL 60640
(312) 275-5871/561-8183

THE WASHINGTON NEWSPAPER
3833 Stone Way, North
Seattle, Washington 98103

WASHOE NEWSLETTER
Washoe Tribe, 919 Hwy 395 S.
Gardnerville, NV 89410
(702) 265-4191 Fax 265-6240
Tribal newsletter.

WASSO-GEE-WAD-NEE
Council—Marquette Branch Prison
P.O. Box 779 • Marquette, MI 49855

WE SA MI DONG
Route 5, Box 5320
Hayward, Wisconsin 54843

WELLPINIT INDEPENDENT WATCHDOG
P.O. Box 213 • Wellpinit, WA 99040
(509) 238-0667

WHIRLING RAINBOW - VOICE OF THE PEOPLE
Pan-American Indian Association
8335 Sevigny Dr.
N. Fort Myers, FL 33917-1705
(941) 731-7029 or 543-7727

Cindy "Spirit Catcher" Barnard, Editor
Quarterly.

WHISPERING WIND MAGAZINE
Written Heritage
P.O. Box 1390
Folsom, LA 70437-1390
(800) 301-8009; (504) 796-5433 Fax 796-9236
E-mail: whiswind@i-55.com
Website: www.whisperingwind.com
Jack B. Herlard, Editor
Bimonthly magazine of American Indian crafts and material culture. Includes how-to craft articles, old photos, history, powwow dates and reports, and video and book reviews. 24,000 cir. $20/yr.; $35/two yrs Advertising. Began 1967.

WHISPERING WINDS
Tule River Tribal Council
Porterville, CA 93258

WHITE EARTH RESERVATION NEWS
P.O. Box 274
White Earth, MN 56591

WHITE MOUNTAIN APACHE NEWSPAPER
P.O. Box 700
White River, AZ 85941

WHITE MOUNTAIN EAGLE
P.O. Box 1570
Show Low, AZ 85901

THE WICAZO SA REVIEW
(The Red Pencil Review)
University of Minnesota Press
Minneapolis, MN 55455
Journal of American Studies devoted to the development of Native American Studies as an academic discipline. *Contributing editors*: William Willard, Roger Buffalohead, Beatrice Medicine, Larry Evers, Ted Jojola, Cecil T. Joie, A. Blair Stonechild, Jack D. Forbes, Steven J. Crum, Robert Warrior, Gloria Bird, and James Riding In. Bi-annual. 600 cir. $20/year. Begun 1985.

WICOZANNI WOWAPI
Native American Community Board
P.O. Box 572 • Lake Andres, SD 57356
(605) 487-7072 Fax 487-7964
Charon Asetoyer, Editor
Newsletter of the Native American Community Board concerned with Native American issues. No charges; donations accepted. Quarterly.

WI GUABA
Havasupai Tribal Council
P.O. Box 10 • Supai, AZ 86435

WIG-I-WAM
Department of Indian Work
Minnesota Council of Churches
3045 Park Ave. So.
Minneapolis, MN 55407

WIGWAM CLUB MONTHLY
Greater Minneapolis Council of Churches
122 West Franklin Ave.
Minneapolis, MN 55404

WIIGEGABA
Havasupai Tribe
P.O. Box 8010 • Supai, AZ 86435
(520) 448-2731
Tribal newspaper.

WILDFIRE MAGAZINE
Beart Tribe Medicine Society
3750A Airport Blvd. #223
Mobile, AL 36608-1618
Sun Bear, Publisher
Matthew Ryan, Editor
Concerned with healthy living, including in-depth interviews, environmental issues, book reviews, etc. Semiannual. 10,000 cir. $4/copy; $15/year; $23/year, Canada; $27/year, foreign. Library rates: $7.50/year-U.S., $15/year, Canada. $2.50 per copy. Advertising. Begun 1961.

WILLIAM & MARY QUARTERLY
Institute of Early American History & Culture
P.O. Box 8781
Williamsburg, VA 23187-8781
 (757) 221-1120 Fax 221-1047
 Philip Morgan, Editor
 Ann Gross, Managing Editor
Scholarly journal containing articles on American Indians, including Caribbean and Southwestern, in the period up to about 1820—including their relations with other groups in early America. 3,600 circ. $30/year, individuals; $50, institutions; $15, students.

WIN-AWENEN-NISITOTUNG
Sault Ste. Marie Tribe of Chippewa Indians
206 Greenough St., 2nd Floor
Sault Ste. Marie, MI 49783
 (906) 635-4768 Fax 635-7016
 Jennifer Dale, Editor
Tabloid published every three weeks (17 times per year), 24 pages. Contains local, state, national news and features. *Subscription:* $15/year, U.S.; $22/year, Canada; $32/year, other foreign countries. 15,000 circ. Advertising accepted. Begun 1978.

WIND RIVER JOURNAL
Shoshone Tribe
P.O. Box 157
Fort Washakie, WY 82514

WIND RIVER NEWS
P.O. Box J • Lander, WY 82520

WIND RIVER RENDEZVOUS
St. Stephan's Mission Foundation
P.O. Box 278 • St. Stephan, WY 82524
 (307) 856-6797
 Ron Marnot, Editor
Covers the history of Western USA, cultural contribution of the Native American, and pastoral programs for the Arapaho and Shoshoni people at St. Stephens Mission. Quarterly magazine. 41,000 cir. $10/year. Begun 1971.

WINDOW ROCK SCENE
P.O. Box 580 • Window Rock, AZ 86515
 (505) 371-5392

WINDS OF CHANGE
A.I.S.E.S. Publishing, Inc.
P.O. Box 9828
Albuquerque, NM 87119
 (505) 765-1052 Fax 765-5608
 James Weidlein, Editor
Designed to provide positive program information and successful role models for Indian students and professionals of all disciplines (not just science and engineering.) Information about education and career opportunities, as well as tribal culture and events. A new section highlights articles and information about environmental concerns and issues of interest to Native Americans. Quarterly magazine. 50,000 cir. $24/year.

WINNEBAGO INDIAN NEWS
P.O. Box 687 • Winnebago, NE 68071
 (402) 878-3220 Fax 878-2632
 Jerome LaPointe, Editor
 E-mail: winnebagoindiannews@yahoo.com
Biweekly newspaper of the Winnebago Tribe of Nebraska.

WOLF SONGS
The Tiospaye, P.O. Box 200
Wamblee, SD 57577 (605) 462-6544
Quarterly. 4 issues for $10.

WOODLAND VOICE
Mille Lacs Band of Ojibwe
43408 Oodena Dr.
Onamia, MN 56359
 (320) 532-4181 ext. 7486 Fax 532-4209
A quarterly newsletter for the Mille Lacs Ojibwe community, employees of Grand Casino Mille Lacs and Grand Casino Hinckley, the media, tribal government employees, legislators, and state government officials.

WOTANGING IKCHE
E-mail: gars@nanews.org
Web site: www.nanews.org/
Weekly electronic Native American news.

WOTANIN WOWAPI
Fort Peck Assiniboine & Sioux Tribes
P.O. Box 1027 • Poplar, MT 59255
 (406) 768-5155 Ext. 2370
 Bonnie Red Elk, Editor
Weekly newspaper of articles and photos of news pertinent to the Assiniboine and Sioux people residing on the Fort Peck Reservation. Also contains complete tribal government meetings; also a historical review of the tribes. Complimentary copies available upon request. Advertising. Begun 1976.

WUSKUSU YERTUM
Mashantucket Pequot Tribe
Box 160, Indian Town Rd.
Ledyard, CT 06339

WYOMING INDIAN HIGH SCHOOL NEWSLETTER
P.O. Box 145 • Ethete, WY 82520

Y

YA-KA-AMA INDIAN EDUCATION NEWSLETTER
6215 East Side Rd.
Forestville, CA 95436

YAKIMA DRUMBEAT
P.O. Box 365
Wapato, Washington 98951

YAKAMA NATION REVIEW
Yakama Indian Nation
P.O. Box 310 • Toppenish, WA 98948
 (509) 865-5121 Fax 865-2794
 Ronnie Washines, Managing Editor
 E-mail: ynreview@yakima.com
Contains articles pertaining to and affecting Native Americans, human interests involving Native American population, governmental action on national, state and local levels relevant to the Yakama Tribal Government structure. Biweekly newspaper. 5,500 cir. $26/year. Complimentary copies available upon request. Advertising. Begun 1970.

YANKTON SIOUX MESSINGER
P.O. Box 248
Marty, SD 57361

YAQUI BULLETIN
4730 West Calle Tetakusin
Tucson, AZ 85910

YUGTARVIK REGIONAL MUSEUM NEWSLETTER
P.O. Box 338 • Bethel, AK 99559
Monthly.

YUPIIT GANLAUCIAT
Association of Village Council President
Pouch 219
Bethel, AK 99559

Z

ZUNI CARRIER
Zuni Pueblo
Zuni, NM 87327

ZUNI LEGAL AID NEWSLETTER
Zuni, NM 87327

ZUNI TRIBAL NEWSLETTER
Box 339, Zuni Tribal Office
Zuni, NM 87327

ALASKA

ALASKAN TREASURES
1013 E. Dimond #514
ANCHORAGE, AK 99515
  (907) 333-5839;
  Fred, Eva & Angie Larson, Owners
Wholesale, retail. *Products*: Beadwork, clothing, dolls, art, carvings, craft supplies. *Membership*: IACA.

ALONDA STUDIO
3212 West 30th Ave.
ANCHORAGE, AK 99517
  (907) 248-0454
  Helen J. Simeonoff, Owner/Manager
Wholesale, retail. *Products*: Original watercolors of Alaska subject matter, such as Alaska Natives, historical masks.

"OOMINGMAK" - MUSK OX PRODUCERS' COOPERATIVE
604 H St. • ANCHORAGE, AK 99501
  (907) 272-9225
  Sigrun C. Robertson, Manager
  E-mail: oomingmak@qiviut.com
  Web site: www.qiviut.com
Mail order, limited retail. Yupik and Inupiat Alaska Native cooperative. *Products*: Handknitted Qiviut (the underwool of the arctic musk oxen), garments such as caps, scarves, tunics, and nachaqs. Brochure and price list.

SMALL TREASURES
8851 Cordell Circle #5
ANCHORAGE, AK 99502
  (907) 248-9639
  Patrick W. Lind, Owner/Manager
Retail, wholesale; special orders. *Products*: Aleut arts & crafts; paintings; birchwood products.

TAHETA ARTS & CULTURAL GROUP
605 "A" St. • ANCHORAGE, AK 99501
  (907) 272-5829; Rick Lonsdale, Manager
Retail, mail order, wholesale; special orders. Eskimo, Indian & Aleut nonprofit cooperative. *Products*: Ivory, stone, wood, and bone carvings; baskets; ivory carvings; jewelry; masks; etchings, drawings & prints.

WHALE DREAMS STUDIO
P.O. Box 112492 • ANCHORAGE, AK 99511
  (907) 344-6789
  Jerry Laktonen, Owner/Manager
Retail, mail order. Commissions accepted. *Products*: Alutiiq (Sugpiaq) masks and paddles. Brochure and price list, $5.

YUGTARVIK REGIONAL MUSEUM SHOP
P.O. Box 388 • BETHEL, AK 99559
  (907) 543-2098
  Penni K. Abraham, Manager
Wholesale/mail order. *Products*: Baskets, clothing, dolls, jewelry, sculpture, carvings.

YUP'IK GIFT SHOP
P.O. Box 219 • BETHEL, AK 99559
  (907) 543-1819; Mary Romer, Manager
Mail order. Special orders accepted. Nonprofit organization. *Products*: Grass baskets, mats, trays, plates; wooden & ivory masks & carvings; Native made clothing; bead, quill & ivory jewelry; dolls; headdresses; drawings.

ST. LAWRENCE ISLAND ORIGINAL IVORY COOPERATIVE, LTD.
P.O. Box 189 • GAMBELL, AK 99742
  (907) 985-5112/5649 Fax 985-5927
  Clement Ungott, Manager
Mail order. Eskimo Cooperative. *Products*: Eskimo walrus ivory carvings of animal figurines; bracelets; cribbage boards; etchings. Price list.

CHILKAT VALLEY ARTS
209 Willard St., P.O. Box 145 •
HAINES, AK 99827
  (907) 766-2990 Fax 766-3090
  Susan Folletti, Owner/Manager
Retail. *Products*: Silver jewelry, totemic designs of the Northwest Coast Tlingit Indians. *Second shop*: The Far North, Haines, AK.

THE FAR NORTH
111 2nd Ave., P.O. Box 145
HAINES, AK 99827
  (907) 766-3535 Fax 766-3090
  Susan Folletti, Owner/Manager
Retail. *Products*: Fine Eskimo art - ivory and soapstone carvings, baleen and grass baskets, jewelry.

INUA
P.O. Box 4243 • HOMER, AK 99603
  (907) 235-6644
  William E. Lovett, Owner
Retail, wholesale. *Products*: Native crafts from Alaska - Baskets, beadwork, clothing, dolls, art, dreamcatchers, jewelry, miniatures, sculpture, carvings, repair & restoration. *Appraisals*: Baskets, art, sculpture. *Membership*: IACA. *Branch*: Anchorage, AK.

AMOS WALLACE
P.O. Box 478 • JUNEAU, AK 99802
  (907) 586-9000
  Amos Wallace, Owner
Wholesale, mail order. Tlingit crafts. Special orders on totem poles, masks and paddles.

INUCRAFT
P.O. Box 49 • KOTZEBUE, AK 99752
  (907) 442-2800
Retail, mail order. A division of NANA Development Corp. *Products*: Eskimo dolls, masks, birch bark baskets, carvings, jewelry, parkas and mukluks.

NANA MUSEUM OF THE ARCTIC CRAFT SHOP
P.O. Box 49 • KOTZEBUE, AK 99752
  (907) 442-3304/3747
  Pete Schaeffer
Retail, mail order by special request. *Products*: Baskets, clothing, dolls, art, jewelry, sculpture, carvings.

SAVOONGA NATIVE STORE
P.O. Box 100 • SAVOONGA, AK 99769
  Paul Rookok, Sr., Manager
Mail order. *Products*: Eskimo ivory carvings, jewelry. Price list available.

RAVEN ART STUDIO
820 Charles St. • SITKA, AK 99835
  (907) 747-3641; Teri Rofkar, Owner/Manager
  E-mail: cuthbert@ptialaska.net
Retail, limited wholesale; special commissions. *Products*: Tlingit traditional spruce root & cedar bark baskets, recently revived Tlingit Raven's Tail wool weavings.

MARDINA DOLLS
P.O. Box 611 • WRANGELL, AK 99929
  (907) 874-3854; Marleita Wallace, Owner/Manager
Wholesale, mail order. *Products*: Tlingit-Tsimsian art, clothing, dolls. Flyer available.

ARIZONA

JESSE T. HUMMINGBORD
102 Silver St. • BISBEE, AZ 85603
  (520) 432-7305 Fax 432-4306
Retail, wholesale. *Products*: A,H. Original acrylic contemporary paintings of Cherokee and other Native American themes. Brochire & price list. *Memberships*: IACA, SWAI, Intertribal Indian Ceremonial.

NAVAJO ARTS & CRAFTS ENTERPRISE
P.O. Box 464 • CAMERON, AZ 86020
  (520) 679-2244
Retail, wholesale. Tribal Enterprise. *Products*: Art, baskets, beadwork, clothing, dolls, jewelry, kachinas, pottery, sandpaintings, sculpture, carvings, craft supplies, repairs & restoration. Branch shop.

THE BOULDERS
P.O. Box 2090 • CAREFREE, AZ 85377
  (602) 9009 Fax 488-4118
  Melissa Brasch, William Nassikas, Kenneth Humes
Retail. *Products*: Baskets, ornaments, drums, pipes, fetishes, jewelry, kachinas, pottery, rugs. *Membership*: IACA.

D.Y. BEGAY; NAVAJO TEXTILE STUDIO
P.O. Box 1770 • CHINLE, AZ 86503

(201) 391-2236
Retail, by appointment only. *Products*: V. Traditional and contemporary Navajo weavings—rugs, blankets and tapestries. Special orders accepted.

NAVAJO ARTS & CRAFTS ENTERPRISE
P.O. Box 608 • CHINLE, AZ 86503
  (520) 674-5338
Retail, wholesale. Tribal Enterprise. *Products*: Art, baskets, beadwork, clothing, dolls, jewelry, kachinas, pottery, sandpaintings, sculpture, carvings, craft supplies, repairs & restoration. Branch shop.

THUNDERBIRD LODGE
Canyon de Chelly, Box 548
CHINLE, AZ 86503
  (602) 674-5841
  Mary Jones, Owner
Retail. *Products*: All. *Membership*: IACA.

ARROWHEAD TRADING POST
1402 Gold Dust Circle
COTTONWOOD, AZ 86326-4867
  (602) 476-3140
  Dorothea L. Poland
Retail. *Products*: Art, beadwork, boxes, clothing, dolls, drums, fetishes, heishi, jewelry, kachinas, rugs, sandpaintings. *Membership*: IACA.

BLACK MESA TRADERS
2930 E. Matterhorn Dr.
FLAGSTAFF, AZ 86004-2213
  (602) 526-8354 Fax 774-9079
  Rita Alexander & Rodger Berg
Wholesaler. *Products*: Art, baskets, beadwork, ornaments, clothing, dolls, artifacts, jewelry, kachinas, miniatures, sculpture, carvings; repairs & restoration. *Appraisals*: Kachinas. Specializes in Kachinas. *Membership*: IACA. Catalog.

MILT'S INDIAN ARTS
P.O. Box 22007 • FLAGSTAFF, AZ 86002
  (602) 526-0442
  Milton Forsman
Wholesale. *Products*: baskets, rugs, sandpaintings, sculpture, carvings.

DEE'S EXQUISITE JEWELRY
P.O. Box 235 • FREDONIA, AZ 86022
  (602) 643-7093
  Melvin Martin and Dolores Savala
Retail.

MELJOY INDIAN TRADERS
165 Amarilla Dr. • GLOBE, AZ 85501
  (602) 425-0216
  Melvin & Joyce Montgomery
Wholesale, retail. *Products*: Baskets, beadwork, clothing, dolls, miniatures. *Membership*: IACA.

GRAND CANYON SQUIRE INN
Box 130, Hwy. 64/180
GRAND CANYON, AZ 86023
  (520) 638-2681
  Raymond Curley, Manager
Retail. *Products*: Art, baskets, beadwork, drums, pipes, jewelry, pottery, rugs, weavings, sandpaintings, sculpture, carvings.

PRINGLE'S SOUTHWEST, LTD.
P.O. Box 503 • GREEN VALLEY, AZ 85614
  (520) 648-1388
  Don & Phyllis Pringle
Retail. *Products*: Baskets, fetishes, jewelry, miniatures, pottery, rugs, wewavings.

CHEE'S INDIAN STORE, INC.
P.O. Box 66, I-40 Allentown Rd., Exit 351
HOUCK, AZ 86506
  (520) 688-2603
  Clara Chee & Harrison Lauber
  Karen Chee & Paul Schell
Retail. *Products*: All. *Membership*: IACA.

THE GIFT SHOP OF JEROME
P.O. Box 396, 114 Jerome Ave.
JEROME, AZ 86331
  (520) 634-5105
  Anna Rae Adams
Wholesale, retail. *Products*: All. *Membership*: IACA.

NAVAJO ARTS & CRAFTS ENTERPRISE
Hwys. 160 & 163, KAYENTA, AZ 86033
(520) 697-8611
Retail, wholesale. Tribal Enterprise. *Products*: Art, baskets, beadwork, clothing, dolls, jewelry, kachinas, pottery, sandpaintings, sculpture, carvings, craft supplies, repairs & restoration. Branch shop.

McGEE'S INDIAN ART
P.O. Box 607, Hwy. 264
KEAMS CANYON, AZ 86034
(520) 738-2295 Fax 738-5250
William B. & C.F. McGee
Wholesale, retail. *Products*: Art, baskets, beadwork, clothing, dolls, jewelry, kachinas, pottery, sandpaintings, sculpture, carvings, craft supplies, repairs & restoration. *Membership*: IACA.

MORNING STAR INDIAN JEWELRY
P.O. Box 987 • KINGMAN, AZ 86402
(520) 753-6434
Sarah J. Ellis, Owner
Retail. *Products*: All.

SOCKYMA'S HOPICRAFTS
P.O. Box 96 • KYKOTSMOVI, AZ 86039
(928) 734-1050 or 734-6667
Michael & Theodora Sockyma, Owners
Retail. *Products*: Specializes in Hopi overlay jewelry in silver & gold; Hopi kachinas, pottery, baskets, weavings, oil paintings. Brochure.

ALBERT LONG: TRADER/CRAFTSMAN
P.O. Box 40 • LAKE HAVASU CITY, AZ 86405
(520) 453-5925; Albert Long, Owner
Mail order. *Products*: Dolls, jewelry.
Brochure available.

PERCHARO JEWELRY
RR 2, Box 790 • LAVEEN, AZ 85339
(520) 237-4249
Nathaniel & Lisa Percharo, Owners
Retail/mail order. *Product*: P.

HEARTLINE TRADING
911 N. Somerset Cir. • MESA, AZ 85205
(602) 969-6232; Barbara Stechnij, Owner
Retail. *Products*: Beadwork, fetishes, heishi, jewelry, knives, pottery, rugs, craft supplies. *Membership*: IACA.

INDIAN JEWELRY USA
6101 E. Main St. • MESA, AZ 85204-0090
(602) 985-5146; Jack & Ranelle Adam, Owners
Wholesale, retail. *Products*: Art, beadwork, music, books, dolls, drums, pipes, fetishes, heishi, jewelry, kachinas, knives, miniatures, pottery, sandpaintings, sculpture; repair & restoration. *Appraisals*. *Membership*: IACA.

WHITE EAGLE TRADING CO.
911 N. Somerset Cr. • MESA, AZ 85205
(602) 969-6232
Mark & Barbara Stechnij, Owners
Wholesale, retail. *Products*: Baskets, fetishes, jewelry, kachinas, pottery, rugs, sandpaintings.

HUDSON TRADING CO.
P.O Box 1254 • ORACLE, AZ 85623
(602) 896-2901
Raymond & Velveeta Volante, Owners
Wholesale. *Products*: Baskets, beadwork, fetishes, jewelry, kachinas, miniatures, pottery, rugs. *Membership*: IACA.

BLAIR'S DINNEBITO TRADING POST
P.O. Box 2903 • PAGE, AZ 86040
(520) 645-3008; Elijah & James Blair, Owners
Wholesale, retail. *Products*: All. *Membership*: IACA.

WAHWEAP GIFT SHOP
P.O. Box 1597 • PAGE, AZ 86040
(520) 645-2433; Kathy M. Parsons, Manager
Retail. *Products*: All.

**COLORADO RIVER INDIAN
TRIBES LIBRARY/MUSEUM**
Rt. 1, Box 23-B • PARKER, AZ 85344
(602) 669-9211 ext. 335 Fax 669-1246
Betty L. Cornelius, Director/Manager

Retail. *Products*: Beadwork, Navajo rugs, kachina dolls, pottery, bows & arrows, cradleboards.

DRUMBEAT INDIAN ARTS
4143 N. 16th St., Suite 1
PHOENIX, AZ 85016
(602) 266-4823 Fax 265-2402
Bob Nuss, Owner
Retail, wholesale, mail order. *Products*: American Indian recordings (cassettes, CDs, videos) over 2,000 titles; also books, crafts supplies, craft items. Catalog available, $3.

HEARD MUSEUM STORE
22 E. Monte Vista • PHOENIX, AZ 85004
(602) 252-8344
Retail. *Products*: Art, baskets, beadwork, boxes, dolls, fetishes, heishi, jewelry, kachinas, miniatures, pottery, rugs, sandpaintings, sculpture. *Membership*: IACA.

KALLEY KEAMS
P.O. Box 86448 • PHOENIX, AZ 85080
(602) 412-7905
Kalley Keams, Owner
Wholesale. *Products*: Baskets, rugs, weavings.

MUSIAL'S NAVAJO ARTS
P.O. Box 86448 • PHOENIX, AZ 85080
(602) 569-2283
Kalley Musial
Wholesale, retail. *Products*: Baskets, ornaments, dolls, artifacts, reproductions, jewelry, pottery, rugs; repair & restoration. *Membership*: IACA.

NATIVE AMERICAN FASHIONS, INC.
P.O. Box 44802 • PHOENIX, AZ 85064
(602) 956-7581
Margaret Wood, Owner/Manager
Retail, wholesale, mail order. *Products*: Clothing, rugs, wall hangings, sculpture, carvings. Special orders accepted.

NAVAJO SILVERCRAFT
P.O. Box 2725
PHOENIX, AZ 85002
(602) 253-1594
Jane Yikazbaa Popovich
Retail. *Product*: Jewelry.

ROCKING HORSE DESIGNS
2415 W. Glenrosa • PHOENIX, AZ 85015
(602) 265-1061
Lani Randall
Wholesale, retail. *Product*: Jewelry.
Appraisals: Jewelry. *Membership*: IACA.

GILA RIVER ARTS & CRAFTS CENTER
P.O. Box 457 • SACATON, AZ 85247
(602) 963-3981
Bruce Hamana, Manager
Retail, some mail order. Tribe-owned corporation. *Products*: Southwest Indian jewelry, pottary, rugs, kachina dolls, beadwork, basketry.

BROWN'S TURQUOISE SHOP
2248 First Ave. • SAFFORD, AZ 85546
(602) 428-6433
Bernice Brown, Owner
Retail, wholesale. *Products*: Art, baskets, beadwork, clothing, dolls, jewelry, kachinas, pottery, sandpaintings, sculpture, carvings, craft supplies, repairs & restoration. *Membership*: IACA.

PHILLIP TITLA STUDIO
P.O. Box 497
SAN CARLOS, AZ 85550
(602) 475-2361
Phillip Titla, Owner
Retail, mail order. *Products*: Art, dolls, sculpture, carvings. Brochure.

D.Y. BEGAY'S NAVAJO ARTS
6929 E. Jenan Dr.
SCOTTSDALE, AZ 85254
(602) 922-9232 Fax 951-2357
D.Y. Begay, Owner/Manager
Wholesale. Special orders accepted. *Products*: Museum quality traditional and contemporary Navajo weavings by the artist and other Navajo weavers; custom tapestries, rugs, and blankets.

THE EASTERN COWBOYS
4235 N. 86th Pl.
SCOTTSDALE, AZ 85251
(480) 945-9804 (phone & fax)
Jay & Edith Sadow, Owners
E-Mail: EasternCow@aol.com
Web site: www.xylem.web.com/eastcow
Wholesale. *Products*: All. Catalog.

GODBERS JEWELRY, INC.
Box 831, 7542 E. Main
SCOTTSDALE, AZ 85252
(602) 949-1133
Allie Mae & Ken Godber, Owners
Wholesale. *Products*: Art, baskets, dye charts, fetishes, heishi, jewelry, kachinas, pottery, rugs, sandpainting, sculpture. *Membership*: IACA.

GREY WOLF
7239 E. First Ave.
SCOTTSDALE, AZ 85251
(602) 423-0004
Anne & Sid Billings, Owners
Wholesale, retail. *Products*: All.
Membership: IACA.

LEONA KING GALLERY
7171 E. Main
SCOTTSDALE, AZ 85251
(602) 945-1209
Sam & Sue King, Owners
Wholesale, retail. *Products*: Art, baskets, beadwork, clothing, drums, pipes, fetishes, jewelry, kachinas, knives, miniatures, pottery, rugs, sculpture, carvings. *Appraisals*: Art, pottery, sculpture, carvings. *Membership*: IACA.

SAR-JO & ASSOCIATES, INC.
10482 E. Balancing Rock Rd.
SCOTTSDALE, AZ 85262-4521
(602) 502-8021 Fax 502-8022
E-Mail: sarjoassoc@aol.com
Joseph B. Levine, CEO
Wholesale. Southwest arts & crafts. *Products*: Baskets, dolls, drums, pipes, heishi, jewelry, kachinas, miniatures, rugs; repairs & restoration. *Membership*: IACA.

SEWELL'S INDIAN ARTS
7087 5th Ave.
SCOTTSDALE, AZ 85251
(602) 945-0962
Sandy, Sam & Nadiya Daiza, Owners
Retail. *Products*: All. *Appraisals*: Jewelry, kachinas. *Membership*: IACA.

SOUTHWEST EVENTS ETC.
3200 N. Hayden Rd., Suite 100
SCOTTSDALE, AZ 85251-6653
(602) 947-6800 Fax 947-6888
Nancy & Michael Pavlik, Owners
Retail. *Products*: Art, baskets, boxes, ornaments, fetishes, heishi, jewelry, kachinas, knives, miniatures, pottery, rugs, sculpture. *Membership*: IACA.

TRADER GENE
P.O. Box 13413
SCOTTSDALE, AZ 85267
(800) 258-3746
(602) 945-5826 Fax 443-0355
Gene Benner, Owner
Wholesale. *Products*: Dolls, fetishes, jewelry, kachinas, rugs, sandpaintings, sculpture, craft supplies.

TURQUOISE HOGAN, INC.
P.O. Box 657
SCOTTSDALE, AZ 85252-0657
(602) 949-5122 (Phone & Fax)
Judith & Donald Barajas, Owners
Wholesale, retail. *Products*: Fetishes, jewelry; repairs & restoration. *Membership*: IACA.

DAWA'S HOPI ARTS & CRAFTS
P.O. Box 127 (Hopi Reservation)
SECOND MESA, AZ 86043
(520) 734-2430
Bernard Dawahoya, Owner
Retail, mail order. *Product*: P.
Specializes in Hopi overlay silver jewelry.

HONANI CRAFTS-GALLERY
P.O. Box 221
SECOND MESA, AZ 86043
(520) 737-2238
King Honani, Sr., Owner/Manager
Retail, wholesale, mail order. Special orders accepted.
Products: Hopi overlay gold & silver jewelry, pottery,
weavings, paintings, kachinas, baskets; Zuni, Navajo,
and Santo Domingo jewelry; Navajo rugs.

HOPI GALLERY
Hopi Cultural Center
P.O. Box 316
SECOND MESA, AZ 86043
(520) 734-2238
Phil Sekaquaptewa, Owner
Retail, wholesale, mail order. *Products*: Art, baskets,
jewelry, kachinas, pottery, rugs. Brochure, catalog.

**HOPI ARTS & CRAFTS - SILVERCRAFT
COOPERATIVE GUILD**
P.O. Box 37 • SECOND MESA, AZ 86043
(520) 734-2463 Fax 734-6647
Milland S. Lomakema, Manager
Retail, wholesale, mail order. Special orders accepted.
Products: Hopi overlay silver jewelry, basketry, pot-
tery, Hopi kachina dolls, paintings and textiles. Bro-
chure, catalog.

SECAKUKU ENTERPRISES & SHOP
P.O. Box 67 • SECOND MESA, AZ 86043
(520) 734-2401; 737-2632
Dorothy & Ferrell Secakuku, Owners
Retail, wholesale. *Products*: Art, baskets, kachinas,
pottery.

BLUE-EYED BEAR
299 N. Hwy. 89-A
SEDONA, AZ 86336
Bud & Linda Johnson
Retail. *Products*: Fetishes, jewelry, pottery, rugs,
sandpaintings, sculpture, carvings. *Membership*: IACA.

GARLAND'S INDIAN JEWELRY
Box 1848, Indian Gardens Hwy. 89-A
SEDONA, AZ 86336
(520) 282-6632
William T. Garland, Owner
Britt Burns, Manager
Wholesale, retail. *Products*: Baskets, heishi, jewelry,
kachinas, knives, miniatures, pottery, sandpaintings.
Appraisals: Jewelry. *Membership*: IACA.

GARLAND'S NAVAJO RUGS
Box 851, 411 Hwy. 179 • SEDONA, AZ 86336
(520) 282-4070
Daniel J. Garland, Owner
Retail. *Products*: Baskets, kachinas, miniatures, rugs,
sandpaintings. *Appraisals*: Rugs. *Membership*: IACA.

TURQUOISE TORTOISE GALLERY
Hozho Center, 431 Hwy. 179
SEDONA, AZ 86336
(520) 282-2262
Peggy J. Lanning-Eisler, Owner
Wholesale, retail. *Products*: Art, baskets, beadwork,
boxes, clothing, fetishes, heishi, jewelry, kachinas,
miniatures, sandpaintings. *Membership*: IACA.

INDIAN PONY TRADING POST
P.O. Box 767 • SONOITA, AZ 85637
(520) 394-2264
Retail. *Products*: Art, baskets, beadwork, pottery,
sandpaintings, sculpture, carvings.

THE TRADING POST
8817 Montana • SUN LAKES, AZ 85248
(520) 895-6072
Tom & Marilyn DeYoung, Owners
Wholesale, retail. *Products*: Beadwork, fetishes, jewelry, kachinas, knives. *Membership*: IACA.

TEEC NOS POS ARTS/CRAFTS
P.O. Box Z • TEEC NOS POS, AZ 86514
(520) 656-3228
Bill & Kay Foutz, Owners
Wholesale, retail. *Products*: Baskets, beadwork, boxes,
ornaments, dolls, jewelry, kachinas, pottery, rugs,
sandpaintings, sculpture, carvings. *Membership*: IACA.
Catalog.

**ARLENE'S SOUTHWEST TRADING
CO. & ARLENE'S GALLERY**
P.O. Box 340, 400/404/415 Allen St.
TOMBSTONE, AZ 85638
(520) 457-3344
Arlene L. Klein, Owner
Wholesale, retail. *Products*: All. *Membership*: IACA.

HATATHLI GALLERY
Navajo Community College
TSAILE, AZ 86556
(520) 724-6650 Fax 724-3349
Ms. Bert Dempsey, Manager
Wholesale, retail. *Products*: Jewelry, paintings, rugs,
sandpaintings, beadwork, art items. Brochure.

TUBA TRADING POST
Box 247, Main & Moenave Sts.
TUBA CITY, AZ 86045
(520) 283-5441 Fax 283-4144
Mark & Janet Shipley
Wholesale, retail. *Products*: Art, baskets, boxes, cloth-
ing, dolls, drums, pipes, jewelry, kachinas, pottery,
rugs, sandpaintings, sculpture. *Membership*: IACA.

OLD PRESIDIO TRADERS
Box 4023, #14 Tubac Rd.
TUBAC, AZ 85646
(520) 398-9333
Lisa & Garry Hembree
Retail.

TURQUOISE TORTOISE GALLERY
Box 2321, La Pradera Mall, Hwy. 82
TUBAC, AZ 85646 (520) 398-2041
Esther & Larry Fitzpatrick
Retail. *Products*: Art, baskets, beadwork, boxes, cloth-
ing, drums, pipes, flutes, fetishes, heishi, jewelry,
kachinas, rugs, sandpaintings. *Membership*: IACA.

BAHTI INDIAN ARTS
4300 N. Campbell Ave. • TUCSON, AZ 85701
(520) 577-0290; Mark Tomas Bahti, Owner
Retail. *Products*: All. *Membership*: IACA.

BLACK ARROW TRADERS
2400 N. Calle de Maurer
TUCSON, AZ 85749-9582
(520) 749-4119
Sophie & Jack Guth
Wholesale, retail. *Products*: Baskets, beadwork, dolls,
fetishes, heishi, jewelry, kachinas, rugs, sandpaintings.
Membership: IACA.

DESERT SON INDIAN ART
4759 E. Sunrise Dr. • TUCSON, AZ 85718
(520) 299-0818
Steve Osborne, Owner
E-Mail: elrey@azstarnet.com
Web site: www.desertson.com
Retail. *Products*: Hopi kachinas; gold & silver jewlery;
Navajo rugs, baskets, pottery and moccasins. *Member-
ship*: IACA.

GUARDIAN RAINBOW
P.O. Box 32078 • TUCSON, AZ 85751
(520) 885-8369 Fax 722-5872
Keith & Doris Palmer
Wholesale, retail. *Products*: Baskets, fetishes, jewelry,
kachinas, pottery, rugs. *Appraisals*: Jewelry, kachinas,
pottey, rugs. *Membership*: IACA.

K & G CO., INC.
63647 E. Edgeview Ln.
TUCSON, AZ 85737
Gloria Snook
Retail. *Products*: Art, baskets, beadwork, clothing,
dolls, jewelry, kachinas, pottery, sandpaintings, sculpture, carvings, craft supplies. *Membership*: IACA.

MORNING STAR TRADERS, INC.
2020 E. Speedway Blvd.
TUCSON, AZ 85719
(520) 881-2112 Fax 881-5694
Richard (Rick) Rosenthal, Owner
Retail. *Products*: Southwestern Indian jewelry, baskets,
pottery, and old Navajo rugs. Specializing in old pawn
jewelry, old baskets and rugs, collectors items. Hopi
jewelry by Bernard Dawahoya, Wilson Jim and Julian
Lovato. *Membership*: IACA.

NATIVE AMERICAN COLLECTIBLES
2241 S. Double O Pl. • TUCSON, AZ 85713
John & Ruth Gruber
Wholesale, retail. *Products*: Baskets, drums, pipes,
fetishes, heishi, jewelry, kachinas, pottery, rugs. *Appraisals*: Rugs. *Membership*: IACA.

INDIGENA FINE ART PUBLISHING CO.
P.O. Box 13222
TUCSON, AZ 85732-3222
(520) 721-1886 Fax 721-2105
David B. Waine, Owner
Wholesale. *Products*: Contemporary art and historical
Native American folding cards, postcards, posters;
signed limited editions. Catalog to retailers only.

RESERVATION CREATIONS
P.O. Box 27626 • TUCSON, AZ 85726
(520) 622-4900
Carole J. Garcia, Owner/Manager
Retail, wholesale, mail order. *Products*: Art, baskets,
beadwork, boxes, clothing, dolls, pottery, rugs, sculpture.

SO WEST TERRITORIES
186 N. Meyer Ave. • TUCSON, AZ 85701
(800) 851-6153; (520) 623-1871
Linda & Harry Sheraw
E-Mail: harlin@azstarnet.com
Retail. *Products*: Native American and Southwest art.
Membership: IACA.

URSHEL TAYLOR'S OWL EAR STUDIO
2901 W. Sahuaro Divide
TUCSON, AZ 85742
(800) 487-0180; (520) 297-4456 Fax 544-4382
Urshel & Tony Taylor, Owners
Retail, mail order. *Products*: A,N,X. *Membership*: IACA.
Brochure.

TOWAYALANE TRADING CO.
6590 E. Tanque Verde, Suite A
TUCSON, AZ 85715 (520) 886-3542
Joe & Jan Douthitt
Wholesale. *Products*: Art, baskets, beadwork, clothing, dolls, jewelry, kachinas, pottery, rugs,
sandpaintings, sculpture, carvings. *Membership*: IACA.

TREASURE CHEST BOOKS LLC
1802 W. Grant Rd. #101 • TUCSON, AZ 85745
(520) 623-9558 Fax 624-5888
W. Ross Humphreys, Owner
Wholesale, retail, mail order. *Products*: Books.
Membership: IACA. Catalog.

TREASURES & TRIFLES
3030 N. Willow Creek Dr. • TUCSON, AZ 85712
(520) 881-2124; James & Elsie Deer, Owner
Retail. *Products*: Art, baskets, fetishes, heishi, jewelry,
miniatures, craft supplies; repair & restoration. *Appraisals*: Baskets, fetishes, heishi, jewelry, miniatures. *Membership*: IACA.

UWIGA DESIGNS
3420 E. Maxim Pl. • TUCSON, AZ 85739
(520) 825-2830
Retail, Wholesale. *Products*: Clothing.
Native American designs. Catalog, $6.

VINCENT MEIER
P.O. Box 5862 • TUCSON, AZ 85703
(520) 325-3209; Vincent Meier, Owner
Wholesale. *Products*: Baskets, beadwork, dolls,
fetishes, jewelry, kachinas, knives, pottery,
sandpaintings.

BENALLY'S INDIAN ARTS
P.O. Box 780 • WINDOW ROCK, AZ 86515
(520) 871-5727
Ronald F. Benally, Owner
Wholesale.

NAVAJO ARTS & CRAFTS ENTERPRISE
P.O. Box 160 • WINDOW ROCK, AZ 86515
(520) 871-4095 Fax 871-3340
Raymond R. Smith, Manager
Retail, wholesale. Tribal Enterprise. *Products*: Indian
art, jewelry, rugs, pottery. Branch shops in Cameron,
AZ; Chinle, AZ; Kayenta, AZ; Gallup, NM; Magdalena,
NM.

CALIFORNIA

HHS EXPORT TRADING CO.
2305 Roark Dr. • Alhambra, CA 91803-4535
(626) 281-7769 Fax 281-5543
E-mail: hhsetc@worldnet.att.net
Hermann & Maria Schmidt, Owners
Retail, wholesale, mail order. *Products*: Native American jewelry & artifacts; Western and Southwestern apparel, products & accessories. Bison meat & products. *Appraisal*: Art, artifacts, fetishes, heishi, jewelry, kachinas, knives, pottery, sculpture, carvings. *Membership*: IACA. Brochure & catalog. Branch shop: Germany (exporter to Europe & the Pacific Rim countries).

SANTA FE CRAFTS
P.O. Box 298 • Altadena, CA 91003-0298
(800) 421-7661
(818) 398-1789 Fax 398-1575
Barbara Goldeen
Wholesale. *Products*: Baskets, ornaments, dolls, artifacts, fetishes, heishi,, jewelry, kachinas, miniatures, pottery. *Membership*: IACA.

BEAR MOUNTAIN TRADING CO.
P.O. Box 6503, 42626 Moonridge Rd.
Big Bear Lake, CA 92315
(714) 585-9676 Fax 585-0310
Gerry & Patty Taylor
Retail. *Products*: Art, baskets, beadwork, clothing, dolls, jewelry, kachinas, pottery, sandpaintings, sculpture, carvings. *Membership*: IACA.

EASTERN SIERRA TRADING CO.
P.O. Box 731 • Bridgeport, CA 93517
(619) 932-7231
Joe & Mary Lent, Owners
Retail. *Products*: Baskets, beadwork, jewelry, pottery.

KNOTT'S BERRY FARM
8039 Beach Blvd. • Buena Park, CA 90620
(714) 220-5270
Fred Wagner, Mechandise Div.
Retail. *Products*: All. *Membership*: IACA.

THE WRIGHT STUFF
1811 W. Burbank Blvd.
Burbank, CA 91506
(818) 954-8943 Fax 954-9370
Peter & Marcie Wright
Retail. *Products*: Fetishes, jewelry, kachinas, pottery. *Membership*: IACA.

THE WOODEN INDIAN
3019 State St. • Carlsbad, CA 92008
(619) 729-1596 (Phone & Fax)
LaVon & Pete Ritter, Owners
Retail. *Products*: All. *Appraisals*: Art, baskets, beadwork, fetishes, heishi, jewelry, kachinas, pottery, rugs, sandpaintings. *Membership*: IACA.

BUNTE & SHAW TRADING CO.
651 Citadel Ave. • Claremont, CA 91711
(714) 626-0121
Howard Bunte & Theresa Shaw, Owners
Retail. *Products*: Art, fetishes, heishi, jewelry, rugs. *Membership*: IACA.

THREE FLAGS TRADING POST
Walker Rt. 1, Box 115, Hwy. 395
Coleville, CA 96107
(916) 495-2955
Tom & Marlene Stewart, Owners
Retail. *Products*: Art, baskets, beadwork, clothing, dolls, drums, pipes, flutes.

BLACK EAGLE
P.O. Box 621 • Copperopolis, CA 95228
(209) 785-5259
Wholesale. *Products*: Original Shoshone & Northern Plains style artifacts

WHITE PELICAN
34475 Golden Lantern
Dana Point, CA 92629
(714) 240-1991 (phone & fax)
Diana & George Poulos, Owners
Wholesale, retail. *Products*: All. *Membership*: IACA.

DELUNA JEWELERS
521 Second St. • Davis, CA 95616
(916) 753-3351
Richard Luna, Owner
Wholesale, retail, mail order. *Products*: Baskets, beadwork, jewelry, pottery, rugs, sculpture, carvings.

AMERICAN INDIAN STORE
1095 Magnolia • El Cajon, CA 92020
(619) 583-5389
G. Roy Cook, Owner
Mail order. *Products*: A,C,H,P,Q,U,V,Z. Catalog.

INDIAN ARTS GIFT SHOP (NCIDC)
241 F St. • Eureka, CA 95501
(707) 445-8451 Fax 445-8479
Terry Coltra, Manager
Retail, wholesale, mail order. *Products*: Art, baskets, beadwork, clothing, dolls, jewelry, kachinas, pottery, rugs, sandpaintings, sculpture, carvings, craft supplies. *Membership*: IACA. Special orders accepted. Brochure & price list.

KAROK ORIGINALS BY VIT
P.O. Box 3317 • Eureka, CA 95502
(707) 442-8800
Linda C. Vit, Owner
Wholesale, retail, mail order. *Products*: P.V. Special orders accepted. Catalog and wholesale price list.

THE WESTERNER
110 N. Main St. • Fallbrook, CA 92028
(619) 728-1462
Juanita Walden
Retail. *Products*: Art, baskets, beadwork, clothing, dolls, jewelry, kachinas, pottery, rugs, sandpaintings, sculpture, carvings. *Membership*: IACA.

ANCIENT ECHOES
12776 Brookhurst St. • Garden Grove, CA 92640
(714) 638-0908
Mary Ray, Owner
Retail. *Products*: A,D,J,P,Q,X

THE TURQUOISE NUT
321 N. Verdugo Rd. • Glendale, CA 91206
(818) 243-1001
Tom & Helen Snyder
Wholesale, retail. *Products*: All. *Membership*: IACA.

MAR-BILL INDIAN STORE
1620 San Vicente Dr. • Hemet, CA 92543
(509) 996-2470
Mary Luther
Retail. *Products*: Baskets, beadwork, clothing, dolls, jewelry, kachinas, pottery, rugs, sandpaintings, sculpture, carvings, craft supplies. *Membership*: IACA. *Branch*: Winthrop, WA.

GEORGE BLAKE'S STUDIO
P.O. Box 1304 • Hoopa, CA 95546
(916) 625-4619
George N. Blake, Owner
Wholesale, retail. Hupa-Yurok crafts. *Products*: Drums, flutes, pipes, pottery, sculpture, carvings. Large and miniature canoes.

AUTRY MUSEUM OF WESTERN HERITAGE STORE
4700 Western Heritage Way
Los Angeles, CA 90027
(323) 667-2000 FAX 666-4863
E-mail: mstore@autry-museum.org
Web site: www.autry-museum.org
John L. Gray, Executive Director
Susan VanDeVyvere, Director of Merchandising
Kathy Kemp, Manager
Retail. *Products*: All. *Membership*: IACA.

ROCKY MOUNTAIN HOUSE
2574 S. Bundy Dr. • Los Angeles, CA 90064
(310) 393-8912
Ron Daleo, Owner
Wholesale. *Products*: Baskets, beadwork, clothing, drums, pipes, fetishes, jewelry, miniatures, pottery, rugs, sandpaintings. *Membership*: IACA.

TRIBAL ARTS
P.O. Box 19965 • Los Angeles, CA 90019
(213) 292-6808 Fax 295-1045
Judy Cross

Wholesale, retail. *Products*: Heishi, jewelry. *Membership*: IACA.

YO'ZHO
10392 Almayo Ave. • Los Angeles, CA 90064
(213) 858-7700
Paula Palmer
Retail. *Product*: P.

THE INDIAN STORE
Box 308, 50 University Ave.
Los Gatos, CA 95031
(408) 354-9988
Janice L. Benjamin
Retail. *Products*: All. *Membership*: IACA.

FIEGE'S COLLECTIBLES
15236 Lassan St. • Mission Hills, CA 91345
(818) 892-6826
Kathleen & Gary Fiege
Wholesale, retail.

OPHELIA JOHNSON'S INDIAN VARIETY SHOP
10256 Central Ave. • Montclair, CA 91763
(714) 625-2611
Retail/mail order. *Products*: Baskets, beadwork, dolls, jewelry, pottery.

INTERTRIBAL FRIENDSHIP HOUSE GIFT SHOP
523 E. 14th St. • Oakland, CA 94606
(510) 452-1235
Susie Astor, Manager
Retail, wholesale. *Products*: Beadwork, clothing, jewelry, rugs.

OJAI INDIAN SHOP
318 E. Ojai Ave.
Ojai, CA 93023-2739
(805) 646-2631
George & Wendy LaBraque
Retail. *Products*: All. *Appraisals*: Baskets, rugs.

THE SOUTHWEST
P.O. Box 32 • Ontario, CA 91762
(714) 981-5711
Debbie Zugzda, Owner
Retail. *Products*: Baskets, beadwork, boxes, dolls, drums, pipes, flutes, Northwest Coast art, heishi, jewelry, kachinas, miniatures, pottery, rugs.

REDROCK ARTS
1295 Adobe Lane
Pacific Grove, CA 93950
(408) 624-5149
Steve & Carol Bishop, Owners
Retail. *Products*: Ar, baskets, fetishes, heishi, jewelry, pottery, rugs.

INDIAN VILLAGE, INC.
#43 Town & Country Village
Palo Alto, CA 94301-2326
(415) 328-7090
Beth & Ron Hale, Owners
Retail. *Products*: All. *Membership*: IACA.

PALOMAR MOUNTAIN GENERAL STORE & TRADING CO.
P.O. Box 100, Jct. S6 & S7
Palomar Mountain, CA 92060-0100
(619) 742-3496 Fax 742-4233
Brian Beck
Retail. *Products*: Baskets, beadwork, boxes, drums, flutes, pipes, Northwest Coast art, artifacts, fets=ishes, heishi, jewelry, kachinas, pottery, rugs, sculpture, carvings. *Membership*: IACA.

THE INDIAN SHOP
P.O. Box 614 • Pauma Valley, CA 92061
(619) 749-0130
Leo & Monte Calec, Owners
Wholesale, retail. *Products*: Art, baskets, clothing, dolls, pipes, flutes, jewelry, rugs.

MOON DANCER
1706 S. Catalina Ave.
Redondo Beach, CA 90277
(310) 316-7200
Paula Hausvick, Owner
Retail. *Products*: All. *Membership*: IACA.

GALLERY OF THE AMERICAN WEST
121 "K" St. • Sacramento, CA 95814
(916) 446-6662
   Leon W. Hodge, Owner
Retail. *Products*: Art, baskets, beadwork, clothing, dolls, fetsihes, heishi, jewelry, kachinas, pottery, sandpaintings, sculpture, carvings, craft supplies, repairs & restoration. *Appraisals*: Baskets, fetishes, heishi, jewelry, kachinas, pottery, rugs, sandpaintings. *Membership*: IACA.

WAKEDA TRADING POST
1926 H St. • Sacramento, CA 95814
(916) 438-6624 Fax 438-6684
   E-Mail: wakeda7431@yahoo.com
   Website: www.wakeda.com
   Cliff C. Paulsen, President
Retail, wholesale, mail order. *Products*: Native American craft supplies, beads, feathers, clothing, botanicals, books, videos, recodings

BAZAAR DEL MUNDO GALLERY
2754 Calhoun St. • San Diego, CA 92110
(619) 296-3161 Fax 297-2706
   Diane Powers
Retail. *Products*: Art, beadwork, fetishes, jewelry, kachinas, pottery, rugs, sandpaintings, sculpture, carvings. *Membership*: IACA.

ENBEE COLLECTIBLES
6435 Crystalaire Dr. • San Diego, CA 92120
(619) 582-3185
   Norman & Bernice Harris
Wholesale/retail. *Products*: Baskets, pottery, sculpture, carvings.

TRAILS WEST SILVER & LEATHER CO.
821 W. Harbor Dr. • San Diego, CA 92101
(619) 232-0553 Fax 232-3236
   Betty McAdams, Sec./Treasurer
Retail. *Products*: Indian jewelry, implements, drums, kachinas, fetishes, pottery, leather goods. *Appraisals*: P. *Membership*: IACA.

SKY LOOM
502 S. Darwood • San Dimas, CA 91773
(714) 599-3071
   Bob & Deborah Anderson
Wholesale, retail.

AMERICAN INDIAN CONTEMPORARY ARTS GALLERY
23 Grant Ave., 6th Fl. • San Francisco, CA 94108
(415) 989-7003 Fax 989-7025
   Janeen Antoine, Director
Wholesale, retail, mail order. *Products*: Art, baskets, beadwork, jewelry, pottery, rugs, sculpture. Gift shop.

KACHINA
2801 Leavenworth #J-22
San Francisco, CA 94133
(415) 441-2636
   Farideh Petri, Owner
Wholesale, retail. *Membership*: IACA.
Branch: Tiburon, CA.

MAYFLOWER GIFT SHOP
2770 40th Ave. • San Francisco, CA 94116
(415) 982-1890
   Doug & Julie Shinn, Owners
Retail. *Products*: All.

SCRIPSIT
1592 Union St. #356
San Francisco, CA 94123
(415) 586-4202
   Glenn Billy, Owner/Manager
Retail, wholesale, mail order. *Products*: Greeting cards with Indian words, each with an Indian design; calligraphy on paper. Custom orders for certificates, honorary awards. Special orders accepted.

WHITE BUFFALO GALLERY
900 North Point
San Francisco, CA 94109
(415) 931-0665
   Ata Petri, Owner
Retail. *Products*: Art, baskets, beadwork, clothing, dolls, jewelry, kachinas, pottery, sandpaintings, sculpture, carvings. *Membership*: IACA.

REYNA'S GALLERIES
Box 1022, 106 Third St.
San Juan Bautista, CA 95045
(408) 623-2379
   Sonne & Elaine Reyna, Owners
Wholesale, retail. *Products*: All.
Appraisals: All. Catalog.

LA QUINTA TRADING CO., LTD.
P.O. Box 427 • Santa Barbara, CA 93102
(619) 568-4188 Fax 568-6955
   Randy Gillet, Owner
Retail. *Products*: All. *Membership*: IACA.

DONNA GOLD
P.O. Box 55277
Sherman Oaks, CA 91413
(818) 789-2559 Fax 789-1510
   Donna Gold, Owner
Wholesale, retail. *Products*: Art, baskets, beadwork, clothing, dolls, jewelry, kachinas, pottery, rugs, sandpaintings, sculpture, carvings. Northwest Coast Indian masks, rattles, bowls, graphics. Mail order only - pictures available.

TWO BEARS GALLERY
14755 Ventura Blvd. #1-619
Sherman Oaks, CA 91403
(310) 393-4776
   Lou A. Finley, Owner
Retail. *Products*: Art, baskets, boxes, ornaments, clothing, dolls, drums, pipes, Northwest Coast art, heishi, jewelry, pottery, rugs, sculpture. *Membership*: IACA.
Branch: 1205 Montana Ave., Santa Monica, CA.

KACHINA
41 Reed Ranch Rd. • Tiburon, CA 94920
(415) 389-8524
   Farideh Petri, Owner
Wholesale, retail. *Membership*: IACA.
Branch: San Francisco, CA.

CHIEF GEORGE PIERRE TRADING POST
620 The Village (Redondo Beach)
P.O. Box 3202 • Torrance, CA 90510
(213) 372-1048
   Chief George Piere, Owner
Wholesale, retail, mail order. *Products*: Beadwork, jewelry, kachinas, rugs.

AB-ORIGINALS
P.O. Drawer 850 • Trinidad, CA 95570
(707) 677-3738
   Joy & Lisa Sundberg & Elaine Clary, Owners
Wholesale, retail. *Products*: H.P. Fashionable accessories such as chokers, hair pieces, necklaces, earrings, beaded neck ties, belts.

ADOBE ROAD, INC.
1000 Universal Center Dr., Shop 157
University City, CA 91608
(818) 622-3623
   Prudence J. Gallop, Owner
Wholesale, retail. *Products*: All. *Membership*: IACA.

ZUNI PEOPLE
222A Main St. • Venice, CA 90291
(310) 399-7792
Retail, wholesale, mail order. Zuni tribal enterprise.
Products: Zuni turquoise, shell, coral, jet and silver jewelry; pottery; fetishes; contemporary art. Jewelry catalog, $5.

RED FLUTE TRADERS
9620 Las Cruces
Ventura, CA 93004
(805) 647-6437
   Floyd & Sue Beller
Wholesale, retail. *Products*: Baskets, beadwork, heishi,, jewelry, kachinas, rugs. *Membership*: IACA.

KACHINA ART GALLERY
Box 4800, 12301 Whittier Blvd.
Whittier, CA 90607
(213) 941-5635
   Lynn & Mercedes Stermolle
Retail. *Products*: Art, baskets, beadwork, clothing, dolls, jewelry, kachinas, pottery, rugs, sandpaintings, sculpture, carvings. *Membership*: IACA.

MATOSKA TRADING CO.
P.O. Box 2004
Yorba Linda, CA 92686
(909) 393-0647 Fax 614-1165
   Brent Schellhase, Owner
   E-mail: matoska@matoska.com
   Web site: www.matoska.com
Retail, wholesale, mail order. *Products*: Art, beadwork, books, clothing, drums, pipes, rugs. Catalog, $3.

THE ANSEL ADAMS GALLERY
P.O. Box 455, The Village Mall
Yosemite, CA 95389
(209) 372-4413 Fax 372-4714
   Michael & Jeanne Adams
Retail. *Products*: Art, baskets, beadwork, clothing, dolls, jewelry, kachinas, pottery, rugs, sandpaintings, sculpture, carvings. Catalog.

YOSEMITE PARK & CURRY CO.
P.O. Box 578
Yosemite Lodge (209) 372-1438
Ahwahnee Hotel (209) 372-1409
Yosemite, CA 95389
   Cassandra Martin, Manager (Yosemite Lodge)
   Georgine Gray, Manager (Ahwahnee Hotel)
Retail. *Products*: All. *Membership*: IACA.

BARKER'S INDIAN TRADING POST
P.O. Box 2732, 6495 Washington St.
Yountville, CA 94599-2732
(707) 944-8012
   Frank & Wilda Barker
Wholesale/retail. *Products*: Art, baskets, beadwork, jewelry, pottery, rugs, sandpaintings, sculpture. *Membership*: IACA.

GEODES & GEMS
56925 Yucca Trail, Suite A
Yucca Valley, CA 92284
(619) 365-9614
   Robert & Marjorie Clayton
Wholesale, retail. *Products*: All. *Membership*: IACA.

COLORADO

EAGLE PLUME'S
9853 Hwy. 7
Allenspark, CO 80510
(303) 747-2861 (phone & fax)
   Ann Strange Owl-Raben, Nico Strange Owl-Hunt, Dayton Raben, Owners
Retail. *Products*: Baskets, beadwork, jewelry, kachinas, pottery, sculpture, carvings. American Indian arts & crafts.

FOUR WINDS TRADING CO.
685 A S. Broadway
Boulder, CO 80306
(800) 456-5444; (303) 499-4484
   Richard & Cat Carey, Owners
Retail. *Product*: D. *Membership*: IACA.

SANTA FE AMBIANCE
1116 Pearle St.
Boulder, CO 80302
(303) 444-7200
   Deborah Smith-Klein & Melinda Theis, Owners
Retail. *Products*: Art, baskets, beadwork, clothing, dolls, jewelry, kachinas, pottery, rugs, sandpaintings, sculpture, carvings. *Membership*: IACA.

A.M. INDIAN ARTS, INC.
12 E. Bijou St.
Colorado Springs, CO 80903
(719) 471-3235
   Samuel M. Eppley, Owner
Retail. *Products*: Art, baskets, beadwork, pottery, rugs, sandpaintings, sculpture.

ARIZONA ROOM
8085 Edgerton
Colorado Springs, CO 80919
(719) 592-9106
   Linda & Carl Radunsky, Owners
Retail. *Products*: Art, baskets, fetishes, jewelry, kachinas, pottery, rugs, sculpture. *Membership*: IACA.

BROADMOOR DRUG CO.
P.O. Box 1439
Colorado Springs, CO 80901
(719) 577-5740
Ben B. Finch, Owner
Retail. *Products*: Baskets, fetishes,
heishi, jewelry, pottery.

THE FLUTE PLAYER GALLERY
2511 W. Colorado Ave.
Colorado Springs, CO 80904
(719) 632-7702
John & Linda Edwards, Owners
Retail, wholesale. *Products*: Ornaments, fetishes,
heishi, jewelry, kachinas, knives, miniatures, pottery,
rugs, sandpaintings, sculpure. *Appraisals*: Jewelry,
pottery, rugs. *Membership*: IACA.

HIDDEN INN
529 S. 31st St.
Colorado Springs, CO 80904
(719) 632-2303
Al Dickey, Owner
Retail. *Membership*: IACA.

THE SQUASH BLOSSOM & COGSWELL GALLERY
2531 W. Colorado
Colorado Springs, CO 80904
(719) 632-1899
John Cogswell & Chris Jones, Owners
Retail. *Products*: Art, baskets, beadwork, clothing,
dolls, jewelry, kachinas, pottery, rugs, sandpaintings,
sculpture, carvings. *Appraisals*: All products. Gallery
specializes in Pueblo pottery; Navajo weavings; Hopi
kachinas; Kiowa sculptures; Navajo, Hopi and Pima/
Papago baskets; Navajo, Hopi and Zuni jewelry; Zuni
fetishes; Navajo sandpaintings. *Membership*: IACA.
Catalog.

CLIFF DWELLER
Box 9, 1004 E. Main St.
Cortez, CO 81321
(303) 565-3424
J.D. Tipton, Jr., Owner
Retail. *Products*: All. *Membership*: IACA.

DON WOODARD'S INDIAN TRADING POST
27688 E. Hwy. 160 • Cortez, CO 81321-9366
(303) 565-3986
Don Woodard, Owner
Retail. *Products*: All. Appraisals. *Membership*: IACA.

MESA VERDE POTTERY
P.O. Box 9 • Cortez, CO 81321
(800) (303) 565-4492
Jay Tipton, Jr.
Wholesale, retail. *Products*: All. *Membership*: IACA.
Catalog.

TRIBAL DESIGNS
P.O. Box 341 • Crestone, CO 81131
(719) 256-4455
Retail, Wholesale. *Products*: Custom made handbags
made with deer/elk hide, silver conchos, wool, Zapotec
weavings.

THE BLACK BEAR
8753 E. Monmouth Pl.
Denver, CO 80237
(303) 779-1316
John & Mary Claire Walter, Owners
Retail. *Products*: Art, fetishes, heishi, jewelry, kachinas,
miniatures, pottery, rugs, sandpaintings. *Membership*:
IACA.

BOUCHER TRADING CO.
8505 E. Temple Dr. #473
Denver, CO 80237-2542
(303) 770-7718
Robert G. Boucher
Wholesale/retail. *Product*: Jewelry. *Membership*: IACA.

D & H GIFTS
1281 Phillips Dr.
Denver, CO 80233-1259
(303) 457-3606 Fax 457-9944
H. & Diane Yamamoto
Wholesale/retail. *Products*: Jewelry, sandpaintings.
Membership: IACA. *Branch*: 11480 N. Cherokee St.,
Unit I, Denver.

DENVER ART MUSEUM SHOP
100 W. 14th Ave. Pkwy.
Denver, CO 80204
(303) 640-2672
Mary Jane Butler
Retail. *Products*: C,I,N,P,U. *Membership*: IACA.

DENVER MUSEUM OF NATURAL HISTORY SHOP
2001 Colorado Blvd., City Park
Denver, CO 80205-5716
(303) 370-6366 Fax 331-6492
Thielma Gamewell & Ron Veenstra
Retail. *Products*: All. *Membership*: IACA.

FIGHTING BEAR ENTERPRISES
5430 Conley Way • Denver, CO 80222
(303) 758-9177; Fighting Bear, Owner
Retail. Arts and crafts and stained glass.

MILLER STOCKMAN WESTERN WEAR
P.O. Box 5127 • Denver, CO 80217-5127
(800) 688-9888
Retail, wholesale. *Products*: Native American clothing.

MORNING FLOWER PRESS
P.O. Box 11443 • Denver, CO 80211
(303) 477-8442
Susanne Aikman & John Chingman, Owners
Wholesale, retail, mail order. *Products*: Art, sculpture;
rapirs & restoration. Traditional and contemporary
crafts. Repairs beadwork.

SAND CREEK ARTS
5344 Altura St. • Denver, CO 80239
(303) 371-7636
William W. Phillips
Wholesale, retail. *Product*: Art. *Membership*: IACA.

SHALAKO
3023 East 2nd Ave. • Denver, CO 80206
(303) 295-2713
Angie Yava & Mike O'Neil
Retail. *Products*: Art, baskets, beadwork, clothing,
dolls, jewelry, kachinas, pottery, rugs, sandpaintings,
sculpture, carvings. *Membership*: IACA.

THE SQUASH BLOSSOM
1428 Larimer Square • Denver, CO 80202
(303) 572-7979 (phone & fax)
Mark Alexander, Owner
Retail. *Products*: All. *Membership*: IACA. Catalog.

TRADER GENE
451 E. 58th St. #1090 • Denver, CO 80216
(303) 296-6435
Harold Benner & Robert Staab, Owners
Wholesale. *Products*: All. Appraisals.

WESTERN TRADING POST
P.O. Box 9070 • Denver, CO 80209-0070
(303) 423-9446 (phone & fax)
Ronald Eberhart, Owner
Retail, wholesale, mail order. *Products*: All.
Appraisals: B,V, *Membership*: IACA. Catalog.

GLEN COMFORT STORE
2380 Big Thompson Canyon
Drake, CO 80515
(303) 586-3878
Harold M. Tregent, Owner
Retail. *Products*: Baskets, clothing, dolls, jewelry,
kachinas, pottery, rugs, sandpaintings, sculpture, carvings. *Membership*: IACA.

APPALOOSA TRADING CO.
501 Main St. • Durango, CO 81301
(907) 259-1994
Retail, Wholesale. *Products*: Handcrafted leather belts,
buckles, sterling bolos, badges, etc.

DIAMOND CIRCLE INDIAN GIFT SHOP
651 Main Ave. • Durango, CO 81301-5423
Skip & Marsha Wells, Owners
Retail. *Products*: All.

DURANGO TRADING CO.
602 Eagle Pass • Durango, CO 81301
Sharleen & L.D. Daugherty, Owners
Retail, wholesale. *Products*: Pottery, rugs.
Membership: IACA.

HELL BENT LEATHER & SILVER
741 Main Ave. • Durango, CO 81301
(303) 247-9088
Lovvis Downs & Charles Glass, Owners
Retail. *Products*: Beadwork, fetishes, heishi, jewelry,
kachinas, knives, pottery, rugs, craft supplies. *Membership*: IACA.

TOH-ATIN GALLERY
Box 2329, 145 W. 9th St.
Durango, CO 81301
(800) 525-0384; (303) 247-8277 Fax 259-5390
Jackson & Antonia Clark, Owners
Retail, wholesale. *Products*: All. *Appraisals*: Stones.
Catalog.

RED MAN HALL
P.O. Box 608 • Empire, CO 80438
(303) 569-3243
Francine & Richard Frajola, Owners
Retail. *Products*: Art, baskets, beadwork, fetishes, jewelry, kachinas, pottery, sandpaintings, sculpture, carvings. *Membership*: IACA.

CHEBON
1285 Chasm Dr. • Estes Park, CO 80517
(970) 586-5838
Chebon Dacon, Owner/Manager
Web site: www.cdacon.com
Retail, wholesale, mail order. *Products*: Acrylic and
watercolor paintings; limited edition prints, cards, book-
marks; carvings. Special commissions accepted.
Illusrated Catalog.

FALL RIVER TRADING POST
1875 Fall River Rd.
Estes Park, CO 80517
(505) 586-6573
Wendell & Ann Keller, Owners
Retail. *Products*: All. *Membership*: IACA.

GRANDPA'S
Box 861, 230 W. Elkhorn Ave.
Estes Park, CO 80517
(800) 242-4218; (303) 586-3539
Bob & Betty Hockaday, Owners
Retail. *Products*: All. *Membership*: IACA.

NATIONAL PARK VILLAGE NORTH
3450 Fall River Rd. • Estes Park, CO 80517
(303) 586-3183
H.W. Stewart, Owner
Retail. *Products*: baskets, ornaments, dolls, artifacts,
jewelry, pottery, rugs; reapirs & restoration. *Membership*: IACA.

**ROCKY MOUNTAIN NATIONAL
PARK-TRAIL RIDGE STORE**
P.O. Box 2680 • Estes Park, CO 80517
(970) 586-9319 Fax 586-8590
Don Wallace, VP
Retail. *Products*: All. *Winter address*: Forever Resorts,
P.O. Box 29041, Phoenix, AZ 85038-9041. *Member-
ship*: IACA.

SERENDIPITY TRADING CO.
117 E. Elkhorn Ave., Box 3945
Estes Park, CO 80517
(970) 586-8410 Fax 586-0463
E-mail: seren117@aol.com
Web site: www.serendipitytrading.com
John & Karen Ericson, Owners
Retail, wholesale, mail order. *Products*: All.
Membership: IACA.

BENZAV TRADING CO.
P.O. Box 911, 1716 E. Lincoln Ave.
Fort Collins, CO 80522
(303) 482-6397
Steven Pickelner
Wholesale. *Products*: Baskets, beadwork, clothing,
artifacts, heishi, jewelry, pottery, rugs. Appraisals.

SIOUX VILLA CURIO
114 6th St. • Glenwood Springs, CO 81601
(303) 945-6134
John Gilcrest
Retail. *Products*: Beadwork, heishi, jewelry.
Membership: IACA.

BANWARTH ENTERPRISES
8 Zodiac St. • Golden, CO 80401
Kay Dawn Todd
(970) 279-4870
Wholesale, retail. *Product*: P.

SILVER FEATHER TRADING CO.
1209 Washington Ave. • Golden, CO 80401
(970) 279-0595
David & Kay Dawn Todd, Owners
Wholesale, retail. Products: Beadwork, dolls, drums, flutes, pipes, fetishes, jewelry, kachinas, pottery. sandpaintings. *Membership*: IACA.

HARVEY INDIAN GALLERY
P.O. Box 3524, 130 N. 6th St.
Grand Junction, CO 81502
(970) 243-4093
Jim & Nancy Harvey, Owners
Retail. *Products*: All. *Membership*: IACA.

THUNDEROCK
128 N. 5th St. • Grand Junction, CO 81501
(970) 242-4890
Max & Judith Barnstead
Retail. *Products*: All. *Membership*: IACA..

EAGLE DANCER TRADING CO.
P.O. Box 547 • Grand Lake, CO 80447
(303) 726-9209; 627-3394
Dick & Nina Stasser, Owners
Retail. *Products*: All. *Membership*: IACA.
Branch: Winter Park, CO.

BEN NIGHTHORSE STUDIO
P.O. Box 639 • Ignacio, CO 81137
(970) 563-4623
Ben Nighthorse, Owner
Mail order. *Product*: Contemporary gold and silver jewelry. Special orders accepted.

SKY UTE INDIAN GALLERY
P.O. Box 550 • Ignacio, CO 81137
(970) 563-4531
Elise Redd & John Cole
Retail. Tribal Enterprise. *Products*: Art, beadwork, jewelry, pottery, sandpainting, sculpture; repairs & restoration.

SOUTHERN UTE MUSEUM STORE
P.O. Box 737 • Ignacio, CO 81137
(970) 563-4649
Helen Hoskins, Director
Retail. *Products*: Art, beadwork, clothing, jewelry, pottery, rugs. *Appraisals*: All. *Membership*: IACA.

THE SOUTHWESTERN COLLECTION
12600 W. Colfax Ave., Suite A120
Lakewood, CO 80215
(303) 237-2719
Jacqueline B. Aucoin, Owner
Retail. *Products*: Art, baskets, clothing, dolls, jewelry, kachinas, pottery, rugs, sandpaintings, sculpture, carvings. *Membership*: IACA. *Branch*: 6921 Hwy. 73, Evergreen, CO.

WALTON'S
12550 W. Second Dr.
Lakewood, CO 80228
(303) 988-5580
Roger Alan Walton, Owner
Wholesale, retail. *Products*: G,Q,U,X.
Membership: IACA.

BONANZA TRADING
316 Harrison Ave. • Leadville, CO 80461
(719) 486-3020
Clyde & Mary McVicar, Owners
Retail. *Products*: Art, baskets, beadwork, clothing, dolls, jewelry, kachinas, pottery, rugs, sandpaintings, sculpture, carvings. *Membership*: IACA.

SOUTHWESTERN GALLERY
1212 W. Littleton Blvd. • Littleton, CO 80120
(303) 795-7338
Beverly J. Nelson, Owner
Retail, mail order. *Products*: Art, fetishes, jewelry, kachinas, pottery, rugs, sandpaintings, sculpture. *Membership*: IACA.

TOUCH OF SANTA FE
P.O. Box 620549 • Littleton, CO 80162
(303) 730-2408
Ruth Venable, Owner
Retail. *Products*: All.

DEER TRACK TRADERS LTD.
P.O. Box 448 • Loveland, CO 80539-0448
(719) 669-6750 Fax 667-8464
Alpine & Sue Rodman, Owners
Wholesale. *Products*: Art, baskets, beadwork, books, clothing, dolls, jewelry, kachinas, pottery, rugs, sandpaintings, sculpture, carvings. *Membership*: IACA. Catalog.

DENNY HASKEW
540 N. Grant Ave.
Loveland, CO 80537
(970) 663-6375
Wholesale. *Products*: Monumental to maquette bronze, stone sculpture. Corporate, private, and public commissions accepted. By appointment.

ANASAZI TRADING POST
P.O. Box 320 • Lyons, CO 80540
(719) 823-5681
Susan & Daniel Martin, Owner
Retail. *Products*: All. *Membership*: IACA.

ARA MESA VERDE CO.
P.O. Box 277 • Mancos, CO 81328
(303) 533-7731
Bob Marshall, Owner
Retail. *Products*: All. *Membership*: IACA.

MANITOU JACK'S
742 Manitou Ave.
Manitou Springs, CO 80829
(719) 685-5004
Kendra Homer & Dawn Carnel, Owners
Wholesale, retail. *Products*: Art, jewelry, pottery, sandpainting, sculpture, craft supplies; repairs & restoration. *Membership*: IACA.

NAVA SOUTHWEST
61336 Hwy. 90 • Montrose, CO 81401
(970) 325-4850 Fax 249-0733
Douglas & Elizabeth Nava, Owners
Retail, wholesale, mail order. *Products*: Native American arts & crafts, jewelry, pottery, rugs, fetishes. *Summer address*: Box 37, Ouray 81427

RED ROCKS TRADING POST
16351 County Rd. 93
Morrison, CO 80465
(303) 697-8935
William S. Carle
Retail. *Products*: Art, clothing, jewelry, kachinas, pottery. *Membership*: IACA.

WINTERCOUNT
P.O. Box 889
New Castle, CO 81647
(970) 984-3685
Tom & Diane Voight, Owners
Wholesale, retail. *Products*: Art, books, t-shirts & calendars. *Membership*: IACA. Catalog.

BUCKSKIN TRADING CO.
P.O. Box 1876 • Ouray, CO 81427
(303) 325-4044
P. David & Jan Smith
Retail. *Products*: All. *Membership*: IACA.

NORTH MOON
P.O. Box 51 • Ouray, CO 81427
(303) 325-4885
Sandra K. Boles
Retail. *Products*: Beadwork, Northwest Coast art, fetishes, jewelry. *Membership*: IACA. *Branch shop*: Telluride, CO.

TAWA INDIAN GALLERY
P.O. Box 322 • South Fork, CO 81154
Beverly S. Van Horn, Owner
Retail. *Products*: Art, baskets, clothing, fetishes, jewelry, kachinas, pottery, rugs, sandpainting; repairs & restoration. *Summer address*: Box 322, South Fork, CO 81154 (719) 873-5838.

THE COLLECTOR'S ROOM
P.O. Box 3226, Vail National Bank #302
108 S. Frontage Rd. West • Vail, CO 81657
(303) 476-9019
Paul & Betty Numerof, Owners
Retail. *Products*: P. *Membership*: IACA.

SQUASH BLOSSOM, INC.
198 Gore Creek Dr. • Vail, CO 81657
(303) 476-3129 FAX 476-8984
John Cogswell, Owner
Retail. *Products*: All. *Appraisals*: Art, drums, pipes, flutes, artifacts, fetishes, heishi, jewelry, kachinas, knives, miniatures, pottery, rugs, sandpainting. Catalog.

ELK HORN ART GALLERY
P.O. Box 197 • Winter Park, CO 80482
(800) 285-4676; (970) 726-9292 Fax 726-8292
Tom Coblentz, Owner
E-mail: elkhorn@rkymtnhi.com
Web site: elkhorngallery.com
Retail, wholesale, mail order. *Products*: Works of art by Native American artists, Jo Anne Bird, Robert Red Bird, and Michael C. McCullough. Also published limited edition prints with dealerships available. *Menbership*: IACA. Brochure & Catalog available.

CONNECTICUT

SOUTHWEST INDIAN ARTS
98 The Laurels • Enfield, CT 06082
(203) 749-7332 (phone & fax)
Bud August, Owner
Retail. *Products*: Baskets, beadwork, artifacts, fetishes, jewelry, kachinas, pottery, rugs, sandpainting. *Membership*: IACA.

RALPH W. STURGIS
97 Raymond St. • New London, CT 06320
(203) 442-8005
Retail. *Products*: Sculpture, carvings.
Special commissions accepted.

YAH-TA-HEY GALLERY
279 Captains Walk • New London, CT 06320
(203) 443-3204
Dorothy Noga
Retail. *Products*: Art, baskets, boxes, dolls, drums, flutes, pipes, fetishes, jewelry, kachinas, rugs, sandpainting, sculpture. *Membership*: IACA.

TRIBAL WEAR BY SKINZ
27 Summit Rd. • Riverside, CT 06878
(203) 637-7884
Retail, wholesale. *Products*: Native American clothing.

DISTRICT OF COLUMBIA

THE INDIAN CRAFT SHOP
1849 C St., NW, Rm. 1023
Washington, DC 20240
(202) 208-4056 Fax 219-1135
Susan M. Pourian, Shop Director
Retail. *Products*: Over 45 tribal areas represented - jewelry, weavings, basketry, beadwork, pottery, kachinas, sandpaintings, fetishes, books, Alaskan walrus ivory and crafts. *Membership*: IACA.

FLORIDA

SHARED VISIONS GALLERY
10355 Prestwick Rd.
Boynton Beach, FL 33436
(407) 272-4495
Kathleen & Chad Ragland, Owners
Retail, wholesale. *Products*: Art, baskets, dolls, Northwest Coast art, fetishes, jewelry, kachinas, pottery, rugs, sandpaintings, sculpture. *Membership*: IACA. *Branch shop*: 504 E. Atlantic Ave., Delray Beach, FL 33483.

TURTLE ISLAND TRADERS
P.O. Box 9563 • Bradenton, FL 34206
(813) 747-5653
C.G. "Bud" Horton, Owner
Retail. *Products*: Books, artifacts, miniatures, sculpture, carvings. D,M,S,X.

SUNDANCER GALLERY
6 Florida Ave. • Cocoa Village, FL 32922
(407) 631-0092
Joan & Jim McCarthy, Owners
Retail, wholesale. *Products*: Southwest & Native American art & craftwork, and turquoise jewelry. Branch shop: This N' That, Cocoa Village.

THUNDERBIRD SHOP
16754 Willow Creek Dr.
Delray Beach, FL 33484
Louis & Sheila Brilliant, Owners
Retail. *Products*: All.

THE PLAINSMEN GALLERY
542 Douglas Ave. • Dunedin, FL 34698
(813) 446-4396
Betty Brown & Maria Alcoz, Owners
Retail. *Products*: Art, baskets, fetishes, jewelry, kachinas, rugs.

MASSACHUSETTS BAY TRADING CO.
2611 S. 16th St. • Ft. Pierce, FL 34982
(407) 465-2230
Dean & Jacie Davis, Owners
Wholesale, retail. *Products*: Art, clothing, artifacts, fetishes, jewelry, pottery, rugs. *Membership*: IACA.

AMERICAN INDIAN IMAGEMAKERS
6321 N.W. 34th St.
Hollywood, FL 33024
(305) 983-7708
Jo Motlow North, Owner
Retail, wholesale. By appointment only.
Products: Art, clothing, jewelry.

RADFORD BEAD CO.
11451 Old Kings Rd.
Jacksonsville, FL 32219
(904) 765-4886
Robin Radford, Owner
Mail order. Cherokee craftspersons. *Products*: Beadwork, clothing, masks, drums, flutes, pipes, sculpture, carvings. Special orders accepted. Catalog and brochure, $4.

**MICCOSUKEE GIFT SHOP
& CULTURAL CENTER**
Box 440021, Tamiami Station
Miami, FL 33144
(305) 223-8380
Jim Kay, Manager
Retail, wholesale. Miccosukee Tribal Enterprise. *Products*: Baskets, beadwork, clothing & accessories, dolls, sculpture, carvings.

NIZHONI DREAM CATCHERS
5141 Brixton Ct. • Naples, FL 33942
(813) 643-2026
Patricia Sauselein & Ralph Stevens, Owners
Retail. *Products*: Art, baskets, beadwork, clothing, dolls, jewelry, kachinas, pottery, rugs, sandpaintings, sculpture, carvings. *Membership*: IACA.

PRODIGY GALLERY
4320 Gulf Shore Blvd. N., Suite 206
Naples, FL 33940
(813) 263-5881 Fax 263-5882
Karen Weinert-Kim & Sam Miller, Owners
Retail. *Products*: All. *Membership*: IACA.

ME'SHIWI
544 Harrell Dr. • Orlando, FL 32828
(407) 568-5162
Terrence & Olivia Halote, Owners
Retail. *Products*: Art, jewelry, kachinas, pottery. Gold & sterling jewelry. Zuni craftspersons. By appointment only. Special orders accepted.

JOLIMA INDIAN CRAFTS
1403 N. 57th Ave.
Pensacola, FL 32506
(904) 455-0874

John & Marie Varnes, Owners
Retail, wholesale; retail by appointment only. *Products*: Baskets, beadwork, drums, pipes, flutes, jewelry. Special orders accepted.

GREEN'S RINGS & THINGS
4151 Hidden Valley Cir.
Punta Gorda, FL 33982
(813) 695-3559
Jeri & Larry Green, Owners
Retail, wholesale. *Products*: Art, beadwork, clothing & accesories, jewelry, pottery, rugs, sandpaintings.

RED CLOUD
208 Beach Dr. NE
St. Petersburg, FL 33701-3414
(813) 821-5824
Pamela R. Glawe, Owner
Retail. *Products*: All. *Membership*: IACA.

ABORIGINALS: ART OF THE FIRST PERSON
2340 Periwinkle Way • Sanibel, FL 33957
(813) 395-2200 Fax 482-7025
Susanne Waites, Owner
Retail, wholesale. *Products*: Art, baskets, beadwork, books, clothing, dolls, jewelry, kachinas, pottery, rugs, sandpaintings, sculpture, carvings. Appraisals.

INDIAN SUN, INC.
3831 Monica Pkwy. • Sarasota, FL 34235
(941) 366-0023
Joyce Kasanoukwas Syndheim, Owner
Retail, wholesale. Penobscot-Mohawk craftspersons. *Products*: Jewelry, rugs, sandpaintings.

SEMINOLE CULTURAL CENTER
5221 Orient Rd. • Tampa, FL 33610
(813) 623-3549
Leslie Stevens, Manager
Retail, mail order. *Products*: Baskets, beadwork, clothing, sculpture.

PAIRS OF WELLINGTON, INC.
13873 Wellington Trace, Suite B-3
Wellington, FL 33414
(407) 798-5590
Merlin & Pierluigi Nuti, Owners
Retail. *Products*: Fetishes, heishi, jewelry. *Membership*: IACA.

GEORGIA

NATIVE AMERICA GALLERY
195 E. Clayton St. • Athens, GA 30601
(706) 543-8425
Jane M. Scott, Owner
Retail. *Products*: Fetishes, jewelry, moccasins, sandpaintings, books, music, t-shirts. Brochure available. *Membership*: IACA.

COYOTE TRADING CO.
419 Moreland Ave. NE • Atlanta, GA 30307
(404) 221-1512
David Simpson
Retail. *Products*: Art, fetishes, heishi, jewelry, kachinas, pottery. *Membership*: IACA.

OUT OF THE WOODS GALLERY
22-B Bennett St., NW • Atlanta, GA 30309
(404) 351-0446
Deb Douglas
Retail. *Products*: All.

SOUTHWEST INDIAN ARTISANS
P.O. Box 941759 • Atlanta, GA 31141
(770) 840-8111 (phone & fax)
Martha J. Hueglin, Owner
Wholesale, retail. *Products*: Art, baskets, drums, flutes, pipes, fetishes, jewelry, kachinas, pottery, rugs, sculpture, carvings. *Membership*: IACA. Catalog.

RAY'S INDIAN ORIGINALS
90 Avondale Rd.
Avondale Estates, GA 30002
(404) 299-2397/4999
Ray Belcher, Owner
Wholesale/retail. *Products*: art, baskets, kachina dolls, jewelry, pottery, rugs.

CHESTATEE CROSSING
P.O. Box 2064 • Dahlonega, GA 30533
(404) 864-9099
Mary Brogdon & Kitty Jarrard, Owners
Retail. *Products*: Art, beadwork, books, clothing, craft supplies, dolls, jewelry, kachinas, pottery, rugs, sandpaintings, sculpture, carvings. *Membership*: IACA.

OGLEWANAGI GALLERY
9459 Hwy. 5, Suite F-G
Douglasville, GA 30135
(404) 872-4213
Tom Perkins & Vickie Dunken, Owners
Retail. *Products*: Jewelry, kachinas, pottery, rugs.

TEKAKWITHA
P.O. Box 338 • Helen, GA 30545
(404) 878-2938
Ruth Lammers
Retail. *Products*: All. *Membership*: IACA.

STONE BEAR GALLERY
120 Strand Hill Rd. • Tyrone, GA 30290
(404) 631-3424
M. Barry Bartlett
Retail. *Products*: Art, boxes, jewelry, pottery, sculpture, carvings. *Membership*: IACA.

WESTERN HEART
372 Powderhorn
St. Mary's GA 31558
(912) 882-8976
Retail, wholesale. *Products*: Native American clothing.

ANASAZI ARTS & CRAFTS
5347 E. Mountain St.
Stone Mountain, GA 30083
(770) 498-6340 Fax (706) 629-8163
Faye & Al Hart, Owners
Retail. *Products*: All. *Membership*: IACA.

HAWAII

THE SANTA FE COLLECTION
469 Ena Rd. #3004
Honolulu, HI 96815
(808) 947-9169 (Phone & Fax)
Raymond & Louann Suppa
Retail. *Products*: Art, baskets, clothing, dolls, jewelry, kachinas, pottery, rugs, sandpaintings, sculpture, carvings. *Membership*: IACA.

IDAHO

KAMIAKIN KRAFTS
P.O. Box 358 • Fort Hall, ID 83203
(208) 785-2546
Atwice Goudy Osborne, Owner
Retail, mail order. By appointment only. *Products*: Bags, beadwork, clothing/moccasins. Price list available.

TRADING POST CLOTHES HORSE
P.O. Box 368 • Fort Hall, ID 83203
(208) 237-8433 Fax 237-9343
Gayle Shappert, Manager
Retail, wholesale, mail order. Shoshone-Bannock Tribal Enterprise. *Products*: beaded and Native-tanned buckskin, moccasins, drums. Special orders accepted. Brochure and price list available.

MARSH'S TRADING POST
1105 36th St., N. • Lewiston, ID 83501
(208) 743-5778
Lorna Marsh, Owner
Retail, wholesale. *Products*: Contemporary and antique Nez Perce cornhusk bags and beadwork; Klickitat baskets; silver, turquoise, and pink mussel shell jewelry; beads & beading supplies.

HEARTLINE GALLERY
Box X, 317 East Lake • McCall, ID 83638
(800) 736-0231; (208) 634-2544
Elizabeth Cook, Owner
Retail. *Products*: All. *Membership*: IACA.

ILLINOIS

TRIBAL EXPRESSIONS
7 S. Dunton Ave. • Arlington Heights, IL 60005
(847) 590-5390 Fax 590-8634
Rob & Jeri Brooke, Owners
E-mail: rbrooke@tribalexpressions.com
Web site: www.tribalexpressions.com
Retail. *Products*: American Indian jewelry, pottery, baskets, rugs, sculpture, paintings, and other fine art.
Newsletter.

GALL SOUTHWEST SILVER JEWELRY CO.
9014 W. 31st St. • Brookfield, IL 60513
(708) 387-0460
Geraldine M. Gall, Owner
Retail. *Products*: All.

SILVER LINING GALLERY
697 Chancellor Dr.
Edwardsville, IL 62025-5573
(618) 692-1000
Lorraine Levy & Alison Sale, Owners
Retail. *Products*: Art, baskets, beadwork, books, clothing, dolls, jewelry, kachinas, pottery, rugs, sandpaintings, sculpture, carvings. *Membership*: IACA.

NATIVE AMERICAN ART
810 Dempster • Evanston, IL 60202
(708) 864-0400
Mary L. Dwyer, Owner
Retail. Products: All. *Membership*: IACA.

SKYSTONE TREASURES
715 Valley Rd. • Glencoe, IL 60022
(708) 835-3355
Patricia Schwartz, Manager
Retail. *Products*: Art, beadwork, clothing, dolls, jewelry, kachinas, pottery. Appraisals: Jewelry. *Membership*: IACA.

OBELISK, LTD.
5130 Center Ave. • Lisle, IL 60532
(708) 955-0010
Nancy C. Kelly, manager
Retail. *Products*: beadwork, boxes, cards, Eskimo & Inuit art, fetishes, jewelry, kachinas, pottery, rugs, sculpture/carvings.

BEAR PAW, INC.
217 Ferry St. • Rockton, IL 61072
(815) 624-7427
Patricia Davies & Joe Skeen
Wholesale, retail. *Products*: baskets, beadwork, clothing/moccasins/headdresses, drums/pipes/tomahawks, Eskimo & Inuit art, artifacts, fetishes, kachinas, pottery, rugs/weavings/wall hangings.

SOUTHWEST TRADING CO.
203 W. Main St. • St. Charles, IL 60174
(708) 584-5707
Steven & Janet Fabiani
Retail. *Products*: All. *Membership*: IACA..

FOUR FEATHERS
120 Mill St. • Utica, IL 61373
(815) 667-4499
Judith Rigby
Retail. *Products*: Art, baskets, beadwork, clothing, dolls, jewelry, kachinas, pottery, rugs, sandpaintings. *Membership*: IACA.

INDIANA

BRAD HAWIYEH-EHI
4399 E. Moores Pike • Bloomington, IN 47401
(812) 335-1240 (phone & fax)
Bill Roberts, Owner
Retail, wholesale, mail order. Cherokee craftsperson. *Products*: Drums, pipes, flutes, sculpture, carvings. Special orders & commissions accepted. Catalog, $2.

SKYSTONE N' SILVER
1350 S. Lake Park Ave. • Hobart, IN 46342
(219) 942-9022 Pam Phillips, Owner
E-mail: pamskystone@earthlink.net

Website: www.skystone n'silver.com
Retail, mail order. *Products*: All. *Appraisals*: Art, artifacts, jewelry, kachinas, rugs. Brochure.

SOUTHWEST OUTPOST
5302 Madison Ave. •
Indianapolis, IN 46227
(317) 783-3854
I. Sandy Craven, Owner
Retail, mail order, some wholesale.
Products: All. Catalog & price sheet.

ONE EARTH GALLERY & GIFTS
1022 Main St. • Lafayette, IN 47901
(317) 742-7564
David R. Kurtz
Retail. *Products*: All. Price list.

RAINBOW ART & FRAME
1708 S. 25th St. • Terre Haute, IN 47802
(812) 232-1337
Connie Hickman
Retail. *Products*: Art, baskets, beadwork, books, clothing, dolls, jewelry, kachinas, pottery, rugs, sandpaintings, sculpture, carvings.

DAYS PAST
1215 W. Grant St. • Thorntown, IN 46071
(317) 436-7200
Dan Bunderle, Owner
Retail. *Products*: Artifacts, jewelry, kachinas, pottery, rugs, sandpaintings, sculpture, carvings. *Membership*: IACA.

AMERICAN TREASURES
115 N. Chauncey Ave.
West Lafayette, IN 47906
(317) 743-6153
David R. Kurtz, Owner
Retail. *Products*: All. Price list available.

KANSAS

AMERICAN INDIAN ART CENTER
206 S. Buckeye Ave. • Abilene, KS 67410
(913) 263-0090
Patt Murphy, Owner
Retail. Iowa/Sauk craftsperson. *Products*: Traditional and contemporary fine arts and crafts. Specializing in Woodland and Prairie Indian items.

SEES-THE-EAGLE
111 W. Orange • Caney, KS 67333
(316) 879-2634
Margaret Ann Bird, Owner
Bill De Witt, Manager
Mail order. Osage craftsperson. *Products*: Beadwork, artifacts, rugs. Osage, Cherokee, Delaware, Plains, and Woodland Indians traditional clothing for men and women. Restoration and reproductions of museum pieces. Special orders accepted.

CHINOOK WINDS
RR 2, Box 180 • Oskaloosa, KS 66066
(913) 863-2312
Betty & Elden White, Owners
Retail. *Products*: beadwork, jewelry, moccasins, native-tanned buckskin; various other products by other Indian craftsmen.

THE SANTA FE CONNECTION
P.O. Box 7466
Overland Park, KS 66207
(913) 897-4107
William & Sue Park, Owners
Retail. *Products*: Art, baskets, beadwork, clothing, dolls, jewelry, kachinas, pottery, rugs, sandpaintings, sculpture, carvings. *Membership*: IACA.

INDIAN MUSEUM GIFT SHOP
Mid-America All-Indian Center
650 N. Seneca • Wichita, KS 67203
(316) 262-5221 ext. 41 Fax 262-4216
Jerry Martin, Director
Retail. *Products*: Art, baskets, beadwork, dolls, jewelry, kachinas, pottery.

KENTUCKY

BUFFALO ARROW HEADS
6365 Bethel Ch. Rd. • Kevil, KY 42053
(502) 462-3210
Al Puckett, Owner
Mail order. *Products*: Traditional arrow heads & crafts.

LOUISIANA

BAYOU INDIAN ENTERPRISES
P.O. Box 668 • Elton, LA 70532
(318) 584-2653
Bertney Langley, Owner
Retail, wholesale, mail order. Coushatta craftsperson.
Products: A,B,C,E,H.

MAINE

PAM CUNNINGHAM
397 Old Country Rd.
Hampden, ME 04441
(207) 941-9373
Pam Cunningham, Owner
Retail, wholesale, mail order. By appointment only.
Penobscot craftsperson. *Products*: Penobscot brown ash and sweetgrass fancy baskets.

THREE FEATHERS NATIVE BASKETS
P.O. Box 644 • Houlton, ME 04730
(207) 532-0862
Rosella Silliboy, Owner
Retail, wholesale. Micmac craftsperson. *Products*: Traditional brown ash utility and work baskets made by Micmac tribal members.

NOWETAH'S INDIAN STORE & MUSEUM
Rt. 27, Box 40 • New Portland, ME 04954
(207) 628-4981
Ms. Nowetah Timmerman, Owner/curator
Retail, mail order. *Products*: Art, baskets, beadwork, clothing, dolls, jewelry, kachinas, pottery, rugs, sandpaintings, sculpture, carvings. Catalogs available.

CHIEF POOLAW TEPEE TRADING POST
40 Main St. • Old Town, ME 04468
(207) 827-8674
Ann I. Padilla, Owner
Retail, mail order. Penobscot-Kiowa-Maliseet craftsperson. *Products*: Baskets, beadwork, clothing, dolls, drums, pipes, pottery, rugs, sculpture, carvings. Penobscot sweetgrass baskets; Passamoquoddy baskets. Send S.A.S.E. for Price list.

MAINE INDIAN BASKETMAKERS ALLIANCE
P.O. Box 3253 • Old Town, ME 04468
Products: B. Traditional brown ash and sweetgrass baskets made by members of the Maliseet, Micmac, Passamuoddy, and Penobscot tribes. Write for more information.

PENOBSCOT QUILLWORKS
P.O. Box 195 • Old Town, ME 04468
(207) 827-6117
Martin Neptune & Jennifer Sapiel, Owners
Wholesale/retail jewelry.

WABANAKI ARTS
P.O. Box 453 • Old Town, ME 04468
(207) 827-3447
Stan Neptune, Owner
Wholesale/retail/mail order. *Products*: baskets, beadwork, carvings, soapstone peace pipes, totem poles, traditional Penobscot bows and fish spers.

LONGACRE ENTERPRISES, INC.
P.O. Box 196 • Perry, ME 04667
(800) 642-5024; (207) 853-2762
Cliv Dore, Owner
Wholesale, mail order. *Products*: Passamaquoddy baskets, beadwork, boxes, children's items, dolls, drums/pipes, miniatures. Repairs & restoration. Price list available.

BASKET BANK
Aroostook Micmac Council
P.O. Box 772 • Presque Isle, ME 04769
(207) 764-1972
Alice B. Worcester, Manager
Mail order; some wholesale/retail. *Product*: Baskets.
Special orders accepted. Brochure available.

RUNNING WATER CRAFT & GIFT SHOP
R505 Post Rd. • Wells, ME 04090
(207) 646-1206
Barbara (Running Water) Beckwith, Owner/Manager
Retail, mail order. *Products*: Beadwork, boxes, dolls,
clothing, drums, flutes, pipes, jewelry, kachinas,
sandpaintings. Special orders accepted.

THE CENTER OF NATIVE ART
RFD 3, Box 247 • Woolwich, ME 04579
(207) 442-8399
Chuck & Marli Hagen, Owners
Retail. *Products*: Art, baskets, beadwork, clothing,
dolls, jewelry, kachinas, pottery, rugs, sandpaintings,
sculpture, carvings. *Membership*: IACA. Catalog.

MARYLAND

SPIRIT CATCHER
996 Headwater Rd. • Annapolis, MD 21403
(410) 263-1776
Russell & Ellen Jones, Owners
Retail. *Products*: Art, baskets, beadwork, clothing,
dolls, jewelry, kachinas, pottery, rugs, sandpaintings,
sculpture, carvings. *Membership*: IACA.

DIFFERENT
505 Vogts Lane • Baltimore, MD 21221
(410) 391-0163
Carol Sullivan & Littletree Hughes, Owners
Retail, wholesale, mail order. *Products*: Jewelry - custom design, original, and unique creations; contemporary and traditional styles.

THE WHITE BUFFALO
7101 Democracy Blvd.
Bethesda, MD 20817
(301) 469-0859
Lori & Bob Curtis, Owners
Retail. *Products*: All. *Membership*: IACA.

THE INDIAN CONNECTION
P.O. Box 21
Hyattsville, MD 20781-0021
(301) 768-8201
Littletree "Buffy" Hughes, Owner
Retail, wholesale. *Products*: Art, clothing,
jewelry, rugs, sandpaintings.

THE EARTH ART GALLERY
P.O. Box 236 • Woodstock, MD 21163
(301) 465-6106
Jane Goss & Al Finley, Owners
Retail, mail order. *Products*: Art, baskets, Art, baskets,
books, fetsihes, jewelry, miniatures, pottery, sculpture.
Presently working craft shows & pow wows. Catalog.

MASSACHUSETTS

THE WANDERING BULL, INC.
247 S. Main St. • Attleboro, MA 02703
(508) 226-6074 Fax 226-4878
Janyte Bullock, Owner
Mail order. *Products*: Craft supplies: beads,
leathers, bone, feathers, etc.

DANCING SPIRITS
2456 Mass Ave. #103 • Cambridge, MA 02140
(617) 868-7368
Sharon Basch
Retail. *Products*: All. *Membership*: IACA.

SILVER STAR, WAMPANOAG CRAFTS
P.O. Box 402 • Middleboro, MA 02346
(617) 947-4159
Anita G. Nielsen, Owner
Mail order. *Products*: Baskets, beadwork, quillwork,
moccasins, bags and leather pouches.

THE KHALSA COLLECTION
P.O. Box 604 • Millis, MA 02054-0604
(508) 376-2804 Fax 376-0845
Arjankaur Khalsa
Retail, wholesale. *Products*: Books, fetishes, heishi,
jewelry, kachinas, knives. *Membership*: IACA.

PEACEWORK GALLERY & CRAFTS
263 Main St. • Northampton, MA 01060
(413) 586-7033
Robert Nelson & Daisy Mathias, Owners
Retail. *Products*: All. *Membership*: IACA.

NEW ENGLAND TRADERS
P.O. Box 877 • Palmer, MA 01069
(413) 596-3129
Bob & Linda Schultz, Owners
Retail. *Products*: Art, baskets, beadwork, clothing,
dolls, jewelry, kachinas, pottery, rugs, sandpaintings.
Membership: IACA.

THE AMERICAN INDIAN STORE
139 Water St. • Quincy, MA 02169-6535
(617) 328-1951
Arlene F. Roberts, Owner
Retail. *Products*: art, baskets, beadwork, jewelry, pottery. rugs/weavings/wall hangings, sculpture/carvings.
Appraisals.

SUN BASKET
8-1/2 Bearskin Neck
Rockport, MA 01966
(508) 546-7546
Mary Curran, Owner
E-Mail: kalmar@shore.net
Retail. *Products*: Authentic silver & turquoise jewelry,
baskets, fetishes, pottery, etc. *Membership*: IACA.
Brochure.

MOHAWK TRADING POST
874 Mohawk Trail, Rt. 2
Shelburne, MA 01370
(413) 625-2412 Fax 625-8134
Laurene L. York, Owner
E-Mail: LYork@mohawk-trading-post.com
Web site: www.mohawk-trading-post.com
Retail. *Products*: Art, baskets, beadwork, clothing,
dolls, jewelry, kachinas, pottery, rugs, sandpaintings,
sculpture, carvings. *Membership*: IACA.

THE CORNER CAPE
P.O. Box 853 • Wellfleet, MA 02667
(508) 349-9694/9539
Althea Robida, Owner
Retail. *Products*: Beadwork, fetishes, heishi, jewelry,
kachinas, miniatures, pottery, sculpture, carvings.
Membership: IACA.

JOSEPH JOHNS
7 Russell St. • W. Peabody, MA 02535
(617) 535-2426
Joseph Johns, Owner
Special orders only. *Products*: carvings wood, slate or
bone, based on forms and motifs of the Mushkogean
culture. Illustrative material available upon request.

MICHIGAN

BEAR TRACKS DBA BUNDY'S BUNGALOW
125 Irwin St. • Brooklyn, MI 49230
(517) 592-3439 Fax 592-8022
Caryn Howard, Owner
Retail. *Products*: H,P,V. Pendleton blankets,
coats, crafts, Tshirts.

THE CRAFTS OF MANY TRIBES
South Eastern Michigan Indians, Inc.
26641 Lawrence St.
Center Line, MI 48015
(810) 956-1350 Fax 756-1352\
Retail. *Products*: Native American art and crafts.

FLYING FEATHERS
5686 Heights Ravenna Rd.
Fruitport, MI 49415-9770
(517) 484-7093
Rick Hewitt, Owner
Retail. *Products*: books, tapes, crafts supplies.

NOC BAY TRADING CO.
P.O. Box 295 • Escanaba, MI 49829
(800) 652-7192; (906) 789-0505
Website: www.nocbay.com
Mail order craft supplies & materials. Catalog, $3.

INDIAN EARTH ARTS & CRAFTS STORE
Genesee Valley Indian Association
609 W. Court St. • Flint, MI 48503
(313) 239-6621
Cora Starlin, Manager
Retail, wholesale, mail order. *Products*: art, baskets,
beadwork, moccasins, pottery, quillwork.

INDIAN ARTS & CRAFTS STORE
Native American Arts & Crafts Council
Goose Creek Rd. • Grayling, MI 49738
(517) 348-3190
Robin L. Menefee, Executive Director
Retail, mail order by request only. *Products*: art,
baskets, beadwork, boxes, leatherwork.

COYOTE WOMAN GALLERY
339 State St. • Harbor Springs, MI 49740
(419) 636-3300
Terri & John Freudenberger
Retail. *Products*: All. *Membership*: IACA.
Branch: Bryan, OH.

ANNA M. CRAMPTON
14360 Woodbury Rd. • Haslett, MI 48840
(517) 339-8856
Retail (by appointment only).
Products: baskets, beadwork.

MONADNOCK TRADING CO., INC.
309 E. Central Ave., P.O. Box 400
Mackinaw City, MI 49701
(616) 436-5131 Fax 436-5158
Lawrence Goldman, Owner
Retail. *Products*: Art, beadwork, boxes, jewelry, pot-
tery, rugs, sandpaintings, sculpture. *Membership*:
IACA. *Branch office*: P.O. Box 6465, Apache Junction,
AZ 85278.

SOUTHWEST MIRAGE
36643 Suffolk • Mt. Clemens, MI 48043
(313) 791-3384
Frank & Joann Spatafore
Retail. *Products*: dolls, drums/pipes, fetishes,
heishi, jewelry, kachinas, pottery, sandpaintings.

ELI THOMAS
2795 S. Leaton Rd.
Mt. Prospect, MI 48858
(517) 773-4299
Retail, wholesale. *Product*: baskets.

INDIAN HILLS TRADING CO.
& INDIAN ART GALLERY
1581 Harbor Rd. • Petoskey, MI 49770
(616) 347-3789
Victor S. Kishigo, Owner
Retail, mail order (by special request). *Products*: bas-
kets, beadwork, drums, quillwork, jewelry, pottery,
Navajo rugs.

NATIVE WEST - UNIQUE
AMERICAN SOUTHWEST ART
863 W. Ann Arbor Trail • Plymouth, MI 48170
(313) 455-8838
Annette & Ken Horn, Owners
Retail. *Products*: Art, boxes, clothing, dolls, jewelry,
kachinas, pottery, rugs, sandpaintings, sculpture, carvings. *Membership*: IACA.

BAWATING ART GALLERY
2186 Shunk Rd. • Sault Ste. Marie, MI 49783
(906) 632-0530 ext. 53529 Fax 635-4959
Elisabeth Dietz, Manager
Retail. Products: Native artist's paintings, wood & soapstone carvings, dreamcatchers, etc. Artwork is all sizes
and all mediums, including beadwork on birchbark, and
birchbark paintings.

BIG BEAR TRADING POST
1904 Ashmun St. • Sault Ste. Marie, MI 49783
(906) 632-8336
Catherine Boling, Owner
Retail. Products: Native American crafts and supplies.

SWEETGRASS ARTS & CRAFTS
206 Greenough St.
Sault Ste. Marie, MI 49783
(906) 635-6050
Susan Moore, Manager
Wholesale/retail. *Products*: art, baskets, beadwork, quillwork, wood carvings, shawls and quilts.

MINNESOTA

LADY SLIPPER DESIGNS
RR #3, Box 556
Bemidji, MN 56601
(218) 751-0835
Lisa Bruns, Manager
Wholesale. *Products*: Birch bark baskets & canoes. Special orders accepted. Catalog.

**MANITOK FOOD & GIFTS/
KENOO FINE HANDCRAFTS**
Hwy. 59 - Box 97, Ojibwe Tribal Enterprises
Callaway, MN 56521
(800) 726-1863; (218) 375-3425 Fax 375-4765
White Earth Reservation, Owner
Vicki Kappes, Marketing Manager
E-Mail: vicki@manitok
Web site: http://www.manitok.com
Retail, wholesale, mail order. *Products*: baskets, beadwork, books, boxes, drums, pipes, jewelry, miniatures. *Membership*: IACA. Catalog.

ROBERT DESJARLAIT STUDIO/GALLERY
5901 Rhode Island Ave. N. • Crystal, MN 55428
(612) 535-0091
Robert DesJarlait, Owner
Retail. Anishinaabe artist & craftsperson. *Products*: A,D,E,H. Visual art includes murals, original paintings, illustrations and graphics; traditional art includes bone & feather work. Special orders and commissions accepted.

LAKE OF THE WOODS OJIBWE
1535 Willard Ave. • Detroit Lakes, MN 56501
(218) 846-9911
Karen Floan, Owner
Retail, whlolesale. By appointment. Chippewa craftsperson. *Products*: Applique-style hand beadwork of northern Ojibwe designs; other woodsy, lodge-style interior home products.

IKWE MARKETING
Route 1 • Isage, MN 56570
(218) 573-3411/3049
Margaret Smith & Winona LaDuke, Managers
Retail/mail order. *Products*: baskets, beadwork, quillwork, rugs/quilts.

EARTH CIRCLES
4251 Nicolet Ave. So.
Minneapolis, MN 55409
(612) 823-8244
Retail. *Products*: books, tapes, blankets, hides, beads, etc.

WOODLAND INDIAN CRAFTS
1530 E. Franklin Ave. • Minneapolis, MN 55404
(612) 874-7766
Elaine & Charles Stately, Owners
Retail, mail order. *Products*: B,C,H,P,V.

PIPESTONE INDIAN SHRINE ASSOCIATION
Pipestone National Monument
P.O. Box 727 • Pipestone, MN 56164
(888) 209-0418; (507) 825-5463 Fax 825-2903
Maddie Redwing, Business Manager
Caroll Derby, Sales Manager
E-mail: sales@authenticpipestone.com
Website: www.authenticpipestone.com
Retail, wholesale, mail order. *Products*: beadwork, drums, pipes, flutes, jewelry, pottery. Carvings in pipestone (catlinite) including pipes and jewelry; beaded pipe bags. Brochure.

AMBER WOODS STUDIO
810 Summit Ave. • St. Paul, MN 55071
(612) 856-2328
David D. DuBois, Co-owner
Retail. *Products*: Art, sculpture, carvings.

CBR, INC. TOUCH THE EARTH
2040 St. Clair Ave. • St. Paul, MN 55105
(612) 690-1050 Fax 690-0440
Carol Howe, Owner
Retail, wholesale.

PAINTED TIPI, LTD.
725 Snelling Ave. N. • St. Paul, MN 55104
(612) 854-9193 Fax 645-5745
Retail. *Products*: All. *Appraisals*: Art, artifacts, beadwork, books, clothing, dolls, jewelry, kachinas, pottery, rugs. *Membership*: IACA.

STORMCLOUD TRADING CO.
725 Snelling Ave. N. • St. Paul, MN 55104
(612) 645-0343 Fax 645-5745
Sandra Graves, Owner; Jim Priest, Manager
Retail, wholesale, mail order. *Products*: Art, beadwork, books, artifacts, boxes, jewelry, kachinas, pottery, rugs. Appraisals. *Membership*: IACA.

SHAKOPEE TRADING POST & GALLERY
723 1st Ave. West • Shakopee, MN 55379
(612) 496-2263
Marlon & Mary Jean Estenson, Owners
Retail, wholesale. Native American arts & crafts specialty shop. *Products*: Sterling silver & turquoise handmade jewelry, quill work, beaded items, books, etc.

MISSISSIPPI

**CHOCTAW MUSEUM OF THE
SOUTHERN INDIAN GIFT SHOP**
P.O. Box 6010 • Philadelphia, MS 39350
(601) 650-1685
Bob Ferguson, Manager
Retail, mail order. Tribal enterprise. *Products*: Baskets, beadwork, clothing, dolls, jewelry, pottery. Special orders accepted. Send S.A.S.E. for Price list.

SOARING EAGLE INDIAN JEWELRY
906 Spring St. • Waynesboro, MS 39367
(601) 735-1195
Carolyn Stagg-White
Retail. *Products*: Baskets, jewelry, pottery. *Membership*: IACA.

MISSOURI

SOUTHWEST REFLECTIONS
13735 Co. Rd. #6950
Caulfield, MO 65626
(907) 258-9988
Nancy & Weyman Perez, Owners
Retail. *Products*: Art, baskets, boxes, ornaments, clothing, drums, pipes, artifacts, jewelry, kachinas, knives, miniatures, rugs, sandpaintings. *Memebership*: IACA.

TURNER ARTWORKS
14323 Spring Dr. • De Soto, MO 63020
(314) 337-4105
Kevin Skypainter Turner, Owner
Retail, wholesale, mail order. *Products*: Art, jewelry. Brochure, catalog.

MAHOTA HANDWOVENS
67 Horseshoe Dr. • Joplin, MO 64804
(417) 782-7036
Margaret Roach Wheeler, Owner
Retail. By appointment only. Chickasaw-Choctaw craftsperson. *Products*: Clothing & accessories, rugs.

SOUTHWEST STAR FINE ARTS
11123 E. 85 Terrace
Raytown, MO 64138
(800) 992-8939
Roy A. Beers
Wholesale/retail. *Products*: U. *Appraisals*: U. *Membership*: IACA. Catalog.

SILVER FOX TRADING POST
5104 King Hill Ave.
St. Joseph, MO 64504
(816) 238-7560
Retail, wholesale. *Products*: Indian crafted items & artifacts.

MONTANA

BUFFALO CHIPS INDIAN GALLERY
327 S. 24th St. West
Billings, MT 59102-5669
(406) 656-8954
Thom Myers
Retail, wholesale. *Products*: All. *Appraisals*: Beadwork, clothing, dolls, jewelry, rugs; repairs & restoration. Catalog.

SCHNEES BOOTS & SHOES
6597 Falcon Ln. • Bozeman, MT 59715
(800) 922-1562
Retail, wholesale. *Products*: Arrow Moccasin Co. - contemporary hand-sewn heavy moccasins.

BLACKFEET CRAFTS ASSOCIATION
P.O. Box 51 • Browning, MT 59417
Mary F. Hipp, Manager
Retail, mail order. *Products*: Beadwork, clothing, jewelry.

BLACKFEET TRADING POST
P.O. Box 626 • Browning, MT 59417
(406) 338-2050
Nora Lukin, Owner
Retail, mail order. *Products*: Art, baskets, bneadwork, clothing, pottery. Special order accepted.

**NORTHERN PLAINS INDIAN
CRAFTS ASSOCIATION**
P.O. Box E • Browning, MT 59417
(406) 338-5661
Jackie Parsons, Manager
Retail, mail order. Blackfeet craftspersons. *Products*: Baskets, beadwork, clothing, dolls, jewelry. rugs. Send S.A.S.E. for Price List

YELLOWSTONE TRADING POST
Box 1129, Hwy. 212 • Cooke City, MT 59020
(406) 838-2265
Bernie & Phyllis Kiley, Owners
Retail. *Products*: Art, beadwork, clothing dolls, drums, pipes, fetishes, jewelry, kachinas, sandpaintings. *Membership*: IACA.

JAY CONTWAY ART
434 McIver Rd. • Great Falls, MT 59404
(406) 452-7647
Jay Contway, Owner
Wholesale, retail. *Products*: Art, jewelry, rugs, sculpture. *Membership*: IACA. Catalog.

KING KUKA GRAPHICS
907 Ave. "C", NW • Great Falls, MT 59404
(406) 452-4449
King KuKa, Owner
Retail, wholesale, mail order. By appointment. *Products*: Art, sculpture, carvings. Send S.A.S.E. for price list.

FORT BELKNAP VENTURES, INC.
RR 1, Box 66 • Harlem, MT 59526
(406) 353-2205 ext. 403
Frankie Johnson, Manager
Retail, wholesale, mail order. Fort Belknap Gros Ventres and Assiniboine tribal enterprise. *Products*: Art, beadwork, clothing, dolls, jewelry. Quantity orders accepted.

**H. EARL & MARGARET TURNER
CLACK MEMORIAL MUSEUM**
P.O. Box 1484 • Havre, MT 59501
(406) 265-9913
Elinor Clack, Owner
Retail. *Products*: Art, beadwork, dolls, artifacts. *Appraisals*: Beadwork.

NEENEY
P.O. Box 84 • Joplin, MT 59531
(406) 292-3890
Robert Harvey Allen, Owner
Retail. *Products*: Beadwork, fetishes, jewelry.

GREAT PLAINS GALLERY
P.O. Box 126 - Apt. 28
Lame Deer, MT 59043-0126
(800) 249-2296; (406) 477-9418

Donald Hollowbreast, Owner
Retail, wholesale. Northern Cheyenne artist. *Products*: A. Oil paintings, watercolors, pen & ink drawings. Commissions from color photographs and special orders accepted.

**NORTHERN CHEYENNE
ARTS & CRAFTS ASSOCIATION**
Northern Cheyenne Indian Reservation
Lame Deer, MT 59043
Carol A. White Wolf, Manager
Retail, wholesale. *Products*: Beadwork, clothing, jewelry.

COUP MARKS
Box 532 • Ronan, MT 59864
(406) 246-3216
Lorrain Big Crane & Dwight Billedeaux, Managers
Retail. *Products*: A,C,I,J,H,X. Special orders accepted

**FLATHEAD INDIAN MUSEUM,
TRADING POST & ART GALLERY**
P.O. Box 464 • St. Ignatius, MT 59865
(406) 745-2951
L. Doug Allard, Owner
Retail, wholesale, mail order. *Products*: Art, beadwork, clothing, jewelry. Special orders accepted on beadwork and buckskin items.

FOUR WINDS INDIAN TRADING POST
P.O. Box 580 • St. Ignatius, MT 59865
(406) 745-4336 Fax 745-3595
E-Mail: 4winds@bigsky.net
Preston Miller, President
Retail, wholesale, mail order. *Products*: Indian crafts and frontier collectibles. Catalog

ALL SORTS, INC.
P.O. Box 975 • Wolf Point, MT 59201
(406) 653-3011
Retail, wholesale. *Products*: Native American clothing.

HAMILTON STORES, INC.
P.O. Box 250, Yellowstone National Park
West Yellowstone, MT 59758
(406) 646-7325 Fax 646-7323
David Reynolds & Eleanor Hamilton Povah
Retail. *Products*: All. *Membership*: IACA.

NEBRASKA

THE TURQUOISE SHOP
509 E. 5th St.
North Platte, NE 69101-6924
(308) 532-7023
Betty J. Kind
Retail. *Products*: Fetishes, heishi, jrewelry, pottery, sculpture, craft supplies.

NEVADA

LEHMAN CAVES GIFTS
Great Basin National Park
Baker, NV 89311
(702) 234-7221
Tonia T. Harvey
Retail. *Products*: All. *Membership*: IACA.

STEWART INDIAN MUSEUM TRADING POST
5366 Snyder Ave. • Carson City, NV 89701
(702) 882-1808
Suzi Lisa, Manager
Retail. Apache craftsperson. *Products*: Baskets, beadwork, dolls, jewelry, kachinas, rugs. Special orders accepted.

FORUNATE EAGLE'S ROUND HOUSE GALLERY
7133 Stillwater Rd. • Fallon, NY 89406
(702) 423-2220
Adam Fortunate Eagle Nordwall, Owner
Retail. *Products*: Art, beadwork, clothing, drums, pipes, jewelry, pottery, sculpture.

AMERICAN HERITAGE INDIAN ARTS
850 S. Boulder Hwy. #292
Henderson, NV 89015-7564

Cynthia Judd & D.L. Uher, Sr.
Wholesale/retail. *Products*: Clothing, drums, pipes, rugs. *Membership*: IACA. Catalog.

MALOTTE STUDIO
South Fork Reservation
Star Route • Lee, NV 89829
(702) 744-4305
Jack Malotte, Owner
By appointment only. *Products*: Original drawings , graphic design and illustrations.

MOAPA TRIBAL ENTERPRISES
P.O. Box 340, Paiute Tribal Enterprise
Moapa, NV 89025-0340
(702) 865-2787 Fax 379-4012
Vince Pillig, Manager
Wholesale, retail. *Products*: All. *Membership*: IACA.

MAGGI HOUTEN
P.O. Box 265 • Nixon, NV 89424
(702) 476-0205
Margaret Houten, Owner
Mail order. *Products*: Baskets, beadwork.

MICHAEL & SON'S BLACK HILLS TRADING CO.
2002A Harvard Way • Reno, NV 89502
(702) 829-9933
David & Shannon Lorenz
Wholesale, retail. *Products*: Baskets, clothing, dolls, jewelry, kachinas, pottery, sandpaintings, sculpture, carvings; repairs & restoration. *Membership*: IACA.

THE TEPEE
2500 E. 2nd St. #38 • Reno, NV 89595
(702) 322-5599
Irene Ryan, Owner
Retail, mail order. Products: Baskets, jewelry, kachinas, pottery, rugs.

**ARNOLD ARAGON -
SCULPTURE & ILLUSTRATION**
P.O. Box 64 • Schurz, NV 89427
(702) 773-2542
Arnold Aragon, Owner
Retail, wholesale. *Products*: Art, sculpture, carvings. Special orders accepted.

WINTER MOON TRADING CO.
P.O. Box 189 • Schurz, NV 89427
(702) 773-2088
Elvin Willie, Owner
Retail, mail order. *Products*: Art, baskets, beadwork, jewelry. Send S.A.S.E. for price list.

WESTERN INTERNATIONAL
395 Freeport Blvd. #2
Sparks, NV 89431
(800) 634-6737; (702) 359-4400 Fax 359-4439
John & Shirley Fritz, Owners
Wholesale. *Products*: Books. *Membership*: IACA. Catalog.

INDIAN OUTPOST
Box 829, 20 South C St.
Virginia City, NV 89440
(702) 847-9025
Paul & Marilyn Slick, Owners
Wholesale, retail. *Products*: Art, baskets, beadwork, fetishes, jewelry, kachinas, miniatures, pottery, sculpture.

THE INDIAN TRADING POST
Box 671, Virginia City Mall #7
Virginia City, NV 89440
(702) 847-0242
Winson Hong, Owner
Wholesale, retail. *Products*: All. *Membership*: IACA.

NEW HAMPSHIRE

FOUR WINDS TRADING CO.
1 Rhodora Dr.
Amherst, NH 03031-2242
(603) 672-2729
Colleen & Leo Trudeau, Owners
Retail. *Products*: All. *Membership*: IACA.

AMERICAN INDIAN ARTS
P.O. Box 476 • Epsom, NH 03234
(603) 736-9946
Lynn & Gardner Gray, Owners
Retail.

KACHINA JUGGLER
70 Meadow Rd.
Portsmouth, NH 03801-3124
(603) 436-0253
Kevin & Elisa Marconi-Davis
Retail. *Products*: All. *Membership*: IACA.

NEW JERSEY

BLUE ZAT GEMS INDIAN ROOM
130 Atlantic St. • Bridgeton, NJ 08302
(609) 451-8059
Russell & Doris Harris, Owners
Retail, wholesale. *Products*: Art, jewelry, rugs, sandpaintings, sculpture.

ARCHEOCRAFT
22 Rose Terrace • Chatham, NJ 07928
(201) 635-1447
Kenneth O'Brien
Retail. *Product*: Pottery.

JEAN MUIZNIEKS
13 Channing Way • Cranbury, NJ 08512
(609) 799-0448/1793
Jean Muiznieks
Retail, wholesale. *Products*: Beadwork, fetishes, heishi, jewelry.

THE MORNING DANCER COLLECTION
130F The Orchard • Cranbury, NJ 08512
(908) 548-8423
Holly Sandiford & Chip Greenberg
Retail, wholesale. *Products*: Baskets, jewelry, pottery. *Membership*: IACA.

TURQUOISE LADY
10 Horace Court • Cranbury, NJ 08512
(609) 936-1044
Jayne Davis
Retail. *Products*: Jewelry. *Membership*: IACA.

TWO RIVERS TRADING POST
1164 Stuyvesant Ave. • Irvington, NJ 07111
(973) 351-1210
Carl Watson Longbow, Principal Chief
(Cherokee Nation of New Jersey)
Retail. *Products*: Authentic Native American Indian crafts, artifacts and jewelry; Native American herbs and oils.

SOUTHWEST AMERICAN INDIAN JEWELRY
76 Still Well Rd. • Kendall Park, NJ 08824
(609) 799-0448
Jean M. Muiznieks, Owner
Retail, wholesale. *Products*: Beadwork, fetishes, heishi, jewelry. *Membership*: IACA.

SEIDEN AMERICAN INDIAN DESIGNS
P.O. Box 99, 14 Ridgewood Dr.
Livingston, NJ 07039
(201) 992-4788 Fax 994-2795
Matthew & Gella Seiden, Owners
Wholesale, retail. *Products*: Fetishes, jewelry, kachinas, miniatures, rugs. *Membership*: IACA.

CROSSROADS
65 Main St. • Madison, NJ 07940
(201) 514-1616
Jan Keyes, Owner
Retail. *Products*: Art, baskets, beadwork, books, clothing, dolls, jewelry, kachinas, pottery, rugs, sand paintings. All Native-made crafts. *Membership*: IACA. Catalog.

SPIDER WOMAN
141 Idolstone Lane • Matawan, NJ 07747
(908) 583-0829
John & Shaharazad Kleindienst, Owners
Retail. *Products*: Beadwork, dolls, fetishes, heishi,, jewelry, kachinas, knives, pottery. *Membership*: IACA. *Branch*: Secaucus, NJ.

GREY OWL INDIAN CRAFTS
P.O. Box 1185 • Neptune, NJ 07754
(800) 487-2376
(732) 775-9010 Fax 774-9330
E-mail: greyowlinc@aol.com
Web site: www.greyowlcrafts.com
Jim Feldman, Owner
Wesley Cochrane, Manager
Retail, Wholesale, Mail order. *Products*: Native American Indian craft supplies. 4,000+ items. Catalog, $3; free to Native Americans.

LONE BEAR INDIAN CRAFT CO.
300 Main St. #3F • Orange, NJ 07050
James Lone Bear Revey, Owner
Mail order. *Products*: Woodland Indian craftwork.
Price list.

TURQUOIS INDIAN
137 E. State Rt. 4 • Paramus, NJ 07652-5004
(201) 797-1060
Dennis & Ingred Taormina, Owners
Retail. *Products*: All. *Appraisals*: Jewelry.
Membership: IACA.

MOON LAKE INDIAN JEWELRY
175 Hayes Dr. • Saddle Brook, NJ 07662
(201) 797-8367
Bernard Ahrens, Owner
Retail. *Products*: Jewelry, kachinas; repairs
& restoration.

SPIDER WOMAN
700 Plaza Dr. • Secaucus, NJ 07794
(201) 223-1313
John & Shaharazad Kleindienst, Owners
Retail. *Products*: Beadwork, dolls, fetishes, heishi, jewelry, kachinas, knives, pottery. *Membership*: IACA.
Branch: Matawan, NJ.

ADOBE EAST GALLERY
445 Springfield Ave. • Summit, NJ 07901
(908) 273-8282 Fax 277-1483
Tedd & Phyllis Schwartz
Retail. *Products*: Art, jewelry, pottery,
rugs, sculpture. *Membership*: IACA.

COYOTE JUNCTION
7 Glenview Rd. • Towaco, NJ 07082
(201) 299-0506
Joseph & Susan Ascione, Owners
Retail, wholesale. *Products*: Ornaments, fetishes, heishi, jewelry, kachinas, pottery, sandpaintings. *Membership*: IACA.

NEW MEXICO

LILLY'S GALLERY
P.O. Box 342 • Acoma Pueblo, NM 87034
(505) 552-9501
Maria "Lilly" Salvador, Owner
Wayne Salvador, Manager
Retail. *Products*: Traditional Acoma Pueblo
pottery and figurines. *Memberships*: SWAIA.

SQUASH BLOSSOM
822 N. White Sands Blvd.
Alamogordo, NM 88310-7112
(505) 437-8126
Cliff & Sue Hall, Owners
Retail. *Products*: Navaho, Zuni & Hopi jewelry; Hopi kachina dolls; Navaho rugs & sandpaintings; <escalero Apache sculpture, baskets & paintings. *Appraisals*: P,V. *Membership*: IACA.

WOVEN STITCH-INDIAN DESIGN NEEDLEWORK
1828 Corte Del Ranchero
Alamogordo, NM 88310
(505) 437-2934
Mike Mosier, President
Retail, wholesale, mail order. *Products*: Indian designs in crochet, needlepoint, latch hook kits and patterns. Catalog.

AMERICAN HERITAGE INDIAN ARTS
14024 Wind Mountain Rd. NE
Albuquerque, NM 87112-6561
(505) 271-1981

Cynthia Judd, Owner
Wholesale/retail. *Products*: Clothing, drums, pipes, rugs. *Membership*: IACA. Catalog.

AMERICAN WEST TRADING CO.
1208 San Pedro NE, Suite 117
Albuquerque, NM 87110
Ken Kaemmerle
(505) 265-8549
Wholesale. *Products*: Northwest Coast art, kachinas, pottery, rugs, sculpture. *Membership*: IACA.

AMERINJECO TRADING CO.
P.O. Box 13345 • Albuquerque, NM 87192
(800) 874-1976; (505) 293-4727 (phone & fax)
Layne E. Fuller, Director
Wholesale. *Products*: Fetishes, heishi, jewelry, kachinas, knives, pottery, rugs, sandpaintings, sculpture. *Membership*: IACA. catalog available.

ANITRAS, INC.
1701 Central NW • Albuquerque, NM 87104
(800) 824-4149; (505) 242-1060
Anita Becker & William Blythe
Wholesale. *Product*: Jewelry. Catalog available.

ARMADILLO TRADING CO.
201 Wellesley Dr., SE
Albuquerque, NM 87106-1419
(505) 266-7698
Chuck Hall
Wholesaler. *Product*: Pottery. *Membership*:IACA.

BEAR PAW INDIAN ARTS & GALLERY
326 San Felipe, NW, Old Town
Albuquerque, NM 87104
(505) 843-9337
Jim, Michael, Mary & Marian Trujillo, Owners
Retail, wholesale. *Products*: Art, baskets, dolls, drums, pipes, jewelry, pottery, sandpaintings. Special orders accepted.

THE BELL GROUP RIO GRANDE
7500 Bluewater Rd. NW
Albuquerque, NM 87121-1962
(505) 345-8511
Hugh Bell
Wholesale. *Product*: Y. *Membership*: IACA.

BIEN MUR INDIAN MARKETING CENTER
Sandia Pueblo Tribal Enterprise
P.O. Box 91148 • Albuquerque, NM 87199
(800) 365-5400; (505) 821-5400 Fax 821-7674
Retail, wholesale, mail order. *Products*: A,H,N,P,Q,U. Authentic Native American arts & crafts. Special orders accepted. *Membership*: IACA. Brochure.

BING CROSBY'S INDIAN ARTS
2510 Washington St. NE
Albuquerque, NM 87110
(800) 545-6556; (505) 888-4800 Fax 883-6206
Bing Crosby, Owner
Wholesale. *Products*: Art, clothing, dolls, jewelry, kachinas, pottery, rugs, sandpaintings, sculpture, carvings. *Membership*: IACA.

CARLISLE SILVER CO., INC.
P.O. Box 26627, 750 Rankin Rd., NE
Albuquerque, NM 87125
(505) 345-5304 Fax 345-5445
H. William Pollack, III
Retail, wholesale. *Products*: Art, fetishes, heishi, jewelry, kachinas, pottery, rugs, sandpaintings. Catalog available.

CHRISTIN WOLF, INC.
2425 Monroe NE #B (87110)
206 1/2 San Felipe NW (87104)
Albuquerque, NM (505) 242-4222
Jerry McKenzie, Owner
Wholesale/retail. *Products*: Fetishes, heishi, jewelry, knives.

CHRISTOPHER'S ENTERPRISES
P.O. Box 25621
Albuquerque, NM 87125-0621
(505) 294-4581 Fax 294-4585
Christopher & Deborah Cates, Owners
Wholesale. *Products*: Jewelry. *Membership*: IACA.
Catalog available.

CIBOLA TRAIL TRADERS EAST
P.O. Box 3362
Albuquerque, NM 87190-3362
(505) 869-2044
Garry & Sue Zens
Wholesale. *Products*: Fetishes, jewelry, pottery. *Membership*: IACA. *Branch*: P.O. Box 1500, Peralta, NM 87042.

D'ANZE
P.O. Box 27206, 4908 4th St. NW
Albuquerque, NM 87125-7206
(505) 345-2587
Dee Ann Price
Wholesale. *Product*: Jewelry. *Membership*: IACA.

DISTINCTIVE INDIAN JEWELRY
1028 Stuart Rd., NW
Albuquerque, NM 87114
(505) 897-4152
Ted & Randy Brackett
Wholesale. *Products*: Fetishes, heishi, jewelry, kachinas, rugs. *Membership*: IACA.

GERTRUDE ZACHARY, INC.
1613 Second NW • Albuquerque, NM 87102
(505) 243-3711
Gertrude Schmidt
Wholesale. *Products*: Jewelry, kachinas, pottery.

THE GOLDEN FLEECE
10025 Acoma SE
Albuquerque, NM 87123
(505) 294-1604
Raphael Seidel
Wholesale. *Product*: Jewelry. Appraisals.

DOROTHY GRANDBOIS
P.O. Box 2672 • Corrales, NM 87048
(505) 898-3754
Retail. *Products*: Combines photographic
and printmaking to create her Native art.

GRANDFATHER EAGLE
202-A San Felipe NW
Albuquerque, NM 87104
(505) 242-5376
Mark & Sally Ann Blythe
Wholesale, retail. *Products*: Art, clothing, dolls, jewelry, kachinas, pottery, rugs, sandpaintings, sculpture, carvings. *Membership*: IACA. Catalog.

GUS'S TRADING CO.
2026 Central SW • Albuquerque, NM 87104
(505) 843-6381
Wholesale.

HILL'S INDIAN JEWELRY
3004 2nd St., NW
Albuquerque, NM 87107-1418
(800) 545-6500
(505) 345-4110 Fax 345-5208
Martha & Hershel Hill
Wholesale. Navajo handmade sterling silver jewelry.

HOUSE OF THE SHALAKO
First Plaza Galeria #65
Albuquerque, NM 87102
(505) 242-4579
Gary & Sue Zens
Retail. *Products*: Baskets, beadwork, books, clothing, dolls, jewelry, kachinas, pottery, rugs, sandpaintings, sculpture, carvings. *Membership*: IACA.

INDIAN PUEBLO CULTURAL CENTER, INC.
2401 12th St., NW • Albuquerque, NM 87104
(800) 766-4405; (505) 843-7270
Keith Lucero, Manager
Retail, wholesale, mail order. Nonprofit organization of 19 New Mexican Pueblos. *Products*: Baskets, drums, pipes, jewelry, pottery, rugs, sculpture, carvings. Catalog.

JAMES ROGERS SILVERSMITHS
3137 San Mateo Blvd., NE
Albuquerque, NM 87110
(505) 889-9327 Fax 889-9329
James Rogers
Wholesale. *Product*: Jewelry. Catalog available.

JUDY CROSBY'S AMERICANA ARTS
2119 San Mateo Blvd. NE
Albuquerque, NM 87110
(505) 266-2324
Judy Crosby, Owner
Wholesale. *Products*: Fetishes, heishi, jewelry, kachinas, knives, miniatures, pottery, sandpaintings, sculpture, carvings. *Membership*: IACA.

KENNEDY INDIAN ARTS
P.O. Box 6526, 602 Montano NW
Albuquerque, NM 87197
(505) 344-7538
John & Georgiana Kennedy, Owner
Wholesale. *Products*: All. *Membership*: IACA.

KHALSA TRADING CO.
1423 Carlisle NE • Albuquerque, NM 87110
(505) 255-8278 Fax 255-3877
S.S. Gurubachan Khalsa & Kulbir Puri
Wholesale. *Product*: Jewelry.

L.G. KINGS TRADING CO.
900 Coors SW • Albuquerque, NM 87105
(505) 836-2824
Leonard G. King
Wholesale. *Membership*: IACA.

MILAINES SANTA FE SILVER
2013 Ridgecrest Dr. SE
Albuquerque, NM 87108
(505) 268-8073 Fax 255-0659
Wayne Desantis
Wholesale. *Products*: Art, fetishes, dreamcatchers, jewelry, pottery, sculpture, carvings. *Membership*: IACA. Catalog.

NARRANJO'S WORLD OF AMERICAN INDIAN ART
1911 Lomas Blvd. NW
Albuquerque, NM 87104-1207
Stella Naranjo Thompson, Manager
Wholesale/retail/mail order. *Products*: baskets, beadwork, dolls, jewelry, leatherwork, pottery, rugs. Price list available.

NAVAJO GALLERY
323 Romero NW, Suite #1
Albuquerque, NM 87104
(505) 843-7666
Barbara Griffith, Manager
Wholesale/retail/and some mail order. *Products*: paintings, sculpture, lithographs, and drawings by R.C. Gorman.

OLD TOWN TRADING POST
Box 7036, 208 San Felipe NW
Albuquerque, NM 87194-7036
(505) 243-0859; Bruce Mollenkopf
Wholesale, retail. *Products*: All. *Membership*: IACA.

R.L. COX FUR & HIDE CO., INC.
Box 25321, 708 1st St., NW
Albuquerque, NM 87125
(505) 242-4980 Fax 242-6101
R.L. Cox, Owner
Wholesale. *Products*: Tanned furs & leather for chaps, moccasins, garments & crafts. *Membership*: IACA.

SANTA FE SILVER FOX
7000 Louisiana NE #1005
Albuquerque, NM 87109
Joan & Robert Fox
Wholesale, retail. *Products*: Dolls, fetishes, heishi, jewelry, kachinas, pottery. *Membership*: IACA.

SHAFFER'S INDIAN ART
P.O. Box 21700 • Albuquerque, NM 87154
(505) 293-2217/264-0549
Richard L. Shaffer
Wholesale. *Products*: Baskets, boxes, fetishes, jewelry, kachinas, miniatures, pottery. *Membership*: IACA.

SILVER NUGGET
416 Juan Tabo NE • Albuquerque, NM 87123
(505) 293-6861 Fax 292-0367
Gary DePriest
Wholesale/retail. *Products*: Dolls, fetishes, jewelry, kachinas; repairs & restoration. *Membership*: IACA. Catalog.

SILVER SUN
2042 S. Plaza NW
Historic Old Town
Albuquerque, NM 87104
(800) 662-3220
(505) 242-8265/246-9692 Fax 246-9719
Deanna Olson & Kathy Sanchez
Wholesale/retail. *Products*: Children's items, clothing, drums, pipes, fetishes, heishi, jewelry, miniatures. *Branch*: 2011 Central NW, Albuquerque, NM; and Santa Fe, NM. *Membership*: IACA. Catalog.

SOUND OF AMERICA RECORDS (SOAR CORP.)
5200 Constitution Ave. NE
Albuquerque, NM 87110
(505) 268-6110 Fax 268-0237
Tom Bee, President
E-Mail: soar@rt66.com
Retail, wholesale, mail order. *Products*: Contemporary and traditional Native American music on cassette, compact disc, and video. Brochure.

TECOLOTTE TILES & GALLERY
400 San Felipe, NW
Albuquerque, NM 87104-1462
(505) 243-3403 Fax 296-6865
Richard & Priscilla Jupp
Retail. *Products*: Art, boxes, ornaments, dolls, jewelry, pottery. *Membership*: IACA. Catalog.

TRACEY LTD.
2100 Aztec Rd. NE #A
Albuquerque, NM 87107-4204
(800) 458-2500; (505) 883-8868 Fax 883-8806
Ray Tracey & Kristen Middleton
Wholesale. *Products*: Jewelry. *Branch*: 2407 E. Boyd #8A, Gallup, NM. *Membership*: IACA. Catalog.

THE TREASURE TRADERS
6000 Lomas NE • Albuquerque, NM 87110
(505) 268-4343
Arnie & Norma Jean Sidman
Retail. *Products*: art, beadwork, cards, clothing, dolls, drums/pipes, heishi, jewelry, kachinas, knives, miniatures, pottery, sculpture/carvings.

UTILITY SHACK, INC.
11035 Central NE • Albuquerque, NM 87123
(505) 292-0174
Linda & David Stout
Wholesale/retail. *Products*: All.
Appraisals: baskets, jewelry, pottery, rugs.

WADE'S AMERICAN INDIAN TRADERS
627 Fairway NW • Albuquerque, NM 87107
(505) 343-9100 Fax 343-9101
Clare Wade
Wholesale, retail. *Products*: All. *Membership*: IACA.

WRIGHT'S INDIAN COLLECTION
1100 San Mateo Blvd. NE, Suite 21
Albuquerque, NM 87110-6473
(505) 883-6122
Sam Chernoff, Owner; Wayne Bobrick, Director
Retail. *Products*: All. *Membership*: IACA.

YELLOWHORSE
4314 Silver SE
Albuquerque, NM 87108-2723
(505) 266-0600
Artie Yellowhorse
Wholesale. *Product*: P. *Membership*: IACA.

THE ED YOUNGS, INC.
2323 Krogh Ct. NW
Albuquerque, NM 87104-2508
(505) 864-1242
Ed Young, President
Wholesale. *Products*: Beadwork, clothing, dolls, jewelry, kachinas, pottery, rugs, sandpaintings, sculpture, carvings. *Membership*: IACA. Catalog.

ZACH-LOW, INC.
7500 2nd St. NW
Albuquerque, NM 87184
(800) 821-7443; (505) 848-1623
Joe & Katy Lowry
Wholesale. *Products*: Baskets, beadwork, dolls, fetishes, jewelry, kachinas, miniatures, pottery, rugs, sandpaintings. Catalog available.

TA-MA-YA CO-OP ASSOCIATION
Santa Ana Pueblo
Star Route Box 37
Bernalillo, NM 87004
(505) 867-3301
Clara Paquin, President
Wholesale/retail. *Products*: Pueblo pottery, embroidery, weaving and clothing.

SOUTHWEST SUNSET INTERIORS
702 W. Broadway
Bloomfield, NM 87413
(505) 632-3805
Brad & Marcia Magee
Wholesale/retail.

THE INDIAN PONY ART GALLERY
56 Comanche Dr.
Carlsbad, NM 88220-9474
(505) 887-0065 Fax 887-0065
E-mail: ndnpony@cavemen.net
Web site: www.cavemen.net/indianpony
Wanda D. Spencer, Owner
Retail. *Products*: Indian artifacts, baskets, beadwork, jewelry, paintings, prints, posters, pottery, sculpture, textiles and books. *Membership*: IACA.

THE PLAINS COMPANY
P.O. Box 186, 1014 E. Ave.
Carrizozo, NM 88301
(505) 648-2472 Fax 648-2983
Woody Schlegel
Retail. *Products*: Art, jewelry, pottery, rugs, sculpture, carvings. *Membership*: IACA.

CLINES CORNERS OPERATING CO.
#1 Yacht Club Dr.
Clines Corners, NM 87070
(505) 472-5488 Fax 472-5487
Doug Murphy
Retail. *Products*: Art, baskets, beadwork, clothing, dolls, jewelry, kachinas, pottery, rugs, sandpaintings, sculpture, carvings. *Membership*: IACA.

THE BEAR TRACK
P.O. Box 15, 502 Burro Ave.
Cloudcraft, NM 88317
(505) 682-3046
Nita & Donald Lane
Retail. *Products*: All. *Membership*: IACA.

BIG SKY TRADERS
P.O. Box 461 • Corrales, NM 87048
(800) 827-1992; (505) 899-1990
Phil & Margene Gibbs
Wholesale. *Products*: Baskets, drums, pipes, dye charts, fetishes, jewelry, sandpaintings, sculpture. *Membership*: IACA.

CROWNPOINT RUG WEAVERS' ASSOCIATION
P.O. Box 1630 • Crownpoint, NM 87313
(505) 786-5302 or 786-7386
Ena B. Chavez, Manager
Christina Ellsworth, Co-Manager
Navajo rugs sold at auction held monthly.

THE SILVER EAGLE
P.O. Box 158 • Crownpoint, NM 87313
(505) 786-5591 Fax 786-5593
Jim Clinton, Owner
Wholesale/retail. *Products*: Baskets, beadwork, dye charts, jewelry, kachinas, pottery, rugs, sandpaintings. *Membership*: IACA.

APACHE MESA GALLERY & GIFTS
Box 233, Jicarilla Inn, Hwy. 64
Dulce, NM 87528
(505) 759-3663
Eileen Vigil, Manager
Retail, wholesle. *Products*: art, Jicarilla baskets, beadwork, jewelry, pottery, rugs. Special orders accepted.

JICARILLA ARTS & CRAFTS & MUSEUM
P.O. Box 507 • Dulce, NM 87528
(505) 759-3242 ext. 274
Brenda Julian, Director
Retail, mail order. Jicarilla Apache tribal enterprise. *Products*: Art, baskets, beadwork. Send S.A.S.E. for price list and brochure.

PASSAGES EXPRESST
P.O. Box 1184 • Espanola, NM 87532
Char Pully, Owner
Retail, wholesale, mail order. *Products*: dolls, pocupine quill and leatherwork.

SINGING WATER GALLERY
Rt. 1, Box 472-C • Espanola, NM 87532
(505) 753-9663
Joe Baca, Owner
Retail, wholesale. *Products*: Art, clothing, pottery. *Appraisals*: Pottery.

TERESITA NARANJO
Rt. 1, Box 455, Santa Clara Pueblo
Espanola, NM 87532
(505) 753-9655
Retail, wholesale. *Product*: Santa Clara pottery. Special orders accepted.

ARROYO TRADING CO., INC.
2111 W. Apache St. • Farmington, NM 87401
(505) 326-7427
Vince & Helen Ferrari, Owners
Retail, wholesale. *Products*: A,C,E,G,W,X. Author brochure, "Introduction to Sandpainting." Catalog available.

THE FIFTH GENERATION TRADING CO.
232 W. Broadway • Farmington, NM 87401
(505) 326-3211 Fax 326-0097
Joe Tanner, Jr.
Wholesale. *Products*: Baskets, clothing, dolls, jewelry, kachinas, ornaments, pottery, rugs, sandpaintings, sculpture, carvings. *Membership*: IACA.

NAVAJO BEADWORKS
2111 W. Apache • Farmington, NM 87401
(505) 326-7427
Loree Ferari, Owner
Retail, wholesale. *Product*: Navajo beadwork.

RUSSELL FOUTZ INDIAN ROOM
301 W. Main St. • Farmington, NM 87401
(505) 325-9413
Russell Foutz, Owner
Wholesale. *Products*: Baskets, ornaments, dye charts, jewelry, kachinas, rugs, sandpaintings, sculpture. *Membership*: IACA.

ASHCROFT TRADERS
695 County Rd. 6100 • Fruitland, NM 87416
(505) 598-9159
W.L. & Lori Ashcroft
Retail, wholesale. *Products*: Baskets, dye charts, jewelry, rugs, sandpaintings. *Membership*: IACA. *Appraisals*: Rugs. Catalog.

AMERICAN INDIAN FASHIONS
2407 E. Boyd 11-B • Gallup, NM 87301
(800) 377-6837; (505) 722-6837
Virginia Yazzie Ballenger, Owner
Carl H. Ballenger, Manager
Retail, wholesale. Navajo designer.
Products: Clothing, masks.

ANASAZI TRADERS OF GALLUP
400 E. Hwy. 66 • Gallup, NM 87301
(800) 777-6952; (505) 863-9294 Fax 863-2088
Tom Mortensen
Wholesale. *Products*: Art, clothing, dolls, jewelry, kachinas, pottery, rugs, sandpaintings, sculpture, carvings. *Memebership*: IACA. Catalog available.

ANDY'S TRADING CO.
612 W. Wilson • Gallup, NM 87301
(505) 863-3762
Greg & Cambria Masci, Owners
Retail, wholesale. *Products*: Baskets, beadwork, jewelry, kachinas, rugs.

ATKINSON TRADING CO.
P.O. Box 566, 1300 S. 2nd
Gallup, NM 87305
(800) 338-7380
(505) 722-4435 Fax 863-5624
Joe Atkinson, Owner; Roger Morris, Manager
Retail, wholesale. *Products*: Drums, pipes, flutes, dye charts, fetishes, jewelry, kachinas, knives, pottery, rugs. *Membership*: IACA.

CAROLYN BOBELU
731 Kevin Court • Gallup, NM 87301
(505) 722-4939 Carolyn Bobelu, Owner
Retail, wholesale. Zuni-Navajo craftsperson.
Products: P. Special orders accepted.

FELIX INDIAN JEWELRY
P.O. Box 195 • Gallup, NM 87301
(505) 722-5369
Felix Gomez, Owner
Wholesale. *Product*: P. *Membership*: IACA.

FIRST AMERICAN TRADERS
198 Historic Rte. 66 • Gallup, NM 87301
(505) 722-6601 Fax 722-6300
Dominic Biava, Owner
Wholesale, retail. *Products*: Art, dolls, drums, pipes, dye charts, fetishes, heishi, jewelry, kachinas, pottery, rugs, sandpaintings, sculpture. *Membership*: IACA. Catalog available.

GALLUP GALLERY
108 W. Coal Ave. • Gallup, NM 87301
Retail. *Products*: Native American art.

THE INDIAN DEN TRADING CO.
1111 Caesar Dr. • Gallup, NM 87301
(505) 722-4141 Edward Gomez, Owner
Retail, wholesale. *Membership*: IACA.

INDIAN HANDICRAFTS
Southwest Indian Foundation
P.O. Box 86 • Gallup, NM 87305
(505) 863-9568 Fax 863-2760
William McCarthy, Manager
Retail, wholesale, mail order. *Products*: Indian jewelry, clothing, mugs, books and toys. Catalog

INDIAN JEWELERS SUPPLY CO.
601 E. Coal Ave. • Gallup, NM 87305
(505) 722-4451 Fax 722-4172
E-Mail: orders@ijsinc.com
Website: www.ijsinc.com
Retail, wholesle, mail order. *Products*: Precious base metals, jewelry parts, semi-precious stones, tools. Catalog

INDIAN VILLAGE, INC.
2209 W. Hwy. 66 • Gallup, NM 87301
(505) 722-5524 Fax 863-9093
Nathan Ramadoss, Owner
E-Mail: Nathan@cia-g.com
Retail, wholesale, mail order. *Products*: Dolls, fetishes, jewelry, kachinas, pottery, sandpaintings, sculpture. *Membership*: IACA. Catalog.

KIVA GALLERY
200-202 W. Hwy. 66 • Gallup, NM 87301
Retail. *Products*: Native American art.

STEVE LUCAS (KOYEMSI)
301 Calle Pinon • Gallup, NM 87301
Retail, wholesale. *Products*: Traditional and contemporary Hopi pottery.

JOHNNY MURPHY'S TRADING CO.
1206 E. 66th Ave.
Gallup, NM 87301
(505) 722-5088
John E. Murphy, Owner
Retail, wholesale. *Products*: Baskets, beadwork, fetishes, jewelry. *Membership*: IACA.

NAVAJO ARTS & CRAFTS ENTERPRISE
1512 E. Hwy. 66
Gallup, NM 87301
(800) 790-6223
Wholesale Division. Tribal Enterprise. *Products*: Art, baskets, beadwork, clothing, dolls, jewelry, kachinas, pottery, rugs, sandpaintings, sculpture, carvings. Branch shop.

THE NUGGET GALLERY
1302 S. 2nd St.
Gallup, NM 87301-5813
(505) 863-3615
Chet Jones, Owner
Retail, wholesale. *Products*: Baskets, books, dye charts, fetishes, jewelry, kachinas, miniatures, rugs, sculpture.

O.B.'s INDIAN AMERICA
3330 E. Hwy. 66 • Gallup, NM 87301
(505) 722-4431 Fax 722-6394
Bill & Harlene O'Neil, Owners
Wholesale. *Products*: All. *Membership*: IACA.

OUTLAW TRADERS
600 Belle Dr. • Gallup, NM 87301
(505) 722-6703
Diane & Larry Jinks, Owners
Retail, wholesale. *Products*: Art, baskets, beadwork, clothing, dolls, jewelry, kachinas, knives, rugs, sculpture, carvings.

RED SHELL JEWELRY
P.O. Box 764 • Gallup, NM 87305
(505) 722-6963
John Hornbek, Owner
Retail, wholesale. *Products*: B,C,E,G,O,P,Q,V.
Appraisals: B,C,P,V. *Membership*: IACA.

SHAFFER'S INDIAN ART
P.O. Box 5300 • Gallup, NM 87301
(505) 722-2526
Richard L. Shaffer, Owner
Wholesale. *Products*: Art, baskets, boxes, children;s items, dolls, fetishes, jewelry, kachinas, miniatures, pottery.

SUNBURST HANDCRAFTS, INC.
306 County Rd. #1 • Gallup, NM 87301
(505) 863-4541
Lionel McKinney
Wholesale. *Products*: Jewelry.

TOBE TURPEN'S INDIAN TRADING CO.
1710 S. 2nd St. • Gallup, NM 87301-5895
(505) 722-3806
Tobe J. Turpen & Art Quintana
Retail, wholesale. *Products*: Art, baskets, beadwork, clothing, dolls, jewelry, kachinas, pottery, rugs, sandpaintings, sculpture, carvings. *Membership*: IACA.

TRACEY-KNIFEWING, INC.
P.O. Box 443 • Gallup, NM 87305
(505) 863-3635 Fax 722-4218
Ray Tracey & Warren Lyons
Wholesale. *Product*: Jewelry.
Membership: IACA. Catalog.

ANCIENT MESAS GIFTS SOUTHWESTERN
P.O. Box 220 • Grants, NM 87020
(505) 285-4335
Patricia McClure & Kraig Williams, Owners
Retail. *Products*: Art, baskets, beadwork, clothing, dolls, jewelry, kachinas, pottery, rugs. *Membership*: IACA.

LEGACY GALLERY & STUDIO
P.O. Box 418 • Isleta, NM 87022
(505) 869-3317
Spencer Moss & Michael Kirk, Owners
Wholesale. *Product*: Jewelry.

TELLER POTTERY
P.O. Box 135 • Isleta, NM 87022
(505) 869-3118
Stella Teller, Owner
Wholesale. *Product*: U. *Membership*: IACA.

CAROL G. LUCERO-GACHUPIN
P.O. Box 210
Jemez Pueblo, NM 87024
(505) 834-7757
Carol Lucero-Gachupin, Owner
Retail, wholesale. *Products*: Art, ornaments, clothing, pottery, sculpture.

CAROL VIGIL
P.O. Box 443
Jemez Pueblo, NM 87024
Retail, mail order. *Product*: Jemez pottery.

ASHCROFT TRADERS
P.O. Box 1005 • Kirtland, NM 87417
(505) 598-9159
W.L. & Lori Ashcroft, Owners
Wholesale, retail. *Products*: Baskets, dye charts, jewelry, rugs, sandpaintings. *Membership*: IACA. *Appraisals*: Rugs. Catalog.

55 SILVER & SUPPLY
P.O. Box 688 • Kirtland, NM 87417
(505) 598-5322
John & Jacqueline Foutz, Owners
Wholesale, retail. *Products*: Baskets,
jewelry, rugs. *Membership*: IACA.

LAGUNA PUEBLO MART, INC.
P.O. Box 63 • Laguna, NM 87026
(505) 552-9585 Fax 552-7446
Arne & Ron Fernandez, Owners
Retail, wholesale. *Products*: Baskets,
beadwork, kachinas, miniatures, pottery.

MARIE S. TEASYATWHO
P.O. Box 311 • LaPlata, NM 87418
(505) 326-3769
Retail. *Products*: Traditional and contemporary
Navajo weaving and beadwork. Special
commissions accepted.

NAVAJO ARTS & CRAFTS ENTERPRISE
Alamo Trading Post
P.O. Box 1505 • Magdalena, NM 87825
(505) 854-2987
Retail, wholesale. Tribal Enterprise. *Products*: Art,
baskets, beadwork, clothing, dolls, jewelry, kachinas,
pottery, rugs, sandpaintings, sculpture, carvings.
Branch shop.

THE SILVERSMITH, INC.
P.O. Box 531 • Mesilla, NM 88046
(505) 523-5561 Fax 523-5561
Charles & Diane Rogers, Owners
Retail. *Products*: Art, clothing, fetishes, jewelry,
kachinas, miniatures, pottery, sandpaintings. *Membership*: IACA.

THE WILLIAM BONNEY GALLERY
P.O. Box 27, 3 Calle de Parian
Mesilla, NM 88046
(505) 526-8275
Dan & Della McKinney, Owners
Retail. *Products*: Art, baskets, clothing, dolls, jewelry,
kachinas, pottery, rugs, sandpaintings, sculpture, carvings. *Membership*: IACA.

WINDMILL TRADING CO.
Box 1297, 788 Hwy. 22
Pena Blanca, NM 87041-1297
(505) 465-2416
Susan M. Rodin, Owner
Retail, wholesale. *Products*: Heishi, jewelry, rugs.
Membership: IACA.

CHUCK LEWIS EDITIONS
P.O. Box 917 • Questa, NM 87556
(505) 751-2158
Churck Lewis, Owner
Wholesale. Blackfeet craftsperson. *Products*: Art.

SANDS TURQUOIS
P.O. Box 37 • Raton, NM 87740
(505) 445-2737
Worth Wilkins, Owner
Retail. *Products*: Clothing, drums, pipes, flutes, jewelry, pottery, sandpaintings.

NATIVE VISIONS
4110 La Merced • Rio Rancho, NM 87124
(505) 891-0624
Soia Burdette & Doug Gomez, Owners
Retail, wholesale. *Products*: P,U.

TWO SQUAWS
1109 W. Second • Roswell, NM 88201
(505) 623-1921
Pat Mitchell & Garry Zens, Owners
Retail. *Products*: Baskets, beadwork, clothing, dolls,
jewelry, kachinas, pottery, rugs, sandpaintings, sculpture, carvings. *Membership*: IACA.

PUEBLO POTTERY
P.O. Box 366 • San Fidel, NM 87049
(800) 933-5771; (505) 552-6748 (phone & fax)
Arthur & Carol Cruz
Wholesale, retail.*Products*: Art, baskets, beadwork,
clothing, dolls, jewelry, kachinas, pottery, rugs,
sandpaintings, sculpture, carvings. *Appraisals*: Pottery.
Shop located in Acomita, NM. Catalog.

OKE OWEENGE ART & CRAFTS
P.O. Box 1095
San Juan Pueblo, NM 87566
(505) 852-2372
April Crane Star, Manager
Retail, mail order. San Juan Pueblo craftspersons cooperative. *Products*: Art, baskets, beadwork, clothing,
dolls, jewelry, kachinas, pottery, rugs, sandpaintings,
sculpture, carvings. Special orders accepted. Brochure
and price list.

ANASAZI INDIAN ARTS
P.O. Box 319, 1347 Hwy. 76
Santa Cruz, NM 87567-0319
(505) 753-4730
Joe & Belle Becker, Owners
Wholesale. *Products*: Art, pottery, rugs.
Membership: IACA.

AGUILAR INDIAN ARTS
Rt. 5, Box 318C • Santa Fe, NM 87501
Alfred Aguilar, Owner
Retail, some wholesale. San Ildefonso Pueblo
Tewa artist-craftsperson. *Products*: Art, pottery.

CHARLES AZBELL GALLERY
66-70 E. San Francisco St.
Santa Fe, NM 87501 (505) 988-1875
Retail. *Products*: Native American art and sculpture.

**CASE TRADING POST AT
THE WHEELWRIGHT MUSEUM**
P.O. Box 5153, 704 Camino Lejo
Santa Fe, NM 87502
(505) 982-4636 Fax 989-7386
Robb, Lucas, Manager
Web site: http://www.wingspread.com/casetp
Retail. A museum store that is a replica of a turn-of-
the-century trading post. *Products*: Native American
pottery, textiles, jewelry, kachinas, baskets, and folk
art. Also prints, cards, posters, and educational items
for children. Over 2,000 book titles on Native American subject matter.

JOAN CAWLEY GALLERY
133 W. San Francisco St. • Santa Fe, NM 87501
Retail. *Products*: Native American art.

CONTEMPORARY SOUTHWEST GALLERY
123 W. Palace Pl. • Santa Fe, NM 87501
Products: Native American art.

CRISTOF'S
420 Old Santa Fe Trail
Santa Fe, NM 87501-2770
(505) 988-9881 Fax 986-8652
Louis "Buzz" Trevathan, Jr. & Pam Nicosin, Owners
E-Mail: buzzart@cristofs.com
Web site: www.cristofs.com
Retail. *Products*: Jewelry, rugs, sandpaintings, sculpture. Navajo weavings and other Southwest art; Hopi
kachinas; Navajo & Acoma pottery. Brochure; catalog
available on web site.

DEWEY GALLERIES, LTD.
76 E. San Francisco St.
Santa Fe, NM 87501
Retail. *Products*: Native American art.

DISCOVER SANTA FE INDIAN ARTS & CRAFTS
P.O. Box 2847 • Santa Fe, NM 87504
Retail. *Products*: Native American art.

FREE AIR FINE ART
P.O. Box 23285 • Santa Fe, NM 87502
(505) 474-4480
Retail. *Products*: Native American art.

HAND GRAPHICS GALLERY
418 Montezuma Ave. • Santa Fe, NM 87501
Retail. *Products*: Indian handcrafts.

HOGAN IN THE HILTON
100 Sandoval St.
Santa Fe, NM 87504-2131
(505) 984-0932
Paula Hausvick, Owner
Retail. *Products*: Baskets, beadwork, clothing, dolls,
jewelry, kachinas, pottery, rugs, sandpaintings, sculpture, carvings. *Membership*: IACA.

ALLAN HOUSER, INC.
P.O. Box 5217 • Santa Fe, NM 87502
(505) 471-9667
Retail: *Products*: Sculpture garden, gallery, appraisals, resales. Representing the estate of Allan Houser.

**INSTITUTE OF AMERICAN INDIAN
ARTS MUSEUM SHOP**
P.O. Box 20007 • Santa Fe, NM 87504
(505) 988-6281
Marguerite L. Hill, Manager
Retail. *Products*: Art, pottery, sculpture.

KIVA FINE ARTS
102 E. Water St. • Santa Fe, NM 87501
(505) 982-4273
Retail. *Products*: Native American art,
pottery, and Southwestern crafts.

BRUCE LAFOUNTAIN
Rt. 19 Box 111V • Santa Fe, NM 87501
(505) 988-3703
Retail. Native American sculptor.

EDITH LAMBERT GALLERY
707 Canyon Dr. • Santa Fe, NM 87501
Retail. *Products*: Native American art.

MASLAK McLEOD
607 Old Santa Fe Trail
Santa Fe, NM 87501 (505) 820-6389
Retail. *Products*: Inuit, and Native North American.

JOEL C. McHORSE
P.O. Box 1711 • Santa Fe, NM 87504
(505) 989-7716
Joel C. McHorse, Owner
E-Mail: McHorse@ix.netcom.com
Retail, wholesale. *Products*: Micaceous pottery, traditional or contemporary. Silver jewelry and silverwork,
such as miniature picture frames with hand-stamped
designs; various stone sculpture. Special commissions
accepted.

TED MILLER CUSTOM KNIVES
P.O. Box 6328 • Santa Fe, NM 87502
(505) 984-0338
Ted Miller, Owner
Retail, wholesale, some mail order. Price list available.

MORNING STAR GALLERY
513 Canyon Rd. • Santa Fe, NM 87501
(505) 982-8187 Fax 984-2368
Joe Rivera, President
E-Mail: indian@morningstargallery.com
Website: www.morningstargallery.com
Retail, wholesale, mail order. *Products*: Antique
American Indian art. Catalog.

NEW TRENDS GALLERY
225 Canyon Rd. • Santa Fe, NM 87501
(505) 988-1199
Retail. *Products*: Native American art,
sculpture, and crafts.

NOFCHISSEY-McHORSE
P.O. Box 8638 • Santa Fe, NM 87504
(505) 989-7716
Christine C. McHorse, Owner
E-Mail: McHorse@ix.netcom.com
Retail, wholesale. *Products*: Taos style, Navajo
handbuilt micaceous pottery, traditional or contemporary. Silverwork of sandcast animal pins, jewelry, miniature picture frames with hand-stamped designs.

OTTOWI TRADING CO., INC.
P.O. Box 9152 • Santa Fe, NM 87504
(505) 982-6881
Anthony Whitman, Owner
Retail, wholesale. *Products*: Fetishes, heishi, jewelry,
miniatures, pottery, rugs. *Appraisals*: U. *Membership*:
IACA. Catalog.

PACKARDS
61 Old Santa Fe Trail/On the Plaza
Santa Fe, NM 87501
(800) 648-7358; (505) 983-9241 Fax 984-8174
Richard & Carolyn Canon, Owners
Web site: http://www.collectorsquide.com/packards
Retail, mail order. *Products*: Native American jewelry,

pottery, weavings, kachinas and giftware. *Membership*: IACA, SWAIA. Brochure.

PENA STUDIO GALLERY
235 Don Gaspar • Santa Fe, NM 87505
(505) 820-1400
Retail. *Products*: Native American posters, T-shirts, and art.

PEYOTE BIRD TRADING
P.O. Box 99 • Santa Fe, NM 87504-0099
(505) 983-2480 Fax 982-8094
Mark Alexander, Owner
Wholesale. *Products*: Fetishes, heishi, jewelry, pottery. Catalog.

POPOVI DA STUDIO OF INDIAN ART
San Ildefonso Pueblo • Santa Fe, NM 87501
(505) 455-2456
Anita M. Da, Owner
Wholesale, retail. *Prodcuts*: Art, baskets, jewelry, Navjo rugs, Pueblo pottery.

PORTAL PROGRAM OF THE PALACE OF THE GOVERNORS
P.O. Box 2087 • Santa Fe, NM 87504-2087
(505) 827-6474 Fax 827-6521
Sarah Laughlin, Coordinator
Retail. *Description*: Traditional crafts of the 22 recognized New Mexico tribes and pueblos. *Products*: Beadwork, jewelry, stone work, carving, pottery, sandpainting.

RODICH, INC.
903 W. Alameda #114
Santa Fe, NM 87501
(505) 984-1801
Bob & Jane Matthews
Retail. *Products*: Art, fetishes, jewelry, pottery, rugs, sandpaintings, sculpture. *Membership*: IACA.

SCRIPSIT
3089 Plaza Blanca • Santa Fe, NM 87505
(505) 471-1516 Glen Billy, Owner
Retail, wholesale, mail order. *Product*: Calligraphy on paper and leather. Special orders accepted.

SHUSH YAZ TRADING CO.
1048 Paseo de Peralta
Santa Fe, NM 87501
(505) 438-9150 Don Tanner, Owner
Retail. *Products*: All. *Branch shop*: Gallup, NM

SILVER SUN
656 Canyon Rd. • Santa Fe, NM 87501
(800) 562-2036; (505) 983-8743
Deanna Olson, Cheryl Ingram, Kathy Sanchez
Retail, wholesale. *Products*: Art, children's items, fetishes, heishi, jewelry, pottery, sandpaintings. *Membership*: IACA. Catalog.

THE SPANISH & INDIAN TRADING CO.
924 Paseo de Peralta, Suite 1
Santa Fe, NM 87501 (505) 983-6106
(505) 983-6106
Retail. *Products*: Historic American Indian artifacts and jewelry.

SUNBOY GALLERY
622-B Canyon Rd. • Santa Fe, NM 87501
(505) 983-3042 or 266-8900
Terry Sunboy Hunt, Owner
Retail, some wholesale. *Products*: Pueblo-life scenes Indian jewelry; wood sculpture.

SUNSHINE STUDIO
3180 Vista Sandia • Santa Fe, NM 87506
(800) 348-9273
(505) 984-3216 Fax 986-0765
E-mail: sunshine@sunshinestudio.com
Website: www.sunshinestudio.com
Retail. *Products*: Southwest American Indian art; ethnic & natural stone bead jewelry.

TRADE ROOTS
411 Paseo de Peralta • Santa Fe, NM 87501
(800) 477-6687; (505) 982-8168 Fax 982-8688
Jeffrey Lewis, Owner
Retail, wholesale. *Products*: Fetishes, jewelry. *Membership*: IACA. Catalog.

JOE WADE FINE ARTS
102 E. Water St. • Santa Fe, NM 87501
Retail. *Products*: Indian arts & crafts.

ROBERT LONE EAGLE WAYNEE
P.O. Box 15313 • Santa Fe, NM 87506
(505) 466-3456 Fax 466-1248
Robert Waynee, Owner
Retail, wholesale. *Products*: Sculpture, carvings. Special orders accepted.

FOUTZ TRADING CO.
P.O. Box 1894 • Shiprock, NM 87420-1894
(800) 383-0615; (505) 368-5790 Fax 368-4441
Bill & Kay Foutz, Owners
Retail, wholesale. *Products*: Beadwork, clothing, dolls, jewelry, kachinas, pottery, rugs, sandpaintings, sculpture, carvings. *Membership*: IACA. Catalog.

SHIPROCK TRADING CO.
P.O. Box 906, Hwy. 64
Shiprock, NM 87420
(505) 368-4585 Fax 368-5583
Ed Foutz & Jed Foutz, Owners
Retail, wholesale. *Products*: Art, baskets, beadwork, clothing, dolls, jewelry, kachinas, pottery, rugs, sandpaintings, sculpture, carvings. Appraisals. *Membership*: IACA.

TSINNIES GALLERY
Box 537 • Shiprock, NM 87410
(505) 368-5936 Fax 368-4240
Retail. *Products*: Navajo-made jewelry; buckles, squash blossoms, bracelets, earrings, rings, conchos.

MANY NATIONS
46 Burnham St. • Silver City, NM 88061
(505) 538-2471 Fax 538-8561
Rosalie & Robert Baker, Owners
Retail, wholesale. *Products*: All. *Membership*: IACA. Catalog.

ALL ONE TRIBE DRUMS
P.O. Drawer N • Taos, NM 87571
(505) 751-0019 Fax 751-0509
Feeny Lipscomb, Charles Conley
Bruce Ross, Owners
Retail, wholesale. *Products*: Art, baskets, beadwork, clothing, dolls, jewelry, kachinas, pottery, rugs, sandpaintings, sculpture, carvings. *Membership*: IACA. Catalog.

BLUE RAIN GALLERY
115 Taos Plaza • Taos, NM 87571
(505) 751-0066
Retail. *Products*: Native American art, kachinas and crafts, representing Pueblo artists.

BROKEN ARROW INDIAN ARTS & CRAFTS
P.O. Box 1601 • Taos, NM 87571
(505) 758-4304
Joel & Jess Payne, Owners
Retail. *Products*: All. *Membership*: IACA.

CARL'S INDIAN TRADING POST & WHITE BUCKSKIN GALLERY
P.O. Box 813 • Taos, NM 87571
(505) 758-2378
Mary Schlosser, Owner
Retail, wholesale. *Products*: Art, baskets, clothing, dolls, jewelry, kachinas, pottery, rugs, sandpaintings. Papago baskets, Hopi kachinas, Pueblo pottery, Navajo rugs and sandpaintings.

LILLY'S GALLERY
P.O. Box 342 • Taos, NM 87571
(505) 552-9501
Retail. *Products*: Handcrafted Acoma pottery & figurines.

MILLICENT ROGERS MUSEUM STORE
P.O. Box A • Taos, NM 87571
(505) 758-4316 Fax 758-5751
Melody Gladin-Kehoe, Manager
Retail. *Products*: B,D,U,V. *Branch shop*: Millicent Rogers Plaza Store, Taos Plaza, NM.

NATIVE SCENTS
P.O. Box 5639 • Taos, NM 87571
(800) 645-3471

Website: www.nativescents.com
Retail, Mail Order. products: Fine incense, essential oils, herbal teas, bulk botanicals, resins, facial clay, sweetgrass, etc. Catalog.

NAVAJO GALLERY
P.O. Box 1756 • 210 Ledoux St.
Taos, NM 87571
(505) 758-3250 Fax 758-7590
E-mail: navajo@rcgormangallery.com
Web site: www.rcgormangallery.com
R.C. Gorman, Owner; Virginia Dooley, Director
Retail, wholesale, some mail order. *Products*: Complete work of Navajo artist, R.C. Gorman. Brochure & catalog available.

SILVER & SAND TRADING CO.
129 A N. Plaza • Taos, NM 87571
(505) 758-9698
Harold & Wanda Allcorn, Owners
Retail, wholesale. *Products*: All. *Membership*: IACA.

SIX DIRECTIONS
P.O. Box 1042 • Taos, NM 87571
(505) 758-5844
Neva & Otis Wilson, Owners
Retail, wholesale. *Products*: All. *Membership*: IACA.

TAOS DRUMS
P.O. Box 1916 • Taos, NM 87571
(800) 424-3786; (505) 758-3796 Fax 758-9844
Bruce & Pat Allen, Owners
Retail, wholesale. *Products*: Drums, flutes, pipes. *Membership*: IACA.

TEHN-TSA INDIAN ARTS AND CRAFTS
P.O. Box 471 • Taos, NM 87571
(505) 758-0173
Victor Trujillo, Owner
Retail, wholesale. *Products*: Art, beadwork, clothing, heishi. Paintings by Victor Trujillo, pottery.

TONY REYNA INDIAN SHOP
P.O. Box 1892, Taos Pueblo • Taos, NM 87571
(505) 758-3835
Tony Reyna, Owner; Philip Reyna, Manager
Retail. *Products*: Art, drums, pipes, jewelry, kachinas. Navajo, Hopi, and Zuni jewelry.

WESTERN HERITAGE GALLERY
P.O. Box 1042 • Taos, NM 87571
(505) 758-4489
Neva & Otis Wilson, Owners
Retail. *Products*: Art, jewelry, kachinas, pottery, rugs, sandpaintings, sculpture, carvings. *Membership*: IACA.

MILLICENT ROGERS MUSEUM STORE
115 E. McCarthy Plaza • Taos Plaza, NM 87571
(505) 758-4316 Fax 758-5751
Melody Gladin-Kehoe, Manager
Retail. *Products*: Baskets, books, pottery, rugs. *Branch shop*: Millicent Rogers Plaza Store, Taos Plaza, NM.

CONTINENTAL DIVIDE INDIAN HANDCRAFTS
P.O. Box 1059 • Thoreau, NM 87323
(505) 862-7350
Willie Janish
Wholesale. *Product*: Jewelry. *Membership*: IACA..

SOUTHWEST INDIAN SILVERSMITHS
30 Steeplechase Dr. • Tijeras, NM 87059
(505) 281-5276
Channah Pruter-Edwards, Owner
Wholesale. *Products*: Fetishes, heishi, jewelry, pottery. *Membership*: IACA.

THE TEE PEE
P.O. Box 734
Tucumcari, NM 88401
(505) 461-3773
Mike & Betty Callens, Owners
Retail. *Products*: Art, boxes, clothing, jewelry, kachinas, pottery. *Membership*: IACA.

JOE MILO'S TRADING CO.
P.O. Box 296
Vanderwagen, NM 87326
(505) 778-5531 Fax 778-5314
Joe Milosevich, Owner
Retail, wholesale. *Products*: All. *Membership*: IACA.

CIRCLE W PAWN & TRADING CO.
Box 256, 3316 Hwy. 64 • Waterflow, NM 87421
(505) 598-9179
Charles Webb
Reatil, wholesale. *Products*: Baskets, beadwork,
jewelry, rugs, sculpture. *Membership*: IACA.

HOGBACK TRADING CO.
3221 Hwy. 64 • Waterflow, NM 87421
(505) 598-5154/9243
Tom & Ann Wheeler, Owners
Retail, wholesale. *Products*: Art, baskets, clothing,
dolls, jewelry, kachinas, pottery, rugs, sandpaintings,
sculpture, carvings. *Membership*: IACA.

BLUE JAY'S POTTERY & GIFTS
P.O. Box 703 • Zuni, NM 87327
(505) 782-2124
Angelina Medina & Calsue Murray
Wholesale/retail. *Products*: Art, clothing, jewelry,
kachinas, miniatures, pottery, sculpture/carvings.

CAROLYN BOBELU
P.O. Box 443 • Zuni, NM 87327
(505) 782-2773
Carolyn Bobelu, Owner
Retail, wholesale, mail order. *Product*: Jewelry.
Special orders accepted.

PUEBLO OF ZUNI ARTS & CRAFTS
Box 425, Hwy. 53 • Zuni, NM 87327-0339
(505) 782-5531 Fax 782-2136
Lorencita Mahkee, Manager
Retail, wholesale, mail order. Zuni Tribal Enterprise.
Products: Art, beadwork, dolls, jewelry, kachinas, pot-
tery, rugs, sandpaintings, sculpture, carvings. Custom
orders accepted. Catalog, $5. *Branch shops*: Venice,
CA, and San Francisco, CA.

QUANDELACY FAMILY
P.O. Box 266 • Zuni, NM 87327
(505) 782-2797
Faye Quandelacy, Owner
Retail, wholesale. *Products*: Fetishes, jewelry,
sculpture.

**ZUNI CRAFTSMEN
COOPERATIVE ASSOCIATION**
P.O. Box 426, Zuni Pueblo
Zuni, NM 87327
(505) 782-4425/4521
Arvella Latone, Manager
Retail, wholesale, mail order. *Products*: Art,
beadwork, fetishes, jewelry, pottery. Catalog.

ZUNI INDIAN JEWELRY
Drawer F
Zuni, NM 87327
(505) 782-2869
Carlton & Julie Jamon
Retail, wholesale. *Products*: Beadwork, fetishes,
jewelry, rugs, sculpture. *Membership*: IACA.

NEW YORK

DANIEL C. HILL
P.O. Box 22 • Akron, NY 14001
(716) 542-3637
Daniel C. Hill, Owner
Retail, wholesale. *Products*: Traditional carved flutes,
Iroquois silverwork, music recordings, and flute per-
formances.

AMERICAN WEST BOUTIQUE
P.O. Box 58, 475 Main St. • Armonk, NY 10504
(914) 273-4056 Fax 273-5325
Mark & Laura Faller
Retail. *Products*: Art, beadwork, clothing, dolls, jewelry, kachinas, pottery, rugs, sandpaintings, sculpture,
carvings. *Membership*: IACA.

TURQUOISE INDIAN
South Shore Mall, Captree Corners
Bay Shore, NY 11706
(516) 968-5353 Fax 277-1532
John & Jane Fuchs
Retail, wholesale. *Products*: All. *Membership*: IACA.

KIVA TRADING CO.
117 Main St. • Cold Spring Harbor, NY 11724
(516) 367-2875 Fax 367-2834
Richard & Vivian Sutton, Owners
Kristin Quinn, Manager
E-Mail: Kiva1@excite.com
Web site: www.kivatrading.com/
Retail, mail order. *Products*: American Indian handmade crafts, jewelry and fine arts, specializing in Navajo Hopi, Zuni and Pueblo Nations of New Mexico
and Arizona. *Branch shop*: P.O. Box 658, Placitas, NM
87043. *Membership*: IACA. Brochure. Catalog available online.

THE ROCKWELL MUSEUM SHOP
111 Cedar St. • Corning, NY 14830
(607) 937-5386 Fax 974-4536
Juanita M. Malavet, Manager
Retail. *Products*: Native American arts & crafts from
the Southwest. Art reproduction of the permanent collections; books and educational tapes. *Membership*:
IACA. Catalog.

BLITZ ANTIQUE NATIVE AMERICAN ART, LTD.
P.O. Box 400 • Crompond, NY 10517
(914) 739-9683
Retail. *Products*: Specializing in Native American
articles of childhood.

BLACK BEAR TRADING POST
Rt. 9, Box 47 • Esopus, NY 12429
(914) 384-6786
Roy Blackbear, Owner
Retail, wholesale. *Products*: Baskets, beadwork,
clothing, jewelry,, kachinas, sculpture, carvings.

SHELL & STONE TURQUOISE GALLERY
511 E. Genesee St. • Fayetteville, NY 13066-1548
(315) 637-4550
Frank & Rosemary Rodriguez, Owners
Retail. *Products*: All. *Appraisals*: Art, fetishes, jewelry,
kachinas, miniatures, pottery, rugs. *Membership*: IACA.

IROQUOIS BONE CARVINGS
3560 Stony Point Rd. • Grand Island, NY 14072
(716) 773-4974
Stanley R. Hill, Owner
Retail, wholesale, mail order on craftwork only.
Products: C,H,I,J,P,X. Brochure.

AMERICAN INDIAN TREASURES, INC.
P.O. Box 579 • Guilderland, NY 12084-0579
Lillian Samuelson, Owner
Retail. *Product*: A. *Membership*: IACA.

MOHAWK IMPRESSIONS
P.O. Box 20, Mohawk Nation
Hogansburg, NY 13655
(518) 358-2467
Gail General, Pam Brown, Charles Clench, Owners
Retail, wholesale, mail order. *Products*: Art, baskets,
beadwork, dolls, fetishes, jewelry. Iroquois dolls. Spe-
cial orders accepted. Brochure and price list; catalog,
$3.

SWEETGRASS GIFTSHOP
Akwesasne Museum
RR#1 Box 14C, Rt. 37
Hogansburg, NY 13655-9705
(518) 358-2461 Fax 358-2649
Carol White & Sue Dow, Managers
Retail, mail order. *Products*: Mohawk-made black ash
splint and sweetgrass baskets, beadwork, bone jew-
elry. Special orders accepted. Send S.A.S.E. for price
list.

ADOBE ARTS
192 E. Main St. • Huntington, NY 11743
(516) 385-8410
Retail. *Products*: Traditional and contemporary Native
American art, jewelry, pottery, kachinas, fetishes, baskets.

CAYUGA TRADING POST
P.O. Box 523 • Ithaca, NY 14850
(607) 257-3138
Roy Schreck, Owner
Retail, wholesale. *Products*: Baskets, beadwork,
books, children's items, drums, pipes, jewelry, sculpture. *Membership*: IACA.

LITTLE FEATHER TRADING POST
P.O. Box 3165 • Jamaica, NY 11431
(718) 658-0576
Marion Nieves, Owner
Retail, wholesale, mail order. *Products*: beadwork
jewelry and accessories, leatherwork.

SACRED EARTH STUDIOS
197 Longfellow Dr. • Mastic Beach, NY 11951
(516) 399-4539
Jamie Reason, Owner
Retail, wholesale, mail order from dealers only.
Products: carvings, featherwork.

ADIRONDACK ARTWORKS
Rte. 3 Main St. • Natural Bridge, NY 13665
(315) 644-4645
Donn & Nicole Alfredson, Owners
Retail. *Products*: Art, baskets, beadwork, books, cloth-
ing, dolls, jewelry, kachinas, pottery, rugs,
sandpaintings, sculpture, carvings. *Appraisals*: J,P,X.
Membership: IACA.

ONONDAGA INDIAN TRADING POST
Onondaga Indian Reservation
Nedrow, NY 13120
(315) 469-4359
Dewasenta, Owner
Retail, wholesale. *Products*: Iroquois
baskets, beadwork, cornhusk dolls.

AMERICA HURRAH
766 Madison Ave. • New York, NY 10021
(212) 535-1930
Retail, wholesale. *Products*: Pictorial beadwork, Navajo weavings, corn husk bags, and other Native
American articles

**AMERICAN INDIAN COMMUNITY
HOUSE GALERY/MUSEUM**
708 Broadway, 2nd Floor
New York, NY 10003
(212) 598-0100 Fax 598-4909
Joanna O. Bigfeather, Manager
Retail. *Products*: Baskets, books, clothing,
jewelry, pottery.

THE COMMON GROUND, INC.
19 Greenwich Ave.
New York, NY 10014
(212) 989-4178
Retail. *Products*: Antique and contemporary
arts of the North American Indian.

FIRST PEOPLES GALLERY
114 Spring St. • New York, NY 10012
(212) 343-0167
Victoria Torrez
Wholesale, retail. *Products*: Art, baskets, beadwork,
clothing, dolls, jewelry, kachinas, pottery, rugs,
sandpaintings, sculpture, carvings. *Membership*: IACA.

J. CACCIOLA GALLERY
125 Wooster • New York, NY 10012
(212) 966-9177
Retail. *Products*: Contemporary artwork from a
variety of artists including Tony and Elizabeth Abeyta.

KOKOPELLI: SOUTHWESTERN JEWELRY
120 Thompson St.
New York, NY 10012
(212) 925-4411
Retail. *Products*: Contemporary and traditional
Native American jewelry and hand crafted fetishes.

SAKIA
100 LaSalle St., #17D
New York, NY 10027
(212) 866-2193
Eugene A. Cam, Owner
Retail, wholesale.

UNIQUE NATIVE CRAFTS
505 LaGuadia Pl., #19-D
New York, NY 10012
(212) 777-8394
Audrey Bernstein, Owner
Retail. *Products*: Native American jewelry/crafts from
Alaska to Chile since 1989. By appointment. *Member-
ship*: IACA.

VENTURA INDIAN COLLECTION
175 E. 74th St. • New York, NY 10021
(212) 988-8050
Bebe Ventura & Stan Rosenfeld
Retail, wholesale. *Products*: P. *Membership*: IACA.

**NATIVE AMERICAN CENTER
FOR THE LIVING ARTS, INC.**
25 Rainbow Mall • Niagara Falls, NY 14303
(716) 284-2427
Wanda Chew, Manager
Retail, wholesale. *Products*: Art, baskets,
beadwork, clothing, dolls, jewelry, pottery, rugs.

SQUASH BLOSSOM
49 Burd St. • Nyack, NY 10960
(845) 353-0550
Retail. *Products*: Authentic American Indian
jewelry, Hopi kachinas and Pueblo pottery

MINERAL & NEEDLE CRAFT CREATIONS
P.O. Box 614 • Oceanside, NY 11572
(516) 536-2220
Thelma Kirsch, Owner
Retail, wholesale. *Products*: All. *Appraisals*: Art, baskets, beadwork, clothing, dolls, jewelry, kachinas, pottery, rugs, sandpaintings, sculpture, carvings. *Membership*: IACA.

SIX NATIONS INDIAN MUSEUM SHOP
HCR 1, Box 10 • Onchiota, NY 12968
(518) 891-2299
John Fadden, Director
Retail. *Products*: Art, baskets, beadwork, jewelry,
sculpture. Mohawk baskets, acrylic paintings of
Iroquois culture. Brochure.

FULL WOLF MOON
49 Wolden Rd. • Ossining, NY 10562
(914) 762-7083
Jude Westerfield
Retail. *Products*: Jewelry, sculpture.
Membership: IACA.

CHRISJOHN FAMILY ARTS & CRAFTS
RD #2, Box 315 • Red Hook, NY 12571
(914) 758-8238
Richard Chrisjohn, Owner
Retail, wholesale, mail order. *Products*: Clothing,
dolls, drums, pipes, jewelry. Brochure.

M & J ENTERPRISES
42 Eagle Ridge Cir. • Rochester, NY 14617
(716) 342-5225
Mary Catherine Hickey, Owner
Retail. *Products*: Jewelry, rugs, sculpture.
Membership: IACA.

SOUTHWEST STUDIO CONNECTION
P.O. Box 3013
Sag Harbor, NY 11963-0403
(516) 283-9649
Kerry Sharkey-Miller, Owner
Retail. *Products*: Art, ornaments, fetishes, heishi,
jewelry, pottery, sculpture. *Membership*: IACA. .

AMERICAN INDIAN CRAFTS
719 Broad St. • Salamanca, NY 14779
(716) 945-1225
Lane & Lance Hoag, Owners
Retail, wholesale, mail order. *Products*: Mohawk baskets, Seneca beadwork, Navajo and Zuni jewelry, Ute
pottery. Brochure.

**SENECA-IROQUOIS NATIONAL
MUSEUM GIFT SHOP**
794-814 Broad St.
Salamanca, NY 14779
(716) 945-1738
Retail, mail order. Tribal nonprofit organization. *Prod-
ucts*: Baskets, beadwork, clothing, pottery, sculpture.
Brochure. Data sheets and book list.

TUSKEWE KRAFTS
2089 Upper Mountain Rd.
Sanborn, NY 14132
(716) 297-1821 Fax 297-0318
John Wesley Patterson, Jr., Owner
Retail, wholesale, mail order. *Products*: Field lacrosse
and box lacrosse sticks. Brochure/price list.

TROTO-BONO
P.O. Box 34 • Shrub Oak, NY 10588
(914) 528-6604
Retail. *Products*: Indian and Eskimo artifacts
of North America. By appointment.

THE MEXICAN SHACK
Route 100 • Somers, NY 10589
(914) 232-8739 Fax 232-7830
Steven & Mary Delzio
Retail. *Products*: All. *Appraisals*: Jewelry.
Repairs & restoration. *Membership*: IACA.

NATIVE PEOPLES ARTS & CRFATSHOP
P.O. Box 851, 210 Fabius St.
Syracuse, NY 13201
(315) 476-7425 Carol Moses, Manager
Retail, mail order by special request. *Products*: Baskets, clothing, dolls, lacrosse sticks, pottery, sculpture/
carvings.

PETER B. JONES
P.O. Box 174 • Versailles, NY 14168
(716) 532-5993 Roberta & Peter Jones, Owners
Retail, wholesale. Cattaraugus Reservation.
Onondaga artists/craftspersons *Products*: Drims,
pipes, flutes, pottery, rugs, sculpture.

TRADITIONS
7834 North Rd. • Victor, NY 14564
(716) 924-7826 Marty Gingras
Retail. *Products*: Historic American Indian artifacts.

THE VILLAGE POTTER
P.O. Box 220 • Walker Valley, NY 12588
(914) 361-4401 Lois & Charles Garrison
Retail, wholesale. *Membership*: IACA.
Branch: 172 Sullivan St., Wurtsboro, NY 12790.

M. ZACHARY GALLERIES, INC.
347 Maple St. • W. Hempstead, NY 11552
(516) 538-4659 Lorraine & Martin Schmidt, Owners
Retail. *Products*: Baskets, jewelry, kachinas, pottery,
sculpture.

FORTUNOFF
1300 Old Country Rd. • Westbury, NY 11590
(516) 542-4105 Fax 542-4188
Helene & Alan Fortunoff, Owners
Retail. *Product*: Jewelry. Catalog.

NORTH CAROLINA

CROWN DRUGS
400 Commerce Place
Bermuda Quay • Advance, NC 27006
(919) 998-6800 Fax 998-6846
Conrad Stonestreet, Ray Gentry,
Douglas Sprinkle, Owners
Retail, wholesale. *Membership*: IACA.

BIG MEAT POTTERY
Cherokee, NC 28719
(704) 497-9544
Retail. *Product*: Cherokee pottery.

EL CAMINO INDIAN GALLERY
P.O. Box 482 • Cherokee, NC 28719
(704) 497-3600
Nathan Robinson, Owner
Retail. *Products*: Baskets, beadwork, clothing, dolls,
jewelry, sandpaintings, sculpture. Seminole crafts.

QUALLA ARTS & CRAFTS MUTUAL, INC.
Box 310 • Cherokee, NC 28719
(704) 497-3103
Betty DuPree, Manager
Retail. Eastern Cherokee Tribal Enterprise. *Products*:
Baskets, beadwork, dolls, drums, pipes, pottery, sculp-
ture. Catalog, $2.

WHITE BUFFALO
2617 Shady Grove Rd.
Durham, NC 27703-8644
(919) 846-2771 (Phone & Fax)
Donald, Marty & Steve Koehler, Owners
Retail. *Products*: All. *Membership*: IACA.
Branch: Raleigh, NC.

HALIWA-SAPONI TRIBAL POTTERY AND ARTS
P.O. Box 99, Hwy. 561
Hollister, NC 27844
(919) 586-4017
Linda Cooper-Mills, Executive Director
Retail, wholesale, mail order. *Products*: Beadwork,
pottery, rugs, sculpture. Special orders accepted. Price
list.

WAYAH'STI INDIAN TRADITIONS
P.O. Box 130, Rt. 561
Hollister, NC 27844
(919) 586-4519
Patricia & Arnold Richardson, Owners
Mail order. *Products*: Beadwork, clothing, drums, pipes,
pottery, sculpture. Special orders accepted. Price list.

THE MEDICINE BAG
14225 N.C. Highway #18 South
Laurel Springs, NC 28644
(910) 359-2798 Fax 359-8834
Liz Rodgers, Owner
Retail. *Products*: All-natural herbs, smudges,
local honey, and crafts. Brochure.

TUSCARORA INDIAN HANDCRAFT SHOP
Rt. #4, Box 172
Maxton, NC 28364
(919) 844-3352
Leon Locklear, Owner
Retail, mail order. *Products*: Clothing, jewelry.
Special orders accepted. Price list.

NEW BERN NET & CRAFT CO.
2703 Hwy. 70 East
New Bern, NC 28560
(919) 633-2226 Fax 633-5760
Louise & Johnnie Thompson
Retail. Products: Baskets, beadwork, clothing, dolls,
jewelry, kachinas, pottery, rugs, sandpaintings. *Membership*: IACA.

ROBERT D. WAYNEE, SR.
P.O. Box 5232 • New Bern, NC 28560
(919) 637-2546
Retail, wholesale. *Products*: Native American
wood sculptures. Catalog.

WHITE BUFFALO
7909 Falls of Neuse
Raleigh, NC 27615
(919) 846-2771 (phone & fax)
Donald, Marty & Steve Koehler, Owners
Retail. *Products*: All. *Membership*: IACA.
Branch: Durham, NC.

LUMBEE INDIAN ARTS & CRAFTS
Rt. 1, Box 310AA
Rowland, NC 28383
(919) 521-9494
Hope Sheppard & Jane Oxendine, Owners
Mail order. *Products*: Baskets, beadwork.

EARTHWORKS ENVIRONMENTAL GALLERY
110 N. Main St.
Waynesville, NC 28786
(704) 452-9500
Susan & Jerold Johnson, Owners
Retail, wholesale. *Products*: All. *Membership*: IACA.

NORTH DAKOTA

GREAT PLAINS NATIVE AMERICAN ARTS CO-OP
c/o NDIAA • 401 N. Main St.
Mandan, ND 58554-3164
(701) 221-5328
Carol Good Bear, Owner
Wholesale, retail. *Products*: Art, baskets, beadwork,
clothing, dolls, jewelry, kachinas, pottery, rugs,
sandpaintings, sculpture, carvings. *Membership*: IACA.
Catalog.

**THREE AFFILIATED TRIBES
MUSEUM, ARTS & CRAFTS**
P.O. Box 147 • New Town, ND 58763
(701) 627-4477
Retail. *Products*: Art, beadwork, books, rugs.
Misc. items related to Three Tribes.

OHIO

DREAM CATCHERS
262 N. Roanoke
Austintown, OH 44515
(216) 793-7468
Kathleen & Shawne Bowman
Retail, wholesale. *Products*: Art, beadwork, clothing, dolls, jewelry, kachinas, pottery, rugs, sandpaintings, sculpture, carvings. *Membership*: IACA.

COYOTE WOMAN GALLERY
P.O. Box 868, • Bryan, OH 43506
(419) 636-3300
Terri & John Freudenberger
Retail. *Products*: All. *Membership*: IACA.
Branch: Harbor Springs, MI.

QUEMAHONING COLLECTION
8060 Oxford Lane
Chesterland, OH 44026
(216) 247-0430
Retail. *Products*: Art, baskets, beadwork, clothing, dolls, jewelry, kachinas, pottery, rugs, sandpaintings, sculpture, carvings. *Membership*: IACA.

AMERICAN INDIAN ARTS & CRAFTS
3547 Raymar Dr.
Cincinnati, OH 45208
(513) 871-1858
Dan & Pat Stricker
Retail. *Products*: All. *Branch*: 3512 1/2 Erie Ave.
Membership: IACA.

BUFFALO GALLERY
130 E. Main St. • Lebanon, OH 45036
(513) 932-0792
William V. Jordan, Owner
Retail, wholesale. *Products*: All. *Appraisals*: A.
Membership: IACA.

DESERT SUN
101 E. Wayne St.
Maumee, OH 43537
(419) 893-9630
Thomas & Denise Lawson
Retail. *Products*: Art, baskets, beadwork, clothing, dolls, jewelry, kachinas, pottery, rugs, sandpaintings, sculpture, carvings. *Membership*: IACA.

SOUTHWEST EXPRESSIONS OF OHIO, INC.
25576 Mill St.
Olmsted Falls, OH 44138
(216) 235-1177 (phone & fax)
Randi & John MacWilliams, Owners
Retail, wholesale. *Products*: Art, clothing, dolls, jewelry, kachinas, pottery, rugs, sandpaintings, sculpture, carvings. Native American arts & crafts and Southwest home decor. *Membership*: IACA. Brochure.

EARTH SPIRIT-NATIVE AMERICAN ART GALLERY
5758 N. Main #1 • Sylvania, OH 43560
(419) 885-7012
Chris & Pam Clayworth, Owners
Retail. *Products*: Art, books, drums, pipes, flutes, artifacts, jewelry, kachinas, pottery, rugs, sandpaintings. *Membership*: IACA.

OKLAHOMA

BRUCE C. CAESAR
Box 1183, 112 Prairie Village
Anadarko, OK 73005
(405) 247-2303
Retail, wholesale. *Product*: Jewelry. Specilizes in Native Amerian church type ornaments. Special orders accepted.

CIRCLE TURTLE NATIVE SPECIALTIES
P.O. Box 986 • Anadarko, OK 73005
(405) 247-7059
Linda S. Poolaw, Owner
Retail, mail order. *Products*: Southern Plains arts & crafts made to order by local arts and crafts people of S.W. Oklahoma, i.e Kiowa, Comanche, Apache, Ft Sill Apache, Wichita, Caddo and Delaware.

DIXON PALMER HEADDRESSES & TIPIS
Rt. 3, Box 189 • Anadarko, OK 73005
(405) 247-3983
Dixon Palmer, Owner
Retail. By appointment only. *Products*: Headdresses of imitation eagle feathers; painted or plain tipi covers. Special orders only. Send S.A.S.E. for price quotation.

OKLAHOMA INDIAN ARTS & CRAFTS COOP.
Southern Plains Indian Museum Shop
P.O. Box 966 • Anadarko, OK 73005
(405) 247-3486
LaVerna Jane Capes, Manager
Retail, wholesale, mail order. *Products*: Art, clothing, dolls, jewelry. Send S.A.S.E. for price list.

TOEHAY-POTTERY
Route 3 • Anadarko, OK 73005
(405) 247-5268
Thelma Toehay Chapman, Owner
Retail. *Products*: Beadwork, pottery, oil paintings, shawls.

JOYCE L. VINEYARD
330 1/2 W, Main • Anadarko, OK 73005
(405) 247-9770
Retail. *Products*: Beadwork, clothing.
Special orders and commissions accepted.

PAUL HACKER KNIVES & FLUTES
6513 N.W. 20th Dr. • Bethany, OK 73008
(405) 787-8600 (phone & fax)
Paul Hacker, Owner; & Susan Trube, Manager
Retail, wholesale, mail order. *Products*: Art, books, boxes, drums, pipes, knives. *Membership*: IACA. Brochure.

J. BALES STUDIO
P.O. Box 193 • Cookson, OK 74427
(918) 457-4136
Jean E. Bales, Owner; Don Lacy, Manager
Retail, wholesale. By appointment only. *Products*: Art, pottery, sculpture. Special orders accepted.

BAH-KHO-JE ART GALLERY
P.O. Box 221 • Coyle, OK 73027
(405) 466-3101
Frank Murray, Manager
Retail. Iowa Tribe of Oklahoma enterprise.
Products: Art, beadwork, clothing, jewelry, pottery, sculpture.

TOUCHING LEAVES INDIAN CRAFTS
927 Portland Ave. • Dewey, OK 74029
(918) 534-2859
Louise Dean, Owner
Jim Clear-Sky, Manager
Mail order. *Products*: Beadwork, clothing, jewelry. Catalog, $1.

LES BERRYHILL
1800 Bunting Ln.
Edmond, OK 73034
(405) 733-7350 or 330-1951
Les Berryhill, Owner
Retail, wholesale. Yuchi/Creek craftsperson. *Products*: Beadwork, artifacts. Cultural artifact replicas

BILL GLASS, JR., STUDIO
HC64, Box 1410
Locust Grove, OK 74352
(918) 479-8884
Retail, mail order. *Products*: Pottery, sculpture. Special orders accepted.

WAK BOK OLA INTANNAP
P.O. Box 23 • Maysville, OK 73057
(405) 867-5330
Richard Duane Robinson, Owner
Retail, mail order. Choctaw artist. *Products*: Abstract American Indian painting, ceramics, prints, and drawings. American Indian art consulting.

AMERICAN INDIAN HANDICRAFTS
P.O. Box 533 • Meeker, OK 74855
(405) 279-3343
Shalah Rowlen, Owner
Retail, wholesale. *Products*: Beadwork, boxes, clothing. Brochure & price list.

ADAWA TRIBAL GIFT SHOP
Ottawa Tribal Center
P.O. Box 110 • Miami, OK 74355
(918) 549-1536

BUFFALO SUN
P.O. Box 1556 • Miami, OK 74355
(918) 542-8870
Ardina Moore, Owner
Retail, wholesale, mail order. Quapaw-Osage craftsperson. *Products*: Traditional and contemporary Indian fashions and accessories, jewelry, leatherwork. Send S.A.S.E. for brochure.

DOUG MAYTUBBIE
200 E. Lockheed Dr.
Midwest City, OK 73110
(405) 733-8534
Doug & Donna Maytubbie, Owners
Retail, wholesale. *Products*: Art, sculpture. Price list.

SAM KIDD ORIGIALS
Rt. 2, Box 129 • Muldrow, OK 74948
(918) 427-3793
Retail. *Product*: Art.

FIVE CIVILIZED TRIBES MUSEUM TRADING POST
Agency Hill on Honor Hts. Dr. • Muskogee, OK 74401
(918) 683-1701 Fax 683-3070
Mindi Thompson, Manager
Retail, wholesale, mail order. *Products*: Art, baskets, books, ornaments, clothing, jewelry, pottery, sculpture. Brochure.

TIGER ART GALLERY
2110 E. Shawnee St. • Muskogee, OK 74403
(918) 687-7006
Johnny & Peggy Tiger, Owners
Retail, wholesale, mail order. *Products*: Art, clothing, sculpture. Send S.A.S.E. for brochure.

TURTLE WOMAN STUDIO
1106 SE 7th St. • Wagoner, OK 74467
(918) 485-5878
"Nancy" Janet L. Smith, Owner
Retail. By appointment only. *Products*: Art.

THE DANCING RABBIT
814 N. Jones • Norman, OK 73069
(405) 360-0512
Patta LT Joest, Owner
Retail, wholesale. By appointment only.
Products: Beadwork, jewelry. Special orders accepted.

MEMORY CIRCLE STUDIO, INC.
P.O. Box 732 • Norman, OK 73070
(405) 360-0751
George Sullivan, Owner/Manager
Dorothy Sullivan, Cherokee Master Artist
Retail, wholesale, mail order. *Products*: Art. Original paintings/drawings; limited edition prints; greeting cards and mini prints; specializing in art of Cherokee history, culture and legends based on extensive research. *Membership*: IACA. Catalog, $5.

CHOCTAW INDIAN TRADING POST, INC.
1500 N. Portland Ave.
Oklahoma City, OK 73107
(405) 947-2490 Fax 512-0005
Angela A. Askew, Manager
Retail. *Products*: All. *Membership*: IACA

CONNIE SEABOURN STUDIO
P.O. Box 23795
Oklahoma City, OK 73132
(405) 728-3903
Mail order. *Products*: Art.

MAVIS V. DOERING
5918 NW 58th St.
Oklahoma City, OK 73122
(405) 787-6082
Retail. *Product*: Baskets.

MONKAPEME
P.O. Box 457 • Perkins, OK 74059
(405) 547-2948
Remonia O. Jacobsen, Owner
Retail, wholesale. *Product*: Clothing.
Special orders only.

ADAMS STUDIOS
Rt. 3, Box 615A • Ponca City, OK 74604
(405) 765-5086
Jack & Anna Adams, Owners
Retail. *Products*: Art, beadwork, jewelry, knives, pottery. Special orders accepted. Brochure.

CHEROKEE ARTIST STUDIO-GALLERY
Rt. 1, Box 263 • Prague, OK 74864
(405) 567-2856
Ron Mitchell, Owner
Retail, mail order. Call for appointment. Products: Art, Miniatures. Original gouache paintings; limited-edition prints with handmade miniature cultural items. Catalog.

RABBIT STUDIO GALLERY
P.O. Box 34 • Pryor, OK 74362
(800) 613-3716; (918) 825-3788 or 825-3716
Bill & Traci Rabbit, Owners
Retail, wholesale. *Products*: Art, baskets, knives, pottery, sculpture. Catalog.

SNAKE CREEK WORKSHOP
Box 147, Hwy. 33 • Rose, OK 74364
(918) 479-8867
Knokovtee Scott, Owner
Retail, mail order. *Product*: Jewelry. Mussel shell gorget necklaces. Brochure & price list.

MISTER INDIAN'S COWBOY STORE
1000 S. Main • Sapulpa, OK 74066
(918) 224-6511
Bob & Jo Arrington, Managers
Retail, some mail order. *Products*: Art, beadwork, clothing, dolls, jewelry, rugs, sculpture.

KELLY HANEY ART GALLERY
P.O. Box 3817 • Shawnee, OK 74801
(405) 275-2270
Enoch Kelly Haney, Owner
Retail, mail order. Seminole-Creek artist. *Products*: Art, baskets, jewelry, pottery, sculpture. Send S.A.S.E. for brochure.

SUPERNAW'S OKLAHOMA INDIAN SUPPLY
P.O. Box 216, 303
Skiatook, OK 74070
(918) 396-1713
Kugee Supernaw, Owner
Retail, wholesale, mail order. *Products*: Beadwork, boxes, jewelry, pottery, rugs. Catalog.

THE STILWELL COLLECTION
P.O. Box 1287 • Stilwell, OK 74960
(918) 696-3607 Fax 696-3723
Debi Kilgore, Owner
Retail, wholesale. *Products*: Baskets, beadwork, jewelry, rugs. *Membership*: IACA.

CHEROKEE NATION GIFT SHOPS
P.O. Box 948 • Tahlequah, OK 74464
(800) 256-2123; (918) 456-2793
Linda Taylor, Manager
Retail, mail order. Tribal Enterprise. *Products*: Art, baskets, beadwork, clothing, dolls, pottery, rugs, sculpture. Special orders accepted. *Branch shop*: Salisaw, OK. Catalog.

CHEROKEE NATIONAL MUSEUM GIFT SHOP
P.O. Box 515, TSA-LA-GI
Tahlequah, OK 74464
(918) 456-6007
Betty Jo Smith, Manager
Retail, mail order. *Products*: Art, baskets. Price list.

JOYCE JOHNSON
4735 E. Latimer Place
Tulsa, OK 74115
(918) 835-3069
Mail order. *Products*: Baskets. Cherokee baskets. Brochure & price list.

J. BALES STUDIO
One Plaza Soufe
Tahlequah, OK 74464
(405) 247-3993
Jean E. Bales, Owner
By appointment only. *Products*: Art, pottery, sculpture. Special orders accepted.

GILCREASE MUSEUM SHOP
1400 Gilcrease Museum Rd.
Tulsa, OK 74127
(918) 582-2423
Susan Logsdon
Wholesale, retail. *Products*: All.
Membership: IACA. Catalog.

LYON'S INDIAN STORE
401 E. 11th St. • Tulsa, OK 74120
(918) 582-6372 Fax 582-5456
Larry & Janie Lyon, Owners
Retail, mail order. *Products*: Beadwork, clothing, jewelry, rugs. *Membership*: IACA. Brochure; catalog for craft supplies only. *Branch shop*: Woodland Hills Mall, Tulsa, OK.

ZADOKA POTTERY
12515 E. 37th St.
Tulsa, OK 74146
(918) 663-9455
David Thompson, Owner
Retail, wholesale, mail order. *Product*: Earthenware storage vessels, vases and bowls.

WEWOKA TRADING POST
Box 1532, 524 S. Wewoka Ave.
Seminole Nation Historical Society
Wewoka, OK 74884
(405) 257-5580
Retail, mail order. *Products*: Art, beadwork, clothing, dolls, jewelry, rugs. Special orders accepted. Brochure & catalog.

OREGON

RED BEAR CREATIONS
358 N. Lexington Ave. • Bandon, OR 97411
(503) 347-9725
Red She Bear, Owner
Retail, wholesale. *Products*: Traditional star quilts & drum covers made to order. Brochure.

OARD'S
SR2 1604 Buchanan Rd. • Burns, OR 97720
(503) 493-2535
Mavis Oard, Owner
Retail. *Products*: All. *Membership*: IACA.

ART OF THE VINEYARD, INC.
1430 Willamette, #24 • Eugene, OR 97401
William & Jacqueline Kaufman, Owners
Retail. *Products*: Art, baskets, books, Northwest Coast art, jewelry, rugs. *Membership*: IACA.

AMERICAN SHADOWS
1800 SE Hwy. 101, Suite G
Lincoln City, OR 97367
(503) 996-6887
Patricia L. Erickson
Retail. *Products*: Art, baskets, beadwork, clothing, dolls, jewelry, kachinas, pottery, rugs, sandpaintings, sculpture, carvings. *Membership*: IACA.

NADINE'S NATIVE DOLLS
Rt. 1, Box 270 • Pendleton, OR 97801
(541) 276-2566
Nadine Van Mechelen, Owner
Retail, wholesale. By appointment only. Yurok-Karok-Tolowa craftswoman. *Product*: Dolls dressed in authentic Indian costume for collectors. Special orders accepted.

WIND SONG GALLERY
7 SE Court • Pendleton, OR 97801
(541) 276-7993
Nadine Van Mechelen, Owner
Retail, wholesale. *Products*: Art, dolls, jewelry. Dolls dressed in authentic Indian costume for collectors. Special orders accepted.

THE BEAD GOES ON
8721 S.E. Foster Rd.
Portland, OR 97266
(503) 788-9533
Kellie LaBonty, Owner
Retail/wholesale. *Products*: Native American artwork and craft supplies. Special orders accepted.

BLAZE GALLERY
228 SW 1st • Portland, OR 97204
(503) 224-8101
Randall Blaze, Owner; Judi Blaze, Manager
Retail, wholesale, mail order. Oglala Sioux artist. *Products*: Art, jewelry, pottery, sculpture.
Commissions and special orders accepted.

QUINTANA'S GALLERIES
501 SW Broadway
Portland, OR 97205-3425
(503) 223-1729 Fax 223-6030
Cecil & Rose Quintana, Owners
E-mail: qgallery@teleport.com
Web site: www.quintanagalleries.com
Retail, mail order. *Products*: Contemporary Native American Indian art. Specializes in Northwest Coast Indian and Inuit art, masks, totems, bentwood boxes, etc. Also a large collection of Inuit soapstone carvings. Accepts art work on consignment.

PENNSYLVANIA

INDIAN POST
1645 Hausman Rd.
Allentown, PA 18104
(215) 395-5530
Carolyn Foreback, Owner
Connie Foreback, Manager
Retail. *Products*: Art,, baskets, books, clothing, drums, pipes, jewelry, rugs, sandpaintings, sculpture. *Membership*: IACA.

TURTLE ISLAND TREASURERS
Lenni Lenape Historical Society
Museum of Indian Culture
2825 Fish Hatchery Rd.
Allentown, PA 18103-9801
(610) 797-2121 Fax 797-2801
Carla J.S. Messinger, Manager
E-Mail: lenape@comcat.com
Web site: http://www.lenape.org
Retail. *Products*: Art, beadwork, books, books, clothing, dolls, jewelry.

TURQUOISE 'N TREASURES
21 E. High St. • Elizabethtown, PA 17022
(717) 367-1848
Nancy Barnitz, Owner
Retail. *Products*: Art, beadwork, clothing, dolls, jewelry, kachinas, pottery, rugs, sandpaintings. *Membership*: IACA.

EICHER INDIAN MUSEUM SHOP
Ephrata Community Park
P.O. Box 601 • Ephrata, PA 17522
(717) 738-3084
Beverly Flaherty, Manager
Retail. *Products*: Art, baskets, beadwork, clothing, dolls, jewelry, kachinas, pottery, rugs, sandpaintings, sculpture, carvings.

SOUTHWEST SELECTIONS
The Art Works at Doneckers
100 N. State St., Gallery 112
Ephrata, PA 17522-2230
(717) 738-9593
Jeanne Loomis, Owner
Retail. *Products*: Fetishes, heishi, jewelry, kachinas, pottery, rugs, sandpaintings. *Membership*: IACA.

FITCH'S TRADING POST
230 N. 3rd St. • Harrisburg, PA 17101
(717) 233-6832
Delores Fitch-Basehore
Richard & Deirdre Basehore, Owners
Retail, mail order. *Products*: Native American fine art representing 32 tribes in North America and tribe in Central America. *Appraisals*: All. *Membership*: IACA.

WESTERN LEGENDS GALLERY
1311 Old Ford Rd.
Huntingdon Valley, PA 19006
(215) 659-7530
Robert & Annette Griffith, Owners
Retail. *Products*: Art, beadwork, clothing, dolls, jewelry, kachinas, pottery, rugs, sandpaintings, sculpture, carvings. *Membership*: IACA.

THE TURQUOISE SHOPPE
26 E. Main St. • Lititz, PA 17543
(717) 626-1616
Carol Stocker, Owner
Retail. *Products*: Baskets, beadwork, clothing, dolls, jewelry, kachinas, pottery, rugs, sandpaintings, sculpture, carvings. *Membership*: IACA.

SOUTHWEST VISIONS
36 W. Mechanic St. • New Hope, PA 18938
(215) 862-0323 Fax 797-1934
Sandie & Nikki Anthony
Retail. *Products*: Art, baskets, beadwork, clothing, dolls, jewelry, kachinas, pottery, rugs, sandpaintings, sculpture, carvings. *Membership*: IACA. Catalog.

DANDELION
1618 Latimer St. • Philadelphia, PA 19103
(215) 972-0999
Beth Fluke, Owner
Retail. *Products*: Art, beadwork, clothing, dolls, jewelry, kachinas, pottery, rugs, sandpaintings, sculpture, carvings. *Membership*: IACA. *Branch*: 1718 Sansom St., Philadelphia, PA.

BEVERLEY CONRAD
RR 1, Box 159 • Selinsgrove, PA 17870
(717) 374-2647
Beverley Conrad, Owner
Retail, wholesale. St. Regis Mohawk craftsperson. *Products*: Art, beadwork, clothing, fetishes. Reproduction and original Eastern Woodland Indian products. Portraits and commissions accepted; museum work and demonstrations.

SOUTHWEST IMAGES
1041 Hilltown Plaza, Rt. 113
Souderton, PA 18964
(215) 721-9606
Marla & Bill Hammerschmidt, Owners
Retail. *Products*: Art, clothing, dolls, jewelry, kachinas, pottery, sandpaintings, sculpture, carvings. *Membership*: IACA.

SHADY LAMP WORKSHOP
1800 Mearns Rd., Bldg. JJ
Warminster, PA 18974
(215) 672-2350 Fax 672-6401
Eileen & Jack Wilson, Owners
Retail, wholesale. *Products*: Art, baskets, children's items, ornaments, jewelry, rugs. *Membership*: IACA. *Branch shop*: Peddler's Village, Lahaska, PA 18931.

TOMAR SERVICES, INC.
P.O. Box 233 • Wexford, PA 15090
(412) 367-2310
Todd & Mary Grant, Owners
Retail, wholesale. *Products*: Art, baskets, beadwork, dolls, jewelry, kachinas, pottery, rugs, sandpaintings, sculpture, carvings.

RHODE ISLAND

DOVE TRADING POST
390 Summit Rd., Arcadia Village
Exeter, RI 02822-1808
(401) 539-2786 or 539-7795
Eleanor F. Dove, Owner; Dawn Dove, Manager
Retail, wholesale. *Products*: Beadwork, clothing, jewelry, pottery.

SOUTH CAROLINA

SARA AYERS
1182 Brookwood Cr.
West Columbia, SC 29169
(803) 794-5436
Mail order. *Product*: Pottery. Special orders accepted. Price list.

WESTERN VISIONS, INC.
4728 C Hwy. 17 South
North Myrtle Beach, SC 29582
Wolf Creek Gallery, 1315 Celebrity Circle
Myrtle Beach, SC 29577
(800) 745-5691; (803) 272-2698 Fax 272-3798

Grace C. Krueger, Frank Fezzle,
Karen Mattscheck, Owners
E-Mail: wesvis@sccoast.net
Retail. *Products*: Native American jewelry, art, sculpture, drums, reproduction artifacts, books, incense, music. *Membership*: IACA.

SOUTH DAKOTA

FEATHERSTONE PRODUCTIONS
P.O. Box 487 • Brookings, SD 57006
(605) 693-3183
JoAnne & Gordon Bird, Owners
Retail, wholesale, mail order. *Products*: Art.

ST. JOSEPH LAKOTA DEVELOPMENT COUNCIL
St. Joseph's Indian School
Chamberlain, SD 57326
(605) 734-6021 ext. 307
Cy Maus, Manager
Retail, wholesale, mail order. *Products*: Art, beadwork, clothing, dolls, jewelry, rugs. Special order accepted for quilts. Brochure/price list.

GALLERY OF INDIAN ARTS
Mt. Rushmore • Keystone, SD 57751
(605) 574-2515
Charles & Kay Steuerwald, Owners
Retail. *Products*: Art, dolls, drums, pipes, jewelry, pottery, rugs, sandpaintings, sculpture.

THE INDIANS
P.O. Box 162 • Keystone, SD 57751
(605) 666-4864
Eugene & Lucille Jelliffe, Owners
Retail. *Products*: Art, baskets, beadwork, clothing, dolls, jewelry, kachinas, pottery, rugs, sandpaintings, sculpture, carvings.

CHEYENNE CROSSING STORE
HC-37, Box 1220 • Lead, SD 57754
(605) 584-3510
Jim & Bonnie LeMar, Owners
Retail. *Products*: Art, beadwork, clothing, dolls, jewelry, kachinas, pottery, rugs. *Membership*: IACA.

OYATE KIN CULTURAL COOPERATIVE
c/o Wesley Hare, Jr. • Marty, SD 57361
Mail order. *Products*: Beadwork, boxes, clothing, rugs. Special orders accepted.

SZABO STUDIO
P.O. Box 906
Mission, SD 57555
(605) 856-4548
Paul & Linda Szabo, Owners
Retail, wholesale, mail order. Sicangu Lakota craftspersons. *Products*: Handmade Northern Plains style jewelry in 14k gold, sterling silver, and buffalo horn. Custom designs. Special orders accepted.

JACKSON ORIGINALS
P.O. Box 1049 • Mission, SD 57555
(605) 856-2541
Jackie Colomb, Owner
Retail, wholesale, mail order. By appointment only. *Product*: contemporary apparel. Price list.

CRAZY HORSE
P.O. Box 153 • Pringle, SD 57773
(603) 436-3629
Lynn & Gardner Gray
Retail. *Products*: All.

CONTEMPORARY LAKOTA FASHIONS BY GERALDINE SHERMAN
714 Wambli Dr.
Rapid City, OK 57701
(605) 341-7560; Geraldine Sherman, Owner
Retail, wholesale, some mail order. Sioux craftsperson. *Products*: Contemporary fashions.

DAKOTA DRUM COMPANY
603 Main St. • Rapid City, SD 57701
(605) 348-2421
Website: www.dakotadrum.com
Retail, wholesale. *Products*: Authentic Native American drums, hide paintings, bead work, etc.

PRAIRIE EDGE TRADING CO. & GALLARIES
P.O. Box 8303 • Rapid City, SD 57709
(800) 541-2388; (605) 342-3086 Fax 341-6415
Ray Hillenbrand, President
E-Mail: prairie@rapidnet.com
Website: www.prairieedge.com
Retail, wholesale, mail order. *Products*: Plains Indian art and artifacts; jewelry, pottery, beads, craft supplies, books, tapes, CDs, DVDs, videos. Catalog.

SIOUX TRADING POST
415 6th St. • Rapid City, SD 57701
(800) 456-3394 (mail order)
(605) 348-4822 fax 348-9624
Ray Hillenbrand, Manager
Retail, wholesale, mail order. Plains Indian arts & crafts. *Products*: All. *Membership*: IACA. Brochure; catalog, $2. Branch shops: Mission, SD, and Santa Fe, NM.

BRULE SIOUX ARTS & CRAFTS COOPERATIVE
P.O. Box 230 • St. Francis, SD 57572
(605) 747-2019
Retail, wholesale. *Products*: Art, beadwork, boxes, rugs.

WALL DRUG STORE, INC.
Box 401, 510 Main St. • Wall, SD 57790
(605) 279-2175
Ted H. Hustead
Retail. *Products*: Art, baskets, beadwork, books, clothing, dolls, jewelry, kachinas, pottery. *Membership*: IACA.

TENNESSEE

EAGLE FEATHER
144 E. Main St. • Jonesborough, TN 37659
(423) 753-2095
Jane Blair, Owner
Retail, mail order. *Products*: Art, baskets, beadwork, books, clothing, dolls, jewelry, kachinas, pottery, rugs, sandpaintings. *Membership*: IACA.

TEXAS

NATIVE AMERICAN IMAGES, INC.
P.O. Box 156 • Austin, TX 78767
(512) 472-3049
Ted Pearsall
Wholesale. *Product*: Art. *Membership*: IACA.

BONHAM GALLERY
P.O. Box 938 • Burleson, TX 76097
(800) 333-5287; (817) 335-3491
H.E. Eugene Bonham, M.D.
Retail, wholesale. *Product*: Art.

AMERICAN WEST TRADING CO.
1701 Laura Ln. • College Station, TX 77840
Ken Kaemmerle
(505) 265-8549
Wholesale. *Products*: Northwest Coast art, kachinas, pottery, rugs, sculpture. *Membership*: IACA.

THUR-SHAN ARTS & CRAFTS CENTER
305 Yaya Lane • El Paso, TX 79907
(915) 859-5287 Fax 860-8972
Albert Alvidrez, Manager
Retail. Tigua Indian tribal enterprise. *Products*: Pottery, jewelry, and arts & crafts of the Pueblo.

TIGUA INDIAN RESERVATION CULTURAL CENTER
Box 17579, 122 S. Old Pueblo Rd.
El Paso, TX 79917
(915) 859-3916
Pat Gomez, Manager
Retail. Tribal enterprise. Products: Jewelry, pottery.

YSLETA DEL SUR PUEBLO CULTURAL CENTER
122 S. Old Pueblo
El Paso, TX 79907
(915) 859-3916 Fax 859-2889
Vince Munoz, General Manager
Retail, wholesale. Tribal enterprise.
Products: Art, jewelry, kachinas, pottery, rugs.

GUILDHALL, INC.
2535 Weisenberger
Fort Worth, TX 76107
(800) 356-6733
(817) 332-6733 Fax 332-8100
John M. Thompson, III, Owner
Retail, wholesale. *Products*: Art, baskets, beadwork, boxes, clothing, Northwest Coast art, sculpture. *Membership*: IACA.

NATIVE TREASURES
260 Ridgewood Rd. Ext.
Georgetown, TX 78628
(512) 930-5854
Karen M. Bullard, Owner
Retail, mail order. *Products*: Native Americn art and artifacts.

PUEBLO CONNECTION
334 S. Main St. • Grapevine, TX 76051
(817) 481-7724
Patrick & Beverly Fairchild, Owners
Retail. *Products*: All. *Appraisals*: Rugs. *Membership*: IACA.

DINETKAH SILVER GALLERY
351 Memorial City Mall
Houston, TX 77024-2512
Sue O'Dell, Owner
Retail. *Products*: Art, baskets, beadwork, jewelry, kachinas, pottery, rugs, sandpaintings, sculpture, carvings.

DONALD GREENWOOD GIFTS OF THE SPIRIT
c/o Fetch & Send
10414 Autumn Meadow Lane
Houston, TX 77064
(918) 866-2653
Donald "Little Boy" Greenwood, Owner
Retail, mail order, will consider wholesale and special orders. Cherokee craftsperson. *Products*: A,H,P. Brochure and price list, $2.50. *Membership*: IACA.

ZAPOTEC ART/SOUTHWEST SPIRIT
1728 Sunset Blvd.
Houston, TX 77005-1714
(713) 529-0890 Fax 529-0365
Michael C. McBride & Winifred Patton, Owners
Retail, wholesale. *Products*: Drums, pipes, fetishes, jewelry, kachinas, pottery, rugs. *Membership*: IACA. Catalog.

INDIAN CREEK JEWELRY
5920 Lalagray Lane • Hurst, TX 76148
(817) 268-4921
Betty Beaver, Owner
Retail. *Products*: beadwork, fetishes, heishi, jewelry, pottery.

CROW'S NEST ART GALLERY
230 Jefferson * La Porte, TX 77571
(281) 471-4371 Fax 471-2468
Fern Yung, Owner
Retail. *Products*: All. *Membership*: IACA. Brochure.

EAGLE DANCER
159 Gulf Fwy. So.
League City, TX 77573
(713) 332-6028
Joseph Skywolf, Owner
Retail. *Products*: Baskets, beadwork, clothing, dolls, jewelry, pottery, rugs.

L. DAVID EVENING THUNDER CONTEMPORARY NATIVE AMERICAN ART
5926 Indian Springs
Livingston, TX 77351
(409) 563-2655
L. David Eveningthunder, Owner
Retail, wholesale. By appointment only. Products: Art, beadwork, clothing.

TRIBAL ENTERPRISE
Alabama-Coushatta Indian Reservation
Route 3, Box 640 • Livingston, TX 77351
(713) 563-4391; (800) 392-4794 (TX)
Roland A. Poncho, Manager
Retail, mail order. Alabama-Coushatta Tribes of Texas tribal enterprise. *Products*: Baskets, beadwork, clothing, jewelry, pottery.

ANNESLEY STUDIO
P.O. Box 3 • Missouri City, TX 77459
(713) 729-8960
Robert H. Annsley, Owner
Mail order, some wholesale & retail. *Products*: Bronze sculpture, original graphics and drawings, original paintings.

TIGER'S TURQUOISE SHOP
3807 Meeks Dr. • Orange, TX 77630
(409) 886-7906
Abe Tiger, Owner
Retail. *Products*: baskets, beadwork, jewelry, Navajo rugs, pottery.

THE VICTORIAN DREAMER & THE COWBOY
1511 Browning Rd.
Orange, TX 77630
(409) 882-9339
Josephine & Robert Walter
Retail. Products: Art, baskets, clothing, dolls, jewelry, kachinas, pottery, rugs, sandpaintings. *Membership*: IACA.

CRAZY CROW TRADING POST
P.O. Box 847, 1801 N. Airport Rd.
Pottsboro, TX 75076 (800) 786-6210
(903) 786-2287 Fax 786-9059
J. Rex & Ginger Reddick, Owners
E-Mail: info@crazycrow.com
Web site: www.crazycrow.com
Retail, wholesale, mail order. *Products*: Indian craft supplies, beads, buckskin, feathers, needles, thread, simulated and genuine sinew, hides, furs, blankets, books, videos, CDs and cassettes. Special orders accepted. Catalog available, $4.

WHITEWOLF PHOTOGRAPHY
P.O. Box 297 • Redwater, TX 75573
Ron Whitewolf Morgan, Owner
Mail order. *Products*: original photographs of Indian and western themes. Brochure.

GALLERY OF THE SOUTHWEST
13485 Blanco Rd.
San Antonio, TX 78216
(210) 493-3344
R.D. & Ann K. Carlyon, Owners
Retail, wholesale. *Products*: All. *Membership*: IACA.

RATTLESNAKE AND STAR
209 N. Presa
San Antonio, TX 78205
(512) 225-5977
Gustin Aldrete, Owner
Retail. *Products*: Baskets, beadwork, dolls, jewelry, pottery, rugs, sculpture.

THE RESERVATION
8802 Broadway
San Antonio, TX 78217
(210) 820-3916 Fax 820-0633
Matt & Helen Walence, Owners
Wholesale/retail. *Products*: All. *Appraisals*: Jewelry, pottery. *Membership*: IACA. Catalog.

BOB & DOT NATION'S TWO NATIONS TRADING CO.
Box 2441, 109 Shadowyck Ave.
Universal City, TX 78148
(512) 658-1185
Bob & Dot Nation, Owners
Wholesale/retail. *Products*: All. *Membership*: IACA.

BRAZOS ART
P.O. Box 796, 1407 Woodland Hills
Whitehouse, TX 75791
(903) 839-7573
Linda Busby, Owner
Wholesale/reatil. *Products*: Art, baskets, beadwork, clothing, dolls, jewelry, kachinas, pottery, rugs, sculpture, carvings. *Membership*: IACA.

THE TURQUOISE LADY
2310 Brook St.
Wichita Falls, TX 76301-6124
(817) 766-2626 (phone & fax)
Edna Redding, Owner
Retail. *Products*: Art, beadwork, clothing, artifacts, jewelry, pottery. *Appraisals*: jewelry.

UTAH

COW CANYON TRADING POST
P.O. Box 88 • Bluff, UT 84512
(801) 672-2208
Liza Doran, Owner
Retail, wholesale. *Products*: Baskets, beadwork, clothing, artifacts, jewelry, miniatures, pottery, rugs, sculpture.

RUBY'S INN GENERAL STORE
Bryce, UT 84764
(801) 834-5341
Fred Syrett, Manager
Retail. *Products*: All. *Membership*: IACA.

LEMA INDIAN TRADING CO.
Box 474, 60 N. Main & 860 S. Main
Moab, UT 84532
(801) 259-5055/5942/5217
Anthony & Carolyn Lema
Retail, wholesale. *Products*: Art, baskets, beadwork, clothing, dolls, jewelry, kachinas, pottery, rugs, sandpaintings, sculpture, carvings. *Membership*: IACA.

EAGLECRAFTS, INC.
Eagle Feather Trading Post
168 W. 12th St. • Ogden, UT 84404
(801) 393-3991 Fax 745-0903
E-Mail: eglcrafts@aol.com
Website: www.eaglefeathertradingpost.com
Retail, wholesale, mail order. *Products*: Arts & Crafts supplies. Catalog.

BRYCE CANYON TRADING POST
Box 371, 2938 E. Hwy. 12
Panguitch, UT 84759 (435) 676-2688
Barbara Sheen & Gayle Collins, Owners
E-mail: brycetp@color.country.net
Retail. *Products*: Navajo, Zuni, Hopi and Santo Domingo Pueblo pawn jewelry; Navajo rugs, Pueblo pottery, Hopi kachinas, and Navajo sandpaintings. *Membership*: IACA.

RED CANYON INDIAN STORE
Box 717, 3279 Hwy. 12 • Panguitch, UT 84759
(801) 676-2690
Arthur Tebbs, Owner
Retail. *Products*: Baskets, beadwork, clothing, dolls, jewelry, kachinas, pottery, rugs, sandpaintings, sculpture, carvings. *Membership*: IACA.

SOUTHWESTERN EXPRESSIONS
Box 1162, 333 Main St. Mall
Park City, UT 84060
(801) 649-1612
Monty J. Coates, Owner
Retail. *Products*: Art, baskets, clothing, dolls, jewelry, kachinas, pottery, rugs, sandpaintings, sculpture, carvings. *Membership*: IACA.

AIR TERMINAL GIFTS, INC.
AMF Box 22031, 750 N. Airport Rd.
Salt Lake City, UT 84122
(801) 575-2540
Retail. *Products*: All. *Appraisals*: Fetishes, heishi, jewelry. *Membership*: IACA.

ZION NATURAL HISTORY ASSOCIATION
Council Hall/Capitol Hill
Salt Lake City, UT 84116
(801) 538-1398
Mary-Delle Gunn, Owner
Retail. *Products*: Dolls, fetishes, jewelry, pottery, rugs, sandpaintings. *Membership*: IACA.

ZION NATURAL HISTORY ASSOCIATION
Zion National Park • Springdale, UT 84767
(801) 538-1398
Jamie Gentry, Director
Retail. *Products*: Dolls, fetishes, jewelry, pottery, rugs, sandpaintings. *Membership*: IACA.

PIONEER CENTER
391 N. Main St. • Springville, TX 84663
(801) 489-6853
Norma L. Suth, Owner
Retail, wholesale. *Products*: Baskets, jewelry, pottery, rugs. Navajo rugs, Pueblo pottery.

VERMONT

LONG AGO & FAR AWAY
Box 809, Rt. 7A North
Manchester Center, VT 05255
(802) 362-3435
Grant & Betsy Turner, Owners
Retail. *Products*: All. *Appraisals*: Baskets, beadwork, books, Northwest Coast art, jewelry, rugs. *Membership*: IACA

RED ROCK TRADING CO.
P.O. Box 130
Post Mills, VT 05058
Ted & Joan Dunham, Owners
Retail, wholesale. *Products*: All. *Appraisals*: Art, baskets, jewelry, pottery, rugs, sculpture. *Membership*: IACA.

VIRGINIA

TURQUOISE EAGLE
2258 Huntington Ave., Suite S19
Alexandria, VA 22303
(703) 960-3875
Wesley Mathews, Manager
Wholesale, mail order. *Products*: Handmade Native American crafts and jewelry. *Appraisals*: Baskets, Northwest Coast art, jewelry, kachinas, pottery, rugs.

AMERIND GALLERY
885 Roanoke Rd., Box 588
Daleville, VA 24083
(540) 992-1066
Lnda Anderson, Owner
Retail. *Products*: Art, baskets, books, clothing, dolls, jewelry, kachinas, pottery, rugs, sandpaintings, sculpture, carvings. *Membership*: IACA.

FIRST NATIONS ARTS
11917 Main St.
Fredericksburg, VA 22408
(703) 371-5615 Fax 371-3505
Dennis Fox, Jr., Rebecca Adamson, Owners
Wholesale, retail. *Products*: All. *Membership*: IACA; SWAIA, NMAI. Catalog.

PAMUNKEY POTTERY & CRAFTS TRADING POST
Rt. 1, Pamunkey Indian Reservation
King William, VA 23086
(804) 843-2851
Mrs. James Bradby, Manager
Retail. Tribal Enterprise. *Products*: Beadwork, miniaturesm pottery, rugs.

EAGLE SPIRIT
1038 E. Ocean View Ave.
Norfolk, VA 23503
(804) 491-2964
Carol Quanty, Owner
Retail. *Products*: Art, beadwork, books, clothing, dolls, jewelry, kachinas, pottery, rugs, sandpaintings, sculpture, carvings. *Membership*: IACA.

VIA GAMBARO STUDIO, INC.
P.O. Box 1117
Stafford, VA 22554
(703) 659-0130
Retha Walden Gambaro, Owner
Retail. *Products*: Drums, pipes, flutes, rugs, sculpture. Special orders accepted.

GEORGTOWN COTTON & CO.
2070 Chain Bridge Rd., Suite G-99
Vienna, VA 22182
(703) 790-0711 Fax 442-7543
Maureen Donovan & Moses Robbins, Owners
Retail. *Products*: Beadwork, fetishes, heishi, jewelry, miniatures. *Membership*: IACA.

EAGLE DANCER
1505 Brookfield Cove
Virginia Beach, VA 23464
(804) 490-0477
Jacqueline LaCrone, Owner
Retail. *Products*: All. *Membership*: IACA.

EASTERN WIND CRAFTS
Mattaponi Indian Reservation
Rt. 2, Box 233 • West Point, VA 23181
(804) 769-0289
Lionel Custalow, Owner
Retail, wholesale, mail order. *Products*: Beadwork, drums, pipes, pottery.

RIVER OF HIGH BANKS POTTERY SHOP
Mattaponi Indian Reservation
35 Nee-A-Ya Lane • West Point, VA 23181
(804) 769-9331
Christine Rippling Water Custalow, Owner
Retail, wholesale, mail order. *Products*: Hand made pottery, beads and leather items. Brochure.

SNYDER ART STUDIOS
P.O. Box 1565 • Woodbridge, VA 22193
(703) 670-0074
Kim L. Snyder, Owner
Retail, mail order. *Products*: Art, clothing, rugs, sculpture. Special orders and commissions accepted.

WASHINGTON

MARCH POINT INDIAN ARTS
815 S. March Point Rd.
Anacortes, WA 98221
(206) 293-5632
Marvi & Joan Wilbur, Owners
Retail, mail order. *Products*: Baskets, clothing, dolls, jewelry, pottery, rugs, sculpture.

POTLATCH GIFTS
Northwind Trading Co.
P.O. Box 217 • Anacortes, WA 98221
(206) 293-6404
Tim King, Manager
Retail, wholesale, mail order. *Products*: Art, baskets, clothing, jewelry, pottery, sculpture. Special orders accepted on wood carvings and clothing. Brochure & price list.

LELOOSKA FAMILY GALLERY
5618 Lewis River Rd. • Ariel, WA 98603
(206) 225-9522/8828
Patty Fawn, Manager
Retail, some mail order. *Products*: Art, dolls, Northwest Coast art, jewelry, scultpure. All items primarily Northwest Coast.

SONG STICK
P.O. Box 490 • Chimacum, WA 98325
(360) 732-4279
Troy De Roche, Owner
Retail, wholesale, mail order. By appointment only. Blackfeet craftsperson. Products: Traditional handcrafted Native American flutes and accessories; cassettes of originla traditional flute music. Price list and pictures, $1.

M.J.R. ENTERPRISE
126 SW 301 * Federal Way, WA 98023
(206) 941-7333
Ron E. English, Owner
Retail, wholesale. *Products*: Baskets, jewelry, kachinas, sandpaintings.

FRAN & BILL JAMES, LUMMI INDIAN CRAFTSMEN
4339 Lummi Rd. • Ferndale, WA 98248
(360) 384-5292/758-2522
Retail, some mail order. *Products*: Beadwork, Northwest Coast art, rugs. Special orders accepted.

INDIAN ISABELLE'S LUMMI WORKSHOP
4435 Haxton Way • Ferndale, WA 98248
(360) 734-5216
Isabelle Warbus, Owner
Retail. *Products*: Baskets, clothing, jewelry. Special orders accepted.

MAKAH CULTURAL & RESEARCH CENTER
P.O. Box 160 • Neah Bay, WA 98357
(360) 645-2711 Fax 645-2656
Janine Bowechop, Manager
Retail. Makah tribal enterprise. *Products*: Baskets, beadwork, clothing, drums, pipes, Northwest Coast art. Brochure.

TIN-NA-TIT KIN-NE-KI INDIAN ARTS & GIFTS
P.O. Box 1057, 993 Hwy. 20 East
Republic, WA 99166
(509) 775-3077
Ot-Ne-We & Jim Swayne, Owners
Retail. *Products*: Art, baskets, beadwork, clothing, dolls, jewelry, kachinas, pottery, sandpaintings, sculpture, carvings. Brochure.

SACRED CIRCLE GALLERY OF AMERICAN INDIAN ART
c/o Daybreak Star Arts Center
P.O. Box 99100 • Seattle, WA 98199
(206) 285-4425
Steve Charles, Manager
Retail. *Products*: Art, baskets, clothing, knives, pottery, sculpture. Commissions accepted.

SUQUAMISH MUSEUM
P.O. Box 498, Hwy. 305
Port Madison Reservation
Suquamish, WA 98392
(206) 598-3311
Leonard Forsman, Manager
Retail, mail order. *Products*: Baskets, dolls, artifacts, sculpture. Special orders accepted.

TREASURES INDIAN JEWELRY
P.O. Box 64237 • Tacoma, WA 98464
(800) 327-0852; (206) 564-2366
Dave & Judy MacMillan, Owners
Wholesale/retail. *Products*: Art, beadwork, dolls, jewelry, kachinas, pottery, rugs, sandpaintings, sculpture, carvings.

BEAD LADY/CHEROKEE RAINBOWS
315-B Roosevelt
Wenatchee, WA 98801
Dorothea C. Orndorff, Owner
Mail order (special orders only). By appointment only. *Products*: Beadwork, clothing. Beadwork repairs.

WISCONSIN

BEAR TRAP TRADING POST
Rt. 2, Box 419C • Ashland, WI 54806
(715) 682-2209
Retail. *Products*: crafts & supplies.

BUFFALO ART CENTER
Box 51, Hwy. 13
Bayfield, WI 54814
(715) 779-5858
Mardella Soulier, Manager
Retail. *Products*: Art, beadwork, clothing, jewelry, pottery, sculpture.

LIL TP
1114 Woodward Ave.
Beloit, WI 53511
(608) 365-1009
Jim & Katy King, Owners
Retail. *Products*: Beadwork, jewelry.

AMERICAN INDIAN GIFT STORE
132 Main St., Box 73
Hayward, WI 54843
(715) 634-2655
Gerald B. Diamond, Owner
Retail. *Products*: Authentic American Indian made crafts. *Membership*: IACA

C & S LTD.
4303 75th St.
Kenosha, WI 53142-4265
(414) 694-3960
Gayle Chiodo
Retail. *Products*: Art, baskets, beadwork, clothing, dolls, jewelry, kachinas, pottery, rugs, sandpaintings, sculpture, carvings. *Membership*: IACA.

WA-SWA-GON ARTS & CRAFTS
Box 477, Hwy. 47
Lac du Flambeau, WI 54538
(715) 588-7636
Elizabeth Vetterneck, Manager
Mail order. *Products*: Beadwork, boxes, clothing, rugs, sculpture.

TOUCH THE EARTH
220 Main St. • LaCrosse, WI 54601
(608) 785-2980
Dinah & Ron Klemmedson, Owners
Retail. *Products*: hand-crafted silver jewelry
and pottery; art, beads and supplies.

KATY'S AMERICAN INDIAN ARTS
1803 Monroe St. • Madison, WI 53711
(608) 251-5451/0014
Katy Schalles
Retail. *Products*: All. Appraisals: Baskets, fetishes,
heishi, jewelry, kachinas, pottery, rygs, sandpaintings.
Membership: IACA.

WHITE THUNDER WOLF TRADING CO.
320 E. Clybourn St. • Milwaukee, WI 53202
(414) 278-7424 Fax 278-8244
White Thunder Wolf, Owner
Products: Art, jewelry, drums, music, books,
beads & supplies, crafts, gifts.

JO'S LOG CABIN TRADING POST
Box 294, Hwy. 54 • Oneida, WI 54155
(414) 869-2505
Retail. *Products*: Crafts, Leatherwork,
silver turquoise jewelry.

ONEIDA NATION MUSEUM SHOP
P.O. Box 365 • Oneida, WI 54155
(414) 869-2768
Karen S. Brockman, Manager
Retail, wholesale. Tribal enterprise. *Products*: Baskets,
beadwork, books, boxes, clothing, dolls, pottery. Special orders accepted on beadwork and quillwork. Brochure.

TURTLE CLAN TRADERS
1090 Sunlite Dr. • Oneida, WI 54155
(414) 434-6777
Sue Skenandore, Owner
Retail, wholesale. *Products*: Beadwork, clothing, jewelry, rugs.

SHEILA S, SMITH
1795 Poplar Lane • Seymour, WI 54165
(414) 833-7366
Retail. *Products*: Iroquois costumes and accessories.
Special orders accepted.

WINNEBAGO PUBLIC INDIAN MUSEUM
P.O. Box 441 • Wisconsin Dells, WI 53965
(608) 254-2268
Bernadine Tallmadge, Owner
Retail, mail order. *Products*: Winnebago baskets,
beadwork, moccasins, deerskin products; Navajo rugs
and silverwork. Brochure and price list.

WYOMING

**BUFFALO BILL HISTORICAL CENTER
MUSEUM SHOP**
P.O. Box 2630, 720 Sheridan Ave.
Cody, WY 82414-2630
(307) 587-3243 Fax 587-5714
Retail,wholesale. *Products*: All. Catalog available.

LA RAY TURQUOISE CO.
P.O. Box 83 • Cody, WY 82414
(307) 587-9564
Ray & Laura Vallie, Owners
Retail, wholesale, mail order. *Products*: Ojibwa
beadwork, Navajo rugs, silverwork. Special and custom orders accepted.

STEWART'S TRAPLINE GALLERY
P.O. Box 823 • Dubois, WY 82513
(307) 455-2800
Mark & Catherine Stewart, Owners
Retail, wholesale.

FORT WASHAKIE TRADING CO.
P.O. Box 428 • Fort Washakie, WY 82514
(307) 332-3557
Jeri Greeves, Owner
Retail, wholesale, mail order. *Products*: Baskets,
beadwork, clothing, dolls, jewelry, kachinas, pottery,
rugs. Special orders accepted. Brochure.

BOYER'S INDIAN ARTS & CRAFTS
P.O. Box 647 • Jackson, WY 83001
(307) 733-3773
Dick & John Boyer
Retail. *Products*: Baskets, beadwork, books, clothing,
dolls, jewelry, kachinas, pottery, rugs, sandpaintings,
sculpture, carvings. *Membership*: IACA.

RAINDANCE TRADERS
Box 3262, 103 E. Broadway
Jackson, WY 83001-3262
(307) 733-1081
Barbara & Terry Kennedy
Retail. *Products*: All.

TWO GREY HILLS
Box 1252, 110 E. Broadway
Jackson, WY 83001-1252
(307) 733-2677
Gary Mattheis
Retail. *Products*: Baskets, dye charts, fetishes, heishi,
jewelry, kachinas, pottery, rugs, sandpaintings. *Mem-
bership*: IACA.

GRAND TETON NATIONAL PARK
Signal Mountain Lodge
P.O. Box 50 • Moran, WY 83013
(307) 543-2831 Fax 543-2569
Don Wallace, VP Retail
Retail. *Products*: Art, fetishes, jewelry, miniatures,
sandpaintings. *Membership*: IACA. *Winter address*:
Forever Resorts, P.O. Box 29041, Phoenix, AZ.

TW RECREATIONAL SERVICES, INC.
Yellowstone Park, WY 82190
(307) 344-5354 Fax (406) 848-7048
Peter White
Retail. *Products*: All. *Membership*: IACA.

TRIBAL ENTERPRISES

**BIEN MUR INDIAN MARKETING CENTER,
Albuquerque, NM**
(Sandia Pueblo Tribal Enterprise)

KENOO, Callaway, MN
(Ojibwe Tribal Enterprise)

MOAPA TRIBAL ENTERPRISES, Moapa, NV
(Paiute Tribal Enterprises)

**NAVAJO ARTS/CRAFTS ENTERPRISES,
Window Rock, AZ**
(Navajo Tribal Enterprise)

PUEBLO OF ZUNI ARTS & CRAFTS, Zuni, NM
(Zuni Pueblo Tribal Enterprise)

QUALLA ARTS & CRAFTS, Cherokee, NC
(Eastern Cherokee Tribal Enterprise)

**SOUTHERN UTE MUSEUM & GIFT SHOP,
Ignacio, CO**
(Southern Ute Tribal Enterprise)

AUSTRALIA

AMERICAN INDIAN TRADING CO.
P.O. Box 367
Manly, N.S.W. 2095
011-02-938-5278
Ann O'Bryan, Kerry O'Bryan, Suzy Rochester
Wholesale, retail. *Products*: Art, beadwork, clothing,
dolls, jewelry, kachinas, rugs, sandpaintings, sculpture,
carvings. *Membership*: IACA.

THE CORN MAIDEN
P.O. Box 45
Ormeau, 4208 Queensland
011-61-07-210-0518
Kym Quinn, Owner
Wholesale, retail. *Products*: Art, beadwork, clothing,
dolls, jewelry, kachinas, pottery, sandpaintings, sculpture, carvings. *Membership*: IACA. *Branch*: 66 Charlotte St., Brisbane 4000.

THE COWBOY FROM DOWN UNDER
Dolphin Arcade-Surfer's Paradise
Queensland 4217
011-61-07-592-0525
Wholesale, retail. *Products*: Art, clothing, dolls, jewelry, kachinas, rugs, sandpaintings, sculpture, carvings. *Membership*: IACA.

THUNDER DOWN UNDER
P.O. Box 903, 85 Grafton St.
Mareeba, Queensland 4880
011-61-07-051-1040
Greg & Jana Whittaker, Owners
Wholesale, retail. *Products*: Art, beadwork, clothing,
dolls, jewelry, kachinas, rugs, sandpaintings, sculpture,
carvings. *Membership*: IACA.

TWO FEATHERS TURQUOISE GALLERY
1 The Crescent
Sassafras 3787, Victoria
011-61-03-755-1072 (Phone & Fax)
Jacqueline & Paul Johnson, Owners
Wholesale, retail. *Products*: All. *Membership*: IACA.

VELVET IMPORTS
P.O. Box 349 Donacster
Melbourne, Victoria
011-61-03-848-2207
Bob & Zandra Heywood, Owners
Retail. *Products*: Art, beadwork, clothing, dolls, jew-
elry, kachinas, rugs, sandpaintings, sculpture, carv-
ings. *Membership*: IACA.

BELGIUM

SPRL. CURIOS
36 Rue de Dampremy
6000 - Charleroi
011-32-07-132-1339 Fax 136-0324
Leon Gobillon, Owner
Wholesale, retail. *Products*: Jewelry, miniatures, s
culpture. *Membership*: IACA.

CANADA

ARCTIC CO-OPERATIVES LTD.
1741 Wellington Ave.
Winnipeg, Manitoba R3H 0G1
(204) 786-4481
Terry Thompson, Owner
Wholesale. *Membership*: IACA.

WOLFWALKER ENT.
30 Hatt St.
Dundas, Ontario L9H 2E8
(416) 627-1400
Wolf & Myrna Prudek, Owners
Wholesale, retail. *Products*: Art, Northwest Coast art,
fetishes, jewelry, kachinas, pottery, sculpture. *Membership*: IACA.

GERMANY

VONHAND DESIGN
Frankfurter Str. 8
61118 Bad Vilbel
011-49-61-018-7938
Oliver Will & Isolde Eberle, Owners
Wholesale, retail. *Products*: Art, beadwork, clothing,
dolls, jewelry, kachinas, pottery, rugs, sandpaintings.
Membership: IACA.

ARIZONA-GALERIE GAST & MORTELL GMBH
Grosse Bockenheimer
Strasse 37
6000 Frankfurt/Main 1
011-49-06-928-7379 Fax 928-3362
Anja & Hildegard Gast, Owners
Retail. *Products*: Art, beadwork, clothing, dolls, jewelry, kachinas, pottery, rugs, sandpaintings, sculpture,
carvings. *Membership*: IACA.

NAVAJO SILVER
Schmiedstrasse 2
3342 Gields
  011-49-05-339-541 Fax 339-740
  Hans-Jurgen & Le-Thu Grimm, Owners
Wholesale, retail. *Products*: Art, beadwork, clothing, dolls, jewelry, kachinas, sandpaintings, sculpture, carvings. *Membership*: IACA. *Branch Shop*: Weenderstrasse 75, 3400 Gottingen.

TRADING POST
Wilstorfer Str. 72
21073 Hamburg
  011-49-40-765-9699 Fax 765-6879
Wholesale, retail. *Products*: Beadwork, clothing, dolls, jewelry, kachinas, sandpaintings, sculpture, carvings. *Membership*: IACA.

CHEROKEE WIGWAM
Ringseestr 9
85053 Ingolstadt-Sud
  0-11-49-03-416-9541
  A. Weger, Liselotte Nichols, Owners
Wholesale/retail. *Products*: Jewelry, sandpaintings. *Membership*: IACA.

RIO GRANDE
Yantener Str. 42
Meerbusch-Strl"mp 40670
  02159-6466
  Carl Shroeter, Owner
Retail, wholesale. Products: All Indian arts & crafts. Brochure & catalog. Branch shops.

HHS EXPORT TRADING CO., WINZLAR
Westerfeld 18
31547 Rehburg-Loccum
  05037-3513
  Hermann & Maria Schmidt, Owners
Wholesale, retail, mail order. *Products*: Native American, Western and Southwestern products. *Appraisal*: Art, jewelry, kachinas, pottery, sandpaintings, sculpture, carvings. *Membership*: IACA. Brochure & catalog. Branch shop: Germany.

RED CLOUD INDIAN STORE
Rossbachstr. 16
88212 Ravensburg
  011-47-7-511-3755 (phone & fax)
  Michael Gribulis & Katharina Meyer
Wholesale, retail. Products: Art, beadwork, clothing, dolls, jewelry, kachinas, sandpaintings, sculpture, carvings. *Membership*: IACA.

AMERICAN ART GALLERY
Bahnhofstrasse 29
D-6632 Saarwellingen
  011-49-6-838-6791
  Hubert & Marlene Masloh
Wholesale, retail. *Product*: Art. *Membership*: IACA.

JAPAN

GALLERY SEDONA
16-61 Kita 5-Chome, Higashikaigan
Chigasaki, Kanagawa-Pref. 253
  011-81-0467-87-0811 Fax 0467-88-0058
  Shigeo Niida, Owmer
Retail, some mail order. *Products*: Art, beadwork, clothing, dolls, jewelry, kachinas, pottery, rugs, sandpaintings. *Membership*: IACA. Brochure. Kamakura branch shop: Goshoudou Bld. 2-8-16, Komachi, Kamakura, Kanagawa. 248

INDIAN CRAFT CO., LTD.
5-5-10 Akasada
Minato, Tokyo 107
  011-81-03-586-3737
  Ms. Ayako Umemoto & Sumie Matsuda
Wholesale. *Products*: Heishi, jewelry, pottery, rugs, sandpaintings. *Membership*: IACA.

JIMMIE D. WARNELL
U.S. Embassy, Tokyo, Japan
Unit 45004, Box 201 • APO AT 96337-5004
  Jimmie D. Warnell, Owner
Retail, mail order. Cherokee craftsperson.
Products: Silver products, sterling silver jewelry.

NETHERLANDS

CLASSIC WESTERN HOUSE
Kalverstraat 154
1012 XE Amsterdam
  011-31-020-622-3329
  Henk & Ilona Stots
Retail. *Products*: Art, beadwork, clothing, dolls, jewelry, kachinas, rugs. *Membership*: IACA.

NATIONAL INDIAN GAMING ASSOCIATION
224 2nd Ave., SE • Washington, DC 20003
(202) 546-7711 Fax 546-1755
Rick Hill, Chairperson
Jacob Coin, Executive Director
Activities: Holds Indian Gaming Enterprise and Management Law Seminars; and Annual Convention and Trade Show. Professional training for tribal casino management, staff, and for tribal start up operations.

**NATIONAL INDIAN GAMING
& HOSPITALITY INSTITUTE**
College of the Menominee Nation
P.O. Box 1179 • Keshena, WI 54135
(715) 799-5600 Fax 799-1308
Dr. Verna Fowler, Contact
Purpose: To explore and address economic, social and cultural issues related to the development of gaming enterprises on American Indian reservations; to provide certificate and associate degree education programs designed to expand the trained workforce with expertise in Indian gaming nationally; to establish a central clearinghouse and library; and a new gaming product development center.

INDIAN OWNED CASINOS
& BINGO HALLS

ALABAMA

CREEK TRIBE CASINO & BINGO PALACE
Hwy. 21 South at Poarch Rd.
ATMORE, AL 36502
(800) 826-9121; (251) 368-8007
Website: www.creekbingo.com

ARIZONA

At least 14 Arizona tribes have signed gaming compacts with the state of Arizona. 17 casinos are open or in the planning stage. The only legal casino gaming in Arizona is conducted by Indian tribes.

CLIFF CASTLE CASINO
555 Middle Verde Rd., P.O. Box 56677
CAMP VERDE, AZ 86322 (800) 381-7568
(928) 567-7999 Fax 567-3994
Website: www.cliffcastle.com
Owned by the Pascua Yaqui Tribe. *Location*: in Camp Verde. *Facility*: 10,000 sq. feet. 475 slots, video poker, poker tables. 82 hotel rooms.

LONE BUTTE CASINO
1200 S. 56th St., P.O. Box 5074
CHANDLER, AZ 85226 (800) 946-4452
(520) 796-7777 Fax 796-7712
Website: wingilariver.com
Owned and operated by the Gila River Pima-Maricopa Indian Community. *Location*: 25 miles southeast of Phoenix. *Facility*: 30,000 sq. ft. 300 slots; video poker/blackjack/keno. Bingo. Open 24 hours, 7 days a week.

WILD HORSE PASS CASINO
5550 W. Wild Horse Pass
CHANDLER, AZ 85226 (800) 946-4452
(520) 796-7777 Fax 796-7712
Website: wingilariver.com
Owned and operated by the Gila River Pima-Maricopa Indian Community. Facility: 750 slots; 100 video poker/blackjack/keno/roulette. Bingo.

FORT McDOWELL CASINO
Fort McDowell Rd. & State Rd. 87
P.O. Box 11839
FOUNTAIN HILLS, AZ 85269
(602) 837-1427 Fax 837-0844
(800) 843-3678, Betty Humphries, Contact
Website: www.fortmcdowellcasino.com
Owned by the Fort McDowell Yavapai Nation. *Location*: 20 miles east of Phoenix. *Facility*: 120,000 sq. feet. 475 slots; video poker/blackjack/keno; 40 poker tables. Bingo. Open 24 hours, 7 days a week.

PIPE SPRINGS RESORT & CASINO
HC 65, Box 3 • FREDONIA, AZ 86022
(520)643-7777 Fax 643-7260
(800) WIN-7477
Owned by the Kaibab-Paiute Indian Community. *Location*: 200 miles northwest of Flagstaff, north of Grand Canyon National Park, 4 miles from Utah border on Hwy. 89. *Facility*: 7,000 sq. feet. Slots, video poker/keno.

VEE QUIVA CASINO
6443 N. Komatke Ln. • LAVEEN, AZ
(800) 946-4452; (520) 796-7777
Website: www.wingilariver.com
Owned and operated by the Gila River Pima Maricopa Indian Community. *Location*: Off I-10 West at the corner of 51 Ave and Komatke Lane. *Facility*: 69,000 sq. ft. 500 slots; ten poker tables; 6 blackjack tables; bingo; live keno.

HARRAH'S PHOENIX AK-CHIN CASINO
15406 N. Maricopa Rd. • MARICOPA, AZ 85239
(800) 427-7247; (480) 802-5000 Fax 802-5050
Martin J. Antone, Sr., Contact
Website: www.harrahs.com
Owned by the Ak-Chin Indian Tribe. Operated by Harrah's. *Location*: 35 miles south of Phoenix, I-10 exit 162A. *Facility*: 72,000 sq. feet, with a gaming area of 29,500 sq. feet. 475 slots, 40 table games. Open 24 hours.

HUALAPAI CASINO
Grand Canyon West
P.O. Box 761 • MEADVILLE, AZ 86444
(602) 699-4161
Owned by the Hualapai Indian Tribe. *Location*: 50 miles north of Kingman, Ariz. *Facility*: Slots, video poker/keno.

SPIRIT MOUNTAIN CASINO
8555 S. Hwy. 95, P.O. Box 6588
MOHAVE VALLEY, AZ 86440
(928) 346-2000 Fax 326-2468
Website: www.spiritmountainmojave.casinocity.com
Owned by the Fort Mojave Indian Tribe. *Location*: South of Bullhead City, Arizona, off I-40 on Hwy. 95, 1 mile northeast of the Needles bridge. *Facilities*: 6,500 sq. ft. 200 slots; video poker/keno.

BLUE WATER RESORT & CASINO
11300 Resort Dr. • PARKER, AZ 85344
(888) 243-3360; (928) 669-7000 Fax 669-5910
Website: www.bluewaterfun.com
Owned by the Colorado River Indian Tribes. *Location*: In Parker, 160 miles west of Phoenix on the Colorado River. *Facility*: 20,000 sq. ft. 470 slots; 50 video blackjack games; live poker, keno, bingo. Conference Center and amphitheater.

MAZATZAL CASINO
Hwy. 87, P.O. Box 1820
PAYSON, AZ 85547
(800) 777-7529; (928) 474-6044 Fax 474-4238
Website: www.777play.com
Owned by the Tonto Apache Tribe. *Location*: One-half mile south of Payson, 75 miles northeast of Phoenix on Hwy. 87. *Facility*: 35,000 sq. feet. 400 slots, video poker/keno; live poker & blkackjack, keno. Bingo.

HON-DAH CASINO
777 Hwy. 260, P.O. Box 3250
PINETOP, AZ 85953 (800) 929-8744
(928) 369-0299 Fax 369-0382
Website: www.hon-dah.com
Owned by the White Mountain Apache Tribe. *Location*: 190 miles northeast of Phoenix on Hwy. 73 & 260. *Facility*: 4,200 sq. feet. 600 slots, 54 video poker, 8 video keno, 12 seat keno, 8 video blackjack. blackjack tables; 2 poker tables. Hotel with 128 rooms.

BUCKY'S CASINO
1500 E. Hwy. 69 • PRESCOTT, AZ 86301
(800) 756-8744; (928) 778-7909
Website: www.buckyscasino.com
Owned by the Yavapai Prescott Indian Tribe. *Location*: 96 miles north of Phoenix, east of downtown Prescott Junction off Hwy. 69 & 89. *Facility*: 300 slots; blackjack and roulette tables. Open 24 hours, 7 days. 161 room Prescott Resort Hotel.

YAVAPAI CASINO
1501 E. Hwy 69
PRESCOTT, AZ 86301
(928) 445-5767; (800) 756-8744
Website: www.buckyscasino.com
Owned by the Yavapai Prescott Indian Tribe. *Location*: 96 miles north of Phoenix, east of downtown Prescott Junction off Hwy. 69 & 89. *Facility*: 175 video and reel slots, video poker, video keno, 2,000 seat bingo (Tue.-Sun.)

APACHE GOLD CASINO RESORT
P.O. Box 1210
SAN CARLOS, AZ 85550
(800) APACHE-8; (520) 425-7692 Fax 425-7696
Website: www.apachegoldcasinoresort.com
Owned by the San Carlos Apache Tribe. *Location*: 5 miles east of Globe and 110 miles east of Phoenix on Hwy. 70. *Facility*: 12,000 sq. feet. 500 video and reel slots; video poker, keno, and blackjack; and table games. Convention Center and Best Western Hotel.

CASINO ARIZONA AT INDIAN BEND/SALT RIVER
P.O. Box 10099
SCOTTSDALE, AZ 85256
(480) 850-7777
Website: www.casinoaz.com
Owned by the Salt River Pima-Maricopa Indian Community.

DESERT DIAMOND CASINO I-19
1100 West Pima Mine Rd.
SELLS, AZ 85634
(520) 294-7777; (866) DDCWINS
Website: www.desertdiamond.com
Owned by the Tohono O'Odham Nation,

COCOPAH BINGO & CASINO
15136 S. Ave, Box G
SOMERTON, AZ 85350
(800) 23-SLOTS; (520) 726-8066 Fax 344-8010
Website: www.casinosun.com
Owned by the Cocopah Tribe. *Location*: 13 miles southwest of Yuma on Hwy. 95. *Facility*: 32,000 sq. feet. 475 slots, video poker and keno; bingo. Open Sun-Thurs. 6 am - 2 am; Fri-Sat., 24 hours.

CASINO OF THE SUN
7406 Camino de Oeste Rd.
TUCSON, AZ 85746
(800) 344-9435; (520) 883-1700 Fax 883-0983
Owned by Pascua Yaqui Indian Tribe. *Location*: South of downtown Tucson. *Facility*: 24,500 sq. feet. 400 slots, 15 poker tables, video keno and poker; keno; 15 poker & blackjack tables; bingo. Open 24 hours, 7 days.

DESERT DIAMOND CASINO
7350 S. Nogales Hwy.
TUCSON, AZ 85734
(520) 294-7777; (866) DDCWINS
Website: www.desertdiamond.com
Bruce Phillips, Contact
Owned by the Tohono O'Odham Nation. *Location*: South of Tucson. *Facilities*: 45,000 sq. feet. 2,600 slots, video poker/keno; keno, poker, blackjack, craps.

THE WHITE MOUNTAIN APACHE CASINO
P.O. Box 700 • WHITERIVER, AZ 85941
(520) 338-4346
Owned by the White Mountain Apache Tribe. *Location*: South of Show Low, AZ, on Hwy. 60. *Facility*: 1,800 electronic gaming machines.

FORT YUMA QUECHAN PARADISE CASINO
450 Quechan Dr. • YUMA, AZ 85366
(888) 777-4946; (760) 572-7777
Website: www.paradise-casinos.com
Owned by the Quechan Tribe. *Facilities*: 735 gaming machines for video keno, reel slots, video poker and 8 poker tables, live keno and blackjack tables. 5 bingo rooms.

GOLDEN HA:SAN CASINO
Highway 86 • WHY, AZ 85730
(866) 332-9467; (520) 362-2746
Operated by the Tohono O'odham Tribe. *Location*: On the way to Organ Pipe National Park and Rocky Point, Mexico. *Facilities*: Slot machines.

CALIFORNIA

VIEJAS CASINO & TURF CLUB
5000 Willows Rd. • ALPINE, CA 91901
(800) 847-6537; (619) 445-5400
Website: www.viejas.com
Owned by the Viejas Tribe of Indians. *Location*: 30 miles east of San Diego off Interstate Hwy. 8 on the Viejas Indian Reservation. *Facility*: 100,000 sq. ft. 25 gaming tables. Open 24 hours, 7 days.

ALTURAS CASINO
901 County Rd. 56
ALTURAS, CA 96101
(530) 233-3141 Fax 233-3170
Owned by the Pit River Tribe of Alturas Rancheria. *Location*: In Northern California, Modoc County, 170 miles north of Reno, Nevada on U.S. 395. *Facility*: 5,000 sq. ft; 88 slots; 2 tables; bingo.

CAHUILLA CREEK RESTAURANT & CASINO
52702 Hwy. 371 • ANZA, CA 92539
(909) 763-1200; Website: www.cahuilla.com
Owned by the Cahuilla Band of Mission Indians. *Location*: Minutes from Palm Springs, an hour from San Diego, and a half hour from Riverside. *Facilities*: 225 slots; video poker; multi-game machines and table games.

MONO WIND CASINO
37302 Rancheria Ln. • AUBERRY, CA 93602
(559) 855-4350 Fax 855-4351
Owned by the Mono Indians of the Big Sandy Rancheria. *Facilities*: 10,000 sq. ft. casino. 329 slots; 10 table games.

PAIUTE PALACE CASINO
2742 N. Sierra • BISHOP, CA 93514
(888) 372-4883; (760) 873-4150
Owned by the Bishop Paiute Tribe. *Location*: In the Owens Valley, north of Bishop on U.S. Hwy. 395 off I-15 and I-80. *Facilities*: 300 video slots, 38 video poker machines, gaming tables.

BLUE LAKE CASINO
P.O. Box 1128 • BLUE LAKE, CA 95525
(707) 668-5101
Website: www.bluelakecasino.com
Owned by the Blue Lake Rancheria.

CACHE CREEK BINGO & CASINO
14455 State Hwy. 16
P.O. Box 65 • BROOKS, CA 95616
(530) 796-3400 Fax (916) 796-2112
Website: www.cachecreek.com
Owned by the Rumsey Indian Rancheria. *Location*: On Interstate 5 & 505. *Facility*: 45,000 sq. feet. 250 slots, blackjack, poker, bingo. Open 24 hours.

PIT RIVER CASINO
20265 Tamarack Ave.
BURNEY, CA 96013
(888) 245-2992; (530) 335-2334
Owned by thew Pit River Tribe of California. Facilities: 8,600 sq. ft. casino. 130 slots, blackjack tables. Bingo.

MORONGO CASINO
49750 Seminole Dr.
P.O. Box 366 • CABAZON, CA 92230
(800) 252-4499; (714) 849-3080
Website: www.casinomorongo.com
Owned by the Morongo Band of Cahuilla Indians. *Location*: I-10, between Banning and Palm Springs. *Facility*: 100,000 sq. ft. 2,000 slots; 46 blackjack tables, 35 poker tables. Open 24 hours, 7 days a week.

COYOTE VALLEY SHODAKAI CASINO
P.O. Box 388 • CALPELLA, CA
(707) 485-0700 Fax 485-0730

AUGUSTINE CASINO
84-001 Avenue 54
COACHELLA, CA 92236
(888) PLAY 2 WIN; (760) 391-9500 Fax 398-4447
Website: www.augustinecasino.com
Owned by the Augustine Band of Cahuilla Indians. *Location*: East of PGA West on Avenue 54 at Van Buren.

TRUMP 29 CASINO
46-200 Harrison St.
COACHELLA, CA 92236
(760) 775-5566 Fax 775-4637
Owned by the Twenty Nine Palms Band of Mission Indians. *Location*: Interstate 10 at Dillon Rd. *Facility*: 74,000 sq. feet. 24 tables, poker, bingo. Open 24 hours.

COLUSA INDIAN BINGO & CASINO
3770 Hwy. 45, P.O. Box 1267
COLUSA, CA 95932
(800) 655-8946; (530) 458-8844 Fax 458-2018
Website: www.colusacasino.com
Owned by the Cachil DeHe Band of Wintun Indians of the Colusa Indian Community. *Facility*: 300 slots, poker, keno; Bingo.

ELK VALLEY CASINO
2500 Howland Hill Rd.
CRESCENT CITY, CA 95531
(888) 574-2744; (707) 464-1020 Fax 464-5188
Website: www.elkvalleycasino.com
Owned by the Yurok and Tolowa Nation of the Elk Valley Rancheria. *Facility*: 280 slots; gaming tables. Bingo.

SYCUAN INDIAN GAMING CENTER
5469 Dehasa Rd.
EL CAJON, CA 92019
(619) 445-2613 Fax 445-1961
Website: www.sycuancasino.com
Owned by the Sycuan Band of Mission Indians. *Location*: 18 miles east of San Diego on Interstate Hwy. I-8. *Facility*: 70,000 sq. feet. 368 slots, 25 poker tables; 40 video blackjack, 36 video keno, bingo. Open 24 hours.

TABLE MOUNTAIN CASINO
8184 Table Mountain Rd.
P.O. Box 445 • FRIANT, CA 93626
(559) 822-7777; (800) 541-3637
Website: www.tmcasino.com
Owned by the Yokut Tribe of the Table Mountain Rancheria. *Facility*: 250,000 sq. ft. 2,000 slots; blackjack & poker tables; bingo.

RIVER ROCK CASINO
3250 Hwy. 128
GEYSERVILLE, CA 95441
(707) 857-2777
Website: www.river-rock-casino.com
Owned by the Dry Creek Rancheria Band of Pomo Indians.

HAVASU LANDING RESORT & CASINO
P.O. Box 1707
HAVASU LAKE, CA 92363
(800) 307-3610
Website: www.havasulanding.com
Owned by the Chemehuevi Tribe.
Location: The western shores of th Lake Havasu.

SAN MANUEL INDIAN BINGO & CASINO
5797 N. Victoria Ave.
HIGHLAND, CA 92346
(800) 359-2464
(909) 864-5050 Fax 862-3405
Website: www.sanmanuel.com
Ownd by the San Manuel Band of Mission Indians. *Location*: 7 miles from downtown San Bernadino, off Hwy. 30 E. *Facility*: 2,000 slots, 45 poker tables; bingo. Open 24 hours, 7 days a week. Opened in 1986.

HOPLAND SHOKAWAH CASINO & BINGO
13101 Nakomis Rd.
HOPLAND, CA 95449
(888) 745-5292
(707) 744-1395 Fax 744-1698
Website: www.shokawah.com
Owned by the Shokawah Band of Pomo Indians of the Hopland Reservation. *Location*: 45 minutes north of Santa Rosa in Northern California. *Facilities*: 1,200 slots, 16 table games. Bingo.

LUCKY BEAR CASINO & BINGO
P.O. Box 1348 • HOOPA, CA 95546
(530) 625-4211 Fax 625-4594
Owned by the Hoopa Valley Tribe of the Hoopa Valley Indian Reservation.

FANTASY SPRINGS CASINO
84-245 Indio Springs Dr.
INDIO, CA 92203
(800) 827-2964
(760) 342-5000 Fax 347-7880
Website: www.fantasyspringsresort.com
Dan Comiskey, Executive Director
Joe DeRosa, General Manager
Owned by the Cabazon Band of Mission Indians. *Location*: 24 miles east of Palm Springs on Hwy. I-10. *Facility*: 265,000 sq. feet. 2,000 slots, 39 poker tables. 800 video games (poker, keno, blackjack). Bingo.

SPOTLIGHT 29 CASINO
46-200 Harrison St.
INDIO, CA 92201
(619) 775-5566 Fax 775-4638
Owned by the Cabazon Band of Mission Indians. *Location*: 25 miles east of Palm Springs on Interstate Hwy. I-10. *Facility*: 105,000 sq. feet. 24 poker tables; bingo

JACKSON INDIAN BINGO & CASINO
12222 New York Ranch Rd.
P.O. Box 1390
JACKSON, CA 95642
(800) 822-WINN
(209) 223-1677 Fax 223-5371
Website: www.jacksoncasino.com/index.htm
Owned by the Jackson Rancheria Band of Me-wuk Indians. *Location*: Off Hwy. 88 or Hwy. 49. *Facility*: 5 poker tables; bingo. Open 24 hours.

CHICKEN RANCH BINGO
16929 Chicken Ranch Rd.
JAMESTOWN, CA 95327
(800) 75-BINGO
(209) 984-3000 Fax 984-4158
Owned by the Chicken Ranch Band of Me-wuk Indians. *Facility*: 100,000 sq. feet. 100 slots; bingo.

KONOCTI VISTA CASINO RESORT & MARINA
2755 Mission Rancheria Rd.
LAKEPORT, CA 95453
(800) 386-1950; (707) 262-1900
Owned by the Pomo Indians of Big Valley & Scotts Valley Rancherias.

BARONA VALLEY RANCH RESORT & CASINO
1932 Wildcat Canyon Rd.
LAKESIDE, CA 92040
(888) 7-BARONA
(619) 443-2300 Fax 443-2856
Website: www.barona.com
E-mail: info@barona.com
Owned by the Barona Band of Mission Indians. *Location*: Located in the Barona Valley, 21 miles east of San Diego on Hwy. 67. *Facilities*: 115,000 Sq. feet. Bingo. 2,000 slots; 63 table games; 400-room hotel, golf course and event center. Open 24 hours, 7 days a week.

RED FOX CASINO
200 Cahto Dr.
LAYTONVILLE, CA 95454
(888) 473-3369
(707) 984-6800 Fax 984-6500
Owned by the Cahto Tribe of the Laytonville Rancheria. *Facility*: 3,600 sq. ft. 93 slots.

PALACE INDIAN GAMING CENTER
172225 Jersey Ave.
P.O. Box 308 • LEMOORE, CA 93245
(209) 924-7751 Fax 924-7526
Website: www.thepalace.net
Owned and operated by the Tachi Yokut of the Santa Rosa Rancheria. *Facilities*: 2,000 gaming devices; table games & bingo. Open 24 hours, 7 days a week.

TWIN PINE CASINO
P.O. Box 789
MIDDLETOWN, CA 95461
(707) 987-2958
Website: www.twinpine.com
Owned by the Lake Miwok Indian Nation of the Middletown Rancheria.

ROBINSON RANCHERIA BINGO & CASINO
1545 E. Hwy. 20 • NICE, CA 95464
(800) 809-3636; (707) 275-9000 Fax 275-9440
Website: www.robinsonrancheria.biz
Owned by the Robinson Rancheria Pomo Indians. *Location*: 30 miles east of Hwy. 101 between Nice and Upper Lake. *Facility*: 37,500 sq. feet. 285 slots; video poker, keno; 12 table games, poker & blackjack; Bingo. Open 24 hours a day, 7 days a week.

FEATHER FALLS CASINO
3 Alverda Dr.
OROVILLE, CA 95966
(800) 652-4646 Fax (530) 533-4465
Website: www.featherfallscasino.com
Owned by the Concow and Maidu Tribes of the Mooretown Rancheria. *Facilities*: 1,000 slots, gaming tables, poker rooms.

GOLD COUNTRY CASINO
4020 Olive Hwy.
OROVILLE, CA 95966
(530) 534-3859 Fax 534-9173
Owned by the Tyme Maidu Tribe of the Berry Creek Rancheria.

SPA RESORT & CASINO
401 E. Amado Rd.
PALM SPRINGS, CA 92262
(800) 258-2946; (760) 883-1000
Website: sparesortcasino.com
Owned by the Agua Caliente Band of Mission Indians. *Location*: Downtown Palm Springs. *Facility*: 40,000 sq. ft. casino. 900 slots; 30 gaming tables. Hotel & Mineral Springs Spa has 228 rooms.

EAGLE MOUNTAIN CASINO
P.O. Box 1659
PORTERVILLE, CA 93258
(209) 788-6220 Fax 788-6223
Owned by the Yokut Indians of the Tule River Reservation.

AGUA CALIENTE CASINO
32-250 Bob Hope Dr.
RANCHO MIRAGE, CA 92270
(760) 321-2000
Website: www.hotwatercasino.com
Owned by the Agua Caliente Band of Cahuilla Indians. *Location*: Intersection of Bob Hope Dr. and Ramon Rd. at I-10 in Rancho Mirage, minutes from downtown Palm Springs. *Facility*: 45,000 sq. ft. casino. 1,100+ reel slots, video poker and progressives; 10 poker tables and 32 gaming tables. Bingo.

WIN-RIVER CASINO BINGO
2100 Redding Rancheria Rd.
REDDING, CA 96001
(530) 225-8979 FAX 243-0337
Website: www.win-river.com
Owned by the tribes of the Redding Rancheria.

SOBOBA-LEGENDS CASINO
23333 Soboba Rd.
SAN JACINTO, CA 92583
(866) 4-SOBOBAZ; (909) 665-1000
Owned by the Soboba Band of Mission Indians. *Location*: Between Ramona Expressway and Interstate 10. *Facility*: 75,000 sq. feet; 2,000 slots, 21 gaming tables, blackjack, poker; bingo. Open 24 hours, 7 days a week.

CHUMASH CASINO RESORT
3400 Hwy. 246
SANTA YNEZ, CA 93460
(877) CHUMASH; (800) 728-9997
(805) 686-0855
Owned by the Santa Ynez Chumash Indians. *Location*: In Santa Barbara County on Hwy 101 to Solvang exit then 6 miles east to Resort. *Facility*: 2,000 slots; blackjack tables, 14 poker tables; bingo. Hotel with 106 rooms. Open 24 hours, 7 days a week.

LUCKY 7 CASINO
350 N. Indian Rd.
SMITH RIVER, CA 95567
(707) 487-9255 Fax 487-5077
Owned by the Tolowa Tribe of the Smith River Rancheria.

SUSANVILLE CASINO
900 Skyline Dr.
SUSANVILLE, CA 96130
(916) 257-6264 Fax 252-111
Owned by the Susanville Indian Rancheria.

PECHANGA RESORT & CASINO
45000 Pechanga Pkwy.
P.O. Box 9041
TEMECULA, CA 92589-9041
(877) 711-2WIN; (909) 693-1819 Fax 695-7410
Website: www.pechanga.com
E-mail: info@pechanga.com
Norman Pico, Contact
Owned by the Pechanga Band of Luiseno Mission Indians. *Location*: In the Temecula Valley just 20 miles from the Pacific Ocean. *Facility*: 88,000 square foot casino; 2,000 slots, 60 tables, 27-table poker room; 700-seat bingo. *Activities*: Fourth of July weekend Powwow.

CHER-AE HEIGHTS CASINO
P.O. Box 610, 1 Cher-Ae Lane
TRINIDAD, CA 95570
(800) 684-2464; (707) 677-3611
Website: www.cheraeheightscasino.com
Owned by the Cher-Ae Heights Indian Community of The Trinidad Rancheria.

BLACK OAK CASINO
19400 Tuolumne Rd. North
TUOLUMNE, CA 95379 (877) 747-8777
(209) 928-9300
Website: www.blackoakcasino.com
Owned by the Tuolumne band of Me-Wuk Indians of the Tuolumne rancheria. Location: 8 miles east of Sonora off Hwy. 108.

BLACK BART CASINO
100 Kawi Place • WILLITS, CA 95490
(707) 459-7330 Fax 459-7337
Website: www.blackbartcasino.com
Owned by the Pomo Indians of the Sherwood Valley Rancheria. Location: On U.S. Hwy 101, 140 miles north of San Francisco. Facility: 185 slots.

COLORADO

SKY UTE LODGE & CASINO
P.O. Box 340 • IGNACIO, CO 81137
(800) 876-7017; (888) 842-4150
(970) 563-3000 Fax 563-9546
Website: www.skyutecasino.com
Owned by the Southern Ute Indian Tribe. *Location*: 25 miles south of Durango on Hwy. 172. *Facility*: 24,000 sq. feet. 400 slots; table games. 36 room hotel and conference center. Open 24 hours, 7 days a week

UTE MOUNTAIN CASINO, HOTEL & RESORT
3 Weeminuche Dr.
TOWAOC, CO 81334
(800) 258-8007; (970) 565-8800 Fax 565-7276
Owned by the Ute Mountain Ute Indians. *Location*: 11 miles south of Cortez on Hwy. 160 & 666, 425 miles southwest of Denver. *Facility*: 30,000 sq. feet. 373 slots; table games; bingo. Open 8 am - 4 am daily.

CONNECTICUT

FOXWOODS RESORT & CASINO
39 Norwich-Westerly Rd.
P.O. Box 410
LEDYARD, CT 06339
(800) FOXWOODS ; (860) 312-3000
Website: www.foxwoods.com
G. Michael Brown, President
Owned by the Mashantucket Pequot Tribe. *Location*: Southeastern Connecticut, northeast of New London, Connecticut, 8 miles west of I-95 off exit 92 on State Road 2. *Facility*: 250,000 sq. ft. 6,500 slots; 237 table games; 400 video poker; 140 blackjack tables; 60 poker tables, 24 crap tables; 26 roulette tables; 4 mini-baccarat. 320 room hotel. 3,200 seat Bingo hall. Open 24 hours.

MOHEGAN SUN CASINO
Mohegan Sun Blvd., P.O. Box 548
UNCASVILLE, CT 06382
(888) 226-7711; (860) 204-8000 Fax 204-7419
Website: www.mohegansun.som
Owned by the Mohegan Indian Tribe. *Location*: 15 miles west of Ledyard and Foxwoods; One mile from the interchange of I-395 and CT Rt. 2. *Facility*: 300,000 sq. feet. New delux Indian hotel casino complex with 1,176 rooms and 175 suites. 6,300 slots, 300 video poker, 141 table games; 10,000-seat arena for sporting events and concerts. Open 24 hours.

FLORIDA

SEMINOLE CASINO-BRIGHTON CREEK
West of Okeechobee, Hwy. 721
OKEECHOBEE, FL
(866) 2-CASINO; (954) 977-6700
Website: www. seminoletribe.com
Owned by the Seminole Tribe of Florida. *Facility*: 240 machines, 10 poker tables; 500-seat bingo hall. Opened daily at 10 a.m. Tues.-Sunday.

SEMINOLE CASINO-COCONUT CREEK
5550 Northwest 40th St.
COCONUT CREEK, FL
(866) 2-CASINO; (954) 977-6700
Website: www. seminoletribe.com
Owned by the Seminole Tribe of Florida.

SEMINOLE INDIAN CASINO-IMMOKALEE
506 1st St. • IMMOKALEE, FL 33934
(800) 218-0007; (941) 658-1313 Fax 658-1515
Website: www.seminoletribe.com
Owned by the Seminole Indian Tribe. *Location*: 25 miles southwest of Ft. Myers Airport. *Facility*: 525 video gaming machines, 15 poker tables; 500-seat high stakes bingo. Open 24 hours.

SEMINOLE CASINO-HOLLYWOOD
4150 N. State Rd. 7
HOLLYWOOD, FL 33021
(800) 323-5452; (954) 961-3220
Website: www.seminoletribe.com
Owned by Seminole Tribe of Florida. *Location*: 5 miles southwest of Ft. Lauderdale. *Facility*: 1,000 slots, video pull tabs, low 33 poker tables; 800-seat high stakes bingo hall. Open 24 hours, 7 days a week.

MICCOSUKEE RESORT & GAMING
500 SW 177th Ave. • MIAMI, FL 33194
(800) 741-4600; (877) 242-6464; (305) 925-2555
Website: www.miccosukee.com
Owned by the Miccosukee Tribe of Florida. *Facility*: 1,000 slots, Video pull tabs, 58 poker yables, 1,300-seat bingo hall. Open 24 hours, 7 days a week.

SEMINOLE HARD ROCK HOTEL & CASINO-TAMPA
5223 N. Orient Rd. • TAMPA, FL 33610
(800) 282-7016; (813) 627-7625
Website: www.seminoletribe.com
Owned by the Seminole Indian Tribe. *Facility*: 90,000 sq. ft. 1,850 slots; video pull tabs, 32 poker tables. Open 24 hours, 7 days a week.

IDAHO

KOOTENAI RIVER INN & CASINO
Kootenai River Plaza, Hwy. 95
BONNERS FERRY, ID 83805
(800) 346-5668' (208) 267-8511
Website: www.kootenairiverinn.com
Owned by the Kootenai Tribe of Idaho. *Location*: 27 miles from the Canadian border on U.S. Hwy. 95. *Facility*: 400 slots. bingo, and video pull-tabs

SHOBAN CAINO-EXIT 80 CASINO
Exit 80 off I-15 • FORT HALL, ID 83203
(800) 497-4231; (208) 237-8778
Website: www.sho-ban.com
Owned and operated by the Shoshone Bannock Tribes of the Fort Hall Reservation. *Location*: Five miles north of Pocatello. *Facilities*: Slots, 800-seat bingo room.

IT'SE-YE-YE BINGO & CASINO
404 Main St. • KAMIAH, ID 83536
(877) 678-7423; (208) 935-1019
Website: www.crcasino.com
Owned and operated by the Nez Perce
Tribal Gaming Enterprise.

CLEARWATER RIVER CASINO
17500 Nez Perce Rd.
LEWISTON, ID 83501
(877) NP-TRIBE; (208) 746-0723
Website: www.crcasino.com
Owned and operated by the Nez Perce Tribal Gaming
Enterprise. *Facility:* 18,000 sq. ft. Slots, bingo, video
lottery terminals. Open 24 hours, 7 days a week.

COEUR D'ALENE CASINO RESORT HOTEL
P.O. Box 236 • WORLEY, ID 83876
(800) 523-2464; (208) 686-0248 Fax 686-1503
Website: www.cdacasino.com
Owned by the Coeur d'Alene Tribe. *Location:* Northern Idaho on U.S. Hwy. 95, 30 miles south of Coeur
d'Alene and I-90. *Facility:* 41,700 sq. ft. casino; 1,400+
Video slots, video pull-tabs, tables; high stakes bingo.
11,000 sq. ft. convention & meetin center. Open 24
hours, 7 days a week. *Activities:* Annual Tribe Encampment and Pow Wow in July in Post Falls, Idaho, the
largest outdoor Pow Wow in the Northwest.

IOWA

CASINO OMAHA
17214 21-th St., P.O. Box 89
ONAWA, IA 51040
(800) 858-UBET; (712) 423-3700
Owned by the Omaha Tribe of Nebraska. *Location:* 32
miles south of Sioux City, Iowa; or 60 miles north of
Omaha Nebraska. *Facility:* 30,000 sq. feet. 450 slots;
25 table games. Open 24 hours weekends; 8 am - 2
am weekdays.

WINNAVEGAS
1500 330th St., P.O. Box AE
SLOAN, IA 51055
(800) 468-9466; (712) 428-9466
Owned by the Winnebago Tribe of Nebraska. *Location:* 20 miles south of Sioux City, 3 miles west of Hwy.
I-29 exit 127. *Facility:* 45,000 sq. feet. 715 slots, video
poker & keno; 25 tables. Open 24 hours.

MESQUAKI BINGO & CASINO
1504 305th St. • TAMA, IA 52339
(800) 728-4263 (515) 484-2108
Owned by the Sac & Fox Indian Tribe of Mississippi in
Iowa. *Location:* 40 miles west of Cedar Rapids, Iowa.
Facility: 577 Slots and table games. Open 24 hours daily.

KANSAS

GOLDEN EAGLE CASINO
1121 Goldfinch Rd., Rte. 1, Box 149
HORTON, KS 66439
(888) GO-4-LUCK; (785) 486-6601
Website: www.goldeneaglecasino.com
Owned by the Kickapoo Tribe. *Location:* 45 miles north
of Topeka off U.S. Hwy. 75 on K20 5 miles west of
Horton. *Facility:* Slots & video poker; table games;
poker.

HARRAH'S PRAIRIE BAND CASINO
14880 "K" Rd. • MAYETTA, KS 66509
(785) 966-2255 Fax 966-7640
Website: www.harrahs.com
Owned by the Prairie Band Potawatomi Tribe. *Location:* Off Hwy. 75 west of Mayetta. *Facility:* 60,000 sq.
feet. Slots & video poker; table games; bingo.

SAC & FOX CASINO
Rt. 1, Box 105A • POWHATTAN, KS
(785) 467-8070 Fax 467-5001
Owned and operated by the Sac & Fox
Nation of Missouri.

CASINO WHITE CLOUD
Rt. 1 Box 58A
WHITE CLOUD, KS 66094
(785) 595-3258 Fax 595-6610
Website: www.casinowhitecloud.com
Owned by the Iowa of Kansas & Nebraska Tribe. *Lo-
cation:* Northeast corner of Kansas on the Missouri
River near the Nebraska border. *Facility:* Slots, table
games; bingo.

LOUISIANA

CYPRESS BAYOU CASINO
832 Martin Luther King Rd.
P.O. Box 519
CHARENTON, LA 70523
(800) 284-4386; (337) 923-7284
Website: www.cypressbayou.com
Owned by Chitimacha Indian Tribe. *Location:* 45 miles
south of Lafayette, off US Hwy. 90, exit 83 east to
baldwin. *Facility:* 45,000 sq. ft. 1,200 slots, video poker
and table games.

GRAND CASINO COUSHATA
777 Coushatta Dr.
KINDER, LA 70648
(800) 584-7263; (337) 738-1300 Fax 738-7340
Owned by the Coushatta Tribe of Louisiana. *Location:*
25 miles north of I-10 on U.S. Hwy. 165, exit 44, five
miles north of Kinder. *Facility:* 100,000 sq. ft. with 3,250
slots & 80 table games.

PARAGON CASINO RESORT
711 Paragon Pl.
MARKSVILLE, LA 71351
(318) 253-1946 (800) WIN-1-WIN
Website: www.paragoncasinoresort.com
Owned by the Tunica-Biloxi Tribe of Louisiana. Location: 35 miles northeast of Alexandria, Louisiana, on
Hwy 1 in Marksville. *Facility:* 120,000 sq. ft. 2,100 slots
& 80 table games; bingo. Hotel with 335 rooms.

MICHIGAN

Michigan has 13 full-scale Nevada style Indian tribe
casinos. They were in operation before the National
Gaming Act of 1988. All have completed compact
agreements with the state of Michigan. In November
1996 Michigan voters approved the establishment of
three casinos in the city of Detroit.

OJIBWA CASINO RESORT
797 Michigan Ave. • BARAGA, MI 49944
(800) 323-8045; (906) 353-6333 Fax 353-7618
Website" www.ojibwacasino.com
Owned by the Keweenaw Bay Indian Community of
the L'Anse Reservation. *Location:* 5 miles north of
Baraga in Upper Michigan on M-38. *Facility:* 17,000
sq. ft. 400 slots, 11 game tables; 450-seat bingo hall.
40 room hotel. Open 24 hours, 7 days a week.

BAY MILLS RESORT & CASINO
11386 Lakeshore Dr.
P.O. Box 249 • BRIMLEY, MI 49715
(888) 422-9645; (906) 248-3715
Website: www.4baymills.com
Owned by the Bay Mills Indian Community. *Location:*
On the Lakeshore, along the bank of the St. Mary's
River. *Facility:* 17,000 sq. ft with 1,000 slots, video
poker and tables, Caribbean stud poker & keno; Bingo.
144-room hotel. Open 24 hours.

KINGS CLUB CASINO
12140 Lakeshore Dr.
Rt. 1, Box 313 • BRIMLEY, MI 49715
(800) 575-5493; (906) 248-3227 Fax 248-3283
Owned by the Bay Mills Indian Community. *Location:*
17 miles west of Sault Ste. Marie. *Facility:* 5,000 sq.
feet. 275 slots, 8 table games.

KEWADIN CASINO - CHRISTMAS
Rt. 2, Box 223
CHRISTMAS, MI49862
(800) KEWANDIN; (906) 387-5475 Fax 387-5477

Website: www.kewadin.com
Owned by the Sault Ste. Marie Ojibwe (Chippewa)
Tribe. *Location:* 40 miles east of Marquette in the Upper Peninsula of Michigan on the shores of Lake Superior. *Facility:* 1,266 sq. feet. with 80 slots and 4
tables.

CHIP IN'S ISLAND RESORT & CASINO
W 399 HWY. 2 & 41
P.O. Box 351 • HARRIS, MI 49845
(906) 486-2941 Fax 486-2949
Owned by the Hannahville Indian Community-
Potawatomi Tribe. *Location:* 13 miles west of Escanaba
and Lake Michigan's western shore on US Hwy. 41.
Facility: 55,000 sq. ft. 1,000 slots, video poker and 49
table games; 350-seat bingo room. 113-room hotel.
Open 24 hours, 7 days a week.

KEWADIN CASINO - HESSEL
3 Mile Rd. P.O. Box 789
HESSEL, MI 49745
(800) KEWADIN; (906) 484-2903 Fax 484-3248
Website: www.kewadin.com
Owned by Sault Ste. Marie Tribe of Ojibwe (Chippewa)
Indians. *Location:* In Michigan's Upper Peninsula on
Hwy 134, 14 miles east of Interstate Hwy. 75 on the
shore of Lake Huron. *Facility:* 3,850 sq. feet. 120 slots,
4 tables.

LITTLE RIVER CASINO
2700 Orchard Hwy.
MANISTEE, MI 49660
(888) 568-2244; (231) 723-1535
Ownd by the Little River Band of Ottawa Indians at
Manistee. *Facilities:* 1,000 slots, video poker and table
games. Open 24 hours, 7 days a week.

KEWADIN CASINO - MANISTIQUE
P.O. Box 189
MANISTIQUE, MI 49854
(800) KEWANDIN; (906) 341-5510 Fax 341-2951
Website: www.kewadin.com
Owned by Sault Ste. Marie Tribe of Ojibwa (Chippewa)
Indians. *Location:* In Michigan's Upper Peninsula on
the northern shore of Lake Michigan on Hwy. 2 east of
Escanaba. *Facility:* 1,266 sq. feet. 80 slots, 4 tables.

OJIBWA CASINO MARQUETTE
105 Acre Trail • MARQUETTE, MI 49855
(888) 560-9905; (906) 249-4200
www.ojibwacasino.com
Owned and operated by the Keweenaw Bay Indian
Community of the L'Anse Reservation.Facilities:
10,000 sq. ft. 300 slots, 10 tables. Bingo. Open 24
hours, 7 days a week.

SOARING EAGLE CASINO & BINGO HALL
6800 Soaring Eagle Blvd.
MT. PLEASANT, MI 48858
(888) 7EAGLE7; (989) 775-5777 Fax 775-3040
Website: www.soaringeaglecasino.com
Owned by the Saginaw Ojibwa (Chippewa) Tribe. *Location:* 75 miles north of Lansing on Hwy. 20. *Facility:*
210,000 sq. ft.casino with 4,700 slots, 80 table games;
bingo. 3,260-seat showroom, 54,000 sq. ft. expo space
and 26,000 sq. ft. of meeting space. 512-room hotel
resort. Slots open 24 hours.

VICTORIES CASINO & HOTEL
1967 U.S. 131 South
PETOSKEY, MI 49770
(877) 442-6464
Website: www.victories-casino.com
Owned and operated by the Little Traverse Bay Bands
of Odawa Indians. Facilities: 850 slots and video poker
machines; table games; 128-room hotel.

KEWADIN CASINO ST. IGNACE
3039 Mackinaw Trail
ST. IGNACE, MI 49781
(800) 539-2346; (906) 643-7071 Fax 643-8472
Website: www.kewadin.com
Owned by Sault Ste. Marie Ojibwa (Chippewa) Tribe.
Location: Upper Peninsula at the north end of the
Mackinac Bridge, across the Straits of Mackinaw from
Mackinaw City. *Facility:* 56,000 sq. ft. with 2,400 slots,
video poker, keno &30 table games. Hotel with 320
rooms. Open 24 hours.

KEWADIN CASINO SAULTE STE. MARIE
2186 Skunk Rd.
SAULTE STE. MARIE, MI 49783
(800) 539-2346
(906) 632-0530 Fax 635-9155
Website: www.kewadin.com
Owned by the Sault Ste. Marie Ojibwa (Chippewa) Tribe. *Location*: Upper peninsula on the Canadian border and the International bridge to Ontario. *Facility*: 85,000 sq. feet. with 1,000 slots, video poker & keno & 37 table games; bingo. 52 room hotel. Open 24 hours daily.

LEELANAU SANDS CASINO & BINGO
2521 NW Bayshore Dr.
SUTTON BAY, MI 49682
(800) 922-2WIN
(231) 271-4104 Fax 271-4136
Website: www.casino2win.com
Owned by the Grand Traverse Band of Ottawa and Ojibwe (Chippewa) Indians. *Location*: Lower peninsula on the coastline of Lake Michigan, 20 miles northe of Traverse City minutes from Suttons Bay. *Facility*: 75,000 sq. ft. with 850 slots, video poker, video keno & 40 table games. The Leelanau Sands Casino Lodge has 51 rooms.

LEELANAU SUPER GAMING PALACE
2649 NW Bayshore Dr.
SUTTON BAY, MI 49682
(800) 922-2WIN; (616) 271-6852 Fax 271-4208
Owned by the Grand Traverse Band of Ottawa and Ojibwe (Chippewa) Indians. *Location*: 4 miles north of Sutton Bay. *Facility*: 6,000 sq. feet. with 437 slots, video poker, video keno & 5 tables.

LAC VIEUX DESERT CASINO
446 Choate Rd., P.O. Box 249
WATERSMEET, MI 49969
(800) 583-3599; (906) 358-4226 Fax 358-0288
Website: www.lacvieuxdesert.com
Owned by the Lac Vieux Desert Band of Lake Superior Chippewa Indians. *Location*: East of U.S. Hwy. 45, just east of Land O' Lakes, Wisconsin. *Facility*: 25,000 sq. ft. 678 slots, video poker & 15 table games. Bingo. Hotel with 135 rooms. Open 24 hours.

TURTLE CREEK CASINO
7741 M-72 East • WILLIAMSBURG, MI
(888) 777-UWIN
Website: www.casino2win.com
Owned by the Grand Traverse Band of Ottawa and Chippewa Indians. Facilities: 60,000 sq. ft. 1,200 slots, 30 table games, 24 blackjack tables. 83-room hotel.

MINNESOTA

There are 16 Indian gaming facilities operating in Minnesota. The compact agreements are all based on the National Indian Gaming Act of 1988. The tribes offer slots, blackjack, and bingo.

BLACK BEAR CASINO & HOTEL
1785 Hwy. 210
CARLTON, MN 55718
(888) 771-0777; (218) 878-2317 Fax 878-2414
Website: www.blackbearcasinohotel.com
Owned by the Fond du Lac Band of Lake Superior Ojibway (Chippewa) Indians. *Location*: 20 minutes south of Duluth at intersection of I-35 and Hwy. 210. *Facility*: 60,000 sq. feet. 1,200 slots, video poker/blackjack/craps, 32 blackjack tables; bingo. 158-room hotel. Open 24 hours.

THE PALACE BINGO & CASINO
6280 Upper Cass Frontage Rd. NW
CASS LAKE, MN 56633
(800) 228-6676; (877) 9-PALACE
(218) 335-6787 Fax 335-6899
Website: www.palacecasino.com
Owned by the Leech Lake Reservation Ojibwe (Chippewa) Tribe. *Location*: 2.5 miles northwest of Cass lake; 12 miles east of Bemidji on U.S. Hwy. 2. *Facility*: 30,000 sq. ft. 500 slots, video poke & keno, and 6 blackjack tables; 800 seat bingo hall. 80-room hotel. Open 24 hours.

WHITE OAK CASINO
45830 U.S. Hwy. 2
DEER RIVER, MN 56636
(800) 653-2412
Website: whiteoakcasino.com
Owned and operated by the Leech Lake band of Ojibwe. Facilities: 204 slots, blackjack tables.

FOND-DE-LUTH CASINO
129 E. Superior St. • DULUTH, MN 55802
(800) 873-0280; (218) 722-0280 Fax 722-7505
Website: www.fondduluthcasino.com
Owned by the Fond du Lac Band of Lake Superior Chippewa Tribe. *Location*: Downtown Duluth. *Facility*: 20,000 sq. ft. 341 slots & 16 table games; bingo hall. Open 24 hours.

GRAND PORTAGE LODGE & CASINO
70 Grand Portage Dr.
GRAND PORTAGE, MN 55605
(800) 543-1384; (218) 475-2401 Fax 475-2309
Website: www.grandportage.com
Owned by the Grand Portage Chippewa Indian Tribe. *Location*: On Lake Superior, 5 miles south of the Canadian border on Lake Superior. *Facility*: 15,300 sq. feet. 400 slots & 8 blackjack tables; bingo hall. 100-room hotel. Open 24 hours daily.

PRAIRIE'S EDGE CASINO RESORT
Rt. 2, Box 96 • GRANITE FALLS, MN 56241
(866) 293-2121; (320) 564-2121 Fax 564-2547
Website: www.prairiesedgecasino.com
Owned by the Upper Sioux Community. *Location*: On Hwy. 67 miles east of Granite Falls, 130 miles west of Minneapolis. *Facility*: 24,000 sq. feet. 600 slots, 8 blackjack tables. 89-room hotel. Open 24 hours daily.

TREASURE ISLAND RESORT & CASINO
P.O. Box 75 • RED WING, MN 55066
(800) 222-7077; (651) 388-6300
E-mail: info@ticasino.com
Website: www.treasureislandcasino.com
Owned by the Prairie Island Indian Community of Minnesota Mdwewakanton Dakota. Facilities: 2,500 slots; 44 blackjack tables; 550-seat bingo hall. 800-seat showroom/event center.

GRAND CASINO HINCKLEY
777 Lady Luck Dr., RR 3 Box 15
HINCKLEY, MN 55037 (800) 472-6321
(320) 384-7777 Fax 449-7757
Website: www.grandcasinosmn.com
Owned by Mille Lacs Band of Ojibwe (Chippewa). *Location*: 76 miles east of Duluth, on Hwy. 48, 1 mile east of I-35. *Facility*: 140,000 sq. ft.; 2,000 slots; 50 blackjack tables; 388 video poker machines. 281 rooms at the Grand Hinckley Inn. Open 24 hours daily.

SHOOTING STAR CASINO
777 Casino Blvd., Box 418
MAHNOMEN, MN 56557
(800) 453-STAR
(218) 935-2711 Fax 935-2701
Owned by the White Earth Band of Ojibwe (Chippewa) Indians. *Location*: 35 miles north of Detroit Lakes, on U.S. Hwy. 59. *Facility*: 50,000 sq. ft. 1,300 slots, 150 video poker games, and 32 blackjack tables. 350-room hotel and event center with 1,600 seat capacity. Open 24 hours daily.

JACKPOT JUNCTION CASINO HOTEL
39375 County Road 24, P.O. Box 420
MORTON, MN 65270 (800) WIN-CASH
(507) 644-3000 Fax 644-2645
Website: www.jackpotjunction.com
Owned by the Lower Sioux Indian Community. *Location*: 6 miles east of Redwood Falls, on US Hwy. 71 in southwest Minnesota. *Facility*: 325,000 sq. feet. 1,650 slots, keno, poker, and 38 blackjack tables; 375-seat bingo hall. 276-room on-site lodge.Open 24 hours daily

GRAND CASINO MILLE LACS
777 Grand Ave., P.O. Box 240 HCR 67
ONAMIA, MN 56359 (800) 626-5825
(320) 532-7777 Fax 449-5992
Website: www.grandcasinosmn.com
Owned by Mille Lacs Band of Ojibwe (Chippewa) Indians. *Location*: 90 miles north of Minneapolis, on US

Hwy. 169, 8 miles south of Garrison. *Facility*: 130,000 sq. ft. 1,200 slots, 333 video poker & 35 blackjack tables; 350-seat bingo hall. 284-room hotel. Open 24 hours daily.

MYSTIC LAKE CASINO & HOTEL
2400 Mystic Lake Blvd.
PRIOR LAKE, MN 55372
(800) 262-7799; (952) 445-9000 Fax 496-7280
Website: www.mysticlake.com
Leonard Prescott, CEO
Owned by the Shakopee Mdewakanton Dakota Tribe. *Location*: 25 miles southwest of Minneapolis off I- 35 on the Shakopee Mdewakanton Dakota Reservation. *Facility*: 375,000 sq. ft. 4,800 slots & 88 blackjack tables; 1,100 seat bingo hall. 416-room hotel. Open 24 hours daily.

RED LAKE CASINO -SEVEN CLANS CASINO
P.O. Box 574 • RED LAKE, MN 56671
(888) 679-2501; (218) 679-2111 Fax 679-2666
Owned by the Red Lake Band of Ojibwe (Chippewa) Indians. *Location*: 25 miles north of Bemidji, on Hwy. 1 near Red Lake. Facility: 20,000 sq. feet. 86 slots, 3 blackjack tables; bingo.

SEVEN CLANS CASINO
20595 Center St. E.
THIEF RIVER FALLS, MN
(800) 568-6649; (218) 681-4062 Fax 681-8370
Owned by the Red Lake Band of Ojibway (Chippewa) Indians. *Location*: County Rd. 3 off Hwy. 59, 8 miles south of Thief River. *Facility*: 11,800 sq. feet. 750 slots, 8 blackjack tables. 151-suite hotel with 40,000 sq. ft. indoor water park. Open 24 hours, Wed. - Sat.; 8:30 am - 1 am, Sun.-Tues.

FORTUNE BAY CASINO & BINGO HALL
1430 Bois Forte Rd. • TOWER, MN 55790
(800) 992-PLAY; (218) 753-6400 Fax 753-6404
Website: www.fortunebay.com
Owned by the Bois Forte Band of Ojibway (Chippewa) Indians. *Location*: 5 miles west of Tower, on US Hwy. 169, on the Bois Forte Reservation. *Facility*: 40,000 sq. ft. 246 slots & 16 blackjack tables; bingo hall. Open 24 hours.

NORTHERN LIGHTS CASINO & HOTEL
6800 Y Frontage Rd. NW
WALKER, MN 56484 (877) 544-4879
(218) 547-2744 Fax 547-1368
Website: www.northernlightscasino.com
Owned by the Leech Lake Band of Chippewa Indians. *Location*: On the Leech Lake Reservation, 4 miles south of Walker at junction of Hwys. 200 & 371. *Facility*: 14,000 sq. ft. 1,000 slots & 12 blackjack tables; bingo hall; 9,000 sq ft event center. 116-room motel. Golf course; 34-site RV park. Open 24 hours daily.

SEVEN CLANS CASINO - WARROAD
1012 E. Lake St.
WARROAD, MN 56763
(800) 815-8293; (218) 386-3381 Fax 386-2969
Owned by the Red Lake Band of Ojibway (Chippewa) Indians. *Location*: Off Hwy. 11 at Lake of the Woods, 7 miles south of the Canadian border. *Facility*: 14,000 sq. feet. 500 slots, video poker, keno, and 10 blackjack tables. 42 room motel.

TREASURE ISLAND CASINO
5734 Sturgeon Lake Rd.
P.O. Box 75 • WELCH, MN 55089
Owned by Prairie Island Mdewakanton Dakota Tribe. *Location*: 45 miles southeast of St. Paul, 4 Miles south of US Hwy. 61 between Red Wing and Hastings. *Facility*: 100,000 sq. ft. 1,300 slots & 53 blackjack tables; bingo hall. Open 24 hours daily.

MISSISSIPPI

PEARL RIVER RESORT -
SILVER STAR HOTEL & CASINO
GOLDEN MOON HOTEL & CASINO
P.O. Box 6048 • CHOCTAW, MS 39350
(866) 44-PEARL; (601) 656-3400 Fax 656-1992
Owned by the Mississippi Choctaw Indians. *Location*:

40 miles north of Meridian on Hwy. 16W. *Facility*: 40,000 sq. feet. 4,000 slots, 100+ gaming tables. Bingo. 1,000+ hotel rooms. Golf course, water park. Open 24 hours daily.

MISSOURI

BORDER TOWN BINGO & CASINO
129 West Oneida St.
P.O. Box 350 • SENECA, MO 64865
 (800) 957-2435
 Website: www.easternshawnee.org
Owned and operated by the Eastern Shawnee Tribe of Oklahoma.

MONTANA

FOUR C's CASINO
544 Rural Road 1
BOX ELDER, MT 59521
 (406) 395-4863
Owned by the Rocky Boy Indian Tribe. *Location*: On the Rocky Boy Indian Reservation. *Facility*: 8,000 sq. ft. with video poker, video keno and bingo.

GLACIER PEAKS CASINO
209 N. Piegan St.
BROWNING, MT 59417
 (406) 338-5751
Owned by the Blackfeet Tribe and operated by Siyeh Development, Inc. *Facilities*: 160-seat bingo amd video bingo

LITTLE BIG HORN CASINO
P.O. Box 580
CROW AGENCY, MT 59022
 (406) 638-4000
Owned by the Crow Indian Tribe. *Location*: 55 miles southeast of Billings, on the Big Horn River and US Hwy. 90. *Facility*: 100 slots, video poker, video keno, and 200-seat bingo hall.

CHARGING HORSE CASINO & BINGO
P.O Box 1259
LAME DEER, MT 59043
 (406) 477-6677
Owned by the Northern Cheyenne Indian Tribe. *Location*: On Hwy. 212 southeast of Billings. *Facility*: 100 video keno and poker machines, and 500-seat bingo.

KWATAQNUK RESORT & CASINO
303 U.S. Hwy. 93 East
POLSON, MT
 (406) 883-3636
 Website: www.kwataqnuk.com
Owned by the Confederated Salish & Kootenai Tribes of the Flathead Reservation. Facilities: 46 poker and keno tables. 112-room hotel; 350-seat meeting hall.

NEBRASKA

OHIYA CASINO
RR2, Box 163
NIOBRARA, NE 68760
 (402) 857-2302 Fax 857-2393
Owned by the Santee Sioux Tribe of Nebraska

NEVADA

AVI RESORT & CASINO
10000 Aha Macav Pkwy.
LAUGHLIN, NV
 (800) 430-0721; (702) 535-5555
 E-mail: info@avicasino.com
 Website: www.avicasino.com
Owned and operated by the Fort Mojave Tribe. *Facilities*: 25,000 sq. ft. 800 slots, 20 game tables, keno lounge, bingo. 455-room hotel and spa.

NEW MEXICO

In New Mexico 13 tribes and pueblos have signed compacts with the state for Class III gaming. We have included information on eight of the thirteen which have started operations. The five not mentioned are:Pueblo of Santa Clara, Pueblo of Taos, Pueblo of San Felipe, Pueblo of Nambe, and the Jicarilla Apache Tribe.

SKY CITY CASINO
P.O. Box 310 • ACOMA, NM 87034
 (800) 747-0181; (505) 552-6017 Fax 552-9256
 Website: www.skycitycasino.com
Owned by Acoma Pueblo. *Location*: 55 miles west of Albuquerque on I-40 exit 102. *Facility*: 600 slots, video poker, video keno, poker tables. 134-room hotel. Open 24 hours daily.

ISLETA CASINO & RESORT
11000 Broadway SE
ALBUQUERQUE, NM 87105
 (800) 843-5156; (505) 724-3800
 Website: www.isleta-casino.com
Owned by Isleta Pueblo. *Location*: Exit 215 south on I-15 in Albuquerque. *Facility*: 100,000 sq. ft. 1,700 slots, 300 video poker, 48 blackjack tables, 24 poker tables. Golf course & showroom.

SANDIA CASINO
30 Rainbow Rd, NE
ALBUQUERQUE, NM 87184
 (800) 526-9366; (505) 897-2173 Fax 897-1117
 Website: www.sandiacasino.com
Owned by Sandia Pueblo. *Location*: On I-25 & Ramsey Rd. 8 miles north of downtown Albuquerque, nestled between the base of the Sandia Mountains and the Rio Grande River. *Facility*: 65,000 sq. feet. 1,700 slots, video poker, 15 poker tables, 28 blackjack tables; keno, high stakes bingo. Outdoor amphitheater. Open 24 hours, 7 days a week.

SANTA ANA STAR CASINO
54 Jemez Dam Canyon
P.O. Box 9201 • BERNALILLO, NM 87004
 (505) 867-0000 Fax 867-1472
 Website: santanaanastar.com
Owned by Santa Ana Pueblo. *Location*: Off I-25, 17 miles north of Albuquerque. *Facility*: 20,000 sq. feet. VIdeo slots, video poker; live poker. Open 24 hours daily.

DANCING EAGLE CASINO
I-40 exit 108 • CASA BLANCA, NM
 (877) 440-9969; (505) 552-7777
Owned and operated by the Pueblo of Laguna and the Laguna Development Corp. Location: 40 minutes west of Albuquerque and 20 minutes east of Grants. Facilities: 25,000 sq. ft. 500 slots, table games.

APACHE NUGGET CASINO
Narrow Gauge St.
P.O. Box 650 • DULCE, NM 87528
 (505) 759-3777
Owned by the Jicarilla Apache Tribe. *Location*: On Hwy. 64, near the Colorado border,, 150 miles northwest of Santa Fe. *Facility*: Video slots, video poker, live poker, blackjack, roulette & craps. Best Western Jicarilla Inn nearby. Open 24 hours.

CASINO APACHE
Carrizo Canyon Rd.
P.O. Box 205 • MESCALERO, NM 88340
 (877) 277-5677
  Website: www.innofthemountaingods.com/ casino_apache.htm
Owned by the Mescalero Apache Tribe.

INN OF THE MOUNTAIN GODS CASINO & RESORT
Carrizo Canyon Rd. • P.O. Box 269
MESCALERO, NM 88340
 (800) 545-9011; (505) 257-5241 Fax 257-6173
 Website: www.innofthenountaingods.com
Owned by the Mescalero Apache Tribe. *Location*: On I- 70, 26 miles northeast of Alamagordo. *Facility*: 200 video slots, video poker, video keno, live poker, blackjack tables. Scheduled to be opened in April 2005.

CASINO HOLLYWOOD
25 Hagan Rd.
SAN FELIPE PUEBLO, NM 87001
 (877) 529-2946; (505) 867-6700
Owned by the Pueblo of San Felipe. *Location*: Between Albuquerque and Santa Fe on I-25, exit 252. *Facilities*: 100,000 sq. ft. 700 slots, gaming tables; 1,250-seat celebrity showroom. Open 24 hours, 7 days a week.

OH KAY CASINO & RESORT
P.O. Box 1270
SAN JUAN PUEBLO, NM 87566
 (877) 829-2865; (505) 747-1668 Fax 852-4026
Owned by the San Juan Pueblo. *Location*: 2 miles north of Espanola Hwy., 28 miles north of Santa Fe, nestled between the Sangre de Cristo and Jemez Mountains. *Facility*: 80,000 sq. ft. with 575 video slots & video poker; blackjack, poker, bingo. 101-room hotel. Open 24 hours, 7 days a week.

CAMEL ROCK GAMING
Rt. 11, Box 3A • SANTA FE, NM 87501
 (800) 462-2635; (505) 984-8414 Fax 989-9234
 Website: www: camelrockcasino.com
Owned by the Pueblo of Tesuque. *Location*: 10 miles north of Santa Fe. *Facility*: 60,000 sq. feet. with 600 gaing devices, video slots, video poker, live poker; bingo. Open 24 hours daily.

CITIES OF GOLD CASINO
Rt. 11, Box 21-B • SANTA FE, NM 87501
 (800) 455-3363; (505) 455-3313 Fax 455-7188
Owned by Pueblo of Pojoaque. *Location*: Located just outside Santa Fe. *Facility*: 60,000 sq. ft. with video slots, video poker, video keno, video blackjack, live poker, and bingo. Open 24 hours daily.

TAOS MOUNTAIN CASINO
P.O. Box 777 • TAOS, NM 87571
 (505) 758-4460 Fax 751-0578
 Website: taosmountaincasino.com
Owned by Taos Pueblo. *Location*: 70 miles north of Santa Fe. *Facility*: Video slots and video poker only. Open 24 hours daily.

NEW YORK

ST. REGIS CASINO
St. Regis Indian Reservation
Route 37, P.O. Box 670
AKWESASNE, NY 13655
 (877) 992-2746; (518) 358-2222 Fax 358-3203
 Website: www.akwesasnemohawk.com
Owned and operated by the St. Regis Mohawk Indian Tribe. *Location*: in Massena, NY about 50 miles southwest of Montreal. *Facility*: 50,000 sq. ft. 280 slots, 35 table games: dice, roulette and card games; Bingo Palace.

SENECA ALLEGANY CASINO
725 Broad St. • SALAMANCA, NY 14779
 (716) 945-3200
 E-mail: info@satg.com

SENECA NIAGARA CASINO
310 Fourth St.
NIAGARA FALLS, NY 14303
 (877) 873-6322; (716) 299-1100
 Website: www.senecaniagaracasino.com
 E-mail: info@snfgc.com
Owned and operated by the Seneca Nation. *Location*: Just blocks from the Niaraga Falls. *Facility*: 105,000 sq. ft. casino. 2,900 slots, 114 gaming tables. 426-seat showroom-style theater.

TURNING STONE RESORT & CASINO
5218 Patrick Rd., P.O. Box 126
VERONA, NY 13478
 (800) 771-7711; (315) 361-7711 Fax 361-7901
 Website: www.turning-stone.com
Owned by the Oneida Indian Nation. *Location*: Upstate New York, 35 miles east of Syracuse off Hwy. I-90. *Facility*: 95,000 sq. ft. Table games; 1,600 seat bingo hall; spa and 5,000-seat, 30,000 sq. ft. events center; 98-room hotel. Golf course.

NORTH CAROLINA

HARRAH'S CHEROKEE
SMOKEY MOUNTAIN CASINO
777 Casino Dr., P.O. Box 1959
CHEROKEE, NC 28719
  (828) 497-7777 Fax 497-5076
  Website: www.cherokee-wnc.com
Owned by the Eastern Band of Cherokee Indians. *Location*: 35 miles southeast of Ashville, NC at the base of the Great Smoky Mountains. *Facility*: 50,000 sq. feet. 2,300 video slots, 800 multi-game machines. No table games. High stakes bingo. 1,500-seat Pavillion Theater

NORTH DAKOTA

SKY DANCER CASINO & RESORT
P.O. Box 1449, Hwy. 5 W
BELCOURT, ND 58316
  (866) BIG-WINS; (701) 477-3281
  Website: www.skydancercasino.com
Owned by the Turtle Mountain Band of Chippewa Indians. *Location*: On Hwy. 281 & Hwy. 5 W, 8 miles west of Belcourt in north central North Dakota near the Canadian border. *Facility*: 25,000 sq. ft. 417 slots & 10 blackjack and 4 poker tables; bingo. 200-room hotel. Open 24 hours.

PRAIRIE KNIGHTS CASINO & RESORT
1806 Hwy. 24
FORT YATES, ND 58538
  (800) 425-8277; (701) 854-7777 Fax 854-7785
Owned and operated by the Standing Rock Sioux Tribe. *Location*: In south central North Dakota on the Standing Rock Reservation, south of Bismarck on the Missouri River, 44 miles south of Mandan. *Facility*: 75,000 sq. feet. 600 slots, high-stakes blackjack and gaming tables, video poker & keno. Convention & meeting center and entertainment facility. Open 24 hours daily.

4 BEARS CASINO & LODGE
P.O. Box 579
NEW TOWN, ND 58763
  (800) 294-5454; (701) 627-4018 Fax 627-4012
  Website: 4bearcasino.com
Owned by the Three Affiliated Tribes - Mandan, Hidatsa & Arikara. *Location*: 4 miles west of New Town on Hwy. 23 and Lake Sakakawea, part of the Missouri River. *Facility*: 30,000 sq. feet. 500 reel slots, blackjack tables, roulette and poker tables; 1 crap table; bingo. 97- room lodge.

DAKOTA MAGIC CASINO & HOTEL
16849 102ND ST. SE
HANKINSON, ND 58370
  (800) 325-6825; (701) 634-3000
  Website: www.dakotamagic.com
Owned and operated by the Sisseton-Wahpeton Oyate Tribe. *Location*: On I-29, Exit 1 on the border of North & South Dakota. *Facility*: 50,000 sq. ft. casinoi; 700 slots & table games; bingo. Hotel and convention center. Golf course. Open 24 hours daily.

SPIRIT LAKE CASINO & RESORT
7889 Hwy. 57
SPIRIT LAKE, ND 58370
  (800) WIN-U-BET; (701) 766-4747 Fax 767-4900
  Website: www.spiritlakecasino.com
  E-mail: chalgren@spiritlakecasino.com
Owned by the Devil's Lake Sioux Tribe. *Location*: Six miles south of Devil's Lake on Hwy. 57. *Facility*: 40,000 sq. ft. with 500 slots, video poker & keno, gaming tables. 124-room hotel

OKLAHOMA

ADA GAMING CENTER
P.O. Box 1340 • ADA, OK 74820

GOLD RIVER BINGO & CASINO
P.O. Box 806 • ANADARKO, OK 73005

  (866) 499-3054; (405) 247-6979
Owned by the Apache Tribe of Oklahoma. *Location*: 2 miles north of Anadarko on Hwy. 281. *Facilities*: 250 slots; gaming tables. 300-seat bingo hall.

BRISTOW INDIAN BINGO
121 W. Lincoln
BRISTOW, OK 74010

CHOCTAW CASINO
1790 S. Park Dr.
BROKEN BOW, OK
  (580) 584-5450
Owned by the Choctaw Tribe of Oklahoma.
Facilities: Slots, gaming tables; bingo hall.

CHEROKEE BINGO & CASINO
I44 & 193rd St. • CASTOOSA, OK
  (800) 760-6700
  Website: www.cherokeecasino.com
Owned by the Cherokee Tribe of Oklahoma.
Facilities: Slots, gaming tables; bingo hall.

LUCKY STAR CASINO
7777 N. Hwy. 81
CONCHO, OK 73022
  (405) 262-7612; (580) 323-6599
Owned by the Cheyenne and Artapaho Tribes of Oklahoma.Location: 20 miles northwest of Oklahoma City. Facilities: 40,000 sq. ft casino. 600 Vegas-style themed games; high-stakes bingo; blackjack tables. Also has a location in Clinton, OK.

CHOCTAW BINGO & CASINO
1790 S. Park Dr.
P.O. Box 1919
DURANT, OK 74702
  (800) 788-2464
  Website: www.choctawcasinos.com
Owned by the Choctaw Tribe of Oklahoma.
Facilities: Slots, gaming tables; bingo hall.

CHOCTAW BINGO & CASINO
Hwy. 271 • GRANT, OK
  (580) 326-8397
  Website: www.choctawcasinos.com
Owned by the Choctaw Tribe of Oklahoma.
Facilities: Slots, gaming tables; bingo hall.

CHOCTAW BINGO & CASINO
1425 SE Washington St.
IDABEL, OK 74702
  (800) 634-2582
  Website: www.choctawcasinos.com
Owned by the Choctaw Tribe of Oklahoma.
Facilities: Slots, gaming tables; bingo hall.

COMANCHE NATION GAMES
402 SE I-44, P.O. Box 347
LAWTON, OK 73502
  (866) 354-2500
  Website: www.comanchenationgames.com
Owned by the Comanche Tribe of Oklahoma.

CHOCTAW BINGO & CASINO
1638 S. George Nigh Expressway
McALESTER, OK 74702
  (877) 904-8444
  Website: www.choctawcasinos.com
Owned by the Choctaw Tribe of Oklahoma.
Facilities: Slots, gaming tables; bingo hall.

KAW NATION BINGO
P.O. Box 171
NEWKIRK, OK 74647

THUNDERBIRD WILD WILD WEST CASINO
15700 E. State Hwy. 9
NORMAN, OK 73071
  (800) 259-5825; (405) 360-9270
Owned by the Absentee Shawnee Tribe of Oklahoma. *Location*: A few miles south of Oklahoma City. *z*: 800 touch screen video gaming machines; high-stake bingo.

GOLDSBY GAMING CENTER
Rte. 1 Box 104P
NORMAN, OK 73072

CREEK NATION OKMULGEE BINGO
P.O. Box 790
OKMULGEE, OK 74447

CIMARRON BINGO CASINO
P.O. Box 190
PERKINS, OK 74059

CHOCTAW BINGO & CASINO
3400 Choctaw Rd. • POCOLA, OK
  (800) 590-5825
  Website: www.choctawcasinos.com
Owned by the Choctaw Tribe of Oklahoma.
Facilities: Slots, gaming tables; bingo hall.

7 CLANS PARADISE CASINO
7500 Hwy. 177 • RED ROCK, OK 74651
  (580) 723-4005
Owned by the Otoe-Missouria Tribe. *Facilities*: Slots, gaming machines. *Activities*: Annual tribal pow wow held 3rd weekend in July.

CHEROKEE BINGO & CASINO
P.O. Box 1000 • ROLAND, OK 74954
  (800) 256-2338
  Website: www.cherokeecasino.com
Owned by the Cherokee Tribe of Oklahoma.
Facilities: Slots, gaming tables; bingo hall.

POTAWATOMI BINGO
9101 S. Gordon Cooper Dr.
SHAWNEE, OK 74801

CHEROKEE BINGO & CASINO
U.S. Hwy. 412 & OK Hwy. 59
SILOAM SPRINGS, OK 74954
  (800) 754-4111
  Website: www.cherokeecasino.com
Owned by the Cherokee Tribe of Oklahoma.
Facilities: Slots, gaming tables; bingo hall.

CHOCTAW BINGO & CASINO
895 N. Highway 69 • STRINGTOWN, OK
  (580) 346-7862
  Website: www.choctawcasinos.com
Owned by the Choctaw Tribe of Oklahoma.
Facilities: Slots, gaming tables; bingo hall.

SULPHUR GAMING CENTER
West First & Muskogee
SULPHUR, OK 73086

UNITED KEETOOWAH BINGO
2450 S. Muskogee Ave.
TAHLEQUAH, OK 74465

TOUSO ISHTO GAMING CENTER
P.O. Box 149
THACKERVILLE, OK 73459

CREEK NATION TULSA BINGO
P.O. Box 700833
TULSA, OK 74170

OREGON

SEVEN FEATHERS HOTEL & CASINO RESORT
146 Chief Miwaleta Ln.
CANYONVILLE, OR 97417
  (800) 548-8461; (541) 839-1111 Fax 839-4300
  Website: www.sevenfeathers.com
  Peter Ingenito, General Manager
Owned by the Cow Creek Band of Umpqua Tribe of Indians of Oregon. *Location*: In southern Oregon at exit 99 on I-5, north of Medford and south of Eugene. *Facility*: 29,000 sq. ft. 1,000 slots, video poker, blackjack & poker tables; video keno; bingo. 146-room hotel. 22,000 sq. ft. convention center. Open 24 hours daily.

KLA-MO-YA CASINO CORP.
P.O. Box 490
CHILOQUIN, OR 97624
  (541) 783-2219 Fax 783-2029
  Website:: www.klamathtribes.org
Owned by the Klamath Tribes of Oregon.

SPIRIT MOUNTAIN CASINO & RESORT
27100 SW Salmon River Hwy.
P.O. Box 39
GRANDE RONDE, OR 97347
  (800) 760-7977
  (503) 879-2350 Fax 879-2486
  Website: www.spirit-mountain.com
Owned by the Confederated Tribes of the Grand Ronde
Community. *Location*: In northwest Oregon, on Hwy.
16, 60 miles southwest of Portland. *Facility*: 60,000
sq. feet. 800 slots, 85 video poker, 36 blackjack and
poker tables, keno; bingo. Open 24 hours, 7 days a
week.

CHINOOK WINDS CASINO
1777 NW 40th St.
LINCOLN CITY, OR 97367
  (888) 244-6665; (541) 996-5825 Fax 996-5491
  Website: www.chinookwindscasino.com
Owned by the Confederated Tribes of Siletz Indians
of Oregon. *Location*: On the Pacific Ocean Hwy. 101,
80 miles southwest of Portland. *Facility*: 1,350 slots,
blackjack and poker tables, keno; bingo. 20,000 sq. ft.
convention center. Open 24 hours, 7 days a week.

THE MILL CASINO
3201 Tremont
NORTH BEND, OR 97429
  (800) 953-4800; (541) 756-8800 Fax 756-0431
  Website: www.themillcasino.com
Owned by the Coquille Indian Tribe of Oregon. *Location*: On Pacific Coast Hwy. 101 on Oregon's southwest coast. *Facility*: 250 video slots, blackjack and
poker tables, keno; 1,200 seat bingo hall. Open 24
hours daily.

WILD HORSE RESORT & GAMING CENTER
72777 Hwy. 331, P.O. Box 638
PENDLETON, OR 97801
  (800) 654-9453
  (541) 278-2274 Fax 276-3873
  Website: www.wildhorseresort.com
  John Barkley, General Manager
Owned by the Confederated Tribes of the Umatilla Indians of Oregon. *Location*: In northeast Oregon 5 just
south of I-84, 5 miles east of Pendleton. *Facility*: 40,000
sq. ft. 300 slots & 16 table games; 800 seat high stakes
bingo. 100-room motel.

INDIAN HEAD CASINO
Kah-Nee-Ta Resort, P.O. Box 720
6823 Hwy. 8 • WARM SPRINGS, OR 97761
  (800) BET-N-WIN; (541) 553-6123
  Website: www.kahneetaresort.com
Owned by Confederated Tribes of Warm Springs Reservation of Oregon. *Location*: In north central Oregon
on US Hwy. 25, 95 miles southeast of Portland. *Facility*: 25,000 sq. ft. 130 slots, video poker & keno; blackjack & poker tables, keno. 675-people theatre; banquet rooms; 169-room hotel.

SOUTH DAKOTA

ROYAL RIVER CASINO & BINGO
607 S. Veterans St., P.O. Box 326
FLANDREAU, SD 57028
  (800) 833-8666; (605) 997-3746 Fax 997-2388
  Website: www.royalrivercasino.com
Owned by the Flandreau Santee Sioux Tribe. *Location*: On the Santee Sioux Reservation, 7 miles off I-
29, 35 miles north of Sioux Falls. *Facility*: 15,000 sq.
feet. 240 slots, blackjack & poker tables. Motel. Open
24 hours, 7 days a week.

LODE STAR CASINO
P.O. Box 140 • FORT THOMPSON, SD 57339
  (605) 245-6000 Fax 245-2240
  Website: www.lodestar.com
Owned by the Crow Creek Sioux Tribe. *Location*: 50
miles southeast of Pierre on Hwy. 35 & 47. *Facility*:
13,000 sq. ft. 244 slots, blackjack and poker tables.

GOLDEN BUFFALO CASINO & RESORT
321 Sitting Bull St., P.O. Box 204
LOWER BRULE, SD 57548
  (605) 473-5577

Owned by the Lower Brule Sioux Tribe. *Location*: 45
miles southeast of Pierre, on the Lower Brule Sioux
Reservation. *Facility*: 9,000 sq. ft. with 125 slots & 15
table games. 38-room motel.

ROSEBUD CASINO
P.O. Box 21 • MISSION, SD 57642
  (800) 786-7673; (605) 378-3800
  Website: www.rosebudcasino.com
Owned by the Rosebud Sioux Tribe. *Location*: In south
central SD, 18 miles north of the Nebraska border, 22
miles south of Mission, SD on Hwy. 83. *Facility*: 7,000
sq. ft. Slots, video poker, blackjack and poker tables.
60-room hotel and event center featuring music, pow
wows and rodeos. 24 hours, 7 days a week.

GRAND RIVER CASINO
P.O. Box 639 • MOBRIDGE, SD 57601
  (800) 475-3321; (605) 845-7104 Fax 845-3090
  Website: www.grandrivercasino.com
Owned by the Standing Rock Sioux Tribe. *Location*:
On the Missouri River in north central SD. *Facility*:
20,000 sq. ft. 250 slots, video poker, blackjack & poker
tables.

PRAIRIE WIND CASINO
HC 49, Box 10 • PINE RIDGE, SD 57770
  (800) 705-9463; (605) 867-6300
Owned by the Oglala Sioux Tribe. *Location*: Just north
of the Nebraska border in southwest SD on Hwy. 18
between Oglala and Oelrichs. *Facility*: Slots, video
poker, blackjack and poker tables.

DAKOTA CONNECTION CASINO
I-29 & Hwy. 10, Veterans Memorial Dr.
P.O. Box 569 • SISSETON, SD 57262
  (800) 542-2876; (605) 698-4273 Fax 698-4271
  Wevsite: www.dakotaconnection.net
Owned and operated by the Sisseton-Wahpeton Oyate
Sioux Tribe of South Dakota. *Location*: In northeast-
ern SD, 3 miles west of I-29 on Hwy. 10. *Facility*: 20,000
sq. ft. 50 slots, video poker, blackjack & poker tables;
bingo.

FORT RANDALL CASINO HOTEL
Highway 46 West • WAGNER, SD 57380
RR 1, Box 100 • LAKE ANDES, SD 57356
  (800) 553-3003; (605) 487-7871 Fax 487-7354
  Website: www..fortrandallcasino.com
  Sam Weddel & Raymond Stone, Contacts
Owned and operated by the Yankton Sioux Tribe. *Location*: on Hwy. 46, in East Pickstown, 50 miles west
of Yankton on the Missouri River near the Nebraska
border. *Facility*: 24,000 sq. ft. 250 slots, video poker,
blackjack and poker tables; 150-seat bingo. 57-room
hotel. Open 24 hours daily.

DAKOTA SIOUX CASINO
16415 Sioux Conifer Rd.
WATERTOWN, SD 57201
  (605) 882-2051; (800) 658-4717
  Website: www.dakotasioux.com
  Wiley Shepher, Contact
Owned by the Sisseton-Wahpeton Oyate Sioux Tribe
of South Dakota. *Location*: In northeast SD on I-29,
32 miles from the Minnesota border. *Facility*: 7,400
sq. ft. 250 slots, poker & blackjack tables. Open 24
hours daily.

TEXAS

SPEAKING ROCK CASINO
122 S. Old Pueblo
EL PASO, TX 79907
  (915) 860-7777
Owned by the Ysleta Del Sur Pueblo Tribe. *Location*:
In west Texas on the Rio Grande River. *Facility*: Slots
& tables; bingo. Open 24 hours.

KICKAPOO LUCK EAGLE CASINO
7777 Lucky Eagle Dr.
EAGLE PASS, TX 78852
  (210) 758-1995
Owned by the Kickapoo Tribe of Texas. *Location*: In
south Texas on the Rio Grande River. *Facility*: Slots,
tables, poker, bingo.

WASHINGTON

NORTHERN QUEST CASINO
100 N. Hayford Rd., P.O. Box 1300
AIRWAY HEIGHTS, WA
  (888) 603-7051; (509) 242-7000
  Website: www.northernquest.net
Owned by the Kalispel Indian Tribe. *Facility*: 625 slots;
30 live table games; keno and poker room.

NORTHERN LIGHTS CASINO
837 Casino Dr., P.O. Box 628
ANACORTES, WA 98221
  (800) 293-9344; (360) 293-2691 Fax 273-1273
  Website: www.swinomishcasino.com
  Claudine Bruner, Contact
Owned by the Swinomish Indian Tribal Community. *Lo-
cation*: Off Hwy. 20, 9 miles west of I-5 along Skagit
Bay in northwest Washington. *Facility*: 63,000 sq. ft.
with blackjack, craps, roulette and poker tables.

MUCKLESHOOT INDIAN CASINO
2402 Auburn Way South
P.O. Box 795
AUBURN, WA 98002
  (800) 804-4944; (206) 804-4444 Fax 939-7702
  Website: www.muckleshootcasino.com
Owned and operated by the Muckleshoot Indian Tribe.
Location: On Hwy. 164 in western Washington, between Seattle and Tacoma minutes from I-5. *Facility*:
95,000 sq. ft. 2,000 slots, 70 blackjack, craps, roulette and poker tables; bingo.

LUMMI CASINO
2559 Lummi View Dr.
BELLINGHAM, WA 98226
  (800) 776-1337; (360) 758-7559 Fax 758-7545
Owned by the Lummi Indian Tribe. *Location*: 10 miles
off I-5 near Bellingham. *Facility*: 10,000 sq. ft. 41 blackjack, craps, roulette and poker tables. Open 24 hours
daily.

SKAGIT VALLEY CASINO RESORT
5984 N. Dark Lane • BOW, WA 98232
  (877) 275-2448; (360) 724-7777
  Website: www.scasinoresort.com
Owned by the Upper Skagit Indian Tribe. *Location*: In
northwest Washington 16 miles south of Bellingham.
Facility: 64,000 sq. ft. 600 slots, 50 gaming tables; 800-
seat bingo.

DOUBLE EAGLE CASINO
2539 Smith Rd.
CHEWELAH, WA 99109
  (509) 935-4406
Indian owned. *Location*: 50 miles north of Spokane.
Facility: Slots, video poker, craps, roulette, poker, pull
tabs.

COULEE DAM CASINO
515 Birch St.
COULEE DAM, WA 99155
  (800) 556-7492; (509) 633-0766
  Website: www.colvillecasinos.com
Owned and operated by the Colville Tribal Enterprise
Corporation. *Location*: In eastern Washington on the
Columbia River west of Spokane. *Facility*: Slots, video
poker, video keno, blackjack, pull tabs.

TWO RIVERS CASINO
6828B, Hwy. 25 S. • DAVENPORT, WA
  (800) 722-4031; (509) 722-4000 Fax 722-4015
Owned by the Spokane Tribe. *Location*: Where the Columbia and Spokane River meet. *Facility*: 400 reel
slots; table games.

NOOKSACK RIVER CASINO
5048 Mount Baker Hwy.,
P.O. Box 157
DEMING, WA 98244
  (877) 935-9300; (360) 592-5472 Fax 592-5753
  Website: www.nooksackcasino.com
  E-mail: info@nooksackcasino.com
Owned by the Nooksack Indian Tribe. *Location*: 14
miles off I-5, east of Bellingham on Hwy. 542 near
Deming. *Facility*: 25,000 sq. ft. 400 slots; 25 black-
jack, craps, roulette and poker tables; bingo.

SILVER REEF CASINO
4876 Haxton Way
FERNDALE, WA 98248
 (866) 383-0777; (360) 383-0777
 Website: www.silverreefcasino.com
Owned by the Nooksack Indian Tribe. *Location*: On I-5 exit 260. *Facility*: 28,000 sq. ft. 550 slots, gaming tables.

QUILEUTE CASINO
P.O. Box 279
LA PUSH, WA 98350
 (206) 374-6163
Owned by the Quileute Indian Tribe. *Location*: Off Hwy. 110 on the Pacific coast on the Olympic peninsula. *Facility*: 15,000 sq. ft. with blackjack, craps, roulette and poker tables; Bingo.

POINT NO POINT CASINO
31912 Little Boston Rd. NE
KINGSTON, WA 98346
 (360) 297-2646 Fax 297-7097
 Website: www.pointnopointcasino.com
Owned by the Port Gamble S'Klallam Tribe. *Location*: Located in the northern end of the Kitsap Peninsula in Kitsap County in Washington State. *Facility*: Slots, table games, bingo.

MILL BAY CASINO
455 E. Wapato Lake Rd.
MANSON, WA 98831
 (800) 648-2946; (509) 826-8050
 Website: www.colvillecasinos.com
 Website: www.millbaycasino.com
Owned and operated by the Colville Tribal Enterprise Corporation. *Location*: In north central Washington on Lake Chelan. Facility: 9,000 sq. ft. 200 slots; blackjack, craps, roulette and poker tables.

TULALIP CASINO & BINGO
10200 Quil Cedar Blvd.
TULALIP, WA 98271
 (888) 272-1111
 (360) 651-1111 Fax 651-2234
 Website: www.tulalipcasino.com
 Steve Griffis, General Manager
Owned and operated by the Tulalip Tribe. *Location*: 30 miles north of Seattle off I-5, 5 miles north of Everett, Wash. In Snohomish County. *Facility*: 15,000 sq. ft. 2,000 slots; 50 blackjack, craps, roulette and poker tables. Bingo.

QUINAULT BEACH RESORT & CASINO
78 State Rt. 115, P.O. Box 2107
OCEAN SHORES, WA 98587
(360) 374-6163 Fax 374-6311
Website: www.quinaultbeachresort.com
Owned and operated by the Quinault Indian Tribe. *Location*: On the Pacific Ocean in Clallam County. *Facility*: 16,000 sq. ft. Slots; gaming tables; live keno, bingo. 150-room hotel with full spa.

RED WING CASINO
12819 Yelm Hwy. SE
OLYMPIA, WA 98513
 (360) 456-5221 Fax 438-8618
 Website: www.redwingcasino.net
Owned and operated by the Nisqually Indian Tribe. *Location*: Located in Thurston County. *Facility*: Slots, table games, live keno, bingo

OKANOGAN BINGO & CASINO
41 Appleway Rd.
OKANOGAN, WA 98840
 (800) 559-4643; (509) 422-4646
Owned and operated by the Colville Tribal Enterprise Corporation. *Location*: In north central Washington northwest of Spokane. *Facility*: Slots, video poker, tables, bingo.

LOWER ELWHA S'KLALLAM TRIBE CASINO
2851 Lower Elwha Rd.
PORT ANGELES, WA 98363
 (360) 452-8471 Fax 452-3428
Owned by the Lower Elwha S'Kallam Tribe. *Location*: In Port Angeles across from Victoria, British Columbia, Canada. *Facility*: 36,800 sq. feet. Blackjack, craps, roulette and poker tables; keno bingo.

LUCKY EAGLE CASINO & BINGO
12888 188th Road SW
ROCHESTER, WA 98579
 (800) 720-1788; (360) 273-2000
 Website: www.luckyeagle.com
Owned by the Confederated Tribes of the Chehalis Reservation in Washington. *Facility*: 50,000 sq. ft. 350 slots, blackjack, craps, roulette, poker, keno, pull tabs, bingo.

HARRAH'S SKAGIT VALLEY CASINO
2284 Community Plaza
SEDRO WOOLLEY, WA 98284
 (360) 856-5501 Fax 856-3175
Owned by the Upper Skagit Indian Tribe. *Location*: 70 miles north of Seattle, 30 miles southeast of Bellingham. *Facility*: 30,000 sq. feet. Blackjack, craps, roulette and poker tables. 800-seat bingo, keno.

7 CEDARS CASINO
2070756 Hwy. 101 E.
SEQUIM, WA 98382
 (800) 4-LUCKY-7
 (360) 683-7777 Fax 683-4366
 Website: www.7cedarscasino.com
Owned by the Jamestown S' Klallam Tribe. *Location*: On the Olympic Peninsula 17 miles east of Port Angeles, 5 miles east of Sequim. *Facility*: 30,000 sq. ft. with 33 tables: blackjack, craps, roulette and poker; bingo, keno.

LITTLE CREEK CASINO & HOTEL
W. 91 Hwy. 108 • SHELTON, WA 98584
 (800) 667-7711
 (360) 427-7711 Fax 427-7868
 Website: www.little-creek.com
Owned by the Squaxin Island Tribe. *Location*: Northwest of Olympia on Hwy. 108. *Facilities*: 100,000 sq. ft. Slots, gaming tables, bingo. 92-room hotel.

CLEARWATER CASINO
15347 Suquamish Way, NE
SUQUAMISH, WA 98392
 (800) 375-6073; (360) 598-8700
 Website: www.clearwatercasino.com
Owned by the Suquamish Indian Tribe of the Port Madison Reservation. *Location*: Across from Puget Sound 15 miles west via the Bainbridge Ferry. *Facility*: 500+ video slots, blackjack, craps, roulette, poker; 300-seat bingo, pull tabs.

EMERALD QUEEN RIVERBOAT CASINO
2102 Alexander Ave.
TACOMA, WA 98404
 (888) 831-7655; (253) 594-7777
 Website: www.emeraldqueen.com
Owned by the Puyallup Tribe. Location: On the Puget Sound. *Facility*: 1,500 slots, lackjack, roulette, craps, poker, pull tabs.

YAKAMA LEGENDS CASINO
580 Fort Rd.
TOPPENISH, WA 98948
 (877) 726-6311; (509) 865-8800 ext. 217
 Website: www.legendscasino.com
Owned and opereated by the Yakama Nation. Location: On Yakama Reservation in Toppenish. Facility: 675 slots, table games, 600-seat bingo hall. 80-site campground. Annual Rodeo and Pow Wow in August.

WISCONSIN

HO-CHUNK CASINO
S3214 A Hwy. 12
BARABOO, WI 53913
 (800) 746-2486
 (608) 356-0279 Fax 355-4035
 Website: www.ho-chunk.com
Owned by the Ho-Chunk Nation. *Location*: On Hwy. 12, south of Lake Delton, 40 miles north of Madison. *Facility*: 85,000 sq. ft. 1,200 slots and video poker 48 poker & blackjack tables. Open 24 hours.

ISLE VISTA CASINO
Hwy. 13 North, Rt. 3 Box 3365
BAYFIELD, WI 54891

 (800) 226-8478
 (715) 779-3712 Fax 779-3715
Owned by the Red Cliff Band of Lake Superior Ojibway (Chippewa). *Location*: In northern Wisconsin on the shores of Lake Superior, 70 miles east of Duluth, Minn. *Facility*: 15,000 sq. ft. with 175 slots, video poker, video keno, blackjack tables, pull-tabs, bingo.

MAGIC PINES BINGO & CASINO
Hwy. 54, Rte. 5, Box 433-G
BLACK RIVER FALLS, WI 54615
 (800) 657-4621
 (715) 284-9098 Fax 284-9739
 Gordon Thunder, Contact
Owned by the Wisconsin Winnebago Indian Tribe. *Location*: 110 miles northwest of Madison, 44 miles southeast of Eau Claire 4 miles east of I-94 on Hwy. 54. *Facility*: 14,000 sq. ft. 246 slots & video poker; video keno, bingo.

MOHICAN NORTH STAR CASINO & BINGO
W12180A County Rd. A
BOWLER, WI 54416
 (800) 952-0195; (715) 787-3110 Fax 787-3129
 Website: www.mohican.com
 Louis Rawinkle, Contact
Owned by the Stockbridge-Munsee Mohican Indians. *Location*: 50 miles northwest of Green Bay, north of Hwy. 29. *Facility*: 16,000 sq. ft. with 1,000 slots, video poker and keno; 18 blackjack tables. High-stakes bingo. 53-site RV park. Konkapot LodgeOpen 24 hours Fri.-Sat. 10am-2am, Sun.-Thurs.

MOLE LAKE CASINO, BINGO & HOTEL
Rte. 1, Box 625
CRANDON, WI 54520
 (800) 236-9466
 (715) 478-5565 Fax 478-5275
 Website: www.molelake.com
Owned by the Sokoagan Ojibwe (Chippewa) Indian Tribe. *Location*: East of Rhineland, 7 miles south of Crandon on Hwy. 55. *Facility*: 30,000 sq. ft. 450 slots & video poker, and 20 blackjack tables.

HOLE IN THE WALL CASINO
P.O. Box 98 • DANBURY, WI 54830
 (800) BET-UWIN; (715) 656-3444 Fax 656-3434
Owned by the St. Croix Ojibwe Indians. *Location*: On Hwys. 77 & 35, 45 miles south of Duluth, Minnesota. *Facility*: 65,000 sq. feet. 300 slots & video poker; keno, bingo, and 84 blackjack tables.

ONEIDA BINGO & CASINO
2100 Airport Dr., P.O. Box 365
GREEN BAY, WI 54155
 (800) 238-4263
 (414) 494-4500 Fax 497-5803
 Website: www.oneidabingoandcasino.net
 Louise King, Contact
Owned by the Oneida Tribe of Indians of Wisconsin. *Location*: Near Green Bay airport on Hwy. 172 just off U.S. Hwy 43 & 41. *Facility*: 65,000 sq. ft. 2,500 slots & video poker & keno; and 84 blackjack tables; off-track betting; high-stakes bingo. 300-room Radisson Inn. Open 24 hours, 7 days a week.

LAC COURTE OREILLES CASINO
13767 W County Rd. B
Rte. 5, Box 505 • HAYWARD, WI 54843
 (800) 422-2175
 (715) 634-5643 Fax 634-6111
 Website: www.lcocasino.com
Owned by the Lac Courte Orielles Band of Lake Superior Ojibwe. *Location*: Northwest Wisconsin, 55 miles east of Duluth, Minnesota; on County Rd. E, 9 miles south of Hayward. *Facility*: 60,000 sq. feet. 450 slots & video poker; video keno and 12 blackjack tables.

MENOMINEE NATION CASINO
Hwy. 47, Box 7060 • KESHENA, WI 54135
 (800) 343-7778
 (715) 799-3600 Fax 799-4051
 Website: www.menomineecasinoresort.com
Owned by the Menominee Indian Tribe of Wisconsin. *Location*: 40 miles northwest of Green Bay on Hwy. 47. *Facility*: 27,500 sq. feet. 850 slots & 12 blackjack tables. 400-seat bingo hall. Conference and meeting center. 100-room hotel.

LAKE OF THE TORCHES RESORT & CASINO
510 Old Abe Rd.
LAC DU FLAMBEAU, WI 54538
 (800) 25-8672; (715) 588-7070
 Website: www.lakeofthetorches.com
Owned by the Lac du Flambeau Band of Lake Superior Chippewa. *Location*: On Hwy. 47, 160 miles northwest of Green Bay. *Facility*: 15,000 sq. ft. 800 slots; video poker & keno; 12 blackjack tables; high-stakes bingo hall. 101-room hotel. Open 24 hours, 7 days a week.

DeJOPE BINGO
4002 Evan Acres Rd.
MADISON, WI 53718
 (888) 248-1777
 (608) 223-9576 Fax 224-1110
 Website: www.dejope.com
 Joyce Warner, General Manager
Owned by the Ho-Chunk Nation. High-stakes bingo.

POTAWATOMI BINGO CASINO
1721 W. Canal St.
MILWAUKEE, WI 53233
 (800) PAYSBIG
 (414) 645-6888 Fax 645-6866
 Website: www.paysbig.com
Owned by the Potawatomi Tribe of Wisconsin. *Location*: The western shore of Lake Michigan. *Facility*: 200 slots, video poker & keno; 2,000-seat High Stakes Bingo.

RAINBOW CASINO & BINGO
949 County Rd. G, P.O. Box 460
NEKOOSA, WI 54615
 (800) 782-4560
 (715) 886-4560 Fax 886-4551
 Website: www.ho-chunk.com
Owned by the Wisconsin Winnebago Indian Tribe. *Location*: In central Wisconsin on the Wisconsin River south of Stevens Point; 14 miles off Hwy. 13. *Facility*: 37,000 sq. ft. 600 slots; video poker & keno; 24 blackjack and poker tables.

BAD RIVER LODGE & CASINO
US Hwy. 2, P.O. Box 8
ODANAH, WI 54861
 (800) 777-7449; (715) 682-7121
Owned by the Bad River Band of Lake Superior Tribe of Ojibwe (Chippewa) Indians. *Location*: 10 miles east of Ashland on US Hwy. 2 near Lake Superior. *Facility*: 20,000 sq. ft. casino. 500 slots, video poker & keno; 6 blackjack & poker tables; bingo. 600-seat theater.

ST. CROIX CASINO & HOTEL
777 US Hwy. 8 W
TURTLE LAKE, WI 54889
 (800) 846-8946
 (715) 987-4777 Fax 986-2800
 Website: www.stcroixcasino.com
Owned by the St. Croix Ojibwe (Chippewa) Indians of Wisconsin. *Location*: In northwest Wisconsin on US Hwy. 8, 25 miles east of the Minnesota border. *Facility*: 65,000 sq. feet. 1,20 slots, video poker & keno; 20 blackjack tables. 158-room hotel. Open 24 hours daily.

NORTHERN LIGHTS CASINO,
POTAWATOMI BINGO
Hwy. 32, P.O. Box 140
WABENO, WI 54566
 (800) 487-9522
 (715) 473-2021 Fax 886-4551
Owned by the Forest County Potawatomi Indian Community. *Location*: In northeast Wisconsin, 65 miles north of Green Bay on Hwy. 32. *Facility*: 12,000 sq. feet. 420 slots & video poker, and 13 blackjack tables; bingo. 70 room lodge.

WYOMING

789 BINGO & CASINO
10369 Hwy. 789 • RIVERTON, WY
 (307) 856-3964
Owned and operated by the Northern Arapaho Tribe of the Wind River Reservation. High-stakes bingo; progressive bingo machines; Lotto machines.

CANADA

MANITOBA

ASENESKAK CASINO
OPASKWAYAK, THE PAS
P.O. Box 10250 • OPASKWAYAK, MB
 (204) 627-2276
Owned by a concortium of six First Nations of Cree . *Location*: 5 minutes north on Hwy. 10 from the town of The Pas, on the Opaskwayak Cree Nation reserve. *Facilities*: 177 slots; 8 table games.

ONTARIO

The Ontario Gaming Control Board regulates the two First Nation casinos which opened in 1995 & 1996. Other future casinos maybe planned for Toronto, London, Niagara Falls, and Sault Ste. Marie.

GOLDEN EAGLE CHARITABLE
CASINO & ENTERTAINMENT CENTRE
P.O. Box 2860 • KENORA, ON P9N 3X8
 (800) 336-4202; (807) 548-1331 Fax 548-5831
Owned by the Wauzhushk Onigum First Nation. *Location*: On the north shore of Lake of the Woods in northwest Ontario on Canada Hwy. 17. *Facility*: 7,500 sq. feet. No slots. 27 blackjack, roulette and poker tables.

CASINO RAMA RESORT
P.O. Box 178 • ORILLA, ON L0K 1T0
 (705) 329-3325 Fax 329-3329
Owned by the Rama Chippewas First Nation. *Location*: 90 miles north of Toronto on Canada Hwy. 12. *Facility*: 50,000 sq. feet. 1,800 slots, 36 blackjack, roulette and poker tables. Hotel.

SASKATCHEWAN

BEAR CLAW CASINO
White Bear Golf Course
P.O. Box 221
KENOSEE LAKE, SK S0C 2S0
 (306) 577-4577 Fax 577-4899
Owned by the White Bear Indian Community. *Location*: In southeast Saskatchewan on Hwy. 9, 137 miles southeast of Regina. *Facility*: 10,000 sq.ft. with blackjack tables, roulette, bingo.

GOLDEN EAGLE CASINO
11906 Railway St.
N. BATTLEFORD, SK S9A 3K7
 (306) 446-3833 Fax 446-7170
First Nations casino. *Location*: 88 miles northwest of Saskatoon. *Facility*: 128 slots and 12 tables.

NORTHERN LIGHTS CASINO
153 S. Industrial Dr.
PRINCE ALBERT, SK S6V 7L7
 (306) 764-4777 Fax 922-1000
First Nations casino.

(Please call to confirm dates & locations)

JANUARY

New Year's Indoor Contest Powwow
Amigos Indoor Sports Arena
So. Tucson, Arizona (602) 622-4900
Dates: 1st week in January

Santa Monica Indian Show-Sale-Powwow
Civic Auditorium, 1855 Main St.
Santa Monica, California (310) 430-5112
Dates: 2nd week in January

Colorado Indian Market & Western Showcase
Denver/Boulder, Colorado
(303) 447-9967
Dates: 2nd week in January

Festival of the Buffalo
1052 Hwy. 92 West
Auburndale, Florida (863) 665-0062
Dates: 2nd weekend in January

Mystic Eagle PowWow
Scherer State Park
Osprey, Florida (941) 485-9072
E-mail: jno8363406@aol.com
Dates: 4th week in January

Discover Native America
Vinoy Park • St. Petersburg, Florida
(813) 966-6300 ext 1468
Dates: 4th week in January

Native American Powwow
St. Petersburg, Florida
(800) 683-7800 ext. 1467
(888) 762-2409
Dates: 4th week in January

Annual Florida Everglades Powwow
West Palm Beach, Florida
(561) 927-2382
Dates: 1st week in January

Apoctowi New Moon Celebration
Tippecanoe Co. Fairgrounds
Lafayette, Indiana (317) 589-8546
Dates: 3rd week in January

Morning Star Celebration
John Carroll School, Bel Aire, Maryland
(410) 838-8333 ext. 14
Dates: 2nd weekend in January

Greater Lowell Indian Cultural Association
Midwinter Powwow
VA Hospital • Bedford, Massachusetts
(508) 453-7182
Dates: 3rd week in January

Papsaquoho Powwow
Thyer Academy • Braintree, Massachusetts
(617) 884-4227
Dates: 3rd week in January

Mashpee Wampanoag
Winter Social & Potluck
Mashpee United Church
Village Community Center
Mashpee, Massachusetts
(508) 477-0208
Dates: Monthly

American Indianist Society Powwow
Quinsigamond Village Community Center
16 Greenwood St.
Worcester, Massachusetts
(508) 852-6271
Dates: Second week in January

Parkslope Native American Dance Festival
Park Slope, Brooklyn, New York
(718) 499-0912
Dates: Third week in January

Thunderbird American Indian Dancers Powwow
McBurney YMCA, 215 W. 23rd St.
New York, New York (201) 587-9633
Louis Mofsie, Contact
Dates: Monthly

Algonquin Intertribal Society Social
Providence, Rhode Island
(401) 231-9280
Dates: 2nd Saturday of each month

Sinte Gleska Founders' Day Celebration
Traditional & Contest Wacipi
Wakinyawanbi Multipurpose Center
Mission, South Dakota (605) 856-4463

TIHA Powwow
San Antonio, Texas (817) 498-2873
Dates: Third Saturday in January

University of Washington
Annual Winter Powwow
Native American Student Council
Seattle, Washington (206) 543-4635
Dates: 2nd week in January

FEBRUARY

Annual O'Odham Tash
Casa Grande, Arizona
(602) 836-4723
Dates: 2nd week in February

Casa Grande Outdoor Indian Market
Casa Grande, Arizona (520) 538-2471
Dates: 3rd week in February

All Indian Day
Graham County Fairgrounds
Safford, Arizona (602) 428-6260
Dates: 4th week in February

Annual Tony White Cloud Memorial
World Champion Hoop Dance Competition
The Heard Museum • Phoenix, Arizona
(602) 252-8840 ext. 512 or 545
Dates: 3rd week in February

Annual Ira H. Hayes Recognition Day
Veteran's Park • Sacaton, Arizona
(602) 562-3310
Date: February 20th

American Indian, Old West
& Tribal Art Show & Sale
Scottsdale, Arizona
(520) 836-4723 Fax 287-2734
Dates: 3rd week in February

Southwest Indian Art Fair
University of Arizona
Arizona State Museum • Tucson, Arizona
Website: www.statemuseum.arizona.edu
Dates: Last weekend in February

Annual Grossmont College Powwow
Viejas & Barona Band of Kumeyaay Indians
El Cajon, California (619) 644-7529
Date: 3rd or 4th Saturday in February.

American Indian Exposition & Sale
Alameda Fairgrounds • Pleasanton, California
(209) 221-4355 Fax 221-0844
Dates: 2nd week in February

United Native American Tribes Annual Powwow
Porterville Fairgrounds
Porterville, California
(209) 781-1706
Dates: 2nd week in February

Iron Eyes Cody Parade & Powwow
Warman Park, Desert Hot Springs, Calif.
Joyce Running Deer
(619) 251-1677
Dates: 1st week in February

Brighton Field Day & Rodeo
Brighton Reservation, Florida
(305) 966-6300 ext. 1468
Dates: 3rd week in February

Immokalee Powwow
Seminole Indian Reservation
Immokalee, Florida
(305) 966-6300 ext. 1468
Dates: 1st week in February

Seminole Tribal Fair & Rodeo
Bergeron Rodeo Grounds
4271 Davie Rd. • Davie, Florida
(954) 364-4221
Rodeo, Festival, Alligator Show, Dance Troops,
Craft Booths. Dates: 2nd weekend in February

Vero's 'Thunder on the Beach' PowWow
Indian River County Fairgrounds
Vero Beach, Florida (772) 567-1579
E-mail: deedee1579@aol.com
Dates: February 25-27

New England NAI Powwow
Sturbridge, Massacusetts
(508) 886-6073
Dates: 1st week in February

Hosaga Annual PowWow
Springfield College-Dana Gym
Springfield, Massachusetts
(413) 783-3428
Dates: 1st week in February

Michigan State University PowWow
West Lansing, Michigan (517) 353-7745
Dates: 3rd week in February

Honor Our Ancestors
Traditional Powwow
Negaunee Community Center
Negaunee, Michigan (906) 249-3153
Dates: 2nd week in February

Council of Indian Students
Traditional Winter PowWow
Bemidji State University
Bemidji, Minnesota
(218) 755-2094
Dates: 2nd week in February

New Hampshire Inter-
Tribal Council PowWow
Mt. Valley Mall, Rte. 16
North Conway, New Hampshire
(603) 528-3005
Dates: Washington's Birthday weekend

Native American Indians
Traditional PowWow
UAW Hall, 1440 Bellefontaine Ave.
Lima, Ohio (419) 228-1097
Dates: 3rd week in February

Red Earth Winter Expo
Kirkpatrick Center
Oklahoma City, Oklahoma
(405) 427-5228 Fax 427-8079
Dates: 1st week in February

Self-Government
Sovereignty Celebration
Warm Springs, Oregon
(541) 553-3393
Dates: 1st week in February

Sinte Gleska College Founders Day Powwow
Sinte Gleska College
Rosebud, South Dakota
(605) 747-2263
Dates: 1st week in February

Annual Native American Heritage Assn
of Radford University PowWow
Radford, Virginia
(703) 633-1871
Dates: 3rd week in February

Stanley Purser Powwow
Port Gamble Tribal Center
Port Gamble, Washington
(360) 297-2253
Dates: 4th week in February

Washington's Birthday Celebration
Toppenish Community Center
Toppenish, Washington (509) 865-5121
Dates: Washington's Birthday weekend

Three Fires Society
Winter Ceremonies
Lac Courte Oreilles Reservation,
Hayward, Wisconsin (715) 634-1442/4078
Dates: 3rd week in February

Nindinawe Maaganag Nimiwin
Competitive PowWow
North Pines High School
Eagle River, Wisconsin (715) 588-3346
Dates: 3rd week in February

United Amerindian Center PowWow
Washington Commons
Green Bay, Wisconsin (920) 436-6630
dates: 1st weekend in February

MARCH

Gathering of the Clans
Metlakatla, Alaska
(907) 886-6332 ext. 310
Dates: 1st week in March

Indian Festival Bazaar
St. John Indian School
Laveen, Arizona (602) 550-2400
Dates: 1st week in March

Annual Heard Museum Guild
Indian Fair & Market
The Heard Museum • Phoenix, Arizona
(602) 252-8840
Dates: 1st weekend in March

Apache Gold Casino PowWow
San Carlos Apache Reservation
San Carlos, Arizona (800) APACHE8
(928) 475-7800
Dates: 2nd weekend in March

Native Arts & Crafts Show & Sale
Scottsdale, Arizona (602) 569-0728
Dates: 3rd weekend in March

Scottsdale All Indian Powwow
Salt River Reservation
Scottsdale, Arizona (602) 569-0728
Dates: 4th weekend in March

Waila Festival
Arizona Historical Society Museum
Tucson, Arizona (520) 622-808
Dates: 4th week in March

WA AK Powwow
St. Xavier Mission
Tucson, Arizona (520) 294-5727
Dates: 1st week in March

Annual Homestead Intertribal PowWow
Homestead High School
Cupertino, California (408) 241-7999
Dates: 3rd week in March

American Indian Exposition & Sale
Monterey Grounds, Monterey, California
(209) 221-4355 Fax 221-0844
Dates: 3rd week in March

North American Indian
Student Alliance Powwow
Montezuma Hall Aztec Center, SDSU
San Diego, California (619) 594-6991/4251
Dates: 2nd week in March

Cal State U.-Long Beach, Powwow
1250 Bellflower • Long Beach, California
(310) 985-5293
Dates: 2nd week in March

Early Spring Celebration PowWow
Sponsored in part by the Fort Yuma
Quechan Paradise Casino.
Winterhaven, California
Faron Owl (760) 572-0222 ext. 2228
Date: 1st week in March

Crafton Hill Powwow
Yucaipa, California (714) 785-4377
Dates: First week in March

Carmel American Indian Festival
Carmel, California (408) 623-2379
 Attn: Sonny/Elaine Reyna
Dates: First week in March

Rimrock Rendezvous & Powwow
"A Celebration of Contemporary
& Traditinal Native American Art"
Chico Mall • Chico, California (916) 343-0696
Dates: First week in March

American Indian Festival & Market
Museum of Natural History of LA County
900 Exposition Blvd. • Los Angeles, California
(213) 744-3488 Attn: Shelley Stephens
Dates: 3rd week in March

Annual American Indian Powwow
Cal State University-Stanislaus
Turlock, California (800) 828-7733
Dates: 4th week in March

Annual Denver March Powwow
Denver Coliseum • Denver, Colorado
(303) 936-4826
Dates: 3rd weekend in March

Withlacoochee PowWow
Withlacoochee River Park
Dade City, Florida (352) 583-3388
Dates: 2nd weekend in March

Florida Indian Hobbyist Association Powwow
Indian River Community College
Fort Pierce, Florida (407) 464-4973
Dates: 3rd weekend in March

E-Peh-Tes Powwow
Lapwai, Idaho (208) 843-2253
Dates: 2nd weekend in March

College Park Powwow
University of Maryland
College Park, Maryland (301) 270-2991
Dates: 1st weekend in March

Birthday Celebration for Slow Turtle
National Guard Armory
Middle Burrow, Massachusetts
(617) 884-4227
Date: 3rd week in March

American Indian Students Association Powwow
University of Massachusetts
Amherst, Massachusetts (617) 413-5103
Dates: 4th week in March

Massachusetts Center for Native American
Awareness Day Celebration
South Shore, Massachusetts (617) 884-4227
Dates: 1st week in March

Ann Arbor Contest Powwow
Chrysler Arena • Ann Arbor, Michigan
(313) 763-9044
Dates: 3rd week in March

Traditional Powwow
Dominic Jacobetti Center
Michigan University Campus
Marquette, Michigan (906) 227-2138
Dates: 4th week in March

Spring Powwow
Leech Lake Reservation
Cass Lake, Minnesota (218) 335-6211
Dates: 3rd week in March

Traditional Intertribal Powwow
Armed Forces Armory
Rochester, Minnesota (507) 281-4772
Dates: 4th week in March

Heart of the Earth Contest Powwow
Minneapolis Convention Center
Minneapolis, Minnesota (612) 331-8862
Dates: 4th week in March

Annual Natchez Powwow
Grand Village of the Natchez Indians
Natchez, Mississippi (601) 446-6502
Dates: Weekend before Easter

Inter-Tribal Powwow
MSU • Billings, Montana
(406) 657-2561
Dates: 4th week in March

Great Falls Native American
Art Association Exhibit & Sale
Ponderosa Inn • Great Falls, Montana
(406) 791-2212
Dates: 3rd week in March

Celebration of Sobriety & Powwow
College of Great Falls, MacLaughlin Center
Great Falls, Montana
Dates: 3rd week in March

Sugar Row Powwow
Laconia Indian Historical Association
Laconia, New Hampshire (603) 783-9922
Dates: 4th week in March

St. Joseph's Feast Day
Laguna Pueblo Plaza
Laguna Pueblo, New Mexico
(505) 552-6654
Date: 3rd week in March

Carolina Indian Circle Powwow
University of North Carolina
Chapel Hill, North Carolina
(919) 929-0883
Date: 3rd week in March

First Nations of the Woodlands
& High Plains Powwow
Fargo, North Dakota (701) 231-7314
Dates: 1st week in March

Miami Valley Council for Native Americans
Annual Benefit Powwow
Dayton, Ohio (513) 275-8599
Dates: 1st week in March

Students of Five Civilized Tribes
Heritage Art Show
Five Civilixed Tribes Museum
Muskogee, Oklahoma (918) 683-1701
Dates: 2nd week in March

NASA Spring Contest Powwow
Oklahoma State University
Stillwater, Oklahoma (405) 744-5481
Dates: 3rd week in March

Sucker Ceremony
Chiloquin High School, Chiloquin, Oregon
(503) 783-2219 ext. 162
Dates: 4th week in March

Salem Area Spring Powwow
Polk County Fairgrounds
Richreal, Oregon (503) 623-8971
Dates: 4th week in March

Edisto Indian Cultural Festival
Summerville, South Carolina
(803) 871-2126
Dates: 4th week in March

Indian Awareness Powwow
Crow Creek High School
Stephan, South Dakota (605) 852-2258
Date: 3rd week in March

American Indian Festival & PowWow
University Campus • Murfreesboro, Tennesee
(615) 898-2872
Dates: 1st week in March

Texas Indian Market
Arlington Convention Center
Arlington, Texas (806) 355-1610
Dates: 3rd week in March

Yakama Nation Cultural Center
Toppenish, Washington (509) 865-5121
Dates: 2nd weekend in March

Speelyi Mi Arts & Crafts Fair
Yakima, Washington (509) 865-5121
Dates: 2nd weekend in March

Native American Awareness Day PowWow
Northland College • Ashland, Wisconsin
(715) 682-1240
Date: 3rd weekend in March

**Forest County Potawatomi
Recreation Winters End PowWow**
Crandon, Wisconsin (715) 478-7420
Dates: 3rd weekend in March

Bear River Benefit
Lac du Flambeau, Wisconsin (715) 588-3286
Dates: 2nd week in March

**United Indians of Milwaukee
Traditional Powwow**
State Fair Park • Milwaukee, Wisconsin
(414) 384-8070
Dates: 3rd week in March

Central Wisconsin Indian Center Powwow
Rothchild Pavilion • Rothchild, Wisconsin
(715) 845-2613
Dates: 1st week in March

Spring Powwow
University of Wyoming • Laramie, Wyoming
Dates: 4th weekend in March

APRIL

Native Solutions Annual PowWow
Heflin Football Field
Heflin, Alabama (256) 835-0110
Dates: 4th weekend in April

Cocopah Indian Patent Day
Sommerton, Arizona (602) 627-2102
Dates: 2nd week in April

Navajo Community College Powwow
Tsaile, Arizona (605) 724-3311 ext. 219
Dates: 2nd week in April

Annual ASU Spring Competition Powwow
Arizona State University • Tempe, Arizona
Attn: Lee Williams (602) 965-2230
Dates: 3rd week in April

All Indian Days Powwow
Scottsdale Community College
Scottsdale, Arizona (602) 946-4228
Dates: 3rd week in April

Annual Powwow
Mills College • Oakland, California (510) 430-2080
Dates: 4th week in April

**Annual Honoring of the Elders & 1st Annual
SANAI Powwow**
University of Santa Cruz
Santa Cruz, California (408) 459-2296
Dates: 2nd week in April

American Indian Powwow
West Valley College • Saratoga, Califonia
(408) 867-2200 ext. 5601
Dates: 3rd weekend in April

American Indian Days Powwow
Chico State University
Chico, California (916) 895-5396
Dates: 3rd weekend in April

Annual Powwow
Humboldt State University
Arcata, California (707) 826-4994
Dates: 1st week in April

Keeper of the Earth Spring Powwow
Fullerton Union High School Stadium
Fullerton, California
(800) 428-3872
Dates: 4th week in April

Lancaster, California (619) 873-5396
Dates: 1st week in April

**UC Davis Native American Cultural Days
& D-Q University Powwow**
Davis, California (916) 758-0470
Attn: Karen Bohay
Dates: 1st week in April

Cultural Awareness Powwow
Napa Valley College • Napa, California
(707) 226-5075 Attn: Charlie Toledo
Dates: 2nd week in April

**Annual Tewaquchi American Indian Club
Powwow**
California State University-Fresno
Fresno, California (209) 278-3277
Dates: 2nd weekend in April

**Annual Sherman High School
Intertribal Powwow**
Riverside, California
(714) 276-6309 Attn: Mary Basquez
Dates: 3rd week in April

ITSC Powwow
University of California-Berkeley
Berkeley, California
(510) 642-6613 Attn: Ruth Hopper
Dates: 3rd week in April

Agua Caliente Indian Heritage Festival
Palm Springs, California (619) 778-1079
Dates: 4th week in April

Oyate/AISES Spring Powwow
University of Colorado
Boulder, Colorado (303) 492-8874
Dates: 2nd week in April

Annual NASA Powwow
Colorado State University
Fort Collins, Colorado
(303) 491-8946 Attn: Debra Wadena
Dates: 4th week in April

Hart Springs Pow Wow
Hart Springs, Florida
(352) 463-7321
Helen Blair, Contact
Dates: 4th weekend in April

North Florida Indian Cultural Assn. Powwow
Orange Springs, Florida
(904) 799-7981
Dates: 1st weekend in April

**Annual Octagon American Indian Preservation
Society Powwow**
Fort Myers, Florida (813) 543-1130
Dates: 3rd weekend in April

Annual Spring Traditional Powwow
UAW 933 Hall • Indianapolis, Indiana
(317) 545-5057
Dates: 4th weekend in April

Annual AIC Spring Traditional PowWow
Boone County 4H Grounds
Lebanon, Indiana (765) 482-3315
Dates: Last week of April

Redbud Trail Rendezvous
Rochester, Indiana
(219) 223-4436
Dates: Last weekend in April

Annual Indian Creek Traders Expo
Midlands Mall • Council Bluffs, Iowa
(712) 325-1770
Dates: 1st week in April

University of Iowa Powwow
Iowa City, Iowa (319) 335-8298
Dates: 2nd week in April

Annual Indian Awareness Day Powwow
Morningside College Campus
Sioux City Iowa (712) 274-5147
Dates: 2nd weekend in April

Kansas City Indian Market
Overland, Kansas
(806) 355-1610 Attn: Randy Wilkerson
Dates: 1st weekend in April

Mantle Rock PowWow
Mantle Rock Cherokee
Native Education & Cultural Center
Marion, Kentucky (270) 965-9432
Kamama Sutton, Contact
Dates: Last week in April

Red Heart American Indian Festival
Fair Hill Fairgrounds
Elkton, Maryland (410) 885-2800
Dates: Last week in April

Northern Virginia Powwow
White Oak, Maryland (703) 451-8617
Dates: 1st week in April

American Indian Day
Boston Children's Museum
Boston, Massachusetts (617) 426-6500 ext. 261
Date: 1st week in April

Native American Awareness Day Celebration
Wellesley Middle School
Wellesley, Massachusetts (617) 884-4227
Dates: 2nd week in April

Native American Ponatom
Natick, Massachusetts (617) 884-4227
Dates: 2nd week in April

Annual New England NAI Powwow
Foxboro, Massachusetts (508) 791-5007
Dates: 4th week in April

Annual Central Michigan University Powwow
Mt. Pleasant, Michigan (517) 772-5700
Dates: 1st week in April

**Annual 1st Peoples International Trade Expo &
Powwow**
Macomb Community College
Warren, Michigan (313) 756-1350
Dates: 2nd week in April

Annual University of Minnesota-Duluth Powwow
Sports Arena • Duluth, Minnesota
(218) 726-8141
Dates: 4th week in April

Annual Traditional Powwow
Itasca Community College
Grand Rapids, Minnesota (218) 327-4491
Dates: 2nd week in April

St. Cloud State Traditional Powwow
St. Cloud State University
St. Cloud, Minnesota (320) 308-5449
E-mail: siouxgrass@hotmail.com
Dates: in April

American Indian Club Powwow
Montana State University
Bozeman, Montana
(406) 994-4880/3751
Dates: 1st week in April

Annual Kyi-Yo PowWow
University of Montana
Missoula, Montana
(406) 243-5302
E-mail: powwow@kyiyo.com
Website: www.kyiyo.com
Dates: 4th weekend in April

Annual American Indian Week
Indian Pueblo Cultural Center
Albuquerque, New Mexico (800) 288-0721
Dates: 4th week in April

Annual Southwest Nations Powwow
New Mexico State University
Las Cruces, New Mexico (505) 646-4207
Dates: 2nd week in April

**"Gathering of Nations" Powwow
Miss Indian World Pageant**
University of New Mexico
The Pit, Albuquerque, New Mexico
(505) 836-2810
Dates: 4th weekend in April

Nighthawk Dancers Annual Powwow
Little Falls High School
Little Falls, New York
(315) 823-2570
Date: 1st weekend in April

Annual Haliwa-Saponi
Haliwa School • Hollister, North Carolina
(919) 586-3787
Dates: 3rd weekend in April

Annual Raleigh Powwow
Raleigh, North Carolina
(919) 821-7400
Dates: 1st weekend in April

**Annual Native American
Cultural Awareness Weekend**
North Carolina State University
Raleigh, North Carolina (919) 839-2214
Dates: 1st weekend in April

Annual Woodlands & High Plains PowWow
North Dakota State University
Fargo, North Dakota (701) 231-1029
Dates: Last weekend of April

Celebrating Life Not Genocide Powwow
Ohio State University
Columbus, Ohio (614) 443-6120
Dates: 4th week in April

Kent State University PowWow
Kent, Ohio (330) 672-0150
Lauren Yates, Contact
E-mail: nasaksupowwow@yahoo.com
Website: www.geocities.com/nasaksupowwow
dates: 3rd weekend in April

"Art Under the Oaks" Indian Market
Five Civilized Tribes Museum
Muskogee, Oklahoma (918) 683-1701
Dates: 3rd weekend in April

Annual Tulsa Indian Art Festival
Expo Square Pavilion
Tulsa, Oklahoma (918) 838-3875
Dates: 1st week in April

Celilo-Wyam Salmon Feast
Celilo, Oregon (503) 298-1559
Dates: 2nd week in April

South Umpaqua Powwow
Myrtle Creek, Oregon
(503) 863-4942
Dates: 4th week in April

**Northwest Indian Youth
Conference & PowWow**
Rushmore Plaza Civic Center
Rapid City, South Dakota
(605) 867-5161
Melanie Two Eagle, Contact
Dates: last week in April

Quanah Parker Comanche Pow Wow
Back Forty Pavilion
Fort Worth Stockyards
Fort Worth, Texas (580) 429-8229
Robert Tippeconnie, Contact
E-mail: bradlyn@charter.net
Dates: 4th weekend of April

Texas Gulf TIA-PIAH Powwow
Sallas County Park
New Carey, Texas
(713) 523-0583 Attn: Janelle Walker
Dates: 4th week in April

Annual Native American Spring Festival
Virginia Wesleyan College
1518 Wesleyan Dr. • Norfolk, Virginia
(804) 481-7342
Date: 1st week in April

Annual Davis Lake Powwow
Suffolk, Virginia
(804) 539-1191
Dates: 2nd week in April

Rock Creek Annual Salmon Feast
Rock Creek, Washington (509) 773-3787
Dates: 3rd week in April

Annual Chief Seattle Powwow
Connolly Center-Seattle Unversity
Seattle, Washington
(206) 296-6000 ect. 6076
Dates: 1st week in April

**Annual Northwest Indian
Youth Conference Powwow**
Seattle, Washington (206) 343-3111
Dates: 2nd week in April

Annual NASA Powwow
Eastern Washington University
Cheney, Washington (509) 359-2441
Dates: 3rd weekend of April

Annual South Beach Sobriety Powwow
Westport, Washington
(206) 267-6212 Attn: Rose Shipman
Dates: 3rd weekend in April

Annual Powwow
Western Washington State University
Bellingham, Washington (206) 676-3000
Dates: 3rd weekend in April

Annual Native Arts & Crafts Show
Suquamish Tribal Center
Suquamish, Washington (206) 598-3311
Dates: 3rd weekend in April

Annual Eau Claire Traditional Powwow
Eau Claire, Wisconsin
(715) 836-3367
Dates: 4th weekend in April

A.I.R.O. Powwow
University of Wisconsin-Stevens Point
Stevens Point, Wisconsin (715) 346-3576
Dates: 4th weekend in April

Superior Annual Indian Awareness Powwow
University of Wisconsin
Superior, Wisconsin (715) 394-8358
Dates: 2nd weekend in April

Annual Spring Powwow
University of Wyoming
Laramie, Wyoming
(307) 766-6189
Dates: 1st weekend in April

CANADA

**Saskatchewan Indian Federated College
Powwow**
Agridome Exhibition Park
Regina, Saskatchewan, Canada
(306) 584-8333
Dates: 1st week in April

May

Annual Lakeside Intertribal PowWow
Lakeside RV Park, 3509 Hwy. 411 North
Gadston, Alabama (877) 546-8044
Dates: 2nd week in May

Mother's Day Indian Festival
Troy, Alabama (334) 562-9013
Ruth Pace, Contact
Dates: Mother's Day weekend

Creek Indian Removal Remembrance Festival
Spring Park • Tuscumbia, Alabama
(800) 344-0783 (256) 383-0783
Website: www.colbertcountytourism.org
Dates: 1st weekend in May

Annual Zuni Artists Exhibition
Museum of Northern Arizona
Flagstaff, Arizona (520) 774-5213
Dates: 4th week in May

Tse-Ho-Tso Intertribal Powwow
Window Rock High School
Fort Defiance, Arizona (602) 729-5704
Dates: 2nd weekend in May

Annual Inter-Agency Committee PowWow
Bishop, California
(619) 873-6394 Attn: Leslie Davis
Dates: 4th weekend in May

Annual De Anza College Powwow
21250 Steven Creek Blvd.
Cupertino, California
(408) 486-8355 ext. 871
E-mail parkergerri@fhda.edu
Dates: 3rd weekend in May

Annual Intertribal Gathering & PowWow
Fontana, California (714) 984-6215
Dates: 2nd week in May

YA-KA-AMA Spring Fair
6215 Eastside Rd.
Forrestville, California
(707) 887-1541
Dates: 4th weekend in May

Annual Wildflower Festival
Tule Indian Reservation
near Fresno, California
(209) 781-1519 Attn: Leona Dabney
Dates: 1st week in May

Annual Red Road PowWow
Casa de Fruta, near Hollister, California
(831) 425-4404
Dates: Memorial Day weekend

Annual Memorial Weekend Celebration
Cecil B. DeMille Middle School
7025 Parkcrest Ave.
Long Beach, California (714) 785-4377
Dates: 4th weekend in May

Annual UCLA PowWow
Los Angeles, California (310) 206-7513
E-mail: thstew@ucla.edu
Dates: 1st week in May

Annual Strawberry Festival
Kule Koklo Village, Point Reyes
Marin County, California (415) 663-1092
Dates: 1st week in May

Annual Northern & Southern Winds PowWow
Avenida Cesar Chavez
Monterey Park, California
(323) 377-3523
Dates: 2nd weekend in May

Annual Eagle Point PowWow
Ojai, California (805) 494-1558
Dates: 3rd week in May

Feather River Festival
Native American Village
Oroville, California (916) 538-7986
Dates: 2nd weekend in May

Cupa Days
Pala Cultural Center
Pala Reservation, California
(619) 742-1590
Dates: 1st weekend in May

American Indian Arts & Crafts Festival
Indian Canyon Way • Palm Springs, California
(619) 329-3407
Dates: 4th week in May

Medicine Ways Conference & PowWow
University of California
Riverside, California (909) 787-4143
E-mail: tryond@watmail.ucr.edu
Dates: Memorial Day weekend

Nisenan-Maidu Bigtime
Roseville, California (916) 785-5144
Dates: 4th week in May

California Indian & World Culture Festival
Annual American Indian Spring Market
Mission San Juan Bautista
San Juan Batista, California (408) 623-2379
Dates: First weekend in May

American Indian Cultural Days
Balboa Park • San Diego, California
(619) 281-5964
Dates: 3rd weekend in May

Annual San Francisco State University PowWow
San Francisco, California (415) 338-1929
Dates: 1st week in May

Palomar College PowWow
San Marcos, California
(619) 744-1150 ext. 2425
Dates: 2nd week in May

Honoring Powwow for American Indian Children
Rancho Santiago Community College
Santa Ana, California (714) 360-1025
Date: May 29th

Annual Stanford PowWow
Eucalypotus Grove • Stanford, California
(650) 72506947
Dates: 2nd weekend in May

Mother's Day PowWow
Lassen Community College
Susanville, California (916) 257-5222
Dates: 2nd weekend in May

Southern Ute Bear Dance
Ignacio, Colorado (303) 563-4525
Dates: First weekend in May

Indian Nations Rendezvous & Trade Fair
Denver, Colorado (303) 238-7540
Dates: 3rd weekend in May

Annual Fort Garland PowWow
The Old Fort
Fort Garland, Colorado
(719) 384-4850 Attn: Sherry Manyik
Dates: 4th weekend in May

Chehaw National Indian Festival
Albany, Georgia (912) 436-1625
Dates: 3rd weekend in May

Annual Augusta PowWow
3J Road • Augusta, Georgia
Nill Medeiros(706) 771-1221
Dates: 2nd weekend in May

Annual Cherokee County PowWow
Canton, Georgia (404) 735-6275
Dates: 1st week in May

Mat'Alyma Root Festival
Kamiah, Idaho (208) 935-2144
Dates: 3rd weekend in May

Root Festival
Lapwai, Idaho (208) 843-2253
Dates: 2nd weekend in May

Indian PowWow
Rockome Gardens
5 miles west of Arcola, Illinois
(217) 268-4106 Attn: Jeane Lambeth
Dates: 4th week in May

Annual Aurora University
Schingoethe Center for Native American
Cultures Traditional PowWow
Aurora, Illinois (630) 844-7843
Dates: Memorial Day weekend

Annual Contemporary Indian Art Exhibition
(benefits Crow Canyon Archaeological Center)
Chicago, Illinois (708) 234-3310
Dates: 1st week in May

Aniwim Center Spring Pow Wow
Benedict Parish Hall
2215 W. Irving Park Rd.
Chicago, Illinois (773) 561-6155
Dates: 1st weekend in May

Annual NAC Powwow
Lake County Fairgrounds
Grays Lake, Illinois (708) 740-9270
Dates: 4th week in May

Annual Potawatomi Trail PowWow
Christian County Fairgrounds
Taylorville, Illinois (217) 245-0409
Dates: 3rd weekend in May

Indiana Indian Movement PowWow
Black Swan Lake Campground
Hwy. 50 • Bedford, Indiana
(812) 279-2335
Dates: 2nd weekend in May

Haskell Commencement PowWow
Haskell Indian Nations University
Lawrence, Kansas (785) 749-8437
Dates: 2nd weekend in May

Louisiana Indian Heritage
Association PowWow
Folsom, Louisiana (504) 244-5866
Dates: 1st weekend in May

Tunica-Biloxi PowWow
Tunica-Biloxi Indian Reservation
Marksville, Louisiana
(800) 946-1946 ext. 20304
John Barbry, Contact
Dates: 3rd weekend in May

Choctaw-Apache Traditional PowWow
Ebarb Community • 7 miles west of Zwolle
Zwolle, Louisiana (318) 645-2588
Dates: 1st weekend in May

Two Nations Gathering
Century Sportsman's Club Rte.
Auburn, Massachusetts (508) 892-8884
Dates: 1st weekend in May

First Light Singers PowWow
1475 Route 2, Mohawk Trail
Charlemont, Massachusetts
(413) 664-7364
Dates: 1st weekend in May

Wampanoag New Year Ceremony
& Indian Gathering
Wampanoag Indian Reservation
Freetown, Massachusetts (508) 947-7466
Dates: 1st week in May

Native American Awareness Day Powwow
Massachusetts Center for
Native American Awareness
Middleboro, Massachusetts (617) 884-4227
Dates: 3rd weekend in May

Abenaki Nation & State Parks Dept. Powwow
Salisbury State Park
Salisbury, Massachusetts
(508) 682-4511
Dates: 4th week in May

Nipmuck Council Planting Moon
Ceremony & Potluck
Nipmuck Reservation
Webster, Massachusetts (508) 943-4569
Dates: 2nd week in May

GLICA Spring Planting Festival
Tyngsborough State Forest
Tyngsboro, Massachusetts (508) 453-7182
Dates: 3rd week in May

Friends of Native Americans &
Mystic River Association Powwow
Lake Winchester, Massachusetts
(617) 646-0743
Dates: 2nd week in May

Annual Gissiwas Creek Powwow
Tribal Bldg. • Marion, Michigan
(616) 281-3640
Dates: 4th week in May

Gissiwas Creek Powwow
Marion, Michigan (616) 281-3640
Dates: Memorial Day weekend

Annual Bemidji State PowWow
Bemidji, Minnesota
Beemus Goodsky (218) 760-9221
Dates: 1st weekend in May

Annual Grand Casino Powwow
Hinckley, Minnesota (612) 384-7771
Dates: 4th week in May

Leech Lake Nation Spring PowWow
Leech Lake Veterans Memorial Grounds
Leech Lake, Minnesota (218) 335-7400
Dates: Memorial Day weekend

Mankato State University Powwow
Mankato, Minnesota (507) 389-5230
Dates: 2nd week in May

Annual Spring Challenge Powwow
Minneapolis, Minnesota (612) 721-9800
Dates: 1st week in May

AISA University of Minnesota Annual Powwow
Minneapolis, Minnesota (612) 624-2555
Dates: 3rd week in May

Annual Celebration of Sobriety
Red Lake, Minnesota (218) 679-3392
Dates: 4th week in May

Winona State University
Intertribal Powwow
Winona, Minnesota
(507) 457-5098/5230
Dates: 1st week in May

American Indian Festival & Powwow
Jackson, Mississippi (601) 371-8242
Linda Swindoll, Contact
Dates: 1st week in May

Montana State University Annual Powwow
Bozeman, Montana (406) 994-3881
Dates: 2nd weekend in May

Mother's Day All Indian Rodeo
Browning, Montana (406) 338-7406
Date: 2nd Sunday in May

Northern Montana College Powwow
Havre, Montana (406) 265-3700 ext. 3040
Dates: First week in May

Omaha Memorial Day Celebration
Macy, Nebraska (402) 837-5391
Dates: Memorial Day weekend

Red Mountain Powwow & Indian Rodeo
Fort McDermitt, Nevada (702) 532-8259
Dates: 3rd weekend in May

Snow Mountain PowWow
Las Vegas Paiute Indian Reservatioin
Route 95 north at exit 95
Las Vegas, Nevada
(800) 771-2833 ext. 147
(702) 658-2660 ext. 143
E-mail: jdubray@lvpaiute.com
Dates: Memorial Day weekend

Pyramid Lake Spring Powwow
Tribal Gym, State Route 447
Nixon, Nevada (775) 574-0110
Dates: 3rd week in May

Annual Dartmouth PowWow
On the Green • Hanover, New Hampshire
(603) 646-3792
Dates: 2nd week in May

LIHA Annual Auction & PowWow
Laconia, New Hampshire (603) 783-9922
Dates: 2nd week in May

New Hampshire Intertribal Council PowWow
Tamworth Camping area off Rte. 16
Tamworth, New Hampshire (603) 787-4143
Dates: 4th week in May

Annual New Jersey Indian Center PowWow
Old Bridge, New Jersey (908) 525-0066
Dates: 3rd week in May

Spring Juried Arts Festival
Rankocus Indian Reservation
Rancocas, New Jersey (609) 261-4747
Dates: Memorial Day weekend

Call to Cream Ridge PowWow
Cream Ridge Winery
Cream Ridge, New Jersey
(908) 475-3872
Dates: 4th week in May

Native People's Spring Celebration of the Eagle
South Mountain Reservation
Montclair, New Jerey (717) 420-0351

Santa Fe Powwow & Indian Art Market
Pojoaque Pueblo (13 miles north of
Santa Fe, New Mexico (505) 983-5220
Dates: Last weekend in May

Annual All Indian Rodeo & Dance
Sky City Casino (800) 747-0181
Acoma, New Mexico
Website: www.skycitycasino.com
Dates: 3rd week in May

Otsinigo Indian Powwow
Apalachin, New York (607) 625-2221
Dates: 4th week in May

Annual Yonkers PowWow
JFK Memorial Park & Marina
Warburton Ave. & Kennedy Blvd.
Yonkers, New York (914) 668-5493
Dates: Memorial Day weekend

Annual Powwow
Turtle Center for the Living Arts
Niagara Falls, New York (716) 284-2427
Dates: 1st week in May

**Native American Indian Association
Annual Powwow**
Metrolina Indian Center
Charlotte, North Carolina (704) 331-4818
Dates: 1st week in May

Lumbee-Cheraw Spring PowWow
Lumberton, North Carolina (910) 521-8602
Dates: 3rd weekend in May

Tuscarora Nation Annual PowWow & Gathering
Tribal Grounds • Maxton, North Carolina
(910) 844-3352; E-mail: native1027@aol.com
Dates: 3rd weekend in May

Native American Club PowWow
Hamlet, North Carolina (919) 582-7071
Dates: 3rd weekend in May

United Tribes Indian Art Expo & Market
Bismarck, North Dakota (701) 255-3285
Dates: In May

Memorial Day Wacipi Tradition 30
Standing Rock Sioux Tribe
Kenel, North Dakota (701) 854-7202
Dates: Memorial Day weekend

**Moon When the Ponies Shed
Traditional Powwow**
Ohio State University
Canton, Ohio (614) 443-6120
Dates: 2nd week in May

Fort Defiance PowWow
Defiance, Ohio (800) 686-4382
Dates: 3rd week in May

NAICCO Moon When the Ponies Shed PowWow
Franklin County Fair Grounds
Exit 13 off I-270
Columbus, Ohio (800) 294-9343
Dates: Memorial Day weekend

Annual May PowWow
Franklin County Fairgrounds
Hilliard, Ohio (614) 443-6120
Dates: Memorial Day weekend

**Munsee Delaware Nation
Gathering & Festival**
Rt. 22 Vista Lane
Winterset, Ohio (330) 386-1121
Dates: 1st weekend in May

Kiowa Black Leggins Ceremonial
Indian City Dance Grounds
Anadarko, Oklahoma (405) 247-6651
Dates: 2nd weekend in May

Vietnam Veterans Celebration PowWow
Wichita Tribal Park
Anadarko, Oklahoma (405) 247-2425 ext. 133
Website: www.anadarko.org
Dates: Memorial Day weekend

Spavinaw Days
Spavinaw, Oklahoma (918) 589-2758
Dates: 4th week in May

**Annual Delaware Contest
Powwow & Stomp Dancing**
Copan, Oklahoma (918) 336-4925
Dates: 4th week in May

Choctaw Annual Rodeo
Jones Academy
Hartshorne, Oklahoma (405) 924-8280
Dates: Memorial Day weekend

Annual Spring PowWow
University of Oregon
Eugene, Oregon (503) 346-3723
Dates: 3rd week in May

Klamath Memorial PowWow
Klamath Falls, Oregon (503) 883-7466
Dates: 4th week in May

Mother's Day Celebration & PowWow
Eastern Oregon University
La Grande, Oregon (541) 962-3741
Dates: 2nd week in May

**Annual Spring PowWow
Portland State University**
Portland, Oregon (503) 725-4452
Dates: 2nd weekend in May

Salem, Oregon PowWow
(503) 399-5721
Dates: 2nd weekend in May

Tygh Valley All Indian Rodeo
Tygh Valley, Oregon (503) 553-1161 ext. 214
Attn: Ginger Smith
Dates: 3rd weekend in May

Corn Planting Ceremony
Lenni Lenape Historical Society
Allentown, Pennsylvania (215) 797-2121
Date: 1st Sunday in May

De-Un-Da-Ga Memorial Day PowWow
Custalogatown Scout Reserve
Carlton, Pennsylvania (814) 833-3235
Website: www.lagundowi.org
Dates: Memorial Day weekend

**Eastern Delaware Nations
Whispering Maples PowWow**
Lovelton Baseball Field
Lovelton, Pennsylvania (570) 833-4279
Dates: Memorial Day weekend

Memorial Day Powwow
Mt. Pocono, Pennsylvania (717) 420-0351
Dates: Memorial Day weekend

DE-UN-DA-GA Powwow
Yellow Creek State Park
Penn Run, Pennsylvania
(412) 547-8442
Dates: 4th weekend in May

Annual Heal Mother Earth Powwow
Fairgrounds • York, Pennsylvania
(804) 929-6911 Attn: George Whitewolf
Dates: Second week in May

Latimore Valley Powwow
York Springs, Pennsylvania
(717) 632-5246
Dates: Memorial Day weekend

**Annual Traditional Wacipi
Honoring All Mothers**
Simmons Jr High School
Aberdeen, South Dakota
Attn: Stella Flute (605) 226-2533
Dates: 2nd week in May

Annual H.V. Johnston Cultural Center Powwow
Eagle Butte, South Dakota
(605) 964-2542 Attn: Matt Uses Knife
Dates: 3rd week in May

Kenel Powwow
Kenel, South Dakota (701) 854-7231
Dates: Memorial Day weekend

Takini Skyhawk & Stampede & Wacipi
Takini School • Howes, South Dakota
(605) 538-4399
Dates: 3rd week in May

Annual Championship Dance Contest
Pierre Indian Learning Center
Pierre, South Dakota
(605) 224-8661
Dates: 4th week in May

Annual Tribal Elder Day Celebration
Ghost Hawk Park
Rosebud, South Dakota
(605) 747-2381
Dates: 4th week in May

EITL American Indian Celebration & Powwow
Knoxville Convention/Exhibition Center
Knoxville, Tennessee (865) 693-0079
Dates: 2nd weekend in May

Annual Texas Gulf Coast Championship Powwow
Traders Village, NW Hwy. 290
Houston, Texas (713) 890-5500
Dates: 4th week in May

Weber State University Powwow
Ogden, Utah (801) 626-7330
Dates: 1st weekend in May

Annual University of Utah Powwow
Jon Huntsman Center
Salt Lake City, Utah (801) 581-8151
Dates: 4th week in May

Abenaki Celebration Powwow
Highgate, Vermont (802) 748-2559
Dates: In May

Heritage Annual Festival & PowWow
Occoneechee State Park
Clarksville, Virginia (434) 374-2436
Dates: 2nd week in May

Annual Monacan PowWow
Rte. 130 • Elon, Virginia
(434) 946-0389 Fax 946-0390
E-mail: mnation@aol.com
Dates: 3rd weekend in May

Fredericksburg Powwow
Fredericksburg, Virginia (410) 675-3535
Dates: 4th week in May

Annual Native American Festival
Virginia Beach, Virginia (804) 471-7654
Dates: 1st week in May

Upper Mattaponi Native American PowWow & Spring Festival
Tribal Grounds SR-30, 1 mi.. SE of SR-360
King William, Virginia (804) 769-3854
Dates: Memorial Day weekend

Native American Awareness Day
Grays Harbor Community College
Aberdeen, Washington
(800) 562-4839 ext. 211 Attn: Patty Smith
Dates: 4th week in May

Annual Spring Powwow
Green River Community College
Muckleshoot Tribal Center
Auburn, Washington (206) 226-2589
Dates: 4th weekend in May

Annual In Honor of Our Children Powwow
Coweeman Jr. High School, 200 Allen St.
Kelso, Washington (360) 575-7437
Dates: 3rd weekend in May

Annual United Community PowWow
Omak Longhouse, Paschal Sherman School
Omak, Washington (509) 826-7006
Dates: 2nd weekend in May

Annual Spring Powwow
Native American Student Council
University of Washington
Seattle, Washington (206) 543-4635
Dates: In May

Upper Skagit Cultural Day
2284 Community Plaza
Sedro Wooley, Washington
(206) 856-5501
Dates: 4th week in May

Spokane Falls PowWow
Spokane Falls Community College
Sopkane, Washington (509) 533-4105
Dates: 3rd week in May

Weaseltail Powwow
White Swan Pavilion
White Swan, Washington (509) 865-5121
Dates: Memorial Day weekend

Ho-Chunk Wazijaci Memorial PowWow
Red Cloud Memorial PowWow Grounds
Black River Falls, Wisconsin
(608) 847-5694
Dates: 4th week in May

Heart of the Circle Powwow
St. Croix Tribal Center • Hertel, Wisconsin
Dates: 4th weekend in May

Annual Mt. Scenario PowWow
American Indian Program
Mt. Scenario College • Ladysmith, Wisconsin
(715) 532-5511 ext. 272
Dates: 2nd weekend in May

Annual Veterans Memorial PowWow
Keshena, Wisconsin
(715) 799-5168
Dates: 4th weekend in May

Madison Area Technical College Traditional Powwow
Madison, Wisconsin
(608) 246-6584 Attn: Karen Martin
Dates: First week in May

Oneida Vietnam Veterans Powwow
Norbert Hill Center
Oneida, Wisconsin (414) 869-1261
Dates: Fourth week in May

St. Croix Casino Spring Powwow
Hwy. 63 & 8 mi. W. of Turtle Lake
Turtle Lake, Wisconsin (800) 846-8946
Dates: In May

Annual Northwest College PowWow
NWC, Cabre Gymnasium
Powell, Wyoming (307) 754-6138
Dates: 1st week in May

JUNE

Blackwater Creek Traditional PowWow
Blackwater Park
Jasper, Alabama (205) 648-2529
Dates: 1st weekend in June

Mowa Choctaw Indian PowWow
Choctaw Reservation • Mt. Vernon, Alabama
(334) 829-5500
Dates: 3rd weekend in June

Flagstaff All Indian Days Powwow
Flagstaff, Arizona (520) 774-1330
Dates: 3rd week in June

Enduring Creations Sales Exhibition of Hopi, Navajo & Zuni Art
Museum of Northern Arizona
Flagstaff, Arizona (520) 774-5213
Dates: June thru September

Annual Festival of Native American Arts
Cococino Center for the Arts
Flagstaff, Arizona (520) 779-6921
Dates: 4th week in June

Annual Sam Yazzi, Jr. Memorial Powwow
Lukachukai, Arizona (602) 787-2301
Dates: 3rd week in June

Hon-dah Resort PowWow in the Pines
3 miles south of Pinetop, Arizona
(928) 369-7568
Dates: 2nd weekend in June

Annual Yavapai Prescott All Indian Powwow
Prescott, Arizona (520) 445-8790
Dates: 3rd week in June

Standing Bear PowWow
Bakersfield College Campus
Bakersfield, California (661) 589-8414
Dates: 1st weekend in June

Native American Festival & PowWow
Turpentine Creek Wildlife Refuge
Eureka Springs, Arkansas (479) 253-5841
Dates: 3rd weekend in June

Indian Intertribal Agency Committee Powwow
Bishop, California (619) 873-6394
Dates: 1st week in June

DQ University Graduation Powwow
Davis, California (916) 758-0470
Dates: 2nd week in June

Four Moons Powwow
California Steel & Arts Foundation
Fontana, California (714) 624-1072
Dates: 1st weekend in June

YA-KA-MA Spring Festival
Forestville, California (707) 887-1541
Dates: 1st weekend in June

Klamath Salmon Festival
Klamath, California (707) 482-5585
Dates: 2nd week in June

San Joaquin Indian Council Powwow
Manteca, California (209) 858-2421
Dates: Last weekend in June

Annual Southern Cascades Powwow
Intermountain Fairgrounds
McArthur, California
(916) 243-1741 Attn: Bev LeBeau
Dates: 2nd week in June

Annual Trade Feast
Miwok Park • Novato, California
(415) 897-4064
Dates: 2nd weekend in June

Annual Silver Star Powwow & Indian Market
Kaiser Convention Arena
Oakland, California (510) 763-1495
Dates: 3rd weekend in June

American Indian Music Festival
Oakland, California (510) 452-1235
Dates: 4th week in June

San Luis Rey Band of Luiseno Mission Indians Inter-Tribal PowWow
San Luis Rey Mission Grounds
Oceanside, California (760) 724-8505
Dates: 2nd weekend in June

Richmond Title V Indian Program Powwow
Richmond, California (510) 237-1643
Dates: 1st week in June

Museum of Man - Annual Indian Fair
Balboa Park • San Diego, California
(619) 239-2001 Attn: Carla Edwards
Dates: 2nd week in June

Honoring of Elders Gathering & Powwow
Santa Clara County Park
Santa Clara, California (408) 728-8471
Dates: 1st week in June

Santa Monica Indian Ceremonial Show-Sale Powwow
Santa Monica Civic Auditorium
Santa Monica, California (310) 430-5112
Dates: 1st week in June

Indian Hills Powwow
Tehachapi, California (805) 822-4623
Dates: 3rd week in June

Tehachapi Powwow
Tehachapi, California (805) 822-1118
Dates: 4th week in June

Annual Yosemite Indian Days Big Time
Yosemite Valley, California
(209) 372-0294 Attn: Jay Johnson
Dates: 3rd week in June

Annual PowWow
Siskiyou County Fairgrounds
Yreka, California (916) 842-9200
Dates: 1st week in June

Ute Legacy Celebration & PowWow
Glenwood Springs, Colorado (303) 945-6644
Dates: In June

Sky Ute Casino Contest PowWow
Southern Ute Indian Tribe
Ignacio, Colorado (970) 563-3000
  Molly Cotton, Contact
Activities: Drum & dance contests.
Dates:3rd weekend in June

Annual Chipeta Park PowWow
Chipeta Park • Nederland, Colorado
(303) 258-0224
Dates: 2nd week in June

Ute Mountain Bear Dance
Towaoc, Colorado (303) 565-3751 ext. 200
Dates: 1st week in June

Chief Flying Eagle Annual PowWow
Brooklyn Creamery & Bison Farm
Route 395, Exit 91 off I-95
Brooklyn, Connecticut (860) 267-7695
Dates: 4th weekend in June

Connecticut River Powwow Society
Strawberry Moon Powwow
Rocky Hill, Connecticut (203) 684-5407
Dates: 3rd week in June

Lower Creek Muscogee Tribe
Memorial Day Powwow
Lynn Haven, Florida (904) 763-6717
Dates: First week in June

Chief Joseph & Warriors Memorial Powwow
Lapwai, Idaho (208) 843-2525
Dates: 3rd weekend in June

Return to Pimiyeoui PowWow
Edwards, Illinois (309) 694-4876
Dates: 1st weekend in June

Return to Pimitoui Powwow
Peoria, Illinois (309) 685-7843
Dates: 2nd week in June

Summer Powwow
Harford City, Indiana (317) 348-1223
Dates: 3rd week in June

Eiteljorg Museum Indian Market
Indianapolis, Indiana (317) 636-9378
Dates: 4th week in June

Native American Museum Festival
Terre Haute, Indiana (812) 877-6007
Dates: In June

APOCTOWI Woodland Indian Powwow
West Lafayette, Indiana (317) 589-8546
Dates: 2nd weekend in June

Prairie Band Potawatomi Nation PowWow
Mayetta, Kansas (877) 715-6789 ext. 3999
E-mail: powwow@pbpnation.org
Dates: 2nd weekend in June

Veteran's PowWow
Togus VA Hospital, Route 17
Augusta, Maine (207) 623-0338
E-mail: baxterr689@aol.com
Dates: 4th weekend in June

Annual Festival & Powwow
Maryland Indian Heritage Society
Brandywine, Maryland (301) 372-1932
Dates: 1st weekend in June

AIITCO Powwow
Frederick, Maryland (301) 869-9381
Dates: 4th week in June

Eagles Nest at Perry Point VA Hospital PowWow
Perry Point VA Hospital
Perryville, Maryland (410) 885-2800
Dates: 1st week in June

Quiet Bear Memorial PowWow
Lions Mouth Road
Amesbury, Massachusetts (978) 297-1228
Dates: 3rd weekend in June

Wollomononuppoag Indian Council Powwow
LaSalette Shrine Fairgrounds, Rt. 118
Attleboro, Massachusetts (508) 822-5492
Dates: 2nd week in June

Indian Plaza Gift Shop PowWow
1475 Route 2, Mohawk Trail
Charlemont, Massachusetts (413) 339-4096
Dates: 1st weekend in May

Abenaki Gathering
Franklin, Massachusetts (508) 528-7629
Dates: 1st weekend in June

Worcester Intertribal Center Powwow
Rutland, Massachusetts (508) 754-4994
Dates: 1st weekend in June

Worcester Indian Cultural
Art Lodge Powwow
Sterling, Massachusetts (508) 754-3300
Dates: 3rd week in June

Woods People Summer Solstice PowWow
Clark memorial Recreation Field
Winchendon, Massachusetts (978) 297-1228
Dates: 3rd weekend in June

First Peoples Powwow
Camp Rotary, Michigan (313) 756-1350
Dates: 2nd weekend in June

Day of the Eagle Powwow
East Jordan, Michigan (616) 536-7583
Dates: 1st week in June

Buffalo PowWow
Lowell Fairgrounds
Grand Rapids, Michigan (616) 364-4697
Dates: 3rd weekend in June

Homecoming of the Three Fires
Comstock Riverside Park
Grand Rapids, Michigan (616) 774-8331
Dates: 3rd week in June

Traditional Powwow
Comstock Riverside Park
Grand Rapids, Michigan (616) 487-5409
Dates: 2nd weekend in June

Great Lakes Powwow
Hannahville, Michigan (906) 466-2342
Dates: 4th week in June

Lansing Indian Center Powwow
Lansing, Michigan (517) 487-5409
Dates: 1st week in June

Mackinac Bands of Chippewa
& Ottawa Indian PowWow
Mackinac Island, Michigan (906) 643-8152
E-mail: mackinacband@yahoo.com
Dates: 3rd weekend in June

First Peoples Powwow
Mt. Clemens, Michigan (810) 756-1350
Dates: In June

Two Worlds Lodge Spring Gathering
Medicine Bear Lodge Rendezvous
Benson Farms, between Morley
& Stanwood, Michigan (231) 856-4451
Dates: 3rd weekend in June

Grand Casino Celebration
Hinckley, Minnesota
(800) Grand-21 ext. 4743
Dates: 3rd week in June

Lower Sioux Indian Community
Traditional Wacipi
Lower Sioux Reservation
Morton, Minnesota (507) 697-6185
Dates: 2nd weekend in June

Warroad Traditional PowWow
Warroad City Park
Warroad, Minnesota (218) 689-3393
Dates: 2nd week in June

Annual White Earth Powwow
Tribal Grounds • White Earth, Minnesota
(218) 983-3285
Dates: 2nd week in June

Carthage Powwow
Carthage, Missouri (417) 358-4974
Dates: 3rd week in June

All Indian Rodeo
Birch Creek, Montana (406) 338-7521
Dates: Father's Day weekend

Red Bottom Celebration
Pow wow Grounds
Frazer, Montana (406) 477-6284
Dates: 2nd weekend in June

Cheyenne Homecoming Powwow
Lame Deer, Montana (406) 477-6284
Dates: 2nd week in June

Big Sky Indian Art Market
Native American Cultural Institute of Montana
Eastern Montana College
Billings, Montana (406) 657-2200
Dates: 4th week in June

Badlands Celebration
Brockton, Montana (406) 768-5151
Dates: 4th weekend in June

Fort Missoula 1st Nations Powwow
Missoula, Montana (406) 721-3051
Dates: 4th weekend in June

Intertribal Gathering
Fort Robinson State Park
Crawford, Nebraska (308) 632-1311
Dates: 2nd weekend in June

Santee Annual Wacipi
Santee, Nebraska (402) 857-3509
Dates: 4th week in June

Father's Day Powwow & Arts & Crafts Fair
Stewart Indian Cultural Center
Carson City, Nevada (702) 882-1808
Dates: Father's Day weekend

Red Mountain Powwow
Ft. McDermitt, Nevada
(702) 532-8259 Attn: Helen Snapp
Dates: 3rd week in June

Spring Festival
Duckwater Reservation
Duckwater, Nevada (702) 863-0227
Dates: 2nd weekend in June

Monadnock Valley Indian Festival & Powwow
Keene, New Hampshire (603) 647-5374
Dates: 4th week in June

nanticoke Lenni Lenape Indian PowWow
Salem County Fairgrounds, Route 40
Woodstown, New Jersey (856) 455-6910
Dates: 2nd weekend in June

NIYC Annual Powwow
Southwestern Indian Polytechnic Institute
Albuquerque, New Mexico (505) 247-2251
Dates: 1st week in June

Gathering of Native Americans
Arts & Crafts Show
Albuquerque, New Mexico
(505) 768-3466
Dates: 2nd week in June

The Spirit Lives on Contest PowWow
Sanostee, New Mexico (505) 368-3962
E-mail: raynahkai@redvalley.bia.edu
Dates: 2nd weekend in June

Annual Otiningo PowWow
Broome County's Otiningo Park
Binghamton, New York (607) 729-0016
Dates: 2nd week in June

Gateway to the Nations Powwow
Native American Heritage Celebration
Gateway National Recreation Area
Floyd Bennett Field
Brooklyn, New York (718) 686-9297
Dates: 4th weekend in June

Rebirth of the Traditional Spiritual Gathering
North Carolina Indian Cultural Center
Pembroke, North Carolina (910) 521-4178
Dates: Father's Day weekend

AICA of NC Annual Powwow
Van Hoy Family Campground
Union Grove, North Carolina (704) 464-5579
Website: www.vanhoyfarms.com
E-mail: kdh1993@yahoo.com
Dates: 3rd week in June

Native American Powwow
Machapunga Tuscarora Indian Tribal Assn.
Williamson, North Carolina (919) 793-1359
Dates: 2nd week in June

Flag Day Celebration PowWow
Standing Rock Sioux Tribe
Cannon Ball, North Dakota
(701) 544-3430
Dates: 2nd week in June

Porcupine Powwow
Standing Rock Sioux Tribe
Porcupine District
Shields, North Dakota (701) 854-7202
Dates: 3rd week in June

Twin Buttes Celebration & Powwow
Campgrounds, 20 miles north of Halliday
Twin Buttes, North Dakota (701) 938-4396
Dates: 2nd weekend in June

Annual Competition PowWow
American Indian Education Center
Edgewater Park
Cleveland, Ohio (216) 351-4488
Dates: 3rd weekend in June

Annual "Keeping the Traditions" Powwow
Miami Valley Council for Native Americans
Xenia, Ohio (513) 275-8599
Dates: 4th week in June

Chalepah Apache Blackfeet Society
Anadarko, Oklahoma (405) 247-6651
Dates: 2nd week in June

Peoria Tribe Annual PowWow
PowWow Grounds, SH137 & College Farm Rd.
Miami, Oklahoma (918) 540-2535
Dates: 4th week in June

Five Tribes Competitive Art Show
Five Civilized Tribes Museum
Muskogee, Oklahoma (918) 683-1701
Dates: Last weekend in June

Annual American Indian
Film & Video Competition
Oklahoma City, Oklahoma
(918) 747-8276
Dates: 2nd week in June

Red Earth Festival
Oklahoma State Fair Park
Oklahoma City, Oklahoma (405) 427-5228
Website: www.redearth.org
A gathering of Native American tribes in a festival of
art and dance. Dates: 1st week in June

Creek Nation Festival
Okmulgee, Oklahoma (405) 756-8700
Dates: 3rd weekend in June

Annual Potowatomi Powwow
Shawnee, Oklahoma (405) 964-3855
Dates: 4th week in June

Trail of Tears Art Show
Cherokee Historical Society
Tahlequah, Oklahoma (918) 456-6007
Dates: 3rd weekend in June

Sac & Fox All Indian Pro Rodeo
Stroud, Oklahoma (918) 273-0579
Dates: 2nd weekend in June

Delta Park Powwow & Encampment
Delta Park • Portland, Oregon
(503) 788-9360
Dates: 3rd weekend in June

Coquille Indian Tribe Powwow
Brandon, Oregon (503) 888-4274
Dates: 4th week in June

PI-UME-SHA Treaty Days & Powwow
Warm Springs, Oregon (503) 553-1161
Dates: 4th weekend in June

Carlisle Powwow
Carlisle, Pennsylvania (919) 257-5383
Dates: 4th week in June

Eastern Delaware Nations Powwow
Sullivan County Fairgrounds
Forksville, Pennsylvania (570) 924-9082
Dates: 3rd weekend in June

Strawberry Moon Festival
Heffenreffer Museum
Bristol, Rhode Island (401) 253-8388
Dates: 2nd week in June

Annual Wakeby Lake Powwow
Glen Farms • Portsmouth, Rhode Island
(401) 683-5167
Dates: 3rd weekend in June

Graduation Powwow
Oglala Lakota College
Kyle, South Dakota (605) 455-2321
Dates: 4th weekend in June

Fort Randall Casino Contest & PowWow
Fort Randall Casino & Hotel
Pickstown, South Dakota (605) 487-7871
Dates: 3rd weekend in June

Red Cloud Indian Art Show
Heritage Center • Pine Ridge, South Dakota
(605) 867-5491 Attn: Brother Simon
Dates: mid June thru mid August

Ring Thunder Traditional PowWow
St. Francis Indian School
Rosebud, South Dakota
(605) 747-2381 ext. 120
Dates: 3rd weekend in June

St. Francis Indian Day Celebration
St. Francis Indian School
Rosebud, South Dakota
(605) 747-2298
Dates: 4th week in June

Big Foot Memorial Riders Honoring Wacipi
Soldier Creek, South Dakota
(605) 747-2336
Dates: 3rd weekend in June

NAIA PowWow
Halle Stadium • Memphis, Tennessee
(901) 276-4741
Dates: 3rd week in June

American Indian Association
Annual de ha lu yi PowWow
USA Baseball Stadium
Millington, Tennessee
(901) 876-3900
E-mail: ritasevenflowers@aol.com
Dates: 2nd week in June

Alabama Coushatta PowWow
Indian Village Ball Park
Livingston, Texas (936) 563-4391
Dates: 1st week in June

TIHA Summer Powwow
Robinson Park
Llano, Texas (936) 653-3116
Dates: 3rd weekend in June

Annual Heber City PowWow
Heber City, Utah (801) 359-6906
Dates: 4th weekend in June

Windsor-Mt. Ascutney Chamber of Commerce
Native American PowWow
South Windsor fair Grounds
Windsor, Vermont (802) 674-6410
Dates: 1st weekend in June

Monacan Indian Powwow
Big Island, Virginia (804) 929-6911
Attn: George White Wolf
Dates: 2nd weekend in June

Gathering of Veterans PowWow
American Legion Field • Salem, Virginia
E-mail: white_buffalo_woman@yahoo.com
Dates: 1st weekend in June

Virginia Indian Heritage Festival
Jamestown Settlement
Williamsburg, Virginia (757) 253-4838
Dates: 3rd weekend in June

Annual Eagle Mountain Powwow
Ferndale, Washington (360) 647-6238
Dates: 3rd weekend in June

Stommish Water Festival
Lummi Stommish Grounds
Ferndale, Washington (360) 758-2101
Dates: 3rd weekend in June

Annual All My Relations Powwow & Feast
Swinomish Gym • La Conner, Washington
(360) 466-3906
Dates: 3rd weekend in June

Tulalip Veteran's PowWow
Tulalip Community Center
Marysville, Washington (360) 651-4470
Dates: 1st weekend in June

Winds of the Northwest PowWow
Frank's Landing Indian Community
Olympia, Washington (360) 456-1311
Dates: 3rd weekend in June

Four Winds Contest Powwow
Indian Heritage High School
Seattle, Washington (206) 725-8830
Dates: 2nd week in June

Annual Treaty Day Commemoration
Pow Wow Gathering & Rodeo
Confederated Tribes & Bands of the Yakama Nation
Toppenish, Washington (White Swan)
Contact (509) 865-6262
Dates: 1st weekend in June

Tiinowit Annual International Powwow
Yakama, Washington (509) 877-4093
Dates: 1st weekend in June

Annual Sokaogon Traditional Powwow
Crandon, Wisconsin (715) 478-5190
Dates: 3rd weekend in June

Wisconsin Indian Arts Festival
Chippewa Valley Museum
Eau Claire, Wisconsin
(715) 834-7871
Dates: 1st two weeks in June

Annual Anishinaabe Way Powwow
Hayward, Wisconsin (715) 634-3041/5841
Dates: 4th week in June

LCO Ojibwe School Contest Powwow
Hayward, Wisconsin (715) 634-8924
Dates: 1st week in June

Honor the Firekeepers
Traditional PowWow
Dunn Field • Lake Geneva, Wisconsin
(262) 248-2784
Dates: 3rd weekend in June

Annual Traditional Gathering
Powwow Grounds • Mole Lake, Wisconsin
(715) 478-3957
Dates: 3rd week in June

St. Croix Casino & Hotel PowWow
Makoode Arena • Turtle Lake, Wisconsin
(800) 846-8946 ext. 3046
Dates: 4th weekend in June

Community Powwow
Arapahoe, Wyoming (307) 856-6117
Dates: Father's Day weekend

Plains Indian Powwow
Buffalo Bill Historical Center
Cody, Wyoming (307) 587-4771
Dates: 3rd weekend in June

Big Wind Crowheart Powwow
Crowheart, Wyoming (307) 856-1117
Dates: 2nd weekend in June

Nath.nahdo PowWow
Ethete, Wyoming (307) 856-8712
Dates: 2nd weekend in June

Shoshone Indian Days &
Treaty Days Celebration
Fort Washakie, Wyoming (307) 332-4173
Dates: Last weekend in June

CANADA

Eskasoni Powwow
Nova Scotia, Canada (902) 379-2800
Dates: 2nd weekend in June

Redbank Reserve Powwow
New Brunswick, Canada
(506) 836-7529
Dates: 4th weekend in June

Montreal's First Peoples' Festival
Montreal, Ontario, Canada
Website: www.nativelynx.qc.ca
Dates: June 10 to 21
June 21 - National Aboriginal Day in Canada
Native arts of the Americas; celebrating
Indigenous cultures

JULY

Midnight Sun Inter-Tribal PowWow
Tanana Valley Fairgrounds
Fairbanks, Alaska (907) 456-2245
Website: www.midnightsunpowwow.org
Dates: July 4th weekend

Verde Valley PowWow
Cliff Castle Casino 555 Camp Verde, AZ 86322
(928) 567-4363 or 300-9485
Pauline jackson
Website: www.cliffcastle.com
Special activities: Dance competition & drum
contest. Dates: 2nd weekend in July.

Navajo Artists Exhibition
Museum of Northern Arizona
Flagstaff, Arizona (602) 774-5213
Dates: Last weekend in July

Native American Heritage Festival
Pinetop-Lakeside, Arizona
(928) 367-4290 (800) 573-4031
Dates: 3rd weekend in July

July 4th Celebration
Hopi Reservation
Oraibi, Arizona (520) 734-2441
Dates: July 4th weekend

Chief Joseph Encampment & Rodeo
Joseph, Oregon (503) 432-1015
Dates: Fourth weekend in July

Annual White Mountain Native American Art
Festival & Indian Market
Blue Ridge School
Pinetop, Arizona (602) 367-4290
Dates: 4th weekend in July

July 4th Celebration
Tonto Apache Reservation
Payson, Arizona (520) 474-5000
Dates: July 4th weekend

July 4th Celebration Powwow & Rodeo
Window Rock, Arizona
(520) 871-6645/6702/6478
Dates: July 4th weekend

4th of July Celebration in Hoopa Valley
Hoopa, California (916) 625-4211/4239
Dates: July 4th weekend

Annual 4th of July Powwow
Three Rivers Indian Lodge
Manteca, California (209) 858-2421
Dates: July 4th weekend

Lake Casitas Inter-Tribal PowWow
Ojai, California (805) 496-6036
Dates: 4th weekend in July

Annual Chumash Intertribal Powwow
Santa Ynez, California (805) 686-1416
Dates: July 4th weekend

Wa-She-Shu-It-Deh Basket Festival
So. Lake Tahoe, California (702) 888-0936
Dates: Fourth week in July

Pechanga Powwow
Pechanga Resort & Casino
Pechanga Indian Reservation
Temecula, California (909) 303-2523
Dates: July 4th weekend

Annual Big Time Festival
Kule Loklo Village
Pt. Reyes, California (415) 663-1092
Dates: Third week in July

Colorado Indian Market
Currigan Hall • Denver, Colorado
(303) 447-9967
Dates: 2nd week in July

Annual Aspen/Snowmass Celebration
Snowmass Village, Colorado

American University Wins PowWow
Friedheim Quadrangle
4400 Massachusets Ave., NW
Washington, DC (800) 853-3076
2nd weekend in July

Coeur d'Alene Tribe Pow Wow
Julyamsh Committee-Coeur d'Alene Casino
Greyhound Park • Post Falls, Idaho
(800) 523-2464 Ext. 7281
Dates: Last weekend in July

National Powwow
Iroquois County Fairgrounds
Crescent City, Illinois (708) 969-7131
Dates: 2nd week in July

Kekionga Gathering of the People
Fort Wayne, Indiana (219) 459-2112
Dates: Last weekend in July

Kickapoo Tribe of Kansas Powwow
Horton, Kansas (913) 486-2131
Dates: Third week in July

Kansas City Indian Club Powwow
Wyandotte County Fairgrounds
Kansas City, Kansas (816) 331-2823
Dates: 3rd week in July

Annual Indian Art Show
Owens, Kentucky (812) 547-4881
Dates: Last weekend in July

Native American Festival
College of the Atlantic
Route 3, Bar Harbor, Maine
(207) 288-3519 or 859-9722
Largest annual celebration of traditional Wabanaki
art, sponsored by Maine Indian Basketmakers
Alliance and the Abbe Museum. Dates: First
Saturday after the 4th of July

Ghostbear Lodge Elwood Kingbury PowWow
Clinton Fairgrounds, I-95, Exit 37, Rt. 100
Clinton, Maine (207) 426-9637
Dates: 2nd weekend in July

Eastern Woodland Inter-Tribal PowWow
River Rd. (off Route 202)
Lebanon, Maine (207) 457-1955
E-mail: nightfeather@gwi.net
Dates: July 4th weekend

Passamaquoddy Tribe Annual Indian Days
Peter Dana Point • Princeton, Maine
(207) 796-2301 ext. 15
Dates: 2nd week in July

Inter-Tribal Council
& Wells Beach PowWow
Wells Beach, Maine (603) 528-3005
Dates: 3rd weekend in July

Howard County Maryland PowWow
Howard County Fairgrounds, West
Friendship, Maryland (252) 257-5383
Barry Richardson, Contact
Dates: 2nd weekend in July

AIICO Powwow
McHenry, Maryland (301) 963-7284
Dates: July 4th weekend

Native American Indian Powwow
Indian Plaza Mohawk Trail
Charlemont, Massachusetts (413) 339-4096
Dates: July 4th weekend

Annual Native American Fair & Powwow
80 Brigham Hill Rd., Hassanamisco Reservation
Grafton, Massachusetts (508) 393-8860
Dates: 4th week in July

Wesget-Sipu Inter-Tribal Gathering
North-Perley Brook Rd., South
Mashpee, Massachusetts (508) 477-0208
Dates: July 4th weekend

Heat Moon Festival & Potluck
Nipmuck Reservation
Webster, Massachusetts (508) 943-4569
Dates: 1st week in July

American Indian Federation Annual Powwow
Richmond, Massachusetts (508) 372-6754
Dates: Last weekend in July

Council Oak Powwow
Somerset, Massachusetts (508) 669-5008
Dates: 3rd week in July

MCNAA Native American Powwow
Walpole, Massachusetts (617) 884-4227
Dates: Last weekend in July

Annual Keewanaw Bay Traditional Powwow
Ojibway Campground • Baraga, Michigan
(906) 353-8164
Dates: Fourth week in July

Bay City Powwow
Bay City, Michigan (517) 772-5700
Dates: Third week in July

Little River Band of Odawa PowWow
Little River Casino
Manistee, Michigan (888) 723-8288
Dates: July 4th weekend

Honoring Our Heritage Powwow
Genessee County Fair Grounds
Mt. Morris, Michigan (313) 239-6621
Dates: July 4th weekend

Annual Litle Elk's Retreat
Mt. Pleasant, Michigan (517) 772-5700
Dates: Last weekend in July

Sault Ste. Marie Tribe of Chippewa Indians - Homecoming PowWow
Sault Ste. Marie, Michigan (906) 635-4755
dates: July 4th weekend

Annual Traditional Chippewa PowWow
Sault Ste. Marie, Michigan (906) 635-4768
Dates: July 4th weekend

Leech Lake 4th of July Powwow
Leech Lake Veterans Memorial Grounds
Cass Lake, Minnesota (218) 335-7400
Dates: July 4th weekend

Fond du Lac Veterans PowWow
Mash ka Wisen Grounds
Cloquet, Minnesota (218) 879-4593
Dates: 2nd weekend in July

Prairie Island PowWow
15 miles north of Red Wing
Prairie Island, Minnesota
(800) 554-5473 ext. 3023
Dates: 2nd weekend in July

Arlee Powwow & 4th of July PowWow
Confederated Salish & Kootenai Tribes
Arlee, Montana (406) 745-3525
Dates: July 4th weekend

North American Indian Days
Browning, Montana (406) 338-7521
Dan Yellow Owl, Contact
Dates: 2nd weekend in July

Standing Arrow Powwow
Confederated Salish & Kootenai Tribes
Elmo, Montana (406) 849-5541
Dates: 3rd weekend in July

Milk River Powwow
Fort Belknap, Montana (406) 535-2621
Dates: Fourth weekend in July

Fort Kipp Celebration
Fort Kipp, Montana (406) 786-3369
Dates: July 4th weekend

Bitteroot Valley All Nations PowWow
Hwy. 93 South • Hamilton, Montana
(406) 363-5383
Website: www.allnationsmt.homestead.com
Date: 4th weekend in July

Hays Powwow
Hays, Montana (406) 358-2205
Dates: 2nd weekend in July

Annual Northern Cheyenne Powwow
Lame Deer, Montana (406) 477-6284
Dates: July 4th weekend

Early Summer Greasy Grass No Water Districts Powwow
Amateur Rodeo & Celebration
Lodge Grass, Montana (406) 638-2601
Dates: 1st week in July

Annual Native American Exhibition
Red Lodge, Montana (406) 446-1370
Dates: Fourth week in July

Annual Homecoming Celebration
Veterans Park • Winneabgo, Nebraska
(402) 878-2272/2772
Dates: 4th week in July

Native American Festival
Elko, Nevada (702) 753-3794
Dates: 4th week in July

Nevada Indian Days Rodeo & PowWow
Fallon Paiute Shoshone Tribe
Churchill County Fairgrounds
Fallon, Nevada (775) 423-6075
Website: www.fpst.org
Activities: Native American Arts & Crats; dance.
Dates: 3rd weekend in July

Shoshone Paiute Annual Powwow
Owyhee, Nevada (702) 757-3161
Dates: July 4th weekend

Arts & Crafts Fair
Indian Pueblo Cultural Center
Albuquerque, New Mexico (505) 843-7270
Dates: July 4th weekend

Annual Feast
Cochiti Pueblo, New Mexico (505) 465-2244
Dates: 3rd week in July

Annual Eastern Navajo Fair
Crownpoint, New Mexico (505) 786-5244
Dates: 4th weekend in July

Little Beaver Powwow
Jicarilla Apache Tribe
Dulce, New Mexico (505) 759-3242
Dates: 3rd week in July

Annual 4th of July Celebration
Mescalero Apache Reservation
Mescalero, New Mexico (505) 671-4495
Dates: July 4th weekend

Nambe Waterfall Ceremonial
Nambe Pueblo, New Mexico
(505) 455-2036
Dates: July 4th

Annual Eight Northern Indian Pueblos Artist & Craftsman Show
San Juan Pueblo, New Mexico
Attn: Leon Tafoya (505) 852-4265 ext. 112
Dates: 3rd week in July

Taos Powwow
Taos Pueblo Buffalo Field
Taos, New Mexico (800) 732-TAOS
(505) 758-9593
Dates: 2nd weekend in July

Indian League of Americas Powwow
Barrysville, New York (718) 836-6255
Dates: 2nd weekend in July

Thunderbird Dancers PowWow
Queens County Farm Museum
Floral Park, New York (201) 587-9633
Dates: 4th week in July

Celebration of the Big Indian
Indian Trading Post
Big Indian, New York (845) 254-5782
Dates: 2nd weekend in July

Calico Dancers Annual Good Time PowWow
Monroe Recreation Park, Rt. 32
Glen Falls, New York (518) 793-1693
Dates: July 4th weekend

Keeper of the Western Door PowWow
St. Bonaventure University
Olean, New York (716) 945-4971
Dates: Third week in July

Allegany Indian PowWow
Salamanca, New York (716) 945-2034
Dates: 3rd week in July

North American Iroquois Veterans Association PowWow
Veteran's Park, Broad St.
Salamanca, New York (716) 283-0084
Dates: 3rd weekend in July

Charlotte Native American Festival
Charlotte, North Carolina (704) 527-7187
Dates: 3rd week in July

Cherokee of Hoke County & Maxton NC Tuscaroras Powwow
Davis Bridge, North Carolina (910) 875-0222
Dates: 3rd week in July

Fort Totten Annual Wacipi
Fort Totten, North Dakota (701) 766-4221
Dates: Fourth weekend in July

Mandaree Celebration & Powwow
Mandaree, North Dakota (701) 759-3311
Dates: Third week in July

Village Indian Trade Days
Knife River Indian Villages
Stanton, North Dakota
(701) 745-3309 Attn: Fred Armstrong
Dates: Fourth week in July

Arikara Celebration & Powwow
White Shield, North Dakota (701) 743-4244
Dates: 2nd weekend in July

Traditional Intertribal Powwow & Living History Encampment
Dover, Ohio (303) 364-1298
Dates: 3rd week in July

Great Mohican Indian Powwow
Loudonville, Ohio (419) 994-4987
Dates: 2nd week in July

Kiowa Gourd Clan Celebration
Carnegie, Oklahoma (405) 726-2996
Dates: July 4th weekend

Kaw Nation Powwow
Kaw City, Oklahoma (405) 269-2552
Dates: Last weekend in July

Annual Celebration of the Feast Day of the Blessed Katerai Tekakwitha
Miami, Oklahoma (918) 674-2587
Dates: 2nd week in July

Indian Hill Powwow
Oklahoma City, Oklahoma (405) 391-9580
Dates: Last weekend in July

Annual Pawnee Indian Veterans Homecoming & Powwow
Pawnee, Oklahoma (918) 762-2108
Dates: July 4th weekend

Quapaw Tribal Powwow
Beaver Springs Park on Future Farmer Rd.
Quapaw, Oklahoma (918) 542-1853
(888) O-GAH-PAH
Dates: July 4th weekend

Sac & Fox Nation Annual Powwow
Tribal PowWow Grounds
Stroud, Oklahoma (918) 968-3526
Dates: 2nd weekend in July

Tonkawa Powwow
Tonkawa, Oklahoma (405) 628-2561
Dates: 2nd weekend in July

Comanche Homecoming
Walters, Oklahoma (405) 492-4988
Dates: 3rd week in July

Apache Tears Spirit Powwow
Crescent, Oregon (503) 433-2461
Dates: 2nd week in July

Wildhorse Resort & Casino PowWow
Confederated Tribes of the Umatilla Reservation
PowWow Grounds • Pendleton, Oregon
(800) 654-WILD ext. 1510
Dates: July 4th weekend

York Powwow
York, Pennsylvania (919) 257-5383
Dates: July 4th weekend

Mountain Springs Powwow & Festival
Shartlesville, Pennsylvania (215) 488-6859
Dates: July 4th weekend

Algonquin Indian School PowWow
Roger Williams Park
Providence, Rhode Island
(401) 781-2626
Dates: 2nd week in July

Rhode Island Indian Council Powwow
Providence, Rhode Island (401) 521-2410
Dates: 3rd week in July

Narragansett & Pequot Nations Powwow
Westerly, Rhode Island (401) 346-1100
Dates: 2nd weekend in July

Sisseton-Wahpeton Oyate Wacipi
Sisseton-Wahpeton Ceremonial Grounds
Agency Village, South Dakota
Lisa Red Wing (605) 698-4901
E-mail: talentsearch25@hotmail.com
Dates: July 4th weekend

Wakpamni Lake Powwow
Batesland, South Dakota (605) 867-5821
Dates: July 4th weekend

Iron Lightning Powwow
Eagle Butte, South Dakota (605) 964-2542
Dates: July 4th weekend

Traditional Mdewankanton Wacipi
Flandreau Santee Sioux Tribe
Royal River Casino, Ray Redwing, Contact
Flandreau, South Dakota
(605) 997-3891 Fax 997-3878
Dates: 2nd weekend in July

Fort Randall Powwow
Lake Andes, South Dakota (605) 384-3641
Dates: Last weekend in July

Little Eagle Monument Celebration
Little Eagle, South Dakota (701) 854-7564
Dates: 4th week in July

Bear Soldier Powwow
Standing Rock Sioux Tribe
MacLaughlin, South Dakota
(701) 854-7202
Dates: July 4th weekend

Little Hoop Traditional Powwow
Mission, South Dakota (605) 747-2342
Dates: 2nd weekend in July

Antelope Powwow
Mission, South Dakota (706) 613-6104
Dates: 3rd weekend in July

Afraid of His Horse Ceremonial
Pine Ridge, South Dakota (605) 867-5670
Dates: 2nd weekend in July

International Brotherhood Days
Porcupine, South Dakota (412) 331-6129
Dates: 2nd week in July

**Annual Black Hills & Northern Plains
Powwow & Art Expo**
Rushmore Plaza Civic Center
Rapid City, South Dakota (605) 341-0925
Dates: 2nd week in July

Annual Corn Creek Traditional Powwow
Rosebud, South Dakota (605) 462-6281
Dates: 3rd week in July

Wososo Wakpala District Celebration
He Dog & Upper Cutmeat, South Dakota
(605) 747-2263
Dates: Last weekend in July

West Bend Annual PowWow
Crow Creek Sioux Tribe
West Bend, South Dakota
(605) 875-3506
Dates: 4th weekend in July

Annual Northern Ute PowWow & Rodeo
Uintah Ouray Reservation
Fort Duchesne, Utah (435) 545-2146
Dates: July 4th weekend

All My Relations Inter-Tribal PowWow
The Old Lantern
Charlotte, Vermont (802) 479-0594\
Dates: 2nd weekend in July

**Annual Rising-Falling Water
Festival & Powwow**
Tribal Grounds • Fredericksburg, Virginia
(804) 769-1018
Dates: 4th week in July

Rising Water Falling Water Festival & Powwow
Richmond, Virginia (804) 443-4221
Dates: Fourth weekend in July

**Muckleshoot Indian Tribe
Annual Sobriety PowWow**
Muckleshoot Ballfield
Auburn, Washington (253) 804-8752
Dates: Last week in July

Quileute Days
La Push, Washington (206) 374-6163
Dates: 3rd weekend in July

4th of July PowWow & Open Rodeo
Nespelem, Washington (509) 634-4711
Dates: 4th of July

Annual Seafair Indian Days Powwow
Daybreak Star, Discovery Park
Seattle, Washington (206) 285-4425
Dates: Last weekend in July

Chief Taholah Days
Taholah, Washington (206) 276-8211
Dates: July 4th weekend

Toppenish PowWow & Rodeo
Yakama Indian Reservation
Toppenish, Washington (509) 865-5121
E-mail: leafarm@inreach.com
Dates: July 4th weekend

**Takozakpaku Intertribal
Return of the Eagles Powwow**
Vancouver, Washington
(206) 696-4061 ext. 3413
Dates: Last week in July

Indian Days Encampment & PowWow
White Swan, Washington
(509) 865-5121
Dates: July 4th weekend

Ho-Chunk Nesh-la PowWow
North Reedsburg Road
Baraboo, Wisconsin
(800) 746-2486 ext. 2141
Dates: 3rd weekend in July

Honor the Earth Powwow
Hayward, Wisconsin (715) 634-2100
Dates: 2nd week in July

Bear River Powwow
Lac du Flambeau, Wisconsin
(715) 588-3286
Dates: 2nd weekend in July

Red Cliff Traditional PowWow
Red Cliff, Wisconsin (715) 779-3701
Dates: July 4th weekend

Annual Oneida Contest PowWow
Norbert Hill Center
Oneida, Wisconsin (920) 496-7897
Dates: July 4th weekend

Cheyenne Frontier Days
Cheyenne, Wyoming (800) 227-6336
Dates: 3rd week in July

Ethete Powwow
Ethete, Wyoming (307) 332-2056
Dates: 3rd weekend in July

CANADA

Ermineskin PowWow & Hand Games
Maskwacis Cultural Park
Ermineskin, Alberta, Canada (780) 585-3741
Dates: July 4th weekend

Mississauga Powwow
Mississauga, Ontario, Canada
(705) 356-2568
Dates: 3rd weekend in July

Grand River Powwow
Six Nations Reserve
Ohsweken, Ontario, Canada (519) 445-4391
Dates: July 4th weekend

Munsee-Delaware Nation Gathering
Munsee-Delaware Nation Park
Munsee, Ontario, Canada (519) 289-5396
Dates: July 4th weekend

Tekakwitha Island Powwow
Kahnawake, Quebec, Canada (514) 632-8667
Dates: 2nd week in July

AUGUST

Festival of Pai Arts
Museum of Northern Arizona
Flagstaff, Arizona (602) 774-5213
Dates: Last week in August

Annual Native American Festival
Prescott, Arizona
(602) 445-1270 Attn: Ann Hale
Dates: 2nd week in August

Native American Craft Days
Bridgeport, California (619) 934-3342
Dates: 1st weekend in August

Southern California Indian Powwow
Orange County Fairground
Costa Mesa, California (714) 962-6673
Website: www.indiancenter.net
Dates: 4th week in August

YA-KA-AMA Acorn Festival
Forrestville, California (707) 887-1541
Dates: 1st weekend in August

Hoopa Sovereignty Day Celebration
Hoopa, California (916) 625-4211
Date: 2nd Saturday in August

Barona PowWow
Barona Indian Reservation
Barona Ball Field, past Barona Casino
Lakeside, California (619) 561-5560
Dates: 4th weekend in August

**United Lumbee Nations High Eagle
Warrior Society Pow Wow**
Round Mountain, California
Attn: Jim Johnson (916) 234-2038
Dates: 1st weekend in August

Intertribal Powwow
Santa Rosa, California (707) 869-8233
Dates: 4th weekend in August

Indian Days Fair & Powwow
Sierra Mono, California (209) 877-2115
Dates: 1st weekend in August

Squaw Valley Powwow
Squaw Valley, California (209) 338-3119
Dates: 2nd weekend in August

Saquache Powwow
Sagauche, Colorado
(719) 655-2699 Attn: Ruth Horn
Dates: 2nd weekend in August

Connecticut River Powwow
Farmington Polo Grounds
Farmington, Connecticut (203) 388-3391
Dates: 3rd weekend in August

Quinnetuqut
Haddam, Connecticut (203) 282-1404
Dates: 3rd weekend in August

**Schemitzun "Feast of the
Green Corn" PowWow**
The Miner Farm
North Stonington, Connecticut
(860) 396-6531
Dates: Dates: 4th weekend in August

Mohegan Wogwam Powwow
Fort Shantok • Uncasville, Connecticut
(800) MOHEGAN (860) 862-6277
Dates: 3rd weekend in August

Shoshone-Bannock Festival & Rodeo
Fort Hall, Idaho (208) 238-3804
Dates: 2nd weekend in August

Annual Cataldo Mission Pilgrimage
Mass Feast & Powwow
Cataldo, Idaho (208) 274-5871
Dates: 3rd weekend in August

Chief Looking Glass Powwow
Nez Perce Reservation
Kamiah, Idaho (208) 935-0716
Dates: 3rd weekend in August

Annual O-Sa-Wan Powwow
Marengo, Illinois (815) 568-7997
Dates: 3rd weekend in August

Honoring All Veterans Powwow
Lebanon, Indiana (317) 482-3315
Dates: 3rd week in August

AICI Annual Traditional Powwow
Lebanon, Indiana (317) 482-3315
Dates: 3rd weekend in August

Mesquakie Powwow
Tama, Iowa (515) 484-4678
Dates: 1st weekend in August

Sac & Fox Annual Powwow
Tama, Iowa (515) 484-4678/5358
Dates: 2nd weekend in August

**Arroostook Band of Micmacs
Mawiomi of Tribes**
Spruce Haven, Doyle Rd.
Caribou, Maine (207) 764-1972
Dates: 3rd weekend in August

**Sipayik Annual Indian Days Celebration
Annual Passamaquoddy Powwow**
Pleasant Point Reservation
Passamaquoddy Tribe
Perry, Maine (207) 581-1904
Date: 1st weekend in August

Mawiomi of Tribes (Gathering of Tribes)
Aroostook Band of Micmacs
Presque Island, Maine (207) 764-1972
Date: 3rd weekend in August

Annual American Indian Powwow
Baltimore, Maryland (301) 675-3535
Dates: 4th weekend in August

Mohawk Trail Powwow
Indian Plaza, Rt. 2 Mohawk Trail
Charlemont, Massachusetts (413) 339-4096
Dates: 3rd weekend in August

Honor Thy Earth Powwow
Northampton, Massachusetts
(413) 253-7788
Dates: 1st weekend in August

Roaming Buffalo Singers Annual Powwow
Plainfield, Massachusetts (508) 226-5712
Dates: 2nd weekend in August

Lake Quinsigamond Powwow
Worcester, Massachusetts (508) 832-8173
Dates: 4th weekend of August

MCNAA Apsqe Powwow
Walpole, Massachusetts (617) 884-4227
Dates: Fourth week in August

**Annual Leonard J. Pamp
Memorial Traditional Powwow**
Burlington, Michigan (616) 729-9434
Dates: 2nd week in August

International Traditional Summer Powwow
Climax, Michigan (313) 763-8631
Dates: Fourth weekend in August

**Annual Anishinabeg Mom Weh Traditional
Powwow**
Rapid River, Michigan (906) 786-0556
Dates: Fourth weekend in August

American Indian Heritage Powwow
MSU • East Lansing, Michigan
(800) 935-FEST
Dates: In August

Little Elk's Retreat Pow Wow
Saginaw Chippewa Campgrounds
7529 E. Tomah Rd.
Mt. Pleasant, Michigan (989) 775-4059
Dates: 1st week in August

Annual Muskegon Traditional Powwow
Muskegon, Michigan (616) 759-7016
Dates: Fourth week in August

Blue Water Indian Celebration/Contest Powwow
Port Huron, Michigan (810) 982-0891
Dates: 2nd week in August

**Celebrating Our Traditions
Annual Peshawbestown Powwow**
Grand Traverse Band of Ottawa & Chippewa Indians
Suttons Bay, Peshawbestown, Michigan
(616) 271-7230 Tanya
Dates: Third weekend in August

Annual LacVieux Desert Powwow
Waters Meet, Michigan (906) 358-4106
Dates: 2nd week in August

Annual NiMiW Intertribal Powwow
Spirit Mountain • Duluth, Minnesota
(218) 722-2781
Dates: Third week in August

Mille Lacs Powwow
Mille Lacs, Minnesota
(612) 532-4181 ext. 810
Dates: Third week in August

Annual Elders & Youth Powwow
Pipestone National Monument
Pipestone, Minnesota (612) 724-3129
Dates: 2nd Sunday in August

Shakopee Mdewakanton Sioux PowWow
Mystic Lake Casino
Prior Lake, Minnesota (952) 445-8900
Dates: 3rd weekend in August

Red Lake Nation Powwow
Red Lake, Minnesota (218) 679-3341
Dates: In August

**Mash-ka-wisen
Annual Sobriety PowWow**
Mash-ka-wisen Treatment Center
Sawyer, Minnesota (218) 879-6731
Dates: 1st weekend in August

Clear Creek All Indian Powwow
Nevada, Missouri (417) 944-2745
Dates: 2nd week in August

Thunderbird Society Powwow
Vandalia, Missouri (618) 876-3321
Dates: 1st weekend in August

Heart Butte Society Day Celebration
26 miles south of Browning, Montana
Dates: 2nd weeken in August

**Annual Crow Fair Celebration
PowWow & All Indian Rodeo**
Crow Reservation
Crow Agency, Montana (406) 638-3793
Dates: 3rd weekend in August

Heart Butte Indian Days
Heart Butte, Montana (406) 338-7276
Dates: 2nd weekend in August

Big Sky Powwow
Helena, Montana (800) 654-9085
Dates: In August

**Rocky Boy's Indian Reservation
Chippewa Cree Tribe**
Annual Sybil Sangrey-Colliflower Memorial Rodeo
Rocky Boy, Montana (406) 395-4736
Michelle Billy or Charlene Big Knife
Dates: 1st week in August

Rocky Boy Powwow
Rocky Boy PowWow Grounds
Rocky Boy Agency • Havre, Montana
Lloyd Top Sky (406) 395-4478
Dates: 1st weekend in August

United Peoples Powwow & Cultural Rendezvous
Ft. Missoula Historical Museum
Missoula, Montana (406) 728-2180
Dates: 2nd weekend in August

Annual Harvest Dance
Omaha Indian Reservation
Macy, Nebraska (402) 837-5391
Dates: 4th week in August

Omaha Tribal Powwow
Macy, Nebraska (402) 837-5391
Dates: Full moon Aug. weekend

Massacre Canyon Powwow
Trenton, Nebraska
(308) 285-3322
Dates: 1st week in August

Annual Inter-Tribal Indian Ceremonial
Church Rock, New Mexico (800) 233-4528
Dates: 2nd week in August

Intertribal Indian Ceremonial
Red Rock State Park
Gallup, New Mexico (888) 685-2564
Website: www.gallupnm.org
Dates: 1st weekennd in August

Annual Festival
Pojoaque Pueblo, New Mexico
(505) 455-2278
Dates: 1st weekend in August

Santa Fe Indian Market
Santa Fe, New Mexico (505) 983-5220
Dates: Third weekend in August

Annual Fiesta
Zia Pueblo, New Mexico (505) 867-3304
Dates: 2nd week in August

Zuni Arts Cultural Expo
Zuni Pueblo, New Mexico (505) 782-2869
Dates: 2nd week in August

Paumanauke Powwow
Tanner Park
Copiaque, New York (212) 757-0207
Dates: 2nd weekend in August

Bear Mountain Series One PowWow
Harriman State Park
Harriman, New York (718) 686-9297
Website: www.redhawkarts.home.mindspring.com
Dates: 1st weekend in August

Native American Festival
Whiteface Mountain • Wilmington, New York
(518) 523-1655
Dates: 1st weekend in August

Appalachian State University Annual Powwow
Boone, North Carolina (704) 256-2724
Dates: 4th week in August

Standing Rock Wacipi
Standing Rock Sioux Tribe
Fort Yates, North Dakota (701) 854-7451
Dates: 1st week in August

Little Shell Powwow
New Town, North Dakota (701) 627-3838
Dates: 2nd weekend in August

Three Affiliated Tribes Powwow
New Town, North Dakota (701) 627-4307
Dates: 2nd weekend in August

Delaware Indian Heritage Festival & Powwow
Dover, Ohio (216) 343-1047
Dates: Fourth week in August

American Indian Expo
Caddo County Fairgrounds
Anadarko, Oklahoma (580) 365-4707
Dates: 1st weekend in August

Wichita Annual Dance
Wichita Tribe • Anadarko, Oklahoma
(405) 247-2425
Dates: 2nd week in August

Kiowa All Indian Rodeo
Andora, Oklahoma (405) 654-2300
Dates: 1st weekend in August

Cheyenne & Arapaho Annual Summerfest
P.O. Box 38 • Concho, Oklahoma
(800) 247-4612
(405) 262-0345 Fax 262-0745
Dates: In August

Annual Ponca Powwow
White Eagle • Ponca City, Oklahoma
(405) 762-8104
Dates: 4th week in August

Seminole Intertribal Powwow
Seminole Municipal Park
Seminole, Oklahoma (405) 257-6573
Dates: Fourth week in August

Annual IICOT Powwow of Champions
Tulsa State Fairgrounds, OK State Expo Bldg.
Tulsa, Oklahoma (918) 836-1523
Website: www.iicot.org
Dates: 2nd weekend in August

Klamath Treaty Days Celebration
Chiloquin, Oregon (503) 783-2005/2219
Dates: 3rd week in August

Grand Ronde Powwow
Grand Ronde, Oregon (800) 422-0232
(503) 879-5211
Dates: 3rd week in August

AITPC Spirit of People Celebration & Trade Fair
Grants Pass, Oregon (541) 474-6394
Dates: 1st weekend in August

Nesika Illahee Powwow
Pauline Ricks Memorial PowWow Grounds
Siletz, Oregon (800) 922-1399 or
(541) 444-2532 ; Website: www.ctsi.nsn.us
Dates: 2nd weekend in August

Roasting Ears of Corn Feast
Lenni Lenape Historical Society
Allentown, Pennsylvania (215) 797-2121
Dates: 2nd week in August

Thunder Mountain Lenape Nation
Native American Festival
Avonmore, Pennsylvania (724) 459-5276
dates: Dates: 3rd weekend in August

United Indian of Delaware Valley Powwow
Fairmont Park, Pennsylvania (215) 574-9020
Dates: 1st weekend in August

Native American Powwow & Western Festival
Honedale, Pennsylvania (717) 226-9366
Dates: Last week in August

American Indian Gathering
Community College of Beaver County
Monaca, Pennsylvania
Dates: 2nd week in August

Council of Three Rivers Powwow
Indian Center-200 Charles St.
Pittsburgh, Pennsylvania (412) 782-4457
Dates: 4th weekend in August

Mountain Springs
Indian PowWow & Festival
Mountain Springs Arena
Shartlesville, Pennsylvania (610) 488-6859
Dates: 2nd weekend in August

Narragansett Indian Powwow
Charleston, Rhode Island (401) 364-9832
Dates: 2nd Sunday in August

American Indian Federation Powwow
University of Rhode Island
West Greenwich, Rhode Island
(401) 231-9280
Dates: 1st weekend in August

Rock Creek Victory Over Japan
Celebration Powwow
Bullhead, South Dakota (701) 854-7202
Dates: 2nd weekend in August

Cherry Creek Powwow
Cherry Creek, South Dakota
(605) 964-2542
Dates: 4th week in August

Crow Creek Sioux Wacipi
Fort Thompson, South Dakota
(605) 245-2221
Dates: 3rd weekend in August

Standing Rock Wacipi
Fort Yates, South Dakota
(701) 854-7451/3431
Dates: 1st weekend in August

Wazi Paha Oyate Festival
Kyle, South Dakota (605) 455-2321
Dates: 3rd week in August

Yankton Sioux Tribe PowWow
Lake Andes, South Dakota (605) 384-3641
Dates: 1st week in August

Kul-Wicasa Oyate Fair & Wacipi
Iron Elk Memorial Arena
Lower Brule, South Dakota (605) 473-5599
Dates: 2nd weekend in August

Parmalee Traditional Powwow
Parmalee, South Dakota (605) 747-2136
Dates: 2nd weekend in August

Oglala Nation Powwow & Rodeo
Pine Ridge, South Dakota (605) 867-5821
Dates: 1st weekend in August

Red Scaffold Powwow
Red Scaffold, South Dakota (605) 964-4594
Dates: 4th week in August

Annual Rosebud Fair & Wacipi Rodeo
Rosebud, South Dakota (605) 747-2381
Dates: 4th weekend in August

Annual Crow Creek Powwow
Stephan, South Dakota (605) 245-2305/2434
Dates: 2nd week in August

Wakpala Traditional PowWow
Standing Rock Sioux Tribe
Wakpala, South Dakota (701) 854-7231
Dates: 3rd weekend in August

White River Powwow
White River, South Dakota (605) 259-3670
Dates: 3rd weekend in August

Annual West Texas Homecoing Powwow
Amarillo, Texas (806) 273-6504
Dates: 2nd weekend in August

Houston Indian Market
Houston, Texas (806) 355-1610
Dates: 1st week in August

Native American Veterans Memorial Association
Powwow
Salt Palace • Salt Lake City, Utah
(801) 825-3639
Dates: 4th week in August

Annual Family PowWow
Route 58 • Evansville, Vermont
(802) 754-6305
Website: www.clanofthehawk.org
Dates:1st week in August

Annual Virginia Native American
Cultural Center Powwow
Ashland, Virginia (919) 257-5383
Dates: 2nd week in August

Nansemond Indian Tribal Festival
Chuckatuck, Virginia (804) 485-9809
Dates: 3rd week in August

Stillighamish Festival of the River PowWow
Riverbend Park • Arlington, Washington
(206) 435-2755
Dates: 1st weekend in August

Kitsap County Indian Center Annual Powwow
Chico, Washington (360) 692-7470
Dates: 1st weekend in August

Annual Makah Days
Neah Bay, Washington (360) 645-2205
Dates: 3rd week in August

Omak Stampede
Omak, Washington (800) 933-6625
Dates: 2nd weekend in August

Eagle Spirit Celebration
Satus, Washington (509) 865-5121
Dates: 3rd weekend in August

Spokane Falls Northwest Indian Encampment & Powwow
Riverfront Park • Spokane, Washington
(509) 634-4711 Attn: Eddie Palmenteer
Dates: 4th weekend in August

Annual Chief Seattle Days
Suquamish, Washington (206) 598-3311
Dates: 3rd weekend in August

Annual Rodeo & Pow Wow
Yakama Nation Legends Casino & Events Center
Confederated Tribes & Bands of the Yakama Nation
Toppenish, Washington 98948
(509) 865-8800 ext. 217
Dates: 1st week in August.

Kalispel Powwow
Usk, Washington
(509) 445-1147 Attn: Susan Finley
Dates: 1st weekend in August

Annual South Charleston Powwow
South Charleston, West Virginia (501) 253-7364
Dates: Fourth week in August

Mohican Contest Powwow
Stockbridge-Munsee Reservation
Bowler, Wisconsin
(715) 793-4111/4270
Dates: 2nd week in August

Menominee Nation Contest Powwow
Keshena, Wisconsin (715) 799-3341
Dates: 1st weekend in August

Annual Bad River Powwow
New Odanah Powwow Grounds
Odanah, Wisconsin (715) 682-7111
Dates: 4th week in August

Annual St. Croix Wild Rice Powwow
Webster, Wisconsin (715) 349-2195
Dates: 4th week in August

Native American Heritage Days
Fort Laramie Treaty Days
Fort Laramie National Historic Site, Wyoming
(307) 837-2221
Dates: 4th week in August

CANADA

International Native Arts Festival
Calgary, Alberta, Canada (403) 233-0022
Dates: In August

First Peoples Festival
Victoria, British Columbia, Canada
(604) 387-3701
Dates: 1st weekend in August

Big Grassy River PowWow
PowWow Grounds
Big Grassy, Ontario, Canada
(807) 488-5614
Dates: 1st weekend in August

Whitefish River PowWow
Sunshine Alley, Birch Island
Ontario, Canada (705) 285-4321
Dates: 3rd weekend in August

Lake of the Eagle Traditional Powwow
Eagle River, Ontario, Canada
(807) 755-5526
Dates: 1st weekend in August

SEPTEMBER

Trail of Tears Festival Powwow
Waterloo, Alabama (205) 767-6081
Dates: 2nd weekend in September

Zuni Market Place
Museum of Northern Arizona
Flagstaff, Arizona (520) 774-5213
Dates: 2nd week in September

White Mountain Apache Tribal Fair & Rodeo
White River, Arizona (520) 338-4346
Dates: Labor Day weekend

Annual Navajo Nation Fair
Window Rock, Arizona (520) 871-6659
Dates: Labor Day weekend

Annual Arkansas Festival
Eureka, Arkansas (501) 253-7364
Dates: Labor Day weekend

California Indian Day Celebration
Auberry, California (209) 855-8523
Dates: 4th week in September

Eastern Shawnee PowWow
Seneca, Missouri (918) 666-2435
Dates: 2nd week in September

Maidu-Miwok Big Time Powwow
Auburn, California (916) 885-2752
Dates: 2nd weekend in September

Sycuan Band of Kumeyaay Nation Traditional Gathering & Annual Powwow
5459 Sycuan Rd., Sycuan Indian Reservation
El Cajon, California (619) 445-7776
Dates: 2nd weekend in September

Pacific Coast Indian Club Powwow
Barona Indian Reservation
Lakeside, California (619) 484-4784
Dates: Labor Day weekend

American Indian Cultural Festival
Monterey, California (408) 623-2379
Dates: 3rd weekend in September

Annual Honoring of the Youth Powwow
Custom House Plaza • Monterey, California
(408) 375-0095
Dates: 3rd week in September

California Indian Council Foundation Powwow
Newberry, California (310) 457-5496
Dates: 2nd weekend in Sept.

Tule River & Yokuts Powwow
Porterville, California (209) 781-8797
Dates: 4th week in September

Redding Stillwater PowWow
Redding Convention Center
Redding, California (530) 275-1513
Dates: 2nd weekend in September

California Indian Days
Roseville, California (916) 920-0285
Dates: 4th week in September

Camp Pollock Powwow
Sacramento, California
(916) 485-9838
Dates: Labor Day weekend

Indian Summer Festival
San Jose, California
(408) 971-9622
Dates: 2nd week in September

Annual California Indian Days Celebration
Balboa Park • San Diego, California
E-mail: ihrc@aol.com (619) 281-5964
Dates: 4th weekend in September

California All Indian Market Mission
San Juan Bautista, California
(408) 623-2379
Dates: 1st weekend in September

Santa Rosa Junior College Powwow
Santa Rosa, California (707) 528-6170
Dates: 2nd week in September

Stockton, California Indian Days
Edison High School • Stockton, California
(209) 952-6931
Dates: Labor Day weekend

Council Tree PowWow & Cultural Festival
Delta, Colorado (800) 874-1741
(970) 874-1718
Dates: 3rd weekend in September

White Buffalo Council Powwow
Denver, Colorado (303) 936-2688
Dates: Labor Day weekend

Annual Southern Ute Tribal Fair & Powwow
Ignacio, Colorado (800) 772-1236
Dates: 2nd week in September

Ute Mountain Casino Hotel & Resort PowWow
Towaoc, Colorado (970) 565-8800 ext. 237
Dates: 2nd weekend in September

Traditional Intertribal Powwow
Black Rock State Park
Watertown, Connecticut (203) 729-0035
Dates: 4th week in September

Eagle Wing Press American Indian Powwow
Watertown, Connecticut (203) 238-4009
Dates: 4th week in September

Nanticoke Indian PowWow
Rt. 24 & Rt. 5 • Millsboro, Delaware
(302) 945-3400
Dates: 2nd weekend in September

First Americans Festival Indian Market
Smithsonian Institution
National Museum of the American Indian
750 9th St., NW, Suite 4100
Washington, DC 20560-0953
(202) 275-1615
Website: www.americanindian.si.edu
Located on the terraces of the Smithsonian National
Air & Space Museum adjacent to the National Mall
and the new National Museum of the American
Indian opened in Sept. 2004. A six-day festival
which features over 400 performers adn artists.
Dates: 3rd week of Sept.

Labor Day Powwow
Pembroke Pines, Florida
(561) 476-7672
Dates: Labor Day weekend

Labor Day Powwow
C.B. Smith Park, Pembroke Pines, Florida
(561) 476-7672
Dates: Labor Day weekend

Running Water Powwow
Rome, Georgia (404) 295-4382
Dates: Labor Day weekend

Native American Foundation Powwow
Waimea, Hawaii (808) 885-5569
Dates: Fourth week in September

Annual All Nations Powwow
Rock Island, Illinois (309) 788-9063
Dates: 1st week in September

Paw Paw Moon Festival Powwow
Springfield, Illinois (419) 663-4345
Dates: 3rd weekend in September

Indian Ceremonial Harvest Dancers & Feast
Starved Rock, Illinois (815) 667-4976
Dates: 2nd weekend in September

Native American Festival
Swiss Heritage Village
Berne, Indiana (219) 589-8007
Dates: 2nd weekend in September

Angel Mounds S.H.S. Native American Days & Indian Market
8215 Pollack Ave.
Evansville, Indiana (812) 853-3956
Dates: 4th weekend in September

Kee-Boon-Mein-Kaa Powwow
South Bend, Indiana (616) 782-6323
Dates: Labor Day weekend

Festival of the Turning Leaves
Thornton, Indiana (317) 436-2202
Dates: 4th weekend in September

Tecumseh Lodge Powwow
Tipton County Fairgrounds
Tipton, Indiana (317) 745-2858
Dates: Labor Day weekend

Annual Frontier Day & Powwow
Council Bluffs, Iowa (712) 325-1770
Dates: 2nd week in September

Fall Festival & Intertribal Contest Powwow
Sioux City American Indian Center
Sioux City, Iowa (712) 255-8957
Dates: 4th weekend in September

Outdoor Indian Art Market
Haskell Indian Nations University
Lawrence, Kansas (913) 864-4245
Dates: 2nd week in September

Indian Nations of Kansas Powwow
Lake Shawnee • Topeka, Kansas
(913) 272-5489
Dates: Labor Day weekend

Baxoje Fall Powwow
White Cloud, Kansas (913) 595-3367
Dates: 4th weekend in September

Trail of Tears Inter-Tribal Powwow
Trail of Tears Commemorative Park
Hopkinsville, Kentucky (270) 886-8033
Website: www.trailoftears.org
Dates: 2nd weekend in September

Cannes Brulee PowWow
Rivertown • Kennar, Louisiana
(504) 468-7231 ext. 220
Website: www.rivertown.com
Dates: Labor Day weekend

First Light Gathering & Festival
Athens, Maine (207) 654-3981
Dates: Labor Day weekend

Glica: Bedford VA PowWow
VA Hospital Grounds
Bedford, Maine (978) 453-1348
Dates: 3rd weekend in September

Native American Appreciation Day PowWow
Ossippe Valley Fairgrounds
Cornish & So. Hiram, Maine
(207) 339-9520
Dates: 2nd weekend in September

Native American Appreciation Day & Cultural Exchange Powwow
Cumberland, Maine (603) 647-5374
Dates: 2nd weekend in September

Ghostbear Lodge et Deux PowWow
Topsham Fairgrounds, I-95, exit 24B
Topsham, Maine (207) 426-9637
Dates: 2nd weekend in September

AISSI Annual Festival & Powwow
Brandywine, Maryland (301) 372-1932
Dates: 3rd weekend in September

University of Massachusetts at Amherst PowWow
Campus Pond Lawn
Amherst, Massachusetts (413) 577-0970
Dates: 3rd weekend in September

Native American Indian Powwow
Indian Plaza Rte. 2 Mohawk Trail
Charlemont, Massachusetts (413) 339-4096
Dates: Labor Day weekend

First Light Drum Intertribal Powwow
Indian Plaza, Rte. 2 Mohawk Trail
Charlemont, Massachusetts (413) 664-7364
Website: www.firstlightdrum.com
Dates: 3rd weekend in September

GLICA Maple Syrup Festival
Tyngsborough, Massachusetts
(508) 453-7182
Dates: 3rd weekend in September

Chief Red Blanket Memorial Powwow
Haverhill, Massachusetts (617) 884-4227
Dates: 2nd weekend in September

Sly Fox Intertribal Wautta Reservation Powwow
Blakek Park • Ipswich, Massachusetts
(508) 373-0403
Dates: Labor Day weekend

Harvest Moon Festival & PowWow
Lake Cochituate State Park
Natick, Massachusetts (978) 283-0105
Dates: 4th weekend in September

Annual Nipmuck Powwow
Oxford, Massachusetts (508) 943-4569
Dates: 2nd weekend in September

Seacoke Wampanoag Tribe
Harvest Moon Festival & PowWow
Rehoboth, Massachusetts (401) 723-1563
Dates: Labor Day weekend

Native People's Closing of the Seasons Gathering
Worcester, Massachusetts (508) 791-7290
Dates: 4th week in September

Annual Michigan Celebration
University of Michigan
Dearborn, Michigan (313) 593-5390
Dates: 4th week in September

Grand Valley American Indian Lodge Powwow
Riverside Park • Grand Rapids, Michigan
(616) 791-4014 Attn: Ike Peters
Dates: 2nd weekend in September

Frank Bush Memorial Walk in the Spirit PowWow
Charlton Park • Hastings, Michigan
(269) 945-3435
Dates: 3rd week in September

Western Michigan State University Powwow
Kalamazoo, Michgian (616) 375-5376
Dates: Fourth week in September

Michinemackinong Powwow
Marquette Museum
St. Ignace, Michigan
(906) 643-8173
Dates: 1st week in September

Annual Children's Powwow
Hannahville Reservation
Wilson, Michigan (800) 682-6040
Dates: 3rd week in September

Wee-Gitchie-Ne-Me-E-Dim Big Dance Powwow
Leech Lake Reservation
Cass Lake, Minnesota (218) 335-7400
Dates: Labor Day weekend

Annual AIM Powwow
Fort Snelling, Minnesota (612) 724-3129
Dates: Labor Day weekend

Annual Moberly Powwow
Rothwell Park • Moberly, Missouri
(816) 263-3009
Dates: 2nd week in September

Annual American Indian Days
O'Fallon, Missouri (314) 272-1964
Dates: Third week in September

St. Louis Indian/Western Art Show & Sale
Gateway Indian Art Club
St. Louis, Missouri (314) 938-6130
Dates: 4th week in September

North American Indian Alliance PowWow
Butte Civic Center
Butte, Montana (406) 782-0461
Dates: 3rd weekend in September

Poplar Indian Day Powwow
Poplar, Montana (406) 768-5155
Dates: Labor Day weekend

Ponca WowWow
Pow Wow Grounds
Niobrara, Nebraska (402) 857-3519
Dates: Labor Day weekend

Omaha Urban Indian Powwow
Omaha, Nebraska (402) 451-8026
Dates: Labor Day weekend

La Ka Le'l Be Powwow
Carson Indian Colony
Carson City, Nevada (702) 885-6818
Dates: 2nd week in September

Annual Daow-Aga Powwow
Lake Tahoe, Nevada (800) 225-6382
Dates: 2nd week in September

Numaga Indian Days Celebration
Reno-Sparks Indian Colony
Reno, Nevada (712) 324-4600
Dates: Labor Day weekend

Reno-Sparks Indian Colony
Reno, Nevada (702) 329-2936
Dates: Labor Day weekend

All Indian Rodeo
Walker River Paiute Reservation
Schurz, Nevada (702) 773-2306
Dates: 3rd weekend in September

Annual Apigsigtag Ta PowWow
University of New Hampshire
Durham, New Hampshire (603) 862-0231
Dates: Last weekend in September

New Hampshire Inter-Tribal Council PowWow
4-H Fairgrounds
Belmont/Laconia, New Hampshire
(603) 528-3005
Dates: 3rd week in September

Annual Powwow
Camp Calumet, Lake Ossipee
New Hampshire (603) 647-5374
Dates: Labor Day weekend

Laconia Indian Historical Association Labor Day PowWow
Dulac Land Trust, Osgood Rd.
Sanborton, New Hampshire (603) 527-1385
Dates: Labor Day weekend

Traditional Gathering
Cliffwood Beach, New Jersey (908) 390-1642
Dates: 4th week in September

Lenni Lenape Festival
Lebanon, New Jersey (215) 797-2121
Dates: 2nd weekend in September

Four Winds Powwow
Mahwah, New Jersey (201) 529-1171
Dates: In September

Sky City Casino PowWow
Acoma Pueblo, New Mexico
(505) 552-6017
Dates: 3rd week in September

Gojiiya Feast Day
Jicarilla Apache Reservation
Dulce, New Mexico (505) 759-3242
Dates: 2nd week in September

Festival of San Jose De Los Lagunas
& Arts & Crafts Fair
Old Laguna Pueblo, New Mexico
0(505) 552-6654
Dates: 3rd week in September

Indian Arts & Crafts Market
Santo Domingo Pueblo, New Mexico
(505) 465-2812
Dates: Labor Day weekend

Stone Lake Powwow
Jicarilla Apache Reservation
Stone Lake, New Mexico (505) 759-3242
Dates: 3rd week in September

Ironworkers Festival
Oneida Nation Homelands
Canastota, New York (315) 829-8399
Dates: 3rd week in September

Mountain Eagle Festival
Hunter Mountain
Catskill, New York (315) 363-1315
Dates: Labor Day Weekend

Iroquois Indian Festival
Cobleskill, New York (518) 296-8949
Dates: 1st week in September

Iroquois Indian Festival
Iroquois Indian Museum
Howes Cave, NY (518) 296-8949
Dates: Labor Day weekend

Seneca Indian Fall Festival
Irvine, New York (716) 532-4900
Dates: 2nd week in September

Annual Seneca Intertribal Powwow
Kenneth Young Gallery
Lawtons, New York (716) 337-3946
Dates: Labor Day weekend

Mount Vernon PowWow
Mt. Vernon Memorial Stadium
Mt. Vernon, New York (914) 665-2400
Dates: Labor Day weekend

Annual Iroquois Arts Festival
Dutchess County Fairgrounds
Rhinebeck, New York (914) 758-6526
Dates: 2nd weekend in September

Keepers of the Circle PowWow
1180 Main St.
Rotterdam Juntion, New York
E-mail: ckeepers@aol.com
Dates: 2nd weekend in September

Shinnecock Indian PowWow
Shinnecock Reservation
Southampton, New York (631) 283-6143
Dates: Labor Day weekend
Description: Contains about 100 stands
of Native arts, crafts & foods.

Hudson Valley Native American
Festival PowWow
FDR State Park
Yorktown Heights, N ew York
(718) 686-9297
Website: www.redhawks.home.mindspring.com
Dates: 3rd week in September

Kituwah-American Indian
National Arts Exposition & Powwow
Asheville, North Carolina
(704) 252-3880 Attn: Gail Gomez
Dates: 4th week in September

Coharie Powwow
Clinton, North Carolina (910) 564-6909
Dates: 2nd week in September

Native American Celebration
Durham, North Carolina (919) 686-3588
Dates: In September

First Light Singers
Intertribal PowWow
Greensboro County Park
Greensboro, North Carolina
(336) 273-8686
Dates: 3rd week in September

Indian Trail Powwow
Indian Trail, North Carolina
(704) 331-4818
Dates: 4th week in September

Guilford Native American Association
Cultural Festival & Powwow
Jamestown, North Carolina
(919) 273-8686
Dates: 3rd week in September

United Tribes Indian Art Exposition
Bismarck Civic Center • Bismarck, North Dakota
(701) 255-3285 ext. 360
Dates: 2nd week in September

United Tribes International
Championship Powwow
United Technical College
Bismarck, North Dakota
(701) 255-3285 ext. 360
Dates: 2nd week in September

Turtle Mountain
Ni-Mi-Win Celebration
Dunseith, North Dakota
(701) 477-6451 ext. 126
Dates: Labor Day weekend

NAICCO Labor Day Weekend
Traditional PowWow
Heimat Haus, 4555 Jackson Pike, Rt. 104
Grove City, Ohio (614) 443-6120
E-mail: naicco@aol.com
Website: www.naicco.tripod.com
Dates: Labor Day weekend

Great Mohican Indian Powwow
Loudonville, Ohio (419) 994-4987
Dates: 3rd week in September

Fort Sill Apache Tribe PowWow
Tribal Complex • Apache, Oklahoma
(580) 588-2298
Dates: 3rd weekend in September

Indian Summer Festival
Bartlesville, Oklahoma
(918) 336-2787
Dates: 3rd weekend in September

Labor Day Weekend Powwow
Caddo Tribal Grounds
Binger, Oklahoma (405) 656-2344
Dates: Labor Day weekend

Choctaw Powwow
Canadian, Oklahoma (405) 924-8280
Dates: 3rd weekend in September

Cheyenne & Arapaho Powwow
Colony, Oklahoma (405) 323-3542/4877
Dates: Labor Day weekend

Eufaula Powwow
Eufaula, Oklahoma (918) 689-5066
Dates: Labor Day weekend

Annual Choctaw Intertribal Association
Pittsburg County Powwow
McAlester, Oklahoma (918) 423-2667
Dates: 3rd week in September

Ottawa Powwow & Celebration
Odawa Park • Miami, Oklahoma
(918) 540-1536
Dates: Labor Day weekend

Sapulpa Indian Day Powwow
Sapulpa, Oklahoma (918) 224-9322
Dates: 4th week in September

Cherokee National Holiday
& Inter-Tribal Powwow
Cultural Grounds
Tahlequah, Oklahoma (918) 456-0671
Dates: Labor Day weekend

Choctaw Nation Labor Day Festival
Choctaw Capital Grounds
Tushkahoma, Oklahoma
(580) 924-8280 ext. 2134
Dates: Labor Day weekend

Seminole Nation Day Powwow
Miccosukee Mission
Wewoka, Oklahoma (405) 257-6287
Dates: 2nd weekend in September

Pendleton Roundup
Pendleton, Oregon (800) 524-2984
Dates: 3rd week in September

Grants Pass Intertribal Powwow
Pottsville, Oregon (541) 474-3770
Dates: 2nd week in September

Council of Three Rivers Powwow
Dorceyville, Pennsylvania (412) 782-4457
Dates: 4th week in September

Traditional Native American Festival
City Island • Harrisburg, Pennsylvania
(717) 566-9644
Dates: Labor Day weekend

Annual Kit-Han-Ne Powwow
West Kittanning, Pennsylvania
(412) 548-8823
Dates: Second weekend in September

Cheyenne River Sioux Fair & Rodeo
Eagle Butte, South Dakota
(605) 964-4426
Dates: Labor Day weekend

Bull Creek Traditional Powwow
Dixon, South Dakota (506) 747-2381
Dates: Labor Day weekend

Bad River Gathering
Fort Pierre, South Dakota
Dates: Last week in September
Website: www.fortpierre.com

Northern Plains Tribal Arts Show
University of Sioux Falls Campus
Sioux Falls, South Dakota (800) 658-4797
Dates: 4th weekend in September

Raccoon Mountain Indian Festival
Chattanooga, Tennessee (706) 735-6275
Dates: 2nd week in September

Rocky Mountain Indian Festival
Chattanooga, Tennesssee (770) 735-6275
Dates: 2nd weekend in September

Annual Middle Tennessee Powwow
Lebanon, Tennessee (615) 444-4899
Dates: 4th week in September

TIHA Powwow
Llano City Park
Llano, Texas (817) 498-2873
Dates: 3rd weekend in September

Annual Championship Powwow
Grand Prairie, Texas
(214) 647-2331 Attn: Doug Beich
Dates: 2nd week in September

Ogden Powwow
Fort Buenaventura State Park
Ogden, Utah (801) 621-4414
Dates: 3rd week in September

**Eastern Great Basin
Indain Days Powwow**
Tooele, Utah (801) 882-8109
Dates: 4th week in September

Spirit of the Indian Crozet Powwow
Charlottesville, Virginia (804) 929-6911
Dates: 4th week in September

Nansemond Indian Tribal Festival
Chuckatuck, Virginia (804) 485-9809
Dates: 1st week in September

**Rebirth of a Nation
Native American Powwow**
Dublin, Virginia (540) 382-6753
Dates: Labor Day weekend

Indian Heritage Festival & Powwow
Martinsville, Virginia (703) 666-8600
Dates: 2nd weekend in September

Chickahominy Fall Festival & PowWow
Tribal Grounds • Providence Forge, Virginia
(804) 829-2261 or 829-2027
Website: www.hewalkstall@cs.com
Dates: 4th weekend in September

Kla How Ya Days (Tulalip Powwow)
Marysville, Washington (206) 653-4585
Dates: Labor Day weekend

Eagle Plume Society Powwow
Nespelem, Washington (509) 634-4711
Dates: 3rd weekend in September

Snoqualmie Tribal Gathering & Powwow
North Bend, Washington (206) 333-6551
Dates: In September

Salmon Homecoming Celebration
Seattle, Washington (206) 386-4300
Dates: 3rd weekend in September

Annual Black Eagle Powwow
Spanaway, Washington (206) 535-3888
Dates: 4th week in September

**Puyallup Tribe's Annual
Powwow & Salmon Bake**
2002 E. 28th • Tacoma, Washington
(206) 597-6200
Dates: Labor Day weekend

Spokane Tribal Arbor Day Powwow
Wellpinit, Washington
(509) 258-4581 ext. 22
Dates: Labor Day weekend

National Indian Days Powwow
White Swan, Washington (509) 865-5121
Dates: 3rd weekend in September

**Bob Eaglestaff Back to School
Memorial Powwow**
Indian Heritage School
Seattle, Washington (206) 725-8830
Dates: 1st week in September

Cultural Center Celebration
Yakama Nation Cultural Heritage Center
Toppenish, Washington (509) 865-2800
Dates: 2nd weekend in September

National Indian Days Celebration
Confederated Tribes &
Bands of the Yakama Nation
White Swam, Washington
(509) 865-5121 ext. 4343
Lonnie Selam, Sr., Contact
Dates: 3 days Last week in September

Annual WVNAC/NASC Intertribal Powwow
West Virginia University
Morgantown, West Virginia (304) 363-8151
Dates: 2nd weekend in September

Ho-Chunk Wazijaci Labor Day PowWow
Red Cloud Memorial PowWow Grounds
Black River Falls, Wisconsin
(800) 294-9343
Dates: Labor Day weekend

Protect the Earth Powwow
Lac Courte Oreilles Reservation
Hayward, Wisconsin (715) 766-2725
Dates: Labor Day weekend

Indian Summer Festival Powwow
henry Maier Festival Park
200 N. Harbor Dr.
Milwaukee, Wisconsin (414) 604-1000
Dates: 2nd week in September

The Mounds Traditional Powwow
Whitewater, Wisconsin (414) 563-4860
Dates: 4th week in September

Labor Day Powwow
Ethete, Wyoming (307) 856-6117
Dates: Labor Day weekend

Shoshone Indian Fair
Fort Washakie, Wyoming (307) 323-9423
Dates: Labor Day weekend

CANADA

Six Nations Fall Fair & Powwow
Ohsweken, Ontario, Canada
(519) 445-0733
Dates: 2nd weekend in September

OCTOBER

Creek Powwow
Rogersville, Alabama (205) 729-1968
Dates: in October

Indian Summer Powwow
Camden, Arkansas (501) 231-4205
Dates: 1st weekend in October

Apache Days
Globe, Arizona (520) 425-4495
Dates: 3rd weekend in October

Mesa Powwow
Mesa Southwest Museum
Mesa, Arizona (520) 644-2230
Dates: 3rd weekend in October

National Indian Days Powwow
Parker, Arizona • (602) 669-9211/2357
Dates: Last weekend in October

Native American Student Art Show
The Heard Museum • Phoenix, Arizona
(602) 252-8840
Dates: 2nd week in October

Amigos Social Powwow
Tucson, Arizona (602) 622-4900
Dates: 4th weekend in October

NASA Powwow
University of Arkansas
Fayetteville, Arkansas
Dates: 4th weekend in October

Wolf Moon Powwow
Lucerne Valley, California (619) 248-7048
Dates: 1st weekend in October

Fort Mojave Days
Needles, California (602) 326-4591
Dates: 2nd weekend in October

Bay Area Indian Alliance Powwow
Oakland, California (510) 452-1235
Dates: 2nd weekend in October

San Manuel Powwow
Cal State University
San Bernadino, California (909) 864-8933
Dates: 2nd week in October

Annual Mesa College Powwow
San Diego, California (619) 627-2706
Dates: 1st weekend in October

Annual Chumash Intertribal Powwow
Santa Ynez, California (805) 686-1416
Dates: 2nd week in October

Annual West Valley College Powwow
Saratoga, California
(408) 867-2200 ext. 3642
Dates: 1st weekend in October

**Paucatuck Eastern Pequot
Harvest Moon Powwow**
North Stonington, Connecticut
(860) 572-9899
Dates: 2nd week in October

Fire Hawk & Blue Sky Annual Powwow
Pomfret, Connecticut (203) 429-2668
Dates: 2nd weekend in October

Harvest Festival PowWow
Homosassa Civic Club
Homosassa, Florida (352) 563-5423
Dates: 3rd weekend in October

Okiciyapo Festival
Lawrenceville, Georgia (404) 921-4840
Dates: 1st weekend in October

Harvest Outreach American Indian Powwow
Walker County, Georgia (706) 226-7995
Dates: 2nd weekend in October

Cherokees of Georgia Gathering & Powwow
Tribal Grounds • St. George, Georgia
(904) 275-2953
Dates: 1st weekend in October

American Indian PowWow
Thomas Square
Honolulu, Hawaii (808) 734-5171
Dates: 1st week in October

Four Nations Powwow
Lewiston, Idaho (208) 843-2003
Dates: 3rd weekend in October

Rainbow Dancer Powwow
Springfield, Illinois (217) 525-2698
Dates: 1st weekend in October

Annual Indian Arts Expo
Merrillville, Indiana
Dates: Last weekend in October

Feast of the Hunter's Moon
West Lafayette, Indiana (317) 742-8411
Dates: 1st week in October

Day of the Wolf Intertribal Powwow
Louisville, Kentucky (606) 546-9091
Dates: 1st weekend in October

Man-es-ayd'ik Canoe Race
Wabanaki Tribe, Maine (207) 288-3519
Open to public participation.
Date: Early October (call for exact date)

Native American Powwow
Hagerstown, Maryland (410) 675-3535
Attn: Barry Richardson
Dates: In October

Native American Indian Powwow
Charlemont, Massachusetts (413) 339-4096
Dates: 2nd week in October

Council Oaks Powwow
Dighton, Massachusetts (508) 669-5008
Dates: 1st weekend in October

Dine Intertribal PowWow
Newburyport, Massachusetts (508) 346-8901
Dates: 1st weekend in October

Dighton Intertribal Council Powwow
Somerset, Massachusetts (508) 669-5008
Dates: 1st weekend in October

Harvest Moon Festival & PowWow
Nipmuck Reservation
Lake Cochituate State Park
So. Natick, Massachusetts (978) 283-0105
E-mail: menahan@aol.com
Dates: 3rd week in October

Homecoming PowWow
American Indianist Society
Spencer, Massachusetts (508) 852-6271
Dates: 1st weekend in October

Harvest Festival
Greater Lowell Indian Cultural Association
Tyngsborough, Massachusetts
(508) 453-7182
Dates: 2nd weekend in October

Spirit Walk PowWow
311 Lincoln Ave., Winchendon,
Massachusetts (978) 297-1228
E-mail: ppotatobear@aol.com
Dates: 3rd weekend in October

Western Michigan University Powwow
Kalamazoo, Michigan (616) 349-5387
Dates: 1st weekend in October

Two Rivers Native Film & Video Festival
Holiday Inn Metrodome
Minneapolis, Minnesota (612) 292-3221
Dates: 1st weekend in October

**Reservationwide
Championship Wardancing**
St. Ignatius, Montana (406) 745-3523
Dates: 3rd weekend in October

Wa-She-Shu Powwow
Carson Indian Colony
Carson City, Nevada (702) 885-6818
Dates: Last week in October

Las Vegas Indian Days
Community College, Pecos & Cheyenne
No. Las Vegas, Nevada (702) 642-6674
Dates: 4th weekend in October

Annual Juried Arts Festival
Rankocas Reservation
Rancocas, New Jersey (609) 261-4747
Dates: 2nd week in October

New Jersey Indian Powwow
Sandy Hook, New Jersey (908) 525-0066
Dates: 1st weekend in October

All Children's PowWow
Wheelwright Museum of the American Indian
Santa Fe, New Mexico (505) 982-4636
(800) 607-4636
Dates: 2nd week in October

Shiprock Navajo Fair
Shiprock, New Mexico (505) 368-5108
Dates: 1st weekend in October

**Northeastern Native American
Association PowWow**
Jamaica, New York (718) 978-7057
Dates: 1st weekend in October

**Best of the Best Powwow &
Native American Arts Festival**
Rockland Community College
Suffern, New York (914) 357-8424
Dates: 4th weekend in October

Meherrin Indian Tribe Powwow
Meherrin Tribal Grounds on Hwy. 11
Ahoskie, North Carolina (252) 398-3321
Dates: 4th weekend in October

Waccamaw Siouan Powwow
Buckhead Bolton, North Carolina
(910) 655-8778
Dates: 3rd weekend in October

Annual Cherokee Heritage Art Show
Museum of the Cherokee Indian
Cherokee, North Carolina (704) 497-3481
Dates: October 2-30

Cumberland Native American Powwow
Fayetteville, North Carolina
(919) 483-8442
Dates: 1st weekend in October

Lumbee-Cheraw Fall Powwow
North Carolina Indian Cultural Center
Pembroke, North Carolina (910) 521-8602
Dates: 2nd weekend in October

Meherrin Indian Tribe Powwow
Winton, North Carolina (919) 348-2166
Dates: 4th weekend in October

Annual AITA Powwow
Tribal Center • Toledo, Ohio
(419) 249-2601
Dates: 4th weekend in October

Annual Intertribal Arts Experience
Dayton, Ohio (513) 376-4358
Dates: 2nd week in October

AITA Powwow
Toledo, Ohio (419) 249-2601
Dates: 3rd weekend in October

**Kiowa Black Leggins
Ceremonial Society PowWow**
Kiowa Tribe of Oklahoma
Indian City USA • Anadarko, Oklahoma
(580) 654-2300
Website: www.anadarko.org
Dates: 2nd weekend in October

Five Civilized Tribes Masters Show
Five Civilized Tribes Museum
Muskogee, Oklahoma (918) 683-1701
Dates: In October

Annual Powwow
Nowata, Oklahoma (918) 273-3821
Dates: 1st weekend in October

**Oklahoma Federation of
Indian Women Youth Powwow**
State Fairgrounds
Oklahoma City, Oklahoma
Dates: Last weekend in October

Spirit of the People Powwow
Oklahoma City, Oklahoma
(800) 375-3737
Dates: 2nd weekend in October

Comanche War Dance & Powwow
Walters, Oklahoma (405) 492-4988
Dates: 4th weekend in October

Mid Columbia River Powwow
Celilo, Oregon • (503) 298-1559
Dates: Last weekend in October

**Honoring Our Relatives
Celebration & Trade Fair**
Grants Pass, Oregon (541) 474-6394
Dates: 1st week in October

Timutla Art Exposition & Fashion Show
Umatilla Tribal Complex
Pendleton, Oregon (503) 278-0552
Dates: 3rd weekend in October

Salem Area Fall Powwow
Polk Co. Fairgrounds • Rickreal, Oregon
(503) 623-8971 Attn: Cookie Spencer
Dates: 2nd week in October

A Time of Thanksgiving
Lenni Lenape Historical Society
Museum of Indian Culture
Allentown, Pennsylvania (215) 797-2121
Dates: 2nd Sunday in October

American Indian Gathering
College Dome-Community College
of Beaver County, Monaca, Pennsylvania
(412) 775-8561 ext. 157 Attn: Alex Gladis
Dates: 2nd week in October

Columbus Day Weekend Powwow
Mt. Pocono, Pennsylvania (717) 420-0351
Dates: 2nd week in October

Annual Fall Festival
Philadelphia, Pennsylvania (215) 574-9020
Dates: 1st weekend in October

Narragansett Nation Annual Fall Festival
Indian Long House Rt. 2
Charlestown, Rhode Island (401) 364-1100
Dates: 1st week in October

Providence Intertribal Social
Providence, Rhode Island (401) 423-0888
Dates: 2nd week in October

Annual Native American Powwow
Pee Dee Trade School
McCall, South Carolina
(803) 523-5269/6790
Dates: 2nd weekend in October

Chicora Powwow
Andrews, South Carolina (803)221-5640
Dates: 2nd weekend in October

**He Sapa Wacipi-Black Hills
PowWow & Indian Market**
Rushmore Plaza Civic Center
Rapid City, South Dakota (605) 341-0925
Dates: 2nd week in October

Fall Festival & Powwow
Native American Indian Assn of Tennessee
Nashville, Tennessee (800) 497-3231
Dates: 3rd weekend in October

**Coastal Bend Council
Intertribal Powwow**
Corpus Christi, Texas (512) 883-9980
Dates: 1st weekend in October

**Annual American Indian Art
Festival & Market**
Dallas, Texas (214) 891-9640
Dates: in October

Annual South Texas Powwow
McAllen, Texas
(210) 686-6696 Attn: Robert Soto
Dates: 3rd weekend in October

**Annual Native American
Heritage Festival & Powwow**
Roanoke, Virginia (703) 342-5714
Dates: 3rd weekend in October

"Lady of the Drum"
Memorial Mini Powwow
Skagit Valley College
Mt. Vernon, Washington (206) 428-1261
Dates: 2nd weekend in October

Monacan Indian Tribal Bazaar
Amherst, Virginia (804) 946-2531
Dates: 1st weekend in October

Annual Intertribal Powwow
United Indians of Virginia
Chicahominy Reservation
Providence Forge, Virginia
(804) 865-6814
Dates: 2nd weekend in October

Indian Summer Powwow
West Salem, Virginia (804) 929-6911
Dates: 2nd weekend in October

Annual Sacred Beginnings Powwow
South Puget Sound Community College
Olympia, Washington (206) 866-7642
Dates: 1st weekend in October

Wakichipi American Indian PowWow
Martinsburg Youth Fairgrounds
Martinsburg, West Virginia
Barry Richardson (252) 257-5383
E-mail: powwow@vance.net
1st weekend in October

Autumn PowWow
University of Wisconsin-Milwaukee
Milwaukee, Wisconsin (414) 229-5880
Dates: 3rd weekend in October

CANADA

First Nations Cultural Festival
Calgary, Alberta, Canada (403) 273-9855
Dates: 2nd weekend in October

Imagine Native Film & Media Arts Festival
401 Richmond St. West, Suite 417
Toronto, Ontario, M5V 3A8 Canada
(416) 585-2333
E-mail: info@imagineNative.org
Website: www.imagineNative.org
Dates: 3rd weekend in October

Toronto International Powwow
Toronto, Ontario, Canada (519) 751-0040
Dates: 4th weekend in October

Native Cultural Festival
Montreal, Quebec, Canada (514) 499-1854
Dates: In October

Northern Lights Casino PowWow
Prince Albert Communplex
Prince Albert, Sask. Canada (306) 764-4777
E-mail: paul.lomheim@siga.sk.ca
Website: www.siga.sk.ca
Dates: 2nd week in October

NOVEMBER

Oeme Dam Victory Celebration
Fort McDowell Tribal Community
Fort McDowell, Arizona (520) 837-5121
Dates: In November

Pima Maricopa Art Festival
Sacaton, Arizona (602) 963-4323
Dates: 1st weekend in November

Veterans Day Memorial Powwow
Hopi Civic Center • Oraibi, Arizona
(520) 734-2441 ext. 215
Dates: Veterans Day weekend

American Indian Market
Phoenix, Arizona (602) 252-1594
Dates: 4th weekend in November

Native American Month Social
Powwow & Indian Market
Tucson, Arizona (602) 622-4900
Dates: Last weekend in November

Veterans Day Rodeo & Fair
San Carlos Apache Reservation
San Carlos, Arizona (520) 475-2361
Dates: Veterans Day weekend

Carmel American Indian Festival
Carmel, California (408) 623-2379
Dates: 1st weekend in November

Veterans Powwow
DQ University • Davis, California
(916) 758-0470 Fax 758-4891
Dates: 2nd week in November

AITPC Native American Arts Festival
Red Bluffs, California (541) 474-6394
Dates: Last weekend in November

Thanksgiving Powwow
Indland Native American Association
San Bernardino, California
(714) 889-2444
Dates: Thanksgiving weekend

Rimrock Rendezvous & Powwow
"A Celebration of Contemporary
& Traditional Native American Arts"
Redding, California (916) 873-4834
Dates: In November

American Indian Exposition & Sale
Monterey, California, (209) 221-4355
Dates: 1st weekend in November

Pomona Valley Indian Ceremonial
Show/Sale/Powwow
Pomona, California (310) 430-5112
Dates: 2nd weekend in November

American Indian Festival
Presidio • Monterey, California
(408) 623-2379
Dates: 2nd weekend in November

Annual American Indian Film Festival
San Francisco, California (415) 554-0525
Dates: 2nd weekend in November

Netop of E'Chota PowWow
DeSuniak Springs, Florida
(904) 892-7459
Dates: 1st weekend in November

AIA Orlando PowWow
Central Florida Fairgrounds
Orlando, Florida (407) 656-2170
E-mail: aiaofflorida@hotmail.com
Website: www.aiaofflorida.org
Dates: 2nd weekend in November

Bobby's Thanksgiving Festival
East Tampa, Florida
(813) 623-5470
Dates: Weekend before Thanksgiving

Chicago American Indian Center Powwow
Chicago, Illinois (312) 275-5871
Dates: 2nd week in November

NIU PowWow
Northern Illinois University
Student Recreation Center
DeKalb, Illinois (815) 753-0722
Rita Reynolds, Contact
Website: www.sa.niu.edu/nations
Dates: Veterans Day weekend

White Star Gourd Dance
Society & Social
Clermont Lions Club
Clermont, Indiana
(812) 327-6875
Dates: 2nd weekend in November

Veterans Day Powwow
Blue Earth Indian Nation
Council Bluffs, Iowa (712) 325-1770
Dates: Veterans Day weekend

Coffeyville Intertribal
PowWow & Indian Market
Field Kindley High School Gym
Coffeyville, Kansas (620) 252-6819
Dates: 1st weekend in November

Twin Eagles Indian Powwow
Shreveport, Louisiana (318) 688-6980
Dates: 2nd week in November

National Native American Cultural Arts Festival
Baltimore American Indian Center
Baltimore, Maryland (410) 675-3535
Dates: Last weekend in November

Annual Veterans Powwow
University of Maryland
College Park, Maryland (301) 540-0966
Dates: 1st weekend in November

Mashpee Wampanoag Winter Social & potluck
Mashpee, Massachusetts (508) 477-0208
Dates: 3rd week in November

National Native American
Heritage Day Powwow
Concord, Massachusetts (617) 884-4227
Dates: 3rd week in November

Spiritual Gathering
Dighton, Massachusetts (407) 862-9676
Dates: 1st weekend in November

Annual Eastern Michigan Powwow
Ypsilanti, Michigan (313) 487-2377
Dates: 1st weekend in November

Spirit of the North Celebration
Shooting Star Casino Lodge & Event Center
Mahnomen, Minnesota (218) 846-0957
Dates: 1st weekend in November

Indian Arts & Crafts Exhibition & Sale
Stewart Museum • Carson City, Nevada
(702) 882-1808
Dates: November & December

Veteran's Powwow
Duck Valley Reservation
Owyhee, Nevada (702) 757-3161
Dates: In November

Pyramid Lake Rodeo & Elders Day
Pyramid Lake Reservation
Nixon, Nevada (702) 574-0140
Dates: In November

Veterans Day Powwow
Owyhee, Nevada (702) 757-3161
Dates: Veterans Day weekend

Morristown Powwow
Morristown, New Jersey (908) 257-5383
Dates: 2nd week in November

Native American Film & Video Cultural Festival
Huntington, New York (516) 385-7459
Dates: Weekend before Thanksgiving

National Museum of the
American Indian Powwow
New York, New York (212) 598-0100 ext. 29
Dates: 2nd week in November

Guilford Native American Association
Cultural Festival
Greensboro, North Carolina (910) 273-8686
Dates: 1st weekend in November

Town Creek Indian Mound
Festival & Pow Wow
Mt. Gilead, North Carolina (910) 439-6802
Dates: 1st weekend in November

Oglewanagi Powwow
Akron, Ohio
(216) 225-3416 Attn: Donna Seward
Dates: Second weekend in November

Pawnee Veterans Day Gathering & Dance
Pawnee, Oklahoma (918) 762-3621
Dates: 2nd week in November

All Nations Indian Youth Powwow
Tulsa, Oklahoma (918) 762-3962
Dates: 3rd week in November

Veterans Day Powwow
Chemawa Indian School
Salem, Oregon (503) 399-5721
Dates: Veterans Day weekend

Restoration Celebration
Siletz, Oregon (503) 444-2532
Dates: 2nd week in November

**Annual Indoor Native
Arts & Crafts Show**
Bloomsburg, Pennsylvania
(717) 389-4574
Dates: 2nd week in November

Yap Ye Iswa Festival
1536 Tom Steven Rd.
Rock Hill, South Carolina
(803) 328-2427 ext. 223
Dates: 2nd weekend in November

Great Plains Indian Art Show & Sale
Sioux Falls, South Dakota (605) 336-4007
Dates: Mid-November

Red Nations Powwow
Dallas, Texas (214) 263-4039
Dates: 2nd week in November

Annual Powwow
Fort Duchesne, Utah (801) 722-5141
Dates: Thanksgiving weekend

Fredericksburg PowWow
Fredericksburg Fairgrounds
Fredericksburg, Virginia (252) 257-5383
Dates: 1st weekend in November

Great American Indian Expo
Richmond, Virginia (919) 257-5383
Dates: 1st weekend in November

Veterans Day Celebration
Toppenish, Washington (509) 865-5121
Dates: Veterans Day weekend

Veterans Day Powwow
Nespelem, Washington (509) 634-4711
Dates: Veterans Day weekend

Veterans Powwow
LCO Ojibwe Reservation
Hayward, Wisconsin (715) 799-5100/5166
Dates: 2nd week in November

CANADA

Native Arts & Crafts Show & Sale
Aboriginal Artisan Art & Craft Society
Edmonton, Alberta, Canada (403) 486-0069
Dates: 4th weekend in November

DECEMBER

All Indian Rodeo
Colorado River Reservation
Parker, Arizona (520) 669-2357
Dates: 1st weekend in December

New Year's Indoor Contest Powwow
Tucson, Arizona (520) 622-4900
Dates: December 27-31

Winter Powwow
DQ University • Davis, California
(916) 758-0470
Dates: 2nd week in December

American Indian Exposition & Sale
San Jose, California (209) 221-4355
Dates: 1st weekend in December

Quinnipiac Dancers Winter Dance
Milford, Connecticut (203) 263-3610
Dates: 1st weekend in December

Native American Indian Festival Powwow
Melbourne, Florida (321) 749-3692
E-mail: south-wind75@aol.com
Dates: 2nd weekend in December

Miccosuke Art Festival
Miccosukee Reservation
Miami, Florida (305) 223-8380 ext. 346
Dates: Dec. 26 - Jan 1

Annual Maine Indian Basketmakers Market
Hudson Museum, University of Maine
Orono, Maine (207) 581-1904
Date: 2nd Saturday in December

AIM on the Red Road
Minneapolis, Minnesota (612) 724-3129
Dates: December 29-31

Annual Powwow
University of St. Thomas
St. Paul, Minnesota (612) 872-6523
Dates: 1st weekend in December

Indian Arts & Crafts Exhibition & Sale
Stewart Museum • Carson City, Nevada
(702) 882-1808
Dates: November & December

**Native American Christmas
Art & Crafts Market & Powwow**
Reno Sparks Indian Colony
Reno, Nevada (702) 853-7444
Dates: In December

Celebrating the Holidays in Indian Territory
Five Civilized Tribes Museum
Muskogee, Oklahoma (918) 683-1701
Dates: Month of December

Christmas Powwow
Portland State University
Portland, Oregon (503) 725-4425
Dates: Christmas Day

This section lists Indian-related films, videos, recordings, filmstrips, picture-sets, & maps. Films & videos are color/sound unless otherwise stated in the listing. Entries are arranged alphabetically by title. At the end of each entry there are code letters which correspond to the distributor listed at the end of the section.

FILMS & VIDEOS

ABENAKI: THE NATIVE PEOPLE OF MAINE
Jay Kent, Producer/Director/Writer;
Michel Chalufour, Editor
Chronicles the history of the Penobscot, Maliseet, Passamaquoddy & Micmac. The land claims suit of the Passamaquoddy & Penobscot tribes of Maine. Members of the tribe discuss issues, from educational systems hostile to Indian culture to tourism. Produced for the Maine Tribal Governors, Inc. 1982. Grades 7 and up. 29 minutes, color. Purchase: 16mm, $525; video, $149.95. CC.

ABORIGINAL RIGHTS:
I CAN GET IT FOR YOU WHOLESALE
TV Ontario, Producer
Historical photos and on-sight footage trace the history of aboriginal rights in North America from Mexico to Canada. 1976. 60 minutes, color. Video. Rental: $80/week. NAPBC.

ACORNS: STAPLE FOOD
OF CALIFORNIA INDIANS
Clyde B. Smith, Producer
A film on the gathering, storing and processing of acorns, a staple food of the Pomo Indians. Includes scenes showing original primitive methods. 1962. Grades 7 and up. 28 minutes, color. Purchase: 16mm, $560; video, $195. Rental: $50. UC & PSU.

ACTS OF DEFIANCE
Documents the long dispute over sovereign rights between the Mohawk of Kanesatake & the Province of Quebec. 1992. 104 mins, color. VHS. Rental, $29. IU.

ADAM: MINORITY YOUTH
Adam, an American Indian youth, speaks candidly about his cultural heritage and his place in today's society. 1971. Grades 4 and up. 10 minutes, color. Purchase: 16mm, $225; video, $135. 16mm rental, $31. PHOENIX.

ADVENTURE OF YOUNG BRAVE
Two kids go on the trail to solve the mystery of a fortune in buried gold receive help from the spirit of Horton Laughing Feather. 92 mins. 1997. VHS, $14.99; DVD, $19.99. ME.

AGAIN, A WHOLE PERSON I HAVE BECOME
Will Sampson, Narrator
Three American Indian tribal leaders describe the wisdom of their shared culture. Grades 7 and up. 19 mins, color. Video. Purchase: $245; rental, $45. SH. Rental, $21. SH, PSU.

AGE OF THE BUFFALO
An indictment of the mass slaughtering of buffalos & systematic subduing of the Indians. Uses live footage & rare paintings to tell its story. 1964. Grades 4-8. 14 mins, color. Rental: $14. UCT.

AIDS AND THE NATIVE AMERICAN FAMILY
Addresses people's needs for cultural and family support. Includes preventive AIDS information for all ages. 1989. 11 minutes, color. Video. Purchase: $50. UP.

SUZANNE AKIMNACHI MAKES
A BURCH-BARK BERRY BASKET
David E. Young, Trudy Nicks &
David Strom, Producers
A Beaver Indian from northern Alberta, Suzanne documents in detail the entire production process. 1989. 23 minutes, color. Video. Purchase: $70; rental, $20. UADA.

AKWESASNE: ANOTHER POINT OF VIEW
A portrait of the Mohawk people as they confront two

choices: survival or assimilation. Explores some of the social, political, and legal obstacles faced by traditional Mohawks in recent years in their struggle to retain traditional rights. 1981. 28 minutes, color. Purchase: 16mm, 3/4" U-matic; $495, video, $290; rental, 16mm, $50. ICARUS.

THE ALASKA NATIVE CLAIMS
SETTLEMENT ACT SERIES
Bob Walker, Director
In five educational programs, explores the terms and implications of this major legislation. Examines its history; how it has settled native land claims and established native corporations; and what its impact may be in the future. 1979. 16-30 minutes, color. Video. In Inupiaq or English. NATC.

ALASKA: SETTLING A NEW FRONTIER
National Geographic Society
Recounts the history of Alaska and views life in Eskimo villages. 1966. Grades 3 and up. 22 minutes, color. For grades 3 and up. 16mm. Rental, $17.50. PSU.

ALASKA: THE YUP'IK ESKIMOS
Susan Duncan, Executive Producer; Larry Lansburgh & Gail Evanari, Co-producers; Gail Evanari, Writer
Focuses on charges in Yup'ik culture and way of life, with commentary provided by people from four communities: Bethel, Eek, Chevak, and Tooksook Bay. Also depicts changes in village life. For grades 7-12; suitable for adult audiences. A study guide in English or Yup'ik is available. 1985. 27 minutes, color. Video. CHE (free loan).

THE ALASKAN ESKIMO
Sarah Elder & Len Kamerling, Producers
A series of four films produced jointly with village councils to ensure authentic Alaskan Eskimo material and point of view. Now available on video. DER.

DENNIS ALLEY WISDOM DANCERS VIDEO
Dennis Alley presents eight dances, including hoop, Northern traditional, shield and spear, eagle, and war dance. Introduction by Willie Nelson. 30 minutes, color. Video. Purchase: $19.95. CAN.

AMERICA'S GREAT INDIAN LEADERS
Stories of four heroic Native American leaders and their respective tribes. Crazy Horse, Chief Joseph, Geronimo, Quanah Parker. 1995. VHS. 65 mins. $49. CHAR. $29.95. ME.

AMERICA'S GREATEST INDIAN NATIONS
History of all six great Indian Nations, dramatically filmed on location at their native tribal lands across America. The Iroquois, Seminole, Shawnee, Navajo, Cheyenne, and Lakota Sioux. Grades 7 to adult. VHS. 65 mins. $49. CHAR. $29.95. ME.

AMERICA'S INDIAN HERITAGE:
REDISCOVERING COLUMBUS (OHIO)
Roger Kennedy, director of the Smithsonian's National Museum of American History focuses on Columbus, Ohio and the earthworks, moundbuilders of ancient North America. This documentary ties together the connections across thousands of miles and thousands of years of ideas. 56 minutes, color. Video. 1992. Purchase: $159; rental, $75. FH.

THE AMERICAN AS ARTIST:
A PORTRAIT OF BOB PENN
SD ETV, Producer
Penn offers his insights into the essence of being an artist and a Native-American in the U.S. 1976. 29 minutes, color. Video. Rental, $40. NAPBC.

THE AMERICAN EXPERIENCE:
GERONIMO & THE APACHE RESISTANCE
Neil Goodwin
Portrays the profound transformation of a once-proud Indian society faced with the loss of its land and traditions. 1988. Grades 9 and up. 58 minutes, color. Video. Rental, $12. PSU.

THE AMERICAN EXPERIENCE:
INDIANS, OUTLAWS, & ANGIE DEBO
Barbara Abrash & Martha Sandlin
Recounts the life of Angie Debo (1890-1988), a cou-

rageous maverick scholar whose work in behalf of Native American tribal sovereignty and land rights is considered the cornerstone of Indian history. Grades 9 and up. 58 mins, color. 1988. VHS. Rental, $12. PSU.

THE AMERICAN INDIAN
Center for Educational Telecommunications
Examines the history of the American Indian from the turn of the century to the present day. 28 minutes. 1980. 3/4" VHS. DT.

THE AMERICAN INDIAN -
AFTER THE WHITE MAN CAME
Examines the profound impact white expansion had upon the many tribes of Native-Americans. The formation of U.S. governmental policies as well as contemporary social issues are discussed. Narrated by Iron Eyes Cody. 1972. 27 minutes, color. VHS. Rental: $16. UCT.

AMERICAN INDIAN ARTISTS: Parts I & II
Tony Schmitz and Don Cirillo, Directors
Part I: Six programs, profiling seven contemporary Native American artists: Grace Medicine Flower and Joseph Lonewolf, potters; Fritz Scholder, R.C. Gorman, and Helen Hardin, painters; Allen Houser, sculptor; and Charles Loloma, jeweler. 1976. Part II: Three programs—Larry Golsh's artistry in gold and precious stones; James Quick-To-See Smith, painter; and Dan Namingha, artist, 1984. 30 minutes each, color. Video. Part 1 - Rental: $40 each artist, $200/series; Part 2 - Purchase: $150/series; Rental: $80/series. NAPBC.

THE AMERICAN INDIAN DANCE THEATRE -
FINDING THE CIRCLE
Includes dances from many Indian tribes as performed on stage and at outdoor pow wows on their U.S. and international tours. Includes hoop dance, eagle dance, Apache Crown dance, Zuni rainbow dance, pow wow dances, plains snake and buffalo dance and others. 1990. 60 minutes, color. Video. Purchase: $35. CAN.

THE AMERICAN INDIAN DANCE THEATRE #2:
DANCES FOR THE NEW GENERATION
The company performs dances from the Makah, Kwakiutl, Seneca and Penobscot, and Plains Nations. 1996. 60 minutes. Color. Video. $35. CAN & OY.

AMERICAN INDIAN IN TRANSITION
A North American Indian mother, living on a reservation, describes her family & tribal problems-relating her past & her dreams for the future. 1976. 22 minutes, color. 16mm. Rental: $11. UCT.

THE AMERICAN INDIAN INFLUENCE ON THE U.S.
Albert Saparoff, Producer
Narrated by Barry Sullivan, this film depicts how life in the U.S. today has been influenced by the American Indian. Discusses the Pueblo Indians and the Spanish, Chief Massasoit and the Pilgrims, Hiawatha, Sitting Bull, General Custer, Buffalo Bill, President Jackson, Sequoyah, Will Rogers, Jim Thorpe and Buffy St. Marie. 1972. Grades 5 and up. 20 minutes, color. 16mm & video. Purchase: $495; rental: $40. DP. Rental: $20. UK & UMN.

AMERICAN INDIAN OF TODAY
(LOS INDIOS NORTAMERICANOS DE HOY)
Examines current trends that are shaping the future of American Indians in their adjustment to new ways of making their living. 1957. 16 mins. Spanish edition. 16mm. UA.

AMERICAN INDIAN PROPHECIES I & II
Dr. A.Chuck Ross, Narrator
I - Discover how to prepare for the coming earth changes, how the Black Hills can be returned, and more; II - Dr. Ross discusses the prophecies presented in the first video. Video. $20 each. CAN.

AMERICAN INDIAN RHYTHMS
Documentary of Indian dancers from various tribes show authentic Indian dances. 1930. 10 mins, bxw. EG.

THE AMERICAN INDIAN SPEAKS
Documentary lets the Indian speak about his people & heritage, about the white man & the future. Visits

with the Muskogee, Cree, Sioux & Nisqually. 1973. Grades 7 and up. 23 mins, color. 16mm. Purchase: BF. Rental: IU, PSU, UCLA & UMN.

AMERICAN INDIAN SWEAT LODGE CEREMONY
Shows the entire ceremony. A little hut of the woods used as a sauna/steambath. Also shows the sacred pipe ceremony. With Bill Elwell. 1989. 90 mins, color. VHS, $34.95. ME.

THE AMERICAN INDIAN TODAY
This is a lesson which contains material on American Indians circa 1969. 30 minutes. 1969. 1/2" reel. NETV.

AMERICAN INDIANS AS
SEEN BY D.H. LAWRENCE
His wife Frieda speaks intimately about his beliefs & thoughts. Aldous Huxley presents selections from Lawrence, which reveal his deep insights into the religious & ceremonial impulses of Indian culture as shown by various ritual dances. 1966. Grades 7 and up. 14 mins, color. Rental: $8. UCT.

AMERICAN INDIANS BEFORE
EUROPEAN SETTLEMENT
David Baerreis, Ph.D.
Where they came from, how they lived, and unique aspects of their cultures as related to their environment are examined. 1959. 11 mins. Grades 7 to 12. Purchase: 16mm, $270; video, $59. PHOENIX. Rental: UA & UCT.

AMERICAN INDIANS OF TODAY
Describes the achievements and problems of Indians. 1957. Grades 3 and up. 16 minutes, bxw. 16mm. Rental: PSU & UCT.

AMERICAN INDIANS: YESTERDAY & TODAY
Don Klugman
Shows that various Indian tribes have different histories and ways of life. A young Shoshone-Paiute man from the Owens Valley in California, an elderly Northern Cheyenne man from Lame Deer, Montana, and a young Seneca woman from New York State tell about their history and modern lifestyles of their tribes. 1982. 19 minutes, color. Grades K-8. 16mm. Purchase: $375; Rental: $40. FF.

AMERINDIAN LEGACY
Explores the many important contributions first made by the Amerindians. 1992. Grades 4 and up. 29 minutes, color. Purchase: 16mm, $525; video, $285. Rental: 16mm, $55. PHOENIX.

AMIOTTE
Bruce Baird, KUSD-TV, Producer
Explores Sioux painter Arthur Amiotte's art and the reasons for returning to his native culture and religion. 1976. 29 minutes, color. Video. Rental: $40. NAPBC.

AMISK
Alanis Obomsawin, Director/Producer
The traditional lands of the Cree of Misstassini in northern Quebec are being threatened by a Hydro-Electric Power project. Shows a festival, with Cree music and dance, to raise money to fight against this project. 1977. 38 minutes, color. 16mm. NFBC.

ANASAZI: THE ANCIENT ONES
Questions and answers to the ancestors of the Navajo. 29 mins. VHS, $19.99. ME.

THE ANASAZI: BUILDERS
OF AMERICA'S FIRST CITIES
Explores their cliff cities in the American Southwest between 700 BC and 1600 AD. Through live action footage of their ruins, the Anasazi lifestyle takes form.VHS. 1996. 19 minutes. Teacher's guide and seven blackline masters. $95. UL.

THE ANASAZI & CHACO CANYON
This program looks at the fascinating finds at Chaco Canyon, the home of the Anasazi, ancestors of the Navajo. Also, the possible explanation for the disappearance of the highly advanced Anasazi culture. 1993. 43 minutes, color. Purchase: $149; rental: $75. FH.

ANCESTRAL VOICES
Joy Harjo & Mary Tall Mountain
Native American Poetry. 60 minutes. Video. $59.95. PBS

ANCIENT INDIAN CULTURES
OF NORTHERN ARIZONA
Explores the ruins and ancient cultures of the Sinagua and Anasazi of Montezuma Castle, Wupatki, Tuzigoot, Walnut Canyon and Sunset Crater. 27 minutes, color. Video, $29.95. VVP. CH.

ANCIENT PLACES
Focuses on the Native American cultures of the Southwest. 1981. 30 minutes. 16mm. KS.

ANCIENT SPIRIT. LIVING WORD -
THE ORAL TRADITION
The presentations and opinions of the Native Americans featured in this program culminate in a portrait of oral tradition, how it works and where it leads. 1983. 58 minutes, color. Video. Purchase: $150; Rental: $80. NAPBC.

THE ANCIENTS OF NORTH AMERICA
A dry cave/rock shelter with human remains was discovered in southeastern Utah. The site, dated 5500 BC,offers a unique opportunity to examine the culture & remains of a people more than 7000 years old. 28 minutes, color. Video. Purchase: $149; rental: $75. FH.

...AND THE MEEK SHALL INHERIT THE EARTH
Examines the American Indians of Menominee County, Wisconsin. 1972. 59 minutes, color. 16mm. Rental: $25.25. IU & UMN.

...AND WOMAN WOVE IT IN A BASKET
Bushra Azzouz & Marlene Farnum, Directors/Prods.
The spiritual & cultural importance of basketweaving to Oregon's Klickitat Indians is explored in this portrait of master craftswoman Nettie Kuneki. 1989. 70 minutes, color. Video & 16mm. Purchase: $350. WMM.

ANGOON - 100 YEARS LATER
Laurence Goldin, Producer/director/writer
Provides the history and culture of the Tlingit Indians while telling of the 1882 destruction of the Tlingit Indian village of Angoon, Alaska, by U.S. Naval forces. 1982. 30 minutes, color. Video. Rental: $40. NAPBC.

ANGOTEE: STORY OF AN ESKIMO BOY
Douglas Wilkinson, Director
A documentary account of an Indian boy's life from infancy to maturity. 1953. 31 minutes, color. Grades 6 and up. In English or French. Purchase: 16mm, $525; video, $385. Rental, $35. PSU.

ANNIE & THE OLD ONE
Miska Miles, Writer
A dramatized film for young people with non-professional Navajo actors, about the relationship between a ten-year-old girl and her grandmother (the Old One.) 1976. Grades 1-8. 15 minutes, color. Purchase: 16mm, $320; Video, $190; rental, $44. PHOENIX. Rental: UA, UCT & IU.

ANNIE MAE—BRAVE HEARTED WOMAN
Lan Brookes Ritz, Writer/producer/director
A documentary portrait of Annie Mae Pictou Aquash, a young Native American woman and activist for human rights, found dead on the prairie in South Dakota in 1974, a year after the Wounded Knee uprising. Explores the events leading up to her death and investigates her unsolved murder. 1982. 80 minutes, color. 16mm; Purchase: $1,090. Rental: $150. BBP and NAPBC.

ANOTHER WIND IS MOVING: THE OFF-
RESERVATION INDIAN BOARDING SCHOOL
A documentary film about how difficult it is for Native Americans to learn about their culture. 59 minutes, color. 1986. Video. Purchase: $195; rental: $60. UC & STULL.

APACHE - GERONIMO ON THE WARPATH
Two videos containing many photos detailing the life and times of the great Indian warrior. 1993. 90 mins. VHS. $12.99. ME.

THE APACHE INDIAN
Shows the life of Apache Indians on their reservation in the White Mountains of Wyoming; their ancient ceremonies, and contemporary education, work, and the role of the tribal council in determining the direction of tribal affairs. 1975 revised edition. 10 minutes, color. Grades K-6. Purchase: 16mm, $265; video, $59. PHOENIX. Rental: 16mm, $9. UA & IU.

APACHE MOUNTAIN SPIRITS
John H. Crouch, Producer; Bob Graham, Director
An explanation of the role of the "Gaan", the Mountain Spirits who are the source of sacred power for the Apache. 1985. 58 minutes, color. Video. In English and Apache with English subtitles. NAPBC.

ARCHAEOLOGY: PURSUIT OF MAN'S PAST
15 minutes. 16mm. Rental. UA.

ARCHAEOLOGY: QUESTIONING THE PAST
Betty Goerke, Producer
Includes two sequences of digging, one at an ancient Indian site in northern California and the other at Sand Canyon, an Anasazi pueblo site near Mesa Verde National Park in Colorado. Designed for students in introductory archaeology classes. 1988. 25 minutes, color. Video. Purchase, $195; Rental, $50. UC.

ARCHAEOLOGY SERIES
Three, 20-minute tapes explores various aspects of the archaeology of Yup'ik Eskimo sites throughout Southwest Alaska, including an examination of the Smithsonian Museum's huge collection of artifacts collected by Edward Nelson. 1983. 60 mins, color. Video. Purchase: $24.95. KYUK.

ARCTIC SPIRITS
Katherine Marielle & Peter Raymont, Producers; Peter Raymont, Director
An investigation of the rise of evangelical Christianity in Inuit villages in the Canadian Arctic. Follows three Canadian evangelists on their crusades in Arctic Quebec and the Northwest Territories. Interview Inuit. 1983. 27 mins, color. 16mm & video. IP.

ARROW TO THE SUN
Gerald McDermott
From the Acoma Pueblo in New Mexico comes this classic tale of a boy's search for his father: the universal search for identity, purpose, and continuity. 1973. Grades K-8. 12 mins, color. 16mm & video. Purchase: Video, $79. Fl. Rental: 16mm, UCT.

ARROWHEADS, BLADES & KNIVES
Explores the world of flint arrowheads, blades and kniuves found in the heart of America-from Oklahoma to the southwest. VHS. 30 mins. $19.95. VIP.

THE ART OF BEING INDIAN: FILMED ASPECTS
OF THE CULTURE OF THE SIOUX
SD-ETV, Producer
Presents an overview of the cultural heritage of the Sioux from their early days in the Northeast to the Dakotas. Illustrates with paintings and sketches by George Catlin, Seth Eastman, and Karl Bochner; photography by Edward S. Curtis, Stanley Morrow, and the St. Francis Mission; and contemporary paintings by Sioux artist Bob Penn. 1976. 30 mins, color. Video. Rental: $40. NAPBC.

THE ART OF NAVAJO WEAVING
Explores the traditional art of Navajo weaving and its origins. Shows the Durango Collection. 56 mins. VHS, $29.95. CH.

AS LONG AS THE GRASS IS GREEN
A summer experience with the children of the Woodland Indians of North America. Non-narrative. 11 mins, color. 1973. VHS. AP.

AS LONG AS THE GRASS SHALL GROW
Lynn Brown, Writer/Producer
A series of eight programs designed for classroom use with pre-school age children. Combines elements of Seneca life to teach children to count to ten in Seneca, and at the same time helps build positive self-images. 1978. 15 mins each, color. Video. The SN.

AT THE TIME OF WHALING
Leonard Kamerling & Sarah Elder
Depicts an Eskimo whale hunt at Gambell, Alaska, a Yup'ik-speaking community on St. Lawrence Island in the Bering Sea. 1974. 38 mins. color. Purchase: 16mm, $675, video, $195; rental, $70; video, $40. DER.

AUGUSTA
Anne Wheeler, Director
Portrait of Augusta Evans, an 88 year-old granddaughter of a Shuswap chief, who lives alone in a cabin in the caribou country of British Columbia, Canada. She discusses her past and present. 1978. 17 mins. color. Purchase: 16mm, $300; Video, $195; rental, $25. PHOENIX & NFBC.

A BALANCE OF CULTURES
Looks at differences in western medicine and traditional Native healing practices. 1995. 26 mins. VHS. $145. CHAR.

THE BALLAD OF CROWFOOT
Willie Dunn, Director
Graphic history of the Canadian West created by a film crew of Canadian Indians who reflect on the traditions, attitudes, and problems of their people. 1970. 11 mins, bxw. Grades 4 and up. 16mm. Rental: PSU, UCT & IU.

BARROW, ALASKA "A TRUE STORY"
Narrated by Jana Har-charek
Represents the voice of the Inupiaq people from Barrow, Alaska, featuring: The Subsistence Way of Life - a Whaling Culture; local craftspeople creating traditional art work; how we provide communications, water and other services in the Arctic; traditional Eskimo dancing; and local wildlife. Video, 30 mins. SH.

BASIC CHEYENNE BEADWORK
Vicki Little Coyote
Learn bead selection and sizing, plus application and placement; learn how to develop patterns; and garment decorations used by the Southern Cheyenne. VHS. 42 mins. $19.95. VIP.

BASKETRY OF THE POMO
Clyde B. Smith, Producer
A series of three 1962, color films. An "Introductory Film," shows Indians gathering raw materials for baskets, and demonstrates, in slow motion and animation, the ten Pomo basketmaking techniques. 30 minutes. Purchase: 16mm, $600; video, $195. Rental: 16mm, $50. "Techniques": A more detailed film on Pomo basketry techniques, showing precisely how the various weaves were executed. 33 minutes. Purchase: 16mm, $660; video, $195. Rental: 16mm, $50. "Forms and Ornamentation": Illustrates the great variety of shapes, sizes, and design elements of Pomo baskets. 21 mins. Purchase: 16mm, $420; video, $195. Rental: 16mm, $50. UC Rental only, IU.

BEAUTIFUL TREE—CHISHKALE
Clyde B. Smith, Producer
The Southwestern Pomo called the tan oak chishkale (the beautiful tree.) Cooking methods and processing techniques used in making acorn bread are demonstrated. 1965. 20 mins, color. Purchase: 16mm, $410; video, $195. Rental, $50. UC & PSU. Rental only, IU.

BEADWORK: A PRIMER
The art and history of Native American beadwork is shown and taught in this instructional video by Suzanne Aikman, VHS with booklet. 1990. 30 mins. $39. CHAR.

BEAVERTAIL SNOWSHOES
Depicts the construction of traditional beavertail snowshoes by the Eastern Cree Indians of Misyassini Lake, Quebec. VHS. 40 mins. $99. TR.

BEFORE THE WHITE MAN CAME
John E. Maple
A feature film made in the Big Horn Mountains of Montana and Wyoming in the early 1920's with the cooperation of the Crow. An all-Indian cast presents authentic rites and ceremonies. 50 mins, bxw. 16mm. UUT.

BE-TA-TA-KIN
A cliff-dwelling of the Indians who lived in Arizona at the time of the Crusades. Shows the canyons and mesas of these early Indians; their lives, agriculture, and industry. 11 mins, color. Grades 9 and up. Rental, $13.50. NYU and PSU.

THE BELL THAT RANG TO AN EMPTY SKY
William Farley
A film essay using animation techniques and suggestive cutting to make a comment on the relationship between the expansion of white society onto Indian territories and the increase of wealth in the Federal Treasury. Commentary by Russell Means. 1977. Five mins. 16mm. CANYON.

BETWEEN TWO RIVERS
Tells the story of the Indians' continuing battle for identity. The tragedy of Thomas Whitehawk caught between the world of the white man and the Indian. 1970. 26 minutes, color. 16mm. Rental: UCT & UMN.

BETWEEN TWO WORLDS
Peter Raymont; Producer;
Barry Greenwald, Director
Reviews the tragedies and contradictions of Canada's colonization of the Inuit people; in particular, the effects upon the life of Joseph Idlout, one of the world's most famous Inuit. 1991. 58 minutes, color. Purchase: 16mm, $895, video, $390; rental, 16mm, $125. ICARUS.

BETWEEN TWO WORLDS
Gryphon Productions
Two part video which looks at four young single Native mothers and their struggle to find support. Focuses on different programs which are available. 1995. Part 1, 33 mins. Part 2, 30 mins. VHS. Set. $150. CHAR.

BEYOND THE SHADOWS
Documentary about the legacy of Native American boarding schools. 1995. 30 mins. VHS. $145. CHAR.

BEYOND TRADITION - CONTEMPORARY INDIAN ART & ITS EVOLUTION
Presents more than 300 examples of prehistoric, historic and contemporary American Indian art. Carvings, paintings, sculptures, baskets, rugs, jewelry and pottery.The evolution of Indian art is traced through the centuries. 1989. 45 mins, color. Video. Purchase: $29.95. NP, CAN. Rental: $16. UMN.

BIG BEAR
The Government and settlers staking claim to the Cree ancestral lands and hunting grounds, the Cree are forced from the land and torn between loyalty to their leader, Chief Big Bear and the white man. With Gordon Tootoosis & Michael Grayyeyes. 1998. VHS & DVD, $39.99. ME.

BIG CITY TRAIL: THE URBAN INDIANS OF TEXAS
Focuses on the 20,000 American Indian living in the Dallas/Ft. Worth area. Discusses the challenges these people face as they adjust to urban life, while resisting its homogenization. 28 mins. Teacher's guide. $35. UT-ITC.

BILL REID
Jack Long, Director
Haida carver and jewelry-maker, Bill Reid, speaks of his work and what his Haida heritage has meant for him as an artist. 1979. 28 mins. 16mm. NFBC.

THE BIRTH OF CALIFORNIA
A documentary of the prehistory & history of California in the early days of exploration. 1927. 22 mins, bxw. EG.

THE BISON HUNTERS
The painter George Catlin describes his enchantment with the life of the Plains Indians. 13 mins, color. Video. Purchase: $69.95. FH.

BLACK COAL, RED POWER
Shelly Grossman, Producer
Examines the effects coal strip-mining has had on the Navajo and Hopi reservations in Arizona. 1972. 41 mins, color. 16mm. Rental. IU & UA.

THE BLACK HILLS ARE NOT FOR SALE
Sandra Osawa, Producer
Taped at the 1980, International Survival Gathering in South Dakota, Sioux people tell why the Black Hills are not for sale. Provides historical background on the Laramie Treaty of 1868 which guaranteed the Sioux ownership of their lands. 1980. 28 mins, color. Video. UP.

THE BLACK HILLS: WHO OWNS THE LAND?
NETV, Producer
A two-part program examines the roots of this problem, presenting the facts and beliefs that have fueled over a century of debate. Part 1. The Treaty of 1868 - Focuses on the original treaties; Part 2. Black Hills Claim - Highlights the physical and legal battles waged to gain and regain the Black Hills of South Dakota. 30 mins each. Color. Video. Purchase: $50 per program; $70 for series. NETV.

BLACK INDIANS: AN AMERICAN STORY
Steven Heape & Chip Richie, Producer/Director
An introduction to the blending of Native Americans and African Americans. 2000. VHS & DVD. 60 mins. $24.95. RICH & ME.

BLUNDEN HARBOR
Shows a group of Pacific Northwest Kwakiutl Indians living in Blunden Harbor and sustaining themselves by the sea. Includes the Legend of Killer Whale, and a dance ceremony. 1951. Grades 7 and up. 20 mins, bxw. Rental, $14. PSU.

BOLDT DECISION: IMPACTS & IMPLEMENTATION
A discussion of the court ruling by U.S. Judge George Boldt who ruled that treaty Indians in Washington are entitled to half the harvestable catch of salmon and steelhead. 1976. 60 mins. 3/4" U-matic. UW.

BOLDT DECISION: UPDATE
A look at the impact of the Boldt decision. 60 mins, color. 1977. 3/4" U-matic. UW.

BOWS & ARROWS
Jim Hamm
Describes the art of making bows & arrows. 59 mins. VHS, $26.95. CMM.

BOX OF TREASURES
Chuck Olin, Producer/director
In 1921 the Kwakiutl people of Alert Bay, British Columbia, Canada, held their last secret potlatch. Fifty years later, the masks, blankets, and copper heirlooms that had been confiscated by the Canadian government were returned. The Kwakiutl built a cultural center to house these treasures & named it U'Mista something of great value that has come back. 1980. 28 mins, color. Purchase: 16mm, $480; video, $195. Rental. 16mm, $55; video, $35. DER (U.S.); CFDW (Canada).

BOY OF THE NAVAJOS
Depicts life among the Navajos as seen through the eyes of Tony, a present day Navajo Indian boy. Revised 1975 edition. Grades K-6. 11 mins, color. Purchase: 16mm, $270; video, $59. PHOENIX. Rental. UA, IU.

BOY OF THE SEMINOLES
(INDIANS OF THE EVERGLADES)
Wendell W. Wright, PhD
A visit to the Seminole tribe in the Everglades of Florida. 1956. Grades K-6. 11 mins. Purchase: 16mm, $270; video, $190. PHOENIX.

BRAVEHEART
Indian tries to make it in white man's world, falls in love with white woman, alienates his tribe. Finally returns to Indian ways. 1925. 68 mins, bxw. EG.

THE BROKEN CORD WITH LOUISE ERDRICH AND MICHAEL DORRIS
Two Native American authors share their insights into the traditions & conditions of Native America today. 30 mins. Video. $39.95. PBS.

BROKEN JOURNEY
Gary Robinson, Producer
A documentary which looks at the disease of alcohol

through the personal stories of Native American in-mates, men and women who have been incarcerated because of alcohol-related problems. 1986. 30 mins, color. Purchase: $150; Rental: $40. NAPBC.

BROKEN RAINBOW
Victoria Mudd & Maria Florio, Producers/writers/eds; Victoria Mudd, Director
A feature length documentary narrated by Martin Sheen, this film is concerned with the relocation of traditional Navajo from their homes in Big Mountain, Arizona. It provides a sympathetic view of the Navajo perspective on the history of the lands in dispute. Won the Academy Award for best documentary in 1985. 70 minutes, color. 16mm & video. DC.

BROKEN TREATY AT BATTLE MOUNTAIN
Joel Freedman, Director; narrated by Robert Redford
Shows the dramatic story of the traditional Western Shoshone Indians of Nevada and their struggle to re-gain 24 million acres of land stolen from them by the U.S. Government. Also, a portrait of the traditional In-dian way of life. 1974. 60 mins, color. 16mm & video. Purchase: $250. CIN. Rental. UN & UW.

BRYAN BEAVERS: A MOVING POTRAIT
A Maidu Indian of California talks about his past, In-dian spirits, his ancestral history, & his life. 1969. 30 mins, color. Grades 9 & up. 16mm rental, $15.90. IU

BUCKEYES: FOOD OF CALIFORNIA INDIANS
Clyde B. Smith, Producer
Shows harvesting, stone boiling, & leaching of buck-eyes (horse chestnuts) by Niseanan Indians, a centu-ries-old method of changing poisonous nuts into ed-ible mush or soup. 1961. 13 mins, color, 16mm, $280; video, $195. Rental, 16mm, $40. UC & PSU.

BUFFALO, BLOOD, SALMON & ROOTS
George Burdeau, Writer/Director
Filmed at the Flathead, Kalispel and Coeur d' Alene Reservations in western Montana, the Idaho pan-handle and eastern Washington, this film shows the old tribal ways of gathering and preserving food. 1976. 28 mins, color. 16mm & video. NAPBC and PBS.

THE BUFFALO SOLDIERS
Documentary revealing the exploits and heroism of black soldiers who fought Indians and pacified a great deal of the American West after the Civil War. 1992. 47 mins. VHS, $24.99. ME.

BUILDING AN ALGONQUIN BIRCHBARK CANOE
Their techniques are demonstrated by presen t day inhabitants of Maniwaki, Quebec. VHS. 54 minutes. $99. TR.

THE BUSINESS OF FANCY DANCING
written & directed by Sherman Alexie
A modern "life on the rez" drama based on a Sherman Alexie short story. With Evan Adam & Michelle St. John. 2002. VHS, 19.98, DVD, $24.98. ME.

4-BUTTE-1: A LESSON IN ARCHAEOLOGY
Clyde B. Smith and Tony Gorsline
Shows the excavations and analyzes the artifacts of a Maidu Indian village in California Sacramento Valley. 1968. 33 mins, color. Purchase: 16mm, $660; VHS, $195, Rental: $50. UC. Rental only: 16mm, $24.50; VHS, $24. PSU.

BY NO MEANS CONQUERED PEOPLE
Verity Lund and John Moore;
Richard Erdoes, photography
Presents issues that the Longest Walk, 1978, was or-ganized around. The Walk was made across the U.S. to demonstrate their concern about proposed legisla-tion: eleven bills, one of which would abrogate all trea-ties between the U.S. and Indian tribes. Dick Gregory and Clyde Bellacourt were speakers at the gathering. 1979. 26 mins, bxw. VHS. HSS.

BY SPIRITS MOVED
Explores spiritual beliefs & rituals of the Inuit (Eskimo) & other tribal people, and compares the role of the shaman with leadership in Western culture. 20 mins. VHS. $50. TOP.

BY THE WORK OF OUR HANDS
Designed to be used with the text of the same name. However, it can be used independently. Focuses on drum making, and both oak and cane basket making. Teacher's guide. 30 minutes. Grades 3-8. Purchase: video, $85. Rental, $10/two weeks. CHP.

BY THIS SONG I WALK: NAVAJO SONG
Larry Evers with Andrew Natonabah
Natonabah sings as he travels through Canyon de Chelly where the Navajo believe the songs were origi-nally created and he discusses the songs and their origin. In Navajo with English subtitles. 1978. 25 mins, color. Video. Purchase: $175. NR. Rental, $52.50. ATL.

CAHOKIA LEGACY
Cahokia Mounds and Cahokia Archaeology. 20 mins, color. Video, $10. CMM.

CAHOKIA MOUNDS: ANCIENT METROPOLIS
Traces the origins, people, places and products of the Mississippian culture. Story of the ancient mounds just east of St. Louis. Video. 60 mins. $19.95. CMM, VIP & ME.

CAHOKIA MOUNDS VIDEO LIBRARY
Cahokia: A Prehistoric Legacy, 17 minutes, color; The Cahokia Arrow Point, 13 minutes, color; Woodhenge Dedication Lectures, 1985; In Search Of...Ancient In-dian Astronomies, series, 84 minutes, color; 1987 Cahokia Culture Lecture Series, 155 mins, color. 2 week rentals, $2 per tape. CMM.

THE CALIFORNIA MISSIONS
Philomen Long, Director/writer;
Martin Sheen, Narrator
Documentary exploring the heritage of the California missions, emphasizing the clash pf cultures between the Spanish Franciscan missionaries and the native California Indians. 1990. 22 mins. Purchase: 16mm, $450; video, $195; rental, $50. UC.

CALIFORNIA RIVIERA
Looks at the history, culture, archaeology, and oceanographyof southern California. Includes an in-terview with the present members of the Juaneno In-dian tribe. 50 mins. 1989. VHS and Beta. NU.

CALUMET, PIPE OF PEACE
Discusses rituals surrounding the calumet or peace pipes. Describes Indian use of pipes and tobacco, and shows traditional Indian methods of fashioning, deco-rating and consecrating pipe bowl and stem. 1964. 23 mins, color. Purchase: 16mm, $460; video, $195. Rental: $50. UC. Rental only: PSU.

CANADA: PORTRAIT OF A NATION
Covers the environmental problems, and the social & political gains being made by the country's native In-dians & Inuits. Grades 4-8. 5 VHS cassettes. 16 mins each. $49. each. SVE.

CANADA'S ORIGINAL PEOPLES: THEN & NOW
TV Ontario, Producer
Contrasts the life of native Canadians before the ar-rival of Europeans with contemporary native life in Canada. 1977. 20 mins, color. Video. Rental, $40. NAPBC.

CANYON de CHELLY & HUBBELL TRADING POST
Visits both national parks containing Anasazi cliff dwell-ings and Navajo craftsmen. 30 mins. 1979. VHS & Beta. VVP.

CATLIN
Documents, through his paintings, the customs and drama of Native Americans. Scenes of daily life: tribal camps, buffalo hunts, war parties, feasts, and ritual ceremonies. 16mm. 6 mins. Free rental. NGA.

CELEBRATION & THE PIPE IS THE ALTAR
Chris Spotted Eagle, Producer/director
Two companion pieces presents aspects of contem-porary Native American culture for Indians living in the Minneapolis-St. Paul area. CELEBRATION (1979), filmed at the Honor the Earth Pow Wow held annually on the Lac Courte Oreilles Reservation in Wisconsin, depicts the strengths of Native American life: pow wow

dancing, feasting, Indian sports, give-aways, etc. In THE PIPE IS THE ALTAR (1980) spiritual leader Amos Owen, a Sioux Indian living on the Prairie Island Res-ervation near Red Wing, Minnesota, shares his daily prayer ritual using the ceremonial pipe. 26 mins, color. Video (VHS, Beta). IN, MAI.

CELEBRATION OF THE RAVEN
Ken Kuramoto
Bill Reid is the acknowledged master of contempo-rary art in the ancient native tradition of the Haida. Since 1959, he has created a series of large works of sculpture, culminating in his 1980 masterwork, The Raven and the First Men. Traces the evolution of this work of art. 1981. 12 mins, color. Video. CFDW.

A CENTURY OF SILENCE...
PROBLEMS OF THE AMERICAN INDIAN
Correlates the current problems of the American In-dian to the past 100 years of contact with the white culture. Also addresses issues of cultural conflict, as-simation, and activism within the Indian community. 28 mins, color. 1978. VHS and Beta. AP.

CESAR'S BARK CANOE
Bernard Gosselin, Director
Cesar Newashish, a Cree Indian, peels the bark from a birch tree and with his pocket knife and axe, con-structs a canoe. Subtitles in Cree, French and English. 1971. 58 mins, color. Grades 7-adult. EDC.

THE CHACO LEGACY
Graham Chedd, Director
Explores the excavations of the first monumental stone ruins discovered in North America, the Pueblo Bonito community in Chaco Canyon, New Mexico. Teachers guide. 1980. 16mm & up. 59 minutes, color. Pur-chase: 16mm, $600. Rental, $60. DER. Purchase: Video, $59.95. PBS. Rental: 16mm, $24; video, $12. PSU and IU.

A CHANGE FOR CHANGE
Depicts a young Native man caught between the city streets, his culture and family as he decides to get an AIDS test. Includes lesson guide & quiz. 1990. Grades 8-12. 30 mins. VHS. $145. CHAR.

CHARLES KILLS ENEMY, MEDICINE MAN
This film shows Kills Enemy in a Sweat Lodge Cer-emony and a Lowanpi Ceremony. 30 mins, color. 16mm. Purchase: $300; rental: $30. AICRC.

CHARLEY SQUASH GOES TO TOWN
An animated, imaginative simplification of the accul-turation-identity crisis of an Indian. 1969. Grades 6 and up. 5 minutes, color. 16mm. Rental: UA & UCT.

CHEROKEE
Philip Hobel, Executive Producer
Examines the modern Cherokee's efforts to preserve native traditions. Cherokees are shown performing cer-emonies and activities of the past, & discusses their heritage and hopes for the future. 1975. 26 mins. 16mm, $400; video, $340. Rental, $55 each. CG.

THE CHEROKEE ARTISTS SERIES
Jerome Tiger: The Man & His Legacy. 35 mins.; Willard Stone: Against the Odds. 28 mins. Bill Rabbit: Master Artist. 28 mins.; Woodrow Haney: Flutemaker. 28 mins.; Charles Banks Wilson. 28 mins. SH.

CHEROKEE BASKETMAKER
Ella Mae Blackbear
The life of a traditional Cherokee basketmaker; from gathering and dyeing to selling baskets at a museum store. Includes history of everyday Cherokee life in northeastern Oklahoma. VHS. 24 mins. $19.95. VIP.

CHEROKEE GENERAL
The Cherokee Nation and the Civil War. 1998. 30 mins. VHS, $24.95. ME.

THE CHEROKEE NATION:
THE STORY OF NEW ECHOTA
Recorded at the New Echota historical site in Gordon Co. Georgia, the one time capital of the Cherokee Nation where the constitution was written, & many other events. VHS. 15 mins. $14.95. VIP.

CHEYENNE AUTUMN
Based on an actual incident, this film tells of the valiant efforts of the Cheyenne Indians to escape to their Wyoming homeland from their wretched Oklahoma lands. With Richard Widmark & James Stewart. 1964. 156 minutes. VHS, $19.99. ME.

CHIEF MOUNTAIN HOTSHOTS
Blackfeet firefighters identify with traditional warrior societies. 2001. VHS, $24.95. ME.

*CHIEF SEATTLE TELLS HIS OWN STORY
An actor depicts the hisoric personality, explaining the time he lived in; the political, social, & ethical battles they fought, and the contributions he made. Grades 4-8. 20 mins. VHS, $89. SVE.

CHIEFS
Documentary on a winning Arapahoe basketball team. 2002. VHS, $24.95. ME

CHILDREN OF THE LONG-BEAKED BIRD
  Peter Davis and Swedish TV
Portrait of Dominic Old Elk, a 12 year old Crow Indian, exploring his life and interests; a view of Native American life and history. Seeks to erase many stereotypes. 1976. 29 minutes, color. Grades 3 and up. Purchase: 16mm, 485; Video, $100; Rental: $50. BULL. Rental: $40. NAPBC.

CHILDREN OF THE PLAINS INDIANS
A view of Indian life on the Great Plains before the arrival of white settlers, featuring scenes of tribal activities. 20 mins, bxw. 1962. Video. CRM. Rental: UCT.

CHILDREN OF WIND RIVER
Traces the history of Shoshone and Arapaho family life and shows how the introduction of boarding schools disrupted traditional child rearing. Uses interviews and images from the reservation. 1989. 30 mins. VHS. $49. CHAR.

CHOCTAW HERITAGE VIDEO
  William Brescia, Producer
By the Work of Our Hands - Documents tribal members expert in making crafts: split-oak baskets, cane baskets, and drums. 1983. 30 mins; *More Than Just a Week of Fun* - Shows events of the Choctaw Fair, held on the reservation every summer. 1984. 12 minutes; and *Choctaw Tribal Government* - Explains the structure and functions of Mississippi Choctaw tribal government, and a view of life on the Choctaw reservation today. 1985. Grades 5 and up. 17 mins, color. Video. CVP.

CHOCTAW STORY
  Bob Ferguson
Highlights the achievements of the tribal administration of Chief Phillip Martin, since 1979. 1985. 28 mins, color. Video. CVP.

THE CIRCLE
Drama tells the story of a Native American youth who has turned to alcohol to escape his anger and painful childhood memories. Includes a traditional healing circle and innovative programs. 1992. Grades 7 and up. 30 mins. VHS & Guide. $95. CHAR.

CIRCLE OF LIFE, Parts 1 & 2
American Indian youth on teenage pregnancy. Stresses the importance of education, prenatal care, and family planning. Part 1, 43 mins; Part 2, 32 mins, color. Video. Rental: $16. UMN.

CIRCLE OF LIFE: THE ALABAMA-COUSHATTAS
Documentary exploring the cultural identity of the Alabama-Coushattas. 24 mins. Teacher's guide. $35. UT-ITC.

CIRCLE OF SONG
  Cliff Sijohn and George Burdeau
Presents the Indian concept of the Circle of Life on which important life events and the songs and dances associated with them are point. In two parts. 1976. 28 mins each, color. 16mm & video. NAPBC & PBS.

CIRCLE OF THE SUN
  Colin Low, Director
Documents the life and ceremonial customs of the Blood Indians of Alberta, Canada, and contrasts their present existence on the reservation. 1960. Grades 7 and up. 30 mins, color. 16mm & video. $27. NFBC. Rental: UA, IU & UMN.

CIRCLE OF WARRIORS
Featurs nine Native Americans living with HIV infections and AIDS, discussing various aspects of their lives. A discussion guide is provided with the video. 27 mins, color. VHS. Purchase: $185; rental, $45. SH & NNA.

A CIRCLE OF WOMEN
Modern women meet women elders of Native American tribes in an effort to link their cultures. 60 mins, color. 1991. IVA.

CIRCLES
Native justice mshows an alternative approach to justice in the Yukon, focusing on ways to heal an offender, a victim, and the community. 1997. 58 mins. VHS. $139. CHAR.

CIVILIZED TRIBES
  Philip Hobel, Executive Producer
Life is reconstructed at the Seminole Reservation in Florida to simulate that of their Seminole ancestors. Also focuses on their present conditions. 26 minutes, color. 1972. Purchase: 16mm, $400; video, $340. Rental, $55 each. CG. 16mm rental only, IU.

CLASH OF CULTURES
  Scott Nielsen and Dick Blofson
Four elders from the Lakota tribe, drawing on the oral tradition of Indian life in the late 19th-century, explain the cultural attitudes of the Indians and the clash of attitudes with white settlers. 28 minutes. 1978. 16mm & VHS. UMA & KS.

CLASH OF CULTURES ON THE GREAT PLAINS (1865-1890)
Describes the traditional relationship of the Lakota people to their environment & explore conflicts with outsiders who moved into the area during the 1860s & 1870s. Grades 9-12. Teacher's guide. 20 mins. VHS, $125. AIT.

CLOUDED LAND
  Randy Croce, Producer
A sensitive examination of Native American land claims of the White Earth Reservation in Minnesota. 1987/1989. 58 minutes, color. Purchase: 3/4" $160; 1/2" VHS - $110. Rental: IN & UMN.

CLUES TO ANCIENT INDIAN LIFE
Discusses the kind of clues ancient indians left behind, and the importance of preserving these artifacts for study. 1962. 10 mins. Video. AIMS.

COLLIDING WORLDS
The lives of the Mono women, representing three generations, are intertwined to form the body of this film. Shows how traditional Mono ways have clashed & collided with modern technology. 1978. 30 mins, color. 16mm. Rental: $37. UCLA.

COLOURS OF PRIDE
  Henning Jacobson
Four Indian artists of Canada are interviewed in their home studios by Tom Hill, a Seneca from the Six Nations Reserve in Ontario. 1974. 24 minutes, color. 16mm. NFBC.

COLUMBUS CONTROVERSY:
CHALLENGING HOW HISTORY IS WRITTEN
  Nick Kaufman, Director
Examines the Columbus controversy using footage from the classroom of Bill Bigelow, along with historians John Mohawk and William McNeil. 1991. 24 minutes, color. Video. Purchase: $89. SRA.

COLUMBUS DIDN'T DISCOVER US
  Robbie Leppzer, Director; Wil Echevarria, Producer
Features interviews with indigenous activists, filmed at the Quincentennial gathering in 1990 in Ecuador of 300 native peoples of North, South and Central America. A moving testimony of the impact of the Columbus legacy on the lives of indigenous peoples resulting from the European invasion. 1992. 24 minutes, color. Video. Purchase: institutions, $89.95; community groups, $39.95; and indigenous organizations, $29.95. Rental: institutions, $45; community groups, $20. TTP & OY.

COME FORTH LAUGHING:
VOICES OF THE SUQUAMISH PEOPLE
  Suquamish Tribal Cultural Center, Producer
Provides an account of the life of the Suquamish Indian Tribe living in the Puget Sound region of Washington State over the past one hundred years. 1983. 15 minutes. Color and b&w. 16mm and video. SUQ.

A COMMON DESTINY
  Gayil Nalls, Producer/Director; John Steele, Producer
Comprised of two shorter films: "Walk in Both Worlds" - Jewell Praying Wolf James, a Lummi tribesman speaks of his ancestors and presents the 1853 message of Chief Seattle. "We do not own the freshness of the air or the sparkle of the water. How Can you buy them from us? ..."; also talks of the white man's reltaionship to the earth; and that Native American knowledge and needs are being ignored. And, "The Hopi Prophecy" - Thomas Banyacya, now in his 80s, is a spokesman for Hopi high religious leaders, interprets the prophetic symbols of a sacred petroglyph in Arizona for visitors from other tribes, & speaks about the damage that industry has caused on the reservation. 1990. 52 mins, color. VHS, $24.95. MFV.

COMPLETING OUR CIRCLE
Looks at the tradityions of the Plains and West Coast Indians, the Inuit, and the first Europeans and settlers in Western Canada. Presents their arts and crafts. 1978. 27 mins, color. VHS. CRM. Rental: 16mm, $23. UMN.

CONCERNS OF AMERICAN INDIAN WOMEN
  Will George, Director
Interviews with Marie Sanchez, North Cheyenne judge, and Dr. Connie Uri, Choctaw-Cherokee physician and law student. 1977. 30 mins, color. Video. MAI.

THE CONQUERED DREAM
Features sequences on Eskimo art and folklore, traditional hunting methods, health problems and education of today's Eskimo. 51 mins. CEN.

CONQUISTA
  Narrated by Richard Boone
A look at how the history of Old West was affected by the fateful meeting of the Plains Indian and the horse. 1974. 20 mins, color. Video. CFH. Rental: 16mm, $14. UCT.

CONSONANTS WITH COYOTE
Animated Navajo language film. Consonants with common sounds to both Navajo & English. 9 mins. All grades. 16mm & video. SAN.

CONTRARY WARRIORS: A STORY OF THE CROW TRIBE
  Connie Poten & Pamela Roberts, Producers;
  narrated by Peter Coyote
An award-winning documentary on the Crow people of southeastern Montana, as told by the members of the tribe, documents the life of 97-year-old Robert Yellowtail as a focus for the telling of Crow history. 1985. 60 mins, color. 16mm & video. Purchase: $250. DC. Rental: 16mm, $47.50. UMN.

CONTRASTS
Portrays the Plains Indians warriors and the U.S. Cavalrymen that faced off against each other in the 1870's. Filmed at the actual site of the Reno retreat crossing at the Battle of the Little Big Horn. 45 minutes, color. Video. Purchase: $25. OAP.

A CONVERSATION WITH VINE DELORIA, JR.
  Larry Evers, University of Arizona
The writer discusses the gulf between Indian and non-Indian culture and the schizophrenia of white expectations for the Indian. 1978. 29 minutes, color. Purchase: Video, $175. NR. Rental, video. $37.50. ATL.

1987 COOK INLET FRIENDSHIP POTLATCH
Highlights of Alaska Native traditional dances, music, Native Olympic games & other activities. 1988. 12 minutes, color. Video. $7. NDM.

COPPERMINE
Ray Harper, Director
Story about the clash of cultures. The Copper Inuit lived in Canada's central arctic until early 1900's when southern Canadians, Americans & British moved into the area. 1993. 56 minutes, color. Purchase: 16mm, $775; video, $250. Rental: $80.

**CORN & THE ORIGINS OF
SETTLED LIFE IN MESO-AMERICA**
Jack Churchill, Director
Presents the work of three scholars, Michael Coe, Paul Mangelsdorf, and Richard MacNeish. 1964. 40 minutes. 16mm. EDC.

COWTIPPING: THE MILITANT INDIAN WAITER
Randy Redroad
A Cherokee cafe waiter faces customers and their ignorance about American Indians. 1992. VHS. 17 minutes, color. Purchase: $175; rental, $50. TWN.

COYOTE TALES
Don Mose, Director; Kent Tibbitts, Producer
A series of five animated Navajo language and culture-based curriculum films in the Navajo language. 5 legendary coyote stories: Coyote and Beaver, 4 minutes; Coyote and Lizard, 7 minutes; Coyote & Rabbit, 10 mins; Coyote and Skunk, 9 mins; and Coyote and Toad, 8 mins, color. 16mm & video. SAN.

COYOTE WAITS
Robert Redford & Rebecca Eaton, Producers
Based on mystery novel by Tony Hillerman set on navajo reservation. With Wes Studi and Adam Beach. 97 mins. 2003. DVD, $24.95; VHS, $19.95. ME.

CRAZY HORSE - THE LAST WARRIOR
A&E Home Video
Story of Crazy Horse, leader of the Sioux. 1993. 50 mins. VHS, $16.99. ME.

CRAZY HORSE
Turner Network Production
Story of the Oglala Sioux leader. Fine dream sequences. With Michael Greyeyes, Irene Bedard, Wes Studi, et al. 93 mins. 1996. VHS, $59.99. ME.

A CREE HEALER
Consists of interviews with the healer and shows segments where he prepares for the sweatlodge ceremony. The interview concerns the issues and controversies encountered by this native healer in openly discussing the subject. 22 mins, color. VHS. UADA.

CREE HUNTERS OF MISTASSINI
Tony Ianzelo and Boyce Richardson, Directors
The setting up of a winter camp by 16 Cree Indians. Indian life is observed in the bush. 1974. Grades 7 and up. 58 mins, color. 16mm & Video. Purchase: Video, $245; rental, $60; 16mm, $70. DER & NFBC. Rental only: DEC, PSU, UCT & UMN.

CREE WAY
Tony Ianzelo and Boyce Richardson, Director
Provides a view of a successful bilingual education project which connects Cree children to their past and future. 1977. 28 minutes. 16mm. NFBC.

CREEK NATION VIDEO
Gary Robinson, Producer/director
For the past decade The Muscogee Creek Nation Communications Center, located in Okmulgee, Oklahoma, has been producing videotapes to present accurate and contemporary views of the Creek Nation. 17 programs on culture, history, and current affairs have been produced. A copy of any program is available at no charge, if a cassette is supplied. For a complete list of titles and information about production services offered contact MCN.

CROOKED BEAK OF HEAVEN
David Attenborough, Writer/Narrator
A Haida chief bestows lavish gifts on his tribesmen and then smashes his most valuable possessions, a potlatch ceremony. Contrasted with footage made of the Kwakiutl by Edward S. Curtis in 1912. 1976. 52 mins, color. 16mm. Rental: TW, UCLA, UCT, UI & UMN.

CROW DOG
Mike Cuesta and David Baxter, Directors
Documentary portrait of Sioux medicine man, Leonard Crow Dog, the spiritual leader of 89 American Indian tribes and the spokesman for the traditionalists. 1979. 57 mins, color. Purchase: 16mm, $795; video, $350. Rental, $95. CG. Rental only, $30. UT.

CROW DOG'S PARADISE
A look at a Sioux Indian enclave where the Crow Dog family preserves the spiritual and intellectual heritage of their traditional American Indian culture. 1979. Grades 9 and up. 28 minutes. 16mm & video. Purchase: VHS, $89; 3/4", $119. CC. Rental: VHS, $16; 16mm, $21.75. UMN.

1994 & 1995 CROW FAIR AND POW WOW
Views the pow wow dancing and parades at the Crow Fair, Crow Agency, Montana. The celebration of Crow lifeways through their unique music and songs. Two 60 minute color videos. CAN.

**CROW/SHOSHONE SUNDANCE...
A TRADITIONAL CEREMONY**
Documents the traditional Crow Lifeways & philosophies through authentic & legendary Crow/Shoshone Sundance Ceremony. 1991. 56 mins, color. Video. Rental: $16. UMN.

CRY OF THE YUROK
Details the Yuroks, California's largest Native American tribe,with the many problems that beset them as they try to survive. 58 minutes, color. Purchase: $149; rental, $75. FH.

CULTURAL CHANGES
The pre-reservation life of the buffalo hunting Indians of the southern Plains is told through the use of pictographic drawings made by Kiowa & Cheyenne young men imprisoned in Fort Marion, Florida, in 1875. 1970. 17 minutes, color. 16mm. Rental: $13. UMN.

**THE CUP'IK OF ALASKA—ESKIMOS:
A CHANGING CULTURE**
Despite many technological & material changes, their resources are the same as their ancestros, and they still depend on ancient knowledge that helps them adjust to their environment. 1992. Grades 4 and up. 32 minutes, color. Purchase: 16mm, $615; video, $375. Rental: $16mm, $95. PHOENIX.

CUSTER'S LAST FIGHT
Thomas Ince, Producer
The 1925 release of the 1912 Ince film, with two reels added to fill out the story. 45 minutes, color.Video. Purchase: $25. OAP.

THE DAKOTA CONFLICT
Floyd Red Crow Westerman
& Garrison Keillor, Narrators
Recounts the war (sometimes called "the Great Sioux Uprising") that began the 30 year struggle for the Great Plains, a struggle that continued at the Little Big Horn and ended at Wounded Knee. Uses diaries, old photographs, sketchbooks, newspaper archives, trail transcripts, and oral histories passed down through the generations. 1993. 60 mins, color. VHS. $20.95. ME. Rental: $16. UMN.

DAKOTA EXILE
The story of the Dakota people's brave struggle to survive in 1862 after being expelled from Minnesota and the U.S.'s largest mass execution that occurred then. Robbie Robertson narrates. 1995. 60 mins. VHS, $20.95. ME.

DANCE TO GIVE THANKS
Looks at the 184th annual He-De-Wa-Chi (Festival of Joy) of the Omaha Indian Tribe. Learn aboiut the history of the festival and see traditional dance by tribal members. 30 mins. VHS & 3/4" U-matic. NAPBC.

DANCES WITH WOLVES
Kevin Costner
Saga of a disallusioned soldier and his capture and joining the Lakota Sioux tribe. With Graham Greene, Rodney Grant & Kevin Costner as the soldier. 1990. VHS, $16.99; DVD, $29.99. ME.

DANCING FEATHERS
Paul Stephens; Producer/Writer;
Eric Jordan, Director
In this "Spirit Bay" program, Tafia, a young Ojibway girl, is apprehensive about performng a jingle dance at an upcoming powwow in Toronto. 1983. Grades 3-8. 28 mins, color. 16mm & video. Purchase: $149. ALT.

**DANCING IN MOCCASINS: KEEPING
NATIVE AMERICAN TRADITIONS ALIVE**
Examines the needs & problems of today's Native Americans, both those who live on the reservation & those who have chosen the mainstream. The conclusion focuses on celebration & survival as reflected in the continuing tradition of the Pow Wow. 49 mins, color. Video, Purchase: $149; rental: $75. FH.

A DANCING PEOPLE
Dancers & musicians from nine Yup'ik Eskimo villages gathered in the Yukon town of St. Mary's for 'Yupiit Yuraryariat.' Three days of dancing, gift-giving, and contests. 1983. 30 minutes, color. Video. $24.95. KYUK.

DANCING TO GIVE THANKS
NETV, Producer; JR Mathews, Host
Celebrates the traditions and family customs of the Omaha Indian Tribe. Filmed at the Omaha Tribal headquarters near Macy, Nebraska. 1988. 30 minutes, color. Video. Rental: $20. GPN. Purchase: $150; Rental: $40. NAPBC.

DAUGHTERS OF THE ANASAZI
John Anthony
The legendary Acoma potter, Lucy Lewis, and her daughters Emma & Delores demonstrate the traditional way of making fine pottery from grinding the clay to forming the coils & bowls, polishing, painting & firing. 1990. 28 minutes, color. Video. Purchase: $24.95. FI. Rental: $16. UMN.

DAUGHTERS OF THE COUNTRY
Norma Bailey, Producer
Focuses on four women of Native American heritage who find themselves drawn into the world of the white man and then rejected by it. Their stories move from 18th century to present day. Includes: Part 1 - "Ikwe," an Indian girl who lives in a remote area of North America in 1770; Part 2 - "Mistress Madeleine," she is half Native American in 1850; Part 3 - "Places Not Our Own," about a family in pre-Depression era in North America; and Part 4 - "The Wake," about Joan in 1985, a single American Indian parent with two small children whose father deserted them. 1987. 57 minutes each, color. Purchase: 16mm, $775 each; VHS, $150 each. Rental: $80 each. NFBC.

ROBERT DAVIDSON
Michael Brodie & Bill Roxborough, Directors/Prods.
Features one of the best known of contemporary artists, Robert Davidson. He is shown making a deer skin drum, with the entire process well portrayed. Discusses his technique, the philosophy behind the art of the Haida, and his personal connection to it. 1981. 29 minutes, color. In English or French. Video. MVS & VOI.

**THE DAWN RIDERS:
NATIVE AMERICAN ARTISTS**
Robert and Dona DeWeese
Three prominent Indian painters, Woody Crumbo (Potawatomi), Blackbear Bosin (Kiowa-Comanche) and Dick West (Cheyenne), talk about their work and influences on their art. 1969. 27 minutes. 16mm. LF.

DE GRAZIA
Ted De Grazia, well-known Arizona artist, discusses how his life among the Indians and Mexicans of the Southwest is reflected in his work. 1967. 29 minutes. 16mm. Rental. UA.

DEAD MAN
Johnny Depp, a young vet who has a price on his head, travels through the Badlands with a philosophical Indian, Gary Farmer , as his guide, who teaches him to face the dangers that follow a "dead man." 120 mins. b&w. 1996. VHS, $16.99; DVD, $29.99. ME.

THE DEATH MARCH OF DE SOTO
Archaeologists chart the conquistador's trail across Florida's Gulf Coast to the Gulf of the Mississippi and uncover now-extinct Native American cultures, their people victims of brutality, disease, and neglect. 1993. 28 mins, color. VHS. $149; rental: $75. FH.

THE DEATH OF THE BISON
The stories of the Indian chiefs, of Crazy Horse and Sitting Bull and their great battles to the events at Wounded Knee in 1973 demonstrates that the conflicts of the past have yet to be resolved. 13 mins, color. Video. Purchase: $69.95. FH.

THE DENNIS ALLEY WISDOM DANCERS
Two concerts featuring the Dennis Alley Wisdom Dancers. 25 mins each, color. Video. $22.50. CAN.

DESERT DANCE
Includes single voice chanting with Native American flute by Carlos Nakai, drums, rattles, wind & rain. Cassette, $12. CH.

DESERT PEOPLE (PAPAGO)
1949. 25 minutes. Rental. UA.

DESERT REGIONS: NOMADS & TRADERS
A look at the Navajo Indians of Monument Valley and Bedouins of Jordan. 1980. 15 mins, color. Video. PHOENIX.

DETOUR
    Deron Twohatchet
Two mismatched drifters, Jim and James are on a voyage discovering the contours of homo/hetero, red/white, personal/political in an experimental narrative feast. In a critiiiique of the exotized American Trickster figure. 28 minutes. Color & B&W. Video. Purchase: $175; rental, $60. TWN.

DIABETES: LIFETIME SOLUTIONS
Documentary about the prevention, care and maintenance of diabetes in Native American communities. Looks at the history and present day factors contributing to the disease amongst Native North Americans. 1999. 30 mins. VHS. $148. CHAR.

DIABETES: NOTES FROM INDIAN COUNTRY
Lorelei DeCora, a Winnebago publuc health nurse visits the Winnebago Indian Reservation in Nebraska, the Rosebud Sioux Tribe and the Porcupine Lakota community in South Dakota to present community solutions to this health care crisis. 1999. 20 mins. VHS. $50. CHAR.

DIARY: NATIVE AMERICAN MINNESOTANS
Documents the personal stories of several Native Americans living in Minnesota. Describes the process of getting in touch with their roots & fitting into the white American culture. 1992. 35 minutes, color. Video. Rental: $16. UMN.

A DIFFERENT DRUM
The story of a young Comanche boy who is torn between his family's desire for him to attend college and his own natural aptitude for auto mechanics. 1974. 21 minutes. Rental. UK.

DINEH: THE PEOPLE
    Jonathan Reinis & Stephen Hornick
Documentary focusing on the impending relocation of several thousand Navajo from a joint-use land area surrounding the Hopi Reservation which is located in the midst of the Navajo Reservation. Portrays the cultural and economic conditions under which the Navajo attempt to survive while striving to preserve their traditional values. 1976. 77 minutes, color. Video. Purchase: $150; Rental: $80/week. NAPBC.

DISCOVERING AMERICAN INDIAN MUSIC
    Bernard Wilets
Songs and dances of tribes from various parts of the country performed in authentic costumes. Featuring Louis Ballard, Cherokee composer's percussion ensemble combining natural instruments of numerous tribes. 1971. Grades 4 and up. 24 mins., color. SH. Rental: IU, UMN, UCLA, UCT, UT & UK.

THE DISPOSSESSED
Sympatheic view of the Pit River Indians' struggle to regain lands in northern California taken from them in 1853 and now controlled by Pacific Gas & Electric Co.Shows the Indians' impoverished living conditions, and describes how PG&E dams have destroyed salmon runs on which they depend. Traces the legal history of the land dispute. 1970. 33 minutes, color. 16mm. Rental: UCLA.

DISTANT VOICE...THUNDER WORDS
Discusses the role of the oral tradition in modern Native American literature. Includes interviews with storytellers and other experts. 1990. 60 mins, color. VHS. NAPBC.

THE DIVIDED TRAIL:
A NATIVE AMERICAN ODYSSEY
    Jerry Aronson & Michael Goldman
Follows the lives of three Chippewa as they moved from various stages of activism and discontent into vocational alternatives. 1977. 30 mins, color. 16mm, $495; Video, $345; Rental; $42.50. PHOENIX. Rental: Video, $19.65. IU; 16mm, $24.25. UMN

DO WE WANT US TO?
The story about the heritage of the Tlinget Indians. 1979. Grades 7 and up. 20 minutes, color. Video. NAC. Rental: $10. UCT.

DOCTOR, LAWYER, INDIAN CHIEF
    Carol Geddes, Director; Gail Valaskakis, Narrator
Focuses on five Native Indian women from across Canada; each talks about her personal difficulties in getting to where she is today, and about her life experiences. Includes: Sophie Pierre, the chief of St. Mary's Band in B.C.; Lucille McLeod, job-counselor for native women; Margaret Joe, the first native women to have become a minister in the Yukon government; Corrine Hunt, of the Kwakiutl Nation, operates the hydraulic equipment on a commercial fishing boat off the coast of B.C.; and Roberta Jamieson, Canada's first native Indian woman lawyer. 1987. 29 minutes, color. Purchase: 16mm, $550; VHS, $250. Rental: $60. NFBC.

DOE BOY
james Duval, a half Cherokee, mistakingly kills a doe and is nicknamed "Doe Boy". His grandfather teaches him the difference between hunting & killing. With Gordon Tootossis. 87 mins. 2002. VHS, $9.98; DVD, $14.98. ME.

DREAM DANCES OF THE KASHIA POMO
    Clyde B. Smith, Producer
Pomo women dance the Bole Maru nearly a century after it first evolved, blending the native Kaksu cult with the Maru or dream religion. Five dances are shown. The shaman expresses her religious beliefs in her own words. 1964. 30 minutes, color. 16mm, $600; video, $195. Rental: $50. UC. Rental: IU & PSU.

DREAMKEEPERS
    with Nathaniel Arcand & Gerald Auger
American Indian legend told on film. DVD. 180 mins. 2003. ME. $19.99.

DREAMSPEAKER
An emotionally disturbed boy runs away from an institution and is adopted by an old Indian shaman. The Indian vision of life and death are reviewed. 1977. 75 mins, color. Grades 9 and up. Rental, $42. PSU.

THE DRUM
    Alaska Native Human Resource Development Project
Shows a Native American ritual. Grades 4-12. 1987. 15 mins, color. VHS. $260. NDM

THE DRUM IS THE HEART
    Randy Croce, Producer
Narrated entirely by Indian participants, ranging from children to elders, this film focuses on the Blackfeet, Blackfoot, Blood and Peigan tribes that make up the Blackfoot Nation at their celebrations, speaking about their contemporary lives and traditional values. 1982. 29 mins, color. Video. Purchase: 3/4" - $120; 1/2" - $80. Rental: 3/4" - $45; 1/2" - $30. IN.

THE DRUMMAKER
Presents an Ojibwa Indian, William Bineshi Baker, Sr., on the Lac Court Oreilles Reservation in northern Wisconsin, one of the last of his people to continue the art of drummaking. Step-by-step he constructs a dance drum, and expresses his beliefs about tradition, as well as frustrations. 1978. 37 minutes, bxw. Purchase: 16mm, $390; VHS, $175. Rental. 16mm, $22; VHS, $12.50. PSU.

THE DRUMMER
    Thomas Vennum, Jr.
William Bineshi Baker, Jr., an Ojibwa, living on the Lac Courte Oreilles Reservation in northern Wisconsin constructs a drum step-by-step. 1978. 37 mins, bxw. Purchase: 16mm. PSU.

DRUMS OF THE AMERICAN INDIAN
Suitable for practicing traditional dance steps. Cassette, $12. CH.

THE DRUMS OF WINTER (UKSUUM CAUYAI)
    Sarah Elder & leonard Kamerling
A dcoumentary exploring the traditional dance, music and spiritual world of the Yup'ik Eskimo people of Emmonak, a remote village at the mouth of the Yukon River on the Bering Sea coast. 1988. 90 minutes, color. Purchase: 16mm, $1300; video, $345. Rental: 16mm, $140; video, $80. DER.

THE EAGLE & THE CONDOR
    KBYU-TV, Provo Utah, Producer
Examines the interaction between the Native American cultures of North and South America. Native American entertainers of BYU's Laminite Generation tour South America performing and discussing differences and similarities in cultures. 1975. 29 minutes, color. Video. Purchase: $150; Rental: $40. NAPBC.

THE EAGLE & THE MOON
    Wango Weng, Director
An animated Haida story presenting elements of Haida culture such as the class and their totem poles. 1971. 10 minutes. 16mm. WALL.

THE EAGLE & THE RAVEN
Profiles the story of Native American Tlingit teenagers who were sentenced by their tribal court for robbery and the program and healing process. Grades 6 and up. 1996. 80 mins. VHS. $49. CHAR.

EARL'S CANOE: A TRADITIONAL OJIBWE CRAFT
    Tom Vennum, Charles Weber, with Earl Nyholm
The making of a birchbark canoe and what it means to the Ojibwe people of Wisconsin. 1999. 27 minutes. Purchase: $145; rental, $40. DER.

THE EARLY AMERICANS
Traces the rise of man from his arrival in North America as an ice age wanderer, to builder of complex societies more than 2,000 years before Columbus. 1976. 42 minutes, color. Grades 9 and up. Video. Rental, $18. UA & PSU.

THE EARLY AMERICANS, 1776
    Daniel Wilson Productions
Describes the lifestyles of Americans west of the Appalachians in 1776 in New Mexico, Hawaii, Alaka & the Spanish Mission of California. Grades 7 and up. 28 minutes, color. Rental: $10. UCT.

EARLY MAN IN NORTH AMERICA
A film about early man in North America. 1972. 12 mins. VHS. FILMS.

EARTH CIRCLES
Emphasizes the traditional closeness with nature that is a fundamental aspect of Native American life.Images are from Woodlands Indian prints & photos of wildlife in natural habitat. Study guide included. 10 minutes. VHS. $50. TOP.

THE EARTH IS OUR HOME
    Elizabeth Patapoff, Producer/writer
Produced in cooperation with members of the Burns Paiute tribe in Oregon to preserve a record of their traditional way of life and skills. 1979. 29 minutes, color. 16mm & video. MP

EARTHSCAPE
Artists on the Copper River Delta/Alaska. Documents watercolorists, photographers, and sculptors as they travel to Alaska's Copper River Delta to paint and sculpt. Video. 20 mins. SH.

EARTHSHAPERS

A look at the sacred mounds created by the Woodland Native people. Grades 7 and up. 14 minutes, color. Video. NAPBC. Rental: $10. UCT.

EASTER IN IGLOOLIK: PETER'S STORY
Paulle Clark, Producer
A photographed look at Inuit life in a modern Arctic community, Igloolik, in Canada's Northwest Territories. 1987. Grades 7 and up. 24 minutes, color. Purchase: 16mm, $495; Video, $350; Rental: $50. BULL.

EDUCATION OF LITTLE TREE
Story of 8-year old Little Tree who goes to live with his Cherokee grandparents during the depression. He learns his culture and way of life. With Graham Greene, James Cromwell, Joseph Ashton, and Tantoo cardinal. 180 mins. VHS, $19.99. ME.

EDUCATIONAL VIDEO
Two videos in one. Time Journey - explores the prehistoric time period of North America; and, Indian Diversity - examines the life of modern Indian cultures, Choctaw, Ponca, Pueblo, and Peoria/Miami. Plus two Indian stories. Includes handbook. $14. CMM.

THE ELDERS SPEAK..."NOW I LISTEN
Elders from around the country speak out on the needs of Native American, Native Alaskan & Native Hawaiian elders. 20 minutes. Video. Purchase: $245; rental: $45. SH.

ELEGANT VISIONS: NATIVE AMERICAN WOMEN'S CLOTHING
44 models representing 24 tribes show 70 different outfits, including: Woodland tunics and ribbonwork; a Navajo wedding dress; and a Tlingit blanket. VHS. 30 minutes. $19.95. VIP.

ELLA MAE BLACKBEAR: CHEROKEE BASKETMAKER
Scott & Sheila Swearingen, Producers/directors/eds; Fran Ringold, Narrator
Ella Mae Blackbear practices the ancient art of Cherokee basketmaking as it has survived in Oklahoma after the Cherokees' removal to the Indian Territory in the late 1830's. 1982. 25 minutes, color. Video. WH.

EMERGENCE
Barbara Wilk, Producer/writer/animator
Tells the story of the events leading to the entrance of the Dineh, the Navajo people, onto the surface of this earth through a number of underworlds. The traditional chants heard in the film are versions of the origin myths sung as part of certain Navajo healing rituals. 1981. 14 minutes. Color animation. 16mm, video. Purchase: VHS, $89; 3/4", $119. CC & PR.

EMERGENCE: A GRASS ROOTS ACCOUNT OF INDIAN ACTIVISM
Walter Verbanie
Documents how the Potawatomi in Kansas lost lands through disadvantageous treaties and divisions in the tribe between members of the Mission & Prairie bands. 1977. 35 mins. 16mm. MAI.

THE EMERGING ESKIMO
Deals with the impact of the white man upon the native Eskimos. 15 minutes. Grades 1-8. Rental. UK.

THE ENCHANTED ARTS: PABLITA VELARDE
Irene-Aimee Depke, Producer/director
Presents a portrait of Santa Clara Pueblo, Pablita Velarde, one of the first Indian women to pursue painting professionally. 1977. 28 mins, color. Video. DEPKE.

END OF THE TRAIL: THE AMERICAN PLAINS INDIANS
Surveys the westward movement in America during the last century & the tragic impact of that movement on the American Indians. 1967. Grades 6 & up. 53 mins, b&w. 16mm. CRM. Rental: IU, UA, UCT & UMN.

ESKIMO ARTIST - KENOJUAK
John Geeney, Director
Inuit artist Kenojuak shows the sources of her inspiration and methods used to transfer her carvings to stone. 1964. 20 minutes, color. Grades 7 and up. Purchase: 16mm, $410; and video, $300. Rental: $50. NFBC. Rental: $17. UK and PSU.

ESKIMO CHILDREN
Portrays the activities of a typical Eskimo family living on Nunivak Island off the Alaskan coast. 1941. 11 minutes, bxw. Grades 4 and up. In English & Spanish. 16mm. Rental only. IU, UA & UK.

ESKIMO: FIGHT FOR LIFE
Asen Balikci, Advisor and Narrator
Shows the careful division of tasks among the different members of a group of Netsilek Eskimos camped together during the winter seal hunting season. 1970. Grades 7 and up. 51 minutes. 16mm. EDC & UW.

ESKIMO HUNTERS
Presents the life of the Eskimos who live in the cold areas of Northwestern Alaska. 1949. 21 minutes, bxw. 16mm. Rental only. IU & UK.

THE ESKIMO IN LIFE & LEGEND
Shows how the Inuit's way of life, his legends, and his art of stone carving are interrelated. 1960. 22 minutes. Grades 7 and up. Rental. UA.

THE ESKIMO SEA HUNTERS
How Eskimo people live in regions where the weather is always cold. 1949. 20 minutes/bxw. Rental. UK.

ESKIMOS: A CHANGING CULTURE
Wayne Mitchell
Examines the lives of two generations of Inuit Eskimos who live on Nunivak Island in the Bering Sea off the coast of Alaska. 1971. 17 minutes, color. Grades 4 and up. Purchase: 16mm, $355; video, $225. Rental, $53. PHOENIX. Rental only, IU & BYU.

THE ESKIMOS OF POND INLET
Hugh Brody
Studies the Inuits (Eskimos) of Pond Inlet, Baffin Island. 1977. 52 minutes, color. Video. Purchase: FI. Rental: $19. PSU.

ESTE MVSKOKE/THE MUSCOGEE PEOPLE
Marty Fulk & Gene Hamilton, Associate producers; Gary Robinson, Script; Tim Bigpond, Narrator
Beginning with the "origin of clans," this program provides an overview of the history, culture, and modern achievements of the Creek Nation. 1985. 24 minutes, color. Video. MCN & ODE.

THE ETERNAL DRUM
Don Priest, Producer
Looks at the social & spiritual significance of the contemporary American Indian Pow Wow & explains the traditions & the altruistic foundations of the American Indian societies. Grades 6 and up. 25 minutes. VHS. $195. SH, NDM

EVERY DAY CHOICES: ALCOHOL & AN ALASKA TOWN
Sarah Elder, Producer/director/editor
Shows how insidious, destructive, and pervasive the problem of alcohol is in native communities in the north, Yup'ik Eskimo villages in the Bethel, Alaska area. The film addresses stereotyped ideas of Native American alcoholism. 1985. 93 mins, color. 16mm & video. NH.

EVERYONE COUNTS
Looks at the problem of prescrtiotion drug misuse in one Native American community. Part 2 of a 2 part series. 2000. 24 mins. VHS. $75. Part 1, "Knowledge Is the Best Medicine." CHAR.

EVERYTHING HAS SPIRIT
Explored the historical roots of Native American religious persecution and examines contemporary issues including preservation of sacred sites, First Amendment protection and the use of peyote in the Native American Church. Adult. VHS. 30 mins. $69. CHAR.

EXCAVATION OF MOUND 7
Archaeology work in the field and in the lab to piece together the mysteries of the Pueblo Indians of New Mexico. 1973. 44 minutes. VHS, U-matic. NAC.

THE EXILES
Kent Mackenzie, Producer
Classic depiction of one anguished but typical night in the lives of three young American Indians who have left the reservation and come to live in downtown Los Angeles. 1961. 72 minutes. bxw. 16mm & video. Purchase: $250; rental: $75. UC. Rental: UA, UCLA, UMN, UK, IU & PSU.

EXPEDITION ARIZONA: MISSIONS OF OLD ARIZONA
Reviews the buildings of San Xavier del Bac which is still used by the Papago people after 260 years, and the contributions of Father Kino to Indian culture. 1960. 27 minutes, bxw. Rental. UA.

EXPEDITION ARIZONA: SHARDS OF THE AGES
Shows three ancient cultures: the Hohokam of the desert, the Mogollon of the mountains, and the Anasazi of the plateau regions of Arizona. 1960. 27 minutes, bxw. Rental. UA.

EYANOPAPI: THE HEART OF SIOUX
Details the historical and religious significance of the South Dakota Black Hills to the Sioux Nation. Grades 9 and up. 30 minutes. Purchase: VHS, $250; 3/4", $280. CC.

EYES OF THE SPIRIT
Corey Flintoff, Producer/writer; Alexie Isaac, Director/camera; Ina Carpenter, Narrator
Documents the work of a group of dancers, the Bethel Native Dancers, and their struggle, in preserving and teaching Yup'ik Eskimo traditions and reviving the use of masks in Native dancing. 1983. 30 minutes. Color. VHS. $24.95. KYUK.

THE FACE OF WISDOM: STORIES OF ELDER WOMEN
Catherine Busch-Johnston, Producer/Director hosted by Julie Harris
Series of 8 videotapes, including one entitles: "Nellie Red Owl," a Native American elder of the Sioux tribe of South Dakota. Born only 16 years after her tribe's massacre at Wounded Knee, she lives with the conviction that her land & native traditions must never again be compromised. 1993. 30 mins, color. VHS. $125. PHOENIX.

FACE TO FACE
Contains 5 extended interviews with Native Americans living with AIDS. Each discusses various aspects of their lives. A discussion guide is priovidd with the video. 58 mins. VHS. Purchase: $100. NNA. Rental, $45. SH

FACES OF CULTURE: 22 - NEW ORLEANS' BLACK INDIANS: A CASE STUDY IN THE ARTS
Follows the Black Indian tribes of New Orleans, a blend of American Indians and blacks. 1983. 30 minutes, color. Video. Rental, $14. PSU.

THE FAITHKEEPER
Betsy McCarthy, Producer/director
Relates the guding philosophy of Native Americans to our own today. Bill Moyers is the guest of Oren Lyons, who taks about the past and future of Native American peoples. Lyons is chief of the Turtle Clan of the Onondaga Nation and a prominent member of the environmental movement. He describes how the U.S. democracy was modelled on the Iroquois Federation; discusses respect for nature; Native American prophecies about the environmental disasters we now face; and recounts the legends of his clan. 1992. 58 mins, color. Video. Purchase: $29.95. MFV.

FAMILY LIFE OF THE NAVAJO INDIANS
Fries, Kluckhohn & Woolf, Producers
Highlights some of the ways in which the Navajo child develops into adulthood. 1943. 31 mins, bxw. 16mm. Rental, $15. NYU & UT.

A FAMILY OF LABRADOR
Kent Martin, Director
A story of corporate development and changing ways of life for Indian, Inuit and people of mixed ancestry. 1978. 59 minutes, color. Video. $27. NFBC.

FANCY DANCE
Full Circle Communications
Close up and slow motion sequences show champion dancers in exciting contests. 30 mins. VHS. $19.95. WH.

THE FAST RUNNER
Love murder and revenge in the Arctic Circle centuries ago. An all Native cast speaking Inuit language. 2001. DVD, $26.99; VHS, $99.99. ME.

FAT CITY: OBESITY
Roger Bingham
Looks at obesity on the Pima Indian Reservation in Arizona. Grades 7 and up. 1990. 28 mins. VHS. $70. CHAR.

FEATHERS
Larry Littlebird, Writer;
Frank Marrero (WGBH), Producer
Dramatizes personal and social problems encountered by teenagers over how far they, as Indians, should go in joining the mainstream of American life. Emphasizes the closeness of family and community life. 1980. 30 minutes, color. Video. WGBH.

FEDERAL INDIAN LAW
Joel Freedman; Joan Kaehl, Writer
Traces the development of federal Indian law through treaties, statutes, and court decisions. By using real life examples, it illustrates the impact that federal Indian law can have on tribal economics and community lifestyles, and how law can be made to work for your tribe. Narrated by Kirke Kickingbird, Kiowa attorney and founder of the Institute for the Development of Indian Law. 1980. 19 minutes. 16mm. IDIL.

THE FEMININE: ANCIENT VISION, MODERN WISDOM
Wabun Wind
Discusses matriarchy, patriarchy, women's power, moon cycles and menstrual cycles, stereotyping of women, sexuality, relationships, and raising children. 65 minutes. Video. Purchase: $29.95. BTP & CH.

THE FIGHTING CHEYENNE
Depicts the Cheyenne Indians' battles with white travelers on the trail. Relates the historic tale of Dull Knife and his Cheyenne band. 30 minutes. 16mm. Rental. UT.

FINDING THE CIRCLE:
AMERICN INDIANS DANCE THEATRE
Native American dancing with all its colors and sacred ritual. 56 minutes, color. Video. Purchase: $36. CH.

FIRES OF SPRING
Henry T. Lewis, Ph.D., Writer/Producer
Shows how, among the Slavey and Beaver tribes of northern Alberta, Canada, fire was used to carefully maintain and improve selected habitats of plants, game and furbearing animals. 1980. 33 minutes. Purchase: 16mm, $250 (Canadian); video, $125. BINS. Rental: 16mm, $17.50. PSU; $20.50, UMN.

THE FIRST AMERICAN MELTING POT
The gradual arrival of new Indian groups on the Plains and their clash with bison-hunting horse culture. 1981. 30 minutes, color. Video. KS.

THE FIRST AMERICANS
Story of Raymond Tracey, a young Indian man trying to get back to his roots & determine who the American Indians are. Grades 3-8. Produced in 1989 by Children's Television International & American Indian Heritage Foundation. In six 15-minute programs. $29.95 each, $131.70/set. Teacher's Guide, $2. GPN.

THE FIRST AMERICANS
Studies the major Indian tribes of the U.S.- their customs, culture and the land that belonged to them. Students will explore the special characteristics of individual tribes. Grades 4-6. 1988. 60 minutes. Video. Purchase: $129.95. Also available as filmstrips and cassettes. TA.

THE FIRST AMERICANS
In two parts. Part I: And Their Gods— (20 minutes, color) The migration of people into the Americas and the eventual setting and differentiating of these people into tribes. 11 minutes. Part II: Some Indians of the Southlands— (32 minutes, color) Depicts customs & beliefs of certain Indians in the southern half of U.S.: Natchez, the Moundbuilders, the Hopi, Zuni and Na-

vajo. Grades 4-9. 1969. Purchase: 16mm, Part 1-$220; Part 2-$300; Video, 2 parts, $250. IFF; UT - 16mm rental, $20. Rental only, 16mm. IU & UCT.

THE FIRST AMERICANS
Discusses the 30,000 years of cultural development of the American Indian. 1979. 30 minutes. 3/4" U-matic. CET.

THE FIRST AMERICANS-
SOME INDIANS OF THE SOUTHLAND
The customs, beliefs and history that shaped the daily patterns of life in the early cultures of the Natchez, the "Moundbuilders," the Hopi, the Zuni, and the Navajo. 1976. 18 minutes, color. Grades 7 and up. 16 mm. Rental, $14. IU.

FIRST NATION BLUE
Documentary narrated by Graham Greene uncovering the changiung attitudes of the police officers serving Native American communities. 1996. 48 mins. VHS. $150. CHAR.

FIRST FRONTIER
Chronicles the long process of defeat and destruction of the Native American community beginning with the 1540 penetration into North America by DeSoto and his forces, then the French and British. Made with the cooperation of the Mississippi Band of Choctaw and the Poarch Band of Creek Indians. 58 minutes, color. Video. Purchase: $250. BE.

FIRST NATION BLUE
Documentary narrated by Graham Greene about police officers serving Native American communities. VHS. 47.5 mins. $150. CHAR.

THE FIRST NORTHWESTERNERS:
THE ARCHAEOLOGY OF EARLY MAN
Louis and Ruth Kirk, Producers
Examines the first northwest environment of more than 10,000 years ago and the first humans known to have lived there. 1979. 29 minutes, color. Purchase: 16mm, $425; beta, $225; VHS, $215. UW.

FIRST PEOPLES
Explain how ancient people came to North America and compare their lifestyles before Europeans arrived. Myths & legends are included. Grades 4-8. 15 minutes. VHS, $125. AIT.

FISH HAWK
Fish Hawk (Will Sampson), an aging Indian hunter in turn-of-the-century rural America, struggles to overcome the lure of the bottle and local towns people.1994. 95 mins. VHS. $14.99. ME.

A FISHING PEOPLE: THE TULALIP TRIBE
Heather Oakson
Tells the story of their history as a fishing people and provides an overview of the tribe's current involvement with fishing as an industry. 1980. 17 minutes, color. The TT.

FOLKLORE OF THE
MUSCOGEE (CREEK) PEOPLE
Rex Daugherty, Exec. producer;
Gary Robinson, Writer
Host Dr. Ruth Arrington (Creek Nation) describes the nature of folklore within Creek culture, and explains the breakdown of folklore into three categories: legends, myths and fables. Grades 3-12. 1983. 29 mins, color. VHS. $150; Rental: $40. MCN & NAPBC.

FOLLOWING THE STAR
Story of Russian Orthodox Christmas as practiced by the Yup'ik Eskimos of the Kuskokwim River Delta. 1987. 30 minutes, color. VHS. $24.95. KYUK.

FONSECA: IN SEARCH OF COYOTE
Mary Louise King & Fred Aronow, Producers
Noted Native American artist Harry Fonseca relates the development of his "Coyote" series of paintings and drawings; shows how Fonseca's anthropomorphic coyote grew out of traditional North American India art forms and legends surrounding the famous "trickster." 1983. 30 minutes. Video. Purchase: $95; rental, $50. UC. Rental: $16. UMN.

FOREST SPIRITS
NEWIST, Producer
A series of seven 30-minute programs on the Oneida & Menominee tribes of Wisconsin. 1: To Keep a Heritage Alive—Oneida children learn their native tongue, religious code and moral ethic. 2: The Learning Path—The educational system and the Native American. 3: Land Is Life—Documents Oneida's troubles over land. 4: Ancestors Of Those Yet Unborn—Menominee lifestyle. 5: Living With Tradition—Menominee traditions and reaffirmation of heritage. 6 & 7: Dreamers With Power—Part 1: Explores stereotypes and truths about Menominee Reservation life; and Part 2: Menominee's history. Grades 4 and up. 1975-76. Color. Video. Purchase: $350/series; $65/program. Rental: $17.50/program. Teacher's Guide, $1. NAPBC & GPN.

FOREVER IN TIME:
THE ART OF EDWARD S. CURTIS
Robert W. Mull, Producer
Curtis (1868-1952), one of the world's foremost photographers, captured in photos and on film the culture and lifestyle of the American Indian. He recorded tribal chants, narratives of Indian life and vocabulary translations. This documentary chronicles Curtis's career, featuring interviews with surviving family members, and blending his motion picture footage, sound recordings and photographic portraits, and an original music score. 1990. 50 minutes, color & bxw. Video. Purchase: $295; rental, $75. CG. Rental: $20. UMN.

FORGET THE FISH...CULTURAL ASPECTS
OF NURSING CARE FOR NAVAJOS
Reality-based story about a new nurse, Ann Davis, and her experiences with a Navajo patient & his wife. Her encounter with a medicineman helps her learn how to work with Navajo medicine people within the hospital setting. 1984. 25 mins, color. VHS. Rental: $18.50. UMN.

THE FORGOTTEN AMERICAN
A documentary filmed in the Southwest and in the urban Indian communities of Los Angeles and Chicago. Shows the impoverishment of the American Indian, his loss of identity and self-respect. 1968. 25 minutes, color. 16mm. Purchase/rental: MAI-CFV. Rental: PSU, UA, UCT & UCLA.

FORGOTTEN FRONTIER
KAET-TV Phoenix, Producer
Documents Spanish mission settlements of southern Arizona, & the conversion and teaching of skills to Indians. 1976. 30 mins, color. VHS. Rental, $40/week. NAPBC.

FORT PHIL KEARNEY:
THE HATED POST ON THE LITTLE PINEY
A tour of Fort Phil Kerney, Fetterman Hill and the Wagon Box Fight, where the Sioux under Red Cloud clashed with the U.S. Army for control of northern Wyoming's Powder River Country and the Bozeman Trail. 30 minutes. Video, $30. OAP.

FORTY-SEVEN CENTS
Lee Callister & Wendy Carrel, Producers
Focuses on the land claims of the Pit River Indians in northern California and the processes by which Indians are unfairly treated. 1973. 25 minutes, bxw. 16mm & video. Purchase: $95; rental: $50. UC. Rental: 16mm, $14.75. UMN.

FOSTER CHILD
Gil Cardinal, Director
At age 35, Gil Cardinal searches for his natural family and an understanding of the circumstances that led to his coming into foster care as an infant. This is a documentary about the process of that discovery and a renewed sense of his Metis culture. 1988. 43 mins, color. 16mm, $650; video, $300. Rental: $70. NFBC.

THE FOUR CORNERS:
A NATIONAL SACRIFICE AREA?
Christopher McLeod, Glenn Switkes & Randy Hayes, Producers/directors
The Four Corners area of Utah, Colorado, New Mexico, and Arizona is rich in the history for Native Americans

and also rich in coal, oil shale, and uranium. This film raises questions about the "hidden costs" of energy development in the Southwest. Features interviews with region's inhabitants and leaders - Navajo uranium miners, tribal officers, governors, ranchers, energy company spokesmen, and federal government officials. 1983. Grades 9 and up. 58 minutes, color. Purchase: 16mm, $850; Video, $450; Rental: $85. BULL.

FOUR CORNERS OF EARTH
Bureau of Florida Folklife & WFSU-TV
Explores the roles and culture of Seminole women whose traditional values keep pace with the forces of today's technology. 1985. 30 minutes, color. Rental: $40/week. NAPBC.

FRANZ BOAS, 1852-1942
T.W. Timreck
A profile of Franz Boas, his work with Northwest American Indian tribes and his teaching of anthropology. 1980. 59 minutes, color. Purchase: Beta or VHS, $250; rental, $90/week. PBS. Purchase: 16mm, $600; rental, $60. Educator's guide. DER. Rental: 16mm, $24. PSU. Video rental, $14.65. IU.

FROM THE ELDERS
Katrina Waters, Producer & Director
A series of films from the Alaska Native Heritage Film Project presenting the stories and thoughts of one of three highly regarded Alaska Native elders. Provides a window of understanding into the Eskimo experience. Joe Sun - Immaluuraq (Joe Sun in English) tells of the legendary Inupiaq prophet, Maniilaq, who was his great uncle. 19 mins, color. Purchase: 16mm, $390, VHS, $200. Rental: 16mm, $35, video, $30. In Iirgu's Time - an elder from the Siberian Yup'ik Eskimo village of Hambell on St. Lawrence Island. Purchase: 16mm, $390, video, $200. Rental: 16mm, $35, video, $30. The Reindeer Thief - Pelaasi, an elder from Gambell speaks Siberian Yup'ik and tells about Chukchi, the Reindeer People. 13 minutes, color. Purchase: 16mm, $260, video, $150. Rental: 16mm, $25, video, $20. 1988. DER.

FROM THE FIRST PEOPLE
Leonard Kamerling and Sarah Elder
Shows change and contemporary life in Shungnak, a village on the Kobuk River in northwestern Alaska. An old man shares his feelings about the changes he has seen. 1976. 45 minutes. Purchase: 16mm, $675; video, $245; Rental, $70; video, $40. DER. Rental: 16mm & video, $22.50. PSU.

FROM HAND TO HAND:
BETHEL NATIVE ARTIST PROFILES
Gretchen McManus, Producer/camera/editor;
Martha Larson, Narrator
Collection of short profiles of Yup'ik Eskimo artists and their work. Features practitioners who discuss the place of their art in traditional Yup'ik culture. Storyknifing, Lucy Beaver, Skin Sewer, Nick Charles, Carver, & Uncle John, Carver. 1985. 45 mins. In Yup'ik or English. VHS. $24.95. KYUK.

FULFILLING THE VISION "OYATE IGLUKININI"
Examines the struggle of the Sioux generation that came of age in the 70's and 80's to redefine the nation's identity. Addresses contemporary socioeconomic issues, spirituality and traditional wisdom. Depicts Lakota spirituality as expressed in the Vision Quest and Sun Dance. 30 minutes. Color. Video. $35. CAN.

FULL CIRCLE
Maria Gargiulo & John de Graaf
Documentary which relates the success story of Native American tribes of Washington state by depicting the diverse lives of tribal elders, business leaders, traditional artists, environmental activists, salmon fisherman, and innovative teachers. 1990. 50 minutes, color. Video. Purchase: $295; rental, $60. UC.

GAME OF STAVES
Clyde B. Smith, Producer
Pomo boys demonstrate the game of staves, a variation of the dice game using six staves and 12 counters, played by most of the Indian tribes of North America. Explains the individualized pyrographic ornamentation of the staves and counters. 1962. 10 minutes, color.

Purchase: 16mm, $220; video, $195. Rental: $45. UC. Rental only: PSU.

GANNAGARO
Alexandra J. Lewis-Lorentz, Producer
The Seneca, one of the five Iroquois nations of New York State, lived at Gannagaro, an ancient Seneca village located just outside of Victor, New York. It was destroyed by the French in July, 1687. This film pieces together life at this 17th century Seneca village. 1986. 30 mins, color. Video. $150; Rental: $40. NAPBC.

GATHERING OF NATIONS
The largest indoor powwow in North America recorded at Albuquerque, NM in 2004. 60 mins. VHS, $27.95. ME.

12th ANNUAL 1995 GATHERING OF NATIONS POW WOW
One of the largest pow wows in America, this video includes excerpts of the Miss Indian World Pageant. CAN.

GATHERING UP AGAIN: FIESTA IN SANTA FE
Jeanette DeBouzek, Director
Examines the Santa Fe Fiesta; documents preparation for the fiesta; shows the formation of ethnic identities, the ongoing impact of the cultures of conquest on Native Americans in the region. 1992. Grades 7-12. Purchase: $275; rental: $75. CG.

GATECLIFF: AMERICAN INDIAN ROCK-SHELTER
Led by Dr. David Hurst Thomas, amateur archaeologists attempt to discover the identity of ancient inhabitants of this shallow rock-shelter in Monitor Valley, Nevada. Teacher's guide. 1974. 24 minutes. Purchase: 16mm, $345; video, $315. NGS.

GERONIMO: AN AMERICAN LEGEND
Geronimo leads a small band of warriors in escape. With Wes Studi, Rodney Grant, Matt Damon, Robert Duvall, Gene Hackman, et al. 1994. 115 mins. VHS. $14.99. ME.

GERONIMO & THE APACHE RESISTANCE
Dscendants of those Apaches who fought so long ago tell their story, explaining the mysteries of Apache power. The story of Geronimo and his people is told, and his battles and broken promises that provoked them are discussed. 1988. 60 mins, color. VHS, $19.99. ME.

GERONIMO: THE FINAL CAMPAIGN
Host Will Rogers, Jr. draws viewers into Geronimo's fascinating history. Grades 9 and up. 30 mins, color. Purchase: VHS, $250; 3/4", $280. CC. Rental: Video, $17.75. IU.

GERONIMO: THE LAST RENEGADE
A&E Home Video
Biography of Geronimo. 1996. 50 mins. VHS, $19.99. ME.

GERONIMO JONES
A young American Indian of Apache & Papago descent, living on a reservation with his mother and grandfather, explores the conflicts he faces, torn between pride in his heritage and his future in modern American society. 1970. 21 mins, color. 16mm & video. Purchase: $250; rental, $75. PHOENIX. Rental: UCT & UMN.

THE GIFT OF THE SACRED DOG
Cecily Truett, Producer; Larry Lancit, Director; LeVar Burton, Series host; Michael Ansara, Narrator
The narrator reads the book Gift of the Sacred Dog, written and illustrated by Paul Goble, as its illustrations are shown, presenting a tale of ancient times told with minor variations by several tribes of the Great Plains, in which a boy brings to his people the first horse, known to some tribes as the "sacred dog." A documentary film sequence presents Dan Old Elk and his family who live at Crow Agency, Montana, and shows them perparing for and participating in the festivities of the annual Crow Indian Fair, including tipi raising and powwow dancing. 1983. 30 mins, color. Video. GPN.

GIFT OF THE WHALES
A Native American boy discovers a naturalist studying

whales off the coast of his small Alaskan village. Grade 1-5. 30 mins. Video. $19.95. VC.

GIFTS OF SANTA FE
Marguerite J. Moritz, Producer
Tells the story of the Santa Fe Indian Market, the largest and most prestigious competition of Native Amerian artists in the world. 1988. 22 mins, color. Video. Purchase: $150; Rental: $40. NAPBC.

GILA - CLIFF DWELLINGS
Explores the story of the cliff dwellers, a people who lived centuries ago. VHS. 15 mins. $17.95. VIP.

GIRL OF THE NAVAJOS
Norman Nelson
A story about two Navajo girls who become friends. 1977. Grades K-6. 15 mins, color. Purchase: video, $59. PHOENIX. Rental: 16mm, $16.50. UMN.

GIVEAWAY AT RING THUNDER
Jan Wahl, Producer/writer;
Christine Lesiak, Writer/narrator/editor
Documents a giveaway held during the annual Ring Thunder powwow on the Rosebud Sioux Reservation in South Dakota. The Menard family is celebrating the giving of Indian names to three children. Opens with archival photographs of Lakota Sioux life and a reflection on traditional customs in earlier times. 1982. 15 minutes, color. Video. NETV.

GLOOSCAP
India legend of how humans and animals were created to live in peace and plenty, and how evil intervened. 26 mins, color. Video, Purchase: $89.95. FH.

GLOOSKAP
Recounts the Canadian Indian legend of the creation, as told by Glooskap, Father of all Indian children. He shows them how to survive and how to live in peace with man and nature. 1971. 12 minutes, color. Grades 4-9. Purchase: 16mm, 260; Video, $160; rental, $37. PHOENIX.

GONE WEST
In Two Parts: Part I - The Lewis and Clark Expedition; Part II - The gold rush begins a mass migration west. Both parts show the affect of white migrations on Indian nations. 1972. 26 minutes each. Rental. UK.

A GOOD DAY TO DIE
Old Army Press, Producer
Computer graphics combine with aerial photographs to show Custer Battlefield; scenes from the Indian village; re-created by re-enactors including Sioux & Cheyenne Indians. 60 minutes, color. Video. Purchase: $25. OAP.

GOOD MEDICINE
Chris Gaul, Writer/Producer
Documentary on Native American medicine, narrated by John Bolindo, Kiowa-Navajo who was at the time of the film the executive director of the National Indian Health Board. Emphasizes the holistic nature of Indian medicine. Settings include the Rosebud and Navajo Reservations. 1979. 59 minutes, color. Video. WQED.

THE GOOD MIND
Robert Stiles, Producer; Steve Charleston, Narrator
Explores the similarities between Christian and Native American beliefs and practices of traditional Native American tribes in the words and life styles of contemporary Indians. 1983. 30 mins. VHS, U-matic. NAPBC.

GRAND CANYON
Dr. Joseph Wood Krutch journeys on mule down the canyon to the Colorado River. The Havasupai Indian settlement at Bright Angel Creek is compared with the outside world. 1966. 26 mins. Rental. UA.

THE GRAND CIRCLE
Richard Ray Whitman & Pierre Lobstein
Two brothers and a friend take a cross-country journey through Indian Territory in Oklahoma and Georgia. 12 mins. Color. Video. 1995. Purchase: $135; rental, $50. TWN.

GRANDFATHER SKY
A look at contemporary Native Americn life, with Charlie Lone Wolf, a young Navajo/Lakota street fighter, fighting to protect his identity on the streets of Denver. Drama explored role of cultural identity and traditional ways. Grades 7 and up. 1993. 50 mins. VHS & Guide. $89. CHAR.

GREAT AMERICAN INDIAN HEROES
The personal stories of leaders and chiefs who won the trust of their people and inspired their tribes in war and peace. Includes Tecumseh, Osceaola, Black Hawk, Pontiac, Chief Joseph, Sitting Bull, Geronimo, and Joseph Brant. Grades 4-6. 1988. Video. Purchase: $176. Also available as filmstrips and cassettes. TA.

THE GREAT MOVIE MASSACRE
Narrated by Wil Sampson
Explores the motion picture image of the Indian warrior. 1982. VHS, Beta, U-matic. VT.

THE GREAT SPIRIT WITHIN THE HOLE
Chris Spotted Eagle, KTCA, Producer/director
A narrative around the words of Indian people in our nation's prisons. The movie demonstrates how freedom of Indian religious practice aids in rehabilitation. Narrated by Will Sampson, with original soundtrack by Buffy Sainte-Marie. 1983. 60 mins. color. Purchase: video, 3/4" - $160; 1/2" - $110. Rental, 3/4" - $60; 1/2" - $40. IN. Rental: 16mm, $16. UMN.

THE GREEN CORN FESTIVAL
Gary Robinson, Producer/director
Mike Bigler, Narrator
Describes and explains the Green Corn Festival ceremonial activities practiced today by the Creek Indians of Oklahoma. Opens with archival footage shot in the 1940's, underscoring the longevity of the ceremonial. 1982. 20 minutes, color. Video. MCN.

JOHNNY GREYEYES
A story of a Native American woman struggling to maintain strength, love, and spirit. Since the shooting death of her father, Johnny has spent most of her life in prison. 2001. 76 mins. VHS, $39.95; DVD, $24.95. ME.

HAA SHAGOON
Joe Kawaky, Producer
Documents a day of Tlingit Indian ceremony held along the Chilkoot River, ancestral home of the Chilkoot Tlingit of Alaska. Ceremony consists of time-honored prayers, songs and dances. 1983. 29 minutes, color. English & Tlingit with English subtitles. Purchase: 16mm, $580; video, $195. Rental, $50. UC.

HAD YOU LIVED THEN: LIFE IN THE WOODLANDS BEFORE THE WHITE MAN CAME
Indians show how there ancestors lived before the white man came and how deer were important in the survival of the Indians.1976. 12 mins. VHS, U-matic. AIMS.

HAIDA CARVER
Richard Gilbert, Director
Shows a young Haida Indian artist on the Pacific coast of Canada shaping miniature totems from argillite, a soft dark slate. 1964. Grades 9 and up. 12 minutes, color. Purchase: 16mm, 225; video, $195. Rental: UA & UCLA.

HAIRCUTS HURT
Randy Redroad
A Native American woman andher son encounter racism in a barbershop. 1992. 10 minutes. color. Purhcase: $300, 16mm, $200, VHS; Rental: $45, 16mm & VHS. TWN.

HANDS OF MARIA
A pictorial study of Maria Martinez, an Indian potter, and of her work which has brought fame to her and to her pueblo. 1968. 17 minutes. Rental. UA.

HAROLD OF ORANGE
Dianne Brennan, Producer
Richard Weise, Director; Gerald Vizenor, Writer
Confronts with ironic humor the issue of the interconnection between reservation communities and the powerful bureaucracies on which they often must rely,

presenting both a group of young Indian "tricksters" and a well-intentioned, though woefully paternalistic, white institution. 1983. 32 minutes, color. 16mm & Video. FIC.

HASKIE
Jack L. Crowder
The story of a young Navajo Indian boy, who wants to become a medicine man but instead attends a boarding school to meet the requirements of compulsory education. 1970. 25 minutes, color. 16mm. Rental, $15.90. IU.

HAT CREEK
Amarcord Productions
Hat Creek, a small community near Lillooet, British Columbia, Canada faces major environmental changes because of strip-mining and a coal-fired generating plant. Shows the affect it has had on the largely Indian population. 1981. 28 minutes, color. Video. CFDW.

HAUDENOSAUNEE: WAY OF THE LONGHOUSE
Robert Stiles & John Akin, Producers/directors;
Oren Lyons, Narrators
Documents the traditional culture of the six nations of the Iroquois Confederacy, the League of Haudenosaunee. Also documents the resiliency of Iroquois culture in the face of pressures to assimilate. 1982. Grades 6-9. 13 minutes, color. Purchase: 16mm, $245, video, $160; rental, 16mm, $35. ICARUS.

HE WO UN POH:
RECOVERY IN NATIVE AMERICA
Beverly Singer
The filmmaker, a member of the Santa Clara Tewa Pueblo, introduces us to the experiences of seven Native Americans on the road to recovery from alcohol abuse. 54 minutes. Color. Video. Purchase: $225; rental, $75. TWN.

HEALING THE HURTS
Phil Lucas, Producer
The people of Alkali Lake, Albert, Canada participate in a ceremonial healing process focused on healing the hurt and shame of residential schools across North America. 60 minutes. Video. Purchase: $150. FOUR.

A HEALING OF NATIONS
Documentary of cultural revival in Native American communities. Focuses on youth empowerment, the value of traditional ceremonies and teachings. 1993. Grades 7 and up. 49 mins. VHS. $155. CHAR.

HE WO UN POH: RECOVERY IN NATIVE AMERICA
A series of vivid portraits of Native Americans in recovery from alcohol abuse. 1994. 55 mins. VHS. $74. CHAR.

HEALTH CARE CRISIS AT ROSEBUD
South Dakota ETV, Producer
Explores and offers some possible solutions to a serious shortage of physicians on the Rosebud Sioux Reservation in South Dakota. 1973. 20 minutes. Color. VHS. Rental: $40/week. NAPBC.

HEART OF THE EARTH SURVIVAL SCHOOL and CIRCLE OF THE WINDS
Chris Spotted Eagle, Producer/director
Presents aspects of contemporary Native American culture for Indians living in the Minneapolis-St. Paul area. Heart of the Earth Survival School (1980) documents an alternative Native American school in Minneapolis; and Circle of the Winds (1979) documents a Native American student art exhibition. 32 minutes, color. Video. IN.

HEART OF THE NORTH
Presents the ideas & traditions of five contemporary artists from the Woodlands & Plains in their own words & images. Issues impoertant to Indian artists are discussed while the five are shown quarrying, carving, painting, and designing. Includes study guide. 24 minutes. VHS. $50. TOP.

THE HEART OF WETONA
Chief's daughter is wronged by white man. 1918. 69 mins, bxw. EG.

HER GIVEAWAY: A SPIRITUAL JOURNEY WITH AIDS
Mona Smith, Producer/director
A candid portrait of Carole Lafavor, member of the Ojibwe tribe, activist, mother, registered nurse & person with AIDS. 1988. 21 minutes, color. Video. Purchase: $195. WMM. Rental: $16. UMN.

HERITAGE
Provides an overview of early Native American life, before Columbus. Introduces us to oral traditions of Indian people and through slides tells of the differences and similarities in Native art, music, and religion, before the time of Columbus. 28 minutes, color. Grades 9 and up. Video, Purchase: $55. UP.

HERITAGE IN CEDAR: NORTHWEST COAST: INDIAN WOODWORKING, PAST & PRESENT
Louis and Ruth Kirk
From Oregon to Alaska, tribesmen lived in houses built of cedar planks and traveled in canoes hollowed from cedar logs. This film explores the Northwest Coast Indian legacy by going to abandoned villages and to living villages, to archaeological digs and to museums. 1979. 29 minutes, color. Purchase: 16mm, $425; or VHS, $215. UW.

HERITAGE OF THE SEA:
MAKAH INDIAN TREATY RIGHTS
Louis and Ruth Kirk
Examines fishing as the Makahs presently practice it, regard it, and view it historically. In two parts: Part I - Makah reminiscenses about the past and comments on the future of their tribal salmon management programs. Part II - Represents comments by Makah fisherman and elders. 29 mins each, color. Purchase: 16mm, $425 each; beta, $225, or VHS, $215 each. UW.

HERMAN RED ELK: A SIOUX INDIAN ARTIST
South Dakota ETV, Producer;
Bill Hopkins, Project Director
Red Elk speaks of his lifelong interest in art and of the influences of his grandfather's teachings. Points out the role of skin painting in Plains Indian history. 1975. 29 minutes, color. Video. Rental: $40/week. NAPBC.

HIDALGO
A Disney film portraying the ghost dance and Wounded Knee Massacre with Viggo Mortensen as Dakota Territory horseman and racer Frank T. Hopkins, who worked for the U.S. Cavalry as a dispatch rider. 2004. DVD & VHS. ME.

HIGH HORSE
Randy Redroad
A provocative narrative on the concept of "home" for Native Americans. Dislocated Native People search for and sometimes find their figurative - and literal - homes. 1995. VHS. 40 minutes. Color. Purchase: $200; rental: $85. TWN.

HISATSINOM - THE ANCIENT ONES
The history of an Anasazi outpost, Kayenta. People & culture are discussed. A portrait of the Anasazi historical sites at the Navajo National Monument. Grades 7 and up. 24 minutes, color. Rental: $10. UCT.

HISTORY OF SOUTHERN CALIFORNIA
In two parts: Part I, From Prehistoric Times to the Founding of Los Angeles - major sequences include, prehistoric life, Indian economy, European explorations, and establishment of pueblos, missions and presidios; Part II, Rise and Fall of the Spanish and Mexican Influences. 1967. Grades 4-9. 17 minutes each. Rental. UA.

HOHOKAM: AT PEACE WITH THE LAND
Bill Land
The archaeologist Emil Haury discusses his excavations at the earliest Hohokam site, Snaketown, which dates from approximately 2,000 years ago, and their descendants, the Pima and Papago, who still live in the region near Phoenix and Arizona. 1976. 20 minutes, color. 16mm. UA.

HOLLOW WATER
National Film Board of Canada

Sexual abuse, violence, healing, and restorative justice in Hollow Water, an isolated Ojibway Cree village in Northern Manitoba. 1999. 44 mins. VHS. $139. CHAR.

HOME OF THE BRAVE
Helena Solberg-Ladd, Producer/director
David Meyer, Writer
This documentary examines the contemporary plight of Indian peoples of North and South America, focusing on the impact of development on native people, the crisis of identity, and the prospects for political organization to protect Indian lives and land. Includes interviews with numerous Indian leaders.1985. 53 minutes, color. Purchase: 16mm, $850; video, $350. Rental, $90. CG.

HONORABLE NATIONS
Chana Gazit & David Steward, Directors/writers
For 99 years the residents of Slamanca, a town in upstate New York, rented the land beneath their homes from the Seneca Nation for $1 a year under the terms of a lease agreement imposed by Congress. This documentary charts the conflicts that arose when the lease's impendent expiration pitted the town's citizenry against the Seneca Nation. 1991. 54 minutes, color. Video. Purchase: $395. FIL. Rental: $20. UMN.

HONORED BY THE MOON
Provides examples of traditional roles & beliefs of Indian women & men. Covers homosexuality & homophobia in the Indian community. 1989. 15 minutes, color. Video. Rental: $16. UMN.

THE HONOUR OF ALL
Phil Lucas, Producer/director
Two part series that recreates the story of the Alkali Lake Indian Band's heroic struggle to overcome and conquer its widespread alcoholism. Narrated by Andy Chelsea, Chief of the Alkali Lake Indian Band of British Columbia, Canada. In 2 parts: Part 1: (56 minutes) examines the problem; Part 2: (43 minutes) outlines the community development process. 1987. Video. Purchase: $150/series; $75/program. NAPBC & GPN.

THE HOPI
Museum of Northern Arizona, Producer
Scenes of family life, work and rituals as seen through the role of corn in Hopi daily life. Shows how communal values and survival skills that have kept their culture alive for centuries are passed on. 15 mins, color. Purchase: $19.95. CAN.

THE HOPI INDIAN
Observes Hopi men and women in daily routines and in special celebrations, such as the secret Hopi wedding ceremony. Revised 1975. 11 minutes, color. Grades K-6. Purchase: 16mm, $270; video, $59. PHOENIX. Rental: 16mm, $16.50. UA, PSU & IU.

HOPI INDIAN ARTS & CRAFTS
1945 & 1975 Editions. Shows traditional skills as the Hopi work at weaving, basket-making, silversmithing and ceramics. Grades K-6. 11 minutes, color. Purchase: 16mm, $250; video, $175. Rental, $40. PHOENIX, IU & UA.

THE HOPI INDIAN & THE NAVAJO INDIANS
Documentary. 1925. 10 minutes, bxw. EG.

HOPI KACHINAS
Shows an artisan in the complete process of carving, assembling and painting a doll; also, Hopi life and dance. 1960. 10 minutes. 16mm. UA.

HOPI SNAKE DANCE
Preparation of dancers, handling of snakes, costumes and part of a dance. 1951. 10 minutes, bxw. 16mm. UW.

HOPI: SONGS OF THE FOURTH WORLD
Pat Ferrero, Producer/director
narrated by Ronnie Gilbert
The study of the Hopi that captures their deep spirituality and reveals their integration of art and daily life. In two parts: Part I - Story of emergence into 4th world; explanation of corn (color and directions) and planting; Hopi courtship and marriage ceremonies; Hopi kachinas. Part II - Hopi religion; interviews with Hopi

painter and potter; women's roles; child-raising and traditional education; games, clowns and Hopi humor. A study guide/resource book. 1983. Grades 4 and up. 16mm, 58 minutes, color. 30 minute version for high school audiences-video only. Purchase: $350. NDF. Rental. UN, UMN & UW.

THE HOPI WAY
Shelly Grossman; Mary Louise Grossman, Writer
The history of the Hopi is briefly discusses by David Mongnongyi who shows pictographs made by Hopi ancestors. Presents a concise picture of Hopi traditionalism and current threats to that way of life. 1972. Grades 4 and up. 23 minutes. 16mm. Purchase. FILMS. Rental, $16.20. UA.

HOPIIT
Victor Masayesva, Jr., Producer/director/camera; Ross Macaya & Victor Masayesva, Sr., Narrators
Provides an impressionistic view of a year in the Hopi community, including ordinary scenes of Hopi life. 1982. 15 minutes, color. Purchase: Video, 3/4" - $120, and 1/2" - $80; Rental: 3/4" - $45, 1/2" - $30. IN & IS. Rental: ATL.

HOPIS—GUARDIANS OF THE LAND
Dennis Burns, Producer
Explores the traditional Hopi way of life and the threat of men's desecration of the land and life they have known. 1971. 10 minutes, color. Purchase: 16mm, $150; VHS, $89. FF. Rental: $13. FF & UMN.

HOW BEAVER STOLE FIRE
Caroline Leaf
A retelling, through animation, of a Northwest American Indian legend of how the Animal People all worked together to capture fire from the Sky People. 1972. Grades K-4. 12 minutes, color. 16mm. Purchase: AIMS. Rental: UCT, BYU & UI.

HOW MAN ADAPTS TO HIS PHYSICAL ENVIRONMENT
The film uses as examples the Pueblo Indians, Navahos, and the early Caucasians. 1970. 20 minutes. Rental. UA & IU.

HOW PANTHER GOT TEAR MARKS
Presentation of a traditional Karuk story is told in both English & the Karuk language. Grades 4-6. 11 minutes. VHS. $59.95. CB.

HOW TO BEAD: NATIVE AMERICAN STYLE
Full Circle Communications
Learn how to create your own designs; includes instructions on how to make a loom. VHS. Vol. 1 - Loom; Vol. 2 - Lazystitch; Vol. 3 - Peyote Stitch; Vol. 4 - Medallions; Vol. 5 - Needle Applique. 30 minutes each. VHS. $19.95 each. CAN, VIP & WH.

HOW TO BUILD AN IGLOO
Douglas Wilkinson, Director
Two Inuit Eskimos give a step-by-step demonstration of Igloo construction. 1950. Grades K-8. 11 minutes, bxw. Purchase: 16mm, $275; VHS, $200. Rental: $40. NFBC.

HOW TO DANCE: NATIVE AMERICAN STYLE: BEGINNING STEPS
Full Circle Communications
Learn the parts of a war dance song and master the basic steps by dance instructors Mike Pasetopah & Nancy Fields; learn how to dance "on the song." Suitable for ages 5 and up. VHS. 30 minutes. $19.95. CAN, VIP & WH.

HOW TO MAKE MOCCASINS: VOL. 1 - HARD SOLE
Full Circle Communications
Simple teaching methods show how to make a pattern, how to adapt for men & women; any size and how to adapt to high top moccasins. Moccasin maker Annabelle Medicinechips (Cheyenne/Caddo) demonstrates. VHS. 30 minutes. $19.95. WH.

HOW TO MAKE A NATIVE AMERICAN DANCE SHAWL
Full Circle Communications
Step-by-step from selecting materials, cutting cloth and tying fringe. Ribbonwork techniques are also demonstrated. VHS. 30 minutes. $19.95. WH.

HOW TO TRACE YOUR NATIVE AMERICAN HERITAGE
Rich Heape
How to obtain a CDIB card, tribal memebership, internet sites and a list of over 500 federally recognized tribes. VHS & DVD. 35 mins. $24.95. ME, WH & RICH.

HOW THE WEST WAS WON...& HONOR LOST
Ross Devenish, Producer
A re-enactment, using photographs, paintings and newspaper accounts, telling the story of the white man's treatment of American Indians in the westward push for land. Broken treaties, railroad building, decimation of the buffalo, and the massacre at Wounded Knee. 1970. 25 minutes, color. 16mm. PSU & IU.

HOW THE WEST WAS LOST
Discovery Channel
Comprehensive video history and eyewitness account free of popular myth and Hollywood stereotypes. Traces four centuries of American history. In siix videos: Navajo: A Clash of Cultures; Cheyenne: The Only Good Indian Is a Dead Indian; Seminoles: The Unconquered; Nez Perce: "I Will Fight No More Forever"; Apache: Always the Enemy; Iroquois: "Divided We Fall." 2000. $19.95 each. T-L.

HOW THE WEST WAS LOST
Document Associates and BBC, Co-Producers
Highlights the prime of Plains Indian civilization and focuses upon the temporary Indian effort to maintain a sense of their own identity. 1972. 26 minutes, color. Purchase: 16mm, $400; video, $295. Rental, $55 each. CG.

HOW THE WEST WAS LOST
Documentary of the epic struggle for the American West; witnesses the tragic plight of five Native American Nations: the Navajo, Nez Perce, Apache, Cheyenne & Lakota. In three volumes: Vol. 1 - Navajo & Nez Perce; Vol. 2 - Apache & Cheyenne; & Vol. 3 - Lakota & Northern Cheyenne. 100 minutes each, color. Video. Rental: $10 each; $25/set. HO.

HUNGER IN AMERICA
CBS, Producer
A researched study of hunger and malnutrition in the U.S., showing views of Navajo Indians in Arizona, as well as other impoverished groups. 1968. Grades 7 and up. 58 minutes, color. 16mm. Rental, $31. UT.

RICHARD HUNT CARVES A BEAR MASK
A Kwakiutl artist from British Columbia, carves a bear mask. Documents in detail the entire production process. 1988. 25 minutes, b&w. Video. Purchase: $70; rental, $20. UADA.

HUICHOL INDIAN CEREMONIAL CYCLE: RESCUING IMAGES AT THE EDGE OF OBLIVION
A documentary based on the 1934 film by anthropologist, Robert Zingg. Interprets several aboriginal Huichol rituals. 1997. 44 minutes, b&w. 120 page booklet. PSU.

HUICHOL SACRED PILGRIMAGE TO WIRIKUTA
Larain, Boyll
Documentary following the anual pilgrimage and peyote hunt of the Huichol Indians of western Mexico. Focuses on the sacred sites, the traditional Huichol shamans and elders. Includes songs and music. 1991. 29 mins, color. Video. $195; rental, $50. UC.

HUNTERS & BOMBERS: THE INNU FIGHT BACK
The Innu, indigenous inhabitants of Labrador-Quebec in northeast Canada, are fighting back against the Dutch, German, and British air forces which use the region for supersonic low-level bomber training. 52 minutes, color. Video. Purchase: $149; rental: $75. FH.

HUPA INDIAN WHITE DEERSKIN DANCE
Portrays the 10-day deerskin ceremony still held by the Hupa Indians of northwestern California. 1958. Grades 4 and up. 11 mins, color. 16mm. Rental: UCLA.

HUTEETL: KOYUKON MEMORIAL POTLATCH
Curt Madison, Producer/director/editor; Catherine Attla & Eliza Jones, Narrators
A documentary of an Athapascan Indian potlatch in

interior Alaska. 1983. 60 minutes. Color. In English and Koyukon Athabascan with English subtitles. Video. Purchase: $150; Rental: $80. KYUK and NAPBC.

I AM DIFFERENT FROM MY BROTHER: DAKOTA NAME-GIVING
Tony Charles, Director
A real-life docu-drama depicting the Name-Giving Ceremony of three young Flandreau Dakota Sioux Indian children. 1981. Grades 3-9. 20 minutes, color. Video. Purchase: $150; Rental: $40/week. NAPBC.

I HEARD THE OWL CALL MY NAME
Roger Gimbel, Director
A story about how an Anglican priest, who with a short time to live learns acceptance of death from the Indians. 1974. Grades 7 and up. 78 minutes, color. 16mm. Rental: Video, $20; 16mm, $50.50. UA & UMN.

I KNOW WHO I AM
Sandra Sunrising Osawa, Producer
Focuses on cultural values important to Indian tribes of the Pacific coast and was shot on the Makah, Puyallup and Nisqually reservations. 1979. 28 minutes, color. Video. UP.

I WILL FIGHT NO MORE FOREVER
Richard T. Efron, Director; Stan Margulies, Producer
A dramatization of the struggle of the Nez Perce Indians and their leader Chief Joseph, who attempted to take his people to Canada to avoid being placed on a reservation. 1975. 106 minutes, color. 16mm. FILMS & UA. Video, $29.95. CH. VHS. $19.99. ME.

I'D RATHER BE POWWOWING
George P. Horse Capture, Producer
Larry Littlebird, Director
Presents an unstereotyped portrait of a contemporary Indian, Al Chandler (a Gros Ventre from the Fort Berthold Indian Reservation in North Dakota) a senior technical representative for a large corporation and explores the values that are central to his identity. Chandler and his son travel to a powwow celebration at the Rocky Boys Reservation near Havre, Montana. 1983. 27 minutes, color. 16mm & video. Purchase: $50. BB.

ICE PEOPLE
An anthropological study showing that the modern Eskimo must adapt again. 1970. Grades 6 and up. 23 minutes, color. 16mm. Rental. IU & UA.

IHANBLA WAKTOGLAG WACIPI
Henry Smith
A dance showcasing Solaris, a modern dance theatre company, and Sioux Indian dancers drawn from the nine reservations of the Lakota Nation in South Dakota. 1981. 60 minutes, color. Video. SO.

I'ISAW: HOPI COYOTE STORIES
Larry Evers, University of Arizona
With Helen Sekaquaptewa. In Hopi with English subtitles. 1978. 18 minutes. VHS. Purchase: $150. NR. Rental (with Nawatniwa: A Hopi Philosophical Statement) - two programs on one tape, $52.50. ATL.

I'M NOT AFRAID OF ME
A true story of a young American Indian mother and daughter and AIDS. 28 minutes. Video. Purchase: $245; rental, $45. SH.

THE IMAGE MAKER & THE INDIANS
George I. Quimby, Bill Holm and David Gerth
Shows how the famous pioneer cinematographer, Edward S. Curtis, made the first full-length documentary film of Native Americans among the Northwest Coast Indians of 1914. Edited and restored in 1973. 17 minutes; color/bxw. Purchase: 16mm, $275; and VHS, $165. UW.

IMAGES OF INDIANS
Robert Hagopian & Phil Lucas, Producers/Directors/Writers
A five-part series, narrated by Will Sampson, examines the stereotypes drawn by the movies and questions what the effect of the Hollywood image has been on the Indian's own self-image. (1) "The Great Movie Massacre - Indian's warrior image." (2) "Heathen Injuns and the Hollywood Gospel" - The distortion and mis-representation of Indian religion and values in Hollywood movies. (3) "How Hollywood Wins the West" - Deals with the one-sided presentation of Indian history despite the frequent use of Indian culture in Hollywood films. (4) "The Movie Reel Indians" - The image of Indians as savage murderers is commented on by Dennis Banks & Vine Deloria. (5) "Warpaint and Wigs" - Examines how the movie, Nobel Savage and the Savage-Savage, has affected the Native American self-image. 1980. Curriculum package contains a curriculum guide, student resource pages, video, and other learning resources (map, books, posters). Grades 7 and up. Video, 30 minutes each. Video. Purchase: $56.95 each, $237.50 for series. OY, FOUR, GPN & NAPBC.

IMAGINING INDIANS
Victor Masayesva, Jr.
Visits tribal communities in Arizona, Montana, New Mexico, South Dakota, Washington, and the Amazon. 1992. 60 minutes, color. Video. Purchase: $245; rental: $60. DER.

IN THE BEST INTEREST OF THE CHILD
Will Sampson, Narrator
Documents the legal issues involved in Indian child welfare cases. Trys to educate the public to the Indian Child Welfare Act. 1981. Grades 9 and up. 15 minutes, color. Video. Purchase: $245; rental: $45. SH. Rental, $21. PSU.

IN THE HEART OF BIG MOUNTAIN
Captures an intimate portrait of the traumatic consequences of relocation on one Navajo family. Through Katherine Smith's eyes and words, as a Navajo matriarch, the viewer experiences life on one of the most remote and traditional places in Indian country - Big Mountain, Arizona. Grades 5 and up. 1988. 28 minutes, color. Video. Purchase: $30. OY.

IN THE LAND OF THE WAR CANOES: KWAKIUTL INDIAN LIFE ON THE NORTHWEST COAST
Edward S. Curtis; Edited and Restored by George Quimby and Bill Holm
A saga of Kwakiutl Indian life filmed in 1914 in Vancouver Island, British Columbia, Canada. 43 minutes, bxw. Purchase: 16mm, $650; Beta, $425, VHS, $400. UW. Rental: 16mm, $26. UA & PSU.

IN OUR OWN BACKYARDS: URANIUM MINING IN THE U.S.
Pamela Jones & Susanna Styron
Explores the impact of uranium mining on the environment in the Southwest, and on the health of workers and nearby residents. 1981. Grades 7 and up. 29 minutes, color. Purchase: 16mm, $515; Video, $100; Rental: $50. BULL.

IN SEARCH OF THE LOST WORLD
Traces the origins of the lost civilizations of the Americas; tells the story of Indian cultures: complex, urbane & ancient. 1972. 52 minutes, color. 16mm. Rental. UA & UCLA.

IN THE WHITE MAN'S IMAGE
Covers the policies, methods, and tragic long-term consepquences of attempts to "civilize" Native Americans in the 1870s. 1992. 60 minutes, color. Video. Purchase: $59.95. NAPBC. Rental: $10. HO; $16. UMN.

INCIDENT AT OGLALA: THE LEONARD PELTIER STORY
Michael Apted, Director; Robert Redford, Producer
Documentary. 1992. DVD, 24.99; VHS, $29.99. ME.

INDIAN AMERICA
The story of the American Indian and his desperate struggle against extinction. Indian activists, tribal leaders, and poor sheep herders tell about themselves and their heritage. 1970. Grades 4-adult. 80 minutes, color. VHS. Rental. UA & UMN.

INDIAN ARTIFACTS OF THE SOUTHWEST
Examines the arts and crafts of several Southwestern tribes, including: Zuni, Hopi and Navajo. Stresses the history and tradition which are apparent in the objects. 1972. 15 minutes. 16mm. Rental. IU.

INDIAN ARTISTS OF THE SOUTHWEST
Deals with the history of American Indian paintings and its rich heritage from petroglyphs to the modern artists. Shows techniques, symbolism and style. 1972. 15 minutes, color. Grades 4 and up. 16mm. Rental; $23. IU, PSU & UA.

INDIAN ARTS AT THE PHOENIX HEARD MUSEUM
KAET-TV Phoenix, Producer
Dick Peterson, Director
Explores six major areas of Native American Art: 1: Basketry - Naomi White, guest; 2: Painting - Larry Golsh and Pop Chalee, guests; 3: Pottery - Mabel Sunn, guest; 4: Textiles - Martha Began and Lillian Dineyazhe; 5: Jewelry - John E. Salaby; and 6: Katchinas. 1975. 30 minutes each, color. Video. Purchase: $150 each. Rental, $40 each/week. NAPBC.

INDIAN BOY IN TODAY'S WORLD
Presents a picture of life on the Makah Reservation and shows how the way of life on the Reservation is changing as a result of interaction with the outside world—the conflict of Indian and non-Indian cultures. 1971. Grades 4 and up. 14 minutes, color. Rental. UA & IU.

INDIAN BOY OF THE SOUTHWEST
Toboya, a Hopi Indian boy, tells of his life and his home on a high mesa in the Southwestern desert of the U.S. 1983 revised edition. Grades 4-9. 19 minutes, color. Purchase: 16mm, $400; Video, $260; Rental: $58. PHOENIX. Rental only: UA.

THE INDIAN BROTHERS
A sympathetic portrait of the American Indian. 1911. Directed by D.W. Griffith. 12 minutes, bxw. EG.

INDIAN CANOES ALONG THE WASHINGTON COAST
Louis and Ruth Kirk
This film demonstrates how and with what tools a canoe is carved; also, river and salt water races are shown. 1971. 18 minutes. Purchase: 16mm, $250; beta, $175; and VHS, $165. UW.

INDIAN CONVERSATION
Portrays two Indians, one raised in an urban environment, the other on a reservation. Both are college graduates and explore their identities as Indians. 1974. 13 minutes. 16mm. Rental. UK.

INDIAN COUNTRY?
Document Associates and BBC
Indian journalist, Richard LaCourse, discusses the revolution of attitudes within the younger American Indians creating a new mood of militancy. Also, interviews with Indian educators discussing the efforts to preserve the integrity of the Native American culture. 1972. 26 minutes, color. Purchase: 16mm, $400; Video, $295; Rental, $55 each. CG.

INDIAN CRAFTS: HOPI, NAVAJO, AND IROQUOIS
Nancy Creedman, Producer
Illustrates the wide range of arts practiced by the Indians: basketweaving, pottery-making, kachina carving, weaving, jewelry-making, and mask carving by the Hopi, Navajo and Iroquois. 1980. 11 minutes, color. Grades 4-9. Purchase: 16mm, $255; video, $150. Rental, $35. PHOENIX.

INDIAN DIALOGUE
David Hughes, Director
Indians of Canada discuss many problems that cause them concern. 1967. 28 minutes, bxw. Video. $27. NFBC.

INDIAN FAMILY OF LONG AGO: BUFFALO HUNTERS OF THE PLAINS
Tells the story of the Sioux Indian buffalo hunters who roamed the great western plains of the U.S. more than 200 years ago. 1957. Grades 4-9. 15 minutes, color. 16mm. Rental: UA, UCT & UMN.

INDIAN FAMILY OF THE CALIFORNIA DESERT
A woman from the Cahuilla Indian Tribe from the desert of Palm Springs recalls her primitive life and illustrates her tribe's culture. 1967. 16 minutes. Grades 4-9. 16mm. UA.

INDIAN FOR A CHANGE
Uses portraits of five Indian men and women to show the life of the American Indian as it really is, as opposed to the romanticized stereotype commonly accepted. 1970. 28 minutes, color. 16mm & video. Purchase: 16mm, $295; video, $110. NAC. Rental: Video, $10. UCT.

INDIAN HIDE TANNING
Illustrates the methods used by the Eastern Cree Indians of Mistassini, Quebec in the tanning of moose and caribou hides. VHS. 38 minutes. $99. TR.

INDIAN HOUSE: THE FIRST AMERICAN HOME
Remnants of the dwellings of Indians in the Southwest represent the oldest homes in America. 1950. 11 minutes/bxw. 16mm. Rental. UA.

INDIAN HUNTER-GATHERERS
OF THE DESERT: KILIWA
R.C. Michelsen, J. Albrecht & V.W. Kjonegaard
Focuses on subsistence activities of Baja California Indians. 1975. 14 minutes, color. 16mm. Rental, $15. PSU.

INDIAN INFLUENCES IN THE U.S.
David A. Baerreis, Ph.D.
Presents many aspects of Indian heritage in the mainstream of American society today, in music, art and the foods we eat. 1964. Grades 4-9. 11 minutes, color. 16mm. Rental. IU, UA & UK.

INDIAN LAND: THE NATIVE
AMERICAN ECOLOGIST
Herbert McCoy, Jr., Director/Producer
American Indians discuss their traditional veneration for the Earth. 21 minutes; color/bxw. FILMS.

INDIAN LEGENDS: GLOOSCAP
Records a segment of the creation myth of the North American Micmac Indians. 1985. 26 minutes, color. Video. Rental, $29. PSU.

INDIAN LEGENDS OF CANADA
Daniel Bertolino, Director
This series of 15 films (13 parts) provides an authentic backdrop against which to study the first native peoples of Canada. The Winter Wife (Ojibwa); The Windigo (Montagnais); The Invisible Man, Megmuwesug and Magic Box (MicMac); The Path of Souls (3 films, Ojibwa); Moowis, Where Area You Moowis (Algonguian), and The Return of the Child (Carrier); Mandamin, Or the Legend of Corn (Ojibwa); Pitchie the Robin and The Path Without End (Ojibwa); The Spirit of the Dead Chief (Chippewa); Glooscap (Abnaki).1981-1983. 26 minutes each. Color. Available in Native languages with English or French narration. Purchase: 16mm, $675 each; and VHS, $450 each. Rental: $65 each; series, $8,450. ITFE, FH & THA.

INDIAN MAINSTREAM
Thomas Parsons
Emphasizes rediscovery of language and rituals which have been suppressed over the last three generations, and the need to pass on the Indian heritage to the young before it is forgotten. Sponsored by the Dept. of Labor to regenerate the Indian culture of the tribes in northern California, specifically the Hupa, Karok, Tocowa, and Yurok tribes. 1971. Grades 9 and up. 25 minutes, color. Video. Purchase: $245; rental, $45. SH. Rental, $18. SH, PSU.

INDIAN PAINT
Norman Foster, Director
The heroic efforts of a 15-year-old Indian boy, son of a tribal chief, to raise a "painted" colt. The portrayal of Indian life in the far West before the coming of the white man. 1965. 91 minutes, color. 16mm. Rental: UCT.

INDIAN POTTERY OF SAN ILDEFONSO
Rick Krepela
Documentary of renowned Pueblo artist Maria Martinez making hand fired black pottery using techniques redeveloped after they had fallen from use. Maria, in her mid-eighties at the time, works closely with her son Popovi Da at San Ildefonso Pueblo, New Mexico. 1972. 27 minutes, color. 16mm & video. Purchase: 16mm, $285; video, $110. NAC. Rental: UCT.

INDIAN RELOCATION: ELLIOT LAKE: A REPORT
Probes the Canadian government's experiment to move 20 Indian families from their rugged northern Ontario reserves to a new town. Questions the wisdom of the program. 1967. 30 minutes, bxw. 16mm. Rental: $28. UCLA.

INDIAN RIGHTS, INDIAN LAW
Joseph and Sandra Consentino, Directors
Film documentary focusing on the Native American Rights Fund, its staff and certain casework. 1978. 60 minutes. Grades 10-adult. 16mm. Rental, $24. IRA, FILMS, PSU.

INDIAN SELF-RULE: A PROBLEM OF HISTORY
Selma Thomas, Producer
Michael Cotsones, Director
Traces the history of white-Indian relations from 19th century treaties through the present, as tribal leaders, historians, teachers, and other Indians gather at a 1983 conference organized to reevaluate the significance of the Indian Reorganization Act of 1934. The experience of the Flathead Nation of Montana, the Navajo Nation of the Southwest, and the Quinault people of the Olympic Peninsula, Washington, illustrates some of the ways Indians have dealt with shifting demands upon them. 1985. 58 minutes, color. Video. Purchase: $400; rental, $60. DER.

INDIAN SPEAKS
Reveals some of the general cultural deprivation of Indians in Canada & depicts aspects of life on a reserve. Describes the gradual disappearance of the Indian culture & the plight of individual Indians who wish to preserve it. 1967. Grades 7 and up. 41 minutes, color. 16mm. Rental: $15.55. UMN.

INDIAN STEREOTYPES IN PICTURE BOOKS
This video & accompanying script is about stereotypic images as a process over time; and learning to recognize these images. 25 minutes, color. Video. Rental: $10. HO.

INDIAN SUMMER
A summer experience of Chippewa Indian children on a woodland reservation, their relationship to animals & to the environment. 1975. Grades K-4. 11 minutes, color. Rental: $8. UCT.

INDIAN TIME
Native Multi-media Productions, Inc.
Presents Shingoose, Buffy Sainte-Marie, Charlie Hill, Laura Vinson, Tom Jackson, Bill Brittain and special guest, Max Gail in a variety special of America's finest Native American entertainers. 1988. 48 minutes, color. Purchase: $150; Rental: $80. NAPBC.

INDIAN TO INDIAN
Shows Indians who are part of the work force explaining their lives and work. Describes how, though part of the work force, they retain their tribal heritages. 1970. 26 minutes, color. 16mm & Video. Purchase: 16mm, $275; video, $110. NAC.

INDIAN TREATY RIGHTS BY THE
RIGHT REV. WILLIAM WANTLAND
Rev. Wantland (Seminole), an attorney & Episcopol Bishop, gives a 30 minute summary on "What is Soveignty." Video. Purchase: $20; rental: $10. HO.

INDIAN TRIBAL GOVERNMENT
Filmed at the Gila River Indian Reservation, this film shows how effective tribal governments operate and what tribal members should expect from their governments. 1980. 16 minutes, color. 16mm. IDIL.

THE INDIANS
The story of the conflict between the Indian and the white man in the Colorado Territory during the time when white traders, trappers and settlers moved into the Great Plains. 1969. 31 minutes. Grades 4-12. Purchase: VHS, $99. GA. Rental. UA.

INDIANS IN THE AMERICAS
Surveys (using panoramas, still photos, and paintings) the development of the American Indian civilizations from the first nomadic hunter to the European explorers. Revised 1985 edition. 22 minutes, color. Grades 4-12. Purchase: 16mm, $475; video, $285. Rental:

16mm, $55. PHOENIX. Rental: 16mm, $25; video, $23.50. IU & PSU.

INDIANS, THE NAVAJOS
A contemporary motion picture report that examines the winds of change that have been sweeping across the lives of 140,000 Navajos on the largest Indian reservation in the world. 1975. 14 minutes, color. 16mm. Rental: $9. UCT.

INDIANS OF CALIFORNIA
Tells the story of a primitive people as they lived before the white man came to the Pacific Coast. In two parts: Part 1, Village Life - includes trading, house building, basket-making, use of a tule boat, the sweat house, songs and dances. 15 minutes. Part 2, Food - includes bow and arrow making, a deer hunt, gathering and preparing acorns, a family meal, and the story teller. 14 minutes. 1955. Also, a LP record, California Indian Songs, $5. UA.

INDIANS OF EARLY AMERICA
Classifies all of the Indians of early America according to four general geographic regions, and represents each region by one dominant and characteristic tribe. 1957. Grades 4 and up. 22 minutes, bxw. In English & Spanish. 16mm. Rental: $13. IU, UA, PSU & UMN.

INDIANS OF THE EASTERN WOODLANDS:
THE LEGACY OF THE AMERICAN INDIANS
Camera One, Producer; hosted by Wes Studi
Examines the Effigy Mounds, ancient structures & the Woodland Indians; examines the legends & cultures of the various tribes. Ancient America Series. 1994. Video. 60 minutes, color. $20. CAN, CMM, VIP & WKV.

INDIAN OF NORTH AMERICA
John K. White, Consultant; produced by SVE
A series of three, 20 minute VHS cassettes exploring the diverse cultures of Native Americans. Grades 4-6. Volume 1: Indians of the Northeast/Southest; Volume 2: Indians of the Plains/Northwest Coast; Volume 3: Indians of the Southwest/Far North. $SVE, $89 each.

INDIANS OF NORTH AMERICA
Schlessinger Video Productions
Twenty, 30-minute programs portray the history & culture of particular Indian communities, with insights and commentary from historians & contemporary tribal members attacking myths & stereotypes that remain even today. Includes photographic images, sketchings, portraits, and maps. *Programs*: The Apache; The Aztec; The Cherokee (Southeast); The Cheyenne; The Comanche; The Iroquois; The Maya; The Navajo; The Seminole; The Yankton Sioux; The Chinook; The Creek; The Crow, The Huron; The Lenape; The Menominee; The Narragansett; The Potawatomi; The Pueblo; and A History of Native Americans. 1993-94. Grades 4 to adult. Closed captioned for the hearing impaired. Purchase: $39 each; $699 per set. CHAR.

INDIANS OF THE NORTHWEST:
THE LEGACY OF THE AMERICAN INDIANS
Camera One, Producer; hosted by Wes Studi
The origin of the totem pole; examines the legends & cultures of the various tribes. Ancient America Series. 1994. 60 minutes. $20. CAN & WKV.

INDIANS OF THE PLAINS: LIFE IN THE PAST
This film describes how the Plains Indians depended on the buffalo for almost all the necessities of life. Also, quillwork, beadwork and painting are presented. 11 minutes. 16mm. Rental. UT & PSU.

INDIANS OF THE PLAINS:
SUN DANCE CEREMONY
Pictures erection of the tepee or tent for lodging. Features the Sweat Lodge, Sun Dance Ceremony and Grass Dance. 1954. Grades 4 and up. 11 minutes, color. 16mm. Rental: $15. UMN, UT & PSU.

INDIANS OF THE SOUTHWEST:
THE LEGACY OF THE AMERICAN INDIANS
Camera One, Producer; hosted by Wes Studi
From Anasazi to Hohokam to Navajo & Pueblo; examines the legends & cultures of the various tribes. Ancient America Series. 1994. VHS. 60 minutes, color. $20. CAN, VIP & WKV.

INDIANS OF THE SOUTHWEST

Focuses on the history and culture of the Indians of the Southwest; their descendants, the Pueblos, and other tribes that settled in the Southwest, including the Navajos, Hopi and Zuni. 16 minutes. Grades 4-9. 16mm. FILMS.

INDIANS OF THE UPPER MISSISSIPPI SERIES

This three part program documents the success of two tribes of Native Americans, the Winnebago & Menominee. Interviews reveal how these tribes won their struggle to stay on their ancestral lands & retain their culture & heritage. 86 minutes. VHS, $275. Parts: History, 28 minutes, $99.95; Culture, 29 minutes, $99.9; Politics, 29 minutes, $99.95. CC.

INDIANS, OUTLAWS & ANGIE DEBO

95-year-old Angie Debo, an early 20th century scholar and pioneer, recalls her life as the daughter of 19th century Oklahoma homesteaders. Deb unearthed troubling documents regarding a criminal conspiracy by major political figures to rob the Five Civilized Indian Tribes of Oklahoma of their mineral-rich lands. 1988. 60 minutes, color. Video. Purchase: $59.95. PBS. Rental: $10. HO; $16. UMN.

THE INDIANS WERE THERE FIRST

Shows the path of the ancestors of the first North American Indians across the landbridge from Asia; the various tribes and some of their characteristics; and in particular, the distribution of Iroquois at the end of the 16th-century and the nature of their social and political organization. 13 minutes, color. Video. Purchase, $69.95. FH.

INSTITUTE FOR THE DEVELOPMENT OF INDIAN LAW

A series of five seven minute films providing a review of vital areas of federal Indian law and their effect on tribal government. They include: A Question of Indian Sovereignty, Indian Treaties, Indians and the U.S. Government, Indian Jurisdiction, & The Federal-Indian Trust Relationship. Purchase: 16mm, $550/set. IDIL.

INTO THE CIRCLE: AN INTRODUCTION TO NATIVE AMERICAN POWWOWS

Full Circle Communications
Witness the powwow, dance styles; interviews with tribal elders, dancers, singers, plus historic photos of early powwow. VHS. 60 minutes. $19.95. VIP & WH.

INUIT

Bo Boudart, Director
Documents the first Inuit Circumpolar Conference of 1977. Provides an overview of the issues that concern Native peoples in the Arctic. 1978. 28 minutes, color. 16mm. BO.

INUIT KIDS

Paulle Clark, Producer/Director
Helps children get the feel of Arctic life by sharing moments in the lives of two 13-year-old Inuit boys who are friends. 1986. 15 minutes, color. Grades 2-8. Purchase: 16mm, $315; Video, $245; Rental: $30. BULL.

INUPIAT ESKIMO HEALING

Nellie Moore, Producer;
Daniel Housberg, Director/camera/editor
Looks at the practice of medicine in northern Alaska today by following several traditional doctors and their patients in three Inupiat villages. 1985. 30 minutes, color. In English and Inupiaq with English subtitles. Video. NATC.

THE IRON LODGE

Documentary about Native American men behind bars. 2003. VHS, $24.95. ME.

IROQUOIS SOCIAL DANCE I & II

Nick Manning
Presents, in 2 parts, social dances of the Mohawk Indians, filmed on the Reserve at St. Regis, Canada. Part I, 15 minutes; Part II, 11 minutes. Teacher's guide. Video. Purchase: $49 (both). SH, RM.

IS THERE AN AMERICAN STONEHENGE?

Mayer, Producer
Relates Dr. John Eddy's efforts to prove his theory of a Wyoming solar observatory built and used by an-

cient American Indians. Grades 4-adult. 1982. 30 mins, color. Rental. IU & UT.

ISHI IN TWO WORLDS

Richard Tomkins, Producer
The story of the Yahi Indians of California. Ishi, the last of the Yahi, was the last person in North America known to have lived a totally aboriginal existence. 1967. Grades 9 and up. 19 mins, color. Rental: UCLA, UT, PSU & UA.

ISHI, THE LAST YAHI

Linda Hunt, Narrator
The story of Ishi, the last wild Indian in North America. For more than 40 years, Ishi had lived in hiding with a tiny band of survivors in northern California. He suddenly appeared in 1911, & was the last Yahi Indian alive. Yahi stories. Using Alfred Kroeber's notes & recordings taken at the time, the film provides a unique look at indigenous life in America before the arrival of Europeans. 1994. VHS. 57 mins. $19.95. VIP & ME.

IT COULD HAVE BEEN PREVENTED

Substance abuse/boating...a deadly combination. Filmed primarily in Kotzebue, Alaska on the Noatak River with Native people. 17 mins. Purchase: $100; rental, $25. SH.

ITAM HAKIM, HOPIIT

Victor Masayesva, Jr., Producer/director/camera
Ross Macaya, one of the last members of the Hopi tribal storytelling clan, recounts his life story and various epochs in Hopi history. 1984. 60 mins. Color. In Hopi or English. Purchase: Video 3/4" - $200, and 1/2" -$140. Rental: 3/4" - $75, 1/2" - $50. ISP (sales); IN (sales & rentals).

IT'S NOT JUST A TIME FOR FUN

Looks at the annual Choctaw Fair held every June on the Choctaw Reservation. Introduces all the activities of the Fair. All grades. 15 minutes. Purchase: VHS, $85; rental, $10 (two weeks). CHP.

IYAHKIMIX, BLACKFEET BEAVER BUNDLE CEREMONY

Sacred bundles are collections of artifacts and sacred natural objects belonging to clan ancestors and passed on to their descendants. The ritual consists of dancing with the chanting to the bundle's individual parts. Presents the religion's ritual in its entirety. 58 mins. 16mm. UAB.

JAUNE QUICK-TO-SEE SMITH

Jack Peterson, Producer; Anthony Schmitz, Dir.
Joy Harjo, Writer; N. Scott Momaday, Narrator
An imaginative introduction to the work and thought of an outstanding contemporary Native American painter. It conveys Jaune's personal vision & its relation to her painting. 1983. 29 mins, color. 16mm & video. NAPBC.

JOE KILLS RIGHT—OGLALA SIOUX

Jon Alpert (DTC-TV)
Portrait of a young Sioux man living in New York City. Scenes of Joe living in one of New York City's worst neighborhoods. He loses his job, begins drinking and using drugs, then enters a treatment center. After, he returns to the reservation. Includes dialogue of educational and health services on the reservation. 1980. 25 minutes. beta and VHS. DTC.

JOHN CAT

Based on the story by W.P. Kinsella. An encounter with an older Indian leads two younger ones to a painful awareness of racial prejudice. 26 minutes, color. Video. Purchase: $149. BE.

JOHN KIM BELL

Anthony Azzopardi, Producer
Tells the story of a talented and passionate young man who has broken through social barriers and stepped into the limelight. Bell is the first Native American pursuing a career as a symphonic conductor. Film tracks Bell's early interest and development in music. 1983. 36 1/2 minutes. Color. Video. Purchase: $150; Rental: $40. NAPBC.

JOHNNY FROM FORT APACHE

Records the readjustments in lifestyle the Russells, an Indian family, experience when they move from the

reservation to San Francisco. 1971. 15 minutes. Grades 4-adult. 16mm. Rental. UA and IU.

JOSHUA'S SOAPSTONE CARVING

Joshua Qumaluk, an Eskimo, helps his Uncle Levi hunt, fish and trap. He learns to carve soapstone sculptures to sell. 23 minutes. Grades 4 and up. Purchase: 16mm, $495; video, $290. Rental: $60. PHOENIX.

JOURNEY HOME

Gryphon productions
Looks at the lives of three Native Americans living with AIDS/HIV and examines ways in which they are finding help and support. 1994. 39 mins. VHS. $145. CHAR.

JOURNEY TO THE SKY: A HISTORY OF THE ALABAMA COUSHATTA INDIANS

Robert Cozens, & KUHT-TV, Executive Producers
Paul Yeager, Director/writer/camera
Marcellus Bearheart
Williams, and Robert Symonds, Narrators
Alabama Chief, Fulton Battise relates in his native dialect the fantasy tale of three youths traveling to the ends of the earth and beyond. Describes the struggle of a people to preserve their way of life. 1982. 53 minutes. Color. Video. Rental: $80/week. NAPBC.

JUST DANCING

Eskimo dancing. 1987. 60 minutes.
VHS. $24.95. KYUK.

KAINAI

Raoul Fox, Director
On the Blood Indian Reserve, near Cardston, Alberta, Canada, a pre-fab factory has been built to employ the residents. 27 minutes. 16mm. NFBC.

KAMIK

Elise Swerthone
Inuit, Ulayok Kavlok, a hunter & seamstress, makes seal skin boots called Kamik. 15 minutes. Purchase: 16mm, $350; VHS, $200. Rental: $40. NFBC.

KAMINURIAK: CARIBOU IN CRISIS

Inuit Broadcasting Corp. &
Don Snowden, Producers
Focuses on the ecological and cultural practices in the North which has affected the Caribou herds in the Inuit regions of Northern Canada. 33 interviews, 4-20 minutes each, presenting both sides of the issue and contrasting approaches to wildlife management. 1982-3. Color. Video. In Inuktitut & English. IBC.

KANEHSATAKE: 270 YEARS OF RESISTANCE

Alanis Obomsawin, Producer
Documents the confrontation between Mohawks & Canadian government forces in Quebec in 1990, outside the town of Oka. Raises vital questions about basic social injustices, the role of politicians, police, the military, and the press. 120 minutes, color. Video. Purchase: $275; rental: $90. BULL.

KARUK BASKET MAKERS, A WAY OF LIFE

Shows women & girls engaged in learning the art of basketmaking from Karuk elders who still practice it. Types & uses of baskets are discussed. Grades 4-6. 22 minutes. VHS. $69.95. CB.

KASHIA MEN'S DANCES: SOUTHWESTERN POMO INDIANS

Clyde B. Smith, Producer
Preserves four authentic Pomo dances as performed in full costume on the Kashia Reservation on the northern California coast. 1963. 40 minutes, color. Purchase: 16mm, $800; video, $195. Rental: $60. UC. Rental: IU, PSU & UCLA.

KECIA: WORDS TO LIVE BY

Gryphon Productions
15 year-old Kecia speaks of her expereicnes—how she contracted the HIV virus, and her pride in her Native American traditions. 1991. Grades 8 and up. 30 mins. $145. CHAR..

KEEP YOUR HEART STRONG: LIFE ALONG THE POW WOW TRAIL

Deb Wallwork, Producer
Provides an inside view of contemporary Native Ameri-

can culture in its most accessible and popular form - the Pow Wow. 1986. 58 minutes, color. Video. Purchase: $150; Rental: $80. NAPBC. Rental: $16. UMN.

KEEPER OF THE WESTERN DOOR
Eight short films made on the Cattaraugus and Allegany Reservations in western New York. Each program investigates Seneca life. The Music and Dance of the Senecas, 11 minutes; A Seneca Language Class, 11 minutes; Preparing Seneca Food, 18 minutes; The Seneca People—Past and Present, 13 minutes; A Visit to the Basketmaker, 12 minutes; A Visit to the Beader, 15 minutes; A Visit to the Seneca Museum, 15 minutes; A Visit With a Seneca Artist, 17 minutes. 1980. Video. SN.

KEVIN ALEC
Beverly Shaffer, Director
Kevin, an 11 year-old Indian boy from the Fountain Indian Reserve in British Columbia, Canada, whose parents are dead, lives with his grandmother. He leaves, participates and builds pride in the value of tribal life. 1976. 16 minutes. Grades 1-8. Purchase: 16mm, $290; video, $145; rental, $28. MG.

KLEENA
H. Leslie Smith, Director/camera
Dann Firehouse, Writer
A small group of Kwakiutl Indians, organized by Peter Knox, the grandson of a famed carver Mungo Martin, sets out from their community at Alert Bay to participate in a traditional fishing activity. Narration gives economic & social facts related to kleena, the oil extracted from the oil-rich eulachon fish, a feast food for potlatches. 1981. 20 mins, color. 16mm & VHS. CFDW.

KNOWLEDGE IS THE BEST MEDICINE
Looks at the correct use of prescription drugs as it applies to life in Native American communities. Part 1 of a 2 part series. 2000. 15 mins. VHS. $55. Part 2, "Everyone Counts." CHAR.

KWA' NU' TE': MICMAC & MALISEET ARTISTS
Catherine Martin & Kimberlee McTaggart, Directors
Interviews with eight Native American artists at work talking about the power of creation. 1993. 42 minutes, color. Purchase: 16mm, $650; VHS, $250. Rental: $70. NFBC.

THE KWAKIUTL OF BRITISH COLUMBIA
Franz Boas; Bill Holm, Editor
A documentary film made by noted anthropologist Dr. Franz Boas, in 1930 at Fort Rupert on Vancouver Island. Includes scenes depicting traditional Kwakiutl dances, crafts, games, oratory and actions of a shaman. 1950. 55 minutes. Silent/bxw. Purchase: 16mm, $500; beta, $350; VHS, $340. UW. Rental, $19. IU.

KYUK VIDEO
John A. McDonald, Executive producer
Located in Bethel, Alaska, KYUK-TV, begun in 1972, has produced works on the lifestyles and native culture of the Yukon-Kuskokwim Delta, both in English and Yup'ik. Documentaries focusing on the Yup'ik Eskimo way of life and the people's viewpoints on contemporary events and the continuation of their cultural traditions. Several productions include: Eyes of the Spirit; From Hand to Hand: Bethel Native Artist Profiles; A Matter of Trust; They Never Asked Our Fathers; Yupiit Yuraryarait/A Dancing People; Just a Small Fishery; Old Dances, New Dancers; Parlez-Vois Yup'ik; People of Kashunuk. For a complete list of video programs contact KYUK.

LA CROSSE STICK MAKER
Jack Ofield, Director/Producer
Helen-Maria Erawan, Writer/Narrator
Onondaga craftsmen of the sovereign Onondaga Nation, located in New York State, demonstrate the ancient craft of steaming and binding wood to make lacrosse sticks. They discusses tools and techniques, play a game and reflect on their cultural heritage and lifestyle. 1974. Grades 5 and up. 9 minutes, color. Purchase: 16mm, $125; video, $50. Rental: $30 each. NPP & BGF.

THE LAKOTA: ONE NATION ON THE PLAINS
Fran Cantor
Narrated by N. Scott Momaday, this film opens by evoking traditional Lakota philosophy, and conveys history as it is understood in the Lakota tradition. 1976. 29 minutes, color. 16mm & video. UMA & KS.

LAKOTA QUILLWORK: ART & LEGEND
H. Jane Nauman, Producer/director/editor
A documentary on Lakota quillworking, demonstrated and explained, with a re-enactment scene as it might have appeared 150 years ago. Two well-known quillworkers demonstrate sewn and wrapped quilling. 1985. 27 minutes, color. In English & Lakota. 16mm & video. $24.95. SDF & WH.

LAKOTA WOMAN
The life of Lakota activist Mary Crowdog and how she took a stand at Wounded Knee in 1973. 1994. 113 mins. VHS, $199.99. ME.

LAMENT OF THE RESERVATION
Thames TV, Producer
Discusses the living conditions of the 600,000 Indians on barren reservations, pointing out high infant mortality and suicide rates. Grades 7 and up. 23 minutes, color. 16mm. Rental. UT & IU.

THE LAND IS OURS
Laurence A. Goldin, Producer/director/editor
An historical documentary that tells the story of the Tlingits and Haidas, coastal Indians of southeast Alaska. Takes us into the Native's mystical aboriginal opast with time lapse photography and special effects. 57 minutes. Video & 16mm. 1996. AF.

LAND OF THE EAGLE
BBC & WNET's Nature Series
George Page, host & narrator
An 8-part series presenting an account of European colonization of North America. Narratives from American Indians communicate the spiritual naturalism - harmony between man and nature that existed until the "White Man" arrived. 1991. 8/60 minute programs. Video. Individual programs, $39.95. $249.95 complete. A 32-page teacher guide is provided free with series purchase. PBS.

THE LAST DAYS OF OKAK
Anne Budgell & Nigel Markham, Directors
Shows what happens to a community (the Inuit of Labrador) when a disaster (1918-19 flu epidemic) that overwhelms its people also largely destroys the values by which they lived. 1985. 24 minutes, color. Purchase: 16mm, $500; video, $225. Rental: $50. NFBC.

THE LAST MENOMINEE
Describes what is happening to the Menominee Indians of Menominee County, Wisconsin. 1966. Grades 10 and up. 30 minutes, bxw. 16mm. Purchase: $250; rental, $12.15. IU.

THE LAST MOOSESKIN BOAT
Raymond Yakeleya, Director
The Shoteah Dene of the Northwest Territories built mooseskin boats to carry their families and cargo downriver to trading posts. A member of the Dene constructs the last boat of this type to be housed in a museum in Yellowknife. 1982. 28 minutes. Video. Purchase: $27. NFBC.

THE LAST OF THE CADDOES
Ken Harrison, Producer/director/writer/editor
Set in rural Texas in the 1930s, this film follows James Edward Hawkins through a summer of self-discovery. Jimmy, age 12, learns that he is part Indian and seeks to learn about his heritage. 1982. 29 minutes, color. Purchase: 16mm, $525; video, $315. Rental, $52.50. PHOENIX.

LAST OF HIS TRIBE
The story about Ishi (Graham Greene) the last of the Yahi Tribe of California and the secrets of his people. With John Voight as Dr. Kroeber. 1992. 90 mins. VHS. $19.99. ME.

LAST OF THE MOHICANS
James Fenimore Cooper's classic tale of romance in colonial America. With Daniel; Day Lewis, Russell Means, West Studi, Eric Schweig, et al. 1992. 114 mins. VHS, $16.99; DVD, $29.99. ME.

LAST SALMON FEAST OF THE CELILO INDIANS
Produced prior to the Dalles Dam inundation of the last major salmon fishery of the Wy-am Pum, a branch of lower Deschute Indians, the Yakimas and the Warm Springs, and other central Oregon tribes. 1955. 18 mins, bxw. Purchase: 16mm, $150; rental, $10. OHS.

LAST STAND AT LITTLE BIGHORN
N. Scott Momaday, Narrator
Re-examines the Battle of the Little Bighorn from both the white & Native American perspectives. 1992. 54 mins, color. VHS, $19.99. ME. Rental: $10. HO.

THE LEARNING PATH
Loretta Todd, Director
Native control of Native education in Canada, to preserve their languages and identities. Schools in Edmonton and nearby Saddle Lake Reserve. 1991. 57 mins., color. VHS. Purchase: $27. NFBC.

LEGACY
Contemporary portrait of American Indian elders, their daily lives and their struggle with a legacy of poverty. 1994. 40 mins. VHS. $95.

LEGACY
directed by Chief Roy Crazy Horse & Jeff Baker
Examines the perpetuation of the romantic myths surrounding Christopher Columbus' "Discovery of the New World" in 1492. 1993. 22 mins., color. VHS. Purchase: $195. Rental, $50. CG.

LEGACY; NATIVE AMERICAN PHOTOGRAVURES & MUSIC
Historical look at the photogravure work of Edward C. Curtis. 2003. DVD, $19.99. ME.

THE LEGACY OF GENERATIONS: POTTERY BY AMERICAN INDIAN WOMEN
narrated by performer, Buffy Sainte-Marie
Set against the landscape of the American Southwest, this film showcases the art of master potters. 30 mins, color. $19.95. PMI.

LEGACY OF MOUND BUILDERS
Story of a lost civilization born in the heartland of America over 2,000 years ago. VHS. 17 mins. $14.95. VIP.

LEGEND OF THE BOY & THE EAGLE
The Hopi legend of Tutevina, the young Indian boy who is banished from his tribe for freeing the sacrificial bird. 21 mins. 16mm. WD.

THE LEGEND OF THE BUFFALO CLAN
A lesson for teaching traditions, proper behavior, cultural history, and spiritual beliefs. The Buffalo chief does an authentic healing ceremony, reviving the child. 1993. 29 mins., color. Purchase: 16mm, $525; video, $285. Rental: 16mm, $55. PHOENIX.

LEGEND OF THE MAGIC KNIVES
A totem village in the Pacific Northwest provides the setting for this portrayal of an ancient Indian legend, recountered by means of figures on a totem pole and authentic Indian masks. 1970. 11 minutes, color. Grades 4 and up. 16mm. Rental, $14. PSU & IU.

LEGENDS & LIFE OF THE INUIT
Richard Robesco, Director
Animated film looks at life today in an Inuit community and presents five legends. 1978. 58 minutes, color. Video. Purchase: $27. NFBC.

LEGENDS OF THE INDIANS
These stories of various Native American tribes are re-enacted by Native Americans to remember who they are and what they believe. The Return of the Child (Algonquin); The Legend of the Corn (Ojibway); The Winter Wife (Chippewa); Moowis, Where Are You, Moowis? (Algonquin); The Path of the Souls (Ojibway); Glooscap, Creation Legend; The World Between & The Path of Life. 26 minutes each, color. Video. Purchase: Complete series, $675; $89.95 each. FH.

LEGENDS OF THE SIOUX
Filmed in South Dakota, this film relates many of the legends of the Sioux Indians. 27 minutes. 16mm. Rental. UK.

LENAPE: THE ORIGINAL PEOPLE
Thomas Agnello, Producer/director/editor
David Oestreicher, Research coordinator
Briefly sketches Delaware, or Lenape history; focuses on two elders living in Dewey, Oklahoma, who retain the language and knowledge of old customs and beliefs. Edward Thompson describes his participation in a Big House Ceremony in 1924; and Nora Thompson Dean, also know as Touching Leaves Woman. Scenes of the first reunion of Lenape held in 1983 are included. 1986. 22 minutes, color. Purchase: 16mm, $325; video, $95. Rental: $45. AG.

LETTER FROM AN APACHE
Barbara Wilk, Producer/writer/animator
Fred Hellerman, Narrator
An animated film presenting experiences of a Yavapai Indian of the early 20th century. The narration is adapted from a letter written by Carlos Montezuma, M.D., known as Wassajah, to Frederick W. Hodge to provide autobiographical information for the 1907 Handbook of American Indians. 1983. Grades 4-9. 11 mins. 16mm, $240; VHS, $89; 3/4", $119. CC.

LEWIS & CLARK AT THE GREAT DIVIDE
CBS News; hosted by Walter Cronkite
The expedition nearly ends prematurely in 1805 when a young Indian girl turns out to be a Shoshoni chief's sister. Grades 3-8. 22 minutes, color. 16mm & video. Purchase: 16mm, $490; video, $285; rental, $72. PHOENIX.

LEWIS & CLARK: KEN BURNS PRESENTS THE JOURNEY OF THE CORPS OF DISCOVERY
Film documentary of the expedition led by Meriweather Lewis & William Clark and the Corps of Discovery into the heart of America in the early 19th century, and the aid they received from Indians along the way. 1997. 10 hours. VHS & DVD, $29.99. ME.

LEWIS & CLARK: EXPLORERS OF THE NEW FRONTIER
A&E Home Video
Documents the Lewis & Clark expedition. 2000. 50 mins. VHS, $15.95. ME.

LEWIS & CLARK: GREAT JOURNEY WEST
National Geographic
Brings to life the scientific expedition of the Corps of Discovery. 2002. 45 mins. VHS & DVD, $19.99. ME.

A LIFETIME OF CARING
Looks at the issues facing many seniors in many Native communities, including different forms of elder abuse and neglect. and promotes ways of providing improved care-giver services. Grades 9 and up. 1995. 25 mins. VHS. $145. CHAR.

LIGHTING THE SEVENTH FIRE
Salmon Run Productions
The spear-fishing treaty rights in Wisconsin and the Ojibway prophecy of the Seventh Fire, and profiles some of the people trying to bring back the tradition of spear fishing. Documents contemporary racism against Native peoples in the U.S. 1995. Grades 5 and up. 48 minutes. Color. Video. $50. OY.

LIKE THE TREES
Rose, a Metis Indian from northern Alberta, leaves the city to find her roots among the Woodland Cree. 15 minutes. 16mm. NFBC.

A LITTLE WHILE MORE YET
Jan Marie Martell
Stephen Charleson, from the Hesquiat Band of the West Coast of Vancouver Island, talks about the difficulties in making the transition from his native community to a city environment. 1976. 15 minutes. 16mm or video. Purchase or rental. CFDW.

LITTLE WHITE SALMON INDIAN SETTLEMENT
Harry Dawson, Director
Leo Alexander, Advisor/narrator
Cooks Landing, the site of one of the oldest Indian fishing villages in North America, is the subject of this documentary produced in cooperation with members of the Yakima Indian Tribe. 1972. Grades 9 and up. 30 minutes, color. 16mm. Rental: PSU & UCLA.

LIVE AND REMEMBER
Henry Smith, Producer
Using some footage of Vision Dance, as well as new interviews and footage shot on Rosebud Reservation in South Dakota, this film examines the role and sacred nature of dance, music and oral tradition in Lakota culture and what it means to be Indian living in America today. 1986. Grades 9 and up. 29 minutes, color. Video. $35. CAN & NAPBC. Rental: $21. UMN.

THE LIVING STONE
John Freeney, Director
Contemporary Inuit Eskimos of Cape Dorset on Baffin Island continue an ageless tradition of creative craftsmenship carving stone into evocative portrayals of Inuit life. 1958. Grades 7 and up. 33 minutes, color. Purchase: 16mm, $550; video, $350. Rental, $60. NFBC. Rental. IU.

LIVING TRADITIONS: FIVE INDIAN WOMEN ARTISTS
Denise Mayotte, Kathee Prokop and Fran Belvin, Producers/directors/editors; Sherry Wilson, Narrator
The relationship between traditional Indian values and the handiwork of five Indian women artists from Minnesota is examined. Shows the role of culture handed down from generation to generation. 1984. 27 minutes, color. Video. IN.

THE LONG WALK OF FRED YOUNG
Michael Barnes
The story of a child, Fred Young, who only spoke the Ute and Navajo languages, went to a medicine man when he was sick. Today, he is Dr. Frederick Young a nuclear physicist. 1979. 58 minutes. 16mm & video, WGBH. Rental: 16mm, $27.50. UMN.

THE LONGEST TRAIL
Alan Lomax, Producer
Alan Lomax & Forrestine Paulay, Editors
Exploration of the dance traditions of the American Indian showing more than 50 Native American dances. Focuses on Native America, showing patterns of movement linking dances of Indians and Inuit from the Arctic Circle to Tierra del Fuego into one tradition. Also seeks to demonstrate a connection between these cultures and indigenous cultures in Siberia. 1986. 58 minutes, color. Purchase: 16mm, $995; video, $295. Rental, $60. UC. Rental: $23. UMN.

THE LONGEST WALK: S.F. TO D.C. 1978
A documentary of the spiritual and political walk across the nation from Alcatraz Island to Washington, D.C. to protest anti-Indian legislation and inform local communities about eleven bills then currently before Congress. 60 minutes. Also available are three 20 minute videotapes which are supplemental reference information: John Trudell—Pueblo Rally Speech; A Look Behind Indian Legislation; and, Dennis Banks—AIM Leader in Exile. Video. Purchase: $170 (Documentary), $75 (each supplement.) Rental: $50 (Documentary), $35 (each supplement.) CLP.

THE LONGEST WAR
Diane Orr, Director
An interview with Dennis Banks, founder of the American Indian Movement (AIM). Shows scenes of the occupation of Wounded Knee and the burning of the Courthouse at Custer, South Dakota in 1973. Interviews with participants at Wounded Knee. 1974. 30 minutes, color. 16mm & video. BF.

THE LONGHOUSE PEOPLE
Tom Daly, Producer
The life and religion of the Iroquois today. Shows a rain dance, a healing ceremony, and a celebration of a new chief. 1951. Grades 9 and up. 24 minutes, color. Purchase: 16mm, $500; video, $300. Rental, $50. NFBC. Rental: IU & UCLA.

THE LOON'S NECKLACE
Crawley Films, Producer
A Spanish language film recreating a Salish legend which tells how the loon came to receive his distinguished neckband. Authentic ceremonial masks establish the characters of the story. 1949, restored, 1990. 11 minutes, color. Grades 4 and up. 16mm & video. Rental, $14. PSU, UMN, UT & IU.

LORD OF THE SKY
Ludmila Zeman & Eugen Spaleny, Director
Based on the legends of the Native poeples of the Pacific Northwest, this animated film is an artistic unity of form & content. An environmental parable. 13 minutes. Purchase: 16mm, $350; VHS, $200. Rental: $40. NFBC.

LOS INDIOS NAVAJOS
A Spanish language film which shows the Navajo people in their own environment. 1939. 11 minutes; bxw. Grades 4-8. UA.

LOST IN TIME
Bruce G. Kuerten & Maryanne G. Culpepper, Producers; Dennis King, Narrator
Observes the work of archaeologists in the Tennessee Valley. Traces the history of the early native peoples, describing American prehistory beginning with the migration of Paleolithic hunters into the New World over the Bering land bridge. Briefly discusses the changes of Indian culture leading to the complex settled lifestyles of the Indians who built the great mounds of the Black Warrior River Valley in Alabama. 1985. 60 minutes, color. Purchase: video, $250. AT & BE. Edited version, 30 minutes, $195. BE.

LOUISE ERDRICH & MICHAEL DORRIS
Bill Moyers, Host
Native American husband & wife team who write novels together. Their writings & beliefs in family, community & lifestyle reflect their heritage. 1988. 27 minutes, color. Video. Rental: $16. UMN.

LOVING REBEL
A documentary profile of Helen Hunt Jackson, one of the 19th-century's foremost advocates of Native American rights and one of its most celebrated writers. This video features readings from her writings as well as rare photographs & drawings of her world. 1987. Grades 7 and up. 27 minutes, color. Purchase: VHS & Guide, $69; CHAR.

LUCY COVINGTON: NATIVE AMERICAN INDIAN
Steve Heiser, Director
Filmed on the Colville Reservation in eastern Washington, Lucy Covington, chairperson of the Colville tribe and granddaughter of Chief Moses, gives an account of her part in the effort to prevent federal termination of the tribe. She talks about the Indian heritage and Indian identity, and how the land is central to these. 1978. Grades 7 and up. 15 minutes, color. 16mm. Rental: Video, $12. PSU & UCT.

LUCY SWAN
An Indian woman born on the Rosebud Reservation at the turn of the century remembers the old ways but does not entirely discount the new. 16mm. Purchase: $300; rental: $30. AICRC.

LUMAAQ - AN ESKIMO LEGEND
Co Hoedeman, Director
Lumaaq tells the story of a legend widely believed by the Povungnituk Inuit. 1975. Grades 7 and up. 8 minutes, color. Video. Purchase: $22. NFBC.

MAGIC IN THE SKY
Peter Raymont, Director/Writer
An examination of the impact of Canadian (CBC) TV on Inuit Eskimos on the Arctic coast of Quebec, and their efforts to establish their own network. Mirrors the struggle of any culture to preserve its unique identity. 1981. Grades 7 and up. 57 minutes, color. 16mm, $775; video, $350. Rental: $80. NFBC.

MAKE MY PEOPLE LIVE: THE CRISIS IN INDIAN HEALTH CARE
Linda Harrar, Producer/director/writer
Lee Grant, Narrator
Investigates the state of health care for Indians. Details Native American life in four vastly different regions and discusses legislative and other issues, providing an introduction not only to health concerns but also to contemporary life of Native Americans across the country. Sites visited range from the impoverished Rosebud Sioux Reservation to the Tlingit villages of Alaska; and from the Navajo Nation to the Creek Nation of Oklahoma. 1984. 60 minutes, color. 16mm (sales only),

3/4" video (sales & rentals). Rental, 1/2' video, $11. UT; 16mm rental, $37.50. PSU.

MAKE PRAYERS TO THE RAVEN
Mark Badger, Producer/camera/editor
Barry Lopez, Narrator
Public television series introducing the lifeways and traditions of interior Alaska's Koyukon Indians. Focuses on their relationship to the land, and explores their spiritual beliefs. Includes the Koyukon communities of Alatna, Allakaket, Hughes, and Huslia - located just below the Arctic Circle. Color. All video formats. KUAC.

THE MAKING OF A PORKY ROACH
with Kris Woerpol
Noc Bay Publishing
The Porky Roach, worn by male dancers, is the universal headdress worn today in the powwow arena. A complete guide to construction includes sorting deer and porky hair, making of a handwoven base, tying on the hair and care of the finished roach. 30 minutes. VHS. $19.95. WH.

MAKOCE WAKAN: SACRED EARTH
Robby Romero, Director/writer
Focuses on Native American sacred sites & their importance to Native American culture. Personal & poitical insights on the importance of protecting Native American sacred sites: Ben Nighthorse Campbell (Cheyenne); Richard Moves Camp (Oglala Lakota); Audrey Shenandoah (Onondaga); Franklin Stanley (San Carlos Apache); Suzan Shown Harjo (CVheyenne/Hodulgee Muscogee); Ola Cassadore (San Carlos Apache); and Leon Shenandoah (Iroquois). 1993. 30 minutes. VH-1.

THE MAN & THE GIANT: AN ESKIMO LEGEND
Co Hoedeman, Director
An Inuit legend acted out by the Inuit people themselves. They use their traditional form of singing, katadjak, or throat singing. 1978. 8 minutes, color. Video. Purchase: 16mm, $225; Video, $125. Rental. $17. PHOENIX & NFBC.

MAN OF LIGHTNING
Gary Moss, Producer
Based on two Cherokee Indian legends, this film is a drama of the long-vanished world of the Cherokee years before European contact. 1982. 29 minutes, color. Video. Rental: $40/week. NAPBC.

MAN ON THE RIM: THE PEOPLING
OF THE PACIFIC, 4 - FLAMING ARROWS
Over 20,000 years ago Siberian hunters crossed the Bering Strait land bridge into Alaska and poured ito the American prairie. The Indian emerged in North America. 1988. 58 minutes, color. Video. Rental, $24. PSU.

MARIA! INDIAN POTTERY OF SAN ILDEFONSO
National Park Service
Indian pottery maker Maria Martinez demonstrates the traditional India ways of pottery making. 27 minutes. Video, $29.95. CH.

MARIA & JULIAN'S BLACK POTTERY
Arthur E. Baggs, Jr.
Shows famous potters Maria and Julian Martinez in the step-by-step process of creating the famed black-on-black pottery that revived at San Ildefonso Pueblo, New Mexico. 1938/1977. 11 minutes, color. 16mm/silent. Purchase, 16mm, $190; VHS, $105. Rental: 16mm, $14; VHS, $13. PSU.

MARIA OF THE PUEBLOS
The life of the famous Pueblo potter, Maria Martinez. Provides an understanding of the culture, philosophy, art and economic condition of the Pueblo Indians of San Ildefonso, New Mexico. 1971. Grades 4 and up. 15 minutes, color. Purchase: 16mm, $345; video, $240. Rental: $50. PHOENIX. Rental: 16mm, $14. UCT.

MARKS OF THE ANCESTORS:
ANCIENT INDIAN ROCK ART OF ARIZONA
Echo Productions
Produced in cooperation with the Museum of Northern Arizona, this video explores six different rock art sites. 40 minutes, color. VHS. $24.95. TC.

THE MARMES ARCHAEOLOGICAL DIG
Louis & Ruth Kirk, Producers
Presents the oldest fully documented discovery of early man in the Western Hemisphere. 1971. 18 mins, color. Purchase: 16mm, $250; beta, $175; VHS, $165. UW.

MASHPEE
Maureen McNamara & Mark Gunning, Producers/directors/writers/editors
Illustrates the land claims of the Mashpee Wampanoags of Massachusetts since 1976. Provides the complex background of the controversy, with interviews of Mashpee leaders, real estate developers, historians, legal experts, & trial lawyers presenting their sides of the story. 1985. 50 mins, color. Video. McN.

THE MASKS OF CULTURE
Gryphon Productions
Explains the importance the wooden mask in tribal ceremonies. Grades 8 & up. 25 mins. VHS. $250. NDM.

A MATTER OF CHOICE
The Hopi Nation and their efforts to find a place In the modern world. 60 minutes, color. Video. Purchase: $60. PBS.

A MATTER OF PROMISES
Introduces students to members of Native American tribes who describe their struggles to maintain their cultural identity and political sovereignty. 60 minutes, color. Video. Purchase: $60. PBS.

A MATTER OF TRUST
Bill Sharpsteen, Producer/writer/editor/host
Bryan Murray, Narrator
Focuses on the Alaska Native Claims Settlement Act passed by Congress in 1971 and the problems it has posed for Alaska's Indians and Inuit. 1983. 28 minutes, color. Video. KYUK.

MATTHEW ALIUK: ESKIMO IN TWO WORLDS
Bert Sulzman, Writer/Director
The relationship of an Eskimo boy assimilated into the city life of Anchorage. Tells the story of a proud people's struggle for cultural survival in a changing world. 1973. 18 mins, color. 16mm, $270. Rental, $25. LCA.

MEDICINE FIDDLE
Documentary celebrates the fiddling & dancing traditions of Native & Metis families on both sides of the U.S. & Canadian border. Features Ojibwe, Menominee, Metis & Ottawa fiddlers & dancers. 1990. 81 minutes, color. Video. Purchase: $295; rental: $75. UC.

MEDICINE LINE
Ken Mitchell, Director
A brief acount of Chief Sitting Bull of the Lakota Sioux during his years in exile in Canada. 1987. 10 mins. Video. Purchase: $22. NFBC.

THE MEDICINE WHEEL
Native American spirituality/healing. Visually moving segments highlight the Sweat Lodge and Pipe Ceremonies. Grades 7 and up. 1996. 24 mins. VHS. $100. CHAR.

MEDOONAK, THE STORMMAKER
Les Krizsan, Director
A MicMac Indian legend. 1975. Grades 7-12. 13 mins, color. Purchase: 16mm, $250; video, $210. Rental, $17.50. UA.

MEET THE SIOUX INDIAN
Shows the transient life of the Sioux Indians. 1949. Grades K-6. 11 mins, color. Rental: UCT.

MENOMINEE
This documentary examines the historical development of the many social and political problems faced by the Menominee Indians of northwestern Wisconsin. 1974. 59 mins, color. Video. Rental: $80/week. NAPBC.

MESA VERDE
The story of ancient America and the Pueblo builders. 1997. 60 mins. VHS, $19.99. ME.

MESA VERDE
National Park Service
Mesa Verde's cliff dwellings is interpreted. 23 mins, color. Video. Purchase: $29.95. CH.

MESA VERDE: MYSTERY OF THE SILENT CITIES
Views (using extensive aerial photography) the ruined cities and multiply family cliff dwellings of the 13th-century Indians of the Mesa Verde. 1975. 14 mins, color. 16mm. Rental, $11.20. IU.

MESQUAKIE
Alan Weber and Michael Bartell
Looks at the Mesquakie Indian settlement at Tama, Iowa, where carious activities of the traditional days are shown through old photographs and present-day film footage. 1976. 10 minutes. ISU.

MIGHTY WARRIORS
During the mass migration west, the white man encountered the Plains Indians. Familiar battles are depicted in the light of the true facts. 1964. Grades 4 and up. 30 mins, bxw. 16mm. Purchase: $250; rental, $12.15. IU. Rental only, $16. PSU.

MI'KMAQ
A series of five programs recreating, in dramatized form, the seasonal round of Micmac life in Nova Scotia, Canada, before European contact as it might have been experienced by a single, extended Micmac family. Performed by Native people in the Micmac language. Available in French and English. Teacher's guide. Grades 6-adult. Video. NS.

MILLENIUM: TRIBAL WISDOM
& THE MODERN WORLD
Biniman Productions & Adrian Malone Productions
Filmed in 15 countries, this ten-hour series tells the stories of people in 11 tribal cultures across the globe in an attempt to discover different ways of thinking about life as the turn of the century approaches. Two of the cultures covered include the Mohawk, and the Navajo. #6 - Touching the Timeless (Navajo); and #9 - The Tightrope of Power ((Mohawk & Ojibwe-Cree). 1992. 60 mins each. VHS. Purchase: PBS. Rental, $14 each. PSU.

MINORITIES IN AGRICULTURE:
THE WINNEBAGO
Ralph A. Swain, Briar Cliff College
Highlights the economic development programs of the Winnebago Tribe of Nebraska. 1984. 29 mins, color. Video. Rental: $40/week. NAPBC.

MINORITY YOUTH: ADAM
The narration of a teenage American Indian's view of himself, his race, and his cultural heritage that is in danger of being lost. 1971. 10 minutes, color. 16mm. Rental, $9. IU.

MISS INDIAN AMERICA
KBYU-TV, Provo, Utah
Covers the 20th annual Miss Indian America Pageant in 1973 at Sheridan, Wyoming. Contest represents 30 American Indian tribes from all over the U.S. 59 mins, color. VHS. $150; Rental: $80/week. NAPBC.

THE MISSING
Ron Howard, Director
Lots of Apache spoken in this film. With Tommy Lee Jones & Cate Blanchett. 130 mins. 2003. DVD, 28.99; VHS, $70.99. ME.

MISSION LIFE: ALTA CALIFORNIA 1776
22 minutes. 16mm. Rental. UA.

MISSION OF FEAR
Fernand Dansereau, Director
The story of the Jesuit martyrs who lived with their Huron converts, Indians of Midland, Ontario. 79 minutes, bxw. NFBC.

MISSION SAN XAVIER DEL BAC
33 minutes. 16mm. Rental. UA.

MISSIONS OF CALIFORNIA:
NEW WAYS IN NEW WORLD
21 minutes. 16mm. Rental. UA.

MISSIONS OF THE SOUTHWEST
15 minutes. 16mm. Rental. UA.

MITAKUYE OYASIN - "WE ARE ALL RELATED"
Dr. A. Chuck Ross, Narrator
Dr. Ross, a Santee Dakota educator and spiritual guide provides an introduction to Sioux religion and philosophy as detailed in his book "We Are All Related." 60 minutes, color. Video. $22.50. CAN.

MOCCASIN FLATS
A young boy learns to come to terms with his Native American heritage, and learns to be proud of his background and finally claims his Native American name, Moccasin Flats. 26 minutes. Purchase, VHS, $149. CC.

MOCCASIN MAKING
Frank E. White
Step-by-step instructions for making a side-seam moccasin. List of necessary tools and equipment, patternmaking, leather selection, advanced sewing techniques. VHS. 55 minutes. $19.95. WP.

MODOC
Peter Winograd
By the use of archival photos by Edward S. Curtis and news clippings, this film tells the story of the Modoc Indians of California and their struggle to remain on their own lands. 1979. 15 minutes. bxw. 16mm and beta. EM.

MOHAWK BASKETMAKING:
A CULTURAL PROFILE
Frank Semmens, Producer
Features a sensitive and personal look at the life and work of master basketmaker Mary Adams. 1980. 28 minutes. Color. Purchase: 16mm, $385; rental, $22; video, $70; rental, $12.50. PSU.

MOMADAY: VOICE OF THE WEST
Scott Momaday's prose uniquely reflects the Native American experience. Momaday gives viewers a rare glimpse into the human dilemma that led to his strong identification with the land. 30 minutes. Color. Video. $40. PBS.

MONUMENT VALLEY: LAND OF THE NAVAJOS
Shows the life of the Navajo Indians in the four-corner area where Arizona, New Mexico, Colorado and Utah meet. 1959. 17 minutes. Grades 6-adult. 16mm. UA.

THE MOON'S PRAYER
Stories of the Northwest tribes struggles to reverse the unsound environmental practices that have been inflicted upon their land. 60 minutes, color. Video. Rental: $10. HO.

MORE LEGENDS OF THE INDIANS
These are authentic stories from various Indian tribes, told by Native Americans to remember who they are and what they believe. 8-part series: Windigo; The Pleiades; The Magic Box; Pitchie the Robin; The Spirit of the Dead Chief; The Path Without End; The Invisible Man; & Megmoowesoo. 26 mins each, color. Purchase: $89.95 each; $685 for all 8 parts. FH.

MORE THAN BOWS & ARROWS:
THE LEGACY OF THE AMERICAN INDIANS
Roy Williams, Director; narrated by
N. Scott Momaday; produced by Camera One
Documents the contributions of Native Americans to the development of the U.S. & Canada. N. Scott Momaday is a prominent Kiowa Indian writer and educator. 1994. VHS. 58 mins, color. $19.95. ME, CAN, CMM, VIP & WKV; rental: VHS, $10. UMN, PSU & HO.

MOTHER CORN
KBYU-TV, Provo, Utah
Examines the historical significance of various types of corn among Native American cultures. 1977. 29 mins, color. Video. Purchase: $150; Rental: $40/week. NAPBC.

MOTHER OF MANY CHILDREN
Alanis Obomsawin, Director
Agatha Marie Goodine, 108 year-old member of the

Hobbema tribe, contrasts her memories with the conflicts that most Indian and Inuit woman face today. 1977. 58 mins, color. Grades 9 and up. Purchase: 16mm, $775; VHS, $350. Rental, $80. NFBC.

A MOTHER'S CHOICE
Examines the root causes of FAS/FAE (Fetal Alcohol Syndrome/Fetal Alcohol Effects) from the perspective of Native mothers. 1995. 28 mins. VHS. $145. CHAR.

MOUNTAIN WOLF WOMAN: 1884-1960
Naomi Russell, Narrator
Tells the life story of an American Indian in her own words & narrated by her granddaughter. Based on the book by Nancy Oestreich Lurie. Includes an authentic Winnebago wedding song, baskets, beads, wigwams, & scenes from a powwow. 1990. 17 minutes, color. Video. Rental: $16. UMN.

MOVABLE FEAST
Presents Indian & Eskimo ways of hunting, gathering, preparing, and celebrating food, through images by Native artists from all over North America. Includes study guide. 30 minutes, color. Video. $50. TOP.

MUNGO MARTIN:
A SLENDER THREAD/THE LEGACY
Barb Cramer/The U'Mista Cultural Society
From the time of his birth, Mungo Martin was exposed to cultural rituals and traditions of his people. At a young age he learned the basic skills of designing, carving and painting in the Northwest Coast traditional style of the Kwakwakawakw. 1991. 17 minutes, color. Purchase: VHS, $195. CFDW.

MUSIC & DANCE OF THE MOHAWK
Frank Semmons, Producer/director/camera/editor
Traces the origin, development and meaning behind Iroquois social songs; and the making of Iroquois musical instruments. 1983. 25 minutes, color. 16mm & video. AM & IM.

MUSIC & DANCE OF THE SENECAS
Covrs various aspects of the Seneca Indian culture. Introduces a variety of musical instruments with explanations. of how each one was taken from nature. 1981. 20 minutes, color. 3/4" U-matic. Rental: $25. UCLA.

MY FATHER CALLS ME SON:
RACISM & NATIVE AMERICANS
David Fanning, Executive Producer for KOCE-TV
Examines the problem of discrimination and some of the parallel pressures against Indian people to give up their uniqueness and become more like whites. 1975. 29 minutes, color. Video. PBS.

MY HANDS ARE THE TOOLS OF MY SOUL:
ART & POETRY OF THE AMERICAN INDIAN
Arthur Barron & Zina Voynoz
A survey of American Indian achievements in poetry, music, sculpture, philosophy and history. Dialogue in tribal language as well as English. 1975. 52 minutes, color. 16mm & video. FI & TF. Rental: 16mm, PSU & UCT.

THE MYSTERY OF THE ANASAZI
Russ Morash, Director; WGBH, Producer
A study of the ruins of the Anasazi, the builders, ancestors of the Navajo. 1973. 50 minutes, color. 16mm & video. TW & ISU. 16mm rental, $31. PSU.

THE MYSTERY OF THE LOST RED PAINT PEOPLE:
THE DISCOVERY OF A PREHISTORIC NORTH AMERICAN SEA CULTURE
T.W. Timreck & William Goetzmann, Producers
Follows U.S., Canadian, and European scientists from the barrens of Labrador - where archaeologists uncover an ancient stone burial mound - to sites in the U.S., France, England, Denmark and Norway where monumental standing stones testify to links among seafaring cultures across immense distances. 1987. Grades 9 and up. 57 minutes, color. Purchase: 16mm, $895; Video, $495; Rental: $90. BULL. Rental: 16mm, $39. PSU.

THE MYTHICAL TRIBE
History of the Sioux tribe from their victory at Little Big

Horn to their defeat at Wounded Knee. 1981. 30 minutes, video. KS.

MYTHS AND THE MOUNDBUILDERS
Graham Chedd, WGBH, Producer
Archaeologists probe mysterious mounds in the Eastern U.S. uncovering clues about a lost Indian civilization. Educator's guide. 1981. Grades 9 and up. 58 minutes, color. 16MM & Video. Purchase: 16mm, $750; Video, $145. Rental: 16mm, $70; Video, $40. NDM, PBS, DER, CAN & CH. Rental only: $20. PSU & IU.

NANOOK OF THE NORTH
Robert Flaherty
A documentary studying the life of an Eskimo hunter and his constant struggle for survival against the menaces of nature. 1948. 65 minutes, 16mm/bxw/silent. Grades 4 and up. Original silent version, MMA. Purchase: 16mm, $26; video, $12.50. PSU. 1975 (51 minutes) restored version with musical score-rental, $22. PSU. 16mm rental, $20.25. IU.

NANOOK REVISITED
This program revisits the site of Flaherty's filming, and learns that he staged much of what he filmed, sired children to whose future he paid no heed, and is himself part of Inuit myth. 60 mins, color. Purchase: $149; rental: $75. FH.

NATIONS WITHIN A NATION
Dept of Sociology, OK State U.
Examines the historical, legal and social backgrounds of the issue of the right of sovereignty-self-government. Examples of tribal government in operation are drawn from Taos Pueblo, the Mescalero Apache Tribe, the Muscogee (Creek) Nation and the Sac and Fox Tribe. 1986. 59 mins, color. Video. Purchase: $150; Rental: $80. NAPBC.

NATIVE AMERICAN ARTS
Indian Arts and Crafts Board
The development of Native American arts in the U.S. Shows that contemporary artists and craftsmen (Indian Eskimo and Aleut) are making unique and significant contributions to the cultural life of our nation. 1974. 20 mins, color. 16mm & video. Purchase: 16mm, $210. Rental: UCT & NAC.

NATIVE AMERICAN FOLKTALES
Tales from four different Native American tribes: Seneca, Pacific Coast Miwok, Pawnee, Pueblo. Grades 4-8. 1997. 22 mins. VHS & Guide. $95. CHAR.

NATIVE AMERICAN HEALING IN THE 21ST CENTURY: ANCIENT REMEDIES NOW ENDORSED BY MODERN MEDICINE
(produced by Rich-Heape Films)
VHS & DVD. 40 mins. $24.95. WH & RICH.

NATIVE AMERICAN HERBS
Discover the healing properties & preparation of herbs. 2000. VHS. $24.95. ME.

NATIVE AMERICAN HISTORY:
Part 1, THE WILDERNESS; Part 2, CIVILIZATION
Lionheart Television
Part 1, The Wilderness: Examines historical and contemporary attitudes toward Native Americans and reveals the extent to which the European invasion altered life for all Native Americans. Part 2, Civilization: Examines the way the U.S. Government handled Native Americans after the battle at Wounded Knee in 1890. Grades 9-12. 50 mins each. VHS. $99 each. PHOENIX.

NATIVE AMERICAN IMAGES
Carol Patton, Producer
Profiles the lives, philosophies and works of Paladine H. Royce (Ponca), Donald Van (Cherokee) and Steve Forbes, three artists living in Austin, Texas. Forbes is a non-Indian who has devoted himself to the portrayal of contemporary Native Americans. 1984. 29 mins. Color. Video. Rental: $40. NAPBC.

NATIVE AMERICAN INDIAN SACRED PURIFICATION SWEAT LODGE CEREMONY
42 minute version of "American Indian Sweat Lodge Ceremony." Video. Purchase: $24.95. AV.

NATIVE AMERICAN MASTER
ARTISTS VIDEO SERIES
Cherokee Basketmaker: Ella Mae Blackbear. VHS. 24 mins. **The Strength of Life: Knokovtee Scott, Creek Shellworker.** VHS. 28 mins. **Ribbons of the Osage: Art & Life of Georgeann Robinson.** VHS. 28 mins. **$17.95 each.** WH.

NATIVE AMERICAN MEDICINE
Explores the link between naturpathic medicine & native ceremony. 2001. DVD or VHS, $19.95. ME.

NATIVE AMERICAN MEN'S
& WOMEN'S DANCE STYLES
Full Circle Communications
An hour of dancing, highlighting the styles of champion dancers. In 2 Vols. Vol. 1: Men's Straight Dance, Nothern Traditional, Grass Dance, Fancy, Women's Southern Cloth, Buckskin, Jingle Dress, Fancy Shawl. Vol. 2: Hoop Dance, Gourd Dance, Rabbit Dance, Two-Step, Round Dance, Team dancing. VHS. 60 mins each. $19.95 each. VIP & WH.

NATIVE AMERICAN MYTHS
An animated film introduced by Native American narrator Ned Romero, who briefly explains the relevant background information for each of five authentic myths: Sky Woman, a Seneca myth; How Raven Gave Daylight to the World, Haida myth; The First Strawberry, Cherokee myth; The People Came Out of the Underworld, Hopi myth. 1976. 23 minutes. Color. Grades 4-12. 16mm. Rental, $21. PSU & UT.

THE NATIVE AMERICAN POWWOW
An introduction to the powwow and information guide on how to enjoy a powwow. Illustrates the variety of dances; history of the powwow, interviews with tribal elders. 1994. 58 mins. VHS, $29.95. AUDIO.

THE NATIVE AMERICAN SERIES
Consists of three films, helps young people understand the origin of the American Indians, and the effect the coming Europeans had on the Indians. Indian Origins - The First 50,000 Years; Indian Cultures - From 2000 B.C. to 1500 A.D.; and The Indian Experience - After 1500 A.D. 19 mins each, color. Video. Purchase: $305 each. BE.

NATIVE AMERICAN TALES
Video 1: The Dancing Stars (Iroquois) & The Friendly Wolf (Plains Indians); Video 2: The Fire Bringer (Paiute) & How Saynday Brought the Buffalo to the Indians (Kiowa); Video 3: The Angry Moon (Tlingit); Video 4: Coyote & Cottontail & Coyote and the Beaver People (Navajo). Grades K-5. Teacher's guide. 15 mins each. $125 each. AIT.

A NATIVE AMERICAN'S VIEW:
COLUMBUS & EUROPEAN SETTLEMENT
Native American storyteller, Helen Herrara Anderson, answers 9 questions about Columbus & European explorers commonly asked her by her students. Grades 4-7. 8 mins. VHS. 1992. $145. SH, NDM.

NATIVE AMERICAN WOMAN ARTISTS
A documentary, 2 vol. set explores southwestern art of pottery and textiles. 1998. 60 mins. VHS, $24.95. ME.

NATIVE AMERICANS
TBS Productions
The history of Native American peoples as told by Native American people. 8 hrs. VHS. Native Americans, P.O. Box 2203, S. Burlington, VT 05407.

NATIVE AMERICANS: MYTHS & REALITIES
Young Native men & women from various tribes are shown trying to change some of the stereotypes attributed to them throughout the years. Grades 6 and up. 1997. 16 mins. VHS. $95. CHAR.

NATIVE GRACE
A selection of prints of Native American peoples, landscapes, creatures and plants done by famous artists who recorded the earliest days of exploration in North America. 30 mins. $29.95. CH.

NATIVE INDIAN FOLKLORE
a 5-video compilation: Christmas at Moose Factory (James Bay); The Man, the Snake and the Fox (Ojibway legend); Medoonak the Stormmaker (Micmac legend); Salmon People (West Coast Indians); Summer Legend (Micmac legend). 1986. 71 minutes. Video. Purchase: $35. NFBC.

NATIVE LAND
How the history & legacy of these peoples have survived through their myths & art. 58 mins. 1999. VHS, $14.95. ME.

NATIVE LAND; NOMADS OF THE DAWN
Alvin H. Perlmutter, Producer
John Peaslee, Director
Jamake Highwater, Writer/host
Examines the history and culture of the Native Americans who discovered and civilized the North and South American continents. Focuses on the function of myths as the basis of cosmology of ancient (and contemporary) society. 1986. 58 minutes, color. Video. Purchase: $350; rental, $95. CG. Rental: $27.50. UMN.

NATURALLY NATIVE
Three enterprising Americn Indian women start a cosmetics line. With Irene Bedard & Valerie Red Horse. 1998. VHS, $29.95. ME.

NATWANIWA: A HOPI
PHILOSOPHICAL STATEMENT
Larry Evers, University of Arizona
With George Nasoftie, a ceremonial leader, talks of cultivation of the land—how every crop and action has significance for his future life. In Hopi with English subtitles. 27 minutes. Video. $175. NR.

NAVAJO
KBYU, Provo, Utah
Teaching children the way and heritage of the Navajo people. 1979. 29 minutes, color. Video. Purchase: $150; Rental: $40/week. NAPBC.

NAVAJO
The Navajos of the Grand Canyon. 16 minutes. Grades 7-12. 16mm. FILMS.

THE NAVAJO
Museum of Northern Arizona, Producer
Navajos tell their story of survival in northern Arizona. A child learns to tend sheep, a mother teaches how to card, spin, dye & weave wool for rugs. A family sacrifices a sheep. Story is cast against their history & vital role of women in religious, social & cultural life. 1990. 15 mins, color. Video. Purchase: $19.95. CAN.

THE NAVAJO
A visit to the Navajo Reservation in northeastern Arizona to discover the values held by this indigenous community. Navajo medical practices, religious rituals and beliefs are compared to modern practices, with a discussion of the problems of reconciling traditional Navajo ways with modern technology. 1959. 58 minutes, bxw. Grades 9 and up. Rental. UA & IU.

THE NAVAJO
Fred J. Pain, Jr.
The history, customs, and life of the Navajo Indian Nation (15 million acres within the Southwestern part of the U.S.) are described in this film. 1972. 21 mins, color. 16mm. Purchase: $300; video, $180. Rental: 16mm, $13.40. IU.

NAVAJO CANYON COUNTRY
Depicts the way of life of the Navajos and provides some of the historical background of Indian life in Arizona and New Mexico. 1954. 13 minutes. 16mm. Rental. IU & PSU.

NAVAJO CHILDREN
Deals with the semiannual migration of a Navajo family to its summer home. 1938. 11 mins, bxw. 16mm. Rental. UK.

NAVAJO CODE TALKERS
Tom McCarthy
Documentary using interviews and archival footage to show the vital role a small group of Navajo Marines

played in the South Pacific during World War II. Interviews with Peter McDonald, Navajo Chairman; Carl Gorman, artist & scholar; and R.C. Gorman, Taos artist. 1986. 28 mins, color. VHS, $24.95. ME, CAN, NAPBC, NMFV. Rental: $10. UMN.

NAVAJO COUNTRY
Shows the nomadic life of the Navajo Indian in northwestern Arizona. 1951. Grades 1-6. 10 mins, color. 16mm & video. Rental. UA & IU.

NAVAJO COYOTE TALES: LEGEND TO FILM
Animate in English and Navajo. Shows how coyote films were animated on computer. 1972. Grades 6 and up. 18 mins, color. 16mm. Purchase: 16mm, $260. SAN. Rental: SAN & UCLA.

NAVAJO FILMS THEMSELVES SERIES
Sol Worth & John Adair
Concerned with seeing how Navajo Indians, taught the technology of filmmaking might show a definite Navajo perspective in their films. Five films are descriptive of processes; two are concerned with man's relationship to nature. "A Navajo Weaver," by Susie Benally; "A Navajo Silversmith," by Johnny Nelson; "Old Antelope Lake," by Mike Anderson; "The Shallow Well Project," by Johnny Nelson; "Second Weaver," by Alta Kahn; and, "The Spirit of the Navajo," by Maxine & Mary Jane Tsosie. 1966. Grades 9 and up. 9-27 mins, bxw. Video. Purchase: $420 (3 cassettes); $85/title. MMA.

NAVAJO GIRL
Life on an Indian reservation in northeast Arizona. Focuses on the life of a ten year old girl and her family. 1973. 20 minutes. Grades 3-12. Purchase: VHS, $99. GA.

THE NAVAJO INDIAN
Provides a picture of the changing life styles of the Navajos who live on an Arizona reservation. 1975 revised edition. 10 mins, color. Grades K-6. Purchase: 16mm, $265; video, $59. PHOENIX. Rental only, $16.50. PSU; $9. IU.

NAVAJO INDIANS
Portrays the Navajos in their native environment. 1939. 11 minutes. Grades 4-9. 16mm/bxw. Rental. UA, PSU, UK & IU.

NAVAJO LIFE
Shows the National Monument of Canyon de Chelly, describing the life of the Navajo Indians living in the canyon. 1961. 9 mins, color. 16mm. Rental, $9.35. IU.

NAVAJO MEDICINE
hosted by West Studi
Documentary profiles Navajo health care by telling the stories of Navajo health care workers as they travel to remote health linics and care for their people. 1993. 30 mins. VHS. $89. CHAR.

NAVAJO MOON
This documentary-type story, photographed on the Navajo reservation in New Mexico, provides an inside look at the lives of three Navajo children. 28 minutes, color. Purchase: $89.95. FH.

THE NAVAJO MOVES
INTO THE ELECTRONIC AGE
Briefly describes the background of the Navajo before World War II. Then points out how the tribal council invested income from oil discoveries into projects to benefit the entire tribe. 19 minutes. 16mm. Rental. UK and UA.

NAVAJO NIGHT DANCES
Walter P. Lewisohn, Producer
Deals with a Navajo family at the Nine Day Healing Chant, a feast, and the Arrow, Feather and Fire Dance rituals. 1957. 12 minutes. 16mm. Rental: UK & UA.

NAVAJO - A PEOPLE BETWEEN TWO WORLDS
Francis R. Line
Effects of modern culture upon the largest remaining Indian tribe on a reservation in Arizona. 1958. 18 minutes. 16mm. Rental, $14. PSU.

NAVAJO, RACE FOR PROSPERITY
Document Associates & BBC
Offers a contemporary view of life on the Navajo reservation and focuses upon the development of industries on the reservation. 1972. 26 minutes, color. Purchase: 16mm, $400; video, $340. Rental, $55. CG.

NAVAJO ROUND DANCE
A group of Navajo high school students perform the traditional Navajo Round Dance. Navajo music soundtrack, no narration. 1971. 3 minutes, color. 16mm. Rental: $18. UCLA.

NAVAJO RUG WEAVING
Shows how the Navajo Indians weave their famous rugs. Explains the different operations; Provides a clase view of the weaving technique. 10 minutes, color, silent. 16mm. Rental: $21. UCLA.

NAVAJO: SHEPHERDS OF THE DESERT
Describes a day in the life of a typical Navajo family. 1970. 9 mins. Grades 4 and up. 16mm. Rental. UA.

NAVAJO SILVERSMITH
Traces a Navajo artisan's creation of some small Yeibachai figures from the mining of the silver to the finished works. 21 minutes, bxw. Grades 9 and up. Rental: 16mm, $15. PSU.

NAVAJO SILVERSMITHING
Focuses on a Navajo craftsman, Tom Burnside, on an Arizona reservation, who has come to grips with modern technology while still maintaining the values of his own culture. 1961. Grades 7 and up. 11 minutes, color. Rental: PSU, UCT & UA.

NAVAJO: A STUDY IN CULTURAL CONTRAST
Portrays the culture, social organization, and physical environment of the Navajo Indian. 1969. Grades 6 and up. 15 minutes, color. 16mm. Rental: PSU, UCT & IU.

NAVAJO: THE LAST RED INDIANS
Michael Baines
Contains scenes of Navajo ceremonies including diagnosing illnesses by trance-like hand trembling and a sing or healing ceremony. The integration of traditional healing practices with those of white doctors is shown. 1972. 35 mins, color. 16mm & video. TW & UA.

THE NAVAJO WAY
Robert Northshield, Director
Survival as a tribe within American society is said to come from the involvement with tradition, the Navajo way. Reflects the spiritual life of the traditional community. 1975. 52 minutes, color. 16mm. FILMS.

THE NAVAJOS & ANNIE WAUNEKA
Annie Wauneka, awarded the Freedom Medal by President Kennedy for her achievements in public health education among her fellow Navajo Indian, visits the homes of her people instructing them in simple health measures. 1965. 26 minutes. Grades 9-adult. 16mm. Rental. UA.

NAVAJOS OF THE 70's
Deals with the customs, history, economics, current problems and future prospects of the Navajo Indians. Grades 1-8. 15 minutes. 16mm. Rental: UK.

NAWATNIWA: A HOPI PHILOSOPHICAL STATEMENT
George Nasoftie
Ceremonial leader from Shongopavi relates the Hopi ceremonial cycle to agriculture and the sacred teachings. 1978. 20 minutes. Video. With I'isaw: Hopi Coyote Stories - two programs on one tape. Rental, $52.50. ATL.

NEHI CHEII TOAD COUNTS HIS CORN
Math concept of place value taught using coyote and toad. Available in English and Navajo version. Animated. Ten minutes. Grades 2-8. 16mm & video. Rental, $10/week. SAN.

NESHNABEK: THE PEOPLE
Gene Bernofsky; Donald Stull, Project Director
Based on footage of the Prairie Band Potawatomi of Kansas by amateur anthropologist Floyd Schultz between 1927-1941, this film was edited & supplied with a soundtrack based on recent interviews with elderly Potawatomi. Covers reservation life, culture and the people. 1979. 30 mins, 16mm, bxw. STULL, UK & KS.

NETSILIK ESKIMO 1
Gilles Blais, Director
A 2-part video: 1) The Eskimo: Fight for Life, 51 minutes - This ethnographic documentary studies the traditional forms of play, work and education of the Netsilik Inuit during their last migratory camp in the 1960s; and 2) The Netsilik Eskimo Today, 18 minutes - shows the actual life of an Eskimo family in the settlement of Pelly Bay inside the Arctic Circle. Purchase: $35. NFBC.

NETSILIK ESKIMO SERIES
Quenten Brown, Ph.D., Director
Nine films in 21 half-hour parts. Titles include: "At The Autumn River Camp": Two Parts: Part 1, In late autumn, the Inuit travel through soft snow and build karmaks in the river valley. Fishing through ice. 26 minutes. Part 2, The men build an igloo, make a sleigh; women work on parka; children play. 33 minutes. "At The Caribou Crossing Place": Two Parts: Part 1, Early autumn; caribou hunting and skins. 30 minutes. Part 2, Caribou hunting. 29 minutes. "At The Spring Sea Ice Camp": Three Parts: Part 1, Two Inuit families travel across the wide sea ice; build small igloos. 27 minutes. Part 2, The men hunt seal through ice, then skin it. 27 minutes. Part 3, Hunting and fishing; women sewing; breaking camp moving ashore to tents for summer. 27 minutes. "At The Winter Sea Ice Camp": Four Parts: Part 1, Seal hunting; making camp for winter. 36 minutes. Part 2, Women with furs; men hunting; children play; games. 36 minutes. Part 3, Community igloos; games; hunting and fishing. 30 minutes. Part 4, Family activities; games and music. 35 minutes. "Building A Kayak": Two Parts: Part 1, Summer, ice melts, time to build a kayak. 33 minutes. Part 2, Building a Kayak. 33 minutes. "Stalking Seal On The Spring Ice": Two Parts. Part 1, Seal hunt and skinning; use of fur and meat. 25 minutes. Part 2, Seal hunt. 34 minutes. "The Eskimo: Fight For Life; "People of the Seal: Eskimo Summer/Winter"; "Yesterday, Today: The Netsilik Eskimo". 1969. Grades 7-adult. 16mm & video. Purchase: $145 each; rental: $30. DER, CDA & UEVA. Rental: UCT, IU & PSU.

THE NEW CAPITALISTS: ECONOMICS IN INDIAN COUNTRY
Portrays developments on some 30 reservations from Alaska to Florida. Examines the quantum leap into the 20th century being made by Native Americans. Provides insight into Native American culture. Narrated by Eric Sevareid. Adult. 1984. 60 minutes. Color. 3/4" and 1/2" Video. Free loan to Indian organizations and the business and investment community. Purchase: 3/4" - $75, 1/2" $55. OP.

THE NEW INDIANS
Shows a young Creek woman as she attends an intertribal conference; a Kwakiutl chief; a Navajo woman attorney; etc. 1977. 59 minutes. Purchase: 16mm, $595; video, $545. NGS.

THE NEW PEQUOT - A TRIBAL PORTRAIT
Connecticut Public Television, Producer
A documentary exploring the history & future of Connecticut's Mashantucket Pequot Indians. 1989. 60 mins. Color. Video. $150; Rental: $80. NAPBC.

NEZ PERCE - PORTRAIT OF A PEOPLE
Deals with the cultural heritage of the Nez Perce and shows how the Nez Perce National Historical Park has influenced and preserved that culture. 23 minutes, color. Rental: Video, $10. UCT.

NI'BTHASKA OF THE UMONHON - A SERIES
Chet Kincaid, Producer
A three-program series about a 13 year-old boy from the Omaha tribe as he goes through the first summer of his manhood. Program 1: Turning of the Child; Program 2: Becoming a Warrior; Program 3: The Buffalo Hunt. 1987. 30 minutes each. Color. Purchase: $150 each; Rental: $40 each, $80/series. NAPBC.

NINOS NAVAJOS
Spanish language film. 11 mins. 16mm/bxw. Rental. UA.

NINSTINTS: SHADOW KEEPERS OF THE PAST
Spreitz-Husband Productions
'Ninstints' located on Anthony Island, is the site of the last stand of totem poles anywhere on the Northwest Coast still remaining in their original location. The Haida abandoned the village in the late 1800's after falling prey to the white man's diseases and the intrusion of his lifestyle into the wider Haida culture. A study guide is available with the film. 1983. 28 mins. 16mm & video. Purchase or rental. CFDW.

NISHNAWBI-ASKI: THE PEOPLE & THE LAND
Phyllis Wilson, Director
Illustrates the different ways the Cree and Ojibway of the Nishnawbi-Aski region are reacting to change. 1977. 28 minutes. Video. Purchase: $27. NFBC.

NO ADDRESS
Alanis Obomsawin, Director/writer
Focuses on the young native people who are homeless in Montreal. Describes three organizations that are helping the homeless of Montreal: the Montreal Native Friendship Centre, Dernier Recours, and La Mission Colombe. 1988. 56 minutes, color. Purchase: 16mm, $775; VHS, $350. Rental: $80. NFBC.

NOMADIC INDIANS OF THE WEST: THE LEGACY OF THE AMERICAN INDIANS
Camera One, Producer; hosted by Wes Studi
The world of the Plains Indians; examines the legends & cultures of the various tribes. Ancient America Series. 1994. 60 minutes. $20. CAN & WKV.

THE NORTH AMERICAN INDIAN
Narrated by Marlon Brando
In three parts: Part 1: Treaties Made, Treaties Broken—presents the conflict between the Nisqually and Washington State over fishing rights. 18 minutes. Part 2: How the West Was Won, And Honor Lost—presents a chronology of Indian-white relations from the landing of Columbus to the defeat of Geronimo in 1866. 25 minutes. Part 3: Lament of the Reservation—presents the living conditions of the Sioux Indians on Pine Ridge Reservation in the Badlands of South Dakota. Also looks at another reservation in Washington State where suicide is above the national average. 1970. 24 minutes. Music by Buffy St. Marie. Grades 6 and up. 16mm. Rental: $18 each. UMN, IU & PSU.

NORTH AMERICAN INDIAN ARTS & CRAFTS SERIES
Geoff Voyce
Commissioned by the Canadian National Indian Arts & Crafts Corporation, these film shows individual artists in their local setting and their artistic processes examined. The following films are available in English, French and Indian languages. A collection of ethnographic documentaries on outstanding Native American artists & artisans. Each artist recounts the history of their people and their craft while they work. A Teacher's Guide contains 200+ pp. of craft activities, history, maps, glossaries, print & non-print bibliographies (free with purchase of two or more videos. The titles include: A Pair of Moccasins for Mary Thomas, 15 minutes, (Shuswap); A Corn Husk Doll by Deanna Skye, 11 minutes (Cayuga); A Malecite Fancy Basket, 12 minutes (Malecite-Canada); A Moon Mask by Freda Deising, 10 minutes (Haida); Beads & Leather of Manitoba, 18 minutes (Cree-Canada); A Willow Basket by Florine Hotomani, 11 minutes (Assiniboine-Canada); Tony Hunt, a Kwakiutl Artist, 10 minutes; Joe Jacobs - Stone Carver, 11 minutes (Cayuga); Porcupine Quill Work, 11 minutes (Odawa-Canada); A Micmac Scale Basket, 12 minutes (Micmac-Canada); A Ceremonial Pipe by Guy Siwi, 10 minutes (Abenaki); Robert Bellegard, a Prairie Artist, 12 minutes (Cree-Canada); Sara Smith, Mohawk Potter, 18 minutes (Mohawk); Birch Bark Biting by Angelique Mirasty, 6 minutes (Cree-Canada); Wooden Flowers of Nova Scotia by Matilda Paul, 14 minutes (Micmac-Canada); Iroquoian Pottery by Bill Parker, 18 minutes; A Silver Chalice by Jeff Gabriel, 10 minutes (Mohawk); Fort Albany Carver, Lawrence Mark, 14 minutes (Cree-Canada). 1977-1979. Purchase: VHS, $49 each; 16mm, $129 each. Rental: $40 each. AMP & ITFE.

NORTH AMERICAN INDIAN LEGENDS
Dramatizes several Indian legends with special effects photography to emphasize their mythical quality. 1973.

21 mins, color. Grades 1-8. 16mm, $435; VHS; $275; Rental, $65. PHOENIX. Rental. IU and UA.

NORTH AMERICAN INDIAN TODAY
Covers contemporary attitudes of Indians as well as their cultural past. 1977. 25 minutes. Purchase: 16mm, $395; video, $360. NGS.

NORTH AMERICAN INDIANS & EDWARD S. CURTIS
Teri C. McLuhan, Producer/director
Focuses on Edward S. Curtis (1868-1952), photographer, whose life work was concerned with preserving a record of North American Indians & Alaskan Eskimos. 1985. 30 mins. Color. 16mm, 3/4" video. PHOENIX.

NORTH OF 60: DESTINY UNCERTAIN
TV Ontario, Producer
Five 30 minute programs exploring areas of Canada's Northwest Territories, the Yukon and Alaska. Depicts the reality of life in the far north, and the future of this land and the culture of its original inhabitants. 1983. 28 1/2 mins each. Color. See NAPBC for titles & prices.

NORTHERN GAMES
Traditional games of the Inuit. 1981. 25 mins. VHS. $27. NFBC.

THE NORTHERN LIGHTS
Alan Booth, Director
Explores the phenomenon of the aura borealis and illustrates how the legends & tales of the indigenous people of the north have helped us to understand the lights. 1993. 48 minutes. Purchase: 16mm, $710; VHS, $300. Rental: $70. NFBC.

NORTHWEST ARCTIC VIDEO
Bob Walker, Director
The Northwest Arctic Television Center at Kotzebue, Alaska, produces programs about cultural, social, and political issues pertinent to the region, including documentaries of traditional skills, public affairs programs, and looks at specific aspects of cultural transition in Inupiat Eskimo culture; programs on Inuit studies are also available. Series include: The Alaska Native Claims Settlement Act Series; Inupiat Legends of the Northwest Arctic Series; Traditional Inupiat Eskimo Health Series; Traditional Inupiat Eskimo Technology Series. For a complete list of programs contact NATC.

NORTHWEST COAST INDIANS: A SEARCH FOR THE PAST
Louis and Ruth Kirk
Archaeologists and students reconstruct the Ozette Indian Village at Cape Alava, Washington, an abandoned seafaring hunter's village site. 1973. 26 mins. Purchase: 16mm, $340; VHS, $200; VHS, $200. UW.

NORTHWEST INDIAN ART
Walter P. Lewisohn, Producer
Shows material collected from six different museums, including double-faced mechanical masks. 1966. Ten minutes. 16mm. Rental. UK.

NORTHWESTERN AMERICAN INDIAN WAR DANCE CONTEST
Covers an annual contest portraying The War Dance, The Feather Dance, The Fancy Dance, and The Hoop Dance. 1971. 12 minutes. Purchase: 16mm, $200; VHS, $150; VHS, $140. UW.

NOW & FOREVER
Shows scenes of Oregon Indians from 1915 to 1945. 80 minutes/bxw. Rental. OHS.

NOW THAT THE BUFFALO'S GONE
Shows how Europeans, who came to America looking for freedom of speech and religion, forgot those freedoms when it came to the Indians. 1991. 20 mins, color. Video. $149; rental, $75. FH. Rental: 16mm, $13.40.

NOW THAT THE BUFFALO'S GONE
Ross Deveish, Director
Analyzes the history of massacres, broken promises, worthless treaties, and land-grabbing that the Indian nations as a whole have suffered. Narrated by Marlon Brando. 1969. 65 minutes, color. Grades 9 and up. Purchase: 16mm, $995; video, 225. Rental, $80/3

days. MG. Rental only: 16mm, $35.50; VHS, $23. PSU.Rental: 16mm, $20. UCLA.

NUHONIYEH: OUR STORY
Mary & Allen Code
Explores the history & current circumstances of the Sayisi Dene, "a people of the ecological & cultural borderlands between Tundra & forest in Canada. 1993. 55 minutes. VHS. Purchase: $245; rental: $60. DER.

OBSIDIAN POINT-MAKING
Clyde B. Smith, Producer
A Tolowa Indian demonstrates an ancient method of fashioning an arrow point from obsidian. Describes various tribes' folklore customs connected with obsidian-chipping and explains the significance, history, and uses of obsidian points. 1964. 13 minutes, color. Purchase: 16mm, $280; video, $195. Rental: 16mm, $45. UC. Video rental, $19.50. PSU.

OJIBWAY & CREE CULTURAL CENTRE VIDEO
Dennis Austin, Executive Producer
Since 1979, the Ojibway and Cree Cultural Centre in Timmins, Ontario, has produced over 25 videotapes which portray traditional craft techniques, tales, and profiles of elders. The programs reflect the heritage of Indians in eastern Canada. For a complete list of programs contact O&C.

OLD DANCES, NEW DANCERS
Documents the first annual Young People's Eskimo Dance Awareness Festival organized at Chevak, Alaska. 1984. 30 minutes. VHS. $24.95. KYUK.

OMAHA TRIBE - FILM SERIES
David Conger, Director
Documentary of Native American life on a reservation presented through portraits of several Omaha people of
different ages. The Land, The People, and The Family. 1979. 30 minutes each. Color. 16mm and video. Purchase: $50 each; $105/series. GPN, NETV.

ON THE PATH TO SELF-RELIANCE
Peter J. Barton Productions
Narrated by James Billie, Chairman of the Seminole Tribe of Florida, this film provides an overview of tribal history and current tribal economic development. 1982. 45 minutes. Color. Video. Rental: $80/week. NAPBC.

ON THE SPRING ICE
Walrus as well as whales are hunted by the Eskimos of Gambell on St. Lawrence Island. 45 minutes, color. Purchase: 16mm, $700; video, $245. Rental: 16mm, $70; video, $40. DER.

1,000 YEARS OF MUSCOGEE (CREEK) ART
Gary Robinson, Producer
Traces the development of Creek Indian art forms from the prehistoric period of the mound-builders to the present. Examines over 175 examples of Creek art. 1982. 28 minutes. Color. Video. Rental: $40/week. NAPBC.

ONENHAKENRA: WHITE SEED
Frank Semmons, Producer/director/camera
Explores the development of Iroquois culture; focuses on corn and people's reflections on its use as a way of presenting the audience with a view of Mohawk traditions. Features local people of Akwesasne. 1984. 20 minutes. Color. 16mm, 3/4" and 1/2" video. AM.

THE ORIGIN OF THE CROWN DANCE: AN APACHE NARRATIVE & BA'TS'OOSEE: AN APACHE TRICKSTER CYCLE
Larry Evers, University of Arizona
With Rudoplh Kane. In Apache with English subtitles. 40 minutes. VHS. Purchase: $220. NR. Rental: $52.50. ATL.

ORIGINS
Takes the viewer across the continent looking at the history, geography, language and circumstance, and the roles each had in naming the places we all know. Includes the legacy of Indian languages (26 of the United States have Indian names.) 1989. 30 minutes, color. Video. Purchase: $30. COP.

OSCAR HOWE: THE SIOUX PAINTER
KUSD-TV, Producer
Vincent Price adds his narrative to the personal commentary of Oscar Howe, focusing on his art, philosophy and cultural heritage, as he designs and paints the brilliant Sioux Eagle Dancer. 1973. 27 minutes. Color. Grades 9-adult. 16mm and video. PHOENIX. Purchase: $150; Rental: $40. NAPBC.

THE OTHER SIDE OF THE LEDGER: AN INDIAN VIEW OF THE HUDSON'S BAY COMPANY
Martin Defalco and Willie Dunn, Directors
Presents the view of spokesmen for Canadian Indian and Metis groups. With archival materials and contemporary examples, this film includes scenes from a conference in which Hudson's Bay Co. officials respond to Native people's objections. 1972. 42 minutes. Video. Purchase: $27. NFBC.

OUR LAND, OUR TRUTH
Maurice Bulbulian, Director
Ethnographic description of the Inuit of James Bay. 1983. 54 minutes. Video. Purchase: $27. NFBC.

OUR LIVES IN OUR HANDS
Karen Carter & Harold Prins, Producers
Karen Carter, Director
Presents the story of the Micmac basketmakers of Aroostook Co., Maine, focusing on Donald Sanipass, and members of his extended family.Touches on survival of their language and tribal lands. 1986. 49 minutes, color. Purchase: 16mm, $700; video, $145. Rental: 16mm, $70; video-3/4" and 1/2", $40. DER.

OUR PROUD LAND
Written and narrated from the Navajo point of view, this film presents a number of sequences of modern day life of the Navajo Indians. 30 minutes. 16mm. Rental. UK.

OUR SACRED LAND
Chris Spotted Eagle, Producer/director
Focuses on the story of the continuing struggle of the Sioux to regain the Black Hills of South Dakota. Examines the reasons why many Sioux have refused to accept the $105 million recently awarded by the Federal Government for the lands confiscated. 1984. 28 minutes, color. 16mm & Video. Purchase: $290. NAPBC & SE. Rental: $10. HO & IN.

OUR SONGS WILL NEVER DIE
Yurok, Karuk & Tolowa cultural summer camps are established for the purpose of reconstructing early village dance sites. 35 minutes. Video. Purchase: $245; rental: $45. SH.

OUR TOTEM IS THE RAVEN
Features Chief Dan George in a contemporary tale of a young Indian boy's initiation into manhood and his acceptance of his Indian heritage. 1972. 21 mins, color. Purchase: 16mm, 435; Video, $250; Rental, $58. PHOENIX. Rental: $14. IU & UMN.

OUR YOUTH, OUR FUTURE
About a bicultural drug and alcohol treatment center in Shiprock, New Mexico that serves Native American youth. 2000. 35 mins. VHS. $100. CHAR.

OURS TO CARE FOR
Emphasizes the special importance of good nutrition during pregnancy for the contemporary Native American woman. 6 mins. VHS. $75; renatl, $25. SH.

THE OWL & THE LEMMING: AN ESKIMO LEGEND
Co. Hoedeman, Director
An example of the Inuit art and folklore. 1971. 6 mins. All ages. Purchase: 16mm, $150; video, $150. Rental, $35. NFBC. 16mm rental only, $8.70. IU.

THE OWL & THE RAVEN: AN ESKIMO LEGEND
Co Hoedeman, Director
An Inuit legend is retold using puppets of sealskin in traditional Inuit design and accompanied by a music track of Inuit songs. 1974. 7 mins. Grades 1-6. All ages. 16mm, $200; VHS, $150. Rental, $35. NFBC.

THE OWL WHO MARRIED A GOOSE:
AN ESKIMO LEGEND
Caroline Leaf, Director
An example of commitment and love. 1974. 8 mins, b&w. All ages. 16mm & video. C M. Rental, $14. PSU.

PABLITA VELARDE
Irene-Aimee Depke, Producer
Santa Clara Indian artist Pablita Velarde reminisces about her childhood at the Pueblo, her struggling years in a medium traditionally closed to Indian women, her philosophy and her existence in the white man's world, away from the pueblo. She demonstrates her "earth painting" technique, which begins with her gathering the stones and minerals from New Mexico soil. She closes with a visit to a classroom of first-graders, where she tells them a Santa Clara legend, "Why the Coyote Bays at the Moon." 29 mins, color. Video. DEPKE.

PADDLE TO SEATTLE
Mark Mascarin, Producer/Director
Documents a cooperative project undertaken by the Quileute & Hoh peoples of La Push, Washington, namely to embark on a journey made many times by their ancestors - a six day, 170 mile "paddle to Seattle." 1990. Grades 9-12. 45 mins, color. Video. Purchase: $78. QTS.

PAGES ON THE PAST
A series of four films which tell the story of the peoples of the Pacific Northwest from the time of the Ice Age to the coming of Lewis and Clark. An Age of Ice: How the peoples of the Northwest adapted and endured; After the Flood: Floods 13,000 years ago signalling the end of the Ice Age; Landmarks In Time: The time of the eruption of Mt. Mazama about 7,000 years ago; and, History In the Making: Portrays the expansion of Native American civilization throughout the region up to the coming of Lewis and Clark. Study guide and maps. 30 mins each. Grades 9 and up. Purchase: 16mm, (An Age of Ice only) $450; video, $250 each ($900/series). Rental: 16mm & video, $50/week. TBM.

PAHA SAPA: THE STRUGGLE
FOR THE BLACK HILLS
Mel Lawrence, Director; Cis Wilson, Exec. Producer
Story of the Lakota Sioux' struggle to get their sacred lands back. Told by Lakota Sioux and Cheyenne storytellers. The speakers recount the legends, customs, and history of their people. Includes archival paintings, photos, early documentaries and newsreels. Nominated for an Emmy in 1993. 60 mins. Color. VHS. $34.95. MFV.

CYNTHIA ANN PARKER: BLUE EYED COMANCHE
Jillian Preet, Writer/ Editor/Narrator
Story about a settler child who was abducted by the Comanche Indians. Archival photos & paintings evoke the triumph & tragedy of the American frontier. 1987. Grades 4 and up. 12 mins, color. Video. Purchase: $49. FI.

THE PATH OF OUR ELDERS
Several Pomo elders portray a way of life that has been handed down throughout the generations. 1986. Grades 4 and up. 20 mins, color. Video. Purchase: $245; rental: $45. SH. Rental: $20.50. UMN.

PAUL KANE GOES WEST
Gerald Budner, Director
Artist Paul Kane traveled Canada in the mid-19th century depicting the Indians through his sketches and paintings. 1972. 14 mins. Grades 4-12. Video. NFBC.

PEACEFUL ONES
Shows life and customs of the Hopi in the painted desert, including cultivating the land, harvesting crops, weaving, kachinas, and snake dance. 1953. 12 mins. Grades 4-adult. 16mm. Rental. UT, PSU and UA.

THE PEOPLE (INDIAN)
An analysis of Indian literature. 1981. 30 mins, video. KS.

THE PEOPLE AT DIPPER
Richard Gilbert, Jack Olfield
Shows life among the Chippewayan Indians of a reserve in northern Saskatchewan. 1966. 18 mins. Video. Purchase: $27. NFBC.

PEOPLE OF THE BUFFALO
Austin Campbell
Dramatic contemporary paintings of life on the Western Plains, portray the unique relationship between the Indians and buffalo. 1968 revised edition. 14 minutes, color. Grades 5 and up. Rental. PSU, IU, & UA.

PEOPLE OF THE FIRST LIGHT
WGBY-TV Springfield, Mass.
7-29 minute films about Native Americans living in Rhode Island, Massachusetts and Connecticut: The Narragansetts, Pequots, Wampanoags, Mohegans, Nipnucs and Paugausetts, descendents of the original Eastern Woodland Algonquin Indians. Indians In Southern New England (The Survivors); The Wampanoags of Gay Head (Community Spirit and Island Life); The Boston Indian Community (Change and Identity); The Narragansett (Tradition); Indians of Connecticut (The Importance of Land); The Indian Experience: Urban and Rural (Survival); The Mashpee Wampanoags (Tribal Identity.) 1979. Color. Video. GPN and NAPBC.

PEOPLE OF KASHUNUK
A family portrait through sight & sound of the Yup'ik Eskimo village of Chevak. 1983. 30 minutes. VHS. $24.95. KYUK.

PEOPLE OF THE MACON PLATEAU
Introduction to the Indian cultures of the Macon Plateau with emphasis on the Mississippian Indian culture. Grades 7 and up. 12 mins, color. Video. RentaL $10. UCT.

PEOPLE OF THE SEAL
Michael McKennirey & George Pearson, Producers
Part I: Eskimo Summer - Documents the summer activities of th Netsilik Inuit, which take place on the land. Part II: Eskimo Winter - Search for seal holes; building igloos; seal hunting. 1971. 52 mins each. Grades 7-adult. Video. Purchase: $27 each. NFBC. 16mm & video, EDC.

PEOPLE OF THE SUN: THE TIGUAS OF YSLETA
Documentary surveying the history of the Tigua Indians as they struggle to gain recognition as a tribe & walk the fine line between being Texans in El Paso & Pueblo Indians. Teacher's guide. 56 mins. $45. UT-ITC.

PEPPER'S POW POW
Salmon Run Productions
Documents the enduring musical and cultural legacy of Jim Pepper, a contemporary jazz musician who was an innovator in jazz-rock fusion as well as world music. 1995. Grades 5 and up. 57 mins. Color. Video. $50. OY.

THE PEYOTE ROAD
Gary Rhine, Producer/Director
A feature length documentary exploring the history of the use of the cactus Peyote as a religious sacrament by North American Indigenous people. Interviews with experts Dr. Huston Smith, Dr. Milner Ball and NAC Roadman Reuben Snake. 1993. 60 mins, color. VHS. $29.95. ME. Rental, $45. KF.

PETROGLYPHS: IMAGES IN STONE
Marianne Kaplan
A documentary focusing on the petroglyphs of the Coastal Salish, Kwakiutl and West Coast People and uses the carvings to depict their rituals and myth. 1985. 10 mins. 16mm or video. Purchase or rental. CFDW.

PINE NUTS
Clyde B. Smith, Producer
Members of the Paviotso and Paiute tribes demonstrate how the pine nut, from the pinon tree, were harvested and prepared as food, using ancient techniques. 1961. 13 mins, color. Purchase: 16mm, $280; video, $195. Rental: 16mm, $45, UC. Rental only: Video, $15.50. PSU.

PLAINS INDIAN WAR BONNET:
HISTORY & CONSTRUCTION
Full Circle Communications
Explores the tradition and significance of this honored symbol of Native America. Includes the history and development along with close-ups of bonnets from the Gilcrease Collection. Construction is shown step-by-step. 45 minutes. VHS. $19.95. WH.

PLAINS MOCCASINS
Vicki Little Coyote
Step-by-step procedure to making moccasins worn by the Southern Cheyenne. She demonstrates simple techniques. VHS. 86 minutes. $19.95. VIP.

PLAY & CULTURAL CONTINUITY:
Part 4, MONTANA INDIAN CHILDREN
On the Flathead Indian Reservation and surrounding countryside, the play of Indian children ranges from the universal domestic activities and monster play themes of those mirroring individualistic cultural elements, such as wrapping of babies, drumming, singing, and hunting. 1975. 29 minutes, color. 16mm rental, $17.50. PSU.

POCAHONTAS
A&E Home Video
Biography. 1995. 50 mins. VHS. $19.99. ME.

POINTY SIDE UP: AN EASY
WAY TO SET UP YOUR TIPI
Step-by-step video. VHS. 60 mins. $17.95. WH.

POMO BASKETWEAVERS:
A TRIBUTE TO THREE ELDERS
This three-part series provides an in-depth introduction to the culture, history, and basketweaving traditions of the Pomo. Part 1: The People, the Baskets - presents an overview of Pomo culture & features a portrait of basketweaver, Laura Somersal. An introduction to Pomo basketweaving, showing the varies types of styles & different techniques. Part 2: A History of Change, a Continuing Tradition - recounts the history of the Pomo & explores the changes in the art & traditions of Pomo basketweaving. Features a biographical tribute to Elsie Allen, one of the most revered of all Pomo basketweavers. Part 3: The People, the Plants, and the Rules - examines the close relationship of the Pomo to their environment & explores the spiritual rules & responsibilities of the Pomo to the natural world. Features a portrait of Mabel McKay, a famed dream weaver & Indian doctor. 1994. 29 minutes each. Video. Purchase: $175 each; rental: $50 each. UC.

POMO SHAMAN
William Heick, Producer
A shortened version of the complete research documentary, "Sucking Doctor." The second and final night of a shamanistic curing ceremony among the Kashia group of Southwestern Pomo Indians. 1964. 20 minutes, bxw. Purchase: 16mm, $410; Video, $195. Rental, $50. UC. 16mm rental: $14,50. PSU & IU.

PORTAGE
Reviews the history of Canadian fur trapping and shows the building of a birch bark canoe by Indian craftsmen. 1941. 22 minutes, color. Grades 6 and up. 16mm. Rental, $12.75. IU.

PORTRAIT OF LUCY SWAN
Elderly Lucy Swan, Cheyenne River Sioux, reminisces about family and tribal history. Illustrates past/present living conditions on the reservation. Adult. 30 minutes. 16mm. Rental, $15. NILB.

POSITIVELY NATIVE
Portrays stereotypes and how Indians really live through the eyes of two teens, a Native American boy and his friend Sam of Korean descent. Grades 4-7. 1992. 15 mins. VHS. $95. CHAR.

POTLATCH PEOPLE
Document Associates & BBC
Presents the Indians of the Pacific Northwest and the ceremonial potlatch feast. 1972. 26 minutes, color. Purchase: 16mm, $400; video, $340. Rental, $55. CG.

POTLATCH: A STRICT LAW BIDS US DANCE
Dennis Wheeler, Director
Features the outlawed Kwakiutl Potlatch ceremony. The confiscation of an enormous and valuable collection of dancing masks and costumes. Shows a Potlatch given by the Cranmer family. Narrated by Gloria Cranmer Webster. 1975. 53 minutes. 16mm & video. Purchase or rental. CFDW.

POUNDMAKER'S LODGE: A HEALING PLACE
Alanis Obomsawin, Director
Drug and alcohol abuse and treatment in St. Albert, Alberta. 1987. 29 minutes. Video. Purchase: $27. NFBC.

POW-WOW!
Displays North American Indian dances at a gathering of more than 20 tribes. Chiricahua Apaches perform their ancient sacred Fire Dance; Comanches execute the Gourd Dance; the Intertribal Dance; and, the War Dance. Indians speak of their traditions, ceremonies and heritage. Grades 7-12. 1980. 16 minutes. Purchase: 16mm, $375; video, $59. PHOENIX. Rental: $16mm, $20. UMN.

POW WOW: A NATIVE AMERICAN GATHERING
Documentary of intertribal gathering...ceremonies and traditions. Grades 5 and up. 30 mins. $70. CHAR.

POWWOW AT DUCK LAKE
Bonnie Sherr Klein, Director
A discussion at Duck Lake, Saskatchewan, where Indian-Metis problems are openly and strongly presented before a gathering of Metis Indians and Whites. 1967. 14 minutes. Video. Purchase: $22. NFBC.

POWWOW TRAIL SERIES
11 episodes filmed over a 2-year period produced for Canada's CBC-TV network, an episode every two months. Episode 1: The Drum, 60 mins. 2004; Episode 2: The Songs, 60 mins. 2004; The Dance, 60 mins. 2004; Episode 4: The Grand Entry, 60 mins. 2004; seven more episodes to follow throughout 2005. DVD only, $18.99 each. ME.

THE POWER OF THE WORD WITH BILL MOYERS: 3 - ANCESTRAL VOICES
Features three poets with distinctive heritages that ionfluence their work: Joy Harjo (Creek-Cherokee), Garrett Hongo (Japanese-American), and Mary TallMountain (Native American born in Alaska.) 1989. 58 minutes, color. Video rental, $12. PSU.

POWERLESS POLITICS
Sandy Johnson Osawa—KNBC-TV, Producer
Provides an overview of the legal relationship between the U.S. and Indian tribes showing how shifts and emphasis in the government Indian policy have had far reaching effects on Indian life. 1975. 28 minutes. Video. Purchase: $55. BYU-N.

PREHISTORIC MAN
Traces the development of the Indians in the American West. 1967. Grades 7 and up. 17 minutes, color. Rental. UA & UCT.

PRIDE, PURPOSE & PROMISE: PAIUTES OF THE SOUTHWEST
Mitchell Fox, Producer/writer
Interviews with tribal leaders and members of the Kaibab Reservation in Arizona, the Shivwits Reservation in Utah, and the Moapa Reservation in Nevada. Discusses Southern Paiute tribal self-determination, tribal lands, history, education and economic development, and the present day Indian reservation life. 1984. 28 mins, color. VHS. Rental: $40. NAPBC.

THE PRIMAL MIND
Alvin H. Perlmutter, Producer
Jamake Highwater, Writer/host
Documentary which explores the basic differences between Native American and Western cultures, while examining two cultures' contrasting views of nature, time, space, art, archaeology, dance and language. 1984. 58 mins, color. VHS, $19.99. ME. Rental: 16mm, $100. CG. Rental: VHS, $39. SH, PSU.

PRINCESS OF THE POW-WOW
A documentary focusing on Ella Aquino, a Lummi Indian woman, who has devoted her life toward the advancement of Indian culture and concerns. Examines issues of battles over land and fishing rights on behalf of the Puget Sound Indians. 22 mins. Color. Video. Purchase: $50. GPN.

THE PROBABLE PASSING OF ELK CREEK
Rob Wilson, Director
Documentary focusing on the controversy between a

little town, Elk Creek, and the Grindstone Indian Reservation over a government planned reservoir. 1983. 60 mins, color. Purchase: 16mm, $895; 3/4" and 1/2" video, $350. Rental, $95. CG. NAPBC (members only).

THE PSORIASIS RESEARCH PROJECT - A CREE HEALER
Documents the healer's treatment practices under controlled conditions in a western health clinic. It also shows treatment of the same patients in a more traditional sweatlodge ceremony. 1985. 35 minutes. Color. Video-3/4" U-Matic, $125; VHS, Beta, $100. In A CREE HEALER, which serves as an introduction to the psoriasis video, Russell Willier talks about traditional native medicine and the controversies he has encountered in openly discussing this subject. 1985. 22 minutes. Color. Video. 3/4" U-Matic, $100; VHS, Beta, $75. Combines on One Tape, 3/4" U-Matic, $200, and VHS, Beta, $150. UADA.

PUEBLO BOY
Tells the story of a young Indian boy being instructed in the ancient and modern ways and traditions of his people, the Pueblos of the Southwest. 24 minutes. 16mm. Rental. UK.

PUEBLO INDIANS OF TAOS, NM
1927 documentary of of the lives, customs and characters of the Pueblos of the area and some of the whites who lived among them. 10 minutes, bxw. EG.

THE PUEBLO PEOPLES: FIRST CONTACT
George Burdeau, Director; co-produced
with Larry Walsh; hosted by Conroy Chino
Describes the early encounter between this peaceful Indian tribe and the distructive Spanish explorer Coronado. Told through the images and legends of the Pueblo people. 1990. 30 minutes, color. Video. Purchase: $50. PBS. Rental: Video, $14. PSU.

THE PUEBLO PRESENCE
Hugh and Suzanne Johnston, WNET-13
Examines the continuity of ancient Pueblo civilization into the present. Zuni historian Andrew Napetcha discusses the ancestry of Pueblo peoples. Art, religion, ceremonials, language, architecture, and daily activities and relationship to the natural world. 1981. 58 minutes. 16mm and VHS. JOHNSTON.

PUEBLO RENAISSANCE
Philip Hobel, Executive Producer
Provides an authentic view of the sacred traditions, ancient religious and agricultural ceremonies of the Pueblo people. 1972. 26 minutes, color. Purchase: 16mm, $400; video, $295. Rental, $55. CG and IU.

THE PUEBLO EXPERIENCE: MAKING A NEW WORLD
Richard Marquand, Director/Producer
The story of a 17 year-old girl, Charity, in Puritan Massachusetts in 1640. Captured by the Indians then returned, Charity rebels against the Puritan doctrine and treatment of the Indians. 1975. 31 minutes. All ages. Purchase: 16mm, $425; rental, $40. LCA.

QAGGIQ
Zacharias Kunuk, Producer/director
A drmatization of past Arctic life, directed by an Inuit videomaker & improvised by Igloolik community members, far-flung families arrive via dogsled for a joyful reunion. 1989. 58 minutes, color. Video. Purchase: $1,250. IIP.

QUEEN VICTORIA & THE INDIANS
Animated film adaptation is based on a true story by noted American artist George Catlin. In the late 1840's a small group of Ojibwes journeyed to London to dance at the opening of the Indian Gallery. Grades 4-9. 11 minutes. Purchase: 16mm, $240; VHS, $89; 3/4", $119. CC.

THE RAINBOW OF STONE
When drought threatens the grazing lands of the Navajos, an old chief tells his grandson the tribal legend of a wonderful country beyond The Rainbow of Stone. 1949. 23 minutes, color. 16mm. Rental: UCT & UT.

RAMONA: A STORY OF PASSION & PROTEST
Helen Hunt Jackson's novel of 1884 crystalized opin-

ion about whites' maltreatment of Indians. This film uses feature film clips to recap the plot & historical sources & sites. 28 minutes, color. Video. Purchase: $89.95. FH.

REAFFIRMATION & DISCOVERY" THE FIRST POW-WOW ON HAWAII
Story of two women whose lives & vision come together in the creation of the first pow wow on the big island, Hawaii - of the connection made between Native Americans & Native Hawaiians, 29 minutes. Video. Purchase: $250; rental: $45. SH.

THE REAL PEOPLE SERIES
KSPS-TV Spokane, Washington
Nine, 30-minute programs on Indian tribes of Northwest. The Colville, the Flathead, the Couer d' Alene, the Kalispel, the Kootenai, the Nez Perce and the Spokane. Examines the lifestyles, culture and lore of these seven tribes. Teacher's guide. 1976. Color. Grades 5-adult. 16mm & video. Purchase: $450/series, $65/program. Rental: $17.50/program. GPN & NAPBC.

RED BLOOD
The mob and Jimmy White Cloud and his reservation in Arizona where he rediscovers his heritage. With David Mid Thunder & Lee White Star. 90 mins. 2003. DVD, $24.99; VHS, $49.99. ME.

THE RED DRESS
Michael Scott, Director
Tells the story of conflicting loyalties to the past, the demands of the present day, traditional values and family affections. 1978. 28 minutes. Grades 7-adult. 16mm, $500; video, $300. Rental, $50. NFBC.

THE RED ROAD TO SOBRIETY
DreamCatchers Sobriety Fund
Documents the contemporary Native American sobriety movement currently flourishing throughout the Indian communities of North America. 1995. 90 mins. Color. VHS, $34.95; Video Talking Circle is the companion video featuring many respected Native therapists and healers. 8 15-minute segments. To be used as a prevention and recovery tool by individualss, clinics, programs, schools, and youth groups. 1995. 120 mins. Color. VHS, $34.95. ME.

RED ROAD - TOWARD THE TECHNO-TRIBAL
KBDI-TV, Producer
Documentary presenting and exploring contemporary views of Native American philosophy, spirituality and prophecy. 1984. 27 minutes. Color. Video. Purchase: $150; Rental: $40. NAPBC.

RED SUNDAY
John McIntyre, Narrator
The story of the Custer battle, told in art work, photographs, modern re-enactment and aerial photography. 1975. 28 minutes, color. Purchase: Video, $25. OAP. Rental: 16mm, $15. IU.

REDISCOVERY: THE EAGLE'S GIFT
Peeter Prince
On a remote island off the Northwest coast of British Columbia, native and non-native youth learn about the unique Haida culture. They explore ancient villages, caves, totem and burial grounds, as they learn the drum song, dances and drama of the "Haida Potlatch". 1984. 29 minutes. 16mm and video. Purchase or rental. CFDW.

RELOCATION & THE NAVAJO-HOPI LAND DISPUTE
Victoria Mudd, Director/producer
In 1974, Congress passed the Navajo-Hopi Land Settlement Act, partitioning 1.8 million acres of disputed land i Arizona equally between the Navajo and Hopi Indian tribes. This film examines the historical and political forces behind the land dispute, and documents the struggle of 9,000 displaced Navajos to retain their homes, their culture, and their dignity. 1981. 23 minutes, 16mm rental, $20. PSU.

RETURN OF THE RAVEN - THE EDISON CHILOQUIN STORY
Barry Hood Films, Producer
In 1954, in a policy which became known as "Klamath

Termination," the Klamath Tribe of Oregon joined over 100 tribes throughout the country in loss of federal recognition. This is the true story of Klamath Termination and Edison Chilquin's ten-year struggle to preserve traditional values. 1985. 47 minutes. Color. Video. Rental: $80. NAPBC.

RETURN OF THE SACRED POLE
Michael Farrell, Producer/director/writer
narrated by Roger Welsch
Documentary charting the return of a treasured religious object to the Omaha people, the sacred pole (Washabagel) that forms the center of Omaha spiritual life. 1990. 28 mins, color. Video. $39.95. GPN.

RETURN TO THE CIRCLE
Illustrates the philosophy of recovery which the American Indian Family Healing Center has successfully implemented for over 25 years, and is now practicing for the treatment of women and children. 12 minutes. Video. Purchase: $90; rental, $25. SH.

RETURN TO SOVEREIGNTY: SELF-DETER-MINATION & THE KANSAS KICKAPOO
Donald D. Stull, Producer/writer
David M. Kendall, Director/writer/editor;
Bernard Hirsch, Writer/narrator
A documentary film about the Kickapoo Indians of Kansas and their struggle to regain control of their future. Explores Indian self-determination & the Education Assustance Acts. 1987. 46 minutes, color. Video. Purchase, $95; and rental, $50. UC. KS (loan).

1492 REVISITED
Provides an alternative, "indigenous" perspective on the quincentennary of Columbus' arrival. Features artwork from the touring national exhibition Counter Colon-Ialismo as well as challenging commentary by artists & scholars. Also raises important questions about the nature of history and its construction. 1993. 28 mins, color. Video. Purchase: $225; rental: $50. UC.

REVIVAL
Michael Brodie & Bill Roxborough, Producers/dirs.
Doreen Jensen, Narrator
Presents four contemporary artists of the Northwest Coast: Reg Davidson and Dorothy Grant, both Haida; Nishga artist Norman Tait overseas the printing of a silkscreen design of the beaver; and Noreen Jensen, Gitskan carver. These artists look to the artists of old to interpret the design vocabulary of the Northwest Coast tradition. 1983. 29 minutes. Color. 3/4" and 1/2" video. MBP and VOI.

REZ-ROBICS
Exercise videos for and by Indians. 2 VHS videotapes. Free to Indian communities. Send Self-addressed box or padded envelope and $5 for shipping. DR.

RIBBONS OF THE OSAGE: THE ART & LIFE OF GEORGEANN ROBINSON
Relates the history of the Osage and stresses the importance of maintaining the traditions. Teacher's guide. VHS. 28 mins. $19.95. VIP.

RICHARD CARDINAL: CRY FROM A DIARY OF A METIS CHILD
Alanis Obomsawin, Director/writer
Based on the diary of a young man who committed suicide at 17 years of age. Richard had lived in 28 foster homes, group homes, shelters and lockups throughout Alberta. The new Alberta Welfare Act is, in part, Richard's legacy, whereby numerous tribes are now administering their own social services. 1986. 29 mins, color. $550; VHS, $250. Rental: $60. NFBC.

RICHARD'S TOTEM POLE
Richard Harris, 16, is a Gitskan Indians living in British Columbia, Canada, while helping his father a master totem pole carver, he begins to take an interest in his heritage. Through his carving he discovers his roots, culture and family traditions. 25 minutes. Grades 4-adult. Purchase: 16mm, $495; video, $290. Rental, $60. PHOENIX.

THE RIGHT TO BE MOHAWK
George Hornbein, Lorna Rasmussen
& Anne Stanaway, Producers/Directors
Members of the Mohawk Nation at Akwesasne de-scribe their efforts to maintain identity & sovereignty in an ever-changing society. 1989. Grades 9-12. 17 mins, color. 16mm & video. Purchase: $250. NDF.

RIO GRANDE: WHERE FOUR CULTURES MEET
Explores the cultural and economic interdependence and interaction of Mexican, Spanish, Indian, and Anglo-American peoples of the Rio Grande Valley. Grades 7 and up. 15 mins. 16mm. Rental, $15. UT.

RITA JOE: THE SONG SAYS IT ALL
About the life & work of the contemporary Micmac poet, Rita Joe. 1988. 27 mins. Video. NS.

RIVER PEOPLE
The Pima Indians reconstruct their old ways of life for this film. 1949. 25 mins. Grades 4-adult. Rental. UA.

RIVER PEOPLE: BEHIND THE CASE OF DAVID SOHAPPY
Michael Conford, Michele Zacchero
narrated by Ruby Dee
Focuses on the case of David Sohappy, a Yakima spiritual leader, who was sentenced to a five-year prison term for selling 317 salmon out of season. Claiming an ancestral right to fish along the Che Wana, the indigenous name for the Columbia River, Sohappy openly defied state & federal fishing laws and has become a symbol of resistance for Native peoples of the Northwest. 1990. 50 mins., color. Video. Purchase: $395. FIL.

ROAD TO INDEPENDENCE
Transportation & independence for elders. A story of how the need is being met by the Chickasaw Nation & Delaware Tribe of Oklahoma. 14 mins. Video. Purchase: $100; rental: $25. SH.

THE ROADS LESS TAKEN
OPBS/Dorothy Velasco, Producer
The travels & travails of the pioneers who journeyed west in the mid-1840's are documented, with the focus on the exploration of less traveled routes and the impact on the Native Americans along the way. 1993. Grades 7 and up. 26 mins. Purchase: VHS, $260. NDM

ROCK ART TREASURES OF ANCIENT AMERICA: THE CALIFORNIA COLLECTION
Dave Caldwell, Producer/director
Scott Beach, Narrator
Focuses on three major types of rock art - carvings, paintings, and ground figures - at three sites in southern California. Also contemporary Indian storytellers from tribes near these sites. 1983. 25 mins. Color. 16mm, 3/4" and 1/2" video. DCP.

ROOTS TO CHERISH
Evaluates young Indian pupils. A concept film designed to identify & illustrates consequences of cultural differences upon school performance; ways to conduct a more appropriate evaluation; and suggestions for program modifications. 30 mins. Video. purchase, $245; rental, $45. SH.

ROPE TO OUR ROOTS
Bo Boudart, Producer/director/writer
Presents the Inuit Circumpolar Conference, an international organization of Eskimos and Inuit from Alaska, Canada, and Greenland founded in 1977. Discusses the commonalities and differences in life styles and concerns of the delegates. 1981. 30 minutes. Color. 16mm, 3/4" and 1/2" VHS. BO.

ROSEBUD TO DALLAS
Jed Riffe and Robert Rouse
Tells the story of five families who come to Dallas from the Rosebud Sioux Reservation in South Dakota to make a better life through vocational education and on the job training. 1977. 60 mins. VHS. THRC.

ROUND DANCE
A group of dancers perform a round dance. Three minutes. All grades. Purchase: 16mm, $110. Rental, $10/week. Also available in video. SAN.

THE RUNAWAY
NETV, Producer
14 year-old Darlene Horse runs away from a difficult home situation. Social workers and a Native American alcoholism counselor help the family through appreciation of their culture and use of counseling groups. 1989. 29 mins. Color. Video. Purchase: $150; Rental: $40. NAPBC.

RUNNING ON THE EDGE OF THE RAINBOW: LAGUNA STORIES & POEMS
Larry Evers, University of Arizona
With Leslie Marmon Silko—reflects on the nature of Laguna storytelling, its functions and the problems she has faced as an Indian poet. 28 mins. Purchase: VHS & Beta, $175. NR. Rental: VHS, $37.50. ATL.

SACAGAWEA
Reenacts her journey in her own words. 80 min. 2004. DVD, $19.99. ME.

SACAJAWEA
Neil Affleck
A 16 year-old Shoshone girl joins the Lewis & Clark Expedition. Still photos and drawings offer scope to the land they travelled while animation brings to life Sacajawea and the adventures she shared. She is followed into her later years as a traveller, mediator between Indian and white man and speaker in the councils of her tribe. 1991. 18 mins, color. Grades 4-9. VHS, $95; CHAR.

SACAJAWEA
A young Indian guide of Lewis & Clark Expedition to the Pacific Northwest. Sacajawea recounts the events prior to the sighting of the Pacific Ocean in 1805. 24 mins, color. Video. Purchase: $79. FH.

THE SACRED CIRCLE
Donald K. Spence, Producer/director
Adrian Hope, Narrator
In two parts: Part I: Invites the viewer through a bold series of symbolic imagery to participate in the mystical harmony of the Native world. Culminates in the ritual expression of the Sun Dance. The film combines animation, documentary photographs, paintings and on location realism, augmented by lyrical narrative. Part II: Recovery—moves from the frontal assault on Native culture by missionaries and others in the last century to a series of vignettes reflecting its contemporary face, while conveying the tragedy of cultural loss. 1980. 29 mins each. Color. VHS. UAL.

SACRED GROUND
The story of the North American Indian's relationship to the land. Their intimate involvement and reverence for places throughout the land that hold a special religious and traditional significance for their race. Provides a detailed look at the specific geographic places all over America that are and always were sacred to the American Indian. Original music by Dr. Louis Ballard, and narrated & hosted by Cliff Robertson. 50 mins. Video, $19.95. NV.

THE SACRED TREE
Curriculum package including text, four videos, six resource books, posters and other visual aids. Presents many of the universal concepts and teachings handeed down through the ages in Native societies throughout North America concerning the nature, purposes and possibilities of human existence. $450. FOUR.

ST. MARY'S POTLATCH
Three vilages participated in this huge potlatch, celebrating the traditional Yup'ik Eskimo Messenger feast, at which young people are honored as they come of age. 1981. 30 minutes. VHS. $24.95. KYUK.

SANANGUAGAT: INUIT MASTERWORKS OF 1,000 YEARS
Derek May, Director
An exhibition of Inuit carvings from public and private collections. Views of daily life in the Iglootik settlement of the Northwest Territories. 1974. 25 minutes, color. Grades 7 and up. Purchase: 16mm, $500; video, $300. Rental, $50. NFBC. Rental, $19.50. PSU.

SCHOOL IN THE BUSH
Dennis Sawyer, Producer
Tony Ianzelo, Photographer
Cree values & culture. Touches on the jarring dichoto-

mies experienced by (Canadian) Native children in city schools. Uses excerpts from two documentaries, "Cree Hunters of the Mistassini," & "Our Land is Our Life." 1986. Grades 7-12. 15 minutes, color. 16mm & video. Purchase: $200. NFBC.

THE SEA IS OUR LIFE
Bo Boudart
Inuit speak out about the effects of offshore drilling. Shows the growing political awareness and their efforts to organize. 1979. 16 minutes. 16mm. BO.

THE SEARCH FOR THE FIRST AMERICANS
This program follows the trail of America's first inhabitants. 1993. 60 mins, color. VHS. $89.95. FH.

SEASONS OF THE NAVAJO
John Borden, Producer/camera
Will Lyman, Narrator
Documentary on the lifestyles & traditions of modern Navajo families in Canyon de Chelly, Arizona - sacred songs, ceremonies and oral traditions. Aspects of Navajo life rarely seen on film are shown. Also filmed is the kinaalda, the ritual for young women. 1984. 60 mins, color. In English & Navajo with English subtitles. VHS, $15.95. ME.

SEASONS OF THE SALISH: SACRED ENCOUNTERS
Father De Smet and the Indians of the Rocky Mountain West examines tyhe collision of catholic and Native worlds in Montana and Idaho. 1996. 30 mins. VHS, $25.95. ME.

SECRETS OF THE LITTLE BIGHORN
By retracing the pattern of bullets & cartridge cases across the battlefield, archaeologists have been able to generate a computer simulation of the final, fatal moments of the Battle of the Little Bighorn. The reconstyruction shows a Native American triumph rather than Custer's defeat. 1993. 28 mins, color. Video. Purchase: $149; rental: $75. FH..

SEDNA; THE MAKING OF A LEGEND
John Paskievich, Director
Follows a team of Inuit carvers and a white man from Vancouver as they craft the first monumental sized Inuit sculpture for a private corporation. 1992. 58 mins. VHS. Purchase: $27. NFBC.

SEEKING THE FIRST AMERICANS
Graham Chedd
Archaeologists from Texas and Arkansas search for clues to the identity of the first North Americans. 58 minutes, color. Adult. Purchase: 16mm, $750; rental, $60. Educator's guide. Purchase: VHS, $145; rental, $40. DER & PBS. Rental only, IU.

SEEKING THE SPIRIT: PLAINS INDIANS IN RUSSIA
Dr. Bea Medicine & Dr. Liucija Baskaiskas
Russians interested in Native American culture. 1999. 27 mins. Video. Purchase: $145; rental, $40. DER.

THE SENECAS
Ron Hagell
Through interviews and narration, this film views the contemporary Seneca Indian of New York State and their history. 1980. 29 minutes. VHS. WXXI.

SEPARATE VISIONS
Peter Blystone & Nancy Tongue, Producers
Profiles four pioneering American Indian artists: Baje Whitethorne, a Navajo painter: Brenda Spencer, a Navajo weaver; John Fredericks, a Hopi kachina carver; and Nora Naranjo-Morse, a Santa Clara sculptor. 1989. 40 minutes, color. Video. Purchase: $195; rental, $50. UC. Rental: $16. UMN.

SEQUOYAH
The story of the Cherokee Indian who developed the first written American Indian language. 15 mins. 16mm. WD.

SERVING NATIVE AMERICAN PEOPLE
Guidelines for health care providers. Illustrates the spiritual needs unique to traditional Native People, the meaning of healing and the role of the extended family. 30 minutes. Video. $125; rental: $45. SH.

THE SETTLERS
Allied Film Artists, Inc., Producer
Explores the reasons for and history and impact of America's westward expansion. Including the destruction of Native American cultures. 1978. 22 mins, color. 16mm, $450; Video, $275; Rental, $62. PHOENIX.

SEYEWAILO: THE FLOWER WORLD
Larry Evers, University of Arizona
Yaqui Deer Songs as they are sung and danced to at a fiesta, the pahko. Yaqui with English subtitles. 51 minutes. Purchase: VHS & Beta, $290. NR. Rental: VHS, $52.50. ATL.

THE SHADOW CATCHER: EDWARD S. CURTIS & THE NORTH AMERICAN INDIAN
T.C. McLuhan, Director/Producer
A film about Edward S. Curtis, photographer, anthropologist and filmmaker.Features marked Kwakiutl dancers, a Navajo Yebechai Ceremony, and Curtis' own initiation into the Hopi Snake Fraternity. Soundtrack features original Indian music and contemporary Comanche variations. 1975. 88 minutes, color. Grades 9 and up. Purchase: 16mm, 975; video, $585; Rental, $100. SH, PHOENIX. Rental: IRA, PSU, IU, UCT, UK, UMN, UCLA & UA.

SHAMANISM
Serge King & Terry Eaton, Producers
Terry Eaton discusses Native American spiritual values and traditions. 57 minutes. VHS video. TPH.

SHEM PETE MEMORIAL POTLATCH
Highlights of potlatch held in Tyonek, Alaska on October 7, 1989. Remarks by Bonnie McCord, Emil McCord, Sr., Jim Kari, Jim Fall, et al. Features the Tyuonek Dancers, the Northern Lights Intertribal Pow-wow Club, Paul Theodore of Knik & the Dena'Ina Indian cloth ceremony. 1990. 45 minutes. VHS. $15. NDM.

SHENANDOAH FILMS
Vern & Carole Korb, Producers
Carole Korb, Director
A Yurok-owned production company, which has made numerous films, filmstrips, and slide tapes about Indian culture, particularly in northern California. Focuses on improving the education, employment skills, and cultural pride of Indian children and youth. Among the productions are: "Again, A Whole Person I Have Become" - Narrated by Will Sampson, this film features a Wintu medicine woman, a Karok spiritual leader, and a Tolowa headman who speak of wisdom of the old ways. 1985, 20 minutes; "In the Best Interest of the Child: Indian Child Welfare Act" - Narrated by Will Sampson, this film depicts an Indian child's removal from his home, to be placed in a non-Indian foster home. Tells of the problems of foster care and the provisions of the Act. 1984, 20 minutes; "Our Songs Will Never Die" - Narrated by Juni Donahue. Yurok, Karok, and Tolowa summer camps have been established in California, where young people work together with tribal elders. 1983, 35 minutes; "The Path of Our Elders" - Narrated by Pat Tswelmaldin. Pomo elders show how traditions are passed on, demonstrating traditional song and dance and the preparation and weaving of basketry. 1986, 20 minutes, video only; and "Roots to Cherish" - Directed by Marilyn Miles & Don Mahler, narrated by Carl Degado. A concerned mother, a Maidu educator, a traditional Hupa teacher, and a guidance counselor speak of the consequences their cultural differences have for Indian students. 1983, 30 minutes, color. 16mm & video. For a complete list of titles contact SH.

SHINNECOCK: THE STORY OF A PEOPLE
Dana Rogers, Producer
Joseph E. Miller, Director/writer
The Indians of the East Coast region who were the first to come into contact with the white man, when the original settlers arrived from Europe. Consequently, these Indians were the first to lose much of their own culture. 1976. 20 minute, color. Purchase: 16mm, $375; video, $215; Rental, $35. PHOENIX.

SHUNGNAK: A VILLAGE PROFILE
Daniel Housberg, Director
Focuses on a tiny Inupiat Eskimo community in northwest Alaska, 75 miles north of the Arctic Circle. Villag-

ers discuss their subsistence practices, and the contrast between past and present. 1985. 30 minutes. Color. 3/4" & 1/2" video. NATC.

18th ANNUAL SIFC POW WOW 1996
The Saskatchewan Indian Federated College indoor pow wow is one od Canada's largest. 25 drum groups and 600 dancers performed during the pow wow. CAN.

THE SILENT ENEMY
H.P. Carver
Chief Yellow Robe, a noted Sioux, who acts in the film, points out the usefulness of the film in preserving an authentic image of the old days. Documents a band of Ojibwa in winter. 1930. 88 minutes. 16mm/bxw. FCE.

SINCE 1634: IN THE WAKE OF NICOLET
In 1634, French explorer Jean Nicolet explores Wisconsin and details the subsequent history of the Native American tribes that Nicolet found when he got there - the Menominee and the Winnebago. 90 minutes. Color. Video. $25. CAN.

SINEW-BACKED BOW & ITS ARROWS
Clyde B. Smith, Producer
Follows the construction of a sinew-backed bow, by a Yurok craftsman. Also demonstrates the making of arrows. 1961. 24 minutes, color. Purchase: 16mm, $480; video, $195. Rental, $50. UC. Rental: 16mm, $20. PSU.

SINGERS OF TWO SONGS
A story of Indian artists as they live in two worlds: traditional & contemporary. 25 minutes. Video Purchase: $245; rental: $45. SH.

SINUMWAK
Jim & Justine Bizzocchi
Follows the (Bella Coola) process from catching oolichan (fish) to feasting on the result, while the many uses of oolichan grease are discussed. 1979. 20 minutes. Purchase: 16mm, $325; and video, $225. CFDW.

THE SIOUX
The Sioux were a people of war. Forced onto the grasslands by woodland tribes in the east, they had to fight to survive. The Sioux war ethic was a noble assertion of individuality. 25 minutes. Color VHS. $99.95. AVP.

SIOUX LEGENDS
Charles & Jane Nauman
Recreates some of the legends closest to the philosophy and religion of the Sioux culture. Demonstrates the Indian feeling of identification with the forces of nature. 1973. Grades 4 and up. 20 minutes, color. Purchase: 16mm, $415; video, $70; rental: $30. AIMS. Rental: $24.95. WH.

SITTING BULL & THE GREAT SIOUX NATION
History Channel Production
Shows us how the Sioux changed their tactics and defeated Custer. 1993. 50 mins. VHS, $16.99. ME.

SITTING BULL: A PROFILE IN POWER
The tragic but heroic saga of Indian/U.S. relations in this interview with Sitting Bull, portrayed by August Schellenberg. 1977. 26 minutes, color. Purchase: 16mm, $325; rental, $30. LCA. Rental: 16mm, $20. UMN.

THE SIX NATIONS
Nick Gosling, Director
The President of the Seneca Nation and the Mayor of the town of Salamanca discuss the various aspects of Indian and white coexistence. The Iroquois League consists of the Mohawk, Oneida, Onondaga, Seneca, Cayuga and Tuscarora India tribes. Grades 7 and up. 1976. 26 minutes, color. Purchase: 16mm, $400; video, $295. Rental, $55. CG. Rental: $30. UT.

SKINS
Chris Eyre, Director
Drama about the painful legacy of Indian existence. With Graham Greene & Eric Schweig. 2002. 87 mins. DVD, $24.95; VHS, $19.99. ME.

SKINWALKERS
Chris Eyre, Director; Robert Redford, Producer
Based on mystery novel by Tony Hillerman set on

Navajo reservation. With Wes Studi & Adam Beach. 2002. 97 mins. DVD, $24.95; VHS, $19.95. ME.

SKOKOMISH INDIAN BASKETS:
THEIR MATERIALS & TECHNIQUES
Documents the varied techniques of basket-making by the Skokomish Indians from the Puget Sound region in western Washington State. 1977. 28 minutes/ bxw/silent. Super 8mm and video. Rental. UW.

SMOKE SIGNALS
A comedy which depicts contemporary reservation life. With Adam Beach, Evan Adams & Irene Bedard. 1998. 89 mins. VHS, $12.99; DVD, $24.99. ME.

SNAKETOWN
This study of the Snaketown archaeological excavation in southern Arizona, explores the Hohokam Indian culture. 1969. 40 minutes, color. Video. Purchase: $95; rental, $50. UC.

SOMEDAY, I'LL BE AN ELDER
Narrated by Will Sampson
This film is about a pilot substance prevention program, "Project Renewal." A story featuring Karuk tribal members as they conduct a 3 week summer camp program which emphasizes the renewal of traditional ways & values. 25 minutes. Purchase: Video, $245; rental, $45. SH.

SOMEPLACE YOU DON'T WANT TO GO
Vivid scenes show hardcore drug & alcohol abuse. Designed to educate elementary & high school Indian youth to drug & alcohol abuse. 22 minutes. Video. Purchase: $245; rental: $45. SH.

SOMETIMES WE FEEL
William Maheras, Director
Brad Stanley, Writer/Producer
A young Indian tells of a life of sorrow, poverty, neglect, and isolation on an Arizona reservation. Ten minutes. 16mm. Rental. UA.

SOMEWHERE BETWEEN
Hy Perspectives Media Group
Looks at the history of Canadian government legislation affecting Indian women and their traditional role in Indian society. 1982. 50 minutes. 16mm & video. Purchase or rental. CFDW.

A SONG FOR DEAD WARRIORS
Examines the reasons for the Wounded Knee occupation in the Spring of 1973 by Oglala Sioux Indians. Features many of the personalities involved, including Russell Means, tribal chairman Dick Wilson, Chief Charley Red Cloud, & Medicine Man Frank Fools Crow. 1973. 25 mins, color. 16mm. Rental: UCLA & UNI.

SONGS IN MINTO LIFE
Curt Madison, Producer/director
A documentary which explores the creativity and tradition in the songs of Tanana Indians living near Minto Flats, Alaska. Shows activities during the four seasons, with elders singing both contemporary songs and traditional khukal'ch'leek songs. 1985. 30 minutes, color. In English & Tanana Athapascan. Video. Purchase: $56.95. KYUK, NAPBC & RTP.

SONGS OF MY HUNTER HEART:
LAGUNA STORIES & POEMS
Harold Littlebird
Author sings traditional and popular Pueblo songs. Includes his song-poem Talking 49 which describes the singing which takes place around a drum after a powwow. 1978. 34 minutes in Engliush and Keres. VHS. Rental, $52.50. ATL.

SONGS OF MY HUNTER HEART:
LAGUNA SONGS & POEMS
Larry Evers, University of Arizona
Harold Littlebird continues the oral tradition of his people by incorporating contemporary themes into his work which retains the Pueblo reverence for the Spoken word. 1978. 34 minutes. Video, $220. NR.

SOUTHWEST CULTURAL VIDEO SERIES
Designed & developed to help the classroom teacher. Four videos: *Storytelling in Clay & Language* - Native American sculptor Dorothy Trujillo demonstrating how

to make a clay storyteller doll. 26 minutes. *Creating Portraits in Art & Language* - Sam English, a Native American painter, is shown demonstrating the art of self-portraiture to 3rd & 4th graders. 17 minutes. *Space in Dance & Poetry* - Jerome Marcus, a Taos Pueblo Indian, demonstrates the grass dance for 5th & 6th graders, and Jennifer Predock-Linnell, a modern dancer, is shown demonstrating a variety of creative dance movements to these students. 26 minutes. *Mask, Dance & Character* - Rosalie Jones, artistic director of Daystar Dancers, demonstrates Native American dance steps & use of costumes, masks, and button blankets for theatrical production. 17 minutes, color. VHS. Purchase: $49.95 each; $100 each with curriculum package. ALA.

SOUTHWEST INDIAN ARTISTS SERIES
Seven videos introduces various arts & crafts of the Southwest. Baskets (Papago & Hopi); Kachina Dolls (Hopi); Pottery (Pueblo & Navajo); Jewelry (Navajo, Hopi & Zuni); Navajo Rug Makers; Sandpaimting (Navajo); Pueblo Storytellers. VHS. 40 minutes each. $19.95 ea. set of seven, $99.95. WH.

SOUTHWEST INDIAN ARTS & CRAFTS
Shows techniques in Navajo rug-making; San Ildefonso and Acoma pottery; Hopi and Zuni jewelry and kachina dolls; and Pima and Papago basket-making. 1973. 14 mins. Grades K-12. 16mm, $320; video, $225; Rental, $40. PHOENIX. Rental. IU and UK.

SOUTHWEST INDIAN OF EARLY AMERICA
Uses Indian actors, dioramas, and narration to help recreate what life might have been like about 600 years ago for the Hohokam and Anasazi Indians of northern Arizona and New Mexico. 1973. 14 minutes. Grades 4-8. Purchase: 16mm, $350; video, $245. PHOENIX. Rental. IU and UK.

SOVEREIGNTY & THE U.S. CONSTITUTION
By Senator Daniel S. Inouye, Chairman of the Senate Select Committee on Indian Affairs. 20 minutes, color. Video. Purchase: $20; rental: $10. HO.

SPEECHES COLLECTION
A sample of heartfelt addresses from Sitting Bull. 1997. 35 mins. VHS, $19.98. ME.

SPIRIT BAY SERIES
Eric Jordan & Paul Stephens, Producers/directors
Keith Leckie, Director
An entertainment series of 13 films which reflect some of the reality of reserve life and debunks stereotypes about Indians. Filmed on the Rocky Bay Reserve in Ontario, it depicts a remote northern Indian community through the experiences of its children, and shows how its residents have adapted to white society while retaining ties to the land. 1982-86. Grades 4 and up. 28 minutes each, color. In English, French, or Ojibwa. Video. $149 each. ALT & BE (U.S.); ML (Canada).

SPIRIT IN THE EARTH
The legend of a Western Indian tribe, describing the phenomenon of Old Faithful in terms of the Plains' Indians concept of original sin. 22 minutes. Rental. UK.

THE SPIRIT OF CRAZY HORSE
Milo Yellow Hair, Narrator
Reveals the modern Sioux struggle to regain their heritage, and how places like Wounded Knee became sites for a fight that continues still. Presents the militant confrontations of the 1960's & 1970's, the explosive results of 100 years of confinement on Indian reservations. 1989. 58 minutes, color. Purchase: Video, $19.95. CAN. Purchase: Video, $25. AUDIO; $40. PBS. Rental: Video, $10. HO, UMN & PSU.

SPIRIT OF THE HUNT
Narrated by Will Sampson, this film features a spiritual search for the essential elements of what the Buffalo meant historically and in the present to people of the Chippewa, Cree and Dogrib tribes. Historical footage combined with a modern hunt, illustrates the central concept. 1982. Grades 9 and up. 29 minutes, color. Purchase: 16mm, $675. TC. Purchase: VHS, $160; 3/ 4", $190. CC. Rental: 16mm, $20.50. UMN.

THE SPIRIT OF THE MASK
Peter von Puttkamer, Director; Gryphon Productions

Documentary explores the spiritual & psychological powers of the masks of the Northwest Coast Native people. Features ceremonies as well as commentary by important Indian spiritual leaders, Relates the colonial history of the Northwest Coast Indians.1992. 50 minutes, color. Video. Purchase: $295; rental: $70. UC.

SPIRIT OF THE WHITE MOUNTAINS
Documents the activities of the White Mountain Apaches, and how they support themselves by developing the natural resources of their reservation. 1959. 13 minutes. Grades 4-9. 16mm. Rental. IU & UA.

SPIRIT RIDER
Raised in foster homes, 16-year-old Native American Jesse Threebears is reluctantly repatriated to the reservation of his birth. 1993. Grades 4 and up. 98 minutes, color. Video. Purchase: $29.95. FI.

SPIRIT OF THE WILD
A mystical grandfather transforms the life of a modern day boy through the legends of Seeks-to-Hunt-Great. Michael Horse tracks a mountain lion for many months, learns from it and eventually gains its trust. The struggle to survive the hardships and dangers of living in the wild. Based on Native American folklore and the Medicine Wheel Way, this video brings an awareness of the important relationship with our environment. 30 minutes, color. Video. CAN.

THE SPIRIT WITHIN
Gil Cardinal & Wil Campbell, Directors
Story of how Native prisoners in four western Canadian correctional facilities have won the right to practice their traditional spirituality. 1990. 51 minutes, color. 16mm, $775; VHS, $350. Rental: $80. NFBC.

SPIRITS OF THE CANYON:
ANCIENT ART OF THE PECOS INDIANS
Artist Amado Pena & archaeologists analyze the paintings & pictographs on the walls of the majestic southwest Texas canyons that date from about 3000 BC until the arrival of the conquistadors in the 16th century. 1992. 30 minutes, color. Video, Purchase: $149; rental: $75. FH.

SQUANTO: A WARRIOR'S TALE
A young Indian warrior is kidnapped by 17th century English traders and exhibited as a wild man back in England. He escapes and returns home. 1994. With Adma Beach, Eric Scweig, Alex Norton, mandy Pantinkin. 97 mins. VHS, $12.99. ME.

STANDING ALONE
Colin Low, Director
25 years ago, Pete Standing Alone was the subject of a film by Colin Low which stressed the conflicts facing a young man of the Blood tribe caught between Indian and the white ways. Now middle-aged, Standing Alone lives on the Blood Indian Reserve in Alberta and is active in family and tribal affairs. Through his eyes are seen many aspects of contemporary Blood life. Also considers the economic and political pressures which affect Indian tribes. 1983. 58 minutes. Color. 16mm, 3/4" and 1/2" video. Purchase: 16mm, $775; VHS, $150. Rental: $80. NFBC

STANDING BUFFALO
Joan Henson, Director
An account of rug-making cooperative organized by Sioux Indian women of the Standing Buffalo Reserve in the Qu'Appelle Valley of southern Saskatchewan. 1968. 23 miutes. Video. Purchase: $27. NFBC.

STANDING STRONG AGAINST
THE CANCER ENEMY
Old Man Coyote Productions
Promotes healthful traditional practices of Native Americans as effective cancer prevention and control practices. Grades 5 and up. 1993. 30 mins. VHS. $49. CHAR.

STAR LORE
Faith Hubley, Producer/director
An animated, original and visually dynamic rendering of six Native American sky myths. Stories chosen include: an Inuit tale, and a Pawnee tale. 1984. 8 1/2 minutes. Color. 16mm, 3/4" video. PFV.

STARBLANKET
Donald Brittain, Director
Video about Noel Starblanket and his methods of learning the political process. Looks at his Canadian reserve and what life was like for his people. 1973. 27 minutes. Purchase: $27. NFBC.

STARTING FIRE WITH GUNPOWDER
David Poisey & William Hansen, Directors
Chronicles the origins and achievement of the Inuit Broadcasting Corp. Explores how Inuit TV is a critical element in the creation of a modern Inuit nation in Canada's Arctic. 1991. 57 mins. Video. Purchase: $27. NFBC.

STEVE CHARGING EAGLE
A film about an American Indian man from Red Scaffold, South Dakota. Quiet, proud, a man of responsibility, he performs in a War Dance competition. 30 minutes, color. 16mm. Purchase: $300; rental: $30. AICRC.

STICKS & STONES WILL BUILD A HOUSE
Traces the development of Indian architecture in the Southwestern U.S. 1970. 30 mins. Rental, $19. IU.

STONE AGE AMERICANS
Jules Powers and Daniel Wilson, Producers
Discovery Series, NBC
Introduces the vanished Indians of the Mesa Verde in Colorado. The film presents the history of these farmer Indians by examining the cliff dwellings and artifacts discovered in 1888. 21 minutes. 16mm. Rental. UA.

STOP RUINING AMERICA'S PAST
Covers the problem of the destruction of archaeological sites by urban and industrial expansion, as illustrated by the case histories of two prehistoric Indian communities in Illinois - Cahokia Mounds and Hopewell Mounds. 1968. 22 mins, bxw. 16mm. Rental: UA.

STORIES OF NORTH AMERICA. Part II
Includes Stories of Native American Peoples - Joe Bruchac tells "The Earth on Turtle's Back" & "The Race With the Buffalo." 30 mins, color. Video. Purchase: $70. NGS.

THE STORY OF TUKTU SERIES
Lawrence Hyde, Director
A children's adventure series, starring Tuktu, an Inuit boy, in 13 film adventures. 1966-1968. Approximately 14 minutes each. Grades 1-8. FILMS.

STORYTELLER
A documentary, focusing on an important Pueblo tradition, this video tells the story of the increasingly popular clay sculpture of Helen Cordero of Cochiti Pueblo, New Mexico. Grades 7 and up. 23 minutes, color. Purchase: VHS, $79; 3/4", $109. CC.

THE STRENGTH OF LIFE
Scott & Sheila Swearingen, and Gary Robinson, Producers/directors/writers/editors
Portrays Creek-Cherokee artist Knokovtee Scott reviving an ancient art form of producing jewelry made with engraved shells, its motifs based on the incised shell tradition of the moundbuilder cultures of the ancient Southeast. 1984. 26 mins. Color. VHS. $19.95. VIP, WH, NAPBC.

SUCKING DOCTOR
William Heick, Producer
A documentary presenting the final night of a curing ceremony held by the Kashia group of Southwestern Pomo Indians. The Indian Sucking Doctor is a prophet of the Bole Maru religion, spiritual head of the Kashia community. 1964. 45 mins, bxw. Video. Purchase: $295; rental $60. UC. Rental: 16mm, PSU & UCLA.

THE SUMMER OF JOHNSON HOLIDAY - NAVAJO BOY
Johnson Holiday lives in Monument Valley. During the summer he herds the family sheep and goats; during the winter he attends the white man's school. 12 mins. Grades 1-8. Rental. UK.

SUMMER OF THE LOUCHEUX: PORTRAIT OF A NORTHERN INDIAN FAMILY
Graydon McCrae, Producer/director
Profiles the Andre family, a Loucheux or Kutchin, one of the northernmost Indian peoples, living in both Canada and Alaska. 1983. Grades 7 and up. 28 mins, color. 16mm & video. In English or Loucheux. TAM (Canada, sales only.) 16mm rental, $27.50. UMN & PSU.

SUN BEAR: ON POWER & EARTH CHANGES
"On Power" - Sun Bear, medicine teacher and founder of the Bear Tribe, teaches people the first steps toward finding their own path of power. "Earth Changes" - Sun Bear draws on his own visions and Native prophecies to help people understand and come into harmony with these times of change. 65 mins each. VHS & Beta. $29.95 each.

THE SUN DAGGER
Anna Sofaer, Producer/Writer
Albert Ihde, Director/Editor
Tells the story of Anna Sofaer, A Washington, DC artist who having climbed to the top of a high butte in Chaco Canyon, New Mexico, saw a dagger of light pierce an ancient spiral rock carving. After careful study, she found that the dagger marks solstices, equinoxes, and the 19-year lunar cycle. Narrated by Robert Redford, this film explores the Anasazi culture that produced this calendar and thrived over 1,000 years ago in the Chaco Canyon environment. 1982. Grades 7 and up. 60 & 30 min. versions. Color. Purchase: 16mm; $550; video, $250; Rental: $50. BULL. Rental: 30 minute-16mm version, UCT, UT & PSU. Video rental (30 minute version): $40. NAPBC.

SUN, MOON & FEATHER
Bob Rosen & Jane Zipp, Producers/directors
Documentary about three Native American sisters growing up in Brooklyn during the 1930s & 1940s. Blends musical theater (song & dance reenactments of family & tribal stories) and personal memoir (scenes filmed in Brooklyn home). 1989. 30 mins, color. Purchase: 16mm, $425; video, $250. Rental: $55. CG.

SUNFLOWER JOURNEYS
Explores the heritage of Kansas. Each 30-minute video contains three separate stories. Includes: Native Americans (#209-200 Series, 1989); Glaciated Region - Iowa Tribe Powwow (#303-300 Series, 1990); Natives & Newcomers - Medicine Lodge Peace Treaty & Indian Self Determination (#502-500 Series, 1992); Indian Art Market (#513-500 Series, 1992); Artifacts of Culture - Sacred Spaces (#607-600 Series, 1993); Native Americans (#704-700 Series, 1994); Three Dimensional Art (#705-700 Series, 1994). KS.

THE SUNRISE DANCE
Gianfranco Norelli
A documentary showing an ancient, sacred Apache ritual that has never before been filmed. The Sunrise Ceremony marks the passage from adolescence to adulthood for young Apache women. 28 mins. Color. Video. 1994. Purchase: $145; rental, $40. DER.

SURVIVING COLUMBUS
Chronicles the Pueblo Indians' 450 years of contact with Europeans and their long struggle to preserve their culture, land & religion. Includes stories of Pueblo elders, interviews with Pueblo scholars & leaders, historical accounts as told by the Pueblo Indians of New Mexico & Arizona. VHS. 1992. Grades 7 and up. 120 mins, color. Purchase: $100. PBS & NAPBC. Rental, $14. UMN & PSU.

SWEATING INDIAN STYLE: CONFLICTS OVER NATIVE AMERICAN RITUAL
Susan Smith
A documentary about a group of non-Native women's search for self in "other". The focus is on a spoecific group of New Age women in Ojai, California who construct a new sweat lodge and perform their own ceremony. 57 mins. Color. Video. 1994. Purchase: $145; rental, $40. DER.

TAHTONKA: PLAINS INDIANS BUFFALO CULTURE
Charles and Jane Nauman, Producers
A re-enactment of the Plains Indian's culture from the pre-horse era to the time of the Wounded Knee massacre. 1966. 30 mins, color. Grades 4-adult. Purchase: 16mm, $495 and video, $70. Rental, $50. AIMS & NILB. Rental: $24.95, WH.

TAKING TRADITION TO TOMORROW
N. Scott Momaday, Ph.D., Narrator
A video presentation and study guide, featuring significant cultural and scientific contributions that American Indians have made to society. Grades 7-college level. 32-page study guide. 30 mins. Video. $69.95. AISES.

TALES OF THE TUNDRA
Traditional Yup'ik Eskimo storytellers explore the legends of Southwest Alaska. 1992. 30 mins. VHS. $24.95. KYUK.

TALES OF WESAKECHAK
Marla Dufour, Storytellers Production
A series of 13 fifteen-minute programs based on well known Canadian Cree legends. Wesakechak, the teacher of the first Indian people. 1984. Color. Rental: $300/series; $40 each. NAPBC.

TALES OF WONDER, I & II
Gregory Howard
Howard (Cherokee/Powhatan) tells traditional Native American stories for children. VHS & DVD. 60 mins each. $24.95. CD Soundtrack available for $15.95. WH, ME & RICH.

TALKING HANDS
Demonstrates the sign language of the Plains Indians. Tells the story of the Battle of the Washita in sign language with background narration. 20 mins. 16mm. Rental: $15. UT.

THE TAOS PUEBLO
Paulle Clark, Producer/Director
Spend a day at the 1000-year-old pueblo in Toas, New Mexico to discover more about the traditions that the resident Indians are trying to preserve. See young children doing ceremonial dances; learn about building homes with adobe clay; breadbaking; & making pottery. Includes study guide. 1986. 9 mins, color. Grades 2-8. Purchase: 16mm, 225; video, $165. Rental: $20. BULL.

TEACHING INDIANS TO BE WHITE
Reviews the issues surrounding schooling of Native American children, where native children find it nearly impossible to balance the white view they are taught with the language & values they learn at home. The Seminole in Florida resist being integrated, the Miccosukee decided not to fight, and the Cree took back their own schools. 1993. 28 mins, color. Video. Rental: $16. UMN.

TEARS OF THE RAVEN
Examines the dissolution of Alaskan indigenous culture, suicide and alcoholism among Alaska's Natives, and explores some of the things the Natives are doing to bring health and hope back to their communities. 1993. 30 mins. VHS. $49. CHAR.

TECUMSEH, THE LAST WARRIOR
About Shawnee warrior, Tecumseh and his attempt to win back the West. With Jesse Borrego, Tantoo Cardinal. 1995. 94 mins. VHS, $79.99. ME.

TEN THOUSAND BEADS FOR NAVAJO SAM
Focuses on Sam Begay, a full-blooded Navajo, who has left the reservation to make a new alien, but secure, life for himself and his family in Chicago. 1971. 25 mins, color. 16mm. Rental. IU & UCLA.

TENACITY
Chris Eyre, Cheyenne/Arapaho Productions
The story of two Indian boys who encounter rednecks on a reservation road. Short narrative filmed in the Onondaga Territory near Nedrow, New York. 1995. VHS. 10 mins. Color. $175; rental: $50. TWN.

THAT ONE GOOD SPIRIT - AN INDIAN CHRISTMAS STORY
Larry Cesspooch, Writer/Director
A clay animated tale of a young Ute Indian boy. 1981. 16 mins. Color. Grades K-3. VHS. Rental: $40/week. NAPBC.

THE THEFT OF FIRE
Title V Indian Education Program staff
Based on a traditional Yurok story retold by elder

Jimmie James, this video version features a running translation in Yurok & English. *Curriculum Unit*: discusses the traditional use of fire as a land management tool by Native Americans. Illus. by Frank Tuttle (Pomo/Maidu). Grades 6-8. 14 mins. VHS. $59.95 (includes Curriculum Unit). CB.

THESE ARE MY PEOPLE
Michael Mitchell, Director
Two Mohawk spokesmen explain historical and other aspects of Longhouse religion, culture and government which are interwoven. 1969. 13 mins. Video. Purchase: $22. NFBC.

THEY NEVER ASKED OUR FATHERS
Corey Flintoff, Producer/writer; John A. McDonald, Director/editor; John Active, Narrator
Through interviews and scenes of various aspects of Yup'ik life on Nunivak Island, 20 miles from the mainland of southwest Alaska, this video presents the situation of a native people whose daily affairs are dominated by the federal government located thousands of miles away. 1980. 60 minutes. In English and Yup'ik with English subtitles. VHS. $24.95. KYUK.

THEY PROMISED TO TAKE OUR LAND
Document Associates & BBC
Discusses the misunderstanding by the white man of the value of land to the Indian. 1976. 26 mins, color. Purchase: 16mm, $400; video, $295. Rental, $55. CG. Rental, $30. UT.

THIEVES OF TIME
Gerald Richman
Describes the problems of pot hunters looting valuable archaeological sites in Arizona. 1995. 30 mins. VHS. $15.95. ME.

THIS SIDE OF THE RIVER
Monona Wali
Focuses on concerns of Onondaga Indians of New York State. Discusses social problems and political awareness. 1978. 30 mins. VHS; bxw. WALI.

THIS WAS THE TIME
Eugene Boyko and William Brind, Directors
A recreation of Haida Indian life in a village in the Queen Charlotte Islands. Portrays the potlatch and totems which existed. 16 mins. 16mm. NFBC.

THIS WORLD IS NOT OUR HOME
Introduction to the history, culture, and traditions of the Pomo people of northern California, as seen through the eyes of Elvina Brown, a tribal elder. 1993. 13 mins, color. Video. $125; rental $40. UC.

THOSE BORN AT MASSET:
A HAIDA STONEMOVING AND FEAST
Covers the Haida ritual, the modern equivalent of the traditional memorial potlatch. 1976. 70 mins/bxw. 16mm and video. UW.

THREE WARRIORS
Keith Merrill, Director
Portrays the problems encountered by a 13 year-old on the Warm Springs Indian Reservation in Oregon, and his coming to terms with his heritage. 1977. 105 minutes, color. 35mm & 16mm. ZAENTZ.

THROUGH THIS DARKEST NIGHT
Susan Malins, Producer; Daniel Salazar, Director; Vivian Locust & Richard Peters, Narrators/advisors
Presents Indian people's experiences during the early reservation period, including some drawn from period accounts. Three speakers: a man speaks of the upheaval experienced when the buffalo were finally gone; a woman describes how she used her strength and traditional skills to ensure that her family would survive; and a third speaker tells of being sent to boarding school and the isolation and humiliation of that experience. 1986. 12 mins, color. Video. ADL & DAM.

THUNDER IN THE DELLS
Lance Tallmadge, a Wisconsin Winnebago, presents the history of his tribe and their legal struggle to remain in the Wisconsin Dells area in the mid-19th Century. Shows the effects of over 120 years of tourism on the Winnebagos, and discusses the importance of their traditional songs and dances to their well-being

and survival. Also the preparation and weaving of black ash wood baskets. 1989. Grades 7 and up. 28 mins, color. Video. $20. CAN.

THUNDERHEART
An FBI agent is sent to solve a murder on a Sioux Indian reservation. He learns of his Native culture and soon believes the U.S. government framed an innocent man. 1992. With Val Kilmer, Graham Greene, Chief Ted Thin Elk, Sam Shepard. 118 mins. VHS, $19.99. ME.

TI EKIYE: FINDING THE WAY HOME
Native American Advocacy Project, SD
This educational and training video with facilitator's guide addresses mental illness in Native American communities and the providing of culturally sensitive services. 1994. 60 mins. VHS & Guide. $55. CHAR.

THE LISA TIGER STORY
Educational video of a 29-year old, Muscogee Creek/Cherokee from Oklahoma, who is HIV positive, offers strength and inspiration for Native American youth with HIV and a message of prevention and protection for others. 1993. 27 mins. VHS. $50. CHAR.

TIKINAGAN
Gil Cardinal
Account of the difficulties along the path to Native self-determination. Foster care and a child welfare agency in Northwestern Ontario, Canada. 1991. 57 mins, color. Video. $27. NFBC.

TIME IMMEMORIAL
Hugh Brody, Director
Native land claims in Canada today; Aboriginal rights in Canada. Takes place in Nass Valley where the Nishga'a people bear witness to their struggle and that of their ancestors. 1991. 57 mins, color. Video. Purchase: $27. NFBC.

TIME OF THE CREE
Bob Rodgers and Gail Singer
Records a salvage archaeological dig near Southern Indian Lake on the Churchill River in northern Manitoba, Canada. Shows a Cree family in the area living a traditional way of life. 1974. 26 mins. 16mm. RODGERS.

A TIME TO BE BRAVE
Eric Jordan, Producer/editor
Paul Stephens, Director/writer
Filmed in Ontario, Canada, this film focuses on the Shibagabo family - living on their trapline in winter. Scenes of the family at home and of tracking and trapping establish a good sense of daily life. 1982. 28 mins, color. 16mm & video. BE.

TIWA TALES: LITTLE FILTH & THE TLACHEES
Chuck Banner, Maggie Banner &
Joseph Leonard Concha, Producers/Directors
A grandfather relates an ancient story. Interwoven with claymation live-action & video effects, bring to life the tale. 1990. Grades 2-8. 17 mins, color. Video. Purchase: $31.95. MP.

TO EVERY NATION...FROM EVERY TRIBE
An Episcopol film about the history of mission work among Indians to the present day. 28 minutes, color. Video. Rental: $10. HO.

TO FIND OUR WAY/FIRST STEPS
Two programs on one tape dealing with domestic violence in Native American communities. 1992. 32 mins. VHS. $150. CHAR.

TOBACCO FABLE
"DOLPHIN MEETS OL' COYOTE"
A children's story on the effects of smoking abd chewing. 14 mins. Video. $200; rental, $45. SH.

TOM SAVAGE: BOY OF EARLY VIRGINIA
Dramatizes the story of a boy given to the Indians. Depicts his new life, and his learning of their language, skills and tribal customs. 1958. Grades 4-9. 22 mins. Rental: UA.

TOMORROW'S YESTERDAY
KBYU-TV Provo, Utah, Producer
Shows how the Pueblo people adapt to the challenges of modern civilization while maintaining their identity and culture. 1971. 29 minutes, color. Video. Rental: $40/week. NAPBC.

TOTEM POLE
Clyde B. Smith, Producer
Illustrates the seven types of totem poles and relates each to a social system and mythology that laid great stress on kinship, rank, and ostentatious displays of wealth. The carving of a pole by Mungo Martin, a famous carver and chief of the Kwakiutl is shown. 1963. 27 minutes, color. Purchase: 16mm, $540; video, $195. Rental, $50. UC. Rental: 16mm, $27; video, $26. PSU.

TOTEMS
Shows the enormous cedar totems, with their ritualistic & religious carvings, made by the Wes Coast Indians of British Columbia. 1944. 11 minutes, color. 16mm. Rental: $19. UCLA.

TRADITIONAL USE OF PEYOTE
Gary Rhine, Producer/Director
A Summary of the Native American Church Crisis. The U.S. Supreme Court "Smith Decision." 17 minutes, color. Video. Purchase: $19. KF. Rental: $10. HO.

TRAGEDY & TRIUMPH -
THE CHEROKEE STORY
The history of the Eastern Band of Cherokee told through tradition and a glimpse of their lives today in Western North Carolina. 30 mins. Video. $29.95. CH.

TRAIL OF BROKEN TREATIES
Document Associates & BBC, Producer
Examines the past and present injustices and focuses on the attempt of Indian leaders to improve the situation. 1972. 26 minutes, color. Purchase: 16mm, $400; video, $295. Rental, $55. CG.

TRAIL OF THE BUFFALO
Eight minutes. 16mm. Rental. UA.

THE TRAIL OF TEARS
Traces westward expansion and the damage created to Indian culture. 13 mins, color. $69.95. FH.

TRAIL OF TEARS
WETA-TV Washington, D.C.
Focuses on the forced removal of the Cherokees from their homelands and their exodus to the West, and the Cherokee's struggle to maintain their identity & their heritage. 20 mins. Grades 7-12. 16-page teacher's guide, $1.95. Purchase: 16mm, $300; video, $150. AIT.

TRANSITIONS: DESTRUCTION
OF MOTHER TONGUE
Darrell Kipp & Joe Fisher
This program explores the relationship between language, thought & culture, and the impact of language disappearance in Native American communities. 1991. 25 minutes, color. Video. Rental: $10. HO.

TRAVELING THE DISTANCE
The colors, sounds, sights and essence of the Pow Wow, featuring dancers ablaze in colorful regalia, representing spirits, animals and tribal affiliations. Native Americans from across the U.S. and Canada tell in their own words what the pow wow means to them. The days that follow on the Shinnecock Indian reservation grounds on Long Island, NY, are inspirational. 1997. Won the Best Feature Documentary Award from the Long Island Film Festival. Video. 52 mins. SH.

THE TREASURE: INDIAN HERITAGE
Two teenage Indian brothers, after their father is arrested for defending tribal fishing rights, begin to weigh the worth of their heritage against today's commercial considerations. 1970. 13 minutes, color. Purchase: 4280; video, $175; Rental, $38. PHOENIX.

TREASURY OF CALIFORNIA INDIAN BASKETRY
Dr. Gregory Schaaf
Illustrates hundreds of baskets in their natural environments. 1990. VHS. CIAC.

TREATIES
Sandra Osawa, Writer/Producer
Julian Finkelstein, Director
Retraces Indian treaty history from Colonial times to the present. Discusses the treaty as a legal concept and historical reality. A speech made by Chief Seattle during a treaty session in 1855 is dramatized by host, Nez Perce actor, John Kauffman. 1975. 28 minutes. Video. Purchase: $55. UP and BYU-N.

TREATIES MADE—TREATIES BROKEN
Discusses the land grabbing, broken promises and treaties made by the white man with the Nisqually Indian tribe of Washington State. 1970. 18 minutes, color. 16mm. Rental. UT and IU.

TREATIES, TRUTH & TRUST
Presents 10 of the most commonly asked questions on treaty rights. The answers are given by Wisconsin tribal leaders & religious leaders from various communities. 14 minutes, color. Video. Purchase: $20; rental: $10. HO.

TREATY 8 COUNTRY
Anne Cubitt and Hugh Brody, Producers/directors
Documents subsistence hunting of the Beaver Indians of the Halfway River Band in northeast British Columbia, and records their views on the current situation over the abrogation of their treaty rights. 1982. 44 minutes. Color. 16mm (sales and rentals); 3/4" and 1/2" (sales only). CFDW.

THE TREATY OF 1868
NETV, Producer
Examines the roots of the dispute over the Lakota Sioux claim to the Black Hills of South Dakota. A series, two 30-minute videos. Program 1: The Treaty of 1868; Program 2: The Black Hills Claim. 1987. Color. Rental: $65/series; $40 each. NAPBC.

THE TREE IS DEAD
Describes one of the last Indian reservations in the State of Minnesota, Red Lake, and the disintegration of their own culture. 1955. Grades 4 and up. 11 minutes, bxw. 16mm. Rental: $13. UMN.

THE TRIAL OF STANDING BEAR
NETV, Producer
Tells the story of one man's struggle of self-determination in th 1879 court case "Standing Bear vs. Crook. The dramatic portrayal of the courageous Ponca Chief Standing Bear explores the personal side of the story as the Poncas were forced from their home on the Niobrara River (now northern Nebraska) to inhospitable Territory that is now modern-day Oklahoma. 1988. 120 minutes. Color. Video. Purchase: $40. GPN & NAPBC.

TRIBAL LAW
Title V Indian Education Program staff
Demonstrates students resolving a problem using the classroom system, and gives background information on underlying cultural valuesm as well as practical discussion for using a dispute resolution system based on the traditional "sttleup" compensation principals of the tribes of Northwest California. Grades 4-6. 15 minutes. VHS. $59.95 (includes Curriculum Unit). CB.

THE TRIBE & THE PROFESSOR:
OZETTE ARCHAEOLOGY
Louis and Ruth Kirk, Producers
Professor Richard Daugherty and his students from Washington State University returned to Ozette Indian Village to resume archaeological investigation begun in 1966. Results in the reconstruction of the Makah's past. Revised 1978 edition. 44 minutes. Purchase: 16mm, $550; beta, $425; VHS, $400. UW.

TRIBE OF THE TURQUOISE WATERS
Records the life of the Havasupai Indians in Arizona, and how their lives are shaped by their environment. Shows food preparation & the use of sweat lodges. 1952. Grades 6 and up. 13 minutes, color. 16mm. Rental: UA & UCLA.

TRUST FOR NATIVE AMERICAN
CULTURES AND CRAFTS VIDEO
Todd Crocker, Producer/narrator/editor;
Henri Vaillancourt, Director/writer/camera/editor

Documents aspects of the material culture of northern Native Americans i Eastern Canada. Programs include: Beavertail Snowshoes - the construction of traditional Cree Indian beavertail snowshoes, 1981, 40 minutes; Building an Algonquin Birchbark Canoe, 1984, 57 minutes; and Indian Hide Tanning -the Cree of northern Quebec show s moose and caribou hide tanning process, 1981, 35 minutes. Color. 3/4" & 1/2" video. In English and native languages. TR.

TUBUGHNA, THE BEACH PEOPLE
Emil McCord, Sr., Film Coordinator
Documentary about life in the Athabascan village of Tyonek, Alaska from 1964 to 1984. 1988. 57 minutes. VHS. $29.95. CIRI.

TUKTU STORIES
Lawrence Hyde, Writer/Editor
A series of 13 stories on Inuit culture. 1969. 14 minutes each. 16mm. Grades 3-9. See FILMS for titles and prices.

TULE TECHNOLOGY: NORTHERN PAIUTE USES
OF MARSH RESOURCES IN WESTERN NEVADA
Thomas Vennum, Jr., Producer
Louella George, Narrator
A film about Northern Paiute Indian people who have lived near the Stillwater marshes of western Nevada for generation. Focuses on Wuzzie George and members of her family constructing a duck egg bag, cattail house, duck decoy, and tule boat. 1983. 42 minutes, color. Purchase: 16mm, $420; video, $70. Rental: 16mm, $23; video, $12.50. PSU.

TUNUNEREMIUT: THE PEOPLE OF TUNUNAK
Portrays aspects of the lives of the people (Eskimos) of Tununak, a village on the southwestern coast of Alaska. 1973. 35 minutes, color. 16mm, $550; video, $195. Rental: 16mm, $60; video, $40. DER.

TURNAROUND
Moira Simpson, Prod./dir.; Janet Wright, Narrator
Aurora House provides a 6-12 week program for overcoming both chemical and physical dependencies. This film is about women who are learning to face painful truths with courage. One of the women is Marlene, who grew up in an environment of poverty and neglect. A Native Indian, she is committed to her work within the Native community. Four short films (Recovery Series) reflects the ongoing life of an Aurora House client after she has left treatment. 1984. 47 minutes. Color. 16mm, video. NFBC.

TURTLE SHELLS
Gary Robinson, Producer
Christine Hanneha, a Muscogee Creek Indian of Oklahoma demonstrates an ancient method of fashioning turtle shell leg rattles. 1987. 26 minutes. Color. Video. Purchase: $150; Rental: $40. NAPBC.

THE 21ST ANNUAL WORLD
ESKIMO-INDIAN OLYMPICS
Skip Blumberg, Producer/Director
Portraits of two Inupiat Eskimo athletes preparing for the Olympics and speaking of their Eskimo heritage. 1983. 27 minutes, color. Video. Purchase: $200. EIA.

TWO INDIANS - RED REFLECTIONS OF LIFE
Documentary study of two North American Indian high school students and their classmates. 1973. 26 mins. 16mm. Rental. UK.

TWO SPIRITS: NATIVE AMERICAN
LESBIANS & GAYS
T. Osa Hidalgo-Dela Riva
Royal Eagle Bear Productions
A documentary exploring one Native belief in human adrogyny. Compiles interviews with First People throughout the Americas. 28 mins. Color. VHS, $225; rental, $75. TWN.

UMEALIT: THE WHALE HUNTERS
John Angier (WGBH)
The Inuit and the controversy of whale hunting for subsistence versus the international effort to save the whales. 1980. 58 minutes. video. WGBH.

UNDERSTANDING A.I.R.F.A.
Gary Rhine, Producer/Director
A summary of the 1993 Congressional Amendment to the American Indian Religious Freedom Act which concerns protection of the use of sacred sites, eagle feathers and Peyote, and guarantees prisoner's rights. Features testimony by Indian law professor Vine Deloria, Native American rights attorney Walter Echo-Hawk, and Senator Daniel Inouye, Chair of the Senate Select Committee on Indian Affairs. 15 minutes, color. VHS. Purchase: $19. KF. Rental: $10. HO.

UNIVERSITY OF CALIFORNIA:
AMERICAN INDIAN FILM SERIES
Samuel A. Barrett and Clyde Smith
Each of 12 films uses the memories and oral traditions of contemporary Indians as well as anthropological records to document their cultural skills. Tribes filmed include: Southwestern Pomo, Kwakiutl, Yurok, Paviotso, Washo, Tolowa, Nisenan, and Brule Sioux. See UC for titles & prices.

UNLEARNING INDIAN STEREOTYPES
VHS tape & discussion guide. A teaching unit for elementary teachers & children's librarians contains: a study of stereotyping in picture books; 10 classroom don'ts for teachers; guidelines for publishers, illustrators, & writers; role playing strategies; Native American perspectives on Columbus Day, Thanksgiving, & Washington's Birthday. Rental: $10. HO.

URBAN ELDER
Documentary of Vern Harper, an urban Indian elder talking about traditional Indian culture and modern urban life. VHS. 28 mins. $139 with Guide. CHAR.

URBAN FRONTIER
Seattle Indian Center, Producer
Narrated by Dr. John Fuller and Will Sampson, this film provides an insight into the historical problems that have confronted Indian culture, and that have set the stage for the difficulties of adaptation in today's fast-paced society. A story which is told by Indians themselves, and illustrates how Indians have banded together in cities to form urban Indian centers; how they are putting their traditional values to work to help solve their problems. Two versions, 26 minutes & 17 minutes. Purchase: 16mm—27 minute version, $290; video, $65; 16mm—17 minute version, $215; video, $45. Rental (16mm only): 26 minute version, $30; 17 minute version, $20. COP. Rental: 16mm (26 min.), $16. UMN.

URBAN INDIANS
The story of Joe Killsright, an Oglala Sioux Indian from Pine Ridge Reservation who comes to New York City for a job and the problems he encounters as a result.20 minutes. Color. Video. Purchase: $175; Rental, $40. DTC.

UTE INDIAN TRIBE VIDEO
Larry Cesspooch, Producer/director
Sincer 1979, the Ute Indian Tribe, from the Uintah and Ouray Ute Reservation in Colorado, has been documenting Ute traditions and tribal concerns on video. Includes interviews, historical photographs, and other materials to illustrate this decisive period in Ute history. Programs include: Ute Bear Dance Story - 1983, 15 minutes; NOOdtVweep/Ute India Land - 1986, 18 minutes. Color. 3/4" and 1/2" video. UTE.

THE VANISHING AMERICAN
Richard Dix
Indian pre-history is the prelude to the story of Reservation Indians who are cheated by the Indian Agent, even after the Indians go fight in WW I. 1926. Grades 7 and up. 110 minutes, bxw. EG. Rental: $16. UMN.

1994 VIDEOBOOK
Beverly Singer
In this video diary, Singer, a documentarian, video artist and member of the Santa Clara Tewa Pueblo, has created an introspective examination of her life and her memories. 6 minutes. color video. 1994. Purchase: $225; rental: $50. TWN.

VILLAGE OF NO RIVER
Barbara Lipton, Writer/Director/Producer
Yup'ik Eskimo film, 1935-1940 and 1979-1980, illus-

trating change and continuity in the culture. Discusses present problems and concerns. 1981. 58 minutes. 16mm/bxw. In English and Yup'ik with English subtitles. NM.

VILLAGES IN THE SKY
Shows life in the high mesa villages of the Hopi. Women are shown making baskets and pottery, and baking; also, dances. 1952. Grades 6 and up. 12 mins, color. 16mm. Rental: UT, UA & UCLA.

A VIOLATION OF TRUST
Bill Jersey, Producer/director
Jim Belson, Producer/writer
Presents a conference, the American Indian International Tribunal, which indicts the U.S. government for its violation of trust relationship guaranteed by treaties. American Indian activists (Bob Gregory-Inupiat Eskimo; the late Philip Deere-Muscogee Creek; Oren Lyons-Onondaga; Janet McCloud-Tulalip-Duwamish; Dennis Banks-Ojibwa; and Matthew King-Oglala Sioux) forcefully articulate their aims and goals. 1982. 26 minutes, color. Video. CAT.

VISION DANCE
Henry Smith & Skip Sweeney, Directors
Showcases the talents of SOLARIS Dance Theatre and Lakota Sioux Indian Dancers drawn from nine reservations of the Lakota Nation in South Dakota. Lakota legends, myths and spirit qualities are juxtaposed with modern dance interpretations. 1982. 58 minutes. Purchase: or Video, $300; rental, $75. SOLARIS.

VISION QUEST
Dramatization of the spiritual experience required of 14 year old Western Indian boy before his acceptance as a man and a warrior. Shows phases of Indian life. 1961. 30 minutes, color. Grades 7 & up. 16mm rental, $19. PSU.

A VISIT TO WILD RICE COUNTRY
A visit with the Chippewa Indians shows that harvesting techniques have changed very little in a thousand years. 1975. Grades 1-6. 10 minutes, color. 16mm. Rebtal: $14.35. UMN.

VOICES FROM THE TALKING STICK
Narrated by Robert Davidson, John Yeltarzie and Woodrow Morrison
Story of the past, present and future told by the Haida people, maintaining the oral tradition of their culture, the narrators embark on a journey in four vignettes. Discusses how art, culture, the environment, and family are part of the Haida identity. Video, 20 mins. SH.

WALELA: LIVE IN CONCERT
Benfiting the Sovereign nations Preservations Project Non-Profit Provider of Eduactional Media benefiting Native Americans. With Rita Coolidge, Laura Satterfield and Priscilla Coolidge. 60 mins. 2004. VHS, $24.95; DVD, $27.95. ME.

WALKING IN A SACRED MANNER
Stephen Cross; Joseph Epes Brown, Consultant
Opens with photography by Edward S. Curtis and the words of many Native American orators, this film conveys the respect felt by Native Americans for the natural world. 1982. 23 minutes, color. Purchase: 16mm, $425; video, $340. Rental: UCT, UA & IU.

WALKING WITH GRANDFATHER
Phil Lucas, Producer/director
A series of six,15-minute programs - stories, drawing upon the rich oral traditions of North American Indian people of several tribes. Presents basic human values. Teacher's guide. 1988. Color. Video. Teacher's Guide, $12. Purchase: $325/series; $70/program. FOUR (Canada); GPN (U.S.)

WANAGI IS GONE
Bruce Baird
The uncovering of a massive ancient grave site raises questions about the excavations of such sites as well as examines Indian traditional views as well as scientific significance. 1978. 30 minutes. 2 quad, 1 videotape, VHS. KUSD.

WANDERING SPIRIT SURVIVAL SCHOOL
Marvin Midwicki, Les Holdway, Christopher Wilson
Canadian children learn Indian legends, traditions, languages and crafts. 1978. 28 minutes, color. Video. Purchase: $27. NFBC.

WAR AGAINST THE INDIANS
CBC Production
Explores the impact of our native peoples through conversations, scenery, paintings, photos, drama, and music. 3 tapes, 60 mins. each. VHS, $25.99. ME.

THE WARPATH
Western expansion and the breaking of treaties which led to war between the setlers and Indians. 13 minutes, color. Video. Purchase: $69.95. FH.

WARRIOR CHIEFS IN A NEW AGE
Dean Curtis Bear Claw
As a young man in the late 1800's, Chiefs Plenty Coups & Medicine Crow had prophetic visions concerning the future of the Crow people. This portrait of the transitional leaders tells the story of how these visions helped lead the Crow Indian Nation into the 20th century. 28 minutes, color. Rental: $10. HO.

WARRIORS
Deb Wallwork, Producer
Honoring Native American veterans of the Vietnam War. 1986. 57 minutes, color. Video. Purchase: $56.95. NAPBC. Purchase: 3/4" - $160, 1/2" - $110; Rental: 3/4" - $60, 1/2" - $40. IN.

WARRIORS AT PEACE
Depicts the life of the Apache Indians in eastern Arizona with emphasis on their customs and traditions. 1953. 12 minutes, color. Grades 4 and up. Rental: UA, UCLA & UK.

WARRIORS SONG: POST TRAUMATIC STRESS DISORDER
Explores the legacy of post traumatic stress disorder from a Native American perspective as three therapists and one author share their personal stories. Focuses on the healing challenges facing veterans of war. 1996. 60 mins. VHS. $50. CHAR.

WASHOE
Veronika Pataky
Depicts the transition of the Washoe Tribe in Nevada from traditional customs to the 20th century. 1968. Grades 7 and up. 57 minutes, bxw. 16mm. In Washoe with English narration. Rental: UW, UK, IU, UCLA & UMN.

THE WATER IS SO CLEAR THAT A BLIND MAN COULD SEE
New Mexico's Taos Indians believe that all life (plant and animal) is sacred and live without disturbing their environment. Lumber companies are trying to get permission from the Federal Government to lumber the Taos Indian area. 1970. 30 minutes, color. 16mm. Rental: PSU, UCT & IU.

THE WAY
Sandra Osawa (KNBC-TV)
A sketch of Native American religion and its place in contemporary Indian life. Focuses on the Cherokee, Cheyenne and Ojibwa religious practices, and Indian spirituality. 1975. 28 minutes. VHS. BYU-N.

A WAY OF LIFE
CBC Northern Services, Producer
The lifestyle of Henry Evaluarjuk, Inuit carver, who, with his family and two other families, chose to live on an uninhabited and secluded inlet on Baffin Island. 1983. 28 minutes. 2 quad, 1 videotape, and VHS. Rental, $40/week. NAPBC.

THE WAY WE LIVE
Four, 10-15 minute video tapes showing several aspects of traditional Yup'ik Eskimo culture. 1981. 60 minutes. VHS. $24.95. KYUK.

WAY OF OUR FATHERS
Bradley Wright
Members of several northern California Indian tribes depict unique elements of a way of life as it flourished before the imposition of European culture. 33 minutes,

color. Grades 9 and up. Video. Purchase: $95; rental: $50. UC. Rental: 16mm, $24.50. PSU.

WE ARE ONE
Chet Kincaid, Producer
Eight, 20-minute programs about the life and culture of a Native American family in early 19th century Nebraska/\ Focuses on 13-year-old Ni'bthaska and his younger sister Mi'onbathin and on the daily rituals and rites of passage that make up their lives. 1986. Color. Video. Rental: $250/series; $40 each. NAPBC.

WE ARE A RIVER FLOWING
Nick Clark, Producer
An exploration of Northern Irish and Native American cultures. A Ten-year-old girl from Belfast travels to the Pine Ridge Indian reservation as a part of a program for children of political turmoil. 1985. 28 minutes. Color. Video. Purchase: 3/4" - 120, 1/2" - 80; Rental: 3/4" - 45, 1/2" - 30. IN.

WE ARE THESE PEOPLE
Featuring Will Sampson, this film is designed to foster an appreciation for the richness of Native American cultures & promote social support by reinforcing traditional values. 15 minutes, color. Video. Purchase: $245; rental: $45. SH. Rental: 16mm, $21. UMN.

WE BELONG TO THE LAND
Reaffirms the relationship between Indain & the land; and explores lifestyles in natural resource careers of forestry, game management, range management, & related fields. 30 minutes. Video. Purchase: $245; rental, $45. SH.

WE OF THE RIVER
Documentary chronicles the arrival and the emergence into the 20th century of the Yup'ik Eskimo people who have lived in this area for more than 12,000 years. 1985. 60 minutes. VHS. $24.95. KYUK.

WE OWE IT TO OURSELVES & TO OUR CHILDREN
Video uses cartoon images and live action Native health educators to discuss the causes, symptoms, treatments, and prevention of HIV & STDs. 8 mins. VHS, $5. NNA.

WE PRAY WITH TOBACCO
Focuses on the traditional cultural & ceremonial uses of this herb. 1998. 60 mins. VHS. $24.95. ME.

WE REMEMBER
Raymond Yakeleya
The history of the Dene people as told by Yakeleya, a Slavey Indian, and some of the elders of the Slavey and Loucheau tribes of Canada - their past, present and thoughts for the future. 1979. In two parts. 1979. 30 mins. each. 16mm & VHS. CFMDC.

A WEAVE OF TIME
Susan Fanshel, with John Adair & Deborah Gordon, Producers
Susan Fanshel, Director
Follows the lives of four generations of the Burnsides, a Navajo family from the Pine Springs community in Arizona on the Navajo reservation. In 1938 anthropologist John Adair filmed daily activities and artistic techniques; explores many aspects of Navajo life. 1986. 60 mins. b&w & color. 16mm, 3/4" (sales only) and 1/2" (sales & rentals). SH, DC.

WEAVERS OF THE WEST
A film which shows the Navajo's process of rug-making. 1954. 13 mins, color. Rental, IU.

WEDDING OF PALO
F. Dalsheim and Knud Rasmussen
Rasmussen, the Danish Inuit anthropologist and explorer directed this film based on a traditional Inuit tale about the courtship and marriage of a young man and woman. 1937. 72 mins. 35mm/16mm/bxw. In Inuit with English subtitles. MMA.

WELCOME TO NAVAHO LAND
Paul Auguston
Navajo children's drawings are animated with the children telling the stories their work illustrates. Navajo songs. In two parts: Part I, 12 minutes; Part 2, 20 minutes. video. UMC.

WEMAWE-FETISH CARVING OF THE ZUNI PUEBLO

A documentary of ten exceptional carvers of the Zuni Pueblo and in their own words their view of what carving means to the artists. Video. 26 mins. SH.

THE WEST

Insignia Films & WETA

A 9-part series of American expansionism. Teaches middle school and high school students about Native American tribes, American pioneers and homesteaders, and the steady expansion of the U.S. across the continent. Begins with the arrival of the first Europeans and extends into the 20th century. Includes audio tapes, curriculum package, a printed index, and a promotional poster. 1996. $295. PBS.

WESTWARD EXPANSION

Follows the chain of events leading to the Indian Removal Act, manifest destiny, the Civil War, and the Indian wars. 1969. 25 minutes, color. Grades 6 and up. 16mm. Rental, $15.25. IU.

WHAT MORE CAN I DO?... A NURSE'S EXPERIENCE WITH A NAVAJO CANCER PATIENT

Story of a community health nurse, who through persistence & sensitivity, learns to integrate her own values & perceptions with those of a Navajo cancer patient & his family. 1986. 27 minutes, color. 3/4" U-mat. Rental: $16. UMN.

WHEN THE WHITE MAN CAME

Describes life among the major tribes across the U.S. when the Europeans arrived in the late 15th Century. 13 minutes, color. Video. Purchase: $69.95. FH.

WHERE HAS THE WARRIOR GONE?

Explores the life of Ted Cly, a typical Navajo father living on a reservation in Utah. 13 minutes. Grades 1-8. Rental. UK.

WHERE THE SPIRIT LIVES

Bruce Pittman, Director; music by Buffy St. Marie

The story of Amelia, a young Blackfoot Indian girl, and her plight to escape the horrors that white society has forced upon her. Set in 1937 amid the Canadian Rockies. Amelia was kidnapped from her reserve by the government and placed in an Indian Residential School. 1989. 97 minutes, color. Video. Purchase: $295. BE. Rental: $16. UMN.

WHITE MAN'S WAY

Christine Lesiak & NETV, Producer

Beginning in the late 1800s, an experiment that endeavored to transform the American Indian took place; the federal government built the U.S. Indian School in Genoa, Nebraska, a military-style school for Indian children from more than 20 tribes. Here they taught the white man's language, traditions, lifestyles and were forbidden to practice their own. 1986. 30 minutes, color. Video. Purchase: $40. NAPBC & GPN. Rental: $16. UMN.

WHY COYOTE HAS THE BEST EYES

Discusses the importance of stories & storytelling within Indian culture. An elder of the Hupa tribe shares his knowledge of nature & heritage with Indian children on the Hoopa Reservation. Grades K-3. 10 minutes. $59.95. CB.

WHY DID GLORIA DIE?

NET, Producer

Depicts the tragic life of Gloria Curtis, a Chippewa woman who died of hepatitis at age 17. Deals with the adjustments one must make from reservation to urban life. 1973. 27 minutes, color. 16mm & video. Rental: $20. IU & UMN.

WILD RICE: THE TAMING OF A GRAIN

Waterstone Films, Producer

Traces the history of wild rice, a Native North American food, and the first wild grain to be brought into cultivation in modern history. 1988. Grades 7 and up. 18 minutes. Purchase: VHS, $250. SH, NDM.

WINTER ON AN INDIAN RESERVATION

A film about children on a forest reservation. 1973. Grades K-4. 11 minutes, color. 16mm. Rental: $9. UCT.

RUSSELL & YVONNE WILLIER TAN A MOOSE HIDE

David E. Young, Trudy Nicks, Ruth McConnell, & David Strom, Producers

Russell and Yvonee are Woods Cree Indians from northern Alberta. Documents the entire production process. 1989. 30 minutes, color. Video. Purchase: $70; rental, $20. UADA.

WIND RIVER

Story about Washakie, Chief of the Shoshone. With Wes Studi & Russell Means. 1998. VHS, $16.99; DVD, $24.99. ME.

WINDTALKERS

About WWII Navajo codetalkers and their protection during the war. With Nicholas Cage, Adam Beach. 2002. 134 mins. VHS, $19.99; DVD, $24.99. ME.

WINDS OF CHANGE: A MATTER OF CHOICE

Carol Cotter, Writer/producer

Examines the struggle of Native Americans to maintain individual identities & sovereign Indian nations within the U.S. Hopi tribal members provide insights into the personal side of acculturation & assimilation, focusing on the exodus of their youth to the cities. Original score by R. Carlos Nakai. Hosted by Hattie Kauffman & N. Scott Momaday. 1990. 58 mins, color. Video. Purchase: PBS. Rental: $12. PSU; $16. UMN.

WINDS OF CHANGE: A MATTER OF PROMISES

PBS, Producer

Kiowa author, N. Scott Momaday explores the plight of the American Indian in today's society. A visit to the Onondaga of New York, the Navajo in Arizona, and the Lummi in Washington. 58 mins, color. Video. Purchase: $19.95. PBS & CAN. Rental: $10. HO & PSU; $16. UMN.

WINDWALKER

Story of a dying Cheyenne Indian whose life spans three generations of Cheyenne life. 108 mins. VHS, $19.99. ME.

WINTER WOLF: LEARNING ABOUT NATIVE AMERICAN CULTURE

Follows a young Native American girl as she seeks to understand age-old conflicts between mankind & wolves. 30 mins. Purchase: VHS, $49. GA.

WIPING THE TEARS OF SEVEN GENERATIONS

Gary Rhine, Producer/Director

A documentary that examines U.S. history through the Lakota Sioux perspective, with emphasis on The Wounded Knee Massacre and The Bigfoot Memorial Ride. In English & Lakota with English subtitles. 1992. Grades 4 and up. 57 mins, color. Purchase: VHS, $30. ME. 16mm, $750. Rental: Video, $85; 16mm, $200; 60 mins audiocassette, $11. KF & OY. Rental: $10. HO & UMN.

WITH HEART & HAND

Oak Creek Films, Producer

Documentary on the history of Southwestern Native American art as seen through a selected group of contemporary practitioners & storytellers. 1993. Grades 7 and up. 30 mins. VHS, $25. ME.

WITHIN THE CIRCLE

Dance styles. Powwows. Includes Blacklodge Singers. VHS. 60 minutes. $19.95. WH.

WOMEN IN AMERICAN LIFE

Five videos depicting women's roles in American history. How westward expansion, immigration, the two world wars, and government legislation have affected the lives of Native Americans. 1990. KS.

WOMEN & MEN ARE GOOD DANCERS

Arlene Bowman

Cree language of an intertribal pow wow song. 1994. VHS. 6 minutes, color. Purchase: $125; rental, $50. TWN.

WOODEN BOX: MADE BY STEAMING & BENDING

Clyde B. Smith, Producer

The Indians of the Northwest Pacific Coast developed woodworking; a specialty was steaming and bending of a single wooden slab to form a box. This film follows, carefully, every stage of making the Kwakiutl box. 1962. 33 minutes, color. Purchase: 16mm, $660; video, $195. Rental: $50. UC. Rental only: 16mm, $24.50. PSU.

WOODLAND INDIANS OF EARLY AMERICA

Roy A. Price, Ed.D.

Authentic reconstructions and scenes in the eastern and Great Lakes regions provide settings for this study of Woodland Indian life (Chippewa) prior to European influence. Revised 1980 edition. 10 minutes, color. Grades K-6. Purchase: 16mm, $265; video, $59. PHOENIX. Rental: 16mm, $16.50. IU, UMN & PSU.

WOODLAND TRADITIONS: THE ART OF THREE NATIVE AMERICANS

Features three Woodland Indian artists who tell in their own words how & why they create. Follows the artists step-by-step from the point of inspiration through the actual creation to the final work of art. 1984. 27 minutes, color. Video. Rental: $16. UMN.

WOONSPE (EDUCATION AND THE SIOUX)

SD ETV

Explores the problems of Native American education. 1974. 28 minutes, color. Video. Rental: $40. NAPBC.

WORDS & PLACE: NATIVE LITERATURE FROM THE AMERICAN SOUTHWEST

Denny Carr, Director; Larry Evers, Producer

Series of eight videotapes (produced by the University of Arizona, in cooperation with KUAT (Tucson, 1976-77) focus on traditional & modern Native American literature as told or written by individuals of various Southwestern tribes: Apache, Yaqui and Hopi people speak of their traditional philosophy, rituals & songs. Titles: "By This Song I Walk" (A Navajo Song); "Seyewailo: The Flower World" (Yaqui Deer Songs); "The Origin of the Crown Dance" (An Apache Narrative) & "Ba'ts'oosee" (An Apache Trickster Cycle); "Iisaw" (Hopi Coyote Stories); "Natwaniwa" (A Hopi Philosophical Statement); "Running on the Edge of the Rainbow" (Laguna Stories & Poems); "Songs of My Hunter Heart" (Laguna Songs & Poems); "A Conversation With Vine Deloria, Jr." 18-51 minutes. Video. Purchase: $150 to $290 each, $1425/series. NR. Rentals: see ATL.

A WORLD OF IDEAS WITH BILL MOYERS 1 & 2: LOUISE ERDRICH & MICHAEL DORRIS

Louise Erdrich and Michael Dorris, a Native American wife-husband team who write novels based on their heritage. 1. Discuss the values and difficulties of modern Native Americans, the concept of "ironic survival humor," and the Native American's ability to live on the land in harmony with nature. 29 minutes, color. 2. Observe how alcoholism & despair have shattered the lives of many Native Americans. Grades 9 and up. Rental: video, $11 & $14. PSU & IU.

WOVEN BY THE GRANDMOTHERS: 19TH CENTURY NAVAJO TEXTILES

Narrated by performer Buffy Sainte-Marie

Captures the rhythms of Navajo life; explores the 19th century Navajo textiles collection of the Museum of the American Indian. 30 minutes, color. $19.95. PMI.

YAQUI

Arizona artist Ted De Grazia narrates this filmic story of his paintings that depict the Yaqui Indian Ceremony. 1973. Grades 4 and up. 19 minutes, color. 16mm. Rental: UA.

THE YAQUI CUR

D.W. Griffith, Director

A young Yaqui brave is converted to Christianity, and refuses to fight when his tribe is attacked by Zuni neighbors. He later redeems himself. 1913. 12 minutes, bxw. EG.

YESTERDAY'S CHILDREN

Skokomish youth interview two elders on the Skokomish Reservation on Hood Canal in western Washington State. The elders talk about their lives and changes they have experienced. Teacher's guide and lesson plans. 30 minutes, color. Grades 9 and up. Purchase: Video, $110. Rental: $25. DSP.

YESTERDAY, TODAY: THE NETSILIK ESKIMO
Gilles Blais
Traces the adaptation of the Netsilik from a migratory people to settlers in a government village. Filmed ten years after the documentary film, The Eskimo: Fight for Life. 1974. 58 minutes, color. Grades 7 and up. 16mm. EDC & UA. Video, $27. NFBC.

YOU ARE ON INDIAN LAND
Mort Ransen, Director
Report of a protest demonstration by Mohawk Indians of the St. Regis Reservation on the international Bridge between Canada and U.S. 1969. 36 mins, bxw. Purchase: Video, $27. NFBC. Rental: 16mm, $17.50. PSU.

YOU CHOOSE
Features Nathan Chasing His Horse. Designed to discourage youth from chewing or smoking tobacco. 20 mins, color. Video. Purchase: $245; rental: $45. SH.

YOUR HUMBLE SERPENT:
THE WISDOM OF REUBEN SNAKE
Written & directed by Gary Rhine
Portrait of the late American Indian political and spiritual leader, Reuben A. Snake, Jr., in which he speaks out on ecology, sacredness, intuitive thinking and the "Rebrowning of America." 1996. 60 mins, color. VHS. $29.95. ME & KF.

YUMA CROSSING
Docu-drama Quechan storyteller, Joe Homer, traces the history of the Yuma Crossing in southwestern Arizona from prehistori times until the opening of the Ocean to Ocean Highway Bridge in 1916. Grades 6 to adult. VHS. 28 mins. $69. CHAR.

1987 YUP'IK DANCE FESTIVAL
Villages from the Yukon & Kuskokwim Delta sent dancers to Bethel to participate in one of the largest festivals in recent memory. 1988. 120 mins, color. Video. $24.95. KYUK.

FILMSTRIPS & SLIDES

AKWESASNE RESERVATION SLIDE SHOW
A complete package of slide carousel, tape and script. Includes Iroquois legends, corn husk doll-making, Mohawk basketmaking, Iroquois Wampum & Cradleboards. 1984. 10 minutes. Rental, $15. AM.

AMERICA'S 19th CENTURY WARS
Covers the Indian Wars. Includes teacher's guide. Grades 7-12. Six filmstrips/cassettes. $141. LL.

AMERICAN INDIAN FOLK LEGENDS
Myths and legends of the American Indian. The White Buffalo; The First Tom-Tom; First Winter, First Summer; The Four Thunders, two parts; How Fire Came to Earth. Six filmstrips; records or cassettes. $130. RH.

AMERICAN INDIAN LEGENDS
Four filmstrips: The Magic Food (Iroquois); The Basket Lady (Ute); When the People Lived in the Dark (Cherokee); Mountain Spirit Dance (Mescalero Apache). 4 cassettes, guide. $129. SVE.

AMERICAN INDIAN LEGENDS
Adventure stories showing many customs and rituals of American Indians. Aids vocabulary growth. Grades 3-5. Six filmstrips / cassettes. $119.00; six filmstrips (captioned), $55. RH.

AMERICAN INDIAN LIFE
Nine color filmstrips comparing and contrasting the ways of life of Indians in different sections of the U.S. Grades 1-6. CMC.

AMERICAN INDIAN NATURE LEGENDS
The wonders of nature and reverence for life are interwoven into these American Indian legends. Grades 3-6. 6 filmstrips, 6 cassettes. $132. TA.

AMERICAN INDIAN SONGS
A broad cross-section of American Indian folk songs from every region in the U.S. Filmstrip, cassette & book. $34.95. ALF.

THE AMERICAN INDIAN: A STUDY IN DEPTH
Dr. Ethel J. Alpenfeis traces the history and development of the American Indians over the past 400 centuries. Six color filmstrips/cassettes. PHM.

AMERICAN INDIANS & HOW THEY REALLY LIVED
The heritage and history of American Indians are revealed. Indian crafts and customs are depicted. Includes Hopi and Navajo, Seminoles, Crow, Chinook, and the Iroquois tribes. Grades 3-7. 5 filmstrips. $50; $10, individual. TA.

AMERICAN INDIANS OF
THE NORTH PACIFIC COAST
Their history, arts and crafts, myths and ceremonies. Grades 4-6. Six filmstrips/cassettes. $119. PHOENIX.

AMERICAN INDIANS OF THE NORTHEAST
A study of the rise and fall of the Algonquin and Iroquois Indian empires, migrants from Asia to the Northeastern U.S. and southern Canada. Who they are, their history, religion, handicrafts. Grades 4-6. Six filmstrips/ cassettes. $119. PHOENIX.

AMERICAN INDIANS OF THE PLAINS
Presents the history, tribes, culture, arts and crafts, and religion of the Plains Indians. Grades 4-9. Six filmstrips/cassettes. $119. PHOENIX.

AMERICAN INDIANS OF THE SOUTHEAST
A full-blooded Cherokee explains their life today. Reveals the life of the Southeastern Indian tribes from prehistoric times to the present. Grades 4-9. Six filmstrips/cassettes. $119. PHOENIX.

AMERICAN INDIANS OF THE SOUTHWEST
A history-oriented presentation of the Pueblo tribes, examining their customs and languages. Grades 4-9. Six filmstrips/cassettes. $119. PHOENIX.

AMERICAN MUSEUM OF NATURAL HISTORY—
PHOTOGRAPHIC & FILM COLLECTION
Contains thousands of bxw photographs, color slides, and color transparencies of Native Americans; may be rented for reproduction, or purchased. For films, short footage segments may be available for reproduction upon payment of film/video duplication costs and use fees. AM.

ANCIENT ART OF THE AMERICAN
WOODLAND INDIANS
David Penney (guest curator of the National Gallery) discusses ancient Woodland Indian artifacts and explains their cultural and aesthetic significance. Includes maps showing the Archaic, Woodland, and Mississippian period sites from which the artifacts came. 27 slides; audiocassette & text. 32 mins. Free rental. NGA.

THE BATTLE OF THE LITTLE BIGHORN
A detailed study of the impact of Custer's defeat by the Sioux and Cheyenne. Grades 7-12. Filmstrip/cassette. $26. LL.

BATTLE OF THE LITTLE BIG HORN
A series of 78 slides or filmstripdepicting the Battle which took place in 1876. Includes a booklet, teacher's guide, cassette tape, map and poster. $36.60. SI.

CAHOKIA SLIDE PACKAGE
Seven sets of 5 slides each with a cassette tape and written text, illustrating the history of Indian culture at Cahokia, as well as the archaeological techniques used to explore and study the site. $2 per strip. CMM.

CLIMBING THE HILL
A specialized filmstrip developed for men and women who are interested in following the kind of leadership demonstrated by the old Dakota Holy Men. $15. AICRC.

CONTEMPORARY INDIAN &
ESKIMO CRAFTS OF THE U.S.
74 full-color, 35mm slides with lecture text booklet illustrating the great variety of distinctive craft forms created by numerous contemporary Native American craftsmen. $50. TIPI.

CONTEMPORARY NATIVE AMERICAN MASKS
20 color slides. $30. ATL.

CONTEMPORARY SIOUX PAINTING
77 full-color and bxw, 35mm slides with lecture text booklet. Illustrates the historic development of expressive forms of painting created by Sioux artists during the past 200 years. $50. TIPI.

THE CORPS OF DISCOVERY:
THE LEWIS & CLARK EXPEDITION
An exploration that had a significant impact on opening up Western America. Grades 7-12. Two filmstrips; cassette. $31. LL.

COSTUMES & MASKS OF
THE SOUTHWEST TRIBES
Shows Navajo, Apache, Hopi & Pueblo ceremonial attire, including masks & costumes. 27 slides, no narration. 1977. $10. UCLA.

DAKOTA WAY & THE SACRAMENTS
Filmstrip, with cassette & guide. $10. AICRC.

THE DRUM IS THE HEART
Randy Croce, Producer
Focuses on the Blackfeet, Blackfoot, Blood and Peigan tribes that make up the Blackfoot Nation at their celebrations, speaking about their contemporary lives and traditional values. Filmstrip and slide set. Purchase and rental. BM.

THE EARTH KNOWERS:
THE NATIVE AMERICANS SPEAK
Statements of Indian wise men who relied on religious and cultural experience to deal with technological and social reorganization. Guide. Grades 7-12. Filmstrip/cassette. $26. LL.

ESKIMOS OF ALASKA (ARCTIC LIFE)
Four color filmstrips providing a picture of the life of Eskimos in Alaska. Emphasis is placed on activities of children. Grades 4-8. CMC.

EVERYTHING NEW
Audio tape with slides tells the story of creation; traditional chants and songs include Eskimo, and North American Indian people. 1973. 19 minutes. $7.00. UT.

EXPLORING & COLONIZING
In 4 parts. One filmstrip on the First Americans. 4 filmstrips, 4 cassettes, 28 skill sheets, guide. $89. SVE.

FAMOUS INDIAN CHIEFS
Examines eight famous Indian chiefs: Pontiac (Ottawa), Joseph Brant (Mohawk), Tecumseh (Shawnee), Black Hawk (Sauk), Osceola (Seminole), Chief Joseph (Nez Perce), Sitting Bull (Sioux), and Geronimo (Apache). Grades 4-6. Eight filmstrips; cassettes. $149. PHOENIX.

THE FAR NORTH
Deals with the art and culture of the Alaskan Eskimo Aleuts and the Athapascan and Tlingit Indians, focusing on the art and ways of life. 1975. 48 color slides. Free rental. NGA.

THE FIRST AMERICANS
Six sound filmstrips which studies the major Indian tribes of the U.S. - their customs, culture and the land that belonged to them. Indians of the Northeast, Southwest, Great Lakes, Plains, Southeast, and Northwest. Grades 4-6. $132.00; $22 each. Available os a video. TA.

THE FIRST PEOPLE OF NORTH AMERICA:
INDIANS & INUIT
Presents an historical overview of the various native cultures existing in North America. The distinctive lifestyles of native peoples of differing geographic regions are examined with an emphasis on environmental factors. One filmstrip is devoted to the study of the Inuit of the Arctic. Six filmstrips; cassettes; one sound filmstrip guide with discussion questions; one script booklet. $160. UL.

FOLKTALES OF ETHNIC AMERICA
Includes The Brahman, The Tiger, and The Six Judges (Indian); and The Blind Boy and the Loon (Alaskan.) Grades 3-6. Six filmstrips/cassettes. $119. RH.

THE FRENCH & INDIAN WARS: ROAD TO THE AMERICAN REVOLUTION?
Reviews the outstanding developments which lead to independence, including the French and Indian War 1689-1762. Grades 7-12. Two filmstrips/cassettes. $31. LL.

GHOST DANCE TRAGEDY AT WOUNDED KNEE
66-slide program which brings the Wounded Knee incident of December of 1890 alive — its historical and religious background, and the events of that infamous day when members of the Seventh Cavalry (Custer's old regiment) confronted the Sioux who had gathered at the Pine Ridge agency. Includes booklet, teacher's guide, cassette tape, and 2 maps. $36.60. SI.

GREAT AMERICAN INDIAN HEROES
Personal stories of leaders and chiefs who won the trust of their people and inspired their tribes in war and peace. 8 sound filmstrips: Tecumseh, Osceola, Black Hawk, Pontiac, Chief Joseph, Sitting Bull, Geronimo, and Joseph Brant. Grades 4-6. $176; $22. each. Available as a video. TA.

HOMES OF ANCIENT PEOPLE
A color filmstrip showing the ruins of ancient Indian homes at Mesa Verde, Canyon de Chelly, and Walnut Canyon. Grades 4-8. CMC.

HOW THE INDIANS DISCOVERED A NEW WORLD
Paleo-Indian transition from hunting to farming, trade and communications. Grades 6-12. Two filmstrips; cassettes. $33. RH.

HUNGER WALKS AMONG INDIANS
Indian Ministries Task Force on some of the work they have done to alleviate hunger problems of Native Americans. 85 slides; cassette. Rental, $5. NILB.

INDIAN AMERICANS: STORIES OF ACHIEVEMENT
A four filmstrip set which portrays, in illustrations and soundtracks, the contributions of four great Indian Americans: Hiawatha, Ely S. Parker, Washakie, and Pocahontas. Four records or cassettes; teacher's guide. WD.

INDIAN ART IN AMERICA: THE ARTS & CRAFTS OF THE NORTH AMERICAN INDIANS
51 slides. MAI.

INDIAN HERITAGE
Six color filmstrips that explore the life and culture of the American Indian. Includes: Americans Before Columbus, Indian Children, Indian Homes, Indian Celebrations, Indian Legends, Indians Who Showed the Way. Grades 2-6. $60; $10 each. TA.

AN INDIAN JESUS
Richard West, a Cheyenne Indian, is a Christian and an artist. Through his paintings, he helps us see Jesus through Native American eyes. 42 frames; color. Reading script and guide. Grades 3-12. $10. FP.

INDIAN LEADERS OF TOMORROW
  American Indian Science & Engineering Society, Producer
For encouraging Native American youth to further their education & pursue professional careers. Slide/tape. Purchase: $150; rental: $40. SH.

INDIAN PAINTING
63 subjects (slide sets.) See MAI for ordering information.

INDIAN ROCK ART
Portrays one of the most ancient art forms in New Mexico, illustrating the timeless images of a mysterious art. 12 minute slide-tape program. Available for loan or purchase. MNM.

INDIAN SOVEREIGNTY—INDIAN TREATIES— INDIANS AND THE U.S. GOVERNMENT— INDIAN JURISDICTION FEDERAL INDIAN TRUST RELATIONSHIP
A series of five instructional programs of four filmstrips each, explaining the legal concepts and the history behind many of the present areas of controversy involving Indian tribes. Researched by the Institute for the Development of Indian Law, Inc. Includes response sheet master for practice quizes; trainer's guide for each. Pre/Post tests available, $6 per topic. $120 each; $480 per set. COOK.

INDIAN VALUES IN A NEW WORLD
  Council Energy Resource Tribes, Producer
A teenage brother & sister are troubled by their uncertain future as high school graduation nears. Through their grandfather they meet various role models who apply traditional values in pursuing their post-secondary education. Slide/tape. Purchase: $150; rental: $40. SH.

INDIAN VILLAGE ARCHAEOLOGY
Documents the rediscovery of ancient Ozette by archaeologists. 1972. 88 color frames; teacher's guide and cassette. UW.

THE INDIAN WOMEN OF THE EARLY DAWN
Presents a philosophic view of the Indian woman. Video/slide show; 10-20 minutes. Purchase: $150; rental, $40. SH.

INDIANS OF HISTORIC TIMES
Slide sets on the following areas: Eskimo and Arctic (33 subjects); Northwest Coast (221 subjects); Woodlands and Northeast (118 subjects); Southeast (38 subjects); Plains and Plateau (446 subjects); Southwest (184 subjects); and, Far West (73 subjects). See MAI for ordering information.

INDIANS OF NORTH AMERICA
North America's native peoples from ancient to modern times. A series of five sound filmstrips: The First Americans; The Eastern Woodlands; The Plains; West of the Shining Mountains; and, Indians Today. 13-14 minutes each. Grades 5-12. $99.50. NGS.

INDIANS OF NORTH AMERICA
Six filmstrips: Indians of the Northeast, Southeast, Plains, Northwest Coast, Southwest, Far North. Grades 4-6. Includes 6 cassettes, guide. $179. SVE.

INDIANS: THE SOUTHWEST & THE PLAINS INDIANS
The history of the American Indian people and how they live today. The Southwest Indians and The Sundance People. Two filmstrips, cassettes each, $48 each. Grades 6-8. RH.

INSIDE THE CIGAR STORE: IMAGES OF THE AMERICAN INDIAN
Focuses on the contradictory stereotypes of the American Indian which have been perpetuated by mass media and textbooks, and pleads for the replacement of the inaccurate images with the knowledge about contemporary American Indian people. Filmstrip/cassette. MRC.

IT IS WRITTEN IN THE HEARTS OF OUR PEOPLE
Views contemporary Indian youth and points out their guardianship of the land and customs passed down by the elders. Based around the words of Chief Seattle's 1853 speech. Video/slide show. 10-20 minutes. Purchase: $150; rental, $40. SH.

LEGENDS OF THE MICMAC
The use of puppetry and mask-making in providing an instructive introduction to one of the earliest tribes to settle in North America. Grades 2-5. Four filmstrips, cassettes; teacher's guide. $95. RH.

THE LIFE OF THE AMERICAN INDIAN
Two sound filmstrips: The Eastern Woodlands and the Plains - explains how eastern tribes utilize their environment; and The Northwest Coast and the Southwest - Southwestern Indians farm arid lands and dance for rain, while Northwest Coast Indians fish and hold potlatches. 1977. 13-14 minutes each. Grades K-4. $50. NGS.

THE MAKE-BELIEVE INDIAN: NATIVE AMERICANS IN THE MOVIES
  Gretchen Bataille & Charles L.P. Silet
Demonstrates the influence of early travel narratives, literature, the visual arts, and the wild west shows on the Native American image in the movies. Examples are drawn from silent films, serials, and contemporary feature films. 140 slides and carousel tray; audio-cassette; bibliography; script; suggestions. Purchase: $99; rental, $15/3 days. MRC.

THE MAN FROM DEER CREEK, THE STORY OF ISHI
A Yahi Indian in 1911, the last of his tribe, and the last to grow up without contact with American civilization. Grades 7-12. Two filmstrips, cassette. $41. LL.

THE MARMES MAN DIG
  Louis and Ruth Kirk, Producer
An account of an archaeological discovery in eastern Washington State. The remains of early man in the Western Hemisphere. A graphic exposition of the techniques of archaeology. 1968. 61 color frames. $10. UW.

MICMAC: THE PEOPLE & THEIR CULTURE
A kit of nine filmstrips provide an overview of Micmac culture—structures, transportation, hunting and fishing, recreation and domestic crafts. Grade 6. NOVA.

NAKED CLAY: 3,000 YEARS OF UNADORNED POTTERY OF THE AMERICAN INDIAN
Features American Indian artistry in modelled ceramics. Includes a 72-page catalog. 90 slides. MAI.

NATIVE AMERICAN LITERATURE
Literature by and about the Native American: The writings of John Smith, Cotton Mather, William Byrd; the Noble Savage; Cooper's novels, Longfellow's "Hiawatha;" the characteristics of Indian literature; song, dance, myth & rituals; the Cherokee alphabet; Chief Joseph's oratory; the work of Momaday. Two 15-minute filmstrips. $49.95. FH.

NATIVE PEOPLES OF THE SOUTHWEST
  The Heard Museum
A multi-media instructional materials program designed to develop concepts and skills by focusing on traditional and contemporary Native American cultures. Five levels of instructional units are: Level 2: Inde: The Western Apache, Apache family life; Level 3: Hopi: The Desert Farmers, Hopi communities; Level 4: Anasazi: The Ancient Villagers, archaeology and culture history of livin Pueblo Indians; Level 5: O'odham: Indians of the Sonoran Desert, cultural geography and human adaptations to the desert environment; Level 6: Dine: The Navajo, cultures change and evolve. Each program consists of color slides, audio cassettes, overhead transparencies, 30 student booklets and teacher's guide, and artifacts. $295 each. Complete set, $1472. CA.

NAVAJO CULTURAL FILMSTRIPS & SLIDES
Contains 23 filmstrips with cassettes ranging in time from five minutes to 20 minutes. All grades. See SAN for titles and prices.

NORTH AMERICAN ARCHAEOLOGICAL SLIDE SET SERIES
Paleoindians of Northeastern U.S.: 64 slides, $120; Sloan Dalton Site: 68 slides, $122; Ohio Hopewell: 100 slides, $161; Mississippian Cultures: 85 slides, $151; The Southeastern Ceremonial Complex: 86 slides, $151; Early Caddoan Cultures: 78 slides, $140; Late Caddoan Cultures: 70 slides, $122; Spiro Mounds: 80 slides, $140; The Tunica Treasure: 79 slides, $140; Poverty Point: 63 slides, $120; The Art of the Taino: 59 slides, $110; Weeden Island Culture: 65 slides, $120; Fort Center: 54 slides, $102; The Gulf of Georgia: 80 slides, $140; Stone Sculpture of the Fraser River: 50 slides, $94; Ozette: 58 slides, $110; Hoko River Complex: 80 slides, $140; Mesa Verde: 86 slides, $152; Canyon de Chelly: 78 slides, $140; Chaco Canyon: 65 slides, $120; Native American Rock Art of the Colorado Plateau: 52 slides, $102. PR.

NORTHWEST COAST INDIAN TRADITIONS TODAY: A CONTEMPORARY LOOK AT REMNANTS OF A HERITAGE
  Louis & Ruth Kirk, Producers
Features dugout canoes hollowed from cedar logs, the netting and preparation of fish, baskets made from swamp and saltwater marsh grasses, etc. 1972. 90 color/sound frames. 15 minutes. Cassette/booklet. $25. UW.

OUR HEARTS BEAT AS ONE
Provides an historical view of tribes in Oregon. Two carousel slide trays; 160 slides. Grades 6-adult. Rental, $15. NILB.

OZETTE ARCHAEOLOGY
Louis and Ruth Kirk, Producers
Tells the story of the past and the present as it is being continually uncovered at the Ozette Archaeological Dig, Cape Alava, Washington State. Summarizes the resources available to the Makah Indians living on the Northwest Coast of the Olympic Peninsula. 1979. 153 color; sound frames. 21 minutes. Cassette - booklet. $25. UW.

THE PAINTINGS OF CHARLES BIRD KING
King painted many prominent Amerian Indians. 34 slides. $31. SI.

A POINT OF PARTNERSHIP
Depicts some of the work of the National Indian Lutheran Board. All ages. 12 minutes. Filmstrip/cassette. NILB.

PRE-COLUMBIAN ARCHAEOLOGICAL SITES - NORTH AMERICA
Includes the following sites: Betatakin, AZ (17 slides); Sand Island, UT (8 slides); Hovenweep, UT (33 slides); Mesa Verde, CO (47 slides); Aztec Ruins, NM (19 slides); Salmon Ruins, NM (6 slides); Chaco Canyon, NM (79 slides); El Morro, NM (4 slides); Canyon de Chelly, NM (35 slides); Bandelier, NM (29 slides); Pecos, NM (9 slides); Gran Quivira, NM (19 slides); Quari, NM (5 slides); Abo, NM (4 slides); Gila Cliff Dwellings, NM (23 slides); Tonto Ruins, AZ (14 slides); Casa Grande, AZ (9 slides); Tuzigoot, AZ (10 slides); Montezuma's Castle, AZ (6 slides); Walnut Canyon, AZX (2 slides); Wupatki, AZ (9 slides); Cahokia Mounds, IL (6 slides); Sonotobac Mound, IN (1 slide). $2.45 ea. in sets; $2.95 ea. ordering individually. HLM.

PRE-COLUMBIAN CULTURES
A series of slide sets. United States (231 subjects); Canada (three subjects). All archaeological specimens are of pottery. MAI.

PUEBLO INDIANS OF NEW MEXICO
Examines the history and culture of the Pueblo Indians. Includes images of the people, ancient and modern villages, crafts and ways of life many of which are drawn from the Museum of New Mexico's collection of historic photographs and rare old hand-tinted glass slides. 17 minute slide-tape program. Available for loan or purchase. MNM.

THE PURITAN EXPERIENCE: MAKING A NEW WORLD
Life in Massachusetts—the Higgin's family daughter, a captive of the Indians for a while, resents the Puritans' treatment of the Indians, and challenges strict Puritan authority. Grades 7-12. Two filmstrips, cassettes. $60. LL.

READ ALONG AMERICAN INDIAN LEGENDS
Stimulates reading interest with tales of Indian lore. Vocabulary-building captions. Program guide. Grades 2-5. Six filmstrips, cassettes. $119. RH.

THE SACRED PIPE
A filmstrip of the Sacred Pipe, the central instrument of the Dakota religion. Gives the proper understanding of the origin and use of the Pipe. $15. AICRC.

SANDSTONE COUNTRY: THE CANYONS & INDIANS OF THE SOUTHWEST
Louis and Ruth Kirk, Producers
Arizona and Utah apartment-dwelling Indians before Columbus, reveals the ancient cities and the geological history. Teacher's guide. 1970. 70 color frames. $10. UW.

SICA HOLLOW
An historical and religious filmstrip. One of the old story of the flood—localized on the Sisseton-Wahpeton Reservation. $15. AICRC.

THE SIOUX
Black Elk's words from a broken treaty. Study of the Sioux, past and present, are analyzed to show the In-

dian in confrontation with cultural crisis and identity loss. Includes a script. Grades 7-12. Filmstrip/cassette. $30. LL.

SIX NATIVE AMERICAN FAMILIES
The Life of a Mohawk Family; The Life of a Sioux Family; The Life of a Seminole Family; The Life of a Navajo Family; The Life of a Pueblo Family; The Life of a Kwakiutl Family. Grades K-6. 6 filmstrips, 6 cassettes, guide. $149. SVE.

THE SOUTHWEST: EARLY INDIAN CULTURES: THE SPANISH HERITAGE: THE EARLY ANGLO PERIOD: THE MODERN SOUTHWEST
The influence of the desert environment on the culture and lifestyle of the Indians. Four sound filmstrips, two cassettes. Script/guide. $90. UL.

SOUTHWEST INDIAN FAMILIES
A day in the lives of four real families from four different tribes: Navajo, Zuni, Apache and Hopi. Grades 1-3. Four filmstrips, four cassettes; four filmstrips/captioned. $40. PHOENIX.

SUBMULOC SHOW/COLUMBUS WOHS
Represents the theme of turning back the history of the Columbian legacy. 36 color slides. $60. ATL.

SURVIVAL: A HISTORY OF NORTHWEST INDIAN TREATY FISHING RIGHTS
A slide presentation produced by the Point No Point Treaty Council. Recounts the history of Indian fishing before the arrival of white people in the Northwest, and of treaties and legal decisions culminating in the 1974 Boldt Decision. Teacher's guide and student handouts and worksheets. 20 minutes. Grades 4-adult. Purchase: $195; rental, $30. DSP.

TALES OF THE PLAINS INDIANS
Gives insight into the religion, culture, and relationship to nature of the Blackfeet, Sioux, Pawnee and Cheyeen tribes. Grades 3-5. Six filmstrips, cassettes. $119. RH.

TEXAS INDIANS: THE ALABAMA-
COUSHATTA INDIANS - Presents the early history and present customs of the Alabamas and the Coushattas who have lived together in the Piney Woods of east Texas. 1971. 8 minutes. Filmstrip, $20; Slide set, $40; **THE INDIAN TEXANS** - Tribes of the 20th century who live together in Texas. The Dallas Intertribal Council's annual ceremonials are highlighted in this program. 1971. 7 minutes. Filmstrip, $25; slide set, $45; **THE TIGUA INDIANS: OUR OLDEST TEXANS** - Discusses the early (1680) settlement of the Tigua Pueblo Indians of Ysleta, near present El Paso, Texas, and the progress they are making through the Texas Commission on Indian Affairs to become completely self-sufficient and financially independent. 1971. 8 mins. Filmstrip, $20; slide set, $25. UT-ITC.

TRIBAL ARCHIVES
In two parts: Part 1: An Introduction - Discusses what an archives is, what you need to establish one, and how you will benefit from an archives program. Slide/tape program; 110 slides; 1983, 13 minutes. Part 2: Getting Started - A slide/tape program. Includes a booklet containing script, a bibliography, a glossary, and a list of resources. 1986. Purchase: $80 each; rental, $17 each. SI-OMP.

TWO EAGLES LEGEND
This filmstrip is a morality story; a young man, betrayed by his friend, is saved by two young eagles. (In Dakota tradition, the Eagle is always a symbol of God's presence.) $15. AICRC.

UNLEARNING INDIAN STEREOTYPES
Works with myths and images from books and television. 15 minutes. Grades 3-6. Filmstrip, cassette. Rental, $5. NILB.

A VISIT TO THE FATHER
Authentic Navajo origin legend in four filmstrip episodes. Translated and illustrated by Navajo artist Auska Kee. All ages. $67.50 with cassettes. CEN.

VOICES FROM THE CRADLEBOARD
Slide presentation of traditional child rearing practices,

such as the use of legends and the cradleboard, which emphasizes the importance of children in past and present Indian societies. 30 minutes. Grades 9-adult. Purchase, $185; rental, $30. DSP.

WHITE MAN AND INDIAN: THE FIRST CONTACTS
Depicts the first explorers and their halting, initial contacts with the Indians of Eastern America. Grades 7-12. Two filmstrips, cassettes. $31. LL.

WOLF GIRL
This filmstrip is a morality story. In non-Indian myth, the Wolf is always an evil animal. Indian people, however, have discovered the wolf to be a friend and a helpful animal. $15. AICRC.

WOMEN OF SWEETGRASS, CEDAR & SAGE: CONTEMPORARY ART BY NATIVE AMERICAN WOMEN
20 color slides. ATL.

RECORDINGS

AH-K' PAH-ZAH
Douglas Spotted Eagle & Dan James
Dan James on synthesizer and Douglas Spotted Eagle on Native American flute. 60 minutes. Cassette, $9.98. CAN.

AKA GRAFITTI MAN
John Trudell (Santee)
A unique blend of poetry & music by songwriter/poet John Trudell. Cassette, $10; CD, $17. OY & ICC.

ALASKAN ESKIMO SONGS AND STORIES
Lorraine D. Koranda; illustrated by Robert Mayokok 42 stories and songs on one LP. Sung in Eskimo and told in English. 1971. 50 page booklet. UW.

ALL ONE EARTH: SONGS FOR THE GENERATIONS
Performed by Michael J. Caduto
A new dimension to the lessons of the Keepers books12 songs; 10 original compositions. 47 minutes. 1993. Cassette, $9.95; CD, $14.95. FUL.

AN AMERICAN INDIAN
Kiowa-Apache flute player Andrew Vasquez presents his contemporary vision of tradition by combining musical styles of yesterday and today. CD, $14.98; Cassette, $9.98. MCP.

AMERICAN INDIAN DANCES
Recordings of the following Indian dances: Rabbit Dance, Sun Dance and Omaha Dance (Sioux); Devil Dance (Apache); Eagle Dance (San Ildefonso); Harvest Dance and Rain Dance (Zuni); Squaw Dance (Navajo); War Dance and Dog Dance (Plains); Snake Dance and Pow-Wow Dance (Flathead). LP. $9.98. VIP & CAN.

AMERICAN INDIAN GOSPEL/CHRISTIAN MUSIC
American Indian Hymn Singers - Christian Hymns in Creek - Arbor Shade Singers -Vol. 1: What a Beautiful Day, Vol. 2: Nizhonie Christmas, Vol. 3: Let It Shine; The Chinle Galileans; Country Gospel Singers; Johnny Curtis - Vol. 1: Apache Country Gospel Songs, Vol. 2: Leavin' This Reservation, Vol. 3: Johnny Curtis - With Apache Gospel Sounds, Vol. 4: In Loving Memories, Vol. 5: Spirit of God, Vol. 6: In Loving Memories; Larry Emerson - Vol. 1: Larry Emerson and Skyward -10 gospel songs, Vol. 2: Now is the Tim; The Gospel Light Singers -Volume One - 12 songs, Vol. 2: Jesus Died for Me Long Ago, Vol. 3: To My Mansion in the Sky, Vol. 4: Life's Railway to Heaven, Vol. 5: I'm Bound for that City, Vol. 6: If That Isn't Love; Harvey Family: Vol. 1: The Curtis Harvey Family, Vol. 2: Let's Tell the World; Murphy Platero: Murphy Platero and the Morning Star Band-When Shall It Be; Smith Family: Smith Family Gospel Singers with The Thunders. Cassettes. $7.98 each. CAN.

AMERICAN INDIAN LANGUAGES
Cherokee Phrase Cards (with syllabary pronunciation tape), $12.95; Introduction to Cherokee (2 tapes plus 50-page workbook & glossary), $35.95; Cherokee Dictionary - Durbin Feeling, $18.95; Choctaw Language Sampler (audiotape with booklet), $14.95; Introduction to Choctaw (2 tapes plus 60-page workbook),

$35.95; Choctaw Dictionary - Cyrus Byington, hard cover, $59, soft cover, $39; The Lord's Prayer & 23rd Psalm - read in Choctaw by Charlie Jones (audiocassette with both printed in Choctaw), $9.95; Ontroduction to Chickasaw (2 tapes plus workbook), $35.95; Introduction to Kitoah Cherokee-Eastern dialect (2 tapes, with workbook), $35.95; Chickasaw Language Sampler (audio tape with phrase booklet), $14.95; Chickasaw Glossary - Albert S. Gatchet, 1889, $15.95; Kiowa Language Sampler (audio tape with pronunciation guide), $12.95; Cherokee Syllabary (8 1/2 x 11 aged parchment), $1.95. VIP.

AMERICAN INDIAN LEGENDS
Recorded in both Indian & English. Cherokee: "The Rabbit & the Bear," & "Why the Hog's Tail is Flat" (Sam Hider, storyteller), $12.95; Choctaw: "Choctaw Creation Story," 'The Little People," & "Why the Rabbit's Tail is Short," (Charlie Jones - storyteller), $12.95; Kiowa: "The Little Eagle" (EvaLu Ware Russell, storyteller), $12.95. VIP

AMERICAN INDIAN MEDICINE
Rolling Thunder, a Medicine Man, describes the difficulties Indians have had in preserving their philosophy and culture, while being captives in the white man's society. 60 minutes. cassette. BSR.

AMERICAN INDIAN MUSIC FOR THE CLASSROOM
Dr. Louis Ballard sings 27 songs of 22 Indian tribes in the authentic style of the tribal musician. He analyzes the song content so that the listener acquires an understanding of both the musical and cultural meaning of Indian vocal music. 4 LPs or cassettes. Includes a study guide, 20 study photographs, a complete set of spirit masters, and a bibliography of books for students who wish to pursue a further study of Indian cultures. Grades 1-12. $75. CAN.

THE AMERICAN INDIAN ORAL HISTORY COLLECTION
Dr. Joseph H. Cash & Dr. Herbert Hoover, Gen. Eds In two volumes, the series contains 30 interviews on audiocassettes conducted by historians and anthropologists for students and scholars. The tapes offer a broad account of the experience of being an Indian, from recollections of 19th- century Indian-white relations and indigenous Indian culture to the experience of today's young Indians struggling to survive in White America without sacrificing their ethnic identity. Includes the following: Volume I - The Sundance (Crow); Medicine Men and Women I & II (Cheyenne River Sioux, Crow and Rosebud Sioux); The Buffalo Hunt I & II (Crow); Kinship, I, II & III (Crow); Legends (Chippewa); The Drum Society (Mille Lacs Chippewa); Little Bighorn; The BIA (Oglala Sioux); The BIA (Rosebud Sioux); Indian Students (Oglala Sioux); Life in 1900 (Cheyenne River Sioux). Volume II - A. Traditional Ways of Life: Religion (Rosebud Sioux , Winnebago & Northern Cheyenne, 5 tapes); Traditional Foods (Cheyenne River Sioux); Traditional Social Customs (Sisseton & Yankton Sioux); Legends (Spokane). B. Indian Leaders and Uprisings: Crazy Horse and Struck-by-the-Ree (Sioux); The Minnesota Uprising of 1862, I&II (Sioux). C. Contemporary Indian Problems: The City Vs. The Reservation (Spokane, Winnebago, Sioux); Problems of the Reservation (Crow Creek Sioux); Problems of the Urban Indian (Yankton Sioux & Winnebago); India Schools (Oglala Sioux). 30 minutes each. $15 each; Either Volume (15 tapes), $190; $350 per set (30 tapes). NR.

AMERICAN INDIAN SONGS
Dawley/McLaughlin
A broad cross-section of American Indian folk songs from every region in the U.S. LP or cassette. $9.95; book, $4.95. ALF.

AMERICAN INDIAN STAR TALES: THE FEATHER MOON
Stories told by Lynn Moroney about the sky, the stars, and the planets. Music is composed & performed on a Plains Indian flute. Cassette, $10. CH.

AMERICAN INDIANS IN FACT AND SYMBOL
In two parts by Dr. Joseph Henderson: Part 1: The American Indian and the Jungian Orientation —Dr. Henderson offers an historical sketch of the white man's attitudes and actions toward American Indians. Part 2: The American Indian—A Sioux Shaman — Dr. Henderson speaks of Black Elk, who at the age of nine had a vision which later evolved into the seven secret rites of the soul. Three hours, two tapes. BSR.

ANAPAO
Indian tales. Spoken and written by Jamake Highwater. Cassette. $10.98. FR.

ANCESTRAL VOICES
R. Carlos Nakai and William Eaton
Flute & guitar combo with songs. $11.50. CAN & CMM.

THE ANGRY INDIANS
Documentary on American Indian Conference at the University of Chicago in 1961, whose objectives were to get Indians from all parts of the U.S. together so that they could discuss their common problems and determine what they want from the U.S. Government and people. 26 minutes. Cassette. AUDIO.

ANIMAL STORIES (in English)
Stories colected from the Navajo, Cheyenne, Hopi, Kwakiutl, Tlingit, and Iroquois. Narrated by Gerald Hausman. 1 cassette (60 minutes), $10.95. AUDIO.

ANTHOLOGY OF NORTH AMERICAN INDIAN & ESKIMO MUSIC
A two-record set, compiled by Michael I. Asch, of the music of many of the tribes of North America, including: music of the Plains Indians; Indians of the Southwest; Northwest Coast Indians; Sub-Arctic; Arctic; Northeast Indians; and Southeast Indians. LPs. $19.96. FR.

APACHE INDIAN RECORDS & TAPES
Apache-Cassadore; Remembering Murphy Cassa, 2 Vols.; Songs of the Arizona Apache-San Carlos & White Mountain; Songs of the White Mountain Apache. Cassettes. $7.98 each. CAN.

THE ARCHIVE OF FOLK CULTURE- NATIVE AMERICAN RECORDINGS
Contains the following material: 1) The Jesse Walter Fewkes' 1890 cylinders of Passamaquoddy Indians— earliest field recordings made anywhere in the world; 2) More than 3,500 cylinders assembled between 1895 and 1940 by Francis Densmore and others for the Smithsonian Institution, Bureau of American Ethnology; 3) Several hundred discs and tapes 1940 to 1952 by Willard Rhodes for the Bureau of Indian Affairs; and 4) numerous other collections. The following recordings were edited by William N. Fenton ($8.95 each): Songs From the Iroquois Longhouse; Seneca Songs From Coldspring Longhouse. The following were recorded and edited by Frances Densmore ($8.95 each): Songs of the Chippewa; Songs of the Sioux; Songs of the Yuma, Cocopa, and Yaqui; Songs of the Pawnee and Northern Ute; Songs of the Papago; Songs of the Nootka and Quileute; Songs of the Menominee, Mandan and Hidatsa. The following songs were recorded and edited by Willard Rhodes ($8.95 each): Northwest (Puget Sound); Kiowa; Indian Songs of Today; Delaware, Cherokee, Choctaw and Creek; Great Basin: Paiute, Washo, Ute, Bannock, Shoshone; Plains: Comanche, Cheyenne, Kiowa, Caddo, Wichita, Pawnee; Sioux; Navajo; Apache; Pueblo: Taos, San Ildefonso, Zuni, Hopi; Omaha Indian Music: Historic Recordings from the Fletcher/LaFlesche Collection, $10.95. Copies of most of the Archive's recorded collections can be ordered from: The Archive of Folk Culture, Library of Congress, Washington, D.C. 20540. (202) 707-5510. Photocopies of folklore and ethnomusicology material which are not protected by copyright or other restrictions may also be ordered.

ARCHIVES OF TRADITIONAL MUSIC
Indiana University, Morrison Hall
Bloomington, IN 47405 (812) 335-8632
Dorothy Sara Lee
Maintains extensive recorded material on the North American Indian.

AS LONG AS THE GRASS SHALL GROW
Peter LaFarge sings 13 of his own songs. A 12-page brochure includes words and transcriptions of songs. LP. $9.98. CAN.

AUTHENTIC INDIAN LEGENDS
Each program has an Indian-language version on one side and an English version on the other. The Little Eagle (Kiowa), Creation, Little People, and Rabbit's Short Tail (Choctaw); The Rabbit and the Bear, and Why the Hog's Tail Is Flat (Cherokee); Raccoon (Passamaquoddy). One cassette each (30 minutes). $11.95 each. AUDIO.

AUTHENTIC INDIAN MUSIC #1 & 2
Field recorded in North America in mid 1900s. Two Cassettes. $9.95 each. VIP.

BASIC MEDICAL NAVAJO
An elementary course for physicians & nurses who treat Navajo speakers. Each section consists of dialogues, vocabulary, questions & instructions, grammatical explanations & notes. 1 cassette (60 minutes) and 141 pp. text, $39. AUDIO.

BEARHEART: VISION QUEST
Marcellus (Bearheart) Williams
Journey to the Seven Directions with Lakota medicine man Marcellus Williams. Cassette, $6. ZANGO.

BEGINNING CHEROKEE
Ruth Bradley Holmes & Betty Sharp Smith
Set of 2 cassettes for learning the Cherokee language. 3 hours, 332-page text. $39. CAN, CH & AUDIO.

BEGINNING PASSAMAQUODDY
Provides basic phrases, structures and vocabulary needed to speak Passamaquoddy in everday situations. Includes one cassette for basic phrasework, encyclopedia-type reference text with 3 cassettes for a spoken presentation of the material of the program, and one cassette for mastering the vowel sounds. 3.5 hours, 50 pp. phrasebook & 112 pp. reference text, and vowel sounds booklet. $59.50. AUDIO.

BEGINNING TLINGIT
A sytematic & structural introduction to Tlingit grammar with phrases & conversations for everyday use. 2 cassettes (2 hours) and 208 pp. spiral-bound text in album. $55. AUDIO.

BLACK HILLS DREAMER, JOURNEY TO THE SPIRIT WORLD
Buddy Red Bow (Lakota)
CD. $16.98. OY.

BLACK LODGE SINGERS: KID'S POW-WOW SONGS
The Black Lodge Singers of White Swan, Washington are one of the leading pow-wow drums in North America. Cassette, $6; CD, $9.15. ZANGO.

BLACKFEET GRASS DANCE SONGS
11 grass dance songs sung by Allen White Grass, Pat Kennedy & Stanley Whiteman. Recorded at Browning, Montana, July 2, 1960. Cassette/LP, $10. VIP & AIS.

BLACKFEET RECORDS & TAPES
Blackfeet Pow-Wow Songs; Carlson Singers; From the Land of the Blackfeet (LP); Hand Game Songs - Thomas Big Spring and Floyd Heavy Runner; Heart Butte Singers, 2 Vols.; Kicking Woman Singers, 5 Vols.; Little Corner Singers - Pow Wow Songs; Spotted Eagle Singers - Intertribal Pow Wow Songs; Two Medicine Lake Singers, 2 Vols.; Young Grey Horse Society, 2 Vols.; Black Lodge Singers - Pow Wow Songs, 6 Vols. Cassettes, $7.98 each. CAN.

BLACKSTONE SINGERS - POW-WOW SONGS
Live recordings by the Blackstone Singers (Cree from Saskatchewan, Canada) at the 1991 Ft. Duchesne (Utah) Pow-Wow. 57 minutes. Cassette, $6. CAN.

THE BLESSING WAYS
Sharon Burch (Navajo) and A. Paul Ortega (Mescalero Apache) sing of Navajo culture, especially about women and their ways. Cassette, $10. FTW.

BLOODY KNIFE: CUSTER'S FAVORITE SCOUT
Ben Innis; edited by Richard E. Collin
Audio book tells the story of Bloody Knife. 2 Cassette, 245 pp. $14.98. MCP.

BOAT PEOPLE
R. Carlos Nakai
Musical satire that takes a pointed look at the 500 years since Columbus. Nakai on the cedar flute and trumpet. Accompanied by Larry Yanez on the guitar and bass. 38 minutes. Cassette/CD. CAN.

BOOTS & SADDLES
Book-on-cassette depicting Elizabeth (Libbie) Custer's experiences during her stay in the Dakotas with her husband General George Armstrong Custer. Edited from the original 1886 edition. 2 cassettes, $14.98. MCP.

BREAKTHROUGH NAVAJO
Self-study audiocassette/book programs developed by Alan Wilson to give instruction in the Navajo language and to provide a deeper understanding of the culture & lifestyle of the Navajo. An Introductory Course: 2 cassettes (3 hours) & 234 pp. text, $49; Speak Navajo: Intermediate: 2 cassettes (2 hours) & 180 pp. text, $49. AUDIO.

BUDDY RED BOW
Two albums: "Black Hills Dreamer" - country western songs; and "Journey to the Spirit World". Cassettes, $10 each. CAN and FWT.

BUFFALO BIRD WOMAN - MY LIFE ON THE NOTHERN PLAINS (1840-1890)
Narrative by Buffalo Bird Woman tells how th Hidatsa lived on the Missouri River in western North Dakota during the late 1800's. 2 cassettes, $14.98. MCP.

BUFFALO SPIRIT
Original compositions by Fernando Cellicion. Cassette. $4.50. GDA.

BURNING SKY: CREATION
From the Dine of northern Arizona. Aaron White on guitar and Kelvin Bizahaloni on Native American flute with Michael Bannister on percussion. 39 minutes. Cassette, $6. CAN.

CADDO TRIBAL DANCES
4 turkey dance songs, 4 duck dance songs, 4 green corn dance songs, 4 bell dance songs, 2 fish dance songs, and 2 stirrup dance songs sung by Mr. & Mrs. Houston Edmonds, Mr. & Mrs. Lewis Edmonds, and Lowell Edmonds. Recorded at Anadarko, Oklahoma, March 1955. $9.95. VIP.

CANADIAN INDIAN RECORDS & TAPES
Assiniboine Jr. - 10 pow wow songs recorded in Manitoba, $9.98; Elk's Whistle - 13 pow wow songs recorded in Saskatoon, Saskatchewan, $9.98; Dakota Hotain Singers, Vol. 1 - 14 songs from Sioux Valley, Manitoba, and Vol. 2 - songs of the Dakota, $9.98 each; Whitefish Bay Singers - pow wow songs by a popular Ojibway drum from Whitefish Bay, Ontario, $9.98; Chiniki Lake Singers (from Morley, Alberta) 4 Vols., $7.98 each; Vic Thunderbird and the Thunderchild Singers; Old Agency Drummers-13 grass dance and chicken dance songs from the Blood Reserve, Standoff, Alberta, $7.98. Cassettes. CAN.

CANYON TRILOGY
Carlos Nakai with his Native American flute, journeys to the past, records in a canyon to simulate the ambience of the now abandoned cliff-dwelling villages. Cassette, $12. CAN & CH.

CARRY THE GIFT
R. Carlos Nakai & William Eaton
The harmonies of Nakai's flute with Eaton's guitar. 59 minutes. Cassette/CD. CAN.

CEREMONIAL SONGS & DANCES OF THE CHEROKEE
Kevin Lewis sings 50 songs accompanied by a gourd or drum. 2 vols. Cassette, $11 ea. CAN, CMM, MFP & CH.

CHANGES
Native American flute music by R. Carlos Nakai. 40 minutes. Cassette/CD. CAN.

CHEROKEE CEREMONIAL SONGS
Two cassettes. $9.95 each. VIP.

CHEROKEE LANGUAGE WORKBOOK & INSTRUCTIONAL CASSETTE TAPE
Prentice Robinson
Booklet, 30 pp. and one cassette, $25. CH.

CHEROKEE LEGENDS I
Kathi Smith
30 minute cassette. $9. CH.

CHEYENNE NATION
The music of Joseph Fire Crow...traditional flute and contemporary instrumentation promoting the unity of the Cheyenne people. CD, $14.98; Cassette, $9.98. MCP.

6 CHEYENNE WARRIOR SONGS & 7 CROW GRASS DANCE SONGS
$9.95. VIP.

CHICKASAW
Gregg Howard
Language course containing words, phrases, and sentences around the themes of everyday living. Also includes recipes of authentic dishes; legends & bibliography of information on the Chickasaw Nation. 1994. 2 cassettes & 95-page book. $39.95. AUDIO.

CHICKEN SCRATCH - POPULAR DANCE MUSIC OF THE INDIANS OF SOUTHERN ARIZONA
Chicken Scratch is a couples social dance passed down from generation to generation among the desert tribes of Southern Arizona. The music is primarily polkas and chotes played on guitars, accordions, saxophones, and drums, and is performed at church, fiestas, tribal celebrations, family affairs, and weekend social dances. A series of 42 LPs and cassettes based on the Scratch Dance. See CAN for titles.

CHIPPEWA-CREE CIRCLE DANCE
13 cirlce dance songs sung by Rocky Boy Singers, Paul Eagleman, Charles Gopher, Bill Baker, John Gilbert Meyers, and Windy Boy. Recorded at Crow Agency, Montana, August 1966. Cassette/LP, $10, AIS.

CHIPPEWA-CREE GRASS DANCE
14 grass dance songs sung by Rocky Boy Singers, Paul Eagleman, Charles Gopher, Bill Baker, John Gilbert Meyers, and Windy Boy. Recorded at Crow Agency, Montana, August 1966. Cassette/LP, $10, AIS.

CHOCTAW SINGING
Charlie Jones, Singer
With lyric booklet in Choctaw. Cassette. $14.95. VIP.

COMANCHE CHURCH HYMNS
Traditional hymns in the Comanche language. Cassette. CAN & GDA.
COMANCHE FLUTE MUSIC
Flute songs and narration by Doc Tate Nevaquaya as he discusses the flute and songs. LP. $9.98. CAN.

COMING LIGHT: CHANTS TO HONOR THE MOTHER EARTH
19 original chants on a 45-minute cassette. $10. CH.

THE CONTEST IS ON
Trick dance songs. Vol. 1 - Chiefly Ponca and Pawnee; Vol. 2 - Part of the annual Osage War Dance, Ponca Pow Wow and Ponca Heluska. Cassettes. $7.98 each. CAN & GDA.

COVERSATIONAL LAKOTA
Set of 6 tapes, $60. Set of 6 books (16 pp. each), $30. CAN.

COYOTE LOVE MEDICINE
Jessica Reyes uses the Native American courting flute with ritual percussion instruments & synthesizers. Cassette, $12. CH.

CREATION CHANT
Eric Casillas
A compilation of original chants and captivating stylizations. With Native American drums and West African polyrhythms. Cassette, $6; CD, $9.15. ZANGO.

CROW GRASS & OWL DANCE SONGS
12 grass dance songs & 1 owl dance song sung by Lloyd Old Coyote, Frank Bakcbone, Sr., Robert Other Medicine, & Lindsey Bad Bear; 3 owl dance songs sung by Warren Bear Cloud & John Strong Enemy. Cassette/LP, $10. AIS.

CRY FROM THE EARTH
Music of the North American Indians. 33 songs from 24 different tribes. LP. $14.95. VIP & CAN.

CULTURAL PLURALISM & THE RECOVERY OF THE CLASSIC
Uses poetry of the American Indian and reservation treaties of the 19th century to reveal the wisdom and philosophy of Indian leaders. 1972. 59 minute cassette. NCTE.

CYCLES
Native American flute music by R. Carlos Nakai. The music from Our Voices, Our Land. 33 minutes. Cassette/CD. CAN.

DAKOTA LANGUAGE (SANTEE) BY AGNES ROSS
Beginning language & simple sentence material. CAN.

DAKOTA THEOLOGY
30 minutes, bxw. VHS. $5.00. AICRC.

DANCES WITH RABBITS
R. Carlos Nakai & Jackalope
Musical satire that takes a pointed look at the 500 years since Columbus. Nakai on the flute and trumpet, with Larry Yanez on the keyboards and guitar. 38 minutes. Cassette/CD. CAN.

DANCES WITH WOLVES
John Barry
Soundtrack of film. Cassette, $8; CD, $13.50. ZANGO.

DANCING DAKOTA
Songs & stories of North Dakota singer/songwriter, Chuck Suchy. Cassette, $10; CD, $15. MCP.

DAWN LAND
Joseph Bruchac's first novel on audiocassette. 180 minutes, 2 cassettes. $16.95. FUL.

THE DAWNING: CHANTS OF THE MEDICINE WHEEL
17 original chants on a 60-minute cassette. $10. CH.

DESERT DANCE
Carlos Nakai with his Native American flute, drums, voice, rattles, wind and rain in his ritual expression of nature's beauty. Cassette, $12. CH.

DISTANT SHORES
Gary Stroutsos brings classical, jazz and Native American techniiques to the cedar flute. CD, 14.98; cassette, $9.98. MCP.

DREAM CATCHER
Flute music by Tokeya Inajin (Kevin Locke). Cassette, $10.60; CD, $16. MCP.

DREAM'S FOR YOU
Susan Aglukark (Inuit)
Audiotape. $10. OY.

DREAMS FROM THE GRANDFATHER
Robert Tree Cody
Flutist and singer, Robert Tree Cody, draws on his Dakota-Maricopa heritage as well as Zuni, Lakota and Acoma peoples. 48 minutes. Cassette. CAN.

DRUMS OF THE AMERICAN INDIAN
One side of drum beat; and other side includes a collection of different drums and beats accompanied by shaker, rattle, deer toes or bells. 40 minutes. Cassette. $4.50. GDA.

EARTH SPIRIT
Carlos Nakai presents sounds of the Native American flute and introduces the mysterious & sacred sounds of the eagle bone whistle. 59 minutes. Cassette, $11.50. CAN & CMM.

EARTHLODGE
Mandan-Hidatsa storyteller and performer, Keith Bear, shares songs of his people recorded in an earthlodge built on the Plains of the Dakotas. This enhanced CD

contains a ten minute video about Keith Bear, his life and culture. CD, $14.98; Cassette, $9.98. MCP.

EASTERN INDIANS TAPES
Iroquois Social Dance Songs, 3 Vols.; Beginning Cherokee-book & 2 tapes ($33.93); Songs & Dances of Eastern Indians From Medicine Spring (Cherokee) & Allegany (Seneca); Ceremonial Songs and Dances of the Cherokee. Cassettes, $8.98-9.98 each. CAN.

ECHOES OF THE NIGHT: NATIVE AMERICAN LEGENDS OF THE NIGHT SKY
Tsonakwa & Dean Evanson
Stories from Hopi, Ojibway, Algonkian and other tribal traditions of star knowledge. Cassette, $11; CD, $17. MFP.

ECHOES OF THE UPPER MISSOURI
Flute music by Keith Bear (debut release). Cassette, $10; CD, $15. MCP.

THE ELDERS SPEAK
Dakotah and Ojibway stories of the land told by Mary Louise Defender Wilson (Gourd Woman) and Francis Cree (Eagle Heart). The enhanced CD contains maps and photos of the landmark areas & folk arts described in their stories. CD, $14.98; Cassette, $9.98. MCP.

ELECTRIC WARRIOR
Russell Means
AIM activist brings us what he calls "rap-ajo." Spoken work backed with traditional and contemporary percussion. Cassette. $9.95; $14.95, CD. VIP.

EMERGENCE
Songs of the rainbow by Carlos Nakai (flute music). Cassette, $11.50. CAN & CMM.

ENGLISH & AMERICAN INDIAN STUDIES
Robert Lewis sets forth dos and donts for English teachers who plan to use Native American materials. 1972. 35 minutes. NCTE.

ESKIMO MUSIC OF ALASKA & THE HUDSON BAY
Record and notes by Laura Boulton. LP. $9.98. CAN.

ESKIMO SONGS FROM ALASKA
Twenty contemporary and ancient songs recorded by Miriam C. Stryker on St. Lawrence Island. Edited by Charles Hoffman. Includes an illustrated brochure. LP. $9.98. CAN.

EVERYDAY KIOWA PHRASES
Provides a brief introduction to some of the most common words & phrases used in Kiowa. 1 cassette, $12.95. AUDIO.

FEATHER, STONE & LIGHT
R. Carlos Nakai & William Eaton
Nakai and Eaton, the cedar flute and guitar, respectively, is joined by Will Clipman who adds ethnic percussion to the music. 71 minutes. CD. CAN.

FEATHERSTONE CASSETTES
Gordon Bird Sings Traditional/Contemporary American Indian Songs-12 songs from the Mandan, Hidatsa and Arikara Nations; Dakota Songs by Wahpe Kute-12 traditional/contemporary songs of the Dakota Nation; New Town Singers-Live at Dakota Dance Clan Celebration; Mandaree Singers-Live at New Town, N.D.; Old Scout Singers-Live at White Shield, N.D.; Wahpe Kute-Live at Dakota Dance Clan Celebration, Sisseton, S.D.; Eagle Whistles-Live at Mandaree, N.D.; Leroy Strong and Johnny Smith "The Buckaroos"; Little Earth Singers-Live in the Twin Cities (Minneapolis/St. Paul, MN); Ft. Yates Singers-Live at Ft. Yates, N.D.; Rock Creek Singers-Live at Ft. Yates, N.D.; Mandaree Singers-Live at Bismarck, N.D.-Vol. 2; Eagle Whistles-Live at Bismarck, N.D.-Vol. 2; Assiniboine Singers-Live at Dakota Tipi; Dakota Tipi Live-Minneapolis Buckaroos, Red Nation Singers and the Assiniboine Singers; Red Nation Singers-Live at Ft. Totten Days; Dakota Language (Santee) by Agnes Ross; The White Buffalo Calf Woman as Told by Martin High Bear; Lakota Wiikijo Olowan by Kevin Locke, 2 Vols.; All Nation Singers-Flandreau Indian School; Songs of the People by Georgia Wettlin-Larsen. Cassettes. $8.25 each. GAN.

FIRE CROW
Joseph Fire Crow
Flute and vocals. CD, $14.98; cassette, $9.98. MCP.

THE FIRST FLUTE
Internationally acclaimed traditional flute player, Kevin Locke, interprets centuries-old songs of the Lakota. CD, $14.98; Cassette, $9.98. MCP.

THE FLASH OF THE MIRROR
Flute music by Tokeya Inajin (Kevin Locke). Cassette, $9.98; CD, $14.98. MCP.

THE FLOOD & OTHER LAKOTA STORIES
Kevin Locke
Locke performs traitional Native American flute music between stories he tells. All stories reveal the values and beliefs of the Lakota. 60 minutes. 1993. Cassette. $11. CHA.

FLUTE MUSIC
4 cassettes. Sacred Feelings by Doug Spotted Eagle; Riding the Wind by Ketcheshawno; Moon Spirits by Tsa'ne Dos'e; and Out of the Fire by Tom Minton. $9.95 each. VIP.

FLUTE/NEW AGE TAPES
Each flute artist has his own style influenced by his tribal heritage, personal experiences and feelings. N. Carlos Nakai, Gordon Bird, Fernando Cellicion, Robert Tree Cody, Herman Edwards, Daniel C. Hill, Kevin Locke, Frank Montano, Cornel Pewewardy, John Rainer, Jr., Rainmaker, Stan Snake, Douglas Spotted Eagle, Robert Two Hawks, and Tom Mauchahty-Ware. See CAN for tape titles.

THE FLUTE PLAYER
Traditional Dakota flute music by Bryan Akipa. Cassette, $9.98; CD, $14.98. MCP & MFP.

FLUTE PUEBLO
Traditional Zuni Pueblo flute music of Fernando Cellicion. 10 songs from Zuni, Laguna, Sioux & Acoma tribes. Cassette, $10. CMM.

FOOLS CROW, HOLY MAN
A retrospective of noted Ceremonial Chief & spiritual leader of the Oglala Sioux. Cassette, $10.60. MCP.

FORT OAKLAND RAMBLERS: OKLAHOMA INTERTRIBAL & CONTEST SONGS
Ponca Flag Song, 6 intertribal songs, 2 patriotic giveaway songs, 4 contest songs, & 1 Ponca veterans' song sung by a variety of singers. Recorded at White Eagle, Oklahoma, 1992. Cassette/LP, $10. IH.

THE GIFT OF THE GREAT SPIRIT
Tehanetorens
These lesson stories, including The Story of the Monster Bear, are told by Mohawk Elder Tehanetorens in his inimitable style. 1988. Cassette, $9.95. OY.

GREAT AMERICAN INDIAN SPEECHES
Narrated by Vine Deloria, Jr. and Arthur S. Junalaska. Includes speeches of Geronimo, Standing Bear, Cochise, Black Elk and others. Grades 7-12. Two cassettes. $19.95. LL.

HEALING & PEYOTE SONGS IN SIOUX & NAVAJO
Harmonized chanting without percussion by Verdell Primeaux (Oglala/Yankton Sioux & Ponca), Johnny Mike (Dine) and Robert Attson (Dine). 43 minutes. Cassette. CAN.

HEALING SONGS OF THE AMERICAN INDIANS
Healing songs of the Chippewa, Sioux, Yuman, Northern Ute, Papago, Makah and Menominee Indians. Text included. LP. $14.95. VIP & CAN.

HEART OF THE WORLD
Mary Youngblood with guest Joanne Shenandoah. Double chamber flutes, guitar, percussion, and Joanne's voice. CD, $15.98; cassette, $9.98. SWR.

HEART SONGS OF BLACK HILLS WOMAN
Paula Horne (Dakota Sioux) speaks her prose of each song in English before she sings it in her Native tongue. Cassette, $11; CD, $16. MCP.

HEARTBEAT: VOICES OF 1ST NATIONS WOMEN
Cassette, $10; CD, $15. OY & VIP

THE HERON SMILED
Anishinaabe singer/songwriter Annie Humphrey's contemporary style of love songs and political anthems. John Trudell contributes poetry and vocals. CD, $14.98 & Cassette, $9.98. MCP.

AN HISTORICAL ALBUM OF BLACKFOOT INDIAN MUSIC
Includes Medicine Pipe songs, Sun Dance songs, Owl Dance songs, Gambling songs. Historical recordings dating back to the turn of the century. LP. $9.98. CAN.

HO HWO SJU LAKOTA SINGERS TRADITIONAL SONGS BY THE SIOUX
Includes the Sioux National Anthem, among other traditional songs of the Sioux. Cassette, $10. IH.

HONORABLE SKY
Peter Kater & R. Carlos Nakai. CD, $15.98; cassette, $9.98. SWR.

HOPI KATCINA SONGS
Includes six other songs by Hopi Chanters. 17 songs and dances recorded by Dr. Jesse Walter Fewkes in Arizona in 1924. Text included. LP. $9.98. CAN.

THE HORSES STILL CRY
Native American flute music by Native American flutemaker Paul Hacker. Cedar flutes provide courting songs with sounds of nature background. Cassette, $11 or CD, $16. PH.

HOW THE WEST WAS LOST
Peter Kater & R. Carlos Nakai. Vol. 1 - Original soundtrack from six-hour PBS/Discovery Channel miniseries of 1994; Vol. II - from sequel series on the Discovery Channel. Cassette, $11 each; CDs, $17 each. SWR.

HYMNS OF PRAISE: THE NATIVE AMERICAN CHURCH
Public radio program examining the Peyote religion and way of life. 30 minute audiocassette. $11. KF.

IMPROVISATIONS IN CONCERT
Peter Kater & R. Carlos Nakai. A collection of songs performed live. CD, $15.98; cassette, $9.98. SWR.

IN THE LONG TIME AGO
11 legendary Cherokee stories told by Rogers Clinch, Sr., a Cherokee elder. He explains modern relevance to ancient stories. Cassette, $10. FTW.

INDIAN CHIPMUNKS
Alvin Ahoy-boy and his Indian Chipmunk Singers from Yuk-a-Day, Canada, sing pow wow songs. 2 Vols. Cassettes. $7.98 each. CAN & GDA.

INDIAN COUNTRY-WESTERN
Apache Spirit, 10 Vols. ($8.50 each)Three guys and a girl from Whiteriver, Arizona singing a combination of their own original compositions and popular country-western standards; Cody Bearpaw, 2 Vols. ($7.98 each); Louis Becenti - Eddie's Club in Gallup, NM presents Louis Becenti singing 12 country-western standards ($7.98); El Coochise, 3 Vols. ($7.98 each) - Hopi, Apache, and Navajo musicians provide back up for the vocals of Hopi musician and singer El Coochise; The Fenders, 2 Vols. ($7.98 each) - Navajo country-western band; Bill Johnson & the Jamborees, 3 Vols. (7.98 each) - A Navajo country-western band; Harold Mariano & the Variations, 3 Vols. ($7.98 each); Joe Montana and the Roadrunners, 3 Vols. ($8.98 each) - Hualapai Indian group from Peach Springs, Arizona; Navajo Clan, 3 Vols. ($7.98 each); Navajo Sundowners, 13 Vols. ($8.50 each) - A popular country-western group from Farmington, NM; Night Ryders - Composed of members of the Hopi and White Mountain Apache tribes. ($7.98); Jimi Poyer - Juke Box Music ($7.98); The Rockin' Rebels - Navajo group ($8.50); Sioux Savages - A Sioux-Navajo band from Tuba City, AZ ($7.98); The Thunders, 3 Vols. ($7.98 each); Undecided Takers - Navajo country-western and rock group from Kayenta, AZ ($7.98 each); Wingate Valley Boys - Navajo band from Fort Wingate, NM ($7.98); Zuni Midnighters, 4 Vols. - country-western

dance band from Zuni Pueblo, NM ($7.98 each); Isleta Poorboys - Just Play 'N Good, songs by Clarence Jojola of Isleta Pueblo, NM. ($8.50). Cassettes. CAN.

INDIAN HOUSE RECORDS & TAPES
Includes the following records & cassettes: Round Dance Songs of Taos Pueblo, 2 vols.; Taos Round Dance, 2 parts; Taos Pueblo Round Dance; Ditch-Cleaning & Picnic Songs of Picuris Pueblo; Turtle Dance Songs of San Juan Pueblo; Cloud Dance Songs of San Juan Pueblo; Zuni Fair-Live; Navajo Sway Songs; Night & Daylight Yeibichei; Navajo Skip Dance & Two Step Songs; Navajo Round Dance; Navajo Gift Songs & Round Dance; Navajo Corn Grindings & Shoe Game Songs; Klagetoh Maiden Singers; Navajo Songs About Love - The Klagetoh Swingers, Six volumes; The San Juan Singers - Navajo Skip Dance Songs; Turtle Mountain Singers - Navajo Social Dance Songs, 2 vols.; Navajo Skip Dance & Two-Step Songs - The Rock Point Singers, 2 vols.; Southern Maiden Singers - Navajo Skip Dance & Two-Step Songs; Navajo Peyote Ceremonial Songs, 4 vols.; War Dance Songs of the Ponca, 2 vols.; Ponca Peyote Songs, Three volumes; Cheyenne Peyote Songs, 2 vols.; Comanche Peyote Songs, 2 vols.; Handgame of the Kiowa, Kiowa Apache, & Comanche, 2 vols.; Kiowa Gourd Dance, 2 vols.; Kiowa 49 - War Expedition Songs; Kiowa Church Songs, 2 Vols.; War Dance Songs of the Kiowa—O-ho-mah Lodge Singers, 2 vols.; Flute Songs of the Kiowa & Comanche - Tom Mauchahty-Ware; Kiowa & Kiowa-Apache Peyote Songs; Songs of the Muskogee Creek, 2 parts; Stomp Dance - Muskogee, Seminole, Yuchi, 4 vols.; Blackfoot A-1 Club Singers, 2 vols; Old Agency Singers of the Blood Reserve, 2 parts; The Badland Singers -Assiniboine-Sioux Grass Dance; Sounds of the Badland Singers; The Badland Singers - Live at Bismarck; The Badland Singers at Home; Kahomini Songs - The Badland Singers; The Badland Singers, Live at United Tribes, 2 vols.; Ashland Singers - North Cheyenne War Dance; Ho Hwo Sju Lakota Singers - Traditional Songs of the Sioux; Love Songs of the Lakota, performed on Flute by Kevin Locke; Ironwood Singers - Songs of the Sioux, Live at the 106th Rosebud Sioux Fair; Yankton Sioux Peyote Songs, 8 vols.; Songs of the Native American Church - Sung by Rev. Joseph M. Shields; Rocky Boy Singers: Grass Dance & Jingle Dance Songs, 2 Vols.; Rocky Boy Chippewa-Cree Grass Dance Songs; Red Earth Singers, Live at Bismarck, 2 vols.; Sounds of Indian America - Plains & Southwest; Pueblo Songs of the Southwest; Turtle Mountain Singers-Welcome to Navajo Land & Early This Morning I Heard My Horse Calling; Eagle Society-Blackfoot Grass Dance Songs, Siksika Nation; Red Earth Singers of Tama, Iowa - "Live". American Indian Soundchiefs: Blackfeet Grass Dance Songs; Crow Grass Dance & Owl Dance Songs; Ponca & Pawnee Warriors Dance Songs; Ponca Tribal Songs; Caddo Tribal Dances; Kiowa-Comanche Peyote Songs; Cassette or LP recordings available for most selections. $10 for each cassette or LP. See HI for further information.

INDIAN KILLER
Sherman Alexie. Sherman reads from his novel. 3 hours. 1996. $21.95. OY.

INDIAN MUSIC OF THE CANADIAN PLAINS
Recordings of the Blood, Cree, Blackfoot and Assiniboine Indians made on the reservation. Includes war songs, greeting songs, stick games, Dance songs, etc. LP. $9.98. CAN.

**INDIAN MUSIC OF THE
PACIFIC NORTHWEST COAST**
A two-record set containing 27 songs and dances recorded by Dr. Ida Halpern, mostly from the Kwakiutl Tribe with Nootka and Tlingit songs and dances included. LP. $19.96. CAN.

INDIAN MUSIC OF THE SOUTHWEST
Includes Hopi, Zuni, Navajo, Taos, San Ildefonso, Santa Ana, Mohave, Papago, Pima and Apache music. Record and notes by Dr. Laura Boulton. LP. $9.98. CAN.

INDIAN ROCK MUSIC
Hamana (2 LPs-$7.98 each): Hamana, and Butchamana and the Big Bang Brothers Band; Many Hogans: American Clan; Mr. Indian and Time: Medi-

cine Dream; Redbone (2 LPs-$7.98 each): Message from a Drum, and Beaded Dreams Through Turquoise Eyes; Sand Creek: Endless Flight ($7.98); Winterhawk (3 cassettes-$8.50 each): Electric Warriors, Dog Soldier, and Winterhawk; XIT (7 cassettes-$8.98 each): Plight of the Redman, Silent Warrior, Entrance, Backtrackin', Relocation, Drums Across the Atlantic, and Tom Bee-Color Me Red. CAN.

INDIAN THEME CONTEMPORARY
B.Y.U. Musical Production - Lamanite Generation, 1985, Go My Son, and From the Eagle's Bed; Vincent Craig, Vol. 1 - (Navajo performer), and The Navajo Code Talker Song (45 rpm record); A. Paul Ortega - Mescalero Apache: Two Worlds, Three Worlds, and Blessing Ways; Buddy Red Bow - Journey to the Spirit World; Floyd Westerman: Custer Died for Your Sins, and The Land is Your Mother; Francis Country: The Peyote Dream; Homeland - 10 songs by Bugs Moran; Burt Lambert and the Northern Express: Just Arriving (LP-$7.98); Billy Thunderkloud and the Chieftones: Off the Reservation (LP-$5.98), and What Time of Day. Cassettes. $8.98 each. CAN.

INDIAN WISDOM STORIES
Dramatized legends recorded and produced by American Indians with authentic Salish Indian language chants, drum songs, and sound effects. Told by Jay Silverheels, Mohawk Indian actor. Includes 2 cassettes; four color filmstrips, a script for each story; a teacher's guide by Dr. Jerry Blanche (Choctaw Indian educator). Grades 4-6. CAN.

INSPIRIATIONS OF THE GREAT SPIRIT
Richard Bell. Lyric tales of the Tahue people. Cassette, $6; CD, $10. ZANGO.

INTERTRIBAL GROUPS & COLLECTIONS
Bala Sinem Choir, 2 Vols. (American Indian Songs for Choir & Walk in Beauty My Children); Crow Celebration-10 Great Drums at Crow Fair; Denver Indian Singers-Arikara & Sioux (LP); Great Plains Singers & Songs; Hopi Sunshield Singers-Northern Style Pow Wow Songs; Kyi-Yo Pow Wow-9 Northern Plains Drums; Omak Pow Wow 1980 (Washington)-6 Drums from the Northwest; Pow Wow Songs - Music of the Plains Indians ($9.98-LP); The Song of the Indian-8 Tribal Groups & Soloists; White Eagle Singers-Intertribal Pow Wow Songs and Love Songs, 5 Vols.; Santa Fe Pow Wow, 2 Vols; Songs of the Earth, Water, Fire and Sky; Pow Wow Songs-Music of the Plains Indians. Cassettes, $7.98-$9.98 each; also available on compact disc, $16.98 each. CAN.

INTRODUCTION TO CHOCTAW
Provides a brief introduction to some of the most common words and phrases used in Choctaw. The seections revolve around the themese of everyday living, The native speaker is Charles G. Jones, past president of the Choctaw Indian Council. 2 cassettes (2 hours, 20 minutes); 60 pp. looseleaf binder album, $32.95. AUDIO.

INTRODUCTORY LAKOTA
All recordings are by native speakers; text contains 15 lessons, the last lesson being a comprehensive review. Exercises for written practice are included, using the English alphabet. 15 cassettes (12 hours), 102 pp. text, 9 pp final exam. Purchase: $175. AUDIO.

IROQUOIS SOCIAL DANCE SONGS
Traditional Iroquois social dance songs from the Six Nations Reserve in Ontario, Canada. Singers are: George Buck, Raymond Spragge, Jacob Thomas and Wm. Guy Spittal. 3 Vols. Cassettes. $7.98 each. CAN.

IROQUOIS STORIES
Joseph Bruchac. 1988. All Grades. Cassette, $9.95. OY.

ISLAND OF BOWS
Flute music by R. Carlos Nakai. Recorded in a Buddhist temple in Kyoto, Japan. 48 minutes. Cassette/CD. CAN.

JACKALOPE
R. Carlos Nakai. The Native American flute and trumpet by Larry Yanez. 50 minutes. Cassette/CD. CAN.

JIM BOYD
Two albums: "Reservation Bound" - first solo album, and "Unity" - original songs deal with a variety of issues concerning Native Americans today. Cassette, $6 each; CD, $9.75 each. ZANGO.

JOHNNY DAMAS & ME
John Trudell (Santee). The music of John Trudell, with the Graffiti Band. Cassette, $10; CD, $12. ICC.

JOURNEYS
Native American flute music. R. Carlos Nakai performs on several wooden flutes. 54 minutes. Cassette, $11.50. CAN & CMM.

**KEEPERS OF THE ANIMALS
& KEEPERS OF THE EARTH**
Told by Joseph Bruchac, featuring the complete, unabridged stories from "Keepers of the Animals" and Keepers of the Earth" Represents the art of traditional Native American storytelling, performing stories drawn from the native cultures of North America. 110 & 133 minutes, respectively (two tapes each). Cassette, $16.95 each. FUL.

KEEPERS OF THE DREAM
Flute music by Tokeya Inajin (Kevin Locke). Cassette, $10.60; CD, $16. MCP.

KEVIN LOCKE (TOKEYA INAJIN)
"Dream Catcher," "Flash of the Mirror," "Keepers of the Dream," "Love Songs of the Lakota," "Open Circle." Traditional songs of the Meskwaki Dakota, and Lakota People, Native flute, voice, and drum. Cassettes, $6 each; CD, $9.75 each. ZANGO.

KIOWA CIRCLE & TWO-STEP SONGS
12 round dance songs sung by Leonard Cozad, Jasper Sankadota, Oscar Tahlo & Laura Tahlo. Recorded in 1964. Cassette/LP, $10. AIS.

KIOWA & COMANCHE PEYOTE SONGS
13 songs sung by Nelson Big Bow. Recorded at Crow Agency, Montana, August 1966. Cassette/LP, $10. AIS.

KIOWA-COMANCHE PEYOTE SONGS
6 songs sung by Nelson Big Bow, 6 songs sung by Edgar Gouladdie, 4 songs sung by Harding Big Bow & 7 songs sung by Walter Ahhaity. Cassette/LP, $10. VIP & AIS.

KIOWA FLAG SONG
Oklahoma Round Dance, Kiowa War Mothers & Comanche "49". Cassette. $45. GDA.

KIOWA HYMNS
Traditional church hymns for solo voice in the Kiowa language sung by Ralph Kotay. 2 cassettes. $15.95. CAN. $9. GDA.

**KIOWA & KIOWA-APACHE
PEYOTE RITUAL SONGS**
4 songs sung by Emmett Williams, 4 songs sung by Nathan Doyebi, 4 songs sung by Edgar Gouladdie, & 8 songs sung by Nelson Big Bow. Cassette/LP, $10, AIS.

KIOWA MYTHS & LEGENDS
Kiowa Jill Momaday brings these traditional Native American tales to life. Each is accompanied by authentic tribal music. 2 cassettes (180 minutes), $21. AUDIO.

KIOWA PEYOTE MEETING
Documents the vision-producing peyote ritual. Recorded with the Anadarko, Oklahoma tribes and consists of both words & syllables with emotional connotations. 3 LP record set. Edited by Harry E. Smith. $29.94. CAN.

KIOWA PEYOTE RITUAL SONGS
18 ritual songs sung by the following: James Aunguoe, Ernest Redbird, Allen Tsontokoy, Francis Tsontokoy, and Oscar Tahlo. Cassette/LP, $10. AIS.

KIOWA PEYOTE RITUAL SONGS
15 Kiowa songs sung by Edward Hunmmingbird. Recorded at Crow Agency, ontana, in August 1966. Casette/LP, $10. AIS.

KIOWA ROUND DANCE SONGS
16 round dance songs, 2 Comanche 49 songs, 2 Kiowa War Mother's songs and a Kiowa Flag Song. Cassette. $7.98. CAN.

KIOWA SONGS & DANCES
Dance and war songs of the Kiowa Indians. LP. $9.98. CAN.

KIOWA STORYTELLER
Stories in the age-old oral tradition told by master storyteller & Pulitzer-Prize winner, N. Scott Momaday (Kiowa). 1 cassette (60 minutes), $10.95. AUDIO.

KOKOPELLI DREAMS
Flute music by Fernando Cellicion. Cassette/CD, $4.50. GDA.

KOKOPELLI'S CAFE
Flute music by R. Carlos Nakai Quartet. Cassette/CD. CAN.

KWAKIUTL INDIAN MUSIC OF THE PACIFIC NORTHWEST
25 songs including Raven, Hagok, Hamatsa, Thunderbird, Potlatch, Whale and others. Two LP records. $19.96. CAN.

LAKOTA LOVE SONGS & STORIES
Flute music by Tokeya Inajin (Kevin Locke). Cassette, $10. MCP.

LAUGHTER: THE NAVAJO WAY
Humorous stories of the Navajo. Each story is presented in Navajo with a word-for-word translation, colloquial English equivalents, and an explanation of the story with cultural notes. 1 cassette (80 minutes) and 143 pp. text, $39. AUDIO.

LEARN TO PLAY NATIVE AMERICAN FLUTE
Dave Powell. Instruction for playing the Native American wood flute. Includes instructions and demonstrations, and lessons for playing four tunes are also included. 32 minutes. Cassette. $9.95. CAN.

THE LEGACY OF REUBEN SNAKE: NATIVE AMERICAN ELDER
Public radio portrait of Mr. Snake's life and work. 30 minute audiocasette. $11. KF.

LEGENDS OF NORTH AMEICAN INDIANS
Music by Jackie Crow Hiendlmayr. Cassette, $10.50. CMM.

LENAPE LANGUAGE LESSONS
Introductory-level course of the language of the Lennape (Delaware Indians) consists of 4 lessons on 2 audio cassettes (71 minutes) and two 30 pp. texts. $29.50. AUDIO.

LET'S 49!
25 singers record 49 songs from Oklahoma. Cassette. CAN & GDA.

LET'S SPEAK MOHAWK
Beginning-level course in conversational Mohawk provides the pronunciation, grammar, structures, and vocabulary needed to communicate in everday situations. 3 cassettes, and 102 pp. text. $39.95. AUDIO.

LETTER FROM THE END OF THE 20TH CENTURY
Joy Harjo & Poetic Justice. Six piece band with lyrics by Harjo. CD, $15.98; cassette, $9.98. SWR.

LIBRARY OF CONGRESS
LPs: Seneca Songs from the Coldspring Longhouse; Songs of the Yuma, Cocopa, Yaqui; Songs of the Pawnee & Northern Ute; Songs of the Papago; Songs of the Nootka & Quiliute; Songs of the Menominee, Mandan & Hidatsa. Cassettes: Songs of the Kiowa; Indian Songs of Today; Songs of the Paiute, Washo, Ute, Bannock, Shoshone; Songs of the Comanche, Cheyenne, Kiowa, Caddo, Wichita, Pawnee; Songs of the Sioux; Songs of the Navajo; Songs of the Apache; Pueblo: Taos, San Ildefson, Zuni, Hopi; Omaha Indian Music. Cassettes & LPs, $9.98 each. CAN.

LIFE BLOOD
Joanne Shenandoah with Peter Kater. Ancient Iroquois melodies...piano with synthesizer, shakuhachi, bass, guitar, and percussion. CD, $15.98; cassette, $9.98. SWR.

KEVIN LOCKE CASSETTE SERIES
Three of Kevin Locke's first recordings. 3 cassettes, $24.98. MCP.

LONG AGO TIME
Cassette, $10. CMM.

LOVE FLUTE
Audio companion to Paul Goble's book put to the music of Bryan Akipa's flute. Cassette, $11; CD, $16. MCP.

LOVING WAYS
Joanne Shenedoah (Oneida) and A. Paul Ortega (Mescalero Apache) sing songs which reflect Native American philosophy and culture. 41 minutes. Cassette, $8.98. CAN & FWT.

MAKE ME A HOLLOW REED
Flute music by Tokeya Inajin (Kevin Locke). Cassette, $10. MCP.

MATRIARCH: IROQUOIS WOMEN'S SONGS
Joanne Shenandoah. Recorded at ancient village sites on Iroquois land. SWR.

MESA MUSIC CONSORT
Ben Tavera King, Joe Trevino & Eric Casillas. Drum, flute and keyboards. Three albums: "Medicine Flutes," "Spirit Feathers," and "Spirits of the Wild." Cassette, $6 each; CD, $9.15 each. ZANGO.

MIDWEST INDIANS RECORDS & TAPES
Chippewa War Dance Songs; Chippewa Grass Dance Songs; The Kingbird Singers; Mesquakie Bear Singers with War Dance Songs; Songs of the Chippewa; White Earth Pow-Wow; Winnebago Songs; Ojibway Music from Minnesota ($9.98); Honor the Earth Pow Wow - Songs of the Great Lakes Indians (Cassette, $9.98; compact disc, $16.98). Cassettes, $7.98 each. CAN.

MIGRATION
Peter Kater & R. Carlos Nakai. Piano & flute. CD, $15.98; cassette, $9.98. SWR.

MIGRATIONS
Ia Tulip. First album by flutist Ia Tulip of Sedona, Arizona. Cassette, $9.98. CAN.

MITAKUYE OYASIN: LAKOTA SUNDANCE SONGS
16 songs with booklet of words in Lakota and English. 2 cassettes. $16. BOND.

MORNING STAR
Flute music by Tom Marchanty-Ware, featuring, "Crazy Horse Song." Cassette, $4.50. GDA.

MUSIC OF THE ALASKAN KUTCHIN INDIANS
Traditional Athabascan language songs including love, medicine, crow and other plus jigs, reels and square dances played on a violin. Recorded in 1972 in the Fort Yukon area of Alaska. LP. $9.98. CAN.

MUSIC OF THE ALGONKIANS
19 songs, most of them about hunting. Includes those of the Woodland Indians: Cree, Montagnais, Naskapi. LP. $9.98. CAN.

MUSIC OF THE AMERICAN INDIANS OF THE SOUTHWEST
Includes the Navajo, Zuni, Hopi, San Ildefonso, Taos, Apache, Yuma, Papago, Walapai and Havasupai tribal music. Recorded by Willard Rhodes in cooperation with the Bureau of Indian Affairs. Notes by Harry Tschopik, Jr. and Willard Rhodes. LP. $9.98. CAN.

MUSIC OF THE PAWNEE
Contains 45 Pawnee Indian songs sung by Mark Evarts and recorded in 1935 by Dr. Gene Weltfish. Reflects all aspects of Pawnee life. LP. $9.98. CAN.

MUSIC OF THE PLAINS APACHE
15 songs recorded and edited by Dr. John Beatty. Includes children's songs, lullabies, church songs, dance songs, hand game songs, and peyote songs. Notes and background of songs included. LP. $9.98. CAN.

MUSIC OF THE PUEBLOS, APACHE, AND NAVAJOS
Recorded by David P. MacAllester and Donald N. Brown. 12 LP. TM.

MUSIC OF THE SIOUX AND THE NAVAJO
Sioux recordings include, among others, Rabbit Dance, Sun Dance, love songs; Navajo recordings include: Squaw Dance, Night Chant, riding song, etc. Notes included. Recorded by Willard Rhodes in cooperation with the Bureau of Indian Affairs. LP. $14.95. VIP.

MYTH, MUSIC, & DANCE OF THE AMERICAN INDIAN
De Cesare. An introduction to the Native American culture. The teacher's resource book provides pronunciations, tribe information, maps and instructions on making Indian instruments. Cassette & teacher's resource book, $19.95; student's songbook, $4.95; student's workbook, $3.95. ALF.

CARLOS R. NAKAI - NATIVE AMERICAN FLUTE MUSIC
Includes the following cassettes: Winter Dreams, Changes, Trilogy, Natives, Cycles, Journeys, Earth Spirit, Carry the Gift, Sundance, Desert Dance. $15 each tape. RC.

NATIVE AMERICAN CURRENTS
Joanne Shenandoah, R. Carlos Nakai & Peter Kater, Robert Mirabal, Joy Harjo & Poetic Justice. CD, $15.98; cassette, $9.98. SWR.

NATIVE AMERICAN FLUTE MUSIC
Kevin Locke: Lakota Wiikijo Olowan, 2 Vols. ($8.25 each); Tom Mauchahty-Ware: The Traditional & Contemporary Indian Flute of Tom Mauchahty-Ware ($7.98); Carlos Nakai: Changes - Native American Flute Music, Vol. 1, Cycles - Native American Flute Music, Vol. 2, and Journeys: Native American Flute Music, Vol. 3 ($8.98 each); Stan Snake: Dan of Love ($8.98). Cassettes. CAN.

NATIVE AMERICAN LANGUAGES
Self-study audiocassette/book programs celebrating the languages, lives, legends and music of the Navajo, Lakota, Kiowa, Cherokee, Choctaw, Lenape, and Passaquoddy Indians; and Hawaiian Natives. Separate programs include: *Navajo* - Breakthrough Navajo-2 cassettes (3 hours) and 234 pp. text, $49; Laughter: The Navajo Way (humorous stories of the Navajo-1 cassette (80 minutes), and 143 pp. text, $39; Basic Medical Navajo-1 cassette (1 hour), and 141 pp. text, $39. *Lakota* - Introductory Lakota-15 cassettes (12 hours), and 102 pp. text, $175. *Kiowa*-1 cassette, $12.95. *Cherokee* - Beginning Cherokee-2 cassettes (3 hours), and 332 pp. text, $39.00. *Lenape* - Lenape Language Lessons-2 cassettes (71 minutes), and 2-30 pp. text., $29.50. *Passamaquoddy* - Beginning Passamaquoddy-5 cassettes (3.5 hours), 50 pp. phrasebook, 112 pp. text and vowel sounds booklet, $59.50. *Hawaiian* - Let's Speak Hawaiian-8 cassettes (8.5 hours), and 430 pp. text, $95. AUDIO.

NATIVE AMERICAN LISTEN & COLOR LIBRARY
Library of educational coloring books with accompanying cassettes portrays the symbols, settings, dress, & tribal decorations of 95 Indian tribes grouped into six major division: Northeast, Northwest, Southwest, Plains, Southeast, California. Each tribe is described and illustrated. 1994. Six, 32-page booklets, six, 60-minute cassettes. $39.95. AUDIO.

NATIVE AMERICAN MUSIC
Authentic music of four Native American tribes. Songs of the Cherokee, Songs of the Lenape, Songs of the Navajo, Songs of the Sioux. $11.95 each. AUDIO.

NATIVE AMERICAN SOUNDTRACK
Robbie Ribertson & Red Road Ensemble. From TBS series "Native Americans." Cassette, $12; CD, $20. MFP.

NATIVE AMERICAN WISDOM
Kent Nerburn & Louise Mengelkoch, Editors
Features flute music by R. Carlos Nakai. Read by Kent Nerburn, Paula Bruce & Marc Allen. The unabridged reading of the book, and the Native American oral tradition. Speeches and writings of peoples from many tribes. 1993. Cassette, 83 minutes. $10.95. NWL & MFP.

THE NATIVE HEART
Gary Stroutsos
The wooden flute with piano & hand percussion...world jazz with American Indian influences. CD, $14.98; cassette, $9.98. MCP.

NATIVE TAPESTRY
Collaboration between R. Carlos Nakai and composer James DeMars. Traditional Native American flute music combined with African percussion, piano, cello, sax and chamber orchestra. 59 minutes. Cassette/CD. CAN.

NATIVES
Peter Kater and Carlos Nakai with an improvisational exploration and expression of the seven directions. CD, $15.98; cassette, $9.98. SWR.

NAVAJO
Alan Wilson. Self-study audio-cassette/book programs on the Navajo language. Also provides a deeper understanding of the Navajo culture and life style. Includes the following programs: Breakthrough Navajo: An Introductory Course, 2 cassettes (3 hrs.) and 234-page text, $49; Speak Navajo: Intermediate, 2 cassettes (2 hrs.) and 180-page text, $49; Laughter: The Navajo Way (Humorous Stories of the Navajo), 1 cassette (80 mins.) and 143-page text, $39; and Basic Medical Navajo, 1 cassette (60 mins.) and 141-page text, $39. AUDIO.

NAVAJO CREATION STORIES
Sacred Twins & Spider Woman (stories); accompanied by drums & song, Geri Keams, Streak-of-Black-Forest Navajo Clan, brings listener into the circle & beauty way. 1994. Cassette, 60 mins. $11.95. AUDIO.

NAVAJO & ENGLISH CASSETTES
20 cassettes. Grades K-6.
See SAN for titles and prices.

NAVAJO EXPERIENCE STORIES
24 cassettes and booklets. Grades 1-6.
See SAN for titles and prices

NAVAJO INDIAN RECORDS & TAPES
Beclabito Valley Singers, Vol. 3&4; Bita Hochee Travelers, Vols. 1,3&4; Chinle Valley Boys, 4 Vols.; Chinle Valley Singers, 2 Vols.; Chinle Valley Traditional Song and Dance Festival, 2 Vols.; Cove Nava-Tune Singers; Dennehotso Swinging Wranglers, 3 Vols.; Dine' Ba'Aliil of Navajoland (Navajo Songs and Dances)(LP); Four Corners Singers (Teec Nos Pos, Navajo Two Step & Love Songs), 7 Vols.; Four Corners Yei-Be-Chai; Lupton Valley Singers ($8.98); Memories of Navajoland; Davis Mitchell, 3 Vols.; Nanaba Midge Sings Traditional Navajo Songs; Natay, Navajo Singer; Navajo - Songs of the Dine; Navajo Squaw Dance Songs; Rock Point Singers, Vols. 3&4; San Juan Singers; Toh-Den-Nas-Shai Singers; Traditional Navajo Songs; Tsi Yi-Tohi Singers (Woodspring), 2 Vols.; Yei-Be-Chai Songs; Sweethearts of Navajoland, 2 Vols.; D.J. Nez, 2 Vols.Chinle Swingin' Echoes, 2 Vols.; Lupton Valley Singers, Vol. 1; Navajo Nation Swingers; Whippoorwill Singers, Vol. 1; Navajo Songs from Canyon de Chelly; Southwestern Singers. Cassettes & Compact discs. $7.98-$9.98; compact discs available, $16.98 each. CAN.

NAVAJO NIGHTS
Gerald Hausman. Navajo healing stories.
50 minutes. Cassette, $11.95. AUDIO.

NAVAJO PLACE NAMES
Arranged in alphabetical order, non-Navajo name first, then the Navajo name followed by literal translation of the complete Navajo term. 1 cassette & 100-page text which includes pronunciation guide and entire text of place names. $16.95. AUDIO.

THE NEW KICKING WOMAN SINGERS, Vol. 5
Intertribal Pow Wow Songs recorded live at Many Farms, AZ Pow Wow. 1988. Cassette, $7.98. CAN.

NEW WORLD RECORDS
A series of recordings compiled by Charlotte Heth, an ethnomusicologist and member of the Cherokee tribe. Includes: Songs of Love, Luck, Animals and Music - music of the Yurok and Tolowa Indians of Northern California; Songs and Dances of the Eastern Indians from Medicine Spring and Allegany - ritual, ceremonial and social music from the Cherokee (Oklahoma) and Seneca (Iroquois-Salamanca, NY); Oku Shareh - turtle dance songs recorded at San Juan Pueblo, NM; Songs of Earth, Water, Fire and Sky - an anthology of nine tribes: San Juan Pueblo, Seneca; Northern Arapaho; North Plains; Creek, Yurok, Navajo, Cherokee, and Southern Plains; Pow Wow Songs - Music of the Plains Indians. Cassettes. CAN.

NIGHT RIDERS & SKY BEINGS
Tsonakwa's second tape contains magical tales of the unseen world of the spirit told with warmth & power. 42 minutes. Cassette. $9.95. TOP & CH.

NOOTKA - INDIAN MUSIC OF THE PACIFIC NORTHWEST COAST
Includes canoe paddling songs, medicine songs, various animal songs, potlatch songs. Two LP record set. $19.96. CAN.

NORTH AMERICAN INDIAN & ESKIMO MUSIC
$14.95. VIP

NORTHERN PLAINS RECORDS & TAPES
Arapaho War Dance Songs and Round Dances; Arikara Grass Songs - White Shield Singers (LP); Cree Pow-Wow Songs, 2 Vols. - By the Parker Singers from Rocky Boy's Reservation; Flathead Stick Game Songs; Hays Singers - Gros Ventre Songs; Hidatsa Songs - By the Little Shell Singers (LP); The Mandaree Singers - Contemporary Pow-Wow Songs, 2 Vols.; Pow-Wow Songs from Rocky Boy, 2 Vols.; Social Songs of the Arapaho Sun Dance - By Wind River Singers; Stick Game Songs; War Dances of the Crow; Sage Point Singers; Music of the Nez Perce; Nez Perce Stories. Cassettes, $7.98-$9.98 each. CAN.

NORTHWEST INDIAN RECORDS & TAPES
Canyon Wellpinit Singers - Spokane WA; The Chemiwai Singers; Songs & Stories from Neah Bay Makah (LP); Songs of the Warm Springs Indian Reservation; Songs of a Yakima Encampment; Stick Game Songs by Joe Washington - Lummi; Treaty of 1855 - Intertribal Pow-Wow Songs; Umatilla Tribal Songs; Yakima Nation Singers of Satus Longhouse. Cassettes, $7.98. CAN.

OBSIDIAN BUTTERFLY
Alice Gomez with Madalyn Blanchett & Marilyn Rife. Flutes with percussion. CD, $15.98; cassette, $9.98. SWR.

THE OFFERING
Mary Youngblood (Aleut & Seminole) plays the flute. CD, $15.98; Cassette, $9.98. SWR.

OJIBWAY MUSIC FROM MINNESOTA: A CENTURY OF SONG FOR VOICE & DRUM
booklet by Thomas Vennum, Jr. 15 songs; 15-page booklet on Ojibway music and pow wows. Cassette & booklet, $9.95. CAN.

OJIBWE INTERMEDIATE VOCABULARY
Ojibwe Mekana. One, 60-minute tape & translation book. $21. ICC.

OJIBWE VOCABULARY FOR ADVANCED LEARNERS
Ojibwe Mekana. Two, 60-minute language tapes; Ojibwe/English booklet. $33. ICC.

OJIBWE VOCABULARY FOR BEGINNERS
Ojibwe Mekana. One, 60-minute language tape; Ojibwe/English work manual. $22. ICC.

OKLAHOMA POWWOW
18 specialty dance songs, including, "Eagle Dance." Cassette, $4.50. GDA.

ONCE IN A RED MOON
Joanne Shenandoah. Joanne opened Woodstock '94 with songs from this album. Songs deal with Native American issues. Includes the hit song, "America," performed at the White House and on TNT. 42 mins. Cassette. CAN.

OPEN CIRCLE
The flute by Kevin Locke. CD, $14.98; cassette, $9.98. MCP.

ORENDA
Joanne Shenandoah and Lawrence Laughing. Songs are primarily from the Iroquois tradition. CD, $15.98; cassette, $9.98. SWR.

OUT OF THE FIRE
Tom Minton flute music. Cassette. $9.95. VIP.

PAPAGO-PIMA INDIAN RECORDS & TAPES
Papago Dance Songs (Chelkona & Keihina Dance Songs) (LP); Songs from the Pima; Traditional Papago Music; Traditional Pima Dance Songs. Cassettes. $7.98 each. CAN.

PASSAMAQUODDY BRIEF HISTORIES
One cassette (30 minutes) in Passamaquoddy & bilingual, with 20 pp. booklet. $11.95. AUDIO.

PETER LA FARGE—ON THE WARPATH
Includes 14 contemporary protest songs by Peter La Farge, accompanied by Nick Navarro, Indian drums. LP. $9.98. CAN.

PEYOTE CANYON
Paul Guy, Jr. and Teddy Allen (Navajos) sing peyote songs. Cassette, $10. FTW.

PEYOTE MUSIC
Peyote - A Collection; Chants of Native American Church, Vol. 2 (LP); Intertribal Peyote Chants-Bill Denny, 5 Vols.; Kiowa Peyote Songs; Lord's Prayer Songs-Alfred Armstrong; Navajo Wildcat Peak-Peyote Songs, 5 Vols.; Navajo Wildcat Peak-Youth; Peyote Healing Chants of Native American Church (LP); Peyote Prayer Songs, 2 Vols.; Peyote Songs, Vol. 2.; Billy Nez-Peyote Songs from Navajoland; Nez & Yazzie-Peyote Voices; Guy and Allen. Cassettes. $7.98-$9.98 each. CAN.

PLIGHT OF THE REDMAN
by XIT. Cassette, $9.95; CD, $14.95. VIP.

PONCA TRIBAL SONGS
Songs sung by Lamont Brown, Sylvester Warrior, Alberta Waters, & henry Snake. Recorded in 1967. Cassette/LP, $10. AIS.

PONCA WARRIORS DANCE SONGS & PAWNEE WARRIORS DANCE SONGS
10 Ponca warrior dance songs vy Sylvester Warrior, Albert Waters & Francis Eagle; Pawnee Flag Song & 12 warrior dance songs sung by Frank Murrie, Lamont Pratt, Phillip Jim & Mrs. Jacob Leader. Cassette/LP, $10. AIS.

POW WOW SONGS
American Pow Wow by the Cathedral Singers; Pow-wow Highway Songs & Pow Wow Peple, both by Black Lodge Singers; and Pow Wow Season by the Indian Creek Singers. Cassettes & CDs. $9.95 each. VIP.

POW WOW SONGS FROM OKLAHOMA
32 War Dance Songs from the O-Ho-Mah Lodge, Cheyenne, Pawnee and Ponca tribes sung by Tom Ware, Millard Clark, et al. 2 Vols. Cassettes. $15.96. CAN & GDA.

POW WOW SONGS OF THE MENOMINEE
Summer Cloud Singers in honor of the life of "Nepenanakwat" Johnson Awonohopay. Cassette, $12. ICC.

POW WOW & SPECIALTY DANCE SONGS FROM OKLAHOMA
18 songs including Comanche Flag Song, round, gourd, war eagle, hoop, etc. dance songs. Kiowa and Comanche singers. Cassette, $10. CMM & CAN.

POWWOW SONGS
1 audiocassette (48 minutes), $10.95. AUDIO.

PUEBLO INDIAN TAPES
Hopi Butterfly; Hopi Social Dance Songs, 2 Vols.; Songs from Laguna; Pueblo Indian Songs from San Juan; Zuni - Ceremonial Songs; Grand Canyon Hopi Dancers, recorded 1958-15 minutes ($6.95). Cassettes, $7.98 each. CAN.

RED TAIL CHASING HAWKS: BROTHER HAWK
 Calvin Standing Bear & James Torres
Native American flute and keyboards. Cassett, $6.; CD, $9.15. CAN.

REFLECTIONS
Tsonakwa tells stories & reminisces about his early life. 11 short tales told in "intimate leisurely style. 53 minutes. Cassette, $9.95.

THE RENAISSANCE OF THE AMERICAN INDIAN
Describes the social barriers the American Indian has had to face; his experiences in various careers, and the anachronistic traditions of Indian culture that confuses his progress. 1968. Cassette. AUDIO.

RESERVATION BLUES: THE SOUND TRACK
 Jim Boyd & Sherman Alexie
Sherman Alexie (Spokane/Coeur D'Alene writer, author of the novel Reservation Blues) and Jim Boyd (Colville Confederated Tribes) collaborate on this soundtrack. Cassette, $6; CD, $10. OY.

ROBERT TREE CODY:
LULLABIES & TRADITIONAL SONGS
Native American flute music. Cassette, $12. CH.

ROCK POINT SINGERS, Vol. 4
Traditional love tunes. 14 skip and two-step dance songs. Cassette, $7.98. CAN

ROUND DANCE SONGS WITH ENGLISH LYRICS
48 songs. By Tom Mauchahty-Ware & Millard Clark. 4 LPs. $7.98 each. CAN & GDA.

SACRED FEELINGS
Douglas Spotted Eagle combines the nature sounds of the earth-mother with Native American flute. Cassette, $12. CH.

SALISH
Language course for beginners in the Salish language, spoken today principally in British Columbia. 30 lessons providing vocabulary, phrases, and sentences on subjects of everyday interest, such as work, weather, directions, food & money. 1994. 2 cassettes & 88-page text which includes 22 pp. index. $29.95. AUDIO.

SAN XAVIER FIDDLE BAND
O'odham old time fiddle music. 12 polkas, chotes and mazurkas. Cassette, $7.98. CAN

SELF-DETERMINATION FOR AMERICAN INDIANS:
1) DEVELOPMENT OF THEIR LANDS
2) CULTURES IN CONFLICT
Recorded and edited by Henry W. Hough: 1) Traces the history of reservations and discusses the present development of resources on Indian reservations. 2) Why Indians cling to their way of life although proud of their American citizenship. 1968. Cassettes, 25 minutes each. AUDIO.

SELU: SEEKING THE CORN MOTHR'S WISDOM
 Awiakta
In this companion to her book of the same name, Awiakta leads all who will listen along a deer trail that spirals into the Great Smokey Mountains to the Corn Motehr herself—and to her wisdoms. 3 hours. 1995. $16.95. OY.

SEMINOLE INDIANS OF FLORIDA
Dr Frances Densmore on cylinders. Includes corn dance, Cypress Swamp hunting and buffalo dance songs; plus songs for treatment of the sick and songs concerning removal of Seminole to Oklahoma. LP. $9.98. CAN.

SENECA SOCIAL DANCE MUSIC
30 songs from Allegany Reservation, Cattaraugus Co., New York. Recorded by M.F. Reimer. LP. $9.98. CAN.

SENECA SONGS FROM
COLDSPRING LONGHOUSE
Songs include the Drum Dance, Bear Society, Fish Dance, and others. Recorded and edited in 1941-1945 by Willard N. Fenton. 16-page brochure. LP. $8.98, LC and $9.98. CAN.

THE SEVENTH DIRECTION
Flute music by Tokeya Inajin (Kevin Locke). Cassette, $10. MCP.

SHENANDOAH
 JoAnne Shenandoah
Country tunes with contemporary ballads about Native American life. 40 minutes. Cassette/CD. CAN.

SIGNALS FROM THE HEART
Collection of "49" and round dance love songs using traditional drumming and style. Performed by Common Man Singers of the Standing Rock Sioux Reservation in North Dakota. Cassette, $11; CD, $17. MCP & MFP.

SILENT WARRIOR
by XIT. Cassette, $9.95; CD, $14.95. VIP.

SIOUX RECORDS & TAPES
Celebration on an Indian Theme; Denver Dakota Singers -Pow Wow Songs; Fort Kipp Celebration; Fort Kipp '77 Live; Fort Kipp Sioux Singers; Grass Dance Songs from Devil's Lake - By the Lake Region Singers; Ironwood Singers; Montana Grass Songs - By the Fort Kipp Singers; Porcupine Singers, 6 Vols. - At Ring Thunder, Traditional Sioux Songs, Concert in Vermillion, At the University of South Dakota, Rabbit Songs; Rock Creek Singers - Hunkpapa Sioux; Sioux Favorites; Sioux Grass Songs and Round Dances; Sioux Songs From Devils Lake - By the Lone Buffalo Singers; Sioux Songs of War and Love; Sisseton-Wahpeton Songs (LP); and Songs of the Sioux. Rock Creek Singers; Sioux-Assiniboine Singers, 2 Vols.; Red Nation Singers; Taku Wakan: Lakota Sundance Songs; Taku Skanskan: Lakota Yuwipi Songs. Cassettes, $7.98-9.98 each. CAN.

A SKY OF DREAMS
Neoprimitive solos for flutes of the world. By Barry Stramp of the Coyote Oldman duo. Cassette, $10; compact disc, $15. FTW & CH.

SMOKESIGNS
 Rick Eby
Flute & synthesizer music. Cassette. $12.95. VIP.

SONG CARRIER
Robert Mirabal. Flute. CD, $15.98; cassette, $9.98. SWR.

SONGS & DANCES OF THE FLATHEAD INDIANS
A complete musical culture of the Salish people. Illustrated notes included. LP. $9.98. CAN.

SONGS & DANCES OF THE
GREAT LAKES INDIANS
Music of the Algonquins and Iroquois. Recorded in Iowa, Wisconsin, Michigan and New York State by Gertrude P. Kurath. Text included. LP. $9.98. CAN.

SONGS FROM THE IROQUOIS LONGHOUSE
Selections include: Creator's Songs; Midwinter Festival Chants; Medicine Men's Celebration (Onondaga.) Recorded and edited by William N. Fenton in cooperation with the Smithsonian Institution. 34-page brochure. LP. $8.95, LC and $9.98, CAN.

SONGS OF THE CHEROKEE
Ceremonial songs & dances (caasette); songs & dances of the Cherokee of North Carolina & the Seneca (cassette). $11.95 each. AUDIO.

SONGS OF EARTH, WATER, FIRE & SKY
Traditional dance songs recorded on location by Pueblo, Seneca, Arapaho, Plains, Creek, Yurok, Navajo & Cherokee tribes. Cassette, $12. CH.

SONGS OF THE NATIVE AMERICAN CHURCH
Peyote songs by Billy McClellan. 2 Vols. $9. GDA.

SONGS OF THE NAVAJO
 Traditional Navajo songs (cassette); traditional Sioux songs (cassette); Taku Wakan: Lakota Sundance Songs (cassette). $11.95 each. AUDIO.

SONGS, POEMS AND LIES
Lorenzo Baca (Isleta Pueblo/Mescalero Apache) sings songs with traditional chants and original poetry. Cassette, $10. FTW.

SONGS & STORIES FROM NEAH BAY - MAKAH
Legends and little songs by a favorite Makah storyteller, Helen Peterson. LP. $7.98. CAN.

SOUND OF AMERICAN RECORDS (SOAR)
Specializes in contemporary & traditional Native music from throughout North America. Contains hundred of recordings on CD and cassette as well as videos and audio books on cassette. SOAR.

SOUNDS OF INDIAN AMERICA —
PLAINS & SOUTHWEST RECORDED
LIVE AT THE GALLUP CEREMONIALS
Includes the Buffalo Dance, Jemez Eagle Dance, Ute Bear Dance, San Juan Butterfly Dance, Zuni Rain Song Dance by the Olla Maidens, Taos Belt Dance, Pawnee Ghost Dance, Zuni Doll Dance, Crow Sun Dance, Kiowa Attack Dance. Cassette, $10. IH.

SOUTHERN PLAINS-OKLAHOMA
INDIANS RECORDS & TAPES
Brave Scout Singers-Northern Style Otoe, Missourian & Pawnee; Gourd Dance Songs of the Kiowa-Koomsa Tribal Singers; Kiowa Back Leggings Society Songs-Bill Kaulaity; Kiowa Gourd Dance Songs; Kiowa "49" & Round Dance Songs; Kiowa Scalp & Victory Dance Songs-Koomsa Tribal Singers; Ponca War Dances-Ponca India Singers; Pow Wow - Southern Style War Dances; Songs of the Caddo, 2 Vols. (LP). Cassettes. $7.98 each. CAN.

SOUTHERN SCRATCH:
WAILA OF THE TOHONO O'ODHAM
Popular dance music of the native peoples of southern Arizona. 53 minutes. Cassette. CAN.

SOUTHERN THUNDER:
INTERTRIBAL SONGS OF OKLAHOMA
Osage Flag Song, 14 intertribal songs, 2 Pawnee veterans' songs, & 1 Pawnee war dance song sung by a few different singers. Recorded at Hominy, Oklahoma, 1992. Cassette/LP, $10. IH.

SOUTHERN THUNDER: REACHIN' OUT
14 intertribal songs by a number of singers. Recorded at Hominy, Oklahoma, 1993. Cassette/LP, $10. IH.

SPACE AGE INDIAN
 Tiger Tiger
Cassette, $9.95; CD, $14.95. VIP.

SPIRIT HORSES
R. Carlos Nakai with traditional cedar flute and contemporary concerto for Native American flute and chamber orchestra. Cassette, $12. CAN & CH.

SPIRIT JOURNEY - CORNEL PEWEWARDY
Dr. Pewewardy (Comanche/Kiowa) demonstrates his talents of singer, flute player & keeper of the drum. Cassette, $11; CD, $17. MCP & MFP.

SPIRIT OF SONG
Original digital recording of the "Spirit of Song" singers from the spring of 1990. The voices of Sissy & Credric Goodhouse, Earl & Tom Bullhead, Dave Archambault, et al. on the Lakota culture. CD, $14.98; Cassette, $9.98. MCP.

SPIRITS OF THE PRESENT:
THE LEGACY FROM NATIVE AMERICA
Focuses on Native American histories, cultures, and modern realities. Explores American Indian religious freedom, the sovereignty of Native nations, stereotyping of Native people by sports teams and other com-

mercial entities, and Native American art. 1991. 5 audiocassettes. $29.95. PUSA (800) 253-6476.

STAR LORE
Lynn Moroney (Cherokee/Chickasaw), tells the star lore to be found in the myths of Native Americans. Authentic music by Native American flute player. The Feather Moon, 1 casette; The Star Husband, 1 casette. 1994. 45 minutes each. $10.95 each. AUDIO.

STARGAZER
Gerald Hausman
Navajo supernatural myths & divination stories. 60 minutes. Cassette, $11.95. AUDIO.

STORYTELLER
N. Scott Momaday
Stories in the Native American oral tradition shared by a storytelling master of the Kiowa origin. 60 minutes. Cassette, $9.95. AUDIO.

SUNRISE
Flute music by Tom Mauchanty-Ware, featuring, "Zuni Sunrise Song." Cassette. $4.50. GDA.

SYMBOLIC SHAMANISM:
A STUDY OF NAVAJO MEDICINE MEN
Dr. Donald Sandner describes the healing process of medicine men and attempts to explain the sandpaintings, how they are made, how images are evoked for each patient, and how cures are performed. Two hours/two cassettes. BSR.

SYMBOLS OF HOPI
Jill McManus, a jazz musician, has created a jazz album by arranging two songs each by a pair of Hopi composers who work within their own dance music tradition, and added three originals in the spirit of Hopi and Pueblo music. Includes two Hopi ceremonial songs, "Corn Dance" and "Cloud Blessing." Louis Mofsie, director of the famed Thunderbird Dance Troup, opens Mark Lomayestewa's Corn Dance on the cottonwood drum. CJ.

TAOS TALES
Robert Mirabal. In song, chant and music, Mirabal tells stories of the land known as Taos using flute, cello, guitar and percussion. CD, $15.98; cassette, $9.98.

TEAR OF THE MOON
Coyote Old Man. Compositions on Native American flute & Incan Pan Pipes. Cassette, $12. CH.

THE THIRD CIRCLE -
SONGS OF LAKOTA WOMEN
Traditional & contemporary Lakota women's songs sung by Sissy Goodhouse. Cassette, $9.98; CD, $14.98. MCP.

THUNDER CHORD
Coyote Oldman. Native American flutes and panpipes. Cassette, $12. CH.

THUNDERDRUMS
Scott Fitzgerald uses drums from both Native America and Africa for sounds of nature. Cassette, $10; compact disc, $16. FTW.

TIWAHE
Sissy Goodhouse, her family and friends sing traditional and contemporary Lakota songs celebrating the meaning of family. CD, $14.98; cassette, $9.98. MCP.

TO THOSE WHO'VE GONE BEFORE US
Native flute music. Paul Hacker and son, Jason, team up for a duet of Native American flute traditional and gospel. Cassette, $11 or CD, $16. PH

TOUCH THE EARTH
A unique performance of words and music on the sacredness of land and life by twelve distinguished Native American actors, musicians, artists, writers and spiritual leaders, based on T.C. McLuhan's best-selling book, Touch the Earth. 60 minutes. Audiocassette. $10.95. MFV.

TOUCH THE FIRE
Native American poetry by Bob Annesley. Cassette, $4.50. GDA.

TOUCH THE SWEET EARTH
Sharon Burch
Her songs focus on the importance of the maternal relationship to the Dine. In Navajo with some English. 1996. 36 minutes. Cassette. $6; CD, $9.15. CAN.

TRACKS WE LEAVE
16 impressionistic compositions featuring William Eaton, with R. Carlos Nakai, Rich Rodgers, Claudia Tulip, Arvel Bird & Udi Arouh. Notes on the instruments and performers included. 55 minutes. Cassette, $8.98; compact disc, $14.98. CAN & CH.

THE TRADITIONAL & CONTEMPORARY
INDIAN FLUTE
Flute music by Tom Mauchanty-Ware. Cassette. $4.50. GDA.

THE TRADITIONAL & CONTEMPORARY
INDIAN FLUTE
Flute songs by Fernando Cellicion. Cassette, $4.50. GDA.

TRADITIONAL INDIAN FLUTE
OF FERNANDO CELLICION
10 flute songs. Cassette, $4.50. GDA.

TRIBAL MUSIC INTERNATIONAL
Music from the Hopi; Music from San Juan Pueblo; Red Eagle Wing Pow Wow Songs; Flute and Prayer Songs; Music from the Alliance West Singers; and 65th Inter-Tribal Ceremonial-Gallup Ceremonial; Music from Zuni Pueblo. Cassettes. $8.98 each. CAN.

TRIBAL SONGS
Ceremonial and social songs and dances of eight Native American Indian tribes: Tohono O'odham (Papago), Apache, Sioux, Navajo, Crow, Ute, Shawnee, and New Taos. 1 cassette. $12.95. AUDIO.

TURTLE ISLAND ALPHABET
Gerald Hausman's anthology of myths & stories which study the symbols & images central to the Native American culture. Cassette (90 mins), $10.95. AUDIO.

TURTLE MOUNTAIN SINGERS: EARLY THIS
MORNING I HEARD MY HORSE CALLING
10 Navajo social dance songs sung by John Comanche, Jimmie Castillo, Samuel Harrison, & Kee Trujillo, . Recorded at Taos, New Mexico, 1990. Cassette/LP, $10. IH.

TURTLE MOUNTAIN SINGERS:
WELCOME TO NAVAJO LAND
10 Navajo social dance songs sung by John Comanche, Jimmie Castillo, Samuel Harrison, Ernest Chavez, Kee Trujillo, Johnny B. Dennison & Benson Trujillo. Recorded at Lybrook, New Mexico, 1990. Cassette/LP, $10. IH.

UNDER THE GREEN CORN MOON:
NATIVE AMERICAN LULLABIES
Performers represent 14 different Indian Nations, and include Joanne Shenandoah and Robert Mirabal. CD, $15.98; Cassette, $9.98. SWR.

UNITED TRIBES INTERNATIONAL POWWOW
Powwow recording featuring some of the best drum groups in the nation singing their best songs. 2 CD set, $19.98; 2 cassette set, $12.98. MCP.

UP WHERE WE BELONG
Buffy Sainte-Marie (Cree)
Cassette, $10. OY.

UTES
Includes six northern war dance songs, three bear dances, and three sun dance songs. Singers from Ignacio, Colorado, and from the White Mesa, Utah. Cassette, $7.98. CAN.

VASQUEZ
Andrew Vasquez's flute. CD, $14.98; Cassette, $9.98. MCP.

VETERANS SONGS
Lakota Thunder
Songs honoring warriors from past to present. Included are songs of Sitting Bull, the Battle of the Little Big-

horn, World Wars, Korean and Vietnam Wars. CD, $14.98; Cassette, $9.98. MCP.

A VOICE FOR THE AMERICAN INDIAN
A program on Indian culture and history, and the current struggles for political rights and power. Produced by Pacifica, KPFA. 1971. 54 minutes. AUDIO.

WALKING THE RED ROAD
Earl Bullhead, a Lakota of the Standing Rock Reservation in North Dakota, sings traditional Lakota songs recorded in a contemporary style. Cassette, $10.60; CD, $16. MCP.

WAR WHOOPS AND MEDICINE SONGS
33 songs collected at the Upper Dells of the Wisconsin River where more than 200 American Indians from five different tribes assembled for the annual Star Rock Indian Ceremonial. Includes an illustrated brochure. Edited by Charles Hoffman. LP. $9.98. CAN.

WARRIOR MAGICIAN
Robert Mirabal. Flute music. CD, $15.98; cassette, $9.98. SWR.

WASHO PEYOTE SONGS: SONGS OF
THE AMERICAN INDIAN NATIVE CHURCH
Recorded by Dr. Warren d'Azevedo. LP. $9.98. CAN.

WEAVINGS
R. Carlos Nakai
Nakai on the Native American flute and trumpet is joined by Larry Yanez on synthesizer with percussion and guitar. 49 minutes. Cassette/CD. CAN.

WESTERN CANADIAN INDIAN RECORDS & TAPES
A-1 Club Singers - Vol. 2; Blackfoot A-1 Singers; Blackfoot Oldtimers - Songs from the Past; Calgary Drummer; Chiniki Lake Drummers; Crowfoot Drummers - Blackfoot, Alberta; The Drums of Poundmaker - With the Tootoosis Family, 2 Vols. (LP); Fraser Valley Spotted Lake Inter-Tribal Singers; Little Pine Singers - Cree Pow-Wow Songs; Pigeon Lake Singers - Cree Tribal Songs, 2 Vols.; Pow Wow Songs - Treaty 6 Ermine Skin Band; Sarcee Broken Knife Singers, 2 Vols.; Sarcee Oldtimers; Pezhin Wachipi (Grass Dance) (LP); Scalp Lock Singers; Sioux Pow-Wow Songs; Songs from the Blood Reserve - Kaispai Singers; Songs from the Battleford Pow-Wow; Songs of the Sarcee (LP); Stony Pow-Wow Songs - Eden Valley Pow-Wow Club; Two Nation Singers - Round Dance Songs; Little Boy Singers - Pow Wow Songs, 2 Vols.; Northern Cree Singers, Vols. 3 - Live at Fort Duchesne; Blackstone Singers, Vol. 1 - Contest Songs - Live at Fort Duchesne; Sioux Assiniboine - Dakota Kahomini Songs; The Red Bull Singers, 2 Vols.; Dakota Hotain Singers, 2 Vols.; Cathedral Lakes Singers, 2 Vols.; Whitefish Bay Singers, 2 Vols.; Plains Ojibway Singers, Vol. 1; Stoney Eagle. Cassettes & LPs, $7.98-$9.98 each. CAN.

WHEN THE EARTH WAS LIKE NEW
Chesley Goseyun Wilson &
Ruth Longcor Harnisch Wilson
Songs and stories of the Apache. WMP.

WHISPERING TREE:
ANISHINAABE STORIES & SONGS
Traditional stories and contemporary situations about friendship, hope, joy and trust by Annie Humphrey, John Trudell, Pato Hoffman, Larry Long and author Anne Dunn and friends. CD, $14.98. MCP.

THE WHITE BUFFALO CALF WOMAN
AS TOLD BY MARTIN HIGH BEAR
Cassette, $8.25. CAN.

WHITE EAGLE SINGERS, Vol. 5
11 intertribal pow wow songs recorded live at the Numaga Indian Days in Reno-Sparks, Nevada. Cassette, $7.98. CAN.

WHITE FISH BAY SINGERS, Vol. 6
One of Canada's most popular traditional drum groups. Powwow singing. Cassette, $11. MFP.

WIND RIVER
Andrew Vasquez's flute with friends, Rodney Grant and Rita Coolidge. CD, $14.98; Cassette, $9.98. MCP.

WINDS OF HONOR
Gary Stroutsos
Joining Stroutsos are various artists including Epaminondas Trimis, Jovano Santos Neto, the Goodhouse family with traditional vocals, and Joseph Fire Crow on vocals and hand drum. CD, $14.98; cassette, $9.98. MCP.

WINDS OF THE PAST, Vol. I & II
Flute music by Choctaw/Cherokee flutemaker Paul Hacker. Blend of traditional and contemporary. Cassette, $11; CD, $21. PH

WINTER DREAMS
Native American Christmas music. R. Carlos Nakai and William Eaton arranged these old traditional European Christmas songs. Cassette, $12. CAN & CH.

WITHOUT REZERVATION
Urban Native Americans rapping a politico-ethnic funk about the struggle of the red brother and red sister. Features Chris LaMarr, Kevin Nez and Cory Aranaydo. 42 minutes. Cassette. CAN.

WIYUTA: ASSINIBOINE STORYTELLING WITH SIGNS CD
CD, $100. UTP.

WOLVES (Original Soundtrack)
Film score by Michael Cusson. Songs by Bruce Cockburn, Robbie Robertson, Sacred Spirits, Joanne Shenadoah, Walela, Paul Winter and Mary Youngblood. CD only, $15.98.

WOODLAND WINDS - THE WOODLAND CONSORT
Fusion of Native & Western instruments, with Ojibway flute. Cassette, $11; CD, $16. MCP.

WOPILA - A GIVEAWAY: LAKOTA STORIES
Dovie Thompson
Features the traditional flute music of Kevin Locke within the prose of tha artist. Grades PS-4. Cassette, $10.60. MCP.

THE WORLD IN OUR EYES
Storyteller Reuben Silverbird's view of the essence of our country's most ancient heritage. Tells of the Great Spirit, Mother Earth, Father Sky, the circle, the rain, the eagle and other elements of the creation stories. Two cassettes, $18; CD, $29. MFP.

A YAQUI WAY OF KNOWLEDGE
The group Wild Strawberries in a series of tone poems inspired by Carlos Castaneda's best-selling book of the same title. Cassette, $10; compact disc, $16. FTW.

YAZZIE GIRL
Sharon Burch
Her songs focus on the importance of the maternal relationship to the Dine. In Navajo with some English. 36 minutes. Cassette. $6; CD, $9.15. CAN.

YOUNG EAGLE'S FLIGHT
Robert Tree Cody
Collection of solo Native American flute contains nine traditional (Lakota and Dakota) and five original songs. 46 minutes. Cassette. CAN.

ZANGO MUSIC DISTRIBUTION
Zango Music is a wholesale distribution company specializing in Native American music. Their Tribal Fires catalog is a comprehensive and useful guide for ordering tapes and compact discs. They carry over 800 titles of flute, traditional, contemporary and pow-wow music. Half of these titles are given detailed reviews with pictures of the album accompanying them. The catalog has advertising from many different independent and Native-owned labels; also include a best seller page to take the confusion out of ordering. Free demos are available on almost all selections. Wholesale only. Catalog. ZANGO.

PRINTS & PHOTOGRAPHS, PICTURE SETS, POST CARDS, CALENDARS, POSTERS, CRAFT KITS, FLAGS

ALASKAMEUT '86
Exhibition poster features masks by John Kailukiak, Kathleen Carlo and James Schoppert. 24x18", full color. $8.50, postpaid. IANA.

ALL-NEW NATIVE AMERICAN BRACELETS
by Geri Dawn Weitzman
This kit includes 750 seed beads, embroidery floss, felt, and a 16-page full-color book wioth step-by-step instructions. $7.95. TA.

AMERICAN INDIAN CUT & USE STENCILS
Ed Sibbett, Jr.
64 pp. $6.95. DOV.

AMERICAN INDIAN PORTRAIT POSTCARDS
Charles Bird King
24 postcards. 9 x 12" $4.95. DOV & WH.

ARTS FROM THE ARCTIC
Exhibition poster featuring the artwork of Alvin Amason. 18x22", full color. $12.50, postpaid. IANA.

ATHABASCAN OLD-TIME FIDDLING POSTER
Features musicians and dancers. 18x24", black and silver duotone. $7.50, postpaid. IANA.

THE BEAUTY OF NATIVE AMERICAN CHURCH-POSTER
By Haroldton Begaye. 21 x 17. $3.95. CAN.

BENDING TRADITION
Exhibition poster featuring bentwood art by traditional and contemporary artists. 24" x 18" full color. Institute of Alaska Native Arts, $8.50, postpaid. IANA.

BLACKFOOT INDIAN PORTRAITS
Winold Reiss
A portfolio of 6 self-matted full-color prints. 9x12. $3.95. DOV.

BOSTON CHILDREN'S MUSEUM BORROW A KIT
The Indians Who Met the Pilgrims: Presents the Wampanoag people of Massachusetts past and present; Hopi Culture: Describes a public kachina dance and its connection to contemporary Hopi culture. These two kits may be used as curriculum units, include cultural objects, oral history, texts and guides, A-V materials, and classroom activities; prepared with the participation of Native American people. Two other kits, The Navajo and Northwest Coast Indians, contain cultural objects and related labels for classroom exhibit. CMB.

CAHOKIA ARTIFACTS POSTER
Full color poster showing artifacts found at Cahokia Mounds site. 38" x 25". $10. CMM.

CAHOKIA MOUNDS MURAL
Entrance scene in new Interpretive Center - artists conception of ancient city. 20" x 37". $10. CMM.

CATLIN'S NORTH AMERICAN INDIAN PORTFOLIO
The 1845 American edition is supplemented with six additional prints from the original British edition. Each set contains 31 plates measuring 16x22". Strictly limited to 950 sets. 1989. $1,250. A.

CHEROKEE POEM
8.5" x 11 poster. $2.50. VIP.

CHEROKEE POSTER
Kevin Smith, artist
17" x 21". $7.95. VIP.

CHOCTAW T-SHIRT
Kevin Smith, artist
$13.95. VIP.

CLOVIS CULTURE
Poster. $15. CMM.

CRAFT SUPPLIES
Beads, needles, thread, metal items, shawl fringe, feathers, herbs, books. CAN.

CUSTER'S FIGHT
Poster. 29" x 21" full color; flat. $1.50. DOV.

EARLY PALEO INDIAN PERIOD
Poster. $15. CMM.

EARLY TEXAS INDIAN MURAL POSTERS
George Nelson
Series of posters, full-color photographs of the actual 24" x 10" murals on the Institute of Texan Cultures' Floor. "A Caddo Farming Community in East Texas"; "Desert Farmers of Southwest Texas: The Mogollon Culture"; An Apache Encampment in the Texas Hill Country." Each poster, 36" x 21". $10 each; $25 for all three. UT-ITC.

EDUCATIONAL AID KITS
Children's touchable exhibits contained in a large footlocker-type trunk. Artifacts are compiled from the Museum of New Mexico's collections and various other sources in Santa Fe. Includes: Anglo Pioneer Family; Apache Family; Navajo Family; Pueblo Indian Family; and Spanish Frontier Family. Grades 1-6. Available for loan in the State of New Mexico only. Free one month rental. MNM.

GEORGE CATLIN'S NORTH AMERICAN INDIANS
Box of 20 5x7" notecards & envelopes. 4 different designs. $11.95. A.

HOOP DANCER PRINT
Milton Denny, artist
$2.50. VIP.

HOPI KACHINAS: A POSTCARD COLLECTION
Cliff Bahnimptewa, illustrator
20 full-color postcards. Illus. $7.95. NP.

HOWARD ROCK & HIS LEGACY
Exhibition poster featuring *The Dance of Kakirnok*, a painting by the late Howard Rock. 16x20", full color. $7.50, postpaid. IANA.

INDIAN DWELLING & HOMES OF THE U.S. POSTER
Revised 1984. 29" x 23". $5.25. CMM.

INDIAN PHOTOGRAPHS FROM THE SMITHSONIAN
There are four sets of five prints each. Set 1) Selected portraits: Kicking Bear, Geronimo, Chief Joseph, Quanah Parker, and Wolf Robe; Set 2-4) Lifestyles, Northwestern Indians - Southwestern Indians - Plains Indians. 11 x 14. SI.

INDIAN POW-WOW CALENDAR
NACO.

THE INDIANS OF THE PLAINS
Contains 46, 11 x 14 photographs explaining the Plains Indians culture, government, society and habits; and how they were discovered in 1805. $73.50. DPA.

INTERWOVEN EXPRESSIONS
Exhibition poster featuring 20 Alaska Native baskets representative of all of the Alaska Native cultures. 24x18", full color. $8.50, postpaid. IANA.

KIOWA EAGLE PRINT
Ruth Blaylock Jones, artist
$3. VIP.

LIBRARY OF CONGRESS PRINTS & PHOTOGRAPHS DIVISION
Recently completed the processing and cataloging of 3,500 images of American Indians photographed over an 85-year period ending in the 1940s. Also an extensive collection of Edward S. Curtis photographs, more than 1,600 photos. The images are now accessible to researchers in the division's reading room in the Library's Madison building in Washington, DC. LC.

CARL MOON PHOTOGRAPHS
see publisher MPC for details and prices.
MUSEUM OF THE AMERICAN

INDIAN-PHOTOGRAPHIC ARCHIVES
Covers all areas and aspects of Native American life in the Western Hemisphere. Includes photographs by Curtis, Matteson and Jackson; Pepper, Wildschut and Verrill. 42,000 negatives, 28,000 bxw prints, and 5,000 color transparencies and slides; bxw prints, 5x7 or 8x10 format; 35mm color slides; and 4x5 color transparencies. A slide list is available for a modest fee. MAI.

MUSEUM OF NEW MEXICO
PHOTOGRAPHIC PORTFOLIOS
Includes three Native American photographic portfolios: Pueblo Indians of New Mexico; Apache Indians of New Mexico; and, Navajo Indians of New Mexico. Each set contains 16 photographs illustrating important aspects of the subject group's life and history during the late 19th and early 20th centuries. Large bxw photographs printed on heavy glossy paper. Each portfolio also contains a brief history of the group plus a vocabulary list, bibliography, and descriptive captions for the photographs. $6.95 each. MNM.

NATIVE AMERICAN CRAFT KITS
Dream Catchers, $7.95.; Kachinas, $7.95; Clay Pots, $7.95. All-New Native American Bracelets, $7.95; Sand Painting, $6.95. TA & CLD.

NATIVE AMERICAN FLAG
3' x 5'. $25. NACO.

NATIVE AMERICAN IMAGES
Exhibit posters and limited edition prints by Donald Vann, and original stone lithographs by Steve Forbes. NAI.

NATIVE AMERICAN VISIONS CALENDAR
12 exquisite Sam English (Ojibwa artist) full-color prints; calendar with 10x14 print and appointment calendar below; and selected quotes from historic and present-day tribal leaders. Available in August for upcoming year. $10.95. FUL.

NAVAJO CURRICULUM MATERIALS -
DRUGS & ALCOHOL
"Drug & Alcohol Myths" - poster set, 11x17-3 colors - 12 posters drawn with Indian people depicting common myth about drug and alcohol use and abuse. $5.10 per set; $8.95 laminated; "Fetal Alcohol Syndrome" - poster set, 11x17-2 color - 8 posters stating facts about fetal alcohol syndrome and its effect on new born babies. $3.40 per set; $6.80 laminated. SAN.

NAVAJO DESIGN GIFTWRAP PAPER
  Elaine Norman
4 sheets, 9x12. $3.95. DOV.

NAVAJO GUIDES, CULTURAL
MANUALS, & TEXTBOOKS
See SAN for titles and prices.

NAVAJO INDIAN CULTURAL
CARD SETS & POSTERS
Contains 16 in all. All grades.
See SAN for titles and prices.

NAVAJO INSTRUCTIONAL PROGRAMS,
KITS & PACKETS
See SAN for titles and prices.

NAVAJO RUG STIK-WITHIT NOTECUBES
  Self Stick
Full color. 600 sheets, 3.5 x 3". $12. NP.

NEW TRADITIONS
Exhibition poster features The Hunter, by the late Sam Fox of Dillingham, AK. 18x30", blue & black duotone. $7.50, postpaid. IANA.

NORTH AMERICAN INDIAN
DESIGN GIFTWRAP PAPER
  Gregory Mirow
4 sheets. 9x12. $3.95. DOV.

NORTH AMERICAN INDIAN DESIGNS
LASER-CUT PLASTIC STENCILS
  Charlene Tarbox
8 designs. $7.95. DOV.

OLD WOMAN PRINT
  Milton Denny, artist
$3. VIP.

PAINTINGS OF AMERICAN WEST POSTCARDS
  Eiteljorg Museum
16 pp. $3.95. DOV.

PEYOTE PRAYER-POSTER
By Doug Standing Rock. 28 x 21". $3.95. CAN.

THE PLAINS INDIANS
Two sets of 18 different photographs, featuring the fully captioned art of Howard Terpning, renowned painter of Plains Indian history. $44 each; $78 for both. DPA.

POSTCARDS OF HISTORIC TAHLEQUAH
BxW postcards of the capital of the Cherokee Nation. 4 sets available. $6 for each set of 6 views, all 4 sets, 24 cards, $10. VIP.

POW WOW: PORTRAITS OF NATIVE AMERICANS
  photos by Ben Marra
Includes a personal statement from each Native American dancer. 2005. $12.99.

POWWOW
  photos by Chris Roberts
Captures the energy of powwow dancers. 2005 calendar. $12.95. ME.

PUEBLO PEOPLE CALENDAR:
A PHOTOGRAPHIC PORTFOLIO
OF PUEBLO INDIANS
  Marcia Keegan
$12. CL.

SACRED PEYOTE WATER BIRD-POSTER
By Doug Standing Rock. 21 x 14". $3.95. CAN.

SELECTED PORTRAITS OF PROMINENT
NORTH AMERICAN INDIANS
8x10 glossy or matte prints. SI.

SIX INDIAN CRAFTS POSTCARDS
  Eiteljorg Museum
Full-color postcards of items on display at the Eiteljorg Museum of American Indian and Western Art in Indianapolis, Indiana. 6 cards, $1. TC.

SOUTHWEST INDIAN CALENDAR
  Marcia Keegan
Large-format color pictures of life among the Pueblo Indians of New Mexico. 12 1/2 x 10 1/4". $12. NAV.

SOUTHWEST INDIAN GIFTWRAP PAPER
  Muncie Hendler
2 sheets. 9x12" $1.75. DOV.

SOUTHWEST INDIAN STICKERS
  Madeleine Orban-Szontagh
24 full-color, pressure-sensitive, designs adapted from the Hopi, Navajo and Pueblo tribes. 8 pp. $1. TC.

STORY IN STONE
Artifacts poster. 24" x 36". $10. CMM.

SUN RIVER WAR PARTY
Poster. 33" x 21" full color...flat. $1.50. DOV.

TEACHING RESPECT FOR NATIVE PEOPLES
A brief list of how, and how not to, teach about Native peoples in the classroom. 18" x 24". $10. OY.

A TREASURED HERITAGE
Exhibition poster featuring 11 works by Alaska Native artists representative of Yup'ik and Inupiaq Eskimo, Tlingit, Haida, Tsimshian and Athabascan Indian cultures. 24x18", full color. $8.50, postpaid. IANA.

TRIBAL PROFILE POSTER SERIES
3 wall displays of federally recognized U.S. tribes and bands. Packaged in 5 mil. lamination, comered and graumetted. TDR.

TRUST FOR NATIVE AMERICAN
CULTURES & CRAFTS
a 17" x 22.5" poster featuring many of the traditional skills (canoe, snowshoe making, hide tanning, the

manufacture of skin clothing, etc.) Represented are the Montagnais, Cree, Algonquin, and Attikamek groups. Color on one side and black & white on the reverse. $8. TR.

WHEN EARTH BECOMES AN "IT"
A poem, about what will happen if Mother Earth continues not to be respected, was a gift to us from Cherokee/Appalachian poet Awiakta. 11" x 14". $10. OY.

WOVOKA POSTER
16 1/2 x 23" poster of the Northern Paiute Ghost Dance Prophet. $5.00. YPT.

XIT RELOCATION POSTER
23 x 35". $1.95. CAN.

MAPS

AMERICAN INDIAN HISTORY MAP
Documents the last 500 years of American Indian history. 24 x 36" full color shaded relief map with matte finish, printed on two sides. Informational booklet. $3.50. ATL.

AMERICAN INDIAN NATIONS
A composite graphic of contemporary Indian America. 24x36" full-color shaded relief map. Illustrates the diminished land base as Indians were forced westward be encroahing settlers. Locations of over 300 federally recognized reservations. Reservations with gaming facilities are indicated. $13 postpaid. TE.

ATLAS OF THE NORTH AMERICAN INDIANS
  Carl Waldman; Map & illus. by Molly Braun
1989. $16.95. FOF.

COLOR MAP
Shows the distribution of Indian tribes in New York City and vicinity during the 17th century. $1.50. MAI.

CONOZCA SUS RAICES / KNOW YOUR ROOTS:
A MAP OF THE INDIGENOUS PEOPLES OF
MEXICO & CENTROAMERICA
  Dolan H. Eargle, Jr., Editor
A full color, 18"x24" poster, bilingual - Spanish & English with color-coded legend of contemporary ethnic homelands grouped by linguistic families. Mexico to Panama. Biblio. Trees Company Press, $5.

DISTRIBUTION OF INDIAN
TRIBES OF NORTH AMERICA
Map by Dr. A.L. Kroeber. 21x28" map of the time of first contact with white men. SM.

EARLY INDIAN TRIBES, CULTURE
AREAS, & LINGUISTIC STOCK
  William Sturtevant-U.S. Geological Survey
Multi-colored map, shows geographic extent of major an minor Indian tribes, their culture areas, and 18 linguistic stocks for Alaska and the 48 states. Biblio. $3.10. WE.

THE GABRIELINO INDIANS AT THE
TIME OF THE PORTOLA EXPEDITION
Map by Allen M. Welts. 22x15 map showing locations of ancient Indian villages in southern California. SM.

HISTORICAL MAP, WARM SPRINGS
INDIAN RESERVATION
Map by Ralph M. Shane and Ruby D. Leno, showing historical trails, sites and modern Kah-Nee-Ta. 15x18 color. OHS.

INDIAN COUNTRY MAP
  George Russell
24x36" map representing a geographic history of 500 years of the American Indian. Identifies military forts & dates of activity, major battles & dates, and today's Indian tribes, nations, lands & reservations. The margins contain texts that discuss various topics & time periods. Accompanied with a pamphlet, 1998. Rolled, $12; folded, $8. TE.

INDIAN GAMING MAP
18X24" The map shows the Interstate Highway system & the geographical location of each gaming facil-

ity listed alfabetically by state. The map roster Lists the name, address, & telephone number of all 223 Indian gaming facilities. Endorsed by Indian Gaming magazine. $12. TE.

INDIAN LAND AREAS—GENERAL
Official map of the Bureau of Indian Affairs. A multicolor map that indicates the location and size of Federal Indian reservations, Indian groups, etc. $10. NACO.

INDIAN RESERVATIONS MAP
Black and white map of the U.S. showing where the Indian tribes, reservations, and settlements are located. IRA.

**INDIAN TRIBES & LANGUAGES
OF OLD OREGON TERRITORY**
22x33 color map. OHS.

INDIANS OF NORTH AMERICA
An archaeological and ethnological map. 32x37" with ethnological descriptive notes and illustrations. 1979. NGS.

**MAP'N'FACTS: NATIVE PEOPLES
OF NORTH AMERICA**
Two full-color maps show—before Columbus—and today. 23x35. Two bxw maps on reverse set forth population and language groups. $4.50. FP.

MAP OF NORTH AMERICAN INDIANS
16 x 20 color map on durable enamel finished paper, $2.95; laminated, $4.95. CH.

NATIVE AMERICAN INDIAN TRIBES - MAP
Shows four geographical areas. 20" x 16". $3. CMM.

**NATIVE LANGUAGES & LANGUAGE
FAMILIES OF NORTH AMERICA**
Ives Goddard, Editor
A map which shows the locations and distriubution of the known languages spoken by Native peoples across North America at the time of first contact. University of Nebraska Press, $14.95, folded study map; $19.95, wall display map. UNP.

NATIVE TRIBES MAP
Alfred L. Kroeber
$5.95. UCP.

NAVAJOLAND
A full-color illustrated map of the Southwestern U.S. where the Navajos live. Covers four states and 16 million acres. KC.

NORTHWEST INDIAN GUIDE AND MAP
Features Native attractions, arts and businesses. Affiliated Tribes of Northwest Indians (ATNI), 1995. $2.

THREE MAPS OF INDIAN COUNTRY
Haskell Indian Junior College, Lawrence Kansas 66044. No charge.

MICROFILM & MICROFICHE

AKWESASNE NOTES
Vols. 1-9, 1969-1981. 168 fiches. $588. KM.

AMERICAN CIVIL LIBERTIES UNION ARCHIVES
Contains issues surrounding the rights of Native Americans and the ACLU's work with them are included throughout. The BIA and Indian Rights Association are also subjects. 293 rolls of 35mm microfilm, $115 per roll, $33,695. SR.

**AMERICAN CULTURE SERIES I
(ACSI), 1493-1806**
Series I: A Compact Overview of American Books & Pamphlets - 1493-1806 - this collection includes accounts of Indians and Indian captives. Microfilm. UM.

**THE AMERICAN INDIAN
COLLECTION, 1647-1940**
Printed matter, manuscripts, photographs, and typescripts, 1647-1940, relating to Native Americans. Also

the Mohegan Indian case in Connecticut, 1740-1750. 1 roll of 35mm microfilm with guide, $115. SR.

**AMERICAN INDIAN CORRESPONDENCE:
THE PRESBYTERIAN HISTORICAL SOCIETY
COLLECTION OF MISSIONARIES' LETTERS,
1833-1893**
Letters describe 60 years of ministry to 39 tribes all over America - from the Seneca of New York to Arizona's Navajo. All aspects of Indian and missionary life are detailed. 35 rolls of 35mm microfilm and guide. $4,025. SR.

AMERICAN INDIAN PERIODICALS
From the State Historical Society of Wisconsin. Tribal news, political issues, humor, community services, scholarly research. Silver halide film; 12 reels (approximate) 35mm silver halide microfilm. $585. From the Princeton University Library on Microfiche. Part 1, 96 titles: 2,068 fiche and two reels 35mm film, $5,000; Part 2, 34 titles: 401 fiche and two reels 35mm film, $1,000. See NR for individual titles and prices.

**AMERICAN THEOLOGICAL
LIBRARY ASSOCIATION (ATLA)**
Mainstream Protestant publications dealing with missions to native Americans: The Baptist Home Mission Monthly (from 1878-1909 - 7 rolls of 35mm microfilm, $805); The American Missionary (1857-1933 - 19 rolls of 35mm microfilm, $2,185); Missionary Monthly (1939-1958 - 4 rolls of 35mm microfilm, $460); Presbyterian Home Missionary (1872-1886 - 3 rolls of 35mm microfilm. $345. SR.

AMERINDIAN: AMERICAN INDIAN REVIEW
Vols. 1-23, 1952-1974. 23 fiches, $80.50. KM.

**APPLICATIONS FOR ENROLLMENT &
ALLOTMENT OF WASHINGTON INDIANS,
1911-1919**
Reproduces the bulk of records relating to Special Agent Charles Roblin's enrollment of those Native Americans in western Washington State. National Archives Record Group 75. 6 rolls of 35mm microfilm, $204. SR.

**APPLICATIONS FOR ENROLLMENT
OF THE COMMISSION TO THE FIVE
CIVILIZED TRIBES, 1898-1914**
Reproduced the application forms filled out by persons seeking official enrollment in the Five Civilized Tribes (Cherokee, Chickasaw, Choctaw, Creek and Seminole). National Archives Record Group 75. 468 rolls of 35mm microfilm, $15,912. SR.

**APPLICATIONS FROM THE BIA, MUSKOGEE AREA
OFFICE, RELATING TO ENROLLMENT IN THE FIVE
CIVILIZED TRIBES UNDER THE ACT OF 1896**
54 rolls of 35mm microfilm, $1,836. SR.
Reproduced the application forms filled out by persons seeking official enrollment in the four of the Five Civilized Tribes (Cherokee, Chickasaw, Choctaw and Creek). National Archives Record Group 75. 54 rolls of 35mm microfilm, $1,836. SR.

**ARCTIC EXPEDITION DIARIES OF
VILHJALMUR STEFANSSON, 1878-1925**
An Account of Eskimo Life and Culture Preserved on Microfilm. A record of native Arctic culture and geography with detailed documentation of Eskimo life before it was altered by white cultural values. Chronicles three expeditions made by V. Stefansson between 1906 and 1918. Provides factual and insightful accounts of Eskimo hunting trips, religious beliefs, legends and family traditions. Includes translations of Eskimo words and phrases, extensive charts and maps; and sketches illustrating Eskimo clothes. 5 reels of 35mm microfilm. UM.

THE BEYNON MANUSCRIPT
The Literature, Myths and Traditions of the Tsimshian People - Represents the most extensive body of Tsimshian literature available for linguistic, anthropological and theological scholarship. Provides documentation on North American Indian myths and traditions. The Tsimshian people, native to the territory along the international border between Alaska and British Columbia, originated the totem pole and other art forms characteristic of the Pacific Northwest coastal region.

William Beynon was a native speaker of the Tsimshian language. He recorded the history, ethnography and literature of his people. Includes narratives of clan histories and myths, and descriptions of traditional ceremonies, practices and beliefs. 4 reels of 35mm microfilm. UM.

**BUREAU OF INDIAN AFFAIRS RECORDS
CREATED BY THE SANTA FE INDIAN SCHOOL,
1890-1918**
National Archives Record Group 75.
38 rolls of 35mm microfilm, $1,292. SR.

**CANADIAN DEPARTMENT OF INDIAN
AFFAIRS ANNUAL REPORTS, 1880-1936**
Library of Congress microfilm. 10 rolls of 35mm, $420. SR.

CHEROKEE ALMANAC
1838-1860. Text in English and Cherokee.
1 reel, 35mm. $50. KM.

**CLAIMS FOR GEORGIA MILITIA CAMPAIGNS
AGAINST INDIANS ON THE FRONTIER, 1792-1827**
National Archives Record Group 217.
5 rolls of 35mm microfilm, $170. SR.

THE JOHN COLLIER PAPERS, 1922-1968
The Author of a Sweeping Federal Indian Reform Strategy - Assimilation was the U.S. Indian policy from the late 1880's through the 1920's, and provoked widespread animosity as it eroded tribal culture, religion, history, and freedom. Collier's accomplishments in effecting major Indian rights reforms as executive secretary of the American Indian Defense Association and later as Commissioner of Indian Affairs during FDR's administration marked a turning point in federal Indian policy. His Indian New Deal proposed tribal self-government, culture preservation, and religious freedom for native Americans. Includes correspondence, speeches, government documents, court records and news clippings which record Collier's private thoughts and public impact during those years. 59 reels of 35mm microfilm. UM.

**CONSTITUTION & LAWS
OF THE AMERICAN INDIAN**
Includes a hardbound copy of A Bibliography of the Constitution and Laws of the American Indian, and a listing of titles filmed. 157 separate constitutions. 7 reels, 35mm. $360. Contact KM for a complete list of tribes and nations included.

**CORRESPONDENCE OF THE OFFICE OF
THE ADJUTANT GENERAL (MAIN SERIES)**
Letters relate to Indian matters. See SR for titles and prices.

DUKE INDIAN ORAL HISTORY COLLECTION
Consists of the tape-recorded verbal testimonies of knowledgeable Indian people, members of most of the Indian tribes of Oklahoma, concerning their history, culture and philosophy of life. 310 fiches with Index on 8 reels. 35mm. $1,450. KM.

**EASTERN CHEROKEE APPLICATIONS OF
THE U.S. COURT OF CLAIMS, 1906-1909**
National Archives Record Group 123. 348 rolls. of 35mm microfilm. $11,832. SR.

ENCYCLOPEDIA ARCTICA
16 volumes of articles on the Arctic Region written by leading specialists from around the world. Compiled by by noted explorer and scholar Vilhjalmur Stefansson. Features articles and information on: The Sciences, Trade, Biographies, and Maps, diagrams and charts. 27 reels of 35mm microfilm. UM.

**ENROLLMENT CARDS OF THE
FIVE CIVILIZED TRIBES, 1898-1914**
Reproduced the enrollment cards prepared by the staff of the Commission to the Five CXivilized Tribes betweem 1898 and 1914. National Archives Record Group 123. 93 rolls. of 35mm microfilm. $3,162. SR.

FBI FILE ON OSAGE INDIAN MURDERS
Several dozen Osage Indians were murdered in the 1920s and the FBI was brought in on the investigation. 3 rolls of 35mm microfilm with guide, $345. SR.

VIOLA E. GARFIELD ALBUMS ON TOTEM ART
Anthropologist Viola E. Garfield (1899-1983) amassed a collection of 26 volumes of photographs and information on the totem art of the Native Americans of the Pacific Northwest Coast from Seattle to southeastern Alaska. Microfiche-60 sheets, $60 per set. UWL.

GEORGE BIRD GRINNELL PAPERS
Contains letterbooks, correspondence, and subject files, including photographs and writings, which document the life and work of naturalist and conservationist George Bird Grinnell. 47 rolls of 35mm microfilm with guide. $5,405. SR.

HISTORY OF THE PACIFIC NORTHWEST & CANADIAN NORTHWEST
Microfilm collection which makes available a number of rare primary source materials on the early history of the two regions. 511 texts, from reports of expeditions to political pamphlets. 50 reels, $2,325. 20-page microfilm reel index and Table of Contents, $30. RP.

INDEX TO LETTERS RECEIVED BY THE COMMISSION TO THE FIVE CIVILIZED TRIBES, 1897-1913
National Archives Record Group 75. 23 rolls of 35mm microfilm, $782. SR.

INDIAN CENSUS ROLLS
Contains biographies of Native Americans compiled each year by agents or supts. in charge of Indian reservations spanning the years 1885-1940. National Archives Record Group 75. 692 rolls of 35mm microfilm, $23,528. SR.

INDIAN CULTURE & HISTORY
A new microform index to Wisconsin Native American periodicals, 1879-1981. Edited by James P. Danky. Six computer-output microfiche; 42:1 reduction ratio. 1984. $30. GP.

INDIAN HISTORIAN
American Indian Historical Society. New series: Vols. 1-12, 1967-1979. 48 fiches. $168. KM.

INDIAN PIONEER PAPERS: 1860-1935
Consists of interviews of elderly early day settlers in Oklahoma collected in the late 1930's. Consists of typescripts of 7105 interviews. A subject index is included. 1019 fiches. $3.057. KM.

INDIAN RIGHTS ASSOCIATION PAPERS, 1864-1973
Documents the struggle for American Indian civil liberties, and includes information on Indian affairs, and supported federal and state court cases in its efforts to secure basic rights for Native Americans. Includes correspondence, printed materials, Herbert Welsh Papers, 1877-1934, photographs, and Council on Indian Affairs Papers, 1943-1968. 136 reels of 35mm microfilm. UM.

INDIAN RIGHTS ASSOCIATION PAPERS, 1885-1901
26 rolls of 35mm microfilm, $2,990. SR.

INDIAN TRUTH
Indian Rights Association. Nos. 1-260, 1924-1984. 59 fiches. $177. KM.

INDIAN'S FRIEND
National Indian Association. Vols. 1-63, 1888-1951. 3 reels, 35mm. $150. KM.

INDIANS - U.S. GOVERNMENT PRINTING OFFICE PUBLICATIONS
1927-1970. 168 fiches. $588. Contact KM for complete list of titles.

INDIANS OF NORTH AMERICA
1760-1952. Includes works by James B. Finley, Hampton Institute, and Peter Williamson. 2 reels, 35mm. $100. KM.

IROQUOIS INDIANS: A DOCUMENTARY HISTORY
Provides 8,000 reproductions of records from the early 1600s to the 1840s compiled by the D'Arcy McNickle Center for the History of the American Indian at the Newberry Library. Focuses on the Mohawk, Oneida,

Onondaga, Cayuga, Seneca and Tuscarora nations comprising the Iroquois Confederacy. Includes a guide with chronological calendar and index of names, places, and tribes cited. 35mm microfilm. 1984. RP.

THE SHELDON JACKSON COLLECTION, 1855-1909
Papers of the missionary and U.S. general agent of education, Sheldon Jackson. He organized pioneer Presbyterian churches in the West and Alaska. 41 rolls of 35mm microfilm with guide, $4,715. SR.

THE LAKE MOHONK CONFERENCE OF FRIENDS OF THE INDIAN
From 1883 to 1916 the center of the movement to reform federal Indian policy was the annual Lake Mohonk Conference, and its significance on Indian-white relations in the U.S. Details the opinions and programs of a distinguished group of American reformers. Microfiche (80 fiche), $200. Index volume, $25. NR.

LETTERS RECEIVED BY THE U.S. GEOLOGICAL SURVEY, 1879-1901
National Archives Record Group 57. Includes a survey and investigation of irrigation on Indian reservations and disputes over the western boundary of the Yakima Reservation and the Seminole border. 118 rolls of 35mm microfilm, $4,012. SR.

LETTERS SENT BY THE OFFICE OF INDIAN AFFAIRS, 1824-1881
Contains correspondence from all sources concerning Indian lands, emigration, treaty negotiations, subsistence, conflicts, claims, education, etc. National Archives Record Group 75. 962 rolls of 35mm microfilm. SR.

LETTERS SENT TO THE OFFICE OF INDIAN AFFAIRS BY THE PINE RIDGE AGENCY, 1875-1914
National Archives Record Group 75. 52 rolls of 35mm microfilm, $1,768. SR.

MISCELLANEOUS LETTERS SENT BY THE AGENTS OF SUPERINTENDENTS AT THE PINE RIDGE INDIAN AGENCY, 1876-1914
National Archives Record Group 75. 76 rolls of 35mm microfilm, $2,584. SR.

NATIVE AMERICANS OF THE PACIFIC NORTHWEST: A PHOTOGRAPHIC RECORD
A comprehensive graphic documentation of Pacific Northwest and Alaska Native Americans. Over 4,000 images were selected resulting in a 17,000 entry catalog. Microfiche-112 sheets, $115 per set. UWL.

THE PACIFIC NORTHWEST TRIBES INDIAN LANGUAGE COLLECTION OF THE OREGON PROVINCE ARCHIVES OF THE SOCIETY OF JESUS, 1853-1960
Edited by Robert C. Carriker. Includes the materials amassed by the Oregon Province Archives on 12 different Indian languages: Assiniboine, Blackfoot/Piegan, Chelan, Coeur d'Alene, Columbia/Moses, Colville, Crow, Gros Ventre, Kalispel, Kootenai, Nez Perce, and Yakima. 21 rolls. of 35mm microfilm with guide, $2,415. SR.

THE PACIFIC NORTHWEST TRIBES MISSIONS COLLECTION OF THE OREGON PROVINCE ARCHIVES OF THE SOCIETY OF JESUS, 1853-1960
Edited by Robert C. Carriker. Papers and records of the Jesuit missions and missionaries in Oregon, Washington, Idaho, and western Montana from 1853 to 1960. Provides much insight on the Northwest tribes. 34 rolls. of 35mm microfilm with guide, $3,910. SR.

THE PAGAENT OF AMERICA
A vital, authentic pictorial history of the U.S. Volume 1: Adventures in the Wilderness - covers the early navigators, settlers, and explorers as they fought Native Americans and each other for mastery of the New World; Volume 6: The Winning of Freedom - from the early struggles with the Indians through the War of 1812. Microfiche. Each volume begins with an essay or outline. UM.

THE PAPERS OF CARLOS MONTEZUMA, M.D.
Edited by John W. Larner, Jr. Montezuma (1867-1923) speeches and monthly newsletter, *Wassaja*, promot-

ing the Indian cause. 9 rolls of 35mm microfilm with guide, $1,035. SR.

THE PAPERS OF PANTON, LESLIE & CO.
Ethnographic collection for the study of the American Indians of the Southwest. Documents trading activities with the Cherokee, Chickasaw, Choctaw, and Creek Nations, and is a key collection for the study of the origins and early development of the Seminole Indians. Includes a guide to listed documents. 35mm microfilm; approximately 10,000 documents on 26 reels. $2,400. RP.

THE PAPERS OF JOHN PEABODY HARRINGTON IN THE SMITHSONIAN INSTITUTION, 1907-1957
Consists of over 750,000 pages of his documents. Includes a detailed guidebook giving the contents of each reel. Individual reels, $75. See KM for titles and prices.

PAPERS OF THE SOCIETY OF AMERICAN INDIANS, 1906-1946
Edited by John W. Larner, Jr. 5,600 documents from 45 repositories across the country. 10 rolls of 35mm microfilm with guide, $1,150. SR.

PARRAL PAPERS
Spanish-American History of the Southwest and Mexico - spanning the years 1631-1821, this Spanish-written collection includes official records, directives, treaties, court transcripts, wills, letters, and other documents relating to the Spanish Colonial Era. Includes information on Indian uprisings, plus an account of the 1720 peace treaties with the Apaches and the Texans. 324 reels of 35mm microfilm. Includes index in English or Spanish. UM.

PRE-1900 CANADIANA
Primary resource materials which preserve and document printed materials from Canada's past. Covers Canadian culture, politics, ethnology, sociology, history, geography, art, economics, literature, religion and natural sciences. 35mm microfilm. UM.

THE PROFESSIONAL CORRESPONDENCE OF FRANZ BOAS
Franz Boas (1858-1942) anthropologist. Covers over 50,000 items, dating from 1881 through 1942, including correspondence with Margaret Mead, Albert Einstein, Alexander Granahm Bell, and Presidents, Taft, Wilson and Roosevelt. 44 rolls. of 35mm microfilm with guide, $5,060. SR.

RATIFIED INDIAN TREATIES, 1722-1869
National Archives Record Group 11. 16 rolls of 35mm microfilm, $544. SR.

RECORDS CREATED BY BIA FIELD AGENCIES HAVING JURISDICTION OVER THE PUEBLO INDIANS, 1874-1900
National Archives Record Group 75. 32 rolls of 35mm microfilm, $1,088. SR.

RECORDS OF THE ALASKA DIVISION OF THE BIA CONCERNING METLAKATLA, 1887-1933
National Archives Record Group 75. 14 rolls of 35mm microfilm, $476. SR.

RECORDS OF THE CREEK FACTORY OF THE OFFICE OF INDIAN TRADE OF THE BIA, 1795-1821
National Archives Record Group 75. 13 rolls of 35mm microfilm, $442. SR.

RECORDS OF FIELD JURISDICTIONS
National Archives Record Group 75. See SR for number of rolls of 35mm microfilm and prices.

RECORDS OF HEADQUARTERS, ARMY OF THE SOUTHWESTERN FRONTIER, & HEADQUARTERS, SECOND & SEVENTH MILITARY DEPTS., 1835-1853
National Archives Record Group 393. 8 rolls of 35mm microfilm, $272. SR.

RECORDS OF THE MORAVIAN MISSION AMONG THE INDIANS OF NORTH AMERICA
Microfilm collection of the Indian missionary records at the archives of the Moravian Church in Bethlehem, PA, provides important information on the history and activities of the Moravian Church in North America. Includes a 111-page Guide and two-volume, 135,000

entry index. 35mm microfilm. 40 reel;s, $19.10; 2-volume Index, $400. RP.

RECORDS OF THE U.S. INDIAN CLAIMS COMMISSION

Includes 550,000 pages—6,140 silver halide microfiche, $12,000. Historical, anthropological and economic reports of the American Indian. The Decisions, Volumes 1-47 & Appeals, 355 fiche, $750; Expert Testimony, 400 volumes, 100,000 pages, 1,270 fiche, $2,500/Supplement 1: 48 titles on 125 fiche, $250;2: 97 titles on 209 fiche, $400. Transcripts of Oral Expert Testimony, 400 volumes, 100,000 pages, 1,398 fiche, $2,800/Supplement; 77 titles, 420 fiche, $850. The Briefs, 3,000 volumes, 125,000 pages, 1,536 fiche, $3,000. GAO Reports, 80 volumes, 25,000 pages, 300 fiche, $600/Supplement; 11 titles, 34 fiche, $75. Index to Decisions, $25. Index to Expert Testimony, $25. Legislative History of the Indian Claims Commission Act, 12 fiche, $35. Docket Books, 41 fiche, $80. Journal, 32 fiche, $60. NR.

REPORTS OF INSPECTION OF THE FIELD JURISDICTIONS OF THE OFFICE OF INDIAN AFFAIRS, 1873-1900

Contains the Indian inspector's records pertaining to the conditions of Indians. National Archives Record Group 48. 60 rolls of 35mm microfilm, $2,040. SR.

RECORDS OF MILITARY DIVISIONS, DEPARTMENTS & DISTRICTS

National Archives Record Group 393. Letters in this publication revolve around problems in Indian-white relations. Describes scouting activities and armed expeditions against. Apache, Ute, Navajo, Kiowa and Comanche Indians. see SR for titles and prices.

REPORT BOOKS OF THE OFFICE OF INDIAN AFFAIRS, 1838-1885

Contains correspondence sent by the Office of Indian Affairs to members of the president's cabinet, and copies of letters to the president, members of Congress, and other government officials. National Archives Record Group 75. 53 rolls of 35mm microfilm, $1,802. SR.

REPORT...INDEX TO THE ANNUAL REPORTS, 1894-1905

Annual reports of the Dawes Commission and its successors from 1893-1920, with an index for the years, 1894-1905. The Commission was appointed by the president to negotiate with the Five Civilized Tribes to divide tribal property, to procure the concession of remaining tribal lands, and to prepare tribal rolls of citizenship. 2 rolls of 35mm microfilm, $84. SR.

HENRY ROWE SCHOOLCRAFT PAPERS

Schoolcraft (1793-1864, was the foremost pioneer in Indian studies. Includes his work as an ethnologist, Indian agent, explorer, mineralogist, geologist, and writer. 69 rolls of 35mm microfilm with guide, $2,898. SR.

SELECTED NATIVE AMERICAN PERIODICALS

The Red Man - an illustrated magazine printed by Indians, 1909-1917. 2 rolls of 35mm microfilm, $84; The Native American - devoted to Indian education, 1900-1931. 8 rolls, $336; The Indian's Friend - organ of the Women's National Indian Association - 1888-1940 (changed to National Indian Association in 1902). 14 rolls, $588. SR.

SELECTED RECORDS OF THE BIA RELATING TO THE ENROLLMENT OF INDIANS ON THE FLATHEAD RESERVATION, 1903-1908

National Archives Record Group 75. 3 rolls of 35mm microfilm, $102. SR.

SELECTED WORKS BY AMERICAN INDIAN AUTHORS

12 titles, 1860-1939. 2 reels, 35mm. $100. Contact KM for complete listing of authors.

SMITHSONIAN INSTITUTION BUREAU OF AMERICAN ETHNOLOGY BULLETINS & ANNUAL REPORTS

Includes primary sources of information on the culture and history of North and South American Indian Tribes.

Includes material on the prehistory, language, society and culture of many extinct tribal groups. Focuses on the history f Indian tribes within the U.S., with substantive information on the Indian tribes of Alaska, Hawaii, Mexico, Central America, and Canada. 42 reels of 35mm microfilm. Comes with a guide to Microfilm Edition of Smithsonian Publications Relating to the North American Indian. UM.

SUPERINTENDENTS' ANNUAL NARRATIVE & STATISTICAL REPORTS FROM FIELD JURISDICTIONS OF THE B.I.A., 1907-1938

Documents the operations and accomplishments at the agencies under the BIA, schools, hospitals, and other field jurisdictions. National Archives Record Group 75. 174 rolls of 35mm microfilm, $5,916. SR.

SURVEY OF THE CONDITIONS OF THE INDIANS OF THE U.S.

In Feb 1928, the U.S. Senate directed its Committee on Indian Affairs to study conditions among Native Americans, the effects of laws passed by Congress, and the effects of the policies of the BIA on Native American health, improvement and welfare. 9 rolls of 35mm microfilm, $378. SR.

U.S. BOARD OF INDIAN COMMISSIONERS. ANNUAL REPORT OF THE BOARD OF INDIAN COMMISSIONERS TO THE SECRETARY OF THE INTERIOR

Reports 1-63, 1869-1932. 3 reels, 35mm. $150. KM.

U.S. BUREAU OF INDIAN AFFAIRS

17 titles, 1966-1970. 17 fiches, $59.50. Contact KM for complete listing of titles.

WASAJA/THE INDIAN HISTORIAN. A NATIONAL NEWSMAGAZINE OF INDIAN AMERICA

Vols. 1-19, 1973-1982. 82 fiches. $287. KM.

WESTERN AMERICANA

Includes federal and state documents, directories, guidebooks, state and regional histories, memoirs, reminiscences and travel accounts, and conventional and secondary histories of the West. Two sub-collections may be purchased separately: Indians, and Other Ethnic Influences. Microfiche. UM.

WESTERN AMERICANA: FRONTIER HISTORY OF THE TRANS-MISSISSIPPI WEST, 1550-1900

Includes a broad selection of printed sources relating to the discovery, exploration, settlement, and development of North America. Provides information on Indian/White relations including missions, trade, government relations, and Indian wars. A 2-volume guide and index accompanies each order. 35mm microfilm. 617 reels; divided into 11 units of 56-57 reels each, $2,880 each. RP.

THE WILLIAM WIRT PAPERS

Edited by John B. Boles. William Wirt (1772-1834) author and historian, attorney general from 1817 to 1829. Involved in the Cherokee cases of 1831-32 and was devoted to Indian causes throughout his life. 24 rolls of 35mm microfilm with guide, $2,760. SR.

COMPUTER NETWORK

INDIAN NATION NETWORK (INN) ELECTRONIC BULLETIN BOARD (EBB)

Devoted entirely to issues affecting and relating to Indian country. Access INN with a phone line, modem, computer, and communications software. Features such issues as religious freedom, environmental degradation on Indigenous lands, stereotypes, and treaty rights. INN equips users with tools necessary for meaningful advocacy and action by offering Congressional bills significant to Native Americans, hearing write-ups, Federal Register Notices relating to Indian country, listing of federally recognized tribes, telephone/addresses of Congressional Committees, events in Indian Country, and more. $25/year. HO.

CD-ROMs, SOFTWARE & DATABASES

THE AMERICAN INDIAN CD-ROM

CD-ROM consisting of a library of Indian resources: Federal treaties; American State papers (through 1826); artistic view of the images and scenes-over 700 engravings; Books by Black Hawk and Right Hand Thunder; accounts from original observers. Includes Henry R. Schoolcraft's Archives of Aboriginal Knowledge; League of the Iroquois; Wigwam Evening-Sioux Folk Tales Retold; extensive data on Chippewa, Cherokees, Sioux, and many other tribes; linguistic coverage-large vocabulary lists, including a highly detailed analysis of Algonquin by Schoolcraft. The artwork of George Catlin's Letters and Notes on the Manners, Customs and Conditions of the North American Indians. For IBM compatible multimedia PCs. $75. TP.

THE AMERICAN INDIAN: A MULTIMEDIA ENCYCLOPEDIA

Version 2.0. Covers more than 150 tribes of native peoples of the U.S., Canada, and northern Mexico - focusing on the history, culture, words, images, legends, and leaders. Includes the complete texts of four titles: Atlas of the North American Indian; Who Was Who in Native American History; Encyclopedia of Native American Tribes; and Voices of the Winds. There are sound bites of authentic Indian songs, over 900 VGA photographs, over 1,000 biographies, 250 color illustrations, the full text of over 250 documents from the 18th and 19th centuries, mor than 100 legends from over 60 tribes, maps, time lines, and lsitings of tribal locations, historical societies, and museums. 1996. $150 for single user; $500 for lab pack (allows 5 users simulatneously). FOF.

BIBLIOGRAPHY OF NATIVE NORTH AMERICANS ON DISC - CD-ROM

Timothy O'Leary & M. Marlene Martin, Editors The Human Relations Area File's Ethnographic Bibliography of North America. Semiannual. CD-ROM or Network. IBM compataible. $1,045 for annual subscription for CD; $1,306 for one person network. SP.

ETHNIC NEWSWATCH

A full text multicultural general reference database on CD-ROM. Contains more than 70 newspapers published by the ethnic and minority press in America. Contains about 90,000 fully ndexed articles from more than 100 newspapers and magazines. Includes Native American newspapers, i.e., News From Indian Country, Navajo TimesSho-Ban News, Seminole Tribune, Tundra Times, Cherokee Advocate, Lakota Times, et al. SII.

INDIAN COUNTRY ADDRESS BOOK DATABASE

Database of about 15,000 names from the book, Indian Country Address Book, including individuals, tribal businesses, organizations, tribal nations, schools, colleges, government agencies, museumscasinos and bingo halls, publishers, book and video distributors. $75 per thousand names. 5,000 name minimum. TP.

INVENTING THE SOUTHWEST: THE FRED HARVEY COMPANY & NATIVE AMERICAN ART

Kathleen L. Howard & Diana F. Pardue Based on the exhibit of the Heard Museum. 90 color & 50 bxw photos. Biblio. 168 pp. Paper. $17.95. CD-ROM. $29.95. NP.

THE NATIONAL TRIBAL DIRECTORY SOFTWARE

The Standard Edition provides education and connectivity for the tribes themselves as well as for those entities that serve and assist them. Includes contact, membership, culture, profile and history information on over 550 federally recognized and non-recognized U.S. tribes and bands in the U.S. and basic contact information for over 200 non-recognized tribes that are currently in the process of petitioning the U.S. Dept. of the Interior for "recognition" status. The Business Edition database includes all of the information and features of the "standard" edition, plus, contact information for all of the 645+ First Nations & bands of Canada and includes over 10,000 Native American Service and Enterprise contacts; also BIA and other

Federal agency offices. Updates are provided by a web-based "live update" system downloaded from the TDR server. $499. TDR.

NORTH AMERICAN INDIANS - CD-ROM
A database of text and image on the history of Native Americans. Includes information on leadership, tribal heritage, religion, family life, and customs. IBM compatible. 1991. $69.95. QP.

REFERENCE ENCYCLOPEDIA OF THE AMERICAN INDIAN DATABASE
We have available approximately 15,000 listings from this book available in database format. Separate sections available. 5,000 name minimum. $75 per thousand names. TP.

WEB SITES

INDIANVILLAGE.COM
(970) 247-3100 Fax 259-6020
E-mail: info@indianvillage.com
Web site: www.indianvillage.com
Lists authentic Native American Indian stores, galleries, stores, events, news and gaming.

NATIVE AMERICAN INTERNET GUIDE
Listing of about 1,200 Native groups, organizations, nations, businesses and individuals and their web sites. 96 pages. $30. Available on diskette. TP.

A TIME OF VISIONS: INTERVIEWS WITH NATIVE AMERICAN ARTISTS
Table of Contents: Rick Bartow, Sara Bates, Patricia Deadman, Joe Feddersen, Anita Fields, Harry Fonseca, Bob Haozous, Melanie Printup Hope, Bobby Martin, Gerald McMaster, George Morrison, Shelley Niro, Joanna Osburn-Bigfeather, Diego Romero, Mateo Romero, Bently Spang, Ernie Whiteman, Richard Ray Whitman, Alfred Young Man. Available on the web site: www.britesites.com/native_artist_interviews

COMPUTER GRAPHICS

NATIVE AMERICAN CLIP ART COLLECTIONS
Art Bernstein
For IBM PC & Macintosh: **The Santa Fe Collection** - Pueblo Indians and Spanishinfluence, $179; **Plains Collections** - Indians of the Great Plains, $149; **Northwest Collections** - tribes of the Northwest to Alaska. 500 EPS images, 125 EPS borders. RT.

GAMES

POW WOW! THE GAME
Sarah Seeney Sullivan
A Native American board game featuring Native American concepts and designs that will challenge and entertain family members ages 8 and up. Includes Native American trivia cards. $19.95. LE.

GIFT ITEMS

HOPI KACHINAS
Edwin Earle and Edward A. Kennard
Second edition. Illus. 50 pp. National Museum of the American Indian, 1971. $12.50. Portfolio of 28 color plates from the book, $3.50.

HOPI KACHINAS: A POSTCARD COLLECTION
Cliff Bahnimptewa, illustrator
20 full-color postcards. Illus.
Northland Publishing, $7.95.

NAVAJO RUG STIK-WITHIT NOTECUBES
Self Stick
Full color. 600 sheets, 3.5 x 3".
Northland Publishing, $12.

TRAVELING EXHIBITS

AKWESASNE TRAVELLING EXHIBITS
Teionkwahontasen Basketmakers of Akwesasne: Ten panel, color and bxw photo display detailing the history of basketry. *Tsinikaiatotenne Ne Akwesasne - A Portrait of Akwesasne*: Ten panel bxw historical photo display of Akwesasne family, religion, sports and lifestyles of the Mohawk of Akwesasne. *Our Strength Our Spirit*: Art exhibit by contemporary artists of Akwesasne. Catalog available. Cost negotiable. AM.

THE BUFFALO TOUR
The Institute for the Study of Natural Systems
P.O. Box 637 • Mill Valley, CA 94942
(415) 383-5064
James A. Swan, Project Director
Pete Sears, Musical Director
To support bison restoration on Indian reservations, a musical concert tour program is being produced by a coalition of Indian leaders, entertainers and ecologists. The tour will begin in 1992 and hold a series of concerts around the U.S. which will culminate in the first annual Buffalo Festival, which will be held in late July of 1993, in the LaCrosse, Wisconsin, area in cooperation with the first International Bison Conference. Each concert will include Indian and non-Indian artists, as well as educational materials and programs, Indian arts and crafts sales, and a chance for local community involvement.

CAHOKIA TRAVELING DISPLAYS
A large free-standing exhibit on Cahokia with texts, photos and artifacts. Depicts the phases of Illinois prehistory. A booklet, Illinois Archaeology, is included. Two weeks, no charge. Must be picked up by the borrower. CMM.

MUSEUM OF NEW MEXICO TRAVELING EXHIBITS
Maintains the following traveling exhibits: Art of the Rainmakers: Prehistoric Indian Art and Architecture; Crystal to Burnt Water: Navajo Regional Style Textiles; People of the Sun: Photographs by Buddy Mays; The Portrait: Historic Photographs of New Mexicans; Sacred Paths: Aspects of the Native American and Hispanic Religious Experience in the Southwest; Traditions in Transition: Contemporary Basket Weaving of the Southwestern Indians; and, Turquoise and Tobacco: Trade Systems in the Southwest. The exhibits include historical and contemporary artifacts, drawings, prints, photographs, and paintings which have been assembled for exhibition in museums, libraries, community and art centers, and any other public space with controlled access. Pieces in the exhibitions are framed and matted with descriptive or interpretive labels printed directly on the mats and faced with plexiglass. In addition, each exhibition contains a title and statement panel. The exhibitions are offered free of charge and are transported in sturdy, custom-built crates. MNM.

TEXAS INDIANS WHO LIVED IN HOUSES
Students can learn to cook Indian bread, make an adobe brick, or plant a garden. The trunk contains artifact reproductions, filmstrips, activity cards, audio cassettes, and books. Grades 3-8. Rental fee: $100 (30 days) UT-ITC.

FESTIVALS OF NATIVE AMERICAN FILM & VIDEO

AMERICAN INDIAN FILM FESTIVAL & VIDEO EXHIBITION
333 Valencia St., Suite 322
San Francisco, CA 94103
(415) 554-0525
Michael Smith, Contact
Held in November, this festival is the oldest international film exhibition dedicated to the presentation of Native Americans in cinema. It is competitive and features seven categories: documentary feature; documentary short, feature, docudrama, live short subject, animated short subject & industrial. Founded 1975.

AMERICAN INDIAN FILM & VIDEO COMPETITION
2101 N. Lincoln, Jim Thorpe Bldg., Rm. 640
Oklahoma City, OK 73105
(405) 521-2931
Patrick Whelan, Contact
All entries are publicly presented at the Red Earth Festival in Oklahoma City. Finalists in each category are screened & awards presented at the University of Tulsa during the conference. Founded 1992.

DREAMSPEAKERS: THE FIRST PEOPLES WORLD FILM CELEBRATION
9914 76th Ave. • Edmonton, Alberta
Canada T6E 1K7 (403) 439-3456 Fax 439-2066
Russell Mulvey, Contact
Held in September, this noncompetitive event includes around 60 hours of public screenings. Also a Professional Development Symposium component each year.

NATIVE AMERICAN FILM & VIDEO FESTIVAL
Film & Video Center, George Gustav Heye Center
National Museum of the American Indian
Smithsonian Institution • 1 Bowling Green
New York, NY 10004 (212) 283-2420
Millie Seubert & Elizabeth Weatherford, Contacts
A noncompetitive showcase of film, video & audio productions with a focus on works by independent & tribal community leaders. Each festival screens about 40 documentaries, short features & animations, introduced by their producers & members of the native communities represented. Established in 1979.

TWO RIVERS NATIVE FILM & VIDEO FESTIVAL
Native Arts Circle • 1433 E. Franklin
Minneapolis, MN 55404 (612) 870-7173
Juanita Espinoza, Contact
Presents a prize known as the "New Visionary" Award. Established in 1991.

TRIBAL FILM/VIDEO PRODUCERS

CHICKASAW NATION
c/o Cultural Center
P.O. Box 1548
Ada, OK 74820
(405) 436-2603 Fax 436-4287
Glenda Galvan, Contact
More than 200 oral histories have been recorded (a portion of these exist on audio only). Established 1986.

CHOCTAW VIDEO PRODUCTION (CVP)
P.O. Box 6010 • Philadelphia, MS 39350
(601) 656-5251 Fax 656-6696
Bob Ferguson, Contact
In addition to 3/4" documentary & instructional videos on Choctaw history & culture, this production unit also does contract work for other tribes, including the Creek of Alabama, the Seneca of New York, and the Tunica-Biloxi of Louisiana. CVP also maintains a 24-hour TV station. Established 1983.

CREEK NATION VIDEO
c/o Muskogee Creek Nation Communication Center
P.O. Box 580 • Okmulgee, OK 74447
(918) 758-8700 Fax 758-0824
Produces documentaries containing various archival material & video shot in the last 20 years on the history of the Creek people. The collection is divided into a four-volume video history; each volume contains 5-7 titles.

OJIBWAY & CREE CULTURAL CENTER
152 3rd Ave. • Timmins, Ontario
Canada P4N 1C6
(705) 267-7911 Fax 267-4988
Esther Wesley, Contact
Produces documentaries on tribal practices, crafts & oral histories of elders, which are ideal for general audiences & classroom use. Maintains a catalog of about 20 titles with an average running time of 20 minutes. Established 1978.

SUQUAMISH MUSEUM
c/o Suquamish Tribal Cultural Center
P.O. Box 498 • Suquamish, WA 98392
(206) 598-3311 Fax 598-4666
Marilyn Jones or Alan Preston, Contacts

The Suquamish do not currently mantain an active video production unit, but the museum does hold several self-produced educational titles including "Come Forth Laughing," which features oral histories of Suquamish elders, and "Waterborne," which illustrates the processes involved in making canoes. Titles run under 30 minutes each.

TULALIP TRIBE
6700 Totem Beach Rd. • Marysville, WA 98271
(206) 653-0255; Lita Sheldon, Contact
Video production within the tribe is divided nto two categories: industrial (public relations) video & domentation of oral histories. The public relations tapes are brief introductions to Tulalip culture: "My Indian People" (1991, 7 minutes); and "Tulalip Tribe: Administration for Native Americans" (1990, 10 minutes). Also oral history shorts. Established 1989.

UTE INDIAN TRIBE
c/o Audio-Visual Dept.
P.O. Box 190 • Fort Duchesne, UT 84026
(801) 722-3736 Fax 722-4023
Larry Cesspooch, Contact
Approximately half of the 250 videotapes produced functions as legal documentation of meetings & agreements with local, staff and federal officials. The remainder serves as educational preservation of Ute history & culture practices. Much of this work is intended for audiences ages 5-13. Includes many oral histories as well as a variety of tribal ceremonies. Working on a low-power television station. Established 1979.

AUDIO-VISUAL AIDS DISTRIBUTORS

(A) Abbeville Press, 488 Madison Ave., New York, NY 10022 (800) 278-2665
(ADL) Anti-Defamation League of B'nai Brith, 823 United Nations Plaza, New York, NY 10017 (212) 490-2525
(AF) Aurora Films, P.O. Box 022955, Juneau, AK 99802-0164 (907) 586-6696
(AG) Agnello Films, 31 Maple St., Ridgefield, NJ 07660 (201) 933-6698
(AICRC) American Indian Culture Research Center, Blue Cloud Abbey, P.O. Box 98, Marvin, SD 57251 (605) 432-5528
(AIMS) AIMS Media, 9710 DeSoto Ave., Chatsworth, CA 91311 (800) 367-2467; in CA, AK & HI (818) 785-4111 Fax (818) 376-6405
(AIS) American Indian Soundchiefs, Box 472, Taos, NM 87571 (505) 776-2953
(AISES) American Indian Science & Engineering Society, Video Department, 1630 30th St., Suite 301 Boulder, CO 80303 (303) 492-8658 Fax 492-7090
(AIT) Agency for Instructional Technology, Box A, Bloomington, IN 47402 (800) 457-4509
(ALA) A.L. Atkins, Special Projects, 223 Onate Hall, Universityof New Mexico, Albuquerque, NM 87131 (505) 277-5204
(ALF) Alfred Publishing Co., Inc., P.O. Box 10003, Van Nuys, CA 91410 (818) 891-5999 Fax 891-2369
(ALT) The Altschul Group, 1560 Sherman Ave., #100, Evanston, IL 60201 (800) 323-5448; Fax (708) 328-6706
(AM) Akwesasne Museum, RR 1 Box 14C, Hogansburg, NY 13655 (518) 358-2240
(AMNH) American Museum of Natural History, Dept. of Library Services, Central Park West at 79th St., New York, NY 10024 (212) 873-1300 ext. 346/347
(AMP) Arthur Mokin Productions, P.O. Box 71, Issaquah, WA 98027
(AP) Atlantis Productions, 1252 La Granada Dr., Thousand Oaks, CA 91360 (805) 495-2790
(AT) Auburn Television, Auburn University, Auburn, AL 36849 (205) 826-4110
(ATL) ATLATL, P.O. Box 34090, Phoenix, AZ 85067 (602) 277-3711 Fax 277-3690
(ATNI) Affiliated Tribes of Northwest Indians, 222 N.W. Davis, Suite 403, Portland, OR 97209 (503) 241-0070 Fax 241-0072
(AUDIO) Audio-Forum, Jeffrey Norton Publishers, 96 Broad St., Guilford, CT 06437 (800) 243-1234; Fax (203) 453-9774
(AV) Artistic Video, 87 Tyler Ave., Sound Beach, NY 11789 (516) 744-0449 Fax 744-5993

(AVP) Ambrose Video Publishing, 28 W. 44th St., Suite 2100, New York, NY 10036 (800) 526-4663; Fax (212) 768-9282; Website: www.ambrosevideo.com
(BB) Buffalo Bill Historical Center, Education Dept., Box 1000, Cody, WY 82414 (307) 587-4771 Fax 587-5714
(BBP) Brown Bird Productions, 1971 N. Curson Ave., Hollywood, CA 90068 (213) 851-8928
(BE) Beacon Films, 1560 Sherman Ave., #100, Evanston, IL 60201 (800) 323-5448; Fax (708) 328-6706
(BF) Britannica Films, 310 S. Michigan Ave., Chicago, IL 60604 (312) 347-7958 Fax 347-7966
(BGF) Bowling Green Films; Dist. by Jack Ofield Productions, P.O. Box 12792, San Diego, CA 92112 (619) 462-8266
(BINS) Boreal Institute for Northern Studies, U. of Alberta, CW-401 Biological Sciences Bldg., Edmonton, AB, Canada T6G 2E9 (403) 432-4409
(BM) Blackfeet Media, P.O. Box 850, Browning, MT 59417 (406) 338-7179 ext. 268
(BMP) Bishop Museum Press, P.O. Box 19000A, Honolulu, HI 96817 (808) 848-4134
(BO) Bo Boudart Films, 1032 Marker Ave., Palo Alto, CA 94301 (415) 856-2004
(BOND) Jim Bond, I.T., 35113 Brewster Rd., Lebanon, OR 97355 (503) 258-3645
(BTP) Bear Tribe Publishing, 3750A Airport Blvd. #223, Mobile, AL 36608
(BYU) Brigham Young University, Educational Media Center, 101 Fletcher Bldg., Provo, UT 84602 (801) 378-2713
(BYU-N) Brigham Young University— Native American Series, Multi-Cultural Education Dept., 115 BRMB, Provo, UT 84602
(BULL) Bullfrog Films, P.O. Box 149, Oley, PA 19547 (800) 543-3764; Fax (610) 370-1978
(CA) Cloud Associates, P.O. Box 39016, Phoenix, AZ 85069 (800) 888-7820; (602) 866-7820
(CAN) Canyon Records & Indian Arts, 4143 N. 16th St., Phoenix, AZ 85016 (602) 266-4823
(CANYON) Canyon Cinema, 2325 3rd St., Suite 338, San Francisco, CA 94107 (415) 626-2255
(CAT) Catticus Corporation, 2600 10th St., Berkeley, CA 94710 (510) 548-0854
(CB) Cook's Books, P.O. Box 650, Hoopa, CA 95546 (916) 625-4222
(CC) Centre Communications, 1800 30th St., Suite 207, Boulder, CO 80301 (800) 886-1166; (303) 444-1166
(CDA) Curriculum Development Associates, 1211 Connecticut Ave., NW, Suite 414, Washington, DC 20036 (202) 293-1760
(CEN) Centron Productions, 416 Rock Fence Place, Lawrence, KS 66049
(CET) Center forEducational Telecommunications, 9596 Walnut St., Dallas, TX 75243 (214) 952-0303
(CFDW) Canadian Filmmakers Distribution West, 1131 Howe St., Suite 100, Vancouver, BC, Canada V6Z 2L7 (604) 684-3014
(CFH) Center for Humanities, Communication Park, Box 1000, Mt. Kisco, NY 10549 (800) 431-1242; (914) 666-4100
(CG) The Cinema Guild, 1697 Broadway, Suite 506, New York, NY 10019 (800) 723-5522; Fax (212) 246-5525 E-Mail: thecinemag@aol.com; Website: www.cinemaguild.com/cinemaguild
(CH) Cherokee Publications, P.O. Box 256, Cherokee, NC 28719 (704) 488-2988
(CHA) Caedmon: Harper-Audio Div. of HarperCollins, 10 E. 53 St., New York, NY 10022 (212) 207-7000
(CHAR) Chariot Distribution, 1274 Lambert Cir., Lafayette, CO 80026 (866) 243-6414; (303) 666-4558 Fax 666-5808. Website: www.chariotdist.com. E-mail: info@chariotdist.com.
(CHE) Chevron USA, Community Affairs, 575 Market St., San Francisco, CA 94105 (415) 894-5193; Study Guide: Chevron USA, 742 Bancroft Way, Berkeley, CA 94710
(CIAC) Center for Indigenous Arts & Cultures, P.O. Box 8627, Santa Fe, NM 87504 (505) 473-5375 Fax 424-1025. E-mail: indians@nets.com Website: www.indianartbooks.com
(CIMA) CIMA, 52 E. 1st St., New York, NY 10003 (212) 673-1666
(CIN) Cinnamin Productions, 19 Wild Rose Rd., Westport, CT 06880 (203) 221-0613 (phone & fax)
(CIRI) The CIRI Foundation, P.O. Box 93330, Anchorage, AK 99509 (907) 274-8638

(CJ) Concord Jazz, Inc., Box 845, Willow Pass Rd., Concord, CA 94522 (415) 682-6770
(CL) Clear Light Publishers, 823 Don Diego Santa Fe, NM 87501 (800) 253-2747; Fax (505) 989-9519 E-mail: ordercl@aol.com Website: www.clearlightbooks.com
(CM) Churchill Media, 6677 N. Northwest Hwy., Chicago, IL 60631 (800) 334-7830
(CMB) The Children's Museum, Boston, Museum Wharf, 300 Congress St., Boston, MA 02210 (617) 426-6500
(CMM) Cahokia Mounds Museum Society, Video Rental, P.O. Box 382, Collinsville, IL 62234 (618) 344-9221
(COOK) Cook School, 708 S. Lindon Lane, Tempe, AZ 85281
(COP) Camera One Productions, 8523 15th Ave., NE, Seattle, WA 98115 (800) 726-3456; Fax (206) 523-3668
(CRM) CRM/McGraw Hill Films, 2233 Faraday Ave., Carlsbad, CA 92008 (619) 431-9800
(CT) Coast Telecourses, 11460 Warner Ave., Fountain Valley, CA 92708 (714) 241-6109
(CVP) Choctaw Video Productions, Choctaw Tribe, P.O. Box 6010, Philadelphia, MS 39350 (601) 656-5251
(DAR) Denver Art Museum, Education Dept., 100 W. 14th Ave. Parkway, Denver, CO 80204 (303) 575-2312
(DC) Direct Cinema Limited, P.O. Box 10003, Santa Monica, CA 90410 (800) 525-0000; Fax (310) 396-3233
(DCP) Dave Caldwell Productions, 26934 Halifax Pl., Hayward, CA 94542 (415) 538-4286
(DEPKE) Irene-Aimee Depke, 5627 N. Neva Ave., Chicago, IL 60631 (312) 774-2589
(DER) Documentary Educational Resources, 101 Morse St., Watertown, MA 02472 (800) 569-6621; Fax (617) 926-9519. E-mail: docued@der.org. Web site: www.der.org/docued
(DOV) Dover Publications, 31 E. 2nd St., Mineola, NY 11501 (800) 223-3130; Fax (516) 742-5049.
(DP) Dana Productions, 6249 Babcock Ave., N. Hollywood, CA 91606 (213) 877-9246
(DR) Dreamcatchers, Inc., 23852 PCH #766, Malibu, CA 90265; Website: www.dreamcatchers.org
(DPA) Documentary Photo Aids, P.O. Box 952137, Lake Mary, FL 32795 (800) 255-0763; Fax (904) 383-5679
(DSP) Daybreak Star Press Film & Video, United Indians of All Tribes Foundation, Daybreak Star Cultural/Educational Center, Discovery Park, P.O. Box 99253, Seattle, WA 98199 (206) 285-4425
(DT) Dallas Telecourses, 9596 Walnut St., Mesquite, TX 75243 (214) 952-0303 Fax 952-0329
(DTC) DTC-TV Downtown Community Television, 87 Lafayette St., New York, NY 10013 (212) 966-4510
(EDC) Education Development Center, 55 Chapel St., Newton, MA 02158 (800) 225-4276; in MA (617) 969-7100
(EG) Em Gee Film Library, 6924 Canby, #103, Reseda, CA 91335 (818) 881-8110 Fax 981-5506
(FF) FilmFair Comunications, Gregg Ohara Films, P.O. Box 2187, Beverly Hills, CA 90213
(FH) Films for the Humanities, P.O. Box 2053, Princeton, NJ 08543 (800) 257-5126; (609) 275-1400 Fax 275-3767
(FI) Films Incorporated Video, 5547 N. Ravenswood Ave., Chicago, IL 60640 (800) 343-4312; Fax (312) 878-0416
(FIC) Film in the Cities, 2388 University Ave., St. Paul, MN 55114 (612) 646-6104 Fax 646-3879
(FIL) Filmakers Library, 124 E. 40th St., New York, NY 10016 (212) 808-4980 Fax 808-4983
(FILMS) Films, Inc., 5547 N. Ravenswood Ave., Chicago, IL 60640 (800) 323-4222
(FL) Flower Films, 10341 San Pablo Ave., El Cerrito, CA 94530 (415) 525-0942
(FM) Facets Multimedia, 1517 W. Fullerton Ave., Chicago, IL 60614 (312) 281-9075
(FOF) Facts on File, 11 Penn Plaza, New York, NY 10001 (800) 322-8755 Fax (212) 967-9196
(FOUR) Four Worlds Development Project, Faculty of Education, The University of Lethbridge, 4401 University Dr., Lethbridge, AB, Canada T1K 3M4 (403) 329-2065 Fax 329-3081

(FP) Friendship Press Distribution Office,
P.O. Box 37844, Cincinnati, OH 45237 (513) 761-2100
(FU) Fulton Films, 64 Orchard Hill Rd.,
Newton, CT 06070 (203) 426-2580
(FUL) Fulcrum Publishing, 350 Indiana St., Suite 350,
Golden, CO 80401 (800) 992-2908 Fax (303) 279-7111
E-mail: info@fulcrum-books.com;
Web site: www.fulcrum-books.com
(FWT) Four Winds Trading Co., P.O. Box 1887,
Boulder, CO 80306 (800) 456-5444; (303) 499-4484
(GA) Guidance Associates, P.O. Box 1000,
Mt. Kisco, NY 10549 (800) 431-1242;
Fax (914) 666-5319
(GAUL) Chris Gaul, 1919 Old Turkey Point Rd.,
Baltimore, MD 21211 (301) 686-7273
(GDA) Gray Deer Arts, P.O. Box 2341,
Edmond, OK 73083 (405) 340-6323
(GP) Greenwood Press, 88 Post Rd. West,
Box 5007, Westport, CT 06881
(GPN) Great Plains National, P.O. Box 80669, Lincoln,
NE 68501 (800) 228-4630; or (402) 472-2007 Fax
(402) 472-1785
(HLM) H.L. Murvin, 500 Vernon St.,
Oakland, CA 94610
(HO) HONOR, Inc., 6435 Wiesner Rd.,
Omro, WI 54963 (414) 582-7142
(HSS) Henry Street Settlement, 265 Henry St.,
New York, NY 10002 (212) 766-9200
(IANA) Institute of Alaska Native Arts, P.O. Box 70769,
Fairbanks, AK 99707 (907) 456-7491
(IBC) Inuit Broadcasting Corp., 251 Laurier Ave., West,
Suite 703, Ottawa, ON, Canada K1P 5J6 (613) 235-1892
(ICARUS) Icarus-First Run Films, 153 Waverly Place,
6th Floor, New York, NY 10014 (800) 876-1710; Fax
(212) 989-7649
(IDIL) Institute for the Development of Indian Law, 1104
Glyndon St., SE, Vienna, VA 22180 (703) 938-7822
(IF) Image Film, 37 Burkhart Place, Rochester,
New York, NY 14620 (716) 473-8070
(IFF) International Film Foundation, 155 W. 72nd St.,
Rm. 306, New York, NY 10023 (212) 580-1111
(IH) Indian House, P.O. Box 472, Taos, NM 87571
(800) 545-8152; in NM (505) 776-2953
(IIP) Igloolik Isuma Productions, P.O. Box 223, Igloolik,
NWT, Canada X0A 0L0 (819) 934-8809 Fax 934-8782
(IM) Image Film, 132 Hampshire Dr.,
Rochester, NY 14618 (716) 473-8070
(IN) Intermedia Arts Minnesota, 2822 Lyndale Ave. S.,
Minneapolis, MN 55408 (612) 627-4444
(IP) Investigative Productions, 48 Major St.,
Toronto, ON, Canada M5S 2L1 (416) 968-7818
(IRA) Indian Rights Association, Film Rental Program,
c/o Janney Montgomery, 1601 Market St.,
Philadelphia, PA 19103 (215) 665-4523
(IS) IS Productions, P.O. Box 747, Hotevilla, AZ 86030
(ISU) Iowa State University, Media Resources
Center, 121 Pearson Hall, Ames IA 50010
(515) 294-1540
(ITFE) International Tele-Film Enterprises,
47 Densley Ave., Toronto, ON, Canada M6M 5A8
(416) 241-4483
(IU) Indiana University, Instructional Support
Services, Bloomington, IN 47405 (800) 552-8620;
Fax (812) 855-8404
(IVA) Island Visual Arts, 8920 Sunset Blvd., 2nd Floor,
Los Angeles, CA 90069 (213) 288-5382 Fax 276-5476
(JOHNSTON) Hugh and Suzanne Johnston, 16 Valley Rd., Princeton, NJ 08540 (609) 924-7505
(KC) KC Publications, Box 14883,
Las Vegas, NV 89114 (703) 731-3123
(KF) Kifaru Productions, 23852 PCH #766,
Malibu, CA 90265 (800) 400-8433; (310) 457-1617
Fax 457-2688. E-mail: kifaru@aol.com;
Website: www.dreamcatchers.org
(KM) Kraus Microform, Route 100, Millwood, NY 10546
(800) 223-8323; Fax (914) 762-1195
(KS) Kansas State Historical Society, 6425 S.W. Sixth
St., Topeka, KS 66615 (800) 766-3777
(KUAC) KUAC-TV, University of Alaska,
Fairbanks, AK 99775 (907) 474-7492
(KUHT) KUHT-TV, 4513 Cullen Blvd.,
Houston, TX 77004 (713) 749-7371
(KUSD) KUSD-TV, 414 E. Clark St.,
Vermillion, SD 57069 (605) 677-5861
(KUTV) KUTV, Promotion Dept., P.O. Box 30901,
Salt Lake City, UT 84301 (801) 973-3375
(KYUK) KYUK Video Productions, Pouch 468,
Bethel, AK 99559 (907) 543-3131

(LC) Library of Congress, Motion Picture,
Broadcasting & Recorded Sound Division;
and Prints & Photographs Division, Washington,
DC 20540 (202) 707-8572 Fax 707-2371
(LCA) Learning Corporation of America;
Distributed by PHOENIX
(LE) Lenapehoking Enterprises, P.O. Box 310,
Cheswold, DE 19936 (800) 897-4263
(LL) Listening Library, P.O. Box L,
Old Greenwich, CT 06870 (800) 243-4504
(LV) Library Video Co., P.O. Box 1110,
Bala Cynwyd, PA 19004 (800) 843-3620;
Fax (610) 667-3425
(MAI) National Museum of the American Indian,
Film & Video Archives & Photographic Archives,
The George Gustav Heye Center-Smithsonian Institution, Alexander Hamilton U.S. Customs House, One
Bowling Green, New York, NY 10004 (212) 283-2420
(MAN) Robert N. Manning, 53 Hamilton Ave.,
Staten Island, NY 10301
(MB) Margaret Brandon, 140 Ridgeway Rd.,
Woodside, CA 94062 (415) 369-0139
(MBP) Michael Brodie Productions, 590 Transit Rd.,
Victoria, BC, Canada V8S 4Z5 (604) 598-2308
(McN) Maureen McNamara, 12 Vincent St.,
Cambridge, MA 02140 (617) 661-0402
(MC) Meadowlark Communications, P.O. Box 7218,
Missoula, MT 59807 (888) 728-2180 ; (406) 728-2180
Fax 549-3090 E-mail: info@powwowcountry.com
Website: www.powwowcountry.com
(MCN) Muscogee Creek Nation Community Center,
P.O. Box 580, Okmulgee, OK 74447 (918) 756-8700
(MCP) Makoche Recordings, P.O. Box 2756, Bismarck,
ND 58502 (800) 637-6863; Fax (701) 255-8287.
Website: www.makoche.com
(ME) Meadowlark Media, P.O. Box 7218,
Missoula, MT 79807 (888) 728-2180 Fax
(406) 549-3090. E-mail: info@powwowcountry.com;
Website: www.powwowcountry.com.
(MFP) Morning Flower Press, P.O. Box 114433,
Denver, CO 80211 (303) 477-8442
(MFV) Mystic Fire Video, 524 Broadway, Suite 604,
New York, NY 10012 (800) 292-9001; (212) 941-0999
Fax 941-1443
(MG) The Media Guild, 11562 Sorrento Valley Rd.,
Suite J, San Diego, CA 92121 (619) 755-9191
(ML) Magic Lantern Communications, Ltd.,
775 Pacific Rd., Unit #38, Oakville, ON, Canada L6L
6M4 (416) 827-1155 in Canada (800) 263-1717
(MMA) Museum of Modern Art, 11 West 53rd St.,
New York, NY 10019 (212) 956-4204
(MNM) Museum of New Mexico, Programs &
Education A-V Specialist, Santa Fe, NM 87503
(505) 827-2770
(MP) Mixtech Productions, P.O. Box 1100-304,
Taos, NM 87571 (505) 758-9052
(MPC) Maurose Publishing Co., P.O. Box 2153,
Moscow, PA 18444 (800) 391-0011
Fax (570) 842-4716; E-mail: maurose1@aol.com;
Web site: www.carlmoon.com
(MRC) Media Resources Center, 121 Pearson Hall,
Iowa State University, Ames, IA 50011 (515) 294-1540
(NACO) Native American Co-op, P.O. Box 27626,
Tucson, AZ 85726 (520) 622-4900
(NAI) Native American Images, P.O. Box 746,
Austin, TX 78767 (800) 531-5008; (512) 472-7701
(NAPBC) Native American Public Broadcasting
Consortium, P.O. Box 83111, Lincoln, NE 68501
(402) 472-3522
(NATC) Northwest Arctic Television Center,
P.O. Box 51, Kotzebue, AK 99752 (907) 442-3472
(NAV) Native Voices, P.O. Box 180, Summertown,
TN 38483 (800) 695-2241 Fax (931) 964-2291.
E-mail: catalog@usit.net
(NCTE) National Council of Teachers of English,
1111 Kenyon Rd., Urbana, IL 61801
(NDF) New Day Films, 121 W. 27th St., Suite 902,
New York, NY 10001 (212) 645-8210 Fax 645-8652
(NDM) New Dimension Media, 85803 Lorane Hwy.,
Eugene, OR 97405 (800) 288-4456
(NETCHE) NETCHE is now NETV
(NETV) Nebraska Educational Television,
P.O. Box 83111, Lincoln, NE 68501
(800) 228-4630; in HI & NE (402) 472-2007
(NFBC) National Film Board of Canada,
22D Hollywood Ave., Hohokus, NJ 07423
(800) 542-2164; Fax (201) 652-1973
(NGA) National Gallery of Art,
Extension Services, Washington, DC 20565

(NGS) National Geographic Society,
Educational Services, P.O. Box 98018, Washington,
DC 20090 (800) 368-2728; Fax (301) 921-1575
(NH) Northern Heritage Films (For information
on distribution and new productions contact MAI)
(NM) The Newark Museum, 49 Washington St.,
Newark, NJ 07101 (201) 733-6600
(NMFV) New Mexico Film & Video, Box 272,
Tesuque, NM 87574 (505) 983-3094
(NNA) National Native American AIDS Prevention
Center, 3515 Grand Ave., Suite 100, Oakland,
CA 94610 (510) 444-2051 Fax 444-1593.
(NOVA) Nova Scotia Department of Education,
Education Media Services, 6955 Bayers Rd.,
Halifax, NS, Canada B3L 4S4 (902) 453-2810
(NP) Northland Publishing, P.O. Box 1389, Flagstaff,
AZ 86002 (800) 346-3257 Fax (800) 257-9082
(NPP) New Pacific Productions, P.O. Box 12792,
San Diego, CA 92112 (619) 462-8266
(NR) Norman Ross Publishing, 330 W. 58th St.,
New York, NY 10019 (800) 648-8850;
Fax (212) 765-2393
(NU) New & Unique Videos, 2336 Summac Dr.,
San Diego, CA 92105 (619) 282-6126 Fax 283-8264
(NV) New Visions, P.O. Box 599, Aspen, CO 81612
(303) 925-2640 Fax 925-9369
(NWL) New World Library, 58 Paul Dr., San Rafael
CA 94903 (800) 972-6657; Fax (415) 472-2100
(NYU) New York University Film Library,
26 Washington Pl., New York, NY 10003
(O&C) Ojibway & Cree Cultural Center, 84 Elm South,
Timmons, ON, Canada P4N 1W6 (705) 267-7911
(OAP) Old Army Press, P.O. Box 2243,
Fort Collins, CO 80522 (800) 627-0079
(ODE) Oklahoma Dept. of Education,
Media Resources, Oliver Hodge Bldg.,
Oklahoma City, OK 73105
(OHS) Oregon Historical Society,
Education Dept., 1230 S.W. Park Ave.,
Portland, OR 97205 (503) 222-1741 ext. 36
(OP) Odyssey Productions, 2800 NW Thurman St.,
Portland, OR 97210 (503) 223-3480
(OY) Oyate, 2702 Mathews St., Berkeley, CA 94720
(510) 848-6700 Fax 848-4815
(PBS) PBS Video, 1320 Braddock Place, Alexandria,
VA 22314 (800) 344-3337; Fax (703) 739-5269
(PFV) Pyramid Film & Video, Box 1048,
Santa Monica, CA 90406 (800) 421-2304
(PH) Paul Hacker Knives & Flutes, 6513 N.W. 20th
Dr., Bethany, OK 73008 (405) 787-8600 (phone & fax)
(PHOENIX) Phoenix/BFA Films, 2349 Chaffee Dr., St.
Louis, MO 63146 (800) 221-1274; Fax (314) 569-2834
(PIE) Pacific International Enterprises, 1133 S. Riverside, Suite 1, Medford, OR 97501 (503) 779-0990
(PMI) Public Media, Inc., Home Vision Arts,
4411 N. Ravenswood Ave., Chicago, IL 60640
(800) 826-3456; Fax (773) 878-0416
(PR) Pictures of Record, 119 Kettle Creek Rd.,
Weston, CT 06883 (203) 227-3387 Fax 222-9673
(PSU) The Pennsylvania State University,
Audio-Visual Services, Special Services Bldg.,
1127 Fox Hill Rd., University Park, PA 16803
(800) 826-0132; In PA, HI & AK (814) 865-6314
(PUSA) Penguin USA, Academic Marketing Dept.,
375 Hudson St., New York, NY 10014 (800) 253-6476
(QP) Quanta Press, 1313 Fifth St. SE, Minneapolis,
MN 55414
(QTS) Quileute Tribal School, Old Coast Guard Rd.,
P.O. Box 39, La Push, WA 98350 (206) 374-6163
Fax 374-6311
(RC) Reservation Creations, P.O. Box 27626,
Tucson, AZ 85726 (602) 622-4900
(RH) Random House—School Division, Dept. 9020,
400 Hahn Rd., Westminster, MD 21157
(800) 638-6460; in MD (800) 492-0782;
in AK & HI (301) 876-2286
(RICH) Rich-Heape Films, Inc., 5952 Royal Lane,
Suite 254, Dallas, TX 75230 (888) 600-2922; (214)
696-6916 Fax 696-6306. E-mail: orders@richheape.
com; Website: www.rich-heape.com
(RITZ) Lan Brook Ritz, Brown Bird Productions, 1971
N. Curson Ave., Hollywood, CA 90046 (213) 851-8928
(RM) Robert N. Manning, 53 Hamilton Ave.,
Staten Island, NY 10301 (718) 981-0120
(RP) Research Publications, 12 Lunar Dr./Drawer AB,
Woodbridge, CT 06525 (800) 732-2477;
in CT call collect; in AK & HI (203) 397-2600;
Fax (203) 397-3893

(RODGERS) Distributed by Gail Singer Films, 82 Willcocks St., Toronto, ON, Canada M5S 1C8 (416) 923-4245

(RT) RT Computer Graphics, 602 San Juan de Rio, Rio Rancho, NM 87124 (800) 891-1600; (505) 891-1600 Fax 891-1350

(RTP) River Tracks Productions, Box 9, Manley Hot Springs, AK 99756

(SAN) San Juan School District Media Center, Curriculum Division, 28 West 200 North (15-7), Blanding, UT 84511 (801) 678-2281

(SDF) Sun Dog Films, Box 232, Custer, SD 57730 (605) 673-4065,

(SE) Spotted Eagle Productions, 2524 Hennepin Ave. So., Minneapolis, MN 55405 (612) 377-4212

(SH) Shenandoah Film Productions, 538 G St., Arcata, CA 95521 (707) 822-1030 Fax 822-5334 Website: www.northcoast.com/~vern

(SHSW) State Historical Society of Wisconsin, 816 State St., Madison, WI 53706

(SI) Smithsonian Institution, Services Branch, National Anthropological Archives, Washington, DC 20560 (202) 357-4560

(SI-OMB) Smithsonian Institution, Office of Museum Programs, A-V Loan Program, Washington, DC 20560 (202) 357-3101

(SII) Softline Information, Inc., 20 Summer St., Stamford, CT 06901 (800) 524-7922; Fax (203) 975-8347

(SM) Southwest Museum, Highland Park, Los Angeles, CA 90042 (323) 221-2164 Fax 224-8223; E-mail: dking@annex.com; Web site: www.southwestmuseum.org

(SN) Seneca Nation of Indians, P.O. Box 442, Salamanca, NY 14779 (716) 945-1738

(SO) Solaris, 264 West 19th St., New York, NY 10011 (212) 741-0778

(SOAR) Sound of America Records (SOAR), P.O. Box 8606, Albuquerque, NM 87198 (505) 268-6110 Fax 268-0237; E-mail: soar@rt66.com; Web site: www.soundofamerica.com

(SP) SilverPlatter, 100 River Ridge Dr., Norwood, MA 02062 (800) 343-0064

(SR) Scholarly Resources, 104 Greenhill Ave., Wilmington, DE 19805 (800) 772-8937; (302) 654-7713 Fax 654-3871. E-mail: sales@scholarly.com; Web site: www.scholarly.com

(SRA) Science Research Associates, P.O. Box 543, Blacklick, OH 43004 (800) 843-8855

(STULL) Donald D. Stull, 2900 Westdale Rd., Lawrence, KS 66044 (913) 842-8055

(SUPT) Superintendent of Documents, G.P.O., Washington, DC 20402

(SUQ) Suquamish Museum, P.O. Box 498, Suquamish, WA 98392 (206) 598-3311

(SVE) Society for Visual Education, N. Northwest Hwy., Chicago, IL 60631 (800) 829-1900 Fax (800) 624-1678

(SWR) Silver Wave Records, Inc., P.O. Box 7943, Boulder, CO 80306 (800) 745-9283 Fax (303) 443-0877; E-mail: info@silverwave.com - Web site: www.silverwave.com

(TA) Troll Associates, Instructional Materials, 100 Corporate Dr., Mahwah, NJ 07430 (800) 526-5289; Fax (201) 529-9347

(TAM) Tamarack Films, 11032-76 St., Edmonton, AB, Canada T5B 2C6 (403) 477-7958

(TC) Treasure Chest, P.O. Box 5250, Tucson, AZ 85703 (800) 969-9558

(TE) Russell Publications, 9027 N. Cobre Dr. Phoenix, AZ 85028-5317 (800) 835-7220 Fax (602) 493-4691 Web site: www.indiandata.com

(TL) Time-Life Video, 1450 East Parham Rd., Richmond, VA 23280

(TM) Taylor Museum, Colorado Springs Fine Arts Center, 30 West Dale, Colorado Springs, CO 80903

(TBM) Thomas Burke Memorial, Washington State Museum, DB-10, University of Washington, Seattle, WA 98195 (206) 543-5884

(TDR) Tribal Data Resources, 2576 Hartnell Ave. Suite 5, Redding, CA 96002 (530) 222-2964 Fax 222-8413. E-mail: tdr@tdronline.com; Web site: www.tdronline.com

(THA) Thomas Howe Associates Ltd., 1100 Homer St., Vancouver, BC, Canada V6B 2X8 (604) 687-4215

(THRC) Texas Human Resources Center, University of Texas, Arlington, Library, P.O. Box 19497, Arlington, TX 76019 (817) 273-2767

(TIPI) Tipi Shop, P.O. Box 1542, Rapid City, SD 57709

(TOP) The Origins Program, 4632 Vincent Ave. S.,

Minneapolis, MN 55410

(TPH) Theosophical Publishing House, 306 W. Geneva Rd., Wheaton, IL 60189 (800) 654-9430; in IL (312) 665-0123

(TR) The Trust for Native American Cultures & Crafts, P.O. Box 142, Greenville, NH 03048 (603) 878-2944

(TT) Tulalip Tribe, 3901 Totem Beach Rd., Marysville, WA 98270 (206) 653-0220

(TTP) Turning Tide Productions, P.O. Box 864, Wendell, MA 01379 (508) 544-8313

(TW) Time-Warner Video, P.O. Box 4367, Huntington Station, NY 11750 (800) 854-7200

(TWN) Third World Newsreel, 545 8th Ave. 10th Fl., New York, NY 10018 (212) 947-9277 Fax 594-6417 E-mail:twn@twn.org

(UA) University of Arizona, Media Services- Film Library, Tucson, AZ 85706 (602) 626-3282

(UAB) University of Alberta, Motion Picture Division, Edmonton, AB, Canada (403) 432-3302

(UADA) University of Alberta, Dept. of Anthropology, 13-15 HM Tory Bldg., Edmonton, ON T6G 2H4 Canada (403) 432-3879

(UAL) University of Alberta, Audio Visual Services, L2-6A Humanities Bldg., Edmonton, AB, Canada T6G 2E1 (403) 432-4962

(UC) University of California, Extension Media Center, 2000 Center St., Berkeley, CA 94704 (510) 642-0460; Fax 643-9271

(UCLA) University of California, Los Angeles, Instructional Media Library, Powell Library-46, Los Angeles, CA 90024 (310) 825-0755

(UCP) University of California Press, orders to: California/Princeton Fulfillment Services, 1445 Lower Ferry Rd., Ewing, NJ 08618 (800) 777 4726 Fax (800) 999-1958 Website: www.ucpress.edu

(UCT) University of Connecticut, Film Library, U-1, Storrs, CT 06268 (203) 486-2530

(UI) University of Illinois Film Center, 506 S. Wright St. #378, Urbana, IL 61801 (800) 367-3456

(UK) University of Kansas, Audio Visual Center, 645 New Hampshire St., Lawrence, KS 66044 (913) 864-3352

(UL) United Learning, 6633 W. Howard St., P.O. Box 48718, Niles, IL 60714 (800) 424-0362

(UM) University Microfilms International, 300 North Zeeb Rd., An Arbor, MI 48106 (800) 521-0600; (313) 761-4700 ext. 789

(UMA) University of Mid-America (See GPN)

(UMC) Utah Media Center, 20 South West Temple, Salt Lake City, UT 84101

(UMN) University of Minnesota, Film & Video, 1313 Fifth St. SE, Suite 108, Minneapolis, MN 55414 (800) 847-8251; in MN (612) 373-3810

(UN) University of Nevada Film Library, Getchell Library, Reno, NV 89557 (702) 784-6037

(UNP) University of Nebraska Press, P.O. Box 880484, Lincoln, NE 68588 (800) 755-1105

(UP) Upstream Productions, 420 1st Ave. W., Seattle, WA 98119 (206) 281-9177 Fax 284-6963

(UT) University of Texas, Film Library, Education Annex G-5, 20th at San Jacinto, Austin, TX 78713-7448 (512) 471-3572

(UTE) Ute Indian Tribe Audio-Visual, P.O. Box 129, Fort Duchesne, UT 84026 (801) 722-5141

(UTFL) The University of Texas Film Library, Drawer W, Austin, TX 78711 (512) 471-3573

(UT-ITC) The University of Texas, Institute of Texan Cultures at San Antonio, P.O. Box 1226, San Antonio, TX 78294-1226 (800) 776-7651; (210) 558-2235 Fax 558-2205

(UTP) University of Texas Press, P.O. Box 7819, Austin, TX 78713 (800) 252-3206 Fax (800) 687-6046 (512) 471-7233 Fax 320-0668. Web site: www.utexas.edu/utpress

(UUT) University of Utah , Instructional Media Center, 207 Milton Bennion Hall, Salt Lake City, UT 84112 (801) 581-3170

(UW) University of Washington, Instructional Media Services, 23 Kane Hall, DG-10, Seattle, WA 98195 (206) 543-9909

(UWL) University of Washington Libraries, Special Collection Division—Microforms, Suzzallo Library, FM-25, Seattle, WA 98195

(VC) The Video Catalog, P.O. Box 64428, St. Paul, MN 55164-0428 (800) 733-2232

(VH) VH-1, 1515 Broadway, New York, NY 10036 (212) 258-7800

(VIP) VIP Publishing, P.O. Box 1788, Fayetteville, AR 72702 (800) 776-0842

(VOI) Video Out International, 1160 Hamilton St., Vancouver, B.C., Canada V6B 2S2 (604) 688-4336

(VT) Video Tech, 19346 3rd Ave. NW, Seattle, WA 98177 (206) 546-5401

(VVP) Victorian Video Productions, P.O. Box 1540, Colfax, CA 95713 (800) 848-0284; (916) 346-6184

(WALI) Monona Wali, 886 S. Bronson Ave., Los Angeles, CA 90005 (213) 650-7341

(WALL) Alfred Wallace, 420 Riverside Dr., New York, NY 10025 (212) 865-8817

(WD) Walt Disney Educational Media Co., 500 South Buena Vista, Burbank, CA 91521

(WE) World Eagle, Inc., 64 Washburn Ave., Wellesley, MA 02181

(WGBH) WGBH Distribution Office, 125 Western Ave., Boston, MA 02134 (617) 492-2777

(WH) Written Heritage, P.O. Box 1390, Folsom, LA 70437 (800) 301-8009 Fax (504) 796-9236 E-mail: whiswind@i-55.com Web site: www.whispering wind.com

(WKV) Wood Knapp Video, 5900 Wilshire Blvd., Los Angeles, CA 90036 (800) 521-2666; Fax (213) 930-2742

(WMM) Women Make Movies, 462 Broadway, 5th Floor, New York, NY 10013 (212) 925-0606 Fax 925-2052

(WNET) WNET-13 Video Distribution, 356 W. 58th St., New York, NY 10019 (212) 560-3045

(WP) White Publishing, P.O. Box 342, Arlee, MT (406) 726-3627

(WQED) WQED-TV, Distribution Department, 4802 Fifth Ave., Pittsburgh, PA 15213 (412) 622-1356

(WXXI) WXXI-TV, 280 State St., P.O. Box 21, Rochester, NY 14601 (716) 325-7500

(YPT) Yerington Paiute Tribe Publications, 171 Campbell Lane, Yerington, NV 89447

(ZAENTZ) The Saul Zaentz Productions Co., 2600 Tenth St., Berkeley, CA 94710 (800) 227-0602

CANADIAN RESERVES & BANDS

This section contains a listing of Canadian Indian Reserves and Bands, with land areas of at least 1,000 acres. Many bands have more than one reserve in each province. Arranged alphabetically by Reserve and Province.

ALBERTA

FIRST NATIONS

ALEXANDER FIRST NATION
P.O. Box 3419 • Morinville, AB T0G 1P0
(780) 939-5887 Fax 939-6166
Joseph Stanley Arcand, Chief

ALEXIS FIRST NATION
P.O. Box 7 • Glenevis, AB T0E 0X0
(780) 967-2225 Fax 967-5484
Howard Mustus, Chief

ATHABASCA CHIPEWYAN FIRST NATION
P.O. Box 366 • Fort Chipewyan, AB T0P 1B0
(780) 697-3730 Fax 697-3500
Patrick Marcel, Chief

BEAVER FIRST NATION
P.O. Box 270 • High Level, AB T0H 1Z0
(780) 927-3544 Fax 927-3496

BEAVER LAKE FIRST NATION
P.O. Box 960 • Lac La Biche, AB T0A 2C0
(780) 623-4549 Fax 623-4523
Alphonse Lameman, Chief

BIGSTONE CREE NATION
P.O. Box 960 • Desmarais, AB T0G 0T0
(780) 891-3836 Fax 891-3942
Eric Alook, Chief

CHIPEWYAN PRAIRIE FIRST NATION
General Delivery • Chard, AB T0P 1G0
(780) 559-2259 Fax 559-2213

COLD LAKE FIRST NATIONS BAND
P.O. Box 1769 • Grand Centre, AB T0A 1T0
(780) 594-7183 Fax 594-3577
Baptiste Blackman, Chief

DENE THA' TRIBE BAND
P.O. Box 120 • Chateh, AB T0H 0S0
(780) 321-3842 Fax 321-3886
Harry Chonkolay, Chief

DRIFTPILE INDIAN BAND #450
General Delivery • Driftpile, AB T0G 0V0
(780) 355-3868 Fax 355-3650
Eugene Germain Laboucan, Chief

DUNCAN'S NATION
P.O. Box 148 • Brownvale, AB T0H 0L0
(780) 597-3777 Fax 597-3920
Donald Testawich, Chief

ENOCH CREE FIRST NATION #440
P.O. Box 29 • ENOCH, AB T7X 3Y3
(780) 470-4505 Fax 470-3380
Howard Peacock, Chief

ERMINESKIN FIRST NATION
P.O. Box 219 • Hobbema, AB T0C 1N0
(780) 585-3941 Fax 585-2550
John Baptiste Ermineskin, Chief

FORT McKAY FIRST NATION
P.O. Box 5360 • Fort McMurray, AB T9H 3G4
(780) 828-4220 Fax 828-4393
Mary Dorothy McDonald, Chief

FORT McMURRAY #468 FIRST NATION
P.O. Box 6130 • Fort McMurray, AB T9H 4W1
(780) 334-2293 Fax 334-2457
Robert Cree, Chief

FROG LAKE FIRST NATION
General Delivery • Frog Lake, AB T0A 1M0
(780) 943-3737 Fax 943-3966
Elmer Thomas Abraham, Chief

HEART LAKE FIRST NATION
P.O. Box 447 • Lac La Biche, AB T0A 2C0
(780) 623-2130 Fax 623-3505
Eugene Monias, Chief

HORSE LAKE FIRST NATION
P.O. Box 303 • Hythe, AB T0H 2C0
(780) 356-2248 Fax 356-3666
Dale Robert Horseman, Chief

KAINAIWA/BLOOD FIRST NATION
P.O. Box 60 • Standoff, AB T0L 1Y0
(780) 737-3753 Fax 737-2336
Roy Fox, Chief

KAPAWE'NO FIRST NATION
P.O. Box 10 • Gouard, AB T0G1C0
(780) 751-3800 Fax 751-3864

KEHEWIN CREE NATION
P.O. Box 6218 • Bonnyville, AB T9N 2G8
(780) 826-3333 Fax 826-2355
Gordon Gadwa, Chief

LITTLE RED RIVER CREE FIRST NATION
P.O. Box 1165 • High Level, AB T0H 1Z0
(780) 759-3912 Fax 759- 3780
A.J. Sewepagaham, Chief

LOON RIVER CREE NATION
P.O. Box 189 • Red Earth Creek, AB T0G 1X0
(780) 649-3883 Fax 649-3873

LOUIS BULL FIRST NATION
P.O. Box 130 • Hobbema, AB T0C 1N0
(780) 585-3978 Fax 585-3799
Simon Threefingers, Chief

LUBICON LAKE FIRST NATION
P.O. Box 6731 • Peace River, AB T8S 1S5
(780) 629-3945
Bernard Ominayak, Chief

MIKISEW CREE FIRST NATION
P.O. Box 90 • Fort Chipewyan, AB T0P 1B0
(780) 697-3740 Fax 697-3826
Archie Waquan, Chief

MONTANA FIRST NATION
P.O. Box 70 • Hobbema, AB T0C 1N0
(780) 585-3744 Fax 585-3264
Leo Cattleman, Chief

O'CHIESE FIRST NATION
P.O. Box 1570 • Rocky Mtn. House, AB T0M 1T0
(403) 989-3943 Fax 989-3795
Caroline Beaver Bones, Chief

PAUL FIRST NATION
P.O. Box 89 • Duffield, AB T0E 0N0
(780) 892-2691 Fax 892-3402
Walter Rain, Chief

PEIGAN FIRST NATION
P.O. Box 70 • Brocket, AB T0K 0H0
(403) 965-3940 Fax 965-2030
Leonard Walter Bastien, Chief

SADDLE LAKE FIRST NATION
P.O. Box 100 • Saddle Lake, AB T0A 3T0
(780) 726-3829 Fax 726-3788
Carl Quinn, Chief

SAMSON CREE FIRST NATION
P.O. Box 159 • Hobbema, AB T0C 1N0
(780) 421-4926 Fax 585-2700
Victor Buffalo, Chief

SAWRIDGE FIRST NATION
P.O. Box 326 • Slave Lake, AB T0G 2A0
(780) 849-4311 Fax 849-3446
Walter Patrick Twinn, Chief

SIKSIKA NATION
P.O. Box 1100 • Siksika, AB T0J 3W0
(780) 734-5100 Fax 734-5110
Strater Crow Foot, Chief
Cultural/Education Centre
(780) 734-3862 Fax 734-2709
Floria Duck, Coordinator

STONEY BEARSPAW FIRST NATION
P.O. Box 40 • Morley, AB T0L 1N0
(403) 881-3770 Fax 881-2187
Johnny Ear, Chief

STONEY CHINIKI FIRST NATION
P.O. Box 40 • Morley, AB T0L 1N0
(403) 881-3770 Fax 881-2187
Kenneth Soldier, Chief

STONEY WESLEY FIRST NATION
P.O. Box 40 • Morley, AB T0L 1N0
(403) 881-3770 Fax 881-2187
John Snow, Chief

STURGEON LAKE FIRST NATION
P.O. Box 757 • Valleyview, AB T0H 3N0
(780) 524-3307 Fax 524-2711
Ronald Sunshine, Chief

SUCKER CREEK FIRST NATION
P.O. Box 65 • Enilda, AB T0G 0W0
(780) 523-4426 Fax 523-3111
Jim Badger, Chief

SUNCHILD CREE FIRST NATION
P.O. Box 747 • Rocky Mountain House, AB T0M 1T0
(403) 989-3740 Fax 989-2533
Harry Goodrunning, Chief

SWAN RIVER FIRST NATION
P.O. Box 270 • Kinuso, AB T0G 1K0
(780) 775-3536 Fax 775-3796
Charles Henry Chalifoux, Chief

TALLCREE FIRST NATION
P.O. Box 100 • Fort Vermillion, AB T0H 1N0
(780) 927-3727 Fax 927-4375
Bernard John Meneen, Chief

TSUT'INA K'OSA NATION (SARCEE)
9911 Chula Blvd. #200 • Tsuu T'ina, AB T2W 6H6
(403) 281-4455 Fax 251-6061
Roy Albert Whitney, Chief

WHITEFISH LAKE FIRST NATION #128
P.O. Box 271 • Goodfish Lake, AB T0A 1R0
(780) 636-7000 Fax 636-7006
Ernest Houle, Chief

WHITEFISH LAKE FIRST NATION #459
General Delivery • Atikameg, AB T0G 0C0
(780) 767-3914 Fax 767-3814
Eddie Tallman, Chief

WOODLAND CREE FIRST NATION
General Delivery • Cadotte Lake, AB T0H 0N0
(780) 629-3803 Fax 629-3898
John Cardinal, Chief

METIS NON-STATUS

BUFFALO LAKE METIS SETTLEMENT
P.O. Box 20 • Castan, AB T0A 0R0
(780) 689-2170 Fax 689-2024

EAST PRAIRIE METIS SELLEMENT
P.O. Box 1289 • High Prairie, AB T0G 1E0
(780) 523-2594 Fax 523-2777

ELIZABETH METIS SETTLEMENTS
P.O. Box 420 • Cold Lake, AB T9M 1P1
(780) 594-5026 Fax 594-5452

FISHING LAKE METIS SETTLEMENT
General Delivery • Sputinow, AB T0A 3G0
(780) 943-2202 Fax 943-2575

FORT McKAY METIS #122
General Delivery • Fort McKay, AB T0P 1C0
(780) 828-4086 Fax 828-4111

GIFT LAKE METIS SETTLEMENTS
P.O. Box 60 • Gift Lake, AB T0G 1B0
(780) 767-3894 Fax 767-3888

KIKINO METIS SETTLEMENTS
General Delivery • Gift Lake, AB T0G 1B0
(780) 623-7868 Fax 623-7080

METIS NATION OF ALBERTA (Headquaters)
#100 11738 Kingsway Ave. • Edmonton, AB T5G
O4R
(780) 455-2200 Fax 452-8946
in AB only (800) 252-7553

METIS SETTLEMENTS GENERAL COUNCIL
3rd Floor, 10525 - 170 St. • Edmonton, AB T5P 4W2
(780) 427-1122 Fax 489-9558

PADDLE PRAIRIE METIS SETTLEMENT
General Delivery • Paddle Prairie, AB T0H 2W0
(780) 981-2227 Fax 981-3737

PEAVINE METIS SETTLEMENTS
P.O. Box 238 • High Prairie, AB T0G 1E0
(780) 523-2557 Fax 523-5616

BRITISH COLUMBIA

FIRST NATIONS

ADAMS LAKE FIRST NATION
P.O. Box 588 • Chase, BC V0E 1M0
(250) 679-8841 679-8813
Harvey Jules, Chief

AHOUSAHT FIRST NATION
General Delivery • Ahousaht, BC V0R 1A0
(250) 670-9563 Fax 670-9696
Louie M. Frank, Sr., Chief

AITCHELITZ FIRST NATION
8150 Aitken Rd. • Sardis, BC V2R 1A9
(604) 792-2404 Fax 858-7692
Johnny George, Chief

ALEXANDRIA FIRST NATION
c/o Tsilhoqot'in National Government
51D S. Fourth Ave. • Williams Lake, BC V2J 1J6
(250) 993-4324 Fax 398-5798
Thomas Billboy, Chief

ALEXIS CREEK FIRST NATION
P.O. Box 69 • Chilanko Forks, BC V0L 1H0
(250) 481-3335 Fax 481-1197
Irvine Charleyboy, Chief

ASHCROFT FIRST NATION
P.O. Box 440 • Ashcroft, BC V0K 1A0
(250) 453-9154 Fax 453-9156
Mae Boomer, Chief

BEECHER BAY FIRST NATION
3843 E. Sooke Rd., RR 1, Box 1
Sooke, BC V0S 1N0
(250) 478-3535 Fax 478-3585
Patricia Ann Chipps, Chief

BLUEBERRY RIVER FIRST NATION
P.O. Box 3009 • Buick Creek, BC V0C 2R0
(250) 630-2584 Fax 630-2588
Joe Apsassin, Chief

BONAPARTE FIRST NATION
P.O. Box 669 • Cache Creek, BC V0K 1H0
(250) 457-9624 Fax 457-9550
Nels Terry Porter, Chief

BOOTHROYD FIRST NATION
P.O. Box 295 • Boston Bar, BC V0K 1C0
(604) 867-9211 Fax 867-9747
Wilfred Campbell, Chief

BOSTON BAR FIRST NATION
S.S. #1 • Boston Bar, BC V0K 1C0
(604) 867-8844 Fax 867-9317
Herman Phillips, Chief

BRIDGE RIVER FIRST NATION
P.O. Box 190 • Lillooet, BC V0K 1V0
(250) 256-7423 Fax 256-7999
Susan James, Chief

BURNS LAKE FIRST NATION
P.O. Box 9000 • Burns Lake, BC V0J 1E0
(250) 692-7717 Fax 692-4214
Robert Charlie, Chief

CAMPBELL RIVER FIRST NATION
1400 Weiwaikum Rd.
Campbell River, BC V9W 5W8
(250) 286-6949 Fax 287-8838
Roy Roberts, Chief

CANIM LAKE FIRST NATION
P.O. Box 1030 • 100 Mile House, BC V0K 2E0
(250) 397-2227 Fax 397-2769
Gabriel Roy Christopher, Chief

CANOE CREEK FIRST NATION
General Delivery • Dog Creek, BC V0L 1J0
(250) 440-5645 Fax 440-5679
William Harry, Chief

CAYOOSE CREEK FIRST NATION
P.O. Box 484 • Lillooet, BC V0K 1V0
(250) 256-4136 Fax 256-4030
Perry Redan, Chief

CHAWATHIL FIRST NATION
P.O. Box 1659 • Hope, BC V0X 1L0
(604) 869-9994 Fax 869-7614
Herman W. Dennis Peters, Chief

CHEAM FIRST NATION
52130 Old Yale Rd. • Rosedale, BC V0X 1X0
(604) 794-7924 Fax 794-7456
Theodore (Sam) Douglas, Chief

CHEHALIS INDIAN BAND
RR 1, Chehalis Rd. • Agassiz, BC V0M 1A0
(604) 796-2116 Fax 796-3946
Virginia Peters, Chief

CHEMAINUS FIRST NATION
RR 1 • Ladysmith, BC V0R 2E0
(250) 245-7155 Fax 245-3012
Robert Daniels, Chief

CHESLATTA CARRIER NATION
P.O. Box 909 • Burns Lake, BC V0J 1E0
(250) 694-3334 Fax 694-3632
Marvin Charlie, Chief

COLDWATER FIRST NATION
P.O. Box 4600 • Merritt, BC V0K 2B0
(250) 378-6174 Fax 378-5351
Gordon Antoine, Chief

COLUMBIA LAKE FIRST NATION
P.O. Box 130 • Windermere, BC V0B 2L0
(250) 342-6301 Fax 342-9693
Joseph Nicholas, Chief

COMOX FIRST NATION
3320 Comox Rd. • Courtenay, BC V9N 3P8
(250) 339-7122 Fax 339-7053
Norman Frank, Chief

COOK'S FERRY FIRST NATION
P.O. Box 130 • Spences Bridge, BC V0K 2L0
(250) 458-2224 Fax 458-2312
Percy Minnabarriet, Chief

COWICHAN FIRST NATION
5760 Allenby • Duncan, BC V9L 5J1
(250) 748-3196 Fax 748-1233
Dennis Alphonse, Chief

COWICHAN LAKE FIRST NATION
P.O. Box 1376 • Lake Cowichan, BC V0R 2G0
(250) 749-4301 Fax 743-6800
E. Cyril Livingstone, Chief

DEASE RIVER FIRST NATION
General Delivery • Good Hope Lake, BC V0C 2Z0
(250) 239-3000 Fax 239-3003
Roy Carlick, Chief

DITIDAHT FIRST NATION
P.O. Box 340 • Port Alberni, BC V9Y 7M8
(250) 745-3333 Fax 745-3332
G. Jackie Thompson, Chief

DOIG RIVER FIRST NATION
P.O. Box 55 • Rose Prairie, BC V0C 2H0
(250) 827-3776 Fax 827-3778
Gerry Attachie, Chief

DOUGLAS FIRST NATION
7311 James St., Unit B • Mission, BC V2V 3V5
(604) 820-3082 Fax 820-3020
E-mail: dfnc@uniserve.com
Neil Phillips, Chief

EHATTESAHT FIRST NATION
P.O. Box 59 • Zeballos, BC V0P 2A0
(250) 761-4155 Fax 761-4156
Earl J. Smith, Chief

ESKETEMC FIRST NATION
P.O. Box 4479 • Williams Lake, BC V2G 2V5
(250) 440-5611 Fax 440-5721

ESQUIMALT FIRST NATION
1000 Thomas Rd. • Victoria, BC V9A 7K7
(250) 381-7861 Fax 384-9309
Andrew Benedict Thomas, Chief

FORT NELSON FIRST NATION
RR 1, Mile 293 Alaska Hwy.
Fort Nelson, BC V0C 1R0
(250) 774-7257 Fax 774-7260
Sally Behn, Chief

GINGOIX FIRST NATION
1304 Broad St. • Kincolith, BC V0V 1B0
(250) 326-4212 Fax 326-4208

GITANMAAX FIRST NATION
P.O. Box 440 • Hazelton, BC V0J 1Y0
(250) 842-5297 Fax 842-6364
Garry Patsey, Sr., Chief

GITANYOW FIRST NATION(KITWANCOOL)
P.O. Box 340 • Kitwanga, BC V0J 2A0
(250) 849-5222 Fax 849-5787
Elmer Derrick, Chief

GITLAKDAMIX FIRST NATION
P.O. Box 233 • New Aiyansh, BC V0J 1A0
(250) 633-2215 Fax 633-2271
Herbert Morven, Chief

GITSEGUKLA FIRST NATION
36 Cascade Ave., RR #1
South Hazelton, BC V0J 2R0
(250) 849-5490 Fax 849-5492
Donald Ryan, Chief

GITWANGAK FIRST NATION
P.O. Box 400 • Kitwanga, BC V0J 2A0
(250) 849-5591 Fax 849-5353
Glenford Williams, Chief

GITWINKSIHLKW FIRST NATION
P.O. Box 1 • Gitwinksihlkw, BC V0J 3T0
(250) 633-2294 Fax 633-2539
Harry Nyce, Chief

GLEN VOWELL FIRST NATION
P.O. Box 157 • Hazelton, BC V0J 1Y0
(250) 842-5241 Fax 842-5601
Marvin N. Sampson, Chief

GWA'SALA-'NAKWAXDA'ZW FIRST NATION
P.O. Box 998 • Port Hardy, BC V0N 2P0
(250) 949-8343 Fax 949-7402
Paddy Walkus, Chief

HAGWILGET FIRST NATION
P.O. Box 460 • New Hazelton, BC V0J 2J0
(250) 842-6258 Fax 842-6924
Jack Sebastian, Chief

HALALT FIRST NATION
RR 1 • Chemainus, BC V0R 1K0
(250) 246-4736/7 Fax 246-2330
George Norris, Chief

HALFWAY RIVER FIRST NATION
P.O. Box 59 • Wonowon, BC V0C 2N0
(250) 787-4452 Fax 785-2021
Gerry Hunter, Chief

HARTLEY BAY FIRST NATION
445 Yayimisaxaa Way • Hartley Bay, BC V0V 1A0
(250) 841-2500/25 Fax 841-2581
William Clifton, Chief

HEILTSUK FIRST NATION
P.O. Box 880 • Waglisa, BC V0T 1Z0
(250) 957-2381 Fax 957-2544
Cecil Reid, Chief

HESQUIAHT FIRST NATION
P.O. Box 2000 • Tofino, BC V0R 2Z0
Fax (250) 724-8570
Richard Lucas, Sr., Chief

HIGH BAR FIRST NATION
P.O. Box 45 • Clinton, BC V0K 1K0
(250) 392-2510 Fax 392-2570
Rosemarie Haller, Chief

HOMALCO FIRST NATION
1218 Butte Crescent
Campbell River, BC V9H 1G5
(250) 923-4979 Fax 923-4987
Richard Harry, Chief

HUU-AY-AHT FIRST NATION
P.O. Box 70 • Bamfield, BC V0R 1B0
(250) 728-3414 Fax 728-1222

ISKUT FIRST NATION
P.O. Box 30 • Iskut, BC V0J 1K0
(250) 234-3331 Fax 234-3200
Louis Louie, Chief

KAMLOOPS FIRST NATION
315 Yellowhead Hwy.
Kamloops, BC V2H 1H1
(250) 828-9700 Fax 372-8833
Clarence Thomas Jules, Chief

KANAKA BAR FIRST NATION
P.O. Box 210 • Lytton, BC V0K 1Z0
(250) 455-2279 Fax 455-2772
James Frank, Chief

KATZIE FIRST NATION
10946 Katzie Rd.
Pitt Meadows, BC V3Y 2G6
(250) 465-8961 Fax 465-5949
Ed Pierre, Chief

KINCOLITH BAND COUNCIL
General Delivery • Kincolith, BC V0V 1B0
(250) 326-4212 Fax 326-4208
Stuart Doolan, Chief

KISPIOX FIRST NATION
RR #1, P.O. Box 25
Kispiox, BC V0J 1Y0
(250) 842-5248 Fax 842-5604
Brian Williams, Chief

KITAMAAT FIRST NATION
Haisla, P.O. Box 1101
Kitamaat, BC V0T 2B0
(250) 639-9382 Fax 632-2840
Gerald Victor Amos, Chief

KITASOO FIRST NATION
General Delivery • Klemtu, BC V0T 1L0
(250) 839-1255 Fax 839-1256
Percy Star, Chief

KITKATLA FIRST NATION
General Delivery • Kitkatla, BC V0V 1C0
(250) 848-2214 Fax 848-2238
Francis Lewis, Chief

KITSELAS FIRST NATION
4562 Queensway • Terrace, BC V8G 3X6
(250) 635-5084 Fax 635-5335
Melville Stanley Bevan, Chief

KITSUMKALUM FIRST NATION
House of Sim-Oi-Ghets
P.O. Box 544 • Terrace, BC V8G 4B5
(250) 635-6177/8 Fax 635-4622
Steve Roberts, Chief

KLAHOOSE FIRST NATION
P.O. Box 9, Squirrel Cove
Manson's Landing, BC V0P 1K0
(250) 935-6536 Fax 935-6997
Arlene Hope, Chief

KLUSKUS FIRST NATION
P.O. Box 4639 • Quesnel, BC V2J 3J8
(250) 992-8186 Fax 992-3929
Roger Jimmie, Chief

KWA-WA-AINEUK FIRST NATION
P.O. Box 344 • Port McNeill, BC V0N 2R0
(250) 949-8732; Charlie Williams, Chief

KWAKIUTL FIRST NATION
P.O. Box 1440 • Port Hardy, BC V0N 2P0
(250) 949-6012 Fax 949-6066
Alfred Hunt, Chief

KWANTLEN FIRST NATION
P.O. Box 108 • Fort Langley, BC V1M 2R4
(604) 888-2488 Fax 888-2442
Alfred J. Gabriel, Chief

KWAYHQUITLUM FIRST NATION
65 Colony Farm Rd. • Coquitlam, BC V3C 3V4
(604) 540-0680 Fax 525-0772

KWIAKAH FIRST NATION
1440 Island Hwy.
Campbell River, BC V9W 2E3
(250) 286-1295; Stephen G. Dick, Chief

**KWICKSUTAINEUK-AH-KWAW-AH-MISH
FIRST NATION**
General Delivery • Simoon Sound, BC V0P 1S0
(250) 974-8099 Fax 974-8100
Alice Smith, Chief

KYUQUOT FIRST NATION
General Delivery • Kyuquot, BC V0P 1J0
(250) 332-5259 Fax 332-5210
Richard H. Leo, Chief

LAKAHAHMEN FIRST NATION
41290 Lougheed Hwy., RR #1
Deroche, BC V0M 1G0
(604) 826-7976 Fax 826-0362
George Campo, Chief

LAKALZAP FIRST NATION
General Delivery • Greenville, BC V0J 1X0
(250) 621-3212 Fax 621-3320
Henry Moore, Chief

LAKE BABINE FIRST NATION
P.O. Box 879 • Burns Lake, BC V0J 1E0
(250) 692-7555 Fax 692-7559
Wilf Adams, Chief

LAX-KW-ALAAMS FIRST NATION
206 Shashaak St. • Port Simpson, BC V0V 1H0
(250) 625-3474 Fax 625-3246
Lawrence Helin, Chief

LHEIDI T'ENNEH FIRST NATION
1041 Whenum Rd.
Prince George, BC V2K 5G5
(250) 563-8451 Fax 563-8324
Peter Quaw, Chief

LILLOOET FIRST NATION
P.O. Box 615 • Lillooet, BC V0K 1V0
(250) 256-4118 Fax 256-4544
William Machell, Chief

LITTLE SHUSWAP FIRST NATION
P.O. Box 1100 • Chase, BC V0E 1M0
(250) 679-3203 Fax 679-3220
Felix Arnouse, Chief

LOWER KOOTENAY FIRST NATION
RR#2, 42 Centre Rd. • Creston, BC V0B 1G2
(250) 428-4428 Fax 428-7686
Wayne Louie, Chief

LOWER NICOLA FIRST NATION
73 Shulus, Hwy. 8 • Merritt, BC V1K 1N2
(250) 378-5157 Fax 378-6188
Darryl C. Moses, Chief

LOWER SIMILKAMEEN FIRST NATION
P.O. Box 100 • Keremeos, BC V0X 1N0
(250) 499-5528 Fax 499-5335
Barnett Allison, Chief

LYACKSON FIRST NATION
5360 Mission Rd. RR #6 • Duncan, BC V9L 4T8
(250) 245-5091 Fax 246-5049
Gordon Thomas, Chief

LYTTON FIRST NATION
P.O. Box 20 • Lytton, BC V0K 1Z0
(250) 455-2304 Fax 455-2291
Byron James Spinks, Chief

MALAHAT FIRST NATION
P.O. Box 111 • Mill Bay, BC V0R 2P0
(250) 743-3231 Fax 743-3251
Randolph Daniels, Chief

**MAMALELEQALA QWE'QWA'SOT'ENOX
FIRST NATION**
1400 Weiwakum Rd.
Campbell River, BC V9W 5W8
(250) 287-2955 Fax 287-4655
Robert Sewid, Chief

MATSQUI FIRST NATION
Box 10 • Matsqui, BC V0X 1S0
(604) 826-6145 Fax 826-7009
David McKay, Chief

McLEOD LAKE FIRST NATION
General Delivery • McLeod Lake, B.C. V0J 2G0
(250) 750-4415 Fax 750-4420
Harry Chingy, Chief

METLAKATLA FIRST NATION
Box 459 • Prince Rupert, BC V8J 3R1
(250) 628-9294 Fax 628-9205
Danny V. Leighton, Chief

MORICETOWN FIRST NATION
RR 1, Site 15, Box 1• Moricetown, BC V0J 2N0
(250) 847-2133 Fax 847-9291
Stanislaus G. Nikal, Chief

MOUNT CURRIE FIRST NATION
P.O. Box 165 • Mount Currie, BC V0N 2K0
(604) 894-6115 Fax 894-6841
Fraser Andrew, Chief

MOWACHAHT FIRST NATION
P.O. Box 459 • Gold River, BC V0P 1G0
(250) 283-2532 Fax 283-2335
Lawrence Andrews, Chief

MUSQUEAM FIRST NATION
6370 Salish Dr. • Vancouver, BC V6N 2C6
(604) 263-3261 Fax 263-4212
Wendy Grant, Chief

N'QUATQUA FIRST NATION
P.O. Box 88 • D'Arcy, BC V0N 1L0
(604) 452-3221 Fax 452-3295

NADLEH WHUTEN FIRST NATION
P.O. Box 36 • Fort Fraser, BC V0J 1N0
(250) 690-7211 Fax 690-7316
Ernie Nooski, Chief

NAK'AZDLI FIRST NATION
P.O. Box 1329 • Fort St. James, BC V0J 1P0
(250) 996-7171 Fax 996-8010
Leonard Thomas, Chief

NAMGIS FIRST NATION
P.O. Box 210 • Alert Bay, BC V0N 1A0
(250) 974-5556 Fax 974-5900
Patrick Alfred, Chief

NANAIMO FIRST NATION
1145 Totem Rd. • Nanaimo, BC V9R 1H1
(250) 753-3481 Fax 753-3492
Robert E. Thomas, Chief

NANOOSE FIRST NATION
209 Mallard Way • Lantzville, BC V0R 2H0
(250) 390-3661 Fax 390-3365
Leonard W. Edwards, Chief

NAZKO FIRST NATION
3574 Hillborn Rd. • Quesnel, BC V2J 3P7
(250) 992-9085 Fax 992-7982
Stanley Boyd, Chief

NEE-TAHI-BUHN FIRST NATION
RR 2, Box 28 • Burns Lake, BC V0J 1E0
(250) 694-3492 Fax 694-3530
Pius Jack, Chief

NESKONLITH FIRST NATION
P.O. Box 608 • Chase, BC V0E 1M0
(250) 679-3295 Fax 679-5306
Madene Joyce Manuel, Chief

NEW WESTMINSTER FIRST NATION
105 - 3680 Rae Ave.
Vancouver, BC V5R 2P5
(604) 451-0531 (Phone & Fax)

NICOMEN FIRST NATION
P.O. Box 328 • Lytton, BC V0K 1Z0
(250) 455-2279 Fax 455-2772
Cyril H. Spence, Chief

NOOAITCH FIRST NATION
18 Shackelly • Merritt, BC V0K 2B0
(250) 378-6141 Fax 378-3699
Linday May Shackelly, Chief

NORTH THOMPSON FIRST NATION
P.O. Box 220 • Barriere, BC V0E 1E0
(250) 672-9995 Fax 672-5858
Nathan L. Matthew, Chief

NUCHATLAHT FIRST NATION
P.O. Box 40 • Zeballos, BC V0P 2A0
(604) 724-8609 (Phone & Fax)
Walter Michael, Chief

NUXALK NATION
P.O. Box 65 • Bella Coola, BC V0T 1C0
(604) 799-5613 Fax 799-5426
Edward Moody, Chief

OKANAGAN FIRST NATION
Site 8, Comp. #20, RR #7
Vernon, BC V1T 7Z3
(250) 542-4328 Fax 542-4990
Albert Saddleman, Chief
E-mail: ewrnet:okinband@junction.net

OLD MASSET VILLAGE COUNCIL
P.O. Box 189 • Old Masset, BC V0T 1M0
(250) 626-3337 Fax 626-5440
Michael Nicoll, Chief

OPETCHESAHT FIRST NATION
P.O. Box 211 • Port Alberni, BC V9Y 7M7
(250) 724-4041 Fax 724-1232
Daniel Watts, Chief
E-mail: opet@island.net

OREGON JACK CREEK FIRST NATION
P.O. Box 940 • Ashcroft, BC V0K 1A0
(250) 453-9098 Fax 453-9097
Robert S. Pasco, Chief

OSOYOOS FIRST NATION
Comp. 1, Box 1, RR 3 • Oliver, BC V0H 1T0
(250) 498-4906 Fax 498-6577
Clarence Louie, Chief

OWEEKENO FIRST NATION
P.O. Box 3500 • Port Hardy, BC V0N 2P0
(250) 949-2107 Fax 949-2112
Frank Johnson, Chief

PACHEENAHT FIRST NATION
General Delivery • Port Renfrew, BC V0S 1K0
(250) 647-5521 Fax 647-5561
Kenneth Jones, Chief

PAUQUACHIN FIRST NATION
8960 W. Saanich Rd. • Sidney, BC V8L 5W4
(250) 656-0191 Fax 656-6134
Edwin Mitchell, Chief

PAVILION FIRST NATION
P.O. Box 609 • Cache Creek, BC V0K 1H0
(250) 256-4204 Fax 256-4058
Marvin Bob, Chief

PENELAKUT FIRST NATION
P.O. Box 360 • Chemainus, BC V0R 1K0

(250) 246-2321 Fax 246-2725
Earl Wilbur Jack, Chief

PENTICTON FIRST NATION
RR 2, Site 80, Comp. 19
Penticton, BC V2A 6J7
(250) 493-0048 Fax 493-2882
Archie Jack, Chief

PETERS FIRST NATION
Peters Rd., RR 2 • Hope, BC V0X 1L0
(604) 794-7059 Fax 794-7885
Frank Peters, Chief

POPKUM FIRST NATION
Bldg. #1 - 7201 Vedder Rd.
Chilliwack, BC V2R 4G5
(604) 794-7924 Fax 798-4790
James Murphy, Chief

PROPHET RIVER FIRST NATION
P.O. Box 3250 • Fort Nelson, BC V0C 1R0
(250) 773-6555 Fax 773-6556
Liza Wolf, Chief

QUALICUM FIRST NATION
5850 River Rd.
Qualicum Beach, BC V9K 1Z5
(250) 757-9337 Fax 757-9898
Robert M. Recalma, Chief

QUATSINO FIRST NATION
P.O. Box 100 • Coal Harbour, BC V0N 1K0
(250) 949-6245 Fax 949-6249
Stephen Clair, Chief

RED BLUFF FIRST NATION
1515 Arbutus Rd., P.O. Box 4693
Quesnel, BC V2J 3J9
(250) 747-2900 Fax 747-1341
Frank Boucher, Chief

SAIK'UZ FIRST NATION
RR#1, Site 12, Comp. 26
Vanderhoof, BC V0J 3A0
(250) 567-9293 Fax 567-2998

SAMAHQUAM FIRST NATION
P.O. Box 456 • Mount Currie, BC V0N 2K0
(604) 894-5262 Fax 894-6188
Allan Smith, Chief

SAULTEAU FIRST NATION
P.O. Box 414 • Chetwynd, BC V0C 1J0
(250) 788-3955 Fax 788-9158
Stewart Cameron, Chief

SCOWLITZ FIRST NATION
P.O. Box 76 • Lake Errock, BC V0M 1N0
(604) 826-5813 Fax 826-6222
Clarence Martin Pennier, Chief

SEABIRD ISLAND FIRST NATION
P.O. Box 650 • Agassiz, BC V0M 1A0
(604) 796-2177 Fax 796-3729
Archie Charles, Chief

SECHELT FIRST NATION
P.O. Box 740 • Sechelt, BC V0N 3A0
(604) 688-3017 Fax 885-3490
Thomas Paul, Chief

SEMIAHMOO FIRST NATION
RR 7, 16010 Beach Rd.
White Rock, BC V4B 5A8
(604) 536-1794 Fax 536-6116
Bernard Charles, Chief

SETON LAKE FIRST NATION
Site 3, Box 76 • Shalalth, BC V0N 3C0
(250) 259-8227 Fax 259-8384
Rooney J. Louie, Chief

SHACKAN FIRST NATION
37 - Hwy. 8 Shulus • Merritt, BC V1K 1M9
(250) 378-5410 Fax 378-5219
Percy Anthony Joe, Chief

SHUSWAP FIRST NATION
P.O. Box 790 • Invermere, BC V0A 1K0

(250) 342-6361 Fax 342-2948
Paul Ignatius Sam, Chief

SHXW'OW'HAMEL FIRST NATION
RR#2, Site 22, Comp. 4 • Hope, BC V0X 1L0
(604) 869-2627 Fax 869-9903

SISKA FIRST NATION
P.O. Box 519 • Lytton, BC V0K 1Z0
(250) 455-2219 Fax 455-2539
Guy Dunstan, Chief

SKAWAHLOOK FIRST NATION
Bldg. #1 - 7201 Vedder Rd.
Chilliwack, BC V2R 4G5
(604) 858-3366 Fax 824-2424
Ana Delores Chapman, Chief

SKEETCHESTN FIRST NATION
P.O. Box 178 • Savona, BC V0K 2J0
(250) 373-2493 Fax 373-2494
Ronald Eric Ignace, Chief

SKIDEGATE FIRST NATION
P.O. Box 1301 • Haidi Gwaii, BC V0T 1S1
(250) 559-4496 Fax 559-8247
Paul E. Pearson, Chief

SKOOKUMCHUCK FIRST NATION
P.O. Box 190 • Pemberton, BC V0M 2L0
(604) 894-5262 Fax 894-6188
Paul Williams, Chief

SKOWKALE FIRST NATION
P.O. Box 2159 • Sardis, BC V2R 2R2
(250) 792-0730 Fax 792-1153
Sam Archie, Chief

SKUPPAH FIRST NATION
P.O. Box 116 • Lytton, BC V0K 1Z0
(250) 455-2279 Fax 455-2772
John McIntyre, Chief

SKWAH FIRST NATION
P.O. Box 178 • Chilliwack, BC V2P 6H7
(604) 792-9204 Fax 792-1093
Leslie Williams, Chief

SKWAY FIRST NATION
P.O. Box 364 • Chilliwack, BC V2R 6J4
(604) 792-9316 Fax 792-9317
Cecelia James, Chief

SLIAMMON BAND OFFICE
RR 2, 6690 Sliamon Rd.
Powell River, BC V8A 4Z3
(604) 483-9646 Fax 483-9769
Gene Louie, Chief

SNUNEYMUXW FIRST NATION
1145 Totem Rd. • Nanaimo, BC V9R 1H1
(250) 753-3481 Fax 753-3492
E-mail: nfntno@islans.net

SODA CREEK FIRST NATION
Site 15, Comp. 2, RR 4
Williams Lake, BC V2G 4M8
(250) 297-6323 Fax 297-6300
Beverly Ann Sellers, Chief

SONGHEES BAND OFFICE
1500 A-Admirals Rd. • Victoria, BC V9A 2R1
(250) 386-1043 Fax 386-4161
John P. Albany, Chief

SOOWAHLIE FIRST NATION
4070 Swoowahie Rd.
Cultus Lake, BC V2R 4Y2
(604) 858-4603 Fax 858-2350
William Commodore, Chief

SPALLUMCHEEN FIRST NATION
P.O. Box 3010 • Enderby, BC V0E 1V0
(250) 838-6496 Fax 838-2131
Cindy Williams, Chief

SPUZZUM FIRST NATION
RR 1 • Yale, BC V0K 2S0
(604) 863-2395 Fax 863-2218
James Johnson, Chief

SQUAMISH FIRST NATION
P.O. Box 86131 • N. Vancouver, BC V7L 4J5
(604) 980-4553 Fax 980-4523
Joseph Mathias, Chief

SQUIALA FIRST NATION
8528 Ashwell Rd. • Chilliwack, BC V2P 7Z9
(604) 792-8300 Fax 792-4522
Robert B. Jimmie, Chief

ST. MARY'S FIRST NATION
Site 15, SS #1, Comp. 55 • Cranbrook, BC V1C 6H3
(250) 426-5717 Fax 426-8935
Agnes McCoy, Chief

STELLAT'EN FIRST NATION
P.O. Box 760 • Fraser Lake, BC V0J 1S0
(250) 699-8747 Fax 699-6430
Robert Mitchell, Chief

STONE FIRST NATION
General Delivery • Hanceville, BC V0L 1K0
(250) 394-4295/6 Fax 394-4407
Tony Myers, Chief

SUMAS FIRST NATION
3092 Sumas Mountain Rd.
Abbotsford, BC V2S 4N4
(604) 852-4040 Fax 852-3834
Lester Vernon Ned, Chief

T'LT'KIT FIRST NATION
P.O. Box 615 • Lillooet, BC V0K 1V0
(250) 256-4118 Fax 256-4544

T'SOU-KE FIRST ANTION
P.O. Box 307 • Sooke, BC V0S 1N0
(250) 642-3957 Fax 642-7808

TAHLTAN FIRST NATION
P.O. Box 46 • Telegraph Creek, BC V0J 2W0
(250) 235-3241 Fax 235-3244
Ronnie Carlick, Chief

TAKLA LAKE FIRST NATION
Suite 345 - 1460-6th Ave.
Prince George, BC V2L 3N2
(250) 564-9321 Fax 564-3704
Roy French, Chief

TAKU RIVER TLINGIT FIRST NATION
P.O. Box 132 • Atlin, BC V0W 1A0
(250) 651-7615 Fax 651-7714
Sylvester Jack, Sr., Chief

TANAKTEUK FIRST NATION
P.O. Box 330 • Alert Bay, BC V0N 1A0
(250) 974-2179 Fax 974-2109
William McKenzie, Chief

TLA-O-QUI-AHT FIRST NATIONS
P.O. Box 18 • Tofino, BC V0R 2Z0
(250) 725-3223/34 Fax 725-4233
Francis F. Frank, Chief

TLATLASIKWALA FIRST NATION
c/o Whe-La-La-U Area Council
P.O. Box 270 • Alert Bay, BC V0N 1A0
(250) 974-2000 Fax 974-2010
Thomas Wallace, Chief

TL'AZT'EN NATION FIRST NATION
P.O. Box 670 • Fort St. James, BC V0J 1P0
(250) 648-3212 Fax 648-3266
Edward John, Chief

TL'ETINQOX-T'IN GOVERNMENT OFFICE
P.O. Box 168 • Alexis Creek, BC V0L 1A0
(250) 394-4212/3 Fax 394-4275
Andrew Harry, Chief

TLOWITSIS-MUMTAGILA FIRST NATION
P.O. Box 121 • Akert Bay, BC V0N 1A0
(250) 974-5546 Fax 974-5595
John Smith, Chief

TOBACCO PLAINS FIRST NATION
P.O. Box 76 • Grasmere, BC V0B 1R0
(250) 887-3461 Fax 887-3424
Josephine Shottanana, Chief

TOOSEY FIRST NATION
P.O. Box 80 • Riske Creek, BC V0L 1T0
(250) 659-5655 Fax 659-5601
Francis Laceese, Chief

TOQUAHT FIRST NATION
P.O. Box 759 • Ucluelet, BC V0R 3A0
(250) 726-4230 Fax 726-4403
Burt Mack, Chief

TSARTLIP FIRST NATION
P.O. Box 70 • Brentwood Bay, BC V0S 1A0
(250) 652-3988 Fax 652-3788
Daniel Sam, Sr., Chief

TSAWATAINEUK FIRST NATION
General Delivery • Kingcome Inlet, BC V0N 2B0
(250) 974-3013 Fax 974-3005
Patricia Dawson, Chief

TSAWOUT FIRST NATION
P.O. Box 121 • Saanichton, BC V0S 1M0
(250) 652-9101 Fax 652-9114
Louie Claxton, Chief

TSAWWASSEN FIRST NATION
Bldg. #132, N. Tsawwassen Dr.
Delta, BC V4M 4G2
(604) 943-2112 Fax 943-9226
Frederick A. Jacobs, Chief

TSAY KEH DENE BAND
#11 - 1839 First Ave. • Prince George, BC V2L 2Y8
(250) 562-8882 Fax 562-8899
Gordon Pierre, Chief

TSESHAHT FIRST NATION
P.O. Box 1218 • Port Alberni, BC V9Y 7M1
(250) 724-1225 Fax 724-4385
Adam Shewish, Chief

TSEYCUM FIRST NATION
1210 Totem Lane • Sidney, BC V8L 4C1
(250) 656-0858 Fax 656-0868
David Bill, Chief

TSLEIL-WAUTUTH (BURRARD) FIRST NATION
3082 Ghum-lye Dr. • N. Vancouver, BC V7H 1B3
(604) 929-3455 Fax 929-4714
Leonard George, Chief

TZEACHTEN FIRST NATION
45855 Promontory Rd. • Chilliwack, BC V2R 4E2
(604) 858-3888 Fax 858-3382
Kenneth Malloway, Chief

UCHUCKLESAHT FIRST NATION
P.O. Box 1118 • Port Alberni, BC V9Y 7L9
(250) 724-1832 Fax 724-1806
Charlie Cootes, Chief

UCLUELET FIRST NATION
P.O. Box 699 • Ucluelet, BC V0R 3A0
(250) 726-7342 Fax 726-7552
Robert Mundy, Chief

ULKATCHO FIRST NATION
P.O. Box 3430 • Anahim Lake, BC V0L 1C0
(250) 742-3260 Fax 742-3411
Jimmy Stillas, Chief

UNION BAR FIRST NATION
P.O. Box 788 • Hope, BC V0X 1L0
(604) 869-9466 (phone & fax)
Andrew Alex, Chief

UPPER NICOLA FIRST NATION
P.O. Box 3700 • Merritt, BC V0K 2B0
(250) 350-3342/3 Fax 350-3311
George Saddleman, Chief

UPPER SIMILKAMEEN FIRST NATION
P.O. Box 310 • Keremeos, BC V0X 1N0
(250) 499-2221 Fax 499-5117
Edward Allison, Chief

WE WAI KAI FIRST NATION
P.O. Box 220 • Quathiaski Cove, BC V0P 1N0
(250) 285-3316 Fax 285-2400
Ralph Dick, Sr., Chief

WEST MOBERLY LAKE FIRST NATION
P.O. Box 90 • Moberly Lake, BC V0X 1X0
(250) 788-3663 Fax 788-9792
George Desjarlais, Chief

WESTBANK FIRST NATION
301 - 515 Highway 97 South
Kelowna, BC V1Z 3J2
(250) 769-4999 Fax 769-4377
Robert Louie, Chief

WET'SUWET'EN FIRST NATION
P.O. Box 760 • Burns Lake, BC V0J 1E0
(250) 698-7309 Fax 698-7480

WHISPERING PINES-CLINTON FIRST NATION
RR 1, Site 8, Comp. 4 • Kamloops, BC V2C 1Z3
(250) 579-5772 Fax 579-8367
Richard LeBourdais, Chief

WILLIAMS LAKE FIRST NATION
RR 3, Box 4 • Williams Lake, BC V2G 1M3
(250) 296-3507 Fax 296-4750
Eric M. Gilbert, Chief

XAXLI'P FIRST NATION
P.O. Box 1330 • Lillooet, BC V0K 1V0
(250) 256-4800 Fax 256-7505
Roger Adolf, Chief

YAKWEAKWIOOSE FIRST NATION
7176 Chilliwack River Rd., RR 2
Sardis, BC V2R 4M1
(604) 824-0826 FAX 824-5326
Frank Malloway, Chief

YALE FIRST NATION
P.O. Box 1869 • Hope, BC V0X 1L0
(604) 863-2443 Fax 863-2467
Robert Hope, Chief

YEKOOCHE FIRST NATION
1527 - 3rd Ave. #200
Prince George, BC V2L 3G3
(250) 648-3267 (Phone & Fax)

METIS NON-STATUS

COWICHAN METIS ASSN.
2699 Sahilton Rd. • Kosilah-Duncan, BC V0R 2C0
(250) 746-6146 Fax 746-5864

THE EMMA DONAHUE METIS ASSN.
Suite 302, 1368 Pandora Ave.
Victoria, BC V8R 3A2 (250) 384-3773

MANITOBA

FIRST NATIONS

BARREN LANDS CREE NATION
General Delivery • Brochet, MB R0B 0B0
(204) 323-2300 Fax 323-2275
Fred Bighetty, Chief

BERENS RIVER FIRST NATION
Berens River P.O. • Berens River, MB R0B 0A0
(204) 382-2161 Fax 382-2297
Lester O. Everett, Chief

BIRDTAIL SIOUX FIRST NATION
P.O. Box 22 • Beulah, MB R0M 0B0
(204) 568-4540 Fax 568-4687
Henry Skywater, Chief

BLACK STURGEON FIRST NATION
P.O. Box 1150 • Lynn Lake, MB R0B 0W0
(204) 356-2439 Fax 356-8282

BLOODVEIN FIRST NATION
General Delivery • Bloodvein, MB R0C 0J0
(204) 395-2148 Helen Cook, Chief

BROKENHEAD FIRST NATION
General Delivery • Scanterbury, MB R0E 1W0
(204) 766-2494 Fax 766-2306
Wendell Sinclair, Chief

BUFFALO POINT FIRST NATION BAND
P.O. Box 1037 • Buffalo Point, MB R0A 2W0
(204) 437-2133 Fax 437-2368
James Thunder, Chief

CANUPAWAKPA DAKOTA FIRST NATION
P.O. Box 146 • Pipestone, MB R0M 1T0
(204) 854-2959 Fax 854-2525

CHEMAWAWIN FIRST NATION
P.O. Box 9 • Easterville, MB R0C 0V0
(204) 329-2161 Fax 329-2017
Alpheus Brass, Chief

CROSS LAKE INDIAN BAND
Cross Lake, MB R0B 0J0
(204) 676-2218 Fax 676-2117
Sydney Garrioch, Chief
Cultural/Education Centre
John Paupanekis, Coordinator

DAKOTA OJIBWAY TRIBAL COUNCIL
702 Douglas St. • Brandon, MB R7A 5V2
(204) 725-3560 Fax 726-5966
Hubert Pierre, Director
Cultural/Education Center

DAKOTA PLAINS FIRST NATION
P.O. Box 110 • Portage La Prairie, MB R1N 3P1
(204) 252-2288 Fax 252-2525
Ernie Smoke, Chief

DAKOTA TIPI INDIAN FIRST NATION
P.O. Box 1569 • Portage La Prairie, MB R1N 3P1
(204) 857-4381 Fax 239-6384
Dennis Pashe, Chief

DAUPHIN RIVER OJIBWAY NATION
P.O. Box 58 • Gypsumville, MB R0C 1J0
(204) 659-5370 Fax 659-4458
Emery Stagg, Chief

EBB & FLOW OJIBWAY FIRST NATION
General Delivery • Ebb & Flow, MB R0L 0R0
(204) 448-2134 Fax 448-2305
Alfred Beaulieu, Chief

FAIRFORD INDIAN RESERVE
Fairford, MB R0C 0X0
(204) 659-5705 Fax 659-2068
Edward Anderson, Chief

FISHER RIVER FIRST NATION
P.O. Box 367 • Koostatak, MB R0C 1S0
(204) 645-2171 Fax 645-2745
Lorne Cochrane, Chief

FOX LAKE FIRST NATION
P.O. Box 369 • Gilliam, MB R0B 0L0
(204) 486-2463 Fax 486-2503
Robert Wavey, Chief

GAMBLERS FIRST NATION
P.O. Box 293 • Binscarth, MB R0J 0G0
(204) 532-2464 Fax 532-2495
Louis Tanner, Chief

GARDEN HILL FIRST NATION
Island Lake, MB R0B 0T0
(204) 456-2085 Fax 456-2338
Geordie Little, Chief

GOD'S LAKE NARROWS FIRST NATION
God's Lake Narrows, MB R0B 0M0
(204) 335-2130 Fax 335-2400
Peter Watt, Chief

GOD'S RIVER CREE NATION
God's River, MB R0B 0N0
(204) 335-2011 Fax 366-2282
Marcel Okimaw, Chief

GRAND RAPIDS CREE NATION
P.O. Box 500
Grand Rapids, MB R0C 1E0
(204) 639-2219 Fax 639-2503
Harold Turner, Chief

HOLLOW WATER FIRST NATION
Wanipigow, MB R0E 2E0

(204) 363-7278 Fax 363-7418
Roderick Bushie, Chief

INTERLAKE RESERVES TRIBAL COUNCIL
P.O. Box 580 • Ashern, MB R0C 0E0
(204) 659-4465 Fax 659-2147
Rene E. Toupan, Tribal Administrator
Cultural/Educational Program

JACKHEAD FIRST NATION
Dallas, MB R0C 0S0
(204) 394-2366 Fax 394-2271
Bert Traverse, Chief

KEESEEKOOWENIN OJIBWAY FIRST NATION
P.O. Box 100 • Elphinstone, MB R0J 0N0
(204) 625-2004 Fax 625-2042
Randy Bone, Chief

LAKE MANITOBA FIRST NATION
Vogar, MB R0C 3C0
(204) 768-3492 Fax 768-3036
Raymond Swan, Chief

LAKE ST. MARTIN FIRST NATION
P.O. Box 69 • Gypsumville, MB R0C 1J0
(204) 659-4539 Fax 659-2034
David E. Traverse, Chief

LITTLE BLACK RIVER FIRST NATION
General Delivery • O'Hanley, MB R0E 1K0
(204) 367-4411 Fax 367-2741
Franklin Abraham, Chief

LITTLE GRAND RAPIDS FIRST NATION
Little Grand Rapids, MB R0B 0V0
(204) 397-2264 Fax 397-2340
Oliver Owens, Chief

**LITTLE SASKATCHEWAN
OJIBWAY FIRST NATION**
General Delivery • St. Martin, MB R0C 2T0
(204) 659-4584 Fax 659-2071
Hector Shorting, Chief

LONG PLAINS FIRST NATION
P.O. Box 430
Portage La Prairie, MB R1N 3B7
(204) 252-2731 Fax 252-2012
Peter Yellowquill, Chief

MATHIAS COLOMB FIRST NATION
Pukatawagan, MB R0B 1G0
(204) 553-2090 Fax 553-2419
Pascal Bighetty, Chief

MOSAKAHIKEN CREE NATION
Moose Lake, MB R0B 0Y0
(204) 678-2113 Fax 678-2292
Jim Tobacco, Chief

NELSON HOUSE CREE NATION
General Delivery
Nelson House, MB R0B 1A0
(204) 484-2332 Norman Linklater, Chief

NORTHLANDS DENE FIRST NATION
General Delivery • Lac Brochet, MB R0B 2E0
(204) 337-2001 Fax 337-2110
Simon Samuel, Chief

NORWAY HOUSE INDIAN BAND
P.O. Box 250 • Norway House, MB R0B 1B0
(204) 359-6786 Fax 359-4186
Alan James Ross, Chief

O-CHI-CHAK-KO-SIPI FIRST NATION
General Delivery • Crane River, MB R0B 0J0
(204) 732-2490 Fax 732-2596
John H. MacDonald, Chief

OAK LAKE FIRST NATION
P.O. Box 146 • Pipestone, MB R0M 1T0
(204) 854-2959 Fax 854-2525
Marcel Yuhada, Chief

OPASKWAYAK CREE NATION
P.O. Box 297 • The Pas, MB R9A 1K4
(204) 623-5483 Fax 623-5263
Francis Flett, Chief

OXFORD HOUSE FIRST NATION
General Delivery • Oxford House, MB R0B 1C0
(204) 538-2156 Gabriel Hart, Chief

PAUINGASSI FIRST NATION
P.O. Box 60 • Pauingassi, MB R0B 2G0
(204) 397-2371 Fax 397-2145
David Owen, Chief

PEGUIS FIRST NATION
P.O. Box 219 • Hodgson, MB R0C 1N0
(204) 645-2359 Fax 645-2360
Louis J. Stevenson, Chief

PINE CREEK INDIAN BAND
P.O. Box 70 • Camperville, MB R0L 0J0
(204) 524-2478 Fax 524-2801
Clifford McKay, Chief

POPLAR RIVER FIRST NATION
General Delivery • Negginan, MB R0B 0Z0
(204) 244-2267 Fax 244-2690
Vera Mitchell, Chief

RED SUCKER LAKE FIRST NATION
Red Sucker Lake, MB R0B 1H0
(204) 469-5041 Fax 469-5325
Fred Harper, Chief

ROLLING RIVER INDIAN BAND
P.O. Box 145 • Erickson, MB R0J 0P0
(204) 636-2211 Fax 636-7823
Dennis Whitebird, Chief

ROSEAU RIVER ANISHINABE FIRST NATION
P.O. Box 30 • Ginew, MB R0A 2R0
(204) 427-2312 Fax 427-2584
Lawrence Henry, Chief

SAGKEENG FIRST NATION
P.O. Box 280 • Fort Alexander, MB R0E 0P0
(204) 367-2287 Fax 367-4315
Jerry Fontaine, Chief

SANDY BAY OJIBWAY FIRST NATION
P.O. Box 109 • Marius, MB R0H 0T0
(204) 843-2462 Fax 843-2706
Angus Starr, Chief

SAPOTAWEYAK CREE NATION (SHOAL RIVER)
General Delivery
Pelican Rapids, MB R0L 1L0
(204) 587-2012 Fax 587-2072
Ronald Cook, Chief

SAYISA DENE FIRST NATION
General Delivery
Tadoule Lake, MB R0B 2C0
(204) 684-2069 Fax 684-2069
Peter Thorassie, Chief

SHAMATTAWA FIRST NATION
P.O. Box 102 • Shamattawa, MB R0B 1K0
(204) 565-2340 Fax 565-2321
Tommy McKay, Chief

SIOUX VALLEY DAKOTA FIRST NATION
P.O. Box 38 • Griswold, MB R0M 0S0
(204) 855-2671 Fax 855-2436
Robert J. Bone, Chief

ST. THERESA POINT CREE FIRST NATION
St. Theresa Point, MB R0B 1J0
(204) 462-2106 Fax 462-2646
Jack Flett, Chief

SWAN LAKE OJIBWAY FIRST NATION
P.O. Box 368 • Swan Lake, MB R0G 2S0
(204) 836-2101 Fax 836-2255
Roy McKinney, Chief

VALLEY RIVER FIRST NATION
General Delivery • Shortdale, MB R0L 1W0
(204) 546-3334 Fax 546-3090
Mervin Lynxleg, Sr., Chief

WAR LAKE CREE NATION
General Delivery • Ilford, MB R0B 0S0
(204) 288-4315 Fax 288-4371
Alex Ouskan, Chief

WASAGAMACK FIRST NATION
Wasagamack, MB R0B 1Z0
(204) 457-2337 Fax 457-2255
Elijah Knott, Chief

WATERHEN FIRST NATION
P.O. Box 106 • Skownan, MB R0L 1Y0
(204) 628-3478 Fax 628-3435
Harvey Nepinak, Chief

WAYWAYSEECAPPO FIRST NATION
P.O. Box 9 • Rossburn, MB R0J 1V0
(204) 859-2879 Fax 859-2403
Murray Clearsky, Chief

WUSKWI SIPIHK FIRST NATION
P.O. Box 220 • Birch River, MB R0L 0E0
(204) 236-4201 Fax 236-4786
Charles Audy, Chief

YORK FACTORY FIRST NATION
York Landing, MB R0B 2B0
(204) 342-2180 Fax 342-2322
Eric Saunders, Chief

METIS NON-STATUS

MANITOBA METIS FEDERATION, INC.
412 McGregor St. • Winnipeg, MB R2W 1X4
(204) 586-8474 Fax 947-1816

NEW BRUNSWICK

FIRST NATIONS

BIG COVE FIRST NATION
P.O. Box 1, RR 1, Site 11 • Rexton, NB E0A 2L0
(506) 523-9183 Fax 523-8230
Albert Levi, Vice-Chief

BOUCTOUCHE MICMAC FIRST NATION
RR 2 Kent Co. • Buctouche, NB E0A 1G0
(506) 743-6493 Fax 743-8731
William Sanipass, Chief

BURNT CHURCH FIRST NATION
RR 2 • Lagaceville, NB E0C 1K0
(506) 776-1200 Fax 776-1215
Wilbur Dedam, Chief

EEL GROUND FIRST NATION
47 Church Rd. • Eel Ground, NB E1V 4B9
(506) 627-4600 Fax 627-4602
Roger J. Augustine, Chief

EEL RIVER FIRST NATION
P.O. Box 1660 • Dalhousie, NB E0K 1B0
(506) 684-3360 Fax 684-5101
Thomas Everett Martin, Chief

FORT FOLLY FIRST NATION
Box 21, RR 1 • Dorchester, NB E0A 1M0
(506) 379-6224 Fax 379-6641
Dave Thomas, Chief

INDIAN ISLAND FIRST NATION
RR 2 Box 1 • Rexton, NB E0A 2L0
(506) 523-9795 Fax 523-8110
Wendall Paul Barlow, Chief

KINGSCLEAR INDIAN BAND
Comp. 19, RR 6, Site 6
Fredericton, NB E3B 4X7
(506) 363-3028/9 Fax 363-4324
Stephen Sacobie, Chief

MADAWASKA MALISEET FIRST NATION
RR 2 • St. Basile, NB E0L 1H0
(506) 739-9765 Fax 735-0024

OROMOCTO FIRST NATION
P.O. Box 417 • Oromocto, NB E2V 2J2
(506) 357-2083 Fax 357-2628
Rupert J. Sacobie, Chief
Cultural Education Program
Bob Atwin, Director

PABINEAU FIRST NATION
RR 5, Box 385 • Bathurst, NB E2A 3Y8
(506) 548-9211 Fax 548-9849
Benjamin Peter Paul, Chief

RED BANK FIRST NATION
P.O. Box 293 • Red Bank, NB E9E 2P2
(506) 836-2366 Fax 836-7593
Michael Ward, Chief
Arts and Crafts Committee
Marlene Ward, Contact

ST. MARY'S FIRST NATION
35 Dedham St. • Fredericton, NB E3A 2V7
(506) 472-9511 Fax 452-2763
Richard "Sonny" Polchies, Chief

TOBIQUE FIRST NATION
19 Band Office Lane
Tobique First Nation, NB E7H 1C6
(506) 273-5400 Fax 273-3035
Stewart Paul, Chief

WOODSTOCK INDIAN FIRST NATION
3 Wulastook Ct. • Woodstock, NB E7M 4K6
(506) 328-3303 Fax 328-2420
Len Tomah, Chief

NEWFOUNDLAND

FIRST NATIONS

BENOITS COVE BAND COUNCIL
General Delivery • John's Beach, NF A0L 1A0
(709) 789-3404

CASTOR RIVER NORTH BAND COUNCIL
Box 2A7 • Castor River North, NF A0K 2W0
(709) 847-4251

CLARKES HEAD BAND COUNCIL
General Delivery • Gander Bay, NF A0G 2G0
(709) 676-2178

CORNER BROOK BAND COUNCIL
Box 834 • Corner Brook, NF A2H 6H6
(709) 785-2101

EXPLOITS BAND COUNCIL
5 Kenmore Ave. • Grandfalls, NF A2B 1A9
(709) 489-6436

FLAT BAY BAND COUNCIL
P.O. Box 4, Site 5 • St. George, NF A0N 1Z0
(709) 647-3445

GLENWOOD BAND COUNCIL
Geberal Delivery • Glenwood, NF A0H 2K0
(709) 679-2075

MIAWPUKEK FIRST NATION (MICMACS)
P.O. Box 10, Baie d'Espoir
Conne River, NF A0H 1J0
(709) 882-2146 Fax 882-2292
Shayne McDonald, Chief

MUSHUAU INNU FIRST NATION
P.O. Box 107
Davis Inlet, Labrador, NF A0P 1A0
(709) 478-8827 Fax 478-8936
Prote Poker, Chief

PORT-AUX-PORT EAST BAND COUNCIL
General Delivery
Port-Aux-Port East, NF A0N 1T0
(709) 648-2713

SHESHATSHUI INNU BAND COUNCIL
P.O. Box 160
Northwest River, Labrador NF A0P 1M0
(709) 497-8522 Fax 497-8757
Daniel Ashini, Chief

ST. GEORGES BAND COUNCIL
Steel Mountain Rd. • St. Georges, NF A0N 1Z0
(709) 647-3124

STEPHENVILLE CROSSING BAND COUNCIL
P.O. Box 149
Stephensville Crissong, NF A0N 1C0
(709) 646-5305

METIS NON-STATUS

LABRADOR METIS ASSOCIATION
P.O. Box 2164 Sta. B
Happy Valley, NF A0P 1E0
(709) 896-0592 Fax 896-0594

INUIT

HAPPY VALLEY INUIT COMMUNITY
P.O. Box 40 Sta B
Happy Valley, NF A0P 1E0
(709) 896-8582 Fax 896-5834

HOPEDALE INUIT COMMUNITY
P.O. Box 103 • Hopedale, NF A0P 1G0
(709) 933-3777 Fax 933-3746

LABRADOR INUIT ASSOCIATION
General Delivery • Rigolet, NF A0P 1P0
(709) 947-3383 Fax 947-3371

MAKKOVIK INUIT COMMUNITY
P.O. Box 132 • Makkovik, NF A0P 1J0
(709) 923-2365 Fax 923-2366

TOWN COUNCIL OF NAIN
P.O. Box 50 • Nain, NF A0P 1L0
(709) 922-2941 Fax 922-2295

POSTVILLE INUIT COMMUNITY
P.O. Box 74 • Postville, NF A0P 1N0
(709) 479-9880 Fax 479-9891

NORTHWEST TERRITORY

FIRST NATIONS

AKLAVIK FIRST NATION
P.O. Box 118 • Klavik, NT X0E 0A0
(867) 978-2340 Fax 978-2937
Eugene Pascal, Chief

BEHDZI AHDA' FIRST NATION
General Delivery • Colville Lake, NT X0E 0V0
(867) 709-2200 Fax 709-2202
Richard Kochon, Chief

DECHI LAO'TI DENE COUNCIL
P.O. Box 69 • Wekweti, NT X0E 1W0
(867) 713-2010 Fax 713-2030
Joseph Judas, Chief

DEH GAH GOT'IE DENE COUNCIL
General Delivery • Fort Providence, NT X0E 0L0
(867) 699-3402 Fax 699-3401
Joachim Bonnetrouge, Chief

DELINE BAND
P.O. Box 158 • Deline, NT X0E 0G0
(867) 589-3151 Fax 589-4208

DENINU K'UE FIRST NATION
P.O. Box 1899
Fort Resolution, NWT X0E 0M0
(867) 394-4335 Fax 394-5122
Bernadette Unka, Chief

DOGRIB RAE BAND
P.O. Box 8 • Rae Edzo, NT X0E 0Y0
(867) 392-6581 Fax 392-6150
Edward Erasmus, Chief

EHDITAH GWICH'IN COUNCIL
P.O. Box 2770 • Inuvik, NT X0E 0T0
(867) 979-3344 Fax 979-3090
Cece McCauley, Chief

FORD FITZGERALD FIRST NATION
P.O. Box 1470 • Fort Smith, NT X0E 0P0
(867) 872-3345 (phone & fax)
Henry Beaver, Chief

FORT GOOD HOPE FIRST NATION
General Delivery
Fort Good Hope, NT X0E 0H0
(867) 598-2231 Fax 598-2024
Everett Kakfwi, Chief

FORT LIARD BAND COUNCIL
General Delivery • Fort Liard, NT X0G 0A0
(867) 770-4141 Fax 770-3555
Harry Deneron, Chief

FORT NORMAN BAND
General Delivery • Fort Norman, NT X0E 0K0
(867) 588-3341 Fax 588-3613
David Etchinelle, Chief

GAMETI FIRST NATION
P.O. Box 1 • Red lakes, NT X0E 1R0
(867) 997-3441 Fax 997-3411

GWICHA GWICH'IN COUNCIL
P.O. Box 4 • Tsiigehtchic, NT X0E 0B0
(867) 953-3201 Fax 953-3302

HAY RIVER DENE RESERVE No. 1
P.O. Box 1638 • Hay River, NT X0E 0R0
(867) 874-6701 Fax 874-3229
Pat Martel, Chief

INUVIK NATIVE BAND
P.O. Box 2570 • Inuvik, NT X0E 0T0
(867) 777-3344 Fax 777-3090

JEAN MARIE RIVER DENE NATION
General Delivery
Jean marie River, NT X0E 0N0
(867) 695-9801 Fax 809-2002

KA'A'GEE TU FIRST NATION
P.O. Box 4428 • Hay River, NT X0E 1G3
(867) 825-2000 Fax 825-2002
Lloyd Chicot, Chief

LIIDLI KUE FIRST NATION
P.O. Box 469 • Fort Simpson, NT X0E 0N0
(867) 695-3131 Fax 695-3132
Jim Antoine, Chief

LUTSEL K'E DENE INDIAN BAND
General Delivery • Lutsel K'e, NT X0E 1A0
(867) 370-3551 Antoine Michel, Chief

NAHANNI BUTTE NATION
General Delivery • Nahanni Butte, NT X0E 0N0
(867) 602-2900 Fax 602-2910

PEHDZEH K'I FIRST NATION
General Delivery • Wrigley, NT X0E 1R0
(867) 581-3321 Fax 581-3229
Alma Ekenale, Chief

SALT RIVER FIRST NATION
P.O. Box 960 • Fort Smith, NT X0E 0P0
(867) 872-2986 Fax 872-3550

SHAMAHQUAM FIRST NATION
General Delivery • Trout Lake, N.W.T. X0E 1E0
(867) 695-9800 Fax 695-2038
Edward Jumbo, Chief

TETLIT GWICH'IN COUNCIL
P.O. Box 30 • Fort McPherson, NT X0E 0J0
(867) 952-2330 Fax 952-2212
James Ross, Chief

WEST POINT FIRST NATION
#1-47031 Mackenzie Hwy.
Hay River, NT X0E 0R9
(867) 874-6677 Fax 874-6677

WHA'TI FIRST NATION
P.O. Box 92 • Wha'Ti, NT X0E 1P0
(867) 573-3012 Fax 573-3075
Isidore Zoe, Chief

YELLOWKNIVES DENE BAND (DETTAH)
P.O. Box 2514 • Yellowknife, NT X1A 2P8
(403) 873-4307 Fax 873-5969
Jonas Sangris, Chief

YELLOWKNIVES DENE BAND (NDILO)
P.O. Box 2514 • Yellowknife, NT X1A 2P8
(403) 873-8951 Fax 873-8545
Darrel Beaulieu, Chief

INUIT

AKLAVIK HAMLET
P.O. Box 88 • Aklavik, NT X0E 0A0
(867) 978-2351 Fax 978-2834

ARCTIC BAY HAMLET
General Delivery • Arctic Bay, NT X0A 0A0
(867) 439-9917 Fax 439-8767

ARCTIC RED RIVER SETTLEMENT
General Delivery • Arctic Red River, NT X0E 0B0
(867) 953-3201 Fax 953-3302
Peter Ross, Chief

ARVIAT HAMLET
General Delivery • Arviat, NT X0C 0E0
(867) 857-2841 Fax 857-2519

BAKER LAKE HAMLET
P.O. Box 149 • Baker Lake, NT X0C 0A0
(867) 793-2874 Fax 793-2509

BATHURST INLET
Cambridge Bay, NT X0C 0C0
(867) 983-7262

HAMLET OF BROUGHTON ISLAND
General Delivery • Broughton Island, NT X0A 0B0
(867) 927-8832 Fax 927-8120

CAMBRIDGE BAY HAMLET
P.O. Box 16 • Cambridge Bay, NT X0E 0C0
(867) 983-2337 Fax 983-2193

CAPE DORSET HAMLET
General Delivery • Cape Dorset, NT X0A 0C0
(867) 897-8943 Fax 897-8030

CHESTERFIELD INLET HAMLET
General Delivery
Chesterfield Inlet, NT X0C 0B0
(867) 898-9951 Fax 898-9108

CLYDE RIVER HAMLET
General Delivery • Clyde River, NT X0A 0E0
(867) 924-6220 Fax 924-6293

COPPERMINE HAMLET
P.O. Box 271 • Coppermine, NT X0E 0E0
(867) 982-4471 Fax 982-3060

CORAL HARBOUR HAMLET
General Delivery
Coral Harbour, NT X0C 0C0
(867) 925-8867 FAX 925-8233

HAMLET OF GJOA HAVEN
General Delivery • Gjoa Haven, NT X0E 1J0
(867) 360-7141 Fax 360-6309

HAMLET OF HALL BEACH
General Delivery • Hall Beach, NT X0A 0K0
(867) 928-8829 Fax 928-8945

HAMLET OF FORT FRANKLIN (DELINE)
Mayor Gina Dolphus • Deline, NT X0E 0G0
(867) 589-4800 FAX 589-4106
Raymond Taniton, Chief

HAMLET OF HOLMAN
General Delivery • Holman, NT X0E 0S0
(867) 396-3511 Fax 396-3256

HAMLET OF IGLOOLIK
General Delivery • Igloolik, NT X0A 0T0
(867) 934-8700 Fax 934-8757

LAKE HARBOUR HAMLET
General Delivery • Lake Harbour, NT X0A 0N0
(867) 939-2247 Fax 939-2045

MUNICIPAL OF SANIKILUAQ
General Delivery • Sanikiluaq, NT X0A 0W0
(867) 266-8874 Fax 266-8903

HAMLET OF PANGNIRTUNG
P.O. Box 253 • Pangnirtung, NT X0A 0R0
(867) 473-8953 Fax 473-8832

HAMLET OF PAULATUK
General Delivery • Paulatuk, NT X0E 1N0
(867) 580-3531 Fax 580-3703

HAMLET OF PELLY BAY
General Delivery • Pelly Bay, NT X0E 1K0
(867) 769-6281 Fax 769-6069

HAMLET OF POND INLET
General Delivery • Pond Inlet, NT X0A 0S0
(867) 899-8934 Fax 899-8940

HAMLET OF RANKIN INLET
General Delivery • Rankin Inlet, NT X0C 0G0
(867) 645-2953 Fax 645-2146

HAMLET OF REPULSE BAY
Repulse Bay, NT X0C 0H0
(867) 462-9952 Fax 462-4144

HAMLET OF RESOLUTE BAY
General Delivery • Resolute Bay, NT X0A 0V0
(867) 252-3616 Fax 252-3749

HAMLET OF SACHS HARBOUR
General Delivery • Sachs Harbour, NT X0E 0Z0
(867) 690-4351 Fax 690-4802

HAMLET OF TALOYOAK
General Delivery • Taloyoak, NT X0E 1B0
(867) 561-6341 Fax 561-5057

HAMLET OF TUKTOYAKTUT
P.O. Box 120 • Tuktoyaktut, NT X0E 1C0
(867) 977-2286 Fax 977-2110

HAMLET OF WHALE COVE
General Delivery • Whale Cove, NT X0C 0J0
(867) 896-9961 Fax 896-9109

METIS NON-STATUS

HAY RIVER METIS ASSOCIATION
St. 1 - 8 Gagnier St. • Hay River, NT X0E 1G1
(867) 896-9961 Fax 874-6888

NOVA SCOTIA

FIRST NATIONS

ACADIA FIRST NATION (Main Office)
RR 4, P.O. Box 5914C • Yarmouth, NS B5A 4A8
(902) 742-0257 Fax 742-8854
Diana D. Robinson, Chief
Head Office: South Brookfield,
Queens Co., NS B0T 1X0
(902) 682-2150 Fax 682-3112

AFTON FIRST NATION
RR 1 • Afton, NS B0H 1A0
(902) 386-2881 Fax 386-2043
Noel Francis, Chief

ANNAPOLIS VALLEY FIRST NATION
P.O. Box 89 • Cambridge Station, NS B0P 1G0
(902) 538-7149 Fax 538-7734
Lawrence Leo Toney, Chief

BEAR RIVER FIRST NATION
P.O. Box 210 • Bear River, NS B0S 1B0
(902) 467-3802 Fax 467-4143
Frank S. Meuse, Jr., Chief

CHAPEL ISLAND FIRST NATION
P.O. Box 538 • St. Peters, NS B0E 3B0
(902) 535-3317 Fax 535-3004
George W. Johnson, Chief

ESKASONI FIRST NATION
RR 2, East Bay • Cape Breton, NS B0A 1H0
(902) 379-2800 Fax 379-2172
Leonard Paul, Chief

HORTON FIRST NATION
P.O. Box 449 • Hantsport, NS B0P 1P0
(902) 684-9788 Fax 684-9890
Joseph B. Peters, Chief

INDIAN BROOK FIRST NATION
P.O. Box 350 • Shubenacadie, NS B0N 2H0
(902) 758-2049 Fax 758-2017
Stephen J. Knockwood, Chief

MEMBERTOU FIRST NATION
111 Membertou St. • Sydney, NS B1S 2M9
(902) 564-6466 Fax 539-6645
Terrance Paul, Chief

MILLBROOK FIRST NATION
P.O. Box 634 • Truro, NS B2N 5E5
(902) 897-9199 Fax 893-4785
Lawrence Alexander Paul, Chief

PICTOU LANDING FIRST NATION
Site 6, Box 55, RR2 • Trenton, NS B0K 1X0
(902) 752-4912 Fax 755-4715

WAGMATCOOK FIRST NATION
P.O. Box 237 • Baddeck, NS B0E 1B0
(902) 295-2598 Fax 295-3398
Francis Pierro, Chief

WHYCOCOMAGH FIRST NATION
P.O. Box 149 • Whycocomagh, N.S. B0E 3M0
(902) 756-2337/2440 Fax 756-2060
Roderick A. Googoo, Chief

ONTARIO

FIRST NATIONS

ALDERVILLE FIRST NATION
P.O. Box 4 • Roseneath, ON K0K 2X0
(905) 352-2011 Fax 352-3242
Nora Bothwell, Chief

ALGONQUINS OF PIKWAKANGAN FIRST NATION
P.O. Box 300 • Golden Lake, ON K0J 1X0
(613) 625-2800 Fax 625-2332
Clifford Milnese, Chief

AROLAND FIRST NATION
P.O. Box 390 • Nakina, ON P0T 2H0
(807) 329-5970 Fax 329-5750
William Magiskan, Chief

ANISHINABEK FIRST NATION
General Delivery • Grassy Narrows, ON P0X 1B0
(807) 329-5970 Fax 329-5750

ATTAWAPISKAT FIRST NATION
P.O. Box 248 • Attawapiskat, ON P0L 1A0
(705) 997-2166 Fax 997-2116
Reg Louttit, Chief

BEARSKIN LAKE FIRST NATION
P.O. Box 25 • Bearskin Lake, ON P0V 1E0
(807) 363-2518 Fax 363-1066
Steven Fiddler, Chief

BEAUSOLEIL FIRST NATION
Cedar Point P.O. • Christian Island, ON L0K 1C0
(705) 247-2051 Fax 247-2239
Jeffrey Monaque, Chief

BEAVERHOUSE FIRST NATION
P.O. Box 1022 • Kirkland lake, ON P2N 3L1
(705) 567-2022 Fax 567-1143
Isaac Mathias, Chief

BIG GRASSY FIRST NATION
General Delivery • Morson, ON P0W 1J0
(807) 488-5552 Fax 488-5533
Fred Copenace, Chief

BIG ISLAND FIRST NATION
General Delivery • Morson, ON P0W 1J0
(807) 488-5602 Fax 488-5942
Pauline Big George, Chief

BRUNSWICK HOUSE FIRST NATION
P.O. Box 1118 • Chapleau, ON P0M 1K0
(705) 864-0174 Fax 864-1960
Joseph Saunders, Sr., Chief

CALDWELL FIRST NATION
10297 Talbot Rd. • Blenheim, ON N0P 1A0
(519) 692-3442 Fax 695-3920
Larry Johnson, Chief

CAT LAKE FIRST NATION
2 Back Rd. West • Cat Lake, ON P0V 1J0
(807) 347-2100 Fax 347-2116
Albert Wesley, Chief

CHAPLEAU CREE FIRST NATION
P.O. Box 400 • Chapleau, ON P0M 1K0
(705) 864-0784 Fax 864-1760
Doreen Cachagee, Chief

CHAPLEAU OJIBWAY FIRST NATION
P.O. Box 279 • Chapleau, ON P0M 1K0
(705) 864-2910 Fax 864-2911
Joanne Nakogee, Chief

CHIPPEWAS OF GEORGINA ISLAND FIRST NATION
RR 2 Box 12 • Sutton West, ON L0E 1R0
(705) 437-1337 Fax 437-4597
Eric Charles, Chief

CHIPPEWAS OF KETTLE POINT & STONY POINT
RR 2, 55 Indian Lane • Forest, ON N0N 1J0
(519) 786-2125 Fax 786-2108
Thomas S. Bressette, Chief

CHIPPEWAS OF NAWASH FIRST NATION
RR 5 • Wiarton, ON N0H 2T0
(519) 534-1689 Fax 534-2130
Ralph Akiwenzie, Chief

CHIPPEWAS OF SARNIA
978 Tashmoo Ave. • Sarnia, ON N7T 7H5
(519) 336-8410 Fax 336-0382
Phillip Maness, Chief

CHIPPEWAS OF SAUGEEN
RR 1 • Southampton, ON N0H 2L0
(519) 797-2781 Fax 797-2978
Vernon Roote, Chief

CHIPPEWAS OF THE THAMES FIRST NATION
RR 1 • Muncey, ON N0L 1Y0
(519) 289-5555 Fax 289-2230
Delbert Riley, Chief

CONSTANCE LAKE FIRST NATION
General Delivery • Calstock, ON P0L 1B0
(705) 463-4511 Fax 463-2222
Mark Spence, Chief

COUCHICHING FIRST NATION
RRA#2, RMB 2027 • Fort Frances, ON P9A 3M3
(807) 274-3228 Fax 274-6458
Joan Mainville, Chief

CURVE LAKE FIRST NATION
P.O. Box 100 • Curve Lake, ON K0L 1R0
(705) 657-8045 Fax 657-8708
Mel Jacob, Chief

DEER LAKE FIRST NATION
Deer Lake, ON P0V 1N0
(807) 775-2141 Fax 775-2220
Fred Meekis, Chief

DELAWARE NATION (MORAVIAN OF THE THAMES)
RR #3 • Thamesville, ON N0P 2K0
(519) 692-3936 Fax 692-5522

DOKIS FIRST NATION
Dokis Bay • Monetville, ON P0M 2K0
(705) 763-2200 Fax 763-2087
Tim Restoule, Chief

EABAMETOONG FIRST NATION
P.O. Box 298 • Fort Hope, ON P0T 2H0
(807) 242-7361 Fax 242-1440
Harvey Yesno, Chief

EAGLE LAKE INDIAN BAND
P.O. Box 10 • Eagle River, ON P0V 1S0
(807) 755-5526 Fax 755-5696
Arnold Gardner, Chief

FLYING POST FIRST NATION
P.O. Box 460 • Nipigon, ON P0T 2J0
(807) 887-3071 Fax 887-1138
Frances Ray, Chief

FORT ALBANY FIRST NATION
P.O. Box 1 • Fort Albany, ON P0L 1H0
(705) 278-1044 Fax 278-1193
Edmund Metatawabin, Chief

FORT SEVERN FIRST NATION
Fort Severn, ON P0V 1W0
(807) 478-2572 Fax 478-1103
Elias (Ennis) Crow, Chief

FORT WILLIAM FIRST NATION
P.O. Box 786 • Thunder Bay, ON P7C 4W6
(807) 623-9543 Fax 623-5190
Christi Pervais, Chief

GARDEN RIVER FIRST NATION
P.O. Box 7, Site 5, RR 4
Graden River, ON P6A 5K9
(705) 946-6300 Fax 945-1415
Darrell E. Boissoneau, Chief

GINOOGAMING FIRST NATION
P.O. Box 89 • Long Lac, ON P0T 2A0
(807) 876-2242 Fax 876-2495
Leslie O'Nabigon, Chief

GULL BAY FIRST NATION
General Delivery • Gull Bay, ON P0T 1P0
(807) 982-2101 Fax 982-2290
John Roger King, Chief

HENVEY INLET FIRST NATION
General Delivery • Pickerel, ON P0G 1J0
(705) 857-2331 Fax 857-3021
Charlotte Contin, Chief

HIAWATHA FIRST NATION
RR#2 • Keene, ON K0L 2G0
(705) 295-4421 Fax 295-4424

HORNEPAYNE FIRST NATION
P.O. Box 1553 • Homepayne, ON P0M 1Z0
(807) 868-2040 Fax 868-2050
Dave Taylor, Chief

KASABONIKA LAKE FIRST NATION
P.O. Box 124 • Kasabonika, ON P0V 1Y0
(807) 535-2547 Fax 535-1152
Jeremiah McKay, Chief

KASHECHEWAN FIRST NATION
P.O. Box 240 • Kashechewan, ON P0L 1S0
(705) 275-4440 Fax 275-1023
Dan Koosees, Chief

KEE-WAY-WIN FIRST NATION
General Delivery • Sandy Lake, ON P0V 1V0
(807) 774-1210 (phone & fax)
Halum (Alijum) Kakepetum, Chief

KINGFISHER LAKE FIRST NATION
Kingfisher Lake, ON P0V 1Z0
(807) 532-2067 Fax 532-2063
James Mamawka, Chief

KITCHENUHWAYKOOSIB FIRST NATION
General Delivery
Big Trout Lake, ON P0V 1G0
(807) 537-2263 Fax 537-2574
Stanley Sainnawap, Chief

KOOCHECHING FIRST NATION
P.O. Box 32 • Sandy Lake, ON P0V 1V0
(807) 774-1576 Fax 774-1082

LAC DES MILLES LACS INDIAN BAND
3-116 Syndicate Ave.
Thunder Bay, ON P7E 1C6
(807) 622-4044 Fax 622-9655
Kevin Chicago, Chief

LAC LA CROIX FIRST NATION
P.O. Box 640 • Fort Frances, ON P9A 3N9
(807) 485-2431 Fax 485-2583
Steve Jourdain, Chief

LAC SEUL FIRST NATION
P.O. Box 100 • Lac Seul, ON P0V 2A0
(807) 582-3211 Fax 582-3493
Roger Southwind, Chief

LAKE HELEN FIRST NATION (RED ROCK)
P.O. Box 1030 • Nipigon, ON P0T 2J0
(807) 887-2510 Fax 887-3446
Betty Paakunainen, Chief

LAKE NIPIGON OJIBWAY FIRST NATION
P.O. Box 120 • Beardmore, ON P0T 1G0
(807) 875-2785 Fax 875-2786
Joseph Thompson, Chief

LONG LAKE #58 FIRST NATION
P.O. Box 609 • Long Lac, ON P0T 2A0
(807) 876-2292 Fax 876-2757
Sydney Abraham, Chief

MAGNETAWAN FIRST NATION
P.O. Box 15, RR 1 • Britt, ON P0G 1A0
(705) 383-2477 Fax 383-2566
Joan Noganosh, Chief

MARTIN FALLS FIRST NATION
Ogoki Post • Nakina, ON P0T 2L0
(807) 349-2509 Fax 349-2511
Eli Moonias, Chief

MATACHEWAN FIRST NATION
P.O. Box 208 • Matachewan, ON P0K 1M0
(705) 565-2230 Fax 565-2585
Barnie Batisse, Chief

MATTAGAMI FIRST NATION
P.O. Box 99 • Gogama, ON P0M 1W0
(705) 894-2072 Fax 894-2887
GeraldLuke, Chief

McDOWELL LAKE FIRST NATION
P.O. Box 740 • Red Lake, ON P0V 2M0
(807) 727-1168 (phone & fax)
Albert James, Chief

MICHIPICOTEN FIRST NATION
P.O. Box 1, Site 8, RR 1 • Wawa, ON P0S 1K0
(705) 856-4455 Fax 856-1642
Evelyn Stone, Chief

MISSANABIE CREE FIRST NATION
RR#4 Hwy 17E, Bell's Point
Garden River, ON P6A 5K9
(705) 254-2702 Fax 254-3292
Arthur Nolan, Spokesperson

MISSISSAUGA #8 FIRST NATION
P.O. Box 1299 • Blind River, ON P0R 1B0
(705) 356-1621 Fax 356-1740
Douglas Daybutch, Chief

MISSISSAUGAS OF NEW CREDIT NATION
RR #6 • Hagersville, ON N0A 1H0
(905) 768-1133 Fax 768-1225
Maurice LaForme, Chief

MISSISSAUGAS OF SCUGOG NATION
RR #5 • Port Perry, ON L9L 1B6
(905) 985-3337 Fax 985-8828
Yvonne Edgar, Chief

MNJIKANING FIRST NATION (RAMA)
P.O. Box 35 • Rama, ON L0K 1T0
(705) 325-3611 Fax 325-0879

MOCREBEC INDIAN GOVERNMENT
P.O. Box 4 • Moose Factory, ON P0L 1W0
(705) 658-4769 Fax 658-4487
Randy

MOHAWKS OF AKWESASNE FIRST NATION
P.O. Box 579 • Cornwall, ON K6H 5T3
(613) 575-2250 Fax 575-2181
Michael Mitchell, Chief

MOHAWKS OF THE BAY OF QUINTE
RR 1 • Deseronto, ON K0K 1X0
(613) 396-3424 Fax 396-3627
Earl Hill, Chief

MOOSE CREE FIRST NATION
P.O. Box 190 • Moose Factory, ON P0L 1W0
(705) 658-4619 Fax 658-4734
Norman F. Wesley, Chief

MOOSE DEER POINT FIRST NATION
P.O. Box 119 • Mactier, ON P0C 1H0
(705) 375-5209 Fax 375-0532
Edward Williams, Chief

MUNSEE-DELAWARE NATION FIRST NATION
RR 1 • Muncey, ON N0L 1Y0
(519) 289-5396 Fax 289-5156
Leroy Dolson, Chief

MUSKRAT DAM FIRST NATION
General Delivery
Muskrat Dam, ON P0V 3B0
(807) 471-2573 Fax 471-2540
Frank Beardy, Chief

NAICATCHEWENIN FIRST NATION
P.O. Box 15, RR 1 • Devlin, ON P0W 1C0
(807) 486-3407 Fax 486-3704
Roseanna Councillor, Chief

NEW POST FIRST NATION
RR #2, Box 3310 • Cochrane, ON P0L 1C0
(705) 272-5685 Fax 272-6352
Peter Archibald, Sr., Chief

NIBINAMIK FIRST NATION
Via Pickle Lake
Summer Beaver, ON P0T 3B0
(807) 593-2131 Fax 593-2270
Sandy Yellowhead, Chief

NICIKOUSEMENECANING FIRST NATION
P.O. Box 68 • Fort Francis, ON P9A 3M5
(807) 481-2536 Fax 481-2511
Kelvin Morrison, Chief

NIPISSING FIRST NATION
RR #1 • Sturgeon Falls, ON P0H 2G0
(705) 753-2050 Fax 753-0207
Phil Goulais, Chief
Tribe in residence: Ojibway. *In residence*: 1,971.
Area: 52,000 acres. *Activities*: Annual Pow-wow,
feast, elders gathering. Library.

NISHNAWBE-ASKI NATION
P.O. Box 755 • Thunder bay, ON P7C 4W6
(807) 623-8228 Fax 623-7730
Bentley Cheechoo, Grand Chief

NORTH CARIBOU LAKE FIRST NATION
Weagamow Lake, ON P0V 2Y0
(807) 469-5191 Fax 469-1315
Caleb Sakchekapo, Chief

NORTH SPIRIT LAKE FIRST NATION
Box 70 • Cochenour, ON P0V 1L0
Peter Campbell, Chief

NORTHWEST ANGLE #33 FIRST NATION
Angle Inlet, MN 56711
(807) 733-2200 Fax 733-3148
Kenneth Sandy, Chief

NORTHWEST ANGLE #37 FIRST NATION
P.O. Box 267 • Sioux Narrows, ON P0X 1N0
(807) 226-5353 Fax 226-1164
Joseph Powassin, Chief

**OCHIICHAGWE BABIGO'INING
(DALLAS) FIRST NATION**
P.O. Box 88 • Kenora, ON P9N 3X7
(807) 759-0914 Fax 759-9171

OJIBWAYS OF BATCHEWANA FIRST NATION
236 Frontenac St.
Sault Ste. Marie, ON P6A 5K9
(705) 759-0914 Fax 759-9171
Harvey Bell, Chief

OJIBWAYS OF HIAWATHA FIRST NATION
RR #2 • Keene, ON K0L 2G0
(705) 295-4421 Fax 295-4424
Frank Frank Cowie, Chief

OJIBWAYS OF ONEGAMING FIRST NATION
P.O. Box 160 • Nestor Falls, ON P0X 1K0
(807) 484-2162 Fax 484-2737
Anthony Copenace, Chief

OJIBWAYS OF THE PIC RIVER FIRST NATION
General Delivery • Heron Bay, ON P0T 1R0
(807) 229-1749 Fax 229-1944
Roy Michano, Chief

OJIBWAYS OF SUCKER CREEK FIRST NATION
RR #1, Box 21 • Little Current, ON P0P 1K0
(705) 368-2228 Fax 368-3563
Patrick Madahbee, Chief

OJIBWAYS OF WALPOLE ISLAND
RR #3 • Wallaceburg, ON N8A 1R0
(519) 627-1481 Fax 627-0440
Robert L. Williams, Chief

ONEIDA NATION OF THE THAMES
RR #2 • Southwold, ON N0L 2G0
(519) 652-3244 Fax 652-9287
Alfred L. Day, Chief

PAYS PLAT FIRST NATION
P.O. Box 849 • Schreiber, ON P0T 2S0
(807) 824-2541 Fax 824-2206
Aime Bouchard, Chief

PIC MOBERT FIRST NATION
General Delivery • Mobert, ON P0M 2J0
(807) 822-2131/4
James Kwissiwa, Chief

PIKANGIKUM FIRST NATION
Pikangikum, ON P0V 2L0
(807) 773-5578 Fax 773-5536
John James Suggashie, Chief

POPLAR HILL FIRST NATION
P.O. Box 315 • Poplar Hill, ON P0V 2M0
(807) 772-8838 Fax 772-8876
Gary Owen, Chief

RAINY RIVER FIRST NATION
P.O. Box 450 • Emo, ON P0W 1E0
(807) 482-2479 Fax 482-2603
Willie Wilson, Chief

RED ROCK FIRST NATION
P.O. Box 1030 • Nipigon, ON P0T 2J0
(807) 887-2510 Fax 887-3446

ROCKY BAY FIRST NATION
MacDiarmid, ON P0T 2P0
(807) 885-3401 Fax 885-3231
James Hardy, Chief

SACHIGO LAKE FIRST NATION
Sachigo Lake, ON P0V 2P0
(807) 595-2577 Fax 595-1119
Titus Tait, Chief

SAGAMOK ANISHNAWBEK FIRST NATION
P.O. Box 610 • Massey, ON P0P 1P0
(705) 865-2421 Fax 865-3307
Nelson Toulouse, Chief

SAND POINT FIRST NATION
600 Victoria Ave. • Thunder Bay, ON P7C 5Y7
(807) 344-3841 Fax 344-4593
Dan R. McGuire, Chief

SANDY LAKE FIRST NATION
Sandy Lake, ON P0V 1V0
(807) 774-3421 Fax 774-1040
Jonas Fiddler, Chief

SAUGEEN FIRST NATION
General Delivery
Savant Lake, ON P0V 2S0
(807) 584-2989 Fax 584-2243
Edward Machimity, Chief

SEINE RIVER FIRST NATION
P.O. Box 124 • Mine Centre, ON P0W 1H0
(807) 599-2224 Fax 599-2865
Andrew Johnson, Chief

SERPENT RIVER FIRST NATION
48 Indian Rd. • Cutler, ON P0P 1B0
(705) 844-2418 Fax 844-2757
Earl Commanda, Chief

SHAWANAGA FIRST NATION
RR #1 • Nobel, ON P0G 1G0
(705) 366-2526 Fax 366-2740
Howard Pamajewon, Chief

SHEGUIANDAH FIRST NATION
P.O. Box 101 • Sheguiandah, ON P0P 1W0
(705) 368-2781 Fax 368-3697
Maxie Assinewai, Chief

SHESHEGWANING FIRST NATION
P.O. Box C-1 • Sheshegwaning, ON P0P 1X0
(705) 283-3292 Fax 283-3481
Joseph Endanawas, Chief

SHOAL LAKE No. 40 FIRST NATION
Kejick P.O. • Shoal Lake, ON P0X 1E0
(807) 733-2315 Fax 733-3115
Lloyd Redsky, Chief

SIX NATIONS OF THE GRAND RIVER FIRST NATION
P.O. Box 5000 • Ohsweken, ON N0A 1M0
(519) 445-2201 Fax 445-4208
Roberta Jamieson, Chief
Canada's most populous Aboriginal community.

SLAT FALLS FIRST NATION
General Delivery • Slate Falls, ON P0V 3C0

STANJIKOMING FIRST NATION
Box 609 • Fort Frances, ON P9A 3M9
(807) 274-2188 Fax 274-4774
Janice Henderson, Chief

TEMAGAMI FIRST NATION
Bear Island P.O., ON P0H 1C0
(705) 237-8943 Fax 237-8959
Gary Potts, Chief

THESSALON FIRST NATION
P.O. Box 9, R.R. #2
Thessalon, ON P0R 1L0
(705) 842-2323 Fax 842-2332
Alfred Bisaillon, Chief

WABAUSKANG FIRST NATION
Box 418 • Ear Falls, ON P0V 1T0
(807) 529-3174 Fax 529-3007
Barney Petiquan, Chief

WABIGOON LAKE OJIBWAY FIRST NATION
Site 112, Box 24
Dinorwic P.O., ON P0V 1P0
(807) 938-6684 Fax 938-1166
John Kooshet, Chief

WAHGOSHIG FIRST NATION
P.O. Box 722 • Matheson, ON P0K 1N0
(705) 567-4891 (phone & fax)
Clifford Diamond, Chief

WAHNAPITAE FIRST NATION
P.O. Box 1119 • Capreal, ON P0M 1H0
(705) 858-0610 Fax 693-7987
Norman Recollect, Chief

WAHTA MOHAWKS
P.O. Box 327 • Bala, ON P0C 1A0
(705) 762-3343 Fax 762-5744

WAPEKEKA INDIAN BAND
Angling Lake, ON P0V 1B0
(807) 537-2315 Fax 537-2336
Norman Brown, Chief

WASAUKSING FIRST NATION (PARRY ISLAND)
P.O. Box 253 • Parry Sound, ON P2A 2X4
(705) 746-2531 Fax 746-5984
John I. Rice, Chief

WASHAGAMIS BAY INDIAN BAND
General Delivery • Keewatin, ON P0X 1C0
(807) 543-2532 Fax 543-2964
Alfred Sinclair, Chief

WAUZHUSHIK ONIGUM FIRST NATION
P.O. Box 1850 • Kenora, ON P9N 3X7
(807) 548-5663 Fax 548-4877
George Kakeway, Chief

WAWAKAPEWIN FIRST NATION
Long Dog Lake, ON P0V 1G0
(807) 442-2567
Jermiah Nanokeesic, Chief

WEBEQUI FIRST NATION
P.O. Box 176 • Webequi, ON P0T 3A0
(807) 353-6531 Fax 353-1218
Roy Spence, Chief

WEENUSK FIRST NATION
P.O. Box 1 • Peawanuck, ON P0L 2H0
(705) 473-2554 Fax 473-2503
Joseph Bird, Chief

WEST BAY FIRST NATION
P.O. Box 2 • West Bay, ON P0P 1G0
(705) 377-5362 Fax 377-4980
Stewart Roy, Chief

WHITEFISH LAKE FIRST NATION
P.O. Box 39 • Naughton, ON P0M 2M0
(705) 692-3423 Fax 692-5010
Larry Naponse, Chief

WHITEFISH RIVER FIRST NATION
General Delivery • Birch Island, ON P0P 1A0
(705) 285-4335 Fax 285-4532
Leona Nahwegahbow, Chief

WHITESAND FIRST NATION
P.O. Box 68 • Armstrong, ON P0T 1A0
(807) 583-2177 Fax 583-2170
Doug Sinoway, Chief

WHITEWATER LAKE FIRST NATION
RR#4, 115A Mountain Rd.
Thunder Bay, ON P7C 4Z4
(807) 622-0894 Fax 622-0687

WIKWEMIKONG FIRST NATION
P.O. Box 112 • Wikwemikong, ON P0P 2J0
(705) 859-3122 Fax 859-3851
Henry Peltier, Chief

WUNNUMIN LAKE FIRST NATION
P.O. Box 105 • Wunnumin Lake, ON P0V 2Z0
(807) 442-2555 Fax 442-2627
Simon Winnepetonga, Chief

ZHIIBAAHAASING (COCKBURN ISLAND) FIRST NATION
General Delivery • Silverwater, ON P0P 1Y0
(705) 283-3963 Fax 283-3964

METIS NON-STATUS

METIS NATION OF ONTARIO
141 Holland Ave. • Ottawa, ON K1Y 0Y2
(800) 263-4889; (613) 798-1488 Fax 722-4225
E-mail: tonyb@metisnation.con.ca
Web site: www.metistraing.org

METIS NATIONAL COUNCIL
350 Sparks St. #309 • Ottawa, ON K1P 7S9
(613) 232-3216 Fax 232-4262
E-mail: mnc@storm.ca
Web site: www.sae.ca/mbc

PRINCE EDWARD ISLAND

FIRST NATIONS

ABEGWEIT INDIAN BAND
P.O. Box 220 • Cornwall, PEI C0A 1H0
(902) 675-3842 Fax 892-3420
George James Sark, Chief

LENNOX ISLAND FIRST NATION
P.O. Box 134 • Lennox Island, PEI C0B 1P0
(902) 831-2779 Fax 831-3153
Jack J.T. Sark, Chief

QUEBEC

FIRST NATIONS

ABENAKIS DE WOLINAK
Reserve indienne de Wolinak
4850, rue Mikowa • Becancour, PQ G0X 1B0
(819) 294-6696 Fax 294-6697
Raymond Bernard, Chief

ABITIBIWINNI (ALGONQUIN)
45, rue Migwan • Pikogan, PQ J9T 3A3
(819) 732-6591 Fax 732-1569
Harry McDougall, Chief

ATTIKAMEKS DE MANOUANE
135, Kicik • Manouane, PQ J0K 1M0
(819) 971-8813 Fax 971-8848
Henri Ottawa, Chief

BARRIERE LAKE (ALGONQUIN) FIRST NATION
Rapid Lake
Parc de la Verendrye, PQ J0W 2C0
(819) 824-1734 (phone & fax)
Jean-Maurice Matchewan, Chief

CONSEIL DES BANDE DES BETSIAMITES
2, Rue Ashini, CP 40
Betsiamites, P.Q. G0H 1B0
(418) 567-2265 Fax 567-8528
Jean-Louis Bacon, Chief

CREE NATION OF CHISASIBI
P.O. Box 150 • Chisasibi, P.Q. J0M 1E0
(819) 855-2878 Fax 855-2875
Violet Pachano, Chief

CONSEIL DE BANDE D'OBEDJIWAN
Reserve Indienne d'Obedjiwan
Via Roberval, PQ G0W 3B0
(819) 974-8837 Fax 974-8828
Paul Mequish, Chief

CONSEIL DE BANDE D'ODANAK
102, rue Sibosis • Odanak, PQ J0G 1H0
(514) 568-2810 Fax 568-3553

CREE NATION OF EASTMAIN
Eastmain, PQ J0M 1W0
(819) 977-0211 Fax 977-0281
Ted Moses, Chief

CONSEIL DE BANDE DE GASPE (MICMAC)
P.O. Box 69, Fontenelle • Gaspe, PQ G0E 1H0
(418) 368-6005 Fax 368-1272
Placide Jeannotte, Chief

GRAND LAC VICTORIA (ALGONQUIN)
C.P. 35 • Louvicourt, PQ J0Y 1Y0
(819) 825-1466 Fax 824-1931
Henri Papatisse, Chief

KENESATAKE MOHAWK NATION
681 Ste. Philomene • Kanesatake, PQ J0N 1E0
(514) 479-8373 Fax 479-8249
James Gabriel, Grand Chief

EAGLE VILLAGE FIRST NATION KIPAWA (ALGONQUIN)
P.O. Box 756 • Eagle Village, PQ J0Z 3R0
(819) 627-3455 Fax 627-9428
Jimmy Constant, Chief

KITIGAN ZIBI ANISHINABEG FIRST NATION
P.O. Box 309 • Maniwaki, PQ J9E 3C9
(819) 449-5170 Fax 449-5673
Jean-Guy Whiteduck, Chief

LAC SIMON (ALGONQUIN) FIRST NATION
Lac Simon, PQ J0Y 3M0
(819) 736-4501 Fax 736-7311
Louis Jerome, Chief
Centre Amikwan-Jeanette Papatie, Coordinator

LONG POINT (ALGONQUIN) FIRST NATION
P.O. Box 1 • Winneway River, PQ J0Z 2J0
(819) 722-2441 Fax 722-2579
Jerry Polson, Chief

LES ATIKAMEKW DE MANOUANE
331, rue Simon Ottawa
Manouane, PQ J0K 1M0
(819) 971-8813 Fax 971-8848
Henri Ottawa, Chief

MICMACS OF GESGAPEGIAG
Maria Indian Reserve
P.O. Box 1280 • Maria, PQ G0C 1Y0
(418) 759-3441/2 Fax 759-5856
Douglas Martin, Chief
John Martin, Education Director

BANDE INDIENNE DE MINGAN
P.O. Box 319 • Mingan, PQ G0G 1V0
(418) 949-2234
Jean-Charles Pietacho, Chief

MISTISSINI INDIAN BAND
187 Main St. • Mistissini , PQ G0W 1C0
(418) 923-3461 Fax 923-3115
Henry Mianscum, Chief

MOHAWKS OF KAHNAWAKE
P.O. Box 720 • Kahnawake, PQ J0L 1B0
(514) 632-7500 Fax 638-5958
Joseph Norton, Grand Chief
Grand Chief and 11 council chiefs. *Tribe served*:
Mohawk of the Six Nations Iroquois Confederacy. *In residence*: 5,500. *Total acreage*: 12,500. *Boundaries*: Triangular i shape, bounded on north by St. Lawrence River with survey boundaries east & west. *Special programs*: Social services; alcohol and drug abuse prevention; heath services program; social assistance; economic and financial services; community development; human resource development. Mohawk Council.

CONSEIL DES MONTAGNAIS DES ESCOUMINS
27, rue de la Reserve, C.P. 820
Les Escoumins, PQ G0T 1K0
(418) 233-2509 Fax 233-2888
Denis Ross, Chief

CONSEIL DES MONTAGNAIS DE LA ROMAINE
La Romaine, PQ G0G 1M0
(418) 229-2917 Fax 229-2921
Georges Bacon, Chief

CONSEIL DES MONTAGNAIS DE PUKUA SHIPI
St-Augustin, PQ G0G 2R0
(418) 947-2253 Fax 947-2622
Charles Mark, Chief

CONSEIL DES MONTAGNAIS DE SCHEFFERVILLE
C.P. 1390 • Schefferville, PQ G0G 2T0
(418) 585-2601 Fax 585-3856
Alexandre McKenzie, Chief

CONSEIL DES MONTAGNAIS DE UASHAT ET MALIOTENAM
1084 Rue dequen, C.P. 4000
Sept-Iles, PQ G4R 4L9
(418) 968-0107 Fax 968-0937
Elie Jacques Jourdain, Chief

CONSEIL DES MONTAGNAIS DE NATASHQUAN
Natashquan, PQ G0G 2E0
(418) 726-3529
Joseph Tettaut, Chief

CONSEIL DES MONTAGNAIS DU LAC ST-JEAN
1671, rue Quiatchouan
Mashteuiatsh, PQ G0W 2H0
(418) 275-2473 Fax 275-6212
Remi Kurtness, Chief

CONSEIL DES NASKAPIS OF SCHEFFERVILLE INDIAN BAND
P.O. Box 1390
Schefferville, PQ G0G 2T0
(418) 585-2601 Fax 585-3856
Alexandre McKenzie, Chief

CONSEIL DE LA NATION HURONNE-WENDAT
255, Place Chef Michel Laveau
Wendake, PQ G0A 4V0
(418) 843-3767 Fax 842-1108
Max (Magella) Gros-Louis, Grand Chief
Elected chiefs: Roger Picard, Reine Laine, Rene Duchesneau, Arold Bastien, Michel Picard, Raymond Gros Louis. *Tribe served*: Huron - Wendat. *In residence*: 850. *Total acreage*: 300. School and museum.

NEMASKA (CREE) INDIAN BAND
Lac Champion • Nemiscau, PQ J0Y 3B0
(819) 673-2512 Fax 673-2542
Lawrence Jimiken, Chief

CONSEIL DES D'OBEDJIWAN
Reserve indienne d'Obedjiwan
Obedjiwan, PQ G0W 3B0
(819) 974-8837 Fax 974-8828
Hubert Clary, Chief

ODANAK (ABENAQUIS)
58, rue Wabanaki • Odanak, PQ J0G 1H0
(514) 568-2810 Fax 568-3553
Albert O'Bomsawin, Chief

CREE NATION OF WEMINDJI
P.O. Box 60 • Wemindji, PQ J0M 1L0
(819) 978-0264 Fax 978-0258
Walter Hughboy, Chief

RESTIGOUCHE (MICMAC) INDIAN BAND
P.O. Box 298, 17 Riverside West
Listujug, PQ G0C 2R0
(418) 788-2136 Fax 788-2058
Ronald Jacques, Chief

TEMISKAMING (ALGONQUIN) FIRST NATION
P.O. Box 336
Notre-Dame-Du-Nord, PQ J0Z 3B0
(819) 723-2335 Fax 723-2353
Carol McBride, Chief

PREMIER NATION OF MALECITE DE VIGER
112, Avenue de la Greve, c.p. 10
Cacouna, PQ G0L 1G0
(418) 860-2393 Fax 867-3418
Gaetane Aubin, Grand Chief

CREE NATION OF WASKAGANISH
P.O. Box 60 • Waskaganish, PQ J0M 1R0
(819) 895-8650 Fax 895-8901
Billy Diamond, Chief

CREE NATION OF WASWANIPI
Waswanipi River, PQ J0Y 3C0
(819) 753-2587 Fax 753-2555
Allan Happyjack, Chief

BANDE INDIENNE DE WEYMONTACHIE
Reserve indienne de Weymontachie
Comte Laviolette, PQ G0A 4M0
(819) 974-8837 Fax 974-8828
Marcel Boivin, Chief

WHAPMAGOOSTUI CREE NATION
P.O. Box 390 • Hudson Bay, PQ J0M 1G0
(819) 929-3384 Fax 929-3203
Robbie Dick, Chief

WOLF LAKE FIRST NATION
P.O. Box 998
Temiscamingue, PQ J0Z 3R0
(819) 627-3628 627-9428
Harold St. Denis, Chief

INUIT

VILLAGE OF AKULIVIK
P.O. Box 61 • Akulivik, PQ J0M 1V0
(819) 496-2552 Fax 496-2200

VILLAGE OF AUPALUK
Aupaluk, PQ J0m 1X0
(819) 491- 7005 Fax 491-7035

VILLAGE OF INUKJUAK
P.O. Box 254 • Inukjuak, PQ J0m 1M0
(819) 254-8845 Fax 254-8779

VILLAGE OF IVUJIVIK
P.O. Box 120 • Ivujivik, PQ J0m 1H0
(819) 922-9944 Fax 922-3045

VILLAGE OF KANGIQSUJJUAQ
P.O. Box 60 • Kangiqsujjuaq, PQ J0m 1K0
(819) 338-3342 Fax 338-3237

VILLAGE OF KANGIQSUALUJJUAQ
Kangiqualujjuaq, PQ J0m 1N0
(819) 337-5271 Fax 337-5200

VILLAGE OF KANGIRSUK
P.O. Box 90 • Kangirsuk, PQ J0M 1A0
(819) 935-4388 Fax 935-4287

REGIONAL GOVERNMENT OF KATIVIK
C.P. 9 • Kuujjuaq, PQ J0M 1C0
(819) 964-2961 Fax 261-2956

NORTHERN VILLAGE OF CHISASIBI
P.O. Box 92 • Chisasibi, PQ J0m 1E0
(819) 855-2657 Fax 855-2875

NORTHERN VILLAGE OF PUVIRNITUQ
Puvirnituk, PQ J0M 1P0
(819) 988-2828 Fax 988-2751

NORTHERN VILLAGE OF QUAQTAQ
P.O. Box 107 • Quaqtaq, PQ J0M 1J0
(819) 492-9912 Fax 492-9935

NORTHERN VILLAGE OF SALLUIT
P.O. Box 240 • Salluit, PQ J0M 1S0
(819) 255-8953 Fax 255-8802

NORTHERN VILLAGE OF TASIUJAQ
Tasiujaq, PQ J0M 1T0
(819) 633-9924 Fax 633-5026

NORTHERN VILLAGE OF UMIUJAQ
P.O. Box 108 • Umiujaq, PQ J0M 1Y0
(819) 331-7000 Fax 331-7057

SASKATCHEWAN

FIRST NATIONS

AHTAHKAKOOP BAND OF THE CREE NATION
P.O. Box 220 • Shell Lake, SK S0J 2G0
(306) 468-2326 Fax 468-2344
Barry Ahenakew, Chief

ASIMAKANISEEKAN ASKIY RESERVE
100 103A Packham Ave.
Saskatoon, SK S7N 4K4
(306) 374-8118 Fax 374-7377

BEARDY'S & OKAMASIS FIRST NATION
P.O. Box 340 • Duck Lake, SK S0K 1J0
(306) 467-4523 Fax 467-4404
Richard J.H. Gamble, Chief

BIG RIVER INDIAN BAND
P.O. Box 519 • Debden, SK S0J 0S0
(306) 724-4700 Fax 724-2161
John Keenatch, Chief

BIRCH NARROWS FIRST NATION
Tumor Lake, SK S0M 3E0
(306) 894-2030 Fax 894-2060
Jean Campbell, Chief

BLACK LAKE DENESULINE NATION
P.O. Box 27 • Black Lake, SK S0J 0H0
(306) 284-2044 Fax 284-2101
Daniel Robillard, Chief

BUFFALO RIVER FIRST NATION
General Delivery • Dillon, SK S0M 0S0
(306) 282-2033 Fax 282-2102
Gordon Billette, Chief

CANOE LAKE CREE NATION
General Delivery • Canoe Narrows, SK S0M 0K0
(306) 829-2150 Fax 829-2101
Frank Iron, Chief

CARRY THE KETTLE FIRST NATION
P.O. Box 57 • Sintaluta, SK S0G 4N0
(306) 727-2135 Fax 727-2149
James L. O'Watch, Chief

CLEARWATER RIVER DENE NATION
P.O. Box 389 • La Loche, SK S0M 1G0
(306) 822-2021 Fax 822-2212
Frank Piche, Chief

COTE FIRST NATION
P.O. Box 1659 • Kamsack, SK S0A 1S0
(306) 542-2694 Fax 542-3735
Hector Badger, Chief

COWESSESS FIRST NATION
P.O. Box 100 • Cowessess, SK S0G 5L0
(306) 696-2520 Fax 696-2767
Lionel Sparvier, Chief

CUMBERLAND HOUSE CREE NATION
P.O. Box 220 • Cumberland House, SK S0E 0S0
(306) 888-2226 Fax 888-2084
Pierre Settee, Chief

DAY STAR FIRST NATION
P.O. Box 277 • Punnichy, SK S0A 3C0
(306) 835-2834 Fax 835-2724
Cameron Kinequon, Chief

ENGLISH RIVER FIRST NATION
General Delivery • Patuanak, SK S0M 2H0
(306) 396-2055 Fax 396-2155
Louis George, Jr., Chief

FISHING LAKE FIRST NATION
P.O. Box 508 • Wadena, SK S0A 4J0
(306) 338-3838 Fax 338-3635
Allan Paquachan, Chief

FLYING DUST FIRST NATION
8001 Flying Dust Reserve
Meadow Lake, SK S0M 1V0
(306) 236-4437 Fax 236-3373
Richard Gladue, Chief

FOND DU LAC DENESULINE NATION
P.O. Box 211 • Fond du Lac, SK S0J 0W0
(306) 686-2102 Fax 686-2040
Napolean Mercredi, Chief

GORDON FIRST NATION
P.O. Box 248 • Punnichy, SK S0A 3C0
(306) 835-2232 Fax 835-2036
Wayne Morris, Chief

HATCHET LAKE DENE NATION
General Delivery • Wollaston Lake, SK S0J 3C0
(306) 633-2003 Fax 633-2040
Joe Tsannie, Chief

ISLAND LAKE FIRST NATION
P.O. Box 460 • Loon Lake, SK S0M 1L0
(306) 837-2188 Fax 837-2266
Ernest Crookedneck, Chief

JAMES SMITH CREE NATION
P.O. Box 1059 • Melfort, SK S0E 1A0
(306) 864-3636 Fax 864-3336
Walter Constant, Chief

JOSEPH BIGHEAD FIRST NATION
P.O. Box 309 • Pierceland, SK S0M 2K0
(306) 839-2277 FAX 839-2323
Ernest Sundown, Chief

KAHKEWISTAHAW FIRST NATION
P.O. Box 609 • Broadview, SK S0G 0K0
(306) 696-3291 Fax 696-3201
Louis Taypotat, Chief

KAWACATOOSE FIRST NATION
P.O. Box 640 • Raymore, SK S0A 3J0
(306) 835-2125 Fax 835-2178
Richard Poorman, Chief

KEESEEKOOSE FIRST NATION
P.O. Box 1120 • Kamsack, SK S0A 1S0
(306) 542-2516 Fax 542-2586
Albert James Musqua, Chief

KEY FIRST NATION
P.O. Box 70 • Norquay, SK S0A 2V0
(306) 594-2020 Fax 594-2545
Dennis O'Soup, Chief

KINISTIN FIRST NATION
P.O. Box 2590 • Tisdale, SK S0E 1T0
(306) 873-5590 Fax 873-5235
Albert Scott, Chief

LAC LA RONGE FIRST NATION
P.O. Box 480 • La Ronge, SK S0J 1L0
(306) 425-2183 Fax 425-2590
Harry Cook, Chief

LITTLE BLACK BEAR FIRST NATION
P.O. Box 40 • Goodeve, SK S0A 1C0
(306) 334-2269 Fax 334-2721
Clarence A. Bellegarde, Chief

LITTLE PINE FIRST NATION
P.O. Box 70 • Paynton, SK S0M 2J0
(306) 398-4942 Fax 398-2377
Johnson Kakum, Chief

LUCKY MAN CREE NATION
225-103B Packham Ave.
Saskatoon, SK S7N 2T7
(306) 374-2828 Fax 934-2853
Andrew King, Chief

MAKWA SAHGAIEHCAN FIRST NATION
P.O. Box 340 • Loon Lake, SK S0M 1L0
(306) 837-2102 Fax 837-4448
Gerald Kisyeinwakup, Chief

MISTAWASIS INDIAN BAND
P.O. Box 250 • Leask, SK S0J 1M0
(306) 466-4800 Fax 466-2299
Noel Daniels, Chief

MONTREAL LAKE CREE NATION
P.O. Box 106
Montreal lake, SK S0J 1Y0
(306) 663-5349 Fax 663-5320
Edward Henderson, Chief

MOOSOMIN INDIAN BAND
P.O. Box 98 • Cochin, SK S0M 0L0
(306) 398-2206 Fax 398-2098
Gerald SwiftWolfe, Chief

**MOSQUITO GRIZZLY BEAR'S HEAD
FIRST NATION**
P.O. Box 177 • Cando, SK S0K 0V0
(306) 937-7707 Fax 937-7747
Jenny Spyglas, Chief

MUSCOWPETUNG FIRST NATION
P.O. Box 1310
Fort Qu'Appelle, SK S0G 1S0
(306) 723-4747 Fax 723-4710
Paul Poitras, Chief

MUSKEG LAKE FIRST NATION
Asimakaniseekan Asiky Reserve
#100-103A Packham Ave.
Saskatoon, SK S7N 4K4
(306) 374-8118 Fax 374-7377

MUSKEG LAKE FIRST NATION
P.O. Box 248 • Marcelin, SK S0J 1R0
(306) 466-4959 Fax 466-4951
Harry Lafond, Chief

MUSKODAY FIRST NATION
P.O. Box 9 • Birch Hills, SK S0J 0G0
(306) 764-1282 FAX 764-7272
Austin Bear, Chief

MUSKOWEKWAN FIRST NATION
P.O. Box 249 • Lestock, SK S0A 2G0
(306) 274-2061 Fax 274-2110
Albert Pinacie, Chief

NEKANEET FIRST NATION
P.O. Box 548
Maple Creek, SK S0N 1N0
(306) 662-3660 Fax 662-4160
Gordon Oakes, Chief

OCEAN MAN FIRST NATION
P.O. Box 157 • Stoughton, SK S0G 4T0
(306) 457-2697 Fax 457-2933
Laura Big Eagle, Chief

OCHAPOWACE FIRST NATION
P.O. Box 550 • Whitewood, SK S0J 5C0
(306) 696-3160 Fax 696-3146
Denton George, Chief

OKANESE FIRST NATION
P.O. Box 759 • Balcarres, SK S0G 0C0
(306) 334-2532 Fax 334-2545
Marie Ann Daywalker, Chief

ONE ARROW FIRST NATION
P.O. Box 147 • Bellevue, SK S0K 3Y0
(306) 467-2337 Fax 467-2339
Richard John, Chief

ONION LAKE FIRST NATION
P.O. Box 100 • Onion Lake, SK S0M 2E0
(306) 847-2200 Fax 847-2226
Donald Cardinal, Chief

PASQUA FIRST NATION
P.O. Box 968 • Fort Qu'Appelle, SK S0G 1S0
(306) 332-5697 Fax 332-5199
Lindsay Cyr, Chief

PEEPEEKISIS FIRST NATION
P.O. Box 518 • Balcarres, SK S0G 0C0
(306) 334-2573 Fax 334-2280
Enoch Poitras, Chief

PELICAN LAKE FIRST NATION
P.O. Box 399 • Leoville, SK S0J 1N0
(306) 984-2313 Fax 984-2029
Leo Thomas, Chief

PETER BALLANTYNE FIRST NATION
General Delivery
Pelican Narrows, SK S0P 0E0
(306) 632-2125 Fax 632-2275
Ronald Michel, Chief

PHEASANT RUMP NAKOTA NATION
P.O. Box 238 • Kisbey, SK S0C 1L0
(306) 462-2002 Fax 462-2003
Kelvin J. McArthur, Chief

PIAPOT FIRST NATION
General Delivery • Zehner, SK S0G 5K0
(306) 781-4848 Fax 781-4853
Art Kaiswatum, Chief

POUNDMAKER CREE NATION
P.O. Box 220 • Paynton, SK S0M 2J0
(306) 398-4971 Fax 398-2522
Teddy Antoine, Chief

RED EARTH FIRST NATION
P.O. Box 109 • Red Earth, SK S0E 1K0
(306) 768-3640 Fax 768-3440
Philip Head, Chief

RED PHEASANT FIRST NATION
P.O. Box 70 • Cando, SK S0K 0V0
(306) 937-7717 Fax 937-7727
Mike Baptiste, Chief

SAKIMAY FIRST NATION
P.O. Box 339 • Grenfell, SK S0G 2B0
(306) 697-2831 Fax 697-3565
Samuel Bunnie, Chief

SAULTEAUX FIRST NATION
P.O. Box 159 • Cochin, SK S0M 0L0
(306) 386-2424 Fax 386-2444
Gabriel Gopher, Chief

SHOAL LAKE CREE NATION
P.O. Box 51 • Pakwaw Lake, SK S0E 1G0
(306) 768-3551 Fax 768-3486
Dennis Whitecap, Chief

STANDING BUFFALO FIRST NATION
P.O. Box 128 • Fort Qu'Appelle, SK S0G 1S0
(306) 332-4685 Fax 332-5953
Mel Isnana, Chief

STAR BLANKET CREE NATION
P.O. Box 456 • Belcarres, SK S0G 0C0
(306) 334-2206 Fax 334-2606
Irvin Starr, Chief

STURGEON LAKE FIRST NATION
P.O. Box 5, Site 12, RR #1
Shellbrook, SK S0J 2E0
(306) 764-1872 Fax 764-1877
Wesley Daniels, Chief

SWEETGRASS FIRST NATION
Box 147 • Gallivan, SK S0M 0X0
(306) 937-2990 Fax 937-7010
Edward Standinghorn, Chief

THUNDERCHILD FIRST NATION
P.O. Box 600 • Turtleford, SK S0M 2Y0
(306) 845-3424 Fax 845-3230
Charles Paddy, Sr., Chief

WAHPETON LAKE FIRST NATION
P.O. Box 128 • Prince Albert, SK S6V 3B0
(306) 764-6649 Fax 764-6637
Lorne Waditaka, Chief

WATERHEN LAKE FIRST NATION
P.O. Box 9 • Waterhen Lake, SK S0M 3B0
(306) 236-6717 Fax 236-4866
Robert Fiddler, Chief

WHITE BEAR FIRST NATION
P.O. Box 700 • Carlyle, SK S0C 0R0
(306) 577-4553 Fax 577-2108
Bernard Shepherd, Chief

WHITECAP DAKOTA/SIOUX FIRST NATION
Site 507, Box 28, RR #5 • Saskatoon, SK S7K 3J8
(306) 477-0908 Fax 374-5899
Charles R. Eagle, Chief

WITCHEKAN LAKE FIRST NATION
P.O. Box 879 • Spiritwood, SK S0J 2M0
(306) 883-2787 Fax 883-2008
Mike Fineday, Chief

WOOD MOUNTAIN FIRST NATION
P.O. Box 104 • Wood Mountain, SK S0H 4L0
(306) 266-4422 Fax 266-2023
William Goodtrack, Chief

YELLOWQUILL (NUTT LAKE) FIRST NATION
P.O. Box 40 • Rose Valley, SK S0E 1M0
(306) 322-2281 Fax 322-2304
Henry Neapetung, Chief

YOUNG CHIPPEWAYAN FIRST NATION
P.O. Box 220 • Shell Lake, SK S0J 2G0
(306) 468-2326 Fax 468-2344
Barry L. Ahenakew, Chief

METIS NON-STATUS

METIS NATION OF SASKATCHEWAN
2nd Floor, 219 Robin Crescent
Saskatoon, SK S7L 6M8
(306) 343-8285 Fax 343-0171

YUKON

FIRST NATIONS

CARCROSS/TAGISH FIRST NATIONS
P.O. Box 130 • Carcross, YU Y0B 1B0
(867) 821-4251 Fax 821-4802
Doris McLean, Chief

CHAMPAGNE/AISHIHIK FIRST NATION
P.O. Box 5309
Haines Junction, YU Y0B 1L0
(867) 634-2288 Fax 634-2108
Paul Birckel, Chief

FIRST NATION OF NA-CHO NY'A'K DUN
P.O. Box 220 • Mayo, YU Y0B1M0
(867) 996-2265 Fax 996-2107
Robert Hager, Chief

KLUANE FIRST NATION
P.O. Box 20 • Burwash Landing, YU Y1A 1V0
(867) 841-4274 Fax 841-5900
Agnes Johnson, Chief

KWANLIN DUN FIRST NATION
35 McIntyre • Whitehorse, YU Y1A 5A5
(867) 667-6465 Fax 668-5057
Ann Smith, Chief

LIARD RIVER FIRST NATION
P.O. Box 328 • Watson Lake, YU T0A 1C0
(867) 536-2131 Fax 536-2332
Dixon Lutz, Chief

LIARD RIVER INDIAN RESERVE #3
P.O. Box 489 • Watson Lake, YU T0A 1C0
(867) 779-3161 Fax 779-3371
George Miller, Deputy Chief

LITTLE SALMON/CARMACKS FIRST NATION
P.O. Box 135 • Carmacks, YU Y0B 1C0
(867) 863-5576 Fax 863-5710

LOWER POST FIRST NATION
P.O. Box 489 • Watson lake, YU Y0A 1C0
(250) 779-3161 Fax 779-3371

ROSS RIVER FIRST NATION
General Delivery • Ross River, YU Y0B 1S0
(403) 969-2278/9 Fax 969-2405
Clifford McLeod, Chief

SELKIRK FIRST NATION
P.O. Box 40 • Pelly Crossing, YU Y0B 1P0
(403) 537-3331 Fax 537-3902
Patrick Van Bibber, Chief

TA'AN KWACH'AN COUNCIL
P.O. Box 32081 • Whitehorse, YU Y1A 5P9
(403) 668-3613 Fax 667-4295
Glenn Grady, Chief

TESLIN TLINGIT FIRST NATION
P.O. Box 133 • Teslin, YU Y0A 1B0
(403) 390-2532 Fax 390-2204
David Keenan, Chief

TR'ON DEK HWECH'IN FIRST NATION
P.O. Box 599 • Dawson City, YU Y0B 1G0
(403) 993-5385 Fax 993-5753
Steve Tailor, Chief

TWALNJIK DAN FIRST NATION
P.O. Box 135 • Carmacks, YU Y0B 1C0
(403) 863-5576 Fax 863-5710
Roddy Blackjack, Chief

VUNTUT GWITCHIN TRIBAL COUNCIL
General Delivery • Old Crow, YU Y0B 1N0
(403) 966-3261 Fax 966-3800
Roger Kaye, Chief

WHITE RIVER FIRST NATION INDIAN BAND
General Delivery • Beaver Creek, YU Y0B 1A0
(403) 862-7802 Fax 862-7806
Billy Blair, Chief

NATIONAL ASSOCIATIONS/ ORGANIZATIONS

ASSEMBLY OF FIRST NATIONS (AFN) NATIONAL INDIAN BROTHERHOOD
1 Nicholas St., Suite 1002 • Ottawa, ON K1N 7B7
(613) 241-6789 Fax 241-5806
Phil Fontaine, National Chief
Web site: www.afn.ca
Head Office: Territory of Akwesasne, Hamilton's Island, Summerstown, ON K0C 2E0   (613) 241-6789 Fax 241-5806. *Ontario Regional Chiefs*: 22 College St., 2nd Floor, Toronto, ON M5G 1K2 (416) 972-0212 Fax 972-0217. Harry Alen, Northern Region (403) 667-7631; Gordon Peters, Ontario Region (416) 972-0212; Konrad Sioui, Quebec and Labrador Region (418) 842-5020; Leonard Tomah, Atlantic Region (506) 328-3304; Ken Young, Manitoba Region (204) 956-0610; Bill Wilson, British Columbia Region (604) 339-6605;

Roland Crowe, Saskatchewan Region (306) 721-2822. There are approximately 650 First Nations groups across Canada. *Purpose*: To represent the views and interests of Canada's First Nations in discussions with other levels of government on the issues: education, housing, economic development, health, and forestry; to inform other Canadians about the opportunities and issues relating to First Nation's self-government. *Activities*: The AFN Resource Centre; Educational scholarships; Awards in honour of "Heroes of Our Time". *Publications*: AFN Bulletin, $18/year. Library. Founded 1969.

CANADA—DEPT. OF INDIAN AFFAIRS NORTHERN DEVELOPMENT
Ottawa, ON K1A 0H4
(819) 997-0811 Fax 997-0511
Andy Mitchell, Minister

CANADIAN ABORIGINAL AIDS NETWORK
#2-324 Somerset St. W. • Ottawa, ON K2P 0J9
(888) 285-2226; (613) 567-1817 Fax 567-4652

CANADIAN ABORIGINAL SCIENCE & ENGINEERING ASSOCIATION
22 Colege St., 2nd Fl. • Toronto, ON G1K 2K3
(416) 972-0212 Fax 972-0217

CANADIAN ALLIANCE IN SOLIDARITY WITH THE NATIVE PEOPLES
Box 574, Station "P" • Toronto, ON M5S 2T1
(416) 972-1573 Fax 972-6232
Catherine Jerrall, Coordinator
Membership: 1,250. Native and non-native people working together to bring a better understanding to non-native people. *Purpose*: To bring awareness issues to the public as identified by native people. *Committees*: Aboriginal Rights, Child Welfare Native, Focus on the Canadian Constitution, Justice, Native Rights, and Prisons. *Publications*: Phoenix, quarterly journal; Resource/Reading List; Indian Giver: A Legacy of North American Native Peoples; Native Rights in Canada, Third Edition. Maintains small resource center. Annual meeting. Established 1960.

CANADIAN COUNCIL FOR ABORIGINAL BUSINESS
204A St. George St., Coach House
Toronto, ON M5R 2N5 (416) 961-8663 Fax 961-3995
E-mail: ccab@io.org

CONGRESS OF ABORIGINAL PEOPLES
65 Bank St., 4th Floor • Ottawa, ON K1P 5N2
(613) 238-3511 Fax 230-6273

FIRST NATIONS HEALTH MANAGEMENT INSTITUTE
c/o Mohawk Council of Akwesasne
Box 579 • Cornwall, ON K6H 5R7
(613) 575-2341 Fax 575-1311

FIRST NATIONS NATIONAL GAMING COUNCIL
Suite 50, 666 Burrard St. • Vancouver, BC V6C 3H3
(800) 267-3216; (604) 687-3216 Fax 683-2780
Ferguson Gifford, Director

FIRST NATIONS SUMMIT
#208-1999 Marine Dr. • N. Vancouver, BC V7P 3J3
(604) 990-9939 Fax 990-9949
E-mail: fns@istar.ca

FIRST NATIONS TRIBAL JUSTICE INSTITUTE
P.O. Box 3730 • Mission, BC V2V 4L2
(250) 826-3691 FAX 826-9296

FIRST NATIONS WELLNESS SOCIETY
International Plaza Towers
1959 Marine Dr. #365
N. Vancouver, BC V7P 3G1
(604) 986-7424 Fax 984-0124

GRAND COUNCIL OF THE CREES (OF QUEBEC)
24 Bayswater Ave. • Ottawa, ON K1Y 2E4
(613) 761-1655 Fax 761-1388

GRAND COUNCIL OF TREATY No. 3 ASSN. OF OJIBWAY CHIEFS
Box 1720 • Kenora, ON P9N 3X7
(807) 548-4214 Fax 548-5041

INDIGENOUS BAR ASSOCIATION IN CANADA
408 Queen St. • Ottawa, ON K1R 5A7
(613) 233-8686 Fax 233-3116
Web site: nahnad@comnet.ca

INDIGENOUS LAW PROGRAMS
4th Floor law Centre, U. of Alberta
Edmonton, AB T6G 2H5
(780) 492-7749 Fax 492-4924

**INSTITUTE OF HUMAN IDEAS ON
ULTIMATE REALITY & MEANING**
St. Paul's College, University of Manitoba
70 Dysart rd. • Winnipeg, MB R3T 2M6
204-474-2351 Fax 275-5421
Joan F. Perry, Editor
e-mail: perrygf@cc.umanitoba.ca
web site: www.uofs.edu/urem
Purpose: See listing below for International Society.
Publication: Ultimate Reality and Meaning, newsletter. Established 1970.

**INTERNATIONAL NETWORK OF
INDIGENOUS PEOPLES ASSOCIATION**
54 Lockearnest St.
Hamilton, ON L8R 1W1
(905) 523-7356

**INTERNATIONAL SOCIETY OF HUMAN
IDEAS ON ULTIMATE REALITY & MEANING**
St. Regis College, 15 St. Mary St.
Toronto, ON M4Y 2R5 (416) 922-2476
Tibor Horvath, General Editor
Purpose: Interdisciplinary research on human effort to find meaning in our world; specifically how 63 North American and 72 South American Indian linguistic families with their 474 and 505 members respectively expressed the meaning of their lives and their concepts of ultimate reality and meaning. *Activities*: Biennial meetings and publications of essays in journal; scholars-experts in any of 979 American Indian groups listed in the Outline of the Research are welcome to submit essays following the guidelines of the Institute. *Publication*: Ultimate Reality and Meaning, newsletter. Library. Established 1970.

INTERTRIBAL CHRISTIAN COMMUNICATIONS
P.O. Box 3765, Sta. B • Winnipeg, MB R2W 3R6
(204) 661-9333 George McPeek, Director
Purpose: To assist the Indian church in its broadest sense to speak to the social, cultural and spiritual concerns of its own native people. *Activities/programs*: Seminars dealing with grief resolution. *Publications*: Indian Life Magazine; The Grieving Indian; Christian education curricula for Native youth.

INUIT ART FOUNDATION
2081 Merivale Rd.
Nepean, ON K2G 1G9
(800) 830-3293; (613) 224-8189 Fax 224-2907

INUIT BROADCASTING CORPORATION (IBC)
Box 700 • Iqaluit, NT X0A 0H0
(867) 979-6231 Fax 979-5853

INUIT CIRCUMPOLAR CONFERENCE
544-170 Laurier Ave. West
Ottawa, ON K1P 5V5
(613) 563-2642 Fax 565-3089
Mary Simon, President

INUIT TAPIRISAT OF CANADA
510-170 Laurier Ave. West
Ottawa, ON K1P 5V5
(613) 238-8181 Fax 234-1991
Rosemarie Kuptana, President
Purpose: National voice of Inuit in Canada. Activities: Lobby for Inuit rights, self-government, economic development, environment, and cultural preservation & development. Publication: Inuktitut Magazine. Library. Founded 1971.

METIS NATIONAL COUNCIL
350 Spark St. #309 • Ottawa, ON K1P 7S9
(613) 232-3216 Fax 232-4262
E-mail: mnc@storm.ca

METIS NATIONAL COUNCIL OF WOMEN
#500 - 1 Nicholas St. • Ottawa, Ontario K1N 7B7
(613) 241-6028 Fax 241-6031

**NATIONAL ABORIGINAL
ACHIEVEMENT FOUNDATION**
70 Yorkville Ave. #33A • Toronto, ON M5R 1B9
(800) 329-9780; (416) 926-0775 Fax 926-7554
E-mail: naaf@star.ca Web site: www.naaf.ca

**NATIONAL ABORIGINAL
BUSINESS ASSOCIATION**
c/o Neegan Enterprises, Inc.
Box 5566 • Fort McMurray, AB T9H 3G5
(780) 791-0654 Fax 791-0671

**NATIONAL ABORIGINAL
COMMUNICATIONS SOCIETY**
47 Clarence St., Suite 430
Ottawa, ON K2P 1M3
(613) 230-6244 Fax 230-6227

**NATIONAL ABORIGINAL
FORESTRY ASSOCIATION**
875 Bank St. • Ottawa, ON K1S 3W4
(613) 233-5563 Fax 233-4329
E-mail: nafa@web.net
Web site: www.omnimage.ca/clients/nafa/n

NATIONAL ABORIGINAL VETERAN ASSN.
32 Moore Pl. • Saskatoon, SK S7L 3Z8
(306) 384-0565 Fax 382-6587

**NATIONAL ASSN. OF CULTURAL
EDUCATION CENTRES**
191 Prominade du Portage #500
Hull, PQ J8X 2K6
(819) 772-2331 Fax 772-1826
E-mail: gmorris@fox.nstn.ns.ca

**NATIONAL ASSOCIATION
OF FRIENDSHIP CENTRES**
275 MacLaren St. • Ottawa, ON K2P 0L9
(613) 563-4844 Fax 594-3428
Jerome Berthelette, Executive Director
Purpose: To act in the capacity of social advocate for Canadian Native Peoples in an urban setting by qualifying or lobbying for special projects funding in the areas of Native self-sufficiency, alcohol, drug and solvent abuse counseling, courtwork representation, etc. *Activities*: Handles core support to new and satellite centres, as well as training support, capital constructions, and renovations of existing centres. *Publication*: Monthly newsletter. Library.

NATIONAL INDIAN ARTS & CRAFTS CORP.
Les Artisans Indiens du Quebec
540 Max Gros-Louis • Village des Hurons
Wendake, PQ G0A 4V0
(418) 845-2150
Wellington Staats, President
A national native owned non-profit development organization. *Purpose*: To develop Indian arts and crafts industry; the promotion and development of viable native arts and crafts enterprises and industries. *Activities/programs*: Maintains a business referral and information service (BRS) answering inquiries from producers, distributors and other interested parties; sponsors exhibitions. *Publication*: Canadian Indian Artscraft, a national quarterly trade magazine. Library - maintains a collection of resource material including artists profiles, reference books and trade magazines; a series of video tapes entitled "NIACC Indian Arts and Crafts Film Series" available for viewing through a separate distribution company, titles available upon request. Established 1975.

NATIONAL INDIAN FINANCIAL CORPORATION
P.O. Box 2377 • Prince Albert, SK S6V 6Z1
(306) 763-4712 Fax 763-3255
#217-103B Packham Ave.
Saskatoon, SK S7N 4K4
(800) 667-4712; (306) 955-4712 Fax 477-4554

**NATIONAL INDIAN & INUIT COMMUNITY
HEALTH REPRESENTATIVES ORGANIZATION**
P.O. Box 1019
Kahnawake, PQ J0L 1B0
(514) 632-0892 Fax 632-2111

NATIONAL INUIT YOUTH COUNCIL
#510-170 Laurier Ave. West
Ottawa, ON K1P 5V5
(613) 238-8181 Fax 234-1991

**NATIONAL NATIVE ALCOHOL
& DRUG ABUSE PROGRAM**
20 3rd St. E.
Portage La Priaire, MB R1N 1N4
(204) 857-6178

**NATIONAL NATIVE ASSOCIATION
OF TREATMENT DIRECTORS**
8989 MacLeod Trail S.W. #410 •
Calgary, AB T2H 0M2
(403) 253-6232 Fax 252-9210
Betty Bastien, Executive Director

NATIVE AMATEUR SPORTS ASSOCIATION
836 Lorne Ave. • Brandon, MB R7A 0T8
(204) 725-4686

**NATIVE INVESTMENT &
TRADE ASSOCIATION (NITA)**
Suite 410 • 890 W. Pender St.
Vancouver, BC V7T 1J9
(800) 337-7743
(604) 684-0880 Fax (888) 684-0881
Calvin Helin, President
E-mail: nita@bc.synpatico.ca
Web site: www.native-invest-trade.com
Purpose: To promote the health and well-being of First Nations citizens by creating wealth through commercial enterprise. *Activities*: Trade shows; business conferences.

NATIVE LANGUAGE INSTITUTE
Lakehead University, Faculty of Education
955 Oliver Rd. • Thunder Bay • ON P7B 5E1
(807) 343-8198 Fax 346-7746

NATIVE LAW STUDENTS ASSOCIATION
U. of British Columbia-Faculty of Law
1822 East Mall • Vancouver, BC V6T 1Z1
(604) 822-3151 Fax 822-8108

NATIVE LAW CENTRE
University of Saskatchewan
150 Diefenbaker Centre
Saskatoon, SK S7K 3S9
(306) 966-6189
Don Purich, Director
Purpose: To provide a head start program for people of native ancestry who wish to enter law school; to research problems related to native legal rights, e.g. land claims; to provide a resource to lawyers and researchers working in the area of native law; and, to back up the courses in native law taught in the College of Law, University of Saskatchewan. *Activities*: Summer program of legal study for native people; research. *Prizes*: Harvey Bell Memorial Prize, $1,000 for a student graduating from law school; Native Law Students Association Writing Competition, $200 book prize; book prize to student in summer program, $150. *Publication*: Canadian Native Law Reporter, quarterly journal; books for sale. Library.

**NATIVE MENTAL HEALTH
ASSOCIATION OF CANADA**
Box 242 • Chillwack, BC V2P 6J1
(604) 793-1983 Fax 793-4557
Clare Clifton Brant, Chairperson
Purpose: To provide mental health care services to Native peoples of Canada. *Activities*: Workshops; training programs; and information and referral services.

NATIVE PHYSICIANS ASSOCIATION OF CANADA
Box 8427, Sta. "D" • Ottawa, ON K1G 3H8
(613) 445-1676 Fax 445-1678

NATIVE SPORTS DEVELOPMENT PROGRAM
Box 1240 Sta. "M" • Calgary, AB T2P 2L2
(403) 818-6085 Fax 261-5676
Web site: wwwaboriginalnet.com/sports

NATIVE WOMEN IN THE ARTS
101-141 Bathhurst St. • Toronto, ON M5V 2R2
(416) 392-6800 Fax 392-6920

NATIVE WOMEN'S ASSOCIATION OF CANADA
P.O. Box 185 • Ohsweken, ON N0A 1M0
9 Mellrose Ave. • Ottawa, ON K1Y 1T8
(800) 461-4043; (613) 722-3033 Fax 722-7687
Gail Stacey-Moore, Speaker
Goals: To enhance, promote and foster the social,

econimic, cultural and political well-being of First Nations and Metis women with First Nations and Canadian societies. Awards granted. Founded 1974.

NATIVE THEATRE SCHOOL INDIGENOUS THEATRE CELEBRATION
Association for Native Development in the Performing & Visual Arts
27 Carlton St. # 208 • Toronto, ON M5B 1L2
(416) 977-2512

CANADA (REGIONAL)

ALBERTA

ABORIGINAL OPPORTUNITIES COMMITTEE
Calgary Chamber of Commerce
517 Centre St. S. • CALGARY, AB T2G 3C4
(403) 750-0400 Fax 266-3413

ASSEMBLY OF FIRST NATIONS OF ALBERTA
c/o Grand Council of Treaty No. 7
Suite 310, 6940 Fisher Rd. SE
CALGARY, AB T2H 0W3
(403) 927-3727 Fax 927-4375

CALGARY ABORIGINAL AWARENESS SOCIETY
Suite 360, 1207 11th Ave. SW
CALGARY, AB T3C 0M5
(403) 296-2227 Fax 296-2226

CALGARY ABORIGINAL URBAN AFFAIRS COMMITTEE
c/o City of Calgary, Box 2100, Sta. "M"
CALGARY, AB T2P 2M5
(403) 268-5188 Fax 268-5696

CALGARY NATIVE FRIENDSHIP SOCIETY
140 - 2nd Ave. SW • CALGARY, AB T2P 0B9
(403) 777-2263 Fax 265-9275
Laverna McMaster, Executive Director

CALGARY URBAN INDIAN YOUTH
1139 Riverdale Ave. S.W. • CALGARY, AB T2S 0Y9
(403) 243-1876

FIRST NATIONS CONFERENCES, INC.
P.O. Box 1240, Sta. "M"
CALGARY, AB T2P 2L2
(403) 261-3022 Fax 261-5676
E-mail aboriginalcongress@discoveryweb.com
Web site: www.aboriginalnet.com/congress

INDIGENOUS PEOPLES RESOURCE ASSOCIATION
221-1011 17th Ave., SW
CALGARY, AB T2T 0A8
(403) 228-9683

NATIVE COUNSELING SERVICES OF ALBERTA
#640, 615 MacLeod Trail, SE
CALGARY, AB T0K 0H0
(403) 237-7850 Fax 237-7857

PLAINS INDIAN CULTURAL SURVIVAL SCHOOL
1723 33 St. S.W. • CALGARY, AB T3C 1P4
(403) 246-5378

TSUT'INA K'OSA
Sarcee Cultural Program, Box 135
3700 Anderson Rd., SW
CALGARY, AB T2W 3C4
(403) 238-2677; Fax 251-5871
Jeanette Starlight, Director

ABORIGINAL AFFAIRS/ALBERTA
Rm. 1301, 10155-102nd St.
EDMONTON, AB T5J 4L4
(780) 427-2008 FAX 427-4019

ABORIGINAL MULTI-MEDIA SOCIETY OF ALBERTA (AMMSA)
15001, 112 Ave. • EDMONTON, AB T5M 2V6
(780) 455-2700 Fax 455-7639
Fred Didzena, President
Bert Crowfoot, General Manager
Newspaper: Windspeaker - Gary Gee, Editor

ALBERTA HERITAGE ABORIGINAL SOCIETY
12728 66th St. • EDMONTON, AB T5C 0A3
(780) 475-1699 Fax 472-1873

ALBERTA INDIAN ARTS & CRAFTS SOCIETY
501, 10105-109th St.
EDMONTON, AB T5J 1M8
(780) 426-2048 Leonie Willier, President

ALBERTA NATIVE NEWS
330 - 10036 Jasper Ave.
EDMONTON, AB T5J 2W2
(780) 421-7966 Fax 424-3951

ALBERTA NATIVE FRIENDSHIP CENTRE ASSOCIATION
10534 - 124 St. #104
EDMONTON, AB T5N 1S1
(780) 482-5196 Fax 482-2032
Fred Campiou, President

ALBERTA NATIVE RIGHTS FOR NATIVE WOMEN
14211 - 130th Ave. • EDMONTON T5L 4K8
(780) 453-2808 or 454-8462

CANADIAN NATIVE FRIENDSHIP CENTRE
11205-101 ST. • EDMONTON, AB T5G 2A4
(780) 479-1999 Fax 479-0043

COUNCIL FOR THE ADVANCEMENT OF NATIVE DEVELOPMENT OFFICERS
Suite 240-10036 Jasper Ave.
EDMONTON, AB T5J 2W2 (800) 463-9300
(780) 990-0303 Fax 429-7487
E-mail: cando@ccinet.ab.ca
Web site: www.incentre.net/cando

FIRST NATIONS COUNSELLING CENTRE
201-10010 106 St.
EDMONTON, AB T5J 2L8
(780) 944-0172 Fax 944-0176

FIRST NATIONS RESOURCE COUNCIL
11748 Kingsway Ave. #101
EDMONTON, AB T5G 0X5
(780) 453-6114 Fax 453-6150

METIS NATION OF ALBERTA
#100-11738 Kingsway Ave
EDMONTON, AB T5G 04R
(800) 252-7553; (780) 455-2200 Fax 452-8948

NATIVE COUNCIL OF CANADA
10426-124th St., NW
EDMONTON, AB T5N 1R6
(780) 917-1203 Fax 488-2741
Doris Ronnenberg, President

NATIVE COUNSELLING SERVICES OF ALBERTA-EDMONTON
#800, Highfield Pl., 10010-106th St.
EDMONTON, AB T5J 3L8
(780) 423-2141 Fax 424-0187

INDIAN ASSOCIATION OF ALBERTA
P.O. Box 159 • HOBBEMA, AB T0C 1N0
(800) 661-2579;
(780) 585-3793; Fax 585-4700
Roy Louis, President
Purpose: To advance the social and economic welfare of the Treaty Indians of Alberta; to promote programs designed to serve the educational and cultural interests of the Native people's it represents; to work in conjunction with other Indian bands and/or chiefs and councils to work with with Federal, Provincial and Local Governments for the benefit of the Treaty Indians of Alberta. Established 1944.

ABORIGINAL RADIO & TELEVISION SOCIETY
Box 2250 • LAC LA BICHE, AB T0A 2C0
(780) 447-2393 Fax 454-2820

INDIAN NEWS MEDIA
Box 120
STANDOFF, AB T0L 1Y0
(780) 653-3301
Gerri Manyfingers, Executive Director
Marie Smallface Marule, President
Blackfoot Radio Network; Bull Horn Video
Newspaper: Kainai News-Mary Weasel Fat, Editor

BRITISH COLUMBIA

U'MISTA CULTURAL CENTRE
Box 253 • ALERT BAY, BC V0N 1A0
(250) 974-5403 Fax 974-5499
Wendy Jakobsen, Administrator

BELLA COOLA-NUXALK EDUCATION AUTHORITY
P.O. Box 778
BELLA COOLA, BC V0T 1C0
(250) 799-5453/5911
Stewart Clellamin, Coordinator

SAANICH NATIVE HERITAGE SOCIETY
Saanich Cultural Education Centre
Box 28 • BRENTWOOD BAY, BC V8M 1R3
(250) 652-5980 Fax 652-5957
Philip Paul, Director

TANSI FRIENDSHIP CENTRE
P.O. Box 418 • CHETWYND, BC V0C 1J0
(250) 788-2996 Fax 788-2353
Bev Davies, Executive Director

NAWICAN FRIENDSHIP CENTRE
1320 - 102 Ave.
DAWSON CREEK, BC V1G 2C6
(250) 782-5202 Fax 782-8411
Keith Hall, Executive Director

FORT NELSON-LIARD NATIVE FRIENDSHIP SOCIETY
P.O. Box 1266
FORT NELSON, BC V0C 1R0
(250) 774-2993 Fax 774-2998
Don Potkins, Executive Director

FORT ST. JOHN FRIENDSHIP SOCIETY
10208 - 95th Ave.
FORT ST. JOHN, BC V1J 1J2
(250) 785-8566 Fax 785-1507
Shirley Churchill, Executive Director

B.C. NATIVE WOMEN'S SOCIETY
Box 392 • KEREMMEOS, BC V2L 5B8
(250) 562-9106 fax 562-0360
Janet Gottfriedson, President

INTERIOR INDIAN FREINDSHIP CENTRE
125 Palm St. • KAMLOOPS, BC V1J 8J7
(250) 376-1296 Fax 376-2275
Ruth Williams, Executive Director

SECWEPEMC CULTURAL EDUCATION SOCIETY
345 Yellowhead Hwy.
KAMLOOPS, BC V2H 1H1
(250) 828-9779 Fax 372-1127
Muriel Sasakamoose, Executive Director

CENTRAL OKANAGAN FRIENDSHIP SOCIETY
442 Leon Ave. • KELOWNA, BC V1Y 6J3
(250) 763-4905 Fax 861-5514
Tillie Goffic, Executive Director

LILLOOET FRIENDSHIP CENTRE
P.O. Box 1270 • LILLOOET, BC V0K 1V0
(250) 256-4146 Fax 256-7928
Susan James, Executive Director

ED JONES CULTURAL/EDUCATION CENTRE
Box 189 • MASSET, BC V0T 1M0
(250) 626-3337 Fax 626-5440
John Enrico, Director

CONAYT FRIENDSHIP CENTRE
P.O. Box 1989 • MERRITT, BC V1K 1B8
(250) 378-5107 Fax 378-6676
Ross Albert, Executive Director

NATIVE WOMEN'S ASSN. OF CANADA - WEST REGION
Box 213 • MERRITT, BC V0K 2V0
(250) 378-5969 Sharon McIvor, Director

MISSION INDIAN FRIENDSHIP CENTRE
33150 A First Ave. • MISSION, BC V2V 1G4
(250) 826-1281 Fax 826-4056
Christina Cook, Executive Director

TILLICUM HAUS SOCIETY
927 Haliburton St. • NANAIMO, BC V9R 6N4
(250) 753-8291 Fax 753-6560
Grace Nielson, Executive Director

ABORIGINAL COUNCIL OF B.C.
Box 52038 • N. VANCOUVER, BC V7J 3T2
(604) 987-6225 Fax 987-6683

NATIVE ARTS & CRAFTS
445 W. 3rd St. • N. VANCOUVER, BC V7M 1G9
(604) 986-7321 Fax 990-9403

NATIVE BROTHERHOOD OF B.C.
415B W. Esplanade
N. VANCOUVER, BC V7M 1A6
(604) 987-9115 Fax 987-4419

PORT ALBERNI FRIENDSHIP CENTRE
3555 4th Ave., Box 23
PORT ALBERNI, BC V9Y 4H3
(888) 723-7232; (250) 723-8281 Fax 723-1877
Wally Samuel, Executive Director

UNITED NATIVE NATIONS
5060 Argyle St. #144
PORT ALBERNI, BC V9Y 2A7
(250) 723-8131 Fax 723-8132
Ron George, President

B.C. WOMEN OF THE METIS NATION
409 - 3rd Ave. • PRINCE GEORGE, BC V2L 3C1
(250) 564-9794 Fax 564-9793

**PRINCE GEORGE NATIVE
FRIENDSHIP CENTRE**
1600-3rd Ave.
PRINCE GEORGE, BC V2L 3G6
(250) 564-3568 Fax 563-0924
Dan George, Executive Director

FIRST NATIONS WOMEN'S GROUP
Box 921 • PRINCE RUPERT, BC V8J 4B7
(250) 624-3200

**FRIENDSHIP HOUSE ASSOCIATION
OF PRINCE RUPERT**
P.O. Box 512 • PRINCE RUPERT, BC V8J 3R5
(250) 627-1717 Fax 627-7533
Fred Anderson, Executive Director

**QUESNEL TILLICUM SOCIETY
FRIENDSHIP CENTRE**
319 N. Fraser Dr. • QUESNEL, BC V2J 1Y9
(250) 992-8347 Fax 992-5708
Doug Sanderson, Executive Director

B.C. ASSN. OF INDIAN FRIENDSHIP CENTRES
#3-2475 Mt. Newton X Rd.
SAANICHTON, BC V8M 2B7
(250) 652-0210 Fax 652-3102
Marie Anderson, President
Florence Wylie, Coordinator
E-mail: bcaafc@pinc.com

**FIRST NATIONS TRAINING
& CONSULTING SERVICES**
P.O. Box 69 • SAANICHTON, BC V8M 2C3
(250) 652-7097 Fax 652-7039

FIRST PEOPLE'S CULTURAL FOUNDATION
7-2475 Mt. Newton X Rd.
SAANICHTON, BC V8M 2B7
(250) 652-2426 Fax 652-3431

**COQUALEETZA CULTURAL
EDUCATION CENTRE**
P.O. Box 2370 • SARDIS, BC V2R 1A7
(604) 858-7196 Fax 858-8488
Shirley D. Leon, Manager

DZEL K'ANT FRIENDSHIP CENTRE
P.O. Box 2920 • SMITHERS, BC V0J 2N0
(250) 847-8959 Fax 847- 8974
E-mail: dzelkant@mailbulkley.net

KERMODE FRIENDSHIP SOCIETY
3313 Kalum St. • TERRACE, BC V8G 2N7
(250) 635-4906 Fax 635-3013
Sadie Parnell, Executive Director

ASSEMBLY OF FIRST NATIONS/B.C.
Suite 205-675 W. Hastings St.
VANCOUVER, BC V6B 1N2
(604) 609-0114 Fax 609-0124

ASSN. FOR FIRST NATIONS WOMEN
#204-96 E. Broadway
VANCOUVER, BC V5T 4N9
(604) 873-1833 Fax 872-1845

ALLIED INDIAN METIS SOCIETY
2716 Clark Dr. • VANCOUVER, BC V5N 3H6
(604) 874-9610 Fax 876-3858
Marge White, Executive Director

B.C. ABORIGINAL DIRECTORY
#410-890 W. Pender St.
VANCOUVER, BC V6C 1J9
(800) 337-7743;
(604) 684-0880 Fax (888) 684-0881

**B.C. ABORIGIAL PEOPLES' FISHERIES
COMMISSION**
Box 52038 • N. VANCOUVER, BC V7J 3Y2
(604) 987-6225 Fax 987-6683
Ken Malloway, Chairperson

CANADIAN INDIAN VOICE SOCIETY
429 E. 6th St. • N. VANCOUVER, BC V7L 1P8

FIRST NATIONS CONGRESS OF B.C.
403-990 Homer St. • VANCOUVER, BC V6B 2W6
(604) 682-8516 Fax 682-8057
Bill Wilson, Vice-Chief

FIRST NATIONS FOCUS PROGRAM
403-318 Homer St. • VANCOUVER, BC V6B 2V2
(604) 681-6536 Fax 681-2117
E-mail: ala47738@bc.sympatico.ca

FIRST NATIONS HEALTH CAREERS
First Nations House of Learning
U.B.C., 1985 West Mall
VANCOUVER, BC V6T 1Z2
(604) 822-2115 Fax 822-8944

INDIAN ARTS & CRAFTS SOCIETY OF B.C.
540 Burrard St. #505 • VANCOUVER, BC V6C 2K1
(604) 682-8988 Noel C. Derriksan, President

**INDIAN HOMEMAKERS ASSOCIATION
OF BRITISH COLUMBIA**
102 - 423 W. Broadway
VANCOUVER, BC V5Y 1R4
(604) 876-4929

NATIVE BROTHERHOOD OF B.C.
#200 - 1755 E. Hastings
VANCOUVER, BC V5L 1T1
(604) 255-3137 Fax 251-7107
Robert Clifton, President

NATIVE COMMUNICATIONS SOCIETY OF B.C.
1161 W. Georgia St.
VANCOUVER, BC V6E 3H4
(604) 684-7375 Fax 684-5375
Emma Williams, President
Tim Isaac, Managing Editor
Publication: Kahtou, newspaper.

NATIVE EDUCATION CENTRE
Urban Native Education Society
285 E. 5th Ave. • VANCOUVER, BC V5T 1H2
(604) 873-3761 Fax 873-9152

TILLICUM NATIVE CENTRE
2422 Main St. • VANCOUVER, BC V5T 3E2
(604) 873-3767 (phone & fax)

UNITED NATIVE NATIONS SELF-GOVERNBMENT
736 Granville St., 8th Fl
VANCOUVER, BC V6Z 1G3
(800) 555-9756; (604) 688-1821 Fax 688-1823

**UNION OF B.C. INDIAN CHIEFS
RESOURCE CENTRE**
342 Water St., 4th Fl.
VANCOUVER, BC V6B 1B6
(604) 602-3433 Fax 684-0231
Saul Terry, President

VANCOUVER INDIAN CENTRE SOCIETY
1607 E. Hastings St.
VANCOUVER, BC V5L 1S7
(604) 251-4844 Fax 251-1986
Art Paul, Executive Director

ALLIED INDIAN & METIS SOCIETY
R.R. #7, Comp. 24, Site 11
VERNON, BC V1T 7Z3
(250) 549-7413
Dave Parker, Executive Director

UNITED NATIVE FRIENDSHIP CENTRE
2902 - 29th Ave. • VERNON, BC V1T 1S7
(250) 542-1247 Fax 542-3707
Bertha Phelan, Executive Director
E-mail: fnfc@junction.net

B.C. INDIAN LANGUAGE PROJECT
171 Bushby St. • VICTORIA, BC V8S 1B5
(250) 384-4544 Fax 384-2502

VICTORIA NATIVE FRIENDSHIP CENTRE
220 Bay St. • VICTORIA, BC V8W 3K5
(250) 384-3211 Fax 384-1586
Edmond Constantineau, Executive Director

HEILTSUK CULTURAL EDUCATION CENTRE
Box 880 • WAGLISLA, BC V0T 1Z0
(250) 957-2381/2626 Fax 957-2544
Jennifer Carpenter, Program Manager

CARIBOO FRIENDSHIP SOCIETY
99 3rd Ave. S. • WILLIAMS LAKE, BC V2G 1J1
(250) 398-6831 Fax 398-6115
Gail Madrigga, Executive Director

MANITOBA

BRANDON FRIENDSHIP CENTRE
303 - 9th St. • BRANDON, MB R7A 4A8
(204) 727-1407 Fax 726-0902
Louise Phaneuf-Miron, Executive Director

DAUPHIN FRIENDSHIP CENTRE
210 First Ave. NE • DAUPHIN, MB R7A 1A7
(204) 638-5707 • 638-4799
Stan Guiboche, Executive Director

WEST REGION TRIBAL COUNCIL
Indian Cultural Education Program
21-4th Ave., N.W. • DAUPHIN, MB R7N 1H9
(204) 638-8225 FAX 638-8062
Wally Swain, Program Head

**FLIN FLON INDIAN & METIS
FRIENDSHIP CENTRE**
Box 188 • FLIN FLON, MB R8A 1M7
(204) 687-3900 Fax 687-5328
Marcie Johnson, Executive Director

LYNN LAKE FRIENDSHIP CENTRE
Box 460 • LYNN LAKE, MB R0B 0W0
(204) 356-2445 Fax 356-8223
Vicki Stoneman, Executive Director

PORTAGE FRIENDSHIP CENTRE
Box 1118
PORTAGE LA PRAIRIE, MB R1N 3C5
(204) 239-6333 Fax 239-6534
Richard Chaske, Executive Director

KA-WAWIYAK FRIENDSHIP CENTRE
Box 74 • POWERVIEW, MB R0E 1P0
(204) 367-2892
Rhonda Houston, Exec. Director

**NATIVE WOMEN'S ASSOCIATION
OF MANITOBA**
P.O. Box 177
RIVERTON, MB R0C 2R0
(204) 373-2396/378-2460

**RIVERTON & DISTRICT
FRIENDSHIP CENTRE**
P.O. Box 359 • RIVERTON, MB R0C 2R0
(204) 378-2927 Fax 378-5705
Marlane Monkman, Executive Director

**INDIAN COUNCIL OF FIRST NATIONS
OF MANITOBA, INC.**
Box 13, Group 10, R.R. #2
SAINT ANNE, MB R0A 1R0
(204) 422-5193 Fax 422-8860
Andrew Kirkness, Grand Chief

BROKENHEAD CULTURAL CENTRE
SCANTERBURY, MB R0E 1W0
(204) 766-2494 FAX 766-2270
Harvey Olson, Director

INDIAN & METIS FRIENDSHIP CENTRE
347 Phyllis St. • SELKIRK, MB R1A 2J5
(204) 482-5896 Elsie Bear, Exec. Directort

SELKIRK FRIENDSHIP CENTRE
425 Eveline St. • SELKIRK, MB R1A 2J5
(204) 482-7525 Fax 785-8124
Jim Sinclair, Executive Director

**SWAN RIVER INDIAN &
METIS FRIENDSHIP CENTRE**
Box 1448 • SWAN RIVER, MB R0L 1Z0
(204) 734-9301 Fax 734-3090
Elbert Chartrand, Executive Director

**INDIAN COUNCIL OF FIRST NATIONS OF
MANITOBA, INC.**
P.O. Box 2857 • THE PAS, MB R9A 1M6
(204) 623-7227 Fax 623-4041

MANITOBA METIS WOMEN'S ALLIANCE
Box 1503 • THE PAS, MB R9A 1L4
(204) 623-7881

THE PAS FRIENDSHIP CENTRE
Box 2638 • THE PAS, MB R9A 1M3
(204) 623-6459 Fax 623-4268
Judy Elaschuk, Executive Director

MA-MOW-WE-TAK FRIENDSHIP CENTRE, INC.
122 Hemlock Crescent • THOMPSON, MB R8N 0R6
(204) 778-7337 Fax 677-3195
Larry Soldier, Executive Director
Cathy V. Menard, Program Coordinator
A social service organization existing to administer
and implement programs to meet the neds of native
people either migrating to or living in urban areas.
Special programs: Counseling and referral service;
social and recreational programs; cultural awareness and community development. Native Resource
Library: consisting of audio/visual and reading
material. Publication: Interagency Quarterly
Newsletter. Founded 1976.

MANITOBA KEEWATINOWI OKIMAKANAK
3 Station Rd. • THOMPSON, MB R8N 0N3
(204) 778-4431 Fax 778-7655
Chief Robert Wavey, Chairperson

ABORIGINAL COUNCIL OF WINNIPEG
181 Higgins Ave. • WINNIPEG, MB R3B 3G1
(204) 989-6380 Fax 942-5795

THE ABORIGINAL WOMEN OF MANITOBA
78 Grey Friars • WINNIPEG, MB R3T 3J5
(204) 269-0033 Pauline Busch, President

ASSEMBLY OF FIRST NATIONS OF MANITOBA
Assembly of Manitoba Chiefs
200-260 St. Mary Ave. • WINNIPEG, MB R3C 0M6
(204) 956-0610 Fax 943-2369
Ovide Mercredi, Vice-Chief

FIRST NATIONS CONFEDERACY
333 Garry St., 2nd Fl. • WINNIPEG, MB R3B 2G7
(204) 944-8245; 075-5238 Telex
Chief Ken Courchene, Chairperson

INDIAN & METIS FRIENDSHIP CENTRE
45 Robertson St. • WINNIPEG, MB R2W 5H5
(204) 586-8441 Fax 582-8261
Stirling Ranville, Executive Director

INDIAN CRAFTS & ARTS MANITOBA, INC.
348 Hargrave St. • WINNIPEG, MB R3B 2J9
(204) 944-1469
Pat Bruderer, President

**INDIGENOUS WOMEN'S COLLECTIVE
OF MANITOBA, INC.**
120-388 Donald St. • WINNIPEG, MB R2B 2J4
(204) 944-8709/10 Fax 949-1336
Winnie Greisbretch, President

**MANITOBA ABORIGINAL
RESOURCE ASSOCIATION**
286 Smith St., 5th Fl.
WINNIPEG, MB R3C 1K4
(204) 947-1647 Fax 942-3687

**MANITOBA ASSOCIATION
OF FRIENDSHIP CENTRES**
P.O. Box 716 • WINNIPEG, MB R3C 2K3
(204) 942-6299 Fax 942-6308
David Chartrand, President

**MANITOBA FIRST NATIONS
REPATRIATION PROGRAM**
#704, 167 Lombard Ave.
WINNIPEG, MB R3B 0B3
(800) 665-5762; (204) 957-0037 Fax 944-1015

**MANITOBA INDIAN CULTURAL
EDUCATION CENTRE**
119 Sutherland Ave.
WINNIPEG, MB R2W 3C9
(204) 942-0228 Fax 947-6564
Dennis Daniels, Executive Director

MANITOBA METIS FEDERATION
412 McGregor St. • WINNIPEG, MB R3B 1X4
(204) 586-8474 Fax 947-1816

WINNIPEG COUNCIL OF FIRST NATIONS
201 - 286 Smith St. • WINNIPEG, MB R2C 1K4
(204) 946-0804 Fax 946-0075

WINNIPEG NATIVE ALLIANCE
510 King St. • WINNIPEG, MB R2W 5L2
(204) 582-4127 Fax 586-1698

NEW BRUNSWICK

**ASSEMBLY OF FIRST NATIONS
COUNCIL OF ELDERS**
R.R. #9 • FREDERICTON, NB E3B 4X9
(506) 457-2129 Fax 451-9386
Wallace Labillois, Chairperson

FREDERICTON NATIVE FRIENDSHIP CENTRE
361 King St. • FREDERICTON, NB E3B 1C8
(506) 459-5283 Fax 459-1756

**NEW BRUNSWICK ABORIGINAL
PEOPLES COUNCIL**
320 St. Mary's St. • FREDERICTON, NB E3A 2S5
(506) 458-8422/3 Fax 450-3749
Phil Fraser, President
Raymond Gould, Vice President

**NEW BRUNSWICK INDIAN
ARTS & CRAFTS ASSOCIATION**
212 Queen St. #402
FREDERICTON, NB E3V 1A7
(506) 459-7312
David Paul, President

**NEW BRUNSWICK NATIVE INDIAN
WOMEN'S COUNCIL**
65 Brunswick St.
FREDERICTON, NB E3A 2V5
(506) 458-1114 Fax 451-9386
Carol Wortman, President

UNION OF NEW BRUNSWICK INDIANS
385 Wilsey Rd. Comp. 43 • FREDERICTON, NB
E3B 5N6
(506) 458-9444 Fax 458-2850
Ronald Perley, President

**ASSEMBLY OF FIRST NATIONS/NEW
BRUNSWICK/P.E.I.**
5 Sunrise Ct. • WOODSTOCK, NB E7M 4K4
(506) 324-8184 Fax 328-4589
Leonard Tomah, Vice-Chief

NEWFOUNDLAND

FEDERATION OF NEWFOUNDLAND INDIANS
Box 956 • CORNER BROOK, NF A2H 6J3 1Z0
(709) 634-0996 Fax 634-0997
Gerard Webb, President

LABRADOR INUIT DEVELOPMENT CORP.
P.O. Box 1000, Sta. B
GOOSE BAY, NF A0P 1E0
(709) 896-8505 Fax 896-5834

LABRADOR METIS ASSOCIATION
Box 2164, Sta. B • GOOSE BAY, NF A0P 1E0
(709) 896-0592 Fax 896-0594
Reg Michelin, President
Ruby Durno, Vice-President

LABRADOR INUIT ASSOCIATION
Box 909, Sta. B • HAPPY VALLEY, NF A0P 1E0
(709) 896-8582 Fax 896-2610

LABRADOR NATIVE FRIENDSHIP CENTRE
P.O. Box 767, Station "B"
HAPPY VALLEY/GOOSE BAY, NF A0P 1E0
(709) 896-8302 Fax 896-8731
Renne Simms, Executive Director

LABRADOR NATIVE WOMEN'S ASSOCIATION
Box 542, Station "B"
HAPPY VALLEY, NF A0P 1M0
(709) 896-9420 Fax 896-0736
Annette Blake, President

LABRADOR INUIT ASSOCIATION
P.O. Box 70 • NAIN, NF A0P 1L0
(709) 922-2942; Fax 922-2931
Joe Dicker, President

OKALAKATIGET SOCIETY
P.O. Box 160 • NAIN, NF A0P 1L0
(709) 922-2955 Fax 922-2293
Fran Williams, President

TORNGUSOK CULTURAL INSTITUTE
P.O. Box 40 • NAIN, NF A0P 1L0
(709) 922-2158 Fax 922-2863
Gary Baikie, Director

LABRADOR INUIT ASSOCIATION
95 Lemarchant Rd. #302
ST. JOHN'S, NF A1C 2H1
(709) 754-2587 Fax 754-2364

ST. JOHN'S NATIVE FRIENDSHIP CENTRE
61 Cashen Ave. • ST. JOHN'S, NF A1E 3B4
(709) 726-5902 Fax 726-3557
Myrtle Blandford, Executive Director

NASKAPI-MONTAGNAIS INUIT ASSOCIATION
Box 119 • SHESHATSHIU, NF A0P 1N0
(709) 497-9800 Greg Penashue, President

NORTHWEST TERRITORY

INUIT CULTURAL INSTITUTE
Bag 2000 • ARVIAT, NT X0E 0E0
(867) 857-2803 Fax 857-2740
Roy Goose, Executive Director

KITIKMEOT INUIT ASSOCIATION
P.O. Box 88
CAMBRIDGE BAY, NT X0E 0C0
(867) 983-2458 Fax 983-2158
John Maksagak, President

ZHAHTI KOE FRIENDSHIP CENTRE
General Delivery
FORT PROVIDENCE, NT X0E 0L0
(867) 699-3801 Fax 699-4355
Esther Lazore, Executive Director

DEH CHO SOCIETY FRIENDSHIP CENTRE
Box 470 • FORT SIMPSON, NT X0E 0N0
(867) 695-2577 Fax 695-2141
Bertha Norwegian, Executive Director

UNCLE GABE'S FRIENDSHIP CENTRE
Box 957 • FORT SMITH, NT X0E 0P0
(867) 872-3004 Fax 872-5313
Roger Rawlyk, Executive Director

BAFFIN REGION INUIT ASSOCIATION
P.O. Box 219
FROBISHER BAY, NT X0A 0H0
(867) 979-5391

SOARING EAGLE FRIENDSHIP CENTRE
Box 396 • HAY RIVER, NT X0E 0R0
(867) 874-6581 Fax 874-3362
Abby Crook, Executive Director

**COMMITTEE FOR ABORIGINAL \
PEOPLE'S ENTITLEMENT (COPE)**
Box 2000 • INUVIK, NT X0E 0T0
(867) 979-3510
Inuit Association.

**N.W.T. COUNCIL OF FRIENDSHIP CENTRES
INGAMO HALL FRIENDSHIP CENTRE**
Box 1293 • INUVIK, NT X0E 0P0
(867) 979-2166 Fax 979-2837
Shirley Kisoun, Executive Director

BAFFIN REGIONAL INUIT ASSOCIATION
Box 219 • IQALUIT, NT X0A 0H0
(867) 979-5391 Fax 979-4325

KAKIVAK ASSOCIATION
Box 1419 • IQALUIT, NT X0A 0H0
(867) 979-0911 Fax 979-3707

BAFFIN REGIONAL INUIT ASSOCIATION
Box 219 • PROBISHER BAY, NT X0L 0G0
(867) 979-5391 Fax 979-4325
Louis Tapardjuk, President

RAE EDZO FRIENDSHIP CENTRE
Box 85 • RAE-EDZO, NT X0E 0Y0
(867) 392-6000 Fax 392-6093
Bertha Rabesca, Executive Director

INUIT BROADCASTING CORP.
Box 178 • RANKLIN INLET, NT X0C 0G0
(867) 645-2678 Fax 645-2937

KEEWATIN INUIT ASSOCIATION
Box 340 • RANKLIN INLET, NT X0C 0G0
(867) 645-2800 Fax 645-2885
Jack Anawak, President

SAPPUJJIJIT FRIENDSHIP CENTRE
Box 429 • RANKLIN INLET, NT X0C 0G0
(867) 645-2488 Fax 645-2538
Cecilia Papak, Executive Director

ASSEMBLY OF FIRST NATIONS
Dene Nation, P.O. Box 2338
4701 Franklin Ave., Northway Bldg.
YELLOWKNIFE, NT X1A 2P7
(867) 873-3310 Fax 920-2254

DENE CULTURAL INSTITUTE
Box 207 • YELLOWKNIFE, NT X1A 2N2
(867) 873-6617 Fax 873-3867
Joanne Barnaby, Executive Director

DENE NATION
Box 2338, Northway Bldg.
YELLOWKNIFE, NT X1A 2P7
(867) 873-4081 Fax 920-2254

METIS ASSOCIATION OF THE N.W.T.
P.O. Box 1375
YELLOWKNIFE, NT X1A 2P1
(867) 873-3505
Gary Bohnet, President

**NATIVE COMMUNICATION SOCIETY
OF WESTERN N.W.T.**
Box 1919 • YELLOWKNIFE, NT X1A 2P4
(867) 920-2277 Fax 920-4205

NATIVE WOMEN'S ASSOCIATION OF N.W.T.
P.O. Box 2321 • YELLOWKNIFE, NT X1A 2P7
(867) 873-5509 Fax 873-3152
Helen Hudson-MacDonald, President

NUNASI CORPORATION
5022 49th St. #260
YELLOWKNIFE, NT X1A 3R7
(867) 920-4587 Fax 920-4592

TREE OF PEACE FRIENDSHIP CENTRE
Box 2667 • YELLOWKNIFE, NT X1A 2P9
(867) 873-2864 Fax 873-5185
Tom Eagle, President

N.W.T. NATIVE ARTS & CRAFTS SOCIETY
Box 2765 • YELLOWKNIFE, NT X1A 2R1
(867) 920-2854
Sonny McDonald, President

YELLOWKNIVES DENE BAND CORP.
Box 1287 • YELLOWKNIFE, NT X1A 2N2
(867) 873-6680 Fax 873-5969

NOVA SCOTIA

MICMAC NATIVE FRIENDSHIP CENTRE
2158 Gottingen St. • HALIFAX, NS B3K 3B4
(902) 420-1576 Fax 423-6130
Gordon V. King, Executive Director
Purpose: To provide Native Indians with an education
and occupational training in computer technology and
office automation. A licensed trade school granting a
Certificate to all students who graduate. Small library.

ASSEMBLY OF FIRST NATIONS/NS & NF
P.O. Box 327 • SHUBENACADIE, NS B0N 2H0
(902) 758-2142 Fax 758-1759

UNION OF NOVA SCOTIA INDIANS
Box 400 • SHUBENACADIE, NS B0N 2H0
(902) 758-2346

**MICMAC ASSOCIATION
OF CULTURAL STUDIES**
Box 961 • SYDNEY, NS B1P 6J4
(902) 539-8037 Fax 539-6645
Peter Christmas, Executive Director

**NATIVE COMMUNICATIONS
SOCIETY OF NOVA SCOTIA**
Box 344 • SYDNEY, NS B1P 6H2
(902) 539-0045 Fax 564-0430

NATIVE COUNCIL OF NOVA SCOTIA
75 Dodd St. • SYDNEY, NS B1P 1T7
(902) 567-1240 Fax 564-1123
Dwight Dorey, President

UNION OF NOVA SCOTIA INDIANS
P.O. Box 961 • SYDNEY, N.S. B1P 6J4
(902) 539-4107 Fax 539-6645
Alex Christmas, President

**NOVA SCOTIA MICMAC
ARTS & CRAFTS SOCIETY**
Box 978 • TRURO, NS B2N 5G7
(902) 892-7128

NOVA SCOTIA NATIVE WOMEN'S ASSOCIATION
P.O. Box 805 • TRURO, NS B2N 5E8
(902) 893-7402 Fax 897-7162
Clara Gloade, President

ONTARIO

ATIKOKAN NATIVE FRIENDSHIP CENTRE
P.O. Box 1510
ATIKOKAN, ON P0T 1C0
(807) 597-1213 Fax 597-1473
Roberta McMahon, Executive Director
Purpose: To help create a better quality of life for urban Natives. *Special programs*: Youth programs; craft
teachings, Pow Wow's; traditional teachings;
fundraising activities. Founded 1983.

BARRIE NATIVE FRIENDSHIP CENTRE
175 Bayfield St. • BARRIE, ON L4M 3B4
(705) 721-7689 Fax 721-4316
Ken Geroux, Director

UNITED INDIAN COUNCILS
7 Pinsent Ct. • BARRIE, ON L4N 6E5
(705) 739-8422 Fax 739-8423
PINE TREE CENTRE OF BRANT
25 King St. • BRANTFORD, ON N3T 3C4
(519) 752-5132 Fax 752-5612
Nancy Hill, President

**WOODLAND INDIAN CULTURAL
EDUCATION CENTRE**
P.O. Box 1506 • BRANTFORD, ON N3T 5V6
(519) 759-2650 Fax 759-8912
Joanna Bedard, Executive Director

ININEW FRIENDSHIP CENTRE
P.O. Box 1499 • COCHRANE, ON P0L 1C0
(705) 272-4497 Fax 272-3597
Howard Restoule, Executive Director

AKWESASNE COMMUNICATIONS SOCIETY
Box 1496 • CORNWALL, ON K6H 5V5
(613) 938-1113

DRYDEN NATIVE FRIENDSHIP CENTRE
53 Arthur St. • DRYDEN, ON P8N 1J7
(807) 223-4180 Fax 223-7136
Irene St. Goddard, Executive Director

FORT ERIE INDIAN FRIENDSHIP CENTRE
796 Buffalo Rd. • FORT ERIE, ON L2A 5H2
(905) 871-8931 Fax 871-9655
Wayne Hill, Executive Director

UNITED NATIVE FRIENDSHIP CENTRE
P.O. Box 752 • FORT FRANCIS, ON P9A 3N1
(807) 274-3207 Fax 274-4110
Frank Bruyere, Executive Director

THUNDERBIRD FRIENDSHIP CENTRE
P.O. Box 430 • GERALDTON, ON P0T 1M0
(807) 854-1060 Fax 854-0861
Terry Dowhank, Executive Director

SIX NATIONS ARTS COUNCIL
RR 2 • HAGERSVILLE, ON N0A 1H0
(905) 768-4965

SIX NATIONS ARTS & CRAFTS ASSN.
RR 6 • HAGERSVILLE, ON N0A 1H0
(905) 445-2451

HAMILTON REGIONAL INDIAN CENTRE
712 Main St. E. • HAMILTON, ON L8M 1K8
(905) 548-9593 Fax 545-4077
Cathy Staats, Executive Director

KAPUSKASING INDIAN FRIENDSHIP CENTRE
P.O. Box 26 • KAPUSKASING, ON P5N 1A8
(705) 337-1935 Fax 335-6789
Dorothy Wynne, Executive Director

GRAND COUNCIL TREATY No. 3
Box 1720 • KENORA, ON P7N 3X7
(800) 665-3384; (807) 548-4215 Fax 548-5041
Robin Greene, Grand Chief

**LAKE OF THE WOODS
g1OJIBWAY CULTURAL CENTRE**
Box 159 • KENORA, ON P9N 3X3
(807) 548-5744 Fax 548-1591
Joseph Tom, Director

NE'CHEE FRIENDSHIP CENTRE
P.O. Box 241 • KENORA, ON P9N 3X3
(807) 468-5440 Fax 468-5340
Joe Seymour, Executive Director

KATAROKWI FRIENDSHIP CENTRE
28 Bath Rd., 2nd Fl. • KINGSTON, ON K7L 1H4
(613) 548-1500 Fax 548-1847

ASSEMBLY OF FIRST NATIONS-ONTARIO
536 Queens Ave. • LONDON, ON N6B 1Y8
(519) 660-6171 FAX 439-0467

N'AMERIND FRIENDSHIP CENTRE
260 Colborne St. • LONDON, ON N6B 2S6
(519) 672-0131 Fax 672-0717
Rossalyn McCoy-Mestes, Executive Director

GEORGIAN BAY NATIVE FRIENDSHIP CENTRE
175 Yonge St. • MIDLAND, ON L4R 2A7
(705) 526-5589 Fax 526-7662
Fred Jackson, Executive Director

MOOSONEE NATIVE FRIENDSHIP CENTRE
P.O. Box 478 • MOOSONEE, ON P0L 1Y0
(705) 336-2808 Fax 336-2929
Bill Morrison, Executive Director

NIAGARA REGIONAL NATIVE CENTRE
RR #4, Queenston & Taylor Rd.
NIAGARA-ON-THE-LAKE, ON L0S 1J0
(905) 688-6484 Fax 688-4033
Vince Hill, Executive Director

NORTH BAY INDIAN FRIENDSHIP CENTRE
980 Cassells St. • NORTH BAY, ON P1B 4A6
(705) 472-2811 Fax 472-5251
Bill Butler, Executive Director

UNION OF ONTARIO INDIANS
c/o Nipissing First Nation
P.O. Box 711 • NORTH BAY, ON P1B 8J8
(705) 497-9127 Fax 497-9135

METIS NATION OF ONTARIO
141 Holland Ave. • OTTAWA, ON K1Y0Y2
(800) 263-4889; (613) 798-1488 Fax 722-4225
E-mail: tonyb@metisnation.con.ca
Web site: www.metistraing.org

NATIVE BUSINESS INSTITUTE OF CANADA
2055 Carling Ave. #101
OTTAWA, ON K2A 1G6
(613) 761-9734 Fax 725-9031

ODAWA NATIVE FRIENDSHIP CENTRE
12 Stirling Ave. • OTTAWA, ON K1Y 1P8
(613) 722-3811 Fax 722-4667
Jim Eagle, Executive Director
E-mail: trinan@odawa.on.ca
Web site: www.odawa.on.ca

PARRY SOUND FRIENDSHIP CENTRE
13 Bowes St. • PARRY SOUND, ON 92A 2K7
(705) 746-5970 Fax 746-2612
Vera Pawis-Tabobondung, Executive Director

PETERBOROUGH NATIVE FRIENDSHIP CENTRE
65 Brock St.
PETERBOROUGH, ON K9H 3L8
(705) 876-8195 Fax 876-8806

RED LAKE INDIAN FRIENDSHIP CENTRE
Box 244 • RED LAKE, ON P0V 2M0
(807) 727-2847 Fax 727-3253
Donna Prest, Executive Director

METIS NATION OF ONTARIO
244-143-A Great Northern Blvd.
SAULT STE. MARIE, ON P6B 4X9
(705) 256-6146 Fax 256-6936

ONTARIO METIS ABORIGINAL ASSOCIATION
452 Albert St. E.
SAULT STE. MARIE, ON P6A 2J8
(800) 461-5112; (705) 946-5900 Fax 946-1161
Olaff Bjornaa, President

**SAULT STE. MARIE INDIAN
FRIENDSHIP CENTRE**
122 East St. • SAULT STE. MARIE, ON P6A 3C6
(705) 256-5634 Fax 942-3227
Mary Desmoulin, Executive Director

NISHNAWBE-GAMIK FRIENDSHIP CENTRE
P.O. Box 1299 • SIOUX LOOKOUT, ON P8T 1B8
(807) 737-1903 Fax 737-1805
Laura Wynn, Executive Director

WAWATAY NATIVE COMMUNICATIONS SOCIETY
P.O. Box 1180 • SIOUX LOOKOUT, ON P0V 2T0
(807) 737-2951 Fax 737-3224

ASSOCIATION OF IROQUOIS & ALLIED INDIANS
Oneida Reserve, RR 2
SOUTHWOLD, ON N0L 2G0
(519) 652-3251 Fax 652-9287
Harry Dixtator, President

N'SWAKAMOK NATIVE FRIENDSHIP CENTRE
110 Elm St. W. • SUDBURY, ON P3C 1T5
(705) 674-2128 Fax 671-3539
Marie Meawasige, Executive Director
Established to help Native people to help themselves. Founded 1972.

NATIVE ARTS & CRAFTS
McIntyre Centre, 1886 Memorial Ave.
THUNDER BAY, ON P7B 5K5
(807) 622-5731

ONTARIO NATIVE WOMEN'S ASSOCIATION
977 Alloy Dr. #7 • THUNDER BAY, ON P7B 5Z8
(800) 667-0816; (807) 623-3442 Fax 623-1104
Carol Nobigan, President

THUNDER BAY FRIENDSHIP CENTRE
401 N. Cumberland St.
THUNDER BAY, ON P7A 4P7
(807) 345-5840 Fax 344-8945
Ann Cox, Executive Director

OJIBWAY & CREE CULTURAL CENTRE
#304-210 Spruce St. S.
TIMMINS, ON P4N 2C7
(705) 267-7911 Fax 267-4988
E-mail: ojcc@opnlink.net
Esther Wesley, Director
Purpose: To encourage and support Native People's involvement in the development of self-determination of the Nishnawbe-Aski Nation; to Involve and provide opportunities for people; to support and maintain the use of Native languages; to produce and circulate educational printed and audio-visual material; to promote and ancourage the establishment of a library and information services in the community. *Activities/programs*: Native Language program; Ojibway Cree Resource Center; Ojibway Cree media productions; Indian education programs. Grand Council Treaty #9 - Signed between the crown, the Provincial Government and the Cree-Ojibway of what is now known as Northern Ontario in 1905-06. This was one of a number of treaties made across Canada, following the Royal Proclamation of 1763. The area under Treat #9 covers about 210,000 square miles. There are over 40 Indian commuties scattered throughout the area. 30 of these are accessible by air only. The Indian People of the Treat #9 area are known as the Nishnawbe-Aski. *Publications*: Catalogue of Materials Available for Sale. Library. Established 1976.

TIMMINS NATIVE FRIENDSHIP CENTRE
316 Spruce St. • TIMMINS, ON P4N 2M9
(705) 268-6262 Fax 268-6266
Christine Cummings, Executive Director

ABORIGINAL URBAN ALLIANCE OF ONTARIO
Box 46035, 444 Yonge St.
TORONTO, ON M5B 2L8
(416) 516-8836

CHIEFS OF ONTARIO
344 Bloor St. W. #602
TORONTO, ON M5G 3A7
(416) 972-0212 Fax 972-0217
Andrea Chrisjohn, Executive Director
Gordon Peters, ON Regional Chief

COUNCIL FIRE NATIVE CULTURAL CENTRE
252 Parliament St. • TORONTO, ON M5A 3A4
(416) 360-4350 Fax 360-5978

NATIVE CANADIAN CENTRE OF TORONTO
16 Spadina Rd. • TORONTO, ON M5R 2S7
(416) 964-9087 Fax 964-2111
Gayle Mason, Executive Director
Publication: Native Canadian.

**NATIVE CHILD & FAMILY SERVICES
OF METRO TORONTO**
101-22 College St. • TORONTO, ON M5G 1K2
(416) 969-8510 Fax 969-9251

**ONTARIO FEDERATION OF
INDIAN FRIENDSHIP CENTRES**
290 Shute St. • TORONTO, ON M5A 1W7
(416) 956-7575 Fax 956-7577
Vera Pawis Tabobondung, President
Sylvia Maracle, Executive Director

Assists and supports the 18 Indian Centres under its membership in Ontario. Promotes development of new centres, and provides programs and services to its member centres. Publications. Library.

UNION OF ONTARIO INDIANS
27 Queen St. East, 2nd Floor
TORONTO, ON M5C 1R2
(416) 693-1305 Fax 693-1620
Joe Miskokomon, President
K. Gayle Mason, Executive Director
Represents 40 Indian bands and their 35,000 members. A political organization offering technical and support services to member bands. Library.

OJIBWE CULTURAL FOUNDATION
P.O. Box 278, West Bay Indian Reserve
WEST BAY, ON P0P 1G0
(705) 377-4902 Fax 377-5460
Mary Lou Fox, Director

THE ONTARIO ARCHAEOLOGICAL SOCIETY
126 Willowdale Ave.
WILLOWDALE, ON M2N 4Y2
(416) 730-0797
Christine L. Caroppo, Director
Purpose: To preserve, promote, investigate record and publish an archaeological record of the Province of Ontario. *Activities/progams*: Excavations; workshops; annual Symposium; tours and trips; public lectures; volunteer program "Passport to the Past."*Publications*: Ontario Archaeology - refereed journal; Monographs in Ontario Archaeology - periodic; special publications - directories, etc. Founded 1950.

CAN AM INDIAN FRIENDSHIP CENTRE
1684 Ellrose Ave. • WINDSOR, ON N8Y 3X7
(519) 258-8954 Fax 258-3795
Terry Doxtator, Executive Director

PRINCE EDWARD ISLAND

**ABORIGINAL WOMEN'S
ASSOCIATION OF P.E.I., INC.**
P.O. Box 213
CHARLOTTETOWN, PEI C1A 7K4
(902) 892-0928 Fax 894-3854
Mary Moore, President

NATIVE COUNCIL OF PRINCE EDWARD ISLAND
CHARLOTTETOWN, PEI C1A 4S5
(902) 892-5314 Fax 368-7464
Graham Tuplin, President

**LENNOX ISLAND CULTURAL
EDUCATIONAL CENTRE**
Box 134 • LENNOX ISLAND, PEI C0B 1B0
(902) 831-2779 Fax 831-3153
Charles Sark, Director

QUEBEC

CREE INDIAN CENTRE
95 rue Jaculet • CHIBOUGAMAU, PQ G8P 2G1
(418) 748-7667 Fax 748-6954
Judy Parceaud, Executive Director

**JAMES BAY CREE CULTURAL
EDUCATION CENTRE**
Box 291 • CHISASIBI, PQ J0M 1M0
(819) 855-2473 Jane Pachano, Director

**NATIVE ALLIANCE OF QUEBEC &
LAURENTIAN ALLIANCE OF METIS
& NON-STATUS INDIANS**
21 Brodeur Ave. • HULL, PQ J8Y 2P6
(819) 770-7763 Fax 770-6070
Rheal Boudrias, President

AVATAQ CULTURAL INSTITUTE, INC.
INUKJUAK J0M 1M0
(819) 254-8919 Fax 254-8148
Johnny Epoo, President
office: #404-650 32nd Ave.
LACHINE, PQ H2X 1A4

(800) 361-5029; (514) 637-9883 Fax 637-9707
Arantxa Comas, Contact
Purpose: To preserve and promote Nunavik (Northern Quebec) Inuit language and culture. *Activities/programs*: Building a community museum; language program; traditional medicine project; place name project; genealogy project; photo exhibits; retrieval of anthropological material; transcribe and translate recorded information. Documentation Center comprises historical photographs colection, interview with elders, and library and archives.

**KANIEN'KEHAKA: RAOTITIONHKWA
CULTURAL CENTRE**
Kahnawake Indian Band
Box 1988 • KAHNAWAKE, PQ J0L 1B0
(450) 638-0880 Fax 638-0920
Jessica Hill, Coordinator

QUEBEC NATIVE WOMEN'S ASSOCIATION
P.O. Box 44 • KAHNAWAKE, PQ J0L 1B0
(514) 632-7452

KANESATAKE CULTURAL CENTRE
681 "C" Ste. Philomene
KANESATAKE, PQ J0N 1E0
(514) 479-1783 Fax 479-8249
Chief George Martin, Contact

KATIVIK REGIONAL DEVELOPMENT COUNCIL
P.O. Box 239 • KUUJJUAQ, PQ J0M 1C0
(819) 964-2035 Fax 2611

**CENTRE D'AMITIE AUTOCCHTONE
DE LA TUQUE**
C.P. 335, 544 St. Antoine
LA TUQUE, PQ G9X 3P3
(819) 523-6121 Fax 523-8637
Rosanne Petiquay, Executive Director

CENTRE D'AMITIE AUTOCCHTONE DE QUEBEC
234, rue St-Louis
LORETTEVILLE, PQ G2B 1L4
(418) 843-5818 Fax 843-8960
Jocelyn Gros-Louis, Executive Director

JAMES BAY CREE COMMUNICATION SOCIETY
75 Riverside St.
MISTASSINI LAKE, PQ G0W 1C0
(418) 923-3191 Fax 923-2088

CENTRE FOR NATIVE EDUCATION
1455 de Maissonneuve West
MONTREAL, PQ H3G 1M8
(514) 838-7326 Fax 848-3599

NATIVE FRIENDSHIP CENTRE OF MONTREAL
2001 Boulevard St. Laurant
MONTREAL, PQ H2X 2T3
(514) 499-1854 Fax 499-9436
Ida Williams, Executive Director

QUEBEC NATIVE WOMEN'S ASSOCIATION
460 Ste. Catherine W., Suite 503
MONTREAL, PQ H3A 1A7
(800) 363-0322; (514) 954-9991 Fax 954-1899
Michele Rouleau, President

CREE REGIONAL AUTHORITY COUNCIL
2 Lakeshore Rd. • NEMASKA, PQ J0Y 3B0
(819) 673-2600 Fax 673-2606

**RESTIGOUCHE ECONOMIC
DEVELOPMENT COMMISSION**
Restigouche Indian Band
Box 298, 17 Riverside W.
RESTIGOUCHE, PQ G0C 2R0
(418) 788-2136 Ext. 56 Fax 788-2058
Romey Labillois, Director

CENTRE FOR INDIGENOUS SOVEREIGNTY
Mohawks of Akwesasne
McDonald Rd. • ST. REGIS, PQ H0M 1A0
(613) 575-1731 Fax 575-1443

CENTRE D'AMITIE AUTOCHTONE
910, 10e Ave., C.P. 1769
SENNETERRE, PQ J0Y 2M0
(819) 737-2324 Fax 737-8311
Louis Bordeleau, Executive Director

INNU FRIENDSHIP CENTRE
100 Laure Blvd., #100 • SEPT-Ies, PQ G4R 1Y1
(418) 968-2026

ALGONQUIN COUNCIL OF WESTERN QUEBEC
351 Central Ave. • VAL D'OR, PQ J2P 1P6
(819) 770-7763 Fax 770-6070
Roger Brindamour, Director

CENTRE D'AMITIE AUTOCHTONE
1272, 7th St. • VAL D'OR, PQ J9P 3W4
(819) 825-6857 Fax 825-7515
Diane Decoste, Executive Director

GRAND COUNCIL OF THE CREES
1462 rue de la Quebecoise
VAL D'OR, PQ J9P 5H4
(819) 825-3402 Fax 825-6892
Matthew Coon-Come, Grand Chief

ASSEMBLY OF FIRST NATIONS/QUEBEC
430 Koska • WENDAKE, PQ G0A 1B6
(418) 842-5020 Fax 842-2660

**INSTITUT EDUCATIF ET CULTUREL
ATTIKAMEK-MONTAGNAIS**
7-40, rue Francois Gros-Louis
WENDAKE, PQ G0A 4V0
(418) 843-0258 Fax 843-7313
Johanne Robertson, Director

LES ARTISANS INDIENS DU QUEBEC
540 Max Gros-Louis St., Village des Hurons
WENDAKE, PQ G0A 4V0 (418) 845-2150
Therese Sioui, President

NATIVE CONSULTING SERVICES
50 boul. Maurice Bastien #100
Village des Hurons • WENDAKE, PQ G0A 4V0
(418) 847-0322 Fax 843-7339

**REGROUPMENT DES CENTRES D'AMITIE
AUTOCHTONE DU QUEBEC**
30 rue de l'ours, Village des Hurons
WENDAKE, PQ G0A 4V0
(418) 842-6354 Fax 842-9795
Ida Williams, President

**SECRETARIAT OF FIRST NATIONS
OF QUEBEC & LABRADOR**
430 Koska, Village des Hurons
WENDAKE, PQ G0A 4V0
(418) 842-5020 Fax 842-2660
Konrad Sioui, Vice-Chief

SASKATCHEWAN

NATIVE COUNCIL OF SASKATCHEWAN
P.O. Box 132 • GREEN LAKE, SK S0M 1B0
(306) 888-2125 Fax 288-4622
Harvey Young, President

QU'APPELLE VALLEY FRIENDSHIP CENTRE
P.O. Box 240 • FORT QU'APPELLE, SK S0G 1S0
(306) 332-5616 Fax 332-5091
J. Peter Dubois, Executive Director
Personnel: W. Arliss Dellow, Program Director; Robyn Donsion, Coordinator (Youth Alternative Measures Program). *Purpose*: To identify and cater to the social, cultural, and recreational needs of the Indian and Metis people of Fort Qu'Appelle and District; to enhance community participation by the people of Indian descent; and to promote better understanding and relations between Native and non-Native citizens. *Programs*: Youth Alternative Measures; Identification Program (fingerprinting children); Drug & Alcohol Counseling; Literacy, et al. *Publication*: Qu'Appelle Valley Quill, quarterly newsletter.

KIKINAHK FRIENDSHIP CENTRE, INC.
Box 254 • LA RONGE, SK S0J 1S0
(306) 425-2051 Fax 425-3359
Norm Bouvier, Executive Director

NORTHWEST FRIENDSHIP CENTRE
P.O. Box 1780 • MEADOW LAKE, SK S0M 1V0
(306) 236-3766 Fax 236-5451
Gladys Joseph, Executive Director

MOOSE JAW NATIVE FRIENDSHIP CENTRE
42 High St. E.
MOOSE JAW, SK S6H 0B8
(306) 693-6966 Fax 692-3509
Ed Pelletier, Executive Director

**BATTLEFORDS INDIAN &
METIS FRIENDSHIP CENTRE**
12002 Railway Ave. E.
N. BATTLEFORD, SK S9A 3W3
(306) 445-8216 Fax 445-6863
Daryl Larose, Executive Director

**ABORIGINAL WOMEN'S COUNCIL
OF SASKATCHEWAN**
#101-118, 12th St. E.
PRINCE ALBERT, SK S6V 1B6
(306) 763-6005 Fax 922-6034
Lil Sanderson, Contact

INDIAN & METIS FRIENDSHIP CENTRE
1409 1st Ave.
PRINCE ALBERT S6V 2B2
(306) 764-3431 Fax 763-3205
Eugene Arcand, Executive Director

NATIVE INDIAN FINANCIAL CORPORATION
P.O.Box 2377
PRINCE ALBERT, SK S6V 6Z1
(306) 763-4712 Fax 763-3255

**FEDERATION OF SASKATCHEWAN
INDIAN NATIONS**
1692 Albert St. • REGINA, SK S4P 2S6
(306) 721-2822 Fax 721-2707
Alphonse Bird, Chief

FIRST NATIONS EMPLOYMENT CENTRE
3639 Sherwood Dr. • REGINA, SK S4R 4A7
(306) 924-1606 Fax 949-0526

INDIAN & METIS FRIENDSHIP CENTRE
303 McGee Crescent
REGINA, SK S4R 6K8
(306) 543-2745
Walter Schoenthal, Exec. Director

REGINA FRIENDSHIP CENTRE
1440 Scarth St. • REGINA, SK S4R 2E9
(306) 525-5459 Fax 525-3005
Sharon Ironstar, President
Dona Racette, Executive Director

**SASKATCHEWAN INDIAN
ARTS & CRAFTS CORPORATION**
2431-8th Ave. • REGINA, SK S4R 5J7
(306) 352-1501 Dorothy Thomas, President

**SASKATCHEWAN INDIAN
HOUSING COMMISSION**
109 Hodsman Rd.
REGINA, SK S4N 5W5
(800) 721-2707; (306) 721-2822 Fax 775-2994

ASSEMBLY OF FIRST NATIONS
#200 - 103A Packham Ave.
SASKATOON, SK S7N 4K4
(306) 665-1215 Fax 244-4413

**FEDERATION OF SASKATCHEWAN
INDIAN NATIONS**
#200-103A Packham Ave.
SASKATOON, SK S7N 4K4
(306) 956-6916 Fax 955-0950

NATIONAL INDIAN FINANCIAL CORPORATION
#217, 103B Packham Ave.
SASKATOON, SK S7N 4K4
(800) 667-4712; (306) 955-4712 Fax 477-4554

SASKATCHEWAN ARCHAEOLOGICAL SOCIETY
#5 - 816 1st Ave. N. • SASKATOON S7K 1Y3
(306) 664-4124 Fax 665-1928
Tim Jones, Executive Director
Purpose: To actively promote and encourage the study, preservation and proper use of the archaeological resources of Saskatchewan. *Activities*: Educational programs; field school; seminars; field trips; Certification program; operates the Regional Archaeology Volunteers Program. Member Funding Grants - 4 grants for

members to complete special projects. *Publication*: Tracking Ancient Hunters: Prehistoric Archaeology in Saskatchewan; Avonlea, Yesterday and Today, Annotated Bibliography of Saskatewan Archaeology and Prehistory; Bimonthly newsletter; annual Journal. Founded 1963.

SASKATCHEWAN INDIAN CULTURAL CENTRE
205-103B Packham Ave.
SASKATOON, SK S7K 4K4
(306) 244-1146 Fax 665-6520
Linda Pelly-Landrie, President

SASKATCHEWAN NATIVE COMMUNICATIONS SOCIETY
104-219 Robin Cres.
SASKATOON, SK S7N 6M8
(306) 244-7441 Fax 343-0171

SASKATOON INDIAN & METIS FRIENDSHIP CENTRE
168 Wall St. • SASKATOON, SK S7K 1N4
(306) 244-0174 Fax 664-2536
Maurice J. Blondeau, Director

SASKATOON NATIVE THEATRE
919 Broadway Ave.
SASKATOON, SK S7N 1B8
(306) 244-7779

ABORIGINAL FRIENDSHIP CENTRES OF SASKATCHEWAN
c/o Yorktown Friendship Centre
139 Dominion Ave. • YORKTON, SK S3N 1P7
(306) 782-2822 Fax 782-6662
Ivan Cote, Executive Director

YUKON

COUNCIL FOR YUKON FIRST NATIONS
11 Nisutlin Dr. • WHITEHORSE, YUKON Y1A 3S5
(403) 667-7631 Fax 668-6577
Judy Gingell, Chairperson

SKOOKUM JIM FRIENDSHIP CENTRE
3159 - 3rd Ave. • WHITEHORSE, YU Y1A 1G1
(403) 668-4465 Fax 668-4725
Ruby Van Bibban, Executive Director

YE SA TO COMMUNICATIONS SOCIETY
22 Nisutlin Dr. • WHITEHORSE, YU Y1A 3S5
(403) 667-2775 Fax 667-6923

YUKON INDIAN ARTS & CRAFTS CO-OPERATIVE LIMITED
4230-4th Ave.
WHITEHORSE, YU Y1A 1K1
(403) 668-5955 Fax 668-6466
Stan Peters, President

YUKON INDIAN DEVELOPMENT CORP.
409 Black St.
WHITEHORSE, YU Y1A 2N2
(403) 668-3908 Fax 668-3127

YUKON INDIAN CULTURAL EDUCATION SOCIETY
11 Nisultin Dr.
WHITEHORSE, YU Y1A 3S5
(403) 667-4616 Fax 668-6577
Pat Martin, Coordinator

YUKON INDIAN WOMEN'S ASSOCIATION
11 Nisutlin Dr. • WHITEHORSE Y1A 3S4
(403) 667-6162 Fax 668-7539
Nina Bolton, President'

CANADA

ALBERTA

LUXTON MUSEUM
Box 850 • BANFF, AB T0L 0C0
(403) 762-2388 Fax 760-2803
Western Canadian Indian museum.

OLDMAN RIVER CULTURAL CENTER
P.O. Box 70 • BROCKET, AB T0K 0H0
(403) 965-3939 Fax 965-2087
Reggie Crow Shoe, Director
Opened in 1973.

TSUU T'INA MUSEUM & ARCHIVES
Box 135 • CALGARY, AB T2W 3C4
(403) 238-2677 Fax 251-0980
Jenette Starlight, Director
Description: Dedicated to the preservation of Tsuu T'ina culture and history.

PROVINCIAL MUSEUM OF ALBERTA
Archaeology & Ethnology Section
12845 - 102 Ave.
EDMONTON, AB T5N 0M6
(780) 453-9147 Fax 454-6629
John W. Ives, Manager, Archaeology & Ethnology
E-mail: jives@mcd.gov.ab.ca
Susan J. Berry, Curator-Ethnology
Description: Collections focus on the material culture and lifeways of indigenous peoples of Alberta (Beaver, Slavey, Chipewyan, Northern and Plains Cree, Blackfoot, Blood, Peigan, Sarsi, Assiniboine, Kutenai, Sauteaux, Metis) and other groups relevant to the histories of indigenous peoples in Alberta (e.g. Iroquois.) Contains approximately 12,000 items, strong in both functional and religious Plains materials; tipis and moccasins are extensive; Inuit clothing and other items from the Canadian Arctic. *Special programs*: Research and collecting projects—Native lifeways and material cultures in Alberta, focusing on 20th century items. *Publications*: Storyteller, monthly; books for sale. Library.

MASKWACHEES CULTURAL COLLEGE
P.O. Box 360 • HOBBEMA, AB T0C 1N0
(403) 585-3925 Fax 585-2080
Steve Skikum, Director
Opened in 1974.

NAKODA LODGE/CULTURAL INSTITUTE
P.O. Box 149 • MORLEY, AB T0L 1N0
(403) 881-3949 Fax 881-3901
Dave Drews, Director
Opened in 1988.

SIKSIKA NATION MUSEUM
Old Sun Community College
P.O. Box 1250
SIKSIKA NATION, AB T0J 3W0
(403) 734-3862
Opened in 1977.

NINASTAKO CULTURAL CENTER
P.O. Box 232 • STANDOFF, AB T0L 1Y0
(403) 737-3774 Fax 737-3786
Gloria Wells, Director
Opened in 1974.

BRITISH COLUMBIA

U'MISTA CULTURAL CENTRE
P.O. Box 253 • ALERT BAY, BC V0N 1A0
(604) 974-5403 Fax 974-5499
E-mail: umista@north.island.net
Linda Manz, Director
Description: Houses one of the finest collections of carved masks depicting the Potlatch Ceremony of the Kwak'wala-speaking peoples. Exhibits of contemporary arts and crafts, including artifacts, audio & video, photographs, library and archival resources. Opened in 1980.

ATLIN MUSEUM
Fourth & Trainor Sts. • ATLIN, BC
Exhibits Tlingit Indian artifacts.

SAANICH NATIVE HERITAGE SOCIETY
P.O. Box 28
BRENTWOOD BAY, BC V0F 1A0
(250) 652-5980 Fax 652-5957
Adelynne Claxton, Director

CAMPBELL RIVER MUSEUM
Box 101 • CAMPBELL RIVER, BC
Indian museum displaying Northwest Coast material.

COQUALEETZA EDUCATION TRAINING CENTRE
7201 Vedder Rd. Bldg. #1
CHILLIWACK, BC V2R 4G5
(604) 858-3366 Fax 824-5226
Shirley Leon, Director

COWICHAN NATIVE VILLAGE/ NATIVE HERITAGE
200 Cowichan Way • DUNCAN, BC V9L 4T8
(250) 746-8119 Fax 746-4143
John Parker, Director

'KSAN MUSEUM
P.O. Box 326 • HAZELTON, BC V0J 1Y0
(250) 842-5544 Fax 842-6533
Eve Hope, Director & Curator
Description: Museum is part of a reconstructed Indian village. Maintains a collection of Northwest Coast Indian artifacts, specifically Gitksan. *Special program*: Kitanmax School of Northwest Coast Indian Art - a 2-year program in wood carving, design, tool making, serigraph. *Publications*: Weget Wanders On - prints and legends; Gathering What the Great Nature Provided; Robes of Dover. Opened in 1959.

KAMLOOPS MUSEUM & ARCHIVES
207 Seymour St.
KAMLOOPS, BC V2C 2E7
(250) 828-3576 Ken Favrholdt, Director & Curator
Description: General history collection related to the natural and human history of the Kamloops district including artifacts and exhibits related to Native Indians of area. *Special collection*: Extensive archives including files on interior Salish Indians and local Shuswap Indians.Exhibits Indian artifacts, mostly Shuswap Indians, with some material relevant to other tribes of the Interior Salish. *Publication*: The Dispossessed (Salish Indians); local history publications. Archives and library. Opened in 1937.

SECWEPMEMC MUSEUM & NATIVE HERITAGE PARK
355 Yellowhead Hwy.
KAMLOOPS, BC V2H 1H1
(250) 828-9801 Fax 372-1127
Ken Favrholdt, Director; Linda Jules, Curator
Description: Portrays the history and culture of the Secwepmemc (Shuswap) Nation of south-central British Columbia from prehistoric to contemporary times. Includes archives, gift shop, and a 12-acre heritage park including a 2,000 year old village site. Contains canoes, a tule mat lodge, archaeological material, baskets, church and religious artifacts, photos, beadwork, trade items, leatherwork. *Programs*: Educational; Language; Trades training; Communications; workshops & conferences. *Publication*: Secwepmemc News - monthly newspaper. Library. Opened in 1985.

OKANAGAN INDIAN EDUCATIONAL RESOURCES SOCIETY
257 Brunswick St.
PENTICTON, BC V2A 5P9
(250) 493-7181 Fax 493-5302
Jeanette Armstrong, Director
E-mail: jarmstrg@web.net
Opened in 1980.

MUSEUM OF NORTHERN BRITISH COLUMBIA
P.O. Box 669
PRINCE RUPERT, BC V8J 3S1
(250) 624-3207 Elaine Moore, Curator/Director
Description: Exhibits a collection of ethnographic artifacts representing Tsimshian native people (coast, Gitksan and Nisgha) and Haida and Tlingit to a lesser extent; Northwest Coast Indian artifacts, and other cultural remains relating to regional history. *Publication*: The Curator's Log, quarterly newsletter; Arts of the Salmon People; Totem Poles of Prince Rupert", illustrated guide; Guide to the Collection. Library.

KWAGIULTH MUSEUM & CULTURAL CENTRE
P.O. Box 8 • QUATHIASKI, BC V0P 1N0
(604) 285-3733 Fax 285-2400
Estelle Inman, Executive Director
Opened in 1979.

ED JONES HAIDA MUSEUM
Second Beach Skidgate
QUEEN CHARLOTTE CITY, BC V0T 1S0
(250) 559-4643

UNIVERSITY OF BRITISH COLUMBIA
MUSEUM OF ANTHROPOLOGY
6393 N.W. Marine Dr.
VANCOUVER, BC V6T 1W5
 (250) 228-5087
Description: Major research and study collections include Northwest Coast archaeology and ethnology, and ethnological specimens from other North American Indian cultures. *Publications*: Anthropology at the Academy, newsletter; The Elkus Collection of Southwestern Indian Art; Hopi Kachina: Spirit of Life. Library.

THE VANCOUVER MUSEUM
1100 Chestnut • VANCOUVER, BC V6J 3J9
 (250) 736-4431 Dr. David Hemphill, Director
 Lynn Maranda, Curator of Anthropology
Special collections: Lipsett Native Indian collection; Ryan Collection of Haida argillite carvings. *Publication*: Muse News. Library. Founded 1894.

HEILSTUK CULTURAL EDUCATION CENTRE
P.O. Box 880 • WAGLISLA, BC V0T 1Z0
 (604) 957-2626 Fax 957-2780
 Jennifer Carpenter, Director
 E-mail: jcarp@unix.infoserve.net
 Opened in 1978.

MANITOBA

ESKIMO MUSEUM
James St. • CHURCHILL, MB R0B 0E0

CROSS LAKE CULTURAL/EDUCATION CENTRE
Cross Lake Indian Reserve
CROSS LAKE, MB R0B 0J0
 (204) 676-2268/2218

NORWAY HOUSE CULTURAL EDUCATION
CENTRE
Norway House Cree Nation
P.O. Box 250 • NORWAY HOUSE, MB R0B 1B0
 (204) 359-6296 Fax 359-6262
 Myra Saunders, R&D Coordinator
 Opened in 1990.

CULTURAL CENTER
Fort Alexander Band
P.O. Box 1610 • PINE FALLS, MB R0E 1M0
 (204) 367-8740

SAGKEENG CULTURAL EDUCATION CENTRE
Box 749 • PINE FALLS, MB R0E 1M0
 (204) 367-2612 Art Boubard, Director
 Opened in 1998.

MANITOBA INDIAN CULTURAL
EDUCATION CENTRE
119 Sutherland Ave. • WINNIPEG, MB R2W 3C9
 (204) 942-0228 Fax 947-6564
 Ron Missyabit, Director
Description: Maintains a collection of artifacts of native peoples of Manitoba. Library of books, films, tape/slides, and audio-visual presentations, artifacts, educational kits. *Publications*: Manitoba Elders, $6; Lifestyles of Manitoba Indians, $2 coloring book. Opened in 1975.

MANITOBA MUSEUM OF MAN & NATURE
190 Rupert Ave. • WINNIPEG, MB

NORTHWEST TERRITORIES

INUMMARIT COMMITTEE - SOD HOUSE
MUSEUM
c/o Hamlet of Arctic Bay, General Delivery
ARCTIC BAY, NT X0A 0A0
 Dorothee Komangapik, Director

INUIT SILATTUQSARVINGAT
Inuit Cultural Institute
ESKIMO POINT, NT X0C 0E0
 (819) 857-2803 Luke Suluk, Director

DENE MUSEUM/ARCHIVES
c/o General Delivery
FORT GOOD HOPE, NT X0E 0U0

AUGMARLIK INTERPRETIVE CENTRE
P.O. Box 225 • PANGNIRTUNG, NT X0A 0R0
 (819) 473-8737 Fax 473-8685
 Sheila Garpik, Director
 Opened in 1987.

SIPALASEEQUTT MUSEUM SOCIETY
PANGNIRTUNG, NT X0A 0R0
 Koaguk Akulujuk, Director

DENE CULTURAL INSTITUTE
P.O. Box 207 • YELLOWKNIFE, NT X1A 2N2
 (403) 873-6617
 Joanne Burnaby, Executive Director

NOVA SCOTIA

NOVA SCOTIA MUSEUM
1747 Summer St. • HALIFAX, NS B3H 3A6
 (902) 429-4610
 Candace Stevenson, Director
Description: Contains an extensive collection and exhibit of Micmac material culture—stone tools, basketry, birchbark objects, quill boxes, and bone implements. *Publications*: Micmac Quillwork; Elitekey; Red Earth; Withe Baskets, Traps and Brooms. Library.

ONTARIO

WOODLAND CULTURAL CENTRE
P.O. Box 1506, 184 Mohawk St.
BRANTFORD, ON N3T 5V6
 (519) 759-2653 Fax 759-2445
 Tom Hill, Director
 E-mail: tomhill@museumat.woodland-centre.on.ca
 Opened in 1972.

JOSEPH BRANT MUSEUM
1240 North Shore Blvd. • BURLINGTON, ON
Description: A collection of Joseph Brant (Iroquois) memorabilia; general material on the Iroquois culture. Library.

NORTH AMERICAN INDIAN TRAVELLING
COLLEGE
RR #3 • CORNWALL ISLAND, ON K6H 5R7
Mail: P.O. Box 273, Hogansburg, NY 13655
 (613) 932-9452 Fax 932-0092
 Barbara Barnes, Director
 Opened in 1968.

GOLDEN LAKE ALGONQUIN MUSEUM
P.O. Box 28 • GOLDEN LAKE, ON K0J 1X0

LAKE OF THE WOODS
OJIBWAY CULTURAL CENTRE
P.O. Box 159 • KENORA, ON P9N 3X3
 (807) 548-5744 Fax 548-1591
 Donald Kavanaugh, Director
 E-mail: ojibwaycc@voyageur.ca
 Opened in 1977.

THE McMICHAEL CANADIAN ART COLLECTION
10365 Islington Ave.
KLEINBERG, ON L0J 1C0
 (416) 893-1121
 Jean Blodgett, Curator of Native
  Indian and Inuit Art
Description: Collection includes contemporary Canadian Woodland and Plains paintings, drawings and sculpture; some Northwest Coast Indian material culture. *Special program*: School program and resource package entitled: "Contemporary Expressions: Indian Art." *Publications*: Quarterly newsletter; exhibition catalogs. Library. Founded 1965.

MUSEUM OF INDIAN ARCHAEOLOGY
University of Western Ontario, Lawson-Jury Bldg.
LONDON, ON N6G 3M6 (519) 473-1360
 William D. Finlayson, Ph.D., Executive Director
 Debra Bodner, Curator
Description: Large (over one-half million specimens) archaeological collections from throughout southern Ontario; small ethnographic collection from Ontario, Canadian Plains, and the Arctic. *Lawson Prehistoric Indian Village*: An open-air facility featuring excava-

tion, reconstruction and interpretation of a prehistoric Neutral village. *Programs*: Exhibition Gallery; study and layout space; tours and lectures; Research Associate Program; Archaeological Contracting and Consulting Services; archaeological field schools and courses. *Publications*: Newsletter; Bulletin; Research Reports. Library.

OJIBWA CULTURAL FOUNDATION
Excelsior Post Office, West Bay
MANITOULIN ISLAND, ON T0P 1G0
 (705) 377-4902/4899

CHIEFSWOOD MUSEUM
P.O. Box 5000
OHSWEKEN, ON N0A 1M0
 (519) 752-5005 Fax 752-9578
 Paula Whitlow, Director
 Opened in 1998.

NATIONAL MUSEUM OF MAN
NATIONAL MUSEUMS OF CANADA
OTTAWA, ON K1A 0M8
 (819) 994-6113 (Archaeological Survey of Canada)
 (613) 996-4540 (Canadian Ethnological Service)
 Ian G. Dyck, Ph.D., Chief-Archaeology
 A. McFadyen Clark, Chief Ethnologist
Archaeological Collection: Contains approximately 2,500,000 specimens from Canada and Alaska; collections from the Eastern Woodlands (Ontario eastward to the Atlantic Provinces) and the Eskimo (Arctic) areas; the Arctic Coast, Northwest Coast, Plateau, western Boreal forest, and Plains. *Ethnological Collection*: Approximately 50,000 artifacts, 90 of which are Canadian Indian and Inuit material (including modern works of Indian and Inuit art) with emphasis on Inuit and Pacific Coast Indian traditional material culture. *Programs*: Responsible for the survey and rescue of Canada's prehistoric sites; to record the languages and cultures of Canadian Indians, Inuit and Metis. Publications. Library.

LAURENTIAN UNIVERSITY
MUSEUM & ARTS CENTRE
John St. • SUDBURY, ON P3E 2C6
 (705) 674-3271 Pamela Krueger, Director/Curator
Description: Collection areas relate to contemporary native and Inuit artists of Canada, and native and Indian artists of Northern Ontario; over 800 works by over 600 Canadian artists, historical and contemporary; over 25 diffferent exhibitions are presented each year. *Special programs*: Talks and tours; lectures; art courses; film series. *Publications*: Communique, published every six weeks; exhibition catalogues. Library. Founded 1967.

OJIBWAY & CREE CULTURAL CENTRE
210 Spruce St. S., Suite 304
TIMMINS, ON P4N 2M7
 (705) 267-7911 Fax 267-4988
 Bertha Metat, Director
 E-mail: ojccc@onlink.net
Description: Exhibits materials describing the history of the Cree, Oji-Cree, and Ojibway of the Treaty #9 area of Northern Ontario. The Center has over 200 photographs both archival and contemporary, and 182 objects which include traditional dress, games, tools, and contemporary craftwork. Opened in 1975.

ROYAL ONTARIO MUSEUM
100 Queens Park
TORONTO, ON M5S 2C6
 (416) 586-5724 Fax 586-5863
 Mima Kapches, Chairperson
 E-mail: mimak@rom.on.ca
Ethnology: Collections of material for the following geographical areas and tribes: Arctic—Eastern Canadian Eskimo, Netsilik Eskimo, Copper Eskimo, Western Canadian Eskimo; Northwest Coast—Kwakiutl, Tsimshian, Haida, Gitskan, Bella Bella; Northeast Coast—Iroquois, Cree Ojibwa, Montagnais-Naskapi; Plains—Blackfoot, Cree and Saulteaux, Canadian Plains. *Archaeology*: Provincial collections of Ontario archaeological material; and material from the rest of Canada; material from the U.S., including the Southwest and Mississippi Valley cultures. *Publications*: Archaeological Newsletter; Rotunda, quarterly magazine; Monographs and Papers; Round Lake Ojibwa (monograph); contemporary native arts catalogs; Native People of Canada (7 booklets); books for sale. Library.

QUEBEC

CANADIAN MUSEUM OF CIVILIZATION
P.O. Box 3100 Station "B" • HULL, PQ J8X 4H2
(819) 776-8430 Web site: www.civilization.ca
Andrea Laforet, Director
Morgan Baillargeon, Curator-
  Plains Indian Ethnology
Gerald McMaster, Curator-Contemporary Indian Art
Description: Concerned with the national representation of artwork, artifacts and documentation relative to archaeology, ethnology, physical anthropology, folk culture and history. Reference Library.

AVATAQ CULTURAL INSTITUTE, INC.
P.O. Box 230 • INUKJUAK, PQ J0M 1M0
(819) 254-8919 Fax 254-8148
Opened in 1992.

**KANIEN'KEAKA RAOTITIONKWA
CULTURAL CENTRE**
P.O. Box 969 • KAHNAWAKE, PQ J0L 1B0
(514) 638-0880 Fax 638-0920
Kana Pakta, Director
Description: To promote, preserve, and maintain the culture of the Kanien'kehaka and the Iroquois. Maintains a library, cultural exhibit, and photographic archives. Annual Proud Nation Powwow in July. Opened in 1978.

KANEHSATAKE CULTURAL CENTRE
681 Ste. Philomene
KANEHSATAKE, PQ J0N 1E0
(514) 479-1783 Fax 479-8249
Steven L. Bonspille, Director
E-mail: cultural@netc.net
Opened in 1978.

LISTUGUJ ARTS & CULTURAL CENTRE
2 Riverside West • LISTUGUJ, PQ G0C 2R0
(418) 788-9088 Fax 788-5980
Olitha Isaac, Director
Opened in 1990.

**KITIGAN ZIBI CULTURAL
EDUCATION DISPLAYS CENTRE**
41 Kikinamage Mikan • MANIWAKI, PQ J9E 3B1
(819) 449-1798 Gilbert Whiteduck, Director
Opened in 1979.

MUSEE AMERINDIEN DE MASHTEWIATSH
1787 rue Amishk
MASHTEWIATSH, PQ G0W 2H0
(418) 275-4842 Fax 275-7494
Florent Begin, Director

MUSEE DES ABENAKIS
108 Waban-aki St. • ODANAK, PQ J0G 1H0
(514) 568-2600 Fax 568-5959
Nichole O'Bomsawin, Director
E-mail: abenakis@enternet.com
Opened in 1962.

AMERINDIAN MUSEUM
406 Amisk • POINTE-BLEUE, PQ G0W 2H0
Carmen Gill Casavante, Director

**INSTITUT EDUCATIF ET CULTUREL
ATTIKAMEK-MONTAGNOMIS**
40 rue Francois Gros-Louis, No. 7
VILLAGE DES HURONS, PQ G0A 4V0
(418) 968-4424 Fax 968-1841
Luc Anbre, Director

SASKATCHEWAN

**BATTLEFORD NATIONAL
HISTORIC PARK MUSEUM**
P.O. Box 70 • BATTLEFORD, SK

PRAIRIE PIONEER MUSEUM
P.O. Box 273 • CARIK, SK

MOOSE JAW ART MUSEUM
Crescent Park • MOOSE JAW, SK

SASKATCHEWAN INDIAN CULTURAL CENTRE
P.O. Box 3085
SASKATOON, SK S7K 0S2
(306) 244-1146 Fax 665-6520
Linda Pelly-Landrie, Director
E-mail: sicc@sasknet.sk.ga
Opened in 1972.

**THE SASKATOON GALLERY
& CONSERVATORY MUSEUM**
Mendel Art Gallery
950 Spadina Crescent E. • SASKATOON, SK

VIGFUSSON MUSEUM
University of Saskatchewan
Room 69, Arts Bldg. • SASKATOON, SK

LIBRARIES

ALBERTA

HISTORICAL RESOURCES LIBRARY
Provincial Archives of Alberta
12845 102 Ave. • EDMONTON T5N 0M6
(403) 427-1750 Fax 454-6629
Margaret E. Bhatnagar, Librarian
Description: A collection of 20,000 volumes on local history (Alberta), western Canadian history, archaeology and ethnology. *Publications*: Bibliography and Literature Guide. Interlibrary loans. Open to public.

**UNIVERSITY OF ALBERTA
COLLEGE OF ST. JEAN LIBRARY**
8406 91st St. • EDMONTON T6C 4G9
Description: Maintains a collection of 50,000 volumes, many of which are on the anthropology and ethnology of North American Indians.

BRITISH COLUMBIA

UNIVERSITY OF BRITISH COLUMBIA LIBRARY
Humanities and Social Sciences Division
1956 East Mall
VANCOUVER, BC V6T 1W3
(604) 228-2725 Fax 228-6465
Description: Maintains a strong academic collection, specializing in the Indians of the Northwest Pacific Coast (especially British Columbia) but also Canadian aboriginal peoples in general. Interlibrary loans. Open to the public.

MANITOBA

ESKIMO MUSEUM LIBRARY
242 La Verendrye St.
CHURCHILL, MB R0B 0E0
(204) 675-2541
A collection of ethnographic material on the Eskimos.

**DEPARTMENT OF CULTURAL AFFAIRS
& HISTORICAL RESOURCES
PROVINCIAL ARCHIVES**
200 Vaughan St. • WINNIPEG, MB R3C 0V8
Focus Program: A collection of master tapes and duplicates made with Indian people in Manitoba.

NEWFOUNDLAND

MEMORIAL UNIVERSITY OF NEWFOUNDLAND
Centre for Newfoundland Studies
Elizabeth Ave.
ST. JOHNS, NF A1B 3Y1
(709) 737-7476 Fax 737-3188
Anne Hart, Librarian
Description: Holdings include materials on Beothuk, Naskapi-Montagnais, Micmac, Dorset, Innu, Maritime Archaic, and Inuit peoples. Also an archives, holding a small collection of manuscript material on some of these peoples.

NOVA SCOTIA

**DALHOUSIE UNIVERSITY MARITIME
SCHOOL OF SOCIAL WORK LIBRARY**
6420 Coburg Rd. • HALIFAX, NS B3H 3J5
Special collection: Native Peoples Collection—books and journals on Indians, Eskimos and Metis.

NOVA SCOTIA MUSEUM LIBRARY
1747 Summer St. • HALIFAX, NS B3H 3A6
Description: Contains a collection of books on Micmac material culture and ethnography.

ONTARIO

**ASSEMBLY OF FIRST NATIONS -
RESOURCE CENTRE**
One Nicholas St. #1002
OTTAWA, ON K1N 7B7
(613) 241-6789 Fax 241-5808
Kelly Whiteduck, Coordinator
Description: Maintains a collection of 10,000 volumes on treaty and aboriginal rights, with special collections on education, alcohol and drug abuse, lands revenue & Trust Review, etc.; books and monographs (unpublished reports); 100 Native-American periodicals; and law cases. Open to public as a reference library - Monday-Friday, 9 AM - 5 PM.

**CANADA—DEPT. OF INDIAN AFFAIRS
NORTHERN DEVELOPMENTAL LIBRARY**
OTTAWA, ON K1A 0H4
(819) 997-0811 Fax 997-0511
Mrs. Ramma Kamra, Librarian
Holdings include over 51,000 titles (200,000 volumes); 20,000 bound periodical volumes; 1,200 current subscriptions; 3,500 government documents; 3,000 reels of microfilm; 6 drawers of microfiche. Subject coverage: Canadian native peoples; the Canadian North, the environment, natural resources, Canadian history, and economic development. books on North American Indians and Eskimos.

**THE NATIONAL MUSEUMS
OF CANADA LIBRARY**
360 Lisgar St. • OTTAWA, ON K1A 0M8
Description: Maintains a collection of 35,000 volumes on anthropology, including many on the Indians and native peoples of Canada. Museocinematography: Ethnographic Film Programs.

**LAURENTIAN UNIVERSITY MUSEUM
& ARTS CENTRE LIBRARY**
Laurentian University
Dept. of Cultural Affairs • SUDBURY, ON P3E 2C6
(705) 675-1151 Fax 674-3065
Pamela Krueger, Librarian
Description: A collection of books covering all areas of art with special sections on native and Inuit peoples. Open to the public.

ROYAL ONTARIO MUSEUM LIBRARY
100 Queen's Park • TORONTO, ON M5S 2C6
Description: A collection of 50,000 volumes, and 20 journals of anthropological interest; many books on the Indians and native peoples of Canada.

QUEBEC

**CANADIAN MUSEUM OF
CIVILIZATION MEDIATHEQUE**
P.O. Box 3100 • HULL, PQ J8X 4H2
(819) 953-6456 Fax 953-4378
M. Boudreau, Reference Librarian

SASKATCHEWAN

NATIVE LAW LIBRARY
Native Law Centre, University of Saskatchewan
150 Diefenbaker Centre
SASKATOON, SK S7N 0W0

(306) 966-6189
Linda Fritz, Native Law Librarian
Description: A collection of 6,000 books, journals and legal decisions in all areas of native law including self-government, constitutional developments, membership rights, child welfare and international law. A major retrospective cataloguing project has recently been completed, making historical documents from various native organizations and older published works accessible. Archival collection of materials from the Mackenzie Valley Pipeline Inquiry; and a complete collection of native law cases.

PERIODICALS

ABORIGINAL VOICES MAGAZINE
116 Spadina Ave. #201
Toronto, ON M5V 2K6
(416) 703-4577 Fax 703-7996
E-mail: abvoices@inforamp.net

ACHIMOWEN
Box 90 • Fort Chipewyan, AB T0P 1B0
(780) 697-3740 Fax 697-3826

AFN BULLETIN
Assembly of First Nations
One Nicholas St. #1002
Ottawa, ON K1N 7B7
(613) 241-6789 Fax 241-5808
Bi-monthly newsletter. $18.00/year.

AKWESASNE NOTES
Mohawk Nation
Box 30 • St. Regis, PQ H0M 1A0
(613) 575-9531 Fax 575-2935

ALBERTA NATIVE NEWS
530-10036 Jasper Ave.
Edmonton, AB T5J 2W2
(403) 421-7966 Fax 424-3951

ALBERTA SWEETGRASS
15001-112 Ave. • Edmonton, AB T5M 2V6
(403) 455-2945 Fax 455-7639

ANISHINABE NEWS
Nipissing First Nation
Box 711 • North Bay, ON P1B 8J8
(705) 497-9127 Fax 497-9135

ANTHROPOLOGICAL JOURNAL OF CANADA
Anthropological Association of Canada
1575 Forlan Dr. • Ottawa, ON K2C 0R8

ARTSCRAFT
The National Indian Arts and Crafts Corporation
1 Nicholas St. # 1106
Ottawa, ON K1N 7B6 - Canada
(613) 232-2436 Claudette Fortin, Editor
A quarterly publication which includes feature articles on Indian arts and crafts; regional profiles and artist's profiles; and book reviews. No advertising. Subscription, $16 per year. Begun 1989.

ASSOCIATION FOR NATIVE DEVELOPMENT IN THE PERFORMING & VISUAL ARTS NEWSLETTER
27 Carlton St. #208 • Toronto, ON M5B 1L2

AWA'K'WIS NEWSPAPER
Box 2490 • Port Hardy, BC V0N 1P0
(604) 949-9433 Fax 949-9677

BATCHEWANA FIRST NATION NEWSLETTER
236 Frontenac St.
Sault Ste. Marie, ON P6A 5K9
(705) 759-0914 Fax 759-9171
Darlene Syrette, Editor

BLOOD TRIBE NEWS
Box 410 • Standoff, AB T0L 1Y0
(403) 737-2121 Fax 737-2336

BROTHER OF TIME
Native Brotherhood of Millhaven
P.O. Box 280 • Bath, ON K0H 1G0

CANADIAN ETHNIC STUDIES
Research Centre for Canadian Ethnic Studies
University of Calgary, 2500 University Dr., N.W
Calgary, AB T2N 1N4
(403) 220-7257 Fax 282-8606
J.S. Frideres, Editor
Book reviews. Triannual journal. 1,250 cir. $30/year; institutions, $36/year. Begun 1969.

CANADIAN INDIAN ARTCRAFTS
National Indian Arts & Crafts Corporation
One Nicholas St. #1106 • Ottawa, ON K1N 7B6
Published quarterly.

CANADIAN JOURNAL OF NATIVE EDUCATION
University of Alberta , 5-109 Education N. Bldg.
Edmonton, AB T6G 2G5
(403) 492- 2769 Fax 492-0762
Carl Urion, Editor
Semiannual. Covers the education of native peoples in North America with special focus on Canada. Includes Inuit, Metis and Indian people. Book reviews. 750 cir. $8/copy; $15/year. Advertising. Begun 1973.

CANADIAN JOURNAL OF NATIVE STUDIES
Dept. of Native Studies, Brandon University
Brandon, MB R7A 6A9 Samuel W. Corrigan, Editor
An international refereed periodical published twice annually. It is the official publication of the Canadian Indian/Native Studies Association.

CANADIAN NATIVE LAW REPORTER
Native Law Centre
University of Saskatchewan
Rm. 141, Diefenbaker Centre
Saskatoon, SK S7N 0W0
(306) 966-6189
Zandra MacEachern, Editor
Contributing editors: Donald Purich, Phil Lancaster, Norman K. Zlotkin, and Nancy Ayers.
A specialized law report series, providing full, comprehensive coverage of native law judgements in Canada. Research features: subject index, statutes judicially considered; year end cumulative indexes; articles and case comments. Advertising. Published quarterly (March, June, September and December.) Subscription: $50/year (Canadian). Back issues: 1984-1985, $45/year; 1979-1983, $30/year. Begun 1978.

THE CARIBOU
Box 375 • St. George's, NF A0N 1Z0
(709) 647-3723

CENTRAL OKANAGON FRIENDSHIP SOCIETY NEWSLETTER
442 Leon Ave. • Kelowna, BC V1Y 6J3
(604) 861-4905 Fax 861-5514

CHIPPEWA TRIBUNE
978 Tashmoo Ave. • Sarnia, ON N7T 7H5
(519) 336-8410 Fax 336-0382

CLICKS & BITS COMMUNICATIONS, INC.
1902b - 11th St. S.E. • Calgary, AB T2G 3G2
(403) 265-5361 Fax 234-7061

COUNCIL FIRES
Box 2049 • Blind River, ON P0R 1B0
(705) 356-1691 Fax 356-1090

CREE AJEMON
James Bay Cree Communications Society
MISTASSINI, PQ G0W 1C0
(418) 923-3191
Diane Reid, Editor
Bulletin.

DAKOTA TIMES
Box 151 • Griswold, MB R0M 0S0
(204) 855-2250

DAN SHA NEWS
Ye Sa to Communications Society
22 Nisutlin Dr. • Whitehorse YT Y1A 3S5
(403) 667-2775 Fax 668-6577
Joanne MacDonald, Publisher
Eric Huggard, Editor
Monthly newspaper covering Yukon Indian issues and community events. 2,700 cir. $12/year, individuals; $25/year, institutions. Advertising. Begun 1973.

DANNZHA
Ye Sa To Communications Society
22 Nisutlin Dr.
Whitehorse, Yukon Y1A 3S5
(403) 667-7636/2775

THE EAGLE'S VOICE
Box 2250 • Lac La Biche, AB T0A 2C0
(403) 453-6100 Fax 453-6259

EASTERN DOOR
Box 326 • Kahnawake, PQ J0L 1B0
(514) 635-3050 Fax 635-8479

ENOCH ECHO
Enoch Tribal Administration
Box 2, Site 2, RR 1
Winterburn, AB T0E 2N0
(403) 470-4505

ESKIMO
P.O. Box 10 • Churchill, MB R0B E0E
(204) 675-2252
Guy Mary-Rousselier, Editor
Semiannual magazine on missionary history in the central and eastern Canadian Arctic and Inuit traditions. Published in French. Begun 1944.

ESQUIMALT NEWS
542C Fraser St. • Victoria, BC V9A 6H7
(604) 381-5664 Fax 361-9283

ETHNIC DIRECTORY OF CANADA
Western Publishers
Box 30193, Sta. B • Calgary, AB
(403) 289-3301 Vladimir Markotic, Editor
Published once every few years.
Complimentary copies available.

ETUDES/INUIT/STUDIES
Inuksiutit Katimajiit Association
Dept. of Anthropology, Laval University
Quebec, P.Q. G1K 7P4
(418) 656-2353 Fax 656-3023
Francois Therien, Editor
Semiannual journal devoted to the study of Inuit societies of Siberia, Greenland, and Canada, either traditional or contemporary, in the perspective of social sciences and humanities: archaeology, linguistics, symbolism, demography, ethnohistory and law. Contains articles in French and English on the Inuit culture, language and history . Book reviews. 750 cir. $12/copy; $27/year, individuals; $43/year, institutions. Back issues available. Advertising. Begun 1976.

THE FIRST PERSPECTIVE
209 - 65 Dewdney Ave.
Winnipeg, MB R3B 0E1
(204) 988-9400 Fax 988-9407

FIRST NATIONS COMMUNICATIONS, INC.
#2 - 875 Bank St. • Ottawa, ON K1S 3W4
(800) 387-2532; (613) 231-3858 Fax 231-6613

FIRST NATIONS DRUM
2104 West 13th Ave. • Vancouver, BC V6K 2S1
(604) 669-5539 (phone & fax)

FIRST NATIONS FREE PRESS
110 Athabasca Pl., 80 Chippewa Rd.
Sherwood Park, AB T8A 3Y1
(403) 449-1803 Fax 449-1807

FIRST NATIONS LAW
c/o Ferguson Gifford, Barristers & Solicitors
666 Burard St., #500
Vancouver, BC V6C 3H3
(800) 267-3216; (604) 687-3216 Fax 683-2780

FIRST NATIONS MAGAZINE
CKND-TV, 603 St. Mary's Rd.
Winnipeg, MB R2M 4A5
(204) 233-3304 Fax 233-5615

FIRST NATIONS STUDENTS VOICE
University of Manitoba
Box 02, University Centre
Winnipeg, MB R3T 2N2
(204) 582-1522 Fax 989-2017

FIRST PEOPLES BUSINESS MAGAZINE
204-1111 Monroe Ave. • Winnipeg, MB R2K 3Z5

THE FIRST PERSPECTIVE
Brokenhead Ojibway Nation
General Delivery • Scanterbury, MB R0E 1W0
(204) 766-2686

FOUR WORLDS EXCHANGE
Box 143 • Pincher Creek, AB T0K 1W0
(403) 627-4411
Michael Bopp, Editor

FRIENDSHIP CENTRE NEWS
16 Spadina Rd. • Toronto, ON M5R 2S7
(416) 964-9087

**GATHERINGS: THE EN'OWKIN JOURNAL
OF FIRST NORTH AMERICAN PEOPLES**
Theytus Books Ltd.
P.O. Box 20040 • Penticton, BC V2A 8K3
Published annually by the En'owkin Centre of the International School of Writing, a Native writer's school in Canada, affiliated with the University of Victoria. Contents are poetry and fiction. 300 pages.

HA-SHILTH-SA
Box 1383 • Port Alberni, BC V9Y 7M2
(604) 724-5757 Fax 723-0463

HOLMAN ESKIMO PRINTS
Canadian Arctic Producers Limited
P.O. Box 4132. Postal Station E
Ottawa, ON K1S 5S2

INDIAN & INUIT GRADUATE REGISTER
Canada Department of Indian
Affairs & Northern Affairs
10 Wellington, • Ottawa, ON K1A 0H4

INDIAN ECHO
Canadian Department of Justice
Penitentiary Branch • Ottawa, ON

INDIAN FREE PRESS N'AMERIND
London's Indian Friendship Centre
613 Wellington St. • London, ON

INDIAN LIFE MAGAZINE
P.O. Box 3765 Sta. B
Winnipeg, MB R2W 3R6

INDIAN LIFE MINISTRY
Intertribal Christian Communications
Box 3765 Sta. B • Winnipeg, MB R2W 3R6
(204) 661-9333 Fax 661-3982
George McPeek, Director
Jim Uttley, Editor & Publisher
Bimonthly. Contains feature news, first-person articles, photo features, family-life material and legends. Focus is primarily on dealing with problems and issues within contemporary North American Indian society. 150,000 cir. $1.50/copy; $7/year. Advertising. Begun 1967.

INDIAN MAGAZINE NEWSLETTER
Canadian Broadcasting Company, Publishers
Box 500, Station A • Toronto 116, ON

INDIAN NEWS
Canada Department of Indian Affairs
and Northern Development
10 Wellington • Ottawa, ON K1A 0H4

INDIAN RECORD
480 Aulneau St. • Winnipeg, MB R2H 2V2
(204) 233-6430
Rev. G. Laviolette, OMI, Editor
Contains articles on the Canadian Indians from coast to coast. Published four times per year. Advertising. Subscription: $4/year, $7/two years, $10/three years.

INDIAN TIME
Mohawk Nation
Box 189 • St. Regis, PQ H0M 1A0
(518) 358-9531; (613) 575-2063 Fax 575-2935

THE INDIAN VOICE
Canadian Indian Voice Society
429 East 6th St. N. • Vancouver, BC V7L 1P8

(604) 876-0944 Donna Doss, Editor
Quarterly newsletter covering areas affecting the native Indian. 2,800 cir. $1/copy; $7/year. Advertising. Begun 1969.

INDIAN WORLD MAGAZINE
Union of British Columbia Indian Chiefs
440 W. Hastings, 3rd Fl. • Vancouver, BC V6B 1L1
(604) 684-0231

INDIANS OF QUEBEC
c/o Coalition of Nations. P.O. Box 810
Caughnawaga, PQ J0L 1B0
(514) 632-7321

THE INDIGENOUS TIMES
#250 - 103C Packham Ave.
Saskatoon, SK S7N 4K4
(306) 975-3969 Fax 975-3759

INUKTITUT
Inuit Tapirisat of Canada
170 Laurier W. • Ottawa, ON K1P 5V5
(613) 238-8181 Fax 234-1991
John Bennett & Alootook Ipellie, Editors
Quarterly magazine promoting the exchange of cultural information among Inuit groups in Canada and to inform non-Inuit about Iuit life. 10,000 cir. $7/copy. Advertising. Begun 1959.

INUVIALUIT
Committee for Original People's Entitlement
P.O. Box 200 • Inuvik, NT X0E 0T0

JOURNAL OF ABORIGINAL TOURISM
Aboriginal Tourism Authority
Box 1240, Sta. "M" • Calgary, AB T2P 2L2
(403) 261-3022 Fax 261-5676
E-mail: tourism@istar.ca
Web site: www.aboriginalnet.com/tourism

JOURNAL OF INDIGENOUS STUDIES
Gabriel Dumont Institute of
Native Studies & Applied Research
121 Broadway Ave. E. • Regina, SK S4N 0Z6
(306) 522-5691 Fax 565-0809
Catherine I. Littlejohn, Editor
Semiannual. 200 cir. Individuals, $10/copy; $20/year; Institutions, $15/copy, $30/year. Begun 1989.

KAHTOU COMMUNICATIONS, INC.
Native Communications Society of BC
203-540 Burrard St. • Vancouver, BC V6C 2K1
(604) 684-7375 Fax 684-5375
Tim Isaac, Managing Editor
Biweekly newspaper. $15/year.

**KAHTOU NEWS: THE VOICE
OF BC FIRST NATIONS**
K'Watamus Publications
P.O. Box 192 • Sechelt, BC V0N 3A0
(604) 885-7391 Fax 885-7397

KAINAI NEWS
Indian News Media
P.O. Box 120 • Standoff, AB T0L 1Y0
(403) 653-3301 Fax 653-3437
Mary Weasel Fat, Editor
A weekly newspaper that covers issues of interest to status, non-status and Metis people of southern Alberta. Extensive coverage of the Treaty 7 tribes located in southern Alberta. The tribes are Blackfoot, Blood, Peigan, Carcee and Stoney. Coverage is extended to the urban cities of Calgary and Lethbridge. Advertising accepted. Complimentary copies are available upon request. Maintains a Calgary Bureau locate at Calgary Friendship Centre. $20/year; 50¢ per copy. Begun 1968.

KATERI
P.O. Box 70 • Kahnawake, PQ J0L 1B0
(514) 525-3611
Rev. Henri Bechard, S.J., Editor
"Its aim is to promote the canonization of Blessed Kateri Tekakwitha; articles on life of the Beata, nes concerning the native peoples of North America, with special emphasis on her own people, the account of favors due to her intercession." Published quarterly. Subscription: $3/year. No advertising. Complimentary copies available upon request. Begun 1949.

KINATUINAMOT ILENGAJUK
Okalakatiget Society
Box 160 • Nain, Labrador, NF A0P 1E0
(709) 922-2955 Fax 922-2293
Ken Todd, Editor
Newsletter.

THE LABRADORIAN
Box 39, Station "B" • Goose Bay, NF A0P 1E0
(709) 896-3341 Fax 896-8781

LE CHEWITAN
Cree Indian Centre
95 rue Jaculet • Chibougamau, PQ G8P 2G1
(418) 788-2136 Fax 748-6954

LE METIS
410 McGregor St. • Winnipeg, MB R2W 4X5
(204) 589-4327 Fax 586-6462

**LISTUGUJ WI'GATIGN
COMMUNITY NEWSLETTER**
17 Riverside West • Listuguj, PQ H2V 4S0
(514) 788-2136 Fax 788-2058

MACKENZIE TIMES
Box 499 • Fort Simpson, NT X0E 0N0
(403) 695-3330 Fax 695-2922

MAL-I-MIC NEWS
320 St. Mary's St. • Fredericton, NB E3A 2S4
(506) 458-8422 Fax 450-3749

**MANITOBA ASSOCIATION OF
NATIVE LANGUAGES NEWSLETTER**
119 Sutherland Ave. • Winnipeg, MB R2W 3C9
(204) 943-3707 Fax 947-6564

**MANITOBA INDIAN EDUCATION
ASSOCIATION NEWSLETTER**
305 - 352 Donald Ave.
Winnipeg, MB R3B 2H8
(204) 947-0421 Fax 942-3067

MASENAYEGUN NEWSPAPER
45 Robinson St. • Winnipeg, MB R2W 5H5
(204) 586-8441 Fax 582-8261

MAWIO'MI JOURNAL
240 - 10036 Jasper Ave.
Edmonton, AB T5J 2W2
(800) 463-9300; (403) 990-0303 Fax 429-7487

MESSENGER
William Head Institute, Indian Education Club
Box 10 • Metochosin, BC
M. Walkus, Editor
Quarterly newsletter. $1/year. Begun 1970.

METIS ONTARIO NEWSLETTER
193 Holland Ave. • Ottawa, ON K1Y 0Y3
(800) 263-4889; (613) 798-1488 Fax 722-4225

MICMAC NEWS
Nova Scotia Native Communications Society
Box 344 • Sydney, NS B1P 6H2
(902) 539-0045 Fax 564-0430
Roy Gould, Publisher
Brian Douglas, Editor
Bimonthly newspaper containing local provincial and national issues on Canadian Indians. $7.00 per year.

MICMAC-MALISEET NEWS
Confederacy of Mainland Micmacs
Box 1590 • Truro, NS B2N 5V3
(902) 895-6385 Fax 893-1520

THE MIDDEN
Archaeological Society of British Columbia
Box 520, Sta. A
Vancouver, BC V6C 2N3
Kathryn Bernick, Editor
Contains articles, book reviews, news items related to British Columbia archaeology—prehistoric and historic periods. Published five times per year. Subscription: $10/year; $12/year, overseas.

MIRAMICHI NEWS
Miramichi Indian Agency
P.O. Box 509 • Chatham, NB

MOOSE TALK
Box 125 • Moosonee, ON P0L 1Y0
(705) 336-2510

MOSAIK
696 Buckingham Rd.
Winnipeg, MB R3R 1C2
(204) 888-8245
Ted Alcuitas, Editor & Publisher
Monthly tabloid of news and views on multicultural
events and issues that impact on the multicultural
community, Book reviews. 3,500 cir. $35/year; $45/
year, foreign. Advertising. Begu 1983.

**MUSEUM OF INDIAN
ARCHAEOLOGY NEWSLETTER**
University of Western Ontario
Lawson-Jury Bldg. • London, ON N6G 3M6
(519) 473-1360
Debra Bodner, Editor

THE NATION
Box 151 • Chisasibi, PQ J0M 1E0 (head office)
Box 48036 • Montreal, PQ H2V 4S0
(514) 278-9914 (phone & fax)

NATIVE ALLIANCE FOR RED POWER
P.O. Box 6152 • Vancouver, BC

NATIVE BROTHERHOOD NEWS
P.O. Box 60 • Mission, BC V2Y 4L1

NATIVE BROTHERHOOD NEWSCALL
Saskatchewan Pentitentiary
P.O. Box 160 • Prince Albert, SK S6V 5R6

NATIVE CANADIAN
c/o Native Canadian Centre of Toronto
16 Spadina Rd. • Toronto, ON M5R 2S7
(416) 964-9087 Fax 964-2111

NATIVE HEROES
#3, 10032 - 29A Ave. • Edmonton, AB T6N 6H4
(403) 448-3715Fax 448-3964

NATIVE ISSUES
Native Peoples Support Group
of Newfoundland and Labrador
Box 582, Sta. C • St. John's, NF A1C 5K8

NATIVE ISSUES MONTHLY
816 E. 10th Ave. • Vancouver, BC V5T 2B1
(604) 873-1408 Fax 873-1920

NATIVE JOURNAL
P.O. Box 49039 • Edmonton, AB T5L 4R8
(403) 448-9693 Fax 448- 9694

NATIVE NETWORK NEWS
13140 St. Albert Trail
Edmonton, AB T5L 4H4
(403) 454-7076 Fax 452-3468

NATIVE NEWS NETWORK
Social Science Center, 3rd Floor, Rm. 3254
London, ON N6A 5C2

NATIVE PERSPECTIVE
Box 2550 • LacLa Biche, AB T0A 2C0
(403) 623-3333

NATIVE PRESS
Native Communications Society
of the Western N.W.T.
P.O. Box 1919, Aquarius Bldg.
Yellowknife, NT X1A 2P4
(403) 873-2661 Fax 920-4205
Lee Selleck, Editor
Weekly newspaper serving 26 communities in the
Western Northwest Territories. Book reviews. 5,600
cir. $1/copy; $25/year. Advertising. Begun 1971.

NATIVE SCENE MAGAZINE
202-115 Bannatyne Ave.
Winnipeg, MB R3B 0R3
(204) 943-6475 Fax 942-1380

THE NATIVE SISTERHOOD
P.O. Box 515 • Kingston, ON K7L 4W7

NATIVE SPORTS NEWS
205-15517 Stony Plain Rd.
Edmonton, AB T3P 3Z1
(403) 486-7766

NATIVE STUDIES REVIEW
University of Saskatchewan
Native Studies Dept., 104 McLean Hall
Saskatoon, SK S7N 0W0
(306) 966-6208 Fax 966-6242
Semiannual journal.

THE NATIVE VOICE
200 - 1755 E. Hastings St.
Vancouver, BC V5L 1T1
(604) 255-4696 Fax 251-7107

NATIVE WOMEN IN THE ARTS JOURNAL
#101 - 141 Bathurst St.
Toronto, ON M5V 2R2
(416) 392-6800 Fax 392-6920

NATIVE WOMEN NEWSPAPER
10032-29A Ave. • Edmonton, AB T6N 1A8
(403) 448-3715
Monthly.

NATIVE YOUTH NEWS
90 Sioux Rd. • Sherwood Park, AB T8A 3X5
(403) 449-1803 Fax 449-1807

NATIVEBEAT
Box 1260 • Forest, ON N0N 1J0
(519) 786-2142 (phone & fax)

NATOTAWIN NEWS
c/o The Pas First Nation
Box 197 • The Pas, MB R9A 1K4
(204) 623-5483 Fax 623-5263

NDOODEMAK (MY FRIENDS/RELATIVES)
Manitoba Association for Native Languages
119 Sutherland Ave.
Winnipeg, MB R2W 3C9
(204) 943-3707 Fax 943-9312

NEECHEE CULTURE MAGAZINE
273 Selkirk Ave. • Winnipeg, MB R2W 2L5
(204) 586-3667 Fax 586-5165

NEIGHBOURHOOD PROFILE
Box 2868 • Winnipeg, MB R3C 4B4
(204) 256-2699 Fax 254-5302

NEW BREED MAGAZINE
#204 - 845 Broad St. • Regina, SK S4R 8G9
(306) 569-9995 Fax 569-3533

NEWS & VIEWS
Canada Department of Indian Affairs
and Northern Development
10 Wellington • Ottawa, ON K1A 0H4

NEWS OF THE NORTH
Box 2820 • Yellowknife, NT X1A 2R1
(403) 873-4031 Fax 873-8507

NICOLA INDIAN
Nicola Valley Indian Administration
P.O. Box 188 • Merritt, BC V0K 2B0
(604) 378-6441/4235

NORTHERN REPORTER
Box 310, Sta. "B" • Goose Bay, NF A0P 1E0
(709) 896-2595

THE NORTHERN STAR
Box 2212 • Yellowknife, NT X1A 2P6
(403) 873-2719 Fax 920-7719

NORTHWEST EAGLE
P.O. Box 2139 • Meadow Lake, SK S0M 1V0

NUNATSIAQ NEWS
Box 8 • Iqaluit, NT X0A 0H0
(819) 979-5357 Fax 979-4763

OMUSHKEGOW ARROW
Box 370 • Moose Factory, ON P0L 1W0
(705) 658-4222 Fax 658-4250

ONTARIO ARCHAEOLOGY
The Ontario Archaeological Society
126 Willowdale Ave. • Willowdale, ON M2N 4Y2
(416) 730-0797 Charles Garrad, Admin.
A learned refereed journal dedicated to the
archaeoogy and prehistory of Ontario and the
Northeast. Back issues are available for sale.
Included in membership. Begun 1956.

ONTARIO INDIAN
Union of Ontario Indians
27 Queen St. E., 2nd Fl.
Toronto, ON M5C 2M6
(416) 366-3527 Dennis Martel, Editor
Published monthly. $10.00 per year. Began 1978.

ONTARIO NATIVE EXPERIENCE
Ontario Federation of Friendship Centres
234 Eglinton Ave., E. #203
Toronto, ON M4P 1K5

**ONTARIO NATIVE WOMEN'S ASSOCIATION
NEWSLETTER**
115 N. May St. • Thunder Bay, ON P7C 3N8
(807) 623-3442 Fax 623-1104

OWNEWS
Original Women's Network, Inc.
A-356 Stella Ave. • Winnipeg, MB R2W 2T9
(204) 582-2383 Fax 582-6468

PAPERS OF THE ALGONQUIAN CONFERENCE
Carleton University, Dept. of Linguistics
Ottawa, ON K1S 5B6 (613) 788-2809
William Cowan, Editor
Publishes papers given at annual Algonquian
Conference. 300 cir. $25/copy. Begun 1974.

PEACE HILLS COUNTRY NEWSPAPER
Box 509 • Hobbema, AB T0C 1N0
(403) 474-6283 Fax 477-1699

PENTICTON INDIAN BAND NEWSLETTER
RR 2, Site 50, Comp. 8
Penticton, BC V2A 6J7
(604) 493-0048 Fax 493-2882

THE PHOENIX
Canadian Alliance in Solidarity With the Native
Peoples
Box 574, Station "P" • Toronto, ON M5S 2T1
(416) 972-1573 Fax 972-6232
Quarterly magazine. Curent issues seen from a
Native perspective; also poetry and book reviews.
$20/year.

PRAIRIE FORUM
Canadian Plains Research Center
University of Regina • Regina, SK S4S 0A2
(306) 585-4795 Fax 586-9862
Alvin Finkel, Editor
Semiannual journal of research relating to the
Canadian Plains. Book reviews. 400 cir. $13/copy;
$20/year, individuals; $25/year, institutions.
Advertising. Begun 1976.

RECHERCHES AMERINDIENNES AU QUEBEC
Societe de Recherches Amerindiennes au Quebec
6742 rue St. Denis • Montreal, PQ H2S 2S2
(514) 277-6178 Carole Levesque, Editor
Quarterly journal on the Native peoples of Quebec with
an anthropological perspective. Text mainly in French.
Book reviews. 1,500 cir. $8/copy. $24/year, individuals; $30/year, institutions. Advertising. Begun 1971.

RED ROAD MAGAZINE
c/o Ken Davis, #121B - 621 E.7th Ave.
Vancouver, BC V5T 1N9 (604) 877-0444

RENCONTRE
Secretariat aux Affaires Autochtones
875 Grande Allee est. • Quebec, PQ G1R 4Y8
(418) 643-3166 Ann Picard, Publisher
Quarterly government publication for Quebec's
Amerindian and Inuit peoples. Begun 1979.

REX MAGAZINE
443 W. 3rd St. • N. Vancouver, BC V7M 1G9
(604) 985-0799 Fax 980-3861

**THE RUNNER: NATIVE MAGAZINE
FOR COMMUNICATIVE ARTS**
c/o ANDPVA, 39 Spadina Rd., 2nd Fl.
Toronto, ON M5R 2S9
(416) 972-0871 Fax 972-0892
Gary Farmer, Editor/Publisher
Promotes the talents, products and services of established and upcoming Native individuals and groups in the arts and communication fields. Includes news for Native writers, actors, film makers and radio and television people. Quarterly. $20/yr., individuals; $24/yr., institutions.

THE SACRED FIRE
2-Spirited People of the First Nation
202-476 Parliament St. • Toronto, ON M4X 1P2
(416) 961-4725 Fax 944-8381

**SASKATCHEWAN ARCHAEOLOGICAL
SOCIETY NEWSLETTER**
Saskatchewan Archaeological Society
816 1st Ave. North #5 • Saskatoon, SK S7K 1Y3
(306) 664-4124 Jim Finnigan, Editor
A bi-monthly publiction. No advertising.
Included in membership. Begun 1963.

SASKATCHEWAN ARCHAEOLOGY
Saskatchewan Archaeological Society
816 1st Ave. North #5 • Saskatoon, SK S7K 1Y3
(306) 664-4124 Terry Gibson, Editor
An annual publication. Included with membership.
Begun 1980.

SASKATCHEWAN INDIAN
c/o ABCOM Publishers
215 - 103B Packham Ave.
Saskatoon, SK S7N 4K4
(306) 242-2372 Fax 664-8851
Alex Greyeyes, Publisher
Doug Cuthand, Editor
Monthly magazine providing communication among Saskatchewan's almost 50,000 Treaty Indians through information news, stories and editorial opinion. Book reviews. 8,500 cir. $15/year; $3/copy. Advertising. Begun 1987.

**SASKATCHEWAN INDIAN
FEDERATED COLLEGE JOURNAL**
College W. Bldg., 127 • Regina, SK S4S 0A2
(306) 584-8333 Joel Demay, Editor
Semiannual. $15/year, individuals; $25/year, institutions. Begun 1984.

THE SCOUT
Indian-Metis Friendship Centre
Brandon Friendship Centre
836 Lorne Ave. • Brandon, MB R7A 0TB

SECWEPEMC NEWS
Secwepemc Cultural Education Society
345 Yellowhead Hwy. • Kamloops, BC V2H 1H1
(604) 828-9784 Fax 372-1127
Newspaper of the Shuswap Nation containing current political, social and economic issues and events affecting their lives and promoting the preservation of Shuswap history, language and culture. Published six times per year.

STO:LO NATION NEWS
Box 370 • Sardis, BC V2R 1A7
(604) 858-9431 Fax 858-8488

STRAIT ARROW
#16 - 1630 Crescent View Dr.
Nanaimo, BC V9S 2N5 (604) 754-5155

SWEETGRASS GROWS ALL AROUND HER
Native Woman in the Arts
401 Richmond St. #363 • Toronto, ON M5V1X3
(416) 598-4078 Fax 340-8458
Annual.

TANSAI JOURNAL
207- 13638 Grosvenor Rd. • Surrey, BC V3R 5C9
(604) 581-2522 Fax 582-4820

TAQRALIK
Northern Quebec Inuit Association
P.O. Box 179 • Fort Chimo, PQ J0M 1C0

THE TALKING LEAVES
Native Brotherhood Association
P.O. Box 880 • Kingston, ON

TAWOW MAGAZINE
First Nations Communications
#2, 875 Bank St. • Ottawa, ON K1A 3W4
(800) 387-8357; (613) 231-3858 Fax 231-6613

TEKAWENNAKE NEWSPAPER
Tekawennake Publications
Box 130 • Ohsweken, ON N0A 1M0
(519) 445-2238 Fax 445-2434
Roberta Green, Editor
Weekly tabloid. Advertising.

**TEKAWENNAKE SIX NATIONS
NEW CREDIT REPORTER**
Woodland Indian Cultural Education Center
184 Mohawk St., Box 1506
Brantford, ON N3T 5V6 (519) 753-5531
Roberta Green, Editor & Publisher
Weekly native newspaper for and about native peoples. Book reviews. 1,550 cir. $30/year; $1/copy. Advertising. Begun 1967.

THREE SISTER'S MULTI-MEDIA
Box 1260 • Forest, ON N0N 1J0
(519) 786-2142 (phone & fax)

TORONTO NATIVE TIMES
16 Spadina Rd. • Toronto, ON M5R 2S8
(416) 964-9087

TREATY No. 3 COUNCIL FIRE
37 Main St. S. • Kenora, ON P9N 1S8

TRENT NATIVE NEWS
Dept. of Native Studies, Trent University
Petersborough, ON K9J 7B7

TRIBAL INDIAN NEWS N'AMERIND
London's Indian Friendship Centre
613 Wellington St. • London, ON

TUSAAYAKSAT (Newspaper)
Inuvialuit Communications Society
Box 1704, McKenzie Rd., Semmler Bldg.
Inuvik, NT X0E 0T0
(403) 979-2067; 977-2202
Vincent Teddy, Editor & President

TYENDINAGA TERRITORY NEWSLETTER
c/o Mohawk Band Office
RR 1 • Deseronto, ON K0K 1X0
(613) 396-3424 Fax 396-3627

UNITY
Association of Iroquois and Allie Indians
R.R. 2 • Southwold, ON N0L 2G0
Shelly Bressette, Editor
Quarterly newsletter covering news and issues of importance to the Indian peoples.

**WA-WA-TAY CREE
COMMUNICATIONS NETWORK**
Fort Albany, ON P0L 1H0
(705) 278-1147

WAWATAY NATIVE NEWS
Wawatay Communications Society
Box 1180, 16-5th Ave.
Sioux Lookout, ON P0V 2T0
(807) 737-2951 Fax 737-3224
Megan Williams, Editor
Bilingual, semi-monthly newspaper which carries all types of news for and about Nishnawbe-Aski Nation. Advertising accepted. Circulation 10,000/ \Subscription: $11/year (individuals) in Canada; $12, U.S., and $16, foreign. Begun 1973.

WEETAMAH
P.O. Box 178 • Winnipeg, MB R3C 3G9
(204) 944-9517 Fax 944-9521

THE WESTERN CANADIAN ANTHROPOLOGIST
University of Saskatchewan
Dept. of Anthropology/Archaeology
Saskatoon, SK S7N 0W0
(306) 966-4175 Satya Sharma, Editor

Annual journal cotaining material of interest to anthropologists. Book reviews. 400 cir. $10/copy. Begun 1968.

WESTERN NATIVE NEWS
530-10036 Jasper Ave.
Edmonton, AB T5J 2W2
(403) 421-7966 Fax 424-3951
office: 201-1593 W. 3rd St. Vancouver, BC V6J 1J8
(604) 736-3015

WHISPERING PINES
Northern Association of Community Councils
504-63 Albert St. • Winnipeg, MB R3B 1G4
(204) 947-2227 Fax 947-9446

WINDSPEAKER
Aboriginal Multi-Media Society of Alberta
15001 112th Ave. • Edmonton, AB T5M 2V6
(403) 455-2700 Fax 455-7639
Gary Gee, Publisher
Biweekly newspaper. 10,000 cir. $26/year; $40, foreign. Advertising. Begun 1983.

WINNIPEG INDIAN TIMES
Indian and Metis Friendship Centre
73 Princess St. • Winnipeg 3, MB

UNIVERSITIES & COLLEGES

ALBERTA

UNIVERSITY OF CALGARY
Native Studies Dept. • CALGARY, AB T2N 1N4
Faculty: Jean-Guy Goulet, PhD

UNIVERSITY OF ALBERTA
School of Native Studies
11023 90th Ave. • EDMONTON, AB T6G 1A6
(780) 492-2991 Fax 492-0527

UNIVERSITY OF ALBERTA
Faculty of Medicine
2J2.11 W.C. MacKenzie Sciences Centre
EDMONTON, AB 6G 2R7
(780) 492-6350 Fax 492-7303
Anne-Marie Hodes, Coordinator
Program: Native Health Care Career Program

UNIVERSITY OF ALBERTA
Faculty of Law, 4th Floor, Law Centre
EDMONTON T, AB 6G 2H5
(780) 492-7749 FAX 492-4924
Programs: Indigenous Law Program.

GRANT MacEWAN COMMUNITY COLLEGE
City Centre Campus 5-174
10700 104th Ave.
EDMONTON, AB T5J 4S2
(780) 497-5646 Fax 497-5630
Program: Native Communications Program.

OLD SUN COMMUNITY COLLEGE
P.O. Box 339 • GLEICHEN, AB T0J 1N0
(780) 734-3862; 264-9658
Blackfoot Cultural Centre
Gerald Sitting Eagle, Coordinator

MASKWACHEES CULTURAL COLLEGE
P.O. Box 360 • HOBBEMA, AB T0C 1N0
(403) 585-3925 Fax 585-2080
Dr. Fred Carnew, Director

UNIVERSITY OF LETHBRIDGE
Department of Native American Studies
4401 University Dr.
LETHBRIDGE, AB T1K 3M4
(403) 329-2635 Fax 329-2085
Don Frantz, Chairperson

UNIVERSITY OF LETHBRIDGE
School of Management-Indian
Inuit & Metis Peoples
4401 University Dr.
LETHBRIDGE, AB T1K 3M4
(403) 329-2114 Fax 329-2038

BLUE QUILLS FIRST NATIONS COLLEGE
Box 189 • SADDLE LAKE, AB T0A 3T0
(403) 645-4455 FAX 645-5215

BRITISH COLUMBIA

SIMON FRASER UNIVERSITY
Native Indian Teachers Education Program-UBC
345 Yellowhead Hwy. • KAMLOOPS, BC V2H 1H1
Chief Ron Ignace, Co-chair
Muriel Sasakamoose, Executive Director
(250) 828-9817 Fax 828-9780
Currently in its first year of offering a university program for Native Indian students with focus on social science research and Native studies.

**UNIVERSITY OF NORTHERN
BRITISH COLUMBIA**
Dept. of First Nations Studies
3333 University Way
PRINCE GEORGE, BC V2N 4Z9
(250) 960-5772 Fax 960-5545
James A. McDonald, Chairperson
Instructors: Antonia Mills, PhD, Avis Mysyk, PhD, Bruce Low, MA, Kathrine Dennig, PhD, Mike Evans, PhD, Ellen facey, PhD, Jo-Anne Fiske, PhD, Margaret S. Anderson, PhD.

UNIVERSITY OF BRITISH COLUMBIA
Dept. of Anthropology
6303 N.W. Marine Dr.
VANCOUVER, BC V6T 1Z1
(604) 822-2878 Fax 822-6161
Instructors: David F. Aberle, PhD, Harry B. Hawthorn, PhD (Indians of Canada); J.E. Michael Kew, PhD (Indians of Canada), Bruce G. Miller, PhD (Indian-white relations); William Robin Ridington, PhD (Native American cosmology); Ruth Phillips, PhD (director of Museum of Anthropology; Iroquoian & Anishnabe art & culture); James V. Powell, PhD (linguistics). *Special program*: Summer Field School in Archaeology. *Special facilities*: Research laboratories in archaeology, ethnomethodology and socio-linguistics, and ethnography; Museum of Anthropology.

UNIVERSITY OF BRITISH COLUMBIA
Museum of Anthropology
6393 N.W. Marine Dr. • VANCOUVER V6T 1W5
(604) 228-5087
Michael M. Ames, Ph.D., Director/Professor
Moya Waters, Administrative Officer
Special programs: Anthropology and archaeology of Northwest Coast of British Columbia, indigenous arts, material culture, ceramics, & development of innovative teaching pograms in museology and the arts. *Financial aid*: The Lois McConkey Memorial Fellowship for Native Indian Work-Study Program - a fellowship for secondary school & university students of North American Indian descent. Research results published occasionally in professional journals & books; also publishes notes, catalogues, & museum visitory profiles.

UNIVERSITY OF BRITISH COLUMBIA
First Nations Health Careers
1985 West Mall • VANCOUVER, BC V6T 1Z2
(604) 822-2115 Fax 822-8944

UNIVERSITY OF BRITISH COLUMBIA
Native Indian Teachers Education Program
1985 West Mall • VANCOUVER, BC V6T 1Z2
(604) 822-5240 FAX 822-8944
345 Yellowhead Hwy. • Kamloops, BC V2H 1H1
(604) 828-9817 Fax 828-9780

UNIVERSITY OF BRITISH COLUMBIA
First Nation Legal Studies Program,
1822 East Mall • VANCOUVER, BC V6T 1Z1
(604) 822-5559 Fax 822-8108

UNIVERSITY OF BRITISH COLUMBIA
Synala Honours Program, 1985 West Mall
VANCOUVER, BC V6T 1Z2   (604) 822-9697

UNIVERSITY OF BRITISH COLUMBIA
TS'KEL Program (MEd, MA, EdP, PhD)
Faculty of Education • VANCOUVER, BC V6T 1Z4
(604) 822-5857 Fax 822-6501

VANCOUVER SCHOOL OF THEOLOGY
Native Ministries Program
6000 Iona Dr. • VANCOUVER, BC V6T 1L4
(604) 228-9031 Fax 228-0189

UNIVERSITY OF VICTORIA
Dept. of Anthropology
P.O. Box 3050 • VICTORIA V8W 3P5
(250) 721-7046 Fax 721-6215
Instructors: Michael Asch, PhD, Kathleen A. Berthiaume, PhD, Leland H. Donald, PhD, Eric A. Roth, PhD, Andrea N. Walsh, MA. *Special facilities*: Provincial Archives and Museum; archaeological, ethnological and linguistic (especially in Coast Salish languages through the Lingistics Department) field training; Pacific Studies; and Interdisciplinary Studies Program.

UNIVERSITY OF VICTORIA
Administration of Aboriginal Governments Program
School of Public Administration
P.O. Box 1700 • VICTORIA, BC V8W 2Y2
(250) 721-8089 Fax 721-8849
E-mail: stheiss@hsd.univ.ca

UNIVERSITY OF VICTORIA
First Nations Tax Administrators' Institute
School of Public Administration
P.O. Box 1700 • VICTORIA, BC V8W 2Y2
(250) 721-8083 Fax 472-4163
E-mail: fntai@lsd.univ.ca

MANITOBA

UNIVERSITY OF BRANDON
Department of Native Studies
270 18th St. • BRANDON, MB R7A 6A9
(204) 727-7349

UNIVERSITY OF BRANDON
Aboriginal Heritage Committee
270 18th St. • BRANDON, MB R7A 6A9
(204) 727-7349

UNIVERSITY OF BRANDON
Northern Teachers Education Program
Rm. 13, Education Bldg.
270 18th St. • BRANDON, MB R7A 6A9
(204) 727-9669 Fax 727-0942

INTER-UNIVERSITIES NORTH
494 Princeton Dr.
THOMPSON, MB R8N 0A4
(800) 442-0462
(204) 677-6740 Fax 677-6589

UNIVERSITY OF MANITOBA
Aboriginal Focus Programs
188 Continuing Education
WINNIPEG, MB R3T 2N2
(800) 432-1960 ext. 7401
(204) 474-6720 Fax 474-7660
E-mail: shuttle@bldgarts.lan1.umanitoba.ca

UNIVERSITY OF MANITOBA
Continuing Education Division/Native Focus
Rm. 188, Continuing Education Complex
WINNIPEG, MB R3T 2N2
(204) 474-9921 Fax 474-7661

UNIVERSITY OF MANITOBA
Dept. of Anthropology
WINNIPEG, MB R3T 2N2
(204) 474-9361
Instructors: Louis Allaire, PhD, David H. Pentland, PhD, Linguistics, Kevin Russell, PhD, Joan B. Townsend, PhD, H. C. Wolfart, PhD (Linguistics), (Linguistics), Jillian E. Oakes, PhD (Native Studies); John D. Nichols, PhD (Native Studies), William W. Koolage, PhD (Cultural Anthropology); Gregory Monks, PhD (Archaeology); Dwight A. Rokala, PhD (Physcial Anthropology); and David H. Stymeist, PhD (Social Anthropology). *Special programs*: Population biology and medical anthropology of North American Indians; indigenous languages of Canada, especially Siouan and Algonquian (Cree Language Project). *Special facilities*: Anthropology Laboratories; The Provincial Archives.

UNIVERSITY OF MANITOBA
Department of Native Studies
532 Fletcher Ave. • WINNIPEG, MB R3T 2N2
(204) 474-6333 Fax 275-5781
E-mail: fred_shore@umanitoba.ca
Freda Ahenakew, PhD, Chairperson
Instructors: Freda Ahenakew, PhD, Jilian E. Oakes, PhD, Emma LaRocque, PhD, Paul L.A.H. Chartrand, PhD, Fred Shore, PhD, John D. Nichols, PhD, H. C. Wolfart, PhD (Linguistics), Kevin Russell, PhD (Linguistics). *Publications*: Algonquian and Iroquoian Linguistics, quarterly; Algonquian and Iroquoian Memoirs (monograph series.)

UNIVERSITY OF MANITOBA
Engineering Access Program
Rm. 107, Engineering Bldg.
WINNIPEG, MB R3T 5V6
(204) 474-7518 Fax 474-7518
E-mail: bmathia@cc.umanitoba.ca

UNIVERSITY OF WINNIPEG
Department of Anthropology
515 Portage Ave. • WINNIPEG R3B 2E9
(204) 786-9382
Instructors: Gary R. Granzberg, PhD, George Fulford, PhD, Peter Dawson, PhD. *Special program*: Archaeological Field School. *Special facilities*: Algonkian ethnological collections; Hudson's Bay Company Archives Research Centre; ethnology, archaeology, and physical anthropology laboratories.

NEW BRUNSWICK

UNIVERSITY OF NEW BRUNSWICK
Dept. of Anthropology
FREDERICTON E3B 5A3
(506) 453-4975 Fax 453-3569
Instructors: William G. Dalton, PhD, Vincent O. Erickson, PhD, Peter R. Lovell, PhD, and Gail R. Pool, PhD. *Special resources*: Local fieldwork opportunities (Maliseet-Micmac Indian communities); archaeology-anthropology laboratory. Archives. Library.

UNIVERSITY OF NEW BRUNSWICK
Micmac-Maliseet Institute
Bag Service 45333 • FREDERICTON E3B 5A3
(506) 453-4840 Fax 453-3569

NEWFOUNDLAND

MEMORIAL UNIVERSITY OF NEWFOUNDLAND
Dept. of Anthropology • ST. JOHN'S A1C 5S7
(709) 737-8870
Instructors: Gordon Inglis, PhD, John C. Kennedy, PhD, Thomas F. Nemec, PhD, Adrian Tanner, PhD, and James A. Tuck, PhD. Special foci: Field research programs—Arctic, Subarctic, and circumpolar (especially Lapps, Algonquin, Inuit and white settlers); northern North Atlantic (Newfoundland, Labrador, Baffin, Iceland.) *Special facility*: Killam Arctic Library.

ONTARIO

**NORTH AMERICAN INDIAN
TRAVELLING COLLEGE**
R.R. 3 • CORNWALL ISLAND, ON K6H 5R7
(613) 932-9452 Fax 932-0092
Barbara Barnes, President

UNIVERSITY OF GUELPH
GUELPH, ON N1G 2W1
(519) 824-4120 Fax 837-2940

McMASTER UNIVERSITY
Indigenous Studies Program
Rm. 228-1280 Main St W.
HAMILTON, ON L8B 4K1
(905) 525-9140 Fax 540-8443

UNIVERSITY OF WESTERN ONTARIO
Faculty of Education • LONDON, ON N6G 1G7
(519) 661-3430 Fax 661-2157

Program: Native Language Teaching. *Instructors*: Chet Creider, PhD, Margaret Seguin, PhD (Director-Center for Research and Teaching of Candian Native Languages), Michael W. Spence, PhD, and Lisa Valentine, PhD. *Special facilities*: Center for Research and Teaching of Canadian Native Languages, administered within the Department, offers research funds and facilities for faculty and students working on Canadian Native languages; publishes a monograph series on interpretations of texts and occasional papers, and offers training in linguistics for Canadian native persons. Recent research and publication have had a particular emphasis on Mohawk. Library. London Museum of Archaeology.

UNIVERSITY OF WESTERN ONTARIO
Journalism Program for Native People
Middlesex College • LONDON, ON N6A 5B7
(519) 661-3380 Fax 661-3292

UNIVERSITY OF NIPISSING
100 College Dr.
NORTH BAY, ON P1B 8L7
(705) 474-3450 Ext. 4239 Fax 474-1947
Program: Native Teacher Certification Program

YORK UNIVERSITY
Faculty of Environmental Studies
Native/Canadian Relations Dept.
4700 Keele St.
NORTH YORK, ON M3J 1P3
(416) 736-5252 Fax 736-5679
Peter Homenuck, Director
Program: "Native/Canadian Relations (masters level program) focuses on the multi-faceted, unique, bicultural relationships, between, on the one hand, the Native community and its organizations and, on the other, the broader Canadian society and its institutions, together with the issues that result from the relationships. An important component of Native/Canadian Relations is research conducted on the expressed need of Bands, Native communities, Native organizations, and government departments."

CARLETON UNIVERSITY
Centre for Aboriginal Education, Research & Culture
Rm. 2207 Dunton, 1125 Colonel By Drive
OTTAWA, ON K1B 5B6
(613) 520-4494 Fax 520-2512

TRENT UNIVERSITY
Department of Native Studies
PETERBOROUGH, ON K9J 7B8
(705) 748-1416 Fax 748-1613
Joan M. Vastokas, PhD, Chairperson
E-mail: jvastokas@trentu.ca
Web site: www.trentu.ca/academic/anthro/
Instructors: Julia Harrison, DPhil, Susan M. Jamieson, PhD, Evelyn M. Todd, PhD, and Joan M. Vastokas, PhD, Cath Oberholtzer, PhD. *Special facility*: Archaeological Centre.

ALGOMA UNIVERSITY COLLEGE
Ojibway Language, 1520 Queen St. E.
SAULT STE. MARIE, ON P6A 2G4
(705) 949-2301 Ext. 203

LAURENTIAN UNIVERSITY
Native Institute of Research & Learning
Native Studies Department
Ramsey Lake Rd.
SUDBURY, ON P3E 2C6
(705) 673-5661
Instructors: Roger Spielmann, PhD, Patrick J. Julig, PhD, Kathryn T. Molohon, PhD.

LAKEHEAD UNIVERSITY
Dept. of Anthropology
THUNDER BAY, ON P7B 5E1
(807) 343-8632
Special programs: Native Studies; Boreal Studies. Instructors: Paul Driben, PhD, and Joe D. Stewart, PhD (Chair).

LAKEHEAD UNIVERSITY
School of Engineering
THUNDER BAY, ON P7B 5E1
(807) 343-8399 Fax 343-8013
E-mail: nape@lakeheadu.ca
Program: Native Access Program for Engineering

LAKEHEAD UNIVERSITY
Faculty of Education, Native Language Intsitute
955 Oliver Rd. • THUNDER BAY, ON P7B 5E1
(807) 343-8003 Fax 346-7746
Program: Native Language Instructors Program & Native Teacher Education Program

LAKEHEAD UNIVERSITY
School of Nursing
THUNDER BAY, ON P7B 5E1
(807) 343-8446 Fax 343-8246
Program: Native Nurses Entry Program

UNIVERSITY OF TORONTO
Aboriginal Health Professions Program
First Nations House, 563 Spadina Ave., 3rd Fl.
TORONTO, ON M5S 1A8
(416) 978-8227 Fax 978-1893

UNIVERSITY OF TORONTO
Dept. of Anthropology, Sidney Smith Hall
TORONTO, ON M5S 3G3 (416) 978-5416
Instructors: Gary Coupland, PhD, Ivan Kalmer, PhD, Martha A. Latta, PhD, Richard B. Lee, PhD, Krystyna Siesiechowicz, PhD, and Rosamund Vanderburgh, PhD, Mima Kapches, PhD, Alexander Von Gernet, PhD. *Special program*: Northern Yukon Research Project; excavations at historic and prehistoric Huron villages and older sites in Ontario; research among Canadian Indians, rural and urban.

UNIVERSITY OF WATERLOO
Dept. of Anthropology • WATERLOO N2L 3G1
(519) 885-1211 ext. 2520
Courses: Prehistoric man in America/Great Lakes area - A survey; Inuit and Eskimo cultures; the contemporary Canadian Indian scene; comparative policies on native minorities; early man in the new world. *Instructors*: Thomas S. Abler, PhD, and Sally M. Weaver, PhD. *Award*: Graham Goddard Anthropology Medal—silver medal awarded annually to a 3rd and 4th year anthropology major or honours student who has demonstrated an interest in native peoples of North America.

QUEBEC

McGILL UNIVERSITY
Dept. of Anthropology
855 Sherbrooke St. W.
MONTREAL H3A 2T7
(514) 398-4300 Fax 398-7476
Special programs: Canadian Studies Program; Northern Studies Minor; a group of Iroquoian archaeologists forms a core of an intimate group in archaeology. *Instructors*: Carmen Lambert, PhD, Toby Morantz, PhD, and Colin Scott, PhD, George Wenzel, PhD.

McGILL UNIVERSITY
Faculty of Education, 3700 McTavish St.
MONTREAL, PQ H3A 1Y2
(514) 398-4533 Fax 398-4679
Program: Native and Northern Education.

UNIVERSITY OF MONTREAL
Department of Anthropology
CP 6128, Succursale 'A'
MONTREAL H3C 3J7 (514) 343-6560
Instructors: Franklin Auger (Doct. en Anth), Asen Balikci, PhD, Pierre Beaucage, PhD, Claude Chapdelaine, PhD, Norman Clermont, PhD, Louise I. Paradis, PhD, Remi Savard (Doct. en Ethnol.), Gilles Lefebvre, Ph.D. (Linguistics), and Marcel Rioux, M.A. (Sociology). *Special programs*: Northeast archaeology; Summer Field Programs (Inuit and Canadian Indian areas—ethnology.)

UNIVERSITE LAVAL
Department of Anthropologie
Cite Universitaire • STE-FOY G1K 7P4
(418)656-5867
Courses: ethnologie des Amerindiens; ethnologie des Inuit; dossiers autochtones contemporains. Instructors: Paul Charest, Gerry McNulty, Bernard Saladin d'Anglure, Francois Trudel, PhD, Louis-Jacques Dorais, Pierre Miranda, and Yvan Simonis. *Special programs*: North American Indian; Canadian Inuit. *Special facility*: Centre d'etudes nordiques. *Publications*: Etudes Inuit Studies; Anthropologie et Societes.

SASKATCHEWAN

GABRIEL DUMONT INSTITUTE
48 12th St. E
PRINCE ALBERT, SK S6V 1B2
(306) 764-1797 Fax 764-3995
Program: Saskatchewan Urban Native Teacher Education program (SUNTEP)

GABRIEL DUMONT INSTITUTE
48 12th St. E • REGINA, SK S4N 0Z6 1B2
(306) 347-4108
Program: Saskatchewan Urban Native Teacher Education program (SUNTEP)

SASKATCHEWAN INDIAN FEDERATED COLLEGE
University of Regina
118 College West • REGINA, SK S4S 0A2
(306) 584-8333 Fax 584-8334
Dr. Oliver Brass, President
Prof. Paul J. Dudgeon, V.P. Academic
Programs: Undergraduate and graduate degree programs within an environment of Indian cultural affirmation. Elders are available to provide counseling and advice based on traditional Indian values. *Personnel*: Gloria Mehlmann, Director, Research and Development; Richard Laye, Director, Public Relations; Rolando Ramirez, Director, Centre for International Indigenous Studies and Development; Blair Stonechild, Dean; Brian Opikokew, Dean of Students; Robert Anderson, Registrar; Phyllis Lerat, Librarian. *Department Heads*: Bob Boyer, Indian Fine Arts; Edgar Epp, School of Social Work; Dr. Brent Galloway, Indian Languages, Literature & Linguistics; Dr. Pam Janz, Indian Education; David Reed Miller, PhD, Indian Studies. *Publication*: Saskatchewan Indian Federated College Journal, Bi-annual.

UNIVERSITY OF REGINA
Dept. of Anthropology
REGINA, SK S4S 0A2
(306) 584-4189 Richard K. Pope, Head
Instructors: George W. Arthur, PhD, Head; J.J. McHugh, PhD, Richard K. Pope, and C.R. Watrall, PhD, David Reed Miller, PhD, Patrick Douard, PhD. *Special facilities*: Canadian Plains Research Centre; Saskatchewan Archives; Saskatchewan Indian Federated College. Publications.

SASKATCHEWAN INDIAN CULTURAL COLLEGE
University of Saskatchewan Campus
SASKATOON, SK S7K 3S9
(306) 244-1146

UNIVERSITY OF SASKATCHEWAN
College of Education. McLean Hall
#7-106 Wiggins Rd.
SASKATOON, SK S7N 5E6
(306) 975-7095 Fax 975-1108
Program: Indian Teachers Education Program

UNIVERSITY OF SASKATCHEWAN
College of Nursing
Health Science Bldg., 107 Wiggins Rd.
SASKATOON, SK S7N 5E5
(800) 463-3345; (306) 966-6224 Fax 966-6703
Programs: National Native Access Program to Nursing; Indian Health Careers Program

UNIVERSITY OF SASKATCHEWAN
Dept. of Anthropology & Archaeology
SASKATOON, SK S7K 5B1
(306) 966-4181 Fax 966-5640
David Meyer, PhD, Head
Special Program: Native Studies and Ethnicity. *Instructors*: Alexander M. Ervin, PhD, Mary C. Marino, PhD, Ernest G. Walker, PhD, Robert G. Williamson, PhD, Urve Linnamae, PhD (part-time), and James B. Waldram, PhD (Native Studies Dept.). *Special programs*: Emphasis is given to research in the Prairie Provinces of western Canada, Arctic, Subarctic and Northwest Territories of Canada; summer fieldwork in archaeology and ethnology in Saskatchewan and/or NWT. *Special facilities*: Indian and Northern Curriculum Resources Centre, College of Education, with a specialized collection in North American Indian and crosscultural education; Saskatchewan Provincial Archives; Reference Library.

UNIVERSITY OF SASKATCHEWAN
Native Law Centre, 101 Diefenbaker Centre
SASKATOON, SK S7N 5B8
(306) 966-6189 Fax 966-6207
E-mail: hendrsny@duke.usak.ca
Donald J. Purich, JD, Director
Established in 1973 to promote the development of
the law and the legal system in ways which would better accommodate the advancement of native communities in Canadian society. One of the Centre's best
known activities is its annual pre-law orientation and
screening program for native students, the Program
of Legal Studies for Native People. Instructors: Linda
Fritz, JD, Norman K. Zlotkin, JD, Donald J. Purich, JD,
Fergus J. O'Connor, JD, and Zandra MacEachern, JD.
Special programs: Research - aboriginal land rights;
rights of indigenous peoples in international law; Indians and taxation and other areas. Summer program.
Publications: The Canadian Native Law Reporter,
quarerly journal, which provides full text reporting of
current native law cases; Canadian Native Law Cases,
9 volumes. Library.

UNIVERSITY OF SASKATCHEWAN
Native Studies Dept., 104 McLean Hall
SASKATOON, SK S7N 0W0 (306) 966-6208

YUKON

YUKON COLLEGE PROGRAM
Box 2799 • WHITEHORSE, YU Y1A 5K4

MEDIA

ALBERTA

CKUA - AM/FM
Native Voice of Alberta. On the Air 4:30 PM, Sunday,
in the following cities: Edmonton, Grand Prairie, Medicine Hat, Lethbridge, Red Deer, and Peace River.

'YR' RADIO
Native Voice of Alberta. On the Air 9:30 AM, Sunday,
in the following cities: Hinton, Whitecourt, Edson, Jasper, Grand Cache.

CFAC - FM
CALGARY, AB
Treaty No. 7 Radio Program; News Information
Program. On the Air 10:30 to 10:45 AM, Sunday.

CFWE RADIO (NATIVE PERSPECTIVE)
Aboriginal Multi Media Society of Alberta
15001 112th Ave.
EDMONTON, AB T5M 2V6
(800) 661-5469
(780) 455-2700 Fax 455-7639
Fred Didzena, President
Bert Crowfoot, Gen. Mgr.
Thomas Droege, Host/Producer
Gary Gee, Editor (Windspeaker-newspaper)

GREAT NORTH PRODUCTIONS
300-10359 82nd Ave.
EDMONTON, AB T6E 1Z9
(780) 439-1260 Fax 431-0197

GREAT PLAINS PRODUCTIONS
202-10138 81st Ave.
EDMONTON, AB T2E 1X1
(780) 439-4600 Fax 432-7354

CJOK - FM
FORT McMURRAY, AB
Native Voice of Alberta.
On the Air 7:30 PM, Sunday.

SIKSIKA COMMUNICATIONS/FM 90
P.O. Box 1490
GLEICHEN, AB T0J 1N0
(780) 734-5248 Fax 734-2355

CREE TV
Box 539 • HOBBEMA, AB T0C 1N0
(780) 585-2021 Fax 585-2393
CFWE - 89.9 FM (CATCH THE SPIRIT)
Aboriginal Multi Media Society of Alberta
P.O. Box 2250
LAC LA BICHE, AB T0A 2C0
(780) 623-3333 Fax 623-2811
Ray Fox, Host, Station Manager
Program: Native Perspective. Aboriginal programming
- news magazine format. Cree/English 50/50 split.
Broadcast 6-9 AM, Monday-Friday, via satellite.
Alberta's only aboriginal radio station, rebroadcasts
in 29 Native communities in Northern Alberta as well
as across Canada and the U.S.

CILA - FM (RED ROCK RADIO)
LETHBRIDGE, AB
Native Rock Program.
On the Air 1:00 to 2:00 PM, Sunday.

CJOC - FM
LETHBRIDGE, AB
Native-American Radio Program catering to tribes of
southern Alberta. On the Air 11:30 AM to 12:00 PM,
Sunday.

CKMR - 88.1 FM
MORLEY, AB

CIOK - FM
ST. PAUL, AB
Native Voice of Alberta.
On the Air 8:00 PM, Sunday.

COKI - 103.1 FM
SIKSIKA COMMUNICATIONS
P.O. Box 1490 • SIKSIKA, AB T0J 3W0
(403) 734-5248

INDIAN NEWS MEDIA
Box 120 • STANDOFF, AB T0L 1Y0
(780) 653-3301
Marrie Smallface Marule, President
Gerri Manyfingers, Executive Director
Mary Weasel Fat, Editor (Kainai News)
Blackfoot Radio Network; Bull Horn
Audio Video; Newspaper.

CKTA - FM
TABOR, AB
Native-American Elders Program.
On the Air 10:30 to 11:00 AM, Sunday.

BRITISH COLUMBIA

NUXALK COMMUNICATIONS SOCIETY
Box 368 • BELLA COOLA, BC V0T 1C0
(250) 799-5418

NNB-BC RADIO
Northern Native Broadcasting
Box 1090 • TERRACE, BC V8G 4V1
(250) 638-8137 Fax 638-8027
Ray Jones, General Manager

THE NATIVE CANADIAN MEDIA CORPS.
600-444 Robson St.
VANCOUVER, BC V6B 2B5
(604) 688-3877

CITR - NATIVE RADIO STATION
233-6138 Sub Blvd.
VANCOUVER, BC V6T 1Z1
(604) 822-3017 Fax 822-9364

THE NATIVE VOICE
200-1755 E. Hastings St.
VANCOUVER, BC V5L 1T1
(604) 255-3137

NATIVE VOICE BROADCAST SYSTEM
533 Yates St.
VICTORIA, BC V8W 1K7
(604) 383-3211 Fax (384-1586
Radio & TV broadcasting.

MANITOBA

CFNC NATIVE BROADCASTING
Box 129 • CROSS LAKE, MB R0B 0J0
(204) 676-231 Fax 676-2911

PIMICKAMAK MULTICHANNEL TV
Box 118 • CROSS LAKE, MB R0B 0J0
(204) 676-2146 Fax 676-2540

PINESIW PRODUCTIONS, INC.
CROSS LAKE, MB R0B 0J0
(204) 676-2146 Fax 676-2540

POPLAR RIVER RADIO STATION
NEGGINAN, MB R0B 0Z0
(204) 244-2123 Fax 244-2690

CJNC (RADIO) NORWAY HOUSE
Norway House Communications, Inc.
Box 311 • NORWAY HOUSE, MB R0B 1B0
(204) 359-6775 Fax 359-6191

NATIVE MEDIA NETWORK
Box 848
PORTAGE LA PRAIRIE, MB R1N 3C3
(204) 239-1920

NATIVE COMMUNICATIONS, INC.
76 Severn Cres.
THOMPSON, MB R8N 1M6
(204) 778-8343 Fax 778-6559
E-mail: nci@nor.comb.mb
Ron Nadeau, Chairperson & CEO
Henry Wilson, Dirctor of Broadcasting

BLIND TREK
9-819 Grant Ave.
WINNIPEG, MB R3M 1Y1
(204) 287-2311
30 minute live phone in show, Ch. 11

CHIKAK COMMUNICATIONS
316 St. Mary's Rd.
WINNIPEG, MB R2H 1J8
(204) 237-1170 Fax 233-5562

CKND TV
603 St. Mary's Rd.
WINNIPEG, MB R2M 3L8
(204) 233-3304 Fax 233-5615

FIRST CITIZEN TV TALK SHOW
517 Craig St. • WINNIPEG, MB R3G 3C2
(204) 774-8432

NATIVE COMMUNICATIONS, INC.
Unit C-130, 1666 St. James St.
WINNIPEG, MB
(204) 774-5939 Fax 774-5939

NATIVE MEDIA NETWORK
204-424 Logan Ave.
WINNIPEG, MB R3A 0R4
(204) 943-6475 Fax 942-1380

NATIVE MULTIMEDIA PRODUCTIONS
CKND TV, 6 Elm Park Blvd.
WINNIPEG, MB R2M 0V9
(204) 231-1524 Fax 233-5615

OUR NATIVE LAND TV
CBC Radio, Box 160 • WINNIPEG, MB

THETA PRODUCTIONS, INC.
205-698 Corydon Ave.
WINNIPEG, MB R3M 0X9
(204) 284-0398

URBAN EAGLES
204 - 825 Sherbrook St.
WINNIPEG, MB R3A 1M5
(204) 772-6967 FAX 786-0860

WOODSMOKE & SWEETGRASS
CKY TV, Polo Park
WINNIPEG, MB R3G 0L7
(204) 775-0371 Fax 783-4841

NEW BRUNSWICK

C.F.N.T. - 104.5 FM
Maliseet Nation at Tobique Radio
P.O. Box 695 • PERTH ANDOVER, NB E0J 1V0
(506) 273-4307 Fax 273-9697

NEWFOUNDLAND

ATJIQANGITUT &LABRADORIMUIT
Box 160 • NAIN, NF A0P 1L0
(709) 922-2955 Fax 922-2293
Radio & TV, respectively.

OKALAKATIGET SOCIETY
P.O. Box 160 • NAIN, NF A0P 1L0
(709) 922-2896 Fax 922-2293
Robert Lyall, President
Ken Todd, Executive Director
Radio, TV. *Publication*: Kinatuinamot Ilengajuk
(newsletter).

NORTHWEST TERRITORIES

CKQN-FM RADIO
BAKER LAKE, NT X0C 0A0
(867) 793-2962

SUDLIQVALUK RADIO SOCIETY
CORAL HARBOUR, NT X0C 0C0
(867) 925-9940

ARCIAQPALUK RADIO SOCIETY
ESKIMO POINT, NT X0C 0E0
(867) 857-2810

HALL BEACH RADIO SOCIETY
HALL BEACH, NT X0A 0K0
(867) 928-8852

INUVIALUIT COMMUNICATIONS SOCIETY
P.O. Box 1704 • INUVIK, NT X0E 1C0
(867) 979-2067 Fax 979-2744
Vincent Teddy, President

CFFB RADIO STATION
Canadian Broadcasting Corp.
IQALIUT, NT X0A 0H0
(867) 979-6100

IBC-TV - INUIT BROADCASTING CORP.
P.O. Box 700 • IQALIUT, NT X0A 0H0
(867) 979-6231 Fax 979-5853
Jobi Weetaluktuk, Executive Producer
Lynda Gunn, Regional Manager

TELEVISION NORTHERN CANADA (TVNC)
Box 1630 • IQALIUT, NT X0A 0H0
(867) 979-1707 Fax 979-1708

ALLANIQ RADIO SOCIETY
PANGNIRTUNG, NT X0A 0R0
(867) 473-8903

CBC KIVALLIQ
RANKIN INLET, NT X0C 0G0
(867) 645-2885

INUIT BROADCASTING CORP.
P.O. Box 178 • RANKIN INLET, NT X0C 0G0
(867) 645-2678 Fax 645-2937
Radio & television programs.

CBC NORTH
Northern Services Program
Box 160 • YELLOWKNIFE, NT X1A 2N2
(867) 920-5465 Fax 920-5440

CKLB RADIO
Native Communications Society of the Western
NWT
Box 1919 • YELLOWKNIFE, NT X1A 2P4
(867) 920-2277 Fax 920-4205

CKNM-FM
Native Communications
Society of the Western NWT
Box 1919 • YELLOWKNIFE, NT X1A 2P4
(867) 873-2661 Fax 920-4205
Percy Kinney, Radio Manager
Lee Selleck, Editor
Publication: Native Press (newspaper)

NCS-TV LTD.
Native Communications
Society of the Western NWT
Box 1919 • YELLOWKNIFE, NT X1A 2P4
(867) 920-2277 Fax 920-4205

TELEVISION NORTHERN CANADA (TVNC)
5120-49th St., Box 3
YELLOWKNIFE, NT X1A 1P8
(867) 669-7299 Fax 669-7930
E-mail: tvncda@arcticdata.nt.ca
Web site: www.tvnc.ca

NOVA SCOTIA

**NATIVE COMMUNICATIONS
SOCIETY OF NOVA SCOTIA**
P.O. Box 344 • SYDNEY, NS B1P 6H2
(902) 539-0045 Roy A. Gould, Exec. Director

**NATIVE COMMUNICATIONS SOCIETY OF NOVA
SCOTIA**
P.O. Box 1005 • TRURO, NS B2N 5G7
(902) 895-6217 Brian Douglas, Editor
Publication: Micmac News.

ONTARIO

BEARSKIN LAKE RADIO STATION
BEARSKIN LAKE, ON P0V 1E0
(807) 363-2578

CKON - FM 97.3
Box 1496 • CORNWALL, ON K6A 5B7
(613) 575-2100 Fax 575-2935

"SMOKE SIGNALS" RADIO PROGRAM
Unit 61 - 1290 Sandford St.
LONDON, ON N5V 3X9
(519) 659-4682 Fax 453-3676

CHMO - AM
James Bay Broadcasting Corp.
P.O. Box 400 • MOOSONEE, ON P0L 1Y0
(705) 336-2301 Fax 336-3153

**FIRST NATIONS, INC.
CABLE TV & COMMUNICATIONS**
Box 905 • OHSWEKEN, ON N0A 1M0
(519) 445-2981 Fax 445-4084

CHFN 100.3 FM
RR#5 • OHSWEKEN, ON N0H 2T0
(519) 534-1003 Fax 524-2130

CKRZ 100.3 FM
Box 189 • OHSWEKEN, ON N0A 1M0
(519) 445-4140 Fax 445-0177
E-mail: ckrz@worldchat.com

INUIT BROADCASTING CORP. (IBC)
703-251 Laurier Ave. • OTTAWA, ON K1P 5J6
(613) 235-1892 Fax 230-8824
E-mail: ibcicsl@sonetis.com
Doug Saunders, President
Debbie Brisebois, Executive Director

TV NORTHERN CANADA (TVNC)
1412 - 130 Albert St. • OTTAWA, ON K1P 5g4
(613) 567-1550 Fax 567-1834
E-mail: tvno@sometis.com
Web site: www.tvnc.ca

CKWE 105.9 FM
general Delivery • SHANNONVILLE, ON K0K 3A0
(613) 967-0463 (Phone & Fax)

WAWATAY COMMUNICATIONS SOCIETY
Box 1180, 15 - 5th Ave.
SIOUX LOOKOUT, ON P0V 2T0
(807) 737-2951 Fax 737-3224
E-mail: wawatay@sl.lakeheadedu.ca
Lawrence Martin, Executive Director
Megan Williams, Editor - WaWaTay (newspaper)
MOOSE FACTORY, ON P0L 1W0
(705) 658-4556
Vern Cheechoo, Sr. Producer (Radio & TV)

CIUT - 89.5 FM
91 St. George St.
TORONTO, ON M5S 2E8
(416) 595-0909 Fax 595-5604

CFRZ 91.5 FM
RR#3 • WALLACEBURG, ON N8A 4K9
(519) 627-6272 Fax 627-6074

WIKY TV5 VIDEO PRODUCTIONS
P.O. Box 112
WIKWEMIKONG, ON P0P 2J0
(705) 869-3200 Fax 859-3851

FIRST PEOPLES FREE RADIO
334 Askin Ave.
WINDSOR, ON N9B 2X2
(519) 254-8596

**MOCCASIN TELEGRAPH
NATIVE RADIO PROGRAM**
38 Burwick Ave.
WOODBRIDGE, ON L4L 1J7
(905) 856-5962 Fax 975-0466

QUEBEC

**CHISASIBI TELECOMMUNICATIONS
ASSOCIATION**
Chisasibi First Nation
CHISASIBI, PQ J0M 1E0
(819) 855-2527

TAQRAMIUT NIPINGAT, INC.
Administrative Centre
185 Dorval Ave. #501
DORVAL, PQ H9S 5J9
(514) 631-1394 Fax 631-6258

CKRK-103.7 MOHAWK RADIO STATION
Box 1050 • KAHNAWAKE, PQ J0L 1B0
(450) 638-1313 Fax 638-4009

CKHQ KANESATAKE RADIO
P.O. Box 747
KANASATAKE, PQ J0N 1E0
(514) 479-8321

QAJJALIK FM STATION
KANGIQSUALUJJUAQ, PQ J0M 1A0
(819) 935-4258

TAQRAMIUT NIPINGAT, INC.
Television Production Centre
Box 360 • KUUJJUAQ, PQ J0M 1C0
(819) 964-2565 Fax 964-2252

CHME-FM 94.9
c/o Montagnais de les Escoumins
20 rue de la Reserve, Box 820
LES ESCOUMINS, PQ G0T 1K0
(418) 233-2700 Fax 233-3326

CHRQ FM RADIO STATION
Riverside East • LISTUGUJ, PQ G0C 2R0
(418) 788-2449 Fax 788-2653

CKWE RADIO
Bande de la riviere Deserte
C.P. 10, rue Bitobi • MANIWAKI, PQ J9E 3B3
(819) 449-5097

JAMES BAY CREE COMMUNICATIONS SOCIETY
75 Riverside St.
MISTASSINI LAKE, PQ G0W 1C0
(418) 923-3191 Fax 923-2088

JAMES BAY CREE COMMUNICATIONS SOCIETY
1, Place Ville Marie, Suite 3434
MONTREAL, PQ H3B 3N9
   (514) 861-5837 Fax 861-0760
   Soloman Awashish, Radio Director
   Diane Reid, Director General
Publication: Cree Ajemon.

**SANS RESERVE COMMUNICATIONS
AUTOCHTONES**
3575, boul. Saint-Laurent
MONTREAL, PQ H2X 2T7
   (514) 843-6098

MONT NATASHQUAN RADIO
NATASHQUAN, PQ G0G 2E0
   (418) 726-3327

NEMASKA RADIO STATION
NEMASKA, PQ J0Y 3B0
   (819) 673-2046 Fax 673-2542

CREE COMMUNITY RADIO STATION
POSTE-DE-LA-BALEINE, PQ J0M 1G0
   (819) 929-3397

CKPV FM RADIO
QUAQTAQ, PQ J0M 1J0
   (819) 492-9946

TAQRAMIUT NIPINGAT, INC.
Television & Radio Production Centre
Box 120 • SALLUIT, PQ J0M 1S0
   (819) 255-8822 (radio) Fax 255-8891
   (819) 255-8901 (television)
   George Kakayuk, President

RADIO KUESHAPETSHEKEN/CKU 104.5 FM
1089, rue Dquen, C.P. 8000
SEPT-LIES, PQ G4R 4L9
   (418) 927-2440 Fax 927-2800

TEWEGAN COMMUNICATIONS SOCIETY
351 Central Ave. • VAL D'OR, PQ J9P 1P6
   (819) 825-5192 Fax 631-6528
   Noe Mitchell, Executice Director

WASWANIPI COMMUNICATIONS SOCIETY
20 Popular St. • WASWANIPI, PQ J0Y 3C0
   (819) 753-2557 Fax 753-2555

WEMIDJI RADIO STATION
Reserve Indienne Wemidji
WEMIDJI, PQ J0M 1L0 (819) 978-0264 ext. 245

RADIO COMMUNAUTAIRE
545, Chef Thomas Martin, Village des Hurons
WENDAKE, PQ G0A 4V0
   (418) 843-3937

SOCAM - AM RADIO
Societe de Communications Atikamekw Montagnais
85 Boul. Chef Maurice Bastien
C.P. 329, Village des Hurons
WENDAKE, PQ G0A 4V0
   (418) 843-3873 Fax 845-4198
   Bernard Hervieau, Producer
   Diane Savard, General Manager

SASKATCHEWAN

CILX RADIO - BELANGER'S COMMUNICATIONS
P.O. Box 208
ILE-ALA-CROSSE, SK S0M 1C0
   (306) 833-2173 Fax 833-2310

MISSINIPI BROADCASTING CORP.
Box 1529 • LA RONGE, SK S0J 1L0
   (306) 425-4003 Fax 425-3755
   Robert Merasty, Executive Director
   Rick Laliberte & William Dumais, Directors
Radio: Missinipi Atchimowin

RAM REBROADCASTING, INC.
Box 3075
PRINCE ALBERT, SK S6V 3M4
   (306) 763-0396

**SASKATCHEWAN NATIVE
COMMUNICATIONS CORP.**
2526 Eleventh Ave.
REGINA, SK S4P 0K5
   (306) 653-2253
   Gary Laplante, Chairperson
   Ona Fiddler-Bertelg, Editor/Manager
Publication: New Breed

CJUS - FM
SASKATOON, SK
Native Voice of Alberta.
On the Air 4:30 PM, Sunday.

GEMINI PRODUCTIONS, INC.
Box 7773
SASKATOON, SK S7K 4R5
   (306) 665-8575 Fax 665-0008

MOCCASIN TELEGRAPH
c/o Saskatchewan Indian
1630 Idylwyld Dr.
SASKATOON, SK S7K 3S9

QUEST
c/o Saskatchewan Indian
Institute of Technologies
Moose Woods Reserve
RR 5, GB 139
SASKATOON, SK S7K 3J8
   (306) 244-4444 Fax 244-1391

**SASKATCHEWAN NATIVE
COMMUNICATIONS SOCIETY**
104, 219 Robin Cres.
SASKATOON, SK S7L 6M8
   (306) 244-7441 Fax 343-0171

O & O BROADCASTING, INC.
Thunderchild Reserve
TURTLEFORD, SK S0M 2Y0
   (306) 845-3170

YUKON

CHON-FM
Northern Native Broadcasting of Yukon
4228-A 4th Ave.
WHITEHORSE, YU Y1A 1K1
   (867) 688-2420 Fax 668-6612
   Ken Kane, Chairperson
   Marion Telep, Radio Director
Radio broadcasting.

KEYAH PRODUCTIONS
4228-A 4th Ave.
WHITEHORSE, YU Y1A 1K1
   (867) 668-2420 Fax 668-6612
   E-mail: nnby@yknet.yk.ca
Radio & TV productions.

YE SA TO COMMUNICATIONS SOCIETY
Council of Yukon Indians, 22 Nisutlin Dr.
WHITEHORSE, YU Y1A 3S5
   (867) 668-5477 Fax 667-6923
   Elizabeth Jackson, President
Publication: Dan Sha (newspaper).

An alphabetical listing of about 6,000 in-print books relating to Indians of North America. In each listing —where sufficient material has been provided—the title, author or editor, information on pagination, whether illustrated, indexed, etc., name of publisher, the year of publications, and price. The address of the publishers are contained in the Publishers Index. An asterisk (*) preceding a title indicates it is of primarily juvenile or young adult interest; the specific age group for which such titles are intended has been noted, if available. If you require material on a particular subject or interest area, refer to the subject listings in the Subject Classifications section, located at the end of this section.

A

*A,B,C'S THE AMERICAN INDIAN WAY
Children learn the alphabet while learning about American Indians. Grades K-2. Illus. Paper. Sierra Oaks, $7.95.

*ABC'S OF OUR SPIRITUAL CONNECTION
Kim Soo Goodtrack
First Nations people's common ethics and cultural values that identify them in their everday lives. Grades 3-8. Illus. 56 pp. Paper. Theytus, 1994. $9.95.

A.D. 1250: ANCIENT PEOPLES OF THE SOUTHWEST
Lawrence W. Cheek
Focuses on the cultures of the Anasazi, Sinagua, Mogollon, Hohokam, and Salado. 176 pp. University of Arizona Press, 1994. $49.95.

*THE ABENAKI
Colin G. Calloway
Grades 5 and up. Illus. 104 pp. Chelsea House, 1988. $17.95.

*THE ABENAKI
Elaine Landau
Grades 5-8. Illus. 64 pp. Franklin Watts, 1996. $22; paper, $6.95.

*ABENAKI CAPTIVE
M.L. Dubois
Grades 4-7. 144 pp. Lerner, 1994. $16.95.

ABENAKI WARRIOR, THE LIFE & TIMES OF CHIEF ESCUMBUIT: BIG ISLAND POND, 1665-1727 FRENCH HERO! BRITISH MONSTER! INDIAN PATRIOT
Alfred E. Kayworth; Adolph Case, Editor
Illus. 260 pp. Branden Publishing Co., 1998. $22.95.

ABORIGINAL AMERICAN INDIAN BASKETRY: STUDIES IN TEXTILE ART WITHOUT MACHINERY
Otis Tufton Mason
Reprint of 1904 ed. Illus. 688 pp. The Rio Grande Press, $40.

ABORIGINAL INDIAN BASKETRY
Otis T. Mason
Reprint of 1904 edition. Illus. 688 pp. Rio Grande, $35.

ABORIGINAL MONUMENTS OF THE STATE OF NEW YORK
E.B. Squier
Reprint of 1849 edition. Illus. 200 pp. Sourcebook, $18.95.

ABORIGINAL ONTARIO: HISTORICAL PERSPECTIVES ON THE FIRST NATIONS
Edward S. Rogers & Donald B. Smith, Editors
14 contributing authors review the historical experience of the First Nations of Ontario. 448 pp. University of Toronto Press, 1994. $25.

ABORIGINAL PEOPLE & COLONIZERS OF WESTERN CANADA TO 1900
Sarah Carter
History of Canada's aboriginal peoples after European contact.152 pp. U. of Toronto Press, 1999. $45; paper, $14.95.

ABORIGINAL PEOPLE & OTHER CANADIANS: SHAPING NEW RELATIONSHIPS
edited by Martin Thornton & Roy Todd
University of Toronto Press, 2001. $22.95.

THE ABORIGINAL PIPES OF WISCONSIN
West
Reprint of 1905 article. 130 pp. Paper. Hothem House. $12.50.

ABORIGINAL PLANT USE IN CANADA'S NORTHWEST BOREAL FOREST
Robin J. Marles, et al
Describes the traditional Aboriginal uses of over 200 plants from Canada's boreal forest. Illus. 256 pp. UBC Press, 1999. $75.

ABORIGINAL REMAINS OF TENNESSEE
J. Jones
Reprint of 1880 edition. Illus. 186 pp. Sourcebook, $16.95.

ABORIGINAL SLAVERY ON THE NORTHWEST COAST OF NORTH AMERICA
Leland Donald
Illus. 379 pp. University of California Press, 1997. $42.50.

ABORIGINAL SOCIETY IN SOUTHERN CALIFORNIA
William D. Strong
Reprint of 1929 edition. Paper. Malki Museum Press, $37.50.

ABORIGINAL SUBSISTENCE TECHNOLOGY ON THE SOUTHEASTERN COASTAL LAIN DURING THE LATE PRE-HISTORIC PERIOD
Lewis H. Larson
Illus. Maps. Biblio. 260 pp. University Press of Florida, 1980. $29.95.

ABORIGINAL & TREATY RIGHTS IN CANADA
Michael Asch, Editor
Paper. UBC Press, 1997. $25.95.

AN ABRIDGEMENT OF THE INDIAN AFFAIRS CONTAINED IN FOUR FOLIO VOLUMES
Peter Wraxall
Transacted in the Colony of New York from the Year 1687 to 1751. Reprint of 1915 edition. Ayer Co., $24.50.

*ABSALOKA
Council for Indian Education, 1971. 75¢.

ABSARAKA: HOME OF THE CROWS
Margaret I. Carrington
Illus. 285 pp. University of Nebraska Press, 1983. $22.50; paper, $6.95.

ACCESS FIRST NATIONS
Directory for American Indian artists and craftspeople listing businesses that carry such arts and crafts, and more. $32.95. Order from Access First Nations, 69 Kelley Rd., Falmouth, VA 22405 (703) 371-5615.

AN ACCOUNT OF THE ANTIQUITIES OF THE INDIANS: CHRONICLES OF THE NEW WORLD ENCOUNTER
Fray Ramon Pane; Jose Juan Arrom, Editor
Illus. 128 pp. Duke University Press, 2000. $39.95.

ACCULTURATION IN SEVEN INDIAN TRIBES
Ralph Linton
Reprint. Peter Smith, $13.25.

ACOMA
H.L. James
Revised edition. Presents Acoma, the "sky city" of New Mexico. Illus. 96 pp. Paper. Schiffer, $14.95.

ACOMA
Tryntje Van Ness Seymour
Text & original photographs tell the story of Acoma. Limited edition of 75. Illus. 64 pp. Lime Rock Press, 1980. $295. Delux edition of 25 signed copies available, $750.

ACOMA & LAGUNA POTTERY
Rick Dillingham; with Melinda Elliott
Traces the development of pottery making at the two pueblos. Illus. Maps. Biblio. 256 pp. Paper. University of Washington Press & School of American Research, 1994. $24.95.

ACORN SOUP
L. Frank
Cartoons depicting the ancient life of native California and challenging stereotypes about California Indians. Illus. 64 pp. Paper. Heyday Books, $7.95.

ACROSS ARCTIC AMERICA, NARRATIVE OF THE FIFTH THULE EXPEDITION
Knud Rasmussen
Reprint of 1927 edition. Greenwood, $35.

*ACROSS THE TUNDRA
Marjorie Vandervelde
Tale of two Eskimo boys hunting alone. Grades 4-9. 40 pp. Council for Indian Education, 1972. $9.95; paper. $3.95.

ACTS & RESOLUTIONS OF INDIAN NATIONS-TRIBAL COUNCILS
A series of books on laws, treaties and unions among Indians of certain nations. See Scholarly Resources for titles and prices.

A.D. 1250: ANCIENT PEOPLES OF THE SOUTHWEST
text by Lawrence W. Cheek
Details ancient cultures such as the Anasazi, Mogollon, etc. 200 full-color photos and drawings. 176 pp. Treasure Chest, 1994. $49.95.

ADA, OKLAHOMA, QUEEN CITY OF THE CHICKASAW NATION: A PICTORIAL HISTORY
Marvin Kroeker & Guy Logsdon
Donning, 1998.

ADAMS: THE MANUFACTURING OF FLAKED STONE TOOLS AT A PALEOINDIAN SITE IN WESTERN KENTUCKY
Thomas N. Sanders
Illus. 165 pp. Paper. Persimmon Press & Hothem House, 1990. $15.95.

THE ADKINS SITE: A PALAEO-INDIAN HABITATION & ASSOCIATED STONE STRUCTURE
Richard M. Gramly
Illus. 130 pp. Paper. Persimmon Press & Hothem House, 1988. $13.95.

ADOBE WALLS: THE HISTORY & ARCHAEOLOGY OF THE 1874 TRADING POST
Lindsay Baker & Billy Harrison
Illus. 430 pp. Texas A&M University Press, 1986. $39.50.

*ADOPTED BY INDIANS: A TRUE STORY
Thomas Jefferson Mayfield; Malcolm Margolin, Editor
Gives younger readers a close-up view of traditional California Indians life and early California. Grades 4 and up. Illus. 192 pp. Paper. Heyday Books, $10.95.

ADVENTURES IN STONE ARTIFACTS
Livoti & Kiesa
A family guide to hunting and collecting Indian artifacts. Illus. 254 pp. paper. Hothem House, 1997. $15.95.

*ADVENTURES IN STORYTELLING
Set of three titles with accompanying audiocassette. *The Animals' Ballgame, Loon and Deer Were Traveling,* and *Naughty Little Rabbit and Old Man Coyote.* Grades K-4. Illus. 24-48 pp. Childrens Press, $37.

ADVENTURES ON THE WESTERN FRONTIER
Maj. Gen. John Gibbon
A record of the lives of the Indians, soldiers and white settlers; Indian warfare; Sioux Campaign of 1876.Illus. 288 pp. Indiana University Press, 1994. $24.95.

AFRICANS & CREEKS: FROM THE COLONIAL PERIOD TO THE CIVIL WAR
Daniel F. Littlefield, Jr.
Illus. Greenwood Publishing, 1979. $35.

AFRICANS & SEMINOLES: FROM REMOVAL TO EMANCIPATION
Daniel F. Littlefield, Jr.
Documents the interrelationship of two racial cultures in antebellum Florida and Oklahoma. Originally published in 1977. Illus. Paper. University Press of Mississippi, 2001. $18.

AFTER & BEFORE THE LIGHTNING
Simon J. Ortiz
Prose & verse poems of winter in South Dakota on the Rosebud Sioux Reservation. 134 pp. Paper. University of Arizona Press, 1994. $17.95.

AFTER COLUMBUS: THE SMITHSONIAN CHRONICLE OF THE NORTH AMERICAN INDIANS
Herman J. Viola
The facts & implications of Indian & white interaction in America. Illus. 288 pp. Paper. Smithsonian Institution Press, 1991. $24.95.

AFTER REMOVAL: THE CHOCTAW IN MISSISSIPPI
Samuel Wells & Roseanna Tubby, Editors
Illus. 154 pp. University Press of Mississippi, 1986. $32.50.

AFTER THE TRAIL OF TEARS: THE CHEROKEES' STRUGGLE FOR SOVEREIGNTY, 1839-1880
William G. McLoughlin
450 pp. University of North Carolina Press, 1994. $49.95; paper, $19.95.

AGAINST BORDERS: PROMOTING BOOKS FOR A MULTICULTURAL WORLD
Hazel Rochman
Illus. 288 pp. Paper. ALA Books, 1993. $16.95.

AGAINST CULTURE: DEVELOPMENT, POLITICS, & RELIGION IN INDIAN ALASKA
Kirk Dombrowski
Tlingit & Haida life in Southeast Alaska today. Illus. Map. 247 PP. University of Nebraska Press, 2001. $60; paper, $19.95.

*AGALIHA': INDIAN SELF-ESTEEM CURRICULUM ACTIVITY BOOK
Indian Developed Curriculum & Publishing Corp.
Encourages Indian students to feel pride in their heritage. Grades 1-8. 62 pp. Daybreak Star Press, $12.95.

THE AGATE BASIN SITE: A RECORD OF THE PALEOINDIAN AGENTS OF REPRESSION: THE FBI's SECRET WARS AGAINST THE BLACK PANTHER PARTY & THE AMERICAN INDIAN MOVEMENT
Ward Churchill & James V. Wall
325 pp. South End Press, 1988. $30.00; paper, $15.

AGRICULTURAL TERRACING IN THE ABORIGINAL NEW WORLD
Robin Donkin
Illus. 196 pp. Paper. University of Arizona Press, 1979. $8.50.

AH MO: INDIAN LEGENDS FROM THE NORTHWEST
Arthur Griffin, Editor
Illus. 64 pp. Paper. Hancock House, 1990. $7.95.

AHTNA ATHABASKAN DICTIONARY
James Kari, Editor
Contains 6,000 Ahtna language entries. 700 pp.
Alaska Native Language Center, 1990. $50; paper, $25.

AIDS REGIONAL DIRECTORY:
RESOURCES IN INDIAN COUNTRY
Laurie McLemore, MD, Director
Association of Native American Medical Students, 1994,
2nd Ed. $23, postpaid.

AIRLIFT TO WOUNDED KNEE
Bill Zimmerman
Illus. 348 pp. Ohio University Press, 1976. $14.95.

AKWE:KON LITERARY ISSUE
An anthology of new fiction and poetry from 14
Native American authors. Akwe:kon Press, $8.

AKWESASNE HISTORICAL POSTCARDS;
PEACEMAKER & HIAWATHA POSTERS
Akwesasne Museum, 50/postcard; 75/poster.

ALAAWICH
Lucy Arvidson
Paper. Malki Museum Press, 1978. $3.

THE ALABAMA-COUSHATTA INDIANS
Jonathan Hook
Photos. 208 pp. Texas A&M University Press, 1995. $29.95.

ALASKA DAYS WITH JOHN MUIR
Samuel Hall Young
Illus. 240 pp. Paper. Gibbs Smith, 1991. $9.95

THE ALASKA ESKIMOS: A SELECTED
ANNOTATED BIBLIOGRAPHY
Arthur Hippler & John Wood
Paper. University of Alaska, 1977. $15.

ALASKA 1899: ESSAYS FROM
THE HARRIMAN EXPEDITION
George Bird Grinnell
Records Grinnell's observations of native Alaskans. Illus.
136 pp. Paper. University of Washington Press, 1994. $14.95.

ALASKA: A HISTORY OF THE 49TH STATE
Claus M. Naska & Herman Slotnick
Second edition. Photos. Maps. 368 pp. Paper.
University of Oklahoma Press, $18.95.

ALASKA HISTORY SERIES
Richard Pierce, Editor/Publisher
See Limestone Press for complete list of titles and prices.

*ALASKA IN THE DAYS THAT WERE BEFORE
Tanya Hardgrove
A Native elder tells stories from his life. Grades 3-10. 31 pp.
Council for Indian Education, 1985. $8.95; paper, $2.95.

ALASKA NATIVE ARTS & CRAFTS
Alaska Geographic
In-depth review of the art and artifacts of Alaska's Native people.
210 pp. Alaska Natural History Association & The Alaska Geographic Society, $19.95.

THE ALASKA NATIVE CLAIMS SETTLEMENT ACT,
1991, & TRIBAL GOVERNMENT
Thomas A. Morehouse
Illus. 29 pp. University of Alaska, Institute of Social
and Economic Research, 1988. $2.

ALASKA NATIVE LAND RIGHTS: HEARING BEFORE THE
COMMITTEE ON ENERGY & NATURAL RESOURCES,
U.S. SENATE, 150TH CONGRESS
USGPO Staff
64 pp. USGPO, 1998.

ALASKA NATIVE LANGUAGE CENTER PUBLICATIONS
Contains numerous titles covering the Inupiaq Eskimo, Cen-
tral Yup'ik Eskimo, Alutiiq (Sugpiaq) Eskimo, Aleut, Siberian
Yup'ik EskimoAhtna Athabaskan, Tanaina Athabaskan, Ingalik
(Deg Hit'an) Athabaskan, Holikachuk Athabaskan, Upper
Kuskokwim, Koyukon Athabaskan, Han Athabaskan, Lower
Tanana Athabaskan, Tanacross Athabaskan, Upper Tanana
Athabaskan, Kutchin (Gwich'in) Athabaskan, Eyak, Tlingit, and
Haida. Also research papers, maps, and other sources of ma-
terials. Alaska Native Language Center.

ALASKA NATIVE LANGUAGES: PAST-PRESENT-FUTURE
Michael E. Krauss
Illus. 110 pp. Paper. Alaska Native Language Center, 1980.
$6.

ALASKA NATIVE POLICY IN THE TWENTIETH CENTURY
Ramona E. Skinner
140 pp. Garland, 1997. $44.

ALASKA NATIVES & AMERICAN LAWS, 2ND ED.
David S. Case & David A. Voluck
A review & analysis of legal principles applicable to Alaska
Natives in several substantive areas. 566 pp. University of
Alaska Press, 2002.

ALASKA NATIVES: A GUIDE TO CURRENT REFERENCE
SOURCES IN THE RASMUSON LIBRARY
Mark C. Goniwiecha
78 pp. Paper. University of Alaska, Rasmuson Library. $10.

ALASKA'S NATIVE PEOPLE
Lael Morgan, Editor
Illus. 304 pp. Paper. Alaska Northwest & The Alaska
Geographic Society, 1979. Album style, $24.95.

ALASKA'S SOUTHERN PANHANDLE
Alaska Geographic
Explores the southern tip of southeastern Alaska including the
Tlingit, Haida and Tsimshian Native groups. 96 pp. Paper.
Alaska Geographic Society, 1997. $19.95.

ALASKAMEUT '86
Exhibition catalog featuring interviews with and the artwork of
14 maskmakers representative of Aleut, Yup'ik, Inupiaq, Tlingit
and Athabascan cultures. Illus. 48 pp. Paper. Institute of Alaska
Native Arts, 1986. $10.50, postpaid.

ALASKAN ESKIMO LIFE IN THE 1890S: AS SKETCHED
BY NATIVE ARTISTS
George Phebus, Jr.
Illus. Map. 168 pp. Paper. University of Alaska Press, 1995.
$18.95.

*ALASKAN IGLOO TALES
Keithahn; illus. by Ahgupuk
Grades 3 and up. Paper. Graphic Arts Center, $12.95.

ALASKAN NATIVE FOOD PRACTICES,
CUSTOMS & HOLIDAYS
Karen Halderson
Paper. American Dietetic Assocaition, 1991. $10.

ALBERNI PREHISTORY
Alan D. McMillan & Denis St. Claire
Archaeological & ethnographic investigations on Western
Vancouver Island. Illus. 221 pp. Paper. Theytus, 1982. $9.95.

ALCATRAZ: INDIAN LAND FOREVER
Troy R. Johnson, Editor
144 pp. UCLA, American Indian Studies Center, 1994.
$25; paper, $12.

ALCATRAZ! ALCATRAZ:
THE INDIAN OCCUPATION OF 1969-71
Adam Fortunate Eagle
A personal account written by one of the organizers. 160 pp.
Paper. Heyday Books, $9.95.

ALEUT DICTIONARY
Knut Bergsland, Compiler
Documents all the recorded vocabulary of the Aleut language;
1,600 Aleut place names are plotted on 33 maps; over 600
Aleut men's names; English index qith 14,000 Aleut words &
suffixes. 739 pp. Paper. Alaska Native Language Center, 1994.
$37.50.

ALEUT TALES & NARRATIVES
Waldemar Jochelson; edited by Knut Bergsland & Moses Dirks
Aleut folklore in Aleut with English translations. 87 stories. Illus.
715 pp. Alaska Native Language Center, 1990. $25.

ALEUTS: SURVIVORS OF THE BEPING LAND BRIDGE
William S. Laughlin
Paper. Holt, Rinehart & Winston, 1981. $9.95.

*ALGONKIAN: LIFESTYLE OF THE NEW ENGLAND
INDIANS
Bob Eaton
Grades PS-4. Illus. Paper. One Reed Publications, 1998.
$11.95.

*ALGONQUIAN
Rita & Mary D'Apice
Grades 5-8. Illus. 32 pp. Rourke Corp., 1990. $9.95.

ALGONQUIN APPRENTICE: DISCOVERING THE
HISTORY & LEGEND OF THE BIRCHBARK CANOE
David Gidmark
Illus. 224 pp. Paper. Stackpole Press, 1995. $15.95.

ALGONQUIN LEGENDS
Charles G. Leland
Study of myths & folklore of the Micmac, Passamaquoddy
& Penobscot tribes. Illus. 416 pp. Paper. Dover, $8.95.

THE ALGONQUIAN PEOPLES OF LONG ISLAND
FROM EARLIEST TIMES TO 1700
John A. Strong
356 pp. Heart of the Lakes Publishing, 1997. $40.

*THE ALGONQUIANS
Patricia R. Quiri
Grades 4-6. Illus. 64 pp. Franklin Watts, 1992. $22.

THE ALGONQUIN BIRCH BARK CANOE
Gidmark
Contains the history of canoes and tips on making and main-
taining a birch bark canoe. Paper. Smoke & Fire Co., $9.50.

*ALL ABOUT ARROWHEADS & SPEAR POINTS
Howard E. Smith, Jr.
Grades 4-7. Illus. 80 pp. Henry Holt & Co., 1989. $14.95.

ALL MY RELATIONS: AN ANTHOLOGY OF
CONTEMPORARY CANADIAN NATIVE FICTION
Thomas King, Editor
220 pp. Paper. University of Oklahoma Press, 1992. $15.95.

ALL MY SINS ARE RELATIVES
W.S. Penn
Investigation of mixed-race identity. Illus. 268 pp. paper.
University of Nebraska Press, 1995. $25.

ALL-NEW NATIVE AMERICAN BRACELETS
Geri D. Weitzman
Paper. Troll Communications, 1997. $7.95.

ALL ROADS ARE GOOD:
NATIVE VOICES ON LIFE & CULTURE
Foreword by W. Richard West, Jr.
& Preface by Clara Sue Kidwell
23 accomplished figures from diverse indigenous cultures
throughout the Americas selects objects of cultural, spiritual,
artistic, or personal significance from the National Museum of
the American Indian's collection & reflects on their cultural heritage. Illus. 224 pp. Paper. Smithsonian Institution Press, 1994.
$34.95.

ALL THAT REMAINS: A WEST VIRGINIA
ARCHAEOLOGISTS DISCOVERIES
Robert Pyle; Betty L. Wiley, Editor
Illus. Paper. Cannon Graphics, 1991.

ALLAN HOUSER
Barbara H. Perlman
The art of Allan Houser. 133 color & 183 bxw illus.
266 pp. Smithsonian Institution Press, 1991. $75.

THE ALLEGANY SENECAS & KINZUA DAM: FORCED RE-
LOCATION THROUGH TWO GENERATIONS
Joy A. Bilharz
Illus. Maps. 204 pp. Paper. University of Nebraska Press, 1998.
$24.95.

ALMANAC OF THE DEAD
Leslie Marmon Silko
Fiction. 792 pp. Paper. Penguin USA, $13.

ALWAYS GETTING READY, UPTERRLAINARLUTA:
YUP'IK ESKIMO SUBSISTENCE IN SOUTHWEST ALASKA
James H. Barker
Illus. 144 pp. Paper. University of Washington Press, 1993.
$29.95.

THE AMAZING DEATH OF CALF SHIRT & OTHER
BLACKFOOT STORIES: THREE HUNDRED YEARS OF
BLACKFOOT HISTORY
Raymond J. DeMallie & Alfonso Ortiz
Maps. 250 pp. Paper. University of Oklahoma Press, 1996.
$13.95.

THE AMBIGUOUS IROQUOIS EMPIRE:
THE COVENANT CHAIN CONFEDERATION
OF INDIAN TRIBES WITH ENGLISH COLONIES
Francis Jennings
Reprint. Illus. 464 pp. Paper. W.W. Norton & Co., $16.95.

AMERICA BEFORE THE EUROPEAN INVASIONS
Alice Beck Kehoe
Longman, 2002.

AMERICA ON PAPER: THE FIRST HUNDRED YEARS
Lynn Glaser
Revised and enlarged edition. Illus. 288 pp. Associated Anti-
quaries, 1989. $32.50.

AMERICA STREET: A MULTICULTURAL
ANTHOLOGY OF STORIES
Anne Mazer, Editor
Persea Books, 1993.

AMERICA'S ANCIENT TREASURES
Folsom & Folsom
Guide to Canadian and U.S. archaeological sites. Photos.
4th Edition. 459 pp. Paper. Hothem House, 1993. $15.95.

AMERICA'S BLACK & TRIBAL COLLEGES: THE COMPRE-
HENSIVE GUIDE TO HISTORICALLY & PREDOMINANTLY
BLACK & AMERICAN INDIAN COLLEGES & UNIVERISITIES
J. Wilson Bowman
3rd revised edition. Illus. 328 pp. Paper. R.J. Enterprises, 1998.
$21.95.

AMERICA'S FASCINATING INDIAN HERITAGE
Readers Digest Editors
Synthesis of North American Indian heritage. Illus. Photos. 416
pp. Reader's Digest & Cherokee Publications, 1978. $29.50.

AMERICA'S FIRST FIRST WORLD WAR:
THE FRENCH & INDIAN WAR, 1754-1763
Timothy Todish; Monte Smith, Editor
Illus. 120 pp. Paper. Eagles View Publishing, 1987. $10.95.

AMERICA'S INDIAN STATUES
Marion Gridley
Paper. Brown Book Co., 1966. $3.95.

AMERICA'S INDIANS: UNIT STUDY OUTLINE
Donna R. Fisher
11 pp. Paper. Hewitt Research Foundation, 1993. $2.95.

**AMERICA'S SECOND TONGUE: AMERICAN INDIAN
EDUCATION & THE OWNERSHIP OF ENGLISH, 1860-1900**
Ruth Spack
Examines the implementation of English-language instruction
and its effects on Native students. Illus. 231 pp. University of
Nebraska Press, 2002. $45.

*AMERICAN ARTIST. VOL. 1: NATIVE AMERICANS
Shanon Fitzpatrick
Grades 4-8. Illus. 36 pp. Paper. Creative Teaching Press, 1994.
Student edition, $11.98.

**AMERICAN BEGINNINGS: THE PREHISTORY
& PALEONTOLOGY OF BERINGIA**
Frederick H. West, Editor
Illus. Photos. Maps. 576 pp. University of Chicago Press, 1996.
$75; paper, $35.

*AMERICAN BISON
Ruth Berman
Grades 2-5. Photos. Lerner, 1992. $16.95.

THE AMERICAN BUFFALO IN TRANSITION
John Rorabacher
North Star Press, $6.50.

THE AMERICAN EAGLE
Tom & Pat Leeson, photographers
Photos of the eagle with text exploring the historic symbolism,
the Native American traditions & myths, and the legends which
comprise the portrait of the bald eagle. Illus. 88 color photos.
128 pp. Beyond Words Publishing, $39.95; paper, $24.95.

AMERICAN ENCOUNTERS
Howard Morrison
Illus. 80 pp. Paper. National Museum of American History, 1992.

**AMERICAN FOLK MASTERS:
THE NATIONAL HERITAGE FELLOWS**
Steve Siprin, Editor
Documents in text and photographs the winners and their skills,
including numerous Native American artists. Pottery, baskets,
weavings, and musical instruments are shown. 256 pp. Harry
N. Abrams, 1992. $49.50.

**AMERICAN FRONTIERS: CULTURAL
ENCOUNTERS & CONTINENTAL CONQUEST**
Gregory H. Nobles
Illus. 304 pp. Hill & Wang, 1997. $24; paper, $13.

AMERICAN GYPSY: SIX NATIVE AMERICAN PLAYS
Diane Glancy
Collection of six plays invoking the myths and realities of mod-
ern Native American life. Illus. 224 pp. University of Oklahoma
Press, 2002. $34.95.

THE AMERICAN INDIAN
Raymond F. Locke, Editor
Paper. Mankind, 1976. $1.75.

AMERICAN INDIAN
Lee F. Harkins, Editor
Reprint. Liveright, 1970. Slipcased, $99.99.

THE AMERICAN INDIAN
Clark Wissler
Reprint of 1938 edition. Illus. Photos. Maps. 466 pp.
High-Lonesome Books, $30.

**AMERICAN INDIAN ACTIVISM:
ALCATRAZ TO THE LONGEST WALK**
edited by Troy Johnson, Joane Nagel & Duane Champagne
368 pp. University of Illinois Press, 1997. $36.95; paper, $19.95.
Also available from The Falmouth Institute, $20

**AMERICAN INDIAN & ALASKA NATIVE HEALTH:
BIBLIOGRAPHY: JAN. 1990 THROUGH SEPT. 1996**
Mary Conway, Editor
Reprint. 123 pp. Paper. Diane Publishing, 1999. $40.

**THE AMERICAN INDIAN & ALASKA NATIVE
HIGHER EDUCATION FUNDING GUIDE**
Gregory W. Frazier
100 pp. Arrowstar, 1990. $21.90.

**AMERICAN INDIAN & ALASKA NATIVE NEWSPAPERS
& PERIODICALS, 1826-1924/1925-1970**
Daniel Littlefield, Jr. and James Parins
Two volumes. 482 pp. 577 pp. Greenwood Publishing, 1984/
86. $85 each.

**AMERICAN INDIAN & ALASKA NATIVE
TRADERS DIRECTORY**
Gregory Frazier
140 pp. Arrowstar, 1990. $21.45.

**AMERICAN INDIAN/ALASKA NATIVE TRIBAL
& VILLAGE HIV-1 POLICY GUIDELINES**
48 pp. National Native American AIDS Prevention Center, 1991.

**AMERICAN INDIAN & ALASKAN NATIVES
IN POSTSECONDARY EDUCATION**
Michael D. Parvel
Illus. 426 pp. Paper. U.S. Government Printing Office, 1998.
$33.

THE AMERICAN INDIAN: THE AMERICAN FLAG
Richard A. Pohrt
Illus. 152 pp. Flint Institute of Arts, $12.50; paper, $9.

AMERICAN INDIAN ARCHERY
Reginald & Gladys Laubin
Reprint of 1980 edition. Illus. 190 pp. University
of Oklahoma Press, 2002. $29.95; paper, $19.95.

**AMERICAN INDIAN ARCHIVAL MATERIAL:
A GUIDE TO HOLDINGS IN THE SOUTHEAST**
R. Chepesiuk & A. Shankman, Editors
325 pp. Greenwood Publishing, 1982. $69.50.

**AMERICAN INDIAN AREAS &
ALASKA NATIVE VILLAGES, 1980**
38 pp. Supt. of Documents, 1984. $2.75.

AMERICAN INDIAN ART, 1920-1972
Paper. Peabody Museum, 1973. $2.

**AMERICAN INDIAN ARTIFACTS: HOW TO IDENTIFY,
EVALUATE & CARE FOR YOUR COLLECTION**
Ellen Woods
232 pp. paper. Seven Locks Press, 1997. $18.95.

AMERICAN INDIAN ARTS & CRAFTS SOURCE BOOK
Anthony J. Cusmano, Editor
Paper. Media Publications, 1987. $6.95.

AMERICAN INDIAN ART SERIES
Gregory Schaaf, Ph.D.,
Vol. 1: Hopi-Tewa Pottery. 500 Artist Biographies. 199 pages,
500 illustrations in color and black & white. (sold
out, except a few copies of the Collectors Edition bound in
buffalo, gold embossments, slip case, limited to 200 copies,
signed and numbered - $250; **Vol. 2: Pueblo Indian Textiles.**
750 Artist Biographies." 296 pages, 600 illustrations in color
and black & white. Featuring Tewa potters from Santa Clara,
San Ildefonso, San Juan, Tesuque, Nambe and Pojoaque. $55
hardback, Collectors Edition- $250. **Vol. 3: American Indian
Textiles:** 2,000 Artist Biographies. 320 pages, 700 illustrations
in color and black & white. Featuring over a 1,000 textiles created during the past 200 years by Navajo rug weavers, Hopi,
Zuni, Rio Grande Pueblo, Apache, Cherokee, Osage,
Comanche, Northwest Coast and other Native American textile artists, including 500 photographs of weavers holding their
rugs and twenty years of auction records. $69.95 hardback,
postpaid; Collectors Edition $250).

**THE AMERICAN INDIAN AS SLAVEHOLDER
& SUCCESSIONIST**
Annie Heloise Abel; intro. by Theda Perdue & Michael D. Green
Reprint of 1919 edition. Illus. Map. 394 pp. Paper. University of
Nebraska Press, 1992. $25.

AMERICAN INDIAN BALLERINAS
Lili Cockerille Livingston
Biography of four 20th century American Indan ballerinas: Maria
Tallchief, Rosella Hightower, Marjorie Tallchief, and Yvonne
Chouteau. Photos. Biblio. 352 pp. University of Oklahoma
Press, 1997. $34.95; paper, $17.95.

AMERICAN INDIAN BASKETRY
Otis Tufton Mason
Reprint. Illus. 800 pp. Paper. Hothem House & Dover, 1988.
$17.95.

**AMERICAN INDIAN BASKETS:
1,200 ARTIST BIOGRAPHIES**
Gregory Schaaf; Richard M. Howard, Editor
Illus. 450 pp. Center for Indigenous Arts &
Cultures (CIAC) Press, 2004. $50.

**THE AMERICAN INDIAN:
BRONZE SCULPTURE BY GRIFFIN**
Hampton Chiles
Illus. Paper. Hampton Chiles, 1997. $35.

**THE AMERICAN INDIAN, 1492-1976:
A CHRONOLOGY & FACT BOOK**
Henry C. Dennis
Second edition. 177 pp. Oceana Publications, 1977. $8.50.

AMERICAN INDIAN BOOKS
Joe Thompson
A mail order catalog listing of over 100 books on Indians
and archaeology. American Indian Books, No charge.

THE AMERICAN INDIAN CD-ROM
Guild Press
Includes original 1850s encyclopedia on American Indians,
edited by Henry Schoolcraft, over 4200 pages of first hand ac-

counts, history, essays, and more; collection of authentic myths;
Federal Treaties; American State Papers through 1826; Notebooks of George Catlin; guides to National Archives; lives of
famous Indian chiefs. Illus. 10,000 pp. of text. Todd Publications, 1999. $75.

**AMERICAN INDIAN CEREMONIES: A PRACTICAL
WORKBOOK & STUDY GUIDE TO THE MEDICINE PATH**
Hawk Medicine & Grey Cat
Reprint. Illus. 144 pp. Inner Light, $15.

AMERICAN INDIAN CHILDREN AT SCHOOL, 1850-1930
Michael C. Coleman
Study revealing white society's program of civilizing Indian
schoolchildren. 230 pp. University Press of Mississippi, 1993.
$39.50.

*THE AMERICAN INDIAN COLORING BOOK
Tom Underwood
Reprint of 1969 edition. Grades 1-4. 24 pp. Paper.
Cherokee Publications, $3.

**AMERICAN INDIAN COOKING:
RECIPES FROM THE SOUTHWEST**
Carolyn Niethammer
Features 150 recipes and detailed illustrations of dozens of
edible wild plants and their history; mail order sources. Illus.
Map. 191 pp. Paper. University of Nebraska Press, 1998.
$16.95.

AMERICAN INDIAN COOKING & HERB LORE
J. Ed Sharpe & Thomas Underwood
Contains dozens of recipes. Illus. 32 pp. Paper. Written
Heritage, VIP Publishing & Cherokee Publications, $5.

THE AMERICAN INDIAN CRAFT BOOK
Marz Minor and Nono Minor
Illus. 416 pp. Paper. University of Nebraska Press, 1978.
$15.

AMERICAN INDIAN DESIGN & DECORATION
Leroy H. Appleton
Reprint of 1971 edition. Illus. 280 pp. Paper.
Dover & Written Heritage, $10.95.

AMERICAN INDIAN ECOLOGY
Donald J. Hughes
Revised Second Edition. Illus. Biblio. 190 pp.
Texas Western Press, 1995. $20.

**AMERICAN INDIAN EDUCATION: DIRECTORY
OF ORGANIZATIONS & ACTIVITIES IN AMERICAN
INDIAN EDUCATION**
ERIC/CRESS, $4.50.

**AMERICAN INDIAN EDUCATION:
GOVERNMENT SCHOOLS & ECONOMIC PROGRESS**
Evelyn C. Adams
Reprint of 1946 edition. Ayer Co. $16.

AMERICAN INDIAN EDUCATION: A HISTORY
Jon Reyhner & Jeanne Eder
Comprehensive history of American Indian education from co-
lonial times to the present. Illus. Map. 368 pp. University of
Oklahoma Press, 2004. $29.95.

**THE AMERICAN INDIAN & THE END
OF THE CONFEDERACY, 1863-1866**
Annie Heloise Abel; intro. by Theda Perdue & Michael D. Green
Reprint of 1919 edition. Illus. Map. 419 pp. Paper. University of
Nebraska Press, $12.95.

AMERICAN INDIAN ENCYCLOPEDIA - CD-ROM
3 reference books on CD-ROM; text, pictures, sound.
Facts-on-File, $295.

**AMERICAN INDIAN ENERGY
RESOURCES & DEVELOPMENT**
Roxanne D. Ortiz, Editor
Includes Transnational Energy Corporations and American In-
dian Development, by Richard Nafziger, and The Role of Policy
in American Indian Mineral Development, by Lorraine Turner
Ruffing. 80 pp. Paper. University of New Mexico, Native Ameri-
can Studies, 1980. $5.

AMERICAN INDIAN ENGLISH
William L. Leap
Documents and examines the diversity of English in American
Indian speech communities. 352 pp. Paper. University of Utah
Press, 1993. $20.

**AMERICAN INDIAN ENVIRONMENTS: ECOLOGICAL
ISSUES IN NATIVE AMERICAN HISTORY**
C. Vecsy & R.W. Venables, Editors
Reprint of 1980 edition. Illus. 236 pp. Paper.
Syracuse University Press, $16.95.

*THE AMERICAN INDIAN EXPERIENCE
(American Historic Places series)
Explores Native Amerian cultures through the study of existing
historical sites. Illus. 160 pp. Grades 5-12. Facts on File, 1997.
$18.95.

AMERICAN INDIAN FACTS OF LIFE:
A PROFILE OF TODAY'S TRIBES & RESERVATIONS
George Russell
Contemporary American Indian demographics with regard to
population, tribes and reservation. Includes maps, reservation
roster, graphics, tables, and reference sources. 80 pp. Paper.
Russell Publications, $10.

AMERICAN INDIAN FAMILY SUPPORT SYSTEMS &
IMPLICATIONS FOR THE REHABILITATION PROCESS:
THE EASTERN BAND OF CHEROKEE INDIANS & THE
MISSISSIPPI BAND OF CHOCTAW INDIANS: EXECUTIVE
SUMMARY & FINAL REPORT
C.A. Marshall & L.K. Cerveny
Executive Summary, 16 pp. Final Report, 78 pp.
Northern Arizona University, 1994.

AMERICAN INDIAN FOOD:
SIXTY-ONE INDIAN RECIPES
Imogene Dawson
25 pp. Paper. Holitopa, 1993. $4.95.

*AMERICAN INDIAN FOODS
Jay Miller
Grades 4 and up. 48 pp. Children's Press, 1996.
$21; paper, $6.95.

AMERICAN INDIAN FOODS & VEGETABLES
Harriet L. Smith
Illus. Paper. SSS Publishing, 1982. $4.50.

*AMERICAN INDIAN GAMES
Jay Miller
Grades 4 and up. 48 pp. Children's Press, 1996.
$21; paper, $6.95.

AMERICAN INDIAN GENESIS:
THE STORY OF CREATION
Percy Bullchild
Reprint. Illus. 200 pp. Ulysses Press, $22.95.

AMERICAN INDIAN GHOST DANCE, 1870 & 1890:
AN ANNOTATED BIBLIOGRAPHY
Shelley Osterreich
110 entries. 96 pp. Greenwood, 1991. $37.95.

AMERICAN INDIAN GRANDMOTHERS:
TRADITIONS & TRANSITIONS
Marjorie M. Schweitzer, Editor
Essays. Illus. 248 pp. University of New Mexico Press, 1999.
$45; paper, $19.95.

AMERICAN INDIAN HEALING ARTS: HERBS, RITUALS
& REMEDIES FOR EVERY SEASON OF LIFE
Barrie Kavasch & Karen Baar
352 pp. Bantam Books, 1999. $17.95.

AMERICAN INDIAN HOLOCAUST & SURVIVAL:
A POPULATION HISTORY SINCE 1492
Russell Thornton
Reprint of 1987 edition. Illus. Maps. 292 pp. Paper.
University of Oklahoma Press, 2002. $24.95.

AMERICAN INDIAN IDENTITY:
TODAY'S CHANGING PERSPECTIVES
Clifford E. Trafzer
Seven American Indians provide essays. 51 pp. Paper.
Sierra Oaks Publishing, 1986. $10.95.

THE AMERICAN INDIAN IN
ALABAMA & THE SOUTHEAST
John F. Phillips
Illus. 213 pp. American Indian Books, 1986.
$10.95; paper, $8.95.

*THE AMERICAN INDIAN IN AMERICA, Vol. II
Jayne Clark Jones
Grades 5 and up. Illus. 96 pp. Paper. Lerner, $5.95.

THE AMERICAN INDIAN IN THE CIVIL WAR, 1862-1865
Annie Heloise Abel; intro. by Theda Perdue & Michael D. Green
Reprint of 1919 edition. Illus. Map. 403 pp. Paper. University of
Nebraska Press, 1992. $29.95.

AMERICAN INDIAN IN ENGLISH
LITERATURE OF THE 18th CENTURY
Benjamin H. Bissell
Reprint of 1925 edition. Illus. 225 pp. Gordon Press, $59.95.

THE AMERICAN INDIAN IN FILM
Michael Hilger
Illus. 206 pp. Scarecrow Press, 1986. $21.

THE AMERICAN INDIAN IN GRADUATE STUDIES:
A BIBLIOGRAPHY OF THESES AND DISSERTATIONS
Frederick J. Dockstader
Two volumes. Paper. National Museum of the American Indian,
1973. $10 each; $18 per set.

THE AMERICAN INDIAN IN NORTH CAROLINA
Douglas L. Rights
Illus. 298 pp. Paper. John F. Blair, Publisher, $14.95.

THE AMERICAN INDIAN IN SHORT FICTION:
AN ANNOTATED BIBLIOGRAPHY
Peter G. Beidler and Marion F. Egge
215 pp. Scarecrow Press, 1979. $18.50.

AMERICAN INDIAN IN THE U.S., PERIOD 1850-1914
Warren K. Moorehead
Facsimile of 1914 edition. Bibliographies Reprint Series.
Ayer Co., $35.

THE AMERICAN INDIAN & WESTERN THOUGHT:
THE DISCOURSE OF CONQUEST
Robert A. Williams, Jr.
368 pp. Paper. Oxford University Press, 1992. $19.95.

THE AMERICAN INDIAN IN THE WHITE MAN'S PRISONS:
A STORY OF GENOCIDE
Art Solomon, et al
Illus. 447 pp. Paper. Uncompromising Books, 1993. $25.

AMERICAN INDIAN INDEX:
A DIRECTORY OF INDIAN COUNTRY
Gregory W. Frazier
Contains listings for American Indian and Alaska Native groups.
325 pp. Arrowstar Publishing, 1985. $21.45.

AMERICAN INDIAN & INDO-EUROPEAN STUDIES:
PAPERS IN HONOR OF MADISON S. BELLER
Kathryn Klar, et al, Editors
495 pp. Mouton, 1980. $82.

AMERICAN INDIAN INTELLECTUALS
OF THE 19TH & 20TH CENTURIES
Margot Liberty
Biographical sketches of major American Indian intellectuals.
288 pp. Paper. University of Oklahoma Press, 2003. $19.95.

AMERICAN INDIAN ISSUES IN HIGHER EDUCATION
206 pp. UCLA, American Indian Studies Center, 1981. $14.

AMERICAN INDIAN JEWELRY:
2,000 ARTIST BIOGRAPHIES
Gregory Schaaf; Richard M. Howard, Editor
Illus. 450 pp. Center for Indigenous Arts & Cultures (CIAC)
Press, 2004. $50.

AMERICAN INDIAN LACROSSE,
LITTLE BROTHER OF WAR
Thomas Vennum, Jr.
An account of the Native American game, and its functions in
Indian life. Illus. 376 pp. Paper. Smithsonian Institution Press
& Written Heritage, 1994. $16.95.

AMERICAN INDIAN: LANGUAGE & LITERATURE
Jack W. Marken
Paper. Harlan Davidson, 1978.

AMERICAN INDIAN LANGUAGE SERIES
Includes: Mayan Linguistics, 267 pp., $5.00; Hualapai Refer-
ence Grammar, 575 pp., $17.50; and Chem'ivillu' (Let's Speak
Cahuilla), 316 pp., $17.50. UCLA, American Indian Studies
Center.

AMERICAN INDIAN LANGUAGES, Vol. 5
William Bright, Editor
585 pp. Mouton de Gruyter, 1989. $99.

AMERICAN INDIAN LANGUAGES:
CULTURAL & SOCIAL CONTEXTS
Shirley Silver & Wick R. Miller
433 pp. University of Arizona Press, 1998. $65; paper,
$29.95.

AMERICAN INDIAN LAW
Clinton, et al
3rd edition. 1,378 pp. LEXIS Law Publishing, 1991. $52.
1996 Supplement, 213 pp. $8.

THE AMERICAN INDIAN LAW DESKBOOK
Conference of Western Attorney General Staff
2nd Edition. 502 pp. University Press of Colorado, 1998. $75.

AMERICAN INDIAN LAW IN A NUTSHELL
William C. Canby, Jr.
2nd edition. 336 pp. Paper. 1988. $17. 3rd edition, 250 pp.
1998. $25.95. West Publishing & The Falmouth Institute.

THE AMERICAN INDIAN LAW SERIES
A series of seven pamphlets: Indian Sovereignty; Indian Trea-
ties; Indians and the U.S. Government; Indian Jurisdiction; The
Federal Indian Trust Relationship; Indian Water Rights; and
Introduction to Oil and Gas. Institute for the Development of
Indian Law.·

AMERICAN INDIAN LEADERS: STUDIES IN DIVERSITY
R. David Edmunds, Editor
Illus. Maps. 257 pp. Paper. University of Nebraska Press, 1980.
$12.

AMERICAN INDIAN LEGAL MATERIALS: A UNION LIST
Laura N. Gasaway, et al
Lists important works of Indian law, history, and policy. 200 pp.
E.M. Coleman, 1979. $49.50.

AMERICAN INDIAN LEGAL STUDIES
TEACHER'S MANUAL & TEXT
Institute for the Development of Indian Law. $20 each.

AMERICAN INDIAN LIFE
Elsie C. Parsons, Editor
Reprint of 1967 edition. Illus. 425 pp. Paper.
University of Nebraska Press, $32.

AMERICAN INDIAN LINGUISTICS & ETHNOGRAPHY
IN HONOR OF LAURENCE C. THOMPSON
Anthony Mattina & Timothy Montler
497 pp. University of Montana, 1993. $25; paper, $15.

AMERICAN INDIAN LINGUISTICS & LITERATURE
William Bright
159 pp. Mouton de Gruyter, 1984. $41.25.

AMERICAN INDIAN LITERATURE: AN ANTHOLOGY
Alan R. Velie
Revised 1991 edition. Illus. 374 pp. University of Oklahoma
Press, 2001. $27.95.

AMERICAN INDIAN LITERATURE, ENVIRONMENTAL
JUSTICE, & ECOCRITICISM: THE MIDDLE PLACE
Joni Adamson
Discussions of such writers as Simon Ortiz, Louis Erdrich, Joy
Harjo, and Leslie Marmon Silko. 214 pp. Paper. University of
Arizona, 2001. $19.95.

AMERICAN INDIAN LITERATURE & THE SOUTHWEST:
CONTEXTS & DISPOSITIONS
Eric Gary Anderson
Illus. Paper. University of Texas Press, 1999. $35; paper,
$17.95.

AMERICAN INDIAN LITERATURES: AN INTRODUCTION,
BIBLIOGRAPHIC REVIEW, & SELECTED BIBLIOGRAPHY
LaVonne Brown Ruoff
Includes journals, films & videos, and Indian authors and their
works. Also provides and index and chronology of notable
American Indian events. 200 pp. Paper. Modern Language As-
sociation, 1990. $19.50.

*AMERICAN INDIAN LIVES (SERIES)
Scholars, Writers, and Professionals, by Claire Wilson &
Jonathan Bolton, 1994. 160 pp.; **Spiritual Leaders,** by Paul
Robert Walker, 1994. 160 pp.; **Political Leaders and Peace-**
makers, by Victoria Sherrow, 1994. 160 pp.; **Artists and**
Craftspeople, by Arlene Hirschflder, 1994. 160 pp.; **Perform-**
ers, by Liz Sonneborn, 1995. 128 pp.; **Athletes,** by Nathan
Aaseng, 1995. 144 pp.; **Reformers and Activists,** by Nancy
J. Neilen, 1997. 144 pp.; **Healers,** by Deanne Durrett, 1997.
144 pp. Illus. Grades 5-12. Facts on File. $7.95 each.

AMERICAN INDIAN MAGIC: SCARED POW WOWS & HOPI
PROPHECIES
Brad Steiger
Illus. 210 pp. Paper. Global Communications, 1986. $17.95.

AMERICAN INDIAN MARRIAGE RECORD
DIRECTORY FOR ASHLAND CO., WISC.
Michael D. Munnell
279 pp. Paper. Chippewa Heritage Publications, 1993. $21.

THE AMERICAN INDIAN & THE MEDIA
Mark Anthony Rolo
Essays that explain many of the struggles facing Native people.
Native American Journalists Association, $15.

AMERICAN INDIAN MEDICINE
Rolling Thunder
Sweetlight Books, 1972. $10.

AMERICAN INDIAN MEDICINE
Virgil J. Vogel
The contribution of the American Indian to pharmacology &
medicine. Reprint of of 1977 edition. Illus. 622 pp. Paper. University of Oklahoma Press, 1999. $29.95.

THE AMERICAN INDIAN:
A MULTIMEDIA ENCYCLOPEDIA - CD-ROM
Incorporates four Facts on File publications: Atlas of the North
American Indian; Native American Legends; Indians & Non-
Indians from Early Contacts through 1900; and Encyclopedia
of Native American Tribes. Also over 1,000 reproductions of
images and maps from NARA publications and documents.
Facts on File, 1993. $295.

*AMERICAN INDIAN MUSIC & MUSICAL INSTRUMENTS
George S. Fichter
Grades 5-10. David McKay, 1978. $8.95.

AMERICAN INDIAN MYTHOLOGY
Alice Marriott and Carol K. Rachlin
Illus. 210 pp. Paper. New American Library, 1972. $3.95.

AMERICAN INDIAN MYTHS & LEGENDS
Richard Erdoes & Alfonso Ortiz
160 tales from 80 tribal groups from across North America.
Illus. 528 pp. Paper. Cherokee Publications, $17.

AMERICAN INDIAN NEEDLEPOINT DESIGNS
Roslyn Epstein
Illus. 38 pp. Paper. Dover & Written Heritage, $4.50.

AMERICAN INDIAN PAINTERS:
A BIOGRAPHICAL DIRECTORY
Jeanne Snodgrass
National Museum of the American Indian, 1968.

AMERICAN INDIAN PAINTING & SCULPTURE
Patricia Janis Broder
Survey of work by this century's leading Native American artists. 74 full-color illustrations, including 4 gatefolds. 168 pp. Abbeville Press, $45.

THE AMERICAN INDIAN PARFLECHE:
A TRADITION OF THE ABSTRACT PAINTING
Gaylord Torrence
Illustrate with over 100 examples of parfleches in full color. Written Heritage, $39.95.

THE AMERICAN INDIAN: PAST & PRESENT
Roger L. Nichols
5th edition. 300 pp. Paper. McGraw-Hill, 1999. $21.

AMERICAN INDIAN PERSISTENCE & RESURGENCE
Karl Kroeber, Editor
352 pp. Duke University Press, 1994. $49.95; paper, $17.95.

THE AMERICAN INDIAN: PERSPECTIVES
FOR THE STUDY OF SOCIAL CHANGE
Fred Eggan
185 pp. Cambridge University Press, 1981. $37.50.

AMERICAN INDIAN POETRY:
AN ANTHOLOGY OF SONGS & CHANTS
George W. Cronyn
336 pp. Paper. Fawcett Book Group, 1991. $10.

AMERICAN INDIAN POLICY
Theodore W. Taylor
Illus. 230 pp. Lomond, 1983. $23.50. Microfilm, $12.95.

AMERICAN INDIAN POLICY & AMERICAN REFORM:
CASE STUDIES OF THE CAMPAIGN TO ASSIMILATE
THE AMERICAN INDIANS
Christine Bolt
228 pp. Paper. Routledge, 1987. $34.95.

AMERICAN INDIAN POLICY & CULTURAL VALUES:
CONFLICT & ACCOMMODATION
Jennie R. Joe, Editor
169 pp. Paper. UCLA, American Indian Studies Center, 1987. $10.

AMERICAN INDIAN POLICY IN THE FORMATIVE YEARS:
THE INDIAN TRADE & INTERCOURSE ACTS, 1790-1834
Francis P. Prucha
310 pp. Paper. University of Nebraska Press, 1970. $5.95.

AMERICAN INDIAN POLICY IN THE JACKSONIAN ERA
Ronald N. Satz
Illus. Maps. 368 pp. Paper. University of Oklahoma Press, 2001. $19.95

AMERICAN INDIAN POLICY IN THE TWENTIETH CENTURY
Vine Deloria, Jr., Editor
272 pp. University of Oklahoma Press, 1985. $24.95; paper. $15.95.

AMERICAN INDIAN POLICY: SELF-GOVERNANCE &
ECONOMIC DEVELOPMENT
Lyman H. Legter & Fremont J. Lyden, Editors
240 pp. Greenwood, 1993. $59.95.

AMERICAN INDIAN POPULATION BY TRIBE
FOR THE U.S., REGIONS, DIVISIONS, & STATES
Illus. 69 pp. Paper. Diane Publishing, $45.

AMERICAN INDIAN POPULATION
RECOVERY IN THE 20TH CENTURY
Nancy Shoemaker
176 pp. University of New Mexico Press, 1999. $39.95.

AMERICAN INDIAN PORTRAIT POSTCARDS
Charles Bird King
Color prints; paintings on postcard format. Smoke & Fire Co., $4.95.

AMERICAN INDIAN POTTERY
Sharon Wirt
Studies pottery styles of the early natives and their significance. Illus. 32 pp. Paper. Hancock House, 1984. $3.95.

AMERICAN INDIAN POTTERY:
AN IDENTIFICATION & VALUE GUIDE
John W. Barry
Second Edition. Illus. 214 pp. Apollo Books, 1984. $29.95.

AMERICAN INDIAN PRAYERS & POETRY
J. Edward Sharpe, Editor
Illus. 32 pp. Paper. Cherokee Publications, 1985. $3.

AMERICAN INDIAN PROPHETS: RELIGIOUS
LEADERS & REVITALIZATION MOVEMENTS
Clifford E. Trafzer
138 pp. Paper. Sierra Oaks, 1986. $11.95.

AMERICAN INDIAN QUOTATIONS
Howard J. Langer
288 pp. Greenwood, 1996. $55.

THE AMERICAN INDIAN READER SERIES
Jeannette Henry, Editor
Five volumes covering separate subject areas: Anthropology, 174 pp.; Education, 300 pp.; Literature, 248 pp.; History, 149 pp.; and Current Affairs, 248 pp. Paper. The Indian Historian, 1972-75. $4.50 each.

AMERICAN INDIAN REFERENCE BOOKS
FOR CHILDREN & YOUNG ADULTS
Barbara Kuipers
An annotated bibliography of 200 entries for grades 3-12. 190 pp. Libraries Unlimited, 1991. $25. Available on diskette.

AMERICAN INDIAN RESOURCE
MANUAL FOR PUBLIC LIBRARIES
Illus. 200 pp. paper. Diane Publishing, 1994. $45.

AMERICAN INDIAN RESOURCE MATERIALS
IN THE WESTERN HISTORY COLLECTION
Donald DeWitt
Illus. 290 pp. University of Oklahoma Press, 1990. $39.95.

AMERICAN INDIAN SOCIETIES: STRATEGIES &
CONDITIONS OF POLITICAL & CULTURAL SURVIVAL
Duane Champagne, Editor
2nd revised edition. 160 pp. Cultural Survival, 1989. $19.95; paper, $10.

AMERICAN INDIAN SONGS
Dawley & McLaughlin
American Indian folk songs from every region of the U.S. Paper. Alfred Publishing. $4.95. LP, $9.95; filmstrip/cassette/book, $34.95.

AMERICAN INDIAN SPORTS HERITAGE
Joseph B. Oxendine
Traditional Indian games and explores the apex of Indian sports during the early 20th century and the decline since. Illus. 334 pp. Paper. University of Nebraska Press, 1995. $35.

AMERICAN INDIAN SOVEREIGNTY & THE U.S.
SUPREME COURT: THE MASKING OF JUSTICE
David E. Wilkins
421 pp. University of Texas Press, 1997. $40; paper, $24.95.

AMERICAN INDIAN STEREOTYPES IN THE WORLD
OF CHILDREN: A READER & BIBLIOGRAPHY
Arlene B. Hirschfelder, et al.
2nd Ed. 384 pp. Paper. Scarecrow Press, 1999. $32.50.

*AMERICAN INDIAN STORIES
A 12 book series on the lives & achievements of great Native Americans: Carlos Montezuma, Geronimo, Hole-in-the-Day, Ishi, Jim Thorpe, John Ross, Maria Tallchief, Osceola, Plenty Coups, Sarah Winnemucca, Sitting Bull, and Wilma Mankiller. Grades 4-5. Illus. Raintree, 1993. $19.95 each.

AMERICAN INDIAN STORIES
Zitkala-Sa (Red Bird)
Presents the pain and difficulty of growing up Indian in a white man's world. 196 pp. Paper. University of Nebraska Press, 1985. $10.95.

AMERICAN INDIAN STUDIES: AN INTERDISCIPLINARY
APPROACH TO CONTEMPORARY ISSUES
Diane Morrison, Editor
456 pp. Paper. Peter Lang Publishing, 1997. $59.95; paper, $29.95.

AMERICAN INDIAN TEXTILES:
2,000 ARTIST BIOGRAPHIES
Gregory Schaaf; Richard M. Howard, Editor
Illus. 400 pp. Center for Indigenous Arts & Cultures (CIAC) Press, 2001. $60.

AMERICAN INDIAN THEATER IN PERFORMANCE:
A READER
edited by Hanay Geiogamah & Jaye T. Darby
Presents the views of leading scholars, playwrights, directors, and educators in contemporary Native theater. 414 pp. Paper. The Falmouth Institute, 2000. $20.

AMERICAN INDIAN TOMAHAWKS
Peterson
Reprint of 1965/71 edition. Illus. 142 pp. Hothem House. $49.95.

AMERICAN INDIAN TRADITIONS & CEREMONIES
Karen Berman
Illus. 128 pp. Diane Publishing, 1998. $45.

AMERICAN INDIAN TREATIES:
THE HISTORY OF A POLITICAL ANOMALY
Francis P. Prucha
University of California Press, 1994. $50; paper, $21.95.

THE AMERICAN INDIAN TREATY SERIES
Compiles treaties and agreements made between the U.S. Government and Indian Tribes. Nine volumes. Separate books for treaties and agreements of the Sioux Nation, the Pacific Northwest, the Northern Plains, eastern Oklahoma, the Southwest (western Oklahoma), the Five Civilized Tribes, the Chippewa, and the Great Lakes region. 102-278 pp each. Institute for the Development of Indian Law, 1973-1975.

AMERICAN INDIAN TRIBAL COURTS:
THE COSTS OF SEPARATE JUSTICE
American Bar Foundation Staff
153 pp. Paper. American Bar Association, 1978. $5.

AMERICAN INDIAN TRIBAL GOVERNMENTS
Sharon O'Brien
Examines the impact of federal policies on Indian tribes. Illus. Maps. Biblio. 368 pp. Paper. University of Oklahoma Press, 1989. $24.95.

*AMERICAN INDIAN TRIBES
The first book "Indians," is an overview of the Indian Tribes; tribes covered: Choctaw, Apache, Cherokee, Chippewa, Eskimo, Hopi, Navajo, Seminole, Sioux, Cheyenne, Shoshone, Nez Perce, Anasazi, Cayuga, Crow, Mandans, Mohawk, Oneida, Onandaga, Pawnee, Seneca, Tlingit, Tuscarora. Grades 2-3. Illus. Photos. 48 pp. each. Paper. Childrens Press, $.95 each; $125/set of 27 books.

*AMERICAN INDIAN TRICKSTER TALES
Richard Erdoes & Alfonso Ortiz, Editors
Grades 4-8. 352 pp. Viking Penguin, 1998. $24.95.

THE AMERICAN INDIAN & THE U.S.:
A DOCUMENTARY HISTORY
Wilcomb E. Washburn, Editor
Four volumes. Greenwood Press, 1973. $195 per set; $50 each.

AMERICAN INDIAN UTENSILS: HOW TO
MAKE BASKETS, POTTERY & WOODENWARE
WITH NATURAL MATERIALS
Evelyn Wolfson
Illus. David McKay Co., 1979. $8.95.

AMERICAN INDIAN WARRIOR CHIEFS: TECUMSEH,
CRAZY HORSE, CHIEF JOSEPH, GERONIMO
Jason Hook
Illus. 210 pp. Sterling Publishing, $24.95; paper, $14.95.

AMERICAN INDIAN WARS
Philip Katcher
Paper. Stackpole Books, 1989. $10.95.

AMERICAN INDIAN WATER RIGHTS
& THE LIMITS OF LAW
Lloyd Burton
Illus. 174 pp. University Press of Kansas, 1991. $29.95; paper, $14.95.

AMERICAN INDIAN & WHITE CHILDREN:
A SOCIOPSYCHOLOGICAL INVESTIGATION
R.J. Havighurst and B.L. Neugarten
Reprint of 1969 edition. University of Chicago Press, $17.

AMERICAN INDIAN WOMEN: A GUIDE TO RESEARCH
Gretchen M. Bataille & Kathleen M. Sands
Contains over 1,500 annotated citations to resources and materials pertaining to American Indian women. 423 pp. Garland, 1991. $57.

AMERICAN INDIAN WOMEN: TELLING THEIR LIVES
Gretchen M. Bataille & Kathleen Mullen Sands
211 pp. Paper. University of Nebraska Press, 1984. $13.95.

AMERICAN INDIAN WOMEN'S CALENDAR
12 beautiful women representing 18 different tribes. 10x13" Annual. Elan Marketing, $12 postpaid.

THE AMERICAN INDIAN:
YESTERDAY, TODAY & TOMORROW
Calif. Dept. of Education Staff
Illus. 88 pp. Paper. California Dept. of Education, 1991. $8.75.

*AMERICAN INDIANS
Grades Preschool-12. Aerial Photography Services, $2.85.

AMERICAN INDIANS
Describes the Federal Government's economic policy affecting Indian tribes and Alaska natives. 45 pp. Paper. Supt. of Documents, 1984. $2.50.

*AMERICAN INDIANS
Bearl Brooks
Grades 4-6. 24 pp. ESP, 1977. Workbook, $5.

*AMERICAN INDIANS
J. Philip Di Franco
Grades 5 and up. 120 pp. Paper. Chelsea House, 1995. $9.95.

*THE AMERICAN INDIANS
Roland W. Force
Grades 7-12. Illus. 112 pp. Chelsea House, 1990. $17.95.

*AMERICAN INDIANS
Patricia Kindle & Susan Finney
Grades 4-8. Illus. 64 pp. Workbook. Good Apple, 1985. $6.95.

AMERICAN INDIANS
William T. Hagan
Revised 3rd edition. A history of the relationship between the white man and the Indian. Illus. 240 pp. Paper. University of Chicago Press, 1993. $37; paper, $14.95.

*THE AMERICAN INDIANS
Time-Life Book Editors
A series of books which reveals the customs & cultures, myth, magic & folklore of the American Indian. The titles in the series are: *The First Americans, The Spirit World, European Challenge, People of the Desert, The Way of the Warrior, The Buffalo Hunter, Realm of the Iroquois, The Mighty Chieftains, Keeper of the Totem, Cycles of Life, The War of the Plains, Tribes of the Southern Woodlands, The Indians of California, People of the Ice & Snow, People of the Lakes, Tribes of the Atlantic Coast, The War of the West II, Plains Indians II, The Way of Beauty, Indians of the Western Range,* & *Villagers and Cliff Dwellers.* Grades 4 and up. Illus. 176 pp. each. Paper. Time-Life Books, $14.95 each.

THE AMERICAN INDIANS
Edward H. Spicer
176 pp. Paper. Harvard University Press, 1982. $6.95.

AMERICAN INDIANS
Herman J. Viola
Random House, 1997. $25.

AMERICAN INDIANS, AMERICAN JUSTICE
Vine Deloria, Jr. & Clifford M. Lytle
Reprint of classic indictment of mistreatment of Indian peoples.
278 pp. Paper. University of Texas Press, 1983. $14.95.

AMERICAN INDIANS:
ANSWERS TO TODAY'S QUESTIONS
Jack Utter
Second edition. Illus. Photos. Maps. 528 pp. Paper.
University of Oklahoma Press, 2001. $21.95.

AMERICAN INDIANS & CHRISTIAN MISSIONS:
STUDIES IN CULTURAL CONFLICT
Henry W. Bowden
256 pp. Paper. University of Chicago Press, 1981. $17.95.

AMERICAN INDIANS: A CULTURAL GEOGRAPHY
Thomas E. Ross, et al, Editor
2nd edition. Illus. 300 pp. Karo Hollow Press, 1995. $39.95.

AMERICAN INDIANS DISPOSSESSED: FRAUD IN LAND CESSIONS FORCED UPON THE TRIBES
Walter H. Blumenthal
Facsimile of 1955 edition. Ayer Co., $20.95.

AMERICAN INDIANS: FACTS & FUTURE TOWARD ECONOMIC DEVELOPMENT FOR NATIVE AMERICAN COMMUNITIES
Subcommittee on Economy in Government
Reprint of 1969 edition. Ayer Co., $13.

AMERICAN INDIANS: THE FIRST OF THIS LAND
C. Matthew Snipp
450 pp. Paper. Russell Sage, 1989. $49.95.

*THE AMERICAN INDIANS IN AMERICA: VOLUME II:
THE LATE 18TH CENTURY TO THE PRESENT
Jayne Clark Jones
Grades 5 and up. 72 pp. Lerner Publications, 1991. $11.95; paper, $5.95.

AMERICAN INDIANS IN COLORADO
Donald J. Hughes
Illus. Paper. Pruett, 1987. $8.95.

AMERICAN INDIANS & THE LAW
Lawrence Rosen
Reprint of 1976 edition. 230 pp. Transaction Publishers, $24.95.

AMERICAN INDIANS IN THE LOWER MISSISSIPPI VALLEY: SOCIAL & ECONOMIC HISTORIES
Daniel H. Usner, Jr.
Illus. Maps. 256 pp. Paper. University of Nebraska Press, 1998. $29.95.

AMERICAN INDIANS & NATIONAL PARKS
Robert H. Keller & Michael F. Turek
Examines Federal policy and park/Indian relations. Illus.
340 pp. Paper. University of Arizona Press, 1998. $19.95.

AMERICAN INDIANS IN SILENT FILM:
MOTION PICTURES IN THE LIBRARY OF CONGRESS
compiled by Karen C. Lund
Library of Congress, 1995.

AMERICAN INDIANS IN U.S. HISTORY
Roger L. Nichols
The history of tribes throughout the U.S. Illus. 288 pp.
University of Oklahoma Press, 2003. $29.95; paper, $17.95.

AMERICAN INDIANS OF THE SOUTHEAST
Michael G. Johnson
Southeastern history and material culture; clothes & weapons.
Color photos. Illus. Biblio. 48 pp. Paper. Written Heritage & Smoke & Fire Co., $14.95.

AMERICAN INDIANS OF THE SOUTHWEST
Bertha P. Dutton
Revised edition. Illus. Photos. 317 pp. Paper. University of New Mexico Press, 1983. $18.95.

AMERICAN INDIANS ON FILM & VIDEO:
DOCUMENTARIES IN THE LIBRARY OF CONGRESS
Compiled by Jennifer Brathode
Library of Congress, 1992.

AMERICAN INDIANS: A SELECT CATALOG OF NATIONAL ARCHIVES MICROFILM PUBLICATIONS
Revised 1984 edition. 91 pp. Paper. National Archives, 1998. $3.50.

AMERICAN INDIANS, TIME & THE LAW: NATIVE SOCIETIES IN A MODERN CONSTITUTIONAL DEMOCRACY
Charles F. Wilkinson
Examines Indian law from pre-Columbian times to the present.
227 pp. Paper. Yale University Press, 1987. $14.

AMERICAN INDIANS TODAY:
ANSWERS TO YOUR QUESTIONS
Bureau of Indian Affairs
Pamphlet providing an overview of the role of federal government and its relationship to Native Americans. Includes general statistics, map, and bibliography. 36 pp. Paper. U.S. Government Printing Office, 1991.

*AMERICAN INDIANS TODAY: ISSUES & CONFLICTS
Judith Harlan
Grades 7 and up. Illus. 128 pp. Franklin Watts, 1987. $12.90.

AMERICAN INDIANS & WORLD WAR II:
TOWARD A NEW ERA IN INDIAN AFFAIRS
Alison R. Bernstein
Illus. 264 pp. Paper. University of Oklahoma Press, 1991. $17.95.

AMERICAN INDIANS IN WORLD WAR I: AT WAR & AT HOME
Thomas A. Britten
Illus. 264 pp. Paper. University of New Mexico Press, 1999. $19.95.

AMERICAN NATIONS: ENCOUNTERS IN INDIAN COUNTRY, 1850-2000
Frederick E. Hoxie (co-edited with James Merrell & Peter Mancall)
Routledge, 2001.

AMERICAN PROTESTANTISM & U.S. INDIAN POLICY, 1869-1882
Robert H. Keller, Jr.
Illus. 400 pp. University of Nebraska Press, 1983. $32.50.

*THE AMERICAN PUEBLO INDIAN ACTIVITY BOOK
Walter C. Yoder, PhD
Grades 3 and up. 40 pages of activities. 48 pp. Paper. Sunstone Press & Clear Light, $7.95.

AMERICAN PURITANISM & THE DEFENSE OF MOURNING: RELIGION, GRIEF, & ETHNOLOGY IN MARY WHITE ROWLANDSON'S CAPTIVITY NARRATIVE
Mitchell Breitwieser
224 pp. University of Wisconsin Press, 1990. $40.00; paper, $15.50.

THE AMERICAN RACE: A LINGUISTIC CLASSIFICATION & ETHNOGRAPHIC THE AMERICAN REVOLUTION IN INDIAN COUNTRY
Colin G. Calloway
Cambridge University Press, 1995.

THE AMERICAN REVOLUTION IN INDIAN COUNTRY: CRISIS & DIVERSITY IN NATIVE AMERICAN COMMUNITIES
Colin G. Calloway
Illus. 353 pp. Cambridge University Press, 1995. $69.95; paper, $18.95.

*THE AMERICAN REVOLUTIONARIES:
A HISTORY IN THEIR OWN WORDS
Milton Meltzer
Grades 7 and up. Illus. 256 pp. Harper & Row, Junior Books, 1987. $13.89.

AN AMERICAN URPHILOSOPHIE: AN AMERICAN PHILOSOPHY - BP (BEFORE PRAGMATISM)
Robert Bunge
218 pp. University Presses of America, 1984. $27.25.

THE AMERICAN WEST
Paper. Mankind, 1991. $1.75.

THE AMERICAN WEST
Dee Brown
An account of the demise of the Native Americans of the Plains.
Illus. 304 pp. Scribners, 1994. $25.

THE AMERICAN WEST IN THE TWENTIETH CENTURY:
A BIBLIOGRAPHY
Richad W. Etulain & co-editors
Compiled over 8,000 entries focusing on the West after 1900.
464 pp. University of Oklahoma Press, 1994. $67.50.

AMERICAN WOODLAND INDIANS
Michael Johnson
Biblio. 48 pp. Paper. Written Heritage & Smoke & Fire Co., 1990. $14.95.

AMERICANIZING OF THE AMERICAN INDIANS:
WRITINGS BY THE FRIENDS OF THE INDIAN, 1880-1900
Francis P. Prucha, Editor
368 pp. Paper. University of Nebraska Press, $6.95.

AMERINDIANS & THEIR PALEO-ENVIRONMENTS IN NORTHEASTERN NORTH AMERICA, Volume 288
Walter Newman and Bert Salwen
New York Academy of Science, 1977. $37.

AMONG THE APACHES
Frederick Schwatka
Facsimile of the 1887 articles. Collected observations of several visits to the Apache Indian agencies. Tells of life as it was.
Illus. 32 pp. Paper. Filter Press, 1974. $4.

AMONG THE CHIGLIT ESKIMOS
E. Petitot
202 pp. Paper. CCI, 1981. $10.

AMONG THE MESCALERO APACHES:
THE STORY OF FATHER ALBERT BRAUN
Dorothy Emerson
224 pp. Paper. University of Arizona Press, 1973. $22.95.

*AMONG THE PLAINS INDIANS
Lorenz Engel
Based upon the journals of the German explorer Maximilian, as well as upon the records of George Catlin during the early 1830's. Grades 5-12. Illus. 112 pp. Lerner, 1970. $9.95.

AMONG THE SIOUX OF DAKOTA: EIGHTEEN MONTHS EXPERIENCE AS AN INDIAN AGENT, 1869-70
D.C. Poole
Reprint of 1881 edition. Illus. Photos. Map. 241 pp. Paper.
Minnesota Historical Society, 1988. $8.95.

ANASAZI
Pike
Paper. Random House, $17.

*THE ANASAZI
Grades K-4. Illus. 48 pp. Childrens Press, $11.45.

ANASAZI AMERICA: SEVENTEEN CENTURIES ON THE ROAD FROM CENTER PLACE
David E. Stuart
Illus. 264 pp. Paper. University of New Mexico Press, 2002. $17.95.

*ANASAZI, THE ANCIENT VILLAGERS
Susan Shaffer
Grade 4. Illus. with 30 student booklets and teacher's manual; transparencies, slides & audiocassette. Heard Museum, 1987. $295.

ANASAZI ARCHITECTURE & AMERICAN DESIGN
Baker H. Morrow & V.B. Price
Illus. Paper. University of New Mexico Press, 1999. $19.95.

*ANASAZI COLORING BOOK:
THE STORY OF THE ANCIENT ONES
Sandra Stemmler
Grades 4 and up. Illus. 28 pp. Paper. Clear Light, $3.95.

*ANASAZI LEGENDS, SONGS OF THE WIND DANCER
Lou Cuevas
Grades 4 and up. 176 pp. Paper. Naturegraph, 1999. $12.95.

ANASAZI OF MESA VERDE & THE FOUR CORNERS
William M. Ferguson
Paper. University Press of Colorado, 1996. $34.95.

ANASAZI PLACES: THE PHOTOGRAPHIC VISION OF WILLIAM CURRENT
Jeffrey Cook
Illus. 101 bxw photos. 152 pp. University of Texas Press, 1992. $45.

ANASAZI POTTERY
Robert H. Lister & Florence C. Lister
Illustrates ten centuries of prehistoric southwestern pottery.
Illus. 100 pp. Paper. University of New Mexico Press & Clear Light, $16.95.

ANASAZI REGIONAL ORGANIZATION AND THE CHACO SYSTEM
Edited by David E. Doyel
Illus. 208 pp. Paper. Maxwell Museum of Anthropology, 2002. $29.95.

ANASAZI RUINS OF THE SOUTHWEST IN COLOR
William M. Ferguson & Arthur H. Rohn
Illus. Color photos. 310 pp. Paper. University of
New Mexico Press & Clear Light, 1987. $32.50.

*AN ANASAZI WELCOME
Kay Matthews; illus. by Barbara Belknap
Grades Preschool-3. Illus. 40 pp. Paper. Red Crane Books,
$6.95.

*ANCESTOR'S FOOTSTEPS
T. Moore
Two stories of young men who prove themselves. Grades 6 to
9. Illus. 40 pp. Council for Indian Education, 1978. $9.95; pa-
per, $3.95.

**THE ANCESTORS: NATIVE AMERICAN
ARTISANS OF THE AMERICAS**
edited by Anna C. Roosevelt & James G.E. Smith
Illus. 197 pp. Paper. National Museum of the American Indian,
1979. $17.50.

ANCESTRAL HOPI MIGRATIONS
Patrick D. Lyons
142 pp. Paper. University of Arizona Press, 2003. $16.95.

**ANCESTRAL VOICE: CONVERSATIONS
WITH N. SCOTT MOMADAY**
edited by Charles L. Woodard
He explores his individual & Kiowa tribal identity, his philosophies on language & literature, and his painting theories & practices. Illus. 230 pp. Center for Western Studies, $21.50; paper,
$9.95. Paper. University of Nebraska Press, $9.95.

ANCIENT AMERICA
Marian Wood
Facts on File, 1990. $17.95.

ANCIENT ANCESTORS OF THE SOUTHWEST
Gregory Schaaf
Graphic Ats Center Publishing Co., 1996.

ANCIENT ARCHITECTURE OF THE SOUTHWEST
William N. Morgan
Explores concurrent Mogollon, Hohokam & Anasazi architec-
ture. Illus. 339 pp. University of Texas Press, 1994. $60.

ANCIENT ART OF THE AMERICAN WOODLAND INDIAN
David S. Brose
Illus. 240 pp. Detroit Institute of Arts, $29.95. Harry N. Abrams,
1985. $35.

THE ANCIENT AMERICAS: THE MAKING OF THE PAST
Earl H. Swanson, et al
Illus. 160 pp. Peter Bedrick Books, 1989. $24.95; paper, 16.95.

ANCIENT ART OF OHIO
Lar Hothem
Reviews most of the artifact types in all of Ohio's prehistoric
periods. Illus. 272 pp. Hothem House, 1994. $53, postpaid.

**ANCIENT BURIAL PRACTICES IN THE AMERICAN
SOUTHWEST: ARCHAEOLOGY, PHYSICAL ANTHRO-
POLOGY, & NATIVE AMERICAN PERSPECTIVES**
Edited by Douglas R. Mitchell & Judy L. Brunson-Hadley
Illus. Maps. Paper. University of New Mexico Press, 2001.
$32.95.

ANCIENT CHIEFDOMS OF THE TOMBIGBEE
John H. Blitz
256 pp. Paper. University of Alabama Press, 1993. $24.95.

THE ANCIENT CHILD
N. Scott Momaday
Novel which juxtaposes Indian lore and wild west legend.
336 pp. Paper. Clear Light, $13.50.

**ANCIENT DRUMS, OTHER MOCCASINS:
NATIVE NORTH AMERICAN CULTURAL ADAPTATION**
Harriet J. Kupferer
Illus. 352 pp. Prentice-Hall, 1988. $34.67.

**ANCIENT ECHOES: NATIVE AMERICAN
WORDS OF WISDOM**
Patricia Martin
64 pp. Great Quotations, 1994. $6.50.

**ANCIENT INDIAN POTTERY OF
THE MISSISSIPPI RIVER VALLEY**
Hathcock
2nd Edition. Illus. 236 pp. Hothem House, 1988.
$48, postpaid.

*ANCIENT INDIANS: THE FIRST AMERICANS
Roy Gallant
Grades 5-11. 128 pp. Enslow Publishers, 1989. $15.95.

ANCIENT LIFE IN THE AMERICAN SOUTHWEST
Edgar Lee Hewett
Reprint of 1948 edition. Illus. 392 pp. High-Lonesome
Books & Biblo-Moser, $30.

ANCIENT MODOCS OF CALIFORNIA & OREGON
Carrol Howe
Reprint of 1979 edition. Illus. 264 pp. Paper.
Binford & Mort, $12.95.

ANCIENT MONUMENTS OF THE MISSISSIPPI VALLEY
Squier & Davis
Covers earthworks in Ohio and Mississippi valleys. Diagrams
& maps. 316 pp. Hothem House, 1998. $63, postpaid.

**ANCIENT NORTH AMERICA:
THE ARCHAEOLOGY OF A CONTINENT**
Brian M. Fagan
Revised edition. Paper. Thames & Hudson, 1995. $31.95.

ANCIENT PEOPLE OF THE ARCTIC
Robert McGhee
UBC Press, 1996. $35.95.

**ANCIENT ROAD NETWORKS & SETTLEMENT
HIERARCHIES IN THE NEW WORLD**
Charles Trombold
300 pp. Cambridge University Press, 1991.

**ANCIENT RUINS OF THE SOUTHWEST:
AN ARCHAEOLOGICAL GUIDE**
David Grant Noble
90 bxw photos. 18 maps & diagrams. 232 pp. Paper.
Northland Publishing, $14.95.

ANCIENT SOCIETY
Lewis H. Morgan
The primitive institutions of the Indians. Reprint of 1877
edition. 608 pp. Paper. University of Arizona Press, $19.95.

**ANCIENT TREASURES: A GUIDE TO ARCHAEOLOGICAL
SITES & MUSEUMS IN THE U.S. & CANADA**
Franklin Folsom & Mary Elting
3rd Edition. University of New Mexico Press, 1983.

ANCIENT TRIBES OF THE KLAMATH COUNTRY
Carol B. Howe
Illus. Paper. Binford-Metropolitan, 1968. $9.95.

**ANCIENT VISIONS: PETROGLYPHS & PICTOGRAPHS OF
THE WIND RIVER & BIGHORN COUNTRY, WYOMING &
MONTANA**
Julie E. Francis & Lawrence L. Loendorf
University of Utah Press. $35.

**ANCIENT VOICES, CURRENT AFFAIRS:
THE LEGEND OF THE RAINBOW WARRIORS**
Steven McFadden
Explores the myth of the rainbow warriors through the teach-
ings of indigenous peoples of the Americas, Australia, and Ti-
bet. Illus. 176 pp. Paper. Bear & Co., $9.95.

ANCIENT WALLS: INDIAN RUINS OF THE SOUTHWEST
Chuck Place & Susan Lamb
100 color photos. 112 pp. Fulcrum Publishing
& Clear Light, 1991. $34.95; paper, $19.95.

**ANCIENT WASHINGTON: INDIAN CULTURES
OF THE POTOMAC VALLEY, Vol. 6**
Robert Humphrey & Mary Chambers
George Washington University, $5.

**AND EAGLES SWEEP ACROSS THE SKY: INDIAN
TEXTILES OF THE NORTH AMERICAN WEST**
Dena S. Katzenberg
Illus. Baltimore Museum, 1977. $6.98.

***AND IT IS STILL THAT WAY: LEGENDS
TOLD BY ARIZONA INDIAN CHILDREN**
Byrd Baylor
Grades K-6. Demco, 1976. $13.05.

**ANGEL SITE: AN ARCHAEOLOGICAL,
HISTORICAL, AND ETHNOLOGICAL STUDY**
Glenn A. Black
Excavations of Angel Mounds community in southwestern In-
diana. 2 Vols. Illus. 620 pp. Indiana Historical Society & Hothem
House, 1967. $80.

ANGELS TO WISH BY
Joseph Juknialis
Paper. Resource Publications, 1984. $7.95.

**THE ANGUISH OF SNAILS: NATIVE AMERICAN
FOLKLORE IN THE WEST**
Barre Toelken
Examines Native American visual arts, dance, oral tradition
(story & song), humor, & patterns of thinking & discovery. 270
pp. Utah State University Press, 2002. $39.95; paper, $22.95.

**THE ANIMALS CAME DANCING: NATIVE AMERICAN
SACRED ECOLOGY & ANIMAL KINSHIP**
Howard L. Harrod
170 pp. Paper. University of Arizona Press, 2000. $18.95.

ANISHINABE: SIX STUDIES OF MODERN CHIPPEWA
J. Anthony Paredes, Editor
Illus. 447 pp. University Press of Florida, 1980. $41.95.

*ANNA'S ATHABASKAN SUMMER
Arnold Griese; Illus. by Charles Ragins
Grades PS-2. Illus. Boyds Mills Press, 1995. $14.95.

**ANNALS OF SHAWNEE METHODIST MISSION
& INDIAN MANUAL LABOR SCHOOL**
Martha B. Caldwell
Reprint of 1939 edition. Illus. 120 pp. Paper.
Kansas State Historical Society, $3.

**ANNIKADEL: THE HISTORY OF THE UNIVERSE AS
TOLD BY THE ACHUMAWI INDIANS OF CALIFORNIA**
Istet Woiche; edited by C. Hart Merriam
Reprint of 1928 edition. 166 pp. Paper.
University of Arizona Press, $14.95.

**AN ANNOTATED BIBLIOGRAPHY OF AMERICAN INDIAN
& ESKIMO AUTOBIOGRAPHIES**
H. David Brumble, III
182 pp. University of Nebraska Press, 1981. $16.50.

**AN ANNOTATED BIBLIOGRAPHY
OF AMERICAN INDIAN PAINTING**
Doris O. Dawdy
50 pp. Paper. National Museum of the American Indian, 1968.
$2.50.

**ANOTHER AMERICA: NATIVE AMERICAN
MAPS & THE HISTORY OF OUR LAND**
Mark Warhus
Illus. 224 pp. St. Martins Press, 1997. $29.95.

*ANPAO: AN AMERICAN INDIAN ODYSSEY
Jamake Highwater
Grades 5-9. Harper & Row Junior Books, 1977.
$13.50; paper, $3.95.

**ANSWERED PRAYERS: MIRACLES
& MILAGROS ALONG THE BORDER**
Eileen Oktavec
Explains the use of the tiny metal tokens depicting objects for
which miracles are sought. Illus. 256 pp. University of Arizona
Press, 1995. $36; paper, $17.95.

ANSWERING CHIEF SEATTLE
Albert Furtwangler
208 pp. University of Washington Press, 1997. $27.50.

**ANTHROPOLOGICAL PAPERS
OF UNIVERSITY OF ALASKA**
Linda Ellanna, Editor of Series
See Dept. of Anthropology, University of Alaska, Fairbanks, AK
99775 (907) 474-7288 for a complete listing with prices.

**ANTHROPOLOGICAL STUDIES ON THE
QUICHUA & MACHIGANGA INDIANS**
Harry B. Ferris
Reprint of 1921 edition. Paper. Elliots Books.

ANTHROPOLOGY & THE AMERICAN INDIAN
Report of a symposium held in 1970 by the American Anthropological Association on the issues raised by Vine Deloria's
book, Custer Died for Your Sins. 125 pp. Paper. Indian Historian Press, 1973. $2.50.

ANTHROPOLOGY ON THE GREAT PLAINS
W. Raymond Wood and Margot Liberty, Editors
Illus. 310 pp. University of Nebraska Press, 1980. $27.95.

ANTHROPOLOGY OF THE NORTH PACIFIC RIM
William Fitzhugh & Valerie Chaussonnet, Editors
Investigates the anthropology, history, and art of the North pa-
cific rim. Illus. 368 pp. Smithsonian Institution Press, 1993. $55.

ANTS & ORIOLES: SHOWING THE ART OF PIMA POETRY
Donald Bahr, Lloyd Paul & Vincent Joseph
Illus. University of Utah Press, $29.95.

ANY OTHER COUNTRY EXCEPT MY OWN
Hadley A. Thomas
The evolution of the Dine from prehistory to the present. The
story of the Navajo. Illus. 270 pp. paper. Cross Cultural Publications, 1994. $19.95.

AOBE NABING
M.T. Bussey
Text. Michigan Indian Press.

APACHE
Will L. Comfort
274 pp. Paper. University of Nebraska Press, 1985. $7.95.

*APACHE
Barbara McCall
Grades 5-8. Illus. 32 pp. Rourke Corp., 1990. $9.95.

*THE APACHE
Patricia McKissack
Grades K-4. Illus. 48 pp. Childrens Press, $11.45.

*THE APACHE
Michael Melody
Grades 5 -up. Illus. 104 pp. Paper. Chelsea House, 1988. $9.95.

APACHE
Christine Ronan
Addison-Wesley Educational Publishers, 1998. $9.95.

APACHE AGENT: THE STORY OF JOHN P. CLUM
W. Clum
Illus. 300 pp. Gordon Press, 1977. $59.95 (library binding.)

APACHE AUTUMN
Robert Skimin
Novel deals with the struggle of the Apaches to maintain their way of life against insurmountable odds. 427 pp. St. Martins Press, 1993. $22.95.

AN APACHE CAMPAIGN IN THE SIERRA MADRE
John G. Bourke
Illus. 150 pp. Paper. University of Nebraska Press, 1987. $4.95.

*APACHE CHILDREN & ELDERS TALK TOGETHER
Barrie E. Kavasch
Grades 4 and up. Rosen Group, 1998. $18.

APACHE DAYS & AFTER
Thomas Cruse; E. Cunningham, Editor
Illus. 364 pp. University of Nebraska Press, $27.95; paper, $9.95.

THE APACHE DIARIES: A FATHER-SON JOURNEY
Grenville Goodwin & Neil Goodwin
Illus. Maps. 304 pp. Paper. University of Nebraska Press, 2000. $16.95.

APACHE GOLD & YAQUI SILVER
J. Frank Dobie
Legend & lore. Explores the mysterious and alluring sagas of lost mines and adventure. Illus. 380 pp. Paper. University of Texas Press, $15.95.

APACHE INDIAN BASKETS
Clara Lee Tanner
Illus. 204 pp. University of Arizona Press, 1982. $42.

THE APACHE INDIANS
Frank C. Lockwood
Illus. Maps. 388 pp. Paper. University of Nebraska Press, 1987. $18.95.

APACHE LEGENDS: SONGS OF THE WIND DANCER
Lou Cuevas
Illus. 128 pp. Naturegraph, $8.95.

AN APACHE LIFE-WAY: THE ECONOMIC, SOCIAL, & RELIGIOUS INSTITUTIONS OF THE CHIRICAHUA INDIANS
Morris E. Opler; intro. bu Charles R. Kraut
Reprint of 1941 edition. Based on the author's two years of field work. Illus. Maps. 530 pp. Paper. University of Nebraska Press, 1996. $29.95.

APACHE: THE LONG RIDE HOME
Grant Gall
Story of a Mexican boy captured by Apaches and adopted into the tribe. 112 pp. Paper. Sunstone Press, 1998. $9.95.

APACHE MEDICINE-MEN
John G. Bourke
Intensive studies of 19th century American Indian life. Reprint. Photos. Illus. 176 pp. Paper. Dover, $7.95.

APACHE MOTHERS & DAUGHTERS: FOUR GENERATIONS OF A FAMILY
Ruth McDonald Boyer & Narcissus Duffy Gayton
Family history of four generations of Chiricahua Apache women from 1848 to the present. Illus. Maps. 416 pp. University of Oklahoma Press, 1993. $27.95; paper, $16.95.

APACHE, NAVAHO & SPANIARD
Jack D. Forbes
Apache & Navaho response to Spanish advance in the 17th century into northern mexico and the Southwest U.S. 2nd Edition. Illus. Maps. Biblio. 328 pp. Paper. University of Oklahoma Press, 1994. $15.95.

APACHE NIGHTMARE: THE BATTLE OF CIBECUE CREEK
Charles Collins
Illus. Maps. University of Oklahoma Press, 1998. $27.95.

APACHE ODYSSEY: A JOURNEY BETWEEN TWO WORLDS
Morris E. Opler; intro. by Philip J. Greenfield
In 1933, Opler recorded the life story of a Mescalero Apache he called Chris. Illus. Maps. 302 pp. Paper. University of Nebraska Press, 2002. $18.95.

APACHE RESERVATION: INDIGENOUS PEOPLES & THE AMERICAN STATE
Richard J. Perry
Discusses reservation issues and the historical development of the reservation system. Illus. Maps. 276 pp. University of Texas Press, 1993. $37.50; paper, $18.95.

APACHE, THE SACRED PATH TO WOMANHOOD
John Annerino
The right of passage for Apache young women. Illus. 128 pp. Marlowe & Co., $43.50; paper, $29.95.

APACHE SHADOWS
Albert R. Booky
Story of two Mescalero Apache brothers and the settlement of the West. 159 pp. Paper. Sunstone Press, 1998. $10.95.

APACHE VOICES: THEIR STORIES OF SURVIVAL AS TOLD TO EVE BALL
Sherry Robinson
Illus. 288 pp. University of New Mexico Press, $34.95; paper, $19.95.

APACHE WARS: AN ILLUSTRATED BATTLE HISTORY
E. Lisle Reedstrom
Illus. 256 pp. Sterling, 1990. $24.95.

APACHE WOMEN WARRIORS
Kimberly M. Buchanan
Illus. 62 pp. Paper. Texas Western Press, 1986. $12.50.

APACHEAN CULTURE HISTORY & ETHNOLOGY
Keith H. Basso & Morris E. Opler, Editor
Reprint of 1971 edition. Illus. 176 pp. Paper. University of Arizona Press, $26.95.

APACHES AT WAR & PEACE: THE JANOS PRESIDIO, 1750-1858
William B. Griffen
Illus. 313 pp. University of New Mexico Press, 1988. $35.

THE APACHES: A CRITICAL BIBLIOGRAPHY
Michael Melody
96 pp. Paper. Indiana University, 1977. $6.95.

APACHES DE NAVAJO: 17TH CENTURY NAVAJOS IN THE CHAMA VALLEY OF NEW MEXICO
Curtis F. Schaafsma
Illus. University of Utah Press. $55.

THE APACHES: EAGLES OF THE SOUTHWEST
Donald Worcester
Illus. Maps. 407 pp. Paper. University of Oklahoma, 1979. $19.95.

APACHES: A HISTORY & CULTURE PORTRAIT
James L. Haley
Illus. 544 pp. Maps. Paper. University of Oklahoma Press, 1997. $24.95.

*THE APACHES & NAVAJOS
Craig & Katherine Doherty
Grades 3 and up. Illus. 64 pp. Paper. Franklin Watts, 1991. $4.95.

THE APALACHEE INDIANS & MISSION SAN LUIS
John H. Hann & Bonnie McEwan
208 pp. University Press of Florida, 1998. $49.95; paper, $19.95.

APALACHEE: THE LAND BETWEEN THE RIVERS
John H. Hann
Illus. Biblio. 464 pp. University Press of Florida, 1988. $39.95.

APOLOGIES TO THE IROQUOIS
Edmund Wilson
Illus. 356 pp. Paper. Syracuse University Press, $17.95.

APPALACHIAN INDIAN FRONTIER: THE EDMOND ATKIN REPORT AND PLAN OF 1755
Edmond Atkin; Wilbur R. Jacobs, Editor
Illus. 125 pp. Peter Smith, 1967. $11.25. Paper. University of Nebraska Press, $3.95.

APPALACHIAN MOUNTAIN ANIYUNWIYA
A bibliographic research source which documents and discusses original tribal identities, traditions, culture, social and political configuration of the aboriginal people of the Appalachian mountain region and Piedmont of the eastern U.S. David Michael Wolfe.

APPALACHIAN MOUNTAIN CHEROKEE
David Michael Wolfe
Booklet specifically to Cherokee people of the present day Appalachian Mountain region encompassing the mountainous regions of West Virginia, Kentucky, Ohio and Pennsylvania. 24 pp. David. M. Wolfe.

APAUK: CALLER OF BUFFALO
James W. Schultz
Reprint. Illus. 227 pp. Time-Life, 1993. $21.99.

APOCALYPSE OF CHIOKOYHIKOY: CHIEF OF THE IROQUOIS
edited by Robert Griffin & Donald A. Grinde, Jr.
A dramatic Iroquois prophecy accompanied by a literary and historical commentary. 274 pp. Published by Les Presses de L'niversite Laval in Quebec, 1997. Available from The Falmouth Institute, $27.

APPLICATION OF A THEORY OF GAMES TO THE TRANSITIONAL ESKIMO CULTURE
Robert G. Glassford
Reprint of the 1976 edition. Ayer Co., $23.50.

APPLIQUE PATTERNS FROM NATIVE AMERICAN BEADWORK DESIGNS
Dr. Joyce Mori
Floral applique patterns in full size patterns and instructions. Illus. 96 pp. Paper. Written Heritage, $14.95.

APPROACHES TO TEACHING MOMADAY'S THE WAY TO RAINEY MOUNTAIN
Kenneth M. Roemer, Editor
175 pp. Modern Language Association, 1988. $32.00; paper, 17.50.

APPROACHING FOOTSTEPS: PUGET SOUND INDIANS - BAINBRIDGE ISLAND SAWMILLS
Velma H. Basworth
113 pp. Paper. Panpress, 1998. $19.95.

*THE ARAPAHO
Loretta Fowler
Grades 5 and up. Illus. Chelsea House, 1989. $17.95.

THE ARAPAHO
Alfred L. Kroeber
Discusses Arapaho culture; dance and design, Indian symbolism. Illus. 480 pp. University of Nebraska Press, 1983. $10.95.

ARAPAHO DIALECTS
A.L. Kroeber
Reprint oif 1916 edition. 67 pp. Paper. Coyote Press, $7.81.

THE ARAPAHO INDIANS: A RESEARCH GUIDE & BIBLIOGRAPHY
Zdenek Salzmann, Compiler
Greenwood, 1988. $35.

ARAPAHOE POLITICS, 1851-1978: SYMBOLS IN CRISES OF AUTHORITY
Loretta Fowler
Illus. Maps. 375 pp. Paper. University of Nebraska Press, 1982. $14.

THE ARAPAHOES, OUR PEOPLE
Virginia C. Trenholm
Illus. Map. Paper. University of Oklahoma Press, 1986. $21.95.

ARARAPIKVA: TRADITIONAL KARUK INDIAN LITERATURE FROM NORTHWESTERN CALIFORNIA
translated & introduced by Julian Lang
Bilingual text. 122 pp. Heyday Books, 1994. $10.95.

THE ARBITRARY INDIAN: INDIAN ARTS & CRAFTS ACT OF 1990
Gail K. Sheffield
An in-depth analysis of the act, revealing its historical, legal, and social implications and exposing its fundamental flaws. 232 pp. University of Oklahoma Press, 1997. $27.50.

ARCHAEOASTRONOMY IN THE NEW WORLD: AMERICAN PRIMITIVE ASTRONOMY
A.F. Aveni, Editor
230 pp. Cambridge University Press, 1982. $39.50.

ARCHAEOLOGICAL GEOLOGY OF NORTH AMERICA
N.P. Lasca & J. Donahue, Editors
Illus. Geological Society of America, 1990. $62.50.

ARCHAEOLOGICAL INVESTIGATIONS IN THE UPPER SUSQUEHANNA VALLEY, NEW YORK STATE (VOLUME 1)
Robert E. Funk
Illus. 400 pp. Persimmon Press, 1994. $66.95.

THE ARCHAEOLOGICAL INVESTIGATIONS OF FORT KNOX II, FORT KNOX CO., INDIANA, 1803-1813
Marlesa Gray
Illus. 312 pp. Paper. Indiana Historical Society, 1988. $32.00.

ARCHAEOLOGICAL INVESTIGATIONS OF THE KIOWA & COMANCHE INDIAN AGENCY COMMISSARIES
Daniel J. Crouch
Illus. Paper. Museum of the Great Plains, 1978. $11.30.

ARCHAEOLOGICAL PERSPECTIVES ON THE BATTLE OF LITTLE BIGHORN: THE FINAL REPORT
Douglas D. Scott
Illus. 328 pp. University of Oklahoma Press, 1989. $31.95.

ARCHAEOLOGICAL RECONNAISSANCE OF FORT SILL, OKLAHOMA
C.R. Ferring
Illus. Paper. Museum of the Great Plains, 1978. $20.30.

AN ARCHAEOLOGICAL STUDY OF THE MISSISSIPPI CHOCTAW INDIANS
John H. Blitz
Illus. 120 pp. Paper. Mississippi Department of Archives and History, 1985. $7.50.

ARCHAEOLOGY AS ANTHROPOLOGY: A CASE STUDY
William Longacre
Focuses on organizational and behavioral aspects of societies which emerged approximately 1500 B.C. through 1350 AD. 57 pp. Paper. University of Arizona Press, 1970. $5.95.

**ARCHAEOLOGY & CERAMICS
AT THE MARKSVILLE SITE**
Alan Toth
Illus. Paper. University of Michigan,
Museum of Anthropology, 1975. $4.

**ARCHAEOLOGY & ETHNOHISTORY OF THE
OMAHA INDIANS; THE BIG VILLAGE SITE**
John M. O'Shea & John Ludwickson
Illus. 380 pp. University of Nebraska Press, 1992. $40.

**ARCHAEOLOGY, HISTORY, & CUSTER'S LAST BATTLE:
THE LITTLE BIGHORN REEXAMINED**
Richard Allan Fox, Jr.
Illus. Maps. 416 pp. University of Oklahoma Press, 1993.
$32.95; paper, $15.95. Video-VHS, $29.95; & PAL, $29.95.

**ARCHAEOLOGY IN THE CITY: A HOHOKAM
VILLAGE IN PHOENIX, ARIZONA**
Michael H. Bartlett, et al
Describes the process of salvage archaeology as it interprets
artifacts. 80 pp. Paper. University of Arizona Press, 1986.
$10.95.

ARCHAEOLOGY IN VERMONT
John C. Huden, Editor
Illus. Paper. Charles E. Tuttle, 1970. $6.50.

**ARCHAEOLOGY OF ABORIGINAL CULTURE CHANGE IN
THE INTERIOR SOUTHEAST: DEPOPULATION DURING
THE EARLY HISTORIC PERIOD**
Marvin T. Smith
Illus. Biblio. 198 pp. University Press of Florida, 1987.
$29.95; paper, $16.95.

THE ARCHAEOLOGY OF ANCIENT ARIZONA
Jefferson Reid & Stephanie Whittlesey
Overview of prehistoric peoples: HOhokam, Patayan, Mogollon,
Anasazi, Sinagua, and Salado. Illus. 310 pp. University of Ari-
zona Press, 1997. $45; paper, $17.95.

**ARCHAEOLOGY OF BANDELIER NATIONAL MONUMENT:
VILLAGE FORMATION ON THE PAJARITO PLATEAU, NEW
MEXICO**
Edited by Timothy Alan Kohler
Essays summarize the results of new excavation and survey
research in Bandelier. 288 pp. University of New Mexico, 2004.
$59.95.

THE ARCHAEOLOGY OF CAPE NOME, ALASKA
John Bockstoce
Illus. 133 pp. Paper. University of Pennsylvania Museum, $25.

**ARCHAEOLOGY OF EASTERN NORTH AMERICA:
PAPERS IN HONOR OF STEPHEN WILLIAMS**
James B. Stoltman, Ed.
Illus. 382 pp. Paper. Mississippi Dept. of Archives & History,
$20.

ARCHAEOLOGY OF THE FROBISHER VOYAGES
William Fitzhugh & Jacqueline S. Olin, Editors
An account of the Frobisher voyage into the Canadian Arctic,
1576-1578. Illus. Maps. 368 pp. Smithsonian Institution Press,
1993. $45.

ARCHAEOLOGY OF THE LOWER OHIO RIVER VALLEY
Jon Muller
Paper. Academic Press, 1986. $47.50.

ARCHAEOLOGY OF MISSISSIPPI
Calvin S. Brown
Reprint of 1926 edition. Illus. 230 pp. University Press
of Mississippi, 1993. $42; paper, $19.95.

THE ARCHAEOLOGY OF NAVAJO ORIGINS
Ronald H. Towner, Editor
Illus. Maps. University of Utah Press. $45.

*THE ARCHAEOLOGY OF NORTH AMERICA
Dean R. Snow
Grades 7-12. Illus. 128 pp. Chelsea House, 1989. $17.95.

ARCHAEOLOGY OF THE LOWER OHIO RIVER VALLEY
Jon Muller
Paper. Academic Press, 1986. $ 47.50.

ARCHAEOLOGY OF PRECOLUMBIAN FLORIDA
Jerald T. Milanich
Illus. Maps. Biblio. 456 pp. University Press of Florida, 1994.
$24.95.

**ARCHAEOLOGY OF PREHISTORIC NATIVE AMERICA:
AN ENCYLCOPEDIA**
Guy Gibbon, Editor
Survey of the early cultures of North America. Illus. Photos.
36 maps. 2 vols. 900 pp. Garland, 1998. $165.

**AN ARCHAEOLOGY OF THE SOUL:
NORTH AMERICAN INDIAN BELIEF & RITUAL**
Robert L. Hall
240 pp. University of Illinois Press, 1997. $49.95.

ARCHAEOLOGY OF THE SOUTHWEST
Linda Cordell
Paper. Academic Press, 1997. $45.

**THE ARCHAEOLOGY OF SUMMER ISLAND: CHANGING
SETTLEMENT SYSTEMS IN NORTHERN LAKE MICHIGAN**
David S. Brose
Illus. Paper. University of Michigan, Museum of Anthropology,
1970. $3.

**THE ARCHAEOLOGY OF THREE SPRINGS VALLEY:
A STUDY IN FUNCTIONAL CULTURAL HISTORY**
Brian D. Dillon & Matthew A. Boxt, Editors
Illus. 200 pp. Paper. University of California, Los Angeles, 1989.
$19.

**ARCHITECTURE OF ACOMA PUEBLO: THE 1934 HISTORIC
AMERICAN BUILDINGS SURVEY PROJECT**
Peter Nabokov
Illus. 144 pp. Paper. Ancient City Press, $15.95.

THE ARCHITECTURE OF GRASSHOPPER PUEBLO
Charles R. Riggs
Reconstructs the Pueblo and everyday life of the community.
Illus. Univesity of Utah Press. $40.

**THE ARCHITECTURE OF SOCIAL INTEGRATION
IN PREHISTORIC PUEBLOS**
William Lipe & Michelle Hegmon, Editors
Illus. 175 pp. Paper. Crow Canyon Archaeological Center, 1990.
$21.95.

ARCHIVES OF CALIFORNIA PREHISTORY
A series of 41 volumes on the archaeology of California.
See Coyote Press for titles and prices.

ARCTIC ART: ESKIMO IVORY
James G. Smith
Examples of Eskimo art from the Museum's collection. The text
discusses the people of the Arctic. 127 pp. Paper. National Museum of the American Indian, $19.95.

ARCTIC ARTIST
C. Stuart Houston, Editor
The journal and paintings of George Back, midshipman with
Sir John Franklin, 1819-1822, Arctic explorer. Covers various
native peoples. Illus. 392 pp. McGill-Queen's University Press,
$45.

ARCTIC DREAMS
Alootook Ipellie
Inuit mythology. Illus. 200 pp. Paper. Theytus, 1993. $16.95.

**ARCTIC HANDBOOK OF NORTH AMERICAN INDIANS,
Vol. 5**
David Damas & William C. Sturtevant, Editors
Illus. 862 pp. Smithsonian, 1985. $29.00.

*ARCTIC HUNTER
Diane Hoyt-Goldsmith
An Inupiat experiences ancient & modern cultures. Grades 4-
6. Illus. 32 pp. Holiday House, 1992. $15.95; paper, $6.95.

ARCTIC LIFE: CHALLENGE TO SURVIVE
M. Jacobs and J. Richardson, III, Editors
Illus. 208 pp. Paper. Carnegie Museum, 1982. $17.50.

*ARCTIC MEMORIES
Normee Ekoomiak
Bilingual - English/Inuit. Grades 3 and up. Illus. 32 pp.
Henry Holt & Co., 1988. $15.95.

**ARCTIC SCHOOLTEACHER:
KULUKAK, ALASKA, 1931-1933**
Abbie Morgan Madenwald
Story of Abbie Morgan's experiences teaching Eskimo children
in the Alaskan village of Kulukak in 1931. Reprint. Illus. Maps.
196 pp. University of Oklahoma Press, $24.95; paper, $13.95.

ARCTIC SKY: INUIT ASTRONOMY, STAR LORE, & LEGEND
John MacDonald
Interviews with Inuit elders & historical records of arctic explor-
ers. Illus. 348 pp. Paper. University of Toronto Press, 1998.
$29.95.

ARCTIC VILLAGE: A 1930s PORTRAIT OF WISEMAN, AK
Robert Marshall
Illus. Maps. 400 pp. University of Alaska Press, 1991. $28; pa-
per, $20.

**ARIKARA NARRATIVE OF CUSTER'S CAMPAIGN
& THE BATTLE OF THE LITTLE BIGHORN**
Orin G. Libby, Editor
Illus. Map. Paper. University of Oklahoma Press, 1998. $9.95.

ARIZONA TRAVELER: INDIANS OF ARIZONA
Eleanor H. Ayer
Illus. 48 pp. Paper. Renaissance House Publishers, 1999.
$4.95.

ARK OF EMPIRE: THE AMERICAN FRONTIER
Dale Van Every
Reprint of 1963 edition. Ayer Co. Publishers, $17.

*ARKANSAS INDIANS: LEARNING & ACTIVITY BOOK
Berna Love
Paper. August House, 1996. $4.95

**ARMS, INDIANS & THE MISMANAGEMENT
OF NEW MEXICO**
D. Vigil; David Weber, Ed. & Translator
Texas Western, $10.00; paper, $5.00.

**THE ARMY & THE NAVAJO: THE BOSQUE REDONDO
RESERVATION EXPERIMENT, 1863-1868**
Gerald Thompson
Chronicles the federal government's attempt to find solutions
to problem of raids by Navajo and Apache Indians. 196 pp.
Paper. University of Arizona Press, 1976. $7.50.

**AROUND THE WORLD IN FOLKTALE & MYTH:
AMERICAN INDIAN**
Lu Keatley; H.E. & L.K. Fraumann, Editors
96 pp. Paper. Specialty Books International, 1989. $99.87.

ARROWHEADS & PROJECTILE POINTS
Lar Hothem
2nd Edition. Illus. Photos. 224 pp. Paper. Hothem House, 1983.
$7.95.

**ARROWHEADS & SPEAR POINTS OF THE PREHISTORIC
SOUTHEAST: A GUIDE TO UNDERSTANDING CULTURAL
ARTIFACTS**
Linda Crawford Culberson
Illus. 118 pp. 230 pp. University Press of Mississippi, 1993.
$29.95; paper, $13.95.

**ARROWHEADS & STONE ARTIFACTS:
A PRACTICAL GUIDE FOR THE SURFACE
COLLECTOR & AMATEUR ARCHAEOLOGIST**
C.G. Yeager
A handbook for identifying various stone artifacts. The Arrow-
heads Video shows where to look and what to look for. VHS or
Beta, 30 minutes. Illus. 158 pp. Paper. Pruett Publishing &
Hothem House (book only), 1986. $12.95; video, $22.95.

THE ARROYO HONDO ARCHAEOLOGICAL SERIES
Douglas W. Schwartz, General Editor
5 volumes. Illus. Biblio. Paper. School of American Research,
1990. $10-15.

ART & ENVIRONMENT IN NATIVE AMERICA
M.E. King and I.R. Traylor, Jr. Editors
Illus. 169 pp. Paper. Texas Tech Press, 1974. $8.

**ART & ESKIMO POWER: THE LIFE &
TIMES OF ALASKAN HOWARD ROCK**
Lael Morgan
Illus. 260 pp. Paper. Epicenter Press, 1988. $24.95; paper,
$16.95.

ART IN THE LIFE OF THE NORTHWEST COAST INDIANS
Describes the Rasmussen Collection of Northwest Coast In-
dian art. Published by the Portland Art Museum, 1219 SW Park
Ave., Portland, OR 97205 (503) 226-2811.

ART OF THE AMERICAN INDIAN
Levin, et al: Vandervelde, Editor
Paper. Council for Indian Education, 1973. $1.95.

THE ART OF AMERICAN INDIAN COOKING
Yeffe Kimball & Jean Anderson
Recipes divided into culktural areas. 224 pp.
Paper. Lyons Press,, $12.95.

**ART OF THE AMERICAN INDIAN FRONTIER:
THE CHANDLER-POHRT COLLECTION**
David Penney, Editor
Illustrates the many objects in the collection. Includes mem-
oirs, essay, and text. Illus. Photos. 368 pp. Paper. University of
Washington Press, 1992. $39.95.

**ART OF THE AMERICAN INDIAN FRONTIER:
A PORTFOLIO**
David W. Penney & Detroit Institute of Arts
Introduction to the art and culture of Native Americans in a
portfolio format. 24 pp. booklet and 24 full-color plates. W.W.
Norton & Co., $18.95.

**ART OF CLAY: TIMELESS POTTERY
OF THE SOUTHWEST**
Lee M. Cohen
Works of 20 southwestern potters, including Maria Martinez,
Nampeyo, Popovi Da, Margaret Tafoya, and Al Qoyawayma.
Illus. 96 color photos. 139 pp. Clear Light, $39.95.

***ART OF THE FAR NORTH: INUIT SCULPTURE,
DRAWING & PRINTMAKING**
Carol Finley
Grades 5-8. Color photos. Maps. Biblio. 60 pp. Lerner, 1998.
$17.95.

**ART OF THE HOPI: CONTEMPORARY
JOURNEYS ON ANCIENT PATHWAYS**
Lois Jacka; photos by Jerry Jacka
158 color photos. 176 pp. Paper. Northland Publishing
& Clear Light, $21.95.

THE ART OF THE INDIAN BASKET IN NORTH AMERICA
Carol Fallon
Illus. 56 pp. Paper. Spencer Museum of Art, 1975. $2.50.

THE ART OF NATIVE AMERICAN BASKETRY:
A LIVING LEGACY
Frank W. Porter, III, Editor
Illus. Greenwood Publishing, 1990. $49.95.

ART OF THE NATIVE AMERICAN FLUTE
R. Carlos Nakai & James DeMars
With additional material by David P. McAllester & Ken Light. A summation of R. Carlos Nakai's years as an educator, performer and student of the Native American flute. Includes 16 transcriptions of songs fro Nakai's recordings, plus two DeMars compositions. 132 pp. Canyon Records Productions, 1995.

ART OF THE NORTH AMERICAN INDIANS:
THE THAW COLLECTION
Gilbert T. Vincent, Sherry Brydon & Ralph T. Coe, Editors
770 Illus. 550 pp. University of Washington Press, 1999. $85.

ART OF THE OSAGE
Garrick Bailey & Daniel C. Swan; with E. Sean Standing Bear & John W. Nunley
Two centuries of Osage art, tracing the material culture, social organizations, cosmology, aesthetics, and rituals of the Osage. Illus. 232 pp. University of Washington Press, 2004. $40.

ART OF THE RED EARTH PEOPLE:
THE MESQUAKIE OF IOWA
Gaylord Torrence & Robert Hobbs
Illus. 144 pp. University of Washington Press, 1989. $50; paper, $24.95.

THE ART OF THE SHAMAN: ROCK ART OF CALIFORNIA
David S. Whitley
Illus. Maps. University of Utah Press. $45.

THE ART OF SIMULATING EAGLE FEATHERS
Bob Gutierrez
How to create realistic imitation golden & bald eagle feather. Color photos. 32 pp. Paper. Written Heritage, $8.50.

ART OF THE TOTEM
Marius Barbeau
Explains the historic origins & the significance of totem art among northwest tribes. Illus. 64 pp. Paper. Hancock House, 1984. $6.95.

ART OF A VANISHED RACE:
THE MIMBRES CLASSIC BLACK-ON-WHITE
Victor Giamattei & Nanci Reichert
Mimbres art of the 10th century Southwest. Illus. 2nd Ed. 100 pp. Paper. High-Lonsome Books, 1990. $11.95.

THE ART & STYLE OF WESTERN INDIAN BASKETRY
Hancock House, $7.95.

ARTIFACTS OF THE NORTHWEST COAST INDIANS
Hilary Stewart
Illus. 172 pp. Paper. Hancock House, $12.95.

ARTISTIC TASTES: FAVORITE RECIPES
OF NATIVE AMERICAN ARTISTS
Barbara Harjo
Illus. 140 pp. Kiva Publishing, 1998. $12.95.

ARTISTRY IN NATIVE AMWERICAN MYTH
Karl Kroeber
Analyzes stories and forms of oral storytelling. 292 pp. University of Nebraska Press, 1998. $70; paper, $30.

THE ARTISTS BEHIND THE WORK
Suzi Jones, Editor
Features the life history & craft of four Alaska Native artists: Nicholas Charles, a Yup'ik Eskimo; Frances Demientieff, an Athabaskan bead worker & skin sewer; Lena Sours, an Inupiat skin sewer; and Jennie Thlunaut, a Chilkat Tlingit basket & blanket maker. Illus. Maps. Photos. Paper. University of Alaska Museum, 1986. $17.50.

ARTS & CRAFTS OF THE CHEROKEE
Rodney Leftwich
Illus. 146 photos. 160 pp. Paper. The Book Publishing Co., Written Heritage & Cherokee Publications, $9.95.

ARTS FROM THE ARCTIC
An exhibition catalog documenting the Arts from the Arctic exhibition. Illus. 80 pp. Institute of Alaska Native Arts, 1993. $22.50, postpaid.

THE ARTS IN SOUTH DAKOTA:
A SELECTIVE, ANNOTATED BIBLIOGRAPHY
Ron MacIntyre, Rebecca Bell, Arthur Amiotte, et al
A companion volume to An Illustrated History of the Arts in South Dakota. A section on Dakota/Lakota arts. Illus. 282 pp. Center for Western Studies, $12.50.

ARTS OF THE INDIAN AMERICAS: NORTH, CENTRAL & SOUTH: LEAVES FROM THE SACRED TREE
Jamake Highwater
Illus. 320 pp. Paper. HarperCollins, 1985. $22.50.

THE ARTS OF THE NORTH AMERICAN INDIAN:
NATIVE TRADITIONS IN EVOLUTION
Edwin L. Wade, Editor
Illus. 320 pp. Hudson Hills Press, 1986. $50; paper, $27.50.

AS LONG AS THE GRASS SHALL GROW & RIVERS FLOW:
A HISTORY OF NATIVE AMERICANS
Clifford E. Trafzer
Harcourt Brace, 2000.

AS LONG AS THE RIVERS RUN: HYDROELECTRIC
DEVELOPMENT & NATIVE COMMUNITIES IN
WESTERN CANADA
James B. Waldram
Paper. University of Toronto Press, 1993. $19.95.

AS LONG AS THE WATERS FLOW:
NATIVE AMERICANS IN THE SOUTH & EAST
Frye Gaillard; photos by Carolyn DeMeritt
Illus. John F. Blair, Publisher, 2000. $21.95.

AS MY GRANDFATHER TOLD IT: TRADITIONAL STORIES
FROM THE KOYUKUK / SITSY YUGH NOHOLNIK TS'IN
Catherine Attla
University of Alaska Press, $12.

AS WE ARE NOW: MIXEDBLOOD ESSAYS
ON RACE & IDENTITY
W.S. Penn
University of California Press, 1998. $45; paper, $17.95.

THE ASCENT OF CHIEFS: CAHOKIA & MISSISSIPPIAN
POLITICS IN NATIVE NORTH AMERICA
Timothy R. Pauketat
Analysis of the origins of Cahokia. 256 pp. Paper. University of Alabama Press, 1994. $28.95.

ASHES & SPARKS
R. Dell Davis
Illus. 185 pp. J. Franklin Publishers, 1989. Includes audiotape. $24.95.

AN ASIAN ANTHROPOLOGIST IN THE SOUTH: FIELD
EXPERIENCES WITH BLACKS, INDIANS & WHITES
Choong S. Kim
University of Tennessee Press, 1977. $17.95; paper, $8.95.

ASSESSMENT OF AMERICAN INDIAN
HOUSING NEEDS & PROGRAMS: FINAL REPORT
C. Thomas Kinglsey, et al.
Illus. 268 pp. Paper. Diane Publishing, 1997. $50.

ASSESSMENT OF A MODEL FOR DETERMINING
COMMUNITY-BASED NEEDS OF AMERICAN INDIANS
WITH DISABILITIES THROUGH CONSUMER INVOLVEMENT
IN COMMUNITY PLANNING & CHANGE
C.A. Marshall, et al
Northern Arizona University, 1990.

AN ASSUMPTION OF SOVEREIGNTY: SOCIAL
& POLITICAL TRANSFORMATION AMONG THE
FLORIDA SEMINOLES
Harry A. Kersey, Jr.
Illus. 278 pp. University of Nebraska Press, 1996. $45.

ASPECTS OF UPPER GREAT LAKES ANTHROPOLOGY:
PAPERS IN HONOR OF LLOYD A. WILFORD
Elden Johnson, Editor
Illus. 190 pp. Paper. Minnesota Historical Society, 1974. $9.50.

THE ASSAULT ON INDIAN TRIBALISM: THE GENERAL
ALLOTMENT LAW (DAWES ACT) OF 1887
Wilcomb E. Washburn
88 pp. Paper. Krieger Publishing, 1975. $7.50.

AT THE DESERT'S GREEN EDGE:
AN ETHNOBOTANY OF THE GILA RIVER PIMA
Amadeo M. Rea
Discusses the Piman people, environment, language, and botanical knowledge of 240 plants. Illus. 430 pp. University of Arizona Press, 1997. $65.

AT HOME WITH THE BELLA COOLA INDIANS:
T.F. McILWRAITH'S FIELD LETTERS, 1922-24
edited by John Barker & Douglas Cole
Illus. Map. 224 pp. Paper. University of Washington Press, 2002. $24.95.

*AT THE MOUTH OF THE LUCKIEST RIVER
Arnold Griese; Illus. by Glo Coalson
Grades 1-4. Illus. Boyds Mills Press, 1996 reissue. $7.95.

*ATARIBA & NIGUAYONA
adapted by Harriet Rohmer & Jesus Guerrero;
illus. by Consuelo Mendez
Taino tales. Grades 1-6. Illus. Children's Book Press, $13.95.

THE ATHABASKAN LANGUAGES: PERSPECTIVE
ON A NATIVE AMERICAN LANGUAGE FAMILY
Theodore Fernald & Paul Platero, Editors
352 pp. Oxford University Press, 1999. $55.

ATHAPASKAN LINGUISTICS
Eung-Do Cook, Editor
Current perspectives on a language family. 645 pp. Mouton de Gruyter, 1989. $125.

ATHABASCAN OLD-TIME FIDDLING
COMMEMORATIVE BOOKLET
Festival booklet featuring musicians, dancers and history. Illus. 20 pp. Institute of Alaska Native Arts, 1992. $8.50, postpaid.

ATHABASKAN STORIES FROM ANVIK
COLLECTED BY JOHN W. CHAPMAN
James Kari, retranscribed by
16 stories. 186 pp. Alaska Native Language Center, 1981. $12.

ATHAPASKAN VERB THEME CATEGORIES: AHTNA
James Kari
230 pp. Paper. Alaska Native Language Center, 1979. $10.

THE ATHABASKANS:
PEOPLE OF THE BOREAL FOREST
Richard K. Nelson
Focuses on the Athabaskans' implements, translated tales & poems, and describes their significance. Illus. Maps. 68 pp. paper. University of Alaska Museum, 1983. $9.95.

ATKA, AN ETHNOHISTORY
OF THE WESTERN ALEUTIANS
Lydia T. Black
Illus. 219 pp. Limestone, 1984. $26.

ATLAS OF AMERICAN INDIAN AFFAIRS
Francis P. Prucha
Graphically presents the history of Native Americans in 109, full-page, black & white maps. Includes references. Illus. Biblio. 190 pp. University of Nebraska Press, 1990. $47.50.

ATLAS OF GREAT LAKES INDIAN HISTORY
Helen Hornbeck Tanner, Editor
Illus. Maps. 240 pp. University of Oklahoma Press, 1987. $90; paper, $49.95.

ATLAS OF INDIANS OF NORTH AMERICA
Gilbert Legay
Grades 8 and up. Illus. 96 pp. Barron's Educational Series, 1995. $16.95.

ATLAS OF THE NORTH AMERICAN INDIAN
Carl Waldman; map & illus. by Molly Braun
Revision of the 1985 title provides a series of overviews on Native American history, culture, and locations of Native Americans in North & Central America. Extensive text, numerous illustrations, and more than 100 b&w maps on the . Illus. 385 pp. Facts on File, 2000. $45; paper, $21.95.

ATTITUDES OF COLONIAL POWERS
TOWARD THE AMERICAN INDIAN
Howard Peckham and Charles Gibson, Editors
Paper. University of Utah Press, 1969. $9.95.

THE ATTRACTION OF PEYOTE: AN INQUIRY INTO
THE BASIC CONDITIONS FOR THE DIFFUSION OF
THE PEYOTE RELIGION IN NORTH AMERICA
Ake Hultkrantz
232 pp. Paper. Coronet Books, 1997. $49.50.

*AUNT MARY, TELL ME A STORY
as told by Mary Chiltoskey
28 Cherokee legends & tales. Grades 3 and up. Illus. 82 pp. Paper. Cherokee Publications, $3.50.

AUTHENTIC ALASKA: VOICES OF ITS NATIVE WRITERS
Susan B. Andrews & John Creed
Collection of essays and stories. Illus. Map. 180 pp. Paper. University of Nebraska Press, 1998. $16.95.

AUTHENTIC AMERICAN INDIAN
BEADWORK & HOW TO USE IT
Pamela Stanley-Millner
Illus. 48 pp. Paper. Smoke & Fire Co., $4.95.

AUTHENTIC INDIAN DESIGNS
Maria Naylor, Editor
2,500 illustrations from reports of the Bureau of American Ethnology. Reprint of 1975 edition. Illus. 219 pp. Paper. Hothem House, Written Heritage, $11.95.

AUTHENTIC MEMOIRS OF
WILLIAM AUGUSTUS BOWLES, ESQ.
W.A. Bowles
He was the ambassador from the United Nations of Creeks and Cherokees to the Court of London. A classic adventure story casting light on conditions along the troubled southern frontier during the 1780s & 1790s. Reprint of 1791 edition. Ayer Co., $19.95.

*AUTHENTIC NORTH AMERICAN INDIAN
CLOTHING FOR SPECIAL TIMES SERIES
Little Bears Go Visiting Series. Preschool -3. Arctic Circle; California; Columbia River Plateau; Columbia River Plateau Yakima; Great Basin; Oregon; Pacific Northwest Coast; Plains; Southeast; Southwest; and Woodlands. See Celia Totus Enterprises for prices.

*AUTHENTIC NORTH AMERICAN INDIAN CRADLEBOARDS
Baby Bears Go Visiting Series. Columbia River Plateau and California; Great Basin, Southeast and Southwest; Pacific Northwest Coast, Woodlands & Arctic Circle; and Plains. See Celia Totus Enterprises for prices.

AUTOBIOGRAPHY OF RED CLOUD:
WAR LEADER OF THE OGLALAS
R. Eli Paul
Illus. 240 pp. Paper. Montana Historical Society, 1999. $15.95.

THE AUTOBIOGRAPHY OF A WINNEBAGO INDIAN
Paul Radin
Reprint of 1920 edition. 91 pp. Paper. Dover, $4.95.

AUTOBIOGRAPHY OF A YAQUI POET
Refugio Savala; Kathleen M. Sands, Editor
Yaqui culture. 228 pp. Paper. University of Arizona Press, 1980. $22.95.

AWAY FROM HOME: AMERICAN INDIAN BOARDING
SCHOOL EXPERIENCES, 1878-2000
Edited by Margaret L. Archuleta, K. Tsianina Lomawaima & Brenda J. Child
Illus. 144 pp. Paper. Heard Museum, 2000. Also available from the Museum of New Mexico Press, $29.95.

B

*BABY RATTLESNAKE
told by Te Ata; adapted by Lynn Moroney
Folktale. Grades K-6. Illus. Childrens Press, $13.95.

BACAVI: A HOPI VILLAGE
Peter Whitely
144 pp. Paper. Northlan, 1988. $14.95.

BACKGROUND OF TREATY-MAKING
IN WESTERN WASHINGTON
Barbara Lane
32 pp. Institute for the Development of Indian Law, $15.

BACONE INDIAN UNIVERSITY
Howard Meredith & John Williams
A history of the nation's oldest continuing Indian institution of higher learning from 1880 to 1980. Illus. 163 pp. Indian University Press, 1980. $14, postpaid.

BACKWARD: AN ESSAY ON INDIANS,
TIME & PHOTOGRAPHY
Will Baker
Illus. 420 pp. North Atlantic, 1983. $24.95; paper, $12.95.

BAD MEDICINE & GOOD: TALES OF THE KIOWAS
Wilbur S. Nye
Illus. Maps. 320 pp. Paper. University of Oklahoma Press, 1997. $24.95.

BAD MEN & BAD TOWNS
Wayne C. Lee
Chronicles the violent events in Nebraska from 1823-1925, including Indian conflicts. Illus. paper. The Caxton Printers, 1994. $14.95.

*A BAG OF BONES: LEGENDS OF THE
WINTU INDIANS OF NORTHERN CALIFORNIA
Marcelle Masson
Grades 4 and up. Illus. Photos. Map. Paper. Naturegraph, 1966. $8.95.

BAGS OF FRIENDSHIP: BANDOLIER
BAGS OF THE GREAT LAKES INDIANS
Richard Pohrt, Jr. & David W. Penney
Illus. 32 pp. Paper. Morning Star Gallery, 1996. $20.

BANDELIER NATIONAL MONUMENT
Patricia Barey
History of Bandelier canyons & mesas of the Pajarito Plateau in northern New Mexico. Color photos. 48 pp. Paper. Clear Light, $7.95.

*DENNIS BANKS: NATIVE AMERICAN ACTIVIST
Karyn Cheatham
Grades 6 and up. Illus. 112 pp. Enslow Publishers, 1997. $19.95.

THE BARK CANOES & SKIN BOATS OF NORTH AMERICA
Edwin Adney & Howard Chapelle
Reprint of 1964 second edition. Illus. 242 pp. Paper. Smithsonian Institution Press, $29.95.

WILLIAM BARTRAM ON THE SOUTHEASTERN INDIANS
edited by Gregory A. Waselkov & Kathryn E. Holland Braund
Illus. Maps. 343 pp. Paper. University of Nebraska Press, 1995. $25.

BASHFUL NO LONGER: AN ALASKAN
ESKIMO ETHNOHISTORY, 1778-1988
W.H. Oswalt
Illus. Maps. 270 pp. University of Oklahoma Press, 1990. $24.95.

BASIC CALL TO CONSCIOUSNESS
Oren Lyons, et al, Editors
A collection of position papers delivered to the United Nations by the traditional Six Nations Council in 1977. Illus. Photos. 120 pp. Paper. The Book Publishing Co. & Clear Light, $7.95.

BASIC GUIDE TO INDIAN COMMUNITY ADVOCACY
Institute for the Development of Indian Law, $7.50.

BASIN-PLATEAU ABORIGINAL SOCIOPOLITICAL GROUPS
Julian H. Steward
Ethnographic study of the Western Shoshoni and some of their Northern Paiute, Ute, and Southern Paiute neighbors. Paper. University of Utah Press, $19.95.

BASKET WEAVERS FOR THE CALIFORNIA
CURIO TRADE: ELIZABETH & LOUISE HICKOX
Marvin Cohodas
Illus. 464 pp. University of Arizona Press, 1997. $45.

BASKETMAKER CAVES IN THE PRAYER
ROCK DISTRICT, NORTHEASTERN ARIZONA
Elizabeth A. Morris
158 pp. Paper. University of Arizona Press, 1980. $13.95.

BASKETRY
F.J. Christopher
Covers selection of material, patterns and weaving procedures are explained and illustrated. 130 pp. Paper. Cherokee Publications, $2.95.

BASKETRY & CORDAGE FROM HESQUIAT HARBOUR
Kathryn Bernick
Illus. 160 pp. paper. UBC Press, 1998. $14.95.

BASKETRY OF THE PAPAGO & PIMA INDIANS
Mary Lois Kissell
Reprint of 1916 edition. Illus. 158 pp. Rio Grande Press, $15.

BASKETRY OF THE SAN CARLOS APACHE INDIANS
Helen H. Roberts
Reprint of 1929 edition. Illus. 105 pp. Paper. Rio Grande Press, $10.

BATTLE CANYON
Robert Hilgardner
Illus. 110 pp. Paper. Mid-America Publishing House, 1986. $8.95.

BATTLE OF THE LOXAHATCHEE RIVER:
THE SEMINOLE WAR
John B. Wolf
Illus. 32 pp. Paper. Florida Classics, 1996. $2.95.

BATTLE OF THE LITTLE BIGHORN
Mari Sandoz
Illus. Maps. 191 pp. Paper. University of Nebraska Press & Clear Light, 1978. $7.95.

BATTLE OF THE ROSEBUD:
PRELUDE TO THE LITTLE BIGHORN
Neil C. Mangum
Illus. 200 pp. Upton & Sons, 1987. $35.

THE BATTLE OF WISCONSIN HEIGHTS
Crawford B. Thayer, Editor
Illus. 416 pp. Paper. Thayer Associates, 1983. $9.95.

BATTLE ROCK, THE HERO'S STORY
Bert & Margie Webber, Editors
A true account-Oregon Coast Indian attack. Illus. Maps. Biblio. 75 pp. Paper. Webb Research Group, $8.95.

BATTLEFIELD & CLASSROOM: FOUR DECADES
WITH THE AMERICAN INDIAN, 1867-1904
Richard H. Pratt; Robert Utley, Editor;
foreword by David W. Adams
Pratt's meoirs about the carlisle Indian school which he founded in the late 1800s. Originally published in 1964. Illus. Maps. 416 pp. Paper. University of Oklahoma Press, 2004. $24.95.

*BATTLEFIELDS & BURIAL GROUNDS:
THE INDIAN STRUGGLE TO PROTECT
ANCESTRAL GRAVES IN THE U.S.
Roger C. Echohawk & Walter R. Echohawk
Examines the historical & cultural roots behind the double standard perpetuated by American society. Grades 7 and up. Illus. Color photos. 80 pp. Lerner, 1993. $22.60; paper, $9.95.

BATTLES & SKIRMISHES OF THE GREAT
SIOUX WAR, 1876-1877: THE MILITARY VIEW
Jerome A. Greene, Editor
Illus. Maps. 256 pp. Paper. University of Oklahoma Press, 1993. $14.95.

BAYONETS IN THE WILDERNESS: ANTHONY WAYNE'S
LEGION IN THE OLD NORTHWEST
Alan D. Gaff
How the U.S. Army conquered the first American frontier, the 1790s Indian confederacy of the Ohio River Valley. Illus. Maps. 416 pp. University of Oklahoma Press, 2004. $39.95.

BAYOU SALADO
Virginia M. Simmons
Illus. 280 pp. Paper. Century One, 1982. $8.95.

BEAD ON AN ANTHILL: A LAKOTA CHILDHOOD
Delphine Red Shirt
146 pp. Paper. University of Nebraska Press. 1997. $11.95.

*THE BEADED MOCCASINS
Lynda Durant
Grades 5-8. 185 pp. Houghton Mifflin, 1998. $15.

BEADS & BEADWORK OF THE AMERICAN INDIAN
William C. Orchard
Revised 1929 second edition. Illus. 168 pp. Paper. Eagle's View Publishing, $9.95.

BEADS TO BUCKSKINS
Peggy Sue Henry
Annual from 1989. Illus. 96 pp. each. Paper. Beads to Buckskins, Vol. 1-9, $10.95 each; Vol. 10 and up, $12.95 each.

A BEADWORK COMPANION
Jean Heinbuch
Step-by-step, illustrated projects designed to teach Native American beadwork. Illus. 112 pp. Paper. Eagle's View Publishing & Smoke & Fire Co., 1992. $12.95.

BEAR CHIEF'S WAR SHIRT
James W. Schultz and Wilbur Betts
Illus. 240 pp. Paper. Mountain Press, 1984. $8.95.

BEAR HEART: THE HEIRSHIP CHRONICLES
Gerald Vizenor
Sentiments of Manifest Destiny. 260 pp. University of Minnesota Press, 1990. $24.95; paper, $12.95.

THE BEAR RIVER MASSACRE
Newell Hart
Illus. 300 pp. Cache Valley, 1982. $35.

THE BEAR SHAMAN TRADITION
OF SOUTHERN CALIFORNIA INDIANS
Cheryl Hinton
Barona Cultural Center & Museum, 2002.

*THE BEAR THAT TURNED WHITE;
& OTHER NATIVE TALES
Maurine Grammer, retold by
Stories with messages intended to teach young people about various aspects of Native American culture or tradition. Grades 4-10. Illus. 108 pp. Northland Publishing, $11.95.

THE BEAR TRIBE'S SELF-RELIANCE BOOK
Sun Bear, Wabun & Nimimosha
Contains Native American philosophy, legends and prophecy. Illus. 202 pp. Paper. Prentice Hall Press, 1989. $8.95.

THE BEAUTIFUL & THE DANGEROUS:
ENCOUNTERS WITH THE ZUNI INDIANS
Barbara Tedlock
Illus. 336 pp. Paper. University of New Mexico Press, $24.95.

JIM BECKWOURTH: BLACK MOUNTAIN
MAN & WAR CHIEF OF THE CROWS
Elinor Wilson
Reprint of 1972 edition. Illus. maps. Biblio. 248 pp. University of Oklahoma Press, $14.95.

BECOMING BRAVE: THE PATH
TO NATIVE AMERICAN MANHOOD
Laine Thom, Editor
Illus. 120 pp. Chronicle Books, 1992. $29.95; paper, $18.95.

BECOMING & REMAINING A PEOPLE: CONTINUITY &
CHANGE AMONG NATIVE AMERICAN RELIGIONS ON THE
NORTHERN PLAINS
Howard L. Harrod
Religious developments of the Mandans and the Hidatsas. 152 pp. University of Arizona Press, 1995. $31.95; paper, $18.95.

BEDBUGS' NIGHT DANCE & OTHER
HOPI TALES OF SEXUAL ENCOUNTER
Ekkehart Malotki
Illus. 390 pp. Paper. University of Nebraska Press & Clear Light, 1995. $16.95.

*BEFORE COLUMBUS
Muriel Batherman
Daily life of earliest inhabitants, based on archaeological findings. Focus on Pueblos. Illus. Paper. Houghton Mifflin Co., 1990. $4.95.

BEFORE THE GREAT SPIRIT: WAR, RIVALRY
& IRREVERENCE AMONG THE SIOUX
Julian Rice
Illus. 172 pp. University of New Mexico Press, $45; paper, $22.50.

BEFORE THE LONG KNIVES CAME
Millie House
Illus. 94 pp. Kennebec River Press, 1987.

BEFORE MAN IN MICHIGAN
R. Ray Baker
Reprint. Paper. George Wahr Publishing, $12.50.

***BEFORE THE STORM: AMERICAN INDIANS
BEFORE COLUMBUS**
Allison Lassieur
Grades 7 and up. Illus. 150 pp. Facts on File, 1998. $19.95.

**BEFORE THE WILDERNESS: ENVIRONMENTAL
MANAGEMENT BY NATIVE CALIFORNIANS**
Tom Blackburn & Kat Anderson
Includes the full text of *Patterns of Indian Burning*. Illus.
476 pp. Ballena Press, 1994. $41.50; paper, $31.50.

BEGINNING CHEROKEE
Ruth Bradley Holmes & Betty Sharp Smith
A Cherokee language grammar. Revised edition. Illus. 346 pp.
Paper. University of Oklahoma Press, 1977. $29.95. Set of two
cassettes, $25.

BEGINNING CREEK: MVSKOKE EMPONVKV
Pamela Innes, Linda Alexander, Bertha Tilkens
Basic intriduction to the language and culture of the Muskogee
(Creek) and Seminole Indians. Illus. Tables. 256 pp. Paper.
University of Oklahoma Press, 2004. $29.95.

BEGINNING WASHO
William H. Jacobsen, Jr.
Nevada State Museum, 1996.

**BEHIND THE FRONTIER: INDIANS IN 18TH
CENTURY EASTERN MASSACHUSETTS**
Daniel R. Mandell
Illus. Maps. 257 pp. Paper. University of Nebraska Press, 1996.
$19.95.

**BEHIND THE TRAIL OF BROKEN TREATIES:
AN INDIAN DECLARATION OF INDEPENDENCE**
Vine Deloria, Jr.
Historical review of Indian political recognition and land title
with respect to other nations. 310 pp.
Paper. University of Texas Press, 1985. $14.95.

**BEING & BECOMING INDIAN: BIOGRAPHICAL
STUDIES OF NORTH AMERICAN FRONTIERS**
James A. Clifton, Editor
337 pp. Wadsworth, 1988. $32.95. Paper. Waveland Press,
$14.95.

**BRING IN BEING: THE COLLECTED WORKS
OF SKAAY OF THE QQUUNA QIIGHAWAAY**
Edited and trans. by Robert Bringhurst
Haida myths. Illus. Map. 397 pp. University of Nebraska Press,
2002. $37.95.

**BEING COMANCHE: A SOCIAL HISTORY
OF AN AMERICAN INDIAN COMMUNITY**
Morris W. Foster
Won the 1992 Erminie Wheeler-Voegelin Prize of the Ameri-
can Society of Ethnohistory. Illus. Paper. University of Arizona
Press, 1991. $18.95.

BEING & VIBRATION
Joseph Rael & Mary E. Marlow
A Native American visionary shares information on rise of hu-
man consciousness. 175 pp. Paper. VIP Publshing. $14.95.

BELIEF & WORSHIP IN NATIVE NORTH AMERICA
Ake Hultkrantz; Christopher Vecsey, Editor
358 pp. Syracuse University Press, 1981. $30.

**BELIEFS & HOLY PLACES: A SPIRITUAL
GEOGRAPHY OF THE PIMERIA ALTA**
James S. Griffith
The Tohono O'odham, their places and traditions are covered.
218 pp. Paper. University of Arizona Press, 1992. $18.95.

***BELLE HIGHWALKING: THE NARRATIVE
OF A NORTHERN CHEYENNE WOMAN**
Katheryne Weist, Editor
Grades 5-12. 66 pp. Council for Indian Education, 1979. $9.95;
paper, $3.95.

BENDING TRADITION
Exhibiton catalog featuring traditional and contemporary
bentwood containers, Aleut headgear and sculptures. Illus. 48
pp. Institute of Alaska Native Arts, 1990. $12.50, postpaid.

**THE BENTEEN-GOLDIN LETTERS
ON CUSTER & HIS LAST BATTLE**
John M. Carroll
Illus. Paper. Amereon Ltd., 1985. $18.95.

*THE BENTWOOD BOX
Nan McNutt
Grades 3-8. Illus. 35 pp. Paper. N. McNutt Associates, 1989.
$9.95.

**O.E. BERNINGHAUS - TAOS, N.M., MASTER PAINTER
OF AMERICAN INDIANS AND FRONTIER WEST**
Gordon E. Sanders
Illus. 152 pp. Taos Heritage Press, 1985. $40.

**BEST OF THE BEST - INDIAN ARTIFACTS
OF THE DEEP SOUTH**
Prehistoric artifacts of the Southeast including chipped points
and blades, stone artifacts and pottery. Color photos. 220 pp.
Hothem House, 1998. $60; paper, $24.95.

BETRAYING THE OMAHA NATION, 1870-1916
Judith A. Boughter
Illus. 304 pp. University of Oklahoma Press, 1998. $27.95.

**A BETTER KIND OF HATCHET: LAW, TRADE,
DIPLOMACY IN THE CHEROKEE NATION**
John P. Reid
262 pp. Penn State University Press, 1975. $27.50.

***BETWEEN EARTH & SKY - LEGENDS
OF NATIVE AMERICAN SACRED PLACES**
Joseph Bruchac; illus. by Thomas Locker
A young boy learns that everything living and inanimate has its
place, should be considered sacred, and given respect. Grades
3-6. Meadowlark Communications, $16; paper, $7.

**BETWEEN INDIAN & WHITE WORLDS:
THE CULTURAL BROKER**
Margaret Connell Szasz
14 portraits of cultural brokers between the Indians & non-Indi-
ans. Illus. Maps. Biblio. 400 pp. Paper. University of Oklahoma
Press, 1994. $19.95.

***BETWEEN SACRED MOUNTAINS:
NAVAJO STORIES & LESSONS FROM THE LAND**
Sam & Janet Bingham, Editors
Grades 4-12. Illus. 290 pp. University of Arizona Press, $35;
paper, $25.95.

**BETWEEN TWO CULTURES:
KIOWA ART FROM FORT MARION**
Moira F. Harris; with Rodney C. Loehr
Reproduction of the drawings by Wo-Haw completed during
his imprisonment. Illus. 148 pp. Pogo Press, 1989. $39.95.

**BETWEEN WORLDS: INTERPRETERS,
GUIDES, & SURVIVORS**
Frances Karttunen
Tells the story of 16 men & women who served as interpreters
& guides to explorers, soldiers, anthropologists, missionaries,
and conquerors. Includes the stories of Sacajawea, Sarah
Winnemucca, Charles Eastman, and Ishi. Rutgers University
Press, 1994. $24.95.

**BEYOND THE COVENANT CHAIN: THE IROQUOIS
& THEIR NEIGHBORS IN INDIAN NORTH AMERICA,
1600-1800**
Daniel Richter & James Merrell, Editors
Illus. 288 pp. Syracuse University Press, 1987. $27.50.

**BEYOND THE FOUR CORNERS OF THE WORLD:
NAVAJO WOMAN'S JOURNEY**
Emily Benedek
Paper. University of Oklahoma Press, 1998. $$14.95.

**BEYOND THE FRONTIER:
EXPLORING THE INDIAN COUNTRY**
Stan Hoag
Reprint. Illus. Maps. 352 pp. University of Oklahoma Press,
$17.95.

**BEYOND THE HUNDRETH MERIDIAN: JOHN WESLEY
POWELL & THE SECOND OPENING OF THE WEST**
Wallace Stegner
Exploration of the Colorado River, the Grand Canyon, and
homeland of Indian tribes of the American Southwest. Illus.
464 pp. Paper. Penguin USA, $12.

**BEYOND THE RESERVATION: INDIANS, SETTLERS,
& THE LAW IN WASHINGTON TERRITORY, 1853-1889**
Brad Asher
Maps. Biblio. 288 pp. University of Oklahoma Press, 1999.
$34.95.

**BEYOND THE RIVER & THE BAY:
THE CANADIAN NORTHWEST IN 1811**
Eric Ross
Illus. Paper. University of Toronto Press, 1970. $9.95.

**BEYOND TRADITION: CONTEMPORARY
INDIAN ART & ITS EVOLUTION**
Lois Jacka; photos pby Jerry Jacka
203 color photos. 216 pp. Northland, 1988. $40; paper, $20.

**BEYOND THE VISION: ESSAYS
ON AMERICAN INDIAN CULTURE**
William K. Powers
Illus. 200 pp. University of Oklahoma Press, 1987. $37.95.

**A BIBLIOGRAPHICAL GUIDE TO THE HISTORY
OF INDIAN-WHITE RELATIONS IN THE U.S.**
Francis P. Prucha
Lists and discusses more than 9,000 items including materials
in the National Archives. Paper. University of Chicago Press,
1977. $12.

**BIBLIOGRAPHY: NATIVE AMERICAN
ARTS & CRAFTS OF THE U.S.**
A selection of books and pamphlets chosen and annotated for
their pertinence to the field of contemporary Native American
arts and crafts of the U.S. 8 pp. Indian Arts and Crafts Board.
No charge.

**BIBLIOGRAPHY OF ARTICLES & PAPERS
ON NORTH AMERICAN INDIAN ART**
Anne D. Harding and Patricia Bolling
Reprint of 1938 edition. Gordon Press, 1980.
Library binding, $75.

A BIBLIOGRAPHY OF THE ATHAPASKAN LANGUAGES
Richard T. Parr
Paper. National Museum of Canada, $3.95.

BIBLIOGRAPHY OF THE BLACKFOOT
Hugh Dempsey & Lindsey Moir
255 pp. Scarecrow Press, 1989. $35.

BIBLIOGRAPHY OF THE CATAWBA
Thomas J. Blumer
575 pp. Scarecrow Press, 1987. $65.

BIBLIOGRAPHY OF THE CHICKASAW
Anne Kelley Hoyt
230 pp. Scarecrow Press, 1987. $30.

**A BIBLIOGRAPHY OF CONTEMPORARY NORTH
AMERICAN INDIANS: SELECTED & PARTIALLY
ANNOTATED WITH STUDY GUIDES**
William H. Hodge; intro. by Paul Prucha
320 pp. Interland Publishing, 1976. $27.50.

**BIBLIOGRAPHY OF THE INDIANS OF SAN DIEGO
COUNTY: THE KUMEYAAY, DIEGUENO, LUISENO,
AND CUPENO**
Phillip M. White & Stephen D. Fitt
288 pp. Scarecrow Press, 1997. $58.

**BIBLIOGRAPHY OF LANGUAGE ARTS MATERIALS FOR
NATIVE NORTH AMERICANS, 1975-1976: WITH SUPPLE-
MENTAL ENTRIES FROM 1965-1974**
G. Edward Evans, Karin Abbey & Dennis Reed
A list of language art materials for 1975-76 and earlier years to
supplement the 1977 *Bibliography*. 120 pp. Paper. UCLA, Ameri-
can Indian Studies Center, 1977. $5.

**BIBLIOGRAPHY OF LANGUAGE ARTS MATERIALS FOR
NATIVE NORTH AMERICANS, BILINGUAL, ENGLISH AS A
SECOND LANGUAGE & NATIVE LANGUAGE MATERIALS,
1965-1974**
G. Edward Evans, Karin Abbey & Dennis Reed
A compilation of Native language and bilingual education
sources. 283 pp. Paper. UCLA, American Indian Studies Cen-
ter, 1977. $5.

**BIBLIOGRAPHY OF LANGUAGES OF NATIVE CALIFORNIA:
INCLUDING CLOSELY RELATED LANGUAGES OF ADJA-
CENT AREAS**
William Bright
234 pp. Scarecrow Press, 1982. $20.

**BIBLIOGRAPHY OF NATIVE NORTH AMERICANS
ON DISC - CD-ROM**
Timothy O'Leary & M. Marlene Martin, Editors
The Human Relations Area File's Ethnographic Bibliography
of North America. Semiannual. CD-ROM or Network. IBM
compatable. SilverPlatter, $1,045 for annual subscription for
CD; $1,306 for one person network.

**BIBLIOGRAPHY OF NORTH AMERICAN INDIAN
MENTAL HEALTH**
Dianne Kelso and Carolyn Attneave, Editors
Illus. 404 pp. Greenwood Publishing, 1981. $46.95.

BIBLIOGRAPHY OF THE OSAGE
Terry P. Wilson
172 pp. Scarecrow Press, 1985. $25.

BIBLIOGRAPHY OF THE SIOUX
Jack W. Marken & Herbert T. Hoover
388 pp. Scarecrow Press, 1980. $35.

*THE BIG AMERICAN SOUTHWEST ACTIVITY BOOK
Walter C. Yoder, PhD
The Southwest multicultural environment. Grades 3 and up.
Illus. 64 pp. Paper. Clear Light & Sunstone Press, $8.95.

BIG BEAR: THE END OF FREEDOM
Hugh A. Dempsey
Illus. 227 pp. Paper. University of Nebraska Press, 1985. $8.95.

BIG CYPRESS: A CHANGING SEMINOLE COMMUNITY
M. Garbarino; Spindler, Editors
131 pp. Paper. Waveland, 1972. $8.50.

BIGHORSE THE WARRIOR
Tiana Bighorse; Noel Bennett, Editor
Stories of the sufferings of the Navajo people. 115 pp.
Paper. The University of Arizona Press, 1990. $15.95.

BILINGUAL EDUCATION FOR AMERICAN INDIANS
U.S. Bureau of Indian Affairs
Francesco Cordasco, Editor
Reprint of 1971 edition. Ayer Co. Publishers, $22.

*BILL RED COYOTE IS A NUT
Hap Gilliland
Grades 1-8. 32 pp. Paper. Council for Indian Education, 1981.
$8.95; paper, $2.95.

THE BINGO PALACE
Louise Erdrich
A novel of gaming & competetion dancing and traditional
Anishinabe culture. HarperCollins, 1994.

**A BIO-BIBLIOGRAPHY OF NATIVE AMERICAN WRITERS,
1772-1925: SUPPLEMENT**
Daniel F. Littlefield, Jr. & James W. Parsons
350 pp. Scarecrow Press, 1985. $35.

**BIOGRAPHICAL DICTIONARY OF INDIANS
OF THE AMERICAS**
Contains nearly 2,000 detailed biographies of significant Indians past and present, and over 900 portraits. Second edition.
2 vols. 882 pp. American Indian Publishers, 1998. $385 per
set.

**THE BIOGRAPHICAL DIRECTORY
OF NATIVE AMERICAN PAINTERS**
Patrick D. Lester, Editor
700 pp. University of Oklahoma Press, 1995. $49.95.

**BIOGRAPHICAL & HISTORICAL INDEX OF AMERICAN
INDIANS & PERSONS INVOLVED IN INDIAN AFFAIRS**
U.S. Dept. of the Interior
Biographical material on Native Americans who were involved
in any way with the U.S. government up to 1965. G.K. Hall,
1966.

**BIOGRAPHY OF FRANCIS SLOCUM, THE LOST SISTER OF
WYOMING: A COMPLETE NARRATIVE OF HER CAPTIVITY
& WANDERINGS AMONG THE INDIANS**
John F. Meginness
Reprint of 1891 edition. 260 pp. Ayer Co., $21.

THE BIRCH: BRIGHT TREE OF LIFE & LEGEND
John L. Peyton
Illus. 74 pp. Paper. McDonald & Woodward Publishing, 1994,
$9.95.

BIRCHBARK CANOES OF THE FUR TRADE
Kent
Examination of watercraft of the North American fur trade era.
Sketches, photos. 2 Vols. 670 pp. Paper. Hothem House, 1997.
$50 per set.

**BIRDS, BEADS & BELLS: REMOTE SENSING
OF A PAWNEE SACRED BUNDLE**
Diane Good
Illus. 25 pp. Kansas State Historical Society, 1989. $7.95.

THE BIRTH OF AMERICA
R.F. Locke
Mankind, $1.75.

**BISON CULTURAL TRADITIONS
OF THE NORTHERN PLAINS**
Lauren M. McKeever
A report on the bison cultural presentationnn June 17, 1993 at
Ethete, Wyoming on the Wind River Indian Reservation. Book-
let. The InterTribal Bison Cooperative, 1993.

BITTERNESS ROAD: THE MOJAVE, 1604-1860
Lorraine Sherer; Sylvia Vane & Lowell Bean, Editors
126 pp. Paper. Ballena Press, 1995. $13.95.

**BLACK, BROWN & RED: THE MOVEMENT FOR FREEDOM
AMONG BLACK, CHICANO, LATINO & INDIAN**
John Alan, Editor
Illus. 78 pp. Paper. News & Letters, $9.95.

BLACK EAGLE CHILD
Ray A. Young Bear
Facepaint Narratives. 261 pp. University of Iowa Press, $24.95.

**BLACK ELK & FLAMING RAINBOW: PERSONAL MEMO-
RIES OF THE LAKOTA HOLY MAN & JOHN NEIHARDT**
Hilda Neihardt
Illus. Map. 158 pp. Paper. University of Nebraska Press, 1995.
$15.95.

BLACK ELK: HOLY MAN OF THE OGLALA
Michael F. Steltenkamp
Portrays the Sioux spiritual leader as a victim of Western subjugation. Illus. 240 pp. Maps. University of Oklahoma Press,
1993. $22.95; paper, $11.95.

**BLACK ELK LIVES: CONVERSATIONS
WITH THE BLACK ELK FAMILY**
Esther Black Elk DeSersa, Olivia Black Elk Pouier, et al.
Description of the lives of the grandchildren and great grand-
children of the Lakota holy man. Illus. 176 pp. Paper. Univer-
sity of Nebraska Press, 2000. $12.95.

*BLACK ELK: A MAN WITH VISION
Carol Greene
Grades K-3. Illus. 50 pp. Childrens Press, 1990. $11.95.

**BLACK ELK'S RELIGION:
THE SUN DANCE & LAKOTA CATHOLICISM**
Clyde Holler
282 pp. Syracuse University Press, 1998.
$39.95; paper, $16.95.

BLACK ELK: THE SACRED WAYS OF A LAKOTA
Wallace Black Elk & William Lyon
225 pp. Paper. HarperCollins & VIP Publishing, 1992. $9.95.

BLACK ELK SPEAKS
as told through John C. Neihardt
Story of Lakota visionary and healer Nicholas Black Elk (1863-
1950) and his people. This special edition features three pref-
aces by Neihardt, a map, a reset text, a listing of Lakota words
newley translated. Illus. 246 pp. University of Nebraska Press,
2000. $50; paper, $14.95.

BLACK ELK'S WORLD (Website)
Full text of Black Elk Speaks; history and culture of the Lakotas;
Native biographies and memoirs. www.blackelkspeaks.uni.edu
University of Nebraska Press.

**BLACK EYES ALL OF THE TIME: INTIMATE VIOLENCE,
ABORIGINAL WOMEN, AND THE JUSTICE SYSTEM**
Anne McGillivray & Brenda Comaskey
Based on the 1995 Winnipeg, Canada, study between the au-
thors and 26 aboriginal women. 208 pp. University of Toronto
Press, 1999. $55; paper, $18.95.

BLACK HAWK: AN AUTOBIOGRAPHY
Donald Jackson, Editor
Reprint of 1955 edition. Maps. 177 pp. Paper.
University of Illinois Press, $5.95.

*BLACK HAWK & JIM THORP
Greison Bloom & Hap Gilliland
Biographies of two Salk heros. Grades 5-12.
71 pp. Paper. Council for Indian Education. $4.95.

THE BLACK HAWK WAR, 1831-1832
Ellen M. Whitney, Editor
Two volumes. Illinois State Historical Library.

**THE BLACK HAWK WAR, INCLUDING
A REVIEW OF BLACK HAWK'S LIFE**
Frank E. Stevens
A detailed history of the war, with data on many participants.
Illus. 323 pp. Paper. Heritage Books, $22.

THE BLACK HAWK WAR, WHY?
Lloyd H. Efflandt
Illus. 40 pp. Paper. Rock Island Arsenal Historical Society, 1987.
$1.95.

BLACK HAWK'S AUTOBIOGRAPHY
Roger L. Nichols, Editor
Iowa State University Press, 1999.

**THE BLACK HILLS; OR, THE LAST
HUNTING GROUND OF THE DACOTAHS**
Annie D. Tallent
Reprint of 1899 edition. Illus. 594 pp. Brevit Press, limited
leather edition, $50. Facsimile edition. Illus. Ayer Co., $62.

BLACK HILLS: SACRED HILLS
Tom Charging Eagle & Ron Zeilinger
Illus. 60 pp. Paper. VIP Publishing. 1987. $6.95.

**BLACK HILLS/WHITE JUSTICE: THE SIOUX NATION
VERSUS THE U.S., 1775 TO THE PRESENT**
Edward Lazarus
Case study in the history of Indian/white relations in North
America. Illus. Maps. 500 pp. Paper. University of Nebraska
Press, 1999. $22.

BLACK INDIAN GENEALOGY RESEARCH
Angela Walton-Raji
180 pp. Paper. Heritage Books, 1993. $18.50.

**BLACK, RED & DEADLY: BLACK & INDIAN
GUNFIGHTERS OF THE INDIAN TERRITORIES**
Art Burton
Illus. 288 pp. Eakin Press, 1992. $19.95.

**BLACK ROBE FOR THE YANKTON SIOUX:
FR. SYLVESTER EISENMAN, O.S.B. (1891-1948)**
Mary E. Carson
Illus. 295 pp. Paper. Tipi Press, 1989. $11.95.

BLACK SAND: PREHISTORY IN NORTHERN ARIZONA
Harold S. Colton
Reprint of 1960 edition. Illus. 132 pp. Greenwood, $35.

BLACK SUN OF THE MIWOK
Jack Burrows
University of New Mexico Press. $19.95.

**THE BLACKFEET: ARTISTS OF THE NORTHERN PLAINS:
THE SCRIVER COLLECTION OF BLACKFEET INDIAN AR-
TIFACTS & RELATED OBJECTS, 1894-1990**
Bob Scriver
406 color plates. 320 pp. Lowell Press & Written Heritage, 1992.
$60.

**BLACKFEET & BUFFALO:
MEMORIES OF LIFE AMONG THE INDIANS**
James W. Schultz; Keith Seele, Editor
Reprint of 1962 edition. Illus. Maps. Biblio. Paper.
University of Oklahoma Press, 2002. $21.95.

BLACKFEET CRAFTS
John C. Ewers
Reprint of 1945 edition. Illus. 68 pp.
Paper. R. Schneider, Publishers, $6.95.

BLACKFEET INDIAN STORIES
George Bird Grinnell
Reprinted from 1913 ed. With original N.C. Wyeth
painting, Spring, on front cover. Illus. 224 pp. Paper.
Globe Pequot Press, $10.95.

BLACKFEET INDIANS
W. Reiss and F.B. Linderman
Reprint. Gordon Press, 1977. $75.95.

**THE BLACKFEET: RAIDERS
ON THE NORTHWESTERN PLAINS**
John C. Ewers
Reprint of 1958 edition. Illus. Maps. 377 pp. Paper.
University of Oklahoma Press, 2000. $24.95.

BLACKFEET TALES FROM APIKUNI'S WORLD
James Willard Schultz
Tales of author's experiences with the Blackfeet. Illus.
320 pp. University of Oklahoma Press, 2002. $34.95.

BLACKFEET: THEIR ART & CULTURE
John C. Ewers; Herb Bryce, Editor
Illus. 96 pp. Paper, Hancock House, 1985. $6.95.

*BLACKFOOT CHILDREN & ELDERS TALK TOGETHER
Barrie E. Kavasch
Grades 4 and up. Rosen Group, 1998. $18.

**THE BLACKFOOT CONFEDERACY, 1880-1920:
A COMPARATIVE STUDY OF CANADA & U.S.
INDIAN POLICY**
Hana Samek
Illus. 248 pp. University of New Mexico Press, 1987. $27.50.

BLACKFOOT CRAFTWORKER'S BOOK
Adolf & Beverly Hungry Wolf
A collection of photos of traditional clothing, accessories,
utensils, cradleboards, etc. Illus. 80 pp. Paper. The Book
Publishing Co., $11.95.

BLACKFOOT GRAMMAR
Donald G. Frantz
200 pp. University of Toronto Press, 1991. $45.

**BLACKFOOT LODGE TALES:
THE STORY OF A PRAIRIE PEOPLE**
George B. Grinnell
Reprint of 1892 edition. 322 pp. Paper.
University of Nebraska Press, 2003. $14.95.

**THE BLACKFOOT MOONSHINE REBELLION OF 1881:
THE INDIAN WAR THAT NEVER WAS**
Ron Carter
112 pp. Harbour Books & Mountain Press, 1997. $12.95

**BLACKFOOT MUSICAL THOUGHT:
COMPARATIVE PERSPECTIVES**
Bruno Nettl
214 pp. Kent State University, 1989. $21.

BLANKET WEAVING IN THE SOUTHWEST
Joe Ben Wheat; edited by Ann Lane Hedlund
Describes the evolution of southwestern textiles-
Pueblo, Navajo & Spanish American blankets. Illus.
444 pp. University of Arizona Press, 2003. $75.

**BLANKETS & MOCASSINS: PLENTY COUPS
& HIS PEOPLE, THE CROWS**
G. Wagner & W. Allen
Illus. 304 pp. University of Nebraska Press, 1987.
$24.95; paper, $8.95.

**BLESSED ASSURANCE: AT HOME
WITH THE BOMB IN AMARILLO TEXAS**
A.G. Mojtabai
Illus. 259 pp. Paper. University of New Mexico Press, 1988.
$10.95.

**BLESSING FOR A LONG TIME: THE
SACRED POLE OF THE OMAHA TRIBE**
Robin Ridington & Dennis Hastings
Illus. 260 pp. Paper. University of Nebraska Press, 1997.
$18.

BLESSINGWAY
Leland C. Wyman
The central rite of Navajo religion. Presents Navajo origin myths and ritual poetry. Illus. 688 pp. University of Arizona Press, 1970. $50.

BLOOD AT SAND CREEK: THE MASSACRE REVISITED
Bob Scott
Illus. Biblio. 256 pp. Paper. The Caxton Printers, 1994. $8.95.

BLOOD MONSTER: THE NEZ PERCE COYOTE CYCLE
Deward E. Walker, Jr.
240 pp. Mountain Press. $32.50.

BLOOD & VOICE: NAVAJO WOMEN CEREMONIAL PRACTITIONERS
Maureen Trudelle Schwarz
Explores Navajo women's role in age-old ceremonies. 186 pp. University of Arizona Press, 2003. $50; paper, $24.95.

BLOODLINES: ODYSSEY OF A NATIVE DAUGHTER
Janet Campbell Hale
Autobiographically-based book of essays traces the life experiences of the author and her family, members of the Coeur d'Alene tribe. Reprint of 1993 edition. 187 pp. Paper. University of Arizona Press. $17.95.

THE BLUE GOD: AN EPIC OF MESA VERDE
An epic poem based on the legends of the Zuni Indians who inhabited parts of Colorado 7 centuries ago. 256 pp. High-Lonesome Books, $35.

BLUE SKY, NIGHT THUNDER: THE UTES OF COLORADO
Jess McCreede
416 pp. Affiliated Writers of America, $19.95.

BLUE HORSES RUSH IN: POEMS & STORIES
Luci Tapahonso
A Navajo woman's life. 120 pp. University of Arizona Press, 1997. $22.95; paper, $12.95.

*BLUE JACKET: WAR CHIEF OF THE SHAWNEES
Allen W. Eckert
Grades 7-adult. 177 pp. Paper. Landfall Press, 1983. $5.95.

BLUE JACKET: WARRIOR OF THE SHAWNEES
John Sugden
Illus. Maps. 400 pp. Paper. University of Nebraska Press, 2000. $19.95.

BLUE STAR: THE STORY OF CORABELLE FELLOWS, TEACHER AT DAKOTA MISSIONS, 1884-1888
Kunigunde Duncan
A church-sponsored teacher among the Sioux and Cheyenne in the Dakota Territory in the 1880s. Illus. 216 pp. Photos. Map. Paper. Minnesota Historical Society Press, 1990. $8.95.

*BLUE THUNDER
Richard Throssel
Grades 5-12. 32 pp. Paper. Council for Indian Education, 1976. $8.95; paper, $2.95.

BO'JOU, NEEJEE!: PROFILES OF CANADIAN INDIAN ART
Ted J. Brasser
Source of ethnographic information on central Indian artifacts. Illus. 204 pp. Paper. National Museums of Canada and University of Chicago Press, 1976. $19.95.

BOARDING SCHOOL SEASONS: AMERICAN INDIAN FAMILIES, 1900-1940
Brenda J. Child
Illus. 154 pp. Paper. University of Nebraska Press, 1998. $14.95.

*BOAT RIDE WITH LILLIAN TWO BLOSSOM
Patricia Polacco
A story which explores the magic of myth. Illus. 32 pp. Philomel, 1989. $14.95.

FRANZ BOAS: THE EARLY YEARS, 1858-1906
Douglas Cole
Illus. Bibliog. 484 pp. University of Washington Pres, 1999. $50.

BONE DANCE: NEW & SELECTED POEMS, 1965-1993
Wendy Rose
Poetry anthology of a Native American author's work. 108 pp. Paper. University of Arizona Press, 1994. $13.95.

BONE GAME
Louis Owens
A novel (murder mystery) by Louis Owens, of Choctaw-Cherokee-Irish descent. 256 pp. Paper. University of Oklahoma Press, 1994. $14.95.

BONES, BOATS, AND BISON: ARCHAEOLOGY & THE FIRST COLONIZATION OF NORTH AMERICA
E. James Dixon
Illus. Maps. 320 pp. University of New Mexico Press, 1999. $49.95; paper, $24.95.

BOOK OF AUTHENTIC INDIAN LIFE CRAFTS
Oscar E. Norbeck
Revised edition. Illus. 260 pp. Galloway, 1974. $10.95.

BOOK OF THE ESKIMOS
Peter Freuchen
Paper. Fawcett, 1981. $2.95.

BOOK OF THE FOURTH WORLD: READING THE NATIVE AMERICAS THROUGH THEIR LITERATURE
Gordon Brotherstein
Illus. 494 pp. paper. Cambridge University Press, 1995. $24.95.

BOOK OF THE HOPI
Frank Waters
Reveals the Hopi view of life, kept secret for generations. Illus. 360 pp. Paper. Penguin USA, 1977. $9.95.

THE BOOK OF INDIAN CRAFTS & INDIAN LORE
Julian H. Salomon
A general discussion of the Indians of the U.S. Reprint. Illus. Biblio. Index. 418 pp. Gordon Press, $69.95.

THE BOOK OF THE NAVAJO
Raymond Friday Locke
Navajo history and legends. The Navajo's own history taken from the authentic Navajo "Singer" folktales & extensive historical and anthropological research. 5th Ed. Illus. 512 pp. Paper. Mankind Publishing, $6.95.

THE BOOK OF ONE TREE
Annette R. Schober
Fiction. Story of of the struggle many Native Americans have today as they cope with urban life. 64 pp. Northland Publishing, $9.95.

A BOOK OF TALES, BEING MYTHS OF THE NORTH AMERICAN INDIANS
Charles E. Woods
Reprint. Gordon Press, $59.95.

THE BOOK OF WOODCRAFT & INDIAN LORE
Ernest T. Seton
Illus. 590 pp. Paper. Stevens Publishing, 1994. $29.95.

A BOOKMAN'S GUIDE TO THE INDIANS OF THE AMERICAS
Richard A. Hand
A compilation of over 10,000 catalogue entries with prices and annotations. 764 pp. Scarecrow Press, 1989. $80.

BOOKS ON AMERICAN INDIANS & ESKIMOS
Mary J. Lass-Woodfin
American Library Association, 1977. Text edition, $25.

BOOKS WITHOUT BIAS: THROUGH INDIAN YES
Beverly Slapin & Doris Seale, Editors
Illus. 2nd Edition. 470 pp. Oyate, $25.

"BOOTS & SADDLES": OR, LIFE IN DAKOTA WITH GENERAL CUSTER
Elizabeth B. Custer
Reprint of the 1961 edition. Illus. Maps. 388 pp. Paper. University of Oklahoma Press, $12.95.

BORDER TOWNS OF THE NAVAJO NATION
Aaron Yava
Second edition. Illus. 80 pp. Paper. Holmgangers, 1975. $4.

BORDERLANDER: LIFE OF JAMES KIRKER, 1793-1852
Ralph Adam Smith
Indian fighter. Illus. Maps. Biblio. 416 pp. University of Oklahoma Press, 1999. $32.95.

BORN A CHIEF: THE NINETEENTH CENTURY HOPI BOYHOOD OF EDMUND NEQUATEWA, AS TOLD TO ALFRED F. WHITING
edited by P. David Seaman
193 pp. Paper. University of Arizona Press, 1993. $19.95.

BOSQUE REDONDO: A STUDY OF CULTURAL STRESS AT THE NAVAJO RESERVATION
Lynn R. Bailey
Illus. 275 pp. Westernlore, $8.50.

HENRY BOUCHA - STAR OF THE NORTH
Mary Halverson Schofield
Biography about a Native American Olympic & NHL hockey player. Photos. Paper. Snowshoe Press, $14.95.

BOUNDARIES BETWEEN: THE SOUTHERN PAIUTES, 1775-1995
Martha C. Knack
The history of the Southern Paiutes. Illus. Maps. 471 pp. University of Nebraska Press, 2001. $55.

BOUNDARIES & PASSAGES: RULE & RITUAL IN YUP'IK ESKIMO ORAL TRADITION
Ann Fienup-Riordan
Traditional Yup'ik rules and rituals. Illus. Maps. Biblio. 390 pp. Paper. University of Oklahoma Press, 1994. $19.95.

BOWS, ARROWS & QUIVERS OF THE AMERICAN FRONTIER
John Baldwin
Describes hundreds of bows, arrows, quivers, and bow cases. 40 photos. 96 pp. Writen Heritage, 1999. $69.95.

BOWS & ARROWS OF THE NATIVE AMERICANS
Jim Hamm
Illus. 156 pp. Paper. Hothem House & Written Heritage, 1989. $14.95.

*A BOY BECOMES A MAN AT WOUNDED KNEE
Ted Wood & Wanbli N. Afraid
Grades 3-7. Illus. 48 pp. Paper. Walker & Co., 1995. $6.95.

*THE BOY WHO DREAMED OF AN ACORN
Leigh Casler; illus. by Shonto Begay
Based on a Native American rite known as the Spirit Quest. Grades PS-3. Illus. 32 pp. Putnam, 1994. $15.95.

*THE BOY WHO LIVED WITH THE SEALS
Rafe Nartin; illus by David Shannon
A Chinook Indian tale about loss & redemption. Grades PS-3. Illus. 32 pp. Putnam, 1993. $14.95.

*THE BOY WHO MADE DRAGONFLY: A ZUNI MYTH
Tony Hilleman
Grades 4 and up. Illus. 21 drawings. 87 pp. Paper. University of New Mexico Press. $9.95

THE BOZEMAN TRAIL: HISTORICAL ACCOUNTS OF THE BLAZING OF THE OVERLAND BRAIDED LIVES: AN ANTHOLOGY OF MULTICULTURAL WRITING
Minnesota Humanities Commission, copiler
Illus. Paper. Minnesota Humanities Commission, 1992.

BRAID OF FEATHERS: AMERICAN INDIAN LAW & CONTEMPORARY TRIBAL LIFE
Frank Pommershein
Paper. University of California Press, 1997. $16.95.

THE BRAINERD JOURNAL: A MISSION TO THE CHEROKEES, 1817-1823
Joyce B. Phillips & Paul Gary Phillips, Editors
Illus. Maps. 586 pp. University of Nebraska Press, 1998. $70.

JOSEPH BRANT, 1743-1807: A MAN OF TWO WORLDS
Isabel Thompson Kelsay
Illus. Map. 792 pp. Paper. Syracuse University Press, 1996. $22.50.

MOLLY BRANT: A LEGACY OF HER OWN
Lois M. Huey & Bonnie Pulis
Paper. Smoke & Fire Co., $12.

JOSEPH BRANT: IROQUOIS ALLY OF THE BRITISH
Robert A. Hecht; D. Steve Rahmas, Editor
32 pp. SamHar Press, 1975. $3.95; paper, $2.50.

BRAVE ARE MY PEOPLE: INDIAN HEROES NOT FORGOTTEN
Frank Waters
Biographies and history. Illus. 180 pp. Clear Light, 1994. $24.95.

*BRAVE BEAR & THE GHOSTS: A SIOUX LEGEND
Grades 1-5. Illus. Paper. Troll Associates, 1992. $4.95.

BRAVE EAGLE'S ACCOUNT OF THE FETTERMAN FIGHT
Paul Goble, Writer & Illus.
Illus. 64 pp. Paper. University of Nebraksa Press, 1992. $9.95

BREAD & FREEDOM
Ted Zuern
160 pp. Paper. Tipi Press, 1991. $11.95.

BREAKING THE IRON BONDS: INDIAN CONTROL OF ENERGY DEVELOPMENT
Marjane Ambler
Tribal resource management. 352 pp. Illus. Maps. Paper. University Press of Kansas, 2001. $19.95.

BREAKING NEW GROUND FOR AMERICAN INDIAN & ALASKA NATIVE YOUTH AT RISK: PROGRAM SUMMARIES
Illus. 102 pp. Paper. Diane Publishing, 1995. $35.

BREATH OF THE INVISIBLE
John Redtail Freesoul
Illus. 226 pp. Paper. Theosophical Publishing House, 1986. $8.95.

BREATHTRACKS
Jeannette C. Armstrong
Poetry by an Okanagan author/artist. Illus. 112 pp. Theytus, 1991. $9.95.

A BRIEF HISTORY OF THE COEUR D'ALENE INDIANS, 1806-1909
Jerome Peltier
94 pp. Paper. Ye Galleon Press, $6.95.

A BRIEF HISTORY OF THE INDIAN PEOPLES
William W. Hunter
Ayer Co., $16.75.

A BRIEF HISTORY OF THE PEQUOT WAR
John Mason
Facsimile of 1736 edition. Ayer Co., $9.

A BRIEF & TRUE REPORT OF THE NEW FOUND LAND IN VIRGINIA
Thomas Harriot
Reprint of 1588 edition. Illus. 106 pp. Paper. Dover, $8.95.

BRIEFCASE WARRIORS: STORIES FOR THE STAGE
E. Donald Two-Rivers
Six plays presenting contemporary American Indian urban life. 298 pp. University of Oklahoma Press, $27.95.

THE BRIGHT EDGE: A GUIDE TO THE NATIONAL PARKS OF THE COLORADO PLATEAU
Stephen Trimble
Illus. 76 pp. Paper. Museum of Northern Arizona, 1979. $5.95.

BRINGING HOME ANIMALS: RELIGIOUS IDEOLOGY & MODE OF PRODUCTION OF THE MISTASSINI CREE HUNTERS
Adrian Tanner
St. Martin's Press, 1979. $27.50.

THE BRINGING OF WONDER: TRADE & THE INDIANS OF THE SOUTHEAST, 1700-1783
Michael P. Morris
176 pp. Greenwood Publishing, 1999. $55.

BRINGING THEM UNDER SUBJECTION: CALIFORNIA'S TEJON INDIAN RESERVATION AND BEYOND, 1852-1864
George Harwood Phillips
Illus. Maps. 384 pp. University of Nebraska Press, 2004. $59.95.

THE BROKEN CIRCLE
Rodney Barker
A true story of murder and magic in Indian country. 367 pp. 1992. Shenandoah Books, $24.50.

THE BROKEN CORD
Michael Dorris
Story about an Indian family's ordeal with "Fetal Alcohol Syndrome." 300 pp. Paper. Paper. Harper Perennial, Greenfield Review Press or Cherokee Publications, $11.

*BROKEN ICE
Hap Gilliland
Grades 1-8. 35 pp. Paper. Council for Indian Education, 1972. $8.95; paper, $2.95.

BROKEN PATTERN - SUNLIGHT & SHADOWS OF HOPI HISTORY
Vada Carlson
The intrusion of the Spanish; life of the Hopi. Illus. 208 pp. Paper. Naturegraph, $8.95.

THE BROKEN RING: THE DESTRUCTION OF THE CALIFORNIA INDIANS
Van H. Sarner
Illus. Westernlore, 1982. $13.95.

*BROTHER EAGLE, SISTER SKY
Susan Jeffers
Grades 4 and up. Text based on the famous Chief Seattle speech of the mid-1950's. Illus. 26 pp. Four Winds Trading Co., $15.

BROTHERHOOD TO NATIONHOOD: GEORGE MANUEL & THE MAKING OF THE MODERN INDIAN MOVEMENT
Peter McFarlane
Biography of George Manuel a prominent leader of Canada's modern Indian movemewnt. Paper. University of Toronto press, $15.95.

BROTHERS OF LIGHT, BROTHERS OF BLOOD: THE PENITENTS OF THE SOUTHWEST
Marta Weigle
Illus. 320 pp. Paper. Ancient City Press, 1988. $12.95.

SAMUEL J. BROWN IN CAPTIVITY
Samuel J. Brown
Details the capitivity by the Sioux Indians during the Massacre and War of 1862. Reprint. 37 pp. Paper. Ye Galleon Press, $4.95.

BRULE: THE SIOUX PEOPLE OF THE ROSEBUD
Paul Dyck
Reprint. Illus. Center for Western Studies, $50.

BRUSHED BY CEDAR, LIVING BY THE RIVER: COAST SALISH FIGURES OF POWER
Crisca Bierwert
314 pp. University of Arizona Press, 1999. $40.

BUCKSKIN HOLLOW REFLECTIONS
Maggie Culver Fry
Book of poetry by the author who was a former Oklahoma poet laureate. 95 pp. The Five Civilized Tribes Museum. $4.50.

THE BUCKSKINNER'S COOKBOOK
Over 200 authentice recipes of Indian, Canadian, Alaskan, etc. cooking; food at trading posts. Illus. The Fur Press, $5.

BUFFALO BIRD WOMAN'S GARDEN: AGRICULTURE OF THE HIDATSA INDIANS
Buffalo Bird Woman as told to Gilbert Wilson
Reprint of 1917 edition. Illus. 129 pp. Paper. Minnesota Historical Society Press, 1987. $8.95.

BUFFALO HEARTS
Sun Bear
An account of Native American history, culture, and religion from a Native viewpoint. Illus. 128 pp.Paper. Bear Tribe Publishing, 1976. $5.95.

BUFFALO HUMP & THE PENATEKA COMANCHES
Jodyce & Thomas Schilz
Illus. 78 pp. Texas Western Press, 1989. $12; paper, $7.50.

*BUFFALO HUNT
Russell Freedman
The Plains Indians and the buffalo. Grades 4-6. Illus. 52 pp. Holiday House, 1988. $18.95.

*BUFFALO & INDIANS ON THE GREAT PLAINS
Noel Grisham & Betsy Warren
Grades K-4. Illus. Eakin, 1985. $8.95.

*THE BUFFALO JUMP
Peter Roop; illus. by Bill Farnsworth
Native American tale. Ages 6-8. Illus. 32 pp. Northland, $14.95.

THE BUFFALO: THE STORY OF AMERICAN BISON & THEIR HUNTERS FROM PREHISTORIC TIMES TO THE PRESENT
Francis Haines
Illus. Biblio. Paper. University of Oklahoma Press, 1995. $14.95.

BUFFALO TIGER: A LIFE IN THE EVERGLADES
Buffalo Tiger & Harry A. Kersey, Jr.
Observations of Buffalo Tiger, the first tribal chairperson of the Miccosukees. Illus. Map. 184 pp. University of Nebraska Press, 2002. $27.95.

BUFFALO WOMAN COMES SINGING
Brooke Medicine Eagle
The Spirit Song of the Rainbow Medicine Woman. Illus. 495 pp. Paper. Ballantine Publishing, $12.50.

*BUILDING A BRIDGE
Lisa Shook Begaye; Illus. by Libba Tracy
Picture book. Ages 5-8. Illus. 32 pp. Paper. Northland, $7.95.

BUILDING A CHIPPEWA INDIAN BIRCHBARK CANOE
Robert E. Ritzenhaler
Second revised edition. 42 pp. Milwaukee Public Museum, 1984. $4.

BUILT LIKE A BEAR
James P. Dowd
Historical biography of the Illinois Indian chief, Shabbona, born about 1775, a friend of the whites in the Black Hawk War of 1831. 190 pp. Ye Galleon, 1979. $19.95.

BULL CREEK
Jesse D. Jennings and Dorothy Sammons-Lohse
Paper. University of Utah Press, 1982. $15.

BULLYING THE MOQUI
Charles F. Lummis; edited by Robert Easton & Mackenzie Brown
Reprints articles that Lummis published in "Out West" in 1903. Text is a story of the attempts to forcibly "civilize" the Hopi Indians of Arizona. Illus. 132 pp. Center for Anthropological Studies, $30.

THE BURDEN OF HISTORY: COLONIALISM & THE FRONTIER MYTH IN A RURAL COMMUNITY
Elizabeth Furniss
Ethnographic case study; Aboriginal land claims and place of Aboriginal people in Canadian society. 288 pp. UBC Press, 1999. $75.

BURIAL MOUNDS OF THE RED RIVER HEADWATERS
Lloyd A. Wilford
Illus. 36 pp. Paper. Minnesota Historical Society, 1970. $2.

BURIED ROOTS & INDESTRUCTIBLE SEEDS: THE SURVIVAL OF AMERICAN INDIAN LIFE IN STORY, HISTORY & SPIRIT
Mark A. Linquist & Martin Zanger
Illus. 160 pp. University of Wisconsin Press, 1995. $45; paper, $17.95.

BURY MY HEART AT WOUNDED KNEE: AN INDIAN HISTORY OF THE AMERICAN WEST
Dee Brown
Illus. 480 pp. Henry Holt & Co., 1971. $24.95. Juvenile edition. Demco, 1991. $20.

THE BUSINESS OF BENEVOLENCE: INDUSTRIAL PATERNALISM IN PROGRESSIVE AMERICA
Andrea Tone
Cornell University Press, 1997. $43.50.

THE BUSINESS OF FANCYDANCING
Sherman Alexie
Stories and poems. 84 pp. Hanging Loose Press, $18.00; paper, $10.

BUTTERFLY LOST
David Cole
A Hopi's granddaughter is missing. 373 pp. Paper. HarperCollins, 1999. $5.99.

*THE BUTTON BLANKET
Nan McNutt
Grades K-3. Illus. 2nd Edition. 45 pp. Paper. Workshop Publications, $7.95.

BY CANOE & MOCCASIN. SOME NATIVE PLACE NAMES OF THE GREAT LAKES
Basil Johnston
Illus. Greenfield Review Press, $10.95.

BY CHEYENNE CAMPFIRES
George B. Grinnell
A collection of war stories, mystery stories, tales of creation. Illus. 319 pp. Paper. University of Nebraska Press, 1971. $10.95.

BY THE POWER OF THE DREAMS: SONGS, PRAYERS & SACRED SHIELDS OF THE PLAINS INDIANS
Maureen E. Mansell
Illus. 96 pp. Chronicle Books, 1994. $16.95.

BY THE PROPHET OF THE EARTH: ETHNOBOTANY OF THE PIMA
L.S.M. Curtin
Reprint of 1949 edition. Illus. 156 pp. Paper. University of Arizona Press. $10.95.

C

THE CADDO CHIEFDOMS: CADDO ECONOMICS & POLITICS 700-1835
David La Vere
Map. 199 pp. University of Nebraska Press, 1998. $55.

THE CADDO INDIANS: TRIBES AT THE CONVERGENCE OF EMPIRES, 1542-1854
E. Todd Smith
Maps. 240 pp. Texas A&M University Press, 1997. $24.95.

CADDO INDIANS: WHERE WE COME FROM
Cecile Elkins Carter
Illus. Maps. 432 pp. University of Oklahoma Press, 1995. $50; paper, $19.95.

CADDO NATION: ARCHAEOLOGICAL & ETHNOHISTORIC PERSPECTIVES
Timothy K. Perttula
Illus. 352 pp. Paper. University of Texas Press, 1992. $19.95.

CADDO VERB MORPHOLOGY
Lynette R. Melnar
Illus. 244 pp. University of Nebraska Press, 2004. $75.

CADDOAN, IROQUOIAN & SIOUIAN LANGUAGES
Wallace L. Chafe
98 pp. Paper. Mouton de Gruyter, 1976. $20.

CADDOS, THE WICHITAS, & THE U.S., 1846-1901
E. Todd Smith
History of reservation life among the tribes. Maps. 198 pp. Texas A&M University Press, 1998. $29.95.

CAHOKIA & THE ARCHAEOLOGY OF POWER
Thomas E. Emerson
Paper. University of Alabama Press, 1997. $29.95.

CAHOKIA CHIEFDOM: THE ARCHAEOLOGY OF A MISSISSIPPIAN SOCIETY
George R. Milner
Illus. 216 pp. Smithsonian Press, 1998. $40.

CAHOKIA: CITY OF THE SUN
Mink, Iseminger, Corley
About Cahokia Mounds. Illus. Full color. 76 pp. Paper. Cahokia Mounds Museum Society, 1992. $9.95.

CAHOKIA: DOMINATION & IDEOLOGY IN THE MISSISSIPPIAN WORLD
Timothy R. Pauketat & Thomas E. Emerson, Editors
Essays. Illus. 360 pp. University of Nebraska Press, 1997. $60; paper, $25.

*THE CAHUILLA
Lowell Bean & Lisa Bourgeault
Grades 5 and up. Illus. 112 pp. Chelsea House, 1989. $17.95.

*THE CAHUILLA
Craig & Katherine Doherty
Grades 4-8. 32 pp. Rourke Publications, 1994. $22.60.

CAHUILLA DICTIONARY
Hansjakob Seiler & Kojiro Hioki
Paper. Malki Museum Press, 1979. $14.95.

CAHUILLA GRAMMAR
Hansjakob Seiler & Kojiro Hioki
Paper. Malki Museum Press, 1979. $12.

THE CAHUILLA INDIANS OF SOUTHERN CALIFORNIA
John L. Bean & Harry W. Lawton
Paper. Malki Museum Press, 1965. $2.

THE CAHUILLA LANDSCAPE: THE SANTA ROSA & SAN JACINTO MOUNTAINS
Lowell J. Bean, Sylvia Brakke Vane & Jackson Young
Illus. 116 pp. Ballena Press, 1991. $19.95; paper, $14.95.

CALENDAR HISTORY OF THE KIOWA INDIANS
James Mooney
Reprint of 1895 17th Annual Report of the BIA. Illus. 460 pp.
Paper. Smithsonian, $24.95.

CALIFORNIA
Robert F. Heizer, Editor
Illus. 800 pp. Smithsonian, $25.

CALIFORNIA ARCHAEOLOGY
Michael J. Moratto
Paper. Academic Press, 1984. $45.

CALIFORNIA'S CHUMASH INDIANS
Santa Barbara Museum of Natural History
Extracted from The Chumash Peoples. Illus.
72 pp. Paper. EZ Nature Books. $5.95.

CALIFORNIA INDIAN COUNTRY: THE LAND & THE PEOPLE
Dolan H. Eargle, Jr., Editor
A pictorial guide to contemporary Native American peoples and places of California. 1st edition. Maps. 180 pp. Paper. Trees Company Press, 1992. $10.

CALIFORNIA INDIAN NIGHTS ENTERTAINMENT
E. Gifford and G. Block, Compilers
Reprint of 1930 edition. Illus. 325 pp. Paper.
University of Nebraska Press, $9.95.

CALIFORNIA INDIAN SHAMANISM
Lowell J. Bean, Editor
Illus. 274 pp. Ballena Press, 1992. $33; paper, $27.50.

CALIFORNIA INDIAN WATERCRAFT
Richard W. Cunningham
Illus. Paper. E Z Nature Books, 1989. $12.95.

*CALIFORNIA INDIANS
C.L. Keyworth
Grades 5-8. Illus. 95 pp. Facts on File, 1990. $18.95.

*CALIFORNIA INDIANS: AN EDUCATIONAL COLORING BOOK
Linda Spizzirri & staff, Editors
Grades 1-8. Illus. 32 pp. Paper. Spizzirri Publishing, 1981.
Read & Coloring Book, $1.95; Cassette/book, $6.95.

CALIFORNIA INDIANS & THE ENVIRONMENT
News from Native California
Special Report #1. Greenfield Review Press, $5.

*CALIFORNIA'S INDIANS & THE GOLD RUSH
Clifford E. Trafzer
Grades 4-7. Illus. 60 pp. Paper. Sierra Oaks, 1990. $10.95.

CALIFORNIA INDIANS: PRIMARY RESOURCES
Sylvia Vane & Lowell J. Bean
A guide to manuscripts, artifacts, documents, serials, music, and illustrations. Illus. 300 pp. Paper. Ballena Press, 1990. $33.

*THE CALIFORNIA NATIVE AMERICAN TRIBES
Mary Null Boule
A series of 26 individual books on each tribe of California.
Pre-European tribal life of each tribe. Grades 2-6. Illus.
Paper. Merryant Publishers, boxed sets, $108.

CALIFORNIA'S GABRIELINO INDIANS
Bernice Johnston
Illus. 198 pp. Southwest Museum, 1962. $12.50.

CALIFORNIA INDIAN COUNTRY: THE LAND & THE PEOPLE
Dolan Eargle
Trees Co. Press, 1992.

CALIFORNIA INDIAN SHAMANISM
Lowell J. Bean & Sylvia B. Vane, Editors
Illus. 274 pp. Ballena Press, 1992. $ 33; paper, $27.50.

CALIFORNIA INDIAN WATERCRAFT
Richard Cunningham
A summary of all known forms of primitive water transport n the Indian Californias up to mid-19th century. Illus.128 pp. EZ Nature Books. $12.95.

CALIFORNIA JOE: NOTED SCOUT & INDIAN FIGHTER
Joe E. Milner & Earle R. Forrest
Illus. 400 pp. University of Nebraska Press, 1987.
$28.95; paper, $9.95.

*CALIFORNIA MISSIONS
Seven volume series examines California's early history. Organized regionally into siix volumes and a book on projects and layouts. An account of the establishment of the missions and their impact on existing cultures. Titles include: *Projects and Layouts* by Libby Nelson; *Missions of the Central Coast* by June Behrens; *Missions of the Inland Valleys* by Pauline Brower; *Missions of the Los Angeles Area* by Dianne MacMillan; *Missions of the Monterey Bay Area* by Emily Abbink; *Missions of the San Francisco Bay Area* by Tekla White; *Missions of the Southern Coast* by Nancy Lemke. Grades 4-7. Illus. Photos. Maps. 80 pp. each. Lerner, 1996. $17.95 each; paper, $9.95 each.

*THE CALIFORNIA NATIVE AMERICAN TRIBES
Mary N. Boule
Grades 1-8. Illus. Paper. Merryant Publishers, 1991.
$68.95; boxed edition.

CALIFORNIA PLACE NAMES: THEIR ORIGIN & ETYMOLOGY OF CURRENT GEOGRAPHICAL NAMES
Erwin G. Gudde
380 pp. University of California Press, 1998. $45

1500 CALIFORNIA PLACE NAMES: THEIR ORIGIN & MEANING
William Bright
Map. 172 pp. University of California Press, 1998. $12.95.

CALIFORNIA POWWOWs
Karen Doris Wright
Powwow dates and locations in the state of California.
Annual. 90 pp. California Powwow. $10.

*CALIFORNIA TRIBES
Ed Castillo
Grades 4-6. Two vols. Bellerophon Books, 1996. $3.95 each.

CALUMET & FLEUR-DE-LYS; ARCHAEOLOGY OF INDIAN & FRENCH CONTACT IN THE MIDCONTINENT
John Walthal & Thomas Emerson, Editors
Illus. 320 pp. Smithsonian Institution Press, 1992. $45.

CAMBRIDGE HISTORY OF THE NATIVE PEOPLES OF THE AMERICAS
Stuart Schwartz & frank Salomon, Editors
Illus. 1,500 pp. Cambridge University Press, 1998. $150.

CAMP BEALE'S SPRINGS AND THE HUALAPAI INDIANS
Dennis G. Casebier
Illus. 240 pp. Tales Mojave Rd., 1980. $18.50.

CAMPAIGNING WITH CUSTER & THE NINETEENTH KANSAS VOLUNTEER CAVALRY ON THE WASHITA CAMPAIGN, 1868-69
David L. Spotts
Illus. 215 pp. University of Nebraska Press, 1988.
$19.95; paper, $6.95.

CAMPAIGNING WITH KING: CHARLES KING, CHRONICLER OF THE OLD ARMY
Don Russell; Paul Hedrin, Editor
Illus. 215 pp. University of Nebraska Press, 1991. $25.

BEN NIGHTHORSE CAMPBELL
Herman J. Viola
Biography of the Native American, U.S. Congressman from Colorado. Illus. Random House, $23.

THE CAMPO INDIAN LANDFILL WAR: THE FIGHT FOR GOLD IN CALIFORNIA'S GARBAGE
Dan McGovern
Illus. 352 pp. University of Oklahoma Press, 1995. $26.95.

CAN THE RED MAN HELP THE WHITE MAN?
Sylvester M. Morey, Editor
130 pp. Illus. Paper. Myrin Institute, 1970. $3.50.

*CANADA: THE LANDS, PEOPLE, & CULTURES SERIES
Bobbie Kalman, Editor
4 vols. Canada: The Land; Canada: The People; Canada: The Culture; and Canada Celebrates Multiculturalism. Grades 3-9. Ilus. 32 pp. each. Crabtree, 1993. $20.60 each.

CANADA'S FIRST NATIONS: A HISTORY OF FOUNDING PEOPLES FROM EARLIEST TIMES
O.P. Dickason
Illus. Maps. 590 pp. University of Oklahoma Press, 1992.
$45; paper, $19.95.

CANADA'S INDIANS: CONTEMPORARY CONFLICTS
J. Frideres
Paper. Prentice-Hall, 1974. $12.95.

CANADIAN INDIAN POLICY: A CRITICAL BIBLIOGRAPHY
Robert J. Surtees
Illus. 120 pp. Paper. Indiana University Press, 1982. $4.95.

CANADIAN INDIAN POLICY & DEVELOPMENT PLANNING THEORY
Alain Cunningham
Garland Publishing,1998. $50.

THE CANADIAN IROQUOIS & THE SEVEN YEARS' WAR
D. Peter MacLeod
Looks at the social and economic impact of the war on both men and women in Canadian Iroquois communities. Illus. 300 pp. University of Toronto Press, 1996. $30.

CANADIAN NATIVE LAW CASES
Brian Slattery and Linda Charlton
Three volumes. Volume 1, 1763-1869, 478 pp, 1980, $50; Volume 2, 1870-1890, 634 pp., 1981, $65; Volume 3, 1891-1910, 663 pp., 1985, $65. Native Law Centre Publications.

CANADIAN PREHISTORY SERIES
Each book includes time charts, graphs, maps, photos and drawings which picture the life of native peoples of Canada before the arrival of Jacques Cartier. The titles are: Canadian Arctic Prehistory, by Robert McGhee, the prehistoric ancestors of the Inuit. 136 pp., $8.50; The Dig, by George MacDonald and Richard Inglis, the story of the Coast Tsimshian people. 102 pp., $7.50; Maritime Provinces Prehistory, by James A. Tuck, the story of the Micmacs nd Malecites. 112 pp., $12.95; Newfoundland and Labrador Prehistory, by James A. Tuck. 135 pp. $5.50; Six Chapters of Canada's Prehistory, by J.V. Wright. 118 pp. $5.50; Quebec Prehistory, by J.V. Wright. 128 pp. $5.50; Ontario Prehistory, by J.V. Wright. 132 pp. Paper. $5.50. Paper. National Museums of Canada.

THE CANADIAN SIOUX
James H. Howard
210 pp. University of Nebraska Press, 1984. $18.95.

T.C. CANNON: HE STOOD IN THE SUN
Joan Frederick in cooperation with Walter Cannon
Words & works of a contemporary Native American artist.
70 color & 15 bxw photos. 45 sketches. 224 pp. Northland, $40.

A CANNNONEER IN NAVAJO COUNTRY: JOURNAL OF PRIVATE JOSIAH M. RICE, 1851
Richard H. Dillon, Editor
Illus. Old West, 1970. $17.50.

THE CANOE ROCKS: ALASKA'S TLINGIT & THE EURAMERICAN FRONTIER, 1800-1912
Ted C. Hinkley
476 pp. University Press of America, 1995. $59.

CANOEING WITH THE CREE
Eric Sevareid
Reprint of 1935 edition. Illus. 206 pp. Paper.
Minnesota Historical Society, $6.95.

CANTE OHITIKA WIN (BRAVE-HEARTED WOMEN): IMAGES OF LAKOTA WOMEN FROM THE PINE RIDGE RESERVATION, SOUTH DAKOTA
Caroline Reyer
With the writings of Beatrice Medicine & Debra Lynn White Plume; photos by Thomas Gleason and Tom Casey. Illus. 90 pp. Dakota Press, $19.95; paper, $13.95.

CANYON DE CHELLY: ITS PEOPLE & ROCK ART
Campbell Grant
290 pp. Paper. University of Arizona Press, 1978. $19.95.

CANYON DE CHELLY: THE STORY BEHIND THE SCENERY
Charles Supplee, et al
Photos. Maps. 48 pp. Paper. KC Publications, $6.95.

CAPTAIN JACK, MODOC RENEGADE
Doris P. Payne
Illus. Paper. Binford & Mort, 1979. $9.95.

CAPTIVITY OF THE OATMAN GIRLS: AMONG THE APACHES & MOJAVE INDIANS
Royal B. Stratton
Reprint of 1857 edition. Illus. 240 pp. Paper.
University of Nebraska Press & Dover, $7.95.

CAPTIVITY TALES: AN ORGINIAL ANTHOLOGY
Reprint of 1974 edition. Illus. Ayer Co. Publishers, $20.

CAPTURED BY THE INDIANS: 15 FIRSTHAND ACCOUNTS, 1750-1870
Frederick Drimmer, Editor
180 pp. Paper. Hothem House & Smoke & Fire Co., 1985.
$9.95.

CAPTURED HERITAGE: THE SCRAMBLE FOR NORTHWEST COAST ARTIFACTS
Douglas Cole
Paper. University of Oklahoma Press, 1998. $16.95.

CAPTURED IN THE MIDDLE: TRADITION & EXPERIENCE IN CONTEMPORARY NATIVE AMERICAN WRITING
Sidner Larson
224 pp. University of Washington Press, 1999. $27.95.

CARBINE & LANCE: THE STORY OF OLD FORT SILL
Wilbur S. Nye
Reprint of the 1969 Centennial edition. Illus. Maps. 426 pp.
Paper. University of Oklahoma Press, 1997. $24.95.

KIT CARSON & HIS THREE WIVES: A FAMILY HISTORY
Marc Simmons
His biography finds his first wife was an Arapaho and his second wife was Cheyenne. He adopted several Indian children and was an Indian agent for many years. Illus. 224 pp. University of New Mexico Press, $24.95.

KIT CARSON & THE INDIANS
Thomas W. Dunlay
Biography. Illus. 537 pp. University of Neb. Press, 2000. $50.

STOKES CARSON: TWENTIETH-CENTURY TRADING ON THE NAVAJO RESERVATION
Willow Roberts
246 pp. University of New Mexico Press, 1987. $24.95; paper, $13.95.

CARTIER'S HOCHELAGA & THE DAWSON SITE
James Pendergast & Bruce Trigger
Illus. 470 pp. University of Toronto Press, 1972. $34.95.

CARTOGRAPHIC ENCOUNTERS: PERSPECTIVES ON NATIVE AMERICAN MAPMAKING & MAP USE
G. Malcolm Lewis, Editor
51 figures. 318 pp. University of Chicago Press, 1998. $60.

CARTOGRAPHIES OF DESIRE: CAPTIVITY, RACE, & SEX IN THE SHAPING OF AN AMERICAN NATION
Rebecca Blevins Faery
Illus. Biblio. 288 pp. Paper. University of Oklahoma Press, 1999. $18.95.

CARVED HISTORY: A GUIDE TO THE TOTEM POLES OF SITKA NATIONAL HISTORICAL PARK
Alaska Natural History Association.

CARVING THE NATIVE AMERICAN FACE
Terry Kramer
Offers the wood carver a method for creating realistic Native American faces in wood. 250 color photos. 64 pp. Paper. Schiffer Books. $12.95.

THE CASAS GRANDES WORLD
edited by Curtis F. Schaafsma & Carroll L. Riley
The history & meaning of the great site, covering Chihuahua, Sonora, New Mexico, Texas and Arizona. Illus. Maps. University of Utah Press. $60.

CASE & AGREEMENT IN INUIT
Reineke Bok-Bennema
308 pp. Mouton de Gruyter, 1991. $75.

THE CASE OF THE SENECA INDIANS IN THE STATE OF NEW YORK
Reprint of 1980 Edition. 366 pp. E.M. Coleman. $32.50.

A CASE STUDY OF A NORTHERN CALIFORNIA INDIAN TRIBE: CULTURAL CHANGE TO 1860
Robert M. Peterson
R & E Research Associates, 1977. $11.95.

CARLOS CASTANEDA, ACADEMIC OPPORTUNISM, & THE PSYCHEDELIC SIXTIES
Jay Courtney Fikes
Illustrates the chronic ignorance about Native American religions. 275 pp. Madison Books, 1992. $24.95; paper, $14.95.

CATAWBA NATION
Charles Hudson, Jr.
152 pp. Paper. University of Georgia Press, 1970. $8.50.

***THE CATAWBAS**
James H. Merrell
Grades 7-12. Illus. 112 pp. Chelsea House, 1989. $17.95.

CATCH THE WHISPER OF THE WIND
Cheewa James
Compilation of 70 quotations from U.S. and Canadian tribes, with an accompanying cassette of songs in original tribal languages. Illus. Revised edition. 128 pp. Cassette and book. BookWorld, 1994. $24.95; book only, $12.95.

CATHECHISM & GUIDE: NAVAHO-ENGLISH
Berard Haile
Reprint 1937 ed. Paper. St. Michaels Historical Museum, $3.

CATHLAMET ON THE COLUMBIA
Thomas N. Strong
New edition. Illus. 178 pp. Binford & Mort, 1981. $12.95.

GEORGE CATLIN
Joseph R. Millichap
Illus. Paper. Boise State University, 1977. $2.95.

THE GEORGE CATLIN BOOK OF AMERICAN INDIANS
Hassrick
Reproductions of Catlin's famous paintings. 48 color & 121 bxw illustrations. 203 pp. Hothem House, 1988. $35 postpaid.

CATLIN'S NORTH AMERICAN INDIAN PORTFOLIO
George Catlin
Reprint. Illus. Abbeville Press, 1989. $1,250.

CATLIN'S NORTH AMERICAN INDIAN PORTFOLIO: A REPRODUCTION
George Catlin
Reprint of 1845 edition. Ohio University Press, $250.

CATLINITE PIPES
Lars Hothem
Basic booklet on Catlinite pipestone and the smoking instruments made from it. 38 photos of Plains and related pipes. 48 pp. Paper. Hothem House, 1998. $8.95.

CAVALIER IN BUCKSKIN: GEORGE ARMSTRONG CUSTER & THE WESTERN MILITARY FRONTIER
Robert M. Utley
Illus. Maps. 250 pp. Paper. University of Oklahoma Press, 1991. $14.95.

***THE CAYUGA**
Grades K-4. Illus. 48 pp. Childrens Press, $11.45.

THE CAYUSE INDIANS: IMPERIAL TRIBESMEN OF THE OLD OREGON
Robert Ruby & John Brown
Illus. 350 pp. Paper. Pacific Northwest National Parks, 1989. $11.95.

CEDAR SMOKE ON ABALONE MOUNTAIN
Norla Chee
Poetry. 49 pp. Paper. The Falmouth Institute, 2001. $12.

CELEBRATE NATVE AMERICA! AN AZTEC BOOK OF DAYS
Richard Balthazar
Explains the complex Aztec count of days. Illus. 80 pp. Paper. Five Flower Press, $18.95.

***CELEBRATING THE POWWOW**
Bobbie Kalman
Grades 2 to 5. Illus. 32 pp. Paper. Crabtree, 1997. $19.96; paper, $5.95.

A CELEBRATION OF BEING
Susanne Page
Illus. 175 pp. Paper. Northland Press, $24.95.

CELILO TALES: WASCO MYTHS, LEGENDS, TALES OF MAGIC AND THE MARVELOUS
Donald M. Hines
Illus. 266 pp. Great Eagle Publishing. $21.95.

CELLULOD INDIANS: NATIVE AMERICANS & FILM
Jacquelyn Kilpatrick, Editor
Overview of Native American representation in film over the past century. Illus. 261 pp. Paper. University of Nebraska Press, 1998. $21.95.

CENTENNIAL CAMPAIGN: THE SIOUX WAR OF 1876
John S. Gray
Illus. Maps. 396 pp. Paper. University of Oklahoma Press, 1988. $18.95.

THE CENTRAL ESKIMO
Franz Boas
A record of Eskimo life in the 1880s. Reprint of 1884 edition. Illus. 280 pp. Paper. University of Nebraska Press, $9.95.

CENTURIES OF DECLINE DURING THE HOHOKAM CLASSIC PERIOD AT PUEBLO GRANDE
edited by David R. Abbott
Illus. 265 pp. University of Arizona Press, 2003. $47.50.

A CENTURY OF DISHONOR: A SKETCH OF THE U.S. GOVERNMENT'S DEALING WITH SOME OF THE INDIAN TRIBES
Helen Jackson
Reprint of 1888 edition. 552 pp. Paper. University of Oklahoma Press, $19.95.

CERAMIC PRODUCTION IN THE AMERICAN SOUTHWEST
Barbara J. Mills & Patricia L. Crown, Editors
376 pp. University of Arizona Press, 1995. $46.

CEREMONIES OF THE PAWNEE
James R. Murie; Douglas R. Parks, Editor
Reprint of 1981 edition. Illus. 500 pp. Paper. University of Nebraska Press, $19.95.

CEREMONY
Leslie Marmon Silko
A novel which captures the search for the identity of the American Indian. 262 pp. Paper. Penguin USA, $8.

***CEREMONY IN THE CIRCLE OF LIFE**
White Deer Autumn (Gabriel Horn)
A tale of how Little Turtle is visited by the Star Spirit and taught the mysteries of life through love & understanding pf Mother Earth & her four seasons. Grades 1-5. Illus. 32 pp. Levite of Apache, $14.95. Paper. Morning Flower Press & Beyond Words Publishing, $8.95.

CEV'ARMIUT QANEMCIIT QULIRAIT-LLU: ESKIMO NARRATIVES & TALES FROM CHEVAK, ALASKA
Anthony C. Woodbury, Editor
5 Chevak Yup'ik elders tell of traditional life, shamans, and history of the people of Chevak. Illus. 88 pp. Paper. University of Alaska Press, 1989. $9.

THE CHACO ANASAZI: SOCIOPOLITICAL EVOLUTION IN THE PREHISTORIC SOUTHWEST
Lynne Sebastian
Illus.195 pp. Cambridge University Press, 1992. $64.95; paper, $20.95.

CHACO CANYON: ARCHAEOLOGY & ARCHAEOLOGISTS
Robert & Florence Lister
Illus. 298 pp. Paper. University of New Mexico Press, $20.95.

CHACO CANYON: A CENTER & ITS WORLD
Photos by Mary Peck
Essays by Stephen H. Lekson, Simon Ortiz, & John R. Stein. Archaeological ruins of Chaco Canyon are portrayed and essays exploring Chaco's unique role in the Anasazi world. Illus. Maps. 80 pp. Paper. Museum of New Mexico Press, 2000. $24.95.

CHACO: A CULTURAL LEGACY
Michele Strutin
Color photos. 64 pp. Paper. Clear Light, $9.95.

CHACO CULTURE NATIONAL HISTORICAL PARK
David Peterson
Childrens Press, 1999. $21.50.

THE CHACO HANDBOOK: AN ENCYCLOPEDIC GUIDE
R. Gwinn Vivian & Bruce Hilpert
Related sites, place-names & architectural features. Illus. University of Utah Press. $55; paper, $17.95.

CHACO & HOHOKAM: PREHISTORIC REGIONAL SYSTEMS IN THE AMERICAN SOUTHWEST
Patricia Crown & W. James Judge
Illus. 380 pp. School of American Research, 1991. $35; paper, $15.95.

THE CHACO MERIDIAN: CENTERS OF POLITICAL POWER IN THE ANCIENT SOUTHWEST
Stephen H. Lekson
Illus. 256 pp. Paper. AltaMira Press, 1998. $23.95.

THE CHACOAN PREHISTORY OF THE SAN JUAN BASIN
R. Gwinn Vivian
525 pp. Academic Press, 1990. $85.

CHAHTA ANUMPA: A GRAMMAR OF THE CHOCTAW LANGUAGE (CD-ROM)
Marcia Haag & Loretta Fowler
CD-ROM. University of Oklahoma Press, 2001. $29.95.

CHAIN OF FRIENDSHIP: NORTH AMERICAN INDIAN TRADE SILVER
Carter
Study of historic silver objects made for, and treasured by, the Indians. Photos. Canadian edition. 256 pp. Paper. Hothem House, 1988. $23.95.

CHAINBREAKER: THE REVOLUTIONARY WAR MEMOIRS OF GOVERNOR BLACKSNAKE
Chainbreaker; Benjamin Williams & Thomas Abler, Editors
Illus. Maps. 310 pp. University of Nebraska Press, 1989. $35.

CHALLENGE: THE SOUTH DAKOTA STORY
Robert Karolevitz
Illus. 325 pp. Brevet Press, $19.95; paper, $12.95.

CHAMPIONS OF THE CHEROKEES: EVAN & JOHN B. JONES:
William G. McLoughlin
492 pp. Princeton University Press, 1989. $35.

CHANCERS: A NOVEL
Gerald Vizenor
Centered on the issue of repatriation of Native American skeletal remains. 168 pp. University of Oklahoma Press, 2001. $19.95; paper, $14.95.

CHANGING MILITARY PATTERNS OF THE GREAT PLAINS INDIANS
Frank R. Secoy
Historical study of tribal change, conflicts and movements. Maps. 120 pp. Paper. University of Nebraska Press, $7.95.

CHANGING NUMBERS, CHANGING NEEDS: AMERICAN INDIAN DEMOGRAPHY & PUBLIC HEALTH
National Research Council
Illus. 315 pp. Paper. National Academy Press, 1996. $49.

CHANGING PRESENTATION OF THE AMERICAN INDIAN: MUSEUMS & NATIVE CULTURES
W. Richard West, et al
Six prominent museum professionals examine the ways in which Indians and their cultures have been represented by museums in North America. Illus. 120 pp. University of Washington Press, 1999. $25.

CHANGING WOMAN: THE LIFE & ART OF HELEN HARDIN
Jay Scott
Native American art. 64 color & 10 bxw photos.
176 pp. Paper. Northland, $19.95.

*CHANT OF THE RED MAN
Hap Gilliland
A fable for Americans. Grades 7-adult. Illus. 84 pp. Paper.
Council for Indian Education, 1976. $10.95; paper, $4.95.

***CHARLES EASTMAN: PHYSICIAN, REFORMER,
& NATIVE AMERICAN LEADER**
Grades 4 and up. Illus. 128 pp. Childrens Press, $13.95.

*CHARLIE YOUNG BEAR
Katherine Van Ahnen & Joan Azure Young Bear
Grades K-3. 48 pp. Paper. Roberts Rinehart, 1994. $4.95.

*THE CHARM OF THE BEAR CLAW NECKLACE
Margaret Zehmer Searcy
2 Stone Age Indian siblings living in what is now the Southeastern U.S. Grades 3-8. Illus. 80 pp. Pelican Publishing,
$13.95; paper, $6.95.

**CHASING APACHES & YAQUIS ALONG
THE U.S. - MEXICAN BORDER, 1876-1911**
Shelley B. Hatfield
202 pp. University of New Mexico Press, 1998. $35.

**CHASING SHADOWS: APACHES & YAQUIS
ALONG THE U.S.-MEXICO BORDER, 1876-1911**
Shelley Bowen Hatfield
Illus. Maps. 216 pp. Paper. University of New Mexico Press,
1999. $15.95.

**CHEHALIS RIVER TREATY COUNCIL
& THE TREATY OF OLYMPIA**
Robert & Barbara Lane
75 pp. Institute for the Development of Indian Law, $15.

CHEMEHUEVI INDIANS OF SOUTHERN CALIFORNIA
Ronald Miller & Peggy Miller
Paper. Malki Museum Press, 1979. $2.

CHEM'IVULLU: LET'S SPEAK CAHUILLA
316 pp. Paper. UCLA, American Indian Studies Center, 1982.
$17.50.

*THE CHEROKEE
Emilie U. Lepthien
Grades K-4. Illus. 48 pp. Childrens Press, $11.45.

*THE CHEROKEE
Barbara McCall
Grades 5-8. Illus. 35 pp. Rourke Corp., 1989. $9.95.

*THE CHEROKEE
Theda Perdue
Grades 7-12. Illus. 112 pp. Chelsea House, 1988.
$17.95; paper, $9.95.

*CHEROKEE ABC COLORING BOOK
Daniel Pennington
Words in English & Cherokee characters with phoentic
pronunciations. Grades K-3. Paper. VIP Publishing &
Cherokee Publications, $5.

CHEROKEE ADAIRS
Mary Adair & Family members
A historical and genealogical book. 1,000+ pp. Illus.
Adair Reunion Assoc., 2003. $66.

**CHEROKEE AMERICANS: THE EASTERN BAND
OF CHEROKEES IN THE 20TH CENTURY**
John R. Finger
Illus. Maps. 250 pp. Paper. University of Nebraska Press, 1991.
$14.95

CHEROKEE ANIMAL STORIES
George F. Shear
Reprint. 80 pp. Paper. Clear Light & VIP Publishing. $7.95.

**CHEROKEE ARCHAEOLOGY:
A STUDY OF THE APPALACHIAN SUMMIT**
Bennie C. Keel
Illus. 290 pp. Paper. Cherokee Publications & University of Ten-
nessee Press, 1975. $14.95.

**CHEROKEE BY BLOOD: RECORDS OF EASTERN
CHEROKEE ANCESTRY IN THE CHEROKEE CROWN
OF TANNASSY**
William O. Steel
Sir Alexander Cuming's effort to charm the Cherokees into loy-
alty to England before the Revolutionary War. 162 pp. Chero-
kee Publications, $7.95.

**CHEROKEE BY BLOOD: RECORDS OF EASTERN
CHEROKEE ANCESTRY IN THE U.S. COURT OF
CLAIMS, 1906-1910**
Jerry Wright Jordan
Series presents detailed abstracts of those applications includ-
ing numerous verbatim transcriptions of affidavits by the appli-
cants. 8 vols. Heritage Books, 1988-1992. $25 each.

**THE CHEROKEE CASES: THE CONFRONTATION
OF LAW & POLITICS**
Jill Norgren
Paper. McGraw-Hill, 1995. $14.

**THE CHEROKEE CASES: TWO LANDMARK FEDERAL
DECISIONS IN THE FIGHT FOR SOVEREIGNTY**
Jill Norgren; foreword by Kermit L. Hall & Melvin I. Urofsky
Explores two landmark U.S. Supreme Court cases of the early
1830s. Maps. 224 pp. Paper. University of Oklahoma Press,
2004. $21.95.

**CHEROKEE CAVALIERS: FORTY YEARS OF CHEROKEE
HISTORY AS TOLD IN THE CORRESPONDENCE OF THE
RIDGE-WATIE-BOUDINOT FAMILY**
Edward E. Dale & Gaston Litton
Reprint of 1939 edition. Illus. Map. 320 pp. Paper.
University of Oklahoma Press, $15.95.

CHEROKEE CONNECTIONS
Myra V. Gormley
Revised edition.Illus. 64 pp. Paper. Family Historian Books,
1995. $9.95.

CHEROKEE COOKLORE
Contains many Cherokee recipes; chart of herbs; Cherokee
food preparation and a menu from a Cherokee Indian Feast.
Reprint of 1949 edition. Illus. 72 pp. Paper. VIP Publishing &
Cherokee Publications, $5.

**CHEROKEE DANCE:
CEREMONIAL DANCES & COSTUMES**
Donald Sizemore
How-to-do book. Color illus. 176 pp. Paper. Clear Light
& Written Heritage, $24.95.

CHEROKEE DANCE & DRAMA
Frank G. Speck & Leonard Broom
Reprint of 1951 edition. Illus. 112 pp. University of Oklahoma
Press, $9.95

CHEROKEE DICTIONARY
Durbin Feeling
Paper. VIP Publishing, $22.95.

CHEROKEE DRAGON: A NOVEL
Robert J. Conley
304 pp. Paper. University of Oklahoma Press, $14.95.

**CHEROKEE EDITOR: THE WRITINGS
OF ELIAS BOUDINOT**
Theda Perdue
256 pp. Paper. University of Georgia Press, 1996. $15.95.

**CHEROKEE-ENGLISH INTERLINER, FIRST
EPISTLE OF JOHN OF THE NEW TESTAMENT**
Ralph E. Dawson, III and Shirley Dawson
25 pp. Indian University Press of Oklahoma, 1982.
Spiral binding, $5.

**THE CHEROKEE EXCAVATIONS: HOLOCENE ECOLOGY
& HUMAN ADAPTATIONS IN NORTHEASTERN IOWA**
Duane C. Anderson and Holmes Semken, Editors
Academic Press, 1980. $54.50.

A CHEROKEE FEAST OF DAYS, 2 VOLS.
Joyce Sequichie Hifler
Philosophy & history of the Cherokee and other tribes.
2 Vols. 400 pp. each. Paper. Clear Light, $10.95 each.

**CHEROKEE FOLK ZOOLOGY: THE ANIMAL
WORLD OF A NATIVE AMERICAN PEOPLE**
Arlene Fradkin
Reprint. 583 pp. Garland Publishing, $10.

**THE CHEROKEE FREEDMEN: FROM
EMANCIPATION TO AMERICAN CITIZENSHIP**
Daniel F. Littlefield, Jr.
Greenwood Press, 1978. $35.

*CHEROKEE FUN & LEARN BOOK
J. Ed Sharpe
Grades 4-6. 20 pp. Cherokee Publications, 1970. $3.

THE CHEROKEE GHOST DANCE
William G. McLoughlin
525 pp. Mercer University Press, 1984. $34.95.

CHEROKEE GLOSSARY
Over 900 words with pronunciation guide.
VIP Publishing. $9.95.

CHEROKEE HERITAGE
Duane King, Editor
The official guidebook to the Museum of the Cherokee Indian.
Photos. 130 pp. Paper. Cherokee Publications, $4.

**THE CHEROKEE INDIAN NATION:
A TROUBLED HISTORY**
Duane H. King
Illus. 276 pp. University of Tennessee Press
& Cherokee Publications, 1979. $16.95.

**CHEROKEE LANGUAGE WORKBOOK
& INSTRUCTIONAL CASSETTE TAPE**
Prentice Robinson
30 pp. & cassette. Cherokee Publications, $25.

*CHEROKEE LEGENDS & THE TRAIL OF TEARS
Tom Underwood
Grades 4-12. Illus. 32 pp. VIP Publishing
& Cherokee Publications, 1956. $5.

***CHEROKEE LITTLE PEOPLE:
THE SECRETS OF THE YUNWI TSUNSDI**
Lynn Lossiah
Depicts the little people, elf-like beings of Cherokee life & cul-
ture. Grades 4 and up. Illus. 152 pp. Paper. Clear Light, $23.95.

CHEROKEE MESSENGER
Althea Bass
Illus. Map. 354 pp. Paper. University of Oklahoma Press, 1996.
$17.95.

CHEROKEE NATION CODE ANNOTATED
Reviewed by Joan S. Howland
New edition. Recodification of the Cherokee Nation statutes.
Contains tribal legislation passed through 1992. Two vols. West
Publishing, 1993. $55.

***CHEROKEE NATION VS. GEORGIA:
NATIVE AMERICAN RIGHTS**
Victoria Sherrow
Grades 6 and up. 128 pp. Enslow Publishers, 1997.

CHEROKEE NEW TESTAMENT
American Bible Society
In the Cherokee language. 408 pp. Paper.
Cherokee Publications, $3.95.

THE CHEROKEE NIGHT & OTHER PLAYS
Lynn Riggs
Plays by the only active American Indian dramatist during first
half of 20th century. 368 pp. Paper. University of Oklahoma
Press, 2003. $24.95; leather edition, $69.95.

**THE CHEROKEE PEOPLE: THE STORY OF THE
CHEROKEES FROM EARLIEST ORIGINS TO
CONTEMPORARY TIMES**
Thomas E. Mails
Illus. 368 pp. Paper. Written heritage, 1992. $26.95.

THE CHEROKEE PERSPECTIVE
L. French & J. Hornbuckle, Editors
The Cherokee today. Photos. 244 pp. Paper.
Cherokee Publications, $7.95.

CHEROKEE PLANTS
Hamel & Chiltoskey
Resource dictionary for plants and their uses by the Cherokee
in food, medicine & religion. Illus. 72 pp. Paper. VIP Publishing
& Cherokee Publications, $5.

**CHEROKEE PREHISTORY: THE PASGAH
PHASE IN THE APPALACHIAN SUMMIT REGION**
Roy S. Dickens, Jr.
Illus. 260 pp. University of Tennessee Press, 1976. $26.95.

THE CHEROKEE PERSPECTIVE
Laurence French & Jim Hornbuckle, Editors
Illus. 245 pp. Appalachian Consortium & Cherokee
Publications, 1981. $7.95.

A CHEROKEE PRAYERBOOK
Howard Meredith and Adeline Smith
44 pp. Paper. Indian University Press, 1981. $2.

**CHEROKEE PROUD: A GUIDE TO TRACING &
HONORING YOUR CHEROKEE ANCESTORS**
Tony Mack McClure
2nd Ed. 336 pp. Chu Nan Nee, 1999. $29.95; paper, $22.95.

CHEROKEE PSALMS, A COLLECTION OF HYMNS
J. Ed Sharpe; Daniel Scott, translated by
Illus. 33 pp. Cherokee Publications, 1991. $3.

CHEROKEE REMOVAL: BEFORE & AFTER
William L. Anderson, Editor
Maps. 176 pp. Paper. University of Georgia Press, 1991.
$12.95.

**CHEROKEE REMOVAL: THE WILLIAM PENN ESSAYS
& OTHER WRITINGS BY JEREMIAH EVARTS**
Francis P. Prucha, Editor
320 pp. University of Tennessee Press, 1981. $28.95.

CHEROKEE RENASCENCE, 1794-1833
William G. McLaughlin
472 pp. Princeton University Press, 1987. $29.50.

CHEROKEE ROOTS
Bob Blankenship
Trace your Cherokee ancestry. Includes over 15,000 name
entries from 1835 to 1924. Two vols. Vol. 1, Eastern Cherokee
Rolls (164 pp.), $12; and Vol. 2, Western Cherokee Rolls (306
pp.), $18. Paper. 1992. Both vols. $25. Also the 1898 Dawes

Roll "Plus", 275 pp. 1994. Paper, $25; and 1909 Gujon Miller
Roll "Plus", 62,769 names and related information. 225 pp.
1994. Paper, $30. Cherokee Roots, VIP Publishing & Heritage
Books.

CHEROKEE SONG BOOK
Agnes Cowen
A collection of favorite songs and hymns written in the Chero-
kee language. 112 pp. Paper. Cherokee Publications, $5.95.

**THE CHEROKEE STRIP LIVE STOCK ASSOCIATION:
FEDERAL REGULATION & THE CATTLEMAN'S
LAST FRONTIER**
William W. Savage, Jr.
Documents the role of federal governmental agencies in deal-
ing with both white ranhcers & Indian entrepreneurs. Illus. Map.
152 pp. Paper. University of Oklahoma Press, $14.95.

*CHEROKEE SUMMER
Diane Hoyt-Goldsmith
A proud Cherokee girl lives in two worlds. Grades 4-6. Illus.
32 pp. Holiday House, 1993. $15.95.

THE CHEROKEE TRAIL
O.K. Armstrong
260 pp. Paper. Indian University Press, 1994.
$18.50, postpaid.

**CHEROKEE TRAGEDY: THE RIDGE FAMILY
& THE DECIMATION OF A PEOPLE**
Thurman Wilkins
Reprint of 1970 revised second edition. Illus. Maps.
432 pp. Paper. University of Oklahoma Press, $16.95.

CHEROKEE VISION OF ELOH'
Howard Meredith & Virginia E. Milan;
Wesley Proctor, Translator
A legendary histor of the Cherokee people. Bilingual in Chero-
kee and English. 49 pp. Paper. Indian University Press, 1981.
$10.50, postpaid.

**CHEROKEE VOICES: ACCOUNTS
OF CHEROKEE LIFE BEFORE 1900**
Vicki Rozema
Cherokee life, customs and historical events during the 18th
century and first half of the 19th century. 128 pp. Paper. John
F. Blair, Publisher, 2002. $9.95.

**CHEROKEE WOMEN: GENDER
& CULTURE CHANGE, 1700-1835**
Theda Perdue
Examines the roles and responsibilities of Cherokee women
during the 18th & 19th centuries. 254 pp. Paper. University of
Nebraska Press, 1998. $15.95.

CHEROKEE WORDS
Mary Ulmer Chitoskey
A simplified, illustrated Cherokee/English dictionary.
72 pp. Paper. Cherokee Publications, $3.50.

THE CHEROKEES
Grace Steele Woodward
Reprint of 1963 edition. Illus. Maps. 376 pp. Paper.
University of Oklahoma Press, $18.95.

*THE CHEROKEES
Elaine Landau
Grades 5-8. Illus. 64 pp. Paper. Franklin Watts, 1992. $6.95.

**THE CHEROKEES & CHRISTIANITY, 1794-1870:
ESSAYS ON ACCULTURATION & CULTURAL
PERSISTENCE**
William G. McLoughlin; edited by Walter H. Comser, Jr.
Examines how the process of religious acculturation worked
wityhin the Cherokee Nation during the 19th century. 368 pp.
University of Georgia Press, 1994. $45.

CHEROKEES AT THE CROSSROADS
John Gulik
With a new chapter by Sharlotte N. Williams. The cultural patterns of the Eastern Cherokees during 1956-1958. 222 pp. Institute for Research in Social Science, 1973. $7.

CHEROKEES, AN ILLUSTRATED HISTORY
Billy M. Jones & Odie B. Faulk
Overview of the Cherokee people, 1735 to 1984. Illus.
166 pp. The Five Civilized Tribes Museum, 1984. $25.

**CHEROKEES IN TRANSITION: A STUDY OF CHANGING
CULTURE & ENVIRONMENT PRIOR TO 1775**
Gary C. Goodwin
Illus. Paper. University of Chicago, Dept. of Geography, 1977.
$10.

CHEROKEES & MISSIONARIES, 1789-1839
William G. McLoughlin
376 pp. Yale University Press, 1984. $37.50;. Paper.
University of Oklahoma Press, 1995. $18.95.

THE CHEROKEES OF THE SMOKEY MOUNTAINS
Horace Kephart
Photos. Map. 48 pp. Paper. Cherokee Publications, $3.50.

THE CHEROKEES - PAST & PRESENT
J. Edward Sharpe
Illus. 32 pp. VIP Publishing & Cherokee Publications, 1970.
$5.

THE CHEROKEES: A POPULATION HISTORY
Russell Thornton
Illus. Maps. 240 pp. Paper. University of Nebraska Press, 1990.
$18.95.

*CHEYENNE
Sally Lodge
Grades 5-8. Illus. 35 pp. Rourke Corp., $9.95.

*THE CHEYENNE
Dennis B. Fradin
Grades K-4. Illus. 48 pp. Childrens Press, 1988. $11.45.

*THE CHEYENNE
Stanley Hoig
Grades 7-12. Illus. 112 pp. Chelsea House, 1989.
$17.95; paper, $9.95.

*CHEYENNE AGAIN
Eve Bunting; illus. by Irving Toddy
Grades 4 and up. Illus. 32 pp. Clear Light, $14.95.

CHEYENNE & ARAPAHO MUSIC
Frances Densmore
Reprint of 1936 edition. 111 pp. Southwest Museum, $5.

**THE CHEYENNE & ARAPAHO ORDEAL: RESERVATION
& AGENCY LIFE IN THE INDIAN TERRITORY, 1875-1907**
Donald J. Berthrong
Illus. Maps. Biblio. 418 pp. Paper. University of Oklahoma Press,
1976. $17.95.

CHEYENNE AUTUMN
Mari Sandoz
The story of the Northern Cheyennes, who fled the reservation
in 1878 to return to their ancestral hunting grounds. Illus. Map.
290 pp. Paper. University of Nebraska Press, 1992. $14.95.

**CHEYENNE DOG SOLDIERS: A LEDGERBOOK
HISTORY OF COUPS & COMBAT**
Jean Afton, et al
Illus. 434 pp. University Press of Colorado, 1997.
$49.95; paper, $37.50.

***CHEYENNE FIRE FIGHTERS:
MODERN INDIANS FIGHTING FOREST FIRES**
Henry Tall Bull and Tom Weist
Grades 4-12. Paper. Council for Indian Education, 1973. $1.95.

**CHEYENNE FRONTIER DAYS, THE FIRST 100 YEARS:
A PICTORIAL HISTORY**
Illus. Wyoming Tribune-Eagle, 1996. $45.99.

CHEYENNE INDIANS, THEIR HISTORY & WAYS OF LIFE
George B. Grinell
Reprint of 1923 edition. Two vols: Vol. 1, 402 pp.; Vol. 2, 478
pp. Illus. Map. Paper. University of Nebraska Press, $15.95,
Vol. 1, $19.95, Vol. 2.

*CHEYENNE LEGENDS OF CREATION
Henry Tall Bull and Tom Weist
Grades 4-9. Paper. Council for Indian Education, 1972. $1.95.

CHEYENNE MEMORIES
John & Margot Liberty Stands in Timber
2nd Edition. Illus. 384 pp. Paper. Yale University Press,1998.
$16.

**CHEYENNE MEMORIES OF THE CUSTER FIGHT:
A SOURCE BOOK**
Richard G. Hardorff
Illus. Maps. 189 pp. Paper. University of Nebraska Press, 1998.
$10.

**THE CHEYENNE NATION:
A SOCIAL & DEMOGRAPHIC HISTORY**
John H. Moore
Illus. 390 pp. University of Nebraska Press, 1987. $32.50.

*CHEYENNE SHORT STORIES
Grades 3-8. 32 pp. Council for Indian Education, 1977.
$8.95; apper, $2.95.

*CHEYENNE WARRIORS
Henry Tall Bull and Tom Weist
Grades 2-12. 32 pp. Paper. Council for Indian Education, 1976.
$8.95; paper, $2.95..

**THE CHEYENNE WAY: CONFLICT & CASE LAW
IN PRIMITIVE JURISPRUDENCE**
Karl Llewellen and E. Adamson Hoebel
Reprint of 1941 edition. Illus. 375 pp. University of Oklahoma
Press, $37.95; paper, $19.95.

CHEYENNES AT DARK WATER CREEK
William Y. Chalfant
Cheyenne life on the southern plains. Illus. 256 pp.
University of Oklahoma Press, 1997. $27.95.

**CHEYENNES & HORSE SOLDIERS: THE 1857
EXPEDITION & THE BATTLE OF SOLOMON'S FORK**
William Chalfant; Illus,. by Roy Grinnell
Illus. 12 maps. 416 pp. University of Oklahoma Press, 1989.
$29.95.

THE CHEYENNES: INDIANS OF THE GREAT PLAINS
E. Adamson Hoebel
A portrait of the Cheyenne Indians. Second edition. 125 pp.
Paper. Holt, Rinehart, 1978. $9.95.

**THE CHEYENNES, MA HEO O'S PEOPLE:
A CRITICAL BIOGRAPHY**
Peter J. Powell
Illus. 160 pp. Paper. Indiana University Press, 1980. $4.95.

THE CHEYENNES OF MONTANA
Thomas Marquis; Tom Weist, Editor
Reference Publications, 1978. $19.95.

*THE CHEYENNES: PEOPLE OF THE PLAINS
Nancy Bonvillain
Grades 4-6. Illus. 64 pp. Millbrook Press, 1996. $21.90.

**THE CHICAGO AMERICAN INDIAN COMMUNITY,
1893-1988: AN ANNOTATED BIBLIOGRAPHY &
GUIDE TO SOURCES IN CHICAGO**
David Beck
Illus. 296 pp. Paper. Academy Chicago Publishers, 1989.
$39.95.

*THE CHICKASAW
Duane Hale
Grades 5 and up. Illus. Chelsea House, 1989. $17.95.

*THE CHICKASAW
Craig & Katherine Doherty
Grades 4-8. 32 pp. Rourke Publications, 1994. $22.60.

CHICKASAW: AN ANALYTICAL DICTIONARY
Pamela Munro & Catherine Willmond
The first scholarly dictionary of the Chickasaw language. Biblio.
540 pp. Paper. University of Oklahoma Press, 1994. $21.95.

CHICKASAW GLOSSARY
Albert S. Gatchet
Reprint of 1889 edition. VIP Publishing, $15.95.

THE CHICKASAWS
Arrell M. Gibson
Reprint of the 1971 edition. Illus. Maps. 339 pp.
Paper. University of Oklahoma Press, $19.95.

**CHIEF CORNPLANTER (GY-ANT-WA-KIA)
OF THE SENECAS**
Joseph A. Francello
277 pp. Glasco Publishing, 1998. $39.95.

CHIEF JOSEPH
Matthew Grant & Dan Zadra
Creative Education, 1987. $16.45.

**CHIEF JOSEPH COUNTRY:
LAND OF THE NEZ PERCE**
Bill Gulick
Reprint of 1981 edition. Illus. 27 maps. Biblio. 316 pp.
The Caxton Printers, $39.95.

CHIEF JOSEPH: GUARDIAN OF THE NEZ PERCE
Jason Hook
Illus. 52 pp. Sterling, 1989. $12.95.

*CHIEF JOSEPH & THE NEZ PERCES
Robert A. Scott
Grades 7-12. Illus. 144 pp. Facts on File, 1993. $17.95.

***CHIEF JOSEPH OF THE NEZ PERCE INDIANS:
CHAMPION OF LIBERTY**
Grades 4 and up. Illus. 130 pp. Childrens Press, $13.95.

**CHIEF JOSEPH & THE NEZ PERCES:
A PHOTOGRAPHIC HISTORY**
Bill & Jan Moeller
Photos. 96 pp. Paper. Mountain Press. $15.

**CHIEF JOSEPH'S ALLIES: THE PALOUSE
INDIANS & THE NEZ PERCE WAR OF 1877**
Richard D. Scheuerman
Illus. Paper. Sierra Oaks, 1987. $10.95.

***CHIEF JOSEPH'S OWN STORY AS TOLD
BY CHIEF JOSEPH IN 1879**
Foreword by Donald McRae
Autobiography. Grades 4 and up. 38 pp. Paper.
Ye Galleon Press, $5.95.

**CHIEF JUNALUSKA OF THE
CHEROKEE INDIAN NATION**
John F. Phillips
Biography. Illus. 90 pp. American Indian Books, 1988.
$9.00; paper, $6.

CHIEF LEFT HAND: SOUTHERN ARAPAHO
Margaret Coel
Biography. Illus. Maps. 338 pp. Paper. University of Oklahoma Press, 1981. $14.95.

*CHIEF PLENTY COUPS:
LIFE OF THE CROW INDIAN CHIEF
Flora Hatheway
Grades 4-12. 36 pp. Council for Indian Education, 1971. $8.95; paper, $2.95.

CHIEF POCATELLO, THE "WHITE PLUME"
Brugham D. Madsen
Illus. 142 pp. Paper. University of Utah Press, 1986. $6.95.

*CHIEF SARAH: SARAH WINNEMUCCA'S
FIGHT FOR INDIAN RIGHTS
Dorothy N. Morrison
Grades 4 and up. Illus. 195 pp. Paper.
Oregon Historical Society Press, 1990. $5.95.

CHIEF SEATTLE'S UNANSWERED CHALLENGE
John M. Rich
Speech delivered by Chief Seattle in Seattle. Reprint of 1970 edition. 61 pp. Paper. Ye Galleon Press, $9.95.

*CHIEF STEPHEN'S PARKY
Ann Chandonnet; Hap Gilliland, Editor
Historical fiction looks at 1898 Alaska and a year in the life of Athapascan Chief Stephen's wife, Olga. Grades 4 and up. Illus. 72 pp. Paper. Council for Indian Education & Roberts Rinehart, 1993 ed. $7.95.

CHIEF WASHAKIE
Mae Urbanek
Illus. 150 pp. Urbanek, $5.

CHIEFDOMS & CHEIFTAINCY IN THE AMERICAS
Elsa M. Redmond, Editor
416 pp. University Press of Florida, 1998. $55.

CHIEFLY FEASTS: THE ENDURING
KWAKIUTL POTLATCH
Aldona Jonaitis
Portait of Kwakiutl culture. Illus. 300 pp.
University of Washington Press, 1991. $60.

THE CHIEFS HOLE-IN-THE-DAY
OF THE MISSISSIPPI CHIPPEWA
Mark Diedrich
Legends recounting the lives of four generations of Chippewa leaders. Photos. Map. Biblio. 58 pp. Paper. Coyote Books, $14.95.

CHIEFS & WARRIORS: NATIVE NATIONS
Christopher Cardozo; Robert Janjigan, Editor
Illus. 96 pp. Callaway Editions, 1996. $13.95.

CHIHULY'S PENDLETONS
Chihuly
University of Arizona Press, $65.

*CHII-LA-PE & THE WHITE BUFFALO
John Nicholson
Adventures of a young Crow Indian boy. Grades 2-10.
44 pp. Paper. Council for Indian Education. $4.95.

A CHILD'S ALASKA
Claire Rudolf Murphy
Photos by Charles W. Mason. Children's photo-essay.
Grades K-4. Illus. Photos. 48 pp. Graphic Arts Center, $14.95.

CHILDHOOD & FOLKLORE: A PSYCHOANALYTIC
STUDY OF APACHE PERSONALITY
L. Bryce Boyer
Illus. Paper. Psychohistory Press, 1979. $10.95.

CHILDHOOD & YOUTH IN JICARILLA APACHE SOCIETY
Morris E. Opler
Reprint of 1946 edition. Illus. 180 pp. Paper. Southwest Museum, $5.

CHILDREN IN THE PREHISTORIC
PUEBLOAN SOUTHWEST
edited by Kathryn A. Kamp
Ethnographic evidence of children. Illus. Map. University of Utah Press. $35.

CHILDREN AT RISK: MAKING A DIFFERENCE THROUGH
THE COURT APPOINTED SPECIAL ADVOCATE PROJECT
Michael Blady
ILLUS. 318 pp. NCJW, 1982. Workbook, $7.50.

*CHILDREN INDIAN CAPTIVES
Roy D. Holt
Grades 4-7. Eakin Publications, 1980. $6.95.

THE CHILDREN OF AATAENTSIC:
A HISTORY OF THE HURON PEOPLE TO 1660
Bruce G. Trigger
An analysis of the internal dynamism of Huron culture. Reprint of 1976 edition. Illus. University of Toronto Press, $80; paper, $29.95.

CHILDREN OF THE CIRCLE
Adolf & Star Hungry Wolf
A photographic history of Native American children from 1870s to 1920s. Includes over 20 tribes from American West. 90 photos. 160 pp. Paper. Center for Western Studies, Written Heritage, The Book Publishing Co., $9.95.

CHILDREN OF COTTONWOOD: PIETY &
CEREMONIALISM IN HOPI INDIAN PUPPETRY
Armin Geertz & Michael Lomatuway'ma
Illus. 412 pp. University of Nebraska Press, 1987. $24.95; paper, $14.95.

CHILDREN OF THE DRAGONFLY: NATIVE AMERICAN
VOICES ON CHILD CUSTODY & EDUCATION
edited by Robert Bensen
Documents Native Americans' struggle for cultural survival in the face of placement of their children in residential schools and in foster or adoptive homes. 280 pp. University of Arizona Press, 2001. $47; paper, $19.95.

*CHILDREN OF THE EARTH & SKY: FIVE STORIES
ABOUT NATIVE AMERICAN CHILDREN
Stephen Krensky
Grades PS-3. 40 pp. Demco, 1991. $10.15. Paper. Scholastic, $4.99.

CHILDREN OF THE FIRST PEOPLE:
A PHOTOGRAPHIC ESSAY
Dorothy Haegart
Illus. 127 pp. Paper. Left Bank, 1984. $18.95.

CHILDREN OF THE FUR TRADE: FORGOTTEN
METIS OF THE PACIFIC NORTHWEST
John C. Jackson
342 pp. Paper. Mountain Press, $15.

CHILDREN OF GRACE: THE NEZ PERCE WAR OF 1877
Bruce Hampton
Illus. Maps. 407 pp. Paper. University of Nebraska Press, 2002. $19.95.

*CHILDREN OF THE MORNING LIGHT:
WAMPANOAG TALES AS TOLD BY MANITONQUAT
Story Medicine
Grades 1 and up. Illus. 80 pp. Macmillan, 1994. $16.95.

CHILDREN OF SACRED GROUND:
AMERICA'S LAST INDIAN WAR
Catherine Feher-Elston
Illus. 256 pp. Northland, 1988. $19.95.

CHILDREN OF THE SALT RIVER
Mary R. Miller
Paper. Resource Center for Language Semiotic, 1977. $11.

*CHILDREN OF THE TLINGIT
Frank J. Staub
Grades 4-7. Illus. Color photos. 48 pp. Lerner, 1999. $19.95.

CHILDREN OF THE TWILIGHT:
FOLK TALES OF INDIAN TRIBES
Emma-Lindsay Squier
Gordon Press, 1977. $34.95.

*CHILDREN'S ATLAS OF NATIVE AMERICANS
Provides an in-depth view of Native American cultures; origins, cliff dwellers and mound builders, and the great civilizations of Central & South America, e.g. Mayans, Aztecs, and Incas. Grades 3-7. Illus. Maps. 80 pp. Rand McNally, $14.95.

CHILIES TO CHOCOLATE: FOOD
THE AMERICAS GAVE THE WORLD
Nelson Foster & Linda Cordell, Editors
The foods Native Americans enjoyed before the arrival of the Europeans. 191 pp. Paper. University of Arizona Press, 1992. $14.95.

THE CHILKAT DANCING BLANKET
Cheryl Samuel
Illus. Map. Biblio. 234 pp. Paper. University of Oklahoma Press, 1982. $27.95.

CHILLS & FEVER: HEALTH & DISEASE
IN THE EARLY HISTORY OF ALASKA
Robert Fortuine
Illus. 395 pp. University of Alaska Press, 1989. $29.95.

CHINIGCHINICH
Geronimo Boscana
Malki Museum Press, 1978. $27.50.

CHINIGCHINIX, AN INDIGENOUS
CALIFORNIA INDIAN RELIGION
James R. Moriarty
Illus. Maps. 70 pp. Southwest Museum, 1969. $12.50.

CHINLE TO TAOS
R.C. Gorman
Exhibition catalog-retrospective of R.C. Gorman at the Millicent Rogers Museum in June 1988. Illus. 64 pp. Navajo Gallery, $20.

*CHINOOK
Jessie Marsh
Grades K-6. 32 pp. Paper. Council for Indian Education, 1976. $8.95; paper, $2.95.

CHINOOK: A HISTORY & DICTIONARY
Edward Thomas
Second edition. 184 pp. Binford & Mort, $12.95.

THE CHINOOK INDIANS: TRADERS
OF THE LOWER COLUMBIA RIVER
Robert H. Ruby & John A. Brown
Illus. Maps. 374 pp. Paper. University of Oklahoma Press, 1988. $19.95.

*THE CHINOOK - NORTHWEST
Clifford L. Trafzer
Grades 7-12. Illus. 112 pp. Chelsea House, 1990. $17.95.

*THE CHIPPEWA
Alice Osinski
Grades K-4. Illus. 48 pp. Childrens Press, 1987. $13.27; paper, $3.95.

CHIPPEWA & DAKOTA INDIANS
Subject catalog of books, pamphlets, periodical articles and manuscripts in the Minnesota Historical Society. 131 pp. Paper. Minnesota Historical Society, 1970. $7.50.

CHIPPEWA & THEIR NEIGHBORS:
A STUDY IN ETHNOHISTORY
Harold Hickerson; G. and L. Spindler, Editors
Reprint of the 1970 edition. 151 pp. Paper. Waveland Press, $9.50.

CHIPPEWA CHILD LIFE & ITS CULTURAL BACKGROUND
M. Inez Hilger
Reprint of 1951 edition. Illus. Photos. Biblio. 204 pp. Paper. Minnesota Historical Society, $10.95.

*CHIPPEWA CUSTOMS
Frances Densmore
Authoritative source for tribal history, customs, legends, traditions, art, music, economy & leisure activity of the Chippewa (Ojibway) Indians of the U.S. & Canada. Reprint of 1929 edition. Illus. Biblio. 204 pp. Paper. Minnesota Historical Society, $9.95.

CHIPPEWA FAMILIES: A SOCIAL STUDY
OF WHITE EARTH RESERVATION, 1938
M. Inez Hilger
Illus. 204 pp. Paper. Minnesota Historical Society, 1998. $12.95.

CHIPPEWA MUSIC
Francis Densmore
Reprint of 1911 & 1913 editions. 2 vols in 1. 110 pp.
Da Capo Press, $20.

CHIPPEWA TREATY RIGHTS: THE RESERVED
RIGHTS OF WISCONSIN'S CHIPPEWA INDIANS
IN HISTORICAL PERSPECTIVE
Ronald N. Satz
History of the Chippewa's treaty rights in Wisconsin. Illus. 272 pp. Paper. Wisconsin Academy of Sciences, 1994. $17.95. GLIFWC, 1991.

1826 CHIPPEWA TREATY WITH THE U.S. GOVERNMENT
Robert Keller
45 pp. Institute for the Development of Indian Law, $10.

THE CHIPPEWAS OF LAKE SUPERIOR
Edmund J. Danziger, Jr.
Illus. Maps. 264 pp. Paper. University of Oklahoma Press, 1979. $16.95.

*THE CHIPEWYAN
James G. Smith
Grades 5 and up. Illus. Chelsea House, 1989. $17.95.

THE CHIRICAHUA APACHE, 1846-1876: FROM WAR TO
RESERVATION
D.C. Cole
Illus. 225 pp. University of New Mexico Press, 1988. $32.50.

THE CHIRICAHUA APACHE PRISONERS
OF WAR: FORT SILL, 1894-1914
John A. Turcheneske, Jr.
Illus. 232 pp. University Press of Colorado, 1997. $32.50.

JESSE CHISHOLM: TEXAS TRAIL BLAZER
& PEACEMAKER
Ralph B. Cushman
Illus. 288 pp. Eakin Press, 1992. $22.95.

*CHOCOLATE CHIPMUNKS & CANOES:
AN AMERICAN INDIAN WORDS COLORING BOOK
written & illus. by Juan Alvarez
Grades Preschool-3. Illus. 32 pp. Paper.
Red Crane Books, 1991. $3.95.

*THE CHOCTAW
E. Lepthien
Grades K-4. Illus. 48 pp. Childrens Press, 1987. $11.45.

*THE CHOCTAW
Jesse O. McKee
Grades 5 and up. Illus. Chelsea House, 1989. $17.95.

*A CHOCTAW ANTHOLOGY, I & II
Papers written by Choctaw high school and college prep students on Choctaw history, culture and current events. Grades 7-12. Choctaw Heritage Press, I—$2.75; II—$7.00. $8.50/set.

THE CHOCTAW BEFORE REMOVAL
Carolyn K. Reeves, Editor
University Press of Mississippi, 1985. $27.50.

CHOCTAW CLAIMANTS & THEIR HEIRS
Joe R. Goss
193 pp. Paper. Oldbuck Press, 1995. $26.

CHOCTAW DICTIONARY
Cyrus Byington
Paper. VIP Publishing. $32.

CHOCTAW GENESIS, 1500-1700
Patricia Galloway
Illus. Maps. 413 pp. Paper. University of Nebraska Press, 1995. $30.

CHOCTAW LANGUAGE AWARENESS TEACHERS MANUAL
Developed in cooperation with Choctaw Nation. 112 pp. manual and 6 audio tapes. Grades K-3. VIP Publishing. $59.95.

CHOCTAW LANGUAGE & CULTURE: CHAHTA ANUMPA
Marcia Haag & Henry Willis; foreword by Grayson Noley
Illus. 400 pp. Paper. University of Oklahoma Press, 2001. $29.95

THE CHOCTAW LAWS
Reprint . Scholarly Resources, $11.

CHOCTAW LEGENDS WITH TEACHER'S GUIDE
With audio tape. VIP Publishing. $9.95.

CHOCTAW MUSIC
Frances Densmore
Reprint of 1943 edition. Illus. 110 pp. Da Capo Press, $22.50.

CHOCTAW MUSIC & DANCE
James H. Howard & Victoria Lindsay Levine
Discusses all aspects of Choctaw dances and songs.Illus. 30 musical transcriptions, 144 pp. Paper. University of Oklahoma Press, 1989. $13.95.

CHOCTAW VERB AGREEMENT & UNIVERSAL GRAMMAR
William D. Davies
Kluwer Academic, 1986. $48; paper, $19.50.

CHOCTAWS AT THE CROSSROADS: THE POLITICAL ECONOMY OF CLASS & CULTURE IN THE OKLAHOMA TIMBER REGION
Sandra Faiman-Silva
Illus. Maps. 285 pp. Paper. University of Nebraska Press, 1997. $24.

CHOCTAWS & MISSIONARIES IN MISSISSIPPI, 1818-1918
Clara Sue Kidwell
Explores how the Choctaws changed and adapted to U.S. policy of assimilation in their efforts to preserve their independence. Illus. 288 pp. Maps. Paper. University of Oklahoma Press, 1995. $14.95.

THE CHOCTAWS IN A REVOLUTIONARY AGE, 1750-1830
Greg O'Brien
Story of the Choctaws through the lives of Taboca and Franchimastabe, two leaders. Map. 160 pp. University of Nebraska Press, 2002. $45.

CHOTEAU CREEK: A SIOUX REMINISCENCE
Joseph Iron Eye Dudley
Growing up on the Yankton Sioux Reservation in South Dakota. 1993 Christopher Award Winner. Illus. 180 pp. Paper. University of Nebraska Press, 1992. $15.95.

CHRISTIAN HARVEST
Bill B. DeGeer
104 pp. Carlton Press, 1988. $8.95.

CHRISTIAN INDIANS & INDIAN NATIONALISM, 1855-1950: AN INTERPRETATION IN HISTORICAL & THEOLOGICAL PERSPECTIVES
George Thomas
271 pp. Peter Lang, 1979. $41.

CHRISTIANITY & NATIVE TRADITIONS: INDIGENIZATION & SYNCRETISM CHRONICLES OF AMERICAN INDIAN PROTEST
Antonio R. Gualtieri
The actual views of Arctic missionaries of various denominations. 200 pp. Cross Cultural Publications, $19.95.

CHRONICLES OF BORDER WARFARE: HISTORY OF THE SETTLEMENTS BY WHITES OF NORTHWESTERN VIRGINIA
Alexander S. Withers
Reprint of 1895 edition. Ayer Co., $36.

CHRONOLOGY OF THE AMERICAN INDIAN
Examination of Indian history. Revised edition. Illus. 300 pp. American Indian Publishers, 1994. $85.

CHRONOLOGY OF NATIVE NORTH AMERICAN HISTORY FROM PRE-COLUMBIAN TIMES TO THE PRESENT
edited by Duane Champagne
Details important people, places, and events in the history of Native peoples. 574 pp. The Falmouth Institute, 1994. $70.

TO THE CHUKCHI PENINSULA & TO THE TLINGIT INDIANS 1881/1882: JOURNALS & LETTERS BY AUREL & ARTHUR KRAUSE
translated by Margot Krause McCaffrey
The expedition that brought knowledge of southern Alaska and its people the Tlingit. Illus. Maps. 230 pp. Paper. University of Alaska Press, 1993. $17.50.

*THE CHUMASH
Robert O. Gibson
Grades 5 and up. Illus. 105 pp. Paper. Chelsea House, 1989. $9.95.

THE CHUMASH & COSTANOAN LANGUAGES
A.L. Kroeber
Reprint oif 1910 edition. 35 pp. Paper. Coyote Press, $4.06.

CHUMASH HEALING
Phillip L. Walker & Travis Hudson
Medical & healing practices of a California Indian tribe—the Chumash of the Santa Barbara area. Illus. 161 pp. Malki Museum Press, 1993. $16.95; paper, $12.95.

*CHUMASH INDIAN GAMES
Travis Hudson & Jan Timbrook
Reprint. Grades 2-6. Illus. 20 pp. Paper. Santa Barbara Museum, $4.95.

THE CHUMASH INDIANS OF SOUTHERN CALIFORNIA
Eugene Anderson
Paper. Malki Museum Press, 1973. $2.

THE CHUMASH PEOPLE
Santa Barbara Museum of Natural History
Revised reprint. Illus. 96 pp. EZ Nature Books. $12.95.

CHUMASH: A PICTURE OF THEIR WORLD
Bruce W. Miller, III
Illus. 144 pp. Paper. Sand River Press, 1988. $8.95.

THE CHUMASH & THEIR PREDECESSORS: AN ANNOTATED BIBLIOGRAPHY
Marie S. Holmes & John R. Johnson
240 pp. paper. Santa Barbara Museum, 1998. $32.50.

CHURCH PHILANTHROPY FOR NATIVE AMERICANS & OTHER MINORITIES
Phyllis A. Meiners, Editor
Profiles over 50 grant programs & more than 25 loan programs from church & religious institutions for Native American, Hispanic, and other minority groups. 11 denominations are included; each listing includes contact persons, special interests, sample grants, application deadlines & procedures, etc. CRC Publishing, 1994. $118.95.

CHURCHMEN & THE WESTERN INDIANS, 1820-1920
Clyde Milner, II, and Floyd O'Neil
Illus. Maps. 264 pp. University of Oklahoma Press, 1985. $28.95.

THE CIBECUE APACHE
Keith H. Basso
106 pp. Paper. Waveland Press, 1970. $8.50.

THE CIRCLE IS SACRED: A MEDICINE BOOK FOR WOMEN
Scout Cloud Lee
Guide to women's ceremonies. Includes aboriginal medicine woman, Alinta, Cherokee Princess Moon Feathers, Spider Red-Gold, and Seneca elder, Grandmother Kitty. 137 bxw photos. 256 pp. Paper. Clear Light, $17.95.

A CIRCLE OF NATIONS: VOICES & VISIONS OF AMERICA INDIANS
John Gattuso
Reflection of the lives of contemporary American Indians through the eyes of well known Indian writers & photographers including Paula Gunn Allen, Leslie Marmon Silko, Joy Harjo, Simon ortiz, White Deer of Autumn, David Neel, Monty Roessel & Ken Blackbird. Illus. 128 pp. Beyond Words Publishing, $39.95. Available in two-tape audiocassette, $15.95.

A CIRCLE OF POWER
William Higbie
Story of a Plains Indian boy seeking manhood. Illus. 90 pp. Eagle's View, 1991. $13.95; paper, $7.95.

*THE CIRCLE OF THANKS: NATIVE AMERICAN POEMS AND SONGS OF THANKSGIVING
Joseph Bruchac; Illus. by Murv Jacob
Thanksgiving prayers of 14 Native American cultures. Grades PreK-3. Illus. 32 pp. BridgeWater Books, 1997. $11.21.

*CIRCLE OF WONDER: A NATIVE AMERICAN CHRISTMAS STORY
N. Scott Momaday, writer & illustrator
Illus. 18 color photos. 44 pp. University of New Mexico Press, 2001. Book, $19.95; audio tape, $5.95; book & tape package, $24.95.

THE CIRCLE WITHOUT END: A SOURCEBOOK OF AMERICAN INDIAN ETHICS
Gerald & Francis Lombardi
Illus. 212 pp. Paper. Naturegraph, 1980. $8.95.

CIRCLES, CONSCIOUSNESS & CULTURE
James A. Mischke
Native American religious activities. Paper. Dine College Press, 1984. $2.50.

CIRCLES OF POWER
Ronald McCoy
Devoted to shields. Illus. 32 pp. Paper. Four Winds Trading Co., $6.

CIRCLES OF THE WORLD: TRADITIONAL ART OF THE PLAINS INDIANS
Richard Conn
Illus. 152 pp. Paper. Denver Art Museum, 1982. $14.95.

CLAIMING BREATH
Diane Glancy
Focuses on contemporary life of American Indians. 1993 American Book Award Winner. 119 pp. Paper. University of Nebraska Press, 1992. $12.

*CLAMBAKE, A WAMPANOAG TRADITION
Russell M. Peters
Grades 3-6. Illus. 48 pp. Lerner, 1992. $14.95.

*CLAMSHELL BOY: A MAKAH LEGEND
Terri Cohlene
Grades 1-5. Illus. Paper. Troll Associates, 1992. $4.95.

WILLIAM CLARK: JEFFERSONIAN MAN ON THE FRONTIER
Jerome O. Steffen
Reprint of 1977 edition. Illus. University of Oklahoma Press, $16.95; paper, $7.95.

CLASSIFICATION & DEVELOPMENT OF NORTH AMERICAN INDIAN CULTURES: A STATISTICAL ANALYSIS OF THE DRIVER-MASSEY SAMPLE
Harold E. Driver and James L. Coffin
Illus. Paper. American Philosophical Society, 1975. $15.

CLASSROOM ACTIVITIES ON WISCONSIN INDIAN TREATIES & TRIBAL SOVEREIGNTY
Ronald N. Satz
500 pp. Paper. Wisconsin Dept. of Public Instruction, 1995. $54.

CLOTHED-IN-FUR & OTHER TALES: AN INTRODUCTION TO AN OJIBWA WORLD VIEW
Thomas W. Overholt and J. Biard Callicott
198 pp. University Presses of America, 1982. $32.25; paper, $14.25.

*CLOUDWALKER: CONTEMPORARY NATIVE AMERICAN STORIES
Joel Monture; illus. by Carson Waterman
Grades 3 and up. Illus. 64 pp. Fulcrum Publishing, $15.95.

CLOWNS OF THE HOPI: TRADITION KEEPERS & DELIGHT MAKERS
Barton Wright; photos by Jerry Jacka
Looks at Hopi clowns, their purposes and historical backgrounds. Illus. 30 color photos. 148 pp. Northland Publishing, $14.95.

*CLUES FROM THE PAST: A RESOURCE BOOK ON ARCHAEOLOGY
Pam Wheat & Brenda Whorton, Editors
Grades 3 and up. Illus. 200 pp. Paper. Hendrick-Long, 1990. $17.95.

COAST SALISH
Reg Ashwell
Illus. 88 pp. Paper. Hancock House, $4.95.

THE COAST SALISH OF BRITISH COLUMBIA
Homer Barnett
Reprint of 1955 edition. Illus. 320 pp. Greenwood, $25.

*THE COAST SALISH PEOPLE
Frank W. Porter
Grades 5 and up. Illus. Chelsea House, 1989. $17.95.

COASTAL INDIANS: READY-TO-USE ACTIVITIES & MATERIALS
Dana Newmann
Illus. 200 pp. Paper. Center for Applied Research in Education, 1996. Teacher edition, $24.95.

COCHISE: CHIRICAHUA APACHE CHIEF
Edwin R. Sweeney
Biography of Cochise, the most resourceful & most feared Apache chief. Illus. Maps. Biblio. 502 pp. Paper. University of Oklahoma Press, 1991. $24.95.

THE COCHISE CULTURAL SEQUENCE IN SOUTHEASTERN ARIZONA
E.B. Sayles, et al
192 pp. Paper. University of Arizona Press, 1983. $15.95.

COCHITI: A NEW MEXICO PUEBLO, PAST & PRESENT
Charles H. Lange
Illus. 650 pp. Paper. University of New Mexico Press, 1990. $22.50.

*COCHULA'S JOURNEY
Virginia Pounds Brown
The effect of the Spanish entrada upon Southeastern Indian culture as told through a young Indian woman taken captive by Spanish explorer DeSoto in 1539. Grades 6-8. 160 pp. Black Belt Press, 1996. $18.

COCOPA ETHNOGRAPHY
William H. Kelly
A study of the Cocopa Tribe of the Colorado River Delta during the late 1880s. Paper. University of Arizona Press, 1977. $13.50.

CODE OF FEDERAL REGULATIONS, TITLE 25: INDIANS
U.S. Dept. of the Interior
Presents regulations relating to Native Americans administered by the U.S. Dept. of Interior in the areas of human services, education, tribal government, finance, land & water, energy & minerals, fish & wildlife, housing, heritage preservation, Indian arts & crafts, gaming, and relocation. 1,157 pp. Bernan Publciations, 2002. $60.

THE COEUR D'ALENE INDIAN RESERVATION
Glen Adams
Government documents between government and the Coeur d'Alene tribe describing the sale of about 185,000 acres of tribal land in 1898. Reprint. 92 pp. Paper. Ye Galleon Press, $9.95.

THE COEUR D'ALENE INDIAN RESERVATION &OUR FRIENDS THE COEUR D'ALENE INDIANS
Lawrence Palladino
Two booklets in one binding...facsimile 1967 ed. 46 pp. Ye Galleon Press, $7.95.

COEUR D'ALENE, OKANOGAN & FLATHEAD INDIANS
James Teit & Franz Boas
From the 45th annual report of the Bureau of American Ethnology, 1927-28. 382 pp. Ye galleon, $25.95; paper, $17.95.

COGEWEA, THE HALF-BLOOD
Mourning Dove
302 pp. Paper. University of Nebraska Press, 1981. $13.95.

FELIX S. COHEN'S HANDBOOK OF FEDERAL INDIAN LAW
Felix S. Cohen
Facsimile of 1942 edition. 950 pp. University of New Mexico Press, $25.

THE COLD-AND-HUNGER DANCE
Diane Glancy
The process and problems of language for modern Native authors. Illus. 114 pp. Paper. University of Nebraska Press, 1998. $17.95.

MICHAEL COLEMAN
Illus. Paper. University of Nebraska Press, 1979. $12.95.

THE COLLECTED WORKS OF EDWARD SAPIR
William Bright & Philip Sapir, Editors
Vol. V: American Indian Languages, 584 pp., 1990; Vol. VI: American Indian Languages, 559 pp. 1991; Vol. VII: Wishram Texts & Ethnography, 518 pp. 1990; Vol. X: Southern Paiute & Ute Linguistics & Ethnography, 932 pp. 1993. Mouton de Gruyter.

COLLECTING AUTHENTIC INDIAN ARTS & CRAFTS: TRADITIONAL WORK OF THE SOUTHWEST
IACA
Information on identifying and collecting contemporary Indian art. Color photos. 124 pp. Paper. Clear Light, $16.95.

COLLECTING INDIAN KNIVES
Lar Hothem, Editor
Reprint. Illus. 152 pp. Hothem House, 1986. $11.70 postpaid.

COLLECTING NATIVE AMERICA, 1870-1960
Shepard Krech, III & Barbara A. Hail
Photos. 288 pp. Smithsonian Institution Press, 1999. $45.

COLLECTING NORTH AMERICAN INDIAN KNIVES
Lar Hothem
Illus. 300 pp. Paper. Hothem House, 1986. $14.95.

COLLECTING THE NAVAJO CHILD'S BLANKET
Joshua Baer
Illus. 60 pp. Paper. Morning Star Gallery, 1986. $21.

COLLECTING SHAWNEE POTTERY: A PICTORIAL REFERENCE & PRICE GUIDE
Mark Supnick
Illus. 64 pp. Paper. M. Supnick, 1983. $12.95.

COLLECTING THE WEST: THE C.R. SMITH COLLECTION OF WESTERN AMERICAN ART
Richard H. Saunders
Illus. 224 pp. University of Texas Press, 1988. $35.

COLLECTIONS OF SOUTHWESTERN POTTERY
Allan Hayes & John Blom
Candlestickls to Canteens, Frogs to Figurines. Anasazi to Zuni. 52 color photos. Paper. Northland Press & Clear Light, $9.95.

COLLECTOR'S GUIDE TO INDIAN PIPES: IDENTIFICATION & VALUES
Lar Hothem
Study of American Indian pipes of all major classes. 1,000 photos, 700 in color. 225 pp. Paper. Hothem House & Collector Books, 1998. $29.95.

COLLECTIVE WILLETO: THE VISIONARY CARVINGS OF A NAVAJO ARTIST
Essays by Shonto Begay, Walter Hopps, Lee Kogan, and Greg Lachapelle; photos by Bruce Hucko. Illus. 120 pp. Museum of New Mexico Press, 2000. $45; paper, $29.95.

JOHN COLLIER'S CRUSADE FOR INDIAN REFORM, 1920-1954
Kenneth R. Philp
Commissioner of Indian Affairs under FDR, Collier rejected the idea of Americanizing Indians in favor of preserving their traditions. 304 pp. Paper. University of Arizona Press, 1977. $8.95.

COLONIAL DISCOURSES, COLLECTIVE MEMORIES, & THE EXHIBITION OF NATIVE AMERICAN CULTURES & HISTORIES IN THE CONTEMPORARY U.S.
C. Richard King
250 pp. Garland, 1998. $50.

COLONIAL INITMACIES: INDIAN MARRIAGE IN EARLY NEW ENGLAND
Ann Marie Plane
Cornell University Press, 2000. $45; paper, $17.95.

COLONIZING BODIES: ABORIGINAL HEALTH & HEALING IN BRITISH COLUMBIA, 1900-1950
Mary-Ellen Kelm
Looks at the impact of government policy on the health of native people. 272 pp. Paper. University of Washington Press, 1999. $25.95.

COLLOQUIAL NAVAJO: A DICTIONARY
Robert W. Young & William Morgan
A practical guide to colloquial terms and idiomatic expressions of the Navajo language. 461 pp. Paper. Hippocrene Books, 1994. $16.95.

THE COLORADO PLATEAU: THE LAND & THE INDIANS
K.C. Compton, Editor; photos by Tom Till & Stephen Trimble
An overview of the geology and the indigenous cultures of the Colorado Plateau region of Colorado, Utah, Arizona and New Mexico—the Four Corner states...members of the Pueblo, Ute, Navajo, Jicarilla Apache, and Paiute cultures. Inclndes historical photographs from museums and from the famous Pennington collection of Durango, Colorado. Illus. 86 pp. Thunder Mesa Publishing, 1999. $14.95.

*A COLORING BOOK OF AMERICAN INDIANS
Grades K-3. Paper. Bellerophon, $3.95.

*A COLORING BOOK OF HIDATSA INDIAN STORIES
Roberta Krim & Thomas Thompson
Grades K-3. 32 pp. Paper. Minnesota Historical Society Press, $3.50.

*COLORS OF THE NAVAJO
Emily Abbink
Introduces children to the history, traditions, and daily life of the Navajo. Grades 1-4. Illus. Map. Paper. Lerner, 1998. $5.95.

THE COLOUR OF RESISTANCE: A CONTEMPORARY COLLECTION OF WRITING BY ABORIGINAL WOMEN
Connie Fife
A collection of writing by 45 Native women from throughout North America , some of the strongest voices in Native literature. Paper. Sister Vision Press, 1993.

THE COLUMBIA GUIDE TO AMERICAN INDIANS IN THE SOUTHEAST
Theda Perdue
Columbia University Press, 2001.

COLUMBIA RIVER BASKETRY: GIFT OF THE ANCESTORS, GIFT OF THE EARTH
Mary Dodds Schlick
The material culture of the Columbia River region. Includes traditional designs and techniques of construction. Color photos. Illus. 240 pp. Biblio. Paper. Written Heritage, $35.

COLUMBUS & BEYOND: VIEWS FROM NATIVE AMERICANS
A look at Columbus by prominent Native writers including Paula Gunn Allen, Lee Francis III, Linda Hogan, Simon Ortiz, Carter Revard & Ray Young Bear. Southwest Parks & Monuments, $7.95.

*COLUMBUS DAY
Vicki Liestman; illus. by Rick Hanson
Grades K-3. Deals with the mistreatment of the Indians by Columbus & the Spaniards. Illus. 50 pp. Lerner, 1991. $15.95; paper, $5.95

COLUMBUS: HIS ENTERPRISE: EXPLODING THE MYTH
Hans Koning
Depicts Columbus for who he was and describes the consequences of his actions on the Native people and the environment. Monthly Review Press, 1991. $8.95.

COLUMBUS ON TRIAL
Anthology. A look at Coluiimbus and his crimes against Native society. Greenfield Review Pres, $10.

COLUMBUS & OTHER CANNIBALS
Jack Forbes
Collection of essays dealing with some past & contemporary problems that have come about & continued in America since Columbus. Published by Autonomedia. Available from Greenfield Review Press, $10.

*THE COMANCHE
Willard Rollings
Grades 7-12. Illus. 112 pp. Chelsea House, 1989. $17.95; paper, $9.95.

COMANCHE DICTIONARY & GRAMMAR
Lile Robinson & James Armagost
Paper. Summer Institute of Linguistics, 1990.

COMANCHE MOON: A PICTURE NARRATIVE ABOUT CYNTHIA ANN PARKER, HER TWENTY-FIVE YEAR CAPTIVITY AMONG THE COMANCHE INDIANS-AND HER SON QUANAH PARKER, THE LAST CHIEF OF THE COMANCHES
Jack Jackson
129 pp. Paper. Texas State Historical Association, 1979. $5.95.

COMANCHE POLITICAL HISTORY: AN ETHNOHISTORICAL PERSPECTIVE 1706-1875
Thomas W. Kavanagh
Illus. Maps. 586 pp. University of Nebraska Press, 1996. $47; paper, $20.

COMANCHE TREATIES DURING THE CIVIL WAR
R.J. DeMallie
30 pp. Institute for the Development of Indian Law, $10.

COMANCHE TREATIES: HISTORICAL BACKGROUND
R.J. DeMallie
20 pp. Institute for the Development of Indian Law, $7.50.

COMANCHE TREATIES OF 1835 WITH THE U.S.
R.J. DeMallie
20 pp. Institute for the Development of Indian Law, $7.

COMANCHE TREATIES OF 1846 WITH THE U.S.
R.J. DeMallie
16 pp. Institute for the Development of Indian Law, $6.50.

COMANCHE TREATIES OF 1850, 1851, 1853 WITH THE U.S.
R.J. DeMallie
60 pp. Institute for the Development of Indian Law, $12.50.

COMANCHE TREATIES WITH THE REPUBLIC OF TEXAS
R.J. DeMallie
20 pp. Institute for the Development of Indian Law, $7.50.

COMANCHE VOCABULARY
Manuel Garcia Rejon
106 pp. Paper. University of Texas Press, 1995. $25; paper, $10.95.

*COMANCHE WARBONNET
Troxey Kemper
Fiction. About famous Comanche chief Quanah Parker. Paper. Dine College Press, $12.50.

THE COMANCHERO FRONTIER: A HISTORY OF NEW MEXICAN-PLAINS INDIAN RELATIONS
Charles L. Kenner
History of the Comancheros, or Mexicans who traded with the Comanche Indians in the early Southwest. Illus. Maps. Biblio. 270 pp. Paper. University of Oklahoma Press, 1994. $15.95.

THE COMANCHES: A HISTORY, 1706-1875
Thomas W. Kavanaugh
In-depth historical study of Comanche social and political groups. Illus. 588 pp. Paper. University of Nebraska Press, 1999. $20.

COMANCHES IN THE NEW WEST, 1895-1908: HISTORIC PHOTOGRAPHS
Stanley Noyes, et al
Photos. 120 pp. University of Texas Press, 1999. $24.95.

THE COMANCHES: LORDS OF THE SOUTH PLAINS
Ernest Wallace and E. Adamson Hoebel
Reprint of 1952 edition. Illus. Map. 400 pp.
University of Oklahoma Press, $19.95.

COMANCHES & MENNONITES
ON THE OKLAHOMA PLAINS
Marvin E. Kroeber
Illus. 196 pp. Paper. Kindred Productions, 1997. $18.95.

"COME, BLACKROBE":
DE SMET & THE INDIAN TRAGEDY
John J. Killoren, S.J.
Evaluation of DeSmet, known as "Blackrobe," an evangelist
among the Coeur d'Alenes, the Flatheads, the Kalispels, the
Blackfeet, and the Kutenais. Illus. Maps. Biblio. 448 pp. Paper.
University of Oklahoma Press, 1994. $18.95.

*COME TO OUR SALMON FEAST
Martha F. McKeown
Grades 4-9. Illus. 80 pp. Binford & Mort, 1959. $7.95.

COMEUPPANCE AT KICKING HORSE CASINO
& OTHER STORIES
Charles Brashear
200 pp. Paper. UCLA, American Indian Studies Center, 2000.
$15. Also available from The Falmouth Institute.

COMMAND OF THE WATERS: IRON TRIANGLES,
FEDERAL WATER DEVELOPMENT, & INDIAN WATER
Daniel McCool
Reprint of 1987 edition. Illus. 321 pp. Paper.
University of Arizona Press, 1994. $19.95.

*THE COMING OF COYOTE
Donald J. Boon
Grades 4 and up. Illus. 64 pp. Paper.
American Literary Press, 1994. $9.95.

THE COMING OF THE SPIRIT OF PESTILENCE: INTRO-
DUCED INFECTIOUS DISEASES & POPULATION DECLINE
AMONG NORTHWEST COAST INDIANS, 1774-1874
Robert Boyd
Illus. Maps. 428 pp. Univ. of Washington Press, 1999. $50.

COMING TO LIGHT: CONTEMPORARY TRANSLATIONS
OF THE NATIVE LITERATURES OF NORTH AMERICA
edited by Brian Swann
Native American narratives and poetry. 525 pp. University of
Nebraska Press, $60; paper, $24.50.

THE COMMISSIONERS OF INDIAN AFFAIRS, 1824-1977
Robert Kvasnicka & Herman Viola
Discusses the leaders of the Bureau of Indian Affairs. Illus. Uni-
versity of Nebraska Press, 1977.

COMMON & CONTESTED GROUND: A HUMAN & ENVIRON-
MENTAL HISTORY OF THE NORTHWESTERN PLAINS
Theodore Binnema
History of northwestern plains between A.D. 200 and 1806.
Illus. Maps. 288 pp. University of Oklahoma Press, 2001.
$29.95.

COMMON THREADS: PUEBLO & NAVAJO
TEXTILES IN THE SOUTHWEST MUSEUM
Kathleen Whitaker
64 pp. Paper. Southwest Museum, 1998.

COMMONERS, TRIBUTE, & CHIEFS: THE DEVELOPMENT
OF ALGONQUIAN CULTURE IN THE POTOMAC VALLEY
Stephen R. Potter
Archaeological and documentary information on the
Indianpeoples who lived in the Potomac Valley from A.D. 200
to 1650. 280 pp. University Press of Virginia, 1993. $29.95.

COMMUNICATING EFFECTIVELY WITH
NON-INDIAN SERVICE PROVIDERS
A handbook for Indian parents that summarizes five effective
communication skills to use when talking with non-Indian professionals. Southwest Communication Resources, $10.00.

COMMUNICATION & DEVELOPMENT:
A STUDY OF TWO INDIAN VILLAGES
Y.V. Rao
Reprint of 1966 edition. Paper. Books on Deamnd, $38.

COMMUNITY-BASED RESEARCH:
A HANDBOOK FOR NATIVE AMERICANS
Susan Guyette
358 pp. Paper. UCLA, American Indian Studies Center, $15.

A COMPANY OF HEROES:
THE AMERICAN FRONTIER, 1775-1783
D. Van Every
Reprint of 1962 edition. Ayer Co. Publishers, $17.

COMPARATIVE HOKAN-COAHUILTECAN STUDIES
Margaret Langdon
Illus. 114 pp. Paper. Mouton, 1974. $58.50.

COMPARATIVE STUDIES IN AMERINDIAN LANGUAGES
Esther Matteson, et al
251 pp. Paper. Mouton, 1972. $55.75.

A COMPARATIVE STUDY OF LAKE IROQUOIAN ACCENT
Karin Michelson
Kluwer Academic, 1988. $89.

THE COMPLETE BOOK OF NATURAL SHAMANISM
Robert J. Titus
Snowbird Publishing Co., $11.45 postpaid.

THE COMPLETE BOOK OF SEMINOLE PATCHWORK
Beverly Rush & Lassie Wittman
Illus. 128 pp. Paper. Dover, $7.95.

THE COMPLETE GUIDE TO TRADITIONAL
NATIVE AMERICAN BEADWORK
Joel Monture
A definitive study of authentic tools, materials, techniques
& styles. Illus. Greenfield Review Press, $14.

THE COMPLETE HOW-TO BOOK OF INDIAN CRAFT
W. Ben Hunt
68 projects. Illus. 186 pp. Written Heritage, 1973. $13.95.

COMPLETE NATIVE AMERICAN RESOURCE LIBRARY:
READY-TO-USE ACTIVITIES & MATERIALS
Dana Newmann
4 vols. Coastal Indians; Desert Indians; Plains Indians, and
Woodland Indians. Illus. 200 pp. each; Paper. Center for Ap-
plied Research in Education. 1996. $24.95 each.

COMPLETING THE CIRCLE
Virginia Driving Hawk Sneve
Stories of Native American women. Illus. 120 pp.
University of Nebraska Press, 1995. $25; paper, $8.95

CONCERNING THE LEAGUE: THE IROQUOIS LEAGUE
TRADITION AS DICTATED IN ONONDAGA BY JOHN
ARTHUR GIBSON
Hanni Woodbury, Editor
Paper. Syracuse University Press, 1993. $80.

A CONCISE DICTIONARY OF MINNESOTA OJIBWE
John D. Nichols & Earl Nyholm
An expanded, revised edition. University of Minesota Press,
1994. $19.95; paper, $9.95.

A CONCISE DICTIONARY OF
INDIAN TRIBES OF NORTH AMERICA
Barbara Leitch et al; Keith Irvine, Editor
Revised 2nd edition. Reference Publications, 1995. $75.

CONCISE ENCYCLOPEDIA OF THE AMERICAN INDIAN
Bruce Grant
Over 800 entries covering legends, lore, weapons and wars,
beliefs, tools, information on each tribe. Illus. 352 pp. Cherokee Publications, 1989. $7.99.

THE CONCISE LAKHOTA DICTIONARY:
ENGLISH TO LAKHOTA
Cheyenne River Sioux Tribal Members
Features over 4,000 entries of words from the Lakhota dialect
of the ancient Sioux language. 70 pp. Paper. Todd Publica-
tions, 2000. $25.

CONFLICT & SCHISM IN NEZ PERCE ACCULTURATION
Deward Walker
Illus. 171 pp. Paper. University of Idaho Press, 1968. $10.95.

THE CONFLICT OF EUROPEAN & EASTERN ALGONKIAN
CULTURES, 1504-1700:STUDY IN CANADIAN CIVILIZATION
Alfred Bailey
Second edition. Paper. University of Toronto Press, 1969. $9.95.

CONFLICTING VISIONS IN ALASKA EDUCATION
Richard Dauenhauer
The education of Natives in Alaska. Published by Tlingit Read-
ers, Inc. 48 pp. Paper. University of Alaska Press, 1997. $6.50.

CONFOUNDING THE COLOR LINE: THE INDIAN-BLACK
EXPERIENCE IN NORTH AMERICA
Edited by James F. Brooks
Illus. Map. Univ. of Nebraska Press, 2002. $70; paper, $29.95.

CONOZCA SUS RAICES / KNOW YOUR ROOTS:
A MAP OF THE INDIGENOUS PEOPLES OF MEXICO
& CENTROAMERICA
Dolan H. Eargle, Jr., Editor
A full color, 18"x24" poster, bilingual - Spanish & English with
color-coded legend of contemporary ethnic homelands grouped
by linguistic families. Mexico to Panama. Biblio. Trees Com-
pany Press, $5.

THE CONQUEST OF THE KARANKAWAS
& THE TONKAWAS, 1821-1859
Kelly F. Himmel
Explores how geopolitical factors, economic factors and cul-
tural differences as a major cause of the groups' destructions.
224 pp. Texas A&M University Press, 1999. $32.95.

THE CONQUEST OF PARADISE: CHRISTOPHER
COLUMBUS & THE COLUMBIAN LEGACY
Kirkpatrick Sale
Reexamination of colonialism and its wake of ecological
destruction. 464 pp. Paper. Penguin USA, 1993. $12.95.

CONRAD WEISER & THE INDIAN
POLICY OF COLONIAL PENNSYLVANIA
Joseph S. Walton
Reprint of 1900 edition. Ayer Co., $34.95.

CONSERVATION & INDIAN RIGHTS
David W. Felder
48 pp. Paper. Wellington Press, 1996. $8.95.

CONSERVATISM AMONG THE IROQUOIS
AT THE SIX NATIONS RESERVE
Annemarie Shimony
Ethnography. Includes the practices of the Longhouse religion,
the events of the Iroquoian life cycle, the use of folk medicine,
witchcraft, and rituals of death & burial. 348 pp. Paper. Syracuse University Press, 1994. $18.95.

CONQUERING HORSE
Frederick Manfred
370 pp. Paper. University of Nebraska Press, 1983. $8.95.

CONQUEST & CATASTROPHE: CHANGING
RIO GRANDE PUEBLO SETTLEMENT
Elinore M. Barrett
Maps. 192 pp. University of New Mexico Press, 2001. $39.95.

CONQUEST OF APACHERIA
Dan Thrapp
Illus. 406 pp. Maps. University of Oklahoma Press, 1967.
$19.95.

CONQUEST OF THE KARANKAWAS
& THE TONKAWAS, 1821-1859
Kelly F. Himmel
224 pp. Texas A&M University Press, 1999. $32.95.

CONQUISTADOR IN CHAINS: CABEZA DE VACA
& THE INDIANS OF THE AMERICAS
David A. Howard
Illus. 240 pp. Paper. Universityof Alabama Press, 1997. $29.95.

CONSERVATISM AMONG THE IROQUOIS
AT THE SIX NATIONS RESERVE
Annemarie Shimony
Reprint. 344 pp. Paper. Syracuse University Press, $19.95.

CONSIDERATIONS ON THE PRESENT STATE
OF THE INDIANS & THEIR REMOVAL TO THE
WEST OF THE MISSISSIPPI
Lewis Cass
Reprint of 1828 edition. Ayer Co. Publishers, $13.50.

CONSPIRACY OF INTERESTS: IROQUOIS
DISPOSSESSION & THE RISE OF NEW YORK STATE
Laurence M. Hauptman
Photos. Maps. Biblio. 272 pp. Syracuse University Press, 1999.
$34.95.

THE CONSTITUTION & LAWS OF THE CHOCTAW NATION
Reprint. 3 vols. Scholarly Resources, $12.

CONSTITUTION, LAWS & TREATIES OF THE CHICKASAWS
Reprint. Scholarly Resources, $17.

THE CONSTITUTION OF THE FIVE NATIONS -
THE IROQUOIS BOOK OF THE GREAT LAW
Arthur C. Parker
Paper. The Greenfield Review Press, $5.95.

CONSTITUTIONALISM & NATIVE AMERICANS, 1903-1968
John R. Wunder, Editor
Reprint. Illus. 408. Garland, $77.

THE CONSTITUTIONS & LAWS
OF THE AMERICAN INDIAN TRIBES
This program presents the complete collection of the written
constitutions and laws of the American Indian tribes to 1906
when tribal governments in Indian territory were abolished. The
constitutions for the following tribes are included: The
Chickasaw, Osage, Cherokee, Choctaw, Muskogee, Creek, and
Sac and Fox. Two series. 53 volumes. See Scholarly Resources
for titles, descriptions and prices.

CONSUMER'S GUIDE TO SOUTHWESTERN
INDIAN ARTS & CRAFTS
Mark T. Bahti
Guide to determining the quality and authenticity of rugs, blankets, jewelry, and pottery. Includes buying tips, and a list of
hallmarks of well known silversmiths. Illus. 32 pp. Paper. Treasure Chest, $3.

THE CONSUMER'S RIGHTS UNDER WARRANTIES
Institute for Development of Indian Law, $3.50.

CONTEMPORARY AMERICAN INDIAN LITERATURES
& THE ORAL TRADITION
Susan Berry Brill de Ramirez
272 pp. University of Arizona Press, 1999. $42; paper, $20.95.

CONTEMPORARY ARCHAEOLOGY:
A GUIDE TO THEORY & CONTRIBUTIONS
Mark P. Leone, Editor
Illus. 476 pp. Paper. Southern Illinois Univ. Press, 1972. $17.95.

CONTEMPORARY ARTISTS & CRAFTSMEN OF THE CHEROKEE INDIANS
Illus. 145 pp. Qualla Arts & Crafts & Cherokee Publications, 1990. $9.95.

CONTEMPORARY FEDERAL POLICY TOWARD AMERICAN INDIANS
Emma R. Gross
165 pp. Greenwood Publishing, 1989. $39.95.

CONTEMPORARY INDIAN ART FROM THE CHESTER & DAVID HERWITZ FAMILY COLLECTION
Thomas W. Sokolowski
Illus. 88 pp. Paper. Grey Art Gallery Study Center, 1985. $15.

CONTEMPORARY INDIAN ARTISTS: MONTANA, WYOMING & IDAHO
Catalog of an exhibition presented at the Museum of the Plains Indian in Browning, Montana. Reviews the diversity of paintings by contemporary Indian artists of the Northern Plains region. Illus. Map. 80 pp. Northern Plains Indian Crafts Association, 1972. $7, postpaid.

CONTEMPORARY NATIVE AMERICAN AUTHORS: A BIOGRAPHICAL DICTIONARY
Kay Juricek & Kelly J. Morgan
320 pp. Fulcrum Publishing, $95.

CONTEMPORARY NATIVE AMERICAN CULTURAL ISSUES
edited by Duane Champagne
328 pp. AltaMira Press, 1998. $52; paper, $24.95.
Also available from The Falmouth Institute, $25.

CONTEMPORARY NATIVE AMERICAN POLITICAL ISSUES
Troy Johnson, Editor
328 pp. Alta Mira Press, 1998. $52; paper, $24.95.
Also available from The Falmouth Institute, $25.

CONTEMPORARY NAVAJO AFFAIRS
Norman Eck
243 pp. Navajo Curriculum, 1982. $15.

CONTEMPORARY NAVAJO WEAVING; THOUGHTS THAT COUNT
Ann Lane Hedlund
Discusses what it means to be a Navajo weaver, including history of the rugs, their designing and making, buying & collecting, and the future of weaving. Illus. 32 pp. Paper. Museum of Northern Arizona, $6.95.

CONTEMPORARY SOUTHERN PLAINS INDIAN METALWORK
Explores an important tradition of distinctive jewelry and ornamentation created of nickel-silver by modern tribal craftsmen of the Southern Plains region. Illus. Map. 80 pp. Catalog. Oklahoma Indian Arts & Crafts Cooperative, $8, postpaid.

CONTEMPORARY SOUTHERN PLAINS INDIAN PAINTING
An historic survey of contemporary painting by Indian artists of the tribally diverse Southern Plains region. Illus. Map. 80 pp. Catalog. Oklahoma Indian Arts & Crafts Coop., 1972. $7.

CONTENT & STYLE OF AN ORAL LITERATURE: CLACKAMAS CHINOOK MYTHS & TALES
Melville Jacobs
285 pp. University of Chicago Press, 1959. $17.50.

CONTEST FOR EMPIRE, 1500-1775
Essays by George Waller, James Brown, John Tepaske, George Rawlyk, Jack Sosin, and Thomas Clark. 95 pp. paper. Indiana Historical Society, 1975. $2.75.

CONTESTED GROUND: COMPARATIVE FRONTIERS ON THE NORTHERN & SOUTHERN EDGES OF THE SPANISH EMPIRE
Donna J. Guy & Thomas E. Sheridan, Editors
Indian-White relations. 275 pp. University of Arizona Press, 1998. $52; paper, $29.95.

CONTINENT LOST - A CIVILIZATION WON: INDIAN LAND TENURE IN AMERICA
J.P. Kinney; Dan C. McCurry & Richard E. Rubinstein, Editors
Reprint of 1937 edition. Illus. 336 pp. Ayer Co., $36.50.

CONTINENTS IN COLLISION: THE IMPACT OF EUROPE ON THE NORTH CONTINUITIES OF HOPI CULTURE CHANGE
Richard O. Clemmer
Paper. Acoma Books, 1978. $9.50.

CONTRACTS & YOU
Institute for Development of Indian Law, $3.50.

CONTRARY NEIGHBORS: SOUTHERN PLAINS & REMOVED INDIANS IN INDIAN TERRITORY
David La Vere
Illus. Map. 304 pp. University of Oklahoma Press, 2000. $21.95.

CONTRIBUTIONS TO ANTHROPOLOGY: SELECTED PAPERS OF A. IRVING HALLOWELL
A. Irving Hallowell
University of Chicago Press, 1976. $40.

CONTRIBUTIONS TO THE ARCHAEOLOGY & ETHNOHISTORY OF GREATER MESOAMERICA
William J. Folan, Editor
368 pp. Southern Illinois University Press, 1985. $28.95.

CONTRIBUTIONS TO THE ETHNOGRAPHY OF THE KUTCHIN
Cornelius Osgood
Reprint of 1936 edition. 190 pp. Paper. HRAF Press, $15.

CONVERGING CULTURES: ART & IDENTITY IN SPANISH AMERICA
Diana Fane
The Brooklyn Museum, 1996.

A CONVERSATIONAL DICTIONARY OF KODIAK ALUTIIQ
Jeff Leer, Editor
119 pp. Paper. Alaska Native Language Center, $4.

CONVERSATIONS WITH THE HIGH PRIEST OF COOSA
Edited by Charles M. Hudson
University of North Carolina Press, 2003.

CONVERSATIONS WITH LOUISE ERDRICH & MICHAEL DORRIS
Allan Chavkin & Nancy Feyl Chavkin, Editors
224 pp. University Press of Mississippi, 1994. $39.50; paper, $15.95.

CONVERTING THE WEST: A BIOGRAPHY OF NARCISSA WHITMAN
Julie Roy Jefffrey
Pioneer missionary to the Cayuse Indians of Oregon Territory. Illus. Maps. 238 pp. Paper. University of Oklahoma Press, $12.95.

COOKING WITH SPIRIT; NORTH AMERICAN INDIAN FOOD & FACT
Lisa Railsback & Darcy Williamson
Cookbook, healing guide & folklore anthology. Illus. 111 pp. Paper. Cherokee Publications & Four Winds Trading Co., $12.95.

COPING WITH THE FINAL TRAGEDY: DYING & GRIEVING IN CROSS CULTURAL PERSPECTIVE
David & Dorothy Counts, Editors
285 pp. Baywood , 1992. $34.95; paper, $24.95.

COPPER ARTIFACTS IN LATE EASTERN WOODLAND PREHISTORY
Goodman
Illus. 104 pp. Hothem House, 1984. $17.75 postpaid.

COPPER PALADIN: THE MODOC TRAGEDY
Walter H. Palmberg
Looks at some of the leading figures in one of the most costly Indian wars. 194 pp. Dorrance Publishing, 1982. $12.

THE COPPERS OF THE NORTHWEST COAST INDIANS: THEIR ORIGIN, DEVELOPMENT, & POSSIBLE ANTECEDENTS
Carol F. Jopling
Illus. Paper. American Philosophical Society, 1987. $25.

THE COQUILLE INDIANS: YESTERDAY, TODAY & TOMORROW
Roberta L. Hall
Illus. 250 pp. Paper. SSS Publishing, 1984. $9.95.

CORBETT MACK: THE LIFE OF A NORTHERN PAIUTE
Michael Hittman
Illus. Maps. 400 pp. Paper. University of Nebraska Press, 1996. $18.

CORN AMONG THE INDIANS OF THE UPPER MISSOURI
George F. Will and George E. Hyde; intro. by Douglas R. Parks
Originally published in 1964. Illus. 323 pp. Paper. University of Nebraska Press, 2002. $17.95.

CORN RECIPES FROM THE INDIANS
Frances G.W. Altney
Illus. 32 pp. Paper. Smoke & Fire Co., $5.

CORNHUSK BAGS OF THE PLATEAU INDIANS
Cheney Cowles Memorial Museum
Microfiche. Illus. University of Chicago Press, 1976. $36.

THE CORPORATE & FOUNDATION FUNDRAISING MANUAL FOR NATIVE AMERICANS
A step-by-step guide to securing private sector grants, outlining basic fundraising and research procedures. Helps Native American planners diversify their funding base with private sector dollars. 3rd Ed. 288 pp. Paper. CRC Publishing, 1996. $129.95.

THE CORPORATION & THE INDIAN: TRIBAL SOVEREIGNTY & INDUSTRIAL CIVILIZATION IN INDIAN TERRITORY, 1865-1907
H. Craig Minor
Illus. Map. 236 pp. Paper. University of Oklahoma Press, 1976. $14.95.

THE COSMOLOGY OF THE GITA
Institute for Indian Studies Staff, Editors
187 pp. Foundation for Classical Reprints, 1986. $127.45.

COUGAR WOMAN
Jane E. Hartman
Captured at age 10, she was keenly attuned to nature and her adopted tribe's struggle for survival. Illus. 188 pp. Paper. Clear Light, $16.

*COULD IT BE OLD HIARI
Marjorie Vandervelde
Grades 5-9. 30 pp. Council for Indian Education, 1975. $8.95; paper, $2.95.

COUNCIL FIRES ON THE UPPER OHIO
Randolph C. Downs
Illus. Paper. University of Pittsburgh Press, 1969. $8.75.

COUNCIL OF THE RAINMAKERS ADDRESS BOOK
David Dawangyumptewa, artist
24 paintings of Hopi artist David Dawanyumptewa's paintings. 110 pp. Northland Publishing, 1993. $12.95.

COUNSELING AMERICAN INDIANS
Laurence A. French
216 pp. Univ. Press of America, 1997. $52.50; paper, $32.50.

THE COUNSELLING SPEECHES OF JIM KA-NIPITEHTEW
Freda Ahenakew & H.C. Wolfart, Edited & tr. by
A highly respected orator speaks of his concern for young people and the proper performance of rituals. Paper. University of Toronto Press, 1998. $24.95.

A COUNTRY BETWEEN: THE UPPER OHIO VALLEY & ITS PEOPLES, 1724-1774
Michael N. McConnell
History of Indians in Upper Ohio Valley. Illus. Maps. 359 pp. University of Nebraska Press, 1992. $55; paper, $20.

*COURAGEOUS SPIRITS: ABORIGINAL HEROES OF OUR CHILDREN
Joann Archibald; editorial by Richard Wagamese
Grades 4 and up. Illus. 76 pp. Paper. Theytus, 1993. $9.95; teachers guide, $5.95.

THE COVENANT CHAIN: INDIAN CEREMONIAL & TRADE SILVER
Jaye Frederickson and Sandra Gibb
Reprint of 1980 edition. Illus. 168 pp. Paper. University of Chicago Press & Hothem House, $27.50.

THE COYOTE: DEFIANT SONGDOG OF THE WEST
Francois Leydet
Revised 1988 ed. Illus. 224 pp. Paper. University of Oklahoma Press, $11.95.

*COYOTE & THE FISH
Lorna Garrod
A Mimbre Indian trickster story tells how the first rainbow trout got its colors. Grades 3-7. Illus. 36 pp. Filter Prss, 1993. $4.

*COYOTE & THE GRASSHOPPERS: A POMO LEGEND
Terri Cohlene
Grades 4-8. Illus. 48 pp. Paper. Rourke Corp., Troll Associates & Clear Light, 1992. $4.95.

*COYOTE & KOOTENAI
Louie Gingras and Jo Rainboldt
Grades 2-6. Paper. Council for Indian Education, 1977. $1.95.

*COYOTE & LITTLE TURTLE
as told by Hershel Talashoema; edited & translated by Emory Sekaquaptewa & Barbara Pepper
A traditional Hopi tale. Grade 1-4. Illus. 95 pp. Clear Light, 1995. $14.95; paper, $9.95.

COYOTE MEDICINE: LESSONS FROM NATIVE AMERICAN HEALING
Lewis Mehl-Madrona
Simon & Schuster, 1997. $23.50.

*COYOTE & NATIVE AMERICAN FOLK TALES
Joe Hayes; illus. by Lucy Jelinek
10 tales about the origins of Native American myth & spirituality. Grades 4 and up. 80 pp. Paper. Clear Light, $11.95.

*COYOTE STEALS THE BLANKET: A UTE TALE
Janet Stevens
Grades K-3. Illus. 32 pp. Holiday House, 1993. $15.95; paper, $5.95.

*COYOTE STORIES
Mourning Dove
Reprint of 1933 edition. Grades 4 and up. Illus. 246 pp. University of Nebraska Press, 1990. $12.95.

*COYOTE STORIES FOR CHILDREN: TALES FROM NATIVE AMERICA
Susan Strauss; illus by Gary Lund
Coyote tales with true-life anecdotes about coyotes & Native wisdom. Grades 1-6. Illus. 50 pp. Beyond Words Publishing, $10.95; paper, $6.95.

*COYOTE TALES
Evelyn Dahl Reed
Collection of tales from the Indian Pueblos. Grades 4 and up.
64 pp. Paper. Sunstone Press, $8.95.

*COYOTE TALES OF THE MONTANA SALISH
as told by Pierre Pichette; transcribed by
Harriet Miller & Elizabeth Harrison
13 folk tales about the mischievous & amazing folk hero. Grades
4 and up. Illus. Maps. 80 pp. Paper. Northern Plains Indian
Crafts Association, 1972. $7, postpaid.

**COYOTE: A TRICKSTER TALE
FROM THE AMERICAN SOUTHWEST**
Gerald McDermott
Grades Pre-school to 3. Illus. 32 pp. Harcourt Brace. Dist.
by Meadowlark Communications, 1994. $14.95; paper, $6.

*COYOTE & THE WINNOWING BIRDS
as told by Eugene Sekaquaptewa; edited & translated
by Emory Sekaquaptewa & Barbara Pepper
A traditional Hopi tale. Grades 1-4. Illus. 100 pp.
Clear Light, 1995. $14.95; paper, $9.95.

**COYOTE WOMAN: A CONTINUING
JOURNAL OF MY LIFE AS AN ARTIST**
Tina Le Marque
8 color plates. 214 pp. Paper. Clear Light, $18.95.

**COYOTE'S COUNCIL FIRE: CONTEMPORARY
SHAMANS ON RACE, GENDER, & COMMUNITY**
Loren Cruden
Leading Native American and non-Native members of the
American shamanic community share their thoughts on bring-
ing shamanism into the modern era. 176 pp. Paper. Inner Tra-
ditions, $14.95.

*COYOTE'S POW-WOW
Hap Gilliland
Grades K-4. 31 pp. Paper. Council for Indian Education, 1972.
$8.95; paper, $2.95.

**COYOTEWAY: A NAVAJO HOLYWAY
HEALING CEREMONIAL**
Karl W. Luckert
Includes more than 100 photos, plus song and prayer texts.
Illus. 243 pp. Paper. University of Arizona Press, 1979. $13.95.

CRAFT MANUAL OF ALASKAN ESKIMO
George M. White
Eskimo culture and handcraft. 80 pp. paper. White Publishing,
$5.55.

***CRAFT MANUAL OF NORTH AMERICAN
INDIAN FOOTWEAR**
George M. White
Grades 4 and up. Includes 28 moccasin designs and patterns,
sewing instructions. 72 pp. Paper. White Publishing, 1992. $6.

CRAFT MANUAL OF NORTHWEST INDIAN BEADING
George M. White
Beading methods. Photos. 164 pp. paper. White Publishing,
$17.55.

CRAFT MANUAL OF YUKON TLINGIT
George M. White
Instructions for making dolls, snowshoes, moosehide boats,
woodcarvings and bonework. Short history. 56 pp. Paper. White
Publishing, $4.85.

***CRAFTS OF THE NORTH AMERICAN INDIANS:
A CRAFTSMAN'S MANUAL**
Richard C. Schneider
Grades 9-12. Reprint of 1972 edition. Illus. 325 pp.
Paper. R. Schneider, Publishers, $21.95.

**CRANIOMETRY OF SOUTHERN
NEW ENGLAND INDIANS**
Marian V. Knight
Reprint of 1915 edition. Paper. Elliots Books, $150.

**CRANIOMETRIC RELATIONSHIPS AMONG PLAINS
INDIANS: CULTURAL, HISTORICAL & EVOLUTIONARY
IMPLICATIONS**
Patrick J. Key
204 pp. Paper. University of Tennessee Press, 1983. $21.

**CRASHING THUNDER: THE AUTOBIOGRAPHY
OF AN AMERICAN INDIAN**
Paul Radin, Editor
250 pp. Paper. University of Nebraska Press, 1983. $8.95.

CRAZY HORSE
Larry McMurtry
Biography. 148 pp. High-Lonesome Books, 1999.$15.

*CRAZY HORSE
Judith St. George
An account of the Sioux Wars and the character of the Plains
people; and the life story of Crazy Horse. Grades 6 and up.
Illus. 192 pp. Putnam, 1994. $16.95.

CRAZY HORSE CALLED THEM WALK-A-HEAPS
Neil Baird Thompson
The story of the foot soldier in the Prairie Indian Wars.
Illus. North Star Press, $9.95.

**CRAZY HORSE & CUSTER: THE PARALLEL
LIVES OF TWO AMERICAN WARRIORS**
Stephen E. Ambrose
Illus. 544 pp. Paper. New American Library, 1986. $15.

CRAZY HORSE, HOKA HEY: IT IS A GOOD TIME TO DIE!
Vinson Brown
Personal study of Crazy Horse. 192 pp. Paper. Naturegraph,
$9.95.

**CRAZY HORSE & KORCZAK: THE STORY
OF AN EPIC MOUNTAIN CARVING**
Robb DeWall
Illus. 154 pp. Crazy Horse Memorial Foundation,
$15.95; paper, $7.95.

CRAZY HORSE MEMORIAL, 40TH ANNIVERSARY
Illus. Crazy Horse Memorial Foundation.

CRAZY HORSE: SACRED WARRIOR OF THE SIOUX
Illus. 52 pp. Sterling, 1989. $12.95.

CRAZY HORSE: THE STRANGE MAN OF THE OGLALAS
Mari Sandoz
50th Anniversary Edition. Illus. Map. 428 pp. Paper.
University of Nebraska Press, 1992. $14.95.

THE CRAZY HORSE SURRENDER LEDGER
Thomas R. Buecker, Editor
Illus. Paper. Nebraska State Historical Society, 1994.

CRAZY HORSE'S PHILOSOPHY OF RIDING RAINBOWS
Louis Hooban
Indian Heritage Publishing, 2001.

**CREATING CHRISTIAN INDIANS:
NATIVE CLERGY IN THE PRESBYTERIAN CHURCH**
Bonnie Sue Lewis
Illus. Maps. 304 pp. University of Oklahoma Press, 2003.
$34.95.

**CREATING & USING THE LARGER NATIVE AMERICAN
FLUTES**
Lew P. Price
Illus. Paper. Lew Paxton Price, 1998. $10.

**CREATING & USING THE NATIVE AMERICAN
CONCERT FLUTE**
Lew P. Price
Illus. 54 pp. Paper. Lew Paxton Price, 1996. $10.

**CREATING & USING THE NATIVE AMERICAN LOVE
FLUTE**
Lew P. Price
Illus. Paper. Lew Paxton Price, 1994. $10.

**CREATING & USING THE VERY SMALL NATIVE
AMERICAN FLUTES**
Lew P. Price
Illus. Paper. Lew Paxton Price, 1998. $12.

CREATION MYTHS OF PRIMITIVE AMERICA
Jeremiah Curtin
Ayer Co., 1980. $31.00.

***CREATION OF A CALIFORNIA TRIBE:
GRANDFATHER'S MAIDU INDIAN TALE**
Paper. Sierra Oaks Publishing, $6.95.

*CREATION TALES FROM THE SALISH
W.H. McDonald
Grades 3-9. Paper. Council for Indian Education,
1973. $1.95.

**CREATION'S JOURNEY: NATIVE AMERICAN
IDENTITY & BELIEF**
Tom Hill & Richard W. Hill, Sr.
Draws on the vast collections of the National Museum of the
American Indian to retell the story of native life from the Arctic
to the Tierra del Fuego. Illus. 256 pp. Smithsonian Institution
Press, 1994. $45.

CREATORS OF THE PLAINS
Thomas E. Mails; Anthony Meisel, Editor
Illus. 96 pp. Paper. Council Oaks Books, 1997. $10.95.

**CREE LEGENDS & NARRATIVES FROM
THE WEST COAST OF JAMES BAY**
told by Simeon Scott, et al; edited & tr. by C. Douglas Ellis
Annotated texts in James Bay Cree. University of Toronto Press,
1995. $75. Set of 6 cassette tapes, $65.

*THE CREEK
Michael D. Green
Grades 5 and up. Illus. 104 pp. Chelsea House, 1989. $17.95.

*CREEK CAPTIVES AND OTHER ALABAMA STORIES
Helen F. Blackshear; Illus. by Thomas Raymond

Actual events fro the early American (Southeastern Indians)
frontier and told from the viewpoint of a fictional young boy.
Grades 5-12. Illus. 112 pp. Paper. Black Belt Press, 1995. $9.95.

**CREEK INDIAN HISTORY: A HISTORICAL NARRATIVE OF
THE GENEALOGIES, TRADITIONS & DOWNFALL OF THE
ISPOCOGA OR CREEK INDIAN TRIBE OF INDIANS BY ONE
OF THE TRIBE**
George Stiggins; Virginia P. Brown, Editor
Illus. 160 pp. Birmingham Public Library, 1989. $24.95.

**CREEK INDIAN MEDICINE WAYS:
THE ENDURING POWER OF MVSKOKE RELIGION**
David Lewis, Jr. & Ann T. Jordan
Illus. 224 pp. University of New Mexico Press, $29.95

**CREEK (MUSKOGEE)
NEW TESTAMENT CONCORDANCE**
Lee Chupco, Rev. Ward Coachman, et al
The first New Testamint Concordance printed for an American
Indian language. 167 pp. Indian University Press, 1982. $11,
postpaid.

CREEK RELIGION & MEDICINE
John R. Swanton; intro. by James T. Carson
Reprint. Illus. 213 pp. Paper. University of Nebraska Press,
2000. $45.

THE CREEK VERB
Henry O. Harwell & Deloris T. Harwell
A linguistic study of the Creek (Muskogee) verb and grammar.
57 pp. Indian University Press, 1981. $8.50, postpaid.

**A CREEK WARRIOR FOR THE CONFEDERACY:
THE AUTOBIOGRAPHY OF CHIEF G.W. GRAYSON**
G.W. Grayson; W. David Baird, Editor
Illus. Maps. 182 pp. Paper. University of Oklahoma Press, 1988.
$15.95.

**CREEKS & SEMINOLES: THE DESTRUCTION &
REGENERATION OF THE MUSCOGULGE PEOPLE**
J. Leitch Wright, Jr.
Illus. Maps. 383 pp. Paper. University of Nebraska Press, 1987.
$19.95.

**THE CRESCENT HILLS
PRHISTORIC QUARRYING AREA**
David J. Ives
35 pp. Paper. Museum of Anthropology,
University of Missouri, 1975. $1.80.

***CRICKETS & CORN: FIVE STORIES ABOUT
NATIVE NORTH AMERICAN CHILDREN**
Peg Black
Five Native American children make important discoveries
about it means to be Native people. paper. Friendship Press,
$3.50.

**CRIMINAL JURISDICTION ALLOCATION
IN INDIAN COUNTRY**
Ronald B. Flowers
126 pp. Associate Faculty Press, 1983. $17.50.

CRIMSONED PRAIRIE: THE INDIAN WARS
S.L. Marshall
Reprint of 1972 edition. Illus. 285 pp. Paper.
Da Capo Press, $10.95.

**CRITICAL FICTIONS: THE POLITICS OF
IMAGINATIVE WIRITING**
Philomena Mariani, Editor
292 p. Paper. Bay Press, $15.95.

**THE CROOKED STOVEPIPE: ATHAPASKAN FIDDLE
MUSIC & SQUARE DANCING IN NORTHEAST ALASKA
& NORTHWEST CANADA**
Craig Mishler
Illus. 248 pp. University of Illinois Press, 1993. $29.95.

**CROOKED TREE: INDIAN LEGENDS
OF NORTHERN MICHIGAN**
John Wright
Reprint. 2nd edition. Illus. 170 pp. Paper.
Tunder Bay Press, 1996. $15.95.

**CROSSBLOODS: BONE COURTS, BINGO,
& OTHER REPORTS**
Gerald Vizenor
From reservation treaties to cultural schizophrenia and the rise
of the American Indian Movement. Illus. 335 pp. University of
Minnesota Press, 1990. $34.95; paper, $14.95.

**CROSSCURRENTS ALONG THE COLORADO: THE IMPACT
OF GOVERNMENT POLICY ON THE QUECHEN INDIANS**
Robert Bee
184 pp. Paper. University of Arizona Press, 1981. $7.50.

**CROSSING THE POND: THE NATIVE AMERICAN
EFFORT IN WORLD WAR II**
Jere Bishop Franco
Photos. 336 pp. Texas A&M University Press, 1999. $29.95.

CROSSROADS ALASKA, NATIVE CULTURES OF ALASKA & SIBERIA
Valerie Chaussonnet
Photos. 112 pp. Paper. Smithsonian Inst. Press, 1995. $24.95.

*THE CROW
Frederick E. Hoxie
Grades 5 and up. Illus. Chelsea House, 1989. $17.95.

*THE CROW
Ruth Hagman
Grades K-4. Illus. 50 pp. Childrens Press, 1990.
$14.60; paper, $4.95.

*THE CROW
Craig & Katherine Doherty
Grades 4-8. 32 pp. Rourke Publications, 1994. $22.60.

*CROW CHIEF
Paul Goble
Grades PS-3. Illus. 32 pp. Orchard Books, $15.

*CROW CHILDREN & ELDERS TALK TOGETHER
Barrie E. Kavasch
Grades 4 and up. Rosen Group, 1998. $18.

CROW DOG: FOUR GENERATIONS OF SIOUX MEDICINE MEN
Leonard Dog & Richard Erdoes
Illus. 272 pp. Paper. HarperCollins, 1996. $13.

CROW DOG'S CASE: AMERICAN INDIAN SOVEREIGNTY, TRIBAL LAW & U.S. LAW IN THE 19TH CENTURY
Sidney L. Harring
Illus. 317 pp. Cambridge University Press, 1994.
$69.95; paper, $19.95.

THE CROW & THE EAGLE: A TRIBAL HISTORY FROM LEWIS & CLARK TO CUSTER
Keith Algier
Relates the saga of the Crow Nation in the 1800s. Illus. Maps.
Biblio. 399 pp. Paper. The Caxton Printers, 1994. $14.95.

CROW INDIAN ART: PAPERS PRESENTED AT THE CROW INDIAN ART SYMPOSIUM SPONSORED BY THE CHANDLER INSTITUTE
R. Pohrt, Jr. and B. Lanford;
F. Dennis Lessurd, Editor
Illus. 68 pp. Paper. Chandler Institute, 1984. $12.

CROW INDIAN BEADWORK
William Wildschut & John C. Ewers
A descriptive and historical study. 2nd edition.
Illus. 108 pp. Paper. Eagles View, $10.95.

CROW INDIAN MEDICINE BUNDLES
William Wildschut; John C. Ewers, Editor
Reprint of 1960 edition. Illus. 187 pp. Paper.
National Museum of the American Indian, $9.95.

CROW INDIAN PHOTOGRAPHER: THE WORK OF RICHARD THROSSEL
Peggy Albright
80 photos. Biblio. 231 pp. University of
New Mexico Press, $70; paper, $37.95.

THE CROW INDIANS
Robert H. Lowie; intro by Phenocia Bauerle
Reprint of 1935 edition. Illus. 384 pp. Paper.
University of Nebraska Press, 2004. $17.95.

CROW MAN'S PEOPLE: THREE SEASONS WITH THE NAVAJO
Nigel Pride
Illus. 222 pp. Universe Books, 1985. $15.

CROWFOOT: CHIEF OF THE BLACKFEET
Hugh A. Dempsey
Reprint of 1972 edition. Illus. Maps. 226 pp.
Paper. University of Oklahoma Press, $13.95.

CRY FOR LUCK: SACRED SONG & SPEECH AMONG THE YUROK, HUPA & KAROK INDIANS FO NORTHWESTERN CALIFORNIA
Richard Keeling
University of California Press, 1992. $45.

A CRY FROM THE EARTH: MUSIC OF THE NORTH AMERICAN INDIANS
John Bierhorst
Illus. 113 pp. Paper. Ancient City Press, 1992.
$15.95. Cassette, $10.95.

CRY OF THE EAGLE: ENCOUNTERS WITH A CREE HEALER
David Young & Grant Ingram
University of Toronto Press, $22.50; paper, $14.95.

CRY OF THE THUNDERBIRD: THE AMERICAN INDIAN'S OWN STORY
Charles Hamilton
Reprint of 1971 edition. Illus. Paintings by George Catlin. Map.
Biblio. 284 pp. Paper. University of Oklahoma Press, $18.95.

CRYING FOR A DREAM
Richard Erdoes
Focus is on the natural & sacred world of North America's indigenous peoples, includes elements of the Sioux ceremonial cycle & portraits of native peoples from the plains, mesas, and deserts. Describe the sun dance, sacred pipe, yuwipi, the vision quest. Illus. 128 pp. Paper. Bear & Co., 1989. $24.95.

*THE CRYING FOR A VISION
Walter Wangerin, Jr.
Saga of Wask Mani - a Lakota orphan with a mysterious past & powers. Grades 7-up. 288 pp. Simon & Schuster, 1994. $15.

CRYING FOR A VISION: A ROSEBUD SIOUX TRILOGY 1886-1976
John Anderson, Eugene Buechel, S.J. & Don Doll, S.J.
Photos cover nearly a century of life in the Rosebud country of South Dakota. Illus. Morgan & Morgan, $19.95.

CRYSTALS IN THE SKY: AN INTELLECTUAL ODYSSEY INVOLVING CHUMASH ASTRONOMY, COSMOLOGY & ROCK ART
Travis Hudson & Ernest Underhay
Illus. 165 pp. Paper. Ballena Press, 1978. $18.95.

CUCKOO FOR KOKOPELLI
Dave Walker
40 color photos. 64 pp. Paper. Clear Light, $7.95.

DELFINA CUERO: HER AUTOBIOGRAPHY & HER ETHNOBOTANIC CONTRIBUTIONS
Florence Shipek
Includes "The Autobiography of Delfina Cuero." Illus.
120 pp. Ballena Press, 1991. $16; paper, $12.

CULTIVATING A LANDSCAPE OF PEACE: IROQUOIS-EUROPEAN ENCOUNTERS IN SEVENTEENTH-CENTURY AMERICA
Matthew Dennis
Illus. 296 pp. Cornell University Press, 1993.
$57.95, paper, $19.95.

CULTURAL CHANGE AND CONTINUITY ON CHAPIN MESA
Arthur H. Rohn
Illus. 330 pp. University Press of Kansas, 1977. $29.95.

CULTURAL DIVERSITY & ADAPTATION: THE ARCHAIC, ANASAZI & NAVAJO OCCUPATION OF THE SAN JUAN BASIN
Lori S. Reed & Paul F. Reed, Editors
Illus. 182 pp. Bureau of Land Management, 1992. $8.

CULTURAL ENCOUNTERS IN THE EARLY SOUTH: INDIAN & EUROPEANS IN ARKANSAS
Jeannie M. Whayne
Illus. 240 pp. University of Arkansas Press, 1995. $28.

CULTURAL & ENVIRONMENTAL HISTORY OF CIENEGA VALLEY, SOUTHEASTERN ARIZONA
Frank W. Eddy and Maurice E. Cooley
62 pp. University of Arizona Press, 1983. $7.95.

CULTURAL PERSISTENCE: CONTINUITY IN MEANING & MORAL RESPONSIBILITY AMONG THE BEARLIKE ATHAPASKANS
Scott Rushforth with James Chisholm
Ethnographic description of Athapaskan-speaking Indians of Canada's Northwest Territories. 187 pp. University of Arizona Press, 1991. $42.

THE CULTURAL TRANSFORMATION OF A NATIVE AMERICAN FAMILY & ITS TRIBE, 1763-1995: A BASKET OF APPLES
Joel H. Spring
248 pp. Lawrence Erlbaum Associates, 1996. $45.

CULTURE, CHANGE & LEADERSHIP IN A MODERN INDIAN COMMUNITY: THE COLORADO RIVER INDIAN RESERVATION
Katherine E. Blossom
101 pp. Paper. Cherokee Publications, 1979. $6.

CULTURES IN CONTACT: THE EUROPEAN IMPACT ON NATIVE CULTURAL INSTITUTIONS IN EASTERN NORTH AMERICA A.D. 1000-1800
William W. Fitzhugh, Editor
Illus. 326 pp. Paper. Smithsonian Institution Press, 1985.
$29.95; paper, $17.95.

CURRENT RESEARCH IN INDIANA ARCHAEOLOGY & PREHISTORY: 1987 & 1988
Christopher S. Peebles
Illus. 51 pp. Paper. Indiana Historical Society, 1989. $2.75.

EDWARD S. CURTIS & THE NORTH AMERICAN INDIAN PROJECT IN THE FIELD
Edited with intro. by Mick Gidley
Illus. 224 pp. University of Nebraska Press, 2003. $49.95.

CUSHING AT ZUNI: THE CORRESPONDENCE & JOURNALS OF FRANK HAMILTON CUSHING, 1879-1884
Jesse Green, Editor
Illus. 450 pp. University of New Mexico Press, 1990. $45.

CUSTER & THE BATTLE OF THE LITTLE BIGHORN: AN ENCYCLOPEDIA OF THE PEOPLE, PLACES, EVENTS, INDIAN CULTURE & CUSTOMS, INFORMATION SOURCES, ART & FILMS
Thom Hatch
Photos. Maps. 248 pp. McFarland, 1996. $45.

CUSTER BATTLEFIELD, A HISTORY & GUIDE TO THE BATTLE OF THE LITTLE BIGHORN
Robert M. Utley
Illus. 112 pp. Paper. U.S. Government Printing Office, 1988.
$4.75.

CUSTER, BLACK KETTLE, & THE FIGHT ON THE WASHITA
Charles J. Brill; foreword by Mark L. Gardner
Illus. Maps. 328 pp. Paper. University of Oklahoma Press, 2002.
$17.95.

CUSTER & COMPANY: WALTER CAMP'S NOTES ONTHE CUSTER FIGHT
Bruce R. Liddic & Paul Harbaugh, Editors
Illus. Maps. 189 pp. Paper. Clear Light, $13.

*CUSTER & CRAZY HORSE
Jim Razzi
Grades 3-7. Paper. Scholastic, Inc., 1989. $2.75.

CUSTER DIED FOR YOUR SINS: AN INDIAN MANIFESTO
Vine Deloria, Jr.
Federal Indian policy from a Native American perspective. Reprint of 1988 edition. 292 pp. Paper. University of Oklahoma Press, $19.95.

CUSTER & THE LITTLE BIGHORN: A COLLECTION OF WALTER MASON CAMP'S RESEARCH PAPERS ON GENERAL GEORGE A. CUSTER'S LAST FIGHT
Richard G. Hardorff
Illus. 135 pp. Upton & Sons, 1997. $50.

CUSTER LIVES
James P. Dowd
Personal sketches of individuals on both sides of the Little Bighorn. Reprint. Map. 264 pp. Ye Galleon Press, $16.95.

THE CUSTER MYTH: A SOURCE BOOK OF CUSTERIANA
Col. W.A. Graham
A complete account of what happened at Little Bighorn with narrative Indian and soldier accounts. Reprint of 1953 edition. Photos. Maps. High-Lonesome Books, $25.

THE CUSTER STORY: THE LIFE & INTIMATE LETTERS OF GENERAL GEORGE A. CUSTER & HIS WIFE ELIZABETH
Marguerite Merington, Editor
Reprint of 1950 edition. 340 pp. Chatham Pres, $9.95.

THE CUSTER TRAGEDY: EVENTS LEADING UP TO & FOLLOWING THE LITTLE BIG HORN CAMPAIGN OF 1876
Fred Dustin
Reprint of 1939 edition. Illus. 310 pp. Upton & Sons, $45.

CUSTER'S CHIEF OF SCOUTS: THE REMINISCENCES OF CHARLES A. VARNUM
Charles A. Varnum; John M. Carroll, Editor
Illus. 192 pp. University of Nebraska Press, 1987. $18.95; paper, $6.95.

CUSTER'S DEFEAT & OTHER CONFLICTS IN THE WEST
Illus. 110 pp. Paper. Sunflower University Press, 1979. $15.

CUSTER'S FALL: THE NATIVE AMERICAN SIDE OF THE STORY
David H. Miller
Presents an interpretation of the Battle of the Little Big Horn, and of the death of General Custer. Illus. 288 pp. Paper. Penguin USA, $10.

CUSTER'S LAST BATTLE
Richard A. Roberts
60 pp. Paper. Monroe County Library, 1978. $8.

CUSTER'S LAST CAMPAIGN: MITCH BOYER & THE LITTLE BIGHORN
John S. Gray
Illus. Maps. 446 pp. Paper. Clear Light, $17.95.

*CUSTER'S LAST STAND
Quentin Reynolds
Grades 5-9. Illus. 160 pp. Random House, 1964.
$8.99; paper, $2.95.

CUSTER'S PRELUDE TO GLORY
Herbert Krause & Gary Olson
Illus. 280 pp. Brevet Press, $19.95.

CUSTER'S SEVENTH CAVALRY & THE CAMPAIGN OF 1873
Lawrence A. Frost
Illus. 255 pp. Upton & Sons, 1986. $45.

*A CYCLE OF MYTHS: NATIVE LEGENDS FROM SOUTHEAST ALASKA
John E. Smelcer, Editor
Grades 7 and up. Illus. 116 pp. Paper. Salmon Run, 1993.
$12.95.

CYCLES OF CONQUEST: THE IMPACT OF SPAIN, MEXICO & THE U.S. ON INDIANS OF THE SOUTHWEST, 1533-1960
Edward H. Spicer
More than 400 years of cultural history of some 25 Southwestern tribes. Illus. 609 pp. Paper. University of Arizona Press, 1962. $28.95.

CYCLORAMA OF GEN. CUSTER'S LAST FIGHT: A REPRODUCTION OF THE ORIGINAL DOCUMENT COMPLETE IN ALL RESPECTS
John M. Carroll, intro by
Reprint of 1889 edition. Illus. 104 pp. Upton & Sons, $30.

D

DAHCOTAH: OR, LIFE & LEGENDS OF THE SIOUX AROUND FORT SNELLING
Mary Eastman
Facsimile of 1849 edition. Illus. Ayer Co., $24.50.

DAILY AFFIRMATIONS FROM THE DIVINE CREATOR
Willie C. Hooks
75 pp. Paper. JTE Associates, 1990. $7.95.

*DAILY LIFE IN A PLAINS INDIAN VILLAGE, 1868
Michael Bad Hand Terry
Grades 3 to 5. 130 color photos. 48 pp. Paper. Written heritage, 1999. $9.95.

*THE DAKOTA
Brief history of the Dakota. Grades 6 and up. Illus. 32 pp. Minnesota Historical Society Press, 1984. $3.50.

DAKOTA CROSS-BEARER: THE LIFE & WORLD OF A NATIVE AMERICAN BISHOP
Mary E. Cochran; intro by Raymond Bucko & Martin Brokenleg
Biography of Harold S. Jones, the first Native American bishop. Illus. 264 pp. University of Nebraska Press, 2000. $35.

A DAKOTA-ENGLISH DICTIONARY
Stephen R. Riggs
Reprint of 1852 edition. 680 pp. Paper. Minnesota Historical Society Press, $24.95.

DAKOTA GRAMMAR, TEXTS & ETHNOLOGY
Stephen R. Riggs; Edited by James Owen Dorsey
Reprint of 1893 edition. 232 pp. Ross & Haines or Shenandoah Books, $30.

*DAKOTA INDIANS COLORING BOOK
Chet Kozlak
Grades 1-3. Map. 32 pp. Paper. Minnesota Historical Society Press, $3.50.

*DAKOTA & OJIBWE PEOPLE IN MINNESOTA
Frances Densmore
Grades 6 and up. Illus. 55 pp. Paper. Minnesota Historical Society Press, 1977. $3.50.

THE DAKOTA OR SIOUX IN MINNESOTA: AS THEY WERE IN 1834
Samuel W. Pond
192 pp. Paper. Minnesota Historical Society Press, 1986. $8.95.

DAKOTA ORATORY: GREAT MOMENTS IN THE RECORDED SPEECH OF THE EASTERN SIOUX, 1695-1874
compiled & illus. by Mark Diedrich
Illus. Biblio. 102 pp. Paper. Coyote Books, 1989. $18.95.

DAKOTA PANORAMA
J. Leonard Jennewein & Jane Boorman
Illus. 468 pp. Paper. Brevet Press, $14.95.

DAKOTA SIOUX INDIAN DICTIONARY
Paul Warcloud
English to Sioux translations of over 4,000 words. Developed for beginners interested in the Sioux language by artist and author Paul Warcloud. 192 pp. Paper. Center for Western Studies, $5.95.

DAKOTA: A SPIRITUAL GEOGRAPHY
Kathleen Norris
An evokation of the Great Plains, this book weaves together the lives of farmers, townsfolk, Native Americans, and a community of Benedictine monks. 224 pp. Paper. Houghton Mifflin, 1994. $9.95.

DAKOTA TEXTS
Ella C. Deloria
Reprint of 1932 edition. Paper. Dakota Press, $10.95.

DAKOTA WAR WHOOP
H.E. McConkey
Reprint of 1864 edition. Ross & Haines, $15.

DAKOTA WAY OF LIFE SERIES
Incorporates Indian legends & culture with Christian teaching. using Indian designs, Indian art & photographs of Indian people. Pre-school, Teacher's Guide, $7.50; Grades 1-12, Student text, $2.50; Teacher Guide, $4.75. American Indian Culture Research Center.

DAKSI
An introductory multicultural educational resource which challenges the ethnocentric cultural stereotypes. David Michael Wolfe.

DAMMED INDIANS: THE PICK-SLOAN PLAN & THE MISSOURI RIVER SIOUX, 1944-1980
Michael L. Lawson
Reprint of 1982 edition, with a new preface by the author, and a new foreword by Vine Deloria, Jr. Illus. 262 pp. Paper. University of Oklahoma Press, $15.95.

THE DANCE HOUSE: STORIES FROM ROSEBUD
Joseph Marshall, III (Sicangu Lakota)
Essays and short stories based on incidents or events which took place on the Rosebud (Sicangu Lakota) Indian Reservation in South Dakota. 214 pp. Paper. Red Crane Books, 1998. $13.95.

DANCES OF THE TEWA PUEBLO INDIANS: EXPRESSIONS OF LIFE
Jill D. Sweet
Illus. 100 pp. Paper. School of American Research, 1985. $9.95.

DANCES WITH WOLVES
Blake
Plains Indian struggle for survival during the late 1800s. Illus. Center for Western Studies, 1989. $16.95.

DANCING COLORS: PATHS OF NATIVE AMERICAN WOMEN
C.J. Brafford & Laine Thom
Illus. 120 pp. Chronicle Books, 1992. $29.95; paper, $18.95.

*DANCING DRUM: A CHEROKEE LEGEND
Terri Cohlene
Grades 4-8. Illus. 48 pp. Demco & Rourke, 1990. $16.95; paper, $10.15

DANCING GHOSTS: NATIVE AMERICAN & CHRISTIAN SYNCRETISM IN MARY AUSTIN'S WORK
Mark Hoyer
224 pp. University of Nevada Press, 1998. $34.95.

DANCING GODS: INDIAN CEREMONIALS OF NEW MEXICO & ARIZONA
Erna Fergusson
The Corn Dance, Deer Dance and Eagle Dance as well as various dances at Zuni; also describes the Hopi bean-planting and Niman Kachina ceremonies in a ddition to the Snake Dance, the navajo Mountain Chant and Night Chant, and several Apache ceremonies. 328 pp. Paper. University of New Mexico Press, 2001. $19.95.

THE DANCING HEALERS: A DOCTOR'S JOURNEY OF HEALING WITH NATIVE AMERICANS
Carl Hammerschlag
128 pp. Harper & Row, 1988. $14.45.

DANCING IN THE PATHS OF THE ANCESTORS
Book Two of the Pueblo Children of the Earth Mother
Thomas E. Mails
Overview of the Pueblo Indians of New Mexico and Arizona. Illus. 544 pp. Marlowe & Company, 1998. $46.50; paper, $29.95.

DANCING ON COMMON GROUND: TRIBAL CULTURES & ALLIANCES ON THE SOUTHERN PLAINS
Howard L. Meredith
Illus. 222 pp. University Press of Kansas, 1995. $29.95.

DANCING ON THE RIM OF THE WORLD: AN ANTHOLOGY OF CONTEMPORARY NORTHWEST NATIVE AMERICAN WRITING
Andrea Lerner, Editor
266 pp. Paper. University of Arizona Press, 1990. $19.95.

*DANCING TEPEES: POEMS OF AMERICAN INDIAN YOUTH
Virginia Sneve
Grades K-3. Illus. 32 pp. Holiday House, 1989. $15.95; paper, $5.95.

DANCING WITH CREATION
Martha Kirk
Paper. Resource Publications, 1983. $7.95.

DANCING WITH INDIANS
Angela Shelf Medearis
An African-American family attends a Seminole celebration & participants. Illus. 32 pp. Holiday House, 1991. $14.95; paper, $5.95.

DANGEROUS PASSAGE: THE SANTA FE TRAIL & THE MEXICAN WAR
William Y. Chalfant
Tells the story of the Santa Fe Trail and the Indians who onces lived on it. Ilus. Photos. Biblio. University of Oklahoma Press, 1994. $29.95.

DARING DONALD McKAY: OR, THE LAST WAR TRIAL OF THE MODOCS
Keith and Donna Clark, Editors
Illus. Paper. Oregon Historical Society, 1971. $2.95.

*DARK ARROW
Lucille Mulcahy; Illus. by Herbert Danska
Prehistoric cliff-dwelling people. Grades 4 and up. Illus. 210 pp. Paper. University of Nebraska Press, 1995. $7.95.

DARK LADY DREAMING
Amy Cordova
A contemporary Native American/Hispanic artist discusses the methods and spiritual commitments inher work. Illus. 15 pp. The origins Program, $5.95.

*THE DARK SIDE OF THE MOON
Tom Kovach
Grades 1-4. Illus. 32 pp. Council for Indian Education, $8.45; paper, $2.45.

DAUGHTERS OF THE BUFFALO WOMEN: MAINTAINING THE TRIBAL FAITH
Beverly Hungry Wolf
First hand accounts of reservation life. Photos. 144 pp. Paper. Clear Light & Written Heritage, $14.95.

THE DAWES COMMISSION & THE ALLOTMENT OF THE FIVE CIVILIZED TRIBES, 1893-1914
Kent Carter
Ancestry, 1998. $29.95.

DAWN IN ARCTIC ALASKA
Diamond Jenness
Illus. Maps. 220 pp. Paper. University of Chicago Press, 1985. $11.95.

DAWN LAND
Joseph Bruchac
First novel by a Native American storyteller. 332 pp. Fulcrum Publishing, 1992. $19.95; paper, $12.95. Also on audiocassettes, $16.95.

THE DAWN OF THE WORLD: MYTHS & TALES OF THE MIWOK INDIANS OF CALIFORNIA
C. Hart Merriam, Editor
Illus. Maps. 273 pp. University of Nebraska Press, 1993. $30; paper, $9.95.

*DAWN RIDER
Jan Hudson
Details of tribal life. Fiction. Grades 4-8. 192 pp. Philomel, 1990. $14.95.

DAWNLAND ENCOUNTERS: INDIANS & EUROPEANS IN NORTHERN NEW ENGLAND
Colin G. Calloway
Illus. 300 pp. Paper. University Press of New England, 1991. $15.95.

*THE DAY OF THE OGRE KACHINAS: A HOPI INDIAN FABLE
Peggy Spence
Grades 1-6. Illus. 48 pp. Paper. Council for Indian Education & Roberts Rinehart, 1994. $4.95.

*A DAY WITH A CHEYENNE
Franco Meli; illus. by Giorgio Bacchin
Grades 4-7. Illus. Color photos. 48 pp. Lerner, 1998. $19.95.

*A DAY WITH A CHUMASH
Franco Meli; illus. by Giorgio Bacchin
Grades 4-7. Illus. Color photos. 48 pp. Lerner, 1998. $19.95.

*A DAY WITH A MIMBRES
Franco Meli; illus. by Giorgio Bacchin
Grades 5-7. Illus. Color photos. 48 pp. Lerner, 1998. $22.60.

*A DAY WITH A PUEBLO
Franco Meli; illus. by Giorgio Bacchin
Grades 4-7. Illus. Color photos. 48 pp. Lerner, 1998. $19.95.

DEAD TOWNS OF ALABAMA
W. Stuart Harris
176 pp. Ilus. University of Arizona Press, 1977. $10.95.

DEAD VOICES: NATURAL AGONIES IN THE NEW WORLD
Gerald Vizenor
Using tales drawn from traditional tribal stories, this book illuminates the centuries of conflict between American Indians & Europeans. 144 pp. Paper. University of Oklahoma Press, 1992. $10.95.

DEADLY INDIAN SUMMER
Leonard A. Schonberg
Navajo medicine men. 184 pp. Sunstone Press, 1997. $24.95.

DEADLY MEDICINE: INDIANS & ALCOHOL IN EARLY AMERICA
Peter C. Mancall
Illus. 296 pp. Paper. Cornell University Press, 1997. $18.95.

DEATH IN THE DESERT: THE FIFTY YEARS' WAR FOR THE GREAT SOUTHWEST
Paul Wellman
Illus. 318 pp. University of Nebraska Press, 1987. $27.95; paper, $8.95.

THE DEATH OF BERNADETTE LEFTHAND
Ron Querry
Alcohol & witchcraft and a mysterious murder in Navajo terri-
tory. 232 pp. Red Crane Books, 1993, $23.95; paper, $12.95.
Poster available.

THE DEATH OF CRAZY HORSE:
A TRAGIC EPISODE IN LAKOTA HISTORY
edited by Richard G. Hardorff
Interviews describe the surrender & death of Crazy Horse in
1877. Illus. Maps. 288 pp. Univ. of Nebraska Press, 2001.
$14.95.

THE DEATH OF JIM LONELY
James Welch
Novel about a modern American Indian, with no tribe and no
real home. 192 pp. Paper. Penguin USA, $8.

*THE DEATH OF JIMMY LITTLEWOLF:
AN INDIAN BOY AT BOYS RANCH
R.L. Templeton
Grades 4-7. Eakin Publications, 1980. $6.95.

DEATH ON THE PRAIRIE: THE THIRTY YEARS'
STRUGGLE FOR THE WESTERN PLAINS
Paul I. Wellman
Illus. 322 pp. University of Nebraska Press, 1987.
$27.95; paper, $8.95.

THE DEATH & REBIRTH OF THE SENECA
Anthony F. Wallace
416 pp. Paper. Random House, 1972. $6.36.

DEATH STALKS THE YAKIMA: EPIDEMIOLOGICAL
TRANSITIONS & MORALITY ON THE YAKIMA INDIAN
RESERVATION, 1888-1964
Clifford E. Trafzer
220 pp. Paper. Michigan State University Press, 1997. $24.95.

DEATH, TOO, FOR THE HEAVY-RUNNER
Ben Bennett
Illus. 192 pp. Paper. Mountain Press, 1982. $7.95.

DEBATING DEMOCRACY: NATIVE AMERICAN
LEGACY OF FREEDOM
Bruce E. Johansen
Chapters by Donald A. Grinde, Jr. and Barbara A. Mann. The
Iroquois Confederacy and its influence on the founding fathers
of the U.S. 224 pp. Clear Light, 1995. $24.95; paper, $14.95.

DEBERT: A PALEO-INDIAN SITE IN CENTRAL
NOVA SCOTIA
George MacDonald
Third revised edition. Illus. 205 pp. Paper. Persimmon, 1985.
$13.95.

ANGIE DEBO: PIONEERING HISTORIAN
Shirley A. Leckie
Illus. 256 pp. University of Oklahoma Press, 2000.
$29.95; paper, $14.95.

DECEMBER'S CHILD: A BOOK
OF CHUMASH ORAL NARRATIVES
Thomas Blackburb, Editor
360 pp. Univerity of California Press, 1976. $25; paper, $10.95.

DECEPTION ON ALL ACCOUNTS
Sara Sue Hoklotubbe
Native American (Oklahoma Cherokee) mystery novel.
210 pp. University of Arizona Press, 2003. $14.95.

DECIPHERING ANASAZI VIOLENCE: WITH REGIONAL
COMPARISONS TO MESO AMERICAN & WOODLAND
CULTURES
Peter Bullock, et al
Illus. 150 pp. Paper. Historical Research & Mapping, 1998.
$20.

DECORATIVE ART OF THE SOUTHWESTERN INDIANS
Dorothy S. Sides
Reprint of 1962 edition. Illus. 100 pp. Paper. Dover, $5.95.

DEEPER THAN GOLD: INDIAN LIFE
ALONG CALIFORNIA'S HIGHWAY 49
Brian Bibby; photos by Dugan Aguilar
Photos. 192 pp. Paper. Heyday Books, 1999. $16.

DEER DANCER: YAQUI LEGENDS OF LIFE
Stan Padilla
Traditional Yaqui myths and legends. 112 pp. Paper.
Clear Light, $11.95.

DEER TRACK: A LATE WOODLAND VILLAGE
IN THE MISSISSIPPI VALLEY
Charles McGimsey & Michael Conner, Editors
Illus. 134 pp. Paper. Center for American Archaeology, 1985.
$7.95.

DEERSKINS & DUFFELS: THE CREEK INDIAN
TRADE WITH ANGLO-AMERICA, 1685-1815
Kathryn E. Holland Braund
Illus. Maps. 310 pp. Paper. University of Nebraska Press, 1993.
$29.95.

*THE DEFENDERS
Ann McGovern
Grades 3-7. Illus. 128 pp. Paper. Scholastic, Inc., 1987. $2.50.

DEFENDING THE DINETAH: PUEBLITOS
IN THE ANCESTRAL NAVAJO HEARTLAND
Ronald H. Towner
Explores the origins of the Navajo. Illus. 208 pp.
University of Utah Press, 2003. $35.

DELFINA CUERO: HER AUTOBIOGRAPHY
Florence C. Shipek
Illus. 101 pp. Ballena Press, 1991. $16; paper, $12.

THE DELAWARE INDIANS: A BRIEF HISTORY
E.J. Adams
History, language, legends, government. Reprint of 1906
edition. 80 pp. Paper. Library Research Associates, $8.95.

THE DELAWARE INDIANS: A HISTORY
C.A. Weslager
570 pp. Paper. Rutgers University Press, 1990. $19.95.

DELAWARE REFERENCE GRAMMAR
John O'Meara
168 pp. University of Toronto Press, 1998. $30.

THE DELAWARE & SHAWNEE ADMITTED TO CHEROKEE
CITIZENSHIP & THE RELATED WYANDOTTE & MORAVIAN
DELAWARE
Toni Jollay Prevost
Contains information on migration patterns; missionary school
data; 1860 & 1870 federal census of Wyandotte County, Kan-
sas. 129 pp. Paper. Heritage Books, 1992. $21.50.

DELAWARE TRAILS: SOME TRIBAL RECORDS, 1842-1907
transcribed by Fay Louise Smith Arellano
Collection of records pertaining to the Delaware Indians.Illus.
527 pp. Paper. Clearfield Co., 1996. $55.

THE DELAWARES: A CRITICAL BIBLIOGRAPHY
C.A. Weslager
Paper. Indiana University Press, 1978. $4.95.

DELIBERATE ACTS: CHANGING HOPI
CULTURE THROUGH THE ORAIBI SPLIT
Peter M. Whiteley
373 pp. University of Arizona Press, 1988. $52.

DELIGHT MAKERS
Adolph F. Bandelier
A fictional reconstruction of prehistoric Indian culture in the
American Southwest by a 19th century archaeologist. Illus. 490
pp. Paper. Harcourt Brace, 1971. $12.95.

DEMONSTRATION OF BUILDING INDIAN
HOUSING IN UNDERSERVED AREAS
Housing Assistance Council Staff
19 pp. Housing Assistance, 1993. $4.

DENA'INA LEGACY K'TL'EGH'I SUKDU:
THE COLLECTED WRITINGS OF PETER KALIFORNSKY
Peter Kalfornsky; edited by James Kari & Alan Boraas
Illus. Photos. Maps. 485 pp. Paper. CIRI & Alaska Native
Language Center, 1991. $16.

DENA'INA NOUN DICTIONARY
James Kari, Compiled by
Illus. 355 pp. Paper. Alaska Native Language Center, 1977.
$8.

DENE NATION: THE COLONY WITHIN
Mel Watkins
Paper. University of Toronto Press, 1977. $12.95.

DENETSOSIE
B. Johnson and S.M. Callaway, Editors
Revised edition. Illus. 51 pp. Navajo Curriculum, 1974. $5.

FRANCES DENSMORE & AMERICAN INDIAN MUSIC
Charles Hofmann
127 pp. Paper. National Museum of the American Indian, 1968.
$5.

THE DEPT. OF INTERIOR'S DENIAL OF THE WISCONSIN
CHIPPEWA'S CASINO APPLICATIONS: HEARINGS BE-
FORE THE COMMITTEE ON GOVERNMENT REFORM &
OVERSIGHT, HOUSE OF REPS, 150TH CONGRESS, SEC-
OND SESSION
U.S. Staff
U.S. Government Printing Office, 1998.

DEPREDATIONS & MASSACRE
BY THE SNAKE RIVER INDIANS
Edward R. Geary
17 pp. Paper. Ye Galleon Press, 1966, $4.95.

DESCENDANTS OF NANCY WARD:
A WORKBOOK FOR FURTHER RESEARCH
David K. Hampton
448 pp. Paper. Arc Press, 1997. $60.

DESCRIPTION — NATURAL HISTORY
OF THE COASTS OF NORTH AMERICA
N. Denys; W.F. Ganong, Editor
Reprint of 1908 edition. Greenwood Press, $42.

DESCRIPTION OF A JOURNEY &
VISIT TO THE PAWNEE INDIANS
Dottlieb Oehler & David Smith
Reprint of 1851 edition. 34 pp.
Ye Galleon Press, $9.95; paper, $4.95.

DESERT FORAGERS & HUNTERS:
INDIANS OF THE DEATH VALLEY REGION
William J. & Edith Wallace
Illus. Paper. Acoma Books, 1979. $3.25.

DESERT IMMIGRANTS: THE MEXICAN
OF EL PASO, 1880-1920
Mario T. Garcia
Illus. 328 pp. Yale University Press, 1981.
$32.50; paper, $11.95.

THE DESERT IS NO LADY: SOUTHWESTERN
LANDSCAPES IN WOMEN'S WRITING & ART
Vera Norwood & Janice Monk, Editors
Reprint of 1987 edition. Illus. 340 pp. Paper. University of Ari-
zona Press, $19.95.

THE DESERT LAKE: THE STORY
OF NEVADA'S PYRAMID LAKE
Sessions S. Wheeler
Prehistory and history of the basin, including its famous Indian
battles. Illus. Biblio. 139 pp. Paper. The Caxton Printers, $7.95.

DESERT LIGHT: MYTHS & VISIONS
OF THE GEAT SOUTHWEST
John Miller, Editor
Illus. 120 pp. Paper. Chronicle Books, 1990. $18.95.

THE DESERT SMELLS LIKE RAIN:
A NATURALIST IN PAPAGO INDIAN COUNTRY
Gary P. Nabhan
176 pp. Paper. North Point Press, 1987. $8.95.

DESERT INDIAN WOMAN: STORIES & DREAMS
Frances Manuel & Deborah Neff
Basket weaver, storyteller, and tribal elder, Frances Manuel is
a living preserver of Tohono O'odham culture. Speaking in her
own words, she shares the story of her life and tells of O'odham
culture and society. Illus. 240 pp. Paper. University of Arizona
Press, 2001. $17.95.

THE DESERT SMELLS LIKE RAIN:
A NATURALIST IN O'ODHAM COUNTRY
Gary Paul Nabhan
The everyday life and perseverance of the Tohono O'odham.
Originally published in 1982. Illus. 148 pp. Paper. University of
Arizona Press, 2002. $16.95.

DESIGNING WITH THE WOOL
Noel Bennett
Illus. 128 pp. Paper. Northland, 1979. $8.95.

DESIGNS & FACTIONS: POLITICS, RELIGION,
& CERAMICS ON THE HOPI THIRD MESA
Lydia Wyckoff
Illus. 210 pp. Paper. University of New Mexico Press, 1990.
$24.95.

DESIGNS OF THE NIGHT SKY
Diane Glancy
Fiction. Cherokee theme. 157 pp.
University of Nebraska Press, 2002. $24.95.

DESIGNS ON PREHISTORIC HOPI POTTERY
Jesse W. Fewkes
Reprint. Illus. 290 pp. Paper. Dover, 1973. $9.95.

THE DESTRUCTION OF AMERICAN INDIAN FAMILIES
Steven Unger, Editor
Paper. Association on American Indian Affairs, 1977. $4.25.

THE DESTRUCTION OF CALIFORNIA INDIANS
edited by Robert F. Heizer; intro. by Albert L. Hurtado
Reveals how thousands of California natives died from 1847
to 1865. Illus. 321 pp. Paper. University of Nebraska Press,
1993. $19.95.

DEVELOPING REHABILITATION RESEARCHERS IN THE
AMERICAN INDIAN COMMUNITY: A TECHNICAL REPORT
OF CONSUMER-RESEARCHER TRAINING
C.A. Marshall & George S. Gotto
Paper. Northern Arizona University, 1998. $7.50.

THE DEVELOPMENT OF CAPITALISM IN THE
NAVAJO NATION: A POLITICAL-ECONOMIC HISTORY
Lawrence D. Weiss
180 pp. MEP Publications, 1984. $29.95; paper, $10.95.

THE DEVELOPMENT OF
SOUTHEASTERN ARCHAEOLOGY
Jay K. Johnson, Editor
352 pp. Paper. University of Alabama Press, 1993. $29.95.

THE DEVIL IN THE NEW WORLD:
THE IMPACT OF DIABOLISM IN NEW SPAIN
Fernando Cervantes
Reveals how Native American reinterpreted the view of Christianity presented to them. He deals with the social history of the interaction between the two cultures. Illus. 192 pp. Yale University Press, 1994. $22.50.

DEVIL SICKNESS & DEVIL SONGS:
TOHONO O'ODHAM POETICS
David L. Kozak & David L. Lopez
Illus. Maps. 224 pp. Smithsonian Institution Press, 1999. $45.

DEZBA, NAVAJO WOMAN OF THE DESERT
Gladys A. Reichard
Illus. 220 pp. Paper. Rio Grande Press, $12.

DIABETES EPIDEMIC HEARING BEFORE THE
COMMITTEE ON INDIAN AFFAIRS, U.S. SENATE,
105TH CONGRESS
USGPO taff
1st Session on Diabetes Epidemic Among American Indians & Others in the Gallup Area, April 4, 1997, Gallup, NM. 33 pp. Paper. USGPO, 1998.

DIABETES IN NATIVE AMERICANS:
THE EASTERN TRIBES
Illus. 126 pp. Paper. Diane Publishing. $35.

DIALOGUES WITH ZUNI POTTERS
Milfred Nahohai & Elisa Phelps
Illus. 102 pp. Paper. University of New Mexico Press, $19.95.

THE DIARIO OF CHRISTOPHER COLUMBUS'S
FIRST VOYAGE TO AMERICA 1492-1493
trans. by Oliver Dunn & James Kelley, Jr.
Illus. 492 pp. University of Oklahoma Press, 1989. $70; paper, $27.95.

DICTIONARY OF THE ALABAMA LANGUAGE
Cora Sylestine, Heather Hardy & Timothy Montler
The language of the Alabama-Coushatta Indian Reservation in Polk County, Texas. Over 8,000 entries. 765 pp. University of Texas Press, 1993. $35.

DICTIONARY OF THE AMERICAN INDIAN
John Stoutenburgh, Jr.
Sourcebook of American Indian history and lore. 480 pp. Cherokee Publications, $9.95.

DICTIONARY OF THE BILOXI & OFO LANGUAGES
Dorsey & Swanton
340 pp. Reprint Services, 1995. $99.

DICTIONARY CATALOG OF THE EDWARD E. AYER
COLLECTION OF AMERICANA & AMERICAN INDIANS
Newberry Library Staff
16 Volumes and First Supplement. G.K. Hall, 1970. $1,280.00; First Supplement, $365.

DICTIONARY OF THE CHOCTAW LANGUAGE
Cyrus Byington
611 pp. Reprint Services, 1995. $149.

DICTIONARY OF CREEK/MUSKOGEE
Jack B. Martin & Margaret McKane Mauldin
Illus. Map. 359 pp. University of Nebraska Press, 2000. $65.

DICTIONARY OF DAILY LIFE
OF INDIANS OF THE AMERICAS
2 vols. 2,000 pp. American Indian Publishers, 1982. $165. per set.

DICTIONARY OF INDIAN TRIBES OF THE AMERICAS
2nd edition. 3 vols. Illus. 2,000 pp. American Indian Publishers, 1981. $375 per set.

DICTIONARY OF MESA GRANDE DIEGUENO
Ted Couro & Christina Hutcheson
First dictionary published of a Yuman Indian language. Paper. Malki Museum Press, 1979. $7.50.

DICTIONARY OF NATIVE AMERICAN HEALING
William S. Lyon
Explores the various aspects of Native American healing. Includes Canadian and Eskimo cultures. 360 pp. ABC-CLIO, 1996. $70.

DICTIONARY OF NATIVE AMERICAN MYTHOLOGY
Sam D. Gill & Irene F. Sullivan
Describes past & present rituals, traditions, and myths of over 100 Native American cultures. Biblio. 425 pp. ABC-Clio, 1992. $69.50.Paper. Illus. 456 pp. Oxford University Press, $18.95.

DICTIONARY OF THE OJIBWAY LANGUAGE
Frederica Baraga
Compiled nearly 150 years ago. Reprint of 1878 edition. 736 pp. Paper. Minnesota Historical Society Press, $24.95.

DICTIONARY OF THE OSAGE LANGUAGE
Francis La Flesche
406 pp. Reprint Services, 1994. $60. Native American Book Publishers, $59; paper, $39.

A DICTIONARY OF PAPAGO USAGE
M. Mathiot
504 pp. Mouton de Gruyter, $50.

DICTIONARY OF POWHATAN
William A. Strachey; Frederic W. Gleach, Editor
Reprint. 100 pp. Evolution Publishing & Manufacturing, $24.

DIGEST OF AMERICAN INDIAN LAW:
CASES & CHRONOLOGY
H. Barry Holt & Gary Forrester
140 pp. Fred B. Rothman & Co., 1990. $35.

DINE BAHANE': THE NAVAJO CREATION STORY
Paul G. Zolbrod
368 pp. Paper. University of New Mexico Press, 1984. $17.95.

DINE BIBLIOGRAPHY TO THE 1990s: A COMPARISON
TO THE NAVAJO BIBLIOGRAPHY OF 1969
Howard M. Bahr
Contains over 6,300 entries covering Navajo literature from 1970 to 1990, as well as newly discovered literature. Includes health-related, artistic, economic, religious, social, scientific, and other literature on the Navajo. 736 pp. Scarecrow Press, 1999. $95.

DINE: A HISTORY OF THE NAVAJOS
Peter Iverson
Winner of the Western Writers of America 2003 Spur Award for Nonfiction-Contemporary. Illus. 3 maps. 432 pp. University of New Mexico Press, 2003. $45; paper, $21.95.

*DINE, THE NAVAJO
Suan L. Shaffer, Editor
Grade 6. Illus. Includes 30 student booklets, one teacher's resource binder which includes transparencies, color slides and audiocassette. Heard Museum, 1987. $295.

DINETAH: AN EARLY HISTORY OF THE NAVAJO
Lawrence D. Sundberg
A chronicle of the early band Navajo people. 128 pp. Paper. Sunstone Press, $12.95.

DINETAH: NAVAJO HISTORY
Robert A. Roessel; T.L. McCarty, Editor
Volume III. Illus. 180 pp. Navajo Curriculum, 1983. $15.

DIPLOMATS IN BUCKSKINS: A HISTORY OF
INDIAN DELEGATIONS IN WASHINGTON CITY
Herman J. Viola; foreword by Ben Nighthorse Campbell
Originally published in 1981. Illus. 58 photos. 234 pp. University of Oklahoma Press, 1996. $19.95.

DIRECTORY OF AMERICAN INDIAN
CASINOS & BINGO HALLS
Sheryl & Bruce Mason
70 pp. Paper. The Lone Star Connection, 1997. $12.95.

DIRECTORY OF AMERICAN INDIAN LAW ATTORNEYS
150 pp. Native Word Research and Publishing, 1990-91. $35.

DIRECTORY OF NATIVE AMERICAN
PERFORMING ARTISTS
Lists artists and groups available for booking and performances. Includes storytellers, musicians, dancers, poets, singers, and craft demonstrators. Atlatl, 1991. $3.

DIRECTORY OF NATIVE AMERICAN TRIBES OF THE U.S.
Jes Lujan
81 pp. Paper. Apache Arts, 1995. $19.50.

DIRECTORY OF NATIVE EDUCATION
RESOURCES IN THE NORTHWEST REGION
Lists about 600 organizations in the 5-state region that provide educational services to Native Americans and Alaska Natives. 73 pp. paper. NWREL, 1994. $7.

DISCIPLINED HEARTS: HISTORY, IDENTITY &
DEPRESSION IN AN AMERICAN INDIAN COMMUNITY
Theresa Deleane O'Neil
Illus. 265 pp. University of California Press, 1996. $40.

*DISCOVER AMERICAN INDIAN WAYS:
A CARNEGIE ACTIVITY BOOK
Pamela Soeder
Grades 2-6. Illus. 28 pp. Roberts Rinehart, 1998. $4.95.

DISCOVER INDIAN RESERVATIONS:
A VISITOR'S WELCOME GUIDE
Veronica Tiller
Lists reservations by state, providing a tribal profile, location, sites, events, etc. for each. Paper. Council Publications, 1992. $19.95.

DISCOVERED LANDS, INVENTED PASTS:
TRANSFORMING VISIONS OF THE AMERICAN WEST
Jules David Prown, et al
Presents a major reinterpretation of western American art of the past three centuries. Includes depictions of Indians by early explorers. Illus. 232 pp. Yale University Press, 1992. $40; paper, $25.

DISCOVERY OF THE YOSEMITE & THE INDIAN
WAR OF 1851 WHICH LED TO THE EVENT
Lafayette H. Bunnell
Original source history of Yosemite Valley. Reprint of 1911 edition. 340 pp. Paper. Yosemite Association, $9.95.

DISEASE & DEMOGRAPHY IN THE AMERICAS
John W. Verano & Douglas Ubelaker
Illus. 352 pp. Paper. Smithsonian Institution Press, 1992. $34.95.

DISEASE, DEPOPULATION & CULTURE CHANGE
IN NORTHWESTERN NEW SPAIN, 1518-1764
Daniel T. Reff
Illus. 415 pp. University of Utah Press, 1990. $30.

THE DISPOSSESSED: CULTURAL GENOCIDE OF THE
MIXED-BLOOD UTES, AN ADVOCATE'S CHRONICLE
Parker M. Nielson
Illus. Maps. Biblio. 384 pp. University of Oklahoma Press, 1998. $34.95.

DISPOSSESSING THE AMERICAN INDIAN:
INDIAN & WHITES ON THE COLONIAL FRONTIER
Wilbur R. Jacobs
Illus. Maps. 246 pp. Paper. University of Oklahoma Press, 1972. $15.95.

DISPOSSESSING THE WILDERNESS: INDIAN REMOVAL,
NATIONAL PARKS & THE PRESERVATIONIST IDEAL
Mark D. Spence
Illus. 208 pp. Oxford University Press, 1999. $35.

DISPOSSESSION BY DEGREES: INDIAN LAND
& IDENTITY IN NATICK, MA, 1650-1790
Jean M. O'Brien
Illus. Maps. 224 pp. Paper. University of Nebraska Press, 2003. $29.95.

THE DISPOSSESSION OF THE
AMERICAN INDIAN, 1887-1934
Janet A. McDonnell
Illus. 176 pp. Indiana University Press, 1991. $20.

DISPUTED WATERS: NATIVE AMERICA
& THE GREAT LAKE FISHERY
Robert Doherty
184 pp. University Press of Kentucky, 1990. $24.

DISTORTED IMAGES OF THE
APPALACHIAN MOUNTAIN CHEROKEE
A bibliographic historic and ethnologic survey of the Eurocentric stereotyping of original AniYunwiya history, identity, culture and social mechanisms concerning the original people of the Appalachian mountains @ 1500 B.C. to the present historic era. David Michael Wolfe.

DIVING FOR NORTHWEST RELICS
James S. White
Illus. Binfort-Metropolitan, 1979. $8.95; paper, $6.50.

DIVISIVENESS & SOCIAL CONFLICT:
AN ANTHROPOLOGICAL APPROACH
Alan R. Beals and Bernard J. Siegel
185 pp. Stanford University Press, 1966. $19.50.

DO YOU SEE WHAT I MEAN? PLAINS INDIAN
SIGN TALK & THE EMBODIMENT OF ACTION
Brenda Farnell
Illus. 400 pp. University of Texas Press, 1995. $40.

DOCTORS OF MEDICINE IN NEW MEXICO: A HISTORY
OF HEALTH & MEDICAL PRACTICE, 1886-1986
Jake W. Spidle, Jr.
Illus. 400 pp. University of New Mexico Press, 1986. $29.95.

DOCUMENTS OF AMERICAN INDIAN DIPLOMACY:
TREATIES, AGREEMENTS, & CONVENTIONS, 1775-1979
Vine Deloria, Jr. & Raymond DeMallie
Biblio. 1,536 pp. Two vols. University of Oklahoma Press, 1999. $125.

DOCUMENTS OF U.S. INDIAN POLICY
Francis P. Prucha, Editor
Selection of primary documents important in Indian-white relations. The 2nd edition was published in 1990. Illus. 3rd Edition. 396 pp. University of Nebraska Press, 2000. $50; paper, $25.

*DOG PEOPLE: NATIVE DOG STORIES
Joseph Bruchac; illus. by Murv Jacob
Grades 3 and up. Illus. 64 pp. Fulcrum Publishing, $14.95.

DOG SOLDIER SOCIETIES OF THE PLAINS
Thomas E. Mails
Account of the warrior societies and cults of the Plains Indians. Illus. 384 pp. Marlowe & Co. & Written Heritage, $46.50; paper, $29.95.

THE DOG'S CHILDREN: ANISHINAABE TEXTS
told by Angeline Williams; edited by Leonard Bloomfield
In Ojibwe, with English translations by Bloomfield. Ojibwe-English glossary. Paper. University of Toronto Press, 1991. $37.50.

DOING FIELDWORK: WARNINGS & ADVICE
Rosalie H. Wax
Reprint of 1971 edition. 396 pp. Paper.
University of Chicago Press, $20.

DOLLS & TOYS OF NATIVE AMERICA
Don & Debra McQuiston
Indian dolls of North American including Alaska.
Historic color & b&w photos. 119 pp. Chronicle Books,
Hothem House & Written Heritage, 1995. $19.95.

**DOMINION & CIVILITY: ENGLISH IMPERIALISM,
NATIVE AMERICA & THE FIRST AMERICAN
FRONTIERS, 1585-1685**
Michael L. Oberg
Cornell University Press, 1999. $44.50; paper, $24.95.

**DON'T BLAME THE INDIANS: NATIVE AMERICANS
& THE MECHANIZED DOORS OF PERCEPTION**
Aldous Huxley
Paper. Harper & Row, 1970. $3.95.

*THE DOUBLE LIFE OF POCAHONTAS
Jean Fritz
Dispels myths & describes the life of the girl whose active conscience made her a pawn, exploited by her own people and
the white world. Grades 4-8. Illus. 96 pp. Putnam, 1983. $13.95.

**THE DOVE ALWAYS CRIED:
NARRATIVES OF INDIAN SCHOOL LIFE**
Marguerite Bigler Stoltz
Author's experiences as a teacher in schools for Indian
children in the 1920s-30s, plus tales by some of her pupils.
36 photos, 7 maps. Paper. Pocahontas Press, 1994. $9.95.

**DR. JOHN McLOUGHLIN, MASTER OF
FORT VANCOUVER, FATHER OF OREGON**
Nancy Wilson; Bert Webber, Editor
Treatment of Indians is included. Illus. Maps.
Biblio. Paper. Webb Research Group, $12.95.

DRAGONFLY'S TALE
Kristina Rodanas
Native American folklore. Paper. Clarion Books, 1993.
$14.95.

**DRAMATIC ELEMENTS IN
AMERICAN INDIAN CEREMONIALS**
Virginia S. Heath
Paper. Haskell House, 1970. $22.95.

**DRAWINGS OF THE SONG ANIMALS;
NEW & SELECTED POEMS**
Duane Niatum
Poetry. Drawing on his native heritage, Niatum interweaves the
themes of aging and human community. 136 pp. Holy Cow!
Press, 1994. $18.95; paper, $10.95.

*DREAM FEATHER
Stan Padilla
Story of a young boy's spiritual awakening. Grades 5 and up.
Illus. 60 pp. Paper. The Book Publishing Co., 1991. $11.95.

*DREAM QUEST: STORIES FROM SPIRIT BAY
Amy J. Cooper
Grades 3 to 7. Illus. 128 pp. Firefly Books, 1996.
$7.95; paper, $4.95.

**THE DREAM SEEKERS: NATIVE AMERICAN
VISIONARY TRADITIONS OF THE GREAT PLAINS**
Lee Irwin
Demonstrates the central importance of visionary dreams as
sources of empowerment and innovation in Plains Indian reli-
gion. Biblio. 306 pp. Paper. University of Oklahoma Press, 1994.
$14.95.

*DREAMCATCHER
Audrey Osofsky; illus. by Ed Young
Free verse text with glimpses of Ojibwe life.
Grades PS-3. Illus. 32 pp. Orchard Books, $15.

DREAMING THE DAWN
E.E. Caldwell, Editor
Collection of interviews with twelve leading artists and activ-
ists. Illus. 136 pp. University of Nebraska Press, 1998. $22.50.

*DREAMPLACE
George Ella Lyon
When a young girl visits the Pueblo where the Anasazi lives,
she sees images of its past inhabitants' history. Grades PS-3.
Illus. 32 pp. Orchard Books, $16.

**DREAMER-PROPHETS OF THE COLUMBIA
PLATEAU: SMOHALLA & SKOLASKIN**
Robert Ruby & John Brown
Illus. Maps. 272 pp. University of Oklahoma Press, 1989.
$24.95.

DREAMERS WITH POWER: THE MENOMINEE
George & Louise Spindler
Reprint of 1971 edition. Illus. 208 pp. Paper.
Waveland Press, 1984. $9.95.

**DREAMING OF THE DAWN: CONVERSATIONS
WITH NATIVE ARTISTS & ACTIVISTS**
E.K. Caldwell
Illus. 145 pp. University of Nebraska Press, 1999. $30.

**DREAMING WITH THE WHEEL: HOW TO INTERPRET
YOUR DREAMS USING THE MEDICINE WHEEL**
Sun Bear & Wabun Wind
320 pp. paper. Simon & Schuster, 1994. $12.

**DREAMS & THUNDER: STORIES, POEMS,
AND *THE SUN DANCE OPERA***
Zitkala-Sa; edited by P. Jane Hafen
Zitkala-Sa (Red Bird)(1876-1938), a Yankton Sioux teacher,
artist, activist, and violin soloist presents previously unpublished
material. Illus. 174 pp. University of Nebraska Press, 2001.
$22.95.

DRESS CLOTHING OF THE PLAINS INDIANS
Ronald P. Koch
Illus. 220 pp. Paper. University of Oklahoma Press, 1977.
$15.95.

**DRESSING IN FEATHERS: THE CONSTRUCTION
OF THE INDIAN AMERICAN POPULAR CULTURE**
Elizabeth S. Bird, Editor
Paper. Westview Press, 1996. $25.

**DRINKING BEHAVIOR AMONG THE SOUTHWESTERN
INDIANS: AN ANTHROPOLOGICAL PERSPECTIVE**
Jack Waddell & Michael Everett, Editors
248 pp. Paper. University of Arizona Press, 1980. $19.50.

**DRINKING CAREERS: A 25-YEAR STUDY
OF THREE NAVAJO POPULATIONS**
Stephen J. Kunitz & Jerrold E. Levy
Illus. 296 pp. Yale University Press, 1994. $32.50.

DRIFTING THROUGH ANCESTOR DREAMS
Ramson Lomatewama
Poetry. Illus. 72 pp. Northland Publishing, $9.95.

**DRINKING CAREERS: A 25-YEAR STUDY
OF THREE NAVAJO POPULATIONS**
Stephen J. Kunitz & Jerrold E. Levy
First long-term follow-up study of alcohol use among Native
Americans. 300 pp. Yale University Press, 1994. $28.50.

DROWNING IN FIRE
Craig S. Womack
Novel of sexual and cultural identity. 294 pp. University of Ari-
zona Press, 2001. $35; paper, $17.95.

DRUM SONGS: GLIMPSES OF DENE HISTORY
Kerry Abel
Examines the history of the Dene, one of the aboriginal peoples
of Canada's western subarctic. Illus. Maps. McGill-Queen's University Press, 1993. $44.95; paper, $19.95.

***DRUMBEAT....HEARTBEAT:
A CELEBRATION OF THE POWWOW**
Susan Braine
Grades 4-8. Illus. 50 pp. Lerner Publications
& Meadowlark Communications, $6.95.

DRUMS ALONG THE MOHAWK
Walter D. Edmonds
616 pp. Paper. Syracuse University Press, $19.95.

DRY BONES, DAKOTA TERRITORY REFLECTED
John & Pauline Gregg
Ancient diseases in the northern Plains; problems concerning
the prehistory of the Great Plains native populations. Paper.
Dakota Press, 1987. $25.

**THE DULL KNIFES OF PINE RIDGE:
A LAKOTA ODYSSEY**
Joe Starita
An account of four generations of Lakota Sioux family. Illus.
Map. 392 pp. Paper. University of Nebraska Press, 2002.
$17.95.

**THE DUST ROSE LIKE SMOKE:
THE SUBJUGATION OF THE ZULU & THE SIOUX**
James O. Gump
Illus. Maps. 180 pp. Paper. University of Nebraska Press, 1994.
$19.95.

THE DUTCH & THE IROQUOIS
Rev. C.H. Hall
Reprint of 1882 edition. 55 pp. paper. Library Research Asso-
ciates, $8.95.

**DWELLERS AT THE SOURCE: SOUTHWESTERN
INDIAN PHOTOGRAPHS OF A.C. VROMAN**
William Webb & Robert Weinstein
Illus. 223 pp. University of New Mexico Press, 1987.
$42.50; paper, $27.50.

***DWELLINGS: A SPIRITUAL
HISTORY OF THE LIVING WORLD**
Linda Hogan
16 essays. Grades 7 and up. Oyate, 1995. $21.

**THE DYNAMICS OF GOVERNMENT PROGRAMS
FOR URBAN INDIANS IN THE PRAIRIE PROVINCES**
Raymond Breton and Gail Grant
628 pp. Paper. Gower, 1984. $19.95.

DYNAMICS OF SOUTHWEST PREHISTORY
Linda Cordell & George Gumerman, Editors
Illus. 390 pp. Smithsonian Press, 1989. $39.95.

E

*EAGLE DRUM
Robert Crum
Grades 3 to 5. A 9-year-old boy's involvement in powwows as
he changes from traditional dancing to grass dancing. Meadowlark Communications, $16.95.

*EAGLE FEATHER FOR A CROW
Alice Durland Ryniker
Grades Grades 2-6. A Crow Indian boy growing up.
Illus. 80 pp. The Lowell Press, $9.95.

AN EAGLE NATION
Carter Revard
Poetry. 125 pp. Paper. University of Arizona Press, 1993.
$15.95.

**EARLIEST HISPANIC-NATIVE AMERICAN
INTERACTION IN THE AMERICAN SOUTHEAST**
Jerald T. Milanich, Editor
528 pp. Garland Publishing, 1991. $30.

**EARLY AMERICAN INDIAN DOCUMENTS:
TREATIES & LAWS, 1607-1789**
Alden T. Vaughan
20 vols. 7,000 pp. University Publications of America, 1987.
$2,435 per set.

EARLY AMERICAN WRITINGS
Giles Gunn, Editor
Includes writings from Cherokee, Hopi, and other Amerindian
genesis legends. 720 pp. Penguin USA, 1994. $12.95.

**EARLY ENCOUNTERS - NATIVE AMERICANS & EUROPE-
ANS IN NEW ENGLAND FROM THE PAPERS OF W. SEARS
NICKERSON**
Delores Bird Carpenter, Editor
19 essays from the papers of Warren Sears Nickerson (1880-
1966), New England historian, antiquarian, and genealogist.
Illus. 200 pp. Michigan State University Press, $28.85.

EARLY EXPLORERS OF NORTH AMERICA
C. Keith Wilbur, MD, Editor
Recreates the clash of two dissimilar cultures.
144 pp. Paper. Gobe Pequot Press, $11.95.

**EARLY FUR TRADE ON THE NORTHERN PLAINS:
CANADIAN TRADERS AMONG THE MANDAN &
HIDATSA INDIANS, 1738-1818**
W. Raymond Wood & Thomas D. Thiessen
Reprint. Illus. Maps. Biblio. 376 pp. Paper.
University of Oklahoma Press, $26.95.

**EARLY HISTORY OF THE CREEK INDIANS
& THEIR NEIGHBORS**
John R. Swanton
Reprint. 508 pp. Paper. University Press of Florida, 1998.
$29.95.

*EARLY INDIAN PEOPLE
Roots Magazine back issue
Petroglyphs, tools and bone fragments and how early Indians
before European arrivals lived. Grades 4 and up. Illus. 32 pp.
Minnesota Historical Society Press, 1979. $3.50.

EARLY INDIAN TRADE GUNS: 1625-1775
T.M. Hamilton
Illus. Paper. Museum of the Great Plains, 1968. $6.95.

**EARLY INTERVENTION WITH AMERICAN INDIAN
FAMILIES: AN ANNOTATED BIBLIOGRAPHY**
Readings provide information about the influence of Indian
culture and its affect on Indian families whose young children
have health impairments or disabilities. Southwest Communication Resources, $10.

**EARLY LATE WOODLAND OCCUPATIONS IN THE
FALL CREEK LOCALITY OF THE MISSISSIPPI VALLEY**
David T. Morgan & C. Russell Stafford, Editors
Illus. 145 pp. Paper. Center for American Archaeology, 1987.
$7.95.

EARLY MAN IN THE NEW WORLD
Richard J. Shutler, Jr., Editor
Illus. 200 pp. Sage, 1983. $32.00; paper, $16.95.

**EARLY POTTERY IN THE SOUTHEAST: TRADITION
& INNOVATION IN COOKING TECHNOLOGY**
Kenneth E. Sassaman
312 pp. Paper. University of Alabama Press, 1993. $27.95.

**EARLY PREHISTORIC AGRICULTURE
IN THE AMERICAN SOUTHWEST**
W.H. Wills
Illus. 196 pp. School of American Research, $27.50.

**EARLY PUEBLOAN OCCUPATIONS:
TESUQUE BY-PASS & UPPER RIO GRANDE VALLEY**
Charles McNutt
Illus. Paper. University of Michigan,
Museum of Anthropology, 1969. $3.

**EARLY SPANISH, FRENCH & ENGLISH
ENCOUNTERS WITH THE AMERICAN INDIANS**
Anne Paolucci, et al; John H. Ryan, Editor
Illus. 192 pp. Paper. Griffon House, 1997. $25.

**AN EARLY AND STRONG SYMPATHY:
THE INDIAN WRITINGS OF WILLIAM GILMORE SIMMS**
Edited by John C. Guilds & Charles M. Hudson
University of South Carolina Press, 2003.

**EARLY TREATIES WITH THE
SOUTHERN CHEYENNE & ARAPAHO**
Raymond J. DeMallie
35 pp. Institute for the Development of Indian Law, $10.

**EARLY WHITE INFLUENCE UPON PLAINS INDIAN
PAINTING: GEORGE CATLIN & CARL BODMER
AMONG THE MANDAN, 1832-34**
John C. Ewers
Illus. Paper. Territorial Press, 1989. $4.50.

**THE EARLY YEARS OF NATIVE AMERICAN ART HISTORY:
THE POLITICS & SCHOLARSHIP OF COLLECTING**
Janet Catherine Berlo, Editor
Anthology of academic essays on the development of Native
American artifact collections and the historiography of Native
American material culture. Illus. 244 pp. University of Wash-
ington Press, 1993. $30.

**EARNEST GENEALOGY: INDIAN EVE & HER
DESCENDANTS, AN INDIAN STORY OF BEDFORD CO.**
Emma A. Replogle
Reprint. Illus. 128 pp. Paper. Higginson Book Co., $31.

*EARTH DAUGHTER: ALICIA OF ACOMA PUEBLO
George Ancona
Follows Alicia and her family as they make pottery. Preschool
and up. Illus. 40 pp. Simon & Schuster & Oyate, 1995. $16.

EARTH ELDER STORIES
Alexander Wolfe
Stories by a Salteaux leader who lived in Canada's Northwest
Territories and the U.S. Great Plains in the 1800s. Greenfield
Review Press, $9.95.

**EARTH FIRE: A HOPI LEGEND OF
THE SUNSET CRATER ERUPTION**
E. Malotki & M. Lomatuway'ma
Illus. 150 pp. Paper. Northland, 1987. $19.95.

**EARTH IS MY MOTHER, SKY IS MY FATHER: SPACE,
TIME & ASTRONOMY IN NAVAJO SANDPAINTING**
Trudy Griffin-Pierce
Illus. 8 color photos, 50 drawings. Paper.
University of New Mexico Press, $21.95.

**THE EARTH IS OUR MOTHER: A GUIDE TO THE INDIANS
OF CALIFORNIA, THEIR LOCALES & HISTORIC SITES**
Dolan Eargle, Jr.
4th Ed. Illus. Photos. Maps. 200 pp. Paper.
Trees Co. Press, 1996. $10.

**EARTH MAGIC: SKY MAGIC:
NORTH AMERICAN INDIAN TALES**
Rosalind Kerven
Illus. 95 pp. Cambridge University Press, 1991.
$12.95; paper, $7.95.

**EARTH MEDICINE: ANCESTOR'S WAYS
OF HARMONY FOR MANY MOONS**
Jamie Sams
364 daily offerings organized according to the cycles of the
moon. Insights into the spirituality of the earth. 400 pp. Paper.
Treasure Chest, 1994. $12.

**EARTH POWER COMING: SHORT FICTION
IN NATIVE AMERICAN LITERATURE**
Simon J. Ortiz
Contemporary fiction by 30 contemporary Native American
writers. Paper. Dine College Press, $16.

**THE EARTH SHALL WEEP:
A HISTORY OF NATIVE AMERICA**
James Wilson
496 pp. Grove-Atlantic, 1999. $27.

**EARTHDIVERS: TRIBAL NARRATIVES
ON MIXED DESCENT**
Gerald Vizenor
A series of stories that convey the oral tradition of modern
American Indian life. Illus. 195 pp. University of Minnesota
Press, 1981. $14.95.

***EARTHMAKER'S LODGE: NATIVE AMERICAN
FOLKLORE, ACTIVITIES & FOODS**
E. Barrie Kavasch
Grades PS-4. Illus. 160 pp. Paper. Cobblestone, $17.50.

***EARTHMAKER'S TALES: NORTH AMERICAN INDIAN
STORIES ABOUT EARTH HAPPENINGS**
Gretchen W. Mayo
Grades 5 and up. Illus. 96 pp. Walker & Co., 1989. $11.95.

EARTHQUAKE WEATHER
janice Gould
Work by a California Maidu Indian. 96 pp. University
of Arizona Press, 1996. $24.95; paper, $12.95.

THE EARTHSHAPERS
Karen Speerstra
Details of daily life, great tribal gfestivals, and reasons behind
the gigantic mounds. Illus. 80 pp. Paper. Naturegraph, 1977,
$5.95.

THE EASTERN BAND OF CHEROKEES, 1819-1900
John R. Finger
Illus. 304 pp. Paper. University of Tennessee Press
& Cherokee Publications, 1984. $14.50.

EASTERN OJIBWA-CHIPPEWA-OTTAWA DICTIONARY
Richard Rhodes
623 pp. Mouton de Gruyter, $125.

EASTERN SHORE INDIANS OF VIRGINIA & MARYLAND
Helen C. Rountree & Thomas E. Davidson
352 pp. University Press of Virginia, 1998.
$49.50; paper, $16.95.

EASTERN WOODLAND INDIAN DESIGNS
Caren Calloway
Illus. 48 pp. paper. Paper. Stemmer House, $5.95.

EASTMAN JOHNSON'S LAKE SUPEROR INDIANS
Patricia Condon Johnson
Paintings and drawings of the native Ojibwe at Lake Superior
in 1856 & 1857. Illus. 72 pp. Johnston Publishing, $12.95.

**ECOCIDE OF NATIVE AMERICA: ENVIRONMENTAL
DESTRUCTION OF INDIAN LANDS & PEOPLES**
Donald A. Grinde, Jr. & Bruce E. Johansen
Offers the environmental perspectives through the testimony
of Native North Americans. Illus. 224 pp. Clear Light, 1995.
$24.95; paper, $14.95.

**AN ECOLOGICAL ANALYSIS INVOLVING THE
POPULATION OF SAN JUAN PUEBLO, NM**
Richard I. Ford
Illus. 360 pp. Garland, 1992, $10.

THE ECOLOGICAL INDIAN: MYTH & HISTORY
Shepard Krech, III
A look at historical truths and romantic falsehoods about
Native Americans and nature. 318 pp. Written Heritage, $27.95.

**ECOLOGY, SOCIOPOLITICAL ORGANIZATION &
CULTURAL CHANGE ON THE SOUTHERN PLAINS:
A CRITICAL TREATISE IN THE SOCIOCULTURAL
ANTHROPOLOGY OF NATIVE NORTH AMERICA**
Michael G. Davis
214 pp. Truman State University Press, 1996. $45.

**ECONOMIC DEVELOPMENT ON
AMERICAN INDIAN RESERVATIONS**
Roxanne D. Ortiz, Editor
157 pp. Paper. University of New Mexico,
Native American Studies, 1979. $8.95.

**THE ECONOMICS OF SAINTHOOD: RELIGIOUS
CHANGE AMONG THE RIMROCK NAVAJOS**
Kendall Blanchard
Illus. 244 pp. Fairleigh Dickinson, 1976. $22.50.

**EDUCATION & THE AMERICAN INDIAN:
THE ROAD TO SELF-DETERMINATION SINCE 1928**
Margaret C. Szasz
Illus. 3rd Ed. 336 pp. Paper. University of New Mexico Press,
1999. $19.95.

**EDUCATION ASSISTANCE FOR AMERICAN INDIANS
& ALASKA NATIVES**
Master of Public Health Program
for American Indians
School of Public Health, 1994. Free.

**EDUCATION & CAREER
OPPORTUNITIES HANDBOOK**
The CIRI Foundation
Lists over 200 scholarships, grant & loan programs for
which Alaska Natives may be eligible. Annual. CIRI, $5.

**EDUCATION FOR EXTINCTION: AMERICAN INDIAN
& THE BOARDING SCHOOL EXPERIENCE, 1875-1928**
David Wallace Adams
Illus. University Press of Kansas, 1995. $40; paper, $17.95.

*THE EDUCATION OF LITTLE TREE
Forrest Carter
A moving account of a Cherokee as he grows up with his grand-
parents. Grades 3 and up. 220 pp. University of New Mexico
Press, Reprint. $21.95; paper, $13.95.

***AN EDUCATIONAL AMERICAN INDIAN
COLORING BOOK**
Reginald Oxendine
Grades PS-3. Illus. 31 pp. Paper. Arrow Publishing, 1994.
$5.95.

**EDWARD SHERIFF CURTIS:
VISIONS OF A VANISHING RACE**
Florence Curtis Graybill & Victory Boesen
Paper. Houghton Mifflin, $19.95.

**THE EFFECT OF EUROPEAN CONTACT & TRADE
ON THE SETTLEMENT PATTERN OF INDIANS IN
COASTAL NEW YORK, 1524-1665**
Lynn Ceci
360 pp. Garland Publishing, 1991. $10.

EFFECTIVE PRACTICES IN INDIAN EDUCATION
Floy Pepper
Techniques and ideas to help teachers of Indian children. 211
pp. Teacher's Monograph, 211 pp. $14.80; Curriculum Mono-
graph, 186 pp. $24.45; and Administration Monograph, 86 pp.
$11.30. NWREL.

THE ELDER AMERICAN INDIAN
Frank Dukepoo
South Dakota State University Press, 1978. $3.50.

THE ELDERS: PASSING IT ON
Essays, art, photos, and poetry by Native American artists
about their elders. Illus. 31 pp. Paper. The Origins Program,
$5.95.

**ELDERBERRY FLUTE SONG,
CONTEMPORARY COYOTE TALES**
Peter Blue Cloud
Illus. Greenfield Review Press, $10.

THE ELDERS ARE WATCHING
Dave Bouchard; illus. by Roy H. Vickers
Environmental message. Illus. 66 pp. Paper.
Fulcrum Publishing, 1993. $12.95.

**ELEVEN YEARS A CAPTIVE
AMONG THE SNAKE INDIANS**
James Kimball
13 pp. Paper. Ye Galleon Press, 1986. $4.95.

**JOHN ELIOT'S INDIAN DIALOGUES:
A STUDY IN CULTURAL INTERACTION**
J. Eliot; H.W. Bowden & J. Rhonda, Editors
Illus. 173 pp. Greenwood Publishing, 1980. $35.

THE ELKUS COLLECTION: SOUTHWEST INDIAN ART
Dorothy K. Washburn, Editior
Illus. 222 pp. Paper. California Academy of Sciences, 1986.
$19.95.

E-MAIL NAMES FOR INDIAN COUNTRY
Martha Crow
Lists about 9,000 E-mail addresses of Native Americans,
organizations, companies, and Indian-related addresses.
96 pp. Todd Publications, 1999. $75.

ELNGUQ
Anna W. Jacobson
The first novel written in Yup'ik. Reflects a traditional Native
Alaskan way of life. 114 pp. Alaska Native Language Center,
$13.50, postpaid.

**THE EMIGRANT INDIANS OF KANSAS:
A CRITICAL BIBLIOGRAPHY**
William E. Unrau
Illus. 96 pp. Paper. Indiana University Press, 1980. $4.95.

**EMIL W. HAURY'S PREHISTORY
OF THE AMERICAN SOUTHWEST**
Emil W. Haury; J. Jefferson Reid & David Doyel, Editors
A collection of Haury's published works. 506 pp. Paper.
University of Arizona Press, 1986. $17.50.

**EMOTIONAL EXPRESSION AMONG THE CREE INDIANS:
THE ROLE OF PICTORIAL REPRESENTATIONS IN THE
ASSESSMENT OF PSYCHOLOGICAL MINDEDNESS**
Nadia Ferrara
Jessica Kinglsey, 1998 $59.95; paper, $26.95.

**EMPIRE OF FORTUNE: CROWNS, COLONIES, &
TRIBES IN THE SEVEN YEARS WAR IN AMERICA**
Francis Jennings
W.W. Norton & Co., 1988. $27.

**EMPIRE OF SAND: THE SERI INDIANS & THE
STRUGGLE FOR SPANISH SONORA, 1645-1803**
Thomas E. Sheridan
493 pp. University of Arizona Press, 1997. $32.

EMPOWERING NORTHERN & NATIVE COMMUNITIES FOR SOCIAL, POLITICAL & ECONOIC CONTROL: AN ANNOTATED BIBLIOGRAPHY OF RELEVANT LITERATURE
M.G. Stevenson, C.G. Hickey
Inuit literature on models for community empowerment.
64 pp. Paper., CCI, 1994. $15.

EMPTY NETS: INDIANS, DAMS, AND THE COLUMBIA RIVER
Roberta Ulrich
The Columbia River Indians' fight to maintain their livelihood and culture. Illus. Maps. 256 pp. Paper. UBC Press, 1999. $29.95.

ENCYCLOPEDIA OF AMERICAN INDIAN BIOGRAPHY
Donald A. Grinde, Jr. & Bruce E. Johansen
UCLA, American Indian Studies Center, 1997.

ENCYCLOPEDIA OF AMERICAN INDIAN CIVIL RIGHTS
James S. Olson, et al, Editors
448 pp. Greenwood, 1997. $65.

ENCYCLOPEDIA OF AMERICAN INDIAN COSTUME
Josephine Paterek
Illus. Biblio. 516 pp. Paper. Written Heritage, $19.95.

ENCYCLOPEDIA OF FRONTIER BIOGRAPHY
Dan L. Thrapp, Editor
Contains over 5,500 biographies of the men and women who have played major roles in frontier history. From the earliest European explorers to contemporary historians. Includes Indians and Indian agents. 4 vols. The Arthur H. Clark Co. The original three-volume work was published in 1988 and costs $195; paper, $60. Volume 4, Supplemental, 1993. $65.

ENCYCLOPEDIA OF MULTICULTURALISM
Examines American history and society through the experiences of ethnic groups, including Native Americans. 6 Vols. More than 2,000 entries. Cross-referenced. Illus. 2,500+ pp. Bibliographies. Marshall Cavendish Corp., 1992. $460.

ENCYCLOPEDIA OF NATIVE AMERICA
Trudy Griffin-Pierce
Illus. 192 pp. Paper. Viking Penguin, 1995. $25.

ENCYCLOPEDIA OF NATIVE AMERICAN BIOGRAPHY: 600 LIFE STORIES OF IMPORTANT PEOPLE, FROM POWHATAN TO WILMA MANKILLER
Donald A. Grinde & Bruce E. Johansen
Grades 9 and up. Illus. 512 pp. Henry Holt & Co., 1998. $50.

ENCYCLOPEDIA OF NATIVE AMERICAN BOWS, ARROWS & QUIVERS
Vol. 1 - Northeast, Southeast, & Midwest
Steve Allely & Jim Hamm
100 historic bows, scores of arrows, and quivers from 38 tribes. Illus. 144 pp. Writen Heritage, $29.95.

ENCYCLOPEDIA OF NATIVE AMERICAN CEREMONIES
Michelene Pesantubbee
ABC-Clio, 1996. $65.

ENCYCLOPEDIA OF NATIVE AMERICAN HEALING
William S. Lyon
Explores, explains, and honors the healing practices of Native Americans throughout North America. Illus. Maps. 416 pp. Paper. ABC-Clio, $70. Paper. W.W. Norton, $14.95.

THE ENCYCLOPEDIA OF NATIVE AMERICAN LEGAL TRADITION
Bruce E. Johansen
424 pp. Greenwood Publishing, 1998. $95.

ENCYCLOPEDIA OF NATIVE AMERICAN RELIGIONS
Arlene Hirschfelder & Paulette Molin
Ceremonies, individuals, places, and concepts from Native American groups across America. 1,200 entries. Includes biographies of religious leaders and Christian missionaries. Illus. 367 pp. Facts on File & Written Heritage, 1992. $49.95.

ENCYCLOPEDIA OF NATIVE AMERICAN SHAMANISM: SACREED CEREMONIES OF NORTH AMERICA
William S. Lyon
468 pp. ABC-Clio, 1998. $65.

*ENCYCLOPEDIA OF NATIVE AMERICAN TRIBES
Carl Waldman
Contains concise descriptions on history and culture for more than 150 Indian tribes in the U.S., Canada, and Mexico; also a glossary of terms and classified bibliography. Reprint of 1987 edition. Grades 7-12. Illus. 324 pp. Diane Publishing, $45. Paper. Facts on File, $19.95.

ENCYCLOPEDIA OF WORLD CULTURES,
Vol. 1 - North America
An overview of American Indian cultures. Articles of traditional cultural practices and beliefs. G.K. Hall, 1991.

THE END OF INDIAN KANSAS: A STUDY OF CULTURAL REVOLUTION, 1854-1871
H. Craig Miner & William E. Unrau
Illus. 196 pp. Paper. University Press of Kansas, 1977. $9.95.

ENDURING CULTURE: A CENTURY OF PHOTOGRAPHY OF THE SOUTHWEST INDIANS
Marcia Keegan
88 photos, 44 color Illus. 120 pp. Clear Light, 1991. $29.95.

THE ENDURING INDIANS OF KANSAS: A CENTURY & A HALF OF ACCULTURATION
Joseph B. Herring
Illus. 248 pp. University Press of Kansas, 1990. $25; paper, $12.95.

THE ENDURING NAVAHO
Laura Gilpin
Illus. 243 photos. 321 pp. University of Texas Press, 1968. $70; paper, $34.95.

ENDURING SEEDS: NATIVE AMERICAN AGRICULTURE & WILD PLANT CONSERVATION
Gary P. Nabhan
Native ecology, seeds, and roots. Reprint of 1989 edition. 225 pp. Paper. University of Arizona Press, 2002. $19.95.

THE ENDURING SEMINOLES: FROM ALLIGATOR WRESTLING TO ECOTOURISM
Patsy West
Illus. 192 pp. University Press of Florida, 1998. $24.95.

THE ENDURING STRUGGLE
George H. Phillips, Jr.; N. Hundley and John Schutz, Editors
Illus. 110 pp. Paper. Boyd & Fraser, 1981. $6.95.

ENDURING TRADITIONS: ART OF THE NAVAJO
Lois Essary Jacka; photos by Jerry Jacka
Presents modern-day crafts from 192 Navajo artists. 205 full-color photos. 200 pp. Northland Publishing & Clear Light, 1994. $40.

ENDURING VISIONS: ONE THOUSAND YEARS OF SOUTHWESTERN INDIAN ART
D. Erdman and P.M. Hortstein, Editors
Illus. Paper. Aspen Center for Visual Arts, 1979. $12.95.

ENGENDERED ENCOUNTERS: FEMINISM & PUEBLO CULTURES, 1879-1934
Margaret D. Jacobs
Explores changing relationships between Anglo-American women and Pueblo Indians before and after the turn of the century. Illus. Map. 284 pp. University of Nebraska Press, 1999. $55; paper, $27.50.

ENDURING HARVESTS: NATIVE AMERICAN FOODS & FESTIVALS FOR EVERY SEASON
E. Barrie Kavasch
Illus. 352 pp. Paper. Globe Pequot, 1995. $24.50.

ENGLISH—CHEYENNE DICTIONARY
163 pp. Paper. Council for Indian Education, 1976. $14.95.

ENGLISH-DAKOTA DICTIONARY
John P. Williamson
Reprint of 1902 edition. 288 pp. Paper.
Minnesota Historical Society Press, $12.95.

ENGLISH—ESKIMO, ESKIMO—ENGLISH DICTIONARY
P. Shalom Publications, $24.50; thumb-index edition, $29.50.

ENGLISH-ESKIMO, ESKIMO-ENGLISH DICTIONARY
A. Thibert
Revised edition. Paper. IBD Ltd., $18.75.

ENGLISH TO CHOCTAW & CHOCTAW TO ENGLISH DICTIONARIES
Cyrus Byingtons
Choctaw Museum.

ENGLISH-ESKIMO & ESKIMO-ENGLISH VOCABULARIES
R. Wells, Compiler; John Kelly, Translator
72 pp. Paper. Charles E. Tuttle, 1982. $6.95.

ENGLISH-MICMAC DICTIONARY
Silas T. Rand
286 pp. IBD Ltd., 1994. $62.50.

*ENGLISH-NAVAJO CHILDREN'S PICTURE DICTIONARY
Roman de los Santos; illus. by Raymond Johnson
Seected words and phrases. Grades 4-8. Paper.
Dine College Press. $19.95.

ENWHISTEETKWA: WALK IN WATER
Jeanette Armstrong
An Okanagan child of 11 in 1860 encounters non-Indian people. Grades K-4. Illus. 44 pp. Paper. Theytus, 1982. $5.95.

ESCAPE FROM INDIAN CAPTIVITY
John Ingles; Roberta Steele, Editor
39 pp. Paper. Roberta Ingles Steele, 1982. $3.50.

*THE ESKIMO
Jean Aigner
Grades 5 and up. Illus. Chelsea House, 1989. $17.95.

*THE ESKIMO
Alice Osinski
Grades 2-3. Illus. 45 pp. Childrens Press, $13.27; paper, $4.95.

THE ESKIMO ABOUT BERING STRAIT
Edward W. Nelson
The Alaskan Eskimos of the 19th century. Reprint of 1899 edition. Illus. 520 pp. Paper. Smithsonian Institution Press, $29.95.

ESKIMO ARCHITECTURE: DWELLING & STRUCTURE IN THE EARLY HISTORIC PERIOD
Molly Lee & Gregory L. Reinhardt
Illus. Maps. Biblio. 200 pp. University of Alaska Press, 2002.

*THE ESKIMO: ARCTIC
Jean S. Aigner
Grades 5 and up. Illus. Chelsea House, 1989. $17.95.

ESKIMO ARTISTS
Hans Himmelheber
The cultural and artistic heritage of the Yup'ik Eskimo in southwestern Alaska during the late 1930s. Illus. Photos. Map. 90 pp. Paper. University of Alaska Press, 1993. $15.

ESKIMO CAPITALISTS: OIL, POLITICS & ALCOHOL
Samuel Z. Klausner and Edward A. Foulks
Illus. 360 pp. Rowman & Littlefield, 1982. $43.50.

ESKIMO ESSAYS: YUP'IK LIVES & HOW WE SEE THEM
Ann Fienup-Riordan
Illus. 232 pp. Rutgers University Press, 1990. $30; paper, $15.

*AN ESKIMO FAMILY
Bryan and Cherry Alexander
Grades 2-5. Illus. 39 pp. Lerner Publications, 1985. $8.95.

*THE ESKIMO: INUIT & YUPIK
Grades K-4. Illus. 48 pp. Childrens Press, $11.45.

ESKIMO LIFE OF YESTERDAY
Revellion Freres
48 pp. Paper. Hancock House, $3.95.

ESKIMO MEDICINE MAN
Otto George
Illus. 324 pp. Paper. Oregon Historical Society, 1979. $7.95.

ESKIMO OF NORTH ALASKA
Norman A. Chance
Paper. Holt, Rinehart & Winston, 1966. $9.95.

ESKIMO POEMS FROM CANADA & GREENLAND
Tom Lowenstein, Translator
University of Pittsburgh Press, 1973. $17.95.

ESKIMO SCHOOL ON THE ANDREAFSKY: A STUDY OF EFFECTIVE BICULTURAL EDUCATION
Judith S. Kleinfeld
209 pp. Praeger Publishers, 1979. $36.95.

THE ESKIMO STORYTELLER: FOLKTALES FROM NOATAK, ALASKA
Edwin S. Hall, Jr.
Illus. 510 pp. Originally published by the University of Tennessee Press, 1975. Paper. University of Alaska Press, 1999. $24.95.

THE ESKIMOS
Ernest S. Burch, Jr.; photos by Werner Forman
Illus. Map. 128 pp. 302 p. University of Oklahoma Press, 1988. $29.95.

*ESKIMOS
Kate Petty
Grades 1-3. Illus. 32 pp. Franklin Watts, 1987. $10.40.

*ESKIMOS
Nancy M. Davis
Preschool-5. Illus. 32 pp. Paper. DaNa Publications, 1986. $4.95.

*ESKIMOS
Derek Fordham
Grades 5 and up. Silver Burdette, $13.96.

ESKIMOS & ALEUTS
Don E. Dumond
Illus. 180 pp. Paper. Thames & Hudson, 1977. $11.95.

ESKIMOS: AN EDUCATIONAL COLORING BOOK
Grades 1-8. Illus. 32 pp. Paper. Spizzirri Publishing, 1981.
Read & Coloring Book, $1.95; Cassette/book, $6.95.

ESKIMOS & EXPLORERS
Wendell H. Oswalt
2nd Edition. Illus. Maps. 341 pp. Paper.
University of Nebraska Press, 1999. $19.95.

*ESKIMOS - THE INUIT OF THE ARCTIC
J.H. Smith
Grades 4-8. Illus. 48 pp. Rourke Corp., 1987. $12.66.

THE ESKIMOS OF BERING STRAIT, 1650-1898
Dorothy Jean Ray
Oral tradition of this region. Quotes & details of cross-cultural contact for the past 250 years. Illus. Maps. 360 pp. Paper. Alaska Natural History Association, $16.95.

ESKIMOS, REVISED
Jill Hughes
Illus. 32 pp. Franklin Watts, 1984. $11.90.

ESSAYS IN ANTHROPOLOGY PRESENTED TO A.L. KROEBER IN CELEBRATION OF HIS SIXTIETH BIRTHDAY, JUNE 11, 1936
Alfred L. Kroeber
Facsimile of the 1936 edition. Ayer Co., $27.50.

ESSAYS IN NORTH AMERICAN INDIAN HISTORY
Gillis
255 pp. Paper. Kendall-Hunt, 1990. $24.95.

ESSAYS ON THE ETHNOGRAPHY OF THE ALEUTS
R.G. Liapunova
Illus. Photos. Map. 256 pp. Paper. University of Alaska Press, 1996. $18.

ESSIE'S STORY: THE LIFE & LEGACY OF A SHOSHONE TEACHER
Esther Burnett Horne & Sally McBeth
Infomative narrative about education and identity. Illus. Map. 275 pp. Paper. University of Nebraska Press, 1998. $13.95.

ESTHETIC RECOGNITION OF ANCIENT AMERINDIAN ART
George Kubler
Illus. 300 pp. Yale University Press, 1991. $32.50.

ESTIYUT OMAYAT: CREEK WRITING
Lewis Oliver
Illus. 17 pp. Paper. Indian University Press, 1985. $3.60, postpaid.

ETERNAL ONES OF THE DREAM: MYTH & RITUAL, DREAMS & FANTASIES - THEIR ROLE IN THE LIVES OF PRIMITIVE MAN
Geza Roheim
Paper. International Universities Press, $19.95.

ETHICS: ATTORNEY VS. TRIBE, WHO'S IN CONTROL
Panel discussion materials discuss ethical considerations of representing Indian tribes from the tribal perspective. 75 pp. Federal Bar Association, 1988. $15.

ETHNIC HERITAGE IN MISSISSIPPI
Barbara Carpenter, Editor
Essays. Illus. 192 pp.University Press of Mississippi, 1993. $35; paper, $15.95.

THE ETHNOBOTANY OF THE COAHUILLA INDIANS OF SOUTHERN CALIFORNIA
David P. Barrows
Reprint of 1900 edtition. Paper. Malki Museum Press, $12.

ETHNOBOTANY OF THE MENOMINEE INDIANS
Huron H. Smith
Reprint of 1923 edition. Greenwood, $35.

ETHNOBOTANY OF THE RAMAH NAVAHO
Paul A. Vestal
Reprint of 1952 edition. Paper. Redwood Seed, $9.50.

ETHNOGRAPHIC BIBLIOGRAPHY OF NORTH AMERICA
J. O'Leary; supplement by Martin & O'Leary
5 vols. of original publication by geographic areas, subdivided by tribe. 1975. Supplement is arranged by author, with extensive subject and tribal indexes. 1990. HRAF Press.

AN ETHNOGRAPHY OF DRINKING & SOBRIETY AMONG THE LAKOTA
Beatrice Medicine, Editor
University of Nebraska Press, 1994.

ETHNOGRAPHY & FOLKLORE OF THE INDIANS OF NORTHWESTERN CALIFORNIA: A LITERATURE REVIEW & ANNOTATED BIBLIOGRAPHY
Joan Berman; G. Breschini & T. Haversat, Editors
120 pp. Paper. Coyote Press, 1986. $7.45.

ETHNOGRAPHY OF FRANZ BOAS: LETTERS & DIARIES OF FRANZ BOAS WRITTEN ON THE NORTHWEST COAST FROM 1886-1931
Franz Boas; Ronald P. Rohner, Editor
Reprint. Illus. University of Chicago Press, $16.

AN ETHNOGRAPHY OF THE HURON INDIANS, 1615-1649
Elisabeth Tooker
Reprint of 1964 edition. 195 pp. Syracuse University Press, $39.95; paper, $15.95.

ETHNOGRAPHY OF THE NORTHERN UTES
Anne M. Smith
Illus. Paper. Museum of New Mexico Press, 1974. $14.95.

ETHNOGRAPHY OF THE TANAINA
Cornelius Osgood
A study of the Tanaina of Cook Inlet, Alaska. Reprint of 1937 edition. Illus. 229 pp. Paper. HRAF Press, $15.

ETHNOHISTORY IN THE ARCTIC: THE BERING STRAITS ESKIMO
Dorothy J. Ray; Richard A. Pierce, Editor
Illus. 280 pp. Limestone Press, 1983. $27.

ETHNOLOGICAL RESULTS OF THE POINT BARROW EXPEDITION
John Murdock
The only major early ethnography of northern Alaskan Eskimos. Reprint of 1892 9th Annual Report of the BIA. Illus. 480 pp. Paper. Smithsonian Institution Press, $29.95.

THE ETHNOLOGY OF THE SALINAN INDIANS
J. Alden Mason
Reprint of 1912 edition. 143 pp. Paper. Coyote Press, $15.63.

ETHNOLOGY OF THE YUCHI INDIANS
Frank G. Speck; intro by Jason Baird Jackson
Reprint. Illus. 192 pp. Paper. University of Nebraska Press, 2004. $29.95.

THE EUROPEAN CHALLENGE
Time-Life Books Editors
176 pp. Time-Life Books, 1993. $19.95.

THE EUROPEAN & THE INDIAN: ESSAYS IN THE ETHNOHISTORY OF COLONIAL NORTH AMERICA
James Axtell
Illus. 256 pp. Oxford University Press, 1982. $27.50; paper, $9.95.

EUROPEAN & NATIVE AMERICAN WARFARE
Armstrong Starkey
Illus. Biblio. 160 pp. University of Oklahoma Press, 1998. $39.97; paper, $17.95.

EVA: AN ARCHAIC SITE
Thomas Lewis and Madeline Lewis
Illus. Paper. University of Tennessee Press, 1961. $5.95.

EVERYDAY LAKOTA: AN ENGLISH-SIOUX DICTIONARY FOR BEGINNERS
Joseph S. Karol & Stephen L. Rozman
Includes 3,800 entries, 300 phrass, idiom drills, expressions of time, coinage, native birds, etc.Intended to enable speakers of English to begin to learn Lakota. 122 pp. Paper. VIP Publishing. $12.95.

EVERYDAY LIFE OF THE NORTH AMERICAN INDIAN
Jon M. White
Illus. 256 pp. Holmes & Meier, 1979. $24.50.

THE EVOLUTION OF THE CALUSA: A NON AGRICULTURAL CHIEFDOM ON THE SOUTHWEST FLORIDA COAST
Randolf J. Widmer
Illus. 393 pp. Paper. University of Alabama Press, 1988. $18.95.

THE EVOLUTION OF NORTH AMERICAN INDIANS
David Hurst Thomas, Editor
A 31-volume series of outstanding dissertations. Garland Publishing, $2,230/set; also sold separately.

EVOLUTION OF THE ONONDAGA IROQUOIS: ACCOMODATING CHANGE, 1500-1655
James Bradley
Illus. 288 pp. Syracuse University Press, 1987. $24.95.

EXCAVATIONS AT MAGIC MOUNTAIN
Cynthia Irwin-Williams
Paper. Denver Museum of Natural History, 1966. $4.95.

EXCAVATION OF MAIN PUEBLO AT FITZMAURICE RUIN
Franklin Barnett
Illus. 178 pp. Paper. Museum of Northern Arizona, 1974. $7.50.

EXCAVATIONS AT SNAKETOWN: MATERIAL CULTURE
Harold S. Gladwin, et al
Reconstructs the building of the Hohokam civilization. Reprint of 1965 edition. 305 pp. University of Arizona Press, $19.95.

EXCAVATIONS, 1940, AT UNIVERSITY INDIAN RUIN
Julian Hayden
Illus. Maps. 234 pp. Paper. Southwest Parks and Monuments, 1957. $2.

EXECUTIVE ORDERS ESTABLISHING THE PAPAGO RESERVATIONS — WITH A BRIEF CHRONOLOGICAL HISTORY
Lynn Kickingbird & Curtis Berkey
57 pp. Institute for the Development of Indian Law, $12.

EXECUTIVE ORDERS RELATING TO INDIAN RESERVATIONS FROM 1855-1912; AND FROM 1912-1922
Reprint of 1922 edition. Two volumes in one. Scholarly Resources, $45.

EXEMPLAR OF LIBERTY: NATIVE AMERICAN & THE EVOLUTION OF AMERICAN DEMOCRACY
Donald A. Grinde, Jr. & Bruce E. Johansen
320 pp. Paper. UCLA, American Indian Studies Center, 1991. $15.

EXILED IN THE LAND OF THE FREE: DEMOCRACY, THE INDIAN NATIONS & THE U.S. CONSTITUTION
8 essays - Oren Lyons, John Mohawk, Vine Deloria, Jr., Laurence Hauptman, Howard Berman, Donald Grinde, Jr., Curtis Berkey, and Robert Venables. Preface by Sen. Daniel K. Inouye; Foreword by Peter Matthiessen. Illus. Maps. 427 pp. Clear Light, 1992. $24.95; paper, $14.95.

EXILED: THE TIGUA INDIANS OF YSLETA DEL SUR
Randy L. Eickhoff
300 pp. Paper. Wordware Publishing, 1996. $12.95.

EXILES OF FLORIDA
Joshua R. Giddings
Facsimile of 1858 edition. Illus. Ayer Co., $15.

EXPANDING THE VIEW OF HOHOKAM PLATFORM MOUNDS: AN ETHNOGRAPHIC PERSPECTIVE
Mark D. Elson
Illus. 160 pp. paper. University of Arizona Press, 1998. $16.95.

EXPANSION & AMERICAN INDIAN POLICY, 1783-1812
Reginaldo Horsman
Reprint. 210 pp. Paper. University of Oklahoma Press, 1992. $16.95.

EXPEDITION TO THE SOUTHWEST: AN 1845 RECONNAISSANCE OF COLORADO, NEW MEXICO, TEXAS & OKLAHOMA
James William Albert
Map. 144 pp. Paper. University of Nebraska Press, 1999. $10.

EXPLORATION INTO WORLD CULTURES: AN "ORAL HISTORY" BIOGRAPHY OF HAP GILLILAND
Heather Logan
The author's experiences with Yanoamo Indians of Venzuela, the Cheyenne of Montana, and the Papuans of New Guinea. 112 pp. Council for Indian Education, 1995. $9.95.

EXPLORING ANCIENT NATIVE AMERICA: AN ARCHAEOLOGICAL GUIDE
David H. Thomas
Illus. 336 pp. Prentice Hall Books, 1994. $25. Paper. Routledge, 1999. $18.99.

EXPLORING IOWA'S PAST: A GUIDE TO PREHISTORIC ARCHAEOLOGY
Lynn M. Alex
Illus. 180 pp. Paper, University of Iowa Press, 1980. $8.95.

EXPLORING THE OUTDOORS WITH INDIAN SECRETS
Allan A. Macfarlan
Illus. 224 pp. Paper. Stackpole, 1982. $12.95.

EXPLORING THE WEST
Herman J. Viola
Story of those who risked everything to open upo the West. Includes the Lewis & Clark Expedition. Illus. 256 pp. Smithsonian Books, $24.96.

EXPLORING YOUR CHEROKEE ANCESTRY: A BASIC GENEALOGICAL RESEARCH GUIDE
Tom Mooney
58 pp. Paper. VIP Publishing & Cherokee Publications, $12.50.

EXTERMINATE THEM: WRITTEN ACCOUNTS OF THE MURDER, RAPE & ENSLAVEMENT OF NATIVE AMERICANS DURING THE ALIFORNIA GOLD RUSH, 1848-1868
Clifford E. Trafzer
Paper. Michigan State University Press, 1999. $22.95.

*EXTRAORDINARY AMERICAN INDIANS
Grades 4 and up. Illus. Biblio. 150 pp. Childrens Press, $22.95.

*THE EYE OF THE NEEDLE: BASED ON A YUP'IK TALE TOLD BY BETTY HUFFMAN
Teri Sloat, retold by & Illus.
Grades Preschool-4. E.P. Dutton, 1990. $13.95.

THE EYES OF CHIEF SEATTLE
The Suquamish Museum
The lives and experiences of the original inhabitants of northwest Washington state. Color photos. 56 pp. Paper. Clear Light, $16.95.

EYEWITNESS AT WOUNDED KNEE
Richard E. Jensen, R. Eli Paul, and John E. Carter
Illus. Maps. 210 pp. Oyate & University of Nebraska Press, 1991. $55.

F

A FACE IN THE ROCK: THE TALE OF A GRAND ISLAND CHIPPEWA
Loren R. Graham
Illus. 172 pp. Paper. University of California Press, 1998. $12.95.

FACES IN THE MOON
Betty Louise Bell
Story of three generations of Cherokee women. 192 pp. University of Oklahoma Press, 1994. $19.95; paper, $10.95.

*FACES IN THE FIRELIGHT
Joh L. Peyton
Legends and traditional life ways of the northern Ojibway. Grades 6 to 8. Illus. 267 pp. Paper. University of Nebraska Press, 1992. $14.95.

FACES OF A RESERVATION: A PORTRAIT OF THE WARM SPRINGS INDIAN RESERVATION
Cynthia D. Stowell
Illus. 220 pp. Oregon Historical Society, 1987. $29.95.

FACING WEST: THE METAPHYSICS OF INDIAN HATING & EMPIRE-BUILDING
Richard Drinnan
Makes connection between suppression of native nations and suppression of liberation movements throughout the world. Illus. 608 pp. Paper. University of Oklahoma Press, 1997. $19.95.

THE FAITHFUL HUNTER & OTHER ABENAKI STORIES
Joseph Bruchac
Abenaki traditional legends. Illus. Bowman Books, $7.95.

THE FALCON: A NARRATIVE OF THE CAPTIVITY & ADVENTURES OF JOHN TANNER
Louise Erdrich, Editor
John Tanner was captured by the Shawnee Indians in 1789 and ultimately sold to and adopted by the Ojibwas. 304 pp. Penguin USA, 1993. $12.50.

THE FALL OF NATURAL MAN: THE AMERICAN INDIAN & THE ORIGINS OF COMPARATIVE ETHNOLOGY
Anthony Pagden
272 pp. Cambridge University Press, 1982. $49.50.

THE FALSE FACES OF THE IROQUOIS
William N. Fenton
Illus. 522 pp. University of Oklahoma Press, 1987. $98.50; paper, $39.95.

*FAMILY, CLAN, NATION
Grades 4-5. 50 pp. Capstone Press, 1989. $10.95.

FAMILY MATTERS, TRIBAL AFFAIRS
Carter Revard
Osage writer. 224 pp. Paper. University of Arizona Press, 1998. $17.95.

*FAMINE WINTER
John W. Schultz
Grades 4-10. Paper. Council for Indian Education, 1984. $1.

*FAMOUS AMERICAN INDIAN LEADERS
Bearl Brooks
Grades 4-6. 24 pp. ESP. Workbook, $5.

FAMOUS FLORIDA! SEMINOLE INDIAN RECIPES
Marina Polvay & Joyce LaFray
29 pp. SeaSide Publishing, 1996. $5.95.

FAMOUS INDIAN CHIEFS
Charles Johnston
Reprint of 1909 edition. Ayer Co., $30.

FAMOUS INDIANS OF NORTHWEST NEBRASKA
Dr. James A. Hanson
Biographies of 12 famous chiefs including Red Cloud and Crazy Horse. Illus. 40 pp. The Fur Press, $2.

FANTASIES OF THE MASTER RACE: LITERATURE, CINEMA & THE COLONIZATION OF AMERICAN INDIANS
Ward Churchill
Examines the connection between culture & genocide in the 500 years since Columbus. Essays on Tony Hillerman's novels, Sun Bear and Dances With Wolves. Revised edition. 192 pp. Paper. City Lights, 1998. $16.95.

THE FAR WEST & THE GREAT PLAINS IN TRANSITION, 1859-1900
Rodman W. Paul
Paper. University of Oklahoma Press, 1998. $17.95.

FAREWELL MY NATION: THE AMERICAN INDIAN & THE U.S., 1820-1890
Philip Weeks
264 pp. Paper. Harlan Davidson, 1990.

FARMERS, HUNTERS, & COLONISTS: INTERACTION BETWEEN THE SOUTHWEST & THE SOUTHERN PLAINS
Katherine A. Spielmann, Editor
217 pp. University of Arizona Press, 1991. $40.

FATHER FRANCIS M. CRAFT, MISSIONARY TO THE SIOUX
Thomas W. Foley
Illus. Maps. 195 pp. University of Nebraska Press, 2002. $45.

FATHER PETER JOHN DE SMET: JESUIT IN THE WEST
Robert C. Carriker
Illus. Maps. 266 pp. 302 p. University of Oklahoma Press, 1995. $26.95; paper, $13.95.

FATHERS & CROWS: VOL. 2 OF SEVEN DREAMS: A BOOK OF NORTH AMERICAN LANDSCAPES
William T. Vollmann
Fictional history of the clash of Indians & Europeans in the New World. 1,008 pp. Paper. Penguin USA, $14.

THE FAUNEL REMAINS FROM ORROYO HONDO, NEW MEXICO
Richard W. Lang and Arthur Harris
Illus. 150 pp. Paper. Scholarly American Research, 1984. $15.

A FEAST FOR EVERYONE
Grades 4-5. 50 pp. Capstone Press, 1989. $10.95.

FEASTING WITH CANNIBLAS: AN ESSAY ON KWAKIUTL COSMOLOGY
Stanley Walens
Illus. 236 pp. Princeton University Press, 1981. $20.00.

FEASTING WITH MINE ENEMY: RANK & EXCHANGE AMONG NORTHWEST COAST SOCIETIES
Abraham Rosman & Paula Rubel
Illus. 221 pp. Paper. Waveland Press, 1986. $9.95.

THE FEATHERED SUN: PLAINS INDIANS IN ART & PHILOSOPHY
Frithjof Schuon
165 pp. World Wisdom Books, 1990. $37.50; paper, $25.

FEATHERING CUSTER
W.S. Penn
W.S. Penn, a noted Nez Perce fiction writer and critic, considers how modern scholarship has affected the ways Native Americans and others see themselves and their world. 240 pp. University of Nebraska Press, 2001. $35.

*FEATHERS IN THE WIND: THE STORY OF OLIVE OATMAN
Lillian M. Fisher
Account of capture of two young pioneer girls by Apaches. Grades 5-10. Illus. Biblio. 184 pp. Paper. Pocahontas Press, 1992. $12.95.

FEDERAL CONCERN ABOUT CONDITIONS OF CALIFORNIA INDIANS 1853-1913: EIGHT DOCUMENTS
Robert F. Heizer
Paper. 152 pp. Ballena Press, 1979. $7.95.

FEDERAL INDIAN LAW: CASES & MATERIALS
David H. Getches, et al
3rd & 4th editions. Richard West, $54 & $60.

*FEDERAL INDIAN POLICY
Lawrence C. Kelly
Grades 5 and up. Illus. Chelsea House, 1989. $17.95.

FEDERAL INDIAN TAX RULES: A COMPILATION OF IRS RULES RELATING TO INDIANS
Hans Walker, Jr.
240 pp. Paper. Institute for the Development of Indian Law, 1989. $50.

THE FEDERAL-INDIAN TRUST RELATIONSHIP
Institute for Development of Indian Law, 1981. $12.

FEDERAL PERSONNEL: PUBLIC HEALTH SERVICE COMMISSIONED CORPS OFFICERS' HEALTH CARE FOR NATIVE AMERICANS
Larry H. Endy
Illus. 59 pp. Paper. Diane Publishing, 1998. $25.

FEDERAL PROGRAMS OF ASSISTANCE TO AMERICAN INDIANS: A REPORT PREPARED FOR THE SENATE SELECT COMMITTEE ON INDIAN AFFAIRS OF THE U.S. SENATE
Roger Walke, Editor
335 pp. U.S. Government Printing Office, Dec. 1991. No charge.

FEMININE FUR TRADE FASHIONS
Patterns for Indian dresses and moccasins from the Crees to the Pueblos. Illus. 48 pp. Paper. The Fur Press, $2.

FEMINIST READINGS OF NATIVE AMERICAN LITERATURE: COMING TO VOICE
Kathleen M. Donovan
Analyzes texts of well-known writers, N. Scott Momaday, Joy Harjo, Paula Gunn Allen, and others. 182 pp. Paper. University of Arizona Press, 1998. $17.95.

FETISHES & CARVINGS OF THE SOUTHWEST
Oscar T. Branson
Illus. Paper. Treasure Chest & Hothem House, 1976. $9.95.

FIELD GUIDE TO THE FLINT ARROWHEADS & KNIVES OF THE NORTH AMERICAN INDIAN
Tully
Illus. 175 pp. Paper. Hothem House, 1997. $9.95.

A FIELD GUIDE TO MYSTERIOUS PLACES OF THE WEST
Salvatore Michael Trento
Includes many Native American sites. Illus. 256 pp. Paper. Pruett Publishing, 1994. $18.95.

FIELD GUIDE TO SOUTHWEST INDIAN ARTS & CRAFTS
Jake & Susanne Page
Paper. Random House, 1998. $17.

*FIELD MOUSE GOES TO WAR
Edward Kennard; illus. by R. Kabotie
Traditional Hopi stories. Grades 2-5. Illus. 74 pp. Paper. Filter Press, $5.

FIELD OF HONOR
D.L. Birchfield
A novel about a secret underground civilization of Choctaws, deep beneath the Ouachita Mountains of southeastern Oklahoma. 224 pp. University of Oklahoma Press, 2004. $27.95.

FIFTEEN FLOWER WORLD VARIATIONS: A SEQUENCE OF SONGS FROM THE YAQUI DEER DANCE
Jerome Rothenberg
Illus. 60 pp. Paper. Membrane Press, 1985. $12.00.

FIFTH ANNUAL INDIAN LAW SEMINAR
Federal Bar Association Conference of 1980.
100 pp. Federal Bar Association, $15.

THE FIFTH WORLD OF FORSTER BENNETT: PORTRAIT OF A NAVAJO
Vincent Crapanzano
Ethnographic account of the author's time spent with a Navajo man and his community. 245 pp. Paper. University of Nebraska Press, 2003. $15.95.

FIFTY YEARS BELOW ZERO
Charles D. Brower
Reprint of 1942 edition. Illus. Dodd-Mead, $12.95.

FIG TREE JOHN: AN INDIAN IN FACT & FICTION
Peter G. Beidler
152 pp. Paper. University of Arizona Press, 1977. $4.95.

*THE FIGHT FOR FREEDOM, 1750-1783
N. Farr and D. Postert; L. Block, Editor
Grades 4-12. Illus. Pendulum, 1976. $2.95; paper, $1.25.

FIGHT WITH FRANCE FOR NORTH AMERICA
A.G. Bradley
Reprint of 1900 edition. Illus. Ayer Co. Publishers, $25.50.

FIGHTIN': NEW & COLLECTED STORIES
Simon Ortiz
Collection of contemporary short stories.
Thunder's Mouth Press, 1983. $6.95.

THE FIGHTING CHEYENNES
George F. Grinnell
Reprint of 1956 edition. Illus. Map. 468 pp. Paper. University of Oklahoma Press, 1997. $24.95.

FIGHTING TUSCARORA: THE AUTOBIOGRAPHY OF CHIEF CLINTON RICKARD
Barbara Graymont, Editor
Reprint of 1973 edition. Illus. Maps. 328 pp. Paper. Syracuse University Press, $15.95.

A FINAL PROMISE: THE CAMPAIGN TO ASSIMILATE THE INDIANS, 1880-1920
Frederick E. Hoxie
Originally published in 1984. 350 pp. Paper. University of Nebraska Press. New preface edition, 2001. $22.

FINAL REPORT OF THE U.S. DE SOTO EXPEDITION COMMISSION
John R. Swanton
Report of the Indians' and Spaniards' actions, their societies, and the ecology; early southeastern American life. Reprint of 1939 congressional committee report. 12 maps. 400 pp. Smithsonian Institution Press, $29.95.

FINAL YEAR EXCAVATIONS AT THE EVANS MOUND SITE
Walter A. Dodd
Paper. University of Utah Press, $15.

FINANCIAL AID FOR NATIVE AMERICANS
Gail Schlachter & R. David Weber
A list of scholarships, fellowships, loans, grants, awards, and internships open primarily or exclusively to Native Americans. 500 pp. Reference Service Press, 1999-2001. $45.

FINDING THE CENTER: THE ART OF THE ZUNI STORYTELLER
Dennis Tedlock, tr.
Translated from live performances in Zuni by Andrew Peynetsa and Walter Sanchez. 2nd Ed. Illus. Maps. 337 pp. University of Nebraska Press, 1998. $55; paper, $16.

FINDING A WAY HOME: INDIAN & CATHOLIC SPIRITUAL PATHS OF THE PLATEAU TRIBES
Patrick J. Twohy
Reprint. Illus. 296 pp. Paper. P.J. Twohy, 1990. $12.

THE FINE ART OF CALIFORNIA INDIAN BASKETRY
Brian Bibby, Editor
Presents 62 baskets in full color. 128 pp. Paper. Heyday Books, $20.

FINGER WEAVING: INDIAN BRAIDING
Alta R. Turner
Illus. 48 pp. Paper. Cherokee Publications, 1989. $4.

FIRE ALONG THE SKY
Robert Moss
350 pp. St. Martin's Press, $19.95.

FIRE & THE SPIRITS: CHEROKEE LAW FROM CLAN TO COURT
Rennard Strickland
Reprint of 1975 edition. Illus. Maps. 280 pp. Paper. University of Oklahoma Press, $16.95.

FIRESTICKS: A COLLECTION OF STORIES
Diane Glancy
Drama, poetry & Cherokee history. 148 pp. University of Oklahoma Press, 1993. $24.95.

FIRST AMERICAN ART: THE CHARLES & VALERIE DIKER COLLECTION OF AMERICAN INDIAN ART
Bruce Bernstein, Gerald McMaster, Donald Kuspit, Margaret Dubin
Works from many tribal traditions across Canada and the U.S. Illus. 272 pp. Universityof Washington Press, 2004. $60.

THE FIRST AMERICANS
William H. Goetzmann; compiled by Owen Andrews
Illus. Photos from The Library of Congress. 144 pp. Fulcrum Publishing & Starwood Publishing, $34.95.

*THE FIRST AMERICANS COLORING BOOK
William Sauts &Netamuxwe Bock
Grades 3-5. Illus. Paper. 64 pp. Middle Atlantic Press, $4.95.

*FIRST AMERICANS SERIES, 8 Vols.
Provides an overview of Native American history and culture. Each volume covers a region of the U.S. Grades 5-8. Illus. 768 pp. Facts on File, 1990-91. $18.95/volume.

*THE FIRST AMERICANS: TRIBES OF NORTH AMERICA
Jane W. Watson
Grades 1-4. Illus. Pantheon, 1980. $6.95.

*FIRST BOOKS
A series of books for Grades 3-5 covering history & culture of various tribes. Titles are: The Chippewa, by Jacqueline D. Greene; The Inuits, by Shirlee P. Newman; The Pawnee, by Arthur Myers; The Pueblos, by Suzanne Powell; and The Zunis, by Craig & Katherine Doherty. Illus. Franklin Watts, 1993.

THE FIRST CANADIANS
Pauline Comeau & Aldo Santin
2nd revised edition. 220 pp. Paper. Formac Distributing, 1995. $19.95.

FIRST ENCOUNTERS: SPANISH EXPLORATIONS IN THE CARIBBEAN & THE U.S., 1492-1570
Jerald T. Milanich & Susan Milbrath, Editors
Illus. Maps. Biblio. 222 pp. University Press of Florida, 1989. $49.95; paper, $22.95.

FIRST FISH, FIRST PEOPLE: SALMON TALES OF THE NORTH PACIFIC RIM
Judith Roche & Meg Mehutchison
204 pp. Paper. University of Washington Press, 1998. $24.95.

FIRST HORSES: STORIES OF THE NEW WEST
Robert Franklin Gish
Collection of original short stories on multi-ethnic complexities of the 1950s and 1960s in Albuquerque, NM. Illus. 134 pp. University of Nevada Press, 1993. $19.95; paper, $10.95.

FIRST HOUSES: NATIVE AMERICAN HOMES & SACRED STRUCTURES
Ray Williamson & Jean Monroe
Illus. 160 pp. Houghton Mifflin, 1993. $16.

FIRST HUNTERS - OHIO'S PALEO-INDIAN ARTIFACTS
Lar Hothem
Photos & sites. 163 pp. Paper. Hothem House, 1990. $13.95.

THE FIRST KOSHARE
Alicia Otis
Story of Koshare clown figure in Native American humor. 128 pp. Paper. Sunstone Press, $8.95.

FIRST LESSONS IN MAKAH
William H. Jacobsen, Jr.
Revised ed. Makah Cultural & Research Center, 1999.

FIRST MAN WEST
A. Mackenzie; W. Sheppe, Editor
Reprint of 1962 edition. Illus. 366 pp. Greenwood, $35.

FIRST NATIONS OF BRITISH COLUMBIA
Robert J. Muckle
Illus. 146 pp. Paper. University of Washington Press, 1998. $19.95.

FIRST NATIONS TRIBAL DIRECTORY
Canadian aboriginal directory of tribal groups and organizations. Includes U.S. tribal listings, gaming and internet listings. 2nd Ed. 1996. 630 pp. Paper. Arrowfax , Inc., $44.

FIRST PEOPLE: THE EARLY INDIANS OF VIRGINIA
Keith Egloff & Deborah Woodward, Editors
Grades 5-8. Illus. 68 pp. Paper. University Press of Virginia, 1992. $11.95.

FIRST PEOPLE OF MICHIGAN
Wilbert B. Hinsdale
Reprint of 1930 edition. Paper. George Wahr Publishing, $12.95.

FIRST PEOPLES: A DOCUMENTARY SURVEY OF AMERICAN INDIAN HISTORY
Colin G. Calloway
Bedford Books, 1999 & 2004.

FIRST PEOPLES, FIRST CONTACTS: NATIVE PEOPLES OF NORTH AMERICA
J.C.H. King
Paper. Harvard University Press, 1999. $24.95.

FIRST PERSON, FIRST PEOPLES: NATIVE AMERICAN COLLEGE GRADUATES TELL THEIR LIFE STORIES
Andrew Garrod & Colleen Larimore, Editors'
Contains stories of Native American college students struggling for survival. 250 pp. Paper. Cornell University Press, 1997. $47.95; paper, $17.95.

FIRST SCALP FOR CUSTER: THE SKIRMISH AT WARBONNET CREEK, NEBRASKA, JULY 17, 1876
Paul L. Hedrin
Illus. 106 pp. University of Nebraska Press, 1981. $12.95; paper, $5.95.

THE FIRST SOCIAL EXPERIMENTS IN AMERICA
Lewis Hanke
Peter Smith, 1964. $11.25.

*THE FIRST THANKSGIVING
Jean Craighead George
Its hero is Squanto, a Pawtuxet man, once kidnapped by European traders. Grades PS-3. Illus. 32 pp. Philomel, 1993. $15.95.

FIRST TO FIGHT
Henry Mihesuah; edited by Devon Abbott Mihesuah
The life story of Henry Mihesuah, a Comanche of the Quahada band. Illus. 118 pp. University of Nebraska Press, 2002. $26.95.

FIRST WHITE FROST: NATIVE AMERICANS & UNITED METHODISM
Homer Noley
276 pp. Paper. Abingdon, 1991. $8.97.

*FIRST WOMAN & THE STRAWBERRY: A CHEROKEE LEGEND
Terri Cohlene
Grades 1-5. Illus. Paper. Troll Associates, 1992. $4.95.

FISH DECOYS OF THE LAC DU FLAMBEAU OJIBWAY
Art & Brad Kimball
Illus. 96 pp. Paper. Aardvark Publications, 1988. $19.50.

FISH IN THE LAKES, WILD RICE & GAME IN ABUNDANCE: TESTIMONY ON BEHALF OF MILLE LACS OJIBWE HU
James McClurken
Michigan State University Press, 1999. $34.95.

FISHING AMONG THE INDIANS OF NORTHWESTERN CALIFORNIA
A.L. Kroeber & S.A. Barrett; J.H. Rowe, etal, Editors
Reprint of 1960 edition. Illus. 216 pp. Paper. Coyote Press, $23.

THE FIVE CIVILIZED TRIBES
Grant Foreman
A brief history. Reprint of 1934 edition. Illus. 478 pp. Paper. University of Oklahoma Press, 2000. $19.95.

FIVE CIVILIZED TRIBES
Grant Foreman
Documents the removal of the Cherokee, Choctaw, Chickasaw, Creek & Seminole tribes from their ancestral homes in the southeast to the Indian territory west oif the Mississippi. Reprint. 478 pp. Paper. University of Oklahoma Press, 2001. $19.95.

THE FIVE CIVILIZED TRIBES: A BIBLIOGRAPHY
Library Resources Div.
Paper. Oklahoma Historical Society, 1991. $5.

THE FIVE CROWS LEDGER: BIOGRAPHIC WARRIOR ART OF THE FLATHEAD INDIANS
James D. Keyser
Series of 13 ledger-art drawings described and annotated by Fr. Pierre-Jean De Smet. Illus. Map. University of Utah Press. $24.95.

500 NATIONS CD-ROM
Interactive version of mini-series produced by Kevin Costner. VIP Publishing. $39.

FIVE INDIAN TRIBES OF THE UPPER MISSOURI: SIOUX, ARICKARAS, ASSINIBOINES, CREES & CROWS
Edwin T. Denig
Reprint of 1961 edition. Illus. Map. 260 pp. Paper. University of Oklahoma Press, 2001. $19.95.

FLAG & EMBLEM OF THE APSAALOOKA NATIVE
Mickey Old Coyote Lloyd G. & Helene Smith
Illus. 75 pp. Paper. MacDonald-Sward, 1995. $14.95.

THE FLAG IN AMERICAN INDIAN ART
Toby Herbst & Joel Kopp
Illus. 120 pp. University of Washington Press, 1993. $40; paper, $24.95.

FLAGS OF THE NATIVE PEOPLES OF THE U.S.: THEIR DESIGN, HISTORY, & SYMBOLISM
Donald T. Healy
Details the story of the flags of 135 sovereign American Indian nations. 242 pp. Photo of each flag. Paper. Written Heritage, $24.95.

*14 FLAGS OVER OKLAHOMA
Lucilia Wise
Illus. The Five Civilized Tribes Museum, 1984. $1.

FLANDREAU PAPERS TREASURE TROVE FOR MIXED BLOOD DAKOTA INDIAN GENEALOGY
Alan Woolworth & Charles E. Flandreau
Paper. Park Genealogical Books, 1997. $15.95.

THE FLIGHT OF THE NEZ PERCE
Mark H. Brown
Illus. 408 pp. Paper. University of Nebraska Press, 1982. $10.95.

*FLIGHT OF THE NEZ PERCE
Bill Schneider
Grades 4 and up. Illus. 33 pp. Paper. Council for Indian Education & Falcon Press, 1988. $5.95.

FLIGHT OF THE SEVENTH MOON: THE TEACHING OF THE SHIELDS
Lynn F. Andrews
Illus. 208 pp. Harper & Row, 1984. $13.50.

*FLINT'S ROCK
Hap Gilliland
A young Cheyenne boy must leave his home on the Montana reservation to live with his sister in the city. Grades 4-8. 87 pp. Paper. Council for Indian Education & Roberts Rinehart, 1995. $8.95.

*THE FLOOD
Grades 3-12. Paper. Council for Indian Education, 1976. $2.95.

FLORIDA'S INDIANS FROM ANCIENT TIMES TO THE PRESENT
Jerald T. Milanich
Illus. 224 pp. University Press of Florida, 1998. $39.95.

FLORIDA INDIANS & THE INVASION FROM EUROPE
Jerald T. Milanich
Illus. 304 pp. University Press of Florida, 1995. $29.95.

THE FLORIDA SEMINOLE & THE NEW DEAL, 1933-1942
Harry Kersey, Jr.
Illus. Biblio. 230 pp. University Press of Florida, 1989. $25.95.

FLORIDA'S PREHISTORIC STONE TECHNOLOGY: A STUDY OF THE FLINTWORKING TECHNIQUES OF EARLY FLORIDA STONE IMPLEMENT-MAKERS
Barbara Purdy
Illus. 165 pp. University Press of Florida, 1981. $31.95.

FLORIDA'S SEMINOLE INDIANS
Wilfred Neill & E. Ross Allen
Illus. Photos. 128 pp. Paper. Great Outdoors, 1965. $4.95.

*THE FLUTE PLAYER: AN APACHE FOLKTALE
Michael Lacapa
Picture book. Ages 6-8. Illus. 48 pp. Paper. Northland Press & Clear Light, 1990. $7.95.

*FLYING WITH THE EAGLE, RACING THE GREAT BEAR: STORIES FROM NATIVE NORTH AMERICA
Joseph Bruchac
Grades 5-8. Illus. 144 pp. Bridgewater, $13.95; paper, $5.95.

FLUTES OF FIRE: ESSAYS OF THE LANGUAGES OF NATIVE CALIFORNIA
Leanne Hinton
Collection of essays on Native California languages.
264 pp. Heyday Books, 1994. $18.

*FLYING WITH THE EAGLE, RACING THE GREAT BEAR
Joseph Bruchac
16 Native American tales. Grades 5-8. Illus. 144 pp.
BridgeWater Books, 1993. $10.46; paper, $5.95.

FOLK MAMMALOGY OF THE NORTHERN PIMANS
Amadeo M. Rea
Knowledge held about animals by Pima-speaking Native Americans. Illus. 285 pp. University of Arizona Press, 1998. $50.

FOLK MEDICINE OF THE DELAWARE & RELATED ALGONKIAN INDIANS
Gladys Tantaquidgeon
Illus. 145 pp. Pennsylvania Historical & Museum Commission, 1972. $7.50; paper, $5.50.

FOLKLORE OF THE WINNEBAGO TRIBE
David Lee Smith
The oral tradition of the Winnebago, or Ho-Chunk, people ranges from creation myths to Trickster stories and histories of the tribe. 224 pp. University of Oklahoma Press, 1997. $22.95.

FOLLOWING THE GAME: HUNTING TRADITIONS OF NATIVE CALIFORNIANS
Malcolm Margolin
Illus. 192 pp. Heyday Books, $27.95; paper, $18.

FOLLOWING THE GUIDON: INTO THE INDIAN WARS WITH GENERAL CUSTER & THE SEVENTH CAVALRY
Elizabeth B. Custer
Covers the period between 1867 to 1869 when Custer engaged in extensive military activity against the Plains Indians. Reprint of 1967 edition. Illus. 368 pp. Paper. University of Oklahoma Press, $12.95.

FOLLOWING THE INDIAN WARS: THE STORY OF THE NEWSPAPER CORRESPONDENTS AMONG THE INDIAN CAMPAIGNERS
Oliver Knight
Illus. Maps. 364 pp. Paper. University of Oklahoma Press, $18.95.

FOLLOWING THE SUN & MOON: HOPI KACHINA TRADITION
Alph H. Secakuku
Presents the Hopi kachina ceremonial calendar.
120 color photos. 152 pp. Northland, $19.95.

FOOD PLANTS OF COASTAL FIRST PEOPLES
Nancy J. Turner
Illus. 176 pp. Paper. UBC Press, 1996. $24.95.

FOOD PLANTS OF INTERIOR FIRST PEOPLES
Nancy J. Turner
Illus. 176 pp. Paper. UBC Press, 1997. $24.95.

FOOD PLANTS OF THE SONORAN DESERT
Wendy C. Hodgson
Information on 540 edible plants used by over 50 traditional cultures o the Sonoran desert. Illus. 313 pp. University of Arizona Press, 2001. $75.

FOOLS CROW
James Welch
Novel. Illus. Paper. Penguin USA, $10.

FOOLS CROW: WISDOM & POWER
Thomas E. Mails
Teton Sioux holy man Frank Fools Crow describes his life. Illus. Maps. 294 pp. Paper. University of Nebraska Press, $1990. 14.95.

FOOTSTEPS OF THE CHEROKEES: A GUIDE TO THE EASTERN HOMELANDS OF THE CHEROKEE NATION
Vicki Rozema
Illus. Maps. 300 pp. Paper. John H. Blair, Publisher, 1995. $17.95.

FOR AN AMERINDIAN AUTOHISTORY
Georges E. Sioul
The author, a Huron, presents guidelines for the study of Native history from an Amerindian point of view. McGill-Queen's University Press, 1992. $29.95.

THE FORGOTTEN ARTIST: INDIANS OF ANZA-BORREGO & THEIR ROCK ART
Manfred Knaak; Rose Houk & Harry Daniel, Editors
Illus. 128 pp. Anza-Borrego, 1988. $36.95; paper, $24.95.

THE FORGOTTEN CENTURIES: INDIANS & EUROPEANS IN THE AMERICAN SOUTH, 1521-1704
Charles Hudson & Carmen Chaves Tesser, Editors
17 Essays of the history of the early South. Illus. Maps. 496 pp. University of Georgia Press, 1994. $50; paper, $25.

FORGOTTTEN FIRES: NATIVE AMERICANS & THE TRANSIENT WILDERNESS
Omer C. Stewart
Native hunter-gatherers and their uses of fire. Originally published in 1955. Illus. 352 pp. University of Oklahoma Press, 2003. $39.95.

THE FORGOTTEN PEOPLE
Tony Williams
Studies the history of Madoc, a 12th century prince of Wales and his interactions with the Sioux people in North American lands before the time of Columbus. Photos. 203 pp. Paper. Beekman Publishers, $14.95.

THE FORGOTTEN SIOUX: AN ETHNOHISTORY OF THE LOWER BRULE RESERVATION
Ernest L. Schusky
Illus. 272 pp. Nelson-Hall, 1975. $23.95.

THE FORGOTTEN TRIBES, ORAL TALES OF THE TENINOS & ADJACENT MID-COLUMBIA RIVER INDIAN NATIONS
Donald M. Hines
Umatilla, Tenino, and Cascades Indians' myths, legends and tales. Illus. 176 pp. Great Eagle Publishing. $10.95.

FORGOTTEN TRIBES: UNRECOGNIZED INDIANS & THE FEDERAL ACKNOWLEDGEMENT PROCESS (FAP)
Mark Edwin Miller
Examines the FAP as viewed by four once unrecognized tribal communities & their battles to gain indigenous rights under federal law. Map. 464 pp. Univ. of Nebraska Press, 2004. $59.95.

FORKED TONGUES: SPEECH, WRITING & REPRESENTATION IN NORTH AMERICAN INDIAN TEXTS
David Murray, Editor
188 pp. Indiana University Press, 1991. $39.95; paper, $14.50.

FORLORN HOPE: THE BATTLE OF WHITEBIRD CANYON AND THE BEGINNING OF THE NEZ PERCE WAR
John D. McDermott
Illus. 230 pp. Idaho State Historical Society, 1978. $9.95; paper, $4.95.

FORMAL EDUCATION IN AN AMERICAN INDIAN COMMUNITY: PEER SOCIETY & THE FAILURE OF MINORITY EDUCATION
Murray Wax, Rosalie Wax & Robert Dumont, Jr.
Revised edition. 145 pp. Paper. Waveland Press, 1989. $8.95.

THE FORMATIVE CULTURES OF THE CAROLINA PIEDMONT
J.L. Coe
Reprint of 1964 edition. American Philosophical Society, $12.

FORMULATING AMERICAN INDIAN POLICY IN NEW YORK STATE, 1970-1986
Laurence Hauptman
Illus. 288 pp. State University of New York Press, 1988. $57.50; paper, $19.95.

FORT CHIPEWYAN HOMECOMING: A JOURNEY TO NATIVE CANADA
Morningstar Mercredi
12-year-old boy learns about the traditional ways of the Chipewyan, Cree and Metis of Canada. Photos by Darren McNally. Paper. Meadowlark Communications, $6.95.

FORT GIBSON HISTORY
Grant Foreman
A brief history of Fort Gibson in Indian Territory.
The Five Civilized Tribes Museum. Booklet, $2.50.

FORT GIBSON: TERMINAL ON THE TRAIL OF TEARS
Brad Agnew
Reprint of 1980 edition. Illus. Maps. 274 pp. Paper. University of Oklahoma Press, $13.95.

FORT LARAMIE & THE GREAT SIOUX WAR
Paul L. Hedren
Paper. University of Oklahoma Press, 1998. $15.95.

FORT LARAMIE & THE SIOUX
Remi Nadeau
Illus. 375 pp. Paper. University of Nebraska Press, 1982. $9.95.

FORT LIMHI: THE MORMON ADVENTURE IN OREGON TERRITORY, 1855-1858
David L. Bigler
Includes Indian battles; and proselyting among the Shoshone, Bannock, Nez Perce and other tribes. Illus. Maps. Paper. Utah State University Press, 2004. $24.95.

FORT MEADE & THE BLACK HILLS
Robert Lee
An authoritative history of the fort that served the northern plains from the Indian Wars until World War II. 321 pp. Center for Western Study. $40.

FORT SUPPLY, INDIAN TERRITORY: FRONTIER OUTPOST ON THE PLAINS
Robert Carriker
Illus. Maps. 258 pp. University of Oklahoma Press, 1970. $26.95; paper, $13.95.

FOUNDATIONS OF ANASAZI CULTURE: THE BASKETMAKER-PUEBLO TRANSITION
edited by Paul F. Reed
Illus. University of Utah Press. $60; paper, $30.

FORTY MILES A DAY ON BEANS & HAY: THE ENLISTED SOLDIER FIGHTING THE INDIAN WARS
Don Rickey, Jr.
Reprint of 1963 edition. Illus. Maps. Paper.
University of Oklahoma Press, $16.95.

*FOUR ANCESTORS: STORIES, SONGS, & POEMS FROM NATIVE NORTH AMERICA
Joseph Bruchac
Stories and songs of the four elements: fire, earth, water and air. Grades 2-5. Illus. 96 pp. BridgeWater Books, 1996. $14.21.

FOUR DAYS IN A MEDICINE LODGE
Walter McClintock
Facsimile reprint. 21 pp. Paper. Shoreys Bookstore, $2.95.

FOUR GREAT RIVERS TO CROSS: CHEYENNE HISTORY, CULTURE & TRADITIONS
Patrick M. Mendoza, et al
Illus. 131 pp. Teacher Ideas Press, 1998. $20.

THE FOUR HILLS OF LIFE: NORTHERN ARAPAHO KNOWLEDGE & LIFE MOVEMENT
Jeffrey D. Anderson
Illus. 360 pp. University of Nebraska Press, 2001. $55.

400 YEARS: ANGLICAN/EPISCOPAL MISSION AMONG AMERICAN INDIANS
Owanah Anderson
Illus. 416 pp. Paper. Forward Movement, 1997. $12.95.

FOUR MASTERWORKS OF AMERICAN INDIAN LITERATURE
John Bierhorst, Editor
Reprint of 1974 edition. 371 pp. Paper.
University of Arizona Press, 1984. $19.95.

FOUR SEASONS OF CORN: A WINNEBAGO TRADITION
Sally M. Hunter; photos by Joe Allen
A photographic essay where a 12-year-old Ho Chunk (Winnebago) boy learns the traditions of corn from his grandfather. Illus. 40 pp. Lerner Publications, 1997. $20.95; paper, $6.95

FOUR WINDS: POEMS FROM INDIAN RITUALS
Gene M. Hodge
36 pp. Paper. Sunstone Press, 1979. $4.95.

FOUR WINDS CATALOG
Richard & Cat Carey
Catalog of Native American titles, periodicals and audio tapes.
Four Winds Trading Co.

FOURTEEN FAMILIES IN PUEBLO POTTERY
Rick Dillingham
Introduced seven new families and explores the development of the craft. Illus. 275 color plates; 209 halftones. 309 pp. Paper. University of New Mexico Press. $39.95.

THE FOURTH BIENNIAL NATIVE AMERICAN FINE ARTS INVITATIONAL, OCTOBER 21, 1989-SPRING 1990
Margaret Archuleta
Illus. 32 pp. Paper. The Heard Museum, 1989. $5.

THE FOURTH WORLD OF THE HOPIS: THE EPIC STORY OF THE HOPI INDIANS AS PRESERVED IN THEIR LEGENDS & TRADITIONS
Harold Courlander
Illus. 239 pp. Paper. University of New Mexico Press, 1987. $15.95.

*FOX SONG
Joseph Bruchac; illus. by Paul Morin
Story of a modern Abenaki child learning to accept death.
Grades PS-3. Illus. 32 pp. Oyate & Philomel, 1993. $14.95.

THE FOX WARS: THE MESQUAKIE CHALLENGE TO NEW FRANCE
R. David Edmunds & Joseph L. Peyser
The Foxes occupied central Wisconsin, where for a long time they had warred with the Sioux. Struggling to maintain their identity in the face of colonial New France, the Foxes were eventually defeated and took sanctuary among the Sac Indians. Illus. Maps. 282 pp. University of Oklahoma Press, 1993. $29.95.

THE FREEING OF THE DEER & OTHER NEW MEXICO INDIAN MYTHS
Carmen Espinosa
Illus. 93 pp. Paper. University of New Mexico Press, 1985. $9.95.

THE FREMONT CULTURE: A STUDY IN CULTURE DYNAMICS ON THE NORTHERN ANASAZI FRONTIER
James H. Gunnerson
Paper. Peabody Museum, 1969. $15.

FRENCH & INDIAN WAR BATTLE SITES: A CONTROVERSY
Bob Bearor
New York French & Indian War sites. Paper. Smoke & Fire Co., $17.50.

THE FRENCH & INDIAN WAR IN PENNSYLVANIA, 1753-1763
Louis M. Waddell & Bruce D. Bomberger
List of all the forts built during that time period. Illus. Maps. Paper. Smoke & Fire Co., $14.95.

FRIENDS OF THUNDER: FOLKTALES OF THE OKLAHOMA CHEROKEES
Jack F. & Anna G. Kilpatrick
202 pp. Paper. University of Oklahoma Press, 1995. $12.95.

*FROM ABENAKI TO ZUNI: A DICTIONARY OF NATIVE AMERICAN TRIBES
Evelyn Wolfson
Grades 4-7. Illus. 216 pp. Paper. Walker & Co., 1995. $11.95.

*FROM THE ASHES
Pat Ramsey Beckman
Brothers are abducted and raised separately by the Shawnee in 1794. Grades 4-10. 160 pp. Council for Indian Education. $9.95

FROM THE DEEP WOODS TO CIVILIZATION: CHAPTERS IN THE AUTOBIOGRAPHY OF AN INDIAN
Charles A. Eastman
Illus. 255 pp. Paper. University of Nebraska Press, 1977. $7.95.

FROM DROUGHT TO DROUGHT
Florence H. Ellis
Illus. 220 pp. Paper. Sunstone, 1988. 1988. $14.95.

FROM THE EARTH TO BEYOND THE SKY: NATIVE AMERICAN MEDICINE
Evelyn Wolfson
Illus. 112 pp. Houghton Mifflin, 1993. $16.

FROM FINGERS TO FINGER BOWLS
Helen Walker Linsenmeyer
History of California cooking, including Indian cooking, with recipes and lore. Illus. 152 pp. Paper. EX Nature Books. $14.95.

FROM THE GLITTERING WORLD: A NAVAJO STORY
Irvin Morris
Navajo creation story. 272 pp. Paper. University of Oklahoma Press, 1997. $14.95

FROM THE HEART OF CROW COUNTRY
Joseph Medicine Crow; foreword by Herman J. Viola
The Crow Indians' own stories. Illus. Photos. 138 pp. Paper. University of Nebraska Press, 2000. $10.

FROM THE HEART: VOICES OF THE AMERICAN INDIAN
Lee Miller, Editor
Alfred A. Knopf, 1995. $24; Paper. Random House, $15.

FROM INDIAN LEGENDS TO THE MODERN BOOKSHELF
Edith Mosher & Nella Williams
Reprint of 1931 edition. Paper. George Wahr Publishing, $12.95.

FROM INDIANS TO CHICANOS: THE DYNAMICS OF MEXICAN-AMERICAN CULTURE
James D. Virgil
Illus. 245 pp. Paper. Waveland Press, $9.95.

FROM MASSACRE TO MATRIARCH: SIX WEEKS IN THE LIFE OF FANNY SCOTT
Clara Talton Fugate
Illus. 50 pp. 19 drawings, 3 maps. Paper. Pocahontas Press, 1989. $8.95.

FROM THE LAND OF SHADOWS: THE MAKING OF GREY OWL
Donald Smith
Paper. University of Washington Press, $17.95.

FROM THE LAND OF THE TOTEM POLES: THE NORTHWEST COAST INDIAN ART COLLECTION AT THE AMERICAN MUSEUM OF NATURAL HISTORY
Aldona Jonaitis
Illus. 272 pp. Paper. University of Washington Press, 1988. $40.

FROM MISSION TO METROPOLIS: CUPENO INDIAN WOMEN IN LOS ANGELES
Diana Meyers Bahr
Illus. 184 pp. University of Oklahoma Press, 1993. $24.95.

FROM REVIVALS TO REMOVALS: JEREMIAH EVERTS, THE CHEROKEE NATION & THE SEARCH FOR THE SOUL OF AMERICA
John A. Andrew
Illus. 432 pp. University of Georgia Press, 1992. $45.

FROM SAND CREEK
Simon J. Ortiz
96 pp. Paper. University of Arizona Press, 2000. $11.95.

FROM THE SANDS TO THE MOUNTAIN: A STUDY OF CHANGE & PERSISTENCE IN A SOUTHERN PAIUTE COMMUNITY
Pamela Bunte & Robert Franklin
350 pp. University of Nebraska Press, 1987. $22.95.

FROM SAVAGE TO NOBLEMAN: IMAGES OF NATIVE AMERICANS IN FILM
Michael Hilger
Covers over 800 films, inclding many silents and all relevant sound films. Index. 296 pp. Scarecrow Press, 1995. $57.50.

FROM THIS EARTH: THE ANCIENT ART OF PUEBLO POTTERY
Stewart Peckham
Illus. 180 pp. Museum of New Mexico Press, 1990. $39.95.

FROM TIME IMMEMORIAL: INDIGENOUS PEOPLES & STATE SYSTEMS
Richard J. Perry
Maps. University of Texas Press, 1993. $37.50; paper, $16.95.

FROM VILLAGE, CLAN AND CITY
Alyce Sadongei, Editor
A chapbook of eleven Native American writers. Includes poetry and short stories. ATLATL, 1989. $3.

FROM YORKTOWN TO SANTIAGO WITH THE SIXTH U.S. CAVALRY
W.H. Carter
Reprint of 1900 edition. Illus. 335 pp. State House Press, $24.95.

FRONTIER CHILDREN
Linda Peavy & Ursula Smith
Illus. Photos. 176 pp. University of Oklahoma Press, 1999. $24.95.

FRONTIER DIPLOMATS: ALEXANDER CULBERTSON & NATOYIST-SIKSINA' AMONG THE BLACKFEET
Lesley Wischmann
Dual biography. Illus. Map. 400 pp. Paper. University of Oklahoma Press, 2004. $24.95.

A FRONTIER DOCUMENTARY: SONORA & TUCSON, 1821-1848
Kieran McCarty, Editor
165 pp. University of Arizona Press, 1997. $32.

FRONTIER PATROL: THE ARMY & THE INDIANS IN NORTHEASTERN CALIFORNIA, 1861
Loring White
28 pp. Association of Northern California Records, 1974. $4.

FRONTIER REGULARS: THE U.S. ARMY & THE INDIAN, 1866-1891
Robert M. Utley
Reprint of 1977 edition. Illus. 500 pp. Paper. University of Nebraska Press, $12.95.

FRONTIERS OF HISTORICAL IMAGINATION: NARRATING THE EUROPEAN CONQUEST OF NATIVE AMERICA, 1890-1990
Kerwin Lee Klein
Explores the traditions through which historians, philosophers, anthropologists, and literary critics have understood America's origin story. 388 pp. University of California Press, 1997. $55; paper, $19.95.

*FRONTIERSMEN
Gail Stewart
Grades 3-8. Illus. 32 pp. Rourke Corp., 1990. $12.95.

FRY BREADS , FEAST DAYS & SHEEPS
Kris Hotvedt
48 pp. Paper. Sunstone, 1987. $6.95.

FUGITIVE POSES: NATIVE AMERICAN INDIAN SCENES OF ABSENCE & PRESENCE
Gerald Vizenor
Essays. 240 pp. Paper. University of Nebraska Press, 1998. $16.95.

FUNDAMENTALS OF AGE-GROUP SYSTEMS
Frank H. Stewart
Academic Press, 1977. $39.50.

FUNNY, YOU DON'T LOOK LIKE ONE: OBSERVATIONS FROM A BLUE-EYED OJIBWAY
Drew H. Taylor
132 pp. Paper. Orca Book Publishers, 1997. $10.95.

*FUR TRADE
Roots Mag. back issue
How fur companes and their trade with Indians helped shape Minnesota's history. Grades 6 and up. Illus. 32 pp. Minnesota Historical Society Press, 1981. $3.50.

FUR TRADE & EXPLORATION: OPENING THE FAR NORTHWEST, 1821-1852
Theodore J. Karamanski
Illus. Maps. Biblio. 330 pp. Paper. University of Oklahoma Press, 1983. $17.95.

THE FUR TRADE IN CANADA
Harold A. Innis
Social history through the clash between colonial and aboriginal cultures. 496 pp. Paper. University of Toronto Press, 1999. $24.95.

*FUR TRAPPERS & TRADERS: THE INDIANS, THE PILGRIMS & THE BEAVER
Beatrice Siegel
Grades 3-7. Illus. 64 pp. Walker & Co., 1981. $11.85.

THE FUS FIXICO LETTERS: A CREEK HUMORIST IN EARLY OKLAHOMA
Alexander Posey; Edited by Daniel F. Littlefield & Carol A. Pretty Hunter; foreword by A. LaVonne Brown Ruoff
Humorous articles by Posey, the Creek political humorist. Reprint. Illus. Map. 352 pp. Paper. University of Oklahoma Press, 2002. $19.95.

G

THE GABRIELINO
Bruce W. Miller
A historical look at the Indians of the Los Angeles Basin. Illus. 120 pp. Paper. Sand River Press, $7.95.

GAGIWDULAT: BROUGHT FORTH TO RECONFIRM THE LEGACY OF A TAKU RIVER TLINGIT CLAN
Elizabeth Nyman & Jeff Leer
Ancient legends and traditional stories of the Tlingit of the Taku region. Illus. Photos. 261 pp. Alaska Native Language Center, $26.95.

GALE ENCYCLOPEDIA OF NATIVE AMERICAN TRIBES
Vol. 1: Northeast & Southeast; Vol. 2: Great Basin & Southwest; Vol. 3: Arctic, Subarctic, Plateau & Great Plains; Vol. 4: Pacific Northwest &California. The Gale Group, 1997-98. $349 per set.

GALENA & ABORIGINAL TRADE IN EASTERN NORTH AMERICA
John A. Walthall
Illus. 66 pp. Paper. Illinois State Museum, 1981. $2.50.

GAMBLING & SURVIVAL IN NATIVE NORTH AMERICA
Paul Pasquaretta
Explores the impact of reservation gambling on the development of contemporary tribal communities and the survival of indigenous cultural traditions. 220 pp. University of Arizona Press, 2003. $40.

THE GAMES OF AMERICAS: A BOOK OF READINGS
Brian Sutton-Smith
Reprint of 1975 edition. Illus. Ayer Co., $42.

GAMES OF THE NORTH AMERICAN INDIANS
Stewart Culin
Reprint of 1907 edition. Two vols. Illus. 402 pp. **Vol. 1: Games of Chance;** Illus. 490 pp. **Vol. 2: Games of Skill.** Paper. University of Nebraska Press, 1992. $15.95 each.

GATHERING THE DESERT
Gary Paul Nabhan; illus. by Paul Mirocha
Reveals how Southwestern desert peoples have used indigenous plants over the centuries. 209 pp. Paper. University of Arizona Press, 1985. $19.95.

A GATHERING OF RIVERS: INDIANS, METIS, & MINING IN THE WESTERN GREAT LAKES, 1737-1832
Lucy Eldersveld Murphy
Traces the history of Indian, multi-racial, and mining communities in the western Great Lakes region, 1737-1832. Illus. Maps. 231 pp. University of Nebraska Press, 2000. $50.

A GATHERING OF SPIRIT: WRITING & ART BY NORTH AMERICAN INDIAN WOMEN
Beth Brant, Editor
Illus. 240 pp. Paper. Sinister Wisdom Books, 1984. $9.50.

GATHERING OF WISDOMS: TRIBAL MENTAL HEALTH - A CULTURAL PERSPECTIVE
Jennifer F. Clarke, Editor
Illus. 514 pp. Paper. Swinomish Indian, 1991. $19.95.

GATHERINGS II
Greg Young-Ing, Editor
Features the works of several high profile First Nations authors and artists. Illus. 240 pp. Paper. Theytus, 1991. $12.95.

GATHERINGS III
Greg Young-Ing, Editor
Features a wide array of work by First Nation authors from across North America. Illus. 240 pp. Paper. Theytus, 1992. $12.95.

GATHERINGS IV: RE-GENERATION: EXPANDING THE WEB TO CLAIM OUR FUTURE
Don Fiddler, Editor
Poetry, short fiction, essays, songs, oratory, pictograph writing, drama, criticism, biography, artworks and cartoons. 250 pp. paper. Theytus, 1993. $12.95.

GENERAL & AMERINDIAN ETHNOLINGUISTICS: IN REMEMBRANCE OF STANLEY NEWMAN
Mary Key & Henry Hoenigwald, Editors
500 pp. Mouton de Gruyter, 1989. $125.

GENERAL CROOK IN THE INDIAN COUNTRY
John G. Bourke & F. Remington
Two accounts of soldiers of the Indian wars, written by contemporary observers. Reprint of 1974 edition. Illus. 44 pp. Paper. Filter Press, $4.

GENERAL GEORGE WRIGHT: GUARDIAN OF THE PACIFIC COAST, 1803-1865
Carl P. Schlicke
Illus. Maps. Biblio. University of Oklahoma Press, 1988. $34.95.

GENERAL ORDERS OF 1757 ISSUED BY THE EARL OF LOUDON & PHINEAS LYMAN IN THE CAMPAIGN AGAINST THE FRENCH
Loudon and Lyman
Facsimile of 1899 edition. Ayer Co. Publishers, $14.

GENERAL REQUIREMENTS & PARAMETERS FOR VENDOR LICENSING
Casino & Industry Relations Dept. of NIGA
Directed to the Gaming Commissions and companies who wish to do business with Indian Nations. Offers general parameters and guidelines for issuance of vendor licensees. National Indian Gaming Association (NIGA), $20, members; $40, non-members.

GENERAL STAND WATIE'S CONFEDERATE INDIANS
Frank Cunningham
Paper. University of Oklahoma Press, 1998. $14.95.

GENERATION TO GENERATION
Edward Benton-Benai
Ojibway traditional teaching story. Illus. 24 pp. Indian Country Communication, 1991. $6.

THE GENETIC RELATIONSHIP OF THE NORTH AMERICAN INDIAN LANGUAGES
Paul A. Radin
Reprint of 1919 edition. 13 pp. Paper. Coyote Press, $1.88.

THE GENIUS OF SITTING BULL: 13 HEROIC STRATEGIES FOR TODAY'S BUSINESS LEADERS
Emmett C. Murphy with Michael Snell
Illus. 340 pp. Prentice Hall, 1993. $18.95.

GENOCIDE AGAINST THE INDIANS: ITS ROLE IN THE RISE OF U.S. CAPITALISM
George Novak
Reprint of 1970 edition. 31 pp. Booklet. Pathfinder Press, $3.

GENOCIDE OF THE MIND: NEW NATIVE AMERICAN WRITING
edited by Marijo Moore; foreword by Vine Deloria, Jr.
Collection of essays, stories & poetry that describes the struggles of American Indian to maintain an authentic identity within an evolving world. Thunder's Mouth Press.

GENUINE NAVAJO RUGS: HOW TO TELL
Noel Bennett
Illus. 24 pp. Paper. Filter Press, 1979. $4.

GEOGRAPHIA AMERICAE WITH AN ACCOUNT OF THE DELAWARE INDIANS
Peter Linderstrom
Based on Surveys & Notes Made in 1654-1656. Reprint of 1925 edition. Ayer Co., $37.

GEOGRAPHICAL NAMES OF THE KWAKIUTL INDIANS
Franz Boas
Reprint of 1934 edition. Illus. 124 pp. Paper. Coyote Press, $13.75.

GEORGE WASHINGTON GRAYSON & THE CREEK NATION, 1853-1920
Mary Jane Warde
Illus. Maps. Biblio. 384 pp. University of Oklahoma Press, 1999. $25.95.

GEORGIA VOICES, Vol. Two: Nonfiction
Hugh Ruppersburg, Editor
Includes selections from Native American writers. 592 pp. University of Georgia Press, 1994. $40; paper, $19.95.

GERANIUMS FOR THE IROQUOIS: A FIELD GUIDE TO AMERICAN INDIAN MEDICINAL PLANTS
Daniel E. Moerman; Keith Irvine, Editor
Illus. Reference Publications, 1982. $24.95.

GERMAN ARTIST ON THE TEXAS FRONTIER: FRIEDRICH RICHARD PETRI
William K. Newcomb, Jr.
Illus. 250 pp. University of Texas Press, 1978. $35.

GERMANS & INDIANS: FANTASIES, ENCOUNTERS, PROJECTIONS
Edited by Colin G. Calloway, Gerd Gemunden & Susanne Zantop
Historical and cultural roots of the interactions between Germans and Indians. Illus. Maps. 351 pp. University of Nebraska Press, 2002. $75; paper, $29.95.

GERONIMO
Alexander B. Adams
Illus. 380 pp. Da Capo Press, $14.95.

*GERONIMO
Russell Shorto
Grades 5-7. Illus. 144 pp. Silver Burdette, 1989. $11.98; paper, $7.95.

GERONIMO CAMPAIGN
Odie B. Faulk
Illus. Oxford University Press, 1969. $27.95.

GERONIMO & THE END OF THE APACHE WARS
C.L. Sonnichson, Editor
Illus. 140 pp. Paper. University of Nebraska Press, 1990. 6.95.

GERONIMO: LAST RENEGADE OF THE APACHE
Jason Hook
Illus. 52 pp. Sterling, 1989. $12.95.

GERONIMO: THE MAN, HIS TIME, HIS PLACE
Angie Debo
Reprint of 1976 edition. Illus. Maps. 500 pp. Paper. University of Oklahoma Press, 2002. $24.95.

GERONIMO'S KIDS: A TEACHER'S LESSONS ON THE APACHE RESERVATION
Robert S. Ove & H. Henrietta Stockel
Photos. 200 pp. Texas A&M University Press, $24.95.

GERONIMO'S STORY OF HIS LIFE
Geronimo; S.M. Barrett, Editor
Illus. 122 pp. Paper. Alexander Books, 1998. $14.95.

GETTING SENSE: THE OSAGES & THEIR MISSIONARIES
James D. White
Illus. 389 pp. Paper. Sarto Pres, 1997. $21.95.

GHOST DANCE
David H. Miller
Illus. 325 pp. University of Nebraska Press, 1985. $27.95; paper, $8.95.

GHOST DANCE MESSIAH: THE JACK WILSON STORY
Paul Bailey
Westernlore, $12.95.

GHOST DANCE RELIGION
Alice B. Kehoe
190 pp. Paper. Harcourt Brace College Publishers, 1989. $23.50.

GHOST-DANCE RELIGION & THE SIOUX OUTBREAK OF 1890
James Mooney; Anthony Wallace, Editor
Reprint. Illus. Maps. 483 pp. University of Nebraska Press, 1991. $80; paper, $39.95.

THE GHOST-DANCE RELIGION & WOUNDED KNEE
James Mooney
Explores messianic cult behind Indian resistance. Reprint. Illus. 544 pp. Paper. Dover, $12.95.

GHOST DANCING THE LAW: THE WOUNDED KNEE TRIALS
John W. Sayer
320 pp. Harvard University Press, 1997. $31.

GHOST VOICES
Donald M. Hines
Yakima Indian myths, legends, humor and hunting stories. Illus. 435 pp. Biblio. Great Eagle Publishing, 1993. $23.95.

*GIANTS OF THE DAWNLAND: ANCIENT WABANAKI TALES
Alice Mead & Arnold Neptune, Editors
Grades 4 and up. Illus. 76 pp. Paper. Loose Cannon, 2000, $8.

FORT GIBSON HISTORY
Grant Foreman
A brief history of Fort Gibson in Indian territory. Booklet. Five Civilized Tribes Museum, $2.50.

THE GIFT OF AMERICAN NATIVE PAINTINGS FROM THE COLLECTION OF EDGAR WILLIAM & BERNICE CHRYSLER GARBISCH
Illus. 68 pp. Paper. Chrysler Museum, 1975. $5.00.

*THE GIFT OF CHANGING WOMAN
Tryntje Van Ness Seymour
Describes the Apache girl's puberty ceremony. Grades 5-9. Illus. 40 pp. Henry Holt & Co., 1995. $16.95.

THE GIFT OF THE GILA MONSTER: NAVAJO CEREMONIAL TALES
Introduced & retold by Gerald Hausman
Mythology/ceremonial songs of the Navajo. Illus. 224 pp. Paper. Simon & Schuster, 1993. $11.

GIFT OF POWER: THE LIFE & TEACHINGS OF A LAKOTA MEDICINE MAN
Archie Fire Lame Deer & Richard Erdoes
Illus. 304 pp. Bear & Co., 1992. $21.95; paper, $14.95.

THE GIFT OF THE SACRED PIPE
Vera L. Drysdale and Joseph Epes Brown
Illus. 128 pp. Paper. University of Oklahoma Press, 1982. $27.95.

THE GIFT OF SPIDERWOMAN: SOUTHWESTERN TEXTILES, THE NAVAJO TRADITION
Joe B. Wheat
Illus. 48 pp. Paper. University of Pennsylvania, 1984. $14.95.

GIFTS OF PRIDE & LOVE: KIOWA & COMANCHE CRADLES
Barbara Hail, Editor
History of the origins of latice cradles and essays by cradle makers. Originally published by Smithsonian Press in hardcover in 2000. Illus. 136 pp. Paper. University of Oklahoma Press, 2004. $29.95.

*GIFTS OF THE SEASON: LIFE AMONG THE NORTHWEST INDIANS
Carol Batdorf
Grades 1-6. Illus. 25 pp. Hancock House, 1990. $5.95.

GIGYAYK VO JKA! (WALK STRONG!) YUMAN POETRY WITH MORPHOLOGICAL ANALYSIS
Lucille Watahomigie & Akira Yamamoto, Editors
Poetry. 141 pp. Paper. Malki Museum Press, 1983. $12.

*THE GIRL WHO MARRIED THE MOON: TALES FROM NATIVE NORTH AMERICA
Told by Joseph Bruchac & Gayle Ross
Grades 5-8. 127 pp. BridgeWater Books, 1994. $10.46; paper, $5.95.

GIVE OR TAKE A CENTURY: AN ESKIMO CHRONICLE
Joseph E. Senungetuk
The first professional, full-length work to be published by an Eskimo author. Illus. Map. 206 pp. Paper. The Indian Historian Press, 1971. $6.

GIVING: OJIBWAY STORIES & LEGENDS FROM THE CHILDREN OF CURVE LAKE
Curve Lake Reserve, Canada
Paper. Greenfield Review Press, $7.95.

*GIVING THANKS: A NATIVE AMERICAN GOOD MORNING MESSAGE
Jake Swamp
Reprint. Grades K-5. Illus. 24 pp. Paper. Lee & Low Books, 1997. $5.95.

GIVING VOICE TO BEAR: NORTH AMERICAN INDIAN MYTHS, RITUALS, & IMAGES OF THE BEAR
David Rockwell
Stories, both oral and written, in which rituals describe the bear as central to initiation, shamantic rites, healing & hunting ceremonies, and new year celebrations. Illus. 224 pp. Roberts Rinehart Publishers, 1994. $25; paper, $14.95.

THE GLACIAL KAME INDIANS
Converse
Photos of shell and slate artifacts. 159 pp. Hothem House, 1979. $20.

GLEN CANYON: AN ARCHAEOLOGICAL SUMMARY
Jesse D. Jennings
A valuable perspective on Pueblo culture. Illus. Maps. Paper. University of Utah Press, $14.95.

GLEN CANYON REVISITED
Phil R. Geib
Illus. Paper. University of Utah Press, $34.50.

GLIMPSES OF THE ANCIENT SOUTHWEST
David E. Stuart
Describes the prehistoric life in Chaco Canyon, Folsom, esa Verde, Bandelier, Mibres, and other sites. Illus. Maps. 128 pp. Paper. Ancient City Press & Clear Light, $10.95.

THE GLORIOUS QUEST OF CHIEF WASHAKIE
Mary H. Tillman & Ralph Tillman
Illus. 60 pp. Paper. Filter Press, 1998. $8.95.

GOD IS RED: A NATIVE VIEW OF RELIGION
Vine Deloria, Jr.
On Native American religious views. Revised edition. 320 pp. Fulcrum Publishing & Clear Light, $22.95; paper, $16.95.

GOING NATIVE: AMERICAN INDIAN COOKERY
165 pp. Paper. Seattle Indian Services Commission, 1991. $14.95.

**GOING NATIVE: INDIANS IN THE
AMERICAN CULTURAL IMAGINATION**
Shari M. Huhndorf
Paper. Cornell University Press, 2001. $16.95.

**THE GOLDEN WOMAN: THE COLVILLE
NARRATIVE OF PETER J. SEYMOUR**
Anthony Mattina, Editor
Northwest Indian version of a European folktale.
357 pp. University of Arizona Press, 1985. $34.95.

**A GOOD CHEROKEE, A GOOD ANTHROPOLOGIST:
PAPERS IN HONOR OF ROBERT K. THOMAS**
edited by Steve Pavlik
Collection of essays and personal anecdotes that illuminate
the writings and life of Bob Thomas. 390 pp. The Falmouth
Institute, 1998. $40; paper, $25.

**A GOOD MEDICINE COLLECTION;
LIFE IN HARMONY WITH NATURE**
Adolph Hungry Wolf
Legends, lore, and spiritual seeking of North America's Native
people. Illus. 200 pp. Paper. The Book Publishing Co., 1990.
$9.95.

*THE GOOD RAINBOW ROAD
Simon J. Ortiz; illus. by Michael Lacapa
Story of two boys and how they saved their village. In the tradition of Native American oral storytelling. Grades 3 and up. Illus.
64 pp. University of Arizona Press, 2004. $16.95.

**THE GOOD RED ROAD:
PASSAGES INTO NATIVE AMERICA**
Kenneth Lincoln and Al Logan Slagle
Illus. 286 pp. Paper. University of Nebraska Press, 1997.
$13.

**A GOOD YEAR TO DIE: THE STORY
OF THE GREAT SIOUX WAR**
Charles M. Robinson, III
Illus. Maps. Photos. Biblio. 428 pp. Paper.
University of Oklahoma Press, 1996. $16.95.

*GOODBIRD THE INDIAN: HIS STORY
Edward Goodbird as told to Gilbert L. Wilson
Grades 7 and up. Illus. 110 pp. Paper.
Minnesota Historical Society Press, 1985. $5.95.

**GRENVILLE GOODWIN AMONG THE WESTERN APACHE:
LETTERS FROM THE FIELD**
Morris E. Opler, Editor
Reprint of the 1973 edition. 104 pp. University of Arizona Press,
$19.95.

R.C. GORMAN'S ENGAGEMENT CALENDAR
10.5 x 12.5". Clear Light, $12.

R.C. GORMAN'S NUDES & FOODS: IN GOOD TASTE
R.C. Gorman; compiled & edited by Virginia Dooley
Cookbook. 55 color art reproductions. 142 pp. Clear Light, 1993.
$34.95.

*THE GOSPEL OF THE GREAT SPIRIT
Joshua M. Bennett
Grades 8 and up. Illus. Morning Star Publishing, 1990. $21.

THE GOSPEL OF THE REDMAN
Ernest T. Seton
Reprint of 1930 edition. Compilation of Indian thought
& culture. Illus. 126 pp. Paper. Naturegraph, $5.95.

GOVERNMENTS OF THE WESTERN HEMISPHERE
Susan D. Gold
Grades 5 and up. 96 pp. Millbrook Press, 1997. $21.40.

**A GRAMMAR & DICTIONARY
OF THE TIMUCUA LANGUAGE**
Julian Granberry
Describes the grammar and lexicon of the extinct 17th-century
Timucua language of Central and North Florida. 352 pp. Pa-
per. University of Alabama Press, 1993. $29.95.

A GRAMMAR OF BELLA COOLA
Philip W. Davis & Ross Saunders
Describes the major syntactic and morphological patterns of
Bella Coola (NuXalk), a Salishan laguage of British Columbia.
190 pp. paper. University of Montana, 1997. $20.

A GRAMMAR OF COMANCHE
Jean Ormsbee Charney
288 pp. University of Nebraska Press, 1994. $35.

A GRAMMAR OF MISANTLA TOTONAC
Carolyn MacKay
Grammar of the Totonac-Tepehua language in English.
Illus. Maps. University of Utah Press. $55.

**GRAND ENDEAVORS OF AMERICAN INDIAN
PHOTOGRAPHY**
Paula Richardson Fleming & Judith Lynch Luskey
Illus. Smithsonian Institution Press, $39.95.

GRAND MOUND
Michael K. Budak
Minnesota historic site of Woodland people 2,500 years ago.
Photos. 32 pp. Paper. Minnesota Historical Society Press, 1995.
$7.50.

THE GRAND PORTAGE STORY
Carolyn Gilman
History of legendary fur-trade crossroads in northern
Minnesota. Illus. Photos. Maps. Biblio. 168 pp. Paper.
Minnesota Historical Society Press, $9.95.

**THE GRAND VILLAGE OF THE
NATCHEZ INDIANS REVISITED**
Robert Neitzel; Patricia Galloway, Editor
215 pp. Paper. Mississippi Dept. of Archaeology, 1983. $15.

*GRANDCHILDREN OF THE LAKOTA
LaVera Rose
Young readers learn how Lakota children live.
Grades 3-6. Color photos. Lerner, 1999. $16.95.

*GRANDFATHER GREY OWL TOLD ME
Althea Bass
Grades 4 and up. Paper. Council on Indian Education, 1973.
$1.95.

*GRANDFATHER & THE POPPING MACHINE
Henry Tall Bull & Tom Weist
Grades 2-12. 32 pp. Council for Indian Education, 1970.
$8.95; paper, $2.95.

***GRANDFATHER ORIGIN STORY:
THE NAVAJO INDIAN BEGINNING**
Richard Redhawk
Grades 3-6. 34 pp. Paper. Sierra Oaks, 1988. $6.95.

*GRANDMOTHER FIVE BASKETS
Lisa Larrabee & Lori Sawyer
12-year old Anna finds it fun to help Grandmother Five
Baskets basket weave (Poarch Creek). Grades 3-7. 64 pp.
Harbinger House, $14.95; paper, $9.95.

GRANDMOTHER, GRANDFATHER, & OLD WOLF
Clifford E. Trafzer
Collection of oral literature presented by Plateau Indian
men and women. Michigan State University Press, 1997.

***GRANDMOTHER SPIDER BRINGS THE SUN:
A CHEROKEE STORY**
Geri Keams; Illus. by James Bernardin
Picture book. Ages 5-8. Illus. Paper. Northland Press
& Clear Light, 1992. $7.95.

***GRANDMOTHER STORIES:
NORTHWESTERN INDIAN TALES**
Nashone
Grades 5-12. Illus. Paper. Sierra Oaks, 1987. $5.95.

***GRANDMOTHER'S CHRISTMAS STORY:
A TRUE QUECHAN INDIAN STORY**
Grades 3-7. Illus. Paper. Sierra Oaks Publishing, $6.95.

**GRANDMOTHER'S GRANDCHILD:
MY CROW INDIAN LIFE**
Alma Hogan Snell; edited by Becky Matthews
Illus. Maps. 215 pp. Paper. University of Nebraska Press, 2000.
$12.95.

**GRANDMOTHERS OF THE LIGHT:
A MEDICINE'S WOMAN'S SOURCEBOOK**
Paula Gunn Allen
250 pp. Paper. Beacon Press, 1991. $19.95.

**GRANDPA WAS A COWBOY &
AN INDIAN & OTHER STORIES**
Virginia Driving Hawk Sneve
A Lakota storyteller and stories based on oral traditions.
116 pp. Paper. University of Nebraska Press, 2000. $11.95.

**GRASS GAMES & MOON RACES:
CALIFORNIA INDIAN GAMES & TOYS**
Jeannine Gendar
Dozens of traditional games are described through personal
accounts, anecdotes, photographs, and drawings. Photos. Illus.
128 pp. Paper. Heyday Books, $12.95.

GRASS HEART: A NOVEL
M.M.B. Walsh
In 1837, a smallpox epidemic devastated the Mandan Indians
of the Great Plains. This novel shows the horrifying reality of
the epidemic Sioux slavery, cultural plundering by anthropologists, and exile. 176 pp. University of New Mexico Press, 2001.
$22.95.

**GRASSHOPPER PUEBLO: A STORY
OF ARCHAEOLOGY & ANCIENT LIFE**
Jefferson Reid & Stephanie Whittlesley
Life & times of Mogollon community of the 14th century in the
American Southwest. Illus. 192 pp. University of Arizona Press,
1999. $16.95.

**GRAVE CONCERNS, TRICKSTER TURNS:
THE NOVELS OF LOUIS OWENS**
Chris LaLonde
Illus. 240 pp. University of Oklahoma Press, 2002. $34.95.

**GRAVE INJUSTICE: THE AMERICAN INDIAN
REPATRIATION MOVEMENT & NAGPRA**
Kathleen S. Fine-Dare
Illus. 250 pp. University of Nebraska Press, 2002.
$60; paper, $19.95.

GREAT AMERICAN INDIAN BIBLE
Homer "Louis" Hooban, Editor
Indian Heritage Publishing, 1990.

*GREAT BALL GAME OF THE BIRDS & ANIMALS
Deborah L. Duvall; illus. by Murv Jacob
Vol. 1 of the Grandmother Stories. Cherokee history & legend.
Winner of the 2003 Olahoma Book Award for Design and Illus-
tration. All ages. Illus. 32 pp. University of New Mexico Press,
$13.95.

GREAT BASIN ATLATL STUDIES
T.R. Hester; R.F. Heizer, Editor
Illus. 60 pp. Paper. Ballena Press, 1974. $6.95.

**GREAT BASIN INDIAN POPULATION FIGURES
(1873 TO 1970) & THE PITFALLS THEREIN BOUND
WITH BIG SMOKEY VALLEY SHOSHONI**
Joy Leland
Illus. 276 pp. 2 Vols. University of Nevada Systems,
1976. $11.00 per set.

GREAT BLACK ROBE
Jean Pitrone
Illus. Daughters of St. Paul, 1965. $4; paper, $3.

*THE GREAT CHANGE
White Deer of Autumn (Gabriel Horn)
A tale of a wise grandmother explaining a meaning of death to
her questioninf granddaughter. Grades 3 and up. Illus. 36 pp.
Levite of Apache & Beyond Words Publishing, 1992. $14.95.

*THE GREAT CHIEFS
B. Capps
Grades 7-12. Illus. Silver Burdette, 1975. $19.94.

THE GREAT CHIEFS
William W. Johnson
Illus. 240 pp. Time-Life Books, 1975. $14.95.

**GREAT EXCAVATIONS: TALES OF EARLY
SOUTHWESTERN ARCHAEOLOGY, 1888-1939**
Melinda Elliott
Stories of the early Southwestern archaeologists. Illus.
230 pp. School of American Research, 1995.

**THE GREAT FATHER: THE U.S. GOVERNMENT
& THE AMERICAN INDIANS**
Francis Paul Prucha
Detailed chronological overview of the interaction between the
federal government and Indian tribes. 2 vols. Illus. Maps. 1,355
pp. Paper. University of Nebraska Press, 1984. $60.

GREAT INDIAN CHIEFS
Albert Britt
Facsimile of 1938 edition. 280 pp. Ayer Co. Publishers, $21.50.

*GREAT INDIAN CHIEFS
50 stories of the great chiefs. Grades 3-5. Illus.
Paper. Bellerophon, $3.95.

*GREAT INDIANS OF CALIFORNIA
Maurice Vallejo, et al
Coloring book. Grades K-3. 48 pp. Paper. Bellerophon, 1981.
$4.95.

**THE GREAT JOURNEY: THE PEOPLING
OF ANCIENT AMERICA**
Brian Fagan
Illus. 288 pp. Paper. Thames & Hudson, 1987. $12.95.

THE GREAT KIVA
Phillips Kloss
Poetry. Illus. 112 pp. Sunstone Press, $50
(limited edition-signed); paper, $14.95.

**THE GREAT LAW & THE LONGHOUSE: A POLITICAL
HISTORY OF THE IROQUOIS CONFEDERACY**
William N. Fenton
Illus. Maps. 808 pp. University of Oklahoma Press, 1998. $75.

*GREAT NATIVE AMERICANS COLORING BOOK
Peter F. Copeland
Grades K-2. 48 pp. Paper. Dover, $2.95.

GREAT NORTH AMERICAN INDIANS
Frederick Dockstader
Van Nostrand Reinhold, 1977.

GREAT PLAINS: NATIVE NATIONS
Christopher Cardozo; Robert Janjigan, Editor
Illus. 96 pp. Callaway Editions, 1997. $13.95.

A GREAT PLAINS READER
Zitkala-Sa, Editor
Illus. Paper. University of Nebraska Press, 2003.

GREAT SALT LAKE TRAIL
H. Inman and W.F. Cody
Reprint of 1897 edition. Illus. Ross & Haines, $15.

THE GREAT SIOUX TRAIL
Joseph Altsheler
Amereon Ltd., $20.95.

THE GREAT SIOUX WAR: THE BEST FROM MONTANA, THE MAGAZINE OF WESTERN HISTORY
Paul L. Heden
Illus. 330 pp. Montana Historical Society Press, 1991. $27.50; paper, $11.95.

THE GREAT SOUTHWEST OF THE FRED HARVEY COMPANY & THE SANTA FE RAILWAY
Marta Weigle & Barabara Babcock, Editors
Illus. 270 pp. Paper. University of Arizona Press, 1996. $24.95.

GREAT WESTERN INDIAN FIGHTS
Potomac Coral of the Westerners
Illus. 352 pp. Paper. University of Nebraska Press, 1966. $7.95.

*GREEN MARCH MOONS
Mary TallMountain; illus. by J.E. Senungetuk
Details Native Alaskan life. Grades 5 and up. Illus. Paper. New Seed Press, $7.95.

GREENGRASS PIPE DANCERS
Lionel Little Eagle
Story of trips to sundances with Crazy Horse's pipe bag. 256 pp. Paper. Naturegraph, 1999. $14.95.

GROS VENTRE OF MONTANA
Regina Flannery
Reprint of 1956 edition. Two volumes: Vol. 1: Social Life; Vol. 2: Religion & Ritual. Illus. Gros Ventre Treaty, $21 per set.

THE GROWING PATH
Describes traditional Indian infant stimulation practices. Illus. 16 pp. Southwest Communication Resources, $10.

*GROWING UP IN SIOUXLAND
Arthur R. Huseboe & Sandra Looney
Grades 4 and up. Illus. 74 pp. Paper. Center for Western Studies, $5.

GROWING UP INDIAN
Evelyn Wolfson
Illus. 96 pp. Paper. Walker & Co., 1986. $11.95; paper, 8.95.

GROWING UP NATIVE AMERICAN
Patricia Riley
336 pp. Demco Media, 1993. $17. Avon, paper, $12.

*GUARDIAN SPIRIT QUEST
Ella Clark
Grades 5-10. 36 pp. Paper. Council for Indian Education,1974. $4.95.

GUESTS NEVER LEAVE HUNGRY: THE AUTOBIOGRAPHY OF JAMES SEWID, A KWAKIUTL INDIAN
James Sewid; James P. Spradley, Editor
Reprint of 1969 edition. Illus. 310 pp. University of Toronto Press, 1969. $16.95.

GUIDE TO AMERICAN INDIAN DOCUMENTS IN THE CONGRESSIONAL SERIAL SET: 1817-1899
Steven L. Johnson
503 pp. N. Ross, 1977. $35.

A GUIDE TO AMERICA'S INDIANS: CEREMONIALS, RESERVATIONS & MUSEUMS
Arnold Marquis
Illus. Maps. 268 pp. Paper. University of Oklahoma Press, 1974. $19.95.

A GUIDE TO THE ANASAZI & OTHER ANCIENT SOUTHWEST INDIANS
Eleanor Ayer
Illus. Map. 48 pp. Paper. Renaissance House, 1991. $4.95.

A GUIDE TO CHEROKEE DOCUMENTS IN FOREIGN ARCHIVES
William L. Anderson and James A. Lewis
768 pp. Scarecrow Press, 1983. $40.

A GUIDE TO CHEROKEE DOCUMENTS IN THE NORTHEASTERN U.S.
Paul Kutsche
541 pp. Scarecrow Press, 1986. $79.50.

A GUIDE TO COMMUNITY EDUCATION
Institute of the Development of Indian Law, $7.50.

GUIDE TO CONTEMPORARY SOUTHWEST INDIANS
Bernard Fontana
Illus. 96 pp. Paper. Southwest Parks & Monuments, 1998. $10.95.

GUIDE TO THE CULIN ARCHIVAL COLLECTION
Deirdre E. Lawrence & Deborah Wythe, Editors
The Brooklyn Museum, 1996.

GUIDE TO FEDERAL FUNDING FOR GOVERNMENTS & NONPROFITS: NATIVE AMERICAN EDITION
Describes general assistance funds for which Native Americans are eligible. Covers federal programs that are relevant to Indian Tribal governments, Indian villages, nonprofits serving Native American needs, and state and local governments encompassing Native American populations. 3 Volumes. 2,456 pages. Government Information Services. $329.95. includes 12 monthly grant updates.

GUIDE TO THE 400 BEST CHILDREN'S & ADULT'S MULTICULTURAL BOOKS OF PEOPLE OF NATIVE AMERICAN DESCENT
Anna D. Friedler
60 pp. Lift Every Voice, 1997. $24.

GUIDE TO INDIAN ARTIFACTS OF THE NORTHEAST
Roger W. Moeller
Illus. 32 pp. Paper. Hancock House, 1984. $3.95.

GUIDE TO INDIAN HERBS
Ray Stark; Margaret Campbell
Illus. 48 pp. Paper. Hancock House, 1984. $7.95.

GUIDE TO INDIAN QUILLWORKING
C. Ann Hensler
Illus. 64 pp. Paper. Hancock House, 1989. $8.95.

GUIDE TO INDIAN ROCK CARVINGS OF THE PACIFIC NORTHWEST COAST
Illus. 48 pp. Paper. Hancock House, 1984. $5.95.

A GUIDE TO THE INDIAN TRIBES OF THE PACIFIC NORTHWEST
Robert H. Ruby & John A. Brown
Illus. Maps. 310 pp. Revised edition. Paper. University of Oklahoma Press, 1992. $24.95.

A GUIDE TO THE INDIAN TRIBES OF OKLAHOMA
Muriel H. Wright
Reprint of 1951 edition. Illus. 320 pp. Paper. University of Oklahoma Press, 1997. $19.95.

A GUIDE TO THE INDIAN TRIBES OF THE PACIFIC NORTHWEST
Robert Ruby & John Brown
Illus. Maps. 304 pp. Paper. University of Oklahoma Press, 1986. $19.95.

A GUIDE TO THE INDIAN WARS OF THE WEST
John D. McDermott
Illus. Map. 211 pp. Paper. University of Nebraska Press, 1998. $19.95.

GUIDE TO MULTICULTURAL RESOURCES, 1995-96
Alex Boyd, Editor
Current information on multicultural organizations, services and trends. Lists over 3,000 organizations including many Native American associations, institutions, and government agencies. 512 pp. Paper. Highsmith Press, $49.

GUIDE TO NATIVE AMERICAN MUSIC RECORDINGS
Lists thousands of available recordings. Cassettes & CDs. 150 pp. VIP Publishing. $14.95.

GUIDE TO NAVAJO RUGS
Susan Lamb
Describes and depicts the 17 most common Navajo rug styles and includes quotes by some of the weavers. Color photos. 48 pp. Paper. Clear Light, $4.95.

GUIDE TO NAVAJO RUGS
Kent McManis & Robert Jeffries
Illus. over 50 rug types available to the collector today. Illus. Paper. Clear Light, $9.95.

GUIDE TO THE PALAEO-INDIAN ARTIFACTS OF NORTH AMERICA
Richard M. Gramly
2nd revised edition. An authoritative treatment of the variety of stone, bone, ivory and antler artifacts at North American Palaeo-Indian sites from Alaska to Florida. Illus. 90 pp. Paper. Persimmon Press & Hothem House, 1992. $15.95.

GUIDE TO PREHISTORIC RUINS OF THE SOUTHWEST
Oppelt
Surveys many prehistoric sites, and provides background facts. Illus. 208 pp. Paper. Pruett Publishing, $12.95.

A GUIDE TO PROPOSAL WRITING
Institute of the Development of Indian Law, $7.50.

A GUIDE TO PUEBLO POTTERY
Susan Lamb
Color photos and full descriptions of the 18 most collectible pottery styles of the Southwest. 48 pp. Paper. Clear Light, $3.95.

GUIDE TO THE RECORDS AT THE NATIONAL ARCHIVES-LOS ANGELES BRANCH GUIDE TO RECORDS IN THE NATIONAL ARCHIVES RELATING TO AMERICAN INDIANS
Edward E. Hill, Compiler
Illus. 468 pp. Illus. 368 pp. Smithsonian Institution Press, 1981. $25.

GUIDE TO THE RECORDS OF THE THE MORAVIAN MISSION AMONG THE INDIANS OF NORTH AMERICA
111 pp. Paper. Primary Source Media, 1983. $80.

GUIDE TO RESEARCH ON NORTH AMERICAN INDIANS
Arlene B. Hirschfelder
A basic guide to the literature for general readers, students, and scholars interested in the study of American Indians. 340 pp. American Library Association, 1983. $75.

GUIDE TO ROCK ART OF THE UTAH REGION: SITES WITH PUBLIC ACCESS
Dennis Slifer
Illus. Photos. 46 maps. 255 pp. Paper. Ancient City Press, 2002. $16.95.

A GUIDE TO UNDERSTANDING CHIPPEWA TREATY RIGHTS
Booklet. GLIFWC, 1991. No charge

A GUIDE TO ZUNI FETISHES & CARVING
Kent McManis
Vol. 1: The Animals & the Carvers. Color photos. 56 pp. Vol. 2: The Materials & the Carvers. Color photos. 64 pp. Paper. Treasure Chest & Clear Light, $8.95 each.

GUNS ON THE EARLY FRONTIERS: A HISTORY OF FIREARMS FROM COLONIAL TIMES THROUGH THE YEARS OF THE WESTERN FUR TRADE
Carl P. Russell
395 pp. University of Nebraska Press, 1980. $28.95.

GUNS OF THE WESTERN INDIAN WAR
Dorsey
Examines Indian weapons froma base collection of 410. Photos. 220 pp. Paper. Hothem House, 1995. $30.

GYAEHLINGAAY: TRADITIONS, TALES, & IMAGES OF THE KAIGANI HAIDA
Carol M. Eastman & Elizabeth A. Edwards
Provides the historical, cultural, and linguistic background of each story. Illus. 138 pp. Paper. University of Washington Press, $22.50.

H

HAA AANI OUR LAND: TLINGIT & HAIDA LAND RIGHTS
Walter Goldschmidt
Paper. University of Washington Press, 1999. $35.

HAA SHUKA, OUR ANCESTORS; TLINGIT ORAL NARRATIVES
Nora Marks & Richard Dauenhauer, Editor
A Tlingit author tells stories that deal with "coming of age, alienation, identity and self concept," etc. Illus. 532 pp. Paper. University of Washington Press, $22.50.

HAA KUSTEEYI, OUR CULTURE: TLINGIT LIFE STORIES
Nora Marks & Richard Dauenhauer, Editor
Introduction to Tlingit social & political history featuring biographies and life histories of over 50 men & women. Illus. 600 pp. University of Washington Press, 1994. $40; paper, $24.95.

HAA TUWUNAAGU YIS, FOR HEALING OUR SPIRIT: TLINGIT ORATORY
Nora Marks & Richard Dauenhauer, Editor
Tlingit texts with English translations and detailed annotations; biographies of the elders. Illus. Biblio. 606 pp. Paper. University of Washington Press, $22.50.

HABOO: NATIVE AMERICAN STORIES FROM PUGET SOUND
Vi Hilbert, Editor & Translator
Illus. 228 pp. Paper. University of Washington Press, 1985. $19.95.

HAIDA ART
George F. MacDonald
Illus. 256 pp. University of Washington Press, 1996. $60.

HAIDA MONUMENTAL ART: VILLAGES OF THE QUEEN CHARLOTTE ISLANDS
George F. MacDonald
Includes about 300 photos of houses & totem poles constructed by the Haida Indians of the Queen Charlotte Islands, British Columbia during the late 19th century. Illus. 240 pp. Paper. University of Washington Press, $39.95.

HAIDA: THE QUEEN CHARLOTTE ISLAND INDIANS: THEIR ART & CULTURE
Leslie Drew
Illus. 112 pp. Paper. Hancock House, $9.95.

HAIDA SYNTAX
John Enrico
Description of the syntax of two Haida dialects. Two vols. Map. 1,387 pp. University of Nebraska Press, 2003. $200.

HAIDA: THEIR ART & CULTURE
Leslie Drew
Illus. 111 pp. Paper. Hancock House, $7.95.

THE HAKO: SONG, PIPE, AND UNITY IN A PAWNEE CALUMET CEREMONY
Alice Fletcher
Illus. 390 pp. Paper. University of Nebraska Press, 1996. $16.95.

HALF-SUN ON THE COLUMBIA: A BIOGRAPHY OF CHIEF MOSES
Robert H. Ruby & John A. Brown
Reprint of 1965 edition. Illus. Maps. 390 pp. Paper. University of Oklahoma Press, $18.95.

HALFBREED
Maria Campbell
A Canadian Metis tells you what it is like to be a half breed woman. 157 pp. Paper. University of Nebraksa Press, 1982. $10.95.

THE HALL OF THE NORTH AMERICAN INDIAN
Hillel Burger & Ian Brown; Barbara Isaac, Editor
Illus. 135 pp. Paper. Peabody Museum, 1990. $25.

HALLMARKS OF THE SOUTHWEST: WHO MADE IT?
Indian Arts & Crafts Association Staff
Illus. 244 pp. Schiffer, 1989. $45.

THE HAN INDIANS: A COMPILATION OF ETHNOGRAPHIC & HISTORICAL DATA ON THE ALASKA—YUKON BOUNDARY AREA
Cornelius Osgood
Paper. Yale University, Anthropology, 1971. $7.50.

HAND TREMBLING, FRENZY WITCHCRAFT, & MOTH MADNESS: A STUDY OF NAVAJO SEIZURE DISORDERS
Jerrold E. Levy, et al
176 pp. Paper. University of Arizona Press, 1987. $21.95.

HANDBOOK OF THE AMERICAN FRONTIER - FOUR CENTURIES OF INDIAN-WHITE RELATIONSHIPS, 5 Vols.
J. Norman Heard
Vol. I: The Southeastern Woodlands - 421 pp. 1987. $45; Vol. II: The Northeastern Woodlands - 417 pp. 1990. $45; Vol. III: The Great Plains - 280 pp. 1993. $36; Vol. IV: The Far West - 400 pp. 1997. $39.50; Chronology, Bibliography, Index - 336 pp. 1998. $57.50. Scarecrow Press.

HANDBOOK OF AMERICAN INDIAN GAMES
Allan & Paulette Macfarlan
150 authentic Indian games. Illus. 288 pp. Paper. Dover & Cherokee Publications, 1985. $7.95.

HANDBOOK OF THE AMERICAN INDIAN LANGUAGES
Franz Boas
Reprint. 4 vols. Reprint Services & Scholarly Press, $360 per set.

HANDBOOK OF AMERICAN INDIAN RELIGIOUS FREEDOM
Christopher Vecsey
175 pp. Paper. Crossroad Publishing, 1991. $17.95.

HANDBOOK OF AMERICAN INDIANS NORTH OF MEXICO, 1907-1910
Frederick Hodge
Reprint of 1912 edition. 2 vols. Illus. Greenwood, $49.60.

A HANDBOOK OF CREEK (MUSCOGEE) GRAMMAR
Anna Bosch
Vocabulary, spelling, and pronunciation. 35 pp. Paper. Indian University Press, 1994 second printing. $7, postpaid.

HANDBOOK OF FEDERAL INDIAN LAW
Felix S. Cohen, Editor
Standard reference work on federal Indian law. Reprint of 1942 edition. 662 pp. William S. Hein, $95.

HANDBOOK OF FEDERAL INDIAN LAW WITH REFERENCE TABLES & INDEX
Felix S. Cohen
Reprint of 1941 edition. 686 pp. William S. Hein, $75.

HANDBOOK OF THE INDIANS OF CALIFORNIA
A. L. Kroeber
Reprint of 1925 edition. Illus. 995 pp. Paper. Hothem House & Dover, $20.95.

HANDBOOK OF NATIVE AMERICAN HERBS
Alma T. Hutchens
Illus. 200 pp. Paper. Random House, 1992. $12.95.

HANDBOOK OF NATIVE AMERICAN LITERATURE
Andrew Wiget, Editor
Essays by over 40 Native American writers provides a guide to the oral and written literatures of Native Americans. Biblio. 616 pp. Paper. Garland, 1996. $24.95.

HANDBOOK OF NORTH AMERICAN INDIANS
William C. Sturtevant & Wilcomb Washburn, Editors
A 20-volume encyclopedia summarizing knowledge about all Native peoples north of Mesoamerica, including cultures, history, languages, prehistory, and human biology. Vol. 4: History of Indian-White Relations, 852 pp., 1989, $51; Vol. 5: Arctic, 862 pp., 1984, $52; Vol. 6: Subarctic, 853 pp., 1981, $51; Vol. 7: Northwest Coast, 795 pp., 1990, $51; Vol. 8: California, 800 pp., 1978, $51; Vol. 9: Southwest - Puebloan Peoples, 701 pp., 1980, $49; Vol. 10: Southwest - Non-Puebloan People, 868 pp., 1983, $52; Vol. 11: Great Basin, 868 pp., 1986, $52; Vol. 12: Plateau, 816 pp., 1998. $61; Vol. 13: Plains. 1392 pp., 2001. $101; Vol. 15: Northeast, 924 pp., 1979, $53 (also available from Hothem House, $58.50 postpaid); Vol. 17: Languages, 957 pp., 1997. $74. Volumes 1-3, 12-14, 16, & 18-20 are not yet published. Illus. Maps. Produced by the Smithsonian Institution. Available from Bernan Publications.

A HANDBOOK OF NORTHEASTERN INDIAN MEDICINAL PLANTS
James A. Duke
Illus. 212 pp. Quarterman, 1986. $30.

THE HANDS FEEL IT: HEALING & SPIRIT PRESENCE AMONG A NORTHERN ALASKAN PEOPLE
Edith Turner
Illus. 240 pp. paper. Northern Illinois University Press, 1996. $20.

THE HANDSOME PEOPLE: A HISTORY OF THE CROW INDIANS & THE WHITES
Charles Crane Bradley
Grades 8-adult. 310 pp. Council for Indian Education, $20.95; paper, $14.95.

HANO: A TEWA INDIAN COMMUNITY IN ARIZONA
Edward P. Dozier
Paper. Holt, Rinehart & Winston, 1966. $9.95.

HARMONY BY HAND: ART OF THE SOUTHWEST INDIANS
Patrick Houlihan
Illus. 108 pp. Paper. Chronicle Books, 1987. $16.95.

HARPER'S ANTHOLOGY OF TWENTIETH CENTURY NATIVE AMERICAN POETRY
Duane Niatum, Editor
Anthology of poetry by 30+ Native Americans. 432 pp. Paper. Clear Light, 1988. $22.

LADONNA HARRIS: A COMANCHE LIFE
LaDonna Harris; edited by H. Henrietta Stockel
Mrs. Harris discusses the importance of her Comanche values and life experiences. Illus. 160 pp. Map. University of Nebraska Press, 2000. $30.

HART'S PREHISTORIC PIPE RACK
Hart
Covers prehistoric Indian pipes for the Mississippi River into the Eastern U.S. Illus. 272 pp. Hothem House, 1978. $52, postpaid.

HASINAI: A TRADITIONAL HISTORY OF THE CADDO CONFEDERACY
Vynola Newkumet & Howard Meredith
Illus. 168 pp. Texas A&M University Press, 1988. $16.95.

THE HASINAIS: THE SOUTHERN CADDOANS AS SEEN BY THE EARLIEST EUROPEANS
Herbert Bolton
Illus. Maps. 208 pp. Paper. University of Oklahoma Press, 1987. $14.95.

A HAUNTING REVERENCE: MEDITATIONS ON A NORTHERN LAND
Kent Nerburn
Reprint. Paper. University of Minnesota Press, 1999. $14.95.

EMIL W. HAURY'S PREHISTORY OF THE AMERICAN SOUTHWEST
Emil W. Haury; J. Reid & D. Doyel, Editors
506 pp. Paper. University of Arizona Press, 1986. $ 28.95.

HAVASUPAI HABITAT: A.F. WHITING'S ETHNOGRAPHY OF A TRADITIONAL INDIAN CULTURE
Steven A. Weber & David P. Seaman, Editors
288 pp. University of Arizona Press, 1985. $39.95.

HAVASUPAI LEGENDS: RELIGION & MYTHOLOGY OF THE INDIANS OF GRAND CANYON
Carma Lee Smithson & Robert C. Euler
Illus. Paper. University of Utah Press, 1994. $12.95.

*HAVASUPAI YEARS
Madge Knobloch
Journal of teacher teching on the Havasupai reservation in the bottom of the Grand Canyon in 1931-33. Grades 6 and up. 124 pp. Paper. Council for Indian Education, $8.95.

HAVSUW BAAJA: PEOPLE OF BLUE GREEN WATER
Lois Hurst
Revised 1985 edition. Havasupai Council, $18.

THE HAWK IS HUNGRY; & OTHER STORIES
D'Arcy McNickle; Birgit Hans, Editor
16 stories by McNickle, one of the most influential Native Americans of this century. 180 pp. Paper. University of Arizona Press, 1992. $17.95.

HE WALKED THE AMERICAS
L. Taylor Hansen
Illus. Amherst Press, 1963. $13.95.

HEAD & FACE MASKS IN NAVAHO CEREMONIALISM
Berard Haile; foreword by James Faris
Reprint 1947 ed. Illus. Paper. University of Utah Press, $15.95.

HEADED UPSTREAM: INTERVIEWS WITH ICONOCLASTS
Jack Loeffler
Illus. 168 pp. Paper. Harbinger House, Inc., 1989. $10.95.

HEALING HERBS OF THE UPPER RIO GRANDE: TRADITIONAL MEDICINE OF THE SOUTHWEST
L.M.S. Curtin
Illus. 280 pp. Paper. Mountain Press. $14.95.

A HEALING PLACE: INDIGENOUS VISIONS FOR PERSONAL EMPOWERMENT & COMMUNITY RECOVERY
Kayleen M. Hazelhurst
Reprint. Illus. 274 pp. Accents Publications, 1996. $29.95.

HEALING PLANTS: MEDICINE OF THE FLORIDA SEMINOLE INDIANS
Alice Micco Snow & Susan Enns Stans
Illus. Photos. 192 pp. University Press of Florida, 1999. $24.95.

HEALING WAYS: NAVAJO HEALTH CARE IN THE TWENTIETH CENTURY
Wade Davies
Illus. 256 pp. University of New Mexico Press, 2001. $39.95.

HEALING WITH PLANTS IN THE AMERICAN & MEXICAN WEST
Margarita Artschwager Kay
Description of 100 plants commonly used today by Native Americans and Mexican Americans of the Southwest. 330 pp. Paper. University of Arizona Press, 1996. $19.95.

THE HEALTH OF NATIVE AMERICANS TOWARDS A BIOCULTURAL EPIDEMIOLOGY
T. Kue Young
Illus. 288 pp. Oxford University Press, 1994. $49.95.

HEALTH OF NATIVE PEOPLE OF NORTH AMERICA: A BIBLIOGRAPHY & GUIDE TO RESOURCES, 1970-1994
Sharon A. Gray
Lists peer-reviewed journals, texts, and reference books. Includes association publications, dissertations, reports, audiovisual materials, and book chapters related to health of native peoples. 400 pp. Scarecrow Press, 1996. $58.

HEAR THE CREATOR'S SONG: A GUIDE TO THE STUDY THEME "NATIVE PEOPLES OF NORTH AMERICA"
Remmelt & Kathleen Hummelen
Includes five study sessions for groups using the book, Stories of Survival," and offers a selection of poetry, myths, songs and artwork of Native cultures across North America. Paper. Friendship Press, $4.50.

HEAR ME MY CHIEFS: NEZ PERCE LEGEND & HISTORY
Lucullus V. McWhorter
Reprint of 1952 edition. Illus. Maps. Biblio. 640 pp. The Caxton Printers, $27.95; paper. $19.95.

HEARD IN THE KITCHEN: THE HEARD MUSEUM GUILD COOKBOOK
Illus. 276 pp. Heard Museum, 1994. $18.95.

THE HEARD MUSEUM: HISTORY & COLLECTIONS
Ann Marshall & Mary Brennan
Illus. 50 pp. Paper. The Heard Museum, 1989. $8.95.

HEART BAGS & HAND SHAKES: THE STORY OF THE COOK COLLECTION
Dorothy Cook Meade
By the granddaughter of Capt." James H. Cook describes the unique friendships which Cook forged with Sioux & Cheyenne families in western Nebraska from the late 1800s to the 1940. Illus. 60 pp. Paper. National Woodlands Publishing, 1994. $10.95.

*HEART BUTTE: A BLACKFEET INDIAN COMMUNITY
John Reyhner
Grades K-4. 18 pp. Paper. Council for Indian Education, 1984. $1.95.

*A HEART FULL OF TURQUOISE: PUEBLO INDIAN TALES
Joe Hayes; illus. by Lucy Jelinek
Grades 4 and up. Illus. 80 pp. Paper. Clear Light, 1988. $11.95.

THE HEART IS FIRE: THE WORLD OF THE CAHUILLA INDIANS OF SOUTHERN CALIFORNIA
Deborah Dozier
Five Cahuilla elders provides an Indian interpretation of the Cahuilla world, past and present. Photos. Illus. Biblio. 169 pp. Paper. Heyday Books, $16.

HEART OF THE DRAGONFLY
  Allison Bird
Discusses the development and history of the cross necklaces worn by Pueblo & Navajo Indians. Illus. Photos. 208 pp. Paper. Avanyu Publishing, $39.95.

*HEART OF NASOAQUA
  Katherine Von Ahnen
In 1823 the Mesquakie Indians are forced to find a new home west of the Mississippi. Nasoaqua is a 12-year-old girl. Grade 4-10. 160 pp. Council for Indian Education. $9.95.

HEART OF THE ROCK:
THE INDIAN INVASION OF ALCATRAZ
  Adam Fortunate Eagle with Tim Findley
Illus. 232 pp. University of Oklahoma Press, 2002. $29.95.

HEEDING THE VOICES OF OUR ANCESTORS:
KAHNAWAKE MOHAWK POLITICS & THE RISE
OF NATIVE NATIONALISM
  Gerald R. Alfred
Illus. 232 pp. Paper. Oxford University Press, 1995. $32.

*HEETUNKA'S HARVEST:
A TALE OF THE PLAINS INDIANS
  retold by Jennifer Berry Jones
Grades 1-6. Illus. 32 pp. Roberts Rinehart, 1994. $15.95.

THE HEILTSUKS: DIALOGUES OF CULTURE
& HISTORY ON THE NORTHWEST COAST
  Michael E. Harkin
Maps. 195 pp. Paper. University of Nebraska Press, 1997. $24.

THE HEIRS OF COLUMBUS
  Gerald Vizenor
190 pp. University Press of New England, 1991. $22.95; paper, $12.95.

HELEN HUNT JACKSON & HER INDIAN REFORM LEGACY
  Valerie Sherer Mathes
Conflict in Indian policy and reform of the period. Illus. Map. 253 pp. University of Texas Press, 1990. $27.95.

HERALDIC POLE CARVERS: NINETEENTH
CENTURY NORTHERN HAIDA ARTISTS
  Robin K. Wright
Illus. 300 pp. University of Washington Press, 2000.

HERE, NOW, AND ALWAYS: VOICES OF
THE FIRST PEOPLES OF THE SOUTHWEST
  Foreword by Rina Swentzell; Preface by Bruce Bernstein
Tells the story of the Southwest's oldest communities. Contributors: Carlotta Penny Bird, Tony Chavarria, Anthony Dorame, Gloria Emerson, Michael Lacapa, Tessie Naranjo, et al. Illus. 96 pp. Museum of New Mexico Press, 2001. $24.95.

*THE HERITAGE
  Nancy Armstrong et al
Grades 3-6. Council for Indian Education, 1977. $2.95.

THE HERITAGE OF KLICKITAT BASKETRY:
A HISTORY & ART PRESERVED
  Nettie Kuneki and Marie Teo
Illus. 48 pp. Paper. Oregon Historical Society, 1982. $4.95.

HERMANITOS COMANCHITOS: INDO-HISPANO
RITUALS OF CAPTIVITY & REDEMPTION
  Enrique R. Lamadrid; photos by Miguel Gandert
Festival of defiance and tribute to the Comanches by the Pueblo and Hispano groups of the Southwest. Illus. 78 halftones, 3 maps. 312 pp. Includes 70-minute CD. University of New Mexico Press, $45; paper, $27.95.

THE HERNANDO DE SOTO EXPEDITION: HISTORY,
HISTORIOGRAPHY, & "DISCOVERY" IN THE SOUTHEAST
  Patricia Galloway, Editor
Essays. Illus. Maps. 457 pp. University of Nebraska Press, 1997. $75.

HERNANDO DE SOTO & THE INDIANS OF FLORIDA
  Jerald T. Milanich & Charles Hudson
Illus. 42 maps. Biblio. 307 pp. University Press of Florida, 1993. $39.95.

THE HERO OF BATTLE ROCK:A TRUE ACCOUNT -
OREGON COAST INDIAN ATTACK
  Bert Webber
Illus. 56 pp. Ye Galleon, 1978. $8.95; paper, $4.95.

*HEROES & HEROINES IN TLINGIT-HAIDA LEGENDS:
& THEIR COUNTERPARTS IN CLASSICAL MYTHOLOGY
  Mary L. Beck
Grades 8 and up. Illus. 120 pp. Paper. Alaska Northwest, 1989. $12.95.

*HEROES & HEROINES, MONSTERS & MAGIC
  Retold by Joseph Bruchac; illus. by Daniel Burgevin
A collection of 30 tales told in the Longhouses of the Iroquois Indians. Grades 3-7. Illus. 200 pp. Paper. The Crossing Press, 1991, $12.95.

HIAPSI WAMI SEEWAM: FLOWERS OF LIFE :
A CURRICULUM GUIDE OF YAQUI CULTURE & ART
  Octaviana V. Trujillo; Wendy Weston-Ben, Editor
Illus. Paper. Atlatl, 1995.

*HIAWATHA
  Megan McCiard & George Ypsilantis
Grades 5-7. Illus. 144 pp. Silver Burdette, 1989. $11.98; paper, $7.95.

*THE HIDATSA
  Mary J. Schneider
Grades 7-12. Illus. 112 pp. Chelsea House, 1989. $17.95.

HIDATSA SOCIAL & CEREMONIAL ORGANIZATION
  Alfred W. Bowers
Extensive personal and ritual narratives. Illus. 530 pp. Paper. University of Nebraska Press, 1992. $15.95.

HIDDEN FACES: NATIVE NATIONS
  Christopher Cardozo; Robert Janjigan, Editor
Illus. 96 pp. Callaway Editions, 1997. $13.95.

THE HIDDEN HALF:
STUDIES OF PLAINS INDIAN WOMEN
  Patricia Albers and Beatrice Medicine
286 pp. University Presses of Ameica, 1983. $31.50; paper, $15.

THE HIDDEN LANGUAGE OF THE SENECA: LANGUAGE
OF THE STONES; LANGUAGE OF THE TREES; ENTERING
THE SILENCE THE SENECA WAY; CHANTS AND DANCES
  Twylah Nitsch
Scriptorium Press, 1987.

THE HILL CREEK HOMESTEAD & THE LATE
MISSISSIPPIAN SETTLEMENT IN THE LOWER
ILLINOIS VALLEY
  Michael D. Connor, Editor
Illus. 239 pp. Paper. Center for American Archaeology, 1985. $9.95.

TONY HILLERMAN'S NAVAJOLAND:
HIDEOUTS, HAUNTS, & HAVENS IN THE
JOE LEAPHORN & JIM CHEE MYSTERIES
  Laurance D. Linford; foreword by Tony Hillerman
Illus. Map. Paper. University of Utah Press. $19.95.

HINDU FESTIVALS IN A NORTH INDIAN VILLAGE
  Stanley & Ruth Freed
Illus. 380 pp. Paper. University of Washington Press, 1998. $34.95.

HIROSHIMA BUGI: ATOMU 57
  Gerald Vizenor
Kabuki novel draws on samurai and native traditions to confront the nuclear age. 224 pp. University of Nebraska Press, 2003. $26.95.

HISTORIC CONTACT: INDIAN PEOPLE & COLONISTS IN
TODAY'S NORTHEASTERN U.S. IN THE 16TH THROUGH
18TH CENTURIES
  Robert S. Grumet
Illus. Maps. Biblio. 514 pp. University of Oklahoma Press, 1995. $49.95.

THE HISTORIC INDIAN TRIBES OF LOUISIANA:
FROM 1542 TO THE PRESENT
  Fred B. Kniffen, et al
Illus. 344 pp. Louisiana State University Press, 1987. $24.95.

HISTORIC NAVAJO WEAVING, 1800-1900:
THREE CULTURES-ONE LOOM
  Tyrone Campbell
Revised edition. Illus. 40 pp. Paper. Avanyu, 1987. $14.75.

HISTORIC POTTERY OF
THE PUEBLO INDIANS, 1600-1800
  Larry Frank & Francis Harlow
Illus. 175 pp. Schiffer, 1989. $35.

HISTORIC ZUNI ARCHITECTURE & SOCIETY
  T.J. Ferguson
Illus. 150 pp. University of Arizona Press, 1996. $14.95.

HISTORICAL ACCOUNT OF THE DOINGS & SUFFERINGS
OF THE CHRISTIAN INDIANS IN NEW ENGLAND IN THE
YEARS 1675, 1676, 1677
  Daniel Gookin
Reprint of 1836 edition. Ayer Co. Publishers, $21.

HISTORICAL ATLAS OF THE AMERICAN WEST
  Warren A. Beck & Ynez D. Haase
Includes a section on aboriginal settings and Native American tribes, European contacts and settlements, etc. 78 maps. 158 pp. Paper. University of Oklahoma Press, 1989. $19.95.

HISTORICAL ATLAS OF ARIZONA
  Henry P. Walker & Don Bufkin
Includes a section on aboriginal settings and Native American tribes. Maps. Biblio. 146 pp. University of Oklahoma Press, 1979. $37.95; paper, $19.95.

HISTORICAL ATLAS OF ARKANSAS
  Gerald T. Hanson & Carl H. Moneyhon
Includes a section on Arkansas' aboriginal setting and Native American tribes, etc. 71 maps. 156 pp. Paper. University of Oklahoma Press, 1989. $19.95.

HISTORICAL ATLAS OF CALIFORNIA
  Warren A. Beck & Ynez D. Haase
Includes a section on aboriginal settings and Native American tribes, etc. Maps. 231 pp. Paper. University of Oklahoma Press, 1974. $23.95.

HISTORICAL ATLAS OF COLORADO
  Thomas J. Noel, et al
Includes a section on Colorado's aboriginal setting and Native American tribes, etc. 60 maps. Biblio. 192 pp. Paper. University of Oklahoma Press, 1994. $19.95.

HISTORICAL ATLAS OF LOUISIANA
  Charles R. Goins & John M. Caldwell
Includes a section on Louisiana's aboriginal setting and Native American tribes, European contacts & settlements, etc. 99 maps. 198 pp. University of Oklahoma Press, 1995. $65; paper, $29.95.

HISTORICAL ATLAS OF MISSOURI
  Milton D. Rafferty
Includes a section on Missouri's aboriginal setting and Native American tribes, European contacts and settlements, etc. 113 pp. of maps. 248 pp. University of Oklahoma Press, 1982. $29.95.

HISTORICAL ATLAS OF NEW MEXICO
  Warren A. Beck & Ynez D. Haase
Includes a section on aboriginal settings and Native American tribes, etc. Reprint of 1969 edition. Maps. 144 pp. Paper. University of Oklahoma Press, 1969. $19.95.

HISTORICAL ATLAS OF OKLAHOMA
  John W. Morris, Charles R. Goins & Edwin C. McReynolds
Includes a section on Oklahoma's aboriginal setting and Native American tribes, European contacts & settlements, etc. 3rd edition. 83 maps. 166 pp. University of Oklahoma Press, 1986. $37.95; paper, $19.95.

HISTORICAL ATLAS OF TEXAS
  A. Ray Stephens & William M. Holmes
Includes a section on Texa's aboriginal setting and Native American tribes, European contacts and settlements, etc. 64 maps. 132 pp. University of Oklahoma Press, 1989. $39.95; paper, $19.95.

HISTORICAL ATLAS OF WASHINGTON
  James W. Scott & Roland L. De Lorme
Maps. 180 pp. University of Oklahoma Press, 1988. $27.95.

HISTORICAL BACKGROUND
OF THE SANTA ANA PUEBLO
  Tom Luebben
25 pp. Institute for the Development of Indian Law, $8.50.

HISTORICAL BACKGROUND TO CHIPPEWA TREATIES
  Robert Keller
25 pp. Institute for the Development of Indian Law, $12.50.

AN HISTORICAL CHRONOLOGY OF THE KIOWA TRIBE
  John Belindo
I2 pp. Institute for the Development of Indian Law, $5.50.

HISTORICAL COLLECTIONS OF GEORGIA
  George White
Reprint of 1920 edition. 787 pp. Genealogical Publishing, $35.

HISTORICAL COLLECTIONS OF
THE INDIANS OF NEW ENGLAND
  Daniel Gookin
Reprint of 1836 edition. Ayer Co., $23.50.

THE HISTORICAL DEVELOPMENT OF THE CONCEPT
OF NUNAVUT: AN ANNOTATED BIBLIOGRAPHY OF
THE LITERATURE SINCE THE 1930'S
  R.L. Minion
Paper. CCI, 1994. $15.

HISTORICAL DICTIONARY OF
NORTH AMERICAN ARCHAEOLOGY
  Edward Jelks & Juliet Jelks
An alphabetical listing of over 1,800 entries providing descriptions for cultures, mounds, ruins, and archaeological sites. Sources of information, and list of references. Biblio. 760 pp. Greenwood, 1988. $95.

AN HISTORICAL JOURNAL OF THE CAMPAIGNS
IN NORTH AMERICA IN THE YEARS 1757-1760
  A.G. Doughty
Facsimile of 1916 edition. 2 vols. Greenwood, $125 per set.

HISTORICAL SKETCH OF
THE FLATHEAD INDIAN NATION
  Peter Ronan
Reprint of 1890 edition. 108 PP. Ross & Haines, $15.

HISTORY & ANNOTATED BIBLIOGRAPHY OF AMERICAN RELIGIOUS PERIODICALS & NEWSPAPERS ESTABLISHED FROM 1730 THROUGH 1830
Gaylor P. Albaugh
2 vols. 1,550 pp. Oak Knoll, 1994. $125.

HISTORY & CULTURE OF IROQUOIS DIPLOMACY: AN INTERDISCIPLINARY GUIDE TO THE TREATIES OF THE SIX NATIONS & THEIR LEAGUE
Francis Jennings & William Fenton, Editors
Illus. Maps. 296 pp. Paper. Syracuse University Press, 1985. $17.95.

HISTORY, ETHNOLOGY, & ANTHROPOLOGY OF THE ALEUT
Waldemar Jochelson
Aleut society 100 years ago. Illus. Paper.
University of Utah Press. $14.95.

HISTORY, EVOLUTION & THE CONCEPT OF CULTURE: SELECTED PAPERS BY ALEXANDER LESSER
Sidney W. Mintz
192 pp. Cambridge University Press, 1989. $34.50.

HISTORY, MANNERS & CUSTOMS OF THE INDIAN NATIONS WHO ONCE INHABITED PENNSYLVANIA & NEIGHBORING STATES
John Heckewelder
Reprint of 1819 edition. Illus. 450 pp.
Heritage Books & Ayer Co., $29.95.

HISTORY, MYTHS & SACRED FORMULAS OF THE CHEROKEES
James Mooney
Primary source book on Cherokee contains 126 legends obtained on the Cherokee Reservation in N.C. in 1887-88. Illus. 768 pp. Paper. Bright Mountain Books, $17.95.

HISTORY OF ALABAMA, & INCIDENTALLY OF GEORGIA & MISSISSIPPI, FROM THE EARLIEST PERIOD
Albert J. Pickett
Reprint of 1851 edition. Illus. Ayer Co., $52.95.

HISTORY OF BEADS: FROM 30,000 B.C. TO THE PRESENT
Lois Sherr Dubin
350 illus. 254 color plates. 8 pp. fold-out time line. 364 pp. Written Heritage, $59.95.

A HISTORY OF THE BUREAU OF INDIAN AFFAIRS & ITS ACTIVITIES AMONG INDIANS
Curtis E. Jackson and Marcia J. Galli
Paper. R & E Research Associates, 1977. $15.

HISTORY OF CANADA, OR NEW FRANCE
F. Du Creaux; J.B. Conacher, Editor
Reprint of 1951 edition. Two vols. Greenwood, $26.75 each.

HISTORY OF THE CATHOLIC MISSIONS AMONG THE INDIAN TRIBES OF THE U.S.
John D. Shea
Reprint. Reprint Services, $75.

HISTORY OF THE CHEROKEE INDIANS & THEIR LEGENDS & FOLKLORE
Emmet Starr
Reprint of 1921 edition. 600+ pp.VIP Publishing, $50.

*A HISTORY OF THE CHEYENNE PEOPLE
Tom Weist
Grades 6 and up. Illus. 227 pp. Paper. Council for Indian Education, 1977. $14.95; paper, $9.95.

HISTORY OF THE CHOCTAW, CHICKASAW & NATCHEZ INDIANS
H.B. Cushman; edited by Angie Debo
512 pp. Paper. University of Oklahoma Press, 1999. $15.95.

HISTORY OF THE FIVE INDIAN NATIONS
Cadwallader Colden
Reprint of 1958 edition. 205 pp. Paper.
Cornell University Press, $11.50.

HISTORY OF INDIAN ARTS EDUCATION IN SANTA FE
Winona Garmhausen
Illus. 144 pp. Paper. Sunstone Press, 1988. $15.95.

A HISTORY OF INDIAN EDUCATION
Jon Reyhner & Jeanne Eder
Overview from first missionaries to present. 150 pp.
Paper. Council for Indian Education. $8.95.

A HISTORY OF INDIAN POLICY: SYLLABUS
Judith Bachman
Paper. National Book, $6.75; cassette recording, $146.10.

A HISTORY OF INDIAN VILLAGES & PLACE NAMES OF PENNSYLVANIA
George A. Donehoo
312 pp. Paper. Wennawoods, 1998. $19.95.

HISTORY OF THE INDIAN WARS
Samuel Penhallow
Reprint of 1726 edition. 208 pp. Corner House, $18.50.

HISTORY OF THE INDIAN WARS IN NEW ENGLAND, FROM THE FIRST SETTLEMENT TO THE TERMINATION OF THE WAR WITH KING PHILIP IN 1677
William Hubbard
Reprint of 1865 edition. 2 vols. in one. 595 pp.
Map. Paper. Heritage Books, $35.

HISTORY OF INDIAN-WHITE RELATIONS, Vol. 4
William Sturtevant; Wilcomb E. Washburn, Editor
Illus. 852 pp. Smithsonian, 1989. $47.

HISTORY OF THE INDIANS OF CONNECTICUT FROM THE EARLIEST KNOWN PERIOD TO 1850
John W. DeForest
Reprint of 1851 edition. 536 pp. Paper.
Native American Book Publishers, $49.

HISTORY OF THE INDIANS OF THE UNITED STATES
Angie Debo
Reprint of 1970 edition. Illus. Maps. 450 pp. Paper.
University of Oklahoma Press, 2000. $24.95.

HISTORY OF THE IROQUOIS CONFEDERACY
William H. Fenton
Illus. Maps. Biblio. 808 pp. University of Oklahoma Press, 1998. $70.

HISTORY OF THE NATIVE AMERICANS
Alvin Josephy, Editor
Six biographies of Native American leaders and the tribes theyu represent. Includes separate books for Hiawatha, King Philip, Geronimo, Sitting Bull, Sequoyah & Tecumseh. Illus. Mapos. 128 -144pp each. Silver Burdett Press, 1993. $10.95 each; paper, $7.95. $65.70/set; paper, $47.70/set.

A HISTORY OF THE NATIVE PEOPLE OF CANADA VOL. I (10,000-1,000 B.C.)
James V. Wright
The first of 3 vols. on the history of Canada's Native people as revealed by the archaeological evidence. Illus. 588 pp. Paper. UBC Press, 1995. $45.

A HISTORY OF THE NATIVE PEOPLE OF CANADA VOL. II (1,000 B.C.-A.D. 500)
James V. Wright
Second of 3 vols. examining the 12,000 years of Native history which preceded the arrival of Europeans in Canada. Illus. Maps. Biblio. 640 pp. Paper. University of Washington Press, 1999. $45.

HISTORY OF THE NAVAJOS: THE RESERVATION YEARS
Garrick & Roberta Bailey
Illus. 376 pp. School of American Research, 1986. $32.50; paper, $17.50.

HISTORY OF NEW FRANCE
Marc Lescarbot
Reprint of 1907 edition. Three vols.
Greenwood, $27.50, $37.75, & $35.25.

HISTORY OF THE NEW YORK INDIANS & INDIANS OF THE PRINTUP FAMILY
A.D. Printup
Illus. 89 pp. DeWitt & Sheppard, 1985. $66.66.

HISTORY OF THE OJIBWAY INDIANS
Peter Jones
Reprint of 1861 edition. Ayer Co., $24.50.

HISTORY OF THE OJIBWAY PEOPLE
William W. Warren
First hand descriptions & stories from relatives, tribal leaders & acquaintances. Reprint of 1885 edition. Illus. 411 pp. Paper. Minnesota Historical Society Press, 1984. $12.95.

THE HISTORY OF OKLAHOMA
Arrell M. Gibson
Illus. Maps. 242 pp. University of Oklahoma Press, 1984. $19.95.

HISTORY OF THE ORIGINAL PEOPLES OF NORTHERN CANADA
Keith J. Crowe
Revised edition. Paper. McGill-Queen's University Press, 1991. $19.95.

HISTORY OF PHILIP'S WAR, COMMONLY CALLED THE GREAT INDIAN WAR OF 1675 & 1676. ALSO OF THE FRENCH & INDIAN WARS AT THE EASTWARD IN 1689, 1690, 1692, 1696, & 1704
Thomas Church, Esq.; notes by Samuel G. Drake
Reprint. 360 pp. Paper. Heritage Books, $23.50.

HISTORY OF THE SANTEE SIOUX: U.S. INDIAN POLICY ON TRIAL
Roy W. Meyer
Reprint of 1967 edition. Illus. Maps. 507 pp. Paper.
University of Nebraska Press, $17.95.

HISTORY OF THE SECOND SEMINOLE WAR, 1835-1842
John K. Mahon
Revised 1967 edition. Illus. Biblio. 391 pp. Paper.
University Press of Florida, $15.95

HISTORY OF THE TRIUMPHS OF OUR HOLY FAITH AMONGST THE MOST BARBAROUS & FIERCE PEOPLES OF THE NEW WORLD
Andres Perez De Ribas; trans. by Daniel T. Reff, Maureen Ahern & Richard K. Dan ford
Colonial encounter in southwestern North America.
761 pp. University of Arizona Press, 1999. $89.

A HISTORY OF UTAH'S AMERICAN INDIANS
Forrest S. Cuch, Editor
Chapters on each of six tribes. Illus. 416 pp. Paper.
Utah State University Press, 2000. $19.95.

HISTORY & PRESENT DEVELOPMENT OF INDIAN SCHOOLS IN THE U.S.
Solomon R. Ammon
Reprint of 1935 edition. Paper. R & E Associates, $10.95.

HIV PREVENTION IN NATIVE AMERICAN COMMUNITIES: A MANUAL FOR NATIVE AMERICAN HEALTH & HUMAN SERVICE PROVIDERS
Updates AIDS: The Basics. It highlights Native American HIV prevention educators and programs. Includes overviews of HIV and AIDS. National Native American AIDS Prevention Center, $20.

HIWASSEE ISLAND: AN ARCHAEOLOGICAL ACCOUNT OF FOUR TENNESSEE INDIAN PEOPLES
Thomas N. Lewis and Madeline Kneberg
Illus. 328 pp. University of Tennessee Press, 1984. $28.50; paper, $14.95.

THE HOE & THE HORSE ON THE PLAINS: A STUDY OF CULTURAL DEVELOPMENT AMONG NORTH AMERICAN INDIANS
Preston Holder
An ethnological study; fieldwork with the Arikara; Plains ethnography. Illus. Maps. 186 pp. Paper.
University of Nebraska Press, 1970. $16.95.

HOGANS: NAVAJO HOUSES & HOUSE SONGS
David & Susan McAllester
Reprint. Illus. 115 pp. Paper. Dine College Press. $15.95.

THE HOHOKAM: ANCIENT PEOPLE OF THE DESERT
David Grant Noble
Illus. Maps. 88 pp. Paper. School of American Research, 1989. $10.95.

HOHOKAM ARTS & CRAFTS
Barbara Granemann; Linda Gregonis, Editor
Reprint. Grades 4 and up. Illus. 48 pp. Paper.
Southwest Learning SDources, 1994. $7.95.

THE HOHOKAM INDIANS OF THE TUCSON BASIN
Linda Gregonis & Karl J. Reinhard
A layman's guide to Hohokam lifeways. 48 pp. Paper.
University of Arizona Press, 1979. $4.95.

HOHOKAM & PATAYAN: PREHISTORY OF SOUTHWESTERN ARIZONA
R. McGuire and M. Schiffer, Editors
Academic Press, 1982. $49.50.

HOKAHEY! A GOOD DAY TO DIE! THE INDIAN CASUALTIES OF THE CUSTER FIGHT
Richard G. Hardorff
Identifies the fallen Indians, by name and the location where they were killed. Illus. 174 pp. Paper. University of Nebraska Press, 1999. $12.95.

THE HOKO RIVER ARCHAEOLOGICAL SITE COMPLEX
Dale R. Croes
Native American site on Washington's Olympic Peninsula. Illus. Maps. Biblio. 272 pp. paper. Washington State University Press, 1996. $50.

*HOKSILA & THE RED BUFFALO
Moses N. Crow
Grades 3 and up. Illus. 40 pp. Paper. Tipi Press, 1991. $5.95.

HOLDING STONE HANDS: ON THE TRAIL OF THE CHEYENNE EXODUS
Alan Boye
Moving account of the Cheyennes' struggle to return to Montana. Illus. 348 pp. Paper. University of Nebraska Press, 1998. $16.

*HOLE-IN-THE-DAY: CHIPPEWA NATIVE AMERICAN INDIAN STORIES
Robert M. Kvasnicka]
Grades 4 and up. Demco, 1996. $10.15.

HOLLOW VICTORY: THE WHITE RIVER EXPEDITION OF 1879 & THE BATTLE OF MILL CREEK
Mark E. Miller
Illus. 224 pp. University Press of Colorado, 1997. $27.50.

HOLY WIND IN NAVAJO PHILOSOPHY
James K. McNeley
115 pp. Paper. University of Arizona Press, 1981. $16.95.

HOME PLACES: CONTEMPORARY NATIVE AMERICAN WRITING FROM SUN TRACKS
Larry Evers & Ofelia Zepeda
Stories, songs, poems and other writings. 97 pp.
Paper. University of Arizona Press, 1995. $12.95.

HOME TO MEDICINE MOUNTAIN
Chiori Santiago; illus. by Judith Lowry
Story of 2 young brothers separated and sent to live at a government-run Indian residential school in the 1930s. Illus. Meadowlark Communications, $15.95.

A HOMELAND FOR THE CREE: REGIONAL DEVELOPMENT IN JAMES BAY, 1971-1981
Richard F. Salisbury
Shows how the first James Bay project was negotiated between the Cree and the Quebec government. McGill-Queen's University Press, 1986. $19.95.

HOMOL'OVI: AN ANCIENT HOPI SETTLEMENT CLUSTER
E. Charles Adams
Illus. 304 pp. University of Arizona Press, 2002. $50.

HOMOL'OVI II: ARCHAEOLOGY OF AN ANCESTRAL HOPI VILLAGE, ARIZONA
E. Charles Adams & Kelley Ann Hays, Editors
Excavations. 139 pp. Paper. University of Arizona Press, 1992. $19.95.

HOMOL'OVI III: A PUEBLO HAMLET IN THE LITTLE COLORADO RIVER VALLEY, ARIZONA
edited by E. Charles Adams
Illus. 400 pp. Paper. University of Arizona Press, 1999. $24.95.

HONOR DANCE: NATIVE AMERICAN PHOTOGRAPHS
John Running
Illus. 176 pp. Paper. University of Nevada Press, 1985. $24.95.

HONORING THE WEAVERS
Gregory Schaaf
Illus. 200 pp. Center for Indigenous Arts & Cultures Press, 1996. $40.

THE HOOP OF PEACE
Jan Havnen-Finley
Kevin Locke, a Lakota, is one of a few hoop dancers. He depicts the sacred Great Hoop of Peace. Illus. Photos. 48 pp. Paper. Naturegraph, $7.95.

*HOPE & HAVE: FANNY GRANT AMONG THE INDIANS
Oliver Optic
Reprint. Grades 3-7. Illus. 264 pp. Paper. Lost Classics, 1997. $14.95.

HOPEWELL VILLAGE: A SOCIAL & ECONOMIC HISTORY OF AN IRON-MAKING COMMUNITY
J.E. Walker
University of Pennsylvania Press, 1966. $26.50; paper, $14.95.

HOPEWELLIAN STUDIES
Joseph Caldwell and Robert Hall, Editors
Facsimile edition. Illus. 156 pp. Illinois State Museum, 1977. $4.

HOPI
Susanne and Jake Page
Illus. 240 pp. Harry N. Abrams, 1982. $55.

*THE HOPI
Ann Tomchek
Grades K-4. Illus. 48 pp. Childrens Press, 1987. $11.45.

*THE HOPI
Nancy Bonvillain
Part of the *Indians of North America* series. Grades 4 and up. Illus. 112 pp. Paper. Chelsea House, 1991. $7.95.

*THE HOPI
Suzanne Freedman
Grades 5-8. Illus. 32 pp. Rourke, 1997. Set V, $21.27

*THE HOPI
Elaine Landau
Tells the story of the Hopi way of life. Part of the *Indian of Americas* series Full-color illustrations. Grades 3 and up. 64 pp. Paper. Franklin Watts, 1994. $5.95.

HOPI ANIMAL STORIES
edited & compiled by Ekkehart Malotki
Illus. 261 pp. Paper. University of Nebraska Press, 2001. $16.95.

HOPI ANIMAL TALES
edited & compiled by Ekkehart Malotki
Illus. 524 pp. University of Nebraska Press, 1998. $50.

THE HOPI APPROACH TO THE ART OF KACHINA DOLL CARVING
Erik Bromberg
Presents the diversity of Hopi Kachina dolls. Illus. 94 pp. Paper. Schiffer, $9.95.

HOPI BASKET WEAVING: ARTISTRY IN NATURAL FIBERS
Helga Teiwes
Illus. 200 pp. University of Arizona Press, 1996. $50; paper, $22.95.

HOPI BIBLIOGRAPHY: COMPREHENSIVE & ANNOTATED
W. David Laird
3,000 sources. 735 pp. Paper. University of Arizona Press, 1977. $38.50.

THE HOPI CHILD
Wayne Dennis
Reprint of 1940 edition. Illus. 232 pp. Ayer Co. Publishers, $16.

HOPI COOKERY
Juanita Tiger Kavena
Includes over 100 authentic Hopi recipes. 115 pp. Paper. University of Arizona Press, 1980. $15.95.

HOPI COYOTE TALES: ISTUTUWUTSI
Ekkehart Malotki & Michael Lomatuway'ma
Illus. 343 pp. Paper. University of Nebraska Press, 1984. $29.95.

*HOPI, THE DESERT FARMERS
Susan L. Shaffer, Editor
Grade 3. Illus. Includes 30 student booklets and teacher's manual with transparencies, slides & audiocassette. The Heard Museum. $295.

HOPI DICTIONARY: HOPI-ENGLISH, ENGLISH-HOPI, GRAMMATICAL APPENDIX
P. David Seaman
208 pp. Paper. Northern Arizona University, 1996. $27.

HOPI DICTIONARY: A HOPI-ENGLISH DICTIONARY OF THE THIRD MESA DIALECT
Hopi Dictionary Project
30,000 entries. 900 pp. University of Arizona Press, 1998. $98.

HOPI DWELLINGS: ARCHITECTURE AT ORAYVI
Catherine M. Cameron
Hopi & Pueblo history. 160 pp. University of Arizona Press, 1999. $42.

HOPI & HOPI-TEWA POTTERY
32 pp. Paper. Museum of Northern Arizona, 1982. $4.

HOPI HOUSES: ARCHITECTURAL CHANGE AT ORAYVI
Catherine M. Cameron
University of Arizona Press, 1999. $39.95.

HOPI INDIAN ALTER ICONOGRAPHY
Armin W. Geertz
Illus. 39 pp. Paper. Brill Academic, 1987. $39.

HOPI KACHINA DOLLS & THEIR CARVERS
Theda Bassman
Illustrates contemporary kachina dolls and the lives of the 25 carvers who make them. Illus. 192 pp. Schiffer, $59.95.

HOPI KACHINA DOLLS WITH A KEY TO THEIR IDENTIFICATION
Harold S. Colton
Revised edition. Illus. 14 color photos; 33 halftones. 160 pp. Paper. University of New Mexico Press, 2002. $15.95.

HOPI KACHINAS
Edwin Earle and Edward A. Kennard
Second edition. Illus. 50 pp. National Museum of the American Indian, 1971. $12.50. Portfolio of 28 color plates from the book, $3.50.

HOPI KACHINAS: THE COMPLETE GUIDE TO COLLECTING KACHINA DOLLS
Barton Wright
Includes buying tips and the history of the cultural roles played by the various figures. Illus. 30 color photos. 152 pp. Northland Publishing & Clear Light, $14.95.

HOPI KACHINAS: A POSTCARD COLLECTION
Cliff Bahnimptewa, illustrator
20 full-color postcards. Illus. Northland Publishing, $7.95.

HOPI KATCINAS
Jesse W. Fewkes
Reprint of 1903 edition. Illus. 150 pp. Rio Grande Press, $25. Paper. Hothem House & Dover, $8.95.

HOPI MUSIC & DANCE
Robert Rhodes
Illus. 36 pp. Paper. Dine College Press, $3.25.

*HOPI MYSTERIES
Jack Woolgar and Barbara J. Rudnicki
Grades 5-9. 32 pp. Council for Indian Education, 1974. $8.95; paper, $2.95.

HOPI PHOTOGRAPHERS—HOPI IMAGES
Victor Masayesva & Erin Younger, Editors
Illus. 111 pp. Paper. University of Arizona Press, 1983. $19.95.

HOPI POTTERY SYMBOLS
Alex Patterson
Based on work by Alexander M. Stephen. Includes tentative meanings and a glossary of Hopi words. Illus. 308 pp. Paper. Johnson Books, $17.95.

HOPI QUILTING: STITCHED TRADITIONS FROM AN ANCIENT COMMUNITY
Carolyn O. Davis
Illus. 128 pp. Paper. Sanpete Publications, 1997. $27.95.

*HOPI SHIELDS & THE BEST DEFENSE
Eugene L. Hartley
Hopi boy learns about their traditional shields and their tradition of peace. Grades 2-6. 32 pp. Paper. Council for Indian Education, $3.95.

HOPI SILVER: THE HISTORY & THE HALLMARKS OF HOPI SILVERSMITHING
Margaret Nickelson Wright
Revised edition. Illus. 24 color photos; 29 halftones. 160 pp. Paper. University of New Mexico Press, 2003. $14.95.

HOPI SNAKE CEREMONIES
Jesse Walter Fewkes
An eyewitness account. Illus. 40 halftones. 160 pp. Paper. University of New Mexico Press. $24.95. Published originally by Avanyu Publishing, 1986.

A HOPI SOCIAL HISTORY: ANTHROPOLOGICAL PERSPECTIVES ON SOCIOCULTURAL PERSISTENCE & CHANGE
Scott Rushforth & Steadman Upham
Illus. 320 pp. paper. University of Texas Press, 1992. $16.95.

HOPI STORIES OF WITCHCRAFT, SHAMANISM, & MAGIC
Ekkehart Malotki & Ken Gary
Illus. 290 pp. University of Nebraska Press, 2001. $29.95.

HOPI TALES OF DESTRUCTION
collected, trans. ed. by Ekkehart Malotki
narrated by Michael Lomatuway'ma, et al
Seven tales about ancient Hopi villages describing village destruction.288 pp. Paper. University of Nebraska Press, 2002. $27.95.

HOPI-TEWA POTTERY: 500 ARTIST BIOGRAPHIES
Gregory Schaaf; Richard M. Howard, Editor
Illus. 200 pp. Center for Indigenous Arts & Cultures Press, 1999. $50.

HOPI TIME
E. Malotki
A linguistic analysis of the temporal concepts in the Hopi Language. 677 pp. Mouton de Gruyter, $125.

HOPI TRADITIONAL LITERATURE
David Leedom Shaul
246 pp. University of New Mexico Press, 2002. $49.95.

THE HOPI VILLAGES: ANCIENT PROVINCE OF TUSAYAN
John W. Powell
Powell describes his 1870 journey and observations of the Hopi way of life. Illus. Maps. 48 pp. Paper. Filter Press, 1972. $4.

HOPI VOICES & VISIONS
Michael Kabotie, et al, Editors
80 pp. Paper. Street Press, 1984. $7.50.

THE HOPI WAY: AN ODYSSEY
Robert Boissiere
Illus. 90 pp. Paper. Sunstone Press, $8.95.

THE HOPI WAY: TALES FROM A CHANGING CULTURE
Mando Sevillano; drawings by Mike Castro
Illus. 102 pp. Paper. Northland Publishing, 1986. $12.95.

TOM HORN, GOVERNMENT SCOUT & INDIAN INTERPRETER
Tom Horn
Reprint of 1904 edition. A first-hand account of the Apache Indian wars of the American Southwest. 318 pp. Paper. The Rio Grande Press, $12.

THE HORSE IN BLACKFOOT INDIAN CULTURE
John C. Ewers
Bound with comparative material from other western tribes. Reprint of 1955 edition. Illus. 374 pp. Paper. Smithsonian Institution Press, $21.

*THE HORSE & THE PLAINS INDIAN
Raymond Schuessler & Tom Weist
Grades 4-10. 32 pp. Council for Indian Education, $8.95; paper, $2.95.

THE HORSEMEN OF THE AMERICAS: AN EXHIBITION FROM THE HALL OF THE HORSEMEN OF THE AMERICAS
Sheila Ohlendorf and William D. Wittliff
Illus. Paper. University of Texas, Humanities, 1968. $5.

*HOSKILA & THE RED BUFFALO
Moses Big Crow
A story from Lakota Sioux traditions. Grades 3 and up. Illus. Paper. Tipi Press, $5.95.

HOSTEEN KLAH: NAVAHO
MEDICINE MAN & SAND PAINTER
Franc J. Newcomb
Reprint of 1964 edition. Illus. Map. 227 pp. Paper.
University of Oklahoma Press, $17.95.

HOTEVILLA: HOPI SRINE OF THE COVENANT/
MICROCOSM OF THE WORLD
Thomas E. mails & Dan Evehema
Illus. 577 pp. marlowe & Co., 1996. $40; paper, $25.

HOUSE MADE OF DAWN
N. Scott Momaday
Pulitzer Prize winning first novel. Reprint of 1968 edition.
192 pp. University of Arizona Press, 1996. $35.

HOUSES BENEATH THE ROCK: THE ANASAZI OF
CANYON DE CHELLY & NAVAJO NATIONAL MONUMENT
David Noble, Editor
Illus. Maps. Photos. 56 pp. Paper. Ancient City Press, 1992.
$8.95.

*HOUSES OF BARK: TIPI, WIGWAM, & LONGHOUSE
Grades 3-7. Illus. 25 pp. Tundra Books, 1990. $12.95.

HOUSES & HOUSE-LIFE OF
THE AMERICAN ABORIGINES
Lewis Henry Morgan
Illus. Paper. University of Utah Press. $19.95.

HOUSING PROBLEMS & NEEDS OF
AMERICAN INDIANS & ALASKA NATIVES
C. Thomas Kingsley, et al
Illus. 162 pp. Paper. Diane Publishing, 1997. $40.

*HOW THE BABY DEER GOT SPOTS:
A STORY BASED ON INDIAN LEGEND
Steven A. Roy
Grades 3 and up. Illus. 17 pp. Paper. Tipi Press, 1996.
$3.95.

HOW CAN ONE SELL THE AIR?
CHIEF SEATTLE'S VISION
Eli Gifford & R. Michael Cook
New edition. Illus. 80 pp. Paper. The Book
Publishing Co. & Clear Light, 1993. $6.95.

*HOW FIRE GOT INTO THE ROCKS & TREES:
A STORY BASED ON INDIAN LEGEND
Steven A. Roy
Grades 3 and up. Illus. 17 pp. Paper. Tipi Press, 1996.
$3.95.

*HOW FOOD WAS GIVEN: AN OKANAGAN LEGEND
illus. by Barb Marchand
Grades K-6. Illus. Paper. Theytus, 1991. $12.95.

HOW GEORGE ROGERS CLARK WON
THE NORTHWEST & OTHER ESSAYS
IN WESTERN HISTORY
R.G. Thwaites
Facsimile of 1903 edition. Ayer Co. Publishers, $21.50.

HOW INDIANS USE WILD PLANTS
FOR FOOD, MEDICINE & CRAFTS
Frances Densmore
Focuses on plants used by the Chippewa. Reprint of 1926-27
edition. Photos. 120 pp. Paper. Cherokee Publications, Writ-
ten Heritage, Hothem House, Dover, $6.95.

*HOW MEDICINE CAME TO THE PEOPLE: A TALE OF
THE ANCIENT CHEROKEES
Deborah L. Duvall; illus. by Murv Jacob
Vol. 2 of the Grandmother Stories...Cherokee history & leg-
end. All ages. Illus. University of New Mexico Press, 2002.
$13.95.

*HOW NAMES WERE GIVEN: AN OKANAGAN LEGEND
Illus. by Barb Marchand
Grades K-6. Illus. Paper. Theytus, 1991. $12.95.

*HOW THE PLAINS INDIANS LIVED
George Fichter
Grades 6 and up. David McKay, 1980. $10.95.

*HOW RABBIT LOST HIS TAIL: A TRADITIONAL
CHEROKEE LEGEND
Deborah L. Duvall; illus. by Murv Jacob
Vol. 3 of the Grandmother Stories...Cherokee history
& legend. All ages. Illus. University of New Mexico Press,
2003. $14.95.

*HOW RABBIT STOLE THE FIRE:
A NORTH AMERICAN INDIAN FOLK TALE
Joanna Troughton, retold by and illus by
Preschool-2. Illus. 28 pp. Peter Bedrick Books, 1986.
$13.95.

*HOW THE STARS FELL INTO THE SKY:
A NAVAJO LEGEND
Jerrie Oughton
Grades K-3. Illus. 32 pp. Houghton Mifflin, 1996.
$16; paper, $5.95.

HOW TO COLLECT NORTH AMERICAN INDIAN ARTIFACTS
Robert F. Brand
Illus. 151 pp. Robert F. Brand and American Indian Books,
$11.95.

HOW TO ENROLL IN AN INDIAN/ALASKA NATIVE TRIBE
A step-by-step plan for an individual who is interested in en-
rolling in a tribe. Includes forms and instructions. Arrowstar Publishing, 1994. $19.95.

HOW TO MAKE CHEROKEE CLOTHING
Donald Sizemore
Detailed instructions and illustrations. Illus.
304 pp. Paper. Written Heritage, $23.95.

HOW TO RESEARCH AMERICAN INDIAN BLOOD LINES
Cecilia S. Carpenter
Illus. 110 pp. Paper. Heritage Quest, 1987. $9.

HOW TO TAKE PART IN LAKOTA CEREMONIES
William Stolzman
A step-by-step guide to the Pipe, Sweatbath, Vision Quest,
Yuwipi, Lowanpi, and Sundance Ceremonies of the Lakota
(Sioux). Illus. 72 pp. Paper. VIP Publishing, $7.95.

HOW TO TAN SKINS THE INDIAN WAY
Evard H. Gibby
Explains brain tanning as it was done by Native Americans.
Photos. 37 line drawings. 32 pp. Paper. Eagle's View Publish-
ing, 1991. $4.50.

HOW TO TEACH ABOUT AMERICAN INDIANS: A GUIDE
FOR THE SCHOOL LIBRARY MEDIA SPECIALIST
Karen D. Harvey, et al
240 pp. Greenwood, 1995. $35.

*HOW TURTLE SET THE ANIMALS FREE:
AN OKANAGAN LEGEND
illus. by Barb Marchand
Grades K-4. Illus. Paper. Theytus, 1991. $12.95.

*HOW WOULD YOU SURVIVE AS AN AMERICAN INDIAN
Scott Steedman
History of the American Indian. Grades 3 and up. Illus.
Paper. Clear Light, $7.95.

HOWARD'S CAMPAIGN AGAINST
THE NEZ PERCE INDIANS, 1878
Thomas A. Sutherland
Reprint of 1878 edition. 62 pp. Ye Galleon Press,
$19.95; paper, $14.95.

HUICHOL INDIAN CEREMONIAL CYCLE
Jay C. Fikes, PhD
120 pp. Millenia Press, 1997.

HUICHOL INDIAN SACRED RITUALS
Mariano Valadez
Revised edition. 112 pp. Paper. Amber Lotus, 1998. $24.95.

HUMAN & CULTURAL DEVELOPMENT
J.T. Robinson, et al
66 pp. paper. Indiana Historical Society, 1974. $2.75.

HUMAN ECOLOGY: ISSUES IN THE NORTH Vols. I & II
R. Riewe & J. Oakes
Volume I - papers from the 1991 lecture series addressing traditional native nutrition and spirituality; health, housing & social problems; Inuit bird skin clothing. 135 pp., 1992; Volume II
- collection of papers featuring presentations in the 1992 & 1993
lecture series focusing on relationships between aboriginal
people & the Alberta government's education system; health &
environmental legislation. 1994. CCI, $15 each.

THE HUMAN SIDE OF HISTORY
R.F. Locke, Editor
Paper. Mankind, $1.75.

*THE HUNT
Samuel Stanley and Pearl Oberg
Grades 5-9. 32 pp. Paper. Council for Indian Education, 1976.
$1.95.

THE HUNT FOR WILLIE BOY:
INDIAN-HATING & POPULAR CULTURE
James A. Sandos & Larry E. Burgess
The story of the Paiute-Chemehuevi Indian, Willie Boy, and
his flight from justice. Illus. 182 pp. Map. Biblio. University
of Oklahoma Press, 1994. $19.95; paper, $12.95.

*THE HUNTER & THE RAVENS
Mary Holthaus
Eskimo legends. Grades K-3. 32 pp. Council
for Indian Education, 1976. $8.95; paper, $2.95.

*THE HUNTER & THE WOODPECKER
Christine Crowl
Grades Preschool-6. Illus. 12 pp. Paper. Tipi Press, 1990.
$2.50.

HUNTERS OF THE BUFFALO
R. Stephen Irwin
Illus. 52 pp. Paper. Hancock House, 1984. $3.95.

HUNTERS OF THE EASTERN FOREST
R. Stephen Irwin
52 pp. Paper. Hancock House, 1984. $3.95.

HUNTERS OF THE ICE
R. Stephen Irwin
Illus. 84 pp. Paper. Hancock House, 1984. $5.95.

HUNTERS OF THE NORTHERN FOREST
R. Stephen Irwin
Illus. 52 pp. Paper. Hancock House, 1984. $3.95.

HUNTERS OF THE NORTHERN FOREST: DESIGNS
FOR SURVIVAL AMONG THE ALASKAN KUTCHIN
Richard K. Nelson
Illus. 320 pp. Second edition. Paper.
University of Chicago Press, 1986. $12.95.

HUNTERS OF THE NORTHERN ICE
Richard K. Nelson
Illus. Paper. University of Chicago Press, 1972. $12.95.

HUNTERS OF THE SEA
R. Stephen Irwin
Illus. 52 pp. Paper. Hancock House, 1984. $3.95.

HUNTING A SHADOW:
THE SEARCH FOR BLACK HAWK
Crawford Thayer
Illus. 496 pp. Paper. Thayer Associates, 1984. $9.95.

HUUPUK"ANUM: THE ART, CULTURE &
HISTORY OF THE NUU-CHAH-NULTH PEOPLE
Alan L. Hoover
110 photos & illus. 400 pp. UBC Press, 1999. $39.95.

HURON: FARMERS OF THE NORTH
B.G. Trigger
Paper. Holt, Rinehart & Winston, 1969. $9.95.

*THE HURON
Craig & Katherine Doherty
Grades 4-8. 32 pp. Rourke Publications, 1994. $22.60.

*THE HURON: GREAT LAKES
Nancy Bonvillain
Grades 5 and up. Illus. Chelsea House, 1989. $17.95.

I

*I AM THE EAGLE FREE (SKY SONG): A SIX NATIONS
LEGEND AS INTERPRETED BY SIMON PAUL-DENE
Grade K-4. Illus. 36 pp. Paper. Theytus, 1992. $10.95.

I AM ESKIMO: AKNIK MY NAME
Paul Green & Abbe Abbott
Reprint of 1959 edition. Illus. 86 pp. Paper.
Alaska Northwest, $12.95.

I AM HERE; TWO THOUSAND YEARS
OF SOUTHWEST INDIAN CULTURE
Stewart Peckham
Museum of New Mexico Press, 1988.
$34.95; paper, $24.95.

I AM LOOKING TO THE NORTH FOR MY LIFE:
SITTING BULL, 1876-1881
Joseph Manzione
What happened to the Sioux after the Little Bighorn.
Illustrates how two countries, the U.S. & Canada, struggled
to control their potentially explosive common border. Illus.
300 pp. Paper. University of Utah Press, 1994. $14.95.

*I AM REGINA
Sally Keehn; illus. by Jan Schoenherr
Fictionalized account of a girl held captive by the
Delaware Indians from 1755 to 1764. Grades 4-8.
Illus. 240 pp. Philomel, 1991. $15.95.

I BECOME PART OF IT: SACRED DIMENSIONS
IN NATIVE AMERICAN LIFE
D.M. Dooling & Paul Jordan-Smith, Editors
Illus. 304 pp. Paper. Parabola, 1989. $14.95.

I FOUGHT WITH GERONIMO
Jason Betzinez & Wilbur Nye
Illus. 214 pp. University of Nebraska Press, 1987.
$19.95; paper, $7.95.

I HAVE COME TO STEP OVER YOUR SOUL:
A TRUE NARRATIVE OF MURDER & INDIAN JUSTICE
Charles W. Sasser
298 pp. Scarborough House, 1987. $17.95.

I HAVE SPOKEN: AMERICAN HISTORY
THROUGH THE VOICES OF THE INDIANS
Virginia I. Armstrong, Editor
Paper. Swallow Press, 1971. $7.95.

**I HEAR THE TRAIN: REFLECTIONS,
INVENTIONS, REFRACTIONS**
Louis Owens
Illus. 288 pp. University of Oklahoma Press, 2001. $29.95.

I'ISHIYATAM (DESIGNS)
K.S. Saubel & A. Galloway
Paper. Malki Museum Press, 1978. $3.

I SEND A VOICE
Evelyn Eaton
A first person account of what actually transpires inside of an
Amerindian Sweat Lodge. Illus. 180 pp. Theosophical Publish-
ing House, 1978. $12.95; paper, $4.95.

**I, THE SONG: CLASSICAL POETRY
OF NATIVE NORTH AMERICA**
A.L. Soens
Illus. University of Utah Press, $50; paper, $19.95.

**I STAND IN THE CENTER OF THE GOOD: INTERVIEWS
WITH CONTEMPORARY NATIVE AMERICAN ARTISTS**
Lawrence Abbott
Illus. 330 pp. University of Nebraska Press, 1994. $65.

**I TELL YOU NOW: AUTOBIOGRAPHICAL
ESSAYS BY NATIVE AMERICAN WRITERS**
Brian Swann & Arnold Krupat
283 PP. Paper. University of Nebraska Press, 1987. $12.

I WILL DIE AN INDIAN
E. Richard Hart, Editor
116 pp. Paper. Howe Brothers, $5.95.

**I WILL FIGHT NO MORE FOREVER:
CHIEF JOSEPH & NEZ PERCE WAR**
Merrill D. Beal
Reprint of the 1963 edition. Illus. 384 pp. Paper.
University of Washington Press, $16.95.

**ICE WINDOW: LETTERS FROM A
BERING STRAIT VILLAGE 1898-1902**
edited by Kathleen Loop Smith & Verbeck Smith
A teacher and a student helping a generation of Native Inupiat
adjust to the white culture being thrust upon them while learning their language and lifeways. Illus. Maps. Photos. 392 pp.
University of Alaska Press, 2002. $34.95; paper, $24.95.

**IDENTIFYING OUTSTANDING TALENT IN AMERICAN
INDIAN & ALASKAN NATIVE STUDENTS**
Illus. 84 pp. Diane Publishing, 1995. $30.

IDONAPSHE, LET'S EAT: TRADITIONAL ZUNI FOODS
A:shiwi A:wan Museum & Heritage Center
Illus. Paper. University of New Mexico Press, 1999. $16.95.

*IF YOU LIVED WITH THE SIOUX INDIANS
Ann McGovern
Grades K-3. Illus. 96 pp. Paper. Scholastic, Inc., 1974. $2.95.

IF YOU POISON US: URANIUM & NATIVE AMERICANS
Peter H. Eichstaedt
Story of how America's frantic entry into the nuclear age im-
pacted Native American communities. Illus. 32 color photos.
272 pp. Red Crane Books, 1994. $19.95.

**IF YOU TAKE MY SHEEP...THE EVOLUTION &
CONFLICTS OF NAVAJO PASTORALISM, 1630-1868**
Lynn R. Bailey
Illus. 304 pp. Westernlore, $14.95.

**IGNOBLE SAVAGE: AMERICAN LITERARY RACISM,
1790-1890**
Louise Barnett
220 pp. Greenwood, 1976. $29.95.

*IKTOMI & THE BERRRIES: A PLAINS INDIAN STORY
Paul Goble
Grades PS-3. Illus. 32 pp. Orchard Books, 1989. $15.

*IKTOMI & THE BOULDER
Paul Goble
Grades PS-3. Illus. 32 pp. Orchard Books, 1990. $15.

*IKTOMI & THE BUFFALO SKULL: A PLAINS INDIAN STORY
Paul Goble, as told by & Illus.
Grades PS-3. Illus. 32 pp. Orchard Books, 1991. $15.

*IKTOMI & THE DUCKS
Paul Goble
Grades PS-3. Illus. 32 pp. Orchard Books, 1992. $15.

*IKWA OF THE MOUND-BUILDER INDIANS
Margaret Zehmer Searcy
Story of a young Indian girl living in the Southeastern U.S.
before colonization. Grades 3-8. Illus. Map. Photos. 800 pp.
Pelican Publishing, $13.95; paper, $6.95.

**I'LL GO & DO MORE: ANNIE DODGE WAUNEKA,
A NAVAJO LEADER & ACTIVIST**
Carolyn Niethammer
The story of Annie Dodge Wauneka (1918-1997). Illus.
Map. 291 pp. University of Nebraska Press, 2001. $29.95.

**I'LL SING 'TIL THE DAY I DIE: CONVERSATIONS
WITH TYENDINAGA ELDERS**
Beth Brant
Elders speak social and political history to Mohawk author, Beth
Brant. Illus. 132 pp. Paper. University of Toronto Press, $11.95.

THE ILLINOIS & INDIANA INDIANS
H.W. Beckwith

**AN ILLUSTRATED HISTORY OF
THE ARTS IN SOUTH DAKOTA**
Arthur R. Huseboe
With a major section on Sioux arts by leading Lakota artist Arthur
Amiotte. Illus. 396 pp. Center for Western Studies, $24.95.

**ILLUSTRATED MYTHS OF NATIVE AMERICA:
THE SOUTHWEST, WESTERN RANGE, PACIFIC
NORTHWEST & CALIFORNIA**
Tim McNeese
Illus. 160 pp. Blandford Press, 1999. $27.95.

**IMAGERY & CREATIVITY: ETHNOAESTHETICS
& ART WORLDS IN THE AMERICAS**
Dorothea S. Whitten & Norman E. Whitten, Jr.
377 pp. University of Arizona Press, 1993.
$34.95; paper, $24.95.

**IMAGES FROM THE INSIDE PASSAGE:
AN ALASKAN PORTRAIT BY WINTER & POND**
Vicoria Wyatt
A catalog for an exhibition documenting the work of Lloyd Win-
ter and E. Percy Pond. Includes photos of Alaskan natives,
landscapes and village scenes. 144 pp. University of Alaska
Press, 1989. $40; paperback, $19.95.

**IMAGES IN OSAGE: AN ILLUSTRATED GUIDE
TO THE SYLVESTER J. TINKER COLLECTION**
Diane L. Good
Paper. Kansas State Historical Society, 1990. $5.95.

IMAGES OF A PEOPLE: TLINGIT MYTHS & LEGENDS
Mary Helen Pelton & Jacqueline DiGennaro, Editors
22 Tlingit legends. Illus. 150 pp. Libraries Unlimited, 1992. $22.

**IMAGES OF A VANISHED LIFE: PLAINS INDIAN
DRAWINGS FROM THE COLLECTION OF THE
PENNSYLVANIA ACADEMY OF FINE ARTS**
John C. Ewers, et al
Illus. 50 pp. Pennsylvania Academy of Art, 1985.

**IMAGINING INDIANS IN THE SOUTHWEST:
PERSISTENT VISIONS OF A PRIMITIVE PAST**
Leah Dilworth
Illus. 304 pp. Smithsonian Institution Press, 1996.
$34.95; paper, $16.95.

JOSEPH IMHOF: ARTIST OF THE PUEBLOS
Nancy Hopkins Reily
Biography of a famous painter in the American Southwest.
Illus. 448 pp. Sunstone Press, 1999. $60.

*THE IMMIGRANT EXPERIENCE
David Reimers
Grades 5 and up. Illus. 112 pp. Chelsea House, 1989. $17.95.

**THE IMPACT OF DISLOCATION: THE AMERICAN INDIAN
LABOR FORCE AT THE CLOSE OF THE 20th CENTURY**
Patricia Kasari
Garland Publishing, 1999.

**IMPERFECT VICTORIES: THE LEGAL
TENACITY OF THE OMAHA TRIBE, 1945-1995**
Mark R. Scherer
Details the postwar federal legislation that transferred control
over Indian affairs to state authorities. Illus. 166 pp. University
of Nebraska Press, 1999. $50.

**THE IMPERIAL OSAGES: SPANISH—INDIAN
DIPLOMACY IN THE MISSISSIPPI VALLEY**
Gilbert Din and Abraham P. Nasatir
Illus. Maps. 432 pp. University of Oklahoma Press, 1983.
$49.95.

**IMPLEMENTATION OF THE INDIAN GAMING
REGULATORY ACT: SURVEY & AUDIT REPORTS**
Harold Bloom, Editor
Illus. 62 pp. Paper. Diane Publishing, 1998. $25.

**IMPLEMENTING THE NATIVE AMERICAN GRAVES
PROTECTION & REPATRIATION ACT (NAGPRA)**
Roxana Adams
American Association of Museums, 2001.

**IMPROVING AMERICAN INDIAN HEALTH CARE:
THE WESTERN CHEROKEE EXPERIENCE**
William C. Steeler
Illus. Map. 168 pp. University of Oklahoma Press, 2001.
$34.95.

**IN THE ABSENCE OF THE SACRED: THE FAILURE OF
TECHNOLOGY & THE SURVIVAL OF THE INDIAN NATIONS**
Jerry Mander
Reprint. 464 pp. Paper. Four Winds & Sierra Club Books, $14.

**IN A BARREN LAND: AMERICAN INDIAN
DISPOSSESSION & SURVIVAL**
Paula M. Marks
Illus. 451 pp. William Morrow, 1998. $27.50.

*IN THE BEGINNING
Ella Clark, Editor
Grades 5-12. Paper. Council for Indian Education, 1977.
$2.95.

IN THE BEGINNING: THE NAVAJO GENESIS
Jerrold E. Levy
Navajo religion, myths & rituals. 325 pp. University
of California Press, 1998. $45; paper, $16.95.

***IN A CIRCLE LONG AGO: A TREASURY
OF NATIVE LORE FROM NORTH AMERICA**
Nancy Van Laan
Grades PS-3. Illus. 128 pp. Random House, 1995. $21.95.

**IN COMPANY: AN ANTHOLOGY
OF NEW MEXICO POETS AFTER 1960**
Edited by Lee Bartlett, V.B. Price & Dianne Edwards
Collection of poetry including poetry of: Joy Harjo, Jimmy
Santiago Baca, N. Scott Momaday, and Arthur Sze. 544 pp.
University of New Mexico Press, 2004. $34.95.

**IN THE DAYS OF VICTORIO: RECOLLECTIONS
OF A WARM SPRINGS APACHE**
Eve Ball
Records an Apache's own account of their history from 1878-
1886. Reprint of 1970 edition. 222 pp. Paper. University of Ari-
zona Press, 1970. $15.95.

**IN DEFENSE OF MOHAWK LAND: ETHNOPOLITICAL
CONFLICT IN NATIVE NORTH AMERICA**
Linda Pertusati
Illus. 166 pp. State University of New York Press, 1997.
$44.50; paper, $14.95.

IN THE HANDS OF THE SENECAS
Walter D. Edmonds
233 pp. Paper. Syracuse University Press, $14.95.

**IN HONOR OF EYAK:
THE ART OF ANNA NELSON HARRY**
Michael E. Krauss
Illus. 157 pp. Paper. Alaska Native Language Center, 1982.
$10; two cassettes, $9.

**IN HONOR OF MARY HAAS: FROM THE HAAS FESTIVAL
CONFERENCE ON NATIVE AMERICAN LINGUISTICS**
William Shipley, Editor
826 pp. Mouton, 1988. $175.

**IN THE LAND OF THE GRASSHOPPER SONG:
TWO WOMEN IN THE KLAMATH RIVER INDIAN
COUNTRY, 1908-1909**
Mary Arnold and Mabel Reed
Illus. 313 pp. Paper. Naturegraph, 1980. $13.95.

IN MAD LOVE AND WAR
Joy Harjo
Poetry. Illus. 70 pp. Paper. University Press of New England,
1990. $10.95.

**IN MOHAWK COUNTRY: EARLY NARRATIVES
ABOUT A NATIVE PEOPLE**
Dean R. Snow, Charles T. Gehring
& William A. Starna, Editors
38 narratives written between 1634 and 1810 about the Mohawk
Valley and its Iroquois residents. Maps. Biblio. Syracuse Uni-
versity Press, 1998. $39.95; paper, $16.95.

**IN MY OWN WORDS: THE STORIES, SONGS,
& MEMORIES OF GRACE McKIBBEN, WINTU**
Alice Shepherd
Bilingual collection of the songs, stories, and traditional tales of
the Wintu. Photos. 172 pp. Paper. Heyday Books, $14.

**IN PURSUIT OF THE PAST: AN ANTHROPOLOGICAL &
BIBLIOGRAPHIC GUIDE TO MARYLAND & DELAWARE**
Frank W. Porter, III
268 pp. Scarecrow, 1986. $27.50.

***IN A SACRED MANNER I LIVE:
NATIVE AMERICAN WISDOM**
Neil Philip, Editor
Grades 6 and up. Illus. 96 pp. Houghton Mifflin, 1997. $20.

**IN A SACRED MANNER WE LIVE: PHOTOGRAPHS
OF THE AMERICAN INDIAN AT THE BEGINNING
OF THE TWENTIETH CENTURY**
Don D. Fowler
Illus. 196 pp. Paper. Barre, 1972. $5.95.

**IN SEARCH OF THE WILD INDIAN: PHOTOGRAPHS
& LIFE WORKS BY CARL & GRACE MOON**
Tom Driebe
230+ color & 200 bxw photos. 432 pp.
Maurose Publishing, $85.

IN THE SHADOW OF THE SUN: CONTEMPORARY CANADIAN INDIAN & INUIT ART
Gerhard Hoffmann
Illus. 600 pp. University of Chicago Press, 1989. $60.

IN THE SPIRIT OF CRAZY HORSE
Peter Matthiessen
American Indian Movement and the Leonard Peltier case.
688 pp. Paper. Penguin USA, 1992. $14.

IN THE SPIRIT OF MOTHER EARTH: NATURE IN NATIVE AMERICAN ART
Jeremy Schmidt & Laine Thom
Illustrates the relationship between art and nature.
100 full-color & 15 bxw photos. 120 pp. Chronicle Books, 1994. $35; paper, $19.95.

*IN THE TRAIL OF THE WIND: AMERICAN INDIAN POEMS & RITUAL ORATIONS
John Bierhorst, Editor
Grades 8 and up. Paper. Farrar, Strauss & Giroux, 1987. $3.50.

IN VAIN I TRIED TO TELL YOU: ESSAYS IN NATIVE AMERICAN ETHNOPOETICS
Dell Hymes
Showcases the methodology and theory of ethnopoetics focusing on Native storytelling traditions of the Pacific Northwest. Reprint of 1981 edition. 424 pp. Paper. University of Nebraska Press, 2004. $29.95.

IN THE WORDS OF THE ELDERS: ABORIGINAL CULTURES IN TRANSITION
Peter Kulchyski, Don McCaskill & David Newhouse
First Nations cultures. Illus. 480 pp. University of Toronto Press, 1999. $70; paper, $29.95.

INCOME & HEALTH IN A NORTH INDIAN VILLAGE
Mike Shepperdson
200 pp. Gower, 1987. $49.95.

INCONSTANT SAVAGE: ENGLAND & THE NORTH AMERICAN INDIANS, 1500-1660
H.C. Porter
588 pp. Biblio Distribution Centre, 1979. $34.95.

*THE INCREDIBLE ESKIMO
Raymond Coccola & Paul King; J. Cameron, Editor
Life among the Barren Land Eskimo. Grade 9. Illus.
435 pp. Paper. Hancock House, 1986. $16.95.

*INDE, THE WESTERN APACHE
Susan L. Shaffer
Grades 5 and up. Illus. Includes 30 student booklets and teacher's resource binder with overhead transparencies, slides, audiocassette. The Heard Museum, 1987. $295.

INDEH: AN APACHE ODYSSEY
Eve Ball, et al
Illus. Maps. 360 pp. Paper. University of Oklahoma Press, 1988. $21.95.

INDEPENDENT LIVING OUTCOMES FOR AMERICAN INDIANS WITH DISABILITIES
P.L. Sanderson
40 pp. Paper. Northern Arizona University, 1996. $10.

INDEX TO THE DECISIONS OF THE INDIAN CLAIMS COMMISSION
Norman A. Ross
168 pp. N. Ross, 1973. $25.

INDEX TO THE EXPERT TESTIMONY PRESENTED BEFORE THE INDIAN CLAIMS COMMISSION
Norman A. Ross
112 pp. N. Ross, 1973. $25.

INDEX TO LITERATURE ON THE AMERICAN INDIAN
Jeanette Henry, Editor
Four volumes. Paper. The Indian Historian Press, 1975. $12 each.

INDEX TO THE RECORDS OF THE MORAVIAN MISSION AMONG THE INDIANS OF NORTH AMERICA
Carl J. Fliegel, Compiler
4 vols. 1,400 pp. Research Publications, 1970. $400 per set.

INDIAN AFFAIRS
Larry Woiwode
320 pp. Farrar, Straus & Giroux, 1991. $18.95.

INDIAN AFFAIRS IN COLONIAL NEW YORK: THE 17TH CENTURY
Allen W. Trelease
Illus. Maps. 381 pp. Paper. University of Nebraska Press, 1997. $16.95.

INDIAN AFFAIRS IN OREGON & WASHINGTON TERRITORIES
James Buchanan
23 pp. Paper. Ye Galleon Press, 1988. $4.95.

INDIAN AFFAIRS LAWS & TREATIES: U.S. LAWS, STATUTES, ETC.
Charles J. Kappler, Editor
Reprint edition. 7 vols. 6,000 pp. William S. Hein, $490.

INDIAN AGENTS OF THE OLD FRONTIER
Flora W. Seymour
Reprint of 1941 edition. Octagon Books, 1973. $27.50.

INDIAN AGRICULTURE IN AMERICA: PREHISTORY TO THE PRESENT
R. Douglas Hurt
Illus. 304 pp. Paper. University Press of Kansas, 1988. $17.95.

INDIAN AMERICA: A GEOGRAPHY OF NORTH AMERICAN INDIANS
M. Wallace Ney
Illus. Maps. 56 pp. Paper. VIP Publishing & Cherokee Publications, 1977. $6.

INDIAN AMERICANS: UNITY & DIVERSITY
Murray L. Wax
Prentice-Hall, 1971. $21.

INDIAN ANTIQUITIES OF THE KENNEBEC VALLEY
Charles Willoughby; Arthur E. Spiess, Editor
Illus. 160 pp. Maine State Museum, 1980. $22.

INDIAN ARROWHEADS - IDENTIFICATION & PRICE GUIDE
Overstreet & Peake
5th edition. Illus. 950 pp. Hothem House, 1997. $24, postpaid.

INDIAN ART & CULTURE
Della Kew and P.E. Goddard
Reprint of 1978 second edition. Illus. 96 pp.
Paper. Hancock House, $9.95.

INDIAN ART IN THE ASHMOLEAN MUSEUM
J.C. Harle & Andrew Topsfield
Illus. 128 pp. University of Chicago Press, 1988.
$50; paper, $22.50.

INDIAN ART OF ANCIENT FLORIDA
Barbara Purdy
Illus. 152 pp. University Press of Florida, 1996. $34.95.

INDIAN ART OF THE U.S.
F.H. Douglas and R. D'Harmoncourt
Reprint of 19451 edition. Illus. Ayer Co., $20.00.

INDIAN ART TRADITIONS ON THE NORTHWEST COAST
Roy L. Carlson, Editor
Illus. 214 pp. Paper. University of Washington Press, 1984. $14.95.

INDIAN ARTIFACTS
Russell
Flint & stone artifacts, with identification & classification.
Illus. 170 pp. Hothem House, 1981. $14.45, postpaid.

INDIAN ARTIFACTS OF THE EAST & SOUTH: AN ID GUIDE
Swope
Many clkasses are described and hundreds of artifacts are shown. 148 pp. Paper. Hothem House, 1982. $14.

INDIAN ARTIFACTS OF THE MIDWEST
Lar Hothem
Covers six states: KY, OH, IN, IL, MO, IA. 2nd edition. Illus. 206 pp. Paper. Hothem House, 1993. $16.95, postpaid.

INDIAN ARTIFACTS OF THE MIDWEST - BOOK I, II & III
Lar Hothem
Book I covers six states: KY, OH, IN, IL, MO, IA. Illus. 206 pp. 1993, $16.95 postpaid; Book II, Illus. 1994, $18.985 postpaid; Book III, 1997, $21.45. Illus. Paper. Hothem House. $18.95, postpaid.

INDIAN ARTISTS AT WORK
Ulli Steltzer
Illus. 144 pp. University of Washington Press, 1977. $30; paper, $14.95.

INDIAN ARTS & CRAFTS BOARD - SOURCE DIRETORY
A directory of Native American owned & operated businesses located throughout the U.S. that market a wide range of authentic contemporary Native American arts & crafts. Illus. 48 pp. Indian Arts & Crafts Board. No charge.

*THE INDIAN AS A SOLDIER AT FORT CUSTER, MONTANA, 1890-1895: LT. SAMUEL C. ROBERTSON'S FIRST CAVALRY CROW INDIAN CONTINGENT
Richard Upton
Grades 7-12. Illus. 147 pp. Upton Sons, 1985. $27.50.

INDIAN ATROCITIES: NARRATIVES OF THE PERILS & SUFFERINGS OF DR. KNIGHT & JOHN SLOVER
Dr. John Knight & John Slover
Facsimile of 1867 edition. 72 pp. Ye galleon, $9.95.

THE INDIAN AWAKENING IN LATIN AMERICA
Yves Materne, Editor
Friendship Press, $5.95.

INDIAN AXES & RELATED STONE ARTIFACTS
Lar Hothem
2nd edition. Illus. 214 pp. Paper. Hothem House, 1993. $24.50, postpaid.

INDIAN BASKET WEAVING
Navajo School of Indian Basketry
Illus. 104 pp. Paper. Dover, 1971. $5.95.

INDIAN BASKETMAKERS
Larry Dalrymple
Two-volume slipcased set containing *Indian Basketmakers of California and the Great Basin* and *Indian Basketmakers of the Southwest*. Paper. Museum of New Mexico Press, 2001. $60.

INDIAN BASKETMAKERS OF CALIFORNIA & THE GREAT BASIN
Larry Dalrymple
Features the baskets and basketmakers of the Hupa, Yurok, Karuk, Tolowa, Western Mono or northern California, and the Great Basin tribes including the Western Shoshoni, Northern paiute, Washoe and Chemehuevi. Illus. Map. 88 pp. Paper. Museum of New Mexico Press, 2001. $24.95.

INDIAN BASKETMAKERS OF THE SOUTHWEST
Larry Dalrymple
Features the baskets and basketmakers of the Hualapai, Havasupai, Yavapai, Western Apache; Jicarilla Apache, the Ute, San Juan Paiute, Navajo, Tohono O'odham; Pueblos of New Mexico and Hopi of Arizona. Illus. Map. 156 pp. Paper. Museum of New Mexico Press, 2001. $29.95.

INDIAN BASKETRY
George W. James
Reprint. Illus. 271 pp. Paper. Hothem House & Dover, $7.95.

INDIAN BASKETRY, & HOW TO MAKE BASKETS
George W. James
Enlarged 1903 edition. 2 vols. in 1. Illus.
Biblio. 424 pp. The Rio Grande Press, $30.

INDIAN BASKETS
Sarah & William Turnbaugh
Illus. 256 pp. Paper. Schiffer, $24.95.

INDIAN BASKETS & CURIOS
Reproduction of 1902 Frohman Trading Co. Illus.
28 pp. catalog. Paper. Binford & Mort, $6.50.

INDIAN BASKETS OF THE PACIFIC NORTHWEST & ALASKA
Lobb; photos by Al Wolfe
Illus. 130 pp. Graphic Arts Center Publishing, 1990. $29.50.

INDIAN BASKETS OF THE SOUTHWEST
Clara Lee Tanner
Illus. 242 pp. University of Arizona Press, 1983. $60.

INDIAN BATTLES ALONG THE ROGUE RIVER: ONE OF AMERICA'S WILD AND SCENIC RIVERS
Frank K. Walsh
Second edition. Illus. 32 pp. Paper. Te-Cum-Tom, 1972. $4.95.

INDIAN BATTLES, MURDERS, SEIGES, & FORAYS IN THE SOUTHWEST: THE NARRATIVE OF COLONEL JOSEPH BROWN
Joseph Brown
Illus. Paper. Territorial Press of Tennessee, 1989. $4.50.

INDIAN BATTLES & SKIRMISHES ON THE AMERICAN FRONTIER, 1790-1898
Joseph P. Peters, Compiler
Reprint of 1966 edition. 256 pp. Ayer Co., $33.95.

*INDIAN BEAD—WEAVING PATTERNS: CHAIN WEAVING DESIGNS & BEAD LOOM WEAVING—AN ILLUSTRATED HOW—TO GUIDE
Horace R. Goodhue
Grades 3-12. Illus. 80 pp. Paper. Bead Craft, 1984. $9.95.

THE INDIAN BILL OF RIGHTS
John R. Wunder, Editor
Reprint of 1968 edition. 344 pp. Garland, $70.

INDIAN BLANKETS & THEIR MAKERS
George W. James
Reprint. Illus. Biblio. 352 pp. The Rio Grande Press, $40. Paper. Hothem House & Dover, $10.95.

*INDIAN BOYHOOD
Charles A. Eastman
Grades 3 to 7. 190 pp. Paper. Dover, $5.95.

*INDIAN CANOEING
Pierre Pulling with Hap Gilliland
Grades 6 and up. Illus. 55 pp. Paper.
Council for Indian Education, 1976. $4.95.

THE INDIAN CAPTIVE: A NARRATIVE OF THE ADVENTURES & SUFFERINGS OF MATTHEW BRAYTON, IN HIS 34 YEARS OF CAPTIVITY AMONG INDIANS OF NORTHWEST U.S.
John H. Bone
Reprint. 65 pp. Ye Galleon Press, $16.95.

THE INDIAN CAPTIVE: OR, A NARRATIVE OF THE CAPTIVITY & SUFFERINGS OF ZADOCK STEELE
Zadeck Steele
Reprint of 1908 edition. Ayer Co., $14.

THE INDIAN CAPTIVITY OF O.M. SPENCER
O.M. Spencer
112 pp. Paper. Dover, $6.95.

INDIAN CEREMONIAL AND TRADE SILVER
Gibb
Illus. 168 pp. Paper. Hothem House, 1980. $29, postpaid.

*INDIAN CHIEFS
H. Upton
Grades 3-8. Illus. 32 pp. Rourke Corp., 1990. $17.26.

*INDIAN CHIEFS
Russell Freedman
Six western chiefs. Grades 4-6. Illus. Photos. Map. 160 pp. Holiday House, 1987. $18.95; paper, $9.95.

INDIAN CHIEFS OF PENNSYLVANIA
C. Hale Sipe
Reprint of 1927 edition. Illus. 569 pp. Paper. Wennawoods Publishing. $24.95.

INDIAN CHIEFS OF SOUTHERN MINNESOTA
Thomas Hughes
Reprint. Ross & Haines, $10.

THE INDIAN CHILD WELFARE ACT HANDBOOK: A LEGAL GUIDE TO THE CUSTODY & ADOPTION OF NATIVE AMERICAN CHILDREN
248 pp. Paper. American Bar Association, 1995. $69.95.

*INDIAN CHILDREN PAPER DOLLS
Phyllis Hughes
Author and artist Phyllis Hughes has drawn Pueblo, Navajo and Apache boys and girls in authentic detail. A brief text shows the closeness of Indian families in daily and ceremonial life. Grades PS-2. Illus. Paper. Red Crane Books, $5.95.

THE INDIAN CHRONICLES
Jose Barreiro
Historical novel that recounts the invasion of the Americas by the Spaniards as seen by Christopher Columbus's adopted Indian son. 303 pp. Arte Publico Press, $19.95.

INDIAN CLOTHING BEFORE CORTES: MESOAMERICAN COSTUMES FROM THE CODICES
Patricia R. Anawalt
Illus. 232 pp. University of Oklahoma Press, 1981. $65; paper, $39.95.

INDIAN CLOTHING OF THE GREAT LAKES: 1740-1840
Sheryl Hartman; Monte Smith, Editor
Illus. 134 pp. Eagles View & Smoke & Fire Co., 1988. $14.95.

INDIAN COOKING
Traditional recipes. Illus. 64 pp. Paper. Cherokee Publications, $3.50.

INDIAN CORN OF THE AMERICAS: GIFT TO THE WORLD
Jose Barreiro, Editor
Explores the meaning of corn to Indian people through tradition, myth, agriculture, economics, histry, and language. Akwe:kon Press, $10.

*INDIAN COSTUMES
Robert Hofsinde (Gray-Wolf)
Grades 3-7. Illus. 96 pp. William Morrow, 1968. $11.80.

INDIAN COUNTRY
Peter Matthiessen
350 pp. Peter Smith, 1984. $24.95. Paper. Penguin USA, $11.

INDIAN COUNTRY ADDRESS BOOK 2003
Barry Klein, Editor
Names, addresses, phone & fax numbers, e-mail addresses and websites of Indian organizations, groups, programs, institutions, government agencies, tribes & nations, and individuals. 15,000 entries. 400 pp. Todd Publications, 4th Edition, 2003. $95.

INDIAN COUNTRY: A GUIDE TO NORTHEASTERN ARIZONA
Tom Dollar
Provides an overview of Indian arts & crafts. Illus. Maps. 64 pp. Paper. University of Arizona Press, 1993. $9.95.

*INDIAN COUNTRY: A HISTORY OF NATIVE PEOPLE IN AMERICA
Karen D. Harvey & Lisa D. Harjo
Excerpts from Ada Deer and M. Scott Momaday. Complete lesson plans utilizing a whole-language approach. Grades 4-9.

Illus. 360 pp. Paper. Fulcrum Publishing, 1998. $26.95; Teacher's Guide - additional lesson plans &support materials including maps, graphs, documents. $12.95.

INDIAN COUNTRY, L.A. MAINTAINING ETHNIC COMMUNITY IN A COMPLEX SOCIETY
Joan Weibel-Orlando
Illus. 384 pp. University of Illinois Press, 1991. $34.95.

INDIAN COUNTRY: TRAVELS IN THE AMERICAN SOUTHWEST, 1840-1935
Martin Padget
Analyzes the works of Anglo writers and artists who encountered American Indians in the course of their travels in the Southwest during a 100 year period. Illus. 320 pp. University of New Mexico Press, 2004. $37.95.

*INDIAN CRAFTS
Janet and Alex D'Amato
Grades 1-4. Illus. Lion Press, $11.95.

THE INDIAN CRAFTS OF WILLIAM & MARY COMMANDA
David Gidmark
Illus. 144 pp. Paper. Stackpole Press, 1995. $15.95.

INDIAN CRISIS: THE BACKGROUND
J.S. Hoyland
Reprint of 1943 edition. Ayer Co., $17.00.

INDIAN CULTURE & EUROPEAN TRADE GOODS: THE ARCHAEOLOGY OF THE HISTORIC PERIOD IN THE WESTERN GREAT LAKES REGION
George I. Quimby
Reprint of 1966 edition. Greenwood Press, 1978. $22.50.

INDIAN DANCES OF NORTH AMERICA: THEIR IMPORTANCE TO INDIAN LIFE
Reginald & Gladys Laubin
Reprint of 1977 edition. Illus. 538 pp. Paper. University of Oklahoma Press, 1997. $24.95.

*INDIAN DANCING COLORING BOOK
Connie Asch
Grades 2-4. Illus. 32 pp. Paper. Clear Light, $3.50.

INDIAN DAYS OF LONG AGO
Edward S. Curtis
Reprint of 1978 edition. Illus. 221 pp. Ten Speed Press, $8.95; paper, $5.95.

INDIAN DEPREDATION CLAIMS, 1796-1920
Larry C. Skogen
Illus. 290 pp. University of Oklahoma Press, 1996. $35.95.

INDIAN DEPREDATIONS IN TEXAS
J.W. Wilbarger
Reprint. Illus. 690 pp. Eakin Press, $32.95.

INDIAN DESIGNS
David & Jean Villasenor
Shows quilt patterns, applique, needlepoint, stitchery, fabric painting, etc. Illus. 48 pp. Paper. Naturegraph, 1983. $8.95.

*INDIAN DESIGNS STAINED GLASS COLORING BOOK
John Green
Grades K-3. 32 pp. paper. Dover, $3.95.

INDIAN DOCTOR: NATURE'S METHOD OF CURING & PREVENTING DISEASE ACCORDING TO THE INDIANS
Poisons, Ailments & Herbs. Plants to use for treatment and how to prepare; dictionary of herbs and what to use them for. Reprint. Illus. 60 pp. Paper. Clear Light, $7.50.

INDIAN EDUCATION
Jack Rudman
Three vols. Elementary, Secondary and Guidance. 1989. Paper. National Learning Corp., $16.00 each.

INDIAN EMPLOYMENT, TRAINING & RELATED SERVICES DEMONSTRATION ACT
U.S. Governemnt
157 pp. U.S. Government Printing Office, 1998.

INDIAN, ESKIMO & ALEUT BASKETRY OF ALASKA
Gogol
Basketry items of the Attu, Yakutat, Tlingit, Haida and Tsimshian. Vol. 6 of American Indian Basketry, 1982. Illus. 34 pp. Hothem House, $7.95, postpaid.

INDIAN, ESKIMO, ALEUT OWNED & OPERATED ARTS BUSINESSES SOURCE DIRECTORY
Indian Arts and Crafts Board.

INDIAN & ESKIMO ARTIFACTS OF NORTH AMERICA
Reginald P. Bolton
Outlet Book Co., 1981. $9.98.

*INDIAN FAIRY TALES
Jacobs
Grades 3 and up. Peter Smith.

INDIAN FIGHTING IN THE FIFTIES IN OREGON & WASHINGTON TERRITORIES
Philip Sheridan
Reprint. 93 pp. Paper. Ye Galleon Press, $14.95; paper, $9.95.

INDIAN FIGHTS & FIGHTERS
Cyrus Brady
Illus. 495 pp. University of Nebraska Press, 1971. $33.95; paper, $8.95.

INDIAN FISHING: EARLY METHODS ON THE NORTHWEST COAST
Hilary Stewart
Illus. 450 drawings, 75 photos. 182 pp. Paper. University of Washington Press, 1977. $24.95.

INDIAN FLINTS OF OHIO
Lar Hothem
Covers prehistoric tools and weapons of the eastern Midwest. 165 artifact types with names and descriptions. Illus. 188 pp. Paper. Hothem House, $11.95.

*INDIAN FOLK TALES FROM COAST TO COAST
Jessie Marsh
Grades 3-6. Illus. Paper. Council for Indian Education, 1978. $1.95.

THE INDIAN FRONTIER, 1763-1846
R. Douglas Hurt
Illus. 35 halftones. 10 maps. 318 pp. Paper. University of New Mexico Press, 2001. $21.95.

THE INDIAN FRONTIER OF THE AMERICAN WEST, 1846-1890
Robert M. Utley
Revised edition. 90 bxw Illus. 344 pp. Paper. University of New Mexico Press, 2003. $22.95.

INDIAN GAMES & DANCES WITH NATIVE SONGS
Alice Fletcher
Musical scores. Illus. 140 pp. Paper. University of Nebraska Press, 1994. Written Heritage, $5.95.

THE INDIAN GAMING HANDBOOK
Levine & Associates
Portable briefcase/desk reference on Indian gaming. In two vols. Vol. I: The Little Red Book" - The Indian Gaming Regulatory Act (IGRA); Vol. II: "The Little Yellow Book" - The National Indian Gaming Commission (NIGC) bulletins, advisory opinions, management contract and background investigation requirements, etc. National Indian Gaming Association, $50 each, $90 per set.

INDIAN GAMING & THE LAW
Judy Cornelius & William Eadington, Editors
2nd ed. Reprint. 298 pp. Paper. Univ. of Nevada, 1998. $14.95.

INDIAN GAMING: WHO WINS?
edited by Angela Mullis & David Kamper
Explores American Indian gaming practices on many U.S. Indian reservations today. 189 pp. Paper. UCLA, American Indian Studies Center, 2000. Also available from The Falmouth Institute. $15.

INDIAN GIVERS: HOW THE INDIANS OF THE AMERICAS TRANSFORMED THE WORLD
Jack M. Weatherford
Native Americans "gave" Europeans food, the idea of a federal government system, and many other innovations that are thought of as European. 272 pp. Crown, 1989. $18.95; paper, $9.95. Paper. Morning Flower Press, $10.

INDIAN HANDCRAFTS
C. Keith Wilbur, M.D.
How to craft dozens of practical objects using traditional Indian techniques. Illus. 144 pp. Paper. Globe Pequot, 1989. $14.95.

INDIAN HEALING; SHAMANIC CEREMONIALISM IN THE PACIFIC NORTHWEST TODAY
W.G. Jilek
Reprint. Illus. 184 pp. Paper. Hancock House, $17.95.

INDIAN HEALTH SERVICE: IMPROVEMENTS NEEDED IN CREDENTIALING TEMPORARY PHYSICIANS
IHS
Illus. 43 pp. Paper. Diane Publishing, 1996. $25.

INDIAN HERBALOGY OF NORTH AMERICA
Hutchens
An illustrated encyclopedic guide to over 200 medicinal plants found in North America. 382 pp. Paper. Cherokee Publications, $17.

INDIAN HERITAGE OF AMERICA
Alvin M. Josephy, Jr.
Enlarged 1968 edition. 450 pp. Paper. Houghton Mifflin, 1991. $15.

THE INDIAN HERITAGE OF AMERICANS
John Frank Phillips
The tools of the American Indians are examined;
some achievements of the American Indians. 54 pp.
Paper. American Indian Books, 1981. $2.95.

*INDIAN HEROES & GREAT CHIEFTAINS
Charles A. Eastman
Grades 3 to 7. Illus. 254 pp. Paper. University of
Nebraska Press, 1991. First published in 1918. $15.95.

INDIAN & HIS PROBLEM
Francis E. Leupp
Reprint of 1910 edition. Ayer Co., $24.50.

INDIAN HISTORY, BIOGRAPHY & GENEALOGY:
PERTAINING TO THE GOOD SACHEM MASSASOIT
OF THE WAMPANOAG TRIBE, & HIS DESCENDANTS
E.W. Pierce
Reprint of 1878 edition. Ayer Co., $21.

THE INDIAN HISTORY OF BRITISH COLUMBIA
Wilson Duff
Illus. Paper. UBC Press, 1997. $14.95.

THE INDIAN HISTORY OF THE MODOC WAR
Jeff C. Riddle
Illus. 292 pp. Urion Press, 1975. $14.95; paper, $7.95.

THE INDIAN HOUSEHOLD MEDICINE GUIDE
J.I. Lighthall
152 pp. Paper. Fly Eagle, 1996. $14.95.

INDIAN HOUSING IN THE USA: A HISTORY
Housing Assistance Council
96 pp. Housing Assistance, 1988. $8.25.

THE INDIAN HOW BOOK
Arthur C. Parker
Authentic history & information on American Indian crafts, customs, food, clothing, religion & recreation. Reprint. Illus. 335
pp. Paper. Hothem House, Cherokee Publications & Dover,
$6.95.

THE INDIAN HUNTERS
R. Stephen Irwin, MD; illus. by J.B. Clemens
The lives of the first North American hunters. 296 pp.
Paper. Hancock House, 1994. $16.95.

INDIAN HUNTING, TRAPPING & FISHING RIGHTS
IN THE PRAIRIE PROVINCES OF CANADA
Kent McNeil
64 pp. University of Saskatchewan, 1983. $20.00.

INDIAN HUNTS & INDIAN HUNTERS OF THE OLD WEST
F. Hibben; as told to him by Juan de Dios
An account of the old West as told to him by Juan de Dios, a
Navajo captured by the Spanish in a slaving raid. Reprint. Illus.
Photos. 228 pp. Safari Press, 1989. $24.95.

THE INDIAN IN AMERICA
Wilcomb Washburn
Illus. 330 pp. Harper & Row, 1975. $19.45; paper, $8.95.

THE INDIAN IN AMERICAN HISTORY
William T. Hagan
32 pp. Paper. American Historical Association, 1971.
$3.50.

THE INDIAN IN AMERICAN LITERATURE
Albert Keiser
Gordon Press, $59.95.

*THE INDIAN IN THE CUPBOARD
Lynne Reid Banks
Grades 4 and up. Illus. 224 pp. Paper. Scholastic, 1995.
$4.95.

AN INDIAN IN WHITE AMERICA
Mark Monroe; edited by Carolyn Reyer
Autobiography of Mark Monroe, A Lakota Sioux Indian who
overcame his personal struggles to help his communty. Illus.
256 pp. Temple University Press, 1994. $49.95; paper, $18.95.

INDIAN INTERNATIONAL MOTORCYCLE DIRECTORY
Gregory Frazier
Paper. Whole Earth Motorcycle Center, 2001.

INDIAN ISSUES
E.B. Eiselein
Presents a brief introduction to current issues facing both
urban and reservation Indians. Spiral bound. Spirit Talk
Press, 1993. $12.

INDIAN JEWELRY OF THE AMERICAN SOUTHWEST
William & Sarah Turnbaugh
Illus. 96 pp. Paper. Schiffer, $12.95.

INDIAN JEWELRY ON THE MARKET
Peter Schiffer
Price guide. Color photos. 144 pp. Paper.
Schiffer Books. $19.95.

THE INDIAN JOURNALS, 1859-1862
Lewis Henry Morgan; L. White & C. Walton, Editors
Morgan's researches among the tribes of Kansas & Nebraska.
Reprint of 1958 edition. Paper. Dover, $10.95.

INDIAN JUSTICE: A CHEROKEE MURDER
TRIAL AT TAHLEQUAH IN 1840
John Howard Payne
First newspaper account of an Indian trial in Indian Territory.
First published in "The New York Journal of Commerce" on
April 17 & April 29, 1841. Illus. Map. 136 pp. Paper. University
of Oklahoma Press, 2002. $17.95.

INDIAN JUSTICE: A RESEARCH BIBLIOGRAPHY
Vincent J. Webb
CPL Biblios, 1976. $6.50.

INDIAN KILLER
Sherman Alexie
Novel by a Spokane/Coeur d'Alene writer.
Grades 9 and up. Oyate, 1996. $22.

INDIAN LAND CESSIONS IN THE UNITED STATES
Charles C. Royce
Reprint of 1900 edition. Illus. Ayer Co., $75.

INDIAN LAND LAWS
S.T. Bledsoe; Stuart Bruchey, Editor
Reprint of 1909 edition. Ayer Co., $47.50.

INDIAN LAND TENURE: BIBLIOGRAPHICAL
ESSAYS & A GUIDE TO THE LITERATURE
Irme Sutton
300 pp. Illus. N. Ross, 1975. $25.00.

INDIAN LANDS
Malcom Rosholt
Illus. 352 pp. Paper. Krause Publications, $17.50.

INDIAN LAW CONFERENCE SERIES
Federal Bar Assn. Editors
Material includes annual updates of legislation and litigation;
jurisdictional issues, bibliographies, etc. 1977-92. See the Federal Bar Association for editions and prices.

INDIAN LAW - RACE LAW:
A FIVE HUNDRED YEAR HISTORY
James E. Falkowski
192 pp. Greenwood, 192. $45.

THE INDIAN LAWYER
James Welch
A young American Indian lawyer is torn between the trappings
of his profession and his Indian heritage. Illus. 352 pp. Paper.
Penguin USA, $8.95.

INDIAN LEADERSHIP IN THE WEST
Walter Williams, Editor
92 pp. Paper. Sunflower University Press, 1984. $15.

INDIAN LEGACY OF CHARLES BIRD KING
Herman J. Viola
Illus. 152 pp. Smithsonian, 1976. $27.50.

*INDIAN LEGENDS
Johanna R. Lyback
Grades 3 and up. Reprint. Illus. 279 pp. Paper.
Tipi Press, $7.95.

INDIAN LEGENDS FROM THE NORTHERN ROCKIES
Ella E. Clark
Reprint of 1966 edition. Illus. Map. 356 pp.
Paper. University of Oklahoma Press, 1995. $19.95.

INDIAN LIFE AT THE OLD MISSIONS
Edith B. Webb
Reprint of 1952 edition. Illus. 385 pp. University
of Nebraska Press, $35.

*INDIAN LIFE IN PRE-COLUMBIAN NORTH AMERICA
John Green
Grades K-3. 48 pp. Paper. Dover, $2.95.

INDIAN LIFE OF THE YOSEMITE REGION:
MIWOK MATERIAL CULTURE
S.A. Barrett & E.W. Gifford
Study of the Miwok Indian culture based upon data obtained
from Miwok informants shortle after 1900. Reprint of 1933 edi-
tion. Illus. Maps. Biblio. 261 pp. Paper. Yosemite Association,
$7.50.

INDIAN LIFE ON THE UPPER MISSOURI
John C. Ewers
Reprint of 1968 edition. Illus. 228 pp. Paper.
University of Oklahoma Press, 1968. $14.95.

INDIAN LIFE: TRANSFORMING AN AMERICAN MYTH
William Savage, Editor
Illus. 286 pp. Paper. University of Oklahoma Press, 1977.
$12.95.

INDIAN LIVES: ESSAYS ON 19th & 20th
CENTURY NATIVE AMERICAN LEADERS
L.G. Moses & Raymond Wilson
Illus. 232 pp. University of New Mexico Press, 1985.
$19.95; paper, $10.95.

INDIAN LIVES: A PHOTOGRAPHIC RECORDS
FROM THE CIVIL WAR TO TO WOUNDED KNEE
Ulrich W. Hiesinger
Illus. 140 pp. te Neues, 1994. $35.

THE INDIAN MAN: A BIOGRAPHY OF JAMES MOONEY
L.G. Moses
Illus. 248 pp. Paper. University of Nebraska Press, 2002.
$29.95.

INDIAN MEDICINE POWER
Brad Steiger; Marah Ren, Editor
224 pp. Schiffer Publishing & Cherokee Publications, 1984.
$12.95.

INDIAN MINIATURE PAINTINGS & DRAWINGS:
THE CLEVELAND MUSEUM OF ART CATALOGUE
OF ORIENTAL ART
L. York Leach
Part One. Illus. 350 pp. Indian University Press, 1986. $65.

INDIAN MOUNDS OF THE ATLANTIC COAST
Jerry McDonald & Susan Woodward
A guide to the prehistoric mounds and mound-like features of
the Atlantic Coast region. 2nd Edition. Illus. Photos. Maps. 200
pp. Paper. McDonald & Woodward Publishing Co., 2000.
$16.95.

INDIAN MOUNDS OF THE MIDDLE OHIO VALLEY:
A GUIDE TO MOUNDS & EARTHWORKS OF THE
ADENA, HOPEWELL, & LATE WOODLAND PEOPLE
Jerry McDonald & Susan Woodward
Adena and Hopewell Mounds and earthworks of the region.
2nd Edition. Illus. Maps. Photos. 200 pp. Paper. University of
Nebraska Press, 2001. $19.95.

INDIAN MOUNDS YOU CAN VISIT: 165 ABORIGINAL
SITES ON FLORIDA'S WEST COAST
I. Mac Perry
Illus. Photos. 320 pp. Paper. Great Outdoors Publishing, 1995.
$12.95.

INDIAN MYTH & LEGEND
D. Mackenzie
Reprint of 1913 edition. Longwood, $50.00.

INDIAN MYTHS
Ellen Emerson
Gordon Press, $59.95.

*INDIAN MYTHS FROM THE SOUTHEST
Beatrice Levin
Grades 4-12. Council for Indian Education, 1974. $1.95.

INDIAN NATION
Homer "Louis" Hoban
Indian Heritage Publishing, 1991.

INDIAN NATION: NATIVE AMERICAN
LITERATURE & 19TH CENTURY NATIONALISM
Cheryl Walker
Illus. 264 pp. Duke University Press, 1'997. $49.95.

INDIAN NEW ENGLAND BEFORE THE MAYFLOWER
Howard S. Russell
Illus 384 pp. Paper. University Press of New England, 1980.
$19.95.

INDIAN NOTES & MONOGRAPHS:
A REPORT FROM NATCHITOCHES IN 1807
John Sibley; Annie H. Abel, Editor
Reprint. 105 pp. Paper. Dogwood Press, $15.

INDIAN OLD MAN STORIES: MORE
SPARKS FROM WAR EAGLE'S LODGE-FIRE
Frank B. Linderman
Stories collected from Blackfeet, Chippewa and Cree elders
and first published in 1920. Illus. 170 pp. Paper. University of
Nebraska Press, 1996. $12.95.

INDIAN ORATORY: FAMOUS SPEECHES
BY NOTED INDIAN CHIEFTAINS
W.C. Vanderwerth
Reprint of 1971 edition. Illus. 291 pp. Paper.
University of Oklahoma Press, $16.95.

INDIAN OUTBREAKS
Daniel Buck
Reprint of 1965 edition. Ross & Haines, $12.50.

THE INDIAN PAPERS OF TEXAS
& THE SOUTHWEST, 1825-1916
Dorman H. Winfrey & James M. Day, Editors
Reprint. 5 vols. Illus. Texas State Historical Association, 1995.
$95.

INDIAN PEACE MEDALS IN AMERICAN HISTORY
Francis Paul Prucha
Reprint of 1971 edition. illus. 186 pp. Paper. Hothem House,
Written Heritage & University of Oklahoma Press, $19.95.

**THE INDIAN PEOPLES OF EASTERN AMERICA:
A DOCUMENTARY HISTORY OF THE SEXES**
James Axtell, Editor
Illus. 256 pp. Paper. Oxford University Press, 1981. $12.95.

INDIAN PLACE NAMES IN ALABAMA
William A. Read
Illus. 128 pp. University of Alabama Press, 1984.
$20.00; paper, $8.95.

INDIAN PLACE NAMES IN ILLINOIS
Virgil J. Vogel
Paper. Illinois State Historical Society, 1963. $2.

INDIAN PLACE NAMES IN MICHIGAN
Virgil J. Vogel
Illus. 224 pp. University of Michigan Press, 1986.
$29.50; paper, $14.95.

INDIAN PLACE NAMES OF NEW ENGLAND
John C. Huden
408 pp. Paper. National Museum of the American Indian, 1962.
$7.50.

**INDIAN PLACE-NAMES: THEIR ORIGINS, EVOLUTION, &
MEANINGS, COLLECTED IN KANSAS FROM THE SIOUAN,
ALGONQUIAN, SHOSHONEAN, CADDOAN, IROQUOIAN,
AND OTHER TONGUES**
John Rydjord
Illus. Maps. 380 pp. Paper. University of Oklahoma Press,
$19.95.

**INDIAN POPULATION DECLINE: THE MISSIONS
OF NORTHWESTERN NEW SPAIN, 1687-1840**
R. Jackson
241 pp. Paper. University of New Mexico Press, 1995. $16.95.

INDIAN PORTRAITS OF THE PACIFIC NORTHWEST
George M. Cochran
Third edition. Illus. 64 pp. Paper. Binford & Mort, 1987. $5.95.

INDIAN POTTERY
Toni Roller
Step-by-step photographs and explanations of traditional Santa
Clara Pueblo pottery making. Photos. 64 pp. paper. Sunstone
Press, $12.95.

**INDIAN POTTERY OF THE SOUTHWEST:
A SELECTED BIBLIOGRAPHY**
Marcia Muth
Illus. 35 pp. Paper. Sunstone Press, 1991. $6.95.

INDIAN PUEBLO COLOR BOOK
O.T. Branson
32 pp. Paper. Treasure Chest, 1984. $1.95.

INDIAN QUILLWORKING
Christy A. Hensler
Illus. 64 pp. Paper. Hancock House, $6.95.

*INDIAN READING SERIES
A supplementary reading program for elementary classrooms
representing the oral tradition of 16 Northwest tribes in Idaho,
Montana, Oregon & Washington. Contains 99 booklets written
at six reading levels, teacher's manuals, and a parent/teacher
guide. Stories and legends. Sundance Educational Publishers.
$403 (postpaid) for complete series.

INDIAN RECIPE BOOK
United Tribes Technical College
Authentic recipes. Illus. Arrow Graphics, $6., postpaid.

**THE INDIAN REFORM LETTERS OF
HELEN HUNT JACKSON, 1879-1885**
Helen Hunt Jackson
Illus. Map. 400 pp. University of Oklahoma Press, 1998. $39.95.

**INDIAN RELICS OF NORTHEAST
ARKANSAS & SOUTHEAST MISSOURI**
Dethrow
Summary of prehistoric artifacts in stone, bone, etc.
Also pottery. Illus. 152 pp. Hothem House, 1985. $20.

**INDIAN REMOVAL: THE EMIGRATION OF
THE FIVE CIVILIZED TRIBES OF INDIANS**
Grant Foreman; foreword by Angie Debo
Reprint of 1932 ed. Illus. 423 pp. University of Oklahoma Press,
2001. $19.95.

INDIAN REORGANIZATION ACT: CONGRESS & BILLS
Vine Deloria, Jr.
464 pp. University of Oklahoma Press, 2001. $75.

INDIAN RESERVATIONS: A STATE & FEDERAL HANDBOOK
Confederation of American Indians Staff
Alpha-geographical listing of reservations with information on
land status, culture, government, facilities, recreation, and vital statistics for each. 330 pp. McFarland & Co., 1986. $45.

**INDIAN RESERVED WATER RIGHTS: THE WINTERS DOC-
TRINE IN ITS SOCIAL & LEGAL CONTEXT, 1880s-1930s**
John Shurts
Illus. Maps. 350 pp. Paper. University of Oklahoma Press, 2003.
$39.95; paper, $21.95.

**THE INDIAN RIGHTS ASSOCIATION:
THE HERBERT WELSH YEARS, 1882-1904**
William T. Hagan
301 pp. University of Arizona Press, 1985. $45.

INDIAN RIGHTS MANUALS
A Manual for Protecting Indian Natural Resources, 151 pp.,
$25.00; A Self-Help Manual for Indian Economic Development,
300 pp., $35.00; A Manual on Tribal Regulatory Systems, 110
pp., $25.00; Handbook of Federal Indian Laws, 130 pp., $15.00.
Native American Rights Fund.

INDIAN ROCK ART IN WYOMING
Mary H. Hendry
Illus. 240 pp. Hendry Publications, 1983. $25.

INDIAN ROCK ART OF THE SOUTHWEST
Polly Schaafsma
Reprint of 1980 edition. Illus. Color & bxw photos. Maps. 390
pp. Paper. University of New Mexico Press & Clear Light, $35.

INDIAN ROCK CARVINGS
Beth Hill
Illus. 50 pp. Paper. Hancock House, 1990. $4.95.

INDIAN ROOTS OF AMERICAN DEMOCRACY
Jose Barreiro, Editor
Book version of best selling special issue of *Akwe:kon Journal.*
Explores the influence of the Iroquois Great Law of Peace on
the formation of U.S. democracy. New and previously published
works by Donald Grinde, Richard Hill, Sally Roesch Wagner
and others. Akwe:kon Press, $12.

**INDIAN RUNNING: NATIVE AMERICAN
HISTORY & TRADITION**
Peter Nabokov
2nd edition. Illus. Map. 208 pp. Paper.
Ancient City Press, 1987. $15.95.

INDIAN SANDPAINTING OF THE GREATER SOUTHWEST
David Villasenor
An excerpt from Tapestries in Sand. 32 pp. Paper.
Naturegraph. $4.95.

INDIAN SCHOOL DAYS
Basil H. Johnston
Map. 256 pp. Paper. University of Oklahoma Press, 1989.
$19.95.

INDIAN SCOUT CRAFT & LORE
Charles Eastman
Reprint. Illus. 190 pp. Paper. Dover, $5.95.

**INDIAN SELF-DETERMINATION
& EDUCATION ASSISTANCE ACT**
P.L. 93-638, as amended
This handbook is a comprehensive overview of the ISDEAA,
covering Titles I, II, IV, V and VI, and includes applicable regulations and selected legislative history. The handbook, which
is updated annually, provides useful information for tribal leaders and others working with tribes and tribal organizations on
self-determination and self-governance matters. Hobbs, Straus,
Dean & Walker, LLP. $20.

**INDIAN SELF RULE: FIRST HAND ACCOUNTS OF INDIAN-
WHITE RELATIONS FROM ROOSEVELT TO REAGAN**
Kenneth R. Philp, Editor
Illus. 350 pp. Paper. Utah State University Press, 1985. $19.95.

THE INDIAN'S SIDE OF THE INDIAN QUESTION
William Barrows
Reprint of 1887 edition. Ayer Co. Publishers, $13.

INDIAN SIDE OF THE WHITMAN MASSACRE
T.E. Jessett
Reprint. 45 pp. Paper. Ye Galleon Press, $6.95.

INDIAN SIGN LANGUAGE
William Tomkins
Illus. 110 pp. Paper. Dover, $3.95.

THE INDIAN SIGN LANGUAGE
W.P. Clark
Map. 443 pp. Paper. University of Nebraska Press, 1982.
$18.95.

*INDIAN SIGN LANGUAGE
Robert Hofsinde (Gray-Wolf)
Shows how to form more than 500 words in Indian sign language; 200 drawings. Grades 5 and up. 96 pp. William Morrow, 1956. $11.88.

INDIAN SIGN LANGUAGES
William Tomkins
Original title: Universal Sign Language of the Plains Indians of
North America. Reprint of 1969 edition. Illus. 108 pp. Paper.
VIP Publishing & Cherokee Publications, $4.95.

INDIAN SILVER JEWELRY OF THE SOUTHWEST, 1868-1930
Larry Frank, with Millard Holbroo, II
Color photos. Illus. 224 pp. Paper. Schiffer, 1989.
$19.95. High-Lonesome Press, $12.

**INDIAN SLAVE TRADE IN THE SOUTHWEST: A STUDY OF
SLAVE-TAKING & THE TRAFFIC IN INDIAN CAPTIVES
FROM 1700-1935**
L.R. Bailey
Reprint of 1966 edition. Illus. Westernlore, $12.95.

INDIAN SLAVERY IN THE PACIFIC NORTHWEST
Robert H. Ruby & John A. Brown
Illus. Maps. Biblio. 336 pp. The Arthur H. Clark Co., $37.50.

**INDIAN SLAVERY, LABOR, EVANGELIZATION, &
CAPTIVITY IN THE AMERICAS: AN ANNOTATED
BIBLIOGRAPHY**
Russell M. Magnaghi
Focuses on the history of the imposition of policies upon
Native Americans by the governments of other people.
768 pp. Scarecrow Press, 1998. $110.

**THE INDIAN SOUTHWEST, 1580-1830:
ETHNOGENESIS & REINVENTION**
Gary Clayton Anderson
Illus. Maps. Biblio. University of Oklahoma Press, 1999. $39.95.

**INDIAN STORIES & LEGENDS OF THE
STILLAGUAMISH, SAUKS, & ALLIED TRIBES**
Nels Bruseth
Upper Puget Sound Indian material. 35 pp. Paper.
Ye Galleon Press, 1977. $9.95.

**INDIAN STORIES FROM THE PUEBLOS:
TALES OF NEW MEXICO & ARIZONA**
F.G. Applegate
Reprint of 1929 edition. Illus. 198 pp. Paper.
The Rio Grande Press, 1977. $10.

INDIAN STORY & SONG FROM NORTH AMERICA
Alice C. Fletcher
Illus. 126 pp. Paper. University of Nebraska Press, 1995. $6.95.

**INDIAN SUMMER: TRADITIONAL LIFE AMONG
THE CHOINUMNE INDIANS OF CALIFORNIA'S
SAN JOAQUIN VALLEY**
Thomas Jefferson Mayfield
Photos. Illus. Maps. 144 pp. Paper. Heyday Books, $16.

**INDIAN SUMMERS: WASHINGTON STATE COLLEGE
& THE NESPELEM ART COLONY, 1937-41**
J.J. Creighton
Illus. Photos. Map. 88 pp. Washington State University Press,
2000. $35.95; paper, $22.95.

**INDIAN SURVIVAL ON THE CALIFORNIA
BORDERLINE FRONTIER, 1819-60**
Albert Hurtado
Yale University Press, 1988. $25.

*INDIAN TALES
J. De Angulo
Reprint of 1962 edition. Grades 5-12. Illus. 256 pp.
Paper. Farrar, Straus & Giroux, $7.95.

INDIAN TALES FROM PICURIS PUEBLO
Collected by John P. Harrington
Illus. Photos. 104 pp. Paper. Ancient City Press, 1989.
$11.95.

INDIAN TALES & LEGENDS
J.E. Gray
Illus. 230 pp. Over 35 stories. Demco, $18.05. Paper.
Diane Publishing, $13.

*INDIAN TALES OF THE NORTHERN PLAINS
Sally Old Coyote and Joy Yellow Tail Toineeta
Grades 2-5. Council for Indian Education, 1972. $1.95.

INDIAN TALES & OTHERS
John G. Neihardt
306 pp. Paper. University of Nebraska Press, 1988. $22.

***INDIAN TALK: HAND SIGNALS OF
THE NORTH AMERICAN INDIANS**
Iron Eyes Cody
A silent language developed by the Plains tribes. Grades 1-12.
Illus. Photos. 112 pp. Paper. Naturgraph, 1970. $7.95.

INDIAN TERMS OF THE AMERICAS
Lotsee Patterson & Mary Ellen Snodgrass
Defines a variety of terms from Native American history; a compendium of vocabulary, people, places and events. Illus. 275
pp. Libraries Unlimited, 1994. $35.

**INDIAN TERRITORY & THE U.S., 1866-1906: COURTS, GOV-
ERNMENT, & THE MOVE FOR OKLAHOMA STATEHOOD**
Jeffrey Burton
Shows how the U.S. used judicial reform to surpress the Five
Tribes' governments and clear the way for Oklahoma state-
hood. 314 pp. Maps. University of Oklahoma Press, 1995.
$29.95; paper, $13.95.

THE INDIAN TESTIMONY
Amiya Chakravarty
Paper. Pendle Hill, 1983. $2.50.

THE INDIAN TIPI: ITS HISTORY, CONSTRUCTION & USE
Reginald & Gladys Laubin
Reprint of 1977 2nd ed. Illus. 384 pp. Paper.
University of Oklahoma Press, 2001. $24.95.

INDIAN TRADE GOODS
Arthur Woodward
Trade goods used in exchange with Indians of the Pacific North-west, and the way natives adapted these to their own use. Second edition. Illus. 40 pp. Paper. Binford & Mort, $5.95.

INDIAN TRADE GOODS & REPLICAS
Miller & Corey
Color photos of historic era artifacts and goods from the fur trade period. Illus. 192 pp. Paper. Hothem House, 1998. $29.95.

INDIAN TRADERS ON THE MIDDLE BORDER:
THE HOUSE OF EWING, 1827-1854
Robert A. Trennert, Jr.
Illus. 280 pp. University of Nebraska Press, 1981. $23.95.

INDIAN TRADERS OF THE SOUTH-WESTERN SPANISH BORDER LANDS: PANTON & FORBES CO. 1783-1847
W.S. Coker and T.D. Watson
Illus. Maps. Biblio. 448 pp. University Press of Florida, 1985. $44.95.

INDIAN TREATY-MAKING POLICY
IN THE U.S. & CANADA, 1867-1877
Jill St. Germain
Illus. Maps. 253 pp. University of Nebraska Press, 2001. $45.

THE INDIAN TRIAL: THE COMPLETE STORY OF THE WARREN WAGAN TRAIN MASSACRE & THE FALL OF THE KIOWA NATION
Charles Robinson
Illus. 210 pp. Arthur H. Clark, 1997. $27.50.

INDIAN TREATIES
Institute for the Development of Indian Law, 1980. $12.

INDIAN TREATIES, 1778-1883
C.J. Kappler, Editor
Contains a listing of every treaty and agreement made between the U.S. & Native Americans. Reprint of 1904 edition. Illus. Map. 1,100 pp. Interland, $75.

INDIAN TRIBAL CLAIMS DECIDED IN THE COURT OF CLAIMS OF THE U.S.: BRIEFED & COMPILED JUNE 30, 1947
E.B. Smith, Editor
2 Volumes. Greenwood, 1976. $65 each.

INDIAN TRIBES AS SOVEREIGN GOVERNMENTS:
A SOURCEBOOK ON FEDERAL-TRIBAL HISTORY,
LAW & POLICY
Christine L. Miklas, Editor
156 pp. Paper. American Indian Lawyer Training Program, 1991. $12.50.

*INDIAN TRIBES OF THE AMERICAS
Archaeological searches for the ruins of Chaco Canyon.
Grades 4 and up. Photos. 120 pp. Chelsea House, $19.95.

INDIAN TRIBES OF HUDSON'S RIVER
E. Ruttenber
Two vols. Vol. I to 1700...all NY tribes-origins, legends, history, 208 pp. Vol. II to 1850, with 100 appendix of language & bios. 246 pp. paper. Library Research Associates, $12.95 each.

INDIAN TRIBES OF THE LOWER MISSISSIPPI VALLEY & ADJACENT COAST OF THE GULF OF MEXICO
John R. Swanton
Reprint. Illus. 387 pp. Higginson Book Co., $42.
Paper. Dover, $14.95.

INDIAN TRIBES OF OHIO
Warren King Moorehead
History starts in the mid-1'5th century and ends with the War of 1812. Paper. Smoke & Fire Co., $10.50.

*INDIAN TRIBES OF NORTH AMERICA:
COLORING BOOK
Peter F. Copeland
Grades K-2. 48 pp. Paper. Dover, $2.95.

INDIAN TRIBE OF THE NORTHWEST
Reg Ashwell
Illus. 64 pp. Paper. Hancock House, 1990. $8.95.

INDIAN TRIBES OF NORTH AMERICA
Joseph Sherman
Random House, 1996. $17.95.

INDIAN TRIBES OF NORTH AMERICA
John R. Swanton
Outlines tribal histories. Reprint of 1952 edition. Illus. Biblio. 726 pp. Paper. Smithsonian Institution Press, $35.

INDIAN TRIBES OF NORTH AMERICA WITH BIOGRAPHICAL SKETCHES & ANECDOTES OF THE PRINCIPAL CHIEFS
McKenney & Hall
3 vols. Scholarly Press, 1974. $275.

INDIAN TRIBES OF THE NORTHERN ROCKIES
Adolf Hungry Wolf
Illus. Maps. Biblio. 135 pp. Paper.
The Book Publishing Co., $9.95.

INDIAN TRIBES OF WASHINGTON, OREGON & IDAHO
John R. Swanton
Reprint. Pocket guide for Pacific Northwest Indian tribes. 81 pp. Ye Galleon Press, $9.95; paper, $6.95.

INDIAN TRIBES OF WASHINGTON TERRITORY
George Gibbs
56 pp. Paper. Ye Galleon, 1978. $4.95.

INDIAN UPRISING ON THE RIO GRANDE:
THE PUEBLO REVOLT OF 1680
Franklin Folsom
144 pp. Paper. University of New Mexico Press, $13.95.

INDIAN USE OF THE SANTA FE NATIONAL FOREST:
A DETERMINATION FROM ETHNOGRAPHIC SOURCES
Eva Friedlander & Pamela Pinyan
Illus. Maps. 51 pp. Center for Anthropological Studies, 1980. $8 (postpaid).

INDIAN USES OF NATIVE PLANTS
Describes the uses and documents the plants, giving detailed descriptions and methods of preparation. Includes traditional recipes, dictionary of plants. Illus. 81 pp. Paper. Cherokee Publications, $6.95.

INDIAN VILLAGES OF THE ILLINOIS COUNTRY:
HISTORIC TRIBES & SUPPLEMENT
Wayne C. Temple
Facsimile edition. Illus. 218 pp. Paper. Illinois State Museum, 1977. $5.00. Supplement, 4 pp. 39 maps. $5.00.

INDIAN VOICES: THE NATIVE AMERICAN TODAY
Jeanette Henry, Editor
The Second Convocation of Indian Scholars, 1971, discussing education, health and medicine, communications, etc. of American Indians. 250 pp. Paper. The Indian Historian Press, 1974. $9.95.

INDIAN WAR SITES: A GUIDEBOOK TO BATTLEFIELDS, MONUMENTS & MEMORIALS, STATE BY STATE WITH CANADA & MEXICO
Steve Rajtar
Illus. 352 pp. Mcfarland & Co., 1999. $39.95, boxed set.

INDIAN WAR IN THE PACIFIC NORTHWEST:
THE JOURNAL OF LT. LAWRENCE KIP
Lawrence Gip; intro. by Clifford E. Trafzer
Map. 151 pp. paper. University of Nebraska Press, 1999. $9.95.

INDIAN WARS, 1850-1890
Richard H. Dillon
Photos. Illus. 128 pp. High-Lonesome Books, 1984. $18.

THE INDIAN WAR OF 1864
Capt. Eugene F. Ware
Illus. Center for Western Studies, $25.

*INDIAN WARRIORS & THEIR WEAPONS
Robert Hofsinde (Gray-Wolf)
Grades 4-7. Illus. 96 pp. William Morrow, 1965. $11.88.

*THE INDIAN WARS
Richard B. Morris; illus. by Leonard E. Fisher
Grades 5 and up. Illus. 74 pp. Lerner, 1985. $13.50.

INDIAN WARS
Robert Utley & W. Washburn
Illus. 317 pp. Paper. Houghton Mifflin & Cherokee Publications, 1985. $10.95.

INDIAN WARS OF NEW ENGLAND
H.M. Sylvester; R.H. Kohn, Editor
Reprint of 1910 edition. 3 vols. Ayer Co., $121.50 per set.
528 pp. Paper. Library Research Associates, $37.

INDIAN WARS OF PENNSYLVANIA
C. Hale Sipe
Reprint of 1929 edition. Illus. 908 pp.
Wennawoods Publishing. $49.95.

INDIAN WARS OF THE RED RIVER VALLEY
William Leckie
Illus. 135 pp. Paper. Sierra Oaks, 1987. $11.95.

INDIAN WARS OF THE WEST
Timothy Flint
Reprint of 1833 edition. Ayer Co., $26.95

INDIAN WARS & PIONEERS OF TEXAS
John H. Brown
Reprint of 1896 edition. Illus. 775 pp. State House Press, $100.

INDIAN WATER, 1985: COLLECTED ESSAYS
Richard B. Collins, et al
137 pp. Paper. American Indian Lawyer Training Program, 1986. $6.

INDIAN WATER IN THE NEW WEST
Thomas R. McGuire, et al
Collection of essays on Indian water rights. 260 pp.
University of Arizona Press, 1993. $38.

*INDIAN WAY: LEARNING TO COMMUNICATE
WITH MOTHER EARTH
Gary McLain
Grades 3 and up. Illus. 110 pp. Paper. John Muir, 1990. $9.95.

INDIAN WEAVING, KNITTING, & BASKETRY
\OF THE NORTHWEST COAST
Elizabeth Hawkins
Illus. 32 pp. Paper. Hancock House, 1978. $3.50.

INDIAN—WHITE RELATIONS IN THE U.S.:
A BIBLIOGRAPHY OF WORKS PUBLISHED, 1975-1980
Francis P. Prucha
180 pp. Paper. University of Nebraska Press, 1982. $12.

INDIAN-WHITE RELATIONS: A PERSISTENT PARADOX
Jane Smith & Robert Kvasnicka, Editors
278 pp. Howard University Press, 1976. $15; paper, $6.95.

INDIAN—WHITE RELATIONSHIPS
IN NORTHERN CALIFORNIA, 1849-1920
Norris Bleyhl
109 pp. Association of Northern California Records, 1978. $12.

INDIAN & WHITE: SELF—IMAGE & INTERACTION
IN A CANADIAN PLAINS COMMUNITY
Niels W. Braroe
Illus. 206 pp. Stanford University Press, 1975.
$22.50; paper, $7.95.

INDIAN & THE WHITEMAN IN CONNECTICUT
Chandler Whipple
Illus. 95 pp. Paper. The Berkshire Traveller, 1972. $3.50.

INDIAN WHY STORIES: SPARKS
FROM WAR EAGLE'S LODGE-FIRE
Frank B. Linderman
Illus. 236 pp. Paper. University of Nebraska Press, 1996. $14.95.

*AN INDIAN WINTER
Russell Freedman
The culture of the Mandan & Hidatsa. Grades 4-6. Illus. 96 pp. Holiday House, 1992. $21.95.

INDIAN WISDOM & ITS GUIDING POWER
Brad & Sherry Steiger
Illus. 176 pp. Paper. Schiffer, 1991. $12.95.

INDIAN WOMEN CHIEFS
Carolyn T. Foreman
Reprint of 1954 edition. Zenger, $15.95.

INDIANCRAFT
Chief McIntosh & Harvey Shell
Concise instruction in the art of Indiancraft.
Illus. 144 pp. Paper. Naturegraph, $9.95.

*INDIANS
Teri Martini
Grades K-4. Illus. 48 pp. Childrens Press, 1982. $11.45.

*THE INDIANS
Ben Capps
Grades 7 and up. Illus. Silver Burdette, 1973.
$19.94; Time-Life Books, $14.95.

*INDIANS
Nancy Davis & Teresa Moon
Grades K-5. Illus. 33 pp. Paper. DaNa Publications, 1986. $4.95.

*INDIANS
Edwin Tunis
Revised 1959 edition. Grades 5-12. Illus.
Harper & Row, Junior Books, $24.89.

INDIANS
Rich Steber
Illus. 60 pp. Paper. Bonanza, 1987. $4.95.

*INDIANS: AN ACTIVITY BOOK
John Artman
Grades 4-8. Good Apple, 1981. $6.95.

INDIANS & ALCOHOL IN EARLY AMERICA
Peter C. Mancall
Explores the liquor trade's devastating impact on the Indian communities of colonial America. Cornell University Press, 1995. $29.95.

INDIANS ALONG THE OREGON TRAIL:
THE TRIBES OF NEBRASKA, WYOMING,
IDAHO, OREGON, WASHINGTON IDENTIFIED
Bert Webber
Includes village locations, language groups, populations to
1989. Illus. Biblio. 208 pp. Paper. Webb Research, 1989 ex-
panded edition. $17.95.

INDIANS, THE AMERICAN HERITAGE LIBRARY
William Brandon
Chronicles 20,000 years of Indian history. 420 pp. Paper.
Cherokee Publications, $10.95.

INDIANS & THE AMERICAN WEST
IN THE TWENTIETH CENTURY
Donald L. Parman
Follows the Indians' continuing struggle to hold on to their land,
their resources, and their identity. Illus. 256 pp. Indiana Uni-
versity Press, 1994. $29.95; paper, $12.95.

INDIANS, ANIMALS, & THE FUR TRADE:
A CRITIQUE OF KEEPERS OF THE GAME
Shepard Krech, Editor
210 pp. Paper. University of Georgia Press, 1981. $10.

INDIANS & ANTHROPOLOGISTS: VINE DELORIA, JR.
& THE CRITIQUE OF ANTHROPOLOGY
Thomas Biolsi & Larry Zimmerman, Editors
Essays examining how the relationship between anthropolo-
gists and Indians have changed in the past 25 years since Vine
Deloria, Jr.'s book, "Custer Died for Your Sins" was published.
240 pp. University of Arizona Press, 1997. $48; paper, $21.95.

INDIANS & ARCHAEOLOGY OF MISSOURI
Chapman & Chapman
Revised edition. Paper. University of Missouri Press, $17.95.

INDIANS ARE US? CULTURE & GENOCIDE
IN NATIVE NORTH AMERICA
Ward Churchill
Discusses the commercialization of Native American cultures
which is threatening the indigenous struggles for sovereignty
and freedom. 400 pp. Common Courage Press, 1993. $29.95;
paper, $14.95.

INDIANS & ARTIFACTS IN THE SOUTHEAST
Bierer
Over 1,000 illustrations, many artifact types. Includes trails,
maps, and tribal data. 506 pp. Paper. Hothem House, 1980.
$28.50.

INDIANS AT HAMPTON INSTITUTE, 1877-1923
Donald F. Lindsey
336 pp. University of Illinois Press, 1994. $39.95.

THE INDIANS' BOOK
Natalie Curtis
Lore, music, narratives, drawings by Indians. 149 songs in full
notation. Reprint. Illus. 584 pp. Paper. Dover & Cherokee Publications, $14.95.

INDIANS & BUREAUCRATS: ADMINISTERING THE
RESERVATION POLICY DURING THE CIVIL WAR
Edmund J. Danziger, Jr.
250 pp. University of Illinois Press, 1974. $22.95.

INDIANS, BUREAUCRATS & LAND: THE DAWES ACT
& THE DECLINE OF INDIAN FARMING
Leonard A. Carlson
231 pp. Greenwood Press, 1981. $35.

*THE INDIANS & THE CALIFORNIA MISSIONS
Linda Lyngheim
Grades 4-6. Illus. Revised edition. 160 pp.
Langtry Publications, 1990. $14.95; paper, $10.95.

INDIANS & A CHANGING FRONTIER:
THE ART OF GEORGE WINTER
Sarah E. Cooke & Rachel Ramadhyani, Editors
Watercolors & drawings of the Potawatomi Indians in northern
Indiana just before their removal west of the Mississippi in the
mid 1800's. Illus. 270 pp. Indiana University Press, 1993.
$39.95.

INDIANS & COLONISTS AT THE CROSSROADS
OF EMPIRE: THE ALBANY CONGRESS OF 1754
Timothy J. Shannon
Cornell University Press, 1999. $45; paper, $17.95.

INDIANS & CRIMINAL JUSTICE
Laurence French, Editor
224 pp. Rowman & Littlefield, 1982. $23.95.

INDIANS & ENGLISH: FACING OFF IN EARLY AMERICA
Karen Ordahl Kupperman
Paper. Cornell University Press, 2000. $18.95.

INDIANS & EUROPE: AN INTERDISCIPLINARY
COLLECTION OF ESSAYS
edited by Christian F. Feest
Essays on the relationship between European and Native
peoples. Illus. Map. 643 pp. Paper. University of Nebraska
Press, 1999. $33.

INDIANS, FIRE & LAND IN THE PACIFIC NORTHWEST
Robert Boyd, Editor
Illus. 320 pp. Paper. Oregon State University Press, 1999.
$34.95.

INDIANS, FRANCISCANS, & SPANISH COLONIZATION:
THE IMPACT OF THE MISSION SYSTEM ON CALIFORNIA
INDIANS
Robert H. Jackson & Edward Castillo
Illus. 222 pp. Paper. University of New Mexico Press, 1999.
$21.95.

INDIANS FROM NEW YORK IN WISCONSIN & ELSWHERE:
A GENEALOGY REFERENCE
Toni J. Prevost
228 pp. Paper. Heritage Book, 1995. $27.

INDIANS IN AMERICAN HISTORY: AN INTRODUCTION
Frederick Hoxie & Peter Iverson
2nd Edition. Illus. 304 pp. Harlan Davidson, 1998. $16.95.

THE INDIANS IN AMERICAN SOCIETY: FROM
THE REVOLUTIONARY WAR TO THE PRESENT
Francis P. Prucha
University of California Press, 1985. $38; paper, $13.95.

INDIANS IN THE FUR TRADE: THEIR ROLES AS
TRAPPERS, HUNTERS & MIDDLEMEN IN THE
LANDS SOUTHWEST OF HUDSON BAY, 1660-1870
Arthur J. Ray
Revised edition. Illus. 320 pp. University of Toronto Press, 1998.
$50; paper, $21.95.

INDIANS IN THE MAKING: ETHNIC RELATIONS &
INDIAN IDENTITIES AROUND THE PUGET SOUND
Alexandria Harmon
Illus. Photos. Maps. 405 pp. University of California Press, 1999.
$45; paper, $19.95.

INDIANS IN MINNESOTA
Elizabeth Ebbott; Judith Rosenblatt, Editor
Survey of contemporary experience of Ojibway & Dakota Indi-
ans on and off the reservations in Minnesota. Illus. 330 pp.
Paper. University of Minnesota Press, 1985. $13.95.

*INDIANS IN NEW YORK STATE
Kenneth Job; Bernard Whitman, Editor
Grades 4-7. Illus. 50 pp. Paper. IN Education, Inc., 1989. $5.

THE INDIANS IN OKLAHOMA
Rennard Strickland
Reprint of 1980 edition. Illus. Maps. 187 pp. Paper.
University of Oklahoma Press, 2002. $14.95.

INDIANS IN OVERALLS
Jaime De Angulo
Revised edition.120 pp. Paper. City Lights, 1990. $6.95.

INDIANS IN PENNSYLVANIA
Paul A. Wallace
Illus. 200 pp. Pennsylvania Historical & Museum
Commission, 1981. $8.95; paper, $5.95.

INDIANS IN PRISON: INCARCERATED
NATIVE AMERICANS IN NEBRASKA
Elizabeth S. Grobsmith
Illus. 265 pp. University of Nebraska Press, 1994. $37.50.

INDIANS IN 17th CENTURY VIRGINIA
Ben C. McCary
Reprint of 1957 edition. 93 pp. Paper.
University Presses of Virginia, $3.95.

INDIANS IN THE FUR TRADE
Arthur J. Ray
Illus. 320 pp. Paper. University of Toronto Press, 1998.
$21.95.

INDIANS IN THE MAKING: ETHNIC RELATIONS
& INDIAN IDENTITIES AROUND PUGET SOUND
Alexandra Harmon
University of California Press, 1999. $40.

INDIANS IN THE U.S. & CANADA:
A COMPARATIVE HISTORY
Roger L. Nichols
Illus. Maps. 393 pp. Paper. University of Nebraska Press, 1998.
$25.

INDIANS IN YELLOWSTONE NATIONAL PARK
Joel C. Janetski
Revised edition. Paper. University of Utah Press. $12.95.

INDIANS & INDIAN AGENTS
George Harwood Phillips
The origins of the reservation system in California, 1849-1852.
Illus. Maps. 238 pp. University of Oklahoma Press, 1997.
$27.95.

INDIANS, INDIAN TRIBES & STATE GOVERNMENT:
MAJOR LEGAL ISSUES
79 pp. Paper. Diane Publishing, 1994. $30.

THE INDIANS & INTRUDERS IN
CENTRAL CALIFORNIA, 1769-1849
George Harwood Phillips
Illus. Maps. 224 pp. University of Oklahoma Press, 1993.
$27.95.

THE INDIANS' LAND TITLE IN CALIFORNIA:
A CASE IN FEDERAL EQUITY, 1851-1942
Ruth C. Dyer
Paper. R & E Research Associates, 1975. $10.95.

INDIANS' NEW SOUTH: CULTURAL CHANGE
IN THE COLONIAL SOUTHEAST
James Axtell
Illus. 120 pp. Paper. Louisiana State University Press, 1997.
$11.95.

THE INDIAN'S NEW WORLD: CATAWBAS & THEIR
NEIGHBORS FROM EUROPEAN CONTACT THROUGH
THE ERA OF REMOVAL
James H. Merrell
Illus. 382 pp. University of North Carolina Press, 1989. $45;
paper, $13.25.

*INDIANS OF AMERICA
PS-12. Aerial Photography. $2.85.

*INDIANS OF AMERICA SERIES
Indian Crafts; Indian Festivals; Indian Homes; Indians of th East-
ern Woodlands; Indians of the Plains; and Indian of the West.
Grades 4-6. Paper. VIP Publishing. $5 each.

*INDIANS OF AMERICA: GERONIMO, CRAZY HORSE,
OSCEOLA, PONTIAC, SQUANTO, CHIEF JOSEPH
Dan Zadra
Grades 2-4. 6 volumes. Creative Education. 1987.
$19.95 each; paper, $13.95 each.

INDIANS OF THE AMERICAN SOUTHWEST
Steven Walker
Discusses different prehistoric & presentday cultures.
Photos & Illus. 64 pp. Paper. Treasure Chest, $8.95.

INDIANS OF THE AMERICAS
National Geographic Society
An illustrative record of Indians like the Navajo, Tarascan,
Eskimo, et al. Illus. Photos. 430 pp. High-Lonesome Books,
$10.

*INDIANS OF THE AMERICAS COLORING BOOK
Connie Asch
Grades K-6. Illus. 32 pp. Paper. Treasure Chest, 1987. $1.95.

INDIANS OF THE AMERICAS: SELF-DETERMINATION
& INTERNATIONAL HUMAN RIGHTS
Roxanne D. Ortiz
360 pp. Praeger, 1984. $38.95; paper, $13.95.

INDIANS OF ARIZONA:
A GUIDE TO ARIZONA'S HERITAGE
Eleanor H. Ayer
Illus. Map. 48 pp. Paper. Renaissance House, 1990. $4.95.

INDIANS OF CALIFORNIA: THE CHANGING IMAGE
James J. Rawls
Illus. 310 pp. Paper. University of Oklahoma Press, 1984.
$19.95.

THE INDIANS OF CALIFORNIA:
A CRITICAL BIBLIOGRAPHY
Robert F. Heizer
Paper. 80 pp. Indiana University Press, 1976. $4.95.

THE INDIANS OF CANADA
Diamond Jenness
Sixth Edition. Paper. University of Toronto Press, 1963. $17.95.

INDIANS OF CANADA: CULTURAL DYNAMICS
J. Price
Illus. 262 pp. Paper. Sheffield, Wisc., 1979. $8.95.

THE INDIANS OF THE CHICAGO AREA
Terry Straus
2nd Edition. 185 pp. Paper. American Indian Press, 1990.
$16.95.

THE INDIANS OF CONNECTICUT
Harold C. Bradshaw
64 pp. Paper. Fawcett, $8.95.

INDIANS OF THE FEATHER RIVER: TALES & LEGENDS
OF THE CONCOW MAIDU OF CALIFORNIA
Donald Jewell; Sylvia Vane & Lowell Bean, Editors
Illus. 184 pp. Paper. Ballena Press, 1987. $12.95.

INDIANS OF THE FOUR CORNERS:
THE ANASAZI & THEIR PUEBLO DESCENDANTS,
A HISTORY OF YOUNG ADULTS
Alice Marriott
Account of the Anasazi culture, including accounts of every-
day life. Illus. 48 drawings. Map. 187 pp. Paper. Ancient City
Press, $13.95.

**INDIANS OF THE GREAT BASIN:
A CRITICAL BIBLIOGRAPHY**
Omer C. Stewart
152 pp. Paper. Indiana University Press, 1982. $5.95.

THE INDIANS OF THE GREAT PLAINS
Norman Bancroft-Hunt; photos by Werner Foreman
Presents a vivid image of the lives of the the Great Plains
Indians. Reprint of 1982 edition. Illus. 128 pp. Paper.
University of Oklahoma Press, $24.95.

*INDIANS OF THE GREAT PLAINS STENCILS
Mira Bartok & Christine Ronan
Five easy-to-do art projects that explore the myths, legends
and festivals of the Plains Indians. Grades 3 and up. 32 pp.
Paper. Harper & Row, $9.95.

***INDIANS OF THE GREAT PLAINS:
TRADITIONS, HISTORY, LEGENDS & LIFE**
Courage Book Staff
Grades 4 and up. Illus. 64 pp. Courage Books, 1997. $9.98.

**INDIANS OF THE HIGH PLAINS: FROM THE PREHISTORIC
PERIOD TO THE COMING OF EUROPEANS**
George E. Hyde
Reprint of 1959 edition. Illus. Maps. 246 pp. Paper.
University of Oklahoma Press, 1976. $14.95.

**INDIANS OF KANSAS: THE EURO-AMERICAN
INVASION & CONQUEST OF INDIAN KANSAS**
William E. Unrau
Paper. Kansas State Historical Society, 1991. $10.95.

*THE INDIANS OF LOUISIANA
Fred B. Kniffen
Legends and tales. A list of tribes in Louisiana, and a glossary
of state Indian names are included with the history. Grades 3-
8. Illus. 112 pp. Pelican Publishing, $13.95.

**INDIANS OF THE LOWER HUDSON REGION:
THE MUNSEE**
Julian Harris-Salomon
Illus. 95 pp. Rockland County Historical Society, 1983.
$15.95; paper, $8.95.

**THE INDIANS OF MAINE & THE ATLANTIC PROVINCES:
A BIBLIOGRAPHIC GUIDE**
Roger B. Ray
Reprint of 1972 edition. Paper. Maine Historical Society, $5.

**THE INDIANS OF NEW ENGLAND:
A CRITICAL BIBLIOGRAPHY**
Neal Salisbury
128 pp. Paper. Indiana University Press, 1982. $4.95.

THE INDIANS OF NEW JERSEY
Gregory E. Dowd
New Jersey Historical Commission, 1992. $9.

***THE INDIANS OF NEW JERSEY:
DICKON AMONG THE LENAPE**
M.R. Harrington
Grades 4-6. Illus. 352 pp. Paper. Rutgers University Press,
1963. $12.95.

INDIANS OF NEW MEXICO
Richard C. Sandoval & Ree Sheck, Editors
Color photos. 182 pp. Paper. Clear Light, $14.95.

*THE INDIANS OF NORTH AMERICA SERIES
Dr. Frank W. Porter, III, Editor
Grades 4 and up. Illus. Maps. 96-144 pp. each. Chelsea House,
1987. 49 Hardcover titles, $19.95 each, $977.55 per set; 21
paper titles, $9.95 each; $208.95per set.

INDIANS OF NORTH AMERICA
Harold E. Driver
Second revised edition. Illus. 668 pp. High-Lonesome books,
$50. Paper. University of Chicago Press, 1961. $29.95.

**INDIANS OF NORTH AMERICA - LIFE, HEALTH, CULTURE
& DISEASE CONDITIONS: INDEX OF NEW INFORMATION
WITH AUTHORS, SUBJECTS & BIBLIOGRAPHICAL REF-
ERENCES**
Swedlo A. Sampos
150 pp. Paper. Abbe Publishers Assn., 1996. $47.50.

**INDIANS OF NORTH AMERICA: SURVEY
OF TRIBES THAT INHABIT THE CONTINENT**
Paula Franklin
Illus. David McKay, 1979. $12.95.

*INDIANS OF THE NORTH AMERICAN PLAINS
Virginia Luling
Grades 6 and up. 64 pp. Silver Burdette, $13.96.

INDIANS OF THE NORTH PACIFIC COAST
Tom McFeat, Editor
Examines the culture of the Tlingit, the Haida, the Tsimshian,
the Bella Coola, the Kwakiutl, the Nootka, and the Salish
peoples of the Northwest Coast. 286 pp. Paper. University of
Washington Press, $10.95.

**INDIANS OF NORTH & SOUTH AMERICA:
BIBLIOGRAPHY BASED ON THE COLLECTION
AT THE WILLARD E. YAGER LIBRARY-MUSEUM,
HARTWICK COLLEGE, ONEONTA, NY**
Carolyn E. Wolf & Karen R. Folk
496 pp. Scarecrow Press, 1997. $59.50.

INDIANS OF THE NORTHEAST
Karin Badt
Illus. 60 pp.Paper. Discovery Enterprises, Ltd., 1997. $5.95.

INDIANS OF NORTHEAST NORTH AMERICA
Christian F. Feest
Illus. 50 pp. Paper. Brill Academic, 1986. $48.

***INDIANS OF THE NORTHEAST:
TRADITIONS, HISTORY, LEGENDS & LIFE**
Courage Book Staff
Grades 4 and up. Illus. 64 pp. Courage Books, 1997.
$9.98.

INDIANS OF THE NORTHWEST
Rochelle Cashdan, Editor
Illus. 64 pp. Paper. Discovery Enterprises, Ltd., 1998.
$5.95.

*INDIANS OF THE NORTHWEST
Coloring book. Grades K-3. Paper. Bellerophon, $4.95.

*INDIANS OF NORTHWEST CALIFORNIA
Title V program staff & tribal resource people
A currciulum book dealing with Native American culture; information on tribal groups in Northwest California which can be
integrated into language, literature, social studies, science &
math curriculum. Videos available. Grades K-5. Illus. 325 pp.
binder. Cook's Books. $49.95, institutions; $39.95, individuals.

INDIANS OF THE NORTHWEST COAST
D. Allen
Photographic study of the northwest people, their land, houses,
dances, totem poles, and artifacts. 32 pp. Paper. Hancock
House, $4.95.

INDIANS OF THE NORTHWEST COAST
Peter R. Gerber & Max Bruggmann
Covers the Tlingit, Haida, Nootka, Coast Salish, Tsimishian,
Kwakiutl, and other tribes, detailing each group's history, cul-
ture, language, religion, and art forms. Illus. 232 pp. Facts on
File, 1989. $45.

INDIANS OF THE NORTHWEST COAST
Pliny Goddard
The material culture, social & political organization, religion and
art of the Indians of the Northwest Coast. Reprint of 1924 edition. Photos. Illus. Maps. 76 pp. High-Lonesome Books, $22.

***INDIANS OF THE NORTHWEST:
TRADITIONS, HISTORY, LEGENDS & LIFE**
Courage Book Staff
Grades 4 and up. Illus. 64 pp. Courage Books, 1997.
$9.98.

*INDIANS OF OKLAHOMA
Lucilia Wise
Illus. The Five Civilized Tribes Museum. $1.

*INDIANS OF THE PACIFIC NORTHWEST
Karen Liptak
Grades 5-8. Illus. 96 pp. Facts on File, 1990. $18.95.

INDIANS OF THE PACIFIC NORTHWEST: A HISTORY
Robert H. Rubie and John A. Brown
Illus. Maps. 304 pp. Paper. University of Oklahoma Press,
1981. $24.95.

INDIANS OF PECOS PUEBLO
Ernest A. Hooton
Elliots Books, 1930. $200.

INDIANS OF THE PIKE'S PEAK REGION
Irvin Howbert
An account of the Sand Creek massacre of 1864, with material
on the Ute Indians of the area east of the Rockies. Reprint of
1914 edition. Illus. Maps. 262 pp. Rio Grande Press, $15.

*INDIANS OF THE PLAINS
Elaine Andrews
Grades 5-8. Illus. 96 pp. Facts on File, 1991. $18.95.

*INDIANS OF THE PLAINS
Ruth Thompson
Grades K-4. Illus. 32 pp. Franklin Watts, 1991. $11.40.

INDIANS OF THE PLAINS
Robert H. Lowie
Reprint. 250 pp. University of Nebraska Press,
$21.00; paper, $7.95.

**THE INDIANS OF PUGET SOUND:
THE NOTEBOOKS OF MYRON EELS**
Myron Eels; George Castile, Editor
Illus. 496 pp. University of Washington Press, 1985. $40.

**INDIANS OF THE RIO GRANDE DELTA:
THEIR ROLE IN THE HISTORY OF SOUTHERN
TEXAS & NORTHEASTERN MEXICO**
Martin Salinas
Maps. 207 pp. Paper. University of Texas Press, 1990.
$11.95.

INDIANS OF THE SOUTH
Maxine Alexander, Editor
Illus. 120 pp. Paper. Institute of Southern Studies, 1985. $4.

INDIANS OF THE SOUTHEASTERN U.S.
John Swanton
Reprint of 1946 edition. Illus. 13 maps. 1,068 pp.
Greenwood Publishing, $59.50. Paper. Smithsonian
Institution Press, $29.95.

**INDIANS OF THE SOUTHEASTERN U.S.
IN THE LATE 20TH CENTURY**
J. Anthony Paredes, Editor
Surveys American Indian communities still surviving in
the southeastern U.S. from Virginia to Florida. 256 pp.
Paper. University of Alabama Press, 1992. $21.95.

INDIANS OF SOUTHERN ILLINOIS
Irvin Peithman
Photocopy spiral edition. Illus. 172 pp.
Charles C. Thomas, 1964. $14.50.

*INDIANS OF THE SOUTHWEST
Karen Liptak
Grades 5-8. Illus. 96 pp. Facts on File, 1990. $18.95.

INDIANS OF THE SOUTHWEST
Pliny E. Goddard
Reprint of 1913 edition. 248 pp. The Rio Grande Press,
$20.

**INDIANS OF THE SOUTHWEST: A CENTURY
OF DEVELOPMENT UNDER THE U.S.**
Edward E. Dale
Reprint of 1949 edition. Illus. Maps. Paper.
University of Oklahoma Press, $16.95.

***INDIANS OF THE SOUTHWEST:
TRADITIONS, HISTORY, LEGENDS & LIFE**
Courage Book Staff
Grades 4 and up. Illus. 64 pp. Courage Books, 1997. $9.98.

**THE INDIANS OF THE SUBARCTIC:
A CRITICAL BIBLIOGRAPHY**
June Helm
104 pp. Paper. Indiana Unviersity Press, 1976. $6.95.

**THE INDIANS OF TEXAS: AN ANNOTATED
RESEARCH BIBLIOGRAPHY**
Michael L. Tate
514 pp. Scarecrow Press, 1986, $60.

**THE INDIANS OF TEXAS: FROM
PREHISTORIC TO MODERN TIMES**
W.W. Newcomb, Jr.
Reprint of 1961 edition. Illus. 422 pp. Paper.
University of Texas Press, $14.95.

***INDIANS OF THE TIDEWATER COUNTRY:
OF MD, VA, DE & NC**
Thelma Ruskin; Carol Buchanan & Robert Ruskin, Editors
Grades 4-5. Illus. 132 pp. Maryland Historical Press, 1986. $15.

**INDIANS OF THE U.S.: FOUR CENTURIES
OF THEIR HISTORY & CULTURE**
Clark Wissler
Paper. Doubleday, 1966. $6.95.

INDIANS OF UPPER CALIFORNIA
F.P. Wrangell
Reprint. 25 pp. Paper. Ye Galleon Press, $3.95.

INDIANS OF THE UPPER TEXAS COAST
Laurence Aten
338 pp. Academic Press, 1983. $44.50.

THE INDIANS OF WASHTENAW COUNTY, MICHIGAN
Wilbert B. Hinsdale
Reprint of 1927 edition. Paper. George Wahr, $12.95.

INDIANS OF THE WESTERN GREAT LAKES, 1615-1760
W. Vernon Kinietz
Reprint of 1965 edition. 440 pp. Paper. Hothem House
& University of Michigan Press, $18.95.

THE INDIANS OF YELLOWSTONE PARK
Joel Janetski
Illus. 116 pp. Paper. University of Utah Press, 1987. $8.95.

**INDIANS: OR, NARRATIVES OF MASSACRES &
DEPREDATIONS ON THE FRONTIER IN WAWASINK
& ITS VICINITY DURING THE AMERICAN REVOLUTION**
Abraham G. Bevier
Reprint of 1846 edition. 90 pp. Paper.
Library Research Associates, $4.50.

INDIANS, SETTLERS, & SLAVES IN A FRONTIER EXCHANGE ECONOMY: THE LOWER MISSISSIPPI VALLEY BEFORE 1783
Daniel H. Usner, Jr.
Examines the economic and cultural interactions among the Indians, Europeans & slaves of colonial Louisiana. 320 pp. University of North Carolina Press, 1991. $32.50; paper, $12.95.

THE INDIAN'S SIDE OF THE INDIAN QUESTION
W. Barrows
Reprint of 1887 edition. Ayer Co., $13.

THE INDIANS & THEIR CAPTIVES
James Levermier and Henry Cohen, Editors
Greenwood Press, 1977. $35.

THE INDIANS & THE U.S. CONSTITUTION
Institute for the Development of Indian Law, $7.95.

INDIANS & THE U.S. GOVERNMENT
Institute for the Development of Indian Law, 1977. $12.

*INDIANS WHO LIVED IN TEXAS
Betsy Warren
Reprint of 1970 edition. Grades 2-12. Illus. 48 pp. Hendrick-Long, $9.95.

INDIGENIZING THE ACADEMY: TRANSFORMING SCHOLARSHIP & EMPOWERING COMMUNITIES
edited by Devon Abbott Mihesuah & Angela Cavender Wilson
Anthology. 256 pp. University of Nebraska Press, 2004. $50; paper, $19.95.

INDIGENOUS AESTHETICS: NATIVE ART, MEDIA, AND IDENTITY
Steven Leuthold
Illus. 240 pp. University of Texas Press, 1998. $30; paper, $16.95.

INDIGENOUS AMERICAN WOMEN: DECOLONIZATION, EMPOWERMENT, ACTIVISM
edited by Devon Abbott Mihesuah
Anthology. 268 pp. Paper. University of Nebraska Press, 2003. $16.95.

INDIGENOUS COMMUNITY-BASED EDUCATION
Stephen May, Editor
Collection provides examples of indigenous community-based initiatives from around the world. Includes programs among Native Americans in the U.S. and Canada. 182 pp. University of Toronto Press, 1999. $59.95.

INDIGENOUS ECONOMICS: TOWARD A NATURAL WORLD ORDER
Jose Barreiro, Editor
Iroquois, Anishnabe, Algonquin, Dene Indian, among other, viewpoints are represented in this book that features Fourth World analysis of environment and developmnent issues. Akwe:kon Press, $10.

INDIGENOUS LANGUAGES OF THE AMERICAS: A BIBLIOGRAPHY OF DISSERTATIONS & THESES
Robert Singerman
Compiled citations to over 1,600 dissertations and master's theses from American, Canadian and British institutions. 346 pp. Scarecrow Press, 1996. $75.

INDIGENOUS PEOPLES & TROPICAL FOREST: MODELS OF LAND USE & MANAGEMENT FROM LATIN AMERICA
Jason Clay
116 pp. Cultural Survival, 1988. $19.95; paper, $8.

INDIGENOUS WOMEN'S HEALTH BOOK, WITHIN THE SACRED CIRCLE
edited by Charon Asetoyer, Katharine Cronk, Samanthi Hewakapuge
Assists Native Amnerican women in developing self-advocacy skills; healthcare choices, policies, and politics. 323 pp. Paper. Indigenous Women's Press, $32.,95.

INGALIK MATERIAL CULTURE
C. Osgood
Reprint of 1940 edition. Illus. Biblio. 500 pp. Paper. HRAF Press, $25.

INHABITED WILDERNESS: INDIANS, ESKIMOS & NATIONAL PARKS IN ALASKA
Catton
285 pp. Paper. University of New Mexico Press, 1997. $22.95.

*ININATIG'S GIFT OF SUGAR: TRADITIONAL NATIVE SUGARMAKING
Laura Waterman Wittstock; photos by Dale Kakkak
Grades 3-7. Photos. Paper. Lerner Publications & Meadowlark Communications, $6.95.

INSECTS AS FOOD: ABORIGINAL ENTOMOPHAGY IN THE GREAT BASIN
Mark Q. Sutton; Thomas C. Blackburn, Editor
Illus. 115 pp. Paper. Ballena Press, 1988. $17.95.

*INSIDE THE CULTURE
A series of teacher and student workbooks. "American Indian Astronomy," "American Indian Communicating Systems," American Indian Timekeeping Devices," and "American Indian Toys and Games." These lessons were designed for 5th grade students. Illus. Paper. Oyate, $4.95 each.

INSIDE PASSAGE: LIVING WITH KILLER WHALES, BALD EAGLES & KWAKIUTL INDIANS
Michael Modzelewski
Illus. 215 pp. HarperCollins, 1991. $19.95.

INSIGHT GUIDE: NATIVE AMERICA
A travel guide to Indian reservations, historic sites, festivals and ceremonies. Houghton Mifflin, $19.95.

THE INSISTENCE OF THE INDIAN: RACE & NATIONALISM IN 19TH CENTURY AMERICAN CULTURE
Susan Scheckel
184 pp. 492 pp. Princeton University Press, 1998. $49.50; paper, $16.95.

THE INSTITUTE OF AMERICAN INDIAN ARTS, ALUMNI EXHIBITION
Intro. by Lloyd K. New
Illus. 72 pp. Paper. Amon Carter Museum, 1974. $3.25.

INTELLECTUAL PROPERTY RIGHTS FOR INDIGENOUS PEOPLES: A SOURCE BOOK
Tom Greaves, Editor
274 pp. Paper. Society of Appllied Anthropology, 1994. $18.

INTERIOR LANDSCAPES: AUTOBIOGRAPHICAL MYTHS & METAPHORS
Gerald Vizenor
Illus. 280 pp. University of Minnesota Press, 1990. $17.95.

INTERIOR SALISH TRIBES OF BRITISH COLUMBIA: A PHOTOGRAPHIC COLLECTION
Leslie H. Tepper
Illus. 277 pp. Paper. University of Chicago Press, 1988. $17.95.

INTERPRETING THE INDIAN: TWENTIETH-CENTURY POETS & THE NATIVE AMERICAN
Michael Castro
222 pp. Paper. University of Oklahoma Press, 1991. $15.95.

INTO THE AMERICAN WOODS: NEGOTIATORS ON THE PENNSYLVANIA FRONTIER
James H. Merrill
Illus. 320 pp. W.W. Norton, 1999. $27.95; paper, $14.95.

INTRODUCTION TO AMERICAN INDIAN ART
O. LaFarge, et al
Reprint of 1932 edition. 2 vols. in one. Illus. 200 pp. Paper. The Rio Grande Press, $17.50.

INTRODUCTION TO CHEROKEE: A CHEROKEE LANGUAGE STUDY COURSE
Sam Hider
Teaches the fundamental of the language using tapes and work book. Also a history of the language. 44 pp. CD OR 2 cassette tapes. VIP Publishing, $19.95.

INTRODUCTION TO CHOCTAW: A CHOCTAW LANGUAGE STUDY COURSE
Sam Hider
Teaches the fundamental of the language using tapes and work book. Also a history of the language. 44 pp. CD or 2 cassette tapes. VIP Publishing, $19.95.

INTRODUCTION TO CRIMINAL JURISDICTION IN INDIAN COUNTRY
Gilbert L. Hall
52 pp. Paper. American Indian Lawyer Training Program, 1981. $6.

INTRODUCTION TO HANDBOOK OF AMERICAN INDIAN LANGUAGES by Franz Boas and **INDIAN LINGUISTIC FAMILIES OF AMERICA NORTH OF MEXICO** by J.W. Powell
Reprint. Two vols. in one. 221 pp. Paper. University of Nebraska Press, 1991. $16.50.

INTRODUCTION TO HOPI POTTERY
Francis H. Harlow
32 pp. Illus. Paper. Museum of Northern Arizona, 1978. $2.50.

AN INTRODUCTION TO THE LUISENO LANGUAGE
Villiana Hyde
Paper. Malki Museum Press, 1979. $8.

AN INTRODUCTION TO NATIVE NORTH AMERICA
Sutton
Paper. Allyn & Bacon, 1999. $32.

AN INTRODUCTION TO THE PREHISTORY OF INDIANA
James H. Kellar
Revised 1983 edition. Illus. Biblio. 78 pp. Paper. Indiana Historical Society, $4.95.

AN INTRODUCTION TO THE SHOSHONI LANGUAGE: DAMMEN DAIQWAPE
Drusilla Gould & Christopher Loether
A basic information on the phonology & grammar of the language. University of Utah Press, $50; paper, $24.95; 4 cassettes, $20; paperback & cassettes, $39.95.

INTRODUCTION TO THE STUDY OF INDIAN LANGUAGES WITH WORDS, PHRASES, & SENTENCES TO BE COLLECTED
J.W. Powell
Gordon Press, 1977. $69.95.

INTRODUCTION TO THE STUDY OF SOUTHWESTERN ARCHAEOLOGY
Alfred V. Kidder
Illus. Paper. Yale University Press, 1962. $16.95.

*INTRODUCTION TO TRIBAL GOVERNMENT
Yerington Paiute Tribe
Grades 9-12. 94 pp. Paper. Yerington Paiute Tribe Publications, $13.

INTRODUCTION TO WISCONSIN INDIANS: PREHISTORY TO STATEHOOD
Carol I. Mason
Illus. 321 pp. Paper. Sheffield Publishing, 1988. $15.50.

AN INTRODUCTORY GUIDE TO ENTREPRENEURSHIP FOR AMERICAN INDIANS
Enid, et al, Editors
50 pp. American Association for Community & Junior Colleges, 1990. $11.

THE INTRUDERS: THE ILLEGAL RESIDENTS OF THE CHEROKEE NATION,1866-1907
Nancy N. Sober
3rd Edition. Illus. 222 pp. Cherokee Books, 1991. $24.95.

*INTRUDERS WITHIN: PUEBLO RESISTANCE TO SPANISH RULE & THE REVOLT OF 1680
Louis Baldwin
Grades 7-12. Illus. 128 pp. Franklin Watts, 1995. $24.

INUA: SPIRIT WORLD OF THE BERING SEA ESKIMOS
William Fitzhugh & Susan Kaplan
Illus. 296 pp. Smithsonian, 1982. $35.00; paper, $19.95.

*INUIT
Elizabeth Hahn
Grades 5-8. Illus. 32 pp. Rourke Corp., 1990. $13.26.

INUIT ARTISTS PRINT WORKBOOK
Sandra B. Barz, Editor
Illus. 324 pp. Paper. Arts and Culture of the North, 1981. $58.

INUIT GLIMPSES OF AN ARCTIC PAST
David Morrison & George Hebert Germain
Illus. UBC Press, 1995. $34.95.

INUIT: THE NORTH IN TRANSITION
Ulli Steltzer
Illus. 224 pp. Paper. University of Chicago Press, 1983. $22.50.

THE INUIT PRINT, L'ESTAMPE INUIT
Helga Goetz
The art of the Canadian Inuit. Illus. 267 pp. University of Chicago Press, 1977. $24.95; paper, $17.95.

INUIT WOMEN ARTISTS
Odette Leroux, et al
Reminiscences of 12 Inuit women artists. Illus. 256 pp. University of Washington Press, 1994. $45.

INUIT YOUTH: GROWTH & CHANGE IN THE CANADIAN ARCTIC
Richard Condon
275 pp. Paper. Rutgers University Press, 1987. $15.

INUPIALLU TANNILLU UQALUNISA ILANICH: ABRIDGED INUPIAQ & ENGLISH DICTIONARY
Edna A. MacLean
Illus. 168 pp. Paper. Alaska Native Language Center, 1981. $10.

INUPIAQ ESKIMO NATIONS OF NORTHWEST ALASKA
Ernest S. Burch, Jr.
A social geography. Illus. Maps. Biblio. 473 pp. University of Alaska Press, 1998. $49.95; paper, $31.95.

THE INUPIAQ & ARCTIC ALASKA: AN ETHNOGRAPHY OF DEVELOPMENT
Norman Chance
250 pp. Paper. Holt, Rinehart & Winston, 1990. $10.

THE INVASION OF AMERICA: INDIANS, COLONIALISM, & THE CHANT OF CONQUEST
Francis Jennings
Illus. 384 pp. Paper. W.W. Norton, 1976. $9.95.

INVASION OF INDIAN COUNTRY IN THE 20TH CENTURY: AMERICAN CAPITALISM & TRIBAL NATURAL RESOURCES
Donald L. Fixico
Paper. University Press of Colorado, 1998. $24.95.

THE INVENTED INDIAN: CULTURAL FICTIONS & GOVERNMENT POLICIES
James A. Clifton, Editor
388 pp. Paper. Transaction Publishers, 1990. $24.95.

INVENTING THE SAVAGE: SOCIAL CONSTRUCTION OF NATIVE AMERICAN CRIMINALITY
Luana Ross
Illus. 326 pp. University of Texas Press, 1998.
$35; paper, $17.95.

INVENTING THE SOUTHWEST: THE FRED HARVEY COMPANY & NATIVE AMERICAN ART
Kathleen L. Howard & Diana F. Pardue
Based on the exhibit of the Heard Museum. 90 color & 50 bxw photos. Biblio. 168 pp. Paper. Northland, $17.95. CD-ROM, $29.95.

THE INVENTION OF THE CREEK NATION, 1670-1763
Steven C. Hahn
Explores the political history of the Creek Indians of Georgia and Alabama. Map. 392 pp. University of Nebraska Press, 2004. $59.95.

THE INVENTION OF NATIVE AMERICAN LITERATURE
Robert Dale Parker
Focuses on issues of gender and literary form. Examines, among others, the following writers: Thomas King, John Joseph Mathews, D'Arcy McNickle, Leslie Marmon Silko and Ray A. Young Bear. 250 pp. Cornell University Press, 2003. $49.95, paper, $18.95.

THE INVENTION OF PROPHECY: CONTINUITY & MEANING IN HOPI INDIAN RELIGION
Armin W. Geertz
Illus. 39 pp. Paper. Brill Academic Publishing, 1987. $54.50.

THE INVENTIVE MIND: PORTRAITS OF RURAL ALASKA TEACHERS
G. Williamson McDiarmid, Judith S. Kleinfeld & Wm. H. Parrett
180 pp. Paper. University of Alaska Press, 1988. $10.

AN INVENTORY OF THE MISSION INDIAN AGENCY RECORDS
James Young, Dennis Moristo & G. David Tanenbaum
66 pp. Paper. UCLA, American Indian Studies Center, 1976. $5.

AN INVENTORY OF THE PALA INDIAN AGENCY RECORDS
James Young, Dennis Moristo and G. David Tanenbaum
66 pp. Paper. UCLA, American Indian Studies Center, 1976. $5.

THE INVISIBLE CULTURE: COMMUNICATION IN CLASSROOM & COMMUNITY ON THE WARM SPRINGS INDIAN RESERVATION
Susan Urmston Philips
A classic in the field of educational anthropology & sociolinguistics. 147 pp. Paper. Waveland Press, 1993. $9.95.

INVISIBLE INDIGENES: THE POLITICS OF NONRECOGNITION
Bruce Granville Miller
320 pp. University of Nebraska Press, 2003. $49.95.

THE INVISIBLE MUSICIAN
Ray A. Young Bear
Poetry. Draws upon ancient traditions while creating dramatic versions of the harshness of modern tribal life. 120 pp. Holy Cow! Press, $15; paper, $8.95.

INVISIBLE NATIVES: MYTH & IDENTITY IN THE AMERICAN WEST
Armando Jose Prats
Cornell University Press, 2002. $49.95; paper, $21.95.

INVOLVEMENT OF CANADIAN NATIVE COMMUNITIES IN THEIR HEALTH CARE PROGRAMS: A REVIEW OF THE LITERATURE SINCE THE 1970'S
D.E. Young & L.L. Smith
Identifies ovber 60 models of Native community involvement in health care in Canada. 90 pp. paper. CCI, 1993. $15.

IOWA INDIANS
O.J. Fargo
Two vols. Book 1, 51 pp.; Book 2, 71 pp. Paper. Green Valley Area Education Agency, 1988. $1.50 each.

THE IOWAY INDIANS
Martha R. Blaine
Illus. Maps. 364 pp. Paper. University of Oklahoma Press, 1979. $19.95.

THE IROQUOIS
Dean R. Snow
Illus. 288 pp. Paper. Blackwell Publishers, 1998. $28.95.

THE IROQUOIS
Frank G. Speck
Second edition. Illus. 95 pp. Paper. Cranbrook Institute, 1955. $4.50.

*THE IROQUOIS
Barbara Graymont
Grades 7-12. Illus. 104 pp. Chelsea House, 1989.
$17.95; paper, $9.95.

*THE IROQUOIS
Craig & Katherine Doherty
Grades 4-8. 64 pp. Franklin Watts, 1994. $22; paper, $6.95.

*THE IROQUOIS
Barbara McCall
Grades 5-8. Illus. 32 pp. Rourke Corp., 1989. $13.26.

IROQUOIS: ART & CULTURE
Carrie Lyford
Illus. 100 pp. Paper. Hancock House, $6.95.

IROQUOIS CORN IN A CULTURE-BASED CURRICULUM
Carol Cornelius
Illus. 288 pp. State University of New York Press, 1998. $65; paper, $21.95.

IROQUOIS CRAFTS
Carrie A. Lyford
Reprint of 1945 edition. Illus. 100 pp. Paper. R. Schneider, Publishers, $5.95.

IROQUOIS CULTURE & COMMENTARY
Doug George-Kanentiio
Perspectives on the life, traditions, and current affairs of the peoples of the Iroquois Confederacy. Illus. Photos. 224 pp. Clear Light, $14.95.

THE IROQUOIS EAGLE DANCE: AN OFFSHOOT OF THE CALUMET DANCE
William Fenton
Illus. 324 pp. Paper. Syracuse University Press, 1991. $17.95.

THE IROQUOIS & THE FOUNDING OF THE AMERICAN NATION
Donald A. Grinde, Jr.
UCLA, American Indian Studies Center, 1992.

IROQUOIS IN THE AMERICAN REVOLUTION
Barbara Graymont
Illus. Maps. 370 pp. Paper. Syracuse University Press, 1972. $16.95.

THE IROQUOIS IN THE CIVIL WAR: FROM BATTLEFIELD TO RESERVATION
Laurence M. Hauptman
The ware and effects of the war on the Iroquois families at home. Illus. Maps. 240 pp. Paper. Syracuse University Press, 1993. $29.95.

THE IROQUOIS IN THE WAR OF 1812
Carl Benn
Illus. Maps. 288 pp. University of Toronto Press, 1998. $50; paper, $21.95.

IROQUOIS INDIANS: A DOCUMENTARY HISTORY - GUIDE TO THE MICROFILM COLLECTION
Mary Druke, Editor
718 pp. Research Publications, 1985. $180.

IROQUOIS LAND CLAIMS
Christopher Vecsey & William Starna, Editors
Illus. Maps. 240 pp. Syracuse University Press, 1988. $45; paper, $16.95.

IROQUOIS MEDICAL BOTANY
James W. Herrick & Dean R. Snow
A guide to understanding the use of herbal medicines in traditional Iroquois culture. Illus. 240 pp. Syracuse University Press, 1994. $29.95; paper, $19.95.

IROQUOIS MUSIC & DANCE: CEREMONIAL ARTS OF TWO SENECA LONGHOUSES
Gertrude P. Kurath
Reprint of 1964 edition. Reprint Services, $49.

THE IROQUOIS & THE NEW DEAL
Laurence Hauptman
Illus. 276 pp. Syracuse University Press, 1988. $24.95; paper, $10.95.

THE IROQUOIS RESTORATION: IROQUOIS DIPLOMACY ON THE COLONIAL FRONTIER, 1701-1754
Richard Aquila
Illus. Maps. 285 pp. Paper. University of Nebraska Press, 1997. $18.95.

AN IROQUOIS SOURCEBOOK
Elisabeth Tooker, Editor
Reprint. Three volumes. Vol. 1, Political and Social Organization, 400 pp. $55; Calendric Rituals, 292 pp. $40; and Medicine Society Rituals, 360 pp. $50. Garland Publishing.

IROQUOIS STUDIES: A GUIDE TO DOCUMENTARY & ETHNOGRAPHIC RESOURCES FROM WESTERN NEW YORK & THE GENESEE VALLEY
Russell A. Judkins, Editor
Illus. 98 pp. Paper. State University of New York at Geneseo.

THE IROQUOIS STRUGGLE FOR SURVIVAL: WORLD WAR II TO RED POWER
Laurence Hauptman
44 photos. Maps. 344 pp. Paper. Syracuse University Press, 1986. $16.95.

THE IROQUOIS TRAIL: DICKON AMONG THE ONONDAGAS & SENECAS
Mark Harrington
215 pp. Paper. Rutgers University Press, 1991. $9.95.

IRREDEEMABLE AMERICA: THE INDIANS' ESTATE & LAND CLAIMS
Imre Sutton
Illus. University of New Mexico Press, 1985.

*IS MY FRIEND AT HOME? PUEBLO FIRESIDE TALES
John Bierhorst
Grades 3-8. Illus. 32 pp. Simon & Schuster Childrens, $14.95.

ISHI IN THREE CENTURIES
Edited by Karl Kroeber & Clifton Kroeber
Illus. 416 pp. University of Nebraska Press, 2003. $49.95.

ISHI IN TWO WORLDS
Theodora Kroeber
Reprint of 1961 edition. 255 pp. Paper. University of California Press, 1961. $45; paper, $16.95. Illus. edition. 296 pp. 1976. $50.

*ISHI: THE LAST OF HIS PEOPLE
Grades 2-4. Illus. 32 pp. Childrens Press, $10.95.

ISHI, THE LAST YAHI: A DOCUMENTARY HISTORY
Robert F. Heizer & Theodora Kroeber
Illus. Maps. 251 pp. Paper. University of California Press, 1979. $18.95.

ISHI MEANS MAN
Thomas Merton
Five essays about Native American Indians. Illus. 75 pp. Unicorn, 1976. $17.50; paper, $6.95.

ISHI'S JOURNEY—FROM THE CENTER TO THE EDGE OF THE WORLD
James A. Freeman
Ishi tale, the last Yahi Indian. Illus. Photos. 224 pp. Paper. Naturegraph, $10.95.

ISLAND BETWEEN
Margaret E. Murie
Fiction. Saga of Toozak the Eskimo, his people, his early years, marriage and manhood. Illus. 228 pp. University of Alaska Press, 1977. $9.95.

ISLAND IMMIGRANTS
J.D. Cleaver
40 pp. Paper. Oregon Historical Society, 1986. $2.95.

ISLANDS OF TRUTH: THE IMPERIAL FASHIONING OF VANCOUVER ISLAND
Daniel W. Clayton
Native people of Vancouver Island's early encounters with Europeans. Illus. 256 pp. UBC Press, 1999. $75.

ISSUES FOR THE FUTURE OF AMERICAN INDIAN STUDIES
Susan Guyette
267 pp. Paper. UCLA, American Indian Studies Center, 1985. $10.

ISSUES IN NATIVE AMERICAN CULTURAL IDENTITY
Michael K. Green
320 pp. Paper. Peter Lang Publishing, 1998. $29.95.

IT IS A GOOD DAY TO DIE: INDIAN EYEWITNESSES TELL THE STORY OF THE BATTLE OF THE LITTLE BIG HORN
Herman J. Viola, with Jan Shelton Danis
Accounts of Crow, Lakota, and Cheyenne warriors who triumphed at Little Bighorn. Illus. Maps. Paper. University of Nebraska Press, 2001. $12.95.

IT WILL LIVE FOREVER: TRADITIONAL YOSEMITE ACORN PREPARATION
Bev Ortiz
Photos. Biblio. 160 pp. Paper. Heyday Books, $12.95.

IT'S YOUR MISFORTUNE & NONE OF MY OWN: A NEW HISTORY OF THE AMERICAN WEST
Richard White
Illus. Maps. 664 pp. University of Oklahoma Press, 1991. $45; paper, $26.95.

ITCH LIKE CRAZY
Wendy Rose
Poetry which addresses concerns with personal identity. Illus. 121 pp. University of Arizona Press, 2002. $15.95.

J

HELEN HUNT JACKSON & HER INDIAN REFORM LEGACY
Valerie Sherer Mathes
Illus. Map. Biblio. 256 pp. Paper. University of Oklahoma Press, 1997. $19.95.

WILLIAM JACKSON, INDIAN SCOUT
James W. Schultz
Reprint of 1976 edition. 200 pp. Borgo Press, $19.95.

*JAMES AT WORK
Looks at reservation life through the eyes of a Choctaw Indian boy. Grades P-3. 14 pp. Choctaw Heritage Press, $2.75.

JAMES RIVER CHIEFTDOMS: THE RISE OF SOCIAL INEQUALITY IN THE CHESAPEAKE
Martin D. Gallivan
Explores the Powhatan and Monacan societies met by Jamestown colonists in 1607. Illus. 320 pp. University of Nebraska Press, 2003. $55.

*JAMES JOE
As told to Susan Thompson
Autobiography of a present-day Navajo Medicine Man. Grades 4 and up. 32 pp. Paper. Council for Indian Education, 1995. $4.95.

JEFFERSON'S AMERICA: 1760-1815
Norman Risjord
350 pp. Madison House, 1991. $32.95; paper, $17.95.

THOMAS JEFFERSON & THE CHANGING WEST: FROM CONQUEST TO CONSERVATION
James P. Ronda
University of New Mexico Press, $29.95; paper, $16.95.

JEFFERSON & THE INDIANS: THE TRAGIC FATE OF THE FIRST AMERICANS
Anthony F.C. Wallace
Illus. Maps. 416 pp. Harvard University Press, 1999. $29.95.

JEFFERSON & SOUTHWESTERN EXPLORATION: THE FREEMAN & VUSTIS ACCOUNTS OF THE RED RIVER EXPEDITION OF 1806
Thomas Freeman & Peter Custis
Illus. Maps. Biblio. 386 pp. Paper. University of Oklahoma Press, 1984. $18.95.

MARY JEMISON: WHITE WOMAN OF THE SENECA
Rayna M. Gangi
True story of the famous Indian captive. 152 pp. Clear Light, 1996. $22.95; paper, $12.95.

THE JEROME AGREEMENT BETWEEN THE KIOWA, COMANCHE & APACHE TRIBES & THE U.S.
R.J. DeMalle
38 pp. Institute for the Development of Indian Law, $11.

THE JESUIT MISSION TO THE LAKOTA SIOUX: PASTORAL MINISTRY & THEOLOGY, 1885-1945
Ross A. Enochs
188 pp. Paper. Sheed & Ward, 1996. $12.95.

THE JESUS ROAD: KIOWA, CHRISTIANITY, & INDIAN HYMNS
Luke Lassiter, Clyde Ellis, Ralph Kotay
Christian faith among the Kiowas of southwestern Oklahoma. Illus. 152 pp. University of Nebraska Press, 2002. $65; paper, $24.95.

JEWELRY BY SOUTHWEST AMERICAN INDIANS: EVOLVING DESIGNS
Nancy Schiffer
Illus. 256 pp. Schiffer, 1990. $59.95.

JEWELS OF THE NAVAJO LOOM: THE RUGS OF TEEC NOS POS
Ruth K. Belikove
Illus. 38 pp. Paper. Museum of New Mexico Press, 2000. $14.95.

JICARILLA APACHE TRIBAL CODE
The Michie Co., 1987.

THE JICARILLA APACHE TRIBE: A HISTORY, 1846-1970
Veronica E. Tiller
Revised edition. Illus. Photos. Maps. 300 pp. Paper. University of New Mexico Press, 1991. $24.95.

THE JICARILLA APACHES: A STUDY IN SURVIVAL
Dolores Gunnerson
Illus. 327 pp. Northern Illinois University Press, 1973. $22.

*JIM THORPE: WORLD'S GREATEST ATHLETE
Grades 4 and up. Illus. 130 pp. Childrens Press, $13.95.

*JOHN HAWK: A SEMINOLE SAGA
Beatrice Levin
A novel recounting the horror and the hostilities of the Seminole wars. Grades 7 and up. Illus. 182 pp. Paper. Council for Indian Education & Roberts Rinehart, 1994. $9.95.

JOHN ROSS: CHEROKEE CHIEF
Gary E. Moulton
Biography. 292 pp. Paper. University of Georgia Press, $11.95.

JOHNSON OF THE MOHAWKS
Arthur Pound & Richard E. Day
Reprint of 1930 edition. Ayer Co., $44. Gordon Press, $59.95.

*PHILIP JOHNSTON & THE NAVAJO CODE TALKERS
Syble Lagerquist
Grades 4 and up. 32 pp. Paper. Council for Indian Education, 1990. $4.95.

JOSANIE'S WAR: A CHIRICAHUA APACHE NOVEL
Karl H. Schlesier
University of Oklahoma Press, 1998. $22.95

*JOSEPH: CHIEF OF THE NEZ PERCE
Dean Pollock
Grades 5 and up. Illus. 64 pp. Paper. Binford & Mort, 1990. $7.95.

*ALVIN JOSPEHY'S HISTORY OF THE NATIVE AMERICANS SERIES
Alvin M. Josephy, Jr.
Grades 5-7. Six books. Illus. 864 pp. Silver Burdette Press, 1989. $71.88 per set; paper, $47.70 per set.

THE JOURNAL AND ACCOUNT BOOK OF PATRICK GASS: MEMBER OF THE LEWIS & CLARK EXPEDITION
Carol Lynn MacGregor, Editor
Illus. Maps. 384 pp. Mountain Press, 1997. $30; paper, $18.

JOURNAL OF THE ADVENTURES OF MATTHEW BUNN
Matthew Bunn
Facsimile of the 1962 edition. Paper. Newberry Library Center, $2.

JOURNAL OF CHEROKEE STUDIES
Issues of the Journal (official publication of the Museum of the Cherokee) 1976-1986. Illus. 4 Vols. 1,200 pp. Cherokee Publications, $125/set.

THE JOURNAL OF...NARRATING AN ADVENTURE FROM ARKANSAS THROUGH INDIAN TERRITORY, ETC.
Jacob Fowler
A trip from Arkansas to New mexico and encounters with the Cherokee, Kiowa, Pawnee & Arapaho. Reprint of 1898 edition. 183 pp. Ross Haines, $15.

THE JOURNEY OF NATIVE AMERICAN PEOPLE WITH SERIOUS MENTAL ILLNESS: FIRST NATIONAL CONFERENCE
A. Marie Sanchez & Frank D. McGuirk
Illus. 137 pp. Paper. Diane Publishing, 1996. $35.

THE JOURNEY OF NAVAJO OSHLEY: AN AUTOBIOGRAPHY & LIFE HISTORY
Robert S. McPherson, Editor
Oshley's narrative is woven with vivid and detailed portraits of Navajo culture. Illus. 235 pp. Utah State University Press, 2000. $39.95; paper, $19.95.

A JOURNAL OF SIBLEY'S INDIAN EXPOSITION DURING THE SUMMER OF 1863 AND RECORD OF THE TROOPS EMPLOYED
Arthur M. Daniels
Reprint. Illus. 154 pp. Thueson, $30.

THE JOURNALS OF THE LEWIS & CLARK EXPEDITION
Meriwether Lewis & William Clark; Gary Moulton, Editor
Three volumes. Illus. University of Nebraska Press, 1987. $40.00 each.

JOURNALS OF JOSEPH N. NICOLLET: 1836-1837
Martha Bray; Andre Fertey, Translator
Illus. 288 pp. Minnesota Historical Society Press, 1970. $16.50.

JOURNALS OF THE MILITARY EXPEDITION OF MAJOR GENERAL JOHN SULLIVAN: AGAINST THE SIX NATIONS OF INDIANS IN 1779
Maj. Gen. John Sullivan
Reprint of 1887 edition. Ayer Co., $39.

JOURNEY FROM PRINCE OF WALES' FORT IN HUDSON'S BAY TO THE NORTHERN OCEAN, 1769-1772
Samuel Hearne
Reprint of 1795 edition. Illus. Maps. 437 pp. Charles E. Tuttle, $20; Greenwood Press, $32.75.

A JOURNEY INTO MOHAWK & ONEIDA COUNTRY, 1634-1635: THE JOURNAL OF HARMEN MEYNDERTSZ VAN DEN BOGAERT
Charles Gehring
Illus. 120 pp. Paper. Syracuse University Press, 1988. $16.95.

THE JOURNEY OF NAVAJO OSHLEY: AN AUTOBIOGRAPHY & LIFE HISTORY
Robert S. McPherson, Editor
Portraits of Navajo culture: clan relationships, marriages and children, ceremonies, trading, etc. 235 pp. Utah State University Press, 2000. $39.95; paper, $21.95.

JOURNEY SONG: A SPIRITUAL LEGACY OF THE AMERICAN INDIAN
Celinda Reynolds Kaelin
Illus. 250 pp. Paper. Four Directions Publishing, 1998. $14.95.

JOURNEY TO ALASKA IN 1868
E. Teichmann
Reprint of 1925 edition. Argosy, $20. Delux edition, $50.

JOURNEY TO THE ANCESTRAL SELF: TAMARACK SONGS
Teaches that the lifeways of all native peoples are essentially one. Illus. 224 pp. Paperback. Teaching Drum Outdoor School, $14.95. With voice cassette, $26.

JOURNEY TO THE ANCESTRAL SELF: THE NATIVE LIFEWAY GUIDE TO LIVING IN HARMONY WITH EARTH MOTHER
Tamarack Song
264 pp. Paper. Station Hill Press, 1994. $14.95.

*JOURNEY TO CAHOKIA
Iseminger, Steele
Story about Ancient Cahokia (A.D. 1200) as seen through the eyes of a young boy. Grades 4-6. Illus. 32 pp. Paper. Cahokia Mounds Museum Society, 1995. $2.95.

*JOURNEY TO CENTER PLACE
Viola R. Gates
Anasazi life through a 12-year-old Anasazi girl. Grades 3-7. 144 pp. Council for Indian Education, $10.95.

JOURNEY TO THE FOUR DIRECTIONS: TEACHINGS OF THE FEATHERED SERPENT
Jim Berenholtz
Ceremoial musician & visionary traveler Jim Berenholtz shares the story of his mystical awakening & remarkable training. Illus. Map. 288 pp. Paper. Bear & Co., $14.95.

JOY BEFORE NIGHT: EVELYN EATON'S LAST YEARS
Terry Eaton
Illus. 173 pp. Paper. Theosophical Publishing House, 1988. $6.95.

THE JUAN PARDO EXPEDITION; EXPLORATION OF THE CAROLINAS & TENNESSEE, 1566-1568
Charles Hudson, Editor
Illus. 354 pp. Smithsonian Institution Press, 1990. $42.

JUH, AN INCREDIBLE INDIAN
Dan L. Thrapp
Juh was a chief and Geronimo only a war leader. The full account of his Apache shadowy life & career. Illus. Map. 42 pp. Paper. Texas Western Press, 1993. $12.50.

THE JUMANOS: HUNTERS & TRADERS OF THE SOUTH PLAINS
Nancy Parrott Hickerson
Describes encounters with Native North Americans by Spanish explorers. Illus. Maps. 340 pp. Paper. University of Texas Press, 1994. $17.95.

*THE JUNIOR LIBRARY OF AMERICAN INDIANS
Grades 2 and up. Illus. 72-80 pp. each. Chelsea House Publishers, 1992. 30 hardcover titles, $16.95 each, $508.50 per set; 12 paperback titles, $9.95 each, $119.40 per set.

*JUST TALKING ABOUT OURSELVES: VOICES OF OUR YOUTH, Vol. 2
Marlena Dolan
Stories, poetry, and visual art by Native young people of British Columbia. Grades 4 and up. Paper. Oyate, 1994. $10.95.

*JUST A WALK
Jordan Wheeler; illus. by Bill Cohen
Children's stories by a Cree author. Grades K-4. Illus. 50 pp. Paper. Theytus, 1994. $8.95.

K

*KA-HA-SI & THE LOON: AN ESKIMO LEGEND
Terri Cohlene
Grades 1-5. Illus. Paper. Troll Associates, 1992. $4.95.

FRED KABOTIE: HOPI INDIAN ARTIST
Fred Kabotie and Bill Belknap
Illus. 150 pp. Museum of Northern Arizona, $24.95; Northland Press, 1977. $35.00.

KACHINA CEREMONIES & KACHINA DOLLS
Martina M. Jacobs
Illus. 72 pp. Paper. Carnegie, 1980. $1.50.

THE KACHINA & THE CROSS: INDIANS & SPANIARDS IN THE EARLY SOUTHWEST
Carroll Riley
History of the conflict between the Pueblos and the Franciscan Order in the 17th century. Illus. Maps. University of Utah Press, 1999. $34.95; paper, $16.95.

*THE KACHINA DOLL BOOK I & II
Donna Greenlee
Grades 1-5. I - Explains the meaning of 14 ceremonial dolls of the Hopi Indians. II - tells about 13 more Hopi dolls with two special pages of Indian symbols. Illus. 32 pp. Paper. Fun Publishing, \$4.95 each.

KACHINA DOLLS: THE ART OF HOPI CARVERS
Helga Teiwes
Provides an understanding of the secular contexts of contemporary Hopi kachina wood sculpture. Illus. 161 pp. University of Arizona Press, 1991. \$34.95; paper, \$29.95.

*KACHINA DOLLS: AN EDUCATIONAL COLORING BOOK
Grades 1-8. Illus. 32 pp. Paper. Spizzirri Publishing, 1981. Read & Coloring Book, \$1.95;

THE KACHINA DOLLS OF CECIL CALNIMPTEWA: THEIR POWER, THEIR SPLENDOR
Theda Bassman; photos by Gene Balzer
Features 127 dolls in full-color. Includes a biography of the author. Illus. 112 pp. Treasure Chest, 1993. \$70.

KACHINA: A SELECTED BIBLIOGRAPHY
Marcia Muth
Over 100 references to kachinas and an essay. Illus. 32 pp. Paper. Sunstone Press, \$4.95.

KACHINA TALES FROM THE INDIAN PUEBLOS
Gene Meany Hodge, Editor
Illus. 96 pp. Paper. Sunstone Press, \$8.95.

KACHINAS: A HOPI ARTIST'S DOCUMENTARY
Barton Wright; illus. by Cliff Bahnimptewa
237 color plates. Illus. 272 pp. Paper. Northland Publishing & Clear Light, 1973. \$29.95.

KACHINAS IN THE PUEBLO WORLD
edited by Polly Schaafsma
14 scholars examine the vital role of kachinas in the cultures of the Rio Grande, Zuni, and Hopi Pueblos. Illus. Paper. University of Utah Press. \$19.95.

KACHINAS: A SELECTED BIBLIOGRAPHY
Marcia Muth
Illus. 32 pp. Paper. Sunstone Press, \$4.95.

KACHINAS: SPIRIT BEINGS OF THE HOPI
Neil David, Sr, J. Brent Ricks & Alexander E. Anthony, Jr.
Based on 79 paintings by Neil David, Sr., Hopi Indian artist and Kachina carver. Illus. Photos. 196 pp. Avanyu Publishing, 1993. \$50.

KAHBE NAGWIWENS - THE MAN WHO LIVED IN THREE CENTURIES
Carl A. Zapffe
Illus. 100 pp. Paper. Historical Heart Associates, 1975. \$10.

KAHTNUHT'ANA QENAGA: THE KENAI PEOPLE'S LANGUAGE
Peter Kalifornsky; James Kari, Editor
Second edition. Illus. 140 pp. Paper. Alaska Native Language Center, 1982. \$6.

PAUL KANE, THE COLUMBIA WANDERER: SKETCHES, PAINTINGS & COMMENT, 1846-1847
Thomas Vaughan, Editor
Illus. 80 pp. Paper. Oregon Historical Society, 1971. \$3.95.

PAUL KANE'S GREAT NOR-WEST
Diane Eaton & Sheila Urbanek
Photos. Paper. UBC Press, 1995. \$29.95.

KANIENKEHAKA (MOHAWK NATION): STATE POLICIES & COMMUNITY RESISTANCE
Donna Goodleaf
Account of the "Oka Crisis" with Mohawk perspective of the issues & events. 250 pp. Paper. Theytus, 1993. \$12.95.

KANSAS INDIANS: A HISTORY OF THE WIND PEOPLE, 1673-1873
William E. Unrau
Illus. Maps. 262 pp. University of Oklahoma Press, 1971. \$16.95.

THE KARANKAWA INDIANS OF TEXAS: AN ECOLOGICAL STUDY OF CULTURAL TRADITION & CHANGE
Robert A. Ricklis
Illus. 236 pp. University of Texas Press, 1996. \$35; paper, \$17.95.

KARNEE: A PAIUTE NARRATIVE
Lalla Scott
Story of Northern Paiute Indian life in Nevada as told by Annie Lowry, a Paiute/Caucasion woman who lived with the Paiute tribe near Lovelock, Nevada. 168 pp. Paper. University of Nevada Press, 1966. \$11.95.

KARUK: THE UPRIVER PEOPLE
Maureen Bell
The history of the Karuk; also present-day Karuk life & culture are presented. Photos. 144 pp. Paper. Naturegraph, \$8.95.

KASHAYA POMO PLANTS
Jennie Goodrich, Claudia Lawson, Vana Parrish Lawson
Describes 150 common plants growing in Kashaya Pomo territory that have long been an important part of the tribe's culture. Illus. Glossary. 176 pp. Paper. Heyday Books, \$12.95.

KASKA INDIANS: AN ETHNOGRAPHIC RECONSTRUCTION
John J. Honigmann
163 pp. Paper. HRAFP, 1964. \$15.

KATHLAMET TEXTS
Franz Boas
Reprint. Scholarly Press, \$49.

K'ETAALKKAANEE: THE ONE WHO PADDLED AMONG THE ANIMALS
Catherine Attla
University of Alaska Press, \$12.

KEEPER OF THE DELAWARE DOLLS
Lynette Perry & Manny Skolnick
The Delaware culture and dollmaking craft. Illus. Map. Paper. University of Nebraska Press, 1999. \$12.

*KEEPER OF FIRE
James Magorian
Grades 4-12. Illus. 78 pp. Paper. Council for Indian Education, 1984. \$6.95.

*KEEPERS OF THE ANIMALS: NATIVE AMERICAN STORIES & WILDLIFE ACTIVITIES FOR CHILDREN
Michael Caduto & Joseph Bruchac; illus. by John Kahionhes Fadden
Grades 1-7. Illus. 286 pp. paper. Fulcrum Publishing, 1991. \$19.95. Native American Animal Stories, Illus. 160 pp. paper, \$12.95; Teacher's Guide, 66 pp. paper, \$9.95; 2 audiocassettes, \$16.95.

KEEPERS OF THE CENTRAL FIRE ISSUES IN ECOLOGY FOR INDIGENOUS PEOPLES
Stephen Kunitz & Jerrold Levy
Illus. 191 pp. University of Arizona Press, 1991. \$39.

KEEPERS OF THE CULTURE: WOMEN IN A CHANGING WORLD
Janet Mancini Billson
Explores women's lives in seven distinct and intact North American cultures: Iroquois, Inuit, Blood, mennonite, West Indian, Chinese & Ukranian. 350 pp. Lexington Books, 1995. \$23.'

KEEPERS OF THE DREAM
Patricia Wyatt
Illus. 72 pp. Pomegranate, 1995. \$24.

*KEEPERS OF THE EARTH: NATIVE AMERICAN STORIES & ENVIRONMENTAL ACTIVITIES FOR CHILDREN
Michael Caduto & Joseph Bruchac; illus. by John Kahionhes Fadden
Grades K-12. Illus. 240 pp. Paper. Fulcrum Publishing, 1988. \$19.95. Native American Stories, Illus. 160 pp. paper, \$12.95; Teacher's Guide, 52 pp. paper, \$9.95; two audiocassette, \$16.95.

KEEPERS OF THE GAME: INDIAN-ANIMAL RELATIONSHIPS & THE FUR TRADE
Calvin Martin
Illus. Paper. University of California Press, 1978. \$16.95.

*KEEPERS OF LIFE: DISCOVERING PLANTS THROUGH NATIVE AMERICAN STORIES AND EARTH ACTIVITIES FOR CHILDREN
Michael Caduto & Joseph Bruchac; illus. by John Kahionhes Fadden
Grades K-12. Illus. 288 pp. Paper. Fulcrum Publishing, 1994. \$22.95. Native Plant Stories, 160 pp. paper, \$12.95; Teacher's Guide, 48 pp. paper, \$9.95; 2 audiocassette, \$16.95.

*KEEPERS OF THE NIGHT: NATIVE AMERICAN STORIES & NOCTURNAL ACTIVITIES FOR CHILDREN
Michael Caduto & Joseph Bruchac; illus. by John Kahionhes Fadden
Grades K-12. Illus. 168 pp. Paper. Fulcrum Publishing, \$15.95.

KE-MA-HA: THE OMAHA STORIES OF FRANCIS LA FLESCHE
Francis La Flesche; edited by Daniel Littlefield & James Parins
135 pp. Paper. University of Nebraska Press, 1995. \$10.

KENEKUK, THE KICKAPOO PROPHET
Joseph B. Herring
Illus. Maps. 170 pp. University Press of Kansas, 1988. \$19.95.

A KEY INTO THE LANGUAGE OF AMERICA
Roger Williams
Reprint. 232 pp. Paper. Applewood, \$12.95.

A KEY INTO THE LANGUAGE OF WOODSPLINT BASKETS
Ann McMullen & Russell Handsman, Editors
Illus. 196 pp. Paper. American Indian Archaeological Institute & Hothem House, 1987. \$22.50.

*THE KEY TO THE INDIAN
Lynn R. Banks
Grades 2-5. Paper. Avon, 1999. \$4.95.

THE KICKAPOO INDIANS, THEIR HISTORY & CULTURE: AN ANNOTATED BIBLIOGRAPHY
Phillip M. White
152 pp. Greenwood Publishing, 1999. \$55.

THE KICKAPOOS: LORDS OF THE MIDDLE BORDER
Arrell M. Gibson
History of the tribe. Reprint. Illus. Map. Biblio. 408 pp. Paper. University of Oklahoma Press, \$25.95.

KIIKAAPOA: THE KANSAS KICKAPOO
Donald D. Stull
Illus. 214 pp. Paper. Kickapoo Tribal Press, 1984. \$12.

KILIWA DICTIONARY
Mauricio J. Mixco
207 pp. Paper. University of Utah Press, 1985. \$25.

KILIWA TEXTS: WHEN I HAVE DONNED MY CREST OF STARS
Mauricio J. Mixco
Illus. 250 pp. Paper. University of Utah Press, 1983. \$25.

THE KILLING OF CHIEF CRAZY HORSE
Robert A. Clark, Editor
Three eyewitness accounts of the killing of Crazy Horse. Illus. 152 pp. Paper. University of Nebraska Press, 1988. \$9.95.

KILLING TIME WITH STRANGERS
W.S. Penn
Nez Perce's family's struggle to fit into a white world. 283 pp. University of Arizona Press, 2000. \$23.95.

KILLING US QUIETLY: NATIVE AMERICANS & HIV/AIDS
Irene S. Vernon
Discusses prevention strategies and educational resources. 138 pp. University of Nebraska Press, 2001. \$40; paper, \$14.95.

KILLING THE WHITE MAN'S INDIAN: REINVENTING NATIVE AMERICANS AT THE END OF THE CENTURY
Fergus M. Bordewich
400 pp. Paper. Doubleday, 1997. \$14.

KINAALADA: A NAVAJO PUBERTY CEREMONY
Shirley M. Begay and Verna Clinton-Tullie
Illus. 171 pp. Navajo Curriculum, 1983. \$15; paper, \$11.

KINAALDA: A STUDY OF THE NAVAHO GIRL'S PUBERTY CEREMONY
Charlotte Johnson Frisbie
Illus. Paper. University of Utah Press, \$24.95.

KING ISLAND TALES - UGIUVANGMIUT QULIAPYUIT
Eskimo history & legends from the Bering Strait. University of Alaska Press, \$19.95.

KING OF THE DELAWARES: TEEDYUSCUNG, 1700-1763
Anthony F.C. Wallace
Reprint of 1949 edition. 328 pp. Maps. Paper. Syracuse University Press, \$16.95.

KINSHIP & THE DRUM DANCE IN A NORTHERN DENE COMMUNITY
M.L. Asch
Illus. 113 pp. CCI, \$25; paper, \$15.

KINSMEN OF ANOTHER KIND: DAKOTA—WHITE RELATIONS IN THE UPPER MISSISSIPPI VALLEY, 1650-1862
Gary C. Anderson
Reprint. 383 pp. Paper. Minnesota Historical Society, 1997. \$15.95.

KINSMEN THROUGH TIME: AN ANNOTATED BIBLIOGRAPHY OF POTAWATOMI HISTORY
David R. Edmunds
237 pp. Scarecrow Press, 1987. \$27.50.

KIOWA, APACHE, & COMANCHE MILITARY SOCIETIES: ENDURING VETERANS, 1800 TO THE PRESENT
William C. Meadows
Photos. 576 pp. University of Texas Press & Written Heritage, 1999. \$65.

*THE KIOWA: GREAT PLAINS
John Wunder
Grades 5 and up. Illus. Chelsea House, 1989. \$17.95.

KIOWA MEMORIES; IMAGES FROM INDIAN TERRITORY, 1880
Ron McCoy
Illus. 67 pp. Morning Star Gallery, 1987. \$21.

THE KIOWA TREATY OF 1853
R.J. DeMallie
60 pp. Institute for the Development of Indian Law, \$12.50.

*KIOWA VOICES: CEREMONIAL DANCE, RITUAL & SONG
Maurice Boyd
Grades 3 and up. Illus. 165 pp. Paper. Texas Christian
University Press, 1981. $29.95.

*KIOWA VOICES: MYTHS, LEGENDS & FOLKTALES
Maurice Boyd
Grades 3 and up. Volume II. Illus. 323 pp. Texas Christian
University Press, 1983. $39.95.

KIOWA: A WOMAN MISSIONARY IN INDIAN TERRITORY
Isabel Crawford
Illus. 241 pp. Paper. University of Nebraska Press, 1998. $12.

THE KIOWAS
Mildred P. Mayhall
Revised 1971 edition. Illus. Map. Paper.
University of Oklahoma Press, $18.95.

**KITCHI-GAMI: LIFE AMONG
THE LAKE SUPERIOR OJIBWAY**
Johann G. Kohl; trans. by L. Wraxall
Illus. 477 pp. Paper. Minnesota Historical Society Press, 1985.
$12.95.

KIVA ART OF THE ANASAZI AT POTTERY MOUND, N.M.
Frak Hibben
Illus. 145 pp. KC Publications, 1975. $35; paper, $14.95.

**KIVA, CROSS, & CROWN: THE PECOS
INDIANS & NEW MEXICO, 1540-1840**
John L. Kessell
Illus. 304 pp. Paper. Clear Light, $19.95.

THE KLICKITAT INDIANS
Selma M. Neils
Illus. 240 pp. Paper. Binford & Mort, 1985. $12.95.

**KNOWLEDGE OF THE ELDERS: THE IROQUOIS
CONDOLENCE CANE TRADITION**
A study guide designed for high school students.
Looks at a living tradition of the Eastern Woodlands
as told by Jacob Thomas, and elder of the Cayuga
Nation. Akwe:kon Press, $8.

**KNOWLEDGE & SECRECY IN AN ABORIGINAL
RELIGION**
Ian Keen
Illus. 368 pp. Paper. Oxford University Press, 1998. $29.95.

KOASATI DICTIONARY
Geoffrey Kimball
407 pp. University of Nebraska Press, 1994. $60.

KOKOPELLI: FLUTE PLAYER IMAGES IN ROCK ART
Dennis Slifer & Jim Duffield
Extensive survey of rock art depictions of the humpbacked flute
player. Photos. Illus. maps. Paper. 210 pp. Ancient City Press
& Clear Light, 1994. $16.95.

KOKOPELLI: THE MAKING OF AN ICON
Ekkehart Malotki
Story of the mythical flute player. Illus. 200 pp.
University of Nebraska Press, 2000. $35; paper, $19.95.

**KOKOPELLI'S COOKBOOK:
AUTHENTIC RECIPES OF THE SOUTHWEST**
James R. Cunkle & Carol Cunkle
112 pp. Golden West Publishing, 1997. $9.95.

KOMANTCIA
Harold Keith
A tale of captivity by the Comanche Indians. 300 pp.
Levite of Apache, $17.

**KONAWA, INDIAN TERRITORY: TWO PIONEER
FAMILIES, HAMMONS & TROBAUGH**
Chester Kennedy
Illus. 225 pp. Oldbuck Press, 1993. $36.95.

KOOTENAI WHY STORIES
Frank B. Linderman
Illus. 173 pp. Paper. University of Nebraska Press, 1997.
$9.95.

KORCZAK: STORYTELLER IN STONE
The biography of Korczak Ziolkowski, the sculpture of
Crazy Horse from Thunderhead Mountain. Illus. 80 pp.
Paper. Crazy Horse Memorial Foundation, $3.25.

KOSSATI GRAMMAR
Geoffrey Kimball
Illus. 640 pp. University of Nebraska Press, 1991. $70.

*KOU-SKELOWH "WE ARE THE PEOPLE"
Barb Marchand, Editor & Illus.
Entirely done by Okanagan First Nation people.
Grades K-4. Illus. 28 pp. Paper. Theytus, 1990. $12.95.

KTUNAXA LEGENDS
Kootenai Cultural Committee
Legends from the Confederated Salish & Kotenai Tribes.
Paper. UBC Press, 1997. $41.95.

KUMTUX
Jeanette Mills, Editor
A monthly calendar of events in and related to Indian Country
in Washington State. Native American Task Force, Church
Council of Greater Seattle. $18/yr.

MORT KUNSTLER'S OLD WEST: INDIANS
Mort Kunstler
Illus. 192 pp. Rutledge Hill Press, 1998. $ 12.95.

*KUNU: WINNEBAGO BOY ESCAPES
Kenneth Thomasma; Jack Brouwer. Illus.
Historical novel of the forced migration of Winnebago Indians
in 1863. Grades 4 and up. Illus. Baker Book House, $10.99;
paper, $6.99.

**KUSIQ: AN ESKIMO LIFE HISTORY
FROM THE ARCTIC COAST OF ALASKA**
Waldo Bodfish, Sr.
Illus. Photos. Maps. 330 pp. Paper.
University of Alaska Press, 1991. $21.

*THE KWAKIUTL
Stanley Walens
Grades 5 and up. Illus. Chelsea House, 1989. $17.95.

KWAKIUTL ETHNOGRAPHY
Franz Boas; Helen Codere, Editor
Illus. University of Chicago Press, 1967. $30.

KWAKIUTL: INDIANS OF BRITISH COLUMBIA
R.P. Rohner and E. Rohner
111 pp. Paper. Waveland Press, 1970. $8.50.

KWAKIUTL STRING FIGURES
Julia Averkieva & Mark Sherman
Study of 112 string figures and tricks collected among the
Kawkiutl Indians by Averkieva. Illus. 164 drawings. 232 pp. Uni-
versity of Washington Press, $35.

A KWAKIUTL VILLAGE AND SCHOOL
Harry F. Wolcott
Reprint of 1967 edition. Illus. 132 pp. Paper.
Waveland Press, 1984. $7.95.

KWAKWAKA'WAKW SETTLEMENT SITES, 1775-1920
Robert Galois
Demographics & settlement patterns of the Kawakiutl in British
Columbia betweem 1775 and 1920. 60 maps. 350 pp. Univer-
sity of Washington Press, $60.

*KWULASULWUT: STORIES FROM THE COAST SALISH
Ellen White; illus. by David Neel
Grades K-6. Illus. 76 pp. Paper. Theytus, 1992. $12.95.

*KWULASULWUT: SALISH CREATION STORIES
Ellen White; illus. by David Neel
Grades K-6. Illus. 25 pp. Paper. Theytus, 1995. $9.95.

L

**LABORING IN THE FIELDS OF THE LORD:
SPANISH MISSIONS & SOUTHEASTERN INDIANS**
Jerald T. Milanich
Photos. Maps. 210 pp. Smithsonian Institution Press,
1999. $26.95.

**LACHLAN McGILLIVRAY, INDIAN TRADER: THE
SHAPING OF THE SOUTHERN COLONIAL FRONTIER**
Edward J. Cashin
The career of the Indian trader from 1736 to 1776.
Illus. 352 pp. University of Georgia Press, $45.

LAKE PERTHA & THE LOST MURALS OF CHIAPAS
J. David Wonham
Illus. 19 pp. Paper. Pre-Columbian Art, 1985. $10.

LAKOTA BELIEF & RITUAL
James R. Walker
Illus. 370 pp. Paper. University of Nebraska Press,
1980. $18.95.

LAKOTA CEREMONIAL SONGS
Book & tape. VIP Publishing. $19.95.

LAKOTA CEREMONIES
Alice C. Fletcher
Paper. VIP Publishing. $7.95.

**LAKOTA & CHEYENNE: INDIAN VIEWS
OF THE GREAT SIOUX WAR, 1876-1877**
Jerome A. Greene, Editor
Illus. Map. 164 pp. University of Oklahoma Press, 1994.
$26.95.

LAKOTA CULTURE, WORLD ECONOMY
Kathleen Ann Pickering
Interviews with residents of Pine Ridge and Rosebud
Reservations to present an in-depth look at the modern
economy of the Lakotas. Illus. Maps. 179 pp. University of
Nebraska Press, 2000. $45.

*LAKOTA & DAKOTA ANIMAL WISDOM STORIES
Mark W. McGinnis
Grades 6 and up. Illus. 24 pp. Paper. Tipi Press, 1994.
$11.98.

**LAKOTA DICTIONARY:
LAKOTA-ENGLISH/ENGLISH-LAKOTA**
compiled & edited by Eugene Buechel & Paul Manhart
Over 30,000 entries, examples of word usage; overview of
Lakoat grammar. 530 pp. University of Nebraska Press,
2002. $65; paper, $27.50.

LAKOTA GRIEVING: A PASTORAL RESPONSE
Stephen Huffstetter
157 pp. Paper. Tipi Press, 1998. $7.95.

LAKOTA LIFE
Ron Zeilinger
Illus. 74 pp. Paper. Tipi Press, 1986. $3.95.

LAKOTA MYTH
James R. Walker; edited by Elaine A. Jahner
428 pp. Paper. University of Nebraska Press, 1983. $16.95.

LAKOTA NAMING: A MODERN-DAY HUNKA CEREMONY
Marla N.Powers
History of the Hunka and a description of a contemporary
Naming ceremony. 37 photos. Paper. Written Heritage, $11.95.

**LAKOTA NOON: THE INDIAN NARRATIVE
OF CUSTER'S DEFEAT**
Gregory Michno
325 pp. Mountain Press, $30; paper, $16.

**LAKOTA RECOLLECTIONS OF THE CUSTER FIGHT:
NEW SOURCES OF INDIAN-MILITARY HISTORY**
Richard G. Hardorff, Editor
A collection of sixteen interviews with participants in the Battle
of the Little Big Horn. Illus. Maps. 211 pp. Paper. University of
Nebraska Press & Clear Light, $12.95.

**THE LAKOTA RITUAL OF THE SWEAT LODGE:
HISTORY & CONTEMPORARY PRACTICE**
Raymond A. Bucko
Illus. 340 pp. Paper. University of Nebraska Press,
1998. $17.95.

*LAKOTA SIOUX CHILDREN & ELDERS TALK TOGETHER
Barrie E. Kavasch
Grades 4 and up. Rosen Group, 1998. $18.

LAKOTA SOCIETY
James R. Walker; Raymond J. DeMallie, Editor
Illus. 243 pp. Paper. University of Nebraska Press,
1982. $13.95.

LAKOTA SONGS
Isaac Brave Eagle
100 pp. Sky & Sage Books, 1996. $17 includes audio cassette.

**THE LAKOTA SWEAT LODGE CARDS:
SPIRITUAL TEACHINGS OF THE SIOUX**
Chief Archie Fire Lame Deer & Helene Sarkis
The powerful imagery and sacred wisdom of the inipi—the
sweat lodge ceremony used for centuries by the Lakota people
for healing and purification. Boxed set: 192-page book and 50
full-color cards. Inner Traditions, $29.95.

LAKOTA TALES & TEXTS IN TRANSLATION
Eugene Buechel & Paul manhart
2 vols. Tipi Press, 1998. $39.95.

LAKOTA WARRIOR
Joseph White Bull; James H. Howard, Editor/Translator
Illus. 108 pp. Paper. University of Nebraska Press, 1998.
$15.

LAKOTA WOMAN
Mary Crow Dog
Illus. 275 pp. Paper. HarperCollins, 1991. $9.95.

**LAMAR ARCHAEOLOGY: MISSISSIPPIAN
CHIEFDOMS IN THE DEEP SOUTH**
Mark Williams & Gary Shapiro, Editors
256 pp. Paper. University of Alabama Press, 1990. $20.95.

**LAME DEER: SEEKER OF VISIONS:
THE LIFE OF A SIOUX MEDICINE MAN**
John Fire/Lame Deer and Richard Erdoes
Chief Lame Deer, the chief medicine man for the western
Sioux tribes, tells of the modern Indianexperience. Paper.
Simon & Schuster, 1972. $11.

**THE LANCE & THE SHIELD:
THE LIFE & TIMES OF SITTING BULL**
Robert M. Utley
Biography of a great Sioux leader. Henry Holt, 1993.
$19.95.

THE LAND OF THE CLIFF—DWELLERS
Frederick H. Chapin
Reprint of 1892 edition. Paper.
University of Arizona Press, $9.95.

LAND OF THE FOUR DIRECTIONS
Frederick J. Pratson
A photographic portrayal of American Indians of Maine.
Illus. 140 pp. Paper. Chatham Press, $3.95.

THE LAND OF THE OJIBWE
MHS Education Dept.
Describes the movement of the Ojibwe throughout the
Western Great Lakes region and beyond. Maps. 48 pp.
Paper. Minnesota Historical Society Press, 1973. $1.50.

**THE LAND OF PREHISTORY: A CRITICAL
HISTORY OF AMERICAN ARCHAEOLOGY**
Alice B. Kehoe
256 pp. Routledge, 1998. $80; paper, $22.99.

**THE LAND OF RED CLOUD:
AMONG NORTH AMERICA'S INDIANS**
Peter Korniss
136 pp. International Specialized Book Service, 1982.
$19.95.

**LAND OF THE SPOTTED EAGLE:
PORTRAITS OF THE RESERVATION SIOUX**
Luther Standing Bear
Illus. 260 pp. Paper. University of Nebraska Press,
1978. $14.95.

LAND RIGHTS OF INDIGENOUS CANADIAN PEOPLES
Brian Slattery
478 pp. University of Saskatchewan, 1979. $70.

LANDLORD TENENT RELATIONS
Institute for the Development of Indian Law, $3.50.

**LANDSCAPE OF THE SPIRITS: HOHOKAM
ROCK ART AT SOUTH MOUNTAIN PARK**
Todd W. Bostwick; photos by Peter Krocek
Illus. 252 pp. University of Arizona Press, 2002.
$60; paper, $27.95.

LANGUAGE & ART IN THE NAVAJO UNIVERSE
Gary Witherspoon
Illus. 234 pp. University of Michigan Press, 1977.
$24.95; paper, $15.95.

**LANGUAGE, CULTURE & HISTORY:
ESSAYS BY MARY R. HAAS**
Mary R. Haas; Anwar S. Dil, Editor
398 pp. Stanford University Press, 1978. $32.50.

**LANGUAGE, HISTORY, & IDENTITY:
ETHNOLINGUISTIC STUDIES OF THE ARIZONA TEWA**
Paul V. Kroskrity
289 pp. University of Arizona Press, 1993. $56.

**LANGUAGE OF THE ROBE:
AMERICAN INDIAN TRADE BLANKETS**
Robert W. Kapoun with Charles Lohrmann
Resource for trade blanket owners and collectors.
Color photos. 200 pp. Written Heritage, $26.95.

THE LANGUAGE OF THE SALINAN INDIANS
J. Alden Mason
Reprint of 1918 edition. 154 pp. Paper. Coyote Press, $16.88.

**LANGUAGE RENEWAL AMONG
AMERICAN INDIAN TRIBES**
Robert N. St. Clair and William L. Leap
176 pp. Paper. National Clearinghouse Bilingual
Education, 1982. $8.95.

LANGUAGE SAMPLER SERIES
Western Cherokee Language; Eastern Cherokee Language;
Choctaw Language; Chickasaw Language. 12 pp. Paper. VIP
Publishing. $5 each.

**LANGUAGES OF THE ABORIGINAL SOUTHEAST:
AN ANNOTATED BIBLIOGRAPHY**
Karen M. Booker
265 pp. Scarecrow Pres, 1991. $37.50.

**A LANGUAGE OF OUR OWN: THE GENESIS OF MICHIF,
THE MIXED CREE-FRENCH LANGUAGE OF THE
CANADIAN METIS**
Peter Bakker
Illus. 336 pp. Oxford University Press, 1997. $80.

**LANGUAGE SHIFT AMONG THE NAVAJOS:
IDENTITY POLITICS & CULTURAL CONTINUITY**
Deborah House
121 pp. University of Arizona Press, 2002. $35.

**THE LANGUAGES OF THE COAST OF CALIFORNIA
NORTH OF SAN FRANCISCO**
A.L. Kroeber
Reprint of 1911. 164 pp. Paper. Coyote Press, $11.56.

**THE LANGUAGES OF THE COAST OF CALIFORNIA
SOUTH OF SAN FRANCISCO**
A.L. Kroeber
Reprint of 1911. 103 pp. Paper. Coyote Press, $11.56.

**LANGUAGES OF NATIVE AMERICA:
HISTORICAL & COMPARATIVE ASSESSMENT**
Lyle Campbell and Marianne Mithun, Editors
1,040 pp. University of Texas Press, 1979. $35.

**THE LAST CONTRARY: THE STORY OF
WESLEY WHITEMAN (BLACK BEAR)**
Warren Schwartz
Illus. 146 pp. Center for Western Studies, 1990. $12.95.

**LAST CRY: NATIVE AMERICAN PROPHECIES;
TALE OF THE END TIMES**
Robert Ghostwolf
319 pp. Paper. Wolf Lodge, 1997. $21.95.

LAST DAYS OF THE SIOUX NATION
Robert M. Utley
Historical study of the reaction of the Sioux to the reservation
system in the mid 1800s. Illus. Maps. Biblio. 314 pp. Paper.
Center for Western Studies & Yale University Press, 1963. $15.

**THE LAST LIGHT BREAKING:
LIVING AMONG ALASKA'S INUPIAT ESKIMOS**
Nick Jans
Map. 224 pp. Graphic Arts Center, 1994. $21.95.

**THE LAST OF THE INDIAN WARS, THE SPANISH
AMERICAN WAR, THE BRINK OF THE GREAT WAR,
1881-1916**
Randy Steffen
Illus. 268 pp. Paper. University of Oklahoma Press,
1978. $39.95.

*THE LAST OF THE MOHICANS
James Fenimore Cooper; illus. by N.C. Wyeth
Grades 5 and up. Illus. 400 pp. Paper.
Center for Western Studies, $5.95.

**LAST RAMBLES AMONGST THE INDIANS
OF THE ROCKY MOUNTAINS & THE ANDES**
George Catlin
Reprint of 1867 edition. Reprint Services, $79.

THE LAST SHALL BE FIRST
Murray Angus
96 pp. Paper. University of Toronto Press, 1991. $9.95.

*THE LAST WARRIOR
Suzanne Pierson Ellison
Story of a young warrior apprentice to Geronimo.
Ages 12 and up. 240 pp. Northland, $12.95; paper, $6.95.

**THE LAST WARRIOR: PETER MACDONALD
& THE NAVAJO NATION**
Peter MacDonald
Crown Publishing, 1993. $25.

THE LAST YEARS OF SITTING BULL
Herbert Hoover
Paper. VIP Publishing. $4.95.

**THE LASTINGS OF THE MOHEGANS:
THE STORY OF THE WOLF PEOPLE**
Melissa J. Fawcett
2nd Edition. Illus. 68 pp. Paper. Little People Publications,
1995. $10.

**LATE WOODLAND SITES IN THE
AMERICAN BOTTOM UPLANDS**
Charles Bentz, et al
Illus. Paper. University of Illinois Press, 1988. $17.50.

**LATE WOODLAND SOCIETIES: TRADITION &
TRANSFORMATION ACROSS THE MIDCONTINENT**
edited by Thomas E. Emerson, Dale L. McElrath
& Andrew C. Fortier
Sites, artifacts, and prehistoric cultural practices of Late Woodland lifestyle across the Midwest. Illus. Maps. 736 pp. University of Nebraska Press, 2000. $60.

LAUGHING BOY
Oliver La Farge
A novel about a young Navajo lover & his mate. Winner of
the 1929 Pulitzer Prize. 192 pp. Paper. Penguin USA, $4.95.

AUGUSTINE LAURE, S.J. MISSIONARY TO THE YAKIMAS
Victor Garrard
56 pp. Paper. Ye Galleon Press, 1977. $9.95.

THE LAUREL CULTURE IN MINNESOTA
James B. Stoltman
Illus. 146 pp. Paper. Minnesota Historical
Society, 1973. $5.50.

**LAW & THE AMERICAN INDIAN:
READINGS, NOTES AND CASES**
Monroe E. Price and Robert Clinton
Second edition. 800 pp. Michie Co., 1983. $28.50.

**LAW ENFORCEMENT ON INDIAN RESERVATIONS
AFTER OLIPHANT V. SUQUAMISH INDIAN TRIBES**
Institute for the Development of Indian Law, $2.

**LAWS & JOINT RESOLUTIONS
OF THE CHEROKEE NATION**
Reprint of 1975 edition. Scholarly Resources, $22.

**LAWS & JOINT RESOLUTIONS OF THE
NATIONAL COUNCIL, PASSED 1870 & 1876**
Reprint of 1975 edition. Scholarly Resources, $12 each.

LAWS OF THE CHEROKEE NATION: PASSED 1845
Reprint of 1975 edition. Scholarly Resources, $12.

LAWS OF THE CHICKASAW NATION
Reprint of 1975 edition. Scholarly Resources, $12.

LAWS OF THE CHOCTAW NATION
Reprint of 1975 edition. Scholarly Resources, $12.

LEAGUE OF THE IROQUOIS
L.H. Morgan
Reprint of 1904 edition. 477 pp. Peter Smith. $15.50.

*LEARN ABOUT TEXAS INDIANS
Georg Zappler; illus. by Elena T. Ivy
Grades 4 and up. Illus. 48 pp. Paper.
University of Texas Press, 1985. $7.95.

**LEASING INDIAN WATER: UPCOMING
CHOICES IN THE COLORADO RIVER BASIN**
Gary Weatherford & Mary Wallace
66 pp. Paper. Conservation Forum, 1988. $10.50.

**LEAVING EVERYTHING BEHIND: THE SONGS
& MEMORIES OF A CHEYENNE WOMAN**
Bertha Little Coyote & Virginia Giglio
Illus. 192 pp. University of Oklahoma Press, 1997.
$29.95; compact disc, $12.95; book and CD, $40.

LEFT BY THE INDIANS
E. Fuller & C. Schlicke
Reprint. 61 pp. Ye Galleon Press, $14.95; paper, $9.95.

**LEFT HANDED, SON OF OLD MAN HAT:
A NAVAHO AUTOBIOGRAPHY**
By Left Handed; recorded by Walter Dyk
Anthropological study. 378 pp. Paper.
University of Nebraska Press, 1967. $16.95.

**THE LEGACY OF ANDREW JACKSON: ESSAYS
ON DEMOCRACY, INDIAN REMOVAL & SLAVERY**
Robert Remini
120 pp. Paper. Louisiana State University Press, 1990. $6.95.

THE LEGACY OF MARIA POVEKA MARTINEZ
Richard L. Spivey; photos by Herbert Lotz
Illus. 198 four-color photos. 208 pp. Museum of
New Mexico Press, 2001. $60.

**LEGACY OF A MASTER POTTER:
NAMPEYO & HER DESCENDANTS**
Mary Ellen Blair & Laurence Blair
Illus. Paper. Treasury Chest Books, 1999.

**THE LEGACY OF SHINGWAUKONSE:
A CENTURY OF NATIVE LEADERSHIP**
Janet E. Chute
Examines the careers of the Ojibwa chief Shingwaukonse and
of two of his sons. Illus. 359 pp. University of Toronto Press,
1998. $60; paper, $24.95.

**THE LEGACY: TRADITION & INNOVATION
IN NORTHWEST COAST INDIAN ART**
Peter Macnair, Alan Hoover & Kevin Neary
Illus. 194 pp. Paper. University of Washington Press, $26.95.

LEGAL INFORMATION SERVICE
32 vols. on Canadian Indian legal affairs. See
University of Saskatchewan for titles and prices.

LEGAL ISSUES IN INDIAN JURISDICTION
63 pp. National Attorney's General, 1976. $3.50.

LEGAL PROCESS & THE RESOLUTION OF INDIAN CLAIMS
Eric Golvin
Studies in Canadian aboriginal rights. 29 pp.
University of Saskatchewan, 1981. $6.50.

*A LEGEND FROM CRAZY HORSE CLAN
Big Crow & Moses Nelson; Renee S. Flood, Editor
Grades 3 and up. Illus. 36 pp. Paper. Tipi Press &
Center for Western Studies, 1987. $4.95.

*THE LEGEND OF THE BLUEBONNET, retold
Tomie dePaola
An old tale of Texas..a courageous little Comanche girl sacri-
fices her most beloved possession, Grades PS-3. Illus. 32 pp.
Putnam, 1983. $14.95; paper, $5.95.

*THE LEGEND OF THE INDIAN PAINTBRUSH, retold
Tomie dePaola
An Indian brave dreams of creating a painting that will capture
the beauty of a sunset. Grades PS-3. Illus. 40 pp. Putnam,
1988. $14.95.

*LEGEND OF THE LITTLE DEER
Wade Blevins
Grades 2 and up. Illus. 49 pp. Ozark Publishing, 1993. $12.95.

THE LEGEND OF NATURAL TUNNEL
Clara Talton Fugate; illus. by Caren Ertmann
A tale of love and war and Indian customs, set in the southern
Appalachians before white settlement. Illus. 40 pp. 16 draw-
ings, 3 maps. Paper. Pocahontas Press, 1986. $5.95.

*THE LEGEND OF TOM PEPPER & OTHER STORIES
Arthur Griffin
Grades 2-5. Illus. 100 pp. Bainbridge Press, 1990.

LEGENDS IN STONE, BONE & WOOD
Tsonakwa
Abenaki legends, history, and photographed works of art.
The Greenfield Review Press, $10.95.

*LEGENDS OF CHIEF BALD EAGLE
Harry B. Shows and Hap Gilliland
Grades 2-10. Paper. Council for Indian Education, 1977. $2.95.

LEGENDS OF THE COWLITZ INDIAN
Roy I. Wilson
400 pp. Demco, 1998. CSS Publishing, 1998.

LEGENDS OF THE DELAWARE INDIANS
& PICTURE WRITING
Richard C. Adams; edited by Deborah Nichols
Illus. 128 pp. Syracuse University Press, 1998. $25.95.

*LEGENDS OF THE GREAT CHIEFS
Emerson N. Matson
Authentic legends and little-known incidents recalled during
first-hand interviews with actual descendants of some of the
most famous chiefs. Grades 8-12. Illus. 144 pp. Paper.
Storypole, 1972. $5.95.

LEGENDS OF THE IROQUOIS
Tehanetorens
Stories presented in pictograph form with English
translation. 112 pp. Paper. Clear Light, $9.95.

LEGENDS OF THE IROQUOIS
William W. Canfield
Yestermorrow Press, 1998. $26.95.

LEGENDS OF THE LAKOTA
James LaPointe; illus. by Louis Amiotte
Illus. 184 pp. The Indian Historian Press, 1975. $11; paper, $6.

LEGENDS OF THE LONGHOUSE
Jesse Cornplanter
Iroquois tales told by Jesse Corplanter. Illus.
Greenfield Review Press, $10.

LEGENDS OF THE MIGHTY SIOUX
Montana Lisle Reese, Editor
45 traditional legends of the Sioux written by elders on the
Rosebud & Yankton reservations. Reprint of 1941 edition. Center for Western Studies, $14.95; paper, $6.95. Paper. VIP Publishing. $6.95.

LEGENDS OF OUR NATIONS
Collection of traditional Native tales from across
Canada & U.S. Paper. Greenfield Review Press, $6.

LEGENDS OF OUR TIMES: NATIVE COWBOY LIFE
Morgan Baillargeon & Leslie Tepper
UBC Press, 1998. $45.

LEGENDS OF THE YOSEMITE MIWOK
Frank LaPena, Craig D. Bates & Steven P. Medley, Editors
Revised edition. Illus. 64 pp. Paper. Yosemite Association,
1993. $10.95.

LEGENDS TOLD BY THE OLD PEOPLE
Adolph Hungry Wolf
Illus. 80 pp. Paper. Cherokee Publications
& The Book Publishing Co., 1990. $5.95.

THE LEMHI: SACAJAWEA'S PEOPLE
Brigham Madsen
Illus. Maps. Biblio. 214 pp. Paper. The Caxton Printers,
1980. $7.95.

THE LENAPE
Herbert Kraft
Illus. 300 pp. New Jersey Historical Society, 1987. $24.95.

*THE LENAPE: MIDDLE ATLANTIC
Robert Grumet
Grades 5 and up. Illus. Chelsea House, 1989. $17.95.

LENAPE HISTORY & NUMBERS POSTERS
The Middle Atlantic Press, $5 each.

LENAPE INDIAN TEACHING KIT 2:
LENAPE LORE/FOLK MEDICINES
Karen Waldauer
Includes teacher's guide, charts, quizzes. Illus. Middle Atlantic
Press, $24.95.

LESCHI, LAST OF THE NISQUALLIES
Cecilia Carpenter
Illus. 56 pp. Paper. Heritage Quest, 1986. $5.

LESSONS FROM CHOUTEAU CREEK:
YANKTON MEMORIES OF DAKOTA INTRIGUE
Renee Sansom-Flood
Reprint. Illus. Paper. Center for Western Studies, $10.95.

LESSONS IN HOPI
Milo Kalectaca; Ronald W. Langacker, Editor
30 grammar lessons, ten exemplary dialogs, and
Hopi—English, English—Hopi lexicons. 234 pp.
Paper. University of Arizona Press, 1978. $11.95.

LET ME BE FREE: THE NEZ PERCE TRAGEDY
David Lavender
Illus. Maps/ 432 pp. Paper. University of Oklahoma Press,
1999. $17.95.

*LET ME TELL YOU A STORY
Yerington Paiute Tribe
Grades 2-8. Illus. 95 pp. Paper. Yerington Paiute Tribe
Publications, $8. Companion Activity Workbook, 105 pp.
$10.

LET MY PEOPLE KNOW: AMERICAN INDIAN
JOURNALISM, 1828-1978
James E. and Sharon M. Murphy
300 pp. The Indian Historian Press, 1979. $19.95.

*LET'S REMEMBER...INDIANS OF TEXAS
Betsy Warren
Grades 3-8. Illus. 32 pp. Paper. Hendrick-Long, $4.50.

LET'S TALK CHEYENNE: AN AUDIO CASSETTE
TAPE COURSE OF INSTRUCTION IN THE CHEYENNE
LANGUAGE
Ted Risingsun & Wayne Leman
57 pp. Paper. Wolf Moon, 1999. $15.95 includes audio.

LETTER FROM THE SECRETARY OF THE INTERIOR -
INFORMATION IN RELATION TO THE EARLY LABORS
OF THE MISSIONARIES
90 pp. Paper. Ye Galleon Press, 1988. $7.50.

LETTERS FROM WUPATKI
Courtney Reeder Jones; edited by Lisa Rappoport
Story of National Park Service caretakers in 1938 and their
Navajo neighbors. 184 pp. Paper. University of Arizona Press,
1995. $15.95.

LETTERS FROM THE ROCKY MOUNTAIN
INDIAN MISSIONS
Father Philip Rappagliosi; edited by Robert Bigart
Letters from a Jesuit (1841-78) about daily lives, customs, and
beliefs of Nez Perces, Kootenais, Salish Flatheads, Coeur
d'Alenes, Pend d'Oreilles, Blackfeet, and Canadian Metis. Illus.
Map. 200 pp. University of Nebraska Press, 2003. $49.95.

LETTERS OF THE LEWIS & CLARK EXPEDITION,
WITH RELATED DOCUMENTS, 1783-1854
Donald Jackson, Editor
2nd Ed. 2 vols. 832 pp. University of Illinois Press, 1978.
$49.95.

LETTERS & NOTES ON THE MANNERS, CUSTOMS
& CONDITIONS OF THE NORTH AMERICAN INDIANS
George Catlin
Reprint of 1841 edition. Two vols. 300 paintings. 572 pp.
Paper. Hothem House & Written Heritage, $19.90;
Dover, $15.95.

LETTERS TO HOWARD: AN INTERPRETATION
OF THE ALASKA NATIVE LANDS CLAIM
Fred Bigjim
Collection of 24 letters on critical issues of the Alaska
Native Land Claims. Greenfield Review Press, $12.

LEWIS & CLARK AMONG THE INDIANS
James P. Ronda
Bicentennial edition. Illus. Maps. 310 pp. Paper.
University of Nebraska Press, 2002. $17.95.

THE LEWIS & CLARK EXPEDITION
Patrick McGrath
Grades 5 and up. Illus. 64 pp. Silver Burdette, 1985.
$14.96; paper, $7.95.

LEWIS & CLARK TERRITORY: CONTEMPORARY
ARTISTS REVISIT PLACE, RACE, & MEMORY
Rock Hushka & Thomas Owl Haukaas
Reevaluates the expedition and its impact on American cul-
ture. Includes contemporary works in traditional & innovative
Native Americn techniques, such as carving, beadwork, and
basketry. Illus. 80 pp. Paper. University of Washington Press,
2004. $21.95.

LEWIS & CLARK'S WEST: WILLIAM CLARK'S 1810
MASTER MAP OF THE AMERICAN WEST
William Clark
Collector's edition. Illus. Maps. University Press of
New England, 2004. $50, map only, $14.95.

*MERIWEATHER LEWIS & WILLIAM CLARK:
SOLDIERS, EXPLORERS, & PARTNERS IN HISTORY
David Petersen & Mark Coburn
Grades 4 and up. Illus. 152 pp. Childrens Press, 1988.
$15.95.

LEWIS & CLARK: VOYAGE OF DISCOVERY
Dan Murphy
Illus. 64 pp. Paper. KC Publications , 1977. $4.50.

LEXICAL ACCULTURATION IN
NATIVE AMERICAN LANGUAGES
Cecil H. Brown
272 pp. Oxford University Press, 1999. $55.

LICENSE FOR EMPIRE: COLONIALISM
BY TREATY IN EARLY AMERICA
Dorothy V. Jones
University of Chicago Press, 1982. $25.

LIES MY TEACH TOLD ME: EVERYTHING YOUR
AMERICAN HISTORY TEXTBOOK GOT WRONG
James W. Loewen
Illus. 384 pp. W.W./ Norton, 1995. $24.95. Paper.
Simon & Schuster, $14.95.

LIFE & ADVENTURES OF JAMES P. BECKWOURTH,
MOUNTAINEER, SCOUT & PIONEER, & CHIEF OF
THE CROW NATION OF INDIANS
J. Beckwourth; T.D. Bonner, Editor
Reprint of 1856 edition. 650 pp. Ayer Co., $36.95.
Paper. University of Nebraska Press, $10.95.

LIFE AMONG THE APACHES
John C. Cremony
322 pp. Paper. University of Nebraska Press, 1983. $8.50.

LIFE AMONG THE INDIANS: OR, PERSONAL
REMINISCENCES & HISTORICAL INCIDENTS
ILLUSTRATIVE OF INDIAN LIFE & CHARACTER
James Finley; D.W. Clark, Editor
Facsimile of the 1857 edition. Ayer Co., $31.

LIFE AMONG THE MODOCS: UNWRITTEN HISTORY
Joaquin Miller
Reprint of 1873 edition. 446 pp. Paper.
Urion Press & Heyday Books. $15.95.

LIFE AMONG THE PAIUTES: THEIR WRONGS & CLAIMS
Sarah Winnemucca Hopkins
Reprint of 1883 edition. Autobiography which deals with her
life as a Paiute princess and the plight of the Paiutes. 272 pp.
Paper. University of Nevada Press. $13.95.

LIFE AMONG THE TEXAS INDIANS: THE WPA NARRATIVES
David La Vere
Detail about the life among the Kiowas, Comanches, Wichitas,
Caddos, Tonkawas, and Lipan Apaches who lived in Texas
around 1830. Photos. 288 pp. Texas A&M University Press,
1999. $29.95.

LIFE & ART OF THE NORTH AMERICAN INDIAN
John Warner
Book Sales, 1990. $15.98.

LIFE & DEATH IN MOHAWK COUNTRY
Bruce E. Johansen; illus. by John Kahionhes Fadden
Disputed land claims along the U.S. & Canadian border.
Illus. 202 pp. North American Press, 1992. $23.95.

THE LIFE I'VE BEEN LIVING
Moses Cruikshank
Biography of Moses Cruikshank, an Athabaskan elder and
skilled storyteller from Interior Alaska. Reprint of 1986 edition.
Illus. 132 pp. Paper. University of Alaska Press, $9.95.

LIFE IN CUSTER'S CAVALRY: DIARIES & LETTERS
OF ALBERT & JENNIE BARNITZ, 1867-1868
Albert & Jennie Barnitz; Robert Utley, Editor
Illus. 302 pp. Paper. University of Nebraska Press, 1987.
$7.95.

LIFE IN THE PUEBLOS
Ruth Underhill; edited by Willard Beatty
Interprets Pueblo lifestyles for the general public. Illus.
Maps. 168 pp. Paper. Ancient City Press, $15.95.

LIFE, LETTERS & SPEECHES
George Copway
The biography of a Canadian Ojibwe writer and lecturer.
Map. 255 pp. University of Nebraska Pres, 1997. $40.

LIFE, LETTERS & TRAVELS OF FATHER
PIERRE JEAN DE SMET, S.J., 1801-1873
Pierre Jean de Smet
Missionary Labors & Adventures Among the Wild Tribes of the
North American Indians. Reprint of the 1905 edition. 4 vols.
Ayer Co., $96.95.

THE LIFE & TIMES OF DAVID ZEISBERGER:
THE WESTERN PIONEER & APOSTLE OF THE INDIANS
Edmund De Schweinitz
Reprint of 1870 edition. Ayer Co., $39.

**LIFE LIVED LIKE A STORY: LIFE STORIES
OF THREE YUKON NATIVE ELDERS**
Julie Cruikshank
Illus. Maps. 404 pp. Paper. University of Nebraska Press,
1991. $39.95.

LIFE OF GEORGE BENT: WRITTEN FROM HIS LETTERS
George E. Hyde; Savoie Lottinville, Editor
Reprint of 1968 edition. Illus. Maps. 390 pp. Paper.
University of Oklahoma Press, $19.95.

LIFE OF BLACK HAWK
Black Hawk
128 pp. Dover, $6.95.

THE LIFE OF BLACKHAWK, DICTATED BY HIMSELF
J.B. Patterson
Enlarged facsimile of the 1834 edition. 156 pp.
Ye Galleon Press, $15.95; paper, $9.95.

**THE LIFE OF HAROLD SELLERS COLTON:
A PHILADELPHIA BRAHMIN IN FLAGSTAFF**
Jimmy Herbert Miller
Paper. Dine College Press, 1991. $15.95.

**LIFE OF TECUMSEH & HIS BROTHER THE PROPHET:
WITH AN HISTORICAL SKETCH OF THE SHAWANOE
INDIANS**
B. Drake
Reprint of 1841 edition. Ayer Co., $21.95.

**LIFE OF TOM HORN, GOVERNMENT SCOUT &
INTERPRETER, WRITTEN BY HIMSELF, TOGETHER
WITH HIS LETTERS & STATEMENTS BY HIS FRIENDS:
A VINDICATION**
Tom Horn
272 pp. Paper. University of Oklahoma Press, 1964.
$12.95.

**THE LIFE & TIMES OF LITTLE TURTLE:
FIRST SAGAMORE OF THE WABASH**
Harvey L. Carter
Illus. 296 pp. University of Illinois Press, 1987. $24.95.

**LIFE & TIMES OF DAVID ZEISBERGER:
WESTERN PIONEER & APOSTLE OF THE INDIANS**
Edmund De Schweinitz
Reprint of 1870 edition. Ayer Co., $39.

LIFE UNDER THE SUN
Charles Lovato
Lithograph art. Illus. Sunstone Press, $35;
signed & numbered hard cover edition, $125.

LIFE WITH THE ESKIMO
Illus. 16 pp. Paper. Hancock House, $2.95.

LIFE WOVEN WITH SONG
Nora Marks Dauenhauer
Prose, poetry and plays from a woman from Alaska. 139 pp.
University of Arizona Press, 2000. $32; paper, $17.95.

LIGHT ON THE LAND
Art Davidson; photos by Art Wolfe
Landscape photography with essays and Native writings from
around the world. Illus. 100 color photos. 196 pp. Beyond Words
Publishing, 1994. $75.

THE LIGHT PEOPLE: A NOVEL
Gordon Henry, Jr.
A young Chippewa boy is trying to learn the whereabouts of
his parents. 226 pp. Paper. University of Oklahoma Press, 1994.
$13.95.

**LIGHTING THE SEVENTH FIRE: THE SPIRITUAL WAYS,
HEALING, & SCIENCE OF THE NATIVE AMERICAN**
F. David Peat
322 pp. Birch Lane Press, 1994. $19.95.

***LIGHTNING INSIDE YOU: & OTHER
NATIVE AMERICAN RIDDLES**
John Bierhorst, Editor
Grades 2 and up.William Morrow, 1992. $14.

**THE LIGHTNING STICK: ARROWS,
WOUNDS, AND INDIAN LEGEND**
H. Henrietta Stockel
History of the bow and arrow; brings together a broad range of
significant people and events, spiritual usages, medicinal treat-
ments. Illus. 176 pp. University of Nevada Press, 1995. $24.95.

THE LIGHTNING WITHIN
Alan R. Velie, Editor
An Anthology of Contemporary American Indian fiction: N. Scott
Momaday, James Welch, Louise Erdich, and Michael Doris.
170 pp. University of Nebraksa Press, 1991. $22; paper, $9.95.

**LIKE BEADS ON A STRING: A CULTURE HISTORY OF
THE SEMINOLE INDIANS IN NORTH PENINSULA FLORIDA**
Brent Weisman
Illus. 216 pp. Paper. University of Alabama Press, 1989.
$15.95.

**LIKE A BROTHER: GRENVILLE GOODWIN'S
APACHE YEARS, 1928-1939**
Neil Goodwin
Unpublished field notes, diaries, and letters. Illus. 280 pp.
Paper. University of Arizona Press, 2004. $19.95.

**LIKE A HURRICANE: THE INDIAN MOVEMENT
FROM ALCATRAZ TO WOUNDED KNEE**
Paul C. Smith & Robert A. Warrior
An account of a defining period of Native American radical
protest. 400 pp. W.W. Norton & Co., $25; paper, $14.95.

**THE LILLOOET LANGUAGE:
PHONOLOGY, MORPHOLOGY, SYNTAX**
Jan VanEijk
279 pp. University of Washington Press, 1997. $75.

LINCOLN & THE INDIANS: CIVIL WAR POLICY & POLITICS
David A. Nichols
256 pp. University of Missouri Press, 1978. $26.

**LINKING ARMS TOGETHER: AMERICAN INDIAN
TREATY VISIONS OF LAW & PEACE, 1600-1800**
Robert A. Williams, Jr.
Illus. 208 pp. Oxford University Press, 1997. $32.

*LINDA'S INDIAN HOME
Grades 3-7. Illus. Binford & Mort, 1969. $6.95.

THE LIPAN APACHES IN TEXAS
Thomas F. Schilz
Illus. 58 pp. Texas Western, 1987. $10; paper, $5.

***LISTEN & READ FAVORITE NORTH
AMERICAN INDIAN LEGENDS**
Philip Smith, Editor
Grades 5 and up. Illus. 96 pp. Dover, 1997.
$5.95 includes audiotape.

**LISTEN TO THE DRUM: BLACKWOLF SHARES HIS
MEDICINE**
Gina & Blackwolf Jones
Illus. 224 pp. Paper. Commune-A-Key, 1995. $12.95.

**LISTENING TO OUR GRANDMOTHER'S STORIES:
THE BLOOMFIELD ACADEMY FOR CHICKASAW
FEMALES, 1852-1949**
Amanda J. Cobb
Tells the story of the school and its students. American Book
Award from the Before Columbus Foundation. Illus. Maps. 192
pp. University of Nebraska Press, 2000. $40. 2001

**LITERATURE BY & ABOUT THE AMERICAN INDIAN:
AN ANNOTATED BIBLIOGRAPHY**
Anna L. Stensland, Compiler
Describes more than 775 books on Native American experi-
ences, new and old. Second edition. 382 pp. Paper. National
Council of Teachers of English, 1979. $10.95.

**THE LITERATURE OF CALIFORNIA, VOL. 1:
NATIVE AMERICAN BEGINNINGS TO 1945**
edited by Jack Hicks, James Houston,
Maxine Hong Kingston & Al Young
Ranges from Native American origin myth to Hollywood novels
dissecting the American dream. Illus. Map. 653 pp. University
of California Press, 2000. $60; paper, $24.95.

**LITTLE BIG HORN DIARY:
CHRONICLE OF THE 1876 INDIAN WAR**
James Willert
Second Edition. Illus. 520 pp. J. Willert, 1982. $60.

**LITTLE BIG HORN REMEMBERED, THE UNTOLD
INDIAN STORY OF CUSTER'S LAST STAND**
Herman J. Viola
Smithsonian Institution Press, 1999.

LITTLE BIG MAN
Thomas Berger
480 pp. Amereon, $30.95; Paper. Dell, $13.95.

**LITTLE BIT KNOW SOMETHING:
STORIES IN A LANGUAGE OF ANTHROPOLOGY**
Robin Ridington
Illus. 300 pp. University of Iowa Press, 1990.
$28.50; paper, $10.95.

**A LITTLE BIT OF WISDOM:
CONVERSATIONS WITH A NEZ PERCE ELDER**
Horace Axtell & Margo Aragon
Confluence Press, 1997. $25.

***LITTLE BOY WITH THREE NAMES:
STORIES OF TAOS PUEBLO**
Ann Nolan Clark
Reprint. Grades 3 and up. Illus. 80 pp. Paper.
Ancient City Press, $8.95.

LITTLE CROW, SPOKESMAN FOR THE SIOUX
Gary Anderson
Illus. Photos. Maps. 259 pp. Paper. Minnesota Historical
Society Press, 1986. $10.95.

*LITTLE FIREFLY: AN ALGONQUIAN LEGEND
Terri Cohlene
Grades 4-7. Illus. 48 pp. Paper. Troll Communications, $4.95.

*LITTLE HERDER IN AUTUMN
Ann Nolan Clark
Reprint. Grades 3 and up. Illus. 96 pp. Paper.
Ancient City Press, $9.95.

***LITTLE (SOUTHWEST/PLAINS/SOUTHEAST)
INDIAN GIRLS PAPERDOLL**
Kathy Allert
Outfits represent Navajo, Pueblos, and Apache tribes.
Grades 3 and up. 16 pp. Paper. Dover, $1.

A LITTLE WAR OF DESTINY
John C. Jackson
Reprint. Manuscript om the Yakima Indian War of 1855-56 and
the Cayuse Indian War soon after. 202 pp. Ye Galleon, $24.95;
paper, $14.95.

***LITTLE WATER & THE GIFT OF THE ANIMALS:
A SENECA LEGEND**
C.J. Taylor
Grades 5 and up. Illus. 24 pp. Paper. Tundra Books, 1997.
$6.95.

THE LITTLE WATER MEDICINE SOCIETY OF THE SENECAS
William N. Fenton
Ceremonies of the medicine society of the Iroquois Indians of
western New York. Illus. 256 pp. University of Oklahoma Press,
2003. $39.95.

**LIVING IN BALANCE: THE UNIVERSE
OF THE HOPI, ZUNI, NAVAJO & APACHE**
Dorothy K. Washburn
Illus. 92 pp. Paper. University of Pennsylvania Museum Publi-
cations, 1995. $12.95.

**LIVING LIFE'S CIRCLE:
MESCALERO APACHE COSMOVISION**
Claire R. Farrer
Illus. Paper. University of New Mexico Press, $18.95.

**LIVING LIKE INDIANS: A TREASURY OF NORTH
AMERICAN INDIAN CRAFTS, GAMES & ACTIVITIES**
Allan A. Macfarlan
Illus. 320 pp. Paper. Dover, 1999. $8.95.

**LIVING THE SKY: THE COSMOS
OF THE AMERICAN INDIAN**
Ray A. Williamson
Illus. Maps. 382 pp. Paper. University of Oklahoma Press, 1987.
$24.95.

**LIVING THE SPIRIT: A GAY AMERICAN INDIAN
ANTHOLOGY**
Will Roscoe, Editor
Illus. 240 pp. St. Martin Press, 1988. $16.95.

THE LIVING TRADITION OF MARIA MARTINEZ
Susan Peterson
Revised edition. Illus. 300 pp. Kodansha, 1989.
$70; paper, $34.95.

LIVING WISDOM: NATIVE NORTH AMERICA
Larry Zimmerman
Illus. 184 pp. Paper. Little, Brown & Co., 1997. $15.95.

*LIVING WITH THE ESKIMOS
Grades K-5. Illus. 40 pp. Childrens Press, $11.45.

THE LIVINGSTON INDIAN RECORDS, 1666-1723
Lawrence H. Leder, Editor
Reprint of 1956 edition. 240 pp. E.M. Coleman, $25.

LOGS OF THE CONQUEST OF CANADA
W. Wood, Editor
Reprint of 1909 edition. Greenwood, $29.

**LONE WOLF V. HITCHCOCK: TREATY RIGHTS &
INDIAN LAW AT THE END OF THE 19TH CENTURY**
Blue Clark
Places the Kiowas at center stage in the drama, as prime
movers in determining their own fate. Illus. 198 pp. Paper.
University of Nebraska Press, 1995. $18.95.

**LONG BEFORE COLUMBUS: HOW THE
ANCIENTS DISCOVERED AMERICA**
Hans Holzer
Illus. 160 pp. Paper. Bear & Co., $12.95.

**THE LONG BITTER TRAIL:
ANDREW JACKSON & THE INDIANS**
Anthony F. Wallace
144 pp. Paper. Hill & Wang, 1993. $7.95.

**THE LONG DEATH: THE LAST DAYS
OF THE PLAINS INDIANS**
Ralph K. Andrist
The subjugation of the Plains Indians. Illus. 392 pp.
Paper. University of Oklahoma Press, 2001. $19.95.

LONG JOURNEY TO THE COUNTRY OF THE HURONS
G. Sagard-Theodat; George M. Wrong, Editor
Reprint of 1939 edition. Greenwood, $29.25.

LONG LANCE
Chief Buffalo Child Long Lance (Sylvester Long)
A fictional account of the Blackfoot Indians' last days of freedom. 320 pp. University Press of Mississippi, 1995. $45; paper, $16.95.

LONG LANCE: THE TRUE STORY OF AN IMPOSTER
Donald B. Smith
Illus. 325 pp. Paper. University of Nebraska Press, 1983. $8.95.

LONG RIVER
Joseph Bruchac
Novel. Sequel to "Dawn Land." 312 pp. Fulcrum Publishing, 1996. $19.95.

*THE LONG SEARCH
Richard A. Boning
Grades 5-11. Illus. 48 pp. B. Loft, 1972. $7.95.

*LONG SHADOWS: INDIAN LEADERS STANDING IN THE PATH OF MANIFEST DESTINY 1600-1900
Jack Jackson
Grades 6 and up. Illus. 128 pp. Paramount, 1985. $17.95.

A LONG & TERRIBLE SHADOW: WHITE VALUES & NATIVE RIGHTS IN THE AMERICAS, 1492-1992
Thomas R. Berger
Surveys and examines the history of the Americas since their discovery by Europeans. Illus. 196 pp. Paper. University of Washington Press, 1993. $17.95.

THE LONG WALK: HISTORY OF THE NAVAJO WARS, 1846-1868
Lynn R. Bailey
Illus. 300 pp. Westernlore, $10.95.

A LONG WAY FROM HOME: THE TUBERCULOSIS EPIDEMIC AMONG THE INUIT
Pat S. Grygier
Illus. 272 pp. Paper. CUP Services, 1997. $19.95.

LOOK TO THE MOUNTAIN: AN ECOLOGY OF INDIGENOUS EDUCATION
Gregory Cajete, PhD
Studies indigenous educational philosophy by a Native American scholar. Looks to Indian education for tomorrow and into the 21st century. Illus. Biblio. 248 pp. Paper. Kivaki Press, 1994. $16.95.

LOOKING AT INDIAN ART OF THE NORTHWEST COAST
Hilary Stewart
Illus. 112 pp. Paper. University of Washington Press, 1979. $14.95.

LOOKING AT THE LAND OF PROMISE: PIONEER IMAGES OF THE PACIFIC NORTHWEST
William H. Goetzmann
Contains the work of many important early artists who painted and drew scenes in the Pacific Northwest. Some of the artists recorded th customs of the American Indians. Illus. Biblio. 122 pp. Washington State University Press, 1988. $35; paper, $20.

LOOKING AT TOTEM POLES
Hilary Stewart
Guide to totem poles in outdoor locations accessible to tourists and interested viewers; with legends most often associated with the poles. Illus. 100 drawings, 30 photos. 192 pp. Paper. University of Washington Press, $14.95.

LOOKING AT THE WORDS OF OUR PEOPLE
Jeanette Armstrong, Editor
An anthology of First Nation literary criticism. 150 pp. Paper. Theytus, 1993. $12.95.

LOOKING BOTH WAYS: HERITAGE & IDENTITY OF THE ALUTIIQ PEOPLE
edited by Aron L. Cromwell, Amy F. Steffian & Gordon L. Pullar
Illus. Maps. Photos. Glossary. Biblio. 266 pp. University of Alaska Press, 2001. $49.95; paper, $24.95.

LOOKING FOR LOST BIRD: A JEWISH WOMAN'S DISCOVERY OF HER NAVAJO ROOTS
Yvette Melanson & Claire Safran
240 pp. Avon, 1999. $22.

LOOKING HIGH AND LOW: ART & CULTURAL IDENTITY
Brenda Jo Bright & Liza Bakewell, Editors
Essays on Native American art & culture. 208 pp. University of Arizona Press, 1995. $43; paper, $18.95.

LOON LEGENDS
Corrine A. Dwyer
Illus. North Star Press, $9.95.

LOON: MEMORY, MEANING, & REALITY IN A NORTHERN DENE COMMUNITY
Henry S. Sharp
Aspects of Chipewyan life in the Northwest Territories of Canada. 216 pp. University of Nebraska Press, 2001. $55.

LORD OF THE ANIMALS: A MIWOK INDIAN CREATION MYTH
Fiona French
Grades K-3. Illus. 32 pp. Millbrook Press, 1997. $22.50.

LORE OF THE GREAT TURTLE: INDIAN LEGENDS OF MACKINAC RETOLD
Dirk Gringhuis
Illus. 96 pp. Paper. Mackinac Island State Park, 1970. $3.75.

LOS COMANCHES: THE HORSE PEOPLE, 1751-1845
Stanley Noyes
Paper. University of New Mexico Press, $16.95.

THE LOST BAND: A NOVEL
Don Coldsmith
272 pp. University of Oklahoma Press, 2000. $24.95

LOST BIRD OF WOUNDED KNEE: SPIRIT OF THE LAKOTA
Renee S. Flood
Reprint. Illus. 392 pp. Paper. Da Capo Press, $15.95.

LOST COPPER
Wendy Rose
Poetry. 127 pp. Paper. Malki Museum Press, 1980. $12.

THE LOST FIELD NOTES OF FRANKLIN R. JOHNSTON'S LIFE & WORK AMONG THE AMERICAN INDIANS
Franklin R. Johnston
Reprint. Illus. 200 pp. First Glance, 1997. $22.95.

LOST HARVESTS: PRAIRIE INDIAN RESERVE FARMERS & GOVERNMENT POLICY
Sarah Carter
350 pp. University of Toronto Press, 1990. $34.95.

THE LOST UNIVERSE: PAWNEE LIFE & CULTURE
Gene Weltfish
Illus. 525 pp. University of Nebraska Press, 1977. $35; paper, $10.95.

LOUD HAWK: THE U.S. VERSUS THE AMERICAN INDIAN MOVEMENT
Kenneth S. Stern
Explains what happened to the American Indian Movement (AIM). Documents official government misconduct on the Pine Ridge Reservation in 1975. Originally published in 1994. Illus. 374 pp. Paper. University of Oklahoma Press, 2002. $19.95.

LOUDON'S INDIAN NARRATIVES
Archibald Loudon
Originally published in 1808 & 1811. Two vols. in one. 658 pp. Wennawoods Publishing. $49.95.

*LOUISIANA INDIAN TALES
Elizabeth Butler Moore & ASlice Wilbert Couvillon
Tales for children to learn of Louisiana Indian heritage. Grades 3-8. Illus. 112 pp. Pelican Publishing, $11.95.

*LOVE FLUTE
Paul Goble
Story of a shy young man, incorporating the traditional Native American flute, Plains Indian culture, and the beauty of a legend. Paintings. Grades K-3. Illus 32 pp. Meyer Creative Productions, $15.95.

*LUCY LEARNS TO WEAVE: GATHERING PLANTS
Virginia Hoffman
Grades 1-4. Illus. 46 pp. Paper. Navajo Curriculum Center Press, 1974. $2.75.

LULU LINEAR PUNCTATED: ESSAYS IN HONOR OF GEORGE IRVING QUIMBY
Robert Dunnell & Donald Grayson
Illus. 354 pp. Paper. University of Michigan, Museum of Anthropology, 1983. $12.

*THE LUMBEE
Karen Blu
Grades 5 and up. Illus. Chelsea House, 1989. $17.95.

LUMBEE INDIAN HISTORIES: RACE, ETHNICITY & INDIAN IDENTITY IN THE SOUTHERN U.S.
Gerald M. Sider
336 pp. Paper. Cambridge University Press, 1994. $18.95.

THE LUMBEE PROBLEM: THE MAKING OF AN AMERICAN INDIAN PEOPLE
Karen I. Blu
Illus. 298 pp. Paper. University of Nebraska Press, 2001. $24.95.

*LUMBERMAN
Gail Stewart
Grades 3-8. Illus. 32 pp. Rourke Corp., 1990. $17.26.

LUMINARIES OF THE HUMBLE
Elizabeth Woody
Collection of poems focusing on the land & people of the Pacific Northwest. 128 pp. University of Arizona Press, 1994. $38; paper, $16.95.

CHARLES F. LUMMIS: THE CENTENNIAL EXHIBITION
Daniela P. Moneta, Editor
Illus. 82 pp. Paper. Southwest Museum, 1985. $14.95.

LURE OF THE ARCTIC
Bernice Chappel; Marjorie Klein, tr
Illus. 256 pp. Paper. Wilderness Adventure.

LUSHOOTSEED CULTURE & THE SHAMANIC ODYSSEY: AN ANCHORED RADIANCE
Jay Miller
Overview of the Native people of Puget Sound. Illus. Map. 185 pp. University of Nebraska Press, 1999. $55.

LUSHOOTSEED DICTIONARY
Dawn Bates, Thom Hess & Vi Hilbert
Update of *Thom Hess's Dictionary of Puget Salish* (1976). 406 pp. Paper. University of Washington Press, $30.

LUSHOOTSEED READER WITH INTRODUCTORY GRAMMAR
Thomas M. Hess
4 stories from Edward Sam. Vol. 1. 200 pp. University of Montana , 1995. $20.

M

MAASAW: PROFILE OF A HOPI GOD
E. Malotki & M. Lomatuway'ma
Illus. 275 pp. University of Nebraska Press, 1987. $24.95; paper, $ 14.95.

MAD BEAR: SPIRIT, HEALING, AND THE SACRED IN THE LIFE OF A NATIVE AMERICAN MEDICINE MAN
Doug Boyd
Profiles Mad Bear, a Tuscarora Indian, renowned medicine man, and dynamic Indian-rights activist during the 1960s and 1970s. He died in 1985. 352 pp. Paper. Simon & Schuster, 1994. $12.

MADAM DORIAN
Jerome Peltier
Reprint. The first woman to cross the Plains and settle in Oregon. 44 pp. Ye Galleon Press, $9.95; paper, $6.95.

MADCHILD RUNNING
Keith Egawa
A novel about a young girl caught up in urban violence. The author is a Lummi Indian from Seattle, Wash. 200 pp. Red Crane Books, 1999. $23.95; paper, $14.95.

MADONNA SWAN: A LAKOTA WOMAN'S STORY
as told through Mark St. Pierre
Biography of a Lakota Sioux woman from the Cheyenne River Sioux Reservation. Illus. Maps. 210 pp. Center for Western Studies, $19.95. Paper. University of Oklahoma Press, $11.95.

MAGIC IMAGES: CONTEMPORARY NATIVE AMERICAN ART
Edwin Wade and Rennard Strickland
Illus. 125 pp. Paper. Southwestern Art Association & University of Oklahoma Press, 1982. $16.95.

MAGIC IN THE MOUNTAINS, THE YAKIMA SHAMAN: POWER & PRACTICE
Donald M. Hines
Account of the Yakima shaman observed from 1872 to 1882 plus first-hand accounts from shamans or their patients. Illus. 253 pp. Great Eagle Publishing. $17.95.

*THE MAGIC LAKE: A MYSTICAL HEALING LAKE OF THE CHEROKEE
Tom Underwood
Grades 1-3. Illus. 20 pp. VIP Publishing & Cherokee Publications, 1982. $5.

*THE MAGIC WEAVER OF RUGS
Jerrie Oughton
Grades K-3. Illus. 32 pp. Houghton Mifflin, 1994. $14.95.

THE MAGIC WORLD: AMERICAN INDIAN SONGS & POEMS
William Brandon
Reprint. Ohio University Press, $26.95.

THE MAIDU INDIAN MYTHS & STORIES OF HANC'IBYJIM
William Shipley, editor & translator
192 pp. Paper. Heyday Books, $12.95.

MAIDU MYTHS & TALES
Hanc'ibyjim
Illus. Heyday Books, $12.

THE MAIN STALK: SYNTHESIS OF NAVAJO PHILOSOPHY
John R. Farella
221 pp. Paper. University of Arizona Press, 1984. $18.95.

*MAISONS D'ENCORE: TIPI, WIGWAM ET LONGUE MAISON
Bonnie Shemie
Grades 3-7. Illus. 25 pp. Tundra Books, 1990. $12.95.

MAJOR RICHARDSON'S SHORT STORIES
David Beasley, Editor
Ottawa Indian novelist of the mid-1800s. 134 pp.
Paper. Theytus, 1985. $6.95.

THE MAKAH INDIANS
Elizabeth Colson
Reprint of 1953 edition. Illus. 308 pp. Greenwood, $25.

MAKE PRAYERS TO THE RAVEN
Richard Nelson
Ethnographic study of the Koyukon Athabascan people.
292 pp. Paper. University of Chicago Press, 1983. $15.

**MAKERS & MARKETS: THE WRIGHT COLLECTION
OF TWENTIETH-CENTURY NATIVE AMERICAN ART**
edited by Penelope Ballard Drooker
Paper. University of New Mexico Press, $30.

MAKING ARROWS THE OLD WAY
Doug Wallentine
How to make Native American arrows. Illus. 28 pp. Paper.
Eagle's View Publishing, & Smoke & Fire Co., $4.50.

MAKING THE ATTIKAMEK SNOWSHOE
Henri Vaillancourt
Describes the design, construction, and use of the Attikamek
sh=nowshoe. Illus. Photos. 176 pp. The Trust for Native American Cultures & Crafts, 1995. $34, postpaid.

**MAKING HISTORY: ALUTIIQ/SUGPIAQ LIFE ON THE
ALASKA PENINSULA**
Patricia Partnow
Illus. Photos. Maps. Biblio. University of Alaska Press, 2002.

MAKING INDIAN BOWS & ARROWS...THE OLD WAY
Doug Wallentine
Explores in detail acquiring tools and wood, designing, and
making Native American bows and arrows. Illus. 98 pp. Paper.
Eagle's View Publishing & Smoke & Fire Co., $12.95.

**MAKING IT THEIR OWN: SEVEN OJIBWE
COMMUNICATIVE PRACTICES**
Lisa P. Valentine
Illus. 272 pp. University of Toronto Press, 1995.
$55; paper, $19.95.

MAKING NATIVE AMERICAN POTTERY
Michael Simpson
How indigenous people gathered & processed clay; designs,
finishes, firing pottery, etc. Photos. 80 pp. Paper. Naturegraph,
$9.95.

**MAKING PEACE WITH COCHISE: THE 1872 JOURNAL
OF CAPTAIN JOSEPH ALTON SLADEN**
Edwin R. Sweeney, Editor
Illus. Maps. 208 pp. University of Oklahoma Press,
1997. $24.95.

**MAKING TWO WORLDS ONE & THE STORY
OF ALL-AMERICAN INDIAN DAYS**
Hila Gilbert
Illus. 60 pp. Paper. Connections Press, 1986. $8.

MALAESKA; THE INDIAN WIFE OF THE WHITE HUNTER
Anna S. Stephens
Fiction. A portrait of the early Dutch settlers of New York
and the Indians they encountered. Reprint of 1929 edition.
Ayer Co., $17.

**MAN CORN: CANNIBALISM & VIOLENCE
IN THE AMERICAN SOUTHWEST & MEXICO**
Jacqueline A. Turner
Illus. Maps. University of Utah Press, 1998. $65.

**MAN OF THE PLAINS: RECOLLECTIONS
OF LUTHER NORTH, 1856-1882**
Luther North; Donald Danker, Editor
Illus. 350 pp. University of Nebraska Press, 1961. $25.

**A MAN OF DISTINCTION AMONG THEM: ALEXANDER
MCKEE & BRITISH-INDIAN AFFAIRS ALONG THE OHIO
COUNTY FRONTIER, 1754-1799**
Larry L. Nelson
Kent State University Press, 1999. $35.

THE MAN TO SEND RAIN CLOUDS
Kenneth Rosen, Editor
18 stories, including the work of Leslie Marmon Silko, Simon J.
Ortiz, Anna Lee Walters, and Larry Littlebird & members of the
Circle Films. 192 pp. Paper. Penguin USA, $9.

MAN WHO KILLED THE DEER
Frank Waters
Reprint of 1974 edition. 266 pp. Ohio University Press,
$9.95; paper, $6.95.

**MAN'S KNIFE AMONG THE ESKIMO: A STUDY IN
THE COLLECTION OF THE U.S. NATIONAL MUSEUM**
Otis Mason
Reprint. Illus. 20 pp. Paper. Shorey's Bookstore, $1.95.

**MAN'S KNIFE AMONG THE NORTH AMERICAN INDIANS:
A STUDY IN THE COLLECTION OF THE U.S. NATIONAL
MUSEUM**
Otis Mason
Reprint of 1897 edition. Illus. 20 pp. Paper. Amereon, $16.95.

**MAN'S KNIFE AMONG THE NORTH AMERICAN INDIANS:
A STUDY IN THE MAN'S RISE TO CIVILIZATION: THE CUL-
TURAL ASCENT OF THE INDIANS OF NORTH AMERICA**
Peter Farb
Illus. Maps. Biblio. 336 pp. Paper. Penguin USA, $16.95.

**MAN'S RISE TO CIVLIZATION: THE CULTURAL
ASCENT OF THE INDIANS OF NORTH AMERICA**
Peter Farb
Illus. Photos. Maps. Biblio. 336 pp. Paper.
Penguin USA, $12.95.

MANDAN & HIDATSA MUSIC
F. Densmore
Reprint of 1923 edition. Illus. 236 pp. Da Capo Press, $27.50.

*THE MANDANS
Emilie Lepthien
Grades K-4. 50 pp. Childrens Press, 1989. $11.45.

**MANIFEST MANNERS: NARRATIVES
OF POSTINDIAN SURVIVANCE**
Gerald Vizenor
191 pp. Paper. University of Nebraska Press, 1999. $15.

*WILMA MANKILLER
Linda Lowery; Illus. by Janice Lee Porter
Grades 1-3. Illus. 56 pp. Lerner, 1996. $11.95.

*WILMA MANKILLER
Gini Holland
Grades 4 and up. Illus. 32 pp. Raintree/Steck-Vaughn
Publishers, 1997. $21.40.

*WILMA MANKILLER: CHIEF OF THE CHEROKEES
Grades 2-4. Illus. 32 pp. Childrens Press, $10.95.

MANKILLER: A CHIEF & HER PEOPLE
Wilma Mankiller & Michael Wallis
An autobiography by the Principal Chief of the Cherokee
Nation. 293 pp. St. Martin's Press, 1993. $22.95; paper, $13.95.

*WILMA P. MANKILLER: CHIEF OF THE CHEROKEE
Biography of her childhood to the present, 1992. Includes list
of important dates and an index. Grades 3-7. Illus. 20 pp. Cherokee Publications, $3.

**RAY MANLEY'S COLLECTING SOUTHWESTERN
INDIAN ARTS & CRAFTS**
Clara L. Tanner, et al
Third revised edition. Illus. Paper. Ray Manley, 1979. $6.

RAY MANLEY'S "THE FINE ART OF NAVAJO WEAVING"
Steve Getzwiller
Illus. Paper. Ray Manley, 1984. $9.95.

RAY MANLEY'S HOPI KACHINA
Clara L. Tanner
Illus. Paper. Ray Manley, 1980. $6.

RAY MANLEY'S INDIAN LANDS
Clara L. Tanner
Illus. Ray Manley, 1979. $10; paper, $7.95.

THE MANY FACES OF MATA ORTIZ
Lowell, Hills, Quintana, Parks, Wisner
The ancient art of ceramics. 260 color photos. 208 pp.
Paper. Clear Light, $29.95.

*MANY NATIONS: AN ALPHABET OF NATIVE AMERICA
Joseph Bruchac; Illus. by Robert Goetzl
From Anishinabe artists making birch bark bowls to Zuni
elders saying prayers. Grades PS-2. Illus. 32 pp. Paper.
BridgeWater Books, Clear Light, $5.95.

**MANY NATIONS: A LIBRARY OF CONGRESS RESOURCE
GUIDE FOR THE STUDY OF INDIAN & ALASKA NATIVE
PEOPLES OF THE U.S.**
LC Staff & Patrick Frazier, Eds.
Library of Congress, 1996.

**MANY SMOKES, MANY MOONS: A CHRONOLOGY OF
AMERICAN INDIAN HISTORY THROUGH INDIAN ART**
Jamake Highwater
130 pp. HarperCollins, 1978. $15.95.

**MANY TENDER TIES: WOMEN IN
FUR-TRADE SOCIETY, 1670-1870**
Sylvia Van Kirk
Reprint of 1983 edition. Illus. Map. 314 pp. Paper.
University of Oklahoma Press, 2000. $21.95.

**MANY TRAILS: INDIANS OF
THE LOWER HUDSON VALLEY**
Catherine C. Brawer, Editor
Illus. 112 pp. Paper. Publishing Center for Cultural
Research, 1983. $14.50.

*MANY WINTERS
Nancy Winters
Grades 6-12. Illus. 80 pp. Doubleday, 1974. $13.95.

**A MAP OF VIRGINIA: THE PROCEEDINGS
OF THE ENGLISH COLONIE IN VIRGINIA**
John Smith
Reprint of 1612 edition. 164 pp. Walter J. Johnson, $18.50.

MAP'N'FACTS: NATIVE PEOPLES OF NORTH AMERICA
Two maps show "then" and "now" in the life of
Native North Americans. Friendship Press, $4.50.

THE MAP OF WHO WE ARE: A NOVEL
Lawrence R. Smith
320 pp. University of Oklahoma Press, 1997. $24.95.

**THE MARCH OF THE MONTANA COLUMN:
A PRELUDE TO THE CUSTER DISASTER**
James Bradley
Reprint of 1961 edition. Illus. Map. 216 pp. Paper.
University of Oklahoma Press, $11.95.

MARIA
Richard L. Spivey
The famous San Ildefonso potter Maria Martinez developed
her legendary black-on-black ware around 1919. Illus. Biblio.
176 pp. Northland Publishing, 1989 revised & expanded edition. $19.95.

MARIA MAKING POTTERY
Hazel Hyde
Illus. 32 pp. Paper. Sunstone Press & Clear Light, $4.95.

*MARIA MARTINEZ: PUEBLO POTTER
Grades 2-4. Illus. 32 pp. Childrens Press, $10.95.

MARIA: THE POTTER OF SAN ILDEFONSO
Alice Marriott
Reprint of 1948 edition. Illus. 294 pp. University of Oklahoma
Press & Clear Light, $27.95; paper, $16.95.

*MARK OF OUR MOCCASINS
Colleen Reece
Grades 5-12. Paper. Council for Indian Education, 1982. $2.95.

MARQUIS DE MORES AT WAR IN THE BAD LANDS
Usher Burdick
27 pp. Paper. Ye Galleon Press, 1986. $4.95.

**VIOLA MARTINEZ, CALIFORNIA PAIUTE:
LIVING IN TWO WORLDS**
Diana Meyers Bahr
Illus. Map. 224 pp. University of Oklahoma Press, 2003.
$29.95.

MARTYRS OF THE OBLONG & LITTLE NINE
Defost Smith
Reprint of 1948 edition. Brown Book Co., $6.

**THE MARU CULT OF POMO INDIANS:
A CALIFORNIA GHOST DANCE SURVIVAL**
Clement W. Meighan and Francis A. Riddele
134 pp. Southwest Museum, 1972. $12.50.

THE MARVELOUS COUNTRY
Samuel Cozzens
Cochise & the Apaches; Indian life, struggles & customs.
Reprint of 1874 edition. 532 pp. Ross & Haines, $20.

MARY & I: FORTY YEARS WITH THE SIOUX
Stephen Riggs
Reprint of 1971 edition. 412 pp. Ross & Haines, $15.
Corner House, $21.

MARXISM & NATIVE AMERICANS
Ward Churchill, Editor
250 pp. South End Press, 1984. $20; paper, $12.50.

**MASCOUTENS OR PRAIRIE POTAWATOMI INDIANS:
SOCIAL LIFE & CEREMONIES**
Alanson Skinner
Reprint of 1924 edition. Greenwood Press, $35.

MASHKIKI: OLD MEDICINE NOURISHING THE NEW
Edwin Haller & Larry Aitken
Examines learning by American Indian & Alaskan Native
students. 214 pp. University Press of America, 1992.
$39.50; paper, $24.50.

THE MASHPEE INDIANS: TRIBE ON TRIAL
Jack Campisi
Illus. 188 pp. Paper. Syracuse University Press, 1991.
$15.95.

THE MASK MAKER
Diane Glancy
Novel. 160 pp. University of Oklahoma Press, 2004. $24.95.

MASKED GODS: NAVAHO & PUEBLO CEREMONIALISM
Frank Waters
Reprint of 1950 edition. 438 pp. Paper.
Ohio University Press, $10.95.

**MASKS OF THE SPIRIT: IMAGE
& METAPHOR IN MESOAMERICA**
  Roberta & Pter Markman
Illus. 375 pp. University of California Press, 1989. $75.

MASSACRE!
  Frank Laumer
Illus. Maps. Biblio. 188 pp. Paper.
University Press of Florida, 1968. $14.95.

**MASSACRE ALONG THE MEDICINE ROAD: A SOCIAL
HISTORY OF THE INDIAN WAR OF 1864 IN NEBRASKA
TERRITORY**
  Ronald Becher
Paper. Caxton, 1999. $22.95.

MASSACRE AT BAD AXE
  Crawford Thayer
Illus. 544 pp. Paper. Thayer Associates, 1981. $9.95.

**MASSACRE AT FORT BULL: THE DELERY
EXPEDITION AGAINST ONEIDA CARRY, 1756**
  Gilbert Hagerty
Illus. Mowbray, 1971. $8.

THE MASSACRE AT SAND CREEK: NARRATIVE VOICES
  Bruce Cutler
The massacre of over 200 Cheyennes in southeast Colorado
Territory. 252 pp. Paper. University of Oklahoma Press, 1994.
$11.95.

**MASSACRE AT THE YUMA CROSSING: SPANISH
RELATIONS WITH THE QUECHANS, 1779-1782**
  Mark Santiago
220 pp. University of Arizona Press, 1998. $37.50.

**MASSACRE ON THE GILA: AN ACCOUNT OF THE
LAST MAJOR BATTLE AMONG AMERICAN INDIANS**
  Clifton Kroeber & Bernard Fontana
232 pp. Paper. University of Arizona Press, 1986. $18.95.

MASSACRE: A SURVEY OF TODAY'S AMERICAN INDIAN
  Robert Gessner
Reprint of 1931 edition. 418 pp. Da Capo Press, $45.

MASSACRE: THE TRAGEDY AT WHITE RIVER
  Marshall Sprague
Illus. 365 pp. University of Nebraska Press, 1980.
$28.95; paper, $8.95.

MASTERWORKS FROM THE HEARD MUSEUM
  Heard Museum Staff
In 3 vols. Illus. 300 pp. (combined). Heard Museum
& Museum of New Mexico Press, $55.

MATERIAL CULTURE & THE STUDY OF AMERICAN LIFE
  Ian M. Quimby
Illus. Paper. W.W. Norton & Co., 1978. $7.95.

**TOMMY McGINTY'S NORTHERN TUCHTONE STORY
OF CROW: A FIRST NATION ELDER RECOUNTS THE
CREATION OF THE WORLD**
  Dominique Legros
Tales of Crow from inland northwestern Canada. Map. Biblio.
268 pp. Paper. University of Washington Press, 1999. $27.95.

McINTOSH & WEATHERFORD, CREEK INDIAN LEADERS
  Benjamin Griffith
Illus. 300 pp. Paper. University of Alabama Press, 1988.
$19.95.

**THE McKENNEY-HALL PORTRAIT
GALLERY OF AMERICAN INDIANS**
Portraits of famous American Indians. First published in 1836,
this new volume includes historical materials and biographical
profiles on each. Illus. 370 pp. Cherokee Publications, $14.95.

**JOHN McMURTRY & THE AMERICAN INDIAN:
A FRONTIERSMAN IN THE STRUGGLE FOR
THE OHIO VALLEY**
  Richard K. McMurtry
Illus. Paper. Current Issues, 1980. $14.95.

**ME & MINE: THE LIFE STORY
OF HELEN SEKAQUAPTEWA**
  as told to Louise Udall
262 pp. Paper. University of Arizona Press, 1969. $15.95.

***ME RUN FAST GOOD: BIOGRAPHIES OF TEWANIMA
(HOPI), CARLOS MONTEZUMA (APACHE) & JOHN HORSE
(SEMINOLE)**
  Beatrice Levin and Marjorie Vanderveld
Grades 5-9. 32 pp. Paper. Council for Indian Education,
1983. $1.95.

**MECHANISMS & TRENDS IN THE DECLINE OF THE
COSTANOAN INDIAN POPULATION OF CENTRAL CALI-
FORNIA: NUTRITION & HEALTH IN PRE-CONTACT CALI-
FORNIA & MISSION PERIOD ENVIRONMENTS**
  Ann Stodder: Gary Breschini & Trudy Harverset, Editors
Illus. 78 pp. Paper. Coyote Press, 1986. $6.20.

**MEDIATION IN CONTEMPORARY
NATIVE AMERICAN FICTION**
  James Ruppert
Focuses on novels by six major contemporary Native Ameri-
can writers: N. Scott Momaday, James Welch, Leslie Silko,
Gerald Vizenor, D'Arcy McNickle, and Louise Erdrich. 174 pp.
University of Oklahoma Press, 1995. $29.95; paper, $11.95.

THE MEDICAL HISTORY OF ISHI
  Saxton T. Pope
Facsimile edition. Illus. 38 pp. Coyote Press, $4.38.

**MEDICINAL & OTHER USES
OF NORTH AMERICAN PLANTS**
  Charlotte Erichsen-Brown
Historical citations document uses of plants with special refer-
ence to the Eastern Indian tribes. Illus. 544 pp. Paper. Dover,
$12.95.

**MEDICINAL USES OF PLANTS
BY INDIAN TRIBES OF NEVADA**
  Percy Train, et al
Reprint of 1957 edition. Quarterman, $30.

**THE MEDICINE BOWS:
WYOMING'S MOUNTAIN COUNTRY**
  Scott Thybony, et al
The region was an important fur trading center and one of the
last refuges of the Cheyenne, Arapaho, and Sioux Indians. Illus.
Biblio. 180 pp. Paper. The Caxton Printers, $7.95.

**MEDICINE CARDS: THE DISCOVERY OF
POWER THROUGH THE WAYS OF ANIMALS**
  Jamie Sams & David Carson
224 pp. Bear & Co., 1988. $26.95.

THE MEDICINE CREEK TREATY OF 1854
  Lynn Kickingbird & Curtis Berkey
31 pp. Institute for the Development of Indian Law, $10.

MEDICINE HAT: A NOVEL
  Don Coldsmith
A love story and the tale of a daring search for spiritual mean-
ing in the American West of the 1700s. 272 pp. University of
Oklahoma Press, 1997. $24.95

*MEDICINE MAN
Grades 4-5. Illus. 48 pp. Capstone Press, 1989. $10.95.

**THE MEDICINE MEN: OGLALA SIOUX
CEREMONY & HEALING**
  Thomas H. Lewis
Describes traditional healing practices of the Oglala Sioux of
Pine Ridge Reservation. Illus. 221 pp. Paper. University of
Nebraska Press, 1990. $10.95.

**MEDICINE MEN OF THE APACHE, A PAPER FROM THE
NINTH ANNUAL REPORT OF THE BUREAU OF AMERICAN
ETHNOLOGY (1887-1888)**
  John Bourke
Reprint of 1970 edition. Illus. 187 pp. The Rio Grande Press,
$22.50.

**MEDICINE OF THE CHEROKEE: THE WAY OF RIGHT
RELATIONSHIP**
  J.T. & Michael T. Garrett
240 pp. Paper. Bear & Co., 1996. $14.

MEDICINE RIVER
  Thomas King
Breaks down stereotypes about Indians. A young Blackfoot
Indian returns to his birthplace in Alberta. 480 pp. Paper. Pen-
guin USA, $11.

**MEDICINE TRAIL: THE LIFE & LESSONS
OF GLADYS TANTAQUIDGEON**
  Melissa Jayne Fawcett
Autobiography of Gladys Tanataquidgeon (100 year-old medi-
cine woman) with Mohegan traditional knowledge and ways of
life. Illus. 179 pp. Paper. University of Arizona Press, 2000.
$17.95.

**MEDICINE WAY: HOW TO LIVE THE TEACHINGS
OF THE NATIVE AMERICAN MEDICINE WHEEL:
A SHAMANIC PATH TO SELF-MASTERY**
  Kenneth Meadows
256 pp. Paper. Element Books, 1997. $17.95.

MEDICINE WHEEL: EARTH ASTROLOGY
  Sun Bear & Wabun
Learn about the different moons, totems, powers of the direc-
tions and elemental clans. Illus. 228 pp. Paper. Simon &
Schuster, $10.

MEDICINE WHEEL CEREMONIES
  Vicki May & C.V. Rodberg
Ancient philosophies for use in modern day life.
48 pp. Paper. Naturegraph, 1995. $9.95.

THE MEDICINE WHEEL: EARTH ASTROLOGY
  Sun Bear & Wabun
Illus. 203 pp. Paper. Cherokee Publications, $8.95.

**MEDICINE WHEELS: NATIVE AMERICAN
VEHICLES OF HEALING**
  Roy I. Wilson
154 pp. Paper. Crossrad Publishing, 1994. $14.95.

MEDICINE WOMEN, CURANDERAS & WOMEN DOCTORS
  Bobette Perrone, et al
Illus. 272 pp. Paper. University of Oklahoma Press, 1989.
$19.95.

**MEDICINE TRAIL: THE LIFE & LESSONS
OF GLADYS TANTAQUIDGEON**
  Melissa Jayne Fawcett
Paper. University of Arizona Press, 1999. $16.95.

**MEDITATION WITH NATIVE AMERICANS:
LAKOTA SPIRITUALITY**
  Paul Steinmetz
The songs & thoughts of the Lakota, along with a section
on the Native American Church & Christian influences.
Illus. 144 pp. Paper. Bear & Co., 1984. $7.95.

**MEDITATIONS WITH ANIMALS:
A NATIVE AMERICAN BESTIARY**
  Gerald Hausman
Shows the healing roles animals have played since the
beginning. Illus. 144 pp. Paper. Bear & Co., 1986. $7.95.

MEDITATIONS WITH THE HOPI
  Robert Boissiere
The author's interpretation of the essence of Hopi experience.
Illus. 144 pp. Paper. Bear & Co., 1984. $7.95.

MEDITATIONS WITH THE NAVAJO
  Gerald Hausman
Prayer, songs & stories of healing & harmony. Illus.
144 pp. Paper. Bear & Co., 1987. $7.95.

MEET CREE: A GUIDE TO THE CREE LANGUAGE
  C.H. Wolfart and J.F. Carroll
120 pp. University of Nebraska Press, 1981. $12.50.

MEET THE LAKOTA, VOL. ONE: THE PEOPLE
  Rose LaVera
An introduction to the Lakota, written in English & in Lakota by
Alvin Horse Looking. Illus. Paper. The Greenfield Review Press,
$5.95.

*MEET THE NORTH AMERICAN INDIANS
  Elizabeth Paine
Grades 2-6. Illus. Random House, 1965. $8.99; paper, $5.95.

**MEMOIR OF INDIAN WARS & OTHER OCCURENCES
BY THE LATE COLONEL STUART OF GREENBRIER**
  John Stuart; Charles Stuart, Editor
Reprint of 1833 edition. Ayer Co., $11.50.

**MEMOIRS OF A CHICKASAW SQUAW:
A JOURNAL OF THE CHICKASAW REMOVAL**
  Velma Taliaferro; Molly Griffis, Editor
Illus. 65 pp. Paper. Levite of Apache Publishing, 1987. $5.

MEMOIRS OF LT. HENRY TIMBERLAKE
  Henry Timberlake
Reprint of 1927 edition. Ayer Co., $28.95.

MEMOIRS OF A WHITE CROW INDIAN
  Thomas Leforge; Thomas Marquis, Narrator
380 pp. University of Nebraska Press, 1974.
$31.50; paper, $10.95.

MEMOIRS, OFFICIAL & PERSONAL
  Thomas L. McKenney; Herman J. Viola, Editor
Insight into Indian affairs by Thomas McKenney, Director of
Indian Affairs, 1816-1830. 340 pp. Paper. University of Nebraska
Press, 1973. $6.95.

**MEMORY ETERNAL: TLINGIT CULTURE & RUSSIAN
ORTHODOX CHRISTIANITY THROUGH TWO CENTURIES**
  Sergei Kan
Illus. 696 pp. University of Washington Press, 1999. $60.

**MEN AS WOMEN, WOMEN AS MEN: CHANGING
GENDER IN NATIVE AMERICAN CULTURES**
  Sabine Lang
Illus. Maps. 416 pp. University of Texas Press, 1998. $50;
paper $19.95.

MEN ON THE MOON: COLLECTED SHORT STORIES
  Simon J. Ortiz
26 stories drawn from Ortiz's Acoma Pueblo experience.
216 pp. Paper. University of Arizona Press, 1999. $18.95.

**MENDING THE CIRCLE: A NATIVE REPATRIATION
GUIDE:**
  Jack Trope, et al
Includes articles on NAGPRA, the Smithsonian Institution's
repatriation policies and strategies for the private sector.
167 pp. AIRORF, 1997. $40. Supplement. 57 pp. $8.

*THE MENOMINEE
  Patricia Ourada
Grades 5 and up. Illus. Chelsea House, 1989. $17.95.

THE MENOMINI INDIANS OF WISCONSIN
Felix Keesing
304 pp. University of Wisconsin Press, 1987.
$30; paper, $11.95.

MENOMINEE MUSIC
Francis Densmore
Reprint of 1932 edition. Illus. 286 pp. Da Capo Press,
$29.50. Reprint Services, $75.

MEREJILDO GRIJALVA, APACHE CAPTIVE, ARMY SCOUT
Edwin R. Sweeney
Presents a detailed acount of his life. Illus. Map. Biblio.
Paper. Texas Western Press, 1993. $12.50.

MESA VERDE NATIONAL PARK
Ruth Radlauer
Updated edition. Grades 3 and up. Illus. 50 pp.
Childrens Press, 1984. $14.60; paper, $4.50.

MESA VERDE ANCIENT ARCHITECTURE
Jesse W. Fewkes
3 essays on the daily lives of the cliff dwellers of Mesa Verde.
Illus. 240 pp. Paper. University of New Mexico Press & Avanyu
Publishing, 1999. $16.95.

MESA VERDE: THE STORY BEHIND THE SCENERY
Linda Martin
Archaeological sites of Anasazi culture. Photos.
Maps. 48 pp. Paper. KC Publications, $6.95.

MESCALERO APACHES
C.L. Sonnichsen
2nd ed. Illus. Maps. 340 pp. Paper.
University of Oklahoma Press, 1973. $16.95.

MESSAGES FROM MOTHER EARTH:
DAILY AFFIRMATIONS
Willie Hooks
60 pp. Paper. JTE Associates, 1989. $6.95.

METAL WEAPONS, TOOLS & ORNAMENTS
OF THE TETON DAKOTA INDIANS
James A. Hanson
Illus. 118 pp. University of Nebraska Press, 1975. $16.50.

THE MEXICAN KICKAPOO INDIANS
Felipe & Dolores Latorre
Illus. Map. 416 pp. Paper. Dover, $11.95.

THE MIAMI-ILLINOIS LANGUAGE
David J. Costa
Overview of the Miami-Illinois language. 566 pp.
University of Nebraska Press, 2003. $75.

THE MIAMI INDIANS
Bert Anson
Reprint. Illus. Maps. 352 pp. Paper.
University of Oklahoma Press, $25.95.

THE MIAMI INDIANS OF INDIANA:
A PERSISTENT PEOPLE, 1654-1994
Stewart Rafert
Illus. 358 pp. Indian Historical Society, 1996.
$29.95; paper, $14.95.

***MI'CA: BUFFALO HUNTER**
Jane Bendix
Sioux life in the 1740's. Grades 4 and up. 188 pp.
Council for Indian Education. $14.95; paper, $9.95.

MICMAC DICTIONARY
Albert D. DeBlois
98 pp. Paper. University of Washington Press, 1997. $29.95.

THE MICROFILM EDITION OF THE WASHINGTON
MATTHEWS PAPERS & GUIDE
Wheelwright Museum Staff
Illus. 126 pp. University of New Mexico Press, 1985. $15. Mi-
crofilm (ten rolls), $400.

MID-APPALACHIAN FRONTIER: A GUIDE TO HISTORIC
SITES OF THE FRENCH & INDIAN WAR
Robert B. Swift
Paper. Smoke & Fire Co., 1999. $17.95.

THE MIDDLE FIVE: INDIAN SCHOOLBOYS
OF THE OMAHA TRIBES
Francis La Flesche
Illus. 152 pp. University of Nebraska Press, 1978.
$17.50; paper, $4.50.

THE MIDDLE GROUND: INDIANS, EMPIRES, & REPUBLICS
IN THE GREAT LAKES REGION, 1650-1815
Richard White
Illus. 560 pp. Cambridge University Press, 1991.
$69.50; paper, $19.95.

MIDNIGHT & NOONDAY: OR THE INCIDENTAL HISTORY OF
SOUTHERN KANSAS & THE INDIAN TERRITORY, 1871-1890
G.D. Freeman; Richard L. Lane, Editor
Illus. Maps. Biblio. University of Oklahoma Press, 1984. $37.95.

MIGRATION TEARS
Michael Kabotie (Lomawywesa)
Poems dealing with separation, transition, and loss.
54 pp. Paper. The Falmouth Institute, 1987. $10.

BARTLEY MILAM: PRINCIPAL CHIEF
OF THE CHEROKEE NATION
Howard Meredith
157 pp. Paper. Indian University Press, 1985. $5.

THE MILITARY & THE U.S. INDIAN POLICY, 1865-1903
Robert Wooster
268 pp. Paper. University of Nebraska Press, $10.95.

MILLENIUM: TRIBAL WISDOM & THE MODERN WORLD
David Maybury-Lewis
Illus. Penguin USA, $45.

MIMBRES ARCHAEOLOGY AT THE NAN RANCH RUIN
Harry J. Shafer
New information and interpretations of the rise and
disappearance of the ancient Mimbres culture. Illus.
176 halftones, 5 maps. 304 pp. University of New
Mexico Press, $59.95.

THE MIMBRES, ART & ARCHAEOLOGY
Jesse Walter Fewkes; into. by J.J. Brody
Reprint of 1914 edition. Illus. 182 pp. Paper.
Avanyu Publishing, $16.95.

MIMBRES CLASSIC MYSTERIES: RECONSTRUCTING
A LOST CULTURE THROUGH ITS POTTERY
Tom Steinbach, Sr.; illus. by Tom Steinbach, Jr.
& Peter Steinbach
A visual history of the Mimbres people. Illus. 184 pp.
Museum of New Mexico Press, 2001. $45; paper, $29.95.

MIMBRES DESIGNS
Fred Kabotie
Prepared interpretations of 12 Mimbres designs. Draws upon
the traditional beliefs of his tribe. bxw art is printed on heavy
faun-colored all-rag folded sheets. Limited edition of 100. Illus.
64 pp. Lime Rock Press, 1982. $295.

MIMBRES INDIAN TREASURE: IN THE LAND OF BACA
Roy Evans, R. Evelyn & Lyle Ross
Illus. 352 pp. The Lowell Press, 1985. $29.95.

MIMBRES MOGOLLON ARCHAEOLOGY: CHARLES C.
DI PESO'S EXCAVATIONS AT WIND MOUNTAIN
Anne I. Woosley & Allan J. McIntyre
Illus. 480 pp. University of New Mexico Press, 1996.
$34.95.

MIMBRES MYTHOLOGY
Pat Carr
Illus. 78 pp. Texas Western Press, 1989. $12; paper, $7.50.

MINIATURE ARTS OF THE SOUTHWEST
Nancy Schiffer
Arts of American Indian tribes in the Southwest are occasionally made in miniature. This book presents a wide array of these
miniatures of all the major craft styles of the region. Illus. 64
pp. Paper. Schiffer, $12.95.

MINING, THE ENVIRONMENT, AND
INDIGENOUS DEVELOPMENT CONFLICTS
Saleem H. Ali
Examines environmental conflicts between mining
companies and indigenous communities. Illus. 270 pp.
University of Arizona Press, 2003. $50.

MINISTER TO THE CHEROKEES:
A CIVIL WAR AUTOBIOGRAPHY
James Anderson Slover; edited by Barbara Cloud
in 1857 James Anderson Slover rode into Indian Territory as
the first Southern Baptist missionary to the Cherokee Nation.
Illus. 212 pp. University of Nebraska Press, 2001. $50.

THE MINNESOTA ETHNIC FOOD BOOK
Anne Kaplan, Marjorie Hoover, Willard Moore
Includes Ojibway recipes. Illus. 449 pp. Minnesota
Historical Society Press, 1986. $14.95.

THE MI'KMAQ: RESISTANCE,
ACCOMMODATION, & CULTURAL SURVIVAL
Harald E.L. Prins
Explores the historical dynamics that have marked Mi'kmaq
culture over the last 500 years. Paper. 184 pp. Harcourt Brace,
1996.

MIRROR & PATTERN: GEORGE LAIRD'S
WORLD OF CHEMEHUEVI MYTHOLOGY
Carobeth Laird
Myths of the Chemehuevi. 373 pp. Malki Museum Press,
$25.

***THE MISHOMIS BOOK, THE VOICE OF THE OJIBWAY**
Edward Benton-Banai
Ojibway traditions, culture and ceremonies. Grades 4 and up.
Illus. Indian Country Communication, 1988. $19.95. Also, The
Mishomis Coloring Book Series - 5 history coloring books. $4.25
each.

MISSION AMONG THE BLACKFEET
Howard L. Harrod
Examines the effects of catholic and Protestant missionary
activity upon the Blackfeet from the 1840s through the 1960s.
Reprint. Illus. Map. Biblio. 240 pp. Paper. University of Okla-
homa Press, $19.95.

***THE MISSIONS: CALIFORNIA'S HERITAGE**
Mary Null Boule
21 individual booklets of detailed facts of each Mission's
history. Grades 4-6. Illus. Meerant Publishers.

THE MISSIONS OF CALIFORNIA,
A HISTORY OF GENOCIDE
Rupert Costo & Jeanette Henry
Paper. Indian Historian Press, $12.50.

MISSIONS & PUEBLOS OF THE OLD SOUTHWEST
Earle R. Forrest
Reprint of 1929 edition. 398 pp. Paper.
The Rio Grande Press, $12.

MISSISSIPPI CHOCTAWS AT PLAY:
THE SERIOUS SIDE OF LEISURE
Kendall Blanchard
248 pp. University of Illinois Press, 1981. $22.95.

THE MISSISSIPPIAN EMERGENCE
Bruce D. Smith, Editor
Collection of 11 essays examines the evolution of ranked
chiefdoms in the midwestern and southeastern U.S. from 700-
1220 A.D. Illus. 272 pp. Smithsonian Institution Press, 1990.
$45.

MISSISSIPPIAN MORTUARY PRACTICES
Goldstein
Covers burial details and Indian social organization. Illus.
196 pp. Paper. Hothem House, 1980. $12.50, postpaid.

MISSISSIPPIAN STONE IMAGES IN ILLINOIS
Thomas E. Emerson
Illus. 50 pp. Paper. Univerfy of Illinois Archaeology, 1982.
$3.75.

MISSISSIPPIAN TOWNS & SACRED SPACES:
SEARCHING FOR AN ARCHITECTURAL GRAMMAR
R. Barry Lewis
Paper. University of Alabama Press, 1999. $29.95.

MISSISSIPPIAN VILLAGE TEXTILES AT WICKLIFFE (KY)
Drooker
Prehistoric weavings. Illus. 291 pp. Paper.
Hothem House, 1992. $19.95 postpaid.

MITAKUYE OYASIN: WE ARE ALL RLATED
Allen C. Ross
Comparative culture studies. Illus. 215 pp. Paper.
Bear & Center for Western Studies, $12.

MIWOK MATERIAL CULTURE
S.A. Barrett and E.W. Gifford
Illus. 257 pp. Paper. Yosemite, $6.95.

MIXEDBLOOD MESSAGES:
LITERATURE, FILM, FAMILY & PLACE
Louis Owens
Illus. 277 pp. University of Oklahoma Press, 1998.
$29.95; paper, $14.95.

MIXED BLOODS, APACHES & CATTLE BARONS:
DOCUMENTS FOR A HISTORY OF THE LIVESTOCK
ECONOMY ON THE WHITE MOUNTAIN RESERVATION,
ARIZONA
Thomas R. McGuire
Illus. 227 pp. Arizona State Museum, 1980. $13.95.

MIXED BLOOD INDIANS: RACIAL
CONSTRUCTION IN THE EARLY SOUTH
Theda Perdue
University of Georgia Press, 2002.

MIXED-BLOODS & TRIBAL DISSOLUTION:
CHARLES CURTIS & THE QUEST FOR INDIAN IDENTITY
William Unrau
Illus. 224 pp. University Press of Kansas, 1989. $27.50.

MOBILITY & ADAPTATION:
THE ANASAZI OF BLACK MESA, ARIZONA
Shirley Powell
304 pp. Southern Illinois University Press, 1983. $29.95.

THE MOCASSIN MAKER
E. Pauline Johnson
Reprint of 1913 edition. 267 pp. Paper.
University of Arizona Press, 1987. $12.95.

MOCCASINS ON PAVEMENT: THE URBAN INDIAN
EXPERIENCE, A DENVER PORTRAIT
Michael Taylor, et al
Illus. Paper. Denver Museum of Natural History, 1978. $2.50.

MODEL COURT DEVELOPMENT PROJECT: FULL FAITH & CREDIT FOR INDIAN COURT JUDGEMENTS
National Center for State Courts Staff
750 pp. National Center for State Courts, manuscript, $3.12.

MODELS FOR THE MILLENNIUM: GREAT BASIN ANTHROPOLOGY TODAY
Charlotte Beck, Editor
Illus. Maps. 464 pp. University of Utah Press, 1999. $65.

MODERN AMERICAN INDIAN TRIBAL GOVERNMENT & POLITICS: AN INTERDISCIPLINARY STUDY
Howard Meredith
169 pp. Paper. Dine College Press. $16.95.

MODERN BLACKFEET: MONTANANS ON A RESERVATION
Malcolm McFee
Illus. 134 pp. Paper. Waveland Press, 1984. $8.95.

MODERN BY TRADITION: AMERICAN INDIAN PAINTING IN THE STUDIO STYLE
Bruce Bernstein & W. Jackson Rushing
Reproduces over 90 paintings by prominent artists such as Pablita Velarde, Joe H. Herrera, Allan Houser, and Opo Chalee. Illus. 176 pp. Museum of New Mexico Press, 2000. $45; paper, $29.95.

THE MODERN FANCY DANCER
C. Scott Evans & J. Rex Reddick
Traces the evolution of the Fancy dance style, with instructions to make an entire dance outfit. Color photos. Illus. 64 pp. Paper. Meadowlark Communications & Written Heritage, $15.95.

MODERN INDIAN PSYCHOLOGY
John F. Bryde
Paper. Dakota Press, 1971. $9.

MODERN PRIMITIVE ARTS OF MEXICO, GUATEMALA & THE SOUTHWEST
C. Oglesby
Facsimile of 1939 edition. Ayer Co., $16.

MODERN TRANSFORMATIONS OF MOENKOPI PUEBLO
Shuichi Nagata
Illus. 350 pp. Paper. University of Illinois Press, 1970. $10.95.

*THE MODOC
Odie & Laura Faulk
Illus. 104 pp. Chelsea House, 1988. $17.95.

MODOCS & THEIR WAR
Keith A. Murray
Reprint of 1959 edition. Illus. Map. 358 pp. Paper. University of Oklahoma Press, 2001. $29.95.

MOGOLLON CULTURE IN THE FORESTDALE VALLEY, EAST-CENTRAL ARIZONA
Emil W. Haury
Reprint. 454 pp. University of Arizona Press, 1985. $54.

MOHAVE ETHNOPSYCHIATRY & SUICIDE: PSYCHIATRIC KNOWLEDGE & THE PSYCHIC DISTURBANCES OF AN INDIAN TRIBE
George Devereux
586 pp. Reprint Services, 1995. $119.

A MOHAVE WAR REMINISCENCE 1854-1880
A.L. Kroeber & G.B. Kroeber
128 pp. Paper. Dover, $7.95.

*THE MOHAWK
Grades K-4. Illus. 48 pp. Children's Press, $11.45.

MOHAWK FRONTIER: THE DUTCH COMMUNITY OF SCHENECTADY, NEW YORK, 1661-1710
Thomas E. Burke, Jr.
Explores Schenectady's origins and its destruction in 1690. Tells the story of the Indians, French and African slaves, et al. 264 pp. Cornell University Press, $36.95.

MOHAWK, ONE THOUSAND USEFUL WORDS
David K. Maracle
158 pp. Paper. Audio-Forum, 1992. $12.95.

THE MOHAWK THAT REFUSED TO ABDICATE
David P. Morgan
Kalmbach Publishing, 1975. $25.

MOHEGAN INDIAN MAPS OF MONTVILLE, CT
Allen V. Polhemus
Illus. 84 pp. Nutmeg Publishers, 1993. $42.95.

THE MOHICANS OF STOCKBRIDGE
Patrick Frazier
The ethnohistory of the colonial Northeast. Illus. Map. 307 pp. Paper. University of Nebraska Press, 1992. $25.

THE MOHICANS & THEIR LAND: 1609-1730
S.W. Dunn
Ilus. 350 pp. Paper. Library Research Associates, 1994. $24.

MOKI SNAKE DANCE
Walter Hough
Travel guide published in 1899 describes the drama of Snake Dance ceremonial of the Moki (Hopi) Indians of Arizona. Includes the Snake Legend. Illus. Photos. 80 pp. Paper. Avanyu Publishing, $5.95.

MOLDED IN THE IMAGE OF CHANGING WOMAN: NAVAJO VIEWS ON THE HUMAN BODY & PERSONHOOD
Maureen Trudelle Schwarz
292 pp. Paper. University of Arizona Press, 1997. $22.95.

MOLLY MOLASSES & ME: A COLLECTION OF LIVING ADVENTURES
Ssipsis & Georgia Mitchell
Illus. 2nd edition. 75 pp. Paper. Robin Hood Books, $8.

MOLLY SPOTTED ELK: A PENOBSCOT IN PARIS
Bunny McBride
Illus. 360 pp. University of Oklahoma Press, 1995. $24.95; paper, $13.95.

N. SCOTT MOMADAY: THE CULTURAL & LITERARY BACKGROUND
Matthias Schubnell
336 pp. University of Oklahoma Press, 1985. $29.95.

MOMADAY, VIZENOR, ARMSTRONG: CONVERSATIONS ON AMERICAN INDIAN WRITING
Hartwig Isernhagen
304 pp. University of Oklahoma Press, 1999. $34.95; paper, $14.95.

MONACANS & MINERS: NATIVE AMERICAN & COAL MINING COMMUNITIES IN APPALACHIA
Samuel R. Cook
Illus. Maps. 337 pp. University of Nebraska Press, 2000. $65; paper, $29.95.

*THE MONEY GOD
Dolly Hildreth, et al
Grade 6. Paper. Council for Indian Education, 1972. $1.95.

THE MONGREL: A STORY OF LOGAN FONTANELLE OF THE OMAHA INDIANS
Anthony J. Barak; Jim Reisdorff, Editor
Illus. 145 pp. Paper. South Platte Press, 1988. $9.95.

*MONSTORS & MAGIC: MYTHS OF NORTH & SOUTH AMERICA
Stewart Ross
Grades 5 and up. Illus. 44 pp. Millbrook Press, 1998. $23.90.

THE MONTANA CREE: A STUDY IN RELIGIOUS PERSISTENCE
Verne Dusenberry
Illus. Maps. Biblio. 296 pp. Paper. University of Oklahoma Press & Written Heritage, $15.95.

MONTANA'S INDIANS: YESTERDAY & TODAY
William Bryan
Profiles each of Montana's seven reservations and the nations residing there. Illus. 142 pp. 1986 edition distributed by Meadowlark Communications, $24.95.

MONTEREY IN 1786: THE JOURNAL OF JEAN FRANCOIS DE LA PEROUSE
Intro by Malcolm Margolin
Account of Carmel Mission and the relations between the missionaries and the Indian neophytes, shortly after the death of Junipero Sera. Illus. 104 pp. Paper. Heyday Books, $8.95.

MONTEZUMA'S DINNER
Lewis Morgan
Second edition. Paper. New York Labor News, 75¢.

MONUMENT VALLEY: THE STORY BEHIND THE SCENERY
K.C. DenDooven
The story of the Navajo who lived there, the Gouldings who established the trading post, and a young photographer in 1937. Illus. Photos. 48 pp. Paper. KC Publications, $6.95.

MOON DASH WARRIOR: THE STORY OF AN AMERICAN INDIAN IN VIETNAM, A MARINE FROM THE LAND OF THE LUMBEE
Delano Cummings
Illus. 266 pp. Signal Tree, 1998. $22.

MOON OF POPPING TREES
Rex Alan Smith
The tragedy of Wounded Knee and the end of the Indian wars, 1851-1891. Maps. 219 pp. Paper. University of Nebraska Press, 1981. $12.95.

MORE AH MO: INDIAN LEGENDS FROM THE NORTHWEST
Tren J. Griffin
New Edition of Ah Mo. Illus. 64 pp. Paper. Hancock House, 1994. $7.95.

LEWIS H. MORGAN ON IROQUOIS MATERIAL CULTURE
Elisabeth Tooker
A collection of 500 Iroquois objects, researched in 1849-50, provides information on Irqouois culture. Illus. 400 pp. University of Arizona Press, 1994. $76; paper, $41.

MORE TECHNIQUES OF BEADING EARRINGS
Deon DeLange
Illus. 80 pp. Paper. Eagle's View Publishing, $9.95.

*MORNING GIRL
Michael Dorris
Grades 3 and up. Illus. Paper. Hyperion. $3.50.

MORNING STAR QUILTS
Florence Pulford
Illus. 80 pp. Dover, $9.95.

THE MORNING THE SUN WENT DOWN
Darryl Babe Wilson
A memoir of rural Native American life. 190 pp. Heyday Books, $22.50; paper, $13.95.

MARY MOSES' STATEMENT
William C. Brown, et al
Biography of Mary Moses, the daughter of the Upper Yakima Chief Owhi who married Chief Moses in the 1860s. 70 pp. Ye Galleon, 1996. $17.95; paper, $12.95.

MOTHER EARTH: AN AMERICAN STORY
Sam D. Gill
196 pp. Paper. University of Chicago Press, 1987. $13.95.

MOTHER EARTH, FATHER SKY: PUEBLO & NAVAJO INDIANS OF THE SOUTHWEST
Marcia Keegan
Reprint of 1974 edition. Illus. 112 pp. Clear Light, 1974. $29.95.

MOTHER EARTH SPIRITUALITY: NATIVE AMERICAN PATHS TO HEALING OURSELVES & OUR WORLD
Ed McGaa & Eagle Man
Illus. 304 pp. Paper. HarperCollins, 1990. $14.95.

MOUND BUILDERS & CLIFF DWELLERS
Time-Life Editors
Illus. 168 pp. Hothem House, 1992. $22, postpaid.

THE MOUNDBUILDERS
Robert Silverberg
276 pp. Paper. Ohio University Press, 1986. $6.95.

MOUNDS FOR THE DEAD
Dragoo
Study of the Adena (Early Woodland) Indians; their lifeway, mounds, burial pratice, artifacts. Reprint of 1963 edition. Illus. 315 pp. Paper. Hothem House, $15.95.

THE MOUNTAIN CHANT: A NAVAJO CEREMONY
Washington Matthews
A nine-day Navajo healing ceremony. Contains the story of the wandering hero and describes each of the days, with original song texts and translations. Reprint of 1897 ed. Illus. 120 pp. Paper. University of Utah Press. $14.95.

THE MOUNTAIN MEADOWS MASSACRE
Juanita Brooks
Story of a wagon train in southern Utah was attacked by Indians & Mormans. Reprint of 1962 edition. Illus. Maps. 352 pp. Paper. University of Oklahoma Press, 2000. $19.95.

MOUNTAIN TOWN: FLAGSTAFF'S FIRST CENTURY
Platt Cline
History of Flagstaff. 175 historic photos. 672 pp. Northland, $35.

MOUNTAIN WINDSONG: NOVEL OF THE TRAIL OF TEARS
Robert J. Conley
A love story and the Cherokee Removal of 1835-1838 from their traditional lands in North Carolina. 218 pp. Paper. University of Oklahoma Press, 2001. $14.95.

MOUNTAIN WOLF WOMAN, SISTER OF CRASHING THUNDER: THE AUTOBIOGRAPHY OF A WINNEBAGO INDIAN
Nancy O. Lurie, Editor
Illus. 164 pp. Paper. University of Michigan Press, 1961. $7.95.

THE MOUNTAINWAY OF THE NAVAJO
Leland Wyman
The examination of a Navajo song ceremonial and its various branches, phases and ritual. Illus. 286 pp. University of Arizona Press, 1975. $35.

MOURNING DOVE: A SALISHAN AUTOBIOGRAPHY
Mourning Dove; edited by Jay Miller
Illus. Map. 267 pp. Paper. University of Nebraska Press, 1990. $15.95.

MOVEMENT FOR INDIAN ASSIMILATION, 1860-1890
Henry E. Fritz
Reprint of 1963 edition. Illus. 244 pp. Greenwood Press, $35.

MOVING WITHIN THE CIRCLE: CONTEMPORARY NATIVE AMERICAN MUSIC & DANCE
Bryan Burton
Features songs, dances, and flute tunes of the Haliwa-Saponi Dancers, R. Carlos Nakai, the Porcupine Singers, and more.

Illus. 176 pp. World Music Press, Book & CD or Book & Tape Set, $29.95; with optional slides, $63.

*MUCKWA: THE ADVENTURES OF A CHIPPEWA INDIAN BOY
Wilson G. Dietrich
Illus. Winston-Derek, $6.95.

*THE MUD FAMILY
Betsy James; illus. by Paul Morin
Story depicting the lives of the Anasazi, ancestor of the Pueblo peoples of the Southwest. Grades PS-3. Illus. 32 pp. Putnam, 1994. $15.95.

MUD WOMAN: POEMS FROM THE CLAY
Nora Naranjo-Morse
Poetry by a noted Pueblo potter. Illus. 127 pp. Paper. University of Arizona Press, 1992. $17.95.

MULEWETAM: THE FIRST PEOPLE
Jane H. Hill & Rosinda Nolasquez
Paper. Malki Museum Press, 1991. $18.

MULTICULTURAL RESOURCE BOOK & APPOINTMENT CALENDAR
Detailed entries marking birthdays, historical/cultural events, and days of religious observance associated ith over 30 different cultural and religious tradition, including 30 entries dealing with Native Americans. Book, 6"X9"; Resource Calendar, 11"x17". Biblio. Index. Annual. Amherst Educational Publishing, $21.95 each.

MULTIDISCIPLINARY RESEARCH AT GRASSHOPPER PUEBLO, ARIZONA
W.A. Longacre and S.J. Holbrook, Editors
138 pp. Paper. University of Arizona Press, 1982. $12.95.

MUMIGCISTET KALIKAIT: A YUP'IK LANGUAGE TERM BOOK
Oscar Alexie, et al, Editors
175 pp. Paper. University of Alaska, Fairbanks Center, 1990.

*MARY MUSGRAVE: GEORGIA INDIAN PRINCESS
Helen Todd
Grades 6-12. 152 pp. Paper. Cherokee, 1981. $6.95.

MUSHROOM STONES OF MESO-AMERICA
Karl H. Meyer
Illus. Paper. Acoma Books, 1977. $4.95.

MUSIC & DANCE OF THE AMERICAN INDIAN
Ruth DeCesare
Paper. Alfred Publishing, 1997. $21.95 includes audio CD.

MUSIC & DANCE RESEARCH ON THE SOUTHWESTERN INDIANS
Charlotte Frisbie
109 pp. Harmonie Park Press, 1977. $18.

MUSIC OF ACOMA, ISLETA, COCHITI & ZUNI PUEBLOS
Francis Densmore
Reprint of 1957 edition. Illus. 142 pp. Da Capo Press, $25.

MUSIC OF THE INDIANS OF BRITISH COLUMBIA
Francis Densmore
Reprint of 1943 edition. Illus. 118 pp. Da Capo Press, $21.50.

MUSIC OF THE NATIVE NORTH AMERICAN FOR FLUTE & RECORDER
Daniel Chazanoff
Music notation book with spiral binding; includes melodies from the Great Lakes and Eastern Woodlands Indians, Southeast, Plains, Southwestern, Pueblo, Great Basin-Plateau, Northwest and California Indians. 32 pp. $9.95. Canyon Records & Indian Arts. See Audio-Visual Distributors under CAN.

THE MUSIC OF THE NORTH AMERICAN INDIAN
Francis Densmore
13 volumes. Da Capo Press, 1972. $325 per set.

MUSKOGEE CITY & COUNTY
Odie B. Faulk
History through the 1970s of the Muskogee area of Oklahoma. Illus. 197 pp. The Five Civilized Tribes Museum, 1984. $19.95.

MY ADVENTURES IN ZUNI
Frank H. Cushing
Hist story of life in the Zuni Pueblo in 1867. Illus. 58 pp. Filter Press, 1967. $8; paper, $5.

MY FRIEND THE INDIAN
James McLaughlin
Illus. 475 pp. Paper. University of Nebraska Press, 1989. $11.50.

MY GRANDFATHER'S HOUSE: TLINGIT SONGS OF DEATH & SORROW
David Cloutier
Illus. 40 pp. Paper. Holmgangers, 1980. $3.

MY HEART SOARS
Chief Dan George
Illus. 96 pp. Paper. Hancock House, $7.95.

MY INDIAN BOYHOOD
Chief Luther Standing Bear
Illus. 200 pp. University of Nebraska Press, 1988. $19.95; paper, $6.95.

*MY LIFE AS AN INDIAN: THE STORY OF A RED WOMAN & A WHITE MAN IN THE LODGES OF THE BLACKFEET
James W. Schultz
Reprint of 1981 edition. Grades 6 and up. 288 pp. Paper. Dover, $8.95.

MY LIFE ON THE PLAINS; OR, PERSONAL EXPERIENCES WITH INDIANS
George A. Custer; Milo M. Quaife, Editor
Reprint of 1962 edition. Illus. 418 pp. Paper. University of Nebraska Press or University of Oklahoma Press, $12.95.

MY LUISENO NEIGHBORS
Eleanor Beemer
Illus. 91 pp. Acoma Books, 1980. $9.95.

*MY NAVAJO SISTER
Eleanor Schick
Grades 3 to 7. A white girl forms a close bond with a Navajo girl. Meadowlark Communications, $16.

MY PEOPLE THE SIOUX
L. Standing Bear; E.A. Brininstool, Editor
Reprint of 1928 edition. Illus. 288 pp. Paper. University of Nebraska Press, $6.95.

MY SPIRIT SOARS
Chief Dan George
Illus. 96 pp. Paper. Hancock House, $7.95.

MY WORK AMONG THE FLORIDA SEMINOLES
James Glenn; Harry Kersey, Jr., Editor
Illus. Maps. 121 pp. University Press of Florida, 1982. $16.95.

*MYSTERY AT ECHO CLIFFS
Kate Abbott
Story for children contains information about Navajo customs and history. Grades 4-9. Illus. 184 pp. Paper. Red Crane Books, $11.95.

*MYSTERY OF COYOTE CANYON
Timothy Green
Col. Kit Carson's military campaign against the Navajos, artifacts of the Anasazi, and the ruins of Cliff dwellings in Canyon de Chelly are some of the historical themes in this story. Grades 6 and up. Illus. Map. 150 pp. Paper. Ancient City Press, 1994. $12.95.

MYSTERY OF E TROOP: CUSTER'S GRAY HORSE COMPANY AT LITTLE BIG HORN
Gregory Michno
352 pp. Paper. Mountain Press. $16.

*THE MYSTERY OF THE ANASAZI
Leonard E. Fisher
Grades K-4. Illus. 32 pp. Children's Press, 1997. $16.

MYSTERY OF SACAJAWEA: INDIAN GIRL WITH LEWIS & CLARK
Harold P. Howard
Story of Shoshone guide Sacajawea of the Lewis & Clark Expedition. Illus. 200 pp. Paper. Center for Western Studies, $4.95.

*MYSTERY TRACKS IN THE SNOW
Hap Gilliland
Identifies over 100 North American animal tracks. Grades 4 and up. 142 pp. Council for Indian Education, $14.95; paper, $7.95.

THE MYSTIC LAKE SIOUX: SOCIOLOGY OF THE MDEWAKANTONWAN SANTEE
Ruth Landes
Illus. Map. 234 pp. University of Wisconsin Press, 1969. $25.

THE MYSTIC WARRIORS OF THE PLAINS: THE CULTURE, ARTS, CRAFTS, & RELIGION OF THE PLAINS INDIANS
Thomas E. Mails
Documents the lifestyles of the Plains Indians. Illus. 618 pp. Marlowe & Co. & Written Heritage, $46.50; paper, $29.95.

MYSTICS, MAGICIANS, & MEDICINE PEOPLE
Doug Boyd
Simon & Schuster. $12.

*MYTH, MUSIC & DANCE OF THE AMERICAN INDIAN
Ruth DeCesare; Sandy Feldstein, et al, Editors
Grades 4-12. Illus. 80 pp. Teacher's edition, $12.95 with cassette, $19.95; cassette only, $9.95; student edition, 16 pp. $3.95; student songbook, 24 pp., $4.95. Alfred Publishing, 1988.

THE MYTH & PRAYERS OF THE GREAT STAR CHANT & THE MYTH OF THE COYOTE CHANT
Recorded by Mary C. Wheelwright; ed. by David McAllester
Illus. 190 pp. Paper. Dine College Press, 1989. $27.

THE MYTHIC WORLD OF THE ZUNI: AS WRITTEN BY FRANK HAMILTON CUSHING
Barton Wright, Editor
Reprint. Illus. 190 pp. Paper. University of New Mexico Press, $14.95.

THE MYTHICAL PUEBLO RIGHTS DOCTRINE: WATER ADMINISTRATION IN HISPANIC NEW MEXICO
Daniel Tyler
Illus. 65 pp. Texas Western, 1989. $12; paper, $7.50.

MYTHOLOGY OF THE BLACKFOOT INDIANS
compiled & tr. by Clark Wissler & D.C. Duvall
Illus. 168 pp. Paper. University of Nebraska Press, 1995. $13.95.

MYTHOLOGY OF THE LENAPE: GUIDE & TEXTS
John Bierhorst
Synopsis of 218 Lenape narratives on record. 192 pp. Paper. University of Arizona Press, 1995. $20.95.

MYTHOLOGY OF NATIVE NORTH AMERICA
David Leeming & Jake Page
Illus. Map. 224 pp. University of Oklahoma Press, 1998. $24.95; paper, $14.95.

THE MYTHOLOGY OF NORTH AMERICA: INTRO TO CLASSIC AMERICAN GODS, HEROES & TRICKSTERS
John Bierhorst
Illus. 256 pp. Paper. William Morrow, 1986. $6.95.

MYTHOLOGY & VALUES: AN ANALYSIS OF NAVAHO CHANTWAY MYTHS
Katherine Spencer
Reprint of 1957 edition. 248 pp. Paper. University of Texas Press, 1957. $6.95.

MYTHOLOGY OF THE WICHITA
George A. Dorsey
354 pp. University of Oklahoma Press, 1995. $13.95.

MYTHS & FOLKTALES OF THE ALABAMA-COUSHATTA INDIANS
Howard N. Martin
45 stories. The Encino Press, 1982. $10.95.

MYTHS & LEGENDS OF CALIFORNIA & THE OLD SOUTHWEST
Katherine Berry Judson
Zuni, Pima, Paiute Shastika, and Miwok stories of the creation of the universe. Illus. 255 pp. Paper. University of Nebraska Press, 1994. $8.95.

*MYTHS & LEGENDS OF THE HAIDA INDIANS OF THE NORTHWEST
Dr. Reid
Grade 5. Illus. Paper. Bellerophon Books, 1978. $3.95.

*MYTHS & LEGENDS OF THE INDIANS OF THE SOUTHWEST: HOPI, ACOMA, TEWA, ZUNI
Bertha Dutton and Caroline Olin
Grade 5. Illus. Paper. Bellerophon Books, 1978. $3.95.

*MYTHS & LEGENDS OF THE INDIANS OF THE SOUTHWEST: NAVAJO, PIMA & APACHE
Bertha Dutton and Caroline Olin
Grade 5. Illus. Paper. Bellerophon Books, 1978. $3.95.

MYTHS & LEGENDS OF THE NORTH AMERICAN INDIANS
Lewis Spence
474 pp. Paper. Kessinger Press, 1997. $35.

MYTHS & LEGENDS OF THE PACIFIC NORTHWEST
Katherine Berry Judson
Klamath, Nez Perce, Tillamook, Modoc, Shastan, Chinook, Flathead, Clatsop and other Northwest tribes' stories of the creation of the universe. Illus. 195 pp. Paper. University of Nebraska Press, 1997. $12.95.

MYTHS & LEGENDS OF THE SIOUX
Marie L. McLaughlin
38 Sioux legends. Illus. 200 pp. Paper. University of Nebraska Press, 1990. $13.95.

MYTHS & SACRED FORMULAS OF THE CHEROKEES
James Mooney
Obtained on the Cherokee Reservation in NC in 1887-1888 covering daily life and thought of the Cherokee. Reprint. 400 pp. Paper. VIP Publishing & Cherokee Publications, $15.95.

MYTHS & SYMBOLS, OR ABORIGINAL RELIGIONS IN AMERICA
Stephen Peet
Reprint of 1905 edition. Illus. Longwood, $45.

MYTHS & TALES OF THE CHIRICAHUA APACHE INDIANS
Morris E. Opler; into. by Scott Rushforth
Reprint of 1942 edition. 115 pp. Paper. University of Nebraska Press, 1994. $11.95.

MYTHS & TALES OF THE JICARILLA APACHE INDIANS
Morris E. Opler
Reprint of 1938 edition. 407 pp. Paper. University of Nebraska Press, $14.95; Dover, $9.95.

MYTHS & TALES OF THE SOUTHEASTERN INDIANS
John R. Swanton
276 pp. Paper. University of Oklahoma Press, 1995. $13.95.

MYTHS & TALES OF THE WHITE MOUNTAIN APACHE
G. Goodwin, Editor
Reprint of 1938 edition. 223 pp. Paper. University of Arizona Press, $18.95.

MYTHS & TRADITIONS OF THE ARIKARA INDIANS
Douglas R. Parks
Illus. Maps. University of Nebraska Press, 1996. $40; paper, $17.95.

MYTHS OF THE CHEROKEE
James Mooney
Reprint of 1900 edition. 608 pp. paper. Dover, $14.95.

MYTHS OF THE MODOCS: INDIAN LEGENDS FROM THE NORTHWEST
Jeremiah Curtin
Reprint of 1912 edition. Ayer Co.

MYTHS OF THE NEW WORLD INDIANS: A TREATISE ON THE SYMBOLISM & MYTHOLOGY OF THE RED RACE OF AMERICA
D.G. Brinton
Reprint of 1876 edition. Illus. 360 pp. Longwood, $30; Greenwood, $35.

THE MYTHS OF THE NORTH AMERICAN INDIANS
Lewis Spence
Anthology of the myths & legends of the Algonquins, Iroquois, Pawnees & Sioux. Illus. 480 pp. Paper. Dover, Smoke & Fire Co., 1989. $12.95.

MYTHS OF PRE-COLUMBIAN AMERICA
Donald A. Mackenzie
416 pp. Paper. Dover, $9.95.

N

NA YO PISA
A noun recognition book for young readers. Includes three scenes from reservation life are shown, home-school-town. Grades K-3. 7 pp. Choctaw Heritage Press, $3.

NAIRNE'S MUSKHOGEAN JOURNALS: THE 1708 EXPEDITION TO THE MISSISSIPPI RIVER
Capt. Thomas Nairne; Alexander Moore, Editor
Muskhogean society in Colonial white-Indian relations. 92 pp.University Press of Mississippi, 1988. $18.50.

THE NAKED MAN, VOL. 4: MYTHOLOGIQUES
Claude Levi-Strauss; John & Doreen Weightman, translators
Reprint. 760 pp. Paper. University of Chicago Press, 1990. $21.95.

NAME OF SALISH & KOOTENAI NATION: THE 1855 HELL GATE TREATY & THE ORIGIN OF THE FLATHEAD INDIAN RESERVATION
Robert Bigart
Illus. 180 pp. Paper. University of Washington Press, 1996. $14.95.

THE NAMES
N. Scott Momaday
Reprint of 1977 edition. 180 pp. University of Arizona Press, 1987. $35; paper, $13.95.

NAMING CANADA: ESSAYS ON PLACE NAMES FROM CANADIAN GEOGRAPHIC
Alan Rayburn
Native place names are stamped across the entire country, reflecting the First Nations' contributions to Canadian history. Illus. 300 pp. University of Toronto Press, 1994. $55; paper, $18.95.

NAMPEYO & HER POTTERY
Barbara Kramer
Hopi-Tewa Potter. Reprint of 1996 edition. Illus. 224 pp. Paper. University of Arizona Press, 2003. $24.95.

NANA'S RAID: APACHE WARFARE IN SOUTHERN NEW MEXICO
Stephen H. Lekson
Illus. 78 pp. Texas Western Press, 1989. $12; paper, $7.50.

NANISE: A NAVAJO HERBAL
Vernon O. Mayes & Barbara Bayless Lacy
Identifies and illustrates 100 plants found today on the Navajo Reservation. Illus. Paper. Dine College Press, $27.

THE NANTICOKE
Frank Porter
Grades 5 and up. Illus. 104 pp. Chelsea House, 1987. $17.95.

THE NANTICOKE INDIANS
C.A. Weslager
Reprint of 1948 edition. 350 pp. University of Delaware Press, $28.50.

THE NARRAGANSETT
William Simmons
Grades 7-12. Illus. 112 pp. Chelsea House, 1989. $17.95.

THE NARRAGANSETT
Craig & Katherine Doherty
Grades 4-8. 32 pp. Rourke Publications, 1994. $22.60.

NARRATIVE CHANCE: POSTMODERN DISCOURSE ON NATIVE AMERICAN INDIAN LITERATURES
Gerald Vizenor, Editor
224 pp. University of New Mexico Press, 1989. $29.95. Paper. University of Oklahoma Press, $17.95.

A NARRATIVE OF THE CAPTIVITY OF ROBERT EASTBURN
Robert Eastburn
French & Indian War captivity account. 50 pp. Paper. Ye Galleon Press, $8.95.

NARRATIVE OF THE CAPTIVITY OF ISAAC WEBSTER
Isaac Webster
25 pp. Paper. Ye Galleon Press, 1988. $4.95.

A NARRATIVE OF THE CAPTIVITY OF MRS. JOHNSON
Johnson
Rerint of 1814 edition. Illus. 230 pp. Paper. Heritage Book, $18.50.

A NARRATIVE OF THE EARLY DAYS & REMEMBRANCES OF OCEOLA NIKKANOCHEE, PRINCE OF ECONCHATTI, A YOUNG SEMINOLE INDIAN, et al
Andre G. Welch
Reprint of 1841 edition. Illus. 305 pp. University Press of Florida, $19.95.

NARRATIVE OF THE EXPEDITION TO THE SOURCE OF ST. PETER'S RIVER
W.H. Keating
Facsimile of 1825 edition. Illus. Ross & Haines, $20.

NARRATIVE OF HENRY BIRD WHO WAS CARRIED AWAY BY THE INDIANS, AFTER THE MURDER OF HIS WHOLE FAMILY IN 1811
Henry Bird
Reprint. 65 pp. Paper. Ye Galleon, $6.95.

A NARRATIVE OF THE LIFE OF MRS. MARY JEMISON
James E. Seaver
Reprint of 1824 edition. 208 pp. Paper. Syracuse University Press, 1990. $14.95. A new edition edited by June Namias, 208 pp. and published by University of Oklahoma Press. $15.95.

A NARRATIVE OF THE MANNER IN WHICH THE CAMPAIGN AGAINST THE INDIANS, IN THE YEAR 1791, WAS CONDUCTED
Arthur St. Clair
Reprint of 1812 edition. Ayer Co., $29.95.

NARRATIVE OF THE MISSION OF THE BRETHREN AMONG THE DELAWARE AND MOHEGAN INDIANS
J. Heckewelder
Reprint of 1820 edition. Ayer Co., $29.

NARRATIVE OF OCCURENCES IN THE INDIAN COUNTRIES OF NORTH AMERICA
S.H. Wilcocke
Reprint of 1817 edition. Beekman Publishers, $19.95.

NARRATIVE OF WILLIAM BIGGS
William Biggs
Reprint. 35 pp. Paper. Ye Galleon Press, $5.95.

NARRATIVE OF THOMAS BROWN
Thomas Brown
Facsimile of 1760 printing of a French & Indian War booklet. 24 pp. Paper. Ye Galleon Press, $4.95.

NARRATIVE OF MATTHEW BUNN
Matthew Bunn
Captivity account. Reprint of the 1796 edition. 64 pp. Paper. Ye Galleon Press, $7.95.

NARRATIVES OF CAPITIVITY AMONG THE INDIANS OF NORTH AMERICA: A LIST OF BOOKS & MANUSCRIPTS ON THE SUBJECT IN THE EDWARD A. AYER COLLECTION OF THE NEWBERRY LIBRARY
Lists 339 narratives. Reprint of 1912 edition. 185 pp. Omnigraphics, $35.

NARRATIVES OF THE INDIAN WARS, 1675-1699
Charles Lincoln, Editor
Reprint of 1913 ed. 312 pp. Barnes & Noble Imports, $21.50.

NATION IROQUOIS: A 17TH CENTURY ETHNOGRAPHY OF THE (ONEIDA) IROQUOIS
edited & trans. by Jose Antonio Brandao with K. Janet Ritch
The original French transcription of "Nation Iroquois" manuscript; its English translation, an overview of Iroquois culture and of Iroquois-French relations. Map. 128 pp. University of Nebraska Press, 2003. $40.

NATION-STATES & INDIANS IN LATIN AMERICA
Greg Urban & Joel Sherzer
370 pp. University of Texas Press, 1991. $37.50.

NATION WITHIN A NATION: DEPENDENCY & THE CREE
Marie-Anik Gagne
Canadian First Nations and their struggle against economic subjection and oppression. 160 pp. University of Toronto Press, $49; paper, $20.

THE NATIONAL CONGRESS OF AMERICAN INDIANS: THE FOUNDING YEARS
Thomas W. Cowger
A full-length history of the NCAI. Illus. 223 pp. University of Nebraska Press, 1999. $50; paper, $22.

NATIONAL DIRECTORY OF CORPORATE PHILANTHROPY FOR NATIVE AMERICANS
Phyllis A. Meiners, et al, Editors
Profiles about 40 corporate giving programs and corporate foundations each of whom have made multiple grants to Native American tribes and organizations. 250 pp. Paper. CRC Publishing, Irregular. $99.95.

NATIONAL DIRECTORY OF FOUNDATION GRANTS FOR NATIVE AMERICANS
Phyllis Meiners, et al, Editors
Profiles over 55 private foundations considered to be the most prominent funders of Native American programs. 205 pp. Paper. CRC Publishing. $99.95.

NATIONAL DIRECTORY OF PHILANTHROPY FOR NATIVE AMERICANS
Phyllis A. Meiners, et al. Editors
Profiles about 40 private sector (foundations, corporations, and religious institutions) grant makers; prominent funders of Native American programs. 250 pp. CRC Publishing. $125.

NATIONAL DIRECTORY OF SEED MONEY GRANTS FOR AMERICAN INDIAN PROJECTS
Phyllis Meiners, et al, Editors
Sourcebook of private sector seed money grants for start-up and innovative programs managed by Native Americans. Also a section of Native American foundations is included. 220 pp. Paper. CRC Publishing, 1996. $109.95.

NATIONAL INDIAN GAMING ASSOCIATION (NIGA) INDIAN GAMING RESOURCE DIRECTORY
The complete desk-top reference guide for tribal representatives, gaming management, Indian gaming suppliers and gaming enthusiasts including listings of regional gaming associations, Indian gaming facilities, gaming regulatory agencies, Indian gaming lawyers and lobbyists, American Indian entertainment, and Indian gaming suppliers. National Indian Gaming Association, $30, members; $55, non-members.

NATIONAL INDIAN GAMING MINIMUM INTERNAL CONTROL STANDARDS FOR INDIAN CASINOS
adopted by NIGA/NCAI Tribal Leader Task Force & NIGA Membership
Developed by tribal professionals from within the Indian gaming industry as a set of baseline internal control procedures for gaming facilities operated by Indian Nations under the Federal Indian Gaming Regulatory Act, 1998 revised version. National Indian Gaming Association, $30, members; $55, non-members.

NATIONAL MUSEUM OF THE AMERICAN INDIAN, A POSTCARD BOOK
30 full-color photos...images from the book *Creation's Journey: Native American Identity & Belief*. 33 pp. Running Press, $8.95.

NATIONS REMEMBERED: ORAL HISTORY OF THE CHEROKEES, CHICKASAWS, CHOCTAWS, CREEKS, & SEMINOLES, 1865-1907
Theda Perdue
Illus. Maps. 222 pp. Paper. University of Oklahoma Press, 1993. $14.95.

NATIONS WITHIN A NATION: HISTORICAL STATISTICS OF AMERICAN INDIANS
Paul Stuart
Historical statistics on Native American tribes. Biblio. 251 pp. Greenwood, 1987. $45.

THE NATIONS WITHIN: THE PAST & FUTURE OF AMERICAN INDIAN SOVEREIGNTY
Vine Deloria, Jr. and Clifford Lytle
Reprint of 1984 edition. 336 pp. Paper. University of Texas Press, $12.95.

NATIVE AMERICA
John Gattuso
A narrative approach to identify and describe the sites and

activities of the Native American. Includes discussion of Amerian Indian art, Indians and alcohol, and ancestral grounds. Illus. Biblio. 389 pp. Paper. Prentice-Hall, 1992. $19.95.

NATIVE AMERICA: ARTS, TRADITIONS & CELEBRATIONS
Christine Mather
Illus. Crown Publishers, 1990. $40.

NATIVE AMERICA COLLECTED: THE CULTURE OF AN ART WORLD
Margaret Dubin
Examines the ideas and interactions involved in contemporary collecting. Illus. 192 pp. University of New Mexico Press, 2001. $29.95.

NATIVE AMERICA & THE EVOLUTION OF DEMOCRACY
Bruce E. Johansen
184 pp. Greenwood Publishing, 1999. $65.

NATIVE AMERICA IN THE TWENTIETH CENTURY: AN ENCYCLOPEDIA
Mary B. Davis, Editor
Contains 282 signed articles (written by historians, anthropologists, and other specialists - 40% of whom are Native American) on present-day tribal groups providing information on 20th-century American Indians & Alaska Natives. 75 photos. 25 maps. 832 pp. Garland Publishing, 1994. $100; paper, $29.95.

*NATIVE AMERICA MEDICINE: INDIANS OF NORTH AMERICA
Chelsea House Staff
Grades 5 and up. 120 pp. Chelsea House, 1997. $9.95.

NATIVE AMERICA: PORTRAIT OF THE PEOPLES
Duane Champagne, Editor
A selection of articles covering Native American history, religion, arts, language and present-day lifeways and issues. Also hundreds of biographies. Illus. 200 photos and drawings. Maps. 814 pp. Paper. Visible Ink Press, $18.95.

NATIVE AMERICAN AFFAIRS & THE DEPARTMENT OF DEFENSE
Donald Mitchell & David Rubenson
Released from RAND the National Defense Research Institute. 80 pp. Paper. Rand, 1996. $15.

NATIVE AMERICAN AIDS STATISTICS
Statistics from the U.S. CDC on reported cases of AIDS among Native Americans. Graphs. National Native American AIDS Prevention Center. No charge.

THE NATIVE AMERICAN ALMANAC: A PORTRAIT OF NATIVE AMERICA TODAY
Arlene Hirschfelder & Martha Kreipe de Montano
Includes history of Native-white relations, the location & status of tribes, religious traditions & ceremonies, language & literature, and contemporary performers & artists; organizations, Native American landmarks, museums & cultural centers. 100 bxw photos & drawings. 340 pp. The Book Publishing Co., $14.95.

NATIVE AMERICAN ANCESTORS: EASTERN TRIBES
Arlene H. Eakle
50 pp. Paper. Genealogical Institute, 1996. $16.50.

*NATIVE AMERICAN ANIMAL STORIES
told by Joseph Bruchac
24 stories. Grades K-5. Illus. 160 pp. Demco, $18.05. Paper. Fulcrum Publishing, 1991. $12.95. Audiocassette, $16.95.

NATIVE AMERICAN ANNUAL, Vol. I
Margaret Clark-Price
Illus. 100 pp. Native American Publishing, 1985. $8.95.

NATIVE AMERICAN ARCHITECTURE
Peter Nabakov & Robert Easton
307 photos. Illus. 432 pp. Paper. Oxford University Press & Written Heritage, 1988. $29.95.

NATIVE AMERICAN ARCHIVES: AN INTRODUCTION
John A. Fleckner
72 pp. Paper. Society of American Archivists, 1985. $7.

NATIVE AMERICAN ART
David W. Penney & George C. Longfish
Traces the development of American Indian art from the handmade tools of the Archaic Period to contemporary creations. 290 full-color black & white photos, 320 pp. Levin Associates, 1994. $85.

THE NATIVE AMERICAN ART LOOK BOOK
Dawn Weiss and Barbara Zaffran, Editors
An activity book from The Brooklyn Museum. Presents objects from the museum's collection of Native American art—pottery, basketry, and wood carvings. Illus. 48 pp. Paper. W.W. Norton & Co., 1993. $14.95.

NATIVE AMERICAN ART MASTERPIECES
David W. Penney
Illus. 120 pp. Simon & Schuster, 1996. $35.

NATIVE AMERICAN ART AT PHILBROOK
Philbrook Art Center
Paper. Philbrook Art Center,1980. $9.95.

NATIVE AMERICAN ART & THE NEW YORK AVANTE-GARDE
W. Jackson Rushing
The influence Native American art had on American modernist art of 1910-1950. Illus. 272 pp. University of Texas Press, 1994. $39.95.

NATIVE AMERICAN ARTS & CULTURE
Mary Connors & Dona Herweck
Illus. Teacher Created mateials, 1994. $14.95.

NATIVE AMERICAN ARTISANS SURVEY
A survey of American Indian artists in Arizona. Atlatl, 1992. $5.

NATIVE AMERICAN BASKETRY: AN ANNOTATED BIBLIOGRAPHY
Frank W. Porter, III, compiled by
1,000+ entries on all aspetcs of Native American basket making. 249 pp. Greenwood, 1988. $39.95.

NATIVE AMERICAN BASKETRY OF THE SENECA & TLINGIT
Richard C. Schneider, Editor
Reprint of 1941 edition. Illus. Photos. 120 pp. Paper. R. Schneider, Publishers, $8.95.

NATIVE AMERICAN BEADWORK
Georg J. Barth
Covers all aspects of traditional Indian beadwork. Illus. 220 pp. R. Schneider, Publishers, 1993. $27.95; paper, $19.95.

NATIVE AMERICAN BIBLIOGRAPHY SERIES
Jack W. Marken, General Editor
Begun in 1980, titles in this series have focused on individual tribes, geographic areas, literature, languages, and collections of documents. See publisher for titles & prices. Scarecrow Press.

*NATIVE AMERICAN BIOGRAPHIES
3 biographies: Sacajawea, Pocahontas, Sitting Bull. Grades 3-7. Illus. 48 pp. each. Troll Associates, $3.50 each.

*NATIVE AMERICAN BIOGRAPHIES
Series of six biographies: Dennis Banks, 112 pp. Maria Tallchief, 128 pp. Geronimo, 128 pp. Scagawea, 128 pp. Jim Thorpe, 128 pp. & Siting Bull, 112 pp. Grades 6 and up. Illus. Photos. Enslow Publishers, 1997. $17.95 each, $107.70 per set.

*THE NATIVE AMERICAN BOOK OF CHANGE
White Deer of Autumn
Chronicles the struggles of the American Indians since Europeans came into their world. Grades 3-7. Paper. Beyond Words or Greenfield Review Press, $5.95.

*THE NATIVE AMERICAN BOOK OF KNOWLEDGE
White Deer of Autumn
Grades 3-7. Paper. Beyond Words or Greenfield Review Press, $5.95.

*THE NATIVE AMERICAN BOOK OF LIFE
White Deer of Autumn
Grades 3-7. Paper. Beyond Words or Greenfield Review Press, $5.95.

*THE NATIVE AMERICAN BOOK OF WISDOM
White Deer of Autumn
Grades 3-7. Paper. Beyond Words or Greenfield Review Press, $5.95.

NATIVE AMERICAN CHECKLIST
Barbara Beaver, Compiler
Contains over 900 titles relating to Native Americans. Covers art, history, literature, religion, travel, and women's studies. Also audiovisual materials and children's books. 20 pp. Paper. Bookpeople. No charge to schools and lbraries.

*NATIVE AMERICAN CHIEFS & WARRIORS
Deanne Durrett
Grades 4-12. Illus. Lucent Books, 1999. $22.45.

NATIVE AMERICAN COLLECTIBLES
Dawn E. Reno
Covers baskets, clothing, jewelry, photographs and pottery. Illus. 512 pp. Paper. Hothem House, 1994. $16.95 postpaid.

NATIVE AMERICAN COMMUNITIES IN WISCONSIN, 1600-1960
Robert E. Bieder
Illus. 272 pp. Paper. University of Wisconsin Press, 1995. $18.95.

NATIVE AMERICAN COURTSHIP & MARRIAGE TRADITIONS
Leslie Gourse
Includes the Hopi, Navajo, Iroquois, and Oglala Sioux love, courtship, marriage and family traditions. 160 pp. Hippocrene Books, 1999. $22.50.

NATIVE AMERICAN CRAFT INSPIRATIONS
Janet & Alex D'Amato
Illus. 224 pp. Paper. M. Evans, 1992. $11.95.

NATIVE AMERICAN CRAFTS
Suzanne McNeill
Sterling, 1997.

NATIVE AMERICAN CRAFTS DIRECTORY
Diane L. McAlister
A guide for locating craft shops and craft suppliers. Over 1,000 entries to help you locate hard-to-find Native American products, organizations, and resources. 136 pp. 2nd Edition. The Book Publishing Co. & Clear Light, 1998. $9.95.

NATIVE AMERICAN CRAFTS OF CALIFORNIA, THE GREAT BASIN & THE SOUTHWEST
Judith Hoffman-Corwin
Franklin Watts, 1999.

NATIVE AMERICAN CRAFTS OF THE NORTHWEST COAST, THE ARCTIC & THE SUBARCTIC
Judith Hoffman-Corwin
Franklin Watts, 1999.

NATIVE AMERICAN CULTURAL & RELIGIOUS FREEDOMS
John R. Wunder
Reprint. 392 pp. Garland, $75.

*NATIVE AMERICAN CULTURES: A STUDY UNIT TO PROMOTE CRITICAL & CREATIVE THINKING
Rebecca Stark
Grades 4-8. 80 pp. Student edition, 1991. $12.95; Book & Poster, 1998. $12.95. Educational Impressions.

NATIVE AMERICAN CURRICULAR LESSONS
Developed by a diverse group of teachers and educators attending the Native American Curriculum Development Workshop. ITEPP CRC, 1996.

NATIVE AMERICAN DANCE: CEREMONIES & SOCIAL TRADITIONS
Charlotte Heth, General Editor
Collection of essays on Native American dance traditions & their meaning, origin, and evolution. 192 full-color photos & illus. 208 pp. Fulcrum Publishing, Starwood Publishing & Clear Light, 1992. $45; paper, $29.95.

NATIVE AMERICAN DESIGNS
Caren Caraway
Combines five regional books: *Eastern Woodland Indian Designs, Northwest Indian Designs, Plains Indian Designs, Southeastern Woodland Indian Designs,* and *Southwest American Indian Designs.* Illus. 240 pp. Paper. Stemmer House, 1993. $27.95. Regional books, $5.95 each.

NATIVE AMERICAN DESIGNS FOR QUILTING
Joyce Mori
80 pp. Paper. Collector Books, 1998. $14.95.

NATIVE AMERICAN DIRECTORY: ALASKA, U.S. & CANADA
Fred Synder, Editor
Paper. Native American Co-Op. Irregular.

NATIVE AMERICAN DIRECTORY: VITAL RECORDS OF MAINE, MASS., RI, CT, NY & WI
Lorraine Henry
131 pp. Paper. Heritage Books, 1998. $15.

NATIVE AMERICAN DISCOURSE: POETICS & RHETORIC
Joel Sherzer & Anthony Woodbury
Illus. 256 pp. Cambridge University Press, 1987. $44.50.

*NATIVE AMERICAN DOCTOR: THE STORY OF SUSAN LaFLESCHE PICOTTE
Jeri Ferris
Grades 4-7. Biography. Photos. Lerner, 1991. $17.95; paper, $6.95.

NATIVE AMERICAN & THE EARLY REPUBLIC
Frederick Hoxie, et al
University Press of Kentucky, 2000.

NATIVE AMERICAN ESTATE: THE STRUGGLE OVER INDIAN & HAWAIIAN LANDS
Linda S. Parker
256 pp. University of Hawaii Press, 1989. $24.

NATIVE AMERICAN EXPRESSIVE CULTURE
Akwe:kon Press Editors
Essays from 28 Native American writers. 1213 bxw photos. 176 pp. Paper. Fulcrum Publishing, 1996. $17.95.

NATIVE AMERICAN FASHION: MODERN ADAPTATIONS OF TRADITIONAL DESIGNS
Margaret Wood
2nd revised edition. Illus. 128 pp. Paper. Native American Fashion, 1997. $21.95.

NATIVE AMERICAN FLAGS
Donald T. Healy & Peter J. Orenski
Revised edition of *Flags of the Native Peoples of the U.S.* Illus.
325 pp. Paper. University of Oklahoma Press, 2003. $29.95.

NATIVE AMERICAN FOLKLORE, 1879-1979
Frances Malpezzi
Covers all aspects of oral literature, including dance and ritual.
Swallow Press, 1984.

*NATIVE AMERICAN FOODS
Raven Hail
Coloring book showing many of the world's staple foods that
came from Indian America. Grades K-2. Illus. 21 pp. Paper.
Raven Hail, 1986. $3.95.

**NATIVE AMERICAN GARDENING: STORIES,
PROJECTS & RECIPES FOR FAMILIES**
Michael J. Caduto & Joseph Bruchac
Explores the Native American approach to gardening.
Illus. 176 pp. Paper. Fulcrum Publishing, $15.95.

NATIVE AMERICAN GENEALOGICAL SOURCEBOOK
Paula K. Byers, Editor
250 pp. Gale, 1995. $69.

NATIVE AMERICAN HERITAGE, Third Ed.
Merwyn Garbarino & Robert F. Sasso
A text providing a broad overview of the diversity of American
Indian cultures. In 4 parts: prehistory, the construct of culture
areas; various culture traits, and exploring the interactions be-
tween Native Americans and non-natives. Illus. Maps.Paper.
Waveland Press, 1994. $17.95.

NATIVE AMERICAN HIGHER EDUCATION IN THE U.S.
Cary M. Carney
226 pp. Transaction Publishers, 1999. $32.95.

**NATIVE AMERICAN HISTORICAL DEMOGRAPHY:
A CRITICAL BIBLIOGRAPHY**
Henry Dobyns
104 pp. Paper. Indian University Press, 1982. $4.95.

NATIVE AMERICAN HOUSING ASSISTANCE
Diane Publishing Staff
Illus. 246 pp. Diane Publishing, 1998. $45.

**NATIVE AMERICAN HOUSING: INFORMATION ON
HUD'S FUNDING OF INDIAN HOUSING PROGAMS**
Carol Anderson-Gutherie
Illus. 63 pp. Paper. Diane Publishing, 1999. $20.

**NATIVE AMERICAN IDENTITIES: FROM STEREOTYPE
TO ARCHETYPE IN ART & LITERATURE**
Scott B. Vickers
Illus. 192 pp. University of New Mexico Press, 1998.
$40; paper, $19.95.

**NATIVE AMERICAN IN AMERICAN LITERATURE:
A SELECTIVELY ANNOTATED BIBLIOGRAPHY**
Roger O. Rock
225 pp. Greenwood Press, 1985. $36.95.

**THE NATIVE AMERICAN IN LONG FICTION:
AN ANNOTATED BIBLIOGRAPHY**
Joan Beam
Lists novel-length fictional works by and about Native
Americans of the U.S. published between the 1890s and 1990s.
384 pp. Scarecrow Press, 1996. $56.

THE NATIVE AMERICAN INDIAN ARTIST DIRECTORY
Robert Painter
Lists over 1,200 artists, sculptors, potters, rug weavers, basket makers, kachina carvers, bead workers, clothing designers, silversmiths, jewelry makers and other craftspeople from
over 100 tribes across America. Includes names, addresses,
phone numbers, e-mail addresses, tribal affiliations, web sites.
288 pp. Paper. Todd Publications, $19.95.

NATIVE AMERICAN INTERNET GUIDE
Martha Crow
Listing of about 1,200 Native groups, organizations, nations,
businesses and individuals and their web sites. 80 pp. Spiral
bound. Todd Publications, $35.

NATIVE AMERICAN ISSUES: A REFERENCE HANDBOOK
ABC-Clio staff
288 pp. ABC-Clio, 1996. $39.50.

**NATIVE AMERICAN LAW & COLONIALISM
BEFORE 1776 TO 1903**
John R. Wunder, Editor
Reprint. Illus. 352 pp. Garland, 1996. $70.

*NATIVE AMERICAN LEADERS
Profiles 25 great leaders of North American Indian tribes mostly
in the 19th century. Grades 4 and up. Illus. 64 pp. Chelsea
House, $17.95.

*NATIVE AMERICAN LEADERS OF THE WILD WEST
William R. Sanford
7 biographies: Chief Joseph, Crazy Horse, Geronimo, Quanah
Parker, Red Cloud, Sitting Bull, and Osceola. Grades 4-10. Illus.

Maps. Biblio. 48 pp. each. Enslow Publishing, 1994.
$14.95 each; $104.65 per set.

NATIVE AMERICAN LEGENDS
131 legends from many North American Indian tribes and information and background of each legend. Six book set. Illus.
288 pp. Paper. Rourke Corp., 1990, $89.70.

NATIVE AMERICAN LEGENDS & LORE LIBRARY
Troll Book Staff
Paper. Troll Communications, 1999. $59.40.

NATIVE AMERICAN LEGENDS: THE SOUTHEAST
George Lankford
Illus. 268 pp. August House, 1987. $19.95; paper, $9.95.

NATIVE AMERICAN MATHEMATICS
Michael P. Closs
Illus. 439 pp. Paper. University of Texas Press, 1986. $19.95.

NATIVE AMERICAN MUSIC DIRECTORY
Greg Gombert
1,600 listings of traditional flute, vocal, pow wow, peyote, rock,
and country songs in print and available for purchase in the
U.S. and Canada. 176 pp. Triennial. Book Publishing Co., 1997.
$12.95.

**NATIVE AMERICAN MYTH & LEGEND:
AN A-Z OF PEOPLE & PLACES**
Mike Dixon-Kennedy
Illus. 288 pp. Paper. Sterling, 1996. $27.95; paper, $17.95.

**NATIVE AMERICAN ORAL TRADITIONS:
COLLABORATION & INTERPRETATION**
Larry Evers & Barre Toelken, Editors
Native American oral texts with commentary. 256 pp.
Utah State University Press, 2001. $39.95; paper, $21.95.

NATIVE AMERICAN PAINTED BUFFALO HIDES
George P. Horse Capture, Anne Vitart,
& Richard West, Editors
Collection of 100 photos of painted buffalo hides. Includes in-
troductory and historical essays by two Native American art
experts. Illus. 168 pp. W.W. Norton & Co., 1993. $35.

**NATIVE AMERICAN PEDAGOGY & COGNITIVE-BASED
MATHEMATICS INSTRUCTION**
Judith T. Hankes
200 pp. Garland Publishing, 1998. $50.

*NATIVE AMERICAN PEOPLE
Rita D'Apice, et al
Grades 5-8. Illus. 6 book set. 192 pp. Rourke Corp.,
$59.70 per set.

**NATIVE AMERICAN PERIODICALS & NEWSPAPERS, 1828-
1982: BIBLIOGRAPHY, PUBLISHING RECORD & HOLDINGS**
James Danky, Editor; Maureen Hady, Compiler
Lists 1,200 Native American periodicals in 146 libraries in North
America. Illus. 565 pp. Greenwood, 1983. $50.95.

**NATIVE AMERICAN PERSPECTIVES
ON LITERATURE & HISTORY**
Alan R. Velie
136 pp. paper. University of Oklahoma Press, 1995. $14.95.

**NATIVE AMERICAN PICTURE BOOKS OF CHANGE:
THE ART OF HISTORIC CHILDREN'S EDITIONS**
Rebecca C. Benes
Story of children's books of the last century documenting four
decades of these picture books in a readers' series for Pueblo,
Navajo, and Lakota/Dakota children. Illus. 106 color plates. 176
pp. Museum of New Mexico Press, 2004. $45.

NATIVE AMERICAN PLACENAMES OF THE U.S.
William Bright
Dictionary of American placenames derived from Native languages; details the history and culture found in American Indian placenames. 608 pp. University of Oklahoma Press, 2004.
$59.95.

**NATIVE AMERICAN POLITICAL SYSTEMS & THE
EVOLUTION OF DEMOCRACY: AN ANNOTATED
BIBLIOGRAPHY**
Bruce E. Johansen
184 pp. Greenwood, 1996. $67.95.

NATIVE AMERICAN PORTRAITS
Nancy Hathaway
Illus. 120 pp. Paper. Chronicle Books, 1990. $16.95.

NATIVE AMERICAN POSTCOLONIAL PSYCHOLOGY
Eduardo Duran & Bonnie Duran
227 pp. Paper. State University of New York Press, 1995.
$20.95.

**NATIVE AMERICAN PRESS IN WISCONSIN & THE NATION:
PROCEEDINGS OF THE CONFERENCE ON THE NATIVE
AMERICAN PRESS IN WISCONSIN & THE NATION, APRIL,
1982**
James P. Danky and Maureen B. Hady
197 pp. Paper. University of Wisconsin Library School,
1982. $6.50.

**NATIVE AMERICAN PROPHECIES: EXAMINING THE
HISTORY, WISDOM & STARTLING PREDICTIONS OF
VISIONARY NATIVE AMERICANS**
Scott Peterson
256 pp. Paragon House, 1991. $22.95; paper, $12.95.

**NATIVE AMERICAN READER:
STORIES, SPEECHES & POEMS**
Anthology of stories. The Denali Press, $25.

**THE NATIVE AMERICAN REFERENCE COLLECTION:
DOCUMENTS COLLECTED BY THE OFFICE OF
INDIAN AFFAIRS**
University Publications of America, 1994. $3,695.

NATIVE AMERICAN RELIGION
Joel W. Martin
144 pp. Oxford University Press, 1999. $21.

NATIVE AMERICAN RELIGIONS
Sam Gill
192 pp. Paper. Wadsworth, 1982.

NATIVE AMERICAN RELIGIONS: AN INTRODUCTION
Denise Lardner Carmody & John Tully Carmody
Surveys major aspects of the traditional religious lives
of native peoples in all parts of the Americas. Illus.
288 pp. paper. Paulist Press, 1993. $14.95.

**NATIVE AMERICAN RELIGIONS:
A GEOGRAPHICAL SURVEY**
John J. Collins
420 pp. Edwin Mellen Press, 1991. $79.95.

NATIVE AMERICAN RELIGIONS: NORTH AMERICA
Lawrence Sullivan
Macmillan, 1989. $15.95.

*NATIVE AMERICAN RELIGIONS: WORLD RELIGIONS
Paula R. Hartz
Illus. 128 pp. Facts on File & Written Heritage, 1997.
$21.95.

**NATIVE AMERICAN RELIGIOUS ACTION:
A PERFORMANCE APPROACH TO RELIGION**
Sam D. Gill; Frederick Denny, Editor
125 pp. University of South Carolina Press, 1987. $21.95.

**NATIVE AMERICAN REPRESENTATIONS:
FIRST ENCOUNTERS, DISTORTED IMAGES,
& LITERARY APPROPRIATIONS**
Edited by Gretchen M. Bataille
Leading critics examine images in a wide range of media.
265 pp. University of Nebraska Press, 2001. $80; paper, $29.95.

NATIVE AMERICAN RESEARCH INFORMATION SERVICE
William Carmack, et al
292 pp. Paper. UCLA, American Indian Studies Center, 1983.
$15.

**NATIVE AMERICAN RESURGENCE & RENEWAL:
A READER & BIBLIOGRAPHY**
Robert N. Wells, Jr.
Native American self determination. Treaty rights and
tribal soverignty. 671 pp. Scarecrow Press, 1994. $68.50.

*NATIVE AMERICAN RIGHTS
Tamara L. Roleff, Editor
Grades 5-12. 208 pp. Greenhaven, 1997. $26.50;
paper, $16.20.

THE NATIVE AMERICAN RIGHTS MOVEMENT
Mark Grossman & ABC-Clio Staff
Follows the efforts to preserve and recover the civil rights of
American Indians in the U.S. Illus. 400 pp. ABC-CLIO, 1996.
$60.

NATIVE AMERICAN SONGS & POEMS
Swann, Editor
64 pp. Paper. Dover, $1.

NATIVE AMERICAN SPIRIT
Calendar. Pictures taken from book, *The Spirit of
Native America.* 12x12". Chronicle Books, $9.95.

**NATIVE AMERICAN SPIRITUALITY:
A CRITICAL READER**
Lee Irwin
Essays that explore the problems and prsoepcts of understand-
ing and writing about Native American spirituality in the 21st
century. 334 pp. Paper. University of Nebraska Press, 2000.
$24.95.

*NATIVE AMERICAN STORIES
Joseph Bruchac; illus. by John Kahiuonhes Fadden
25 myths. Grades 4 and up. 156 pp. Paper. Fulcrum
Publishing, $12.95; audio tape, $16.95.

**NATIVE AMERICAN STUDIES:
NEW NATIVE AMERICAN STORYTELLERS**
Clifford E. Trafzer
496 pp. Paper. Doubleday, 1996. $14.95.

**THE NATIVE AMERICAN STRUGGLE:
CONQUERING THE RULE OF LAW: A COLLOQUIUM**
Margaret A. Gilbert-Temple, Managing Editor
Speeches, articles and review essays. 226 pp. Paper.
New York University, Review of Law & Social Change.
Volume XX, 1993. $7.

NATIVE AMERICAN STYLE
Elmo Baca & M.J. Van Deventer
Collection of Native and native-inspired designs in art, architecture and interior design. Includes history and tradition og Native American craftsmanship and profiles of modern artisans and craftspeople. Illus. Color photos. 145 pp. Gibbs Smith, Publisher, 1999. $39.95.

**THE NATIVE AMERICAN SUN DANCE RELIGION
& CEREMONY: AN ANNOTATED BIBLIOGRAPHY**
Phillip M. White
144 pp. Greenwood Publishing, 1998. $55.

**NATIVE AMERICAN SWEAT LODGE:
HISTORY & LEGENDS**
Joseph Bruchac
Explains the history, the meaning and the use of the sweat lodge. Paper. Crossing Press & Written Heritage, $12.95.

*NATIVE AMERICAN TALKING SIGNS
The sign language of the North American Indians is explained and placed into context. Grades 4 and up. Illus. 64 pp. Chelsea House, $17.95.

***NATIVE AMERICAN TESTIMONY: AN ANTHOLOGY
OF INDIAN & WHITE RELATIONS, FIRST ENCOUNTER
TO DISPOSSESSION**
Peter Nabokov, Editor
Grades 7-and up. Illus. 220 pp. Harper & Row, 1992. $25.

**NATIVE AMERICAN TESTIMONY: A CHRONICLE
OF INDIAN-WHITE RELATIONS FROM PROPHECY
TO THE PRESENT, 1492-1992**
Peter Nabokov, Editor
Collection of essays by Native Americans. 512 pp.
Paper. Penguin USA, $10.

THE NATIVE AMERICAN TODAY
Joan Isom & Claude Noble, Editors
118 pp. Paper. Northeastern State University, 1986. $6.95.

NATIVE AMERICAN TRADITIONS
Arthur Versluis
Paper. Element Press, 1993. $9.95.

**NATIVE AMERICAN TRIBALISM:
INDIAN SURVIVALS & RENEWALS**
D'Arcy McNickle
Illus. 120 pp. Paper. Oxford University Press, 1973. $9.95.

NATIVE AMERICAN TRADITIONS
Sam Gill
200 pp. Paper. Wadsworth Publishing, 1983. $12.95.

**NATIVE AMERICAN TRUTHS:
PHILOSOPHY OF GOOD MEDICINE**
H.M. Byron
Illus. 72 pp. paper. Dorrance, 1999. $10.

NATIVE AMERICAN VERBAL ART: TEXTS & CONTEXTS
William F. Clements
295 pp. Paper. University of Arizona Press, 1996. $22.95.

NATIVE AMERICAN VISIONS CALENDAR
12 exquisite Sam English (Ojibwa artist) full-color prints; calendar with 10x14 print and appointment calendar below; and selected quotes from historic and present-day tribal leaders. Available in August for upcoming year. Fulcrum Publishing, $10.95.

NATIVE AMERICAN VOICES
David A. Rausch & Blair Schlepp
Native American history and culture from an evangelical perspective. Describes native cultures before the coming of the Europeans. 192 pp. Paper. Baker Book House, 1993. $10.99.

*NATIVE AMERICAN WAY OF LIFE
Grades 4-8. 28 pp. Paper. Council for Indian Education, 1997. $1.95.

NATIVE AMERICAN WEAPONS
Colin F. Taylor
Surveys weapons made and used by American Indians north of Mexico from prehistoric times to the late 19th century. Illus. 128 pp. University of Oklahoma Press, 2001. $24.95.

NATIVE AMERICAN WISDOM
Kent Nerburn & Louise Mengelkoch, Editors
Collection of philosophical and religious thoughts, quotations from Chief Joseph, Sitting Bull, Red Cloud, Black Elk, Ohiyesa, and others. 127 pp. New World Library, 1991. $14. Audiocassette, $10.95. Paper. Morning Flower Press, $4.95.

NATIVE AMERICAN WISDOM, 3 Vols.
Terry P. Wilson, Text by
Hopi: Following the Path of Peace; Lakota: Seeking the Great

Spirit; and *Navajo: Walking in Beauty.* Illus. 64 pp. each. Chronicle Books, 1990. $9.95 each; $29.95/set.

NATIVE AMERICAN WOMEN
Calendar. Features photos from the book,
Native American Portraits. 12x12". Chronicle Books, $9.95.

**NATIVE AMERICAN WOMEN:
A BIOGRAPHICAL DICTIONARY**
Gretchen M. Bataille, Editor
Profiles more than 200 Native American women born in the U.S. and Canada. Covers both historical and contemporary figures; bibliograpies of primary & secondary works. Illus. 352 pp. Garland Publishing, 1993. $55.

**NATIVE AMERICAN WOMEN:
A CONTEXTUAL BIBLIOGRAPHY**
Rayna Green
700 entries about or by Native North American women.
128 pp. Indiana University Press, 1983. $25.

**NATIVE AMERICAN WRITING IN THE SOUTHEAST:
AN ANTHOLOGY, 1875-1935**
Daniel Littlefield, Jr. & James Parins, Editors
The first anthology of Native American literature representing tribes of the Southeastern U.S. 232 pp. University Press of Mississippi, 1995. $40; paper, $16.95.

*NATIVE AMERICANS
Preschool-8. Illus. 32 pp. Paper. Smithsonian, $29.50.

NATIVE AMERICANS
Norman Bancroft-Hunt
Paper. Book Sales, 1998. $12.99.

*NATIVE AMERICANS
William Dudley, Editor
Grades 5-12. Illus. Paper. Greenhaven Press, 1997. $26.20; paper, $16.20.

NATIVE AMERICANS
Dona Herweck & Mari L. Robbins
Illus. Teacher Created Materials, 1994. $14.95.

THE NATIVE AMERICANS
Carter Smith, Editor
Illus. 288 pp. Facts on File, 1990. $14.50.

THE NATIVE AMERICANS
Robert Spencer & Jesse Jennings
The prehistory and ethnology of the pre-Columbian North American Indian, from the Arctic to Middle America. Reprint of 1965 edition. Illus. Maps. 539 pp. High-Lonesome, $25.

**NATIVE AMERICANS: AKWE KON'S
JOURNAL OF INDIGENOUS ISSUES**
Jose Barreiro, Editor
Illus. 64 pp. Akwe Kon Press, 2000. $20.

NATIVE AMERICANS: AN ANNOTATED BIBLIOGRAPHY
Frederick E. Hoxie & Harvey Markowitz
Overview of Native American studies, including introductory texts and popular accounts. 324 pp. Scarewcrow Press, 1991. $42.

NATIVE AMERICANS AS SHOWN ON STAGE, 1753-1916
Eugene Jones
219 pp. Scarecrow Press, 1988. $30.

**NATIVE AMERICANS BEFORE 1492:
MOUNDBUILDING CENTERS OF THE
EASTERN WOODLANDS**
Lynda N. Shaffer
149 pp. M.E. Sharpe, 1992. $54.95; paper, $22.95.

*NATIVE AMERICANS & BLACK AMERICANS
Kim Dramer
Grades 5 and up. 120 pp. Chelsea House, 1997. $9.95.

*NATIVE AMERICANS & CHRISTIANITY
Steve Klotts
Grades 5 and up. 120 pp. Chelsea House, 1996. $19.95; paper, $9.95.

**NATIVE AMERICANS: AN ENCYCLOPEDIA
OF HISTORY, CULTURE & PEOPLES**
Barry Pritzker
2 Vols. Illus. 868 pp. ABC-Clio, 1998. $150.

**NATIVE AMERICANS: ETHNOLOGY & BACKGROUNDS
OF THE NORTH AMERICAN INDIANS**
Robert Spencer
Second edition. Illus. Harper & Row, $38.50.

**NATIVE AMERICANS: FIVE CENTURIES
OF CHANGING IMAGES**
Patricia Trenton & Patrick Houlihan
Illus. 305 pp. Harry N. Abrams, 1989. $49.50.

**NATIVE AMERICANS IN FICTION: A GUIDE TO 765
BOOKS FOR LIBRARIANS AND TEACHERS, K-9**
Vicki Anderson
Works are primarily from 1963-1993. Entries provide author,

publisher, date, grade designation and a brief annotation.
180 pp. McFarland, 1994. $31.50.

NATIVE AMERICANS IN THE SATURDAY EVENING POST
Peter G. Beidler & Marion F. Egge
List references and provide extensive summaries of many of the writings, and in many of the important articles, the authors have quoted excerpts. Also included are reproductions of the images and illustrations fromthe magazine. Illus. 464 pp. Scarecrow Press, 1999. $70.

**NATIVE AMERICANS: THE INDIGENOUS
PEOPLE OF NORTH AMERICA**
Taylor & Sturtevant
Illus. Color photos. Artrifact spreads. 256 pp.
Hothem House, 1991. $24.95.

NATIVE AMERICANS INFORMATION DIRECTORY
Julia C. Furtaw, Editor
Information sources on Native Americans. 371 pp.
Biennial. Gale Research, 1993. $75.

NATIVE AMERICANS: AN INTEGRATED UNIT
Kathy Rogers
Illus. 80 pp. Paper. ECS Learning Systems, 1993. $12.95.

NATIVE AMERICANS & THE LAW
Gary A. Sokolow
ABC-Clio, 1998. $39.50.

**NATIVE AMERICANS & THE LAW: CONTEMPORARY
& HISTORICAL PERSPECTIVES ON AMEIRCAN
INDIAN RIGHTS, FREEDOM & SOVEREIGNTY**
John R. Wunder
6 vols. garland, 1997. $406.

**NATIVE AMERICANS & NIXON: PRESIDENTIAL
POLITICS & MINORITY SELF—DETERMINATION,
1969-1972**
Jack D. Forbes
A study of how the Nixon administration dealt with Indian demands. 2nd edition. 148 pp. Paper. UCLA, American Indian Studies Center, 1982. $12.

NATIVE AMERICANS: NORTH AMERICA
Frederick E. Hoxie & Harvey Markowitz
Illus. 324 pp. Scarecrow, 1991. $40.

NATIVE AMERICANS OF CALIFORNIA & NEVADA
Jack D. Forbes
Revised edition. 240 pp. Illus. Photos. Paper.
Naturegraph, $14.95.

NATIVE AMERICANS: CRIME & JUSTICE
Robert A. Silverman
Paper. Westview Press, 1996. $79.

**NATIVE AMERICANS OF THE NORTHWEST
COAST: A CRITICAL BIBLIOGRAPHY**
Robert S. Grumet
Illus. 128 pp. Paper. Indiana University Press, 1979. $5.95.

NATIVE AMERICANS OF THE PACIFIC COAST
Vinson Brown
Life as it was 300 years ago along the Pacific Coast. Illus. Photos. 272 pp. Paper. Naturegraph, 1979. $14.95.

*NATIVE AMERICANS: THE PEOPLE & HOW THEY LIVED
Eloise Potter & John Funderburg
Grades 4-12. Illus. 80 pp. North Carolina State Museum of Natural Sciences, 1986. $18.95; paper, $14.95.

*NATIVE AMERICANS: A PERSONAL HISTORY BOOK
This interctive workbook includes a chronological overview of the history of an American culture; open-ended exercises for research projects. Index & answer key. SVE, $7.95; package of ten, $69.

NATIVE AMERICANS & PUBLIC POLICY
Fremont Lyden & Lyman Legters, Editors
Illuis. 336 pp. University of Pittsburgh Press, 1988. $49.95; paper, $15.

***NATIVE AMERICANS & THE RESERVATION
IN AMERICAN HISTORY**
Anita Louise McCormick
Grades 5 and up. Illus. 128 pp. Enslow Publishers, 1996. $19.95.

**NATIVE AMERICANS OF THE SOUTHWEST: THE SERIOUS
TRAVELER'S INTRODUCTION TO PEOPLES & PLACES**
Zdenek Salzmann
Paper. Westview Press, 1997. $14.

NATIVE AMERICANS OF TEXAS
Sandra L. Myers
Surveys the history of the Native American people of Texas from prehistoric times to the present. Illus. Map. Biblio. 46 pp. American Press, 1981. $3.95.

***NATIVE AMERICANS OF WASHINGTON STATE:
CURRICULUM GUIDE FOR THE ELEMENTARY GRADES**
A guide to aid the elementary classroom teacher in implement-

ing Native American curriculum in the classroom.
Grades 1-6. 40 pp. Daybreak Star Press, $5.50.

NATIVE AMERICANS ON FILM & VIDEO
Elizabeth Weatherford, with Emilia Seubert, Editors
Detailed descriptions of films and videotapes about Indians
and Inuit of the Americas. Two volumes Volume I, 151 pp., 1981;
Volume II, 112 pp., 112 pp. Paper. National Museum of the
American Indian, $5 & $7.

NATIVE AMERICANS: A PORTRAIT:
THE ART & TRAVELS OF CHARLES BIRD KING,
GEORGE CATLIN & KARL BODMER
Robert J. Moore, Jr.
Illus. 280 pp. Stewart Tabori & Chang, 1997. $60.

NATIVE AMERICANS & PUBLIC POLICY
Fremont J. Lyden & Lyman H. Legters, Editors
17 essays covering such topics as problems of national policy,
questions of legal sovereignty, and Native resources and
economy. Illus. 336 pp. University of Pittsburgh, 1992. $49.95.

NATIVE AMERICANS: A RESOURCE GUIDE
Illus. 55 pp. Paper. Diane Publishing, 1993. $25.

NATIVE AMERICANS: SOCIAL, ECONOMIC
& POLITICAL ASPECTS - A BIBLIOGRAPHY
Joan Nordquist
72 pp. Paper. Reference & Research Services, 1998. $20.

NATIVE AMERICANS: A THEMATIC UNIT
Leigh Hoven
Grades 3-5. Illus. 80 pp. Teacher Created Materials, 1990.
Student edition, $9.95.

NATIVE AMERICANS & WAGE LABOR:
ETHNOHISTORICAL PERSPECTIVES
Alice Livingston & Martha C. Knack
Illus. 368 pp. University of Oklahoma Press, 1996. $32.95.

*****NATIVE ARTISTS OF NORTH AMERICA**
Reavis Moore
Five Native American artists. Grades 8 and up.
Illus. 48 pp. Paper. John Muir, 1991. $14.95.

NATIVE ARTS NETWORK
Atlatl convenes native artists and administrators to discuss issues in the field. Special reports document these biennial conferences. 1986, 1990, 1992, 1994. Atlatl, $5.

NATIVE ARTS OF THE COLUMBIA PLATEAU
Susan E. Harless
Selections from the Doris Swaze Bounds Collection. Illus.
176 pp. Paper. University of Washington Press, $29.95.

NATIVE ARTS OF NORTH AMERICA
Christian F. Feest
Revised edition. Illus. 220 pp. Paper. Thames & Hudson, 1992.
$19.95.

THE NATIVE ARTS OF NORTH AMERICA, AFRICA
& THE SOUTH PACIFIC: AN INTRODUCTION
George Corbin
Illus. 352 pp. Paper. Harper & Row, 1988. $24.95.

NATIVE BASKETRY OF WESTERN NORTH AMERICA
Joan M. Jones
Illus. 72 pp. Paper. Illinois State Museum, 1979. $2.

THE NATIVE BROTHERHOODS: MODERN INTER-TRIBAL
ORGANIZATIONS ON THE NORTHWEST COAST
Peter Drucker
Reprint of 1958 edition. 200 pp. Scholarly Press, $59. Reprint
Services, $79. Paper. Native American Book Publishers, $39.

NATIVE CALIFORNIA GUIDE:
WEAVING PAST & PRESENT
Dolan Eargle
Guide to Native peoples in California, including organizations,
reservations, rancherias, tribes. With history of early life and
interviews with tribal members. Also event calendars-powwows.
Appendices of museums, missions, military posts, traders,
gaming, etc. Illus. Maps. 260 pp. paper. Trees Company Press,
2000. $18.

NATIVE CALIFORNIAN:
A THEORETICAL RETROSPECTIVE
Lowell J. Bean & Thomas Blackburn
Anthology of 16 papers on Native Californians.
453 pp. Paper. Ballena Press, 1976. $21.95.

NATIVE CANADIAN ANTHROPOLOGY
& HISTORY: A SELECTED BIBLIOGRAPHY
Shepard Krech III
Revised edition. 3,000 sources emphasizes recent publications
on Canada's Native peoples. 212 pp. University of Oklahoma
Press, 1994. $34.95.

NATIVE CAROLINIANS: THE INDIANS
OF NORTH CAROLINA
Theda Perdue
Illus. 75 pp. Paper. North Carolina Division of Archives & Chero-
kee Publications, 1985. $4.50.

NATIVE & CHRISTIAN: INDIGENOUS VOICES ON
RELIGIOUS IDENTITY IN THE U.S. & CANADA
James Treat, Editor
248 pp. Routledge, 1996. $75; paper, $19.99.

THE NATIVE CREATIVE PROCESS:
A COLLABORATIVE DISCOURSE
Douglas J. Cardinal & Jeanette Armstrong;
illus. by Greg Young-Ing
Authors share their visions and insights into the creative process from the perspective of their Native ancestry. Illus. 127
pp. Paper. Theytus, 1991. $24.95.

NATIVE CULTURES OF ALASKA:
TRADITIONS THROUGH TIME
L.J. Campbell
Illus. 112 pp. Paper. Alaska Geographic Society, 1996. $19.95.

NATIVE EDUCATION DIRECTORY: ORGANIZATIONS &
RESOURCES FOR EDUCATORS OF NATIVE AMERICANS
Patricia Hammer & Heather Beasley, compilers
2nd edition. 102 pp. Paper. ERIC-CRESS, 1997. $12.

NATIVE FACES; INDIAN CULTURES IN AMERICAN ART
P. Trenton and P.T. Houlihan
Illus. 120 pp. Paper. Southwest Museum, 1984. $15.95.

NATIVE FAMILY: NATIVE NATIONS
Christopher Cardozo; Robert Janjigan, Editor
Illus. 96 pp. Callaway Editions, 1996. $13.95.

NATIVE HARVESTS: RECIPES & BOTANICALS
OF THE AMERICAN INDIAN
Barrie Kavasch
Illus. Paper. Random House, 1979. $7.95.

NATIVE HEALER: INITIATION INTO AN ANCIENT ART
Lake Medicine Grizzlybear
Paper. Theosophical Publishing House, 1991. $10.95.

NATIVE HEART: AN AMERICAN INDIAN ODYSSEY
Gabriel Horn (White Deer of Autumn)
An autobography. One man's sacred journey as he strugles to
live the way of his ancestors in modern America. 304 pp. Paper. New World Library, $13.95.

A NATIVE HERIATGE: IMAGES OF THE
INDIAN IN ENGLISH-CANADIAN LITERATURE
Leslie Monkman
208 pp. University of Toronto Press, 1981. $35.

NATIVE INDIAN WILD GAME,
FISH & WILD FOODS COOKBOOK
David Hunt, Editor
304 pp. Fox Chapel Publishing, 1992. $24.95

NATIVE LAND
Mary Ann Wells
Documented chronicle about the lands that became the state
of Mississippi. Illus. Maps. 256 pp. University Press of Mississippi, 1995. $45; paper, $15.95.

NATIVE LANGUAGES & LANGUAGE
FAMILIES OF NORTH AMERICA
compiled by Ives Goddard
A map which shows the locations and distriubtion of the
known languages spoken by Native peoples across North
America at the time of first contact. University of Nebraska
Press, $14.95, folded study map; $19.95, wall display map.

NATIVE LAW BIBLIOGRAPHY
Linda Fritz
100 pp. University of Saskatchewan, 1984. $20.

NATIVE LIGHT FOR A DARK WORLD
Donald Matheson
272 pp. Carlton Press, 1988. $14.95.

NATIVE NEW ENGLAND: THE LONG JOURNEY
Charles T. Robinson
Illus. 128 pp. Paper. Douglas Charles Ltd., 1996. $16.95.

NATIVE NORTH AMERICA
Larry J. Zimmerman & Brian Leigh Molyneaux
Illus. 184 pp. Paper. University of Oklahoma Press, 2000.
$14.95.

NATIVE NORTH AMERICAN ALMANAC
Duane Champagne, Editor
Covers the range of Native history and culture in the U.S. and
Canada. Includes a chronology, demographic and distribution
descriptions and histories, and discussions. Illus. 1,472 pp.
Gale, 2001. $120.

NATIVE NORTH AMERICAN ART HISTORY—
SELECTED READINGS
Zena Mathews and Adona Jonaitis
Illus. 500 pp. Paper. Peek Publications, 1982. $19.95.

NATIVE NORTH AMERICAN FIRSTS
Karen Swisher & Ancita Benally
Illus. 263 pp. Gale, 1997. $44.95.

NATIVE NORTH AMERICAN FLUTES
Lew P. Price
Illus. Paper. Lew Paxton Price, $5.

NATIVE NORTH AMERICAN MUSIC & ORAL DATA:
A CATALOGUE OF SOUND RECORDINGS, 1893-1976
Dorothy S. Lee
480 pp. Indian University Press, 1979. $25.

NATIVE NORTH AMERICAN SHAMANISM: AN
ANNOTATED BIBLIOGRAPHY
Shelley Anne Osterreich
128 pp. Greenwood Publishing, 1998. $55.

NATIVE NORTH AMERICAN SPIRITUALITY OF THE
EASTERN WOODLANDS: SACRED MYTHS, DREAMS,
VISION SPEECHES, HEALING FORMULAS, RITUALS
& CEREMONIES
Elisabeth Tooker, Editor
302 pp. Paulist Press, 1979. $14.95.

NATIVE NORTH AMERICAN VOICES
Deborah A. Straub
160 pp. Gale, 1996. $39.

NATIVE NORTH AMERICANS:
AN ETHNOHISTORICAL APPROACH
Molly R. Mignon & Daniel Boxberger, Editors
2nd Edition. 508 pp. Paper. Kendall-Hunt, 1997. $42.95.

NATIVE NORTH AMERICANS IN DOCTORAL
DISSERTATIONS, 1971-1975: A CLASSIFIED
& INDEXED RESEARCH BIBLIOGRAPHY
S. Gifford Nickerson
CPL Biblios, 1977. $7.50.

NATIVE PEOPLE IN CANADA:
CONTEMPORARY CONFLICTS
James Frideres
2nd Edition. 344 pp. Prentice-Hall, 1983.

NATIVE PEOPLE, NATIVE LANDS:
CANADIAN INDIANS, INUIT & METIS
Bruce Cox
300 pp. Paper. Oxford University Press, 1988. $16.95.

*****NATIVE PEOPLE, NATIVE WAYS SERIES**
White Deer of Autumn (Gabriel Horn)
Stories about the Native American experience. In 4 vols. *Na-
tive American Book of Knowledge* (Vol. I): stories - "We Have
Always Been Here", & "Prophets, Poets & Peacemakers: Be-
fore Columbus"; *Native American Book of Life* (Vol. II): stories
- "The Children, Always the Children," & "By the Magic of the
Strawberry Moon"; *Native American Book of Change* (Vol. III):
stories- "Prophets, Poets & Peacemakers: After the Conquest,"
& "Dad's Signs, Now Mine"; *Native American Book of Wisdom*
(Vol. IV): stories- "From the Great Mystery: Wakan-Tanka," &
"Medicine Man." 96 pp. Paper. Beyond Words Publishing, $4.95
each.

THE NATIVE PEOPLE OF ALASKA
Steve J. Langdon
Introductory guide to the Eskimos, Indians, and Aleuts. Focus
is on their life-styles, traditions, and culture. Photos. Maps.
Biblio. 90 pp. Revised edition. Paper. Alaska Natural History
Association & Greatland Graphics, 1993. $7.95.

NATIVE PEOPLES OF ALASKA: A TRAVELER'S
GUIDE TO LAND, ART & CULTURE
Jan Halliday & Patricia Petrivelli
320 pp. Paper. Sasquatch Books, 1998. $17.95.

NATIVE PEOPLE OF SOUTHERN NEW ENGLAND,
1500-1650
Kathleen J. Bragdon
Illus. Maps. Biblio. 328 p. University of Oklahoma Press,
1996. $28.95; paper, $16.95.

NATIVE PEOPLES OF THE NORTHEAST WOODLANDS:
AN EDUCATIONAL RESOURCE PUBLICATION
Judith Brundin
Illus. 255 pp. National Museum of the American Indian, 1990.
$29.95.

NATIVE PEOPLES OF THE NORTHWEST:
A TRAVELER'S GUIDE TO LAND, ART & CULTURE
Jan Halliday & Gail Chehak
Guide for travelers to the Northwest. Maps. 291 pp. Paper.
Affiliated Tribes of Northwest Indians & Written Heritage, 1996.
$16.95.

NATIVE PEOPLES OF THE OLYMPIC PENINSULA:
WHO WE ARE
edited by Jacilee Wray
Explores the different tribes of Olympic Peninsula. Illus.
Maps. University of Oklahoma Press, $29.95; paper, $17.95.

NATIVE PEOPLES OF THE SOUTHWEST
Trudy Griffin-Pierce
Scholarly text of the true history of Southwestern American In-
dians. University of New Mexico Press, $49.95; paper, $24.95.

*NATIVE PEOPLES OF THE SOUTHWEST
Susan L. Shaffer, Editor
Grades 2-6. Illus. Includes 150 student booklets with 5 teacher resource binders with overhead transparencies, slides & audiocassette; artifacts, posters, etc. The Heard Museum, 1987. $1,475.

THE NATIVE RACES
H.H. Bancroft
Reprint of 1888 edition. 5 vols. Bancroft Press, $200 per set.

NATIVE RELIGIONS OF NORTH AMERICA
Ake Hultkrantz
144 pp. Paper. Harper & Row, 1988. $7.95.

NATIVE RESISTANCE & THE PAX COLONIAL IN NEW SPAIN
Susan Schroeder, Editor
Overview of Native uprisings in New Spain. Maps. 200 pp. University of Nebraska Press, 1998. $50; paper, $25.

NATIVE ROOTS: HOW THE INDIANS ENRICHED AMERICA
Jack Weatherford
Illus. 300 pp. Paper. Morning Flower Press, $10.

NATIVE SCIENCE: NATURAL LAWS OF INTERDEPENDENCE
Gregory Cajete
The indigenous view of reality. Illus. Photos. 328 pp. Clear Light, $24.95; paper, $14.95.

NATIVE TIME: AN HISTORICAL TIME LINE OF NATIVE AMERICA
Lee Francis
Illus. 352 pp. St. Martins Press, 1996. $35; paper, $19.95.

THE NATIVE TRIBES OF OHIO
Helen Cox Tregillis
Tells the story from the very beginning of the Eries to the later tribes before their removal west of the Mississippi; brief biographies and list of resources. Illus. 130 pp. Maps. Paper. Heritage Books, $15.50.

THE NATIVE UNIVERSE
Clifford E. Trafzer and Gerald McMaster
National Museum of the American Indian, 2004.

NATIVE VISIONS: EVOLUTION IN NORTHWEST COAST ART FROM THE 18TH THROUGH THE 20TH CENTURY
Steven C. Brown
Paper. University of Washington Press, $40.

NATIVE UNIVERSE: VOICES OF INDIAN AMERICA
Gerald McMaster & Clifford Trafzer
Illustrated cultural history of American Indians written exclusively by Native people in collaboration with the new National Museum of the American Indian's opening exhibitions. Illus. Paper. National Geographic Books, 2004. $40.

NATIVE WAYS: CALIFORNIA INDIAN STORIES & MEMORIES
Malcolm Margolin & Yolanda Montijo
80 photos. Illus. Map. 128 pp. Paper. Heyday Books, $8.95.

NATIVE WILD GAME: FISH & WILD FOODS COOKBOOK
340+ recipes from many tribes. 283 pp. Cherokee Publications, $19.95.

NATIVE WRITINGS IN MASSACHUSETTS
Ives Goddard & Kathleen Bragdon
Illus. 838 pp. American Philosophical Society, 1988. $60.

NATIVES & ACADEMICS: RESEARCHING & WRITING ABOUT AMERICAN INDIANS
Devon Abbott Mihesuah, Editor
Anthology. 213 pp. Paper. University of Nebraska Press, 1998. $16.95.

NATIVES & NEWCOMERS: CANADA'S "HEROIC AGE" RECONSIDERED
Bruce G. Trigger
A tale of Canada's early development that finally gives Native people their rightful place. paper. University of Toronto Press, 1986. $22.95.

NATIVES & STRANGERS
Roger L. Nichols, et al.
4th Ed. Oxford University Press, 2003.

*NATOSI: STRONG MEDICINE
Peter Roop
Blackfeet raiding party captures their first horses from the Crows. Grades 3-8. 32 pp. Council for Indian Education, $8.95; paper, $2.95.

A NATURAL EDUCATION: NATIVE AMERICAN IDEAS & THOUGHTS
Stan Padilla, Editor & Illus.
Collection of quotations from traditional Native Americans on the importance of educating young people to the natural way. Revised edition. Illus. 80 pp. Paper. The Book Publishing Co., 1994. $8.95.

THE NATURAL MAN OBSERVED: A STUDY OF CATLIN'S INDIAN GALLERY
William Truettner
Illus. 323 pp. Smithsonian Institution Press, 1979. $47.50.

*NATURAL WORLD OF THE CALIFORNIA INDIANS
Grades 4 and up. Paper. University of California Press, $15.95.

A NATURALIST IN INDIAN TERRITORY: THE JOURNALS OF S.W. WOODHOUSE, 1849-50
John S. Tomer & Michael J. Brodhead
A young Philadelphia physician was appointed surgeon-naturalist of two expeditions to survey Creek-Cherokee boundary in Indian Territory. Illus. Maps. 320 pp. Paper. University of Oklahoma Press, 1994. $17.95.

THE NATURE OF NATIVE AMERICAN POETRY
Norma C. Wilson
Illus. 176 pp. Paper. University of New Mexico Press, 2001. $18.95.

NATURE RELIGION IN AMERICA: FROM THE ALGONKIAN INDIANS TO THE NEW AGE
Catherine L. Albanese
Photos. 268 pp. Paper. University of Chicago Press, 1990. $13.95.

THE NAVAHO
Clyde Kluckhohn and Dorothea Leighton
Revised 1973 edition. Illus. 365 pp. Harvard University Press, $18.50; paper, $8.95.

THE NAVAJO
James F. Downs
The basic themes of their culture and their ability to adjust to new situations and the Anglo culture without losing their identity. Illus. 136 pp. Paper. High-Lonesome Books, 1984. $7.

*THE NAVAJO
S. Stan
Grades 5-8. Illus. 32 pp. Rourke Corp., 1989. $13.26.

*THE NAVAJO
Grades K-4. Illus. 48 pp. Childrens Press, $11.45.

*NAVAJO ABC: A DINE ALPHABET BOOK
Eleanor Schick & Luci Tapahonso
Grades PS and up. Illus. 32 pp. Simon & Schuster, 1995. $16.

NAVAJO AGING: THE TRANSITION FROM FAMILY TO INSTITUTIONAL SUPPORT
Stephen J. Kunitz & Jerrold E. Levy
191 pp. University of Arizona Press, 1991. $42.

NAVAJO ARCHITECTURE: FORMS, HISTORY, DISTRIBUTION
Stephen C. Jett & Virginia E. Spencer
310 pp. University of Arizona Press, 1981. $50.

NAVAHO ART & CULTURE
George T. Mills
Reprint of 1959 edition. Illus. 273 pp. Greenwood, $41.50.

NAVAJO ART, HISTORY & CULTURE
Stephen Wallace, et al
79 pp. Paper. Navajo Curriculum Center Press, 1984. $5.

THE NAVAJO ART OF SANDPAINTING
Douglas Congdon-Martin
Contains over 400 full color photos of sandpaintings. Illus. 64 pp. Paper. Schiffer, 1990. $9.95.

NAVAJO ARTS & CRAFTS
Robert Roessel
Illus. 176 pp. Navajo Curriculum Center Press, 1989. $15.

NAVAJO ARTS & CRAFTS
Nancy Schiffer
Photos and explanations of each craft. Illus. 64 pp. Paper. Schiffer, $12.95.

THE NAVAJO ATLAS: ENVIRONMENTS, RESOURCES, PEOPLES & HISTORY OF THE DINE BIKEYAH
James Goodman
Illus. Maps. 109 pp. Paper. University of Oklahoma Press, 1982. $19.95.

NAVAJO: BASIC MEDICAL
Alan Wilson
141 pp. Paper. Audio-Forum, 1992. $18.95; $39 with audio.

NAVAJO BEADWORK: ARCHITECTURES OF LIGHT
Ellen K. Moore
History of Navajo beadwork - belts & hatbands, baskets & necklaces. Illus. 296 pp. University of Arizona Press. $50.

NAVAJO BLESSINGWAY SINGER: AUTOBIOGRAPHY OF FRANK MITCHELL, 1881-1967
Charlotte Frisbie & David McAllester, Editors
Reprint of 1977 edition. 456 pp. Paper. University of Arizona Press, $39.95.

A NAVAJO BRINGING-HOME CEREMONY: THE CLAUSCHEE SONNY VERSION OF DEERWAY AJILEE
Karl W. Luckert
Illus. 224 pp. paper. University of Nebraska Press and Museum of Northern Arizona, 1980. $14.95.

*THE NAVAJO BROTHERS & THE STOLEN HERD
Maurine Grammer; illus by Fred Cleveland
Story of two Navajo teenagers who regain their family's sheep from thieves. Grades 4-9. Illus. 120 pp. paper. Red Crane Books, $9.95.

NAVAJO: A CENTURY OF PROGRESS, 1868-1968
Martin Link, Editor
Illus. 110 pp. Navajo Tribal Museum, 1968. $6.

NAVAJO CHANGES: A HISTORY OF THE NAVAJO PEOPLE
Teresa McCarty and staff, Editors
107 pp. Navajo Curriculum Center Press, 1983. $10.

NAVAHO CHANTWAY MYTHS
Katherine Spencer
Reprint of 1957 edition. 240 pp. Paper. High-Lonesome Books, $20.

*NAVAJO CHILDREN
Nancy Armstrong
Grades 2-6. Paper. Council for Indian Education, 1975. $1.95.

NAVAJO CODE TALKERS
Doris Paul
Story of Navajo platoon during World War II and of the intricate and unbreakable code language they created. Illus. 171 pp. Dorrance Publishing, 1973. $14.50.

*NAVAJO CODE TALKERS: NATIVE AMERIACAN HEROES
Catherine Jones
Grades 6 and up. 31 pp. Paper. Tudor Publishers, 1997. $7.95.

A NAVAJO CONFRONTATION & CRISIS
Floyd A. Pollock
Traces the development of Navajo-federal relations during the 1930s and 1940s. Dine College Press, $10.

NAVAJO COUNTRY DINE BIKEYAH: A GEOGRAPHIC DICTIONARY OF NAVAJO LANDS IN THE 1930s
A. Richard Van Valkenburgh
Reprint. 2nd edition. Illus. 140 pp. Time Traveler Maps, 1999. $29.95.

*NAVAJO COYOTE TALES
collected by William Morgan
Grades 4 and up. Illus. 53 pp. Paper. Ancient City Press, 1989. $9.95.

*NAVAJO COYOTE TALES: THE CURLY TO AHEEDLIINII VERSION
Father Berard Haile
Ages 7-10. Reprint. Illus. 146 pp. Paper. University of Nebraska Press, 1984. $12.95.

A NAVAJO CRISIS & CONFRONTATION
Floyd A. Pollock
Dine College Press, 1984. $15.

*NAVAJO CULTURAL GUIDES, EXPERIENCE STORIES, & CULTURAL READERS
See San Juan District Media Center for titles, prices and grade levels.

*THE NAVAJO DESIGN BOOK
Donna Greenlee
Grades 1-6. The arts & crafts of the Navajo people... weaving, sand painting, and silver design. Illus. 32 pp. Paper. Fun Publications, 1975. $4.95.

NAVAJO DICTIONARY ON DIAGNOSTIC TERMINOLOGY
Dine Center for Human Development
Paper. Dine College Press, 1991. $10.

NAVAJO EDUCATION IN ACTION: THE ROUGH ROCK DEMONSTRATION SCHOOL
Robert A. Roessel, Jr.
149 pp. Navajo Curriculum Press, 1977. $10.

NAVAJO EDUCATION, 1948-1978: ITS PROGRESS & PROBLEMS
Robert A. Roessel, Jr.
Illus. 339 pp. Navajo Curriculum Press, 1979. $14.95.

*NAVAJO-ENGLISH CHILDREN'S PICTURE DICTIONARY
Roman Delos-Santos; Raymond Johnson, illustrator
Grades 4-8. Navajo Community College Press, 1995.

NAVAJO-ENGLISH DICTIONARY
Leon Wall & William Morgan
Includes over 9,000 entries, a section on Navajo pronunciation, everyday expressions, etc. 164 pp. Paper. Hippocrene Books, $9.95.

THE NAVAHO (OR CORRAL) FIRE DANCE
B. Haile
Reprint of 1946-7 editions. 3 vols. in 1. Paper.
St. Michaels, $7.50.

NAVAJO FOLK ART: THE PEOPLE SPEAK
Chuck & Jan Rosenak
Features 41 artists. 90 color photos. Biblio. 176 pp.
Paper. Northland Press & Clear Light, $14.95.

NAVAHO FOLK TALES
Franc Johnson Newcomb
229 pp. Paper. University of New Mexico Press, $14.95.

NAVAJO FOOD PRACTICES, CUSTOMS & HOLIDAYS
Suzanne Pelican & Karen Bachman-Carter
Paper. American Dietetic Association, 1992. $10.

NAVAJO FOREIGN AFFAIRS: 1795-1846
Frank D. Reeve; ed. by Eleanor Adams & John Kessell
Paper. 54 pp. Dine College Press, 1983. $4.

**NAVAJO GRAVES: AN ARCHAEOLOGICAL
REFLECTION OF ETHNOGRAPHIC REALITY**
Albert E. Ward
Discusses select Navajo burials from northeastern Arizona and
northwestern New Mexico. Illus. 54 pp. Center for Anthropo-
logical Studies, 1980. $8.

THE NAVAJO & HIS BLANKET
Uriah S. Hollister
Reprint of 1903 edition. Illus. 176 pp. The Rio Grande
Press, $17.50.

NAVAJO HISTORY
Ethelou Yazi, Editor
Revised edition. Volume I. Illus. 100 pp. Paper.
Navajo Curriculum Center Press, 1982. $11.

**THE NAVAJO-HOPI LAND DISPUTE: AN AMERICAN
TRAGEDY**
David M. Brugge
Illus. Maps. 320 pp. Paper. University of New Mexico Press,
1999. $19.95.

THE NAVAJO HUNTER TRADITION
Karl W. Luckert
Hunter myths and rituals are examined in conjunction with other
deities and the rise of shamanism. 248 pp. University of Arizona Press, 1975. $35.

*THE NAVAJO INDIAN BOOK
Donna Greenlee
Grades 1-6. Traditional lifestyles of the Navajo.
32 pp. Paper. Fun Publications, 1975. $4.95.

NAVAHO INDIAN MYTHS
Aileen O'Bryan, Editor
Tribal fables & legends recorded in the 1920s from
an elderly chief. Reprint. 187 pp. Paper. Dover, $6.95.

THE NAVAJO INDIANS
Henry F. Dobyns & Robert C. Euler
An account of the Navajo Indians, past and present. Illus.
Maps. 121 pp. Center for Anthropological Studies, $8.

*NAVAJO INDIANS
Leigh Hope Wood
Grades 4-8. Demco, 1991. $12.15.

**NAVAJO INFANCY: AN ETHNOLOGICAL
STUDY OF CHILDREN DEVELOPMENT**
James S. Chisholm
267 pp. Aldine de Gruyter, 1983. $36.95.

NAVAJO JEWELRY: A LEGACY OF SILVER & STONE
Lois Jacka; photos by Jerry Jacka
History of Navajo jewelry-making. 100 color photos. Biblio.
144 pp. Paper. Northland Press & Clear Light, $14.95.

NAVAJO KINSHIP & MARRIAGE
Gary Witherspoon
Illus. 140 pp. Paper. University of Chicago Press, 1975.
$10.95.

NAVAJO THE LAUGHTER WAY
Alan Wilson
143 pp. Paper. Audio-Forum, 1992. $7.95; with audio, $39.

**NAVAJO LAND, NAVAJO CULTURE:
THE UTAH EXPERIENCE IN THE 20TH CENTURY**
Robert S. McPherson
History of the Dine of southeastern Utah. Illus. Map.
University of Oklahoma Press, 2004. $34.95; paper, $19.95.

**NAVAJO LAND USE: AN
ETHNOARCHAEOLOGICAL STUDY**
Klara B. Kelley
Academic Press, 1985. $39.50; paper, $19.50.

NAVAJO LEADERSHIP & GOVERNMENT
Title IV Materials Development Staff
149 pp. Navajo Curriculum Center Press, 1977. $7.50.

NAVAHO LEGENDS
Washington Matthews
Reprint of 1897 ed. Illus. Paper. Univ. of Utah Press, $19.95.

**NAVAJO LIFEWAYS: CONTEMPORARY ISSUES,
ANCIENT KNOWLEDGE**
Maureen Trudelle Schwarz
Illus. 292 pp. University of Oklahoma Press, 2001. $29.95.

**NAVAJO LIVESTOCK REDUCTION:
A NATIONAL DISGRACE**
Ruth Roessel, Editors
Illus. 224 pp. Navajo Community College Press, 1974. $15.

*NAVAJO LONG WALK
Nancy Armstrong
In 1864 thousands of Navajo Indians were forced to leave their
land in Arizona and march nearly 300 miles east. Grades 4-9.
120 pp. Paper. Council for Indian Education & Roberts Rinehart,
1994. $7.95.

*NAVAHO MAGIC OF HUNTING
Elsie Kreischer; illus. by Jin Paddock
Narrative poem telling of a boy's first deer hunt. Grades 4-9.
32 pp. Paper. Council for Indian Education, 1994. $4.95.

**NAVAJO MEDICINE BUNDLES OR JISH: ACQUISITION,
TRANSMISSION & DISPOSITION IN THE PAST & PRESENT**
Charlotte Frisbie
Illus. 627 pp. University of New Mexico Press, 1987. $42.

NAVAJO MEDICINE MAN SAND PAINTINGS
Gladys Reichard
Reprint. Illus. 132 pp. Paper. Dover, $12.95.

NAVAJO MOUNTAIN & RAINBOW BRIDGE RELIGION
Karl W. Luckert
Translated by I.W. Goosen and H. Bilagody, Jr.
Illus. 164 pp. University of Nebraska Press, 1977. $9.95.

**NAVAJO MULTI-HOUSEHOLD SOCIAL UNITS:
ARCHAEOLOGY ON BLACK MESA, ARIZONA**
Thomas R. Rocek
Examines a 150-year-old ethnohistoric and archeological
settlement record. 240 pp. Univ. of Arizona Press, 1995. $52.

**NAVAJO MYTHS PRAYERS & SONGS
WITH TEXTS & TRANSLATIONS**
Washington Matthews; P.E. Goddard, Editor
Facsimile of 1907 edition. 43 pp. Paper. Coyote Press,
$4.69.

THE NAVAJO NATION
Peter Iverson
Illus. 275 pp. Greenwood Press, 1981. $35.
Paper. University of New Mexico Press, $9.95.

NAVAJO NATIVE DYES: THEIR PREPARATION & USE
Nonobah Bryan & Stella Young
How to use native plants of the Southwest to dye yarns for rug
making. Reprint of 1940 ed. Illus. 75 pp. Paper. Filter Press,
$5.

NAVAJO ORAL HISTORY
Alfred W. Yazzie
Gene and Isaac Johnson, Editors
Illus. 56 pp. Paper. Rough Rock Demonstration School, 1984.

NAVAJO ORAL TRADITIONS
Alfred W. Yazzie; Jeri Eck, Editor
Illus. 72 pp. Paper. Navajo Curriculum Center Press, 1984.

**NAVAJO & PHOTOGRAPHY: A CRITICAL HISTORY OF
THE REPRESENTATION OF AN AMERICAN PEOPLE**
James C. Faris
Illus. 392 pp. University of New Mexico Press, $39.95.
Paper. University of Utah Press, 2003. $19.95.

NAVAJO PLACES: HISTORY, LEGEND, LANDSCAPE
Laurance D. Linford
Place-Name guide of the entirety of the traditional Navajo
homeland. University of Utah Press. $60; paper, $24.95.

NAVAJO PICTORIAL WEAVING 1800—1950
Tyrone Campbell & Joel & Kate Kopp
178 full color photos of Navajo rugs. Illus. 128 pp. Paper.
University of New Mexico Press, $24.95.

NAVAJO: PORTRAIT OF A NATION
Joel Grimes
Calendar. 12 full-color photos of the people, places, and land-
scapes from the Navajo Nation. 14x12". Treasure Chest.
$10.95.

NAVAJO POTTERY: TRADITIONS & INNOVATIONS
Russell Hartman & Jan Musial
Illus. Biblio. Paper. Northland Publishing, 1987. $12.95.

**THE NAVAJO PROJECT: ARCHAEOLOGICAL
INVESTIGATIONS PAGE TO PHOENIX 500 KV
SOUTHERN TRANSMISSION LINE**
Donald Fiero, et al
282 pp. Museum of Northern Arizona, 1978. $9.95.

NAVAJO & PUEBLO SILVERSMITHS
John Adair
Reprint of 1944 edition. Illus. Maps. Paper.
University of Oklahoma Pres, $15.95.

NAVAHO RELIGION: A STUDY OF SYMBOLISM
Gladys A. Reichard
Reprint of 1963 edition. 856 pp. Paper.
Princeton University Press, $19.95.

**NAVAJO REPORTER: OFFICIAL REPORTS OF CASES
ARGUED & DECIDED IN THE SUPREME COURT & THE
DISTRICT COURTS IN THE NAVAJO NATION**
Volume 5. Navajo Community College Press. $50.

NAVAJO RESOURCES & ECONOMIC DEVELOPMENT
Philip Reno
Illus. 200 pp. Paper. University of New Mexico Press,
and Native American Studies Center, 1981. $8.95.

NAVAJO RUG STIK-WITH-IT NOTECUBES
Self Stick
Full color. 600 sheets, 3.5 x 3". Northland Publishing, $12.

**NAVAJO RUGS: HOW TO FIND,
EVALUATE, BUY & CARE FOR THEM**
Don Dedra
75 color & 6 bxw photos. 136 pp. Paper.
Northland Press & Clear Light, 1997. $14.95.

NAVAJO RUGS, PAST & PRESENT
Gilbert Maxwell
100 pp. Paper. Treasure Chest, 1987. $7.

NAVAJO SACRED PLACES
Klara Bonsack Kelley & Harris Francis
Illus. Maps. 264 pp. Indiana University Press, 1994.
$29.95; paper. $12.95.

**NAVAJO SADDLE BLANKETS:
TEXTILES TO RIDE IN THE AMERICAN WEST**
Edited by Lane Coulter
Illus. 144 pp. Paper. Museum of New Mexico Press, 2001.
$29.95.

**NAVAJO SANDPAINTING ART: WHERE THE GODS
GATHER**
Mark Bahti
Illus. 56 pp. Paper. Treasure Chest Books, 1999. $15.95.

**NAVAJO SANDPAINTING: FROM
RELIGIOUS ACT TO COMMERCIAL ART**
Nancy J. Parejo
275 pp. Paper. University of New Mexico Press, 1991. $19.95.

NAVAJO SANDPAINTING: THE HUCKEL COLLECTION
Leland C. Wyman
Illus. Paper. Taylor Museum, 1971. $5.

NAVAJO SANDPAINTING ART: WHERE THE GODS GATHER
Mark Bahti & Eugene B. Joe, et al
Illus. Color photos. 32 pp. Paper. Treasure Chest
& Clear Light, 1978. $14.95.

NAVAJO SHEPARD & WEAVER
Gladys Reichard
Reprint of 1936 edition. Illus. 280 pp. Paper.
Rio Grande Press. $12.

*THE NAVAJO: SOUTHWEST
Peter Iverson
Grades 5 and up. Illus. Chelsea House, 1989. $17.95.

**NAVAJO SPOONS: INDIAN ARTISTRY
& THE SOUVENIR TRADE, 1880-1940**
Cindra Kline
Navajo silverwork is explored. 128 pp. Paper.
Museum of New Mexico Press, 2001. $27.50.

NAVAJO STORIES OF THE LONG WALK PERIOD
Compiled by Ruth Roessel
Presents Navajo accounts of the Lonf Walk and the concentration camp life at Fort Sumner in easter New Mexico from 1864-
1868. Paper. Navajo Community College Press. $15.

**NAVAHO SYMBOLS OF HEALING: A JUNGIAN
EXPLORATION OF RITUAL, IMAGE, & MEDICINE**
Donald Sandner, M.D.
A Jungian-trained psychiatrist explores ancient Navaho meth-
ods of healing that use vibrant imagery to bring the psyche into
harmony with the natural forces. 8 color plates. 304 pp. Paper.
Inner Traditions, $14.95.

**NAVAJO TEXTILES: THE WILLIAM
RANDOLPH HEARST COLLECTION**
Nancy J. Blomberg
Illus. 257 pp. Paper. University of Arizona Press, 1988. $36.95.

**NAVAJO & TIBETAN SACRED WISDOM:
THE CIRCLE OF THE SPIRIT**
Peter Gold
Shows the parallels between cultures. 200 color & bxw Illus.
350 pp. Paper. Inner Traditions, 1994. $29.95.

**NAVAJO TRADER: ESSAYS
ON A REGION & ITS LITERATURE**
Gladwell Richardson; edited by Philip Reed Rulon
217 pp. Paper. University of Arizona Press, 1986. $22.95.

NAVAHO TRADING DAYS
Elizabeth Hegemann
Illus. 399 pp. University of New Mexico Press, 1987.
$24.95; paper, $14.95.

NAVAJO TRADING: THE END OF AN ERA
Willow Roberts Powers
Examines trading in the last quarter of the 20th century.
Illus. 320 pp. University of New Mexico Press, 2001. $29.95.

NAVAJO: TRADITION & CHANGE IN THE SOUTHWEST
Wolfgang Lindig; photos by Helga Teiwes
Illus. Photos. Biblio. 240 pp. Facts on File, 1993. $45.

THE NAVAJO TREATY, 1868
K C Publications, 1968. $3.50; paper, $1.

NAVAJO TRIBAL CODE
The Michie Co., 1987. $130.

**THE NAVAJO VERB: A GRAMMAR
FOR STUDENTS & SCHOLARS**
Leonard M. Faltz
University of New Mexico Press, 1996. $60; paper, $29.95.

THE NAVAJO VERB SYSTEM: AN OVERVIEW
Robert W. Young
University of New Mexico Press, 1996. $45.

NAVAJO WAR DANCE
B. Haile
Reprint of 1946 edition. Paper. St. Michaels, $6.

NAVAJO WEAVERS & SILVERSMITHS
W. Matthews
Facsimile of 1968 edition. Illus. 43 pp. Paper. Filter Press. $4.

A NAVAHO WEAVING, ITS TECHNIC & HISTORY
Charles A. Amsden
A comprehensive study of primitive textile weaving. Reprint of
1934 edition. Illus. 460 pp. The Rio Grande Press, $17.50.
Paper, Dover, $8.95.

NAVAJO WEAVING, NAVAJO WAYS
Harriet & Seymour Koenig; Betty Himmel, Editor
56 pp. Paper. Katonah Galleries, 1986. $12.

NAVAJO WEAVING: THREE CENTURIES OF CHANGE
Kate Peck Kent
Illus. 150 pp. Paper. School of American Research, 1985.
$16.95.

NAVAJO WEAVING TODAY
Nancy Schiffer
Full-color photos of contemporary Navajo blankets and rugs,
with text. Illus. 64 pp. Paper. Schiffer, $12.95.

**THE NAVAJO WEAVING TRADITION,
1650 TO THE PRESENT**
Alice Kaufman & Christopher Selser
Detailed history and appreciation of the Navajo weavings. Discusses traders, the weaving process, and contemporary weaving. 200 full-color photos. Illus. 160 pp. Paper. E.P. Dutton &
Clear Light, $29.95.

NAVAJOLAND: FAMILY SETTLEMENT & LAND USE
Clara Kelley & Peter Whitely
Paper. Navajo Community College Press, $14.50.

NAVAJOLAND PLANT CATALOG
Vernon Mayes & James Rominger
List of more than 1,100 plants known to grow on the Navajo
Reservation. 72 pp. Paper. National Woodlands Publishing,
1994. $7.

**NAVAJOLAND: A PORTFOLIO OF NAVAJO
LIFE DURING THE 1940's & 1950's**
Ray Manley
A pictorial study, in bxw, of the Navajo people.
Illus. 52 pp. Paper. Ray Manley, $9.95.

*****THE NAVAJOS**
Peter Iverson
Grades 5 and up. Illus. Chelsea House, 1990.
$17.95; paper, $9.95.

*****THE NAVAJOS**
Virginia Driving Hawk Sneve
The creation myth of the Navajos; history, customs,
& facts about the tribe today. Grades 2-6. Illus. 32 pp.
Holiday House, 1993. $15.95.

THE NAVAJOS
R. Underhill
Reprint of 1956 edition. Illus. Maps. 304 pp. Paper.
University of Oklahoma Press, 2002. $19.95.

THE NAVAJOS: A CRITICAL BIBLIOGRAPHY
Peter Iverson
Paper. Indian University Press, 1976. $4.95.

**THE NAVAJOS IN 1705:
ROQUE MADRID'S CAMPAIGN JOURNAL**
Rick Hendricks & John P. Wilson
Paper. University of New Mexico Press, $15.95.

THE NAVAJOS' LONG WALK FOR EDUCATION
H. Thompson; Broderick Johnson, Editor
Illus. 248 pp. Navajo Community College Press, 1975. $15.

THE NAVAJOS & THE NEW DEAL
Donald L. Parman
Illus. 320 pp. Yale University Press, 1976. $37.50.

*****THE NAVAJOS: PEOPLE OF THE SOUTHWEST**
Nancy Bonvillain
Grades 4-6. Illus. 64 pp. Millbrook Press, 1995. $21.90.

*****NAYA NUKI: SHOSHONE GIRL WHO RAN**
Kenneth Thomasma; Eunice Hundley, Illus.
Indian lore, survival skills, and the Wes before the white man.
Grades 4-9. Illus. Baker Book House, $10.99; paper, $6.99.

**NCH'I-WANA "THE BIG RIVER"
MID-COLUMBIA INDIANS & THEIR LAND**
Eugene S. Hunn
Illus. 384 pp. Paper. University of Washington Press,
1990. $19.95.

THE NEBRASKA INDIAN WARS READER, 1865-77
R. Eli Paul, Editor
Illus. Maps. 290 pp. Paper. University of Nebraska Press,
1998. $19.95.

**A NECESSARY BALANCE: GENDER & POWER
AMONG INDIANS OF THE COLUMBIA PLATEAU**
Lillian A. Ackerman
Illus. Maps. 296 pp. University of Oklahoma Press,
2004. $42.95.

*****NEEKNA & CHEMAI**
Jeanette Armstrong
Two little Okanagan girls teach about the seasonal life
patterns of the Okanagan Indian people. Grades 2-8.
Illus. Paper. Theytus, 1991. $12.95.

**NEETS'AII GWIINDAII: LIVING
IN THE CHANDALAR COUNTRY**
Katherine Peter
Illus. 108 pp. Paper. Alaska Native Language Center, 1992.
$12.

**NEGOTIATORS OF CHANGE: HISTORICAL
PERSPECTIVES ON NATIVE AMERICAN WOMEN**
Nancy Shoemaker, Editor
Collection of articles on th history of women & gender in
American Indian societies. Illus. 320 pp. Routledge, 1994.
$59.95; paper, $17.95.

NEHALEM TILLAMOOK TALES
Melville Jacobs, et al, Editors
275 pp. Oregon State University Press, 1990.
$19.95; paper, $9.95.

NEITHER RED NOR WHITE & OTHER INDIAN STORIES
George A. Boyce
96 pp. Paper. Sunstone Press, $12.95.

**NEITHER WOLF NOR DOG: AMERICAN INDIANS,
ENVIRONMENT & AGRARIAN CHANGE**
David L. Lewis
Illus. 256 pp. Oxford University Press, 1994.
$39.95; paper, $17.95.

**NEITHER WOLF NOR DOG: ON FORGOTTEN
ROADS WITH AN INDIAN ELDER**
Kent Nerburn
A journey into the Native American experience.
224 pp. New World Library, 1994. $14.

**THE NELSON ISLAND ESKIMO: SOCIAL
STRUCTURE & RITUAL DISTRIBUTION**
Norman Chance
Paper. Holt, Rinehart & Winston, 1966. $9.95.

THE NETSILIK ESMIKO
Asen Balikci
Revised edition. Illus. 264 pp. Paper. Waveland, 1989.
$9.50.

*****NEVADA HISTORY COLORING BOOKS:
NEVADA'S NATIVE AMERICANS**
Nancy C. Miluck
Grades K-5. Illus. 48 pp. Paper. Dragon Enterprises, 1992. $4.

*****NEVADA TRIBAL HISTORY & GOVERNMENT**
Yerington Paiute Tribe
Grades 7-12. An introductory social studies unit about Nevada
Tribes. Illus. 32 pp. Yerington Paiute Tribe Publications, $5.

NEVER IN ANGER: PORTRAIT OF AN ESKIMO FAMILY
Jean L. Briggs
Illus. Paper. Harvard University Press, 1970. $10.95.

**NEVER WITHOUT CONSENT: JAMES BAY CREES
STAND AGAINST AN INDEPENDENT QUEBEC**
Grand Council of the Crees Staff
200 pp. Paper. General Distribution Services, 1997.
$21.95.

**THE NEW AMERICAN STATE PAPERS:
INDIAN AFFAIRS, 1789-1860, Subject Set, 13 Vols.**
Loring B. Priest, Ed.; Thomas C. Cochran, Gen. Ed.
Contains reports of the commissioners of Indian Affairs,
personal accounts of Indian life and culture, etc. Facsimile
reprint. Illus. Scholarly Resources, $750 per set.

**THE NEW DEAL & AMERICAN INDIAN TRIBALISM:
ADMINISTRATION OF THE INDIAN REORGANIZATION
ACT, 1934-1945**
Graham D. Taylor
210 pp. University of Nebraska Press, 1980. $18.95.

NEW DIRECTIONS IN AMERICAN INDIAN HISTORY
Colin Calloway, Editor
262 pp. Paper. University of Oklahoma Press, 1988. $15.95.

**NEW DIRECTIONS IN FEDERAL INDIAN POLICY:
A REVIEW OF AMERICAN INDIAN POLICY REVIEW
COMMISSION**
edited by Anthony D. Brown
Collection of articles presented as papers at a 1978 conference sponsored by the UCLA, American Indian Studies Center. 150 pp. Paper. UCLA, American Indian Studies Center,
1979. $10.

**NEW ECHOTA LETTERS: CONTRIBUTIONS OF
SAMUEL L. WORCESTER TO THE CHEROKEE PHOENIX**
Jack & Anna Kilpatrick, Editors
The Phoenix was the first newspaper printed in part in an Ameri-
can Indian language. A white missionary, Worcester, writes of
a crucial period in Cherokee history. 136 pp. SMU Press, 1968.
$14.95.

THE NEW ENGLAND INDIANS
C. Keith Wilbur, MD
Describes how New England's 18 major Indian tribes actually
lived. 400 Illus. Biblio. 110 pp. Paper. Globe Piquot Press, 1978.
$14.95.

NEW ENGLAND'S PROSPECT
W. Wood; Alden T. Vaughan, Editor
Reprint of 1634 edition. Illus. 144 pp. Paper.
University of Massachusetts Press, $11.95.

**NEW HOPE FOR THE INDIANS: THE GRANT PECE
POLICY & THE NAVAJOS IN THE 1870s**
Norman Bender
Illus. 288 pp. University of New Mexico Pres, 1990.

NEW HORIZONS IN AMERICAN INDIAN ART
Illus. 16 pp. Paper. Southwest Museum, 1976. $2.

NEW INDIAN SKETCHES
P.J. DeSmet
Reprint of 1904 edition. 146 pp.
Ye Galleon, $16.95; paper, $11.95.

NEW LIGHT ON CHACO CANYON
David Grant Noble, Editor
Illus. 108 pp. Paper. School of American Research, $11.95.

NEW NATIVE AMERICAN DRAMA: THREE PLAYS
Hanay Geiogamah, Editor
Rep[rint of 1980 edition. Illus. 158 pp. Paper.
University of Oklahoma Press, 2001. $17.95.

NEW & OLD VOICES OF WAH'KON-TAH
Robert Dodge & Jos. McCullough
144 pp. Paper. International Publishers, 1985. $4.95.

NEW PERSPECTIVES ON THE PUEBLOS
A. Ortiz, Editor
Illus. 360 pp. Paper. University of New Mexico Press,
1970. $11.95.

**NEW RELATION TO GASPESIA: WITH THE
CUSTOMS & RELIGION OF THE GASPESIAN INDIAN**
C. Le Clercq
Reprint of 1910 edition. Greenwood, $33.75.

**NEW RESOURCE WARS: NATIVE STRUGGLES
AGAINST MULTINATIONAL CORPORATIONS**
Al Gedicks
Illus. 250 pp. South End Press, 1994. $35; paper, $15.

**NEW TRAILS IN MEXICO: AN ACCOUNT OF ONE YEAR'S
EXPLORATION IN NORTH-WESTERN SONORA, MEXICO,
& SOUTH-WESTERN ARIZONA, 1909-1910**
Carl Lumholtz
An early look at the Papagos. Reprint of 1912 edition.
411 pp. Paper. University of Arizona Press, $18.95.

NEW VOICES FROM THE LONGHOUSE:
ANTHOLOGY OF MODERN IROQUOIS LITERATURE
 Joseph Bruchac
Greenfield Review Press, 1988. $12.95.

NEW VOICES IN NATIVE AMERICAN LITERARY CRITICISM
 Arnold Krupat, Editor
20 critics explore the oral and textual expressions of Native
Americans past and present. 704 pp. Paper. Smithsonian Institution Press, 1993. $34.95.

THE NEW WARRIORS: NATIVE AMERICAN
LEADERS SINCE 1900
 edited by R. David Edmunds
Profiles American Indian men and women who played a significant role in the affairs of their communities and of the nation
in the 20th century. Illus. 356 pp. University of Nebraska Press,
2001. $40.

NEW WORDS, OLD SONGS
 Charles E. Blanchard; illus. by Merald Clark
Understanding the lives of ancient peoples in Southwest Florida
through archaeology. Illus. 136 pp. Paper. IAPS Book. Distributed by Great Outdoors Publishing, $24.95; paper, $14.95.

NEW WORLD ARCHAEOLOGY & CULTURE HISTORY:
COLLECTED ESSAYS & ARTICLES
 Gordon Willey
Illus. 450 pp. University of New Mexico Press, 1990. $39.95.

NEW WORLD BABEL: LANGUAGES
& NATIONS IN EARLY AMERICA
 Edward G. Gray
Princeton University Press, 1999. $35.

NEW WORLDS FOR ALL: INDIANS, EUROPEANS,
& THE REMAKING OF EARLY AMERICA
 Colin G. Calloway
Illus. 216 pp. Johns Hopkins University Press, 1997. $24.95.

NEW WRITERS OF THE PURPLE SAGE
 Russell Martin, Editor
Includes some Native American writers. 368 pp.
Penguin USA, $11.

NEW YORK CITY IN INDIAN POSSESSION
 Reginald P. Bolton
Second Edition. Illus. 170 pp. Paper. National Museum
of the American Indian, 1975. $6.

NEWBERRY LIBRARY/CENTER FOR THE HISTORY
OF AMERICAN INDIAN BIBLIOGRAPHICAL SERIES
 Francis Jennings
A series of bibliographies of Native American groups, geo-
graphic areas, & subjects. Indiana University Press, 1976-84.

NEWE HUPIA: SHOSHONI POETRY SONGS
 Jon P. Dayley, and Beverly & Earl Crum
Written texts of songs in Shoshoni & English, packaged with a
CD with songs by Earl and beverly Crum. 276 pp. Paper & CD.
Utah State University Press, 2001. $24.95.

NEXT STEPS: RESEARCH & PRACTICE
TO ADVANCE INDIAN EDUCATION
 Karen G. Swisher
300 pp. Paper. ERIC-CRESS, 1999. $20.

*****NEZ PERCE**
 Kathi Howes
Grades 5-8. Illus. 32 pp. Rourke Corp., 1990. $9.95.

*****THE NEZ PERCE**
 Clifford E. Trafzer
Historical look at the Nez Perce. Grades 7 and up. Illus.
Chelsea House Publishers, 1993. $7.95.

*****THE NEZ PERCE**
 Virginia Driving Hawk Sneve
The creation myth of the Nez Perce; their history, customs,
and facts about the tribe today. Grades 4-6. Illus. 32 pp.
Holiday House, 1994. $15.95; paper, $6.95.

*****THE NEZ PERCE**
 Alice Osinski
Grade K-4. Illus. 48 pp. Childrens Press, 1984. $11.45.

NEZ PERCE COUNTRY
223 pp. Paper. Nez Perce National Historical Park.

NEZ PERCE COYOTE TALES: THE MYTH CYCLE
 Deward E. Walker
Illus. Maps. Biblio. Paper. University of Oklahoma Press,
1998. $13.95.

NEZ PERCE DICTIONARY
 Haruo Aoki
University of California Press, 1993. $155.

THE NEZ PERCE INDIANS & THE
OPENING OF THE NORTHWEST
 Alvin M. Josephy, Jr.
Abridged edition. Illus. 683 pp. Paper. University of Nebraska
Press, 1979. $14.95.

NEZ PERCE JOSEPH
 O. Howard
Reprint of 1881 edition. Illus. 274 pp. Da Capo Press,
1972. $32.50.

NEZ PERCE NARRATIVES
 Aski Haruo & Deward Walker
Paper. University of California Press, 1989. $64.

*****THE NEZ PERCE: NORTHWEST**
 Peter Nabakov
Grades 5 and up. Illus. Chelsea House, 1989. $17.95.

NEZ PERCE TEXTS
 Haruo Aoki
Paper. University of California Press, 1979. $25.

THE NEZ PERCES SINCE LEWIS & CLARK
 Kate McBeth
Reprint. Illus. 288 pp. Paper. University of Idaho Press,
$15.95.

NEZ PERCES: TRIBESMEN
OF THE COLUMBIA PLATEAU
 Francis Haines
Reprint of 1955 edition. Illus. Paper.
University of Oklahoma Press, $17.95.

NI-KSO-KO-WA: BLACKFOOT SPIRITUALITY,
TRADITIONS, VALUES, & BELIEFS
 Long Standing Bear Chief
Presents an overview of Blackfoot beliefs from a modern
day viewpoint. Paper. Spirit Talk Press, 1992. $9.95.

NICOLAS POINT, S.J.: HIS LIFE &
NORTHWEST INDIAN CHRONICLES
 Cornelius Buckley
356 pp. Loyola University Press, 1989. $15.95.

THE NIGHT CHANT: A NAVAHO CEREMONY
 Washington Matthews
Reprint of 1902 edition. Illus. 376 pp. University of
Utah Press, 1998. $45; paper, $19.95.

NIGHT FLYING WOMAN: AN OJIBWAY NARRATIVE
 Ignatia Broker; illus. by Steven Premo
Life experiences of author's great-great grandmother
from the 1860s through the 1940s. Illus. 135 pp. Paper.
Minnesota Historical Society Press, 1983. $8.50.

*****THE NIGHT THE GRANDFATHERS DANCED**
 Linda Theresa Raczek; Illus. by Katalin Olah Ehling
A tale revolving around a Ute Indian traditional springtime
dance. Ages 5-8. Illus. 32 pp. Paper. Northland Press & Clear
Light, $7.95.

THE NIGHT HAS A NAKED SOUL: WITCHCRAFT
& SORCERY AMONG THE WESTERN CHEROKEE
 Alan Kilpatrick
Traditional Cherokee beliefs & practices regarding the occult.
Maps. 224 pp. Syracuse University Press, 1998. $28.95; pa-
per, $19.95.

*****NIGHT OF THE CRUEL MOON: CHEROKEE**
REMOVAL AND THE TRAIL OF TEARS
 Stanley Hoig
Grades 5-12. Illus. 144 pp. Facts on File, 1996.
$17.95; paper, $9.95.

NIGHT SKY, MORNING STAR
 Evelina Zuni Lucero
229 pp. Paper. University of Arizona Press, $17.95.

NIGHT SPIRITS: THE STORY OF THE
RELOCATION OF THE SAYISI DENE
 Ila Bussidor & Ustun Bilgen-Reinart
Paper. University of Toronto Press, 1997. $18.95.

*****NIGHT WALKER & THE BUFFALO**
 Althea Bass
An old Southern Cheyenne warrior tells stories that relate
the old ways to the new. Grades 5-9. 32 pp. Council for
Indian Education, $8.95; paper, $2.95.

NIGHTLAND: A NOVEL
 Louis Owens
Cherokee ranchers. 224 pp. Paper. University of Oklahoma
Press, $14.95.

THE NIGHTWAY: A HISTORY & A HISTORY OF
DOCUMENTATION OF A NAVAJO CEREMONIAL
 James C. Faris
Paper. University of New Mexico Press, $18.95.

NIHANCAN'S FEAST OF BEAVER: ANIMAL
TALES OF THE NORTH AMERICAN INDIANS
 Edward Lavitt & Robert McDowell
Illus. 120 pp. Paper. Museum of New Mexico Press,
1990. $12.95.

NINE VISITS TO THE MYTHWORLD:
GHANDL OF THE QAYAHL LLAANAS
 translated by Robert Bringhurst

Myths, legends, and everyday stories of the Haidas.
224 pp. University of Nebraska Press, 2000. $35.

NINE YEARS AMONG THE INDIANS, 1870-1879:
THE STORY OF THE CAPTIVITY & LIFE OF A
TEXAN AMONG THE INDIANS
 Herman Lehmann; edited by Marvin Hunter
Paper. University of New Mexico Press, $16.95.

NINSTINCTS: HAIDA WORLD HERITAGE SITE
 George E. MacDonald
Illus. Paper. UBC Press,, 1998. $15.95.

NO MORE INDIANS
 Ralph Taylor & Bearl Brooks
Grades 4-6. 24 pp. Workbook. ESP, Inc., $5.

NO MORE BUFFALO
 Bob Scriver
Illus. 150 pp. Lowell Press, 1982. $35.

*****NO ONE LIKE A BROTHER**
 Hap Gilliland
Grades 4-12. 32 pp. Council for Indian Education, 1970.
$8.95; paper, $2.95.

NO TURNING BACK: A HOPI INDIAN WOMAN'S
STRUGGLE TO LIVE IN TWO WORLDS
 Polingaysi Qoyawayma
187 pp. Paper. University of New Mexico Press, 1977.
$11.95.

NO WORD FOR TIME: THE WAY OF THE ALGONQUIN
 Evan T. Pritchard
Explores Algonquin myth, history, and philosophy.
114 pp. Paper. Clear Light, $12.95.

NOBLE RED MAN: LAKOTA WISDOMKEEPER
MATHEW KING
 Harvey Arden
Illus. 128 pp. Beyond Words Publishing, $16.95.

NOCCALULU: LEGEND, FACT & FUNCTION
 Jeffrey R. Jones; Jerry Pogue & David Underhill, Editors
Illus. 72 pp. Jeffrey & Jones, 1989. $17.00; paper, $7.

THE NOME LACKEE INDIAN RESERVATION, 1854-1870
 Donald L. Hislop
99 pp. Association for Northern California Records, 1978. $7.

NOOTKA & QUILEUTE MUSIC
 F. Densmore
Reprint of 1939 edition. Illus. 416 pp. Da Capo Press, $42.50.

NORTH ALASKA CHRONICLE:
NOTES FROM THE END OF TIME
 John Martin Campbell
Presents Eskimo tribesman Simon Paneak's detailed drawings
of his native culture and life ways. Illus. 160 pp. Museum of
New Mexico Press, 2002. $45; paper, $29.95.

NORTH ALASKAN ESKIMOS:
A STUDY IN ECOLOGY & SOCIETY
 Robert F. Spencer
490 pp. Reprint Services, 1995. $109.

THE NORTH AMERICAN INDIAN
 David Hurst Thomas, Editor
21-volume set reproducing over 375 articles in facsmilie.
Garland Publishing.

*****NORTH AMERICAN INDIAN ACTIVITY BOOK**
 Winky Adam
Grades K-3. 32 puzzles, crosswords, coloring, mazes.
64 pp. paper. Written Heritage, $1.

NORTH AMERICAN INDIAN ALMANAC
 Duane Cjampagne, Editor
Information on the civilization and culture of the indigenous
peoples of the U.S. and Canada. Documentary excerpts, biographies, and 400 maps and illustrations. 800 pp. Gale Research,
1993. $95.

NORTH AMERICAN INDIAN ANTHROPOLOGY:
ESSAYS ON SOCIETY & CULTURE
 Raymond J. De Mallie & Alfonso Ortiz
Essay exploring the blending of structural & historical ap-
proaches to American Indian anthropology. Illus. Maps. 448
pp. Paper. University of Oklahoma Press, 1994. $18.95.

NORTH AMERICAN INDIAN ART
 Peter T. and Jill L. Furst
Illus. 265 pp. Paper. Rizzoli International, 1982. $25.

NORTH AMERICAN INDIAN ARTIFACTS:
A COLLECTOR'S ID & VALUE GUIDE
 Lar Hothem
Revised 6th edition with 500 new color photos and pricing.
Illus. 512 pp. Paper. Hothem House, 1998. $29.95 postpaid.

NORTH AMERICAN INDIAN ARTS: PRICES & AUCTIONS
 Laurence & Maurine Smith
Annual. Artist.

NORTH AMERICAN INDIAN BEADWORK
Smith
Standard text gives good directions on Applique, loom work, lazy stitch, and much more. Illus. Smoke & Fire Co., $13.95.

NORTH AMERICAN INDIAN BEADWORK PATTERNS
Pamela Stanley-Millner
Illus. 48 pp. Paper. Dover, 1985. $4.95.

NORTH AMERICAN INDIAN BORDERS
Charlene Tarbox
55 copyright-free forms. 48 pp. Paper. Dover, $5.95.

NORTH AMERICAN INDIAN BURIAL CUSTOMS
H.C. Yarrow; Monte Smith, Editor
Illus. 150 pp. Paper. Cherokee Publications
& Eagle's View Publishing. $9.95.

*NORTH AMERICAN INDIAN CRAFTS
Peter F. Copeland
Grades K-2. Coloring book. 48 pp. Paper. Dover, $2.95.

NORTH AMERICAN INDIAN DANCES & RITUALS
Copeland
Paper. Dover, 1998. $2.95.

NORTH AMERICAN INDIAN DESIGNS
Caren Caraway
5 titles: *Eastern Woodland Indian Designs, Northwest Indian Designs, Plains Indian Designs, Southeastern Woodland Indian Designs,* and *Southwest American Indian Designs.* 50 pp. each. Paper. Stemmer House Publishers, $6.95 each.

261 NORTH AMERICAN INDIAN DESIGNS
Madeline Orban-Szontagh
Illus. 48 pp. Paper. Dover, $4.95.

*NORTH AMERICAN INDIAN DESIGNS COLORING BOOK
Paul C. Kennedy
Grades K-3. 48 pp. Paper. Dover, $2.95

**NORTH AMERICAN INDIAN DESIGNS
FOR ARTISTS & CRAFTSPEOPLE**
Eva Wilson
128 pp. Paper. Dover & Written Heritage, 1987. $8.95.

**NORTH AMERICAN INDIAN DESIGNS IN FULL
COLOR FOR NEEDLEPOINTERS & CRAFTSPEOPLE**
Dorothy P. Story
Illus. 32 pp. Paper. Dover, $5.95.

NORTH AMERICAN INDIAN DESIGNS/STAINED GLASS
John Green
Paper. Dover, 1995. $3.95.

NORTH AMERICAN INDIAN ECOLOGY
J. Donald Hughes
2nd Edition. Illus. 222 pp. Paper. Texas Western Press, 1996. $20.

NORTH AMERICAN INDIAN ICONS: A CALENDAR BOOK
Beth Garbo
Illus. 106 pp. Especially Books, 1998. $12.95.

**NORTH AMERICAN INDIAN JEWELRY & ADORNMENT:
FROM PREHISTORY TO THE PRESENT**
Lois Sherr Dubin
1200 photos. 50 maps. Biblio. 608 pp. Written Heritage, $59.95.

**NORTH AMERICAN INDIAN LANDMARKS:
A TRAVELER'S GUIDE**
George Cantor
Explores more than 300 sites relevant to American Indian history and culture. Illus. 409 pp. Gale, $45. Reprint of 1993 edition. Paper. Diane Publishing, $18.

**NORTH AMERICAN INDIAN LANGUAGE MATERIALS,
1890-1965: AN ANNOTATED BIBLIOGRAPHY OF
MONOGRAPHIC WORKS**
G. Edward Evans and Jeffrey Clark
An update of James C. Pilling's nine American Indian linguistic bibliographies published for the U.S. Bureau of Ethnology. 187 entries. 153 pp. Paper. UCLA, American Indian Studies Center, 1979. $5.

**NORTH AMERICAN INDIAN LIFE:
CUSTOMS & TRADITIONS OF 23 TRIBES**
Elsie Clews Parsons, Editor
27 fictionalized essays by noted anthropologistss. Studies by Paul Rodin, Robert Lowie, Stewart Culin, Franz Boas, and Elsie Clews Parson. 480 pp. Paper. Dover, $10.95.

NORTH AMERICAN INDIAN LIVES
Nancy O. Lurie
Illus. 72 pp. Paper. Waveland Press, 1985. $6.95.

*NORTH AMERICAN INDIAN MASKS
Frieda Gates
Grades 5 and up. Illus. 64 pp. Walker & Co., 1982. $8.95.

*NORTH AMERICAN INDIAN MEDICINE PEOPLE
Karen Liptak
Grades 5-8. Illus. 65 pp. Franklin Watts, 1990. $11.90.

NORTH AMERICAN INDIAN MOTIFS: CD-ROM & BOOK
Kate
Provides 391 copyright-free designs printed on one side of glossy pages. 32 pp. book and CD-ROM. Hothem House, Dover & Written Heritage, 1996. $5.95, book; $9.95 CD-ROM & book.

**NORTH AMERICAN INDIAN MUSIC: A GUIDE TO
PUBLISHED SOURCES & SELECTED RECORDINGS**
Richard Keeling
420 pp. Garland, 1997. $75.

NORTH AMERICAN INDIAN MYTHOLOGY
Cottie Burland
Illus. 144 pp. Peter Bedrick Books, 1985. $19.95.

NORTH AMERICAN INDIAN POINTS
Lar Hothem
Illus. Second edition. 208 pp. Paper. Hothem House, 1984. $7.95.

**THE NORTH AMERICAN INDIAN PORTFOLIOS
FROM THE LIBRARY OF CONGRESS**
Bodmer, Catlin, McKenney & Hall
Illus. 272 pp. Paper. Abbeville Press, $12.95.

*NORTH AMERICAN INDIAN STORIES
Gretchen Mayo
Grades 5 and up. 4 titles: *Earthmaker's Tales,
More Earthmaker's Tales, Star Tales & More Star Tales.*
Illus. 48 pp. each. Walker & Co., 1991. $5.95 each.

*NORTH AMERICAN INDIAN SURVIVAL SKILLS
Karen Liptak
Grades 5-8. Illus. 65 pp. Fraklin Watts, 1990. $11.90.

NORTH AMERICAN INDIAN TRADE SILVER
Carter
Study of the historic silver objects made for, and treasured by, the Indians. Illus. 256 pp. Paper. Hothem House, 1996. $16.95.

NORTH AMERICAN INDIAN TRAVEL GUIDE
Ralph & Lisa Shanks
U.S. & Canada's Indian & Eskimo events & places of interest. Over 100 tribal offices; over 900 places & events to visit. 5th Ed. Illus. 295 pp. Paper. Costano Books, 1993. $19.95..

NORTH AMERICAN INDIAN WARS
Don Nardo
Greenhaven, 1999. $26.20; paper, $16.20.

NORTH AMERICAN INDIAN WARS - CD-ROM
In the process of being completed. Quanta Press.

*NORTH AMERICAN INDIAN WARS
Grades 6 and up. Illus. Smithmark, $26.95.

NORTH AMERICAN INDIANS
Illus. 32 pp. Paper. Hancock House, $3.

**NORTH AMERICAN INDIANS: PHOTOGRAPHS FROM
THE NATIONAL ANTHROPOLOGICAL ARCHIVES**
Smithsonian Institution
96 frames; 96 fiche; 5,000 illustrations.
University of Chicago Press, 1974. $105.

NORTH AMERICAN INDIANS
George Catlin; Peter Mathiessen, Editor & intro by.
Collection of George Catlin's letters, and illustrated with 50 of his drawings. Reprint. 560 pp. Paper. Penguin USA, $11.

NORTH AMERICAN INDIANS
Paula Fleming & Judith Luskey
256 pp. Harper & Row, 1986. $34.50.

*NORTH AMERICAN INDIANS
Marie Gorsline and Douglas Gorsline
Preschool-2. Paper. Random House, 1978. $1.95.

NORTH AMERICAN INDIANS - CD-ROM
A database of text and image on the history of Native Americans. Includes information on leadership, tribal heritage, religion, family life, and customs. IBM compatible. Quanta Press, 1991. $69.95.

**NORTH AMERICAN INDIANS & ALASKA NATIVES:
ABSTRACTS OF THE PSYCHOLOGICAL & BEHAVIORAL
LITERATURE, 1967-1994**
Joseph E. Trimble & Weldon M. Bagwell, Editors
272 pp. Paper. American Psychological Association, 1995. $27.50.

NORTH AMERICAN INDIANS COLORING ALBUM
Rite Warner, Illustrator
Illus. 32 pp. Paper. Troubador Press, 1978. $3.95.

**NORTH AMERICAN INDIANS:
A COMPREHENSIVE ACCOUNT**
Alice B. Kehoe
2nd Ed. Illus. 625 pp. Paper. Prentice-Hall, 1992. $42.

NORTH AMERICAN INDIANS: A DISSERTATION INDEX
University Microfilms International, 1976. $28.

**NORTH AMERICAN INDIANS
IN HISTORICAL PERSPECTIVE**
Eleanor Burke Leacock & Nancy O. Lurie, Editors
Illus. 498 pp. Paper. Waveland Press, 1988. $18.95.

*NORTH AMERICAN INDIANS OF ACHIEVEMENT
Dr. Frank W. Porter, III
Grades 4 and up. Includes Sitting Bull, Will Rogers, Jim Thorpe, Sarah Winnemucca, Joseph Brant, Quanah Parker, et al. Illus. 104-128 pp. each. Chelsea House, 21 hardcover titles, $19.95, $418.95 per set; 5 paperback titles, $9.95, $49.75 per set.

**THE NORTH AMERICAN INDIANS:
PHOTOGRAPHS BY EDWARD S. CURTIS**
Edward S. Curtis
Illus. 96 pp. Aperture, 1972. $25.

*NORTH AMERICAN MYTHS & LEGENDS
Philip Ardagh
paper. Silver Burdett Press, 1999. $23.

NORTH AMERICAN NATIVE AUTHORS CATALOG
Lists more than 600 titles from over 90 different publishers. Works by American Indian poets, writers, historians, storytellers and performers. Publications range from novels and books of poetry to children's literature, journals and newspapers, sacred traditions and more. Greenfield Review Press, 1995. $2.

**NORTH AMERICAN SUN KINGS:
KEEPERS OF THE FLAME**
Joseph B. Mahan
300 pp. ISAC Press, 1992. $30.

NORTH AMERICAN TRIBAL DIRECTORY
Arrowfax Editors
U.S. and Canadian tribal listings. 630 pp.
Arrowfax, Inc. Annual. $50.

THE NORTH AMERICANS OF YESTERDAY
F.S. Dellenbaugh
A comparative study of North American Indian life, customs and products, on the theory of the ethnic unity of the race. Reprint of 1901 edition. Gordon Press, $69.95.

NORTH CAROLINA'S STATE HISTORIC SITES
Gary L. McCullough
Chronicles more than six centuries of NC history, from the ancient Native American civilization at Town Creek Indian Mound. 96 pp. Paper. John F. Blair, Publisher, 2001. $12.95.

NORTH DAKOTA INDIANS: AN INTRODUCTION
Mary Schneider
275 pp. Paper. Kendall-Hunt, 1986. $19.95.

**FRANK J. NORTH: PAWNEE SCOUT,
COMMANDER AND PIONEER**
Ruby E. Wilson
Illus. 335 pp. Ohio University Press, 1982. $19.95.

NORTH POLE LEGACY: BLACK, WHITE & ESKIMO
S. Allen Counter
Illus. 236 pp. University of Massachusetts Press, 1991. $24.95.

NORTH SLOPE INUPIAQ DIALOGUES
Edna MacLean
13 pp. Paper. Alaska Native Language Center, $2.50.

**NORTH, SOUTH, EAST & WEST:
AMERICAN INDIANS & THE NATURAL WORLD**
Marsha C. Bol
Illus. 176 pp. Paper. Roberts Rinehart, 1998. $24.95.

NORTHEAST INDIANS: EDUCATIONAL COLORING BOOK
Grades 1-8. Illus. 32 pp. Paper. Spizzirri Publishing, 1981. Read & Coloring Book, $1.95; Cassette/book, $6.95.

***NORTHEAST INDIANS FACT CARDS: INDIANS
OF NEW ENGLAND & THE NORTHEAST COAST**
Reeve Chace
Grades 4 and up. Illus. 70 pp. Toucan Valley, 1998. $29.

A NORTHEASTERN ALGONQUIAN SOURCEBOOK
Edward S. Rogers, Editor
364 pp. Garland Publishing, 1985. $50.

NORTHEASTERN INDIAN LIVES, 1632-1816
Robert S. Grumet, Editor
Illus. 408 pp. University of Massachusetts Press, 1996. $55; paper, $19.95.

**NORTHERN ATHABASCAN SURVIVAL:
WOMEN, COMMUNITY, AND THE FUTURE**
Phyllis Ann Fast
Conversations with Athabascan women. Map. 305 pp. University of Nebraska Press, 2002. $55.

NORTHERN ATHAPASKAN ART: A BEADWORK TRADITION
Kate Duncan
Illus. 272 pp. University of Washington Press, 1988. $45.

THE NORTHERN & CENTRAL NOOTKAN TRIBES
Philip Drucker
Reprint. Reprint Services, $75.

*NORTHERN CHEYENNE FIRE FIGHTERS
Henry Tall Bull & Tom Weist
Grades 4-adult. 39 pp. Paper. Council for Indian
Education. $5.95.

THE NORTHERN CHEYENNE INDIAN RESERVATION, 1877-1900
Orlan Svingen
216 pp. Paper. University Press of Colorado, 1997. $22.50.

THE NORTHERN COPPER INUIT: A HISTORY
Richard D. Condon, et al.
Illus. 216 pp. 302 p. University of Oklahoma Press, 1996. $29.95.

THE NORTHERN MAIDU
Marie Potts
Illus. Map. 48 pp. Paper. Naturegraph, 1977. $7.95.

NORTHERN NAVAJO FRONTIER, 1860-1900: EXPANSION THROUGH ADVERSITY
Robert S. McPherson
Navajo tribal history. 144 pp. Paper.
Utah State University Press, 2001. $19.95.

THE NORTHERN PAIUTE LANGUAGE OF OREGON
W.L. Marsden
Reprint of 1923 edition. 19 pp. Paper. Coyote Press. $2.50.

NORTHERN TALES: TRADITIONAL STORIES OF ESKIMO & INDIAN PEOPLES
Howard Norman, Editor
370 pp. Pantheon Press, 1990. $24.95.

THE NORTHERN TRADITIONAL DANCER
C. Scott Evans & J. Rex Reddick
2nd Ed. Illus. 50 pp. Reddick Enterprises, 1998. $12.95.

NORTHERN UTE MUSIC
F. Densmore
Reprint of 1922 edition. Illus. 236 pp. Da Capo Press, $27.50.

NORTHERN VOICES: INUIT WRITING IN ENGLISH
Penny Petrone
Illus. 330 pp. University of Toronto Press, 1988. $27.50.

WALTER NORTHWAY
Yvonne Yarber & Curt Madison, Editors;
Della Northway, et al, trs
Illus. 55 pp. Paper. Alaska Native Language Center, 1987. $7.

NORTHWEST CHIEFS: GUSTAV SOHON'S VIEWS OF THE 1855 STEVENS TREATY COUNCILS
Paper. Washington State Historical Society, 1986. $9.50.

NORTHWEST COAST INDIAN ART: AN ANALYSIS OF FORM
Bill Holm
Illus. 133 pp. Paper. University of Washington Press, 1965. $16.95.

*THE NORTHWEST COAST INDIAN ART SERIES
Nan McNutt
Grades 3-6. Illus. 120 pp. Nan McNutt & Associates, 1991. $29.85.

NORTHWEST COAST INDIAN DESIGNS
Madeleine Orban-Szontagh
48 pp. Paper. Dover, $4.95.

NORTHWEST COAST INDIAN PAINTING: HOUSE FRONTS & INTERIOR SCREENS
Edward Malin
Illus. 200 pp. Timber Press, 1999. $39.95.

*NORTHWEST COAST INDIANS COLORING BOOK
David Rickman
Grades K-2. 48 pp. Paper. Dover, $2.95.

NORTHWEST COAST NATIVE & NATIVE STYLE ART
Lloyd Averill & Daphne Morris
Paper. University of Washington Press, $18.95.

NORTHWEST INDIAN DESIGNS
Caren Caraway
Illus. 48 pp. Paper. Stemmer House, 1996. $6.95.

NORTHWEST INDIAN GUIDE & MAP
Features Native attractions, arts and businesses.
Affiliated Tribes of Northwest Indians (ATNI), 1995. $2.

NORTHWEST INDIANS: AN EDUCATIONAL COLORING BOOK
Grades 1-8. Illus. 32 pp. Paper. Spizzirri Publishing, 1981.
Read & Coloring Book, $1.95; Cassette/book, $6.95.

THE NORTHWEST INDIGENOUS GOLD RUSH HISTORY
Booklet includes seven interviews with tribal elders and historians recounting their memories and stories of the Gold Rush era. from the Karuk, Yurok, Wintu, and Wiyot people of Northern California. 1999. ITEPP CRC.

NORTHWEST NATIVE HARVEST
Carol Batdorf
96 pp. Paper. Hancock House, 1990. $7.95.

NORTHWEST NEBRASKAS INDIAN PEOPLE
Dr. James A. Hanson
Scholarly story of 6 successive tribes in the region including the Kiowa and Apache. Illus. 48 pp. The Fur Press. $2.

NORTHWEST PASSAGE: THE GREAT COLUMBIA RIVER
Wiliam Dietrich
The settlers & Native American struggle over these lands. Maps. 432 pp. Paper. University of Washington Press, 1995. $18.95.

NORTHWESTERN INDIAN IMAGES: A PHOTOGRAPHIC LOOK AT PLATEAU INDIANS
Richard Scheuerman
Illus. Paper. Sierra Oaks, 1989. $9.95.

THE NORTHWESTERN INDIAN TRIBES IN EXILE: MODOC, NEZ PERCE, & PALOUSE REMOVAL TO THE INDIAN TERRITORY
Clifford Trafzer
Illus. 137 pp. Paper. Sierra Oaks, 1987. $11.95.

*NORTHWOOD CRADLE SONG - FROM A MENOMINEE LULLABY
Douglas Wood; illus. by Lisa Destimini
Ullus. Paper. Meadowlark Communications, $5.99.

NOT FOR INNOCENT EARS: SPIRITUAL TRADITIONS OF A DESERT CAHUILLA MEDICINE WOMAN
Ruby Modesto & Guy Mount
Ethnographic portrait of the spiritual beliefs, healing strategies, personal history & cultural heitage of a Desert Cahuila medicine woman & her people. Illus. 128 pp. Paper. Sweetlight, 1980. $9.95.

NOTABLE NATIVE AMERICANS
Sharon Malinowski & George H.J. Abrams, Editors
Biographies of about 275 notable Native Americans from all areas of endeavor, both past and present. 2nd Ed. 490 pp. Gale Research, 1994. $75.

NOTEBOOK ON ART, HISTORY & CULTURE
Stephen Wallace, et al
80 pp. Navajo Curriculum Center Press.

NOTES FROM INDIAN COUNTRY
Tim Giago
Includes columns on communications, culture, education and athletics, government, health, humor, litigation, politics, religion, and people as observed by Giago. Greenfield Review Press, $10.

NOTES OF A TWENTY-FIVE YEARS' SERVICE IN THE HUDSON'S BAY TERRITORY
John McLean; W.S. Wallace, Editor
Reprint of 1932 edition. Greenwood Press, $29.50.

NOTES ON EIGHT PAPAGO SONGS
E.G. Stricklen
Reprint. 6 pp. Paper. Coyote Press, $.95.

NOTES ON THE GYNECOLOGY & OBSTETRICS OF THE ARIKARA TRIBE OF INDIANS
Melvin Gilmore
Paper. Acoma Books, 1980. $2.50.

NOTES ON THE IROQUOIS
Henry Schoolcraft
Reprint. Illus. 500 pp. Higginson Book Co., 1998. $52.50.

NOTES ON THE SETTLEMENT & INDIAN WARS OF THE WESTERN PARTS OF VA & PA FROM 1763 TO 1783
Joseph Doddridge
Reprint. 320 pp. Paper. Clearfield Co., $28.50.

NOTICES OF EAST FLORIDA: WITH AN ACCOUNT OF THE SEMINOLE NATION OF INDIANS
W. Simmons; George Buker, Editor
Reprint of 1822 edition. 123 pp. University Press of Florida, $14.95.

NOTICIAS DE NUTKA: AN ACCOUNT OF NOOTKA SOUND IN 1792
Jose Mozino; Iris Engstrand, Editor
200 pp. Paper. University of Washington Press, 1991. $14.95.

NOW I KNOW ONLY SO FAR: ESSAYS IN ETHNOPOETICS
Dell Hymes
Native North American stories. 512 pp. University of Nebraska Press, 2003. $65; paper, $29.95.

NOW THAT THE BUFFALO'S GONE: A STUDY OF TODAYS AMERICAN INDIANS
Alvin M. Josephy
Illus. 302 pp. Paper. University of Oklahoma, 1984. $18.95.

NOW THE WOLF HAS COME: THE CREEK NATION IN THE CIVIL WAR
Christine Schulz White & Benton R. White

Focuses on teh conflict between the Muskogee bands and the Confederate-allied McIntosh family. Photos. 216 pp. Texas A&M University Press, 1990. $29.95.

NUDES & FOODS, VOLUME II
R.C. Gorman
A new collection of nudes, recipes, and anecdotes by Navajo artist, R.C. Gorman. Illus. 112 pp. Navajo Gallery, 1989. $20.

NUMBERS FROM NOWHERE: THE AMERICAN INDIAN CONTACT POPULATION DEBATE
David Henige
544 pp. University of Oklahoma Press, 1998. $47.95.

*A NUMU HISTORY-THE YERINGTON PAIUTE TRIBE
Michael Hittman
Grades 7-12. Illus. 68 pp. Paper. Yerington Paiute Tribe Publications, $12.50.

*THE NUMU WAY
Yerington Paiute Tribe
Grades 4 and up. Traditional arts, crafts, food, music, medicine, customs, clothing and games of the Yerington Paiute Tribe. 94 pp. Paper. Yerington Paiute Tribe Publications, $8. Workbook, 71 pp., $10.

NUNAVUT ATLAS
Rick Riewe, Editor
The atlas assisted the Inuit in selecting the lands they retained after the settlement of the Nunavut claim. The relationship between Inuit & the natural environment. Illus. Maps. 259 pp. CCI, $15.

O

O BRAVE NEW PEOPLE: THE EUROPEAN INVENTION OF THE AMERICAN INDIAN
John Moffitt & Santiago Sebastian
Illus. 408 pp. Paper. University of New Mexico Press, 1998. $24.95.

O BRAVE NEW WORDS: NATIVE AMERICAN LOANWORDS IN CURRENT ENGLISH
Charles L. Cutler
Covers more than one thousand North American Indian, Eskimo, and Aleut words in the English vocabulary. Surveys the thousands of Native American place-names in North America. Map. Biblio. 286 pp. University of Oklahoma Press, 1994. $19.95.

OBJECTS OF BRIGHT PRIDE: NORTHWEST COAST INDIAN ART FROM THE MUSEUM OF NATURAL HISTORY
Allen Wardwell
Second revised edition. Illus. 130 pp. Paper. American Federation of Arts, 1988. $30.

OBJECTS OF CHANGE: THE ARCHAEOLOGY & HISTORY OF ARIKARA CONTACT WITH EUROPEANS
J. Daniel Rogers
Illus. 336 pp. Smithsonian Press, 1990. $35.

OBJECTS OF MYTH & MEMORY: AMERICAN INDIAN ART AT THE BROOKLYN MUSEUM
Diana Fane, Ira Jacknis & Lise Breen
Illus. 320 pp. The Brooklyn Museum, 1991. $60; paper, $29.95.

OBSERVATIONS OF THE ETHNOLOGY OF THE SAUK INDIANS
A.B. Skinner
Reprint of 1923-1925 edition. Illus. 180 pp. Greenwood Publishing, $35.

THE OCCUPATION OF ALCATRAZ ISLAND: INDIAN SELF-DETERMINATION & THE RISE OF INDIAN ACTIVISM
Troy R. Johnson
Illus. 304 pp. University of Illinois Press, 1996. $49.95; paper, $17.95.

OCCUPATION OF WOUNDED KNEE
Robert Hecht; Siguid C. Rahmas, Editor
32 pp. SamHar Press, 1982. $3.95; paper, $2.50.

OCEAN POWER: POEMS FROM THE DESERT
Ofelia Zepeda
Perceptions of Tohono O'odham woman. 96 pp. Paper. University of Arizona Press, 1995. $13.95.

OCMULGEE ARCHAEOLOGY, 1936-1986
David J. Hally
Illus. Maps. 264 pp. University of Georgia Press, 1994. $40.

ODE SETL'OGHWNH DA': LONG AFTER I AM GONE
Teddy Charlie
Stories of traditional knowledge and skills by Tanana Athabaskan. Illus. Map. 30 pp. Alaska Native Language Center, 1992. $6.50

**THE ODYSSEY OF CHIEF STANDING BUFFALO
& THE NORTHERN SISSETON SIOUX**
Mark Diedrich
Photos. Maps. Biblio. 119 pp. Paper. Coyote Books, 1988.
$18.95.

**OF BREATH & EARTH: A BOOK OF DAYS
WITH WISDOM FROM NATIVE AMERICA**
John Netherton
42 color photos. 120 pp. Northland Publishing, 1995. $14.95.

**OF EARTH & ELDERS: VISIONS &
VOICES FROM NATIVE AMERICA**
Serle Chapman
Traditional & contemporary Native American images, narratives
and ideas. Illus. 218 pp. Paper. Mountain Press, $24.95.

OF EARTH & LITTLE RAIN: THE PAPAGO INDIANS
Bernard L. Fontana
Illus. 170 pp. Paper. University of Arizona Press, 1981.
$16.95.

OF MOTHER EARTH & FATHER SKY
Fred Bia and T.L. McCarthy
Illus. 69 pp. Navajo Curriculum Center Press, 1983.
$17; paper, $12.

OF UNCOMMON BIRTH: DAKOTA SONS IN VIETNAM
Mark St. Pierre
Illus. Map. 320 pp. University of Oklahoma Press, 2003. $27.95.

OFFERING
Diane Glancy
Poetry. Commemorating Indian chief Sequoyah's achievement
in absorbing and transforming a foreign language into his own
native Cherokee. 88 pp. Paper. Holy Cow! Press, $6.95.

**OFFERING SMOKE: THE SACRED PIPE
& NATIVE AMERICAN RELIGION**
Jordan Paper
Illus. 192 pp. Paper. University of Idaho Press, 1989.
$22.95.

**OFFICE OF INDIAN AFFAIRS, 1824-1880:
HISTORICAL SKETCHES**
Edward E. Hill
255 pp. N. Ross, 1974. $25.

**OGLALA LAKOTA CRAZY HORSE: A PRELIMINARY
GENEALOGICAL STUDY & AN ANNOTATED LISTING
OF PRIMARY SOURCES**
Richard G. Hardorff
Illus. Amereon Ltd. $17.95; paper, $11.95.

OGLALA PEOPLE, 1841-1879: A POLITICAL HISTORY
Catherine Price
Illus. Maps. 244 pp. Paper. University of Nebraska Press,
1996. $16.95.

OGLALA RELIGION
William Powers
Illus. 250 pp. Paper. University of Nebraska Press, 1977.
$6.95.

OGLALA WOMEN: MYTH, RITUAL & REALITY
Marla N. Powers
Illus. 242 pp. Paper. University of Chicago Press, 1986. $15.95.

***OHIO'S FIRST SETTLERS: THE INDIANS -
NATIVE AMERICANS**
Nicholas P. Georgiady & Louis G. Romano
Vol. 3, 2nd revised edition. Grades 4-8. Ilus. Paper.
Argee Publishers, 1998. $4.50.

OHIO'S INDIAN PAST
Lar Hothem
Photos. 165 pp. Paper. Hothem House, 1996. $14.95.

OHIYESA: CHARLES EASTMAN, SANTEE SIOUX
Raymond Wilson
Illus. 242 pp. University of Illinois Press, 1983. $10.95.

**THE OHLONE PAST & PRESENT: NATIVE AMERICANS
OF THE SAN FRANCISCO BAY REGION**
Lowell J. Bean & Sylvia B. Vane, Eds.
Illus. 408 pp. Paper. Ballena Press, 1995. $29.95.

**THE OHLONE WAY: INDIAN LIFE IN THE
SAN FRANCISCO & MONTEREY BAY AREAS**
Malcolm Margolin
Illus. 182 pp. Paper. Heyday Books, 1978. $12.95.

OIL & GAS
Institute for the Development of Indian Law, 1980. $12.

OJIBWA CHIEFS, 1690-1890: AN ANNOTATED LISTING
John A. Ilko, Jr., compiler
Illus. 79 pp. Paper. Whitston Publishing, 1995. $6.50.

OJIBWA CRAFTS
Carrie A. Lyford
Reprint of 1943 edition. Illus. 216 pp. Paper. R. Schneider,
Publishers, $8.95.

*THE OJIBWA: GREAT LAKES
Helen H. Turner
Grades 5 and up. Illus. Chelsea House, 1989. $17.95.

THE OJIBWA OF SOUTHERN ONTARIO
Peter S. Schmalz
University of Toronto Press, 1991. $60; paper, $24.95.

**OJIBWA WARRIOR: DENNIS BANKS & THE RISE
OF THE AMERICAN INDIAN MOVEMENT**
Dennis Banks with Richard Erdoes
Illus. Photos. 352 pp. University of Oklahoma Press,
2004. $29.95.

THE OJIBWA OF WESTERN CANADA, 1780 TO 1870
Laura Peers
Illus. 320 pp. Maps. Minnesota Historical Society Press,
1994. $39.95; paper, $19.95.

THE OJIBWA WOMAN
Ruth Landes; intro. by Sally Coles
Study of gender relations in a Native society. 247 pp.
Paper. University of Nebraska Press, 1997. $13.

THE OJIBWAS: A CRITICAL BIBLIOGRAPHY
Helen H. Tanner
88 pp. Paper. Indiana Univerity Press, 1976. $4.95.

OJIBWAY CEREMONIES
Basil Johnston; Illus. by David Beyer
Illus. 188 pp. Paper. University of Nebraska Press,
1990. $13.95.

THE OJIBWAY DREAM
Arthur Shilling
Illus. 48 pp. Tundra Books, 1986. $29.95.

OJIBWAY HERITAGE
Basil Johnston; Illus. by David Beyer
Illus. Map. 170 pp. Paper. University of Nebraska Press,
1990. $11.95.

*OJIBWAY INDIANS COLORING BOOK
Chet Kozlak
Grades 1-6. Map. 32 pp. Paper. Minnesota Historical
Society Press, $2.50.

**OJIBWAY MUSIC FROM MINNESOTA:
A CENTURY OF SONG FOR VOICE & DRUM**
Thomas Vennum, Jr.
LP record/cassette & booklet. Minnesota Historical
Society Press, 1990. $9.95.

OJIBWAY ORATORY
compiled & illus. by Mark Diedrich
Illus. Biblio. 110 pp. Paper. Coyote Books, 1990. $18.95.

OJIBWAY TALES
Basil Johnston
Illus. 188 pp. Paper. University of Nebraska Press,
1993. $13.95.

*THE OJIBWE
Raymond Bial
Grades 5 and up. Illus. 128 pp. Marshall Cavendish,
1999. $22.95.

OJIBWE LANGUAGE BOOK
Coy Eklund
Ojibwe/English translations and phrases. 272 pp. Indian Coun-
try Communications, $24.

**OJIBWE VOCABULARY FOR BEGINNERS; INTERMEDIATE
VOCABULARY; & VOCABULARY FOR ADVANCED LEARN-
ERS**
Ojibwe Mekana
Tape and booklet. Indian Country Communications, Beginners,
$22; Intermediate Vocabulary, $21; Advanced Learners, $33.

OKANAGAN SOURCES
Jean Webber, Editor
Essays by First Nation authors providing historical accounts
of Okanagan Valley. 206 pp. Paper. Theytus, 1990. $16.95.

OKANOGAN HIGHLAND ALBUM
Mary L. Loe, et al
Illus. 510 pp. Statesman-Examimer, 1990. $19.95.

*OKEMOS: STORY OF A FOX INDIAN OF HIS YOUTH
George Fox and Lela Puffer
Grades 3-9. Paper. Council for Indian Education, 1976.
$1.95.

*OKLA APILACI: COMMUNITY HELPERS
Text in Choctaw with English translation.
All participants are Choctaw. Different professions on reservation are featured. Grades Preschool-3. 14 pp. Choctaw Heritage Press, $3.50.

OKLA HANNALI
R.A. Lafferty
The history of the Choctaw Indians. 222 pp. Paper.
University of Oklahoma Press, $12.95.

OKLAHOMA: FOOT-LOOSE & FANCY-FREE
Angie Debo
Illus. 266 pp. Paper. University of Oklahoma Press, $12.95.

OKLAHOMA: A HISTORY OF FIVE CENTURIES
Arrell M. Gibson
Reprint of 1981 edition. Illus. Maps. 262 pp.
Oklahoma: A History of Five Centuries, $29.95.

OKLAHOMA: A HISTORY OF THE SOONER STATE
Edwin C. McReynolds
Reprint of the revised 1964 edition. Illus. Maps. 477 pp.
University of Oklahoma Press, $24.95.

OKLAHOMA: THE LAND & ITS PEOPLE
Kenny Franks & Paul Lambert
Chronicles the history of Oklahoma, its geography and it people
and lore from ancient times to the present. Illus. 104 pp. Paper. University of Oklahoma Press, 1997. $15.95.

OKLAHOMA PLACE NAMES
George H. Shirk
Revised 1974 edition. Maps. Biblio. 268 pp. Paper.
University of Oklahoma Press, 2002. $19.95.

OKLAHOMA SEMINOLES: MEDICINES, MAGIC & RELIGION
James H. Howard and Willie Lena
Illus. 280 pp. Paper. University of Olahoma Press, 1984. $12.95.

OKLAHOMA: THE STORY OF ITS PAST & PRESENT
Edwin C. McReynolds,, Allice Marriott & Estelle Faulconer
Reprint of the 3rd 1971 edition. Illus. Maps. 500 pp. University
of Oklahoma Press, $22.95.

OKLAHOMA TRIBAL COURT REPORTS
Dennis W. Arrow
1,800 pp. 3 vols. Oklahoma City University, $75 each.

*O'KOHOME: THE COYOTE DOG
Hap Gilliland
Grades 4-9. Illus. 47 pp. Paper. Council for Indian Education,
1989. $10.45.

**OLD BETSY: THE LIFE & TIMES OF A
FAMOUS DAKOTA WOMAN & HER FAMILY**
Mark Diedrich
Illus. Photos. Maps. Biblio. 170 pp. Paper.
Coyote Book (MN), 1995. $24.95.

*OLD FATHER STORY TELLER
Pablita Velarde
6 legends from Santa Clara Pueblo. Grades 3 and up.
Illus. 56 pp. Clear Light, 1992. $24.95; paper, $14.95.

OLD FATHER'S LONG JOURNEY
Beulah Karney
Illus. 192 pp. Paper. CLC Press, 1985. $15.95; paper, $7.95.

**OLD FORT KLAMATH: AN OREGON FRONTIER POST,
1863-1890**
Buena Cobb Stone; Bert Webber, Editor
History of the the many military posts in the west over 100
years ago. Fort Klamath and its part in Modoc Indian War. Biblio.
112 pp. Paper. Webb Research Group, $10.95.

**OLD FRONTIERS: THE STORY OF THE CHEROKEE
INDIANS FROM THE EARLIEST TIMES TO THE DATE
OF THEIR REMOVAL TO THE WEST, 1838**
J.P. Brown
Reprint of 1838 edition. Illus. Ayer Co., $38.50.

OLD INDIAN DAYS
Charles A. Eastman
Stories of Sioux bands of the Upper Midwest in pre-reserva-
tion times. 300 pp. Paper. University of Nebraska, $8.95.

OLD INDIAN LEGENDS
Zitkala-Sa (Red Bird)
Illus. 165 pp. Paper. University of Nebraska Press, 1985.
$10.95.

OLD INDIAN TRAILS
Walter McClintock
Records the native customs, legends, religious rites, and daily
life of the Blackfoot. Illus. 400 pp. Paper. Houghton & Mifflin,
1992. $10.95.

OLD MAN COYOTE
Frank B. Linderman
Illus. 254 pp. Paper. University of Nebraska Press,
1996. $11.95.

**OLD NAVAJO RUGS: THEIR DEVELOPMENT
FROM 1900-1940**
Marian E. Rodee
Illus. 96 pp. Paper. University of New
Mexico Press, 1981. $15.95.

**OLD NORTH TRAIL: LIFE, LEGENDS &
RELIGION OF THE BLACKFEET INDIANS**
Walter McClintock
Reprint of 1910 edition. Illus. 540 pp.
University of Nebraska Press, 1999. $18.95.

*THE OLD ONES: A CHILDREN'S BOOK
ABOUT THE ANASAZI INDIANS
J. Brian & Jodi Freeman
Grades K-4. Illus. 65 pp. Paper. Think Shop, Inc., 1986. $2.95.

OLD SHIRTS & NEW SKINS
Sherman Alexie
Poetry. 94 pp. Paper. The Falmouth Institute, 1993. $12.

OLIVER LA FARGE & THE AMERICAN INDIAN:
A BIOGRAPHY
Robert A. Hecht
Illus. Photos. 400 pp. Scarecrow Press, 1991.
$42.50,cloth; paper, $26.50.

OMAHA TRIBE
A. Fletcher and F. LaFlesche
Reprint of 1911 edition. Two vols. Illus. Musical examples. Vol.
1, 312 pp.; Vol. 2, 355 pp. Paper. University of Nebraska Press,
$12.95 each, $25.90 per set.

*OM-KAS-TOE: BLACKFEET
TWIN CAPTURES & ELKDOG
Kenneth Thomasma; Jack Brouwer, Illus.
The Blackfeet tribe in the early 1700s. Grades 4 and up.
Illus. Baker Book House, $10.99; paper, $6.99.

ON THE APACHE INDIAN RESERVATIONS &
ARTIST WANDERINGS AMONG THE CHEYENNES
Frederic Remington
Two stories written and illustrated by Remington in 1889.
Reprint of 1974 edition. Illus. 36 pp. Paper. Filter Press, $4.

ON BEHALF OF THE WOLF & THE FIRST PEOPLES
Joseph Marshall, III (Sicangu Lakota)
Essays providing insight on being a Native American in a white
man's world. 256 pp. Paper. Red Crane Books, 1996. $13.95.

ON THE BLOODY ROAD TO JESUS:
CHRISTIANITY & THE CHIRICAHUA APACHES
H. Henrietta Stockel
Study of the religious legacy of the Chiricahua Apaches annd
its inevitable collision with Christianity. Illus. 336 pp. University
of New Mexico Press, 2004. $29.95.

ON THE BORDER WITH CROOK
John G. Bourke
490 pp. Paper. University of Nebraska Press, 1971. $11.95.

*ON THE CLIFFS OF ACOME
John Dressman
Children's story for all ages outlining the history of the cel-
ebrated New Mexico cliffs. Illus. 48 pp. Paper. Sunstone Press,
$5.95.

ON THE EDGE OF SPLENDOR: EXPLORING GRAND
CANYON'S HUMAN PAST
Douglas W. Schwartz
Illus. 80 pp. Paper. School of American Research, $12.95.

ON THE GLEAMING WAY: NAVAJOS, EASTERN PUEBLOS,
ZUNIS, HOPIS, APACHES & THEIR LAND, & THEIR MEAN-
ING TO THE WORLD
John Collier
Illus. 163 pp. Paper. Ohio University Press, 1962. $5.95.

ON THE LANDING
Michael W. Simpson
A book of poems by a young Indian poet. 49 pp. Paper.
Indian University Press, 1986. $3.60, postpaid.

ON THE MUSIC OF THE NORTH AMERICAN INDIANS
Theodore Baker; Ann Buckley, Translator
Da Capo Press, 1977. $25.

ON NATIVE GROUND: MEMOIRS AND IMPRESSIONS
Jim Barnes
Poetry & prose. 296 pp. University of Oklahoma Press,
1997. $27.95.

ON THE PADRE'S TRAIL
Christopher Vecsey
520 pp. University of Notre Dame Press, 1996. $50.

ON OUR OWN GROUND: THE COMPLETE
WRITINGS OF WILLIAM APESS, A PEQUOT
Barry O'Connell, Editor & intro.
An autobiography by a Native American in the early 1800s.
432 pp. University of Massachusetts Press, $50.00; paper,
$17.95.

*ON THE POWWOW TRAIL COLORING BOOK
Garrett J. Schembri
Grades 1-3. Companion to On the Powwow Trail video.
Focuses on the preservation of Native American Indian
customs, traditional dress and dance. Paper. Meadowlark
Communications, $2.99.

ON TIME FOR DISASTER:
THE RESCUE OF CUSTER'S COMMAND
Edward J. McClernand
Illus. 176 pp. Paper. University of Nebraska Press, 1989. $6.95.

ON THE TRAIL OF SPIDER WOMAN: PETROGLYPHS,
PICTOGRAPHS, AND MYTHS OF THE SOUTHWEST
Carol Patterson-Rudolph
Illus. Charts & Maps. 160 pp. University of New Mexico Press.
$29.95; paper, $16.95.

ON THE TRANSLATION OF
NATIVE AMERICAN LITERATURES
Brian Swann, Editor
23 scholars in linguistics, folklore, English, and anthropology,
provide a working introduction to the history, methods, and problems of translating Native American l;iteratures. Illus. 498 pp.
Smithsonian Institution Press, 1993. $45; paper, $19.95.

ONCE THEY MOVED LIKE THE WIND:
COCHISE, GERONIMO, AND THE APACHE WARS
David Roberts
History of final battlkes of the Indian wars. Illus.
368 pp. Paper. Simon & Schuster. $14.

*ONE GOOD STORY, THAT ONE
Thomas King (Cherokee)
Stories of Native-white relations. Grades 7 and up.
Paper. Oyate, 1993. $14.95.

ONE HOUSE, ONE VOICE, ONE HEART:
NATIVE AMERICAN EDUCATION AT THE
SANTA FE INDIAN SCHOOL
Sally Hyer
Illus. 170 pp. Museum of New Mexico Press, 1990.
$29.95; paper, $22.50.

ONE HUNDRED YEARS OF NATIVE AMERICAN ARTS:
SIX WASHINGTON CULTURES
Delbert McBride; Penelope Loucas, Editor
Illus. 16 pp. Paper. Tacoma Art Museum, 1989. $1.

ONE HUNDRED YEARS OF NAVAJO RUGS
Marian E. Rodee
Illus. Color & bxw photos. 200 pp. Paper.
University of New Mexico Press, $29.95.

ONE HUNDRED YEARS OF OLD MAN SAGE:
AN ARAPAHO LIFE
Jeffrey D. Anderson
Biography of Sherman Sage, an Arapaho. Illus. Map.
168 pp. University of Nebraska Press, 2003. $35.

*ONE INDIAN & TWO CHIEFS: SHORT FICTION
Ralph Salisbury
Grades 4 and up. Short stories. Navajo Community
College Press, 1993. $14.95.

ONE MORE STORY: CONTEMPORARY SENECA TALES
Duwayne Bowen
Tales of the supernatural drawn from modern day Seneca life.
Illus. Bowman Books, $9.95.

ONE NATION UNDER GOD: TRIUMPH
OF THE NATIVE AMERICAN CHURCH
Huston Smith & Reuben Snake, Editors
Includes testimonies offered by Church members from many
different tribes. Describes the prayer meetings, the sacramental use of peyote, and the significance of various practices and
objects of the Native American Church which now has more
than 80 chapters throughout the country. Illus. 174 pp. Clear
Light, 1996. $24.95; paper, $14.95.

ONE OF THE KEYS: 1676-1776-1976:
WAMPANOAG INDIAN CONTRIBUTION
Milton A. Travers
A list of words and definitions from the language of the histori-
cal Indians of southeastern Massachusetts. Illus. 64 pp. Chris-
topher Publishing House, 1975. $8.95.

ONE SMART INDIAN
Robert J. Seidman
Paper. Penguin USA, $13.95.

ONE THOUSAND USEFUL MOHAWK WORDS
Mohawk-English, English-Mohawk dictionary includes words,
idioms, and expressions common in everyday speech. 158 pp.
Audio-Forum, $9.95.

ONE THOUSAND YEARS ON MOUND KEY
R. Schell
Revised 1968 edition. Illus. 125 pp.
Shoeless Publishing, 1997.$12.95.

ONE VAST WINTER-COUNT: THE NATIVE AMERICAN
WEST BEFORE LEWIS & CLARK
Colin G. Calloway
Illus. Maps. 640 pp. University of Nebraska Press, 2003. $39.95

*THE ONEIDA
Grades K-4. Illus. 48 pp. Childrens Press, $11.45.

THE ONEIDA CREATION STORY
Demus Elm & Harvey Antone; tr. & ed. by
Floyd G. Lounsbury & Bryan Gick
Ancient elements of Iroquoian cosmology. Illus. 174 pp.
University of Nebraska Press, 2000. $12.

THE ONEIDA INDIAN EXPERIENCE
Jack Campisi & Laurence Hauptman
245 pp. Paper. Syracuse University Press, 1988. $16.95.

THE ONEIDA LAND CLAIMS: A LEGAL HISTORY
George Shattuck
290 pp. Paper. Syracuse University Press, 1991. $16.95.

ONEIDA VERB MORPHOLOGY
Floyd G. Lounsbury
111 pp. Paper. HRAF Press, 1976. $15.

ONEONTA STUDIES
Guy E. Gibbon and
Robert F. Spencer, Editors
122 pp. Paper. University of Minnesota,
Dept. of Anthropology, 1983. $7.50.

ONLY APPROVED INDIANS: STORIES
Jack D. Forbes
176 pp. University of Oklahoma Press, 1995. $22.95.

THE ONLY LAND I KNOW:
A HISTORY OF THE LUMBEE INDIANS
Adolph Dial & David Eliades
Illus. Biblio. 206 pp. Paper. Syracuse University Press,
1974. $15.95.

THE ONLY LAND THEY KNEW:
AMERICAN INDIANS IN THE OLD SOUTH
J. Leitch Wright, Jr.
Illus. Maps. 388 pp. Paper. University of Nebraska Press,
1999. $19.95.

*ONLY THE NAMES REMAIN:
THE CHEROKEES & THE TRAIL OF TEARS
Alex W. Bealer
Grades 3-7. Illus. 96 pp. Demco Media, $10.
Paper. Little, Brown & Co., 1972. $4.95.

*THE ONONDAGA
Grades K-4. Illus. 48 pp. Childrens Press, $11.45.

ONONDAGA IROQUOIS PREHISTORY:
A STUDY IN SETTLEMENT ARCHAEOLOGY
James A. Tuck
Illus. 256 pp. Paper. Syracuse University Press, $15.95.

ONONDAGA: PORTRAIT OF A NATIVE PEOPLE
Dennis Connors, Editor; photos by Fred R. Wolcott
Collection of photographs & history of the Onondaga people.
Illus. 100 pp. Paper. Syracuse University Press, 1985. $16.95.

O'ODHAM CREATION & RELATED EVENTS:
AS TOLD TO RUTH BENEDICT IN 1927 IN PROSE
edited by Donald Bahr
Origin stories of the O'odham (Pima) Indians of Arizona.
320 pp. The University of Arizona Press, 2001. $45.

*O'ODHAM, INDIANS OF THE SONORAN DESERT
Susan Shaffer
Grades 5 and up. Illus. Includes 30 student booklets and
teacher's resource binder with overhead transparanecies,
slides, and audiocasstte. The Heard Museum, 1987. Student
edition, $149.95; teacher edition, $197.95. Set, $294.43.

OPENING IN THE SKY
Armand Garnet Ruffo
Poetry by an Ojibway person. Explores issues of identity,
alienation, liberation, love and loss. Illus. 64 pp. Paper.
Theytus, 1994. $9.95.

ORACLES: A NOVEL
Melissa Tantaquidgeon Zobel
One Indian family trying to maintain tribal culture in the midst
of rapid transformation. 192 pp. University of New Mexico Press,
2004. $24.95.

ORATORY IN NATIVE NORTH AMERICA
William M. Clements
Examines speeches made by Native North Americans
as recorded by whites. 186 pp. University of Arizona
Press, 2002. $40.

THE ORDEAL OF THE LONGHOUSE: THE PEOPLES OF
THE IROQUOIAN LEAGUE IN THE ERA OF EUROPEAN
COLONIZATION
Daniel K. Richter
Illus. Maps. 580 pp. University of North Carolina Press,
1993. $55; paper, $19.95.

THE ORDEAL OF RUNNING STANDARD
Thomas Fall
Dramatizes the dilemma of two young Indians, Running Standing (Kiowa) and his Cheyenne wife. 320 pp. Paper. University
of Oklahoma Press, 1993. $15.95.

THE ORDERS OF THE DREAMED: GEORGE NELSON
ON CREE & NORTHERN OJIBWA RELIGION & MYTH, 1823
Jennifer S.H. Brown & Robert Brightman
Detailed portrayal of Algonquian religion and ceremonies.
Paper. Minnesota Historical Society Press, 1989. $18.95.

THE OREGON & CALIFORNIA TRAIL:
DIARY OF JANE GOULD IN 1862
Bert Webber, Editor
Indian massacres. 92 pp. paper. Webb Research Group, $7.50.

OREGON INDIANS: CULTURE, HISTORY &
CURRENT AFFAIRS; AN ATLAS & INTRODUCTION
Jeff Zucker & Bob Hogfoss
Second edition. Illus. 192 pp. Paper.
Oregon Historical Society, 1988. $15.95.

OREGON TRAIL
F. Parkman
Grades 6-12. Paper. Airmont, 1964.
$1.50; New American Library, $3.50.

THE OREGON TRAIL & THE CONSPIRACY OF PONTIAC
Francis Parkman
951 pp. Library of America, 1991. $35.

OREGON'S SALTY COAST
James A. Gibbs; with Bert Webber
Details of the Oregon coast from early explore, from what they
found to Indian encounters. Includes all state parks and other
places. Illus. Maps. Biblio. Paper. Webb Research Group,
$14.95.

ORGANIZING THE LAKOTA: THE POLITICAL ECONOMY
OF THE NEW DEAL ON THE PINE RIDGE & ROSEBUD
RESERVATIONS
Thomas Biolsi
Illus. 245 pp. Paper. University of Arizona Press, 1992. $19.95.

THE ORIGIN & DEVELOPMENT
OF THE PUEBLO KATSINA CULT
E. Charles Adams
Examines the concept of the katsina and the religion that de-
veloped around it. 253 pp. Paper. University of Arizona Press,
1991. $17.95.

ORIGIN OF ANCIENT AMERICAN CULTURES
Paul Shao
Illus. 375 pp. Iowa State University Press, 1983. $42.75.

ORIGINAL JOURNALS OF THE
LEWIS & CLARK EXPEDITION
Reuben Thwaites, Editor
Reprint of 1904 edition. 8 vols. Ayer Co., $224. per set.

THE ORIGINS OF A PACIFIC COAST CHIEFDOM:
THE CHUMASH OF THE CHANNEL ISLANDS
edited by Jeanne E. Arnold
Illus. University of Utah Press. $60.

ORIGINS OF PRE-COLUMBIAN ART
Terence Grieder
Illus. 250 pp. University of Texas Press, 1982. $19.95.

THE ORIGINS OF SOUTHWESTERN AGRICULTURE
R.G. Matson
356 pp. University of Arizona Press, 1991. $66.

ORNAMENTAL & CEREMONIAL ARTIFACTS OF
THE NORTH AMERICAN INDIAN: IDENTIFICATION
& VALUE GUIDE
Lar Hothem
Covers many classes of higher-grade and top-quality artifacts.
Illus. 133 pp. Paper. Hothem House, 1990. $27, postpaid.

THE OSAGE
Terry P. Wilson
Grades 5 and up. Illus. 104 pp. Chelsea House, 1988. $17.95.

THE OSAGE CEREMONIAL DANCE I'N-LON-SCHKA
Alice A. Callahan
Illus. Maps. 12 music examples. 172 pp. Paper.
University of Oklahoma Press, 1990. $11.95.

THE OSAGE: CHILDREN OF THE MIDDLE WATERS
John Joseph Matthews
An account of the Sioux Osage tribe from the oral history of his
people in the period before the coming of the Europeans to the
recorded history since, and his own life among them. Reprint
of 1961 edition. Illus. 826 pp. Paper. University of Oklahoma
Press, $27.95.

OSAGE: AN ETHNOHISTORICAL STUDY
OF HEGEMONY ON THE PRAIRIE-PLAINS
Rollings
Paper. University of Missouri Press, $17.95.

OSAGE IN MISSOURI
Wolferman
Paper. University of Missouri Press, $9.95.

OSAGE INDIAN CUSTOMS & MYTHS
Louis F. Burns
Illus. 240 pp. Ciga Press & The Osage Mission, 1984. $20.

THE OSAGE INDIAN MURDERS: A TRUE CRIME STORY
Lawrence J. Hogan
Illus. 296 pp. Paper. Amlex, 1998. $16.95.

OSAGE INDIANS: BANDS & CLANS
Louis F. Burns
196 pp. Ciga Press & The Osage Mission, 1984. $20.

THE OSAGE & THE INVISIBLE WORLD:
FROM THE WORKS OF FRANCIS LA FLESCHE
Francis La Flesche; Garrick A. Bailey, Editor
Illus. Tables. Map. 344 pp. University of Oklahoma
Press & Written Heritage, 1995. $29.95; paper, $16.95.

OSAGE - LIFE & LEGENDS: EARTH PEOPLE -
SKY PEOPLE
Robert Liebert
History of the Osage Tribe. Illus. 144 pp. Paper.
Naturegraph, 1987. $8.95.

OSAGE MISSION BAPTISMS, MARRIAGES,
& INTERMENTS, 1820-1886
Louis Burns, Editor
870 pp. Ciga Press & The Osage Mission, 1986. $35.

THE OSAGES, DOMINANT POWER
OF LOUISIANA TERRITORY
Wallace T. Talbott
96 pp. Carlton Press, 1989. $8.95.

OTOKSHEKAGAPI: (FIRST BEGINNINGS)
SIOUX CREATION STORY
Thomas Simms
Presents the creation mystery legend in English & Lakota.
Illus. 36 pp. paper. VIP Publishing, $6.95.

OTHER DESTINIES: UNDERSTANDING
THE AMERICAN INDIAN NOVEL
Louis Owens
Critical analysis of novels written between 1854 and today by
American Indian authors. Traces how ten Native American au-
thors have come to terms with discovering their identity in con-
temporary America. Biblio. 292 pp. Paper. University of Okla-
homa Press, 2002. $19.95.

THE OTHER SIDE OF NOWHERE
Peter Blue Cloud
Collection of mythic and rythmic coyote stories.
Illus. Greenfield Review Press, $10.

OTHER WORDS: AMERICAN INDIAN
LITERATURE, LAW, & CULTURE
Jace Weaver
381 pp. University of Oklahoma Press, 2001. $34.95.

OTOKAHEKAGAPI (FIRST BEGINNINGS)
SIOUX CREATION STORY
Thomas E. Simms
Grades 5 and up. Illus. 36 pp. Paper. Tipi Press, 1987. $4.50.

OTTAWA & CHIPPEWA INDIANS OF MICHIGAN, 1870-1909
Raymond C. Lantz
Three censuses taken by the BIA. 288 pp. Heritage Books,
1991. $21.

THE OTTAWAS
Elaine Landau
Grades 5-8. Illus. 64 pp. Franklin Watts, 1996. $22; paper,
$6.95.

OUR CHIEFS & ELDERS: WORDS &
PHOTOGRAPHS OF NATIVE LEADERS
David Neel
Series of portraits of Native American chiefs & elders. Illus.
64 duotone photos. 192 pp. University of Washington Press,
$29.95.

OUR FRIENDS: THE NAVAJO
Ruth Roessel, Editor
Formerly *Papers on Navajo Life & Culture.* Illus.
Paper. Navajo Community College Press, 1976. $8.

OUR HEARTS FELL TO THE GROUND: PLAINS
INDIAN VIEWS ON HOW THE WEST WAS LOST
Colin G. Calloway
224 pp. St. Martin's Press, 1996. $39.95; paper, $21.25.

OUR HOME FOREVER: THE HUPA INDIANS
OF NORTHERN CALIFORNIA
Bryon Nelson
Illus. 225 pp. Paper. Howe Brothers, 1988. $9.95.

OUR INDIAN WARDS
G.W. Manypenny
Reprint of 1880 edition. Da Capo Press, $35.

OUR LIVES IN OUR HANDS:
MICMAC INDIAN BASKETMAKERS
Bunny McBridge
Illus. 96 pp. Paper. Tilbury House, 1991. $10.95.

OUR PRAYERS ARE IN THIS PLACE:
CENTURIES OF PECOS PUEBLO IDENTITY
Frances Levine
Illus. Maps. 232 pp. University of New Mexico Press,
1999. $39.95.

OUR RED BROTHERS & THE PEACE POLICY
OF PRESIDENT ULYSSES S. GRANT
Lawrie Tatum
Illus. 375 pp. University of Nebraska Press, 1970. $28.95.

OUR STORIES, OUR LIVES
CIRI Foundation
Collection of personal experiences & traditional stories told by
23 Alaska Native elders—Eskimos, Indians & Aleuts of the Cook
Inley region. Illus. 245 pp. Paper. CIRI, $15.95.

OUR TELLINGS: INTERIOR SALISH STORIES
FROM THE NLHA7KAPMX PEOPLE
Darwin Hanna
Paper. UBC Press, 1995. $25.95.

OUR VOICES: NATIVE STORIES
OF ALASKA & THE YUKON
edited by James Ruppert & John W. Bernet
Showcases 20 storytellers and writers who represent a full
range of Athabaskan and related languages of Alaska and
the Yukon. Maps. 394 pp. Paper. University of Nebraska
Press, 2001. $25.

OUR WILD INDIANS: 33 YEARS PERSONAL EXPERIENCE
AMONG THE RED MEN OF THE GREAT WEST
R.I. Dodge
Reprint of 1883 edition. 657 pp. Ayer Co., $55.

OUR VOICES, OUR LAND
Stephen Tribmle, Editor
Photographic collection shows Native Americans in various
settings. Illus. 176 pp. Northland Publishing, $19.95.

OURAY - CHIEF OF THE UTES
P. David Smith
Illus. 220 pp. Paper. Wayfinder Press, 1986. $9.95.

OUT OF THE MIST: TREASURES OF THE NUU-CHAH-
NULTH CHIEFS
Martha Black
The art, culture and history of the Nuu-chah-culth, Ditidaht-
Pacheenaht and Makah Nations of British Columbia, Canada.
Photos. 112 pp. paper. UBC Press, 1999. $25.

OUT THERE SOMEWHERE
Simon J. Ortiz
Poetry. 158 pp. University of Arizona Press, 2002.
$35; paper, $17.95.

OUTCROPPINGS FROM NAVAJOLAND
David Levering
Poems. Navajo Community College Press, $5.

AN OUTLINE OF BASIC VERB INFLECTIONS
OF OKLAHOMA CHEROKEE
Charles D. Van Tuyl
79 pp. Paper. Indian University Press, 1994. $15.50, postpaid.

AN OUTLINE OF SENECA CEREMONIES
AT COLDSPRING LONGHOUSE
William N. Fenton
Bound with: The Shawnee Female Deity, by C.F. Voegelin;
Human Wolves Among the Navaho, by William Morgan; Musi-
cal Areas in Aboriginal North America, by Helen H. Roberts;
and Rank & Potlatch Among the Haida, by George P. Murdock.
Reprint of 1936 edition. HRAF Press, $15.

OVER A CENTURY OF MOVING TO THE DRUM:
SALISH INDIAN CELEBRATIONS ON THE FLATHEAD
INDIAN RESERVATION
Johnny Arlee; Robert Bigart, Editor
Illus. 104 pp. Paper. Montana Historical Society, 1998. $14.95.

OVERCOMIG OBSTACLES & IMPROVING OUTCOMES:
EARLY INTERVENTION SERVICES FOR INDIAN CHILDREN
WITH SPECIAL NEEDS
Southwest Communication Resources, $10.

OVERLAND TO STARVATION COVE: WITH THE
INUIT IN SEARCH OF FRANKLIN, 1878-1880
Heinrich Klutschak; William Barr, Editor & tr.
Illus. University of Toronto Press, 1987. $30.

LOUIS OWENS: LITERARY REFLECTIONS
ON HIS LIFE & WORK
edited by Jacquelyn Kilpatrick
Essays examining Owen's writings. Contributors include:
Susan Bernardin, David Brande, Renny Christopher,
Neil Harrison, Jesse Peters, et al. Illus. 320 pp. University
of Oklahoma Press, 2004. $39.95.

THE OWL IN THE MONUMENT CANYON,
& OTHER STORIES FROM INDIAN COUNTRY
H. Jackson Clark
Illus. University of Utah Press, $24.95; paper, $14.95.

OWL IN THE CEDAR TREE
N. Scott Momaday; illus. by Don Perceval
Details of Navaho culture and religious beliefs, and the conflict
between traditional and contemporary ways. Grades 4-8. Illus.
125 pp. Paper. University of Nebraksa Press, 1992. $9.95.

*THE OWL'S SONG: A NOVEL
janet Campbell Hale
Grades 4 and up. Paper. University of New Mexico Press,
$12.95

OYATE CATALOG
Bibliography of books for grades K-12. Includes evaluation of
texts, resource materials and fiction; as well as distribution of
children's books, with an emphasis on writing and illustration
by Native people. 20 pp. Oyate.

OZARK BLUFF-DWELLERS
Mark R. Harrington
Reprint of 1960 edition.Illus. 185 pp. Paper.
National Museum of the American Indian, $5.

P

***PACHEE GOYO: HISTORY & LEGENDS
FROM THE SHOSHONE**
Rupert Weeks
Paper. Jelm Mountain Publications, 1981. $6.

PACIFIC NORTHWEST AMERICANA
Charles W. Smith, Editor
Bibliography of 11,000+ books, pamphlets, newspapers,
speeches & historical documents relating to the history of the
Pacific Northwest. Also a listing of libraries. Reprint of 1950
edition. 392 pp. Paper. Supplement, 1949-74 by R.E. Moore &
N.H. Purcell, Eds. Binford & Mort, $20 each.

**PACIFIC NORTHWEST: ITS DISCOVERY &
EARLY EXPLORATION BY SEA, LAND, & RIVER**
Edward W. Nuffield
288 pp. Paper. Hancock House, $16.95.

**PACIFYING THE PLAINS: GENERAL ALFRED TERRY
& THE DECLINE OF THE SIOUX, 1866-1890**
John Bailey
Greenwood Press, 1979. $35.

PAGES FROM HOPI HISTORY
Harry C. James
An authentic account of the Hopi way of life. 258 pp.
Paper. University of Arizona Press, 1974. $17.95.

**PAINTBRUSHES & PISTOLS:
HOW THE TAOS ARTISTS SOLD THE WEST**
Sherry Clayton-Taggett & Ted Schwartz
Illus. 288 pp. Paper. John Muir, 1990. $17.95

**PAINTED TIPIS BY CONTEMPORARY
PLAINS INDIAN ARTISTS**
Explores the esthetic qualities and significance of 12 painted
tipi covers specially created in 1972-73 by contemporary Plains
Indian artists. Illus. Map. 80 pp. Oklahoma Indian Arts & Crafts
Cooperative, $8, postpaid.

**PAINTING THE DREAM: THE VISIONARY ART OF
NAVAJO PAINTER DAVID CHETHLAHE PALADIN**
35 full-color fine art reproductions. Paper. Inner Traditions,
$24.95.

PAINTING OF LITTLE CROW
Frank Blackwell Mayer
Reproduction of an oil painting from the Minnesota Historical
Society, based on a sketch Mayer made of Chief Little Crow in
1851. 20x30" Minnesota Historical Society Press. $6.95.

THE PAIUTE, INDIANS OF NORTH AMERICA
Pamela Bunte & Robert Franklin
350 pp. University of Nebraska Press, 1989. $22.95.

*THE PAIUTE: SOUTHWEST
Pamela Bunte & Robert Franklin
Grades 5 and up. Illus. Chelsea House, 1989. $17.95.

**A PALEO-INDIAN SITE IN EASTERN PENNSYLVANIA:
AN EARLY HUNTING CULTURE**
John Witthoft
Facsimile of the 1952 edition. Illus. 32 pp. Paper.
Persimmon Press, $4.95.

**PALEOINDIAN GEOARCHAEOLOGY
OF THE SOUTHERN HIGH PLAINS**
Vance T. Holliday
Illus. 312 pp. University of Texas Press, 1997.
$50; paper, $24.95.

THE PAMUNKEY INDIANS OF VIRGINIA
Garland Pollard
Reprint of 1894 edition. Reprint Services, $49.

A PAPAGO GRAMMAR
Ofelia Zepeda
190 pp. Paper. University of Arizona Press, 1983. $19.95.

PAPAGO MUSIC
F. Densmore
Reprint of 1929 edition. Illus. 276 pp. Da Capo Press,
$27.50.

THE PAPAGO & PIMA INDIANS OF ARIZONA
Ruth Underhill
Illus. 64 pp. Paper. Filter Press, 1979. $5.

**A PAPAGO TRAVELER: THE MEMORIES
OF JAMES McCARTHY**
James McCarthy; edited by John Westover
Reprint of 1985 edition. 200 pp. University of Arizona
Press, $24.95.

**PAPER MEDICINE MAN: JOHN GREGORY
BOURKE & HIS AMERICAN WEST**
Joseph C. Porter
Illus. 370 pp. Paper. University of Oklahoma Press,
1986. $17.95.

**THE PAPERS OF PANTON, LESLIE & CO.:
GUIDE TO THE MICROFILM COLLECTION**
Documents trading activities with the Cherokee, Chickasaw,
Choctaw and Creek Nations. Over 8,000 documents on 26
reels. 764 pp. Research Publications International, $2,700.

**A PARENT'S GUIDE TO THE BIA
SPECIAL EDUCATION PROCESS**
Handbook for parent's rights. Southwest Communication
Resources, $5.00.

CYNTHIA ANN PARKER: INDIAN CAPTIVE
Catherine T. Gonzales
Eakin Publications, 1980. $6.95.

CYNTHIA ANN PARKER: THE LIFE & LEGEND
Margaret S. Hacker
Recounts her experiences a s a captive of the Comanches
(1836-60). Illus. Biblio. 64 pp. Paper. Texas Western Press,
1990. $12.50.

PARKER ON THE IROQUOIS
Arthur Parker; William Fenton, Editor
Bound with The Code of Handsome Lake, the Seneca prophet;
The Constitution of the Five Nations; and, Iroquois Uses of
Maize and Other Food Plants. Illus. Photos. 482 pp. Paper.
Syracuse University Press, 1968. $16.95.

QUANAH PARKER, COMANCHE CHIEF
William T. Hagan
Presents Parker as a man torn between two worlds. Illus. Maps.
160 pp. Paper. University of Oklahoma Press, $14.95.

*QUANAH PARKER: GREAT CHIEF OF THE COMANCHES
Catherine Gonzales; Melissa Roberts, Editor
Grades 1-5. Illus. 48 pp. Eakin Press, 1987. $9.95.

*FRANCIS PARKMAN & THE PLAINS INDIANS
Jane Shuter
Grades 6-8. Illus. 48 pp. Raintree, 1995. $24.25.

**PARTIAL JUSTICE: FEDERAL INDIAN LAW
IN A LIBERAL-CONSTITUTIONAL SYSTEM**
Petra Shattuck & Jill Norgren
223 p. Berg Publishers, 1991. $50; paper, $15.50.

**PARTIAL RECALL: PHOTOGRAPHS
OF NATIVE NORTH AMERICANS**
Lucy R. Lippard, Editor
Explorations by 12 Native American artists and writers into the
images that have shaped our ideas of "Indianness," and the
complex relationship of photopgraphy to identity. Illus. 100 photos. 200 pp. Paper. W.W. Norton & Co., 1992. $35; paper,
$19.95.

**A PARTICUAR HISTORY OF THE FIVE YEARS FRENCH
& INDIANS WARS IN NEW ENGLAND & PARTS ADJACENT**
Samuel G. Drake
Reprint of 1870 edition. Ayer Co., $19.

**PARTNERS IN FURS: A HISTORY OF THE FUR
TRADE IN EASTERN JAMES BAY, 1600-1870**
Daniel Francis & Toby Morantz
Illus. 205 pp. Paper. University of Toronto Press, 1982. $17.95.

PASCUA: A YAQUI VILLAGE IN ARIZONA
Edward H. Spicer
Reprint of 1940 edition. Illus. 325 pp. Paper.
University of Arizona Press, 1984. $17.95.

*PASSAGE TO LITTLE BIGHORN
Terry Kretzer-Malvehu
Ages 12 and up. 232 pp. Paper. Northland, $6.95.

**PATH BREAKERS: THE EITELJORG FELLOWSHIP
FOR NATIVE AMERICAN FINE ART, 2003**
Lucy R. Lippard, et al.
The 3rd volume in a series that brings the work of Native Ameri-
can fine artists to public attention. Honors artist Kay
WalkingStick (Cherokee) & five fellows: Corwin "Corky"
Clairmont (Salish/Kootenai), Robert Houle (Saulteaux), Nora
Narranjo-Morse (Tewa-Santa Clara Pueblo), Nadia Myre
(Algonquin), & Hulleah Tsinhnahjinnie (Dine/Seminole/
Muscogee). Essays by Lucy Lippard, Margaret Archuleta
(Pueblo/Hispanic), Gail Trenblay (Onandaga/Micmac), Bonnie
Devine (Ojibway), Patricia Deadman (Tuscarora/Mohawk), Jen-
nifer C. Vigil (Navaho/Latina/Ukranian), & Veronica

Passalacqua. Illus. 112 pp. Paper. University of Washington
Press, 2004. $22.50.

THE PATH OF POWER
Sun Bear, Wabun & Barry Weinstock
The life story of Sun Bear, medicine teacher of the Ojibwa and
founder of the Bear Tribe Medicine Society. Illus. 270 pp. Paper. Cherokee Publications, $9.95.

*PATHKI NANA: KOOTENAI GIRL SOLVES A MYSTERY
Kenneth Thomasma; Jack Brouwer, Illus.
Grades 4-8. Illus. Baker Book House, $10.99; paper, $6.99.

THE PATHS OF KATERI'S KIN
Christopher Vecsey
408 pp. University of Notre Dame Press, 1997. $40.

**PATHS OF LIFE: AMERICAN INDIANS OF
THE SOUTHWEST & NORTHERN MEXICO**
Thomas E. Sheridan & Nancy J. Parezo, Editor
Living portraits of 15 Native American groups. Illus.
298 pp. Paper. University of Arizona Press, 1996. $22.95.

**PATHS OF OUR CHILDREN:
HISTORIC INDIANS OF ARKANSAS**
George Sabo
Illus. 144 pp. Paper. Arkansas Archaeological Survey,
1992. $5.

**PATHWAYS TO EXCELLENCE: IMPROVING LIBRARY
& INFORMATION SERVICES FOR NATIVE AMERICAN
PEOPLE**
Report. 2 vols. Gordon Press, 1995. $600.

**PATHWAYS TO SELF-DETERMINATION:
CANADIAN INDIANS & THE CANADIAN STATE**
Leroy Little Bear, et al, Editors
192 pp. Paper. University of Toronto Press, 1984. $12.95.

***PATRICK DES JARLAIT: CONVERSATIONS
WITH A NATIVE AMERICAN ARTIST**
Neva Williams, Editor
Includes photos of his paintings. Grades 1-3. Illus. 56 pp.
Lerner, 1995. $16.95.

**THE PATRIOT CHIEFS: A CHRONICLE
OF AMERICAN INDIAN RESISTANCE**
Alvin M. Josephy, Jr.
Indian resistance to the white man through the stories of nine
outstanding leaders. 384 pp. Paper. Penguin USA, $9.95.

**PATTERNS & CEREMONIALS OF
THE INDIANS OF THE SOUTHWEST**
Moskowitz & Collier
192 pp. Paper. Dover, $14.95.

**PATTERNS OF LIFE, PATTERNS OF ART: THE RAHR
COLLECTIONS OF NATIVE AMERICAN ART - HOOD
PATTERNS & SOURCES OF NAVAJO WEAVING**
W.D. Harmsen
Revised edition. Illus. Harmsen Publishing, 1978.

*THE PAWNEE
Dennis B. Fradin
Revised edition. Grades 2-4. Illus. 48 pp.
Children's Press, 1992. $21; paper, $5.50.

**THE PAWNEE GHOST DANCE HAND GAME:
GHOST DANCE REVIVAL & ETHNIC IDENTITY**
A. Lesser
Reprint of 1933 edition. Illus. 468 pp. University of
Wisconsin, $22.00; paper, $8.95.

**PAWNEE HERO STORIES & FOLKTALES WITH NOTES ON
THE ORIGIN, CUSTOMS & CHARACTER OF THE PAWNEE
PEOPLE**
George Bird Grinnell
Reprint of 1961 edition. Illus. 417 pp. Paper.
University of Nebraska Press, $11.95

THE PAWNEE INDIANS
George E. Hyde
Illus. 372 pp. Paper. University of Oklahoma Press,
1974. $17.95.

PAWNEE & LOWER LOUP POTTERY
Rogert Grange, Jr.
Volume 3. Paper. Nebraska State Historical Society,
1968. $6.00.

PAWNEE MUSIC
F. Densmore
Reprint of 1929 edition. 160 pp. Da Capo Press, $21.50.

THE PAWNEE MYTHOLOGY
George A. Dorsey, Editor
Illus. 546 pp. Paper. University of Nebraska Press, 1997.
$22.

PAWNEE PASSAGE: 1870-1875
Martha Blaine
Illus. 346 pp. University of Oklahoma Press, 1990.
$31.95.

PAWNEES: A CRITICAL BIBLIOGRAPHY
Martha P. Blaine
Illus. 128 pp. Paper. Indiana University Press, 1981. $4.95.

THE PEACE CHIEF: A NOVEL
Robert J. Conley
Originally published in 1999. 352 pp. Paper.
University of Oklahoma Press, 2002. $17.95.

THE PEACE CHIEFS OF THE CHEYENNES
Stan Hoig
Illus. Paper. University of Oklahoma Press, 1980. $19.95.

PEACE WITH THE APACHES OF NEW MEXICO & ARIZONA
V. Colyer
Facsimile of 1872 edition. Ayer Co., $12.

PECOS RUINS: GEOLOGY, ARCHAEOLOGY, HISTORY, & PREHISTORY
David Grant Noble
Describes the development of Pecos Pueblo from prehistoric times to the Anglo period of 19th century. Illus. Maps. Photos. 32 pp. Paper. Ancient City Press, 1990. $7.95.

PELTS, PLUMES & HIDES: WHITE TRADERS AMONG THE SEMINOLE INDIANS, 1870-1930
Harry Kersey, Jr.
Reprint of 1975 edition. Illus. Map. Biblio. 158 pp.
Paper. University Press of Florida, $14.95.

PENHALLOW'S INDIAN WARS
E. Wheelock, Editor
Reprint of 1924 edition. Ayer Co., $20.

PENITENTE SELF-GOVERNMENT: BROTHERHOODS & COUNCILS, 1797-1947
Thomas Steele & Rowena Rivera
Illus. 210 pp. Ancient City Press, 1985. $29.95; paper, $12.95.

***WILLIAM PENN'S OWN ACCOUNT OF LENNI LENAPE OR DELAWARE INDIANS**
Albert C. Myers, Editor
Grades 7 and up. Illus. 96 pp. Paper. Mid Atlantic Press, 1986. $7.95.

***THE PENOBSCOT**
Jill Duvall
Grades K-3. Illus. Childrens Press, 1993.

***THE PENOBSCOT**
Katherine Doherty
Grades 4-6. Reprint. 64 pp. Paper. Franklin Watts, $6.95.

THE PENOBSCOT DANCE OF RESISTANCE: TRADITIONS IN THE HISTORY OF A PEOPLE
Pauleena MacDougall
280 pp. Illus. Paper. University Pres of New England, 2004. $24.95.

PENOBSCOT MAN
Frank G. Speck
Revised edition. Illus. 404 pp. University of Maine Press, 1997. $35; paper, $15.

THE PEOPLE CALLED APACHE
Thomas Mails
Reprint. Illus. Center for Western Studies, $150.

PEOPLE FROM OUR SIDE: A LIFE STORY WITH PHOTOGRAPHS & ORAL BIOGRAPHY
Peter Pitseolak & Dorothy Harley Eber
During his lifetime, Inuit photographer Peter Pitseolak witnessed the arrival of missionaries, fur traders, law, government, and alcohol in the eastern Canadian Arctic. Reprint of 1975 edition. Illus. University of Toronto Press, $39.95; paper, $19.95.

THE PEOPLE: INDIANS OF THE AMERICAN SOUTHWEST
Stephen Trimble, words & illus.
Introduction to the native peoples of the American Southwest. Illus. Maps. 536 pp. Paper. School of American Research, 1994. $29.95.

PEOPLE OF THE LAKES
Time-Life Editors
Overview of the many Indian groups of Great Lakes region. Historic photos. Color illus of artifacts. 192 pp. Hothem House, ,1994. $22, postpaid.

THE PEOPLE NAMED THE CHIPPEWA: NARRATIVE HISTORIES
Gerald Vizenor
History of the Chippewa experience based on memoirs, court records, and the oral tradition of the Anishinaabe. Illus. Map. 175 pp. Paper. University of Minnesota Press, 1984. $12.95.

THE PEOPLE: NATIVE AMERICAN THOUGHTS & FEELINGS
Illus. 64 pp. Paper. The Book Publishing Co., $5.95.

PEOPLE OF THE BLUE WATER: A RECORD OF LIFE AMONG THE WALAPAI & HAVASUPAI INDIANS
Flora G. Iliff
Reprint of 1954 edition. 271 pp. Paper.
University of Arizona Press. $17.95.

***PEOPLE OF THE BUFFALO**
Maria Campbell
Grades 5 and up. Paper. Salem House, $6.95.

PEOPLE OF THE CIRCLE: POWWOW COUNTRY
Chris Roberts
Paper. American World Geographic Publishing, 1998. $21.95

PEOPLE OF THE CRIMSON EVENING
Ruth Underhill
Papago life of long ago. Illus. 64 pp. Paper. Filter Press, $3.

PEOPLE OF THE DALLES: THE INDIANS OF THE WASCOPAM MISSION
Robert Boyd
History and culture of the Chinookan (Wasco-Wishram) and Sahaptan peoples in Oregon. Illus. Maps. 414 pp. University of Nebraska Press, 1996. $55.

PEOPLE OF THE DESERT & SEA: ETHNOBOTANY OF THE SERI INDIANS
Richard Felger & Mary Moser
Illus. 435 pp. Paper. University of Arizona Press, 1984. $40.

***PEOPLE OF THE EARTH**
W. Michael Gear
Grades 2-5. Demco, 1992. $12.

***PEOPLE OF THE FIRE**
W. Michael Gear
Grades 2-5. Demco, 1991. $12.

PEOPLE OF THE HIGH COUNTRY: JACKSON HOLE BEFORE THE SETTLERS
Gary Wright
Illus. 191 pp. Paper. Peter Lang Publishing, 1984. $20.

***PEOPLE OF THE ICE: HOW THE INUIT LIVED**
Heather Siska
Grades 5 and up. Illus. Paper. Salem House, $6.95.

***PEOPLE OF THE LAKES**
W. Michael Gear
Grades 2-5. Demco, 1995. $12.

PEOPLE OF LEGEND: NATIVE AMERICANS OF THE SOUTHWEST
John Annerino
Illus. 144 pp. Sierra Club Books, 1996. $30.

***PEOPLE OF THE LIGHTNING**
Kathleen O'Neal Gear
Grades 2-5. Demco, 1996. $12.

***PEOPLE OF THE LONGHOUSE: HOW THE IROQUOIAN TRIBES LIVED**
Jillian & Robin Riddington
Grades 5 and up. Illus. Paper. Salem House, $9.95

PEOPLE OF THE MESA: THE ARCHAEOLOGY OF BLACK MESA, ARIZONA
Shirley Powell & George Gummerman
Illus. 200 pp. Southern Illinois University Press, 1987. $19.95.

PEOPLE OF THE MIDDLE PLACE: A STUDY OF THE ZUNI INDIANS
Dorothea Leighton & John Adair
189 pp. Paper. HRAF Press, 1966. $15.

PEOPLE OF PASCUA
Edward H. Spicer; edited by Kathleen M. Sands & Rosamond B. Spicer
The history & culture of the Tucson area Yaqui.
331 pp. University of Arizona Press, 1988. $48.

PEOPLE OF THE PEYOTE: HUICHOL INDIAN HISTORY, RELIGION & SURVIVAL
Stacy B. Schaefer & Peter T. Furst
Paper. University of New Mexico Press, $29.95.

PEOPLE OF THE RED EARTH: AMERICAN INDIANS OF COLORADO
Sally Crum
Illus. Maps. Photos. 272 pp. Ancient City Press, 1996. $33.95; paper, $17.95.

***PEOPLE OF THE RIVER**
W. Michael Gear
Grades 2-5. Demco, 1993. $12.

PEOPLE OF THE SACRED MOUNTAIN: A HISTORY OF THE NORTHERN CHEYENNE CHIEFS & WARRIOR SOCIETIES, 1830-1879
Peter Powell
Two vols. Illus. 1,376 pp. Harper & Row, 1981. $125 per set.

THE PEOPLE OF THE SAINTS
George Mills
Illus. Paper. Taylor Museum, 1967. $5.

THE PEOPLE OF SAN MANUEL
Clifford E. Trafzer
San Manuel Tribe, 2003.

***PEOPLE OF THE SEA**
W. Michael Gear
Grades 2-5. Demco, 1994. $11.

PEOPLE OF THE SEVENTH FIRE: RETURNING LIFEWAYS OF NATIVE AMERICA
Dagmar Thorpe
A collection of personal stories from 20 Native American leaders. Illus. Akwe:kon Press, 1996.

PEOPLE OF THE SHINING MOUNTAINS: UTES OF COLORADO
Charles S. Marsh
Illus. 190 pp. Paper. Pruett Publishing, 1984. $11.95.

***PEOPLE OF THE SHORT BLUE CORN, TALES & LEGENDS OF THE HOPI INDIANS**
Harold Coulander
Grades 4-7. Demco Media, 1996. $15.05.

PEOPLE OF THREE FIRES
James Clifton, George Cornell & James McClurken
History, culture & dynamics of Michigan's Indigenous peoples: Ottawa, Potawatomi & Ojibway. Michigan Indian Press & Greenfield Review Press, $14.95.

PEOPLE OF THE TONTO RIM: ARCHAEOLOGICAL DISCOVERY IN PREHISTORIC ARIZONA
Charles L. Redman, Editor
Illus. 224 pp. Paper. Smithsonian Institution Press, 1993. $17.95

PEOPLE OF THE TOTEM: THE INDIANS OF THE PACIFIC NORTHWEST
Norman Bancroft-Hunt & Werner Forman
Reprint of 1979 edition. Illus. Map. 128 pp. Paper. University of Oklahoma Press, $24.95.

***PEOPLE OF THE TRAIL: HOW THE NORTHERN FOREST INDIANS LIVED**
Jillian & Robin Ridington
Grades 5 and up. Illus. Paper. Salem House, $6.95.

PEOPLE OF THE TWILIGHT
Diamond Jenness
Reprint of 1959 edition. Paper. University of Chicago Press, $9.95.

PEOPLE OF THE WIND RIVER: THE EASTERN SHOSHONES, 1825-1900
Henry E. Stamm, IV
Illus. Maps. 272 pp. University of Oklahoma Press, 1999. $27.95.

***THE PEOPLE SHALL CONTINUE**
Simon Ortiz; illus. by Sharol Graves
Epic story of Native American peoples, a "teaching story."
Grades 4-8. Illus. Children's Book Press, 1987. $14.95.

THE PEOPLE SPEAK: NAVAJO FOLK ART
Chuck & Jan Rosenak; photos by Lynn Lown
Guide for collectors of Native American art. Illus. 160 pp. Northland Publishing, $40.

A PEOPLE'S ARMY: MASSACHUSETTS SOLDIERS & SOCIETY IN THE SEVEN YEAR'S WAR
Fred Anderson
Illus. 292 pp. University of North Carolina Press, 1984. $27.50.

A PEOPLE'S ECOLOGY: EXPLORATIONS IN SUSTAINABLE LIVING
Gregory Cajete (Santa Clara Tewa), Editor
Contributors examine the underlying ecology of sustainable living rooted in the historical traditions, environmental practices, and sense of place of Indigenous peoples; and explores possibilities of applying the principles in both non-Native and Native communities. Illus. 283 pp. Clear Light, 1999. $14.95.

THE PEOPLE'S HEALTH: ANTHROPOLOGY & MEDICINE IN A NAVAJO COMMUNITY
John Adair, et al
Illus. 313 pp. University of New Mexico Press, 1988. $27.50; paper, $14.95.

PEOPLES OF THE NORTHWEST COAST: THEIR ARCHAEOLOGY & PREHISTORY
Kenneth M. Ames & Herbert D. Maschner
Illus. 272 pp. W.W. Norton & Co., 1999. $45.

PEOPLES OF THE TWILIGHT: EUROPEAN VIEWS OF NATIVE MINNESOTA, 1823-1862
Christian F. Feest
Afton Historical Society, 1998. $125.

PEOPLING INDIANA: THE ETHNIC EXPERIENCE
Robert Taylor, Jr. & Connie McBirney, Editors
Chapter on Native Americans by Elizabeth Glenn & Stewart Rafert. Illus. 800 pp. Indiana Historical Society, 1996. $39.95.

THE PEQUOT WAR
Alfred A. Cave
Analysis of the Pequot War, 1636-37. 232 pp. University of Massachusetts Press, 1996. $45; paper, $14.95.

THE PEQUOTS IN SOUTHERN NEW ENGLAND:
THE FALL & RISE OF AN AMERICAN INDIAN NATION
Laurence Hauptman & James Wherry
Illus. Maps. 288 pp. Paper. University of Oklahoma Press,
1990. $15.95.

PERFORMING THE RENEWAL OF COMMUNITY:
INDIGENOUS EASTER RITUALS IN NORTH MEXICO
& SOUTHWEST U.S.
Edited by Rosamond B. Spicer & N. Ross Crumrine
Examines the role of the Easter rituals in the Yaqui way of life
in both Arizona & Sonora. 624 pp. University of Press of
America, 1997. $78.50; paper, $61.50.

*PERIL AT THUNDER RIDGE
Anthony Dorame
Myron, a Native American teenager, conveys his people's philosophy that a balanced environment is crucial to man. Grades
6-10. Illus. 128 pp. Paper. Red Crane Books, $9.95.

PERSISTENCE IN PATTERN IN
MISSISSIPPI CHOCTAW CULTURE
Patti C. Black, Editor
Illus. 44 pp. Paper. Mississippi Department of Archives
& University Press of Mississippi, 1987. $9.95.

A PERSISTENT VISION:
ART OF THE RESERVATION DAYS
Richard Conn
Illus. 192 pp. Denver Art Museum, 1986. $35; paper, $19.95.

PERSONAL NARRATIVE OF JAMES O. PATTIE
James O. Pattie; Richard Batman, Editor
Frontier attitudes toward Indians and Mexicans. Illus.
216 pp. Mountain Press, $24.95; paper, $12.95.

PERSONAL RECOLLECTIONS & OBSERVATIONS
OF GENERAL NELSON A. MILES
N.A. Miles
Revised 1896 edition. Illus. Da Capo Press, $69.50.

PERSPECTIVES ON HEALTH CARE DELIVERY
SYSTEMS FOR AMERICAN INDIAN FAMILIES
Article. Southwest Communication Resources, $5.

PERSPECTIVES ON THE SOUTHEAST:
LINGUISTICS, ARCHAEOLOGY, & ETHNOHISTORY
Patricia B. Kwachka
11 essays focusing on questions relating to the
distribution, organization, and relationships of southeastern
Native American groups. Illus. Maps. University of Georgia
Press, 1994. $40; paper, $20.

PETROGLYPHS: ANCIENT LANGUAGE / SACRED ART
Sabra Moore
101 drawings. 192 pp. Clear Light, $19.95.

PETROGLYPHS OF OHIO
James Swauger
Illus. 350 pp. Hothem House & Ohio University Press,
1984. $45.

PETROGLYPHS & PUEBLO
MYTHS OF THE RIO GRANDE
Carol Patterson-Rudolph
Describes individual rock art symbols focusing on their mean-
ing within the context of a language system. Illus. Photos. 162
pp. Paper. Avanyu Publishing, 1991. $29.95.

THE PEYOTE BOOK: A STUDY OF NATIVE MEDICINE
Guy Mount, Compiler/editor
A collection of ancient legends, healing testimonials, spiritual
& philosophical perceptions, songs, stories & illustrations in-
spired by the Good Medicine. 3rd edition. Illus. Biblio. 144 pp.
Sweetlight, 1992. $9.95.

THE PEYOTE CULT
Weston La Barre
Illus. 334 pp. Paper. 5th Ed. University
of Oklahoma Press, 1989. $18.95.

PEYOTE: THE DIVINE CACTUS
Edward F. Anderson
Describes peyote ceremonies and the users' experiences, including use by the Native American Church. 2nd Edition. Illus.
295 pp. University of Arizona Press, 1996. $55.95; paper,
$19.95.

PEYOTE HUNT: THE SACRED JOURNEY
OF HUICHOL INDIANS
Barbara Myerhoff
Illus. 285 pp. Paper. Cornell University Press, 1976. $15.95.

PEYOTE RELIGION: A HISTORY
Omer C. Stewart
Encyclopedic history. Illus. Maps. 454 pp. Paper.
University of Oklahoma Press, 1987. $24.95.

THE PEYOTE RELIGION AMONG THE NAVAHO
David F. Aberle
2nd Ed. Illus. Maps. 528 pp. Paper.
University of Oklahoma Press, 1982. $24.95.

PEYOTISM IN THE WEST: A HISTORICAL
& CULTURAL PERSPECTIVE
Omer Stewart, Editor
Illus. 168 pp. Paper. University of Utah Press, 1984. $17.50.

*PHANTOM HORSE OF COLLISTER'S FIELDS
Gail Johnson
Grades 4-12. Paper. Council for Indian Education, 1974.
$1.95.

PHOENIX. THE DECLINE & REBIRTH
OF THE INDIAN PEOPLE
Wiliam E. Coffer
Illus. 281 pp. Paper. Shenandoah Books, $8.50.

THE PHOENIX INDIAN SCHOOL: FORCED
ASSIMILATION IN ARIZONA, 1891-1935
Robert A. Trennert, Jr.
Illus. 256 pp. University of Oklahoma Press, 1988. $29.95.

PHOENIX INDIAN SCHOOL:
THE SECOND HALF CENTURY
Dorothy R. Parker
History of boarding school from 1930 to 1990. 96 pp.
Paper. University of Arizona Press, 1996. $17.95.

THE PHONETIC CONSITUENTS OF THE NATIVE
LANGUAGES OF CALIFORNIA
A.L. Kroeber
Reprint of 1911 edition. 12 pp. Paper. Coyote Press, $1.56.

THE PHONETIC ELEMENTS
OF THE DIEGUENO LANGUAGE
A.L. Kroeber & J.P. Harrington
Reprint of 1911 edition. Illus. 11 pp. Paper. Coyote Press, $1.75.

THE PHONETIC ELEMENTS
OF THE MOJAVE LANGUAGE
A.L. Kroeber
Reprint of 1911 edition. Illus. 52 pp. Paper. Coyote Press, $6.56.

THE PHONETICS ELEMENTS
OF THE NORTHERN PAIUTE LANGUAGE
T.T. Waterman
Reprint of 1911 edition. Illus. 33 pp. Paper. Coyote Press, $3.75.

PHONOLOGICAL ISSUES IN NORTH ALASKAN INUPIAQ
Lawrence D. Kaplan
280 pp. Paper. Alaska Native Language Center, 1981. $15.

PHONOLOGICAL VARIATION IN WESTERN CHEROKEE
Lawrence Foley
250 pp. Garland, 1980. $35.

PHONOLOGY OF ARIZONA YAQUI WITH TEXTS
Lynne S. Crumrine
Reprint of 1961 edition. 46 pp. University of
Arizona Press, $19.95.

THE PHOTOGRAPH & THE AMERICAN INDIAN
Alfred L. Bush & Lee Clark Mitchell
Illus. 352 pp. Princeton University Press, 1994. $75.

PHOTOGRAPHING NAVAJOS: JOHN COLLIER, JR.
ON THE RESERVATION, 1948-1953
C. Stewart Doty, Dale Sperry Mudge, Herbert John Benally
Photos by John Collier, Jr. Illus. 232 pp. University of New
Mexico Press, $39.95.

PIA TOYA: A GOSHUTE INDIAN LEGEND
Retold and illustrated by the children & teachers of Ibapah
Elementary School. University of Utah Press. $11.95.

PICTOGRAPHIC HISTORY OF THE OGLALA SIOUX
Amos Brad Heart Bull and Helen Blish
Illus. 530 pp. University of Nebraska Press, 1968. $35.

PICTORIAL WEAVINGS OF THE NAVAJOS
Nancy Schiffer
Over 200 photos of pictorial weavings. Paper. Schiffer, $12.95.

*A PICTURE BOOK OF SITTING BULL
David A. Adler; illus. by Samuel Byrd
Grades K-3. Illus. 32 pp. Holiday House, 1993. $15.95.

PICTURE-WRITING OF THE AMERICAN INDIANS
Garrick Mallery
Reprint. Two vols. 1,300 Illus. 822 pp. Paper.
Dover & Written Heritage, $25.90/set.

PICTURES OF OUR NOBLER SELVES: A HISTORY OF
NATIVE AMERICAN CONTRIBUTIONS TO THE MEDIA
Mark N. Trahant
Traces the untold story of tribal and mainstream media begin-
ning with the first Native American newspaper, The Cherokee
Phoenix. Native American Journalists Association, $10.

*PIECES OF WHITE SHELL:
A JOURNEY TO NAVAJOLAND
Terry T. William
Grades 7-12. Illus. 176 pp. Paper. University of
New Mexico Press, $12.95.

A PILLAR OF FIRE TO FOLLOW:
AMERICAN INDIAN DRAMAS, 1808-1859
Priscilla F. Sears
149 pp. Bowling Green University Press, 1982.
$11.95; paper, $5.95.

PIMA INDIAN BASKETRY: ILLUSTRATED WITH
PHOTOGRAPHS FROM THE COLLECTION OF
THE HEARD MUSEUM
H. Thomas Cain
Illus. 40 pp. Paper. The Heard Museum, 1962. $5.

PIMA INDIAN LEGENDS
Anna Moore Shaw
Reprint of 1968 edition. 111 pp. Paper.
University of Arizona Press, $13.95.

THE PIMA INDIANS
Frank Russell
The 1908 ethnography. Reprint of 1975 edition. 496 pp.
University of Arizona Press, $40.

THE PIMA INDIANS: PATHFINDERS FOR HEALTH
Jane Demouy, et al, Editors
Illus. 51 pp. Paper. Diane Publishing, 1998. $15.

*THE PIMA-MARICOPA: SOUTHWEST
Henry Dobyns
Grades 5 and up. Illus. Chelsea House, 1989. $17.95.

A PIMA PAST
Anna Moore Shaw
262 pp. Paper. University of Arizona Press, 1994. $17.95.

A PIMA REMEMBERS
George Webb
Recollections of childhood and Pima Indian lifeways.
126 pp. Paper. University of Arizona Press, 1959. $12.95.

PIMAN & PAPAGO RITUAL ORATORY
Donald M. Bahr
The author's personal relationship with the Pima & Papago.
Illus. Paper. The Indian Historian Press, 1975. $7.

PINE RIDGE 1890
William Fitch Kelley
An eye-witness account of the events surrounding the fighting
at Wounded Knee. Reprint of 1971 edition. Photos. Map. 267
pp. High-Lonesome Books, $30.

PEDRO PINO: GOVERNOR OF ZUNI PUEBLO, 1830-1878
E. Richard Hart; foreword by T.J. Ferguson
Illus. 200 pp. Utah State University Press, 2001.
$36.95; paper, $17.95.

PIONEER MISSIONARY TO THE BERING STRAIT ESKIMOS
Louis Renner, et al
Illus. Binford-Metropolitan, 1979. $12.50.

PIONEERING IN MONTANA:
THE MAKING OF A STATE, 1864-1887
Stuart Granville; Paul Phillips, Editor
Reprint of 1977 edition. Illus. 265 pp. University
of Nebraska Press, $21.50; paper, $7.95.

THE PIONEERS OF NEW FRANCE IN NEW ENGLAND
J.P. Baxter
Reprint of 1894 edition. 450 pp. Heritage Books, $25.

PIPE, BIBLE & PEYOTE AMONG THE OGLALA LAKOTA:
A STUDY IN RELIGIOUS IDENTITY
Paul Steinmetz
270 pp. Paper. Syracuse University Press, 1999. $19.95.

THE PIPE & CHRIST: A CHRISTIAN-SIOUX DIALOGUE
William Stolzman
Reprint. Illus. 4th Edition. 222 pp. Paper. Tipi Press
& Center for Western Studies, 1992. $7.95.

A PIPE FOR FEBRUARY: A NOVEL
Charles H. Red Corn
Novel set against the turn of the century Osage Indians.
Map. 272 pp. University of Oklahoma Press, 2002. $29.95.

THE PIPESTONE QUEST: A NOVEL
Don Coldsmith
Story of Beaver, a member of the Elk-dog People and his quest
to undestand the mystifying power of the red pipestone. 272
pp. University of Oklahoma Press, 2004. $24.95.

PLACE FOR WINTER: PAUL TIULANA'S STORY
Vivian Senungetuk & paul Tiulane
Second edition. Illus. 150 pp. CIRI Foundation, 1989.
$17.95.

PLACE NAMES OF ATLANTIC CANADA
William B. Hamilton
University of Toronto Press, 1996. $60; paper, $24.95.

PLACE NAMES OF ONTARIO
Alan Rayburn
University of Toronto Press, 1997. $55; paper, $21.95.

**PLACE & VISION: THE FUNCTION OF
LANDSCAPE IN NATIVE AMERICAN FICTION**
Robert M. Nelson
Explores the role of physical landscape in three contemporary
Native American novels. 189 pp. Peter Lang, 1994. $39.95.

**A PLAINS ARCHAEOLOGY SOURCEBOOK:
SELECTED PAPERS OF THE NEBRASKA
STATE HISTORICAL SOCIETY**
Wald R. Wedie, Editor
314 pp. Garland, 1985. $40.

**THE PLAINS CREE: TRADE, DIPLOMACY & WAR, 1790
TO 1870**
John S. Milloy
Paper. University of Toronto Press, 1990. $16.95.

*THE PLAINS INDIAN BOOK
Donna Greenlee
Grades 1-5. About the Indians that live in tipis and hunt
Buffalo. Illus. 32 pp. Paper. Fun Publishing, $4.95.

PLAINS INDIAN CULTURE
O.J. Fargo
Illus. 50 pp. Paper. Green Valley Area, 1990. $1.50.

PLAINS INDIAN DESIGNS
Caren Caraway
Illus. 48 pp. Stemmer House, 1984. $5.95.

**PLAINS INDIAN HISTORY & CULTURE;
ESSAYS ON CONTINUITY & CHANGE**
John C. Ewers
Essays on Continuity and Change. Explores the role of women
in Plains Indian life. Illus. Maps. 272 pp. University of Okla-
homa Press, 1997. $29.95; paper, $14.95.

**PLAINS INDIAN & MOUNTAIN MAN ARTS
& CRAFTS I & II: AN ILLUSTRATED GUIDE**
Charles W. Overstreet
Vol. I - Explores the arts, crafts and other accoutrements made
and used by the Plains Indians and Mountain men in the early
1800's. 45 projects ranging from rawhide to an Arapaho saddle.
100s of photos & drawings. Illus. 160 pp. $13.95; Vol. II - Fea-
tures 40 projects ranging from a Blackfoot Fish Trap to a Wolf
Hat in the style of the Wind River Shoshone. 49 photos. 155
illus. 112 pp. Paper. Eagle's View, $12.95.

PLAINS INDIAN MYTHOLOGY
Alice Marriott & Carol Rachlin
A collection of traditional stories gleaned from oral sources,
with poetry. Illus. 224 pp. Paper. Penguin USA, 1975. $4.95.

**THE PLAINS INDIAN PHOTOGRAPHS
OF EDWARD S. CURTIS**
Edward S. Curtis
A collection of photos by Curtis. Illus. 175 pp.
University of Nebraska Press, 2001. $50.

**PLAINS INDIAN RAIDERS: THE FINAL PHASES OF
WARFARE FROM THE ARKANSAS TO THE RED RIVER**
Wilbur S. Nye
Illus. Maps. 418 pp. Paper. University of Oklahoma Press, 1974.
$21.95.

**PLAINS INDIAN SCULPTURE: A TRADITIONAL
ART FROM AMERICA'S HEARTLAND**
John C. Ewers
Illus. 240 pp. Paper. Smithsonian Books, 1986. $27.50.

*PLAINS INDIAN WARRIOR
R.A. May
Grades 3-8. Illus. 32 pp. Rourke Corp., 1990. $14.

*PLAINS INDIANS
Kate Petty
Grades 3 and up. Illus. 32 pp. Franklin Watts, 1988. $10.40.

THE PLAINS INDIANS
Paul H. Carlson
Traces the culture and history of the Plains Indians from 1750
to 1890, relying heavily on Indian voices and an Indian viewpoint. Illus. Maps. 272 pp. Texas A&M University Press, 1999.
$29.95; paper, $15.95.

THE PLAINS INDIANS
Colin F. Taylor
Covers the cultural diversity of many different tribes. Includes
Blackfoot, Cheyenne, Sioux, Comanche, Crow, and others. 250
full-color and b&w illus. 240 pp. Random House, 1994. $25.

**PLAINS INDIANS, A.D. 500-1500:
ARCHAEOLOGICAL PAST OF HISTORIC GROUPS**
Karl H. Schlesler, Editor
Traces Indian ethnic continuity & cultural diversity in the Great
Plains during the millennium preceding European arrival. Illus.
Maps. Biblio. 480 pp. University of Oklahoma Press, 1994.
$42.95; paper, $19.95.

*PLAINS INDIANS COLORING BOOK
David Rickman
Grades K-2. 48 pp. Paper. Dover, $2.95.

PLAINS INDIANS: AN EDUCATIONAL COLORING BOOK
Grades 1-8. Illus. 32 pp. Paper. Spizzirri Publishing,
1981. $1.95.

PLAINS INDIANS OF NORTH AMERICA
Robin May
Grades 4-8. Illus. 48 pp. 6 book set. Rourke Corp.,
$75.96 per set; $12.66 each.

THE PLAINS INDIANS OF THE 20th CENTURY
Peter Iverson, Editor
11 essays dealing with the complex cultural problems of the
20th century Plains Indian reservations. Illus. 288 pp. University of Oklahoma Press, 1985. $24.95; paper, $14.95.

*PLAINS INDIANS PUNCH-OUT PANORAMA
A.G. Smith
Construction of tribal settlement; pieces illustrate their way of
life. 27 full-color pieces, and 4 b&w diagrams. Grades 3 and
up. 12 pp. paper. Dover, $3.95.

*PLAINS INDIANS WARS
Sherry Marker
Chronicles the many battles of the second half of the 19th cen-
tury between Native Americans and the U.S. government.
Grades 5-12. Illus. 128 pp. Facts on File, 1996. $17.95.

**PLANNING FOR BALANCED DEVELOPMENT: A GUIDE
FOR NATIVE AMERICAN & RURAL COMMUNITIES**
Susan Guyette
Uses the creation of the Poeh Center at Pojoaqua Pueblo in
northern New Mexico as a case study. Illus. Photos. 324 pp.
Clear Light, 1996. $24.95; paper, $14.95.

**PLANNING PROCESS ON THE PINE RIDGE
& ROSEBUD INDIAN RESERVATION**
Richard E. Brown
University of South Dakota, Government Research Bureau,
1969. $1.

**PLANTING TAIL FEATHERS: TRIBAL SURVIVAL &
PUBLIC LAW 280**
Carolew Goldberg-Ambrose
246 pp. Paper. UCLA, American Indian Studies Center, 1997.
$15. Also available from The Falmouth Institute.

**PLANTS USED IN BASKETRY
BY THE CALIFORNIA INDIANS**
Ruth Merrill
Reprint. Illus. Acoma Books, 1980. $2.95.

**PLATEAU INDIANS & THE QUEST
FOR SPIRITUAL POWER, 1700-1850**
Larry Cebula
Illus. Maps. 195 pp. University of Nebraska Press, 2003. $49.95.

PLAYING INDIAN
Philip J. Deloria
Illus. 264 pp. Yale University Press, 1998. $30.

A PLEA FOR THE INDIANS
John Beeson
Reprint. 149 pp. Ye Galleon Press, 1998. $16.95; paper, $11.95.

**PLEASING THE SPIRITS: A CATLOGUE OF
A COLLECTION OF AMERICAN INDIAN ART**
Douglas C. Ewing
More than 500 objects of Native American art from across North
America, Illus. 402 pp. University of Washington Press, 1992.
$90.

PLENTY-COUPS, CHIEF OF THE CROWS
Frank B. Linderman; intro by Phenocia Bauerle
& Barney Old Coyote, Jr.
Reprint of 1962 edition. Illus. Map. 225 pp. Paper.
University of Nebraska Press, 2002. $16.95.

PO PAI MO: THE SEARCH FOR WHITE BUFFALO WOMAN
Robert Boissiere
Illus. 96 pp. Paper. Sunstone Press, 1983. $8.95.

POCAHONTAS
Ingri D'Aulaire
Paper. Doubleday, 1989. $7.95.

POCAHONTAS
Grace Steele Woodward
Reprint of 1969 edition. Illus. Map. Biblio. 228 pp.
Paper. University of Oklahoma Press, $14.95.

**POCAHONTAS & CO: THE FICTORIAL AMERICAN INDIAN
WOMAN IN 19th CENTURY LITERATURE: A STUDY OF
METHOD**
Asebrit Sundquist
350 pp. Humanities Press, 1986. $39.95.

*POCAHONTAS COLORING BOOK
Doherty & Kliros
Grades K-3. 48 pp. Paper. Dover, $2.95.

*POCAHONTAS: DAUGHTER OF A CHIEF
Grades K-3. Illus. 48 pp. Childrens Press, $11.95.

*POCAHONTAS, GIRL OF JAMESTOWN
Kate Jassem
Grades 3-7. Illus. 48 pp. Paper. Troll Associates, 1979.
$3.50.

POCAHONTAS: THE LIFE & LEGEND
Frances Mossiker
Reprint. Illus. 424 pp. Paper. Da Capo Press, $15.95.

POCAHONTAS: POWHATTAN PEACEMAKER
Anne Holler
Illus. Biblio. 104 pp. Written Heritage, $14.95.

**POCAHONTAS'S PEOPLE: THE POWHATAN
INDIANS OF VIRGINIA**
Helen Rountree
Illus. 416 pp. University of Oklahoma Press, 1990.
$29.95; paper, $14.95.

THE POINT ELLIOTT TREATY, 1855
Lynn Kickingbird & Curtis Berkey
28 pp. Institute for the Development of Indian Law, $9.

THE POINT-NO-POINT TREATY, 1855
Lynn Kickingbird & Curtis Berkey
29 pp. Institute for the Development of Indian Law, $9.

**POINT OF PINES, ARIZONA: A HISTORY OF THE
UNIVERSITY OF ARIZONA ARCHAEOLOGICAL
FIELD SCHOOL**
Emil W. Haury
140 pp. University of Arizona Press, 1989. $19.95.

POLICING IN INDIAN COUNTRY
Michael Barker
150 pp. Paper. Harrow & Heston, 1998. $22.50.

**THE POLITICAL ECONOMY OF
NORTH AMERICAN INDIANS**
John H. Moore, Editor
Collection of articles on macroeconomics and intercultural con-
flict. Illus. 320 pp. University of Oklahoma Press, 1993.$29.95.

**THE POLITICAL OUTSIDERS: BLACKS &
INDIANS IN A RURAL OKLAHOMA COUNTY**
Brian F. Rader
Paper. R & E Research Associates, 1978. $13.95.

**POLITICAL STRUCTURE & CHANGE IN
THE PREHISTORIC SOUTHEASTERN U.S.**
John F. Scarry, Editor
Illus. 304 pp. University Press of Florida, 1996. $49.95.

**POLITICS & ETHNICITY ON THE RIO YAQUI:
POTAM REVISITED**
Thomas R. McGuire
Yaqui culture. 186 pp. University of Arizona Press, 1986.
$32.

**THE POLITICS OF HALLOWED GROUND: WOUNDED
KNEE & THE STRUGGLE FOR INDIAN SOVEREIGNTY**
Mario Gonzalez & Elizabeth Cook-Lynn
360 pp. University of Illinois Press, 1998. $49.95; paper, $21.95.

**THE POLITICS OF INDIAN REMOVAL:
CREEK GOVERNMENT & SOCIETY IN CRISES**
Michael D. Green
Illus. 250 pp. University of Nebraska Press, 1982. $22.50.

**THE POLITICS OF SECOND GENERATION
DISCRIMINATION IN AMERICAN INDIAN EDUCATION
INCIDENCE, EXPLANATION & MITIGATING STRATEGIES**
David E. Wright, III, et al
192 pp. Greenwood Publishing, 1998. $49.95.

**POLITICS & POWER: AN ECONOMIC & POLITICAL
HISTORY OF THE WESTERN PUEBLO**
Steadman Upham
Academic Press, 1982. $24.50.

THE POLLEN PATH: A COLLECTION OF NAVAJO MYTHS
Retold by M.S. Link
Reprint of 1956 ed. Illus. 210 pp. Stanford University Press,
$19.50.

*THE POMO
Suzanne Freedman
Grades 5-8. Illus. 32 pp. Rourke, 1997. $21.27

**POMO BASKETMAKING -
A SUPREME NATIVE ART FOR THE WEAVER**
Elsie Allen
Step-by-step instructions for recreating beautiful & useful
baskets. Illus. Photos. 67 pp. Paper. Naturegraph, $6.95.

POMO DOCTORS & POISONERS
L.S. Freeland
Reprint of 1923 edition. 18 pp. paper. Coyote Press, $2.19.

POMO INDIAN BASKETRY
S.A. Barrett
Second Edition. Reprint of 1908 edition. 288 pp.
Paper. Rio Grande Press, $10.

*POMO INDIANS OF CALIFORNIA & THEIR NEIGHBORS
Vinson Brown; Albert Alsasser, Editor
Grades 4-12. Illus. Paper. Naturegraph, 1969. $9.95.

POMO LANDS ON CLEAR LAKE
E.W. Gifford
Facsimile edition. 16 pp. Paper. Coyote Press, $2.19.

THE PONCA TRIBE
James H. Howard
Illus. 215 pp. Paper. University of Nebraska Press, 1995.
$16.95.

*PONTIAC: CHIEF OF THE OTTAWAS
Jane Fleischer
Demco, 1979. $8.70.

PONY TRACKS
F. Remington
Reprint of 1961 edition. Illus. 178 pp. Paper.
University of Oklahoma Press, $12.95.

**POPULATION CHANGES AMONG
THE NORTHERN PLAINS INDIANS**
Clark Wissler
Bound with: "Cultural Relations of the Gila River & Lower Colo-
rado Tribes," by Leslie Spier; "Hopi Huntign & Hunting Ritual,"
by Ernest Beaglehole; "Navaho Warfare," by W.W. Hill; "The
Economy of a Modern Teton Dakota Community," by Mekeel
H. Scudder; and "The Distribution of the Northern Athapaskan
Indians." Reprinted from the 1936 edition. HRAF Press, $15.

THE PORTABLE NORTH AMERICAN INDIAN READER
Frederick W. Turner, III
Third Edition. A collection of myths, tales, poetry, speeches,
and passages from Indian autobiographies, and recent writings. 640 pp. Penguin USA, 1977. $9.95.

PORTAGE LAKE: MEMORIES OF AN OJIBWE CHILDHOOD
Maude Kegg; edited & transcribed by John Nichols
A child's view of traditional Anishinaabe lifeways coming into
contact with Euro-American settlers. 272 pp. Paper. University
of Minnesota Press, 1993. $16.95.

PORTFOLIO II
Kathryn Stewart
Illus. 50 pp. American Indian Contemporary Arts, 1988.

**PORTRAIT INDEX OF NORTH AMERICAN INDIANS
IN PUBLISHED COLLECTIONS**
Patrick Frazier, Library of Congress
Identifies and indexes hundreds of pictures, prints, drawings,
and lithographs of Native American portraits contained in 75
sources.Illus. Biblio. 142 pp. Paper. U.S. Government Printing
Office, $16.

**PORTRAITS OF NATIVE AMERICANS: PHOTOGRAPHS
FROM THE 1904 LOUISIANA PURCHASE EXPOSITION**
Charles H. Carpenter
Turn-of-the-century images of Native Americans, in a postcard
format. 48 pp. paper. W.W. Norton & Co., $9.95.

PORTRAITS OF THE WHITEMAN
Keith Basso
130 pp. Paper. Cambridge University Press, 1979. $12.95.

ALEX POSEY: CREEK POET, JOURNALIST, & HUMORIST
Daniel F. Littlefield, Jr.
Illus. Map. 330 pp. Paper. University of Nebraska Press, 1992.
$16.95.

POSTINDIAN CONVERSATIONS
Gerald Vizenor & A. Robert Lee
Collection of in-depth interviews with Gerald Vizenor and his
critical perspectives on important issues affecting Native
peoples in the late 20th century. 192 pp. Paper. University of
Nebraska Press, 1998. $24.95.

*POTAWATOMI
James A. Clifton
Grades 5 and up. Illus. 105 pp. Chelsea House, 1988.
$17.95.

*THE POTAWATOMI: GREAT LAKES
Grades 7-12. Illus. 112 pp. Knowledge Unlimited, $16.95.

**POTAWAOMI INDIANS OF MICHIGAN, 1843-1904,
INCLUDING SOME OTTAWA & CHIPPEWA, 1843-1866,
& POTAWATOMI OF INDIANA, 1869 & 1885**
Raymond C. Lantz
Covers annuity rolls on the Ottawa, Chippewa and Potawatomi
of Michigan abd Indiana. Roll numbers are given. 92 pp. Pa-
per. Heritage Books, 1992. $14.

POTAWATOMI TRAIL OF DEATH - INDIANA TO KANSAS
Shirley Willard & Susan Campbell, Editors
448 pp. Maps. Bib. Paper. Fulton County Historical Society,
2003. $40.

POTAWATOMIS: KEEPERS OF THE FIRE
R. David Edmunds
Illus. 374 pp. University of Oklahoma Press, 1978.
$22.95; paper, $12.95.

**POTLATCH AT GITSEGUKLA:
WILLIAM BEYNON'S 1945 FIELD NOTEBOOKS**
Margaret Anderson & Marjorie Halpin, Editors
Covers 5 totem pole raisings at Gitsegukla and the field notes
he compiled there. Includes a glossary of Gitksan words. Illus.
256 pp. UBC Press, 1999. $75.

**POTLATCH: NATIVE CEREMONY &
MYTH ON THE NORTHWEST COAST**
Mary G. Beck; illus. by Oliver
Paper. Alaska Northwest Books, $12.95.

THE POTLATCH PAPERS: A COLONIAL CASE HISTORY
Christopher Bracken
Photos. Maps. 276 pp. University of Chicago Press, 1997.
$40; paper, $16.95.

**THE POTTERY FROM ARROYO HONDO PUEBLO:
TRIBALIZATION & TRADE IN THE NORTHERN
RIO GRANDE**
Judith A. Habicht-Mauche
Includes *The Stone Artifacts from Arroyo Hondo Pueblo*,
by Carl J. Phagan. Illus. Maps. Biblio. Paper. School of
Americn Research, 1990. $30.

POTTERY OF THE GREAT BASIN & ADJACENT AREAS
Suzanne Griset
Illus. 170 pp. Paper. University of Utah Press, 1986. $17.50.

THE POTTERY OF SANTA ANA PUEBLO
Francis H. Harlow, Duane Anderson & Dwight Lanmon
Museum of New Mexico, 2004.

THE POTTERY OF ZIA PUEBLO
Francis H. Harlow & Dwight Lanmon
Museum of New Mexico, 2003.

POTTERY & PEOPLE: A DYNAMIC INTERACTION
James M. Skibo & Gary M. Feinman
Illus. University of Utah Press, $55; paper, $25.

**POTTERY TECHNIQUES OF NATIVE NORTH AMERICA:
AN INTRODUCTION TO TRADITIONAL TECHNOLOGY**
John K. White
University of Chicago Press, 1976. $46. Includes four-color
text-fiches.

**THE POWER OF KIOWA SONG:
A COLLABORATIVE ETHNOGRAPHY**
Luke E. Lassiter
Illus. 270 pp. University of Arizona Press, 1998.
$42; paper, $18.95.

**POWER OF A NAVAJO: CARL GORMAN:
THE MAN & HIS LIFE**
Henry & Georgia Greenberg; intro. by R.C. Gorman
Biography of artist, merchant, patriot, and respected Navajo
leaders and spokesman. Illus. 224 pp. Paper. Clear Light, 1996.
$14.95.

THE POWER OF SILENCE
Carlos Castaneda; Jane Rosenman, Editor
290 pp. Pocket Books, 1991. $8.95.

**POWER & PERFORMANCE IN GROS VENTRE WAR
EXPEDITION SONGS**
Orin T. Hatton
Illus. 79 pp. Paper. University of Washington Press, $14.95.

POWER QUEST: THE JOURNEY INTO MANHOOD
Carol Betdorf
Illus. 224 pp. Paper. Hancock House, $12.95.

**POWERFUL IMAGES:
PORTRAYALS OF NATIVE AMERICA**
Sara E. Boehme
Paper. University of Washington Press, 1998. $29.95.

**THE POWHATAN INDIANS OF VIRGINIA:
THEIR TRADITIONAL CULTURE**
Helen Rountree
Illus. Maps. 225 pp. Paper. University of Oklahoma Press,
1989. $13.95.

POWHATAN FOREIGN RELATIONS 1500-1722
Helen C. Rountree, Editor
Examines the Powhatans and their relationships with both
European & Indian "foreigners". 321 pp. University Press
of Virginia, 1993. $29.95.

**POWHATAN LORDS OF LIFE & DEATH: COMMAND
& CONSENT IN 17TH CENTURY VIRGINIA**
Margaret Holmes Williamson
Illus. Maps. 323 pp. University of Nebraska Press, 2003.
$55.

**POWHATAN'S MANTLE: INDIANS IN THE
COLONIAL SOUTHEAST**
Peter Wood, Gregory Waselkov & M. Thomas Hatley
Illus. Maps. 355 pp. Paper. University of Nebraska Press,
1989. $22.

**POWHATAN'S WORLD & COLONIAL VIRGINIA:
A CONFLICT OF CULTURES**
Frederic W. Gleach
Illus. 243 pp. Paper. University of Nebraska Press, 1997.
$22.

*THE POWHATAN TRIBES: MIDDLE ATLANTIC
Christina Feest
Grades 5 and up. Illus. Chelsea House, 1989. $17.95.

POW WOW
A young Indian boy, Red Elk, explains what is happening
at the PowWow celebration. Illus. 32 pp. Paper. Cherokee
Publications, $3.95.

*POW-WOW
Mimi Chenfeld and Marjorie Vandervelds
Grades 5-12. Paper. Council for Indian Education, 1972.
$2.95.

POW WOW CALENDAR
Liz Campbell, Editor
Lists, month-by-month, Native American powwows, dances,
crafts fairs and other cultural events. Annual. Illus. 100 pp. The
Book Publishing Co., Clear Light & Meadowlark Communica-
tions, $8.95.

POW WOW CHOW
A cookbook with collection of recipes from women of Five
Tribes heritage. 354 pp. Spiral bound. The Five Civilized
Tribes Museum. $12.95.

THE POW WOW HIGHWAY
David Seals
An up-to-date account of being Indian in America.
304 pp. Paper. Penguin USA, $9.95.

POW WOW: ON THE RED ROAD
Fred Synder
Lists over 870 American Indian events in the U.S. and Canada.
Native American Co-Op, $25.

POW WOW: & OTHER YAKIMA INDIAN TRADITIONS
Helen Willard
23 stories. Illus. 128 pp. Roza Run, 1990. $29.95;
paper, $19.95.

**THE POW WOW TRAIL: UNDERSTANDING &
ENJOYING THE NATIVE AMERICAN POW WOW**
Julia C. White; illus. by Diana E. Stanley
Guide to the activities at pow wows including dances
and dancers. Illus. 112 pp. Clear Light, $8.95.

*POWWOW
George Ancona
Grades 3-5. Young Anthony Standing Rock as he participates
in the Crow Fair in Montana,, as a traditional dancer. Meadowlark Communications, $9.

*POWWOW
Ben Marra
Portraits and words of powwow dancers.
Grades 4 and up. Illus. Paper. Oyate, 1996. $16.95.

*POWWOW ACTIVITY BOOK
Sandy & Jesse Hummingbird
Ages 5-10. Illus. 28 pp. Paper. Clear Light, $4.95.

POWWOW COUNTRY
Chris Roberts
Overview of the powwow circuit and what it means to Indian
people. 100 photos taken at Montana powwows. Text & photos. by Chris Roberts. Paper. Meadowlark Communications,
1993. $19.95.

POWWOW COUNTRY: PEOPLE OF THE CIRCLE
Chris Roberts
A sequel to *Powwow Country*, 1993. Explores the powwow
world. In-depth look at the people, the changes and trends in-
fluencing American Indian culture today. Includes powwow
events and activities from several major national powwows.
120 color photos. Biblio. 128 pp. Paper. Meadowlark Communications, 1998. $21.95.

POWWOW DANCER'S & CRAFTWORKER'S HANDBOOK
Adolf Hungry Wolf
Historical photos of turn-of-century powwows. Illustrations
show step-by-step how to make the outfits worn today.
144 pp. Paper. Written Heritage, $18.95.

*POWWOW: IMAGES ALONG THE RED ROAD
Ben Marra
Grades 4 and up. 105 portraits of powwow dancers.
Meadowlark Communications, $16.95.

***POWWOW SUMMER: A FAMILY
CELEBRATES THE CIRCLE OF LIFE**
Marcie R. Rendon; Cheryl Walsh Bellville, Illus.
Grades 1-5. An Anishinabe (Ojibway) family travel
to two powwows. Illus. 48 pp. Lerner, 1996. $7.95.

A PRACTICAL GRAMMAR OF THE ST. LAWRENCE ISLAND: SIBERIAN YUP'IK ESKIMO LANGUAGE
Steven A. Jacobson
105 pp. Paper. Alaska Native Language Center, 1990. $10.

PRAIRIE CITY: THE STORY OF AN AMERICAN COMMUNITY
Angie Debo; foreword by Rennard Strickland
Reprint. Illus. 276 pp. Paper. University of Oklahoma Press, 1998. $17.95.

*PRAIRIE LEGENDS
M. Earring, et al
Grades 6-9. Paper. Council for Indian Education, 1978. $2.95.

THE PRAIRIE PEOPLE: CONTINUITY & CHANGE IN POTAWATOMI INDIAN CULTURE, 1665-1965
James A. Clifton
Illus. 568 pp. Paper. University of Iowa Press, 1998. $24.95.

*PRAIRIE SMOKE
Melvin R. Gilmore
The life of the Indians of the Missouri Valley, as reflected in their mythology. Grades 7 and up. Reprint of 1929 edition. Illus. 225 pp. Paper. Minnesota Historical Society Press, $7.95.

PRAYER ON TOP OF THE EARTH: THE SPIRITUAL UNIVERSE OF THE PLAINS APACHES
Kay Parker Schweinfurth
University Press of Colorado, 2002. $29.95.

*THE PRAYING FLUTE
Tony Shearer
Grades 4 and up. 112 pp. Paper. Naturegraph, 1988. $7.95.

A PRAYING PEOPLE: MASSACHUSETT ACCULTURA-TION & THE FAILURE OF THE PURITAN MISSION, 1600-1690
Dane Morrison
Revised edition. paper. Peter Lang, $32.95.

PRE-COLUMBIAN ARCHITECTURE, ART & ARTIFACTS SLIDE CATALOG
H.L. Murvin
40 pp. Paper. H.L. Murvin, 1983. $3.95.

PRE-COLUMBIAN ART
Elizabeth P. Benson, Editor
University of Chicago Press, 1976. $25.

PRE-COLUMBIAN ART FROM THE LAND COLLECTION
Alana Cordy-Collins & H.B. Nicholson; L. K. Land, Editor
Illus. 275 pp. Paper. California Academy of Sciences, 1979. $25.'

PRE-SEMINOLE FLORIDA: SPANISH SOLDIERS, FRIARS & INDIAN MISSIONS, 1513-1763
Robert M. Matter
Reprint. 208 pp. Garland, $10.

PREHISTORIC ARCHITECTURE IN THE EASTERN U.S.
Morgan
A source for information on the major prehistoric earthworks east of the Mississippi. Illus. 197 pp. Hothem House, 1980. $19.95.

PREHISTORIC BIOLOGICAL RELATIONSHIP IN THE GREAT LAKES REGION
Richard Wilkinson
Illus. Paper. University of Michigan, Museum of Anthropology, 1971. $3.50.

PREHISTORIC CULTURE CHANGE ON THE COLORADO PLATEAU: TEN THOUSAND YEARS ON BLACK MESA
edited by Shirley Powell & Francis E. Smiley
Study of the ancestral Puebloan and navajo occupation of the Four Corners region. Illus. 221 pp. University of Arizona Press, 2002. $50.

PREHISTORIC HOUSEHOLDS AT TURKEY CREEK PUEBLO, ARIZONA
Julie Lowell
Illus. 110 pp. Paper. University of Arizona Press, 1991. $21.95.

PREHISTORIC HUNTERS OF THE HIGH PLAINS
George Frison
Reprint of 1978 edition. Illus. 2nd Edition. 460 pp. Hothem House, $73.

PREHISTORIC INDIAN ROCK ART: ISSUES & CONCERNS
Jo Anne Van Tilburg & Clement Meighan, Editors
Illus. 66 pp. Paper. UCLA Institute of Archaeology, 1981. $6.

PREHISTORIC INDIANS
Barnes & Pendleton
A guide to understanding the early Indian cultures of the Four Corners (AZ, NM, UT, CO) area. Includes artifacts, cultures, rpck art and ruins. Illus. 256 pp. Paper. Hothem House, 1988. $9.50.

PREHISTORIC INDIANS OF THE SOUTHEAST: ARCHAEOLOGY OF ALABAMA & THE MIDDLE SOUTH
John Walthall
Illus. 288 pp. University of Alabama Press, 1980. $25.

PREHISTORIC INDIANS OF THE SOUTHWEST
H.M. Wormington
Covers the Mogollon, Hohokam & Anasazi cultures. Reprint of 1947 edition. Illus. Photos. Maps. 191 pp. High-Lonesome Books, $10.

PREHISTORIC INDIANS OF WISCONSIN
Robert Ritzenthaler
Third revised edition. Illus. 62 pp. Paper. American Indian Books, and Milwaukee Public Museum, 1985. $7.95.

PREHISTORIC LAND USE & SETTLEMENT OF THE MIDDLE LITTLE COLORADO RIVER VALLEY
Richard C. lange
Survey of the Homolovi Ruins State Park. 175 pp. Paper. University of Arizona Press, 1998. $17.95.

PREHISTORIC LITHIC INDUSTRY AT DOVER, TENN.
Richard M. Gramly
An investigation of quarries and workshops used by lithic crafts-men of the Mississippian archaeological culture, the Flintkappers of Dover. Illus. 150 pp. Paper. Persimmon Press, $21.95.

PREHISTORIC MAN ON THE GREAT PLAINS
Waldo Wedel
Illus. University of Oklahoma, 1961. $28.95.

PREHISTORIC MESOAMERICA
Richard E.W. Adams
Revised 1991 edition. Illus. Maps. Paper. University of Oklahoma Press, $18.95.

PREHISTORIC PAINTED POTTERY OF SOUTHEASTERN ARIZONA
Robert A. Heckman, et al.
Published by Statistical Research, Inc. Illus. 197 pp. Paper. Distributed by The University of Arizona Press, 1999. $35.

THE PREHISTORIC PEOPLES OF MINNESOTA
Elden Johnson
Revised edition. Illus. 35 pp. Paper. Minnesota Historical Society Press, 1988. $3.95.

PREHISTORIC PEOPLES OF SOUTH FLORIDA
William E. McGoun
176 pp. Paper. University of Alabama Press, 1993. $19.95.

PREHISTORIC PIPES
Ahlstrom
Pipes found at northern Ohio's Reeve village site. Photos. 145 pp. Hothem House, 1979. $14, postpaid.

THE PREHISTORIC PUEBLO WORLD, A.D. 1150-1350
Michael A. Adler, Editor
312 pp. Paper. University of Arizona Press, 1996. $26.95.

PREHISTORIC ROCK ART
Barnes
Guide to the prehistoric and historic petroglyphs and pictographs of the Four Corners and Great Basin. Illus. 304 pp. Paper. Hothem House, 1986. $11.25, postpaid.

PREHISTORIC SANDALS FROM NORTHEASTERN ARIZONA: THE EARL H. MORRIS & ANN AXTELL MORRIS RESEARCH
Kelly Ann Hays-Gilpin, Ann Cordy Deegan & Elizabeth Ann Morris
Illus. 168 pp. Paper. University of Arizona Press, 1998. $17.95.

PREHISTORIC SOUTHWESTERN CRAFT ARTS
Clara L. Tanner
Discusses baskets, pottery, textiles, ornaments, and other crafts of the Southwest's prehistoric peoples. Illus. 226 pp. University of Arizona Press, 1976. $27.50.

PREHISTORIC SOUTHWESTERNERS FROM BASKETMAKER TO PUEBLO
C.A. Amsden
Reprint of 1949 edition. Illus. Maps. 165 pp. Paper. Southwest Museum, $5.

PREHISTORIC WARFARE IN THE AMERICAN SOUTHWEST
Steven A. LeBlanc
University of Utah Press, 1998. $34.95.

PREHISTORIC WEAPONS IN THE SOUTHWEST
Stewart Peckham
Illus. Paper. Museum of New Mexico Press, 1965. $1.50.

PREHISTORY IN THE NAVAJO RESERVOIR DISTRICT
Frank W. Eddy
Illus. Paper. Museum of New Mexico Press, 1966. Two parts, $8.95 each.

THE PRE-HISTORY OF THE BURNT BLUFF AREA
James E. Fitting, Editor
Paper. University of Michigan, Museum of Anthropology, 1968. $3.

THE PREHISTORY OF COLORADO & ADJACENT AREAS
Tammy Stone
214 pp. Univesity of Utah Press, 1999. $17.50.

THE PREHISTORY OF FISHTRAP, KENTUCKY
R.C. Dunnell
Paper. Yale University, Anthropology, 1972. $7.

PRESBYTERIAN MISSIONARY ATTITUDES TOWARD AMERICAN INDIANS, 1837-1893
Michael C. Coleman
Based upon correspondence of missionaries in the field. Illus. 222 pp. University Press of Mississippi, 1985. $32.

PRESENT IS PAST: SOME USES OF TRADITION IN NATIVE SOCIETIES
Marie Mauz, Editor
Collection of essays. 250 pp. University of Press of America, 1997. $51.50; paper, $31.

PRESENT STATE OF NEW ENGLAND
Co Mather
Reprint of 1690 edition. Haskell House, $59.95.

PRESERVING TRADITIONAL ARTS: A TOOLKIT FOR NATIVE AMERICAN COMMUNITIES
Susan Dyal
205 pp. UCLA, American Indian Studies Center, 1985. $20.

PRESIDENT WASHINGTON'S INDIAN WAR: THE STRUGGLE FOR THE OLD NORTHWEST, 1790-1795
Wiley Sword
Illus. 432 pp. Paper. University of Oklahoma Press, 1985. $18.95.

PRESSING ISSUES OF INEQUALITY & AMERICAN INDIAN COMMUNITIES
Elizabeth Segal & Keith Kilty, Editors
98 pp. Haworth Press, 1998. $29.95.

THE PRETEND INDIANS - IMAGES OF NATIVE AMERICANS IN THE MOVIES: AN ANALYTICAL SURVEY OF TWENTI-ETH CENTURY INDIAN ENTERTAINERS
Gretchen Bataille & Charles Silent
Iowa State University Press, 1978.

PRETTY-SHIELD, MEDICINE WOMAN OF THE CROWS
Frank B. Linderman; illus by Herbert Morton Stoops
An Indian woman's side of life. Reprint of 1932 edition. Illus. 224 pp. Paper. University of Nebraska Press, 2003. $14.95.

THE PRICE OF A GIFT: A LAKOTA HEALER'S STORY
Gerald Mohatt & Joseph Eagle Elk
Eagle Elk's (1931-91) story of his life, practice, and beliefs. Illus. Map. 230 pp. Paper. University of Nebraska Press, 2000. $14.95.

PRIDE OF THE INDIAN WARDROBE: NORTHERN ATHAPASKAN FOOTWEAR
Judy Thompson
198 pp. University of Toronto Press, 1990. $49.50; paper, $25.

THE PRIMAL MIND: VISION & REALITY IN INDIAN AMERICA
Jamake Highwater
Examines Indian ritual, art, oral traditions, architecture, and ceremonial dance and how it comes into contact and conflict with the "civilized" Western world. 240 pp. Paper. New American Library, $9.95.

PRIMITIVE ART
Franz Boas
Reprint. 376 pp. Paper. Dover, $9.95.

PRIMITIVE ARTS & CRAFTS
Roderick U. Sayce
Reprint of 1993 ed. Illus. Biblio-Moser. $24.

PRIMITIVE MAN IN OHIO
W.K. Moorehead
Reprint of 1892 edition. 246 pp. Hothem House. $46.50, postpaid.

PRIMITIVE PRAGMATISTS: THE MODOC INDIANS OF NORTHERN CALIFORNIA
Verne V. Ray
Illus. University of Washington Press, 1963. $11.50.

PRISON OF GRASS: CANADA FROM A NATIVE VIEWPOINT
Howard Adams
Adams, PhD & leader in the Canadian Native rights movement. Updated edition. Greenfield Review Press, $18.95.

PRIVILEGING THE PAST: RECONSTRUCTING HISTORY IN NORTHWEST COAST ART
Judith Ostrowitz
Illus. 264 pp. University of Washington Press, 1999. $35.

THE PROBLEM OF JUSTICE: TRADITION & LAW IN THE COAST SALISH WORLD
Bruce G. Miller
Ethnographic study of the Coast Salish communities along the northwest coast of North America. Illus. 240 pp. University of Nebraska Press, 2001. $60; paper, $19.95.

**PROCEEDINGS OF THE FORT CHIPEWYAN/
FORT VERMILLION BICENTENNIAL CONFERENCE,
SEPT. 23-24, 1988, EDMONTON, ALBERTA**
Patricia McCormack & R. Geoffrey Ironside, Editors
Focusses on the Aboriginal beginnings, histories, present conditions, and future prospects of the regions. Illus. 319 pp. CCI, $25.

PROCEEDINGS OF THE GREAT PEACE CONFERENCE
Institute for the Development of Indian Law, $10.

PROCEEDINGS OF THE 1973 HOHOKAM CONFERENCE
Donald Weaver, Jr., Susan Burton & Minnabell Laughlin,
Compilers & Editors
Monograph documenting two days of intensive discussions on Hohokam archaeology. Maps. 105 pp. Center for Anthropological Studies, $12 (postpaid).

PROCEEDINGS OF THE HOKAN LANGUAGES WORKSHOP
J.E. Reden, Editor
Reprints. Coyote Press.

**PROCEEDINGS OF THE HOKAN-YUMAN
LANGUAGES WORKSHOP HELD AT THE
UNIVERSITY OF CALIFORNIA**
J.E. Reden, Editor
Reprints. Coyote Press.

**PROFILES IN WISDOM: NATIVE ELDERS
SPEAK ABOUT THE EARTH**
Steven McFadden, Editor
Illus. 256 pp. Paper. Bear & Co., 1991. $12.95.

**PROMISES OF THE PAST:
A HISTORY OF INDIAN EDUCATION**
David H. DeJong
304 pp. North American Press, 1993. $24.95.

PROPERTY CONCEPTS OF THE NAVAHO INDIANS
B. Haile
Reprint of 1954 edition. Paper. St. Michaels, $6.

**PROPHETIC WORLDS: INDIANS &
WHITES ON THE COLUMBIA PLATEAU**
Christopher C. Miller
174 pp. Rutgers University Press, 1985. $35.

**THE PROTECTOR DE INDIOS IN
COLONIAL NEW MEXICO, 1659-1821**
Charles R. Cuttler
Illus. 140 pp. University of New Mexico Press, 1986.
$17.50; paper, $8.95.

**PROTO-ATHAPSKAN VERB STEM VARIATION:
PART ONE: PHONOLOGY**
Jeff Leer
100 pp. Paper. Alaska Native Language Center, 1979. $5.

THE PROTOHISTORIC PUEBLO WORLD, A.D. 1275-1600
edited by Charles Adams & Andrew I. Duff
Describes and interprets this period of southwestern history.
Illus. 260 pp. University of Arizona Press, 2004. $50.

THE PROVIDERS
Stephen Irwin
Illus. 296 pp. Paper. Hancock House, 1984. $12.95.

**PSYCHOCULTURAL CHANGE AND THE AMERICAN
INDIAN: AN ETHNOHISTORICAL ANALYSIS**
Laurence French
Garland, 1987. $34.

**PSYCHOLOGICAL RESEARCH ON AMERICAN INDIAN
& ALASKA NATIVE YOUTH: AN INDEXED GUIDE TO
DISSERTATIONS**
Spero M. Manson, et al, Editors
Illus. 230 pp. Greenwood, 1984. $36.95.

**PSYCHOLOGY OF INDIANS OF NORTH AMERICA:
INDEX OF NEW INFORMATION WITH AUTORS,
SUBJECTS & BIBLIOGRAPHIC REFERENCES**
Swedlo A. Sampos
150 pp. Paper. ABBE Publishers, 1996. $47.50; paper,
$44.50.

*PTEBLOKA; TALES FROM THE BUFFALO
M. Grant Two Bulls
Grades 3 and up. Illus. 20 cartoons. 24 pp. Paper.
Dakota Press, 1991. $3.

*PUEBLO
Mary D'Apice
Grades 5-8. Illus. 32 pp. Rourke Corp., 1990. $9.95.

*THE PUEBLO
Alfonso Ortiz
A history of the people. Grades 7 and up. Illus.
Chelsea House Publishers, $7.95.

*THE PUEBLO
Charlotte Yue
Grades 4-7. Paper. Houghton Mifflin, 1990. $4.95.

**PUEBLO ARCHITECTURE & MODERN ADOBES:
THE RESIDENTIAL DESIGNS OF WILLIAM LUMPKINS**
Joseph Traugott
Pueblo source materials. Illus. 144 pp. Paper.
Museum of New Mexico Press, 2000, $19.95.

PUEBLO ARTISTS: PORTRAITS
Toba Pato Tucker
Essays by Alfred L. Bush, Rina Swentzell, and Lonnie Vigil.
Lives and traditions of over 140 Pueblo artists. 160 pp. Illus.
Museum of New Mexico Press, 2001. $55; paper, $35.

PUEBLO BIRDS & MYTHS
Hamilton A. Tyler
Discusses birds place in Pueblo ritual, ceremony, myth, and folklore. Illus. Biblio. 280 pp. Paper. Northland Press, 1979.
$19.95.

*PUEBLO BOY: GROWING UP IN TWO WORLDS
Marcia Keegan
Grades 3 and up. Illus. 48 pp. Clear Light Publishers, $14.95.

THE PUEBLO CHILDREN OF THE EARTH MOTHER
Thomas E. Mails
Details the history, customs, and accomplishments of the Pueblo Indians of AZ and NM. Illus. 544 pp. 1997. Marlowe & Co., $43.50; paper, $29.95.

PUEBLO CRAFTS
Ruth Underhill; Willard Beatty, Editor
Reprint of 1944 edition. Illus. Map. 148 pp.
Paper. R. Schneider, Publishers, $7.95.

PUEBLO CULTURES
B. Wright
Illus. 30 pp. Paper. Brill, 1986. $36.75.

**PUEBLO DESIGNS: 176 ILLUSTRATIONS
OF THE RAIN BIRD**
H.R. Mera; drawings by Tom Lea
Reprint of 1970 edition. Illus. 115 pp. Peter Smith, $14.25.
Paper. Dover, $7.95.

*PUEBLO GIRLS: GROWING UP IN TWO WORLDS
Marcia Keegan
Grades 3 and up. Illus. 60 color photos. 48 pp.
Clear Light Publishers, $14.95.

PUEBLO GODS & MYTHS
Hamilton Tyler
Reprint of 1964 edition. Illus. Map. 312 pp. Paper. University of Oklahoma Press & Clear Light, $15.95.

**PUEBLO, HARDSCRABBLE, GREENHORN:
SOCIETY ON THE HIGH PLAINS, 1832-1856**
Janet Lecompte
Reprint of 1977 edition. Illus. Maps. 354 pp. Paper.
University of Oklahoma Press, $25.95.

*PUEBLO INDIAN
Steven Cory
Grades 4-7. Illus. 48 pp. Lerner, 1996. $15.95.

PUEBLO INDIAN COOKBOOK
Compiled & edited by Phyllis Hughes
Illus. 64 pp. Paper. Museum of New Mexico Press, $11.95.

PUEBLO INDIAN EMBROIDERY
N.R. Mera
Illus. 80 pp. Paper. Dover, 1975. $6.95.

PUEBLO INDIAN FOLK-STORIES
Charles F. Lummis
Seven elders tell folk-stories. Illus. 257 pp. Paper.
University of Nebraska Press & Clear Light, 1992. $12.

PUEBLO INDIAN POTTERY: 750 ARTIST BIOGRAPHIES
Gregory Schaaf; Richard M. Howard, Editor
Illus. 200 pp. Center for Indigenous Arts & Cultures
(CIAC) Press, 2000. $50.

PUEBLO INDIAN RELIGION
Elsie Clews Parsons
Illus. Map. In 2 vols. Vol. 1, 577 pp., Vol. 2, 760 pp.
Paper. University of Nebraska Press, $25 each.

**PUEBLO INDIAN REVOLT OF 1696 & THE FRANCISCAN
MISSIONS IN NEW MEXICO: LETTERS OF THE MISSIONARIES & RELATED DOCUMENTS**
translated & edited by J. Manuel Espinosa
Portrait of the conflict between Franciscan missionary zeal and the Pueblo holy men. Illus. Maps. 314 pp. Paper. University of Oklahoma Press, $21.95.

PUEBLO INDIAN POTTERY
Francis H. Harlow & Jack Silverman
Silverman Museum, 2001.

PUEBLO INDIAN TEXTILES: A LIVING TRADITION
Kate P. Kent
Illus. 136 pp. Paper. School of American Research & University of Washington Press, 1983. $16.95.

**PUEBLO INDIAN WATER RIGHTS:
STRUGGLE FOR A PRECIOUS RESOURCE**
Charles T. DuMars, Marilyn O'Leary, Albert E. Utton
183 pp. University of Arizona Press, 1984. $32.

THE PUEBLO INDIANS
Joe Sando
The history of the Pueblos; includes the constitution of the All Indian Pueblo Council. Illus. 246 pp. Paper. The Indian Historian Press, 1976. $12.25.

*PUEBLO INDIANS
Liza N. Burby
Grades 4 and up. Demco, 1994. $13.15.

THE PUEBLO INDIANS OF NORTH AMERICA
Edward P. Dozier
Reprint. Illus. 224 pp. Paper. Waveland Press, $9.95.

**PUEBLO & MISSION: CULTURAL ROOTS
OF THE SOUTHWEST**
Susan Lamb; photos by Chuck Place
The events, practices and iconography of the people of the Southwest. 140 color photos. Biblio. 160 pp. Paper. Northland Publishing, 1997. $19.95

**PUEBLO MOTHERS & CHILDREN: ESSAYS
BY ELSIE CLEWS PARSONS, 1915-1924**
Barbara Babcock, Editor
Illus. Maps. 150 pp. Ancient City Press, $29.95; paper, $17.95.

PUEBLO: MOUNTAIN, VILLAGE, DANCE
Vincent Scully
Second edition. Illus. 412 pp. University of Chicago Press, 1989.
$72; paper, $35.

**PUEBLO NATIONS: EIGHT CENTURIES
OF PUEBLO INDIAN HISTORY**
Joe S. Sando
Illus. 49 photos. Maps. 295 pp. Clear Light, 1991.
$24.95; paper, $14.95.

PUEBLO & NAVAJO INDIAN LIFE TODAY
Kris Hotvedt
Revised ed. of *Fry Breads, Feast Days and Sheep.*
Illus. 64 pp. Paper. Sunstone Press, $8.95.

PUEBLO PEOPLE: ANCIENT TRADITIONS, MODERN LIVES
Marcia Keegan
417 color photos. 264 pp. Clear Light, $39.95.

**THE PUEBLO POTTER: A STUDY OF
CREATIVE IMAGINATION IN PRIMITIVE ART**
Ruth L. Bunzel
Reprint of 1926 edition. Illus. 134 pp. Peter Smith, $55.
Paper. Hothem House & Dover, $7.95.

PUEBLO POTTERY DESIGNS
Kenneth M. Chapman
Illus. 208 pp. Paper. Dover, $9.95.

PUEBLO POTTERY OF THE NEW MEXICO INDIANS
Betty Toulouse
Illus. 150 bxw photos; 11 color plates. 96 pp. Paper.
Museum of New Mexico Press, 1977. $12.95.

**PUEBLO PROFILES: CULTURAL IDENTITY
THROUGH CENTURIES OF CHANGE**
Joe S. Sando
Tells the stories of political leaders, educators, and artists who took part in the events and movements that have shaped Pueblo Indian life from the time of the Pueblo Revolt to the present day. Illus. 47 photos. 320 pp. Paper. Clear Light, 1994. $24.95; paper, $14.95.

THE PUEBLO REVOLT
Robert Silverberg; intro. by Marc Simmons
Map. 216 pp. Paper. University of Nebraska Press, 1994.
$14.95.

**THE PUEBLO REVOLT OF 1680: CONQUEST &
RESISTANCE IN 17TH CENTURY NEW MEXICO**
Andrew L. Knaut
Illus. 272 pp. Maps. Paper. University of Oklahoma Press, 1997.
$19.95.

**PUEBLO SHIELDS FROM THE FRED HARVEY
FINE ARTS COLLECTION**
Barton Wright
Illus. 96 pp. The Heard Museum, 1976. $9.50.

*THE PUEBLO: SOUTHWEST
Alfonso Ortiz
Grades 5 and up. Illus. Chelsea House, 1989. $17.95.

PUEBLO STORIES & STORYTELLERS
Mark Bahti
56 pp. Paper. Treasure Chest & Clear Light, 1988. $12.95.

*PUEBLO STORYTELLER
Diane Hoyt-Goldsmith
Grades 3-7. Illus. 32 pp. Holiday House, 1991.
$15.95; paper, $6.95.

THE PUEBLO STORYTELLER: DEVELOPMENT OF A FIGURATIVE CERAMIC TRADITION
Barbara Babcock, et al.
Illus. 201 pp. Paper. University of Arizona Press, 1986.
$26.95.

*A PUEBLO VILLAGE
Hilda Aragon, Illustrator
Preschool-7. Illus. 8 pp. Paper. Pueblo of Acoma Press,
1982. $4.

*THE PUEBLOS
Suzanne Powell
Includes maps, a glossary and bibliography. Part of
Indians of the Americas series. Full-color illustrations.
Grades 3 and up. 64 pp. Paper. Franklin Watts, $5.95.

PUEBLOS: PREHISTORIC INDIAN CULTURES OF THE SOUTHWEST
Sylvio Acatos & Max Bruggman
Illus. 240 pp. Facts on File, 1990. $45.

PUMPKIN SEED POINT: BEING WITHIN THE HOPI
Frank Waters
175 pp. Ohio University Press, 1973. $9.95; paper, $6.95.

THE PUNISHMENT OF THE STINGY & OTHER INDIAN STORIES
George Bird Grinnell
Reprint of 1901 ed. Illus. 265 pp. Paper.
University of Nebraska Press. $9.95.

PURISIMINO CHUMASH PREHISTORY
Michael A. Glassow
Paper. Harcourt Brace College Publishers, 1995. $23.50.

PURITAN JUSTICE & THE INDIAN: WHITE MAN'S LAW IN PURITANS AMONG THE INDIANS: ACCOUNTS OF CAPITIVITY & REDEMPTIONS 1676-1724
Alden Vaughan & Edward Clark
Illus. 352 pp. Harvard University Press, 1981. $23.50.

PUSHED INTO THE ROCKS: SOUTHERN CALIFORNIA INDIAN LAND TENURE, 1769-1986
Florence Shipek
Illus. 230 pp. University of Nebraska Press, 1988. $25.95.

PUSHING THE BEAR: A NOVEL OF THE TRAIL OF TEARS
Diane Glancy (Cherokee)
Story of a young woman and her family surviving the numbing
punishment of the Trail. Grades 9 and up. Oyate, 1996. $22.

Q

QAWIARAQ INUPIAQ LITERACY MANUAL
Lawrence Kaplan
50 pp. Paper. Alaska Native Language Center, 1987. $5.

QUAIL SONG: A PUEBLO INDIAN FOLKTALE
Valerie Carey, retold by
Illus. Putnam, 1990. $14.95.

THE QUALLA CHEROKEE SURVIVING IN TWO WORLDS
Laurence A. French
252 pp. Edwin Mellon Press, 1998. $89.95.

QUALLA: HOME OF THE MIDDLE CHEROKEE SETTLEMENT
T. Walter Middleton
Illus. 287 pp. Paper. WorldComm, 1998. $16.95.

QUANAH: A PICTORIAL HISTORY OF THE LAST COMANCHE CHIEF
Pauline D. Robertson and R.D. Robertson
Illus. 192 pp. Paramount, 1985. $19.95.

*THE QUAPAW INDIANS: A HISTORY OF THE DOWNSTREAM PEOPLE
W. David Baird
Grades 5 and up. Reprint of 1980 edition. Illus.
104 pp. Chelsea House, $17.95.

THE QUAPAW & THEIR POTTERY
Hathcock
The ceramic output of the Quapaw Indians, 1650-1750.
Illus. 176 pp. Hothem House, 1983. $53, postpaid.

*THE QUAPAWS
W.D. Baird
Grades 5 and up. Illus. 105 pp. Chelsea House, 1989.
$17.95.

QUARTER-ACRE OF HEARTACHE
Claude C. Smith
In the words of Big Eagle of the Golden Hill Tribe, Paugussett
Nation, his legal struggle to save the token parcel of land that
remain of the original Paugussett reservation. Illus. Maps. 160
pp. Pocahontas Press, 1985. $21.95; paper, $16.95.

THE QUEEN'S PEOPLE: A STUDY OF HEGEMONY, COERCION & ACCOMMODATION AMONG THE OKANAGAN OF CANADA
Peter Carstens
Illus. 416 pp. University of Toronto Press, 1991. $55.

QUEESTO: PACHEENAHT CHIEF BY BIRTHRIGHT
Chief Charles Jones with Stephen Bosustow
Memoirs of hereditary Chief of the Pacheenaht people
of Vancouver Island's West Coast. 125 pp. Theytus,
1982. $14.95.

*QUEST FOR COURAGE
Stormy Randolph
A lame Blackfeet boy overcomes his handicap by going on a
vision quest. Grades 3-17. Illus. 102 pp. Paper. Roberts
Rinehart, 1993. $8.95.

*QUEST FOR EAGLE FEATHER
John Duncklee
Grades 3-7. Illus. Northland Press, 1997. $12.95.

QUEST FOR THE ORIGINS OF THE FIRST AMERICANS
E. James Dixon
Illus. Maps. 156 pp. Paper. University of New Mexico
Press, 1993. $12.95.

*QUEST FOR QUIVERA
E. Buford Morgan
Historical novel of an Indian known as "the Turk" and his journeys through the Southwest at the time of the Coronado expedition. Grades 9 and up. 189 pp. Council for Indian Education.
$12.95; paper, $6.95.

QUIET PRIDE: AGELESS WISDOM OF THE AMERICAN WEST
J. Bourge Hathaway; photos by Robert A. Clayton
Collectio of photograhs and narration that preserves the stories, wisdom & insight of Native and non-Native American elders. Illus. 80 color photos. 128 pp. Beyond Words Publishing,
1993. $39.95.

QUIET TRIUMPH: FORTY YEARS WITH THE INDIAN ARTS FUND, SANTA FE
Mitchell Wilder
Illus. 18 pp. Paper. Amon Carter Museum, 1965. $2.

QUILL & BEADWORK OF THE WESTERN SIOUX
Carrie A. Lyford
Reprint of 1940 edition. Illus. 116 pp. Paper.
R. Schneider, Publishers, $9.95.

A QUILLWORK COMPANION: AN ILLUSTRATED GUIDE TO TECHNIQUES OF PORCUPINE QUILL EMBROIDERY
Jean Heinbuch
Describes and illustrates all of the basic and advanced designs
used by the American Indian. Also explains birchbark and loom
quillwork. Illus. 92 pp. Paper. Eagle's View Publishing, & Smoke
& Fire Co., $12.95.

*QUILLWORKER: A CHEYENNE LEGEND
Grades 4-8. Illus. Paper. Troll, Demco & Rourke Corp.,
1992. $16.95; paper, $4.95.

QUILTING & APPLIQUE WITH SOUTHWEST INDIAN DESIGNS
Charlotte Bass
Illus. Photos. 96 pp. Paper. Naturegraph, 1998. $15.95.

QUILTING PATTERNS FROM NATIVE AMERICAN DESIGNS
Dr. Joyce Mori
Ready-toUse quilting designs. Illus. 80 pp. Paper.
Written Heritage, $12.95.

QULIAQTUAT MUMIAKRAT ILISAQTUANUN SAVAAKSRIAT
Edna MacLean
Illus. 35 pp. Paper. Alaska Native Language Center, 1986.
$4.

R

*RABBIT & THE BEARS
Deborah L. Duvall; illus. by Murv Jacob
Vol. 4 of the Grandmother Stories. Cherokee history and legend. All ages. Illus. 32 pp. University of New Mexico Press,
2004. $14.95.

A RACE AT BAY: NEW YORK TIMES EDITORIALS ON THE "INDIAN PROBLEM, 1860-1900
Robert G. Hays
304 pp. Southern Illinois University Press, 1997. $39.95.

RACE, DISCOURSE, & THE ORIGIN OF THE AMERICAS, A NEW WORLD VIEW
Vera Lawrence Hyatt & Rex Nettleford
Collection of essays. Photos. 448 pp.
Smithsonian Institution Press, 1994. $29.95.

RACE RELATIONS IN BRITISH NORTH AMERICA, 1607-1783
Bruce Glasrud and Alan Smith
368 pp. Nelson-Hall, Inc., 1982. $27.95.

*RACE WITH THE BUFFALO & OTHER NATIVE AMERICAN STORIES FOR YOUNG READERS
Richard & Judy Young
Grades 4 amd up. Illus. 176 pp. August House, 1993.
$19.95.

RAIN: NATIVE EXPRESSIONS FROM THE AMERICAN SOUTHWEST
Ann Marshall
Photos and textual analysis of cultural objects drawn from the
Heard Museum's extension collections. Illus. 144 pp. Paper.
Museum of New Mexico Press, 2001. $32.50.

*THE RAINBOW BRIDGE: A CHUMASH LEGEND
Tom & Kerry Nechodom
Grades 4 and up. Illus. 32 pp. Paper. Sand River Press, $6.95.

RAINBOW MEDICINE: A VISIONARY GUIDE TO NATIVE AMERICAN SHAMANISM
Wolf Moondance
Teaches self-worth through ancient ceremonies, using ordinary
objects, herbs, and foods. Illus. 192 pp. Paper. Sterling, $12.95.

RAINBOWS OF STONE
Ralph Salisbury
Poems of family tales, tribal history, Cherokee religion.
137 pp. University of Arizona Press, 2000. $16.95.

RAINHOUSE & OCEAN: SPEECHES FOR THE PAPAGO YEAR
Ruth M. Underhill, Donald M. Bahr, et al
Reprint of 1979 edition. Illus. 153 pp. Paper.
University of Arizona Press, $18.95.

THE RAINMAKERS
E.J. Bird
Illus. 150 pp. Lerner, 1993. $19.95.

*RAINY'S POWWOW
Linda Theresa Raczek
Picture book. Ages 5-8. Illus. Northland, $15.95.

*THE RAMILUK STORIES: ADVENTURES OF AN ESKIMO FAMILY IN THE PREHISTORIC ARCTIC
Eugene Vickery
Grades 5 and up. Illus. 125 pp. Stonehaven Publishers,
1989. $16.00; paper, $10.95.

RAMONA
Helen Hunt Jackson : into. by Michael Dorris
Ethical novel of the Native American struggle, and the horror
of the American political past. 384 pp. Paper. Penguin USA,
$3.50.

THE RANGE SITE: ARCHAIC THROUGH LATE WOODLAND OCCUPATIONS
John Kelly, et al
Illus. 480 pp. Paper. University of Illinois Press, 1987. $23.95.

RANGERS & REDCOATS ON THE HUDSON: EXPLORING THE PAST ON ROGERS ISLAND
David S. Starbuck
An account of an archaeological investigation at a major
French & Indian War military encampment. 168 pp. Illus.
Paper. University Press of New England, 2004. $19.95.

RANK & WARFARE AMONG THE PLAINS INDIANS
Bernard Mishkin
Reprint of 1940 edition. 65 pp. Paper.
University of Nebraska Press, $6.95.

THE RAPE OF THE INDIAN LANDS: AN ORIGINAL ANTHOLOGY
Paul Gates and Stuart Bruchey, Editors
Ayer Co., 1978. $23.

THE RAPID CITY INDIAN SCHOOL, 1898-1933
Scott Riney
Illus. Maps. 288 pp. University of Oklahoma Press,
1999. $29.95.

RARE & UNUSUAL ARTIFACTS OF THE FIRST AMERICANS
Ray Parman, Jr.
Illus. 300 pp. Paper. Fred Pruett, 1989. $24.95.

RATIFICATION OF COEUR D'ALENE INDIAN TREATIES
Jerome Peltier
Reprints of government documents telling the tale of the
white man's settlement on Indian's ancestral holdings.
Maps. 117 pp. Paper. Ye Galleon Press, $10.95.

*THE RATTLE & THE DRUM: NATIVE AMERICAN RITUALS & CELEBRATIONS
Lisa Sita
Grades 3-6. Illus. 80 pp. Millbrook Press, 1994. $25.90.

*RAVEN BRINGS TO THE PEOPLE: ANOTHER GIFT:
A STORY BASED ON NATIVE AMERICAN LEGEND
Ann M. Reed
Grades 3 and up. Illus. 18 pp. Tipi Press, 1997. $3.95.

THE RAVEN & THE REDBIRD
A play in three acts of Sam Houston (Raven) and his Cherokee wife (Redbird). 103 pp. Paper. VIP Publishing. $5.95.

THE RAVEN SPEAKS
Raven Hail
Cherokee Indian lore in English with some Cherokee.
Reprint. 192 pp. VIP Publishing. $7.95.

THE RAVEN TALES
Peter Goodchild
Illus. 144 pp. Independent Publishers Group & Chicago
Review Press, 1991. $16.95; paper, $9.95.

RAVEN: A TRICKSTER TALE
FROM THE PACIFIC NORTHWEST
Gerald McDermott
Grades K-3. Illus. Harcourt Brace, 1994. $14.95.

RAVEN'S CRY
Christie Harris; illus. by Bill Reid
Fictionalized retelling of the near destruction of the Haida
Nation. Illus. 196 pp. Paper. University of Washington Press,
$12.95.

RAVEN'S GUIDE TO AIDS PREVENTION RESOURCES
Alaska Native Health Board
Designed to provide infomation & resources available for American Indians and Alaska Natives on AIDS and AIDS prevention.
Includes agencies, programs & servics, books & periodicals,
brochures, videos, posters, and other materials. 42 pp. National Native American AIDS Prevention Center, 1991.

RAVEN'S JOURNEY: THE WORLD
OF ALASKA'S NATIVE PEOPLE
Susan A. Kaplan
Illus. 210 pp. University of Pennsylvania Museum, 1986.
$39.95; paper, $24.95.

RAVEN'S TALES
Raven Hail
Collection of 13 ancient Cherokee legends.
Illus. 49 pp. VIP Publishing. $9.95.

RAVEN'S VILLAGE: THE MYTHS, ARTS, & TRADITIONS OF
NATIVE PEOPLE FROM THE PACIFIC NORTHWEST COAST
Nancy Ruddell
Paper. UBC Press, 1995. $8.95.

RAVENSONG: CHEROKEE INDIAN POETRY
Raven Hail
VIP Publishing. Book, $6.95; tape, $9.95; both, $14.95.

REACHING BOTH WAYS
Helen P. Wolf: Barbara Ketcham, Editor
Illus. 135 pp. Paper. Jelm Mountain, 1989. $9.95.

READERS DIGEST - AMERICA'S
FASCINATING INDIAN HERITAGE
Random House, $30.

READING COMPREHENSION & LANGUAGE
PROFICIENCY AMONG ESKIMO CHILDREN
Virginia Streiff; Francesco Cordasco, Editor
Ayer Co., 1978. $30.

READING THE FIRE: THE TRADITIONAL
INDIAN LITERATURES OF AMERICA
Jarold Ramsey
250 pp. Paper. University of Washington Press. $19.95.

READING THE VOICE: NATIVE AMERICAN
ORAL POETRY ON THE WRITTEN PAGE
Paul Zolbrod
Explores Native American oral poetics. University of Utah Press,
1995. $25.

READINGS IN AMERICAN INDIAN LAW:
RECALLING THE RHYTHM OF SURVIVAL
Jo Carillo, Editor
304 pp. Temple University Press, 1998. $69.95; paper, 29.95.

READING & WRITING THE LAKOTA LANGUAGE
Albert White Hat, Sr.; edited by Jael Kampfe
The effect of language on both cultural deterioration and survival. University of Utah Press, 1998. $50; paper, $24.95. 2
cassettes, $12.95; paperback & cassettes, $34.95.

READINGS ON JAMES BAY
Articles on the hydroelectric projects planned for the James
Bay region of northern Canada where Cree people live.
Akwe;kon Press, $8.

"REAL" INDIANS & OTHERS: MIXED-BLOOD URBAN
NATIVE PEOPLES & INDIGENOUS NATIONHOOD
by Bonita Lawrence
Interviews Canadian mixed-blood, urban Natives from Toronto
and reveals the ways in which they understand their identities

and their struggle to survive. 320 pp. University of
Nebraska Press, 2004. $55; paper, $29.95.

THE REAL ROSEBUD: THE TRIUMPH
OF A LAKOTA WOMAN
Marjorie Weinberg; foreword by Luke Yellow Robe
Illus. 128 pp. University of Nebraska Press, 2004. $19.95.

REBELLION FROM THE ROOTS:
INDIAN UPRISING IN CHIAPAS
John Ross
250 pp. Common Courage Press, 1994.
$29.95; paper, $14.95.

REBIRTH OF THE BLACKFEET NATION, 1912-1954
Paul C. Rosier
Maps. 346 pp. University of Nebraska Press, 2001. $65.

REBIRTH: POLITICAL, ECONOMIC &
SOCIAL DEVELOPMENT IN FIRST NATIONS
Anne-Marie Mawhiney
11 papers published from the 1992 INORD Conference giving
voice to stories about the ways in which First Nations are addressing their own conditions. 256 pp. Paper. University of
Toronto Press, 1993. $18.

RECENT LEGAL ISSUES FOR AMERICAN INDIANS,
1968 TO THE PRESENT
John R. Wunder
Reprint. 344 pp. Garland, $77.

RECENTLY DISCOVERED TALES
OF LIFE AMONG THE INDIANS
James Willard Schultz; Warren L. Hanna, Editor
Collection of stories from Schultz's earliest writings from
1880 to 1894. Illus. 152 pp. Paper. Mountain Press, $10.

RECLAIMING THE VISION: PAST, PRESENT & FUTURE:
NATIVE VOICES FOR THE EIGHTH GENERATION
Lee Francis & James Bruchac, Editors
Illus. 120 pp. Paper. Greenfield Review, 1996. $15.95.

RECKONING WITH THE DEAD, THE LARSEN BAY
REPATRIATION & THE SMITHSONIAN INSTITUTION
Tamara L. Bray & Thomas W. Killion, Editor
Presents the Larsen Baym Alaska, repatriation request of the
Smithsonian. Illus. 352 pp. Paper. Smithsonian Institution Press,
1994. $34.95.

RECONSTRUCTING 18TH CENTURY NAVAJO
POPULATION DYNAMICS IN THE DINETAH
Ronald H. Towner & Byron P. Johnson
Archaeological and Deendrochronological Investigations in
San Rafael Canyon. 150 pp. Paper. University of Arizona Press,
1998. $15.95.

RECONSTRUCTION IN INDIAN TERRITORY
M. Thomas Bailey
A story of avarice, discrimination, and opportunism.
Associated Faculty Press, 1972. $23.95.

RECOVERING THE WORD: ESSAYS
ON NATIVE AMERICAN LITERATURE
Brian Swann & Arnold Krupat, Editors
600 pp. University of California Press, 1987.
$60.00; paper, $17.95.

RED BROTHER
R. Ray Baker
Reprint of 1927 edition. Paper. George Wahr
Publishing, $12.50.

RED CAPITALISM: AN ANALYSIS
OF THE NAVAJO ECONOMY
Larry Galbreath
150 pp. Paper. Books on Deamnd, 1973. $41.80.

RED CHILDREN IN WHITE AMERICA
Ann H. Beuf
168 pp. University of Pennsylvania Press, 1977. $19.95.

*RED CLAY: POEMS AND STORIES
Linda Hogan
Traditional Chickasaw poems and stories.
Grades 7 and up. Paper. Oyate, 1991. $9.95.

RED CLOUD: PHOTOGRAPHS OF A LAKOTA CHIEF
Frank H. Goodyear, III
Illus. Map. 224 pp. University of Nebraska Press, 2003.
$35.

RED CLOUD: WARRIOR STATESMAN
OF THE LAKOTA SIOUX
Robert W. Larson
Biography. Illus. Map. 336 pp. Paper.
University of Oklahoma Press, 1997. $19.95.

RED CLOUD & THE SIOUX PROBLEM
James Olson
Illus. Maps. 400 pp. Paper. University of Nebraska Press,
1965. $12.50.

RED CLOUD'S FOLK: A HISTORY
OF THE OGLALA SIOUX INDIANS
George E. Hyde
Reprint of revised 1957 edition. Illus. 362 pp. Paper.
University of Oklahoma Press, $16.95.

RED CROW: WARRIOR CHIEF
Hugh A. Dempsey
Illus. 256 pp. University of Nebraska Press, 1980. $21.95.

RED EARTH, WHITE LIES: NATIVE AMERICANS
& THE MYTH OF SCIENTIFIC FACT
Vine Deloria, Jr.
On the conflict between mainstream scientific theory about the
world and the ancestral worldview of Native Americans. 288
pp. Paper. Fulcrum Publishing & Clear Light, $16.95.

RED FOX: BRIG.-GENERAL STAND WATIE'S
CIVIL WAR YEARS IN INDIAN TERRITORY
Wilfred Knight
Watie was the last Confederate General in the Civil War to
surrender. He and his Indian troops fought unsung battles in
Indian Territory throughout the war. Illus. Map. Biblio. 320 pp.
The Arthur H. Clark Co., $27.50.

*RED FROG MAN: A HOHOKAM LEADER
Charles Fellers; Maxine Hughes, Editor
Grades 1-6. Illus. 64 pp. Paper. Laughing Fox, 1990. $6.95.

*RED HAWK & THE SKY SISTERS: A SHAWNEE LEGEND
Terri Cohlene
Grades 1-5. Illus. Paper. Troll Associates, 1992. $4.95.

*RED HAWK'S ACCOUNT OF CUSTER'S LAST BATTLE
Paul Goble
Grades 4 and up. Illus. 64 pp. Paper. University of Nebraksa
Press, 1992. $9.95

RED-HEADED RENEGADE —
CHIEF BENGE OF THE CHEROKEE NATION
Clara Talton Fugate
Illus. Paper. Pocahontas Press, 1994.

RED JACKET & HIS PEOPLE
J.M. Hubbard
Reprint of Col. Wm. Stone's The Life & Times of Red Jacket.
356 pp. paper. Library Research Associates, $24.50

RED JACKET: IROQUOIS DIPLOMAT & ORATOR
Christopher Densmore
Biography. Includes his speeches. Illus. Maps. Biblio.
176 pp. Syracuse University Press, 1998. $34.95;
paper, $16.95.

RED JACKET: SENECA CHIEF
Arthur Caswell Parker
Illus. Maps. 228 pp. Paper. University of Nebraska Press,
1998. $10.

THE RED KING'S REBELLION:
RACIAL POLITICS IN NEW ENGLAND, 1675-1677
Russell Bourne
Illus. 304 pp. Paper. Oxford University Press, 1991. $12.95.

RED LAKE COURT OF INDIAN OFFENES:
MANAGEMENT AUDIT
52 pp. National Center for State Courts, 1982. Manuscript, $3.12

RED LAKE COURT OF TRIBAL
OFFENSES COURT MANUAL
450 pp. National Center for State Courts, 1982.

RED LAKE NATION: PORTRAITS OF OJIBWAY LIFE
Charles Brill
Illus. 192 pp. University of Minnesota Press, 1992. $24.95.

RED MAN IN THE U.S.
G. Lindquist
Reprint of 1923 edition. Illus. 487 pp. Augustus M. Kelley, $45.

RED MAN'S AMERICA: A HISTORY
OF INDIANS IN THE U.S.
Ruth Underhill
Revised edition. Illus. Maps. 398 pp. Paper.
University of Chicago Press, 1971. $18.95.

RED MAN'S LAND - WHITE MAN'S LAW: THE PAST
& PRESENT STATUS OF THE AMERICAN INDIAN
Wilcomb E. Washburn
Provides a clear discussion of the legal history of Indian-white
relations. 2nd edition. Illus. 314 pp. Paper. University of Okla-
homa Press, 1995. $21.95.

RED MAN'S RELIGION: BELIEFS & PRACTICES
OF THE INDIANS NORTH OF MEXICO
Ruth Underhill
Illus. Maps. 350 pp. Paper. University of Chicago Press,
1965. $17.

RED MEN IN RED SQUARE
Bud Smith & Chief Big Eagle
Story of Chief Big Eagle of the Golden Hill Tribe of Connecticut
(Quarter-Acre of Heartache, 1985) and his travel to Russia and

discovery of the Indianists-Soviet citizens who study the ways, crafts, and religion of Native American tribes. Illus. Pocahontas Press, 1994. $21.95; paper, $16.95.

RED OVER BLACK: BLACK SLAVERY AMONG THE CHEROKEE INDIANS
R. Halliburton, Jr.
Illus. Greenwood Press, 1977. $35.

RED POWER: THE AMERICAN INDIANS' FIGHT FOR FREEDOM
Alvin M. Josephy, Jr., Joane Nagel & Troy Johnson, Editors
Documentary history of the American Indian activist movement. 2nd Edition. Illus. 300 pp. University of Nebraska Press, 1999. $50; paper, $16.95.

*RED POWER ON THE RIO GRANDE
Franklin Folsom
Pueblo Indian uprising of 1680 against Spanish control in the Southwest. Grades 9 and up. 144 pp. Council on Indian Education, 1989. $12.95; paper, $9.95.

THE RED RECORD: THE OLDEST NATIVE NORTH AMERICAN HISTORY
David McCutchen
Illus. 240 pp. Paper. Avery Publishing, 1992. $14.95.

*RED RIBBONS FOR EMMA
Grades 3-12. Illus. 48 pp. New Seed Press, 1981. $12.

THE RED SWAN: MYTHS & TALES OF THE AMERICAN INDIANS
John Bierhorst, Translator
Reprint of 1976 edition. 386 pp. Paper. University of New Mexico Press, $15.95.

RED, WHITE & BLACK: SYMPOSIUM ON INDIANS IN THE OLD SOUTH
Charles Hudson
Paper. University of Georgia Press, 1971. $8.

RED & WHITE: INDIAN VIEWS OF THE WHITE MAN, 1492-1982
Annette Rosensteil
Illus. 192 pp. Universe Books, 1983. $14.95.

REDSKINS, RUFFLESHIRTS, & REDNECKS: INDIAN ALLOTMENTS IN ALABAMA & MISSISSIPPI, 1830-1860
Mary Elizabeth Young
Illus. Maps. 234 pp. University of Oklahoma Press, 2002. $19.95.

THE GEORGE REEVES SITE: LATE ARCHAIC, LATE WOODLAND, EMERGENT MISSISSIPPIAN, & MISSISSIPPIAN COMPONENTS
Dale McElrath & Fred Finney
Illus. 464 pp. Paper. University of Illinois Press, 1987. $22.95.

REFERENCE LIBRARY OF NATIVE NORTH AMERICA, 4 Vols.
Duane Champagne, Editor
1,920 pp. The Gale Group, 1993. $179.

REFLECTIONS OF THE WEAVER'S WORLD: THE GLORIA F. ROSS COLLECTION OF CONTEMPORARY NAVAJO WEAVING
Ann Lund Hedlund
Illustrates the Denver Art Museum's permanent collection of contemporary Navajo weaving. Illus. 112 pp. Paper. University of Washington Press, $29.95.

REFLECTIONS ON THE ALASKA NATIVE EXPERIENCE: SELECTED ARTICLES/SPEECHES BY ROY M. HUHNDORF
Roy M. Huhndorf
21 selections from a series of articles written by Huhndorf, President of Cook Inlet Region, Inc., for the editorial section of the *Anchorage Times* during the period of 1981 through 1984. 61 pp. CIRI, 1991. No charge.

REFLECTIONS ON NATIVE-NEWCOMER RELATIONS: SELECTED ESSAYS
J.R. Miller
12 essays on First Nations & Metis relationships with newcomers in Canada over the decades. Illus. 320 pp. University of Toronto Press, 2004. $65; paper, $27.95.

REGULARS IN THE REDWOODS: THE U.S. ARMY IN NORTHERN CALIFORNIA, 1852-1861
William F. Strobridge
The clash between settlers and Indians during California's early statehood. Detailed account of the Regular Army's attempts to maintain peace.Illus. Map. Biblio. 283 pp. The Arthur H. Clark Co., $29.95.

BILL REID & BEYOND: EXPANDING ON MODERN NATIVE ART
edited by Karen Duffek & Charlotte Townsend-Gault
Haida art & tradition. 19 contributors write from many perspectives. Illus. 280 pp. University of Washington Press, 2004. $35.

RELIGION & HOPI LIFE IN THE 20TH CENTURY
John D. Loftin
195 pp. Indiana University Press, 1991. $22.95; paper, $8.95.

RELIGION IN NATIVE NORTH AMERICAN
Christopher Vecsey
Illus. 210 pp. Paper. University of Idaho Press, 1990. $22.95.

THE RELIGIONS OF THE AMERICAN INDIANS
Ake Hultkrantz
Paper. University of California Press, 1979. $17.95.

RELIGIOUS MEDICINE: THE HISTORY & EVOLUTION OF INDIAN MEDICINE
Kenneth G. Zysk
340 pp. Transaction Press, 1992. $49.95.

*REMEMBER MY NAME
Sara H. Banks
Deals with the Cherokee Indian Removal of 1838. An 11-year-old Cherokee, Annie Rising Fawn, shows courage and an adventurous spirit. Grades 4 to 9. Illus. 120 pp. Paper. Council for Indian Education & Roberts Rinehart, 1994. $8.95.

REMEMBER NATIVE AMERICA! THE EARTHWORKS OF ANCIENT AMERICA
Richard Balthazar
Documents and illustrates Indian mounds and other earthworks from 23 states. Paper. Five Flower Press, 1993. $14.95.

REMEMBER YOUR RELATIONS: ELSIE ALLEN BASKETS, FAMILY & FRIENDS
Suzanne Abel-Vidor, Dot Brovarney, Susan Billy
Pomo Indian basketry. Full-color photos. 128 pp. Paper. Heyday Books, 1997. $20.

REMEMBER YOUR RELATIVES, YANKTON SIOUX IMAGES, Vol. 1, 1851-1904; Vol. 2, 1865-1915
Renee Sansom-Flood, et al
Illus. Vol. 1, 55 pp.; Vol. 2, 150 pp. Paper. Yankton Sioux Tribe, 1985 & 1989. $8.50 each.

FREDERICK REMINGTON: ARTIST OF THE AMERICAN WEST
Nancy Plain
Silver Burdett, 1999.

REMINGTON & RUSSELL: THE SID RICHARDSON COLLECTION
Brian W. Dippie, Editor
Revised edition. Illus. 240 pp. University of Texas Press, 1994. $70; paper, $34.95.

REMOVAL AFTERSHOCK: THE SEMINOLES' STRUGGLES TO SURVIVE IN THE WEST, 1836-1866
Jane F. lancaster
Illus. 248 pp. University of Tennessee Press, 1994. $32; paper, $16.

REMOVAL OF THE CHEROKEE INDIANS FROM GEORGIA
W. Lumpkin
Reprint of 1907 edition. Ayer Co., $45.50.

THE REMOVAL OF THE CHEROKEE NATION: MANIFEST DESTINY OF NATIOAL DISHONOR
Louis Filler and Allen Guttman, Editors
Reprint of 1962 edition. 128 pp. Paper. Krieger Publishing, $9.50; paper, $7.50.

THE REMOVAL OF THE CHOCTAW INDIANS
Arthur H. DeRosier, Jr.
An accurate account of a major Indian removal with the policies, treaties and agonies that were a part of it. Illus. 210 pp. Paper. Cherokee Publications, $9.95.

REMOVALS: 19TH CENTURY AMERICAN LITERATURE & THE POLITICS OF INDIAN AFFAIRS
Lucy Maddox
216 pp. Oxford Unviersity Press, 1991. $55.

RENEGADE TRIBE: THE PALOUSE INDIANS & THEIR INVASION OF THE INLAND PACIFIC NORTHWEST
Clifford Trafzer & Richard Scheuerman, Editor
Illus. Maps. Biblio. 224 pp. Paper. Washington State University Press, 1986. $17.95.

RENEWING THE WORLD: PLAINS INDIAN RELIGION & MORALITY
Howard L. Harrod
213 pp. Paper. University of Arizona Press, 1987. $19.95.

REPATRIATION READER: WHO OWNS AMERICAN INDIAN REMAINS?
Devon A. Mihesuah
Anthology focusing on issues of repatriation of American Indian remains and artifacts. Illus. 328 pp. Paper. University of Nebraska Press, 2000. $20.

REPORT OF THE BIAS CONSOLIDATED HOUSING INVENTORY
Housing Assistance Council Staff
27 pp. Housing Assistance Council, 1992. $4.50.

REPORT OF CHARLES A. WETMORE, SPECIAL U.S. COMMISSIONER OF MISSION INDIANS OF SOUTHERN CALIFORNIA
Norman Tanis, Editor
Paper. California State University, Northridge, 1977. $10.

REPORT OF THE COMMISSIONER OF INDIAN AFFAIRS FOR THE TERRITORIES OF WASHINGTON, IDAHO & OREGON, 1870
75 pp. Ye Galleon, 1981. $12.

REPORT OF THE MOUND EXPLORATIONS OF THE BUREAU OF ETHNOLOGY
Cyrus Thomas
Reprint of 1894 ed. Illus. 786 pp. Paper. Smithsonian Books, $29.95.

REPORT ON INDIAN MISSIONS
Pierre-Jean DeSmet
Potawatomi Indian missionary material. 67 pp. Ye Galleon, 1985. $14.95.

REPORT TO THE SECRETARY OF WAR OF THE U.S., ON INDIAN AFFAIRS
J. Morse
Reprint of 1822 edition. Illus. 400 pp. Augustus M. Kelley, $45.

REPOSSESSION AND YOU
Institute for the Development of Indian Law, $3.50.

RESEARCH & WRITING TRIBAL HISTORIES
Dr. Duane Hale.
Text. Michigan Indian Press.

THE RESERVATION
Ted C. Williams
Tales of life on the Tuscarora Indian Reservation in New York State, from the late 1930's to the 1950's. Illus. 256 pp. Paper. Syracuse University Press, 1976. $15.95.

THE RESERVATION BLACKFEET, 1885-1945: A PHOTOGRAPHIC HISTORY OF CULTURAL SURVIVAL
William E. Farr
Illus. 240 pp. Paper. University of Washington Press, 1984. $19.95.

RESERVATION TO CITY: INDIAN URBANIZATION & FEDERAL RELOCATION
Elaine M. Neils
200 pp. Paper. University of Chicago, Department of Geography, 1971. $12.

RESERVE MEMORIES: THE POWER OF THE PAST IN A CHILCOTIN COMMUNITY
David W. Dinwoodie
Examines a Northern Athabaskan community. Map. 120 pp. University of Nebraska Press, 2002. $39.95.

RESOURCE READING LIST
Canadian Alliance in Solidarity with Native People
Bibliography of books by and about Native peoples. Paper. Greenfield Review Press, $15.

RESOURCES FOR AMERICAN INDIAN REHABILITATION
T.C. Thomason, Editor
100 pp. paper. Northern Arizona University, 1995.

RESPECT FOR LIFE: THE TRADITIONAL UPBRINGING OF AMERICAN INDIAN CHILDREN
S.M. Morey and O.L. Gilliam, Editors
Illus. 202 pp. Paper. Myrin Institute, 1974. $4.95.

RESTITUTION: THE LAND CLAIM CASES OF THE MASHPEE, PASSAMAQUODDY & PENOBSCOT INDIANS OF NEW ENGLAND
Paul Brodeur
Illus. 160 pp. New England University Press, 1985. $21.95; paper, $9.95.

RESTORING BALANCE: COMMUNITY-DIRECTED HEALTH PROMOTION FOR AMERICAN INDIANS & NATIVE ALASKANS
Beth Howard-Pitney, et al
Illus. 131 pp. Paper. Stanford CRDP, 1992. $15.

RETAINED BY THE PEOPLE: A HISTORY OF AMERICAN INDIANS & THE BILL OF RIGHTS
John R. Wunder
Illus. 312 pp. Paper. Oxford University Press, 1994. $21.95.

RETHINKING AMERICAN INDIAN HISTORY
Donald L. Fixico
149 pp. University of New Mexico Press, 1999. $39.95; paper, $21.95.

RETHINKING HOPI ETHNOGRAPHY
Peter M. Whitely
Photos. Maps. 288 pp. Paper. Smithsonian Institution Press, 1998. $18.95.

THE RETURN OF CHIEF BLACK FOOT
Victoria Mauricio
Illus. 140 pp. Paper. Donning Co., 1981. $5.95.

RETURN OF THE INDIAN:
CONQUEST & REVIVAL IN THE AMERICAS
Phillip Wearne
Chronicles the indigenous resistance in Latin and North America.Illus. 240 pp. Temple University Press, 1996. $19.95.

*RETURN OF THE INDIAN SPIRIT
Vinson Brown
Grades 4 and up. A young Indian boy's coming of age through the beliefs and ways of his people. Illus. 60 pp. Paper. Cherokee Publications, $5.95.

THE RETURN OF LITTLE BIG MAN: A NOVEL
Thomas Berger
448 pp. Little, Brown & Co., $25; paper, $12.95.

THE RETURN OF THE NATIVE:
AMERICAN INDIAN POLITICAL RESURGENCE
Stephen E. Cornell
Illus. 288 pp. Paper. Oxford University Press, 1988. $12.95.

RETURN OF THE SUN: TALES FROM
THE NORTHEASTERN WOODLANDS
Joseph Bruchac
Varies tales illustrating both the wealth of humor and depth of respect for life and earth of the indigenous Northeast American people. Illus. Paper. Crossing Press, $12.95. Written Heritage, $9.95.

RETURN OF THE THUNDERBEINGS
Donn Le Vie, Jr. & Iron Thunderhorse
Illus. 288 pp. Paper. Bear & Co., 1990. $14.95.

RETURN TO CREATION: A SURVIVAL
MANUAL FOR NATIVE & NATURAL PEOPLE
Medicine Story, pseud.
Illus. 210 pp. Paper. Bear Tribe, 1991. $9.95.

RETURNING THE GIFT: POETRY & PROSE FROM THE
FIRST NORTH AMERICAN NATIVE WRITERS' FESTIVAL
Joseph Bruchac, Editor
A collection of submissions by 92 writers at the "Returning the Gift Festival" held in 1992. Bruchac comments on the current state of Native literature. 369 pp. Paper. University of Arizona Press, 1994. $20.95.

REVENGE OF THE PEQUOTS: HOW A SMALL
NATIVE AMERICAN TRIBE CREATED THE WORLD'S
MOST PROFITABLE CASINO
Kim Isaac Eisler
Illus. 267 pp. Paper. University of Nebraska Press, 2002. $13.95.

REVENGE OF THE WINDIGO: THE CONSTRUCTION OF
THE MIND & MENTAL HEALTH OF NORTH AMERICAN
ABORIGINAL PEOPLES
James B. Waldram
The study of Aboriginal mental health. 240 pp. University of Toronto Press, 2004. $45; paper, $24.95.

REVITALIZING COMMUNITIES: INNOVATIVE STATE &
LOCAL PROGRAMS
Kellie J. Dressler, Editor
Illus. 149 pp. Paper. Diane Publishing, 1998. $30.

THE RICHEY CLOVIS CACHE: EARLIEST
AMERICANS ALONG THE COLUMBIA RIVER
Richard M. Gramly
Illus. 70 pp. Paper. Persimmon Press, $12.95.

JOHN ROLLIN RIDGE: HIS LIFE & WORKS
James W. Parins
Paper edition of the 1991 hardcover. Illus. 280 pp. University of Nebraska Press, 2004. $22.

RIDING BUFFALOES & BRONCOS: RODEO & NATIVE
TRADITIONS IN THE NORTHERN GREAT PLAINS
Allison Fuss Mellis
Examines events where American Indians gather to celebrate community and equestrian skills. Illus. Maps. 288 pp. University of Oklahoma Press, 2003. $34.95.

*RIEL'S PEOPLE: HOW THE METIS LIVED
Maria Campbell
Grades 5 and up. Paper. Salem House, $6.95.

RIFLES, BLANKETS & BEADS: IDENTITY, HISTORY,
AND THE NORTHERN ATHAPASKAN POTLATCH
William E. Simeone
Illus. Maps. Biblio. 216 pp. Paper. University of Oklahoma Press, 1995. $19.95.

*RIGHT AFTER SUNDOWN:
TEACHING STORIES OF THE NAVAJO
Marilyne Virginia Mabery; Raymond Johnson, Illustrator
12 short stories. Grades 4 and up. Paper. Dine College Press, 1991. $14.95.

THE RIGHTS OF INDIANS & TRIBES: THE BASIC
ACLU GUIDE TO THE INDIAN & TRIBAL RIGHTS
Stephen L. Pevar
2nd revised edition. 335 pp. Paper. Southern Illinois University Press, 1991. Also available from The Falmouth Institute. $14.95

THE RIGHTS OF INDIGENOUS PEOPLES
Lawrence Rosen
Oxford University Press, 2005.

*THE RINGS ON WOOT-KEW'S TAIL: INDIAN LEGENDS
OF THE ORIGIN OF THE SUN, MOON & STARS
Will Gerber, et al
Grades 3-9. Paper. Council for Indian Education, 1973. $1.95.

RIO DEL NORTE: PEOPLE OF THE UPPER RIO GRANDE
FROM EARLIEST TIMES TO THE PUEBLO REVOLT
Carroll L. Riley
Illus. Maps. Paper. University of Utah Press. $15.95.

RISE & FALL OF THE CHOCTAW REPUBLIC
Angie Debo
Reprint of 1934 edition. 2nd Edition. Illus. Maps. Biblio. 314 pp. Paper. University of Oklahoma Press, 1995. $19.95.

*RISING FAWN & THE FIRE MYSTERY
Marilou Awiakta
Story about the Trail of Tears. Grades 4 and up. Illus. Paper. St. Luke's Press, 1984. $6.95.

RITUAL & MYTH IN ODAWA REVITALIZATION:
RECLAIMING A SOVEREIGN PLACE
Melissa A. Pflug
Illus. Biblio. 304 pp. University of Oklahoma Press, 1998. $28.95.

RITUAL IN PUEBLO ART: HOPI LIFE IN HOPI PAINTING
Byron Harvey, III
Illus. 265 pp. Paper. National Museum of the American Indian, 1970. $10.

THE RIVER & THE HORSEMEN:
A NOVEL OF THE LITTLE BIGHORN
Robert Skimin
The story (part fiction, part fact) of Custer, Sitting Bull, and the Battle of the Little Bighorn. 384 pp. Herodias, 1999. $26.

RIVER OF SORROWS - LIFE HISTORY
OF THE MAIDU-NISENAN INDIANS
Richard Burrill
Historical fiction reveals their lifeways. Illus. Photos. Maps. 192 pp. Paper. Naturegraph, 1978. $8.95.

RIVER OF TEARS
Maud Emery
The events of the massacre at Bute Inlet. Illus. 96 pp. Paper. Hancock House, 1994. $9.95.

*RIVERMAN
Gail Stewart
Grades 3-8. Illus. 32 pp. Rourke Corp., 1990. $17.26.

THE ROAD: INDIAN TRIBES & POLITICAL LIBERTY
Russell Barsh & James Henderson
Paper. University of California Press, 1979. $15.

THE ROAD OF LIFE & DEATH: A RITUAL
DRAMA OF THE AMERICAN INDIANS
Paul Radin
Reprint. 368 pp. Paper. Princeton University Press, $14.95.

THE ROAD ON WHICH WE CAME:
A HISTORY OF THE WESTERN SHOSHONE
Steven J. Crum
Illus. Paper. University of Utah Press, 1993. $19.95.

THE ROAD TO DISAPPEARANCE:
A HISTORY OF THE CREEK INDIANS
Angie Debo
Reprint of 1941 edition. Illus. 400 pp. Paper. University of Oklahoma Press, 2002. $21.95.

THE ROAD TO LAME DEER
Jerry Mader
Memoir. Little Big Horn, Wounded Knee, cultural survival and modern Cheyenne life. Illus. 216 pp. University of Nebraska Press, 2002. $25.

THE ROAD TO NUNAVUT: THE PROGRESS OF THE EAST-
ERN ARCTIC INUIT SINCE THE SECOND WORLD WAR
R. Quinn Duffy
376 pp. University of Toronto Press, 1987. $35.

THE ROAD TO THE SUNDANCE: MY JOURNEY INTO
NATIVE SPIRITUALITY
Manny Twofeathers
240 pp. Paper. Little, Brown & Clear Light 1997. $11.45.

A ROAD WE DO NOT KNOW: A NOVEL
OF CUSTER AT THE LITTLE BIGHORN
Frederick Chiaventone
Paper. University of New Mexico Press, $15.95.

THE ROADS OF MY RELATIONS
Devon A. Mihesuah
19th century Choctaw family forced from Mississippi to Oklahoma. 237 pp. University of Arizona Press, 2000. $36; paper, $17.95.

ROADS TO CENTER PLACE: AN ANASAZI ATLAS
Kathryn Gabriel
Illus. 250 pp. Paper. Johnson Books, 1991. $12.95.

ROADSIDE HISTORY OF ARIZONA
Marshall Trimble
Illus. Maps. Photos. 496 pp. Mountain Press, 1994. $30; paper, $18.

ROADSIDE HISTORY OF ARKANSAS
Alan C. Paulson
Illus. Maps. Photos. 480 pp. Mountain Press, 1995. $30; paper, $18.

ROADSIDE HISTORY OF NEBRASKA
Candy Moullton
Illus. Maps. Photos. 450 pp. Mountain Press, 1997. $30; paper, $18.

ROADSIDE HISTORY OF NEW MEXICO
Francis L. & Roberta Fugate
Illus. Maps. Photos. 484 pp. Mountain Press, 1990. $24.95; paper, $16.

ROADSIDE HISTORY OF OKLAHOMA
Francis L. & Robert B. Fugate
Tales of early explorers. Illus. 472 pp. Mountain Press, 1990. $24.95; paper, $15.95.

ROADSIDE HISTORY OF OREGON
Bill Gulick
Illus. Maps. Photos. 452 pp. Paper. Mountain Press, 1993. $18.

ROADSIDE HISTORY OF SOUTH DAKOTA
Linda Hasslestrom
Illus. Maps. Photos. 480 pp. Mountain Press, 1995. $25; paper, $16.

ROADSIDE HISTORY OF WYOMING
Candy Moullton
Illus. 480 pp. Mountain Press, 1990. $24.95; paper, $15.95.

THE ROARING OF THE SACRED RIVER
Steven Foster with Meredith Little
The wilderness quest for vision and self-healing. Illus. 240 pp. Paper. Prentice Hall Press, $9.95.

ROBERT DAVIDSON: EAGLE OF THE DAWN
Ian Thorn, Editor
On the works of Davidson, master carver of masks and totems, print maker, painter, and jeweler. Illus. 192 pp. University of Washington Press, $50.

ROBES OF SPLENDOR: NATIVE NORTH
AMERICAN PAINTED BUFFALO HIDES
George P. Horse Capture, Anne Vitart & Michael Waldberger
Native American life & artworks. 70 color & bxw photos. 144 pp. Paper. W.W. Norton & Co., $20.

ROCK ART IN NEW MEXICO
Polly Schaafsma
Explores prehistoric rock art of the Anasazi, rock art of the Navajo, the desert peoples of southern New Mexico. Illus. 168 pp. Paper. Museum of New Mexico Press, 2000. $29.95.

ROCK ART OF THE AMERICAN INDIAN
Campbell Grant
Illus. 192 pp. Paper. Outbooks, 1972. $16.95.

ROCK ART OF THE AMERICAN SOUTHWEST
Scott Thybony; photos by Fred Hirschmann
100 color photos of rock art throughout the Southwest. 128 pp. Graphic Arts Center, 1994. $29.50.

ROCK ART OF KENTUCKY
Coy, et al
About 60 petroglyph sites are located and described. Photos. 174 pp. Hothem House, 1997. $34.95.

THE ROCK ART OF TEXAS INDIANS
W.W. Newcomb, Jr.
Paintings by Forrest Kirkland. Illus. University of Texas Press, 1995. $70; paper, $34.95.

THE ROCK ART OF UTAH
Polly Schaafsma
Illus. Paper. University of Utah Press, 1976. $19.95.

ROCK ART OF WESTERN SOUTH DAKOTA
James D. Keyser & linea Sundstrom
An illustrated compendium of prehistoric petroglyphs and pictographs found in caves and on canyon walls throughout western South Dakota. 220 pp. Paper. Center for Western Studies, $9.95.

ROCK, GHOST, WILLOW, DEER: A STORY OF SURVIVAL
Allison Adelle Hedge Coke
Memoir/narrative. Photos. 184 pp.University of Nebraska Press, 2004. $24.95.

ROCK ISLAND: HISTORICAL INDIAN ARCHAEOLOGY IN THE NORTHERN LAKE MICHIGAN BASIN
Ronald Mason
Illus. 275 pp. Paper. Kent State University Press, 1986. $19.95.

ROCK PAINTINGS OF THE CHUMASH
Campbell Grant
Chumash history and culture as well as their rock paintings. Illus. Photos. 186 pp. EZ Nature Books. $35.

THE ROCKS BEGIN TO SPEAK
LaVan Martineau
Illus. 210 pp. K C Publications, 1973. $17.50.

ROCKY MOUNTAIN WEST IN 1867
Louis Simonin; translated by Wilson Clough
Illus. University of Nebraska Press, 1966. $16.95.

*WILL ROGERS
Jane A. Schott
Grades 1-3. Illus. Color photos. 64 pp. Lerner, 1996. $14.95; paper, $5.95.

*WILL ROGERS: AMERICAN HUMORIST
Grades 2-4. Illus. 32 pp. Childrens Press, $10.95.

THE ROGUE RIVER INDIAN WAR & ITS AFTERMATH, 1850-1980
E.A. Schwartz
History of the native peoples of western Oregon. Illus. Maps. 354 pp. University of Oklahoma Press, 1997. $34.95.

*THE ROLLING HEAD: CHEYENNE TALES
Henry Tall Bull and Tom Weist
Grades 3-9. Paper. Council for Indian Education, 1971. $1.95.

ROLLING THUNDER SPEAKS: A MESSAGE FOR TURTLE ISLAND
Rolling Thunder; edited by Carmen Sun Rising Pope
Summation of his teaching in own words. 12 photos. 266 pp. Paper. Clear Light, $14.95.

ROLLING THUNDER: A PERSONAL EXPLORATION INTO THE SECRET HEALING POWER OF AN AMERICAN INDIAN MEDICINE MAN
Doug Boyd
273 pp. Paper. Dell, 1974. $9.95.

THEODORE ROOSEVELT & SIX FRIENDS OF THE INDIAN
William T. Hagan
Illus. 274 pp. University of Oklahoma Press, 1997. $25.95.

ROOTED LIKE THE ASH TREES
Richard Carlson, Editor
Collection of writings by members of New England tribes: the Micmac & Penobscot from Maine, the Paugusset of Connecticut, and the Abenakis of Vermont. Paper. Eagle Wing Press, $5.

THE ROOTS OF DEPENDENCY: SUBSISTENCE, ENVIRONMENT, & SOCIAL CHANGE AMONG THE CHOCTAWS, PAWNEES, & NAVAJOS
Richard White
Illus. Maps. 433 pp. Paper. University of Nebraska Press, 1983. $35.

ROOTS OF OPPRESSION: THE AMERICAN INDIAN QUESTION
Steve Talbot
240 pp. International Publishing Co., 1981. $14; paper, $5.25.

ROOTS OF RESISTANCE: LAND TENURE IN NEW MEXICO (1680-1980)
Roxanne Dunbar Ortiz
A socio-economic interpretation of the history of northern New Mexico focusing on land tenure patterns & changes. 202 pp. The Falmouth Institute, 1980. $15; paper, $8.

ROOTS OF SURVIVAL: NATIVE AMERICAN STORYTELLING & THE SACRED
Joseph Bruchac
Focuses on the relationship of Native traditions to contemporary life. Author traces his own spiritual journey. 224 pp. Fulcrum Publishing, 1997. $24.95.

THE ROOTS OF TICASUK: AN ESKIMO WOMAN'S FAMILY STORY
Emily I. Brown
Illus. Photos. Map. 120 pp. Paper. Alaska Northwest Publishing, 1981. $9.95.

ESTHER ROSS, STILLAGUAMISH CHAMPION
Robert H. Ruby, John A. Brown
Illus. 352 pp. University of Oklahoma Press, 2003. $29.95.

*THE ROUGH-FACE GIRL
Rafe Martin; illus. by David Shannon
An Algonquin tale. Grades PS-3. Illus. 32 pp. Putnam Publishing, 1992. $15.95.

RUGS & POSTS: THE STORY OF NAVAJO WEAVING & THE ROLE OF THE INDIAN TRADER
H.L James
Illus. Maps. 160 pp. Paper. Schiffer, 1988. $19.95.

RUINS & RIVALS: THE MAKING OF SOUTHWEST ARCHAEOLOGY
James E. Snead
Illus. 226 pp. Paper. University of Arizona Press, 2004. $17.95.

*RUNNING EAGLE: WOMAN WARRIOR OF THE BLACKFEET
James W. Schultz
Grades 2-10. 24 pp. Council for Indian Education. $3.95.

RUXTON OF THE ROCKIES
George F. Ruxton; R. LeRoy, Editor
Reprint of 1950 edition. Illus. 326 pp. Paper. University of Oklahoma Press, $14.95.

S

SAANII DAHATAAL - THE WOMEN ARE SINGING: POEMS & STORIES
Luci Tapahonso
95 pp. Paper. University of Arizona Press, 1993. $12.95.

THE SABIN COLLECTION
Selected Americana from Sabin's dictionary of books relating to America from its discovery to the present time. Includes Bibliotheca Americana-over 100,000 entries dating from 1493 to 1890s. See Research Publications for titles and prices.

THE SAC & FOX INDIANS
W.T. Hagan
Reprint of 1958 edition. Illus. 320 pp. Paper. University of Oklahoma Press, $15.95.

*SACAGEWEA: INDIAN INTERPRETER TO LEWIS & CLARK
Grades 4 and up. Illus. 130 pp. Childrens Press, $13.95.

SACAJAWEA
Harold P. Howard; foreword by Joseph Bruchac
Reprint of 1971 edition. Illus. Maps. 214 pp. Paper. University of Oklahoma Press, 2002. $17.95.

*SACAJAWEA—NATIVE AMERICAN HEROINE
Martha F. Bryant
Story of Sacajawea's entire life. Grades 5 and up. 256 pp. Council for Indian Education. $21.95; paper, $15.95.

*SACAJAWEA, WILDERNESS GUIDE
Kate Jassem
Grades 4-6. Illus. 48 pp. Troll Associates & Demco, 1979. $10.95; paper, $3.50.

SACRED BEAUTY: QUILLWORK OF THE PLAINS INDIANS
Mark J. Halvorson
Color photos of crafted quillwork. Paper. Smoke & Fire Co., $6.95.

SACRED BELIEFS OF THE CHITIMACHA INDIANS
Faye Stouff
Illus.81 pp. Neshobatek Press, 1995. $12.95.

SACRED EARTH: THE SPIRITUAL LANDSCAPE OF NATIVE AMERICA
Arthur Versluis
Discussion of how Native American religions compare to traditional religions. 176 pp. Paper. Inner Traditions, $12.95.

SACRED CIRCLES: TWO THOUSAND YEARS OF NORTH AMERICAN INDIAN ART
Ralph Coe
Illus. 260 pp. Paper. Nelson Atkins, $12.95. University of Washington Press, 1977. $15.

SACRED CLOWNS
Tony Hillerman
Novel. Tribal politics and murder. 305 pp. High-Lonesome Books, 1993. $25.

SACRED ENCOUNTERS: FATHER DE SMET & THE INDIANS OF THE ROCKY MOUNTAIN WEST
Jacqueline Peterson; with Laura Peers
Displays the similarities and differences between European Christianity and Native American beliefs. 200 color illustrations and 20 bxw photos. 192 pp. University of Oklahoma Press, 1993. $49.95; paper, $24.95.

SACRED FEATHERS: THE REVEREND PETER JONES (KAHKEWAQUONABY) & THE MISSISSAUGA INDIANS
Illus. 390 pp. University of Nebraska Press, 1987. $22.95.

SACRED FIREPLACE (OCETI WAKAN): LIFE & TEACHINGS OF A LAKOTA MEDICINE MAN
Pete S. Catches, Sr.; edited by Peter V. Catches
The life and traditional teachings of Peter Catches, a Lakota healer and teacher. 240 pp. Paper. Clear Light, 1999. $14.95.

SACRED FOODS OF THE LAKOTA
William & Marla Powers
Descriptions of ceremonies related to eating buffalo meat, wasna, and dog. 168 pp. Paper. Written Heritage, $11.95.

THE SACRED GEOGRAPHY OF THE AMERICAN MOUND-BUILDERS
Maureen Korp
170 pp. Edwin Mellen Press, 1990. $49.95.

SACRED GROUND
Ron Zeilinger
Illus. 152 pp. Paper. Tipi Press, 1986. $5.95.

*THE SACRED HARVEST: OJIBWAY WILD RICE GATHERING
Gordon Regguinti
Grades 3-6. Illus. 48 pp. Lerner, 1992. $21.27.

THE SACRED HOOP: RECOVERING THE FEMININE IN AMERICAN INDIAN TRADITIONS
Paula G. Allen
Essays, poetry, keen insights. 328 pp. Paper. Beacon Press, 1987. $12.95.

THE SACRED JOURNEY: PRAYERS & SONGS OF NATIVE AMERICA
Peg Streep
Illus. 104 pp. Little, Brown & Co., 1995. $12.45.

SACRED LANDS OF THE SOUTHWEST
Harvey Lloyd
4 vols. Illus. 224 pp. Monacelli Press, 1995. $60 each; $240 per set.

SACRED LANGUAGE: THE NATURE OF SUPERNATURAL DISCOURSE IN LAKOTA
William K. Powers
Illus. 248 pp. Paper. University of Oklahoma Press, 1986. $14.95.

SACRED OBJECTS, SACRED PLACES: PRESERVING TRIBAL TRADITIONS
Andrew Gulliford
Paper. University Press of Colorado, 1999. $32.50.

SACRED PATH CARDS: THE DISCOVERY OF SELF THROUGH NATIVE TEACHINGS
Jamie Sams
Illus. 295 pp. HarperCollins, 1990. $29.95; paper, $14.95.

A SACRED PATH: THE WAY OF THE MUSCOGEE CREEKS
Jean Chauhuri & Joyotpaul Chauhuri
191 pp. Paper. The Falmouth Institute, 2001. $15.

THE SACRED PIPE: AN ARCHETYPAL THEOLOGY
Paul B. Steinmetz, S.J.
176 pp. Biblio. Syracuse University Press, 1998. $29.95.

THE SACRED PIPE: BLACK ELK'S ACCOUNT OF THE SEVEN RITES OF OGLALA SIOUX
Joseph Epes Brown, Editor
Reprint of 1953 edition. Illus. 152 pp. University of Oklahoma Press, 2002. $29.95; paper, $12.95.

SACRED PLACES: HOW THE LIVING EARTH SEEKS OUR FRIENDSHIP
James Swan
Discusses varieties of Native American sacred places and the dilemma of sacred places in a modern world, and includes a guide to sacred places on public lands throughout the U.S. Illus. 240 pp. Paper. Bear & Co., 1990. $14.95.

SACRED POWERS
Time-Life Books Editors
Time-Life, 1995. $19.95

SACRED SCROLLS OF THE SOUTHERN OJIBWAY
Selwyn Dewdney
University of Toronto Press, 1974. $30.

SACRED SITES OF THE INDIANS OF THE AMERICAN SOUTHWEST
Raymond Locke
Illus. 130 pp. Roundtable Publishing, 1992. $29.95.

*SACRED SONG OF THE HERMIT THRUSH: AN IROQUOIS TALE
by Tehanetorens
Mohawk legend. Grades 3 and up. Illus. 64 pp. Paper. The Book Publishing Co.. $5.96.

THE SACRED TREE
Four Worlds Development Project
Reflections on Native American spirituality. Paper. Four Winds Trading Co., $9.95.

THE SACRED: WAYS OF KNOWLEDGE, SOURCES OF LIFE
Peggy Beck, Anna Walters & Nia Francisco
Religious concepts of North American Indians. Illus. 384 pp. Dine College Press & Northland, 1977. $19.95.

**SACRED WORDS: A STUDY OF
NAVAJO RELIGION & PRAYER**
  Sam Gill
Illus. 283 pp. Greenwood Press, 1981. $35.

SAGA OF CHIEF JOSEPH
  Helen Addison Howard
The full story opf Chief Joseph and the Nez Perce War. Illus.
Maps. 421 pp. Paper. University of Nebraska Press & Clear
Light, 1978. $16.95.

SAGA OF THE COEUR D'ALENE INDIAN NATION
  Joseph Seltice; Edward J. Kowrach, Intro by
Photos. 372 pp. Ye Galleon Press, 1990. $24.95.

**THE SAGA OF SITTING BULL'S BONES: THE UNUSUAL
STORY BEHIND SCULPTOR KORCZAK ZIOLKOWSKI'S
MEMORIAL TO CHIEF SITTING BULL**
  Robb DeWall
Illus. 320 pp. Paper. Crazy Horse Foundation, 1984. $9.95.

**SAGEBRUSH SOLDIER: PRIVATE WILLIAM EARL
SMITH'S VIEW OF THE SIOUX WAR OF 1876**
  Sherry Smith
Illus. Maps. 158 pp. University of Oklahoma Press,
1989. $19.95.

SAGEBRUSH TO SHAKESPEARE
  Carrol B. Howe
Provides informtion on prehistoric Indian cultures; and the
peope who discovered and developed the region of Southern
Oregon and Northern California. Illus. 216 pp. Paper. Binford
& Mort, 1984. $10.

**SAGWITCH: SHOSHONE CHIEFTAIN,
MORMON ELDER, 1822-1887**
  Scott R. Christensen
Leader of the Northwestern Shoshone and survivor of the Bear
River Massacre. 272 pp. Utah State University Press, 2000.
$29.95.

**SAINT CLAIR PAPERS: THE LIFE & PUBLIC SERVICES OF
ARTHUR ST. CLAIR, WITH HIS CORRESPONDENCE AND
OTHER PAPERS**
  W.H. Smith
Facsimile of 1881 edition. Two volumes. Illus.
Da Capo Press, $115 per set; Ayer Co., $62 each.

**SAINTE MARIE AMONG THE IROQUOIS: A LIVING
HISTORY MUSEUM OF THE FRENCH & THE IROQUOIS
AT ONONDAGA IN THE 17TH CENTURY**
Illus. 118 pp. Paper. E Metz, 1995. $9.95.

**RAMONA SAKIESTEWA - PATTERNED DREAMS:
TEXTILES OF THE SOUTHWEST**
  Suzanne Baizerman
52 pp. Paper. Wheelright Museum, 1989. $9.95.

**SALINAN INDIANS OF CALIFORNIA
& THEIR NEIGHBORS**
  Betty Brusa
History, vocabulary. Illus. 96 pp. Paper.
Naturegraph, 1975. $8.95.

SALINAS: ARCHAEOLOGY, HISTORY, PREHISTORY
  David Grant Noble, Editor
Illus. Maps. Photos. 40 pp. Paper. Ancient City Press,
1990. $8.95.

**SALINAS PUEBLO MISSIONS (ABO, QUARIA,
GRAN QUIVIRA) NATIONAL MONUMENT, NEW MEXICO**
  Dan Murphy
Tells the story of Estancia Basin from Ice Age geology to In-
dian villages, to European invasion to designation as a national
monument. Illus. 64 pp. Paper. Southwest Parks & Monumnets
Association, 1993. $9.95.

*SALISH FOLK TALES
  Katheryn Law
Grades 2-8. Paper. Council for Indian Education, 1972.
$2.95.

SALISH INDIAN SWEATERS
  Priscilla Gibson-Roberts
Dos Tejedoras, 1989. $17.50.

**THE SALISH LANGUAGE FAMILY:
RECONSTRUCTING SYNTAX**
  Paul D. Kroeber
Examines the history of an array of important syntactic
construction in the Salish language family. Map. 464 pp.
University of Nebraska Press, 1999. $60.

THE SALT RIVER PIMA-MARICOPA IDIANS
  John L. Myers & Robert Gryder
Illus. 176 pp. Heritage Publishers, 1988.

**SALVATION AND THE SAVAGE: AN ANALYSIS
OF PROTESTANT MISSIONS & AMERICAN INDIAN
RESPONSE, 1787-1862**
  R.F. Berkhofer
Reprint of 1965 edition. Greenwood, $35.

*SAM & THE GOLDEN PEOPLE
  Marjorie Vandervelde
Grades 5-9. 40 pp. Council for Indian Education, 1972.
$8.95; paper, $2.95.

**SAMPLER QUILT BLOCKS FROM
NATIVE AMERICAN DESIGNS**
  Dr. Joyce Mori
Explores the sample quilt blocks adapted from corn
husk bags Illus. 80 pp.Paper. Written Heritage, $12.95.

**SAN DIEGO COUNTY INDIANS
AS FARMERS & WAGE EARNERS**
  Teo Couro
Paper. Acoma Books, $1.

**SAN GABRIEL DEL YUNGUE
AS SEEN BY AN ARCHAEOLOGIST**
  Florence H. Ellis
Illus. 96 pp. Paper. Sunstone, 1988. $10.95.

SANAPIA: COMANCHE MEDICINE WOMAN
  David E. Jones
Reprint of 1972 edition. 107 pp. Paper. Waveland Press, $7.95.

THE SAND CREEK MASSACRE
  Stan Hoag
Reprint of 1961 edition. Illus. Maps. 231 pp. Paper.
University of Oklahoma Press, 1998. $19.95.

SAND IN A WHIRLWIND: THE PAIUTE INDIAN WAR, 1860
  Ferol Egan
Illus. 316 pp. Paper. University of Nevada Press, 1985. $9.95.

THE SANDAL & THE CAVE: THE INDIANS OF OREGON
  Luther S. Cressman
Illus. 96 pp. Paper. Oregon State University Press, 1981. $6.95.

SANDPAINTINGS OF THE NAVAJO SHOOTING CHANT
  Franc Newcomb & Gladys Reichard
Reprint. Illus. 132 pp. Paper. Dover, $11.95.

SANTA CLARA POTTERY TODAY
  Betty LeFree
Illus. Photos. 126 pp. Paper. University of
New Mexico Press, $14.95.

SANTA FE FANTASY: THE QUEST FOR THE GOLDEN CITY
  Elmo Baca
Full of lore on early Pueblo culture and Spanish colonial trad-
ing. 145 color illustrations. Photos. 109 pp. Clear Light, $34.95.

SANTA FE GUIDE
  Waite Thompson & Richard Gottlieb
Where to go, what to see, cultural activities in town and at sur-
rounding Indian Pueblos. 64 pp. Paper. Sunstone Press, $6.95.

SANTA FE: HISTORY OF AN ANCIENT CITY
  David Grant Noble
Illus. 168 pp. School of American Research, 1990.
$29.95; paper, $16.95.

SANTA FE: A MODERN HISTORY, 1880-1990
  Henry J. Tobias & Charlkes E. Woodhouse
Focuses on what changes over the past 110 years have meant
to the city's inhabitants. Illus. 288 pp. University of New Mexico
Press, 2001. $24.95.

SANTANA: WAR CHIEF OF THE MESCALERO APACHE
  Almer N. Blazer; edited by A.R. Pruit
Photos. 320 pp. Clear Light, 1996. $24.95; paper, $14.95.

**SAPAT'QQAYN: TWENTIETH CENTURY
NEZ PERCE ARTISTS**
72 pp. Paper. Nez Perce National Historical Park.

SASQUATCH: THE APES AMONG US
  John Green
Illus. 492 pp. Paper. Hancock House, $12.95.

SASQUATCH: BIGFOOT: THE CONTINUING MYSTERY
  Thomas N. Steenburg
An Indian legend told to early explorers. Illus Maps.
128 pp. Paper. Hancock House, $11.95.

SAVAGES & CIVILIZATION: WHO WILL SURVIVE?
  Jack M. Weatherford
320 pp. Paper. Fawcett Book Group, 1995. $12.

**THE SAVANAH RIVER CHIEFDOMS: POLITICAL
CHANGE IN THE LATE PREHISTORIC SOUTHEAST**
  David G. Anderson
Illus. 488 pp. Paper. University of Alabama Press, 1994. $39.95.

*SAVINGS
  Linda Hogan
Poems by a Chickasaw woman. Grades 7 and up.
Oyate, 1988. $10.95.

SAYULA POPOLUCA VERB DERIVATION
  Lawrence Clark
80 pp. Paper. Summer Institute of Linguistics, 1983.
$8.50. Microfiche, $2.

**THE SCALPEL & THE SILVER BEAR:THE FIRST
NAVAJO WOMEN SURGEON COMBINES WESTERN
MEDICINE & TRADITIONAL HEALING**
  Lori Alvord & Elizabeth Van Pelt
240 pp. Bantam, 1999. $23.95.

**SCARLET RIBBONS: AMERICAN INDIAN
TECHNIQUE FOR TODAYS QUILTERS**
  Helen Kelley
Reprint of 1987 edition. Illus. 104 pp. Paper.
Written Heritage, 1987. $21.95.

**SCHOLARS & THE INDIAN EXPERIENCE:
CRITICAL REVIEWS OF RECENT WRITINGS
IN THE SOCIAL SCIENCES**
  W.R. Swagerty
280 pp. Indiana University Press, 1984.
$22.50; paper, $9.95.

**SCHOLASTIC ENCYCLOPEDIA
OF THE AMERICAN INDIAN**
  James Ciment
Scholastic, Inc., 1996.

**THE HENRY ROWE SCHOOLCRAFT COLLECTION:
A CATALOGUE OF BOOKS IN NATIVE AMERICAN
LANGUAGES IN THE LIBRARY OF THE BOSTON
ATHENAEUM**
  Robert Kruse
Illus. 90 pp. Boston Athenaeum, 1991.

SCHOOLCRAFT: LITERARY VOYAGER
  Philip Mason, Editor
208 pp. Michigan State University Press, 1962. $5.

SCHOOLCRAFT SERIES
  Philip P. Mason, Editor
Schoolcraft was explorer, historian, and Indian agent. Includes
three volumes: Schoolcraft's Expedition to Lake Itasca;
Schoolcraft's Indian Legends; and Schoolcraft's Narrative Journal of Travels. Reprints. Michigan State University, $35 each;
paper, $16. each

**SCHOOLCRAFT'S INDIAN LEGENDS
FROM ALGIC RESEARCHES**
  H.R. Schoolcraft; M. Williams, Editor
Reprint of 1956 edition. 322 pp. Greenwood Press, $22.50.

**SCHOOLING AT-RISK NATIVE AMERICAN CHILDREN:
A JOURNEY FROM RESERVATION HEAD START TO
PUBLIC SCHOOL KINDERGARTEN**
  Cheryl D. Clay
Revised edition. Illus. 185 pp. Garland Publishing, 1998.
$53.

**SCIENCE ENCOUNTERS THE INDIAN, 1820-1880:
THE EARLY YEARS OF AMERICAN ETHNOLOGY**
  Robert E. Bieder
Illus. 290 pp. University of Oklahoma Press, 1986.
$29.95; paper, $15.95.

**SCIENCE & NATIVE AMERICAN COMMUNITIES:
LEGACIES OF PAIN, VISIONS OF PROMISE**
  edited by Keith James
Gathering of Native American professionals working in the sciences and adavnaced technology and explores the meeting
ground between science and Native American communities.
192 pp. University of Nebraska Press, 2001. $40; paper, $17.95.

SCIENTIST ON THE TRAIL
  A.F. Bandelier; George P. Hammond, Editor
Reprint of 1949 edition. Ayer Co., $17.

**SCOORWA: JAMES SMITH'S
INDIAN CAPTIVITY NARRATIVE**
  James Smith
Reprint. Illus. 176 pp. Paper. Ohio Historical Society, $5.95.

SCOUT & RANGER
  James Pike
Reprint of 1932 edition. Illus. 164 pp. Da Capo Press, $25.

*SCOUTS
  Gail Stewart
Grades 3-8. Illus. 32 pp. Rourke Corp., 1990. $17.26.

SCRAPBOOK OF THE AMERICAN WEST
  E. Lisle Reedstrom
Illus. 260 pp. Paper. The Caxton Printers, 1989. $17.95.

SCULPTURING TOTEM POLES
  Walt Way; Jack Ekstrom, Editor
Illus. 26 pp. Paper. Vestal, 1985. $5.

SEAHB SIWASH
  Leon L. Stock
Illus. 352 pp. Todd & Honeywell, 1981. $15.

*SEAL FOR A PAL
  Paul E. Layman
Grades 4-9. 31 pp. Council for Indian Education, 1972.
$8.95; paper, $2.95.

THE SEARCH FOR AN AMERICAN INDIAN IDENTITY: MODERN PAN-AMERICAN MOVEMENTS
Hazel W. Hertzberg
Illus. 362 pp. Paper. Syracuse University Press, 1971. $16.95.

*SEARCH FOR IDENTITY
Hap Gilliland, et al
5 stories of Indian youth attempting to find their place in life. Grades 6-10. Council for Indian Education, 1991. $10.95; paper, $4.95.

SEARCH FOR THE NATIVE AMERICAN PUREBLOODS
Charles B. Wilson
77 pencil portraits of pureblood American Indians. 3rd edition. Illus. 64 pp. Paper. University of Oklahoma Press, 2004. $17.95.

SEARCHING FOR THE BRIGHT PATH: THE MISSISSIPPI CHOCTAWS FROM PREHISTORY TO REMOVAL
James Taylor Carson
Illus. 185 pp. Paper. Univ. of Nebraska Press, 1999. $29.95.

SEASONS OF THE KACHINA: PROCEEDINGS OF THE CALIFORNIA STATE UNIVERSITY HAYWOOD CONFERENCES ON THE WESTERN PUEBLOS, 1987-1988
Lowell J. Bean
Illus. 175 pp. Ballena Pres, 1989. $32.95; paper, $21.95.

THE SECOND CIVIL WAR: EXAMINING THE INDIAN DEMAND FOR ETHNIC SOVEREIGNTY
David Price
219 pp. Paper. Second Source, 1998. $14.95.

THE SECOND LONG WALK: THE NAVAJO-HOPI LAND DISPUTE
Jerry Kammer
258 pp. Paper. University of New Mexico Press, 1980. $12.95.

THE SECRET GUIDE TO MOHEGAN SUN
Sandra J. Eichelberg, Editor; Melissa J. Fawcett, Translator
Illus. 40 pp. Paper. Little People Publications, 1998. $5.

SECRET NATIVE AMERICAN PATHWAYS: A GUIDE TO INNER PEACE
Thomas E. Mails
A guide to discovering the power of traditional medicine ways and applying spiritual practices in your daily life. Illus. 312 pp. Paper. Council Oak Books, 1988. $24.95, includes audio.

THE SECRET SAGA OF FIVE-SACK
Henry L. Reimers
25 pp. Paper. Ye Galleon Press, 1975. $4.95.

SECRETS FROM THE CENTER OF THE WORLD
Joy Harjo & Stephen Strom
Prose. 76 pp. Paper. University of Arizona Press, 1989. $13.95.

SECRETS OF ESKIMO SKIN SEWING
Edna Wilder
Instructions, drawings, photographs. 140 pp. Paper. University of Alaska Press, 1998. $12.95.

SECRETS OF THE SACRED WHITE BUFFALO: NATIVE AMERICAN HEALING REMEDIES, RITES & RITUALS
Gary Null
Illus. 320 pp. Paper. Prentice Hall, 1997. $15.

SEEDS OF CHANGE: A QUINCENTENNIAL COMMEMORATION
Herman J. Viola & Carolyn Margolis, Editors
Illus. 352 pp. Smithsonian Books, 1991. $39.95.

SEEDS OF EMPIRE: THE AMERICAN REVOLUTIONARY CONQUEST OF THE IROQUOIS
Max M. Mintz
New York University Press, 1999. $29.95.

SEEDS OF EXTINCTION: JEFFERSONIAN PHILANTHROPY & THE AMERICAN INDIAN
Bernard Sheehan
320 pp. University of North Carolina Press, 1973. $30. Paper. W.W. Norton, $9.95.

SEEING THE WHITE BUFFALO
Robert B. Pickering
Illus. 160 pp. Paper. Johnson Books, 1997. $16.95.

SEEING WITH THE NATIVE EYE: CONTRIBUTIONS TO THE STUDY OF NATIVE AMERICAN RELIGION
Walter H. Capps
Paper. Harper & Row, 1976. $6.95.

SELECTED PREFORMS, POINTS & KNIVES OF THE NORTH AMERICAN INDIANS, VOL. I
Perino
Sketches of over 400 types includes description, age, and distribution range. Reprint of 1985 edition. 404 pp. Hothem House, $70.50, postpaid.

SELECTION OF SOME OF THE MOST INTERESTING NARRATIVES OF OUTRAGES COMMITTED BY THE INDIANS IN THEIR WARS WITH THE WHITE PEOPLE
Archibald Loudon
Reprint of 1808 edition. 2 vols. in 1. Ayer Co., $45.

SELF-DETERMINATION & THE SOCIAL EDUCATION OF NATIVE AMERICANS
Guy B. Senese
248 pp. Greenwood, 1991. $52.95.

SELF RELIANCE VS. POWER POLITICS: AMERICAN & INDIAN EXPERIENCES IN GUILDING NATION-STATES
J. Ann Tickner
282 pp. Columbia University Press, 1987. $52.50.

SELF & SAVAGERY ON THE CALIFORNIA FRONTIER: A STUDY OF THE DIGGER STEREOTYPE
Allan Lonnberg
Illus. 98 pp. Paper. Coyote Press, 1980. $10.

SELLING THE INDIAN: COMMERCIALIZING & APPROPRIATING AMERICAN INDIAN CULTURE
edited by Carter Jones Meyer & Diana Royer
8 articles, original contributions that consider the selling of American Indian culture and how it affects the native community. Illus. 279 pp. University of Arizona Press, 2001. $45; paper, $22.95.

SELU: SEEKING THE CORN-MOTHER'S WISDOM
Marilou Awiakta; illus. by Mary Adair
Presents the Corn-Mother's wisdoms as traditionally taught by representative Native peoples. Illus. 352 pp. Fulcrum Publishing & Clear Light, 1993. $19.95; paper, $14.95.

THE SEMANTICS OF TIME; ASPECTUAL CATEGORIZATION IN KOYUKON ATHABASKAN
Melissa Axelrod
Athabaskan studies. 200 pp. University of Nebraska Press, 1993. $40.

*THE SEMINOLE
B. Brooks
Grades 5-8. Illus. 32 pp. Rourke Corp., 1989. $13.26.

*THE SEMINOLE
Merwin Garbarino
Grades 7-12. Illus. 112 pp. Paper. Great Outddors Publishing & Chelsea House, 1989. $8.95.

*THE SEMINOLE
Emilie U. Lepthien
Grades 2-4. Illus. 48 pp. Childrens Press, 1985. $11.45.

THE SEMINOLE BAPTIST CHURCHES OF OKLAHOMA: MAINTAINING A TRADITIONAL COMMUNITY
Jack M. Schultz
Illus. Map. Biblio. 288 pp. University of Oklahoma Press, 1999. $29.95.

SEMINOLE BURNING: A STORY OF RACIAL VENGEANCE
Daniel F. Littlefield
True stories of mob vengeance on two innocent Indian teenagers in Oklahoma. 3 maps. Biblio. 208 pp. University Press of Mississippi, 1996. $26.

*THE SEMINOLE INDIANS
Phillip Koslow
Large-print book traces the history and culture of the Seminoe Indians from pre-Colombian times. Grades 2-5. Illus. 80 pp. Demco, 1994. $12.15. Paper. Great Outdoors Publishing, $6.95.

SEMINOLE INDIANS OF FLORIDA, 1850-1874
Raymond C. Lantz
Annuity & per capita rolls of the BIA and National Archives. 415 pp. Paper. Heritage Books, 1994. $30.

A SEMINOLE LEGEND: THE LIFE OF BETTY MAE TIGER JUMPER
Betty Mae Tiger Jumper & Patsy West
Florida Seminole woman's life and family history. Illus. Photos. Maps. University Press of Florida, 2001. $24.95.

THE SEMINOLE & MICCOSUKEE TRIBES: A CRITICAL BIBLIOGRAPHY
Harry A. Kersey, Jr.
Examines over 200 major works relating to the ethnohistorical development of the Seminole and Miccosukee tribes of Florida. 116 pp. Paper. Indiana University Press, 1987. $7.95.

SEMINOLE MUSIC
F. Densmore
Reprint of 1956 edition. Illus. 276 pp. Da Capo Press, $27.50.

SEMINOLE PATCHWORK
Margaret Brandenbourg
Illus. 96 pp. Paper. Sterling, 1987. $10.95.

SEMINOLE PATCHWORK BOOK
Cheryl G. Bradkin
Illus. 48 pp. Paper. Burdett Design, 1980. $7.50.

SEMINOLE PATCHWORK: THE COMPLETE BOOK
Beverly Rush with Lassie Wittman
How-to on Seminole patchwork for decoration and shirt and dress making. Illus. 80 pp. Paper. Writtenm Heritage, $7.95.

THE SEMINOLE SEED
Robert N. Peck
420 pp. Pineapple Press, 1983. $14.95.

A SEMINOLE SOURCEBOOK
W.C. Sturtevant, Editor
856 pp. Garland Publishing, 1985. $90.

*THE SEMINOLE: SOUTHEAST
Grades 7-12. Illus. 112 pp. Knowledge Unlimited, $16.95.

*THE SEMINOLES
Martin Lee
Grades 3 and up. Illus. 64 pp. Paper. Franklin Watts, 1991. $4.95.

*THE SEMINOLES
Virginia Driving Hawk Sneve
The creation myth of the Seminoles; history, customs, and facts about the tribe today. Grades 2-6. Illus. 32 pp. Holiday House, 1994. $15.95.

SEMINOLES
Edwin McReynolds
Reprint of 1957 edition. Illus. Maps. Paper. University of Oklahoma Press, $16.95.

SEMINOLES: DAYS OF LONG AGO
Kenneth W. Mulder
2nd Edition. Illus. 32 pp. Mulder Enterprises, 1996. $5.

THE SEMINOLES OF FLORIDA
James W. Covington
History of the Florida Seminoles. Illus. Maps. Biblio. 416 pp. University Press of Florida, 1994. $49.95; paper, $18.95.

*THE SENECA
Grades K-4. Illus. 48 pp. Childrens Press, $11.45.

SENECA MYTHS & FOLK TALES
Arthur C. Parker
Reprint of 1923 edition. Illus. 485 pp. Paper. University of Nebraska Press, $15.

SENECA THANKSGIVING RITUALS
Wallace L. Chafe
Reprint. Reprint Services, $75.

THE SENECA & TUSCARORA INDIANS: AN ANNOTATED BIBLIOGRAPHY
Marilyn L. Haas, Editor
Citations to journal articles, books, theses, and government documents published up to 1992. 465 pp. Scarecrow Press, 1994. $58.

THE SENECA WORLD OF GA-NO-SAY-YEH
Joseph A. Francello
225 pp. Peter Lang, 1989. $37.10.

SEPARATE REALITY
Carlos Castaneda; Jane Rosenman
275 pp. Pocket Books, 1991. $8.95; paper, $4.95

SEQUOYAH
Grant Foreman
The life of the creator of the Cherokee alphabet. Reprint of 1938 edition. Illus. 90 pp. Paper. University of Oklahoma Press, $9.95.

*SEQUOYAH
Robert Cwiklik; Nancy Furstinger, Editor
Grades 5-7. Silver Burdett Press, 1989. $11.98; paper, $7.95.

SEQUOYAH & THE CHEROKEE ALPHABET
Robert Cwiklik
Illus. 130 pp. Paper. Cherokee Publications, $7.95.

SEQUOYAH - COMPUTERIZED SYLLABARY LEARNING PROGRAM - DOS
Diskette. VIP Publishing. $14.95.

*SEQUOYAH: FATHER OF THE CHEROKEE ALPHABET
David Petersen
Grades 2-4. Illus. 32 pp. Childrens Press, $10.95. Paper. Cherokee Publications, $3.95.

*SEQUOYAH & HIS MIRACLE
William Roper
Biography of the Cherokee who invented writing for his people. Grades 5-12. 32 pp. Council for Indian Education, $8.95; paper, $2.95.

THE SERI INDIANS OF SONORA
Bernice Johnston
Illus. 16 pp. Paper. University of Arizona Press, 1980. $3.95.

THE SERPENT & THE SACRED FIRE: FERTILITY IMAGES IN SOUTHWEST ROCK ART
Dennis Slifer
Illus. 208 pp. Museum of New Mexico Press, 2000. $35; paper, $16.95.

THE SERPENT'S TONGUE: PROSE, POETRY & ART OF THE NEW MEXICAN PUEBLOS
Nancy Wood, Editor
256 pp. New American Library, 1997. $210.

THE SERRANO INDIANS OF SOUTHERN CALIFORNIA
Frank Johnston
Malki Museum Press, 1967. $1.75.

SERRANO SONGS & STORIES
Guy Mount
Recorded at Morongo Indian Reservation in southern California by Sarah Martin, Louis Marcus and Magdalina Nombre. Introduction to Serrano culture is provided by author, Guy Mount. Sweetlight Books, 1993. $5.

SETTING IT FREE: AN EXHIBITION OF MODERN ALASKAN ESKIMO IVORY CARVING
Dinah Larsen & Terry Dickey, Editors
Illus. Map. Paper. University of Alaska Museum, 1982. $10.

SETTLEMENT PATTERN STUDIES IN THE AMERICAS: FIFTH YEARS SINCE VIRU
Brian Billman & Gary Feinman
Illus. Smithsonian Institution Press, 1999. $65.

SETTLEMENT, SUBSISTENCE, & SOCIETY IN LATE ZUNI PREHISTORY
Keith W. Kintigh
132 pp. Paper. University of Arizona Press, 1985. $19.95.

SEVEN ARROWS
Hyemeyohsts Storm
The story of the Shield and the Medicine Wheel. A teaching story. Illus. 375 pp. Paper. Cherokee Publications, $14.95.

SEVEN CLANS OF THE CHEROKEE SOCIETY
Marcelina Reed
Contains clan names, information on the matrilineal system, marriage systems, governments, etc. Reprint. Illus. Paper. VIP Publishing. $5.

SEVEN FAMILIES IN PUEBLO POTTERY
Maxwell Museum of Anthropology
Illus. 116 pp. University of New Mexico Press, 1974. $7.95.

SEVEN ROCK ART SITES IN BAJA CALIFORNIA
Clement W. Meighan & V.L. Pontoni, Editors
Illus. 236 pp. Paper. Ballena Press, 1979. $10.95.

THE SEVEN VISIONS OF BULL LODGE
told by his daughter Garter Snake
George Horse Capture, Editor
A record of the spiritual life of Bull Lodge (1802-86). Illus. 125 pp. Paper. University of Nebraska Press, 1992. $10.95.

SEVENTH GENERATION: AN ANTHOLOGY OF NATIVE AMERICAN PLAYS
Mimi Gisolfi D'Aponte, Editor
Collection of contemporary Native American writing for the theatre. Paper. Theatre Communications Group (TCG), 1999. $18.95.

THE SEVENTH GENERATION: IMAGES OF THE LAKOTA TODAY
David Seals
Illus. 144 pp. PowerHouse Cultural Entertainment, 1999. $45.

SEVERING THE TIES THAT BIND: GOVERNMENT REPRESSION OF INDIGENOUS RELIGIOUS CEREMONIES ON THE PRAIRIES
Katherine Pettipas
Illus. 336 pp. Paper. University of Toronto Press, 1994. $19.95.

SHADOW COUNTRY
Paula G. Allen
149 pp. Paper. UCLA, American Indian Studies Center, 1982. $7.50.

SHADOW DISTANCE: A GERALD VIZENOR READER
Gerald Vizenor
340 pp. University Press of New England, 1994. $40; paper, $17.95.

SHADOW OF THE HUNTER: STORIES OF ESKIMO LIFE
Richard K. Nelson
Illus. 282 pp. Paper. University of Chicago Press, 1980. $12.95.

SHADOW OF THE WOLF: AN APACHE TALE
Harry James Plumlee
Historical novel of an Apache Shaman. Map. 206 pp. University of Oklahoma Press, 1997. $21.95.

SHADOWCATCHERS
Steve Wall
Teachings of Native American elders from 13 different tribes. Illus. 288 pp. Harper & Row, 1994. $27.50.

THE SHADOW'S HORSE
Diane Glancy
Collection of poems. 58 pp. Paper. University of Arizona Press, 2003. $15.95.

SHADOWS IN GLASS: THE INDIAN PHOTOGRAPHS OF BEN WITTICK
Patricia Broder
Rowman & Littlefield, 1990. $39.95.

SHADOWS OF THE BUFFALO: A FAMILY ODYSSEY AMONG THE INDIANS
Adolf and Beverly Hungry Wolf
Pat Golbitz, Editor
Illus. 288 pp. Paper. William Morrow, 1985. $6.95.

SHADOWS OF THE INDIAN: STEREOTYPES IN AMERICAN CULTURE
Raymond Stedman
Illus. 282 pp. University of Oklahoma Press, 1982. $38.95; paper, $17.95.

SHADOWS ON THE KOYUKUK: AN ALASKAN NATIVE'S LIFE ALONG THE RIVER
Huntington & Rearden
Illus. Map. Paper. Alaska Northwest Books, $12.95.

SHAKIN' THE BUSHES
Vietzen
Covers paleo to historic peoples in northern Ohio with excavation results, artifact descriptions, and mound reports. Photos. 277 pp. Hothem House, 1976. $52, postpaid.

THE SHAMAN & THE MEDICINE WHEEL
Evelyn Eaton
Illus. 206 pp. Theosophical Publishing, 1982. $13.95.

THE SHAMAN: PATTERNS OF RELIGIOUS HEALING AMONG THE OJIBWAY INDIANS
John A. Grim
Reprint of 1983 edition. Illus. Maps. Biblio. Paper. University of Oklahoma Press, 1997. $19.95.

THE SHAMAN'S TOUCH: OTOMI INDIAN SYMBOLIC HEALING
James Dow
Illus. 180 pp. University of Utah Press, 1986. $13.95.

SHAMANIC ODYSSEY: THE LUSHOOTSEED SALISH JOURNEY TO THE LAND OF THE DEAD
Jay Miller; Sylvia Vane, Editor
Illus. 217 pp. Ballena Press, 1988. $39.95; paper, $28.95.

SHAMANISM
Piers Vitebsky
Illus. Maps. 184 pp. University of Oklahoma Press, 2001. $14.95.

SHAMANS & KUSHTAKAS: NORTH COAST TALES OF THE SUPERNATURAL
Mary Beck; illus. by Oliver
Illus. 128 pp. Paper. Alaska Northwest Books, 1991. $12.95.

SHAMANS & RELIGION: AN ANTHROPOLOGICAL EXPLORATION IN CRITICAL THINKING
Alice B. Kehoe
Waveland, 2000.

SHANDAA: IN MY LIFETIME
told by Belle Herbert; edited by Bill Pfisterer & Jane McGary
19th century life on the upper Yukon River. Stories are in Gwich'in Athabaskan with English translations. Illus. 207 pp. Paper. University of Alaska Press, 1988. $14.95.

*SHANNON: AN OJIBWAY DANCER
Grades 3-8. Lerner Publications.

SHAPESHIFT
Sherwin Bitsui
Poetry with Navajo persepctive. 80 pp. University of Arizona Press, 2003. $15.95.

THE SHAPING OF AMERICAN ETHNOGRAPHY: THE WILKES EXPLORING EXPEDITION, 1838-1842
Barry Alan Joyce
The story of the expedition and the observations of indigenous peoples they encountered. Illus. Map. 197 pp. University of Nebraska Press, 2001. $45.

SHARED SYMBOLS, CONTESTED MEANINGS: GROS VENTRE CULTURE & HISTORY, 1778-1984
Loretta Fowler
Paper. Cornell University Press, 1987. $19.95.

SHARED VISIONS: NATIVE AMERICAN PAINTERS & SCULPTORS IN THE TWENTIETH CENTURY
Margaret Archuleta & Rennard Strickland, Editors
Presents works by Native American artists influenced by Euro-American conceptions of art. Prepared by The Heard Museum. Illus. 112 pp. Paper. W.W. Norton & Co., 1992. $20.

SHARING THE DESERT: THE TOHONO O'ODHAM IN HISTORY
Winston P. Erickson
Traces the development of relations between the tribe and other peoples. 182 pp. Paper. University of Arizona Press, 1994. $19.95.

SHARING A HERITAGE: AMERICAN INDIAN ARTS
Charlotte Heth
214 pp. Paper. UCLA, American Indian Studies Center, 1984. $12.

*SHARING OUR WORLDS
A photographic documentary of children from three families sharing their multicultural experiences. Grades 2-6. Illus. 32 pp. Daybreak Star Press, $4.75.

THE SHARPEST SIGHT: A NOVEL
Louis Owens
Mystery. 272 pp. Paper. University of Oklahoma Press, 1992. $17.95.

*SHASTA INDIAN TALES
Rosemary Holsinger
Myths. Illus. 48 pp. Paper. Naturegraph, 1978. $5.95.

THE SHASTA INDIANS OF CALIFORNIA & THEIR NEIGHBORS
Elizabeth Renfro
Shasta origins, shamanism, mythology, philosophy, ceremonies, etc. Illus. Photos. 128 pp. Naturegraph, $16.95; paper, $8.95.

SHAWNEE: THE CEREMONIALISM OF A NATIVE AMERICAN TRIBE & ITS CULTURAL BACKGROUND
James Howard
Illus. 460 pp. Ohio University Press, 1981. $28.95; paper, $14.95.

SHAWNEE HOME LIFE: THE PAINTING OF ERNEST SPYBUCK
Lee Callander and Ruth Slivka
Illus. 32 pp. Paper. National Museum of the American Indian, 1984. $8.95.

THE SHAWNEE PROPHET
R. David Edmunds
Illus. 275 pp. University of Nebraska Press, 1983. $23.50; paper, $7.95.

SHE HAD SOME HORSES
Joy Harjo
Collection of poetry exploring physical & mythic landscapes. 74 pp. Thunder's Mouth Press, $15.95; paper, $10.95.

SHE'S TRICKY LIKE COYOTE: ANNIE MINER PETERSON, AN OREGON COAST INDIAN WOMAN
Lionel Youst
Illus. 320 pp. Maps. University of Oklahoma Press, 1997. $29.95.

THE SHEEPEATERS
W.A. Allen
The Sheepeater Indians of Wyoming & Idaho who died out long ago from diseases brought by whites. Reprint of 1913 edition. 121 pp. Ye Galleon, $14.95; paper, $8.95.

THE SHEFFIELD SITE: AN ONEONTA SITE ON THE ST. CROIX RIVER
Guy E. Gibbon
Illus. 62 pp. Paper. Minnesota Historical Society, 1973. $4.

SHELL SHAKER
LeAnne Howe
Novel. Aunt Lute Books, 2002.

SHEM PETE'S ALASKA
James Kari & James Fall, Editors
Geography of the Cook Inlet region of Alaska. Contains over 700 Dena'ina place names of the western Cook Inlet region. Illus. Maps. 330 pp. Paper. CIRI & Alaska Native Language Center, 1987. $15.

*SHINGEBISS: AN OJIBWAY LEGEND
Nancy Van Laan
Grades PS-3. Illus. 32 pp. Houghton Mifflin, 1997. $16.

SHINGWAUK'S VISION: A HISTORY OF NATIVE RESIDENTIAL SCHOOLS
J.R. Miller
Illus. 582 pp. Paper. University of Toronto Press, 1996. $29.95.

SHONTO: STUDY OF THE ROLE OF THE TRADER IN A MODERN NAVAJO COMMUNITY
W.Y. Adams
Reprint of 1963 edition. Reprint Services, $75.

SHOOTING BACK FROM THE RESERVATION: A PHOTO-GRAPHIC VIEW OF LIFE BY NATIVE AMERICAN YOUTH
Jim Hubbard
A look at the varied worlds of Native Americn children through their eyes. Paper. W.W. Norton & Co., $17.

A SHORT ACCOUNT OF THE DESTRUCTION OF THE INDIES
Bartlome de las Casas; translated by Nigel Griffin
Eyewitness record & protest of Spanish atrocities in the territory of Columbus. Reprint. Illus Maps. 192 pp. Paper. Penguin USA, $9.95.

A SHORT BIOGRAPHY OF JOHN LEETH; WITH AN ACCOUNT OF HIS LIFE AMONG THE INDIANS
E. Jeffries; R.G. Thwaites, Editor
The experiences of a trade-hunter in the Indian country of Pennsylvania & Ohio. Ayer Co., $18.

A SHORT HISTORY OF THE INDIANS OF THE U.S.
Edward H. Spicer
Reprint of 1969 edition. 320 pp. Paper. Krieger Publishing, $11.95.

SHORT-TERM SEDENTISM IN THE AMERICAN SOUTHWEST: THE MIMBRES VALLEY SALADO
Ben Nelson & Steven LeBlanc
Illus. 315 pp. Paper. University of New Mexico Press, 1986. $35.

SHOSHONE GHOST DANCE RELIGION: POETRY SONGS & GREAT BASIN CONTEXT
Judith Vander
656 pp. University of Illinois Press, 1996. $65.

*SHOSHONE INDIANS OF NORTH AMERICA
Kim Dramer
Grades 5 and up.120 pp. Paper. Chelsea House, 1996. $9.95.

SHOSHONE TALES
collected & edited by Anne M. Smith
Collected in 1939, from the Shoshone oral tradition. Illus. 188 pp. Paper. University of Utah Press, 1993. $14.95.

*THE SHOSHONI
Alden Carter
Grades 3-5. Illus. 65 pp. Franklin Watts, 1989. $11.90.

*THE SHOSHONI
Dennis Fradin
Revised edition. Grades 2-4. Illus. 48 pp. Children's Press, 1992. $21; paper, $5.50.

THE SHOSHONI-CROW SUN DANCE
Fred W. Voget
Illus. Maps. 348 pp. Paper. University of Oklahoma, 1984. $14.95.

THE SHOSHONI FRONTIER & THE BEAR RIVER MASSACRE
Brigham D. Madsen
Illus. Maps. 336 pp. Paper. University of Utah Press, 1985. $17.95.

SHOSHONI GRAMMAR
Jon P. Dayley
Boise State University Press, 1993.

SHOSHONI TEXTS
Jon P. Dayley
Boise State University Press, 1997.

THE SHOSHONIS: SENTINELS OF THE ROCKIES
V. Trenholm and M. Carley
Reprint of 1964 edition. Illus. Maps. Biblio. Paper. University of Oklahoma Press, $19.95.

SHOTO CLAY: FIGURINES & FORMS FROM THE LOWER COLUMBIA
Robert Slocum & Kenneth Matsen
Descriptions and classifications of the clay work done by the little-known Shoto Indians, who once lived in the lower Columbia near Vancouver, Wash. Illus. 32 pp. Paper. Binford & Mort, $5.95.

A SHOVEL OF STARS: THE MAKING OF THE AMERICAN WEST, 1800 TO THE PRESENT
Ted Morgan
The forced removal of the Indians to reservations in Oklahoma. Illus. Maps. 544 pp. Simon & Schuster, 1995. $30.

SHOWDOWN AT THE LITTLE BIGHORN
Dee Brown
Reprint of 1964 edition. Illus. 224 pp. Paper. University of Nebraska Press, 2004. $13.95.

THE SHUSWAP LANGUAGE
A.H. Kuipers
297 pp. Paper. Mouton de Gruyter, 1974. $81.55.

SIBERIAN YUP'IK ESKIMO: THE LANGUAGE & ITS CONTACTS WITH CHUKCHI
Willem J. de Reuse
Examines a number of interrelated grammatical subsystems of Central Siberian Yup'ik, an Eskimo language, spoken on St., Lawrence Island, Alaska. 424 pp. University of Utah Press, 1994. $50.

SIEGE & SURVIVAL: HISTORY OF THE MENOMINEE INDIANS, 1634-1856
David R.M. Beck
Illus. Maps. 294 pp. University of Nebraska Press. 2002. $49.50.

SIGN LANGUAGE AMONG NORTH AMERICAN INDIANS COMPARED WITH THAT OF OTHER PEOPLES & DEAF-MUTES
Garrick Mallery, with A.L. Kroeber & C.F. Voegelin
318 pp. Mouton de Gruyter, 1972.

SIGN LANGUAGE: CONTEMPORARY SOUTHWEST NATIVE AMERICA
Skeet McAuley
Illus. 80 pp. Aperture, 1989. $24.95.

SIGNALS IN THE AIR: NATIVE BROADCASTING IN AMERICA
Michael C. Keith
200 pp. Greenwood Publishing, 1995. $55.

THE SIGNIFICANT TIES EXCEPTION TO THE INDIAN CHILD WELFARE ACT: JUDICIAL DECISION-MAKING OR INCORPORATING BIAS INTO LAW
Raquelle Myers; Nancy Thorington & Joseph Myers, Editors
Illus. 46 pp. Paper. National Indian Justice, 1998. $10.

SIGNS FROM THE ANCESTORS: ZUNI CULTURAL SYMBOLISM & PERCEPTIONS OF ROCK ART
Jane M. Young
Illus. 333 pp. Paper. University of New Mexico Press, 1988. $24.95.

SIGNS OF LIFE: ROCK ART OF THE UPPER RIO GRANDE
Dennis Slifer
200 photos & illus. 287 pp. Ancient City Press & Clear Light, 2002. $29.95; paper, $16.95.

*SIGNS OF SPRING
Patrick J. Quinn
A young boy whose family moves from the city to the Minnesota woods. Grades 4-10. 152 pp. Council for Indian Education, 1996. $7.95.

*SILAS & THE MAD-SAD PEOPLE
Grades 1-5. New Seed, 1981. $5.

SILENT ARROWS: INDIAN LORE & ARTIFACT HUNTING
Earl F. Moore
Third Edition. Illus. Tremaine, 1973. $12.95.

SILKO: WRITING STORYTELLER & MEDICINE WOMAN
Brewster E. Fitz
Examines Silko's award-winning literature. 304 pp. University of Oklahoma Press, 2004. $34.95.

LESLIE MARMON SILKO: A COLLECTION OF CRITICAL ESSAYS
edited by Louise K. Barnett & James L. TYhorson
13 essays by a Native American writer. 336 pp. Paper. University of New Mexico Press, 2001. $24.95.

THE SILVER ARROW & OTHER INDIAN ROMANCES OF THE DUNE COUNTRY
E.H. Reed
Gordon Press, 1977. $59.95.

SILVER HORN: MASTER ILLUSTRATOR OF THE KIOWAS
Candace Greene
Biographical portrait of the Kiowa artist. Illus. 360 pp. University of Oklahoma Press, 2004. $59.95.

SILVER IN THE FUR TRADE, 1680-1820
Martha W. Hamilton
Photos & illus. on 250 trade silver maker's marks and their biographies. Summarizing the historic trading routes of North America. 235 pp. Paper. Hothem House & Smoke & Fire Co., 1995. $45.

SINCE THE TIME OF THE TRANSFORMERS: THE ANCIENT HERITAGE OF THE NUU-CHAH-NULTH, DITIDAHT & MAKAH
Alan D. McMillan
Illus. 264 pp. UBC Press, 1999. $85.

SINEWS OF SURVIVAL: THE LIVING LEGACY OF INUIT CLOTHING
Betty Kobayashi Issenman
Illus. UBC Press, 1997. $49.95.

SINGING AN INDIAN SONG: A BIOGRAPHY OF D'ARCY McNICKLE
Dorothy R. Parker
Traces the course of D'Arcy McNickle's life. Illus. 330 pp. University of Nebraska Press, 1992. $35.

SINGING FOR POWER: THE SONG MAGIC OF THE PAPAGO INDIANS OF SOUTHERN ARIZONA
Ruth M. Underhill
Reprint of 1938 edition. 158 pp. Paper. University of Arizona Press, $12.95.

SINGING THE SONGS OF MY ANCESTORS: THE LIFE & MUSIC OF HELMA SWAN, MAKAH ELDER
Linda J. Goodman
Illus. 368 pp. University of Oklahoma Press, 2004. $44.95.

SINGING FOR A SPIRIT: A PORTRAIT OF THE DAKOTA SIOUX
Vine Deloria, Jr.
True stories, legends, songs, and descriptions of traditional Dakota Sioux life. Photos. 223 pp. Clear Light, $24.95; paper, $14.95.

THE SINGING SPIRIT: EARLY STORIES BY NORTH AMERICAN INDIANS
Bernd Peyer, Editor
Native American fiction. 175 pp. Paper. University of Arizona Press, 1990. $13.95.

*THE SIOUX
Virginia Driving Hawk Sneve
Their creation myth, history, beliefs & ways of life. Grades 4-6. Illus. 32 pp. Holiday House, 1994. $15.95; paper, $6.95.

*THE SIOUX
B. Brooks
Grades 5-8. Illus. 32 pp. Rourke Corp., 1989. $12.67.

THE SIOUX
Royal B. Hassrick; with Dorothy Maxwell & Cile Bach
Illus. Paper. University of Oklahoma Press, $17.95.

*THE SIOUX
Elaine Landau
Grades 3-6. Illus. 64 pp. Franklin Watts, 1989. $22; paper, $6.95.

*THE SIOUX
Alice Osinski
Grades K-4. Illus. 48 pp. Children's Press, 1984. $11.45.

*THE SIOUX
Virginia Driving Hawk Sneve
The creation myth of the Sioux; history, customs, and facts about the tribe today. Grades 2-6. Illus. 32 pp. Holiday House, 1993. $15.95.

A SIOUX CHRONICLE
George E. Hyde
Reprint of 1956 edition. Illus. Maps. 356 pp. Paper. University of Oklahoma Press, $16.95.

SIOUX COLLECTIONS
T. Emogene Paulson, Editor
Dakota Press, 1982. $14.95.

SIOUX CREATION STORY
Thomas Simms
Illus. 36 pp. Paper. Tipi Press, 1987. $3.50.

SIOUX INDIAN RELIGION: TRADITION & INNOVATION
Raymond DeMallie & Douglas Parks, Editors
Illus. 244 pp. Paper. University of Oklahoma Press, 1987. $14.95.

*THE SIOUX INDIANS: HUNTERS & WARRIORS OF THE PLAINS
Sonia Bleeker
Grades 3-6. Illus. Wiliam Morrow, 1962. $11.88.

SIOUX: LIFE & CUSTOMS OF A WARRIOR SOCIETY
R.B. Hassrick, et al
Reprint of 1964 edition. Illus. Maps. 394 pp. Paper. University of Oklahoma Press, $24.95.

THE SIOUX OF THE ROSEBUD: A HISTORY IN PICTURES
Henry & Jean Hamilton
Reprint of the 1971 edition. Illus. Maps. 320 pp. Paper. University of Oklahoma Press, $22.95.

THE SIOUX UPRISING OF 1862
Kenneth Carley
Revised edition. Illus. Photos. Map. 102 pp. Paper. Minnesota Historical Society Press, 1976. $8.50.

SIOUX WINTER COUNT, A 131-YEAR HISTORY
Roberta Carkeek Cheney
Indian calendar of 131 years, from 1796 to 1926. Illus. 64 pp. Paper. Naturegraph, 1998. $8.95.

SISTER TO THE SIOUX: THE MEMOIRS OF ELAINE GOODALE EASTMAN, 1885-1891
Edited by Kay Graber
Illus. Map. 208 pp. Paper. University of Nebraska Press, 2002. $12.95.

SITANKA: THE FULL STORY OF WOUNDED KNEE
Forrest W. Seymour
An account of the major events preceding, during and immediately after the battle of 1890 at Wounded Knee. Christopher Publishing, 1981. $10.75.

SITES OF O'AHU
Elspeth Sterling & Catherine Summers
Study of archaeological & historical sites of O'ahu. Illus. Maps. 372 pp. Paper. Bishop Museum, $29.95.

*SITTING BULL
Sheila Black; Nancy Furstinger, Editor
Grades 5-7. Illus. 144 pp. Silver Burdett, $11.98; paper, $7.95.

SITTING BULL, CHAMPION OF THE SIOUX: A BIOGRAPHY
Stanley Vestal
Reprint of 1957 edition. Illus. 370 pp. Paper.
University of Oklahoma Press, $17.95.

SITTING BULL: THE COLLECTED SPEECHES
Mark Diedrich
Illus. Map. Biblio. 190 pp. paper. Coyote Books, 1998. $29.95.

SITTING BULL & THE PARADOX OF LAKOTA NATIONHOOD
Gary Clayton Anderson
208 pp. Addison-Wesley Educational Publishers, 1996. $16.88.

*SITTING BULL & THE PLAINS INDIANS
John Hook
Grades 4-8. Illus. 65 pp. Frankin Watts, 1987. $12.40.

*SITTING BULL: WARRIOR OF THE SIOUX
Jane Fleischer
Grades 4-6. Illus. 48 pp. Paper. Troll Associates, 1979. $3.50.

SITTING ON THE BLUE-EYED BEAR
Gerald Hausman
Navajo mythology & history. Sunstone Press, $10.

SIX MONTHS AMONG THE INDIANS
Darius B. Cook
Reprint of 1889 edition. Illus. 101 pp. Paper.
Hardscrabble Books, $4.50.

**SIX NATIONS OF NEW YORK:
THE 1892 U.S. EXTRA CENSUS BULLETIN**
intro. by Robert W. Venables
Includes data, details, and photographs of the Six Nations. A report on the condition of the iroquois in 1892. 90 pp. Illus. Photos. Paper. Cornell University Press, 1996. $59.95; paper, $18.95.

SIX NATIONS SERIES
The only curriculum overview currently available for 7th through 12th grade units on New York State Indians. Separate guides available for teachers and students. Akwe:kon Press, Teacher's guide, $15. Student's guide, $4.

**SIX WEEKS IN THE SIOUX TEPEES:
A NARRATIVE OF INDIAN CAPTIVITY**
Sarah F. Wakefield
Bound with other captivity narratives. Reprint of 1863 edition, et al. A fully annotated modern version is edited by June Namias, Illus. Map. 192 pp. University of Oklahoma Press, 1997. $27.95; paper, $14.95.

1676: THE END OF AMERICAN INDEPENDENCE
Stephen Saunders Webb
Presents events from the perspectives of the colonists, Whitehall, and the American Indians. Illus. Maps. 460 pp. Paper. Syracuse University Press, $17.95.

SIXTH ANNUAL INDIAN LAW CONFERENCE: PROCEEDINGS OF THE FEDERAL BAR ASSOCIATION, APRIL 1981
Federal Bar Associatio Staff
113 pp. Federal Bar Association, 1981. $15.

THE SIXTH GRANDFATHER: BLACK ELK'S TEACHINGS GIVEN TO JOHN G. NEIHARDT
Raymond J. De Mallie, Editor
Illus. Maps. 465 pp. University of Nebraska Press & Clear Light, 1984. $50; paper, $15.

SKELETAL BIOLOGY IN THE GREAT PLAINS, MIGRATION, WARFARE, HEALTH, & SUBSISTENCE
Douglas W. Owsley & Richard L. Jantz
Illus. 408 pp. Smithsonian Institution Press, 1994. $45.

SKETCHBOOK '56 THE FRENCH & INDIAN WAR, 1756-1763
Ted Spring
Six volumes of notes, sketches, and dimensions depicting life and artifacts of 1756. Paper. Smoke & Fire Co., $9 each.

SKETCHES OF INDIAN LIFE IN THE PACIFIC NORTHWEST
Alexander Diomedi
Reprint of 1894 edition. 97 pp. Ye Galleon Press, $19.95; paper, $14.95.

SKETCHES OF MISSION LIFE AMONG THE INDIANS OF OREGON
Zachariah Mudge
58 sketches, drawings. 75 pp. Ye Galleon Press, 1983. $14.95.

SKETCHES OF A TOUR TO THE LAKES
Thomas L. McKenney
A sourcebook of early Indian life among the Ojibwe & the Sioux. Reprint of 1827 edition. Illus. 494 pp. Ross & Haines, $25.

SKETCHES OF WESTERN ADVENTURE
John McClung
Reprint of 1832 edition. Ayer Co., $13.

SKULKING WAY OF WAR
Patrick Malone
Madison Books, 1991. $29.95.

*SKUNNY WUNDY: SENECA INDIAN TALES
Arthur C. Parker, Editor; Illus by George Armstrong
Children's tales handed down by Native American storytellers. Grades 4 and up. Illus. 224 pp. Paper. Syracuse University Press, 1994. $15.95.

THE SKY CLEARS: POETRY OF THE AMERICAN INDIANS
Arthur G. Day, Editor
Reprint of 1951 edition. 204 pp. Paper.
University of Nebraska Press, $7.95.

THE SKY IS MY TIPI
Mody Boatright, Editor
Reprint of 1949 edition. Illus. 254 pp.
Southern Methodist University Press, $13.95.

*SKY WATCHERS OF AGES PAST
Malcolm E. Weiss
Grades 5-9. Houghton Mifflin, 1982. $7.95.

SKYSCRAPERS HIDE THE HEAVENS: THE HISTORY OF INDIAN-WHITE RELATIONS IN CANADA
J.R. Miller
3rd Edition. Illus. 500 pp. Paper. University of Toronto Press, 2000. $29.95.

*SKYWOMAN: LEGENDS OF THE IROQUOIS
Joanne Shenandoah & Douglas M. George
Illus. by John & David Fadden
Grades 5 and up. Illus. 128 pp. Clear Light, 1997. $14.95.

SLASH
Jeannette C. Armstrong
A novel which traces the pain, and the alienation felt by the modern First Nation peoples of Canada. 254 pp. Paper. Theytus, 1990. $12.95.

SLAVERY & THE EVOLUTION OF CHEROKEE SOCIETY, 1540-1866
Theda Perdue
Maps. 222 pp. University of Tennessee Press, 1979. $19.95; paper, $9.95.

*SLEEPY RIVER
Hannah Bandes; illus. by Jeanette Winter
Grades PS-3. Illus. 32 pp. Philomel, 1993. $14.95.

SLIM BUTTES, 1876: AN EPISODE OF THE GREAT SIOUX WAR
Jerome A. Greene, Editor
Illus. Maps. Biblio. 192 pp. Paper.
University of Oklahoma Press, 1982. $14.95.

JOHN SLOCUM & THE INDIAN SHAKER CHURCH
Robert H. Ruby & John A. Brown
Illus. Map. Photos. 300 pp. University of Oklahoma Press, 1996. $34.95.

JOHN SIMPSON SMITH, 1810-1871
Stan Hoig
Reprint of 1974 edition. Illus. 30 pp. Arthur H. Clark, $22.50. Paper. Pueblo County Historical Society, $3.50.

SMALL POX & THE IROQUOIS WARS: ETHNOHISTORICAL STUDY OF THE INFLUENCE OF DISEASE & DEMOGRAPHIC CHANGE IN IROQUOIAN CULTURE HISTORY, 1630-1700
Stephen Clark
Illus. 125 pp. Paper. Coyote Press, 1981. $11.25.

SMALL SPIRITS: NATIVE AMERICAN DOLLS FROM THE NATIONAL MUSEUM OF THE AMERICAN INDIAN
Mary Jane Lenz; intro. by Clara Sue Kidwell
Illus. 176 pp. Paper. University of Washington Press, 2004. $24.95.

*SMALL WORLD OF ESKIMOS
Bernard Planche; Sarah Matthews, tr.
Grades K-3. Franklin Watts, 1980. $10.40.

SMITH & OTHER EVENTS: TALES OF THE CHILCOTIN
Paul St. Pierre
Collection of short stories of the Chilcotin Indians of British Columbia, Canada. 318 pp. Paper. University of Oklahoma Press, 1994. $12.95.

THE SMITHSONIAN & THE AMERICAN INDIAN: MAKING A MORAL ANTHROPOLOGY IN VICTORIAN AMERICA
Curtis M. Hinsley
A guide to changing attitudes and values about Indians. Illus. 320 pp. Paper. Smithsonian Institution Press, 1981. $17.95.

SMOKE RISING: THE NATIVE NORTH AMERICAN LITERARY COMPANION
Joseph Bruchac, et al.
Illus. 492 pp. Paper. Visible Ink Press, $17.95.

SMOKING TECHNOLOGY OF THE ABORIGINES OF THE IROQUOIS AREA OF NEW YORK STATE
Edward S. Rutsch
252 pp. Fairleigh Dickinson University Press, 1972. $25.

SMOKY-TOP: THE ART & TIMES OF WILLIE SEAWEED
Bill Holm
Illus. 160 pp. University of Washington Press, 1983. $24.95.

*SNAIL GIRL BRINGS WATER: A NAVAJO STORY
Geri Keams
Picture book. Ages 5-8. Illus. Northland Press & Clear Light, $15.95.

THE SNAKE DANCE OF THE HOPI INDIANS
Earle Forrest
Reprint of 1961 edition. Illus. 175 pp. Westernlore, $10.95.

THE SNAKE DANCE OF THE MOQUIS OF ARIZONA
John G. Bourke
Reprint of 1884 edition. Illus. 371 pp. Paper.
University of Arizona Press, $19.95.

REUBEN SNAKE, YOUR HUMBLE SERPENT
As told to Jay C. Fikes
Autobiography. Indian (Winnebago, 1937-1993) visionary and activist as told to Jay Fikes. Photos. 287 pp. Clear Light, 1996. $24.95; paper, $14.95.

SNOWBIRD CHEROKEES: PEOPLE OF PERSISTENCE
Sharlotte Neely
Examines the Cherokees of Snowbird, North Carolina. Illus. Maps. 192 pp. Paper. University of Georgia Press, $14.95.

A SNUG LITTLE PURCHASE: HOW RICHARD HENDERSON BOUGHT KAINTUCKEE FROM THE CHEROKEES IN 1775
Charles Brashers
Illus. Associated Creative Writers, 1979. $7.95; paper, $4.95.

SOCIAL & ECONOMIC CHANGE AMONG THE NORTHERN OJIBWA
R.W. Dunning
Paper. University of Toronto Press, 1959. $8.95.

THE SOCIAL LIFE OF STORIES: NARRATIVE & KNOWLEDGE IN THE YUKON TERRITORY
Julie Cruikshank
Study of indigenous oral narratives. Illus. 220 pp.
Paper. University of Nebraska Press, 1998. $22.

SOCIAL ORGANIZATION OF THE WESTERN APACHE: LETTERS FROM THE FIELD
edited by Morris E. Opler
Reprint of 1973 edition. 104 pp. University of Arizona Press, $19.95.

SOCIAL ORGANIZATION OF THE WESTERN PUEBLOS
Fred Eggan
Reprint of 1950 edition. Illus. Paper. University of Chicago Press, 1973. $12.50; paper, $2.95.

*SOFT CHILD: HOW RATTLESNAKE GOT ITS FANGS
Joe Hayes & Kay Sather
Tohono O'odham tale. Grades Pre-K-3. Illus. 32 pp.
Paper. Harbinger House, $8.95.

*SOFT RAIN: A STORY OF THE CHEROKEE TRAIL OF TEARS
Corneli Cornellison
Grades 3 to 5. Illus. 128 pp. Bantam Doubleday Dell, Books for Young Readers, 1998. $14.95.

SOLD AMERICAN: THE STORY OF ALASKA NATIVES & THEIR LAND, 1867-1959 - THE ARMY TO STATEHOOD
Donald C. Mitchell
Illus. Photos. Map. 600 pp. Originally published by University Press of New England, 1997. University of Alaska Press, 2002. $45; paper, $29.95.

SOLDIER, SETTLER & SIOUX: FORT RIDGELY & THE MINNESOTA RIVER VALLEY, 1853-1867
Paul N. Beck
History of one of the most important military posts in the Minnesota and Big Sioux River valleys. Illus. 150 pp. Paper. The Center for Western Studies, 2000. $12.95.

SOME KIND OF POWER: NAVAJO CHILDREN'S SKIN-WALKER NARRATIVES
Margaret K. Brady
224 pp. University of Utah Press, 1984. $20.

SOME NEWSPAPER REFERENCES CONCERNING INDIAN—WHITE RELATIONSHIPS IN NORTHEASTERN CALIFORNIA, 1850-1920
Norris Bleyhl
209 pp. Association of Northern California Records, 1979. $9.

SOME SEX BELIEFS & PRACTICES IN A NAVAHO COMMUNITY
F.L. Bailey
Reprint of 1950 edition. Paper. Peabody Museum, $10.

SOME THINGS ARE NOT FORGOTTEN:
A PAWNEE FAMILY REMEMBERS
Martha Royce Blaine
Illus. Map. 286 pp. University of Nebraska Press, 1997. $65.

SOME WARMER TONE: ALASKA
ATHABASKAN BEAD EMBROIDERY
Kate C. Duncan, Editor
Illus. Maps. 64 pp. Paper. University of Alaska Museum,
1984. $12.

*SON OF THE DINE'
J. Walter Wood
Grades 5-9. Paper. Council for Indian Education, 1972. $1.95.

SON OF OLD MAN HAT: A NAVAHO AUTOBIOGRAPHY
Walter Dyk & Left Handed, recorded by
380 pp. Paper. University of Nebraska Press, 1967. $10.95.

*SON OF THUNDER
Stig Holmas
The sole survivor of a Mexican Army massacre is adopted
by Cochise. Grades 7 and up. 128 pp. Harbinger House,
1993. $16.95; paper, $10.95.

SON OF TWO BLOODS
Vincent L. Mendoza
Half Creek and half Mexican, the author's traces his experi-
ence with racism. Illus. 200 pp. Paper. University of Nebraska
Press, 1996. $12.

*SONG OF THE HERMIT THRUSH:
AN IROQUOIS LEGEND
Terri Cohlene
Grades 1-5. Illus. Paper. Troll Associates, 1992. $4.95.

THE SONG OF THE LOOM:
NEW TRADITIONS IN NAVAJO WEAVING
Frederick Dockstader
Illus. 132 pp. Hudson Hills Press, 1987. $35; paper, $25.

*SONG OF THE SEVEN HERBS
Walking Night Bear & Stan Padilla
Grades 3 and up. Illus. 60 pp. Paper. Cherokee Publications
& The Book Publishing Co., $11.95.

SONG OF THE SKY: VERSIONS OF
NATIVE AMERICAN SONG-POEMS
Brian Swann; rev. ed. by Barry O'Connell
Paper. University of Massachusetts Press, 1994. $14.95.

SONG OF THE TURTLE:
AMERICAN INDIAN LITERATURE, 1974-1994
Paula Gunn Allen (Laguna/Lakota)
Anthology of American Indian literature.
Grades 9 and up. Oyate, 1996. $25.

*SONG OF THE WILD VIOLETS
Peggy Thompson, Writer & Illus.
Grades 3 and up. Illus. 36 pp. Paper.
The Book Publishing Co., $5.95.

A SONG TO THE CREATOR: TRADITIONAL ARTS
OF NATIVE AMERICAN WOMEN OF THE PLATEAU
Lillian J. Ackerman, Editor
206 pp. University of Oklahoma Press, 1996.
$29.95; paper, $18.95.

SONGPRINTS: THE MUSICAL EXPERIENCE
OF FIVE SHOSHONE WOMEN
Judith Vander
376 pp. Paper. University of Illinois Press, 1996.
$19.95; $26.95 includes audio.

SONGS
Charley J. Greasybear; Tom Trusky
& Judson Crews, Editors
Paper. Ahsahta Press, 1979. $4.95.

SONGS FROM AN OUTCAST
by John E. Smelcer
Collection of poems in both English and Ahtna Athabaskan
dealing with Native American themes. 95 pp. Paper. The
Falmouth Institute, 2000. $12.

SONGS FROM THIS EARTH ON TURTLE'S BACK:
AN ANTHOLOGY OF POETRY BY AMERICAN INDIAN
WRITERS
Joseph Bruchac
300 pp. Paper. Greenfield Review Press, 1983. $9.95.

*SONGS FROM THE LOOM:
A NAVAJO GIRL LEARNS TO WEAVE
Monty Roessel
Grades 3-8. Illus. 48 pp. Paper. Lerner Pubns, 1995. $6.95.

SONGS OF INDIAN TERRITORY
Illus. 2nd Edition. Includes recorded tape. Paper.
Center of the American Indian, 1991.

SONGS OF THE SPIRIT: SCULPTURE BY DOUG HYDE
Patrick T. Houlihan & Charles Dailey
Essays. 24 pp. Paper. Southwest Museum. $4.95.

SONGS OF THE TETON SIOUX
Harry Paige
Illus. Westernlore, 1969. $9.50.

SONGS OF THE TEWA
Herbert J. Spinden, Editor/Translator
Tewa poetry. Reprint of 1933 edition. Illus.
125 pp. Paper. Sunstone Press, $12.95.

SONGS OF THE WIGWAM
Contains more than a dozen songs portraying native life
and thought in the forest around the Great Lakes. 24 pages.
95 each; 65 each, 15 or more. World Around Songs, $2.45

SONORA: A DESCRIPTION OF THE PROVINCE
Ignaz Pfefferkorn
Ethnographic account of the Pima, Opata, and Eudeve Indians
of the Sonora region. Reprint of 1949 edition. 329 pp. Paper.
University of Arizona Press, $12.95.

SONORA YAQUI LANGUAGE STRUCTURES
John M. Dedrick & Eugene H. Casad
480 pp. University of Arizona Press, 1999. $49.95.

THE SONS OF THE WIND:
THE SACRED STORIES OF THE LAKOTA
D.M. Dooling
Mythology of the Oglala Lakota Sioux. 136 pp. Paper.
Parabola Books, 1984. $8.95.

A SORROW IN OUR HEART: THE LIFE OF TECUMSEH
Allan W. Eckert
862 pp. Bantam Books, $27.50.

SOUL CONCEPTS OF THE NAVAHO
Berard Haile
Reprint of 1964 edition. Paper.
St. Michaels Historical Museum, $6.50.

SOUL & NATIVE AMERICANS
Robert Holland, Editor
Abridged edition of original title: Conceptions of the Soul Among
North American Indians. 234 pp. Paper. Spring Publications,
1997. $18.

THE SOUL OF THE INDIAN; &
OTHER WRITINGS FROM OHIYESA
Charles Eastman; edited by Kent Nerburn
Ohiyesa, a Dakota Indian, has been described as "the Native
American Thoreau." Also known as Charles Alexander
Eastman. 96 pp. New World Library, $15.

THE SOUL OF THE INDIAN: AN INTERPRETATION
Charles A. Eastman
Reprint of 1911 edition. Illus. 170 pp. Paper.
University of Nebraska Press, 1980. $8.95.

*SOUN TETOKEN: NEZ PERCE BOY TAMES A STALLION
Kennth Thomasma; Eunice Hundley, Illus.
Recounts the days of the Nez Perce tribe during the War
of 1877. Grades 4 and up. Illus. Baker Book House,
$10.99; paper, $6.99.

THE SOUND OF RATTLES & CLAPPERS: A
COLLECTION OF NEW CALIFORNIA INDIAN WRITING
Greg Sarris, Editor
Poetry & fiction by 10 Native Americans of California
Indian ancestry documents history. 161 pp. Paper.
University of Arizona Press, 1994. $17.95.

THE SOUND OF STRINGS
Harold Keith
The Comanches during the mid-1800s.
182 pp. Levite of Apache, $17.

SOURCE MATERIAL FOR THE SOCIAL &
CEREMONIAL LIFE OF THE CHOCTAW INDIANS
John R. Swanton
Reprint. Illus. 295 pp. paper. Reprint Services,
$89. Paper. Birmingham Public Library, $25.

SOURCE MATERIAL ON THE HISTORY
& ETHNOLOGY OF THE CADDO INDIANS
John R. Swanton
Maps. Photos. 352 pp. Paper. University of
Oklahoma Press, 1996. $15.95.

SOURCES OF FINANCIAL AID AVAILABLE
TO AMERICAN INDIAN STUDENTS
Leslie A. Kedelty, Editor
Major sources of financial aid, and admissions and financial
aid process information. Includes program reps, BIA area offices, and job opportunities. 78 pp. Annual. Paper. Indian Resource Development (IRD), $5.

SOURCING PREHISTORIC CERAMICS
AT CHODISTAAS PUEBLO, ARIZONA
Maria Nieves Zedeno
Prehistoric pottery identification. Illus. 110 p.
Paper. University of Arizona Press, 1994. $12.95.

SOUTH CAROLINA INDIANS, INDIAN TRADERS &
OTHER ETHNIC CONNECTIONS: BEGINNING IN 1670
Theresa M. Hicks
Reprint Co., 1997.

SOUTH DAKOTA LEADERS: FROM PIERRE
CHOUTEAU, JR. TO OSCAR HOWE
Herbert T. Hoover & Larry Zimmerman
Includes biographies of Sitting Bull and Crazy Horse.
Paper. Dakota Press, 1989. $27.50.

SOUTH FLORIDA'S VANISHED PEOPLE:
TRAVELS IN THE HOMELAND OF ANCIENT CALUSA
Byron Voegelin
Island Press, 1977. $6.95.

*SOUTHEAST INDIANS: COLORING BOOK
Peter F. Copeland
Grades K-3. Illus. 48 pp. Paper. Dover, $2.95.

SOUTHEAST INDIANS: AN EDUCATIONAL
COLORING BOOK
Grades 1-8. Illus. 32 pp. Paper. Spizzirri Publishing, 1981.
Read & Coloring Book, $1.95; Cassette/book, $6.95.

SOUTHEASTERN CEREMONIAL
COMPLEX, ARTIFACTS & ANALYSIS
Patricia Galloway, Editor
Illus. 400 pp. University of Nebraska Press, 1989. $60.

SOUTHEASTERN CEREMONIAL
COMPLEX & ITS INTERPRETATION
J.H. Howard and C.H. Chapman
Illus. 169 pp. Paper. Missouri Archaeological Society,
1968. $4.

SOUTHEASTERN FRONTIERS: EUROPEAN, AFRICANS,
& THE AMERICAN INDIANS, 1513-1840: A CRITICAL
BIBLIOGRAPHY
James H. O'Donnell, III
136 pp. Paper. Indiana University Press, 1982. $4.95.

THE SOUTHEASTERN INDIANS
Charles Hudson
Illus. 573 pp. Paper. Hothem House &
University of Tennessee Press, 1976. $18.95.

SOUTHEASTERN INDIANS SINCE THE REMOVAL ERA
Walter Williams, Editor
Illus. 270 pp. Paper. University of Georgia Press, 1979. $12.

SOUTHEASTERN WOODLAND INDIAN DESIGNS
Caren Caraway
Illus. 48 pp. Paper. Stemmer House, 1985. $5.95.

SOUTHERN ARIZONA FOLK ARTS
James Griffith
235 pp. University of Arizona Press, 1988.
$29.95; paper, $14.95.

SOUTHERN ATHAPASKAN MIGRATION: A.D. 200-1750
128 pp. Dine College Press, 1987. $10.50.

SOUTHERN CADDO: AN ANTHOLOGY
H.F. Gregory & David H. Thomas, Editors
550 pp. Garland, 1986. $75.

SOUTHERN CHEYENNE WOMEN'S SONGS
Virginia Giglio
Book & tape set. Illus. Maps. 34 song transcriptions.
244 pp. University of Oklahoma Press, $29.95 (book);
tape, $9.95; book & tape set, $35.

SOUTHERN CHEYENNES
Donald Berthrong
Reprint of the 1963 edition. Illus. Maps. Biblio. 442 pp.
Paper. University of Oklahoma Press, $18.95.

SOUTHERN FRONTIER, 1670-1732
Verner Crane
Reprint of 1956 edition. Greenwood, $22.50.

SOUTHERN INDIAN MYTHS & LEGEDS
Virginia Borwn & Laurella Owens, Editors
Illus. 160 pp. Paper. Beechwood Books, 1985. $12.95.

THE SOUTHERN INDIANS & BENJAMIN HAWKINS,
1796-1816
Florette Henri
Illus. Maps. Biblio. 378 pp. University of Oklahoma Press,
1986. $34.95.

THE SOUTHERN INDIANS: THE STORY OF
THE CIVILIZED TRIBES BEFORE REMOVAL
R.S. Cotterill
Reprint of 1954 edition. Illus. Maps. 259 pp.
Paper. University of Oklahoma Press, $13.95.

SOUTHERN PLAINS ALLIANCES
Howard Meredith
University Press of Kansas, 1994.

SOUTHERN PLAINS LIFEWAYS: APACHE & WICHITA
Pamphlet on the Apache & Wichita Tribes.
Wichita Tribal Office.

SOUTHERN PUEBLO POTTERY:
2,000 ARTIST BIOGRAPHIES
 Gregory Schaaf; Richard M. Howard, Editor
Illus. 400 pp. Center for Indigenous Arts & Cultures Press,
2002. $60.

SOUTHERN UTE INDIANS OF EARLY COLORADO
 Verner Z. Reed; William Jones, Editor
Illus. Paper. Outbooks, 1980. $3.95.

SOUTHERN UTE WOMEN: AUTONOMY &
ASSIMILATION ON THE RESERVATION, 1887-1934
 Katherine M.B. Osburn
University of New Mexico Press, $45; paper, $19.95.

SOUTHWEST
 Alfonso Ortiz, Editor
Illus. 701 pp. Smithsonian, 1980. $23.

SOUTHWEST AMERICAN INDIAN DESIGNS
 Caren Caraway
Illus. 48 pp. Paper. Stemmer House, 1996. $5.95.

SOUTHWEST COOKS! THE TRADITION
OF NATIVE AMERICAN CUISINES
 Lynn Kirst & Jeanette O'Malley, Editors
Illus. 108 pp. Paper. Southwest Museum, 1991. $14.95.

SOUTHWEST: HANDBOOK
OF NORTH AMERICAN INDIANS
Illus. 868 pp. Smithsonian, 1983. $25.00.

SOUTHWEST INDIAN ARTS & CRAFTS
 Mark Bahti
Illus. 48 pp. KC Publications, 1983. $8.95; paper, $4.50.

SOUTHWEST INDIAN CALENDAR
 Marcia Keegan
13 color pictures of life in the Navajo Nation and among the
Pueblo Indians of New Mexico. 12.5" x 10.25". Clear Light,
$12.

SOUTHWEST INDIAN COOKBOOK:
PUEBLO & NAVAJO IMAGES, QUOTES & RECIPES
 Edited & photos by Marcia Keegan
44 color photos. 120 pp. Paper. Clear Light, $12.95.

SOUTHWEST INDIAN CRAFT ARTS
 Clara L. Tanner
Covers baskets, jewelry, textiles, silver, pottery, carving and
minor crafts of recent and contemporary tribes. Illus. 206 pp.
University of Arizona Press, 1968. $27.50.

*SOUTHWEST INDIAN DESIGN
STAINED GLASS COLORING BOOK
 Carol Krez
Grades K-2. 32 pp. Paper. Dover, $3.95.

SOUTHWEST INDIAN DESIGNS;
WITH SOME EXPLANATIONS
 Mark T. Bahti
Recreates about 200 symbols and their variations. Includes
are symbols and explanations of Zuni, Navajo, Hopi, Tewa,
Acoma, Pueblo, Mimbres, and Hohokam designs. Illus. 32 pp.
Paper. Treasure Chest, 1994. $4.95.

SOUTHWEST INDIAN PAINTING: A CHANGING ART
 Clara L. Tanner
Represents Indian easel art from 200 artists from Arizona
and New Mexico; 300 illustrations. Revised edition.
477 pp. University of Arizona Press, 1980. $50.

SOUTHWEST INDIAN SILVER
FROM THE DONEGHY COLLECTION
 Louise Lincoln, Editor
Illus. 189 pp. University of Texas Press, 1982. $29.95.

*SOUTHWEST INDIANS COLORING BOOK
 Peter Copeland
Ready-to-color depictions and descriptions of Southwest Indi-
ans of the past and present, 1840s-1980s. Grades 1 -4. Illus.
Paper. Dover, $2.95.

*SOUTHWEST INDIANS:
AN EDUCATIONAL COLORING BOOK
 Linda Spizzirri, Editor
Grades 1-8. Illus. 32 pp. Paper. Spizzirri Publishing, 1981.
Read & Coloring Book, $1.95; Cassette/book, $6.95.

SOUTHWEST INDIANS: A PHOTOGRAPHIC PORTRAIT
 Bill Harris
A photographic tour of Native American culture in the South-
west. 100 full-color photos. 128 pp. Random House, $9.95.

SOUTHWEST MUSEUM PUBLICATIONS
Southwest Museum.

SOUTHWEST TRAVELER: A TRAVELERS
GUIDE TO SOUTHWEST INDIAN ARTS & CRAFTS
 Charlotte S. Neyland
Illus. 48 pp. Paper.

SOUTHWESTERN ARTS & CRAFTS PROJECTS
 Nancy Krenz & Patricia Byrnes
Arts & crafts of the Indian and Spanish-American cultures.
145 pp. Paper. Sunstone Press, $12.95.

SOUTHWESTERN INDIAN ARTS & CRAFTS
 Tom Bahti; updated by Mark Bahti
Come to know silverwork, turquoise, beadwork, pottery, bas-
kets, ironwood carvings, Navajo sandpainting, Zuni fetishes,
Hopi kachinas, and Navajo rugs. Illus. Photos. Maps. 48 pp.
Paper. KC Publications, 1997. $7.95.

SOUTHWESTERN INDIAN BASKETS:
THEIR HISTORY & THEIR MAKERS
 Andrew H. Whiteford
Illus. 236 pp. Paper. School of American Research,
1988. $18.95.

SOUTHWESTERN INDIAN CEREMONIALS
 Tom Bahti; updated by Mark Bahti
Illus. Photos. Map. 64 pp. Paper. KC Publications, 1997. $7.95.

SOUTHWESTERN INDIAN DESIGNS
 Madeleine Orban-Szontagh
250 authentic motifs drawn from Navajo jewelry & rugs, Pueblo
pottery, Hopi ceremonial dress, & other sources. Illus. 48 pp.
Paper. Dover, $5.95.

SOUTHWESTERN INDIAN RECIPE BOOK
 Zora G. Hesse
Favorite foods of many tribes. Illus. 60 pp. Paper.
Filter Press, $4.

SOUTHWESTERN INDIAN RITUAL DRAMA
 Charlotte Frisbie
Illus. 372 pp. Paper. Waveland, 1989. $14.95.

SOUTHWESTERN INDIAN TRIBES
 Tom Bahti; updated by Mark Bahti
Covers 32 Southwestern Indian cultures. Illus. Photos.
Maps. 72 pp. Paper. KC Publications, 1997. $7.95.

SOUTHWESTERN POTTERY: AN ANNOTATED
BIBLIOGRAPHY & LIST OF TYPES & WARES
 Norman T. Oppelt
Illus. 333 pp. Scarecrow Press, 1988. $35.

SOUTHWESTERN POTTERY: ANASAZI TO ZUNI
 Allan Hayes & John Blom
130 color photos. Biblio. 200 pp. Northland Press
& Clear Light, $40; paper, $21.95.

SOVEREIGNTY & SYMBOL:
INDIAN-WHITE CONFLICT AT GANIENKEH
 Gail Landsman
Illus. 250 pp. University of New Mexico Press, 1988. $19.95.

SPANISH EXPLORERS IN THE SOUTHERN U.S., 1528-1543
 Frederick Hodge & Theodore Lewis, Editors
Reprint fo 1907 edition. Illus. 410 pp. Barnes & Noble, $21.50.

SPANISH-AMERICAN BLANKETRY: ITS RELATIONSHIP
TO ABORIGINAL WEAVING IN THE SOUTHWEST
 H.P. Mera
Reprint of 1948 edition. Illus. 96 pp. Paper. School of Ameri-
can Research, $14.95.

SPANISH & INDIAN PLACE NAMES OF CALIFORNIA:
THEIR MEANING & THEIR ROMANCE
 Nellie Sanchez; Carlos Cortes, Editor
Reprint of 1930 edition. Illus. Ayer Co., $23.

PANISH FRONTIER IN NORTH AMERICA
 David J. Weber
Definitive history of the Spanish colonial period in North
America. Describes the influences by the Spaniards and the
effect Native North Americans on the Spanish settlers from
Florida to California. Illus. 600 pp. Yale University Press, 1992.
$40; paper, $16.

*SPARK IN THE STONE: SKILLS & PROJECTS
FROM THE NATIVE AMERICAN TRADITION
 Peter Goodchild
Grades 5 and up. Illus. 130 pp. Paper. Cherokee
Publications & Chicago Review Press, 1991. $11.95.

*SPARROW HAWK
 Meridel le Sueur; illus. by Robert DesJarlait
Fictional look at youth and race relations.
Grades 4 and up. 192 pp. Holy Cow! Press, $13.95.

SPEAK TO ME WORDS
 edited by Dean Rader & Janice Gould
Essays on contemporary American Indian poetry. 290 pp.
University of Arizona Press, 2003. $50; paper, $24.95..

SPEAKING FOR THE GENERATIONS:
NATIVE WRITERS ON WRITING
 Simon J. Ortiz, Editor
Includes Gloria Bird and Leslie Marmon Silko describe the
influences on their developments as writers. 248 pp. Paper.
University of Arizona Press, 1998. $17.95.

SPEAKING OF INDIANS
 Ella Deloria; intro by Vine Deloria, Jr.
Describes traditional values, costumes, kinship patterns and
religious attitudes of the Sioux. Reprint of 1944 edition. 163
pp. Paper. University of Nebraska Press, 1998. $11.95.

*SPIDER SPINS A STORY
 Jill Max; illus. by Robert Annesley, et al
Collection of 14 legends from native America. Ages 8-12.
Illus. 72 pp. Northland Press & Clear Light, $16.95.

SPIDER WOMAN STORIES:
LEGENDS OF THE HOPI INDIANS
 G.M. Mullett
Hopi mythology. 142 pp. Paper. University of
Arizona Press, 1979. $13.95.

SPIDERWOMAN: A STORY OF
NAVAJO WEAVERS & CHANTERS
 Gladys Reichard
Reprint of 1934 edition. Illus. 319 pp. Paper.
University of New Mexico Press & Clear Light, $16.95.

SPIDERWOMAN'S DREAM
 Alicia Otis
Southwestern Indian mythology. Illus. 64 pp.
Paper. Sunstone Press, $7.95.

SPIDERWOMAN'S GRANDDAUGHTERS:
TRADITIONAL TALES & CONTEMPORARY
WRITING BY NATIVE AMERICAN WOMEN
 Paula G. Allen, Editor
256 pp. Paper. Fawcett, 1990. $11.95.

SPIRIT CAPTURE: PHOTOGRAPHS FROM THE
NATIONAL MUSEUM OF THE AMERICAN INDIAN
 Tim Johnson, Editor; Foreword by W. Richard West
200 images from the Museum with essays from Native American historians, anthropologists, and curators. 25 color photos.
224 pp. Smithsonian Institution Press & Written Heritage, 1998.
$29.95.

SPIRIT FACES: CONTEMPORARY
MASKS OF THE NORTHWEST COAST
 Gary Wyatt
Paper. University of Washington Press, $24.95.

THE SPIRIT & THE FLESH: SEXUAL DIVERSITY
IN AMERICAN INDIAN CULTURE
 Walter L. Williams
Illus. 364 pp. Paper. Beacon Press & Clear Light, 1988. $16.

SPIRIT HEALING: NATIVE AMERICAN MAGIC & MEDICINE
 Mary Dean Atwood; illus. by Bert Seabourn
A self-help guide to the Native American spiritual growth
process. 160 pp. Paper. Sterling, 1992. $12.95.

SPIRIT HERBS: NATIVE AMERICAN HEALING
 Mary Atwood
160 pp. Paper. Sterling, 2000. $12.95.

SPIRIT IN THE STONE: A HANDBOOK OF SOUTHWEST
INDIAN ANIMAL CARVINGS & BELIEFS
 Mark Bahti
Recounts stories and legends associated with the animals and
other figures represented by these fetish forms. Illus. 147 pp.
Paper. Clear Light, $15.95.

SPIRIT MEDICINE: NATIVE AMERICAN
TEACHINGS TO AWAKEN THE SPIRIT
 Wolf Moondance
Illus. 160 pp. Paper. Sterling, 1995. $12.95.

SPIRIT MOUNTAIN: AN ANTHOLOGY
OF YUMAN STORY & SONG
 Leanne Hinton and Lucille Watahomigie, Editors
344 pp. University of Arizona Press, 1984. $45;
paper, $24.95.

SPIRIT MOVES: THE STORY OF SIX
GENERATIONS OF NATIVE WOMEN
 Loree Boyd
448 pp. Paper. New World Library, 1997. $17.95.

SPIRIT OF THE ALBERTA INDIAN TREATIES
 Richard Price
202 pp. Paper. Gower, 1979. $8.95.

SPIRIT OF BLACK HAWK:
A MYSTERY OF AFRICANS & INDIANS
 Jason Berry; photos by Syndey Byrd
The mystery of how a legendary Indian became one of the
patron saints of a sect of African-American churches in New
Orleans. Illus. 128 pp. University Press of Mississippi, 1995.
$20.

SPIRIT OF THE FIRST PEOPLE: NATIVE AMERICAN MUSIC TRADITIONS OF WASHINGTON STATE
Paper. University of Washington Press, $29.95.

SPIRIT OF THE HARVEST: NORTH AMERICAN INDIAN COOKING
Beverly Cox & Marvin Jacobs
Recipes. Illus. 255 pp. Center for Western Studies & Written Heritage, 1991. $29.95. Four Winds Trading Co., $35.

SPIRIT OF NATIVE AMERICA: BEAUTY & MYSTICISM IN AMERICAN INDIAN ART
Anna Lee Walters
Illus. 120 pp. Paper. Chronicle Books, 1990. $18.95.

SPIRIT OF THE NEW ENGLAND TRIBES: INDIAN HISTORY & FOLKLORE, 1620-1984
William S. Simmons
Map. 330 pp. Paper. University Press of New England, 1986. $19.95.

*SPIRIT OF THE WHITE BISON
Beatrice Culleton
Plains Nations sory of the deliberate destruction of the bison. Grades 4 and up. Illus. 64 pp. Book Publishing Co., 1989. $5.95.

*SPIRIT QUEST: THE INITIATIONS OF AN INDIAN BOY
Carol Batdorf
Grades 4 and up. Illus. 160 pp. Paper. Hancock House, $9.95.

SPIRIT & REASON: THE VINE DELORIA, JR. READER
Barbara Deloria, Kristen Foehner & Sam Scinta, Editors
An anthology of his works. 400 pp. Paper. Fulcrum Publishing & Clear Light, 1999. $17.95.

SPIRIT SINGS: ARTISTIC TRADITIONS OF CANADA'S FIRST PEOPLES
Glenbow Museum Staff
Illus. 265 pp. Firefly Books Ltd., 1990. $50.

SPIRIT VISIONS, VOL. 1: THE OLD ONES SPEAK
Dennison & Teddi Tsosie
Illus. 384 pp. Dolphin Publishing, 1997. $19.95.

SPIRIT WORLD
Time-Life Books Editors
Illus. 184 pp. Time-Life, 1992. $19.95.

SPIRITED RESISTANCE: THE NORTH AMERICAN INDIAN STRUGGLE FOR UNITY, 1745-1815
Gregory Evans Dowd
288 pp. The Johns Hopkins University Press, 1991. $26.95; paper, $16.95..

SPIRITS IN THE ART: FROM THE PLAINS & SOUTHWEST INDIAN CULTURES
james A. Hanson
Over 900 objects are illustrated. 262 color photos. 262 pp. Written Heritage, $94.95.

SPIRITS OF THE EARTH: A GUIDE TO NATIVE AMERICAN SYMBOLS, STORIES & CEREMONIES
Bobby Lake-Thom
Illus. 224 pp. paper. New American Library, 1997. $13.95.

SPIRITUAL DIMENSIONS OF HEALING: FROM NATIVE SHAMANISM TO CONTEMPORARY HEALTH CARE
Stanley Krippner & Patrick Welch
Illus. 302 pp. Irvington, 1992. $19.95; with audio, $39.95.

SPIRITUAL ENCOUNTERS: INTERACTION BETWEEN CHRISTIANITY & NATIVE RELIGIONS IN COLONIAL AMERICA
Nicholas Griffiths & Fernando Cervantes, Editors
304 pp. Paper. University of Nebraska Press, 1999. $30.

SPIRITUAL LEGACY OF THE AMERICAN INDIAN
Joseph Epes Brown
Reprint of 1964 edition. Illus. 135 pp. Paper. Crossroad Publishing, $14.95.

SPIRITUAL WISDOM OF THE NATIVE AMERICANS
John Heinerman
Illus. 170 pp. Paper. Cassandra Press, 1989. $9.95.

THE SPOKANE INDIANS: CHILDREN OF THE SUN
Robert H. Ruby & John A. Brown
Reprint of 1970 edition. Illus. Maps. Biblio. 346 pp. Paper. University of Oklahoma Press, $18.95.

SPOKEN CREE: WEST COAST OF JAMES BAY
C. Douglas Ellis
715 pp. Paper. University of Nebraska Press, 1983. $21.

*SPORTS & GAMES THE INDIANS GAVE US
Alex Whitney
Grades 7 and up. David McKay, 1977. $7.95.

*SPOTTED EAGLE & BLACK CROW: A LAKOTA LEGEND
Emery Bernhard
Betrayed by his brother, a warrior is rescued by eagles. Grades K-3. Illus. 32 pp. Holiday House, 1993. $15.95.

*THE SPOTTED HORSE
Henry Tall Bull
Grades 2-10. 32 pp. Council for Indian Education, 1970. $8.95; paper, $2.95.

SPOTTED TAIL'S FOLK: A HISTORY OF THE BRULE SIOUX
George E. Hyde
Reprint of 1961 edition. Illus. Map.s Biblio. 361 pp. Paper. University of Oklahoma Press, $25.95.

*SQUANTO & THE FIRST THANKSGIVING
Joyce K. Kessel; illus. by Lisa Donze
Grades 1-3. Illus. 56 pp. Lerner, 1983. $15.95; paper, $5.95.

*SQUANTO, FRIEND OF THE PILGRIMS
Clyde Bulla
Grades 4-6. Reprint. 110 pp. Paper. Demco, $9.

STABILITY & VARIATION IN HOPI SONG
George List
205 pp. American Philosophical Society, 1993. $28.

STANDING BEAR & THE PONCA CHIEFS
Thomas H. Tibbles; Kay Graber, Editor
143 pp. Paper. University of Nebraska Press, 1995. $13.95.

STANDING FLOWER: THE LIFE OF IRVING PABANALE, AN ARIZONA TEWA INDIAN
edited by Robert Black
Illus. Maps. University of Utah Press. $24.95.

STANDING IN THE LIGHT: A LAKOTA WAY OF SEEING
Severt Young Bear & R.D. Theisz
Illus. Biblio. Map. 210 pp. Paper. University of Nebraska Press, 1994. $14.

THE STAR LAKE ARCHAEOLOGICAL PROJECT: ANTHROPOLOGY OF A HEADWATERS AREA OF CHACO WASH, NEW MEXICO
Walter Wait and Ben Nelson, Editors
Illus. 480 pp. Southern Illinois University Press, 1983. $24.95.

STAR MEDICINE: NATIVE AMERICAN PATH TO EMOTIONAL HEALING
Wolf Moondance
Illus. 192 pp. Paper. Sterling, 1997. $12.95.

STAR QUILT
Roberta Hill Whiteman
Poetry. Illus. 92 pp. Paper. Holy Cowl Press, $6.95.

*STAR TALES: NORTH AMERICAN INDIAN STORIES ABOUT THE STARS
Gretchen Mayo
Grades 5 and up. 96 pp. Walker & Co., 1987. $11.95.

STAR WARRIOR: THE STORY OF SWIFTDEER
Bill Wahlberg
The story of Harley SiftDeer Reagan, a medicine teacher, the leader of the Deer Tribe Metis Medicine Society. Illus. 196 pp. paper. Bear & Co., 1993. $12.95.

THE STARS ABOVE, THE EARTH BELOW: AMERICAN INDIANS & NATURE
Marsha Bol & Carnegie Museum
Illus. 276 pp. Paper. Robets Rinehart, 1998. $19.95.

STARS OF THE FIRST PEOPLE: NATIVE AMERICAN STAR MYTHS & CONSTELLATIONS
Dorcas S. Miller
Guide to Native American constellations and folklore. 75 star charts, 9 regional mapos, bxw illus. 344 pp. Paper. Clear Light, $19.95.

STARTING FROM HERE: DAKOTA POETRY, POTTERY, & CARING
Jerome W. Freeman
Illus. 108 pp. Paper. Ex Machina, 1996. $12.95.

STARTING YOUR OWN SUCCESSFUL INDIAN BUSINESS
Steve Robinson & Stephen Hogan
160 pp. Paper. Thornsbury Bailey Brown, 1991. $45.

THE STATE OF NATIVE AMERICA: GENOCIDE, COLONIZATION & RESISTANCE
M. Annette Jaimes, Editor
Essays by Native American authors and activists on contemporary Native issues including the quincentenary. 480 pp. Paper. South End Press, 1991. $16.

THE STATE OF SEQUOYAH: AN IMPRESSIONISTIC LOOK AT EASTERN OKLAHOMA
Jerald C. Walker; Daisy Decazes, photos by
Traces the background of what is now eastern Oklahoma. The story of Indian removal, "Trail of Tears", and the development of the state. Illus. 120 pp. The Lowell Press, $25.

STATE & RESERVATION: NEW PERSPECTIVES ON FEDERAL INDIAN POLICY
George Pierre Castile & Robert L. Bee, Editors
Essays focus on the rise, change, and persistence of the Native American reservation system. 259 pp. Paper. University of Arizona Press, 1992. $23.50.

STATE-TRIBAL RELATIONS: INTO THE 21st CENTURY
Judy Zelio & James Reed
Analysis of government-to-government relations; describes the issues and discusses agreements. Case studies. 120 pp. National Conference of State Legislatures, 1993. $25.

STATE-TRIBAL RELATIONSHIPS - REPORTS
"1991 State Legislation Relating to Native Americans," Report, Vol. 16, No. 9 - 19 pp. $5; "State-Tribal Transportation Agreements," Report No. 14, No. 4 - 1989. $5; "States and the Indian Gaming Regulatory Act," Report Vol. 17, No. 16 - 1992, 18 pp. $5; "Promoting Effective State-Tribal Relations: A Dialogue" - examines how states and tribes can work together. 1990. 19 pp. $10; "Jurisdiction Over Nuclear Waste Transportation on Indian Tribal Lands: State-Tribal Relationships," Report Vol. 16, No. 4. 1991. 11 pp. $5. National Conference of State Legislatures.

STATES & THE INDIAN GAMING REGULATION ACT
Pam Greenburg & Judy Zelio
17 pp. Paper. National Conference of State Legislators, 1992. $5.

STATISTICAL RECORD OF NATIVE NORTH AMERICANS
Marlita A. Reddy, Editor
Statistics on all aspects of Native American family life, education, business and industry. Compiled from government records, and private associations. Includes 1,000 charts, graphs, and tables; 200 current and extinct tribes are detailed. Illus. 1,650 pp. Gale Research, 1993. $89.50.

STATUS & HEALTH IN PREHISTORY: A CASE STUDY OF THE MOUNDVILLE CHIEFDOM
Mary Lucas Powell
Illus. 352 pp. Smithsonian Institution Press, 1988. $40.

STONE AGE IN THE GREAT BASIN
Emory Strong
Illus. 280 pp. Paper. Binford & Mort, 1967. $12.95.

STONE AGE OF THE COLUMBIA RIVER
Emory Strong
Illus. Photos and maps. 256 pp. Paper. Binford & Mort, 1967. $9.95.

STONE AGE SPEAR & ARROW POINTS OF THE MIDCONTINENTAL & EASTEN U.S.
Noel D. Justice
A modern survey & reference. Illus. 302 pp. Indiana University Press, 1988. $37.95.

STONE ARTIFACTS OF TEXAS INDIANS - A FIELD GUIDE
Turner & Hester
Points & knivfe types, stone tools and ornaments. 200 sketches. 308 pp. paper. Hothem House, 1985. $14.95.

*THE STONE CANOE & OTHER STORIES
John L. Peyton
12 stories told by the People of the Rapids, the northernmost Ojibway. Grades 2 to 5. Illus. 151 pp. Paper. University of Nebraska Press, 1989. $24.95; paper, $14.95.

STORIED STONE: INDIAN ROCK ART IN THE BLACK HILLS COUNTRY
Linea Sundstrom
Illus. 288 pp. University of Oklahoma Press, 2004. $44.95; paper, $24.95.

STORIES FROM INDIAN WIGWAMS & NORTHERN CAMPFIRES
E.R. Young
Reprint. Gordon Press, 1977. $59.95.

STORIES FROM THE LAND
32 pp. Paper. Museum of Northern Arizona, 1981. $3.

STORIES FOR FUTURE GENERATIONS/QULIRAT QANEMCIT-LLU KINGUVARCIMALRIIT: THE ORATORY OF YUP'IK ESKIMO ELDER PAUL JOHN
trans. by Sophie Shield; edited by Ann Fienup-Riordan
Yup'ik tales and personal experiences of Paul John. Text in Yup'ik & English. Illus. 856 pp. Paper. University of Washington Press, 2004. $35.

STORIES & STONE: WRITING THE ANCESTRAL PUEBLO HOMELAND
edited by Reuben Ellis
Includes essays, stories, travelers' reports, poems, and images of the stone ruins, cliff dwellings, pot shards, and peyroglyphs. Illus. Map. 244 pp. Paper. Univeristy of Arizona Press, 2004. $19.95.

*STORIES IN STONE: ROCK ART: IMAGES FROM THE ANCIENT ONES
Jennifer Owings Dewey
Introduces young readers to the history and mystery of rock art in the Southwest. Ages 7 and up. Illus. 32 pp. University of New Mexico Press, 2003. $14.95.

STORIES OF AWE & ABUNDANCE
Jose Hobday
128 pp. Paper. Continuum, 1999. $9.95.

STORIES OF MAASAW, A HOPI GOD
Ekkehart Malotki & Michael Lomatuway'ma
Illus. 275 pp. University of Nebraska Press, 1987.
$24.95; paper, $14.95.

*STORIES OF OUR BLACKFEET GRANDMOTHERS
Mary C. Boss-Ribs & Jenny Running-Crane
Grades 1-6. Paper. Council for Indian Education, 1984. $1.45.

STORIES OF OUR WAY: AN ANTHOLOGY OF AMERICAN INDIAN PLAYS
edited by Hanay Geiogamah & Jaye T. Darby
Anthology of over 30 years of American Indian theater, including the 1930s classic The Cherokee Night and 11 other plays. 503 pp. The Falmouth Institute, 1999. $60; paper, $20.

STORIES OF THE ROAD ALLOWANCE PEOPLE
Maria Campbell
Collection of short stories about Metis political movement. 127 pp. Paper. Theytus, 1994. $12.95.

STORIES OF THE SIOUX
Luther Standing Bear
Illus. 95 pp. Paper. University of Nebraska Press, 1988. $8.95.

STORIES OF SURVIVAL: CONVERSATIONS WITH NATIVE NORTH AMERICANS
Remmelt & Kathleen Hummelen
Stories that depicty concerns of Native peoples in Northeastern cities, Arctic communities, prairie towns, and reservations. Paper. Friendship Press, $5.95.

STORIES THAT MAKE THE WORLD: ORAL LITERATURE OF THE INDIAN PEOPLES OF THE INLAND NORTHWEST: AS TOLD BY LAWRENCE ARIPA, TOM YELLOWTAIL, AND OTHER ELDERS
Rodney Frey, Editor
Illus. Map. 256 pp. University of Oklahoma Press, 1995. $24.95; paper, $14.95.

STORIES WE LIVE BY / BAAK'AATUGH TS'UHUNITY
Catherine Attla
University of Alaska Press, $18.

*STORM BOY
Paul Owen Lewis
Grades K-2. Illus. 30 pp. Beyond WordsPublishing, 1995.

STORM IN THE MOUNTAIN
Vernon Crow
Story of William H. Thomas' Legion of Cherokee Indians formed during the Civil War. Illus. Photos. Maps. 300 pp. Paper. Cherokee Publications, $7.95.

STORM PATTERNS: POEMS FROM TWO NAVAJO WOMEN
Della Frank & Roberts D. Joe
20 poems. Illus. Dine College Press, 1993. $12.

STORMS BREWED IN OTHER MEN'S WORLDS: THE CONFRONTATIONS OF INDIANS, SPANISH, AND FRENCH IN THE SOUTHWEST, 1540-1795
Elizabeth A.H. John
Maps. 806 pp. Paper. University of Oklahoma Press, 1981. $24.95.

A STORY AS SHARP AS A KNIFE: THE CLASSICAL HAIDA MYTHTELLERS & THEIR WORLD
Robert Bringhurst
Illus. Maps. 527 pp. University of Nebraska Press, 2000. $50; paper, $24.95.

*THE STORY OF BLUE ELK
Gerald Hausman; illus. by Kristina Rodanas
Grades 3-5. Color illus. 32 pp. Clear Light, $15.

THE STORY OF THE CHEROKEE PEOPLE
Tom B. Underwood
Reprint of 1961 edition. Illus. 48 pp. Paper. VIP Publishing & Cherokee Publications, $5.

THE STORY OF CYNTHIA ANN PARKER
Jack C. Ramsay, Jr.
Took into captivity, she had a son, the "white Indian," Quanah, the last and most famous of the Comanche war chiefs. Illus. 225 pp. Eakin Press, $16.95.

STORY OF DEEP DELIGHT
Thomas McNamee
Relates the life stories of three young men - the last Chickasaw Indian chief, a mid-19th century slave, and a present-day artist. 480 pp. Paper. Penguin USA, $11.

*THE STORY OF GERONIMO
Grades 3-6. Illus. 32 pp. Childrens Press, $9.95.

THE STORY OF INDIAN MUSIC: ITS GROWTH & SYNTHESIS
O. Gosvami
Reprint. Scholarly Press, $75.

*THE STORY OF LITTLE BIG HORN
R.C. Stern
Grades 3-6. Illus. 32 pp. Childrens Press, 1983. $9.95.

THE STORY OF THE LITTLE BIG HORN: CUSTER'S LAST FIGHT
W.A. Graham
Illus. Maps. 284 pp. Paper. Clear Light, $13.95.

THE STORY OF LYNX
Claude Levi-Straus
Nez Perce myth. Illus. Maps. 276 pp. University of Chicago Press, 1995. $24.95; paper, $17.95.

THE STORY OF OKLAHOMA
W. David Baird & Danney Goble
The up-t-date history of the Sooner State, including a collection of primary sources on life in Indian Territory. Illus. Maps. Biblio. 512 pp. University of Oklahoma Press, 1994. $28.95.

THE STORY OF THE MEADOWLARK
Scott B. Smith
Illus. 47 pp. Stump Publishing, 1986. $15.

STORY OF THE RED MAN
Flora W. Seymour
Facsimile of 1929 edition. Ayer Co., $27.50.

*THE STORY OF THE TRAIL OF TEARS
R. Conrad Stein
Grades 3-6. Illus. 32 pp. Childrens Press, 1985. $9.95.

*THE STORY OF WOUNDED KNEE
R.C. Stein
Grades 3-6. Illus. 32 pp. Childrens Press, 1983. $9.95.

STORYPOLE LEGENDS
Emmerson H. Matson
Folk stories, fables and legends from the Indians of the Puget Sound area. 108 pp. Council for Indian Education, 1996. $8.95.

STORYTELLERS & OTHER FIGURATIVE POTTERY
Douglas Congdon-Martin
In 1964, Helen Cordero of Cochiti Pueblo created the first storyteller, a clay image of her grandfather with five children clinging to him. This book presents over 400 pieces, by nearly 150 artists, in full color and organized by pueblo. Illus. 144 pp. Paper. Schiffer, $19.95.

STRAIGHT WITH THE MEDICINE: NARRATIVES OF WASHOE FOLLOWERS OF THE TIPI WAY
Warren L. D'Azevedo
Narratives compiled in the 1950s from seven followers of the Native American Church. Illus. 64 pp. Paper. Heyday Books, 1985. $5.95.

STRANGE BUSINESS
Rilla Askew
Short story collection of Choctaw Indians' place in the fictitious town of Cedar, Okla. 192 pp. Paper. Penguin USA, $10.

STRANGE EMPIRE
Joseph Kinsey Howard
Story of the Metis. Illus. 601 pp. Minnesota Historical Society Press, 1994. $16.95.

STRANGE JOURNEY: VISIONS OF A PSYCHIC INDIAN WOMAN
Louise Lone Dog
105 pp. Paper. Naturegraph, $8.95.

A STRANGER IN HER NATIVE LAND: ALICE FLETCHER & THE AMERICAN INDIANS
Joan Mark
Illus. 428 pp. Paper. University of Nebraska Press, 1988. $20.

STRANGERS IN BLOOD: FUR TRADE \COMPANY FAMILIES IN INDIAN COUNTRY
Jennifer S.H. Brown
Reprint of 1953 edition. Illus. 152 pp. 302 p. University of Oklahoma Press, 1996. $28.95; paper, $10.95.

STRANGERS IN A STOLEN LAND: AMERICAN INDIANS IN SAN DIEGO
Richard L. Carrico
Illus. Paper. Sierra Coaks, 1987. $10.95.

STRANGERS IN THEIR OWN LAND: A CHOCTAW PORTFOLIO
Photos by Carole Thompson
A booklet of 30 b&w photos with text showing daily life rituals of the Mississippi Choctaw. 40 pp. Paper. University Press of Mississippi, 1983. $4.95.

STRANGERS IN THEIR OWN LAND: AN AMERICAN INDIAN HISTORY GUIDE
Sandra Sheffield & Jude Urich
55 pp. Paper. Open Book Publishers, 1988. $6.95.

STRANGERS TO RELATIVES: THE ADOPTION & NAMING OF ANTHROPOLOGISTS IN NATIVE NORTH AMERICA
edited by Sergei Kan
Leading anthropologists in the U.S. & Canada focus on the cases of such prominent earlier scholars such as Lewis Henry Morgan and Franz Boas. Illus. Map. 270 pp. University of Nebraska Press, 2001. $55; paper, $24.95.

STRATEGIES FOR SURVIVAL: AMERICAN INDIANS IN THE EASTERN U.S.
Frank W. Porter, III, Editor
248 pp. Greenwood, 1986. $36.95.

STRATEGIES ON SUCCESSFUL INDEPENDENT LIVING SERVICES FOR AMERICAN INDIANS WITH DISABILITIES
P.L. Sanderson & J.A. Clay
109 pp. Paper. Northern Arizona University, 1996. $10.

STRONG HEARTS: NATIVE AMERICAN VISIONS & VOICES
Illus. 128 pp. Aperture, 1995. $44.95.

STRONG HEARTS, WOUNDED SOULS: NATIVE AMERICAN VETERANS OF THE VIETNAM WAR
Tom Holm
The role of military traditions and the warrior ethic in the mid-20th century American Indian life. 254 pp. University of Texas Press, 1996. $35; paper, $14.95.

STRUCTURAL CONSIDERATIONS OF METIS ETHNICITY: AN ARCHAEOLOGICAL, ARCHITECTURAL & HISTORICAL STUDY
David Burley, Gayle Horsfall & John Brandon
Illus. Dakota Press, 1992. $44.95; paper, $25.95.

THE STRUCTURE OF TWANA CULTURE: WITH COMPARATIVE NOTES ON THE STRUCTURE OF YUROK CULTURE
William Elmendorf & A.L. Kroeber
An account of Washington's Twana Indians of the southern coast Salish region. Illus. Maps. Biblio. 576 pp. Paper. Washington State University Press, 1992. $25.

A STRUCTURED APPROACH TO LEARNING THE BASIC INFLECTIONS OF THE CHEROKEE VERB
Durbin D. Feeling
190 pp. Paper. Indian University Press, 1994. $29, postpaid.

STRUGGLE FOR THE LAND: INDIGENOUS RESISTANCE TO GENOCIDE, ECOCIDE & EXPROPRIATION IN CONTEMPORARY NORTH AMERICA
Ward Churchill; preface by Winona LaDuke
Essays. 480 pp. Common Courage Press, $29.95; paper, $17.95.

THE STRUGGLE FOR WATER: POLITICS, RATIONALITY & IDENTITY IN THE AMERICAN SOUTHWEST
Wendy Nelson Espeland
One chapter devoted to the building of a dam and the effects on the Yavapai Tribe. Illus. Map. 282 pp. University of Chicago Press, 1998. $47; paper, $19.

JOHN STUART AND THE SOUTHERN COLONIAL FRONTIER: A STUDY OF INDIAN RELATIONS, WAR, TRADE, LAND PROBLEMS IN THE SOUTHERN WILDERNESS, 1754-1775
J. Alden
Reprint of 1944 edition. Illus. 384 pp. Gordian Press, $40.

STUDIES IN AMERICAN INDIAN LANGUAGES: DESCRIPTION & THEORY
Leanne Hinton & Pamela Munro
Paper. University of California Press, 1998. $35.

STUDIES IN AMERICAN INDIAN LITERATURE: CRITICAL ESSAYS & COURSE DESIGNS
Paula G. Allen
385 pp. Modern Language Association of America, 1983. $35; paper, $18.

STUDIES IN SOUTHEASTERN INDIAN LANGUAGES
James Crawford, Editor
463 pp. Brown Book & Cherokee Publications, 1975. $25.

A STUDY IN THE ETYMOLOGY OF THE INDIAN PLACE NAME
G.A. McAleer
Reprint. Gordon Press, 1977. $59.50.

THE STUDY OF AMERICAN INDIAN RELIGIONS
Ake Hultkrantz
Illus. 142 pp. Scholars Press, 1983. $26.95.

A STUDY OF OMAHA INDIAN MUSIC
Alice C. Fletcher
Reprint of 1893 edition. Includes Omaha songs and scores as well as native words for the songs. 160 pp. Paper. Written Heritage, $5.95.

A STUDY OF PUEBLO ARCHITECTURE: TUSAYAN & CIBOLA BUREAU OF AMERICAN ETHNOLOGY, 8th ANNUAL REPORT
Victor Mindeleff
Illus. 425 pp. Paper. Smithsonian, 1989. $19.95.

A STUDY OF THE SPECIAL PROBLEMS & NEEDS OF AMERICAN INDIANS WITH HANDICAPS BOTH ON & OFF THE RESERVATION
J.C. O'Connell
130 pp. Paper. Northern Arizona University, 1987.

STUDYING NATIVE AMERICA:
PROBLEMS & PROSPECTS
Russell Thornton
438 pp. University of Wisconsin Press, 1998.
$65; paper, $27.95.

STYLIZED CHARACTERS' SPEECH
IN THOMPSON SALISH NARRATIVE
Steven M. Egesdal
126 pp. University of Montana, 1992. $7.

THE SUBARCTIC ATHAPASCANS:
A SELECTED, ANNOTATED BIBLIOGRAPHY
Arthur E. Hippler and John R. Wood
380 pp. Paper. University of Alaska Institute of Social Sciences, 1974. $15.

SUBJUGATION & DISHONOR: A BRIEF HISTORY
OF THE TRAVAIL OF THE NATIVE AMERICANS
Philip Weeks and James B. Gidney
160 pp. Paper. Krieger Publishing, 1981. $8.50.

SUICIDE IN AMERICAN INDIANS
David Lester
237 pp. Nova Science Publishers, 1997. $59.

SUMMER IN THE SPRING:
ANISHINAABE LYRIC POEMS & STORIES
Gerald Vizenor
New edition. Anthology. Includes translations and a glossary of the Anishinaabe (Chippewa) words in which the poems and stories originally were spoken. Illus. with tribal pictomyths. 166 pp. Paper. University of Oklahoma Press, $12.95.

SUMMER MEDITATIONS WITH NATIVE AMERICAN
ELDERS
Don Coyhis
Reprint. 106 pp. Paper. Moh-He-Con-Nuck, $9.95.

SUMMER OF THE BLACK WIDOWS
Sherman Alexie (Spokane/Coeur d'Alene)
Poetry. Grades 9 and up. Paper. Oyate, 1996. $13.50.

SUMMER PEOPLE, WINTER PEOPLE: A GUIDE TO
PUEBLOS IN THE SANTA FE, NEW MEXICO AREA.
Sandra A. Edelman
Illus. 32 pp. Sunstone Press, $4.95.

SUMMONING THE GODS: SANDPAINTING
OF THE NATIVE AMERICAN SOUTHWEST
Ronald McCoy
Illus 32 pp. Paper. Museum of Northern Arizona, 1988. $4.95.

SUN BEAR: THE PATH OF POWER
Sun Bear, et al
Illus. 272 pp. Paper. Bear Tribe, 1984. $9.95.

THE SUN CAME DOWN:
TRADITIONAL BLACKFEET STORIES
Percy Bullchild
Illus. 384 pp. Paper. Harper & Row, 1985. $12.95.

SUN CHIEF: THE AUTOBIOGRAPHY OF A HOPI INDIAN
Leo W. Simmons, Editor
Revised 1963 edition. Illus. Paper.
Yale University Press, $12.95.

SUN CIRCLES & HUMAN HANDS: THE
SOUTHEASTERN INDIANS, ART & INDUSTRIES
E.L. Fundaburk and M.D. Forman, Editors
Reprint of 1957 edition. Illus. 232 pp. Hothem House & Southern Publications, $24.

*SUN DANCE FOR ANDY HORN
Shelly Frome
Grades 9-12. 124 pp. Council for Indian Education, 1990. $12.95; paper, $7.95.

THE SUN DANCE RELIGION:
POWER FOR THE POWERLESS
Joseph G. Jorgensen
Illus. 372 pp. Paper. University of Chicago Press, 1972. $14.95.

SUN DANCER
David London
Describes Native American spirituality. 320 pp. Paper. University of Nebraska Press, 1998. $14.95.

THE SUN GIRL
E. White, pseud.
Reprint of 1941 edition. Illus. 52 pp.
Museum of Northern Arizona. $4.75.

*SUN JOURNEY: A STORY OF ZUNI PUEBLO
Ann Nolan Clark
Grades 8 and up. Illus. 96 pp. Paper. Ancient City Press, 1988. $9.95.

SUN MEN OF THE AMERICAS
Grace Cooke
De Vorss & Co., $6.95.

SUN TRACKS
Ofelia Zepeda, Editor
American Indian literary series sponsored by the American Indian Studies Program, Dept. of English, University of Arizona.

SUNDANCING AT ROSEBUD & PINE RIDGE
Thomas E Mails
Reprint. Illus. Center for Western Studies, Delux edition, $125.

SUNDOGS
Lee Maracle
Novel about a young First Nation's family during 1992 and the Meech Lake Accord and the "Oka Crisis." 214 pp. Paper. Theytus, 1992. $12.95.

SUNDOWN
John Joseph Mathews
A novel of life in the Osage. Illus. 312 pp. Paper. University of Oklahoma Press, 1988. $15.95.

*SUNFLOWER'S PROMISE: A ZUNI LEGEND
Terri Cohlene
Grades 1-5. Illus. Paper. Troll Associates & Clear Light, 1992. $4.95.

*SUNPAINTERS: ECLIPSE OF THE NAVAJO SUN
Baje Whitehorne, Writer/Illustrator
Insight into how Native Americans have traditionallu honored natural phenomena. Picture book. Ages 5-8. Illus. 32 pp. Morning Flower Press & Northland Publishing, 1994. $14.95.

SUNSET TO SUNSET: A LIFETIME
WITH MY BROTHERS, THE DAKOTAS
Thomas L. Riggs, Editor
226 pp. Paper. South Dakota State Historical Society, 1997. $14.95.

SUNSHINE ON THE PRAIRIE:
THE STORY OF CYNTHIA ANN PARKER
Jack C. Tamsay; Edwin Eakin, Editor
Illus. 225 pp. Eakin Press, 1989. $16.95.

A SUPPLEMENT GUIDE TO MANUSCRIPTS: RELATING
TO THE AMERICAN INDIANS IN THE LIBRARY OF THE
AMERICAN PHILOSOPHICAL SOCIETY
Daythal Kendall
American Philosophical Society, 1983. $15.

SUPPLEMENT TO THE HANDBOOK OF MIDDLE
AMERICAN INDIANS, Vol. 1: ARCHAEOLOGY
Victoria R. Bricker & Jeremy A. Sabloff, Editors
Illus. 475 pp. University of Texas Press, 1981. $55.

SUPPLEMENT TO THE HANDBOOK OF MIDDLE
AMERICAN INDIANS, Vol. 2: LINGUISTICS
Victoria Bricker & Munro Edmonson, Editors
224 pp. University of Texas Press, 1984. $35.

SUPPLEMENT TO THE HANDBOOK OF MIDDLE
AMERICAN INDIANS, Vol. 3: LITERATURE
Victoria Bricker & Munro Edmonson, Editors
207 pp. University of Texas Press, 1985. $35.

*SUQUAMISH TODAY
A documentary on the Suquamish of Port Madison Reservation, Washington. Teacher's guide. Grades 4-8. Illus. 21 pp. Daybreak Star Press, $4.50.

THE SURROUNDED
D'Arcy McNickle
315 pp. Paper. University of New Mexico Press, $16.95.

SURVIVAL ARTS OF THE PRIMITIVE PAIUTES
Margaret Wheat
Illus. 140 pp. Paper. University of Nevada Press, 1967. $14.95.

SURVIVAL: LIFE & ART OF THE ALASKAN ESKIMO
The Newark Museum; Text by Barbara Lipton
Text and photographs of Alaska and objects: tools, utensils, dress, art created by the Eskimo. Illus. 96 pp. Paper. Newark Museum Publications, 1977. $7.95.

THE SURVIVAL OF THE BARK CANOE
John McPhee
Illus. 146 pp. Paper. Farrar, Straus & Grioux, 1975. $7.95.

SURVIVAL OF THE SPIRIT:
CHIRICAHUA APACHES IN CAPTIVITY
H. Henrietta Stockel
Relates the struggle for survival of the Chiricahua Apaches after being moved from the Southwest to Florida and Alabama then Oklahoma. Illus. 360 pp. University of Nevada Press, 1993. $24.95.

SURVIVAL & REGENERATION:
DETROIT'S AMERICAN INDIAN COMMUNITY
Edmund Jefferson Danziger, Jr.
Illus. 262 pp. Wayne State University Press, 1991. $9.

SURVIVAL SKILLS OF NATIVE CALIFORNIA
Paul D. Campbell
Over 1,000 instructional illus. 2,000+ skills. 400 pp. Paper. Gibbs Smith, Publisher. 2000. $39.95.

SURVIVAL SKILLS OF THE
NORTH AMERICAN INDIANS
Peter Goodchild
Illus. 244 pp. Paper. Chicago Review Press, 1999. $16.95.

SURVIVAL THIS WAY: INTERVIEWS
WITH AMERICAN INDIAN POETS
Joseph Bruchac
365 pp. Paper. University of Arizona Press, 1987. $19.95.

SURVIVING ARTS: TRADITIONAL
SKILLS OF THE FIRST CALIFORNIANS
Mike Shine
Illus. 256 pp. Paper. Heyday Books, $17.95.

SURVIVING AS INDIANS:
THE CHALLENGE OF SELF-GOVERNMENT
Menno Bolt
384 pp. Paper. University of Toronto Press, 1994. $19.95.

SURVIVING CONQUEST:
A HISTORY OF THE YAVAPAI PEOPLES
Timothy Braatz
Maps. 301 pp. University of Nebraska Pres, 2003. $55.

SURVIVING IN TWO WORLDS:
CONTEMPORARY NATIVE AMERICAN VOICES
Lois Crozier-Hogle & Darryl Babe Wilson
photos by Giuseppe Saitta; edited by Jay Leibold
Interviews 26 Native American leaders, such as: Oren Lyons, Arvol Looking Horse, John Echohawk, William Demmert, Cliford Trafzer, Greg Sarris and Roxanne Swentzell. Illus. 287 pp. University of Texas Press, 1997. $35; paper, $14.95.

*SUSETTE LA FLESCHE:
ADVOCATE FOR NATIVE AMERICAN RIGHTS
Grades 4 and up. Illus. 120 pp. Childrens Press, $13.95.

SUSQUEHANNA'S INDIANS
Barry C. Kent
Illus. 438 pp. Pennsylvania Historical
& Museum Commission, 1984. $15.95.

SWAMP SAILORS: RIVERLINE WARFARE
IN THE EVERGLADES, 1835-1842
George Buker
Illus. Maps. Biblio. 152 pp. University Presses of Florida, 1975. $15.

MADONNA SWAN: A LAKOTA WOMAN'S STORY
Mark St. Pierre, Editor
Illus. Maps. 224 pp. Paper. University of Oklahoma Press, 1991, $17.95.

SWAN AMONG THE INDIANS:
LIFE OF JAMES G. SWAN, 1818-1900
Lucile McDonald
A record of the Makah Indian culture and artifacts. Illus. 280 pp. Binford & Mort, $14.95.

THE SWEET GRASS LIVES ON: FIFTY CONTEMPORARY
NORTH AMERICAN INDIAN ARTISTS
Jamake Highwater
Illus. 192 pp. Harper & Row, 1980. $35.

SWEET MEDICINE: THE CONTINUING ROLE OF THE
SACRED ARROWS, THE SUN DANCE, & THE SACRED
BUFFALO HAT IN NORTHERN CHEYENNE HISTORY
Peter J. Powell
Illus. Maps. 2 vols. 994 pp. Paper.
University of Oklahoma Press, 1969. $55.

*SWEETGRASS
Jan Hudson
A novel set in the 19th century western Canadian prairie. 160 pp. Philomel, 1989. $13.95.

SYMBOL & SUBSTANCE IN AMERICAN INDIAN ART
Zena Mathews; Amy Hobar, Editor
24 pp. Paper. Metropolitan Museum of Art, 1984. $2.95.

SYMBOLIC & DECORATIVE
ART OF THE OSAGE PEOPLE
Illus. The Osage Mission.

SYMBOLIC IMMORTALITY: THE TLINGIT
POTLATCH OF THE 19TH CENTURY
Sergei Kan
The first comprehensive analysis of the mortuary practices of the Tlingit Indians of southeastern Alaska. 2 maps, 2 charts. 384 pp. Smithsonian Institution Press, 1989. $35; paper, $16.95.

SYMBOLS OF NATIVE AMERICA
Heike Owusu
Paper. Sterling, 1999. $13.95.

SYNTAX & SEMANTICS: THE SYNTAX
OF NATIVE AMERICAN LANGUAGES
Eung-Do Cook and Donna B. Gerdts
Volume 16 of Syntax and Semantics. Academic Press, 1984. $75.

**SYSTEMS OF CONSANGUINITY &
AFFINITY OF THE HUMAN FAMILY**
Lewis Henry Morgan
Examines the kinship systems of over 100 cultures. Illus.
604 pp. Paper. University of Nebraska Press, 1997. $40.

T

**TACACHALE: ESSAYS ON THE INDIANS OF FLORIDA
& SOUTHEASTERN GEORGIA DURING THE HISTORIC
PERIOD**
J.T. Milanich & Samuel Proctor, Editors
Illus. Maps. 217 pp. University Press of Florida, 1978. $23.95.

**MARGARET TAFOYA: A TEWA
POTTER'S HERITAGE & LEGACY**
Mary Ellen & Laurence Blair; Susan McDonald, Editor
Illus. 200 pp. Schiffer, 1986. $45.

**TAH-KOO WAH-KAN: OR, THE
GOSPEL AMONG THE DAKOTAS**
S. Riggs
Reprint of 1869 edition. 534 pp. Ayer Co., $33.

***THE TAINOS: THE PEOPLE
WHO WELCOMED COLUMBUS**
Francine Jacobs; illus. by Patrick Collins
Describes the early beginnings of the Tainos' culture.
Grades 6 and up. Illus. 112 pp. Putnam, 1992. $15.95.

TAITADUHAAN: WESTERN MONO WAYS OF SPEAKING
Paul V. Kroskrity, Rosalie Bethel, Jennifer F. Reynolds
CD-ROM providing an introduction to the language & culture
of the Western Mono Indians of Central California. $29.95.

**TAKE MY LAND, TAKE MY LIFE: THE STORY OF
CONGRESS'S HISTORIC SETTLEMENT OF ALASKA
NATIVE LAND CLAIMS, 1960-1971**
Donald Craig Mitchell
Illus. Photos. Map. Biblio. University of Alaska Press,
2001. $45; paper, $29.95.

**TAKING INDIAN LANDS: THE CHEROKEE
(JEROME) COMMISSION, 1889-1893**
William T. Hagan
Illus. Maps. University of Oklahoma Press, 2003. $39.95.

TALES THE ELDERS TOLD: OJIBWAY LEGENDS
Basil H. Johnston; illus. by Shirley Cheechoo
Illus. 64 pp. University of Toronto Press, $15.95.

*TALES FROM THE CHEROKEE HILLS
Jean Starr
33 Cherokee folktales. 94 pp. Paper.
John F. Blair & Cherokee Publications, $8.95.

TALES OF THE ANISHINAUBACK: OJIBWAY LEGENDS
Basil H. Johnston; illus. by Maxine Noel
Native myths. Illus. 80 pp. University of Toronto Press,
$24.95.

TALES OF APACHE WARFARE
James M. Barney
True stories of massacres, fights and raids in Arizona & New
Mexico. Reprint fo 1933 edition. 45 pp. Paper. High-Lonesome
Books, $7.

TALES OF THE BARK LODGES
Bertrand N.O. Walker (Hen-Toh)
12 traditional animal tales that preserve elements of Wyandot
culture. Illus. 160 pp. University Press of Mississippi, 1995.
$35; paper, $14.95.

TALES OF THE BLACK HILLS
Helen Rezatto
Collection of legends, including legends by the Sioux. Illus.
288 pp. Paper. Center for Western Studies, $9.95.

**TALES OF AN ENDISHODI: FATHER BERARD HAILE
& THE NAVAJOS, 1900-1961**
Fr. Murray Bodo, Editor
University of New Mexico Press, $45; paper, $24.95.

TALES OF KANKAKEE LAND
C.H. Bartlett
Reprint of 1907 edition. Hardscrabble Books, $7.50.

TALES OF THE NEZ PERCE
Donald M. Hines
Reprint. 41 tales. 232 pp. Ye Galleon Press,
$19.95; paper, $14.95..

TALES OF NORTH AMERICA: NATIVE AMERICANS
Irene Handberg
Revised edition. 112 pp. Learning Connection, 1995.

TALES OF THE NORTH AMERICAN INDIAN
Stith Thompson, Editor
Illus. 416 pp. Paper. Indiana University Press, 1966. $9.95.

**TALES OF THE NORTHWEST:
ON SKETCHES OF INDIAN LIFE & CHARACTER**
W.J. Snelling
Colection of short stories on Plains Indians.
Reprint of 1830 edition. 288 pp. Ross & Haines, $15.

*TALES OF A PUEBLO BOY
Lawrence J. Vallo
Stories of growing up in an Indian Pueblo. Grades 3-9.
Illus. 48 pp. Paper. Sunstone Press, $5.95.

TALES OF A SHAMAN'S APPRENTICE
Mark Plotkin, PhD
Penguin USA, $22.

TALES OF THE TEPEE
Edward Everett Dale
119 pp. paper. University of Nebraska Press, 1998. $8.

TALES OF TICASUK: ESKIMO LEGENDS & STORIES
Emily Ivanoff Brown
Illus. 135 pp. University of Alaska Press, 1987.
$15; paper, $8.95.

**TALKING BACK TO CIVILIZATION:
INDIAN VOICES FROM THE PROGRESSIVE ERA**
Frederick Hoxie, Editor
Bedford Books (Boston), 2001.

TALKING CHICKASAW DICTIONARY
Vinnie May Humes (Chickasaw Speaker)
Over 7,000 words on CD-ROM. VIP, 2002, $34.95.

**TALKING LEAVES: CONTEMPORARY NATIVE
AMERICAN SHORT STORIES, AN ANTHOLOGY**
Craig Lesley, Editor
Anthology of 38 contemporary Native American short stories.
385 pp. Dell Publishing, Demco & Cherokee Pubns, 1991. $10.

**TALKING MYSTERIES: A CONVERSATION
WITH TONY HILLERMAN**
Tony Hillerman & Ernie Bulow
Author details his early years in Oklahoma, first encounters
with Navajo culture and his life as journalist and author. Illus.
144 pp. Paper. University of New Mexico Press, $13.95.

**TALKING TO THE MOON: WILDLIFE ADVENTURES
ON THE PLAINS & PRAIRIES OF OSAGE COUNTRY**
John Joseph Matthews
Keen & intimate observations of nature; Native American com-
parisons, cowboy reflections & humor. University of Oklahoma
Pres, $16.

**TALKING WITH THE CLAY:
THE ART OF PUEBLO POTTERY**
Stephen Trimble
Illus. 124 pp. Paper. University of Washington Press
& School of American Research, 1987. $15.95.

**TALL WOMAN: THE LIFE STORY OF ROSE MITCHELL,
A NAVAJO WOMAN, @ 1874-1977**
Rose Mitchell; edited by Charlotte Frisbie
University of New Mexico Press, 2000. $65; paper, $29.95.

TANAINA TALES FROM ALASKA
Bill Vaudrin
Reprint of 1969 edition. Illus. 127 pp. Paper.
University of Oklahoma Press, $11.95.

**TANGLED WEBS: INDIANS & THE LAW
IN CANADA'S PACIFIC COAST FISHERIES**
Diane Newell
Illus. 288 pp. University of Toronto Press, 1993.
$40; paper, $18.95.

THE TAOS INDIANS
Blanche C. Grant
Reissue of 1925 edition. Illus. 198 pp. Paper.
Rio Grande Press, $10.

THE TAOS INDIANS & THE BATTLE FOR BLUE LAKE
R.C. Gordon-McCutchan
Story of the Taos Indians' 60 year struggle to regain their sacred tribal lands. Illus. 256 pp. Red Crane Books, 1991. $25.95;
paper, $16.95.

TAOS PUEBLO & ITS SACRED BLUE LAKE
Marcia Keegan
Documents the celebration in 1971 when Taos Pueblo got
the sacred lake back. 53 photos. 63 pp. Clear Light, $14.95.

**TAOS: 1847: THE REVOLT IN
CONTEMPORARY ACCOUNTS**
Michael McNierney, Editor
102 pp. Paper. Johnson Books, 1980. $4.95.

TAOS ARTISTS & THEIR PATRONS, 1898-1950
Dean A. Porter, Teresa Hayes Ebie & Susan Campbell
University of New Mexico Press, $65.

TAOS SOCIETY OF ARTISTS
Robert R. White, Editor
University of New Mexico Press, $16.95.

TAOS TALES
Elsie Clews Parsons
Reprint. 192 pp. Paper. Dover, $7.95.

**THE TAOS TRAPPERS: THE FUR TRADE
IN THE FAR SOUTHWEST, 1540-1846**
David J. Webber
Reprint of the 1971 edition. Illus. Maps. 263 pp.
Paper. University of Oklahoma Press, $16.95.

**TAPESTRIES IN THE SAND:
THE SPIRIT OF INDIAN SANDPAINTING**
David Villasenor
Chiricahua Sun Sandpainting. Illus. 112 pp. Paper.
Naturegraph, $8.95.

**TATL'AHWT'AENN NENN' THE
HEADWATERS PEOPLE'S COUNTRY**
James Kari, et al, Editors
Illus. 220 pp. Paper. Alaska Native Language Center,
1986. $10.

**TAX POLICY: A PROFILE OF
THE INDIAN GAMING INDUSTRY**
Harriet Ganson
Illus. 51 pp. Paper. Diane Publishing, 1998. $20.

**TE ATA: CHICKASAW STORYTELLER,
AMERICAN TREASURE**
Richard Green
Illus. 368 pp. University of Oklahoma Press, 2003. $34.95.

A TEACHER'S GUIDE TO THE LENAPE
Karen Waldauer, Editor
Three separate kits: 1. Introduction to the Lenape, $22.50; 2.
Lenape Lore/Folk Medicines, $15.50; 3. Lenape Lore/Cloth-
ing, Shelter, Crafts, Weapons, Tools & Specialties, $15.50. Illus.
Charts, quizzes, posters. The Middle Atlantic Press.

TEACHING ABOUT AMERICAN INDIANS IN CONNECTICUT
17 pp. University of Connecticut Education, 1982. $2.

TEACHING ABOUT NATIVE AMERICANS
Karen D. Harvey, Lisa D. Harjo, Jane K. Jackson
82 pp. Paper. NCSS Publications, $10.95 (members);
$12.95 (non-members).

TEACHING AMERICAN INDIAN HISTORY
Terry P. Wilson
66 pp. Paper. American Historical Association, 1993. $8.

**TEACHING AMERICAN INDIAN HISTORY:
AN INTERDISCIPLINARY APPROACH**
Larry L. Vantine
Paper. R & E Research Associates, 1978. $11.95.

TEACHING AMERICAN INDIAN STUDENTS
Jon Reyhner
Summarizes the latest research on Indian education, and pro-
vides practical suggestions for teachers, and resources. Map.
Biblio. 328 pp. Paper. University of Oklahoma Press, 1992.
$19.95.

TEACHING GUIDE FOR INDIAN LITERATURE
Diana Campbell
Volume I, 110 pp. Grades 4-6; Volume II, 55 pp. Grades 6
and up. Navajo Curriculum Center, 1983. $4.50 each.

TEACHING THE NATIVE AMERICAN
Hap Gilliland
A guide to adapting instruction to the needs of American
Indian students. Third Edition. 277 pp. Council for Indian
Education. $21.95.

**TEACHING SPIRITS: TOWARDS AN UNDERSTANDING
OF NATIVE AMERICAN TRADITIONS**
Joseph Epes Brown
Oxford University Press, 2001.

**TEACHINGS FROM THE AMERICAN EARTH:
INDIAN RELIGION & PHILOSOPHY**
Dennis & Barbara Tedlock, Editors
Illus. 280 pp. Paper. Liveright, 1975. $10.95.

TEACHINGS OF NATURE
Adolf Hungry Wolf
Illus. 94 pp. Paper. The Book Publishing Co., $8.95.

TEAM SPIRITS: THE NATIVE MASCOTS CONTROVERSY
C. Richard King & Charles Fruehling Springwood, Editors
356 pp. University of Nebraska Press, 2001. $24.95.

TECHNIQUE OF NORTH AMERICAN INDIAN BEADWORK
Monte Smith
Features examples and photos of beadwork from 1835 to the
present time. 200 Illus. Biblio. 106 pp. Paper. Eagle's View
Publishing, $10.95.

**TECHNIQUE OF PORCÚPINE QUILL DECORATION AMONG
THE INDIANS OF NORTH AMERICA**
William C. Orchard; Monte Smith, Editor
Revised 1917 ed. Illus. 88 pp. Paper. Eagles View Publishing,
Written Heritage, Hothem House, Smoke & Fire Co., $9.95.

TECHNIQUES OF BEADING EARRINGS
Deon DeLange
Illus. 72 pp. Paper. Eagle's View Publishing, $9.95.

*TECUMSEH
Grades 3-6. Illus. 32 pp. Childrens Press, $11.45.

*TECUMSEH
Russell Shorto; Nancy Furstinger, Editor
Grades 5-7. Illus. 145 pp. Silver Burdett Press, 1989.
$11.98; paper, $7.95.

TECUMSEH: A LIFE
John Sugden
Illus. 448 pp. St. Martins Press, 1995. $34.95.
Paper. VHPS, 1999. $15.95.

TECUMSEH'S LAST STAND
John Sugden; maps by Frank O. Williams
Illus. Maps. Biblio. Paper. University of Oklahoma Press,
1985. $19.95

TECUMSEH & THE QUEST FOR INDIAN LEADERSHIP
R. David Edmunds
Paper. Scott Foresman & Co., 1984. $7.95.

TECUMSEH & THE SHAWNEE CONFEDERACY
Rebecca Stefoff
Grades 5 and up. Illus. 144 pp. Facts on File, 1998. $19.95.

TECUMSEH: VISIONARY CHIEF OF THE SHAWNEE
Jason Hook
Illus. 52 pp. Sterling, 1989. $12.95.

TEEPEES ARE FOLDED: AMERICAN INDIAN POETRY
Sally Old Coyote
Council for Indian Education, 1991. $5.95.

TEJANO ORIGINS IN 18TH CENTURY SAN ANTONIO
Gerald Poyo & Gilberto Hinojoso
Illus. 200 pp. University of Texas Press, 1991. $19.95.

TELL ME AHNA: ESKIMO FOLKTALES
Susan Towne DeBree
Stories. Illus. 32 pp. Paper. White Publishing, $3.45.

TELL THEM WE ARE GOING HOME:
THE ODYSSEY OF THE NORTHERN CHEYENNES
John H. Monnett
Illus. Maps. 288 pp. University of Oklahoma Press,
2001. $27.95.

TELLICO ARCHAEOLOGY
Jefferson Chapman
12,000 years of Native American occupation in the Little Tennessee and Tellico Rivers region of Tennessee. Illus. 142 pp.
Paper. Hothem House & University of Tennessee Press, 1985.
$15.95.

TELLING A GOOD ONE: THE PROCESS OF A
NATIVE AMERICAN COLLABORATIVE BIOGRAPHY
Theodore Rios & Kathleen Mullen Sands
Sands draws on her partnership with the late Theodore Rios, a
Tohono O'odham narrator and the influence of Tohono O'odham
culture and its tradition of storytelling on Rios's actions and
words. Illus. Map. 378 pp. University of Nebraska Press, 2000.
$60; paper, $29.95.

TELLING OURSELVES: ETHNICITY &
DISCOURSE IN SOUTHWESTERN ALASKA
Chase Hensel
232 pp. Paper. Oxford University Press, 1996. $28.

TELLING STORIES THE KIOWA WAY
Gus Palmer, Jr.
Explores the traditional art of storytelling still practiced by the
Kiowas. 145 pp. University of Arizona Press, 2003. $35; paper,
$17.95.

TEMALPAKH: CAHUILLA INDIAN
KNOWLEDGE & USAGE OF PLANTS
Lowell J. Bean & Katherine Siva Saubel
Paper. Malki Museum Press, 1972. $20; paper, $16.

THE TEN GRANDMOTHERS: EPIC OF THE KIOWAS
A. Marriott
Reprint of 1945 edition. Illus. Map. 305 pp.
Paper. University of Oklahoma Press, $15.95.

*10 LITTLE WHITEPEOPLE
Beverly Slapin & Annie Esposito
Grades 9 and up. Illus. Paper. Oyate, 1995. $5.

TENDERFOOT IN TOMBSTONE, THE PRIVATE JOURNAL
OF GEORGE WHITWELL PARKSONS: THE TURBULENT
YEARS, 1880-1882
Lynn R. Bailey
Illus. Westernlore, 1996. $36.95.

*TENDING THE FIRE: THE STORY OF MARIA MARTINEZ
Juddi Morris
Biography of Maria Martinez, Navajo potter. Ages 8-12.
Illus. 120 pp. Northland, $12.95; paper, $6.95.

*TENDOY, CHIEF OF THE LEMHIS
David Crowder
Grades 5-9. Illus. Paper. Caxton, 1969. $2.75.

TENNESSEE'S INDIAN PEOPLES:
FROM WHITE CONTACT TO REMOVAL,
1540-1840
Ronald N. Satz
Illus. 110 pp. University of Tennessee Press, 1979.
$9.95; paper, $3.50.

TENSION & HARMONY: THE NAVAJO RUG
32 pp. Paper. Museum of Northern Arizona, 1982. $4.

TENTING ON THE PLAINS; OR,
GENERAL CUSTER IN KANSAS & TEXAS
Elizabeth B. Custer
Portrays the aftermath of the Civil War in Texas, and life in
Kansas. Detailed dscriptions of an army officer's home life on
the frontier during theis major period of Indian unrest. Reprint.
Illus. Maps. 388 pp. Paper. University of Oklahoma Press,
$12.95.

TEPEE COOKERY: OR, LET'S CHEW
THE FAT INDIAN STYLE: A COOKBOOK
Gwen Fisher
Illus. 74 pp. Paper. Evans Publications, 1986. $12.

TERMINATION & RELOCATION:
FEDERAL INDIAN POLICY, 1945-1960
Donald L. Fixico
Illus. 286 pp. Paper. University of New Mexico Press, $13.95.

TERMINATION REVISITED: AMERICAN INDIANS
ON THE TRAIL TO SELF-DETERMINATION, 1933-1953
Kenneth R. Philp
Illus. 265 pp. Paper. University of Nebraska Press,
1999. $24.95.

TERMINATION'S LEGACY:
THE DISCARDED INDIANS OF UTAH
R. Warren Metcalf
The reality of identity politics in Indian Country. Illus.
Maps. 311 pp. University of Nebraska Press, 2002. $55.

TETON SIOUX MUSIC & CULTURE
Frances Densmore
Explores the role of music in all aspects of Sioux life. Reprint
of 1918 edition. Illus. 644 pp. Paper. University of Nebraska
Press, $19.95.

TEWA TALES
Esie Clews Parsons
Collection of more than 100 tales. Reprint of 1926 edition.
304 pp. Paper. University of Arizona Press, $19.95.

TEWA WORLD: SPACE, TIME, BEING,
AND BECOMING IN A PUEBLO SOCIETY
Alfonso Ortiz
198 pp. Paper. University of Chicago Press, 1969. $11.

THE TEXAS CHEROKEES:
A PEOPLE BETWEEN FIRES, 1819-1840
Dianna Everett
Illus. Maps. 174 pp. Paper. University of Oklahoma Press,
1990. $13.95.

THE TEXAS KICKAPOO: KEEPERS OF TRADITION
Bill Wright & E. John Gesick, Jr.
Illus. Photos. 213 pp. Texas Western Press, 1996. $45.

TEXTBOOKS & THE AMERICAN INDIAN
Jeanette Henry and Rupert Costo, Editors
269 pp. Paper. The Indian Historian Press, 1969. $5.

TEXTILES IN SOUTHWESTERN PREHISTORY
Lynn S. Teague
University of New Mexico Press, $45.

THANKSGIVING: A NATIVE PERSPECTIVE
Sourcebook of essays, speeches, poetry, stories and activities
will help teachers and students think critically about what has
been taught as the "first" thanksgiving. Illus. 93 pp. Paper.
Oyate, 1996. $8.

THAT'S WHAT SHE SAID: CONTEMPORARY POETRY
& FICTION BY NATIVE AMERICAN WOMEN
Rayna Green, Editor
Illus. 352 pp. Indiana University Press, 1984.
$29.95; paper, $12.95.

THE THEFT OF FIRE: A CURRICULUM UNIT
Title V program staff & tribal resource people
A curriculum book featuring the traditional story theme of steal-
ing fire fromthe sun. Activities highlight the complex Native
American technology of creating fire without matches; 14-
minute videos available. Grades 6-8. Illus. 24 pp. booklet.
Cook's Books. $10, institutions; $7, individuals.

THE THEFT OF THE SPIRIT: THE JOURNEY TO
SPIRITUAL HEALING WITH NATIVE AMERICANS
Carl A. Hammerschlag
256 pp. Simon & Schuster, 1993. $18; paper, $10.

THEIR BEARING IS NOBLE & PROUD
James F. O'Neil, II
Collection of unique narratives regarding the appearance
of Natives from 1740-1815. Two vols. Smoke & Fire Co.,
$18.95 each.

THEIR FIRES ARE COLD
Vietzen
Prehistoric artifacts and metal trade items like axes,
pipe-tomahawks, pipes, knives. Photos & sketches.
192 pp. Hothem House, 1984. $60.

THEIR NUMBER BECOME THINNED: NATIVE AMERICAN
POPULATION DYNAMICS IN EASTERN NORTH AMERICA
Henry F. Dobyns
Illus. 382 pp. University of Tennessee Press, 1983. $34.95;
paper, $16.95.

THEIR SECRETS: WHY NAVAJO
INDIANS NEVER GET CANCER
De Lamar Gibbons
125 pp. Paper. Academy of Health, 1998. $10.

THEIR STORIES OF LONG AGO
Belle Deacon
A bilingual collection of traditional Athabascan tales from Alaska.
Illus. Alaskan Native Language Center, $10.

THEMES IN SOUTHWEST PREHISTORY
George J. Gumerman, Editor
Illus. 370 pp. Paper. University of Washington Press
& School of American Research, 1994. $22.50.

THEODORE ROOSEVELT & SIX FRIENDS OF THE INDIAN
William T. Hagan
Describes the efforts by six prominent individuals and two institutions to influence Indian affairs during the Roosevelt administration. Illus. 288 pp. University of Oklahoma Press, 1997.
$25.95

THEORETICAL PERSPECTIVES
ON NATIVE AMERICAN LANGUAGES
Donna Gerdts & Karin Michelson, Editors
Illus. 290 pp. State University of New York Press, 1989. $24.50;
paper, $12.95.

*THERE STILL ARE BUFFALO
Ann Nolan Clark; Willard Beatty, Editor; illus. by Steve Tongier
Grades 1-6. Illus. 50 pp. Paper. Ancient City Press, 1992. $8.95.

THESE ARE MY CHILDREN
A. Murray
Account of four white families adopted into the Coeur d' Alene
tribe in the 1880s. Reprint. 116 pp. Ye Galleon Press, 1977.
$19.95; paper, $14.95..

*THESE WERE THE SIOUX
Marie Sandoz
The philosophy and practical wisdom of the Sioux Indians, in-
cluding their beliefs and customs. Reprint of 1961 edition.
Grades 6-12. Illus. 118 pp. Paper. University of Nebraska Press,
$74.50; paper, $24.50.

THEY CALL ME AGNES: A CROW NARRATIVE BASED
ON THE LIFE OF AGNES YELLOWTAIL DEERNOSE
Fred W. Voget
Illus. Maps. 220 pp. University of Oklahoma Press,
1993. $25.95; paper, $14.95..

THEY CALLED IT PRAIRIE LIGHT:
THE STORY OF CHILOCCO INDIAN SCHOOL
K. Tsianina Lomawaima
Illus. Maps. 215 pp. Paper. University of Nebraska Press,
1994. $13.95.

THEY DIED WITH CUSTER: SOLDIER'S BONES
FROM THE BATTLE OF LITTLE BIGHORN
Douglas D. Scott, P. Willey & Melissa A. Conner
Illus. Map. University of Oklahoma Press, 1998. $29.95.

THEY HAVE NO RIGHTS
Walter Ehlich
266 pp. Paper. Jefferson National, 1979. $7.95.

THEY LED A NATION
Virginia Driving Hawk Sneve; N. Jane Hunt, Editor
A pictorial and biographical documentation of 20 historic
Sioux leaders. Ilus. 46 pp. Paper. Brevet Press, 1975. $4.95.

THEY SANG FOR HORSES: THE IMPACT OF
THE HORSE ON NAVAJO & APACHE FOLKLORE
LaVerne Harrell Clark; illus. by Ted DFeGrazier
The weaving of the horse into existent mythology of the Na-
vajo and Apache tribes. Reprint of 1966 ed. Illus. 225 pp. Pa-
per. University Press of Colorado, 2001. $26.95.

THEY SAY THE WIND IS RED: THE ALABAMA
CHOCTAW LOST IN THEIR OWN LAND
Jacqueline Anderson Matte
The past and present of a Southeastern Indian Tribe. Foreword by Vine Deloria, Jr. Contains a how-to section on researching Indian genealogy. Illus. 256 pp. Paper. NewSouth Books,
2002.

"THEY TREATED US JUST LIKE INDIANS":
THE WORLDS OF BENNETT COUNTY, SOUTH DAKOTA
Paula L. Wagoner
The story of Bennett County, divided by residents into three
groups - "whites," "fullbloods," and "Mixedbloods." Illus. Maps.
156 pp. University of Nebraska Press, 2002. $50; paper, $19.95.

THEY WALKED BEFORE:
THE INDIANS OF WASHINGTON STATE
Cecilia Carpenter
Illus. Revised edition. 75 pp. Paper. Tahoma Publications, 1989.
$10.

THE THIRD ARROW: A STORY OF
MOSHULATUBBEE, CHOCTAW CHIEF
Maxine W. Barker
166 pp. Paper. Pioneer Publishing, 1998. $18.

THIRTEEN DAYS OF TERROR: THE RUFUS
BUCK GANG IN INDIAN TERRITORY
Glenn Shirley
Illus. 109 pp. Western Publications, 1996. $22.95.

THIRTEEN MOONS ON TURTLE'S BACK
Joseph Bruchac & Jonathan London; illus. by Thomas Locker
Retelling of Native American legends. Storytelling poems. Illus.
30 pp. Morning Flower Press & Philomel Press, 1992. $14.95.

*THIRTY INDIAN LEGENDS OF CANADA
Margaret Bemister
Grades 3-7. Illus. 158 pp. Paper. Publishers Group, 1991. $9.95.

THIS FOOL HISTORY, AN ORAL
HISTORY OF DAKOTA TERRITORY
Sylvia G. Wheeler
A play representing the meeting of Indian & white cultures
in Dakota Territory. Dakota Press, 1991. $19.95.

THIS IS OUR LAND
Val J. McClellan
2 Vols. Vol. 1, 902 pp. 1977. Vol. 2, 927 pp. 1979.
Illus. Western Publishers, $17.95 each.

*THIS LAND IS MY LAND
George Littlechild
Grades 1-6. Story by a Canadian Plains Cree. Illus.
Children's Book Press, $15.95.

THIS LAND WAS THEIRS: A STUDY
OF THE NORTH AMERICAN INDIAN
Wendell H. Oswait
6th edition. Illus. 537 pp. Paper. Mayfield Publishing, 1998.
$38.95.

THIS PATH WE TRAVEL: CELEBRATIONS OF
CONTEMPORARY NATIVE AMERICAN CREATIVITY
National Museum of the American Indian,
Smithsonian Institution
Combining photography with collected observations, this book
documents a group of Native American artists examining the
relationships between native and contemporary and traditional
and innovative artistic endeavors. Illus. 128 pp. Fulcrum Publishing, 1994. $24.95; paper, $18.95.

COQUELLE THOMPSON, ATHABASKAN WITNESS: A CUL-
TURAL BIOGRAPHY
Lionel Youst, William R. Seaburg
Illus. 320 pp. University of Oklahoma Press, 2003. $34.95.

THE THOMPSON LANGUAGE
Laurence C. Thompson & M. Terry Thompson
253 pp. University of Montana, 1992. $20.

THOMPSON RIVER SALISH DICTIONARY
Laurence C. Thompson & M. Tewrry Thompson
1,410 pp. University of Montana, 1996. $45.

THOREAU & THE AMERICAN INDIANS
Robert F. Sayre
Princeton University Press, 1977. $29.50; paper, $13.50.

THOSE TREMENDOUS MOUNTAINS: THE STORY
OF THE LEWSI & CLARK EXPEDITION
David Hawke
Illus. 290 pp. Paper. W.W. Norton & Co., 1985. $7.70.

THOSE WHO CAME BEFORE: SOUTHWESTERN
ARCHAEOLOGY IN THE NATIONAL PARK SYSTEM
Robert & Florence Lister
Prehistoric cultures of the American Southwest as preserved
and interpreted by the NPS in over 37 sites. Photos. 232 pp.
Paper. Clear Light, $16.95.

THOUSAND YEARS OF AMERICAN INDIAN
STORYTELLING
Rupert Costo & Jeanette Henry Costo
Collection of Native American tales. Indian Historian Press,
$12.

THREE STRANDS IN THE BRAND:
A GUIDE FOR ENABLERS OF LEARNING
Paula Underwood
Illus. 78 pp. Paper. Tribe of Two Press, $12.

THREE YEARS AMONG THE COMANCHES: THE
NARRATIVE OF NELSON LEE, THE TEXAS RANGER
Nelson Lee
Reprint of the 1957 edition. Illus. 180 pp. Paper.
University of Oklahoma Press, $11.95.

THREE YEARS ON THE PLAINS:
OBSERVATIONS OF INDIANS, 1867-1870
Edmund B. Tuttle
Illus. Maps. 216 pp. University of Oklahoma Press,
2003. $29.95; paper, $17.95.

THROUGH DAKOTA EYES: NARRATIVE ACCOUNTS
OF THE MINNESOTA INDIAN WAR OF 1862
Gary Anderson; Alan Woolworth, Editor
Illus. Photos. Maps. 316 pp. Minnesota Historical
Society Press, 1988. $24.95; paper, $11.95.

THROUGH THE EYE OF THE DEER: AN ANTHOLOGY
OF NATIVE AMERICAN WOMEN WRITERS
Edited by Carolyn Dunn and Carol Comfort
Aunt Lute Books, 2003.

THROUGH THE EYE OF THE FEATHER:
NATIVE AMERICAN VISIONS
Gail Tuchman
The symbolism of the feather in prose and photographs.
Photos. 95 pp. Paper. Written Heritage, $19.95.

THROUGH INDIAN EYES: THE NATIVE
EXPERIENCE IN BOOKS FOR CHILDREN
Beverly Slapin & Doris Seale, Editors
Articles, stories, poetry, and reviews of books dealing with
Native Americans. Bibliography. 246 pp. Paper. Oyate, 1991.
$24.95. Also available from The Falmouth Institute.

THROUGH INDIAN EYES, VOL. 1: THE WHEEL OF LIFE
Donald & Jean Johnson
Revised edition. Illus. Paper. Center for International
Training & Education, 1985. $8.95.

THROUGH NAVAJO EYES: AN EXPLORATION
IN FILM COMMUNICATION & ANTHROPOLOGY
Sol Worth and John Adair
Illus. 320 pp. Paper. University of New Mexico Press, 1996.
$14.95.

THROUGH WHITE MEN'S EYES:
A CONTRIBUTION TO NAVAJO HISTORY
J. Lee Correll
Illus. 6 vols., 2,832 pp. University of Arizona Press, 1979.
$255 per set.

THROWING FIRE AT THE SUN, WATER AT THE MOON
Anita Endrezze
205 pp. University of Arizona Press, 2000. $32; paper,
$17.95.

THUNDER OVER THE OCHOO, 4 Vols.
Andrew Gale Ontko
The Shoshoni Indian history in 4 vols: Vol. I - covers hundreds
of years from pre-Columbian times to the collapse of the world
fur trade in 1840, Vol. I meets the Shoshoni Indians before
arrival of the Europeans; Vol. II - Covers the 20 year period
between 1840 & 1860; Vol. III - Covers between 1860 and 1869;
and Vol. IV - Covers the 45 year interval between 1867 & 1912.
Illus. 450 pp each. Maverick Publications, $16.95 each.

THUNDER RIDES A BLACK HORSE:
MESCALERO APACHES & THE MYTHIC PRESENT
Claire F. Farrer
A 4-day, 4-night Mescalero Apache girls' puberty ceremonial.
Waveland Press, 1994.

*THUNDER WATERS: EXPERIENCES OF
GROWING UP IN DIFFERENT INDIAN TRIBES
Frances Snow, et al
Grades 3-8. Council for Indian Education, 1975.
$7.95; paper, $1.95.

THE TIGUAS: PUEBLO INDIANS OF TEXAS
Bill Wright
Illus. Photos. Biblio. 179 pp. Texas Western Press, 1993.
$40.

TILLAMOOK INDIANS OF THE OREGON COAST
John Sauter and Bruce Johnson
Illus. Binford-Metropolitan, 1974. $9.95; paper, $6.95.

TILLER'S GUIDE TO INDIAN COUNTRY: ECONOMIC
PROFILES OF AMERICAN INDIAN RESERVATIONS
Veronica Tiller
Summarizes the history, language, culture, natural resource
base, industries, enterpises, etc. for more than 500 reserva-
tions in 36 states including Alaska. Illus. 712 pp. Bow Arrow
Publishing, 1996. Distributed by University of New Mexico
Press, $65.

TIME AMONG THE NAVAJO: TRADITIONAL
LIFEWAYS ON THE RESERVATION
Kathy Hooker
Illus. 100 pp. Paper. Museum of New Mexico Press,
1991. $19.95.

A TIME BEFORE DECEPTION: TRUTH IN
COMMUNICATION, CULTURE, AND ETHICS
Thomas W. Cooper
Describes the practices of tribal culture worldwide and exam-
ines the communication ethic of the Dine (Navajo) of northern
Arizona and the Shuswap people of British Columbia. Illus. 224
pp. Clear Light, 1995. $24.95.

A TIME OF VISIONS: INTERVIEWS WITH
NATIVE AMERICAN ARTISTS
Table of Contents: Rick Bartow, Sara Bates, Patricia Deadman,
Joe Feddersen, Anita Fields, Harry Fonseca, Bob Haozous,
Melanie Printup Hope, Bobby Martin, Gerald McMaster, George
Morrison, Shelley Niro, Joanna Osburn-Bigfeather, Diego
Romero, Mateo Romero, Bently Spang, Ernie Whiteman, Ri-
chard Ray Whitman, Alfred Young Man. Available on the web
site: www.britesites.com/native_artist_interviews

TIME: SPACE & TRANSITION IN ANASAZI PREHISTORY
Michael S. Berry
112 pp. University of Utah Press, 1982. $20.

TIME'S FLOTSAM: OVERSEAS
COLLECTIONS OF CALIFORNIA
Thomas Blackburn & Travis Hudson
Illus. 226 pp. Santa Barbara Museum of Natural History, 1990.
$34.95.

TIMELESS TEXTILES: TRADITIONAL PUEBLO ARTS
1840-1940
Tyrone D. Campbell
Illus. Paper. Museum of New Mexico Press, 2002. $14.95.

TIMELINES OF NATIVE AMERICAN HISTORY
Susan Hazen-Hammond
From 1492-1990s. Illus. Maps. 352 pp. Paper. Berkley Pub-
lishing, 1997. $16.

TIMOTHY: NEZ PERCE CHIEF, LIFE & TIMES, 1800-1891
Rowena Alcorn
78 pp. Paper. Ye Galleon Press, 1986. $8.95.

THE TIMUCUAN CHIEFDOMS OF SPANISH FLORIDA
John E. Worth
2 vols. Vol. I: Assimilation. 288 pp. Vol. II: Resistance & Destruction. 336 pp. Univesitry Press of Florida, 1998. $49.95
each.

*TJATJAKIYMATCHAN (COYOTE)
Alex O. Ramirez
A legend from Carmel Valley. Illus. 12 pp.
Paper. Oyate, 1995. $6.

TLAPACOYA POTTERY IN THE MUSEUM COLLECTION
Muriel Weaver
Illus. 48 pp. Paper. National Museum of the American Indian,
1967. $3.50.

*THE TLINGIT
Grades K-4. Illus. 48 pp. Childrens Press, $11.45.

THE TLINGIT: AN INTRODUCTION
TO THEIR CULTURE & HISTORY
Wallace M. Olson
3rd edition. Illus. 111 pp. Paper. Heritage Research, 1997.
$12.50.

TLINGIT ART & CULTURE
Don Kaiper
Illus. 95 pp. Hancock House, 1990. $4.95.

TLINGIT INDIANS OF ALASKA
Anatoli Kamenski; translated by Sergei Kan; Marvin Falk,
Editor
Illus. Biblio. 166 pp. Paper. University of Alaska Press, 1985.
$15.

THE TLINGIT INDIANS
George Thornton Emmons; Frederica de Laguna, Editor
Illus. 65 drawings, 127 photos. 530 pp. University of Washing-
ton Press, $60.

TLINGIT MYTHS & TEXTS
John R. Swanton
Reprint. 451 pp. Native American Book Publishers, $69;
paper, $49.

TLINGIT TALES: POTLATCH & TOTEM POLES
Lorle K. Harris; told by Robert Zuboff
Illus. 48 pp. Paper. Naturegraph, $6.95.

TO BE INDIAN: THE LIFE OF IROQUOIS-SENECA
ARTHUR CASWELL PARKER
Joy Porter
Illus. 320 pp. University of Oklahoma Press, 2003. $34.95.

TO BE AN INDIAN: AN ORAL HISTORY
Joseph Cash & Herbert Hoover, Eds.
Collection of personal accounts presents the contemporary
Northern Plains Native Americans' view of themselves, their
history, and their world. Reissue of 1971 edition. Photos. 239
pp. Minnesota Historical Society Press, 1995. $11.95.

**TO BE THE MAIN LEADERS OF OUR PEOPLE: A
HISTORY OF THE MINNESOTA OJIBWE POLITICS,
1825-1898**
Rebecca Kugel
Illus. 230 pp. Paper. Michigan State University Press,
1998. $24.95.

**TO THE AMERICAN INDIAN:
REMINISCENCES OF A YOUROK WOMAN**
Lucy Thompson
Photos. Revised 1916 edition. 325 pp. Paper.
Heyday Books, $13.95.

TO THE ARCTIC BY CANOE
C. Stuart Houston
The journal & paintings of Robert Hood, midshipman with Sir
John Franklin, Arctic explorer. Reveals the adverse effects on
Native peoples and their environment of the coming of the
Europeans. Illus. 280 pp. Paper. University of Toronto Press,
1994. $22.95.

**TO BE THE MAIN LEADERS OF OUR PEOPLE: A
HISTORY OF MINNESOTA OJIBWE POLITICS, 1825-1898**
Rebeccs Kugel
Illus. 230 pp. Paper. Michigan State University Press, 1998.
$24.95.

TO BE A WARRIOR
Robert Barlow Fox
Navajo boy taught the old ways of his people.
128 pp. Paper. Sunstone Press, $12.95.

**TO CHANGE THEM FOREVER: INDIAN EDUCATION AT
THE RAINY MOUNTAIN BOARDING SCHOOL, 1893-1920**
Maps. Biblio. 250 pp. The Montana Cree: A Study in
Religious Persistence, 1996. $28.95.

**TO THE CHUKCHI PENINSULA & TO THE TLINGIT
INDIANS 1881/1882: JOURNALS & LETTERS BY
AUREL & ARTHUR KRAUSE**
translated by Margot Krause McCaffrey
Studies & observations of the region's natural history, art and
ethnography. Illus. Maps. 230 pp. Paper. University of Alaska
Press, 1993. $17.50.

**TO DIE GAME: THE STORY OF THE LOWRY BAND,
INDIAN GUERILLAS OF RECONSTRUCTION**
William McKee Evans
Indian guerilla warfare against the Confederates and Klu Klux
Klan during the Civil War. 310 pp. Paper. Syracuse University
Press, $15.95.

**TO DIE IN DINETAH: THE
DARK LEGACY OF KIT CARSON**
John A. Truett
Kit Carson's involvement with the relocation of the Navajo and
the "Long Walk." 256 pp. Paper. Sunstone Press, $14.95.

**TO DO GOOD TO MY INDIAN BRETHREN:
THE WRITINGS OF JOSEPH JOHNSON**
Laura J. Murray, Editor
344 pp. Paper. University of Massachusetts Press, 1998. $60.

**TO FISH IN COMMON: THE ETHNOHISTORY
OF LUMMI INDIAN SALMON FISHING**
Daniel L. Boxberger
Illus. 237 pp. Paper. UBC Press, 1989. $26.95.

**TO HAVE THIS LAND: THE NATURE OF INDIAN/
WHITE RELATIONS, SOUTH DAKOTA, 1888-1891**
Philip S. Hall
Illus. Paper. Center for Western Studies & Dakota Press, 1991.
$10.95.

TO HONOR & COMFORT: NATIVE QUILTING TRADITIONS
Edited by Marsha L. MacDowell & C. Kurt Dewhurst
Native quilters in North America and the Hawaiian Islands featuring more than 80 quilts, essays, photos and profiles of
quilters. Illus. 240 pp. Museum of New Mexico Press, 2001.
$50; paper, $35.

**TO IMAGE & TO SEE: CROW INDIAN PHOTOGRAPHS
BY EDWARD S. CURTIS & RICHARD THROSSEL, 1905-1910**
Tamara Northern & Wendi-Starr Brown
Illus. Hood Museum of Art, 1993. $6.

**TO LIVE IN TWO WORLDS:
AMERICAN INDIAN YOUTH TODAY**
Brent Ashabranner
Grades 7-11. Illus. Putnam Publishing Group, $13.95.

**TO LIVE HEROICALLY: INSTITUTIONAL
RACISM & AMERICAN INDIAN EDUCATION**
Delores J. Huff
211 pp. State University of New York Press, 1997.
$54.50; paper, $17.95.

**TO LIVE ON THIS EARTH:
AMERICAN INDIAN EDUCATION**
Estelle Fuchs and Robert Havighurst
Revised 1983 edition. 408 pp. Paper. University of
New Mexico Press, $11.95.

**TO PLEASE THE CARIBOU: PAINTED CARIBOU-SKIN
COATS WORN BY THE NASPAKI, MONTAGNAIS, & CREE
HUNTERS OF THE QUEBEC-LABRADOR PENINSULA**
Dorothy K. Burnham
Description and illustrations of 60 painted Caribou-skin coats.
Illus. 763 drawings, photos. 328 pp. University of Washington
Press, $60; paper, $35.

**TO PRESERVE A CULTURE: THE TWENTIETH-CENTURY
FIGHT OVER INDIAN REORGANIZATION**
Jon F. Rice, Jr.
Illus. 60 pp. The Committee, 1981. $2.

**TO RUN AFTER THEM: CULTURAL & SOCIAL BASES
OF COOPERATION IN A NAVAJO COMMUNITY**
Louise Lamphere
Reprint of 1977 edition. 246 pp. University of Arizona Press,
$22.50.

**TO SHOW HEART: NATIVE AMERICAN SELF-DETERMI-
NATION & FEDERAL INDIAN POLICY, 1960-1975**
George Pierre Castile
216 pp. Paper. University of Arizona Press, 1998. $18.95.

**TO SING OUR OWN SONGS: COGNITION
& CULTURE IN INDIAN EDUCATION**
Paper. Association on American Indian Affairs, 1985. $2.50.

**TO TOUCH THE WIND: AN INTRODUCTION TO
NATIVE AMERICAN PHILOSOPHY & BELIEFS**
Edward Morton
128 pp. Paper. Kendall-Hunt, 1988. $13.95.

TOBA TUCKER: A SHINNECOCK PORTRAIT
John Strong & Madeleine Burnside
Illus. 25 pp. Paper. Guild Hall, 1987. $7.

**TOBACCO AMONG THE
KARUK INDIANS OF CALIFORNIA**
John P. Harrington
Reprint of 1932 edition. Illus. 357 pp. Coyote Press, $37.50.

TOBACCO, PEACE PIPES & INDIANS
Louis Seig
History of the ceremonial use of tobacco. Illus.
Maps. 51 pp. Paper. Filter Press, 1971. $4.

**TOBACCO, PIPES & SMOKING CUSTOMS
OF THE AMERICAN INDIANS**
G.A. West
Reprint of 1934 edition. Greenwood Press, $57.50.

**TOHONO O'ODHAM/PIMA TO ENGLISH, ENGLISH
TO TOHONO O'ODHAM/PIMA DICTIONARY**
Dean & Lucille Saxton, Susie Enos
2nd Edition. 5,000+ entries, plus appendixes on culture.
145 pp. Paper. University of Arizona Press, 1983. $20.95.

**TOMAHAWK & CROSS: LUTHERAN MISSIONARIES
AMONG NORTHERN PRAIRIE INDIANS, 1858-1866**
Gerhard Schmutterer
Illus. 220 pp. Paper. Center for Western Studies, 1989.
$12.95.

TOMAHAWKS ILLUSTRATED
Kuck
Illus. 112 pp. Paper. Hothem House, 1977. $11.

**TOMAHAWKS - PIPE AXES -
OF THE AMERICAN FRONTIER**
Baldwin
Pipe axes' & tomahawks' origins and distributions. Illus.
128 pp. Hothem House & Written Heritage, 1995. $69.95.

**TOMOCHICHI: INDIAN FRIEND
OF THE GEORGIA COLONY**
Helen Todd
Illus. 208 pp. Cherokee Publishing, 1977. $12.95.

TONKAWA, AN INDIAN LANGUAGE OF TEXAS
Harry Hoijer
Paper. J.J. Augustin, Inc., Publisher, $15.

**THE TONKAWA PEOPLE: A TRIBAL HISTORY
FROM EARLIEST TIMES TO 1893**
Deborah Newlin; Gale Richardson, Editor
Illus. 120 pp. Paper. West Texas Museum, $5.

**TONTO'S REVENGE: REFLECTIONS ON
AMERICAN INDIAN CULTURE & POLICY**
Rennard Strickland
170 pp. Paper. University of New Mexico Press, $19.95.

TOP OF THE HILL
Morris Taylor
Tale that crosses generations and cultures. 64 pp.
Paper. Naturegraph, $4.95.

**TOPOGRAPHICAL DESCRIPTION OF THE STATE
OF OHIO, INDIANA TERRITORY AND LOUISIANA**
Jervis Cutler
Reprint of 1812 edition. Illus. Ayer Co., $17.

TOPOGRAPHICAL MEMOIR
Thomas Cram
Facs.of 1859 edition. Information of mistreatment of
Oregon Indians in the 1850s. 126 pp. Ye Galleon, $18.95.

*TOTEM POLE
Diane Hoyt-Goldsmith
The background of totem poles & the creation of one.
Grades 4-6. Illus. 32 pp. Holiday House, $15.95; paper,
$6.95.

TOTEM POLE CARVING: BRINGING A LOG TO LIFE
Vickie Jensen
Illus. 185 pp. Paper. University of Washington Press,
2004. $22.95.

*TOTEM POLE INDIANS OF THE NORTHWEST
Don E. Beyer
Grades 3 and up. Illus. 64 pp. Paper. Franklin Watts,
1991. $4.95.

*TOTEM POLES
Put the parts together and you will have a pole from floor
to ceiling. Grades 3-5. Paper. Bellerophon, $4.95.

TOTEM POLES: AN ILLUSTRATED GUIDE
Marjorie M. Halpin
Illus. Paper. UBC Press, 1981. $15.95.

TOTEM POLES OF THE NORTHWEST
D. Allen
Illus. 32 pp. Paper. Hancock House, $4.95.

TOTEM POLES OF THE PACIFIC NORTHWEST COAST
Edward Malin
Presents totem poles from the Tlingit settlements of Alaska to
the Kwakiutl villages of Vancouver Island. 54 historic photos,
and 14 color photos of contemporary poles; 199 line drawings.
<aps. 195 pp. Paper. Timber Press, 1994 first paper edition.
$19.95.

*TOTEM POLES TO COLOR & CUT OUT, Vol. 2: Tlingit
Grades 3-5. Paper. Bellerophon, $4.95.

*TOTEM POLES TO COLOR & CUT OUT, Vol. 3: Kwakiutl
Grades 3-5. Paper. Bellerophon, $4.95.

TOTEMISM
C. Levi-Strauss
Paper. Beacon Press, 1963. $9.95.

TOTKV MOCVSE • NEW FIRE: CREEK FOLKTALES
Earnest Gouge; edited & trans. by Jack B. Martin, Margaret
McKane Mauldin & Juanita McGirt; foreword by Craig Womack
Illus. 160 pp. University of Oklahoma Press, 1999. $49.95; paper,
$29.95; DVD, $29.95.

**TOUCH THE EARTH: A SELF-PORTRAIT
OF INDIAN EXISTENCE**
T.C. McLuhan
Staements and writings by North American Indians.
Reprint of 1971 edition. 185 pp. High-Lonesome Books,
$12.

**TOUCHING THE FIRE: BUFFALO DANCERS,
THE SKY BUNDLE, & OTHER TALES**
Roger L. Welsch
Illus. 272 pp. Paper. University of Nebraska Press, 1997.
$12.

TOVANGER
Anne Galloway
Paper. Malki Museum Press, 1978. $3.

TOWARD A NATIVE AMERICAN CRITICAL THEORY
Elvira Pulitano
264 pp. University of Nebraska Press, 2003. $50.

**TOWARDS ABORIGINAL SELF-GOVERNMENT:
RELATIONS BETWEEN STATUS INDIAN PEOPLES
& THE GOVERNMENT OF CANADA**
Anne-Marie Mawhiney
160 pp. Garland, 1993. $15.

**TOWN CREEK INDIAN MOUND:
A NATIVE AMERICAN LEGACY**
Joffre Lanning Coe
An archaeologist's view of a temple mound and mortuary at
Town Creek in Montgomery County, North Carolina. Illus. 338
pp. University of North Carolina Press, 1995. $45, cloth; $18.95,
paper.

TOWN & TEMPLES ALONG THE MISSISSIPPI
David Dye & Cheryl Cox, Editors
Illus. 280 pp. Paper. University of Alabama Press, 1990.
$22.95.

**TRACING ANCESTORS AMONG THE FIVE CIVILIZED
TRIBES: SOUTHEASTERN INDIANS PRIOR TO REMOVAL**
Guide book for genealogists, providing general information
about how to research and locate material. Genealogical Publishing Co. $24.95.

TRACKING PREHISTORIC MIGRATIONS: PUEBLO SETLERS AMONG THE TONTO BASIN HOHOKAM
Jeffrey J. Clark
Evaluates Puebloan migration into the Tonto Basin of east-central Arizona during the early Classic period (A.D. 1200-1325). Illus. 124 pp. Paper. The University of Arizona Press, 1999. $16.95.

THE TRADE GUN SKETCHBOOK
Full-size plans to build seven different Indian trade guns from the Revolution to the Indian Wars. Illus. 48 pp. Paper. The Fur Press, $2.00.

TRADERS OF THE WESTERN MORNING: ABORIGINAL COMMERCE IN PRECOLUMBIAN NORTH AMERICA
John U. Terrell
Illus. Maps. 145 pp. Southwest Museum, 1967. $12.50.

TRADERS' TALES
Elizabeth Vibert
Narratives of cultural encounters in the Columbia Plateau, 1807-1846. Illus. Maps. 366 pp. University of Oklahoma Press, 1997. $29.95.

TRADING BEYOND THE MOUNTAINS: THE BRITISH FUR TRADE ON THE PACIFIC, 1793-1843
Richard S. mackie
Illus. Paper. UBC Press, 1997. $29.95.

TRADING IDENTITIES: THE SOUVENIR IN NATIVE NORTH AMERICAN ART FROM THE NORTHEAST, 1700-1900
Ruth B. Phillips
Paper. University of Washington Press, $40.

TRADING POST GUIDEBOOK: WHERE TO FIND THE TRADING POSTS, GALLERIES, AUCTIONS, ARTISTS, & MUSEUMS OF THE FOUR CORNERS REGION
Patrick Eddington & Susan Makov
115 color & 135 bxw photos. Biblio. 264 pp. Paper. Northland, $17.95.

TRADITION & CHANGE ON THE NORTHWEST COAST: THE MAKAH, NUU CHAH-NULTH, SOUTHERN KWAKIUTL & NUXALK
Ruth Kirk
Illus. 200 photos. 256 pp. Paper. University of Washington Press, 1988. $29.95.

TRADITION & INNOVATION: A BASKET HISTORY OF THE INDIANS OF THE YOSEMITE-MONO LAKE REGION
Craig D. Bates & Martha J. Lee
Study of the history and basketry of the Miwok and Paiute people. Illus. 252 pp. Yosemite Association, 1991. $49.95.

TRADITIONAL CLOTHING OF THE NATIVE AMERICANS
Evard H. Gibby
Patterns and ideas for making authentic traditional clothing, modern buckskin clothing, and a section on tanning buckskin and furs. Illus. Smoke & Fire Co., $17.95.

*TRADITIONAL CRAFTS FROM NATIVE NORTH AMERICA
Florence Temko
Grades 2-5. Illus. Color photos. Lerner Publishing, 1996. $22.60.

TRADITIONAL DRESS
Adolph Hungry Wolf
Illus. 80 pp. Paper. Written Heritage & The Book Publishing Co., 1990. $6.95.

TRADITIONAL INDIAN BEAD & LEATHER CRAFTS
Monte Smith & Michele Van Sickle
Illus. 100 pp. Paper. Eagle's View Publishing, & Smoke & Fire Co., 1987. $9.95.

TRADITIONAL INDIAN CRAFTS
Monte Smith
Illus. 96 pp. Paper. Eagle's View Publishing, 1987. $9.95.

TRADITIONAL LITERATURES OF THE AMERICAN INDIAN: TEXTS & INTERPRETATIONS
Karl Kroeber, Editor
2nd edition. Illus. 161 pp. University of Nebraska Press, 1997. $50; paper, $16.95.

TRADITIONAL NARRATIVES OF THE ARIKARA INDIANS, 4 Vols.
Douglas Parks
Vol. 1, *Stories of Alfred Morsette*, 684 pp; Vol. 2, *Stories of Other Narrators*, 660 pp. University of Nebraska Press, 1991. $125 per set. Audiocassette, $20. Vols. 3 & 4, *Free Translations*. Illus. Maps. 400 pp. & 320 pp. $75.

TRADITIONAL NATIVE AMERICAN HEALING & CHILD SEXUAL ABUSE
David W. Lloyd, Editor
62 pp. Paper. Diane Publishing, 1994. $30.

THE TRADITIONAL NORTHERN DANCER
C. Scott Evans
Features dancers at powwows. Color photos. Illus. 48 pp. Paper. Written Heritage, $11.95.

TRADITIONAL OJIBWA RELIGION & ITS HISTORICAL CHANGES
Christopher Vecsey
American Philosophical Society, 1983. $12.

TRADITIONAL PLANT FOODS OF CANADIAN INDIGENOUS PEOPLES: NUTRITION, BOTANY & USE
Harriet V. Kuhnlein
633 pp. Gordon & Breach, 1991. $118.

TRADITIONAL STORIES & FOODS: AN AMERICAN INDIAN REMEMBERS
Joan L. Wodruff; Yoly Zentella, Editor
Illus. 60 pp. Paper. Esoterica Press, 1991. $10.95.

TRADITIONS IN TRANSITION: CONTEMPORARY BASKET WEAVING OF THE SOUTHWESTERN INDIANS
Barbara Maudlin
Illus. 64 pp. Paper. Museum of New Mexico Press, 1984. $8.95.

TRADITIONS OF THE ARAPAHO
George A. Dorsey and A.L. Kroeber
Reprint of 1903 edition. Illus. 488 pp. Paper. University of Nebraska Press, $22.

TRADITIONS OF THE CADDO
George A. Dorsey
Reprint of 1905 edition. Illus. 132 pp. Paper. University of Nebraska Press, 1997. $10.95.

TRADITIONS OF THE NORTH AMERICAN INDIANS
J.A. Jones
Three volumes. Gordon Press, $300 per set.

THE TRAGEDY OF THE BLACKFOOT
W. McCluntock
Reprint of 1930 edition. Illus. 53 pp. Southwest Museum, $5.

*TRAGEDY OF TENAYA
Allan Shields
Grades 6-and up. 60 pp. Paper. Council for Indian Education, 1974. $9.95; paper, $3.95.

TRAGEDY OF THE WAHKSHUM: THE DEATH OF ANDREW J. BOLON...; ALSO, THE SUICIDE OF GENERAL GEORGE A. CUSTER AS TOLD BY OWL CHILD, EYEWITNESS
Lucullus V. McWhorter; ed. by Donald Hines
Illus. Maps. 105 pp. Great Eagle Publishing. $10.95.

TRAGIC SAGA OF THE INDIANA INDIANS
Harold Allison
350 pp. Turner Publishing Co., 1987. $15.

THE TRAIL OF MANY SPIRITS: PAWS - HOOVES - MOCCASINS
Serle Chapman
Illus. 218 pp. Paper. Mountain Press, 1999. $24.95.

THE TRAIL OF TEARS
John Ehle
Portrays the Cherokee Nation filled with legend, lore and religion. 424 pp. Paper. VIP Publishing. $14.95.

*THE TRAIL OF TEARS
Joseph Bruchac
Grades 4 and up. Illus. Random House, 1999. $11.99; paper, $3.99.

THE TRAIL OF TEARS
Gloria Jahoda
224 pp. Random House, 1995. $9.99.

TRAIL OF TEARS ACROSS MISSOURI
Joan Gilbert
Illus. 136 pp. Paper. University of Missouri Press, 1995. $8.95.

TRAIL OF TEARS: AMERICAN INDIANS DRIVEN FROM THEIR LANDS
Jeanne Williams
Reprint. Illus. 192 pp. Hendrick-Long, $16.95.

*THE TRAIL ON WHICH THEY WEPT: THE STORY OF A CHEROKEE GIRL
Dorothy & Thomas Hoobler
The Trail of Tears through the eyes of a young Cherokee girl. Grades 3-5. Illus. 64 pp. Silver Burdett Press, 1992. $7.95; paper. $3.95

TRANSFORMATION OF BIGFOOT: MALENESS, POWER & BELIEF AMONG THE CHIPEWYAN
Henry Sharp
Illus. 190 pp. Smithsonian, 1988, $22.50.

TRANSFORMATION OF THE SOUTHEASTERN INDIANS
edited by Robbie Ethridge & Charles Hudson
Essays by Charles Hudson, Helen Rountree, Stephen Davis, et al., on how Southeastern Indian culture and society evolved. 350 pp. University Press of Mississippi, 2002. $50.

TRAVELER IN INDIAN TERRITORY: THE JOURNAL OF ETHAN ALLEN HITCHCOCK
Ethan A. Hitchcock
Illus. 288 pp. Paper. University of Oklahoma Press, 1996. $17.95.

TRAVELS & INQUIRIES IN NORTH AMERICA, 1882-1883
Herman ten Kate; trans. & edited by
Pieter Hovens, William Orr, Louis Hieb
Dutch traveler, Ten Kate's studies of the Pima, Hopi, Apache, and Zuni people. Illus. 480 pp. University of New Mexico Press, 2004. $55.

TREASURES OF THE HOPI
Theda Bassman
Outlines history of the tribe and their art. 110 color photos. Biblio. 116 pp. Paper. Northland, $12.95.

TREASURES OF THE NAVAJO
Theda Bassman
Outlines history of the tribe and their art. 105 color photos. Biblio. 124 pp. Paper. Northland, $12.95.

TREASURES OF THE ZUNI
Theda Bassman
Outlines history of the tribe and their art. 104 color photos. Biblio. 116 pp. Paper. Northland, $12.95.

THE TRIAL OF DON PEDRO LEON LUJAN: THE ATTACK AGAINST INDIAN SLAVERY & MEXICAN TRADERS IN UTAH
Sondra Jones
Illus. Maps. 208 pp. University of Utah Press, 2000. $27.50.

TRAIL OF TEARS
John Ehle
Portrayal of the Cherokee Nation, filled with legend, lore & religion. 424 pp. Paper. Cherokee Publications, $11.95.

TREKWAYS OF THE WIND
Nils-Aslak Valkeapaa; trans. by Ralph Salisbury, et al
Studies Native American poetry. 300 pp. University of Arizona Press, 1994. $20.

THE TRIAL OF LEONARD PELTIER
Jim Messersmith
Paper. South End Press, 1991. $12.

THE TRAIL OF TEARS
Gloria Jahoda
355 pp. Brown Book Co., 1975. $12.95.

TRAIL OF TEARS: THE RISE & FALL OF THE CHEROKEE NATION
John Ehle
430 pp. Doubleday, 1988. $19.95. Paper. Cherokee Publications, $10.95.

*THE TRAIL ON WHICH THEY WEPT: THE STORY OF A CHEROKEE GIRL
Dorothy and Thomas Hoobler; pictures by S.S. Burrus
A young girls story of their Trail of Tears. Ages 9-11. Illus. 64 pp. Silver Burdett Press.

TRAILS TO TIBURON: THE 1894 & 1895 FIELD DIARIES OF W.J. McGEE
transcribed by Hazel McFeely Fontana
Journals of McGees expedition to the Papagos (Tohono O'odham). 170 pp. University of Arizona Press, 2000. $36.

TRAITS OF AMERICAN INDIAN LIFE & CHARACTER
Peter S. Ogden
128 pp. Paper. Dover, $6.95.

THE TRANSFORMATION OF BIGFOOT: MALENESS, POWER, & BELIEF AMONG THE CHIPEWYAN
Henry S. Sharp
192 pp. Smithsonian Institution Press, 1988. $30.

*TRAPPERS & TRADERS
Gail Stewart
Grades 3-8. Illus. 32 pp. Rourke Corp., 1990. $17.26.

TRAPS OF THE AMERICAN INDIANS: A STUDY IN PSYCHOLOGY & INVENTION
Otis T. Mason
Reprint. Illus. 15 pp. Paper. Shoreys Bookstore, $2.95.

A TRAVELER IN INDIAN TERRITORY: THE JOURNAL OF ETHAN ALLEN HITCHCOCK
Ethan Allen Hitchcock
Illus. Maps. Photos. Paper. University of Oklahoma Press, 1996. $17.95.

A TRAVELERS GUIDE TO SOUTHWEST INDIAN ARTS & CRAFTS
Charlotte Smith Neyland
Illus. Map. 48 pp. Paper. Renaissance House, 1992. $4.95.

TRAVELS AMONG THE DENA OF ALASKA'S YUKON VALLEY
Frederica de Laguna
Illus. Maps. 368 pp. Univ. of Washington Press, 1999. $29.95.

TRAVELS IN THE GREAT WESTERN PRAIRIES
T.J. Farnham
Reprint of 1843 edition. 2 vols. in 1. 612 pp.
Da Capo Press, $75.

TRAVELS IN NORTH AMERICA, INCLUDING A SUMMER WITH THE PAWNEES
C. Murray
Reprint of 1839 Second Edition. 878 pp. Da Capo Press, $85.

TRAVELS IN A STONE CANOE: THE RETURN TO THE WISDOMKEEPERS
Harvey Arden & Steve Wall
Illus. 320 pp. Simon & Schuster, 1998. $25.

TREADING IN THE PAST: SANDALS OF THE ANASAZI
Utah Museum of Natural History
Essays. 256 color photos. University of Utah Press.
$50; paper, $29.95.

A TREASURED HERITAGE: WORKS OF MASTERS & APPRENTICES
Exhibition catalog featuring biographies and the works of 54 Alaska Native master artists and their apprentices. Illus. 64 pp. Paper. Institute of Alaska Native Arts, 1988. $12.50, post-paid.

TREASURES OF THE HOPI
Theda Bassman
The history and art of the Hopi. Illus. 110 color photos.
116 pp. Northland Publishing & Clear Light, 1997. $12.95.

TREASURES OF THE MOUND BUILDERS
Lar Hothem
Covers 135 Adena and Hopewell mounds in Ohio, with name, location, when and by whom excavated, artifacts found. Photos. Illus. 146 pp. Paper. Hothem House, 1989. $11.95.

TREASURES OF THE NATIONAL MUSEUM OF THE AMERICAN INDIAN
W. Richard West, Jr., et al
Overview of the collection of art from the museum. Illus.
318 pp. (small size). Paper. Abbeville Press, 1996. $11.95.

TREASURES OF THE NAVAJO
Theda Bassman
The history and art of the Navajo. Illus. 105 color photos.
112 pp. Northland Publishing & Clear Light, 1997. $12.95.

TREASURES OF THE ZUNI
Theda Bassman
The history and art of the Zuni. Illus. 104 color photos.
116 pp. Northland Publishing & Clear Light, 1997. $12.95.

A TREASURY OF OUR WESTERN HERITAGE: THE FAVELL MUSEUM OF WESTERN ART & INDIAN ARTIFACTS
Illus. Favell Museum, 1986. $19.75.

TREATIES & AGREEMENTS OF THE INDIAN TRIBES OF THE PACIFIC NORTHWEST
Institute for the Development of Indian Law, $12.

TREATIES ON TRIAL: THE CONTINUING CONTROVERSY OVER NORTHWEST INDIAN FISHING RIGHTS
Fay G. Cohen, et al
Illus. 280 pp. Paper. University of Washington Press, 1986.
$11.95.

TREATISE ON THE HEATHEN SUPERSTITIONS THAT TODAY LIVE AMONG THE INDIANS NATIVE TO THIS NEW SPAIN, 1629
Ruiz de Alarcon; J. Richard Andrews & Ross Hassig, Editors
Illus. Map. 406 pp. Paper. University of Oklahoma Press, 1984. $24.95.

TREATMENT OF INDIANS BY THE CRIMINAL JUSTICE SYSTEM
51 pp. paper. Diane Publishing, 1993. $25.

TREATY MANUSCRIPTS SERIES
A series of treaties. See Institute for the Development of Indian Law for titles and prices.

TREATY OF CANANDAIGUA 1794: 200 YEARS OF TREATY RELATIONS BETWEEN THE IROQUOIS CONFEDERACY & THE U.S.
edited by G. Peter Jemison & Anna M. Schein
Tells the story of the Six Nations and their relationship with the U.S. Among the contributors are Chief Irving Powless, Jr., Chief Leon Shenandoah, Chief Oren Lyons, Chief Bernard Parker, Chief Jake Swamp, et al. Illus. Photos. 352 pp. Paper. Clear Light, $14.95.

TREATY TALKS IN BRITISH COLUMBIA
Christopher McKee
Paper. UBC Press, 1996. $19.95.

TRENDS IN INDIAN HEALTH
Indian Health Service
Annual compendium of tables and charts that describe the IHS program, and health ststaus of American Indian and Alaska Natives. Paper. U.S. Government Printing Office. No charge.

THE TRIAL OF "INDIAN JOE": RACE & JUSTICE IN THE 19TH CENTURY WEST
Clare V. McKanna, Jr.
Illus. 135 pp. University of Nebraska Press, 2003. $35.

TRIBAL ASSETS: THE REBIRTH OF NATIVE AMERICA
Robert White
Henry Holt & Co., 1990. $24.95.

TRIBAL BOUNDARIES IN THE NASS WATERSHED
Neil J. Sterritt, et al.
Illus. Paper. UBC Press,, 1998. $27.95.

TRIBAL DISPOSSESSION & OTHER OTTAWA INDIAN UNIVERSITY FRAUD
William E. Unrau & H. Craig Miner
Illus. Maps. 212 pp. University of Oklahoma Press, 1985. $32.95.

THE TRIBAL FIRES CATALOG
Zango Music
Native American music. 500 titles: cassettes, CDs, albums, etc. Over 200 album reviews. Wholesale only. Zango Music, No charge.

TRIBAL GOVERNMENT: A NEW ERA
Includes Choctaw Tribal constitution and all Choctaw treaties with U.S. Government. Choctaw Heritage Press, $6.

TRIBAL GOVERNMENT OF THE OGLALA SIOUX OF PINE RIDGE, S.D.
Ira Grinnell
University of South Dakota, Government Research Bureau, 1967. $5.

TRIBAL GOVERNMENT TEXTBOOK
National Congress of American Indians.

TRIBAL GOVERNMENT TODAY: POLITICS ON MONTANA INDIAN RESERVATIONS
James J. Lopach, Margery Hunter Brown & Richmond L. Clow
Revised edition. University Press of Colorado, 1998. $34.95.

TRIBAL GOVERNMENT: WIND RIVER RESERVATION
Janet Flynn & Scott Ratliff; Pat Trautman, Editor
2nd revised edition. Illus. 90 pp. Paper. Mortimore Publishing, 1998. $14.95.

*TRIBAL LAW
Scott Prentzas
Grades 4-8. 64 pp. Rourke, 1994. $25.27.

TRIBAL SECRETS: RECOVERING AMERICAN INDIAN INTELLECTUAL TRADITIONS
Robert Allen Warrior
A narrative account of the literary productions and political & cultural interactions of American Indian writers of the 20th century. 192 pp. University of Minnesota Press, 1994. $39.95; paper, $16.95.

TRIBAL SOVEREIGNTY & THE HISTORICAL IMAGINATION: CHEYENNE-ARAPAHO POLITICS
Loretta Fowler
Illus. Maps. University of Nebraska Press, 2002. $55.

*TRIBAL SOVEREIGNTY: INDIAN TRIBES IN U.S. HISTORY
Four scholarly papers which consider the issue of tribal sovereignty. Papers by: Dr. Fay Cohen, Dr. D'Arcy McNickle, Dr. Roger Buffalohead, and Dr. Mary Young. Studies the impact of non-Indian settlement and U.S. Government policy. Teacher's guide. Grades7-12. Illus. 60 pp. Daybreak Star Press, $5.50.

TRIBAL WARS OF THE SOUTHERN PLAINS
Stan Hoig
Indian conflicts from the Spaniards in the 16th century through the U.S.-Cheyenne Battle of the Sand Hills in 1875. Illus. Maps. 344 pp. University of Oklahoma Press, 1993. $34.95.

TRIBALLY CONTROLLED COLLEGES: MAKING GOOD MEDICINE
Wayne J. Stein
History of the early years of the American Indian tribally controlled college movement. 180 pp. Peter Lang Publishing, 1992. $35.95.

TRIBALLY CONTROLLED COMMUNITY COLLEGES
Norman T. Oppelt
History of American Indian higher education. Paper.
Dine College Press, 1991. $20.

TRIBES OF CALIFORNIA
S. Powers
Covers American Indian ethnography of California.
Reprint of 1877 edition. Illus. 482 pp. University of California Press, $45.50; paper, $11.95.

TRIBES THAT SLUMBER: INDIANS OF THE TENNESSEE REGION
T. Lewis and M. Kneberg
Reprint of 1958 edition. Illus. 208 pp. Paper.
Hothem House & University of Tennessee Press, $16.95.

TRIBES, TREATIES, & CONSTITUTIONAL TRIBULATIONS
David E. Wilkins & Vine Deloria, Jr.
Examines relationship between Indians and the U.S. Constitution. Paper. University of Texas Press, 1999.

THE TRICKSTER OF LIBERTY: TRIBAL HEIRS TO A WILD BARONAGE
Gerald Vizenor
Novel of a traditional tribal trickster figure; moves from oral stories into contemporary narrative. Illus. 160 pp. University of Minnesota Press, 1988. $19.95; paper, $9.95.

THE TRICKSTER SHIFT: HUMOUR & IRONY IN CONTEMPORARY NATIVE ART
Allan J. Ryan
160 Illus. 320 pp. University of Washington Press, 1999.
$60.

TRICKSTER: STUDY IN AMERICAN INDIAN MYTHOLOGY
Paul Radin
Reprint of 1956 edition. 223 pp. Greenwood, $35.
New edition. 223 pp. Paper. Shocken Books, 1972. $6.95.

*THE TRICKSTER & THE TROLL
Virginia Driving Hawk Sneve
Grades 4 and up. Illus. 110 pp. Paper.
University of Nebraska Press, 1997. $8.

*A TRIP TO A POW WOW
Grades 3 and up. Paper. Sierra Oaks Publishing, $6.95.

TROOPERS WITH CUSTER: HISTORIC INCIDENTS OF THE BATTLE OF THE LITTLE BIG HORN
E.A. Brininstool
343 ,pp. Paper. Clear Light, $13.95.

TRUE COPY OF THE RECORD OF THE OFFICIAL PROCEEDINGS AT THE COUNCIL IN THE WALLA WALLA VALLEY, 1855
Darrell Scott & Isaac Stevens
125 pp. Ye Galleon, 1985. $19.95; paper, $12.95.

TRUE STORIES OF NEW ENGLAND CAPTIVES CARRIED TO CANADA DURING THE OLD FRENCH & INDIAN WARS
Alice C. Baker
Illus. 420 pp. Paper. Heritage Books, 1991. $27.50.

TRUSTEESHIP IN CHANGE: TOWARD TRIBAL AUTONOMY IN RESOURCE MANAGEMENT
Ed. by Richmond Clow & Imre Sutton
University Press of Colorado, 2001. $59.95; paper, $24.95.

THE TRUTH ABOUT GERONIMO
Britton Davis; M.M. Quaife, Editor
Illus. 293 pp. Paper. University of Nebraska Press, 1976. $7.95.

TSONAKWA & YOLAIKIA: LEGENDS IN STONE, BONE & WOOD
Gerard Rancourt Tsonakwa
Indian stories discussing Native American beliefs about the earth and shared life. Illus. 64 pp. The Origins Program, $10.95.

TSEE-MA'HEONE-NEMEOTOTSE: CHEYENNE SPIRITUAL SONGS
David Graber, Editor
227 pp. Faith & Life, 1982. $29.95.

TS'ILIYAZHI SPUDS BAA HANE
Marie Lewis & Navajo Language Program
Pamphlet. Dine College Press. $2.95.

TSIMSHIAN CULTURE: A LIGHT THROUGH THE AGES
Jay Miller
Illus. 204 pp. Paper. University of Nebraska Press, 1997. $28.50.

THE TSIMSHIAN: IMAGES OF THE PAST; VIEWS FOR THE PRESENT
Margaret Seguin, Editor
Illus. 364 pp. Paper. University of Washington Press, $20.

THE TSIMSHIAN & THEIR NEIGHBORS OF THE NORTH PACIFIC COAST
Jay Miller & Carol Eastman, Editors
Illus. 366 pp. University of Washington Press, 1985. $35.

TUBERCULOSIS AMONG CERTAIN INDIAN TRIBES OF THE U.S.
Ales Hrdlicka
Reprint. Reprint Services, $49.

*TUL-TOK-A-NA: THE SMALL ONE
Kathleen Allan Myer
A Yosemite Indian legend. Grades 1-5. 32 pp.
Council for Indian Education, 1991. $4.95.

TULAPAI TO TOKAY: A BIBLIOGRAPHY OF ALCOHOL USE & ABUSE AMONG NATIVE AMERICANS OF NORTH AMERICA
David R. McDonald & Pat Mail
372 pp. HRAFP, 1981, $25.

*THE TUNICA-BILOXI: SOUTHEAST
Jeffrey Brain
Grades 5 and up. Illus. Chelsea House, 1989. $17.95.

THE TURN TO THE NATIVE:
STUDIES IN CRITICISM & CULTURE
Arnold Krupat
168 pp. Paper. University of Nebraska Press, 1996. $13.

*TURQUOISE BOY: A NAVAJO LEGEND
Grades 4-7. Illus. 48 pp. Paper. Troll Communications,
Rourke Corp. & Demco, 1992. $9.15; paper, $4.95.

TURQUOISE - THE GEM OF THE CENTURIES
Branson
Turquoise types and different kinds of Southwestern Indian
jewelry. Illus. 62 pp. Paper. Hothem House, 1975. $7.95.

TURQUOISE & THE INDIAN
Bennett
Study of raw gem materials, turquoise mines and locations,
and the beginning of gem-working and Indian jewelry style pro-
gression. Reprint of 1970 edition. Illus. 152 pp. Hothem House,
$9.95.

TURQUOISE JEWELRY
Nancy Schiffer
Full color photos of a variety of Southwest Indian-made
jewelry with many types of turquoise. Illus. 64 pp. Paper.
Schiffer, $9.95.

TURQUOISE JEWELRY OF THE
INDIANS OF THE SOUTHWEST
Edna & John Bennett
Illus. Turquoise Books, 1973. $21.

TURQUOISE & THE NAVAJO
Lee Hammons
Illus. 32 pp. Paper. Primer Publishers, $1.95.

THE TURQUOISE TRAIL: NATIVE AMERICAN
JEWELRY OF THE SOUTHWEST
Photos by Jeffrey J. Fox
Illus. Photos. 216 pp. Harry N. Abrams, 1993. $49.50.

TURTLE BOY: A NOVEL
Joel Monture
Covers traditional Mohawk culture. 304 pp. Paper.
University of Oklahoma Press, $14.95.

TURTLE DREAM
Gerald Hausman
Illus. Mariposa Print, 1989. $9.95.

TURTLE ISLAND ALPHABET: A LEXICON OF
NATIVE AMERICAN SYMBOLS & CULTURE
Gerald Hausman
Reprint. Illus. 204 pp. Paper. Diane Publishing, 1999. $14.

TURTLE LUNG WOMAN'S GRANDDAUGHTER
Delphine Red Shirt
Stories of Red Shirt's mother, Lone Woman and her
grandmother Turtle Lung Woman, a medicine woman.
268 pp. Paper. University of Nebraska, 2002. $14.95.

TURTLE MEAT & OTHER STORIES
Joseph Bruchac
18 stories, myths and legends reveal the transforming power
Native American writing in a contemporary world. Illus. 128 pp.
Holy Cow! Press, 1993. $18.95; paper, $10.95.

TURTLES, WOLVES & BEARS:
A MOHAWK FAMILY HISTORY
Barbara J. Sivertson
344 pp. Paper. Heritage Books, 1996. $29.

TUSAYAN KATCINAS & HOPI KATCINA ALTARS
Jesse Walter Fewkes
Discusses the ceremonies of the Tusayan (Hopi) Indians and
the Cibola (Zuni) Indians. Illus. 120 pp. Paper. Avanyu Publishing, 1991. $17.95.

*THE TUSCARORA
Grades K-4. Illus. 48 pp. Childrens Press, $11.45.

THE TUSCARORA LEGACY OF J.N.B. HEWITT:
MATERIALS FOR THE STUDY OF THE TUSCARORA
LANGUAGE & CULTURE
Blair Rudes & Dorothy Crouse
670 pp. Paper. University of Chicago Press, 1988. $39.95.

THE TUSCARAWAS VALLEY IN IDNIAN DAYS, 1750-1797
Booth
329 pp. Hothem House, 1994. $30.50, postpaid.

THE TUTOR'D MIND: INDIAN MISSIONARY-
WRITERS IN ANTEBELLUM AMERICA
Bernd C. Peyer
Traces the development of American Indian literature from the
17th century to the eve of the Civil War. 408 pp. University of
Massachusetts Press, 1997. $70; paper, $19.95.

TWANA GAMES
A handbook of games played by Twana people of the
Skokomish Reservation in western Washington State. Illus. 20
pp. Daybreak Star Press, $3.50.

TWELVE THOUSAND YEARS:
AMERICAN INDIANS IN MAINE
Bruce J. Bourque
Reveals how Penobscot, Abenakis, Passaquoddies, Maliseets,
Micmacs, and other Native communities lived and survived ove
the centuries. Illus. Maps. 369 pp. University of Nebraska Press,
2001. $45.

THE TWENTIETH CENTURY FICTIONAL AMERICAN INDIAN
WOMAN & FELLOW CHARACTERS: A STUDY OF GENDER
& RACE
Asebrit Sundquist
304 pp. Humanities Press, 1991, $39.95.

*TWILIGHT BOY
Timothy Green
Navajo story. Ages 12 and up. 240 pp. Northland,
$12.95; paper, $6.95

THE TWILIGHT OF THE SIOUX
John Neihardt
Reprint of 1971 edition. Vol. II of, "A Cycle of the West."
295 pp. Paper. University of Nebraska Press, $22.

*TWO BEAR CUBS: A MIWOK LEGEND FROM
CALIFORNIA'S YOSEMITE VALLEY
Daniel San Souci, Illus.
Grades K-4. Yosemite Association, 1997. $14.95.

TWO CROWS DENIES IT: A HISTORY OF
CONTROVERSY IN OMAHA SOCIOLOGY
R.H. Barnes
Illus. 288 pp. University of Nebraska Press, 1984. $24.95.

TWO EARLY HISTORIC IROQUOIAN
SITES IN WESTERN NEW YORK
Michael Gramly
Paper. Persimmon Press, 1996. $12.95.

TWO GREAT SCOUTS & THEIR PAWNEE BATTALION:
THE EXPERIENCES OF FRANK J. NORTH & LUTHER
H. NORTH
Georghe Grinnell
Reprint of 1929 edition. Map. 300 pp. Paper.
University of Nebraska Press, $12.

TWO LEGGINGS: THE MAKING OF A CROW WARRIOR
Peter Nabokov
Reprint of 1972 edition. Illus. Map. 242 pp. Paper.
University of Nebraska Press, 1982. $13.95.

*TWO OLD WOMEN: AN ALASKA LEGEND
OF BETRAYAL, COURAGE & SURVIVAL
Velma Wallis
Portrait of Native subsistence life in the boreal forest. Told with
an ecological perspective. Grades 6 and up. Illus. 160 pp.
Graphic Arts Center & Greenfield Review Press, $16.95. Pa-
per. Alaska Natural History Association, $9.

TWO SPIRIT PEOPLE: AMERICAN INDIAN LESBIAN
WOMEN & GAY MEN
Lester B. Brown
120 pp. Haworth Press, 1997. $29.95.

TWO WORLDS: THE INDIAN ENCOUNTER
WITH THE EUROPEAN, 1492-1509
S. Lyman Tyler
275 pp. University of Utah Press, 1988. $25.

U

UGIUVANGMIUT QULIAPYUIT KING ISLAND TALES
Lawrence D. Kaplan
Eskimo history and legends from Bering Strait. Illus. Maps.
258 pp. Paper. University of Alaska Press, 1988. $19.95.

UKOMNO'M: THE YUKI INDIANS
OF NORTHERN CALIFORNIA
Virginia P. Miller
Illus. 108 pp. Paper. Ballena Press, 1979. $8.95.

UKWEHU-WEHNAHA TEKAWXNATE?NEYSE:
AN ONEIDA DICTIONARY
Amos Christjohn and Maria Hinton
665 pp. Oneida Turtle School, 1999. $45.

*THE UNBREAKABLE CODE
Sara Hoagland Hunter; illus. by Julia Miner
Picture book. Ages 6-8. Illus. Northland, $15.95.

UNBROKEN CIRCLES: TRADITIONAL ARTS OF
CONTEMPORARY WOODLAND PEOPLES
Looks at the preservation of culture through the artistic media
that have been used by Native people since before Columbus.
Akwe:kon Press, $10.

UNCAS: FIRST OF THE MOHEGANS
Michael Leroy Oberg
Cornell University Press, 2003. $27.50.

UNCLE SAM'S STEPCHILDREN: THE REFORMATION
OF U.S. INDIAN POLICY, 1865-1887
L.B. Priest
Reprint of 1942 edition. 310 pp. Paper.
University of Nebraska Press, $6.95.

UNCONQUERED PEOPLE: FLORIDA'S
SEMINOLE & MICCOSUKEE INDIANS
Brent R. Weisman
University Press of Florida, 1999. $39.95; paper, $19.95.

THE UNCOVERED PAST: ROOTS
OF NORTHERN ALBERTA SOCIETIES
Patricia A. McCormack & R. Geoffrey Ironside, Editors
Illus. Maps. 290 pp. CCI, $30; paper, $20.

*UNDER THE INDIAN TURQUOISE SKY
Rosemary Davey
Animal fables. Grades 4 and up. Illus. 92 pp.
Ye Galleon Press, 1985. $8.95.

UNDER THE PALACE PORTAL: NATIVE AMERICAN
ARTISTS IN SANTA FE
Karl A. Hoerig
A history of the Portal and the Native American Vendors
Program. Illus. Map. 320 pp. University of New Mexico Press,
2003. $29.95.

UNDER SACRED GROUND: A HISTORY OF NAVAJO OIL
Kathleen P. Chamberlain
University of New Mexico Press. $35.

UNDER YOUR FEET: THE STORY OF THE AMERICAN
MOUND BUILDERS OF THE MISSISSIPPI VALLEY
Blanche Busey King
Reprint of 1939 edition. Ayer Co., $22.

THE UNDERGROUND RESERVATION: OSAGE OIL
Terry P. Wilson
Illus. 263 pp. University of Nebraska Press, 1985. $22.95.

UNDERSTANDING THE ANASAZI
OF MESA VERDE & HOVENWEEP
David Noble, Editor
Illus. Maps. 40 pp. Paper. Ancient City Press, 1992. $8.95.

UNDERSTANDING TOLOWA HISTORIES: WESTERN
HEGEMONIES & NATIVE AMERICAN RESPONSES
James Collins
240 pp. Paper. Routledge, 1997. $23.99.

THE UNDYING WEST: STORIES
FROM MONTANA'S CAMAS PRAIRIE
Carlene Cross
History of western Montana's Camas Prairie. The Salish,
Kootenai, Nez Perce, and Iroquois Indians. 50 bxw photos. 176
pp. Paper. Fulcrum Publishing, 1999. $16.95.

UNEVEN GROUND: AMERICAN INDIAN
SOVEREIGNTY & FEDERAL LAW
David E. Wilkins & K. Tsianina Lomawaima
340 pp. University of Oklahoma Press, 2002. $29.95; paper,
$19.95.

UNHALLOWED INTRUSIONS, A HISTORY OF
CHEROKEE FAMILIES IN FORSYTH CO., GA
Don Shadburn
800 pp. Wolfe Publishing, 1996.

THE UNITED KEETOOWAH BAND OF CHEROKEE
INDIANS IN OKLAHOMA
Georgia R. Leeds
320 pp. Peter Lang Publishing, 1997. $49.95.

U.S. FISCAL YEAR BUDGET HEARING BEFORE
THE COMMITTEE ON INDIAN AFFAIRS, U.S. SENATE
U.S. Government Printing Office.

UNIVERSITY OF CALIFORNIA
ANTHROPOLOGICAL RECORDS
A series of 30 facsimile reprints.
See Coyote Press for titles and prices.

UNIVERSITY OF CALIFORNIA,
ARCHAEOLOGICAL REPORTS
A series of 74 facsimile reprints.
See Coyote Press for titles and prices.

UNIVERSITY OF CALIFORNIA, PUBLICATIONS
IN AMERICAN ARCHAEOLGY & ETHNOLOGY
A series of 49 facsimile reprints.
See Coyote Press for titles and prices.

UNJUST RELATIONS: ABORIGINAL
RIGHTS IN CANADIAN COURTS
Peter Kulchyski, Editor
380 pp. Paper. Oxford University Press, 1994. $32.

THE UNKNOWN INDIAN
G.B. Brown
Gordon Press, 1977. $59.95.

UNLEARNING "INDIAN" STEREOTYPES,
A TEACHING UNIT FOR ELEMENTARY
TEACHERS & CHILDREN'S LIBRARIANS
Racism & Sexism Resource Center for Educators
Council on Interracial Books for Children, 1981. $39.95.
Teaching Guide, $4.95.

THE UNRATIFIED TREATY BETWEEN THE KIOWAS,
COMANCHES & APACHES & THE U.S. OF 1863
R.J. DeMallie
8 pp. Institute for the Development of Indian Law. $5.

UNRAVELLING THE FRANKLIN MYSTERY:
INUIT TESTIMONY
David C. Woodman
This new examination of Sir John Franklin's final Arctic expedition (1845) reconsyructs events surrounding the mysterious loss
of both ships and all hands by giving credence to the testimony of Inuit witnesses. University of Toronto Press, 1991.
$42.95; paper, $19.95.

AN UNSPEAKABLE SADNESS:
THE DISPOSSESSION OF NEBRASKA INDIANS
David J. Wishart
Illus. Maps. 311 pp. University of Nebraska Press, 1995.
$65; paper, $23.95.

*UNSUNG HEROES OF WORLD WAR II:
THE STORY OF THE NAVAJO CODE TALKERS
Deanne Durrett
Grades 6 and up. Illus. 122 pp. Facts on File, 1998. $19.95.

UPPER CHEHALIS DICTIONARY
M. Dale Kinkade
378 pp. University of Montana, 1991. $20.

UPSIDE DOWN: SEASONS AMONG THE NUNAMIUT
Margaret B. Blackman
Essays about the people and the life of Anaktuvuk Pass in north-
ern Alaska. Illus. 224 pp. University of Nebraska Press, 2004.
$27.95.

THE UPSTREAM PEOPLE: AN ANNOTATED
RESEARCH BIBLIOGRAPHY OF THE OMAHA TRIBE
Michael L. Tate, Editor
Maps. 522 pp. Scarecrow Press, 1991. $70.

THE UPWARD MOVING & EMERGENCE WAY;
THE GISHIN BIYE VERSION
Father Berard Haile, O.F.M.
Illus. 250 pp. University of Nebraska Press, 1981. $11.95.

UPWHERE BELONG
Buffy Sainte-Marie
224 pp. Paper. LPC InBook, 1998. $15.95.

URBAN INDIAN EXPERIENCE IN AMERICA
Donald L. Fixico
University of New Mexico Press, $35; paper, $17.95.

*URBAN INDIANS
Donald Fixico
Grades 5 and up. Illus. Chelsea House, 1989. $17.95.

URBAN INDIANS
Center for the History of the American Indian Staff
185 pp. Newberry Library, 1981. $4.

URBAN INDIANS: DRUMS FROM THE CITIES
Describes the plight of over one-half of the Alaska Native &
American Indian population. 600 pp. Arrowstar Publishing,
1994. $19.95.

URBAN INSTITUTIONS & PEOPLE OF INDIAN ANCESTRY
Raymond Breton and Gail Akian
52 pp. Paper. Gower Publishing, 1978. $3.

URBAN VOICES: THE BAY AREA
AMERICAN INDIAN COMMUNITY
edited by Susan Lobo
Essays, photos, stories, and art on the American Indian urban
experience. Illus. 160 pp. University of Arizona Press, 2002.
$21.95.

URBANIZATION OF AMERICAN INDIANS:
A CRITICAL BIBLIOGRAPHY
Russell Thornton, et al
96 pp. Paper. Indiana University Press, 1982. $4.95.

THE URINE DANCE OF THE
ZUNI INDIANS OF NEW MEXICO
John G. Bourke
15 pp. Borgo Press, 1989. $9.95.

USES OF PLANTS BY THE INDIANS
OF THE MISSOURI RIVER REGION
Melvin R. Gilmore
Enlarged edition. Illus. 165 pp. Paper.
University of Nebraska Press, 1991. $11.

UTAH PLACE NAMES
John W. Van Cott
Paper. University of Utah Press, $14.95.

UTAH'S BLACK HAWK WAR
John Alton Peterson
An account of the "secret" war between a band led by Ute tribal
leader Black Hawk and the Mormons. University of Utah Press,
$59.95; paper, $19.95.

*THE UTE
Craig & Katherine Doherty
Grades 4-8. 32 pp. Rourke Publications, 1994. $22.60.

UTE INDIAN ARTS & CULTURE: FROM
PREHISTORY TO THE NEW MILLENNIUM
William Wroth, Editor
Includes interviews and essays by Alden B. Naranjo, Terry G.
Knight, Sr., James A. Goss, Rochard N. Ellis, Catherine S.
Fowler, Craig D. Bates, and Cathy L. Wright. Paper. University
of New Mexico Press, $45.

UTE INDIANS OF COLORADO IN THE 20TH CENTURY
Richard K. Young
Comparative history of the Southern Ute and Ute Mountain Ute
peoples. Illus. Maps. 384 pp. University of Oklahoma Press,
1997. $29.95

THE UTE INDIANS OF UTAH, COLORADO, AND NEW
MEXICO
Virginia McConnell Simmons
Paper. University Press of Colorado, 2001. $23.95.

UTE MOUNTAIN UTES
Robert Delaney
Illus. 150 pp. University of New Mexico Press, 1990.

UTE TALES
collected by Anne M. Smith; foreword by Joseph G. Jorgensen
Illus. Map. Paper. University of Utah Press. $14.95.

*THE UTES
Alice Flanagan
Grades 2-4. 48 pp. Children's Press, 1997. $21.

UTES: THE MOUNTAIN PEOPLE
Jan Pettit
Revised edition. 225 pp. Paper. Johnson Books, $11.95.

UTILIZATION OF GENOGRAMS & ECO-MAPS TO
ASSESS AMERICAN INDIAN FAMILIES WHO HAVE
A MEMBER WITH A DISABILITY
C.T. Goodluck
100 pp. Northern Arizona University, 1990.

UTMOST GOOD FAITH: PATTERNS OF APACHE-MEXICAN
HOSTILITIES IN NORTHERN CHICUAHUA BORDER WAR-
FARE, 1821-1848
William Griffen
Illus. 336 pp. University of New Mexico Press, 1989. $37.50.

UTOPIAN LEGACIES: A HISTORY OF CONQUEST
& OPPRESSION IN THE WESTERN WORLD
John Mohawk
Philosophical analysis of Western history in light of patterns of
utopian thinking. 296 pp. Clear Light, $24.95; paper, $14.95.

V

THE VAIL SITE: A PALEO-INDIAN
ENCAMPMENT IN MAINE
Richard M. Gramley
Ilus. 170 pp. Paper. Buffalo Museum of Science, $13.95.

VALLEY OF THE MISSISSIPPI
Henry Lewis; Bertha Heilbron, Editor
Illus. 423 pp. Minnesota Historical Society, 1967.
$39.75; uncut edition, $50.

VALLEY OF THE SPIRITS: THE UPPER SKAGIT
INDIANS OF WESTERN WASHINGTON
June Collins
Illus. 282 pp. University of Washington Press, 1974.
$20; paper, $9.95.

THE VANISHING AMERICAN: THE EPIC OF THE INDIAN
Zane Grey
Paper. Pocket Books, 1982. $3.50.

THE VANISHING AMERICAN:
WHITE ATTITUDES & U.S. INDIAN POLICY
Brian W. Dipple
Illus. 424 pp. Paper. University Press of Kansas, 1982.
$14.95.

VANISHING HERITAGE
Hooge & Lepper
Archaeology & culture history of Licking County, Ohio. Covers
moundbuilders, including the famous Newark Earthworks. Illus.
100 pp. Hothem House, 1992. $22.50.

THE VANISHING RACE & OTHER ILLUSIONS:
PHOTOGRAPHS OF INDIANS BY EDWARD S. CURTIS
Christopher M. Lymans
Illus. 158 pp. Smithsonian Institution Press, 1982.
$24.95. Paper. Pantheon, $14.95.

THE VANISHING RACE: SELECTIONS FROM
EDWARD S. CURTIS' THE NORTH AMERICAN INDIAN
Mick Gidley, Editor
1977 reprint. Illus. Paper. Univ. of Washington Press, $14.95.

VASCO DE QUIROGA & HIS PUEBLO
HOSPITALS OF SANTA FE
Fintan Warren
Illus. Academy of American Franciscan History, 1963. $10.

VAST DOMAIN OF BLOOD
Don Schellie
289 pp. Westernlore, 1968. $9.95.

VECTORS OF DEATH: THE ARCHAEOLOGY
OF EUROPEAN CONTACT
Ann Ramenofsky
Illus. 360 pp. University of New Mexico Press, 1987. $27.50.

*VEHO
Henry Tall Bull & Tom Weist
Grades 2-6. Paper. Council for Indian Education, 1971. $1.95.

THE VENGEFUL WIFE & OTHER BLACKFOOT STORIES
Hugh A. Dempsey
Illus. Maps. 304 pp. University of Oklahoma Press, 2003.
$34.95.

*THE VERY FIRST AMERICANS
Cara Ashrose; illus. by Byrna Waldman
How first Americans lived. Illus. with paintings depicting clothing, dwellings, art , tools, & other artifacts. Grades PS-3. Illus.
32 pp. Paper. Grosset & Dunlap, 1993. $2.25.

A VICTORIAN EARL IN THE ARCTIC:
THE TRAVELS & COLLECTIONS OF THE
FIFTH EARL OF LONSDALE, 1888-89
Shepard Krech III
Examination and analysis of a collection of native artifacts gath-
ered during an early expedition in Canada & Alaskan Arctic.
Illus. 216 pp. University of Washington Press, $35.

VICTORIO & THE MIMBRES APACHES
Dan L. Thrapp
Illus. Maps. 394 pp. Paper. University of Oklahoma Press,
1980. $14.95.

A VIEW FROM BLACK MESA:
THE CHANGING FACE OF ARCHAEOLOGY
George Gumerman
A synopsis of Anasazi prehistory & cultural ecology.
184 pp. Paper. University of Arizona Press, 1984. $16.95.

THE VIEW FROM OFFICERS' ROW:
ARMY PERCEPTIONS OF WESTERN INDIANS
Sherry L. Smith
263 pp. Paper. University of Arizona Press, 1990. $17.95.

VIEW FROM THE SHORE: AMERICAN INDIAN
PERSPECTIVES ON THE QUINCENTENARY
Jose Barreiro, Editor
A collection of articles, interviews, and essays exploring the
effects of Columbus's arrival on Indigenous people. Akwe:kon
Press, 1992. $12.

A VIEW OF THE AMERICAN INDIANS: GENERAL
CHARACTER, CUSTOMS, LANGUAGE, PUBLIC
FESTIVALS, RELIGIOUS RITES & TRADITIONS
I. Worsley; Moshe Davis, Editor
Reprint of 1828 edition. Ayer Co., $19.

VIEWS FROM THE APACHE FRONTIER: REPORT
ON THE NORTHERN PROVINCES OF NEW SPAIN, 1799
Jose Cortes; Elizabeth John, Editor & John Wheat, tr.
Illus. 192 pp. Paper. Univ. of Oklahoma Press, 1989. $13.95.

VIEWS OF A VANISHING FRONTIER
John C. Ewers, et al
Illus. 150 pp. Univerity of Nebraska Press, 1984.
$29.95. Paper. Joslyn Art, $14.95.

THE VILLAGE INDIANS OF THE UPPER MISSOURI:
THE MANDANS, HIDATSAS & ARIKARAS
Roy W. Meyer
Illus. 355 pp. University of Nebraska Press, 1977. $27.50.

VILLAGES OF HISPANIC NEW MEXICO
Nancy Hunter Warren
Illus. 136 pp. Paper. School of American Research, 1987.
$14.95.

VIOLENCE, RESISTANCE, & SURVIVAL IN THE AMERICAS:
NATIVE AMERICANS & THE LEGACY OF CONQUEST
William B. Taylor & Franklin Pease G.Y.
Documents a variety of roles played by Native Americans in
the westernization of the Americas. Illus. 336 pp. Smithsonian
Institution Press, 1994. $55.

*THE VISION OF THE SPOKANE PROPHET
Rebecca Egbert; Hap Gilliland, Editor
Grades 4 and up. Illus. 36 pp. Paper.
Council for Indian Education, 1989. $5.95.

VISION QUEST
Steven Foster & Meredith Little
Personal transformation in the wilderness. Revised edition.
Illus. 235 pp. Paper. Prentice Hall Press, $9.95.

**VISIONS OF THE NORTH: NATIVE ARTS
OF THE NORTHWEST COAST**
Don & Debra McQuiston
Illus. 120 pp. paper. Chronicle Books, 1995. $19.95.

VISIONS OF OUR NATIVE AMERICAN HERITAGE
Jay Stock
Illus. 192 pp. Jays, Inc., 1994. $79.95.

**VISIONS OF SOUNDS: MUSICAL INSTRUMENTS OF FIRST
NATION COMMUNITIES IN NORTHEASTERN AMERICA**
Beverly Diamond, M. Sam Cronk, Franziska von Rosen
Photos. 222 pp. University of Chicago Press, 1994.
$47.50; paper, $19.95.

**VISIONS & VOICES: NATIVE AMERICAN PAINTING
FROM THE PHILBROOK MUSEUM OF ART**
Lydia L. Wyckoff, Editor
University of New Mexico Press, $70; paper, $37.

*THE VISUAL DICTIONARY OF ANCIENT CIVILIZATIONS
Includes early Native American civilizations. Tribal artifacts &
crafts. Grades 3 and up. Illus. 64 pp. Houghton Mifflin, 1994.
$15.95.

**VITAL SOULS: BORORO COSMOLOGY,
NATURAL SYMBOLISM & SHAMANISM**
J. Christopher Crocker
380 pp. University of Arizona Press, 1985. $29.95.

GERALD VIZENOR: WRITING IN THE ORAL TRADITION
Kimberly M. Blaeser
260 pp. University of Oklahoma Press, 1996. $29.95.

A VOCABULARY OF MOHEGAN-PEQUOT
J. Dyneley Prince & Frank Speck
Reprint. 60 pp. Evolution Publishing & Manufacturing,
1998. $16.

VOCABULARY OF NEW JERSEY DELAWARE
James A. Madison
50 pp. Evolution Publishing & manufacturing, 1998. $16.

VOCABULARY OF THE SHOSHONE LANGUAGE
George W. Hill
Reprint. 2nd edition. 40 pp. Paper. Little Red Hen, $11.97.

A VOCABULARY OF THE TUSCARORA
John A. Lawson
Evolution Publishing & Manufacturing, 1998. $16.

**THE VOCATIONAL REHABILITATION OF AMERICAN
INDIANS WHO HAVE ALCOHOL OR OTHER SUBSTANCE
ABUSE DISORDERS**
R.M. Schacht & L. Gaseoma
45 pp. Northern Arizona University IHD, 1993.

**A VOICE IN HER TRIBE:
A NAVAJO WOMAN'S OWN STORY**
Irene Stewart
Illus. 90 pp. Paper. Ballena Press, 1980. $8.95.

**THE VOICE OF THE CRANE ECHOES AFAR:
THE SOCIOPOLITICAL ORGANIZATION OF
THE LAKE SUPERIOR OJIBWA, 1640-1855**
Theresa M. Schenck
Illus. 142 pp. Garland, 1997. $40.

**THE VOICE OF THE DAWN: AN AUTOHISTORY
OF THE ABENAKI NATION**
Frederick M. Wiseman
Paper. University of New England Press, $19.95.

**VOICE OF INDIGENOUS PEOPLES: NATIVE
PEOPLE ADDRESS THE UNITED NATIONS**
compiled & edited by Alexander Ewen
for The Native American Council
With the U.N. Draft Declaration of Indigenous Peoples Rights.
In an epilogue, Chief Oren Lyons describes events of the International Year of Indigenous People, 1993. 19 Photos. Maps.
120 pp. Paper. Clear Light, 1994. $12.95.

VOICE OF THE GREAT SPIRIT
Kaiser
Paper. Random House, $10.

**VOICE OF THE OLD WOLF: LUCULLUS VIRGIL
McWHORTER & THE NEZ PERCE INDIANS**
Steven Ross Evans
Illus. Photos. Maps. Biblio. 250 pp. Washington State
University Press, 1996. $32; paper, $19.95.

THE VOICE THAT WAS IN TRAVEL: STORIES
Diane Glancy
20 stories reveal insights into contemporary American Indian
life. 128 pp. University of Oklahoma Press, 1999. $19.95.

**THE VOICE OF THE TURTLE: AMERICAN INDIAN
LITERATURE, 1900-1970**
Paula G. Allen, Editor
336 pp. Paper. Ballantine Publishing, 1995. $12.50.

VOICES FROM THE DELAWARE: BIG HOUSE CEREMONY
edited by Robert S. Grumet
Illus. 240 pp. University of Oklahoma Press, 2002. $29.95.

**VOICES FROM FOUR DIRECTIONS: CONTEMPORARY
TRANSLATIONS OF THE NATIVE LITERATURES OF NORTH
AMERICA**
edited by Brian Swann
Stories and songs from 31 Native groups in North America.
632 pp. University of Nebraska Press, $70; paper, $27.50.

*VOICES FROM THE ICE
John L. Peyton
A glimpse of Ojibway life during the early 20th Century. Grades
1-4. Illus. 52 pp. Paper. University of Nebraska Press, 1990.
$9.95.

**VOICES FROM WOUNDED KNEE, 1973,
IN THE WORDS OF THE PARTICIPANTS**
Akwesasne Notes
History of American Indian Movement (AIM). Illus.
Akwesasne Notes, 1974.

VOICES IN THE CANYON
Viele
The story of a Navajo National Monument's amazing cliff dwell-
ings written for laymen and reviewed by professionals. Illus.
50 color photos. Maps. 76 pp. Paper. Southwest Parks and
Monuments, $6.

VOICES IN THE WATERFALL
Elizabeth Cuthand
Poetry. Rhythms & traditions of First Nations people. New edi-
tion featuring ten new poems. 80 pp. Paper. Theytus, 1992.
$11.95.

**VOICES OF AMERICAN INDIAN ASSIMILATION & RESIS-
TANCE: HELEN HUNT JACKSON, SARAH WINNEMUCCA
& VICTORIA HOWARD**
Siobhan Senier
Illus. Map. 272 pp. University of Oklahoma Press, 2004.
$29.95; paper, $17.95.

VOICES OF EARTH & SKY
Vinson Brown
The vision life of the Native Americans. Illus. 184 pp.
Paper. Naturegraph, 1976. $8.95.

**VOICES OF NATIVE AMERICA: NATIVE AMERICAN
INSTRUMENTS & MUSIC**
Douglas Spotted Eagle
Includes information and explanations of traditional and con-
temporary music. Photos. Illus. Music sheets. 120pp. paper.
Eagle's View, 1999. $17.95.

VOICES OF NATIVE AMERICA: NATIVE AMERICAN MUSIC
Douglas Spotted Eagle; Monte Smith, Editor
Includes information and explanations of traditional and con-
temporary music. Photos. Illus. Music sheets. 64 pp. paper.
Eagle's View, 1997. $17.95.

**VOICES OF A THOUSAND PEOPLE: THE
MAKAH CULTURAL & RESEARCH CENTER**
Patricia Pierce Erikson
Illus. Map. 264 pp. University of Nebraska Press, 2002. $45.

**VOICES OF THE WIND: NATIVE AMERICAN FLUTE
SONGS**
Bryan Burton
Illus. 36 pp. World Music Press, 1998.
$20.95 includes CD-ROM

VOICES OF THE WIND: NATIVE AMERICAN LEGENDS
Margot Edmonds & Ella Clark
Illus. 385 pp. Facts on File, 1989. $27.95.

VOICES OF THE WIND: POLYNESIAN MYTHS & CHANTS
Katherine Luomala
The oral traditions of the region is examined. Illus.
209 pp. Paper. Bishop Museum, $15.95.

VOICES OF WOUNDED KNEE
edited by William S.E. Coleman
Brings together all of the available sources — Lakota, military,
and civilian — using accounts of participants and observers,
and reconstructs the massacre. Illus. Maps. 446 pp. Paper.
University of Nebraska Press, 2000. $19.95.

**VOICES THROUGH THE AGES:
A NATIVE AMERICAN ANTHOLOGY**
Written by ITEPP Students at Humboldt State University from
1982-1998. Includes writings from "Our People Speak." 1999.
ITEPP CRC.

*VOICES UNDER ONE SKY
Trish Fox Roman
Contemporary Native literature. Illus. 224 pp.
Paper. The Crossing Press, 1997. $12.95.

***VOSTAAS: THE STORY OF
MONTANA'S INDIAN NATIONS**
White Buffalo & Maxine Ruppel
Covers present day life of seven Montana tribes and
other Plains Indians. Grades 4-10. Paper. Council for
Indian Education, 1970 ed. 68 pp. $4.95; 1990 ed. 80 pp.
$6.95.

W

**THE WABANAKIS OF MAINE & THE MARITIMES:
A RESOURCE BOOK ABOUT PENOBSCOT,
PASSAMOQUODDY, MALISEET, MICMAC & ABENAKI
INDIANS**
Contains over 50 lesson plans for grades 4-8. Illus.
510 pp. Paper. American Friends Service Committee, $20.

WAHEENEE: AN INDIAN GIRL'S STORY
Gilbert L. Wilson
Illus. 190 pp. University of Nebraska Press, 1981.
$17.95; paper, $5.95.

**WAKE OF THE UNSEEN OBJECT: TRAVELS
THROUGH ALASKA'S NATIVE LANDSCAPES**
Tom Kizzia
Map. 286 pp. Paper. University of Nebraska Press,
1998. $15.

**WAKEMAP MOUND: A STRATIFIED SITE
ON THE COLUMBIA RIVER**
Emory Strong, Editor
Illus. 40 pp. Paper. Binford & Mort, $5.95.

WAKING A SLEEPING GIANT
Theodore Kouba
Vantage Pres, 1987. $14.95.

WAKINYAN: LAKOTA RELIGION IN THE 20TH CENTURY
Stephen E. Feraca
Illus. 104 pp. Paper. University of Nebraska Press, 1998.
$12.

WALAPAI (HUALAPAI) TEXTS
Werner Winter
Paper. De Gruyter, 1998.

**WALK FOR JUSTICE: ONE MAN'S SACRIFICE
FOR ANOTHER MAN'S FREEDOM**
Harry Kindness
Illus. 200 pp. Paper. Wo-Pila Publishing, 1999. $19.95.

**WALK IN BALANCE: THE PATH TO HEALTHY,
HAPPY, HARMONIOUS LIVING**
Sun Bear, Crysalis Mulligan, Peter Nufer & Wabun
A holistic pathway to personal enrichment and health. A per-
sonal survival manual. 171 pp. Paper. Prentice Hall Press,
$8.95.

WALK IN BEAUTY: THE NAVAJO & THEIR BLANKETS
Anthony Berlant & Mary Kahlenberg
Illus. 225 pp. Paper. Gibbs Smith, 1991. $29.95.

***WALK IN PEACE: LEGENDS &
STORIES OF THE MICHIGAN INDIANS**
Simon Otto; M.T. Bussey, Editor
Selection of legends and stories in the Anishnabe
(Odawa/Ojibwe) oral tradition. Grades 3-4. 2nd ed. Illus.
56 pp. Paper. University of Nebraska Press, 1992. $9.95.

**WALK IN YOUR SOUL: LOVE INCANTATIONS
OF THE OKLAHOMA CHEROKEES**
Jack and Anna Kilpatrick
Reprint of 1965 edition. Illus. 174 pp. Paper.
Southern Methodist University Press, $6.95.

*WALKER OF TIME
Helen Hughes Vick
Native American mythology & mystery combined in a tale for
young readers. Grades 7 and up. 192 pp. paper. Harbinger
House, 1994. $9.95.

**WALKING IN INDIAN MOCCASINS: THE NATIVE
POLICIES OF TOMMY DOUGLAS & THE CCF**
R. Laurie Brown
Illus. 288 pp. University of Washington Press, 1997. $24.95.

**THE WALKING PEOPLE:
A NATIVE AMERICAN ORAL HISTORY**
Paula Underwood; Barbara McNeill & Jeanne Slobod, Eds.
Illus. 839 pp. Tribe of Two Press, 1993. $48; paper, $28.

**WALKING THE TRAIL: ONE MAN'S JOURNEY
ALONG THE CHEROKEE TRAIL OF TEARS**
Jerry Ellis
Map. 256 pp. Paper. University of Nebraska Press, 2001. $16.

WALKING WHERE WE LIVED:
MEMOIRS OF A MONO INDIAN FAMILY
Gaylen D. Lee
Illus. Maps. 224 pp. Paper. University of Oklahoma Press,
1999. $14.95.

*WALKS IN BEAUTY
Hazel Krantz
Navajo story. Ages 12 and up. 192 pp.
Northland, $12.95; paper, $6.95.

WALKS IN THE SUN
Don Coldsmith
Illus. 245 pp. Bantam Books, $12.50.

*WALKS TWO WORLDS:
A NAVAJO BOY'S COMING OF AGE
Robert B. Fox
Grades 4 and up. 62 pp. Paper. Sunstone Press, $6.95.

THE WALLEYE WAR: THE STRUGGLE FOR
OJIBWE SPEARFISHING & TREATY RIGHTS
Larry Nesper
Spearfishing conflict on the Lac du Flambeau Reservation in
Wisconsin. Illus. Map. 245 pp. University of Nebraska Press,
2002. $60; paper, $19.95.

WALLEYE WARRIORS: AN EFFECTIVE ALLIANCE
AGAINST RACISM & FOR THE EARTH
Rick Whaley & Walter Bresette
Depicts the intimidation and fear that the Anishinabe in northern Wisconsin have endured when the courts upheld their treaty
rights to take fish with spears. Traces the history of the modern
anti-Indian treaty movement in the 1960s & 1970s. Illus. Photos. Maps. Biblio. 288 pp. Paper. New Society Publishers, 1994.
$17.95.

*THE WAMPANOAG
Laurie Weinstein-Farson
Grades 5 and up. Illus. 104 pp. Chelsea House, 1988. $17.95.

*THE WAMPANOAG
Katherine Doherty
Grades 4-6. Reprint. 64 pp. Paper. Franklin Watts, $6.95.

*WAMPANOAG INDIANS
Bill Lund
Grades K-3. Illus. 24 pp. Children's Press, 1997. $14.

*THE WAMPANOAGS
Alice Flanagan
Grades 2-4. Illus. 48 pp. Children's Press, 1997.
$21; paper, $6.95.

THE WAMPANOAGS OF MASHPEE
Russell M. Peters
Historical & cultural portrayal of the Wampanoags of
Mashpee, Mass. Illus. The Greenfield Review Pres, $16.

WAMPUM BELTS & PEACE TREES: GEORGE MORGAN,
NATIVE AMERICANS & REVOLUTIONARY DIPLOMACY
Gregory Schaaf
Illus. 304 pp. Fulcrum Publishing, 1990. $27.95.

WAMPUM, WAR & TRADE
GOODS WEST OF THE HUDSON
Gilbert W. Hagerty
Illus. 310 pp. Heart of the Lakes, 1987. $40.

WANDERINGS OF AN ARTIST AMONG
THE INDIANS OF NORTH AMERICA
Paul Kane
384 pp. Paper. Dover, $10.95.

WANGKA: AUSTRONESIAN CANOE ORIGINS
Edwin Doran, Jr.
Illus. 121 pp. Texas A & M University Press, 1981. $15.

THE WAPPO: A REPORT
Yolande S. Beard
Paper. Malki Museum Press, 1979. $8.50.

WAR CHIEFS
Bill Dugan
A series of five books: Geronimo, Chief Joseph, Crazy Horse,
Quanah Parker, and Sitting Bull. Paper. HarperCollins, 1991-
94. $4.99 each.

WAR DANCE: PLAINS INDIAN
MUSICAL PERFORMANCE
William K. Powers
199 pp. Paper. University of Arizona Press, 1990. $14.95.

*WAR DRUMS AT EDEN PRAIRIE
Gladys Nelson
Fictionalized account of Sioux uprising of 1862.
Grades 6-8. Illus. North Star Press, $5.95.

WAR EAGLE'S FACT OF LIFE
Gary D. Bromley (War Eagle)
Teachings by the author of the ancient red road.
Gary D. Bromley, P.O. Box 1629, Fontana, CA 92334-1629.

WAR EAGLE: A LIFE OF GENERAL EUGENE A. CARR
James T. King
Illus. 325 pp. University of Nebraska Press, 1964. $27.95.

WAR IN THE TRIBAL ZONE:
EXPANDING STATES & INDIGENOUS WARFARE
R. Brian Ferguson & Neil Whitehead, Editors
Native warfare. Illus. 350 pp. School of American
Research, 1989. $35; paper, $15.95.

WAR PAINT: BLACKFOOT & SARCEE PAINTED
BUFFALO ROBES IN THE ROYAL ONTARIO MUSEUM
Arni Brownstone
Blackfoot tradition, art, and culture as told through six historic
buffalo robes. Illus. 96 pp. Paper. University of Toronto Press,
$24.95.

WAR-PATH & BIVOUAC; OR,
THE CONQUEST OF THE SIOUX
John F. Finerty
Detailed account of the Dakota Indian wars of 1876 and the
Nez Perce Indian wars of 1877. Reprint. Illus. Map. 360 pp.
Paper. University of Oklahoma Press, $13.95.

*WAR PONY
D. E. Worcester
Reprint of 1961 edition. Grades 4 and up. Illus. 95 pp.
Texas Christian University Press, $10.95.

WAR WOMAN: A NOVEL
Robert J. Conley
Cherokee based. 368 pp. Paper.
University of Oklahoma Press, $17.95.

THE WARDELL BUFFALO TRAP FORTY EIGHT SU THREE
HUNDRED & ONE: COMMUNAL PROCUREMENT IN THE
UPPER GREEN RIVER BASIN, WY
George C. Frison
Paper. University of Michigan, Museum of Anthropology, 1973.
$3.

THE WARING PAPERS: THE COLLECTED
WORKS OF ANTONIO J. WARING
Stephen Williams
Paper. Peabody Museum, 1977. $22.50.

WARLORDS OF THE WEST:
A STORY OF THE COMANCHE
Preston Harper
Borderlands Pres, 1990. $14.95.

WARPATH: THE TRUE STORY OF THE FIGHTING SIOUX
TOLD IN A BIOGRAPHY OF CHIEF WHITE BULL
Stanley Vestal
Illus. Maps. 291 pp. Paper. University of Nebraska Press, 1984.
$13.95.

WARPATH & CATTLE TRAIL
Hubert E. Collins, et al, Editors
Illus. 296 pp. University Press of Colorado, 1998. $34.95.

WARPATHS: INVASIONS OF NORTH AMERICA
Ian K. Steele
Reprint. Illus. 304 pp. paper. Oxford University Press, $19.95.

THE WARREN WAGONTRAIN RAID
B. Capps
Illus. 328 pp. SMU Press, 1974. $10.95.

WARRIOR IN TWO CAMPS: ELY S. PARKER, UNION
GENERAL & SENECA CHIEF
William H. Armstrong
256 pp. Paper. Syracuse University Press, $15.95.

WARRIOR MAIDEN: A HOPI LEGEND
Ellen Schecter
Grades PS-3. Ilus. 48 pp. Paper. Bantam Press, 1992. $3.99.

WARRIOR OF THE MIST
T.G. Boyden
Biography of the Yakima warrior, Qualchan, son of Chief Owhi.
Reprint. Photos. 372 pp. Ye Galleon, $24.95.

WARRIOR QUEEN OF THE INDIAN
Richard Barry
Follows an Indian woman through her trials, heartaches and
triumphs. 494 pp. Terrich Books, 1993. $17.95; paper, $14.95.

WARRIOR, SHIELD & STAR:
IMAGERY & IDEOLOGY OF PUEBLO WARFARE
Polly Schaafsma
Illus. 224 pp. Paper. Mountain Press, 1999. $24.95.

WARRIORS - NAVAJO CODE TALKERS
Photos by Kenji Kawano
Photos & quotes from 75 of the surviving navajo code talkers.
105 pp. Paper. Northland Press & High-Lonesome Books. $12.

*WARRIORS OF THE RAINBOW: STRANGE &
PROPHETIC DREAMS OF THE INDIAN PEOPLE
William Willoya & Vinson Brown
Grades 4-12. Illus. 94 pp. Paper. Naturegraph, 1962. $7.95.

THE WARS OF THE IROQUOIS:
A STUDY IN INTERTRIBAL TRADE RELATIONS
George T. Hunt
Reprint of 1940 edition. Map. 220 pp. Paper.
University of Wisconsin Press, $14.50.

WASHINGTON STATE PLACE NAMES
Paper. University of Washington Press, $12.95.

WASHINGTON STATE PLACE NAMES:
FROM ALKI TO YELM
Doug Brokenshire
Paper. The Caxton Printers, 1994. $14.95.

WASHAKIE, CHIEF OF THE SHOSHONES
Grace Raymond Hebard
Illus. Maps. 325 pp. Paper. University of Nebraska Press,
1995. $12.

THE WASHAKIE LETTERS OF WILLIE OTTOGARY:
NORTHWESTERN SHOSHONE JOURNALIST & LEADER,
1906-1929
Matthew E. Kreitzer, Editor
Letters describing a society in cultural transition. Illus. 352 pp.
Utah State University Press, 2000. $49.95; paper, $24.95.

WASHITA: THE U.S. ARMY & THE
SOUTHERN CHEYENNES, 1867-1869
Jerome A. Greene
Illus. Maps. 304 pp. University of Oklahoma Press,
2004. $29.95.

THE WASHO LANGUAGE OF EAST CENTRAL
CALIFORNIA & NEVADA
A.L. Kroeber
Reprint oif 1907 edition. 66 pp. Paper. Coyote Press, $7.80.

WASHO SHAMANS & PEYOTISTS: RELIGIOUS
CONFLICT IN AN AMERICAN INDIAN TRIBE
Edgar E. Siskin
Illus. 300 pp. University of Utah Press, 1983. $25.

WASI'CHU: THE CONTINUING INDIAN WARS
Bruce Johansen & Roberto Maestro
Chronicles the history of Native struggles in the U.S.
Illus. 270 pp. Paper. Monthly Review Press, 1980. $10.

WATER ON THE PLATEAU
Paper. Museum of Northern Arizona, 1981. $3.

*WATERLESS MOUNTAIN
Laura A. Armer
Reprint of 1931 ed. Grades 5-8. Illus. David McKay Co., $11.95.

WATERLILY
Ella Cara Deloria
A novel of a Sioux woman's life. 244 pp. Paper.
University of Nebraska Press, 1988. $12.95.

WATERWAY
B. Haile
Reprint. Illus. 155 pp. Paper. Univ. of Nebraska Press, $12.95.

WAUBA YUMA'S PEOPLE: THE COMPARATIVE
SOCIO-POLITICAL STRUCTURE OF THE PAI
INDIANS OF ARIZONA
Henry F. Dobyns & Robert C. Euler
Describes Pai socia structure prior to U.S. reservation policy
that created the contemporary Walapai and Havasupai groups.
Illus. Map. 98 pp. Center for Anthropological Studies, 1970.
$30.

THE WAY IT WAS: AN INDIAN GIRL
LIVING THRU THE DEPRESSION
Wanda S. Brookshire; Jean Starr, Ed.
Illus. 56 pp. Brooks Publishing, 1999. $10.

THE WAY OF THE DEAD INDIANS:
GUARJIRO MYTHS & SYMBOLS
Michael Perrin; Michael Fineberg, tr.
Illus. 230 pp. University of Texas Press, 1987.
$30; paper, $12.95.

THE WAY OF THE MASKS
Claude Levi-Strauss
Study of Northwest Coast Indian culture. Reprint of 1982
edition. Illus. Maps. 276 pp. Paper. UBC Press, $29.95.

THE WAY OF THE SPIRIT
Time-Life Books Editors
Illus. 228 pp. Time-Life, 1997. $29.95.

THE WAY OF THE WARRIOR:
STORIES OF THE CROW PEOPLE
Phenocia Bauerle
Illus. University of Nebraska Press, 2003.

THE WAY TO INDEPENDENCE: MEMORIES
OF A HIDATSA INDIAN FAMILY, 1840-1920
Carolyn Gilman, et al
Account of the evolving culture & environment of Buffalo Bird
Woman's family & her tribe. Illus. Photos. Biblio. 371 pp. Min-
nesota Historical Society Press, 1987. $24.95; paper, $14.95.

THE WAY TO KNOWLEDGE
Carole Yazzie-Shaw; illus by William Yazzie
Pamphlet. Dine College Press. $5.

THE WAY TO MAKE PERFECT MOUNTAINS:
NATIVE AMERICAN LEGENDS OF SACRED MOUNTAINS
Leonard F. Chana
64 pp. Paper. Cinco Puntos, 1997. $9.95.

THE WAY TO RAINY MOUNTAIN
N. Scott Momaday
An account of the historic trek of the Kiowa Indians to Oklahoma. Reprint of 1969 edition. Illus. 90 pp. University of Arizona Press, $27.95. Paper. University of New Mexico Press,
$12.95.

THE WAY TO THE WESTERN SEA:
LEWIS & CLARK ACROSS THE CONTINENT
David Lavender
Illus. 415 pp. Harper & Row, 1988. $22.95.

*THE WAY WAS THROUGH WOODS:
THE STORY OF TOMO-CHI-CHI
Sara H. Banks
Story of a Creek man who adopted what he could from the
white settlers, insuring peace with them. Grades 7 and up. Illus.
92 pp. Paper. Roberts Rinehart, 1994. $7.95.

THE WAY WE LIVED: CALIFORNIA INDIAN
STORIES, SONGS & REMINISCENCES
Malcolm Margolin, Editor
Photos. Maps. 260 pp. Paper. Heyday Books, 1981. $14.95.

THE WAY WE MAKE SENSE
Dawn Karima Pettigrew
Aunt Lute Books, 2002.

ANTHONY WAYNE, A NAME IN ARMS
Anthony Wayne; R.C. Knopf, Editor
Reprint of 1960 edition. Illus. 556 pp. Greenwood, $41.50.

WAYS OF INDIAN MAGIC
Teresa VanEtten
Pueblo Indian legends. 91 pp. Paper. Sunstone, 1985. $8.95.

WAYS OF INDIAN WISDOM
Teresa VanEtten
Pueblo Indian legends. 120 pp. Paper. Sunstone, 1987. $10.95.

WAYS OF KNOWING: EXPERIENCE, KNOWLEDGE,
AND POWER AMONG THE DENE THA
Jean-Guy A. Goulet
Athabaskan ethnology...the study of the Dene Tha of northern
Canada. Illus. Map. 334 pp. University of Nebraska Press, 1998.
$75; paper, $35.

THE WAYS OF MY GRANDMOTHERS
Beverly H. Wolf
224 pp. Paper. William Morrow & Co., 1980. $9.95.

*WAYS OF THE LUSHOOTSEED PEOPLE: CEREMONIES &
TRADITIONS OF THE NORTHERN PUGET SOUND INDIANS
Readings. Written in English and Lushootseed. Grades 7-12.
Illus. 56 pp. Daybreak Star Press, $6.

WE ARE STILL HERE! THE ALGONQUIAN
PEOPLES OF LONG ISLAND TODAY
John A. Strong
105 pp. Heart of the Lakes Publishing, 1996. $12.

WE ARE STILL HERE: AMERICAN INDIANS
IN THE 20TH CENTURY
Peter Iverson
255 p. Paper. Harlan Davidson, 1998. $12.95.

*WE ARE STILL HERE: NATIVE AMERICANS TODAY
A series of books examining Native American cultural tradi-
tions and customs. Titles are: *Children of Clay: A Family of*
Pueblo Potters; Clambake: A Wampanoag Tradition; Ininatig's
Gift of Sugar: Traditional Native Sugarmaking; Kinaalda: A
Navajo Girl Grows Up; The Sacred Harvest: Ojibway Wild Rice
Gathering; and Shannon: An Ojibway Dancer;
Drumbeat...Heartbeat: A Celebration of the Powwow; Four
Seasons of Corn: A Winnebago Tradition; Fort Chipewyan
Homecoming: A Journey to Native Canada; Songs from the
Loom: A Navajo Girl Learns How to Weave; A Story to Tell:
Traditions of a Tlingit Community; Weaving a California Tradi-
tion: A Native American Basketmaker. Grades 3-6. Illus. Pho-
tos. 48 pp. Lerner, 1992-1998. $15.95 each; paper, $6.95 each.

WE, THE FIRST AMERICANS
Dwight Johnson
Illus. 28 pp. Paper. U.S. Government Printing Office,
1989. $1.75.

WE GET OUR LIVING LIKE MILK FROM THE LAND
Okanagan Rights Committee
Historical overview of the Okanagan Nation of Canada.
Illus. Maps. 175 pp. Paper. Theytus, 1993. $9.95.

*WE HAVE ALWAYS BEEN HERE
Grades 4-5. 48 pp. Capstone Press, 1989. $10.95.

WE HAVE THE RIGHT TO EXIST: A TRANSLATION
OF ABORIGINAL THOUGHT: THE FIRST BOOK EVER
PUBLISHED FROM AN AHNISHINABEOTJIBWAY
PERSPECTIVE
Wub-e-ke-niew
Illus. 420 pp. Paper. Black Thistle Press, 1995. $16.

WE JUST TOUGHED IT OUT: WOMEN HEADS OF
*WE LIVE ON AN INDIAN RESERVATION
Hap Gilliland
Grades 1-6. 31 pp. Paper. Council for Indian Education,
1981. $4.95.

*WE RODE THE WIND: RECOLLECTIONS
OF NATIVE AMERICAN LIFE
Jane B. Katz, Editor
The writings of eight notable Native Americans who grews up
onthe Great Plains. Grades 6-9. Illus. Color photos. Glossary.
128 pp. Lerner, 1995. $16.95.

WE TALK YOU YAWN
Fred Bigjim
Native education in Alaska; problems & concerns,
as well as solutions. Greenfield Review Press, $9.95.

WE'LL BE IN YOUR MOUNTAINS, WE'LL BE
IN YOUR SONGS: A NAVAJO WOMAN SINGS
Ellen McCullough-Brabson & Marilyn Help
Includes CD. University of New Mexico Press, 2000.
$24.95.

WE'RE STILL HERE: ART OF INDIAN NEW ENGLAND
Joan Lester
86 pp. Paper. Consortium Books, 1987. $9.95.

THE WEAVER'S PATHWAY: A CLARIFICATION
OF THE "SPIRIT TRAIL" IN NAVAJO WEAVING
Noel Bennett
64 pp. Paper. Northland, 1974. $9.95.

WEAVER'S TALES
Romona Bradley
Collection of Cherokee legends. Illus. 36 pp. Paper.
Cherokee Publications, $3.50.

WEAVERS OF TRADITION & BEAUTY:
BASKETMAKERS OF THE GREAT BASIN
Mary Lee Fulkerson; photos by Kathleen Curtis
Illus. 166 pp. Paper. University of Nevada Press, 1995.
$19.95.

WEAVING ARTS OF THE NORTH AMERICAN INDIAN
Frederick J. Dockstader
Revised edition. Survey of the textile artistry of the Indian tribes
of North America. Illus. 224 pp. HarperCollins, 1994. $22.50.

WEAVING A CALIFORNIA TRADITION:
A NATIVE AMERICAN BASKETMAKER
Linda Yamane; photos by Dugan Aguilar
California Indian basketmaking. Illus. 48 pp.
Oyate & Lerner Publications, 1996. $14.95; paper, $6.95.

WEAVING A NAVAJO BLANKET
Gladys Reichard
Reprint of 1936 edition. Illus. 225 pp. Paper. Dover, $6.95.

WEAVING A WORLD: TEXTILES
& THE NAVAJO WAY OF SEEING
Paul G. Zolbrod & Roseann Willink
Features 70 rugs. 100 color plates. 132 pp.
Paper. Museum of New Mexico Press, $29.95.

WEAVING NEW WORLDS: SOUTHEASTERN
CHEROKEE WOMEN AND THEIR BASKETRY
Sarah H. Hill
Illus. 414 pp. Paper. University of North Carolina Press,
1997. $45; paper, $22.50.

WEAVING OF THE SOUTHWEST
Marian Rodee
Both traditional & modern weaving styles are identified
& explained. Discussion of family styles among weavers
today. Illus. 248 pp. Schiffer, $39.95; paper, $29.95

ANSELM WEBER, O.F.M. MISSIONARY TO THE NAVAJO
Robert Wilken
Reprint of 1955 edition. St. Michaels Press, $12.50.

THE WEISER INDIANS: SHOSHONI PEACEMAKERS
Hank Corless
Reprint. Illus. 170 pp. Caxton Printers, 1996. $14.95.

*WESAKEJACK & THE BEARS
Bill Ballantyne
Grades PS-7. Reprint. Illus. 32 pp. Paper. General Distribution
Services, $12.95 includes audio; paper only, 6.95.

*WESAKEJACK & THE FLOOD
Bill Ballantyne
Grades PS-7. Reprint. Illus. 32 pp. General Distribution
Services, $18.95 includes audio; paper, $12.95 with audio,
and 6.95 alone.

THE WEST AS AMERICA: RE-INTERPRETING
IMAGES OF THE FRONTIER
William H. Truettner, Editor
How the 19th & early 20th century artists depicted and roman-
ticized the often brutal, conflict-ridden history of the westward
expansion. 408 pp. Smithsonian Books, $49.96.

*WEST OF YESTERDAY
Lucilia Wise
Illus. The Five Civilized Tribes Museum. $1.

WEST TO THE PACIFIC: THE STORY
OF THE LEWIS & CLARK EXPEDITION
Ronald Fisher; Merle Wells, Editor
Illus. 152 pp. Paper. Alpha & Omega, 1989. $9.95.

WESTERN ABENAKI DICTIONARY VOL. 2:
ENGLISH-ABENAKI
Gordon M. Day
612 pp. Paper. University of Washington Press, 1995.
$34.95.

THE WESTERN ABENAKIS OF VERMONT, 1600-1800:
WAR, MIGRATION & THE SURVIVAL OF AN INDIAN PEOPLE
C.G. Calloway
Illus. Maps. 346 pp. University of Oklahoma Press,
1990. $34.95; paper, $15.95

WESTERN AMERICAN INDIAN:
CASE STUDIES IN TRIBAL HISTORY
Richard N. Ellis, Editor
Indian-White relations from 1850 to the present. Maps.
203 pp. Paper. University of Nebraska Press, 1972. $4.95.

WESTERN APACHE-ENGLISH DICTIONARY:
A COMMUNITY-GENERATED BILINGUAL DICTIONARY
Dorothy Bray, Editor
528 pp. Paper. Biling Review Press, 1998. $20.

WESTERN APACHE HERITAGE:
PEOPLE OF THE MOUNTAIN CORRIDOR
Richard J. Perry
Illus. Maps. 314 pp. University of Texas Press, 1991. $37.50.

WESTERN APACHE LANGUAGE & CULTURE:
ESSAYS IN LINGUISTIC ANTHROPOLOGY
Keith H. Basso
195 pp. Paper. University of Arizona Press, 1990. $17.95.

WESTERN APACHE MATERIAL CULTURE:
THE GOODWIN & GUENTHER COLLECTIONS
Alan Ferg, Editor
Illus. 176 pp. Paper. University of Arizona Press, 1987.
$28.95.

WESTERN APACHE RAIDING & WARFARE
Grenville Goodwin; edited by Keith Basso
Personal narratives of six Western Apaches. Also discusses
weapons, taboos, leadership, and other aspects of Apache raiding. 330 pp. Paper. University of Arizona Press, 1971. $19.95.

WESTERN APACHE WITCHCRAFT
Keith H. Basso, Editor
Reprint of 1969 edition. 80 pp. Paper.
University of Arizona Press, $21.95.

WESTERN INDIAN BASKETRY
Joan Jones
Illus. 56 pp. Paper. Hancock House, 1990. $7.95.

WESTERN MILITARY FRONTIER, 1815-1846
H.P. Beers
Reprint of 1935 edition. Illus. 230 pp. Porcupine Press, $25.

THE WESTERN ODYSSEY OF JOHN SIMPSON
SMITH: FRONTIERSMAN & INDIAN INTERPRETER
Stan Hoig
Smith served as interpreter for major treaty negotiations and
accompanied three delegatons of chiefs to Washington, DC to
visit presidents. Illus. 256 pp. Paper. University of Oklahoma
Press, 2004. $21.95.

THE WESTERN PHOTOGRAPHS OF
JOHN K. HILLERS: MYSELF IN THE WATER
Don Fowler
Ilus. 160 pp. Smithsonian Press, 1989. $24.95.

WESTERN POMO PREHISTORY: EXCAVATIONS AT ALBION
HEAD, NIGHTBIRDS' RETREAT, & THREE CHOP VILLAGE,
MENDOCINO COUNTY, CALIFORNIA
Thomas Layton
Illus. 230 pp. Paper. University of California, Los Angeles,
Institute of Archaeology, 1990. $17.50.

WESTERN PUEBLO IDENTITIES: REGIONAL
INTERACTION, MIGRATION, & TRANSFORMATION
Andrew I. Duff
Illus. 233 pp. University of Arizona Press, 2002. $48.

WESTERN SHOSHONI GRAMMAR
John P. Dayley
Boise State University, 1993.

MARIETTA WETHERILL: LIFE WITH THE NAVAJOS IN CHACO CANYON
Kathryn Gabriel, Editor
Primitive life in Chaco Canyon at the turn of the century.
Paper. University of New Mexico Press, $16.95.

LEWIS WETZEL, INDIAN FIGHTER
C.B. Allman
Revised 1961 edition. Illus. Devin-Adair, $16.95.

WHAT CAN TRIBES DO? STRATEGIES & INSTITUTIONS IN AMERICAN INDIAN ECONOMIC DEVELOPMENT
edited by Stephen Cornell & Joseph P. Kalt
A guide to successful self-determined economic development on Indian reservations. 336 pp. Paper. The Falmouth Institute, 1992. $15.

WHAT THIS AWL MEANS: FEMINIST ARCHAEOLOGY AT A WAHPETON DAKOTA VILLAGE
Janet D. Spector
Focuses on Little Rapids, a 19th-century Eastern Dakota (Sioux) planting village near present-day Minneapolis. Illus. 158 pp. Minnesota Historical Society Press, 1993. $32.50; paper, $15.95.

WHEN BUFFALO RAN
George Grinnell
Story of Wikis, a Plains Indian who grew up in the mid-1800s as part of the last generation before the white changed the plains forever. Reprint. Illus. Paper. Hancock House, $9.95.

***WHEN CLAY SINGS**
Byrd Baylor; illus by Tom Bahti
Grades P-3. Illus. 32 pp. Charles Scribner'sSons, $12.95.

WHEN CULTURES MEET
Papers given by Florence Ellis, Myra Ekken Jenjins, Richard Ford, Marc Simmons, Orlando Romero, and Jim Sagel at the 1984 Conference at San Juan Pueblo. Illus. 96 pp. Paper. Sunstone Press, $9.95.

WHEN DID THE SHOSHONI BEGIN TO OCCUPY SOUTHERN IDAHO: ESSAYS ON LATE PREHISTORIC CULTURAL REMAINS FROM THE UPPER SNAKE AND SALMON RIVER COUNTIES
B. Robert Butler
30 pp. Paper. Idaho Museum of Natural History, 1981. $5.

WHEN THE EARTH WAS LIKE NEW: WESTERN APACHE SONGS AND STORIES
Chesley Goseyun Wilson, Ruth Longcor-Harnish Wilson & Bryan Burton
Includes 17 musical transcriptions of social traveling and game sngs and Apache violin pieces; 38 archival and contemporary photographs of instruments, ceremonies and social life; traditional legends. Illus. 128 pp. World Music Press, 1994. Book & CD or Book & Tape Set, $29.95.

WHEN GERONIMO RODE
Forrestine C. Hooker
Fictionalized account of Geronimo's campaign. Reprint of 1924 edition. 325 pp. High-Lonesome Books, $20.

***WHEN THE GREAT CANOES CAME**
Mary Louise Clifford
A series of conversations between Cockacoeske, the queen of the Pamunkey Indians, and the adolescents of her tribe. Grades 5 to 9. Illus. Map. Biblio. 144 pp. Pelican Publishing, 1990. $12.95.

WHEN INDIANS BECAME COWBOYS: NATIVE PEOPLES & CATTLE RANCHING IN THE AMERICAN WEST
Peter Iverson
Indian cattle ranching focusing on the northern plains & the southwest. Illus. Map. 266 pp. University of Oklahoma Press, 1994. $26.95; paper, $15.95.

WHEN IS A KIVA: AND OTHER QUESTIONS ABOUT SOUTHWESTERN ARCHAEOLOGY
Watson Smith; Raymond H. Thompson, Editor
273 pp. Paper. University of Arizona Press, 1990. $19.95.

WHEN JESUS CAME, THE CORN MOTHERS WENT AWAY: MARRIAGE, SEXUALITY & POWER IN NEW MEXICO, 1500-1846
Ramon Gutierrez
456 pp. Stanford University Press, 1991. $49.50; paper, $16.95.

WHEN THE LAND WAS YOUNG: REFLECTIONS ON AMERICAN ARCHAEOLOGY
Sharman Apt Russell
Illus. Map. 230 pp. Paper. University of Nebraska Press, 2001. $14.95.

WHEN NAVAJOS HAD TOO MANY SHEEP: THE 1940's
George A. Boyce; Jeanette Henry, Editor
Stock overgrazing led to rapidly eroding farmland. Illus. Map. 288 pp. Paper. The Indian Historian Press, 1974. $12.50.

WHEN NICKELS WERE INDIANS: AN URBAN, MIXED-BLOOD STORY
Patricia Penn Hilden
Discusses folk imagery of blood quantum that defines people's lives. Examines the idea that Native America is once more the destination of souls lost in a "New Age." Photos. 260 pp. Paper. Smithsonian Institution Press, 1997. $17.95.

WHEN THE NIGHT BIRD SINGS
Joyce Sequichie Hifler
BxW line drawings. 171 pp. Clear Light, $19.95.

WHEN NO ONE IS LOOKING
Red Hawk - Pipikwass
50 pp. Paper. Robin Hood Books, 1990. $7.

WHEN OUR WORDS RETURN: WRITING, HEARING, & REMEMBERSING ORAL TRADITIONS OF ALASKA & THE YUKON
Phyllis Morrow & William Schneider, Editors
Collection of essays on Native oral traditions from the North. 264 pp. Utah State University Press, $36.95; paper, $19.95.

WHEN RAIN GODS REIGNED: FROM CURIOS TO ART AT TESUQUE PUEBLO
Duane Anderson
Illus. 156 pp. Museum of New Mexico Press, 2002. $45; paper, $29.95.

WHEN THE RAINBOW TOUCHES DOWN
Tryntje Van Ness Seymour
The artists and stories behind the Apache, Navajo, Rio Grande Pueblo, and Hopi paintings in the William and Leslie Van Ness Denman Collection. Illus. Maps. Biblio. 396 pp. University of Washington Press, 1989. $50.

WHEN STARS CAME DOWN TO EARTH: COSMOLOGY OF THE SKIDI PAWNEE INDIANS OF NORTH AMERICA
Von Del Chamberlain
Illus. 272 pp. Paper. Ballena Press, 1982. $17.95.

***WHEN THUNDERS SPOKE**
Virginia Driving Hawk Sneve; illus. by Oren Lyons
Indian story. Grades 5 and up. Illus. 95 pp. Paper. University of Nebraska Press, 1993. $9.95.

WHEN THE CHENOO HOWLS: NATIVE AMERICAN TALES OF HORROR
James & Joseph Bruchac
Grades 3-7. Illus. 128 pp. Walker & Co., 1998. $17.85.

WHEN WAR EAGLE SPEAKS
Gary D. Bromley (War Eagle)
Teachings by the author of the ancient red road. 36 pp. Paper. Gary D. Bromley, P.O. Box 1629, Fontana, CA 92334. 2003. $19.99.

***WHEN WE WENT TO THE MOUNTAINS**
Hap Gilliland, et al
Grades 1-9. 40 pp. Paper. Council for Indian Education, 1991. $9.95; paper, $3.95.

***WHEN THE WORLD ENDED, HOW HUMMINGBIRD GOT FREE, HOW PEOPLE WERE MADE**
Linda Yamane
Rumsien Ohlone stories. Grades 2-5. Illus. 46 pp. Paper. Oyate, 1995. $10.

WHERE COURAGE IS LIKE A WILD HORSE: THE WORLD OF AN INDIAN ORPHANAGE
Sharon Skolnick & Manny Skolnick
Story of an Apache Indian orphan. 148 pp. Paper. University of Nebraska Press, 1997. $11.95.

WHERE THE ECHO BEGAN: & OTHER ORAL TRADITIONS FROM SOUTHWESTERN ALASKA
Recorded by Hans Himmelheber; edited by Ann Fienup-Riordan
Illus. 262 pp. University of Washington Press & University of Alaska Press, 2000. $39.95.

***WHERE INDIANS LIVE: AMERICAN INDIAN HOUSES**
Nashone
Grades K-6. Illus. 37 pp. Paper. Sierra Oaks, 1989. $6.95.

WHERE LEGENDS LIVE
Douglas Rossman
Illus. 72 pp. Paper. VIP Publishing & Cherokee Publications, 1988. $6.

WHERE THE PAVEMENT ENDS: FIVE NATIVE AMERICAN PLAYS
William S. Yellow Robe, Jr.
Based on the author's experiences on the Fort Peck Indian Reservation. 192 pp. University of Oklahoma Press, 2000. $24.95.

WHERE THE PEOPLE GATHER: CARRVING A TOTEM POLE
Vickie Jensen
Documents the entire process of carving a totem pole. Illus. Photos. 194 pp. University of Washington Press, $29.95.

WHERE THE TWO CAME TO THEIR FATHER: A NAVAJO WAR CEREMONIAL GIVEN BY JEFF KING
Maud Oakes, Editor; commentary by Joseph Campbell
Illus. 120 pp. Paper. Princeton University Press, 1991. $90; paper, $14.95.

***WHERE THERE IS NO NAME FOR ART: ART & VOICES OF THE CHILDREN OF SANTA CLARA, SAN ILDEFONSO, SAN JUAN, POJOAQUA, & NAMBE PUEBLOS**
Bruce Hucko
Grades 4 and up. Illus. Paper. Oyate, 1996. $20.

WHERE TWO WORLDS MEET: THE GREAT LAKES FUR TRADE
Carolyn Gilman
History of the fur trade, and essays on various aspects of the early cross-cultural contacts between Indians and whites. Illus. Photos. Maps. 136 pp. Paper. Minnesota Historical Society Press, & Smoke & Fire Co., 1982. $18.95.

WHERE THE WEST BEGINS: ESSAYS ON MIDDLE BORDER & SIOUXLAND WRITING
Arthur Huseboe and William Geyer, Editors
Illus. Paper. Center for Western Studies, 1978. $3.95.

A WHIRLWIND PASSES: NEWS CORRESPONDENTS & THE SIOUX INDIAN DISTURBANCES OF 1890-1891
George R. Kolbenschlag
Illus. Paper. Dakota Press, 1990. $9.95.

WHISKEY PEDDLER: JOHNNY HEALY, NORTH FRONTIER TRADER
William R. Hunt
263 pp. Paper. Mountain Press. $12.

THE WHISKEY TRADE OF THE NORTHWESTERN PLAINS: A MULTIDISCIPLINARY STUDY
Margaret A. Kennedy
208 pp. Peter Lang Publishing, 1998. $39.95.

***WHISPERS FROM THE FIRST CALIFORNIANS: A STORY OF CALIFORNIA'S FIRST PEOPLE**
Gail Faber & Michele Lasagna
Grades 4-8. Revised edition. Illus. 355 pp. Magpie Publications, 1994. Teacher edition, $34.95; student edition, 268 pp. paper, $14.95.

***THE WHISTLING TREE**
Audrey Penn; illus. by Barbara Gibson
Grades 3 and up. Chronicles a young girl's search for her Cherokee identity. 32 pp. CWLA, 2004. $16.95.

***WHITE BUFFALO WOMEN**
Christine Crowl
Grade 6 and up. Illus. 18 pp. Paper. Tipi Press, 1991. $3.95.

THE WHITE CANOE & OTHER LEGENDS OF THE OJIBWAYS
E. Monckton
Gordon Press, 1977. $59.95.

***WHITE CAPITVES**
Evelyn S. Lampman
Grades 4-7. 192 pp. Atheneum Publishers, 1975. $6.95.

WHITE CLOUD: LAKOTA SPIRIT
Cecilia Brownlow & Leslie Wilner
Native American shamanism. Illus. 96 pp. Paper. Sunstone Press, $10.95.

***THE WHITE DEER: & OTHER STORIES TOLD BY THE LENAPE**
John Bierhorst, Editor
Grades 7 and up. Illus. 160 pp. William Morrow, 1995. $15.

THE WHITE EARTH TRAGEDY; ETHNICITY & DISPOSSESSION AT A MINNESOTA ANISHINAABE RESERVATION, 1889-1920
Melissa L. Meyer
Illus. Maps. 333 pp. Paper. University of Nebraska Press, 1994. $18.95.

WHITE INDIAN BOY
Charles Wilson & Trilba Redding
Revised edition. Bound with The Return of the White Indian. Illus. 395 pp. Charles A. Wilson, 1988. $32.50.

WHITE INDIANS OF COLONIAL AMERICA
James Axtell
38 pp. Paper. Ye Galleon Press, 1991. $5.95.

THE WHITE MAN'S INDIAN: IMAGES OF THE AMERICAN INDIAN FROM COLUMBUS TO THE PRESENT
Robert Berkhofer, Jr.
Illus. Paper. Random House, 1979. $6.26.

WHITE MAN'S LAW: NATIVE PEOPLE IN 19TH CENTURY CANADIAN JURISPRUDENCE
Sidney L. Harring
First Nations legal traditions and culture. 488 pp. University of Toronto Press, 1998. $45.

WHITE MAN'S MEDICINE: GOVERNMENT DOCTORS & THE NAVAJO, 1863-1955
Robert A. Trennert, et al
290 pp. University of New Mexico, School of Medicine, 1998. $39.95.

WHITE MAN'S WICKED WATER: THE ALCOHOL TRADE & PROHIBITION IN INDIAN COUNTRY, 1802-1892
William E. Unrau
Illus. 192 pp. University Press of Kansas, 1996.
$30; paper, $14.95.

WHITE MOUNTAIN REDWARE: A POTTERY TRADITION OF EAST-CENTRAL ARIZONA & WESTERN NEW MEXICO
Roy L. Carlson
Originally published in 1970. Illus. 130 pp.
Paper. University of Arizona Press, 2003. $21.95.

WHITE ON RED: IMAGES OF THE AMERICAN INDIAN
Nancy B. Black & Bette S. Weidman, Editors
Associated Faculty Press, 1976. $26.50.

WHITE ROOTS OF PEACE: THE IROQUOIS BOOK OF LIFE
Paul A.W. Wallace
The story of the founding of the Iroquois League of Nations.
Illus. 156 pp. Clear Light, 1994. $22.95; paper, $12.95.

WHITE SETTLERS & NATIVE PEOPLES: AN HISTORICAL STUDY OF RACIAL CONTACTS BETWEEN ENGLISH-SPEAKING WHITES & ABORIGINAL PEOPLES IN THE U.S., CANADA, AUSTRALIA & NEW ZEALAND
A.G. Price
Reprint of 1950 edition. Illus. 232 pp. Greenwood, $35.

WHITE WEATHER UNIVERSE: NAVAJO SILVER FROM THE FRED HARVEY COLLECTION
Byron Harvey, III, et al
Illus. 53 pp. Paper. Heard Museum, 1981. $5.

WHITE WOLF WOMAN
40+ myths from 30 tribes. 168 pp. Paper.
Cherokee Publications, $8.95.

WHITEHALL & THE WILDERNESS: THE MIDDLE WEST IN BRITISH COLONIAL POLICY, 1760-1775
Jack Sosin
Reprint of 1961 edition. Illus. 318 pp. Greenwood, $38.50.

WHITESTONE HILL: THE INDIANS & THE BATTLE
Clair Jacobson
Story of the bloodiest battle ever fought in eastern Dakota Territory, involving the Yanktonai & Hunkpatina Sioux and the U.S. Army under General Sully. Illus. 120 pp. Center for Western Studies, $11.95.

JIM WHITEWOLF: THE LIFE OF A KIOWA APACHE INDIAN
Charles S. Brant, Editor
Autobiography of Jim Whitewolf. Reprint of 1969 edition.
144 pp. Map. Paper. High-Lonesome Books, $7.

*WHO CAME DOWN THAT ROAD?
George Ella Lyon
Story takes children on a journey through time.
Grades PS-3. Illus. 32 pp. Orchard Books, 1993. $16.

WHO SPEAKS FOR WOLF: A NATIVE AMERICAN LEARNING STORY
Paula Underwood
A story of one people's struggle to live within their environment. The Greenfield Review Press, $8.95.

WHO WAS WHO IN NATIVE AMERICAN HISTORY: INDIANS & NON-INDIANS FROM FIRST CONTACTS THROUGH 1900
Carl Waldman
1,000 brief biographical sketches of Indian and non-Indians active in Indian affairs, culture, and history up to 1900. Illus. 416 pp. Facts on File & Written Heritage, 1990. $49.95.

WHO'S LOOKING FOR WHOM IN NATIVE AMERICAN ANCESTRY
Laurie B. Duffy
155 pp. Paper. Heritage Books, 1997. $16.

WHO'S WHO IN INDIAN RELICS
The top collectors and artifact assemblages across the country. 9th Edition. Published once every 4 years. Illus. 400 pp. Hothem House, 1997. $43, postpaid.

*WHY BUFFALO ROAM
L. Michael Kershen
Original tale in the Comanche oral tradition, written by a ten year old boy. Grades 3-7. Illus. 32 pp. Stemmer House, 1993. $15.

WHY GONE THOSE TIMES? BLACKFOOT TALES
James Willard Schultz; edited by Eugene Lee Silliman
Schultz's experience with the Blackfeet from 1877 to 1947. Illus. 288 pp. paper. University of Oklahoma Press, 2002. $19.95.

*WHY THE POSSUM'S TAIL IS BARE: & OTHER NORTH AMERICAN INDIAN NATURE TALES
James E. Connolly, Editor
Grades 3-12. Illus. 64 pp. Stemmer House, 1985. $15.95; paper, $7.95.

THE WICHITA INDIANS: TRADERS OF TEXAS & THE SOUTHERN PLAINS, 1540-1845
F. Todd Smith
Illus. Texas A&M University Press, 2004.

WICHITA MEMORIES
Pamphlet on the Wichita Tribe. Wichita Tribal Office.

THE WICHITA PEOPLE
W.W. Newcomb, Jr.
Published by Indian Tribal Series, Phoenix, 1976.
Available at the Wichita Tribal Office, $25.

WIDE RUINS: MEMORIES FROM A NAVAJO TRADING POST
Sallie Wagner
Paper. University of New Mexico Press, $16.95.

WIGWAM EVENINGS: SIOUX TALES RETOLD
Charles Eastman & Elaine Goodale Eastman
Traditional Sioux legends. Illus. 255 pp. Paper.
University of Nebraska Press, 1990. $12.95.

*THE WIGWAM & THE LONGHOUSE
Charlotte & David Yue
Grades 4-8. Houghton Mifflin, 1999.

WIGWAM STORIES
M.C. Judd
Gordon Press, 1977. $59.95.

*WILD BROTHERS OF THE INDIANS: AS PICTURED BY THE ANCIENT AMERICANS
Alice Wesche
Grades 3-8. Illus. Paper. Treasure Chest, 1977. $4.95.

WILD INDIANS & OTHER CREATURES
Adrian C. Louis
Collection of short fiction. 200 pp.
University of Nevada Press, 1996. $20.

WILD JUSTICE: THE PEOPLE OF GERONIMO VS. THE U.S.
Michael Lieder & Jake Page
336 pp. Paper. University of Oklahoma Press, 1999. $16.95

WILD LIFE ON THE PLAINS & HORRORS OF INDIAN WARFARE
George A. Custer
Reprint of 1891 edition. Ayer Co., $45.95.

WILD PLANTS OF THE PRAIRIE: AN ETHNOBOTANICAL GUIDE
Kelly Kindscher
Illus. 324 pp. Paper. University Press of Kansas, 1992. $12.95.

WILD RICE & THE OJIBWAY PEOPLE
Thomas Vennum, Jr.
Illus. Photos. Biblio. 358 pp. Minnesota Historical Society Press, 1988. $29.95; paper, $14.95.

WILD WEST SHOWS & THE IMAGES OF AMERICAN INDIANS, 1883-1933
L.G. Moses
Examines the lives of Show Indians from their own point of view. Illus. 384 pp. Paper. University of New Mexico Press, 1999. $18.95.

WILDERNESS EMPIRE
Allan Eckert
Illus. Little, Borwn & Co., 1969. $25.

THE WILDERNESS OF THE SOUTHWEST: CHARLES SHELDON'S QUEST FOR DESERT BIGHORN SHEEP & ADVENTURES WITH THE HAVASUPAI & SERI INDIANS
Neil Carmony & David Brown, Editors
Illus. Paper. University of Utah Press, $14.95.

WILDERNESS POLITICS & INDIAN GIFTS: THE NORTHERN COLONIAL FRONTIER, 1748-1763
Wilbur Jacobs
Reprint. Illus. 208 pp. Peter Smith, $10.75. Paper. University of Nebraska Press, $4.95.

THE WILDERNESS TRAIL
Charles Hanna
Reprint of 1911 edition. Illus. 2 vols. 840 pp.
Wennwoods Publishing, $79.95 per set.

WILLIE BOY: A DESERT MANHUNT
Harry Lawton
Paper. Malki Museum Press, 1979. $10.

JOHN P. WILLIAMSON, A BROTHER TO THE SIOUX
Winifred W. Barton
Reprint of 1919 edition. Illus. 308 pp. Sunnycrest, $10.

THE WILLIAMSON SITE
Peck
Covers the most important early-man paleolithic site in the Southeast (Virginia). Illus. 203 pp. Paper. Hothem House, 1985. $25.

*WILLY WHITEFEATHER'S OUTDOOR SURVIVAL HANDBOOK FOR KIDS
Willy Whitefeather
Outdoor survival guidebook. Grades 3 and up. Illus. 104 pp. Paper. Harbinger House, $9.95.

*WILLY WHITEFEATHER'S RIVER BOOK FOR KIDS
Willy Whitefeather
Grandfather teaches a young Cherokee how to make it on the river of life. Grades 3 and up. 128 pp. Paper. Harbinger House, $11.95.

WIND FROM AN ENEMY SKY
D'Arcy McNickle
269 pp. Paper. University of New Mexico Press. $16.95.

THE WIND IS MY MOTHER: THE LIFE & TEACHINGS OF AN AMERICAN SHAMAN
Bear Heart & Molly Larkin
272 pp. Paper. Berkley Publishing, 1998. $14.

*THE WIND IS NOT A RIVER
Arnold Griese; Illus. by Glo Coalson
Grades 1-4. Illus. Boyds Mills Press, 1996 reissue. $7.95.

THE WIND WON'T KNOW ME: THE HISTORY OF THE NAVAJO-HOPI LAND DISPUTE
Emily Benedek
Illus. Map. 480 pp. Paper. University of Oklahoma Press, 1998. $19.95.

THE WINDING TRAIL: THE ALABAMA—COUSHATTA INDIANS
Vivien Fox
Illus. Eakin Publications, 1983. $7.95.

THE WINDS OF INJUSTICE: AMERICAN INDIANS & THE U.S. GOVERNMENT
Laurence A. French
288 pp. Garland Publishing, 1994. $20.

WINDS OF THE PAST: GUIDE TO PLAYING THE NATIVE AMERICAN FLUTE
By Choctaw/Cherokee flutemaker and recording artist Paul Hacker. Illus. 30 pp. Paper. Paul Hacker Knives & Flutes, $20.

WINDSONG: TEXAS CHEROKEE PRINCESS
Raven Hail
Illus. 140 pp. Paper. VIP Publishing, 1986. $9.95.

THE WINGED SERPENT: AMERICAN INDIAN PROSE & POETRY
Margot Astrov, Editor
Songs, chants, prayers, myths, and speeches from over 50 Native nations throughout North, South & Central America. 392 pp. Paper. Clear Light, $16.

WINGED WORDS: AMERICAN INDIAN WRITERS SPEAK
Laura Coltelli, Editor
Paula Gunn Allen, Michael Dorris, Joy Harjo, Simon Ortiz, N. Scott Momaday, Gerald Vizenor, and othjers. Illus. 215 pp. Paper. University of Nebraska Press, 1990. $9.95.

THE WINNEBAGO TRIBE
Paul Radin
Reprint. Illus. 575 pp. Paper. Univ. of Nebraska Press, $24.

SARAH WINNEMUCCA
Sally Zanjani
Illus. Maps. 366 pp. University of Nebraska Press, 2001. $29.95.

SARAH WINNEMUCCA OF THE NORTHERN PAIUTES
Gae Whitney Canfield
Illus. Maps. 336 pp. University of Oklahoma Press, 1983. $14.95.

WINNERS OF THE WEST: A CAMPAIGN PAPER PUBLISHED IN THE INTERESTS OF THE VETERANS OF ALL INDIAN WARS, THEIR WIDOWS & ORPHAN CHILDREN
Reprint of 1944 ed. 2,040 pp. Amereon Ltd. Microfiche, $197.

WINNING THE DUST BOWL
Carter Revard
Growing up on the Osage Reservation during Oklahoma Dust Bowl times. 212 pp. University of Arizona Press, 2001. $40; paper, $17.95.

WINTER COUNT
Dallas Chief Eagle
Originally published in 1967. Historical novel set during turbulent years leading up to the infamous Wounded Knee Massacre of 1890. Map. 230 pp. Paper. University of Nebraska Press, 2003. $14.95.

*THE WINTER HUNT
Henry Tall Bull and Tom Weist
Grades 3-9. Paper. Council for Indian Education, 1971. $1.95.

WINTER IN THE BLOOD
James Welch
A novel set on a Blackfoot reservation in Montana.
192 pp. Paper. Penguin USA, $8.

WINTER OF THE HOLY IRON
Joseph Marshall, III (Sicangu Lakota)
Novel about the winter of 1750, a holy iron (flintlock rifle) and 2 Frenchmen are thrust into the lives of the Wolf Tail Band of Sicangu Lakota. 304 pp. Red Crane Books, 1994. $19.95. Poster available.

THE WINTU & THEIR NEIGHBORS: A VERY SMALL WORLD-SYSTEM IN NORTHERN CALIFORNIA
Christopher Chase-Dunn & Kelly M. Mann
Case study to compare and contrast systematically an indigenous Native American society with the modern world at large. Illus. 310 pp. University of Arizona Press, 1998. $38.

THE WINTUN INDIANS OF CALIFORNIA & THEIR NEIGHBORS
Peter Knudtson
Ethnographic study. Illus. 96 pp. Paper. Naturegraph, 1977. $8.95.

WISCONSIN CHIPPEWA MYTHS & TALES
Victor Barnouw
Colection of traditional Chippewa legends from Lac Court Oreilles & Lac du Flambeau reservations in Wisconsin between 1941 & 1944. University of Wisconsin Press, 1977.

WISCONSIN'S COUNTY FORESTS: CONFLICT OVER INDIAN TIMBER RIGHTS
Michael F. Sohasky
100 pp. New Past Press, 1994. $9.

THE WISDOM OF THE GREAT CHIEFS
Kent Nerburn, Editor
Includes the Soul of an Indian and Other Writings Ohiyesa and the Great Speeches of Chief Red Jacket, Chief Joseph and Chief Seattle, documenting Native perception and philosophy. 96 pp. New World Library, $12.95.

WISDOM OF THE NATIVE AMERICANS
Kent Nerburn
272 pp. New World Library, 1999. $17.95.

WISDOM SITS IN PLACES: LANDSCAPE & LANGUAGE AMONG THE WESTERN APACHE
Keith H. Basso
Illus. 192 pp. Paper. University of New Mexico Press, $18.95.

WISDOM'S DAUGHTERS: CONVERSATIONS WITH WOMEN ELDERS OF NATIVE AMERICA
Steve Wall
Interviews with Native American spiritual leaders, giving voice to women who discuss their ancestyral knowledge, philosophies and traditions. 100+ b&x photos. Illus. 320 pp. Paper. Harper & Row, $15.

WISDOMKEEPERS: MEETINGS WITH NATIVE AMERICAN SPIRITUAL ELDERS
Steve Wall & Harvey Arden
Spirit journey into the lives, minds, and natural-world philosophy of Native American spiritual elders representing 17 tribes. 128 pp. Beyond Words Publishing, 1990. $39.95; paper, $19.95. Two-tape audio, $16.95.

THE WITCH OF GOINGSNAKE & OTHER STORIES
Robert J. Conley
Stories reflect the range of Cherokee culture. 166 pp. Paper. University of Oklahoma Press, $12.95.

THE WITCH PURGE OF 1878: ORAL & DOCUMENTARY HISTORY IN THE EARLY NAVAJO RESERVATION YEARS
Martha Blue
Paper. Dine College Press. $4.75.

WITCHCRAFT IN THE SOUTHWEST: SPANISH & INDIAN SUPERNATURALISM ON THE RIO GRANDE
Marc Simmons
Illus. 185 pp. Paper. University of Nebraska Press, 1980. $5.95.

WITCHCRAFT & SORCERY OF THE NORTH AMERICAN NATIVE PEOPLE
Deward E. Walker, Editor
Revised edition. 336 pp. Paper. University of Idaho Press, 1989. $23.95.

WITH EAGLE TAIL
Hugh Dempsey & Colin Taylor
Illus. 128 pp. Smithmark Publishers, 1999. $12.98.

WITH GOOD HEART: YAQUI BELIEFS & CEREMONIES IN PASCUA VILLAGE
Muriel Painter; Ed Spicer & WilmaKaemlein, Editors
Illus. 533 pp. University of Arizona Press, 1986. $50.95.

WITH MY OWN EYES: A LAKOTA WOMAN TELLS HER PEOPLE'S HISTORY
Susan Bordeaux Bettelyoun & Josephine Waggoner
Tells the histoy of the 19th century Lakotas. Illus. 200 pp. Paper. University of Nebraska Press, 1998. $16.95.

WITH THE NEZ PERCES: ALICE FLETCHER IN THE FIELD, 1889-1892
E. Jane Gay; Frederick E. Hoxie
and Joan T. Mark, Editors
Illus. Map. 226 pp. Paper. Univ. of Nebraska Press, 1981. $10.95.

WITH PEN AND PENCIL ON THE FRONTIER IN 1851: THE DIARY AND SKETCHES OF FRANK BLACKWELL MAYER
Frank Blackwell Mayer
Presents the signing of the Treaty of Traverse des Sioux. Illus. 256 pp. Minnesota Historical Society Press, 1986. $9.95.

WITHOUT QUARTER: THE WICHITA EXPEDITION & THE FIGHT ON CROOKED CREEK
William Y. Chalfant
The climactic story of the first major U.S. army expedition against the Comanches along the Texas frontier. Illus. Maps. 170 pp. University of Oklahoma Press, 1992. $22.95.

WIYOT GRAMMAR & TEXTS
Gladys Reichard
Reprint fo 1925 edition. 215 pp. Paper. Coyote Press, $23.13.

WIYUTA: ASSINIBOINE STORYTELLING WITH SIGNS CD
Brenda Farnell
University of Texas Press, 1995. $100.

WOKINI
Billy Mills
Billy Mills, (Sioux) Olympic gold medalist, teaches of his personal journey to happiness and self-understanding. Four Winds Trading Co., $12.95.

WO'WAKITA: RESERVATION RECOLLECTIONS
Emily H. Lewis
A people's history of the Allen)old Pass Creek) Issue Station District on the Pine Ridge Reservation of South Dakota. Illus. 294 pp. Center for Western Studies, $19.95.

THE WOLF & THE BUFFALO
Elmer Kelton
570 pp. G.K. Hall, 1989. $19.95.

*WOLF DOG OF THE WOODLAND INDIANS
Margaret Zehmer Searcy
Experiences that propel the young Indian boy quickly into manhood. Grades 3-8. Illus. 112 pp. paper. Pelican Publishing, $6.95.

*WOLF STORIES: MYTHS AND TRUE-LIFE TALES FROM AROUND THE WORLD
Susan Strauss
Grades 1-7. 48 pp. Paper. Beyond Words. $11.95; paper, $7.95.

*WOLF TALES: NATIVE AMERICAN CHILDREN'S STORIES
edited & adapted for children by Mary Powell
Grades 3 and up. Illus. 48 pp. Paper. Ancient City Press, 1992. $9.95.

WOLF THAT I AM: IN SEARCH OF THE RED EARTH PEOPLE
Fred McTaggart
Biblio. 202 pp. Paper. University of Oklahoma Press, 1984. $14.95.

WOLFSONG: A NOVEL
Louis Owens
256 pp. Paper. University of Oklahoma Press, 2002. $17.95.

WOLLASTON: PEOPLE RESISTING GENOCIDE
Miles Goldstick
Natives' struggle in northern Saskatchewan to protect their homes from the effects of uranium mining. Illus. Photos. 315 pp. University of Toronto Press, 1987. $46; paper, $17.

WOLVES FOR THE BLUE SOLDIERS: INDIAN SCOUTS & AUXILLIARIES WITH THE U.S. ARMY, 1860-1890
Thomas Dunlay
Illus. Maps. 320 pp. Paper. University of Nebraska Press, 1982. $25.

THE WOLVES OF HEAVEN: CHEYENNE SHAMANISM, CEREMONIES, & PREHISTORIC ORIGINS
Karl H. Schlesier
Illus. Maps. 232 pp. Paper. University of Oklahoma Press, 1987. $14.95.

WOMAN OF THE GREEN GLADE: THE STORY OF AN OJIBWAY INDIAN LADY
Virginia Soetebier
Illus. 88 pp. Paper. University of Nebraska Press, 1999. $14.95.

A WOMAN OF THE PEOPLE
Benjamin Capps
Captivity tale. 248 pp. paper. Texas A&M University Press, 1966. $15.95.

*WOMEN IN AMERICAN INDIAN SOCIETY
Rayma Green
Grades 5 and up. Ill. Chelsea House, 1989. $17.95.

WOMEN IN PREHISTORY: NORTH AMERICA & MESOAMERICA
Cheryl Classen & Rosemary Joyce, Editors
Illus. 288 pp. University of Pennsylvania Press, 1996. $39.95; paper, $18.50.

WOMEN & INDIANS ON THE FRONTIER, 1825-1915
Glenda Riley
Illus. 350 pp. Paper. University of New Mexico Press, 1984. $13.95.

WOMEN IN HISTORY
D.L. Shepherd, Editor
Mankind, $1.50.

WOMEN IN NAVAJO SOCIETY
Ruth Roessel
Illus. 184 pp. Navajo Curriculum Center Press, 1981. $15.

WOMEN OF THE APACHE NATION: VOICES OF TRUTH
H. Henrietta Stckel
Interviews of Chiricahua Apache women emphasizes the importance of storytelling and ritual in preserving Apache heritage. Illus. 226 pp. Paper. University of Nevada Press, 1993. $14.95.

WOMEN OF THE DAWN
Bunny McBride
Stories of four Wabanaki Indian women. Friends of American Writers Literary Award. Illus. 160 pp. Paper. University of Nebraska Press, 1999. $11.95.

WOMEN OF THE EARTH LODGES: TRIBAL LIFE ON THE PLAINS
Virginia Bergman Peters
Examines the influence and vitality of Plains Indian women. Illus. Map. Paper. University of Oklahoma Press, 2002. $19.95.

WOMEN OF THE FIRST NATIONS: POWER, WISDOM & STRENGTH
Christine Miller & Patricia Chuchryk, Editors
Paper. University of Toronto Press, 1996. $19.95.

WOMEN OF THE NATIVE STRUGGLE
Ronnie Farley
Direct record of author's travels across America based on her photographs of native women in their different environments and her interviews with them. Paper. Orion Books, $22.

WOMEN & POWER IN NATIVE NORTH AMERICA
Laura Klein & Lilian Ackerman
Map. 294 pp. Paper. University of Oklahoma Press, 1995. $19.95

WOODEN LEG: A WARRIOR WHO FOUGHT CUSTER
Thomas Marquis, Translator
New edition. Illus. Maps. 416 pp. Paper. University of Nebraska Press, 2003. $14.95.

A WOODLAND FEAST: NATIVE AMERICAN FOODWAYS OF THE 17TH & 18TH CENTURIES
Carolyn Raine
Illus. 90 pp. Paper. Picton Press & Smoke & Fire Co., 1997. $15.

*WOODLAND INDIANS
Cleary & Taylor
Grades 3-6. Teacher edition. Illus. 48 pp. Paper. DoveTail Books, 1995. $5.95.

WOODLAND INDIANS OF THE WESTERN GREAT LAKES
Robert & Pat Ritzenthaler
Second Edition. Illus. 154 pp. Paper. Waveland Press, 1983. $8.95.

WOODLAND PEOPLES: AN EDUCATIONAL UNIT
Nicholas L. Clark
32 pp. Paper. Minnetrista, 1993.

WOODLAND SITES IN NEBRASKA
M.F. Kivett
102 pp. Paper. Nebraska State Historical Society, 1970. $6.

WOODLAND TRAPPERS: HARE INDIANS OF NORTHWSTERN CANADA
Harold Broch
225 pp. Paper. Barber Press, 1987. $10.95.

*WOODLANDS INDIANS: COLORING BOOK
Peter F. Copeland
Grades K-2. 48 pp. paper. Dover, $2.95.

WOODSMEN, OR THOREAU & THE INDIANS: A NOVEL
Arnold Krupat
134 pp. Paper. University of Oklahoma Press, 1994. $10.95.

WORD DANCE: THE LANGUAGE OF NATIVE AMERICAN CULTURE
Carl Waldman
Illus. 304 pp. Paper. Facts on File, 1996. $15.95.

WORD WAYS: THE NOVELS OF D'ARCY McNICKLE
John Lloyd Purdy
167 pp. University of Arizona Press, 1989. $30.95.

WORDARROWS: INDIANS & WHITES IN THE NEW FUR TRADE
Gerald Vizenor
Focuses on the cultural word wars which dominate the relations of Indians and whites. 170 pp. Paper. University of Minnesota Press, 1978. $12.95.

**WORDARROWS: NATIVE STATES
OF LITERARY SOVEREIGNTY**
Gerald Vizenor
Modern Native American life and the different ways that Native
Americans and whites interact, fight, and resolve their conflicts.
Paper. University of Nebraska Press, 2003. $16.

**WORDS IN THE BLOOD: CONTEMPORARY
INDIAN WRITERS OF NORTH & SOUTH AMERICA**
Jamake Highwater
416 pp. Paper. New American Library, 1984. $9.95.

WORDS OF POWER: VOICES FROM INDIAN AMERICA
Norbert S. Hill, Jr., Editor
Collection of quotations, illustrates views & values. Illus.
72 pp. Paper. Fulcrum Publishing & Clear Light, 1994. $9.95.

THE WORLD OF THE AMERICAN INDIAN
Jules B. Billard, National Geographic Editor
398 pp. Illus. 398 pp. Shenandoah Books, $16.50.

**THE WORLD OF THE CROW INDIANS:
AS DRIFTWOOD LODGES**
Rodney Frey
Illus. Maps. 194 pp. Paper. University of Oklahoma Press,
1987. $13.95.

**A WORLD OF FACES: MASKS OF
THE NORTHWEST COAST INDIANS**
Edward Malin
Classic study of Native American masks from the Pacific North-
west. Explores the rcihes of this ancient tradition, showing out-
standing old masks. 8 color photos, 49 b&w photos. 158 pp.
Paper reprint of 1978 edition. Timber Press. $17.95.

**THE WORLD OF FLOWER BLUE:
POP CHALEE: AN ARTISTIC BIOGRAPHY**
Margaret Cesa
Portrait of a unique Native American artist. Illus.
40 color plates. 288 pp. Red Crane Books, 1999. $49.95.

*WORLD OF THE SOUTHERN INDIANS
Virginia Brown & Laurella Owens
Grades 6-9. Illus. 176 pp. Paper. Beechwood Books,
1983. $15.95.

**THE WORLD TURNED UPSIDE DOWN:
INDIAN VOICES FROM EARLY AMERICA**
Colin G. Calloway, Editor
Bedford Books, 1994.

WORLD WAR II & THE AMERICAN INDIAN
Kenneth W. Townsend
Illus. 284 pp. Paper. University of New Mexico Press.
$18.95.

**WORLD'S RIM: GREAT MYSTERIES
OF THE NORTH AMERICAN INDIANS**
Hartley Alexander
Illus. 260 pp. Paper. University of Nebraska Press
& Written Heritage, 1967. $8.95.

**THE WORLDS BETWEEN TWO RIVERS:
PERSPECTIVES ON AMERICAN INDIANS IN IOWA**
Gretchen Bataille, et al, Editors
Illus. 150 pp. Iowa State University Press, 1987. $5.95.

WOUNDED KNEE 1973: A PERSONAL ACCOUNT
Stanley David Lyman
Illus. Map. 196 pp. Paper. University of Nebraska Press,
1991. $16.

WOUNDED KNEE II
Rolland Dewing
230 pp. Paper. Great Plains Network, 1995. $21.95.

WOUNDED KNEE & THE GHOST DANCE TRAGEDY
Jack Utter
Account of events leading to and includng the infamous
massacre at Wounded Knee, SD, in 1890. 29 pp. Illus.
Maps. Paper. National Woodlands Publishing, 1991. $3.95.

***WOUNDED KNEE: AN INDIAN HISTORY
OF THE AMERICAN WEST**
Dee Brown
Grades 7 and up. 192 pp. Paper. Dell, 1974. $1.50.

WOUNDED KNEE: LEST WE FORGET
Alvin M. Josephy, Jr. & Trudy Thomas
Attempts to tell the true story of the history of Wounded Knee
and the practice of Ghost Dance religion by the Sioux. Illus. 64
pp. Paper. University of Washington Press, $21.95.

**THE WOUNDED KNEE MASSACRE:
FROM THE VIEWPOINT OF THE SIOUX**
James H. McGregor
Reprint. Illus. 131 pp. paper. Center for Western Studies,
$5.95.

**WOUNDED KNEE: THE MEANING & SIGNIFICANCE
OF THE SECOND INCIDENT**
Rolling Dewing
417 pp. Irvington, 1984. $49.50; paper, $19.95.

WOVEN BY THE GRANDMOTHERS
Eulalie H. Bonar, Editor
19th century Navajo textiles from the National Museum of the
American Indian. Illus. 215 pp. Smithsonian Institution Press,
1996. $34.95.

WOVEN STONE
Simon J. Ortiz
The autobiography of Simon J. Ortiz. 350 pp.
University of Arizona Press, 1992. $51; paper, $22.95.

**WOVEN WORLD: BASKETRY FROM
THE CLARK FIELD COLLECTION**
edited by Lydia L. Wyckoff
Weavers and their baskets from eight major cultural areas. A
color map in each chapter with historical information and a dis-
cussion with some interviews. Published by The Philbrook
Museum of Art. Illus. Maps. 246 pp. University of New Mexico
Press, 2001. $75; paper, $39.95.

WOVOKA & THE GHOST DANCE: A SOURCE BOOK
Expanded edition by Michael Hittman; edited by Don Lynch
The known research about Wovoka (Jack Wilson) as the Ghost
Dance Prophet. Illus. Map. 370 pp. Paper. Univ. of Nebraska
Press & Yerington Paiute Tribe Publications, 1997. $22.95.

WOVOKA POSTER
16 1/2" x 23" poster of the Northern Paiute
Ghost Dance Prophet. $5.

**WRITE IT ON YOUR HEART:
WORLD OF AN OKANAGAN STORYTELLER**
Harry Robinson
Okanagan stories. Greenfield Review Press, $18.95.

**WRITERS OF THE PURPLE SAGE: AN ANTHOLOGY
OF RECENT WESTERN WRITING**
Russell Martin & Marc Barash, Editors
Includes some Native American writers. 368 pp.
Paper. Penguin USA, $9.95.

WRITING CHEROKEE
Syllabary practice book. 28 pp. VIP Publishing. $5.

**WRITING THE CIRCLE: NATIVE WOMEN
OF WESTERN CANADA-AN ANTHOLOGY**
Jeanne Perreault & Sylvia Vance
Anthology of contemporary Native Canadian women's writings.
288 pp. Paper. University of Oklahoma Press, 1993. $14.95.

WRITING THE SOUTHWEST
David King Dunaway & Sara Spurgeon
Includes interviews, bibliographies, excerpts, and criticism on
14 of the Southwest's most important authors, including Joy
Harjo, Tony Hillerman, Linda Hogan, Simon Ortiz, et al. Revised edition. 320 pp. University of Arizona Press, 2003. $39.95;
paper, $17.95. Includes 74 min. CD.

**WRITING TO CREATE OURSELVES: NEW APPROACHES
FOR TEACHERS, STUDENTS, & WRITERS**
T.D. Allen
Describes nearly two decades of experience in teaching
writing to Navaho & Eskimo students. 253 pp. University
of Oklahoma Press, 1982. $22.95.

WRITINGS IN INDIAN HISTORY, 1985-1990
Jay Miller, Colin G. Calloway & Richard A. Sattler
Bibliography. 216 pp. University of Oklahoma Press, 1995.
$28.95; paper, $12.95

**WRITINGS OF GENERAL JOHN FORBES
RELATING TO HIS SERVICE IN NORTH AMERICA**
John Forbes
Reprin tof 1938 edition. Ayer Co., $22.

**WUPATKI & WALNUT CANYON: NEW PERSPECTIVES
ON HISTORY, PREHISTORY, AND ROCK ART**
David Grant Noble, Editor
Reveals the remains of the Sinagua culture and contains
sketches of the Navajo who live in Wupatki today. Illus. Maps.
Photos. 48 pp. Paper. Ancient City Press, 1990. $8.95.

WYNEMA: A CHILD OF THE FOREST
S. Alice Callahan; edited by A. LaVonne Brown Ruoff
Originally published in 1891. Illus. Map. 120 pp. Paper.
University of Nebraska Press, 1997. $19.95.

WYOMING PLACE NAMES
Mae Urbanek
238 pp. Paper. Mountain Press Publishing, $10.

Y

*THE YAKIMA: NORTHWEST
Helen Schuster
Grades 5 and up. Illus. Chelsea House, 1989. $17.95.

**YAKIMA, PALOUSE, CAYUSE, UMATILLA, WALLA WALLA,
& WANAPUM INDIANS: AN HISTORICAL BIBLIOGRAPHY**
Clifford E. Trafzer, Editor
Map. 263 pp. Scarecrow Press, 1992. $37.50.

THE YAKAMAS: A CRITICAL BIBLIOGRAPHY
Helen H. Schuster
168 pp. Paper. Indiana University Press, 1982. $5.95.

*THE YANKTON SIOUX
Herbert Hoover
Grades 5 and up. Illus. 104 pp. Chelsea House, 1988.
$17.95.

**YANKTONAI SIOUX WATER COLORS:
CULTURAL REMEMBRANCES OF JOHN SAUL**
Martin Brokenleg & Herbert T. Hoover
John Saul was a Minnesota Sioux (1878-1971). His family was
removed to the Dakota Territory after the Minnesota Dakota
war of 1862. Includes 23 of his drawings in full color; and in-
cludes chapters on Sioux customs, the Yanktonai and their
Sioux relatives, a photographic essay on John Saul, and more.
Illus. 66 pp. Center for Western Studies, $12.95.

YAQUI DEER SONGS: A NATIVE AMERICAN POETRY
Larry Evers & Felipe Molina
239 pp. Paper. University of Arizona Press, 1986.
$19.95. Audiocassette of deer songs, $12.95.

A YAQUI EASTER
Muriel Thayer Painter
Introduction to the ceremony. 40 pp. Paper.
University of Arizona Press, 1971. $8.95.

**A YAQUI LIFE: THE PERSONAL
CHRONICLE OF A YAQUI INDIAN**
Rosalio Moises, et al
Illus. 251 pp. University of Nebraska Press, 1977.
$23.95; paper, $5.95.

YAQUI MYTHS & LEGENDS
Ruth Warner Giddings
61 tales narrated by Yaquis. 180 pp. Paper.
University of Arizona Press, 1968. $14.95.

YAQUI WOMEN: CONTEMPORARY LIFE HISTORIES
Jane Holden Kelley
Illus. 265 pp. University of Nebraska Press, 1978. $32.50.

THE YAQUIS: A CELEBRATION
H.S. Choate
Illus. 102 pp. University of Arizona Press, 1997. $32.95;
paper, $17.95.

THE YAQUIS: A CULTURAL HISTORY
Edward H. Spicer
Reprint of 1980 edition. 406 pp. University of
Arizona Press, $35.

YEAR IN NAM: A NATIVE AMERICAN SOLDIER'S STORY
Leroy TeCube
TeCube, a Jicarilla Apache, spent a year in Vietnam in 1968 as
an infantryman in the U.S. Army. Illus. 288 pp. University of
Nebraska Press, 1999. $30; paper, $14.95.

THE YEAR OF THE HOPI
Tyrone Stewart, et al
Illus. 96 pp. Paper. Rizzoli International, 1982. $14.95.

YELLOW WOLF: HIS OWN STORY
L.V. McWhorter
Nez Perce War. Illus. Map. Biblio. 328 pp.
The Caxton Printers, $19.95; paper, $15.95.

**YELLOWTAIL, CROW MEDICINE MAN &
SUN DANCE CHIEF: AN AUTOBIOGRAPHY**
Michael O. Fitzgerald
Illus. Map. 242 pp. University of Oklahoma Press, 1991.
$11.95.

YELLOW WOLF: HIS OWN STORY
L. McWhorter
Reprint. Illus. 325 pp. Caxton Printers, $19.95; paper, $14.95.

YERINGTON PAIUTE DICTIONARY
118 pp. Paper. Yerington Paiute Tribe Publications, $15.

YERINGTON PAIUTE LANGUAGE GRAMMAR
168 pp. Paper. Yerington Paiute Tribe Publications, $15.

**YOEME-ENGLISH, ENGLISH-YOEME
STANDARD DICTIONARY**
David L. Shaul
Reprint. 350 pp. Paper. Hippocrene Books, $14.95.

YOKUTS DIALECT SURVEY
A.L. Kroeber; J.H. Rowe, et al, editors
Reprint of 1963 edition. 83 pp. Paper. Coyote Press, $9.38.

**THE YOKUTS LANGUAGE OF SOUTH CENTRAL
CALIFORNIA**
A.L. Kroeber
Reprint of 1907 edition. 213 pp. Paper. Coyote Press, $9.38.

YOSEMITE INDIANS
Elizabeth Godfrey
Revised edition. Illus. 36 pp. Paper.
Yosemite Association, 1977. $2.95.

**YOU ARE ON INDIAN LAND:
ALCATRAZ ISLAND, 1969-1971**
edited by Troy R. Johnson
160 pp. UCLA, American Indian Studies Center,
1991. $25; paper, $12.

YOU & THE UTILITY COMPANY
Institute for the Development of Indian Law, $3.50.

*YOUNG POCAHONTAS, INDIAN PRINCESS
Anne Benjamin
Grades K-3. Illus. 32 pp. Paper. Troll Associates,
1992. $3.50.

**YOUR FYRE SHALL BURN NO MORE: IROQUOIS
POLICY TOWARD NEW FRANCE & ITS ALLIES TO 1701**
Jose Antonio Brandao
Historiography of the colonial Northeast. Illus. 377 pp.
Paper. University of Nebraska Press, $19.95.

YOUR NAME IN CHEROKEE
Prentice Robinson
1,000 names listed in English with Cherokee phonetics,
the English phonetics & Cherokee syllabary. 25 pp.
Paper. Cherokee Publications, $6.

YOUR RIGHTS AS AMERICAN INDIANS
Institute for the Development of Indian Law, $7.50.

**YUCHI CEREMONIAL LIFE: PERFROMANCE, MEANING, &
TRADITION IN A CONTEMPORARY AMERICAN INDIAN
COMMUNITY**
Jason Baird Jackson
Illus. Maps. University of Nebraska Press, 2003. $75.

**THE YUCHI GREEN CORN CEREMONIAL:
FORM & MEANING**
W.L. Ballard
81 pp. Paper. UCLA, American Indian Studies Center,
1978. $7.50.

YUKON BIBLIOGRAPHY - UPDATE SERIES
G.A. Cooke, Series Editor
CCI.

**YUKON-KOYUKUK SCHOOL DISTRICT
BIOGRAPHY SERIES**
Curt Madison & Yvonne Yarber, Editors
Interviews of selected individuals and describes the events of
their lives in their own words. Includes historical and contemporary photos. See Spirit Mountain Press for complete list of
individuals profiled and prices.

*THE YUMA: CALIFORNIA
Robert L. Bee
Grades 5 and up. Illus. Chelsea House, 1989. $17.95.

YUMAN & YAQUI MUSIC
F. Densmore
Reprint of 1932 edition. Illus. 272 pp. Da Capo Press,
$27.50.

YUMAN TRIBES OF THE GILA RIVER
Leslie Spier
Reprint of 1933 edition. Illus. 435 pp. Paper. Dover, $8.95.

YUP'IK ESKIMO DICTIONARY
Steven Jacobson
Illus. 755 pp. Paper. Alaska Native Language Center,
1984. $18.

YUP'IK ESKIMO GRAMMAR
Irene Reed, et al
330 pp. Paper. Alaska Native Language Center, 1977. $7.50.

**YUP'IK ESKIMO PROSODIC SYSTEMS:
DESCRIPTIVE & COMPARATIVE STUDIES**
Michael Krauss, et al
Illus. 215 pp. Paper. Alaska Native Language Center,
1985. $15.

**THE YUP'IK ESKIMOS AS DESCRIBED IN THE TRAVEL
JOURNALS & ETHNOGRAPHIC ACCOUNTS OF JOHN &
EDITH KILBUCK**
Ann Fienup-Riordon
Illus. Limestone Press, 1988. $30.

YUROK AFFIXES
T.T. Waterman
Reprint of 1923 edition. 20 pp. Paper. Coyote Press, $2.50.

YUROK MYTHS
A.L. Kroeber
A study of the Yurok Indians. Reprint. 460 pp.
University of California, $37.50; paper, $10.95.

YUWIPI: VISION & EXPERIENCE IN OGLALA RITUAL
William K. Powers
Illus. Maps. 113 pp. Paper. University of Nebraska Press, 1982.
$6.95.

Z

DAVID ZEISBERGER: A LIFE AMONG THE INDIANS
Earl P. Olmstead & David Zeisberger
Kent State University Press, 1997. $39.

A ZUNI ATLAS
T.J. Ferguson and E. Richard Hart
Illus. Maps. 168 pp. Paper. University of Oklahoma
Press & Clear Light, 1985. $21.95.

*ZUNI CHILDREN & ELDERS TALK TOGETHER
Barrie E. Kavasch
Grades 4 and up. Rosen Group, 1998. $18.

ZUNI CONTEMPORARY POTTERY
Marian Rodee & Jim Ostler
Illus. 92 pp. Paper. Maxwell Museum, 1987. $9.95.

ZUNI COYOTE TALES
Frank H. Cushing
Reprint. of 1901 edition. 104 pp. Paper.
University of Arizona Press, $8.95.

ZUNI & EL MORO: PAST & PRESENT
David Grant Noble & Richard B. Woodbury
Illus. Maps. Photos. 40 pp. Paper.
Ancient City Press, 1990. $8.95.

THE ZUNI ENIGMA
Nancy Y. Davis
Illus. 352 pp. W.W. Norton, 2000. $26.95.

ZUNI FETISHES
F.H. Cushing
Illus. 43 pp. Paper. KC Publications, 1966. $3.

**ZUNI FETISHES: USING NATIVE AMERICAN OBJECTS
FOR MEDITATION, REFLECTION, AND INSIGHT**
Hal Zina Bennett
Guide to the fetishes used by the Zuni people of
New Mexico. Illus. 192 pp. paper. Clear Light, $19.

ZUNI FETISHISM
Ruth Kirk
Study of 25 pieces from the Museum of New Mexico.
Illus. 72 pp. Paper. Avanyu Publishing, 1988. $4.75.

ZUNI FOLK TALES
Frank H. Cushing
Reprint of 1901 edition. 474 pp. Paper.
University of Arizona Press, $17.95.

**THE ZUNI INDIANS: THEIR MYTHOLOGY,
ESOTERIC FRATERNITIES & CEREMONIES**
M.C. Stevenson
Reprint of 1904 edition. Illus. 685 pp. Rio Grande Press,
$60.

THE ZUNI INDIANS & THEIR USES OF PLANTS
Matilda Coxe Stevenson
Reprint of 1908 report of the Bureau of American
Ethnology. 80 pp. Paper. Dover, $5.95.

ZUNI JEWELRY
Theda & Michael Bassmann
Presents jewelry of the Zuni Indians of New Mexico.
Both traditional and new styles are shown in full color.
Illus. 64 pp. Paper. Schiffer, $12.95.

ZUNI KATCHINAS
Ruth Bunzel
Reprint of 1932 edition. Illus. 358 pp. Rio Grande Press,
$40.

A ZUNI LIFE: A PUEBLO INDIAN IN TWO WORLDS
Virgil Wyaco; edited by J.A. Jones
University of New Mexico Press, $35; paper, $16.95.

THE ZUNI MAN-WOMAN
Will Roscoe
Paper. University of New Mexico Press, 1992. $17.95.

ZUNI POTTERY
Marian Rodee & Jim Ostler
Illus. 92 pp. Paper. Schiffer, 1987. $9.95.

**ZUNI: SELECTED WRITINGS OF
FRANK HAMILTON CUSHING**
F.H. Cushing; Jesse Green, Editor
Illus. 450 pp. University of Nebraska Press, 1979.
$31.50; paper, $10.95.

ZUNI: A VILLAGE OF SILVERSMITHS
James Ostler, marian Rodee, Milfred Nahohai
University of New Mexico Press, $45; paper, $29.95.
*THE ZUNIS
Alice Flanagan
Grades 2-4. Illus. 48 pp. Children's Press, 1997.
$21; paper, $6.95.

*THE ZUNIS
Katherine M. Doherty & Craig A. Doherty
Includes maps, a glossary and bibliography. Part of *Indians of
the Americas* series. Full-color illustrations. Grades 3 and up.
64 pp. Paper. Franklin Watts, $5.95.

In this section, titles annotated in the alphabetically arranged bibliography are grouped under one or more subject headings.

ABENAKI INDIANS

*The Abenaki
*Abenaki Captive
Abenaki Warrior
The Faithful Hunter & Other Abenaki Stories
*From Abenaki to Zuni: A Dictionary of
  Native American Tribes
The Voice of the Dawn: An Autohistory of the Abenaki Nation
The Wabanakis of Maine & the Maritimes
The Western Abenakis of Vermont
The Wind Eagle

ACTIVISM

Alcatraz! Alcatraz!: The Indian Occupation of 1969-1971
Alcatraz: Indian Land Forever
American Indian Activism: Alcatraz to the Longest Walk
Black Panther Party & the American Indian Movement
Blood of the Land: The Government and Corporate
  War Against the American Indian Movement
Custer Died for Your Sins: An Indian Manifesto
Heart of the Rock: The Indian Invasion of Alcatraz
Like a Hurricane: The Indian Movement from Alcatraz
  to Wounded Knee
Loud Hawk: The U.S. versus the American Indian Movement
The Occupation of Alcatraz Island
Occupation of Wounded Knee
Ojibwa Warrior: Dennis Banks & the Rise of the
  American Indian Movement
Where White Men Fear to Tread: Autobiography
  of Russell Means
You Are On Indian Land: Alcatraz Island, 1969-1971

AGRICULTURE & FARMING

Agricultural Terracing in the Aboriginal New World
Agriculture of the Hidatsa Indians
American Indian Foods & Vegetables
Buffalo Bird Woman's Garden: Agriculture of the
  Hidatsa Indians
Early Prehistoric Agriculture in the American Southwest
Enduring Seeds: Native American Agriculture
  & Wild Plant Conservation
Ethnobotany of the Coahuilla Indians of Southern California
Indian Agriculture in America: Prehistory to the Present
Indians, Bureaucrats & Land: The Dawes Act & the \
  Decline of Indian Farming
Iroquois Corn in a Culture-Based Curriculum
Neither Wolf Nor Dog: American Indians, Environment
  & Agrarian Change

ALABAMA-COUSHATTA INDIANS

Myths and Folktales of the Alabama-Coushatta Indians
The Winding Trail: The Alabama-Coushatta Indians

ALASKA NATIVES - ESKIMOS

Across Arctic America, Narrative of the Fifth Thule Expedition
*Across the Tundra
Against Culture: Development, Politics, & Religion in
  Indian Alaska
Ahtna Athabaskan Dictionary
Alaska Days With John Muir
Alaska: A History of the 49th State
The Alaska Eskimos: A Selected, Annotated Bibliography
Alaska 1899: Essays from the Harriman Expedition
Alaska History Series
*Alaska in the Days That Were Before
Alaska Native Arts & Crafts
Alaska Native Claims Settlement Act, 1991,
  & Tribal Government
Alaska Native Land Rights
Alaska Native Language Center Publications
Alaska Native Languages: Past, Present & Future
Alaska Native Policy in the Twentieth Century
Alaska Natives & American Laws
Alaska Natives: A Guide to Current Reference
  Souces in the Rasmuson Library
Alaska's Native People
Alaska's Southern Panhandle
Alaskameut '86
Alaskan Eskimo Life in the 1890s: As Sketched
  by Native Artists
*Alaskan Igloo Tales
Alaskan Native Food Practices, Customs & Holidays
Aleut Dictionary
Aleut Tales & Narratives
Aleuts: Survivors of the Beping Land Bridge
American Indian & Alaska Native Health:
  Bibliography: Jan. 1990 Through Sept. 1996
The American Indian & Alaska Native Higher
  Education Funding Guide
American Indian & Alaskan Native Newspapers
  & Periodicals, 1826-1924

American Indian & Alaskan Native Traders Directory
*Anna's Athabaskan Summer
An Annotated Bibliography of American Indian & Eskimo
  Autobiographies
Anthologia Anthropologica: The Native Races of America
Anthropological Papers of University of Alaska
Application of a Theory of Games to the Transitional
  Eskimo Culture
The Archaeology of Cape Nome, Alaska
Arctic Art: Eskimo Ivory
Arctic: Handbook of North American Indians, Vol. 5
Arctic Life: Challenge to Survive
Arctic Memories
Arctic Schoolteacher
Arctic Village
Art & Eskimo Power: The Life & Times of Alaskan
  Howard Rock
Art of the Far North: Inuit Sculpture, Drawing & Printmaking
The Artists Behind the Work
Artists of the Tundra and the Sea
At Home With the Bella Coola Indians
Athabaskan Stories from Anvik
Athabaskan Verb Theme Categories: Ahtna
The Athabaskans: People of the Boreal Forest
Authentic Alaska: Voices of Its Native Writers
Bashful No Longer: An Alaskan Eskimo Ethnohistory,
  1778-1988
Being in Being
Book of the Eskimo
Books on American Indians and Eskimos
Boundaries & Passages: Rule & Ritual in Yup'ik Eskimo
  Oral Tradition
Breaking New Ground for AmericanIndian & Alaska
  Native Youth At Risk:
The Central Eskimo
Cev'armiut Qanemciit Qulirait-Ilu: Eskimo Narratives
  & Tales from Chevak, Alaska
*Chief Stephen's Parky: One Year in the Life of an
  Athapascan Girl
*A Child's Alaska
*Children of the Tlingit
Chills & Fever: Health & Disease in the Early
  History of Alaska
Conflicting Visions in Alaska Education
Contemporary Native American Cultural Issues
A Conversational Dictionary of Kodiak Alutiiq
Craft Manual of Alaskan Eskimo
Craft Manual of Yukon Tlingit
Crossroads Alaska, Native Cultures of Alaska & Siberia
Cultural Persistence (Athapaskan)
Dawn in Arctic Alaska
Dena'ina Legacy K'tl'egh'i Sukdu: The Collected
  Writings of Peter Kalifornsky
Dena'ina Noun Dictionary
Education & Career Opportunities Handbook
English-Eskimo & Eskimo-English Dictionary
English-Eskimo & Eskimo-English Vocabularies
*The Eskimo
The Eskimo About Bering Strait
Eskimo Architecture
*The Eskimo: Arctic
*The Eskimo: Arctic Hunters & Trappers
Eskimo Artists
Eskimo Capitalists: Oil, Politics & Alcohol
Eskimo Chilhood and Interpersonal Relationships
Eskimo Essays: Yup'ik Lives & How We See Them
*An Eskimo Family
*The Eskimo: Inuit & Yupik
Eskimo Life of Yesterday
Eskimo Medicine Man
Eskimo of North Alaska
Eskimo Poems from Canada & Greenland
Eskimo School on the Andreafsky: A Study of
  Effective Bicultural Education
The Eskimo Storyteller: Folktales from Noatak, Alaska
*Eskimos
The Eskimos & Aleuts
Eskimos and Explorers
*Eskimos: The Inuit of the Arctic
The Eskimos of Bering Strait, 1650-1898
Eskimos, Revised
Essays on the Ethnography of the Aleuts
Ethnography of the Tanaina
Ethnohistory in the Arctic: The Bering Strait Eskimo
An Ethnohistory of the Western Aleutians
Ethnological Results of the Point Barrow Expedition
*The Eye of the Needle: Based on a Yup'ik Tale
  Told by Bety Huffman
Fifty Years Below Zero
Give or Take a Century: An Eskimo Chronicle
*Green March Moons
Haa Aani Our Land: Tlingit & Haida Land Rights
Haa Shuka, Our Ancestors; Tlingit Oral Narratives
Haa Tuwunaagu Yis, For Healing Our Spirit: Tlingit Oratory
Haida Syntax
The Han Indians: A Compilation of Ethnographic
  & Historical Data
Handbook of North American Indians: Arctic
Heroes & Heroines/Tlingit & Haida Legend
*The Hunter & the Ravens
History, Ethnology, & Anthropology of the Aleut
Hunters of the Northern Ice
I Am Eskimo: Aknik My Name

Ice Window: Letters from a Bering Strait Village 1898-1902
The Immigrant Experience
In Honor of Eyak: The Art of Anna Nelson Harry
*The Incredible Eskimo
Indian Baskets of the Pacific Northwest & Alaska
Indian, Eskimo & Aleut Basketry of Alaska
Indian & Eskimo Artifacts of North America
The Indians of the Subarctic: A Critical Bibliography
Ingalik Material Culture
Inhabited Wilderness: Indians, Eskimos & National
  Parks in Alaska
Inua: Spirit World of the Bering Sea Eskimo
*Inuit
Inuit Artists Print Workbook
Inuit Glimpses of an Arctic Past
The Inuit Life As It Was
Inuit: The North in Transition
The Inuit Print, L'Estampe Inuit
Inuit Women Artists
Inuit Youth
Inupiallu Tannillu Uqalunisa Ilanich: Abridged
  Inupiaq & Engish Dictionary
Island Between
The Inupiaq Eskimo Nations of Northwest Alaska
The Inupiaq & Arctic Alaska
The Inventive Mind: Portraits of Rural Alaska Teachers
Journey to Alaska in 1868
Kahtnuht'ana Qenaga: The Kenai People's Language
Kusiq: An Eskimo Life History from the Arctic Coast of Alaska
Languages & the Schools: Athabaskan, Inupiaq,
  and Central Yup'ik
Last Light Breaking: Living Among Alaska's Inupiat Eskimos
Letters to Howard: An Interpretation of the Alaska
  Native Land Claims
The Life I've Been Living
Life With the Eskimo
Life Woven With Stone
*Living With the Eskimos
Looking Both Ways: Heritage & Identity of the Alutiiq People
Lure of the Arctic
Making History: Alutiiq/Sugpiaq Life on the Alaska Peninsula
Man's Knife Among the Eskimo
Memory Eternal: Tlingit Culture & Russian Orthodox
  Christianity through Two Centuries
The Movies Begin: Making Movies in New Jersey, 1887-1930
My Grandfather's House: Tlingit Songs of Death & Sorrow
Native American Directory: Alaska, Canada,, U.S.
Native American Women: A Contextual Bibliography
The Native Americans
Native Cultures of Alaska: Traditions Through Time
The Native People of Alaska
Native Peoples & Languages of Alaska (Map)
Neets'aii Gwiindaii: Living in the Chandalar Country
The Nelson Island Eskimo: Social Structure &
  Ritual Distribution
Never in Anger: Portrait of an Eskimo Family
Nine Visits to the Mythworld: Ghandl of the Qayahl Llaanas
North Alaska Chronicle: Notes from the End of Time
North Alaskan Eskimos
North Pole Legacy: Black, White & Eskimo
North Slope Inupiaq Dialogues
Northern Athabascan Survival
Northern Athapaskan Art
The Northern Copper Inuit: A History
Northern Tales: Traditional Stories of Eskimo & \
  Indian Peoples
Once Upon an Eskimo Time: A Year of Eskimo's Life
  Before the White Man Came
Ode Setl'oghwnh Da': Long After I Am Gone
Our Stories, Our Lives
Our Voices: Native Stories of Alaska & the Yukon
Overland to Stravation Cove; With the Inuit In Search
  of Franklin, 1878-80
People of the Twilight
Phonological Issues in North Alaskan Inupiaq
Pioneer Missionary to the Bering Strait Eskimos
*Place for Winter: Paul Tiulana's Story
A Practical Grammar of the St. Lawrence Island:
  Siberian Yup'ik Eskimo Language
Proto-Athabaskan Verb Stem Variation: Part One, Phonology
Qawiaraq Inupiaq Literacy Manual
Quliaqtuat Mumiaksrat Ilisaqtuanun Savaaksrat
The Ramiluk Stories: Adventures of an Eskimo Family
  in the Prehistoric Arctic
Raven's Journey: The World of Alaska's Native People
Reading Comprehension and Language Proficiency
  Among Eskimo Children
Reflections on the Alaska Native Experience:
  Selected Articles & Speeches by Roy M. Huhndorf
Bill Reid & Beyond: Expanding on Modern Native Art
Reserve Memories: The Power of the Past in a
  Chilcotin Community
The Road to Nunavut: The Progress of the Eastern
  Arctic Inuit Since the Second World War
The Roots of Ticasuk: An Eskimo Woman's Family Story
*Seal for a Pal
Secrets of Eskimo Skin Sewing
Shadow of the Hunter: Stories of Eskimo Life
Shadows on the Poyukuk: An Alaskan Native's Life
  Along the River
Shamans & Kushtakas
Shandaa: In My Lifetime
Shem Pete's Alaska

APACHE INDIANS

ARAPAHO
(See CHEYENNE & ARAPAHO)

ARCHITECTURE-DWELLINGS

ARMS & ARMOR

ART

Between Two Cultures: Kiowa Art From Fort Marion
Beyond Tradition: Contemporary Indian Art & Its Evolution
Bibliography of Articles and Papers on North American
   Indian Art
Biographical Directory of Native American Painters
Black Sand: Prehistory in Northern Arizona
Blackfeet: Their Art & Culture
The Blackfeet: Artists of the Northern Plains
Bo'Jou, Neejee: Profiles of Canadian Indian Art
T.C. Cannon: He Stood in the Sun
Canyon de Chelly: Its People & Rock Art
Carving the Native American Face
Changing Woman: The Life & Art of Helen Hardin
Chiefly Feasts: The Enduring Kwakiutl Potlatch
Chinle to Taos
Circles of the World: Traditional Art of the Plains Indians
Collecting Authentic Indian Arts & Crafts
Collecting Native America, 1870-1960
Collecting the West: The C.R. Smith Collection of
   Western American Art
Collective Willeto: The Visionary Carvings of a Navajo Artist
The Complete How-To Book of Indian Craft
Consumer's Guide to Southwestern Indian Arts & Crafts
Contemporary Artists and Craftsmen of the Eastern Band
   of Cherokee Indians
Contemporary Indian Art From the Chester & Davida Herwitz
   Family Collection
Converging Cultures: Ar & Identity in Spanish America
Council of the Rainmakers Address Book
The Covenant Chain: Indian Ceremonial & Trade Silver
Crow Indian Art
Dark Lady Dreaming
Decorative Art of the Southwestern Indians
Patrick Des Jarlait: Conversations With a
   Native American Artist
Directory of Native American Performing Artists
Discovered Lands, Invented Pasts: Transforming
   Visions of the American West
Dreaming the Dawn: Conversations with Native
   Artists & Activists
Early White Influence Upon Plains Indian Painting:
   George Catlin & Carl Bodmer Among the Mandans
The Early Years of Native American Art History:
   The Politics & Scholarship of Collecting
The Elders
The Elkus Collection: Southwestern Indian Art
Enduring Traditions: Art of the Navajo
Enduring Visions: One Thousand Years of
   Southwestern Indian Art
Esthetic Recognition of Ancient Amerindian Art
Fetishes and Carvings of the Southwest
First American Art: Charles & Valerie Diker Collection
The Flag in American Indian Art
The Forgotten Artist: Indians of Anza-Borrego
   & Their Rock Art
The Fourth Biennial Native American Fine Arts Invitational,
   Oct. 21,1989- Spring 1990
From the Land of the Totem Poles: The Northwest Coast
Indian Art Collection at the American Museum of
   Natural History
Full-Color American Indian Designs for Needlepoint Rugs
A Gathering of Spirit: Writing and Art by North American
   Indian Women
The Gift of American Native Paintings From the Collection
   of Edgar William & Bernice Chrysler Garbisch
Grand Endeavors of American Indian Photography
The Great Southwest of the Fred Harvey Company
   & the Santa Fe Railway
Guide to the Culin Archival Collection
Haida Art
Haida Monumental Art
Haida: Their Art & Culture
Harmony by Hand: Art of the Southwest Indians
Hopi Kachinas Drawn by Native Artists
Hopis, Tewas, and the American Road
I Stand in the Center of the Good
An Illustrated History of the Arts in South Dakota
Imagery & Creativity
Images of a Vanished Life: Plains Indian Drawings From
   the Collection of the Pennsylvania Academy of Fine Arts
In Search of the Wild Indian
In the Shadow of the Sun: Contemporary Canadian
   Indian & Inuit Art
In the Spirit of Mother Earth: Nature in Native American Art
Indian Art & Culture
Indian Art In the Ashmolean Museum
Indian Art of Ancient Florida
Indian Art of the U.S.
Indian Art Traditions of the Northwest Coast
Indian Artists at Work
*Indian Crafts
Indian Designs
*Indian Designs Stained Glass Coloring Book
Indian & Eskimo Artifacts of North America
Indian Miniature Paintings & Drawings:
   The Cleveland Museum of Art
Indian Rawhide: and American Folk Art
Indian Rock Art in Wyoming
Indan Rock Art of the Columbia Plateau
Indian Rock Art of the Southwest
Indian Rock Carvings
Indian Sandpainting of the Southwest
Indiancraft

Indians & Art History: A Pictorial Survey
Indians & A Changing Frontier: The Art of George Winter
*Indians of the Great Plains Stencils
Indigenous Aesthetics" Native Art, Media, and Identity
The Institute of American Indian Arts, Alumni Exhibition
Introduction to American Indian Art
Inuit Artists Print Workbook
Inventing the Southwest
Fred Kabotie: Hopi Indian Artist
Kiowa Memories: Images From Indian Territory, 1880
Kiva Art of the Anasazi
Korczak: Storyteller in Stone
Lake Pertha and the Lost Murals of Chiapas
The Legacy: Tradition & Innovation in Northwest Coast
   Indian Art
Lewis & Clark Territory: Contemporary Artists Revisit Place,
   Race, & Memory
Life & Art of the North American Indian
Life Under the Sun
*Little Indian Girl Paperdolls
Looking at Indian Art of the Northwest Coast
Looking High & Low: Art & Cultural Identity
Lost Copper
Lost & Found Traditions: Native American Art, 1965-1985
Charles F. Lummis: The Centenial Exhibition
Magic Images: Contemporary Native American Art
Makers & Markets: The Wright Collection of
   Twentieth-Century Native American Art
Ray Manley's Collecting Southwestern Indian Arts & Crafts
The Many Faces of Mata Ortiz
Many Smokes, Many Moons: A Chronology of American
Indian History Through Indian Art
Masterworks From the Heard Museum
Mimbres Indian Treasure: In the Land of Baca
Miniature Arts of the Southwest
Modern by Tradition: American Indian Painting
   in the Studio Style
Native America: Arts, Traditions & Celebrations
Native America Collected: The Culture of an Art World
Native American Art
The Native American Art Look Book
Native American Art Masterpieces
Native American Art & the New York Avant-Garde
Native American Art at Philbrook
Native American Artisans Survey
Native American Beadwork
Native American Identities: From Stereotype to
   Archetype in Art & Literature
The Native American Indian Artist Directory
Native American Painted Buffalo Hides
Native American Picture Books of Change:
   The Art of Historic Children's Editions
Native American Style
Native Americans: Five Centuries of Changing Images
*Native Artists of North America
Native Arts Network
Native Arts of the Columbia Plateau
Native Arts of North America
The Native Arts of North America, Africa,
   & the South Pacific: An Introduction
Native Faces: Indian Cultures in American Art From
   the Collection of the Los Angeles Athletic Club & the
   Southwest Museum
Native North American Art History - Selected Readings
Native Universe: Voices of Indian America
Native Visions: Evolution in Northwest Coast Art from
   the 18th through the 20th Century
Navaho Art and Culture
Navajo Art, History and Culture
Navajo Art of Sandpainting
Navajo Arts & Crafts
Navajo Beadwork
Navajo Folk Art: The People Speak
Navajo Pictorial Weaving 1800-1950
Navajo & Pueblo Silversmiths
Navajo Sandpainting Art
Navajo Sandpainting from Religious Act to Commercial Art
Navajo Weavers & Silversmiths
New Horizons in American Indian Art
North American Indian Art
North American Indian Arts: Prices & Auctions
North American Indian Beadwork
North American Indian Beadwork Patterns
North American Indian Borders
*North American Indian Crafts
North American Indian Designs
261 North American Indian Designs
North American Indian Designs for Artists & Craftspeople
North American Indian Motifs
North American Indian Portfolios from the
   Library of Congress
Northern Athapaskan Art: A Beadwork Tradition
Northwest Coast Indian Art
*The Northwest Coast Indian Art Series
Northwest Coast Indian Designs
Northwest Coast Native & Native Style Art
Northwest Indian Designs
Notebook on Art, History and Culture
Nudes & Foods, Volume II
Objects of Bright Pride: Northwest Coast Indian Art
   From the Museum of Natural History
Objects of Myth & Memory
The Ojibway Dream

One Hundred Years of Native American Arts:
   Six Washington Cultures
One Thousand Years of Southwestern Indian Art
The Owl in Monument Canyon
Paintbrushes & Pistols: How Taos Artists Sold the West
Painting the Dream
Painting of Little Crow
Partial Recall: Photographs of Native North Americans
Path Breakers: The Eiteljorg Fellowship for
   Native American Fine Art 2003
Patterns of Life, Patterns of Art: The Rahr Collection
   of Native American Art
The People Speak: Navajo Folk Art
A Persistent Vision: Art of the Reservation Days
Picture-Writing of the American Indians
Plains Indian Designs
Plains Indian & Mountain Man Arts & Crafts I & II
Plains Indian Painting: A Description of
   Aboriginal American Art
*Plains Indians Punch-Out Panorama
Pleasing the Spirits
Portfolio II
Preserving Traditional Arts: A Toolkit for
   Native American Communities
Primitive Arts & Crafts
Privileging the Past: Reconstructing History in
   Northwest Coast Art
Pueblo Artists: Portraits
Pueblo Designs: 176 Illustrations of the Rain Bird
Quiet Triumph: Forty Years With the Indian Arts Fund
Bill Reid & Beyond: Expanding on Modern Native Art
Remington & Russell: The Sid Richardson Collection
Ritual in Pueblo Art: Hopi Life In Hopi Painting
Robert Davidson: Eagle of the Dawn
Robes of Splendor
Rock Art of the American Indian
Sacred Circles: Two Thousand Years of
   North American Indian Art
Shared Visions: Native American Painters and Sculptors
   in the Twentieth Century
Sharing a Heritage: American Indian Arts
Shawnee Home Life: The Paintings of Ernest Spybuck
Signs From the Ancestors: Zuni Cultural Symbolism
   & Perceptions of Rock Art
Signs of Life: Rock Art of the Upper Rio Grande
Silver Horn: Master Illustrator of the Kiowas
Small Spirits: Native American Dolls
Smoky-Top: The Art and Times of Willie Seaweed
A Song to the Creator: Traditional Art of
   Native American Women of the Plateau
Songs of the Spirit: Sculpture by Doug Hyde
Southeastern Woodland Indian Designs
Southern Arizona Folk Arts
Southwest Indian Arts & Crafts
Southwest Indian Craft Arts
Southwest Indian Designs
Southwest Indian Painting: A Changing Art
Southwest Indian Silver from the Doneghy Collection
*Southwest Indians Coloring Book
Southwestern Arts & Crafts Projects
Southwestern Indian Arts & Crafts
Southwest Indian Design Stained Glass Coloring Book
Southwestern Indian Designs
Spirit & Ancestor: A Century of Northwest Coast Indian
   Art at the Burke Museum
Spirit in the Stone
The Spirit of Native America
Spirits in the Art
The State of Sequoyah
Summoning the Gods: Sandpainting of the
   Native American Southwest
Sun Circles and Human Hands: The Southeastern Indians,
   Art and Industries
Survival: Life and Art of the Alaskan Eskimo
The Sweet Grass Lives On: Fifty Contemporary
   North American Indian Artists
Symbol and Substance in American Indian Art
Taos Artists & Their Patrons, 1898-1950
Taos Society of Artists
Tapestries in Sand
The Techniques of Porcupine Quill Decoration
   Among the Indians of North America
This Path We Travel: Celebrations of Contemporary
   Native American Creativity
A Time of Visions: Interviews with Native American Artists
Trading Identities
Trading Post Guidebook
*Traditional Crafts from Native North America
Treasures of the Hopi
Treasures of the Navajo
Treasures of the Zuni
A Treasury of of Our Western Heritage: The Favell
   Museum of Western Art & Indian Artifacts
Trends in Pueblo Pottery in the Rio Grande & Little Colorado
   Cultural Areas From the 16th to 19th Century
The Trickster Shift: Humour & Irony in
   Contemporary Native Art
Tsimshian Indians and Their Arts
Twelve Classics
Under the Palace Portal: Native American Artists in Santa Fe
Visions of the North: Native Arts of the Northwest Coast
Visions & Voices: Native American Painting
We're Still Here: Art of Indian New England

The Weaver's Pathway: A Clarification of the "Spirit Trail"
in Navajo Weaving
The West: A Treasuryt of Art & Literature
The West As America
When the Rainbow Touches Down
White Influence Upon Plains Indian Painting: George Catlin
& Carl Bodmer Among the Mandan, 1832-34
*Wild Brothers of the Indians: As Pictured by the
Ancient Americans
The World of Flower Blue: Pop Chalee: An Artistic Biography
The Year of the Hopi

ARTIFACTS

Ancient Art of Ohio
Arrowheads & Spear Points of the Prehistoric Southeast
Catlinite Pipes
Collecting Indian Knives: Identification & Values
Collecting North AmericanIndian Knives
Collector's Guide to Indian Pipes
Diving for Northwest Relics
Dolls & Toys of Native America
Field Guide to the Flint Arrowheads & Knives of the
North American Indian
First Hunters - Ohio's Paleo-Indian Artifacts
Guide to Indian Artifacts of the Northwest
Guide to Palaeo-Indian Artifacts of North America
Heartbags & Hand Shakes: The Story of th Cook Collection
How to Collect North American Indian Artifacts
Indian Arrowheads - Identification & Price Guide
Indian Artifacts
Indian Artifacts of the East & South: An ID Guide
Indian Artifacts of the Midwest
Indian Axes & Related Stone Artifacts
Indian & Eskimo Artifacts of North America
Indian Relics of Northeast Arkansas & Southeast Missouri
Indians & Artifacts in the Southeast
North American Indian Artifacts: A Collector's
Identification & Value Guide
North American Indian Points
Ornamental & Ceremonial Artifacts
Stone Age Spear & Arrow Points of the
Midcontinental & Eastern U.S.
Stone Artifacts of Texas Indians
A Victorian Ear in the Arctic
Who's Who in Indian Relics

BASKETRY

Aboriginal American Indian Basketry
Aboriginal Indian Basketry
American Indian Basketry
American Indian Baskets: 1,200 Artist Biographies
American Indian Utensils: How to Make Baskets,
Pottery & Woodenware With Natural Materials
Apache Indian Baskets
The Art of the Indian Basket in North America
The Art of Native American Basketry: A Living Legacy
The Art & Style of Western Indian Basketry
Basketry of the Papago & Pima Indians
Basketry of the San Carlos Apache Indians
Baskets & Basketmakers in Southern Appalachia
Basket Weavers for the California Curio Trade
Basketry & Cordage from Hesquiat Harbour
Columbia River Basketry
The Fine Art of California Indian Basketry
The Heritage of Klickitat Basketry: A History & Art Preserved
Hopi Basket Weaving: Artistry in Natural Fibers
Indian Basket Weaving
Indian Basketmakers
Indian Basketmakers of California & the Great Basin
Indian Basketmakers of the Southwest
Indian Basketry
Indian Basketry & How to Make Baskets
Indian Baskets
Indian Baskets & Curios
Indian Baskets of the Pacific Northwest & Alaska
Indian Baskets of the Southwest
Indian, Eskimo & Aleut Basketry of Alaska
Indian Weaving, Knitting and Basketry of the Northwest
A Key Into the Language of Woodsplint Baskets
Native American Basketry: An Annotated Bibliography
Native Basketry of Western North America
North American Indian Designs for Artists and Craftspeople
Our Lives in Our Hands: Micmac Indian Basketmakers
The Pima and His Basket
Pima Indian Basketry
Plants Used in Basketry by the California Indians
Pomo Basketmaking - A Supreme Art for the Weaver
Pomo Indian Basketry
Remember Your Relations
Southwestern Indian Baskets
Traditions in Transition: Contemporary Basket Weaving
of the Southwestern Indians
Weavers of Tradition and Beauty: Basketmakers
of the Great Basin
Weaving a California Tradition: A Native American
Basketmaker
Weaving New Worlds: Southeastern Cherokee
Women & Their Basketry
Weaving of the Southwest
Western Indian Basketry
Woven Worlds: Basketry from the Clark Field Collection

BIBLIOGRAPHIES

Against Borders: Promoting Books for a Multicultural World
Alaska Natives: A Guide to Current Reference Sources
in the Rasmuson Library
The American Indian in Graduate Studies: A Bibliography
of Theses and Dissertations
American Indian Literatures: An Introduction,
Bibliographic Review, and Selected Bibliography
American Indian Reference Books for Children
& Young Adults
The American Indian in Short Fiction:
An Annotated Bibliography
American Indian: Language and Literature
American Indian Stereotypes in the World of Children:
A Reader & Bibliography
American Indian Women: A Guide to Research
American Indians: A Select Catalog of National Archives
Microfilm Publications
The American West in the Twentieth Century: A Bibliography
An Annotated Bibliography of American Indian and
Eskimo Autobiographies
Annotated Bibliography of American Indian Paintings
The Apaches: A Critical Bibliography
A Bibliographical Guide to the History of Indian-White
Relations in the U.S.
Bibliography of Articles & Papers on
North American Indian Art
Bibliography of the Blackfoot
Bibliography of the Catawba
Bibliography of the Chickasaw
Bibliography of Contemporary North American Indians
Bibliography of the Indians of San Diego County
Bibliography of Language Arts Materials for
Native North Americans
Bibliography of the Languages of Native California
Bibliography of Native North Americans on Disc - CD-ROM
Bibliography of North American Indian Mental Health
Bibliography of the Osage
Bibliography of the Sioux
Biobibliography of Native American Writers, 1772-1925
Bookman's Guide to the Indians of the Americas
Books on American Indians and Eskimos
Books Without Bias: Through Indian Eyes
Canadian Indian Policy: A Critical Bibliography
The Cheyennes, Ma heo o's People: A Critical Bibliography
Chippewa & Dakota Indians: A Subject Catalog
The Delawares: A Critical Bibliography
Dictionary Catalog of the Edward E. Ayer Collection
of Americana & American Indians
Dine Bibliography to the 1990s
The Emigrant Indians of Kansas: A Critical Bibliography
Ethnographic Bibliography of North America
The Five Civilized Tribes: A Bibliography
From Savage to Nobleman: Images of
Native Americans in Film
Guide to Cherokee Documents in Foreign Archives
Guide to Cherokee Documents in the Northeastern U.S.
Guide to the 400 Best Children's & Adult's Multicultural
Books of People of Native American Descent
Guide to Records in the National Archives Relating to
American Indians
Health and Diseases of American Indians North of Mexico:
A Bibliography, 1800-1969
Health of Native People of North America
History & Annotated Bibliography of American
Religious Periodicals & Newspapers
Hopi Bibliography: Comprehensive and Annotated
In Pursuit of the Past: An Anthropological & Bibliographic
Guide to Maryland & Delaware
Index to Literature on the American Indian
Indian Land Tenure: Bibliographical Essays
Indian Slavery, Labor, Evangelization, and Captivity
in the Americas
Indian-White Relations in the U.S.
Indians of California: A Critical Bibliography
Indians of the Great Basin: A Critical Bibliography
The Indians of Maine and the Atlantic Provinces:
A Bibliographic Guide
The Indians of New England: A Critical Bibliography
Indians of North & South America: Bibliography
The Indians of the Subarctic: A Critical Bibliography
The Indians of Texas: An Annotated Research Bibliography
Indigenous Languages of the Americas
Iroquois Indians: A Documentary History-
Guide to the Microfilm Collection
Kinsmen Through Time: An Annotated Bibliography
of Potawatomi History
Languages of the Aboriginal Southeast:
An Annotated Bibliography
Literature By and About the American Indian:
An Annotated Bibliography
Narrative Chance: Postmodern Discourse on
Native American Indian Literatures
Narratives of North American Indian Captivity:
A Selective Bibliography
Native American Archives: An Introduction
Native American Historical Demography:
A Critical Bibliography
The Native American in American Literature:
A Selectively Annotated Bibliography
The Native American in Long Fiction
Native American Women: A Contextual Bibliography

Native Americans: An Annotated Bibliography
Native Americans in Fiction
Native Americans: North America—
An Annotated Bibliography
Native Americans of the Northwest Coast:
A Critical Bibliography
Native Americans: Social, Economic & Political Aspects -
A Bibliography
Native Canadian Anthropology & History:
A Selected Bibliography
Native North Americans in Doctoral Dissertations,
1971-1975: A Classified & Indexed Research Bibliography
Newberry Library/Center for the History of the
American Indian Bibliographical Series
North American Indian Language Materials, 1890-1965
Office of Indian Affairs, 1824-1880: Historical Sketches
Ojibwas: A Critical Bibliography
Pawnees: A Critical Bibliography
Recovering the Word: Essays on Native American Literature
Selected Americana from Sabin's Dictionary of Books
Relating to America from Its Discovery to the Present Time
Seneca & Tuscarora Indians: An Annotated Bibliography
Subarctic Athapascans: A Selected, Annotated Bibliography
Traditional Literatures of the American Indians:
Texts and Interpretations
Tulapai to Tokay: A Bibliography of Alcohol Use and
Abuse Among Native Americans of North America
The Upstream People: An Annotated Research
Bibliography of the Omaha Tribe
Winged Words: American Indian Writers Speak
Writings in Indian History, 1985-1990
Yakima, Palouse, Cayuse, Umatilla, Walla Walla,
and Wanapum Indians: An Historical Bibliography
The Yakimas: A Critical Bibliography

BIOGRAPHIES

American Indian, 1492-1976: A Chronology & Fact Book
American Indian Baskets: 1,200 Artist Biographies
American Indian Intellectuals of the 19th & 20th Century
American Indian Jewelry: 1,200 Artist Biographies
American Indian Textiles: 2,000 Artist Biographies
American Indian Leaders: Studies in Diversity
American Indian Lives series
American Indian Painters: A Biographical Directory
*American Indian Stories
American Indian Textiles: 2,000 Artist Biographies
American Puritanism & the Defense of Mourning:
Mary White Rowlandson's Captivity Narrative
An Annotated Bibliography of American Indian &
Eskimo Autobiographies
Apache Agent: The Story of John P. Clum
Art of the Native American Flute - R. Carlos Nakai
Autobiography of a Kiowa Apache Indian-Jim Whitewolf
Autobiography of Red Cloud
The Autobiography of a Winnebago Indian
*Dennis Banks: Native American Activist
Bartley Milam: Principal Chief of the Cherokee Nation
Being & Becoming Indian: Biographical Studies of
North American Frontiers
Between Worlds
Beyond the Hundredth Meridian
Big Bear: The End of Freedom
Bighorse the Warrior
Biobibliography of Native American Writers, 1772-1924:
A Supplement
Biographical Dictionary of Indians of the Americas
Biographical & Historical Index of American Indian &
Persons Involved in Indian Affairs
Black Elk & Flaming Rainbow
Black Elk: Holy Man of the Oglala
Black Elk Lives
*Black Elk: A Man With Vision
Black Elk: The Sacred Ways of a Lakota
Black Elk Speaks
Black Elk's Religion
Black Elk's World (Website)
The Black Hawk War, Including a Review
of Black Hawk's Life
*Blue Jacket: War Chief of the Shawnees
Blue Jacket: Warrior of the Shawnees
Brave Are My People: Indian Heroes Not Forgotten
Ben Nighthorse Campbell
Borderlander: The Life of James Kirker, 1793-1852
Henry Boucha - Star of the North
Joseph Brant, 1743-1807: A Man of Two Worlds
Joseph Brant, Iroquois Ally of the British
Molly Brant: A Legacy of Her Own
Built Like a Bear
T.C. Cannon: He Stood in the Sun
Kit Carson & His Three Wives: A Family History
Kit Carson & the Indians
Chainbreaker: The Revolutionary War Memoirs
of Governor Blacksnake
*Charles Eastman: Physician, Reformer, and
Native American Leader
Chief Cornplanter (Gy-Ant-Wa-Kia) of the Senecas
Chief Joseph: Guardian of the Nez Perce
*Chief Joseph of the Nez Perce Indians: Champion of Liberty
*Chief Joseph's Own Story As Told by Chief Joseph in 1879
Chief Junaluska of the Cherokee Indian Nation
Chief Left Hand: Southern Arapaho
*Chief Plenty Coups: Life of the Crow Indian Chief

Chief Pocatello, the "White Plume"
Chief Sarah: Sarah Winnemucca's Fight for Indian Rights
Chief Seattle's Unanswered Challenge
Chief Washakie
William Clark: Jeffersonian Man on the Frontier
Cochise: Chiricahua Apache Chief
"Come, Blackrobe" De Smet & the Indian Tragedy
Contemporary Native American Authors: A Biographical Dictionary
Converting the West: A Biography of Narcissa Whitman
Corbett Mack: The Life of a Northern Paiute
Cougar Woman
Coyote Woman
Crashing Thunder: The Autobiography of an American Indian
Crazy Horse
*Crazy Horse
Crazy Horse: Sacred Warrior of the Sioux
The Custer Story: Life & Intimate Letters of General George A. Custer & His Wife Elizabeth
*The Defenders
Dakota Cross-Bearer: The Life & World of a Native American Bishop
Angie Debo: Pioneering Historian
Delfina Cuero: Her Autobiography
Dr. John McLoughlin, Master of Fort Vancouver, Father of Oregon
*The Double Life of Pocahontas
Dreamer-Prophets of the Columbia Plateau: Smohalla & Skolaskin
The Education of Little Tree
Edward Sheriff Curtis: Visions of a Vanishing Race
Encyclopedia of Frontier Biography
Encyclopedia of Native American Biography
Exploration Into World Cultures
*Extraordinary American Indians
*Famous American Indian Leaders
Famous Indian Chiefs
Famous Indians of Northwest Nebraska
Father Francis M. Craft, Missionary to the Sioux
Father Peter John De Smet: Jesuit in the West
Fig Tree John: An Indian in Fact & Fiction
Fighting Tuscarora: The Autobiography of Chief Clanton Richard
First to Fight
Fools Crow
Fools Crow: Wisdom & Power
From the Deep Woods to Civilization
Frontier Diplomats: Alexander Culbertson & Natoyist-Siksina' Among the Blackfeet
George Washington Grayson & the Creek Nation, 1853-1920
Geronimo & the End of the Apache Wars
Geronimo: Last Renegade of the Apache
Goodbird the Indian: His Story
*The Great Chiefs
The Great Chiefs
*Great Indian Chiefs
*Great Indians of California
*Great Native Americans Coloring Book
Great North American Indians
Guests Never Leave Hungry: The Autobiography of James Sewid, a Kwakiutl Indian
Handbook of the American Frontier: Four Centuries of Indian-White Relationships
LaDonna Harris: A Comanche Life
Helen Hunt Jackson & Her Indian Reform Legacy
History of the Native Americans
Hopi-Tewa Pottery: 500 Artist Biographies
How Can One Sell the Air? Chief Seattle's Vision
I Have Come to Step Over Your Soul: A True Narrative of Murder and Indian Justice
I Tell You Now: Autobiographical Essays by Native American Writers
I Will Die an Indian
I'll Go and Do More: Annie Dodge Wauneka, a Navajo Leader & Activist
In Search of the Wild Indian
Indeh: An Apache Odyssey
Indian Biography: North American Natives Distinguished as Orators, Warriors, Statesmen
*Indian Boyhood
*Indian Chiefs
*Indian Heroes & Great Chieftains
An Indian In White America
Indian Lives: Essays on 19th & 20th Century Native American Leaders
Indian Man: A Biography of James Mooney
Indian Women Chiefs
Indians in Overalls
Interior Landscapes: Autobiographical Myths & Metaphors
Ishi in Three Centuries
Ishi in Two Worlds: A Biography of of the Last Wild Indian in North America
Ishi's Journey from the Center to the Edge of the World
*Ishi: The Last of His People
Ishi, the Last Yahi: A Documentary History
Helen Hunt Jackson & Her Indian Reform Legacy
William Jackson, Indian Scout
Mary Jemison: White Woman of the Seneca
The Journey of Navajo Oshley: An Autobiography and Life History
Juh, An Incredible Indian
King of the Delawares: Teedyuscung, 1700-1763
Kitchi-Gami: Life Among the Lake Superior Ojibway

Korczak: Storyteller in Stone
*Susette La Flesche: Advocate for Native American Rights
Lame Deer: Seeker of Visions
*The Last Warrior
The Last Warrior: Peter MacDonald & the Navajo Nation
Left Handed, Son of Old Man Hat: A Navajo Autobiography
Legends of Our Times: Native Cowboy Life
Leschi, Last Chief of the Nisquallies
The Last Contrary: The Story of Wesley Whiteman (Black Bear)
The Last Days of Sitting Bull
Life Among the Indians
Life Among the Paiutes: Their Wrongs and Claims
Life, Letters & Speeches
Life Lived Like a Story: Life Stories of Three Yukon Native Elders
Life of Black Hawk
The Life and Times of Little Turtle: First Sagamore of the Wabash
Life and Times of David Zeisberger
Like A Brother: Greenville Goodwin's Apache Years, 1928-1939
A Little Bit of Wisdom" Conversations With a Nez Perce Elder
Long Lance: The True Story of an Imposter
Mad Bear
Madam Dorian
Madonna Swan: A Lakota Woman's Story
Mankiller: A Chief and Her People
*Wilma P. Mankiller: Chief of the Cherokee
*Maria Martinez: Pueblo Potter
Viola Martinez, California Paiute: Living in Two Worlds
Marietta Wetherill: Life With the Navajos in Chaco Canyon
Me & Mine: The Life Story of Helen Sekaquaptewa
*Me Run Fast Good: Biographies of Tewanima (Hopi), Carlos Montezuma (Apache), and John Horse (Seminole)
Medicine Women, Curanderas & Women Doctors
Medicine Trail: The Life & Lessons of Gladys Tantaquidgeon
Merejildo Grijalva, Apache Captive, Army Scout
Minister to the Cherokees: A Civil War Autobiography
Mixed Bloods & Tribal Dissolution: Charles Curtis & the Quest for Indian Identity
Molly Molasses & Me: A Collection of Living Adventures
Molly Spotted Elk
N. Scott Momaday
The Mongrel: A Story of Logan Fontenelle of the Omaha Indians
Montana's Indians: Yesterday & Today
Moon Dash Warrior
Mary Moses' Statement
Mourning Dove: A Salishan Autobiography
*Mary Musgrave: Georgia Indian Princess
My Indian Boyhood (Chief Luther Standing Bear)
My Life As An Indian
My People the Sioux
Mystery of Sacajawea: Indian Girl with Lewis & Clark
The Names
Narrative of the Life of Mrs. Mary Jemison
Narrative of William Biggs
*Native American Biographies
*Native American Doctor: The Story of Susan LaFlesche Picotte
*Native American Leaders of the Wild West
Native American Portraits: 1862-1918
Native Heart: An American Indian Odyssey
Navajo Blessingway Singer: The Autobiography of Frank Mitchell, 1881-1967
Navajo Trader: Essays on a Region & Its Literature
Navajo Woman of the Desert
New Warriors: Native American Leaders Since 1900
North American Indian Icons
North American Indian Lives
North American Indians of Achievement Series
Walter Northway
Odyssey of Chief Standing Buffalo
Ohiyesa: Charles Eastman, Santee Sioux
Ojibwa Warrior: Dennis Banks & the Rise of the American Indian Movement
Old Father's Long Journey
Oliver La Farge and the American Indian: A Biography
On Our Own Ground: The Complete Writings of William Apess, a Pequot
On Time for Disaster: The Rescue of Custer's Command
The Ordeal of Running Standard
Ouray-Chief of the Utes
Louis Owens: Literary Reflections on His Life & Work
Painting the Dream: The Visionary Art of Navajo Painter David Chethlahe Paladin
Personal Narrative of James O. Pattie
Pedro Pino: Governor of Zuni Pueblo, 1830-1878
Plenty-Coups: Chief of the Crows
Pocahontas
*Pocahontas Coloring Book
*Pocahontas: Daughter of a Chief
*Pocahontas, Girl of Jamestown
Pocahontas: Powhattan Peacemaker
*Pontiac: Chief of the Ottawas
Alex Posey: Creek Poet, Journalist & Humorist
Power of a Navajo: Carl Gorman: The Man and His Life
Pretty Shield, Medicine Woman of the Crows
The Price of a Gift: A Lakota Healer's Story
Pueblo Indian Pottery: 750 Artist Biographies
Quanah: A Pictorial History of the Last Comanche Chief

The Real Rosebud: The Triumph of a Lakota Woman
Red Cloud: Photographs of a Lakota Chief
Red Cloud: Warrior Statesman of the lakota Sioux
Red Crow, Warrior Chief
Red-headed Renegade—Chief Benge of the Cherokee Nation
Red Jacket: Iroquois Diplomat & Orator
Red Jacket: Seneca Chief
John Rollin Ridge: His Life & Works
*Will Rogers
*Will Rogers: American Humorist
Rock, Ghost, Willow, Deer: A Story of Survival
Roots of Survival
Esther Ross, Stillaguamish Champion
John Ross: Cherokee Chief
Ruxton of the Rockies
*Sacagawea
*Sacajawea—Native American Heroine
*Sacajawea, Wilderness Guide
Sacred Fireplace: Life & Teachings of a Lakota Medicine Man
Saga of Chief Joseph
Sagwitch: Shoshone Chieftain, Mormon Elder, 1822-1887
Sanapia: Comanche Medicine Woman
Sequoyah
*Sequoyah
Sequoyah & the Cherokee Alphabet
Sequoyah - Computerized Syllabary Learning Program - DOS
*Sequoyah: Father of the Cherokee Alphabet
*Sequoyah & His Miracle
The Shawnee Prophet
Silko: Writing Storyteller & Medicine Woman
Silver Horn: Master Illustrator of the Kiowas
Singing an Indian Song
Singing the Songs of My Ancestors: The Life & Music of Helma Swan, Makah Elder
*Sitting Bull, Warrior of the Sioux
Reuben Snake: Your Humble Serpent
Sorrow In Our Heart: The Life of Tecumseh
Southern Pueblo Pottery: 2,000 Artist Biographies
Standing Flower: The Life of Irving Pabanale, an Arizona Tewa Indian
*The Story of Geronimo
A Supplement to a Guide to Manuscripts Relating to the American Indian in the Library of the American Philosophical Society
Tall Woman: The Life Story of Rose Mitchell, A Navajo Woman @ 1874-1977
Te Ata: Chickasaw Storyteller, American Treasure
*Tecumseh
Tecumseh: A Life
Tecumseh's Last Stand
Tecumseh & the Quest for Indian Leadership
Tecumseh & the Shawnee Confederacy
Tecumseh: Visionary Chief of the Shawnee
Telling a Good One: The Process of a Native American Collaborative Biography
*Tending the Fire: The Story of Maria Martinez
*Tendoy, Chief of the Lemhis
Coquelle Thompson, Athabaskan Witness: A Cultural Biography
*Jim Thorpe
*Jim Thorpe: World's Greatest Athlete
*Thunder Waters: Experiences of Growing Up In Different Indian Tribes
Timothy: Nez Perce Chief, Life & Times, 1800-1891
To Be Indian: The Life of Iroquois-Seneca Arthur Caswell Parker
*Tomo-Chi-Chi
Uncas: First of the Mohegans
Gerald Vizenor: Writing in the Oral Tradition
Warrior in Two Camps: Ely S. Parker, Union General & Seneca Chief
Warrior of the Mist
The Way It Was: An Indian Girl Living Thru the Depression
The Way Was Through Woods: The Story of Tomo-chi-chi
The Western Odyssey of John Simpson Smith: Frontiersman & Indian Interpreter
When No One Was Looking
Where White Men Fear to Tread: Autobiography of Russell Means
White Indian Boy
Who Was Who in Native American History
Wind Is My Mother: Life & Teachings of American Shaman
With Eagle Tail
Sarah Winnemucca
Sarah Winnemucca of the Northern Paiutes
World of Flower Blue: Pop Chalee: An Artistic Biography
Woven Stone: Autobiography of Simon J. Ortiz
A Yaqui Life: The Personal Chronicle of a Yaqui Indian
Yellowtail: Crow Medicine Man & Sun Dance Chief: An Autobiography
*Young Pocahontas, Indian Princess

BLACK ELK

Black Elk & Flaming Rainbow
Black Elk: Holy Man of the Oglala
Black Elk" A Man With Vision
Black Elk: The Sacred Ways of a Lakota
Black Elk Speaks
The Sixth Grandfather

BLACKFEET INDIANS

Blackfeet: Artists of the Northern Plains
Blackfeet & Buffalo: Memories of Life Among the Indians
Blackfeet Crafts
Blackfeet IndianStories
Blackfeet Indians
Blackfeet: Raiders on the Northwestern Plains
Blackfeet Tales From Apikuni's World
Blackfeet: Their Art & Culture
Crowfoot: Chief of the Blackfeet
Frontier Diplomats: Alexander Culbertson &
 Natoyist-Siksina' Among the Blackfeet
*Heart Butte: A Blackfeet Indian
Mission Among the Blackfeet
Modern Blackfeet: Montanans on a Reservation
Old North Trail: Or, Life, Legends and Religion
 of the Blackfeet Indians
Rebirth of the Blackfeet Nation, 1912-1954
The Reservation Blackfeet, 1885-1945:
 A Photographic History of Cultural Survival
*Running Eagle: Woman Warrior of the Blackfeet
Why Gone Those Times? Blackfoot Tales

BLACKFOOT INDIANS

Amazing Death of Calf Shirt & Other Blackfoot Stories
*Blackfoot Children & Elders Talk Togerther
Blackfoot Confederacy ,1880-1920: A Comparative
 Study of Canada & U.S. Indian Policy
Blackfoot Craftworker's Book
Blackfoot Lodge Tales
The Blackfoot Moonshine Rebellion of 1881
A Blackfoot Sourcebook
Horse in Blackfoot Indian Culture With Comparative
 Material From Other Western Tribes
Long Lance
Mythology of the Blackfoot Indians
The Return of Chief Black Foot
Social Organization and Ritualistic Ceremonies
 of the Blackfoot Indians
The Tragedy of the Blackfoot
The Vengeful Wife & Other Blackfoot Stories
War Paint: Blackfoot and Sarcee Painted Buffalo Robes
 in the Royal Ontario Museum
Wooden Leg: A Warrior Who Fought With Custer

BOATS & CANOES

The Bark Canoes and Skin Boats of North America
The Birch: Bright Tree of Life & Legend
Birchbark Canoes of the Fur Trade
Building a Chippewa Indian Birchbark Canoe
California Indian Watercraft
Canoeing With the Cree
*Indian Canoeing
The Survival of the Bark Canoe
Wangka: Austronesian Canoe Origins

CADDO INDIANS

The Caddo Chiefdoms: Caddo Economics & Politics,
 1700-1835
Caddo Indians
Caddo Indians: Where We Come From
Caddo Nation: Archaeological &
 Ethnohistoric Perspectives
Caddo Verb Morphology
The Caddoan, Iroquoian and Siouan Languages
The Caddos, the Wichitas, & the U.S., 1846-1901
The Hasinais: The Southern Caddoans As Seen
 by the Earliest Europeans
Hasinai: A Traditional History of the Caddo Confederacy
The Hasinais: The Southern Caddoans as Seen
 by the Earliest Europeans
Indian Place-Names
Life Among the Texas Indians: The WPA Narratives
Source Material on the History & Ethnology of the
 Caddo Indians
Southern Caddo: An Anthology
Traditions of the Caddo

CALENDARS

American Indian Women's Calendar
Calendar History of the Kiowa Indians
Calendar of Indian Festivals, Dances, Powwows,
 and Events (California)
California Powwows
R.C. Gorman's Calendar
Kumtux
Multicultural Resource Calendar
Native American Spirit
Native American Visions
Native American Women
Navajo: Portrait of Nation
Papago Calendar Record
Pow Wow Calendar
Pueblo People Calendar
Southwest Indian Calendar

CANADIAN INDIANS

*ABC's of Our Spiritual Connection
The Abnakis and Their History
Aboriginal Ontario
Aboriginal People & Colonizers of Western Canada to 1900
Aboriginal People & Other Canadians:
 Shaping New Relationships
Aboriginal Plant Use in Canada's Northwest Boreal Forest
Aboriginal & Treaty Rights in Canada
Alberni Prehistory
Among the Chiglit Eskimos
Arctic Artist
Arctic Dreams & Nightmares
Arctic Sky: Inuit Astronomy, Star Lore, & Legend
As Long As the Rivers Run
Athapaskan Adaptations: Hunters and Fishermen
 of the Subarctic Forests
Basketry & Cordage from Hesquiat Harbour
Beothuk and Micmac
Beyond the River and the Bay: The Canadian
 Northwest in 1811
Black Eyes All of the Time
Blackfoot Confederacy, 1880-1921: A Comparative Study
 of Canada & U.S. Indian Policy
Bo'Jou, Neejee: Profiles of Canadian Indian Art
Breathtracks
Brotherhood to Nationhood
The Burden of History
*Canada: The Lands, Peoples & Cultures Series
Canada's First Nations
Canada's Indians: Contemporary Conflicts
Canadian Indian Policy: A Critical Bibliography
Canadian Indian Policy & Development Planning Theory
Canadian Iroquois & the Seven Years' War
Canadian Native Law Cases
Canadian Prehistory Series
The Canadian Sioux
Canoeing With the Cree
Children of Aataentsic: A History of the Huron
 People to 1660
Christianity and Native Traditions
Colonizing Bodies: Aboriginal Health & Healing in British
 Columbia, 1900-50
The Conflict of European and Eastern Algonkian Cultures,
 1504-1700
The Counselling Speeches of Jim Ka-Nipitehtew
*Courageous Spirits: Aboriginal Heroes of Our Children
Crown and Calumet: British-Indian Relations, 1783-1815
Dene Nation: The Colony Within
Description—Natural History of the Coasts of North America
Dix-Huits Ans Chez Les Sauvages: Voyages et
 Missions de Monseigneur Henry Faraud
The Dog's Children: Anishinaabe Texts
Drum Songs: Glimpses of Dene History
Dynamics of Government Programs for Urban Indians
 in the Prairie Provinces
Early Fur Trade on the Northern Plains
Emotional Expression Among the Cree Indians
*Enwhisteetkwa: Walk in Water
First Man West
First Nations of British Columbia
First Nations Tribal Directory
Food Plants of Coastal First Peoples
Food Plants of Interior First Peoples
Food Plants of the Sonoran Desert
For an Amerindian Autohistory
The Fourth World: An Indian Reality
The Fur Trade in Canada
Gatherings
Guests Never Leave Hungry: The Autobiography of
 James Sewid, a Kwakiutl Indian
History of Canada, Or New France
*History of the Five Indian Nations of Canada
A History of the Native People of Canada Vol. II
 (1,000 B.C.-A.D. 500)
History of New France
A History of the Original Peoples of Northern Canada
A Homeland for the Cree
*How Food Was Given
*How Names Were Given
*How Turtle Set the Animals Free
Huupuk"anum: The Art, Culture & History of the
 Nuu-chah-nulth People
*I Am the Eagle Free (Sky Song)
In the Shadow of the Sun: Contemporary
 Canadian Indian & Inuit Art
The Indian History of British Columbia
Indian School Days
Indian War Sites
Indian & White: Self-Image and Interaction In a
 Canadian Plains Community
Indians, Animals, and the Fur Trade:
 A Critique of "Keepers of the Game"
The Indians in the U.S. and Canada: A Comparative History
The Indians of Canada
Indians of Canada: Cultural Dynamics
The Indians of the Subarctic: A Critical Bibliography
Inuit Artists Print Workbook
Inuit: The North in Transition
The Inuit Print, L'Estampe Inuit
Islands of Truth: The Imperial Fashioning
 of Vancouver Island

*Just a Walk
Kanienkehaka (Mohawk Valley)
Kinship & the Drum Dance in a Northern Dene Community
Kwakiutl: Indians of British Columbia
A Kwakiutl Village and School
*Kwulasulwut I: Stories from the Coast Salish
*Kwulasulwut II: Salish Creation Stories
The Legacy of Shingwaukonse
Life and Death in Mohawk Country
Logs of the Conquest of Canada
Long Journey to the Country of the Hurons
Looking At the Words of Our People
Loon: Memory, Meaning, & Reality in a
 Northern Dene Community
Lost Harvests: Prairie Indian Reserve Farmers
 & Government Policy
Major Richardson's Short Stories
Tommy McGinty's Northern Tutchone Story of Crow
The Middle Ground: Indians, Empires, & Republics
 in the Great Lakes Region
The Mohawk That Refused to Abdicate
Naming Canada: Essays on Place Names From
 Canadian Geographic
Nation Within a Nation
Native Canadian Anthropology & History:
 A Selected Bibliography
The Native Creative Process
Native People in Canada: Contemporary Conflicts
Native People, Native Lands: Canadian Indians, Inuit & Metis
Natives & Newcomers: Canada's "Heroic Age" Reconsidered
*Neekna & Chemai
New Relations of Gaspesia: With the Customs and
 Religion of the Gaspesian Indians
New Resource Wars
Night Spirits
A Northern Algonquian Sourcebook
Northern Voices: Inuit Writing in English
Noticias de Nutka: An Account of Nootka Sound in 1792
Nunuvut Atlas
The Ojibwa of Southern Ontario
The Ojibwa of Western Canada, 1780 to 1870
Ojibway Heritage
Ojibway on Walpole Island, Ontario: A Linguistic Study
Okanagan Sources
The Orders of the Dreamed
Out of the Mist: Treasures of the Nuu-chah-nulth Chiefs
A Paleo-Indian Site in Central Nova Scotia
Pathways to Self-Determination: Canadian Indians
 and the Canadian State
People From Our Side
People of the Buffalo
People of the Terra Nullius
Place Names of Atlantic Canada
Place Names of Ontario
Plains Cree: Trade, Diplomacy & War, 1790 to 1870
Proceedings of the Fort Chipewyan/Fort Vermilion
 Bicentennial Conference
Queesto: Pacheenaht Chief by Birthright
"Real" Indians & Others" Mixed-Blood Urban Native
 Peoples & Indigenous Nationhood
Rebirth: Political, Economic & Social Development
 in First Nations
Reflections on Native-Newcomer Relations: Selected Essays
Rifles, Blankets & Beads
Sacred Feathers: The Reverend Peter Jones
 (Kahkewaquonaby) and the Mississauga Indians
Severing the Ties That Bind
Skyscrapers Hide the Heavens: The History of
 Indian-White Relations in Canada
Since the Time of the Transformers: The Ancient Heritage
 of the Nuu-chah-nulth, Ditidaht and Makah
Slash
Snares, Deadfalls & Other Traps of the Northern
 Algonquian & Northern Athapaskans
Social and Economic Change Among the Northern Ojibwa
The Spirit of the Alberta Indian Treaties
The Spirit Sings: Artistic Traditions of Canada's First Peoples
Stone Ornaments Used by Indians in the U.S. & Canada
Stories of the Road Allowance People
Structural Considerations of Metis Ethnicity
Sundogs
Tales of the Anishinaubaek: Ojibway Legends
Tales the Elders Told: Ojibway Legends
To the Arctic by Canoe
To Please the Caribou
Travels and Adventures in Canada and the Indian
 Territories Between 1760 and 1776
Treaty Talks in British Columbia
The Uncovered Past: Roots of Northern Alberta Societies
Unravelling the Franklin Mystery: Inuit Testimony
Voices in the Waterfall
War Paint: Blackfoot & Sarcee Painted Buffalo
 Robes in the Royal Ontario Museum
The Way of the Masks
Ways of Knowing; Experience, Knowledge & Power
 Among the Dene Tha
We Get Our Living Like Milk From the Land
White Man's Law: Native People in 19th Century
 Canadian Jurisprudence
Wollaston: People Resisting Genocide
Women of the First Nations
Woodland Trappers: Hare Indians of Northwestern Canada
Yukon Bibliography - Update Series

CAPTIVITIES

Apache: The Long Ride Home
Biography of Francis Slocum, The Lost Sister of Wyoming
The Boy Captives
Samuel J. Brown in Captivity
Captivity of the Oatman Girls
Captivity Tales: An Original Anthology
Captured by the Indians: 15 Firsthand Accounts, 1750-1870
*Children Indian Captives
Eleven Years a Captive Among the Snake Indians
Escape From Indian Captivity
The Falcon: A Narrative of the Captivity & Adventures of John Tanner
*Feathers in the Wind: The Story of Olive Oatman
From Massacre to Matriarch: Six Weeks in the Life of Fanny Scott
History of the Spirit Lake Massacre and of Miss Abigail Gardiner's Three Month's Captivity Among the Indians
Indian Atrocities
Indian Captive: A Narrative of the Adventures and Sufferings of Matthew Brayton
The Indian Captive: Or, A Narrative of the Captivity and Sufferings of Zadock Steele
Indian Captivity of O.M. Spencer
Indians: Or Narratives of Massacres & Depredations
The Indians and Their Captives
Journal of the Adventures of Matthew Bunn
Left By the Indians
The Life of Jacob Persinger
Loudon's Indian Narratives
Merejildo Grijalva, Apache Captive, Army Scout
A Narrative of the Captivity of Robert Eastburn
Narrative of the Capitivity of Isaac Webster
A Narrative of the Captivity of Mrs. Johnson
Narrative of Henry Bird
A Narrative of the Life of Mrs. Mary Jemison
Narrative of Thomas Brown
Narratives of Captivity Among the Indians of North America
Nine Years Among the Indians, 1870-1879
Cynthia Ann Parker: Indian Captive
Cynthia Ann Parker: The Life & Legend
Perils of the Ocean and Wilderness: Narrative of Shipwreck & Indian Captivity
Puritans Among the Indians: Accounts of Captivity and Redemptions 1676-1724
The Redeemed Captive, Returning to Zion
Scoorwa: James Smith's Indian Captivity Narrative
Selection of Some of the Most Intersting Narratives of Outrages Committed by the Indians in Their Wars with the White People
Short Biography of John Leeth, With an Account of His Life Among the Indians
Six Months Among Indians
Six Weeks in the Sioux Tepees
Sketches of Western Adventure
Survival of the Spirit: Chiricahua Apaches in Captivity
Tales of the Northwest: On Sketches of Indian Life and Character
Topographical Description of the State of Ohio, Indiana Territory, & Louisiana
The Torture of Captives by Indians of Eastern North America
True Stories of New England Captives Carried to Canada During the Old French & Indian Wars
*White Captives
A Woman of the People

CATLIN, GEORGE (PAINTER OF INDIANS) 1796-1872

George Catlin
George Catlin Book of American Indians
Catlin's North American Indian Portfolio: A Reproduction
Letters, Notes, on the Manners, Customs & Condition of the North American Indians
The Natural Man Observed: A Study of Catlin's Indian Gallery
White Influence Upon Plains Indian Painting: George Catlin & Carl Bodmer Among the Mandan, 1832-34

CHEROKEE INDIANS

Abstract of Cherokee Claims
After the Trail of Tears: The Cherokees' Struggle for Sovereignty, 1839-1880
The American Indian in North Carolina
Arts and Crafts of the Cherokee
Beginning Cherokee: A Cherokee Language Grammar
A Better Kind of Hatchet: Law, Trade, Diplomacy in the Cherokee Nation
The Brainerd Journal: A Mission to the Cherokees, 1817-1823
Census of Cherokee Indians East of the Mississippi 1835
*The Cherokee
*Cherokee ABC Coloring Book
Cherokee Adairs
Cherokee Americans-Eastern Band of Cherokees in the 20th Century
Cherokee Animal Stories
Cherokee Archaeology
Cherokee Archaeology: A Study of the Appalachian Summit
Cherokee By Blood: Records of Eastern Cherokee Ancestry

The Cherokee Cases: Two Landmark Federal Decisions in the Fight for Sovereignty
Cherokee Cavaliers
Cherokee Cooklore
The Cherokee Crown of Tannassy
Cherokee Dance: Ceremonial Dances & Costumes
Cherokee Dance & Drama
Cherokee Dictionary
Cherokee Dragon: A Novel
Cherokee Editor: The Writings of Elias Boudinot
Cherokee Emigration Records 1829-1835
Cherokee-English Dictionary
Cherokee-English Interliner
The Cherokee Excavations
A Cherokee Feast of Days: Native American Daily Meditations
The Cherokee Freedmen: From Emancipation to American Citizenship
Cherokee Fun & Learn Book
The Cherokee Ghost Dance
Cherokee Glossary
The Cherokee Indian Nation
The Cherokee Indian Nation: A Troubled History
Cherokee Language Workbook & Instructional Cassette Tape
*Cherokee Little People
Cherokee Messenger
Cherokee New Testament
The Cherokee Night & Other Plays
Cherokee Old Settlers Roll 1895
The Cherokee People
The Cherokee Perspective
Cherokee Plants
A Cherokee Prayerbook
Cherokee Prehistory: The Pisgah Phase in the Appalachian Summit Region
Cherokee Proud: A Guide to Tracing & Honoring Your Cherokee Ancestors
Cherokee Psalms, A Collection of Hymns
Cherokee Renascence, 1794-1833
Cherokee Removal: Before & After
Cherokee Removal: The William Penn Essays
Cherokee Roots
Cherokee Song Book
The Cherokee Trail
Cherokee Tragedy: The Ridge Family & the Decimation of a People
Cherokee Vision of Eloh'
Cherokee Voices: Accounts of Cherokee Life Before 1900
Cherokee Women
Cherokee Words
The Cherokees
*The Cherokees
The Cherokees & Christianity, 1794-1870
Cherokees at the Crossroads
Cherokees, An Illustrated History
Cherokees in Transition
Cherokees & Missionaries, 1789-1839
The Cherokees of the Smokey Mountains
The Cherokees - Past & Present
The Cherokees: A Population History
Cherokees "West"
Chief Bowles & the Texas Cherokees
Contemporary Artists & Craftsmen of the Cherokee
Deception on All Accounts: A Novel
Designs of the Night Sky
Early of the Cherokees
The Eastern Band of Cherokees, 1819-1900
*The Education of Little Tree
Exploring Your Cherokee Ancestry
Fire & the Spirits: Cherokee Law from Clan to Court
Footsteps of the Cherokees
Fort Gibson: Terminal on the Trail of Tears
Friends of Thunder: Folktales of the Oklahoma Cherokees
A Good Cherokee, A Good Anthropologist: Papers in Honor of Robert K. Thomas
A Guide to Cherokee Documents in Foreign Archives
History of the Cherokee Indians and Their Legends and Folklore
History, Myths & Sacred Formulas of the Cherokees
How to Make Cherokee Clothing
Index to the Cherokee Freedmen Enrolment Cards of the Dawes Commission, 1901-1906
Introduction to Cherokee: A Cherokee Language Study Course
The Intruders: The Illegal Residents of the Cherokee Nation, 1866-1907
John Ross: Cherokee Chief
Journal of Cherokee Studies
*The Last Cherokee Warriors
The Magic Lake: A Mystical Healing Lake of the Cherokee
*The Magic Lake of the Cherokees
*The Magic Weaver of Rugs
Mankiller: A Chief and Her People
Medicine of the Cherokee: The Way of Right Relationship
Bartley Milam: Principal Chief of the Cherokee Nation
Minister to the Cherokees: A Civil War Autobiography
Mountain Windsong: A Novel of the Trail of Tears
Muskogee City & County
Myths of the Cherokee
Myths & Sacred Formulas of the Cherokees
Nations Remembered: An Oral History of Cherokees, Chickasaws, Choctaws, Creeks, and Seminoles, 1865-1907

Native Caroliniana, The Indians of North Carolina
New Echota Letters: Contributions of Samuel A. Worcester to the Cherokee Phoenix
The Night Has a Naked Soul
*Only the Names Remain: The Cherokees and the Trail of Tears
An Outline of Basic Verb Inflections of Oklahoma Cherokee
The Peace Chief: A Novel
Phonological Variations in Western Cherokee
The Qualla Cherokee Surviving in Two Worlds
The Raven and the Redbird
The Raven Speaks
The Raven's Tales
Ravensong
Red Over Black: Black Slavery Among the Cherokee Indians
Removal of the Cherokee Indians from Georgia
The Removal of the Cherokee Nation: Manifest Destiny or National Dishonor
John Ross and the Cherokee Indians
Sequoyah
Sequoyah & the Cherokee Alphabet
*Sequoyah (Cherokee Hero)
Sequoyah, Father of the Cherokee Alphabet
Slavery and the Evolution of Cherokee Society, 1540-1866
Snowbird Cherokees: People of Persistence
A Snug Little Purchase: How Richard Henderson Bought Kaintuckee from the Cherokees in 1775
Storm in the Mountain
The Story of the Cherokee People
*The Story of the Trail of Tears
A Structured Approach to Learning the Basic Inflections of the Cherokee Verb
Taking Indian Lands: The Cherokee (Jerome) Commission, 1889-1893
Tales of the Cherokee Hills
The Ten Year Treasury of Cherokee Studies
The Texas Cherokees: A People Between Two Fires, 1819-1840
These Are My People, The Cherokees
Trail of Tears
*The Trail on Which They Wept: The Story of a Cherokee Girl
Tribes That Slumber
Unhallowed Intrusions, a History of Cherokee Families in Forsyth Co., GA
Walk in Your Soul: Love Incantations of the Oklahoma Cherokees
Walking the Trail: One Man's Journey Along the Cherokee Trail of Tears
War Woman: A Novel
Weaving New Worlds: Southeastern Cherokee Women and Their Basketry
Where Legends Live
*The Whistling Tree
Windsong
The Witch of Goingsnake & Other Stories
Writing Cherokee
Your Name in Cherokee

CHEYENNE & ARAPAHO INDIANS

The Arapaho Indians: A Research Guide & Bibliography
Arapahoe Politics, 1851-1978: Symbols in Crises of Authority
The Arapahoes, Our People
*Belle Highwalking: The Narrative of a Northern Cheyenne Woman
By Cheyenne Campfires
*The Cheyenne
*Cheyenne Again
Cheyenne & Arapaho Music
Cheyenne & Arapaho Ordeal: Reservation & Agency Life
Cheyenne Autumn
*Cheyenne Fire Fighters: Modern Indians Fighting Forest Fires
Cheyenne Frontier Days, the First 100 Years: A Pictorial History
The Cheyenne Indians: Their History & Ways of Life
*Cheyenne Legends of Creation
Cheyenne Memories
Cheyenne Memories of the Custer Fight: A Source Book
The Cheyenne Nation: A Social & Demographic History
*Cheyenne Short Stories
*Cheyenne Warriors
The Cheyenne Way: Conflict and Case Law in Primitive Jurisprudence
Cheyennes at Dark Water Creek
Cheyennes & Horse Soldiers
The Cheyennes: Indians of the Great Plains
*The Cheyennes: People of the Plains
The Cheyennes, Ma Heo O's People: A Critical Biography
The Cheyennes of Montana
*A Day With a Cheyenne
English-Cheyenne Dictionary
The Fighting Cheyennes
Four Great Rivers to Cross: Cheyenne History, Culture & Traditions
The Four Hills of Life: Northern Arapaho Knowledge & Life Movement
*A History of the Cheyenne People
Holding Stone Hands: On the Trail of the Cheyenne Exodus
Lakota & Cheyenne: Indian Views of the Great Sioux War, 1876-1877
*Northern Cheyenne Fire Fighters
Northern Cheyenne Indian Reservation, 1877-1900

On the Apache Indian Reservations & Artist
  Wanderings Among the Cheyennes
The Peace Chiefs of the Cheyennes
People of the Sacred Mountain
*Quillworker, A Cheyenne Legend
The Road to Lame Deer
*The Rolling Head: Cheyenne Tales
The Southern Cheyennes
Sweet Medicine
Tell Them We Are Going Home: The Odyssey
  of the Northern Cheyennes
Traditions of the Arapaho
Tsee-Ma'Heone-Nemeototse: Cheyenne Spiritual Songs
The Wolves of Heaven: Cheyenne Shamanism,
  Ceremonies & Prehistoric Origins

CHICKASAWS

Bibliography of the Chickasaw
*The Chickasaw
Chickasaw: An Analytical Dictionary
Chickasaw Glossary
The Chickasaws
Memoris of a Chickasaw Squaw
Nations Remembered: An Oral History of Cherokees,
  Chickasaws, Choctaws, Creeks, and Seminoles, 1865-1907
The Papers pf Panton, Leslie & Co.
Te Ata: Chickasaw Storyteller, American Treasure

CHIEF JOSEPH

American Indian Warrior Chiefs: Tecumseh,
  Crazy Horse, Chief Joseph, Geronimo
Chief Joseph
Chief Joseph's Allies
Chief Joseph & the Nez Perces: A Photographic History
Chief Joseph Country: Land of the Nez Perce
Chief Joseph: Guardian of the Nez Perce
Chief Joseph of the Nez Perce Indians
Chief Joseph's Own Story
*Chief Joseph's Own Story as Told by Chief Joseph in 1879
I Will Fight No More Forever: Chief Joseph and the
  Nez Perce War
*Indians of America: Chief Joseph, et al
Joseph, Chief of the Nez Perce
Nez Perce Joseph
Saga of Chief Joseph

CHIEF QUANAH PARKER

Comanche Moon
*Comanche Warbonnet
*Native American Leaders of the Wild Wesr
*North American Indians of Achievement
Quanah Parker, Comanche Chief
*Quanah Parker: Great Chief of the Comanches
Quanah: A Pictorial History of the Last Comanche Chief
War Chiefs

CHILDREN

American Indian Children at School, 1850-1930
American Indian Stereotypes in the World of Children
American Indian & White Children: A Sociopsychological
  Investigation
Childhood & Folklore: A Psychoanalytic Study of
  Apache Personality
Childhood & Youth in Jicarilla Apache Society
Children at Risk: Making a Difference Through the
  Court Appointed Special
Children of the Dragonfly: Native American
  Voices on Child Custody & Education
Advocate Project
Children of the Circle
Children of Cottonwood
*Children of the Earth & Sky
Children of the First People
Children Indian Captives
Children of the Salt River
Children of the Tlingit
Chippewa Child Life and Its Cultural Background
Crickets & Corn: Five Stories About Native
  North American Children
*The Death of Jimmy Littlewolf: An Indian Boy at Boys Ranch
Dolls & Toys of Native America
The Hopi Child
*Indian Boyhood
*Indian Children Paper Dolls
Navajo Infancy: An Ethological Study of Child Development
Overcoming Obstacles and Improving Outcomes
Red Children in White America
Respect for Life: The Traditional Upbringing of
  American Indian Children
Shooting Back from the Reservation
*Thunder Waters: Experiences of Growing Up in
  Different Indian Tribes
*To Live In Two Worlds: American Indian Youth Today
*The Trail on Which They Wept:
  The Story of a Cherokee Girl

CHOCTAW INDIANS

Acts & Resolutions, Constitution & Laws of the Choctaw
  (See Constitution & Laws of the American Indian
  Tribes Series)
Chahta Anumpa: A Grammar of the Choctaw Language
  (CD-ROM)
*The Choctaw
*A Choctaw Anthology, I and II
The Choctaw Before Removal
1830 Choctaw Census "Armstrong Roll"
Choctaw Claimants & Their Heirs
Choctaw Dictionary
Choctaw Genesis, 1500-1700
Choctaw Language Awareness Teachers Manual
Choctaw Language & Culture: Chahta Anumpa
Choctaw Language Sampler
The Choctaw Laws
Choctaw Legends Teacher's Guide
Choctaw Music and Dance
Choctaws at the Crossroads
Choctaws & Missionaries in Mississippi, 1818-1918
The Choctaws in a Revolutionary Age, 1750-1830
Field of Honor: A Novel
Intruders Into the Choctaw & Chickasaw Nations, 1884-1890
Mississippi Choctaws at Play: The Serious Side of Leisure
Nations Remembered: An Oral History of Cherokees,
  Chickasaws, Choctaws, Creeks, and Seminoles, 1865-1907
Okla Hannali
Persistence of Pattern in Mississippi Choctaw Culture
The Removal of the Choctaw Indians
Rise & Fall of the Choctaw Republic
The Roads of My Relations
Searching for the Bright Path: The Mississippi Choctaws
Source Material for the Social & Ceremonial
  Life of the Choctaw Indians
Stranges in Their Own Land: A Choctaw Portfolio
They Say the Wind Is Red: The Alabama Choctaw Lost
  in Their Own Land
Tribal Government: A New Era

CLAIMS

The Alaska Native Claims Settlement Act, 1991
  & Tribal Government
The Case of the Seneca Indians in the State of New York
Indian Claims Commission Act
Indian Tribal Claims Decided in the Court of Claims
  of the U.S.: Briefed & Compiled, 6/30/47
Native Claims & Political Development
Restitution: The Land Claims of the Mashpee,
  Passamaquoddy & Penobscot Indians of New England

CLIFF DWELLERS

*Dark Arrow
The Land of the Cliff-Dwellers
Mesa Verde Ancient Architecture
Mesa Verde National Park
Mesa Verde: The Story Behind the Scenery
The Ozark Bluff Dwellers
The Village of Blue Stone
Voices in the Canyon

COMANCHE INDIANS

Archaeological Investigations of the Kiowa & Comanche
Being Comanche
Buffalo Hump and the Penateka Comanches
*The Comanche
Comanche Dictionary & Grammar
Comanche Moon
Comanche Political History
Comanche Treaties During the Civil War
Comanche Treaties: Historical Background
Comanche Treaties (1835, 1846, 1850, 1851, 1853)
  with the U.S.
Comanche Treaties with the Republic of Texas
Comanche Vocabulary
*Comanche Warbonnet
The Comanchero Frontier
The Comanches: A History, 1706-1875
Comanches in the New West, 1895-1908:
  Historic Photographs
The Comanches: Lords of the South Plains
Comanches & Mennonites on the Oklahoma Plains
Expedition to the Southwest
First to Fight
Gifts of Pride & Love; Kiowa & Comanche Cradles
A Grammar of Comanche
LaDonna Harris: A Comanche Life
The Jerome Agreement Between the Kiowa,
  Comanche, and Apache Tribes of the U.S.
Kiowa, Apache, and Comanche Military Societies
Komantcia
The Legend of the Bluebonnet, retold
Life Among the Texas Indians
Los Comanches: The Horse People, 1751-1845
Cynthia Ann Parker: The Life & Legend
The Plains Indians
Quanah Parker: Comanche Chief

*Quanah Parker: Great Chief of the Comanches
Quanah: A Pictorial History of the Last Comanche Chief
Sanapia: Comanche Medicine Woman
The Sound of Strings
The Story of Cynthia Ann Parker
Three Years Among the Comanhes
Warlords of the West: A Story of the Comanche
*Why Buffalo Roam
Without Quarter: The Wichita Expedition & the
  Fight on Crooked Creek

COMMERCE

Adobe Walls: The History and Archaeology
  of the 1874 Trading Post
American Indian & Alaska Native Traders Directory
American Indian Policy in the Formative Years:
  The Indian Trade and Intercourse Acts, 1790-1834
Ancient Road Networks & Settlement Hierarchies in the
  New World
The Bringing of Wonder: Trade & the Indians
  of the Southeast, 1700-1783
Stokes Carson: 20th Century Trading on the
  Navajo Reservation
Condition of the India Trade in North America, 1767:
  As Described in a Letter to Sir William Johnson
Crown and Calumet: British-Indian Relations, 1783-1815
Early Indian Trade Guns: 1625-1775
Fur Trade
Fur Trappers and Traders
Indian, Animals, and the Fur Trade: A Critique of
  Keepers of the Game
Indian Trade Goods
Indian Traders of the Southwestern Spanish Border Lands:
  Panton and Forbes Co. 1783-1847
Indian Traders on the Middle Border:
  The House of Ewing, 1827-1854
Indians in the Fur Trade
Introductory Guide to Entrepreneurship for American Indians
Metal Weapons, Tools and Ornaments of the
  Teton Dakota Indians
Many Tender Ties: Women in Fur-Trade Society, 1670-1870
Native American Crafts Directory
Navajo Trading Days
Navajo Trading: The End of an Era
Pelts, Plumes and Hides: White Traders Among the
  Seminole Indians, 1870-1930
Rugs and Posts: The Story of Navajo Weaving
  & the Indian Trader
Shonto: Study of the Role of the Trader in a Modern Navajo
Community
Smoke Signals: A Directory of American Indian &
  Alaska Native Businesses in Indian Country
The Southern Frontier, 1670-1732
The Trade Gun Sketchbook
Traders of the Western Morning: Aboriginal
  Commerce in Precolumbian North America
Trading Beyond the Mountains
Trading Post Guidebook
Wampum, War and Trade Goods West of the Hudson
Whiskey Peddler
The Whiskey Trade of the Northwestern Plains

CRAZY HORSE

American Indian Warrior Chiefs
Crazy Horse
*Crazy Horse
Crazy Horse Called Them Walk-A-Heaps
Crazy Horse & Custer
Crazy Horse, Hoka Hey: It Is A Good Time To Die
Crazy Horse & Korczak: The Story of an
  Epic Mountain Carving
Crazy Horse Memorial, 40th Anniversary
Crazy Horse: Sacred Warrior of the Sioux
Crazy Horse: The Strange Man of the Oglalas
The Crazy Horse Surrender Ledger
Crazy Horse's Philosophy of Riding Rainbows
*Custer & Crazy Horse
The Death of Crazy Horse
Famous Indians of Northwest Nebraska
Greengrass Pipe Dancers
In The Spirit of Crazy Horse
Indians of America: Crazy Horse.....
The Killing of Chief Crazy Horse
Korczak: Storyteller in Stone
*A Legend From Crazy Horse Clan
*Native American Leaders of the Wild West
Oglala Lakota Crazy Horse
South Dakota Leaders
War Chiefs

CREE INDIANS

Canoeing With the Cree
The Counselling Speeches of Jim Ka-Nipitehtew
Cree Legends & Narratives from the Wst Coast of
  James Bay
Cry of the Eagle: Encounters With a Cree Healer
A Homeland for the Cree: Regional Development in
  James Bay, 1971-1981
Meet Cree: A Guide to the Cree Language

Mistassini Cree Hunters
Montagnais & Cree Hunters of the
  Quebec-Labrador Peninsula
The Montana Cree: A Study in Religious Persistence
Nation Witin a Nation: Dependency & the Cree
Notes on the Eastern Cree and Northern Salteaux
The Orders of the Dreamed
The Plains Cree: Trade, Diplomacy & War, 1790 to 1870
Spoken Cree: West Coast of James Bay

CREEK INDIANS

Africans & Creeks: From the Colonial Period to the Civil War
Beginning Creek: Myskoke Emponvkv
Camp, Clan & Kin, Among the Cow Creek
  Seminole of Florida
*The Creek
Creek Indian History
Creek Indian Medicine Ways
Creek (Muskogee) New Testament Concordance
Creek Religion & Medicine
The Creek Verb
A Creek Warrior for the Confederacy: The Autobiography
  of Chief G.W. Grayson
Creeks & Seminoles: The Destruction & Regeneration
  of the Muscogulge People
Deerskins & Duffels: The Creek Indian Trade with
  Anglo-America, 1685-1815
Early History of the Creek Indians & Their Neighbors
Estiyut Omayat: Creek Writings
The Fus Fixico Letters: A Creek Humorist in Early Oklahoma
George Washington Grayson & the Creek Nation, 1853-1920
Handbook of Creek (Muscogee) Grammar
Handbook of the Creek Langauge
The Invention of the Creek Nation, 1670-1763
McIntosh & Weatherford, Creek Indian Leaders
Myths & Folktales of the Alabama-Coushatta Indians
Nations Remembered: An Oral History of Cherokees,
  Chickasaws, Choctaws, Creeks, and Seminoles, 1865-1907
Now the Wolf Has Come: The Creek Nation in the Civil War
The Politics of Indian Removal: Creek Government
  and Society in Crises
Red Eagle & the Wars With the Creek Indians of Alabama
The Road to Disappearance: A History of the Creek Indians
A Sacred Path: The Way of the Muscogee Creek
Totkv Mocvse • New Fire: Creek Folktales

CROW INDIANS

*Absaloka: Crow Children's Writing
Absaraka: Home of the Crows
Jim Beckwourth: Black Moutnain Man & War Chief
  of the Crows
*Chief Plenty Coups: Life of the Crow Indian Chief
*The Crow
*Crow Children & Elders Talk Together
The Crow & the Eagle: A Tribal History
Crow Indian Art
Crow Indian Beadwork
Crow Indian Medicine Bundles
Crow Indian Photography
The Crow Indians
From the Heart of Crow Country
The Handsome People: A History of the Crow Indians
  and the Whites
*The Indian as a Soldier at Fort Custer, Montana, 1890-1895
Life and Adventures of James P. Beckwourth
Memoirs of a White Crow Indian
Myths & Traditions of the Crow
Plenty-Coups, Chief of the Crows
Pretty-Shield, Medicine Woman of the Crows
The Shoshini-Crow Sun Dance
The Sun Dance of the Crow Indians
They Call Me Agnes
Two Crows Denies It: A History of Controversy in
  Omaha Sociology
Two Leggings: The Making of a Crow Warrior
The Way of the Warrior: Stories of the Crow People
The World of the Crow Indians: As Driftwood Lodges

CULTURAL ASSIMILATION, INTERACTION & SURVIVAL

Acculturation in Seven Indian Tribes
The American Indian in Film
American Indian Policy & American Reform: Case Studies
  of the Campaign to Assimilate the American Indians
American Indian Policy & Cultural Values:
  Conflict & Accommodation
American Indian Societies: Strategies & Conditions
  of Political & Cultural Survival
American Indian Stereotypes in the World of Children:
  A Reader & Bibliography
American Indian Stories
American Indians: A Cultural Geography
Apache Reservation: Indigenous Poeples and the
  American State
As We Are Now: Mixedblood Essays on Race & Identity
Being and Becoming Indian
Bullying the Moqui
Celluloid Indians: Native Americans & Film
The Cherokee Ghost Dance

Cherokees and Missionaries, 1789-1839
Conflict and Schism in Nez Perce Acculturation:
  A Study of Religion & Politics
Confounding the Color Line: The Indian-Black
  Experience in North America
Contested Ground
The Cultural Transformation of a Native American
  Family & Its Tribe, 1763-1995
Cultures in Contact: The European Impact on Native Cultural
  Institutions in Eastern North America, 1000-1800 A.D.
Daksi
Disciplined Hearts
Dispossession By Degrees
Dress Clothing of the Plains Indians
Early White Influence Upon Plains Indian Painting: George
  Catlin & Carl Bodmer Among the Mandan, 1832-1834
Farmers, Hunters & Colonists
A Final Promise: The Campaign to Assimilate the Indians,
  1880-1920
From Savage to Nobleman: Images of Native Americans
  in Film
Fugitive Poses: Native American Indian Scenes
  of Absence & Presence
Gambling & Survival in Native North America
Genocide of the Mind: New Native American Writing
Geographical Names of the Kwakiutl Indians
Germans & Indians: Fantasies, Encounters, Projections
The Good Red Road'
The Hunt for Willie Boy: Indian-Hating & Popular Culture
In Defense of Mohawk Land
Independent Living Outcomes for American Indians
  with Disabilities
Indian Country, L.A. Maintaining Ethnic Community
  in a Complex Society
Indian Culture and European Trade Goods: The Archaeology
  of the Historic Period in the Western Great Lakes Region
Indian Givers: How the Indians of the Americas
  Transformed the World
Indian Police & Judges: Experiments in
  Acculturation & Control
The Indian Reform Letters of Helen Hunt Jackson,
  1879-1885
Indians Are Us?
The Indians in American Society
Indians in Prison
Indigenizing the Academy
Issues in Native American Cultural Identity
Mining, the Environment, and Indigenous
  Development Conflicts
Mixedblood Messages: Literature, Film, Family & Place
Mixed-Bloods and Tribal Dissolution: Charles Curtis
  & the Quest for Indian Identity
The Movement for Indian Assimilation, 1860-1890
Native American Identities: From Stereotype to
  Archetype in Art & Literature
Native American Perspectives on Literature & History
Native American Representations: First Encounters,
  Distorted Images, & Literary Appropriations
Native Roots: How the Indians Enriched America
Navajo Infancy: An Ethological Study of Child Development
North American Indian Lives
The Phoenix Indian School: Forced Assimilation
  in Arizona, 1891-1935
Playing Indian
Rebellion From the Roots: Indian Uprising in Chiapas
The Round Valley Indians of California
Savages & Civilization: Who Will Survive?
Sovereignty & Symbol: Indian-White Conflict at Ganienkeh
Strategies on Successful Independent Living Services
  for American Indians with Disabilities
Strong Hearts: Native American Visions & Voices
Struggles for the Land
Team Spirits: The Native American Mascots Controversy
They Treated Us Just Like Indians
Urban Indian Experience in America
Urban Indians
Urban Indians: Drums From the Cities
Urban Voices: The Bay Area American Indian Community
Urbaniztion of American Indians
The Vanishing American: White Attitudes & U.S. Indian Policy
Wasi'chu: The Continuing Indian Wars
The Way We Make Sense
Voices of American Indian Assimilation & Resistance:
  Helen Hunt Jackson, Sarah Winnemucca & Victoria Howard
Wordarrows: Indians & Whites in the New Fur Trade
Wordarrows: Native States of Literary Sovereignty

CULTURE

Acculturation in Seven Indian Tribes
The Age of Manufactures, 1700-1820
Alaska in the Days That Were Before
All Roads Are Good: Native Voices on Life & Culture
American Indian Grandmothers
American Indians: The First of This Land
American Indians, Time, and the Law: Native Societies
  in a Modern Constitutional Democracy
Ancestor's Footsteps
Ancient Drums, Other Moccasins: Native North
  American Cultural Adaptation
Angels to Wish By
The Anguish of Snails: Native American Folklore in the West
Apachean Culture: History & Ethnology

Arizona Traveler: Indians of Arizona
Art and Environment in Native America
Basic Call to Consciousness
Between Indian & White Worlds: The Cultural Broker
Between Sacred Mountains: Navajo Stories &
  Lessons from the Land
Beyond the Vision: Essays on American Indian Culture
Bread & Freedom
The Business of Benevolence: Industrial Paternaliam
  in Progressive America
Can the Red Man Help the White Man
The Changing Presentation of the American Indian:
  Museums & Native Cultures
Cherokee Dance and Drama
Colonial Discourses, Collective Memories
Colonial Intimacies: Indian Marriage in Early New England
The Covenent Chain: Indian Ceremonial and Trade Silver
Coyote's Council Fire
Crossbloods: Bone Courts, Bingo, and Other Reports
Cultural Diversity & Adaptation
Culture, Change & Leadership in a Modern Indian
  Community: The Colorado River Indian Reservation
Cultures in Contact: The European Impact on Native Cultural
  Institutions in Eastern North America 1000-1800 A.D.
Cycles of Conquest: The Impact of Spain, Mexico & the
  U.S. on Indians of the Southwest, 1533-1960
Dancing With Creation
Deliberate Acts: Changing Hopi Culture
  Through the Oraibi Split
The Desert Smells Like Rain: A Naturalist in
  Papago Indian Country
*Discover American Indian Ways
Dreaming the Dawn
Earthdivers: Tribal Narratives on Mixed Descent
Enduring Culture: A Century of Photography
  of the Southwest Indians
The Fighting Cheyennes
Finding the Center: The Art of the Zuni Storyteller
First Horses: Stories of the New West
The Fremont Culture: A Study in Culture Dynamics
  on the Northern Anasazi Frontier
Fugitive Poses: Native American Indian Scenes
  of Absence and Presence
*The Gift of Changing Woman
Going Native: Indians in the American Cultural Imagination
The Gospel of the Redman
Growing Up Native American
Guide to Contemporary Southwest Indians
Haida Art
Haida: Their Art & Culture
Handbook of the American Frontier - Four Centuries of
  Indian-White Relationships: The Southeastern Woodlands
Hidatsa Social & Ceremonial Organization
History, Evolution and the Concept of Culture:
  Selected Papers by Alexander Lesser
The Hoe and the Horse on the Plains
Hogans: Navajo Houses and House Songs
The Horse and Dog in Hidatsa Culture
The Horse in Blackfoot Indian Culture; With Comparative
  Material from Other Tribes
How Can One Sell the Air?
Huichol Indian Ceremonial Cycle
I Am Here: Two Thousand Years of Southwest Indian Culture
The Idea of Fertilization in the Culture of the Pueblo Indians
Indian Art & Culture
Indian Dances of North America: Their Importance
  to Indian Life
Indian Givers: How the Indians of the Americas
  Transformed the World
Indian Life of the Yosemite Region: Miwok Material Culture
Indian Tribes of the Northern Rockies
Indians Are Us?
The Insistence of the Indian
Iroquois Music & Dance: Ceremonial Arts of
  Two Seneca Longhouses
John Eliot's Indian Dialogues: A Study in Cultural Interaction
Kinaalada: A Navajo Puberty Ceremony
The Kiowas
Lame Deer: Seeker of Visions
Letters, Notes, on the Manners, Customs & Condition
  of the North American Indians
Living in Balance
Making Two Worlds One and the Story of
  All-American Indian Days
Manifest Manners: PostIndian Warriors of Survivance
Men As Women, Women As Men: Changing Gender
  in Native American Cultures
Mimbres Indian Treasure: In the Land of Baca
Miwok Material Culture
Music & Dance Research of the Southwestern Indians
Native American Discourse: Poetics & Rhetoric
Native American Expressive Culture
Native American Heritage
Native Americans of the Southwest
Native Roots: How the Indians Enriched America
A Natural Education: Native American Ideas & Thoughts
Native Universe: Voices of Indian America
Navaho Art & Culture
Navajo Art, History & Culture
The Navajos
Notebook on Art, History & Culture
Objects of Change: The Archaeology & History of
  Arikara Contact with Europeans

Of Mother Earth & Father Sky
Origin of Ancient American Cultures
Osage Life & Legends: Earth People - Sky People
The People: Native American Thoughts & Feelings
The People of the Saints
People of the Seventh Fire
Persistence in Pattern in Mississippi Choctaw Culture
*Pieces of White Shell: A Journey to Navajoland
The Pipe & Christ
Postindian Conversations
The Powhattan Indians of Virginia: Their Traditional Culture
Preserving Traditional Arts: A Toolkit for
  Native American Communities
Red Earth, White Lies
Red Men in Red Square
Rolling Thunder: A Personal Exploration Into the Secret
  Healing Power of an American Indian Medicine Man
Sacred Ground
Seasons of the Kachina
Seeing the White Buffalo
Selling the Indian
Selu: Seeking the Corn-Mother's Wisdom
Shadows of the Indian: Stereotypes in American Culture
The Sioux of the Rosebud: A History in Pictures
The Stars Above, The Earth Below: American Indians
  & Nature
Stories of Our Blackfeet Grandmothers
A Stranger In Her Native Land: Alice Fletcher
  & the American Indians
Strong Hearts, Wounded Souls: Native American
  Veterans of the Vietnam War
A Study in Culture Contact and Culture Change:
  The Whiterock Utes in Transition
The Sun Dance & Other Ceremonies of the Oglala
  Division of the Teton Dakota
Systems of Consanguity and Affinity of the Human Family
Teachings from the American Earth: Indian Religion
  & Philosophy
The Ten Grandmothers
They Sang for Horses: The Impact of the Horse on
  Navajo & Apache Folklore
Through the Eye of the Feather
To Sing Our Own Songs: Cognition & Culture
  in Indian Education
Tradition & Change on the Northwest Coast: The Makah,
  Nuu-chah-nulth, Southern Kwakiutl, & Nuxalk
Traditional Dress
The Transformation of Bigfoot: Maleness,
  Power & Belief Among the Chipewyan
The Vanishing American: The Epic of the Indian
The Vanishing Race: Selection From Edward S. Curtis'
  The North American Indian
The Way We Make Sense
Women in Prehistory

CURTIS, EDWARD S.

Edward S. Curtis & the North American Indian
  Project in the Field
The North American Indian
The North American Indians: Photographs by
  Edward S. Curtis
The Vanishing Race and Other Illusions: Photographs
  of Indians by Edward S. Curtis
The Vanishing Race: Selections from Edward S. Curtis'
  The North American Indian

CUSTER & THE LITTLE BIGHORN

Battle of the Little Bighorn
Cheyenne Memories
Custer & the Battle of the Little Bighorn
Custer Battlefield, A History & Guide to the Battle
  of the Little Bighorn
Custer, Black Kettle, & the Fight on the Washita
Custer & Company
Custer & Crazy Horse
Custer Died for Your Sins
Custer & the Little Bighorn
Custer Lives
The Custer Myth
The Custer Story
The Custer Tragedy
Custer's Chief of Scouts
Custer's Defeat & Other Conflicts in the West
Custer's Fall: The Native American Side of the Story
Custer's Last Battle
Custer's Last Campaign
Custer's Last Stand
Custer's Prelude to Glory
Custer's Seventh Cavalry & the Campaign of 1873
Hokahey! A Good Day to Die
It Is a Good Day to Die: Indian Eyewitnesses Tell the
  Story of the Battle of the Little Bighorn
Lakota Recollections of the Custer Fight: New Sources
  of Indian-Military History
Showdown at the Little Bighorn
*The Story of Little Big Horn
The Story of the Little Big Horn: Custer's Last Fight
Troopers With Custer
Voices of Wounded Knee

DANCE (See MUSIC & DANCE)

DELAWARE/LENAPE INDIANS

*The First Americans Coloring Book:
  Lenape Indian Drawings
The Delaware Indians: A Brief History
The Delaware Indians: A History
The Delaware & Shawnee Admitted to Cherokee Citizenship
Delaware Trails: Some Tribal Records, 1842-1907
The Delawares: A Critical Bibliography
Folk Medicine of the Delaware and Related
  Algonkian Indians
Geographia Americae With an Account of the
  Delaware Indians
*The Indians of New Jersey: Dickon Among the Lenapes
Keeper of the Delaware Dolls
King of the Delawares: Teedyuscung, 1700-1763
Legends of the Delaware Indians & Picture Writing
The Lenape
Lenape History & Numbers Posters
Mythology of the Lenape
*William Penn's Own Account of the Lenni Lenape
  or Delaware Indians
Religion and Ceremonies of the Lenape
A Teacher's Guide to the Lenape

DIRECTORIES, BIBLIOGRAPHIES & REFERENCE BOOKS

Access First Nations
AIDS Regional Directory: Resources in Indian Country
The American Indian & Alaska Native Traders Directory
American Indian/Alaska Native Tribal & Village HIV-1
  Policy Guidelines
American Indian Education: Directory of Organizations
  & Activities in American Indian Education
American Indian Encyclopedia CD-ROM
American Indian Facts of Life
American Indian Index: A Directory of Indian Country
American Indian Literatures
American Indian Reference Books for Children
  & Young Adults
American Indian Resource Manual for Public Libraries
American Indian Women
American Indians in Silent Films
American Indians on Film and Video
Atlas of American Indian Affairs
Atlas of the North American Indian
Bibliography of Articles and Papers on
  North American Indian Art
Bibliography of Native North Americans on Disc - CD-ROM
Biographical Directory of Native American Painters
Cahuilla Dictionary
Celluloid Indians
*Children's Atlas of Native Americans
Church Philanthropy for Native Americans & Other Minorities
Collecting Authentic Indian Arts & Crafts
Comanche Vocabulary
Contemporary Native American Authors:
  A Biographical Dictionary
Corporate and Foundation Fundraising Manual for
  Native Americans
Demographics of American Indians
Digest of American Indian Law
Directory of American Indian Casinos and Bingo Halls
Directory of American Indian Law Attorneys
Directory of Native American Performing Artists
Directory of Native American Tribes of the U.S.
Discover Indian Reservations USA - A Visitor's Guide
E-Mail Names for Indian Country
Education Assistance for American Indians & Alaska Natives
Encyclopedia of American Indian Biography
Encyclopedia of Frontier Biography
Encyclopedia of Multiculturism
Encyclopedia of Native American Healing
Encyclopedia of Native American Religions
*Encyclopedia of Native American Tribes
Encyclopedia of World Cultures
Federal Programs of Assistance to Native Americans
Financial Aid for Native Americans
First Americans Series
First Nations Tribal Directory
From Savage to Nobleman: Images of
  Native Americans in Film
Guide to American Indian Documents
Guide to America's Indians
Guide to the Anasazi & Other Ancient Southwest Indians
Guide to Cherokee Documents in Foreign Archives
Guide to Cherokee Documents
Guide to Community Education
Guide to Federal Funding for Governments & Nonprofits
Guide to Multicultural Resources, 1995-96
Guide to Research on North American Indians & Others
Guide to Indian Artifacts of the Northeast
Guide to Indian Herbs
Guide to Indian Treaties & Other Documents 1778-1902
Guide to Indian Tribes of Oklahoma
Guide to Indian Tribes of the Pacific Northwest
Guide to Native American Music Recordings
Guide to Palaeo-Indian Artifacts of North America

Guide to Prehistoric Ruins of the Southwest
Guide to Proposal Writing
Guide to the Records at the National Archives
Handbook of American Indian Games
Handbook of American Indian Languages
Handbook of American Indian Religious Freedom
Handbook of American Indians North of Mexico, 1907-1910
Handbook of Creek Grammar
Handbook of Federal Indian Law
Handbook of the Indians of California
Handbook pf Native American Literature
Handbook of North American Indians
Handbook of Northeastern Indian Medicinal Plants
Historical Dictionary of North American Archaeology
Hopi Dictionary: A Hopi-English Dictionary of the
  Third Mesa Dialect
Hopi Dictionary: Hopi-English, English-Hopi,
  Grammatical Appendix
Indian Country Address Book
Indian International Motorcycle Directory
The Indian Question CD-ROM
Indian Reservations: A State & Federal Handbook
Indian Tribes of North America
Indians of Arizona: A Guide to Arizona's Heritage
Indians of the Northwest Coast
National Directory of Minority-Owned Businesses
National Directory of Corporate Philanthropy for
  Native Americans
National Directory of Foundation Grants for
  Native Americans
National Directory of Philanthropy for Native Americans
National Directory of Seed Money Grants for
  American Indian Projects
Nations Within a Nation
Native America
Native American Bibliography Series
Native American Biographies
Native American Checklist
Native American Crafts Directory
Native American Directory: Alaska, U.S. & Canada
Native American Directory: Vital Records of
  ME, MA, RI, CT, NY & WI
Native American Indian Artist Directory
Native American Internet Guide
Native American Music Directory
Native American Wisdom
Native American Women
Native Americans in the Saturday Evening Post
Native Americans Information Directory
Native Americans: A Resource Guide
Native California Guide: Weaving Past & Present
The Native North American Almanac
Navajo Dictionary on Diagnostic Terminology
North American Indian Landmarks: A Traveler's Guide
North American Indian Travel Guide
North American Indian Wars - CD-ROM
North American Indians - CD-ROM
North American Native Authors Catalog
Notable Native Americans
Pacific Northwest Americana
Portrait of North American Indians in Published Collections
Pow Wow Calendar
Pow-Wow On the Red Road
Raven's Guide to AIDS Prevention Resources
Research and Writing Tribal Histories
Resource Reading List
Sources of Financial Aid to American Indian Students
Spirit & Reason: The Vine Deloria, Jr. Reader
Talking Chickasaw Dictionary
Tiller's Guide to Indian Country: Economic Profiles
  of American Indian Reservations
A Travelers Guide to Southwest Indian Arts & Crafts
Trends in Indian Health
Ukwehu-Wehnaha Tekawxnate?neyse: An Oneida Dictionary
Who Was Who in Native American History
Who's Who in Indian Relics

DRAMA

American Gypsy: Six Native American Plays
American Indian Theater in Perfromance: A Reader
Celluloid Indians
Dramatic Elements in American Indian Ceremonials
Native Americans as Shown on the Stage, 1753-1916
New Native American Drama: Three Plays
A Pillar of Fire To Follow: American Indian Dramas,
  1808-1859
Seventh Generation: Anthology of Native American Plays
Stories of Our Way: An Anthology of American Indian Plays

DWELLINGS

Indian Homes
The Indian Tipi: Its History, Construction, & Use
*Where Indians Live: American Indian Houses

EARTH ASTROLOGY

Earth Medicine: Ancestor's Way's of Harmony
  for Many Moons
Medicine Wheel Ceremonies
Medicine Wheel: Earth Astrology

Star Warrior: The Story of Swiftdeer
Stars of the First People
*Star Tales

ECONOMIC CONDITIONS

American Indian Ecology
American Indian Education: Government Schools
& Economic Progress
American Indian Energy Resources and Development
American Indians: Facts — Future Toward Economic
Development for Native American Communities
The Cherokee Strip Live Stock Association
A Community Guide to Money
Contemporary Alaskan Native Economies
Culture, Change and Leadership in a Modern Indian
Community: The Colorado River Indian Reservation
The Development of Capitalism in the Navajo Nation:
Political-Economic History
Ecocide of Native America: Environmental Destruction
of Indian Lands & Peoples
Economic Development on American Indian Reservations
Federal Indian Tax Rules
Gambling Survival in Native North America
If You Poison Us: Uranium & Native Americans
Income and Health in a North Indian Village
Invasion of Indian Country in the 20th Century
Mining, the Environment, and Indigenous
Development Conflicts
Native Americans & Wage Labor
Navajo Energy Resources
Navajo Land Use: An Ethnoarchaeological Study
Navajo Resources and Economic Development
The New Resource Wars: Native and Environmental
Struggles Against Multinational Corporations
A People's Ecology: Explorations in Sustainable Living
*Peril at Thunder Ridge: A Guide for
Native American and Rural Communities
The Political Economy of North American Indians
Pressing Issues of Inequality & American Indian
Communities
Property Concepts of the Navaho Indians
The Re-Establishment of the Indians in Their Pueblo Life
Through the Revival of Their Traditional Crafts:
A Study in Home Extension Education
Red Capitalism: An Analysis of the Navajo Economy
The Roots of Dependency: Subsistence, Environment, &
Social Change Among the Choctaws, Pawnees, & Navajos
The Roots of Oppression: The American Indian Question
Roots of Resistance: Land Tenure in New Mexico
(1680-1980)
San Diego County Indians As Farmers and Wage Earners
Trusteeship in Change: Toward Tribal Autonomy in
Resource Management
The Underground Reservation: Osage Oil
What Can Tribes Do? Strategies & Institutions in
American Indian Economic Development
When Indians Became Cowboys
You Are On Indian Land: Alcatraz Island, 1969-1971

EDUCATION
(STUDY & TEACHING)

*A,B,C's The American Indian Way
America's Indians: Unit Study Outline
The American Indian & Alaska Native Higher
Education Funding Guide
American Indian & Alaskan Natives in
Postsecondary Education
American Indian Education: Government Schools
and Economic Progress
American Indian Education: A History
American Indian Issues in Higher Education
The American Indian Reader
The American Indian Reader: Education
American Indian Reference Books for Children
American Indian Stereotypes in the World of Children:
A Reader and a Bibliography
Amerian Indian Studies: An Interdisciplinary Approach
to Contemporary Issues
The American Indian: Yesterday, Today & Tomorrow
Annals of Shawnee Methodist Mission and Indian
Manual Labor
Away From Home: American Indian Boarding
School Experiences, 1879-2000
Bacone Indian University
Battlefield & Classroom: Four Decades with the
American Indian, 1867-1904
Bilingual Education for American Indians
Classroom Activities on Wisconsin Indian Treaties
& Tribal Sovereignty
*Columbus Day
Community-Based Research: A Handbook for
Native Americans
Complete Native American Resource Library:
Ready-to-Use Activities & Materials
Daksi
*Dine, the Navajo
The Dove Always Cried: Narratives of Indian School Life
Education and the American Indian
Education Assistance for American Indians & Alaska Natives

Education & Career Opportunities Handbook
Education for Extinction: American Indianns and
the Boarding School Experience, 1875-1928
*An Educational American Indian Coloring Book
Effective Practices in Indian Education
The Elders Are Watching
Essie's Story: The Life & Legacy of a Shoshoni Teacher
Formal Education in an American Indian Community
A Guide to Community Education
Guide to Proposal Writing
Guide to Records in the National Archives Relating
to American Indians
Guide to Research on North American Indians
Hear the Creator's Song: A Guide to the Study Theme
*Native Peoples of North America
Hiapsi Wami Seewam: Flowers of Life : A Curriculum
Guide of Yaqui Culture & Art
History of Indian Arts Education in Santa Fe
A History of Indian Education
History & Present Development of Indian Schools in the U.S.
*Hopi, the Desert Farmers
How to Teach About American Indians: A Guide
for the School Library Media Specialist
Identifying Outstanding Talent in American Indian
& Alaskan Native Students
*Inde, the Western Apache
Indian Education - Elementary, Secondary & Guidance
Indian School Days
Indians & Anthropologists: Vine Deloria, Jr.
& the Critique of Anthropology
Indians at Hampton Institue, 1877-1923
Indians of North America: Methods & Sources
for Library Research
Indigenous Community-Based Education
Inside the Culture (Teacher & Student Workbooks)
Issues for the Future of American Indian Studies
Keepers of the Animals
Keepers of the Earth
Lies My Teach Told Me
Look To the Mountain: An Ecology of Indigenous Education
Lost Tribes and Sunken Continents: Myth and Method
in the Study of American Indians
Maskiki: Old Medicine Nourishing the New
Multicultural Education and the American Indian
*Na Yo Pisa
Native American Arts & Culture
*Native American Cultures
Native American Curricular Lessons
Native American Directory: Alaska, U.S. and Canada
Native American Higher Education in the U.S.
Native American Pedagogy & Cognitive-Based
Mathematics Instruction
Native American Periodicals and Newspapers, 1828-1982:
Bibliography, Publishing Record and Holdings
Native American Reader: Stories, Speeches & Poems
Native American Research Information Service
Native Americans
Native Americans: An Integrated Unit
*Native Americans: A Personal History Book
Native Americans: A Thematic Unit
Native Education Directory
*Native Peoples of the Southwest
Natives & Academics: Research & Writing
About American Indians
A Natural Education
Navajo Education in Action: The Rough Rock
Demonstration School
Navajo Education, 1948-1978: Its Progress and Its Problems
The Navajos Long Walk for Education
Next Steps: Research & Practice to Advance
Indian Education
No Turning Back: A Hopi Indian Woman's Struggle
to Live in Two Worlds
Northern Voices: Inuit Writing in English
One House, One Voice, One Heart:
Native American Education
O'Odham, Indians of the Sonoran Desert
A Parent's Guide to the BIA Special Education Process
Pathways to Excellence
Phoenix Indian School: The Second Half Century
The Phoenix Indian School: Forced Assimilation in
Arizona, 1891-1935
The Politics of Second Generation Discrimination
in American Indian Education
Promises of the Past: A History of Indian Education
The Rapid City Indian School, 1898-1933
The Re-Establishment of the Indians in Their Pueblo Life
Resource Reading List
Resources for American Indian Rehabilitation
Respect for Life: The Traditional Upbringing of
American Indian Children
Schooling At-Risk Native American Children
Self-Determination & the Social Education of
Native Americans
Shingwauk's Vision: A History of Native Residential Schools
Studying Native America: Problems & Prospects
Tales of North America: Native Americans
A Teacher's Guide to the Lenape
Teaching About American Indians in Connecticut
Teaching About Native Americans
Teaching American Indian History
Teaching American Indian Students
Teaching Guide for Indian Literature

Teaching the Native American
Thanksgiving: A Native Perspective
They Called It Prairie Light: The Story of
Chilocco Indian School
Three Strands in the Brand: A Guide for Enablers of Learning
Through Indian Eyes: The Native Experience in
Books for Children
To Change Them Forever: Indian Education at the
Rainy Mountain Boarding School, 1893-1920
To Live Heroically: Institutional Racism &
American Indian Education
To Live on This Earth: American Indian Education
To Sing Our Own Songs: Cognition &
Culture in Indian Education
Tribal Dispossession and the Ottawa Indian University Fraud
Tribally Controlled Colleges: Making Good Medicine
The Tribally Controlled Community Colleges
Unlearning "Indian" Stereotypes, A Teaching Unit
for Elementary Teachers & Children's Librarians
The Wabanakis of Maine & the Maritmes
Woodland Peoples: An Educational Unit
Writing to Create Ourselves

ETHICS

The Circle Without End: A Sourcebook of
American Indian Ethics
I Have Come to Step Over Your Soul: A True
Narrative of Murder & Indian Justice

FICTION

All My Relations: An Anthology of Contemporary
Canadian Native Fiction
Almanac of the Dead
The American Indian in Short Fiction:
An Annotated Bibliography
American Indian Life
Ancestral Voice
Apache Autumn
Bearheart: The Heirship Chronicles
The Bingo Palace
Bone Game: A Novel
The Book of One Tree
Bone Game
Butterfly Lost
Ceremony
Chancers: A Novel
Cherokee Dragon: A Novel
Cogewea, The Half-Blood
Comanche Warbonnet
Critical Fictions: The Politics of Imaginative Writings
Daring Donald McKay: Or, The Last War Trial of the Modocs
Dawn Land
The Death of Bernadette Lefthand
The Death of Jim Lonely
Deception on All Accounts
Designs of the Night Sky
Drowning in Fire
Earth Power Coming: Short Fiction in
Native American Literature
Elnguq
Faces in the Moon
Fathers & Crows
Field of Honor
Firesticks: A Collection of Stories
Fools Crow
Four Masterworks of American Indian Literature
The Fus Fixico Letters
Hiroshima Bugi: Atomu 57
House Made of Dawn
The Indian Lawyer
Ishi Means Man
Laughing Boy
The Light People: A Novel
The Lightning Within
Long River
The Lost Band: A Novel
Malaeska
Man Who Killed the Deer
The Map of Who W Are: A Novel
Medicine Hat: A Novel
Medicine River
Mountain Windsong: A Novel of the Trail of Tears
The Native American in Long Fiction
Nightland" A Novel
One Indian and Two Chiefs
Oracles: A Novel
The Pipestone Quest: A Novel
The Portable North American Indian Reader
The Powwow Highay
The Punishment of the Stingy
Ramona
The Sharpest Sight: A Novel
Smith & Other Events: Tales of the Chilcotin
A Story of Deep Delight
Strange Business
The Trickster of Liberty
Turtle Belly: A Novel
War Woman: A Novel
Waterlily
Winter in the Blood

Winter of the Holy Iron
The Wolf and the Buffalo
Wolfsong: A Novel
A Woman of the People
Woodsmen, or Thoreau & the Indians: A Novel
Woven Stone
Charlie Young Bear

FIVE CIVILIZED TRIBES

The Chickasaws
Five Civilized Tribes
The Five Civilized Tribes: A Bibliography
Indian Removal: The Emigration of Five Civilized
  Tribes of Indians
Nations Remembered: An Oral History of the Five
  Civilized Tribes, 1865-1907
Notices of East Florida; With An Account of the
  Seminole Nation of Indians
Pow Wow Chow
Reconstruction in Indian Territory
The Southern Indians: The Story of the Civilized
  Tribes Before Removal

FOOD—COOKING

Alaskan Native Food Practices, Customs & Holidays
American Indian Cooking
American Indian Cooking & Herblore
American Indian Food: Sixty-One Indian Recipes
The Art of American Indian Cooking
Artistic Tastes: Favorite Recipes of Native American Artists
The Buckskinner's Cookbook
Cherokee Cooklore
Cherokee Plants
Cooking With Spirit
Corn Recipes from the Indians
*Earthmaker's Lodge
Enduring Harvests: Native American Foods &
  Festivals for Every Season
Ethno-Botany of the Gosiute Indians of Utah
Famous Florida! Seminole Indian Recipes
Food Plants of Coastal First Peoples
Food Plants of Interior First Peoples
From Fingers to Finger Bowls
Going Native: American Indian Cookery
R.C. Gorman's Nudes & Foods
Guide to Indian Herbs
Handbook of Native American Herbs
Heard in the Kitchen: The Heard Museum Guild Cookbook
Hopi Cookery
How Indians Use Wild Plants for Food, Medicine & Crafts
Idonapshe, Let's Eat: Traditional Zuni Foods
Indian Cooking
Indian Corn of the Americas, Gift to the World
Indian Recipe Book
Indian Foods and Fibers of Arid America
Indian Uses of Native Plants
Insects As Food: Aboriginal Entomophgy in the Great Basin
Kokopelli's Cookbook
Mechanisms & Trends in the Decline of the Costanoan Indian
  Population of Central California: Nutrition & Health in
  Pre-Contact California & Mission Period Environments
The Minnesota Ethnic Food Book
*Native American Foods
Native American Gardening
Native Harvests: Recipes & Botanicals of the
  American Indian
Native American Wild Game, Fish & Wild Foods Cookbook
Native Wild Game: Fish & Wild Foods Cookbook
Navajo Food Practices, Customs & Holidays
Pow Wow Chow
Pueblo Indian Cookbook
Southwest Cooks! The Tradition of Native American Cuisines
Southwest Indian Cookbook
Southwestern Indian Recipe Book
Spirit of the Harvest: North American Indian Cooking
Tepee Cookery
Traditional Plant Foods of Canadian Indigenous Peoples
Traditional Stories & Foods
A Woodland Feast

FRENCH & INDIAN WAR, 1755-1763

America's First First World War: The French & Indian War,
  1754-1763
*The American Revolutionaries: A History
  in Their Own Words
Empire and Liberty: American Resistance to British
  Authority, 1755-1763
Empire of Fortune: Crowns, Colonies, & Tribes in the
  Seven Years War in America
*Fawn
*The Fight for Freedom, 1750-1783
Fight With France for North America
French & Indian War Battle Sites: A Controversy
The French & Indian War in Pennsylvania, 1753-1763
General Orders of 1757, Issued by the Earl of Loudoun
  and Phineas Lyman in the Campaign Against the French
An Historical Journal of the Campaigns in North America
  for the Years 1757-1760
The History of the Indian Wars in New England

The History of Philip's War
How George Rogers Clark Won the Northwest &
  Other Essays in Western History
*The Indian Wars
Jeferson's America: 1760-1815
*The Last of the Mohicans
Logs of the Conquest of Canada
Major General Adam Stephen and the
  Cause of American Liberty
Manuscript Records of the French & Indian War
Massachusetts Officers & Soldiers in the
  French & Indian Wars, 1755-56
Massacre at Fort Bull: The Delery Expedition
  Against Oneida Carry, 1756
Memoirs of Lt. Henry Timberlake
Mid-Appalachian Frontier: A Guide to Historic
  Sites of the French & Indian War
Military Affairs in North America, 1748-1765
Military Journals of Two Private Soldiers, 1758-1775
Montcalm and Wolfe
Narrative of the Captivity of Mrs Johnson
New England Captives Carried to Canada
Ohio Valley in Colonial Days
A Particular History of the Five Years French & Indians
  Wars in New England
A People's Army: Massachusetts Soldiers & Society
  in the Seven Year's War
Pioneers of New France in New England
Rangers & Redcoats on the Hudson
Sketchbook '56 The French & Indian War 1756-1763
Shipping and the American War, 1755-1783:
  A Study of British Transport Organization
Slim Buttes, 1876: An Episode of the Great Sioux War
*Struggle for a Continent: The French & Indian Wars,
  1690-1760
True Stories of New England Captives Carried to Canada
  During the Old French & Indian Wars
Wilderness Empire
Wilderness Politics and Indian Gifts: The Northern
  Colonial Frontier, 1748-1763
Writings of General John Forbes Relating to His
  Service in North America

GAMES

*American Indian Games
American Indian LaCrosse
*Chumash Indian Games
Exploring the Outdoors With Indian Secrets
Games of the North American Indians
Grass Games & Moon Races: California Indian
  Games & Toys
Handbook of American Indian Games
*Indian Games & Crafts
Indian Games & Dances With Native Songs
The Pawnee Ghost Dance Hand Game
*Sports & Games the Indians Gave Us
Twana Games

GAMING

Directory of American Indian Casinos and Bingo Halls
General Requirements & Parameters for Vendor Licensing
The Indian Gaming Handbook
Indian Gaming & the Law
Indian Gaming: Who Wins?
National Indian Gaming Association-NIGA Indian
  Gaming Resource Directory
National Indian Gaming Minimum Internal Control
  Standards for Indian Casinos
Tax Policy: A Profile of the Indian Gaming Industry

GENEALOGY

American Indian Marriage Record Directory
  for Ashland Co., Wisc.
Black Indian Genealogy Research
Catawba Indian Genealogy
Cherokee Connections
Cherokee Proud: A Guide to Tracing & Honoring Your
  Cherokee Ancestors
Cherokee Roots
Choctaw & Chickasaw Early Census Records
Choctaw Claimants & Their Heirs
Descendants of Nancy Ward: A Workbook for
  Further Research
Earnest Genealogy: Indian Eve & Her Descendants,
  an Indian Story of Bedford Co.
Flandreau Papers Treasures Trove for Mixed Blood
  Dakota Indian Genealogy
How to Research American Indian Blood Lines
Indians from New York in Wisconsin & Elsewhere:
  A Genealogy Reference
Native American Ancestors: Eastern Tribes
Native American Directory: Vital Records of
  ME, MA, RI, CT, NY & WI
Native American Genealogical Sourcebook
Ojibwa Chiefs, 1690-1890: An Annotated Listing
Tracing Ancestors Among the Five Civilized Tribes
Turtles, Wolves & Bears: A Mohawk Family History
Unhallowed Intrusions, a History of Cherokee
  Families in Forsyth Co., GA

Utilization of Genograms & Eco-Maps
Who's Looking for Whom in Native American Ancestry

GERONIMO

Bloody Trail of Geronimo
Geronimo
*Geronimo
Geronimo Campaign
Geronimo and the End of the Apache Wars
Geronimo: Last Renegade of the Apache
Geronimo: The Man, His Time, His Place
Geronimo's Kids: A Teacher's Lessons
  on the Apache Reservation
Geronimo's Story of His Life
I Fought With Geronimo
Indians of America: Geronimo
The Story of Geronimo
The Truth About Geronimo
When Geronimo Rode
Wild Justice: The People of Geronimo vs. the U.S.

GHOST DANCE

The American Indian Ghost Dance, 1870 & 1890:
  An Annotated Bibliography
The Cherokee Ghost Dance
Ghost Dance
Ghost Dance Messiah: The Jack Wilson Story
Ghost-Dance Religion & the Sioux Outbreak of 1890
Ghost Dancers in the West: The Sioux at Pine Ridge
  & Wounded Knee in 1891
Last Days of the Sioux Nation
The Maru Cult of the Pomo Indians: A California
  Ghost Dance Survival
The Pawnee Ghost Dance Hand Game:
  Ghost Dance Revival & Ethnic Identity
Wovoka and the Ghost Dance: A Source Book

GOVERNMENT RELATIONS

Agents of Repression: The FBIs Secret Wars Against
  the Black Panther Party & the American Indian Movement
Airlift to Wounded Knee
Alaska Native Policy in the Twentieth Century
American Indian Activism: Alcatraz to the Longest Walk
American Indian Holocaust and Survival:
  A Population History Since 1492
American Indian in the U.S., Period 1850-1914
American Indian Policy & American Reform
Amerian Indian Policy & Cultural Values
American Indian Policy in the Formative Years:
  The Indian Trade and Intercourse Acts, 1790-1834
American Indian Policy in the Jacksonian Era
American Indian Policy in the Twentieth Century
The American Indian Reader: Current Affairs
American Indian Societies
American Indian Treaties: The History of a Political Anomaly
American Indian Tribal Governments
American Indian and the U.S.
American Indians and the Law
American Indians: Facts—Future Toward Economic
  Development for Native American Communities
American Indians & National Parks
American Indians: A Select Catalog of National
  Archives Microfilm Publications
American Protestantism and U.S. Indian Policy, 1869-1882
Americanizing the American Indians: Writings by the
  Friends of the Indian, 1880-1900
Apache Agent: The Story of John P. Clum
Appalachian Indian Frontier: The Edmond Atkin
  Report and Plan of 1755
The Army and the Navajo: The Bosque Redondo
  Reservation Experiment, 1863-1868
Art and Eskimo Power: The Life & Times
  of Alaskan Howard Rock
The Assault of Indian Tribalism: The General Allotment
  Law (Dawes Act) of 1887
Battle Canyon
Behind the Trail of Broken Treaties
Beyond the Reservation
Bibliographical Guide to the History of
  Indian-White Relations in the U.S.
Black Hills, White Justice: The Sioux Nation
  vs. the U.S., 1775 to the Present
The Blackfoot Confederacy, 1880-1920: A Comparative
  Study of Canada & U.S. Indian Policy
Border Towns of the Navajo Nation
Bread & Freedom
The Campo Indian Landfill War
Canadian Indian Policy & Development Planning Theory
The Canoe Rocks: Alaska's Tlingit
A Century of Dishonor: A Sketch of the U.S. Government's
  Dealing with Some of the Indian Tribes
Champions of the Cherokees: Evan & John B. Jones
Chasing Shadows: Apaches & Yaquis Along the
  U.S.-Mexico Border
The Cherokee Cases: Two Landmark Federal
  Decisions in the Fight for Sovereignty
The Cherokee Ghost Dance
The Cheyenne and Arapaho Ordeal:
  Reservation & Agency Life

Chippewa Treaty Rights
Claims for Depredations by Sioux Indians
William Clark: Jeffersonian Man on the Frontier
Code of Federal Regulations, Title 25: Indians
The Coeur d'Alene Indian Reservations
Felix S. Cohen's Handbook of Federal Indian Law
John Collier's Crusade for Indian Reform, 1920-1954
Command of the Waters: Iron Triangles, Federal
    Water Development, & Indian Water
The Commissioners of Indian Affairs, 1824-1977
Conquest of the Karankawas & the Tonkawas, 1821-1859
Considerations on the Present State of the Indians &
    Their Removal to the West of the Mississippi
Crazy Horse & Custer
Crosscurrents Along the Colorado
Crossing the Pond: The Native American
    Effort in World War II
Custer Died for Your Sins: An Indian Manifesto
Dammed Indians: The Pick-Sloan Plan and the
    Missouri River Sioux, 1944-1980
Depredations by Sioux Indians
Diplomates in Buckskins: A History of Indian
    Delegations in Washington City
Dispossessing the American Indian:
    Indian & Whites on the Colonial Frontier
The Dispossession of the American Indian, 1887-1934
Documents of American Indian Diplomacy
Documents of U.S. Indian Policy
Dominion & Civility
The Dynamics of Government Programs for
    Urban Indians in the Prairie Provinces
Early American Indian Documents, Treaties and Laws,
    1607-1789 Volume 11: Georgia Treatise, 1733-1763
The Emigrant Indians of Kansas: A Critical Bibliography
Empty Nets: Indians, Dams, and the Columbia River
The End of Indian Kansas: A Study of Cultural Revolution,
    1854-1871
Executive Orders Relating to Indian Reservations
Expansion and American Indian Policy, 1783-1812
Federal Concern About Conditions of California Indians,
    1853-1913
Federal Indian Law Cases & Materials
The First Canadians
The First Social Experiments in America
Fish in the Lakes, Wild Rice & Game in Abundance
The Florida Seminole and the New Deal, 1933-1942
Forgotten Tribes: Unreconized Indians & the
    Federal Acknowledgement Process
Formulating American Indian Policy in New York State,
    1970-1986
Ghost Dancing the Law: The Wounded Knee Trials
The Great Father: The U.S. Government and the
    American Indians
The Great Law & the Longhouse: A Political History
    of the Iroquois Confederacy
Guide to American Indian Documents in the
    Congressional Serial Set: 1817-1899
Guide to Understanding Chippewa Treaty Rights
Handbook of Federal Indian Law
Heeding the Voices of Our Ancestors
A History of the Bureau of Indian Affairs
    and Its Activities Among Indians
Hollow Victory
Home to Medicine Mountain
Imperfect Victories: The Legal Tenacity of the
    Omaha Tribe, 1945-1995
In a Barren Land: American Indian Dispossession & Survival
Index to the Decisions of the Indian Claims Commission
Index to the Expert Testimony Presented Before
    the Indian Claims Commission
Indian Affairs: Laws & Treaties
Indian Agents of the Old Frontier
Indian and His Problem
Indian Self-Rule
Indian Slave Trade in the Southwest
Indian Territory and the U.S., 1866-1906
The Indian Trial
Indian Treaties
Indian Tribal Claims
IndianTribes As Sovereign Governments: A Sourcebook
    on Federal-Tribal History, Law & Policy
Indian Voices: The Native American Today
Indian-White Relations: A Persistent Paradox
Indian-White Relationships in Northern California, 1849-1920
Indians & Bureaucrats
Indians in the Making: Ethnic Relations & Indian Identities
    Around Puget Sound
The Indians' Land Title in California:
    A Case In Federal Equity, 1851-1942
Indians' New South: Cultural Change in the
    Colonial Southeast
Indians of the Americas: Self-Determination &
    International Human Rights
Indians & the U.S. Government
Into the American Woods
The Intruders: The Illegal Residents of the
    Cherokee Nation,1866-1907
Intruders Within: Pueblo Resistance to Spanish
    Rule & the Revolt of 1680
The Invasion of America
The Invasion of Indian Country in the 20th Century
The Invested Indian: Cultural Fictions & Government Policies
An Inventory of the Mission Indian Agency Records

An Inventory of the Pala Indian Agency Records
Invisible Indigenes: The Politics of Nonrecognition
The Iroquois and the New Deal
Irredeemable America: The Indians' Estate & Land Claims
Thomas Jefferson & the Changing West
Jefferson's America: 1760-1815
Kinsmen of Another Kind: Dakota-White Relations
    in the Upper Mississippi Valley, 1650-1862
Land of the Spotted Eagle
Last Days of the Sioux Nation
The Last Shall Be First
License for Empire: Colonialism by Treaty in Early America
Life Among the Paiutes: Their Wrongs and Claims
Like a Hurricane: The Indian Movement from
    Alcatraz to Wounded Knee
Lincoln and the Indians: Civil War Policy and Politics
Linking Arms Together
Lost Harvests: Prairie Indian Reserve
    Farmers & Government Policy
Loud Hawk: The U.S. Versus the American Indian Movement
Making Peace With Cochise
Massacre: A Survey of Today's American Indian
Massacre at the Yuma Crossing
The Military and the U.S. Indian Policy, 1865-1903
Mixed-Bloods and Tribal Dssolution: Charles Curtis
    & the Quest for Indian Identity
Modern American Indian Tribal Government and Politics
My Friend the Indian
My Nation: The American Indian & the U.S., 1820-1890
Nairne's Muskhogean Journals: The 1708 Expedition
    to the Mississippi River
Name of Salish & Kootenai Nation
Nation-States & Indians in Latin America
The Nations Within: The Past and Future of
    American Indian Sovereignty
Native American Affairs & the Department of Defense
Native American Communities in Wisconsin, 1600-1960
Native American Law & Colonialism Before 1776 to 1903
*Native American Testimony: An Anthology of Indian and
    White Relations, First Encounter to Dispossession
Native American Tribalism: Indian Survivals and Renewals
Native Americans: Akew:Kon's Journal of Indigenous Issues
Native Americans & the Early Republic
Native Americans & Nixon: Presidential Politics
    and Minority Self-Determination
Native Americans & Public Policy
Native People in Canada: Contemporary Conflicts
The New American State Papers: Indian Affairs, 1789-1860
The New Deal and American Indian Tribalism
New Directions in Federal Indian Policy
New Hope for the Indians: The Grant Peace Policy & the
    Navajos in the 1870s
Noble Red Man: LakotaWisdomkeeper Mathew King
The Occupation of Alcatraz Island
Occupation of Wounded Knee
Office of Indian Affairs, 1824-1880: Historical Sketches
Our Indian Wards
Our Red Brothers and the Peace Policy of
    President Ulysses S. Grant
Pathways to Self-Determination: Canadian Indians
    and the Canadian State
The Pawnee Ghost Dance Hand Game
The Political Outsiders: Blacks and Indians in a
    Rural Oklahoma County
The Politics of Hallowed Ground: Wounded Knee
    & the Struggle for Indian Sovereignty
The Politics of Indian Removal: Creek
    Government and Society in Crisis
The Protector de Indios in Colonial New Mexico, 1659-1821
Quarter-Acre of Heartache
Vasco de Quiroga and His Pueblo-Hospitals of Santa Fe
A Race at Bay: NY Times Editorials on the
    "Indian Problem," 1860-1900
Race Relations in British North America, 1670-1783
The Rape of the Indian Lands: An Original Anthology
Red Cloud and the Sioux Problem
The Red King's Rebellion: Racial Politics in
    New England, 1675-78
Red Man's Land, White Man's Law: The Past &
    Present Status of the American Indian
Red Power: The American Indians' Fight for Freedom
Red & White: Indian Views of the White Man, 1492-1982
Report to the Secretary of War of the U.S., On Indian Affairs
Reservation to City: Indian Urbanization and
    Federal Relocation
Retained by the People: A History of American Indians
    & the Bill of Rights
The Return of the Native: American Indian
    Political Resurgence
Rise and Fall of the Choctaw Republic
Theodore Roosevelt & Six Friends of the Indian
Seeds of Empire: The American Revolutionary
    Conquest of the Iroquois
Seeds of Extinction: Jeffersonian Philanthropy
    and the American Indian
The Search for an American Indian Identity:
    Modern Pan-American Movements
Self and Savagery on the California Frontier
Self-Determination & the Social Education
    of Native Americans
Some Newspaper References Concerning Indian-White
    Relationships in Northeastern California, 1850-1920
State Tribal Relations; Into the 21st Century

State-Tribal Relationships-Reports
John Stuart & the Southern Colonial Frontier
Surviving As Indians: The Challenge of Self-Government
Taking Indian Lands: The Cherokee (Jerome)
    Commission, 1889-1893
Termination and Relocation: Federal Indian Policy,
    1945-1960
Termination Revisited
Termination's Legacy: The Discarded Indians of Utah
Theodore Roosevelt & Six Friends of the Indian
They Have No Rights
The Timucuan Chiefdoms of Spanish Florida
To Fish in Common
To Have This Land: The Nature of Indian/White
    Relations in South Dakota
To Preserve a Culture: The 20th Century Fight
    Over Indian Reorganization
To Show Heart: Native American Self-Determination
    and Federal Indian Policy, 1960-1975
Tonto's Revenge
The Trail of Tears
Tribal Assets: The Rebirth of Native America
Tribal Government: The Wind River Reservation
*Tribal Sovereignty: Indian Tribes
Two Worlds: The Indian Encounter with the
    European, 1492-1509
Uncle Sam's Stepchildren: The Reformation
    of U.S. Indian Policy, 1865-1887
Understanding Tolowa Histories
The View from Officers' Row: Army Perceptions
    of Western Indians
Voices from Wounded Knee, 1973, In the Words
    of the Participants
Walking in Indian Moccasins
The Walleye War
Walleye Warriors
Wampum Belts & Peace Trees
Western American Indian: Case Studies in Tribal History
The Western Military Frontier, 1815-1846
The Western Odyssey of John Simpson Smith:
    Frontiersman & Indian Interpreter
A Whirlwind Passes
Who Was Who in Native American History
Wilderness Politics and Indian Gifts: The Northern
    Colonial Frontier, 1748-1763
The Wind Won't Know Me: History of the
    Navajo-Hopi Land Dispute

HAIDA INDIANS

Being in Being
Gyaehlingaay: Traditions, Tales, & Images of the Kaigani
    Haida
Haida Songs and Tsimshian Texts
Haida Texts & Myths
Haida: Their Art & Culture
Nine Visits to the Mythworld: Ghandl of the
    Qayahl Llaanas
Raven's Cry
The Raven Steels the Light
A Story As Sharp As a Knife: The Classical Haida
    Mythtellers & Their World

HAVASUPAI INDIANS

Grand Canyon: Intimate Views
Havasupai Habitat
Havasupai Legends
Havasupai Years
Havsuw Baaja: People of Blue Green Water
People of the Blue Water
Wauba Yuma's People
The Wilderness of the Southwest

HEALTH
(MENTAL HEALTH)

AIDS Regional Directory: Resources in Indian Country
American Indian & Alaska Native Health
American Indian Family Support Systems
American Indian Medicine
Bibliography of North American Indian Mental Health
Changing Numbers, Changing Needs
Community Health & Mental Health Care Delivery for
    North American Indians
Counseling American Indians
Coyote's Council Fire
Crow Indian Medicine Bundles
Death Stalks the Yakima
Diabetes Epidemic Hearing Before the
    Committee on Indian Affairs
Diabetes in Native Americans: The Eastern Tribes
Diagnosis & Treatment of Prevalent Diseases of
    North American Indian Populations, I and II
Disciplined Hearts: History, Identity & Depression
    in an American Indian Community
Disease & Demography in the Americas
Doctors of Medicine in New Mexico: A History of
    Health & Medical Practice, 1886-1986
Drinking Careers: A 25-Year Study of Three
    Navajo Populations

Early Intervention with American Indian Families:
   An Annotated Bibliography
Encyclopedia of Native Ameriacn Healing
Federal Personnel: Public Health Service
Folk Medicine of the Delaware and Related
   Algonkian Indians
Gathering of Wisdoms: Tribal Mental Health -
   A Cultural Perspective
Geraniums for the Iroquois: A Field Guide to
   American Indian Medicinal Plants
The Growing Path
Guide to Indian Herbs
Healing Herbs of the Upper Rio Grand:
   Traditional Medicine of the Southwest
Healing Ways: Navajo Health Care in the Twentieth Century
Health & Diseases of American Indians North of Mexico:
   A Bibliography, 1800-1969
The Health of Native Americans Towards a
   Biocultureal Epidemiology
HIV Prevention in Native American Communities: A Manual
Income and Health in a North Indian Village
Indian Healing
Indian Health Service: Improvements Needed in
   Credentialing Temporary Physicians
Indian Medicine Power
The Journey of Native American People With Serious
   Mental Illness: First National Conference
Keepers of the Central Fire Issues in Ecology for
   Indigenous Peoples
Killing Us Quietly: Native Americans & HIV/AIDS
Lakota Belief and Ritual
A Long Way from Home: Tuberculosis Epidemic
   Among the Inuit
Medicinal Uses of Plants by Indian Tribes of Nevada
The Medicine Man of the American Indian &
   His Cultural Background
Native American AIDS Statistics
Navajo Dictionary on Diagnostic Terminology
Navajo Medicine Man Sand Paintings
Notes on the Gynecology and Obstetrics of the
   Arikara Tribe of Indians
Perspectives on Health Care Delivery Systems for
   American Indian Families
The Pima Indians: Pathfinders for Health
Piman Shamanism and Staying Sickness: Ka:
   Cim Mumkidag
Pretty-Shield, Medicine Woman of the Crows
Profiles in Wisdom: Native Elders Speak About the Earth
Restoring Balance: Community-Directed Health
   Promotion for American Indians & Native Alaskans
Rolling Thunder: A personal Exploration Into the Secret
   Healing Power of an American Indian Medicine Man
Sanapia: Comanche Medicine Woman
The Shaman & the Medicine Wheel
Smallpox and the Iroquois Wars
A Study of Delaware Indian Medicine Practice & Folk Beliefs
Survival Skills of the North American Indians
Their Secrets: Why Navajo Indians Never Get Cancer
Tuberculosis Among Certain Indian Tribes of the U.S.
Vectors of Death: The Archaeology of European Contact
The Vocational Rehabilitation of American Indians Who
   Have Alcohol or Other Substance Abuse Disorders
White Man's Medicine: Government Doctors & The Navajo,
   1863-1955

HISTORY

Adventures on the Western Frontier
After Removal: The Choctaw in Mississippi
All Roads Are Good: Native Voices on Life & Culture
America Before the European Invasions
America On Paper, The First Hundred Years
America's Fascinating Indian Heritage
*American Bison
American Encounters
The American Buffalo in Transition
The American Indian
The American Indian, 1492-1976: A Chronology & Fact Book
American Indian Education: A History
*The American Indian Experience
American Indian Holocaust & Survival
American Indian: Past & Present
American Indian Policy
American Indian Policy in the 20th Century
American Indian Population Recovery in the 20th Century
American Indian Quotations
American Indian Reader
American Indian Resource Materials in the
   Western History Collection
American Indian Studies
American Indian Treaties: The History of a Political Anomaly
American Indian and the U.S.
American Indian Warrior Chiefs
American Indians
*The American Indians
*The American Indians in America—Volume II:
   The Late 18th Century to the Present
American Indians in U.S. History
American Indians & World War II
American Indians in World War I
American Nations: Encounters in Indian Country, 1850-2000
The American Revolution in Indian Country
The American West

Among the Apaches
The Appalachian Indian Frontier
Appalachian Mountain AniYunwiya
As Long As the Grass Shall Grow and the Rivers Flow:
   A History of Native Americans
Atlas of American Indian Affairs
Atlas of Great Lakes Indian History
Atlas of Indians of North America
Attitudes of Colonial Powers Toward the American Indian
Bacavi: A Hopi Village
Bad Men & Bad Towns
Battlefield and Classroom: Four Decades
   With the American Indian, 1867-1904
Battles & Skirmishes of the Great Sioux War, 1876-1877:
   The Military View
Bayonets in the Wilderness: Anthony Wayne's
   Legion in the Old Northwest
Bear Chief's War Shirt
Before the Storm: American Indians Before Columbus
*Between Sacred Mountains: Navajo Stories and
   Lessons from the Land
Beyond the Covenant Chain
Beyond the Hundredth Meridian
The Birth of America
Bitterness Road: The Mojave, 1604-1860
Black, Brown & Red
Black, Red and Deadly: Black and Indian Gunfighters
   of the Indian Territories
Blood At Sand Creek: The Massacre Revisited
Blood of the Land: The Government and Corporate
   War Against the American Indian Movement
Franz Boas: The Early Years, 1858-1906
Bread & Freedom
A Brief History of the Indian Peoples
The Broken Ring: The Destruction of the California Indians
Buffalo Hearts
Buried Roots & Indestructible Seeds
Bury My Heart at Wounded Knee: An Indian
   History of the American West
Cambridge History of the Native Poeples of the Americas
Cartographies of Desire
Celebrate Native America! An Aztec Book of Days
Chainbreaker: The Revolutionary War
   Memoirs of Governor Blacksnake
Cherokee Americans Eastern Band of Cherokees
   in the 20th Century
The Cherokee Freedmen: From Emancipation to
   American Citizenship
The Cherokee Indian Nation: A Troubled History
Cherokee Removal: The William Penn Essays and
   Other Writings by Jeremiah Evarts
Cherokees in Transition: A Study of Changing Culture
   and Environment Prior to 1775
The Chicago American Indian Community, 1893-1988
Chiefs & Challengers
Chinigchinich
The Chippewa and Their Neighbors: A Study in Ethnohistory
Christian Harvest
Chronology of the American Indian
Chronology of Native North American History From
   Pre-Columbian Times to the Present
Colonial Intimacies: Indian Marriage in Early New England
The Comanches: A History, 1706-1875
Common & Contested Ground: A Human & Environmental
   History of the Northwestern Plains
The Conquest of Paradise
Conquistador in Chains
Contest for Empire, 1500-1775
A Country Between: The Upper Ohio Valley
   and Its People, 1724-1774
Cowboys and Indians: An Illustrated History
Creation's Journey: Native American Identity & Belief
Cultural Encounters in the Early South
Cry of the Thunderbird: The American Indian's Own Story
Custer's Fall
The Dakota or Sioux in Minnesota
*Dakota & Ojibwe People in Minnesota
Dangerous Passage: The Santa Fe Trail & the Mexican War
Deadly Medicine: Indians & Alcohol in Early America
The Desert Lake: The Story of Nevada's Pyramid Lake
Dictionary of Daily Life of Indians of the Americas
Dictionary of Indian Tribes of the Americas
Dinetah: Navajo History
The Dispossession of the American Indian, 1887-1934
Distorted Images of the Appalachian Mountain Cherokee
Documents of American Indian Diplomacy
Documents of U.S. Indian Policy
Dreamers With Power: The Menominee
The Dust Rose Like Smoke
Earliest Hispanic-Native American Interaction
   in the American Southeast
Early Encounters—Native Americans &
   Europeans in New England
Early Spanish, French & Engi\lish Encounters
   with the American Indians
The Earth Shall Weep: A History of Native America
The Effect of European Contact & Trade on the Settlement
   Pattern of Indians in Coastal New York, 1524-1665
Encyclopedia of Multiculturalism
The End of Indian Kansas: A Study of Cultural
   Revolution, 1854-1871
The Enduring Indians of Kansas
The Enduring Struggle

Essays in North American Indian History
The European Challenge
The European & the Indian
Exemplar of Liberty: Native American & the Evolution
   of American Democracy
Exiled in the Land of the Free
Exploring the West
Eyewitness at Wounded Knee
The Fall of Natural Man
Fantasies of the Master Race
The Far West & the Great Plains in Transition, 1859-1900
A Final Promise: The Campaign to Assimilate the Indians,
   1880-1920
Final Report of the U.S. DeSoto Expedition Commission
The First Americans
First Encounters: Spanish Explorations
First Peoples: A Documentary Survey of
   American Indian History
*The First Thanksgiving
The Five Civilized Tribes
*14 Flags Over Oklahoma
Fort Gibson History
Fort Lumhi: The Mormon Adventure in Oregon
   Territory, 1855-1858
Fort Supply, Indian Territory
From the Heart: Voices of the American Indian
Frontier Children
Frontier Regulars: The U.S. Army & the Indian, 1866-1891
Frontiers of Historical Imagination
Genocide Against the Indians
Germans & Indians
Great Indian Chiefs
Great Father: The U.S. Government & the American Indians
A Guide to the Indian Wars of the West
The Hall of the North American Indian
Handbook of the American Frontier: Four Centuries
   of Indian-White Relations
Handbook of North American Indians
*The Heritage
Hernando de Soto & the Indians of Florida
Historic Contact: Indian People & Colonists
The Historic Indian Tribes of Louisiana
Historical Account of the Doings & Sufferings of the
   Christian Indians in New England in the Years 1675-1677
Historical Atlas of the American West
Historical Atlas of Arkansas
Historical Atlas of Colorado
Historical Atlas of Louisiana
Historical Atlas of Missouri
Historical Atlas of Oklahoma
Historical Atlas of Texas
Historical Atlas of Washington
History of the Cherokee Indians & Their Legends & Folklore
The History of the Five Indian Nations
History of the Five Indian Nations of Canada
A History of Indian Policy: Syllabus
History of the Indian Wars
History of Indian-White Relations
History of the Indians of the U.S.
History of the Native Americans
History of the Ojibway People
History of the Triumphs of Our Holy Faith
A History of Utah's American Indians
Hope & Have: Fanny Grant Among the Indians
The Human Side of History
I Have Spoken: American History Through the
   Voices of the Indians
In Pursuit of the Past
Indian Affairs in Colonial New York
Indian Affairs Papers: American Revolution
Indian Battles, Murders, Seiges, & Forays in the Southwest
The Indian Chronicles
Indian Country
The Indian Frontier of the American West, 1846-1890
Indian Heritage of America
Indian History of the Modoc War
The Indian in American History
Indian Journals, 1859-1862
Indian Notes & Monographs
Indian Running: Native American History & Tradition
Indian Side of the Whiteman Massacre
Indian Traders of the Southeastern Spanish Borderlands
Indian Tribes of the Lower Mississippi Valley
Indian Tribes of North America
Indian Tribes of Ohio
Indian Women Chiefs
Indians & Alcohol in Early America
Indians & English: Facing Off in Early America
Indians & Europe
Indians & the American West in the Twentieth Century
Indians & Colonists at the Crossroads of Empire
Indians in American History: An Introduction
Indians in Oklahoma
Indians in the U.S. & Canada: A Comparative History
The Indian's New World: Catawbas & Their Neighbors
   from European Contact Through the Era of Removal
*Indians of America: Geronimo, Osceola, Crazy Horse,
   Squanto, Pontiac, Chief Joseph
Indians of California: The Changing Image
Indians of the High Plains: From the Prehistoric Period
   to the Coming of Europeans
Indians of Kansas: The Euro-American
   Invasion & Conquest of Indian Kansas

HISTORY, SOURCES

HOPEWELL CULTURE

HOPI INDIANS

Book of the Hopi
Born A Chief
Broken Pattern - Sunlight & Shadows of Hopi History
Bullying the Moqui
The Changing Pattern of Hopi Agriculture
Children of Cottonwood: Piety & Ceremonialism in
  Hopi Indian Puppetry
Clowns of the Hopi: Tradition Keepers and Delight Makers
A Concise Hopi and English Lexicon
Continuities of Hopi Culture Change
Council of the Rainmakers Address Book
The Coyote: Defiant Songdog of the West
*Coyote & Little Turtle: A Traditional Hopi Tale
*Coyote & the Winnowning Birds: A Traditional Hopi Tale
The Day of the Ogre Kachinas: A Hopi Indian Fable
Deliberate Acts: Changing Hopi Culture
  Through the Oraibi Split
Designs on Prehistoric Hopi Pottery
Drifting Through Ancestor Dreams
Earth Fire: A Hopi Legend of the Sunset Crater Eruption
*Field Mouse Goes to War
Following the Sun & Moon: Hopi Kachina Tradition
The Fourth World of the Hopis
Homol'ovi II
Hopi
*The Hopi
Hopi Animal Stories
Hopi Animal Tales
The Hopi Approach to the Art of Kachina Doll Carving
Hopi Basket Weaving: Artistry in Natural Fibers
Hopi Bibliography
The Hopi Child
Hopi Cookery
Hopi Coyote Tales: Istutuwutsi
*Hopi, The Desert Farmers
Hopi Dictionary: A Hopi-English Dictionary
  of the Third Mesa Dialect
Hopi Dictionary: Hopi-English, English-Hopi,
  Grammatical Appendix
Hopi Dwellings: Architecture at Orayvi
Hopi & Hopi-Tewa Pottery
Hopi Houses
Hopi Indian Altar Iconography
Hopi Kachina Dolls and Their Carvers
Hopi Kachina Dolls With a Key to Their Identification
Hopi Kachinas
Hopi Kachinas: The Complete Guide to
  Collecting Kachina Dolls
Hopi Katchinas Drawn by Native Artists
Hopi Kachinas: A Postcard Collection
Hopi Katchinas
Hopi Music & Dance
*Hopi Mysteries
Hopi Photographers - Hopi Images
Hopi Pottery Symbols
Hopi Shields & the Best Defense
Hopi Silver: The History & Hallmarks
  of Hopi Silversmithing
Hopi Snake Cermonies, an Eyewitness Account
A Hopi Social History
Hopi Stories of Witchcraft, Shamanism & Magic
Hopi Tales of Destruction
Hopi-Tewa Pottery
The Hopi: Their History & Use of Lands in
  New Mexico & Arizona, 1200's to 1900's
Hopi Time
Hopi Traditional Literature
The Hopi Villages
Hopi Voices & Visions
The Hopi Way: Tales From a Changing Culture
Hopi and Zuni Ceremonialism
Hopis, Tewas, and the American Road
Introduction to Hopi Pottery Lessons in Hopi
Kachina Tales From the Indian Pueblos
Kachinas: Spirit Beings of the Hopi
Language, History, & Identity
Maasaw: Profile of a Hopi God
Ray Manley's Hopi Kachina
Me & Mine: The Life Story of Helen Sekaquaptewa
Medititions With the Hopi
Moki Snake Dance
Nampeyo and Her Pottery
The Navajo-Hopi Land Dispute: An American Tragedy
No Turning Back: A Hopi Indian Woman's Struggle to
  Live in Two Worlds
Oraibu Maru Ceremony
Pages From Hopi History
Prehistoric Hopi Pottery Designs
Pumpkin Seed Point: Being Within the Hopi
Religion & Hopi Life in the 20th Century
Rethinking Hopi Ethnography
Ritual in Pueblo Art: Hopi Life in Hopi Painting
The Snake Dance of the Hopi Indians
Spider Woman Stories: Legends of the Hopi Indians
Stories of Maasaw, a Hopi God
Sun Chief: The Autobiography of a Hopi Indian
The Traditions of the Hopi
Treasures of the Hopi
The Wind Won't Know Me: History of the
  Navajo-Hopi Land Dispute
The Year of the Hopi

HOUSING

Assessment of American Indian Housing Needs
  & Programs: Final Report
Demonstration of Building Indian Housing in
  Underserved Areas
Indian Housing in the USA: A History
Native American Housing Assistance
Native American Housing: Information on HUD's
  Funding of Indian Housing Progams
Report of BIAs Consolidated Housing Inventory
Revitalizing Communities

HUALAPAI INDIANS

Camp Beale's Springs and the Hualapai Indians

HUNTING & FISHING

Always Getting Ready, Upterrlainarluta: Yup'ik
  Eskimo Subsistence in Southwest Alaska
Apauk: Caller of Buffalo
Archaic Hunters & Gatherers in the American Midwest
Bringing Home Animals:
The Buffalo: the Story of American Bison & Their Hunters
Disputed Waters: Native Americans & the
  Great Lakes Fishery
Don't Blame the Indians: Native Americans &
  the Mechanized Destruction of Fish & Wildlife
Early Fur Trade on the Northern Plains
First Fish, First People: Salmon Tales of the
  North Pacific Rim
Fish Decoys of the Lac du Flambeau Ojibway
Fishing Among the Indians of Northwestern California
Following the Game: Hunting Traditions of
  Native Californians
*Fur Trappers & Traders: The Indians,
  The Pilgrims, and the Beaver
The Horse in Blackfoot Indian Culture
*The Hunt
Hunters of the Buffalo
Hunters of the Eastern Forest
Hunters of the Ice
Hunters of the Northern Forest
Hunters of the Sea
Indian Fishing: Early Methods of the Northwest Coast
Indian Hunts and Indian Hunters of the Old West
Snares, Deadfalls & Other Traps of the Northern
  Algonquian & Northern Athapaskans
Survival Skills of North American Indians
Traps of the American Indians: A Study in
  Psychology & Invention
Treaties on Trial: The Continuing Controversy
  Over Northwest Indian Fishing Rights
*The Winter Hunt

IMPLEMENTS

Collecting Indian Knives
Collector's Guide to Indian Pipes: Identification & Values
Florida's Prehistoric Stone Technology
Horn & Bone Implements of the New York Indians
Metal Weapons, Tools and Ornaments of the
  Teton Dakota Indians
North American Indian Points

INDIANS OF CALIFORNIA

Aboriginal Society in Southern California
Acorn Soup
*Adopted by Indians: A True Story
Alaawich
Alcatraz! Alcatraz!: The Indian Occupation of 1969-1971
Ancient Modocs of California & Oregon
Annikadel
Ararapikva: Traditional Karuk Indian Literature from
Northwestern California
Archives of California Prehistory
Basket Weavers for the California Curio Trade
The Bear Shaman Tradition of Southern California Indians
Before the Wilderness: Environmental Management
  by Native Californians
Bibliography of the Languages of Native California
Black Sun of the Miwok
Bringing Them Under Subjection: California's Tejon
  Indian Reservation and Beyond, 1852-1864
The Broken Ring: The Destruction of the California Indians
Cahuilla Dictionary
Cahuilla Grammar
The Cahuilla Indians
The Cahuilla Indians of Southern California
The Cahuilla Landscape: The Santa Rosa &
  San Jacinto Mountains
California
California Archaeology
California Indian Country: The Land & the People
California Indian Nights Entertainment
California Indian Shamanism
California Indian Watercraft
*California Indians: An Educational Coloring Book
California Indians: Primary Resources

*The California Native American Tribes
*California's Chumash Indians
California's Gabrielino Indians
California Indian Country: The Land & the People
California Indian Watercraft
California Place Names
1500 California Place Names: Their Origin & Meaning
*California Tribes
A Case Study of a Northern California Indian Tribe:
  Cultural Change to 1860
The Chemehuevi Indians of Southern California
Chemehuevi: People of the Coachilla Valley
Chem'ivillu: Let's Speak Cahuilla
Chinigchinix, An Indigenous California Indian Religion
*The Chumash
Chumash Healing
Chumash
The Chumash Indians of Southern California
The Chumash People
Chumash: A Picture of Their World
The Chumash & Their Predecessors
The Classification and Distribution of the
  Pit River Indian Tribes of California
Crystals in the Sky: Chumash Astronomy,
  Cosmology and Rock Art
*A Day With a Chumash
December's Child: A Book of Chumash Oral Narratives
Deeper Than Gold: Indian Life Along California's Highway 49
Delfina Cuero: Her Autobiography
The Destruction of California Indians
Dictionary of Mesa Grande Diegueno
The Diegueno Indians
Discovery of the Yosemite and the Indian War of 1851
  Which Led to That Event
The Earth Is Our Mother: A Guide to the Indians of California
Earthquake Weather
The Ethno-Botany of the Coahuilla Indians
  of Southern California
Ethnography and Folklore of the Indians of
  Northwestern California
The Ethnology of the Salinan Indians
Federal Concern About Conditions of
  California Indians, 1853-1913
The Fine Art of California Indian Basketry
From Fingers to Finger Bowls
Gabrielino
Gigyayk Vo:jka
Grass Games & Moon Races: California Indian
  Games & Toys
*Great Indians of California
Guide to the Records at the National Archives-
  Los Angeles Branch
Handbook of the Indians of California
The Heart Is Fire: The World of the Cahuilla
  Indians of Southern California
I'isniyatam (Designs)
In My Own Words
Indian Life of the Yosemite Region: Miwok Material Culture
Indian Summer: Traditional Life Among the Choinumne
Indians of California's San Joaquin Valley
Indian Survival on the California Borderland Frontier,
  1819-60
Indian-White Relationships in Northern California, 1849-1920
Indians and Indian Agents
Indians, Franciscans, and Spanish Colonization: The Impact
  of the Mission System on California Indians
Indians & Intruders in Central California, 1769-1849
Indians of California: The Changing Image
Indians of California: A Critical Bibliography
Indians of the Feather River: Tales & Legends
  of the Concow Maidu of California
Indians of Upper California
An Introduction to the Luiseno Language
Ishi in Two Worlds: A Biography of the
  Last Wild Indian in North America
Ishi's Journey from the Center to the Edge of the World
Ishi, the Last Yahi: A Documentary History
It Will Live Forever: Traditional Yosemite Acorn Preparation
Karuk: the Upriver People
Kashaya Pomo Plants
Kiliwa Texts: "Whe I Have Donned My Crest of Stars"
Legends of the Yosemite Miwok
The Literature of California, Vol. 1:
  Native American Beginnings to 1945
Lost Copper
The Maidu Indian Myths & Stories of Hanc'ibyjim
Mirror & Pattern
Viola Martinez, California Paiute: Living in Two Worlds
Massacre at the Yuma Crossing
Mission Indians in California
*The Missions: California's Heritage
The Missions of California, a History of Genocide
Monterey in 1786: The Journals of
  Jean Francois de la Perouse
The Morning the Sun Went Down
Mulewetam: The First People
My Luiseno Neighbors
Native Americans of California & Nevada
Native Americans of the Pacific Coast
Native California Guide: Weaving Past & Present
Native Californians: A Theoretical Retrospective
Native Ways: California Indian Stories & Memories
Natural World of the California Indians

The Nome Lackee Indian Reservation, 1854-1870
The Northern Paiute Indians of California and Nevada
Not for Innocent Ears: Spiritual Traditions of a
  Desert Cahuilla Medicine Woman
The Ohlone Past & Present: Native Americans of the
  San Francisco & Monterey Bay Areas
The Ohlone Way: Indian Life in the San Francisco
  & Monterey Bay Areas
The Origins of a Pacific Coast Chiefdom:
  The Chumash of the Channel Islands
Our Home Forever: The Hupa Indians of Northern California
The People of San Manuel
*The Pomo
Pomo Basketmaking
Pomo Doctors & Poisoners
Pomo Indian Basketry
*Pomo Indians of California & Their Neighbors
Pomo Lands on Clear Lake
The Population of the California Indians, 1769-1970
Purisimeño Chumash Prehistory
Pushed Into the Rocks: Southern California Indian
  Land Tenure
Report of Chas. A. Wetmore, Special U.S. Commissioner
  of Mission Indians of Southern California
River of Sorrows-Life History of the Maidu-Nisenan Indians
Rock Painting of the Chumash
Salinan Indians of California & Their Neighbors
Seasons of the Kachina
The Serrano Indians of Southern California
Serrano Songs & Stories
Seven Rock Art Sites in Baja California
Shasta Indian Tales
Shasta Indians of California & Their Neighbors
Spanish & Indian Place Names of California
Strangers in a Stolen Land: American Indians in San Diego
Studies in Cahuilla Culture
Survival Skills of Native California
Surviving Arts: Traditional Skills of the First Californians
Taitaduhaan: Western Mono Ways of Speaking
Temalpakh: Cahuilla Indian Knowledge and Usage of Plants
Time's Flotsam: Overseas Collections of
  California Material Culture
Tobacco Among the Karuk Indians of California
Tovangar
Tradition & Innovation: A Basket History of the
  Indians of the Yosemite-Mono Lake Region
Tribes of California
Ukomno'm: The Yuki Indians of Northern California
University of California Anthropological Records
University of California, Archaeological Survey Reports
University of California, Publications in American
  Archaeology & Ethnology
Walking Where We Liuved: Memoirs of a Mono Indian Family
The Wappo: A Report
Washo Shamans & Peyotists: Religious Conflict
  in an American Indian Tribe
The Way We Lived: California Indian Stories,
  Songs & Reminiscences
Willie Boy
The Wintu & Their Neighbors
The Wintun Indians of California & Their Neighbors
Yosemite Indians
Yurok Myths

INDIANS OF NORTH AMERICA— GENERAL

After Columbus: The Smithsonian Chronicle of the
  North American Indians
*American Indian
The American Indian & Alaska Native Traders Directory
The American Indian: The American Flag
American Indian Archival Material: A Guide to Holdings
  in the Southeast
The American Indian, 1492-1976: A Chronology and
  Fact Book
*The American Indian Coloring Book
American Indian Ecology
American Indian Encyclopedia - CD-ROM
American Indian Energy Resources and Development
American Indian Identities: Today's Changing Perspectives
American Indian Index
*The American Indian in America
The American Indian in English Literature of the 18th Century
American Indian and Indoeuropean Studies
American Indian Leaders: Studies in Diversity
American Indian Literature: An Anthology
American Indian Persistence & Resurgence
American Indian Population by Tribe
The American Indian: A Rising Ethnic Force
*American Indian Stories
*American Indian Tribes
American Indians
*American Indians
The American Indians
American Indians: The First of This Land
American Indians in America
American Indians in U.S. History
Anthropology and the American Indian
Anthropology on the Great Plains
Arctic: Handbook of North American Indians
Atlas of the North American Indian

Backward: An Essay on Indians, Time and Photography
Becoming Brave: The Path to Native American Manhood
Belief & Worship in Native North America
Cartographic Encounters: Perspectives on Native American
  Mapmaking & Map Use
Chicano & Native American Studies
Chiefs & Warriors: Native Nations
The Collected Works of Edward Sapir
*A Coloring Book of American Indians
A Concise Dictionary of Indian Tribes of North America
Conquering Horse
Constitutions & Laws of the American Indian Tribes.
Cranioetric Relationships Among Plains Indians
Creation's Journey
Dancing Colors: Paths of Native American Women
Dictionary of Indian Tribes of the Americas
Ecocide of Native America: Environmental Destruction
  of Indian Lands & Peoples
The Elder American Indian
Essays in Anthropology Presented to A.L. Kroeber
  in Celebration of the 60th Birthday
Ethnic Studies, Volume II: Chicano &
  Native American Studies
The Evolution of North American Indians
Facing West: The Metaphysics of Indian
  Hating and Empire-Building
Fantasies of the Master Race
*The First Americans: Tribes of North America
*The First Books
First Peoples, First Contacts: Native Peoples
  of North America
Five Indian Tribes of the Upper Missouri
Flags of the Native Peoples of the U.S.
The Great Sioux Trail
A Guide to America's Indians: Ceremonies,
  Reservations & Museums
Guide to Records in the National Archives
  Relating to American Indians
Guide to Research on North American Indians
Handbook of American Indians North of Mexico
Hear the Creator's Song: A Guide to the Study Theme
*Native Peoples of North America
The Heirs of Columbus
History, Manners, and Customs of the Indian Nations Who
  Once Inhabited Pennsylvania and the Neighboring States
How to Enroll In An Indian/Alaska Native Tribe
*How Would Survive As an American Indian
I'll Sing 'Til the Day I Die
Inconstant Savage: England and the
  North American Indian, 1500-1660
Indian Affairs
Indian America: A Geography of North American Indians
Indian Americans: Unity & Diversity
Indian Crisis: The Background
Indian Country
Indian Givers: How the Indians of the Americas
  Transformed the World
The Indian Heritage of Americans
The Indian in America
The Indian in American History
Indian Issues
Indian Leadership
Indian Life: Transforming an American Myth
Indian Oratory: Famous Speeches by
  Noted Indian Chieftains
The Indian Peoples of Eastern America:
  A Documentary History of the Sexes
Indian Population in the U.S. and Alaska, 1910, 1930
The Indian Question - CD-ROM
Indian Removal
Indian Terms of the Americas
*Indian Tribes of the Americas
Indian Tribes of North America
*Indian Tribes of North America: Coloring Book
The Indian's Side of the Indian Question
*Indians
*The Indians
Indians Along the Oregon Trail
Indians in Minnesota
The Indians in Oklahoma
Indians in the U.S. & Canada: A Comparative History
*Indians of America
Indians and Anthropologists
Indians and Europe
Indians and Europeans
Indians of the Americas
*Indians of the Americas Coloring Book
Indians of the Americas: Self Determination
  & International Human Rights
Indians of the Great Basin
Indians of North America
Indians of North America - Life, Health
  Culture & Disease Conditions
Indians of North America: Methods &
  Sources for Library Research
*The Indians of North America Series
Indians of North America: Survey of Tribes
  That Inhabit the Continent
Indians of Ohio, Indiana, Illinois, Southern
  Michigan & Southern Wisconsin
Interpreting the Indians: 20th Century Poets
  and the Native American
*The Junior Library of American Indians Series

Killing the White Man's Indian
The Land of Red Cloud: Among North America's Indians
Last Rambles Amongst the Indians of the Rocky Mountains
Letters and Notes on the Manners, Customs &
  Conditions of the North American Indians
The Life & Adventures of James P. Beckwourth
Life & Art of the North American Indian
Lulu Linear Punctated: Essays in Honor of
  George Irving Quimby
Man's Rise to Civilization
*Many Nations: An Alphabet of Native America
Many Nations: A Library of Congress Resource Guide
Map'N'Facts: Native Peoples of North America
*Meet the North American Indians
The Microfilm Edition of the Washington Matthews
  Papers & Guide
My Life As an Indian
National Indian Arts & Crafts Directory
Native America in the Twentieth Century: An Encyclopedia
Native America: Portrait of the Peoples
Native American Almanac
Native American Annual
*The Native American Book of Change
*The Native American Book of Knowledge
*The Native American Book of Life
*The Native American Book of Wisdom
*Native American Chiefs & Warriors
Native American Directory: Alaska, U.S. & Canada
Native American Flags
Native American Mathematics
Native American Periodicals & Newspapers, 1828-1982
Native American Press in Wisconsin and the Nation
Native American Research Information Service
The Native American Today
*Native Americans
*Native Americans & Black Americans
Native Americans: An Encyclopedia of History,
  Cutlure & Peoples
The Native Americans: An Illustrated History
Native Americans: The Indigenous People of North America
Native North Americans: An Ethnohistorical Approach
The Native Races
Native Carolinians: The Indians of North Carolina
Native North America
Native People, Native Lands: Canadian Indians, Inuit & Metis
*Native People, Native Ways Series
Native Tribes Map
Native Villages & Village Sites
Natives & Academics: Researching & Writing About American
  Indians
Natives & Strangers
No American Indians
The North American Indian
North American Indian Anthropology:
  Essays on Society & Culture
North American Indian Burial Customs
North American Indian Ecology
North American Indian Landmarks: A Traveler's Guide
The North American Indian Travel Guide
North American Indians
*North American Indians
North American Indians - CD-ROM
North American Indians Coloring Album
North American Indians: A Comprehensive Account
North American Indians: A Dissertation Index
North American Indians of Acheivement
The North American Indians: Photographs
  by Edward S. Curtis
North American Native Authors Catalog
North American Tribal Directory
The North Americans of Yesterday
Notes From Indian Country
Now That the Buffalo's Gone: A Study of
  Today's American Indians
O Brave New People: The European Invention
  of the American Indian
Of Breath and Earth: A Book of Days With Wisdom
  From Native America
Our Wild Indians, Etc.
Phoenix: The Decline & Rebirth of the Indian People
Pioneering in Montana: The Making of a State, 1864-1887
The Political Economy of North American Indians
The Portable North American Indian Reader
Portraits of Native Americans
The Primal Mind: Vision & Reality in Indian America
Psychocultural Change & the American Indians:
  An Ethnohistorical Analysis
The Quapaws
Quest for the Origins of the First Americans
Readers Digest - America's Fascinating Indian Heritage
Reclaiming the Vision
Red Children in White America
Red Men in Red Square
Reference Library of Native North America, 4 Vols.
Research and Writing Tribal Histories
The Return of the Native: American Indian
  Political Resurgence
Science Encounters the Indian, 1820-1880
Shadow Country
Shadow Distance: A Gerald Vizenor Reader
Signals in the Air: Native Broadcasting in America
Six Months Among the Indians
The Southeastern Indians

Southeastern Indians Since the Removal Era
Southern Athapaskan Migration: A.D. 200-1750
The Spanish Borderlands Sourcebooks
Spanish Explorers in the Southern U.S.
Spirit Capture: Photographs from the National Museum of the AmericanIndian
A Spirited Resistance: The North American Indian Struggle for Unity, 1745-1815
The State of Native America: Genocide, Colonization and Resistance
Strangers to Relatives: The Adoption & Naming of Anthropologists in Native North America
Sun Bear: The Path of Power
Recently Discovered Tales of Life Among the Indians
Teaching About Native Americans
Tennessee's Indian Peoples: From White Contact to Removal, 1540-1840
Their Bearing Is Noble & Proud
Theoretical Perspectives on Native American Languages
This Path We Travel: Celebrations of Contemporary Native American Creativity
Toward a Native American Critical Theory
*Traditional Crafts from Native North America
Treasures of the National Museum of the American Indian
Tulapai to Tokay: A Bibliography of Alcochol Use & Abuse Among Native Americans of North America
The Unknown Indian
Urban Indians
Urban Indians: Drums From the Cities
Urbanization of American Indians: A Critical Bibliography
The Vanishing Race: Selections from Edward S. Curtis' the North American Indian
Views of a Vanishing Frontier
Voice of Indigenous Peoples: Native People Address the U.N.
*The Wampanoag
Wanderings of an Artist Among the Indians of North America
*We Live on an Indian Reservation
We, The First Americans
When Nickels Were Indians: An Urban, Mixed-Blood Story
The White Man's Indian
Words in the Blood: Contemporary Indian Writers of North and South America
Words of Power: Voices from Indian America
World of American Indian
World War II & the American Indian
The World's Rim: Great Mysteries of the North American Indians

INDIANS OF THE GREAT LAKES REGION (NORTHWEST, OLD)

Acculturation and Personality Among the Wisconsin Chippewa
Anishnabe: Six Studies of Modern Chippewa
Aspects of Upper Great Lakes Anthropology
Autobiography of a Winnebago Indian
Before Man in Michigan
Building a Chippewa Indian Birchbark Canoe
The Chicago American Indian Community: 1893-1988
*The Chippewa
Chippewa Child Life and Its Cultural Background
Chippewa Customs
Chippewa Music
The Chippewas of Lake Superior
*The Chipewyan
Council Fires on the Upper Ohio
The Dept. of the Interior's Denial of the Wisconsin Chippewa's Casino Applications
Dreamers With Power: The Menominee
Ethnobotany of the Menomini Indians
First People of Michigan
Folklore of the Winnebago Tribe
Four Seasons of Corn: A Winnebago Tradition
A Gathering of Rivers: Indians, Metis & Mining in the Western Great Lakes, 1737-1832
History of the Ojibway Indians
The Illinois & Indiana Indians
Indian Chiefs of Southern Minnesota
Indian Villages of the Illinois Country: Historic Tribes
Indians of the Chicago Area
Indians of the Western Great Lakes, 1615-1760
The Illinois & Indiana Indians
The Indians of Washtenaw County, Michigan
Indians of the Western Great Lakes, 1615-1760
Introduction to Wisconsin Indians: Prehistory to Statehood
Journals of Joseph N. Nicollet
Kinsmen Through Time: An Annotated Bibliography of Potawatomi History
Long Journey to the Country of the Hurons
Lore of the Great Turtle: Indian Legends of Mackinac Retold
Menomini Indians of Wisconsin
The Miami Indians
The Miami Indians of Indiana: A Persistent People, 1654-1994
Mountain Wolf Woman, Sister of Crashing Thunder: The Autobiography of a Winnebago Indian
The Native Tribes of Old Ohio
North Dakota Indians: An Introduction
Observations of the Ethnology of the Sauk Indians
The Ojibwas: A Critical Bibliography

Ojibway Oratory
Ottawa & Chippewa Indians of Michigan, 1870-1909
*The Ottawas
The People Named the Chippewa: Narrative Histories
*People of Three Fires
People of the Lakes
Peopling Indiana: The Ethnic Experience
Potawatomi Indians of Michigan
Prehistoric Biological Relationship in the Great Lakes Region
President Washington's Indian War: The Struggle for the Old Northwest
Primitive Man in Ohio
Red Brother
The Sauks and Black Hawk War
Sketches of a Tour to the Lakes
Survival & Regeneration. Detroit's American Indian Community
To Be the Main Leaders of Our People: A History of the Minnesota Ojibwe Politics, 1825-1898
Tragic Saga of the Indiana Indians
The Winnebago Tribe
Woodland Indians of the Western Great Lakes
*Woodlands Indians: Coloring Book
Worlds Between Two Rivers: Perspectives on American Indians in Iowa

INDIANS OF THE GREAT PLAINS

Anthropology on the Great Plains
Becoming & Remaining a People
Beyond the Frontier: Exploring the Indian Country
Bison Cultural Traditions of the Northern Great Plains: Past, Present & Future
The Blackfeet: Raiders on the Northwestern Plains
Bury My Heart at Wounded Knee
Carbine & Lance: The Story of Old Fort Sill
Changing Military Patterns of the Great Plains Indians
Circles of the World: Traditional Art of the Plains Indians
The Comanches: Lords of the South Plains
Common & Contested Ground: A Human & Environmental History of the Northwestern Plains
*Daily Life in a Plains Indian Village, 1868
Dakota: A Spiritual Geography
Dances With Wolves
Do You See What I Mean? Plains Indian Sign Talk...
Dog Soldier Societies of the Plains
Dress Clothing of the Plains Indians
Dwellers at the Source: Southwestern Indian Photographs of A.C. Vroman, 1895-1904
Early Fur Trade on the Northern Plains
Farmers, Hunters, and Colonists
The Feathered Sun: Plains Indian Art & Philosophy
A Guide to the Indian Tribes of Oklahoma
*Heetunka's Harvest: A Tale of the Plains Indians
The Hidden Half: Studies of Plains Indian Women
The History of Oklahoma
*How the Plains Indians Lived
Indian Chiefs of Southern Minnesota
*Indian Tales of the Northern Plains
*Indians of the Great Plains
Indians of the Great Plains
Indians of the High Plains: From the Prehistoric Period to the Coming of Europeans
Indians of the Plains
*Indians of the Plains
Leasing Indian Water
Life on the Plains and Among the Diggings
The Long Death: The Last Days of the Plains Indians
The March of the Montana Column
Marquis de Miores at War in the Bad Lands
Midnight & Noonday
The Mystic Warriors of the Plains
North Dakota Indians: An Introduction
Northwest Indian Images: A Photographic Look at Plateau Indians
Of Uncommon Birth: Dakota Sons in Vietnam
Oklahoma: Foot-Loose & Fancy-Free
Oklahoma: A History of Five Centuries
Oklahoma: A History of the Sooner State
Oklahoma: The Land & Its People
Oklahoma Place Names
Oklahoma Seminoles
Oklahoma: The Story of Its Past & Present
*Francis Parkman & the Plains Indians
*The Plains Indian Book
Plains Indian Culture
Plains Indian History and Culture
Plains Indian Mythology
Plains Indian Raiders
The Plains Indians
*Plains Indians Coloring Book
*Plains Indians: An Educational Coloring Book
The Plains Indians and New Mexico
*Plains Indians Wars
The Planning Process on the Pine Ridge & Rosebud Indian Reservations
Political Organization of the Plains Indians
Population Changes Among the Northern Plains Indians
Prehistoric Man on the Great Plains
Rank and Warfare Among the Plains Indians
Renewing the World: Plains Indian Religion & Morality
The Sac & Fox Indians
Seminole Burning

Sitting Bull & the Plains Indians
Skeletal Biology in the Great Plains
Southern Plains Alliances
The Tribal Government of the Oglala Sioux of Pine Ridge, SD
War Dance: Plains Indian Musical Performance
*We Rode the Wind: Recollections of Native American Life
When Buffalo Ran
The Whiskey Trade of the Northwestern Plains
Wolf That I Am: In Search of the Red Earth People
Women of the Earth Lodges: Tribal Life on the Plains

INDIANS OF THE NORTHEAST

*The Abenaki
An Abridgement of the Indian Affairs Contained in Four Folio Volumes
Akwesasne Historical Postcards
*Algonkian: Lifestyle of the New England Indians
The Algonquian Peoples of Long Island: From Earliest Times to 1700
*The Algonquians
American Indians in Connecticut
AmerInds & Their Paleoenvironments in Northeastern North America
Anthropological Studies of the Quichua & Machiganga Indians
Apologies to the Iroquois
Archaeology of Eastern North America: Papers in Honor of Stephen Williams
Beyond the Covenant Chain: The Iroquois & Their Neighbors in Indian North America
Conrad Weiser and the Indian Policy of Colonial Pennsylvania
*The Cayuga
Clambake: A Wampanoag Tradition
Conrad Weiser & the Indian Policy of Colonial Pennsylvania
The Constitution of the Five Nations
Dawnland Encounters: Indians & Europeans in Northern New England
Drums Along the Mohawk
The Dutch & the Iroquois
An Ethnography of the Huron Indians, 1615-1649
Evolution of the Onondaga Iroquois
Fighting Tuscarora: The Autobiography of Chief Clinton Rickard
First People: The Early Indians of Virginia
Five Civilized Tribes
The Great Law & the Longhouse
Guide to Indian Artifacts of the Northeast
*Heroes & Heroines, Monsters & Magic
The Hidden Language of the Seneca
History, Manners and Customs of the Indian Nations Who Once Inhabited Pennsylvania and the Neighboring States
A History of Indian Villages & Place Names of Pennsylvania
History of the Indians of Connecticut
History of New York Indians and the Printup Family
Horn and Bone Implements of the New York Indians
Huron: Farmers of the North
In Defense of Mohawk Land
In the Hands of the Senecas
Indian Chiefs of Pennsylvania
Indian History, Biography & Genealogy
Indian Place Names of New England
Indian Tribes of Hudson's River
Indian Wars of New England
Indian Wars of Pennsylvania
Indian Wars of New England
Indian & the White Man in Connecticut
Indians in Pennsylvania
The Indians of Connecticut
The Indians of Greater New York and the Lower Hudson
Indians of the Lower Hudson Region: The Munsee
The Indians of Maine and the Atlantic Provinces: A Bibliographic Guide
The Indians of New England: A Critical Bibliography
The Indians of New Jersey
*The Indians of New Jersey: Dickon Among the Lenapes
Indians of the Northeast
Indians of the Northeast North America
*Indians of the Northeast: Traditions, History, Legends & Life
Iroquois
Iroquois: Art & Culture
The Iroquois Eagle Dance
The Iroquois & the Founding of the American Nation
Iroquois in the American Revolution
The Iroquois in the Civil War
Iroquois Indians: A Documentary History
Iroquois Land Claims
Iroquois Music and Dance
The Iroquois & the New Deal
The Iroquois Restoration
An Iroquois Sourcebook
Iroquois Studies
The Iroquois Struggle for Survival: World War II to Red Power
The Iroquois Trail
Journals of the Military Expedition of Major General John Sullivan
A Journey Into Mohawk & Oneida Country, 1634-1635
King of the Delawares: Teedyuscung, 1700-1763
Land of the Four Directions
The Lastings of the Mohegans: The Story of the Wolf People

The Problem of Justice: Tradition & Law in
  the Coast Salish World
Ratification of Coeur D'Alene Indian Treaties
The Raven Tales
Renegade Tribe: The Palouse Indians and the
  Invasion of the Inland Pacific Northwest
Report of Indian Missions
The Reservation Blackfeet
The Rogue River Indian War & Its Aftermath, 1850-1980
Esther Ross, Stillaguamish Champion
Salish Folk Tales
The Salish Language Family
The Sandel & the Cave: The Indians of Oregon
The Sanpoil & Nespelem Salishan Peoples of
  Northeastern Washington
Seahb Siwash
Shapes of Thier Thoughts: Reflections of Culture
  Contact in Northwest Coast Indian Art
The Sheepeaters
Shoto Clay: Figurines & Forms From the Lower Columbia
Sketches of Indian Life in the Pacific Northwest
Spirit and Ancestor: A Century of Northwest Coast
  Indian Art at the Burke Museum
The Spokane Indians: Children of the Sun
Stone Age of the Columbia River
The Structure of Twana Culture
*Suquamish Today
Swan Among the Indians: Life of James G. Swan, 1818-1900
Tanaina Tales from Alaska
*Tendoy, Chief of the Lemhis
These Are My Children
Tillamook Indians
Tillamook Indians of the Oregon Coast
Tlingit Indians
To Fish in Common
Topographical Memoir
Trading Beyond the Mountains
Tradition and Change on the Northwest Coast
Traditions of the Quinault Indians
The Tragedy of the Blackfoot
Traits of American Indian Life
Treaties & Agreements of the Indian Tribes
  of the Pacific Northwest
Treaties on Trial: The Continuing Controversy over
  Northwest Indian Fishing Rights
Tribal Boundaries in the Nass Watershed
Tsimshian Culture
Tsimshian Indians & Their Arts
The Tsimshian and Their Neighbors of the
  North Pacific Coast
Tsimshian Texts
Twana Games
Valley of the Spirits: The Upper Skagit Indians
  of Western Washington
Visions of the North: Native Arts of the Northwest Coast
*Vostaas: The Story of Montana's Indian Nation
The Wappo: A Report
The Way of the Masks
The Ways of My Grandmothers
Wolf of the Raven: Totem Poles of Southeastern Alaska
A World of Faces: Masks of the Northwest Coast Indians
The Yakamas: A Critical Bibliography

INDIANS OF THE SOUTH
& SOUTHEAST

American Indian Archival Material
The American Indian and the End of the
  Confederacy, 1863-1866
The American Indian As Slaveholder & Successionist
The American Indian in Alabama and the Southeast
The American Indian in the Civil War, 1862-1865
American Indians in the Lower Mississippi Valley
The American Indian in North Carolina
American Indians of the Southeast
Ancient Chiefdoms of the Tombigbee
Apalachee: The Land Between the Rivers
Archaeology of Aboriginal Culture Change
  in the Interior Southeast
As Long As the Waters Flow: Native Americans
  in the South & East
The Ascent of Chiefs: Cahokia & Mississippian
  Politics in Native North America
Authentic Memoirs of William Augustus Bowles, Esq.
William Bartram on the Southeastern Indians
Buffalo Tiger: A Life in the Everglades
Cahokia & the Archaeology of Power
Cahokia: City of the Sun
Cahokia: Domination & Ideology in the Mississippian World
Catawba Nation
Chapters of the Ethnology of the Powhatan Tribes of Virginia
Cherokee Americans
The Cherokee People
Cherokee Proud: A Guide for Tracing & Honoring
  Your Cherokee Ancestors
Cherokees & Missionaries, 1789-1839
Choctaws & Missionaries in Mississippi, 1818-1918
The Columbia Guide to American Indians in the Southeast
Conversations With the High Priest of Coosa
Creek Indian History
A Creek Warrior for the Confederacy
Creeks & Seminoles
Deerskins & Duffels

The Development of Southeastern Archaeology
Earliest Hispanic - Native American Interactions
  in the American Southeast
Early Pottery in the Southeast
An Early & Strong Sympathy: The Indian Writings
  of William Gilmore Simms
Ethnic Heritage in Mississippi
Ethnology of the Yuchi Indians
The Evolution of the Calusa: A Non-Agricultural
  Chiefdom on the Southwest Florida Coast
Exiles of Florida
Florida Indians & the Invasion from Europe
Florida Place Names of Indian Origin
The Florida Seminole & the New Deal, 1933-1942
The Florida Wars
Florida's Indians from Ancient Times to the Present
Florida's Prehistoric Stone Technology
Florida's Seminole Indians
The Forgotten Centuries
The Formative Cultures of the Carolina Piedmont
Georgia Voices
General Stand Watie's Confederate Indians
A Grammar & Dictionary of the Timucua Language
The Grand Village of the Natchez Indians Revisited
*John Hawk: A Seminole Saga
Historical Collections of Georgia
History of Alabama, and Incidentally of Georgia
  and Mississippi, from the Earliest Period
The History and Present State of Virginia
*Indian Myths from the Southeast
Indian Place Names in Alabama
Indians in Seventeenth Century Virginia
Indians of the South
Indians of the Southeastern U.S.
Indians of the Southeastern U.S. in the Late 20th Century
The Invention of the Creek Nation, 1670-1763
Lachlan McGillivray, Indian Trader: The Shaping
  of the Southern Colonial Frontier
Laboring in the Fields of the Lord: Spanish Missions
  & Southeastern Indians
Laws of the Choctaw Nation
Lumbee Indian Histories: Race, Ethnicity & Indian
  Identity in the Southern U.S.
A Map of Virginia
Mississippian Towns & Sacred Spaces: Searching
  for an Architectural Grammar
Monacans & Miners: Native American &
  Coal Mining Communities
Myths and Tales of the Southeastern Indians
A Narrative of the Early Days and Remembrances
  of Oceaola Nikkanochee
Native American Legends: The Southeast
Native Land
Negro-Indian Relationships in the Southeast
New Words, Old Songs
North Carolina's State Historic Sites
Notices of East Florida
Ocmulgee Archaeology, 1936-1986
The Only Land I Know: A History of the
  Lumbee Indian of North Carolina
The Only Land They Knew: American Indians
  in the Old South
Only the Names Remain: The Cherokees
  & the Trail of Tears
The Pamunkey Indians of Virginia
The Papers of Panton, Leslie & Co.
Perspectives on the Southeast
Pocahontas's People: The Powhatan Indians of
  Virginia Through the Centuries
Pocahontas: Powhatan Peacemaker
Alex Posey: Creek Poet, Journalist, and Humorist
Powhatan Foreign Relations 1500-1722
Powhatan Lords of Life & Death
Powhatan Indians of Virginia
Powhatan Tribes: Middle Atlantic
Powhatan's Mantle
Powhatan's World & Colonial Virginia
Pre-Seminole Florida: Spanish Soldiers,
  Friars & Indian Missions
Prehistoric Indians of the Southeast
Prehistoric Peoples of South Florida
The Qualla Cherokee Surviving in Two Worlds
Redskins, Ruffleshirts & Rednecks: Indian Allotments
  in Alabama & Mississippi, 1830-1860
Removal of the Cherokee Indians from Georgia
Savanah River Chiefdoms
Searching for the Bright Path: The Mississippi
  Choctaws from Prehistory to Removal
Seminole Indians of Florida, 1850-1874
The Seminole & Miccosukee Tribes
Source Material for the Social & Ceremonial
  Life of the Choctaw Indians
Source Material on the History & Ethnology
  of the Caddo Indians
South Florida's Vanished People
*Southeast Indians: Coloring Book
The Southeastern Ceremonial Complex & Its Interpretation
The Southeastern Frontiers
The Southeastern Indians
Southeastern Indians Since the Removal Era
Southeastern Woodland Indian Designs
*Southern Indian Myths & Legends
The Southern Indians & Benjamin Hawkins, 1796-1816

The Southern Indians: The Story of the Civilized
  Tribes Before Removal
The Spirit of Black Hawk: A Mystery of Africans and Indians
John Stuart and the Southern Colonial Frontier
Studies in Southeastern Indian Languages
Sun Circles & Human Hands: The Southeastern
  Indians, Art & Industries
Sunshine on the Prairie: The Story of Cynthia Ann Parker
Tacachale: Essays on the Indians of Florida &
  Southeastern Georgia During the Historical Period
They Say the Wind Is Red: The Alabama Choctaw
  Lost in Their Own Land
Tomochichi: Indian Friend of the Georgia Colony
Town & Temples Along the Mississippi
The Transformation of the Southeastern Indians
Tribes That Slumber: Indians of the Tennessee Region
Unconquered People: Florida's Seminole
  & Miccosukee Indians
*The World of the Southern Indians
Wynema: A Child of the Forest

INDIANS OF THE SOUTHWEST
(See Apache, Hopi, Navajo, &
Pueblo Indian Classifications)

A.D. Ancient Peoples of the Southwest
American Indians in Colorado
American Indians of the Southwest
Ancient Ancestors of the Southwest
Ancient Burial Practices in the American Southwest
Ancient Life in the American Southwest
Ancient Ruins of the Southwest: An Archaelogical Guide
Ants & Orioles: The Art of Pima Poetry
Apache, Navaho, and Spaniard
*The Apaches & Navajos
Archaeological Explorations on the Middle Chinlee
Basketmaker Caves in the Prayer Rock District,
  Northeastern Arizona
*The Big American Southwest Activity Book
Black Sand: Prehistory in Northern Arizona
Blue Sky, Night Thunder: The Utes of Colorado
Brothers of Light, Brothers of Blood
By the Prophet of the Earth: Ethnobotany of the Pima
The Cahuilla Indians of Southern California
Camp Beale's Springs and the Hualapai Indians
A Celebration of Being
Chaco Culture National Historical Park
Chaco & Hohokam: Prehistoric Regional Systems
  in the American Southwest
The Chaco Meridian: Centers of Political Power
  in the Ancient Southwest
Chulo: A Year Among the Coatimundis
Circles, Consciousness and Culture
Cliff Dwellings of the Mesa Verde
Cocopa Ethnography
The Cochise Cultural Sequence in Southeastern Arizona
Collections of Southwestern Pottery
The Comanchero Frontier: A History of
  New Mexican-Plains Indian Relations
CommonThreads: Pueblo & Navajo Textiles
  in the Southwest Museum
Contributions to Archaeology and Ethnohistory
  of Greater Mesoamerica
Cultural and Environmental History of Cienega Valley,
  Southeastern Arizona
Cycles of Conquest
Dancing Gods: Indian Ceremonials of New Mexico & Arizona
*A Day With a Mimbres
Decorative Art of the Southwestern Indians
Desert Foragers and Hunters
The Desert Is No Lady: Southwestern Landscapes
  in Women's Writing & Art
Desert Light
Disease, Depopulation & Culture Change in
  Northwestern New Spain
Divisiveness and Social Conflict
Doctors of Medicine in New Mexico
The Elkus Collection: Southwestern Indian Art
Enduring Culture: A Century of Photography
  of the Southwest Indians
Enduring Visions: One Thousand Years of
  Southwestern Indian Art
Ethno-Botany of the Gosiute Indias of Utah
The Ethobiology of the Papago Indians
Expedition Into New Mexico Made by Antonio de Espejo
Expedition to the Southwest
Fetishes and Carvings of the Southwest
Field Guide to Southwest Indian Arts & Crafts
Ethno-Botany of the Gosiute Indians of Utah
Expeditions Into New Mexico
Fetishes and Carvings of the Southwest
Four Winds: Poems from Indian Rituals
Freeing of the Deer: And Other New Mexico Indian Myths
From the Sands to the Mountain
A Frontier Documentary: Sonora & Tucson, 1821-1848
Fry Breads, Feast Days and Sheep
Gathering the Desert
Glimpse of the Ancient Southwest
Great Basin Indian Population Figures
Great Excavations: Tales of Early Southwestern
  Archaeology, 1888-1939
Guide to Prehistoric Ruins of the Southwest

INDIANS OF TEXAS

INDUSTRIES

Native American Collectibles
Native American Craft Inspirations
Native American Crafts
Native American Crafts Directory
Native American Crafts of California,
  the Great Basin & the Southwest
Native American Crafts of the Northwest,
  the Arctic & the Subarctic
Native American Designs
Native American Designs for Quilting
Native Basketry of Western North America
Navajo Arts & Crafts
Navajo Native Dyes: Their Preparation & Use
Navajo & Pueblo Silversmiths
Navajo Weavers & Silversmiths
Navajo Textiles
Navajo Weaving: Its Technic & History
Navajo Weaving: Three Centuries of Change
Navajo Weaving Today
North American Indian Designs
261 North American Indian Designs
North American Indian Designs for Artists & Craftspeople
North American Indian Designs in Full Color for
  Needlepointers & Craftspeople
North American Indian Designs/Stanied Glass
North American Indian Trade Silver
Northern Athapaskan Art: A Beadwork Tradition
Ojibwa Crafts
Pictorial Weavings of the Navajos
Plants Used in Basketry by the California Indians
Pomo Indian Basketry
Pueblo Crafts
Pueblo Designs: 176 Illustrations of the Rain Bird
Pueblo Indian Textiles
Quill & Beadwork of the Western Sioux
*Quillworker: A Cheyenne Legend
Quilting & Applique With Southwest Indian Designs
The Re-Establishment of the Indians in Their Pueblo Life
Through the Revival of Their Traditional Crafts:
  A Study in Home Extension Education
Reflections of the Weaver's World
Rugs & Posts, The Story of Navajo Weaving
Silver in the Fur Trade 1680-1820
Songs from the Loom
Southern Arizona Folk Arts
Southwest Indian Arts & Crafts
Southwest Indian Craft Arts
Southwest Traveler
Southwestern Indian Baskets: Their History & Their Makers
Spanish-American Blanketry
Starting Your Own Successful Indian Business
Sun Circles & Human Hands: The Southeastern Indians,
  Art & Industries
To Honor & Comfort: Native Quilting Traditions
Traditional Indian Bead & Leather Crafts
Traditional Indian Crafts
Traditions in Transition: Contemporary Basket Weaving
  of the Southwestern Indians
Turquoise and the Indians
Walk in Beauty: The Navajo & Their Blankets
Wampum and Shell Articles Used by the New York Indians
Weavers of Tradition & Beauty
The Weaver's Pathway: A Clarification
  of the "Spirit Trail" in Navajo Weaving
Weaving Arts of the North American Indian
Weaving a Navajo Blanket
Weaving a World
Weaving New Worlds
Weaving of the Southwest
White Weather Universe: Navajo Silver
  from the Fred Harvey Collection

IROQUOIS INDIANS

The Ambiguous Iroquois Empire
Apocalypse of Chiokoyhikoy: Chief of the Iroquois
The Caddoan, Iroquoian & Siouan Languages
Concerning the League
Conservatism Among the Iroquois at the Six Nations Reserve
Conspiracy of Interests: Iroquois Dispossession
  & the Rise of New York State
The Constitution of the Five Nations
Cultivating A Landscape of Peace: Iroquois-European
  Encounters in 17th-Century America
Debating Democracy: Native American Legacy of Freedom
The Dutch & the Iroquois
Evolution of the Onondaga Iroquois
Extending the Rafters: Interdisciplinary
  Approaches to Iroquois Studies
The False Faces of the Iroquois
The Great Law & the Longhouse: A Political History
  of the Iroquois Confederacy
*Heroes & Heroines, Monsters & Magic
The History & Culture of Iroquois Diplomacy
History of the Five Indian Nations
History of the Five Indian Nations in Canada
History of the Iroquois Confederacy
In Mohawk Country
The Iroquois
Iroquois: Art & Culture
Iroquois Corn in a Culture-Based Curriculum
Iroquois Crafts
Iroquois Culture & Commentary

The Iroquois Eagle Dance
The Iroquois & the Founding of the American Nation
Iroquois in the American Revolution
The Iroquois in the Civil War From
  Battlefield to Reservation
The Iroquois in the War of 1812
Iroquois Indians
Iroquois Land Claims
Iroquois Medical Botany
Iroquois Music & Dance
The Iroquois & the New Deal
The Iroquois Restoration
An Iroquois Sourcebook
Iroquois Studies: A Guide to Documentary & Ethnographic
  Resources from Western New York & the Genesee Valley
The Iroquois Struggle for Survival
The Iroquois Trail
The Iroquois Trail: Dickon Among the
  Onondagas & Senecas
League of the Iroquois
Little Water Medicine Society of the Senecas
Lewis H. Morgan on Iroquois Culture
Nation Iroquois: A 17th Century Ethnography
  of the (Oneida) Iroquois
Notes on the Iroquois
Oneida Verb Morphology
Onondaga: Portrait of a Native People
The Ordeal of the Longhouse
Parker on the Iroquois
Red Jacket & His People
Red Jacket: Iroquois Diplomat & Orator
Red Jacket: Seneca Chief
Sainte Marie Among the Iroquois
Seeds of Empire: The American Revolutionary
  Conquest of theIroquois
The Six Nations of New York
Samllpox and the Iroquois Wars
Smoking Technology of the Aborigines of the
  Iroquois Area of New York State
*Skywoman: Legends of the Iroquois
To Be Indian: The Life of Iroquois-
  Seneca Arthur Caswell Parker
Traditions and Laws of the Iroquois
Treaty of Canandaigua 1794
Two Early Historic Iroquoian Sites in Western New York
White Roots of Peace: Iroquois Book of Life

JEWELRY - COSTUME & ADORNMENT

American Indian Jewelry: 1,200 Artist Biographies
Authentic Indian Designs
Beads and Beadwork of the American Indian
A Beadwork Companion
Chain of Friendship: North American Indian Trade Silver
Crow Indian Beadwork
Dress Clothing of the Plains Indians
Feminine Fur Trade Fashions
Guide to Indian Quillworking
Head and Face Masks in Navaho Ceremonialism
Heart of the Dragonfly
History of Beads
How to Make Cherokee Clothing
How to Tan Skins the Indian Way
Indian Bead-Weaving Patterns
Indian Clothing Before Cortes: Mesoamerican
  Costumes from the Codices
Indian Clothig of the Great Lakes: 1740-1840
*Indian Costumes
Indian Jewelry
Indian Silver Jewelry of the Southwest, 1868-1930
Jewelry by Southwest American Indians: Evolving Designs
Making Arrows the Old Way
Making Indian Bows & Arrows
More Techniques of Beading Earrings
Navajo Jewlery: A Legacy of Silver & Stone
Navajo & Pueblo Silversmiths
Navajo Spoons: Indian Artistry and the
  Souvenir Trade, 1880-1940
Navajo Weavers & Silversmiths
North American Indian Beadwork Patterns
North American Indian Jewelry & Adornment
Pueblo Indian Embroidery
Quill & Beadwork of the Western Sioux
A Quillwork Companion
Sacred Beauty: Quillwork of the Plains Indians
Salish Indian Sweaters
Stone Ornaments Used by Indians in the U.S. & Canada
Techniques of Beading Earrings
The Technique of North American Indian Beadwork
The Technique of Porcupine Quill Decoration
  Among the Indians of North America
Traditional Clothing of the Native Americans
Traditional Dress
Traditional Indian Bead & Leather Crafts
Traditional Indian Crafts
Turquoise Jewelry
The Turquoise Trail: Native American Jewelry
  of the Southwest
Zuni Jewelry
Zuni: A Village of Silversmiths

JOURNALISM

The American Indian & the Media
Let My People Know: American Indian Journalism,
  1828-1978
Native American Press in Wisconsin and the Nation
Native American Representations: First Encounters,
  Distorted Images & Literary Appropriations
Pictures of Our Nobler Selves: A History of
  Native American Contributions to the Media

JUVENILE LITERATURE

*Across the Tundra
*Algonquian
*All About Arrowheads & Spear Points
*American Indian Arts & Crafts Source Book
*The American Indian in America
*American Indian Music & Musical Instruments
*American Indians
*American Indians Today
*Anasazi Legends
*An Anasazi Welcome
*The Animals' Ballgame
*Ancient Indians: The First Americans
*Anna's Athabaskan Summer
*ANPAO: An American Indian Odyssey
*Apache
*The Apaches & Navajos
*Approaches to Teaching Momaday's
  "The Way to Rainy Mountain"
*Arctic Hunter
*Arctic Memories
*Around the World in Folktale & Myth: American Indian
*At the Mouth of the Luckiest River
*Atariba and Niguayona
*Aunt Mary, Tell Me Stories
*Authentic North American Indian Clothing Series
*Authentic North American Indian Cradleboards Series
*Baby Rattlesnake
*A Bag of Bones
*The Beaded Moccasins
*The Bentwood Box
*Between Earth & Sky: Legends of Native American
  Sacred Places
*Bill Red Coyote Is a Nut
*Black Elk: A Man with a Vision
*Blackfeet Crafts
*Blue Jacket: War Chief of the Shawnees
*Blue Thunder
*Boat Ride With Lillian Two Blossom
*A Boy Becomes a Man at Wounded Knee
*The Boy Who Dreamed of an Acorn
*The Boy Who Lived With the Seals
*Brave Bear & the Ghosts: A Sioux Legend
*Broken Ice
*Brother Eagle, Sister Sky
*Buffalo Hunt
*Buffalo Hunter
*Buffalo & Indians on the Great Plains
*The Buffalo Jump
*Building A Bridge
*The Button Blanket
*The Cahuilla
*California Indians
*California Indians: An Educational Coloring Book
*California's Indians & the Gold Rush
*The California Native American Tribes
*The Catawbas
*The Cedar Plank
*Ceremony in the Circle of Life
*Chant of the Red Man
*Charlie Young Bear
*The Charm of the Bear Claw Necklace
*The Cherokee
*Cherokee Legends & the Trail of Tears
*Cherokee Summer
*Cheyenne
*The Cheyenne
*Cheyenne Legends of Creation
*Cheyenne Short Stories
*Cheyenne Warriors
*The Chickasaw
*Chief Joseph
*Chief Joseph's Own Story As Told By Chief Joseph in 1879
*Chief Sarah: Sarah Winnemucca's Fight for Indian Rights
*Chief Stephen's Parky
*The Children, Always the Children
*Children of the Morning Light
*Chinook
*The Chinook: Northwest
*Chocolate Chipmunks & Canoes
*The Choctaw
*The Chumash
*Circle of Thanks
*Circle of Wonder: A Native American Christmas Story
*Clamshell Boy: A Makah Legend
*Cloudwalker: Contemporary Native American Stories
*Clues from the Past: A Resource Book on Archaeology
*Columbus Day
*The Comanche
*Comanche Warbonnet

*Come to Our Salmon Feast
*The Coming of Coyote
*Concise Encyclopedia of the American Indian
*Cottontail and Sun
*Could It Be Old Hiari
*Coyote & the Fish
*Coyote & the Grasshoppers: A Pomo Legend
*Coyote & Kootenai
*Coyote & Little Turtle: A Traditional Hopi Tale
*Coyote Stories
*Coyote Steals the Blanket
*Coyote Stories for Children: Tales from Native America
*Coyote & the Winnowing Birds
*Coyote's Pow-Wow
*Coyote Tales of the Montana Salish
*Coyote & the Winnowning Birds: A Traditional Hopi Tale
*Creation of a California Tribe: Grandfather's
  Maidu Indian Tale
*Creation Tales from the Salish
*The Crow
*The Crying for a Vision
*A Cycle of Myths: Native Legends from Southeast Alaska
*Dakota and Ojibwe People in Minnesota
*Dancing Drum: A Cherokee Legend
*Dancing Teepees: Poems of American Indian Youth
*Dancing With the Indians
*The Dark Side of the Moon
*Dawn River
*The Day of the Ogre Kachinas: A Hopi Indian Fable
*The Defenders
*The Delaware Indians: A History
*Dog People: Native Dog Stories
*Dream Feather
*Dwellings: A Spiritual History of the Living World
*Earth Magic, Sky Magic: North American Indian Tales
*Earthmaker's Tales: North American Indian Stories
  About Earth Happenings
*Encyclopedia of Native American Tribes
*Family, Clan, Nation
*Famine Winter
*A Feast for Everyone
*Federal Indian Policy
*Field Mouse Goes to War
*First Woman & the Strawberry: A Cherokee Legend
*Flint's Rock
*The Flood
*The Flute Player: An Apache Folktale
*Flying with the Eagle, Racing the Great Bear
*Four Ancestors
*Fox Song
*From Abenaki to Zuni: A Dictionary of
  Native American Tribes
*From the Ashes
*From Abenaki to Zuni: A Dictionary of
  Native American Tribes
*Frontiersmen
*Fur Trappers and Traders: The Indians,
  The Pilgrims, and the Beaver
*Geronimo
*Giants of the Dawnland: Ancient Wabanaki Tales
*Gifts of the Season: Life Among the Northwest Indian
*The Girl Who Loved Wild Horses
*The Good Rainbow Road
*Grandfather Grey Owl Told Me
*Grandfather's Origin Story: The Navajo Indian Beginning
*Grandfather and the Popping Machine
*Grandfather's Story of Navajo Monsters
*Grandmother Spider Brings the Sun
*Grandmother Stories
*Grandmother Stories of the Northwest
*Grandmother's Christmas Story:
  A True Quechan Indian Story
*The Great Change
*Great Indians of California
*Growing Up Indian
*Heart Butte: A Blackfeet Indian
*Heart of Nasoaqua
*Heetunka's Harvest: A Tale of the Plains Indians
*Heroes & Heroines in Tlingit-Haida Legends
*Heroes & Heroines, Monsters & Magic
*Hiawatha
*The Hidatsa
*Hoksila & the Red Buffalo
*Hopi Mysteries
*Houses of Bark: Tipi, Wigwam & Longhouse
*How the Baby Deer Got Spots
*How Fire Got Into the Rocks & Trees
*How Food Was Given
*How Names Were Given
*How the Plains Indians Lived
*How Rabbit Stole the Fire: A North American
  Indian Folk Tale
*How the Stars Fell Into the Sky: A Navajo Legend
*The Hunt
*The Hunter and the Ravens
*The Hunter and the Woodpecker
*The Huron: Great Lakes
*I Am Regina
*I Can Read About Indians
*If You Lived With the Sioux Indians
*Iktomi & the Berries: A Plains Indian Story
*Iktomi & the Buffalo Skull: A Plains Indian Story
*Iktomi & the Ducks

*Iktomi Series
*Ikwa of the Mound-Builder Indians
*In the Beginning
*In a Circle Long Ago
*In the Trail of the Wind: American Indian
  Poems & Ritual Orations
*Indian Canoeing
*Indian Chiefs
*Indian Children Paper Dolls
*Indian Crafts
*Indian Fairy Tales
*Indian Folk Tales from Coast to Coast
*The Indian in the Cupboard
*Indian Killer
*Indian Myths from the Southeast
*Indian Tales of the Northern Plains
*Indian Tribes of America
*An Indian Winter
*Indians
*Indians in New York State
*Indians of America Series
*Indians of the Americas
*The Indians of Louisiana
*Indians of North America
*Indians of the Pacific Northwest
*Indians of the Plains
*Indians of the Southwest
*The Iroquois
*Is My Friend At Home? Pueblo Fireside Tales
*Joseph: Chief of the Nez Perce
*Alvin Josephy's History of the Native Americans Series
*Journey to Center Place
*Just Talking About Ourselves: Voices of Our Youth
*Ka-Ha-Si and the Loon: An Eskimo Legend
*Kamache and the Medicine Bead
*Keepers of the Animals
*Keepers of the Earth
*Keepers of Life
*Keepers of the Night
*The Key to the Indian
*King Philip
*The Kiowa: Great Plains
*Kiowa Voices: Ceremonial Dance, Ritual and Song
*Kiowa Voices: Myths, Legends & Folktales
*Kunu: Winnebago Boy Escapes
*The Kwakiutl
*Lakota & Dakota Animal Wisdom Stories
*The Last of the Mohicans
*The Last Warrior
*A Legend from Crazy Horse Clan
*The Legend of the Bluebonnet: An Old Tale of Texas
*The Legend of the Indian Paintbrush
*Legend of the Little Deer
*The Legend of Tom Pepper & Other Stories
*Legends of Chief Bald Eagle
*Legends of the Great Chiefs
*The Lenape: Middle Atlantic
*Let Me Tell You a Story & Workbook
*Let's Remember...Indians of Texas
*Lightning Inside You
*Linda's Indian Home
*Listen & Read Favorite North American Indian Legends
*Little Boy with Three Names: Stories of Taos Pueblo
*Little Herder in Autumn
*Little Firefly
*Little Water & Gift of the Animals: A Seneca Legend
*The Long Search
*Loon and Deer Were Traveling
*Louisiana Indian Tales
*Lucy Learns to Weave: Gathering Plants
*The Lumbee: Southeast
*Lumberman
*The Magic Lake: A Mystical Healing Lake of the Cherokee
*The Mandans
*Mark of Our Moccasins
*Me Run Fast Good
*Medicine Man
*Meet the North American Indians
*The Menominee
*The Money God
*The Moundbuilders
*Mystery at Echo Cliffs
*Mystery of Coyote Canyon
*Myths & Legends of the Haida Indians of the Northwest
*Myths & Legends of the Indian Southwest
*Myths & Legends of the Indians of the Southwest
*Native American Animal Stories
*Native American Legends
*Native American People
*Native American Picture Books of Change: The Art of
  Historic Children's Editions
*Native American Stories
*Native American Tales
*Native Americans
*Native Peoples of the Southwest
*The Naughty Little Rabbit and Old Man Coyote
*The Navajo
*The Navajo Brothers & the Stolen Herd
*Navajo Children
*Navajo Coyote Tales
*The Navajo: Southwest
*The Navajos
*Naya Nuki: Shoshoni Girl Who Ran

*Nez Perce
*The Nez Perce
*The Nez Perce: Northwest
*Night Flying Woman: An Ojibway Narrative
*The Night the Grandfathers Danced
*Nightwalker & the Buffalo
*No One Like a Brother
*North American Indian
*North American Indian Masks
*North American Indian Medicine
*North American Indian Stories
*North American Indian Survival Skills
*North American Indians
*The Northwest Coast Indian Art Series
*The Numu Way & Workbook
*The Ojibwa: Great Lakes
*The Ojibwe
*Okemos: Story of a Fox Indian In His Youth
*O'kohome: The Coyote Dog
*Old Father Story Teller
*Old Lop-Ear Wolf
*The Old Ones Told Me: American Indian Stories for Children
*Om-Kas-Toe: Blackfeet Twin Captures an Elkdog
*One Good Story, That One
*Only the Name Remains the Same
*The Owl's Song: A Novel
*Otokahekagapi: Sioux Creation Story
*Pachee Goyo: History & Legends from the Shoshone
*The Paiute: Southwest
*Passage to Little Bighorn
*Pathki Nana: Kootenai Girl Solves a Mystery
*The Pawnee
*People of the Breaking Day
*People of the Buffalo: How the Plains Indians Lived
*People of the Earth
*People of the Fire
*People of the Ice: How the Inuit Lived
*People of the Lakes
*People of the Longhouse: How the Iroquoian Tribes Lived
*People of the River
*People of the Lightning
*People of the Longhouse
*People of the Sea
*People of the Short Blue Corn
*People of the Trail: How the Northern Forest Indians Lived
*The People Shall Continue
*Phantom Horse of Collister's Fields
*Philip Johnston and the Navajo Code Talkers
*A Picture Book of Sitting Bull
*Pieces of White Shell
*The Pima-Maricopa: Southwest
*Plains Indian Warrior
*Plains Indians
*Plains Indians: An Educational Coloring Book
*Plains Indians of North America
*The Potawatomi: Great Lakes
*Pow Wow
*The Powhatan Tribes: Middle Atlantic
*Prairie Legends
*Prairie Smoke
*Pueblo
*The Pueblo
*Pueblo Storyteller
*A Pueblo Village
*Quest for Eagle Feather
*Quillworker: A Cheyenne Legend
*The Rainbow Bridge
*Rainy's Powwow
*Raven Brings to the People
*Red Frog Man: A Hohokam Leader
*Red Hawk & the Sky Sisters: A Shawnee Legend
*Red Power on the Rio Grande
*Riel's People: How the Metis Lived
*The Rings of Woot-Kew's Tail: Indian Legends
  of the Origin of the Sun, Moon and Stars
*Rising Fawn and the Fire Mystery
*Rivermen
*The Rolling Head: Cheyenne Tales
*The Rough-Face Girl
*Sacagawea
*Sacred Song of the Hermit Thrushs
*Salish Folk Tales
*Sam and the Golden People
*Scouts
*Seal for a Pal
*Search for Identity
*The Seminole
*The Seminole: Southeast
*The Seminoles
*Sequoyah
*Shingebiss: An Ojibway Legend
*The Shoshoni
*Signs of Spring
*The Sioux
*The Sioux Indians: Hunters and Warriors of the Plains
*Sitting Bull
*Sitting Bull and the Plains Indians
*Skunny Wundy: Seneca Indian Tales
*Sky Watchers of Ages Past
*Skywoman: Legends of the Iroquois
*Sleepy River
*Snail Girl Brings Water
*Soft rain: A Story of the Cherokee Trail of Tears

*Son of the Dine'
*Son of Thunder
*Song of the Hermit Thrush: An Iroquois Legend
*Song of the Seven Herbs
*Song of the Wild Violets
*Soun Tetoken: Nez Perce Boy Tames a Stallion
*Southeast Indians: An Educational Coloring Book
*Southern Indian Myths & Legends
*Southwest Indians: An Educational Coloring Book
*The Spark in the Stone
*Spelyi and Other Indian Legends
*Spider Spins a Story
*Spirit of the White Bison
*Spotted Eagle & Black Crow
*The Spotted Horse
*Squanto, Friend of the Pilgrims
*Star Tales: North American Indian Stories About the Stars
*Storm Boy
*The Story of Blue Elk
*The Story of Wounded Knee
*Sun Journey: A Story of Zuni Pueblo
*Sunflower's Promise: A Zuni Legend
*Sunpainters: Eclipse of the Navajo Sun
*Sweetgrass
*Tales From the Cherokee Hills
*The Tarhumara: Middle America
*Tecumseh
*10 Little Whitepeople
*There Still Are Buffalo
*These Were the Sioux
*Thirteen Moons on Turtle's Back
*Thirty Indian Legends of Canada
*This Land Is My Land
*Tjatjakiymatchan (Coyote)
*Totem Pole
*The Totem Pole Indians of the Northwest
*Totem Poles & Tribes
*Tragedy of Tenaya
*The Trail of Tears
*The Trail on Which They Wept: The Story of a Cherokee Girl
*Trappers & Traders
*Trickster & the Troll
*Tul-Tok-A-Na: The Small One
*The Tunica-Biloxi: Southeast
*Turquoise Boy: A Navajo Legend
*Twilight Boy
*Two Bear Cubs: A Miwok Legend from
 California's Yosemite Valley
*The Unbreakable Code
*Urban Indians
*Veho
*The Vision of the Spokane Prophet
*Voices Under One Sky
*Vostaas: The Story of Montana's Indian Nations
*The Wind Is Not a River
*The Winter Hunt
*The Yakima: Northwest
*The Yuma: California
*Walker of Time
*War Pony
*We Have Always Been Here
*Weaver's Tales
*Wesakejack & the Bears
*Wesakejack & the Flood
*When Buffalo Free the Mountains: A Ute Indian Journey
*When Clay Sings
*When Hopi Children Were Bad
*When the Great Canoes Came
*When the World Ended
*When We Went to the Mountains
*The Whistling Tree
*White Buffalo Women
*The White Deer: & Other Stories Told by the Lenape
*Why Buffalo Roam
*Why the Possum's Tail Is Bare: And Other
 North American Indian Nature Tales
*Wolf Dog of the Woodland Indians
*Wolf Stories
*Wolf Tales: Native American Children's Stories
*Women in American Indian Society
*Wovoka
*Yerington Paiute Tribe Coloring Book

KACHINAS

The Hopi Approach to the Art of Kachina Doll Carving
Hopi Kachina Dolls and Their Carvers
Hopi Kachina Dolls With a Key to Their Identification
Hopi Kachinas
Hopi Kachinas: The Complete Guide to
 Collecting Kachina Dolls
Hopi Katchinas Drawn by Native Artists
Kachina Ceremonies & Kachina Dolls
The Kachina & the Cross
*The Kachina Doll Book I & II
Kachina Dolls: The Art of Hopi Carvers
*Kachina Dolls: An Educational Coloring Book
The Kachina Dolls of Cecil Calnimptewa: Their Power,
 Their Struggle
Kachina: A Selected Bibliography
Kachina Tales From the Indian Pueblos
Kachinas: A Hopi Artist's Documentary
Kachinas in the Pueblo World

Kachinas: A Selected Bibliography
Kachinas: Spirit Beings of the Hopi
Ray Manley's Hopi Kachina
Small Spirits: Native American Dolls
Tusayan Katcinas & Hopi Katcina Altars
Zuni Katchinas
Zuni Katcinas, An Analytical Study

KICKAPOO INDIANS

Kenekuk, the Kickapoo Prophet
The Kickapoo Indians, Their History & Culture:
 An Annotated Bibliography
The Kickapoos: Lords of the Middle Border
Kiikaapoi: The Kansas Kickapoo
The Texas Kickapoo: Keepers of Tradition

KIOWA INDIANS

Bad Medicine and Good: Tales of the Kiowas
Calendar History of the Kiowa Indians
Expedition to the Southwest
Gifts of Pride & Love; Kiowa & Comanche Cradles
A Grammar of Kiowa
An Historical Chronology of the Kiowa Tribe
The Jesus Road: Kiowa, Christianity, and Indian Hymns
Kiowa, Apache, and Comanche Military Societies
*The Kiowa: Great Plains
Kiowa Memories: Images From Indian Territory, 1880
The Kiowa Treaty of 1853
*Kiowa Voices: Ceremonial Dance, Ritual and Song
*Kiowa Voices: Myths, Legends & Folktales
Kiowa: A Woman Missionary in Indian Territory
The Kiowas
Law and Status Among the Kiowa Indians
Lone Wolf v. Hitchcock
The Power of Kiowa Song
Silver Horn: Master Illustrator of the Kiowas
Telling Stories the Kiowa Way
The Ten Grandmothers: Epic of the Kiowas

KOOTENAI
(See SALISH & KOOTENAI INDIANS)

KWAKIUTL INDIANS

Chiefly Feasts: The Enduring Kwakiutl Potlatch
Feasting With Cannibals: An Essay on Kwakiutl Cosmology
Guests Never Leave Hungry: The Autobiography
 of James Sewid, A Kwakiutl Indian
Indians of the North Pacific Coast
Inside Passage: Living with Killer Whales,
 Bald Eagles & Kwakiutl Indians
*The Kwakiutl
Kwakiutl Ethnography
Kwakiutl: Indians of British Columbia
Kwakiutl String Figures
A Kawakiutl Village and School
Kwakwakawakw Settlement Sites, 1775-1920
Notes and Observations on the Kwakiutl People
Our Chiefs & Elders
Traditions and Change on the Northwest Coast

LAKOTA/DAKOTA
(SIOUX) INDIANS

Among the Sioux of Dakota
40th Anniversary of Crazy Horse Memorial
Autobiography of Red Cloud
Bead on an Anthill: A Lakota Childhood
Before the Great Spirit: The Many Faces of Sioux Spirituality
Bibliography of the Sioux
Black Elk and Flaming Rainbow
Black Elk: Holy Man of the Oglala
*Black Elk: A Man with a Vision
Black Elk's Religion: The Sun Dance & Lakota Catholicism
Black Elk: The Sacred Ways of the Lakota
Black Elk Speaks
Black Elk: The Sacred Ways of a Lakota
The Black Hills; Or, The Last Hunting Ground
 of the Dacotahs
Black Hills: Sacred Hills
Black Robe for the Yankton Sioux
Blue Star: The Story of Corabelle Fellows,
 Teacher at Dakota Missions, 1884-1888
The Canadian Sioux
Choteau Creek: A Sioux Reminiscence
The Concise Lakhota Dictionary: English to Lakhota
Crazy Horse
*Crazy Horse
Crazy Horse & Custer
Crazy Horse and Korczak
Crazy Horse, The Strange Man of the Oglalas
Crazy horse: Sacred Warrior of the Sioux
Crying for a Vision: A Rosebud Sioux Trilogy 1886-1976
Dacotah: Or, Life and Legends of the Sioux
 Around Fort Snelling
*The Dakota
Dakota Cross-Bearer: The Life & World of a
 Native American Bishop

A Dakota-English Dictionary
Dakota Grammar, Texts & Ethnology
*Dakota Indians Coloring Book
Dakota & Ojibwe People in Minnesota
The Dakota or Sioux in Minnesota As They Were in 1834
Dakota Oratory
Dakota Panorama
Dakota Sioux Indian Dictionary
Dakota: A Spiritual Geography
Dakota Texts
Dakota War Whoop
Dakota Way of Life Series
The Dance House: Stories from Rosebud
The Death of Crazy Horse
An English-Dakota Dictionary
An Ethnography of Drinking & Sobriety Among the Lakota
Father Francis M. Craft, Missionary to the Sioux
Fools Crow
The Forgotten People
The Forgotten Sioux: An Ethnohistory
 of the Lower Brule Reservation
Fort Laramie & the Great Sioux War
Fort Laramie and the Sioux
Ghost-Dance Religion and the Sioux Outbreak of 1890
*Grandchildren of the Lakota
The Great Sioux Trail
The Great Sioux War
*Growing Up in Siouxland
History of the Santee Sioux: U.S. Indian Policy on Trial
Hoskila & the Red Buffalo
How to Take Part in Lakota Ceremonies
*If You Lived With the Sioux Indians
Iktomi and the Ducks and Other Sioux Stories
An Indian in White America
Indians in Minnesota, 4th Edition
The Jesuit Mission to the Lakota Sioux
Lakota Belief and Ritual
Lakota Ceremonial Songs
Lakota Ceremonies
Lakota & Cheyenne: Indian Views of the
 Great Sioux War, 1876-1877
Lakota Culture, World Economy
*Lakota & Dakota Animal Wisdom Stories
Lakota Life
Lakota Myth
Lakota Naming: A Modern-Day Hunka Ceremony
Lakota Noon
The Lakota Recollections of the Custer Fight
The Lakota Ritual of the Sweat Lodge:
 History & Contemporary Practice
*Lakota Sioux Children & Elders Talk Together
Lakota Society
Lakota Songs
The Lakota Sweat Lodge Cards
Lakota Tales & Texts in Translation
Lakota Warrior
Lakota Woman
Land of the Spotted Eagle
Last Days of the Sioux Nation
The Last Years of Sitting Bull
A Legend From Carzy Horse Clan
Legends of the Lakota
Legends of the Mighty Sioux
Lessons from Chouteau Creek
Little Crow, Spokesman for the Sioux
Lost Bird of Wounded Knee: Spirit of the Lakota
Madonna Swan: A Lakota Woman's Story
Mary and I: Forty Years with the Sioux
Meditiations with Native Americans: Lakota Spirituality
Meet the Lakota, Vol. One: The People
My People the Sioux
The Mystic Lake Sioux: Sociology of the
 Mdewakantonwan Santee
Myths & Legends of the Sioux
Noble Red Man: Lakota Wisdomkeeper Mathew King
The Odyssey of Chief Standing Buffalo
 and the Northern Sisseton Sioux
The Oglala Lakota Crazy Horse
Oglala Religion
Oglala Women: Myth, Ritual & Reality
Ohiyesa: Charles Eastman, Santee Sioux
Oktokahekagapi: Sioux Creation Story
Old Indian Days
Old Indian Legends
*Otokahekagapi (First Beginnings) Sioux Creation Story
Pacifying the Plains: General Alfred Terry and the
 Decline of the Sioux, 1886-1890
Pictographic History of the Oglala Sioux
The Price of a Gift: A Lakota Healer's Story
Quill and Beadwork of the Western Sioux
Reading & Writing the Lakota Language
The Real Rosebud: The Triumph of a Lakota Woman
Red Cloud: Photographs of a Lakota Chief
Red Cloud: Warrior Statesman of the Lakota Sioux
Red Cloud and the Sioux Problem
Red Cloud's Folks: A History of the Oglala Sioux Indians
Remember Your Relatives: Yankton Sioux Images,
 1865-1915
Sacred Fireplace: Life & Teachings of a
 Lakota Medicine Man
Sacred Foods of the Lakota
The Sacred Pipe: Black Elk's Account of the
 Seven Rites of Oglala Sioux

The Seventh Generation: Images of the Lakota Today
Singing for a Spirit: A Portrait of the Dakota Sioux
*The Sioux
Sioux Collections
Sioux Indian Religion: Tradition & Innovation
*The Sioux Indians: Hunters and Warriors of the Plains
Sioux: Life and Customs of a Warrior Society
The Sioux of the Rosebud: A History in Pictures
The Sioux Uprising of 1862
Sioux Winter County, 131-Year Calendar of Events
Sister to the Sioux: The Memoirs of Elaine Goodale
  Eastman, 1885-1891
*Sitting Bull
Sitting Bull, Champion of the Sioux: A Biography
Sitting Bull: The Collected Speeches
Sitting Bull & the Plains Indians
*Sitting Bull: Warrior of the Sioux
The Sixth Grandfather: Black Elk's Teachings
  Given to John G. Neihardt
Songs of the Teton Sioux
Spotted Tail's Folk: A History of the Brule Sioux
Standing in the Light: A Lakota Way of Seeing
Starting From Here: Dakota Poetry, Pottery & Caring
Stories of the Sioux
*The Story of Little Bighorn
Sun Dance for Andy Horn
The Sun Dance & Other Ceremonies of the
  Oglala Division of the Teton Dakota
Sun Dancer
Sundancing at Rosebud & Pine Ridge
Teton Sioux Music
*These Were the Sioux
They Led a Nation
Through Dakota Eyes
The Twilight of the Sioux
Wakinyan: Lakota Religion in the 20th Century
War Drums at Eden Prairie
Waterlily
Where the West Begins: Essays on Middle
  Border & Siouxland Writing
A Whirlwind Passes
White Cloud: Lakota Spirit
Wigwam Evenings: Sioux Tales Retold
John P. Williamson, A Brother to the Sioux
Winter Count
With My Own Eyes: A Lakota Woman
  Tells Her People's History
Wiyuta: Assiniboine Storytelling With Signs CD
Wounded Knee 1973
Wounded Knee & the Ghost Dance Tragedy
Wounded Knee Massacre: From the Viewpoint of the Sioux
*The Yankton Sioux
Yellow Wolf: His Own Story
Yuwipi: Vision and Experience in Oglala Ritual

LAND CESSIONS, TENURES, TRANSFERS, REMOVALS & DISPUTES

Alcatraz: Indian Land Forever
American Indians Dispossessed
American Indians & National Parks
Another America: Native American Maps
  & the History of Our Land
Apologies to the Iroquois
Big Bear: The End of Freedom
The Cherokee Cases: The Confrontation of Law & Politics
Cherokee Removal
The Choctaw Before Removal
Considerations on the Present State of the Indians
Continent Lost—A Civilization Won:
  Indian Land Tenure in America
The Corporation and the Indian
The Dawes Commission & the Allotment of the
  Five Civilized Tribes, 1893-1914
Dispossessing the American Indian: Indian & Whites
  on the Colonial Frontier
The Dispossession of the American Indian, 1887-1934
The End of Indian Kansas
Haa Aani Our Land: Tlingit & Haida Land Rights
Indian Land Cessions in the U.S.
Indian Land Laws
Indian Land Tenure: Bibliographic Essays
  and a Guide to the Literature
Indian Lands
Indian Removal: The Emigration of
  Five Civilized Tribes of Indians
Indian Use of the Santa Fe National Forest
Indians, Bureaucrats and Land: The Dawes Act
  and the Decline of Indian Farming
Indigenous Peoples & Tropical Forests
Iroquois Land Claims
Native American Estate
*Native Americans & the Reservation in American History
Navajo Land Use: An Ethnoarchaeological Study
New Resource Wars
The Oneida Land Claims
*Only the Names Remain: The Cherokees
  and the Trail of Tears
Pueblo Indian Land Grants of the "Rio Abajo", NM
Pushed Into the Rocks: Southern California Indian
  Land Tenure

The Rape of the Indian Lands: An Original Anthology
Reconstruction in Indian Territory
Redskins, Ruffleshirts and Rednecks
Removal of the Cherokee Indians from Georgia
The Removal of the Cherokee Nation: Manifest
  Destiny or National Dishonor
Reservation to City: Indian Urbanization
  and Federal Relocation
Searching for the Bright Path
The Second Long Walk: Navajo-Hopi Land Dispute
A Snug Little Purchase
Sold American: The Story of Alaska Natives
  & Their Land, 1867-1959
*The Story of the Trail of Tears
The Taos Indians & the Battle for Blue Lake
Territorial Subdivision and Boundaries of the Wampanoag,
  Massachusett & Nauset Indians
The Trail of Tears
The Wind Won't Know Me

LANGUAGES, DICTIONARIES, GLOSSARIES, ETC.

Absaloka: Crow Chilren's Writing
Ahtna Athabaskan Dictionary
Alaawich
Alaska Native Language Center Publications
Aleut Dictionary
American Indian English
American Indian: Language & Literature
American Indian Language Series
American Indian Languages, Vol. 5
American Indian Languages: Cultural & Social Contexts
American Indian Linguistics & Ethnography in
  Honor of Laurence C. Thompson
American Indian Linguistics & Literature
Arapaho Dialects
The Athabaskan Languages
Athapaskan Linguistics
Beginning Cherokee
Beginning Creek: Myskoke Emponvkv
Beginning Washoe
Bibliography of Language Arts Materials for
  Native North Americans, 1965-1974
Bibliography of the Languages of Native California
Blackfoot Grammar
Caddo Verb Morphology
Cahuilla Dictionary
Case & Agreement in Inuit
Chahta Anumpa: A Grammar of the
  Choctaw Language (CD-ROM)
Chem'ivillu: Let's Speak Cahuilla
*Cherokee ABC Coloring Book
Cherokee Dictionary
Cherokee-English Dictionary
Cherokee-English Interliner, First Epistle
  of John of the New Testament
Cherokee Glossary
Cherokee Language Workbook
Cherokee Syllabary
Cherokee Words
Cheyenne Indians: Sketch of the Cheyenne Grammar
Chickasaw: An Analytical Dictionary
Chickasaw Glossary
Chinook Jargon
Choctaw Dictionary
Choctaw Language & Culture: Chahta Anumpa
Choctaw Language Awareness Teachers Manual
The Chumash & Costanoan Languages
Colloquial Navajo: A Dictionary
Comanche Dictionary & Grammar
Comparative Hokan-Coahuiltecan Studies
Comparative Studies in Amerindian Languages
A Comparative Study of Lake-Iroquoian Accent
A Concise Dictionary of Minnesoita Ojibwe
A Concise Dictionary of Indian Tribes of North America
The Concise Lakhota Dictionary: English to Lakhota
Creek (Muscogee) New Testament Concordance
The Creek Verb
Dakota-English Dictionary
Dakota Grammar, Texts & Ethnology
Dakota Sioux Indian Dictionary
Delaware Reference Grammar
Dictionary of the Alabama Language
Dictionary of the American Indian
Dictionary of the Biloxi & Ofo Languages
Dictionary Catalog of the Edward E. Ayer Collection
Dictionary of the Choctaw Language
Dictionary of Creek/Muskogee
Dictionary of Daily Life of Indian of the Americas
Dictionary of Indian Tribes of the Americas
Dictionary of Mesa Grande Diegueno
Dictionary of Native American Healing
Dictionary of Native American Mythology
Dictionary of the Ojibway Language
Dictionary of the Osage Language
Dictionary of Papago Usage
Dictionary of Powhatan
Eastern Ojibwa-Chippewa-Ottawa Dictionary
Elnguq
English-Cheyenne Dictionary
English-Eskimo & Eskimo-English Vocabularies
English-Micmac Dictionary

English-Navajo Children's Picture Dictionary
The Ethnology of the Salinan Indians
Everyday Lakota: An English-Sioux Dictionary for Beginners
First Lessons in Makah
Forked Tongues: Speech, Writing & Representation
  in North American Indian Texts
General & Amerindian Ethnolinguistics
Grammar & Dictionary of the Timucua Language
A Grammar of Bella Coola
A Grammar of Comanche
A Grammar of Misantla Totonac
Haida Syntax
Handbook of American Indian Languages
Handbook of Creek (Muscogee) Grammar
Handbook of the Creek Language
History, Manners & Customs of the Indian Nations
Hopi Dictionary: Hopi-English, English-Hopi,
  Grammatical Appendix
Hopi Time
I'Ishiyatam
In Honor of Mary Haas
Indian Sign Language
Indigenous Languages of the Americas
Introduction to Cherokee
Introduction to Choctaw
Introduction to Handbook of American Indian
  Languages/Indian Linguistic
Introduction to the Shoshoni Language
Introduction to the Study of Indian Languages
Itza Maya Texts with a Grammatical Overview
Journal of Exploring Tour
Kathlamet Texts
A Key Into the Language of America
Kiliwa Dictionary
Koasati Dictionary
Lakota Dictionary
Lakota Tales & Texts in Translation
Language, Culture and History: Essays by Mary R. Haas
A Language of Our Own: The Genesis of Michif
The Language of the Salinan Indians
Language Renewal Among American Indian Tribes
Language Samplers
Languages of the Aboriginal Southeast:
  An Annotated Bibliography
The Languages of the Coast of California
  North of San Francisco
The Languages of the Coast of California
  South of San Francisco
Languages of the Tribes of the Extreme Northwest
Let's Talk Cheyenne
Lexical Acculturation in Native American Languages
The Lillooet Language
Lushootseed Reader with Introductory Grammar
Making It Their Own: Seven Ojibwe
  Communicative Practices
Meet Cree: A Guide to the Cree Language
The Miami-Illinois Language
Micmac Dictionary
Mohawk, One Thousand Useful Words
Mumigcistet Kalikait: A Yup'ik Language Term Book
Mythology of the Lenape: Guide & Texts
*Na Yo Pisa
Native American Placenames of the U.S.
Native American Verbal Art: Texts & Contexts
Native Languages & Language Families of North America
*Navajo ABC: A Dine Alphabet Book
Navajo Country Dine Bikeyah: A Geographic Dictionary
Navajo Dictionary on Diagnostic Terminology
Navajo-English Children's Picture Dictionary
Navajo-English Dictionary
Navajo Texts
The Navajo Verb: A Grammar for Students & Scholars
The Navajo Verb System: An Overview
New World Babel: Languages & Nations in Early America
Nez Perce Dictionary
Nez Perce Texts
North American Indian Language Materials, 1890-1965
The Northern Paiute Language of Oregon
Notes of a Twenty-Five Years' Service in
  the Hudson's Bay Territory
O Brave New Words: Native American
  Loanwords in Current English
Ojibwe Language
Ojibwe Vocabulary
One of the Keys: 1676-1776-1976:
  The Wampanoag Indian Contribution
One Thousand Useful Mohawk Words
Oneida Verb Morphology
An Outline of Basic Verb Inflections of Oklahoma Cherokee
Passamaquoddy Dictionary
Perspectives onthe Southeast: Linguistics,
  Archaeology & Ethnohistory
The Phonetic Consituents of the Native Languages
  of California
The Phonetics Elements of the Diegueno Language
The Phonetics Elements of the Mojave Language
The Phonetics Elements of the Northern Paiute Language
Phonological Issues of North Alaskan Inupiaq
Proceedings of the Hokan Languages Workshop
Proceedings of the Hokan-Yuman Languages Workshop
Reading & Writing the Lakota Language
The Salish Language Family
Sequoyah

Sequoyah & the Cherokee Alphabet
Sequoyah, Father of the Cherokee Alphabet
The Shuswap Language
Siberian Yup'ik Eskimo
Sign Language Among the North American Indians
The Siouan Indian Language
   (Teton & Santee Dialects) Dakota
Sonora Yaqui Language Structures
A Structured Approach to Learning the Basic Inflections
   of the Cherokee Verb
Studies in American Indian Languages
Studies in Southeastern Indian Languages
Stylized Characters' Speech in Thompson Salish Narrative
Supplement to the Handbook of Middle American Indians:
   Linguistics
Syntax & Semantics: The Syntax of
   Native American Languages
Taitaduhaan: Western Mono Ways of Speaking
Talking Chickasaw Dictionary
Theoretical Perspectives on Native American Languages
The Thompson Language
Thompson River Salish Dictionary
Tlingit Verb Dictionary
Tonkawa, An Indian Language of Texas
Totkv Mocvse • New Fire: Creek Folktales
Tovangar
Traditional Narratives of the Arikara Indians
Turtle Island Alphabet
Upper Chehalis Dictionary
A Vocabulary of Mohegan-Pequot
Vocabulary of New Jersey Delaware
Vocabulary of the Shoshone Language
Vocabulary of the Tuscarora
The Washo Language of East Central California & Nevada
Western Apache-English Dictionary
Western Abenaki Dictionary Vol. 2: English-Abenaki
Where the West Begins: Essays on Middle Border
   and Siouxland Writing
Word Dance: The Language of Native American Culture
Writing Cherokee
Wiyot Grammar & Texts
Yerington Paiute Dictionary
Yerington Paiute Language Grammar
Yoeme-English, English-Yoeme Standard Dictionary
Yokuts Dialect Survey
The Yokuts Language of South Central California
Yup'ik Eskimo Dictionary
Yurok Affixes

LEGAL, LAWS, ETC.

Acts and Resolutions (of National Tribal Councils)
Alaska Natives and American Laws
American Indian Law
American Indian Law In a Nutshell
The American Indian in the White Man's Prisons:
   A Story of Genocide
The American Indian Law Series
American Indian Legal Materials: A Union List
American Indian Legal Studies Teacher's Manual & Text
American Indian Policy in the 20th Century
American Indian Sovereignty & the U.S. Supreme Court:
   The Masking of Justice
American Indian Tribal Courts
American Indian Water Rights & the Limits of the Law
The American Indian & Western Thought:
   The Discourse of Conquest
American Indians, American Justice
American Indians, Time and the Law
The Arbitrary Indian: The Indian Arts & Crafts Act of 1990
Basic Guide to Indian Community Advocacy
Behind the Trail of Broken Treaties
Braid of Feathers:American Indian Law
   & Contemporary Tribal Life
Bread & Freedom
The Case of the Seneca Indians in the State of New York
The Cherokee Cases: Two Landmark Federal Decisions
   in the Fight for Sovereignty
Cherokee Nation Code: Annotated
Cherokee Nation vs. Georgia: Native American Rights
The Cheyenne Way: Conflict and Case Law in
   Primitive Jurisprudence
The Constitution and Laws of the American Indian Tribes
Felix S. Cohen's Handbook of Federal Indian Law
Conservation & Indian Rights
Constitutionalism & Native Americans, 1903-1968
Constitutions, Treaties, and Laws Series
The Consumer's Rights Under Warranties
Contracts & You
Criminal Jurisdiction Allocation in Indian Country
Crow Dog's Case: American Indian Sovereignty...
Digest of American Indian Law: Cases & Chronology
Diplomates in Buckskin
Directory of American Indian Law Attorneys
Documents of U.S. Indian Policy, 3rd Ed.
Early American Indian Documents: Treaties & Laws,
   1607-1789
Encyclopedia of American Indian Civil Rights
Tne Encyclopedia of Native American Legal Tradition
Exiled in the Land of the Free: Democracy,
   Indian Nations & the U.S. Constitution
Federal Indian Law, Cases & Material
The Federal-Indian Trust Relationship

Fifth Annual Indian Law Seminar
A Final Promise: The Campaign to
   Assimilate the Indians, 1880-1920
Grave Injustice: The American Indian
   Repatriation Movement & NAGPRA
Guide to American Indian Documents in the
   Congressional Serial Set: 1817-1899
Handbook of American Indian Religious Freedom
Handbook of Federal Indian Law
Imperfect Victories: The Legal Tenacity
   of the Omaha Tribe, 1945-1995
Implementing the Native American Graves
   Protection and Repatriation Act (NAGPRA)
The Indian Bill of Rights
The Indian Child Welfare Act Handbook
Indian Court Judgements
Indian Employment, Training & Related Services
   Demonstration Act
Indian Gaming & the Law
Indian Gaming: Who Wins?
Indian Justice
Indian Justice: A Research Bibliography
Indian Law - Race Law: A Five Hundred Year History
The Indian Lawyer
Indian Police and Judges: Experiments in
   Acculturation and Control
Indian Reserved Water Rights
The Indian Rights Association:
   The Herbert Welsh Years, 1882-1904
Indian Rights Manual
Indian Treaty-Making Policy in the
   U.S. & Canada, 1867-1877
Indian Water, 1985: Collected Essays
Indians & Criminal Justice
The Indians & the U.S. Constitution
Indians, Indian Tribes & State Government:
   Major Legal Battles
Intellectual Property Rights for Indigenous Peoples:
   A Source Book
Introduction to Criminal Jurisdiction in Indian Country
Jicarilla Apache Tribal Code
Labor Laws, Union, and Indian Self-Determination
Landlord Tenant Relations
Law and the American Indian: Readings, Notes and Cases
Law Enforcement on Indian Reservations
   After Oliphant v. Suquamish Indian Tribes
Law & Identity: Lawyers, Native Americans
   and Legal Practice
Law & Status Among the Kiowa Indians
Laws of the Cherokee Nation
Laws & Joint Resolutions
Leasing Indian Water
Legal Conscience, Selected Papers
Legal Structures for Indian Business
   Development on Reservations
Like a Hurricane: The Indian Movement
   from Alcatraz to Wounded Knee
Linking Arms Together: American Indian Treaty
   Visions of Law & Peace
The Livingston Indian Records, 1666-1723
Mending the Circle: A Native Repatriation Guide
Model Court Development Project
Native American Cultural & Religious Freedoms
Native American Issues: A Reference Handbook
*Native American Rights
The Native American Rights Movement
The Native American Struggle: Conquering
   the Rule of Law A Colloquium
Native Americans: Crime & Justice
Native Americans & the Law
Native Americans & Nixon: Presidential Politics
   & Minority Self-Determination, 1969-1972
Native Americans & Public Policy
Native People in Canada: Contemporary Conflicts
The Navajo-Hopi Land Dispute: An American Tragedy
Navajo Tribal Code
The New Deal & American Indian Tribalism
Oil & Gas
Oklahoma Tribal Courts
Partial Justice" Federal Indian Law in a
   Liberal-Constitutional System
Planting Tail Feathers: Tribal Survival & Public Law 280
Policing in Indian Country
Puritan Justice & the Indian: White Man's Law
   in Massachusetts, 1630-1763
Recent Legal Issues for American Indians,
   1968 to the Present
Quarter-Acre of Heartache
Readings in American Indian Law
Red Lake Court of Tribal Offenses Court Manual
Red Man's Land, White Man's Law: The Past &
   Present Status of the American Indian
Repatriation Reader: Who Owns American Indian Remains?
Repossession and You
The Rights of Indians & Tribes: The Basic ACLU Guide
The Rights of Indigenous Peoples
The Significant Ties Exception to the
   Indian Child Welfare Act
Sixth Annual Indian Law Conference
Standing Bear & the Ponca Chiefs
Tangled Webs
Tonto's Revenge: Reflections on
   American Indian Culture & Policy

Towards Aboriginal Self-Government
Treaties on Trial
Treatment of Indians by the Criminal Justice System
*Tribal Law
The Trial of "Indian Joe"
Tribes, Treaties, and Constitutional Tribulations
Uneven Ground: American Indian Sovereignty & Federal Law
Unjust Relations: Aboriginal Rights in Canadian Courts
Walk for Justice
The Walleye War
Walleye Warriors
Wisconsin's County Forests: Conflict Over
   Indian Timber Rights
You and the Utility Company
Your Rights As American Indians

LEGENDS

Aleut Tales & Narratives
The American Eagle
American Indian Genesis
American Indian Legends
American Indian Linguistics & Literature
American Indian Mythology
American Indian Myths & Legends
American Indian Stories
*American Indian Trickster Tales
*Anasazi Legends
Ancient Voices, Current Affairs:
   The Legend of the Rainbow Warriors
*And It Is Still That Way: Legends
   Told by Arizona Indian Children
Apache Legends: Songs of the Wild Dancer
Artistry in Native American Myths
As My Grandfather Told It: Traditional Stories of the Koyukuk
The Bear That Turned White; & Other Native Tales
Bedbugs' Night Dance & Other Hopi Tales of Sexual
   Encounter
Blackfoot Lodge Tales
Californian Indian Nights
Celilo Tales: Wasco Myths, Legends,
   Tales of Magic & the Marvelous
Cherokee Animal Stories
Cherokee Legends and the Trail of Tears
Cherokee Vision of Eloh'
Cheyenne Memories
Childhood & Folklore
Children of the Twilight: Folktales of Indian Tribes
Choctaw Legends Text & Teacher's Guide
Clothed-in-Fur and Other Tales: An Introduction
   to an Ojibwa World View
Coyote: A Trickster from the American Southwest
Dakota Texts
The Dawn of the World
Dine Bahane': The Navajo Creation Story
Dirty Boy: A Jicarilla Tale of Raid & War
Do Them No Harm
Dragonfly's Tale
Earth Elder Stories
Elderberry Flute Song, Contemporary Coyote Tales
Estiyut Omayat: Creek Writings
Ethnography and Folklore of the Indians
   of Northwestern California
Eye of the Changer: A Northwest Indian Tale
The Faithful Hunter & Other Abenaki Stories
Folk-Tales of the Salishan & the Sahaptin Tribes
The Freeing of the Deer and Other New Mexico Indian Myths
Friends of Thunder: Folktales of the Oklahoma Cherokees
From Indian Legends to the Modern Bookshelf
Ghost Voices: Yakima Indian Myths,
   Legends and Hunting Stories
The Gift of the Gila Monster: Navajo Ceremonial Tales
Giving: Ojibway Stories & Legends from the
   Children of Curve Lake
Giving Voice to Bear
A Good Medicine Collection: Life in Harmony with Nature
The Gospel of the Great Spirit
Grandpa Was a Cowboy & an Indian & Other Stories
*The Great Ball Game of the Birds & Animals
The Great Change
Haa Shuka, Our Ancestors
Haboo: Native American Stories from Puget Sound
Hear My Chief: Nez Perce Legend and History
*A Heart Full of Turquoise: Pueblo Indian Tales
*Heroes & Heroines, Monsters & Magic
*Hole-in-the-Day: Chippewa Native American Indian Stories
Hopi Animal Tales
Hopi Coyote Tales: Istutuwutsi
Hoskila & the Red Buffalo
*How Medicine Came to the People:
   A Tale of the Ancient Cherokees
*How Rabbit Lost His Tail: A Traditional Cherokee Legend
*How Rabbit Stole the Fire
Illustrated Myths of Native America
Indian Legends From the Northern Rockies
Indian Stories from the Pueblos:
   Tales of New Mexico and Arizona
Indian Stories and Legends of the Stillaguamish,
   Sauks & Allied Tribes
Indian Story and Song from North America
Indian Tales
Indian Tales & Legends
Indian Tales and Others

Indians of the Feather River: Tales of the
  Concow Maidu of California
Iroquois Stories
K'etaalkkaanee: The One Who Paddled
  Among the People & the Animals
Kickapoo Tales
Kiowa Voices: Myths, Legends and Folktales
Ktunaxa Legends
The Legend of Natural Tunnell
Legends of the Cowlitz
Legends of the Delaware Indians & Picture Writing
*Legends of the Great Chiefs
Legends of the Iroquois
Legends of the Lakota
Legends of the Longhouse
Legends of the Mighty Sioux
Legend of Our Nations
Legends of Our Times
Legends of the Yosemite Miwok
Legends Told by the Old People
Loon Legends
Lore of the Great Turtle: Indian Legends of Mackinac Retold
Maidu Myths & Tales
The Man to Send Rain Clouds
Mandan-Hidatsa Myths and Ceremonies
Masked Gods: Navaho and Pueblo Ceremonialism
Mimbres Mythology
Mythology of the Blackfoot Indians
Myths & Folktales of the Alabama-Coushatta Indians
Myths & Legends of California and the Old Southwest
Myths & Legends of the Pacific Northwest
Myths & Legends of the Sioux
Myths & Tales of the Chiricahua Apache Indians
Myths & Tales of the Jicarilla Apache Indians
Myths & Tales fo the Southeastern Indians
Myths & Tales of the White Mountain Apache
Myths & Traditions of the Arikara Indians
Myths of the Cherokee
Myths of the Cherokee & Sacred Formulas
Myths of the Modocs: Indian Legends from the Northwest
Myths of the New World Indians
Myths of the North American Indians
Myths of Pre-Columbian America
The Naked Man, Vol. 4: Mythologiques
Native American Legends
Native American Legends & Lore Library
Native American Legends: The Southeast
Native American Stories
Navajo Coyote Tales
Navaho Folk Tales
Navaho Indian Myths
Navaho Legends
Navajo Stories of the Long Walk Period
Nehalem Tillimook Tales
Nez Perce Coyote Tales
Nihancan's Feast of Beaver: Animal Tales
  of the North American Indians
Nine Visits to the Mythworld: Ghandl of the Qayahl Llaanas
Noccalula: Legend, Fact & Function
North Amerian Indian Mythology
Northern Tales: Traditional Stories of
  Eskimo & Indian Peoples
Ojibway Heritage
Ojibway Tales
Oktokahekagapi: Sioux Creation Story
Old Father Story Teller
Old Indian Legends
Old Man Coyote
On the Trail of Spider Woman
One More Story: Contemporary Seneca Tales
The Origin of Table Manners, Vol. 3: Mythologiques
Osage Life & Legends
The Other Side of Nowhere
Pawnee Hero, Stories and Folktales
The Pawnee Mythology
Pia Toya: A Goshute Indian Legend
Plains Cree Texts
Plains Indian Mythology
The Pollen Path: A Collection of Navajo Myths
The Portable North American Indian Reader
Pueblo Indian Folk-Stories
Pueblo Stories and Storytellers
The Punishment of the Stingy & Other Indian Stories
Quail Song: A Pueblo Indian Folktale
*Rabbit and the Bears
Race With the Buffalo & Other Native American
  Stories for Young Readers
Raven Tales
Raven's Cry
The Raven Steels the Light
Recently Discovered Tales of Life Among the Indians
The Red Swan: Myths and Tales of the American Indian
Return of the Sun, Tales From the Northeastern Woodlands
Schoolcraft's Indian Legends from Algic Researches
Seneca Myths & Folk Tales
The Sky Is My Tipi
Some Kind of Power: Navajo Children's
  Skinwalker Narratives
Spider Woman's Granddaughters
Spiderwoman's Dream
Shamans & Kushtakas: North Coast Tales
  of the Supernatural
The Social Life of Stories

Song of the Seven Herbs
Spider Woman Stories: Legends of the Hopi Indians
Spirit in the Stone
Spirit Mountain: An Anthology of Yuman Story & Song
The Silver Arrow and Other Indian Romances
  of the Dune Country
The Stone Canoe
Stories from the Indian Wigwams & Northern Campfires
Stories of the Sioux
Stories We Live By
A Story As Sharp As a Knife: The Classical Haida
  Mythtellers & Their World
The Story of Lynx
Storypole Legends
Tales the Elders Told: Ojibway Legends
Tales of the Anishinaubaek: Ojibway Legends
Tales of the Bark Lodges
Taos Tales
Traditions of the Caddo
Tales of Kankakee Land
Tales of the Mohaves
Tales of the North American Indian
Tales of the Tepee
Teachings of Nature
The Ten Grandmothers
Tewa Tales
Their Stories of Long Ago
Thirteen Moons on Turtle's Back
A Thousand Years of American Indian Storytelling
Tlingit Tales: Potlatch & Totem Poles
Top of the Hill
Totkv Mocvse • New Fire: Creek Folktales
Touching the Fire
Traditional Stories & Foods
The Trickster of Liberty
Trickster: Study in American Indian Mythology
*The Trickster and the Troll
Tsonakwa & Yolaikia: Legends in Stone, Bone & Wood
Turtle Dream
Turtle Meat and Other Stories
Two Old Women: An Alaska Legend of Betrayal,
  Courage & Survival
Under the Indian Turquoise Sky
The Unwritten Literature of the Hopi
Voices of the Winds: Native American Legends
Walk in Peace
The Walking People: A Native American Oral History
Warrior Maiden: A Hopi Legend
The Way to Make Perfect Mountains
The Way to Rainy Mountain
Ways of Indian Magic
Ways of Indian Wisdom
Weavers Tales
When the Chenoo Howls: Native American Tales of Horror
Where Legends Live
The White Canoe and Other Legends of the Ojibways
White Wolf Woman
The Wind Eagle
Wisconsin Chippewa Myths & Tales
The Witch of Goingsnake & Other Stories
Write It On Your Heart: World of an Okanagan Storyteller
Zuni Folk Tales

LEWIS & CLARK EXPEDITION

Among the Sleeping Giants
Do Them No Harm
Exploring the West
How George Rogers Clark Won the West
The Incredible Journey of Lewis & Clark
The Journals tof the Lewis & Clark Expedition
Letters of the Lewis & Clark Expedition
Lewis & Clark Among the Indians
Lewis & Clark: Voyage of Discovery
*The Lewis & Clark Expedition
Lewis & Clark Territory: Contemporary Artists
  Revisit Place, Race, & Memory
Lewis & Clark's West
Meriwether Lewis and William Clark: Soldiers,
  Explorers, & Partners in History
Original Journals of the Lewis & Clark Expedition
Sacagawea: Indian Interpreter to Lewis & Clark
*The Story of the Lewis & Clark Expedition
Those Tremendous Mountains
The Way to the Western Sea
West to the Pacific: The Story of Lewis & Clark Expedition

LITERATURE

American Indian in English Literature of the 18th Century
American Indian Linguistics & Literature
American Indian Literature: An Anthology
American Indian Literature, Environmental Justice,
  & Ecocriticism
American Indian Literatures
American Indian Stories
The Ancient Child
Authentic Alaska" Voices of Its Native Writers
Blue Horses Rush In: Poems & Stories
Book of the Fourth World: Reading the Native Americas
  Through Their Literature
Briefcase Warriors: Stories for the Stage

The Broken Circle
The Broken Cord
Captured in the Middle: Tradition & Experience
  in The The Cherokee Night & Other Plays
Contemporary Native American Writing
Chihuly's Pendletons
A Circle of Nations: Voices & Visions of American Indians
The Cold-and-Hunger Dance
The Colour of Resistance: Contemporary Collection
  of Writing by Aboriginal Women
Comeuppance At Kicking Horse Casino & Other Stories
Coming to Light: Contemporary Translations of the
  Native Literatures of North America
Contemporary American Indian Literatures
  & the Oral Tradition
Conversations With Louise Erdrich & Michael Dorris
Dancing on the Rim of the World
Dawn Land
Dead Voices: Natural Agonies in the New World
Deadly Indian Summer
Dreams & Thunder: Stories, Poems,
  & The Sun Dance Opera
Early American Writings
Earth Power Coming: Short Fiction in
  Native American Literature
Feathering Custer
Feminist Readings of Native American Literature
Fire Sticks: A Collection of Stories
Forked Tongues
Four Masterworks of American Indian Literature
From the Glittering World: A Navajo Story
From Sand Creek
The Girl Who Married the Moon:
  Tales from Native North America
Golden Woman: The Colville Narrative of Peter J. Seymour
Grandmother, Grandfather, & Old Wolf
Grave Concerns, Trickster Turns:
  The Novels of Louis Owens
A Great Plains Reader
Handbook of Native American Literature
The Hawk is Hungry and Other Stories
Tony Hillerman's Navajoland
Home Places: Contemporary Native American
  Writing from Sun Tracks
Hopi Traditional Literature
I Hear the Train: Reflections, Inventions, Refractions
Iktomi and the Ducks and Other Sioux Stories
Index to Literature on the American Indian
The Indian in American Literature
Indian Land Tenure
Indian Nation: Native American Literature
  & 19th Century Nationalism
Indian Old Man Stories
Indian Why Stories
Interpreting the Indian
The Invention of Native American Literature
Ke-Ma-Ha: The Omaha Stories of Francis La Flesche
Kootenai Why Stories
Life Woven With Stone
The Lightning Within
Literature By and About the American Indian
Little Big Man
Long River
Madchild Running
The Man to Send Rain Clouds
The Map of Who We Are: A Novel
The Mask Maker: A Novel
Mediation in Contemporary Native Americn Fiction
Medicine Hat: A Novel
Men on the Moon: Collected Short Stories
N. Scott Momaday: The Cultural & Literary Background
Momaday, Vizenor, Armstrong: Conversations
  On American Indian Writing
The Names
Narrative Chance: Postmodern Discourse on Native
  American Indian Literatures
Native American in American Literature:
  A Selectively Annotated Bibliography
Native American Identites: From Stereotype
  to Archetype in Art & Literature
Native American Writers in the Southeast:
  An Anthology, 1875-1935
A Native Heritage
Natives and Academics
Neither Red Nor White
New Voices from the Longhouse
New Voices in Native American Literary Criticism
New Writers of the Purple Sage
Night Sky, Morning Star
North American Native Authors Catalog
Now I Know Only So Far: Essays in Ethnopoetics
Old Man Coyote
On Behalf of the Wolf and the First Peoples
Only Approved Indians: Stories
Other Destinies: Understanding the American Indian Novel
Other Words: American Indian Literature, Law, & Culture
Louis Owens: Literary Reflections on His Life & Work
A Papago Traveler
The Peace Chief: A Novel
Place & Vision: The Function of Landscape in
  Native American Fiction
Pocahontas & Co: The Fictorial American Indian
  Woman in 19th Century Literature

MAGIC

MAKAH INDIANS

MANDAN & HIDATSA INDIANS

MASKS

MEDICINE/SHAMANISM

MENOMINEE INDIANS

MISSIONS

Native Americans & Christianity

Old Frontiers: The Story of the Cherokee Indians
On the Padre's Trail
Osage Mission Baptisms, Marriages, & Internments, 1820-1886
The Paths of Kateri's Kin
The Pipe & Christ
Red Man in the U.S.
Salvation & the Savage
Sketches of Mission Life Among the Indians of Oregon
Sunset to Sunset: A Lifetime With My Brothers, the Dakotas
Tomahawk and Cross: Lutheran Missionaries Among Northern Prairie Indians, 1858-1866
John P. Williamson: A Brother to the Sioux

MIXED DESCENT

All My Sins Are Relatives
As We Are Now: Mixblood Essays on Race & Identity
Funny, You Don't Look Like One: Observations from a Blue-Eyed Ojibway
Interior Landscapes: Autobiographical Myths & Metaphors
MixedBlood Messages
Mixed Blood Indians: Racial Construction in the Early South
Mixed Bloods, Apaches & Cattle Barons
Mixed-Bloods & Tribal Dissolution: Charles Curtis & the Quest for Indian Identity
Son of Two Bloods
South Carolina Indians, Indian Traders & Other Ethnic Connections: Beginning in 1670
When Nickels Were Indians: An Urban, Mixed-Blood Story
The Zuni Enigma

MODOC INDIANS

Ancient Modocs of California and Oregon
Captain Jack, Modoc Renegade
The Indian History of the Modoc War
Life Amongst the Modocs: Unwritten History
The Modoc
Modocs and Their War
Myths of the Modocs: Indian Legends from the Northwest
Primitive Pragmatists: The Modoc Indians of Northern California

MOHAWK INDIANS

Johnson of the Mohawks
A Journey Into Mohawk & Oneida Country, 1634-1635
The Mohawk That Refused to Abdicate

MOUNDS, MOUND-BUILDERS

Aboriginal Monuments of the State of New York
Angel Site
Burial Mounds of the Red River Headwaters
Cahokia: City of the Sun
Cahokia: Domination & Ideology in the Mississippian World
The Earthshapers
Expanding the View of Hohokam Mounds
Final Year Excavations at the Evans Mound Site
Grand Mound
Indian Mounds of the Atlantic Coast
Indian Mounds of the Middle Ohio Valley
Indian Mounds You Can Visit: 165 Aboriginal Sites on Florida's West Coast
*Journey to Cahokia
Mounds for the Dead
Remember Native America!
Report of the Mound Explorations of the Bureau of Ethnology
The Sacred Geography of the American Mound-Builders
Status & Health in Prehistory: A Case Study of the Moundville Chiefdom
Town Creek Indian Mound
Treasures of the Mound Builders
Under Your Feet
Wakemap Mound

MUSIC & DANCE

American Indian Ballerinas
American Indian Poetry
American Indian Songs
Angels to Wish By
*American Indian Music & Musical Instruments
The American Indians & Their Music
The Art of the Native American Flute
Blackfoot Musical Thought: Comparative Perspectives
Ceremonies of the Pawnee
Cherokee Dance: Ceremonial Dances & Costumes
Cherokee Dance & Drama
The Cherokee Ghost Dance
Cherokee Psalms: A Collection of Hymns
Cheyenne & Arapaho Music
The Chilkat Dancing Blanket
Chippewa Music
Choctaw Music
Choctaw Music & Dance
Creating & Using the Larger Native American Flutes
Creating & Using the Native American Concert Flute
Creating & Using the Native American Love Flute

Creating & Using the Very Small Native American Flutes
The Crooked Stovepipe: Athapaskan Fiddle Music & Square Dancing
Cry for Luck: Sacred Song & Speech Among the Yurok, Hupa & Karok Indians fo Northwestern California
A Cry From the Earth: Music of the North American Indians
Dances of the Tewa Pueblo Indians: Expressions of Life
Dancing Gods: Indian Ceremonials of New Mexico & Arizona
Dancing With Creation
Frances Densmore and American Indian Music
Fifteen Flower World Variations: A Sequence of Songs from the Yaqui Deer Dance
Guide to Native American Music Recordings
The Hoop of Peace
In Vain I Tried to Tell You: Essays in Native American Ethnopoetics
Indian Dances of North America: Their Importance to Indian Life
*Indian Dancing Coloring Book
Indian Games & Dances with Native Songs
Indians' Book
Indian Story & Song from North America
The Iroquois Eagle Dance
Iroquois Music & Dance: Ceremonial Arts of Two Seneca Longhouses
Kokopelli: The Making of an Icon
Lakota Songs
*Love Flute
The Magic World: American Indian Songs & Poems
Mandan & Hidatsa Music
Menominee Music
The Modern Fancy Dancer
Moki Snake Dance
Mother Earth, Father Sky: Ancient Chants by Pueblo & Navajo Indians of the Southwest
Moving Within the Circle: Contemporary Native American Music & Dance
Music & Dance of the American Indian
Music & Dance Research of the Southwestern Indians
Music of Acoma, Isleta, Cochiti & Zuni Pueblos
Music of the Indians of British Columbia
Music of the Native North American for Flute & Recorder
Music of the North American Indian
The Maru Cult of the Pomo Indians
Myth, Music & Dance of the American Indian
Music & Dance Research of the Southwestern Indians
The Music of the North American Indian
Myth, Music & Dance of the American Indian
Native American Dance: Ceremonies & Social Traditions
Native American Music Directory
Native American Songs & Poems
The Native North American Flutes
Native North American Music & Oral Data: A Catalogue of Sound Recordings, 1893-1976
The Navajo (Or Corral) Fire Dance
Navajo Myths Prayers & Songs with Texts & Translations
Navajo War Dance
Nootka & Quileute Music
North American Indian Dances & Rituals
North American Indian Music: A Guide to Published Sources & Selected Recordings
The Northern Traditional Dancer
Northern Ute Music
Notes on Eight Papago Songs
The Oldest Music
On the Music of the North American Indians
The Osage Ceremonial Dance I'n-Lon-Schka
Papago Music
The Pawnee Ghost Dance Hand Game: Ghost Dance Revival & Ethnic Identity
Pawnee Music
The People: Native American Thoughts & Feelings
The Power of Kiowa Song
Power & Performance in Gros Ventre War Expedition Songs
The Sacred Journey: Prayers & Songs of Native America
Seminole Music
The Shoshoni-Crow Sun Dance
Shoshone Ghost Dance Religion: Poetry Songs & Great Basin Context
Singing for Power: The Song Magic of the Papago Indians of Southern Arizona
The Snake Dance of the Hopi Indians
The Snake Dance of the Moquis of Arizona
Songprints: The Musical Experience of Five Shoshone Women
Songs of Indian Territory
Song of the Sky
Songs of the Teton Sioux
Songs of the Tewa
Songs of the Wigwam
Spirit of the First People
Spirit Mountain: An Anthology of Yuman Story & Song
Spirit of the First People: Native American Music Traditions of Washington State
Stability & Variation in Hopi Song
The Story of Indian Music: Its Growth & Synthesis
A Study of Omaha Indian Music
The Sun Dance & Other Ceremonies of the Oglala Division of the Teton Dakota
The Sun Dance of the Crow Indians
Teton Sioux Music & Culture
The Traditional Northern Dancer
The Tribal Fires Catalog

Tsee-Ma'Heone-Nemeototse: Cheyenne Spiritual Songs
The Tsimishian: Their Arts & Music
Upwhere Belong
Visions of Sounds: Musical Instruments of First Nation Communities in Northeastern America
Voices of Native America: Native American Instruments & Music
Voices of the Wind: Native American Flute Songs
War Dance: Plains Indian Musical Performance
We'll Be In Your Mountains, We'll Be in Your Songs: A Navajo Woman Sings
Winds of the Past: Guide to Playing Native American Flute
Yaqui Deer Songs/Maso Bwakam
Yuman & Yaqui Music

NAVAJO (DINE) INDIANS

American Indian Tribal Government & Politics
The Army and the Navajo
Apaches de Navajo
*Between Sacred Mountains: Navajo Stories & Lessons from the Land
Beyond the Four Corners of the World
Bighorse the Warrior
Blessingway
Blood & Voice: Navajo Women Ceremonial Practitioners
The Book of the Navajo
Border Towns of the Navajo Nation
Bosque Redondo: A Study of Cultural Stress at the Navajo Reservation
A Cannoneer in Navajo Country
Canyon De Chelly: The Story Behind the Scenery
Circles, Consciousness & Culture
Colloquial Navajo: A Dictionary
*Colors of the Navajo
CommonThreads: Pueblo & Navajo Textiles in the Southwest Museum
Contemporary Navajo Affairs
Coyoteway: A Navajo Holyway Healing Ceremonial
Crow Man's People: Three Seasons with the Navajo
Denetsosie
Defending the Dinetah
The Development of Capitalism in the Navajo Nation: A Political-Economic History
Dine Bahane', The Navajo Creation Story
Dine Bibliography to the 1990s
Dine: A History of the Navajos
Dinetah: An Early History of the Navajo
Dinetah: Navajo History
Drinking Careers: A 25-Year Study of Three Navajo Populations
Earth Is My Mother, Sky Is My Father
The Economics of Sainthood: Religious Change Among the Rimrock Navajos
The Enduring Navaho
Enduring Traditions: Art of the Navajo
The Fifth World of Forster Bennett: Portrait of a Navajo
From the Glittering World: A Navajo Story
Genuine Navajo Rugs: How to Tell
The Gift of the Gila Monster: Navajo Ceremonial Tales
The Gift of Spiderwoman: Southwestern Textiles, The Navajo Traditions
Guide to Navajo Rugs
A Guide to Navajo Weavings
Hand Trembling, Frenzy Witchcraft, & Moth Madness
Head and Face Masks in Navaho Ceremonialism
Healing Ways: Navajo Health Care in the Twentieth Century
Historic Navajo Weaving: 1800-1900: Three Cultures-One Loom
History of the Navajos: The Reservation Years
Hogans: Navajo Houses and House Songs
Holy Wind in Navajo Philosophy
Hosteen Klah: Navaho Medicine Man and Sand Painter
*How the Stars Fell Into the Sky: A Navajo Legend
If You Take My Sheep...The Evolution and Conflicts of Navajo Pastoralism, 1630-1868
I'll Go and Do More: Annie Dodge Wauneka, a Navajo Leader & Activist
In the Beginning: The Navajo Genesis
Indian Sandpainting of the Southwest
Jewels of the Navajo Loom: The Rugs of Teec Nos Pos
*Philip Johnston and the Navajo Code Talkers
The Journey of Navajo Oshley: An Autobiography and Life History
Kinaalada: A Navajo Puberty Ceremony
Kinaalda: A Study of the Navaho Girl's Puberty Ceremony
Language & Art in the Navajo Universe
Language Shift Among the Navajos
The Last Warrior: Peter MacDonald & the Navajo Nation
Left Handed, Son of Old Man Hat: A Navajo Autobiography
Letters from Wupatki
The Long Walk: A History of the Navajo Wars
The Main Stalk: A Synthesis of Navajo Philosophy
Marietta Wetherill: Life With the Navajos in Chaco Canyon
Masked Gods: Navaho and Pueblo Ceremonialism
Meditations with the Navajo: Prayer Songs & Stories of Healing & Harmony
Molded in the Image of Changing Woman: Navajo Views
Monument Valley: The Story Behind the Scenerey
Mother Earth, Father Sky: Ancient Chants by Pueblo and Navajo Indians of the Southwest
The Mountainway of the Navajo
*My Navajo Sister

The Myth & Prayers of the Great Star Chant & the
  Myth of the Oyote Chant
Mythology and Values: An Analysis of
  Navaho Chantway Myths
Nanise': A Navajo Herbal
*The Navajo
The Navaho
*Navajo ABC: A Dine Alphabet Book
Navajo Aging
Navajo Architecture
Navajo Arts & Crafts
Navaho Art and Culture
The Navajo Art of Sandpainting
The Navajo Atlas: Environments, Resources,
  Peoples & History of the Dine Bikeyah
Navajo: Basic Medical
Navajo Blessingway Singer
A Navajo Bringing-Home Ceremony
Navajo: A Century of Progress
Navajo Changes: A History of the Navajo People
Navaho Chantway Myths
*Navajo Children
Navajo Classification of Their Song Ceremonials
A Navajo Confrontation and Crisis
Navajo Code Talkers
Navajo Country Dine Bikeyah: A Geographic Dictionary
Navajo Coyote Tales
A Navajo Crisis and Confrontation
*Navajo Cultural Guides
*The Navajo Design Book
Navajo Dictionary on Diagnostic Terminology
Navajo Education in Action: The Rough Rock
  Demonstration School
Navajo Education, 1948-1978: Its Progress & Problems
Navajo Energy Resources
Navajo-English Children's Picture Dictionary
Navajo-English Dictionary
The Navaho (Or Corral) Fire Dance
Navajo Folk Art: The People Speak
Navaho Folk Tales
Navajo Foreign Affairs: 1795-1846
Navajo History
The Navajo-Hopi Land Dispute: An American Tragedy
The Navajo Hunter Tradition
*The Navajo Indian Book
*Navajo Indian Coloring Book
Navaho Indian Myths
The Navajo Indians
*Navajo Indians
Navajo Infancy: An Ethological Study of Child Development
Navajo Jewelry: A Legacy of Silver & Stone
Navajo Kinship and Marriage
Navajo Land, Navajo Culture: The Utah
  Experience in the 20th Century
Navajo Land Use: Navajo Leadership & Government
Navajo Leadership & Government
Navaho Legends
Navajo Lifeways: Contemporary Issues, Ancient Knowledge
Navajo Livestock Reduction: A National Disgrace
Navajo Medicine Bundles or Jish
Navajo Medicine Man Sand Paintings
Navajo Mountain and Rainbow Bridge Religion
Navajo Multi-Household Social Units
The Navajo Nation
Navajo Native Dyes
Navajo Oral History Traditions
Navajo Oral Traditions
Navajo & Photography
Navajo Places: History, Legend, Landscape
Navajo Pottery: Traditions & Innovations
Navajo & Pueblo Silversmiths
Navaho Religion: A Study of Symbolism
Navajo Resources and Economic Development
Navajo Rug Stik-Withit Notecubes
Navajo Rugs: How to Find, Evaluate, Buy & Care for Them
Navajo Rugs, Past and Present
Navajo Sacred Places
Navajo Saddle Blankets
Navajo Sandpainting Art: Where the Gods Gather
Navajo Sandpainting From Religious Act to Commercial Art
Navajo Sandpainting: The Huckel Collection
Navajo Shepherd and Weaver
Navajo Spoons: Indian Artistry and the
  Souvenir Trade, 1880-1940
Navajo Stories of the Long Walk Period
Navaho Symbols of Healing
Navajo Textiles
Navajo & Tibetan Sacred Wisdom: The Circle of the Spirit
Navajo Trader: Essays on a Region & Its Literature
Navaho Trading Days
Navajo Trading: The End of an Era
Navajo: Tradition & Change in the Southwest
The Navajo Treaty, 1868
Navajo Tribal Code
The Navajo Verb: A Grammar for Students & Scholars
The Navajo Verb System: An Overview
Navajo War Dance
Navajo Weavers & Silversmiths
A Navaho Weaving, Its Technic and History
Navajo Weaving, Navajo Ways
Navajo Weaving: Three Centuries of Change
Navajo Weaving Today
The Navajo Weaving Tradition

Navajoland: Family Settlement and Land Use
Navajoland Plant Catalog
Navajoland: A Portfolio of Navajo Life
  During the 1940's & 1950's
*The Navajos
The Navajos
The Navajos: A Critical Bibliography
The Navajos in 1705: Roque Madrid's Campaign Journal
The Navajos' Long Walk for Education
The Navajos & the New Deal
*The Navajos: People of the Southwest
The Night Chant: A Navaho Ceremonial
The Nightway: A History and a History of Documentation
  of a Navajo Ceremonial
Northern Navajo Frontier, 1860-1900:
  Expansion Through Adversity
Of Mother Earth and Father Sky
Old Navajo Rugs: Their Development from 1900 to 1940
One Hundred Years of Navajo Rugs
Our Friends: The Navajos
Outcroppings From Navajoland
*Owl in the Cedar Tree
Patterns & Sources of Navajo Weaving
The People Speak: Navajo Folk Art
Photographing Navajos: John Collier, Jr.
  on the Reservation, 1948-1953
Pictorial Weavings of the Navajos
*Pieces of White Shell: A Journey to Navajoland
A Political History of the Navajo Tribe
The Pollen Path: A Collection of Navajo Myths
Prehistory in the Navajo Reservoir District
Property Concepts of the Navaho Indians
Pueblo & Navajo Indian Life Today
Reconstructing 18th Century Navajo Population
  Dynamics in the Dinetah
Red Capitalism: An Analysis of the Navajo Economy
Reflections of Social Life in the Navaho Origin Myth
Right After Sundown: Teaching Stories of the Navajo
Rugs & Posts: The Story of Navajo Weaving
Sacred Words: A Study of Navajo Religion & Prayer
The Scalpel & the Silver Bear:
  The First Navajo Women Surgeon
Shonto: Study of the Role of the Trader
  in a Modern Navajo Community
Son of Old Man Hat
*Songs from the Loom: A Navajo Girl Learns to Weave
Soul Concepts of the Navaho Indians
Storm Patterns: Poems From Two Navajo Women
*Sunpainters: Eclipse of the Navajo Sun
Tales of an Endishodi: Father Berard Haile & the Navajos
Tall Woman: The Life Story of Rose Mitchell,
  A Navajo Woman @ 1874-1977
Talking Mysteries: A Conversation With Tony Hillerman
Tapestries in Sand
Their Secrets: Why Navajo Indians Never Get Cancer
Through Navajo Eyes
Through White Men's Eyes: A Contribution to Navajo History
Time Among the Navajo
To Be a Warrior
To Die in Dinetah: The Dark Legacy of Kit Carson
To Run After Them: Cultural & Social Bases of
  Cooperation in a Navajo Community
Treasures of the Navajo
Ts'iliiyazhi Spuds Baa Hane
Turquoise and the Navajo
*Twilight Boy
Under Sacred Ground: A History of Navajo Oil
A Voice in Her Tribe: A Navajo Woman's Own Story
Voices in the Canyon
Walk in Beauty: The Navajo & Their Blankets
*Walks in Beauty
Warriors - Navajo Code Talkers
The Way to Knowledge
We'll Be In Your Mountains, We'll Be in Your Songs:
  A Navajo Woman Sings
Weaving a Navajo Blanket
Weaving a World: Textiles and the Navajo Way of Seeing
When Navajos Had Too Many Sheep: The 1940's
Where the Two Came to Their Father: A Navaho
  War Ceremonial Given by Jeff King
Wide Ruins: Memories from a Navajo Trading Post
The Wind Won't Know Me: History of the
  Navajo-Hopi Land Dispute
The Witch Purge of 1878: Oral and Documentary
  History in the Early Navajo Reservation Years
Woven by the Grandmothers
Wupatki & Walnut Canyon

NEZ PERCE INDIANS

All My Sins are Relatives
Chief Joseph Country; Land of the Nez Perce
*Chief Joseph and the Nez Perces
*Chief Joseph's Own Story as Told by Chief Joseph in 1879
Children of Grace: The Nez Perce War of 1877
Conflict and Schism in Nez Perce Acculturation
Flight of the Nez Perce
Forlorn Hope
Hear Me My Chiefs: Nez Perce Legend and History
Howard's Campaign Against the Nez Perce Indians, 1878
I Will Fight No More Forever: Chief Joseph
  and the Nez Perce War
Joseph, Chief of the Nez Perce

Let Me Be Free: The Nez Perce Tragedy
A Little Bit of Wisdom" Conversations
  With a Nez Perce Elder
*The Nez Perce
Nez Perce Country
Nez Perce Coyote Tales
The Nez Perce Indians and the Opening of the Northwest
Nez Perce Joseph
Nez Perce Narratives
*The Nez Perce: Northwest
Nez Perce Texts
Nez Perces Since Lewis & Clark
Nez Perces: Tribesmen of the Columbia Plateau
Saga of Chief Joseph
Sapat'qayn: Twentieth Century Nez Perce Artists
The Story of Lynx
Voice of the Old Wolf: Lucullus Virgil McWhorter
  & the Nez Perce Indians
With the Nez Perces: Alice Fletcher in the Field, 1889-1992
Yellow Wolf: His Own Story

OMAHA INDIANS

Betraying the Omaha Nation, 1870-1916
Blessing for a Long Time: The Sacred Pole
  of the Omaha Tribe
Imperfect Victories: The Legal Tenacity
  of the Omaha Tribe, 1945-1995
Ke-Ma-Ha: The Omaha Stories of Francis La Flesche
The Omaha Tribe
The Upstream People: An Annotated Research
  Bibliography of the Omaha Tribe

OJIBWE (CHIPPEWA) INDIANS

Acculturation and Personality Among the
  Wisconsin Chippewa
American Indian Marriage Record Directory
  for Ashland Co., Wisc.
Anishinabe: Six Studies of Modern Chippewa
Building a Chippewa Indian Birchbark Canoe
*The Chipewyan
*The Chippewa
Chippewa Child Life & Its Cultural Background
Chippewa Customs
Chippewa & Dakota Indians: A Subject Catalog of
  Books, Pamphlets, Periodical Articles and Manuscripts
Chippewa Music
The Chippewa & Their Neighbors
The Chippewas of Lake Superior
Clothed-in-Fur and Other Tales: An Introduction
  to an Ojibwa World View
Dictionary of the Ojibway Language
A Face in the Rock: The Tale of a Grand Island Chippewa
*Faces in the Firelight
Generation to Generation
Giving: Ojibway Stories & Legends
  from the Children of Curve Lake
The Grand Portage Story
History of the Ojibwa Indians
History of the Ojibway People
How Indians Use Wild Plants for Food, Medicine & Crafts
How Indians Use Wild Plants for Food, Medicine & Crafts
Indians in Minnesota, 4th Edition
Kitchi-Gami: Life Among the Lake Superior Ojibway
The Land of the Ojibwe
The Mishomis Book: The Voice of the Ojibway
*Muckwa: The Adventures of a Chippewa Indian Boy
Night Flying Woman: An Ojibway Narrative
Ojibwa Crafts
Ojibwa Chiefs, 1690-1890: An Annotated Listing
The Ojibwa of Western Canada: 1780-1870
The Ojibwa Woman
The Ojibwas: A Critical Bibliography
Ojibway Ceremonies
The Ojibway Dream
Ojibway Heritage
Ojibway Indians Coloring Book
Ojbway Music from Minnesota
Ojibway Oratory
The Ojibway of Walpole, Ontario, Canada
Ojibway Tales
*The Ojibwe
Ottawa & Chippewa Indians of Michigan, 1870-1909
The People Named the Chippewa
Portage Lake: Memories of an Ojibwe Childhood
Powwow Summer
Red Lake Nation: Portraits of Ojibway Life
The Sacred Harvest: Ojibway Wild Rice Gathering
Sacred Scrolls of the Southern Ojibway
The Shaman: Patterns of Religious Healing Among the
  Ojibway Indians
A Social Study of One Hundred Fifty Chippewa Indian
  Families of the White Earth Reservation of Minnesota
*The Stone Canoe & Other Stories
To Be the Main Leaders of Our People
Traditional Ojibwa Religion and Its Historical Changes
The Transformation of Bigfoot: Malesness,
  Power & Belief Among the Chipewyan
*Voices from the Ice
Walk in Peace: Legends & Stories of the Michigan Indians
Where Two Worlds Meet

The White Canoe and Other Legends of the
 Ojibways Narrative Histories
Wild Rice & the Ojibway People
Woman of the Green Glade

ONEIDA

A Journey Into Mohawk & Oneida Country, 1634-1635
*The Oneida
The Oneida Creation Story
The Oneida Indian Experience
The Oneida Land Claims
Oneida Verb Morphology
Ukwehu-Wehnaha Tekawxnate?neyse:
 An Oneida Dictionary

ORIGIN

Amerinds and Their Paleoenvironments in
 Northeastern North America
The Antiquity and Origin of Native American
Bones, Boats, and Bison
Discoveries of the Truth
Early Man in the New World
The First Americans
Mitakuye Oyasin: We are All Related
Only the Wind
Quest for the Origins of the First Americans

OSAGE INDIANS

Annals of Osage Mission
Art of the Osage
Beacon on the Plain
Bibliography of the Osage
Family Matters, Tribal Affairs
The First Protestant Osage Missions, 1820-1837
History of Neosho County, Kansas
A History of the Osage People
The Imperial Osages
*The Osage
The Osage Ceremonial Dance I'n-Lon-Schka
Osage: An Ethnohistorical Study of Hegemony
 on the Prairie-Plains
Osage in Missouri
Osage Indian Customs & Myths
The Osage Indian Murders: A True Crime Story
Osage Indians: Bands & Clans
The Osage & the Invisible World
Osage Life & Legends: Earth People - Sky People
Osage Mission Baptisms, Marriages and Interments,
 1820-1886
Osages: Children of the Middle Waters
The Osages, Dominant Power of the Louisiana Territory
A Pipe for February: A Novel
Symbolic and Decorative Art of the Osage People
Talking to the Moon
Traditions of the Osage
Winning the Dust Bowl

PAIUTE INDIANS

Boundaries Between: The Southern Paiutes, 1775-1995
Corbett Mack: The Life of a Northern Paiute
From the Sands to the Mountain
Karnee: A Paiute Narrative
*Let Me Tell You a Story & Workbook
Life Among the Paiutes
Viola Martinez, California Paiute: Living in Two Worlds
The Northern Paiute Indians of California
A Numu History - The Yerington Paiute Tribe
*The Numu Way & Workbook
The Paiute, Indians of North America
The Southern Paiutes
Survival Arts of the Primitive Paiute
Sarah Winnemucca of the Northern Paiutes
Wovoka & the Ghost Dance: A Source Book
Wovoka Poster
Yerington Paiute Dictionary
Yerington Paiute Language Grammar
*Yerington Paiute Tribe Coloring Book

PAWNEE INDIANS

Ceremonies of the Pawnee
Description of a Journey and Visit to the Pawnee Indians
The Dubar-Allis Letters on the Pawnee
The Hako: Song, Pipe and Unity in a Pawnee
 Calumet Ceremony
The Lost Universe: Pawnee Life and Culture
Frank J. North: Pawnee Scout, Commander and Pioneer
*The Pawnee
Pawnee Ghost Dance Hand Game
Pawnee Hero Stories & Folktales
The Pawnee Indians
Pawnee and Kansa (Kaw) Indians
Pawnee and Lower Loup Pottery
Pawnee Music
The Pawnee Mythology
Pawnee Passage, 1870-1875
Pawnees: A Critical Bibliography

Some Things Are Not Forgotten
Travels in North America, Including a Summer
 with the Pawnees
Two Great Scouts and Their Pawnee Battalion
When Stars Came Down to Earth: Cosmology
 of the Skidi Pawnee Indians of North America

PERIODICALS

American Indian
American Indian & Alaska Native Newspapers &
 Periodicals, 1826-1924 & 1971-1985
Let My People Know: American Indian Journalism,
 1828-1978
Schoolcraft: Literary Voyager

PEYOTE, PEYOTISM

Doors of Perception
People of the Peyote
The Peyote Book: A Study of Native Medicine
The Peyote Cult
Peyote: The Divine Cactus
Peyote Hunt: The Sacred Journey of Huichol Indians
The Peyote Religion
Peyote Religion Among the Navaho
Peyotism in the West: A Historical and Cultural Perspective
Pipe, Bible & Peyote Among the Oglala Lakota:
 A Study in Religious Identity
Washo Shamans & Peyotists: Religious Conflict
 in an American Indian Tribe

PHILOSOPHY

An American Urphilosophie: An American Philosophy-
 BP (Before Pragmatism)
An Analysis of Navajo Temporality
The Bear Tribe's Sel-Reliance Book
Classification and Development of North American Indian
 Cultures: A Statistical Analysis of the Driver-
 Massey Sample
Crazy Horse's Philosophy of Riding Rainbows
Daily Affirmations from the Divine Creator
Feasting with Cannibals: An Essay on Kwakiutl Cosmology
Headed Upstream: Interviews with Iconoclasts
Holy Wind in Navajo Philosophy
The Indian Testimony
Joy Before Night: Evelyn Eaton's Last Years
The Main Stalk: A Synthesis of Navajo Philosophy
Messages from the Divine Creator
Messages from Mother Earth: Daily Affirmations
Native American Predictions
Native American Prophecies
Native American Wisdom
Native Americans: A Portrait
Native Light for a Dark World
Neither Wolf Nor Dog: On Forgotten Roads With Indian Elder
Our Chiefs & Elders: Words & Photographs
 of Native Leaders
The Path of Power
The Primal Mind: Vision & Reality in Indian America
Profiles in Wisdom: Native Elders Speak Out About the Earth
The Roaring of the Sacred River
Shadowcatchers
The Soul of an Indian; and Other Writings from Ohiyesa
The Soul of the Indian: An Interpretation
Spirit Healing: Native American Magic & Medicine
Spiritual Wisdom of the Native Americans
Teachings from the American Earth:
 Indian Religion & Philosophy
To Image & To See: Crow Indian Photographs
To Touch the Wind: An Introduction to
 Native American Philosophy & Beliefs
Vision Quest
Walk in Balance
The Wisdom of the Great Chiefs

PICTURE-WRITING

Coffee in the Gourd
The Lenape and Their Legends
Picture-Writing of the American Indians

PICTURES, PHOTOGRAPHS
& PORTRAITS

Ada, Oklahoma, Queen City of the Chickasaw Nation
America on Paper: The First Hundred Years
*Among the Plains Indians
Becoming Brave: The Path to Native American Manhood
O.E. Berninghaus - Taos, New Mexico: Master Painter
 of American Indians and Frontier West
Catlin's North American Indian Portfolio
Children of the First People: A Photographic Essay
Michael Coleman
Comanches in the New West, 1895-1908:
 Historic Photographs
Crazy Horse & Korczak
Crow Indian Photographer
Edward S. Curtis & the North American Indian
 Project in the Field

Crying for a Dream:The Earth Is Our Mother
Crying for a Vision: A Rosebud Sioux Trilogy 1886-1976
Dwellers at the Source: Southwestern Indian Photographs
 of A.C. Vroman, 1895-1904
Seth Eastman: Pictorial Historian of the Indian
Enduring Culture: A Century of Photography
 of the Southwest Indians
German Artist on the Texas Frontier: Friedrich Richard Petri
Grand Endeavors of American Indian Photography
Honor Dance: Native American Photographs
Hopi Photographers—Hopi Images
The Horsemen of the Americas
In a Sacred Manner We Live
The Indian Legacy of Charles Bird King
Indian Lives: A Photographic Records from
 the Civil War to to Wounded Knee
Indian Portraits of the Pacific Northwest
Indians of the American Southwest
The Interior Salish Tribes of British Columbia
Keepers of the Dream
Land of the Spotted Eagle: Portrait of the Reservation Sioux
Korczak, Storyteller in Stone
Native American Portraits: 1865-1918
The Natural Man Observed: A Study of
 Catlin's Indian Gallery
New Indian Sketches
North American Indian Portfolios
North American Indians Coloring Album
The North American Indians:
 Photographs by Edward S. Curtis
People of Legend
Peoples of the Twilight
The Photograph & the American Indian
Pictographic History of the Oglala Sioux
Picture-Writing of the American Indians
The Plains Indian Photographs of Edward S. Curtis
Plains Indian Raiders: The Final Phases of Warfare
 from the Arkansas to the Red River
Portrait Index of North American Indians in
 Published Collections
Powerful Images: Portrayals of Native America
Quanah: A Pictorial History of the Last Comanche Chief
Frederick Remington: Artist of the American West
The Reservation Blackfeet, 1885-1945:
 A Photographic History of Cultural Survival
The Saga of Sitting Bull's Bones
Search for the Native American Purebloods
The Seventh Generation: Images of the Lakota Today
*Sharing Our Worlds
Southwest Indians: A Photographic Portrait
The Story of the Meadowlark
Traditions and Change on the Northwest Coast
The Vanishing Race & Other Illusions: Photographs
 of Indians by Edward S. Curtis
Visions of Our Native American Heritage

PLACE NAMES

By Canoe & Moccasin: Some Native
 Place Names of the Great Lakes
Geographical Names of the Kwakiutl Indians
Indian Place-Names in Alabama
Indian Place-Names in Illinois
Indian Place-Names in Mexico & Central America
Indian Place-Names in Michigan
Indian Place-Names of New England
Indian Place-Names of the Penobscot Valley
 & the Maine Coast
Indian Place Names: Their Origins, Evolution & Meanings
Names of the American Indian
Navajo Places
O Brave New Words
Oklahoma Place Names
Spanish & Indian Place-Names of California
Study in the Etymology of the Indian Place Name
Utah Place Names
Washington State Place Names

POETRY

After & Before the Lightning
American Indian Poetry
American Indian Prayers & Poetry
Ants & Orioles: The Art of Pima Poetry
Bone Dance
*The Book of Medicines
Buckskin Hollow Reflections
The Business of Fancydancing
Cedar Smoke on Abalone Mountain
The Circle of Thanks: Native American Poems
 & Songs of Thanksgiving
Drawings of the Song Animals: New & Selected Poems
Drifting Through Ancestor Dreams
An Eagle Nation
Finding the Center: The Art of the Zuni Storyteller
Four Ancestors: Stories, Songs, & Poems from
 Native North America
Four Winds: Poems from Indian Rituals
From Sand Creek
Home Places: Contemporary Native American
 Writing from Sun Tracks
I, the Song: Classical Poetry of Native North America

In Company: An Anthology of New Mexico Poets After 1960
In Mad Love and War
In the Trail of the Wind: American Indian
   Poems & Ritual Orations
Interpreting the Indian
The Invisible Musician
Itch Like Crazy
Lost Copper
Luminaries of the Humble
*Many Winters
Maria: The Potter of San Ildefonso
Migration Tears
Mud Woman
Sarojini Naidu: An Introduction to Her Life, Work & Poetry
Native American Songs & Poems
The Nature of Native American Poetry
New and Old Voices of Wah'kon-Tah
Now I Know Only So Far: Essays in Ethnopoetics
Ocean Power: Poems from the Desert
Offering: Poetry & Prose
Old Shirts & New Skins
On the Landing
On Native Ground: Memories & Impressions
Out There Somewhere
The Portable North American Indian Reader
Alex Posey
Rainbows of Stone
Reading the Voice: Native American
   Oral Poetry on the Written Page
*Red Clay: Poems and Stories
Saanii Dahataal / The Women Are Singing
*Savings
The Shadow's Horse
Shapeshift
She Had Some Horses
The Sky Clears: Poetry of the American Indians
Song of the Sky
Songs
Songs from an Outcast
Songs of the Tewa
Speak to Me Words
Star Quilt
Storm Patterns: Poems From Two Navajo Women
Summer In the Spring: Anishinaabe Lyric Poems & Stories
Summer of the Black Widows
Survival This Way: Interviews with American Indian Poets
Teepees Are Folded: American Indian Poetry
That's What She Said: Contemporary Poetry
   & Fiction by Native American Women
The Twilight of the Sioux
The Vision: Poetry of Native Americans
When No One Is Looking
Woven Stone
Writing the Circle
Yaqui Deer Songs/Maso Bwakam: A Native American Poetry
Yuman Poetry with Morphological Analysis

POLITICS & GOVERNMENT

After the Trail of Tears
Alaska Native Policy in the 20th Century
Alcatraz! Alcatraz: The Indian Occupation of 1969-71
Alcatraz: Indian Land Forever
American Indian Policy: Self-Governance
   & Economic Development
American Indian Tribal Government & Politics
An Assumption of Sovereignty: Social & Political
   Transformation Among the Florida Seminoles
The Caddo Chiefdoms: Caddo Economics & Politics,
   1700-1835
The Cahokia Chiefdom: The Archaeology
   of a Mississippian Society
The Chaco Anasazi
The Chaco Meridian
Chiefdoms & Chieftaincy in the Americas
The Choctaw Laws
Conservatism Among the Iroquois at the Six Nations Reserve
Conspiracy of Interests: Iroquois Dospossession
The Constitution & Laws of the Choctaw Nation
Constitution, Laws & Treaties of the Chickasaws
The Constitution of the Five Nations
Constitutionalism & Native Americans, 1903-1968
Constitutions & Laws of the American Indian Tribes
Contemporary Native American Political Issues
Controlling Consulting: A Manual for Native American
   Governments & Organization
Dancing on Common Ground: Tribal Cultures &
   Alliances on the Southern Plains
Debating Democracy: Native American Legacy of Freedom
Ecocide of Native America
The Ecological Indian: Myth & History
Ecology, Sociopolitical Organization & Cultural
   Change on the Southern Plains
Exemplar of Liberty: Native America & the Evolution
   of Democracy
Exiled in the Land of the Free
The Fox Wars: The Mesquakie Challenge to New France
Governments of the Western Hemisphere
The Great Law & the Longhouse
In Defense of Mohawk Ethnopolitical Conflict
   in Native North America
In the Spirit of Crazy Horse
Indian Gaming: Who Wins?

Indian Reorganziation Act: Congress & Bills
Indian Self-Determination & Education Assistance Act
Indian Self Rule
Indian Tribes As Sovereign Governments
Indian Tribes of North America With Biographical Sketches
Indians, Indian Tribes & State Government:
   Major Legal Issues
Into the Americn Woods: Negotiators
   on the Pennsylvania Frontier
Last Cry: Native American Prophecies;
   Tale of the End Times
The Last Warrior:Peter MacDonald & the Navajo Nation
The Laws of the Chickasaw Nation
The Laws of the Choctaw Nation
*Long Shadows
Mankiller: A Chief & Her People
*Wilma Mankiller
The Minutes of the Michigan Commission
   on Indian Affairs, 1956-1977
Modern American Indian tribal Govenment & Politics:
   An Interdisciplinary Study
The National Congress of American Indians:
   The Founding Years
The Nations Within: The Past & Future
   of American Indian Sovereignty
Native America & the Evolution of Democracy
Native American Political Systems & the Evolution
   of Democracy: An Annotated Bibliography
The Native American Rights Movement
The Native Brotherhoods
Navajo Foreign Affairs, 1795-1846
The New Resource Wars
The Occupation of Alcatraz Island
Oglala People, 1841-1879: A Political History
Oklahoma Tribal Court Reports, Vol. 3
*One Indian & Two Chiefs: Short Fiction
Organizing the Lakota
The Political Economy of North American Indians
Political Structure & Change in the
   Prehistoric Southeastern U.S.
The Politics of Indian Removal:
   Red Jacket: Iroquois Diplomat & Orator
The Queen's People
Removals: 19th Century American Literature
   & the Politics of Indian Affairs
The Roads of My Relations
The Savanah River Chiefdoms: Political
   Change in the Late Prehistoric Southeast
The Second Civil War: Examining the Indian
   Demand for Ethnic Sovereignty
Self Relaince vs. Power Politics
Settlement Pattern Studies in the Americas
Sitting Bull & the Paradox of Lakota Nationhood
State & Reservation: New Perspectives on
   Federal Indian Policy
Surviving As Indians: The Challenge of Self-Government
To Be the Main Leaders of Our People
To Show Heart: Native American Self-Determination
   & Federal Indian Policy, 1960-1975
Tribal Goivernment Today: Politics on
   Montana Indian Reservations
The United Keetoowah Band of
   Cherokee Indians in Oklahoma
The Voice of the Crane Echoes Afar
Wounded Knee II
You Are On Indian Land: Alcatraz Island, 1969-1971
Your Fyre Shall Burn No More

PONCA INDIANS

The Ponca Chiefs
Ponca Indians
Ponca Reservation, 1877
The Ponca Tribe
Standing Bear & the Ponca Chiefs

POTAWATOMI INDIANS

Ethnobotany of the Forst Potawatomi Indians
Indians and a Changing Frontier:
   The Art of George Winter
Kinsmen Through Time: An Annotated Bibliography
   of Potawatomi History
Mascoutens of Prairie Potawatomi Indians
*Potawatomi
Potawatomi Trail of Death - Indiana to Kansas
The Potawatomis: Keepers of the Fire
The Prairie people

POTLATCH

Bags of Friendship
Chiefly Feasts: The Enduring Kwakiutl Potlatch
Feasting With Mine Enemy: Rank & Exchange
   Among Northwest Coast Societies
Potlatch at Gitsegukla
Potlatch: Native Ceremony & Myth
   on the Northwest Coast
Potlatch Paper: A Colonial Caser History
Rifles, Blankets & Beads
Tlingit Tales: Potlatch & Totem Poles

POTTERY

Acoma & Laguna Pottery
American Indian Pottery
American Indian Pottery: An Identification & Value Guide
Anasazi Pottery
Ancient Indian Pottery of the Mississippi River Valley
Art of Clay: Timeless Pottery of the Southwest
Collecting Shawnee Pottery: A Pictorial
   Reference and Price Guide
Collections of Southwestern Pottery
Decorative Art of the Southwestern Indians
Designs & Factions: Politics, Religion,
   & Ceramics on the Hopi Third Mesa
Designs on Prehistoric Hopi Pottery
Dialogues With Zuni Potters
Early Pottery in the Southeast
*Earth Daughter: Alicia of Acoma Pueblo
Fourteen Families in Pueblo Pottery
From This Earth: The Ancient Art of Pueblo Pottery
A Guide to Pueblo Pottery
Historic Pottery of the Pueblo Indians, 1600-1800
Hopi & Hopi-Tewa Pottery
Hopi Pottery Symbols
Hopi-Tewa Pottery: 500 Artist Biographies
Indian Pottery
Indian Pottery of the Southwest: A Selected Bibliography
Introduction to Hopi Pottery
The Legacy of Maria Poveka Martinez
The Living Tradition of Maria Martinez
Making Native American Pottery
Maria
Maria Making Pottery
Maria Martinez: Pueblo Potter
Maria: The Potter of San Ildefonso
The Mimbres: Art & Archaeology
Mud Woman
Nampeyo and Her Pottery
Navajo Pottery: Traditions & Innovations
The Pottery From Arroyo Hondo Pueblo
Pottery of the Great Basin and Adjacent Areas
The Pottery of Santa Ana Pueblo
The Pottery of Zia Pueblo
Pottery & People: A Dynamic Interaction
Pottery Techniques of Native North America
Prehistoric Hopi Pottery Designs
PrehistoricPainted Pottery of Southeastern Arizona
Pueblo Indian Pottery
Pueblo Indian Pottery: 750 Artist Biographies
The Pueblo Potter: A Study of Creative Imagination
   in Primitive Art
Pueblo Pottery Designs
Pueblo Pottery of the New Mexico Indians
The Quapaw and Their Pottery
Santa Clara Pottery Today
Seven Families in Pueblo Pottery
Southern Pueblo Pottery: 2,000 Artist Biographies
Southwestern Pottery: An Annotated Bibliography
   & List of Types & Wares
Southwestern Pottery: Anasazi to Zuni
Storytellers & Other Figurative Pottery
Margaret Tafoya: A Tewa Potter's Heritage & Legacy
Talking With the Clay: The Art of Pueblo Pottery
*Tending the Fire: The Story of Maria Martinez
Tlapacoya Pottery in the Museum Collection
*When Clay Sings
White Mountain Redware
Zuni Pottery

POWHATAN INDIANS

Chapters of the Ethnology of the Powhatan
   Tribes of Virginia
Dictionary of Powhatan
Pocahontas's People: The Powhatan Indians
   of Virginia Through the Centuries
Pocahontas: Powhatan Peacemaker
Powhatan Foreign Relations 1500-1722
Powhatan Lords of Life & Death
Powhatan Indians of Virginia
Powhatan Tribes: Middle Atlantic
Powhatan's Mantle
Powhatan's World & Colonial Virginia

POWWOWS

California Powwows
Celebrating the Powwow
Drumbeat...Heartbeat: A Celebration of the Powwow
*Eagle Drum
*On the Powwow Trail Coloring Book
People of the Circle: Powwow Country
Pow Wow
*Pow-Wow
Pow Wow Calendar
Pow Wow Chow
The Pow Wow Highway
Pow Wow: On the Red Road
Pow Wow: & Other Yakima Indian Traditions
The Pow Wow Trail
*Powwow
*Powwow Activity Book

Powwow Country
Powwow Country: People of the Circle
Powwow Dancer's & Craftworker's Handbook
*Powwow: Images Along the Red Road
*Powwow Summer
*A Trip to a Pow Wow

PSYCHOLOGY

American Indian & White Children
Bibliography of North American Indian Mental Health
Disciplined Hearts: History, Identity & Depression
  In an American Indian Community
Indian Nation
Modern Indian Psychology
Molded In the Image of Changing Woman
North American Indians & Alaska Natives
Psychocultural Change and the American Indians:
  An Ethnohistorical Analysis
Psychology of Indians of North America
Psychosocial Research on American Indian
  and Alaska Native Youth
Revenge of the Windigo: The Construction of the Mind
  & Mental Health of North American Aboriginal Peoples
Suicide in American Indians

PUEBLO INDIANS

Acoma
*American Pueblo Indian Activity Books
Architecture of Acoma Pueblo
The Architecture of Social Integration in Prehistoric Pueblos
Born a Chief
Cochiti: A New Mexico Pueblo
CommonThreads: Pueblo & Navajo Textiles
  in the Southwest Museum
Conquest & Catastrophe: Changing Rio Grande Pueblo
  Settlement Patterns in the 16th & 17th Centuries
Coyote Tales from the Indian Pueblos
Cushing at Zuni
Dances of the Tewa Pueblo Indians
Dancing in the Paths of the Ancestors
*A Day With a Pueblo
Deliberate Acts: Changing Hopi Culture
  Through the Oraibi Split
*Earth Daughter: Alicia of Acoma Pueblo
Earth Fire: A Hopi Legend of the Sunset Crater Eruption
An Ecological Analysis Involving the Population
  of San Juan Pueblo, NM
Engendered Encounters: Feminism & Pueblo Cultures,
  1879-1934
Excavation of Main Pueblo at Fitzmaurice Ruin
The First Koshare
Fourteen Families in Pueblo Pottery
The Fourth World of the Hopis
The Freeing of the Deer and Other New Mexico Indian Myths
Glen Canyon: An Archaeological Summary
A Guide to Pueblo Pottery
A Guide to Zuni Fetishes & Carvings
Hano: A Tewa Indian Commuity in Arizona
Historic Pottery of the Pueblo Indians, 1600-1880
Historical Background of the Santa Ana Pueblo
Historical Introduction to Studies Among the Sedentary
Indians of New Mexico
Homol'ovi III: A Pueblo Hamlet in the Middle
  Little Colorado River Valley, Arizona
Hopi Bibliography
Hopi Indian Altar Iconography
Hopi Katcinas
*Hopi Mysteries
The Hopi Photographs
Hopi Snake Ceremonies
The Hopi Way: Tales from a Vanishing Culture
Hopis, Tewas, and the American Road
Indian Uprising on the Rio Grande:
  The Pueblo Revolt of 1680
Idonapshe, Let's Eat: Traditional Zuni Foods
Indian Stories from the Pueblos
Indian Tales from Picuris Pueblo
Indians of Pecos Pueblos
Kiva, Cross, & Crown: The Pecos Indians
  & New Mexico, 1540-1840
The Kachina & the Cross: Indians & Spaniards
  in the Early Southwest
Language, History, & Identity
Life in the Pueblos
*Little Boy with Three Names: Stories of Taos Pueblo
Maasaw: Profile of a Hopi God
Masked Gods: Navaho and Pueblo Ceremonialism
Meditations with the Hopi
Men on the Moon: Collected Short Stories
Modern Transformation of Moenkopi Pueblo
Mother Earth, Father Sky: Ancient Chants by Pueblo and
Navajo Indians of the Southwest
Music of Acoma, Isleta, Cochiti and Zuni Pueblos
My Adventures in Zuni
The Mythical Pueblo Rites Doctrine
New Perspectives on the Pueblos
*Old Father Story Teller
The Origin & Development of the Pueblo Katsina Cult
Our Prayers Are In This Place
People of the Middle Place: A Study of the Zuni Indians

Petroglyphs & Pueblo Myths of the Rio Grande
Prehistoric Households at Turkey Creek Pueblo, Arizona
Pedro Pino: Governor of Zuni Pueblo, 1830-1878
*The Pueblo
The Protohistoric Pueblo World, A.D. 1275-1600
Pueblo Architecture & Modern Adobes
Pueblo Artists: Portraits
Pueblo Birds & Myths
*Pueblo Boy: Growing Up in Two Worlds
The Pueblo Children of the Earth Mother
Pueblo Crafts
Pueblo Cultures
Pueblo Designs
*Pueblo Girls: Growing Up in Two Worlds
Pueblo Gods and Myths
Pueblo, Hardscrabble, Greenhorn
*Pueblo Indian
Pueblo Indian Cookbook
Pueblo Indian Embroidery
Pueblo Indian Folk-Stories
Pueblo Indian Religion
The Pueblo Indian Revolt of 1696 and the Franciscan
  Missions in New Mexico
Pueblo Indian Textiles
Pueblo Indian Water Rights
The Pueblo Indians
*Pueblo Indians
The Pueblo Indians of North America
Pueblo & Mission: Cultural Roots of the Southwest
Pueblo Mothers & Children
Pueblo: Mountain, Village, Dance
Pueblo Nations: Eight Centuries of Pueblo Indian History
Pueblo & Navajo Indian Life Today
Pueblo People: Ancient Traditions, Modern Lives
Pueblo People Calendar
The Pueblo Potter
Pueblo Pottery Designs
Pueblo Pottery of the New Mexico Indians
Pueblo Profiles: Cultural Identity Through
  Centuries of Change
The Pueblo Revolt
The Pueblo Revolt of 1680
Pueblo Shields from the Fred Harvey Fine Arts Collection
*The Pueblo: Southwest
Pueblo Stories & Storytellers
The Pueblo Storyteller
*The Pueblo Storyteller
*A Pueblo Village
*The Pueblos
Pueblos: Prehistoric Indian Cultures of the Southwest
The Re-Establishment of the Indians in Their Pueblo
  Life Through the Revival of Their Traditional Crafts
Ritual in Pueblo Art: Hopi Life in Hopi Painting
Salinas Pueblo Missions National Monument
The Serpent's Tongue: Prose, Poetry & Art
  of the New Mexican Pueblos
Seven Families in Pueblo Pottery
Signs from the Ancestors: Zuni Cultural Symbolism
  and Perceptions of Rock Art
Social and Ceremonial Organization of Cochiti
Social Organization of the Western Pueblos
Songs of the Tewa
Standing Flower: The Life of Irving Pabanale,
  an Arizona Tewa Indian
Stories of Maasaw, a Hopi God
Stories & Stone: Writing the Ancestral Pueblo Homeland
A Study of Pueblo Architecture
Talking with the Clay: The Art of Pueblo Pottery
Taos Artists & Their Patrons, 1898-1950
The Taos Indians
The Taos Indians & the Battle for Blue Lake
Taos Pueblo and Its Sacred Blue Lake
Taos Society of Artists
The Taos Trappers
Tewa Tales
Tewa World
The Tiguas: Pueblo Indians of Texas
Tracking Prehistoric Migrations: Pueblo Settlers
  Among the Tonto Basin Hohokam
Trends in Pueblo Pottery
Western Pueblo Identities
When Cultures Meet
When Rain Gods Reigned: From Curios
  to Art at Tesuque Pueblo
*Where There Is No Name for Art
A Zuni Atlas
Zuni Bread Stuff
Zuni Contemporary Pottery
Zuni Coyote Tales
Zuni & El Moro
The Zuni Enigma
Zuni Fetishes
Zuni Fetishism
Zuni Folk Tales
The Zuni Indians
The Zuni Indians & Their Uses of Plants
Zuni Jewelry
Zuni Katchinas
Zuni Katcinas
Zuni Kin and Clan
A Zuni Life: A Pueblo Indian in Two Worlds
The Zuni Man-Woman
Zuni Pottery

Zuni: Selected Writings of Frank Hamilton Cushing
Zuni: A Village of Silversmiths
The Zunis

RELIGION & MYTHOLOGY

The American Indian Ghost Dance, 1870 & 1890:
  An Annotated Bibliography
American Indian Mythology
American Indian Prayers and Poetry
American Indian Prophets: Religious Leaders
  & Revitalization Movements
American Indian Traditions & Ceremonies
Analysis of Coeur D'Alene Indian Myths
Answered Prayers
An Archaeology of the Soul: North American Indian
  Belief & Ritual
The Attraction of Peyote
Becoming & Remaining a People
Before the Great Spirit: War, Rivalry & Irreverence
  Among the Sioux
Birds, Beads & Bells: Remote Sensing of a
  Pawnee Sacred Bundle
Black Elk: Holy Man of the Oglala
*Black Elk: A Man with a Vision
Black Elk's Religion: The Sun Dance & Lakota Catholicism
Black Elk: The Sacred Ways of the Lakota
Black Elk Speaks
Black Hills: Sacred Hills
Blessingway
A Book of Tales, Being Myths of the North American Indians
The Boy Who Made Dragonfly: A Zuni Myth
Brushed by Cedar, Living by the River:
  Coast Salish Figures of Power
By the Power of the Dreams: Songs, Prayers
  & Sacred Shields of the Plains Indians
California Indian Nights
Carlos Castaneda, Academic Opportunism,
  and the Psychedelic Sixties
Cave of the Jagua: The Mythological World of the Tainos
Cherokee Folk Zoology
The Cherokee Ghost Dance
Cherokee New Testament
A Cherokee Prayerbook
Cherokee Psalms, A Collection of Hymns
Cherokee Vision of Eloh'
The Cherokees and Christianity, 1794-1870
Children of Cottonwood
Chinigchinix, An Indigenous California Indian Religion
Christian Indians and Indian Nationalism, 1855-1950
Christianity and Native Traditions
Circles, Consciousness, and Culture
Comanches & Mennonites on the Oklahoma Plains
The Complete Book of Natural Shamanism
Creation Myths of Primitive America
*Creation Tales from the Salish
Creation's Journey: Native American Identity & Belief
Creators of the Plains
Creek Indian Medicine Ways
Creek (Muskogee) New Testament Concordance
Crying for a Dream: The World Through
  Native American Eyes
Dakota Cross-Bearer: The Life & World
  of a Native American Bishop
Dancing Ghosts: Native American & Christian
  Syncretism in Mary Austin's Work
Dancing Gods: Indian Ceremonials of New Mexico & Arizona
The Devil in the New World
Devil Sickness & Devil Songs: Tohono O'Odham Poetics
Dictionary of Native American Mythology
Dramatic Elements in American Indian Ceremonials
The Dream Seekers
Dreaming With the Wheel: How to Interpret Your
  Dreams Using the Medicine Wheel
Earth Fire: A Hopi Legend of the Sunset Crater Eruption
The Economics of Sainthood: Religious Change
  Among the Rimrock Navajos
Encyclopedia of Native American Religions
Encyclopedia of Native American Shamanism
The False Faces of the IroquoisThe Feathered Sun:
  Plains Indians in Art & Philosophy
The Feathered Sun: Plains Indians in Art & Philosophy
Finding a Way Home: Indian & Catholic Spiritual
  Paths of the Plateau Tribes
Flight of the Seventh Moon: The Teaching of the Shields
Following the Sun & Moon: Hopi Kachina Tradition
Fools Crow: Wisdom & Power
The Freeing of the Deer & Other New Mexico Indian Myths
Ghost Dance
Ghost Dance Messiah: The Jack Wilson Story
Ghost Dance Religion
Ghost-Dance Religion & the Sioux Outbreak of 1890
The Ghost-Dance Religion & Wounded Knee
*Giving Thanks: A Native American
  Good Morning Message
Giving Voice to Bear: Native American
  Myths, Images, and Rituals of the Bear
God Is Red: A Native View of Religion
The Gospel of the Great Spirit
The Gospel of the Redman
Grandmothers of Light: A Medicine Woman's Sourcebook
Great American Indian Bible
*Guardian Spirit Quest

Guide to the Records of the the Moravian Mission
  Among the Indians of North America
Haida Texts & Myths
Handbook of American Indian Religious Freedom
The Hands Feel It: Healing & Spirit Presence
  Among a Northern Alaskan People
A Haunting Reverence: Meditations on a Northern Land
The Hidden Language of the Seneca
Hindu Festivals in a North Indian Village
*Hoksila & the Red Buffalo
Hopi Indian Altar Iconography
Hopi Kachina Dolls With a Key to Their Identification
Hopi Kachinas
Hopi & Zuni Ceremonialism
Hotevilla: Hopi Srine of the Covenant/Microcosm
  of the World
How to Take Part in Lakota Ceremonies
I Become Part of It: Sacred Dimensions
  in Native American Life
The Idea of Fertilization in the Culture of the Pueblo Indians
In the Beginning: The Navajo Genesis
*In a Sacred Manner I Live
*Indian Legends
Indian Myths
Indian: Tales & Legends
Indians of Northeastern North America
The Invention of Prophecy: Continuity & Meaning
  in Hopi Indian Relgiion
The Jesus Road: Kiowa, Christianity, and Indian Hymns
Journey to the Four Directions
Journey Song: A Spiritual Legacy of the American Indian
Kenekuk, the Kickapoo Prophet
Knowledge & Secrecy in an Aboriginal Religion
Lakota Belief and Ritual
Lakota & Dakota Animal Wisdom Stories
Lakota Life
Lakota Myth
Lighting the Seventh Fire: The Spiritual Ways....
Living the Sky: The Cosmos of the American Indian
Lord of the Animals: A Miwok Indian Creation Myth
Maasaw: Profile of a Hopi God
Masks of the Spirit: Image & Metaphor in Mesoamerica
Meditation With Native Americans: Lakota Spirituality
Meditations With Animals: A Native American Bestiary
Meditations With the Hopi
Meditations With the Navajo: Prayer-Songs
  & Stories of Healing & Harmony
Mission Among the Blackfeet
*Monstors & Magic: Myths of North & South America
The Montana Cree: A Study in Religious Persistence
Mother Earth: An American Story
Mother Earth Spirituality: Native American
  Paths to Healing Ourselves & Our World
The Mystic Warriors of the Plains
Myth, Music & Dance of the American Indian
The Myth & Prayers of the Great Star Chant
  & the Myth of the Coyote Chant
The Mythology of Native North America
The Mythology of North America
Mythology & Values: An Analysis of Navaho Chantway Myths
Mythology of the Wichita
Myths & Legends of the North American Indians
Myths of the Cherokees & Sacred Formulas
  of the Cherokees
Myths of the Modocs
Myths of the New World Indians
Myths of the New World: A Treatise on the Symbolism
  & Mythology of the Red Race of America
The Myths of the North American Indians
Myths of Pre-Columbian America
Myths & Tales of the Southeastern Indians
Myths & Traditions of the Arikara Indians
The Naked Man, Vol. 4: Mythologiques
Narrative of the Mission of the United Brethren
  Among the Delaware & Mohegan Indians
Native American Cultural & Religious Freedoms
Native American Folklore, 1879-1979
Native American Religion
Native American Religions
Native American Religions: A Geographical Survey
Native American Religions: An Introduction
Native American Religions: North America
*Native American Religions: World Religions
Native American Religious Action
Native American Spirituality: A Critical Reader
Native American Traditions
Native American Truths: Philosophy of Good Medicine
Native American Wisdom
Native & Christian: Indigenous Voices on
  Religious Identity in the U.S. & Canada
Native Healer: Initiation into an Ancient Art
Native North American Spirituality of the Eastern Woodlands
Native Religions of North America
Native American Voices
Nature Religion in America
A Navaho Bringing-Home Ceremony
Navaho Chantway Myths
Navajo Mountain and Rainbow Bridge Religion
Navajo Myths, Prayers & Songs with Texts & Translations
Navaho Religion: A Study of Symbolism
Navajo Sacred Places
Navajo Sandpainting From Religious Act to Commercial Art
Navajo & the Tibetan Sacred Wisdom: The Circle of the Spirit

Ni-Kso-Ko-Wa: Blackfoot Spirituality,
  Traditions, Values, and Beliefs
The Night Has a Naked Soul
North American Myths & Legends
North American Sun Kings: Keepers of the Flame
Not For Innocent Ears: Spiritual Traditions of a
  Desert Cahuilla Medicine Woman
Of Earth & Elders: Visions & Voices from Native America
Oglala Religion
The Old North Trail: Or, Life, Legends & Religion
  of the Blackfeet Indians
On the Bloody Road to Jesus: Christianity
  & the Chiricahua Apaches
On the Padre's Trail
The Orders of the Dreamed
The Paths of Kateri's Kin
The Pawnee Mythology
Peyote: The Devine Cactus
Peyote Hunt: The Sacred Journey of Huichol Indians
Peyote Religion: A History
Pipe, Bible & Peyote Among the Oglala Lakota:
  A Study in Religious Identity
The Pipe & Christ
Plains Indian Mythology
The Pollen Path: A Collection of Navajo Myths
The Power of Silence
Prayer on Top of the Earth: The Spiritual Universe
  of the Plains Apaches
Profiles in Wisdom: Native Elders Speak About the Earth
Pueblo Birds & Myths
Pueblo Cultures
Pueblo God & Myths
Pueblo Indian Religion
Rainhouse & Ocean: Speeches for the Papago Year
*Raven Brings to the People Another Gift
Red Man's Religion: Beliefs & Practices of the Indians
  of North of Mexico
The Red Swan: Myths & Tales of the American Indians
Reflections of Social Life in the Navaho Origin Myth
Religion & Hopi Life in the 20th Century
Religion in Native North America
The Religions of the American Indians
Renewing the World: Plains Indian Religion & Morality
Return of the Indian Spirit
Return of the Thunderbeings
Ritual & Myth in Odawa Revitalization:
  Reclaiming a Sovereign Place
The Road to Sundance: My Journey Into Native Spirituality
Sacred Beliefs of the Chitimacha Indians
Sacred Earth: The Spiritual Landscape of Native America
Sacred Encounters: Father De Smet and the Indians
  of the Rocky Mountain West
The Sacred Geography of the American Mound-Builders
Sacred Ground
Sacred Language: The Nature of Supernatural
  Discourse in Lakota
Sacred Objects, Sacred Places: Preserving Tribal Traditions
Sacred Path Cards: The Discovery of Self
  Through Native Teachings
The Sacred Pipe: An Archetypal Theology
The Sacred Pipe: Black Elk's Account of the
  Seven Rites of the Oglala Sioux
Sacred Places: How the Living Earth Seeks Our Friendship
Sacred Powers
Sacred Scrolls of the Southern Ojibway
Sacred Sites of the Indians of the American Southwest
The Sacred Tree
The Sacred: Ways of Knowledge, Sources of Life
Sacred Words: A Study of Navajo Religion and Prayer
Secret Native American Pathways: A Guide to Inner Peace
Seeing With the Native Eye: Contributions
  to the Study of Native American Religion
Seminole Baptist Churches of Oklahoma:
  Maintaining a Traditional Community
Seneca Indian Myths
A Separate Reality
Seven Visions of Bull Lodge
Severing the Ties That Bind
The Shaman & the Medicine Wheel
The Shaman: Patterns of Religious Healing Among the
  Ojibway Indians
Shamanic Odyssey: The Lushootseed Salish
  Journey to the Land of the Dead
Shamans & Kushtakas: North Coast Tales
  of the Supernatural
Shamans & Religion
The Shamans Touch
Sioux Indian Religion: Tradition & Innovation
The Sixth Grandfather: Black Elk's Teachings
  Given to John G. Neihardt
John Slocum & The Indian Shaker Church
Small Spirits: Native American Dolls
Soul & Native Americans
Southern Indian Myths and Legends
The Spirit of Black Hawk: A Mystery of Africans and Indians
Spirit Healing: Native American Magic & Medicine
Spirit Visions, Vol. 1: The Old Ones Speak
The Spirit World
Spiritual Encounters
Spiritual Legacy of the American Indian
Standing in the Light: A Lakota Way of Seeing
Stories of Awe & Abundance
Stories of Masaw, a Hopi God

Stories of the Sioux
The Story of Lynx
Strange Journey: The Vision Life of a Psychic Indian Woman
The Study of American Indian Religions
Summer Meditations With Native American Elders
The Sun Dance Religion: Power for the Powerless
Sun Dancer
Sun Men of the Americas
Symbols of Native America
Tah-Koo Wah-Kan: Or, The Gospel Among the Dakotas
Tales of a Shaman's Apprentice
Teaching Spirits
Teachings from the American Earth:
  Indian Religion and Philosophy
The Theft of the Spirit: A Journey to Spiritual Healing
To Touch the Wind
Traditional Ojibwa Religion and Its Historical Changes
Traditions of the Arapaho
The Transformation of Bigfoot: Maleness,
  Power & Belief Among the Chipewyan
Travels In A Stone Canoe
Treatise on the Heathen Superstitions
The Trickster of Liberty
Trickster: Study in American Indian Mythology
*The Trickster and the Troll
Tusayan Katchinas & Hopi Altars
The Upward Moving & Energence Way
Vital Souls: Bororo Cosology, Natural Symbolism
  & Shamanism
Voices of Earth and Sky
Wakinyan: Lakota Religion in the 20th Century
Warrior, Shield & Star: Imagery & Ideology of Pueblo Warfare
*Warriors of the Rainbow: Strange & Prophetic
  Dreams of the Indian Peoples
Washo Shamans & Peyotists: Religious
  Conflict in an American Indian Tribe
Waterway
The Way of the Spirit
The Way to Make Perfect Mountains
The Way to Rainy Mountain
*White Buffalo Woman
Wisdom of the Native Americans
Wisdomkeepers: Meetings with Native American
  Spiritual Elders
With Good Heart: Yaqui Beliefs & Ceremonies
  in Pascua, Village
The Wolves of Heaven: Cheyenne Shamanism,
  Ceremonies & Prehistoric Origins
Wovoka and the Ghost Dance: A Source Book
Yurok Myths
Zuni Fetishes

RELOCATION

Dispossessing the Wilderness: Indian Removal,
  National Parks & the Preservationist Ideal
Farewell My Nation: The American Indian
  & the U.S., 1820-1890
In a Barren Land: American Indian Dispossession & Survival
The Long Bitter Trail: Andrew Jackson & the Indians
The Roads of My Relations
A Traveler in Indian Territory: The Journal
  of Ethan Allen Hitchcock
The Trail of Tears
*The Trail of Tears
Trail of Tears Across Missouri
Trail of Tears: American Indians Driven From Their Lands

RESERVATIONS

Ancient Treasures
Bacavi: A Hopi Village
Background History of the Coeur D'Alene Indian Reservation
Bread & Freedom
Crying for a Dream: The Earth is Our Mother
Culture, Change and Leadership in a Modern Indian
  Community: The Colorado River Indian Reservation
Discover Indian Reservations: A Visitor's Welcome Guide
Indian Reservations: A State & Federal Handbook
The Nome Lackee Indian Reservation, 1854-1870
North American Indian Landmarks: A Traveler's Guide
The Reservation
The Reservation Blackfeet, 1885-1945
Quarter-Acre of Heartache

RITES & CEREMONIES

American Indian Ceremonies: A Practical Workbook
  & Study Guide to the Medicine Path Hawk Medicine
American Indian Traditions & Ceremonies
The Attraction of Peyote
Catlinite Pipes
Ceremonies of the Pawnee
Coyoteway: A Navajo Holyway Healing Ceremonial
Dancing Gods: Indian Ceremonials of New Mexico & Arizona
Dramatic Elements in American Indian Ceremonials
The Dream Seekers
Encyclopedia of Native American Ceremonies
First Houses: Native American Homes & Sacred Structures
*Flying With the Eagle, Racing the Great Bear
The Forgotten Artist
*Guardian Spirit Quest

A Guide to Zuni Fetishes & Carving
The Hako: Song, Pipe and Unity in a Pawnee
 Calumet Ceremony
Head & Face Masks in Navaho Ceremonialism
Hogans: Navajo Houses & House Songs
Hopi Snake Ceremonies
How to Take Part in Lakota Ceremonies
Huichol Indian Sacred Rituals
I Send a Voice
Indian Games & Dances with Native Songs
Indian Myth and Legend
The Iroquois Eagle Dance
An Iroquois Sourcebook: Medicine Society Rituals
Journey to the Ancestral Self: The Native Lifeway
 Guide to Living in Harmony With Earth Mother
Kachinas: A Hopi Artist's Documentary
Kinaalada: A Navajo Puberty Ceremony
*Kiowa Voices: Ceremonial Dance, Ritual & Songs
Lakota Grieving: A Pastoral Response
Lakota Life
Lushootseed Culture & the Shamanic Odyssey:
 An Anchored Radiance
Making Two Worlds One and the Story of
 All-American Indian Days
Medicine Wheels: Native American Vehicles of Healing
Mitakuye Oyasin: We Are All Related
Mother Earth, Father Sky: Ancient Chants by Pueblo
 and Navajo Indians of the Southwest
Myths & Symbols, or Aboriginal Religions in America
Native American Religious Action
Native North American Spirituality of the Eastern Woodlands
The Native American Sun Dance Religion & Ceremony:
 An Annotated Bibliography
A Navajo Bringing-Home Ceremony
Navajo Mountain & Rainbow Bridge Religion
Navajo Sandpainting Art: Where the Gods Gather
The Night Chant: A Navaho Ceremonial
The Night Has a Naked Soul
The Nightway: A History and a History of
 Documentation of a Navajo Ceremonial
North American Dances & Rituals
North American Indian Travel Guide
Offering Smoke: The Sacred Pipe &
 Native American Religion
On the Gleaming Way
One Nation Under God: The Triumph of the
 Native American Church
Oraibi Soyal Ceremony & Oraibi Powamu Ceremony,
 and Mishongnovi Ceremonies of the Snake and Antelope
 Fraternities & Oraibi Summer Snake Ceremony
Oraibu Marau Ceremony
The Osage Ceremonial Dance I'n-Lon-Schka
The Peyote Cult
The Pipe & Christ
Pow Wow: And Other Yakima Indian Traditions
The Power of Kiowa Song: A Collaborative Ethnography
*The Praying Flute
Rainhouse & Ocean: Speeches for the Papago Year
The Rattle & the Drum: Native American
 Rituals & Celebrations
Religion & Ceremonies of the Lenape
Rig Veda Americanus
Ritual & Myth in Odawa Revitalization
The Road of Life & Death: A Ritual Drama
 of the American Indians
The Road to Sundance: My Journey Into Native Spirituality
Rolling Thunder: A Personal Explortion Into the Secret
 Healing Power of an American Indian Medicine Man
Rolling Thunder Speaks
Sacred Ground
The Sacred Pipe: Black Elk's Account of the
 Seven Rites of Oglala Sioux
Scalp Ceremonials of Zuni
Secret Native American Pathways
Seneca Thanksgiving Rituals
Source Material for the Social & Ceremonial
 Life of the Choctaw Indians
The Southeastern Ceremonial Complex, Artifacts & Analysis
Southwestern Indian Ceremonials
Southwestern Indian Ritual Drama
Spirit Medicine
Spirits of the Earth
Standing in the Light: A Lakota Way of Seeing
The Story of the Meadowlark
Tobacco, Peace Pipes & Indians
The Urine Dance of the Zuni Indians of New Mexico
*Ways of the Lushootsed People: Ceremonies &
 Traditions of the Northern Puget Sound Indians
Witchcraft & Sorcery of the North American Native Peoples
Witchcraft in the Southwest
With Good Heart: Yaqui Beliefs & Ceremonies
 in Pascua Village
World's Rim: Great Mysteries of the North American Indians
The Yuchi Green Corn Ceremonial
Yuwipi: Vision and Experience in Oglala Ritual
Zuni Fetishism

ROCK ART—PETROGLYPHS

Ancient Visions: Petroglyphs & Pictographs
The Art of the Shaman: Rock Art of California
Canyon de Chelly: Its People and Rock Art
Crystals in the Sky

Cuckoo for Kokopelli
The Forgotten Artist: Indians of
 Anza-Borrego & Their Rock Art
Guide to Indian Rock Carvings
 of the Pacific Nothwest Coast
Guide to Rock Art of the Utah Region:
 Sites With Public Access
Indian Rock Art in Wyoming
Indian Rock Art of the Southwest
Indian Rock Carvings
Kokopelli: FlutePlayer Images in Rock Art
Landscape of the Spirits: Hohokam Rock Art
Marks of the Ancestors
Petroglyphs of Ohio
Prehistoric Rock Art
Rock Art in New Mexico
Rock Art of the American Indian
Rock Art of the American Southwest
Rock Art of Kentucky
The Rock Art of Texas Indians
The Rock Art of Utah
Rock Art of Western South Dakota
Rock Paintings of the Chumash
The Rocks Begin to Speak
The Serpent and the Sacred Fire: Fertility Images
 in Southwest Rock Art
Seven Rock Art Sites in Baja California
Signs From the Ancestors: Zuni Cultural Symbolism
 & Perceptions of Rock Art
Signs of Life: Rock Art of the Upper Rio Grande
Storied Stone: Indian Rock Art in the Black Hills Country
Stories & Stone: Writing the Ancestral Pueblo Homeland
*Stories in Stone: Rock Art: Images From the Ancient Ones

SAC, FOX & IOWA INDIANS

Expedition Against the Sauk and Fox Indians, 1832
Observations of the Ethnology of the Sauk Indians
The Sac and Fox Indians
Sacred Bundles of the Sac and Fox Indians
The Sauks and the Black Hawk War

SACAGAWEA, 1786-1884

The Bird Woman: Sacajawea, Guide to Lewis & Clark
Mystery of Sacajawea
*Sacagawea
*Sacajawea—Native American Heroine
Sacagawea of the Lewis & Clark Expedition
Sacajawea, Wilderness Guide
*The Value of Adventure: The Story of Sacajawea

SALISH & KOOTENAI INDIANS

The Coast Salish People
*Coyote Tales of the Montana Salish
*Creation Tales from the Salish
A Dictionary of Puget Salish
Historical Sketch of the Flathead Nation
Kootenai Why Stories
Ktunaxa Legends
Lushootseed Dictionary
Our Tellings: Interior Salish Stories
Over a Century of Moving to the Drum: Salish Indian
 Celebrations on the Flathead Indian Reservation
The Problem of Justice: Tradition & Law
 in the Coast Salish World
*Salish Folk Tales
The Sanpoil and Nespelem: Salishan Peoples
 of Northeastern Washington
Selish, or Flat-Head Grammar

SANDPAINTING

Earth Is My Mother, Sky Is My Father
Hosteen Klah: Navaho Medicine Man and Sand Painter
Indian Sandpainting of the Southwest
The Navajo Art of Sandpainting
Navajo Medicine Man Sandpaintings
Navajo Sandpainting Art: Where the Gods Gather
Navajo Sandpainting From Religious Act
 to Commercial Art
Navajo Sandpainting: The Huckel Collection
Sandpaintings of the Navajo Shooting Chant
Summoning the Gods: Sandpainting of the
 Native American Southwest
Tapestries in Sand - The Spirit of Indian Sandpainting

SCULPTURE

Sculpturing Totem Poles
Plains Indian Sculpture

SEMINOLE INDIANS

Africans & Seminoles: From Removal to Emancipation
An Assumption of Sovereignty
Big Cypress: A Changing Seminole Community
Complete Book of Seminole Patchwork
Creeks and Seminoles
*Dancing with the Indians

The Enduring Seminoles: From Alligate Wrestling
 to Ecotourism
The Florida Seminole and the New Deal, 1933-1942
Florida's Seminole Indians
Healing Plants: Medicine of the Florida Seminole Indians
History of the Second Seminole War
*John Hawk: A Seminole Saga
My Work Among the Florida Seminoles
Nations Remembered
Oklahoma Seminoles: Medicines, Magic and Religion
Pelts, Plumes and Hides
Removal Aftershock
*The Seminole
The Seminole
The Seminole Baptist Churches of Oklahoma
Seminole Burning: A Story of Racial Vengeance
The Seminole Indians
Seminole Indians of Florida, 1850-1874
A Seminole Legend: The Life of Betty Mae Tiger Jumper
The Seminole & Miccosukee Tribes
Seminole Music
Seminole Patchwork
Seminole Patchwork Book
Seminole Patchwork: The Complete Book
Seminole Music
The Seminole Seed
A Seminole Sourcebook
*The Seminole: Southeast
*The Seminoles
Seminoles
Seminoles: Days of Long Ago
The Seminoles of Florida

SENECA INDIANS

The Allegany Senecas and Kinzua Dam
The Death and Rebirth of the Seneca
The Hidden Language of the Seneca
*Little Water & Gift of the Animals: A Seneca Legend
Red Jacket: Seneca Chief
Seneca Myths & Folk Tales
Seneca Thanksgiving Rituals
The Seneca & Tuscarora Indians: An Annotated Bibliography
The Seneca World of Ga-No-Say-Yeh
*Skunny Wundy: Seneca Indian Tales

SHAWNEE INDIANS

*Blue Jacket: War Chief of the Shawnees
Blue Jacket: Warrior of the Shawnees
*From the Ashes
Shawnee: The Ceremonialism of a Native American
 Tribe and Its Cultural Background
Shawnee Home Life: The Painting of Ernest Spybuck
The Shawnee Prophet
*Tecumseh
Tecumseh's Last Stand
Tecumseh & the Quest for Indian Leadership
*Tecumseh & the Shawnee Confederacy
Tecumseh: Visionary of the Shawnee

SHOSHONI INDIANS

Essie's Story: The Life & Legacy of a Shoshoni Teacher
Great Basin Shoshonean Sourcebook
Newe Hupia: Shoshoni Poetry Songs
The Northern Shoshoni
*Pachee Goyo: History and Legends from the Shoshone
People of the Wind River: The Eastern Shoshones,
 1825-1900
The Road on Which We Came; A History
 of the Western Shoshone
Sagwitch; Shoshone Chieftain, Mormon Elder, 1822-1887
*Shoshone Indians of North America
Shoshone Tales
*The Shoshoni
The Shoshoni-Crow Sun Dance
The Shoshoni Frontier & the Bear River Massacre
The Shoshoni Ghost Dance Religion: Poetry Songs
 and Great Basin Context
Shoshoni Grammar
Shoshoni Texts
The Shoshonis: Sentinels of the Rockies
Thunder Over the Ochoco
Vocabulary of the Shoshone Language
The Washakie Letters of Willie Ottogary: Northwestern
 Shoshone Journalist and Leader, 1906-1929
Western Shoshoni Grammar
When Did the Shoshoni Begin to Occupy Southern Idaho?

SIGN LANGUAGE

Do You See What I Mean?
The Indian Sign Language
Indian Sign Language
*Indian Sign Language
Indian Talk: Hand Signals of the North American Indians
*Native American Talking Signs
*North American Indian Sign Language
Sign Language Among North American Indians
Sign Language: Contemporary Southwest Native America

SITTING BULL -
DAKOTA CHIEF, 1834-1890

The Arrest and Killing of Sitting Bull: A Documentary
The Genius of Siting Bull: 13 Heroic Strategies for
  Today's Business Leaders
I Am Looking to the North for My Life; Sitting Bull, 1876-1881
The Last Years of Sitting Bull
The Saga of Sitting Bull's Bones
Sitting Bull
*Sitting Bull
Sitting Bull, Champion of the Sioux: A Biography
Sitting Bull: The Collected Speeches
Sitting Bull & the Plains Indians
*Sitting Bull, Warrior of the Sioux
*The Story of Little Bighorn

SOCIAL CONDITIONS,
LIFE & CUSTOMS

America Street: A Multicultural Anthology of Stories
American Indian Family Support Systems
American Indian Identity: Today's Changing Perspectives
The American Indian: Perspectives for the
  Study of Social Change
American Indian Sports Heritage
American Indians: Facts - Future Toward Economic
  Development for Native American Communities
American Indians: The First of this Land
The Anguish of Snails: Native American
  Folklore in the West
The Animals Came Dancing
Any Other Country Except My Own
Arapahoe Politics, 1851-1978: Symbols
  in the Crisis of Authority
The Architecture of Social Integration in Prehistoric Pueblos
Assessment of a Model for Determining Community-Based
  Needs of American Indians with Disabilities
Autobiography of a Winnebago Indian
*Battlefields & Burial Grounds: The Indian Struggle
  to Protect Ancestral Graves in the U.S.
*Between Sacred Mountains: Navajo Stories
  and Lessons fromthe Land
Boarding School Seasons
Braided Lives: An Anthology of Multicultural Writing
Breaking New Ground for American Indian
  & Alaska Native Youth...
Briefcase Warriors: Stories for the Stage
California Indian Nights Entertainment
Camp, Clan and Kin Among the Cow Creek Seminole
The Canoe Rocks: Alaska's Tlingit & the
  Euroamerican Frontier, 1800-1912
Cherokee Americans - Eastern Band of
  Cherokees in the 20th Century
The Chief Hole-in-the-Day of the Mississippi Chippewa
Children of the Dragonfly: Native American Voices
  on Child Custody & Education
Chippewa Child Life & Its Cultural Background
Chippewa Customs
Chippewa Families: A Social Study of
  White Earth Reservation, 1938
Claiming Breath
*Come to Our Salmon Feast
Communication and Development:
  A Study of Two Indian Villages
Contemporary Federal Indian Policy
  Toward American Indians
Contemporary Native American Cultural Issues
Contemporary Navajo Affairs
Coping with the Final Tragedy: Dying & Grieving in
  Cross Cultural Perspective
The Coppers of the Northwest Coast Indians
Corn Among the Indians of the Upper Missouri
Cry to the Thinderbird: The American Indian's Own Story
Culture, Change and Leadership in a
  Modern Indian Community
Cynthia Ann Parker: The Story of Her Capture at the
Massacre of the Inmates of Parker's Fort
*Daily Life in a Plains Indian Village, 1868
Daughters of the Buffalo Women
The Destruction of American Indian Families
Dictionary of Daily Life of Indians of the Americas, A to Z
Disciplined Hearts
Economic Development on American Indian Reservations
Enduring Culture
Everyday Life of the North American Indian
The Fall of Natural Man
The False Faces of the Iroquois
Feathering Custer
From Indians to Chicanos: The Dynamics of
  Mexican American Culture
Forgotten Fires: Native Americans & the
  Transient Wilderness
Fundamentals of Age-Group Systems
Gambling & Survival in Native North America
Games of the North American Indians
A Good Medicine Collection
The Grand Village of the Natchez Indians Revisited
Handbook of the American Frontier
Handbook of American Indian Games
A Haunting Reverence: Meditations On a Northern Land
The Havasupai Woman

A Healing Place: Indigenous Visions for Personal
  Empowerment & Community Recovery
Hogans: Navajo Houses and House Songs
Houses & House-Life of the American Aborigines
In the Land of the Grasshopper Song
*Indian Boyhood
Indian Gaming: Who Wins?
Indian Life on the Upper Missouri
Indian Police and Judges: Experiments in
  Acculturation and Control
Indian Running: Native American History & Tradition
*Indian Way: Kearning to Communicate with Mother Earth
Indian-White Relations in the U.S.: A Bibliography of
  Works Published, 1975-1980
The Indian's New World: Catawbas & Their Neighbors
  from European Contact Through the Era of Removal
Indians & Criminal Justice
Indians, Fire & Land in the Pacific Northwest
Indians in the Making: Ethnic Relations & Indian
  Identities Around Puget Sound
Indians in Overalls
Indians' New South
The Tobacco Society of the Crow Indians
The Indians of the Great Plains
The Indians of Puget Sound: The Notebooks of Myron Eells
Indians of the U.S.: Four Centuries of Their History & Culture
Ininatig's Gift of Sugar: Traditional Native Sugarmaking
Introduction to the Study of Mortuary Customs
  of the North American Indians
Inventing the Savage: The Social Construction
  of Native American Criminality
The Invention of Prophecy
Journey to the Ancestral Self: Tamarack Songs
*James At Work
The Kickapoo Indians, Their History & Culture:
  An Annotated Bibliography
Oliver La Farge & the American Indian: A Biography
Lakota Life
The Lakota Ritual of the Sweat Lodge:
  History & Contemporary Practice
Lakota Woman
Life Among the Great Plains Indians
Like Beads on a String: A Culture History of the
  Seminole Indians in North Peninsula Florida
Living the Spirit: A Gay American Indian Anthology
Looking for Lost Bird: A Jewish Woman's
  Discovery of Her Navajo Roots
The Makah Indians
Manifest Manners: Postindian Warriors of Survivance
Marxism and Native Americans
Menominee Music
Moccasins on Pavement: The Urban Indian Experience,
  A Denver Portrait
Models for the Millennium: Great Basin Anthropology Today
Modern Blackfeet: Montanans on a Reservation
Montezuma's Dinner
My Life as an Indian
Native America: Arts, Traditions & Celebrations
Native American Studies: New Native American Storytellers
The Native American Sweat Lodge: History & Legends
Native American Traditions
*Native American Way of Life
Native Americans: The People and How They Lived
Native Cemeteries and Forms of Burial
  East of the Mississippi
Native North American Spirituality of the Eastern Woodlands
Navajo Graves
The Navajo Hunter Tradition
Navajo Kinship Marriage
Navajo the Laughter Way
Navajo Leadership and Government
Nch'i-Wana "The Big River" Mid-Columbia Indians
  & Their Land
North American Indian Burial Customs
North American Indian Travel Guide
Of Earth & Elders: Visions & Voices from Native America
Oglala Religion
The Ojibwa of Western Canada
Ojibwa Woman
Ojibway Oratory
Old Indian Trails
The Old North Trail: Or, Life, Legends &
  Religion of the Blackfeet Indians
Osage Mission Baptisms, Marriages,
  and Interments, 1820-1886
Osages: Children of the Middle Waters
Partners in Furs: A History of the Fur Trade
  in Eastern James Bay
The Pequots in Southern New England
Performing the Renewal of Community
Pima and Papago Ritual Oratory
Political Organization of the Plains Indians
Portraits of the Whiteman
Postindian Conversations
Pow Wow: And Other Yakima Indian Traditions
Pow Wow Calendar
Prehistoric Households at Turkey Creek Pueblo, Arizona
Present is Past
Pressing Issues of Inequality & American Indian
  Communities
The Qualla Cherokee Surviving in Two Worlds
Recently Discovered Tales of Life Among the Indians
Reckoning With the Dead

Red Earth, White Lies
Red Hunters and the Animal People
The Re-Establishment of the Indian in Their Pueblo
  Life Through the Revival of Their Traditional Crafts
Reflections of Social Life in the Navaho Origin Myth
Respect for Life: The Traditional Upbringing of
  American Indian Children
The Return of the Native
Return to Creation: A Survival Manual for
  Native & Natural People
Riding Buffaloes & Broncos: Rodeo & Native Traditions
  in the Northern Great Plains
The Roots of Dependency: Subsistence, Environment, &
  Social Change Among the Choctaws, Pawnees & Navajos
Roots of Oppression: The American Indian Question
Sacred Ground
The Sacred Hoop: Recovering the Feminine in
  American Indian Traditions
Scholars and the Indian Experience
Schooling At Risk Native American Children
The Search for an American Indian Identity
Self and Savagery on the California Frontier
Selling the Indian: Commercializing &
  Appropriating American Indian Culture
Shadows of the Indian: Stereotypes in American Culture
Shonto: A Study of the Role of the Trader in a
  Modern Navaho Community
Silent Arrows
Smallpox & the Iroquois Wars
Social & Ceremonial Organization of Cochiti
Social Organization of the Western Pueblos
A Social Study of 150 Chippewa Indian Families
  of the White Earth Reservation of MN
Son of Old Hat: A Navaho Autobiography
Source Material for the Social & Ceremonial Life
  of the Choctaw Indians
Southwestern Indian Ceremonials
The Spirit & the Flesh: Sexual Diversity in
  American Indian Tradition
*Sports & Games the Indians Gave Us
*Squanto & the First Thanksgiving
*The Story of Wounded Knee
Strangers in Blood
A Study of the Special Problems & Needs
  of American Indians with Handicaps
Subjugation and Dishonor: A Brief History of the
  Travail of the Native Americans
Symbolic Immortality, The Tlingit Potlatch
  of the 19th Century
Talking Leaves
Team Spirits: The Native American Mascots Controversy
*To Live In Two Worlds: American Indian Youth Today
Tobacco, Peacepipes and Indians
Tobacco, Pipes & Smoking Customs
  of the American Indians
Traditions of the North American Indians
Traditions of the Quinault Indians
Traits of American Indian Life & Character
Travels in North America, Including a
  Summer with the Pawnees
The Trial of "Indian Joe": Race & Justice
  in the 19th Century West
Turquoise and the Navajo
Two Crows Denies It: A History of Controversy
  in Omaha Sociology
Two Leggings: The Making of a Crow Warrior
Two Spirit People: American Indian Lesbian
  Women & Gay Men
The Underground Reservation: Osage Oil
Urban Indian Experience in America
*Urban Indians
Urban Indians
Urban Indans: Drums from the Cities
Urban Institutions & People of Indian Ancestry
Urban Voices: The Bay Area American Indian Community
Urbanization of American Indians: A Critical Bibliography
Valley of the Spirits: The Upper Skagit Indian
  of Western Washington
Wake of the Unseen Object
Walk in Your Soul: Love Incantations
  of the Oklahoma Cherokees
The Way of the Dead Indians
The Way We Live: California Indian Reminiscences,
  Stories and Songs
Ways of Knowing: Experience, Knowledge &
  Power Among the Dene Tha
When Jesus Came, the Corn Mothers Went Away
When Nickels Were Indians
Where Courage Is Like a Wild Horse
Whitye Man's Wicked Water
The Winds of Injustice
Woodland Indians of the Western Great Lakes

SUN DANCE

The Native American Sun Dance Religion & Ceremony
The Road to the Sundance
Shoshoni-Crow Sun Dance
*Sun Dance for Andy Horn
The Sun Dance Religion: Power for the Powerless
Sun Dancer
Sundancing at Rosebud & Pine Ridge

SUQUAMISH

*Brother Eagle, Sister Sky
Chief Seattle's Unanswered Challenge
How Can One Sell the Air: Chief Seattle's Vision
*Suquamish Today
Law Enforcement on Indian Reservations After
  Oliphant v. Suquamish Indian Tribes
The Wisdom of the Great Chiefs

SWEAT LODGE

The Lakota Ritual of the Sweat Lodge:
  History & Contemporary Practice
The Lakota Sweat Lodge Cards
The Native American Sweat Lodge: History & Legends

TEXTILE INDUSTRY; CLOTHING FABRICS & FOOTWEAR

American Indian Textiles: 2,000 Artist Biographies
And Eagles Sweep Across the Sky: Indian Textiles
  of the North American West
Blanket Weaving in the Southwest
Collecting the Navajo Child's Blanket
CommonThreads: Pueblo & Navajo Textiles
  in the Southwest Museum
Contemporary Navajo Weaving
Designing with the Wool
Encyclopedia of American Indian Costume
The Gift of Spiderwoman: Southwestern Textiles,
  the Navajo Tradition
Guide to Navajo Rugs
A Guide to Navajo Weavings
Historic Navajo Weaving, 1800-1900:
  Three Cultures-One Loom
Honoring the Weavers
*Indian Bead-Weaving Patterns
Indian Blankets and Their Makers
Indian Clothing of the Great Lakes, 1740-1840
Indian Designs
Indian Foods and Fibers of Arid America
Jewels of the Navajo Loom: The Rugs of Teec Nos Pos
Language of the Robe: American IndianTrade Blankets
The Navajo Design Book
Ray Manley's "The Fine Art of Navajo Weaving"
Native American Fashion: Modern Adaptations
  of Traditional Designs
Navajo Native Dyes: Their Preparation and Use
Navajo Pictorial Weaving, 1800-1950
The Navajo Rug
Navajo Rugs: How to Find, Evaluate, Buy & Care for Them
Navajo Rugs, Past & Present
Navajo Saddle Blankets: Textiles to Ride
  in the American West
Navajo Shepherd & Weaver
Navajo Textiles: The William Randolph Hearst Collection
Navajo Weavers & Silversmiths
Navaho Weaving, Its Technic & History
Navajo Weaving, Navajo Ways
Navajo Weaving: Three Centuries of Change
Navajo Weaving Today
The Navajo Weaving Tradition, 1650 to the Present
Navajo Weaving: Three Centuries of Change
Old Navajo Rugs: Their Development from 1900 to 1940
One Hundred Years of Navajo Rugs
Patterns and Sources of Navajo Weaving
Pictorial Weavings of the Navajos
Pride of the Indian Wardrobe
Pueblo Indian Textiles: A Living Tradition
Ramona Sakiestewa - Patterned Dreams:
  Textiles of the Southwest
Rugs & Posts: The Story of Navajo Weaving
Scarlet Ribbons: American Indian Technique
  for Today's Quilters
Seminole Patchwork
The Seminole Patchwork Book
The Song of the Loom: New Traditions in Navajo Weaving
Textiles in Southwestern Prehistory
Timeless Textiles: Traditional Pueblo Arts 1840-1940
Walk in Beauty: The Navajo and Their Blankets
Weaving Arts of the North American Indian
Weaving a Navajo Blanket
Weaving a World: Textiles and the Navajo Way of Seeing
Weaving of the Southwest
Woven by the Grandmothers

TLINGIT INDIANS

*Children of the Tlingit
Gagiwdulat: Brought Forth to Reconfirm The Legacy
  of a Taku River Tlingit Clan
Haa Kusteeyi, Our Culture: Tlingit Life Stories
Haa Tuwunaagu Yis, for Healting Our Spirit: Tlingit Oratory
*Heroes & Heroines in Tlingit-Haida Legends
Images of a People: Tlingit Myths & Legends
Indians of the North Pacific Coast
Memory Eternal: Tlingit Culture & Russian Orthodox
  Christianity through Two Centuries
My Grandfather's House: Tlingit Songs of Death & Sorrow
Symbolic Imortality, The Tlingit Potlatch of the 19th Century

*The Tlingit
The Tlingit: An Introduction to Their Culture & History
Tlingit Art & Culture
The Tlingit Indians
Tlingit Indians of Alaska
The Tlingit Indians: Results of a Trip to the Northwest
  Coast of America & the Bering Straits
Tlingit Verb Dictionary
Tlingit Tales: Potlatch and Totem Poles

TOHONO O'ODHAM (PAPAGO & PIMA INDIANS)

At the Desert's Green Edge: An Ethnobotany
  of the Gila River Pima
Basketry of the Papago and Pima Indians
By the Prophet of the Earth: Ethnobotany of the Pima
Desert Indian Woman: Stories & Dreams
The Desert Smells Like Rain: A Naturalist in
  O'odham Country
Devil Sickness, Devil Songs, Tohono O'odham Poetics
Folk Mammalogy of the Northern Pimans
Gathering the Desert
New Trails in Mexico
Notes on Eight Papago Songs
Ocean Power: Poems from the Desert
Of Earth and Little Rain: The Papago Indians
O'odham Creation & Related Events: As Told to
  Ruth Benedict in 1927 in Prose
A Papago Grammar
Papago Music
The Papago & Pima Indians of Arizona
Papago/Pima to English, English to Papago/Pima Dictionary
A Papago Traveler
People of the Crimson Evening
Pima Indian Basketry
Pima Indian Legends
The Pima Indians
The Pima Indians: Pathfinders for Health
The Pima-Maricopa: Southwest
Pima & Papago Ritual Oratory
A Pima Past
A Pima Remembers
Piman & Papago Ritual Oratory
Rainhouse & Ocean: Speeches for the Papago Year
The Salt River Pima-Maricopa Indians
Sharing the Desert: The Tohono O'odham in History
Singing for Power: The Song Magic of the Papago
  Indians of Southern Arizona
Sonora
Telling a Good One: The Process of a Native American
  Collaborative Biography
Tohono O'odham/Pima to English, English to Tohono
O'odham/Pima Dictionary
When It Rains: Papago & Pima Poetry

TOTEMS, TOTEMISM

Art of the Totem
Carved History: A Guide to the Totem Poles
  of Sitka National Historical Park
Eternal Ones of the Dream: Myth & Ritual,
  Dreams & Fantasies
From the Land of the Totem Poles
Haida Monumental Art
Heraldic Pole Carvers: 19th Century
  Northern Haida Artists
Looking at Totem Poles
Message of an Indian Relic: Seattle's Own Totem Pole
People of the Totem: Indians of the Pacific Northwest
The Savage and His Totem
Sculpturing Totem Poles
Tlingit Tales: Potlatch and Totem Poles
*Totem Pole
Totem Pole Carving: Bringing a Log to Life
Totem Pole Indians of the Northwest
*Totem Poles
Totem Poles: An Illustrated Guide
Totem Poles of the Northwest
Totem Poles of the Pacific Northwest Coast
*Totem Poles to Color & Cut Out, 3 Vols.
Totemism
Where the People Gather: Carving a Totem Pole
Wolf of the Raven: Totem Poles of Southeastern Alaska

TRAIL OF TEARS

After the Trail of Tears: The Cherokees' Struggle
  for Sovereignty, 1839-1880
Cherokee Legends & the Trail of Tears
The Cherokee Trail
Fort Gibson: Terminal on the Trail of Tears
Mountain Windsong: A Novel of the Trail of Tears
*Only the Names Remain: The Cherokees and the
  Trail of Tears
*The Story of the Trail of Tears
Trail of Tears
*The Trail on Which They Wept:
  The Story of a Cherokee Girl
Walking the Trail: One Man's Journey
  Along the Cherokee Trail of Tears

TRAILS

The Bozemand Trail
Indian Paths of Pennsylvania
Many Trails: Indians of the Lower Hudson Valley
Traders of the Western Morning

TRANSPORTATION

Ancient Road Networks & Settlement
  Hierarchies in the New World
California Indian Watercraft
*Indian Canoeing
The Indian and His Horse
Roads to Center Place: An Anasazi Atlas

TREATIES

The American Indian Treaty Series
The Amerian Indian Under Reconstruction
Background of the Treaty-Making in Western Washington
Behind the Trail of Broken Treaties
Chehalis River Treaty Council & the Treaty of Olympia
Cherokee By Blood
Chippewa Treaty Rights
The 1826 Chippewa Treaty with the U.S. Government
A Chronological List of Treaties & Agreements
Comanche Treaties During the Civil War
Comanche Treaties: Historical Background
Comanche Treaties of 1850, 1851 & 1853
  with the U.S. Government
Comache Treaties with the Republic of Texas
Comanche Treaty of 1846 with the U.S.
Comanche Treaty of 1835 with the U.S.
Constitution & Laws of the American Indian Tribes Series
Documents of American Indian Diplomacy
Early American Indian Documents:
  Treaties and Laws, 1607-1789
Early Treaties with the Southern Cheyenne & Arapaho
Executive Orders Establishing the Papago Reservations
Guide to the Indian Treaties and
  Other Documents 1778-1902
Historical Background to Chippewa Treaties
The History and Culture of Iroquois Diplomacy
Indian Affairs, Laws & Treaties
Indian Treaties
Indian Treaties, 1778-1883
Indian Treaties by Tribe
Indians, Superintendents, and Councils:
  Northwestern Indian Policy, 1850-1855
The Jerome Agreement Between the Kiowa,
  Comanche & Apache Tribes & the U.S.
The Kiowa Treaty of 1853
License for Empire: Colonialism by Treaty in Early America
Lone Wolf v. Hitchcock: Treaty Rights & Indian Law
  at the End of the 19th Century
The Medicine Creek Treaty of 1854
The Navajo Treaty, 1868
Northwest Chiefs: Gustav Sohon's Views
  of the 1855 Stevens Treaty Councils
The Point Elliott Treaty, 1855
The Point-No-Point Treaty, 1855
Proceedings of the Great Peace Commissions
Redskins, Ruffleshirts & Rednecks: Indian Allotments
  in Alabama & Mississippi, 1830-1860
The Spirit of the Alberta Indian Treaties
Treaties, Agreements & Proceedings of the
  Tribes & Bands of the Sioux Nation
Treaties & Agreements of the Chippewa Indians
Treaties & Agreements of the Five Civilized Tribes
Treaties & Agreements of the Indian Tribes\
  of the Great Lakes Region
Treaties & Agreements of the Indian Tribes
  of the Northern Plains
Treaties & Agreements of the Indian Tribes
  of the Pacific Northwest
Treaties & Agreements of the Indian Tribes
  of the Southwest
Treaties for the 1860s with the Southern
  Cheyenne & Arapaho
The Treaties of Puget Sound, 1854-1855
Treaty Manuscript Series
The Treaty of 1842 Between the U.S. & Chippewa Idians
The Treaty of 1836 Between the Ottawa &
  Chippewa Nations of Indians & the U.S.
The Treaty of Medicine Lodge, 1867
Treaty of Medicine Lodge: A Programmed Text
The Treaty on the Littel Arkansas River, 1865
Treaty with the Makah
Treaty with the Quinault & Quileute Indians
A True Copy of the Record of the Official Proceedings
  at the Council in the Walla Walla Valley, 1855
The U.S.-Chippewa Treaty at La Pointe, 1854
The U.S.-Seneca Treaty, 1842
The U.S. Treaty with the Sioux Brule, Oglala, et al.
U.S. Treaty with the Walla Walla
The Unratified Treaty Between the Kiowas,
  Comanches & Apaches & the U.S. of 1863
The Walleye War
Walleye Warriors
Western Washington Treaty Proceedings

TRIBAL GOVERNMENT

The Alaska Native Claims Settlement Act, 1991
  & Tribal Government
American Indian Tribal Governments
American Indian Tribal Courts: The Costs of Separate Justice
Indian Tribes of North America
Introduction to Tribal Government
*Long Shadows
The Nations Within: The Past and Future of
  American Indian Sovereignty
Native Brotherhoods: Modern Intertribal Organizations
  on the Northwest Coast
Nevada Tribal History and Government
Penitente Self-Government: Brotherhoods
  & Councils, 1797-1947
Political History of the Navajo Tribe
Political Organization and Law-Ways of the
  Comanche Indians
Political Organization of the Plains Indians
The Politics of Indian Removal: Creek Government
  and Society in Crisis
Politics and Power
The Road: Indian Tribes and Political Liberty
Tribal Government: A New Era
Tribal Government Textbook
Tribal Government Today: Politics on
  Montana's Indian Reservations
Tribal Sovereignty: Indian Tribes in U.S. History

TSIMSHIAN INDIANS

Tsimshian Culture
The Tsimshian: Images of the Past; Views for the Present
The Tsimshian & Their Neighbors of the North Pacific Coast
The Tsimshian & Their Neighbors of the Northwest Coast
Tsimshian Texts

UTE INDIANS

American Indians in Colorado
Black Hawk: An Autobiography
Black Hawk & Jim Thorpe
The Black Hawk War, 1831-1832
The Black Hawk War, Including a Review
  of Black Hawk's Life
Thje Black Hawk War, Why?
Blue Sky, Night Thunder: The Utes of Colorado
Bull Creek
The Dispossessed: Cultural Genocide
  of the Mixed-Blood Utes
Ethnography of the Northern Utes
Indians of the Pike's \Peak Region
Northern Ute Music
People of the Shining Mountains:
  The Ute Indians of Colorado
Southern Ute Indians of Early Colorado
Utah's Black Hawk War
*The Ute
The Ute Indians of Colorado in the Twentieth Century
The Ute Indians of Utah, Colorado, and New Mexico
Ute Mountain Utes
Ute Tales
*The Utes
Utes: The Mountain People

WARS — GENERAL

American Indian Wars
Americans Woodland Indians
Apache Wars
Apache Women Warriors
Ark of Empire: The American Frontier, 1784-1803
The Battle of Wisconsin Heights
The Bear River Massacre
A Brief of the Pequot War
Bury My Heart at Wounded Knee: An Indian History of the
  American West
Campaigning with King
A Cannoneer in Navajo Country
Cheyenne Dog Soldiers: A Ledgerbook
  History of Coups & Combat
*Cheyenne Warriors
Children of Sacred Ground: America's Last Indian War
Crimsoned Prairie: The Indian Wars
The Conflict Between the California
  Indian & White Civilization
Continents in Collision
Crazy Horse Called Them Walk-A-Heaps: The Story
  of the Foot Soldier in the Prairie Indian Wars
Crimsoned Prairie: The Indian Wars
Dakota War Whoop; Or, Indian Masscres
  and War in Minnesota
Deciphering Anasazi Violence
Death in the Desert: The Fifty Years' War
  for the Great Southwest
The Dust Rose Like Smoke: The Subjugation
  of the Zulu & the Sioux
Forlorn Hope: The Battle of White Bird Canyon
  & the Beginning of the Nez Perce War
The Fox Wars: The Mesquakie Challenge to New France
From Yorktown to Santiago with the Sixth U.S. Cavalry

European & Native American Warfare, 1675-1815
General Crook in the Indian Country
*The Great Chiefs
Great Western Indian Fights
A Guide to the Indian Wars of the West
Hasinai: A Traditional History of the Caddo Confederacy
History of Alabama, and Incidentally of Georgia
  & Mississippi, from the Earliest Period
History of the Indian Wars
History of the Indian Wars in New England
Indian Battles Along the Rogue River: One ofAmerica's
  Wild and Scenic Rivers
Indian Battles, Murders, Sieges, and
  Forays in the Southwest
Indian Battles and Skirmishes on the
  American Frontier, 1790-1898
Indian War Sites: A Guidebook to Battlefields,
  Monuments & Memorials
*Indian Warriors and Their Weapons
Indian Wars
Indian Wars of New England
Indian Wars of Pennsylvania
Indian Wars of the Red River Valley
Indian Wars of the West
*The Last of the Cherokee Warriors
Marquis de Mores at War in the Bad Lands
Memoir of Indian Wars & Other Occurrences
Navajo Roundup
North American Indian Wars
*North American Indian Wars
Origin Legend of the Navaho Enemy Way
Our Indian Wards
The Papers of the Order of the Indian Wars
Penhallow's Indian Wars
Plains Indian Raiders
*Plains Indian Warrior
President Washington's Indian War
Red Eagle & the Wars With the Creek Indians of Alabama
The Sac and Fox Indians
Skulking Way of War
Story of the Red Man
Tribal Wars of the Southern Plains
Vision & Valor: General Oliver O. Howard - a Biography
War in the Tribal Zone: Expanding States
  & Indigenous Warfare
The Wars of the Iroquois
The Wind Won't Know Me: A History of the
  Navajo-Hopi Land Dispute
*Wounded Knee: An Indian History of the American West

WARS, 1600-1800

Africans and Creeks: From Colonial Period to the Civil War
Ark of Empire: The American Frontier, 1784-1803
Bayonets in the Wilderness: Anthony Wayne's Legion
  in the Old Northwest
Joseph Brant: Iroquois Ally of the British
A Brief History of the Pequot War
Cheyennes & Horse Soldiers
Chronicles of Border Warfare
A Company of Heroes: The American Frontier, 1775-1783
Continents in Collision: The Impact of Europe
  on the North American Indian Societies
Empire of Fortune: Crowns, Colonies, & Tribes
  in the Seven Years War in America
*The Fight for Freedom, 1750-1783
Historical Collections of the Indians of New England
History of the Indian Wars in New England
The History of Philip's War
Indian Fighter
Indian Uprising on the Rio Grande:
  The Pueblo Revolt of 1680
Indian Wars of the West
Indians: Or Narratives of Massacres & Depredations
Journal of the Adventures of Mathew Bunn
Journals of the Military Expedition of
  Major General John Sullivan
King Philip
King Philip's War
Loudon's Indian Narratives
A Man of Distinction Among Them:
  Alexander Mckee & British-Indian Affairs
John McMurtry & the American Indian
Narratives of the Indian Wars, 1675-1699
Navajos in 1705: Roque Madrid's Campaign Journal
Notes on the Settlement & Indian Wars of the
  Western Parts of VA & PA from 1763 to 1783
The Old Indian Chronicle
On Time for Disaster
Particular History of the Five Years
  French & Indian War, 1744-1748
Penhallow's Indian Wars
The Pequot War
Present State of New England
President Washington's Indian War
The Red King's Rebellion: Racial Politics in
  New England, 1675-1677
Redeemed Captive Returning to Zion
*Mary Rowlandson and King Philip's War
St. Clair Papers
So Dreadful a Judgement: Puritan Responses
  to King Philip's War, 1667-1677

The Southern Frontier, 1670-1732
Tecumseh and the Quest for Indian Leadership
Anthony Wayne, A Name in Arms
Wept of Wish-Ton-Wish
Wilderness Empire
Winners of the West

WARS, 1800-1900

An Apache Campaign in the Sierra Madre
Apache Days & After
Archaeology, History, & Custer's Last Battle
Arikara Narrative of Custer's Campaign & the
  Battle fo the Little Bighorn
Battle of the Loxahatchee River: The Seminole War
Battle of the Little Bighorn
Battle Rock, The Hero's Story
The Battle of Wisconsin Heights
Battlefield & Classroom: Four Decades
  with the American Indian, 1867-1904
Battles & Skirmishes of the Great Sioux War, 1876-1877
The Bear River Massacre
Before the Little Big Horn
Brave Eagle's Account of the Fetterman Fight
Bury My Heart at Wounded Knee: An Indian
  History of the American West
A Cannoneer in Navajo Country: Journey
  of Private Josiah M. Rice, 1851
Cavalier in Buckskin: George Armstrong Custer
  & the Western Military Frontier
Centennial Campaign: The Sioux War of 1876
Cheyenne Memories of the Custer Fight: A Source Book
Children of Grace: The Nez Perce War of 1877
Conquest of Apacheria
The Conquest of the Karankawas & the Tonkawas,
  1821-1859
Copper Paladin: The Modoc Tragedy
Custer & the Battle of the Little Bighorn
Custer Battlefield
Custer, Black Kettle, & the Fight on the Washita
Custer & Company
Custer & Crazy Horse
Custer Died for Your Sins
Custer & the Little Bighorn
The Custer Story
The Custer Tragedy
Custer's Chief of Scout
Custer's Defeat & Other Conflicts in the West
Custer's Fall: The Native American Side of the Story
Custer's Last Battle
Custer's Last Campaign
Custer's Last Stand
Custer's Prelude to Glory
Custer's Seventh Cavalry & the Campaign of 1873
Dakota War Whoop
Death in the Desert: The Fifty Years' War
  for the Great Southwest
Death on the Prairie: The Thiry Years' Struggle
  for the Western Plains
Death, Too, For the Heavy-Runner
Discovery of the Yosemite & the Indian War of 1851
Exiles of Florida
Eyewitness at Wounded Knee
The Fighting Cheyennes
First Scalp for Custer
The Florida Wars
Following the Guidon: Into the Indian Wars with
  General Custer & the Seventh Cavalry
Following the Indian Wars
Forlorn Hope: The Battle of Whitebird Canyon
  & the Beginning of the Nez Perce War
Fort Gibson History
Fort Gibson: Terminal on the Trail of Tears
Fort Meade & the Black Hills
Forty Miles a Day on Beans & Hay: The Enlisted Soldier
Fighting the Indian Wars
Frontier Regulars: The U.S. Army & the Indian, 1866-1891
Ghost-Dance Religion and the Sioux Outbreak of 1890
A Good Year to Die: The Story of the Great Sioux War
The Great Sioux War
The Hero of Battle Rock
History of the Second Seminole War
Hokahey! A Good Day to Die! The Indian
  Casualties of the Custer Fight
I Will Fight No More Forever: Chief Joseph
  and the Nez Perce War
*The Indian as a Soldier at Fort Custer, Montana,
  1890-1895
Indian Battles Along the Rogue River, 1855-1856
Indian Battles & Skirmishes on the American Frontier,
  1790-1890
Indian Fights & Fighters
The Indian History of the Modoc War
Indian Outbreaks
The Indian War of 1864
Indian War in the Pacific Northwest
Indian Wars 1850-1890
The Iroquois in the Civil War:
  From Battlefield to Reservation
Lakota & Cheyenne: Indian Views of the
  Great Sioux War, 1876-1877
Lakota Noon: The Indian Narrative of Custer's Defeat

Lakota Recollections of the Custer Fight: New Sources
   of Indian-Military History
Last Days of the Sioux Nation
Life and Adventures of Frank Grouard
Life in Custer's Cavalry
Life of George Bent
Life of Tom Horn
Little Big Horn Diary: Chronicle of the 1876 Indian War
Little Big Horn Remembered
A Little War of Destiny
The Long Walk: A History of the Navajo Wars, 1846-1868
Man of the Plains: Recollections of Luther North, 1856-1882
Massacre!
Massacre Along the Medicine Road
The Massacre at Sand Creek: Narrative Voices
Massacre on the Gila
The Modocs and Their War
A Mohave War Reminiscence, 1854-1860
Morning Star Dawn: The Powder Ridge Expedition
   and the Northern Cheyennes, 1876
My Life on the Plains
The Mystery of E Troop
The Nebraska Indian Wars Reader, 1865-77
Old Fort Klamath
On the Border With Crook
Once They Moved Like the Wind
The Oregon Trail & the Conspiracy of Pontiac
Personal Recollection & Observations of
   General Nelson A. Miles
Pine Ridge 1890
Plains Indian Raiders
*Plains Indians Wars
Pony Tracks
Red Fox: Brig. General Stand Watie's
   Civil War Years in Indian Territory
Red Hawk's Account of Custer's Last Battle
Regulars in the Redwoods: The U.S. Army in
   Northern California, 1852-1861
The River & the Horseman
A Road We Do Not Know: A Novel of
   Custer at the Little Bighorn
Sagebrush Soldier
The Sand Creek Massacre
Sand in a Whirlwind: The Paiute Indian War of 1860
Scout and Ranger
Showdown at the Little Bighorn
The Sioux Uprising of 1862
Sitanka: The Full Story of Wounded Knee
Slim Buttes, 1876: An Episode of the Great Sioux War
Soldier, Settler, & Sioux
The Soldiers Are Coming
*The Story of Little Big Horn
The Story of the Little Big Horn: Custer's Last Fight
Swamp Sailors: Riverine Warfare in the Everglades,
   1835-1842
Tales of Apache Warfare
Taos, 1847: The Revolt in Contemporary Accounts
Tecumseh & the Shawnee Confederacy
Tenderfoot in Tombstone, the Private Journal
   of George Whitwell Parksons
Tenting on the Plains; Or, General Custer in Kansas & Texas
They Died With Custer
Through Dakota Eyes: Narrative Accounts of the
   Minnesota Indian War of 1862
Troopers With Custer
Two Great Scouts and Their Pawnee Battalion
Vast Domain of Blood
*War Clouds in the West, Indians & Cavalrymen, 1860-1890
War Eagle: A Life of General Eugene A. Carr
War-Path & Bivouac; Or, the Conquest of the Sioux
The Warren Wagontrain Raid
Washita: U.S. Army & the Southern Cheyennes, 1867-1869
Winners of the West
Without Quarter: The Wichita Expedition
Wolves for the Blue Soldiers
Wooden Leg: A Warrior Who Fought Custer
*Wounded Knee: History of the American West
The Wounded Knee Massacre:
   From the Viewpoint of the Sioux

WASHO

Beginning Washo
Straight With the Medicine: Narratives of
   Washoe Followers of the Tipi Way
The Washo Language of East Central California & Nevada
Washo Shamans & Peyotists: Religious
   Conflict in an American Indian Tribe

WOMEN

American Indian Grandmothers
American Indian Women: A Guide to Research
American Indian Women: Telling Their Lives
American Indian Women's Calendar
Apache Women Warriors
Beyond the Four Corners of the World
Black Eyes All of the Time
Blood & Voice: Navajo Women Ceremonial Practitioners
Molly Brant: A Legacy of Her Own
Buffalo Woman Comes Singing: The Spirit Song
   of a Rainbow Medicine Woman
Cartographies of Desire
Changing Woman: The Life & Art of Helen Hardin
Cherokee Women
Children At Risk
The Circle Is Sacred: A Medicine Book for Women
Claiming Breath
The Colour of Resistance: Contemporary Collection of
   Writing by Aboriginal Women
Completing the Circle
Cougar Woman
Coyote Woman
Dancing Colors: Paths of Native American Women
The Desert Is No Lady: Southwestern
   Landscapes in Women's Writing & Art
Feminist Readings of Native American Literature
From Mission to Metropolis
Engendered Encounters: Feminism &
   Pueblo Cultures, 1879-1934
A Gathering of Spirit: Writing and Art by
   North American Indian Women
*The Gift of Changing Woman
The Hidden Half: Studies of Plains Indian Women
The Indian Captivity Narrative: A Woman's View
The Indian Peoples of Eastern America:
   A Documentary History of the Sexes
Indian Women Chiefs
Indigenous American Women
Indigenous Women's Health Book, Within the Sacred Circle
Mary Jemison: White Woman of the Seneca
Keepers of the Culture: Women in a Changing World
Lakota Woman
Leaving Everything Behind
Life Among the Paiutes: Their Wrongs and Claims
Life Lived Like a Story
Madonna Swan: A Lakota Woman's Story
Many Tender Ties: Women in Fur-Trade Society, 1670-1870
Maria: The Potter of San Ildefonso
Medicine Trail: The Life & Lessons of Gladys Tantaquidgeon
Medicine Women, Curanderas, & Women Doctors
The Moccasin Maker
Molded in the Image of Changing Woman: Navajo Views
Mystery of Sacajawea: Indian Girl with Lewis & Clark
Native American Women: A Contextual Bibliography
Negotiators of Change: Historical Perspectives
   on Native American Women
No Turning Back: A Hopi Indian Woman's
   Struggle to Live in Two Worlds
Oglala Women: Myth, Ritual & Reality
Ojibwa Woman
Po Pai Mo: The Search for White Buffalo Woman
Pocahontas
Pocahontas & Co.
*Pocahontas Coloring Book
*Pocahontas: Daughter of a Chief
*Pocahontas: Girl of Jamestown
*Pocahontas: The Life & Legend
Pocahontas: Powhattan Peacemaker
Pretty Shield, Medicine Woman of the Crows
*Running Eagle: Woman Warrior of the Blackfeet
The Sacred Hoop: Recovering the Feminine
   in American Indian Traditions
Sanapia: Comanche Medicine Woman
The Scalpel & the Silver Bear:
   The First Navajo Women Surgeon
A Seminole Legend: The Life of Betty Mae Tiger Jumper
She's Tricky Like Coyote, Annie Miner Peterson, an Oregon
   Coast Indian Woman
A Song to the Creator: Traditional Art of Native American
   Women of the Plateau
Southern Cheyenne Women's Songs
Spirit Moves: The Story of Six Generations of Native Women
Molly Spotted Elk: Penobscot in Paris
Madonna Swan: A Lakota Woman's Story
Tall Woman: The Life Story of Rose Mitchell,
   A Navajo Woman @ 1874-1977
They Call Me Agnes
Through the Eye of the Deer: An Anthology of
   Native American Women Writers
To the American Indian: Reminiscences of a Yurok Woman
Turtle Lung Woman's Granddaughter
The 20th-Century Fictional American Indian Woman
   & Fellow Characters

A Voice in Her Tribe: A Navajo Woman's Own Story
Waheenee: An Indian Girl's Story
Warrior Queen of the Indian
Waterlily
The Ways of My Grandmothers
Sarah Winnemucca
Sarah Winnemucca of the Northern Paiutes
That's What She Said
Voices of American Indian Assimilation & Resistance:
   Helen Hunt Jackson, Sarah Winnemucca
   & Victoria Howard
Wisdom's Daughters: Conversations
   With Women Elders of Native America
Woman of the Green Glade
Women in History
Women in Navajo Society
Women in Prehistory
Women & Indians on the Frontier, 1825-1915
Women & Power in Native North America
Women of the Apache Nation: Voices of Truth
Women of the Dawn
Women of the Earth Lodges: Tribal Life on the Plains
Women of the First Nations
Women of the Native Struggle
Women & Power in Native North America
Wynema: A Child of the Forest
Yaqui Women: Contemporary Life Histories

YAQUI INDIANS

Autobiography of a Yaqui Poet
Chasing Shadows: Apaches & Yaquis Along the
   U.S.-Mexican Border, 1876-1911
Deer Dancer: Yaqui Legends of Life
Pascua
Pascua: A Yaqui Village in Arizona
People of Pascua
Phonology of Arizona Yaqui with Texts
Politics & Ethnicity on the Rio Yaqui
Sonora Yaqui Language Structures
With Good Heart: Yaqui Beliefs & Ceremonies
   in Pascua Village
Yaqui Deer Songs: A Native American Poetry
A Yaqui Easter
A Yaqui Life
Yaqui Myths & Legends
Yaqui Women: Contemporary Life Histories
Yuman & Yaqui Music
The Yaquis: A Celebration
The Yaquis: A Cultural History

ZUNI INDIANS

The Beautiful & Dangerous: Dialogues With the Zuni Indians
The Blue God: An Epic of Mesa Verde
The Boy Who Made Dragonfly: A Zuni Myth
Cushing at Zuni
Dialogues With Zuni Potters
Finding the Center: The Art of the Zuni Storyteller
*From Abenaki to Zuni
A Guide to Zuni Fetishes & Carvings
Historic Zuni Architecture & Society
Idonapshe, Let's Eat: Traditional Zuni Foods
Music of the Acoma, Isleta, Cochiti & Zuni Pueblos
My Adventures in Zuni
The Mythic World of the Zuni
On the Gleaming Way
People of the Middle Place: A Study of the Zuni Indians
Settlement, Subsistence & Society in Late Zuni Prehistory
Signs From the Ancestors: Zuni Cultural Symbolism
   & Perceptions of Rock Art
*Sun Journey: A Story of Zuni Pueblo
Treasures of the Zuni
The Urine Dance of the Zuni Indians of New Mexico
A Zuni Atlas
*Zuni Children & Elders Talk Together
Zuni Contemporary Pottery
Zuni Coyote tales
Zuni & El Moro: Past & Present
Zuni Fetishes
Zuni Fetishism
Zuni Folk Tales
The Zuni Indians: Their Mythology, Esoteric
   Fraternities & Ceremonies
The Zuni Indians & Their Use of Plants
Zuni Jewelry
Zuni Katchinas
Zuni Katcinas, An Analytical Study
A Zuni Life: A Pueblo Indian in Two Worlds
The Zuni Man-Woman
Zuni Pottery
Zuni: Selected Writings of Frank Hamilton Cushing
Zuni: A Village of Silversmiths
The Zunis

The following is a list of publishers whose books appear in the bibliography. Entries are arranged alphabetically, with complete zip-coded addresses and phone numbers.

A

Aardvark Publications
P.O. Box 252 • Boulder Junction, WI 54512
(715) 385-2862

Abbe Publishers Assn. of Washington DC
4111 Gallows Rd. Virginia Div.
Annandale, VA 22003 Fax (703) 642-5966

Abbeville Press
488 Madison Ave. • New York, NY 10022
(800) 278-2665 Fax (212) 644-5085

ABC-CLIO
P.O. Box 1911 • Santa Barbara, CA 93116
(800) 368-6868 Fax (805) 685-9685
E-mail: library@abc-clio.com
Web site: www.abc-clio.com

Abingdon Press
P.O. Box 801 • Nashville, TN 37202
(800) 251-3320; in TN (615) 749-6347

Harry N. Abrams
100 Fifth Ave. • New York, NY 10011
(800) 345-1359; in NY (212) 206-7715

Academic Press
6277 Sea Harbor Dr. • Orlando, FL 32887
(800) 321-5068 Fax (800) 874
Website: www.academicpress.com

Academy of American Franciscan History
P.O. Box 34440 • Bethesda, MD 20817
(301) 365-1763

Academy Chicago Publishers
213 W. Institute Pl. • Chicago, IL 60610
(800) 248-7323; (312) 751-7302

Academy of Health
811 North, 100 West 33-10
Blanding, UT 84511 (615) 662-8632

Ace Books
200 Madison Ave. • New York, NY 10016
(800) 223-0510; in NY (212) 951-8800

Acoma Books
P.O. Box 4 • Ramona, CA 92065
(619) 789-1288

Adair Reunion Assoc.
Rt. 2, Box 287, Sallisaw, OK 74955
(918) 775-5785
E-mail: maryadair@csweb.net

Addison-Wesley Educational Publishers
One Jacob Way • Reading, MA 01867
(800) 447-2226 Fax (781) 942-1117

Adler's Foreign Books
915 Foster St. • Evanston, IL 60201
(800) 433-9229; in IL (708) 866-6329

Aerial Photography Services
2511 S. Tryon St. • Charlotte, NC 28203
(704) 333-5143

Affiliated Tribes of Northwest Indians
222 N.W. Davis, #403 • Portland, OR 97209
(503) 241-0070 Fax 241-0072

Afton Historical Society
P.O. Box 100 • Afton, MN 55001
(800) 436-8443 Fax (651) 436-7354

Ahsahta Press
Boise State University • Univ. Bookstore
Boise, ID 83725 (208) 385-1404

Airmont Publishing
401 Lafayette St. • New York, NY 10003
(800) 223-5251; in NY (212) 598-0222

AIRORF
American Indian Ritual Object Repatriation Foundation
463 E. 57th St. • New York, NY 10022
(212) 980-9441 Fax 421-2746
E-Mail: circle@repatriationfoundation.org
Website: www.repatriationfoundation.org

Akwe Kon Press
American Indian Program
300 Caldwell Hall, Cornell University

Ithaca, NY 14853 (800) 962-8483
(607) 255-4308 Fax 255-0185
E-mail: native_americas@cornell.edu

Akwesasne Notes
Mohawk Nation, P.O. Box 196
Rooseveltown, NY 13683 (518) 358-9531

The Alaska Geographic Society
P.O. Box 93370 • Anchorage, AK 99509
(907) 562-0164 Fax 562-0479
E-mail: akgeo@customcpu.com

Alaska International Art Institute
26241 Foxgrove Ave. • Sun City, CA 92381

Alaska Native Language Center
University of Alaska
P.O. Box 757680 • Fairbanks, AK 99775
(907) 474-7874 Fax 474-6586
E-mail: fyanip@uaf.edu

Alaska Natural History Association
605 W. Fourth Ave.
Anchorage, AK 99501 (907) 274-8440

Alaska Northwest Books
Graphic Arts Center Publishing Co.
P.O. Box 10306 • Portland, OR 97296
(800) 452-3032 Fax (800) 355-9685
E-mail: sales@grcpc.com

Aldine de Gruyter, Inc.
200 Saw Mill River Rd.
Hawthorne, NY 10532 (914) 747-0110

Alfred Publishing Co., Inc.
P.O. Box 10003 • Van Nuys, CA 91406
(800) 292-6122 Fax (818) 891-2369

Allyn & Bacon, Inc.
200 Old Tappan Rd. • Old Tappan, NJ 07675
(800) 223-1360 Fax (800) 445-6991
Website: www.awl.com

Alta Mira Press
1630 N. Main St. #367 • Walnut Creek, CA 94596
(925) 938-7243 Fax 938-9720
Website: www.altamirapress.com

Amereon, Ltd.
P.O. Box 1200 • Mattituck, NY 11952
(516) 298-5100 Fax 298-5631

American Academy of Political & Social Science
Distributed by Sage Publications

American Antiquarian Society
Distributed by University Press of Virginia

American Association of Museum
1575 Eye St., NW, Suite 400
Washington, DC 20005 (202) 289-1818

American Bar Association
750 N. Lake Shore Dr. • Chicago, IL 60611
(312) 988-5000 Fax 988-6281

American Dietetic Association
P.O. Box 97215 • Chicago, IL 60678
(800) 877-1600 x 5000 Fax (312) 899-1757

American Federation of Arts
41 East 65th St. • New York, NY 10021
(212) 988-7700

American Friends Service Committee
1501 Cherry St. • Philadelphia, PA 19102
(215) 241-7048

American Historical Association
400 A St., SE • Washington, DC 20003
(202) 544-2422 Fax 544-8307

American Indian Archaeological Institute
P.O. Box 1260 • Washington, CT 06793
(203) 868-0518

American Indian Basketry & Other Native Arts
P.O. Box 66124 • Portland, OR 97266
(503) 233-8131

American Indian Books, Joe Thompson
10602 Forest Lawn Ct. • St. Louis, MO 63128
(314) 631-7000

American Indian Contemporary Arts
23 Grant Ave. • San Francisco, CA 94105
(415) 495-7600 Fax 495-7781

American Indian Culture Research Center
Blue Coud Abbey, P.O. Box 98
Marvin, SD 57251 (605) 432-5528

American Indian Lawyer Training Program
319 McArthur Blvd. • Oakland, CA 94610
(510) 834-9333 Fax 834-3836

American Indian Publishers
177F Riverside Ave. • Newport Beach, CA 92663

American Library Association
50 E. Huron St. • Chicago, IL 60611
(800) 545-2433 in IL (800) 545-2444

American Literary Press
8019 Belair Rd. #10 • Baltimore, MD 21236
(800) 873-2003 Fax (410) 882-7703

American Philosophical Society
P.O. Box 40098 • Philadelphia, PA 19106
(215) 440-3400

American World Geographic Publishing
P.O. Box 5630 • Helena, MT 59604
(800) 654-1105 Fax (406) 443-5480

American Press
520 Commonwealth Ave. #416
Boston, MA 02215 (617) 247-0022

Amerind Foundation
P.O Box 400 • Dragoon, AZ 85609
(602) 586-3666

Amherst Press
P.O. Box 296 • Amherst, WI 54406
(715) 824-3214

Amlex
P.O. Box 3495 • Frederick, MD 21705
(301) 694-8821vFax 694-0412
E-mail: amlex@radix.net

Amon Carter Museum
Dist. by University of Texas Press

Ancestry
P.O. Box 476 • Salt Lake City, UT 84110
(800) 262-3787 Fax (801) 426-3501

Anchor Press
Division of Doubleday & Co.

The Anchorage Historical & Fine Arts Museum
121 West 7th Ave. • Anchorage, AK 99501

Ancient City Press
Dist. by University of New Mexico Press

Anthropology Film Center Foundation,
P.O. Box 493 • Santa Fe, NM 87594
(505) 983-4127

Anthropology Resource Center
Distributed by Cultural Survival

Anza-Borrego Desert Natural History Assn.
P.O. Box 311 • Borrego Springs, CA 92004
(619) 767-3052

Apache Arts
21216 132nd Ave. SE • Kent, WA 98042
(206) 630-9774

Aperture; Distributed by Farrar, Straus & Giroux

Apollo Books
(800) 431-5003 Fax (617) 350-7818

Appalachian Consortium
University Hall, Appalachian State U.
Boone, NC 28608 (704) 262-2064

Appleton-Century-Crofts; Div. of Prentice-Hall

Applewood Books
128 The Great Rd. • Bedford, MA 01730
(800) 277-5312 Fax (781) 271-0056

Arc Press
P.O. Box 188 • Cane Hill, AR 72717
(501) 824-3821

Archive of Folk Culture
American Folklife Center
Library of Congress • Washington, DC 20540
(202) 707-6590 Fax 707-2076

Argee Publishers
4453 Manitou • Okemos, MI 48864
(517) 349-1254

Argosy
116 E. 59th St. • New York, NY 10022
(212) 753-4455

Arkansas Archaeological Survey
2475 N. Hatch Ave. • Fayetteville, AR 72704
(501) 575-6539 Fax 575-5453

Arrowfax, Inc.
102-90 Garry St. • Winnipeg, MB
Canada R3C 4H1 (800) 665-0037

Arrowstar Publishing
P.O. Box 100134 • Denver, CO 80250
(303) 715-9292

Arte Publico Press
U. of Houston • Houston, TX 77204
(800) 633-ARTE; Fax 743-2847

Artlist
2824 Chama St. NE
Albuquerque, NM 87110
(505) 881-3248

Arts & Culture of the North
Box 1333, Gracie Sq. Sta.
New York, NY 10028 (212) 879-9019

Aspen Center for Visual Arts
Dist. by Publishing Center for Cultural Resources
625 Broadway • New York, NY 10012

Associated Creative Writers
c/o Brashers, 4618 Terry Ln.
La Mesa, CA 92041 (619) 460-4107

Association for Northern California Records & Research
P.O. Box 3024 • Chico, CA 95927
(916) 895-5710

Association of American Indian Physicians
1235 Sovereign Row, Suite C-7
Oklahoma City, OK 73108
(405) 946-7072 Fax 946-7651

Association on American Indian Affairs
P.O. Box 268, Tekakwitha Complex
Agency Rd. #7 • Sisseton, SD 57262
(605) 698-3998 Fax 698-3316

Association Press
Division of Follett Press
1000 W. Washington Blvd.
Chicago, IL 60607 (312) 666-4300

Atheneum Publishers
Front & Brown Sts. • Riverside, NJ 08075
(800) 257-5755

Audio-Forum
Jeffrey Norton Publishers
96 Broad St. • Guilford, CT 06437
(800) 243-1234 Fax (888) 453-4329
E-mail: info@audioforum.com

August House
P.O. Box 3223 • Little Rock, AR 72203
(800) 284-8784 Fax (501) 372-5579
E-mail: ahinfo@augusthouse.com
Web site: www.augusthouse.com

J.J. Augustin, Publisher
123 Buckram Rd. • Locust Valley, NY 11560
(516) 676-1510

Aunt Lute Books
P.O. Box 410687
San Francisco, CA 94141
(800) 949-5883
E-mail: books@auntlute.com
Website: www..auntlute.com

Avanyu Publishing
P.O. Box 27134 • Albuquerque, NM 87125
(505) 266-6128 or 243-8485
E-mail: brentric@aol.com

Avery Publishing
120 Old Brodaway
Garden City Park, NY 11040
(800) 548-5757 Fax (516) 741-2167
E-mail: averypub@aol.com

Avon Books
P.O. Box 767 • Dresden, TN 38225
(800) 223-0690 Fax (212) 261-6895

Ayer Co. Publishers, Inc.
RR 1 Box 85-1, Lower Mill Rd.
North Stratford, NH 03590
(603) 922-5105 Fax (603) 922-3348

B

Baker Book House
P.O. Box 6287 • Grand Rapids, MI 49506
(800) 877-2665 Fax (616) 676-9573
E-mail: bakerbooks@aol.com
Web site: www.bakerbooks.com

Ballantine Publishing
Div. of Random House

Ballena Press
823 Valparaiso Ave.
Menlo Park, CA 94025 (415) 323-9261

Baltimore Museum of Art Shop
Art Museum Dr. • Baltimore, MD 21218
(301) 396-6316

Bancroft Press
27 McNear Dr. • San Rafael, CA 94901
(415) 454-7094 Fax 459-1227

Bantam/Doubleday/Dell
1540 Broadway • New York, NY 10036
orders to: 2451 S. Wolf Rd.
Des Plaines, IL 60018 (800) 323-9872
E-mail: webmaster@bdd.com
Web site: www.bdd.com

Barona Cultural Center & Museum
1095 Barona Rd. • Lakeside, CA 92040
(619) 443-7003 ext. 2 Fax 443-0173.

Barron's Educational series
250 Wireless Blvd. • Haupppauge, NY 11788
(800) 645-3476 Fax (516) 434-3723
E-mail: barrons@ barronseduc.com

Bay Press
115 W. Denny Way
Seattle, WA 98119 (206) 284-5913

Baywood Publishing Co.
P.O. Box 337 • Amityville, NY 11701
(516) 691-1270

Beacon Press; Div. of Harper & Row

Bead-Craft
P.O. Box 4563
St. Paul, MN 55104 (612) 645-1216

Beads to Buckskins
P.O. Box 296 • Hill City, KS 67642
(785) 421-2333 Fax 421-5583

Bear
P.O. Box 480005 • Denver, CO 80248

Bear & Co.
P.O. Box 2860 • Santa Fe, NM 87504
(800) 932-3277; in NM (505) 983-5968

Bear Claw Press
1407 W. Paterson St.
Flint, MI 48504 (313) 238-2569

Bear Tribe Publishing Co.
3750A Airport Blvd. #223
Mobile, AL 36608

Bedford Books

Bedford Publishers
779 Kirts • Troy, MI 48084 (313) 362-0369

Peter Bedrick Books
Dist. by Publishers Group West

Beechwood Books
Rt. 1, Box 720 • Leeds, AL 35094
(205) 699-6935

Beekman Publishers
2626 Route 212, P.O. Box 888
Woodstock, NY 12498 (888) BEEKMAN
(914) 679-2300 Fax 679-2301
E-mail: beekman@beekman.net
Web site: www.beekman.net

Bellerophon Books
36 Anacapa St. • Santa Barbara, CA 93101
(800) 253-9943 Fax (800) 965-8286

John Benjamins North America
821 Bethlehem Pike
Philadelphia, PA 19118 (215) 836-1200

Berkley Publishing; See Penguin Putnam

Berkshire Traveller Press
P.O. Box 297 • Stockbridge, MA 01262
(413) 298-3636

Bernan Publications
4611-F Assembly Dr. • Lanham, MD 20706
(800) 865-3457 Fax (800) 865-3450
Website: www.bernan.com

Beyond Words Publishing
4443 NE Airport Rd.
Hillsboro, OR 97124 (800) 284-9673
(503) 693-8700 Fax 693-6888

Biblo-Moser Booksellers & Publishers
P.O. Box 302 • Cheshire, CT 06410
(800) 272-8778 Fax (203) 250-1647

Bilingual Press
ASU - Hispanic Research Center
P.O. Box 872702 • Tempe, AZ 85287
(480) 965-3867 Fax 965-8309

Birch Lane Press/Carol Publishing
120 Enterprise Ave. • Secaucus, NJ 07094

Birmingham Public Library
2100 Park Pl. • Birmingham, AL 35203
(205) 226-3611

Bison Books
Dist. by University of Nebraska Press

Black Belt Press
P.O. Box 551 • Montgomery, AL 36101
(800) 789-7733; (800) 959-3245
(334) 265-6753 Fax 265-8880
E-Mail: info@black-belt.com
Web site: www.black-belt.com

Black Letter Press
461 Worth Rd., R.1 • Moran, MI 49760
(906) 292-5513

Black Thistle Press
491 Broadway, 6th Floor
New York, NY 10012
(888) 852-5448 Fax (212) 431-6044

Blackwell Publishers
P.O. Box 20 • Williston, VT 05495
(800) 216-2522 Fax (802) 864-7626

John F. Blair, Publisher
1406 Plaza Dr. • Winston-Salem, NC 27103
(800) 222-9796; (336) 768-1374 Fax 768-9194
E-mail: blairpub@blairpub.com
Website: www.blairpub.com

Blanche P. Browder
5133 Jeffries Rd. • Raleigh, NC 27606
(919) 851-0679

Clark Boardman Co./West Group
P.O. Box 64779 • St. Paul, MN 55164
(800) 328-4880

Boise State University
1910 University Dr. • Boise, ID 83725
(208) 385-1246

Bonanza Publishing, Ltd.
P.O Box 204 • Prineville, OR 97754
(503) 447-6909

Book Publishing Co.
P.O. Box 99 • Summertown, TN 38483
(800) 695-2241 Fax (615) 964-3518
Web site: www.nativeauthors.com

Book Sales, Inc.
114 Northfield Ave. • Edison, NJ 08837
(800) 526-7257

Bookpeople
7900 Edgewater Dr.
Oakland, CA 94621 (510) 632-4700

Borgo Press
P.O. Box 2845 • San Bernardino, CA 92406
(909) 884-5813 Fax 888-4942
E-mail: borgopr@gte.net

Boston Athnenaeum Library
10 1/2 Beacon St. • Boston, MA 02108
(617) 227-0270 Fax 227-5266

Bowman Books
2 Middle Grove Rd.
Greenfield Center, NY 12833 (518) 584-1728

Boyd & Fraser Publishing
1 Main St. • Cambridge, MA 02142 (800) 225-3782

Robert F. Brand
1029 Lake Lane • Pennsburg, PA 18073

Branden Publishing Co.
P.O. Box 843 • Brookline Village, MA 02447
(617) 734-2045 Fax 734-2046

Brevet Press
P.O. Box 1404 • Sioux Falls, SD 57101
(605) 338-7973

BridgeWater Books
Imprint of Troll Communications

Brigham Young University Press
205 UPB • Provo, UT 84602
(801) 378-2809

Bright Mountain Books
138 Springside Rd. • Asheville, NC 28803
(800) 437-3959 Fax (828) 681-1790

Brill Academic Publishing
112 Water St. #400 • Boston, MA 02109
(800) 962-4406 Fax (617) 263-2324
E-mail: brill usa@compuserve.com

Brookfield Publishing Co.
Old Post Rd. • Brookfield, VT 05036
(802) 276-3162

Brookings Institution
1775 Massachusetts Ave., NW
Washington, DC 20036 (202) 797-6250

Brooklyn Museum
Pubns-Mktg. Service
200 Eastern Pkwy. • Brooklyn, NY 11238
(718) 638-5000 ext. 308 Fax 638-3731
E-mail: bklnmus2@metgate.metro.org

Brooks Publishing
6712 NW 11th St. • Oklahoma City, OK 73127
(405) 789-5453

William C. Brown Co., Publishers
2460 Kerper Blvd. • Dubuque, IA 52001
(319) 588-1451

Brown University Press
Alumnae Hall, 194 Meeting St.
Providence, RI 02912 (401) 863-2455

Buffalo Bay Trading Co.
P.O. Box 1350 • Bayfield, WI 54814
(715) 779-3687

Buffalo Bill Historical Center
P.O. Box 1000 • Cody, WY 82414
(800) 533-3838

Buffalo Museum of Science
Publications Office, Humboldt Parkway
Buffalo, NY 14211

Burdett Design Studios
17330 Brookhurst St., Suite 300
Fountain Valley, CA 92708
(800) 634-6048; in CA (714) 897-6177

Bureau of Indian Affairs
Publications Dept.
1951 Constitution Ave., NW
Washington, DC 20242 (202) 343-7445

Bureau of Land Management
P.O. Box 27115 • Santa Fe, NM 87502
(505) 438-7400 Fax 438-7426

Burgess Publishing
7110 Ohms Lane • Edina, MN 55435
(612) 831-1344

C

CLC Press
P.O. Box 478 • San Andreas, CA 95249 (209) 369-2781

CPL Bibliographies
1313 East 60 St., Merriam Center
Chicago, IL 60637 (312) 947-2007

Cahokia Mounds Museum Society
30 Ramey St. • Collinsville, IL 62234 (618) 344-9221

California Academy of Sciences Publications
Golden State Park • San Francisco, CA 94118
(415) 221-5100

California Dept. of Education
P.O. Box 271 • Sacramento, CA 95812
(800) 995-4099 Fax (916) 323-0823

California State University, Northridge Library
18111 Nordhoff St.
Northridge, CA 91330 (818) 885-2271

Callaway Editions
70 Bedford St. • New York, NY 10014
(212) 929-5212 Fax 929-8087

Cambridge University Press
110 Midland Ave.
Port Chester, NY 10573 (800) 227-0247

Campanile Press
The San Diego State University
5189 College Ave.
San Diego, CA 92182 (619) 265-6220

**Canadian Alliance in Solidarity
With the Native Peoples**
16 Spadina Rd.
Toronto, Ontario M5R 2S7 (416) 964-0169

CCI-Canadian Circumpolar Institute
U. of Alberta • Old St. Stephen's College
3rd Fl. North, 8820 - 112 St.
Edmonton, Alberta T6G 2E2
(403) 492-4512 Fax 492-1153

Cannon Graphics, Inc.
418 Lehigh Ter. • Charleston, WV 25302
(304) 346-7602

Canyon Records Productions
4143 North 16th St. • Phoenix, AZ 85016
(602) 266-4823 Fax 265-2402

Capstone Press
P.O. Box 669 • Mankato, MN 56001
(507) 625-2746

William Carey Library Publishers
P.O. Box 40129 • Pasadena, CA 91104
(818) 798-0819

Carolrhoda Books
241 First Ave., N. • Minneapolis, MN 55401
(800) 328-4929; in MN (612) 332-3344

Caxton Printers, Ltd.
312 Main St. • Caldwell, ID 83605
(800) 657-6465; Fax (208) 459-7450

Celestial Arts Publishing Co.
P.O. Box 7327 • Berkeley, CA 94704
(800) 841-2665 in CA (415) 524-1801

Center for American Archaeology
Kampsville Archaeological Center
P.O. Box 366 • Kampsville, IL 62053
(618) 653-4316

Center for Anthropological Studies
P.O. Box 14567 • Albuquerque, NM 87191

Center for Applied Linguistics
1118 22nd St., NW • Washington, DC 20037
(202) 429-9292

Center for Applied Research in Education
P.O. Box 11071 • Des Moines, IA 50381
(800) 288-4745 Fax (515) 284-2607

Center for Archaeological Investigations
Southern Illinois University
Carbondale, IL 62901 (618) 536-5529

Center for Indigenous Arts & Cultures (CIAC) Press
P.O. Box 8627 • Santa Fe, NM 87504-8627
(505) 473-5375 Fax 424-1025
E-mail: greg@indianartbooks.com
Web site: www.indianartbooks.com

Center for International Training & Education
777 United Nations Plaza, Suite 9A
New York, NY 10017 (212) 972-9877

Center for Western Studies
Box 727, Augustana College
Sioux Falls, SD 57197 (605) 336-4007

Center of the American Indian
2100 NE 52nd St. • Oklahoma City, OK 73111
(405) 427-5228

Cherokee Books
1805 Dover Dr. • Ponca City, OK 74604
(405) 762-8517

Chelsea House Publishers
1974 Sprout Rd. #400 • Broomall, PA 19008
(800) 848-2665; Fax (610) 359-1439
E-mail: sales@chelseahouse.com
Web site: www.chelseahouse.com

Cherokee Publications
P.O. Box 430 • Cherokee, NC 28719
(704) 488-8856

Cherokee Publishing
P.O. Box 1730 • Marietta, GA 30061
(404) 424-6210

Cherokee Roots
P.O. Box 525 • Cherokee, NC 28719
(800) 732-0075 Fax (704) 497-4330

Chicago Review Press
814 N. Franklin St. • Chicago, IL 60610
(800) 888-4741 Fax (312) 337-5985
E-mail: crp@ipgbook.com

Children's Book Press
246 1st St. #101 • San Francisco, CA 94105
(415) 995-2200

Children's Press
Div. of Grolier Publishing
90 Sherman Tpke. • Danbury, CT 06816
(800) 621-1115 Fax (203) 797-3657

Chilton Book Co.
School Library Services
Chilton Way, Radnor, PA 19089
(800) 345-1214; in PA (215) 964-4729

Choctaw Heritage Press
Route 7, Box 21
Philadelphia, MS 39350 (601) 656-5251

Choctaw Museum of the Southern Indian
Mississippi Band of Choctaw Indians
Route 7, Box 21
Philadelphia, MS 39350 (601) 656-5251

Christopher Publishing House
24 Rockland St. • Hanover, MA 02339
(781) 826-7474 Fax 826-5556
E-mail: email@cphbooks.com
Web site: www.cphbooks.com

Chronicle Books
85 2nd St., 6th Fl. • San Francisco, CA 94105
(800) 722-6657 Fax (415) 537-4440
E-mail: frontdesk@chronbooks.com

Ciga Press
P.O. Box 654 • Fallbrook, CA 92028
(619) 728-9308

Cinco Puntos Press
2709 Louisville • El Paso, TX 79930
(800) 566-9072; (915) 566-9072

The CIRI Foundation
P.O. Box 93330 • Anchorage, AK 99509
(907) 274-8638 Fax 279-8836

City Lights Books
261 Columbus Ave.
San Francisco, CA 94133
(415) 362-1901 Fax 362-4921

Arthur H. Clark Co.
P.O. Box 14707 • Spokane, WA 99214
(800) 842-9286; in WA (509) 928-9540

Clear Light Publishers
823 Don Diego • Santa Fe, NM 87501
(800) 253-2747; Fax (505) 989-9519
E-mail: clpublish@aol.com
Website: www.clearlightbooks.com

Clearfield Co.
200 E. Eager St. • Baltimore, MD 21202
(410) 625-9004

Cobblestone Publishing
Div. of Pearson Education
30 Grove St., Suite C
Peterborough, NH 03458
(800) 821-0115 Fax (603) 924-7380

Columbia University Press
562 W.113th St. • New York, NY 10025
(212) 666-1000 Fax 316-9422

The Committee
2901 S. King Dr., No. 515
Chicago, IL 60616 (312) 567-9522

Common Courage Press
P.O. Box 702 • Monroe, ME 04951
(800) 497-3207

Comstock Editions
1380 W. Second Ave.
Eugene, Oregon 97402 (503) 686-8001

Concordia Publishing House
3558 S. Jefferson Ave. • St. Louis, MO 63118
(800) 325-3391/3040; (314) 664-1662

Confluence Press
Lewis-Clark State College
500 Eighth Ave. • Lewiston, ID 83501
(208) 799-2336 Fax 799-2850
E-mail: conpress@lcsc.edu

Connections Press
961 Delphi Ave. • Sheridan, WY 82801
(307) 674-6625

Cook's Books
P.O. Box 650 • Hoopa, CA 95546
(916) 625-4222

Cornell University Press
Sage House
512 E. State St. • Ithaca, NY 14850
(607) 255-5096 Fax 255-4179
E-mail: cupressinfo@cornell.edu
Web site: www.cornellpress.cornell.edu

Coronet Books
311 Bainbridge St. • Philadelphia, PA 19147
(215) 925-2762 Fax 925-1912

Corporate Resource Consultants
P.O. Box 22583 • Kansas City, MO 64113
(800) 268-2059; (816) 385-9707 Fax 9708

Costano Books
P.O. Box 355 • Petaluma, CA 94953
(707) 762-4848

Council for Indian Education
2032 Woody Dr. • Billings, MT 59102-2852
(406) 652-7598 Fax 652-0536

Council Publications
Council of Energy Resource Tribes
1999 Broadway, Suite 2600
Denver, CO 80202 (303) 297-2378

Courage Books
125 S. 22nd St. • Philadelphia, PA 19103
(800) 345-5359; Fax (215) 568-2919

Coyote Books (MN)
3926 Lillie Ct., SW • Rochester, MN 55902
(507) 288-6159

Coyote Press
P.O. Box 3377 • Salinas, CA 93912
(408) 422-4912
E-mail: coyote@coyotepress.com
Web site: www.coyotepress.com

Crabtree Publishing Co.
350 Fifth Ave. #3308 • New York, NY 10118
(800) 387-7650 Fax (800) 355-7166
E-mail: orders@crabtree-pub.com
Web site: www.crabtree-pub.com

Cranbrook Institute of Science
P.O. Box 801 • Bloomfield Hills, MI 48303
(810) 645-3256 Fax 645-3050

Crazy Horse Memorial Foundation
Black Hills, Ave. of the Chiefs
Crazy Horse, SD 57730 (605) 673-4681

CRC Publishing Co.-Eagle Rock Books
P.O. Box 222583
Kansas City, MO 64113-2583
(800) 268-2069 Fax (816) 261-2115
E-Mail: crcpub@coop.crn.org-e-mail
Web site: www.crcpub.com

Creative Education, Inc.
P.O. Box 227 • Mankato, MN 56001
(800) 445-6209; in MN (507) 388-6273

Creative Teaching Press
P.O. Box 2723 • Huntington Beach, CA 92647
(714) 895-5047 Fax 995-5173

Cross Cultural Publications
Cross Roads Books
P.O. Box 506 • Notre Dame, IN 46556
(219) 272-3321 Fax 273-5973

The Crossing Press
P.O. Box 1048 • Freedom, CA 95019
(800) 777-1048 Fax (800) 549-0020
E-mail: rossing@aol.com
Web site: www.crossingpress.com

Crossroad Publishing
Dist. by National Book Network

Crow Canyon Archaeological Center
23390 County Rd. K • Cortez, CO 81321
(800) 422) 8975; (303) 565-8975

Crown Publishers
201 E. 50th St. • New York, NY 10022
(800) 733-3000; (212) 572-6142

CSS Publishing
P.O. Box 4503 • Lima, OH 45802
(800) 241-4056 Fax (419) 228-9184

Cultural Survival, Inc.
96 Mt. Auburn St. • Cambridge, MA 02138
E-mail: csinc@cs.org. Website: www.cs.org
(617) 441-5400 Fax 441-5417

CWLA
P.O. Box 932831 • Atlanta, GA 31193
(800) 407-6273; Fax (770) 280-4160
E-mail: order@cwla.org
Website: www.cwla.org/pubs

D

Da Capo Press, Inc.
1 Jacob Way • Reading, MA 01867
(800) 242-7737 Fax (800) 822-4090
Web site: www.harpercollins.com

Dakota Press
University of South Dakota
414 E. Clark • Vermillion, SD 57069
(605) 677-5401

DaNa Publications
1050 Austin Ave. • Idaho Falls, ID 83404
(208) 523-7237

Daughters of St. Paul
50 St. Paul's Ave. • Boston, MA 02130
(617) 522-8911

David & Charles
P.O. Box 257 • N. Pomfret, VT 05053
(800) 423-4525; in VT (802) 457-1911

Dawson & Co.
P.O. Box 40157 • Tucson, AZ 85717
(602) 323-8128

Dawson's Book Shop
535 N. Larchmont Blvd.
Los Angeles, CA 90004 (213) 469-2186

DCA Publishers
6709 Esther Ave., NE
Albuquerque, NM 87109 (505) 823-2914

Delacourte Press
See Bantam/Doubleday/Dell

Dell Publishing
See Bantam/Doubleday/Dell

Demco Media
PO. Box 14260 • Madison, WI 53714
(800) 448-6764

The Denali Press
P.O. Box 021535 • Juneau, AK 99802
(907) 586-6014 Fax 463-6780
E-mail: denalipr@alaska.net
Web site: www.alaska.net/~denalipr

T.S. Denison & Co.
9601 Newton Ave. So.
Minneapolis, MN 55431
(800) 328-3831; in MN (612) 888-1460

Denver Art Museum
Publications Dept.
100 West 14th Ave. Parkway
Denver, CO 80204 (303) 575-5582

Denver Museum of Natural History
City Park • Denver, CO 80205 (303) 370-6302

Devin-Adair Publishing
P.O. Box A • Old Greenwich, CT 06870
(203) 531-7755

DeVorss & Co.
P.O. Box 550 • Marina Del Rey, CA 90294
(213) 870-7478; bookstores (800) 843-5743
in CA (800) 331-4719

Diane Publishing
601 Upland Ave. • Upland, PA 19015
(610) 499-7415 Fax 499-7429
E-mail: dianepub@erols.com
Web site: www.dianepublishing.com

Dine College Press
Tsaile, AZ 86556
(520) 724-6635 Fax 724-3327

Discovery Entperprises, Ltd.
31 Laurelwood Dr. • Carlisle, MA 01741
(800) 729-1720 Fax (978) 287-5402
E-mail: del1jbw@aol.com

Dogwood Press
HC 53, Box 345 • Hemphill, TX 75948
(409) 579-2184

Dorrance Publishing Co.
643 Smithfield St. • Pittsburgh, PA 15222
(800) 788-7654 (412) 288-1786

Doubleday See Random House

Douglas Charles Ltd.
7 Adamsdale Rd. • N. Attleboro, MA 02760
(800) 752-3769 Fax (508) 761-9347

Dover Publications
31 E. Second St. • Mineola, New York 11501
(800) 223-3130; in NY (516) 294-7000

DoveTail Books
24 Harstrom Pl. • Rowayton, CT 06853
(203) 852-1640 Fax 852-1694

Duke University Press
Durham, NC 27708
(919) 688-5134 Fax 688-5474
Web site: www.duke.edu/web/dupress/

Dumbarton Oaks
P.O. Box 4866, Hampden Sta.
Baltimore, MD 21211 (301) 338-6954

E

Eagle's View Publishing
6756 North Fork Rd. • Liberty, UT 84310
(800) 547-3364 (801) 393-4555 Fax 745-0903
E-mail: eglcrafts@aol.com

Eakin Press
P.O. Box 90159 • Austin, TX 78709
(800) 880-8642; Fax (512) 288-1813

ECS Learning Systems
P.O. Box 791437 • San Antonio, TX 78279
(800) 688-3224 Fax (830) 438-4263

Educational Impressions
P.O. Box 77 • Hawthorne, NJ 07507
(800) 451-7450 Fax (973) 423-5569

Elan Marketing
3404 S. McClintock, Suite 905
Tempe, AZ 85282 (602) 892-3033

Element Books
160 N. Washington St. • Boston, MA 02114
(800)(526-0275 Fax (617) 248-0909

Elsevier Science Publishing Co.
P.O. Box 882, Madison Sq. Sta.
New York, NY 10159 (212) 989-5800

Encino Press
510 Baylor St. • Austin, TX 78703
(512) 476-6821 Fax 476-9393

Enslow Publishers, Inc.,
P.O. Box 398 • Berkeley Hts., NJ 07922
(800) 398-2504; Fax (973) 379-7940
E-mail: enslow@enslow.com
Web site: www.enslow.com

Epicenter Press
18821 64th NE • Seattle, WA 98155
(206) 485-6822

ERIC-CRESS
Appalachian Education Laboratory, Inc.
P.O. Box 1348 • Charleston, WV 25325
(800) 624-9120 Fax (304) 347-0487

Lawrence Erlbaum Associates
10 Industrial Ave. • Mahwah, NJ 07430
(800) 926-6579 Fax (201) 236-0072

Esoterica Press
1010 Douglas Ave. Apt. 2
Las Vegas, NM 87701

Especially Books
50 Montauk Ave. • Stonington, CT 06378
(860) 535-1647 Fax 535-2049

M. Evans & Co., Inc.
216 E. 49th St. • New York, NY 10017
(212) 688-2810 Fax 486-4544
E-mail: mevans@sprynet.com

Evans Publications
P.O. Box 999 • Inola, OK 74036
(888) 873-4664 Fax (918) 543-2881

Evolution Publishing & Manufacturing
390 Pike Rd. #3 • Huntingdon Valley, PA 19006
(215) 953-5899 Fax 357-4202

Ex Machina
P.O. Box 448 • Sioux Falls, SD 57101
(605) 334-0869 Fax 339-3219

EZ Nature Books
P.O. Box 4206 • San Luis Obispo, CA 93403
(800) 455-0666; (805) 528-5292 Fax 534-0307

F

Facts on File, Inc.
11 Penn Plaza • New York, NY 10001-2006
(800) 322-8755; (212) 967-8800 Fax 967-9196
E-mail: lmilberg@factsonfile.com
Web site: www.factsonfile.com

Fairleigh Dickinson University Press
285 Madison Ave. • Madison, NJ 07940
(973) 443-8564 (phone & fax)
E-mail: fdupress@fdu.edu

Falcon Press Publishing
P.O. Box 1718 • Helena, MT 59624
(800) 582-2665; in MT (406) 442-6597

The Falmouth Institute
3702 Pender Dr. #300 • Fairfax, VA 22030
(800) 992-4489; (703) 352-2250 Fax 352-2323
Website: www.falmouthinstitute.com

Family Historian Books
404 Tule Lake Rd. • Tacoma, WA 98444
(801) 359-7391

Family History Press
5318 Chelsea St. • La Jolla, CA 92037
(619) 488-2123

Family Service America
11700 W. Lake Park Dr.
Milwaukee, WI 53224 (414) 359-2111

Fantail Native Design
c/o Pacific Science Center
200 2nd Ave., N. • Seattle, WA 98109
(204) 489-4604

Farrar, Straus & Giroux
19 Union Square W. • New York, NY 10003
(800) 638-3030 Fax (212) 633-9385

Favell Museum of Western Art & Indian Artifacts
125 W. Main • Klamath Falls, OR 97601
(503) 882-9996

Fawcett Book Group
201 East 50th St. • New York, NY 10022
(800) 733-3000; in NY (212) 751-2600

Federal Bar Association
1815 H St., NW, Suite 408
Washington, DC 20006 (202) 638-0252

Filter Press
P.O. Box 95 • Palmer Lake, CO 80133
(719) 481-2420
E-mail: filter.press@cwix.com

Firefly Books, Ltd.
P.O. Box 1325, Ellicott Station
Buffalo, NY 14205 (800) 387-5085

First Glance Books
P.O. Box 960 • Cobb, CA 95426
(707) 928-1994 Fax 928-1995

The Five Civilized Tribes Museum
Agency Hill on Honor Hts. Dr.
Muskogee, OK 74401 (918) 683-1701

Five Flower Press
369 Montezuma #254
Santa Fe, NM 87501 (505) 983-9745

Fly Eagle Publishing
3125 N. Mendenhall #422
Memphis, TN 38115
(888) 366-5247 Fax (901) 365-9430

Fogelman Publishing Co.
RD 1 Box 240 • Turbotville, PA 17772
(717) 437-3698

Formac Distributing Ltd.
5502 Atlantic St. • Halifax, NS B3H 1G4
(800) 565-1975

Four Directions Publishing
P.O. Box 24671 • Minneapolis, MN 55424
(612) 922-9322 Fax 922-7163
E-mail: eagleman4@aol.com

Four Winds Trading Co.
P.O. Box 1887 • Boulder, CO 80306
(800) 456-5444

Fox Chapel Publishing
1970 Broad St. • E. Petersburg, PA 17520
(800) 457-9112 Fax (717) 560-4702
E-mail: alan@carvingworld.com

Freshwater Press
1701 E. 12th St., Suite 3KW
Cleveland, Ohio 44114-3201 (216) 241-0373

Friendship Press
P.O. Box 37844 • Cincinnati, OH 45222
(513) 761-2100

Fulcrum Publishing
350 Indiana St. #350 • Golden, CO 80401
(800) 992-2908 Fax (800) 726-7112
E-mail: fulcrum@fulcrum-books.com
Web site: www.fulcrum-books.com

Fulton County Historical Society
Indian Awareness Center
37 E 375 N • Rochester, IN 47975
(574) 223-4436
E-mail: fchs@rtcol.com

Fun Publishing Co.
P.O. Box 2049 • Scottsdale, AZ 85252
(602) 946-2093 (phone & fax)

The Fur Press
303 Paddock • Chadron, NE 69339
(308) 665-1960 (phone & fax)

G

The Gale Group
P.O. Box 9187 • Farmington Hills, MI 48333
(800) 877-4253; (800) 414-5043
E-mail: galeord@gale.com
Web site: www.gale.com

Garland Publishing
19 Union Square West, 8th Floor
New York, NY 10003 (800) 627-6273
(212) 414-0650 Fax (212) 414-0659
E-mail: info@garland.com
Web site: www.garlandpub.com

Genealogical Institute
c/o Family History World
P.O. Box 22045 • Salt Lake City, UT 84122
(800) 377-6058 Fax (801) 250-6717
E-mail: eakle@xmission.com

Genealogical Publishing Co.
1001 N. Calvert St. • Baltimore, MD 21202
(800) 296-6687; (410) 837-8271 Fax 752-8492
E-mail: orders@genealogical.com.

General Distribution Services
85 River Rock Dr. #202 • Buffalo, NY 14207
(800) 805-1083 Fax (800) 481-6207

Geological Society of America, Inc.
P.O. Box 9140 • Boulder, CO 80301
(800) 472-1988

George Washington University
Center for Washington Area Studies
Stuart 106 • Washington, DC 20052

Georgetown University Press
Intercultural Center, Rm. 111
Washington, D.C. 20057 (202) 6687-5889

Georgia Dept. of Archives & History
330 Capitol Ave. • Atlanta, Georgia 30334
(404) 656-2393

Gibbs Smith Publishing
P.O. Box 667 • Layton, UT 84041
(800) 748-5439 Fax (800) 213-3023
info@gibbs-smith.com
Web site: www.gibbs-smith.com

Ginn Press
10 Gould St.
Needham Hts., MA 02194
(800) 428-4466; in MA (617) 455-7000

Glasco Publishing
3842 Sunrise Ave. • Allentown, PA 18103
(610) 434-4367

Glencoe Publishing
Div. of Macmillan

GLIFWC
Public Information Office
P.O. Box 9 • Odanah, WI 54861
(715) 682-6619

Global Communications
P.O. Box 753 • New Brunswick, NJ 08903
(212) 685-4080 (phone & fax)

Globe Pequot Press
P.O. Box 480 • Guilford, CT 06437
(800) 243-0440; in CT (800) 962-0973
Fax (860) 395-3069
E-mail: infoglobe/pequot.com
Web site: www.globe-pequot.com

David R. Godine Publishing
Dist. by American Int'l Distribution Corp.
P.O. Box 80 • Williston, VT 05495
(802) 878-0315

Golden West Publishing
4113 N. Longview Ave. • Phoenix, AZ 85014
(800) 658-5830 Fax (602) 279-6901
E-mail: goldwest@goodnet.com

Good Apple, Inc.
P.O. Box 182627 • Columbus, OH 43216
(800) 876-5507 Fax (614) 771-7364

Gordian Press
P.O. Box 304 • Staten Island, NY 10304
(718) 273-4700

Gordon Press Publishers
P.O. Box 459, Bowling Green Sta.
New York, NY 10004 (212) 624-8419

Government Information Services
4301 N. Fairfax Dr., Suite 275
Arlington, VA 22203 (800) 876-0226
(703) 528-1000 Fax 528-6060

Gower Publishing Co.
Old Post Rd.
Brookfield, VT 05036 (802) 276-3162

Graphic Arts Center Publishing
P.O. Box 10306
Portland, OR 97210 (800) 452-3032
Fax (503) 223-1410

Graphic Impressions
44 Monroe St. • Denver, CO 80206
(303) 458-7475

Great Eagle Publishing
3020 Issaquah-Pine Lake Rd. SE, Suite 481
Issaquah, WA 98029
(206) 392-9136 Fax 391-7812

Great Outdoors Publishing
4747 28th St. North
St. Petersburg, FL 33714 (800) 869-6609
(727) 525-6609 Fax 527-4870

Great Plains Network
P.O. Box 482 • Chadron, NE 69337
(308) 432-5063 Fax 432-6464

Great Quotations
1967 Quincy Ct. • Glendale Hts., IL 60139
(800) 354-4889 Fax (630) 582-2813

Greatland Graphics
P.O. Box 100333 • Anchorage, AK 99510
(907) 337-1234 Fax 337-4567

Green Valley Area Education Agency
1405 N. Lincoln • Creston, IA 50801
(515) 782-8443

Greenfield Press
P.O. Box 176
Southport, CT 06490 (203) 268-4878

Greenfield Review Literary Center
P.O. Box 308 • Greenfield Center, NY 12833
(518) 583-1440 Fax 583-9741
E-Mail: asban@aol.com

Greenhaven Press
P.O. Box 289009 • San Diego, CA 92198
(800) 231-5163 Fax (619) 485-9549

Greenwillow Books
Div. of William Morrow & Co.

Greenwood Publishing
88 Post Rd., W., Box 5007
Westport, CT 06881 (203) 226-3571

Grey Art Gallery Study Center
N.Y.U., 33 Washington Pl.
New York, NY 10003 (212) 998-6780

Griffon House Publications
1401 Pennsylvania Ave., Suite 105
Wilmington, DE 19806 (302) 656-3230
E-mail: griffonhse@aol.com

Gros Ventre Treaty Committee
Fort Belknap Agency
P.O. Box 1294 • Harlem, MT 59526

Grove-Atlantic, Inc.
841 Broadway, 4th Floor
New York, NY 10003
(800) 521-0178 Fax (212) 614-7886

H

Paul Hacker Knives & Flutes
6513 N.W. 20th Dr. • Bethany, OK 73008
(405) 787-8600 (phone & fax)

Hafner Press
Div. of Macmillan

G.K. Hall & Co.
Div. of Macmillan

Raven Hail Books
P.O. Box 804 • Mesa, AZ 85211
(602) 898-7530

Hampton Chiles
1221 Cloncurry Rd. • Norfolk, VA 23505
(757) 423-5466

Hancock House Publishers
1431 Harrison Ave. • Blaine, WA 98231
(800) 938-1114 Fax (800) 983-2262
Web site: www.hancockwildlife.org

Hanging Loose Press
231 Wyckoff St. • Brooklyn, NY 11217
(718) 643-9559

Harbinger House, Inc.
P.O. Box 42948 • Tucson, AZ 85733
(800) 759-9945 Dist. by Mountain Press

Harbour Books
147 Armstrong • Claremont, CA 91711
(909) 399-0204

Harcourt Brace College Publishers
6277 Sea Harbor Dr. • Orlando, FL 32887
(800) 782-4479

Hardscrabble Books
10735 Jones Rd. • Berrien Springs, MI 49103
(616) 473-5570

Harlan Davidson
773 Glenn Ave. • Wheeling, IL 60090
(847) 541-9720 Fax 541-9830

Harlo Press
50 Victor Ave. • Detroit, MI 48203
(313) 883-3600

Harmsen Publishing
3131 E. Alameda Ave.
Denver, CO 80209 (303) 777-4030

Harper & Row
1000 Keystone Industrial Park
Scranton, PA 18512
(800) 242-7737; Fax (800) 822-4090

HarperCollins; Div. of Harper & Row

Harrow & Heston Publishers
P.O. Box 3907, Albany, NY 12203
(518) 456-4894
E-mail: harowhest@aol.com

Harvard University Press
79 Garden St. • Cambridge, MA 02138
(617) 495-2600 Fax 495-5898
E-mail: lulu@hup.harvard.edu
Web site: www.hup.harvard.edu

Haskell Booksellers
P.O. Box 420, Blythebourne Sta.
Brooklyn, NY 11219 (718) 435-7878

Havasupai Tribal Council
P.O. Box 10 • Supai, AZ 86435
(602) 448-2731 Fax 448-2551

Haworth Press
10 Alice St. • Binghamton, NY 13904
(800) 429-6784 Fax (607) 722-3487

Heart of the Lakes Publishing
P.O. Box 299
Interlaken, NY 14847 (800) 782-9687
(607) 532-4997 FAX 532-4684

The Heard Museum
22 E. Monte Vista Rd. • Phoenix, AZ 85004
(602) 252-8840 fax 252-9757

William S. Hein & Co.
1285 Main St. • Buffalo, NY 14209
(800) 828-7571 Fax (716) 883-8100
E-mail: mail@wshein.com

T. Emmett Henderson
130 W. Main St. • Middletown, NY 10940
(914) 343-1038 (phone & fax)

Hendrick-Long Publishing
P.O. Box 25123 • Dallas, TX 75225
(800) 544-3770

Hendry Publications
Lost Cabin Route • Lysite, WY 82642
(307) 876-2647

Heritage Books, Inc.
1540 E. Pointer Ridge Pl.
Bowie, MD 20716
(800) 398-7709 Fax (800) 276-1760

Heritage Publishers, Inc.
2700 Woodlands Blvd.
Flagstaff, AZ 86001 (602) 526-1129

Heritage Quest
P.O. Box 40 • Orting, WA 98360
(800) 442-2029

Heritage Research
Box 210961 • Auke Bay, AK 99821
(907) 789-3311 Fax 789-3434
E-mail: wmolson@ptialaska.net

Herodias
346 First Ave. • New York, NY 10009
(800) 426-1049 Fax (718) 621-4933
E-mail: greatblue@acninc.net
Web site: www.herodias.com

Hewitt Research Foundation
P.O. Box 9 • Washougal, WA 98671
(800) 348-150 Fax (360) 835-8697

Heyday Books
P.O. Box 9145 • Berkeley, CA 94709
(510) 549-3564 Fax 549-1889
E-mail: heyday@heydaybooks.com

Higginson Book Co.
P.O. Box 778 • Salem, MA 01970
(978) 745-7170 Fax 745-8025
E-mail: higginsn@cove.com
Web site: www.higginsonbooks.com

High-Lonesome Books
P.O. Box 878 • Silver City, NM 88062
(800) 380-7323 Fax (505) 388-5705
E-mail: high-lonesomebooks@zianet.com
Web site: www.high-lonesome books.com

Hill & Wang
Div. of Farrar, Straus & Giroux

Hillsdale Educational Publishers, Inc.
39 North St., Box 245
Hillsdale, MI 49242 (517) 437-3179

Hippocrene Books
171 Madison Ave. • New York, NY 10016
(718) 454-2366 Fax 454-1391
E-mail: orders@hippocrenebooks.com
Web site: www.hippocrenebooks.com

Historic Pensacola Preservation Board
Distributed by John C. Pace Library
University of West Florida
Pensacola, FL 32504 (904) 476-9500

Historical Research & Mapping
P.O. Box 31235 • Santa Fe, NM 87594 (505) 984-3183

Hobbs, Straus, Dean & Walker, LLP
Publications Dept.
851 S.W. Sixth Ave., Suite 1650
Portland, OR 97204 (503) 242-1745
E-mail: publications@hsdwdc.com
Website: www.hsdwlaw.com/publications.htm

Holiday House
425 Madison Ave. • New York, NY 10017
(212) 688-0085 Fax 421-6134

Holitopa
P.O. Box 12721 • Oklahoma City, OK 73157
(405)842-8226

Holloway House Publishing
Dist. by All America Distributors
8431 Melrose Pl. • Los Angeles, CA 90069
(213) 651-2650

Holmgangers Press
95 Carson Court, Shelter Cove
Whitehorn, CA 95489 (707) 986-7700

Henry Holt & Co.
123 W. 18th St. • New York, NY 10011
(212) 387-9100 Fax 633-0748
Web site: www.henryholt.com

Holt-Atherton Center for Western Studies
University of the Pacific
Stockton, CA 95211 (209) 946-2404

Holt, Rinehart & Winston
see Harcourt Brace

Holy Cow! Press
Box 3170, Mt. Royal Station
Duluth, MN 55803 (218) 724-1653

Hood Museum of Art
Dartmouth College • Hanover, NH 03755
(603) 646-2808 Fax 646-1400

Hothem House
P.O. Box 458 • Lancaster, OH 43130
(740) 653-9030 Fax 653-2262
E-mail: shothem@greenapple.com

Houghton Mifflin
181 Ballardvale St. • Wilmington, MA 01887
(800) 225-3362

Housing Assistance Council
1025 Vermont Ave., NW Suite 606
Washington, DC 20005
(202) 842-8600 Fax 347-3441
E-mail: hac@ruralhome.org

Howard University Press
2900 Van Ness St., N.W.
Washington, DC 20008 (202) 686-6696

Howe Brothers
P.O. Box 6394 • Salt Lake City, UT 84106
(800) 426-5387

HRAF Press
Human Relations Area Files Press
P.O. Box 2015, Yale Station
New Haven, CT 06520 (203) 777-2337

Hudson Hills Press
Dist. by Rizzoli International Publications

Humanities Press International
171 First Ave. • Atlantic Highlands, NJ 07716
(800) 221-3845

Hunter Publishing
Dist. by Many Feathers Books & Maps
5738 N. Central Ave. • Phoenix, AZ 85012
(602) 266-1043

I

IBD Ltd.
24 Hudson St. • Kinderhook, NY 12106
(800) 343-3531 Fax (518) 758-6702

Idaho Museum of Natural History
Campus Box 8096, Idaho State University
Pocatello, ID 83209 (208) 236-3168

Illinois State Historical Library
Old State Capitol
Springfield, IL 62701 (217) 782-4836

Illinois State Museum Society
Spring & Edwards • Springfield, IL 62706
(217) 782-7386

Independence Press
P.O. Box HH, 3225 S. Noland Rd.
Independence, MO 64055
(800) 821-7550; in MO (816) 252-5010

Independent Publishers Group
814 N. Franklin St. • Chicago, IL 60610
(800) 888-4741

Indian Arts & Crafts Association
122 La Veta NE • Albuquerque, NM 87108
(505) 265-9149

Indian Arts & Crafts Board
USDI, 1849 C St., NW, MS: 2058 MIB
Washington, DC 20240 (888) ART-FAKE
(202) 208-3773 Fax 208-5196

Indian Bibliographic Center
University of Arkansas
P.O. Box 1201 • Fayetteville, AR 72202

Indian Chief Publishing House
P.O. Box 5205 • Tahoe City, CA 95730
(916) 583-8054

Indian Country Communications, Inc.
Route 2, Box 2900-A • Hayward, WI 54843
(715) 634-5226 Fax 634-3243

Indian Heritage Publishing
Box 2302, Henry St.
Moristown, TN 37816 (615) 581-4448

Indian Historian Press
1493 Masonic Ave.
San Francisco, CA 94117 (415) 626-5235

Indian Resource Development
Box 30003, Dept. 3IRD
New Mexico State University
Las Cruces, NM 88003 (505) 646-1347

Indian University Press
Bacone College, 2299 Old Bacone Rd.
Muskogee, OK 74403 (918) 683-4581

Indiana Historical Society
315 W. Ohio St., Rm. 350
Indianapolis, IN 46202
(317) 232-1882 Fax 233-3109

Indiana University Press
Tenth & Morton Sts.
Bloomington, IN 47403 (812) 335-4203

Indigenous Women's Press
P.O. Box 572 • Lake Andes, SD 57356
(605) 487-7072 Fax 487-7964
Website: www.nativeshop.org

Inner Traditions International, Ltd.
1 Park St. • Rochester, VT 05767
(800) 246-8648 Fax (802)767-3726
E-mail: orders@gotoit.com
Web site: www.gotoit.com

Institute for the Development of Indian Law
Oklahoma City U., School of Law
2501 N. Blackwelder • Oklahoma City, OK 73106
(405) 531-5337

Institute for Research in Social Sciences
University of North Carolina, 026A Manning Hall
Chapel Hill, NC 27514 (919) 962-3204

Institute of Alaska Native Arts
P.O. Box 70769 • Fairbanks, AK 99707
(907) 456-7491

Integrated Education Associates
U. of Massachusetts, School of Education
Amherst, MA 01003 (413) 545-0327

Inter-Tribal Indian Ceremonial Association
P.O. Box 1 • Church Rock, NM 87311
(505) 863-3896

International Publishers
239 West 23 St. • New York, NY 10011
(212) 366-9816 Fax 366-9820

International Specialized Book Services
5602 NE Hassalo St.
Portland, OR 97213-3640
(800) 547-7734; in OR (503) 287-3093

International Universities Press
P.O. Box 1524
Madison, CT 06443 (203) 245-4000

Iowa State University Press
2121 S. State Ave. • Ames, IA 50010 (515) 294-5280

Irvington Publishers
Box 286, Cooper Sta. • New York, NY 10276
(800) 472-6037 Fax (212) 861-0998

ISAC Press
Institute for the Study of American Culture
P.O. Box 2707 • Columbus, GA 31902
(404) 571-2102 Fax 571-2650

Island Press Publishers
175 Bahia Via • Ft. Myers Beach, FL 33931
(813) 463-9482 Fax 463-9482

ITEPP CRC
Humboldt State University
Arcata, CA 95521 (707) 826-5199
Website: www.humboldt.edu/~hsuitepp/crc

J

Jefferson National Expansion Historical Assn.
11 N. 4th St.
St. Louis, MO 63102

Jelm Mountain Publications
471 Highway 10
Jelm, WY 82063 (307) 721-5058

Johns Hopkins University Press
701 W. 40th St., Suite 275
Baltimore, MD 21211
(800) 537-5487; in MD (301) 338-7864

Johnson Books
1880 S. 57th Ct. • Boulder, CO 80301
(800) 258-5830 Fax (303) 443-1679

Johnson Publishing
820 S. Michigan Ave.
Chicago, IL 60605 (312) 322-9248

Johnson Publishing Co.
405 Union St. • Murfreesboro, NC 27855

Johnston Publishing
P.O. Box 96 • Afton, MN 55001
(612) 436-7344

Joslyn Art Museum
Dist. by University of Nebraska Press

JTE Associates
1800 Lexington Dr. • Fullerton, CA 92635
(714) 447-9293

K

KC Publications
P.O. Box 98118 • Las Vegas, NV 89193
(800) 626-9673; (702) 433-3415 Fax 456-5334

KMG Publications
290 E. Ashland Lane
Ashland, OR 97520 (503) 488-1302

Kalmbach Publishing
21027 Crossroads Circle
Waukesha, WI 53187 (800) 558-1544
in WI (414) 796-8776 Fax 796-1615

Kansas State Historical Society
6425 S.W. 6th Ave.
Topeka, KS 66615 (913) 272-8681

Karo Hollow Press
P.O. Box 1942 • Southern Pines, NC 28388
(910) 944-9744

Katonah Gallery
28 Bedford Rd.
Katonah, NY 10536 (914) 232-9555

Augustus M. Kelley, Publishers
1140 Broadway, # 901 • New York, NY 10001
(212) 685-7202

Kennebec River Press
Dist. by Harpswell Press
132 Water St. • Gardiner, ME 04345
(207) 582-1899

Kent State University Press
P.O. Box 5190 • Kent, OH 44242
(800) 247-6553 Fax (330) 672-3104

Kessinger Press
P.O. Box 160 • Kila, MT 59920
(406) 756-0167 Fax 257-5051

Jessica Kinglsey
Dist. by Taylor & Francis

Kiva Publishing
21731 E. Buckskin Dr. • Walnut, CA 91789
(800) 634-5482 Fax 909) 860-5424
E-mail: kivapub@aol.com

Kivaki Press
585 East 31st St. • Durango, CO 81301
(800) 578-5904; (303) 385-1767 Fax 385-1974

Kluwer Academic Publishers
P.O. Box 358, Accord Sta.
Hingham, MA 02018-0358 (617) 871-6600

Alfred A. Knopf; Div. of Random House

Knowledge Unlimited
P.O. Box 5222 • Buffalo Grove, IL 60078
(312) 358-4795

Krause Publications
700 E. State St. • Iola, WI 54990
(800) 258-0929; (715) 445-2214 Fax 445-4087
E-mail: info@kraus.com
Website: www.krause.com

Krieger Publishing Co.
P.O. Box 9542 • Melbourne, FL 32902-9542
(407) 724-9542 Fax 951-3671

L

Landfall Press, Inc.
5171 Chapin St. • Dayton, OH 45429
(937) 298-9123

Peter Lang Publishing
275 Seventh Ave. • New York, NY 10001
(800) 770-5264; Fax (212) 647-7707

Lantern Press
6214 Wynfield Ct. • Orlando, FL 32819
(407) 876-7720 Fax 876-7758

League of Women Voters of the U.S.
1730 M St., NW • Washington, DC 20036
(202) 429-1965 Fax 429-0854

Learning Connection
P.O. Box 518 • Frostproof, FL 33843
(800) 338-2282 Fax (941) 635-4676

Leetes Island Books
Dist. by Independent Publishers Group
814 N. Franklin • Chicago, IL 60610 (312) 337-0747

Lerner Publications
1251 Washington Ave. N.
Minneapolis, MN 55401
(800) 328-4929 Fax (800) 332-1132
Web site: www.lernerbooks.com

Levin Associates
Dist. by Simon & Schuster

Levite of Apache Publishing
203 Hal Muldrow Dr., Suite 3
Norman, OK 73069 (405) 366-6442

LEXIS Law Publishing
P.O. Box 7587 • Charlottesville, VA 22906
(800) 446-3410; Fax (800) 643-1280
E-mail: custserv@michie.com
Web site: lexislawpublishing.com

Libraries Unlimited, Inc.
P.O. Box 6633 • Englewood, CO 80155
(800) 237-6124 Fax (303) 220-8843
E-mail: lu-books@lu.com

Library of America
14 E. 60th St. • New York, NY 10022
(212) 308-3360 Fax 750-8352

Library of Congress
Motion Picture, Broadcasting & Recorded Sound Division
Washington, DC 10540-4800
(202) 707-5840 Fax 707-2371

Library of Congress/GPO
101 Independence Ave.
Washington, DC 20540 (202) 512-1800

Library Research Associates
474 Dunderberg Rd., RD 6
Box 41 • Monroe, NY 10950
(800) 914-3379 Fax (914) 362-8376
E-mail: irainc@frontiernet.net

Lift Every Voice
16 Park Ln. • Newton Centre, MA 02459
(617) 244-9808 Fax 964-5432
E-mail: liftever@aol.com
Web site: www.qis.net/~liftever/

Lime Rock Press
Mt. Riga Rd., Box 363
Salisbury, CT 06068 (860) 435- 2236

Limestone Press
Dist. by University of Alaska Press

Lion's Head Publishing Co.
2436 S. U.S. 33
Albion, IN 46701 (219) 635-2165

J.B. Lippincott & Co.
E. Washington Sq.
Philadelphia, PA 19105
(800) 242-7737; in PA (800) 982-4377

Little, Brown & Co.
3 Center Plaza • Boston, MA 02108
(800) 759-0190 Fax 286-9471

Little People Publications
c/o The Mohegan Tribe
67 Sandy Desert Rd. • Uncasville, CT 06382
(860) 204-6107 Fax (704) 848-6115

Little Red Hen, Inc.
P.O. Box 4260 • Pocatello, ID 83201
(208) 233-3755 Fax 233-4083

Liveright Publishing
Dist. by W.W. Norton & Co.

Lomond Publications
P.O. Box 88 • Mt. Airy, MD 21771
(800) 443-6299; Fax (301) 694-5151
E-mail: kesson@msn.com

The Lone Star Connection
P.O. Box 0416 • Lone Star, TX 75668
(903) 656-2985

Longman, Inc.
10 Bank St. • White Plains, NY 10606
(914) 993-5000 (800) 552-2259 or 322-1377

Loose Cannon Press
598 Shore Rd. • Cape Elizabeth, ME 04107

Lost Classics
P.O. Box 1756 • Fort Collins, CO 80522
(970) 493-3793; Fax (888) 211-2665

Louisiana State University Press
Baton Rouge, LA 70893 (504) 388-6666

The Lowell Press
P.O. Box 411877 • Kansas City, MO 64141
(800) 736-7660 Fax (816) 753-4057

Lucent Books
10911 Technology Pl. • San Diego, CA 92127
(800) 231-5163 Fax (619) 485-9549

Lyons Press
123 W. 18th St. • New York, NY 10010
(800) 836-0510 Fax 212) 929-1836
E-mail: lporders@aol.com

M

Mackinac Island State Park Commission
P.O. Box 370 • Mackinac Island, MI 49757
(906) 847-3328 Fax (517) 373-4790

MacRae Publications
P.O. Box 652 • Enumclaw, WA 98022 (360) 825-3737

Madison Books
Subs. of University Press of America
Dist. by National Book Network
4720A Boston Way • Lanham, MD 20706
(800) 462-6420 Fax (301) 459-2118

Magi Books
Dist. by St. Bede's Publications
P.O. Box 9345 • Framingham, MA 01701
(800) 507-1000 Fax (800) 919-5600

Magpie Publications
P.O. Box 636 • Alamo, CA 94507
(800) 624-7435 Fax (925) 838-9287

Maine Historical Society
485 Congress St. • Portland, ME 04111
(207) 774-1822

Maine State Museum Publications
State House Sta. 83 • Augusta, ME 04333
(207) 289-2301 Fax 287-6633

Maine Studies Committee
University of Maine, PICS Bldg.
Orono, Maine 04469 (207) 581-1700

Makah Cultural & Research Center
Makah Indian Tribe
P.O. Box 115 • Neah Bay, WA 98357
(360) 645-2201 Fax 645-2788

Malki Museum Press
11-795 Fields Rd.
Morongo Indian Reservation
Banning, CA 92220 (909) 849-7289

Manitoba Museum of Man and Nature
Education Office, 190 Ruper Ave.
Winnipeg, Manitoba R3B 0N2 Canada

Mankind Publishing
8060 Melrose Ave. • Los Angeles, CA 90046
(213) 653-8060 Fax 655-9452
E-mail: psi@loop.com

Marlowe & Company
632 Broadway, 7th Floor
New York, NY 10012
(212) 460-5742 Fax 460-5796
Web site: www.marlowepub.com

Marquette County Historical Society
213 N. Front St. • Marquette, MI 49855
(906) 226-3571

Marshall Cavendish Corp.
99 White Plains Rd.
P.O. Box 2001 • Tarrytown, NY 10591
(800) 821-9881 Fax (914) 332-1888

Maryland Historical Press
9205 Tuckerman St. • Lanham, MD 20706
(301) 577-5308 Fax 577-8711

Marshall Cavendish Corp.
P.O. Box 2001 • Tarrytown, NY 10591
(800) 821-9881 Fax (914) 332-1888

Maverick Publications
P.O. Box 5007 • Bend, OR 97708
(503) 382-6978 Fax 382-4831

Maxwell Museum of Anthropology
University & Ash, NE • Albuquerque, NM 87131
(505) 277-4404

McDonald & Woodward Publishing Co.
325 Dorrence Rd. • Granville, OH 43023
(800) 233-8787
Web site: www.mwpubco.com

McFarland & Co. Publishers
P.O. Box 611 • Jefferson, NC 28640
(800) 253-2187; (910) 246-4460 Fax 246-5018

McGraw-Hill Book Co.
Princeton Rd. • Hightstown, NJ 08520
(609) 426-5254; or 8171 Redwood Highway,
Novato, CA 94947; or 13955 Manchester Rd.
Manchester, MO 63011; (800) 262-4729
(retail); (800) 338-3987 (college);
(800) 722-4726 (consumer)

David McKay Co.
Orders to Random House
400 Hahn Rd., Westminster, MD 21157
(800) 733-3000; (800) 726-0600

Nan McNutt & Associates
Dist. by Pacific Pipeline, Inc.
19215 66th Ave. S. • Kent, WA 98032
(206) 872-5523 in WA (800) 562-4647
in NV, MT, ID, OR, & no. CA (800) 426-4727

Meadowlark Communications
P.O. Box 7218 • Missoula, MT 59807 (888) 728-2180
(406) 728-2180 Fax 549-3090
E-mail: info@powwowcountry.com
Web site: www.powwowcountry.com

Edwin Mellon Press
415 Ridge St. • Lewiston, NY 14092
(716) 754-2788 Fax 754-4056
E-mail: mellon@ag.net
Web site: www.mellon.com

MEP Publications
University of Minnesota
Physics Bldg., 116 Church St., SE
Minneapolis, MN 55455
(612) 922-7993 Fax 624-4578

Merryant Publishers
7615 SW 257th St. • Vashon, WA 98070
(800) 228-8958 Fax (206) 463-1604

Metropolitan Museum of Art
Orders to: Special Services Office
Flushing, NY 11381 (718) 326-7050

Meyer Creative Productions
208 N. 4th St., Box 1738
Bismarck, ND 58502 (800) 637-6863

The Michie Co.; See LEXIS

Michigan Indian Press
523 Ashmun St. • Sault Ste. Marie, MI 49783
(906) 635-6050 Fax 635-4969
E-mail: qadmin7@northernway.net
Web site: www.legislativeimpact.com/book.htm

Michigan State University Press
1405 S. Harrison Rd., 25 Manly Miles Bldg.
East Lansing, MI 48824 (517) 355-9543
Fax (800) 678-2120; (517) 336-2611

Middle Atlantic Press
714 Interchange Blvd.
Newark, DE 19711
(302) 455-9382 Fax 654-9819

Millbrook Press
2 Old New Milford Rd.
Brookfield, CT 06804 (800) 462-4703
(203) 740-2220 Fax 740-2223

Milwaukee Public Museum
800 W. Wells St. • Milwaukee, WI 53233
(414) 278-2787

Minnesota Historical Society Press
345 Kellogg Blvd. West
St. Paul, MN 55102 (800) 647-7827
(651) 296-2264 Fax 297-1345

Minnesota Humanities Commission
987 Ivy Ave. E. • St. Paul, MN 55106
(612) 224-5739

Minnetrista Cultural Center
1200 N. Minnetrista Pkwy.
Muncie, IN 47303
(765) 282-4848 Fax 741-5110

Mississippi Dept. of Archives & History
P.O. Box 571 • Jackson, MS 39205
(601) 359-6850 Fax 359-6975

Modern Language Assn. of America
10 Astor Pl. • New York, NY 10003
(212) 475-9500

Moh-He-Con-Nuck
6145 Lehman Dr. #200
Colorado Springs, CO 80918
(619) 283-1669 Fax 283-4135

Monacelli Press
10 E. 92nd St. • New York, NY 10128
(212) 831-0248 Fax 410-2059

Monroe County Library System
3700 S. Custer Rd. • Monroe, MI 48161 (313) 241-5277

Montana Historical Society Press
225 N. Roberts St. • Helena, MT 59620
(406) 444-4708

Monthly Review Press
122 West 27th St. • New York, NY 10001
(212) 691-2555

Moody Press
820 N. LaSalle Dr. • Chicago, IL 60610
(800) 621-5111; in IL (800) 621-4323

Morgan & Morgan
145 Palisade St. • Dobbs Ferry, NY 10522
(914) 693-0023

Morning Flower Press
P.O. Box 114433 • Denver, CO 80211
(303) 477-8442

Morning Star Gallery
513 Canyon Rd. • Santa Fe, NM 87501
(505) 982-8187 Fax 984-2368
E-mail: indian@morningstargallery.com

William Morrow & Co.
Wilmor Warehouse
P.O. Box 1219, 39 Plymouth St.
Fairfield, NJ 07007 (800) 843-9389

Mountain Press
P.O. Box 2399 • Missoula, MT 59806
(800) 234-5308; (406) 728-1900 Fax 728-1635
E-mail: mtnpress@montana.com

Mouton de Gruyter
200 Saw Mill River Rd. • Hawthorne, NY 10532
(914) 747-0110 Fax 747-1326

Mulder Enterprises
P.O. Box 320935 • Tampa, FL 33679
(813) 837-6325 Fax 805-2707

H.L. Murvin Publisher
500 Vernon St. • Oakland, CA 94610 (415) 658-7517

Museum of Fine Arts
465 Huntington Ave.
Boston, MA 02115 (617) 267-9300

Museum of the Great Plains
Publications Dept., 601 Ferris, Box 68
Lawton, OK 73502 (405) 353-5675

Museum of New Mexico Press
P.O. Box 2087 • Santa Fe, NM 87504
(505) 827-6454

Museum of Northern Arizona
Rte. 4, Box 720 • Flagstaff, AZ 86001
(602) 774-5211

Museum of Ojibwa Culture
500 N. State St. • St. Ignace, MI 49781
(906) 643-9161

Museum of the Plains Indian
P.O. Box 400 • Browning, MT 59417

Myrin Institute
136 E. 64th St. • New York, NY 10021
(212) 758-6475

N

NAES College
2838 W. Peterson Ave. • Chicago, IL 60659
(773) 761-5000 Fax 761-3808
E-mail: davenaes@aol.com
Website: www.naes.indian.com

NCJW, Inc.
53 W. 23rd St. • New York, NY 10010
(212) 532-1740

National Academy Press
Publications Sales Office
2101 Constitution Ave., NW
Washington, DC 20418 (800) 624-6242

National Archives & Records Administration
Publications Division
Seventh St. & Pennsylvania Ave, NW, Rm. G9
Washington, DC 20408 (202) 523-5611

National Book Co.
Div. of Educational Research Center
P.O. Box 8795 • Portland, OR 97207
(503) 228-6345

National Book Network
P.O. Box 62045 • Baltimore, MD 21264
(800) 462-6420 Fax (800) 338-4550
E-mail: custserv@nbnbooks.com
Web site: nbnbooks.com

National Center for State Courts
300 Newport Ave. • Williamsburg, VA 23187
(804) 253-2000

National Clearinghouse for Bilingual Education
8737 Colesville Rd., Suite 900
Silver Spring, MD 20910-3921 (800) 647-0123

National Conference of State Legislatures
Book Order Dept.
1560 Broadway, #700 • Denver, CO 80202
(303) 830-2054 Fax 863-8003

National Congress of American Indians
2010 Massachusetts Ave. NW, 2nd Floor
Washington, DC 20036
(202) 466-7767 Fax 466-7797

NCSS Publications
National Council for the Social Studies
3501 Newark St., NW, Box P
Washington, DC 20016 (202) 966-7840

National Council of Teachers of English
1111 Kenyon Rd. • Urbana, IL 61801
(217) 328-3870

National Geographic Society
P.O. Box 1640 • Washington, DC 20013
(800) 638-4077

National Indian Gaming Association (NIGA)
224 Second St., SE • Washington, DC 20003
(202) 546-7711 Fax 546-1755
E-mail: sjohns@indiangaming.org
Website: www.indiangaming.org

National Indian Justice Center
McNear Bldg., 7 Fourth St., Suite 46
Petaluma, CA 94952 (800) 966-0662
(707) 762-8113 Fax 762-7681
E-mail: nijc@aol.com
Web site: www.nijc.indian.com

National Indian Law Library
1522 Broadway • Boulder, CO 80302
(303) 447-8760

National Learning Corp.
212 Michael Dr. • Syosset, NY 11791
(800) 645-6337; in NY (516) 921-8888

National Museum of American History
Smithsonian Institution
Constitution Ave. & 12th St., NW Rm. MBB66
Washington, DC 20560 (202) 357-1965

National Museum of the American Indian
The George Gustav Heye Center-Smithsonian Institution
Alexander Hamilton U.S. Customs House
One Bowling Green • New York, NY 10004
(212) 283-2420

National Museums of Canada
Dist. by The University of Chicago Press

National Native American AIDS Prevention Center
2100 Lake Shore Ave., Suite A
Oakland, CA 94606
(510) 444-2051 Fax 444-1593

National Woodlands Publishing Co.
8846 Green Briar Rd. • Lake Ann, MI 49650
(616) 275-6735 Fax 275-6735
E-Mail: nwpc@traverse.com

Native American Book Publishers
5884 Winans Lake Rd. • Brighton, MI 48116
(810) 231-3728

Native American Co-Op
P.O. Box 27626 • Tucson, AZ 85726
(520) 622-4900

Native American Images
P.O. Box 746 • Austin, TX 78767
(800) 252-2331 Fax (512) 472-7754

Native American Journalists Association
3359 36th Ave. S. • Minneapolis, MN 55406
(612) 729-9244 Fax 729-9373
Website: www.naja.com; E-mail: info@naja.com

Native American Pathways Press
P.O. Box 221378 • Cleveland, OH 44122
(800) 707-9906

Native American Studies Center
U. of New Mexico, 1812 Las Lomas N.E.
Albuquerque, NM 87131 (505) 277-3917

Native American Task Force
Church Council of Greater Seattle
4759 15th Ave., NE • Seattle, WA 98105

Native Law Centre
University of Saskatchewan
101 Diefenbaker Place
Saskatoon, SK, Canada S7N 5B8
(306) 966-6189 Fax 966-6207
E-mail: K10tz@duke.usak.ca

Native Word Research & Publishing
P.O. Box 827 • Lyons, CO 80540
(303) 772-8249

Naturegraph Publishers
P.O. Box 1047 • Happy Camp, CA 96039
(800) 390-5353; (530) 493-5353
Fax (530) 493-5240
E-mail: nature@sisqtel.net
Web site: www.naturegraph.com

Navajo Curriculum Center Press
Dist. by Rough Rock Press
P.O. Box 217 • Chinle, AZ 86503
(520) 728-3311

Navajo Gallery
P.O. Box 1756 • Taos, NM 87571
(505) 758-3250

Navajo Nation Museum Press
P.O. Box 1904 • Window Rock, AZ 86515
(520) 871-6673

Nebraska State Historical Society
1500 R St., P.O. Box 82554
Lincoln, NE 68501 (402) 471-4747

Nelson-Atkins Museum of Art
4525 Oak St. • Kansas City, MO 64111
(816) 561-4000

Nelson-Hall
111 N. Canal St.
Chicago, IL 60606 (312) 930-9446

Thomas Nelson, Publishers
P.O. Box 14100 • Nashville, TN 37214
(800) 251-4000; in TN (615) 889-9000

Neshobatek Press
6931 MenloDr. • Baton Rouge, LA 70808
(504) 766-9656

Nevada State Museum
600 N. Carson St. • Carson City, NV 89701
(775) 687-4810 Fax 687-4168
Website: www.nevadaculture.org

New American Library, NAL-Dutton
Div. of Penguin USA
375 Hudson St. • New York, NY 10014
(212) 366-2000

New Jersey Historical Commission
P.O. Box 305 • Trenton, NJ 08625
(609) 292-6062 Fax 633-8168

New Jersey Historical Society
230 Broadway • Newark, NJ 07104
(201) 483-3939

New Mexico Dept. of Development
Tourist Division, 113 Washington Ave.
Santa Fe, NM 87503

New Past Press
P.O. Box 558 • Friendship, WI 53934 (608) 339-7191

New Seed Press
P.O. Box 9488 • Berkeley, CA 94709

New Society Publishers
4527 Springfield Ave. • Philadelphia, PA 19143

New York Academy of Sciences
Publications Dept., 2 East 63 St.
New York, NY 10021 (212) 838-0230

New York Labor News
914 Industrial Ave. • Palo Alto, CA 94303
(415) 494-1532

New World Library
14 Pamaron Way • Novato, CA 94949
(800) 972-6657 (415) 884-2100 Fax 884-2199
Web site: www.nwlib.com

New York University Press
Dist. by Columbia University Press
(212) 316-7100

New York University
Review of Law & Social Change
110 W. 3rd St. • New York, NY 10012

Newberry Library
60 W. Walton St. • Chicago, IL 60610
(312) 943-9090

News & Letters Committees
59 E. Van Buren St., Suite 707
Chicago, IL 60605 (312) 663-0839

NewSouth Books

Nez Perce National Historical Park
P.O. Box 93 • Spalding, ID 83551
(208) 843-2261

North American Press
Div. of Fulcrum Publishing

North Atlantic Books
2800 Woolsey St. • Berkeley, CA 94705
(415) 652-5309

North Carolina Division of Archives & History
109 E. Jones St. • Raleigh, NC 27611
(919) 733-7442

North Carolina State Museum of Natural Sciences
P.O. Box 27647 • Raleigh, NC 27611
(919) 733-7450

North Point Press
Dist. by Farrar, Straus & Grioux

North Star Press
P.O. Box 451 • St. Cloud, MN 56301
(612) 253-1636

Northeastern State University
Div. of Arts & Letters, Phoenix SH 218,
Tahlequah, OK 74464 (918) 456-5511

Northern Arizona University
Dept. of Anthropology, Bookstore
P.O. Box 6044 • Flagstaff, AZ 86011
(520) 523-4041

Northern Arizona University
Institute for Human Development
P.O. Box 5630 • Flagstaff, AZ 86011
(800) 553-0714 Fax (520) 523-9127
E-mail: ihd@.uap@nau.edu

Northern Illinois University Press
DeKalb, IL 60115 (815) 753-1826

Northern Michigan University Press
Bookstore, Don H. Bottum University Center,
Marquette, MI 49855 (906) 227-2480

Northern Plains Indian Crafts Association
Box "E" • Browning, MT 59417

Northland Publishing Co.
P.O. Box 1389 • Flagstaff, AZ 86002
(800) 346-3257 Fax (800) 257-9082
Web site: www.northlandpub.com

NWREL
Northwest Regional Educational Laboratory
101 S.W. Main St., # 500 • Portland, OR 97204
(503) 275-9500 Fax 275-9489

Northwestern Publishing House
1250 N. 113th St. • Milwaukee, WI 53226
(414) 475-6600

W.W. Norton & Co., Inc.
500 Fifth Ave. • New York, NY 10110
(800) 233-4830 Fax (800) 458-6515

Nova Science Publishers
6080 Jericho Tpke. #207
Commack, NY 11725
(516) 499-3103 Fax 499-3146

Nova Scotia Museum Publications
P.O. Box 637
Halifax, Nova Scotia B3S 2T3 Canada

O

Oak Knoll Press
310 Delaware St. • New Castle, DE 19720
(800) 996-2556 Fax (302) 328-7274

Oceana Publications
75 Main St. • Dobbs Ferry, NY 10522
(914) 693-1733

Ohio Historical Society
1982 Velma Ave. • Columbus, OH 43211
(614) 297-2300

Ohio University Press
Orders to C.U.P. Services
P.O. Box 6525 • Ithaca, NY 14851
(614) 593-1155

Oklahoma Indian Arts & Crafts Coop.
P.O. Box 966 • Anadarko, OK 73005

Old West Publishing
1228 E. Colfax Ave.
Denver, CO 80218 (303) 832-7190

Oldbuck Press
P.O. Box 1623 • Conway, AR 72033
(501) 336-8184
E-mail: obsales@aol.com

Omnigraphics, Inc.
2400 Penobscot Bldg.
Detroit, MI 48226 (800) 234-1340

One Reed Publications
P.O. Box 561 • Amherst, MA 01004
(413) 253-9450

Oneida Turtle School
P.O. Box 365 • Oneida, WI 54155
(920) 869-4364 Fax 8769-4440

Open Book Publishers
1400 N. State St., Suite C
Bellingham, WA 98225 (206) 676-4613

Orca Book Publishers
P.O. Box 468 • Custer, WA 98240(800) 210-5277 Fax (250)
380-1892

Orchard Books - Sales Dept.
95 Madison Ave.
New York, NY 10016
(800) 621-1115 Fax (800) 374-4329
Schools & Public Libraries send orders to Franklin Watts

Oregon Historical Society Press
1230 S.W. Park Ave.
Portland, OR, 97205 (503) 222-1741

Oregon State University Press
101 Waldo Hall, OSU
Corvallis, OR 97331 (503) 754-3166

Origins Press
4632 Vincent Ave. S.
Minneapolis, MN 55410 (612) 922-8175

Orion Books
Div. of Random House

O'Sullivan, Woodside & Co.
Distributed by Caroline House Publishers
236 Forest Park Place
Ottawa, IL 61350 (815) 434-7905

The Osage Mission-Neosho Co. Historical Society
P.O. Box 113 • St. Paul, KS 66771

Outbooks
Distributed by Vista Books
P.O. Box 1766 • Morristown, NJ 07962
(908) 604-9702

Outlet Book Co.
Dist. by Random House

Ozark Publishing
P.O. Box 228 • Prairie Grove, AR 72753
(800) 327-5113

Oxford University Press
198 Madison Ave. • New York, NY 10016
(800) 451-7556 Fax (212) 725-2972
E-mail: egt@oup.usa.org
Web site: www.oup-usa.org

Oyate
2702 Matthews St.
Berkeley, CA 94702
(510) 848-6700 Fax 848-4815
E-mail: oyate@oyate.org

P

Pacific Books
P.O. Box 558 • Palo Alto, CA 94302
(415) 965-1980

Pacific Northwest National Parks & Forests Assn.
909 1st Ave., Suite 630
Seattle, WA 98104 (206) 553-7958

Panjandrum Books
Distributed by Bookpeople

Panorama West Books-Pioneer Publishing
P.O. Box 4638 • Fresno, CA 93728
(209) 226-1200

Pantheon Books
400 Hahn Rd. • Westminster, MD 21157
(800) 638-6460

Parabola Books
656 Broadway • New York, NY 10010012
(800) 560-6984 Fax (212) 979-7325
E-mail: parabola@panix.com

Paragon House Publishers
2700 University Ave. W Suite 47
St. Paul, MN 55114 (800) 727-2466

Parents Magazine Press
Distributed by Crown Publishers

Park Genealogical Books
P.O. Box 130968 • Roseville, MN 55113
(651) 488-4416 Fax 488-2653
E-mail: mbakeman@parkbooks.com

Pathfinder Press
410 West St. • New York, NY 10014
(212) 741-0690 Fax 727-0150

Pathfinder Publications
4704 Wilford Way • Minneapolis, MN 55435
(612) 835-1128

Paulist Press
997 MacArthur Blvd. • Mahwah, NJ 07430
(201) 825-7300 Fax 825-8345

Peek Publications
P.O. Box 50123 • Palo Alto, CA 94303
(650) 962-1010

Pelican Publishing
P.O. Box 3110 • Gretna, Louisiana 70053
(800) 843-1724 Fax (504) 368-1195

Pendle Hill Publications
338 Plush Mill Rd. • Wallingford, PA 19086
(215) 566-4514

Pendulum Press
Academic Bldg., Saw Mill Rd.
West Haven, CT 06516 (203) 933-2551

Penguin Putnam
P.O. Box 120 • Bergenfield, NJ 07621
(800) 526-0275 Fax (212) 385-6521
Web site: www.penguin.com/usa

Pennsylvania Academy of the Fine Arts
Broad & Cherry St. • Philadelphia, PA 19102
(215) 972-7600

Pennsylvania Historical & Museum Commission
Publications Sales Program, Dept. BRS
P.O. Box 11466 • Harrisburg, PA 17108
(717) 783-2618

Pennsylvania State University Press
215 Wagner Bldg. • University Park, PA 16802
(814) 865-1327

Persea Books
60 Madison Ave. • New York, NY 10010 (212) 779-7668

Persimmon Press
118 Tillinghast Pl. • Buffalo, NY 14216
(716) 849-0149 Fax852-0093

Philbrook Museum of Art
2727 S. Rockford Rd., Box 52510
Tulsa, OK 74152 (918) 749-7941

Picton Press
P.O. Box 250 • Rockport, ME 04856
(207) 236-6565 Fax 236-6713

Pineapple Press
P.O. Box 3899 • Sarasota, FL 34230
(813) 952-1085

Pioneer Publishing
P.O. Box 408 • Carrollton, MS 38917
(662) 237-6010

Pocahontas Press
P.O. Drawer F • Blacksburg, VA 24063
(800) 446-0467; (540) 951-0467

Pocket Books
Div. of Simon & Schuster; Distributed by Prentice Hall Press

Pogo Press
4 Cardinal Lane • St. Paul, MN 55127
(612) 483-4692

Porcupine Press
310 S. Juniper St. • Philadelphia, PA 19107
(215) 735-0101

PowerHouse Cultural Entertainment
180 Varick St. #1302 • New York, NY 10014
(212) 604-9074 Fax 366-5247
E-mail: info@powerhousebooks.com

Praeger Publishers
Dist. by Greenwood Publishing

Pre-Columbian Art Research Institute
1100 Sacramento St.
San Francisco, CA 94108 (415) 776-0606

Prentice-Hall Books
200 Old Tappan Rd. • Old Tappan, NJ 07675
(800) 223-2336 Fax (800) 445-6991

Lew Paxton Price
P.O. Box 88 • Garden Valley, CA 95633
(530) 333-9470

Primer Publishers
5738 N. Central • Phoenix, AZ 85012
(602) 234-1574

Princeton University Press
41 Williams St.• Princeton, NJ 08540
(800) 777-4726 Fax 999-1958
E-mail: orders@cpfs.pupress.princeton.edu
Website: www.pup.princeton.edu
orders to: California/Princeton Fulfillment Services
1445 Lower Ferry Rd., Ewing, NJ 08618

Pruett Publishing
7464 Arapahoe Rd., Suite A-9
Boulder, CO 80303
(800) 247-8224; Fax (303) 443-9019

Publishers Group West
1700 Fourth St. • Berkeley, CA 94710
(800) 788-3123 Fax (510) 528-3444

Publishing Center for Cultural Resources
50 W. 29th St. #7E
New York, NY 10001 (212) 260-2010

Pueblo County Historical Society
Orders to: Robert Crosby
2615 Seventh Ave. • Pueblo, CO 81003
(719) 545-6003

Pueblo of Acoma Press
P.O. Box 449 • Acomita, NM 87034
(505) 552-9833

The Putnam Publishing Group
200 Madison Ave. • New York, NY 10016
(800) 631-8571

Q

Qualla Arts & Crafts Mutual
P.O. Box 277 • Cherokee, NC 28719
(704) 497-3103

Quarterman Publications
P.O. Box 156 • Lincoln, MA 01773
(617) 259-8047

R

Raintree/Steck-Vaughn Publishers
P.O. Box 690789 • Orlando, FL 32819
(800) 531-5015 Fax (800) 699-9459

Rainy Day Press
1147 E 26th St. • Eugene, OR 97403
(503) 484-4626

Rand Corp.
P.O. Box 2138 • Santa Monica, CA 90407
(310) 393-0411 Fax 3451-6996
E-mail: denise@rand.org

Rand McNally & Co.
P.O. Box 7600 • Chicago, IL 60680 (312) 673-9100

Random House
400 Hahn Rd. • Westminster, MD 21157
(800) 733-3000 Fax (800) 659-2436

Raven Hail
P.O. Box 543 • Asheville, NC 28802
(898) 254-0548

Red Crane Books
2008-B Rosina St. • Santa Fe, NM 87505
(800) 922-3392; (505) 988-7070 Fax 989-7476
E-mail: publish@redcrane.com
Web site: www.redcrane.com

Reddick Enterprises
P.O. Box 847 • Pottsboro, TX 75076
(800) 786-6210 Fax (903) 786-9059
E-mail: crazycrow@texoma.com

Reference Publications
P.O. Box 344 • Algonac, MI 48001
(810) 794-5722 Fax 794-7463

Reference & Research Services
511 Lincoln St. • Santa Cruz, CA 95060
(408) 426-4479

Renaissance House Publishers
P.O. Box 177 • Frederick, CO 80530
(800) 521-9221

Reprint Services Corp.
3972 Barranca Pkwy. #J-412
Irvine, CA 92714
(909) 699-5731 Fax 767-0133

Research Center for Language & Semiotic Studies
Dist. by Indiana University
Goodbody Hall, Rm. 344
Bloomington, IN 47405 (812) 335-1605

Research Publications International
12 Lunar Dr., Drawer AB • Woodbridge, CT 06525
(800) 732-2477; in CT (203) 397-2600

Resource Publications
160 E. Virginia St. • San Jose, CA 95112
(800) 737-7600; in CA (408) 286-8505

The Rio Grande Press
P.O. Box 33 • Glorieta, NM 87535
(505) 757-6275

Rizzoli International Publications
300 Park Ave. • New York, NY 10010
(800) 433-1238; in NY (212) 397-3785

R J Enterprises
P.O. Box 1034 • Skyland, NC 28776
(704) 684-7555

Roberts Rhinehart, Publishers
6309 Monark park Pl. • Niwot, CO 80503
(800) 352-1985; Fax (800) 401-9705
E-mail: books@robertsrinehart.com

Robin Hood Books
RR1, Box 1330 • Thorndike, ME 04986
(207) 722-3112

Rock Island Arsenal Historical Society
605 24th Ave. • Moline, IL 61265
(309) 797-3987

Rock Point Community School
Chinle, AZ 86503 (602) 659-4246

Rockland County Historical Society
20 Zukor Rd. • New City, NY 10956
(914) 634-9629

Rosen Publishing Group
29 E. 21st St. • New York, NY 10010
(800) 237-9932 Fax (888) 436-4643

Ross & Haines, Inc.
411 2nd St. • Hudson, WI 54016
(715) 381-1955

Norman Ross Publishing
330 West 58th St. • New York, NY 10019
(800) 648-8850; Fax (212) 765-2393
E-mail: info@nross.com
Web site: www.nross.com

Fred B. Rothman & Co.
10368 W. Centennial Rd.
Littleton, CO 80127 (800) 457-1986

Rough Rock Demonstration School Board
Star Route 1 • Rough Rock, AZ 86503

Roundtable Publishing
P.O. Box 6488 • Malibu, CA 90264
(310) 457-8433

Rourke Corp.
P.O. Box 3328 • Vero Beach, FL 32964
(800) 775-1200 Fax (561) 234-6622
E-mail: rourke@sunset.net

Routledge
29 W. 35th St. • New York, NY 10001
(800) 634-7064 Fax (800) 248-4724

Rowman & Littlefield
4720 Boston Way
Lanham, MD 20706 (800) 462-6420
(301) 459-3366 Fax 459-2118

Roza Run Publishing Co.
57301 N. McDonald Rd.
Prosser, WA 99350 (509) 973-2444

Running Press Book Publishers
125 S. 22nd St. • Philadelphia, PA 19103
(800) 428-1111; in PA (215) 567-5080

Russell Publications
9027 N. Cobre Dr. • Phoenix, AZ 85028-5317
(800) 835-7220 Fax (602) 493-4691
E-mail: russell@indiandata.com
Web site: www.indiandata.com

Russell & Russell, Publishers
Orders to Charles Scribner's Sons

Rutgers University Press
P.O. Box 5062 • New Brunswick, NJ 08903
(800) 446-9323; (908) 932-7764 Fax 932-7039

Rutledge Hill Press
211 Seventh Ave. N. • Nashville, TN 37219
(800) 234-4234 Fax (615) 244-2978
WEeb site: www.rutledgehillpress.com

S

SSS Publishing
17515 S.W. Blue Heron Rd.
Lake Oswego, OR 97034
(503) 636-2979

Safari Press
The Woodbine Publishing Co.
15621 Chemical Lane, Bldg. B
Huntington Beach, CA 92649
(714) 894-9080 Fax 894-4949

Sage Publications
2111 W. Hillcrest Dr.
Newbury Park, CA 91320 (805) 499-0721

St. Martin's Press
175 Fifth Ave. • New York, NY 10010
(800) 221-7945; in NY (212) 674-5151

St. Michaels Historical Museum
St. Michaels Mission, Drawer D
St. Michaels, AZ 86511 (602) 871-4172

St. Scholastica Priory
Duluth, MN 55811 (218) 728-1817

Salem House Publishers
(800) 242-7737
Orders to Harper & Row

Salmon Run Press
P.O. Box 672130 • Chugiak, AK 99567
(907) 688-4268

SamHar Press
Bindery Lane • Charlottesville, NY 12036
(800) 847-2105

San Bernardino County Museum Association
2024 Orange Tree Lane
Redlands, CA 92373 (714) 792-1334

San Juan District Media Center
Curriculum Division
28 W. 200 North, Box 804
Blanding, UT 84511 (801) 678-2281

San Manuel Tribe
P.O. Box 266, Patton, CA 92369
(909) 864-8933 Fax 864-3370

San Marcos Press
410 Bryn Mawr, SE
Albuquerque, NM 87108 (505)266-4412

Sand River Press
1319 14th St.
Los Osos, CA 93402 (805) 543-3591

Sanpete Publications
2751 W. Monte Vista • Tucson, AZ 85745
(520) 622-6007 Fax 798-1514

Santa Barbara Museum of Natural History
2559 Puesta del Sol Rd.
Santa Barbara, CA 93105
(805) 682-4711 Fax 569-3170

Sasquatch Books
615 Second Ave. #260 • Seattle, WA 98104
(800) 775-0817 Fax (206) 467-4301
E-mai: books@sasquatchbooks.com

Scarborough House
P.O. Box 370
Chelsea, MI 48118 (313) 475-9145

Scarecrow Press
15200 NBN Way, P.O. Box 191
Blue Ridge Summit, PA 17214
(800) 462-6420 Fax (800) 338-4550
E-mail: orders@scarecrowpress.com
Web site: www.scarecrowpress.com

Schenkman Books
Box 119, 118 Main St.
Rochester, VT 05767 (802) 767-3702

Schiffer Publishing
77 Lower Valley Rd.-Rt. 372
Atglen, PA 19310
(610) 593-1777 Fax 593-2002

R. Schneider Publishers
312 Linwood Ave. • Stevens Point, WI 54481
(715) 345-7899 Fax (715) 345-7898

Scholarly Books
P.O. Box 160 • St. CVlair Shores, MI 48080
(810) 231-3728

Scholarly Resources
104 Greenhill Ave. • Wilmington, DE 19805
(800) 772-8937; in DE (302) 654-7713

Scholars Press
P.O. Box 6525 • Ithaca, NY 14851
(800) 666-2211

Scholastic, Inc.
555 Broadway • New York, NY 10012
(800) 325-6149 Fax (212) 343-4535
Web site: www.scholastic.com

School of American Research Press
Dist. by University of Washington Press

School of Public Health
Master of Public Health Program
U.of California, Warren Hall, Rm. 140
Berkeley, CA 94720 (510) 642-3228

Scott, Foresman & Co.
1900 E. Lake Ave. • Glenview, IL 60025
(312) 729-3000

Charles Scribner's Sons
Macmillan Distribution Center
Front & Brown Sts. • Riverside, NJ 08075
(800) 257-5755 Fax (800) 562-1272

The Scriptorium Press
71 S. Main St. • Alfred, NY 14802
(607) 587-9371

SeaSide Publishing
P.O. Box 14441 • St. Petersburg, FL 33733
(813) 321-8840 Fax 321-8910

Second Source, Inc.
350 Ninth Ave. • St.Paul Park, MN 55071
(612) 768-0652 Fax 569-5616

Seminole Nation Museum
P.O. Box 1532 • Wewoka, OK 74884

Seven Oaks Press
405 S. Seventh St. • St. Charles, IL 60174
(312) 377-1098

P. Shalom Publications
5409 18th Ave. • Brooklyn, NY 11204
(718) 256-1954

Sheffield Publishing
P.O. Box 359 • Salem, WI 53168
(414) 843-2281

Shenandoah Books
133 E. Wisconsin Ave.
Appleton, WI 54911
(920) 832-9525

Shoreys Bookstore
1109 N. 36th St. #3 • Seattle, WA 98103
(206) 633-2990

Sierra Club Books
85 Second St., 2nd Floor
San Francisco, CA 94105
(415) 291-1600 Fax 291-1602

Sierra Oaks Publishing
1370 Sierra Oaks Ct.
Newcastle, CA 95658 (916) 663-1474

Signal Tree Publications
P.O. Box 551 • Livermoor, ME 04253
(207) 897-6184

Silver Burdett Press
P.O. Box 1226 • Westwood, NJ 07675
(800) 631-8081; (800) 624-4843

SilverPlatter
100 River Ridge Dr. • Norwood, MA 02062
(800) 343-0064 ext. 744

Simon & Schuster
200 Old Tappan Rd.• Old Tappan, NJ 07675
(800) 223-2336 Fax (800) 445-6991

Sister Vision Press
P.O Box 217, Sta. E • Toronto, ON M6H 4E2
Canada (416) 533-2184

Sitka National Historical Park
P.O. Box 738 • Sitka, AK 99835
(907) 747-6281

Sky & Sage Books
91 Woodland Dr. #26 • Sturgis, SD 57785

Peter Smith Publisher
6 Lexington Ave. • Magnolia, MA 01930
(508) 525-3562 Fax 525-3674

Smithmark Publishers
115 W. 18th St., 15th Fl. • New York, NY 10011
(800) 932-0070 Fax (800) 732-8688

Smithsonian Institution Press
P.O. Box 960 • Herndon, VA 20172
(800) 669-1559; (800) 782-4612

Smithsonian Videos
(800) 322-0344

Smoke & Fire Co.
27 N. River Rd. • Waterville, OH 43522
(800) 766-5334; (419) 878-8535 Fax 878-3653
Website: www.smoke-fire.com
E-mail: store@smoke-fire.com

Snowbird Publishing Co.
P.O. Box 729 • Tellico Plains, TN 37385
(615) 982-7261 Fax 681-3418

Snowshoe Press
P.O. Box 24334 • Edina, MN 55424 (612) 975-0838

Society of American Archivists
600 S. Federal, Suite 504
Chicago, IL 60605 (312) 922-0140

The Sourcebook Project
P.O. Box 107 • Glen Arm, MD 21057
(301) 668-6047

South End Press/LPC Group
c/o Consortium Book Sales
1045 Westgate Dr., Suite 90
St. Paul, MN 55114-1065
(800) 283-3572 Fax (651) 221-0124
E-mail: consortium@cbsd.com
Website: www.cbsd.com

South Platte Press
P.O. Box 163 • David City, NE 68632
(402) 367-4734

Southern Illinois U. Press
P.O. Box 3697 • Carbondale, IL 62902
(618) 453-2281

Southern Methodist U. Press
P.O. Box 415 • Dallas, TX 75275
(214) 692-2263

Southwest Communication Resources
P.O. Box 788 • Bernalillo, NM 87004
(505) 867-3396

Southwest Museum
234 Museum Dr. • Los Angeles, CA 90065
(213) 221-2164 Fax 224-8223
E-mail: swmuseum@annex.com

Southwest Parks & Monuments Assn.
157 W. Cedar St. • Globe, AZ 85502
(520) 425-8184 Fax 425-6560

Southwestern Art Association
P.O. Box 52510 • Tulsa, OK 74152

Specialty Books International
P.O. Box 1785 • Ann Arbor, MI 48106
(517) 456-4764

Spencer Museum of Art
U. of Kansas • Lawrence, KS 66045
(913) 864-4710

Spirit Mountain Press
Dist. by University of Alaska Press

Spirit Talk Press
Drawer V • Browning, MT 59417
(406) 338-2882

Spizzirri Publishing
P.O. Box 9397 • Rapid City, SD 57709
(800) 325-9819 Fax (605) 348-6251
E-mail: spizzpub@aol.com

Springer Publishing
536 Broadway • New York, NY 10012
(212) 431-4370

Stanford (University) CRDP
Center for Research in Disease Prevention
730 Welch Rd. • Palo Alto, CA 94304
(650) 723-0003 Fax 498-7775
distribution@scrdp.stanford.edu

Stanford University Press
Stanford, CA 94305-2235 (415) 723-9434

Starwood Publishing
Dist. by Fulcrum Publishing

State Historical Society of Wisconsin
816 State St. • Madison, WI 53706
(608) 262-1368

State House Press
P.O. Drawer 15247
Austin, TX 78761 (512) 454-1959

State Mutual Book & Periodical Service
521 Fifth Ave., 17th Floor
New York, NY 10017 (212) 682-5844

State University of New York at Geneseo
Dept. of Anthropology
Geneseo, NY 14454 (716) 245-5277

State University of New York Press
P.O. Box 6525 • Ithaca, NY 14851
(800) 666-2211 Fax (607) 277-6292

Statesman-Examiner, Inc.
220 S. Main, Box 271
Colville, WA 99114 (509) 684-4567

Station Hill Press
Station Hill Rd. • Barrytown, NY 12507
(914) 758-5840 Fax 758-8163

Roberta Ingles Steele
P.O. Box 3485 FSS
Radford, VA 24143 (703) 639-6383

Stemmer House Publishers
2627 Caves Rd. • Owing Mills, MD 21117
(800) 345-6665; (410) 363-3690 Fax 363-8459
E-mail: stemmerhouse@home.com
Web site: www.stemmer.com

Sterling Publishing
387 Park Ave. So. • New York, NY 10016
(800) 367-9692 Fax (212) 213-2495
E-mail: customerservice@sterlingpub.com
Web site: www.sterlingpub.com

Stevens Publishing
P.O. Box 160 • Kila, MT 59920
(406) 756-0307 Fax 257-5051

Stonehenge Books
12375 E. Cornell Ave., Unit No. 7
Aurora, CO 80014 (303) 695-4710

Storypole Press
11015 Bingham Ave., E.
Tacoma, WA 98446 (206) 531-2032
Fax (206) 535-3889

Strawberry Press
Box 451, Bowling Green Station
New York, NY 10004

Street Press
P.O. Box 772 • Sound Beach, NY 11789
(516) 928-4958

Stump Publishing Co.
121 N. Sultana Ave.
Ontario, CA 91764 (714) 984-6694

Summer Institute of Linguistics
Academic Publications
7500 W. Camp Wisdom Rd.,
Dallas, TX 75236 (214) 709-2403

Sun Dance Books
Distributed by Borgo Press

Sun Tracks
Dept. of English, University of Arizona
Tucson, AZ 85721

Sundance Educational Publishers
Box 184 • Inchelium, WA 99138

Sunflower University Press
1531 Yuma, Box 1009
Manhattan, KS 66502 (800) 258-1232

Sunnycrest Publishing
Rt. 1, Box 1 • Clements, MN 56224
(507) 692-2246

Sunstone Press
P.O. Box 2321 • Santa Fe, NM 87504
(800) 243-5644; (505) 988-4418
Fax (505) 988-1025
Web site: www.sunstonepress.com

Mark Supnick
8524 NW Second St.
Coral Springs, FL 33071
(305) 755-3448

SVE-Society for Visual Education
55 E. Monroe St., 34th Floor
Chicago, IL 60603
(800) 829-1900

Sweetlight Books
16625 Heitman Rd.
Cottonwood, CA 96022 (916) 529-5392

Syracuse University Press
1600 Jamesville • Syracuse, NY 13244
(800) 365-8929 Fax (315) 443-5545
E-mail: talitz@summon3.syr.edu

T

Tacoma Art Museum
1123 Pacific Ave. • Tacoma, WA 98402
(206) 272-4258

Tales of the Mojave Road Publishing
P.O. Box 307 • Norco, CA 91760
(714) 737-3150

Tamal Land Press
39 Merwin Ave. • Fairfax, CA 94930
(415) 456-4705

Taylor & Francis
1900 Frost Rd. #101 • Bristol, PA 19007
(800) 821-8312 Fax (215) 785-5515

Taylor Museum, The Library
Colorado Springs Fine Arts Center
30 W. Dale St. • Colorado Springs, CO 80903
(303) 634-5581

te Neues Publishing Co.
16 W. 22nd St. • New York, NY 10010
(800) 352-0305 Fax (212) 627-9511

Teacher Created Materials
6421 Industry Way • Westminster, CA 92683
(800) 858-7339 Fax (714) 892-0283

Teacher Ideas Press
Dov. of Libraries Unlimited

Teaching Drum Outdoor School
7124 Military Rd. • Three Lakes, WI 54562
(715) 546-2944

Te-Cum-Tom Enterprises
5770 Fransom Ct. • North Bend, OR 97459
(503) 756—5757

Tejas Art Press
207 Terrell Rd. • San Antonio, TX 78209
(512) 826-7803

Temple University Press
1601 N. Broad St., USB-Rm. 305
Philadelphia, PA 19122 (800) 447-1656
(215) 204-8787 Fax 204-4719

Ten Speed Press
P.O. Box 7123 • Berkeley, CA 94707
(800) 841-2665

Terrich Books
P.O. Box 59 • Guilford, NY 13780
(800) 352-3670

Texas A & M University Press
John H. Lindsey Bldg., Lewis St.
4354 TAMU • College Station, TX 77843
(800) 826-8911; Fax (888) 617-2421
Web site: www.tamu.edu/upress

Texas Christian University Press
Dist. by Texas A&M University Press

Texas State Historical Association
Dist. by Texas A&M University Press

Texas Tech University Press
Sales Office • Lubbock, TX 79409-1037
(800) 832-4042; in TX (806) 742-2468

Texas Western Press
c/o University of Texas Press
P.O. Box 7819 • Austin, TX 79968
(800) 252-3206 Fax (800) 687-6046
Web site: www.utexas.edu/utpress/

Texian Press
P.O. Box 1684 • Waco, TX 76703
(817) 754-5636

Thames & Hudson
Dist. by W.W. Norton & Co.

Thayer & Associates
Dist. Hoard Historical Museum
407 Merchants Ave. • Fort Atkinson, WI 53538
(414) 563-4521

Theatre Communications Group, Inc. (TCG)
355 Lexington Ave. • New York, NY 10017
(212) 697-5230 Fax 983-4847
E-mail: tcg@tcg.org

Theosophical Publishing House
306 W. Geneva Rd.
Wheaton, IL 60189-0270
(800) 654-9430; in IL (312) 665-0123

Theytus Books Ltd.
P.O. Box 20040
Penticton, B.C. Canada V2A 8K3
(604) 493-7181 Fax 493-5302

Think Shop, Inc.
P.O. Box 3754
Albuquerque, NM 87190-3754 (505) 831-5029

Charles C. Thomas, Publisher
2600 S. First St. • Springfield, IL 62794
(217) 789-8980

Thunder Mesa Publishing
208 Sherwood Blvd. • Los Alamos, NM 87544
(505) 672-3108 Fax 672-0231

Thunder's Mouth Press
161 William St., 16th Floor
New York, NY 10003
(646) 375-2570

Tiller Research, Inc.
BowArrow Publishing
6727 Academy Rd. NE, Suite C
Albuquerque, NM 87109
(505) 797-9800 Fax 797-9888
Website: www.tillerresearch.com

Timber Press
133 S.W. Second Ave., Suite 450
Portland, OR 97204 (800) 327-5680
(503) 227-2878 Fax 227-3070

Timberline Books
25890 Weld Rd. 53
Kersey, CO 80644-8802 (303) 353-3785

Time-Life Books
1450 E. Parham Rd.
Richmond, VA 23280 (800) 621-7026

Time Traveler Maps
P.O. Box 30 • Mancos, CO 81328
(800) 753-7388 Fax (970) 533-7879

Tipi Press
St. Joseph's Indian School
Chamberlain, SD 57326
(800) 229-5684 Fax (605) 734-3480

Todd Publications
P.O. Box 635 • Nyack, NY 10960
(866) 896-0916 ext. 7530
Fax (845) 358-6213
E-mail: toddpub@aol.com

Todtri Productions, Ltd.
254 W. 31st St. #13th Floor
New York, NY 10001
(800) 241-4477 Fax (212) 279-1241

Celia Totus Enterprises
P.O. Box 192 • Toppenish, WA 98948
(509) 865-2480

Toucan Valley Publications
142 N. Milpitas Blvd. PMB 260
Milpitas, CA 95035 (800) 236-7946

Trans-Anglo Books
P.O. Box 38 • Corona Del Mar, CA 92625
(714) 645-7393

Transaction Publishers
Rutgers - The State University
390 Campus Dr. • Somerset, NJ 08873
(888) 999-6778 Fax (732) 748-9801
E-mail: transpub@idt.net

Treasure Chest Publications
P.O. Box 5250 • Tucson, AZ 85703
(800) 627-0048

Trees Co. Press
49 Van Buren Way
San Francisco, CA 94131
(415) 334-8352

Tremaine Graphic & Publishing
2727 Front St. • Klamath Falls, OR 97601
(503) 884- 4193

Tribal Press
c/o Lowell Jensen
Rt. 2, Box 599 • Cable, WI, 54821
(715) 794-2247

Tribe of Two Press
P.O. Box 216 • San Anselmo, CA 94979
(800) 995-3320 Fax (415) 457-6543
E-mail: ToTPress@aol.com
Web site: www.members.aol.com/totpress

Troll Communications
100 Corporate Dr.• Mahwah, NJ 07430
(800) 526-5289; (800) 929-8765 Fax (800) 979-8765
Web site: www.troll.com

Troubador Press, Inc.
99 Evans Rd. • Brookline, MA 02146
(617) 734-1416

Truman State University Press
100 E. Normal St. • Kirksville, MO 63501
(800) 916-6802 Fax (660) 785-4181

Trust for Native American Cultures & Crafts
P.O. Box 142 • Greenville, NH 03048
(603) 878-2944

Tudor Publishers
3109 Shady Lawn Dr.
Greensboro, NC 27408

Tundra Books
Dist. by University of Toronto Press

Turner Publishing Co.
P.O. Box 3101 • Paducah, KY 420012
(502) 443-0121

Turquoise Books
1202 Austin Bluffs Pkwy.
Colorado Springs, CO 80918
(719) 598-4174

Charles E. Tuttle Co.
RR 1 Box 231-5 • N. Clarendon, VT 05759
(800) 526-2778; (802) 773-8930 Fax 773-6993

U

UBC Press
University of British Columbia Press
6344 Memorial Rd.
Vancouver, BC Canada V6T 1Z2
Website: www.ubcpress.ubc.ca
E-mail: info@ubcpress.ubc.ca
Orders to: UNIpresses
34 Armstrong Ave.
Georgetown, ON L7G 4R9
(877) 864-8477 Fax (877) 864-4272
(905) 873-9781 Fax 873-6170
E-mail: orders@gtwcanada.com
Web site: www.ubcpress.ubc.ca

Ullysses Press
P.O. Box 3440 • Berkeley, CA 94703
(800) 377-2542 Fax (510) 601-8307
E-mail: Ulypress@aol.com

Uncompromising Books
Div.of Native American Prisoners'
Rehabilitation Research Project
P.O. Box 1760 • Taos, NM 87571
(801) 353-4116

U.S. Catholic Conference
Publications Office
3211 4th St. NE • Washington, DC 20017
(800) 235-8722 Fax (202) 722-8709

U.S. Government Printing Office
Supt. of Documents • Washington, DC 20402
(202) 512-1800 Fax 512-2250
E-mail: gpoaccess@gpo.gov
Web site: www.access.gpo.gov/su_docs/

Universe Books
Dist. by St. Martin's Press

University Microfilms International
P.O. Box 1307 • Ann Arbor, MI 48106
(800) 521-0600; in Canada (800) 343-5299

University of Alabama Press
P.O. Box 870380 • Tuscaloosa, AL 35487
(800) 825-9980 Fax (205) 348-9201

University of Alaska
Institute of Social & Economic Research
3211 Providence Dr. • Anchorage, AK 99508
(907) 786-7710

University of Alaska Press
P.O. Box 756240 • Fairbanks, AK 99775
(888) 252-6657; (907) 474-5831 Fax 474-5502
E-mail: orders.uapress@uaf.edu
Website: www.uaf.edu/uapress

The University of Arizona Press
355 S. Euclid Ave., Suite 103
Tucson, AZ 85719 (520) 626-4218
(800) 426-3797 (phone or fax)
E-mail: orders@uapress.arizona.edu
Website: www.uapress.arizona.edu

University of Arkansas Press
201 Ozark Ave. • Fayetteville, AR 72701
(800) 626-0090 Fax (501) 575-3246

UCLA, American Indian Studies Center
3220 Campbell Hall • Los Angeles, CA 90024
(310) 825-7315 Fax 206-7060
E-mail: aiscpubs@ucla.edu

University of California, Los Angeles
Institute of Archaeology
405 Hilgard Ave. • Los Angeles, CA 90024
(213) 825-7411

University of California Press
2120 Berkeley Way • Berkeley, CA 94720
(800) 777-4726 Fax (800) 999-1958
Website: www.ucpress.edu
orders to: California/Princeton Fulfillment Services
1445 Lower Ferry Rd., Ewing, NJ 08618

University of Chicago
Dept. of Geography, Research Paper
5828 S. University Ave.
Chicago, IL 60637 (312) 962-8314

University of Chicago Press
5801 S. Ellis Ave.• Chicago, IL 60637
(800) 621-2736; (773) 702-7748 Fax 702-9756
Web site: www.press.uchicago.edu

University of Connecticut Education
The Thut World Education Center
School of Education
Storrs, CT 06268 (203) 486-3321

University of Georgia Press
330 Research Dr. • Athens, GA 30602
(706) 369-6130 Fax 369-6131

The University of Hawaii Press
2840 Kolowalu St. • Honolulu, HI 96822
(808) 948-8255

University of Idaho Press
Moscow, ID 83843 (208) 885-6245

University of Illinois Archaeology
109 Davenport Hall, 607 S. Mathews Ave.
Urbana, IL 61801

University of Illinois Press
P.O. Box 4856 • Baltimore, MD 21211
(800) 545-4703

University of Iowa Press
Chicago Distribution Center
11030 S. Langley Ave. • Chicago, IL 60628
(800) 621-8476 or (800) 621-2736

University of Kansas-Museum of Natural History
Dist. by University Press of Kansas

University of Maine Press
5754 N. Stevens Hall, Rm. 101
Orono, ME 04469
(207) 581-1408 Fax 581-1490

University of Massachusetts Press
P.O. Box 429 • Amherst, MA 01004
(413) 545-2219 Fax (800) 488-1144

University of Michigan-
Museum of Anthropology
Publications Dept., 4009 Museum Bldg.
1109 Geddes • Ann Arbor, MI 48109 (313) 764-6867

University of Michigan Press
Distributing Center, 839 Greene St.
Ann Arbor, MI 48106 (313) 764-4392

University of Minnesota
Dept. of Anthropology
215 Ford Hall, 224 Church St., SE
Minneapolis, MN 55455 (612) 373-4614

University of Minnesota Press
111 3rd Ave. So. • Minneapolis, MN 55401
(800) 621-2736; (612) 627-1970 Fax 626-7313
E-mail: poggi001@umn.edu

University of Missouri
Museum of Anthropology
104 Swallow Hall • Columbia, MO 65211
(314) 882-3764

University of Missouri Press
2910 LeMone Blvd. • Columbia, MO 65201
(800) 828-1894 Fax (573) 884-4498
E-mail: order@umsystems.edu
Website: www.system.missouri.edu/upress

University of Montana
Occasional Papers in Linguistics
Linguistics Program • Missoula, MT 59812
(406) 243-2693 Fax 243-4918

University of Nebraska
Omaha Center for Applied Urban Research
1313 Farnam on the Mall
Peter Kiewit Conference Center
Omaha, NE 68182 (402) 554-8311

University of Nebraska Press
233 North 8th St. • Lincoln, NE 68588
(800) 755-1105 Fax (800) 526-2617
(402) 472-3584 (outside U.S.)
E-mail: pressmail@unl.edu
Web site: www.nebraskapress.unl.edu

University of Nevada
College of Business Administration
Reno Bureau of Business & Economic Research
Reno, NV 89557 (702) 784-6877

University of Nevada Press
Mail Stop 166 • Reno, NV 89557-0076
(702) 784-6573 Fax 784-6200

University of New Mexico
Institute for Native American Development
Mesa Vista 3080 • Albuquerque, NM 87131
(505) 277-3917

University of New Mexico Press
1720 Lomas Blvd. NE
Albuquerque, NM 87106
(800) 249-7737 Fax (800) 622-8667
(505) 277-4810 Fax 277-3350
Website: www.unmpress.com
E-mail: unmpress@unm.edu

University of New Mexico-
School of Medicine
c/o Health Science Center
P.O. Box 719 • Albuquerque, NM 87131
(505) 277-3633

University of North Carolina Press
P.O. Box 2288 • Chapel Hill, NC 27514
(800) 848-6224; (919) 966-3561 Fax 966-3829

University of Oklahoma Press
4100 28th Ave., NW • Norman, OK 73069
(800) 627-7377 Fax (800) 735-0476
(405) 325-2000 Fax 364-5798 (local)
Website: www.oupress.com

University of Oregon Books
P.O. Box 3237 • Eugene, OR 97403
(503) 686-3165

University of Pennsylvania
Museum Publications
33rd & Spruce Sts. • Philadelphia, PA 19174
(800) 306-1941 Fax (215) 573-2497

University of Pittsburgh Press
3347 Forbes Ave. • Pittsburgh, PA 15260
(800) 666-2211 (410) 5383-2456 Fax 383-2466

University of South Carolina Press
1716 College St. • Columbia, SC 29208
(803) 777-5243

University of South Dakota
Government Research Bureau
233 Dakota Hall • Vermillion, SD 57069
(605) 677-5702

University of South Dakota
Institute of American Indian Studies
301 East Hall, 414 E. Clark St.
Vermillion, SD 57069 (605) 677-5209

University of Tennessee Press
Orders to CUP Services • P.O. Box 6525
Ithaca, NY 14851 (607) 277-2211

University of Texas
Harry Ransom Humanities Research Center
P.O. Box 7219 • Austin, TX 78713
(512) 471-9113

University of Texas Press
P.O. Box 7819 • Austin, TX 78713
(800) 252-3206 Fax (800) 687-6046
(512) 471-7233 Fax 320-0668
Web site: www.utexas.edu/utpress

University of Toronto Press
5201 Dufferin St. • Downsview, ON M3H 5T8
Canada (800) 565-9523 Fax (800) 221-9985
E-mail: utpbooks@gpu.utcc.utoronto.ca

University of Utah Press
1795 E. South Campus Dr. #101
Salt Lake City, UT 84112 (800) 773-6672
(801) 581-6771 Fax (801) 581-3365
E-mail: info@upress.utah.edu

University of Washington Press
P.O. Box 50096 • Seattle, WA 98145
(800) 441-4115 Fax (800) 669-7993
Foreign: (206) 543-8870 Fax 543-3932
E-mail: uwpord@u.washington.edu
Web site: www.washington.edu/uwpress/

University of Wisconsin Library School
Publications Committee
600 N. Park St. • Madison, WI 53706

University of Wisconsin Press
2537 Daniels St. • Madison, WI 53718
(800) 829-9559; Fax (608) 224-3924
E-mail: uwiscpress@macc.wisc.edu

University Press of America
15200 NBN Way, P.O. Box 191
Blue Ridge Summit, PA 17214
(800) 462-6420 Fax (800) 338-4550

University Press of Colorado
Editorial: 5589 Arapahoe Ave., #206C
Boulder, CO 80303 (720) 406-8849
Sales: c/o University of Oklahoma Press

University Press of Florida
15 NW 15th St. • Gainesville, FL 32611
(800) 226-3822; (352) 392-1351
Fax (800) 680-1955; (352) 392-7302
Website: www.upf.com

University Press of Kansas
329 Carruth • Lawrence, KS 66045

University Press of Kentucky
Orders to CUP Services • P.O. Box 6525
Ithaca, NY 14851 (607) 277-2211

University Press of Mississippi
3825 Ridgewood Rd. • Jackson, MS 39211
(800) 737-7788; (601) 432-6246 Fax 432-6217
E-mail: press@ihl.state.ms.us
Website: www.upress.state.ms.us

University Press of New England
37 Lafayette St. • Lebanon, NH 03766
(800) 421-1561 Fax (603) 643-1540
E-mail: university.press@dartmouth.edu
Website: www.upne.com

University Press of Virginia
P.O. Box 3608 • Charlottesville, VA 22903
(804) 924-3468 Fax 982-2655
E-mail: upress@virginia.edu
Web site: www.upress.virginia.edu

University Publications of America
4520 East-West Hwy. #800
Bethesda, MD 20814 (800) 692-6300
(301) 657-3200 Fax 657-3202
E-mail: info@upapubs.com

Upton & Sons
917 Hillcrest St. • El Segundo, CA 90245
(213) 322-7202

Mae Urbanek
Lusk, WY 82225 (307) 334-2473

Utah State Historical Society
300 Rio Grande • Salt Lake City, UT 84101
(801) 533-6024

Utah State University Press
7800 Old Main Hill • Logan, UT 84322
(800) 239-9974; (435) 797-1362 Fax 797-0313
E-mail: ctarbet@upress.usu.edu
Website: www.usu.edu/usupress

V

Valkyrie Publishing House
8245 26th Ave. N. • St. Petersburg, FL 33710
(813) 345- 8864

Alfred Van Der Marck Edition
Orders to Harper & Row

Van Nostrand Reinhold
7625 Empire Dr. • Florence, KY 41022
(606) 525-6600

Vanguard Press, Inc.
201 E. 50th St., 2nd Floor
New York, NY 10022

Vantage Press
516 W. 34 St. • New York, NY 10001
(800) 882-3273

VHPS, Inc.
16365 James Madison Hwy.
Gordonsville, VA 22942
(800) 488-5233 Fax (540) 672-7664

Viking Penguin
Div. of Penguin USA

VIP (Various Indian Peoples) Publishing Co.
P.O. Box 833216 • Richardson, TX 75083
(800) 776-0842
Website: www.nativelanguages.com

Visible Ink Press
Imprint of The Gale Group

W

Wadsworth Publishing Co.
Distribution Center, 7625 Empire Dr.
Florence, KY 41042 (800) 354-9706

George Wahr Publishing Co.
304 1/2 S. State St.
Ann Arbor, MI 48104 (313) 668-6097

Walker & Co.
435 Hudson St. • New York, NY 10014
(800) 289-2553 Fax (212) 727-0984

Washington State Historical Society
315 N. Stadium Way
Tacoma, WA 98403 (206) 593-2830

Washington State University Press
P.O. Box 645910
Pullman, WA 99164 (800) 354-7360
(509) 335-7880 Fax 335-8568
E-mail: wsupress@wsu.edu
Website: www.wsu.edu/wsupress

Franklin Watts, Inc.
90 Sherman Tpke. • Danbury, CT 06816
(203) 797-3500 Fax 797-3197

Waveland Press
P.O. Box 400 • Prospect Hts., IL 60070
(708) 634-0081 Fax 634-9501

Wayfinder Press
P.O. Box 217 • Ridgway, CO 81432
(303) 626-5452

Wayne State University Press
Leonard N. Simons Bldg., 4809 Woodward Ave.
Detroit, MI 48201 (800) 978-7323
Fax (313) 577-6131
Web site: www.wsupress.wayne.edu

Webb Research Group
P.O. Box 314 • Medford, OR 97501
(800) 866-9721; (503) 664-5205

Wells Publishing
9191 Towne Centre Dr. #550
San Diego, CA 92122

Wennawoods Publshing
RR#2 Box 529C • Lewisburg, PA 17837
(717) 524-4820

West Texas Museum Association
P.O. Box 4499 • Lubbock, TX 79409
(806) 742-2443

Western America Institute for Exploration
1821 E. 9th St. • The Dalles, OR 97058
(503) 296-9414

Western Publishers
1808 River Dr. • New Bern, NC 28560

Western Publishing
P.O. Box 905 • Sturtevant, WI 53177
(800) 235-3089

Westernlore Publications
P.O. Box 35305 • Tucson, AZ 85740
(602) 297-5491

Westview Press
5500 Central Ave. • Boulder, CO 80301
(303) 444-3541 Fax 449-3356

Wheelwright Museum of the American Indian
P.O. Box 5153 • Santa Fe, NM 87502
(505) 982-4636

White Publishing
P.O. Box 342 • Arlee, MT (406) 726-3627

Whitston Publishing Co.
P.O. Box 958 • Troy, NY 12181
(518) 283-4363 Fax 283-8573
E-mail: whitsaton@capital.net

Whole Earth Motorcycle Center
P.O. Box 102125 • Denver, CO 80250
(303) 715-9292 Fax 733-8625
E-mail: gregfrazier@yahoo.com

Wichita Tribal Office
P.O. Box 729 • Anadarko, OK 73005
(405) 247-2425 Fax 247-2005

Wilderness Adventure Books
P.O. Box 217 • Davisburg, MI 48350
(800) 852-8652

John Wiley & Sons
1 Wiley Dr. • Somerset, NJ 08873
(201) 469-4400

Charles Alma Wilson
P.O. Box 278 • Story, WY 82842
(307) 683-2188

Wisconsin Academy of Sciences, Arts & Letters
1922 University Ave. • Madison, WI 53705
(800) 443-6159 Fax (608) 265-3039

Wisconsin Dept. of Public Instruction
P.O. Box 7841 • Madison, WI 53707
(800) 243-8782 Fax (608) 267-9110
E-mail: pubsales@mail.state.wi.us

David Michael Wolfe
4167 Timberlane Dr.
Allison Park, PA 15101 (412) 487-7093
E-Mail: wahya@usaor.net

Wolf Moon Press
P.O. Box 2626 • Frisco, CO 80443
(970) 668-5399 Fax (800) 697-5608

Wolfe Publishing Co.
P.O. Box 8036
Fernandina Beach, FL 32035
(904) 277-0555 Fax 321-0417

Wonder-Treasure Books
360 N. La Cienega Blvd.
Los Angeles, CA 90048
(800) 421-0892; in CA (800) 227-8801

Wo-Pila Publishing
P.O. Box 8966 • Erie, PA 16505
(800) 786-6322 Fax (814) 864-3823

Wordware Publishing
2320 Los Rios Blvd., Suite 200
Plano, TX 75074 (800) 229-4949
E-mail: wordware@connectusa.com

Workbooks Press
P.O. Box 8504 • Atlanta, GA 30306
(404) 874-1044

Workman Publishing Co.
708 Broadway • New York, NY 10003
(800) 722-7202 in NY (212) 254-5900

Workshop Publications
P.O. Box 345 • Interlochen, MI 49643-0345
(616) 946-3712

World Around Songs
20 Colbert's Creek Rd.
Burnsville, NC 28714 (704) 675-5343

World Book, Inc.
525 W. Monore St. • Chicago, IL 60661
(312) 258-3700

World Music Press
P.O. Box 2565 • Danbury, CT 06813
(800) 810-2040; Fax (203) 748-3432

World Vision International
919 W. Huntington Dr.
Monrovia, CA 91016 (818) 303-8811

World Wisdom Books
P.O. Box 2682 • Bloomington, IN 47402
(812) 332-1663

WorldComm
65 Macedonia Rd. • Alexander, NC 28701
(800) 472-0438Fax (828) 255-8719

Written Heritage, Inc.
P.O. Box 1390 • Folsom, LA 70437-1390
(800) 301-8009; (504) 796-5433 Fax 796-9236

Wyoming Tribune-Eagle
702 W. Lincoln Way • Cheyenne WY 82001
((307) 634-3361 Fax 778-7163

Y

Yale University Press
P.O. Box 209040 • New Haven, CT 06520
(203) 432-0960 Fax (203) 432-0948

Yale University Publications in Anthropology
208277 Yale Sta. • New Haven, CT 06520
(203) 432-3670

Yankton Sioux Tribe Elderly Board
Dist. by Dakota West Books
P.O. Box 9324 • Rapid City, SD 57701
(605) 348-1075

Ye Galleon Press
P.O. Box 287 • Fairfield, WA 99012
(800) 829-5586; Fax (509) 283-2422

Yerrington Paiute Tribe Publications
171 Campbell Ln. • Yerington, NV 89447

Yosemite Association
P.O. Box 545 • Yosemite Nat'l Park, CA 95389
(209) 379-2646 Fax (209) 379-2486

A

ABBOTT, ANN
(executive director)
Affiliation: Native American Coalition of Tulsa, 1740 West 41st St., Tulsa, OK 74107 (918) 446-8432.

ABBOTT, DEVON IRENE (Choctaw/Cherokee) 1957-
(professor of history)
Born June 2, 1957, Wichita Falls, Tex. *Education*: Texas Christian University, BA, 1981; MEd, 1982; MA, 1986; PhD, 1989. *Principal occupation*: Assistant professor of history. *Address*: Unknown. *Affiliations*: Secretary, American Indian Center of Fort Worth, 1977-78; Board member, American Indian Center of Dallas, 1984-87; consultant, Texas Historical Commission and the Texas Indian Commission's Committee on the Acquisition and Disposition of Human Remains and Sacred Objects, 1984-89; Texas Director - American Indians Against Desecration, 1987-88; assistant professor of history, Northern Arizona University, Flagstaff, AZ, 1989-91; consultant to Northeastern State University's Archives & Special Collections, 1988-. *Memberships*: Phi Alpha Theta; Southern Association for Women Historians; Oklahoma Historical Society; American Indian Historians' Association; Western History Association; America Society for Ethnohistory. *Awards, honors*: TX Phi Alpha Theta Award for paper, "Health Care at the Cherokee Female Seminary: 1876-1909, 1988; Ford Foundation/National Research Council Doctoral Dissertation Fellowship for Minorities, 1988-89; Phi Alpha Theta/Westerners International Award for Best Dissertation in Western History, 1989; Northern Arizona University Junior Nominee, National Endowment for the Humanities Summer Stipend, 1990. *Interests*: American Indian history; American Indian Women, Education; Desecration of Indian Burial Sites; Athletics. *Publications*: Various articles in journals; Cultivating the Rose Buds: The Cherokee Female Seminary, 1851-1909 (University of Nebraska Press).

ABBOTT, GREG, D.O.
(clinical director)
Affiliation: Holton PHS Indian Health Center, 100 West 6th St., Holton, KS 66436 (913) 364-2177.

ABBOTT, LEO D.
(director of administration)
Affiliation: American Indian Studies Dept., University of Minnesota, 102 Scott Hall, 72 Pleasant St. SE, Minneapolis, MN 55455 (612) 624-1338 Fax 624-3858.

ABEITA, ANDY P. (Isleta Pueblo) 1963-
(artist-stone sculptor)
Born July 24, 1963, Chicago, Ill. *Principal occupation*: Artist-stone sculptor. *Home address*: 2 N. Lake Lane, Peralta, NM 87042 (505) 869-8148; (800) 638-7791 (work). *Affiliation*: Co-owner, Laboraex Enterprises, Peralta, NM, 1986-; co-owner, Denver, CO, 1992-; co-owner, Andy Abeita's Bear Fetish Studio, Santa Fe, NM, 1992-. *Memberships*: Indian Arts & Crafts Association; Heard Museum Guild; American Indian Art Council; Gallup Ceremonial Association; Indian Arts Foundation (advocacy for nature conservancy); Council for Indigenous Arts & Culture (president). *Interests*: "My wife, Roberta, and I are Native American artistans - stone sculptors & fetish carvers. Roberta & I travel roughly 50,000 miles a year promoting our art work and our culture. We average 30 gallery appearances a year and 10 wholesale shows annually. In recent years, I have become quite involved with educational & environmental functions held in many parts of the country. I am also a recognized lecturer/speaker by the Native American Art Council."

ABEITA, JAMES (Pueblo)
(BIA agency supt.)
Affiliation: Superintendent, Northern Pueblos Agency, Bureau of Indian Affairs, P.O. Box 4269, Fairview Station, Espanola, NM 87533 (505) 753-1400.

ABEITA, JOSEPH, JR. (Pueblo)
(Indian school supt.)
Affiliation: Santa Fe Indian School, P.O. Box 5340, Santa Fe, NM 87501 (505) 989-6300 Fax 989-6317.

ABEITA, ROBERTA (Ramah Navajo) 1951-
(artist-stone sculptor)
Born August 13, 1951, Rehobeth, N.M. *Principal oc-*
cupation: Artist-stone sculptor. *Address*: Unknown. *Affiliation*: Co-owner, Laboraex Enterprises, Peralta, NM, 1986-; co-owner Laboraex Enterprises, Denver, CO, 1992-; co-owner, Andy Abeita's Bear Fetish Studio, Santa Fe, NM, 1992-. *Memberships*: Indian Arts & Crafts Association; Heard Museum Guild; American Indian Art Council; Gallup Ceremonial Association; Indian Arts Foundation (advocacy for nature conservancy). *Interests*: "My husband Andy and I are Native American artisans - stone sculptors & fetish carvers. Andy & I travel roughly 50,000 miles a year promoting our art work and our culture. We average 30 gallery appearances a year and 10 wholesale shows annually. In recent years, I have become quite involved with educational & environmental functions held in many parts of the country. I am also a recognized lecturer/speaker by the Native American Art Council."

ABERLE, DAVID F.
(professor of anthropology)
Affiliation: Professor, Dept. of Anthropology, University of British Columbia, 6303 N.W. Marine Dr., Vancouver, B.C. V6T 2B2 (604) 228-2878.

ABEYTA, JOSEPH, Jr.
(school superintendent)
Affiliation: Santa Fe Indian School, 1501 Cerrillos Rd., Santa Fe, NM 87501 (505) 989-6300.

ABNEY, DON (Sac & Fox)
(tribal chief)
Address & Affiliation: Sac & Fox Nation of Oklahoma Business Committee, Rt. 2, Box 246, Stroud, OK 74079 (918) 968-3526 Fax 968-3887.

ABRAHAM, ELMER THOMAS
(Indian band chief)
Affiliation: Frog Lake Indian Band, Frog Lake, Alberta, Canada T0A 1M0 (403) 943-3737.

ABRAHAM, FRANKLIN
(Indian band chief)
Affiliation: Little Black River Indian Band, O'Hanley, Manitoba, Canada R0E 1K0 (204) 367-4411.

ABRAHAM, JOHN
(BIA field rep.)
Affiliation: Coeur D'Alene Tribe BIA Field Office, P.O. Box 408, Plummer, ID 83851 (208) 686-1887 Fax 686-1903.

ABRAHAM, SYDNEY
(Indian band chief)
Affiliation: Long Lake #58 Indian Band, Box 609, Long Lac, Ontario, Canada P0T 2A0 (807) 876-2292.

ABRAMS, GEORGE H.J. (Ha-doh-jus)
(Seneca) 1939-
(anthropologist, museum director)
Born May 4, 1939, Allegany Indian Reservation, Salamanca, N.Y. *Education*: SUNY, Buffalo, BA, 1965, MA, 1967; University of Arizona, PhD program, 1968-1971. *Principal occupation*: Anthropologist. *Address*: Yager Museum, Hartwick College, Oneonta, NY 13820 (607) 431-4480. *Affiliations*: Director, Yager Museum, Hartwick College, Oneonta, NY. Special assistant to the Director, National Museum of the American Indian, Heye Foundation, New York, NY. *Other professional posts*: Member, Board of Directors, American Indian Development, Inc., Denver, CO, 1971-; member, American Indian Advisory Board, Denver Museum of Natural History, Denver, CO, 1971-; member, Board of Trustees, Museum of the American Indian-Heye Foundation, New York, New York, 1977-80, 1982-; chairman, Ad Hoc Committee on the New York State Indian, New York State Archaeological Association, Rochester, NY, 1977-; chairman, North American Indian Museums Association, Salamanca, NY, 1978-89; member, Board of Directors, New York Iroquois Conference, Inc., Buffalo, NY, 1979-81; member, advisory board, Center for the History of the American Indian, The Newberry Library, Chicago, 1980-87; member, Commission on Museums for a New Century, American Association of Museums, Washington, DC, 1981-85; member, National Advisory and Coordinating Council on Bilingual Education, Washington, DC, 1984-85, 1985-87; member, National Advisory Panel, Public Monuments Conservation Program, National Institute for the Conservation of Cultural Property, Smithsonian Institution, Washington, DC, 1985-; member, New York
State Commissioner of Education, Advisory Council on Museums, Albany, NY, 1985-. *Community activities*: Seneca Nation Library, NY (member, board of trustees, 1978-, chairman, 1978-81, 1984-9); Johnson O'Malley (JOM) Local Indian Education Committee, Allegany Indian Reservation (chairman, 1979-83, member, 1983-84); Mohawk-Caughnawaga Museum, Fonda, NY (member, board of advisors, 1980-); Seneca Nation of Indians (member, Board of Education, 1987); member, Internal Taxation Committee, 1989; commissioner, Planning Commission, 1989); Gannagaro Archaeological Site, New York State Division of Historic Preservation, Parks and Recreation (member, advisory group.) Membership: American Association of University Professors, 1972-. *Awards, honors*: John Hay Whitney Fellow, 1968-1969; American Indian Graduate Scholarship Program Grant, School of Law, University of New Mexico, 1971. *Interests*: Teaches contemporary American Indian anthropology; American Indian education; applied anthropology; ethnohistory, museology, Iroquois Indians. *Published works*: The Cornplanter Cemetary (Pennsylvania Archaeologist, 1965); Moving of the Fire: A Case of Iroquois Ritual Innovation (Iroquois Culture, History & Prehistory, 1967); Red Jacket (The World Book Encyclopedia, 1976); The Seneca People (Indian Tribal Series, Phoenix, 1976); The Directory of Indian Museums.

ABRAMS, OLIVER (Seneca)
(member-board of regents)
Affiliation: Member, Board of Regents, American Indian Heritage Foundation, 6051 Arlington Blvd., Falls Church, VA 22044-2788 (703) 237-7500.

ABRAHAMSON, MARK
(IHS health director)
Affiliation: Grand Portage Band, P.O. Box 428, Grand Portage, MN 55605 (218) 475-2235.

ACKERMAN, LILLIAN A. 1928-
(professor of anthropology)
Born April 14, 1928, Detroit, Mich. *Education*: University of Michigan, BA, 1950, MA, 1951; Washington State University, PhD, 1982. *Principal occupation*: Professor of anthropology. *Home address*: 1770 SW View Dr., Pullman, WA 99163 (509) 335-4426 (office). *Affiliations*: Professor of anthropology at Washington State University, Pullman, 1982-. *Other professional post*: Consultant in Plateau & Yup'ik Eskimo cultural anthropology. *Community activities*: Chairperson, Development Services Board of Whitman County, Washington (for developing and overseeing programs for the mentally retarded). *Memberships*: American Anthropological Association, 1950- (Fellow); American Ethnological Society, 1980-; Society for Applied Anthropology (Fellow); Alaska Anthropological Association, 1982-; Sigma Xi, 1982-. *Awards, honors*: Woodrow Wilson Fellowship; American Association of University Women - Dissertation Fellowship; grant from the Phillips Fund of the American Philosophical Society, 1988. *Interests*: Primary research is in the Plateau Culture Area with emphasis on the Colville Indian Reservation; worked on the Coeur d'Alene and Nez Perce Reservations; also, worked among Yup'ik Eskimos of Goodnews Bay, Alaska and the Tlingit Indians of Alaska. Extensive work on gender equality and extended family organization. *Published works*: Sexual Equality in the Plateau Culture Area (PhD dissertation, Washington State University, 1982); "The Effect of Missionary Ideals on Family Structure" and "Women's Roles in Plateau Indian Culture" (in Idaho Yesterdays 32(1-2); 64-73); several short articles on gender equality in the Plateau. "Yup'ik Eskimo Residence and Descent in Southwestern Alaska" (Inter-Nord no. 19, 1990); "Gender Status in Yup'ik Society" (in Etudes/Inuit/Studies 1990); an article in the Handbook of North American Indians (Smithsonian) on gender roles and extended family structure; a book, Women and Power in Native North America, (University of Oklahoma Press, 1995) edited by Laura F. Klein and Lillian A. Ackerman; A Song to the Creator: Traditional Arts of Native American Women of the Plateau (University of Oklahoma Press, 1996); A Necessary Balance: Gender & Power Among Indians of the Columbia Plateau (University of Oklahoma Press, 2004).

ACKERMAN, ROBERT E. 1928-
(professor of anthropology; museum director)
Born May 21, 1928, Grand Rapids, Mich. *Education*:

University of Michigan, AB, 1950, M.A., 1951; University of Pennsylvania, Ph.D., 1961. *Principal occupation*: Professor of anthropology; museum director. *Home address*: 1770 SW View Dr., Pullman, WA 99163 (509) 335-4426 (office). *Affiliations*: Professor of anthropology, Washington State University, Pullman, 1961-. *Other professional posts*: Director, Museum of Anthropology. *Military service*: Airman first class, U.S. Air Force, 1952-56. *Memberships*: American Anthropological Association, 1951-; Society for American Archaeology, 1951-; American Association for the Advancement of Science, 1960-; Arctic Institute of North America, 1969; Sigma Xi, 1968-; Explorers Club, 1980-; Canadian Archaeological Association, 1971-; Pacific Science Association, 1979-; American Quaternary Association, 1978-; Society for Professional Archaeology, 1977-. *Awards, honors*: Research grants for archaeological investigations in southwest and southeast Alaska: Arctic Institute of North America, 1962; National Park Service, 1963-65; National Geographic Society, 1978-81; U.S. Forestry Service, 1985-86; National Science Foundation, 1966-67, 1971, 1973, 1992, 1995; Centennial Lecturer for State of Washington, Centennial '89. Fellowships in the American Anthropological Association, 1964; the American Association for the Advancement of Science, 1969; and the Arctic Institute of North America, 1971; Explorers Club, 1980; Life member, Pacific Science Association for contributions to the discipline of anthropology and Arctic research. *Interests*: Archaeological research in Alaska and Siberia; travel to visit classic sites in Mediterranean, China, Korea, and Japan. *Biographical sources*: Who's Who in the West; Who's Who in the World; American Men of Science; International Scholars Directory; Contemporary Authors; Men of Achievement; Dictionary of International Biography; Who's Who Among Journalists and Authors. *Published works*: Kenaitze Indians (Indian Tribal Series, 1975); Eskimos of St. Lawrence Island (Indian Tribal Series, 1977); *In Progress*: Routes Into the New World (ed.), to be published by Washington State University Press; numerous articles and reports.

ACKLEY, ARLYN (Mole Lake Chippewa)
(tribal council chairperson)
Affiliation: Sokaogon Chippewa Tribal Council, Route 1, Box 625, Crandon, WI 54520 (715) 478-2604.

ADAIR, JOHN WILLIAM (Cherokee of Oklahoma-Deer Clan) 1942-
(company president)
Born June 6, 1942, Sequoyah County, Okla. *Education*: Bacone College, Muskogee, OK, AA, 1962; Northeastern State University, Tahlequah, OK, BA, 1964, MA, 1973. *Principal occupation*: Oil/gas exploration; real estate development. *Home address*: 8309 S. 241st E. Ave., Broken Arrow, OK 74014 (918) 357-1745. jwacherokeegas@cox.net. *Affiliations*: President, OK Land Development Co., Inc., Broken Arrow, OK, 1975-1988; President, Adair Oil Co., Tulsa, OK, 1988-present. *Other professional posts*: Chairperson, Cherokee Nation Election Commission; trustee, Cherokee Nation Museum. *Military service*: Naval Air Reserve, Active duty, 1964-71; Reserves, 1971- (CAPTAIN; Commanding Officer of Naval Reserves of Nuclear Aircraft Carrier USS Carl Vinson CVN-70; flew 225 combat missions in Vietnam-14 Air Medals, two Navy Commendation Medals with Combat V, Air Gallantry Cross, Vietnamese Air Gallantry Medal, Vietnam Service Medal with four Bronze Stars). *Memberships*: Civitan, American Legion, Naval Reserve Association, Combat Pilots Association; Red River Valley Fighter Pilots Association; National Who's Who in Executives & Professionals; Society of Petroleum Engineers. *Interests*: "Descendant of prominent Cherokee family - father was Walthal Corrigan Adair, an original enrollee, grandfather was Oscar F. Adair, a Cherokee Veteran of the Civil War under Cherokee General Stand Watie. Cherokees were last to surrender in War. Oscar F. was later judge of Sequoyah District. Great grandson of Judge John Thompson Adair, the Chief Justice of the Supreme Court of the Cherokee Nation." *Published work*: Article - "New Generation Capacity for Power-Strapped California: Non-traditional Site Selection," (World Energy, Vol. 3 No. 2).

ADAIR, MARY (Cherokee) 1936-
(artist)
Born July 2, 1936, Sequoyah County, Okla. *Education*: Bacone Indian Junior College, AA, 1955; North-

eastern Oklahoma State University, BA, 1957; Tulsa University , BFA, 1967; Northeastern State University, Tahlequah, OK, MF, 1983. *Principal occupation*: Artist. *Address*: Rt. 2, Box 287, Sallisaw, OK 74955 (918) 775-5785. E-mail: maryadair@csweb.net. *Affiliations*: Murrow Indian Children's Home, Muskogee, OK (child care-residence care institution) (executive director, 1973-79); Cherokee Nation of Oklahoma, Tahlequah, OK (education & health positions, 1979-88); Cherokee Nation art and Native American crafts teacher, 1988-2001; artist (in paint and Native crafts), 2001-present. *Other professional posts*: Artist in residence, State Arts Council of Oklahoma, Oklahoma City. *Community activities*: Presbyterian Church; Community Council (board member); Indian Parent Committee; Soroptimist Club; American Baptist Indian Caucus; Oklahoma Association of Children's Institutions and Agencies (secretary-treasurer). *Memberships*: North American Indian Women's Association (past secretary); Daughters of the Earth (a group of eight Indian women artists who displayed their work together in gallery and museum shows); National Indian Education Association (past secretary); Descendants of Nancy Ward Association (board member); Goingsnake Historical Association; Trail of Tears Association; Sequoyah County Historical Society (treasurer) Adair Reunion (treasurer); McCoy Cemetery Association (treasurer). *Awards, honors*: Painting and crafts awards and entries in the following shows: Philbrook Museum - Indian Annual Art Show; Five Tribes Museum - Annual Art Show; Cherokee National Museum Show; Bacone Indian Art Competition; American Indian Exposition Competition; Red Cloud Indian Art Show; Heard Museum; Tsa-La-Gi Museum; Santa Fe Indian Market and others. *Interests*: "I have interest in contemporary American Indian affairs, history, education and art. (I) Have traveled to a number of traditional Indian communities and reservation areas for business and fellowship. I have spent the last 18 years serving the Cherokee Nation of Oklahoma in several areas of interest. A highlight was being able to attend the first joint meeting of the eastern and Oklahoma Cherokee councils, and two later meetings; genealogy, Native American crafts." *Biographical source*: Professional American Indian and Alaska Native Women Directory, 1979; Directory of Native American Painters. *Published works*: Illustrations in "Women of Power" magazine, 1989; Selu: Seeking the Corn Mother's Wisdom, book by Marilou Awiakta (Fulcrum, 1993); illustrations in Native American Gardening by M. Caduto and Joseph Bruchac.

ADAMS, ANNA MARIA *(Henu)* (Winnebago) 1961-
(certified art teacher)
Born April 4, 1961, Washington, D.C. *Education*: Institute of American Indian Arts, AFA, 1981; Oklahoma State University, 1982-83; University of Oklahoma, BFA, 1984. *Principal occupation*: Certified art teacher. *Home address*: 7629 Hunt Rd., Ponca City, OK 74604 (580) 765-5086. E-mail: jibbyup@msn.com. *Affiliations*: Art teacher, Ponc City High School; art club. *Other professional posts*: Owner, Adams & Adams Farms (Registered Paint Horses), Ponca City, OK, 1990-present; owner, Adams Studios, Ponca City, OK, 1986-present. *Community activities*: Standing Bear Education Committee, Standing Bear Park, Ponca City, OK, 1996-present; Pawnee Bill Wild West Show Actor, 1995-99; Parent Coalition, Title VII Program, Ponca City High School; Native American Pow-wows. *Membership*: Ponca City Art Association; Ponca City Art Center; Paint Horse Association; Oklahoma Arts Council Master/Apprentice Program. *Awards, honors*: Who's Who in American Junior Colleges; 1st Miss IAIA Powwow Princess; 1996 "Outstanding Patron" Hideaway Pizza Collage 2001-2004 - An Oklahoma Centennial Project. *Interests*: "I have displayed artwork in New York, Santa Fe, NM, and Oklahoma; training and breeding American Paint Horses; raising & breeding manx cats; four wheelers ATV; boating & fishing. *Work in Progress*: Working on a book of "Ribbonwork and Ribbonwork Designs" of the Native Americans.

ADAMS, BERT, Sr. (Tlingit-Haida)
(AK village council president)
Affiliation: Native Village of Yakutat, P.O. Box 418, Yakutat, AK 99689 (907) 784-3932.

ADAMS, DAVID WALLACE
(professor of education, author)
Affiliation: Professor of Education, Cleveland State

University, Cleveland, OH. *Published work*: Education for Extinction: American Indians & the Boarding School Experience, 1875-1928.

ADAMS, E. CHARLES 1947-
(archaeologist/anthropologist)
Born November 27, 1947, Denver, Colo. *Education*: University of Colorado, BA, 1970, MA, 1973, PhD, 1975. *Principal occupation*: Professor of anthropology. *Address*: Unknown. *Affiliation*: University of Arizona & Arizona State Museum, Tucson, AZ, 1985-present; director, Homolovi Research Program. *Military service*: Army National Guard, 1966-72 (Sergeant). *Community activities*: President, Arizona Archaeological Council, 1978-80. *Memberships*: Society for American Archaeology, 1972-; American Anthropological Association, 1975-; Arizona Archaeological Council, 1977-; Sigma Xi, 1973-; Arizona Archaeological & Historical Society, 1975-. *Awards, honors*: Earl Morris Award (presented to the outstanding archaeology graduate student in the Department of Anthropology, University of Colorado, 1975). *Interests*: The prehistory & history of the Colorado Plateau with emphasis on the Pueblo Indians, especially the Hopi. "I have directed several research expeditions for the Museum of Northern Arizona, Flagstaff, and the Arizona State Museum, Tucson, on the Plateau. "I direct an archaeological research project at the University of Arizona excavating 600-700 year-old pueblos that are ancestral to the Hopi Indians. I have worked with the Hopi Tribe over the years on these research projects and employ Hopi high school students." *Published works*: Walpi Archaeological Project: Synthesis & Interpretation (Museum of Northern Arizona, 1982); Homol'ovi II: The Archaeology of an Ancestral Hopi Village (University of Arizona Press, 1991); The Origin & Development of the Pueblo Katsina Cult (University of Arizona Press, 1991).

ADAMS, EDITH
(BIA agency supt.)
Affiliation: Fort Belknap Agency, Bureau of Indian Affairs, P.O. Box 98, Harlem, MT 59526 (406) 353-2901.

ADAMS, EDMUND S. (Pamunkey)
(tribal chief)
Affiliation: Upper Mattaponi Indian Tribe, P.O. Box 182, King William, VA 23086 (804) 769-0041.

ADAMS, EDWARD J., Sr. (Athapascan)
(AK village council president)
Affiliation: Native Village of Sheldon's Point, Sheldon's Point, AK 99668 (907) 498-4226.

ADAMS, HANK
(association director)
Affiliation: Survival of American Indian Associations, 7803-A Samurai Dr., SE, Olympia, WA 98503 (360) 459-2679.

ADAMS, MARGARET B. *(Bina-doh-clish)* (Navajo) 1936-
(anthropologist-retired)
Born April 29, 1936, Toronto, Ontario, Can. *Education*: Monterey Peninsula College, AA, 1969; San Jose State University, BAS, 1971; University of Utah, MA, 1973. *Principal occupation*: Anthropologist-retired. *Home address*: P.O. Box 192, Cedar Ridge, CA 95924. *Affiliations*: Chief of Museum Branch, Fort Ord Military Complex; and, Head Curator of Fort Ord and Presidio of Monterey Museums, 1974-88. *Other professional posts*: Panel member (Indians in Science) for American Association for the Advancement of Science, 1972-85; reviewer, Project Media of American Indian Education Association. *Community activities*: American Indian Information Center of Monterey Peninsula (co-founder and volunteer executive director, 1973-92); member of Monterey Speaker's Bureau. Memberships: National Indian Education Association; California Indian Education Association; American Anthropological Association; American Association of Museums; Monterey History & Art Association. *Interests*: Higher education for Native Americans, particularly in the sciences; media presentations concerning Native Americans; review of media on Native Americans; observations and reporting of improper excavation of Native American ceremonial and burial sites; preservation of Native American ceremonial, burial, and historical sites. Retired from Government service April, 1988 and currently involved in research on a collection of recipes by contemporary Native American cooks, work-

ing title: The First American Cookbook. *Biographical sources*: Who's Who in America; World's Who Who of Women; The Science Teacher (Journal); Women in the Social Sciences. *Published works*: Indian Tribes of North America and a Brief Chronology of Ancient Pueblo Indian and Old World Events (Monterey Museum of Art, 1975); History of Navajo and Apache Painting (Indian America, Tulsa, 1976); Historic Old Monterey (DeAnza College History Center, 1977); Silver & Sheen—Southwestern Indian Jewelry (Indian America, Tulsa, 1977); and numerous publications on museum exhibits & history for the Federal Government.

ADAMS, RAY (Upper Mattaponi)
(tribal chief)
Affiliation: Chief, Upper Mattaponi Tribe, 106 Kyle Circle, Tabb, VA 23602 (804) 898-3310.

ADAMS, ROXANNA
(museum director)
Affiliation: Totem Heritage Center Museum & Library, 629 Dock St., Ketchikan, AK 99901 (907) 225-5900.

ADAMS, VIVIAN M. (Yakima, Puyallup, Suquamish, Quinault) 1943-
(museum curator)
Born March 21, 1943, Toppenish, Wash. *Education*: Institute of American Indian Art, Santa Fe, AFA, 1981. *Principal occupation*: Museum curator. *Address & Affiliation*: Yakima Nation Cultural Center, P.O. Box 151, Toppenish, WA 98948. *Community activities*: Yakima Agency Employees Club (secretary-treasurer); IAIA Student Senate Representative; Yakima Women's Investor's Club. *Memberships*: Washington State Folklife Council; American Association of State & Local History; Toppenish Chamber of Commerce; Yakima Chamber of Commerce; Washington Museum Association; Yakima Valley Visitors and Convention Bureau; National Trust for Historic Preservation; Native American Task Force, Washington State Centennial; Washington State Native American Task Force, Native American Consortium; Washington State Centennial Heritage Subcommittee of Lasting Legacy. *Awards, honors*: Outstanding Artistic & Academic Achievement, 1980-81; Institute of American Indian Art President's Award; Who's Who Among Students, American Junior Colleges, 1981; Scholastic Achievement Award, Yakima Nation Education, 1982. *Interests*: "My main interest is two-dimensional art (sketching, pen and ink). I love to work with Indian artifacts—those items which are hand made of natural materials. Plus, it is a joy to design ways to display these items which teach a lesson in an aesthetic manner. It is important to present our cultural history and traditions from our (Native American) point of view—to promote a better understanding by other cultures—and to learn from them. Oral history and elders input into telling our ways is extremely important to accomplishing those goals of the museum. Therefore, museology is my second interest, my financial base to a sporadic art career! But being a curator allows me the time to work with objects of art—my main love. My third interest is pursuing conservation techniques: recognizing and maintaining basket weaving, textile weaving, restoration techniques, time allowing I hope to accomplish conservator's training." *Biographical sources*: Yakima Herald Republic news article; Girl Scouts of America; Who's Who Among Students in American Junior Colleges.

ADAMS, WILL
(Indian band chief)
Affiliation: Lake Babine Indian Band, P.O. Box 879, Burns Lake, British Columbia, Canada V0J 1E0 (604) 692-7555.

ADAMSON, REBECCA L. (Eastern Cherokee) 1949-
(association founder/president)
Affiliation: Founder & President, First Nations Development Institute, 2300 Fall Hill Ave., Suite 412, Fredericksburg, VA 22401 (540) 371-5615 Fax 371-3505; Website: www.firstnations.org; E-mail: info@firstnations.org. *Other professional post*: Columnist, Indian Country Today, Canastota, NY.

ADAY, JERRY L.
(executive director)
Affiliation: Mid-American All-Indian Center, 650 N. Seneca, Wichita, KS 67203 (316) 262-5241.

ADDISON, ANTHONY (Arapahoe)
(tribal chairperson)
Affiliation: Arapahoe Tribe, P.O. Box 396, Fort Washakie, WY 82514 (307) 332-6120.

ADKINS, A. LEONARD
(tribal chief)
Affiliation: Chickahominy Indian Tribe, RFD 1, Box 299, Providence Forge, VA 23140 (804) 829-2186.

ADKINS, ARTHUR L. (Lonewolf)
(Chickahominy) 1926-
(tribal chief)
Born October 1, 1926, Charles City Co., VA. *Education*: Bacone College, AA, 1952; Virginia Commonwealth University, BS, MA. *Principal occupation*: Tribal chief. *Home address*: 6801 Lott Cary Rd., Providence Forge, VA 23140 (804) 829-2186. *Affiliations*: Chief, Chickahominy Indian Tribe, Providence Forge, VA; elementary school teacher-retired, Charles City Co., VA School System. *Other profesional post*: Member, Selective Service System. *Military service*: U.S. Army, 1945-47 (PFC, E.T.O., Occupation, Victory). *Community activities*: Chief, Chickahominy Indian Tribe; Charles City-New Kent Heritage Library; Woodmen of the World; V.F.W. *Awards, honors*: Woodmen of the World Fraternalist of the Year and Outstanding Citizen, 1990. *Interests*: "Traveling to see things of nature, museums, historical places."

ADKINS, GLORIA
(association director)
Affiliation: Washington State Indian Education Association, c/o Colville Confederated Tribes, P.O. Box 150, Nespelem, WA 99155 (509) 634-4711.

ADKINS, PRESTON
(dance troops coordinator)
Affiliation: Native American Dance Troops, Chickahominy Red Men Dancers, P.O. Box 473, Providence Forge, VA 23140 (804) 829-2152.

ADOLF, ROGER
(Indian band chief)
Affiliation: Fountain Indian Band, Box 1330, Lillooet, B.C., Canada V0K 1V0 (604) 256-4227.

AGNASSAGA, GEORGE (Eskimo)
(AK village council president)
Affiliation: Wainwright Traditional Council, P.O. Box 184, Wainwright, AK 99782 (907) 763-2726.

AGNUS, SIMON
(AK village council president)
Affiliation: Umkumiut Village Council, General Delivery, Nightmute, AK 99690 (907) 647-6213.

AGOGINO, GEORGE A. 1920-
(anthropologist)
Born November 18, 1920, West Palm Beach, Fla. *Education*: University of New Mexico, BA, 1949, MA, 1951; Syracuse University, PhD, 1958; Harvard University, Wenner-Gren Foundation Post Doctoral Fellowship in Anthropology, 1961-62. *Principal occupation*: Distinguished professor of anthropology, museum director. *Home address*: 1600 S. Main, Portales, NM 88130 (505) 356-8709. *Affiliations*: Instructor in anthropology, Syracuse University, 1956-58; museum director and assistant professor, University of South Dakota, 1958-59; assistant professor of anthropology, University of Wyoming, 1959-62; associate professor of anthropology, Baylor University, 1962-63; Eastern New Mexico University, professor of anthropology, 1963-91, distinguished research professor in anthropology, emeritus, 1991- (anthropology dept. chairman, 1963-80); director of Paleo-Indian Institute, 1968-. *Other professional posts*: Founding director, Blackwater Draw Museum, Miles Museum, and Anthropology Museum of Eastern New Mexico University, Portales, N.M. *Military service*: U.S. Army Signal Corps, 1943-46. *Community activities*: Eastern New Mexico University, Local National Educational Association (president and vice-president, 1976-). *Memberships*: American Anthropological Association (Fellow); American Association for the Advancement of Science (Fellow); Royal Anthropological Institute of Great Britain and Ireland (Fellow); Institute Inter-American (Fellow); Current Anthropology (Associate); Explorers' Club (Fellow); Senator Academico (regent) Academmia Romania de Science ed Arti. *Awards, honors*: PhD Rome (Italy)

Institute of Arts & Sciences; multiple grants from Wenner-Gren Foundation for Anthropology, American Philosophical Society, Sigma Xi; twice Eastern New Mexico University Outstanding Educator, 1972, 1974-75; fourth distinguished professor in 70-year history of Eastern New Mexico University; State of New Mexico awarded Dr. Agogino as one of one hundred "Eminent Scholars" of New Mexico. *Interests*: "Indian religion and culture; North America and Mexico Paleo Indian; Indian physical anthropology, pictoglyphs. Have worked with and published on Navajo, Iroquois, Pueblo, Kickapoo, Seminole, Sioux; in Canada: Cree; and in Mexico: Seri, Yaqui, Aztec, Huichol, Tepecano, Mayo, Maya, Huastica and Otomi Indians. Archaeological work has largely been with our earliest Indians, the Paleo-Indian, the discoverers of the New World. I also work for the federal government as a forensic physical anthropologist, getting maximum information before reburial by their respective tribes." *Travels, expeditions*: Anthropological research in Canada, Mexico, New Guinea and Australia. *Biographical sources*: Who's Who Among Authors and Journalists; Directory of International Biography; Who's Who in the World; Who's Who in America; Who's Who in the Southwest; Who's Who in the West; Who's Who in American Education; Directory of International Biography; Contemporary Authors; Outstanding Educators in America; American Men of Science; Plains Anthropological Society; Who's Who in the World (Tenth Edition). *Published works*: Four monographs, and about 450 articles in professional publications.

AGOYO, HERMAN (Pueblo)
(pueblo governor)
Affiliation: Pueblo of San Juan, P.O. Box 1099, San Juan Pueblo, NM 87566 (505) 852-4400; *Past professional post*: Chairperson, All Indian Pueblo Council, Albuquerque, NM.

AGUILAR, ALFRED (Sa wa pin)
(San Ildefonso Pueblo) 1933-
(artist, teacher)
Born July 1, 1933, San Ildefonso Pueblo, N.M. *Education*: High school. *Principal occupation*: Artist, teacher (Chapter I, 1967). *Home address*: Route 5, Box 318C, Santa Fe, NM 87501 (505) 455-3530 (work). *Affiliation*: Owner, Aguilar Indian Arts, Santa Fe, NM. *Military service*: U.S. Air Force, 1952-56 (Good Service Award). *Community activities*: Pueblo official council member. *Memberships*: Eight Northern Pueblo Art Council; The Indian Pueblo Cultural Center. *Awards, honors*: For painting, pottery, and sculptures from the SWAIA, New Mexico State Fair, Inter-Tribal Ceremonial, Jemez Pueblo, Heard Museum, and New Mexico Fine Arts Museum. *Interests*: Education, art-travel expeditions. Mr. Aguilar specializes in black and red pottery, and is well known by many people around the world with his nativity set and story teller. He sculptures black on black buffalos, and animal and dancing figures on pottery. He has gained versatility in water color, and is adept in depicting Indian dances and in preserving ancient design and symbols on his work.

AGUILAR, MICHELLE PENOZIEQUAH
(executive director)
Affiliation: Governor's Office of Indian Affairs, 1515 S. Cherry St., Box 40909, Olympia, WA 98504 (206) 753-2411.

AGUILAR, JOSE V. (Suwu-Peen)
(Tewa Pueblo) 1924-
(technical graphic artist)
Born January 8, 1924, San Ildefonso, N.M. *Education*: Otis Art Institute, Certificate, 1949; Hill and Canyon School of Art, 1950. *Principal occupation*: Technical graphic artist. *Home address*: 9682 Mt. Damard Dr., Buena Park, CA 90620. *Affiliation*: Project Coordinator, Rockwell International, Downey, CA, 1954-. *Military service*: U.S. Army, 1944-46 (European Theatre Medal; Purple Heart). *Memberships*: National Congress of American Indians, 1954-. *Awards, honors*: Certificate of Merit, Inter-Tribal Indian Ceremonial Association, 1949; First Purchase Award, Philbrook Art Center, 1953; Denver Art Museum Purchase Award; Mary Wartrous Award, 1954; Honorable Mention, Philbrook Art Center, 1959; Lippencott and Wellington Award; Museum of New Mexico Award for Collection of Museum of Contemporary Art; paintings in permanent collections of Philbrook Art Center, Museum of New Mexico, and Museum of the American Indian.

Private collections include: Millard Sheet, artist and educator; Vincent Price, actor and art collector; and Darwin Goody, educator.

AGUILAR, TERRY (San Ildefonso Tewa)
(Pueblo lt. governor)
Affiliation: San Ildefonso Pueblo Council, Rt. 5 Box 315-A, Santa Fe, NM 87501 (505) 455-2273.

AHENAKEW, BARRY
(Indian band chief)
Affiliation: Chief, Ahtahkakoop Indian Band, Box 220, Shell Lake, Saskatchewan, Canada S0J 2G0 (306) 468-2326.

AHENAKEW, WILLARD
(corporation president)
Affiliation: President, Saskatchewan Indian Arts & Crafts Corp., 2431-8th Ave., Regina, Saskatchewan, Canada S4R 5J7 (306) 352-1501.

AHHITTY, GLENDA
(commission director)
Affiliation: Los Angeles City/County Native American Indian Commission, 500 W. Temple St., Rm. 780, Los Angeles, CA 90012 (213) 974-7554.

AHKINGA, ORVILLE (Eskimo)
(AK village council president)
Affiliation: Native Village of Diomede (aka Inalik), P.O. Box 7099, Diomede, AK 99762 (907) 686-3021.

AHSHAPANEK, CAROL LO-ANN (PADDLETY)
(Kiowa/Wichita/Pawnee) 1942-
(community health nurse)
Born June 15, 1942, Lawton, Okla. *Education*: Haskell Indian Nations University, AA, 1975; Washburn University, BS, 1979. *Principal occupation*: Community health nurse. *Home address*: 1008 Mimosa Dr., Anadarko, OK 73005 (405) 247-7153. *Affiliations*: Clinical nurse, Haskell Indian Health Clinic, Lawrence, KS, 1980-84; clinical nurse, Anadarko Indian Clinic, Anadarko, OK, 1984-87; community health nurse, Pawhuska, OK, 1988-90; supervisory community health nurse, Lawton Indian Hospital, Lawton, OK, 1990-91; community health nurse, Anadarko, Indian Clinic, Anadarko, OK, 1991-2000. *Memberships*: Oklahoma State Board of Nursing. *Awards, honors*: Community Health Nurse Internship Program, Salt River Reservation, Scottsdale, AZ, 1987-88. *Interests*: Basketweaving, traditional dancing.

AHSHAPANEK, DON COLESTO (JOHNSON)
(Nanticoke/Delaware) 1932-
(tribal government services officer)
Born April 29, 1932, Milton, Dela. *Education*: Central State University (Edmond, OK), BS, 1956; University of Oklahoma, MS, 1959. *Principal occupation*: Realty specialist, adjunct professor of biological sciences. *Home address*: 1008 Mimosa Dr., Anadarko, OK 73005 (405) 247-7153. *Affiliations*: Associate professor, Emporia State University, Emporia, KS, 1962-71; instructor of life sciences, Haskell Indian Nations University, Lawrence, KS, 1971-91; tribal government services officer, Bureau of Indian Affairs, Anadarko Agency, Anadarko, OK, 1991-2000. *Memberships*: National Indian Education Association; American Indian Science & Engineering Society; Society of Native Americans & Chicanos in Science (board member); Headlands Indian Health Careers Program. *Awards, honors*: Research Assistantship, 1956-61; Research Presenter, 11th International Botanical Congress, Seattle, 1969; Program & Project Director, NIH Minority Biomedical Sciences Program, 1976-79; Outstanding Faculty Award, 1977-78, 1988-89; Program & Project Director, Dept. of Education Sciences Improvement Program, 1982-85; NSF Research Post Doctorate Fellowship, Kansas University (Dept. of Microbiology), 1982, (Dept. of Biochemistry), 1983; University of Oklahoma (Dept. of Microbiology), 1985-87; Keynote Speaker, Native American Research Symposium, Bozeman, MT, 1985. *Published works*: "Mammals Associated with Prehistoric People of Oklahoma," in Proceedings of the Oklahoma Academy of Science, 1960; "Phenology of a Native Tall-Grass Prairie in Central Oklahoma," in Ecology 43:135-138, 1962. *Interests*: Ethnohistory, genealogy, philately, traditional dancing.

AHTONE, DEBORAH (Kiowa) 1947-
(editor)
Born July 2, 1947, Carnegie, Okla. *Education*: Bacone College, AAm 1967; Rocky Mountain College, BA, 1970; University of Oklahoma, Graduate School, 1970-71. *Principal occupation*: Editor. *Home address*: P.O. Box 397, Mountain View, OK 73062 (405) 347-2875. *Affiliations*: Editor, Kiowa Indian News, Carnegie, OK, 1982-; editor/owner, Feather Review News, Mountain View, OK, 1989-. *Other professional posts*: Official photographer for Kiowa Tribe; member, Kiowa Tribal Museum Commission; Instructor, traditional techniques, Institute of American Idian Art (1 year); instructor, Indian studies, Dawson College, Glendive, MT (2 years). *Community activities*: Volunteer to Kiowa Tribal Museum & Kiowa Senior Citizen Center; photographer for 1992 Sovereignty Symposium, Oklahoma City. *Memberships*: Southern Plains Museum Association (chairperson, 1990; treasurer, 1992); Native American Journalists Association; Southwestern Association on Indian Affairs; National Congress of American Indians. *Awards, honors*: First Place, Scottsdale Indian Art Show-Mixed Media; Promising New Artist, Rose State College, 1978. *Interests*: Photography; "Interest in Indian affairs - led to appointment as editor of Kiowa News, which led to the establishment of statewide newspaper, "The Feather Review." Business trips for Dawson College led to contacts with other tribes and tribal leaders throughout the U.S. These contacts have remain crucial in networking the "Feather Review" with news from the tribes. Tribal leaders bestowed nickname "Scoop" to me because I am always out searching for nes and am in attendance of inter-tribal meetings both in Oklahoma and other states." *Biographical sources*: Who's Who in American Colleges & Universities, 1970; biography pamphlet for one man show, Southern Plains Indian Museum.

AIKMAN, SUSANNE (Eastern Cherokee)
(publisher; radio & TV producer)
Address: Owner, Morning Flower Press and Path of the Sun Images, P.O. Box 11443, Denver, CO 80211 (303) 477-8442. E-mail: producer@alterNativeVoices.org. Website: www.alterNativeVoices.org. *Affiliation*: Producer, "alter•Native Voices" - weekly Native radio program aired on KUVO-FM 89.3 in Denver and syndicated on American Indian Radio on Satellite Network (Website: www.airos.org).

AINSLEY, KATHY (Seneca) 1952-
(librarian)
Born January 21, 1952, Youngstown, Ohio. *Education*: BFA, MLS. *Principal occupation*: Librarian. *Home address*: 9145 Zayante Dr., Felton, CA 95018 (831) 335-2122. E-mail: rememberearth@yahoo.com. *Memberships*: American Indian Library Association; Wordcraft Circle of Native Writers and Storytellers. *Interests*: Music and art.

AITKEN, LARRY P.
(college president)
Affiliation: Leech Lake Tribal College, 6530 U.S. Hwy. 2 NW, Cass Lake, MN 56633 (218) 335-4220 Fax 335-4209.

AKERS, RUSS
(AK village president)
Affiliation: Native Village of Chuloonawick, General Delivery, Chuloonawick, AK 99581 (907) 949-1147.

AKINS, VIRGIL, DR.
(BIA agency supt.)
Affiliation: Northern California Agency, Bureau of Indian Affairs, 1900 Churn Creek Rd., Suite 300, Redding, CA 96049 (530) 246-5141 Fax 246-5167.

AKIWENZIE, RALPH
(Indian band chief)
Affiliation: Chief, Chippewas of Nawash Indian Band, R.R. #5, Wiarton, Ontario, Canada N0H 2T0 (519) 534-1689.

ALAMEDA, HENRY C., Sr.
(BIA field station supt.)
Affiliate: Metlakatla Field Station, Bureau of Indian Affairs, P.O. Box 450, Metlakatla, AK 99926 (907) 886-3791.

ALBANY, JAMES (Lenni Lenape)
(historical society president)
Address & Affiliation: President, Lenni Lenape Historical Society & Museum, 2825 Fish Hatchery Rd., Allentown, PA 18103 (610) 797-2121 Fax 797-2801. E-mail: lenape@lenape.org.

ALBANY, JOHN PETER
(Indian band chief)
Affiliation: Songhees Indian Band, 1500 A-Admirals Rd., Victoria, British Columbia, Canada V9A 2R1 (604) 386-1043.

ALBERT, ANNA
(director-Indian medical center)
Affiliation: Director, Phoenix Indian Medical Center, 4212 North 16th St., Phoenix, AZ 85016 (602) 263-1200.

ALBERT, ROBERT STEPHEN (Sakhomenewa)
(Hopi) 1964-
(artist)
Born March 27, 1964, Ganado, Ariz. *Education*: Institute of American Indian Arts, AFA, 1986; National Indian Center, Phoenix, Commercial Arts Degree, 1990. *Principal occupation*: Artist. *Home address*: Resides in Tucson, AZ (602) 770-1921. Art: Kachina doll carver (12 years) and watercolor painter. Gallery and Indian Market Shows include: Heard Museum, Mesa Southwest Museum, Museum of North Arizona, Tohono Chul Park, Gallup Ceremonial. *Awards, honors*: T.C. Cannon nominee, 1986, top five students at Institute of American Indian Arts; "Artist of the Year Award" from Council for Tribal Employment Rights, 1988, for original Acrylic on Canvas painting; Best of Show, categories - Kachina Doll, watercolor painting, pencil drawing, from Pine Bi Keyay Museum Market, Page, AZ, 1989; Third Place, categories Kachina Doll and watercolor painting, from Museum of Northern Arizona "Hopi Show,", Flagstaff, AZ, 1991; First Place, category - Kachina Doll, from American Indian Art Festival and Market, Dallas, TX, 1991.

ALBIETZ, JUDITH KAMMINS
(attorney)
Education: University of Michigan, MPA; University of the Pacific, McGeorge School of Law, JD. *Address & Affiliation*: President, Albietz Law Corporation, 2001 N St., Suite 100, Sacramento, CA 95814 (916) 442-4241 Fax 444-5494. *Other professional posts*: Co-chair of the Natural Resources Subsection of the Real Property Section, California State Bar, 1994-96' co-chair, State Bar of California Sacramento Real Property Roundtable, 1996-97. Ms. Albietz has been involved for over 25 years with environmental, Federal and State public agency law, and real property matters in the private law firm setting and the public sector. Her experience with the Federal government includes environmental, Indian law, and land and energy-related experience. She was Chief of the Division of Conveyances to Alaskan Natives for the Bureau of Land Management ("BLM") in Alaska. *Awards, honors*: Received the "Arthur S. Flemming Award (one of the highest honors in the Federal civil service) for her work on behalf of Alaskan Natives in conveying over 22 million acres of land.

ALCHESAY-NACHU, CARLA
(director-Indian hospital)
Affiliation: Director, Whiteriver Indian Hospital, P.O. BOX 860, Whiteriver, AZ 85941 (602) 338-4911.

ALDERETE, JOHN F.
(executive officer)
Affiliation: Society for Advancement of Chicanos & Native Americans in Science (SACNAS), 1156 High St., Santa Cruz, CA 95064 (408) 459-4272 Fax 459-3156.

ALDRED, DR. LISA
(college professor)
Affiliation: Native American Studies Dept., Montana State University, 2-179 Wilson Hall, P.O. Box 172340, Bozeman, MT 59717 (406) 994-3881 Fax 994-6879. *Interests*: Native American women; Federal Indian policy & law.

ALEX, ANDREW
(Indian band chief)
Affiliation: Union Bar Indian Band, Box 788, Hope, British Columbia, Canada V0X 1H0 (519) 627-3911.

ALEXANDER-JUAREZ, CARLA M. (*Wandering Spirit Woman*) (Ramapough Lenape) 1962-
(director of Indian education)
Born November 3, 1962, Bourne, Mass. *Education*: BS in Criminal Justice. *Principal occupation*: Director of Indian education. *Home address*: 266 Sloatsburg Rd., Ringwood, NJ 07456 (973) 962-7029. *Affiliation*: Director of Indian Education, Ringwood Borough Schools, Ringwood, NJ. *Community activities*: Tribal member; Sunday school teacher for Brook Presbyterian Church; choir member; Hillburn Homework Club director. *Associations*: American Indian Community House (New York, NY); Association on American Indian Affairs.

ALEXANDER, CLARENCE
(village council chief)
Affiliation: Native Village of Fort Yukon, P.O. Box 126, Fort Yukon, AK 99740 (907) 662-2581.

ALEXANDER, KAREN WILKINS (Cherokee/Powhatan) 1954-
(librarian/archivist)
Born March 21, 1954, Ardmore, Okla. *Education*: University of Science & Arts of Oklahoma (Chickasha), BA 1975; MA in Library and Information Studies, University of Oklahoma, Norman, OK, 1997. *Principal occupation*: Librarian/archivist. *Address & Affiliation*: Miami Tribe of Oklahoma, P.O. Box 1326, 202 S. Eight Tribes Trail, Miami, OK 74355 (918) 542-4505; E-mail: miamit8@onenet.net, 1989-. *Interests*: Genealogy, reading & writing.

ALEXANDER, MYRA
(manager-counseling)
Affiliation: Native Americans in Biological Sciences, 306 Life Sciences East, Oklahoma State University, Stillwater, OK 74078 (405) 744-6802.

ALEXANDER, NOME
(museum curator)
Affiliation: Museum of Indian Culture, Lenni Lenape Historical Society, R.D. #2, Fish Hatchery Rd., Allentown, PA 18103 (215) 797-2121.

ALEXIE, ANDREW
(school chairperson)
Affiliation: Chairperson, Tuluksak IRA Contract School, Tuluksak, AK 99679 (907) 695-6212.

ALEXIE , SHERMAN J. (Spokane, Coeur d'Alene)
(poet, short fiction writer)
Address: P.O. Box 376, Wellpinit, WA 99040 (509) 258-4252.

ALEXIS, JOHN
(Indian band chief)
Affiliation: Chief, Tl'azt'en Nation, P.O. Box 670, Fort St. James, BC, Canada V0J 1P0 (604) 648-3212.

ALFONSI, JOHN 1961-
(archaeologist, cultural resources management)
Born January 16, 1961, New York, N.Y. *Education*: University of Alaska, Fairbanks (degree in progress). *Principal occupation*: Archaeologist, cultural resources management. *Home address*: Mile 1403.5 Alaska Hiway, Delta Junction, AK 99737. *Affiliation*: Ahtna, Inc., Fairbanks, AK. *Membership*: AK Anthropological Association, 1984-. *Awards, honors*: Outstanding Senator and Outstanding Student—USUA, University of AK, Fairbanks Student Government, 1984 & 1985, respectively. *Interests*: Hunting, trapping, fishing, building; cultural resource assessments throughout Alaska. *Published works*: (In progress) Ahtna Cultural Resources throughout the region. Work includes mainly archaeological fieldwork and intensive investigation, e.g. on-the-ground archaeological survey of the Copper River Basin. First of its kind.

ALFRED, PATRICK
(Indian band chief)
Affiliation: Nimpkish Indian Band, Box 210, Alert Bay, British Columbia, Canada V0N 1A0 (604) 974-5556.

ALGER, RUSS
(director-Indian health center)
Affiliation: Warm Springs PHS Indian Health Center, P.O. Box 1209, Warm Springs, OR 97761 (503) 553-1196.

ALLARD, JEANINE
(museum director)
Affiliation: Flathead Indian Museum, Flathead Indian Reservation, 1 Museum Lane, St. Ignatius, MT 59865 (406) 745-2951.

ALLARD, L. DOUG (*Anteh*) (Flathead-Confederated Salish & Kootenai) 1931-
(Indian trader & auctioneer)
Born August 30, 1931, St. Ignatius, Mont. *Education*: Montana State University, BA, 1956. *Principal occupation*: American Indian art dealer. *Address*: P.O. Box 460, St. Ignatius, MT 59865 (406) 745-2951 (work). *Affiliations*: Founder, owner & curator, Flathead Indian Museum & Doug Allard Trading Post, St. Ignatius, MT (21 years). *Other professional post*: Owner, Allard Indian Auctions (29 years). *Military service*: U.S. Marine Corps, 1950-53 (Korean War Ribbon, U.N. Medal, two Battle Stars, Good Conduct Medal). *Community activities*: Chairman, Flathead Reservation Pow Wow Committee; chairman, Flathead Constitution Convention Committee; former tribal secretary, Confederated Salish & Kootenai Tribes. *Memberships*: National Association of Appraisers; Indian Arts and Crafts Association (charter member, board of directors); V.F.W.; American Legion; National Auctioneers Association; Salish-Kootenai College Foundation (chairperson). *Interests*: Tribal culture; avid collector of Indian artifacts; consultant to many museums and Indian groups. Nationally known appraiser & auctioneer of American Indian material. *Biographical source*: Who's Who in the West. *Published works*: Many articles, too numerous to mention.

ALLEN, CINDY (Catawba)
(craftsperson)
Address: 1815 Baskins Rd., Rock Hill, SC 29730 (803) 324-5088. *Products*: Traditional 19th century-style Catawba pottery.

ALLEN, JAMES
(chairperson-Indian cultural center)
Affiliation: Yukon Indian Cultural-Education Society Resource Center, Council for Yukon Indians, 22 Nisutlin Dr., Whitehorse, Yukon, Canada Y1A 3S5 (403) 667-7631.

ALLEN, JUDY
(editor)
Affiliation: Bishinik, Choctaw Nation of Oklahoma, P.O. Box 1210, Durant, OK 74702 (405) 924-8280.

ALLEN, LORETTA
(commission chairperson)
Affiliation: California Native American Heritage Commission, 915 Capitol Mall #288, Sacramento, CA 95814 (916) 322-7791.

ALLEN, PATRICIA
(school principal)
Affiliation: John F. Kennedy Day School, P.O. Box 130, White River, AZ 85941 (602) 338-4593.

ALLEN, PAULA GUNN (Laguna Pueblo)
(writer)
Address: 3940 Rose Court, Seal Beach, CA 90740 (310) 493-6493.

ALLEN, RICHARD P. (Santee Sioux)
(tribal executive)
Affiliation: President, Flandreau Santee-Sioux Executive Committee, P.O. Box 283, Flandreau, SD 57028 (605) 997-3891.

ALLEN, WILLIAM RON (Jamestown S'Klallam)
(tribal chairman, executive director)
Born December 14, 1947, Port Angeles, Wash. *Education*: Peninsula College, AA & AAA, 1978; University of Washington, BA (Political Science & Economics), 1982. *Principal occupation*: Tribal chairman, executive director. *Address*: 1033 Old Blyn Highway, Sequim, WA 98382 (360) 683-1109 (work). *Affiliation*: Chairman & Executive Director, Jamestown Band of

S'Klallam Tribe, Sequim, WA, 1978-. *Community activities*: National Indian Policy Center (Co-chair); president, National Congress of American Indians. *Awards, honors*: Student of the Year, Peninsula College; Dedicated Service, Northwest Indian Fisheries Commission. *Published works*: Determining the True Cost of Contracting Federal Programs for Indian Tribes (Affiliated Tribes of Northwest Indians, 1987).

ALLISON, BARNETT
(Indian band chief)
Affiliation: Lower Similkameen Indian Band, Box 100, Keremeos, British Columbia, Canada V0X 1N0 (604) 499-5528.

ALLISON, DAVID L.
(BIA agency supt.)
Affiliation: Uintah & Ouray Agency, Bureau of Indian Affairs, P.O. Box 130, Fort Duchesne, UT 84026 (435) 722-4300 Fax 722-2323.

ALLISON, EDWARD
(Indian band chief)
Affiliation: Upper Similkameen Indian Band, Box 100, Keremeos, British Columbia, Can. V0X 1N0 (604) 499-5528.

ALLISON, HARVEY DALE
(school principal)
Affiliation: Principal, Na'Neelzhiin Ji'Olta (Torreon), HCR 79, Box 9, Cuba, NM 87013 (505) 731-2272.

ALLWOOD, ADOLPH A. (*The Eagle Among Us*) (Oklahoma Cherokee) 1943-
(marketing/public relations consultant)
Born November 11, 1943, Buffalo, N.Y. *Education*: City College of New York, BA (Economics); Fordham University, MBA (Marketing-Management). *Principal occupation*: Marketing/public relations consultant. *Address*: 119-30 199th St., St. Albans, NY 11412 (718) 526-2941. *Affiliation*: Affective Marketing Management Consultants, Queens Village, NY. "As a marketing consultant, I presently have a client, State University of New York, S.U.N.Y. Research Foundation. I develop, for the metropolitan New York area, market sensitive programs to train and re-employ recipients of welfare." *Other professional posts*: Public relations, marketing, management planning, training and development with the following companies: New York Post, The New York Times, Ziff Davis Publishing Co. *Memberships*: American Marketing Association; American Management Association; Public Relations Society of America; Southeastern Cherokee Confederacy of Georgia; Native American Indian Enrollment Agency; Chickamaugan Cherokee Community, Tennessee Riner Band. *Interests*: Adolph has competed as an artist working with sculpture, copper, and painting. Primarily self-taught, all themes are core to the Native American culture. The most pronounced dimention of Adolph's involvement with Native American culture has been directing traditional Native American dance groups. He organized an inter-tribal dance troupe called, International Native American Performers. They perform before various audiences throughout the state. The audiences are often delighted and impressed with the unusually programmed series of performance which often were not the dances popular to audiences of even the pow wow circuit. For example the Cherokee Bogar Man Dance, and the Kiowa or Mandan Buffalo Dances. Often Adolph is requested to provide his expertise to audiences as a lecturer or writer about history and varied cultures of Native Americans. He presently serves as the Native Core Economist of a community publication - The Long Island Courier, as a researcher to Professor E.L. Gilmore's, Institute of Cherokee Studies, Tahlequah, Oklahoma. *Biographical source*: Who's Who Among Young American Professionals, 1988.

ALONZO, NANCY MARTINE
(Indian education contact)
Affiliation: New Mexico State Dept. of Education, Division of Indian Education, 300 Don Gaspar, Santa Fe, NM 87501 (505) 827-6679.

ALPHONSE, DENNIS
(Indian band chief)
Affiliation: Cowichan Indian Band, Box 880, Duncan, British Columbia, Canada V9L 3Y2 (604) 748-3196.

ALVARY, COLLEEN
(health council director)
Affiliation: American Indian Council of Central California, 2210 Chester Ave., Suite A, Bakersfield, CA 93301 (805) 327-2207.

ALVIDREZ, ALBERT (Tigua)
(pueblo governor; tribal enterprise manager)
Affiliations: Ysleta Del Sur Pueblo Council, P.O. Box 17579, Ysleta Sta., El Paso, TX 79917 (915) 859-7913; manager, Thur-Shan Arts & Crafts Center, 305 Yaya Lane, El Paso, TX 79907 (915) 859-5287 Fax 860-8972.

ALVORD, LORI ARVISO, M.D. (Navajo)
(surgeon, professor)
Born in Crownpoint, N.M. *Address & Affiliation*: Professor & Associate Dean, Dartmouth Medical School, Office of Multicultural Affairs, Hanover, NH. *Published work*: Co-author with Elizabeth Cohen Van Pelt, "The Scalpel and the Silver Bear: The First Navajo Surgeon Combines Western Medicine & Traditional Healing." *Interests*: Dr. Alvord is the first Navajo woman surgeon, and an advocate for the use of Native healing philosophies and practices in modern medicine.

AMAROK, BOBBY (Eskimo)
(village president)
Affiliation: Chinik Eskimo Community, P.O. Box 62020, Golovin, AK 99762 (907) 779-3521.

AMBLER, ALLEN W. (Lovelock Paiute) 1962-
(management consultant; programs administrator)
Born March 7, 1962, Reno, Nev. *Education*: University of Nevada, Reno. *Principal occupation*: managment consultant; programs administrator. *Address*: 300 Sawabe Dr., P.O. Box 878, Lovelock, NV 89419 (775) 273-7861 Fax 273-1144. E-mail: bigal@niec.net. *Affiliations*: Chairperson, Lovelock Paiute Tribal Council, Lovelock, NV, 1996-present; secretary of Executive Board, Inter Tribal Council of Nevada; president, Nevada Indian Environmental Coalition, 1997-present; chairperson, Board of Directors, 1st Momentum, Inc., 1997-present. *Community activities*: Headstart Committee; Child Protection Team; Education Committee; Chamber of Commerce; volunteer for Special Olympics; Youth Mentor Program; Stop Domestic Violence Team.

AMBLER, MARJANE
(author)
Resides in Mancos, Colorado. E-mail: mjambler@fone. net. *Publication*: Breaking the Iron Bonds: Indian Control of Energy Development.

AMBROSIA, ALEX
(village council president)
Affiliation: Village of Ouzinkie, P.O. Box 13, Ouzinkie, AK 99644 (907) 680-2259.

AMI, JUDY
(school principal)
Affiliation: Four Winds Community School, P.O. Box 199, Fort Totten, ND 58335 (701) 766-4161.

AMIOTTE, ARTHUR DOUGLAS *(Good Eagle Center)* **(Oglala Sioux) 1942-**
(artist, author, educator)
Born March 25, 1942, Pine Ridge, S.D. *Education*: Northern State University, BsEd, 1964; Montana State University, MIS (Master of Interdisciplinary Studies), 1983. *Principal occupation*: Artist; author; educator. Mr. Amiotte has studied traditional Lakota arts techniques with Christina Standing Bear, 1969-75; Lakota Sacred Traditions with Peter Cathces, Sr. (novice apprentice, 1972-76; assistant, 1977-82. *Home address*: P.O. Box 471, Custer, SD 57730 (605) 673-4373. *Affiliations*: Art teacher, Woodrow Wilson Jr. High School, Sioux City, IA, 1964-66; instructor of art, Northern State College, Aberdeen, SD, 1966-69; Lakota arts/creative writing teacher, Porcupine Day School, BIA, Porcupine, SD, 1969-71; director of curriculum development, BIA, Aberdeen Area Office, 1971-74; Lakota Studies and art specialist, Little Eagle Day School, BIA, 1975-77; chairperson, Lakota Studies Dept., Standing Rock Community College, Fort Yates, SD, 1977-80; Dept. of Native Studies, Brandon University, Brandon, Manitoba, Canada (visiting assistant professor, 1982-

85; adjunct professor of Native Studies, 1985-); artist, writer, consultant on Indian Cultures of the Northern Plains, White Horse Creek, Ltd., Custer, SD, 1985-. Exhibitions, commissions, published art and research, and lectures, too numerous to mention. *Awards, honors*: Recipient of "Outstanding Contribution to Indian Education" Award by State of South Dakota Indian Education Association, 1976; appointed member of the Presidential Advisory Council for the Performing Arts, Kennedy Center, Washington, DC by President Jimmy Carter, 1979-81; recipient of "Excellence in Teaching Award," Native Studies, Standing Rock Community College, Fort Yates, ND, 1980; recipient of State of South Dakota Governor's Award, Biennial Award for Outstanding Creative Achievement in the Arts, Pierre, SD, 1980; recipient of the Bush Leadership Fellowship for advanced study in Native American Sacred Traditions and Native Art History, Bush Foundation, 1980-83; recipient of Distinguished Alumni Award, Northern State College, June 1988; presenter of Richard Thompson Memorial Lecture, Iowa State University, June 1988; appointed four year member of Board, National Foundation for Advancement in the Arts, Miami, FL, June 1988; appointed member of Board of Directors, National Native American Art Studies Association (June 1988); appointed member of Board of Directors, Arts Midwest, Minneapolis, MN (June 1988); appointed member of Planning Committee for Northern Tier States Centennial Symposium Project, Montana State Historical Society, Helena, (June 1988); appointed Commissioner of Indian Arts and Crafts Board (a five commissioner board) by U.S. Secretary of the Interior (June 1988); awarded Honorary Doctorate of Lakota Studies by Oglala Lakota College, June 1988; awarded 14th Annual Artistic Achievement Citation by Board of Trustees, SD Art Museum, April 1989; appointed member of National Board of Directors, Center for Western Studies, Augustana College, Sioux Falls, SD, (Nov. 1990); appointed Senior Advisor to Director, Foundation for the Arts in South Dakota, Rapid City, (Oct. 1990); appointed member of Board of Directors, National Museum of the American Indian, Smithsonian Institute, Washington, DC, (Oct. 1990); co-curator, Plains Section of North American Indian Hall, Museum of Natural History, Smithsonian Institute, Washington, D.C., 1991-; One of 25 artists selected from Western Hemisphere to create a collaborative exhibition, "Celebrations" for the 1993-94 opening of the new National Museum of the American Indian, George Gustave Heye Center, Smithsonian Institute, New York, NY, 1992-. *Published interviews*: Marguerite Mullaney, "Artist Arthur Amiotte" Inside the Black Hills (Fall 1990); Ann Grauvogl, "Artist Keeps Tradition Alive Through Change," Sioux Falls Argus Leader (Sept. 10, 1989); Joan Morrison, "Lakota Artist Reveals His Vision of the World," Rapid City Journal (Aug. 4, 1988); Hattie Clark, "Art That Spans Two Cultures: Contemporary Artist Arthur Amiotte Draws on His Sioux Heritage to Fuel a Creative Life," The Christian Science Monitor (Aug. 11, 1987); Charles Nauman, "Diverse Work of Arthur Amiotte Reflects His Lakota Heritage," Rapid City Journal (Jan. 20, 1987). Films and Television: Interview in "Somewhere, Sometime: Tribal Arts, 1989," (SD Public TV, 1989); "Interpreting Contemporary Northern Plains Art," a documentary video of a formal lecture by Arthur Amiotte, to students and faculty of Dept. of Anthropology, University of Colorado, Boulder, Terri Berman, Producer (Nov. 1985); "Homecomings," Arthur Amiotte as narrator and interpreter of 21 person exhibit of contemporary Native art of nationally known artists with Northern Plains origins. North Dakota Museum of Arts, Laurel Reuter, Director, 1985; "Amiotte," a biographical film including art work and tracing the career of the artist from 1961 to 1976. University of South Dakota Education TV, June, 1977; "Four Portraits," one of four subjects. University of Mid America Production, 1977.

AMMON, DANIEL (Tsnungwe/South Fork Hupa)
(Hupa language/math/computer science instructor)
Address: P.O. Box 368, Salyer, CA 95563 (916) 629-4159 Fax 758-4891; E-mail: ammon@cs.stanford.edu. *Affiliations*: DQ University, Davis, CA, 1995-present; Hoopa Tribal Education Association, Hoopa, CA, 1994-95. *Community activities*: Master/Apprentice Hupa Language Project. *Memberships*: California Professional AISES; National Council of Teachers of Mathematics.

AMOS, DANDY
(Indian band chief)
Affiliation: Chief, Stoney Indian Band (Bearspaw Group), P.O. Box 40, Morley, AB, Canada T0L 1N0 (403) 263-8355.

AMOS, GERALD VICTOR
(Indian band chief)
Affiliation: Kitamaat Indian Band, Haisla, P.O. Box 1101, Kitamaat Village, BC, Canada V0T 2B0 (604) 639-9361.

AMOUSE, FELIX
(Indian band chief)
Affiliation: Chief, Little Shuswap Indian Band, P.O. Box 105, Chase, BC, Canada V0E 1M0 (604) 679-3203.

AMYLEE (Iroquois {Mohawk-Seneca}) 1952-
(consultant, artist, writer)
Born January 3, 1952, Ohio. *Education*: State University of New York, 1976-1979; Kent State University, 1970-1980 (concurrent). *Principal occupation*: Director of Indian organization. *Address*: P.O. Box 550, Zoar, OH 44697. E-mail: webbyfeet@webtv.net. *Affiliations*: Founder and director, American Indian Rights Association, Kent State University, 1970-1983; Licensed Raptor (Bird of Prey) Rehabilitator (ongoing); Medicine Woman Initiate (ongoing). *Other professional posts*: Member of the Board (past director), lecturer and artist for the Native American Indian Resource Center (NAIRC). *Memberships*: National Wildlife Rehabilitators Association; Earthwalker Learning Lodge. *Awards, honors*: Numerous awards for artistic achievement; her work can be found in selected galleries and at festivals celebrating women's culture. *Interests*: AmyLee has appeared with Native American leaders and dignitaries including Sakokwenonkwas of Akwesasne, Mad Bear, Rolling Thunder, Sun Bear, Grandfather Sky Eagle and Vernon Bellecourt. She has also had the opportunity to serve as a script consultant for the Smithsonian Institution and a character actress in the Public Broadcast System's film, Americas Ethnic Symphony. As member of the board for NAIRC, AmyLee travels over 50,000 miles annually offering lectures, workshops and retreats. She donates and devotes time to Native and nature projects including a drug and crime rehabilitation facility for recovering Indian youth. Biographical sources: Chapter-long interview in recently released, Profiles in Wisdom by Steven McFadden; excerpts from her writing and lectures appears in Wabun Wind's, Lightseeds, Kay Gardner's, Sounding the Inner Landscape; to MS. Magazine (November 1991). *Published works*: The Pathfinder Directory: A Guide to Native Americans in the Ohiyo Country (Indian House, 1982); When One Foot Wears the Moccasin, 2000; several articles. Presently she is working on two book manuscripts regarding Native Women's Spirituality and Politics.

ANAWAK, JACK (Nunatsiaq)
(parliament member)
Affiliation: Parliament Bldgs., Ottawa, ON K1A 0A4 (613) 992-4587.

ANAYA, MARIA, MPH
(health program director)
Affiliation: Consolidated Tribal Health Program, 562 South Dora St., Ukiah, CA 95482 (707) 462-0488.

ANAYA, S. JAMES (Parasco Apache)
(attorney-professor)
Address: Unknown. *Past affiliations*: Professor, University of Iowa College of Law, Iowa City, IA 52242; staff attorney, National Indian Youth Council, Albuquerque, NM.

ANASKAN, VERNON ROSS
(Indian band chief)
Affiliation: Chief, Piapot Indian Band, Box 178, Cupar, SK, Canada S0G 0Y0 (306) 561-2701.

ANAWAK, JACK
(association president)
Affiliation: President, Keewatin Inuit Association, Ranklin Inlet, NT, Canada X0C 0G0 (819) 979-5301.

ANDERSON, ANDREW
(Indian band chief)
Affiliation: Fairford Indian Band, Fairford, MB, Canada R0C 0X0 (204) 659-5705.

ANDERSON, CHRIS
(Indian education program director)
Affiliation: Glenwood School District #401, Indian Education Program, P.O. Box 12, Glenwood, WA 98619 (509) 364-3438 Fax 364-3689.

ANDERSON, CURTIS F. (Pomo)
(former rancheria chairperson)
Affiliation: Robinson Rancheria, 1545 E. Hwy. 20, Nice, CA 95464 (707) 275-0527.

ANDERSON, CURTIS (Paiute)
(former tribal chairperson)
Affiliation: Las Vegas Indian Colony, One Paiute Dr., Las Vegas, NV 89106 (702) 386-3926.

ANDERSON, DAVID W.
(Ass't Sec., BIA)
Affiliation: Assistant Secretary, Bureau of Indian Affairs, U.S. Dept. of the Interior, 1849 C St., NW, MS:4140MIB, Washington, DC 20240. *Home address:* 7016 Antrim Rd., Edina, MN 55439

ANDERSON, DR. DUANE
(college vice-president)
Affiliation: School of American Research, Indian Arts Research Center, P.O. Box 2188, Santa Fe, NM 87504 (505) 982-3584 Fax 989-9809.

ANDERSON, EDWARD
(Indian band chief)
Affiliation: Chief, Fairford Indian Band, Fairford, MB, Canada R0C 0X0 (204) 659-5705.

ANDERSON, ESTHER, MD
(chief medical officer)
Affiliation: Aberdeen IHS Area Office, Federal Bldg., 115 Fourth Ave., SE, Aberdeen, SD 57401 (605) 226-7581.

ANDERSON, ESTHER L. (Arapaho) 1950-
(business owner)
Born September 20, 1950, Casper, Wyo. *Education:* Casper College (Associate of Science, 19710. *Principal occupation:* Business owner. *Home address:* 5003 Alcova Rte. #20, Casper, WY 82604 (307) 237-7985 (home); (307) 235-0002 (office). *Affiliation:* Member, Equal Opportunity & DBE Committee for the Associated General Contractors of Wyoming. *Community activities:* Former county coordinator for Farm Bureau, ten years as election clerk. *Membership:* Associated General Contractors of Wyoming, 1985-.

ANDERSON, GENEAL (Paiute)
(tribal chairperson)
Affiliation: Paiute Indian Tribe of Utah, 600 North 100 East, Paiute Dr., Cedar City, UT 84720 (801) 586-1111.

ANDERSON, GREG
(school administrator)
Affiliation: Eufaula Dormitory, Swadsley Dr., Eufaula, OK 74432 (918) 689-2522.

ANDERSON, JOHN
(association president)
Affiliation: Chattanooga Intertribal Association, P.O. Box 71585, Chattanooga, TN 37407 (615) 266-6551.

ANDERSON, KENNY (Paiute)
(Indian colony chairperson)
Affiliation: Las Vegas Indian Colony Council, One Paiute Dr. Las Vegas, NV 89106 (702) 386-3926.

ANDERSON, LARRY
(school principal/supt.)
Affiliation: Two Eagle River School, P.O. Box 362, Pablo, MT 59855 (406) 675-0292.

ANDERSON, LAURA (Cherokee)
(instructor of Native American studies)
Affiliation: Native American Studies Program, University of Oklahoma, 455 W. Lindsey, Rm. 804, Norman, OK 73019 (405) 325-2312.

ANDERSON, LEWIS A.
(bank president & chairperson)
Affiliations: President, Woodlands National Bank, Denver, CO; Chairperson, Native American National Bank (NAB), 165 S. Union Blvd., Suite 1000, Denver, CO 80228 (303) 988-2727 Fax 988-5533.

ANDERSON, MARJORIE (Chippewa)
(tribal chairperson)
Affiliation: Mille Lacs Reservation Business Committee, HRC 67, Box 194, Onamia, MN 56359 (320) 532-4181.

ANDERSON, MICHAEL, MD
(medical director)
Affiliation: Prairie Island Community Council, 1158 Island Blvd., Welch, MN 55089 (612) 385-2554.

ANDERSON, NORMAN (Aleut)
(AK village council president)
Affiliation: Naknek Native Village, P.O. Box 106, Naknek, AK 99633 (907) 246-4210.

ANDERSON, OWANAH (Choctaw)
(secretary-board of directors)
Affiliation: Secretary, Board of Directors, Association on American Indian Affairs, P.O. Box 268, Sisseton, SD 57262 (605) 698-3998.

ANDERSON, RODNEY (Eskimo)
(AK village council president)
Affiliation: Native Village of Chignik Lagoon, P.O. Box 57, Chignik Lagoon, AK 99565 (907) 840-2206.

ANDERSON, WILLIAM L. 1941-
(professor of history)
Born February 18, 1941, Monticello, Ark. *Education:* University of Alabama, Tuscaloosa, B.A., 1963, M.A., 1966, Ph.D., 1974. *Principal occupation:* Professor of history. *Address:* Box 888, Cullowhee, NC 28723 (704) 227-7243 (office). *Affiliation:* Western Carolina University, Cullowhee, NC, 1969-. *Other professional posts:* Editor, "Journal of Cherokee Studies"; member, Advisory Board of Museum of Cherokee Indian, Cherokee, NC. *Memberships:* North Carolina Historical Society; Oklahoma Historical Society. *Awards, honors:* Gustavus Myers Human Rights Award for book, Cherokee Removal: Before & After. *Interests:* Cherokee history. *Published works:* Co-author, Guide to Cherokee Documents in Foreign Archives (Scarecrow Press, 1983); co-author, Southern Treasures (Globe Pequot, 1987); editor, Cherokee Removal: Before and After (University of Georgia Press, 1991); articles on Cherokee history in "North Carolina Historical Review," "Journal of Cherokee Studies", "Georgia Historical Quarterly," "Native Press Research Journal"; and in "The American Revolution: An Encyclopedia"; and "Colonial Wars of North America, 1512-1763, An Encyclopedia."

ANDERSON, WILLIAM, III (Inuit)
(association president)
Affiliation: President, Labrador Inuit Association, P.O. Box 70, Nain, Labrador, Canada A0P 1L0 (709) 922-2942.

ANDREAS CHERYL (Paiute)
(tribal council chairperson)
Affiliation: Big Pine Reservation, P.O. Box 700, Big Pine, CA 93513 (619) 938-2003.

ANDREAS, MARY ANN (Cahuilla)
(tribal chairperson)
Affiliation: Chairperson, Morongo Band of Mission Indians, 11581 Potrero Rd., Banning, CA 92220 (909) 849-4697.

ANDREOLI, ANDREW
(program director)
Affiliation: Indian Teacher & Education Personnel Program, Humboldt State University, Spidell House 85, Arcata, CA 95521 (707) 826-3672.

ANDREW, FRASER
(Indian band chief)
Affiliation: Mt. Currie Indian Band, Box 165, Mt. Currie, BC, Canada V0N 2K0 (604) 894-6115.

ANDREW, TREFIM (Athapascan)
(AK village council president)
Affiliation: Iguigig Village Council, P.O. Box 4008, Iguigig, AK 99613 (907) 533-3211.

ANDREWS, JOSE R., III
(actor, lecturer)
Address: 149 Clarendon St., N. Dartmouth, MA 02747 (508) 994-4745. He's a stage and film actor, does voice

overs, is a stuntsperson, a musician, writer, and lecturer. He was assistance content director of the "People of the First Light" series on New England Native American. Jose has appeared in various soap operas such as "Another World" and "One Life to Live." He also provides Shakespearian workshops.

ANDREWS, LAWRENCE
(Indian band chief)
Affiliation: Mowachant, Box 459, Gold River, BC, Canada V0P 1G0 (604) 283-2532.

ANELON, HARVEY (Athapascan)
(AK village council president)
Affiliation: Native Village of Iliamna Council, P.O. Box 286, Iliamna, AK 99606 (907) 571-1246.

ANGELO, LARRY (Ottawa)
(tribal chief)
Affiliation: Ottawa Tribe of Oklahoma, P.O. Box 110, Miami, OK 74355 (918) 540-1536.

ANGLE, HARVEY (Maidu)
(rancheria chairperson)
Affiliation: Enterprise Rancheria, 1940 Feather River Blvd., Suite B, Oroville, CA 95965 (530) 532-9214.

ANNA, KEITH
(BIA acting agency supt.)
Affiliation: Pima Agency, Bureau of Indian Affairs, P.O. Box 8, Sacaton, AZ 85247 (520) 562-3326.

ANNETTE, FRANKLIN
(BIA agency supt.)
Affiliation: Minnesota Agency, Bureau of Indian Affairs, Rt. 3, Box 112, Cass Lake, MN 56633 (218) 335-6913.

ANNETTE, KATHLEEN, M.D.
(IHS - chief medical officer)
Affiliation: Chief medical officer, Bemidji Area Office, Indian Health Service, 203 Federal Bldg., Bemidji, MN 56601 (218) 759-3412.

ANOATUBBY, BILL (Chickasaw) 1945-
(government administration)
Born November 8, 1945, Tishomingo, Okla. *Education:* Murray State College, AS, 1970; East Central University, BS, 1972. *Principal occupation:* Government administration. *Address:* Office of the Governor, P.O. Box 1548, Ada, OK 74821 (580) 436-7208 Fax 436-4287. *Affiliations:* Chickasaw Nation (director of tribal health services, 1975; director of accounting dept., 1976-78; special assistant to governor & controller, 1978-79; lieutenant governor, 1979-87; governor, 1987-). *Military service:* U.S. Army National Guard, 1963-71 (staff Sgt.). *Community activities:* Inter-Tribal Council of the Five Civilized Tribes, 1978-; United Indian Nations in Oklahoma; Ada Area Chamber of Commerce (board of directors, 1988-); Oklahoma City University (board of trustees, 1991-); Oklahoma State Chamber of Commerce & Industry (board of directors, 1991); 5 Who Care (board of directors); Trail of Tears National Historic Trail Advisory Committee; Oklahoma State Easter Seals and Crippled Children (board of directors, 1995-98); board, Oklahoma Foundation for Excellence; board, Oklahoma Academy of State Goals.. *Memberships:* National Congress of American Indians. *Awards, honors:* Appointed to the Oklahoma Indian Affairs Commission, 1987, by Oklahoma Governor Henry Bellmon; re-appointed by Governor David Walters in 1991; appointed by President Bill Clinton to the board of trustees of the Morris K. Udall Scholarship and Excellence in National Environmental Policy Foundation (1995-); U.S. EPA (Special Study Group, Region VI Advisory Group); Leadership Oklahoma Class III (1997-); A+ Award, City of Ada, 1997; 1997 Governor's Arts Award, Oklahoma Arts Council; 1998 Honoree during Literacy Recognition Banquet, for his work in promoting adult literacy in Oklahoma. *Biographical source:* Who's Who in America.

ANSEL, ERYNNE
(museum director)
Affiliation: Iroquois Indian Museum, P.O. Box 7, Caverns Rd., Howes Cave, NY 12092 (518) 296-8949 Fax 296-8955.

ANSPACH, ALLEN J. (Blackfeet) 1951-
(BIA agency supt.)
Born October 25, 1951, Lander, Wyo. *Education:* Uni-

versity of Arizona, BS, 1975. *Principal occupation*: BIA agency supt. *Address & Affiliation*: Colorado River Agency, Bureau of Indian Affairs, Route 1, Box 9-C, Parker, AZ 85344 (520) 669-7111. *Past professional posts*: Supt., San Carlos Agency, BIA, San Carlos, AZ, 1990-93; Supt., Colorado River Agency, BIA, Parker, AZ, 1993-present. *Other professional posts*: Vocational agricultural instructor, tribal operations specialist, land operations officer. *Awards, honors*: Chosen to participate in the 1982-83 Dept. of Interior, Departmental Manager Development Program. *Interests*: "When not occupied with my job, I enjoy raising my family with the able assistance of my wife Flo. Our children, Michael and Andrea, enjoy the outdoors with us where we like to hunt, fish and camp."

ANTELL, JUDITH A.
(program director)
Affiliation: American Indian Studies Program, University of Wyoming, Rm. 109A, Anthropology Bldg., Laramie, WY 82701 (307) 766-6521 Fax 766-2473. E-mail: antell@uwyo.edu.

ANTELL, WILL D. (Minnesota Chippewa) 1935-
(educational administration)
Born October 2, 1935, White Earth, Minn. *Education*: Bemidji State University, BS, 1959; Mankato State University, MS, 1964; University of Minnesota, Ed.D., 1973. *Principal occupation*: Educational administration. *Address*: Unknown. *Affiliation*: Teacher, Janesville (MN) Public Schools, 1959-63; teacher, School District #834, Stillwater, MN, 1963-68; University of Minnesota Faculty, 1969-73; lecturer, Harvard Graduate School of Education, 1973-74; Minnesota Dept. of Education, Minneapolis, MN (human relations consultant, 1968-69; assistant commissioner of special & compensatory education, 1974-82; assistant commissioner of education for special services, 1982-83; manager, 1983-87; manager, Equal Educational Opportunities, 1987-91; manager, Indian Education, 1991-). *Other professional posts*: Consultant: to BIA and U.S. Dept. of Education, 1968-78; appointed by former Governor Wendell Anderson to serve on Adult Corrections Commissions, 1970-73; consultant to U.S. Dept. of State, 1978; evaluator, North Central Association of Schools, 1983. *Community activities*: American Red Cross (board of directors, 1988-89); Anishinabe Job Developers Board of Directors (president, 1988-); Indian Center School Board of Directors, 1989-90; American Indian Chamber of Commerce (treasurer, board member, 1989-91); American Indian Opportunity Center Fundraiser Committee, 1990-91; Bush Foundation, Selection Committee Judge for Bush Foundation Fellowships, 1990-91; Juel Fairbanks Chemical Dependency Center Fundraiser Committee, 1991-; Commission on Judicial Selection, Supreme Court Appointment for Tenth Judicial District, 1990-91; Trustee and Board of Directors, William Mitchell College of Law, 1990-91; Judge, Bicentennial Competition on the Constitution and the Bill of Rights, 1991. *Memberships*: American Association of School Administrators; Minnesota Association of School Administrators; National Indian Education Association (charter member; president, 1970-72); National Advisory Council on Indian Education (member, 1973-78; chairperson, 1974); Board of Regents, Institute of American Indian Arts (member, 1971-82; president, 1976-78); Phi Beta Kappa, 1988. *Awards, honors*: Minnesota Indian Scholarship Recipient, 1955-59; Federal Indian Scholarship Recipient, 1956-59; NDEA Fellowships: Northern Michigan University, 1965, University of Minnesota, 1968; Bush Fellow, 1972-74; Education Policy Fellowship, 1975; Hubert Humphrey Institute Scholarship, 1983-84; Outstanding Alumni Award, Bemidji State University, 1986. *Published works*: Between Two Milestones, The First Report to the President of the U.S. (National Council of Indian Opportunity, 1972); Designs for Library Services (University of Minnesota, 1972); Indian Educational Leadership, Sr. Editor (ERIC-Cress, 1974); American Indian Leadership Training Programs (ERIC-Cress, 1974); Culture, Psychological Characteristics, and Socio-Economic Status in Educational Program Development Native Americans (ERIC-Cress, 1974); Articles: "Education of the American Indian," Current History (Vol. 67, Dec. 1974); "Definition of the Critical and Unique Problems and Concerns in the Education of American Indians and the Identification of Alternative Solutions to These Problems," College Entrance Examination Board, 1978.

ANTHONY, DICK
(AK village council vice president)
Affiliation: Native Village of Nightmute, Nightmute, AK 99690 (907) 647-6213.

ANTIQUIA, CLARENCE (Tlingit) 1940-
(federal government administrator)
Born April 16, 1940, Sitka, Alaska. *Education*: Sheldon Jackson Junior College, Sitka, Alaska, 1958-59. *Principal occupation*: Federal government administrator. *Home address*: Box 1111, Juneau, Alaska 99802. *Affiliations*: Area director, Bureau of Indian Affairs, Juneau, Alaska, 1965-1975. *Awards, honors*: Outstanding Performance Awards, B.I.A., 1965, 1967, 1970. *Interests*: Public administration, government, personnel management, race relations, Indian affairs.

ANTLE, JACK
(store owner)
Address: Thompson River Trade Co., 223 S. Broadway, Checotah, OK 74426 (918) 473-7363; E-mail: indiantrader@lakewebs.net. Specializes in Native American Indian arts and antiques.

ANTOINE, ELORA
(program coordinator)
Affiliation: American Indian Relief Council, 2230 Eglin St., Rapid City, SD 57703 (800) 370-0872; (605) 399-9905 Fax 399-9908. E-mail: info@airc.org.

ANTOINE, GORDON
(Indian band chief)
Affiliation: Coldwater Indian Band, Bag 4600, Merritt, B.C., Canada V0K 2B0 (604) 378-6174.

ANTOINE, JANEEN
(art gallery director)
Affiliation: American Indian Contemporary Arts Gallery, 23 Grant Ave., 6th Floor, San Francisco, CA 94108 (415) 989-7003 Fax 989-7025.

ANTOINE, JIM
(Indian band chief)
Affiliation: Fort Simpson Indian Band, P.O. Box 469, Fort Simpson, NWT, Canada X0E 0N0 (403) 695-3131.

ANTOINE, MINONQUA (*Greta Gigi*) (Odawa/Oneida)
1934-
(writer, singer)
Born March 5, 1934, Depauville, N.Y. Education: High schooll, some college. Principal occupation: Writer, singer. Address: Odawa Mukwa Dodem, 06185 Behling Rd., East Jordon, MI 49727 (231) 536-2162. E-mail: minonqua2000@yahoo.com. Published work: Medicine Bear; Minokahmeh.

ANTOINE, TEDDY LEE
(Indian band chief)
Affiliation: Poundmaker Indian Band, Box 220, Paynton, SK, Canada S0M 2J0 (306) 398-4971.

ANTONE, DONALD R., SR. (Pima-Maricopa)
(tribal council governor)
Affiliation: Gila River Indian Community Council, P.O. Box 97, Sacaton, AZ 85247 (520) 562-6000.

ANTONE, MARTIN, SR. (Papago/Pima)
(ex-tribal chairperson)
Affiliation: Ak Chin Indian Community Council, 42507 N. Peters & Nall Rd., Maricopa, AZ 85239 (602) 568-2227.

ANTONIO, CHRISTINE
(associate director)
Affiliation: Office of Tribal Activities, Albuquerque Area Indian Health Services, 505 Marquette Ave., NW, Suite 1502, Albuquerque, NM 87102 (505) 766-2151.

ANYON, ROGER (Zuni Pueblo)
(archaeology program director)
Affiliation: Zuni Archaeology Program, Pueblo of Zuni, P.O. Box 339, Zuni, NM 87327 (505) 782-4814.

ANYWAUSH, JOELLEN
(health director)
Affiliation: White Earth Band Clinic, P.O. Box 418, White Earth, MN 56591 (218) 983-3285.

APACHITO, GEORGE (Navajo)
(school chairperson)
Affiliation: Alamo Navajo School, P.O. Box 907, Magdalena, NM 87825 (505) 854-2543.

APACHITO, PATSY (Navajo)
(radio station manager)
Affiliation: KABR - 1500 AM, Alamo Navajo School Board, P.O. Box 907, Magdalena, NM 87825 (505) 854-2632.

APESANAHKWAT (Menominee)
(tribal chairperson)
Affiliation: Menominee Tribe, P.O. Box 910, Keshena, WI 54135 (715) 799-5100.

APODACA, MARY ANN
(BIA special education coordinator)
Affiliation: Northern Pueblos Agency, Bureau of Indian Affairs, P.O. Box 4269, Fairview Station, Espanola,, NM 87533 (505) 753-1465 Fax 753-1475.

APODACA, RAYMOND D. (Ysleta del Sur Pueblo-Tigua Indian Tribe of Texas) 1946-
(administrator)
Born October 15, 1946, Las Cruces, N.M. *Education*: New Mexico State University, BA, 1969, MA, 1976. *Principal occupation*: Administrator. *Address*: Texas Indian Commission, P.O. Box 2960, Austin, TX 78768 (512) 458-1203. *Affiliation*: Executive director, Texas Indian Commission (State of Texas), Austin, Texas (1983-87, 1990-95). *Past professional post*: Ysleta del Sur Pueblo, Ysleta Station, El Paso, TX, 1987-90. *Military service*: U.S. Air Force, 1969-1972. *Community activities*: New Mexico State University All-Indian Adult Advisory Board, 1976-; Citizens' Advisory Board, ETCOM Public Radio (El Paso, Texas), 1980-1985; OPM—Intergovernmental Committee on Indian Affairs, Southwest Region, 1982-; University of Texas, Austin, El Paso, Master of Science in Social Work Program, Advisory Council, 1984-; Texas State Committee on the Protection of Human Remains and Sacred Objects (American Indian) (co-chairman, 1984-). *Memberships*: National Indian Education Association, 1973-1980; National Congress of American Indians, 1973- (coordinator-Religious Freedom Act); Governors' Interstate Indian Council, 1977- (national president, 1985-1986); Texas American Indian Sesquicentennial Association (executive board member, 1985-); Texas State Agency Business Administrators Association, 1982-; North American Indian Museums Association, 1977-1980. *Awards, honors*: Colonel Aide-de-Camp, Governor, State of New Mexico, 1977. *Interests*: History, government, theology, education. *Biographical source*: To Live in Two Worlds, by Brent Ashabrenner (Dodd, Mead & Co., 1984.) *Published work*: Directory of Information on Health Careers for American Indians (ERIC/CRESS, National Education Laboratory Publishers, 1977.)

APOKEDAD, CHRISTOPHER (Aleut)
(AK village council president)
Affiliation: Levelock Village, P.O. Box 70, Levelock, AK 99625 (907) 287-3030.

APOLIONA, HAUNANI (Hawaiian)
(association president)
Affiliation: Alu Like, Inc., 1624 Mapunapuna St., Honolulu, HI 96819 (808) 836-8940.

APPLEGATE, ROGER H., MD
(clinical director)
Affiliation: Fort Hall PHS Indian Health Center, P.O. Box 717, Fort Hall, ID 83203 (208) 238-2400.

APSASSIN, JOE
(Indian band chief)
Affiliation: Chief, Blueberry River Indian Band, P.O. Box 3009, Buick, British Columbia, Canada V0C 2R0 (604) 630-2584.

ARAGON, ARNOLD (Crow-Pueblo) 1953-
(artist)
Born July 9, 1953, Crow Agency, Mont. *Education*: American Indian Art Institute, Santa Fe, N.M. (Art/Sculpture), 1979 graduate; University of Nevada, Reno, 1980-1984. *Principal occupation*: Professional artist. *Home address*: P.O. Box 64, Walker River Reservation, Schurz, NV 89427. *Affiliation*: Rites of Passage Wilderness Camp, Schurz, Nevada. *Other pro-

fessional posts: Art consultant, board member, Nevada Urban Indians—Earth Window. *Interests*: Sculpturing using hand tools. His art includes water colors, pastels and pencil drawings. Arnold's sculptures are in various galleries and museums throughout the West as well as private collections throughout the country. He enjoys travel and the outdoors.

ARAGON, VIDAL (Santo Domingo Pueblo)
(pueblo council governor)
Affiliation: Santo Domingo Pueblo Council, P.O. Box 99, Santo Domingo, NM 87052 (505) 465-2214.

ARCAND, EUGENE
(executive director)
Affiliation: Indian & Metis Friendship Centre, 14th St. & 1st Ave. East, Prince Albert, Saskatchewan, Canada S6V 6Z1 (306) 764-3431.

ARCAND, JOSEPH STANLEY
(Indian band chief)
Affiliation: Alexander First Nation, Box 510, Morinville, Alberta, Canada T0G 1P0 (403) 939-5887.

ARCHAMBAULT, DAVE LEON
(Standing Rock Sioux)
(educational administrator)
Education: Black Hills State College, Spearfish, SD, B.S. (Secondary Education), 1976; Pennsylvania State University, M.S. (Educational Administration), 1982. *Principal occupation*: Educational administrator. *Address*: P.O. Box 519, Fort Yates, ND 58538 (701) 854-7246. *Affiliations*: Assistant principal & Jr. High Principal, Little Wound School, Kyle, SD (8 years); acting recreation director, United Tribes Technical College, Bismarck, ND (3 years); president, Standing Rock College, Fort Yates, ND, 1987-. *Other professional posts*: American Indian Higher Education Consortium, (1972-; vice-president, 1988; president, 1989-); board member, North Dakota Humanities Council; secretary, Sitting Bull Historical Society. *Community activities*: Board member, American Indian College Fund. *Memberships*: National Indian Activities Association, (Board of Directors, 1972-82 & 1987); National Indian Education Association, 1975-; American Association of Colleges & Junior Colleges, 1987-. *Awards, honors*: South Dakota Cross Country Coach of the Year, 1980; South Dakota Indian Educator of the Year, 1982; National Indian Basketball Coach of the Year, 1980. *Interests*: "Most interested in educational reform. Masters degree work was done on rationale and justification to change K-12 systems to better meet the needs of Indian learners. (I am an) advocate of the literacy work done by Paulo Freire, author of "Pedogogy of the Oppressed.""

ARCHAMBAULT, JOALLYN
(Standing Rock Sioux) 1942-
(anthropologist, program director)
Born February 13, 1942, Claremore, Okla. *Education*: University of California, Berkeley, B.A., 1970, M.A., 1971, Ph.D., 1984 (Dissertation topic: "The Gallup Ceremonial," A study of patronage within a contemporary context of Indian-white relationships). *Principal occupation*: Director of American Indian Programs. *Address*: National Museum of Natural History, NHB 112, Smithsonian Institution, Washington, DC 20560 (202) 357-4760 (work). *Affiliations*: Lecturer in Native American Studies, University of California, Berkeley, 1976-1979; Department chairperson & lecturer in Ethnic Studies Program, California College of Arts and Crafts, 1979-1983; research associate, Center for the Study of Race, Crime and Social Policy of Cornell University, 1980-82; field ethnographer, Sonoma State Foundation, 1983-1984; assistant professor in anthropology, University of Wisconsin, Milwaukee, 1983-1986; director, American Indian Programs, Smithsonian Institution, Washington, DC, 1986-. *Other professional posts*: Faculty positions at the University of California, Berkeley, University of New Mexico, University of Wisconsin, Navajo Community College, et al. *Community activities*: Board member: California Indian Education Association, 1967-70; Native American Scholarship Fund, Inc., 1976-77; City of Berkeley Minority Elder Project, 1976-77; Committee to Stop Hanta Yo, 1979-82; advisory council member, Foundation for Illinois Archaeology, Native American Studies Program, 1980-81. *Memberships*: American Anthropological Association; Native American Art Studies Association (vice-president, 1982-85); Society for

Applied Anthropology; American Ethnological Society; Anthropology Society of Washington. *Awards, honors*: Ford Foundation Fellowship; National Endowment for the Humanities Travel Grant; numerous art awards dating from 1969 through 1980; art exhibits (group and one-man shows); examples of art in permanent collection of the Heard Museum, the Navajo Tribal Museum, the Indian Arts & Crafts Board, the Red Cloud Cultural Center, and numerous private collections. *Interests*: "Primary interests are in the areas of art and material culture, political anthropology, ethnic relations, Indian-white relations, and patronage systems. I curated an exhibit titled Plains Indian Arts - Change and Continuity for the National Museum of Natural History. The exhibit traveled nationally in 1989." *Published works*: Articles; In-preparation: An Annotated Bibliography of Sources on Plains Indian Art (G.K. Hall & Co.); and The Uses of Non-Visual Sacred Material in Museums by Contemporary Native Americans (Buffalo Bill Historical Center).

ARCHAMBEAU, MADONNA (Yankton Sioux)
(tribal chairperson)
Affiliation: Yankton Sioux Tribal Business Committee, P.O. Box 248, Marty, SD 57361 (605) 384-3804.

ARCHIBALD, CHARLES
(Indian band chief)
Affiliation: Chief, Seabird Island Indian Band, P.O. Box 650, Agassiz, British Columbia, Canada V0M 1A0 (604) 796-2177.

ARCHIBALD, PETER
(Indian band chief)
Affiliation: Chief, New Post Indian Band, Box 1836, Cochrane, Ontario, Canada P0L 1C0 (705) 272-5795.

ARCHIE, SAM
(Indian band chief)
Affiliation: Skowkale Indian Band, Box 365, Sardis, British Columbia, Canada V2R 1A7 (604) 792-0730.

ARCHULETA, DAVE
(enterprise director)
Affiliation: Shoshone-Bannock Gaming Enterprise, P.O. Box 868, Fort Hall, ID 83203.

ARCHULETA, GLENDA (Kaibab Paiute)
(tribal relations)
Affiliation: Tribal Relations, "RedEarth" Magazine, Council Publications, 695 S. Colorado Blvd., Suite 10, Denver, CO 80246 (303) 282-7576 Fax 282-7584.

ARCHULETA, MANUEL (Picuris Pueblo)
(former Pueblo governor)
Affiliation: Picuris Pueblo, P.O. Box 127, Penasco, NM 87553 (505) 587-2519.

ARGEL, GREG
(BIA field rep.)
Affiliation: Makah Field Office, Bureau of Indian Affairs, P.O. Box 115, Neah Bay, WA 98357 (360) 645-2201 Fax 645-2788.

ARIAS, RONALD
(Indian school principal)
Affiliation: Havasupai School, P.O. Box 40, Supai, AZ 86435 (520) 448-2901 Fax 448-2551.

ARKEKETA, BENNETT (Ponca)
(tribal chairperson; technical programs manager)
Affiliations: Chairperson, Ponca Tribe of Oklahoma Business Committee, 20 White Eagle Dr., Ponca City, OK 74601 (580) 762-8104; technical programs manager, Native Americans in Biological Sciences, 306 Life Sciences East, Oklahoma State University, Stillwater, OK 74078 (405) 744-6802.

ARKEKETA, SUSAN M. (Otoe-Missouria/Muscogee Creek) 1954-
(humanities chair)
Born September 5, 1954, Tulsa, Okla. *Education*: University of Oklahoma, B.A. (Journalism), 1978, M.A. (Communications), 1983. *Principal occupation*: Humanities chair. *Address*: 155 Indian Ave., Lawrence, KS 66046 (913) 749-8431 (work). *Affiliations*: Director, Native American Journalists Association, 1987-90; writer/editor, Native American Rights Fund, Boulder, CO, 1985-91; Haskell Indian Nations University, Lawrence, KS (journalism instructor1991-.94; Humani-

ties Chair, 1994-present) *Other professional posts*: Advisory Board, Winds of Change, Boulder, CO; freelance writer; consultant-proposal writer; writer/editor, public relations. *Community activities*: Lawrence Arts Commission, Lawrence KS; Three Sisters Festival. *Memberships*: Kansas Indian Education Association; Native American Journalists Association; American Association of University Women. *Awards, honors*: Miss Indian America, 1978; Outstanding Young Woman of America, 1982, 1986 & 1987; Indian National Finals, Rodeo Trade Fair.

ARMAGOST, JAMES GRAYHAWK (Mohican) 1945-
(silversmith & lapidary)
Born July 8, 1945, Johnstown, Penn. *Education*: Accredited GRE - two year college. *Principal occupation*: Silversmith and lapidary. *Address*: Unknown. *Affiliation*: Owner, The Silver Phoenix, Oakton, Virginia. The Silver Phoenix has been promoting Native American crafts for 15 years. *Military service*: U.S. Army Special Forces. *Community activities*: American Indian Inter-Tribal Cultural Organization (member, board of directors.) *Memberships*: American Indian Society of Washington, DC; American Indian Intertribal Cultural Association. *Awards, honors*: Numerous first place and Best of Show Awards for his jewelry in assorted regional competitions (Native American and non-Native American). *Art form*: His Navajo leafwork and multi-level chizeled boarders are some of the cleanest to be found. The geometrics in his overlay styles are crisp and exact, and his animals, plants and people are nearly animated. He has also produced breathtaking pieces blending inlaid stone and highly polished metal with flawless skill. He has walked away with top prizes in every competition he has ever entered.

ARMENTA, VINCENT (Chumash)
(tribal chairperson)
Affiliation: Santa Ynez Band of Chumash Mission Indians, P.O. Box 517, Santa Ynez, CA 93440 (805) 688-7997.

ARMSTRONG, BENNIE J. (Suquamish)
(tribal chairperson)
Affiliation: Suquamish Tribal Council, P.O. Box 498, Suquamish, WA 98392 (360) 598-3311.

ARMSTRONG, YVONNE (Leech Lake Ojibwe)
(college instructor)
Affiliation: Leech Lake Tribal College, 6530 U.S. Hwy. 2 NW, Cass Lake, MN 56633 (218) 335-4220 Fax 335-4209.

ARNOLD, DONALD (Pomo)
(rancheria chairperson)
Affiliation: Scotts Valley Rancheria, 149 N. Main #200, Lakeport, CA 95453 (707) 263-4771.

ARNOLD, GREIG W. (Makah)
(tribal council chairperson)
Affiliation: Makah Indian Tribal Council, P.O. Box 115, Neah Bay, WA 98357 (360) 645-2201.

ARNOLD, RICHARD W. (Southern Paiute)
(Indian Center director)
Education: Mt. San Antonio College (Walnut, CA) AA (Police Science), 1973; Cal-State University, Long Beach, BS (Criminal Justice/Administration, Certificate & Minor in American Indian Studies), 1975, MS (Educational Psychology/Counseling), 1977. *Principal occupation*: Executive director. *Address & Affiliation*: Las Vegas Indian Center, 2300 W. Bonanza Rd., Las Vegas, NV 89106 (702) 647-5842 , 1977-present. *Other professional posts*: Nevada State Steering Committee on Indian Education; U.S. Senate appointed Delegate to the White House Conference on Indian Education; Commissioner, Nevada Indian Commission; consultant to: U.S. Dept. of Labor Division of Indian & Native American Programs & U.S. Dept. of Energy; member, Board of Trustees, Nevada Business Services, Nevada State Board of Social Workers-Advisory Committee on Continuing Education; Minority Outreach Council; Delegate to the White House Conference on Indian Education; Chairperson, Nevada State Education Steering Committee; Consultant to Yucca Mountain Cultural Resources Program & Nevada Test Site-American Indian Religious Freedom Act Compliance Program. *Community activities*: Clark County Police Community Relations Board; Preservation Association of Clark County; Federal Emergency Man-

agement Board of Clark County; Comprehensive Housing Affordability Strategy Task Force, City of Las Vegas & Clark County; American Red Cross Long Range Planning Committee, Clark County; Overall Economic Development Plan Committee & Training Conference; Fair Housing Task Force - City of Las Vegas; Affirmative Action Advisory Committee. *Memberships*: National Adult Indian Education Association; Nevada State Board of Social Workers; National Indian Education Association; National Indian Employment & Training Association; National Urban Indian Council. *Awards, honors*: Letters of Commendation: City of Las Vegas, Clark County, Governor-State of Nevada, U.S. Dept. of Energy, National Indian & Native American Employment & Training Conference, Las Vegas Chamber of Commerce; Boulder City Rotary Club. *Interests*: Community development - major area of vocational interest, including facilitating motivational seminars for American Indians; enjoy public speaking and representing American Indian interests in associated issues; enjoy traveling, collecting and restoring antiques.

ARNOUSE, FELIX
(Indian band chief)
Affiliation: Little Shuswap Indian Band, Box 1100, Chase, British Columbia, Canada V0E 1M0 (604) 679-3203.

ARONILTH, WILSON, JR.
(Indian center instructor)
Affiliation: Center for Dine Studies, Dine (Navajo) College, P.O. Box 126, Tsaile, AZ 86556 (520) 724-6671 Fax 724-3327.

ARQUETTE, DAVID (Mohawk) 1963-
(environmental specialist)
Born August 29, 1963, Rochester, N.Y. *Education*: Canton (NY) Agricultural & Technical College, AAS, 1984; Rochester Institute of Technology, B.T., 1991. *Principal occupation*: Environmental specialist. *Affiliation*: Environmentalist, St. Regis Mohawk Tribe, Hogansburg, NY, 1991-. *Memberships*: American Indian Science and Engineering Society (AISES); American Society of Civil Engineers. *Awards, honors*: A.T. Anderson Award, AISES; Frederick Douglas Scholarship, Minority Student Affairs Office, R.I.T.; Merit Award for Excellence in Leadership and Community Service, R.I.T. *Interests*: First National People of Color Environmental Conference, Washington, DC - protecting the rights of minorities and the environment; Jame Bay II - involved in helping the Cree and Inuit people protect their lands and culture from degradation of dams being built by Hydro-Quebec.

ARRINGTON, BOB (Creek)
(store owner)
Affiliation: Mister Indian's Cowboy Store, 1000 S. Main St., Sapulpa, OK 74066 (918) 224-6511.

ARRINGTON, JO (Cheyenne)
(store manager)
Affiliation: Mister Indian's Cowboy Store, 1000 S. Main St., Sapulpa, OK 74066 (918) 224-6511.

ARROW, DENNIS WAYNE 1949-
(professor of law)
Born July 27, 1949, Chicago, Ill. *Education*: George Washington University, BA, 1970; California Western School of Law, JD, 1974; Harvard University, LLM, 1975. *Principal occupation*: Professor of law. *Home address*: 825 N.W. 139th St., Edmond, OK 73013 (405) 521-5361 (work). *Affiliation*: Native American Legal Resource Center, 1988-, Oklahoma City University, Oklahoma City, OK (Professor of Law, 1975-, acting director, 1987-88, associate director, 1988-; associate justice, Supreme Court of the Cheyenne-Arapaho Tribes, Concho, OK, 1995-. *Community activities*: Oklahoma Association of Scholars (president); Oklahoma Constitution Revision Commission (member). *Memberships*: Oklahoma Indian Bar Association (president, Oklahoma City Chapter, 1989-90); American Indian Bar Association. *Awards, honors*: Outstanding Graduate-Level Professor, Oklahoma City University, 1990. *Interests*: American Indian law (sovereignty issues); constitutional law (state and federal); U.S. Supreme Court litigation. *Published works*: Oklahoma Tribal Court Reports (5 vols. to date).

ARROYO de WALKER, CANDACE J.
(WRG president)
Affiliation: President, Walker Research Group (WRG), Ltd., P.O. Box 4147, Boulder, CO 80306 (303) 492-6719. Website: www.walkerresearchgroup.com. Mrs. Arroyo de Walker is majority stockholder in WRG, Ltd. She has extensive research experience in the Hispanic cultures of Colorado and the greater U.S. Southwest, and has served as cultural consultant and official interpreter in a variety of capacities and is of both Hispanic and American Indian descent. She is an expert in the graphic, plastic, and textile arts of the Indigenous cultures of the Southwest.

ARVISO, LORI ALVORD (Navajo)
(assistant director of admissions)
Affiliations: Assistant Director of Admissions, Dartmouth Medical School, Dartmouth-Hitchcock Medical Center, Hanover, NH .

ASETOYER, CHARON (Comanche) 1951-
(executive director)
Born March 24, 1951, San Jose, Calif. *Education*: School of International Training (Masters of International Administration & Masters of International Management), 1983. *Principal occupation*: Executive director. *Address & Affiliation*: Native American Women's Health Education Resource Center, Native American Community Board, P.O. Box 572, Lake Andes, SD 57356 (605) 487-7072 (executive director, 1988-present). *Other professional post*: Editor, Wicozanni Wowapi, newsletter. *Memberships*: National Women's Network (executive board); South Dakota Coalition of Violence & Sexual Assault, Advisory Committee for Girls, Inc. *Awards, honors*: "Women of Vision Award," by Ms Foundation. *Interests*: Reproductive rights for indigenous women. *Biographical sources*: "Moving the Mountain," by Flora Davis in Mother Jones, Jan. 1990; Ms. Magazine, July/Aug. 1991. *Published works*: Women, AIF+DS & Activism (collective of works by women) (South End Press, 1990).

ASHBY, RICKIE (Eskimo)
(AK village council president)
Affiliation: Native Village of Noatak, P.O. Box 89, Noatak, AK 99761 (907) 485-2173.

ASHINI, DANIEL
(Indian band chief)
Affiliation: First Nation Council of North West River, Box 160, Sheshatshit, North West River, Labrador, Newfoundland, Canada A0P 1M0 (709) 497-8522.

ASPA, AMELIA
(tribal librarian)
Affiliation: Colorado River Indian Tribes Public Library, Route 1, Box 23-B, Parker, AZ 85344 (602) 669-9211.

ASSINEWAI, MAXIE
(Indian band chief)
Affiliation: Sheguiandah Indian Band, Box 101, Sheguiandah, ON, Canada P0P 1W0 (705) 368-2781.

ASTOR, SUSIE (Yurok-Chippewa)
(gift shop manager)
Affiliation: Intertribal Friendship House Gift Shop, 523 East 14th St., Oakland, CA 94606 (510) 452-1235.

ATANASOFF, DAVID J.
(school principal)
Affiliation: Lake Valley Navajo School, P.O. Drawer 748, Crownpoint, NM 87313 (505) 786-5392.

ATCITTY, THOMAS
(Indian academy headmaster)
Affiliation: Headmaster, Navajo Mission Academy, 1200 W. Apache, Farmington, NM 87401 (505) 326-6571.

ATENCIO, DR. BENJAMIN
(BIA education administrator)
Affiliation: Southern Pueblos Agency, Bureau of Indian Affairs, P.O. Box 1667, Albuquerque, NM 87103 (505) 346-2431 Fax 346-2408.

ATKINSON, JERRY
(organization president)
Affiliation: Aboriginal Research Club, Dearborn Historical Museum, 915 Brady Rd., Dearborn, MI 48124 (313) 565-3000.

ATLOOKAN, SOLOMON
(Indian band chief)
Affiliation: Chief, Fort Hope Indian Band, P.O. Box 70, Eabamet Lake, via Pickle Lake, Ontario, Canada P0T 1L0 (807) 242-7361.

ATOLE, LEONARD (Jicarilla Apache)
(tribal council president)
Affiliation: Jicarilla Apache Tribal Council, P.O. Box 507, Dulce, NM 87528 (505) 759-3242.

ATORUK, BEN (Eskimo)
(AK village council president)
Affiliation: Kiana Traditional Council, P.O. Box 69, Kiana, AK 99749 (907) 475-2109.

ATTACHIE, GERRY
(Indian band chief)
Affiliation: Doig River Indian Band, Box 55, Rose Prairie, BC, Canada V0C 2H0 (604) 787-4466.

ATTATAYUK, GEORGE
(administrative officer)
Affiliation: Barrow PHS Alaska Native Hospital, Barrow, AK 99723 (907) 852-4611

ATTEAN, PRISCILLA A.
(liaison)
Affiliation: Maine Tribal/State Relations Office, 6 River Rd., Indian Head, ME 04468 (207) 827-7776.

ATTI, WILLIE (Eskimo)
(AK village council president)
Affiliation: Kwigillingok Native Village, P.O. Box 49, Kwigillingok, AK 99622 (907) 588-8114.

ATTOCKNIE, KENNETH
(executive director)
Affiliation: American Indians for Development, P.O. Box 117, 236 W. Main St., Meriden, CT 06450 (203) 238-4009.

ATWELL, CLARENCE, JR. (Yokut)
(tribal chairperson)
Affiliation: Santa Rosa General Council, P.O. Box 8, Lemoore, CA 93245 (209) 924-1278.

ATWINE, RUBY (Ute)
(tribal chairperson)
Affiliation: Uintah & Ouray Tribal Business Council, P.O. Box 190, Fort Duchesne, UT 84026 (801) 722-5141.

AUBIN, GAETANE
(Indian band chief)
Affiliation: Malecites de Viger Indian Band, 3400 boul. Losch, Suite 39, St-Hubert, Quebec, Canada J3Y 5T6 (514) 656-9731.

AUBREY, JOHN
(committee chairperson)
Affiliation: Committee on Library Services for American Indian People, American Indian Library Association, American Library Association, Office of Outreach Services, 50 E. Huron St., Chicago, IL 60611 (312) 944-6780.

AUDY, CHARLES
(Indian band chief)
Affiliation: Chief, Indian Birch Band, Birch River, Manitoba, Canada R0L 0E0 (204) 236-4201.

AUGUSTINE, ROGER J.
(Indian band chief)
Affiliation: Eel Ground Indian Band, Site 3, Box 9, RR #1, Newcastle, New Brunswick, Canada E1V 3L8 (506) 622-2181.

AUSTIN, DR. DIANE
(professor of anthropology)
Affiliation: Dept. of Anthropology, Emil Haury Anthropology Bldg., Rm. 221A, University of Arizona, Tucson, AZ 85721 (520) 621-2585 Fax 621-2088. E-mail: daustin@u.arizona.edu. *Interests*: Native American environmental policy.

AUSTIN, JIM
(village council president)
Affiliation: Hoonah Indian Association, P.O. Box 602, Hoonah, AK 99829 (907) 945-3600.

AUSTIN, PAUL S.
(director-Indian center)
Affiliation: The American Indian Center of Arkansas, 1100 N. University #133, Little Rock, AR 72207-6344 (501) 666-9032 Fax 666-5875.

AUSTIN, THOMAS L.
(IHS tribal operations)
Affiliation: Portland Area Office IHS, 1220 S.W. Third Ave., Rm. 476, Portland, OR 97204 (503) 326-2020.

AVERY, PAUL
(school principal)
Affiliation: Lummi High School, 2522 Kwina Rd., Bellingham, WA 98226 (206) 676-2772.

AVEY, GARY
(founding publisher)
Born June 5, 1940, Phoenix, Ariz. *Education*: Arizona State University, BS, 1965, MA, 1975. *Principal occupation*: Founding publisher. *Home address*: 35 E. Pierson St., Phoenix, AZ 85012 (602) 277-0636; 265-4855 (work). *Affiliation*: Publisher/editor, Native Peoples magazine, Phoenix, AZ, 1987-, and Native Artists magazine in Santa Fe, N.M. *Other professional posts*: Editor-in-chief, Arizona Highways magazine; deputy-director, The Heard Museum, Phoenix. *Military service*: U.S. Army, 1965-67 (Capt. 2nd Armored Cavalry Regiment, East German border). *Community activities*: St. Lukes Hospital (board member); St. Lukes Behavioral Health Center; president, DeGrazia Arts & Cultural Foundation Board; Phoenix Arts Commission; chairman, Environmental Commission; Heard Museum. *Memberships*: Western Publishers Association; Regional Publishers Association; Rotary International. *Awards, honors*: Awards for magazine design from: Western Publishers Association, New York Art Directors Club, Phoenix Society for the Visual Arts, and Regional Publishers Association. *Interests*: "I have been fortunate that my work has allowed me to travel extensively, globally and live in Mexico, 1959-60, Germany, 1965-67, as well as Nevada and Washington. Much of my personal time is spent as a volunteer for substance abuse programs; I prefer to be a worker in Native American programs not a leader." *Published works*: The Eternal Desert, with David Muench, 1990; Sacred Mountain, with Gary Driggs; and about a dozen more as editor or designer and approximately 100 magazine editions.

AVRITT, MICHAEL D. (San Felipe Pueblo) 1949-
(mechanical engineer)
Born August 30, 1949, Albuquerque, NM. *Education*: University of New Mexico, BS, 1973. *Principal occupation*: Mechanical engineer. *Home address*: 118 Crestview Ct., Louisville, CO 80027. *Affiliation*: Staff engineer, Pennant Systems Co. (An IBM Co.), Tucson, AZ, 1974-. *Memberships*: American Indian Science & Engineering Society (current board member; chairperson, 1987-88; vice-chairperson, 1985-87). *Awards, honors*: Informal Awards, IBM, 1977 & 1980; First Invention Achievement Level, IBM Corp, 1980; Second Invention Achievement Level, IBM, 1988; named on five patents. *Interests*: Temporary assignment in Boeblingen, Germany for IBM, Dec. 1988 through June 1990; June 1984 to June 1985 IBM loaned exeutive to American Indian Science & Engineering Society to coordinate annual conference held in Los Angeles, CA. *Biographical source*: AISES role model publication, 1987. *Published works*: Various articles in IBM Technical Disclosure Bulletin; various poems published in Winds of Change magazine and used in AISES brochures.

AWAKUNI-SWETLAND, MARK (Uthixide) 1956-
(university lecturer)
Born April 7, 1956, Lincoln, Neb. *Education*: University of Oklahoma, ABD, PhD, 1999. *Principal occupation*: University lecturer. *Address*: University of Nebraska, Dept. of Anthropology, Bessey Hall 132, Lincoln, NE 68588-0368 (402) 472-3455 Fax 472-9462. E-mail: mawakuni-swetland2@unl.edu. *Affiliations*: DOI, National Park Service, Yosemite, CA, 1983-90; Kalaupapa, HI; lecturer, University of Nebraska, Lincoln, 1990-1996, 1999-present; University of Oklahoma, Norman, 1996-99. *Community activities*: Public speaking on Native American and Great Plains topics, powwows, handgames, Master of Ceremony duties; Traditional War Dancer; Southern Plains Gourd Dancer; Museum exhibit consultant. *Memberships*:

Nebraska State Historical Society; Hawaiian Historical Society; Arizona Memorial Museum Association; Omaha Tia Piah Society. *Interests*: Native language & culture maintenance and revitalization; teaching Omaha language; oral histories; material culture replication. *Published works*: Dance Lodges of the Omaha: Building From Memory - monograph (Routledge, 2001); Umo'ho' Iye of Elizabeth Staber: with an Omaha to English Lexicon (John Mangan Printing, Macy, NE, 1991).

AWIAKTA, MARILOU (Cherokee)
(writer, poet, storyteller)
Born in Oak Ridge, Tenn. *Address*: 35 Belleair Dr., Memphis, TN 38104 (901) 726-4639. *Awards, honors*: Distinguished Tennessee Writer Award in 1989; Outstanding Contribution to Appalachian Literature Award in 1991; profiled in the 1994 Oxford Companion to Women's Writing in the U.S. *Published works*: Abiding Appalachia: Where Mountain and Atom Meet; Rising Fawn and the Fire Mystery; Selu: Seeking the Corn-Mother's Wisdom (Fulcrum Publishing, 1994).

AYERS, NANCY
(editor)
Affiliation: Editor, Canadian Native Law Reporter, Native Law Centre, University of Saskatchewan, Room 141, Diefenbaker Centre, Saskatoon, SK S7N 0W0 (306) 966-6189.

AYRES, SONJA K. (Cherokee) 1946-
(professional artist)
Born May 26, 1946, Fort Smith, Ark. *Education*: High school. *Principal occupation*: Professional artist. *Address*: address unknown. *Affiliation*: Sonjya K. Ayres Studio, Muldrow, OK, 1970-. *Collection*: "Red Earth & Fire" - a unique collection of traditional clay art forms using ancient Native American techniques that capture the mystique & lore of great Woodland Indian Tribes. *Art shows/awards*: "Night of the First Americans" John F. Kennedy Center, Washington, DC, 1982; Smithsonian Institute, Washington, DC, 1982; Annual Trail of Tears Arts Show, Tahlequah, OK (Merit Awards, 1984, 1988); Annual Five Civilized Tribes Museum Art Compettion, Muskogee, OK (Division II Award, 1986; Cherokee Heritage Award, 1988; 2nd Place, 1989; Merit Award, 1990); Cherokee National Holiday Art Show, Tahlequah, OK, Honor Award, 1987; Five Civilized Tribes Museum (Poster Artist, Art Uner the Oaks, Indian Market, 1989; Craft Show: 2nd Place, 1990; 1st, 2nd & Honorable Mention, 1991; Solo Exhibit, 1991); Red Cloud Indian Art Show, Pine Ridge, SD, Woodward Award, 1990; Five Civilized Tribes Museum Art & Craft Competitions, awards for clay pipes & pottery, 1992 & 1993; Cherokee Heritage Art Show, Cherokee, NC, 1992; Cherokee Nation History Art Show, 1992 & 1993 awards for Pottery & Graphics; Illustrator of "A Time for Native Americans" 48 playing card portraits, Aristoplay, LTD. Educational Games. *Interests*: Sonja spends most of her time in her studio and personally attends only select major & one-woman shows each year. She spends much of her time researching Native American customs & history.

AYROSO, AILEEN
(director of admissions & records)
Address & Affiliation: Director of Admission & Records, D-Q University, P.O. Box 409, Davis, CA 95617 (916) 758-0470 (phone & fax).

AYULUK, JAMES (Eskimo)
(ex-AK village president)
Affiliation: Chevak Native Village Council, P.O. Box 5514, Chevak, AK 99563 (907) 858-7428.

AZBILL, JOHN (Pomo)
(tribal council president)
Affiliation: Covelo Indian Community Council, P.O. Box 448, Covelo, CA 95428 (707) 983-6126.

AZEAN, MARTINA (Athapascan)
(AK village president)
Affiliation: Kongiganak Native Village, P.O. Box 5069, Kongiganak, AK 99559 (907) 557-5226.

AZUK, DEAN
(vice-president)
Affiliation: Vice-president, National Coalition for Indian Education, 8200 Mountain Rd. NE #203, Albuquerque, NM 87110 (505) 262-2351.

AZURE, F. SAM (Turtle Mountain Chippewa) 1953-
(school principal)
Born July 25, 1953, Rolette, N.D. *Education*: University of North Dakota, BS, 1974; University of South Dakota, Masters in Administrative Education, 1980. *Principal occupation*: Elementary school principal. *Address*: Theodore Jamison Elementary School, 3315 University Dr., Bismarck, ND 58504 (701) 255-3285 Fax 766-4766. *Affiliations*: Teacher, elementary school, Eagle Butte, SD, 1974-81; Federal Program Coordinator, BIA, Billings, MT, 1981-83; BIA Adult Education, teacher of physical education, math, science, Theodore Jamerson Elementary School, Belcourt, ND, 1983-91; principal, Theodore Jamerson Elementary School, Bismarck, ND, 1991-present. *Other professional post*: Tribal Adult Education, Belcourt, ND, 1991-. *Community activities*: Chairperson of Health Board, Turtle Mountain; Board of Directors, Turtle Mountain Community College. *Memberships*: North Dakota Association of Elementary School Principals. *Interests*: High school official for boys and girls basketball and football, and week-end musician.

AZURE, JANE
(special education coordinator)
Affiliation: Cheyenne River Agency, Bureau of Indian Affairs, P.O. Box 2020, Eagle Butte, SD 57625 (605) 964-8722.

AZURE, SAM
(school principal)
Affiliation: Theodore Jamerson Elementary School, United Tribes Technical College, 3315 University Dr., Bismarck, ND 58504 (701) 255-3285.

AZUYAK, TONY (Eskimo)
(AK village president)
Affiliation: Native Village of Old Harbor, P.O. Box 62, Old Harbor, AK 99643 (907) 286-2215.

B

BAALAM, RANDALL
(village council chief)
Affiliation: Birch Creek Village Council, General Delivery, Birch Creek, AK 99740 (907) 628-6126.

BABBY, FAYETTA
(BIA education administrator)
Affiliation: Sacramento Area Office, Bureau of Indian Affairs, Federal Office Bldg., 2800 Cottage Way, Sacramento, CA 95825 (916) 979-2560 Fax 979-3063.

BABBY, WYMAN D.
(BIA agency supt.)
Affiliation: Fort Peck Agency, Bureau of Indian Affairs, P.O. Box 637, Poplar, MT 59255 (406) 768-5312.

BABCOCK, BARBARA
(professor)
Education: University of Chicago, PhD, 1975. *Affiliation*: American Indian Studies Program, The University of Arizona, Harvill Bldg., Rm. 430, P.O. Box 210076, Tucson, AZ 85721 (520) 621-7108 Fax 621-7952. E-mail: aisp@email.arizona.edu. *Interests*: Southwest Indian cultures, especially Pueblo.

BABCOCK, W. KENNETH (Narragansett)
(tribal council chief sachem)
Affiliation: Chief Sachem, Narragansett Indian Tribal Council, P.O. Box 268, Charleston, RI 02813 (401) 364-1100.

BACA, CECILIA
(BIA education field officer)
Affiliation: Bureau of Indian Affairs, Albuquerque Education Field Office, P.O. Box 26567, Albuquerque, NM 87125 (505) 766-3850.

BACA, JOE *(Seng Weng)* (Santa Clara Tewa) 1940-
(gallery owner)
Born September 10, 1940, Dulce, N.M. *Education*: Highlands University, B.A., 1963; University of New Mexico, MBA, 1975. *Principal occupation*: Gallery owner. *Address*: Rt. 5, Box 472-C, Espanola, NM 87532 (505) 753-9663 (work). *Affiliation*: Owner, Singing Water Gallery, Espanola, NM. *Military service*: U.S. Army, 1963-65 (PFC).

BACA, LAWRENCE R. (Pawnee)
(attorney; association president)
Affiliations: Native American Bar Association, Native American Legal Resource Center, Oklahoma City University Law School, 2501 N. Blackwelder, Oklahoma City, OK 73106 (405) 521-5277. *Other professional post*: Chairperson, Indian Law Section, Federal Bar Association, Washington, DC.

BACA, LORENZO (Isleta Pueblo-Mescalero Apache) 1947-
(visual/literary/performing artist; educator)
Born September 9, 1947, Morenci, Ariz. *Education*: California State University, Long Beach, BA (Art), 1972; UCLA, MA (American Indian Studies), 1986. *Principal occupation*: Visual/literary/performing artist; educator. *Address*: P.O. Box 4353, Sonora, CA 95370 (209) 532-1573. *Affiliations*: Arts/graphics consultant: Sierra Audio Systems, Sonora, CA; Image Maker, James, CA; The Woodwright Shop, Twaine Harte, CA. *Other professional posts*: Artist-in-Residence: Tri-County Consortium of Special Education, Tuolumne County Schools, Sonora, CA, 1986-88; Twaine Harte Elementary School, Twaine Harte, CA, 1988-92. *Shows/Exhibits*: Stanford Pow Wow, Stanford, CA, May 1991; Chaw Se Invitational, Chaw Se State Park, Volcano, CA, Aug. 1991; Buff Show, Anne Saunders Gallery, Jamestown, CA, Feb. 1991, 1992; California Spirit, Calaveras County Arts Council, San Andreas, CA, Feb. 1992; among many others dating back to 1986. *Commissions*: Indian Nations At Risk Task Force, U.S. Office of Education, Washington, DC, March 1991; D. Fregeau, Harmony Center, Graphics, Twaine Harte, CA, Sept. 1991; M. Pelletier, Silver Pendant Design, Truckee, CA, Jan. 1992; B. Lopez, Silver Designs, Sutter Creek, CA, Feb. 1992. Numerous workshops and performances. *Awards, honors*: 1st Place awards: sculpture-Twaine Harte Annual Art Show, 1987; sculpture-Chaw Se Indian Grinding Rock, 1987; photography-Central Sierra Arts Council, 1987; pottery-Durfee Gallery, Scottsdale, AZ, Nov. 1985; among others. *Interests*: "His works, which include fine art, sculpture, poetry, acting and video, are often a contemporary expression of the Native traditions of his Southwestern heritage of storytelling, dance, song and art."

BACON, CAROL
(BIA director)
Affiliation: Office of Management & Administration, Bureau of Indian Affairs, Dept. of the Interior, MS-4657-MIB, 1849 C St., NW, Washington, DC 20240 (202) 208-4174.

BACON, GEORGES
(Indian band chief)
Affiliation: Bande Indienne Montagnais de la Romaine, LaRomaine, Quebec G0G 1M0 (418) 229-2110.

BACON, JEAN-LOUIS
(Indian band chief)
Affiliation: Montagnais de Betsiamites, 20 rue Messek Box 40, Betsiamites, Quebec, Canada G0H 1M0 (418) 567-2265.

BAD MILK, RICHARD (Rosebud Lakota)
(elementary school administrator)
Affiliation: Elementary School Administrator, Sicangu Oyate Ho., Inc., St. Francis Indian School, P.O. Box 379 HCR 59 Box 1A, St. Francis, SD 57572 (605) 747-2297.

BAD MOCCASIN, DONALD "BRUCE"
(Crow Creek Sioux) 1949-
(health care administration)
Born February 3, 1949, Chamberlain, S.D. *Education*: South Dakota School of Mines & Technology, BSCE, 1972, MSCE, 1981. *Principal occupation*: Health care administration. Address unknown. *Affiliations*: Engineer, Bureau of Indian Affairs, Aberdeen, SD (4 years); engineer, Indian Health Service, Oklahoma City, OK, 1977-79, Aberdeen Area, 1979-91, and Phoenix Area, 1991-93; Aberdeen Area Office, 1993-. *Military service*: U.S. Army (commissioned second lieutenant, 1972); 1977-present, currently on active duty with the U.S. Public Health Service with rank of Captain (06). *Memberships*: American Water Works Association, 1985-; Commissioned Officers Association (associate recruiter for PHS with emphasis in recruitment of minorities into the I.H.S.) *Awards, honors*: Outstanding

Service Medal, USPHS, 1989; Area Excellence Award-Phoenix, 1992; Employee-of-the-Year, Aberdeen Area, IHS, 1983. *Interests*: "I am interested in early architecture and woodworking. My hobbies are bowling, basketball, and other sports activities involving running. Recently relocated back to Northern Plains area with IHS. Changed career track from engineering management to health care administration. Currently responsible for directing a comprehensive health care delivery system for American Indians throughout North & South Dakota, Nebraska and Iowa."

BAD WOUND, ELGIN (Oglala Lakota)
(college president)
Affiliation: Oglala Lakota College, P.O. Box 490, Kyle, SD 57752 (605) 455-2321.

BADBEAR, FAITH G. (*One Who Cares for Children*)
(Crow) 1959-
(assistant curator of ethnology)
Born February 23, 1959, Dallas, Tex. *Education*: BSED Art K-12. *Principal occupation*: Assistant curator of ethnology. *Address*: Science Museum of Minnesota, 120 W. Kellogg Blvd., St. Paul, MN 55102 (651) 221-9432 Fax 221-4525. E-mail: badbear@smm.org. *Affiliations*: Buffalo Bill Historical Center, Cody, WY, 1989-92; National Museum of the American Indian, 1992-93; Canadian Museum of Civilization, Hull, Quebec, Canada, 1994; St. Louis Historical Society, St. Louis, MO, 1995; Duluth Children's Museum, Duluth, MN, 1995; Science Museum of Minnesota, 1994-present. *Community activities*: Diabetes Walkathon, Toys for Tots, Ain Dah Yung (support Indian group home); volunteer to give lectures at schools and companies in Minnesota on Indian awareness and women in science. *Memberships*: AAM - Keepers of the Treasurers. *Interests*: Cultures of the World, Native American Graves Protection; Repatriation Act & Museum Management; teaching Indian people all aspects of handling and running a museum.

BADGER, HECTOR
(Indian band chief)
Affiliation: Cote Indian Band, Box 1659, Kamsack, Saskatchewan, Canada S0A 1S0 (306) 542-2694.

BADGER, JIM
(Indian band chief)
Affiliation: Sucker Creek Indian Band, Box 65, Enilda, Alberta, Canada T0G 0W0 (403) 523-4426.

BADGERO, RAY
(organization president)
Affiliation: North American Indian Ministries (NAIM), P.O. Box 151, Point Roberts, WA 98281 (604) 946-1227.

BAHE, FANNIE
(executive officer)
Affiliation: National Council of BIA Educators, 8009 Mountain Rd. Place NE, Albuquerque, NM 87110 (505) 266-6638.

BAHE, ROSE MARIE (Paiute)
(tribal chairperson)
Affiliation: Utu Utu Gwaitu Paiute Tribal Council, Star Route 4, Box 56-A, Benton, CA 93512 (619) 933-2321.

BAHE, VELMA (Kootenai)
(tribal chairperson)
Affiliation: Kootenai Tribal Council, P.O Box 1269, Bonners Ferry, ID 83805 (208) 267-3519.

BAHEE, KEE (Navaho) 1962-
(painter & sculptor)
Born September 6, 1962, Winslow, Ariz. *Education*: Institute of American Indian Arts, Santa Fe, NM (one year); N.E.C. and Scottsdale Artist School (two years). *Principal occupation*: Painter & sculptor. *Other professional post*: Graphic artist. *Awards, honors*: 1st Drawing, 2nd Painting, Museum of Northern Arizona Navaho Show; S.N.A.C.F. 1st Painting, Honorable Mention, Scottsdale; 2nd Mixed Media, 1st Pastel, Most Promising New Artist, Scottsdale, etc. *Interests*: "I sculpt as well as paint, but because of lack of space and finances I'm unable to sculpt. Eventually, I would like to work my way into a situation to where I can do both." *Biographical sources*: Art Talk Magazine; Indian Gaming Magazine; ATLATL Directory of Indian Artists.

BAHR, GARY (Sac & Fox of Missouri)
(former tribal chairperson)
Affiliation: Sac & Fox Nation of Missouri, Rt. 1, Box 60, Reserve, KS 66434 (785) 742-7471.

BAILEY, AREBA ELNORA ABERNATHY
(United Lumbee/Cherokee) 1932-
(homemaker)
Born August 30, 1932, Yell County, Ark. *Principal occupation*: Homemaker. *Home address*: 2481 Alfred Ave., Exeter, CA 93221. *Community activities*: Assembly of God Church (taught Sunday school); United Lumbee Nation (Bear Clan treasurer, 1983-; member, Grand Council, 1984-; vice-chief, 1988-). *Membership*: Native American Wolf Clan, 1978-. *Awards, honors*: 1988 United Lumbee Nation's Silver Eagle Award for outstanding work done for their Nation/Band/Clan or the Indian community at large.

BAILEY, BENTON (*Screaming Eagle*)
(United Lumbee/Cherokee) 1948-
(computer specialist)
Born October 29, 1948, Exeter, Calif. *Education*: Sequoia Jr. College (Visalia, CA) 1990-. *Principal occupation*: Computer specialist. *Home address*: 3724 W. Monte Vista, Visalia, CA 92377 (209) 733-2947. *Affiliation*: United Lumbee Tribe. *Military service*: U.S. Air Force, 1971-75 (Sgt. - disabled veteran; awarded Civil Service Ribbon & Vietnam Combat Ribbon). *Community activities*: Special Olympics wheelchair division; competed in Long Beach, CA, won 2 Silver & 1 Gold Medal, 1990; New Orleans, LA, won 2 Gold & 1 Silver Medal, 1991 racing. *Memberships*: United Lumbee Nation's Bear Clan Councilperson, 1983-85, Chief, 1985-90; Re-elected to Chief, 1992-; editor, United Lumbee Bear Clan Newsletter, 1992-. *Interests*: Computer science, working for my Indian people; Special Olympics; Pow Wows.

BAILEY, DIANE
(Indian band chief)
Affiliation: Chief, Katzie Indian Band, 10946 Katzie Rd., Pitt Meadows, British Columbia, Canada V3Y 1Z3 (604) 465-8961.

BAILEY, ELNORA
(tribal vice chief)
Affiliation: United Lumbee Nation of N.C. & America, P.O. Box 512, Fall River Mills, CA 96028 (916) 336-6701.

BAILEY, GARRICK
(professor of anthropology)
Affiliation: Professor of Anthropology, Dept. of Anthropology, 600 S. College Ave, Harwell Hall, 2nd Floor, University of Tulsa, Tulsa, OK 74104 (918) 631-2348. E-mail: garrick-bailey@utulsa.edu. *Published work*: Art of the Osage, with Daniel C. Swan (University of Washington Press, 2004).

BAILEY, MIKE
(Indian school administrator)
Affiliation: Jones Academy, Route 1, Box 102-5, Hartshorne, OK 74547 (918) 297-2518.

BAINES, DAVID, M.D. (*Nei Goot*) (Tlingit/Tsimpsian)
1955-
(family physician)
Born April 26, 1955 in Mt. Edgecumbe, Alaska. *Education*: Mayo Medical School. *Principal occupation*: Family physician, MD. *Address*: Kamiah Health Center, P.O. Box 473, Kamiah, ID 83536 (208) 935-0733 Fax 935-1005. *Affiliations*: Assistant Professor of Family Medicine, University of Washington School of Medicine; affiliate faculty, Idaho State University Family Practice Residency Program; clinical faculty, University of Nevada, Reno, School of Medicine; staff, St. Maries Family Medicine; fight doctor (professional boxing), Couer D'Alene Tribal Casino; board member, National Native News Program, "Native America Calling." *Community activities*: Chairperson-Ad Hoc Committee for Minority Populations, National Heart, Lung and Blood Institute, National Institutes of Health; member, Clinical Laboratory Improvement Act Advisory Committee at Centers for Disease Control and Prevention; . *Awards, honors*: 1993 Searle Pharmaceutical Co.'s "Gentle Giants of Medicine" award; appointed by the Clinton Administration to a six-member screening committee that selected the new Indian Health

Services director; member, Environmental Justice Committee at the Institute of Medicine, National Academy of Sciences, convened by Executive Order (President Clinton) #12898. *Memberships*: Association of American Indian Physicians (past president); American Academy of Family Physicians (past chairperson); American Medical Association. *Published works*: Special Health Problems of Native Americans (chapter 37) in "Principles and Practices of Clinical Preventive Medicine," edited by Richard S. Lang, MD, MPH (Mosby Medical Books, 1992); Native American Women & health Care (chapter IV.12) in "Behavioral Medicine for Women: A Comprehensive Handbook," edited by Elaine Ann Blechman & Kelly Brownell (Guilford Publications, 1997).

BAIRD, BRUCE RICHARD (Ojibway/Oneida)
(administrator, teacher)
Address: Office of Indian Education, P.O. Box 520, Greenway H.S., Coleraine, MN 55722 (218) 245-1199 Fax 245-2019. *Affiliations*: Univac Corp., 1962-65; Control Data Corp., 1965-69; ISD, Minneapolis, MN, 1969-70; University of South Dakota, 1970-80; ISD 316, Coleraine, MN, 1980-present. *Other professional posts*: Teach part time in community college; video/film producer. *Military service*: U.S. Navy, 1958-62. *Community activities*: Chairman, local Indian council. *Memberships*: American Legion, VFW.

BAIRD, LAWRENCE
(Indian band chief)
Affiliation: Chief, Ucluelet Indian Band, Box 699, Ucluelet, B.C., Canada V0R 3A0 (604) 726-7342.

BAIRD, W. DAVID
(professor of history, author)
Affiliation: Dept. of History, Pepperdine University, Malibu, CA. He is an outstanding authority on the Indian period of Oklahoma's history. *Published works*: Editor - A Creek Warrior for the Confederacy: The Autobiography of Chief G.W. Grayson (University of Oklahoma Press); Peter Pitchlynn: Chief of the Choctaws (University of Oklahoma Press); The Story of Oklahoma, with Danney Goble (University of Oklahoma Press, 1994).

BAJWA, SAJJAN
(director-Indian health program)
Affiliation: Director, Tule River Indian Health Program, P.O. Box 768, Porterville, CA 93257 (209) 784-2316.

BAKER, ARLENE ROBERTA *(Cata) (Ka-nay-how)*
(Seneca-Cayuga, Pueblo-Tewa) 1938-
(library media specialist)
Born April 13, 1938, Albuquerque, N.M. *Education*: Northeast Oklahoma A & M Jr. College, AA, 1969; Missouri Southern State College, BS, 1972; Northeastern State University, MEd, 1982. *Principal occupation*: Library media specialist. *Home address*: 59501 E. Highway 60, Fairland, OK 74343 (918) 676-3518. *Affiliation*: Fairland (OK) High School. *Memberships*: Fairland Education Association; Oklahoma Library Association; Oklahoma Education Association; National Education Association. *Interests*: "Enjoy bowling, embroidery, and our grandchildren."

BAKER, FREDERICK P.
(director-Indian health center)
Affiliation: Director, Fort Berthold PHS Indian Health Center, P.O. Box 400, New Town, ND 58763 (701) 627-4701.

BAKER, GERARD
(national monument supt.)
Affiliation: Little Bighorn Battlefield National Monument, P.O. Box 39, Crow Agency, MT 59022 (406) 638-2621.

BAKER, JIMMY
(BIA education program administrator)
Affiliation: Oklahoma Education Office, BIA, 4149 Highline Blvd., Suite 380, Oklahoma City, OK 73180 (405) 945-6051.

BAKER, JOE *(Waim-Me-Ke-Mon)* (Delaware) 1946-
(artist/associate professor)
Born January 14, 1946, in Okla. *Education*: University of Tulsa, BFA, 1968, MFA, 1978. *Principal occupation*: Artist/associate professor. *Home address*: 277 E. Tuckey Lane, Phoenix, AZ 85012 (602) 279-1318. *Affiliations*: Colorado College, Colorado Springs, CO,

Visual Arts Faculty, The Marie Walsh Sharpe Foundation, 1986-91; Visiting Associate Professor of Art, 1992-; curator of fine arts, The Heard Museum, Phoenix, AZ, 2003-. *Other professional posts*: Visiting Artist-In-Residence, Sun Valley Center for the Arts & Humanities, Sun Valley, ID, 1982, 83, 87, 88; Registered Native American Artisan, Delaware Tribe, Bureau of Indian Affairs, Washington, DC, 1991; lecturer, Colorado Springs Fine Arts Center, Colorado Springs, CO, 1992; East Carolina University, Greenville, NC, Visiting Arts Faculty, Painting & Drawing, 1991-92; "The Carolina Series," Lecture & performance, The School of Art, 1992; Dept. of English Poetry Symposium, 1992. *Military service*: U.S. Air Force, 1968-78. *Community activities*: Minority Coalition, United Parents. *Membership*: College Art Association, 1978-. *Awards, honors*: Arizona Commission of the Arts, Phoenix, AZ (Visual Arts Panelist, 1982-84; Bi-cultural Arts Representative to Mexico, 1983-84; Visual Arts Representative, Western States Arts Foundation, Santa Fe, NM, 1983-84; Nominee, Regional Arts Panelist, national Endowment for the Arts, Washington, DC, 1983-84; Arts Panelist, Idaho Commission on the Arts, Boise, ID, 1986; Arts Panelist, Wyoming Council on the Arts, Cheyenne, WY, 1987. *Exhibitions*: Numerous solo & group exhibitions from 1977 to the present. *Biographical sources*: California Art Review, Los Angeles, CA, 1983; The Complete Book of Country Swing & Western Dance and a Bit About Cowboys, by Peter Livingston (Doubleday, 1981); Love Medicine, by Louise Erdrich (Rowohlt Publishing, Germany, 1984); Signale: Indianischer Kunstler, by Katrina Hartje (Berlinger, Kunstblatt, 1984); The American West: The Modern Vision (New York Graphics Society, 1984); A History & Selections from the Permanent Collections, by Colorado Springs Fine Arts Center (Williams Publishing, 1986); "Art & Life," Calendar (Design Graphics, Phoenix, 1992); "Joe Baker, The Painter," by Eileen Baily (Arizona Trends, Apr. 1992); Joe Baker: The Carolina Series," Catalyst (The Colorado College, 1992); New Art of the West 3, Eiteljorg Museum (Benham Press, 1992). Numerous public collections, such as: Metropolitan Museum of Art, Heard Museum, Smithsonian Institution, Phoenix Art Museum, Fine Arts Museum of New Mexico.

BAKER, PAIGE J.
(BIA agency supt.)
Affiliation: Fort Berthold Agency, Bureau of Indian Affairs, P.O. Box 370, New Town, ND 58763 (701) 627-4707 Fax 627-3601.

BAKER, PERRY J.
(BIA agency supt.)
Affiliation: Wind River Agency, Bureau of Indian Affairs, Fort Washakie, WY 82514 (307) 332-7810 Fax 332-4578. *Past professional post*: Uintah & Ouray Agency, BIA, Fort Duchesne, UT.

BAKER, QUINCEE
(library director)
Affiliation: Fort Berthold Reservation Public Library, P.O. Box 788, New Town, ND 58763 (701) 627-4738.

BAKER, SHERRY (Creek)
(director-tribal health center)
Affiliation: Sapulpa Health Center, Creek Nation of Oklahoma, 1125 E. Cleveland, Sapulpa, OK 74066 (918) 224-9310.

BAKKA, NORMA JEAN (Ojibwe) 1939-
(counseling)
Born February 23, 1939, White Earth Reservation, Minn. *Education*: Bemidji State University, B.A.; University of Wisconsin, Superior, M.A. *Principal occupation*: Counseling. Address unknown. *Affiliations*: Director of Indian Services Program, Mesabi Community College, Virginia, MN (218) 749-7727 (10 years); Counselor, Fond du Lac Community College, 1994-. *Community activities*: Range women's advocate for battered women; Indian awareness week activities, Mesabi College. *Published works*: Native American Cultural Cookbook (JumboJacks, 1991); How to Build a Birch Bark Canoe.

BALBER, MARY AL (Ojibway)
(attorney)
Address: 1573 E. Margaret, St. Paul, MN 55106 (612) 222-5863 (office). Membership: Native American Bar Association (board member).

BALDRIDGE, DAVE
(executive director)
Affiliation: National Indian Council on Aging, 10501 Montgomery Blvd. NE #210, Albuquerque, NM 87111 (505) 888-3302.

BALES, JEAN ELAINE MYERS (Iowa) 1946-
(artist)
Born December 25, 1946, Pawnee, Okla. *Education*: Oklahoma University of Science & Art, BA, 1969; Professional Study, Institute of San Miguel de Allende, Mexico. *Principal occupation*: Artist. *Address*: Unknown. *Community activities*: National Wildlife Federation (member). *Memberships*: Oklahoma Indian Art League, 1973-74; Indian Arts & Crafts Association (lifetime member and past board of directors) *Awards*: Numerous awards from: Santa Fe Indian Market; Cherokee National Museum; O'Odham Tash, Casa Grande, AZ; Hear Museum; Philbrook Art Center; Scottsdale National Indian Art Show; Gallup Inter-Tribal Ceremonial; Museum of the Wester Prairie; and many others. *Honors*: Governor's Oklahoma Cup for Outstanding Indian Artist of the Year, 1973; selected as one of the Oklahomans for Indian Opportunity (OIO) calendar artist for the painting "Oklahoma Open Drum"; 1982 Oklahoma Diamond Jubilee - Outstanding Woman of the Southern Plains; 1984 Citation by the state of Oklahoma, House of Representatives for demonstrating exceptional abilities in the creation of the visual arts, and bringing positive recognition to the state of Oklahoma in its pursuit of excellence in the arts. *Permanent Public collections*: Southern Plains Indian Museum; Denver Museum of Natural History; Museum of Northern Arizona; U.S. Dept. of the Interior; Oklahoma Historical Society, among others. *Permanent Private collections*: Too numerous to list, however, they include collections throughout the U.S., Canada and Europe. *Interests*: Mrs. Bales writes, "I have done and still do lectures and seminars for groups and colleges throughout the U.S. I am very active with school systems throughout Oklahoma. By taking the Indian art forms into the classroom we help students (whether they are Indian or non-Indian) to appreciate the rich American Indian culture we have in Oklahoma. I have worked with the schools planning counselors to plan curriculum to include Indian studies. My works are represented in many private and public collections throughout the U.S., Canada and Europe."

BALLARD, CHARLES (Quapaw, Cherokee)
(poet)
Address: 6701 Francis, Lincoln, NE 68505 (402) 466-3706.

BALLARD, CLAY (Cherokee)
(counselor)
Affiliation: University of California, Davis, 300 South Hall, Davis, CA 95616 (916) 752-0864.

BALLARD, JOYCE (Shoshone-Bannock)
(museum director)
Affiliation: Shoshone-Bannock Tribal Museum, P.O. Box 793, Fort Hall, Idaho 83203 (208) 237-9791.

BALLARD, LOUIS WAYNE *(Honganozhe)*
(Quapaw-Cherokee) 1931-
(composer, educator)
Born July 8, 1931, Miami, Okla. *Education*: University of Oklahoma, 1949-50; Northeast Oklahoma A & M, AA, 1951; University of Tulsa, BME, 1954, MM, 1962; College of Santa Fe, Doc. Mus., h.c. *Principal occupation*: Composer, educator. *Address*: P.O. Box 4552, Santa Fe, NM 87502 (505) 986-3984 Fax 986-9244. E-mail: ogx@earthlink.net; Website: www.nswmp.com. *Affiliations*: Chairman, Music Dept., Institute of American Indian Arts, Santa Fe, 1962-64; chairman, Performing Arts Department, Institute of American Indian Arts, 1964-69; music curriculum specialist, Central Office-Education, BIA, Washington, DC, 1969-79; chairman, Minority Awareness Committee for New Mexico Education Association; project director and composer, First National All Indian Honor Band, Santa Fe, 1977-present; Distinguished Visiting Professor, William Jewell College, Liberty, Mo., Spring 2001. *Other professional posts*: Music consultant and lecturer; president, First American Indian Films, Inc. *Memberships*: ASCAP; American Music Center; American Symphony Orchestra League; National Music Educator's Association; Minority Concerns Commission, MENC (member); Society for Ethnomusicology;

Masonic Lodge. *Awards, honors*: Composer's Assistance Grants, Select Composer's Bicentennial Grant, National Endowment for the Arts; New Mexico American Revolution Bicentennial Commission Grant, 1967-1976; First Marion Nevins MacDowell Award, Chamber Music, 1969 for "Ritmo Indio, a Study in American Indian Rhythms"; Ford Foundation Grant, American Indian Music and Music Education, 1970; Outstanding Indian of the Year, Tulsa Council of the American Indian, 1970; National Indian Achievement Award, Indian Council Fire, 1972; Distinguished Alumnus Award, Tulsa University, 1972; Outstanding Indian of the Year, American Indian Exposition, Anadarko, Oklahoma, 1973; Certificate of Special Achievement, Department of the Interior, 1974; Catlin Peace Pipe Award, National Indian Lore Association, 1976; Annual ASCAP Awards, 1966-89; first Native American composer to have composition performed three (3) times in Carnegie Hall, New York, NY, 1984, 1987 & 1992; first American composer to present entire program of chamber music in the new Beethoven Chamber Music Hall, next to Beethoven's birthplace, Bonn, Germany, June 1, 1989; Lifetime Music Achievement Award from the First Americans in the Arts, Feb. 1997, in Beverly Hills, Calif. *Interests*: Mr. Ballard has traveled extensively throughout the U.S. as music consultant for Volt Technical Corp. headstart programs, to B.I.A. area offices and workshops establishing bicultural music programs from kindergarten to college level. "I have traveled to Eastern Europe, Western Europe, South America, Canada and England for performances of my music. Also, my music has been broadcast on Radio France, Deutsch Welle, Voice of America, Saarlandische Rundfunk, Deutsch Sundwesten Rundfunk, Canadian Broadcasting Corp., National Public Radio and others." He has lectured at numerous colleges and universities, and at the M.E.N.C. Regional Music Conference, Albuquerque, N.M., on a variety of subjects relating to American Indian art & music; Mr. Ballard has been a guest composer at numerous events across the country; and guest conductor: Milwaukee Symphony, New Mexico Symphony, Bicentennial Horizons of American Music in St. Louis, MO, Sioux City Symphony. In 1992, Mr. Ballard's work was featured on the roster of Columbia Artists Concert Association in 16 American cities following a January concert at Carnegie Hall where Ballard and the Quintet of the Americas performed "Ritmo Indio" for the program "Celebration of the Americas." *Biographical sources*: Who's Who in America; Who's Who in the World; ASCAP Biographical Dictionary; Baker's Biography of Musicians; Grove's Dictionary of Music, U.S.A.; The New Grove Dictionary of Music and Musicians, 2nd Ed., 2001; This Song Remembers (Self Portraits of Native Americans in the Arts) (Houghton Mifflin, 1980); "Louis W. Ballard, New World Composer of the Southwest", by Branham & Powers (New Mexico Magazine, 1972); and numerous other articles. *Published works*: The American Indian Sings, Book 1, 1970; American Indian Music for the Classroom, 1973; My Music Reaches to the Sky, Musical Instruments of North American Indians; "Indians, the music of", article for "Scholastic Encyclopedia," Arete Publications; The Last Gladiator, article for University of Tulsa Alumni Magazine; "Syllabus for Kindergarten Music Teachers in Navajo Schools." Music album:Wak-101 Ballard, cassette available from Wakan Records, Santa Fe, NM. Composed: (ballets) Ji-Jo Gweh, Koshare, The Four Moons; (orchestral music) Scenes From Indian Life, Why the Duck Has a Short Tail, Devil's Promenade, Incident at Wounded Knee, Fantasy Aborigine, Nos. I, II, III, IV, V; (chamber music) "Ritmo Indio", Desert Trilogy, Kacina Dances, Rio Grande Sonata, String Trio 1, Rhapsody for Four Bassoons; (choral cantatas) "Portrait of Will Rogers", "The Gods Will Hear", "Thus Spake Abraham"; (band works) "Siouxiana", "Scenes From Indian Life", "Ocotillo Festival Overture", "Nighthawk Keetowa"; (percussion) "Cecega Ayuwipi", "Music for the Earth and the Sky"; "Ritmo Indio" with the Quintet of the Americas (CD-released by Newport Records, 1992). Sheet music of Mr. Ballard's are available from the following publishers: Bourne Music Co., 5 West 37th St., New York, N.Y. 10018; Belwin-Mills Publishing Corp. with Theodore Presser Publishing Co., Bryn Mawr, PA; and The New Southwest Music Publications and Wakan Records, P.O. Box 4552, Santa Fe, NM 87502; Website: www.nswmp.com.

BALLEW, GREGORY
(organization chairperson)
Affiliation: National Center for Great Lakes Native American Culture, 5401 S. Cty. Rd. 900 E., Lafayette, IN 47905 (765) 296-9943 (phone & fax).

BALLOT, JOSEPH A.
(association president)
Affiliation: Maniilaq Association, P.O. Box 256, Kotzebue, AK 99752 (800) 478-3312; (907) 442-3311 Fax 442-2381.

BALLOT, PERCY
(AK village president)
Affiliation: Native Village of Buckland, P.O. Box 67, Buckland, AK 99727 (907) 494-2171.

BALLOUE, JOHN (Cherokee) 1948-
(professional artist)
Born April 19, 1948, Richmond, Calif. Education: Chabot College, Hayward, CA, 1971-73; California State University, Hayward, BA (Art), 1975. *Principal occupation*: Professional artist. *Home address*: 26838 Grandview Ave., Hayward, CA 94542 (510) 538-4003. *Affiliations*: American Indian Traders Guild, Fresno, CA, 1991-; Hayward Arts Council, Hayward, CA. Commissions: Santa Clara Indian Health Center; 1995 Bay Area Powwow Calendar; 1995 American Indian Film Festival, poster artist, San Francisco, CA; Army Air Force Exchange Service, 1995 Native American Cultural Month, poster artist, Dallas, TX; cover artist, "Protectors of the Land," by Richard Burill, 1994. *Military service*: U.S. Army, 1968-69 (Specialist-4, Vietnam Vet; Nationall Defense Service Medal, Vietnam Service Medal, Vietnam Campaign Medal, Army Commendation Medal). *Membership*: Indian Arts & Crafts Association, 1988-; Southwestern Association for Indian Arts. *Awards, honors*: 1992 Indian Arts and Crafts Association, Artist of the Year; over 25 awards for various (Indian and non-Indian) juried art shows. *Interests*: "Photography is closely related to much of my work. I've tried to illustrate dance, costumes, and traditions of contemorary Native America. I attend powwows and various social events, photograph and later translate them into artwork. My work is evolving from a purdy photo - Realistic Nature, to that of images that are more spiritual and historical in nature."." *Biographical sources*: Articles in: The Indian Trader (Gallup, NM, Nov. 1991); The Daily Review (Hayward, CA, April 1985). Work included in: "The Biographical Directory of Native American Painters (Patrick D. Lester); and "The Native Americans, an Illustrated History" (Turner Publications).

BANAI, EDWARD BENTON (Ojibway)
(non-fiction writer)
Address: Rt. 2, Box 2800, Hayward, WI 54842 (715) 634-1442.

BANCROFT, PRISCILLA
(BIA field rep.)
Affiliation: Ute Mountain Ute Field Office, Bureau of Indian Affairs, P.O. Box KK, Towaoc, CO 81334 (970) 565-8473 Fax 565-8906.

BANKS, DENNIS J. *(Nowa Cumig)* (Anishinabe)
(lecturer, author, activist)
Born on the Leech Lake Reservation in northern Minnesota. *Education*: DQ University, A.A. *Principal occupation*: American Indian Movement (AIM), lecturer, author. *Address*: P.O. Box 134, Federal Dam, MN 56641. *Affiliations*: Co-founder & presently National Field Director, American Indian Movement, 1968-present; founder & director, Sacred Run Foundation, 1978-present. *Military service*: U.S. Air Force, 1954-58 (active duty-4 years, inactive duty-8 years). *Awards, honors*: Autobiography, "Sacred Soul," won the non-fiction "Book of the Year Award." *Activities*: In 1968, co-founded the American Indian Movement (AIM), and established it to protect the traditional ways of Indian people and to engage in legal cases protecting treaty rights of natives - such as hunting & fishing, trapping, wild riceing. Among other activities, it participated in the occupation of Alcatraz Island where demands were made that all federal surplus property be returned to Indian control. In 1972, organized and led the Trail of Broken Treaties' caravan across the U.S. to Washington DC calling attention to the plight of Native Americans. Spearheaded the move on Pine Ridge Reservation in South Dakota in 1973 to oust corruption and the U.S. appointed tribal chairman. This led to the occupation of Wounded Knee and a siege of 71 days which received national attention. Banks was the principal negotiator and leader of the Wounded Knee forces. Under the leadership of Dennis Banks, AIM led a protest in Custer (SD) in 1973 against the judicial process that found a white man innocent of murdering an Indian. As a result of his involvement in Wounded Knee and Custer, Banks and 300 others were arrested and faced trial. He was acquitted of the Wounded Knee charges, but was convicted of riot and assault at Custer. Refusing the prison term, Banks went underground, later receiving amnesty in California by then Governor Jerry Brown. In California, from 1976-1983, Banks earned an Associates of Arts degree at Davis University and taught at DQ University (an all Indian-controlled Institution), where he became the first American Indian chancellor. He also established the first spiritual run from Davis to Los Angeles, California in 1978 (now an annual event) and organized the Longest Walk from Alcatraz to Washington, DC that same year. This 3,600 mile walk was successful in its purpose: to gather enough support to halt purposed legislation abrogating Indian treaties with the U.S. government. In the spring of 1979, he taught at Stanford University. After Governor Brown left office, Banks received sanctuary on the Onondaga Nation in upstate New York in 1984. It was while living there that Banks organized the Great Jim Thorpe Longest Run from New York City to Los Angeles, California. A Spiritual run, this event ended in Los Angeles to begin the Jim Thorpe Memorial Games where the gold medals Thorpe had won at the 1912 Olympics were restored to the Thorpe family. In 1985, Banks left Onondaga to surrender to law enforcement officials in South Dakota and served 18 months in prison. When released, he worked as a drug and alcohol counselor on the Pine Ridge Indian Reservation. During 1987, grave robbers in Uniontown, Kentucky were halted in their digging for artifacts after they had destroyed over 1,200 American Indian grave sites. Banks was called in to organize the reburial ceremonies for the uncovered remains. His activities in this state resulted in Kentucky and Indiana passing strict legislation against grave desecration. He revived the idea of traditional spiritual running in 1978 when he began Sacred Run. Since then it has become a multi-cultural, international event with participants from around the world joining Native American runners to carry the message of the sacredness of all Life and of humankind's relationship to the planet, Mother Earth. To date, Banks has led runners over 64,000 miles through the U.S., Europe, Japan, Canada, Australia, Ireland, Scotland, and Aotearoa (New Zealand). In addition to leading and organizing Sacred Runs, Dennis Banks stays involved with American Indian issues, AIM activities, and travels the globe lecturing, providing drug & alcohol counseling, teaching Native traditions, and sharing his experiences. In 1994, Banks led the four-month, "Walk for Justice," from Alcatraz Island in San Francisco to Washington, DC. The purpose was to bring public awareness to current Native issues. Banks agreed to head the "Bring Peltier Home" Campaign in 1996 bringing Native Americans and other supporters together in a national drive for executive clemency for political prisoner Leonard Peltier. A musical tape "Still Strong" featuring Banks' original work as well as traditional Native American songs was completed in 1993 and a musical video with the same name was released in 1995. His autobiography, the "Longest Walk," is in writing now...the publication date is unknown at this time. Key roles in the following movies: "War Party", "The Last of the Mohicans", and "Thunderheart". *Biographical sources*: Too numerous to list. *Published works*: Sacred Soul (autobiography, Ashai, Japan, 1988); forewords to "Native America: Portrait of Peoples"; "Shooting Back From the Reservation;" "Of Earth Elders."

BANISTER, MARVIN
(association president)
Affiliation: National Indian Festival Association, P.O. Box 3492, Albany, GA 31706 (912) 436-1625 Fax 883-7786. E-mail: marvinbb@surfsouth.com.

BAPTISTE, JOHN
(Indian band chief)
Affiliation: Ermineskin, Box 219, Hobbema, Alberta T0C 1N0 (403) 585-3814.

BAPTISTE, MIKE
(Indian band chief)
Affiliation: Red Pheasant Indian Band, Box 70, Cando, Saskatchewan, Canada S0K 0V0 (306) 937-7717.

BARACKER, ROBERT
(BIA regional director)
Affiliation: Southwest Regional Office, Bureau of Indian Affairs, P.O. Box 26567, Albuquerque, NM 87125 (505) 346-7590 Fax 346-7517.

BARBER, JAMES
(former BIA agency supt.)
Affiliations: Papago Agency, Bureau of Indian Affairs, P.O. Box 578, Sells, AZ 85634 (602) 383-3286.

BARBER, WILSON
(former BIA area director)
Affiliation: Navajo Area Office, Bureau of Indian Affairs, P.O. Box 1060, Gallup, NM 87301 (505) 863-8314.

BARBERO, CAROL L.
(attorney)
Education: Allegheny College, BA; Georgetown University Law School, J.D., 1978. *Address & Affiliation:* Hobbs, Straus, Dean & Walker, LLP (Associate, 1982-86; Partner, 1987-present), 2120 L St., NW, Suite 700, Washington, DC 20037 (202) 822-8282. E-mail: cbarbero@hsdwdc.com. She has represented tribal schools and Indian education organizations throughout her tenure with the Firm, and is one of a few attorneys in the country who specializes in Indian education law. She served as one of the lead advocates for the Indian-related amendments to the Elementary and Secondary Education Act in 1988 & 1994, and has been an active participant in the ESEA reauthorization effort in the 106th Congress. Ms. Barbero also has expertise in Indian self-determination law, and Indian health care. *Past professional posts:* Legislative assistant, House of Representatives (six years); associate, Wilkinson, Cragun & Barker. *Memberships:* District of Columbia Bar Association; American Bar Association.

BARBRY, EARL, SR. (Tunica-Biloxi)
(tribal chairperson)
Affiliation: Tunica-Biloxi Indian Tribe, P.O. Box 331, Mansura, LA 71351 (318) 253-9767.

BARCEL, ELLEN
(writer/editor, museum president)
Education: BA, MA. *Affiliation:* President, Southold Indian Museum, 1080 Main Bayview Rd., P.O. Box 268, Southold, NY 11971 (631) 765-5577 (phone & fax). E-mail: ebarcel@aol.com. *Memberships:* New York State Archaeological Association (Long Island Chapter); Society for American Archaeology; Ohio Archaeological Society.

BARELA, RAYNA
(museum director)
Affiliation: Director, Gila County Historical Museum, Box 2891, 1330 N. Broad St., Globe, AZ 85502 (602) 425-7385.

BARKLEY, JOHN
(casino/bingo general manager)
Affiliation: Umatilla Casino & Bingo, P.O. Box 638, Pendleton, OR 97801 (503) 276-3165.

BARLOW, LEO H.
(corporation president & CEO)
Affiliation: Sealaska Corp., 1 Sealaska Plaza #400, Juneau, AK 99801 (907) 586-1512 Fax 586-1826.

BARLOW, WENDALL PAUL
(Indian band chief)
Affiliation: Indian Island Indian Band, P.O. Box 288, RR #1, Rexton, NB, Canada E0A 2L0 (506) 523-9187.

BARNABY, CHARLIE
(Indian band chief)
Affiliation: Chief, Fort Good Hope Indian Band, General Deliver, Fort Good Hope, NT X0E 0J0 (403) 952-2330.

BARNARD, ROGER (*Yonv Unega-White Bear*)
(Amonsoquath Cherokee) 1949-
(spiritual leader, publisher, artist)
Born October 16, 1949, Carrolton, Mo. *Education:*

Daytona Beach Community College; Universal Life Church (theology). *Principal occupation:* Artist, spiritual leader. *Affiliation & Address:* Spiritual Advisor/ Leader-Chief, President, Pan American Indian Association, 8335 Sevigny Dr., N. Fort Myers, FL 33917-1705 (239) 543-7727. E-mail: panamia@msn.com. *Military service:* U.S. Navy (Gator-amphibious), 1969-71. *Community activities:* Adopt-a-Road, Lee County, FL; conduct regular Asi ceremonies, weddings, funeral and other special requests; teen and novice program to introduce individuals to the basic understanding of the American Indian spiritual path of learning to respect, "We are Related, We are One." *Memberships:* Pan American Indian Association (chief); Native American Church; American Indian Defense; Universal Life Church; American Indian Medicine Society; Amonsoquath Cherokee Tribe of Missouri. *Published work:* "Quest of the Shield" & "Basic Instruction for Individual Learning Toward Ceremonie" (self-published).

BARNES, BARBARA
(college president)
Affiliation: President, North American Indian Travelling College, Onake Corporation, R.R. 3, Cornwall Island, Ontario Canada K6H 5R7 (613) 932-9452.

BARNES, JIM (Choctaw)
(professor, writer)
Born in southeastern Oklahoma. *Principal occupation:* Professor of Comparative Literature and Writer-in-Residence, Truman State University, Kirksville, MO. *Other professional post:* Editor, The Chariton Review. *Published work:* On Native Ground: Memoirs and Impressions (University of Oklahoma Press, 1997).

BARNES, LEWIS (Yokut)
(tribal co-chairperson)
Affiliation: Table Mountain Rancheria, P.O. Box 243, Friant, CA 93626 (209) 822-2587.

BARNES, M.J. (Cherokee) 1941-
(business owner)
Born July 27, 1941, San Antonio, Tex. Education: Texas Christian University, BA, 1964; Arizona State University, MA (Indian Education), 1968. *Principal occupation:* Business owner. *Home address:* 8710 Linkmeadow, Houston, TX 77025 (713) 665-3576 Fax 665-3576 (office). E-mail: kivamjb@aol.com. *Affiliation:* Houston Metropolitan Ministries, 1982-89; owner & operator, Kiva Enterprises, Houston, TX, 1989-. *Community activities:* Member, Cherokee Cultural Society of Houston. *Memberships:* The American Indian Chamber of Commerce of Texas; Texas Polio Survivors' Association. *Awards, honors:* Southwest Literature Award, Texas Christian University, 1963; Employee Achievement Award, Houston Metropolitan Ministries, 1985; painting accepted for exhibition, Cherokee National Museum, 1988 (Trail of Tears Sesquicentennial). *Interests:* "Typography, desktop publishing, proofreading, writing, art (painting, drawing, woodcarving); environment, social justice, volunteerism, employment and assistance for homebound people with handicaps." *Published works:* Numerous articles; book manuscript in process; newspaper columns.

BARNETT, JAMES F., Jr.
(director-historic landmark site)
Affiliation: The Grand Village of the Natchez Indians, 400 Jefferson Davis Blvd., Natchez, MS 39120 (601) 446-6502.

BARNETT, JOHN (Cowlitz)
(tribal chairperson)
Affiliation: Cowlitz Indian Tribe, P.O. Box 2547, Longview, WA 98632 (360) 577-8140.

BARNETTE, JOAN
(museum curator)
Affiliation: Red Rock Museum, P.O Box 328, Red Rock State Park, Church Rock, NM 87311 (505) 722-6196.

BARNEY, CHERYL
(director-tribal health center)
Affiliation: Fort McDermitt Tribal Health Center, P.O. Box 457, McDermitt, NV 89421 (702) 532-8259.

BARRACKMAN, LLEWELLYN (Mojave)
(tribal vice-chairperson)
Affiliation: Fort Mojave Tribal Council, 500 Merriman Ave., Needles, CA 92363 (760) 629-4591.

BARREIRO, JOSE (*HATvey*) (Taino Nation) 1948-
(writer, editor, lecturer)
Born June 19, 1948, Camaguey, Cuba. *Education:* University of Minnesota, B.A, 1975; State University of New York, Buffalo, Ph.D. (American Studies), 1988. *Principal occupation:* Editor and writer; lecturer. *Address:* 226 Blackman Hill Rd., Berkshire, NY 13736 (607) 255-1923 (office). *Affiliations:* Editor-in-Chief, Akwe:kon Press, Cornell University; contributing editor, Native Nations Magazine, New York, NY. *Memberships:* Native American Press Association (founding member). *Awards, honors:* Human Rights of Indigenous Peoples of the Americas; Indigenous Community Development; communications networking; Native American Press Association - Best Feature, 1988. *Biographical sources:* New York Times (March, 1983); USA Today, 1988; A.P. National, 1985; Turtle Q, 1991. *Published works:* Native Peoples in Struggle (Akwesasne Notes, 1982); Indian Roots of American Democracy (Cornell University, 1988); Indian Corn of the Americas (Cornell University, 1989); View From the Shore (Cornell University, 1992); Indian Chronicles (Arte Publico Press, 1993).

BARREIRO, KATSI COOK (Mohawk)
(writer)
Address: 226 Blackman Hill Rd., Berkshire, NY 13736 (607) 657-8112.

BARRETT, DAVID, M.D.
(medical director)
Affiliation: Alaska Native Health Center, 255 Gambel St., Anchorage, AK 99501 (907) 279-6661.

BARRETT, JOHN ADAMS (ROCKY), JR.
(Citizen Potawatomi) 1944-
(tribal chairperson; corporate president)
Born March 25, 1944, Shawnee, Okla. *Education:* Princeton University, 1962-64; University of Oklahoma, 1964-65; Oklahoma City University, BS, 1968, MS, 1986. *Principal occupation:* Tribal chairperson; corporate president. *Address:* Citizen Potawatomi Tribal Busines Committee, 1901 S. Gordon Cooper Dr., Shawnee, OK 74801 (405) 275-3121 Fax 275-0198. *Affiliations:* Warehouseman and salesman, U.S. Plywood Corp., Oklahoma City,1966-69; promotion and supervisor of construction, Greenbriar Development Co., Memphis, TN, 1969-70; Barrett Construction Co., Southaven, MS, 1970-71; director, C.T.S.A. Enterprise, Shawnee, Okla., 1971-74 (intertribal organization, under Indian Action Team Training Contract from BIA, whose objective was to trade hard-core unemployed adult Indians in construction trades); Barrett Drilling Co. (family owned business in contract drilling & oil production), 1974-82; self-employed, J. Barrett Co., 1982-83; tribal administrator, Citizen Band Potawatomi Tribe, 1983-85, chairman, 1985-; president, Barrett Refining, Shawnee, Okla., 1985-. In the Fall of 1985, Barrett Refining was awarded a $52 million jet fuel contract from the U.S. Department of Defense—the only Defense contract to go to an Indian. *Other professional posts:* Paid lobbyist for Oklahoma Home Builders Association in the Oklahoma Legislature; Citizen Band Potawatomi Tribe (business committee member, tribal administrator (1983-1985), vice-chairperson, and chairperson (1985-). *Other tribal activities:* Member, board of directors, United Western Tribes (representing 32 tribes in Oklahoma and Kansas); chairman and director, Shawnee Service United Indian Health Service Advisory Board; director, Oklahoma Indian Health Service Advisory Board; president, National Indian Action Contractors Association; delegate to National Tribal Chairman's Association and National Congress of American Indians. *Community activities:* Member, Emanuel Episcopal Church (ordained lay reader); member, board of directors, Shawnee Quarterback Club; Elks (B.P.O.E.); member, Shawnee Citizens Advisory Council, Lions Club, and Boy Scouts of America as troop leader.

BARSE, HAROLD G. (Kiowa/Wichita/Sioux) 1947-
(readjustment counseling therapist)
Born June 30, 1947, Riverside, Calif. *Education:* Black Hills State College, Spearfish, S.D., B.S. (Secondary Education), 1973; University of Oklahoma, Norman, Okla., M.Ed. (Guidance and Counseling), 1979. *Principal occupation:* Readjustment counseling therapist. *Home address:* 1814 Windsor Way, Norman, OK 73069 (405) 270-5184 (work). *Affiliations:* Director, Adult Education Program, Lake Traverse Sisseton-

Wahpeton Sioux Tribe, Sisseton, S.D., 1973-1975; instructor, Sinte Gleska Community College, Rosebud Sioux Reservation, S.D., 1975; director, Inhalent Abuse Treatment Project, Oklahoma City Native American Center, 1977-1980; readjustment counseling therapist, Dept. of Veterans Affairs (Vet Center), Oklahoma City, OK, 1980-. *Other professional post*: Co-chairman, Vet Center's American Indian Working Group. *Military service*: U.S. Army, 1969-1971 (specialist 4th class E-4). *Memberships*: Founder, Vietnam Era Veterans Inter-Tribal Association, 1981-; Kiowa Blacklegging Society (Kiowa Veterans Association), 1985-; Native American Veterans Association. *Awards, honors*: Planned and organized first National Vietnam Veterans Pow-Wow. *Interests*: Working with Vietnam veterans; primary program development specialist for video Shadow of the Warrior: American Indian Counseling Perspectives; appear in video "Warriors."

BARTA, SUSAN C.
(executive director)
Affiliation: Native American Alcoholism Treatment Program, P.O. Box 773, Sargeant Bluff, IA 51054 (712) 277-9416 Fax 277-3144.

BARTON, LOUISE ANN *(Wind Walks Woman)*
(OK Cherokee-Mohawk) 1934-
(educator, author, performer)
Born November 21, 1934, New York, NY. *Education*: Rutgers, Master Gardner Certification, 2003; New York University, MA, 1981; Herbert Lehman College, BA, 1978; Bronx Community College, AAS, 1973. *Principal occupation*: Teacher, lecturer, author, performer. *Home address*: 4A Hancock Dr., Whiting, NJ 08759 (732) 849-1892. *Affiliations*: Retired from various NYC Board of Education-teaching/coordinator posts. Have worked with the Leonard Peltier Defense Committee (NYC), the Native American Education Program (NYC), and the Liberty Correctional Institution's Native Awareness Program (FL). *Other professional posts*: Former positions held at George Washington High School - teacher specialist at Professional Staff Development Center; coordinator of Business Career Center House, School Improvement, Project Achieve, Educational Accountability, Community-Based organizations; and business teacher in Adult Education Programs. *Community activities*: Native American storytelling and lectures in NYC & NJ colleges, public schools and libraries, senior residences, and private organizations; affiliated with The gatherer Institute. *Memberships*: Southeastern Cherokee Confederacy, Inc.; Intertribal Indians of NJ; NJ American Indian Center Organization; Chairperson of Wind Walker Productions (nonprofit, theatrical organization specializing in Native American folk arts presentations) and The Lyme Tyx (variety shows). *Awards, honors*: Artistic Community Enrichment Award, 1993-94, from a subsidiary of the NYC State Council on the Arts; grants awarded for Native American Storytelling in NYC public branch libraries, and other projects; scholastic honor societies: Kappa Delta Pi & Delta Pi Epsilon. *Interests*: "A master storyteller from a family of storytellers, telling Native and other tales in public schools, libraries, and colleges; working to improve education, preserve the ecology, inform people about Native American cultures and political problems, and lobbying to change laws. Engaged in multicultural activities, bringing people from all backgrounds together in common projects to enrich their communities. Enjoy writing , lecturing and performing. I've taught Business Education and computer skills at both secondary and college levels, I have worked in community theater in all capacities, and have appeared at Shakespeare Festivals and at Medieval Fairs." *Published works*: Fiction, non-fiction, Native stories, children's stories, poetry, plays, newspaper articles, CD covers, artist's books, information pamphlets and packets; also, co-author of scholastic mission statements and city-wide guidelines for computer training.

BARZ, SANDRA 1930-
(editor, publisher)
Born August 4, 1930, Chicago, Ill. *Education*: Skidmore College, B.A., 1952. *Principal occupation*: Editor, publisher. *Address*: Resides in New York City. *Affiliation*: Editor, publisher, Arts and Culture of the North (newsletter, journal), 1976-. *Community activities*: Yorkville Civic Council (member of board). *Interests*: Eskimo art—circumpolar; traveled to Alaska, Canada (Arctic) and Greenland, and have lead tours to Arctic Canada

and Greenland; run conferences at major museums in Canada and the U.S. since 1978, where Eskimo art-related activities are taking place. *Published works*: Inuit Artists Print Workbook (Arts and Culture of the North, Vol. I, 1981, Vol. II with biographies, 1990); newsletter/journal Arts and Culture of the North (seven volumes, 1976-1981; 1983-1984).

BASS, BARRY W. *(Big Buck)* **(Nansemond)**
(tribal councilperson)
Affiliation: Nansemond Indian Tribal Association, P.O. Box 9293, Chesapeake, VA 23321 (804) 487-5116.

BASS, EARL L. *(Running Deer)* **(Nansemond) 1909-**
(tribal chief; retired machinist-farmer)
Born August 27, 1909, Norfolk Co., VA. *Education*: Nansemond Indian Public School #9, Norfolk, VA. *Principal occupation*: Retired machinist, farmer. *Home address*: 3429 Galberry Rd., Chesapeake, VA 23323 (804) 487-5116. *Affiliations*: Norfolk Naval Shipyard, Portsmouth, VA (30 years); chief, Nansemond Indian Tribal Association, Chesapeake, VA. *Community activities*: Participate in various city festivals, speaking engagements at public schools, civic leagues, etc. *Memberships*: Masonic Lodge, 1964-; Woodmen of the World, 1938-. *Awards, honors*: Recognition & Certificate from City of Suffolk, City of Portsmouth, various other cities, Governor Brailes of VA.

BASS, KENNETH P. *(Iron Horse)* **(Nansemond)**
(tribal councilperson)
Affiliation: Nansemond Indian Tribal Association, P.O. Box 9293, Chesapeake, VA 23321 (804) 487-5116.

BASS, VINCENT (Winnebago)
(tribal vice-chairperson)
Affiliation: Winnebago Tribal Council, P.O. Box 687, Winnebago, NE 68071 (402) 878-3100. Website: www.winnebagotribe.com.

BASS-BENNETT, NANCY AMELIA (Nansemond) 1934-
(retired-caseworker)
Born September 13, 1934, Lowndes Co., GA. *Education*: Valdosta Technical College. *Principal occupation*: Retired-caseworker. *Address*: 4959 U.S. Hwy. 84 East, Naylor, GA 31641 (229) 242-2780. *Community activities*: Cemetery Restoration Church; genealogy research. *Memberships*: Huxford Genealogy Society; Naylor Baptist Church; Tcinto Sakto Muskogee Tribe. *Interests*: Genealogy research, gardening, hiking, crocheting.

BASSETT, JUDY
(elementary school principal)
Affiliation: Tiospaye Topa School, P.O. Box 537, Howes, SD 57652 (605) 733-2290.

BASSETT, MICHAEL
(editor)
Affiliation: Editor, The Circle, Minneapolis American Indian Center, 1530 E. Franklin Ave., Minneapolis, MN 55404 (612) 871-4749.

BATAILLE, GRETCHEN M. 1944-
(professor)
Born September 28, 1944, Mishawaka, Ind. *Education*: Purdue University, 1962-1965; California State Polytechnic University, B.S., 1966, M.A., 1967; Drake University, D.A., 1977. *Principal occupation*: Professor. *Address*: address unknown. *Affiliation*: Iowa State University, Ames, Iowa, 1967-86; professor, 1986-88, chair/professor, 1988-90, Dept. of English, Associate Dean, College of Liberal Arts and Sciences, 1990-, Arizona State University, Tempe, AZ. *Other professional post*: Editor, "Ethnic Reporter," National Association for Ethnic Studies, Dept. of English, ASU, Tempe, AZ. *Community activities*: Iowa Civil Rights Commission, 1975-1979 (chairman, 1977-1979); Iowa Humanities Board, 1981- (president, 1984-1985.) *Memberships*: National Association for Ethnic Studies (executive council, 1980-; treasurer, 1982-); Association for the Study of American Indian Literature (executive board, 1978-1981; Modern Language Association. *Interests*: "I am interested in American Indian literature as a reflection of the culture, history, and world view of diverse peoples. As a collector of popular culture artifacts representing American Indians, I find the popular view in sharp contrast to the image presented in both the oral tradition and contemporary

literary expressions." *Published works*: The Worlds Between Two Rivers: Perspectives on American Indians in Iowa (Iowa State University Press, 1978); The Pretend Indians: Images of Native Americans in the Movies (Iowa State University Press, 1980); American Indian Literature: A Selected Bibliography for Schools and Libraries (NAIES, Inc., 1981); American Indian Women: Telling Their Lives (University of Nebraska Press, 1984); Images of American Indians in Film: An Annotated Bibliography (Garland Publishing, 1985); American Indian Women: A Guide to Research (Garland, 1991); Native American Women: A Biographical Dictionary (Garland, 1993).

BATEMAN, RON
(school principal)
Affiliation: Alamo Navajo School, P.O. Box 907, Magdalena, NM 87825 (505) 876-2769 Fax 854-2545.

BATES, RUSSELL (Kiowa)
(writer)
Address: 116 W. Texas, Anadarko, OK 73005 (405) 247-5898.

BATES, SARA P. (Oklahoma Cherokee) 1944-
(artist/educator)
Born December 10, 1944, Muskogee, Okla. *Education*: California State University, Bakersfield, BA, 1986; University of California, Santa Barbara, MFA, 1989. *Principal occupation*: Artist/educator. *Address*: Unknown. *Affiliation*: Director of Exhibitions and Programs, American Indian Contemporary Arts, San Francisco, CA (415) 989-7003, 1990-. *Other professional posts*: Artist in Residence/instructor: Cherokee Nation, Tahlequah, OK (summers, 1988-90); UCLA Artsreach (taught drawing, painting & sculpture inside California state prison system), 1989-90); Headlands Center for the Arts, Sausalito, CA, 1992. Numerous exhibitions and public speaking engagements across the country. A few of the latest ones include: Migration of Meaning, Invitational Group Exhibition, Intar Gallary, New York, NY, 1992; Traveling Exhibition: Hollywood Art Museum, 1992; Pittsburgh Center for the Arts, 1992; Lehigh Art Galleries, 1993; Spirit As Source, Invitational Group Exhibition, Bade Museum, Berkeley, CA, 1992; Speaker/Presenter, "Education in a Cultural Context: Whose Responsibility Is It?, No. California Women's Caucus For The Arts Conference, Mills College, Berkeley, CA, 1992; Speaker/Presenter, "Native American Contemporary Art: Reflecting Contemporary Art", American Indian Institute, San Francisco, CA, 1992; among many others. *Awards, honors*: Village Artisans Award, Dorian Society, California State University, 1985; Dorian Society Scholarship, 1986; University of California Regents Scholarship, Santa Barbara, 1987; Johnson O'Mally Grants, Cherokee Nation, Tahlequah, OK, 1988-90.

BATISSE, BARNEY
(Indian band chief)
Affiliation: Matachewan Indian Band, Box 208, Matachewan, ON, Canada P0K 1M0 (705) 565-2288.

BATTISE, JO ANN (Alabama Coushatta)
(tribal administrator)
Affiliation: Alabama-Coushatta Indian Museum, Route 3, Box 640, U.S. Highway 190, Livingston, TX 77351 (713) 563-4391.

BATTISE, KEVIN (Alabama-Coushatta)
(tribal chairperson)
Affiliation: Alabama-Coushatta Tribal Council, Route 3, Box 659, Livingston, TX 77351 (936) 563-1100.

BATTISTE, THOMAS (Mikmaq) 1945
(business development specialist)
Address: 15 Waterloo St., Readville, MA 02136 (617) 361-4813 Fax (401) 331-4494. *Affiliations*: Aroostook Micmac Council, Houlton, MA, 1969-74; Administration for Native Americans, Washington, DC, 1976-86; Gay Head Wampanoag Tribe, Gay Head, MA, 1989-92; North American Indian Center of Boston, Boston, MA, 1992-95; Rhode Island Indian Council, Providence, RI, 1995-present. *Military service*: U.S. Army, 1966-68. *Community activities*: Main Street/Broad St. Project, Providence, RI; Board President, North American Indian Center of Boston; Heritage Harbor Board Member, Providence, RI. *Memberships*: Harvard Club of Boston; Vietnam Indian Veterans Association; Veterans of Foreign Wars.

BATY, LOREN (Mono)
(rancheria chairperson)
Affiliation: Chairperson, Big Sandy Rancheria,
P.O. Box 337, Auberry, CA 93602 (209) 855-4003.

BAUERLE, PHENOCIA (Crow)
(writer/editor)
Publication: Editor, "The Way of the Warrior: Stories
of the Crow People" (University of Nebraska Press,
2003).

BAVILLA, WASSILLIE (Yup'ik Eskimo)
(AK village council president)
Affiliation: Native Village of Kwinhagak, Quinhagak
I.R.A. Council, Quinhakag, AK 99655 (907) 556-8449.

BAXSTROM, PATRICK
(organization president)
Affiliation: Indian Educators Federation, 17997
County Rd. P, Cortez, CO 81321 (970) 320-2060.

BAZAN, S. NICOLE (Rosebud Sioux)
(attorney)
Education: Stanford University, BA (Native American
Political History & Law, an individually designed major), 1995; Harvard Law School, J.D., 1999. *Address
& Affiliation*: Hobbs, Straus, Dean & Walker, LLP (Associate, 1999-present), 2120 L St., NW, Suite 700,
Washington, DC 20037 (202) 822-8282. E-mail:
nbazan@hsdwdc.com. While at Harvard, she was an
officer in the Native American Law Students Association, La Alianza, and the Coalition for Cross-Cultural
Unity (the umbrella organization for student groups of
color). She also served as an editor for the Harvard
Blackletter Law Journal, a research assistant in American Indian Law, and a member of the Harvard Legal
Aid Bureau. Nicole participated in a treaty-drafting
clinic with the Carrier-Sekani Bands of British Columbia and wrote her thesis (Dine Bi Beehaz'aanii: Customary Law in the Navajo Nation) for the Navajo Supreme Court. *Areas of concentration*: Indian Self-Determination and Education Assistance Act; tribal sovereignty; tribal government; Indian health care. *Memberships*: Native American Bar Association; New York
Bar Association; Sicangu Oyate (Rosebud Sioux) Bar
Association.

BEAL, C.
(college lecturer)
Affiliation: Indian Studies, Saskatchewan Indian Federated College, Regina Campus, 118 College West,
University of Regina, Regina, Saskatchewan S4S 0A2
(306) 584-8333.

BEAN, LOWELL JOHN 1931-
(anthropologist, ethnographer, ethnologist)
Born April 26, 1931, St. James, Minn. *Education*: Los
Angeles City College, 1954-55; University of California, Los Angeles, BA, 1958, MA, 1961, PhD, 1970.
Principal occupation: Anthropologist, ethnologist.
Home address: 1555 Lakeside Dr. 64, Oakland, CA
94612. *Affiliations*: Instructor and professor of anthropology (chairman, 1973-79;l professor emeritus), Department of Anthropology, California State University
at Hayward, 1965-92; president, Cultural Systems
Research, Inc., 1978-; vice-president, Ballena Press,
1981-. *Other professional posts*: Consultant on ethnographic films, North American Films, 1963-64; contributing editor, American Indian Historian, 1968-72;
consultant, American Indian Scholars Conference,
American Historical Society, 1969; research fellow,
R.H. Lowie Museum of Anthropology, University of
California, Berkeley, 1971-73; curator, Clarence E.
Smith Museum of Anthropology, CSUH, 1974-78. *Military service*: U.S. Marine Corps, 1951-53. *Community
activities*: American Friends Service, Southwest Indian
Committee (member, advisory Indian committee, 1961-
63); Teaching Institute, American Indian Historical
Society (participant, 1968); American Indian Studies
Curriculum Committee, San Francisco State College
(consultant); Planning Committee for Gabrileno Cultural Center, Rancho Los Alamitos, 1972; Malki Museum (member, board of trustees); Journal of California Anthropology (associate editor); editor, Ballena
Press Anthropological Papers. *Memberships*: American Anthropological Association (Fellow); Society for
California Archaeology; Southwestern Anthropological
Association (president, 1974-75). *Awards, honors*:
George Barker Memorial Grant-in-Aid for research
among American Indian, 1960; National Science Foun-

dation Faculty Research Grant-in-Aid, California State
University, Hayward, 1967-72; Postdoctoral Museum
Fellowship, Wenner-Gren Foundation for Anthropological Research, 1971; Smithsonian Institute (Center for
the Study of Man) Grant to research the history of economic development at Morongo Indian Reservation,
Banning, California, 1972-74; Grant-in-Aid, American
Philosophical Society, 1972; Outstanding Educators
of America Award, 1972; National Geographic Soci-
ety (grantee, 1975; California State University at
Hayward (mini-grantee, 1977). *Interests*: California In-
dians; Ethnographic research; directed field studies
among Miwok, Wintun, Tubatulabal and Chemehuevi
Indians of California. *Published works*: The Romero
Expeditions in California and Arizona, 1823-1826, with
William Mason (Palm Springs Desert Museum, 1962);
Cahuilla Indian Cultural Ecology, Ph.D. dissertation
(University Microfilms, 1970); Temalpah: Cahuilla
Knowledge and Uses of Plants (Malki Museum, 1972);
Mukat's People: The Cahuilla Indians of Southern
California (University of California, Berkeley Press,
1972); Antap: California Indian Policy and Economic
Organization, with T. King (Ballena Press, 1974); Na-
tive American California: Essays on Culture and His-
tory, with T. Blackburn (Ballena Press, 1975); Califor-
nia Indians: Primary Resources, with Sylvia Vane
(Ballena Press, 1976); A Comparative Ethnobotany of
Twelve Southern California Tribes, with Charles Smith;
Ethnography and Culture History of the Southwestern
Kashia Pomo Indians; The Native Californian: A Regional Ethnology; and Madman or Philosopher: Essays on Shamanism, with Rex Jones.

BEANE, TAMARA (Cherokee-Choctaw) 1958-
(potter)
Born April 15, 1958, Idaho Falls, Idaho. *Education*:
Jacksonville State University, Jacksonville, AL, BS,
1979. *Principal occupation*: Potter-reproducing southeastern U.S. prehistoric pottery. *Home address*: Unknown. *Community activities*: Presents programs for
museums, archaeological societies, state and other
parks. *Memberships*: Southeastern Archaeological
Conference; Primative Society; Alabama Archaeological Society. *Interests*: "I reproduce southeastern prehistoric and historic Native American pottery. "I travel,
visit archaeological sites, museums, and labs doing
research."

BEANS, ELMER T., Sr. (Eskimo)
(AK village council president)
Affiliation: Native Village of Mountain Village, P.O. Box
32249, Mountain Village, AK 99632 (907) 591-2048.

BEANS, GEORGE, Sr.
(AK tribal council president)
Affiliation: Andreafksi Tribal Council, P.O. Box 368,
St. Mary's, AK 99658 (907) 438-2312.

BEAR, AUSTIN
(Indian band chief)
Affiliation: John Smith Indian Band, Box 9, Birch Hills,
Saskatchewan, Canada S0J 0G0 (306) 764-1282.

BEAR, BOBBIE
(Indian center co-president)
Affiliation: Indian Awareness Center, Fulton County
Historical Society, 37 E 375 N, Rochester, IN 46975
(574) 223-4436.

BEAR, EVERETTE
(Indian band chief)
Affiliation: Chief, John Smith Indian Band, P.O. Box 9,
Birch Hills, SK, Canada S0J 0G0 (306) 764-1282.

BEAR, LAWRENCE (Goshute)
(tribal chairperson)
Affiliation: Skull Valley General Council, c/o Uintah &
Ouray Agency, B.I.A., P.O. Box 130, Fort Duchesne,
UT 84026 (801) 722-2406.

BEAR, LEON D. (Skull Valley Goshute)
(tribal chairperson)
Affiliation: Skull Valley Band of Goshute Indians, 3359
S. Main St., Salt Lake City, UT 84115 (801) 484-4422.

BEAR, MOONFACE (Pequot)
(tribal leader)
Affiliation: Golden Hill Paugussett Traditional Government, 95 Stanavage Rd., Trumbull, CT 06415 (203)
537-0390.

BEAR, NANCY (Kickapoo)
(tribal chairperson)
Affiliation: Kickapoo of Kansas Tribal Council, P.O. Box
271, Horton, KS 66439 (785) 486-2131.

**BEAR, TOM, JR. (*No-Ko-Se*) (Creek-Seminole)
1931-**
(acting director-Indian hospital)
Born October 31, 1931, Holdenville, Okla. *Education*:
Central Oklahoma University, BS, 1956; University of
Oklahoma, MPH, 1975. *Principal occupation*: Acting
director-Indian hospital. *Home address*: 809 Howard,
Ada, OK 74820 (405) 436-2355. *Affiliation*: Director,
Wewoka PHS Indian Health Center, Wewoka, OK,
1988-93; acting director, Carl Albert Indian Hospital,
1001 North Country Club Dr., Ada, OK 74820 (405)
436-3980. *Other professional posts*: District
Sanatarian; Environmental Health Coordinator; Hospital Safety Committee. *Military service*: U.S. Army,
1952 (Sgt. 1st Class; received the Bronz Star for valor
in the Korean Conflict; Capt. in MC Corps, 1964; discharged from Reserve, 1966). *Community activities*:
Chairman of the Board for Southeastern Indian Recovery Center; Ordained Baptist Minister. *Memberships*: Registered Professional Sanitarian, 1976-; National American Indian Safety Council, Inc., 1976-.
Awards, honors: Awarded the "C. Bradley Bridges
Sanitary Science Award" for Academic Achievement
from Tennessee State, 1972; appointed to the "Sanitarian Career Development Committee" which met
quarterly for a term of three years at IHS Headquarters, Washington, DC, 1977. *Interests*: "Our goal for
the Indian patients is to elevate the health status and
to ensure equity, availability and accessibility of a comprehensive high quality health care delivery system."

BEARD, ANNA
(museum curator)
Affiliation: Curator, Tonkawa Tribal Museum,
P.O. Box 70, Tonkawa, OK 74653 (405) 628-5301.

BEARDEN, MARION TED
(health center director)
Affiliation: Miami PHS Indian Health Center,
P.O. Box 1498, Miami, OK 74354 (918) 542-1655.

BEARDY, ERIC
(Indian band chief)
Affiliation: Chief, Shamattawa First Nation Band,
Shamattawa, Manitoba, Canada R0B 1K0.

BEARDY, FRANK
(Indian band chief)
Affiliation: Chief, Muskrat Dam Indian Band, Muskrat
Dam, via Pickle Lake, Ontario, Canada P0V 3A0.

BEARDY, LARRY
(Indian band chief)
Affiliation: Chief, Split Lake Indian Band, Split Lake,
Manitoba, Canada R0B 1P0 (204) 342-2045.

BEARS GHOST, RICHANDA A.
(administrative officer)
Affiliation: New Sunrise Regional Treatment Center,
P.O. Box 219, San Fidel, NM 87049 (505) 552-6634.

BEARSKIN, LAURA
(project coordinator)
Affiliation: Great Lakes Native Diabetes Project,
2318 W. Merrill St., Milwaukee, WI 53204.

**BEARSKIN, LEAFORD (*Kwa-Hoo-Sha-Ha-Ke -
Flying Eagle*) (Wyandotte-Oklahoma) 1921-**
(tribal chief)
Born September 11, 1921, Wyandotte, Okla. *Educa-
tion*: University of Omaha, 1958-60. *Principal occupa-
tion*: Chief, Wyandotte Tribe of Oklahoma. *Address*:
P.O. Box 250, Wyandotte, OK 74370 (918) 678-2297
Fax 678-2944 (work). *Affiliations*: Chief, Wyandotte
Tribe of Oklahoma, 1983-; president, InterTribal Coun-
cil, Miami, OK, 1984-85; executive committee, United
Indian Nations of Oklahoma, 1984-88. *Other profes-
sional posts*: IHS Board of Directors, Muskogee, OK,
1983-89. *Military service*: USAF, 1939-60 (rank-Lt.
Colonel - Pilot; Distinguished Flying Cross - Air Medal
- Medal for Humane Action, Berlin Airlift, Presidential
Unit Citation.) *Community activities*: Executive com-
mittee, Indian Education, NEO A&M College. *Mem-
bership*: The Retired Officers Association, 1960-;
United Indian Nations of Oklahoma. *Awards, honors*:

Indian Achievement Award, 1986. *Interests*: To work in the interest of Indians, particularly members of his tribe; and working in Indian affairs. A few tribal accomplishments are: Getting a settlement on a judgement claim which was pending for years, affecting a payment of $5.7 million to tribal members and getting a provision in the payment bill for the tribe to receive and control its own money; rewrote the Oklahoma Wyandotte Tribal Constitution and monitored its progress through the B.I.A. in 18-months; obtained a grant to fund the tribe's first economic development project—$325,000 to construct a convenience-store complex on tribal land; also working to gain grants-in-aid for all deserving Wyandotte young people. *Biographical sources*: Indians of Today, 1961-1971.

BEARTUSK, KEITH
(BIA regional director)
Affiliation: Rocky Mountain Regional Office, Bureau of Indian Affairs, 316 North 26th St., Billings, MT 59101 (406) 247-7943 Fax 247-7976.

BEATTY, JOHN J. (*Tewahni tan eken*)
(Mohawk) 1939-
(anthropologist)
Born September 5, 1939, Brooklyn, N.Y. *Education*: Brooklyn College, B.A., 1964; University of Oklahoma, M.A., 1966; City University of New York, Ph.D. (Anthropology), 1972. *Principal occupation*: Anthropologist. *Home address*: 2983 Bedford Ave., Brooklyn, N.Y. 11210. *Affiliations*: Teaching assistant, University of Oklahoma, 1964-65; instructor, Long Island University, 1966-67; professor of anthropology, Brooklyn College, CUNY, 1966-. *Other professional posts*: Founder & director, American Indian Institute of City University of New York; private investigator, Phoenix Investigative Associates, 1982-. *Military service*: New York Guard (captain.) *Major research work*: Ethnographic & linguistic: American Indians in Urban Areas (major U.S. cities) 1963-; Tlingit Language and Culture (in New York and Alaska) 1964-67; Totonac Language and Culture (in New York and Mexico) 1964-67; Kiowa-Apache Language and Culture (Anadarko, Oklahoma) 1965-; Mohawk Language and Culture (New York City and various Mohawk Reserves) 1964-; Japanese & Japanese Americans: Language and Culture, 1973-; Scots and Scottish Americans, 1974-; Cross Cultural Perspectives on Police, 1978-. *Memberships*: American Anthropological Association (Fellow); New York Academy of Sciences (Fellow); American Indian Community House. *Awards, honors*: National Science Foundation Training Grant, University of Oklahoma, 1965 (for research with the Kiowa-Apache); City University of New York and National Science Foundation Dissertation Year Fellowships, 1971 (for research with Mohawk languages); National Science Foundation Grant (U.S. - Japanese Co-operative Program, 1973); Brooklyn College Faculty Award, 1973, for research with Japanese macaques; Faculty Research Award Program, CUNY, 1974 and 1975, for research with chimpanzees and for research on sexual behavior; Department of Health, Education and Welfare: Office of Native American Programs, 1975 grant to work with urban American Indians in New York State; National Endowment for the Arts, 1977, for filming Iroquois social dances; Rikkyoo University (Japan) Research Fellowship, 1986-87, for research on solidarity; Certificate of Appreciation, New York Academy of Sciences; Sigma Xi. *Interests*: Anthropology; linguistics; symbolic anthropology - American Indians; Asia; theatre; forensics; lecture series on American Indians and Japanese culture, 1969-; coach, Brooklyn College Wrestling Team. *Published works*: Kiowa-Apache Music and Dance (Museum of Anthropology, University of Northern Colorado, 1974); Mohawk Morphology (Museum of Anthropology, University of Northern Colorado, 1974); A Guide to New York for Japanese: An Ethnographic Approach (Gloview Press, Tokyo, 1985); Kujira! The Whale in Japanese Culture (AJSU, Japan, 1988); numerous articles. Recording: Music of the Plains Apache (Folkways Records). Films: Iroquois Social Dances, Two parts, with Nick Manning, 1979; and others. *Videotapes*: The American Indian Art Center, 1978; American Indians at Brooklyn College, 1978; Scottish Highland Dances, 1979; Custer Revisited, 1980. Books being developed: Intercultural Communications; The Anthropology of Sexual Behavior; The Nature of Language and Culture; and Cross Cultural Perspectives on Police.

BEAULIEU, ALFRED
(Indian band chief)
Affiliation: Ebb & Flow Indian Band, Ebb & Flow, Manitoba, Canada R0L 0R0 (204) 448-2134.

BEAULIEU, ORAN
(health project director)
Affiliation: Red Lake Comprehensive Health Service, Red Lake, MN 56671 (218) 679-3316.

BEAUVAIS, ARCHIE BRYAN (Rosebud Sioux) 1948-
(educational administrator/instructor)
Born December 30, 1948, Rosebud, S.D. *Education*: Northern Arizona University, Flagstaff, B.S. (Education), 1974, M.A. (Education), 1976; Harvard University, Ed.D., 1982. *Principal occupation*: Education administrator/instructor. *Home address*: P.O. Box 426, Mission, S.D. 57555. E-mail: abeaux@post.harvard.edu. *Affiliation*: Bilingual Director/Grant Writer, St. Francis Indian School, St. Francis, SD 57572 (605) 747-2299 (2002-present). *Past professional posts*: Dean, Academic Affairs & Chair, Graduate Education Program, Sinte Gleska University, Rosebud, SD, 1984-02; consultant, South Dakota Board of Regents for Title II math and science; consultant-evaluator, North Central Association, Chicago, IL. *Military service*: U.S. Army, 1967-1970 (Vietnam, 1968-1969, Specialist Fifth Class, Army Commendation Medal.) *Community activities*: Doctoral representative to Student Association Cabinet, Harvard Graduate School of Education. *Memberships*: School Administrators of S.D.; Ducks Unlimited; Harvard Chapter of Phi Delta Kappa; S.D. Indian Education Association, South Dakota Council for Social Studies. *Awards, honors*: 1988 Alumni Achievement Award, Northern Arizona University, Flagstaff, AZ; Jubilee Year Distinguished Alumnus Award, Northern Arizona University, Flagstaff, AZ, 1990; Executive Proclamation, Office of the Governor, State of South Dakota, Feb. 1991; Trio Achiever, National Council of Educational Opportunity Associations, Sept. 1991; Certificate of Appreciation, Rosebud Sioux Tribe, 2002. *Interests*: "Major interest is developing new and innovative programs which will significantly impact reservation, tribal, and other native communities." *Published works*: Article, "A Unique Masters Program" (Harvard Graduate School of Education- Alumni Bulletin, 1989).

BEAVEN, DARRYL
(school principal)
Affiliation: Cove Day School, P.O. Box 2000, Red Valley, AZ 86544 (520) 653-4457.

BEAVER, B. TOM (Muskogee Creek)
(director of public information)
Born in Muskogee, Okla. *Education*: University of Kansas, B.S., 1972, M.S., 1974. *Address*: Resides in Minneapolis, MN (612) 626-7280 (work). *Affiliations*: WCCO TV, Minneapolis, MN (anchor, producer, reporter, 1973-79; public service director, 1981-86); Special Assistant, Assistant Secretary for Indian Affairs, Dept. of the Interior, Washington, DC, 1979-81; public information officer, Regional Transit Board, St. Paul, MN, 1987-88; host & board member, First Americans Update, KTCI-TV, St. Paul, MN & Westmarc Cable, St. Cloud, MN, 1991-; director of public information, University of Minnesota, Office of the Associate Provost & Associatre Vice President for Academic Affairs, Minneapolis, MN, 1988-. *Other professional posts*: Freelancer, 1985-; columnist, "The Lakota Times," Matin, SD, 1985-86. *Community activities*: Work with community groups to define relevant issues and translate those issues into media events; serves on a variety of commissions, panels and boards of non-profit agencies. *Awards, honors*: Indian Media Award for Outstanding Achievement in Television, Native American Public Broadcasting Consortium, 1984; Volunteer of the Year, Minneapolis Junior League, 1985; Distinguished Service Award, City of Minneapolis, MN, 1986.

BEAVER, CHARLES
(Indian band chief)
Affiliation: Chief, Bigstone Cree Band, General Delivery, Desmarais, Alberta, Canada T0G 0T0 (403) 891-3836.

BEAVER, HENRY
(Indian band chief)
Affiliation: Fort Smith Indian Band, Box 960, Fort Smith, Northwest Territories, Canada X0E 0P0 (403) 872-2986.

BEAVER, R. PERRY (Muscogee Creek)
(principal chief)
Address & Affiliation: Muscogee Creek Nation of Oklahoma, P.O. Box 580, Okmulgee, OK 74447 (918) 756-8700 Fax 758-1434.

BEAVERBONE, CAROLINE
(Indian band chief)
Affiliation: O'Chiese Indian Band, Box 1570, Rocky Mountain House, Alberta, Canada T0M 1T0 (403) 989-3943.

BECENTI, FRANCIS D. (Navajo) 1952-
(higher education administrator)
Born May 18, 1952, Fort Defiance, Ariz. *Education*: Navajo Community College, A.A., 1973; University of California, Berkeley, B.A., 1975. *Principal occupation*: Higher education administrator. *Home address*: Native American Student Services, Colorado State University, 312 Student Services, Fort Collins, CO 80523 (303) 491-1101. *Affiliations*: Director of financial aid, Navajo Community College, 1975-1979; director of financial aid, University of Albuquerque, 1980-1981; director of student services, College of Ganado, 1981-1984; director, Native American Student Services, Colorado State University, Fort Collins, 1984-.

BECHARD, REV. HENRI
(editor)
Affiliation: Editor, Kateri, P.O. Box 70, Kahnawake, Quebec, Canada J0L 1B0 (514) 525-3611.

BECK, DAVID R.M. 1956-
(associate professor)
Born July 14, 1956, Evanston, Ill. *Education*: Northwestern University, BA, 1979; University of Illinois, Chicago, MA, 1987, PhD, 1994. *Principal occupation*: Asscociate professor. *Address*: Native American Studies Dept., University of Montana, 600 University Ave., Missoula, MT 59801 (406) 243-6097 Fax 243-6432. E-mail: davebeck@selway.umt.edu. *Affiliations*: NAES College, Chicago, IL (director, Tribal Research Center, 1992-97; dean & senior resident faculty, 1997-2000); associate professor, Native American Studies Dept., University of Montana, Missoula, MT, 2000-present. *Other professional posts*: Advisor, Americans for Indian Opportunity Ambassador Program, 1993-; consultant, Menominee Indian Nation Historic Preservation Dept., Keshena, WI, 1990-. *Community activities*: Archivist, NAES College, 1987-92; GED instructor for history/culture component, NAES College Employment Enhancement Program, 1994-97; member, Clyde Callan Steering Committee; consultant, Menominee Tribe Historic Preservation Dept.; advisor, Americans for Indian Opportunity; advisor, Piegan Institute, Browning, MT; Missoula American Indian Parent Education Committee, 2000-present (vice president, 2001-02; president, 2002-03). *Memberships*: American Historical Association; Wisconsin Historical Society; Montana Historical Society; Natural Resources Defense Council. *Awards, honors*: Listed in Outstanding Young Men of America, 1988; University Fellowship, University of Illinois at Chicago, 1990-92; Certification of Recognition, Americans for Indian Opportunity Ambassador Program, 1993; Wisconsin Historical Society Book Award of Merit, 2002. *Interests*: Vocational interests are teaching and writing history; avocational interests include travelling. *Published works*: Editor, Contemporary Issues, Reader One (NAES College Press, 1981); The Chicago American Indian Community, 1983-1988, Annotated Bibliography & Guide to Sources in Chicago (NAES College Press, 1988). From Sol Tax's Preface to The Contemporary American Indian Community," this work "may be the best record of first-hand sources of information about any immigrant group in any city in North America;" Siege and Survival: Menominee Indian History, 1634-1856 (University of Nebraska Press, 2002).

BECK, DUDLEY, M.D.
(clinical director)
Affiliation: Tuba City PHS Indian Medical Center, P.O. Box 600, Tuba City, AZ 86045 (602) 283-6211.

BECKER, STEPHEN
(museum director)
Affiliation: Museum of Indian Arts & Culture, Laboratory of Anthropology, P.O. Box 2087, 708 Camino Lejo, Santa Fe, NM 87504 (505) 827-6344.

BECKFORD, LYDIA
(BIA special assistant)
Affiliation: Special assistant, Office of the Assistant Secretary for Indian Affairs, Bureau of Indian Affairs, Dept. of the Interior, MS-4140-MIB, 1849 C St., NW, Washington, DC 20240 (202) 208-7163.

BECKWITH, BARBARA (*Running Water*)
(Penobscot)
(craftsperson)
Affiliation: Owner, Running Water Authentic Indian Crafts, 505 Post Rd., Wells, ME 04090 (207) 646-1206.

BECKWITH, TERRY
(BIA agency supt.)
Affiliation: Palm Springs Field Agency, Bureau of Indian Affairs, P.O. Box 2245, Palm Springs, CA 92262 (619) 322-3086.

BEDEL, JENNIFER
(program coordinator)
Affiliation: American Indian Program ("The Web," newsletter), 300 Caldwell Hall, Cornell University, Ithaca, NY 14853 (602) 255-4308.

BEDROSIAN, TOD 1947-
(publisher)
Born July 21, 1947, San Francisco, Calif. *Education*: University of Nevada, Reno, BA, 1971; University of Denver, MA, 1972. *Principal occupation*: Publisher. *Address*: Resides in Sacramento, CA (916) 421-5121. *Affiliations*: Publisher, The Native Magazine, Sacramento, CA, 1992-2002; owner, Bedrosian & Associates, Sacramento, CA, 1986-. *Other professional posts*: Press secretary, U.S. Congress; Nevada assemblyman; journalist. *Military service*: U.S. Air Force (sgt.). *Community activities*: President of Sacramento Chapter of Public Relations Society of America.

BEECHER, WILBUR (Mono)
(rancheria chairperson)
Affiliation: Big Sandy Rancheria, P.O. Box 337, Auberry, CA 93602 (559) 855-4003.

BEELER, SAMUEL W., SR. (Cherokee) 1927-
(principal chief)
Born December 9, 1929, Buena, VA. *Education*: U.S. Air Force Academy, MA. *Principal occupation*: Principal chief. *Address*: Unknown. *Affiliations*: Principal Chief, Cherokee Tribe of Virginia, Rapidan, VA; Cherokee Confederacy, Albany, GA (22 years). *Military service*: U.S. Army Air Corps, 1946-54; U.S. Air Force, 1954-80. *Community activities*: State appointed representative on the advisory committee of Commonwealth of Virginia-State Water Control Board.

BEELER, SAMUEL W., JR. (Cherokee) 1950-
(vice principal chief)
Born January 29, 1950, Paterson, N.J. *Education*: Passaic County School of Nursing, Wayne, N.J., Nursing Degree; American Indian School on Alcohol & Drug Abuse, Reno, Nev., Certified Counselor. *Principal occupation*: Vice principal chief. *Address*: Unknown. *Affiliations*: Vice Principal Chief, Cherokee Tribe of Virginia, Rapidan, VA; Cherokee Confederacy, Albany, GA (22 years). *Military service*: U.S. Air Force, 1968-70. *Memberships*: National Congress of American Indians; Association of American Indian Social Workers; Vietnam Era Veterans Inter-Tribal Association; Cherokee National Historical Society; American Association of Critical-Care Nurses.

BEEMAN, SANDI
(special education coordinator)
Affiliation: Chinle Agency, Bureau of Indian Affairs, Navajo Rt. 7, P.O. Box 6003, Chinle, AZ 86503 (520) 674-5130 Fax 674-5134.

BEER, R. SHANE (Navajo-Laguna Pueblo) 1953-
(artist)
Born June 25, 1953, Albuquerque, N.M. *Education*: High school. *Principal occupation*: Artist. Resides in Austin, TX. *Native American Art*: Hand crafted jewelry; embossed paper; cartoonist. *Juried Exhibits*: Eight Northern Indian Pueblo Arts and Crafts Show, San Ildefonso, NM, 1990-91; American Indian Art Festival and Market, Dallas, TX, 1990-91; A.I.T.G. Indian Art Expo, Austin, TX, 1991; The American Idian Art Festival, Houston, TX, 1992; Heard Museum, Phoenix, AZ, 1992. *Community activities*: Artists in Education, Texas

Commission on the Arts, 1991-. *Awards, honors*: Gallup Intertribal Indian Ceremonial (1st & 2nd Ribbons, 1975 & 3rd Ribbon, 1977, for handmade silver jewelry). *Biographical sources*: Indian Silver - Volume II, by Dale Stuart King, 1976; article in "Southwest Art", Feb. 1992.

BEESON, ARLIE
(health center director)
Affiliation: Bylas Health Center, P.O. Box 208, San Carlos, AZ 85550 (602) 485-2686.

BEESON, DEBRA, MD
(medical director)
Affiliation: Spokane Urban Indian Health Services, P.O. Box 4598, Spokane, WA 99202 (509) 535-0868.

BEGAY, CATHERINE T. (Navajo)
(school principal)
Affiliation: Greasewood/Toyei Consolidated Boarding School, Ganada, AZ 86505 (602) 654-3331.

BEGAY, D.Y. (Navajo) 1953-
(weaver, textile consultant)
Born September 3, 1953, Ganado, Ariz. *Education*: Rocky Mountain College, 1974; Arizona State University, BA, 1978. *Principal occupation*: Weaver, textile consultant. *Address*: 6929 E. Jenan Dr., Scottsdale, AZ 85254 (602) 922-9232 Fax 951-2357. Website: www.amug.org/~dybegay. *Affiliation*: Owner/Manager, D.Y. Begay's Weaving Studio, Scottsdale, AZ; owner, Navajo Textiles & Arts, Chinle, AZ, 1984-. *Other professional posts*: Textile instructor, lecturer. *Memberships*: Palisades Guild; Indian Education; Museum of Natural History, Museum of the American Indian; Handweavers Guild of America. *Interests*: Have done extensive traveling (Canada, Mexico, Europe and U.S.) All my interest is in the field of textiles (Navajo weaving). *Biographical sources*: A Navajo Weaver (N.Y. Times); Navajo Weaving (Bergen Record). Published works: Co-editor, The Sheep (documentary film), 1982.

BEGAY, EUGENE A., SR. (Lac Courte Oreilles Chippewa) 1933-
(business administration, Indian affairs, mechanical engineer)
Born June 6, 1933, Hayward, Wis. *Education*: North Park College, 1952-54; Illinois Institute of Technology, 1955-59. *Principal occupation*: Business administration, Indian affairs, mechanical engineer. *Address*: Unknown. *Affiliations*: Executive director, United Southeastern Tribes, Inc., Nashville, TN, 1972-76; Associate Native American Ministry, United Presbyterian Church-USA, New York, NY, 1976-99. *Other professional posts*: Consultant, B.I.A. and Indian Health Service, U.S. Government. *Military service*: Illinois National Guard, 1950-52. *Community activities*: Chicago American Indian Center (board of directors); National Indian Review Board (NIAAA/HEW) (chairman); National Indian Board on Mental Health (chairman); National Indian Council Fire (member). *Memberships*: National Congress of American Indians; Research Committee on Mental Health (NIMH/HEW). *Interests*: "Active originally in Indian affairs in the area of developing priority by the Federal Government in mental health and alcoholism programs & services. I have lobbied in Congress & advocated amongst tribes and tribal organizations in the area of economic development, education, nutrition, housing, & health services. I am currently active in Indian rights, treaty rights, jurisdiction, & land issues. I provided White House testimony on these issues at the request of the Vice President."

BEGAY, HAROLD
(school director)
Affiliation: Greyhills High School, P.O. Box 160, Tuba City, AZ 86045 (602) 283-6271.

BEGAY, JIMMIE C. (Navajo) 1948-
(Indian school director)
Born September 4, 1948, Rough Rock, Ariz. *Education*: New Mexico Highlands University, A.S., 1969, B.A., 1972, M.A., 1974. *Principal occupation*: Director-Indian school. *Address*: Rock Point Community School, Hwy. 191, Rock Point, AZ 86545 (520) 659-4221. *Affiliations*: Teacher, principal, executive director, Rough Rock Demonstration School; director, Rock Point Community School, Rock Point, AZ. *Other professional posts*: Native American Studies teacher; coordinator, Black Mesa Day School; president, board

of directors, Association of Community Tribal Schools, Inc., Vermillion, SD. *Community activities*: Navaho Culture Organization (chairman); originator of Navaho psychology classes; sponsor of Black Mesa five mile run. *Memberships*: National Association of Secondary School Principals; Smithsonian Institution; Harvard Education Review; Dine Biolta Association. *Award*: Outstanding Accomplishments, Rough Rock School Board. *Interests*: Betterment in education programs, especially for Indians; travel. (I would like to pursue higher educational goals. *Biographical sources*: Principals and Views About Indian Education, (Rough Rock News); Candidate for NACIE (Navajo Times); History of Rough Rock, by Robert Roessell. *Published works*: Navajo Culture Outline, & Navajo Philosophy of Education.

BEGAY, JOHNNY C. (Navajo)
(Indian school principal)
Affiliation: Aneth Community School, P.O. Box 600, Montezuma Creek, UT 84534 (801) 651-3271.

BEGAY, JONES (Navajo)
(Indian school chairperson)
Affiliation: Black Mesa Community School, P.O. Box 97, Pinon, AZ 86510 (520) 674-3632.

BEGAY, JUDI (Navajo)
(college instructor)
Affiliation: Navajo Community College, P.O. Box 580, Shiprock, NM 87420 (505) 368-5291.

BEGAY, KAREN (Navajo)
(artist)
Address: 1161 W. University Heights Dr. S., Flagstaff, AZ 86001.

BEGAY, KAREN FRANCIS (Navajo)
(student affairs)
Affiliation: Director, Native American Student Affairs, University of Arizona, 1212 E. University Blvd., Nugent Bldg., Rm. 203, Tucson, AZ 85721 (520) 621-3835.

BEGAYE, KELSEY A. (Navajo)
(tribal president)
Affiliation: Navajo Nation, P.O. Box 9000, Window Rock, AZ 86515 (928) 871-66352.

BEGAY, LEROY (Navajo) 1967-
(bookstore manager)
Born February 1, 1967, Shiprock, N.M. *Education*: Navajo Community College, AA, 1990. *Address*: P.O. Box 2892, Shiprock, NM 87420 (505) 368-5291. *Affiliation*: Navajo Community College, Shiprock, NM (financial aid tech., 1988-89; bookstore mgr., 1990-).

BEGAY, LISA (Navajo)
(Indian program administrator)
Born in Fort Defiance on the Navajo Reservation. *Education*: Arizona State University, BS in Communications and a Certificate in Native American Justice Studies. *Principal occupation*: Indian program administrator. *Address & Affiliation*: Council of Indian Nations, P.O. Box 1800, Apache Junction, AZ 85217 (800) 811-6955 Fax (480) 281-0708. E-mail: info@cinprograms.org. Website: www.cinprograms.org. Southwest Program Director for the National Relief Charities. She administers all of the programs for both the Southwest Indian Relief Council and the Council of Indian Nations. *Community activities*: While in high school, she was president of the Native American Youth Leadership Council and vice president and secretary of the United national Indian Tribal Unit. While in college, she started Native American Students United, an organization that was tailored to meet the needs of individual students. One of the projects was to match children from urban schools, with an A.S.U. student of a similar cultural background. The A.S.U. student taught the child various things about their shared culture including language, customs, and traditions so the urban school student would learn more about their cultural ties. Upon graduation from college, Lisa worked as a project coordinator for the Department of Youth Services in Chinle, AZ.

BEGAY, LORRAINE C. (Navajo)
(college instructor)
Affiliation: Instructor, Navajo Community College, Tsaile Rural Post Office, Tsaile, AZ 86556 (602) 724-3311.

BEGAY, MANLEY (Navajo)
(professor)
Education: Harvard University, EdD, 1997. *Affiliation*: Native Nations Institute, University of Arizona, 803 E. 1st St., Tucson, AZ 85719 (520) 621-7108 Fax 621-7952. E-mail: aisp@email.arizona.edu. *Interests*: Tribal economic development, educational leadership.

BEGAY, MEREDITH MAGOOSH
(Mescalero Apache) 1937-
(medicine woman)
Born May 2, 1937, Mescalero, N.M. *Education*: High school. *Home address*: 410 Yucca Dr., P.O. Box 91, Mescalero, NM 88340 (505) 671-4344. *Community activities*: Miss Mescalero Apache Committee; Bent-Mescalero School P.T.A.; Mescalero Indian Health Service (hospital board member); National Federation of Federal Employees Local 1472. *Award*: Bureau of Indian Affairs Special Achievement & Tribal Award. *Interests*: "I am active in my traditional religion and application of holistic medicine for my own tribal people. I have been a "medicine woman" for over twenty years. I am trying to keep up the tribal tradition, culture and heritage, along with other medicine men and women, including the school children. Presently give workshops on traditional medicine in cohesion with Western medicine."

BEGAY, RITA (Navajo)
(Indian school chairperson)
Affiliation: Baca Community School, P.O. Box 509, Prewitt, NM 87045 (505) 876-2310.

BEGAY, RONALD C. (Navajo)
(administrative officer)
Affiliation: Crownpoint Comprehensive Health Care Facility, P.O. Box 358, Crownpoint, NM 87313 (505) 786-5291.

BEGAY, RUTH TRACY (Navajo) 1940-
(family nurse practitioner)
Born May 14, 1940, Ganado, Ariz. *Education*: Loretto Heights College, School of Nursing, Denver, Colo., BSN, 1978. *Principal occupation*: Family nurse practitioner. *Affiliation*: Director, Navajo Community College Health Center, Tsaile, AZ, 1978-90. *Other professional posts*: Member, Navajo Health Authority, Office of Nursing Education Board; member, Navajo Community College Nursing Program Board. *Memberships*: Arizona Nurses Association (council on practice); Arizona Public Health Association; Pacific Coast College Health Association; *Awards, honors*: Two documentary films on Nurse Practitioner on Navajo Reservation by NBC and University of Arizona, School of Medicine, 1973; Navajo Community College 1978 Student Service Employee of the Year Award; Outstanding Young Woman of the Year, 1977. *Interests*: Involvement in local community health-social work among the Navajo people. Travel locally, regionally in college health service and nurses association. Interested in continual growth and development in cross-cultural aspects of a different society integrated with our own Navajo Society. *Biographical sources*: Articles: Arizona Nurses Association Newsletter, 1973; The Navajo Times, 1973; Gallup Independent, 1977.

BEHN, SALLY
(Indian band chief)
Affiliation: Fort Nelson Indian Band, RR 1, 293 Alaska Highway, Fort Nelson, B.C., Canada V0C 1R0 (604) 774-7688.

BEIM, ELIZABETH A.
(editor, director of public information)
Affiliation: The Gustav Heye Center, Museum of the American Indian (Newsletter), Smiothsonian Institution, One Bowling Green, New York, NY 10004 (212) 283-2420.

BEIRISE, JOHN H.
(bank president & chairperson)
Affiliation: President & CEO, Native American National Bank, N.A. (NAB), 165 S. Union Blvd., Suite 1000, Denver, CO 80228 (303) 988-2727 Fax 988-5533.

BELARDO, MARY E. (Cahuilla)
(tribal chairperson)
Affiliation: Torres-Martinez Band of Mission Indians, P.O. Box 1160, Thermal, CA 92274 (760) 397-8144.

BELCOURT, ERNESTINE
(administrative officer)
Affiliation: Rocky Boy's PHS Indian Health Center, P.O. Box 664, Box Elder, MT 59521 (406) 395-4489.

BELGARDE, LARRY (Ma-in-gun)
(Turtle Mountain Chippewa) 1945-
(education administrator)
Born December 13, 1945, Belcourt, N.D. *Education*: University of Minnesota, MEd, 1971; Stanford University, PhD, 1993. *Principal occupation*: Education administrator. *Address*: Resides in Albuquerque, NM. *Affiliation*: Turtle Mountain Community College, Belcourt, ND (president, 1987-95; academic dean, 1993-95). *Other professional posts*: Supt. for Education, Bureau of Indian Affairs, Belcourt, ND (7 years); director of Indian education, Duluth Public Schools, Duluth, MN. *Memberships*: American Educational Research Association; American Indian Higher Education Consortium (officer); National Indian Education Association. *Awards, honors*: Indian Education Fellow (Title V), 1988-92. *Interests*: Indian education; organizational sociology.

BELGARDE, GALENE
(BIA special education coordinator)
Affiliation: Turtle Mountain Agency, Bureau of Indian Affairs, School St., P.O. Box 30, Belcourt, ND 58316 (701) 477-3463 Fax 477-5944.

BELGARDE, PETER, JR.
(Sisseton-Wahpeton Sioux)
(tribal chairperson)
Affiliation: Devil's Lake Sioux Tribal Council, Sioux Community Center, Fort Totten, ND 58335 (701) 766-4221.

BELINDO, JON EDWIN (Gui-tain)
(Kiowa/Pawnee/Choctaw/ Navajo) 1963-
(educator, artist)
Born August 4, 1963, Oklahoma City, Okla. *Education*: East Central University (Ada, OK), BA, 1986; Oklahoma City University, M.Ed., 1994. *Principal occupation*: Educator, artist. *Home address*: P.O. Box 501, Arkansas City, KS 67005-0501. E-mail: jon_468@mail.com. *Affiliations*: Gifted Facilitator, Cowley County Special Services COOP/USD 465, Winfield, KS, 1995-present. *Past professional posts*: Program facilitator, Lawton Johnson O'Malley Program, Lawton, OK, 1986-87; art teacher, Stratford High School, Stratford, OK, 1987-90; art teacher, Tuttle High School, Tuttle, OK, 1990-93; Gifted Facilitator, Putnam City West High School, Oklahoma City, OK, 1994 State Director, Indian Education, Oklahoma State Dept. of Education, Oklahoma City, OK, 1994-95. *Community activities*: Coach, Sunday school teacher; F.C.A. director. *Memberships*: Kasnas Association of Gifted, Talented and Creative, 2004-present; National Education ssociation, 1987-present; Association for Supervision & Curriculum Development, 1987-present. *Community activities*: Tuttle Chamber of Commerce; sign & mural painter; church activity; Little League coach. *Awards, honors*: Susan Peters Art Award, 1981; recognized by ECU faculty (art dept.) as top senior of 1986; ECU Fine Arts Award, 1986; Adolf Van Pelt Scholarship Award for graduate studies in education; Oklahoma Fall Arts Institute Award & Alumnus, 1992; AITTP Scholarship (American Indian Teacher Training Program) for American Indian Research & Development (AIRD) - Full scholarship to get M.Ed in Gifted Education, 1993; Outstanding Student Educator, Oklahoma City University, 1994; Five Year Service Award, Winfield Public Schools, 2000; One Man Art Show, Winfield Art & Humanities Center, 2002; Winfield Art in the Park-Exhibitor Award, 2003-04. *Interests*: "As a teacher, I am active in my community and church. When I find the time, I paint scenes from the Kiowa heritage. I am enrolled in the Kiowa Tribe. As an artist, it's important for my work to have meaning beyond the scope of the work. I tend to romanticize my Indian art at times, but I feel it is important to celebrate the unique and diverse North American Indian heritage. The most influential people to my life and art were my parents, especially my father who is also an artist. My children and grandchildren are also an inspiration to me to continue to make more art - to keep such endeavors alive-art ultimately speaks volumes in regard to a societies values and priorities. I have been listed as a top 2nd Generation Indian Artist in the U.S. My father is a well known Indian artist and leader. I have sold a great number of works to private collectors, and worked on a project with my dad that is currently in Japan (a painted tipi). I have exhibited and sold work in the Annual Trail of Tears Show in Tahlequah, OK and Red Earth in Oklahoma City. As an educator, I have attended workshops and seminars on education and recently traveled to Savannah, Georgia to attend an art teachers workshop. As an artist and educator, I feel it is important to keep up on current trends and to assimilate various influences into your profession. I also enjoy visiting art museums, traveling, sports and fishing. My experience at O.C.U. has broadened my awareness in how to relate to people, how to be a leader, and how to advocate for improvement within a tribe or school system. In art, I have also developed more of a unique personal style in painting & drawing. My future goals are to advocate for Indian education, develop educational materials for Indian children, publish books, and develop a small business that is art related." *Other interests*: Political activism, traveling, conservation, literature, fishing, entertainment.

BELKHAM, JACK
(Indian school principal)
Affiliation: Flandreau Indian School, 1000 N. Crescent, Flandreau, SD 57028 (605) 997-2724.

BELKOFF, MARY (Eskimo)
(AK village council president)
Affiliation: Iqurmuit Tribe, P.O. Box 9, Russian Mission, AK 99657 (907) 584-5511.

BELL, HARVEY (Spotted Eagle-Gishwash)
(Batchewana Ojibway) 1946-
(cultural teacher; traditional medicines; pipe-maker)
Born January 20, 1946, Sault Ste. Marie, Ontario, Canada. *Address*: 35 Pontiac St., Sault Ste. Marie, Ontario, Canada P6A-5K9 (705) 253-4610. *Affiliation*: Batchewana First Nation of Ojibways (counsel-six years; chief-six years). *Community activities*: Founded Nog-da-win-da-min, 1987 (shelter for women and children); member, chiefs of Ontario. *Interests*: "Picking and making medicines, pipe carving and making, firekeeping at lodges or 4-day fires. Work with wife Elisabeth Dietz-Bell with young people and elders."

BELL, KATHRYN (Cheyenne)
(film producer/writer)
Address: P.O. Box 875, Beggs, OK 74421 (918) 267-4940.

BELL, LIBBY FOREHAND
(historic site manager)
Affiliation: Etowah Indian Mounds Historic Site, 813 Indian Mounds Rd., S.W., Cartersville, GA 30120 (404) 387-3737.

BELL, THERESA HAYWARD (Wildflower)
(Mashantucket Pequot) 1952-
(museum director)
Born May 28, 1952, Camp Lejeune, N.C. Education: High school. *Principal occupation*: Museum director. *Address & Affiliation*: Executive Director, Mashantucket Pequot Museum & Cultural Research Center, 110 Pequot Trail, Mashantuckt, CT 06338 (860) 396-7073 Fax 396-6850. E-mail: tbell@mptn-nsn.gov. *Website*: www.pequotmuseum.org. *Awards, honors*: Harriet Tubman Award; Mashantucket Pequot Tribal Representative on the Governor's Task Force on Indian Affairs. *Membership*: National Register's Who's Who in Executives & Professionals.

BELLECOURT, CLYDE (Chippewa)
(administrator)
Address & Affiliation: unknown at time of publication.

BELLECOURT, VERNON (Chippewa)
(Indian activist)
Address & Affiliation: unknown at time of publication.

BELLEGARDE, CLARENCE A.
(Indian band chief)
Affiliation: Chief, Little Black Bear Indian Band, Box 40, Goodeve, SK, Canada S0A 1C0 (306) 334-2306.

BELONE, ELSIE
(Indian school principal)
Affiliation: Kinlichee Boarding School, Ganado, AZ 86505 (602) 755-3430.

BELONE, PHILLIP
(BIA agency supt. for education)
Affiliation: Laguna Agency, Bureau of Indian Affairs, P.O. Box 298, Old Laguna, NM 87026 (505) 552-6086.

BELTRAN, DANIEL D. (Pomo)
(rancheria chairperson)
Affiliation: Lower Lake Rancheria, 131 Lincoln St., Healdsburg, CA 95448.

BEN, WENDY WESTON
(editor)
Affiliation: Native Arts Update," ATLATL, 2303 N. Central, Suite 104, Phoenix, AZ 85004 (602) 253-2731.

BENALLY, EVA M. (Navajo)
(Indian school principal)
Affiliation: Red Rock Day School, P.O. Drawer 10, Red Valley, AZ 86544 (602) 653-4456.

BENALLY, HERBERT (Navajo)
(college instructor)
Affiliation: Navajo Community College, P.O. Box 580, Shiprock, NM 87420 (505) 368-5291.

BENALLY, JONES (FAMILY) (Navajo)
(entertainment)
Born on Big Mountain, Ariz. *Education*: Traditional Navajo. *Principal occupation*: Native American dance & music. *Address*: P.O.Box 1492, Flagstaff, AZ 86002 (928) 527-1041 (phone & fax). E-mail: tacoho@hotmail.com. *Web site*: www.blackfire.net. Affiliations: Indigenous Action Media, 2001-present. *Community activities*: President (Dine Bi Naal Gloosh Baa Ahaa Yaa) a 501-c3 dedicated to preserving cultural heritage; president of Grand Canyon Schools Indian Parent Association, 1988-90; president, Flagstaff Arts Council, 1992-95. *Interests*: "The Jones Benally family is a traditional Native American Dance Troupe consisting of Jones, his daughter Jeneda and sons Klee and Clayson Benally. The family also has an original rock band called Blackfire. Their philosophy is that you can live in both worlds and never lose your heritage or identity." *Awards,honors*: Jones Benally is the first traditional consultant for Winslow Indian Hospital ever, and is the only traditional consultant for IHS at this time; Klee Benally was the youngest "Best of Show" winner at the Museum of Northern Arizona in 1992; the family has done numerous film, television and commercial work; nominated for 1999 NAMI "Best Independent Album.". *Published works*: Albums -Tanz und Fest Compilation 92 (Hei-Deck Records, 1992); Soundtrack to Geronimo (Columbia Records, 1993; Navajo Reflections (Canyon Records, 1994); Blackfire 1994 & 1998 (Tacoho Records); One Nation Under. Film documentaries: Rockin Warriors, '96; Bethel '97.

BENAY, JEFFREY
(commissioner)
Affiliation: The Governor's Advisory Commission on Native American Affairs, Pavilion Office Bldg., 109 State St., Montpelier, VT 05609 (802) 828-3333.

BENCHOFF, DONALD
(hospital director)
Affiliation: Sells PHS Indian Hospital, P.O. Box 548, Sells, AZ 85634 (602) 383-7251.

BENDER, DANIEL F. (Washoe)
(tribal chairperson)
Affiliation: Carson Indian Colony, 2900 S. Curry St., Carson City, NV 89703 (775) 883-6459.

BENDER, NATHAN E. 1957-
(curator for library & archives)
Born September 29, 1957, Ohio. *Education*: Ohio State University, BA; University of Washington, MA (Anthropology); Kent State University, MLS, 1986. *Principal occupation*: Curator for library and archives. *Address & Affiliation*: Housel Curator, McCraken Research Library (1997-present), Buffalo Bill Historical Center, 720 Sheridan Ave., Cody, WY 82414 (307) 578-4059 Fax 527-6042. E-mail: nathanb@bbhc.org. Website: www.bbhc.org. *Awards, honors*: Wyoming State Historic Records coordinator; co-chair of Advisory Board; elected representative for Native Ameican Libraries at the Montana Governor's Conference on Library and Information Services, Helena, MT, Jan. 1991. *Professional Service*: Native Americn Studies Committee,

West Virginia University, 1994-97; publications, book reviews & conference presentations. *Memberships*: American Library Association; American Indian Library Association; Society of American Archives; Council of State Historic Records Managers; American Folklore Society. *Interests*: Montana Native American Press; Native American Syllabaries and Writing Systems.

BENDS, LEONARD
(administrative director-IHS)
Affiliation: Crow Agency PHS Indian Hospital, Crow Agency, MT 59022 (406) 638-2624.

BENEDICT, DANIEL
(school director)
Affiliation: Akwesasne Freedom School, P.O. Box 290, Rooseveltown, NY 13683.

BENEDICT, PATRICIA (Abenaki) 1956-
(executive director)
Born August 11, 1956, Waterbury, Conn. *Education*: Mattatuck Community College, Waterbury, Conn., A.S. (Alcohol and Drug Counseling), 1980. *Principal occupation*: Executive director. *Address & Affiliation*: American Indians for Development, Meriden, CT (203) 238-4009 (social worker, 1975-81; executive director, 1986-). *Other professional post*: Co-editor of American Indians for Development Newsletter; editor of May Wutche Aque'ne, American Indians for Development Journal. *Community activities*: American Indians for Development (past chairman, board of directors); member, Energy Assistance Program Policy Making Board, Meriden, Conn.; member, Federal Regional Support Center, American Indian Committee, New Haven, Conn.; chairperson, A.I.D./Eagle Wing Press Powwow Committee; organized Waterbury Indian community into an organization. *Membership*: Title IV Indian Education Committee, Waterbury, Conn. (chairperson); Governor appointee of Connecticut Legislative Task Force o Indian Affairs; member and one of the incorporators of New England Indian Task Force. *Awards, honors*: Award for work performed on behalf of the Connecticut Indian Community, given by the Connecticut River Powwow Society. *Interests*: Personal interests include: furthering my education in the field of social work, attending and participating in Native American cultural activities, and with the assistance from my staff and Indians in Connecticut, American Indians for Development will once again become a multi-service agency. *Biographical source*: newspaper article, Waterbury Republican, Waterbury, Connecticut.

BENEDICT, SALLI (Mohawk)
(writer)
Address: P.O. Box 35, Rooseveltown, NY 13683 (613) 932-0230.

BENGE, GEORGE (Cherokee of Oklahoma)
(news executive)
Address: c/o Native American Journalists Association (NAJA), 3359 36th Ave. South, Minneapolis, MN 55406 (612) 729-9244 Fax 729-9373. E-mail: benge@naja. com. *Affiliation*: News executive with Gannett Co., Inc. In addition to his corporate news role, he writes columns on American Indian and diversity issues for Gannett News Service. *Other professional post*: Member-board of directors, Native American Journalists Association. *Past professional posts*: Executive editor of gannett newspapers in Asheville, NC, Lafayette, Ind., and Muskogee, Okla; and managing editor in Springfield, MO; editing and management positions at The Sun-Sentinel in Fort Lauderdale, The Dallas Morning News, The Miami Herald, and The Detroit News. *Membership*: Society for Newspaper Design (past president). *Awards, honors*: McCormick Foundation Fellow in the Advanced Executive Program of the Media Management Center; two-time Pulitzer Prize juror.

BENGOCHIA, MONTY (Paiute)
(tribal council chairperson)
Affiliation: Bishop Indian Tribal Council, 50 Tu Su Lane, Bishop, CA 93514 (760) 873-3584.

BENJAMIN, DELBERT (Wintun)
(tribal council chairperson)
Affiliation: Colusa Rancheria, P.O. Box 8, Colusa, CA 95932 (916) 458-8231.

BENJAMIN, MELANIE A. (Ojibwe)
(tribal chairperson)
Affiliation: Mille Lacs Reservation Business Committee, HCR-67 Box 194, Onamia, MN 56359 (320) 532-4181 ext. 7486.

BENN, ROBERT C.
(BIA agency supt.)
Affiliation: Choctaw Agency, BIA, 421 Powell, Philadelphia, MS 39350 (601) 656-1521.

BENNALLEY, LUCINDA Y. (Navajo)
(advisor)
Affiliation: Council of Advisors, American Indian Heritage Foundation, 6051 Arlington Blvd., Falls Church, VA 22044-2788 (703) 237-7500.

BENNETT, BEVERLY (Elwha S'Klallam)
(tribal chairperson)
Affiliation: Elwha S'Klallam Business Council, 2851 Lower Elwha Rd., Port Angeles, WA 98362 (206) 452-8471.

BENNETT, GAREY S. (*Stomping Buffalo*)
(Nansemond, Cherokee, Creek) 1957-
(registered nurse)
Born November 13, 1957, Homerville, GA. *Education*: BS (Nursing). *Principal occupation*: Registered nurse. *Address*: 4959 U.S. Hwy. 84 E., Naylor, GA 31641 (229) 242-2780. *Affiliation*: Staff Nurse, South Georgia Medical Center. *Military service*: U.S. Navy, 1975-82. *Community activities*: Tribal registering agent; tribal genealogist; cemetery restoration, Lowndes County, GA. *Memberships*: Madison County Genealogical Society; Echols County Genealogical Society; Genealogy Unlimited (past vice president); Tcinto Sakto Muskogee Tribe; Lower Muskogee Creek Tribe, Lynn Haven, FL. *Interests*: Genealogy, Native American studies; surface artifact collection; hiking. *Published work*: Ephriam Bass, Genealogy.

BENNETT, GERALD TILMAN (Nansemon, Creek, Cherokee)
(marine maintenance, construction)
Born August 16, 1955. *Education*: High school. *Principal occupation*: Marine maintenance, construction. *Address*: 2035 Sallas Lane, Jacksonville, FL 32233 (904) 241-3429. *Membership*: Tcinto Sakto Muskogee Tribe. *Interests*: Motorcycling, hiking, diving.

BENNETT, GEORGE E. (Ottawa)
(tribal chairperson)
Affiliation: Grand Traverse Band of Ottawa & Chippewa Indians, Peshawbestown Community Center, 2605 NW Bay Shore Dr., Suttons Bay, MI 49682 (231) 271-3538; E-mail: gbennett@gtbindians.com.

BENNETT, JOSEPH
(health center director)
Affiliation: Tishomingo Chickasaw Health Center, 815 E. 6th St., Tishomingo, OK 73460 (405) 371-2392.

BENNETT, NOEL KIRKISH 1939-
(organization director; author, artist, teacher)
Born December 23, 1939, San Jose, Calif. *Education*: Stanford University, B.A. (Art), 1961, M.A., 1962; Navajo Reservation, Weaving Apprenticeship, 1968-1976. *Principal occupation*: Organization director, author, artist, teacher. *Home address*: Resides in New Mexico. *Affiliations*: Lecturer, College of Notre Dame, Belmont, Calif., 1963-1967; lecturer, University of New Mexico, 1971-1976; lecturer, International College, Los Angeles, 1979-1981; founder, Navajo Weaver Restoration Center, 1978-; Director, Shared Horizons, Corrales, N.M. (non-profit, educational, perpetuating the Navajo, Southwest textile art tradition. *Other professional post*: Navajo weaving workshops, lectures, demonstrations to museums, universities, and guilds across the nation, 1971-. *Awards, honors*: Cum Laude graduate and recipient of the Mortimer C. Levintritt Award for outstanding work in Departments of Art and Architecture, Stanford University, 1961; Weatherhead Foundation Grant, 1975 (writing of Navajo weaving beliefs and legends); Tennessee Humanities Council, 1982 (Navajo weaving workshop); Communication Arts Award, Three Looms, One Land: Shared Horizons poster award for concept, copy, photo, 1982; Skaggs Foundation Grants, 1986 for publishing of Halo of the Sun, 1989 for Bighorse — The Warrior; National Endowment for the Arts, 1990 for "A Place in the Wild"; hon-

orary member, Indian Arts and Crafts Association; board member, Navajoland Festival of the Arts (Navajo Tribe). *Interests*: "Painting, tapestry weaving, restoration of Navajo rugs, philosophy. Though intensely involved in my own painting, weaving and writing, the area of Navajo life and weaving continues to provide inspiration and satisfaction. With the nine years that I lived and wove on the Navajo Reservation as a basis, my core goals have been to seek out, internalize and share the beauty of traditional Navajo weaving in three main areas: the pure symmetry and balance of designs, refined through generations of use; the rhythm of effortless techniques, a oneness of self and loom evolving over time; and the underlying sustaining beliefs, legends and taboos that give meaning not only to the activity but beyond, to life itself." *Biographical sources*: Contemporary Authors; World Who's Who of Authors; Dictionary of International Biography; World Who's Who of Women; The Directory of Distinguished Americans; International Book of Honor; Personalities of America; Personalities of the West and Midwest; 5,000 Personalities of the World; International Directory of Distinguished Leadership; International Authors' and Writers' Who's Who. *Published works*: Working With the Wool — How to Weave a Navajo Rug, with Tiana Bighorse (Northland Press, 1971); Genuine Navajo Rug — Are You Sure? (Museum of Navajo Ceremonial Art - Wheelwright Museum - and the Navajo Tribe, 1973); The Weaver's Pathway — A Clarification of the Spirit Trail in Navajo Weaving (Northland Press, 1974); How to Tell a Genuine Navajo Rug (final chapter) Navajo Weaving Handbook (Museum of New Mexico Press, 1974, 1977); Designing With the Wool — Advanced Navajo Weaving Techniques (Northland Press, 1979); Shared Horizons-Navajo Textiles, (catalog of exhibition) with Susan McGreevy & Mark Winter (Wheelwright Museum, 1981); Halo of the Sun — Stories Told and Retold (Northland Press, 1987); Bighorse — The Warrior (University of Arizona Press, 1990); various articles.

BENNETT, PHILLIP (Washoe)
(former tribal chairperson)
Affiliation: Woodfords Community Council, 96 Washoe Blvd., Markleeville, CA 96120 (702) 883-1446.

BENNETT, ROBERT L. (Oneida) 1912-
(former commissioner of Indian Affairs)
Born November 16, 1912, Oneida, Wisc. *Education*: Haskell Institute, A.A. (Business Administration), 1931; Southeastern University, LL.B., 1941. *Home address*: 604 Wagon Train, SE, Albuquerque, N.M. 87123 (505) 298-8635. *Affiliations*: Former area director, Bureau of Indian Affairs; former commissioner of Indian Affairs, Bureau of Indian Affairs, Washington, DC, 1966-69; director, American Indian Law Center, University of New Mexico Law School, Albuquerque, NM, 1970-75. *Military service*: U.S. Marine Corps, (PFC,1943-45; Outstanding Recruit in Training Platoon). *Community activities*: Advisor, Board of Regents, Haskell Indian Jr. College and Southwestern Indian Polytechnic Institute; president, American Indian Athletic Hall of Fame; vice-chairman, Futures for Children; president, ARROW, Inc., Washington, DC; consultant on American Indians. *Memberships*: American Society for Public Administration; Society for Applied Anthropology; American Academy of Political and Social Science, 1960-; American Indian Lawyers Association, Order of the Coif (Study of Law). *Awards, honors*: Indian Achievement Award, Indian Council Fire, 1962; Outstanding American Indian Citizen, 1966; founder of American Indian Graduate Center, 1969; founder of American Indian Athletic Hall of Fame, 1969; Outstanding Member of Oneida Tribe of Wisconsin, 1988. *Interests*: Consultant on American Indians - worked with Indian tribes throughout the U.S. including native peoples of the State of Alaska. Lecturer & instructor at seminars on American Indian affairs. *Biographical sources*: Indians of Today (Indian Council Fire, 1960); Robert Bennett (Dillon Press).

BENNETT, RUTH (Shawnee) 1942-
(ethnographic researcher/technical writer)
Born December 12, 1942. *Education*: Indiana University, B.A., 1964; University of Washington, M.A. (English), 1968; California State University, San Francisco, Standard Secondary Teaching Credential (Multi-Cultural Education), 1973; University of California, Berkeley, Ph.D. (language and reading development with a specialization in bilingual education), 1979. *Princi-*

pal occupation: Ethnographic researcher/technical writer. *Address*: Humboldt State University, The Center for Community Development, Arcata, CA 95521 (707) 826-3711 Fax 826-5258; E-Mail: rsb3@axe. humboldt.edu. *Affiliations*: Teaching assistant, University of Washington, 1964-1966; pre-school teacher, Inner Sunset Neighborhood Cooperative, San Francisco, 1971-1972; teaching assistant, University of California, Berkeley, 1973-1974; children's literature instructor, School of the Arts, Berkeley High School, Calif., 1973-1974; enrichment program instructor, Washington Laboratory School, Berkeley, 1975-1978; resource teacher, Hoopa Elementary School, 1976-; field director, Native Language and Culture Program, 1978-1979, assistant director, 1980-, Center for Community Development; director, Title VII, Institute of Higher Education Training Grant, Bilingual Emphasis Program, Center for Community Development, 1981-; teacher, Department of Education, Humboldt State University, 1981-. *Other professional posts*: evaluator/consultant, Hupa Valley Tribe, Johnson O'Malley K-12 Program, 1994-; language program consultant, Cahto Tribe, Laytonville Rancheria, 1996; phonetics chart consultant, Wiyot Tribe, Table Bluffs Rancheria, 1996. *Community activities*: Volunteer research and curriculum preparation, Indian tribes of Northwest California: Hupa, Yurok, Karuk. *Memberships*: Phi Delta Kappa, Phi Beta Kappa, Alpha Lambda Delta, Alpha Omicron Pi; University of California and Indiana University Alumni Associations. *Interests*: Dr. Ruth Bennett has conducted innovative curriculum work for 15 years, leading to computer uses for curriculum. *Published works*: Downriver Indians' Legends, 1983; Let's Go Now, 1983; 1983 Hupa Calendar, 1982; Karuk Fishing, 1983; Look Inside and Read, 1982; Unifon Update, 1983; 1983-1984 Yurok Unifon Calendar, 1983; Origin of Fire; Songs of a Medicine Woman; Hupa Spelling Book; Legends and Personal Experiences; Ceremonial Dances; Yurok Spelling Book; What Is An Indian?; Karuk Vocabulary Book; Karuk Fishing; Basket Weaving Among the Karuk; Tolowa Legends; Tolowa/English Lesson Units; Ya:na:'a'awh, Four Hupa Songs by Alice Pratt, Elementary School Level, High School Level, Higher Education and Adult Level, 1994; and others (all published by The Center for Community Development, Humboldt State University; numerous articles, including Ph.D. dissertation, Hoopa Children's Storytelling, University of California, Berkeley.

BENNETT, WILLARD (Washoe)
(tribal chairperson)
Affiliation: Alpine Washoe Reservation, Woodfords Community Council, 96 Washoe Blvd., Markleeville, CA 96120 (775) 883-1446.

BENOANIE, EDWARD
(Indian band chief)
Affiliation: Chief, Hatchet Lake Indian Band, Wollaston Lake, Saskatchewan, Canada S0J 3C0.

BENSON, DIANE E. *(Lxeis)* (Tlingit) 1959-
(free-lance writer, talent agent, stage director)
Born October 17, 1959, Yakima, Wash. *Education*: University of Alaska, B.A., 1985. *Principal occupation*: Free-lance writer, talent agent, stage director. *Address*: P.O. Box 770369, Eagle River, AK 99577 (907) 688-1370. *Affiliations*: Alaska Film Group, Anchorage, AK; Chugiak/Eagle River Chamber of Commerce, Eagle River, AK. *Other professional posts*: Founder, Alaska Native performance & Film Commission, 1993; Artist in the Schools Residency Program, 1993-; National Museum of the American Indian Consultant, 1991-92. *Community activities*: Board member, Arctic Moon Stage Co.; Chugiak Dog Mushers Club, Junior Club Chute Judge; founder, Kookeena Improv Troupe, 1985; Out North Theatre (member & guest artist - Anchorage); Artist in the Schools Residency Program, 1993-. *Memberships*: Alaska Press Women; National Congress of American Indians; National Association of the Self-Employed; American Indian Register, 1989-93. *Awards, honors*: University of Alaska Outstanding Alumni, 1990; race marshall, Chugiak Junioir Dog Musher's Club, 1993. *Interests*: Traditional dancing & singing - Tlingit & Haida Dancers of Anchorage, 1987-. First Alumni & first Native American to direct UAA Mainstage, 1993. Public speaing on theater, alcohol & drug recovery & motivation; workshop facilitation in acting & theater & combining cultural concepts, writing, poetry, research. Attended International Native

American Writers, Festival in Oklayoma, 1992; travel to Central America. *Biographical sources*:"Goose Girl Lives in Many Worlds" (Tundra Times, 7/6/83); "Fire in Her Heart" (Anchorage Time, 2/25/90). *Published works*: Rven Tells Stories: An Anthology, edited by Joseph Bruchac (Greenfield Review Press, 1991); Native Amerian Literatures: A Special Issue, 1994. I am currently writing for Gale Research, Multicultural Encyclopedia. *Films*: Sacajawea -animated film received national & international awards (FilmFair Communications, Los Angeles, 1989); White Fang (Disney, 1989). Sister Warrior (feature film) script. Performed in many other local television spots, training video's & radio drama's, in addition, stage acting for 15 years.

BENSON, FOLEY C.
(museum director/curator)
Affiliation: Jese Peter Native American Art Museum, 1501 Mendocino Ave., Santa Rosa, CA 95401 (707) 527-4479.

BENSON, LOUISE (Hualapai)
(tribal chairperson)
Affiliation: Hualapai Tribal Council, P.O. Box 179, Peach Springs, AZ 86434 (928) 769-2216.

BENT BOX, EDWARD (*Red Ute*) (Southern Ute) 1920-
(flutemaker)
Born April 1,, 1920, Bayfield, Colo. *Address*: Red Ute, 14693 Hwy. 172, P.O. Box 224, Ignacio, CO 81137 (970) 563-4128. Red Ute has been making flutes (since the 1950's in his home on the Southern Ute Reservation) out of a variety of hardwoods - walnut, paduk, cherry, ebony as well as traditional red cedar. He decorates his flutes with traditional buckskin fringes and Indian beadwork designs. "The purpose of Indian flute music in contemporary society,' he says, "is to promote the feeling of peace and harmony in both the flute player and his audience." *Memberships*: Indian Arts & Crafts Association; American Indian Science & Engineering Society, 1992-98 Committee of Elders. *Military service*: U.S. Navy, 1942-46.

BENTON, MARIA (Zia Pueblo) 1944-
(health educator)
Born July 17, 1944, Zia Pueblo, N.M. *Education*: Parks College, San Jose, CA (1 Yr.); University of New Mexico, Albuquerque (288 hrs.) Certified Chemical Dependency Health Educator. *Principal occupation*: Health educator. *Address*: Zia Route, Box 3, San Ysidro, N.M. 87053 (505) 766-8418 (work). *Affiliation*: Health educator, Southwestern Indian Polytechnic Institute, Albuquerque, NM, 1989-. *Awards, honors*: Community Service Award, Jemez Springs Municipal School Boards; Dedication & Excellence in Health Delivery Service, Five Sandoval Indian Pueblos.

BENTON, SHERROLE DAWN (*Ay-nah-wayne-shee-Quay*) (Oneida/Ojibwe)1956-
(editor, Native news)
Born December 1, 1956, Green Bay, Wisc. *Education*: University of Wisconsin, Green Bay, BA (Communications & the Arts), 1985. *Principal occupation*: Editor, Native news. *Address*: Address unknown. *Affiliations*: Editor, Regional Native News, WOJB-FM, Hayward, WI. *Other professional post*: Production coordinator, Regional Native News, WOJB-FM. *Community activities*: Parent Advisory Committee, LCO Ojibwe School, Hayward, WI. *Memberships*: Three Fires Society; Mide-wi-win Lodge. *Awards, honors*: Best Radio Feature; Outstanding American Indian Reporter. *Interests*: "My major vocational goal is to provide communication and cultural exchanges between Native American people and mainstream American society to encourage understanding, dialogue, respect and dignity among the different culture groups."

BENTZ, MARILYN
(professor)
Affiliation: American Indian Studies Center, Dept. of Anthropology, University of Washington, C514 Padelford, GN-05, Seattle, WA 98195 (206) 543-5240.

BENYSHEK, DANIEL C.
(professor)
Born July 11, 1963, Belleville, Kans. *Education*: PhD in Anthropology. *Principal occupation*: Assistant professor. *Address & Affiliation*: Dept. of Anthropology & Ethnic Studies, 4505 Maryland Pkwy., Box 455003,

University of Nevada, Las Vegas, NV 89154-5003 (702) 895-2070 Fax 895-4823. E-mail: daniel.deny shek@ccmail.nevada.edu. Website: www.nevada.edu/~benyshek/. *Professional activities*: His academic areas of expertise include medical and nutritional anthropology, ethnomedicine, and Native North America. His primary research interests focus on the political ecology and etiology of type 2 Diabetes, the impact of Diabetes on Native American populations, and community-based interventions generated in response to the epidemic of type 2 diabetes among American Indians. Dr. Benyshek has spent over a decade working with the Havasupai Indian Tribe of northern Arizona in an effort to understand the etiology of diabetes in the community, document local attitudes about the disease, assess community resources to combat the problem, and assess the social, political and economic factors which may be impeding the maintenance of healthy bodyweight & blood glucose levels in the community. He consulted on a multi-year, diabetes prevention/control grant proposal submitted by the Havasupai Tribe & funded (June 1998) by the Indian Health Service, (IHS Special Diabetes Programm for Indians) and has helped organize a tribal diabetes task force to oversee the Indian Health Service grant. *Published works*: He has published articles on these topics in the Journal of American Dietetic Assn, 1997 97(11):1275-1282, the Jr. of Nutrition 2000 130:741-744, & Medical Anthropology 2001 v20(1):25-64.

BERG, LAURA
(editor)
Affiliation: "Wana Chinook Tymoo," Columbia River Inter-Tribal Fish Commission, 729 N.E. Oregon, Suite 200, Portland, OR 97232 (503) 238-0667.

BERG, MERRILL
(college president)
Affiliation: President, Little Hoop Community College, P.O. Box 269, Fort Totten, ND 58335 (701) 766-4415.

BERGEN, RONALD J. (Oglala Sioux) 1946-
(educator)
Born July 8, 1946, Pine Ridge, S.D. *Education*: National College (Rapid City, SD), B.S., 1979. *Principal occupation*: Educator. *Home address*: 1345 Sheridan St., Hot Springs, SD 57747 (605) 745-4145 (work). *Affiliation*: Director, Title IX Indian Education/Peer Tutorial Programs, Hot Springs Public Schools, 1609 University Ave., Hot Springs, SD 57747, 1984-. *Military service*: S.D. National Guard, 1964-68; U.S. Army, 1968-70; U.S. Navy, 1971-73. *Community activities*: Board of Directors, Southern Hills Developmental Services; secretary/treasurer, Hot Springs Child Protection Team; Hot Springs Public Schools Strategic Planning Committee; Hot Springs Youth Soccer Coordinator. *Memberships*: Disabled American Veterans, 1970-; Veterans of Foreign Wars, 1970- (life member).

BERGGREN, KAREN
(park manager)
Affiliation: Homolovi Ruins State Park, 523 W. 2nd St., Winslow, AZ 86047 (602) 289-4106.

BERIKOFF, HARIIET (Eskimo)
(AK village council president)
Affiliation: Unalaska Village (Qualingin), P.O. Box 334, Unalaska, AK 99685 (907) 581-2290.

BERKE, DEBRA
(museum director)
Affiliation: U.S. Department of the Interior Museum, 18th & C Sts., Washington, DC 20240 (202) 208-4743.

BERKEY, CURTIS
(director-Indian law center)
Affiliation: Indian Law Resource Center, Dist. Office, 601 E St., SE, Washington, DC 20003 (202) 547-2800.

BERMAN, DR. TRESSA L.
(assistant professor)
Affiliation: Dept. of Social & Behavioral Sciences, Arizona State University, Tempe, AZ 85287 (602) 965-6213 Fax 965-7671. *Interests*: Native North America; indigenous art. E-mail: tressa.berman@asu.edu

BERNARD, ALLISON M.
(Indian band chief)
Affiliation: Chief, Eskasoni Indian Band, Eskasoni, Nova Scotia, Canada B0A 1J0 (902) 379-2800.

BERNARD, RAYMOND
(Indian band chief)
Affiliation: Abenakis de Wolinak, 4680 boul. Danube, Reserve Indienne de Wolinak, Becanour, Quebec G0X 1B0 (819) 294-6690.

BERNARD, STEPHENSON
(Indian band chief)
Affiliation: Chief, Fort Folly Indian Band, P.O. Box 21, Dorchester, New Brunswick, Canada E0A 1M0 (506) 379-6224.

BERNARDI, JOANNA
(executive director-Indian centre)
Affiliation: Executive director, Woodland Indian Cultural Educational Centre, P.O. Box 1506, Brantford, Ontario N3T 5V6 (519) 759-2653.

BERNIE, CLIFFORD (Dakota)
(poet)
Address: P.O. Box 173, Wagner, SD 57380 (605) 487-7671.

BERNSTEIN, BRUCE
(museum curator)
Affiliation: Museum of Indian Arts & Culture, Laboratory of Anthropology, P.O. Box 2087, 708 Camino Lejo, Santa Fe, NM 87504 (505) 827-6344.

BERRY, ERNEST (Eskimo)
(AK village council president)
Affiliation: Native Village of Shungnak, P.O. Box 63, Shungnak, AK 99773 (907) 437-2170.

BERRY, FRANKLIN L.
(executive director)
Affiliation: Cook Inlet Native Association, Anchorage, AK 99503 (907) 278-4641.

BERRY, JOHN D. (Choctaw/Cherokee) 1951-
(librarian)
Born October 31, 1951, in Stillwater, Okla. *Education*: MLIS, MA. *Principal occupation*: Librarian. *Address*:Ethnic Studies Library, 30 Stephens Hall, #2360, UCB, Berkeley, CA 94720 (510) 642-0941. E-mail: jberry@library.berkeley.edu. *Affiliations*: Oklahoma State University (Library, 1995-99, Graduate College, 1999-2001); Native American Studies/Comparative Ethnic Studies Librarian, Ethnic Studies Library, UCB, Berkeley, CA, 2001-present. *Other professional posts*: Dept. of Defense, 1990-91; FDA Medical Library, 1991-95; tribal library consulting. *Memberships*: American Indian Library Association; American Library Association. *Interests*: Libraries, education, NAGPRA.

BERRY, MARTHA (Cherokee)
(craftsperson)
Address: 14295 County Road 1252, Tyler, TX 75709 (903) 509-3617. *Product*: Decorative beadwork in Woodland and Plains Indian styles, with emphasis on Cherokee history, stories and lore.

BERRYHILL, LES (Yuchi-Creek)
(craftsperson)
Address: 1800 Bunting Lane, Edmond, OK 73034 (405) 733-7350 or 330-2951. *Products*: Cultural artifact replicas, old styles and color beadwork; 19th century beaded knife cases with authentic knives.

BERTHRONG, DONALD J. 1922-
(professor emeritus of history)
Born October 2, 1922, La Crosse, Wisc. *Education*: LaCrosse State Teachers College, LaCrosse, WI, 1940-42; University of Wisconsin, BS, 1947, MS, 1948, PhD, 1952. *Principal occupation*: Professor emeritus of history. *Address*: 5903 Mt. Eagle Dr. #G3-1201, Alexandria, VA 22303. *Affiliations*: Instructor, University of Kansas City; assistant professor, 1952-58, associate professor, 1958-64, professor of history, 1964-70, chair, 1966-70, University of Oklahoma; professor, 1970-91, head, Dept. of History, 1970-.85; professor emeritus, 1991-, Purdue University. *Other professional posts*: Fulbright Professor of History, University of Hong Kong, 1965-66. *Military service*: U.S. Army & Air Force, 1942-44; U.S. Army, 1944-46. *Memberships*: American Historical Association; Association of American Historians; Oklahoma Historical Society; Western History Association; Agricultural History; American Association of University Professors. *Awards, honors*: Phi

Beta Kappa, 1985, Purdue University chapter; Fellowship, Social Science Research Council; Fellowship, American Philosophical Society; Award of Merit, Association for State and Local History, for The Southern Cheyennes. *Interests*: Western U.S. history; expert witness before the Indian Claims Commission; consultant, Native American Rights Fund, 1975-76, 1979-84, 1990, 1994; Fulbright lecturer in American history at the University of Hong Kong and Chinese University (Hong Kong, B.C.C.) *Biographical sources*: Who's Who in America, 1970-; Directory of American Scholars of History. *Published works*: Co-editor, Joseph Redford Walker and the Arizona Adventure (University of Oklahoma Press, 1956); The Southern Cheyennes (University of Oklahoma Press, 1963); A Confederate in the Colorado Gold Fields (University of Oklahoma Press, 1970); Indians of Northern Indiana and Southwestern Michigan (Garland, 1974); The Cheyenne and Arapaho Ordeal: Reservation and Agency Life in the Indian Territory, 1875-1907 (University of Oklahoma Press, 1976).

BERUBE, JERRY
(president-Indian centre)
Affiliation: President: Native Alliance of Quebec, 21 Brodeur Ave., Hull, Quebec, Canada J8Y 2P6 (613) 770-7763.

BETSAKA, JIM
(Indian band chief)
Affiliation: Chief, Nahanni Butte Indian Band, General Delivery, Trout Lake, Northwest Territories X0E 0N0.

BETHMANN-MAHOOTY, BARBARA A.
(Ka Non Sen Ha Wi) (Mohawk) 1933-
(Native American home/school coordinator)
Born September 2, 1933, Irondequoit, N.Y. *Home address*: 24 Pauline Cir., Rochester, NY 14623 (716) 359-4651; 359-5047 (work). *Affiliations*: Native American home/school coordinator, N.Y. State Native American Advisory Committee, Cornell University, Ithaca, NY, 1986-; Chair, American Indians of All Nations, Rochester, NY, 1989-. *Other professional posts*: Past member, NY State Advisory Committee to the Commissioner of Education, Indian Education, Albany, NY; past board member, Native American Cultural Center, Inc., Rochester, NY. *Community activities*: Began 1794 Canadaigua Treaty Committee; Mohawk storyteller, Women's Recognition Committee; switchboard operator in hospital for past 13 years. *Memberships*: AISES; American Indians of All nations. *Awards, honors*: Honored at Women's Recognition Dinner, 1991; honored at Pow Wow, Rochester, NY, Sept. 1993. *Interests*: "Interested in the culture of our people, and present day issues. Married Chester B. Mahooty, noted Zuni silversmith and member of American Indian Dance Theatre, in Nov. 1993. (I) like to travel slowly — see things of interest."

BETTELYOUN, CHARLES
(school chairperson)
Affiliation: Porcupine Day School, P.O. Box 180, Porcupine, SD 57772 (605) 867-5336.

BETTELYOUN, LULU F. (JANIS)
(Oglala Sioux) 1947-
(teacher, social welfare/caseworker)
Born April 10, 1947, Pine Ridge, S.D. *Education*: Northern State College (Aberdeen, SD), 1965-68; Black Hills State College, (Spearfish, SD), B.S. (Education), 1972. *Principal occupation*: Teacher, social welfare/caseworker. *Home address*: P.O. Box 66, Pine Ridge, SD 57770.

BETTIS, RICHARD MACK *(Di-yoTa-Li)*
(United Keetowah Cherokee)1934-
(chief deputy county assessor)
Born March 15, 1934, Spiro, Okla. *Education*: Northeast State University, Tahlequah, OK, BA, 1955; Tulsa University (graduate school, 1955-56); Oklahoma City University Law School, JD, 1967. *Principal occupation*: Chief deputy county assessor. *Home address*: 3739 E. 43rd St., Tulsa, OK 74135 (918) 747-7779. *Affiliation*: Occupational Analyst, Oklahoma Employment Security Commission, 1956-67; Dept. of the Interior, Investigate EEO Complaints, Labor Relations Officer, Assistant Personnel Officer (15 years); chief deputy county assessor, Tulsa County, OK, 1979-. *Other professional posts*: Part time private law practice, 1968-; Mayor appointed member of Tulsa Indian

Affairs Commission and elected chairperson seven consecutive terms; taught federal, state government at Tulsa Junior College Evening Division for its first ten years. Memberships: Oklahoma Bar Association, 1968-; U.S. Civil Rights Commission (Oklahoma Delegate Member, 1989-); Oklahoma Indian Historical Society (charter member, Governor appointee, 1986-); United Keetowah Band of Cherokee Indians of Oklahoma, 1972-. *Awards, honors*: Appointed by Dept. of the Interior to serve on White House Staff Team to change election power marketing agencies of the Interior to new U.S. Dept, of Energy. *Interests*: Church offices, activities; Indian community and art activities; Indian law activities; violin making, restoration, collecting, study & appraisals. *Published works*: "Have written articles on Cherokee Indian history, plus introductons & editing for Smithsonian Cherokee history publications; also articles on violins, history, etc."

BETWEEN LODGES, WILBUR (Oglala Sioux)
(tribal chairperson)
Affiliation: Oglala Sioux Tribal Council, P.O. Box H, No. 468, Pine Ridge, SD 57770 (605) 867-5821.

BEVIN, MELVILLE STANLEY
(Indian band chief)
Affiliation: Chief, Kitselas Indian Band, 4562 Queensway, Terrace, British Columbia, Canada V8G 3X6 (604) 635-5084.

BEVINS-ERICSEN, SUSIE
(institute president)
Affiliation: Institute of Alaska Native Arts, P.O. Box 70769, Fairbanks, AK (907) 456-7491.

BEVITT, EMOGENE A.
(program specialit)
Affiliation: National Park Service, American Indian Liaison Office, U.S. Dept. of the Interior-Cultural Resources, P.O. Box 37127, Washington, DC 20013 (202) 343-3395.

BEYDA, MARY
(Indian education program director)
Affiliation: Alhambra Elementary School District #68, Indian Education Program, 4510 N. 37th Ave., Phoenix, AZ 85019 (602) 336-2944.

BICK, RON
(editor)
Affiliation: Char-Koosta, Confederated Salish & Kootenai Tribes, P.O. Box 278, Pablo, MT 59855 (406) 675-3000.

BIGBOY, EUGENE, SR. (Lake Superior Chippewa)
(tribal chairperson)
Affiliation: Bad River Band of Lake Superior Chippewa, P.O. Box 39, Odanah, WI 54861 (715) 682-7111.

BIGBOY, MARY
(health director)
Affiliation: Bad River Health Services, P.O. Box 39, Odanah, WI 54861 (715) 682-7137.

BIG CROW, FRANCIS X.
(Indian school chairperson)
Affiliation: American Horse School, P.O. Box 660, Allen, SD 57714 (605) 455-2480.

BIG EAGLE, DUANE (Crow Creek Sioux)
(tribal chairperson)
Affiliation: Crow Creek Sioux Tribal Council, P.O. Box 50, Fort Thompson, SD 57339 (605) 245-2221.

BIG EAGLE, DUANE (Osage)
(poet, short fiction writer)
Address: 3809 Spring Hill, Petaluma, CA 94952 (707) 778-3107.

BIG EAGLE, LAURA
(Indian band chief)
Affiliation: Ocean Man Indian Band, Box 157, Stoughton, Saskatchewan, Canada S0G 4T0 (306) 457-2697.

BIG GEORGE, PAULINE
(Indian band chief)
Affiliation: Big Island Indian Band, Morson P.O., Morson, Ontario, Canada P0W 1J0 (807) 488-5602.

BIGFOOT, DOLORES SUBIA (Caddo of Oklahoma)
(psychologist; assistant professor)
Education: PhD (Psychology). *Principal occupation*: Psychologist; assistant professor. *Address*: University of Oklahoma Health Sciences Center, College of Public Health, Dept. of Pediatrics, P.O. Box 26901, Oklahoma City, OK 73190 (405) 271-8858; E-mail: dee-bigfoot@ouhsc.edu. Website: www.ouhhsc.edu. *Affiliation*: Assistant Professor of Research, Dept. of Pediatrics, OU Health Sciences Center, Oklahoma City, OK. *Other professional post*: Project Director, Project Making Medicine, Center om Child Abuse & Neglect, OU Health Sciences Center, Oklahoma City, OK. *Community activities*: Board member, Parents Assistance Center. *Memberships*: American Psychological Assn, American Professional Society on the Abuse of Children, National Indian Child Welfare Association. *Interests*: Storytelling, history, museum, historical & fiction writing. *Published works*: Upon the Back of a Turtle; Project Making Medicine, Training Manual; Head Start curriculum - Prevention of Child Abuse and Neglect.

BIGGS, CURLEY (Ramah Navajo)
(tribal council president)
Affiliation: Ramah Navajo Chapter Council, Rte. 2, Box 13, Ramah, NM 87321 (505) 775-3342.

BIGHETTY, FRED
(Indian band chief)
Affiliation: Barren Lands Indian Band, Brochet, Manitoba, Canada R0B 0B0 (204) 323-2300.

BIGHETTY, PASCAL
(Indian band chief)
Affiliation: Mathias Colomb Indian Band, Pukatawagan, Manitoba, Canada R0B 1A0 (204) 553-2090.

BIGHORN, SPIKE (Assiniboine & Sioux)
(former tribal chairperson)
Affiliation: Fort Peck Tribe, P.O. Box 1027, Poplar, MT 59255 (406) 768-5155.

BIGLER, GREGORY H.
(administrative judge)
Affiliation: Prairie Band Potawatomi Nation Tribal Court, 15498 K Rd., Mayetta, KS 66509 (866) 966-2242 or (785) 966-2242 Fax 966-2662. E-mail: tribalcourt@pbpnation.org. Website: www.pbpnation.org/tribalcourt

BILL, DAVID
(Indian band chief)
Affiliation: Tseycum Indian Band, Box 2501, Sidney, B.C., Canada V8L 4C1 (604) 656-0858.

BILL, JACOB
(Indian band chief)
Affiliation: Chief, Pelican Lake Indian Band, P.O. Box 9, Leoville, Sask., Canada S0J 1N0.

BILL, LARSON (Te-Moak Shoshone)
(tribal chairperson)
Affiliation: South Fork Indian Colony, HC 30, Box B-13, Lee, Spring Creek, NV 89815 (775) 744-4273.

BILL, LONNIE (Mono)
(rancheria chairperson)
Affiliation: Cold Springs Rancheria, P.O. Box 209, Tollhouse, CA 93667 (559) 855-5043.

BILLETTE, GORDON
(Indian band chief)
Affiliation: Chief, Buffalo River Indian Band, Dillon, Sask., Canada S0M 0S0 (306) 282-2033.

BILLIE, JAMES E. (Florida Seminole)
(tribal chairperson)
Affiliation: Seminole Tribal Council, 6300 Stirling Rd., Hollywood, FL 33024 (954) 966-6300.

BILLIE, PAULINE
(school principal)
Affiliation: Jones Ranch Community School, P.O. Box 278, Vanderwagen, NM 87326 (505) 778-5574 Fax 778-5575.

BILLINGTON, JAMES H.
(librarian)
Affiliation: Library of Congress, 1st & Independence, SE, Washington, DC 20540 (202) 707-5522.

BILLIE, LOIS (Florida Seminole)
(Indian school chairperson)
Affiliation: Ahfachkee Day School, Star Route, Box 40, Clewiston, FL 33440 (813) 983-6348.

BILLUM, HARRY (Athapascan)
(AK village council president)
Affiliation: Chitina Village Council, P.O. Box 31, Chitina, AK 99566 (907) 823-2215.

BILLY, BRUCE
(B.I.A. agency chairperson for education)
Affiliations: Chairperson, Shiprock Agency, Bureau of Indian Affairs, P.O. Box 3239, Shiprock, NM 87420 (505) 368-4427 Ext. 321; chairperson, Beclabito Day School, P.O. Box 1146, Shiprock, NM 87420 (602) 656-3555.

BILLY, CHARMAIN *(Me-tigh)* (Ponca of Oklahoma)
(executive director)
Born in Ponca City, Okla. *Education*: University of Oklahoma, B.A., 1985. *Principal occupation*: Executive director. *Address & Affiliation*: Executive Director, Lawrence Indian Center, 1423 Haskell Ave., Lawrence, KS 66044, (913) 841-7202 (work), 1993-present. *Other professional post*: Director, Child Welfare Program, Ponca Tribe of Oklahoma, 1985-86. *Community activities*: Indian Education/Parent Committee (vice-president, secretary, historian), 1980-; Native American Law Enforcement Task Force, 1993-94. *Memberships*: Up With People (Alumni, 1968-); Oklahoma University Native American Alumni Association; Chilocco Alumni Association; Haskell Indian Nations University Alumni Association. *Awards, honors*: Full scholarships to attend "Summer Institute on American Indian Affairs, University of Colorado, Boulder; "Clyde Warrior Institute on American Indian Affairs", Stout University, Menominee, WI. *Interests*: Educational and legal matters as they affect Native Americans. Travels with "Up With People" included countries of Germany, France, Austria, Spain, Japan, and Korea. *Biographical source*: "Journal World", July 25, 1993.

BILLY, GLENN (Pomo)
(artist, calligrapher)
Address: Scripsit, 1592 Union St. #356, San Francisco, CA 94123 (415) 586-4202.

BILLY, PAULINE
(B.I.A. agency education coordinator)
Affiliation: Education coordinator, Eastern Navajo Agency, Bureau of Indian Affairs, P.O. Box 328, Crownpoint, NM 87313 (505) 786-6150.

BILLY, RAMON, Sr. (Pomo)
(tribal chairperson)
Affiliation: Chairperson, Hopland Tribal Council, P.O. Box 610, Hopland, CA 95449 (707) 744-1647.

BILLY, STEVEN (Eskimo)
(AK village president)
Affiliation: Chefornak Village Council, P.O. Box 29, Ekwok, AK 99561 (907) 867-8850.

BILLY, ZERNDORFF
(tribal chairperson)
Affiliation: Alabama-Quassarte Tribal Town, P.O. Box 87, Wetumka, OK 74883 (918) 683-2388 Fax 683-3818

BILLYBOY, THOMAS
(Indian band chief)
Affiliation: Alexandria Indian Band, Box 4, RR 2, Quesnel, B.C., Canada V2J 3H6 (604) 993-4324.

BINNEY, ALLISON C. (Pomo)
(attorney)
Education: California State University, Chico, BA, 1997; Arizona State University Law School, J.D. (Certificate in Indian Law), 2000. Her substantial paper for the certificate program focused on repatriation issues for unrecognized tribes. *Address & Affiliation*: Hobbs, Straus, Dean & Walker, LLP (Associate, 2000-present), 2120 L St., NW, Suite 700, Washington, DC 20037 (202) 822-8282. E-mail: abinney@hsdwdc.com. While at ASU, Ms. Binney seved as the Program Coordinator for the Native American Law Students Association. Her current work includes the areas of Indian educatrion, housing, and legislation affecting Indian tribes and tribal organizations.

BIRCHFIELD, D.L. (Choctaw, Chickasaw)
(poet, writer, editor)
Education: University of Oklahoma, MA, 1972, JD, 1975. *Home address:* 5024 Drexel, Oklahoma City, OK 73119 (405) 681-4886. *Affiliations:* News From Indian Country, Hayward, WI; contributing editor, "Moccasin Telegraph," Fairfax, VA. *Awards, honors:* Won the North American Native Authors first book award for "Oklahoma Basic Intelligence Test," from the Native Writers' Circle of the Americas at the University of Oklahoma. *Published works:* Oklahoma Basic Intelligence Test; Field of Honor: A Novel (University of Oklahoma Press, 2004).

BIRCHUM, JAMES (Shoshone)
(tribal council chairperson)
Affiliation: Yomba Tribal Council, HC61, Box 6275, Austin, NV 89310 (775) 964-2463.

BIRCKEL, PAUL
(Indian band chief)
Affiliation: Champagne/Aishihik Indian Band, Box 5309, Haines Junction, Yukon, Canada Y0B 1L0 (403) 634-2288.

BIRD, JOSEPH
(Indian band chief)
Affiliation: Weenusk (Peawanuk) Indian Band, Box 1, Peawanuk, Ontario, Canada P0L 2H0 (705) 473-2554.

BIRD, MAGEL
(clinic president)
Affiliation: Indian Law Clinic, University of Montana Law School, Missoula, MT 59806 (406) 243-6480.

BIRD, MARGARET ANN (Osage)
(craftsperson)
Affiliation: Owner, Sees-the-Eagle, 111 W. Orange, Caney, KS 67333 (316) 879-2634.

BIRD, MICHAEL
(executive director)
Affiliation: National Native American AIDS Prevention Center, 436 14th St., Suite 1020, Oakland, CA 94609 (510) 444-2051 Fax 444-1593.

BIRD, PEGGY (Santo Domingo Pueblo)
(attorney)
Resides in Albuquerque, NM (505) 368-4377 (work). *Memberships:* New Mexico Indian Bar Association (president); Native American Bar Association; American Bar Association.

BIRD BEAR, DUANE
(BIA agency supt.)
Affiliation: Crow Agency, BIA, Crow Agency, MT 59022 (406) 638-2672. *Past professional post:* Supt., Spokane Agency, Bureau of Indian Affairs, Wellpinit, WA .

BIRDINGROUND, CLIFFORD (Crow)
(tribal council chairperson)
Affiliation: Crow Indian Tribal Council, P.O. Box 400, Crow Agency, MT 59022 (406) 638-2601.

BIRON, THOMAS A. *(Animkii Migizi)* **(Anishnaabe)**
1951-
(college administrator, faculty, free lance journalist)
Born October 16, 1951, Sault Ste. Marie, Ontario, Can. *Education:* Lake Superior State College, B.S., 1973; Northern Michigan University, MPA, 1975; currently working on PhD in socio-cultural anthropology at Michigan State University. *Principal occupation:* College administrator, faculty, freelance journalist. *Address:* Address unknown. *Affiliation:* Administrator/faculty, Native American Leadership Program Program, Lansing Community College, Lansing, MI. *Other professional posts:* Editorial advisory board, Lansing State Journal; deans board of advisors, College of Human Ecology, Michigan State University; President's Advisory Committee, Affirmative Action, Lansing Community College. *Military service:* U.S. Army (Medic - Certificate in Advanced Leadership Training & Race Relations. *Community activities:* Mayor's Human Relations Advisory Committee; board member, Spiritual Healing Lodge-Garden River First Nation, Ontario, Can. *Memberships:* Lansing Human Relations Advisory Committee; Public Administrators Association; Word Craft Circle, Native American Writers Guild. *Interests:* Performing arts, journalism, educational video

production, Anishnaabe issues in the Great Lakes cultural region. Youth leadership through inter-generational programming. *Published works:* Native American Values: Survival & Renewal; article, "Anishinaabe Medicine Community Health Planning."

BISAILLON, ALFRED
(Indian band chief)
Affiliation: Thessalon Indian Band, Box 9, RR 2, Thessalon, Ontario, Canada P0R 1L0 (705) 842-2323.

BISONETTE, TERRI
(editor)
Affiliation: Explore Indian Country, Indian Country Communications, Rte. 2, Box 2900-A, Hayward, WI 54843 (715) 634-5226.

BITSIE, OSCAR (Navajo) 1935-
(teacher)
Born October 30, 1935, Tohatchi, N.M. *Education:* Fort Lewis College, BA, 1964; Northern Arizona University, MA, 1973, post graduate work in school administration, 1974-75. *Principal occupation:* Teacher. *Home address:* P.O. Box 1496, Tohatchi, NM 87325. *Affiliations:* Gallup-McKinley County Schools, Gallup, NM; teacher of social studies, Tohatchi Middle School, Tohatchi, NM. *Other professional posts:* Coordinated Title 7 - Bilingual Education, Johnson-O'Malley Indian Education, Title IV - home/school liaison coordinator. *Military service:* U.S. Army 1958-60 (Expert Rifle; Good Conduct Medal). *Community activities:* Tohatchi Chapter President, 1970-74, Vice President, 1978-82; Public Health Service, Gallup, NM (board member, 1970-80); Public Health Service, Gallup Indian Medical Center (health board president, 1980-); Friendship Service for Alcoholic Recovery Center (board of directors, vice-president, 1982-85). *Memberships:* Christian Reformed Church (delegate to Calvin College in Michigan, 1976); Navajo Tribe. *Awards, honors:* Community service award by Tohatchi Chapter for Community Leadership. *Interests:* Reading books in social studies; travel throughout the Rockies for historical information; political activities in Navajo Tribe, county and state.

BITTEM, ANDREW
(Indian band chief)
Affiliation: Chief, Berens River Indian Band, Berens River P.O., Berens River, Manitoba, Canada R0B 0A0 (204) 382-2161.

BITTLE, CHERYL A.
(health programs director)
Affiliation: Portland Area Office, Bureau of Indian Affairs, 1220 S.W. Third Ave., Rm. 476, Portland, OR 97204 (503) 326-3288.

BLACK BEAR, ROY
(museum owner)
Affiliation: Owner, Black Bear Museum, P.O. Box 47, Esopus, NY 12429.

BLACK, DOUGLAS
(IHS-associate director)
Affiliation: Dept. of Health & Human Services, USPHS, Indian Health Service, Office of Tribal Activities, Rm. 6A-05, 5600 Fishers Lane, Rockville, MD 20857 (301) 443-1104.

BLACK, HERBERT C.
(Indian school principal)
Affiliation: Navajo Mountain Boarding School, P.O. Box 10010, Tonalea, AZ 86044 (602) 672-2851.

BLACK, KENNETH E. (Otoe-Missouria)
(ex-tribal chairperson)
Affiliation: Otoe-Missouria Tribal Council, Rt. 1, Box 62, Red Rock, OK 74651 (405) 723-4434.

BLACK, DR. LYDIA T.
(professor emeritus of Alaskan Native studies)
Affiliation: Department of Alaskan Native Studies, University of Alaska, College of Liberal Arts, Fairbanks, AK 99701 (907) 474-7288.

BLACK, MARY A. (Iroquois) 1955-
(attorney)
Born May 4, 1955, Tulsa, Okla. *Education:* University of Oklahoma, BS, 1978; Oklahoma City University Law School, JD, 1981. *Principal occupation:* Attorney.

Home address: Resides in Shawnee, OK (405) 275-0123 (office). *Affiliation:* Attorney, Private Practice, Shawnee, OK, 1982-. *Other professional posts:* District Judge, Absentee Shawnee Tribe; Supreme Court Justice, Sac & Fox Nation. *Memberships:* American Indian Bar Association; Oklahoma Indian Bar Association (secretary, 1991-92); Oklahoma Bar Association; Oklahoma Trial Lawyers Association; American Trial Lawyers Association; American Bar Association; Lawyer-Pilot Bar Association; Pottawatomie County Bar Association (secretary, 1990; treasurer, 1991, 1992; Law Day Committee, 1984-). *Interests:* "Private practice in law with emphasis in personal injury and Indian law."

BLACK, ROBERT. A.
(professor of Native American studies)
Affiliation: Professor, Native American Studies Department, University of California, Dwinelle Hall, Suite 3415, Berkeley, CA 94720 (510) 642-6717.

BLACK, SHERRY SALWAY
(association vice president)
Affiliation: Vice-president, First Nations Development Institute, The Stores Bldg., 11917 Main St., Fredericksburg, VA 22408 (540) 371-5615 Fax 371-3505.

BLACK, WILLIAM A.
(BIA agency supt.)
Affiliation: Puget Sound Agency, Bureau of Indian Affairs, 2707 Colby Ave. #1101, Everett, WA 98201 (425) 258-2651.

BLACK BEAR, BEN, Jr.
(museum chairperson)
Affiliation: Buechel Memorial Lakota Museum, 350 S. Oak St., Box 499, St. Francis, SD 57572 (605) 747-2745.

BLACK EAGLE (Shoshone-Yokut)
(craftsperson)
Address: P.O. Box 621, Copperopolis, CA 95228 (209) 785-5259. *Interests:* Orginal Shoshone and Northern Plains style artifacts.

BLACKBIRD, ELMER (Omaha)
(tribal chairperson)
Affiliation: Omaha Tribal Council, P.O. Box 368, Macy, NE 68039 (402) 837-5391.

BLACKEYE, HENRY MICHAEL, JR. (Shoshone)
(tribal chairperson)
Affiliation: Duckwater Shoshone Tribal Council, P.O. Box 140068, Duckwater, NV 89314 (775) 863-0227.

BLACKHAWK, JOHN (Winnebago)
(tribal chairperson)
Affiliation: Winnebago Tribal Council, P.O. Box 687, Winnebago, NE 68071 (402) 878-3103. Website: www.winnebagotribe.com. *Other professional post:* Executive Director, Nebraska State Commission on Indian Affairs, Lincoln, NE.

BLACKJACK, RODDY
(Indian band chief)
Affiliation: Chief, Little Salmon-Carmacks Indian Band, General Delivery, Carmacks, Yukon, Canada Y0B 1C0 (403) 863-5576.

BLACKMAN, BAPTISTE
(Indian band chief)
Affiliation: Cold Lake Indian Band, Box 1769, Grand Centre, Alberta, Canada T0A 1T0 (403) 594-7183.

BLACKOWL, ELIZABETH (Pawnee)
(tribal committee chairperson)
Affiliation: Pawnee Tribal Business Committee, P.O. Box 470, Pawnee, OK 74058 (918) 762-3621.

BLACKWATER, NORMAN (Navajo)
(writer)
Address: P.O. Box 1999, Chinle, AZ 86503 (520) 674-5259 Fax 674-3799.

BLAESER, ROBERT A. (White Earth Ojibwe) 1953-
(attorney)
Born December 31, 1953, White Earth, Minn. *Education:* Concordia College, BA, 1976; University of Minnesota Law School, JD, 1979. *Principal occupation:*

Attorney. *Home address*: Resides in Minneapolis, MN area (612) 338-6825 (work). *Affiliation*: Senior partner, Robert A. Blaeser & Associates, Minneapolis, MN, 1980-. *Other professional posts*: Member, Supreme Court Task Force on Racial Bias in the Courts; Supreme Court Implementation Committee on Diversity & Racial Fairness in the Courts. *Memberships*: Minnesota American Indian Bar Association (board of directors, founding member, and past officer); Minnesota Indian Chamber of Commerce; Minnesota Trial Lawyers Association; American Trial Lawyers Association; American Bar Association; Minnesota State Bar Association (board of governors): Hennepin County Bar Association (governing council). *Interests*: "I practice exclusively in the area of civil litigation, concentrating on products liability, personal injury and Workers' Compensation."

BLAINE, SILAS (Crow Creek Sioux)
(BIA education chairperson)
Affiliation: Bureau of Indian Affairs, Crow Creek/Lower Brule Agency, P.O. Box 139, Fort Thompson, SD 57339 (605) 245-2398.

BLAIR, BILLY
(Indian band chief)
Affiliation: White River Indian Band, Beaver Creek, Yukon Y0B 1A0 (403) 862-7802.

BLAKE, GEORGE N. (Hupa-Yurok)
(craftsperson)
Address: George Blake's Studio, P.O. Box 1304, Hoopa, CA 95546 (916) 625-4619.

BLAKE, GRACE
(Indian band chief)
Affiliation: Chief, Arctic Red River Indian Band, General Delivery, Arctic Red River, Northwest Territories X0E 0B0 (403) 953-3201.

BLANCHARD, VICTOR
(Singing Eagle (Potawatomi)
(poet, teacher)
Address & Affiliation: Dept. of English, Eastern Washington University, MS 25G, Cheney, WA 99004 (509) 359-7081.

BLANCHE, JOHN G., III
(executive staff director)
Affiliation: Indian Law Section, Federal Bar Association, 2215 M St., NW, Washington, DC 20037 (202) 638-0252 Fax 775-0295.

BLANKENSHIP, GERALD RAY (United Lumbee)
(artist)
Address: P.O. Box 58, Avinger, TX 75630 (903) 755-3228 Fax 755-2982. *Military service*: U.S. Army, 1959-61.

BLANKENSHIP, LAWRENCE, Jr.
(historic site manager)
Affiliation: Kolomoki Mounds State Park & Historic Site, Route 1, Box 114, Blakely, GA 31723 (912) 723-5296.

BLATCHFORD, EDGAR P.
(government commissioner)
Affiliation: Alaska Dept. of Community & Regional Affairs, P.O Box 112100, Juneau, AK 99811 (907) 465-4700.

BLAZE, RANDALL (Oglala Sioux)
(art gallery owner)
Affiliation: Contemporary Native American Fine Art, 228 SW 1st, Portland, OR 97204 (503) 224-8101.

BLAZER, ARTHUR L.
(BIA agency supt.)
Affiliation: Mescalero Agency, BIA, P.O. Box 189, Mescalero, NM 88340 (505) 671-4423. *Past professional posts*: Supt., Ute Mountain Ute Agency, BIA, Towaoc, CO; supt., Laguna Agency, BIA, Laguna, NM.

BLEVINS, WIN (Cherokee) 1938-
(novelist, book editor)
Born October 21, 1938, Little Rock, Ark. *Education*: M.A., post-doctoral diploma. *Principal occupation*: Novelist, book editor. *Address*: P.O. Box 223, Bluff, UT 84512 (435) 672-2459 Fax 672-2460. *E-mail*: win@winblevins.com. *Website*: www.winblevins.com. *Memberships*: Wordcraft Circle; Pen-America; West-

ern Writers of America; Mystery Writers of America. *Awards, honors*: Spur Award for best novel of the West, 1996; Mountains and Plains Booksellers Award for Best Fiction, 1996, nominated for Pulitzer Prize for "Stone Song, 1995; Wordcraft Circle Writer of the Year, 2003. *Interests*: Music, biking. *Published works*: 13 books - Give Your Heart to the Hawks; Dictionary of the American West; Stone Song; Raven Shadow; Charbonneau; Misadventures of Silk & Shakespeare; So Wild a Dream, et al.

BLODGETT, JEAN
(museum curator)
Affiliation: Curator of Native Indian and Inuit Art, The McMichael Canadian Art Collection, 10365 Islington Ave., Kleinberg, Ontario L0J 1C0 (416) 893-1121.

BLOMQUIST, P.S.
(editor)
Affiliation: Editor, Char-Koosta, Confederated Salish & Kootenai Tribes, P.O. Box 278, Pablo, MT 59855.

BLONDEAU, MAURICE
(executive director)
Affiliation: Saskatoon Indian & Metis Friendship Centre, 168 Wall St., Saskatoon, Saskatchewan, Canada S7K 1N4 (306) 244-0174.

BLONDIN, ETHEL (Western Arctic)
(parliament member)
Affiliation: Canadian Parliament, Parliament Bldgs., Ottawa, ON K1A 0A4 (613) 992-2848.

BLOSSOM, LESLIE L.
(Indian commission director)
Affiliation: Nevada Indian Commission, 4600 Kietzke Lane #B-116, Reno, NV 89503 (702) 789-0347.

BLUE, BETTY
(editor)
Affiliation: Ini-Mi-Kwa-Zoo-Min, Minnesota Chippewa Tribe, P.O. Box 217, Cass Lake, MN 56633.

BLUE, GILBERT (Catawba)
(tribal chairperson)
Affiliation: Catawba Indian Nation, P.O. Box 188, Rock Hill, SC 29704 (803) 366-4792.

BLUE, HELEN
(editor)
Affiliation: The Circle, Boston Indian Council, 105 S. Huntington Ave., Jamaica Plain, MA 02130 (617) 232-0343.

BLUE EARTH, EMMA JEAN
(BIA special education coordinator)
Affiliation: Standing Rock Agency, Bureau of Indian Affairs, Agency Ave., P.O. Box E, Fort Yates, ND 58538 (701) 854-3497 Fax 854-7280.

BLUE EYES, FAYE
(Indian school director)
Affiliation: Shiprock Northwest High School, Shiprock Alternative Schools, P.O. Box 1799, Shiprock, NM 87420 (505) 368-2070 Fax 368-5102.

BLUE SPRUCE, GEORGE, Jr. *(Fon-Tem-Dey-Sten)*
(Laguna/San Juan Pueblo) 1931-
(Assistant Surgeon General, USPHS {retired})
Born January 16, 1931, Santa Fe, N.M. *Education*: Creighton University, D.D.S., 1956; University of California School of Public Health, M.P.H., 1967; Federal Executive Institute, Certificate, 1973. *Principal occupation*: Health systems director. *Address*: Unknown. *Affiliations*: Dental officer, U.S. Navy Dental Clinic, 1956-58; dental officer, U.S.P.H.S. Indian Hospital, Fort Belknap, MT, 1958-60; U.S.P.H.S. Outpatient Clinic, New York, NY (resident, 1960-61; deputy dental director, 1961-63); resident in dental public health, Dental Health Center, San Francisco, CA, 1967-68; consultant in dental health (special assignment), Pan American Health Organization, World Health Organization, Washington, DC, 1968-70; Education Development Branch, Division of Dental Health, National Institutes of Health, Bethesda, MD - chief, Auxiliary Utilization Section, 1971, special assistant to the director for American Indian Affairs, 1971, director, Office of Health Manpower Opportunity, 1971-73; liaison officer for Indian concerns, Health Resources Administration, USPHS, Dept. of HEW, 1973-74; director,

Office of Native American Programs, Office of Human Development, Dept. of HEW, 1976-78; director, Indian Health Manpower Development, Indian Health Service, DHEW, 1978-79; director & assistant Surgeon General, Phoenix Area Indian Health Service, USPHS, 1979-90; president, Society of American Indian Dentists, 1990-. *Other professional posts*: Chairman, Intra-Departmental Council on Indian Affairs (DHEW); chairman, Health Manpower Opportunity Advisory Committee; chairman, Feasibility Study Team for Project: Center for Health Professions Education (Navajo Reservation, Arizona); special consultant, Special Committee for the Socio-economically Disadvantaged, American Dental Hygienist's Association; regional director, Indian Health Service, USPHS. *Military service*: U.S. Navy, 1956-58 (Navy Citation Medal-dentist for Atomic Submarine "Nautilus" prior to underwater/North Pole journey). *Community activities*: Was on the Phoenix City Council; Phoenix Indian Center Board of Directors; president, North American Indian Tennis Association. *Memberships*: National Indian Education Association (board of directors); Health Education Media Association (board of directors, Minority Affairs); American Indian Bank (board of directors); American Fund for Dental Education (member, Selection Committee); Task Force for Medical Academic Achievement Program; Students American Veterinary Medicine Association (member, Selection Committee; Health Manpower Study for American Indians (member, Advisory Committee); Navajo Health Authority (member, board of commissioners, Kellog Scholarship Committee, Dean Selection Committee, Health Professions Education Committee); American Indian School of Medicine - Feasibility Study (member, Advisory Council); Health Professions Education System, Rockville, MD (board of directors); USPHS Commissioned Officers' Association ; American Public Health Association; American Indian Physicians' Association; American Dental Association; American Association of Dental Schools; New Mexico State Dental Society; North American Indian Tennis Association (president); U.S. Lawn Tennis Association; Society of American Indian Dentists; American Indian Science and Engineering Society. *Awards, honors*: Outstanding American Indian for 1972, American Indian Exposition, Inc., Anadarko, Okla.; Outstanding American Indian Achievement Award, 1974, American Indian Council Fire, Inc., Washington, D.C.; Award of Merit, presented by the Association of American Indian Physicians for: Significant Contributions Towards Raising the Level of Health Care of the American Indian and Alaskan Native, August 1980; Alumni of the Year, presented by Creighton University (Omaha, NE) in May 1984, for his distinguished service to his fellow man and his alma mater while keeping with the finest traditions of the University; Annual Association of American Medical Colleges Award for Health Professional contributing to the health of American Indians; Annual Award for Most Outstanding American Indian Health Professional by the American Indian Science and Engineering Society. *Biographical sources*: American Indians of Today; Contemporary American Indian Leaders; Who's Who in the Federal Government, Second Edition; National Indian Directory (National Congress of American Indians); Dictionary of International Biography; Men of Achievement, 1974; Journal of American Indian Science and Engineering Society, 1986. *Interests*: "Have been visiting instructor on health care administration for St. Francis College (Joliet, IL) and Northern Michigan University (Marquet, MI). Am presently consultant to Federal Government in the review of grants for medical schools and Centers of Excellence in dental and pharmacy schools. *Published works*: Articles: Toward More Minorities in Health Professions (National Medical Association Journal, Sept. 1972); Needed: Indian Health Professionals (Harvard Medical Alumni Bulletin, Jan.-Feb. 1972); Health Manpower Grants Open New Opportunities for American Indians (Official Newsletter of the Assn. of American Indian Physicians, Vol. 1, No. 1, Nov. 1972); The American Indian as a Dental Patient (Public Health Reports, Dec. 1961); The Fabrication of Simplified Dental Equipment - A Manual (Pan American Health Organization Publication, pending publication); Development & Testing of a Mobile Dental Care Unit (Public Health Residency Report).

BLUEHOUSE, MILTON, SR. (Navajo)
(former tribal president)
Affiliation: Navajo Nation, P.O. Box 9000, Window Rock, AZ 86515 (520) 871-6352.

BLUEWOLF, JAMES DON (*Csimu Muppah*)
(Oklahoma Choctaw) 1950-
(ANA language grant executive coordinator)
Born March 19, 1950, in Okla. Principal occupation: ANA language grant executive coordinator. *Address*: 750 North High St., Lakeport, CA 95453 (707) 263-1099. Website: www.anoliscircle.com. *Affiliation*: Big Valley band of Pomo Indians, 11/03 to present. *Other professional posts*: Porucer/programmer of Native music and other on Lake County community radio, KPFZ 104.5 FM. Awards, honors: Poet Laureate of Lake County, Calif. 2002-2003. *Community activities*: Board member, Lucy Moore Foundation; member of KPFZ, Lake County Community Radio. *Membership*: Regional caucus leader for the Wordcraft Circle of Native Writers and Storytellers. *Interests*: Writing, language, radio, music, family. Published works: "Sitting By His Bones," 1999, Earthen Vessel (poetry); "Grandpa Says - Stories for a Seventh Generation," 2000, Earthen Vessell (stories).

BLUMER, THOMAS J. (*Fallsapart*) 1937-
(archivist)
Born July 7, 1937, Freeport, N.Y. *Education*: University of Mississippi, BA, 1967, MA, 1968; University of South Carolina, PhD, 1976. *Principal occupation*: Archivist. *Home address*: P.O. Box 302, Edinburg, VA 22824 (540) 984-3922. E-mail: tblumer@shentel.net. *Affiliations*: Archivist, Laura Virginia Hale Archives, Warren Heritage Society, Front Royal, VA, 2001-present. *Past professional posts*: Assistant professor, Tidewater Community College, Portsmouth, VA, 1968-72; Teaching assistant, University of South Carolina, Columbia, S.C., 1972-76; lecturer in English, Winthrop College, Rock Hill, S.C., 1976-77; Data Analyst, Planning Research Corp., McLean, Va., 1977-78; senior editor, European Law Division, Law Library, Library of Congress, 1978-98; Magsitrate, Virginia Supreme Court, Shenandoah Co., 1998-2001. *Consulting work*: consultant, Native American Rights Fund, Boulder, Colo., 1980-; consultant, McKissick Museums, University of South Carolina, 1984-; consultant, Schiele Museum of Natural History, Gastonia, NC, 1984-; editor, American Indian Libraries Newsletter, American Library Association, Chicago, IL, 1984-87; consultant, Pamunkey Indian Museum, King William, Va., 1985-; historian, Catawba Nation Restoration of Justice Project, Rock Hill, SC, 1989-. *Community activities*: Civilian Conservation Corp. Legacy Board, 2001-04. *Military service*: U.S. Navy, 1956-60. *Memberships*: South Carolina Historical Association, 1986-; Cherokee Indian Historical Association, 1980-; York County Genealogical & Historical Society, 1989-. *Interests*: Southeastern Indians, Catawba Indian history, Pamunkey Indian history, Southern Indian pottery traditions (Catawba, Cherokee, Pamunkey); lectures. *Published works*: Bibliography of the Catawba (Scarecrow Press, 1987); "History as a Tool in a Folklife Study of the Catawba Indians of South Carolina" (New York Journal of Folklore, 1983); "Wild Indians and the Devil: The Contemporary Catawba Indian Spirit World" (American Indian Quarterly, 1985); "Catawba Indian Influence on the Cherokee Indian Pottery Tradition" (Appalachian Journal, 1987); Catawba Indian Perspectives (2003); Catawba Indian Pottery: The Survival of a Folk Tradition (Alabama, 2004); and other articles. *Works in Progress*: , book-length study being revised for publication; Catawba Indian Folk History Project, 1980-; Catawba Indian Design Motifs, book-length study.

BLYTHE, FRANK
(executive director)
Affiliation: Native American Public Telecommunications, 1800 North 33rd St., Lincoln, NE 68583 (402) 472-3522 Fax 472-8675. E-mail: fblythe@nativetelecom.org.

BOATMAN, JOHN
(program coordinator)
Affiliation: Native American Studies Program, College of Letters & Sciences, P.O. Box 413, University of Wisconsin, P.O. Box 413, Milwaukee, WI 53201.

BOB, MARVIN
(Indian band chief)
Affiliation: Chief, Pavilion Indian Band, P.O. Box 609, Cache Creek, British Columbia, Canada V0K 1H0 (604) 256-7415.

BOBBISH, JAMES
(Indian band chief)
Affiliation: Chief, Chisasibi Indian Band, P.O. Box 150, Chisasibi, Quebec, Canada J0M 1E0 (819) 855-2878.

BOBELU, CAROLYN (Zuni-Navajo)
(craftsperson)
Address: 731 Kevin Ct., Gallup, NM 87301 (505) 722-4939. *Product*: Jewelry items.

BOBBY, PHILLIP
(AK village council president)
Affiliation: Lime Village Council, Lime Village, AK 99627 (907) 526-5126.

BODIN, LARRY A.
(BIA agency supt.)
Affiliation: Pine Ridge Agency, Bureau of Indian Affairs, P.O. Box 1203, Pine Ridge, SD 57770 (605) 867-5125 Fax 867-1141.

BODNER, DEBRA
(museum curator, editor)
Affiliation: Curator & editor (Newsletter), Museum of Indian Archaeology, University of Western Ontario, Lawson-Jury Bldg., London, Ontario, Canada N6G 3M6 (519) 473-1360.

BOGDA, TED
(school supt.)
Affiliation: St. Francis Indian School, P.O. Box 379, St. Francis, SD 57572 (605) 747-2299.

BOGGS, DONNA
(administrative coordinator)
Affiliation: Administrative coordinator, American Indian Studies Department, San Diego State University, College Ave., San Diego, CA 92182-0387 (619) 594-6991.

BOHAM, RUSSELL
(program director)
Affiliation: Indian Natural Resource-Science & Engineering Program, Humboldt State University, McMahan House 80, Arcata, CA 95521 (707) 826-4994.

BOHAN, RANAE
(Indian program coordinator)
Affiliation: Native Americans Into Medicine Program, Bemidji State University, 1500 Birchmont Dr. NE, Bemidji, MN 56601 (218) 755-3977.

BOHNEE, GARY (Hopi)
(staff director)
Address & Affiliation: Staff director, U.S. Senate Select Committee on Indian Affairs, 838 Hart Senate Office Bldg., Washington, DC 20510 (202) 224-2251.

BOINTY, GRACE
(librarian)
Affiliation: Kiowa Tribal Library, P.O. Box 369, Carnegie, OK 73015 (405) 654-2300.

BOISSIERE, ROBERT (Giapateu-White Feather) 1914-
(retired, writer)
Born December 23, 1914, France. *Education*: Law School, Paris (three years). *Principal occupation*: Retired, writer. *Home address*: Route 11, Box 6B, Santa Fe, NM 87501 (505) 455-2138. *Military service*: World War II, France (two decorations). *Memberships*: Western Writers of America. *Biographical sources*: Contemporary Authors. *Published works*: Po-Pai-Mo - The Search for White Buffalo Woman (Sunstone Press, 1983); The Hopi Way - An Odyssey (Sunstone Press, 1985); Meditations With the Hopi (Bear and Co., 1986); The Return of Pahana (Bear and Co., 1990).

BOISSONEAU, DARRELL E.
(Indian band chief)
Affiliation: Garden River Indian Band, Site 5, Box 7, RR 4, Garden River, Ontario, Canada P6A 5K9 (705) 942-4011.

BOIVIN, MARCEL
(Indian band chief)
Affiliation: Chief, Bande Indienne de Weymont Achie, Reserve indienne de Weymontachie via Sanmaur, Quebec, Canada G0A 4M0 (819) 666-2237.

BOLTON, ANNE E.
(BIA agency supt.)
Affiliation: Michigan Field Office, Bureau of Indian Affairs, 2901.5 I-75 Business Spur, Sault Ste. Marie, MI 49783 (906) 632-6809 Fax 632-0689.

BOLTON, TOMMY (Choctaw & Lipan Apache) 1949-
(offshore drilling safety representative; tribal chief)
Born August 12, 1949, Converse, La. *Principal occupation*: Offshore drilling safety representative. *Address & Affiliation*: Chief, Choctaw-ApacheCommunity of Ebarb Tribal Council, P.O. Box 858, Zwolle, LA 71486 (318) 645-2744. *Military service*: U.S. Navy, 1968-74 (Republic of Vietnam Service & Republic of Vietnam Campaign). *Community activities*: Deputy, Sabine Parish Sheriff's Dept.; past administrative chief, North Sabine Fire Prot. District; VFW; American Legion.

BOLTON, W. CLIFFORD
(Indian band chief)
Affiliation: Chief, Kitsumkalum Indian Band, House of Sim-Oi-Ghets, P.O. Box 544, Terrace, British Columbia V8G 4B5 (604) 635-6177.

BOLVIN, MARCEL
(Indian band chief)
Affiliation: Attikameks de Weymontachie, Reserve indienne de Weymontachie, Comte Laviolette, Quebec, Canada G0A 4M0 (819) 666-2237.

BOMBERRY, VICTORIA
(editor)
Affiliation: Editor, Native Self-Sufficiency, Seventh Generation Fund, P.O. Box 10, Forestville, CA 95436 (707) 887-1559.

BOMMELYN, LOREN J. (Tolowa)
(ex-rancheria chairperson)
Affiliation: Smith River Rancheria Tribal Council, P.O. Box 239, Smith River, CA 95567 (707) 487-9255.

BOND, ALVIN L. (Nansemond)
(tribal councilperson)
Affiliation: Nansemond Indian Tribal Association, P.O. Box 9293, Chesapeake, VA 23321 (804) 487-5116.

BOND, RODNEY
(school principal)
Affiliation: Lukachukai Boarding School, Navajo Route 12, Lukachukai, AZ 86507 (520) 787-2301 Fax 787-2311.

BOND, THOMAS
(BIA director)
Affiliation: Office of American Indian Trust, Bureau of Indian Affairs, Dept. of the Interior, MS-4513-MIB, 1849 C St., NW, Washington, DC 20240 (202) 208-3338.

BONE, RANDY
(Indian band chief)
Affiliation: Keeseekoowenin Indian Band, Box 100, Elphinstone, Manitoba, Canada R0J 0N0 (204) 625-2004.

BONE, ROBERT J.
(Indian band chief)
Affiliation: Sioux Valley Indian Band, Box 38, Griswold, Manitoba, Canada R0M 0S0 (204) 855-2671.

BONGA, DAVID C. (Minnesota Chippewa-White Earth) 1952-
(institute president)
Born June 23, 1952, Monroe, Wash. *Education*: Dartmouth College, B.A., 1974; Gonzaga Law School, J.D., 1982. *Principal occupation*: Institute president. *Home address*: So. 1915 Pierce, Spokane, WA 99206 (509) 445-1147 (work). *Affiliations*: President, Camas Institute, Kalispel Indian Tribe, Usk, WA, 2003-present. *Other professional post*: Judge pro-tem for Spokane, Colville, Coeur d'Alene, Nez Perce and Quinault Indian tribes; magistrate for Kalispel Tribe; guest lecturer, Eastern Washington University, Indian Studies Department, Cheney, WA. *Past professional post*: Tribal planner; in-house counsel, Kalispel Indian Tribe, Usk, WA, 1985-2003. *Memberships*: Washington State Bar Association; Northwest Tribal Judges Association; Intercollegiate Center for Nursing (Native American Advisory Council); University of Idaho President Advisory Council for Native American Studies; Board of

Directors, Gonzaga University Legal Assistance. *Interests*: History & Indian law.

BONNETROUGE, JOACHIM
(Indian band chief)
Affiliation: Fort Providence (Yahti Dewe K'O) Dene Indian Band, General Deliver, Fort Providence, Northwest Territories, Canada X0E 0J0 (403) 699-3401.

BONNEY, CARLA K.
(director-health center)
Affiliation: Tanana Health Center, P.O. Box 93, Tanana, AK 99777 (907) 366-7160.

BONNEY, RACHEL A. 1939-
(professor of anthropology)
Born March 28, 1939, St. Paul, Minn. *Education*: University of Minnesota, B.A., 1961, M.A., 1963; University of Arizona, Ph.D., 1975. *Principal occupation*: Professor of anthropology. *Address*: Dept. of Sociology & Anthropology, University of North Carolina, Charlotte, NC 28223 (704) 687-2252; E-mail: rabonney@email. uncc.edu. *Affiliations*: Assistant professor, Tarkio College, Mo., 1965-67; instructor, University of South Florida, 1967-70; graduate teaching associate, University of Arizona, 1971-73; instructor & professor, University of North Carolina at Charlotte, 1973-. *Other professional posts*: Teacher, guidance, B.I.A., Teec Nos Pos Boarding School, Ariz. (Navajo), 1964. *Community activities*: Charlotte-Mecklenburg Title IV (Indian Education Act) Indian Parent Committee (ex-officio member, 1975-77); Metrolina Native American Association, Charlotte, N.C.; UNCC Phoenix Society (American Indian Student Organization) and Phoenix Dancer (Indian dance team), (advisor). *Memberships*: American Anthropological Association (Fellow) 1963-; American Ethnological Society, 1967-71, 1977-; Southern Anthropological Association, 1973-; National Congress of American Indians, 1972-73; Anthropological Council on Education, 1977-; National Indian Education Association, 1977-; Southeastern Indian Cultural Association, 1977-. *Awards, honors*: HEW Title IX (ethnic heritage studies) Project Grant, 1977-78. *Interests*: Indian studies; multi-ethnic studies; culture change (Catawba land claims case); Indian powwows; powwows with Phoenix Dancers; archaeological projects in Minnesota, New York, New Mexico, and Austria. *Biographical sources*: Who's Who in America - The South (Marquis). Published works: American Indian Studies in the Social Studies Curriculum (Proceedings, North Carolina Association for Research in Education, May, 1975); The Role of Women in Indian Activism (The Western Canadian Journal of Anthropology, Vol. VI, No. 3, 1976); The Role of AIM Leaders in Indian Nationalism (American Indian Quarterly, Vol. 3, No. 3, 1977); Indians of the Americas, Courtship Customs (Encyclopedia of Indians of the Americas, Scholarly Press, 1978); among others.

BONNICHSEN, ROBSON
(center director)
Affiliation: Center for the Study of the First Americans, Oregon State U., Corvallis, OR 97331 (503) 737-4515.

BOOMER, MAE
(Indian band chief)
Affiliation: Ashcroft Indian Band, P.O. Box 440, Ashcroft, BC, Canada V0K 1A0 (604) 453-9154.

BOONE, TERESA (Muckleshoot)
(Indian school principal)
Affiliation: Muckleshoot Tribal School, 39015 172nd Ave., SE, Auburn, WA 98002 (206) 931-6709.

BOOL, HERBERT
(museum president)
Affiliation: The Heard Museum, 22 E. Monte Vista Rd., Phoenix, AZ 85004 (602) 252-8840.

BORAAS, DR. ALAN
(professor of anthropology)
Affiliation: Dept. of Anthropology, University of Alaska, 3211 Providence Dr., Anchorage, AK 99508 (907) 786-6840 Fax 786-6850. *Interests*: Athapaskan prehistory and ethnohistory. E-mail: ifasb@uaa.alaska.edu.

BORDEAUX, CHRIS
(association president)
Affiliation: South Dakota Indian Education Association, P.O. Box 2019, Pine Ridge, SD 57770 (605) 867-5633.

BORDEAUX, DR. LIONEL
(college president)
Affiliation: Sinte Gleska College, P.O. Box 490, Rosebud, SD 57570-0490 (605) 747-2263 Fax 747-2098.

BORDEAUX, ROGER C. (Rosebud Sioux) 1952-
(tribal school supt.)
Born August 20, 1952, Valentine, Neb. *Education*: University of South Dakota, BA, 1974, MA, 1988, Ed.D., 1990. *Principal occupation*: Tribal school supt. *Address & Affiliations*: Executive director, Association of Community Tribal Schools, Inc., 616 4th Ave. W., Sisseton, SD 57262, 1976-present. *Past professional posts*: Teacher, director, St. Francis Indian School, St. Francis, SD, 1980-90; supt., Tiospa zina Tribal School, P.O. Box 719, Agency Village, SD 57262, 1991-present. *Memberships*: South Dakota Indian Education Association. *Awards, honors*: M.A. Student of the Year, 1988, University of South Dakota. *Interests*: Golf, softball, fishing.

BOSTROM, MARGUERITA
(tribal education chairperson)
Affiliation: Puyallup Nation Education System, 1850 E. Alexander Ave., Tacoma, WA 98421 (206) 593-0218.

BOTHWELL, NORA
(Indian band chief)
Affiliation: Alderville Indian Band, RR #4, Roseneath, Ontario, Canada K0K 2X0 (416) 352-2011.

BOTT, JOHN
(editor)
Affiliation: Southwestern Association of Indian Affairs, "Quarterly," Roswell Printing Co., 110 N. Pennsylvania, Roswell, NM 88201 (505) 983-5220.

BOUCHA, HENRY C. (*O'Git'chi'Dah*)
(Ojibway) 1951-
(Indian education director, realtor)
Born June 1, 1951, Warroad, Minn. *Education*: University of Detroit (general business courses); Fond du Lac Community College (Title IX workshops & Johnson O'Malley Workshop) 1993. *Principal occupation*: Indian education coordinator, realtor. *Home address*: 314 Minnesota Ave., NE, Warroad, MN 56763 (218) 386-2834 Fax 386-2430. *E-mail*: henryboucha@means. net. *Affiliations*: Real estate agent, Pahlen Realty, Roosevelt, MN 1986-; Indian education director, Warroad Public Schools, Warroad, MN, 1993-. *Other professional posts*: Former National Hockey League player with the Detroit Red Wings & Minnesota North Stars, 1972-75; Hockey coach for Warroad High School, 1989-; Pacific Northwest Hockey School, Lynwood, WA, 1993-. *Military service*: U.S. Army, 1970-72. *Community activities*: Minnesota Indian Education Board of Directors, 1993-95; advisory board - Warroad Community Education; Minnesota's Planning, Evaluation, and Reporting Board; USA's Diversity Hockey Task Force's Board; Warroad's First Nation Board of Directors; chairperson, Warroad's Annual Traditional Pow Wow (1st weekend in June); chair, Kah-Bay-Kah-Nong, Inc. (non-profit to help young people); chair, United Fund of Roseau County, Inc. (non-profit to help people of Roseau County). *Memberships*: U.S. Olympic Alumni; U.S. National Coaches Association; Detroit Red Wings & Minnesota North Stars Alumni; NHL Players Association Alumni; Minnesota Realtors' Association; National Association of Realtors. *Awards, honors*: 1970 World Hockey Championships - Gold Medal; First American Indian inducted into the U.S. Hockey Hall of Fame, Sept. 16, 1995; honored by the American Indian College Scholarship Fund in Sept. 1995; honored at Gathering of the Nations in Albuquerque, NM as one of ten American Indians ever to play in the Olympics; 1973 Detroit Red Wings Rookie of the Year, broke a 41 year old NHL record, scoring the fastest goal at the start of a NHL game on Jan. 23, 1973; Olympic Silver Medalist, Ice Hockey, Sapporo, Japan in 1972; U.S. National Hockey Teams, 1970 & 1971; inducted into the Warroad Warrior Sports Hall of Fame 1995; number #16 Warroad Warrior Hockey jersey retired. *Interests*: Golf, guitar, fishing, hunting, boating, travel, mountains. *Biographical source*: Subject of an Autobiography, "Henry Boucha, Star of the North," by Mary Halverson Schofield (Snowshoe Press, 2000).

BOUCHARD, AIME
(Indian band chief)
Affiliation: Pays Plat Indian Band, Box 819, Screiber, Ontario, Canada P0T 2S0 (807) 824-2541.

BOUCHARD, RICK
(clinic director)
Affiliation: American Indian Free Clinic, 9500 E. Artesia Blvd., Bellflower, CA 90708 (310) 920-7272.

BOUCHER, FRANK
(Indian band chief)
Affiliation: Red Bluff Indian Band, 1515 Arbutus Rd., Box 4693, Quesnel, British Columbia, Canada V2J 3J9 (604) 747-2900.

BOUCHIER, JIMMY LEONARD
(Indian band chief)
Affiliation: Chief, Fort McKay Indian Band, P.O. Box 5360, Fort McMurray, Alberta, Canada T9H 3G4 (403) 828-4220.

BOULAND, GREGG J. (Cheyenne River Sioux)
(tribal chairperson)
Affiliation: Cheyenne River Sioux Tribal Council, P.O. Box 590, Eagle Butte, SD 57625 (605) 964-4155.

BOULE, MARY NULL
(author, publisher)
Address: c/o Merryant Publishers, Inc., 7615 SW 257th St., Vashon Island, WA 98070 (206) 463-3879 Fax 463-1604. *Affiliations*: California elementary school teacher for 27 years. *Community activities*: Church musician; Island Singers. *Published works*: The Missions: California's Heritage, and The California Native American Tribes; both are written at the 3rd to 5th grade reading level and published by Merryant Publishers; Mission Series (21 vols.); Native American Series (26 vols.).

BOURLAND, GREGG J. (*Wanbli Awanyankapi*)
(Cheyenne River Sioux) 1956-
(tribal chairperson)
Born December 22, 1956, Ash Butte, S.D. *Education*: Black Hills State University, BS. *Principal occupation*: Tribal chairperson. *Affiliation*: Cheyenne River Sioux Tribe, P.O. Box 590, Eagle Butte, SD 57625 (605) 964-4155 Fax 964-4151. *E-mail*: eaglwatc@rapidnet.com. *Other professional posts*: The Lakota O'Tipi Group Home in the early 1980s working with children on the reservation; along with his wife Kay, opened one of the only reservation Indian owned businesses in 1985, a video business called Kay's Video World. *Community activities*: Chairman, Cheyenne River Sioux Tribe Industrial Business Development Committee; chairman, Tribal Tax Commision; board member, South Dakota Rural Development Association; board member, Aberdeen Area Tribal Chairman's Health Board; secretary treasurer, Great Plains Tribal Chairmans Association; board member, American Indian Research & Policy Institute; board member, Trustees Presentation College; chairman, Intertribal Monitoring Association on Indian Trust Funds; member of national Indian Policy Center - National Governance Task Force; board member, Morning Star Foundation; board member, Northwest Area Foundation. *Awards, honors*: Served as the only Chairman of the AATCHB Task Force on Health Care Reform; served on Hillary Clinton's panel on health care reform; chosen by his fellow tribal leaders to speak at the White House Tribal Leaders Summit with President Clinton, VP, Al Gore, and the entire Clinton Cabinet on April 29, 1994. He is in constant demand throughout Indian Country and the Nation as a speaker at various functions. He has authored various congressional bills and various congressional appropriations requests.

BOUSCHOR, BERNARD (Chippewa)
(tribal chairperson)
Affiliation: Sault Ste. Marie Chippewa Tribal Council, 523 Ashmun St., Sault Ste. Marie, MI 49783 (906) 635-6050.

BOWANNIE, MARY
(radio host/producer)
Affiliation: "Indian Voices," KGNU 88.5 FM - Public Radio, P.O. Box 885, Boulder, CO 80306 (800) 737-3030.

BOWECHOP, JANINE (Makah)
(tribal enterprise manager)
Affiliation: Makah Cultural Research Center, P.O. Box 160, Neah Bay, WA 98357 (360) 645-2711 or 645-2712.

BOWEKATY, MALCOLM (Zuni Pueblo)
(pueblo governor)
Affiliation: Zuni Pueblo Tribal Governor, P.O. Box 339, Zuni, NM 87327 (505) 782-4481.

BOWEN, DUWAYNE LESLIE *(Dah-dah-wen-yae)*
(Seneca) 1946-
(museum management)
Born July 7, 1946, Salamanca, N.Y. *Education*: Vale Technical Institute (Blairsville, PA), diploma, 1966; Jamestown (NY) Community College. *Principal occupation*: Museum management. *Home address*: RD Box 71J, Salamanca, NY 14779 (716) 945-2260. *Affiliation*: Seneca-Iroquois National Museum, Salamanca, NY, 1990-. *Community activities*: American Red Cross, Salamanca, NY; Red House Indian Chapel, Jimersontown-Salamanca, NY (trustee); Red House Memorial Church, Jimersontown-Salamanca, NY (secretary-treasurer). *Membership*: Cornplanter Descendants Association, Allegany Indian Reservation-Salamanca, NY (chairperson, 1990-), *Interests*: Local church; museum/history of Seneca people; public speaker on subjects of Iroquois history; professional storyteller of ghost stories/supernatural; movies/stage/ literary. *Published works*: Anthology, New Voices From the Longhouse (Greenfield Review Press, 1990); contributor, A Quaker Promise Kept (Spencer Butte Press, 1990); One More Story (Bowman Books, 1991); short story, "He-Sees-Good" (Akew:kon-Northeast Indian Quarterly, 1991).

BOYD, MERLE (Sac & Fox)
(tribal second chief)
Affiliation: Sac & Fox Nation, Rte. 2, Box 246, Stroud, OK 74079 (918) 968-3526.

BOYD, STANLEY
(Indian band chief)
Affiliation: Nazko Indian Band, Box 4534, Quesnel, British Columbia, Canada V2J 3H8 (604) 992-9810.

BOYD, WILLIAM SONNY *(Crazybull)*
(Assiniboine & Sioux)
(chief, tribal president)
Address: Address unknown. *Affiliations*: Chief-President, Assiniboine & Sioux Tribe, Fort Peck Reservation, Poplar, MT; McKensie River Foundation; president, "Inipi O'yate'ki" - Native American Club, Salem, OR.

BOYER, LEE R. 1938-
(Professor/author, U.S. Indian history)
Born June 1, 1938, Aliquippa, PA. *Education*: Mount Union College, BA, 1959; University of Notre Dame, MA, 1969, PhD, 1972; University of New Mexico, Indian law student, 1978-79; Plains Indian Museum, Indian studies seminar, 1981. *Home address*: 2691 Matteson Lake, Bronson, MI 49028 (313) 487-0053. *Affiliation*: Professor of history, Eastern Michigan University, Ypsilanti, MI, 1972-. *Other professional posts*: Assistant professional specialist, University of Notre Dame, (3 years). *Memberships*: American Association of University Professors; National Council for the Social Studies; Michigan Council for the Humanities. *Awards, honors*: Research grant, Merit award, Eastern Michigan University; experienced Teacher Fellowship, Department of H.E.W. *Interests*: Travel and research to Western states; Federal Indian Reservations - sabbatical study; Neah Bay archaeological dig. *Published works*: Episodes in American History (Ginn, 1972); U.S. Indians: A Brief History (Advocate, 1982).

BOYER, LIONEL (Shoshone-Bannock)
(tribal chairperson)
Affiliation: Fort Hall Business Council, P.O. Box 306, Fort Hall, ID 83203 (208) 238-3700.

BOYER, ROBERT
(Indian fine arts instructor)
Affiliation: Instructor, Indian Fine Arts, Saskatchewan Indian Federated College, University of Regina, 118 College West, Regina, Saskatchewan, Canada S4S 0A2 (306) 584-8333.

BOYIDDLE, LORRAINE (Navajo)
(Indian school principal)
Affiliation: Chinle Boarding School, P.O. Box 70, Many Farms, AZ 86538 (602) 781-6221.

BOYLE, REC. ROBERT J., S.J.
(site director)
Affiliation: Kateri Galleries, The National Shrine of North American Martyrs, Auriesville, NY 12016 (518) 853-3033.

BOZSUM, BRUCE (*Two Dogs*) (Mohegan)
(tribal program manager)
Affiliation: Manager, Cultural & Community Programs, Mohegan Tribe, 5 Crow Hill Rd., Uncasville, CT 06382 (860) 862-6100 Fax 862-6162

BRADBY, MARVIN (*Strong Oak*) (Chickahominy)
(tribal chief)
Affiliation: Chief. Eastern Chickahominy Indian Tribe, 12111 Indian Hill Lane, Providence Forge, VA 23140 (804) 966-2719.

BRADLEY, CARMEN (Paiute)
(tribal chairperson; organization chairperson)
Affiliation: Kaibab Paiute Tribal Council, HC65, Box 2, Fredonia, AZ 86022 (928) 643-7245. *Other professional post*: Chairperson, Council of Energy Resource Tribes (CERT), 695 S. Colorado Blvd., Suite 10, Denver, CO 80202 (303) 282-7576. E-mail: cert1975@aol. com. Website: www.certredearth.com.

BRADLEY, JACQUELYN (Eastern Cherokee)
(craftspersons' coop manager)
Affiliation: Qualla Arts & Crafts Mutual, Inc., P.O. Box 310, Cherokee, NC 28719 (704) 497-3103.

BRADY, KEVIN (Shoshone)
(former tribal chairperson)
Affiliation: Yomba Tribal Council, HC61, Box 6275, Austin, NV 89310 (702) 964-2463.

BRAFFORD, C.J. (*Kimimi La*) (Oglala Lakota Sioux/ Northern Cheyenne) 1959-
(museum director)
Born October 11, 1959, Pine Ridge Indian Reservation, S.D. *Education*: AFA, BS, Master's Certificate in Museum Studies/Anthropology. *Principal occupation*: Museum director. *Address & Affiliation*: Director, Ute Indian Museum, 17253 Chipeta Rd., Montrose, CO 81401 (970) 249-3098. E-mail: cj.brafford@state. co.us. *Past affiliation*: Museum curator, Grand Teton National Park Service, 1988-96. *Commuity activities*: Board member of the Visitor Convention Bureau. *Memberships*: American Indian Museum Association. *Published work*: "Dancing Colors," Paths of Native American Women.

BRAFFORD, HAROLD
(BIA agency supt.)
Affiliation: Central California Agency, Bureau of Indian Affairs, 1824 Tribute Rd., Suite J, Sacramento, CA 95815 (916) 566-7121.

BRAIN, JEFFREY PHIPPS 1940-
(archaeologist)
Born January 4, 1940, New York, N.Y. *Education*: Harvard University, BA, 1961; Yale University, MPhil, 1969, PhD, 1969. *Principal occupation*: Archaeologist. *Home address*: 25 Ridgeway, Needham, MA 02492 (978) 740-3624 (work). *Affiliation*: Peabody Museum, Harvard University, Cambridge, MA, & Peabody Essex Museum, Salem, MA (25 years). *Military service*: U.S. Navy (Lt.), 1962-65). *Memberships*: Society for American Archaeology; Society for Historical Archaeology; Archaeological Institute of America; Southeastern Archaeological Conference (past vice-president and president); and various state archaeological societies. *Awards, honors*: The John M. Goggin Award for Method & Theory in Historical Archaeology (Conference for Historic Sites Archaeology); "I am a descendant of Pocahontas." *Interests*: Indians of North America. *Published works*: Tunica Treasure (Peabody Museum, Harvard, 1979); Excavations at Lake George (Peabody Museum, Harvard, 1983); Tunica Archaeology (Peabody Museum, Harvard, 1988); Winterville (Mississippi Archives & History, 1989); The Tunica-Biloxi (Chelsea House Publishers, 1990); Shell Gorgets (Peabody Museum, Harvard, 1996); The Popham Colony (Maine Archaeological Society, 2003).

BRAINARD, RON (Umpqua & Suislaw)
(tribal chairperson)
Affiliation: Confederated Tribes of Coos, Lower Umpqua & Suislaw Indians, 1245 Fulton Ave., Coos Bay, OR 97420 (541) 888-9577.

BRAINE, SUSAN
(project manager)
Affiliation: American Indian Radio on Satellite, P.O. Box 83111, Lincoln, NE 68501 (402) 472-9333.

BRAMLETTE, ALLAN (Cora-Cherokee-Choctaw)
(archaeologist/heritage resource specialist)
Education: Sonoma State University, BA, 1981, MA, 1989. *Principal occupation*: Archaeologist/heritage resource specialist. *Address*: The Center for Community Development, Graves Annex #30, Humboldt State University, Arcata, CA 95521 (707) 826-3711. *Affiliations*: Senior staff archaeologist, Anthropological Studies Center, Sonoma State University (2 years); currently - archaeologist/heritage resource specialist, The Center for Community Development, Humboldt State University. Mr. Bramlette provides archaeological consultancy and cultural resource management assistance to Northern California Indian communities. He provides technical training in development and management of cultural exhibits, interpretive programs & museum collections & facilities. He also serves as liaison between local Indian communities and the professional archaeologists and other heritage resource personnel who work in Northern California. *Other professional post*: Teaches four courses per year in archaeology-related topics in Native American Studies Dept. of Humboldt State University. *Membership*: Society for California Archaeology.

BRANDOW, CRAIG
(school principal)
Affiliation: Na'Neelzhiin Ji' Olta' (Torreon) Boarding School, HCR 79, Box 9, Cuba, NM 87013 (505) 731-2333 Fax 731-2361.

BRANDT, EDWARD N., II (Chickasaw)
(attorney)
Address: 820 Spyglass Cir., Louisville, CO 80027. *Membership*: Native American Bar Association (First Amendment Bar Association of Texas Representative).

BRANDT, DR. ELIZABETH A.
(anthropological linguist)
Born October 20, 1945, Sanford, Fla. *Education*: Florida State University, BA, 1967; Southern Methodist University, MA, 1969, PhD, 1970. *Principal occupation*: Anthropological linguist. *Home address*: 1810 S. Roberts Rd., Tempe, AZ 85281 (602) 965-6213 (office). E-mail: betsy.brandt@asu.edu. *Affiliations*: University of Illinois, Chicago, 1970-74; Dept. of Anthropology, Arizona State University, Tempe, 1974-present. *Community activities*: AZ Humanities Council (board member); American Indian Institute, ASU (director); ASU American Indian Summer Seminars in the Humanities *Memberships*: Linguistics Society of America, Society for Applied Anthropology, Keepers of the Treasures, 1991; Society for the Study of Indigenous Languages of the Americas; Native American Language Issues Institute. *Interests*: "Assist tribes and traditional elders in researching and preparing nominations to National Register for Traditional Cultural Properties, sacred sites protection, land claims, language presentation and renewal." *Biographical source*: Who's Who in the West. *Published works*: Speaking, Singing & Teaching, Arizona State University Press, 1979); Bilingualism & Language Contact (Teachers College Press, 1980); Navajo Students At Risk (Navajo Nation, 1986).

BRANHAM, ANNA "SPEAKSWELL" (Catawba)
(craftsperson; company owner)
Affiliation: Catawba Indian Traditions, Pottery and Beadwork, Catawba Indian Nation, 2234 Indian Trail, Rock Hill, SC 29730 (803) 366-3317. *Products*: Traditional Catawba pottery and loom beading.

BRANHAM, KENNETH (Monacan)
(tribal council chairperson)
Affiliation: Monacan Tribal Council, P.O. Box 1136, Madison Heights, VA 24572 (804) 946-0389.

BRANHAM, MONTY "HAWK" (Catawba)
(craftsperson; company owner)
Affiliation: Catawba Indian Traditions, Pottery and Beadwork, Catawba Indian Nation, 2234 Indian Trail, Rock Hill, SC 29730 (803) 366-3317. *Products*: Traditional Catawba pottery and loom beading.

BRANHAM, RONNIE L. (Monacan)
(tribal chief)
Affiliation: Monacan Indian Tribe, P.O. Box 1136, Madison Heights, VA 24572 (804) 929-6911.

BRANNAN, RICHARD (Arapahoe)
(tribal council chairperson)
Affiliation: Shoshone & Arapahoe Joint Tribal Business Council, P.O. Box 217, Fort Washakie, WY 82514.

BRANTLEY, WILLA
(tribal education administrator)
Affiliation: Tribal Council of the Mississippi Band of Choctaws, P.O. Box 6010, Philadelphia, MS 39350 (601) 656-5251.

BRASHEAR, CHARLES R. (Cherokee) 1930-
(retired professor of English; writer)
Born December 11, 1930, Martin County, Tex. *Education*: Denver University, PhD, 1962. *Principal occupation*: Retired professor of English, writer. *Address*: 1718 Arroyo Sierra Circle, Santa Rosa, CA 95405-7762 (707) 545-3903. E-mail: brashear@mail.sdsu.edu. *Affiliation*: San Diego State University (retired, 1992). *Military service*: U.S. Army, 1953-55. *Memberships*: Wordcraft Circle of Native American Writers; The Writer's League of Texas; California Writers Club; Western Writers of America. *Interests*: Travel, writing, genealogy. *Published works*: The Other Side of Love, 2 novellas (Alan Swallow, 1963); A Snug Little Purchase, How Richard Henderson Bought Kaintuckee from the Cherokees in 1775 (Associated Creative Writers, 1979); Contemporary Insanities (Press of MacDonald & Reineke, 1990); Killing Cynthia Ann, a novel (Texas Christian University Press, 1999); Comeuppance at Kicking Horse Casino, and Other Stories (UCLA, American Indian Studies, 2000).

BRASS, ALPHEUS
(Indian band chief)
Affiliation: Chief, Chemawawin First Nation Band, Easterville, Manitoba, Can. R0C 0V0 (204) 329-2161.

BRASWELL, DAVID L.
(school principal)
Affiliation: Wingate Elementary School, P.O. Box 1, Fort Wingate, NM 87316 (505) 488-6470.

BRATT, BENJAMIN (Quechua)
(actor, producer)
Affiliation: Narrated & produced, "Ghost Riders," (2003) directed by V. Blackhawk Aamodt (Blackfoot/lakota/Mexican) which documents the participation of Lakota elders and youth in the Bigfoot Memorial Ride, a 300-mile journey on horseback to honor those massacred at Wounded Knee.

BRAUCHLI, ROBERT C. 1945-
(attorney)
Born November 11, 1945, Morristown, N.J. *Education*: American University, BA, 1967; Howard University Law School, JD, 1970. *Principal occupation*: Attorney. *Home address*: 5800 N. Campbell Ave., Tucson, AZ 85718. E-mail: aztuc158@aol.com. *Office address*: 6650 N. Oracle Rd., Suite 110, Tucson, AZ 85704 (520) 742-2191 Fax 742-2179. *Affiliations*: General counsel, Cibecue Community School, Cibecue, AZ on Fort Apache Indian Reservation, 1981-present; tribal attorney and/or special counsel, White Mountain Apache Tribe, Whiteriver, AZ, 1980-87, 1990-present; General Counsel, Tohono O'odham Community College, Sells, AZ, 1999-present. *Past professional posts*: Maricopa County Legal Aid Society, Phoenix & Tempe, AZ, 1970-73; Deputy County Attorney, Pima County, AZ, 1973-78; director, Consumer Fraud Division, Assistant Attorney General, 1978-80; tribal attorney and/or special counsel, Pascua Yaqui Tribe of Arizona, Tucson, 1988-96; *Awards, honors*: Reginald Heber Smith Fellow, 1970-72. *Memberships*: State Bar of AZ, Indian Law Section, 1990-. *Awards, honors*: Arizona Bar Foundation, State Bar of AZ. *Interests*: Hobbies include: skiing, fishing, hiking, travel, and reading.

BRAUKER, SHIRLEY M. (*Moon Bear*) (Odawa) 1950-
(potter, painter, sculptor, print maker)
Born August 11, 1950, Angola, Ind. *Education*: Mid-Michigan Community College, AA, 1979; Central Michigan University, BFA, 1981, MA, 1983; attended the Institute of American Indian Art, Santa Fe, 1990. *Principal occupation*: Potter, painter, sculptor. *Home address*: 1048 Silver Rd., Coldwater, MI 49036 (517) 238-5833 (work) E-mail: moonbear@cbpu.com. *Affiliations*: Secretary, Central Michigan University, 1982-88; taught pottery at continuing education and aboard the traveling "Art Train", 1983; worked on documentary film, "Woodland Traditions - 3 Native Americans", 1983; lectured at Delta College on Native American Art, 1992; participated in Native American Women Artists of the Great Lakes - The Kellogg Project, 1993; owner, Moon Bear Pottery, Coldwater, Mich. *Other professional post*: Teaching art appreciation course at Tri-State University, Angola, IN. *Memberships*: National Collegiate Education of Ceramics; National Honor Society; Phi Kappa Phi; Sisters of the Great Lakes (Indian women artists). *Art Exhibitions*: Bachelor of Fine Arts, Central Michigan University, 1981; Great Lakes Traveling Indian Art Exhibition, Dept. of the Interior, Washington, DC, 1983; Ethnic Art Show, Lansing Art Gallery, 1983; Sacred Circle Gallery, Seattle, WA, American Indian Ceramic Art; Yesterday, Today and Tomorrow Exhibit, 1984; Midland Christmas Arts Festival, 1984; Museum of the Plains Indian, Browning, MT, Contemporary Clay Indian Art exhibit, 1985; Larson Gallery, Grand Rapids, MI; the Hummingbird Gallery at Soaring Eagle Casino, Mt. Pleasant, Mich., the Kalamazoo Valley Art Museum Project "Sky Legends of the 3 Fires" - art donations to Diabetes Association, Santa Fe, 1995-98; Synchronicity Gallery, 2001 Glenn Arbor, MI 1999-01; Indigenous Art Market, 2000, 2001 (Mt. Pleasant, Mich.); Elderhostel Workshop 2001; exhibit: University of Michigan Hospital vistor's gallery, Ann Arbor. *Memberships*: Southwest American Indian Arts; Michigan University Alumni Association. *Awards, honors*: Outstanding Community College Student Scholarship Award, 1980; Mae Beck Indian Artist Scholarship Award, 1982; Potter of the Month, Lansing Art Gallery, 1983; numerous awards for pottery, 1995-98; 3rd Place-Pottery & Honorable Mention, Dayton, OH Indian Market; 1st Place in Pottery at Red Earth, Oklahoma City, OK, 1996; numerous awards & prizes at Santa Fe, NM Indian Market, 1996-01; showed at Heard Museum, Phoenix, AZ, 1996; received "Top 100 Alumni" to attend C.M.U. in last 100 years. *Interests*: Indian history, culture and art work; craft work, doll making, quilting, painting, beadwork; travel and guitar - writing children's stories; grant recipient from Kellogg Foundation "25 Native American Women Artists of the Great Lakes" - traveling show & workshops - spanning one year...ending up at the Field Museum, Chicago, IL; Smithsonian Institute; presenter at the First Annual Story Festival, Central Michigan University, Mt. Pleasant, MI, "Story in Sculpture"; 2md & 3rd place, Santa Fe, NM Indian Market, 2003. *Biographical sources*: Documentary film: Woodland Traditions: The Art of Three Native Americans; American Indian Index; Southwest Art Magazine, "Emerging Artists," 1996; and "The Traveler's Guide to American Art"; Who's Who of International Professionals.

BRAVE EAGLE, DOROTHY (*Mani wakan win*)
(Oglala Lakota) 1940-
(BIA officer-retired)
Born April 18, 1940, Red Water Creek, S.D. *Education*: Western Colorado University, BS, 1972, MA, 1974. *Principal occupation*: Administrative Officer. *Home address*: 7892 W. 1st Pl., Lakewood, CO 80226 (303) 238-3420 Fax 238-0323. *Affiliations*: Supt., Bureau of Indian Affairs, Crow Creek Agency, Fort Thompson, SD, 1986-91; administrative officer, Bureau of Indian Affairs, Golden, CO.,1991-95; *Other professional posts*: Owner, B.E.A.R. Publishing Co.; Director, Denver Indian Center. *Community activities*: Lakota Arts creator, instructor and presenter; Instructor, White Buffalo Council, officer - March Pow-wow committee. *Memberships*: American Indian Traders Guild; Roaming Buffalo Indian Arts; President of the Board, Wiconni Waste "Beautiful Life" (non-profit educational corporation for American Indian culture, history). *Awards, honors*: Selected to display traditional Lakota arts at Santa Fe Indian Market. *Interests*: Traveled to France, Germany, Belgium, and England to display Lakota Arts; mother of twin daughters, three grandchildren and one great grandson. *Published work*: Ehanamani (walks among) (B.E.A.R., 1992).

BRAVE HEART, BASIL (Oglala Sioux)
(school administrator)
Born October 5, 1933, Pine Ridge, S.D. *Education*: Chadron State College, BS, 1957; University of Minnesota, MA, 1976; St. Marys Graduate Center, Minneapolis, MA (Psychology & Counseling), 1986. *Principal occupation*: School administrator. *Home address*: Box 83, White Clay, NE 69365 (605) 867-5121 (office). *Affiliations*: Member, Board of Directors, South Dakota Educational TV, Pierre, S.D. (1 year); National Alcohol & Drug Program, Washington, D.C. (3 years); Agency Supt. for Education, BIA, Pine Ridge, SD, 1988-. *Military service*: U.S. Paratroopers - 187 Regimental Combat Team (11th Airborne Diov. Korea, 1951-54; Combat Infantry Badge, Airborne Wings, 3 Combat Citations). *Community activities*: Pine Ridge, SD YMCA Board. *Awards, honors*: Superior Performance Award, by HUD for efforts during the 1972 flood, Rapid City, SD. *Interests*: Travel, Far East & Korea; Korean conflict, 1951-54. *Biographical sources*: Circle of Life; Teacher Handbook on Cultural Orientation, Minneapolis School System.

BRAY, ETHEL E. (Seneca)
(library director)
Affiliation: The Seneca Nation Library, 1490 Rte. 438, Irving, NY 14081 (716) 532-9449.

BRAYBOY, ANNIE
(IHS treatment center director)
Affiliation: Phoenix/Tucson Area Adolescent Regional Treatment Center, P.O. Box 458, Sacaton, AZ 85247 (602) 562-3801.

BRAYBOY, CONNIE (Lumbee)
(editor)
Born in Robeson County, N.C. *Address*: P.O. Box 1075, Pembroke, NC 28372 (910) 521-2826 Fax 521-1975 (work). E-mail: conneebrayboy@hotmail.com. *Affiliation*: Editor, Carolina Indian Voice (weekly Indian newspaper), Pembroke, NC, 1973-. *Publication*: Pembroke, The Twentieth Century.

BRAYBOY, TERRANCE (Lumbee)
(shop owner)
Affiliation: Sacred Hoop Trading Post, 207 Purefoy Rd. #A, Chapel Hill, NC 27514.

BREAD, MARILYN
(association director)
Affiliation: Kansas Association for Native American Education, Haskell Indian Nations University, P.O. Box H-1304, Lawrence, KS 66044 (913) 749-8468.

BREEN, MIDGE
(administrative officer)
Affiliation: Rapid City PHS Indian Hospital, 3200 Canyon Lake Dr., Rapid City, SD 57702 (605) 348-1900.

BRENNAN, MARY H.
(editor)
Affiliation: "Earthsong," The Heard Museum, 22 E. Monte Vista Rd., Phoenix, AZ 85004 (602) 252-8840.

BRENNEMAN, GEORGE 1934-
(pediatrician, maternal & child health coord.)
Born January 21, 1934, Newport News, VA. *Education*: Eastern Mennonite College, B.S., 1957; University of Virginia, School of Medicine, M.D., 1961. *Principal occupation*: Pediatrician, maternal and child health coordinator, Indian Health Service. *Address*: Indian Health Service, Parklawn Bldg., Rm. 6A-54, 5600 Fishers Lane, Rockville, MD 20857 (301) 443-4644 (work). *Affiliations*: Physician, Indian Health Service Hospital, Albuquerque, NM, 1962-64; physician, 1964-65, 1967-68, staff pediatrician, 1981-84, Alaska Native Medical Center, Anchorage, AK; physician & Tuberculosis Control Office, Bethel, Alaska, 1965-67; pediatrician, Alaska Native Medical Center, Bethel, Ak, 1970-73; clinical director, pediatrician and general physician, 1973-76, chief of pediatrics, 1978-79, Alaska Native Service Hospital, Bethel, AK; medical director, Yukon-Kuskokwim Health Corp., instructor, Community Health Aide Program, Kuskokwim Community College, 1979-80; director, Alaska *Haemophilus influenzae* Vaccine project, co-investigator, Efficacy Trial of a *Haemophilus influenzae* Type b Vaccine in a

High Risk Infant Population, 1984-87; maternal & child health coordinator, Indian Health Service, 1987-. *Memberships*: American Academy of Pediatrics (Fellow, 1972-); Mennonite Medical Association; Physicians for Social Responsibility. *Awards, honors*: Commendation Medal, 1975, Meritorious Service Medal, 1977, USPHS; Certificate of Appreciation for Outstanding Performance, 1976 & 1977, Bethel Service Unit, Alaska Native Health Service; In Sincere Appreciation, Pediatric House Staff, University of Virginia Hospital, 1977-78; The Alaska Health Achievement Award, 1981 from the Alaska Public Health Association; Federal Employee of the Year, Category IV Performance Award, 1982, Federal Executive Association; 1987 Alumnus Distinguished Service Award, Eastern Mennonite College. *Published works*: Articles in "Alaska Medicine, 1967, 1969, July 1979, February 1980; Stethoscope (a biweekly and weekly health related news column), Tundra Drums, 1976-80; and other articles.

BRENNER, M. DIANE
(museum archivist)
Affiliation: Archivist, Anchorage Museum of History and Art, 121 W. 7th Ave., Anchorage, AK 99501 (907) 343-4326.

BRESCIA, WILLIAM, Jr. (Mississippi Choctaw) 1947-
(director, research & curriculum development)
Born November 4, 1947, Chicago, Ill. *Education*: Wartburg College, Waverly, Iowa, BA, 1970; University of Wisconsin, Madison, MS, 1973. *Principal occupation*: Director, research & curriculum development. *Address*: Mississippi Band of Choctaw Indians, P.O. Box 6010 - Choctaw Branch, Philadelphia, MS 39350 (601) 656-5251. *Affiliations*: Editor, Daybreak Star Magazine (Daybreak Star Press, 1976-81; Curriculum coordinator, 1976-78, director, Community Educational Services, 1978-81, United Indians of All Tribes Foundation, Seattle; director, Curriculum Developer, Ethnic Heritage Program, 1981-1982, director, Division of Research and Curriculum Development, Mississippi Band of Choctaw Indians, Philadelphia, MS, 1982-. *Other professional posts*: Computer education consultant, Mississippi State Dept. of Education, 1984-. *Community activities*: D'Arcy McNickle Center, Newberry Library, Chicago (advisor, 1985-); ERIC/CRESS National Advisory Board (American Indian educational specialist, 1984-); The Native American (advisory committee member, 1984-); Indian representative, Washington Urban Rural Racial Disadvantaged Advisory Committee, 1979-80; Indian representative, New Voice Advisory committee, WGBH-TV, Boston, 1977-80; Scientists and Citizens Organized on Policy Issues, Seattle, Wash., 1980-81; Seattle Museum of History and Industry, 1979-81. *Memberships*: American Education Research Association; International Reading Association; National Indian Education Association; National Association for Bilingual Education; Mid-South Educational Research Association; Association for Supervision and Curriculum Development. *Awards, honors*: American Indian Heritage High School (special recognition for work in support of that school and Indian education); Northwest American Indian Women's Circle (special recognition for work in support of National Conference, 1979); Northwest Regional Folklife Festival (for administration of Seattle Pow-Wow, 1978); Ethnic Heritage Employee of the Year, 1981; Choctaw Dept. of Education (Employee of the Year, 1982). *Interests*: Computers in education; curriculum development; learning styles and brain functions; economic education; organic gardening; Choctaw literacy. *Published works*: Co-author, Reeves-Brescia, Developmental Checklist, (Mississippi Band of Choctaw Indians, 1975); script advisor, Yesterdays Children: Indian Elder Oral History, 30 minute video (Daybreak Star Press, 1980); co-author, Development of Native American Curriculum, workbook (Daybreak Star Press, 1979); editor, Ways of the Lushootseed People: Ceremonies and Traditions of the Northern Puget Sound Indians (Daybreak Star Press, 1980); editor, Sharing Our Worlds (Daybreak Star Press, 1980); script advisor, Voices from the Cradleboard, 30 minute slide presentation (Daybreak Star Press, 1980); editor, Indians in Careers (Daybreak Star Press, 1980); editor, Starting an Indian Teen Club (Daybreak Star Press, 1980); co-author, Fisherman on the Puyallup & Teachers Guide (Daybreak Star Press, 1980); co-author, Suquamish Today & Teachers Guide (Daybreak Star Press, 1980); executive editor, Tribal Sovereignty,

Indian Tribes in U.S. History (Daybreak Star Press, 1981); editor, Free Range to Reservation: Social Change on Selected Washington Reservations (Daybreak Star Press, 1981); editor, Outdoor Education for Indian Youth (Daybreak Star Press, 1981); Getting Control of Your Money (Daybreak Star Press, 1981); Knowing Your Legal Rights (Daybreak Star Press, 1981); editor, Daybreak Star Pre-School Activities Book (Daybreak Star Press, 1979); editor, Twana Games (Daybreak Star Press, 1981); editor, Our Mother Corn (Daybreak Star Press, 1981); A'una (Daybreak Star Press, 1981); editor, Washington State Indian History for Grades 4-6, A Teacher's Guide Daybreak Star Press, 1981); editor, O'Wakaga (Daybreak Star Press, 1981); editor, By the Work of Our Hands, co-editor, Teacher's Guide (Choctaw Heritage Press, 1982); editor, Choctaw Tribal Government (Choctaw Heritage Press, 1982); co-author, Looking Around, Na Yo Pisa (Choctaw Heritage Press, 1982); editor, Okla Apilachi (Choctaw Heritage Press, 1982); editor, How the Flowers Came to Be (Choctaw Heritage Press, 1982); executive editor, Choctaw Anthology I, II, and III (Choctaw Heritage Press, 1984); Lowak Mosoli (Choctaw Heritage Press, 1984); editor, Little Pigs - Shokoshi Althiha (Choctaw Heritage Press, 1984); editor, The Tale of the Possum (Choctaw Heritage Press, 1984); editor, Welcome to the Choctaw Fair! (Choctaw Heritage Press, 1984); James at Work (Choctaw Heritage Press, 1984); The Choctaw Oral Traditions Relating to Their Origin, chapter from The Choctaw Before Removal (University of Mississippi Press, 1985).

BRESETTE, JOSEPH N.
(executive director)
Affiliation: Great Lakes InterTribal Council, P.O. Box 9, Lac du Flambeau, WI 54538 (715) 588-3324.

BRESHEARS, GARY P.
(executive officer)
Affiliation: Phoenix Area Indian Health Service, 3738 N. 16th St., Suite A, Phoenix, AZ 85016 (602) 640-2052.

BRESSETTE, THOMAS
(Indian band chief)
Affiliation: Chief, Chippewas of Kettle & Stony Point Indian Band, RR #2, Forest, Ontario, Canada N0N 1J0 (519) 786-2125.

BRETERNITZ, CORY DALE
(center president)
Affiliation: Center for Indigenous Studies in the Americas, 1121 North 2nd St., Phoenix, AZ 85004 (602) 253-4938

BREUNINGER, DANNY
(BIA agency supt.)
Affiliation: Southern Ute Agency, BIA, P.O. Box 315, Ignacio, CO 81137 (970) 563-4511 Fax 563-9321. *Past professional post*: Supt., Truxton Canon Agency, BIA, Valentine, AZ.

BREWER, PATRICIA L.
(executive director)
Affiliation: Poarch Creek Indian Heritage Center, HCR 69A, Box 85B, Atmore, AL 36502 (205) 368-9136.

BREWSTER, HARDING
(alcohol/drug abuse program specialist)
Affiliation: Nashville Area IHS, 711 Stewarts Ferry Pike, Nashville, TN 37214 (615) 736-2400.

BRIDGES, THERESA M. (Puyallup) 1924-
(retail sales manager)
Born January 15, 1924, Mud Bay (Olympia), Wash. *Education*: Chemawa Indian High School, Salem, OR. *Principal occupation*: Retail sales manager. *Home address*: 11117 Conine Ave., SE, Olympia, WA 98503 (206) 459-7491. *Affiliations*: Manager, Franks Landing Smoke Shop, Olympia, WA, 1972-; Board Member, WaHeLut Indian School, 1974-. *Other professional posts*: Member & officer, Puyallup Tribal Council, Tacoma, WA, 1969-77; vice-president, Valmarco Foundation, Olympia, WA, 1982-. *Community activities*: Puyallup Tribal Elders Support Organization (director/officer, 1964-. *Memberships*: Survival of American Indians Association (director & vice-president, 1982-). *Awards, honors*: Jefferson Award (Washington State Winner) by Seattle Post-Intelligencer & American Institue for Public Service; Martin Luther King Award

from Thurston County (WA) Community Service. *Interests*: "Patterned quilt making and sewing; Indian basketry, carvings, artifact, and jewelry collecting; Pacific Northwest Indian archival repository development."

BRIGGS, KARA (Yakama)
(journalist)
Affiliation: The Oregonian, 1320 S.W. Broadway, Portland, OR 97201 (503) 221-8100. E-mail: karabriggs@news.oregonian.com

BRIGGS, LESTER JACK, JR.
(Minnesota Chippewa) 1948-
(college administrator)
Born September 18, 1948, Duluth, Minn. *Education*: Johnson Institute, Duluth, MN, Certificate in Chemical Dependency, 1976; Indian counselor, Alcoholism Training Project, University of Minnesota-Duluth, Certificate of Completion - 300 hours - Chemical Dependency, 1977; Rutgers State University, Alcohol Studies Certificate of Completion, 1977; Rainy River Community College, A.A., 1978; Bemidji State University, B.S. (Community Service), 1980; University of Minnesota-Duluth, MED (Education Administration), 1990. *Principal occupation*: College administrator. *Home address*: 1509 Spring Lake Rd., Cloquet, MN 55720 (218) 879-0804 Fax 879-0814 (work). *Affiliations*: American Indian student advisor and planning assistant, Minnesota Higher Education Coordinating Board, 1978-81, regional director, Services to Indian People Program, Arrowhead Community College Region, 1983-89, Rainy River Community College, International Falls, MN; president, Fond du Lac Tribal & Community College, Cloquet, MN, 1989-2003. *Other professional posts*: Chairperson, Indian Education Advisory Committee, Independent School District 361, International Falls, MN, 1977-79; member/president, Board of Directors, North American Indian Fellowship Center, S. International Falls, MN, 1979-83; professional licensure/school social worker, Minnesota State Dept. of Education (current); member, American Indian Advisory Board, University of Minnesota, Duluth (current); proposal writing for: Dept. of Public Welfare, State of Minnesota; Dept. of HEW; Minnesota State Dept. of Education; Rainy River Community College; and Arrowhead Community College Region. *Community activities*: Co-chairperson, International Pow-wow Committee, International Falls, MN, 1979-83; chairperson, advisory committee, Koochiching Co. Family Services, International Falls, MN, 1980-81; member, Youth Diversion Committee, International Falls Juvenile Program, 1981-83; member, Rainy River Citizen Advisory Committee, International Falls, MN, 1981-82; member, Services to Indian People/Bilingual Ojibwe Specialist Project Advisory Committee, Arrowhead Community College Region (current). *Memberships*: Minnesota Association of Counselors on Alcoholism, 1978-83; Minnesota Indian Education Association (treasurer-current). *Awards, honors*: American Indian Administrator of the Year, 1986 & 1987, by Minnesota Indian Education Association; Distinguished Service Award, President's Award, 1988, by Arrowhead Community College Region. *Interests*: Fishing, hunting, reading, guitar, and home carpentry. *Published works*: Rivers of Life, A Native American Cultural Awareness Resource (Living Waters of Faith Series, contributing author and leader).

BRIGHTMAN, LEHMAN L.
(director-Indian organization)
Affiliation: United Native Americans, 2434 Faria Ave., Pinole, CA 94564 (415) 758-8160.

BRIGHTMAN, ROBERT 1950-
(professor of anthropology)
Born April 23, 1950, Chicago, Ill. *Education*: Reed College, Portland, OR, B.A., 1973; University of Chicago, MA, 1976, Ph.D., 1982. *Principal occupation*: Professor of anthropology. *Address*: Dept. of Anthropology, Reed College, Portland, OR 97202 (503) 771-1112. *Affiliations*: Assistant professor of anthropology, University of Wisconsin-Madison, 1982-88; associate professor of anthropology, Reed College, Portland, OR, 1988-. *Memberships*: American Anthropological Association; Linguistic Society of America; American Society for Ethnohistory. *Interests*: North American Indian cultural anthropology & linguistics; Algonquian linguistics; field research: Pokatawagan, Manitoba, 1977-79, 1986 Cree. *Published works*: Orders of the

Dreamed (University of Winnipeg, 1988); Acad ohkiwina & Acimoina: Traditional Literature of the Rock Cree (Canadian Ethnology Service, 1989); Grateful Prey: Cree Human-Animal Relationships (University of California Press, 1990).

BRILL, PETER SCOTT
(museum curator of exhibits)
Affiliation: George Gustav Heye Center, National Museum of the American Indian, Smithsonian Institution, 1 Bowling Green, New York, NY 10004 (212) 283-2420.

BRINK, JEANNE A. (Abenaki)
(Native American educator, consultant, basketmaker)
Born November 12, 1944, Montpelier, Vt. *Education*: MA with concentration in Native American Studies. *Principal occupation*: Native American educator, consultant, and ash splint & sweetgrass basketmaker. *Address*: 130 Tremont St., Barre, VT 05641-3126 (802) 479-0594. E-mail: azoniz@aol.com. *Affiliations*: Board of Advisors, Robert Hull Fleming Museum, University of Vermont, Burlington, VT, 1993—2000; Board of Trustees, Vermont Historical Society, Montpelier, VT, 1992-98. *Community activities*: Coordinator for Shelburne Museum Intertribal Pow-wow; coordinator and member of W'Abenaki Dancers (traditional Western Abenaki social dancers). *Interests*: Jeanne's performances are on Western Abenaki history, culture, language, dance, family stories, basketry and oral tradition. *Published work*: Alnobaodwa: A Western Abenaki Language Guide, with Gordon M. Day, 1990.

BRINK, YANKO (Eskimo)
(AK village council president)
Affiliation: Native Village of Kasigluk Council, P.O. Box 19, Kasigluk, AK 99609 (907) 477-6927.

BRITO, SYLVESTER (Comanche, Tarascan)
(poet, writer)
Address & Affiliation: Dept. of English, Hoyt Hall, University of Wyoming, Laramie, WY 82071 (307) 766-2125.

BRITT, YVETTE
(Indian education program director)
Affiliation: Mounds Public Schools, Indian Education Program, P.O. Box 189, Mounds, OK 74047 (918) 827-6758 Fax 827-3704.

BRITTAN, MARY ANN
(center director)
Affiliation: Indian Education Technical Assistance Center, 2424 Springer Dr., Suite 200, Norman, OK 73069 (405) 360-1163.

BROCK, GLEN (Eastern Shawnee)
(former tribal chief)
Affiliation: Eastern Shawnee Tribe of Oklahoma, P.O. Box 350, Seneca, MO 64865 (918) 666-2435.

BROCK, MICHAEL
(school principal)
Affiliation: Theodore Roosevelt School, P.O. Box 567, Fort Apache, AZ 85926 (520) 338-4464 Fax 338-1009.

BROCKMAN, KAREN S. (Oneida)
(tribal museum director)
Affiliation: Oneida Nation Museum, P.O. Box 365, Oneida, WI 54155 (920) 869-2768.

BRODY, J.J. 1929-
(author)
Born April 24, 1929, Brooklyn, N.Y. *Education*: The Cooper Union, New York, N.Y. (Certificate of Fine Arts), 1950; University of New Mexico, BA, 1956, MA, 1964, PhD, 1970. *Principal occupation*: Author. *Home address*: 15 Blue Crow Lane, Sandia Park, NM 87047 (505) 281-3579; E-Mail: jjbrody@unm.edu. *Affiliations*: Curator of art, Everhart Museum, Scranton, PA, 1957-58; curator, Isaac Delago Museum of Art, New Orleans, 1958-60; curator, Museum of International Folk Art, Santa Fe, 1960-61; University of New Mexico, Albuquerque (curator & director, Maxwell Museum of Anthropology, 1962-83; professor of anthropology and art history, 1964-89, professor emeritus, 1989-). *Other professional posts*: Research curator, Maxwell Museum of Anthropology; research associate, School of American Research, Santa Fe; Senior Research Associate, Laboratory of Anthropology-Museum of Indian

Art and Culture, Museum of New Mexico, Santa Fe. *Military service*: U.S. Army, 1952-54 (sergeant). *Community activities*: Volunteer Recorder, Petroglyph National Monument. *Memberships*: American Rock Art Research Association; Native American Art Research Association; Archaeological Society of New Mexico; Society for American Archaeology. *Awards, honors*: Popejoy Dissertation Prize, University of New Mexico,1971; non-fiction award for Indian Painters and White Patrons, Border Regional Library Conference, 1971; 1977 Art Book Award for Mimbres Painted Pottery; Award of Honor, New Mexico Historic Preservation Commission, 1978; resident scholar, School of American Research, 1980-81; Honoree, 1992, vol. 18, Papers (in honor of), by the Archaeological Society of New Mexico; Honoree, 1997 Native American Art Studies Association; 1998 Conservation Award, American Rock Art Research Association; Historic Preservation Citation, State of New Mexico for rock art preservation; College of Fine Arts, Distinguished Alumni Award, The University of New Mexico, 2000; New Mexico Endowment for the Humanities, Lifetime Contributions to the Humanities, 2001. *Interests*: Indian art, especially of the Southwest; museology; rock art; education; museum exhibitions. *Biographical sources*: Who's Who in America; Who's Who in the West; Who's Who in American Art. *Published works*: Indian Painters and White Patrons (UNM Press, 1971); Between Traditions (University of Iowa Press, 1976; Mimbres Painted Pottery (School of American Research and UNM Press, 1977); Beatien Yazz: Indian Painter, with Sallie Wagner and B. Yazz (School of American Research, 1983); Mimbres Pottery, with Catherine Scott and Steve LeBlanc (Hudson Hills Press, 1983.); The Anasazi (Rizzoli and Jaca Books, 1990); Beauty From the Earth (University Museum, U. of Pennsylvania, 1990); Anasazi and Pueblo Painting (School of American Research, UNM Press, 1991); To Touch the Past: The Painted Pottery of the Mimbres People, with Rina Swentzel (Hudson Hills Press, 1996); Pueblo Indian Painting: Tradition and Modernism in New Mexico, 1900-1930 (School of American Research Press, 1997). *Museum exhibitions*: "Between Traditions" (University of Iowa Museum of Art and Maxwell Museum, 1976); "Myth, Metaphor & Mimbres Art" (Maxwell Museum & Taylor Museum, 1976-77); "Mimbres Pottery: Ancient Art of the American Southwest" (with others) (American Federation of Arts, 1983-85); "Beauty From the Earth" (University Museum, U. of Pennsylvania, 1990-93); "To Touch the Past" (Weisman Museum of Art, U. of Minnesota, 1996); "Space, Time, Nature, Culture," with Dudley King (Maxwell Museum, UNM, 1996).

BROKAW, JERRE
(Indian education program coordinator)
Affiliation: Sand Springs Public Schools, Indian Education Program, P.O. Box 970, Sand Springs, OK 74063 (918) 245-1088.

BROKENLEG, MARTIN (Rosebud Sioux)
(professor of minority studies)
Affiliation: Associate Professor of Minority Studies, Augustana College, Sioux Falls, SD 57197 (605) 336-4007. *Published works*: with Larry Brendtro & Steve Van Bockern, Reclaiming Youth at Risk: Our Hope for the Future (suggests ways in which Native American and European traditions of child-rearing can be merged to help troubled youth); with Herbert T. Hoover, Yanktonai Sioux Water Colors: Cultural Remembrances of John Saul (Center for Western Studies, 1993).

BROMLEY, GARY D. (*War Eagle*)
(United Lumbee-adopted)
(retired/author)
Born in Fort Edward, N.Y. *Education*: Glendale (CA) Community College, 1984. *Principal occupation*: Retired/author. *Address*: P.O. Box 1629, Fontana, CA 92334-1629. *Affiliations*: United Lumbee Nation, 1954-present (chief; director, Research & Development Dept.; former reporter, United Lumbee Times). *Other professional post*: Acting liaison officer to courts for United Lumbee Nation. *Past professional post*: U.S. Dept. of Labor, Bureau of Mine Safety, Health Administration, 1980-95. *Military service*: National (NY State) Guard (Honorable Discharge, Oct. 1953). *Community activities*: "I have been involved in mail-only contacts with prison inmates with the intent to help them find and walk only the straight good path...it does at times

work." *Membership*: Native American Wolf Clan InterTribal Society (principal chief). *Awards, honors*: The "Silver Eagle Award," from the United Lumbee Nation for outstanding services to the Lumbee Nation and to the Indian community at large. *Interests*: "I am at this time dforming sound goodwill efforts with any tribal leaderships or bands and clans that seriously help or will help elderly and youth. *Published works*: "When War Eagle Speaks," & "War Eagle's Fact of Life," - numerous teachings of ancient red road upgraded and presented in modern American English. Scheduled for print in Spanish & Canadian French in late 2004.

BRONSON, BENNETT
(museum chair-anthropology)
Affiliation: Field Museum of Natural History, Roosevelt Rd. at Lake Shore Dr., Chicago, IL 60605 (312) 922-9410.

BROOKS, ROBERT
(professor of Native American studies)
Affiliation: Native American Studies Program, University of Oklahoma, 455 W. Lindsey, Rm. 804, Norman, OK 73019 (405) 325-2312.

BROOKSHIRE, JAMES
(chief-Indian claims)
Affiliation: Chief, Indian Claims Section, Land and Natural Resources Division, Dept. of Justice, Rm. 648, 550 11th St., NW, Washington, DC 20530 (202) 724-7375.

BROUGHTON, NANCY J. 1948-
(library/archives director)
Born December 17, 1948 in Dubuque, Iowa. *Education*: University of Wisconsin-Platteville, BS, 1971; University of Nevada-Reno, MS, 1983; University of Wisconsin-Madison, MA, 1988. *Principal occupation*: Library/archives director. *Address & Affiliation*: Director, Ruth A. Meyers Library/Ojibwe Archives (1996-present), Fond du Lac Tribal & Community College, Cloquet, MN 55720 (218) 879-0837 Fax 879-0814. E-mail: sam@ezigaa.fdl.cc.mn.us. *Past professional post*: Idaho State University Library, 1991-95. *Community activities*: Council member, Immanual Lutheran Church, Brookston, MN. *Memberships*: Western History Association; Wisconsin Library Association; Wisconsin Association of Academic Librarians.

BROWER, ARCHIE (Eskimo)
(AK village council president)
Affiliation: Kaktovik Village, P.O. Box 8, Kaktovik, AK 99747(907) 640-6120.

BROWER, ARNOLD J. (Eskimo)
(ex-AK village president)
Affiliation: Barrow Village Council, P.O. Box 1139, Barrow, AK 99723 (907) 852-4411.

BROWN, ARLENE
(Indian band chief)
Affiliation: Chief, Klahoose Indian Band, Box 9, Squirrel Cove, British Columbia, Canada V0P 1T0 (604) 935-6650.

BROWN, BOB
(school administrator)
Affiliation: Lummi High School, 2522 Kwina Rd., Bellingham, WA 98266 (360) 384-1489.

BROWN, BRIAN J.
(organization president)
Affiliation: National Relief Charities, 10029 SW Nimbus Ave., Suite 200, Beaverton, OR 97008 (800) 416-8102.

BROWN, CECIL
(Indian band chief)
Affiliation: Chief, Masset Indian Band, P.O. Box 189, Masset, BC, Canada V0T 1M0 (604) 626-3337.

BROWN, CHARLES ASA (*Fus Elle Haco-Muskogee*) (Gos Quillen-Shawnee) (Eagle Star-Cherokee) 1912-
(attorney, farm owner, lecturer)
Born October 17, 1912, Woodsfield, Ohio. *Education*: Virginia Military Institute, AB, 1935; University of Michigan Law School, 1935-37; Western Reserve University Law School, JD, 1938. *Principal occupation*: At-

torney, farm owner, lecturer. *Home address*: 1903 Hutchins St., Portsmouth, OH 45662. *Affiliations*: Self-employed lawyer & farmer, Portsmouth, OH, 1938-; Municipal Prosecuting Attorney, Portsmouth, Ohio, 1946; Assistant Attorney General, State of Ohio, 1963. *Military service*: U.S. Army (active duty, 1941-46; reserve service, 1931-72) (Lt. Colonel; American Defense; European Theater Medal with three battle stars; Purple Heart; Bronz Star with oak leaf cluster; Victory Medal; German Occupation Medal; Distinguished Unit Presidential Citation; Army Reserve Longevity Medal). *Community activities*: Scioto Area Council (executive board); Boy Scouts of America, Portsmouth, Ohio (merit badge counselor, 1946-, commissioner); cofounder, Jaycees, Portsmouth, 1938; Chamber of Commerce, Portsmouth; Bentonville, OH, Anti-Horse Thief Society. *Indian activities*: Member, Cedar River Tulsa Band, Muskogee Indian Tribe, Holdinville, Okla.; honorary councilman, Creek Indian Nation, Tulsa, OK, 1962-69; councilman, Western Black Elk Keetowah, Cherokee Nation; councilman, Federated Indian Tribes. *Memberships*: Scioto County Bar Association (trustee); Ohio State Bar Association; American Indian Bar Association; Phi Delta Phi Legal Fraternity; American Legion; Retired Officers Association and Reserve Officers Association, Washington, DC (life member); U.S. Horse Cavalry Association (life member); Masonic Lodge. *Awards, honors*: Silver Beaver Award, Boy Scouts of America; Vigil Honor, Order of the Arrows; President's Award for Distinguished Service, 1982, Boy Scouts of America; Advisory Chief of Indian Tribes, 1961-80; Master Mason, 1944-; Chief's liaison to visiting persons at ceremonials; Tecumseh was my great-great grandfather. *Interests*: Lecturer on Indian lore throughout the U.S.; writer on many Indian subjects; writer on various Masonic subjects; speaker at many public gatherings of all kinds continually. *Biographical sources*: Who's Who in Freemasonry; Who's Who in the Midwest; Who's Who in the World; Who's Who in Ohio; Distinguished Americans. *Published works*: Numerous articles in various publications.

BROWN, DAN, M.D.
(clinical director)
Affiliation: Scottsdale Salt River Clinic, Rte. 1, Box 215, Scottsdale, AZ 85256 (602) 379-4281.

BROWN, DANIEL JEROME
(Indian band chief)
Affiliation: Chief, Nanaimo Indian Band, 1145 Totem Rd., Nanaimo, British Columbia, Canada V9R 1H1 (604) 753-3481.

BROWN, DAVID QUENTIN *(Dotsuwah)* (Chickamauga-Cherokee)
(raven or war chief)
Born October 7, 1953, Chattanooga, Tenn. *Education*: McKenzie (Chattanooga, TN) ABS. *Principal occupation*: War chief of Tennessee River Band Chicka maugas. *Home address*: #6-9001 Bill Reed Rd., Ooltewah, TN 37363 (423) 855-2801. *Affiliation*: War Chief, Tennessee River Band of Chickamauga Cherokees. *Community activities*: Currently conducts teachings and new moon get together/dances; involved in protecting Moccasin Bend Burial Ground Historic Site. *Membership*: Tennessee River Band of Chickamauga Cherokees. *Activities*: Has led various classes in Native American awareness for children & adults, for summer camps & church groups. He is active in the fight against grave desecrations and environmental issues. Involved in initial meetings with the Hamilton County Sheriffs Dept. in forming the Native American Reserve Force which is a deputized group of Native Americans who protect the burial sites at Moccasin Bend from further desecration. This is the first time in history that a group of Native Americans, off reservation, has been deputized to oversee our ancestor's graves. *Published works*: Articles in the "The New Phoenix," "Pan American News," & "Katuah Journal."

BROWN, DEE ALEXANDER 1908-2002 (Deceased)
(librarian, educator, author)
Born in 1908, Louisiana. *Education*: George Washington University, BS, 1937; University of Illinois, MS, 1951. *Principal occupation*: Librarian, educator, author. *Home address*: 7 Overlook Dr., Little Rock, AR 72207. *Affiliations*: Librarian, Dept. of Agriculture, Washington, DC 1934-42; librarian, Aberdeen Proving Ground, Md., 1945-1948; agricultural librarian, 1948-72, professor, 1962-75, University of Illinois, Urbana. *Military*

service: U.S. Army, 1942-45. *Memberships*: Authors Guild; Society of American Historians; Western Writers of America; Beta Phi Mu. *Published works*: Wave High the Banner, 1942; Grierson's Raid, 1954; Yellowhorse, 1956; Cavalry Scout, 1957; The Gentle Tamers: Women of the Old Wild West, 1958; The Bold Cavaliers, 1959; They Went Thataway, 1960; Fighting Indian of the West, with M.F. Schmitt, 1948; Trail Driving Days, with M.F. Schmitt; The Settler's West, with M.F. Schmitt; Fort Phil Kearny, 1962; The Galvanized Yankees, 1963; Showdown at Little Bighorn, 1964; The Girl From Fort Wicked, 1964; The Year of the Century, 1966; Bury My Heart at Wounded Knee, 1971; The Westerners, 1974; Hear That Lonesome Whistle Blow, 1977; Tepee Tales, 1979; Creek Mary's Blood, 1980; editor: Agricultural History, 1956-58; Pawnee, Blackfoot and Cheyenne, 1961.

BROWN, FRANK, M.D. (Cherokee of Oklahoma) 1958-
(physician, geriatric neuropsychiatrist)
Born February 14, 1958, Searcy, Ark. *Education*: BS, MD, MBA. *Principal occupation*: Physician, geriatric neuropsychiatrist. *Home address*: 1899 E. Gate Dr., Stone Mountain, GA 30087 (404) 728-6690 Fax 728-4963; E-mail: sdpfwb@emory.edu. *Affiliations*: Associate Professor, Emory University, Atlanta, GA; Medical Director, Wesley Woods Geriatric Hospital, Atlanta, GA; Medical Director, Emory Clergy Care, Atlanta, GA. *Military service*: U.S. Army Reserves, 1982-89. *Memberships*: American College of Psychiatrists (Fellow); American Psychiatrists Association; American Association of Geriatric Psychiatrists. *Published works*: Journal articles and book chapters.

BROWN, FRITZ (Quechan)
(tribal council president)
Affiliation: Quechan Tribal Council, P.O. Box 11352, Yuma, AZ 85364 (619) 572-0213.

BROWN, G. MICHAEL
(casino/bingo hall president)
Affiliation: Foxwoods High Stakes Bingo & Casino (Mashantucket-Pequot Tribe), State Rd., Box 410, Ledyard, CT 06339 (203) 885-3000.

BROWN, GINGER E. (Choctaw of Oklahoma) 1952-
(illustrator, fine artist)
Born November 9, 1952, Oklahoma City, Okla. *Education*: Kansas City Art Institute. *Principal occupation*: Illustrator, fine artist. *Home address*: 11407 W. 155th Ter., Overland Park, KS 66221 (913) 897-4873. *Other professional post*: Illustrator of endangered species for World Wildlife Fund, 1992-93. *Memberships*: Choctaw Nation of Oklahoma; Indian Arts & Crafts Association; National Colored Pencil Association; Native American Rights Fund. *Awards, honors*: 1990 Scholarship Award from Kansas City Art Institute. *Interests*: "Depicting and combining wildlife with Native American artifacts and their legends and traditions."

BROWN, IAN
(museum curator)
Affiliation: Peabody Museum of Archaeology & Ethnology, Harvard University, 11 Divinity Ave., Cambridge, MA 02138 (617) 495-2248.

BROWN, LAURA JUNE
(Indian program director)
Affiliation: Coffee County School System, Indian Education Program, 400 Reddoch Hill Rd., Elba, AL 36323 (205) 897-5016.

BROWN, LOUELLA
(hospital director)
Affiliation: PHS Indian Hospital, P.O. Box 60, Cass Lake, MN 56633 (218) 335-2291.

BROWN, MARGARET
(professor, site supt.)
Affiliations: Professor, Dept. of Anthropology, Southern Illinois University, P.O. Box 1451, Edwardsville, IL 62026 (618) 692-2744; Supt., Cahokia Mounds State Historic Site & Museum, P.O. Box 681, Collinsville, IL 62234 (618) 346-5160.

BROWN, MARK F. (Mohegan)
(tribal chairperson)
Affiliation: Mohegan Indian Tribe, 5 Crow Hill Rd., Uncasville, CT 06382 (860) 862-6100.

BROWN, NORMAN
(Indian band chief)
Affiliation: Wapekeka (Angling Lake) Indian Band, Wapekeka, Ontario, Canada P0V 1B0 (807) 537-2315.

BROWN, PAM (Mohawk)
(artist; store co-owner/manager)
Affiliation: Mohawk Impressions, Mohawk Nation, P.O. Box 20, Hogansburg, NY 13655 (518) 358-2467.

BROWN, ROBERT
(Indian school director)
Affiliation: Viejas Indian School, P.O. Box 1389, Alpine, CA 91903 (619) 445-4938 Fax 445-8912.

BROWN, STEPHEN (Pomo)
(rancheria chairperson)
Affiliation: Sulphur Bank Rancheria, Elem Indian Colony Council, P.O. Box 618, Clearlake Oaks, CA 95423 (707) 995-2853.

BROWN, THOMAS (Pomo)
(former rancheria chairperson)
Affiliation: Elem General Council, Sulphur Bank Rancheria, P.O. Box 1968, Clearlake Oaks, CA 95423 (707) 998-3431.

BROWN, TONY
(media producer)
Address & affiliation: Brown Eyes Productions, 933 E. 12th #3, Anchorage, AK 99501 (907) 257-1110 Fax 257-1835.

BROWN, VINSON 1912-1991 (Deceased)
(writer, naturalist, publisher)
Born December 7, 1912, Reno, Nev. *Education*: University of California at Berkeley, AB, 1939; Stanford University, MA, 1947. *Principal occupation*: Writer, naturalist, publisher. *Address*: 3543 Indian Creek Rd., Happy Camp, CA 96039 (916) 493-5353 (office). *Affiliations*: Lecturer on American Indian religions, University of South Dakota, University of Northern Michigan, Myrin Institute, Haskell Institute; field collector in natural history; lecturer. *Travels*: Visits to many Indian tribes in the U.S., Canada, and Alaska, 1960-72; Mr. Brown spent about two years in the mountain jungles of Panama where he collected specimens with the aid of a Guaymi Indian named Chio Jari. He has also traveled extensively throughout the world. *Published works*: Understanding Ancient Life (Science Materials Center, 1958); Warriors of the Rainbow, with William Willoya (Naturegraph, 1965); Pomo Indians of California and Their Neighbors (Naturegraph, 1969); Great Upon the Mountain — Crazy Horse of America (Naturegraph, 1971, cloth ed., Macmillan), now published by Naturegraph (1987) under the title: Crazy Horse: Hoka Hey!; Voices of the Earth and Sky: The Vision-Search of the American Indians (Stackpole, 1974; Naturegraph, 1976); Native Americans of the Pacific Coast (Naturegraph, 1985); and others which pertain to nature.

BROWN, WILFRED
(BIA agency supt.)
Affiliation: Western Navajo Agency, Bureau of Indian Affairs, P.O. Box 127, Tuba City, AZ 86045 (520) 283-4531.

BROWN, WILLIE (Eskimo)
(village president)
Affiliation: Native Village of Eek, P.O. Box 87, Eek, AK 99578 (907) 536-5128.

BROWN-GODFREY, LAURIE
(Indian education program director)
Affiliation: Springfield Public Schools, Indian Education Program, 525 Mill St., Springfield, OR 97477 (503) 726-3430 Fax 726-9555.

BROWNE, DALLAS LA SALLE (Cherokee) 1944-
(associate professor of anthropology)
Born October 9, 1944, Chicago, Ill. *Education*: University of Illinois, Urbana, PhD (Cultural Anthropology), 1983. *Principal occupation*: Associate professor of anthropology. *Address & Affiliation*: Associate professor, Dept. of Anthropology, Box 1451, Southern Illinois University, Edwardsville, IL 62026 (618) 650-2138 Fax 650-3509. E-mail: dbrowne@siue.edu. *Other professional posts*: President, St. Louis Committee on Foreign Relations, St. Louis, MO; Honorary Consul for

Tanzania. *Community activities*: Human Relations Commission, Edwardsville, IL; Board of Directors, Katherine Dunham Museum, East St. Louis, MO; Board of Directors, Eugene Redmond Writers Society, East St. Louis, IL. *Memberships*: American Anthropological Association; Society for Urban Anthropology; Association of Black Anthropologists; World Affairs Council. *Interests*: Urban culture, ritual & performance, symbolism, family and kinship, political anthropology, theory and history, African culture, Latin American culture.

BROWNE, VEE F. *(Elvita)* **(Navajo) 1956-**
(author)
Born September 4, 1956, Ganado, Ariz. *Education*: Cochise Community College, AA, 1977; Northern Arizona University, BS, 1985; Western New Mexico University, MA, 1990. *Principal occupation*: Author. *Address*: Unknown. *Affiliations*: Northland Publishing, Flagstaff, AZ, 1991-; journalist, The Navajo-Hopi Observer, Flagstaff, AZ 1991-. *Other professional posts*: National Caucus (member, board of directors) 1994-96; Wordcraft Circle of Native Writers (mentor)/Apprenticeship. *Memberships*: Society of Southwestern Authors; Society of Children's Book Writers; North American Native Authors; Arizona Press Association - The Navajo-Hopi Observer (newspaper). *Awards, honors*: Western Heritage 1991 - Cowboy Hall of Fame Award - Juvenile Book of the Year; The Buddy Bo Jack Nationwide Award for Humanitarian, 1992 Children's Book Writer; Society of Southwestern Authors, 1993 Published Work Award. *Interests*: Returning of Gift of North America's Native Authors during July each year; enjoy conferences and writer's workshops. I enjoy attending writer's intensive Institute each year. *Published works*: Monster Slayer (1991), Monster Birds (1993), & Neon Powwow Anthology (1993) (Northland Publishing). Bi-weekly newspaper sports articles - "Observer"; Maria Tallchief (Simon & Schuster).

BROZZO, SHIRLEY A.
(Keweenaw Bay Anishinaabe) 1956-
(university administrator)
Born February 4, 1956, Wakefield, Mich. *Education*: BS (Business Administration, 1992); MA (English Writing, 1994). *Principal occupation*: University administrator. *Home address*: 6400 U.S. 41 S., Apt. 1, Marquette, MI 49855 (906) 249-5406 Fax 227-1714 (work). E-mail: sbrozzo@nmu.edu. *Affiliation*: GAP Coordinator, Northern Michigan University, 1994-present. *Other professional post*: Past president, NMU Commission for Women, 1997-99. *Community activities*: Storyteller at local schools. *Memberships*: Wordcraft Circle of Native Writers & Storytellers, 1992-present; NMU Allies (co-founder, 1998-present). *Interests*: Writing, reading, knitting & crocheting, working jigsaw puzzles.

BRUCE, LOUIS R.
(consultant)
Affiliation: President, Native American Consultants, Inc., 725 2nd St., NE, Washington, DC 20002 (202) 547-0576. Branch: 1001 Highland St., Arlington, VA 22201.

BRUCHAC, JAMES (Abenaki) 1966-
(editor, press/center owner)
Born June 24, 1966. *Affiliations*: Owner, Greenfield Review Press, P.O. Box 308, Greenfield Center, NY 12833 (518) 584-1728 Fax 583-9741; co-owner, Northeast Native American Education Center, Greenfield Center, NY.

BRUCHAC III, JOSEPH (Abenaki) 1942-
(writer, storyteller, editor)
Born October 16, 1942, Saratoga Springs, N.Y. *Education*: Cornell University, B.A. (English), 1965; Syracuse University, M.A. (Literature, Creative Writing), 1966; Union Institute Graduate School (Yellow Springs, OH), Ph.D. (Comparative Literature), 1974. *Principal occupation*: Writer, storyteller, editor. *Address*: P.O. Box 308, Greenfield Center, NY 12833 (518) 584-1728 Fax 583-9741. E-mail: nudatlog@earthlink.net. Website: www.josephbruchac.com. *Affiliations*: Founder & Co-editor of The Greenfield Review Press, Greenfield Center, NY, 1969-present; literary editor of "Studies in American Indian Literature" (SAIL), 1989-present; editor of "The Greenfield Review", 1969-87. *Past professional posts*: Board member, National Association for Storytelling (NAPPS), 1992-94; acting

chair, Native Writers Circle of the Americas, 1992-93; advisory board, Wordcraft Circle of Native American Writers, 1992-93; national chair, Returning the Gift Project, 1991-92; board member, Poetry Society of America, 1985-87; COSMEP-National Independent Publishers Association (board member, 1973-74, 1981-85; national chairman, 1984-85); adjunct faculty, SUNY/Albany, 1987-1988; faculty, Hamilton College, 1983, 85, 87; coordinator of program at Great Meadow Prison, 1974-81, editor of "The Prison Writing Review", 1976-85; Skidmore College (English instructor, 1969-73; teacher & liaison officer, Teachers for West Africa: Ghana, 1966-1969. *Awards, honors*: NEA Creative Writing Fellowship (poetry), 1974; CCLM Editors' Fellowship, 1980; Rockefeller Humanities Fellowship, 1982; New York State CAPS Poetry Fellowships, 1973, 1982; NEA/PEN Syndicated Fiction Award, 1983; American Book Award for "Breaking Silence", 1984; Yaddo Residency Fellowships, 1984, 1985; The Cherokee Nation Award (prose), 1986; New York State Council on the Arts Editors Fellowship, 1986; The Hope S. Dean Memorial Award, 1993; Knickerbocker Award, 1995; Body Mind Spirit Magazine Award of Excellence, 1995; 1998 Storyteller of the Year from Wordcraft Circle of Native Writers & Storytellers; Albany (NY) Public Library Author of the Year, 1998; 1999 Lifetime Achievement Award from the Native Writers Circle of the Americas; National Education Association Civil Rights Award, 2003; numerous book awards and honors. *Interests*: The Dawnland Singers (Joe, Jim, Jesse, and Marge Bruchac) offer a variety of performance material, including traditional Native American storytelling, drum songs and chants, contemporary music in Abenaki and English, flute songs, and historical presentations. The group formed in the spring of 1993 for the Abenaki Heritage Festival, and has since performed at the Flynn Theater in Burlington, VT, the Champlain Valley Festival and a number of other locations and festivals. *Published works*: Poems and stories in over 400 magazines; poems & stories anthologized in more than 150 anthologies; translations from Abenaki, Ewe, Iroquois, and Spanish in numerous magazines; articles, essays and book reviews in more than 75 magazines & anthologies. *Anthologies edited*: Native Wisdom (1995) Smoke Rising (1995); Returning the Gift (1994); Singing of Earth (with Diana Landau, The Nature Co., 1993); Raven Tells Stories: Contemporary Alaskan Native Writing (1990); New Voices From the Longhouse: Contemporary Iroquois Writing (1989); Songs From This Earth on Turtle's Back: Contemporary American Indian Poetry (1983); among others. *Drama*: Pushing Up the Sky, Seven Native American Plays for Children (Dial, 2000). *Fiction*: Pocahontas (Harcourt, 2003); Foot of the Mountain (Holy Cow Press, 2003); The Warriors (Darby Creek, 2003); The Winter People (Dial, 2002); Skeleton Man (Harper Collins, 2002); Sacajawea (Harcourt, 2000); Heart of a Chief (Harcourt, 1999); Arrow Over the Door (Dial, 1998); Children of the Longhouse (Dial, 1996); Eagle Song (Dial, 1997); Dog People (Fulcrum, 1996); Long River (Fulcrum, 1995); Gluskabe and the Four Wishes (Cobblehill Books, 1994); Returning the Gift (editor, University of Arizona Press, 1994); A Boy Called Slow (Philomel, 1994); The Great Ball Game (Dial, 1994); Dawn Land (novel, Fulcrum, 1993); Turtle Meat (short stories, Holy Cow Press, 1992); The White Moose (short stories, Blue Cloud Quarterly, 1988); among others. *Non-Fiction*: Our Stories Remember (Fulcrum, 2003); Navajo Long Walk (National Geographic Society Press, 2002); Native Games & Stories, with James Bruchac (Fulcrum, 2000); Seeing the Circle (Richard C. Owens Publishers, 1999); Bowman's Store, an autobiography (Dial, 1997); Lasting Echoes (Harcourt, 1997); Roots of Survival (Fulcrum, 1996); Native American Gradening, with M. Caduto (Fulcrum, 1996); The Native American Sweat Lodge (The Crossing Press, 1994); Keepers of Life: Discovering Plants Through Native American Stories and Earth Activities for Children, with Michael Caduto (Fulcrum, 1994); Keepers of the Night, with M. Caduto (Fulcrum, 1994); The Native American Sweat Lodge in History & Story (The Crossing Press, 1994); Keepers of the Animals: Native American Stories & Wildlife Activities for Children, with Michael Caduto (Fulcrum, 1990); Keepers of the Earth: Native American Stories & Environmental Activities for Children (with Michael Caduto, Fulcrum, 1988); Survival This Way (University of Arizona Press, 1987); among others. *Folk Stories*: How Chipmunk Got His Stripes, with james Bruchac (Dial, 2002); When the Chenoo

Howls, with James Bruchac (Walker, 1998); Makiawisug: The Gift of the Little People, with Melissa Fawcett (Little People, 1997); The Girl Who Married the Moon, with Gayle Ross (Bridgewater, 1994); Native Plant Stories (Fulcrum, 1995); Native American Animal Stories (Fulcrum, 1992); Hoop Snakes,, Hide-Behinds and Sidehill Winders (The Crossing Press, 1991); Native American Stories (Fulcrum, 1991); Return of the Sun (The Crossing Press, 1989); The Faithful Hunter and Other Abenaki Stories (Bowman Books, 1988); Iroquois Stories (The Crossing Press, 1985); among others. *Picture Books*: Seasons of the Circle (Troll, 2003); Squanto's Story (Harcourt, 2000); Crazy Horse's Vision (Lee & Low, 2000); Many Nations (Bridgewater, 1998); Between Earth and Sky (Harcourt, 1997); among others Poetry: Ndakinna/Our Land (West End Press, 2003); Above the Line (West End Press, 2003); No Borders (Holy Cow Books, 1998); among others. *Audio cassettes*: Dawnland (Fulcrum, 1993); Keepers of the Animals (Fulcrum, 1992); Keepers of the Earth (Fulcrum, 1990) , The Boy Who Lived With the Bears (Parabola/Harper Audio, 1990); Gluskabe Stories (Yellow Moon, 1990); Translator's Son (Cross Cultural Communications, 1981). *Children's Books*: The First Strawberries (Dial Books, 1993); Fox Song (Philomel, 1993); Thirteen Moons on Turtle's Back, with Jonathan London (Philomel, 1992).

BRUDERER, PAT
(president-Indian organization)
Affiliation: President, Indian Crafts & Arts Manitoba, Inc., 348 Hargrave St., Winnipeg, Manitoba, Canada R3B 2J9 (204) 944-1469.

BRUGGE, DAVID M. 1927-
(anthropologist)
Born September 3, 1927, Jamestown, N.Y. *Education*: University of New Mexico, BA, 1950. *Principal occupation*: Anthropologist. *Address*: Southwest Cultural Resources Center, National Park Service, 1220 S. St. Francis Dr., Box 728, Santa Fe, NM 87504-0728 (505) 988-6766. *Affiliations*: Various positions, Gallup Community Indian Center, Gallup, NM, 1953-57; salvage archaeologist, Four Corners Pipeline Co., Houston, TX, 1957-58; anthropologist, The Navajo Tribe, Window Rock, AZ, 1958-68. *Other professional posts*: Archaeologist, Museum of Northern Arizona, Flagstaff, AZ, 1957; director, Navajo Curriculum Center, Rough Rock, AZ, 1968; instructor, College of Ganado, AZ, 1973; chief, Branch of Curation, Southwest Cultural Resources Center, National Park Service, P.O. Box 728, Santa Fe, NM, 1985-. *Military service*: U.S. Army, 1945-47. *Community activities*: Sage Memorial Hospital, Ganado, Ariz. (secretary, advisory board); Title I Committee, Ganado Public Schools. *Memberships*: American Anthropological Association; Society for American Archaeology; Archaeological Society of New Mexico (trustee); American Society for Ethnohistory (secretary-treasurer, 1966-68); Arizona Archaeological & Historical Society; New Mexico Historical Society; Northern Arizona Society for Science & Art, Inc.; American Association for the Advancement of Science; Plateau Sciences Society. *Interests*: "Navajo studies, especially in archaeology, ethnohistory and history, and more generally of the greater Southwest. In addition to my work with the Navajos, I have done field work in northwestern Mexico, principally among the Pima Bajo (Lower Pima) of Sonora. My work with the Navajo Tribe involved research for various land disputes such as the Land Claims Case, the Navajo-Hopi boundary dispute, the McCracken Mesa land exchange and Utah school section case and the Huerfano Mesa land exchange." *Biographical sources*: Who's Who in the West; The Official Museum Directory. *Published works*: Navajo Pottery and Ethnohistory (The Navajo Tribe, 1963; Long Ago in Navajoland (The Navajo Tribe, 1965); Navajo Bibliography, with J. Lee Correll and Edith Watson (The Navajo Tribe, 1967); Navajos in the Catholic Church Records of New Mexico, 1694-1875 (The Navajo Tribe, 1968); Zarcillos Largos, Courageous Advocate of Peace (The Navajo Tribe, 1970); The Story of the Navajo Treaties, with J. Lee Correll (The Navajo Tribe, 1971); Navajo and Western Pueblo History (Tucson Corral of Westerners, 1972); The Navajo Exodus (Archaeological Society of New Mexico, 1972.)

BRUGUIER, LEONARD R. (Yankton Sioux) 1944-
(administration)
Born October 9, 1944, Wagner, S.D. *Education*: Uni-

versity of South Dakota, BA, 1984, MPA, 1986; Oklahoma State University, PhD, 1989. *Principal occupation*: Administration. *Address & Affiliation*: Director, Institute of American Indian Studies, University of South Dakota, 414 E. Clark, Vermillion, SD 57069 (605) 677-5209, 1989-. *Other professional post*: Editor, "The Bulletin," Institute of American Indian Studies, University of South Dakota; assistant professor of American history, University of South Dakota; host radio show, "Voices of the Plains," South Dakota Public Radio Network, Vermillion, SD. *Military service*: U.S. Marine Corps, 1963-70 (Sergeant; Combat Action Ribbon, Presidential Unit Citation, Vietnam Service Medal, Vietnam Campaign Ribbon, Armed Forces Expeditionary Medal, National Defense Medal). *Community activities*: Member, Indian Memorial Committee, National Parks Service. *Memberships*: Organization of American Historians, 1986-; Western Historical Association, 1985-; Southern Historical Association, 1988-; Phi Alpha Theta, 1986-; Machinists and Aerospace Workers, 1971-; Vietnam Veterans of America, 1976-. *Awards, honors*: Oklahoma State Regents for Higher Education Minority Doctoral Study Grant; Towsend Memorial Minority Scholarships; Archie B. Gillfillan Award for Creative Writing; History Alumni Award; University of South Dakota Veterans Club. *Interests*: "North & South American comparative studies of "Indians," with a particular interest in plains people and their religion, government, and social institutions. in North America, I am researching the Pipe Religion and its influence in Indian-White relations. Ongoing research of Indian men and women who served in the U.S. Armed Force and their impact on reservation, government, and social patterns. Demographic and statistical information on Indians, both continents." *Biographical source*: "The Yankton Sioux", Indians of North America Series, by Herbert Hoover. *Published works*: Remember Your Relatives (Marty Indian School, 1985; Yankton Sioux Elderly Board, 1989); Conference on Reburials (American Indian Research Project, 1985); The Yankton Sioux (Chelsea House Publishers, 1988); South Dakota Leaders (University of South Dakota Press, 1989).

BRUN, FRANCIS
(BIA field rep.)
Affiliation: Red Lake Field Office, Bureau of Indian Affairs, Red Lake, MN 56671 (218) 679-3361 Fax 679-3691.

BRUNDIN, CLAUDIA
(rancheria chairperson)
Affiliation: Blue Lake Rancheria, P.O. Box 428, Blue Lake, CA 95525 (707) 668-5615 .

BRUNDIN, JUDITH A. 1949-
(museum education department head, editor)
Born December 18, 1949, Columbus, Ohio. *Education*: University of Colorado, BFA, 1972; Colorado College, MAT, 1978; New York University, Graduate Certificate-Museum Studies, 1983. *Principal occupation*: Museum education department head. *Home address*: Resides in NJ Fax (201) 271-0070. *Affiliations*: Instructor, BIA, AZ, 1974-77; technician, Tucson Public Schools, 1978-80; exhibitions designer, Navajo Tribe, AZ, 1980-81; Head, Education Dept., National Museum of the American Indian (NMAI), Smithsonian Institution, New York, NY, 1982-95. *Other professional posts*: Consulting, lectures-presentations. *Awards, honors*: Letter of Commendation, BIA, presented upon resignation, April 1977; Tribal plaque from the Navajo Tribe upon completion of the Navajo Tribal Museum's exhibit installation, 1981. *Published works*: Author - American Indian Dolls, An Educational Resource Kit (NMAI, 1986), and The Native People of the Northeast Woodlands, An Educational Resource Publication (NMAI, 1990); articles - "Navajo Sandpainting," Instructor, 87 (Nov. 1977); "On Your Own With Great Native Americans" exhibit guide (NMAI, 1988); "On Your Own With Native American Cultures" exhibit guide (NMAI, 1989); among many other media & journal articles, 1995-present).

BRUNER, TERRY
(BIA agency supt.)
Affiliation: Anadarko Agency, BIA, P.O. Box 309, Anadarko, OK 73005 (405) 247-6677 Fax 247-9232.

BRUNER, WILLIAM E. (Choctaw)
(Indian school principal)
Affiliation: Bogue Chitto Elementary School, Route 2, Box 274, Philadelphia, MS 39350 (601) 656-8611.

BRUNOE, BRUCE, SR.
(Confederated-Warm Springs)
(tribal chairperson)
Affiliation: Confederated Tribes of the Warm Springs Reservation, P.O. Box C, Warm Springs, OR 97761 (503) 553-1161.

BRUNSELL, ADELINE
(BIA agency supt.)
Affiliation: Fort Berthold Agency, BIA, P.O. Box 370, New Town, ND 58763 (701) 627-4707 Fax 627-3601.

BRUSHBREAKER, DAVID (Rosebud Lakota)
(board vice president)
Address & Affiliation: Board Vice President, Sicangu Oyate Ho., Inc., St. Francis Indian School, P.O. Box 379 HCR 59 Box 1A, St. Francis, SD 57572 (605) 747-2299.

BRUYERE, LOUIS
(council president)
Affiliation: President, Native Council of Canada, 450 Rideau St., 2nd Floor, Ottawa, Ontario, Canada K1N 5Z4 (613) 238-3511.

BRUYERE, RICHARD
(Indian band chief)
Affiliation: Chief, Couchiching Indian Band, P.O. Box 723, Fort Frances, Ontario, Canada P9A 3M9 (807) 274-3228.

BRYANT, CHRISTINA *(Ageya Wahya)*
(Tsalagi Cherokee/Shinnecock) 1948-
(visual artist, puppeteer, poet, teacher, doll artist)
Born March 14, 1948, Kings County, N.Y. *Education*: Pace University (New York, NY) B.A. *Principal occupation*: Storyteller, visual artist, free-lance educator, environmentalist. *Home address*: 105 Lincoln Rd., Apt. 5J, Brooklyn, NY 11225 (718) 462-8128. *Affiliation*: Freelance educator - folkways interpreter of Native American culture, environment, recreation therapist, American Indian arts/crafts teacher, storyteller, Huntington Free Library/Heye Foundation and the Smithsonian Institution (American Indian Library); Henry Street Art in Education, Learning Through an Expanded Arts Program (LEAP); Museum of Natural History - Special Education Dept. and Peoples Center; Arts Horizons, NJ & NY, 1998-. *Community activities*: Teaching Native children about puppetry and use of puppets in theatre setting using Native American stories. *Memberships*: Nuyagi Keetoowah, Inc.; Southeastern Cherokee Confederacy of Georgia; National Outdoor Leadership School; Nitchin Family Awareness Network. *Interests*: Storytelling - speaks annually to hundreds of students in the NYC schools and area private schools; works as free-lance art in education teacher. *Publication*: "Tlanuwa Speaks (book of poetry).

BRYANT, RICHARD M., M.D.
(administrative officer)
Affiliation: Phoenix Indian Medical Center, 4212 North 16th St., Phoenix, AZ 85016 (602) 263-1200.

BRYCELEA, CLIFFORD (Dine) 1953-
(professional artist; painter)
Born September 26, 1953, Shiprock, N.M. *Education*: Fort Lewis College, BA (Art), 1975. *Principal occupation*: Professional artist; painter. *Home address*: 1721 Montano St., Santa Fe, NM 87501 (505) 984-8632. *Affiliations*: Toh-Atin Gallery, Durango, CO (16 years); Spirits in the Wind, Golden, CO (8 years); Long Ago & Far Away, Manchester Center, VT (10 years); Skystone N' Silver, Hobart, IN (12 years); Tekakwitha, Helen, GA (8 years); Blue Gem & Gallery, Midland, TX (15 years). *Memberships*: Indian Arts & Crafts Association (IACA), Albuquerque (member, 1980-; board of directors, 1986-91); Southwestern Association on Indian Affairs (Santa Fe), 1980-. *Awards, honors*: 4 Gold Medals, IACA, San Dimas, CA 1981, 1982 & 1986; 1st Place & Memorial Award, Gallup (NM) Ceremonial; Artist-of-the-Year, 1987 by IACA; and City Poster Award, 1991, Sante Fe, NM. *Interests*: "My work is in contemporary and representational style - paintings

of various cultures, telling the stories and recall the legends of American Indians. It also depicted the mysticism and magical composition (spiritual meaning.) *Biographical sources*: Beyond Tradition, by Jerry & Lois Jacka; The Art Fever, by James Parsons; American Artist by Les Krantz; story by Julie Pearson, June, 1992, Southwest Art Magazine. *Published works*: illus. - American Way (American Airlines, 1976); illus. - Navajo Painting, by Katherin Chase, 1980; Pieces of White Shell (Charles Scribner's Sons, 1984); illus. - Haunted Mesa (Bantam Books, 1987); illus. Beyond Tradition, by Lois & Jerry Jacka, 1988; cover illus. - "Wildfire" magazine, Fall 1990; cover illus. - "San Francisco Chamber of Commerce Magazine, 1991; illus. - The Talking Wind, by Jack Hawkins, 1994; illus. - Enduring Traditions, by Lois & Jerry Jacka, 1994; cover illus. - Fire in the Mind, by George Johnson, 1995; illus. - Moon & Otter & Frog, by Laura Simms, 1995.

BUCHEL, SUSAN J.
(museum curator)
Affiliation: Nez Perce National Historical Park & Museum, P.O. Box 93, Spalding, ID 83551.

BUCK, JIM
(radio host/producer)
Affiliation: "Sequoyah," WBAI - FM, 505 Eighth Ave., New York, NY 10018 (212) 279-0707.

BUCK, TERRI
(tribal health director)
Affiliation: Prairie Island Community Council, 1158 Island Blvd., Welch, MN 55089 (612) 385-2554.

BUCKANAGA, GERTRUDE (Chippewa)
(director-Indian women's project)
Affiliation: Director, American Indian Women Into Media, Migizi Communications, Inc., 3123 E. Lake St., Suite 200, Minneapolis, MN 55406 (612) 721-6631.

BUCKANAGA, JOHN (Ojibwe)
(Indian school administrator)
Affiliation: Circle of Life Survival School, P.O. Box 447, White Earth, MN 56591 (218) 983-3285 ext. 269 Fax 983-3767.

BUCKLEY, THOMAS 1942-
(writer)
Born May 28, 1942, Louisville, KY. *Education*: Harvard University, BA, 1975; University of Chicago, MA, 1977, PhD, 1982. *Principal occupation*: Writer. *Address*: 26 York St., Bath, ME 04530; E-mail: timbuckley@earthlink.net. *Past professional posts*: Anthropology & American Studies, UMass/Boston, MA (professor, 1980-2001; academic director, Native American Resource Center, 1996-2001; director, Native American Studies Concentration, 1997-2001). *Interests*: Field work in Native Northwestern California, among Yurok, Hupa, Karuk and Tolowa Indians, since 1976. Focus on Yurok language and politics, religion, gender. Serve as consultant and as expert witness in fishing and in land use & religious freedom cases. *Published works*: Editor, Blood Magic (University of California Press, 1988); Standing Ground (University of California Press, 2002); numerous articles on the Yuroks and on A.L. Kroeber.

BUECKER, THOMAS R. 1948-
(museum curator)
Born November 14, 1948, Neb. *Education*:University of Nebraska, Kearney, BA, 1973; Chadron State College, MA, 1992. *Principal occupation*: Museum curator. *Address*: P.O. Box 304, Crawford, NE 69339 (308) 665-2919. *Affiliation*: Curator, Fort Robinson Museum, Nebraska State Historical Society, Lincoln, NE, 1977-. *Published works*: The Crazy Horse Surrender Ledger (Nebraska State Historical Society, 1994); Fort Robinson and the American West, 1874-1899 (Nebraska State Historical Society, 1999); Fort Robinson and the American Century, 1900-1948 (Nebraska State Historical Society, 2002).

BUENDIA, IMELDA, MD
(clinical director)
Affiliation: Wewoka PHS Indian Health Center, P.O Box 1475, Wewoka, OK 74884 (405) 257-6281.

BUFFALO, VICTOR
(Indian band chief)
Affiliation: Samson Cree Nation, Box 159, Hobbema, Alberta, Canada T0C 1N0 (403) 421-4926.

BUFFALO-REYES, JEAN (Lake Superior Chippewa)
(tribal chairperson)
Affiliation: Red Cliff Band of Lake Superior Chippewa,
P.O. Box 529, Bayfield, WI 54814 (715) 779-3700.

BUFFALOHEAD, W. ROGER
(Indian center director)
Affiliation: Director, Tribal Research Center, NAES
(Native American Educational Services) College, 2838
W. Peterson Ave., Chicago, IL 60659 (773) 761-5000
Fax 761-3808. *Past professional post*: Director,
Achievement Through Communications Project, Migizi
Communications, Inc., Minneapolis, MN 55406.

BUFORD, BETTIE (LITTLE DOVE) *(Gttigua Cox)*
(Yamasee/ Creek/Cherokee) 1935-
(principal chief)
Born February 20, 1935, Ocoee, Fla. *Principal occu-
pation*: Principal chief. *Address*: P.O. Box 521, Cox-
Osceola Seminole Indian Reservation, Orange
Springs, FL 32182 (904) 546-1386 (home); 546-5525
(tribal office). *Affiliations*: President, Oklavueha Seminole Trading Post, Orange Springs, FL, 1985-; licensed
genealogist & historian (29 years). *Professional post*:
Teacher, Indian culture, Osceola Christian Indian
School. *Military service*: American Red Cross Military
Hospital, Korean conflict. *Community activities*: Principal chief, Oklavueha Band of Seminole Indians,
1979-; Assistant principal of Coe Harjo's Private Christian Indian School, 1986-. *Memberships*: Native American Historical Presentation Service, 1991-; National
Indian Unity Coalition, 1990-; The Concerned Citizens
League of America (president). *Awards*: Marion Education Awards; several awards for teaching Indian culture an crafts. *Interests*: "My major interest is to help
improve the lifestyles of my Indian people and to stop
some of the prejudice against them. To let all people
know what real Indians are, not the stereotypes that
they see in the movies and on television. I would like
to travel to all tribes." *Published works*: Oklavueha #1-
2-3-4-5 Band of Seminoles, 1992-94; Oklawaka People
of the River Indians, 1994; Yamasee Indians - Last
Known as Oklavueha Band of Seminoles, 1994; *In
progress*: Oklavuehas Written Language.

BUHR, GRACE
(coordinator-friendship centres)
Affiliation: Manitoba Association of Friendship Centres,
604 - 213 Notre Dame Ave., Winnipeg, Manitoba,
Canada R3B 2J9 (204) 943-8082.

BULFER, JOE
(executive director)
Affiliation: Southern Indian Health Council,
P.O. Box 2128, Alpine, CA 91903 (619) 445-1188.

BULL, ADAM
(school principal)
Affiliation: Wingate High School, P.O. Box 2, Fort
Wingate, NM 87316 (505) 488-6400 Fax 488-6444.

BULL, ROGER
(Indian band chief)
Affiliation: Lac Seul Indian Band, Hudson,
Ontario, Canada P0V 1X0 (807) 582-3503.

BULLARD, LORETTA
(association president)
Affiliation: Kawerak, Inc., P.O. Box 948,
Nome, AK 99762 (907) 443-5231.

BULLDOG, HARVEY
(Indian band chief)
Affiliation: Boyer River Indian Band, Box 270,
High Level, Alberta, Canada T0H 1Z0 (403) 927-3697.

BULLETTS-BENSON, GLORIA (Kaibab Paiute)
(tribal chairperson)
Affiliation: Kaibab Paiute Tribal Council,
HC65, Box 2, Fredonia, AZ 86022 (520) 643-7245.

BULLOCK, MORRIS (Alabama-Coushatta of Texas)
(former tribal chairperson)
Affiliation: Alabama Coushatta Tribe of Texas, Rt. 3
Box 640, Livingston, TX 77351 (409) 563-4391.

BUNKE, JIM
(museum CEO)
Affiliation: Sebewaing Indian Museum, 612 E. Bay St.,
Sebewaing, MI 48759 (517) 883-3730.

BUNN, NELSON (Sioux)
(Indian band chief)
Affiliation: Birdtail Sioux Indian Band, P.O. Box 75,
Beulah, Manitoba, Canada R0M 0B0 (204) 568-4540.

BUNNER, GRACE (Creek)
(town king-Mekko)
Address & Affiliation: Thlopthlocco Tribal Town, P.O.
Box 188, Okemah, OK 74859 (918) 623-2620 Fax 623-
0419.

BUNNIE, SAMUEL
(Indian band chief)
Affiliation: Sakimay Indian Band, Box 339, Grenfell,
Saskatchewan, Canada S0G 2B0 (306) 697-2831.

BURCELL, SUZANNE M.
(Indian program director)
Affiliation: Indian Teacher & Educational Personnel
Program (ITEPP), Humboldt State University, 1 Harpst
St., Spidell House #85, Arcata, CA 95521 (707) 826-
3672 Fax 826-3675. E-mail: smb7001@humboldt.edu.

BURCH, LEONARD C. (Southern Ute)
(tribal chairperson)
Affiliation: Southern Ute Tribal Council,
P.O. Box 737, Ignacio, CO 81137 (970) 563-0100.

BURDEAU, GEORGE
(film producer/director)
Affiliation: Raleigh Studios, 650 N. Bronson Ave.,
Suite 215, Hollywood, CA 90004 (213) 871-8689.

BURDETTE, ROBYN (Paiute)
(tribal chairperson)
Affiliation: Summit Lake Paiute Council, 655 Anderson St., Winnemucca, NV 89445 (702) 623-5151.

BURDETTE, VIVIAN L. (Tonto Apache)
(tribal chairperson)
Affiliation: Tonto Apache Tribal Council, #30 Tonto
Reservation, Payson, AZ 85541 (928) 474-5000.

BURGESS, MICHAEL
(managing editor)
Affiliation: "Talking Leaf Newspaper," Los Angeles Indian Center, Los Angeles, CA 90017 (213) 413-3156.

BURGESS, (FITCH) NINA VONDELL *(She Who
Barks)* **(United Lumbee) 1934-**
(insurance agent-retired)
Born October 9, 1934, Shoals, Ind. *Principal occupa-
tion*: Insurance agent (licensed-retired) *Education*: Two
years college. *Address*: 3125 Warburton Ave., Santa
Clara, CA 95051. E-mail: ninaburgess@hotmail.com.
Affiliation: Secretary/treasurer, United Lumbee War
Hawkk Band, 1987-present. *Community activities*:
Church of Jesus Christ of Latter Day Saints. *Member-
ships*: United Lumbee (Chief-War Hawk Band, 2002-
present); Epsilon Sigma Alpha; Order of the Amoranth.
Interests: Needlepointing, Native American crafts,
reading, walking.

BURGESS, ROXANNE
(liaison)
Affiliation: Los Angeles American Indian Liaison to the
Mayor, 200 N. Spring St., Los Angeles, CA 90012 (213)
485-8881.

BURGESS, VIOLA
(AK village council president)
Affiliation: Hydaburg Cooperative Association,
P.O. Box 323, Hydaburg, AK 99922 (907) 285-3666.

BURHANSSTIPANOV, LINDA
(executive director)
Affiliation: Native American Cancer Research (NACR),
3022 Nova Rd., Pine, CO 80470 (303) 838-9359 Fax
838-7629.

BURLEY, SILVIA (Miwok)
(rancheria chairperson)
Affiliation: Sheep Ranch Rancheria, 1055 Winter Court,
Tracy, CA 95376 (209) 834-0197.

BURNABY, JOANNE
(museum director)
Affiliation: Dene Cultural Institute, P.O. Box 207,
Yellowknife, Northwest Territories, Canada X1A 2N2
(403) 873-6617.

BURNETT, BILL
(Indian education program director)
Affiliation: South Umpqua School District, Indian Edu-
cation Program, 558 Chadwick Lane, Myrtle Creek,
OR 97457 (503) 863-3118.

BURNS, JAMES
(college instructor)
Affiliation: Native American Studies Dept., Montana
State University, 2-179 Wilson Hall, P.O. Box 172340,
Bozeman, MT 59717 (406) 994-3881 Fax 994-6879.
Interests: Native American education.

BURNS, ROBERT I., S.J. 1921-
(clergyman, historian, educator)
Born August 16, 1921, San Francisco, Calif. *Education*: Gonzaga University, BA, 1945, MA, 1947 (D. Litt.),
1968; Fordham University, MA, 1949; Jesuit Pontifical
Faculty (Spokane, WA, Phil.B., 1946, Phil.Lic., 1947)
(Alma, CA, S.Th.B., 1951, S.Th.Lic., 1953; Postgraduate, Columbia University, 1949, Oxford University,
1956-57; Johns Hopkins University, Ph.D. (summa
cum laude)(History), 1958; University of Fribourg,
Switzerland, Doc. es Sc.Hist. (double summa cum
laude)(History, Ethnohistory), 1961. *Principal occupation*: Clergyman, historian, educator. *Address*: History
Department, Graduate School, University of California, Los Angeles, CA 90024. *Affiliations*: Assistant archivist, Jesuit and Indian Archives of Pacific Northwest
Province, Spokane, 1945-47; instructor, History Department, University of San Francisco, (instructor,
1947-48; assistant professor, 1958-62; associate professor, 1963-66; professor, 1967-76; senior professor, History Dept., U.C.L.A., 1976-. *Other professional
posts*: Director, Institute of Medieval Mediterranean,
Spain, 1976-; staff, UCLA Center for Medieval-Renais-
sance Studies, 1977-; staff, UCLA Near Eastern Center, 1979-. *Editorial work*: Board editor, Trend in History, 1980; co-editor, Viator (UCLA), 1980-90; editorial committee, U.C. Press, 1985. *Memberships*: American Historical Association, Pacific Coast Branch (vice
president, 1978; president, 1978-80; presiding-del-
egate, International Congress of Historical Sciences,
1975, and U.S. Representative, 1980); American
Catholic Historical Association (president, 1976); Medieval Association of the Pacific; Society for Spanish
and Portuguese Historical Studies; Hill Monastic Library; North American Catalan Society; American Bibliographical Center (board, 1982-89). *Awards, honors*:
Five book awards from national historical associations,
including American Historical (Pacific Coast Award),
American Catholic Historical, and American Association for State and Local History, for Jesuits and Indian
Wars, 1965; Dr. Burns gave the keynote address at
the National Park Service's Sesquicentennial of the
sustained Indian-white contact by Americans in the
Pacific Northwest states, the (Protestant) Whitman
Mission, July 1986 at Whitman College. *Interests*: "I
have two fields, allied but distinct, in which I publish
regularly. The medieval field is the moving frontier of
the 13th-century Catalonia, particularly the absorption
by the Catalan peoples of the Valencian kingdom of
the Moslems. The American field is the Pacific Northwest, particularly, Indian-white relations and troubles,
1840-1880, as illumined especially by Jesuit documentation here and in Europe. Ethnohistory and the Pacific Northwest frontier is thus seen not in isolation but
as illumined by other frontier experiences." *Biographical sources*: Who's Who in America; Contemporary
Authors; among others. *Published works*: Co-author, I
lift My Lamp: Jesuits in America, 1955; Indians and
Whites in the Pacific Northwest: Jesuit Contributions
to Peace 1850-1880 (University of San Francisco
Press, 1961); The Jesuits and the Indian Wars (Yale
University Press, 1966); The Jesuits and the Indian
Wars of the Northwest, reissue of 1966 edition (Uni-
versity of Idaho Press, 1985). *Articles include*: North-
west Indian Missions, position essay, Handbook of
North American Indians (U.S. Government Printing
Office, 1978-1990, vol. 4; Jesuit Missions, (North
American Indians) Dictionary of American History
(Charles Scribner's Sons, 1977); "Roman Catholic Missionaries", (to U.S. Indians) in Reader's Encyclopedia
of the American West (Thomas Y. Crowell Co., 1977);
"The Opening of the West," (impact on Pacific Northwest Indians) in The Indian: Assimilation, Integration
or Separation (Prentice-Hall, Canada, 1972); "The Significance of the Frontier in the Middle Ages", in Medieval Frontier Societies, ed. by Robert Bartlett & Angus MacKay (Clarendon Press, 1989) This is an inter-

relating of the U.S. Indian and the Medieval frontiers; article in revised edition of Reader's Encyclopedia of the American West (Yale University Press, 1997).

BURR, DONNA J. (Choctaw)
(educator)
Born in Philadelphia, Miss. *Principal occupation*: Educator. *Education*: University of St. Thomas, MA. *Address*: Onamia School District #480, Indian Education Program, 35465 - 125th Ave., Onamia, MN 56359 (320) 532-4174 Fax 532-4658. *Affiliation*: Instructor, Onamia School District #480, Onamia, MN. Military service: U.S. Air Force, 1980-86. *Community activities*: Chairperson, Onamia Parent Advisory Committee.

BURR, JOYCE
(school administrator)
Affiliation: Circle of Nations Wahpeton Indian Boarding School, 832 8th St. North, Wahpeton, ND 58075 (701) 642-6631 Fax 642-5880.

BURR, LARRY J.
(BIA agency supt.)
Affiliation: Rosebud Agency, BIA, P.O. Box 550, Rosebud, SD 57570 (605) 747-2224.

BURROWS, DUDLEY (Wintun)
(rancheria chairperson)
Affiliation: Grindstone Rancheria, P.O. Box 63, Elk Creek, CA 95939 (530) 968-5365.

BURRUS, S.S. (Ms.) *(Going About Grasshopper Sam)* **(Oklahoma Cherokee)**
(artist)
Born in Okla. *Education*: Central State University, BA. *Principal occupation*: Artist of watercolor, sculpture, fashion designer. *Permanent Collections*: State Trail of Tears Museum - Cape Girardeau, MO, 1987, 1991; A-Eiteljorg Museum - Indianapolis, IN, 1989; Heritage Center - Tahlequah, OK, 1991; Cherokee Museum - Cherokee, NC, 1991; Five Tribes Museum - Muskogee, OK, 1991; Smithsonian - Office of Dr. Rayna Green, 1992; University of Oklahoma - Dr. Rennard Strickland, Director of American Indian Law & Policy Center - Oklahoma City, 1992. *Memberships*: Indian Arts and Crafts Association; Southwestern American Indian Association; Oklahoma Arts Council. *Awards, honors*: Numerous awards including: 1988 - Tulsa Arts Festival, Oklahoma Indian Market; 1989 - Five Tribes Museum, Intertribal Ceremonial; 1990 - Tulsa Idian Festival, Red Earth, Intertribal-Gallup; 1991 - Santa Fe Indian Market, Dallas Market Center, Katowah Intertribal Show, Trail of Tears Art Show; 1992 - Featured Fashion Designer-20th Annual Symposium on the American Indian-March 1992 by N.S.U., Tahlequah, OK. One Woman Shows and Special Exhibits, Invitationals. *Published works*: Prose by S S. Burrus - "Why Do They Whisper" (All My Relations, 1991); five prints (Wintercount Greetin Cards, 1991); cover and content illustrations for "The Trail On Which They Wept" (Cherokee Girl) (Silver/Burdett Press, 1992); 1993 Calendar (Wintercount Greeting Cards 1992); numerous prints and posters.

BURSHEARS, J.F.
(museum director)
Affiliation: Koshare Indian Museum, P.O. Box 580, 115 W. 18th St., La Junta, CO 81050 (719) 384-4411.

BURSHIN, BEN
(BIA field rep.)
Affiliation: Southern Paiute Field Office, Bureau of Indian Affairs, P.O. Box 720, St. George, UT 84771 (435) 674-9720 Fax 674-9714.

BURT, EUGENE C. 1948-
(managing editor)
Born July 31, 1948, Philadelphia, PA. *Education*: Temple University, BA, 1970; University of Washington, MA, 1973, PhD, 1980. P*rincipal occupation*: Managing editor, Ethnoarts Index. *Address*: P.O. Box 30789, Seattle, WA 98103 (206) 783-9580. *Affiliation*: Owner, Data Arts, Seattle, WA, 1983-. *Other professional post*: Higher education teaching positions at various institutions. *Interests*: Non-western art history. *Published works*: Bibliography of Tribal Art Bibliographies (Data Arts, 1986); Native American Art: A 5-Year Cumulative Bibliography (Data Arts, 1990).

BURTON, SANDRA
(Indian education program director)
Affiliation: Eureka City Schools, Indian Education Program, 3200 Walford Ave., Eureka, CA 95501 (707) 441-2454.

BURTON, THOMAS C. (Paiute)
(ex-tribal chairperson)
Affiliation: Fallon Business Council, 8955 Mission Rd, Fallon, NV 89406 (702) 423-6075.

BURTON, WILLIAM
(health systems administrator)
Affiliation: SEARHC Health Center, 3289 Tongass Ave., Ketchikan, AK 99901 (907) 225-4156.

BUSH, BOBBIE LOUISE (Chehalis)
(poet, writer)
Address: P.O. Box 926, Hoodsport, WA 98548 (360) 426-3990.

BUSH, MITCHELL LESTER, Jr. (Onondaga) 1936-
(chief-tribal enrollment, B.I.A.-retired)
Born February 1, 1936, Syracuse, N.Y. *Education*: Haskell Institute, 1951-56. *Principal occupation*: Chief, tribal enrollment, B.I.A. *Home address*: 22258 Cool Water Dr., Ruther Glen, VA 22546. *Affiliation*: Chief, Branch of Tribal Enrollment Services, BIA, Washington, DC, 1956-91. *Other professional post*: Editor, American Indian Society (Washington, DC) Newsletter, 1966-. *Military service*: U.S. Army, 1958-61 (Specialist 4th Class). *Community activities*: DC-MD-VA Chapter of VEVITA (board of directors); American Indian Inaugural Ball (committee member, 1969, '73, '77, '81, '85, '89, '93, '97, 2001); American Indian Society, Washington, D.C. (president, 1966-91); Board of Directors, Governors' Interstate Indian Council, 2002-present. *Awards, honors*: American Indian Society Distinguished Service Award, 1971 & 1990; Maharishi Award conferred by the Maharishi University; appointed by Gov. Gerald L. Baliles to Virginia Council on Indians, 1989; Outstanding Public Service to the U.S.A. certificate from the Dept. of the Interior, May, 1990; Mental Health Association Distinguished Service Award; Certificate of Appreciation from MD Governor Hughes; Points of Light Certificate for Outstanding Volunteer Contributions to the U.S.A. issued by Dept. of the Interior; Certificate of Appreciation from the Presidential Inaugural Committee, Jan. 1981. *Interests*: "Lecturer and Indian dancer for American Indian Society; participant, 1990 Census Planning Conference on Race and Ethnic Items sponsored by the Census Bureau; tour leader to Virginia Indian reservations for Resident Associate Program, Smithsonian Institution; honored at the 1982 Nanticoke (Delaware) Pow Wow; judge at the 1978, '80, '82, '84 & '85 Miss Indian America Pageants held in Sheridan, WY, and Bismarck, ND; photo and bio included in Shadows Caught: Images of Native Americans, by Stephen Gambaro at Gilcrease Institute, Tulsa, Oklahoma. Avocational - roller skating and raising ornamental fowl." *Biographical sources*: To Live in Two Worlds, by Brent Ashabranner; American Indian Wars, by John Tebbel, 1960; Successful Indian Career Profiles, to be published by North American Indian Club, Syracuse, N.Y. *Published works*: Editor, American Indian Society Cookbook (American Indian Society, 1975 and 1984 editions); Movies & Television shows: Lives of the Rich and Famous, segment featuring Connie Stevens; MGM, George Washington TV Mini-Series; Indians, Walt Disney Productions; TNT's "Broken Chain"; and numerous television programs.

BUSHIE, RODERICK
(Indian band chief)
Affiliation: Hollow Water Indian Band, Wanipigow, Manitoba, Canada R0E 2E0 (204) 363-7278.

BUSSEY, RUTH
(health clinic director)
Affiliation: Grand Traverse Ottawa/Chippewa Health Clinic, Route 1, Box 135, Suttons Bay, MI 49682 (616) 271-3882.

BUSSIDOR, ILA
(Indian band chief)
Affiliation: Fort Churchill Indian Band, Tadoule Lake, Manitoba, Canada R0B 0L0 (204) 652-2219.

BUSTOS, BERNIE (Navajo)
(radio station manager)
Affiliation: KTDB - 89.7 FM, Ramah Navajo School Board, P.O. Box 40, Pinehill, NM 87357 (505) 775-3215.

BUTLER, LUVENIA H.
(executive director)
Affiliation: Tennessee Commission on Indian Affairs, 401 Church St., L&C Towers, 10th Floor, Nashville, TN 37243 (615) 532-0745.

BUTLER, MICHAEL
(nature park manager)
Affiliation: Iroquois Indian Museum, P.O. Box 7, Caverns Rd., Howes Cave, NY 12092 (518) 296-8949.

BUTLER, RAYMOND (Otoe-Missouria)
(tribal council chairperson)
Affiliation: Otoe-Missouria Tribal Council, Rt. 1, Box 62, Red Rock, OK 74651 (405) 723-4466.

BUTLER, WILLIAM (Apache)
(Indian school supt.)
Affiliation: Mescalero Elementary School, P.O. Box 230, Mescalero, NM 88340 (505) 671-4431.

BUTTERFIELD, JANIE
(health center director)
Affiliation: Pit River Indian Health Center, P.O. Box 2720, Burney, CA 96013.

BUTTERFIELD, ROBIN A.
(education coordinator))
Affiliations: Coordinator, Oregon Dept. of Education, Indian Education, 700 Pringle Pkwy SE, Salem, OR 97310 (503) 378-3606 Fax 373-7968; President-board of directors, National Indian Education Association, 700 N. Fairfax, Suite 210, Alexandria, VA 22314 (703) 838-2870 Fax 838-1620.

BUTTERFLY, ANDREW
(editor)
Affiliation: Native Sun," Detroit American Indin Center, 22720 Plymouth Rd., Detroit, MI 48239 (313) 535-2966.

BUTTES, DR. BARBARA F.
(professor)
Affiliation: Dept. of American Studies, Arizona State University, Tempe, AZ 85287 (602) 965-6213 Fax 965-7671. *Interests*: Mdewekanton Sioux of Minnesota; tribal gaming. E-mail: barbara.buttes@asu.edu.

BUZZARD, GEORGE
(IHS associate director)
Affiliation: Office of Administration & Management, Department of Health and Human Services, USPHS-IHS, Rm. 6-25 Parklawn Bldg., 5600 Fishers Lane, Rockville, MD 20857 (301) 443-7493.

BUZZARD, MARVIN
(administrative officer)
Affiliation: Haskell Indian Nations University, 155 Indian Ave. #1305, Lawrence, KS 66046 (875) 749-8404 Fax 749-8406.

BYARS, TONY
(museum supt.)
Affiliation: Alabama-Coushatta Indian Museum, Route 3, Box 640, U.S. Highway 190, Livingston, TX 77351 (713) 563-4391.

BYERS, LARRY
(school principal)
Affiliation: Chemawa Indian School, 3700 Chemawa Rd. NE, Salem, OR 97305 (503) 399-5721 Fax 399-5870.

BYRD, DARLENE (Paiute)
(former tribal chairperson)
Affiliation: Lovelock Tribal Council, P.O. Box 878, Lovelock, NV 89419 (702) 273-7861.

BYRD, JOE (Oklahoma Cherokee)
(principal chief)
Address & Affiliation: Cherokee Nation of Oklahoma, P.O. Box 948, Tahlequah, OK 74465 (918) 456-0671 Fax 458-6147.

BYRNES, JIM (Navajo)
(Indian school principal)
Affiliation: To'hajiilee-He (Canoncito) School, P.O. Box 438, Laguna, NM 87026 (505) 831-6426 Fax 836-4914.

C

CABRAL, DARIEN
(association executive director)
Address & Affiliation: Executive director, Indian Arts & Crafts Association, 4010 Carlisle NE, Suite C, Albuquerque, NM 87107 (505) 265-9149 Fax 265-8251.

CACHAGEE, DOREEN
(Indian band chief)
Affiliation: Chapleau Cree, Box 400, Chapleau, Ontario, Canada P0M 1K0 (705) 864-0784.

CADUE, CHERYL
(public information coordinator)
Affiliation: American Indian College Fund, 21 W. 68th St., Suite 1F, New York, NY 10023 (800) 776-3863; (212) 787-6312. E-mail: cadue@collegefund.org.

CADUE, STEVEN (Kickapoo of Kansas)
(school chairperson)
Affiliation: Kickapoo Nation School, P.O. Box 106, Powhattan, KS 66527 (913) 474-3550.

CADUTO, MICHAEL J.
(storyteller, ecologist, educator & musician)
Resides in Vermont. *Education*: University of Michigan, MS in Natural Resources/Environmental Education. *Professional post*: Sr. Education Fellow with the Atlantic Center for the Environment. *Interests*: Travels extensively presenting environmental and cultural programs for adults and children. *Published works*: Keepers of the Animals: Native American Stories and Wildlife Activities for Children; Keepers of the Earth: Native American Stories and Environmental Activities for Children; Keepers of Life: Discovering Plants Through Native American Stories and Earth Activities for Children; and Keepers of the Night: Native American Stories and Nocturnal Activities for Children. (all with Joseph Bruchac); also audiocassette, All One Earth: Songs for the Generations (all published by Fulcrum Publishing).

CAESAR, NILES C.
(BIA regional director)
Affiliation: Alaska Regional Office, Bureau of Indian Affairs, P.O. Box 25520, Juneau, AK 99802 (907) 586-7177 Fax 586-7252.

CAGEY, HENRY (Lummi)
(tribal chairperson)
Affiliation: Chairperson, Lummi Business Council, 2616 Kwina Rd., Bellingham, WA 98226 (360) 734-8180.

CAJERO, JOE (Jemez Pueblo)
(pueblo governor)
Affiliation: Jemez Pueblo Council, P.O. Box 100, Jemez, NM 87024 (505) 834-7359.

CALAC, ROBERT (Luiseno)
(tribal chairperson)
Affiliation: Rincon Band of Mission Indians, P.O. Box 68, Valley Center, CA 92082 (619) 749-1051.

CALDWELL, ALAN JAMES (Menominee-White Earth Chippewa) 1948-
(education program director)
Born May 27, 1948, Shawano, Wisc. *Education*: University of Wisconsin, Green Bay, BS (History), 1976; University of Wisconsin, Superior, 1979-83; University of Wisconsin, Madison, 1986-. *Principal occupation*: Education program director. *Address*: Upward Bound, University of Wisconsin, Stevens Point, WI 54481 (715) 346-3337 (office). *Affiliations*: principal/teacher, Lac Courte Oreilles Ojibwe Schools, Hayward, WI, 1976-81; business manager, Menominee Positive Youth Development Corp., Keshena, WI, 1981-84; education consultant, Wisconsin Department of Public Instruction, Madison, WI, 1984-; director-Upward Bound, University of Wisconsin, Stevens Point, WI, 1991. *Other professional post*: Indian education director, Shawano School District, Shawano, WI. *Military*: U.S. Army, 1969-71, SP/5. *Community activities*: Wisconsin Humanities Committee, 1983-89; past member and chair, board of directors, Menominee Tribal Enterprises; (Wisconsin) American Indian Language and Culture Education Board, 1984. *Memberships*: National Indian Education Association (board of directors, 1977-78); Wisconsin Indian Education Association (president, board of directors, 1986-); National Coalition for Sex Equity in Education; National Bilingual Education Association; Wisconsin Bilingual Education Association; Wisconsin Teachers of English to Speakers of Other Languages. *Awards, honors*: 1988 "Wisconsin Indian Educator of the Year Award" from Wisconsin Indian Education Association; "Outstanding Leadership Award" from UW-Green Bay Ethnic Heritage Program, 1976. *Interests*: "Responsible for American Indian education programs established under Wisconsin Act 31 - 1989-91 biennial budget..., previous responsibility for national origin desegregation program (1984-89). *Published works*: Articles on American Indian history, culture, education, athletics and youth programs.

CALDWELL-WOOD, NAOMI RACHEL (Ramapough) 1958-
(library science)
Born March 31, 1958, Providence, R.I. *Education*: Clarion State College, BS, 1980; Clarion University of Pennsylvania, MSLS, 1982; graduate studies: Texas A&M University, 1986-87, Providence College, 1990-92, University of Pittsburgh, 1992- (Library Science doctoral candidate). *Principal occupation*: Library science. *Address*: Residence unkown at time of publication. *Affiliations*: Microtext Reference Librarian, Sterling C. Evans Library, Texas A&M University, College Station, TX, 1985-87; Library Media Specialist, Nathan Bishop Middle School, Providence, RI, 1987-92; American Indian Library Association (secretary, 1987-90; president, 1990-). *Other professional activities*: Editorial Advisory Board & Reviewer, "MultiCultural Review," Greenwood Publishing, 1991-; Professional Reading Reviewer, "School Library Journal" Cahners/R.R. Bowker, 1991-; Advisory Board, OYATE, Berkeley, CA, 1992-; Advisory Board, "Native American Information Directory," Gale Research, 1992; Screening Committee, Native American Public Broadcasting Consortium, 1993-. *Community activities*: Consultant, Brown University/Providence Drug-Free Schools Project, 1987-91; Rhode Island Children's Book Award Committee, 1990-92. *Memberships*: Ramapough Mountain Indian Tribe; American Library Association (OLOS: Library Services for American Indian People Subcommittee, member, 1986-88, 1990-92, chair, 1992-; ALA Council Committee on Minority Concerns, member, 1991-93, 1994-; ALA Councilor-at-Large, 1992-); American Indian Library Association (secretary, 1987-90; president, 1990-). *Awards, honors*: U.S. Board on Books for Young People (member, Discovery Award Committee, 1994-); honorary delegate to White House Conference on Library & Information Services, Washington, DC, 1991; participant, Native American & Alaskan Native Pre-Conference to the White House Conference on Library & Information Services, March 1991; participant, National Indian Policy Center, Forum on Native American Libraries & Information Services, George Washington University, Washington, DC, May 1991. *Interests*: Native American educational materials and books for children; multicultural literature; library & information services. Numerous presentations, including: "Multicultural Books for Children: The Native American Perspective," Library Science Colloquium, Clarion University of Pennsylvania, Jan. 1994; "Native Americans & Children's Books: Evaluation & Selection," Carnegie Library of Pittsburgh Children's Services Meeting, Jan. 1993; "How to Evaluate Native American Books," Texas Library Association, March 1993; Native American Materials for Children," Dept. of Education, Clarion University of Pennsylvania, Oct. 1992. among others. *Published works*: Checklist of Bibliographies Appearing in the Bulletin of Bibliography, 1897-1987, with Patrick Wood (Meckler Corp., 1988). *Articles*: "I Is Not for Indian: The Portrayal of Native Americans in Books for Young People," with Lisa Mitten, in MultiCultural Review (April 1992); "Native American Images in Children's Books," in School Library Journal (May 1992); "Boxes of Light," in Hungry Mind Review: Children's Review Supplement (Fall 1992). among others.

CALHOUN, JEANETTA L. (Delaware, Lenni Lenape)
(poet, writer)
Address: 1971 Western Ave. #1133, Albany, NY 12203.

CALICA, MARIE (Warm Springs)
(advisor)
Affiliation: Council of Advisors, American Indian Heritage Foundation, 6051 Arlington Blvd., Falls Church, VA 22044-2788 (703) 237-7500.

CALICA, RAYMOND, Sr. (Warm Springs)
(ex-tribal chairperson)
Affiliation: Confederated Tribes of the Warm Springs Reservation, P.O. Box C, Warm Springs, OR 97761 (503) 553-1161.

CALLAHAN, BERNADETTE L.
(IHS-administrative services chief)
Affiliation: Indian Health Service, 5300 Homestead Rd., NE, Albuquerque, NM 87110 (505) 837-4108.

CALLENDER, LEE A.
(museum registrar)
Affiliation: George Gustav Heye Center, National Museum of the American Indian, Smithsonian Institution, 1 Bowling Green, New York, NY 10004 (212) 283-2420.

CALLION, DONALD W.
(Indian band chief)
Affiliation: Sucker Creek Band, P.O. Box 65, Enlida, Alberta, Canada T0H 3N0 (403) 523-4426.

CALLOWAY, COLIN G. 1953-
(college professor, historian)
Born February 10, 1953, Yorkshire, England. *Education*: University of Leeds, England, BA, 1974, PhD, 1978. *Principal occupation*: Historian, professor. *Address*: Dartmouth College, Native American Studies Dept. Sherman House, Box 6152, Hanover, NH 03755-3530 (603) 646-2076; E-mail: colin.calloway @dartmouth.edu. *Affiliations*: Assistant director/editor, D'Arcy McNickle Center for the History of the American Indian, The Newberry Library, Chicago, IL, 1985-87; professor of history, University of Wyoming, Laramie, 1987-95; professor of history and Native American Studies, Dartmouth College, Hanover, NH, 1995-. *Memberships*: Organization of American Historians; American Society for Ethnohistory; Western History Association. *Awards, honors*: 1993 John P. Ellbogen Meritorious Teaching Award, University of Wyoming; John Sloan Dickey Third Century Professor in the Social Sciences, Dartmouth College, 1996-2001. *Interests*: American Indian history; early American history. *Published works*: Crown & Calumet: British-Indian Relations, 1783-1815 (University of Oklahoma Press, 1987); Editor, New Directions in American Indian History (University of Oklahoma Press, 1988); The Abenaki (Chelsea House, 1989); The Western Abenakis of Vermont (University of Oklahoma Press, 1990); Editor, Dawnland Encounters: Indians and Europeans in Northern New England (University Press of New England, 1991); Editor (with Alden T. Vaughn), Early American Indian Documents: Treaties and Laws, 1607-1789: The Confederation Period, 1775-1789 (University Publications of America, 1992); Editor, The World Turned Upside Down: Indian Voices from Early America (Bedford Books, 1994); The American Revolution in Indian Country (Cambridge University Press, 1995); editor, Our Hearts Fell to the Ground: Plains Indian Views of How the West Was Lost (Bedford Books, 1996); editor, After King Philip's War: Presence and Persistence in Indian New England (University Press of New England, 1997); New Worlds for All: Indians, Europeans, and the Remaking of Early America (Johns Hopkins University Press, 1997); First Peoples: A Documentary Survey of American Indian History (Bedford Books, 1999, 2004); One Vast Winter-Count: The Native American West Before Lewis & Clark (University of Nebraska Press, 2003).

CALSOYAS, DR. KYRIL
(Indian school principal)
Affiliation: Seba Dalkai Boarding School, P.O. Box HC63 Box H, Winslow, AZ 86047 (520) 657-3208 Fax 657-3224.

CAMBRA, ROSEMARY
(Ohlone/Costanoan Muwekma)
(tribal chairperson)
Affiliation: Ohlone/Costanoan Muwekma Tribe, San Jose, CA (408) 441-6473.

CAMERON, STEWART
(Indian band chief)
Affiliation: Saulteau Indian band, Box 414, Chetwynd, B.C., Canada V0C 1J0 (604) 788-3955.

CAMPBELL, ANGUS PETER
(Indian band chief)
Affiliation: Ahousaht Indian Band, General Delivery, Ahousaht, B.C., Canada (604) 670-9563.

CAMPBELL, BEN (*Nighthorse*)
(Northern Cheyenne) 1933-
(U.S. Senator; jeweler; rancher)
Born April 13, 1933, Auburn, Calif. *Education:* San Jose State University, 1953-58. *Principal occupation:* Jeweler; rancher; U.S. Senator, D-CO. *Address:* Ben Nighthorse Studio, P.O. Box 639, Ignacio, CO 81137 (970) 563-4623. *Affiliation:* U.S. Senate, Washington, DC. The only Native American member of the U.S. Congress-Senate; Chairman, Senate Select Committee on Indian Affairs. *Military service:* U.S. Air Force, 1951-53 (Airman 2nd Class; Korean Veteran). *Membership:* American Quarter Horse Association; U.S. Brangus Association; American Paint Horse Association; Indian Arts & Crafts Association; U.S. Olympic Committee (former secretary). *Awards, honors:* U.S. Judo Champion, 1961-63, All-American, 1964; 1963 Gold Medal Winner, Pan American Games; Captain, U.S. Olympic Team, 1964; "have also won over 200 awards in art shows for jewelry design." *Interests:* "Have traveled extensively - 40 countries. I'm now a member of a delegation to North Atlantic Assembly." *Biographical sources:* Autobiography now being published by Smithsonian Press; have been in Woman's Day, Arizona Highways, Empire Magazine Southwest, and USA Today. *Published work:* Judo Drill Training (Zenbei Publishing, 1967).

CAMPBELL, BERRY, M.D.
(tribal health center administrator)
Affiliation: Kenaitze Indian Tribe Health Center, P.O. Box 988, Kenai, AK 99611 (907) 283-3633.

CAMPBELL, CURTIS, Sr. (Mdewakanton Sioux)
(tribal council president)
Affiliation: Prairie Island Community Council, 1158 Island Blvd., Welch, MN 55089 (320) 388-2554.

CAMPBELL, ERNEST
(Indian band chief)
Affiliation: Musqueam Indian Band, 6370 Salish Dr., Vancouver, BC, Canada V6N 2C6 (604) 263-3261.

CAMPBELL, GENEVIEVE (Cahto-Pomo)
(rancheria chairperson)
Affiliation: Laytonville Rancheria, P.O. Box 1239, Laytonville, CA 95454 (707) 984-6197.

CAMPBELL, GREGORY R. (Eastern Shawnee)
1955-
(professor of anthropology)
Born August 1, 1955, Cincinnati, Ohio. *Education:* Chaffey Community College, AA, 1976; U.C.L.A., BA (Anthropology & History), 1979; University of Oklahoma, Norman, MA, 1982, PhD (Anthropology), 1987 (Dissertation: The Political Economy of Ill-Health: Changing Northern Cheyenne Health Patterns and Economic Underdevelopment, 1876-1930); Institute of American Cultures, University of California, Los Angeles, Postdoctoral Diploma, 1988. *Principal occupation:* Professor of anthropology. *Home address:* 104 Peery Park Dr., Missoula, MT 59812. *Office address:* Dept. of Anthropology, University of Montana, Missoula, MT 59812 (406) 243-2478 Fax 243-4918. E-mail: greg@selway.umt.edu. *Affiliations:* Professor, Dept. of Anthropology, University of Montana, Missoula, MT, 1988-present (Dept. Chair, 1999-04). *Other professional posts:* Curator of Ethnology, Anthropological Collections, Dept. of Anthropology, University of Montana, Missoula, 1988-04; Peer Reviewer, Articles and Manuscripts for various professional journals and publishers, 1988-04; appointed member (presidential appointment), University of Montana Lewis & Clark Bicentennial Committee, Office of the President, University of Montana, Missoula, 2001-04; Chair Workshop Series, University of Montana, Missoula, 2001-03; Provost Seminar Series "Diversity Within Higher Education," 2002-04. *University & Community Services:* Department of Anthropology, University of Montana (General Student Advisor, 1988-04;

Graduate Student Advisor, 1995-04. *Past professional posts:* Graduate & teaching assistantships, instructor & assistant professor, University of Oklahoma, Dept. of Anthropology, 1979-87; Research associate, Southern Cheyenne Ethnohistory Project, Dept of Anthropology, University of Oklahoma, 1979-82; ethnological curator, Oklahoma Historical Society, State Museum, 1982-85; curatorial consultant, Desert Caballeros Museum, Wickenburg, AZ, 1986-87; acting assistant professor, Dept. of Anthropology & American Indian Studies, UCLA, 1987-88; Symposium chair & organizer, Native American Ethnology, Anthropology Program Section Coordinator, 1989 Western Social Science Association, Albuquerque, NM, 1988-89; (current) Curator of ethnology, Anthropological Collections, Dept. of Anthropology, University of Montana; research affiliate, Center for Population Research, University of Montana; Symposium Chair, "Tribal Preservation and Renewal, 1999, 52nd Annual Northwest Anthropological Conference, April 8-10, Oregon State University, Newport, Oreg. *Ethnographic and Consultation Field Research:* Research Associate, Southern Cheyenne Ethnohistory Project, Dept. of Anthropology, University of Oklahoma, 1979-82; Ethnographic Research, Northern Cheyenne Tribe, Lame Deer, MT, 1984-04; Research Ethnologist/Ethnohistorian Consultant, Association for American Indian Affairs, 1992-97; Research Ethnologist/Ethnohistorian, Fort Lemhi Indian Community, Inc. Federal Recognition Project, Salmon, Idaho, 1996-98; Research & Demographic Consultant, Confederated Salish and Kootenai Tribes, Tribal and Legal Dept., The Confederated Salish & Kootenai Tribes of the Flathead Reservation, 1997-98, 2002; Ethnographic/Ethnohistorical Research, Gila River Indian Community, Sacaton, AZ, 1998-04; Ethnographic Research, Blackfeet Tribe, Browning, Mont, 2000-01; Historic Preservation Consultation, Chippewa Cree Tribe of the Rocky Boy Reservation, Box Elder, Mont., 2001; Ethnographic & Museum Interpretation Consultant, Sacajawea Interpretive Center, Salmon, Idaho, 2001-04; NAGPRA Ethnographic Consultation, Glacier National Park, MT, 2003-04. *Awards, honors:* Antiquarian Bookseller's Association of America Award, UCLA, 1979; Counseling Award, Academic Achievement Program, UCLA, 1979; scholarship, Buffalo Bill Historical Center, Cody, WY, 1981; National Endowment for the Arts Grant, 1984-85; Oklahoma Foundation for the Humanities Grant, 1985; Dr. Robert E. Bell Fund Award, Dept. of Anthropology, University of Oklahoma, 1985; University of Oklahoma Associates' Fund, Dissertation Research Grant, 1986; Postdoctoral Scholar, Institute of American Cultures, Native American Studies Center, U.C.L.A., 1987-88; Merit Awards, Teaching & Research, Dept. of Anthropllogy, University of Montana, Missoula, 1997 & 2001; Publication Awards, The mansfield Library, University of Montana, Missoula, 1999 & 2002. *Memberships:* American Society for Ethnohistory; Plains Anthropological Association; Northwest Anthropological Society; The International & Infectious Disease Study Group, Society for Medical Anthropology; American Anthropological Association; National Association for Ethnic Studies; Museum Association of Montana; American Association for State and Local History; Lambda Alpa, National Anthropology Honor Society. *Research Interests:* Native North America; race & ethnicity, ethnohistory, demographic anthropology, social epidemiology, social organization, political economy. *Published works:* Plains Pictographic Art: An Evolving Tradition; Many Americas: Critical Perspectives on Race, Racism, and Ethnicity (Kendall/Hunt, 1998; revised second edition, 2001); An Ethnohistorical & Ethnographic Evaluation of Blackfeet Religious & Traditional Cultural Practices in East Glacier National Park & the Surrounding Mountains (Browning: The Blackfeet Nation, 2001); Native Peoples of the Northwestern Plains: An Ethnohistory of Cultural Persistence & Change (manuscript in progress, 2004). *Articles:* Numerous reports, book reviews & articles on Native American history & culture; also, conference papers &research presentations.

CAMPBELL, SR. JANET
(school principal)
Affiliation: Indian Island School, P.O. Box 566, 1 River Rd., Old Town, ME 04468 (207) 827-4285.

CAMPBELL, JEANETTE (PRATHER)
(*Buffalo Talker*) (United Lumbee) 1948-
(teacher, rancher, writer & reporter)
Born March 4, 1948, Winfield, Kans. *Education:* BA in

Speech & English, Teaching credentials in English, math & science. *Principal occupation:* Teacher, rancher, writer & reporter. *Address:* P.O. Box 117, Nubieber, CA 96068 (530) 294-5778. E-mail: tipicamp@hdo.net. *Community activities:* Big Valley Chamber of Commerce, 2000-present; member, 50+ Club; M.I. Hummel Club. *Memberships:* United Lumbee Tribe (Deer Clan); California Bison Assn; NRA; MNLRA; FMAC. *Interests:* Bacl powder rendezvous.

CAMPBELL, LEON (Iowa of Kansas)
(tribal council chairperson)
Affiliation: Iowa of Kansas Executive Committee, Route 1, Box 58A, White Cloud, KS 66094 (913) 595-3258.

CAMPBELL, PETER
(Indian band chief)
Affiliation: North Spirit Lake Indian Band, Box 70, North Spirit Lake, ON, Canada P0V 2G0.

CAMPBELL, SUSAN J. (Potawatomi/Menominee)
1944-
(author)
Born December 30, 1944, Wichita, Kans. *Education:* Seattle Pacific University, BA (Biblical Studies). *Principal occupation:* Author. *Home address:* 3200-C Wawae Rd., Kalaheo, HI 96741. E-mail: nokmis@yahoo.com. *Affiliations:* Minnesota Center for Great Lakes Native American Studies, Muncie, IN, 1991-95; Museums at Prophetstown, Lafayette, IN, 1996-2000; National Center for Great Lakes Native American Studies, 2001-03; Wordcraft Circle, 2000-present. *Past professional post:* Associate Pastor, Columbia Baptist Church, 1988-92. *Community activities:* Volunteer, American Cancer Society, Kaua'i. *Interests:* Historical research; writing; Potawatomi language recovery; Potawatomi cultural recovery; beadwork, quillwork. *Published works:* "One Woman's Family and the Footprints It Left Behind," 2001 (a history of the Vieux family and its Native American and French roots); The Trail of Death: The Potawatomi Removal of 1838, co-authored with Shirley Willard, historian (Fulton County Historical Society, 2003).

CAMPBELL, WILFRED
(Indian band chief)
Affiliation: Boothroyd Indian Band, Box 295, Boston Bar, BC, Canada V0K 1C0 (604) 867-9211.

CAMPER, BOB, M.D.
(clinical director)
Affiliation: Fort Peck PHS Indian Health Center, Poplar, MT 59255 (406) 768-3491.

CAMPO, GEORGE
(Indian band chief)
Affiliation: Lakahahmen Indian Band, 41290 Lougheed Hwy., Deroche, British Columbia, Canada V0M 1G0 (604) 826-7976.

CANNON, GORDON
(BIA agency supet.)
Affiliation: Warm Springs Agency, Bureau of Indian Affairs, P.O. Box 1239, Warm Springs, OR 97761 (541) 553-2411.

CANTWELL, DR. ANNE-MARIE
(professor of anthropology)
Affiliation: Native American Indian Studies Program, Dept. of Anthropology, Rutgers University, Douglass College, Box 270, New Brunswick, NJ 08903(908) 932-9886.

CAPES, LAVERNA JANE (Kiowa)
(manager-OK Indian Arts & Crafts Coop)
Affiliation: Oklahoma Indian Arts & Crafts Cooperative, P.O. Box 966, Anadarko, OK 73005 (405) 247-3486.

CAPOEMAN-BALLER, PEARL (Quinault)
(tribal president)
Affiliation: Quinault Business Committee (council member & vice-chairperson, 1975-94; president, 1994-present), P.O. Box 189, Taholah, WA 98587 (360) 276-8211.

CAPPELLUZZO, EMMA 1933-
(professor)
Born July 10, 1933, Boston, Mass. *Education:* Boston University, BA, 1955; University of Arizona, MEd, 1960, EdD, 1965. *Principal occupation:* Professor. *Home*

address: West Rd., Wendell, MA 01379 (508) 544-3583. *Affiliation*: University of Massachusetts, Amherst (Director, Multicultural Education, 1965-; joint professor, Dept. of Anthropology, 1975-). *Other professional posts*: Instructor, University of Arizona; teacher, public schools, Jackson, MI & Tucson, AZ; consultant to Kahnawake Education Dept. (13 years); director of Native American Elementary Placements for U Mass for 25 years in the Northern Pueblos of NM. *Community activities*: Town moderator, Historical Society. *Memberships*: National Education Assn; Cultural Survival; American Anthropological Assn; Council on Education. *Interests*: "Work with many Native communities; to look at and try to plan educational programs for Native schools; travel extensively - Europe & North America."

CAPTAIN, GEORGE J. (BUCK)
(Eastern Shawnee) 1922-
  (Intelligence, U.S. Gov't.; tribal chief)
Born August 14, 1922, Miami, Okla. *Education*: University of Maryland, 1954-56. *Principal occupation*: Intelligence, U.S. Government. *Home address*: Route 4, Box 924, Miami, OK 74354 (918) 542-1408; 666-2435 (work). *Affiliations*: Chief of Eastern Shawnee Tribe of Oklahoma, 1978-. *Other professional posts*: Served as instructor at intelligence training center. *Military service*: Airborne (served as top turret gunner, flew 26 missions; 2 air medals). *Community activities*: Chairman, Intertribal Council, Miami, OK (ten years); chairman, Ottawa County Food Coalition (eight years). *Membership*: Oklahoma Indian Health Bopard (past president). *Awards, honors*: Numerous government awards; will instruct at NEO College starting in 1990 (Shawnee history). *Interests*: "Travel in Europe, Asia, Central America; have taught intelligence principals to many Foreign Nationals all over the Free World."

CAPTAIN, NELIS S. (Eastern Shawnee)
  (chief)
Affiliation: Eastern Shawnee Tribe of Oklahoma, P.O. Box 350, Seneca, MO 64865 (918) 666-2435.

CARDINAL, DONALD
  (Indian band chief)
Affiliation: Onion Lake Indian Band, Box 900, Lloydminster, SK, Canada S9V 2Y0 (306) 344-2107.

CARDINAL, JOHN
  (Indian band chief)
Affiliation: Woodland and Cree Band #474, Cadotte Lake, Alberta T0H 0N0 (403) 629-3803.

CARL, CHESTER
  (housing council chairperson)
Affiliation: National American Indian Housing Council, 900 Second St., NE #305, Washington, DC 20002 (800) 284-9165; (202) 789-1754 Fax 789-1758.

CARLISLE, ED
  (BIA agency supt.)
Affiliation: Chinle Agency, Bureau of Indian Affairs, P.O. Box 7H, Chinle, AZ 86503 (602) 674-5100.

CARLSGAARD, SANDRA
  (special education coordinator)
Affiliation: Aberdeen Area Instructional Coordinator, Bureau of Indian Affairs, 115 4th Ave., SE, Federal Bldg., Aberdeen, SD 57401 (605) 226-7431.

CARLSON, DAWN
  (museum chairperson)
Affiliation: Marin Miwok Museum, P.O. Box 864, Novato, CA 94947 (415) 897-4064.

CARLSON, SUSAN, M.D.
  (clinical director)
Affiliation: SEARHC, Mt. Edgecumbe Hospital, 222 Tongass Dr., Sitka, AK 99801 (907) 966-2411.

CARLYLE, DELIA M. (Papapgo-Pima)
  (tribal chairperson)
Affiliation: Ak Chin Indian Community Council, 42507 W. Peters & Nall Rd., Maricopa, AZ 85239 (520) 568-2227.

CARNEAU, FRED
  (director-Indian college)
Affiliation: Maskwachees Cultural College, Box 360, Hobbema, Alberta, Canada T0C 1N0 (403) 585-3925.

CARNEY, R.
  (editor)
Affiliation: Canadian Journal of Native Education, University of Alberta, Faculty of Eduction, 5-109 Education N., Edmonton, Alberta, Canada T6G 2G5.

CARNEY, VIRGINIA (Eastern Cherokee)
  (college instructor)
Affiliation: Leech Lake Tribal College, 6530 U.S. Hwy. 2 NW, Cass Lake, MN 56633 (218) 335-4220 Fax 335-4209.

CAROLIN, ROBERT (Hopi)
  (BIA project manager)
Affiliation: San Carlos Irrigation Project, BIA, P.O. Box 250, Coolidge, AZ 85228. *Past professional post*: Hopi Agency, Bureau of Indian Affairs, P.O. Box 158, Keams Canyon, AZ 86034 (520) 383-3286.

CARPENTER, CECELIA SVINTH (Nisqually) 1924-
  (retired teacher; author, Indian historian/
  consultant)
Born September 2, 1924, Tacoma, Wash. *Education*: Pacific Lutheran University, BA 1966, MA, 1971; University of Puget Sound, 1993 Honorary Doctorate of Humane Letters. *Principal occupation*: Retired teacher; author, Indian historian/consultant. *Home address*: 9609 S. Sheridan, Tacoma, WA 98444 (206) 537-7877. *Affiliation*: Teacher, Tacoma Public School District, 1966-1982 (retired). *Other professional post*: Owns & operates Tahoma Research Service, 1976-. Community activities: Nisqually Tribal History Committee; State Indian Advisory Board for W.S.H.S.; Pierce County Historical Preservation Board member. *Memberships*: Nisqually Indian Tribe. *Awards, honors*: Award for "Historical Documentation" by Native American Student Association, Pierce College, 1986; "Peace and Friendship Award, 1988, by Washington State Capital Museum Association, Olympia, WA for preservation of Native American history; 1990 "Governor's Ethnic Heritage Award" from state of WA; 1993 "Honorary Doctorate of Humane Letters" from University of Puget Sound; 1994, "Distinguished Alumnus Award," Pacific Lutheran University. *Interests*: "Author, Indian historical researcher & consultant; Indian genealogical research" *Published works*: They Walked Before, Indians of Washington State (Washington State Historical Society, 1977; reprint, Tahoma Research, 1989); How to Research American Indian Blood Lines (Heritage Quest, 1984); Leschi, Last Chief of the Nisquallies (Heritage Quest, 1986); Fort Nisqually, A Documented History of Indian and British Interaction (Tahoma Research, 1986); Where the Waters Begin, The Traditional Nisqually Indian History of Mount Ranier (Mount Ranier National Park Service, 1994); Tears of Internment, The Indian History of Fox Island and the Puget Sound Indian War; numerous articles & research papers; consultant papers, and historical presentations.

CARPENTER, GORDON
  (Indian band chief)
Affiliation: New Slate Falls Indian Band, Slate Falls via Sioux Lookout, Ontario, Canada P0V 2P0.

CARROLL, MARGUERITE
  (editor)
Born January 31, 1955, Syracuse, N.Y. *Education*: Syracuse University, BA in Journalism.*Address & Affiliation*: Editor, Syracuse Post Standard, 1980-84; editor, American Indian Report, The Falmouth Institute, Inc. (1986-present), 3702 Pender Dr., Suite 300, Fairfax, VA 22030 (703) 352-2250 Fax 352-2323. E-mail: mcarroll@falmouthinst.com. *Community activities*: Ventures in Community, Conference for northern Virginia. *Memberships*: Native American Journalists Association; National Congress of American Indians.

CARROLL, THOMAS B.
  (monument supt.)
Affiliation: Salinas National Monument, Rte. 1, Box 496, Mountainair, NM 87036 (505) 847-2585.

CARSON, DALE
  (author, columnist)
Address: P.O. Box 13, Madison, CT 06443. E-mail: nativecooking@aol.com. *Affiliation*: Columnist, Indian Country Today, Canastota, NY. *Interests*: Native cooking. *Published works*: "New Native American Cooking"; "Native New England Cooking"; "A Dreamcatcher Book."

CARTER, GALE
  (site attendant)
Affiliation: Choctaw Chief's House, P.O. Box 165, Swink, OK 74761 (405) 873-2492.

CARTER, TRUMAN (Sac & Fox) 1949-
  (attorney)
Born January 16, 1949, Pawnee, Okla. *Education*: U.S. Indian Police Academy, 1979; University of Oklahoma, BA, 1980, College of Law, JD, 1987. *Principal occupation*: Attorney. *Affiliation & Address*: Attorney at Law, P.O. Box 493, Shawnee, OK 74802 (405) 273-6715 Fax 275-4977 (work). *Current activities*: Attorney General, Kickapoo Tribe in eastern Oklahoma, 1988-, the Cheyenne-Arapaho Tribes in western Oklahoma, 1988-, Iowa Tribe of Oklahoma, 1992-, and Otoe-Missouria Tribe of Oklahoma, 1993-; Chairperson, Otoe-Missouria Tax Commission, 1990-; special prosecutor, Iowa Tribe of Oklahoma, 1991-; Coordinator, Liaison of Sac & Fox law and order and judicial system, 1984-; Treasurer & Assistant Attorney General (Chief, Criminal Division), Sac & Fox Nation, 1987-; justice, Supreme Court, Kickapoo Tribe of Kansas, 1991-, Citizen Band Potawatomi of Oklahoma, 1992-; Prosecutor, BIA Court of Indian Offenses, Chickasaw Agency & Wewoka Agency, 1993-. *Accomplishments*: Appeared before the U.S. Supreme Court as designated co-counsel in 1993 landmark case, Oklahoma Tax Commission v. Sac & Fox Nation, where Court ruled 9-0 decision, state cannot impose motor vehicle & income taxes on tribal members; An elected tribal official, served as chief executive financial officer; developed excellent employee compensation & benefit package; provide training, assist Indian tribal governments in development, preparation, administration, and enforcement of tribal laws, policies, and procedures, 1982 to present; organizer and administrator of comprehensive tribal taxation system; negotiated several tribal cooperative agreements with cities, counties, and state agencies dealing with business development, law enforcement, fire protection services, and joint road improvement programs; organized and developed tribal court systems, police operations and fire department for the Sac & Fox Tribe in 1984. *Memberships*: Native American Bar Association; Oklahoma Indian Bar Association (treasurer-Indian Law Section; legislation committee); Oklahoma Bar Association; Potawatomie County (OK) Bar Association; National District Attorneys Association; Leadership Oklahoma, Inc.

CARVER, LAURA
  (health center director)
Affiliation: Santa Clara PHS Indian Health Center, P.O. Box 1323, Espanola, NM 87532 (505) 653-9421.

CARVEY, ELIZABETH A.
  (museum director)
Affiliation: Hauberg Indian Museum, Black Hawk State Park, Rock Island, IL 61201 (309) 788-9536.

CASAVANTE, CARMEN GILL
  (museum director)
Affiliation: Amerindian Museum, 406 Amisk, Pointe-Bleue, Quebec, Canada G0W 2H0.

CASEY, TOM
  (radio station manager)
Affiliation: KILI - 90.1 FM, Oglala Lakota Sioux, P.O. Box 150, Porcupine, SD 57772 (605) 867-5002.

CASH, MARCELLA
  (research center director)
Affiliation: Lakota Archives & Historical Research Center, Sinte Gleska College, Box 490, Rosebud, SD 57570 (605) 747-2263.

CASSEN, MARGARET ANNE 1946-
  (librarian, teacher)
Born August 27, 1946, Carbondale, Ill. *Education*: University of Oklahoma, BS, 1989. *Principal occupation*: Librarian, teacher. *Address*: P.O. Box 168, Fort Wingate, NM 87316 (505) 488-5989. *Affiliation*: Fort Wingate Elementary School, Fort Wingate, NM, 1989-present. *Other professional post*: Teach New Mexico history. *Memberships*: American Library Association; New Mexico Library Association. *Interests*: American history, special education, and gifted program; expanding the Native American section of our library.

CASSIDY, ANNE W.
(executive director)
Affiliation: American Indian Ritual Object Repatriation Foundation, 463 E. 57th St., New York, NY 10128 (212) 980-9441 Fax 421-2746.

CASTELLANOS, JUAN
(executive director)
Affiliation: Indian Human Resource Center, 4040 30th St., Suite A, San Diego, CA 92104 (619) 281-5964 Fax 281-1466.

CASTILLO, EDWARD D. (Cahuilla-Luiseno) 1947-
(professor of Native American studies)
Born August 25, 1947, San Jacinto, Riverside Co., Calif. *Education*: University of California, Riverside, BA, 1969; University of California, Berkeley, MA, 1976, PhD (Anthropology), 1977. *Principal occupation*: Professor of Native American Studies, Dept. Chair. *Address*: Native American Studies program, Sonoma State University, Rohnert Park, CA 94928 (707) 664-2450. *Affiliations*: Lecturer, Native American Studies Dept., University of California at Berkeley, 1970-71, 1973-77; Associate professor, director, Native American Studies, University of California, Santa Cruz, 1977-82; project director, Title IV, Laytonville Unified School District, 1985-88; Director, Native American Studies, Dept. Chair, Sonoma State University, Rohnert Park, CA, 1989-; curriculum resource specialist, Parents for the Improvement of Community & Education Services, Ukiah, CA. *Other professional posts*: President-Advisory Council, California Indian Education Association, California State Dept. of Education; Chairperson of Native American Advisory Committee to the California State University Chancellor Office. *Memberships*: California Historical Society; American Indian Historical Society. *Awards, honors*: National Endowment for the Humanities, History Teacher Training Grant; Meritorious Performance, Professional Promise Award for Research, 1989, California State University system. *Interests*: Reconstruction of California, Far Western, Borderlands; history of Indian tribes, and Hispanic Colonial institutions, i.e. Missions, Presidios, Civilian Hispanic Pueblos. *Published works*: "History of the Impact of Euro-American Exploration & Settlement on the Indians of California (107 pages) and "Recent Secular Movements Among California Indians, 1900-1973 (15 pages). Both chapters appear in Volume 8 of the Smithsonian Institute's Handbook of North American Indians: California; co-author: The California Missions (American Indian History Society Press, 1987); A Bibliography of California Indian History, edited by Robert Heizer (Ballena Press, 1978); Native American Perspectives on the Hispanic Colonization of Alta California (Garland Publishing, 1990); numerous articles & book reviews.

CASTILLO, JOHN (Fort Sill Apache) 1956-
(administrator)
Born February 14, 1956. *Education*: California State University, Fullerton, BA, 1979; UCLA, MSW, 1981. *Principal occupation*: Executive director. *Address*: Unknown. *Affiliation*: Executive Director, Southern California Indian Center, Fountain Valley, CA. *Other professional post*: California & National Child & Adolescent Service System Program Advisory Committee for Culturally Competent Service for Children & Families. *Community activities*: Orange County Community Developmental Council; Orange County ESP & FEMA Board-Orange Coast College EDP Board; Huntington Beach Adult Advisory Board. *Memberships*: UCLA Chancellors Community Advisory Commission; Los Angeles County American Indian Commission (chairperson, 1987-89); Indian Child Welfare Task Force (chairperson, 1986-89); Los Angeles County American Indian Mental Health Task Force, 1986-87. *Awards, honors*: 1979 Federal Mediation Council Labor/Management Certificate; 1985 County of Los Angeles Affirmative Action Volunteer of the Year; 1985-88 Kellogg National Fellowship Fellow Group 6; 1991 Freedoms Foundation at Valley Forge George Washington Honor Medal. Interests: "International work with indigenous peoples - helping indigenous peoples develop their human and economic resources through the many international programs available." *Published works*: Articles - "Spiritual Foundations of Indian Success," in American Indian Culture and Research Journal (1982, Vol. 6 No. 3); "JPTA: American Indian Success Through Group Consensus and Individual Attention," in Occupational Education Forum (1986, Vol. 15 No. 2);

"American Indians: An Overview of Their Socio Economic and Education Status," in The Journal for Vocational Needs Educations (1988, Vol. 10 No. 3).

CASTRO, VERNON (Yokut)
(rancheria chairperson)
Affiliation: Table Mountain Rancheria, P.O. Box 410, Friant, CA 93626 (209) 822-2587.

CATA, JUANITA O. (San Juan Pueblo)
(BIA supt for education)
Affiliation: Northern Pueblos Agency, BIA, P.O. Box 4269, Fairview Station, Espanola, NM 87533 (505) 753-1465.

CATA, SIMON (San Juan Pueblo)
(pueblo governor)
Affiliation: San Juan Pueblo Council, P.O. Box 1099, San Juan Pueblo, NM 87566 (505) 852-4400.

CATE, RICK
(organization president)
Affiliation: Kiva Club, University of New Mexico, Mesa Vista Hall #1117-A, Albuquerque, NM 87131 (505) 277-8259.

CATTLEMAN, LEO
(Indian band chief)
Affiliation: Montana Indian Band, Box 70, Hobbema, Alberta, Canada T0C 1N0 (403) 585-3744.

CAVENDER, REV. GARY C. *(Shun ghida)*
(Little Red Fox) (Dakota) 1939-
(writer, lecturer, teacher)
Born December 23, 1939, Granite Falls, Minn. (Upper Res. Sioux). *Education*: Minneapolis Community College, 1977-79; University of Minnesota, 1980-81; United Theological Seminary, MDiv., 1984. *Principal occupation*: Writer, lecturer, teacher. *Home address*: 2704 County Rd. 42, Shakopee, MN 55379 (612) 447-6679. *Affiliations*: Chaplain, V.F.W., Prior Lake, MN, 1991-; executive secretary, National Committee on Indian Work, New York, NY, 1990-. *Other professional posts*: Lobbyist, Project Impact, Washington, DC; chairperson, Minnesota Committee Indian Work; chairperson, St. Paul Area Council of Churches, Dept. of Indian Work; instructor, Dakota History, University of Minnesota. *Military service*: U.S. Navy, 1958-62; U.S. Air Force, 1963-67 (U.S. Expedition Forces; Medal Viet-Nam, China Quemoy, Matsue Islands, Bronz Star). *Community activities*: Picture People volunteer; art appreciation teacher, Prior Lake elementary school; volunteer, Crisis Counselor, Prior Lake Reservation. *Memberships*: V.F.W.; Disabled American Veteran. *Interests*: Reading historical books, with focus on American Indian history and prehistory; studies of comparative religions; writing, teaching; eating fried bread & corn soup. *Published works*: Black Hills: Who Are the Modern Indian Youth (Native American Theological Association, June 1986; editor, Where Rivers Flow & Waters Meet by Paul Durand (Merritt Parkway, 1994). *Article*: Episcopal Magazine, Sounding Diocese of Minnesota, "Christianity & the Great Mysterious Dakota Spirituality."

CAWSTON, COLLEEN (Confederated Tribes)
(tribal chairperson)
Affiliation: Colville Business Committee, P.O. Box 150, Nespelem, WA 99155 (509) 634-2200.

CESAR, NILES C.
(BIA area director)
Affiliation: Juneau Area Office, Bureau of Indian Affairs, P.O. Box 25520, Juneau, AK 99802 (907) 586-7177.

CESSPOOCH, LARRY (Ute)
(Native American film producer)
Affiliation: Ute Indian Tribe, Audio-Visual, P.O. Box 190, Fort Duchesne, UT 84026 (801) 722-5141 Ext. 243.

CHALIAK, CHUCK (Eskimo)
(village president)
Affiliation: Native Village of Nunapitchuk, Box 130, Nunapitchuk, AK 99641 (907) 527-5705.

CHALIFOUX, CHARLES HENRY
(Indian band chief)
Affiliation: Swan River Indian Band, P.O. Box 270, Kinuso, Alberta, Canada T0G 1K0 (403) 775-3536.

CHAMBERLAIN, KEVIN (Saginaw-Chippewa)
(former tribal chief)
Affiliation: Saginaw-Chippewa Indian Tribe, 7070 E. Broadway, Mt.Pleasant, MI 48858 (517) 775-4000.

CHAMPAGNE, DUANE W.
(Turtle Mountain Ojibway) 1951-
(professor)
Born May 18, 1951, Belcourt, N.D. *Education*: North Dakota State University, BA, 1973, MA, 1975; Harvard University, PhD, 1982. *Principal occupation*: Professor. *Home address*: 2152 Balsam Ave., Los Angeles, CA 90025-5942. *Office address*: Native Nations Law & Policy Center, UCLA Sociology Dept., 264 Haines Hall, Box 951551, Los Angeles, CA 90095-1551 (310) 475-6475 Fax 475-0235; E-Mail: champagn@ucla. edu. *Affiliations*: UCLA Native Nations Law & Policy Center, 2003-present, UCLA Dept. of Sociology, 1984-present; Honoring Nations, 2000-present; Series Editor, Contemporary American Indian Issues, AltaMira Press, 1998-present. *Past professional posts*: Research consultant for the Smithsonian Institution-Public Radio and the Native American Public Broadcasting Consortium (NAPBC). Developed public radio documentaries for the Quincentenary of Columbus' landing in the New World, 1989-92; Advisory Board Member for the Harvard Project on American Indian Economic Development, Energy & Environmental Policy Center, Harvard University, John F. Kennedy School of Government, 1988-90. Director, UCLA, American Indian Studies Center, 1990-2002; editor, "American Indian Culture and Research Journal," 1986-2003. *Community activities*: National Museum of the American Indian (member of board of trustees), 1987-present; The Los Angeles City/County American Indian Commission (chair, board member), 1990-present; Los Angeles American Indian Commission, 1990-present; Southwest Museum (board member, 1994-96); member, American Indian Women's Health Advisory Board, 1994-96; Project Peacemaker, 1998-present; Public Law 280 Police Enforcement Study, 2000-present; Native Voices at the Autry, 1999-present; Tribal Learning Community & Education Exchange (TLCEE), 2003-present. *Memberships*: American Sociological Association; International Sociological Association; American Indian Professors Association Pacific Sociological Association. *Awards, honors*: American Indian Scholarship, 1973-75; American Sociological Association Minority Fellowship, 1975-78; Rockefeller Postdoctoral Fellowship, 1982-83; University of California Pre-tenure Award, 1986; National Science Foundation (Fellow, 1985-88; Creativity Extension Grant, 1988-90; Ford Foundation Postdoctoral Fellowship, 1988-89; Master for the College of Humanities & Social Sciences, North Dakota State University, 1996; Honoree, National Center for American Indian Enterprise, 1999; Wordcraft Circle of Native Writers & Storytellers, Writer of the Year, 1999. *Published works*: American Indian Societies: Strategies & Conditions of Political & Cultural Survival, revised 2nd edition (Cultural Survival, 1989); Social Order & Political Change: Constitutional Governments Among the Cherokee, the Choctaw, the Chickasaw, and the Creek (Stanford University Press, 1992); The Native North American Almanac (Gale Research, Vol. 1, 1994; Vol. 2, 2001); Native America: Portrait of the People (Visible Ink Press, 1994); The Chronology of Native North American History (Gale Research, 1994); American Indian Activism: Alcatraz to the Longest Walk (University of Illinois Press, 1997) edited with Troy Johnson & Joane Nagel; Contemporary Native American Cultural Issues (AltaMira Press, 1999); Native Amerian Studies in Higher Education: Models for Collaboration Between Universities & Indigenous Nations (AltaMira Press, 2002) edited with Jay Stauss; The Future of Indigenous Studies: Strategies for Survival & Development (UCLA American Indian Studies Center, 2003) edited with Ismael Abu Saad, & 80+ articles, papers, and reports.

CHANDLER, ROBERT S.
(museum supt.)
Affiliation: Tusayan Ruin & Museum, Grand Canyon National Park, P.O. Box 129, Grand Canyon, AZ 86023 (602) 638-7701.

CHANNING, WILLIAM E.
(organization emeritus)
Affiliation: Emeritus, Wings of America, The Earth Circle Foundation, Inc., 1601 Cerrillos Rd., Santa Fe, NM 87505 (505) 982-6761 Fax 988-3879.

CHAPIN, DOROTHY
(director-Indian health program)
Affiliation: Feather River Indian Health Program, 2167 Montgomery St., Oroville, CA 95965 (916) 534-6135.

CHAPMAN, ANA DELORES
(Indian band chief)
Affiliation: Skawahlook Indian Band, Box 1668, Hope, British Columbia, Canada V0X 1L0 (604) 796-9877.

CHAPMAN, LAWRENCE
(Indian band chief)
Affiliation: Lac des Milles Lacs Indian Band, P.O. Box 1365, Station "F", Thunder Bay, Ontario, Canada P7C 4Y1.

CHAPMAN, ROBERT (Pawnee)
(tribal president)
Address & Affiliation: Pawnee Tribe, P.O. Box 470, Pawnee, OK 74058 (918) 762-3621 Fax 762-6446.

CHAPMAN, STEVE (White Earth Chippewa) 1951-
(program administrator)
Born July 3, 1951, Minneapolis, Minn. *Education*: Minneapolis Community College, 1969-70; Augsburg College, BA, 1973; hamline University, MA, 1993. *Princpal occupation*: Program administrator. *Home address*: 3625 24th Ave. S., Minneapolis, MN 55406 (612) 722-2080. *Affiliations*: Special Programs, University of Minnesota, Minneapolis, MN, 1973-77; director, American Indian Studies, Minneapolis Community College, 1977-94; Administrator, Indian Education Programs, Minneapolis Public Schools, 1994-; . *Other professional posts*: Executive director, American Indian OIC, 1981-82; Instructor: American Indian Art History, Augsburg College, University of St. Thomas. *Community activities*: Commissioner, Minneapolis Public Housing Authority (vice chair); Minneapolis Community Development Agency (former commssioner); Minnesota Commission on Affordable Housing (former commissioner); American Indian Business Development; Minnesota Indian Women's Resource Center. *Memberships*: Minnesota Indian Education Association; National Indian Education Association. *Awards, honors*: First American Indian graduate of Augsburg College; Oustanding Alumni Award, 1986, Minneapolis Community College; Scholarship Award, MAPE; Outstanding American Indian Educator, 1999, Minneapolis, Minn. *Interests*: "Beadwork; American Indian art history; refinishing furniture; lecturing on American Indian culture, and helping out when asked." *Published work*: Urban American Indian Views on the U.S. Constitution (Hamline Law Journal, 1986).

CHAPPABITTY, DENNIS G.
(attorney)
Address: P.O. Box 292122, Sacramento, CA 95829 (916) 682-0575. E-mail: chaplaw@earthlink.net. *Professional activities*: Federal Practice - Federal Indian law. Counseling and legal representation of Federal employees before the U.S. Merit Systems Protection Board and Federal Equal Employment Opportunity Commission.

CHAPUT, REV. CHARLES J. (Wambli Waste-Good Eagle, Lakota; Pyet-ta-sen, Potawatomi) 1944-
(Roman Catholic Bishop)
Born September 26, 1944, Concordia, Kans. *Education*: St. Fidelis College, BA, 1967; Capuchin College, MA; University of San Francisco (MA in theology), 1971. *Principal occupation*: Roman Catholic Bishop. *Address*: P.O. Box 678, 606 Cathedral Dr., Rapid City, SD 57701 (605) 343-3541. *Affiliations*: Roman Catholic Bishop, Rapid City, SD. *Awards, honors*: "Served as master of ceremonies for 1987 National Tekakwitha Conference with Pope John Paul, !!, Phoenix, Arizona. *Interests*: Travel.

CHARITY WING (Sioux) 1902-
(home economics)
Born March 9, 1902, Fort Peck Reservation, Mont. *Education*: Haskell Institute, Lawrence, KS, AA, 1926. *Principal occupation*: Nursing, homemaking. *Home address*: P.O. Box 897, Poplar, MT 59255 (406) 768-5436. *Community activities*: Member, Indian Tribal Affairs, Citizens Committee, Fort Peck Sioux Tribe, Poplar, Mt. (20 years); advocate, Fort Peck Sioux Claims Committee for Black Hills (ten years). *Other professional post*: Presbyterian Church Elder; Ladies Aid Healer (70 years; president, three terms). *Awards,*

honors: Woman of the Day, Presbyterian Church, Special Recognition, 1981. *Interests*: "Sewing—starquilt construction; travel; guest lecturer for Indian history, lore, crafts, life styles, method of rearing Indian children; Father Basil Reddoor was first ordained minister of Presbyterian Church on the Fort Peck Reservation in Montana."

CHARLES, AGNES (Athapascan)
(AK village president)
Affiliation: Native Village of Napaimute, P.O. Box 96, Aniak, AK 99557

CHARLES, ARCHIE
(Indian band chief)
Affiliation: Seabird Island Indian band, Box 650, Agassiz, B.C., Canada V0M 1A0 (604) 796-2177.

CHARLES, ARNOLD
(school chairperson)
Affiliation: Casa Blanca Day School, P.O. Box 940, Bapchule, AZ 85221 (602) 315-3489.

CHARLES, BERNARD
(Indian band chief)
Affiliation: Semiahmoo Indian Band, RR 7, 16010 Beach Rd., White Rock, BC V4B 5A8 (604) 536-1794.

CHARLES, BILLY (Eskimo)
(AK village president)
Affiliation: Emmonak Village Council, Emmonak, AK 99581 (907) 949-1720.

CHARLES, ERIC
(Indian band chief)
Affiliation: Chippewas (Georgina Island) Indian Band, Box A-3, RR 2, Sutton West, ON, Can L0E 1R0.

CHARLES, FRANCIS G. (Elwha S'Klallam)
(tribal chairperson)
Affiliation: Elwha S'Klallam Business Council, 2851 Lower Elwha Rd., Port Angeles, WA 98362 (360) 452-8471.

CHARLES, GABRIEL (Eskimo)
(AK village president)
Affiliation: Native Village of Kasigluk, P.O. Box 19, Kasigluk, AK 99609 (907) 477-6927.

CHARLES, JAMES (Navajo) 1950-
(archaeologist; park supt.)
Born March 25, 1950, Ganado, Ariz. *Education*: Fort Lewis College, BA, 1974; Northern Arizona University, MA. *Principal occupation*: Archaeologist, park supt.. *Address*: Navajo National Monument, National Park Service, Tonalea, AZ 86044 (520) 672-2366 Fax 672-2345(work). *Affiliations*: Archaeologist, B.I.A., Phoenix, AZ, 1981-82; archaeologist, B.I.A., Billings, MT, 1982-91; supt., B.I.A., Fort Totten, ND, 1991-96; supt., Navajo National Monument, Tonalea, NM, 1996-. *Membership*: North Dakota Archaeological Society. *Interests*: Archaeology, anthropology, cultural anthropology, Navajo history.

CHARLES, JERRY (Shoshone)
(tribal council chairperson)
Affiliation: Ely Colony Council, 16 Shoshone Cr., Ely, NV 89301 (702) 289-3013.

CHARLES, LARRY (Eskimo)
(AK village president)
Affiliation: Newtok Village Council, P.O. Box WWT, Newtok, AK 99559 (907) 237-2314.

CHARLES, RAMONA
(library director)
Affiliation: Tonawanda Indian Community Library, P.O. Box 326, Akron, NY 14001 (716) 542-5618.

CHARLES, RONALD G. (Port Gamble S'Klallam)
(tribal chairperson)
Affiliation: Port Gamble S'Klallam Tribal Council, 31912 Little Boston Rd., NE, Kingston, WA 98346 (360) 297-2646.

CHARLES, STEVE (Tlingit-Haida)
(art gallery manager)
Affiliation: Sacred Circle Gallery of American Indian Art, P.O. Box 99100, Seattle, WA 98199 (206) 285-4425.

CHARLES-LUTZ, IRENE
(college director/academic advisor)
Affiliation: Dine College East, P.O. Box 580, Shiprock, NM 87420 (520) 368-3501 Fax 368-3519.

CHARLEY, DENNIS (Athapascan)
(AK village council president)
Affiliation: President, Tanana IRA Native Council, Box 77093, Tanana, AK 99777 (907) 366-7160.

CHARLEYBOY, IRVINE
(Indian band chief)
Affiliation: Alexis Creek, Box 69, Chilanko Forks, BC, Canada V0L 1H0 (604) 481-3335.

CHARLIE, JOHN
(Indian band chief)
Affiliation: Burns Lake Indian Band, P.O. Box 9000, Burns Lake, BC, Canada V0J 1E0 (604) 692-3849.

CHARLIE, LYNETTE C. (Navajo) 1966-
(educator)
Born October 28, 1966, Tuba City, Ariz. *Education*: University of New Mexico. *Principal occupation*: Educator. *Home address*: P.O. Box 1815, Tuba City, AZ 86045 (520) 283-5628. *Affiliation*: Director of Recruiting, Native American Scholarship Fund, Albuquerque, NM, 1990-. *Community activities*: "Currently volunteering my personal time helping young Native students get into college and obtain the financial support to continue their education. *Memberships*: National Association of Female Executives, 1994-; National Coalition for Indian Education (board member, 1991; member, 1991-).

CHARLIE, MARVIN
(Indian band chief)
Affiliation: Cheslatta Indian Band, Box 909, Burns Lake, British Columbia, Canada V0J 1E0 (604) 694-3334.

CHARLIE, ROBERT
(Indian band chief)
Affiliation: Burns Lake Indian Band, Box 9000, Burns Lake, British Columbia, Canada V0J 1E0 (604) 692-7097.

CHARTRAND, ELBERT
(executive director)
Affiliation: Swan River Indian & Metis Friendship Centre, 723 Main St., Box 1448, Swan River, Manitoba, Canada R0L 1Z0 (204) 734-9301.

CHASE, CON (Eskimo)
(village chief)
Affiliation: Anvik Village, Anvik, AK 99558 (907) 663-6335.

CHASE, DAVID W.
(museum director)
Affiliation: Wampanoag Indian Program of Plimoth Plantation, P.O. Box 1620, Plymouth, MA 02360 (617) 746-1622.

CHASE, EMMETT, M.D.
(IHS-AIDS coordinator)
Affiliation: Indian Health Service, 5300 Homestead Rd., NE, Albuquerque, NM 87110 (505) 837-4116.

CHASE. FRED A. Karuk)
(tribal chairperson)
Affiliation: Quartz Valley Indian Reservation, 9117 Sniktaw Lane, Fort Jones, CA 96032 (916) 467-3307.

CHASE, JOANNE
(executive director)
Affiliation: National Congress of American Indians, 2010 Mass. Ave, NW, Washington, DC 20036 (202) 466-7767.

CHASE, KEN (Eskimo)
(AK village chief)
Affiliation: Anvik Village, General Delivery, Anvik, AK 99558 (907) 663-6335.

CHASING HORSE, NATHAN (Lakota)
(writer)
Address: 1109 Wambli Dr., Rapid City, SD 57701 (605) 343-5820.

CHASKE, RICHARD
(executive director)
Affiliation: Portage Friendship Centre, 21 Royal South, Box 1118, Portage La Prairie, Manitoba, Canada R1N 3C5 (204) 239-6333.

CHAULIFOUX, CHARLIE
(Indian band chief)
Affiliation: Swan River Indian Band, Box 270, Kinuso, Alberta, Canada (403) 775-3536.

CHAVERS, DEAN (Lumbee) 1941-
(fund raiser)
Born February 4, 1941, Pembroke, N.C. *Education*: University of Richmond, 1960-62; University of California, Berkeley, BA, 1970; Stanford University, MA (Anthropology), 1973, MA (Communications), 1975, PhD (Communications Research), 1976. *Principal occupation*: Fund raiser. *Home address*: 9710 Camino del Sol, NE, Albuquerque, NM 87111 (505) 262-2351 Fax 262-0534. *Affiliations*: Director, Catching the Dream (formerly Native American Scholarship Fund), Albuquerque, NM, 1986-present; founding president, Coalition for Indian Education, Albuquerque, NM, 1987-present (editor, newsletter). *Past professional posts*: Assistant professor, California State University, Hayward, 1972-1974; president, Bacone College, Muskogee, OK, 1978-81; president, Dean Chavers & Associates, 1981-85; member, Advisory Panel for Minority Concerns, The College Board, 1980-85; member, Minority Achievement Program, Association of American Colleges, 1980-84; president, MANAGE, Inc., 1985-86. *Military service*: U.S. Air Force, 1963-68 (Navigator, Captain; Distinguished Flying Cross, Air Medal). *Community activities*: Rotary Club, Muskogee & Broken Arrow, OK; Democratic Party of Bernalillo County, NM ; chairman, Albuquerque Commission on Indian Affairs, 1993-95. *Memberships*: National Indian Education Association (board member, 1983-86, 1987-90); Native American Scholarship Fund (president); National Congress of American Indians, 1972-; International Communication Association; Association of Fund Raising Professionals. *Awards, honors*: Ford Foundation Graduate Fellowship for doctoral study, 1970-74; National Honor Society; Junior Officer of the Quarter, 1971, U.S. Air Force, Travis Air Force Base. *Interests*: Main interest is Indian education, secondary interest is Indian economic development. Have published 12 books and technical manuals in these areas, as well as some 30 journal articles. Main occupation is providing technical assistance in fund raising, financial management, computer software development, and training for Indian tribes, contract schools, and Indian health clinics. *Published works*: The Feasibility of an Indian University (Bacone College, 1979); How to Write Winning Proposals (DCA Publications, 1983 & 1996); Funding Guide for Native Americans (DCA Publications, 1983 & 1985); Grants to Indians (DCA Publications, 1984); The Status of Indian Education (Journal of Thought, 1984); Tribal Economic Development Directory (DCA Publications, 1985); "The Effects of Testing on American Indians," symposium paper for the National Commission on Testing and Public Policy, 1987; The Indian Dropout (Coalition for Indian Education, 1991); Exemplary Programs in Indian Education (Catching the Dream Publications, 4th Ed. 2004).

CHAVEZ,, ENA B. (Navajo)
(craftsperson)
Affiliation: Manager, Crownpoint Rug Weavers' Association, P.O. Box 1630, Crownpoint, NM 87313 (505) 786-5302 or 786-7386. *Product*: Navajo rugs sold at auction.

CHAVIS, AGNES H. (Lumbee)
(consortium director)
Affiliation: North Carolina Consortium on Indian Education, P.O. Box 666, Pembroke, NC 28372 (919) 422-3467.

CHAVIS, ANGELA YELVERTON (Lumbee) 1950-
(dentist)
Born May 11, 1950, Pembroke, N.C. *Education*: Pembroke State University, BS, 1971; University of North Carolina, Chapel Hill, School of Dentistry, DDS, 1980. *Principal occupation*: Dentist. Resides in Pembroke, NC. *Community activities*: Student Health Action Committee; Voter Registration. *Memberships*: North Carolina Association for Preventive Dentistry, 1976-; Ameri-

can Dental Association. *Awards, honors*: Graduated Cum Laude, Pembroke State University, 1971; scholarship from American Fund for Dental Health, 1976-80. *Interests*: My vocational interest is dentistry. I plan to return to my home town and work to better the dental health of the Indian people in my town and surrounding community. *Biographical source*: Who's Who Among Students in American Universities & Colleges, 1971.

CHEATHANE, TRINA
(Indian school principal)
Affiliations: Tucker Elementary School, 126 E. Tucker Circle, Philadelphia, MS 39350 (601) 656-8775 Fax 656-9341.

CHEE, EMERY (Navajo)
(BIA agency supt.)
Affiliation: Eastern Navajo Agency, Bureau of Indian Affairs, P.O. Box 328, Crownpoint, NM 87313 (505) 786-6100

CHEE, MARVIN (Navajo)
(BIA agency chairperson)
Affiliation: Chinle Agency, BIA, P.O. Box 6003, Chinle, AZ 86503 (602) 674-5201 ext. 201; Chinle Boarding School, P.O. Box 70, Many Farms, AZ 86538 (602) 781-6221.

CHEEK, JACKIE
(BIA-director)
Affiliation: Bureau of Indian Affairs, Office of Congressional & Legislative Affairs, MS: 1340-MIB, 1849 C St., NW, Washington, DC 20240 (202) 208-5706.

CHEEK, JOHN W.
(executive director)
Affiliations: National Indian Education Association, 700 N. Fairfax, Suite 210, Alexandria, VA 22314 (703) 838-2870 Fax 838-1620.

CHEEK, WARREN F.
(director)
Affiliation: United Indian Missions International, P.O. Box 36010, Greeley, CO 80633 (970) 330-7788.

CHEKELELEE, EDNA (Eastern Cherokee)
(storyteller)
Address: Rt. 1 Box 151, Robbinsville, NC 28771 (704) 479-6601. Sharing Cherokee songs and stories, Edna works in all educational settings, elementary through high school. She has performed at powwows and Native American festivals. Edna also specializes in Cherokee arts & crafts workshops.

CHELSEA, WILLIAM
(Indian band chief)
Affiliation: Alkali Indian Band, Box 4479, Williams Lake, British Columbia, Canada V2G 2V5 (604) 440-5611.

CHENOWETH, BOB
(museum curator)
Affiliation: Big Hole National Battlefield, P.O. Box 237, Wisdom, MT 59761 (406) 689-3155.

CHERINO, FRANCES
(school chairperson)
Affiliation: Isleta Elementary School, P.O. Box 550, Isleta, NM 87022 (505) 869-2321.

CHEROMIAH, NICHOLAS (Laguna Pueblo)
(school principal)
Affiliation: Laguna Middle School, P.O. Box 268, Laguna, NM 87026 (505) 552-9091 Fax 552-6466.

CHESTNUT, PETER
(attorney)
Address: 121 Tijeras Ave., NE #2001, Albuquerque, NM 87102 (505) 842-5864. *Membership*: New Mexico Bar Association (chair, Indian Law Section).

CHIAGO, ROBERT KEAMS (Navajo-Pima) 1942-
(executive director; tribal planner)
Born June 22, 1942, Los Angeles, Calif. *Education*: Arizona State University, BA, 1965; Northern Illinois University, Dekalb, MS, 1970; University of Utah, 1974-76 (61 hours towards PhD). *Principal occupation*: Executive director; tribal planner. *Addresses*: Unknown. *Past Affiliations*: Associate director, American Indian Culture Center, UCLA, 1970; director, Ramah Navajo

School Board, Inc., Ramah, N.M., 1970-71; director, Navajo Division of Education, Navajo Nation, Window Rock, AZ, 1971-73; consultant, Mesa Consultants, Albuquerque, NM, 1973; editor and founder, Utah Indian Journal, which was a statewide Indian newspaper in 1976 & 1977; visiting assistant professor of humanities, University of Utah, Salt Lake City, 1976-79; director, Native American Studies, University of Utah, 1973-81; director of Indian Teacher/Counselor Education Programs, University of Utah, 1980-84; president, Western Indian Technologies, Salt Lake City, Utah, 1984-92; founder & coordinator, Western Indian Education Conference; consulting; proposal writing and evaluation; Executive director, National Advisory Council on Indian Education (NACIE), 330 C St., SW, Rm. 4072, Washington, DC 20202 (202) 205-8353 Fax 205-8897, 1992-2002; tribal planner, Salt River Pima-Maricopa Indian Tribe, Scottsdale, AZ, 1994-2002. *Military service*: U.S. Marine Corps, 1965-68 (Captain, infantry officer; Presidential Unit Citation, Navy Unit Citation, National Defense Service Medal, Vietnam Service Medal and Campaign Medal). *Community activities*: Presidential appointee, National Advisory Council on Indian Education; gubernatorial appointee to the Utah State Board of Indian Affairs; National Congress of American Indians (resolutions committee chairman, 1976-80); advisory committee for the creation of the Native American Rights Fund, 1971-72; member, State of Utah ESEA Title IV Advisory Council, 1977-79; Community Services Council of Utah (board member, 1974-75; director, Minority Economic Development Council. *Memberships*: National Congress of American Indians; Western Indian Education Conference (coordinator, 1983, '84, '86); National Advisory Council on Indian Education, 1983-86. *Interests*: Major areas of interest include education, economic development, and employment.

CHICAGO, KEVIN
(Indian band chief)
Affiliation: Lac Des Milles Lacs Indian Band, 136 Main St. South, Kenora, Ontario, Canada P2N 1S9 (807) 468-5551.

CHICHARELLO, ELOUISE
(BIA regional director & agency supt.)
Affiliation: Navajo Regional Office, Bureau of Indian Affairs, P.O. Box 1060, Gallup, NM 87305 (505) 863-8314 Fax 863-8324; supt., Western Navajo Agency, BIA, P.O. Box 127, Tuba City, AZ 86045; Chinle Agency, BIA, P.O. Box 7H, Chinle, AZ 86503; supt. Fort Defiance Agency, BIA, Rt. 1, Box 9-C, Fort Defiance, AZ 86504.

CHICKS, ROBERT (Stockbridge-Munsee Mohican)
(tribal chairperson)
Affiliation: Stockbridge-Munsee Band of Mohicans Tribe, N 8476 Mo He Con Nuck Rd., Bowler, WI 54416 (715) 793-4111.

CHIEF, LEROY W.
(Indian school principal)
Affiliation: Wahpeton Indian School, Bureau of Indian Affairs, 832 N. 8th St., Wahpeton, ND 58075 (701) 642-3796.

CHIEF WISE OWL (Tuscarora) 1939-
(medicine man)
Born February 16, 1939, Robeson County, N.C. *Education*: Pembroke State University, 1968. *Principal occupation*: Medicine man, Tuscarora Indian Tribe, Drowning Creek Reservation, 1965-. *Home address*: Route 2, Box 108, Maxton, NC 28364 (919) 844-3827. *Other professional posts*: Businessman; make herbs and powerful medicine bags using herbs, and make herbal liniment. *Community activities*: Built tribal community center. *Membership*: National Congress of American Indians; Sheriffs Association of North Carolina. *Biographical source*: Known worldwide as medicine man of Drowning Creek Reservation.

CHILDRESS, DAVID (Cherokee)
(MIS director)
Address & Affiliation: MIS Director, D-Q University, P.O. Box 409, Davis, CA 95617 (916) 758-0470 (phone & fax). *Military service*: U.S. Army, 1965-69. *Memberships*: AAAS; Association for Supervision Curriculum Development, AISES.

CHILE, CLARENCE (Picuris Pueblo)
(pueblo governor)
Affiliation: Picuris Pueblo Council, P.O. Box 127, Penasco, NM 87553 (505) 587-2519.

CHILTON, JUNE
(director-Indian council)
Affiliation: Indian Action Council of Northwestern California, P.O. Box 1287, 2725 Myrtle Ave., Eureka, CA 95502 (707) 443-8401.

CHINGWA, GERALD V. (Odawa)
(tribal chairperson)
Affiliation: Little Traverse Bay Bands of Odawa Indians, P.O. Box 246, Petoskey, MI 49770 (231) 439-3847.

CHINO, CYRUS J. (Acoma)
(Pueblo governor; indian school principal)
Affiliations: Pueblo of Acoma, P.O. Box 309, Acomita, NM 87034 (505) 552-6604; principal, Sky City Community School, P.O. Box 40, San Fidel, NM 87049 (505) 552-6671.

CHINO, WENDELL (Mescalero Apache)
(former tribal chairperson)
Affiliation: Mescalero Apache Tribal Council, P.O. Box 176, Mescalero, NM 88340 (505) 671-4494.

CHIPPS, PATRICIA ANN
(Indian band chief)
Affiliation: Beecher Bay Indian Band, 3843 East Sooke Rd., Box 2, R.R. #1, Sooke, British Columbia, Canada V0S 1A0 (604) 474-6782.

CHISHOLM, ANITA (Shawnee)
(administration)
Address & Affiliation: Director, American Indian Institute (1975-present), College of Continuing Education, University of Oklahoma, 555 Constitution St., Suite 237, Norman, OK 73072 (405) 325-4127 Fax 325-7757; E-Mail: achishol@cce.occe.ou.edu. *Published works*: Oklahoma's Indian People: Images of Today, Yesterday and Tomorrow; Culture Through Concepts - Five Tribes; Cultural Curriculum Materials on Indian Tribes in Oklahoma; conference proceedings (derived from the 11th National Native American/First Nations Cultural Curriculum Development Workshop) guides I & II.

CHIVIS, TERRY A. (Huron Potawatomi)
(former tribal chairperson)
Affiliation: Nottawasppi Band of Huron Potawatomi, 2221 - 1.5 Mile Rd., Fulton, MI 49052 (616) 729-5151.

CHONKOLAY, HARRY
(Indian band chief)
Affiliation: Dene Tha'Tribe Band, Box 120, Chateh, Alberta, Canada T0H 0S0 (403) 321-3842.

CHOSA, DONALD
(college instructor)
Affiliation: Indian/Minority Services Dept., Mesabi Range Community & Technical College, 1001 Chestnut St. W., Virginia, MN 55792 (218) 749-7727 Fax 749-0318.

CHOTEAU, MITCHELL
(BIA-acting area director)
Affiliation: Anadarko Area Office, Bureau of Indian Affairs, W.C.D. Office Complex, P.O. Box 368, Anadarko, OK 73005 (405) 247-6673.

CHRISJOHN, ANDREA
(executive director-organization)
Affiliation: Chiefs of Ontario, 22 College St., 2nd Floor, Toronto, Ontario, Canada M5G 1K2 (416) 972-0212.

CHRISJOHN, RICHARD (Oneida-Iroquois)
(artist; tribal leader)
Address: RD 2, Box 315, Red Hook, NY 13421.
Affiliation: Oneida Nation of New York, Oneida, NY

CHRISTIAN, RANDY LAVAGHN (Shield Wolf)
(Tcinto Sakto Muscogee) 1959-
(cardiac IUC, RN, PCC)
Born April 12, 1959, Lakeland, Ga. *Education*: Georgia Military College (Milledgeville, GA), AAS-Emergency Medical Technology; Abraham Baldwin Agricultural College (Tifton, GA), AAS Nursing; Valdosta State

University, BS, 2001. *Principal occupation*: Cardiac IUC, RN, PCC. *Home address*: 3895 Shelton Rd., Lake Park, GA 31636 (229) 242-3504 (phone & fax). *Affiliations*: South Georgia Medical Center, Cardiac ICU patient care coordinator; Emergency department RN for 17 years; paramedic for 25 years. *Community activities*: Board of Trustees, Valwood School, 1992-94; wildlife rehabilitation for Georgia; birdofprey educator, handler and rehabilitator, 1995-present. *Memberships*: Georgia EMT Association, 1982-84; Emergency Nurses Association, 1989-90; B.A.S.S. Federation member; Tcinto Sakto Muscogee member. *Awards, honors*: 1977 4-H Georgia Key Award; 1977 Valdosta State College Student Council; 1988 Outstanding Young Men of America; Prayer Blanket & Gord Rattle, Red Feather, 1993. *Interests*: Wildlife protection, environmental protection.

CHRISTIANSON, JILL S.
(Indian education liaison)
Affiliation: Maryland Dept. of Education, Liaison to Indian Education, 200 W. Baltimore St., Baltimore, MD 21201 (410) 333-2234.

CHRISTIANSON, ROBERT (Eskimo)
(ex-AK village president)
Affiliation: Native Village of Port Heiden, P.O. Box 49007, Port Heiden, AK 99624 (907) 284-2218.

CHRISTMAS, PETER
(executive director)
Affiliation: Micmac Association of Cultural Studies, P.O. Box 961, Sydney, NS Can. B1P 6J4 (902) 539-8037.

CHRISTOPHER, GABRIEL ROY
(Indian band chief)
Affiliation: Canim Lake Indian Band, Box 1030, 100 Mile House, British Columbia, Canada V0K 2E0 (604) 397-2227.

CHUCULATE, DENNIS
(BIA agency supt.)
Affiliation: Cherokee Agency, Bureau of Indian Affairs, Cherokee, NC 28719 (828) 497-9131 Fax 497-6715.

CHUCULATE, JERRY
(health center director)
Affiliation: Redbird Smith Health Center, 301 JT Stitkes Aves, Sallisaw, OK 74955 (918) 775-9159.

CHURCH, RICHARD M.
(IHS-associate director)
Affiliation: Office of Information Resources Management, Dept. of Health & Human Services, USPHS-IHS, 5600 Fishgers Lane, Rm. 5A-21, Rockville, MD 20857 (301) 443-0750.

CHURCHILL, EDWARD P., Sr. (Coo - Day)
(Tlingit) 1923-
(fisherman)
Born January 1, 1923, Ketchikan, AK. *Education*: Wrangell High school, 1941. *Principal occupation*: Lifetime fisherman. *Address*: P.O. Box 45, Wrangell, AK 99929 (907) 874-3725. *Affiliations*: Chairman of "Alaska Aquaculture" a Fish Hatchery at Burnett Inlet, Alaska; commissioner of Southeast Alaska Native Fisheries & Natural Resources Commission, 1988-. secretary-treasurer, Salmon Bay Protection Association; councilman, A.N.B., Alaska Native Brotherhood. *Military service*:U.S. Army, 1944-46; U.S. Engineers, 1st Mate Tug Boat, Alaska, 1942-44. *Community activities*: Board member, Wrangell Mental Health; president, Wrangell I.R.A. Indian Rehabilitation Association; Elder, Presbyterian Church, 1981-; member, Wrangell School Board. *Memberships*: Wrangell Tlingit & Haida Association (past president, board member). *Awards, honors*: The only Indian ever to be elected as Mayor of Wrangell. *Interests*: Lobbying for Alaska Land Claim in Washington, DC for years.

CHURCHILL, WARD (Kenis)
(Keetoowah Band Cherokee) 1947-
(professor of American Indian studies)
Born October 2, 1947, Urbana, Ill. *Education*: Sangamon State University, MA in Communications. *Prinicpal occupation*: Professor of American Indian studies. *Address*: Dept. of Ethnic Studies, CB 339, University of Colorado, Boulder, CO 80303 (303) 492-8852 Fax 604-0760 (work). *Affiliation*: Chair, Dept. of Ethnic Studies, University of Colorado at Boulder.

Other professional post: Author, lecturer. *Military service*: U.S. Army, 1966-68. *Community activities*: Leadership Council, American Indian Movement (AIM) of Colorado; board member, Human Rights Research Fund; board member, Institute on Holocaust & Genocide. *Awards, honors*: Former delegate to the International Indian Treaty Council. Interests: Law, history, art, music. *Published works*: Co-author, Culture vs. Economism; co-author (with James VanderWall), Agents of Repression: The FBI's Secret War Against the American Indian Movement, ION, and the Black Panther Party; Acts of Rebellion: The Ward Churchill Reader, 2003. Numerous articles for various journals.

CIVIC, DAVID, M.D.
(clinical director)
Affiliation: Mescalero PHS Indian Hospital, P.O. Box 210, Mescalero, NM 88340 (505) 671-4441.

CLADOOSBY, M. BRIAN (Swinomish)
(tribal chairperson)
Affiliation: Swinomish Indian Senate, P.O. Box 817, LaConnor, WA 98257 (360) 466-3163

CLADOUHOS, JOE
(administrator-Indian clinic)
Affiliation: Juneau SEARHC Medical Clinic, 3245 Hospital Dr., Juneau, AK 99801 (907) 463-4000.

CLAH, HERBERT (Navajo) 1949-
(executive director)
Born June 1, 1949, Farmington, N.M. *Education*: Brigham Young University, BS, 1975, MPA, 1981. *Principal occupation*: Executive director. *Address & Affiliations*: Executive director, Utah Navajo Development Council, P.O. Box 129, Bluff, UT 84512 (801) 678-2285, 1986-present; Dean of Instruction, Navajo Community College, Shiprock, 1990-. *Community activities*: Blanding City Planning Commission; Rural Community Assistance Corporation (board of directors). *Awards, honors*: Outstanding Young Men of America; Jamie Thompson Award; Dean's Leadership Award, BYU; USO National Defense Peace Time Award.

CLAIR, STEPHEN
(Indian band chief)
Affiliation: Quatsino Indian Band, Box 100, Coal Harbor, BC, Canada V0N 1K0 (604) 949-6245.

CLARK, BLUE
(professor of law)
Address & Affiliation: Professor of Law, Oklahoma City University, Oklahoma City, OK. Published work: Lone Wolf v. Hitchcock (University of Nebraska Press, 1999).

CLARK, DON (Edge of the Water) (Navajo) 1955-
(commercial graphic artist)
Born March 22, 1955, Winslow, Ariz. *Education*: Navajo Community College, 1974-75; Northern Arizona University, BFA, 1980. *Principal occupation*: Commercial graphic artist. *Home address*: P.O. Box 3240, Tuba City, AZ 86045 (602) 283-4123. *Other professional post*: Professional jazz guitarist. *Memberships*: Indian Arts & Crafts Association; Inter-tribal Indian Ceremonial Association; SWAIA. *Awards, honors*: 1992 First Place, SWAIA; First Place, Santa Fe Indian Market; First Place in pastel drawings at the Navajo Show, Museum of Northern Arizona; 1993 First Place, Poster Artist Winner at Inter-tribal Indian Ceremonial. among others. *Interests*: A full-time painter since 1986. "I am also known for my, more or less trademark, "blanket series." Each is a portrait of a Native American child or adult wrapped in a colorful Navajo blanket. The background is always black, representing darkness and uncertainty. The blanket means protection and security. It's a symbol of hope, trust and all that is good. One of my goals is to let people know who American Indians are. I'm very proud to American Indian." *Biographical sources*: Navajo-Hopi Observer, Feb. 1988; Intertribal America, 1993 Collectors Edition, page 65.

CLARK, ELMER
(Indian school chairperson)
Affiliation: Winslow Dormitory, 600 N. Alfred Ave., Winslow, AZ 86047 (602) 289-4488.

CLARK, ELMO (Caddo)
(tribal chairperson)
Affiliation: Caddo Tribal Council, P.O. Box 487, Binger, OK 73009 (405) 656-2344.

CLARK, ERNEST
(BIA agency supt.)
Affiliation: Yakima Agency, BIA, P.O. Box 632, Toppenish, WA 98948 (509) 865-2255.

CLARK, FRIEDA
(program director)
Affiliation: National Indian Council on Aging, 10501 Montgomery Blvd. NE #210, Albuquerque, NM 87111 (505) 888-3302.

CLARK, GEORGIA LEE
(organization president/editor)
Affiliation: "Visions," Communications Publishing Group, 3100 Broadway, Suite 225, Kansas City, MO 64111 (816) 756-3039.

CLARK, JOSEPH (Eskimo)
(village president)
Affiliation: Native Village of Clark's Point, P.O. Box 9, Clark's Point, AK 99569 (907) 236-1221.

CLARK, KENNETH S., SR. (Nanticoke)
(association chief)
Affiliation: Nanticoke Indian Association, Rte. 4, Box 107-A, Millsboro, DE 19966 (302) 945-3400.

CLARK, NICHOLAS L. (Alankwia)
(Potawatomi/Cherokee) 1944-
(historian & museologist & cultural consultant)
Born November 16, 1944, Topeka, Kans. *Education:* Washburn University, BA, 1972, MA, 1976; University of Idaho, MA, 1978. *Principal occupation:* Historian, museologist and cultural consultant. *Address:* National Center for Great Lakes Native American Culture, 5401 S. Cty. Rd. 900 E., Lafayette, IN 47905 (765) 296-9943 (phone & fax). E-mail: nlclark1@aol.com & nclark@ncglnac.org. *Affiliation:* Social Studies Chair, St. Marys High School, St. Marys, KS, 1973-76; executive director, Heritage Hill State Park, Green Bay, WI, 1978-83; executive director, Southern Oregon Historical Society, 1983-86; founding president, Minnetrista Cultural Center, Muncie, IN, 1986-95; charter member, Governor's Indiana Native American Council; founding director, Museums At Prophetstown, Battle Ground, IN, 1995-2000; president, Clark Associates, 2000-present; founding president, National Center for Great Lakes Native American Culture, 2000-present. (Clark Associates is a firm that consults with museums, public and private institutions of learning, and government agencies concerning Great Lakes Native American Culture. NCGLNAC is under development and will be a gathering place for those traditions.) *Other professional posts:* Founding Co-Chair, Minnstrista Council for Great Lakes Native American Studies, 1988-95; Founding Chair, Prophetstown Council for Preservation of Great Lakes Native American Culture, 1995-2000; advisor, Miami Nation of Indians of Indiana. *Consultant to:* Time-Life Publishing, The Arts & Entertainment and History Channels; and Houghton Mifflin Publishing. *Interests:* Networking for Woodland Cultural Projects, promoting Great Lakes Native American artists and craftspeople; and organizing Woodland Native American cultural workshops, symposiums, events and exhibits that promote and raise awareness of Woodland Great Lakes Culture. *Memberships:* American Association of Museums, Midwest Museums Association, Midwest Outdoor Museums Coordinating Council, Association of Indiana Museums, and Public Historians of America.

CLARK, ROBERT
(executive officer)
Affiliation: Bristol Bay Area Health Corp., P.O. Box 130, Dillingham, AK 99576 (907) 842-5201.

CLARK-PRICE, MARGARET A. (Tio-ron-ia-te-BrightSky) (Wyandotte-Chippewa-Shawnee) 1944-
(motivational speaker, artist)
Born August 2, 1944, Colville Indian Agency, Nespelem, Wash. *Education:* St. Michael's (AZ) High School, 1962; Sierra Nevada College (3 years). *Principal occupation:* Motivational speaker, artist. *Address:* P.O. Box 1281, Scottsdale, AZ 85252 (602) 483-8212 (work & home). *Affiliation:* Legal secretary & researcher, 1966-77; executive director, Native American Press Association, 1985-87; president/director, Native American Communication & Career Development, Ltd. (NACCD), 1987-; associate editor, Native Peoples Magazine, Phoenix, 1988-92; publisher, Na-

tive American Annual (Native American Publishing Co.); consultant, Scottsdale Community College, Tribal Management Programs, Scottsdale, AZ. *Other professional posts:* Member, board of education, Scottsdale Native American Indian Cultural Foundation. *Community activities:* Advisory committee member: Association for Retarded Citizens of Arizona, Inc., Phoenix; fundraising activities; among others. *Exhibits:* Her pastels, oils, acrylics, watercolors and pencil works hang in galleries in Arizona, California, and Nevada as well as in many private collections throughout the U.S. *Memberships:* National Organization of Native American Women; Association for Education in Journalism & Mass Communications. *Awards, honors:* Six awards and a Grand prize for a large pastel entitled Caught in the Middle, at the 1982 annual Navajo Nation Fair, Window Rock, AZ. *Interests:* "My main interests, obviously, surround the Indian world. I have spent years on my own family genealogy, necessitating journeying across the U.S. and into Canada. I hope to instill such an interest in others through the journey among the pages of the Native American Annual." NACCD, Ltd. focuses on career-development seminars to prepare students for journalism careers as well as fund-raising for schools with Native American students. *Published works:* Native American Annual (Native America Publishing Co., 1985); co-founder & editor, Native Peoples Magazine, 1988-92.

CLARKE, FRANK, M.D. (Hualapai) 1921-
(physician/administrator)
Born November 11, 1921, Blythe, Calif. *Education:* Los Angeles City College (2 years); UCLA, BS, 1946; St. Louis University, School of Medicine, MD, 1950. *Principal occupation:* Physician/administrator. *Home address:* 7909 Rio Grande Blvd., N.W., Albuquerque, NM 87114. *Affiliation:* Clinical director, Albuquerque Service Unit, Public Health Service, Indian Health Service, Albuquerque, N.M., 1975-. *Other professional post:* Secretary, National Council of Clinical Directors. *Military service:* U.S. Navy, 1942-46 (Presidential Unit Citation; 1950-53 (Lt. (MC) USNR). *Memberships:* USPHS Commissioned Officers Association; American Academy of Family Physicians (Charter Fellow); NM Academy of Family Physicians; Association of American Indian Physicians (president, 1973-74). *Awards, honors:* Fellow, John Hay Whitney Foundation, 1950; Indian Achievement Award, Indian Council Fire, Chicago, 1961; Man of the Year, City of Woodlake, 1962; Layman of the Year in Education, Tulane County Chapter of California Teacher's Association. *Interests:* Recruitment of Indian students into health professions; lecturer on alcoholism. *Biographical sources:* Indians of Today; Who's Who in the West; Community Leaders & Noteworthy Americans.

CLARKSON, DICK (Umpqua & Suislaw)
(former tribal chairperson)
Affiliation: Confederated Tribes of Coos Lower Umpqua & Suislaw Indians, 338 Wallace Ave., Coos Bay, OR 97420 (541) 267-5454.

CLARY, THOMAS C. (Miami of Oklahoma) 1927-
(priest, psychotherapist, consultant)
Born March 3, 1927, Joplin, Mo. *Education:* Pace University, BBA; University of Oklahoma, Norman, MA; California Western University, PhD (Psychology). *Principal occupation:* Corporate president. *Address:* Resides in Washington, DC. *Affiliations:* Priest (pastor) & counselor, Free Catholic Church, Washington, DC (3 years); president, TCI, Inc., Washington, DC (20 years). *Other professional posts:* MDiplomate & Certified Sex Therapist, The American Board of Sexology; Fellow, American Academy of Clinical Sexologists; president-elect, DC Mental Health Counselors Association; publisher, "Linkages," TCI, Inc., Washington, DC. *Military service:* U.S. Army, 1945-68 (Lt. Colonel) (Legion of Merit, Army Commendation Medal). *Memberships:* American Board of Sexology; American Society of Sexual Educators, Counselors & Therapists; American Counselors Association; American Mental Health Counselors Association; American Association of Professional Hypnotherapists. *Awards, honors:* Silver Anvil Award for International Community Relations by Public Relations Society of America, 1968; Master Hypnotist by American Council of Hypnotist Examiners, 1983; Urban Mass Transportation Administration Minority Business Enterprise Award, 1985. *Interests:* Teach courses in human sexuality, hypnotherapy, psychic potential, spiritual healing and stress manage-

ment. *Published works:* Script Analysis is a New Approach to OD, chapter 12 of Everybody Wins: Transactional Analysis Applied to Organizations (Addison-Wesley, 1974); How to Live with Stress (NTDS Press, 1977); At the Organizational Precipice (NTDS Press, 1977).

CLAUSEN, MARILYN
(Indian education program director)
Affiliation: Arapahoe School, Fremont County School District #38, Indian Education Program, P.O. Box 9211, Arapahoe, WY 82510 (307) 856-9333. E-mail: mclausen@fremont38.k12.wy.us.

CLAW, CHESTER
(Indian school chairperson)
Affiliation: Flagstaff Dormitory, P.O. Box 609, Flagstaff, AZ 86002 (602) 338-4464.

CLAY, JULIE ANNA (Omaha) 1958-
(administration)
Born November 2, 1958, Flandreau, S.D. *Education:* University of Oklahoma, BA, 1982; OU-Health Sciences Campus (Oklahoma City, OK), MPH, 1984. *Principal occupation:* Administration. *Address:* 52 Corbin Hall, University of Montana, Missoula, MT 59801 (406) 243-5467. *Affiliations:* Research & Training Center on Rural Rehabilitation, University of Montana, Missoula (Project Manager, 1989-92, Program Analyst, 1990-92) Management analyst, Indian Health Service, Rockville, MD, 1992-93; Principal Investigator, Montana University Affiliated Rural Institute on Disabilities, 52 Corbin Hall, University of Montana, Missoula, MT, 1993-. *Other professional posts:* Advisory Board for research project, "VR Independent Living Counselor Effects on Independent Living Outcomes for American Indians with Disabilities;" *Memberships:* American Public Health Association (Advisory Committee); American Association of University Affiliated Programs (Minority Affairs Committee); National Congress of American Indians (Disability Issues Committee); member of the Administration on Developmentally Disabled Multicultural Committee; Advisory Council of the Human Services - Rehabilitation Degree Project, Salish Kootenai Tribal College; Training Advisory Committee, Research & Training Center on Public Policy on Independent Living. *Awards, honors:* Indian Health Service Scholarship, Outstanding OU MPH Indian Student, 1984; All American Indian Student Award of Excellence, Americans with Disabilities Act Award. *Interests:* "My major area of interest is to promote communication & education on American Indians with disabilities and all the attendant issues. I enjoy outdoor recreational activities such as skiing, camping, bicycling, attending pow wows and other tribal gatherings." *Published works:* A Descriptive Study of Secondary Conditions Reported by a Population of Adults with Physical Disabilities Served by Three Independent Living Centers in a Rural State, by J.A. Clay et al (Journal of Rehabilitation, April/May/June 1994); National Council on Disability - Prevention of Disabilities - Meeting the Unique Needs of Minorities with Disabilities; A report to the President & the Congress, April 1993; numerous articles & presentations.

CLAYTON, GERALD L. (Hopi)
(school principal)
Affiliation: Hopi High School, P.O. Box 337, Keams Canyon, AZ 86034 (602) 738-5111.

CLEGHORN, MILDRED (Fort Sill Apache)
(tribal chairperson)
Affiliation: Fort Sill Apache Business Committee, Rt. 2, Box 121, Apache, OK 73006 (405) 588-2298.

CLEMENTS, ANDREW
(museum curator)
Affiliation: Iowa, Sac and Fox Presbyterian Mission, Route 1, Box 152C, Highland, KS 66035 (913) 442-3304.

CLEMMER, JANICE WHITE
(Wasco, Shawnee, Delaware) 1941-
(professor)
Born February 17, 1941, Warm Springs Reservation, Oregon. *Education:* Brigham Young University, BS, 1964; Dominican College of San Rafael, MA (History), 1975; University of San Francisco, MA (Education), 1976; University of Utah, PhD (Cultural Foundation of Education), 1979; PhD (History), 1980' J. Reuben Clark

Law School, BYU, JD, 1993. *Principal occupation*: Professor. *Home address*: 1445 E. Princeton Ave., Salt Lake City, UT 84105. *Affiliations*: Professor, College of Education, Brigham Young University, Provo, Utah, 1980-. *Other professional posts*: Council member, National Association of Ethnic Studies; departmental and college committees; consultant. *Community activities*: Boy Scouts (merit badge counselor); Native American Advisory Board, State of Utah Board of Education (board chairman); Coalition for Minority Affairs, State Office of Education (Board member); Minority Affairs, KUTV-Channel 12 committee member; Utah Endowment for the Humanities (board member); American Indian Services (board member); volunteer, Utah State Heart & Lung Association. Utah Girl Scout Council (board of trustees); Utah Valley Community College, Center of Ethics (board member). *Memberships*: SIETAR (Society for Intercultural Education, Training and Research, International Organization); Native American Historians' Association (founding member); American Studies Association; OHOYO - National Native American Women's Program; Association for Supervision and Curriculum Development; State of Utah Bilingual Association; American Historians Western History Association; Utah State Historical Society; Oregon Historical Society; California Historical Society; National Archives (associate); Jefferson Forum; American Association for State & Local History. *Awards, honors*: University of Utah Danforth Foundation Fellowship Candidate; Distinguished Teaching Award Candidate, University of Utah; Tribal Archives Conference Award Recipient; Consortium for Native American Archives; OHOYO One Thousand, Native American Women Award Listing; American Indian Alumni Award, Brigham Young University; Lamanite Award, American Indian Services, BYU; D'Arcy McNickle, Newberry Library Fellowship Research Award, Chicago, Ill.; Spencer W. Kimball Memorial Award, Private Corporation Endowment & AIS, BYU; Phi Alpha Theta; Phi Delta Kappa; Phi Kappa Phi; Phi Alpha Delta; first Native American woman in U.S. history to earn three doctorates; J. Reuben Clark Law School Service Awards, 1990-91, 1991-92; Law School student organization awards, 1990-93; 1982 Women's Conference Spotlight, outstanding woman faculty member from the College of Student Life, BYU; Multicultural Week Advisor Awards, BYU; Multicultural Programs Awards, BYU. *Interests*: National international travel. *Biographical sources*: University of Utah Public Relations Office, Salt Lake City, Utah regarding the earning of two Ph.D.s; stories in Deseret News, Church News Section, 1980; and in Lifestyle section of the Salt Lake Tribune, Salt Lake City, Spring, 1980; hometown newspapers, Bend Bulletin, Bend, Oregon, Spilya Tymoo, Warm Springs, Oregon, and Madras Pioneer, Madras, Oregon; Brigham Young University Magazine, Feb. 1994. *Published works*: The Good Guys and the Bad Guys, The Utah Indian, Journal, Spring, 1979; Ethnic Traditions and the Family—The Native Americans, Ethnic Traditions and the Family series, Salt lake City Board of Education, Fall, 1980; editor, Minority Women Speak Out; co-editor for the Utah Centennial (1996) Tribal History Project sponsored by the state of Utah, the Utah Historical Society, and Utah Office of Indian Affairs; various book reviews pertaining to Native American topics; printed works primarily in-house curriculum development material, Brigham Young University.

CLENCH, CHARLES (Mohawk)
(artist; store co-owner/manager)
Affiliation: Mohawk Impressions, Mohawk Nation, P.O. Box 20, Hogansburg, NY 13655 (518) 358-2467.

CLIFTON, JAMES A. 1927-
(professor)
Born January 6, 1927, St. Louis, Mo. *Education*: University of Chicago, PhB, 1950; University of Oregon, PhD, 1960. *Principal occupation*: Professor. *Affiliation*: Professor, University of Wisconsin, Green Bay, WI, 1970-. *Military service*: U.S. Marine Corps, 1951-1955 (Captain; Purple Heart). *Memberships*: American Anthropological Association; American Society for Ethnohistory; American Historical Association. *Awards, honors*: Frankenthal Professor of Anthropology and History, University of Wisconsin, Green Bay. *Interests*: Research among Klamath of Oregon, Ute of Colorado, Potawatomi of Kansas, Wisconsin, Michigan, and Canada. Historical research on Wyandot and Indians of the Old Northwest Territory generally; research in

Chile. Expert witness, Indian Claims Commission and Great Lakes Indians Treaty Rights. *Published works*: Klamath Personalities (University of Oregon, 1962); Cultural Anthropology (Houghton Mifflin, 1967); A Place of Refuge for All Time (Museum of Man, 1974); The Prairie People (Kansas University Press, 1977); Star Woman and Other Shawnee Tales (University Press of America, 1983); The Pokagons (University Press of America, 1985).

CLINCHER, BONNIE MARIE (Sioux) 1952-
(editor-tribal newspaper)
Born July 6, 1952, Poplar, Mont. *Education*: Haskell Indian Jr. College, 1973-75. *Principal occupation*: Editor of tribal newspaper. *Home address*: Box 631, Poplar, MT 59255. *Memberships*: Survival of American Indians Association, 1976-. *Interests*: "I am most interested in the media, especially when I can assist in informing and making concerned the Indian people. My travels only go as far as celebrations across the northern Plains, on weekends, to just be among the Indian people and refresh my spirit in the old ways before returning to the new ways; photography."

CLINE, ROBERT E.
(coalition president)
Affiliation: South West Indian Student Coalition, 1812 Los Lomas, Albuquerque, NM 87131 (503) 277-6065.

CLINE, ROSS (Nooksack)
(tribal chairperson)
Affiliation: Nooksack Tribal Council, P.O. Box 157, Deming, WA 98244 (360) 592-5176.

CLINTON, ROBERT
(attorney-professor)
Address & Affiliation: University of Iowa College of Law, Boyd Law Bldg., Melrose & Byington, Iowa City, IA 52242 (319) 335-9032.

CLOUD, CHARLES RILEY
(Oklahoma Cherokee) 1932-
(chief judge)
Born November 20, 1932, Britton (now Oklahoma City), Okla. *Education*: College of William and Mary, BS, 1957, Marshall-Wythe Law School, JD, 1959. *Principal occupation*: Chief judge. *Home address*: 1211 Colonial Ave., Norfolk, VA 23517 (804) 622-6185. *Affiliation*: Chief Judge, Norfolk General District Court. *Other professional posts*: Member, Coordinating Council, Conference of Chief Justices, to resolve disputes between State and Tribal Courts over jurisdiction; co-chairperson, Native American Tribal Courts Committee, National Conference of Special Court Judges, JAD, ABA; trustee, Jamestown-Yorktown Foundation. *Military service*: U.S. Army, 1953-55. *Community activities*: Former chief deputy, Norfolk Commonwealth Attorney's Office; deacon and chairperson of the board, First Christian Church (Disciples of Christ), Norfolk, VA. *Memberships*: National Conference of Special Court Judges, Judicial Administration Division (JAD), American Bar Administration (ABA) (district representative and member of executive committee). *Awards, honors*: Several awards from the ABA, National Conference of Special Court Judges, for outstanding service as Chair of the Native American Tribal Courts Committee, and as a member of the Coordinating Council, Civil Jurisdiction of Tribal Courts & State Courts, and for service to the profession. "Honored by receiving letters of support from Indian leaders, such as Chief Wilma Mankiller and former Chief, Ross Swimmer, Cherokee Nation of Oklahoma; Chief Justices of the Navajo Nation, Chief Justice of Supreme Court of Virginia, and the General Assembly of Virginia leading to nomination as one of two judges of the U.S. to serve on the National Judicial College Board, and as its first Native American member." *Interests*: "Participate in programs, as well as advocating the education of Americans as to the many contributions of Native Americans to our Constitutional form of government and Bill of Rights—also, about the part Native Americans played i the Federation of the original Colonies and the American Revolution."

CLOUD, VALERIE (Leech Lake Ojibwe)
(college instructor)
Affiliation: Leech Lake Tribal College, 6530 U.S. Hwy. 2 NW, Cass Lake, MN 56633 (218) 335-4220 Fax 335-4209.

CLOUDMAN, RUTH
(museum curator)
Affiliation: J.B. Speed Art Museum, 2035 S. Third St., P.O. Box 2600, Louisville, KY 40201 (502) 636-2893.

CLOW, RICHMOND L. 1949-
(professor of Native American studies)
Born May 21, 1949, Sioux Falls, S.D. *Education*: University of South Dakota, BS, 1971, MA, 1972; University of New Mexico, PhD, 1977. *Principal occupation*: Professor of Native American studies. *Home address*: 311 Skyline, Missoula, MT 59802 (406) 543-7504. *Affiliation*: Associate professor, Dept. of Native American Studies, University of Montana, Missoula, 1984-. *Memberships*: Organization of American Historians; Western Historical Association. *Interests*: "I enjoy teaching Native American studies courses which enables me to cover many topics of interest to myself and to my students." *Published works*: Co-author: A Forest in Trust: Three Quarters of a Century of Indian Forestry, 1910-1986, (Washington, D.C.: Litigation Support Services for the Bureau of Indian Affairs, 1986); Tribal Government Today: Politics on Montana's Indian Reservations (Westview Press, 1990).

CODY, GARY
(director-Indian health)
Affiliation: Anadarko PHS Indian Health Center, P.O. Box 828, Anadarko, OK 73005 (405) 247-2458

CODY, IRON EYES (Oklahoma Cherokee-Cree)
(advisor)
Affiliation: Council of Advisors, American Indian Heritage Foundation, 6051 Arlington Blvd., Falls Church, VA 22044 (703) 237-7500.

CODY, ROBERT TREE (*Red Cedar Whistle*)
(Dakota-Maricopa)
(traditional flute player, dancer, actor)
Address: c/o Robert Doyle, Canyon Records, 3131 W. Clarendon Ave., Phoenix, AZ 85017 (602) 266-7835. Robert is an internationally known traditional flute player, dancer and actor. He has traveled extensively and participated in a tour of Asia sponsored by the National Council of Traditional Arts and U.S. Information Service. His programs share music from many native communities including his own Dakota and Maricopa. He is currently under recording contract with Canyon Records.

CODY, RON
(program director)
Affiliation: Junior Achievement's Urban American Indian Program, 3939 W. 69th St., Edina, MN 55435 (612) 927-8354.

COFFEY, PETE, JR. (*Bear Charging/Center Feathers/Spirit Eagle*) (Mandan-Arickara-Hidatsa) 1954-
(public radio broadcasting)
Born October 26, 1954, Garrison, S.D. *Education*: High school. *Principal occupation*: Public radio broadcasting. *Address*: P.O. Box 286, Parshall, ND 58770 (701) 862-3058 or 743-4391. *Affiliation*: KMHA-FM, Newtown, ND, 1984-. *Activities*: Chairman of & contributor to Nation Native News, American Public Radio; Coffey programmed & directed operations of KMHA-FM, the first truly native radio station in North Dakota, and is recognized on the national public broadcasting level. He has been in management position at KMHA since inception in 1984 and has served as operations and program manager of KMHA which is looked to by other fledgling Indian communications programs as a model in regard to programming for Native American audiences. *Awards, honors*: Most Outstanding Broadcaster Award given by Fort Berthold Media Association; named to election board for Fort Berthold Tribal Elections, 1988. *Interests*: "Reading and occasionally writing for local tribal newspaper, The MHA Times & Lakota Times. Other interests include combating the terrible effects of alcohol on the Native Indian population such as serving as speaker at chemical dependency seminars and at forums addressed to youth-young adult audiences. (I am) a follower of Native Spiritual belief system more commonly referred to as "The Red Road" and use the teachings of the Red Road to help combat alcoholism among Native Americans. (I) know that groups such as AA are fine but feel Indian people need help with a program which encompasses Native spirituality as a base."

COFFEE, ROBIN (Cherokee/Creek/Sioux)
(licensed professional counselor)
Born October 5, 1953 in Lawrence, Kans. *Education*: M.S. in Counseling Psychology. *Address*: P.O. Box 124, Tahlequah, OK 74465 (918) 456-1861. *Affiliation*: Cherokee Nation of Oklahoma, Tahlequah, OK, 1995-99. *Membership*: The American Mental Health Counselors Association. *Interest*: Poetry. Published works: "Voices of the Heart" (poetry-1990); "The Eagles Path" (poetry-1991); "Sacred Seasons" (poetry-1995); "Vision of the Winter Sleeping Seed" (poetry-1998); "The Eagles Path" (1998-compact disk-music by Tim Veazy, words by Robin Coffee).

COFFEY, WALLACE E. (Comanche)
(tribal liaison)
Affiliation: Institute of American Indian Arts, 83 Avan Nu Po Rd., Santa Fe, NM 87505 (800) 804-6422; (505) 424-2300 Fax 424-4500.

COFFIN, JAMES L.
(program head-Native American studies)
Affiliation: Native American Studies Program, Ball State University, Muncie, IN 47306 (317) 285-1575.

COHEN, JAMES E.
(Attorney)
Affiliation: California Indian Legal Services, 120 W. Grand Ave., Suite 204, Escondido, CA 92025 (619) 746-8941.

COHN, JOAN
(library director)
Affiliation: Eva Butler Library, Indian & Colonial Research Center, Main St., Rte. 27, P.O. Box 525, Old Mystic, CT 06372 (860) 536-9771. *Website*: www.theicrc.org

COIN, JACOB L. (Hopi)
(executive director)
Affiliation: California Nations Indian Gaming Association, website: www.cniga.com. *Past professional posts*: Founding executive director, Arizona Indian Gaming Association, Phoenix, AZ; executive director, National Indian Gaming Association, Washington, DC.

COKE, ALLISON HEDGE (Huron/Tsalagi) 1958-
(writer, artist, education)
Born August 4, 1958, Amarillo, Tex. *Education*: MFAW & Postgraduate work. *Principal occupation*: Writer, artist, educator. *Address*: c/o SDAC, 804 N. Indiana Ave., Sioux Falls, SD 57103 (605) 338-5058. *E-mail*: aahedgecoke@sio.midco.net. *Website*: www.hedge coke.org. *Affiliations*: SDAC, Arts Corr. *Community activities*: Director, Literary Arts Mentorship for Incarcerated Youth in South Dakota. *Memberships*: Wordcraft Circle; NWCA. *Interests*: Youth; elders; women's issues; survival. *Awards, honors*: American Book Award, 1998, for "Dog Road Woman;" Mentor of the Year, Wordcraft Circle, 2001; Sioux Falls Mayor's Award, 2003. Interests: Youth, elders, women's issues, Native community issues, indigenous representation, mental illness, survival. *Published works*: Dog Road Woman (Coffee House Press, 1997); Rock, Ghost, Willow, Deer (University of Nebraska Press, forthcoming); Off-Season City Pipe (Coffee House Press, forthcoming).

COLE, KEN
(historic site archaeologist)
Affiliation: Towosahgy State Historic Site, Big Oak Tree State Park, P.O. Box 35, East Prairie, MO 63845.

COLE, ZELLA JEANETTE CRAWFORD
(Chief Na-Ye-Hi) **(Cherokee) 1941-**
(administrator)
Born January 14, 1941, Clermont, FL. *Education*: Jarvis Christian College, BA, 1983; Northeastern State University, Tahlequah, OK, MA, 1985. *Principal occupation*: Administrator. *Address*: Unknown. *Affiliations*: Education specialist, Hopi Dept. of Education, Kykotsmovi, AZ, 1986-87; executive, Native American Heritage Preserve, Phoenix, AZ, 1988; assistant manager for administration, U.S. Census, Tuscaloosa, AL, 1989. *Other professional posts*: Free-lance writer, 1980-. *Community activities*: Editor of two newsletters; West Blocton Improvement Committee; present programs on Indians at schools and libraries. *Awards, honors*: Presidential Scholar; many awards for writing and presenting papers; achievement in history. *Inter-

ests*: "I have traveled in 22 states and lived in seven." *Biographical sources*: The National Dean's List; Who's Who; East Texas Historical Society; Wood County Historical Society. *Published works*: A Comparative Analysis of American Indian Tribes (book); Indians of Northeastern Texas (professional paper-award winner); Mixed Bloods (an award-winning poem); Petroglyphs and Pictographs (book); Profiles of Native American Leaders (book); Problems and Complexities of American Indian Law Enforcement (major paper for Cole's class in Indian law); and many other poems, short stories, and papers.

COLEMAN, EVA
(Indian education program director)
Affiliation: Red Oak Public Schools, Indian Education Program, P.O. Box 310, Red Oak, OK 74563 (918) 754-2647.

COLEMAN, GEOFFREY, M.D.
(clinical director)
Affiliation: Menominee Tribal Clinic, P.O. Box 970, Keshena, WI 54135 (715) 799-5482.

COLEMAN, STACI D. (Choctaw of Oklahoma) 1970-
(attorney)
Education: Southern Methodist University, BS (cum laude), 1991; Georgetown University Law School, J.D. (cum laude), 1997. *Principal occupation*: Attorney. *Address & Affiliation*: Hobbs, Straus, Dean & Walker, LLP (2001-present), 117 Park Ave., 2nd Floor, Oklahoma City, OK 73102 (405) 602-9425 Fax 602-9426. *E-mail*: scoleman@hsdwok.com. *Past affiliations*: Patton Boggs, LLP, Washington, DC; McAfee & Taft, Oklahoma City, OK. *Activities*: At Georgetown University Law Center, she was a member of the Georgetown International Environmental Law Journal and founder and president of the Georgetown chapter of the Native American Law Students Association. While earning her law degree, Ms. Coleman served as an intern at the White House, Office of Counsel to the President; and at the U.S. Dept. of Justice, Office of Tribal Justice. She has written several papers on Native American issues, including one on federal trust responsibility, which won first place in the Oklahoma Sovereignty Symposium Writing Competition, and second place in the American Indian Law Review Writing Competition. *Memberships*: Native American Bar Association; Oklahoma Bar Association; and serves as President and a member of the board of Oklahoma Indian Legal Services. *Areas of concentration*: Federal Recognition; Indian gaming; litigation.

COLLIER, L. BILL
(BIA area director)
Affiliation: Anadarko Area Office, Bureau of Indian Affairs, W.C.D. Office Complex, P.O. Box 368, Anadarko, OK 73005 (405) 247-6673.

COLLIER, T. DWAYNE
(monument superintendent)
Affiliation: Malmut Canyon National Monument, Rt. 1, Box 25, Flagstaff, AZ 86001 (602) 526-3367.

COLLINS, CARL
(college president)
Affiliation: American Indian Bible Institute & College, 100020 N. 15th Ave., Phoenix, AZ 85021 (602) 944-3335.

COLLINS, JOE
(school principal)
Affiliation: Nenahnezad Community School, P.O. Box 337, Fruitland, NM 87416 (505) 598-6922 Fax 598-0970.

COLLINS, REBA NEIGHBORS 1925-
(director-Will Rogers Memorial)
Born August 26, 1925. *Education*: Central State University, Edmond, BA, 1958; Oklahoma State University, MS, 1959, EdD (Higher Education in Journalism), 1968. *Principal occupation*: Director, Will Rogers Memorial. *Address*: c/o Will Rogers Memorial, P.O. Box 157, Claremore, OK 74018 (918) 341-0719. *Affiliations*: Instructor, professor of journalism, Central State University, 1958-75; director of public relations, sponsor of alumni publications, school newspaper & college yearbook, Central State University, 1958-75; director, Will Rogers Memorial, Claremore, OK, 1975-. *Community activities*: Edmond Guidance Center (board of

directors); Claremore Chamber of Commerce (board of directors); member, Claremore Ambassadors; member, Governor's mini-cabinet for tourism and recreation. *Memberships*: Delta Kappa Gamma; Sigma Delta Chi; American Association of University Women; Oklahoma Public Relations Association for Higher Education (charter president); Oklahoma Education Association (public relations board); CSU Alumni Association; OK Museum Association (board of directors, treasurer). *Awards, honors*: Outstanding Senior Woman, and Outstanding Future Teacher, Central State University, 1958; (2) First Place Awards, OK Press Association for Best Feature on Education; Outstanding Communicator Award from OK Women in Journalism, 1975; Service Award from VFW, 1971; Okie Award from Governor Dewey Bartlet, 1974; Service Award for Helping Organize First Fourth of July Celebration in Edmond, OK, 1973; Distinguished Former Student Award, Central State University, 1979. *Interests*: Genealogy, travel and travel writing. *Published works*: In the Shadows of Old North, 1974; History of the Janes, Peek Family, 1975, plus three follow up books; Will Rogers Memorial Booklet, 1979; Roping Will Rogers' Family Tree, 1982; Will Rogers and Wiley Post in Alaska, 1983; editorial staff, Photolith magazine (seven years); hundreds of feature articles for state and national magazines.

COLLINS, THELMA LOUISE (*Eagle Eye***)**
(United Lumbee) 1920-
(floor manager)
Born September 11, 1920, Fort Worth, Tex. *Principal occupation*: Floor Manager for Longmont Poultry & Construction. *Address*: 22800 Carson Ave., Exeter, CA 93221 (559) 592-4526. *Affiliations*: NAWIC - National Association of Women in Construction, 1975-85; United Lumbee nation - Council Woman for the Bear Clan, 1997-. *Community activities*: Volunteer at Sequoia Union Elementary School; Church; Bear Clan functions.

COLLISION, CHRISTINE (Eskimo)
(AK village council president)
Affiliation: Ketchikan Indian Corporation, 429 Deermount Ave., Ketchikan, AK 99901 (907) 225-5158.

COLOMBE, BOB
(council president)
Affiliation: American Indian Arts Council, 725 Preston Forest Shopping Center, Suite B, Dallas, TX 75230 (214) 891-9640.

COLOMBE, CHARLES (Rosebud Lakota)
(tribal president)
Affiliation: President, Rosebud Sioux Tribe, P.O. Box 430, Rosebud, SD 57570 (605) 747-2381 Fax 747-2243.

COLOSIMO, THOMAS
(executive director)
Affiliations: ARROW, Inc., 1000 Connecticut Ave., NW, Washington, DC 20036 (202) 296-0685; executive secretary, National American Indian Court Clerk's Association, 1000 Connecticut Ave., NW, Washington, DC 20036.

COLSON, COLLEEN
(liaison)
Affiliation: American Indian Community Liaison, Los Angeles County Dept. of Health, 313 N. Figueroa, Los Angeles, CA 90012 (213) 974-7741.

COLTON, ALFRED (*Qoyawayma***) (Hopi) 1938-**
(professional engineer)
Born 1938, Los Angeles, Calif. *Education*: California State Polytechnic University, BS, 1961; University of Southern California, MS (Mechanical Engineer), 1966, graduate program in water resources and environmental engineering, 1970; Westinghouse International School of Environmental Management, graduate. *Principal occupation*: Professional engineer. *Affiliations*: Project engineer, Litton Systems, Inc., 1961-70; supervisor of the Environmental Dept., Salt River Project, Phoenix, Ariz., 1971-. *Other professional posts*: Advisor, University of New Mexico, Native American Program, College of Engineering (NAPCOE); National Representative, Electric Power Research Institute's (EPRI) Environmental Task Force (1974-77); Bureau of Land Management's (BLM) Arizona Multi-Use Advisory Board (one term). *Community activities*: Western

Systems Coordinating Council (WSCC) Environmental Committee (member, past vice-chairman); American Indian Science and Engineering Society (chairman); American Indian Engineering Council (past associate chairman); Heard Museum Men's Council (board of directors); Museum of Northern Arizona (member); Registered Arizona Lobbyist. Memberships: Arizona Society of Professional Engineers; Institute of Electrical and Electronic Engineers; American Association for the Advancement of Science; American Public Power Association; Edison Electric Institute Environmental Committees. Awards, honors: First Place Popovi Da Memorial Award for pottery, 1976, Scottsdale National Indian Arts Exhibition; two blue ribbon awards, 1976, one blue ribbon, 1977, Heard Museum Indian Arts Exhibition, Phoenix, AZ; pottery work featured at 1977 Arizona Kidney Foundation Auction, Numkena Studio of Indian Art, Phoenix; individual showing at Santa East, Austin, Texas; 1st place and special award at the Museum of Northern Arizona's 1977 Hopi Show; 2nd & 3rd place at Gallup Ceremonial; holds patents in engineering work in the U.S. and several foreign countries. Interests: Pottery & weaving in the Hopi tradition.

COLTRA, TERRY
(executive director)
Affiliation: Northern California Indian Development Center, 241 F St., Eureka, CA 95501 (707) 445-8451 Fax 445-8479.

COMACHO, JUDITH
(executive officer)
Affiliation: Society for Advancement of Chicanos & Native Americans in Science (SACNAS), P.O. Box 8526, Santa Cruz, CA 95061 (831) 459-0170 Fax 459-0194.

COMBRINK, VIRGINIA (Tonkawa)
(tribal council president; museum director)
Affiliation: Tonkawa Business Committee, P.O. Box 70, Tonkawa, OK 74653 (405) 628-2561; Tonkawa Tribal Museum, P.O. Box 70, Tonkawa, OK 74653 (405) 628-5301.

COMELLA, NICHOLAS V. (Cherokee) 1948-
(Indian education)
Born May 5, 1948, Salem, Oreg. Education: Canada College (Redwood City, CA) 1 year. Principal occupation: Indian education. Home address: Title IX, Milpitas Unified School District, 1331 E. Calaveras Blvd., Milpitas, CA 95035 (408) 945-2387 Fax 945-2319 (work); E-Mail: wolfn@fuhsd.org. Affiliations: Liaison-Indian Education, Milpitas Unified School District, Milpitas, CA, 1990-, and Fremont Union High School District, Sunnyvale, CA, 1990-. Other professional posts: Provides Title IX Indian Education Program Services to Berryessa Union School District, Campbell Union High School District, and Oak Grove Elementary School District Military service: U.S. Army, Specialist 4 (Vietnam Service Medal; Army Commendation Medal; Good Conduct Medal). Community activities: American Indian Alliance of Santa Clara County - Education Project participant; contributor to Santa Clara County American Indian Needs Assessment Survey; coordinates New Year's Eve Pow Wow (Annual) and Homestead Pow Wow (Annual); annual Title IX Spring Festival; annual American Indian Students/Family Career Day. Memberships: National Indian Education Association; California Indian Education Association; San Francisco Bay Area Title IX Indian Education Council; Santa Clara Title IX Indian Education Coalition. Interests: "Learning about Native cultures & teaching American Indian people & non-Indians about Native cultures. Preservation of American Indian cultures - writing culturally relevant curriculum for American Indian students grades 8-12."

COMER, FANESSA (Navajo)
(administrative officer-IHS)
Affiliation: Shiprock PHS Indian Hospital, P.O. Box 160, Shiprock, NM 87420 (505) 368-4971.

COMMACK, LOUIE, Jr. (Eskimo)
(AK village council president)
Affiliation: Ambler Traditional Council, P.O. Box 47, Ambler, AK 99786 (907) 445-2180.

COMMANDA, EARL
(Indian band chief)
Affiliation: Serpent River Indian Band, Box 14, 48 Indian Rd., Cutler, Ontario, Can. P0P 1B0 (705) 844-2418.

COMMANDER, BRENDA (Maliseet)
(tribal chairperson)
Affiliation: Houlton Band of Maliseet Indians, 88 Bell Rd., Littleton, ME 04730 (207) 532-4273.

COMMODORE, WILLIAM
(Indian band chief)
Affiliation: Soowahlie Indian Band, Box 696, Vedder Crossing, British Columbia, Canada V0X 1Z0 (604) 858-4603.

COMPLO, JENNIFER
(museum curator)
Affiliation: Eiteljorg Museum of American Indians & Western Art, 500 W. Washington St., Indianapolis, IN 46204 (317) 636-9378.

CONCANNON, JOHN
(Indian school chairperson)
Affiliation: Grand Traverse Band Tribal School, 2605 N. West Bay Shore Dr., Suttons Bay, MI 49682 (231) 271-7505 Fax 271-7510.

CONCHA, MIKE (Taos Pueblo)
(former pueblo governor)
Affiliation: Taos Pueblo, P.O. Box 1846, Taos, NM 87571 (505) 758-9593.

CONGER, ANNIE (Eskimo)
(village president)
Affiliation: Native Village of Brevig Mission, P.O. Box 65, Brevig Mission, AK 99785 (907) 642-4301.

CONNOR, LELAND L. (Chief Thunderhawk)
(Shawnee) 1930-
(Indian lorist/historian)
Born May 9, 1930, Logan, Ohio. Education: Hocking Technical College. Principal occupation: Professional Indian lorist/historian. Home address: 960 Walhonding Ave., Logan, OH 43138 (740) 385-7136 Fax 385-9093. E-mail: lelandconnor@webtv.net. Affiliation: Carborundum Company, Logan, OH (leadman, 1956-66; foreman, 1966-83). Military service: U.S. Army, 1951-53. Community activities: Red Cross Blood Program, Hocking County, OH (publicity agent, 1974-75; chairperson, 1976-77); American Heart Association (volunteer); Hocking Hills Tourism Association (volunteer); Logan City Council (member); Operations Clean Sweep (volunteer); consultant to local school district (Indian lore/history). Memberships: Hocking County Historical Society (president, life member); Continental Confederation of Adopted Indians (life member; continental chief); American Indian Lore Association (life member; national director; defunct 2001); Pipestone Indian Shrine Association (life member). Awards, honors: "Catlin Peace Pipe Award," from American Indian Lore Association, for work in Indian lore; Schiele Museum's "Annual Award for Excellence in Indian Lore"; Carborundum Company's, "Community Involvement Award," for sharing Indian lore with youth groups and charitable organizations; Certificate of Proclamation for work in Indian lore, Ohio House of Representatives. Interests: Conner Indian Show; nature hiking, teaching wilderness survival, camping, visiting Indian reservations; world wide Indian lore consultant, and Indian genealogy consultant; writing, replicating ancient Indian tools, weapons, etc. Biographical sources: Articles - "Hobby Turns Logan Man Into Expert on Indians," Columbus Dispatch, Nov. 14, 1978; "Wabash Powwow Honors Region's Indian Heritage," Fort Wayne, IN Journal-Gazette, June 19, 1983; "Ancient Indians' Kindred Spirits," Messinger, Athens, OH, July 9, 1989; "Logan Man Pleased With (Jim) Thorpe Move," Logan (OH) Daily News; "Indian Skills Kept Alive by Leland Conner," The Free Paper, Logan, OH, Sept. 29, 1989. Published work: author - The Vengeance of Lewis Wetzel (Carleton Press, 1980).

CONQUEST, RAYMOND (Athapascan)
(AK village president)
Affiliation: Native Village of Aleknagik, P.O. Box 115, Aleknagik, AK 99555 (907) 842-2229.

CONRAD, BEVERLEY (St. Regis Mohawk) 1950-
(artist/writer, musician)
Born June 13, 1950, Rochester, N.Y. Education: SUNY College at Buffalo, BA, 1973. Principal occupation: Artist/writer, musician. Address: Salem Swamp, RR1 Box 159, Selinsgrove, PA 17870 (717) 374-2647. Community activities: Volunteer at the Joseph Priestly House Museum, North Cumberland, PA (sew reproduction historical clothing & take part in living history exhibitions.) Membership: Indian Arts & Crafts Association. Interests: Reproduction and original Eastern Woodland Indian products. Ms. Conrad makes Corn Husk Faces as a way of keeping a traditional craft alive in her family. "The Iroquois Indians are the only natives in North America that make medicine "masks" out of corn husk." She also grows corn to use for the Husk Faces she makes. Currently, she is writing & illustrating children's books, and works as a portrait artist accepting commissions as they come in. She is active as a musician in the area as a fiddler of American music. Ms. Conrad lectures on the subject of the Corn Husk Face and also on Native American beadwork. Biographical source: "Through the Corn" by Gregory Burgess (Indian Artifacts Magazine, Jan.-March 1992.) Published works: Doggy Tales - Bedtime Stories for Dogs & Kitty Tales - Bedtime Stories for Cats (Dell Publishing, 1980).

CONRAD, JILL A. (Nez Perce)
(attorney)
Address & Affiliation: Dorsey & Whitney LLP, U.S. Bank Centre, 1420 Fifth Ave., Suite 3400, Seattle, WA 98101 (206) 903-8767. E-mail: conrad.jill@dorseylaw.com. Attorney in the Indian Law practice group since 1997. Represents tribes, tribal corporations and tribal members in tribal and state courts.

CONSTANT, CHARLIE
(executive director-Indian centre)
Affiliation: Manitoba Keewatinowi Okimakanak, 3 Station Rd., Thompson, Manitoba, Canada R8N 0N3 (204) 778-4431.

CONSTANT, JIMMY
(Indian band chief)
Affiliation: Kipawa Indian Band, Kebaoweck Indian Reserve, Box 787, Temiscamingue, Que., Canada J0Z 3R0 (819) 627-3455.

CONSTANT, WALTER
(Indian band chief)
Affiliation: James Smith Indian Band, Box 680, Kinistino, Saskatchewan, Canada S0J 0G0 (306) 864-3636.

CONTI, RICHARD
(health director)
Affiliation: Hoopa Health Association, P.O. Box 1288, Hoopa, CA 95546 (916) 625-4261.

CONTWAY, BRUCE P. (Wan Mni Awacin) (Sisseton-Wahpeton Sioux, Chippewa) 1955-
(artist)
Born October 25, 1955, Havre, Mont. Education: Montana State University, BA, 1979. Principal occupation: Artist. Home address: P.O. Box 920, Whitehall, MT 59759 (406) 287-5122. Bronze sculptor: A second generation artist, Bruce grew up on the Blackfeet Reservation in Northern Montana where his parents taught school. His work reflects his connection to Northern Plains Indians. Community activities: Donated sculptures to Sheriff's Office for crime stoppers, to benefit the Galatin County group home for disabled citizens, and as a first donation to Murton Mckloskey Scholarship Fund for Indian students. Memberships: Professional Rodeo Cowboy Association; Indian Arts & Crafts Association. Awards, honors: 1989 Winner, Calgary Stampede Trophy Bronze Competition; 1989 1st and 2nd Sculpture Division, Colorado Indian Market; 1990 Best of Show, Calgary Stampede Art Show; 1991 & 1994 People's Choice Award, Great Falls Native American Art Show; 2nd Bronze, 1993 Santa Fe Indian Market. Major commissions: Atlantic Richfield Corp., Calgary Stampede Rodeo Trophy Bronzes, Montana Pro Rodeo Association. Major honors: Portrait sculpture of U.S. Senator Ben Nighthorse Campbell of Colorado; permanent collection of Calgary Stampede Museum; in collection of actor Tom Berenger. Interests: "Indian oral history; art-I'm lucky that in going to art shows I get to travel all over the country."

CONWAY, CECIL P.
(IHS-tribal programs)
Affiliation: Indian Health Service, Billings Area Office of Tribal Programs, P.O. Box 2143, Billings, MT 59103 (406) 657-6007.

COOK, HARRY
(Indian band chief)
Affiliation: Lac La Ronge Indian Band, Box 480, La Ronge, Saskatchewan, Canada S0J 1L0 (306) 425-2183.

COOK, HELEN
(Indian band chief)
Affiliation: Bloodvein Indian Band, Bloodvein, Manitoba, Canada R0C 0J0 (204) 395-2148.

COOK, J.R.
(executive director)
Education: Coffeyville Jr. College, A.A.; University of Okalhoma, B.S. (Math); Southwestern Oklahoma State University, MEd. *Address & Affiliation:* Founder & Executive Director (1976-), United National Indian Tribal Youth, Inc. (UNITY), P.O. Box 800, Oklahoma City, OK 73101 (405) 424-3010 Fax 424-3018, E-Mail: unity@unityinc.org. *Other professional posts:* Director, Upward Bound, Weatherford, OK, 1967-75; coordinator, Native American Program, Oklahoma City University. *Community activities:* Founder, Southwest Indian Cultural Center; organizer/coach, UNITY Eagle's men's basketball team promoting healthy lifestyles; coordinator, Atlanta Hawks success seminars/basketball clinics for Indian youth. *Awards & honors:* Commendation, Southwest Association of Student Assistance for ten years of service to youth; Jefferson Award for Outstanding Public Service; 1995 Sporting Goods Manufacturers Association's "Heroes Award"; participant, Carnegie Council on Adolescent Development, Washington, DC; profile, 1997 Strathmore's Who's Who Registry. *Memberships:* St. Luke's United Methodist Church, Oklahoma City, OK; Oklahoma County Cherokee Organization; National Indian Education Association; National Congress of American Indians; and MADD Commission on Youth

COOK, RAY
(executive director)
Affiliation: Indigenous Communications Association, P.O. Box 953, Hogansburg, NY 13655 (518) 358-4185.

COOK, RONALD
(Indian band chief)
Affiliation: Shoal River Indian Band, Pelican Rapids, Manitoba, Canada R0L 1L0 (204) 587-2012.

COOK, WARREN
(director-Indian organization)
Affiliation: Mattaponi-Pamunkey-Monacan JTPA Consortium, Mattaponi Indian Reservation, P.O. Box 360, King William, VA 23086 (804) 769-4767.

COOK-LYNN, ELIZABETH (Crow-Creek Sioux) 1930-
(teacher, writer)
Born November 17, 1930, Fort Thompson, S.D. *Education:* South Dakota State College, BS, 1952; University of South Dakota, MA, 1970; doctoral work at University of Nebraska, Lincoln. *Principal occupation:* Teacher, writer. *Address:* Resides in Rapid City, SD area. *Affiliations:* Newspaper work, editing & writing in S.D., 1952-57; part-time teaching, Carlsbad, NM, 1958-64; secondary teaching, Carlsbad, NM, 1965-68, Rapid City, S.D., 1968-69; Professor Emerita of English & Native American Studies (20 years), Eastern Washington University, Cheney, WA; visiting professor, University of California, Davis, 1990-. *Other professional posts:* Editor, "The Wicazo SA Review," a journal of Native Studies, Eastern Washington University, 1985-. *Professional activities:* Consultant & participant in the curriculum development seminar RMMLA, Flagstaff, Ariz., 1978; project director (planning grant) NEH Media Project: Indian Scholar's Journal; member, National Research Council Panel, National Academy of Science, Washington, DC, 1989. *Memberships:* National Indian Education Association; Writer's Guild; Modern Language Association; Council of Editorts of Learned Journals. *Biographical sources:* "Acts of Survival" by Jamie Sullivan, in The Bloomsbury Review, Vol. 13/Issue 1/Feb. 1993; "Bleak & Beautiful Moments" by John Purdy, in American Book Review, 1992-93 (Dec./Jan.). *Published works:* Short stories, poems, and papers: Problems in Indian Education, (South Dakota Review), A Severe Indictment of Our School Systems, and Authentic Pictures of the Sioux? (Great Plains Observer), 1970; Propulsives in Native American Literatures, paper read at National meeting of Conference of College Composition, and Communications, New Orleans, 1973; The Teaching of Indian Literatures, NCTE, Minneapolis, Minn., 1974; The Image of the American Indian in Historical Fiction, RMMLA, Laramie, Wyoming; Delusion: The American Indian in White Man's Fiction, RMMLA, El Paso, Texas; Three, prose and poetry in Prairie Schooner, Fall, 1976; A Child's Story, short story in Pembroke Magazine, 1976; poems published in Sun Tracks (University of Arizona, 1977), and The Ethnic Studies Journal; The Indian Short Story, and bibliography for Encyclopedia of Short Fiction, edited by Walton Beacham (Salem Press, 1980); The Cure, short story accepted for Anthology of Native American Literature, edited by Berud Pryor, UCLA, Davis, 1980; two short stories, The Power of Horses, and A Good Chance, accepted by Simon J. Ortiz (Pueblo writer and poet) for inclusion in anthology, The Short Story in Native American Literature (Navajo College Press, 1983); "Then Badger Said This," collection of poems (Ye Galleon Press, 1984); 12 poems, entitled, "Seek the House of Relatives" (Blue Cloud Press, 1983); three poems, Harper's Book of Twentieth Century Native American Poetry, 1986, edited by Duane Niatum; among other short stories, articles, and essays; short story collection, entitled, "The Power of Horses and Other Stories" (Arcade-Little, Brown, 1990); novel, "From the River's Edge" (Arcade-Little, Brown, 1991); essays, "Why I Can't Read Wallace Stegner" (University of Wisconsin Press, 1996); poetry, "I Remember the Fallen Trees" (Eastern Washington University Press, 1997).

COOMBS, LINDA (Aquinnah Wampanoag) 1949-
(Indian program director)
Born August 24, 1949, Oak Bluffs, Mass. Education: Lowell State College (now - UMass, Lowell) B.MusicEd., 1971. *Home address:* P.O. Box 1554, Mashpee, MA 02649 (508) 477-7240 Fax 830-6026; E-mail: lcoombs@plimoth.org. *Affiliations:* Associate Director, Wampanoag Indian Program, Plimoth Plantation (1975-84, 1988-present), P.O. Box 1620, Plymouth, MA 02362 (508) 746-1622 ext. 8385 Fax 830-6026; Mashpee Indian Education, Title IV, Mashpee, MA, 1984-88; Boston Children's Museum (Native Advisory Committee, 1975-present); Robbins Museum of Archaeology, Middleboro, MA, 1990-present; Aquinnah Cultural Center, Aquinnah, Martha's Vineyard, MA, (board of directors, 1996-present). *Other professional posts:* Visiting Committee, Peabody Museum, Andover, MA, 1997-present. *Community activities:* Museum committee member, Wampanoag Tribe of Gay Head (Aquinnah); member, Wampanoag Nation Singers and Dancers, 1992-present (performance group - traditional Eastern songs). *Interests:* Wampanoag history and culture fropm traditional times to colonial to present; traditional Wampanoag arts: weaving (bags, mats), clothing (deerskin); beadwork; quilting, embroidery, needlearts. *Published work:* "Powwow" - contemporary childrens' book (Modern Curriculum Press, 1992); "First Gift of Spring," article in "Turtle Quarterly," 1990.

COON-COME, CHIEF MATTHEW (Cree)
(grand chief)
Affiliation: Grand Council of the Crees of Quebec, Canada.

COOPER, ALFRED B. (Snohomish)
(tribal chairperson)
Affiliation: Snohomish Tribe, 1422 Rosario Rd., Anacortes, WA 98221 (206) 293-7716.

COOPER, ANNE
(editor)
Affiliation: Quileute Indian News, Quileute Tribe, P.O. Box 279, La Push, WA 98350 (206) 374-6163.

COOPER, CATHY
(executive director)
Affiliation: Deh Cho Society, P.O. Box 470, Fort Simpson, Northwest Territories X0E 0N0 (403) 695-2511.

COOPER, CHARLES B.
(monument supt.)
Affiliation: Aztec Ruins National Monument, P.O. Box 640, Aztec, NM 87410 (505) 334-6174.

COOPER, KAREN COODY
(Oklahoma Cherokee) 1946-
(museum education)
Born November 10, 1946, Tulsa, Okla. *Education:* Oklahoma College of Liberal Arts, 1965-66; Western Connecticut State University, BA, 1981; University of Oklahoma, MLS, 1996. *Principal occupation:* Museum education. *Home address:* P.O. Box 1355, Chesapeake Beach, MD 20732 (202) 633-8991 Fax 357-3346 (work); E-Mail: cooperk@scems.si.edu. *Affiliation:* Coordinator, Museum Training Program, National Museum of the American Indian, Smithsonian Institution, Washington, DC, 1994-present. *Past professional posts:* American Indian Archaeological Institute, Washington, CT, 1985-89; curator of education, Museum of the Great Plains, Lawton, OK, 1990-93. *Community activities:* Board member, Eagle Wing Press, an American Indian newspaper, 1982-89. *Memberships:* American Association of Museums. *Awards, honors:* Kidder Award, 1987, for Excellence in Museum Education, New England History Teachers Association. *Interests:* Ms. Cooper writes, "I am interested in fingerweaving, an ancient craft of American Indians in the Woodlands, and have won prizes and written articles; I am a published poet; I enjoy black and white photography." *Published works:* Tribal Museum Directory.

COOPER, MARGARET
(clinical director)
Affiliation: Arapaho PHS Indian Health Center, Arapaho, WY 82510 (307) 856-9281.

COOPER, NANCY
(Indian school administrator)
Affiliation: Bug-O-Nay-Ge Shig School, Route 3, Box 1000, Cass Lake, MN 56633 (800) 265-5576; (218) 335-3000 Fax 335-3024.

COOPER, TISH
(museum director)
Affiliation: Toppenish Museum, 1 S. Elm, Toppenish, WA 98945 (509) 865-4510.

COPENACE, ANTHONY
(Indian band chief)
Affiliation: Ojibways of Onegaming (Sabaskong Indian Band, Box 160, Nestor Falls, Ontario, Canada P0W 1K0 (807) 484-2162.

COPENACE, FRED
(Indian band chief)
Affiliation: Big Grassy Indian Band, General Delivery, Morson, Ontario P0W 1J0 (807) 488-5614.

COPENHAVER, VICTORIA
(museum curator)
Affiliation: Eiteljorg Museum of American Indians & Western Art, 500 W. Washington St., Indianapolis, IN 46204 (317) 636-9378.

CORBETT, C.
(executive director)
Affiliation: National Indian Training & Research Center, 1940 N. Rosemont, Mesa, AZ 85205-3203 (480) 967-9484 Fax 325-5288.

CORCORAN, BERT (Chippewa-Cree)
(tribal chairperson)
Affiliation: Rocky Boy's Reservation, Chippewa-Cree Business Committee, RR 1 Box 544, Box Elder, MT 59521 (406) 395-4282.

CORDALIS, RITA JO (Dine') 1954-
(gallery director)
Born March 27, 1954. *Education:* Univesity of Colorado, Boulder, MS (Museum Studies), 2000 *Principal occupation:* Gallery director. *Home address:* 1242 County Rd. #205, Durango, CO 81301 (970) 259-1363. E-mail: cordalis_r@fortlewis.edu. *Website:* www.fortlewis.edu. *Affiliations:* Fort Lewis College, Durango, 1993-; Anasazi Heritage Center, Dolores, CO, 1995-; Gallery 10, Santa Fe, NM, Scottsdale, AZ, 1992-. *Other professional posts:* Instructor, artist. *Membership:* Southwestern Association of Indian Arts (Santa Fe, NM), 1982-present.

CORDERO, CARLOS
(college president)
Affiliation: D-Q University, P.O. Box 409, Davis, CA 95617 (916) 758-0470.

CORDERO, GILBERT (Chuckchansi)
(former tribal chairperson)
Affiliation: Picayune Rancheria, P.O. Box 269, Coarsegold, CA 93614 (209) 683-6633.

CORDOVA, EMILIO
(Indian school principal)
Affiliation: Jicarilla Dormitory, P.O. Box 1009, Dulce, NM 87528 (505) 759-3101 Fax 759-3338.

CORDOVA, GREGG (Pomo)
(former chairperson)
Affiliation: Dry Creek Rancheria, P.o. Box 607, Geyserville, CA 95441 (707) 857-3045.

CORDOVA, NELSON (Taos Pueblo)
(pueblo governor)
Affiliation: Taos Pueblo Council, P.O. Box 1846, Taos, NM 87571 (505) 758-9593.

CORDOVA, SHERRY (Cocopah)
(tribal chairperson)
Affiliation: Cocopah Tribal Council, County 15 & Ave. G, Somerton, AZ 85350 (928) 627-2102.

CORDOVA, VAL
(BIA agency supt. for education)
Affiliation: Bureau of Indian Affairs, Crow Creek/Lower Brule Agency, P.O. Box 139, Fort Thompson, SD 57339 (605) 245-2398.

CORE, M. ALLEN (Osage) 1948-
(attorney)
Born August 4, 1948, Tulsa, Okla. *Education*: University of Oklahoma, BS, 1970, MBA, 1974; University of Oklahoma College of Law, JD, 1988. *Principal occupation*: Attorney. *Home address*: Resides in Oklahoma. *Affiliation*: Oklahoma Bar Association, Oklahoma City, OK, 1988-. *Community activities*: Board of Directors of the Tulsa Indian Heritage Center, and Oklahoma Indian Legal Services. *Memberships*: Oklahoma Indian Bar Association (vice-president); Native American Bar Association (board member); Federal Bar Association; Muscogee Bar Association; Court of Indian Offenses for the Anadarko and Muskogee Area Indian Offices. *Awards, honors*: The Oklahoma Bar Association's Outstanding Senior Law Student, University of Oklahoma College of Law, 1988.

COREY, MARK
(monument supt.)
Affiliation: Ocmulgee National Monument, 1207 Emery Hwy., Macon, GA 31201 (912) 752-8257.

COREY, PETER L.
(museum curator)
Affiliation: Sheldon Jackson Museum, 104 College Dr., Sitka, AK 99835 (907) 747-8981.

CORN, SUE
(director-Indian center)
Affiliation: Native American Center, University of Wisconsin-Stevens Point, Stevens Point, WI 54481 (715) 346-3828.

CORNELIUS, BETTY L.
(executive director)
Affiliation: Colorado River Indian Tribes Library/Museum, Rt. 1, Box 23-B, Parker, AZ 85344 (602) 669-9211 ext. 335.

CORNELIUS, PATRICIA
(Indian school supt.)
Affiliation: Chief Bug-O-Nay-Ge Shig School, Route 3, Box 100, Cass Lake, MN 56633 (218) 665-2282.

CORNELL, RICHARD (Tonkawa)
(tribal business committee president)
Affiliation: Tonkawa Tribal Business Committee, P.O. Box 70, Tonkawa, OK 74653 (405) 628-2561.

CORNELL, STEPHEN
(professor)
Born March 30, 1948, Buffalo, NY. *Education*: University of Chicago, PhD, 1980. *Address*: Udall Center, University of Arizona, 803 East First St., Tucson, AZ 85719 (520) 884-4393. *Affiliations*: Professor of Sociology & Director, Udall Center for Studies in Public Policy, University of Arizona, Tempe, AZ; Co-Director, Harvard Project on American Indian Economic Development, Harvard University, Cambridge, MA. *Interests*: Indigenous economic development and governance, American Indian policy, identity.

CORNSILK, CAROL PATTON
(Oklahoma Cherokee) 1949-
(film producer/director/writer/editor)
Born July 8, 1949, Tulsa, Okla. *Education*: University of Texas, BS (Radio-TV-Film), 1973. *Principal occupation*: Film producer/director/writer/editor. *Address*: c/o Native American Public Telecommunications, P.O. Box 83111, Lincoln, NE 68501 (402) 472-3522 Fax 472-8675. E-mail: native@unl.edu. *Affiliations*: "Austin City Limites," PBS (associate producer, 1979-84, associate producer/editor, 1984-85; producer/director, KLRU-TV, Austin, TX, 1985-87; Sr. producer/director, WDCN-TV, Nashville, TN, 1987-95; Director of Programming and Production, Native American Public Telecommunications, Lincoln, NE, 1996-present. *Community activities*: Member, First Church Unity, Nashville, TN. *Awards, honors*: Certificate of Merit, Chicago International Film/Video Festival 1980 for "Austin City Limits 'Songwriter's Special'" Associate Producer/Publicist; Gold Medal, New York International Film/Video Festival 1982 for Best Network Music Special: "Down Home Country Music" Co-producer; CPB Training Grant, 1984; CPB Professional Development Grants, 1985, 1987; CPB Scriptwriting/Storytelling Fellowship, 1991; Native American Public Broadcasting Consortium Program Screening Panel, 1991; National Endowment for the Humanities Media Panelist, 1991. *Interests*: "Cherokee legends, storytellers and history; travelled extensively in Europe, 1983, 1985, 1987; traveled and lived in the west and southwest - Texas, New Mexico and Colorado. I love music, art, theatre, gardening, travelling, and of late devoting much of my free time to my two-year-old son, James Eagle Pace-Cornsilk."

CORRIGAN, SAMUEL W.
(editor)
Affiliation: Canadian Journal of Native Studies, Brandon University Brandon, Manitoba, Canada R7A 6A9.

CORWIN, GILBERT THUNDER
(radio project coordinator)
Affiliation: Quinault Tribe Radio Project, P.O. Box 332, Taholah, WA 98587 (206) 276-4353.

COSTO, JEANETTE HENRY (Tuscarora, Cherokee)
(director)
Affiliation: American Indian Historian Press, 1493 Masonic Ave., San Francisco, CA 94117 (415) 626-5235.

COTTIER, CHOCKIE
(executive director)
Affiliation: National Native American Chamber of Commerce, 225 Valencia St., San Francisco, CA 94103 (415) 552-1070.

COUCH, JIM, M.D.
(medical director)
Affiliation: Dzilth-Na-O-Dith-Hle PHS Indian Health Center, Star Route 4, Box 5400, Bloomfield, NM 87413 (505) 632-1801.

COULTER, CATHERINE
(association contact)
Affiliation: New Mexico Indian Education Association, P.O. Box 16356, Santa Fe, NM 87506 (505) 989-5569.

COULTER, PhD, JOE DAN
(Citizen Band Potawatomi)
(college program director)
Affiliation & Address: Director, American Indians/Native Americans, Opportunity at Iowa, 1410 Bowen Science Bldg., Iowa City, IA 52242-1109 (319) 335-7766 Fax 335-7198; E-mail: joe-coulter@uiowa.edu.

COULTER, ROBERT T.
(Citizen Band Potawatomi) 1945-
(lawyer)
Born September 19, 1945, Rapid City, S.D. *Education*: Williams College, BA, 1966; Columbia University Law School, JD, 1969. *Principal occupation*: Lawyer. *Address & Affiliation*: Director, Indian Law Resource Center, 602 N. Ewing St., Helena, MT 59601 (406) 449-2006, 1978-. *Memberships*: American Bar Association; American Society of International Law. *Awards, honors*: Harvard Law School, Shikes Visiting Fellow, 1983. *Interests*: Indian law; international human rights law; avocations: cello and double bass playing. *Biographical sources*: Response Magazine, Mar. '89 p. 11, "A Decade of Defending Indian Rights"; Harvard Law School Bulletin, Spring '84 p. 38, "Righting Wrongs". *Published work*: Indian Rights - Human Rights (Indian Law Resource Center, 1984).

COUNCILLOR, ROSEANNA
(Indian band chief)
Affiliation: Naicatchewenin Indian Band, Box 12, RR 1, Devlin, Ontario, Canada P0W 1C0 (807) 486-3407.

COURNOYER, FRANK (Yankton Sioux) 1952-
(visual artist, electronic slot technician)
Born December 26, 1952, Wagner, S.D. *Education*: Las Vegas Gaming & Technical School Graduate Certificate, 1992. *Principal occupation*: Visual artist, electronic slot technician. *Address*: Resides in South Dakota. *Affiliations*: Slot technician, Fort Randall Casino, Yankton Sioux Reservation. *Other professional posts*: Elementary teacher-art & Indian studies; member, Board of Directors, Dakota Plains Institute of Learning, Marty, SD 57361, 1984-; chairman, Board of Directors, Native American National Arts Council, and Oyate Kin Cultural Society, Marty, S.D., 1984-. *Military service*: U.S. Army, 1971-1974 (Specialist E-4, 82nd Airborne Division) (National Defense Ribbon, Expert Rifleman Badge, Jump Wings). *Community activities*: Dakota Plains Institute of Learning is the higher adult education branch of the Yankton Sioux Tribe. *Awards, honors*: Honorable mention (best of show); sang a song for "Dances With Wolves" the movie. *Interests*: Reviving and promoting cultural and contemporary arts & culture for 15 years; "Write poetry and short stories about life and the aboriginal people of this continent; other interests include clay, wood and stone sculpture, and most importantly, the revival of the planet. I go around on reservation land and plant and transplant trees of various variety. Am concerned about the environment and tribal issues concerning the living conditions of my people. I am a traditional singer, pipe carrier and sundancer. I perform sacred sweatlodge ceremonies on my reservation for the health and lives of the people. I have traveled from coast to coast many times promoting my own and the work of others (Indian art work) and have been active in producing, promoting and marketing Indian art for almost ten years."

COURNOYER, GERALD (Oglala Sioux)
(artist)
Education: Institute of American Indian Arts, Santa Fe, NM, 1995; University of South Dakota, BFA, 1999, MA, 2000; University of Oklahoma, MFA candidate. *Address*: Unknown...resides in Norman, OK. E-mail: gerald.m.cournoyer-1@ou.edu or dnbrown99@yahoo.com. *Affiliation*: Coordinator & painting instruct, Oscar Howe Summer Art Institute (2-week program in June at the University of South Dakota, Vermillion). *Exhibitions*: Third place in painting at Northern Plains Tribal Arts show in Sioux Falls, SD; Fred Jones Museum of Art and the Sam Noble Museum of Natural History, Norman, Oklahoma; and a group show "Connected Voices," in Oklahoma City, OK. Mr. Cournoyer is currently represented by RB Ravens Gallery in Taos, NM. to view his work online go to website: www.rbravens.com or contact the MA Doran Gallery in Tulsa, OK (918) 748-8700.

COURNOYER, JAMES (Yankton Sioux)
(hospital director)
Affiliation: Rapid City PHS Indian Hospital, 3200 Canyon Lake Dr., Rapid City, SD 57702 (605) 348-1900.

COURNOYER, ROBERT (Yankton Sioux)
(Indian school chairperson)
Affiliation: Marty Indian School, P.O. Box 187, Marty, SD 57361 (605) 384-5431.

COURNOYER, STEPHEN, JR. (Yankton Sioux)
(former tribal chairperson)
Affiliation: Yankton Sioux Tribe, P.O. Box 248, Marty, SD 57361 (605) 384-3804.

COWIE, FRANK (Ojibway)
(Indian band chief)
Affiliation: Hiawatha (Ojibways) First Nation Band, RR #2, Keene, Ontario, Canada K0L 2G0 (705) 295-4421.

COX, BRUCE (Anishinabe)1934-
(professor)
Born June 29, 1934, Santa Rosa, Calif. *Education:* Reed College, B.A., 1956; University of Oregon, M.A., 1959; University of California at Berkeley, Ph.D., 1968. *Principal occupation:* Professor of anthropology. *Home address:* 140 Kenilworth, Ottawa, Ontario, Canada (613) 788-2604 (office). *Affiliations:* Instructor, Lewis and Clark College, 1964-1965; visiting professor, University of Florida, 1966; assistant professor, University of Alberta, 1967-1969; assistant professor, Carleton University, 1969-. *Memberships:* American Anthropological Association; Canadian Ethnology Association (program chair, 1989 meetings). *Interests:* Dr. Cox writes, "I am interested in the cultural ecology of indigenous North American peoples...particularly the disrupted effects of large-scale energy development projects on such peoples' environments. Here, I have in mind the James Bay hydroelectric project in Quebec, and coal strip-mining on Black Mesa, and I am collecting information on all these areas." *Published works:* Cultural Ecology of Canadian Native Peoples (Carleton Library, 1973); Native People, Native Lands (Carleton University, 1988); A Different Drummer: Readings in Anthropology with a Canadian Perspective (Carleton University, 1989); Los Indios del Canada (Mapre Foundation, Madrid, 1992).

COX, DEBORAH LYNN WHITEWOLF (Unega Waya - White Wolf) (Tcinto Sakto Muskogee) 1957-
(supervisor of elections)
Born February 1, 1957, Elizabeth County, Ky. *Education:* AS in Criminal Justice, BS in Psychology, MS in Sociology, PhD in Psychology. *Principal occupation:* Assistant supervisor of elections, Lowndes County, GA. *Home address:* 318 Crestview Dr., Valdosta, GA 31602 (229) 333-5100 Fax 333-5199. *E-mail:* lcbe@datasys.net. *Affiliations:* Supervisor of Elections, Lowndes County, GA. *Other professional posts:* Native American Artist; assistant manager, Storm of Creations; secretary, Tcinto Sakto Muskogee. *Community activities:* Instructor, Native American Studies. *Military service:* USAF, 1980-91. *Memberships:* American Taekwondo Association; Georgia Election Officials Association. *Interests:* Native American history & art. *Published works:* Correlates of Correctional Institution Suicide, 1989; Post Traumatic Stress Disorder in Police Officers, 1990; When a Cop Kills, 1992; Learning Cherokee: Workbook Series, 1994.

COX, DELTON
(school supt.)
Affiliation: Sequoyah High School, P.O. Box 948, Tahlequah, OK 74464 (918) 456-0631

COX, DONALD D. (Quiet Storm)
(Tcinto Sakto Muskogee) 1950-
(police captain)
Born September 16, 1950, Lakeland, Ga. *Education:* Georgia Military College, AA, 1972; South Georgia Tech (2 years). *Principal occupation:* Police captain. *Home address:* 318 Crestview Dr., Valdosta, GA 31602 (229) 244-9104; 293-3099 (work); *E-mail:* dcox@datasys.net. *Affiliation:* Captain, Administrative Assistant to the Chief, Valdosta Police Department, Valdosta, GA, 1973-. *Community activities:* Emergency medical instructor; firearms instructor (civilian & police); CPR & first aid instructor; instruct Citizens Police Academy classes - general instruction certificate. *Membership:* Georgia Peace Officers Assn; Police Benevolent Assn (former president); Fraternal Order of Police; AIM Chapter leader, Chapter 19, Valdosta, GA; American Board of Hypnotherapy; Georgia Police Academy (member, Advisory Board); Firearms Instructors Assn; Red Feather Society; International Assn of Bomb Technicians & Investigators. *Award:* Medal of Valor, Valdosta Police Dept., 1995. *Published work:* Firearms for Women - A Practical Guide.

COX, S. DIANE (Many Cats)
(Tcinto Sakto Muskogee) 1972-
(curator)
Born November 26, 1972, Valdosta, GA. *Education:* B.S. (English); BS (History), BS (Journalism). *Principal occupation:* Zoo curator. *Address:* 6562 S.W. 92nd

Dr., Jasper, FL 32052. *Affiliation:* Curator-birds of prey, primates and big cats, Silver Springs Zoo. *Interests:* Conservation, preservation, herpetologist.

COX, STEPHEN D. 1948-
(museum curator/administrator)
Born April 24, 1948, Bloomington, Ill. *Education:* Middle Tennessee State University, BS, 1970, MA, 1975. *Principal occupation:* Museum curator-assistant director of collections. *Address & Affiliation:* Tennessee State Museum, 505 Deaderick St., Nashville, TN 37243-1120 (615) 741-2692 Fax 741-7231 (work); senior curator, assistant director of collections and manager, Photographic Archives, 1976-present. *Memberships:* Intermuseum Council of Nashville; Tennessee Association of Museums; American Association for State & Local History; Tennessee Historical Society; Historic Nashville, Inc.; National Trust for Historic Preservation; Mid-Cumberland Archaeological Society; Southeastern Archaeological Conference; Kentucky Historical Society; National Trust for Historic Preservation. *Awards, honors:* American Association for State & Local History "Award of Merit" for the exhibition "The First Tennesseans—Tennessee's Prehistoric Indian Cultures" (for which Cox was the supervising curator) and for book, Art & Artisans of Prehistoric Middle Tennessee (for which he was the editor). *Interests:* Prehistoric Indian cultures in Tennessee. "My great-grandmother was full-blooded Indian and was born in Canada." *Published work:* Art & Artisans of Prehistoric Middle Tennessee (Tennessee State Museum, 1985).

COYHIS, LAURA (Stockbridge-Munsee Mohican)
(ex-tribal chairperson)
Affiliation: Stockbridge-Munsee Tribal Council, 8476 Moh He Con Nuck Rd., Bowler, WI 54416 (715) 793-4111.

COYLE, MARTIN (Seminole of Florida)
(school principal)
Affiliation: Ahfachkee Day School, Star Route, Box 40, Clewiston, FL 33440 (813) 983-6348.

CRAIG, BEN JAMIN
(BIA agency supt.)
Affiliation: Fort Defiance Agency, Bureau of Indian Affairs, P.O. Box 619, Fort Defiance, AZ 86504 (520) 729-7221.

CRAIG, CAROL
(media specialist)
Affiliation: Columbia River Inter-Tribal Fish Commission, 729 N.E. Oregon, Suite 200, Portland, OR 97232 (503) 238-0667.

CRAIG, JESSE
(Indian education program director)
Affiliation: Briggs Elementary School, Indian Education Program, Rt. 3, Box 656, Tahlequah, OK 74464 (918) 456-4221 Fax 456-4049.

CRAIG, JIM
(school principal)
Affiliation: Yakima Tribal School, P.O. Box 151, Toppenish, WA 98948 (509) 865-5121.

CRAIG, LAURA (Pit River)
(tribal chairperson)
Affiliation: Lookout Rancheria Council, P.O. Box 1570, Burney, CA 96013 (916) 335-5421.

CRAIG, RONALD (Nashoba Homma)
(Chickasaw/Cherokee) 1944-
(college instructor)
Born October 10, 1944, Louisville, Ky. *Education:* BA in Sociology, MA & PhD in History. *Address & Affiliation:* Chairperson, Native American Studies, Fort Peck Community College (1993-present), P.O. Box 398, Poplar, MT 59255 (406) 768-5551 ext. 22 Fax 768-5552. *Military service:* U.S. Marine Corps, 1962-66, 1974-76; U.S. Air Force, 1966-72. *Community activities:* Sacred site coordinator with Fort Peck Tribal Government and Bureau of Reclamation; advisor to Sioux Treaty Council; Reservation Historical Preservation. *Memberships:* American Indian Professors' Assn; Western History Assn; Western Outlaw Lawman Historical Assn. *Published works:* The Colberts in Chickasaw History, 1783-1818: A Study of Internal Tribal Dynamics (University of New Mexico, 1998); A History of Fort Peck Indian Reservation, 1999.

CRAIG, TIM (Cherokee)
(attorney)
Address: Unknown. *Memberships:* Native American Bar Association; American Bar Association; Native American Alumni Association of Dartmouth College (National Steering Committee).

CRAIG, VINCENT (Navajo) 1950-
(tribal law & legal research)
Born June 6, 1950, Crownpoint, N.M. *Education:* Northland College, AS (Law Enforcement), 1979; Arizona State University, BS (Criminal Justice), 1982; Universit of New Mexico Law School (lst year student). *Principal occupation:* Tribal law & legal research. *Address:* Unknown. *Affiliations:* Police officer, Navajo Nation, White Mountain Apache Tribe, Salt River Tribe (9 years); Commissioner of Justice, White Mountain Apache Tribe, 1987-90; Chief Probation Officer, Navajo Nation Supreme Court, 1991-. *Other professional posts:* Lietenant Police Academy Director, Tribal Prosecutor, Assistant Editor-Fort Apache Scout, and a Mountain Rescue Team leader. Muttonman Productions - Navajo singer-songwriter, cartoonist, illustrator, humorist, consultant; Self-esteem & motivational workshops for Native American students & educators. *Military service:* U.S. Marine Corps, 1969-73 (Sergeant-Helicopter Test-Cell Operations). *Community activities:* Boy Scoutmaster. *Interests:* Hobbies include rock-climbing, poetry, rodeo, flute-making, silversmithing, illustrating, talking to schools on "self-image & motivation". Vincent has performed for many Indian and non-Indian organizations. "I firmly believe that the greatest asset which Indian Nations have is still untapped...our Indian youth. I foresee the day when we will have Indian actors and performers who are internationally known for their accomplishments in the performing arts. It is our responsibility to nurture our youth not to be afraid to express themselves in music, drama, and literature. I can only be as free as my imagination. My idea of success is to be a sydicated cartoonist, with a law degree hanging on the wall."

CRANDELL, BARBARA (Cherokee) 1929-
(horse trainer)
Born May 15, 1929, Davy, West Virginia. *Education:* High school. *Prinicpal occupation:* Horse trainer. *Address:* 6634 Twp. Rd. 19 N.W., Thornville, OH 43076. *E-mail:* naao@avolve.net. *Affiliation:* Horse trainer (30 years); farmer (50 years); livestock broker (15 years); writer (4 years). *Community activities:* Chair of the Native American Alliance of Ohio; member, "Friends of the Mounds." *Membership:* Native American Rights Fund. *Interests:* Sewing, bead work, family. *Publication:* Sacred Wind.

CRANE, KAREN R.
(museum director)
Affiliation: Sheldon Jackson Museum, 104 College Dr., Sitka, AK 99835 (907) 747-8981.

CRAVEN, KIMBERLY
(executive director)
Affiliation: Governor's Office of Indian Affairs, 531 15th Ave. SE, P.O. Box 40909, Olympia, WA 98504 (360) 753-2411 Fax 586-3653.

CRAWFORD, BEVERLY J.
(BIA education administrator)
Affiliation: Chinle Agency, Bureau of Indian Affairs, Navajo Rt. 7, P.O. Box 6003, Chinle, AZ 86503 (520) 674-5130 Fax 674-5134.

CRAWFORD, JEFFREY A.
(attorney)
Address & Affiliation: President, Minnesota American Indian Bar Association, Minneapolis, MN 55401 (612) 540-3728.

RAZY BULL, CHERYL
(executive director)
Affiliation: Executive director, Sicangu Enterprise Center, P.O. Box 205, Mission, SD 57555 (605) 856-2955 Fax 856-4671. *Past professional posts:* Chief Educational Officer, Sicangu Oyate Ho., Inc., St. Francis Indian School, P.O. Box 379, St. Francis, SD 57572; Vice-president, Sinte Gleska College, Rosebud, SD.

CRAZY HORSE, ROY *(Chief Nemattanew)*
(Powhattan Renape)
　(tribal chief)
　Affiliation: Powhattan Renape Nation, P.O. Box 225, Rancocas, NJ 08073 (609) 261-4747. *Other professional post*: New Jersey Governor's Office, Ethnic Advisory Council, State House CN001, 125 W. State St., Trenton, NJ 08625 (609) 292-6000.

CREAMER, DONALD
　(school principal)
　Affiliation: Chuska Community School, P.O. Box 321, Tohatchi, NM 87325 (505) 733-2280 Fax 733-2222.

CREAMER, MARY HELEN (Navajo)
　(director-health center)
　Affiliation: Director, Alamo Navajo Health Center, P.O. Box 907, Magdalena, NM 87825 (505) 854-2626.

CREE, MARY
　(director-Indian centre)
　Affiliation: Oka Cultural Centre, P.O. Box 640, Oka, Quebec, Canada J0N 1E0 (514) 479-8524.

CREE, ROBERT
　(Indian band chief)
　Affiliation: Fort McMurray Indian Band, Box 8217, Clearwater Station, Fort McMurray, Alberta, Canada T9H 4J1 (403) 334-2293.

CREEL, MATTHEW (Natchez/Kusso-Edisto Tribe) 1939-
　(contractor)
　Born June 15, 1939, Ridgeville, S.C. *Home address*: 215 Indigo Rd., Ridgeville, SC 29472 (803) 871-6740. *Affiliation*: Chief, Four Holes Indian Organization, Ridgeville, SC.

CREELMAN, THOMAS, J., M.D.
　(clinical director)
　Affiliation: Warm Springs PHS Indian Health Center, P.O. Box 1209, Warm Springs, OR 97761 (503) 553-1196.

CREWS, NAPOLEON
　(Indian school administrator)
　Affiliation: Kickapoo Nation School, P.O. Box 106, Powhattan,, KS 66527 (785) 474-3550 Fax 474-3498.

CRIDER-COX, THERESA MICHELLE
(Tcinto Sakto Muskogee) 1977-
　(student)
　Born December 26, 1977, Detroit, Mich. *Education*: Georgia State University, BS (Astro Physics); presently in graduate school for Astro Physics. *Address*: 318 Crestview Dr., Valdosta, GA 31602. *Community activities*: Society of Physics Students. *Memberships*: International Society of Physics Students, National Honor Society. *Interests*: Kempo Karate (Black Belt-1st degree).

CRITTENDEN, DON (Oklahoma Cherokee) 1929-
　(tribal council member)
　Born July 8, 1929, Stilwell, Okla. *Education*: Northeastern State College. *Principal occupation*: Tribal council member. *Address*: RR 1, Box 260, Tahlequah, OK 74464 (918) 772-3238. *Affiliation*: Council member, Cherokee Nation. *Other professional post*: Supt. of schools (retired). *Military service*: U.S. Navy, 1948-50; U.S. Army, 1953-55. *Community activities*: Chairperson, County Supt. Association of Oklahoma. *Interests*: Ranching.

CROMARTY, DENNIS
　(grand chief)
　Affiliation: Nishnawbe Aski Nation, 14 College St., 6th Floor, Toronto, Ontario, Canada M5C 1K2 (416) 920-2376.

CRONE-MORANGE, PAULETTE
　(Indian council chairperson)
　Affiliation: Connecticut Indian Affairs Council, 79 Elm St., Hartford, CT 06106 (860) 424-3066 Fax 424-4058.

CROOKEDNECK, ERNEST
　(Indian band chief)
　Affiliation: Island Lake Indian Band, Box 460, Loon Lake, Saskatchewan, Canada S0M 1L0 (306) 837-4845.

CROOKS, STANLEY R. (Mdewakanton Sioux)
　(tribal chairperson)
　Affiliation: Shakopee Mdewakanton Sioux Community Council, 2330 Sioux Trail, NW, Prior Lake, MN 55372 (612) 445-8900.

CROSIER, JEAN
　(administrative librarian)
　Affiliation: Phoenix Indian Medical Center Health Sciences Library, 4212 North 16th St., Phoenix, AZ 85016 (602) 263-1200.

CROSS, TERRY L. (*Ha-nee-ga-noh*) (Seneca) 1952-
　(social work; professor)
　Born August 20, 1952. *Education*: Grove City College (PA), BA, 1974; Portland State University (OR), MSW, 1977. *Principal occupation*: Social work; professor; executive director. *Address & Affiliation*: Executive Director, National Indian Child Welfare Association, (1987-present), 5100 SW Macadam Ave., Suite 300, Portland, OR 97201 (503) 222-4044 Fax 222-4007. E-mail: tlcross@nicwa.org. *Other professional post*: Adjunct assistant professor, Portland State University, 1979-present. *Community activities*: Member, Minority Resource Committee; CASSP Technical Assistance Center, Georgetown University; chairperson of Monograph Sub-Committee, 1988-present; consultant, The Casey Family Program, 1982-present. *Membership*: Association of Certified Social Workers. *Published works*: Heritage & Helping: A Model Cirriculum for Indian Child Welfare Practice (NWICWI, Parry Cenrter for Children, 1985); Cross-Cultural Skills in Indian Child Welfare: A Guide for the Non-Indian (NWICWI, Parry Center for Children, 1988); Positive Indian Parenting: Honoring Our Children by Honoring Our Traditions (NWICWI, Parry Cenrter for Children, 1987); Towards a Culturally Competent System of Care: A Monograph on Effective Services for Minority Children Who Are Severly Emotionally Handicapped (CASSP Technical Assistance Center, Georgetown University, with Dennis, Bazron, Isaacs and Mason).

CROSS, VIRGINIA (Muckleshoot)
　(tribal council chairperson)
　Affiliation: Muckleshoot Tribal Council, 39015 172nd St., SE, Auburn, WA 98002 (206) 939-3311.

CROUTHAMEL, STEVEN J.
　(professor)
　Affiliation: Chairperson, American Indian Studies Program, Palomar Community College, 1140 W. Mission Rd., San Marcos, CA 92069 (619) 744-1150.

CROW, ENNIS
　(Indian band chief)
　Affiliation: Fort Severn Indian Band, Fort Severn, ON, Can. P0V 1W0 (807) 478-2572.

CROW, MARGARET B.
　(attorney)
　Affiliation: California Indian Legal Services, 510 16th St., Suite 301, Oakland, CA 94610 (510) 835-0284.

CROWDER, JOHN EDWARD *(Brave Bear)*
(Oklahoma Cherokee) 1926-
　(marine chief engineer)
　Born August 20, 1926, Eufaula, Okla. *Education*: Alaska Pacific University, BA, 1961. *Principal occupation*: Marine chief engineer, steam & diesel, unlimited. *Address*: P.O. Box 520348, Big Lake, AK 99652 (907) 892-8203. *Affiliation*: U.S. Dept. of Defense, Alaska locations (26 years). *Other professional post*: Chief engineer for Global Marine Drilling Co's. Drillship Glomar Pacific in Santa Barbara Channel in 1980's. *Military service*: U.S. Navy, 1944-46 (Motor Machinist Third Class - Commendation, Asiatic-Pacific & Victory Medals). *Community activities*: President, Anderson, Alaska Advisory School Board, 1973-74; president, Anchorage Community College Student Body, 1957-58. *Membership*: Veterans of Foreign Wars; American Legion; Sons of Confederate Veterans; Military Order of the Stars & Bars; Freemason Marion-Dunn Lodge #19, Ocala, FL. *Awards, honors*: Outstanding Award, Dept. of Defense, Ft. Greely, AK, 1969; Commendation, U.S. Coast Guard for "Flying Enterprise" disaster in 1952. *Interests*: Built my own house to qualify for an Alaska Homesite in 1983.

CROWE, ALVA
　(association vice-president)
　Affiliation: Chattanooga Intertribal Association, P.O. Box 71585, Chattanooga, TN 37407 (615) 266-6551.

CROWFOOT, BERT (Blackfoot/Salteaux) 1953-
　(publisher; management)
　Born September 19, 1953, Gleichen, Alberta, Can. *Education*: Brigham Young University (3 years). *Principal occupation*: Publisher; management. *Address*: Unknown. *Affiliation*: CEO, Aboriginal Multi-Media Society of Alberta, Edmonton, Alberta, 1983-; publisher, Windspeaker (bi-weekly journal), AMMSA (current). *Community activities*: Coach - Alberta team for Canada Summer Games. *Memberships*: Native American Journalists Association; National Aboriginal Communications Society; Native, Inuit, Indian, Photographers Association. *Awards, honors*: Merit Award from Government of Canada for Community Contribution; Softball Alberta Minor Coach of the Year. *Interests*: Sports psychology, psychology, cultural exchange with republic of S. Korea. *Published works*: Powwow Trail (Bear Ghost Enterprises, 1981); Nation's Ensign, monthly (Society for the Preservation of Indian Identity, 1980-83); Windspeaker, bi-weekly & Sweetgrass, monthly (AMMSA).

CROWFOOT, STRATER
　(Indian band chief)
　Affiliation: Siksika Nation Band, Box 249, Gleichen, AB, Can. T0J 1N0 (403) 734-5100.

CRUM, STEVEN JAMES (Western Shoshone) 1950-
　(associate professor of Native American studies)
　Born December 29, 1950, Phoenix, Ariz. *Education*: Arizona State University, BA, 1975; University of Arizona, MEd, 1977; University of Utah, PhD, 1983. *Principal occupation*: Assistant professor of Native American studies. *Address*: P.O. Box 4763, Davis, CA 95617 (530) 752-6488 (work). E-mail: sjcrum@ucdavis.edu. *Affiliation*: Center for Ethnic and Women's Studies, California State University, Chico (acting coordinator, 1984-85, coordinator, 1985-88, American Indian Studies; lecturer, 1985-85, assistant professor, Dept. of History); associate professor, Native American Studies Department, University of California, Davis, 1990-present. *Memberships*: Western Historical Association; National Indian Education Association; California Indian Education Association; Organization of American Historians. *Awards, honors*: "Outstanding Young Men of America" Award, 1987; "Professional Promise" Award, California State University, Chico, 1988; Ford Foundation Postdoctoral Fellowship for Minorities, Native American Studies, University of California, Davis, 1988-89; Postgraduate Researcher/Visiting Scholar, University of California President's Fellowship Program, Native American Studies, University of California, Davis, 1989-90; Nick Yengich Editors' Choice Award, 1992, Utah State Historical Society, for best article in the "Utah Historical Quarterly." *Published works*: Articles: "The Ruby Valley Indian Reservation of Northeastern Nevada: Six Miles Square," Nevada Historical Quarterly, 30(1), 1987; "The Skull Valley Band of the Goshute Tribe - Deeply Attached to their Native Homeland," Utah Historical Quarterly, 55(3), 1987; "The Western Shoshone People and Their Attachment to the Land: A Twentieth Century Perspective," Nevada Public Affairs Review, 2:15-18, 1987; "Bizzel and Brandt: Pioneers in Indian Studies, 1929-1937," The Chronicles of Oklahoma, 66(2), 1988; "Henry Roe Cloud, a Winnebago Indian Reformer: His Quest for American Indian Higher Education," Kansas History, 11(3), 1988; "The Idea of an Indian College or University in Twentieth Century America," Tribal College: Journal of American Indian Higher Education, 1(1), 1989; "Crow Warrior: Robert Yellowtail," Tribal College, 1(4), 1990; "The White Pine War of 1875: A Case of White Hysteria," Utah Historical Quarterly, 53(3), 1991; "Colleges Before Columbus," Tribal College, 3(2), 1992; "Harold L. Ickes and Idea of a Chair in American Indian History," The History Teacher, 25(1), 1991; "Native American Higher Education: The Twentieth Century," & "The Western Shoshone of the Great Basin in the Twentieth Century," both in the Encyclopedia of Native Americans in the 20th Century, 1994; The Ghost Dance," in Encyclopedia of the American West, 1994. *Books*: The Road on Which We Came: A History of the The Western Shoshone (University of Utah Press, 1994).

CRUTCHER, WILSON (Shoshone-Paiute)
(former tribal council chairperson)
Affiliation: Fort McDermitt Tribal Council, P.O. Box 457, McDermitt, NV 89421 (702) 532-8259.

CRUTCHFIELD, MARIAN (Yurok)
(ex-rancheria chairperson)
Affiliation: Trinidad Rancheria, P.O. Box 630, Trinidad, CA 95570 (707) 677-0211.

CRUZ, VIOLA
(editor)
Affiliation: American Indian Culture & Research Journal, American Indian Studies Center, Room 3220 Campbell Hall, UCLA, 405 Hilgard Ave., Los Angeles, CA 90024 (213) 206-1433.

CTIBOR, LARRY
(Indian school principal)
Affiliation: Arlicaq School, Yupiit School District, P.O. Box 227, Akiak, AK 99552 (907) 765-7212.

CUCH, FOREST S. (Ute) 1951-
(director of Indian affairs)
Born July 8, 1951 on the Uintah and Ouray Ute Indian Reservation in northeastern Utah. *Education:* Westminster College, BA, 1973. *Address & Affiliation:* Executive director, Utah Division of Indian Affairs, 324 S. State St., Suite 500, Salt Lake City, UT 84111 (801) 538-8788 Fax 538-8803. E-mail: fscuch@dced.state.ut.us. *Affiliations:* Education director, Ute Indian Tribe, 1973-88; planner for newly recognized tribe, the Wampanoag Tribe of Gay Head (Aquinnah), Gay Head, Mass., 1988, tribal adminsitrator, 1992-94; Social Studies Dept. Head, Wasatch Academy, Mt. Pleasant, UT, 1994-97; executive director, Utah Division of Indian Affairs, Salt Lake City, UT, 1997-. *Published works:* A History of the Northern Ute People (University of Utah Press, 1982).

CUKRO, GEORGE
(school director)
Affiliation: Black Mesa Community School, P.O. Box 97, Pinon, AZ 86510 (520) 674-3632.

CULLEN, THERESA, MD
(clinical director)
Affiliation: Sells PHS Indian Hospital, P.O. Box 548, Sells, AZ 85634 (602) 383-7251.

CULLO, DIANE L.
(director of development)
Affiliation: American Indian Higher Education Consortium (AIHEC), 121 Oronoco St., Alexandria, VA 22314 (703) 838-0400 Fax 838-0388.

CUMMINGS, DARLENE
(tribal chairperson)
Affiliation: Mooretown Rancheria Council, 1 Alverda Dr., Oroville, CA 95966 (916) 533-3625.

CUMMINGS, VICKI
(museum director)
Affiliation: Museum of Indian Heritage, 500 W. Washington St., Indianapolis, Ind. 46204 (317) 293-4488.

CUNHA, AGNES E. (*White Dove*)
(Paucatuck Eastern Pequot)
(tribal chairperson)
Affiliation: Paucatuck Eastern Pequot Tribe, P.O. Box 370, North Stonington, CT 06359 (860) 448-0492 Fax 448-0715. E:-mail: pepitn@aol.com.

CUNHA, JR., JAMES A. (*Growling Bear*)
(Paucatuck Eastern Pequot) 1962-
(tribal chief/treasurer)
Born May 15, 1962, Warwick, RI. *Principal occupation:* Tribal Chief, Tribal Council Treasurer *Affiliation:* Paucatuck Eastern Pequot Tribe, P.O. Box 370, North Stonington, CT 06359 (860) 448-0492. E:-mail: pepitn @aol.com. *Community activities:* Chairperson, North Stonington Democratic Town Committee; member, Board of Directors, Alliance for the Living; commissioner, N. Stonington Planning & Zoning Commission.

CUNNINGHAM, PAM (Penobscot)
(craftsperson)
Address: 397 Old County Rd., Hampden, ME 04440 (207) 941-9373. *Product:* Penobscot brown ash and sweetgrass fancy baskets.

CUPP, LORI, MD (Navajo) 1959-
(surgeon)
Born in Crownpoint, NM. *Education:* Dartmouth College (majored in psychology, sociology and Native American studies), B.A., 1981; Stanford Medical School, M.D., 1990. *Address & Affiliation:* Gallup Indian Medical Center, P.O. Box 1337, Gallup, NM 87305. *Other professional posts:* Crownpoint PHS Indian Hospital, Crownpoint, NM; National Institutes of Health tas force on recruiting—and keeping—women as clinical research subjects. *Memberships:* Association of American Indian Physicians. *Interests:* Dr. Cupp is the first Navajo woman to become a surgeon.

CURLEY, LARRY
(editor)
Affiliation: Elder Voices, National Indian Council on Aging, 6400 Uptown Blvd., NE #510-W, Albuquerque, NM 87110 (505) 888-3302.

CURRIER, JOHN (Luiseno)
(tribal council chairperson)
Affiliation: Rincon Band of Mission Indians, P.O. Box 68, Valley Center, CA 92082 (760) 749-1051 (760) 749-1051.

CURTIS, JOHNNY (*Yike, e naghaa - "the follower"*)
(San Carlos Apache) 1950-
(minister of the gospel word & song)
Born November 4, 1950, Superior, Ariz. *Prinicipal occuaption:* Minister of the gospel word & song. *Address:* P.O. Box 18527, Fountain Hills, AZ 85269 (480) 816-5059. *Community activities:* Full time ministry; paster & evangelist. "Have received Doctor of Theology by the staff of Harvest Bible College, Detroit, Mich., March, 1998; also received Humanitarian Award from Southern California Motion Picture Council, Dec. 1997."

CURTIS, ROSALYN
(hospital director)
Affiliation: Tuba City PHS Indian Medical Center, Tuba City, AZ 86045 (602) 283-6211.

CURTIS, STANLEY
(school principal)
Affiliation: American Horse School, P.O. Box 660, Allen, SD 57714 (605) 455-2446.

CUSSEN, JAMES
(IHS area director)
Affiliation: Shawnee Indian Health Center, 2001 S. Gordon Cooper Dr., Shawnee, OK 74801 (405) 275-4270.

CUSTALOW, CHRISTINE (*Rippling Water*)
(Mattaponi) 1938-
(potter & teacher)
Born April 28, 1938, Mattaponi Indian Reservation, Virginia. *Education:* Mattaponi Indian School. *Principal occupation:* Potter & teacher. *Address:* 35 Nee-A-ya Lane, West Point, VA 23181 (804) 769-9331. *Affiliation:* Teach pottery, beadwork, leather, and mask making to Indian children for the schools in King William, VA. *Interests:* "I am very proud to be able to bring back the lost art of my ancestors as I have been interested in crafts. Make pottery, beadwork, leather, and masks for shows and pow-wows. I became interested in pottery in 1978 after a training program I was in with Eric Callahan, an archaeologist teaching the old ways of making pottery." Her pottery has been displayed at various craft shows and is on permanent display at the River of High Banks Pottery Shop, Mattaponi Indian Reservation, King William, VA. *Honors, awards:* 3rd Place, Potomac Art League, 1981; 1st Place, Kilmarnock Arts & Crafts Show, 1983; Best in Show, Poquoson Art Show, 1984; Award of Excellence, Poquoson Seafood Festival, 1986.

CUSTALOW, LIONEL (Mattaponi) 1966-
(cabinet maker)
Born December 17, 1966, Richmond, Va. *Education:* High school. *Principal occupation:* Cabinet maker. *Address:* Mattaponi Reservation Circle, West Point, VA 23181. *Community activities:* Councilman, Mattaponi Tribe. *Interests:* "I am lead singer of Native American drum group ("Wahunsunacock Drum Group"), singing our song all through our Indian land.

CUSTALOW, WEBSTER (*Little Eagle*) (Mattaponi)
(tribal chief)
Affiliation: Mattaponi Reservation Circle, West Point, VA 23181.

CUTBANK, RICHARD (Leech Lake Ojibwe)
(college instructor)
Affiliation: Leech Lake Tribal College, 6530 U.S. Hwy. 2 NW, Cass Lake, MN 56633 (218) 335-4220 Fax 335-4209.

CUTHAND, DOUG
(editor)
Affiliation: Saskatchewan Indian, Saskatchewan Indian Media Corporation, 2121 Airport Dr. #201A, Saskatoon, SK, Canada S7L 6W5 (306) 665-2175.

CYPRESS, BILLY (Miccosukee)
(tribal chairperson)
Affiliation: Miccosukee Business Committee, P.O. Box 44021, Tamiami Station, Miami, FL 33144 (305) 223-8380.

CYR, JAMES
(Indian center director)
Affiliation: American Indian Center of Indiana, Inc., 7128 Zionsville Rd., Indianapolis, IN 46268 (317) 347-5160 Fax 347-5166; American Indian Center of Indiana, Inc., 406 N. Broadway, Peru, IN 46970 (765) 473-3010 Fax 473-3018.

CYR, LINDSAY
(Indian band chief)
Affiliation: Pasqua Indian Band, Box 968, Fort Qu'Appelle, SK, Canada S0G 0C0 (306) 332-6202.

D

DACON, CHEBON (*Chebon*) (Creek) 1946-
(artist)
Born November 11, 1946, Oklahoma City, Okla. *Education:* University of Oklahoma, 1965-67. *Principal occupation:* Artist. *Address:* 1285 Chasm Dr., Estes Park, CO 80517 (970) 586-5838. His artwork includes detailed pencil drawings, watercolors and acrylics. Specializes in contemporary Western and Indian art. *Community activities:* Celebrities Golf for Indian Education Tournament. *Memberships:* Indian Arts & Crafts Association; SWIWA. *Awards, honors:* High awards and recognition for ceremonial dancing, as well as his talent for art, brought an invitation from the U.S. Dept. of Commerce to act as Good Will Ambassador to Australia. His art has been shown in several European countries and takes its place in museums, galleries, and a number of private collections throughout the U.S.

DAILEY, CHARLES 1935-
(museum educator/director emeritus)
Born May 25, 1935, Golden, Colo. *Education:* University of Colorado, BFA-Fine Arts, 1961. *Principal occupation:* Native American museum director. *Home Address:* 64 Apache Ridge Rd., RR #3. Santa Fe, NM 87505 (505) 988-6281 ext. 114 (work). *Affiliations:* Curator of Exhibitions, Museum of New Mexico, Santa Fe, NM, 1962-71; Director, Institute of American Indian Arts (IAIA) Museum, Santa Fe, NM; Chairman, Museum Studies Program, Institute of American Indian Arts College, 1989-). *Military service:* U.S. Marine Corps, 1953-56 (Sergeant). *Community activities:* Judge for Indian arts & crafts competitions; National Ski Patrol Member, 1960-83; Professional Ski Patrolman, 1962-70. *Memberships:* American Association for State and Local History, 1956-; MPMA, 1960-80; American Association of Museums, 1960-; New Mexico Association of Museums, 1960-85; Native American Museum Association (charter member). *Awards, honors:* Various artistic painting awards - state & local competitions, 1960-1970; professor of the Year Award from Institute of American Indian Arts, Jr. College, 1974,'76,'82,'86, '90; kayaking - invited to participate in World Championships, Italy, 1961; various whitewater championships, 1958-62. *Interests:* Extensive travel; Native American museums survey, 1965-; research, 8,000 slides inventory; museum training interests, 1956-; various sports activities: kayaking, skiing, mountaineering, camping. *Biographical sources:* Artists in America, 1971, 1972; Santa Fe Artists; 1968; International Men of Achievement; Who's Who in the West; Contemporary Personage in the Arts. *Published works:* Creating a Crowd: Mannikens for Small Muse-

ums, El Pacio, MNM Press, 1969; Museum Training Workbooks - IAIA, DOI, BIA, Bureau of Publications, 1973; Art History; Vol. I/II, IAIA, DOI, BIA BOP, 1974; "How to Start an Indian Museum, BIA, IAIA, 1978; Major Influences, Contemporary Indian Art, IAIA, DOI, BOP, 1982; "Museum Theory" BIA, IAIA, 1984; "Museum Problem Solving" BIA, IAIA, 1990; "T.R.C. Cannon", "Bill Soza" IAIA; also, reviews & articles on various Indian artists, 1978-93.

DAKOTA, FREDERICK (Chippewa)
(tribal chairperson)
Affiliation: Keweenaw Bay Tribal Council, 795 Michigan Ave., Baraga, MI 49908 (906) 353-6623.

DALLAS, FLOYD (Dine-Navajo)
(board vice president)
Affiliation: Phoenix Indian Center, 2601 North 3rd St. #100, Phoenix, AZ 85004 (602) 264-6768 Fax 263-7822

DALME, PAMELA L.
(school principal)
Affiliation: Tucker Elementary School, Rt. 4, Box 351, Philadelp[hia, MS 39350 (601) 656-8775.

DALRYMPLE, KATHRINE C. (Western Cherokee) 1940-
(fashion designer)
Born January 30, 1940, Pryor, Oklahoma. *Education*: Oklahoma State University, BA, 1961. *Principal occupation*: Fashion designer (self-employed). *Home address*: Resides in Oklahoma. *Affiliations*: Associate Home Extension agent for the North Dakota State Extension Service and Standing Rock Sioux Tribe, and taught extension courses at graduate level for University of North Dakota, Grand Forks, 1961-73; selected representative art objects from Native American artisans from all sections of the U.S., 1961-73; co-owner, president, Friendship House, Inc. (gift shop specializing in Native American and American-made crafts), 1975-77; design clothing for specialty shops, catered Native American food, 1977-78; part-time volunteer coordinator, fashion consultant to executive director, American Indian Heritage Foundation, 1978-80; owner, American Naturals (design men and women's clothing, jewelry, and accessories based on traditional and contemporary Native American fashions. *Other professional posts*: Ran own catering and fashion design services, Navajo Reservation, 1961-73; coordinated exhibits featuring her own fashions and jewelry, 1975-77, Arlington, Va. *Community activities*: Taught crafts classes at various schools and youth clubs in the Washington D.C. area, as well as at the Smithsonian Institution, the Capitol Hill Club, and at a number of Embassies. *Memberships*: American Indian Society of Washington, DC.; Pocahontas Club (vice-president). *Awards, honors*: Epsilon Sigma Alpha's Outstanding Woman of the Year for Arizona in 1971; her fashions have received three First Prizes at the Gaithersburg, Maryland Exposition, 1973-78; her fashions have been shown at the Congressional Club, Capitol Hill Club, and the International Club of Washington, DC; her fashions have recently been worn at the Cherry Blossom Parade, Presidential Inaugural Ball and Parade for Ronald Reagan, several White House teas, and Oklahoma Society Gala; In March, 1982, 31 of Mrs. Dalrymple's fashions were worn at the John F. Kennedy Center for the Performing Arts during the Night of the First Americans, an event held in celebration of the contributions of the American Indian people; special exhibition, organized by the Indian Arts & Crafts Board's Southern Plains Indian Museum and Crafts Center, the first comprehensive showing of Mrs. Dalrymple's fashions to be presented in the State of Oklahoma; she made the dress worn by the 1983 American Indian Society Princess; in 1976 & 1983, Kathy's work was featured in the American Indian Society Cookbook; Who's Who in American Colleges (dean's list) 1991. *Interests*: Mrs. Dalrymple writes, "I feel so fortunate to have grown up among the many Native American cultures in Oklahoma, and especially to have known not only my grandparents, but four of my great grandparents and many of their friends as well. Seeing them create, from necessity, beautiful and useful articles for everyday use from whatever was available was the origin of my interest in the arts of the American Indian. As we have lived and worked in many areas of this great land, I've marveled at the resourcefulness and creativity of the people, and of

the women, in particular. No matter how busy and difficult their lives have been, they have always managed to provide many and varied forms of useful, beautiful articles to enrich the lives of the people around them. Trading of ideas, supplies, and patterns as tribes came into contact with each other is greatly apparent. How each group adapted the trade goods brought by the Europeans is a unique and fascinating study of American history. I especially enjoy creating traditional clothing for powwow wear." *Works in Progress*: Currently writing Native American children's books and producing authentic traditional dolls as well as continuing art and writing studies.

DALTON, MARGARET (Miwok)
(rancheria chairperson)
Affiliation: Jackson Rancheria, P.O. Box 1090, Jackson, CA 95642 (209) 223-1935.

DAMPHINNAIS, LOUIS
(school principal)
Affiliation: Turtle Mountain Middle School, P.O. Box 440, Belcourt, ND 58316 (701) 477-6471 Fax 477-6470.

DANA, BARRY (Penobscot)
(tribal governor)
Affiliation: Penobscot Indian Nation, Community Bldg., Indian Island, 6 River Rd., Old Town, ME 04468 (207) 827-7776.

DANAY, RICHARD GLAZER
(Mohawk of Kahnawake, Canada) 1942-
(professor; artist)
Born August 12, 1942, Coney Island, N.Y. *Education*: California State University, Chico, MA, 1972; University of California, Davis, MFA, 1978. *Principal occupation*: Professor; artist. *Home address*: 927 Alta Loma Dr., Corona, CA 91720 (714) 735-4347. *Affiliation*: The Rupert Costo Chair in American Indian History, The University of California, Riverside, 1991-93. *Other professional post*: Professor, Dept. of Art, California State University, Long Beach, 1985-. *Military service*: U.S. Army, Specialist IV, 1961-62; U.S. Army Reserve, 1962-65. *Community activities*: Commissioner, Indian Arts & Crafts Board, U.S. Dept. of the Interior, 1989-. *Memberships*: L'Association Canadienne Des Etudes D'Art Autochtone, 1986-; Native American Art Studies Association, 1983-90; California Indian Education Association, 1970-91. *Awards, honors*: Distinguished Faculty Scholar, California State University, Long Beach, 1990/91. *Interests*: Animal rights activist; exhibited art in over 150 group and one man shows from 1970 to 1992. Art Exhibit/Show Catalogs: "Shared Vision;" Native American Painters and Sculptors in the 20th Century (The Heard Museum, 1991); "Collecting the Twentieth Century," (British Museum, London, 1991-92); "The Human Figure in American Indian Art," (The Institute of American Indian Arts Museum, 1991).

DANFORTH, GERALD (Oneida)
(tribal chairperson)
Affiliation: Oneida Nation, P.O. Box 365, Oneida, WI 54155 (920) 869-2214.

DANIELS, DAVID, M.D.
(clinical director)
Affiliation: Keams Canyon PHS Indian Hospital, P.O. Box 98, Keams Canyon, AZ 86034 (602) 738-2211.

DANIELS, DENNIS
(director-Indian centre)
Affiliation: Manitoba Indian Cultural Education Centre, 119 Sutherland Ave., Winnipeg, Canada R2W 3C9 (204) 942-0228.

DANIELS, JOHN, JR. (Muckleshoot)
(tribal chairperson)
Affiliation: Muckleshoot Tribe, 39015 172nd St., SE, Auburm, WA 98092 (253) 939-3311.

DANIELS, NOEL
(Indian band chief)
Affiliation: Mistawasis Indian Band, Box 250, Leask, Sask., Canada S0J 1M0 (306) 466-4800.

DANIELS, ROBERT
(Indian band chief)
Affiliation: Chemainus Indian Band, RR 1, Ladysmith, British Columbia, Canada V0R 2E0 (604) 245-7155.

DANIELS, WESLEY
(Indian band chief)
Affiliation: Sturgeon Lake Indian Band, Box 757, Valleyview, Alberta, Canada T0H 3N0 (403) 764-1872.

DANKERT, DIANE C.
(editor)
Affiliation: Arizona Tribal Director, Arizona Commission on Indian Affairs, 1645 W. Jefferson, Phoenix, AZ 85007 (602) 255-3123.

DANKERT, MARLA
(museum curator)
Affiliation: Eiteljorg Museum of American Indians & Western Art, 500 W. Washington St., Indianapolis, IN 46204 (317) 636-9378.

DARDEN, RALPH (Chitimacha)
(tribal chairperson)
Affiliation: Chitimacha Tribal Council, P.O. Box 661, Charenton, LA 70523 (318) 923-7215.

DARLING, NEDRA (Potawatomi/Cherokee)
(BIA director of public affairs)
Affiliation: Director of Public Affairs, Bureau of Indian Affairs, 1849 C St., NW, MS 4140-MIB, Washington, DC 20240 (202) 208-3711.

DARROW, RUEY (Fort Sill Apache)
(tribal chairperson)
Affiliation: Fort Sill Apache Tribal Business Committee, Route 2, Box 121, Apache, OK 73006 (580) 588-2298 Fax 588-3133.

DASHENO, WALTER (Pueblo)
(pueblo governor)
Affiliation: Pueblo of Santa Clara, P.O. Box 580, Espanola, NM 87532 (505) 753-7330.

DAUENHAUER, NORA MARKS (*Keixwnei*)
(Tlingit) 1927-
(writer, researcher-language & culture)
Born May 8, 1927, Juneau, AK. *Education*: Alaska Methodist University, Anchorage, BA, 1976. *Principal occupation*: Writer, researcher - language & culture. *Home address*: 3740 N. Douglas Hwy., Juneau, AK 99801 (807) 463-4844 (work). *Affiliations*: Tlingit language researcher, Alaska Native Language Center, University of Alaska-Fairbanks, 1972-73; cultural coordinator, Cook Inlet Native Association, Anchorage, AK, 1978-80; translator and principal investigator, Tlingit Text Translation Project, 1980-81; assistant professor, Alaska Native Studies, University of Alaska, Juneau, 1981-82; principal researcher, Language and Cultural Studies, Sealaska Heritage Foundation, 9085 Glacier Hwy., Juneau, AK, 1983-97. *Community activities*: Member and chair, Russian Orthodox Church and Alaska Native Sisterhood; president, Shax'saani keek' Weavers. *Awards, honors*: Commissioner, Alaska Historical Commission, 1978-81; First Prize in Short Story and Poetry Categories, Southeast Alaska Native Arts Festival, Sitka, AK, 1979; 1980 "Humanist of the Year" by Alaska Humanities Forum (joint award with Richard Dauenhauer); member, Alaska Humanities Forum Committee, 1981-87; 1989 "Governor's Award for the Arts", presented by Alaska Governor Steve Cowper; 1991 American Book Award for Haa Tuwunaagu Yis, for Healing our Spirit: Tlingit Oratory. *Interests*: Tlingit language and literature, poetry, fiction, drama. *Biographical sources*: Directory of American Indian/Alaska Women, 1979. *Published works*: Co-editor, "Because We Cherish Your...": Sealaska Elders Speak to the Future (Sealaska Foundation, 1981); short story anthologized in Earth Power Coming: Short Fiction in Native American Literature, edited by Simon Ortiz (Navajo Community College Press, 1983); Tlingit Spelling Book (revised third edition), with Richard Dauenhauer (Sealaska Heritage Foundation, 1984); poetry anthologized in That's What She Said: Contemporary Poetry & Fiction by Native American Women, edited by Rayna Green (Indiana University Press, 1984); Alaska Native Writers, Storytellers and Orators (special issue of Alaska Quarterly Review, University of Alaska, Anchorage, 1986); Haa Shuka, Our Ancestors: co-editor, Tlingit Oral Narratives (University of Washington Press, 1987); poetry anthologized in Harper's Anthology of 20th Century Native American Poetry, edited by Duane Niatum (Harper & Row, San Francisco, 1988); The Droning Shaman (The Black Current Press, Haines, AK, 1988); Editor, with

Richard Dauenhauer, Haa Tuwunaagu Yis, for Healing our Spirit: Tlingit Oratory (University of Washington Press, 1990; Beginning Tlingit, 3rd Revised Ed., with Richard Dauenhauer (Sealaska Heritage Foundation, 1991); et al.

DAUENHAUER, RICHARD 1942-
(writer)
Born April 10, 1942, Syracuse, N.Y. *Education*: Syracuse University, BA, 1964; University of Texas, Austin, MA, 1966; University of Wisconsin, Madison, PhD (Comparative Literature), 1975. *Principal occupation*: Writer. *Home address*: 3740 N. Douglas Hwy., Juneau, AK 99801 (907) 586-4708. *Affiliations*: Assistant professor, Alaska Methodist University, Anchorage,1969-75; education specialist, Alaska Native Education Board, Anchorage, 1974-76; staff associate, Alaska Native Foundation, Anchorage, 1976-78; associate professor, Alaska Pacific University, Anchorage, 1979-83; program director, Sealaska Heritage Foundation, Juneau, 1983-97. *Community activities*: Reader, parish council officer, St. Nicholas Orthodox Church. *Memberships*: PEN; Poets & Writers. *Awards, honors*: Woodrow Wilson Fellowship, 1964; Fulbright Fellowship, 1966; Named "Humanist of the Year" by Alaska Humanities Forum, 1980 (joint award with Nora Marks Dauenhauer); Poet Laureate of Alaska, 1981-88; 1989 Governor's Award for the Arts, presented by Steve Cowper, Governor of Alaska; 1991 American Book Award for Haa Tuwunaagu Yis, for Healing our Spirit: Tlingit Oratory. *Interests*: Comparative literature, oral literature, Alaska Native literature, languages and linguistics, poetry. *Published works*: Co-editor, Snow in May: An Anthology of Finnish Writing, 1945-72 (Associated University Presses, Cranbury, NJ, 1978); Glacier Bay Concerto (Poetry) (Alaska Pacific University Press, Anchorage, 1980); co-editor, "Because We Cherish You...": Sealaska Elders Speak to the Future (Sealaska Heritage Foundation, 1981; The Shroud of Shaawat Seek' (Poetry) (Orca Press, Sitka, AK, 1983); co-editor, Tlingit Spelling Book (Third revised Edition-Sealaska, 1984); co-editor, Alaska Native Writers, Storytellers and Orators (special issue of Alaska Quarterly Review, 1986); Frames of Reference (Poetry) (The Black Current Press, Haines, AK, 1987); co-editor, Haa Shuka, Our Ancestors: Tlingit Oral Narratives (University of Washington Press, 1987); Editor, with Richard Dauenhauer, Haa Tuwunaagu Yis, for Healing our Spirit: Tlingit Oratory (University of Washington Press, 1990; Beginning Tlingit, 3rd Revised Edition, with Nora Marks Dauenhauer (Sealaska Heritage Foundation, 1991); and numerous other writings.

DAUGHERTY, JOHN (Shawnee-Delaware) 1948-
(health systems administrator)
Born August 9, 1948, Claremore, Okla. *Education*: Northeastern State University, BA, BS, 1976; University of Minnesota, 1986 (Advanced certificate in health administration). *Principal occupation*: Health systems administrator. *Address*: Claremore PHS Indian Hospital, W. Will Rogers & Moore, Claremore, OK 74017 (918) 341-8430. *Affiliation*: Executive director, Native American Coalition of Tulsa, 1978-79; administrator, USPHS Miami Indian Health Center, Miami, OK, 1979-90; Claremore PHS Indian Hospital, Claremore, OK, 1991-. *Military service*: U.S. Air Force, 1969-72 (in Madrid, Spain) (Commendation Medal for Meritorious Service). *Community activities*: Member, Rotary International; chairman, Title IV, Indian Education Parent Committee; officer, Native American Student Association at Northeast Oklahoma A&M Junior College and Northeastern Oklahoma State University, 1973-76. *Awards, honors*: Who's Who Among Students in American Universities and Colleges, 1976-77; golf team; deans honor roll, 1976, NEOSU, Tahlequah; chosen by University of Minnesota Independent Study Program to give presentation on Indian Health in U.S. during International Health Night, July 17, 1985. *Interests*: "My educational and vocational interest is in health care administration. My goals are to better myself in these areas. Indian cultures and the presentation of my tribal ceremonies are of great concern to me. Participating in tribal activities of other tribes, as well as my tribe and encouraging others to participate are very important to me."

DAUGHTERS, DOUGLAS L. (Sioux)
(school principal)
Affiliation: Fort Thompson Elementary School, P.O. Box 139, Fort Thompson, SD 57339 (605) 245-2372.

DAVENPORT, TALBERT (Sac & Fox)
(tribal chairperson)
Affiliation: Sac & Fox Tribe of the Mississippi in Iowa, 349 Meskwaki Rd., Tama, IA 52339 (515) 484-4678.

DAVID, BETTY (Spokane)
(artist-designer)
Address: 2504 Castillo #4, Santa Barbara, CA 93105 (805) 682-5175. *Membership*: Indian Arts & Crafts Association.

DAVID, TERESA
(publisher)
Affiliation: Akwesasne Notes, Mohawk Nation, P.O. Box 196, Rooseveltown, NY 13683 (518) 358-9531.

DAVIS, BRENDA
(organization president)
Affiliation: Inter-Tribal Indians of New Jersey, 21 Village Rd., Morganville, NJ 07751 (732) 591-8335.

DAVIS, DERRICK
(singer, dancer)
Derrick is a Plains Indian style singer and dancer. All performances are done in a fashion that will educate people and correct misconceptions about native American music and dance. Dances include Eagle Dance, Fancy Feather Dance, Hoop Dance, and Round Dance. He can be contacted at (602) 244-8019.

DAVIS, DON J.
(BIA area health director)
Affiliation: Phoenix Area Indian Health Service, 3738 N. 16th St., Suite A, Phoenix, AZ 85016 (602) 640-2052.

DAVIS, E. MORRIS
(executive officer)
Affiliation: Indian Rights Association, 1801 Market St., 10th Floor, Philadelphia, PA 19103 (215) 665-4523.

DAVIS, GARY
(director-Indian health center)
Affiliation: Pawnee PHS Indian Health Center, Rural Route 2, Box 1, Pawnee, OK 74058 (918) 762-2517.

DAVIS, GWEN (Shoshoni)
(tribal chairperson)
Affiliation: Northwestern Band of Shoshoni Nation, 427 N. Main, Suite 101, Blackfoot, ID 83204 (208) 478-5712.

DAVIS, IRMA
(Indian education center director)
Affiliation: Director, Local Indians for Education, P.O. Box 729, Shasta Lake, CA 96019 (916) 275-1513 Fax 275-6260.

DAVIS, JAMES L.
(BIA agency supt. for education)
Affiliation: Turtle Mountain Agency, Bureau of Indian Affairs, P.O. Box 30, Belcourt, ND 58316 (701) 477-6471 ext. 211.

DAVIS, KENNETH W.
(BIA agency supt.)
Affiliation: Turtle Mountain Agency, BIA, P.O. Box 60, Belcourt, ND 58316 (701) 477-3191. *Past professional post*: Supt., Northern Cheyenne Agency, BIA, Lame Deer, MT .

DAVIS, LARRY
(ranger-in-charge-historical monument)
Affiliation: Anasazi Indian Village, State Historical Monument, P.O. Box 1329, Boulder, UT 84716 (801) 335-7308.

DAVIS, MARVIN
(association president)
Affiliation: Inter-Tribal Indians of New Jersey, 21 Village Rd., Morganville, NJ 07751 (908) 591-8335.

DAVIS, MARY B. 1942-
(library director)
Born December 4, 1942, Huntington, WV. *Education*: Beloit College, 1960-62; University of Illinois, Champaign, AB, 1964; University of Michigan, MA, 1969. *Principal occupation*: Library director. *Address & Affiliation*: Huntington Free Library and Reading Room (formerly-Museum of the American Indian Library), 9 Westchester Square, Bronx, NY 10461 (718) 829-7770 Fax 829-4875; E-Mail: hflib1@metgate. metro.org., 1977-. *Community activities*: Peace Corps Volunteer, 1964-66; 1987 panelist, "American Indians, Library Collections & Resources in the Metro Region." *Memberships*: Art Libraries Society of North America (ARLIS); American Library Association; Special Libraries Association; Bronx Library Emergency Consortium. *Awards, honors*: 1995 "Denali Press Award," Native America in the Twentieth Century: An Encyclopedia. *Selected presentations*: ARLIS programs: panelist, "Documenting Native American Culture: Past & Present Resources," 1989); panelist, "Native American Documentation: An Overview," 1992; NYLA program: panelist, Native American Voices: Are They In Your Library?," 1992. *Published works*: Field Notes of Clarence B. Moore's Southeastern Archaeological Expeditions, 1891-1918 (Huntington Free Library, 1987); Papers of the Hemenway Southwestern Archaeological Expedition in the Huntington Free Library, (Huntington Free Library, 1987); Stockbridge Indian Papers in the Huntington Free Library (Huntington Free Library, 1987); The Wabanaki Collection and the Williams Wallace Tooker papers in the Huntington Free Library (Huntington Free Library, 1991); Papers of Constance Goddard Du Bois in the Huntington Free Library (Huntington Free Library, 1994); The Joseph Keppler Iroquois Papers in the Huntington Free Library (Huntington Free Library, 1994); Papers of the Women's National Indian Association in the Huntington Free Library (Huntington Free Library, 1994); editor, Native America in the 20th-Century: An Encyclopedia (Garland Publishing, 1994); book reviews.

DAVIS, MONA (Chuckchansi)
(tribal vice-chairperson)
Affiliation: Picayune Rancheria, P.O. Box 1480, Coarsegold, CA 93614 (209) 683-6633.

DAVIS, OLA CASSADORE (San Carlos Apache)
(organization chairperson)
Affiliation: Apache Survival Coalition, P.O. Box 1237, San Carlos, AZ 85550 (520) 475-2543.

DAVIS, ROBERT, JR. (Marietta Nooksack)
(tribal chairperson)
Affiliation: Marietta Band of Nooksack Indians, 1827 Marine Dr., Bellingham, WA 98226.

DAVIS, ROBERT C. 1922-
(film producer, lecturer)
Born May 7, 1922, Kansas City, Mo. *Education*: High school. *Principal occupation*: Film producer, lecturer. *Home address*: P.O. Box 12, Cary, IL 60013 (847) 639-3068. *Affiliations*: Self-employed selling hand weavings of Maya Indians of Guatemala on a volunteer basis last ten years. *Military service*: U.S. Signal Corps, 1942-45. *Memberships*: Film Lecturer's Association, 1970-. *Interests*: American Indians; community service as volunteers. *Awards, honors*: American Film Festival Awards for Arizona Revealed; Columbus Film Festival Awards for seven other films. *Films produced*: Land of the Crimsoned Cliffs, 1955; Arizona Utopia, 1961; Arizona Revealed, 1964; Arizona Adventure, 1975; many 35mm and 2 x 2 color transparencies of Navajo, Pima and Hopi Indians.

DAVIS, ROBERT E.
(national secretary-organization)
Affiliation: Great Council of U.S. Improved Order of Red Men, P.O. Box 683, Waco, TX 76703 (817) 756-1221.

DAWES, CHARLES (Ottawa)
(tribal chief)
Affiliation: Ottawa Tribe of Oklahoma, P.O. Box 110, Miami, OK 74355 (918) 540-1536.

DAY, DR. DON
(college administrator)
Affiliation: President, Fond du Lac Tribal and Community College, 2101 14th St., Cloquet, MN 55720 (218) 879-0804 Fax 879-0814.

DAY, JOSEPH
(executive director)
Affiliation: Minnesota Indian Affairs Council, 1819 Bemidji Ave., Bemidji, MN 56601 (218) 755-3825.

DAY, KEVIN (Miwok)
(rancheria chairperson)
Affiliation: Tuolumne Rancheria, P.O. Box 699, Tuolumne, CA 95379 (209) 928-3475.

DAYBUTCH, DOUGLAS
(Indian band chief)
Affiliation: Mississauga Indian Band, Box 1299, Blind River, Ontario, Canada P0R 1B0 (705) 356-1621.

DAYLEY, JON P. 1944-
(professor of linguistics)
Born October 8, 1944, Salt Lake City, Utah. *Education*: Idaho State University, BA, 1968, MA, 1970; University of California, Berkeley, MA, 1973, PhD, 1981. *Principal occupation*: Professor of linguistics. *Home address*: 5953 Eastwood Place, Boise, ID 83716 (208) 385-1714 (work). *Affiliations*: Visiting lecturer in linguistics, University of California, Berkeley, 1982; professor of linguistics, Boise State University, Boise, ID, 1982-. *Other professional posts*: Linguista - Projecto Linguistico Francisco Marroquin, Guatemala, 1973-78; writer, researcher, Experiment in International Living, Brattleboro, Vt., 1978-79. *Memberships*: Linguistic Society of America; Society of the Study of Indigenous Languages of America; Berkeley Linguistics Society. *Interests*: American Indian languages and cultures: Mayan language—Tzutujil Maya, Uto-Aztecon languages—Shoshone & Panamint; Creole languages; general linguistics. *Published works*: Belizean Creole Handbook, Vols. I-IV (Experiment in International Living, U.S. Peace Corps, 1979); Tzutujil Grammar (University of California Press, 1985); Tumpisa (Panamint) Shoshone Grammar & Dictionary (2 separate books) (University of California Press, 1989); Western Shoshoni Grammar (Boise State University, 1993); Dictionario Tz'utujil de San Juan la Laguna (Projecto Linguistico Francisco Marroquin, Guatemala, 1994); Shoshoni Texts (Boise State University, 1997); Newe Hupia: Shoshoni Poetry Songs, with Beverly and Earl Crum (Utah State University Press, 2002); and many articles on Mayan languages, Shoshone and general linguistics.

DAYO, DIXIE
(AK village council president)
Affiliation: Manley Hot Springs Village, Manley Hot Springs, AK 99756 (907) 672-3331.

DAWES, CHARLES (Ottawa) 1923-
(manufacturing management; tribal chief)
Born February 7, 1923, Peoria, Okla. *Education*: Missouri Southern University, AA, 1950; University of Arkansas, BS, 1952. *Principal occupation*: Manufacturing management; tribal chief. *Address*: P.O. Box 32, Quapaw, OK 74363 (918) 674-2553. *Affiliations*: Manufacturing engineer, Vickers, Inc., Joplin, MO, 1952-56; plant manager, president, Ingersoll-Rand Co., Ft. Smith, AR; chief, Ottawa Busines Council, P.O. Box 110, Miami, OK 74355 (918) 540-1536 Fax 542-3214. *Military service*: Army Air Corp, 1943-46 (S/Sergeant); Army Infantry School, 1945 (2nd Lt.). *Community activities*: Fort Smith Manufacturing Executives Association (president); United Fund (board member); Abilities Unlimited Sheltered Workshop; St. Edwards Mercy Hospital; Intertribal Council; Claremore Indian Hospital.

DAWSON, KAREN
(Indian school principal)
Affiliation: Tohono O'Odham High School, HC01 Box 8513, Sells, AZ 85634 (520) 362-2400.

DAY, KEVIN (Me-wuk)
(rancheria chairperson)
Affiliation: Tuolumne Rancheria, P.O. Box 699, Tuolumne, CA 95379 (209) 928-3475.

DEACON, HENRY
(AK village president)
Affiliation: Organized Village of Grayling (aka Holikachu) Council, Grayling, AK 99590 (907) 453-5116.

DEAN, S. BOBO
(attorney)
Education: Yale University, BA, 1954, LLB, 1961; Oxford University (Rhodes Scholar), MA, 1956. *Principal occupation*: Attorney. *Address & Affiliation*: Co-founder (in 1982), Hobbs, Straus, Dean & Walker, 2120 L St.,

NW, Suite 700, Washington, DC 20037 (202) 822-8282 Fax 296-8834. E-mail: sdean@hsdwdc.com. *Past professional posts*: Debevoise Plimpton, New York, NY, 1961-65; Strasser, Spiegelberg, Fried, Frank & Kampelman (founded by Felix Cohen whose work in the Indian field was nationally known), 1965-82. His extensive experience in the representation of Indian tribal governments and tribal organizations includes assisting the Miccosukee Tribe of Indians of Florida in negotiating the first contract with the Bureau of Indian Affairs under which an entire BIA agency is administered by a tribal government. Mr. Dean was instrumental in the enactment and implementation of the Indian Self-Determination and Education Assistance Act of 1975, and the 1988 and 1994 amendments to that Act. He served as a member of the Negotiated Rulemaking Committee which prepared regulations under Title I of the Act as a representative of tribes in Alaska. He has represented Indian tribal and Alaska Native organizations in contracting with federal agencies to operate schools, hospitals, and other federal service programs for Indians, and he represents tribes and tribal organizations in administrative appeals and litigation to vindicate tribal self-determination rights. He participated in drafting the bill to reauthorize the Indian Health Care Improvement Act which is now under consideration in the Congress.

DeASIS, PATRICIA A.
(IHS director of communications)
Affiliation: Indian Health Service, 5600 Fishers Lane, Room 6-35, Rockville, MD 20857 (301) 443-3593.

DeBEN, SHERRY
(Indian education tutor, coordinator)
Address & Affiliation: Bark River - Harris School, P.O. Box 350, Harris, MI 49845 (906) 466-5334. *Community activities*: Michigan Works - The Job Force, Summer Youth Program, 1994-96.

DeBOER, ROY J. (Lummi) 1936-
(school principal)
Born July 23, 1936, Bellingham, Wash. *Education*: Olympic Junior College, AA, 1960; Western Washington State University, BA, 1962; University of Puget Sound, Tacoma, Wash., MEd, 1981. *Principal occupation*: School principal. *Home address*: 3528 S.E. Pine Tree Dr., Port Orchard, WA 98366. *Affiliations*: Director of Indian Education, South Kitsap School District, Port Orchard, WA, 1973-80; principal, Wolfe Elementary School, Kingston, WA, 1981-. *Other professional posts*: Seven years on Washington State Advisory Committee, Indian Education to Washington State Supervisor of Schools. *Military service*: U.S. Air Force, 1954-58 (A 1/C). *Community activities*: Pacific Lutheran Theological Seminary (board of directors); Division of Service and Mission in America, American Lutheran Church (board of directors); Chamber of Commerce, Kingston, Wash.; Sons of Norway, Poulsbo, WA. *Memberships*: National Education Association; Washington Education Association; ASCD; ESPA. *Awards, honors*: Outstanding Secondary Teacher of America, 1973; Quill and Scroll Adult Leadership Award, 1969. *Interests*: Reading, travel, photography; singing with Twana Dancers, Skokomish traditional dance group.

DeCAMP, LINDA
(Indian education program coordinator)
Affiliation: Big Bay de Noc School, Indian Education Program, 1250 N. Oaks St., Davison, MI 48423 (810) 591-3531 Fax 591-0918. E-mail: ldecamp@mail. davison.k12.mi.us.

DEER, ADA E. (Menominee) 1935-
(lecturer, social worker)
Born August 7, 1935, Keshena, Wis. *Education*: University of Wisconsin, Madison, BA, 1957; Columbia University, School of Social Work, MSW, 1961. *Principal occupation*: Lecturer, social worker. *Address*: University of Wisconsin, School of Social Work, Madison, WI 53706. *Affiliations*: Lecturer, School of Social Work & Native American Studies Program, University of Wisconsin, Madison, WI, 1977-93; 2000-present; Assistant Secretary, Bureau of Indian Affairs, Washington, DC, 1993-2000; *Other professional posts*: Chairperson, Menominee Restoration Committee, 1973-76; vice president & Washington lobbyist, National Committee to Save the Menominee People and Forest, Inc., 1972-73; chairperson, Menominee Common Stock &

Voting Trust, 1971-73. *Community activities*: American Indian Policy Review Commission (member, 1975-77). *Memberships*: National Association of Social Workers; National Organization of Women; Common Cause; Girl Scouts of America; Democratic Party of Wisconsin; National Congress of American Indians. *Awards, honors*: Doctor of Humane Letters, University of Wisconsin, 1974; Doctor of Public Service, Northland College, Ashland, WI, 1974; White Buffalo Council Achievement Award, Denver, CO, 1974; Pollitzer Award, Ethical Cultural Society, NY, 1975; Fellow, Harvard Institute of Politics, 1977. *Interests*: Social work; community organization and social action; minority rights. *Biographical sources*: I Am the Fire of Time, Jane B. Katz, editor (E.P. Dutton, 1977); Ms Magazine, April, 1973; Indians of Today, 4th Edition; The Circle, Dec. 1977.

DEER SMITH, MARY HELEN
(executive director)
Affiliation: Oklahoma City Indian Clinic, 1214 N. Hudson, Oklahoma City, OK 73101 (405) 232-1526. *Past professional post*: Dallas Inter-Tribal Center, Dallas, TX.

DEER CLOUD, SUSAN ANN (*Deer Cloud*)
(Mohawk/Seneca/Blackfoot) 1950-
(writer; professor of creative writing)
Born October 20, 1950, Livingston Manor, N.Y. *Education*: Binghamton University, BA, 1980, MA, 1982. *Principal occupation*: Writer; professor of creative writing. *Home address*: 45 Vine St., Binghamton, NY 13903 (607) 723-3816. E-mail: sdeercloud@aol.com. *Affiliation*: Binghamton University, Binghamton, NY. *Community activities*: Do readings and talks at the university & in the community; bring Native people to Binghamton University to perform/read. *Membership*: Poets & Writers, AWP, Wordcraft Circle of Native Writers & Storytellers. *Awards, honors*: New York State Foundation for the Arts Poetry Fellowship, 1993. *Poetry honors*: "Indian Interlude," Honorable Mention in New Letters 1990 Poetry Competition; Singularities," 1st Prize, Paterson's Poetry Center's International Poetry Contest; "Potato", finalist in Eve of St. Agnes Competition, 1993; among others. *Interests*: "Primarily interested in writing both stories and poetry that often contain an interweaving of Indian themes. I also like photography, reading, hiking, and traveling to just about anywhere. I am also deeply involved with Indian issues, which I try to express in my work." *Published works*: The Sacred Hoop (Blue Cloud Press, 1988); In the Moon When the Deer Lose Their Horns (Chantry Press, 1993).

DEERINWATER, DAN
(BIA regional director)
Affiliation: Southern Plains Regional Office, Bureau of Indian Affairs, P.O. Box 368, Anadarko, OK 73005 (405) 247-6673 Fax 247-5611.

DEERNOSE, KITTY BELLE (Crow) 1956-
(museum curator)
Born April 14, 1956, Crow Agency, Mont. *Education*: Institute of American Indian Arts, Santa Fe, NM. *Principal occupation*: Museum curator. *Address & Affiliation*: Little Bighorn Battlefield National Monument, P.O. Box 39, Crow Agency, MT 59022 (406) 638-2621 Fax 638-2623. E-mail: kitty-deernose@nps.gov (1990-). *Community activities*: Plenty Coups Museum, Advisory Board member; Little Bighorn College, School-to-Work Governing Board. *Memberships*: American Association of Museums; Museum Association of Montana; Montana Plains Museum.

DEETZ, JAMES L.
(museum curator)
Affiliation: Robert H. Lowie Museum of Anthropology, 103 Kroeber Hall, University of California, Berkeley, CA 94720 (510) 642-3681.

DeFOE, PETER J. (Ojibwe)
(tribal committee president)
Affiliation: Minnesota Chippewa Tribal Executive Committee, P.O. Box 217, Cass Lake, MN 56633 (218) 335-8581.

DeGARMO, RALPH (Paiute)
(tribal chairperson)
Affiliation: Chair, Fort Bidwell Community Council, P.O. Box 129, Fort Bidwell, CA 96112 (916) 279-6310.

DeGENNARO, GAETANA (Tohono O'odham)
(Indian resource center manager)
Affiliation: Resource Center, George Gustav Heye Center, National Museum of the American Indian, Smithsonian Institution, New York, NY 10004 (212) 514-3781.

DeGROAT, ELLOUISE (Navajo) 1939-
(BIA tribal affairs officer)
Born May 12, 1939, Tuba City, Ariz. *Education*: Arizona State University, BS, 1962, MSW, 1966. *Principal occupation*: BIA tribal affairs officer. *Home address*: P.O. Box 526, Fort Defiance (Navajo Nation), AZ 86504. *Affiliation*: Tribal Affairs Officer, Navajo Area Office, BIA, P.O. Box G, Hwy. 264, Window Rock, AZ 86515, 1976-. *Other professional posts*: Consultant, American Child Psychiatry (Committee on Indian Affairs) and the Indian Task Force on Mental Health. *Community activities*: St. Michaels Special Education Association (member); instrumental in staging the First Annual Navajo Health Symposium; involvement with education of Indian children and special concern for the handicapped. *Memberships*: American Indian Health Association; National Association of Social Workers; National Conference of Social Workers (national board member, 1972-74). *Awards, honors*: Distinguished Service Award, The Navajo Tribe, 2nd Annual Navajo Health Symposium. *Interests*: Tribal government; national legislation for Indian tribes; advocate for Indian causes, especially health; American Indian woman; served on the Policy Committee on the Indian Policy Statement on national health insurance. *Published work*: Navajo Medicine Man (Psychiatric Annuals, 1974).

DeHAAS, JAMES
(BIA agency supt.)
Affiliation: Anadarko Agency, BIA, P.O. Box 309, Anadarko, OK 73005 (405) 247-6673. *Past professional post*: Supt., Shawnee Agency, BIA, Shawnee, OK.

DeHOSE, JUDY
(school chairperson)
Affiliations: Cibecue Community School, P.O. Box 80068, Cibecue, AZ 85911 (520) 332-2480.

DEIGH, RICHARD (Eskimo)
(tribal council president)
Affiliation: Egegik Tribal Council, P.O. Box 29, Egegik, AK 99579 (907) 233-2270.

DEKINGER, BILL
(school principal)
Affiliation: Mt. Edgecumbe High School, 1332 Seward, Sitka, AK 99835 (907) 966-2201.

DeLaCRUZ, DOROTHY L. (Quinault)
(health center director)
Affiliation: Taholah PHS Indian Health Center, P.O. Box 219, Taholah, WA 98587 (206) 276-4405.

DeLaCRUZ, JOSEPH (Quinault)
(former tribal chairperson)
Address & Affiliation: Quinault Business Committee (chairperson, 1970-94), P.O. Box 189, Taholah, WA 98587 (206) 276-8211.

DELASHMUTT, HARRY
(law enforcement specialty-BIA)
Affiliation: Division of Law Enforcement Services, Bureau of Indian Affairs, 1849 C St., NW - MS 4443-MIB, Washington, DC 20240 (202) 208-3485.

DeLaTORRE, JOELY (Pechanga Band of Luiseno Indians) 1969-
(assistant professor of American Indian Studies)
Born March 2, 1969, San Bernardino, Calif. *Education*: California State University, Long Beach, BA, 1993; Northern Arizona University, MA, 1995, PhD (Political Science), 1999. *Principal occupation*: Assistant professor of American Indian Studies. *Address*: 1600 Holloway Ave., San Francisco, CA 94132 (415) 338-1934 Fax 338-1739. E-mail: luiseno@sfsu.edu. *Affiliations*: California State University, Long Beach, 1995, 1996; Northern Arizona University, Flagstaff, AZ, 1996-; San Francisco State University, 1996-. *Community activities*: Campaign spokesperson for the "Yes on 5" Campaign: The Indian Self-Reliance Initiative; board member, California Indian Museum. *Memberships*:

American Political Science Association; Native American Caucus.

DELOACHE, BARBARA
(BIA special education coordinator)
Affiliation: Southern Pueblos Agency, Bureau of Indian Affairs, P.O. Box 1667, Albuquerque, NM 87103 (505) 346-2431 Fax 346-2408.

DE LOS ANGELES, ANDY (Snoqualmie)
(tribal chairperson)
Affiliation: Snoqualmie Tribal Council, P.O. Box 280, Carnation, WA 98014 (206) 333-6551.

DEIGH, RICHARD (Eskimo)
(AK village president)
Affiliation: Egegik Village Council, P.O. Box 29, Egegik, AK 99579 (907) 233-2211.

DEL ROSA, PAUL (Pit River)
(tribal chairperson)
Affiliation: Alturas Rancheria, P.O. Box 340, Alturas, CA 96101 (530) 233-5571.

DELABREAU, JOAN (Menominee of Wisconsin)
(tribal chairperson)
Affiliation: Chairperson, Menominee Tribe, P.O. Box 910, Keshena, WI 54135 (715) 799-5100 Fax 799-3373

DELANEY, CHARLES L., II (*Megeso-Soaring Eagle*) (Mazipskwik Abenaki) 1957-
(contractor, missisquoi masonry)
Born March, 21, 1957, Burlington, Vt. *Principal occupation*: Contractor, missisquoi masonry. *Address*: P.O. Box 5862, Burlington, VT 05402-5962 (802) 863-6002. *Affiliations*: Local #6 Masons, Washington, DC, 1977-81; Federal Government sub-contractor, 1982-89; private & Historic Restoration, State of Vermont, General Contractor, 1990-present. *Other professional post*: At-large representative, Missisquoi Abenaki Nation; lecturer in anthropology and social history, Abenaki history at the University of Vermont & Community College of Vermont. *Awards, honors*: Former ambassador to State of Vermont, U.S. Government, Washington, DC. *Community activities*: Property Committee, Unitarian Universalist Society, Burlington, VT; Red Path member; Burlington-BILWI Sister City program (Vermont-Nicararagua); board of directors, Green Mountain Project. *Memberships*: Mazipskwik Abenaki; Director, Waubanawin Society; Aboriginal Non-profit Co-op between First Nations peoples. *Interests*: Indian legal affairs - representing Abenakis on state and federal government affairs; traditional, cultural and religious practices of Abenakis. *Published works*: Wabanawin Society information pamphlet; non-profit public interest letters.

DELASHMUTT, HARRY
(BIA-law enforcement specialist)
Affiliation: Bureau of Indian Affairs, Div. of Law Enforcement Services, MS: 4443-MIB, 1849 C St., NW, Washington, DC 20240 (202) 208-3485.

DELGADO, MICHELLE (Cahuilla)
(ex-tribal chairperson)
Affiliation: Cahuilla Band of Mission Indians, P.O. Box 391760, Anza, CA 92539 (714) 763-5549.

DeLONG, DR. LORETTA
(BIA education administrator)
Affiliation: Turtle Mountain Agency, Bureau of Indian Affairs, School St., P.O. Box 30, Belcourt, ND 58316 (701) 477-3463 Fax 477-5944.

DELORIA, PHILIP S.
(director-Indian law center)
Affiliation: Executive Director, American Indian Law Center, University of New Mexico, School of Law, P.O. Box 4456, Station A, 1117 Stanford, NE, Albuquerque, NM 87196 (505) 277-5462.

DELORIA, VINE, Jr. (Standing Rock Sioux) 1933-
(writer, professor)
Born March 26, 1933, Martin, S.D. *Education*: Iowa State University, BS, 1958; Lutheran School of Theology, M. Sac. Theo., 1963; University of Colorado, School of Law, JD, 1970. *Principal occupation*: Writer, professor. *Home address*: Resides in Boulder, Colorado. *Affiliations*: Welder, McLaughlin Body Company,

Moline, IL, 1959-63; staff associate, United Scholarship Service, Denver, 1963-64; executive director, National Congress of American Indians, Washington, DC, 1964-67; consultant on programs, National Congress of American Indians, FUND, Denver, CO, 1968; lecturer, College of Ethnic Studies, Western Washington State College, Bellingham, 1970-72; lecturer, American Indian Cultural and Research Center, UCLA, 1972-73; executive director, Southwest Intergroup Council, Denver, 1972; special counsel, Native American Rights Fund, Boulder, CO, summer-1972; script writer (Indian series), KRMA-TV, Denver, 1972-1973; American Indian Resource Associates, Oglala, SD, 1973-1974; American Indian Resource Consultants, Denver, 1974-1975. visiting lecturer, Pacific School of Religion, Berkeley, CA, summer, 1975; visiting lecturer, New School of Religion, Pontiac, MI, summer, 1976; visiting lecturer, Colorado College, 1977-1978; professor, Dept. of Political Science, University of Arizona, Tucson, AZ, 1978-95; professor, Dept. of Political Science, University of Colorado, Boulder, 1995-. *Other professional post*: Vice-chairperson, National Museum of the American Indian, Smithsonian Institution, 1990-. *Military Service*: U.S. Marine Corps Reserve, San Diego, CA & Quantico, VA, 1954-56. *Organizational Memberships*: White Buffalo Council, Denver (board of directors, 1964-66); Citizens Crusade Against Poverty, Washington, DC (board of directors, 1965-66); Council on Indian Affairs, Washington, DC (vice-chairman, 1965-68); Board of Inquiry Into Hunger & Malnutrition in the U.S.A., New York, NY, 1967-68; National Office for the Rights of the Indigent, New York, NY (board of directors, 1967-68); Ad-Hoc Committee on Indian Work, Episcopal Church, New York, NY (chairman, 1968-69); Southwest Intergroup Council, Austin, TX (board of directors, 1969-71); Institute for the Development of Indian Law, Washington, DC (chairman & founder, 1971-76); Model Urban Indian Centers Project, San Francisco, CA (board of directors, 1971-73); Oglala Sioux Legal Rights Foundation, Pine Ridge, SD (board of directors, 1971); National Friends of Public Broadcasting, New York, NY, 1971-76; Colorado Humanities Program, Boulder, CO, 1975-77; National Indian Youth Council, Albuquerque, NM (advisory council, 1976); American Civil Liberties Union, Denver, CO (Indian committee, 1976-78); The Center for Land Grant Studies, Santa Fe, 1976; American Lutheran Church, Minneapolis (consultant, 1976-78); Nebraska Educational Television Network, Lincoln, NE (advisory council, American Indian Series, 1976-78); Denver Public Library Foundation, Denver (board of directors, 1977-78); Museum of the American Indian, New York (board of trustees, 1977-82); American Indian Development, Inc., Bellingham, WA 1978-81; Daybreak Films, Denver (board of directors, 1979-81); Field Foundation, New York (board of directors, 1980); Indian Rights Association, Philadelphia (board of directors, 1980); Institute of the American West, Sun Valley, ID (national advisory council, 1981-83); Disability Rights & Education Defense Fund, Berkeley, CA (advisory council, 1981); Save the Children Federation, Westport, CT (national advisory council, 1983). *Professional Memberships*: American Judicature Society, 1970-; Colorado Authors League, 1970-. Editorial Boards and Contributing Editorships: American Indian Historical Society, San Francisco (editorial board, 1971-72); Handbook of North American Indians, Smithsonian Institution (planning committee, 1971-72); The World of the American Indian, (National Geographic Society, 1972-76); Clearwater Press (consultant, advisory board, 1972-78); American Indian Cultural & Research Center Journal, UCLA (editorial board, 1972); Race Relations Information Center (contributing editor, 1974-75); Integrateducation, University of Massachusetts (editorial advisory board, 1975); American Heritage Dictionary of the English Language, Houghton-Mifflin (usage panel, 1976-83); Explorations in Ethnic Studies, LaCrosse, WI, 1977-; Katallagete, Berea, KY (editorial board, 1977); The Historical Magazine of the Episcopal Church, Austin, TX (editorial board, 1977); The Colorado Magazine, Colorado Historical Society, Denver (editorial review board, 1979); National Forum, Phi Kappa Phi, Johnson City, TN (contributing editor, 1979); Studies in American Indian Literature, Columbia University (advisory board, 1981); Adherent Forum, New York, NY (contributing editor, 1981). *Special Activities*: White House Conference on Youth (delegate, 1970); Avco-Embassy Pictures on movie Soldier Blue (consultant, 1970); Educational Challenges, Inc., Washington, DC (consultant, 1971-

72); Senate Committee on Aging, Washington, DC (consultant, 1971-72); Served as expert witness in four trials involving the occupation of Wounded Knee and aftermath as expert on 1868 Fort Laramie treaty and Sioux history (1974); Project 76, National Council of Churches (sponsor, 1974-76); Served as appointed counsel in Consolidated Wounded Knee Cases, treaty hearing in federal court (1975); Colorado Centennial-Bicentennial Commission (commissioner, 1975-77); EVIST, National Science Foundation (advisory board, 1975-78); Robert F. Kennedy Journalism Awards (judge, 1975); Sun Valley Center for the Arts and Humanities, Sun Valley, Idaho (advisory council, 1976-78, 1980-83); Handbook of North American Indians, Volume Two, Indians in Contemporary Society, Smithsonian Institution (editor, 1978-); American Indian Studies Program, University of Arizona (chairman, 1978-81). *Special Honors & Awards*: Anisfield Wolf Award, 1970, for Custer Died for Your Sins; Special Citation, 1971, National Conference of Christians and Jews, for We Talk, You Listen; Honorary Doctor of Humane Letters, 1972, Augustana College; Indian Achievement Award, 1972, Indian Council Fire, Chicago; Named one of eleven Theological Superstars of the Future, 1974, by Interchurch Features, New York, N.Y.; Honorary Doctor of Letters, 1976, Scholastica College, Duluth, Minn.; Distinguished Alumni Award, 1977, Iowa State University; Honorary Professor, 1977, Athabasca University, Edmonton, Can.; Honorary Doctor of Human Letters, 1979, Hamline University, St. Paul, Minn.; 1985 - Distinguished Alumni in the Field of Legal Education, Colorado University School of Law. *Published works*: Books: Custer Died For Your Sins (Macmillan, 1969); We Talk, You Listen (Macmillan, 1970); Of Utmost Good Faith (Straight Arrow, 1971); Red Man in the New World Drama, edited and revised (Macmillan, 1972); God Is Red (Grosset & Dunlap, 1973); Behind the Trail of Broken Treaties (Delacourte, 1974); The Indian Affair (Friendship Press, 1974); Indians of the Pacific Northwest (Doubleday, 1977); The Metaphysics of Modern Existence (Harper & Row, 1979); American Indians, American Justice, with Clifford Lytle (University of Texas Press, 1983); A Sender of Words, editor-The Neihardt Centennial Essays (Howe Brothers, 1984); The Nations Within, with Clifford Lytle (Pantheon Books, 1984); The Aggressions of Civilization, edited with Sandra Cadwalader (Temple University Press, 1984); American Indian Policy in the Twentieth Century, editor (University of Oklahoma Press, 1985). Special Reports: The Lummi Indians, — Center for the Study of Man, Smithsonian Institution, 1972; Legal Problems and Considerations Involved in the Treaty of 1868, prepared for the John Hay Whitney Foundation, 1974; Indian Education Confronts the Seventies, editor and contributor, five volumes, Office of Indian Education, 1974; Contemporary Issues of American Indians, A Model Course, prepared for the National Indian Education Association, 1975; Legislative Analysis of the Federal Role in Indian Education, Office of Indian Education, 1975; A Better Day for Indians, issued by the Field Foundation, 1977. Also, articles as contributing editor, editorials, and introductions to books—too numerous to mention.

DELORIMIERE, GORDON T.
(administration)
Affiliation: Administrative Assistant Secretary, Bureau of Indian Affairs, Dept. of the Interior, MS-4140-MIB, 1849 C St., NW, Washington, DC 20240 (202) 208-5649.

DELORME, GENE
(organization director)
Affiliation: Indians Into Medicine, University of North Dakota, School of Medicine, P.O. Box 9037, Grand Forks, ND 58202 (701) 777-3037 Fax 777-3277.

DELP, PATSY
(school principal)
Affiliation: Santa Rosa Ranch School, HC 02 Box 7570, Sells, AZ 85634 (520) 383-2359 Fax 383-3960.

DeMAIN, PAUL *(Oshscabewis)* **(Oneida/White Earth Ojibway) 1955-**
(editor)
Born October 8, 1955, Milwaukee, Wis. *Education*: University of Wisconsin, Eau Claire, AA, 1975-77. *Principal occupation*: CEO, Indian Country Communications. *Address*: P.O. Box 1500, 8558N County Road

K, Hayward, WI 54843 (715) 634-5226. *Affiliations*: Ass't. manager & manager, Lac Courte Oreilles Graphic Arts, 1979-80; acting director, Great Lakes Indian News Association, 1980-82; self determination information officer, Lac Courte Oreilles Tribal Government, 1981-82; managing editor, Lac Courte Oreilles Journal, Hayward, WI, 1977-82; advisor on Indian affairs policy to Governor Anthony S. Earl, State of Wisconsin, 1983-87; secretary-treasurer, Native Horizons, 1983-; CEO, Indian Country Communications, 8558N County Road K, Hayward, WI 54843, 1987-. *Other professional posts*: Native American Journalists Association (NAJA) (treasurer, 1991-92; president, board of directors, 1992-); president of UNITY 94 & 99, an alliance of the National Association of African American Journalists, Asian American Journalists Association, National Association of Hispanic Journalists, and NAJA. 1999 Green Party Vice Presdiential Campaign Manager for Winona LaDuke. *Community activities*: Governor's representative, State Council on Alcohol and Other Drug Abuse, 1983-87; lay counselor, Lac Courte Oreilles Tribal Court, 1980-; board member, Lac Courte Oreilles Honor the Earth Education Foundation, 1980-; volunteer, WOJB Radio, Hayward, WI, 1980-; representative, Governor's Council on Minority Business Development, 1983-88; planning committee, National Indian Media Conference; Governor's Interstate Indian Council Executive Board, 1986-88; advisory board, Center for Mining Alternatives, 1980-82; member, Northwestern Wisconsin Mining Impact Committee, 1980-82; member, Governor's Study Committee on Equal Rights, 1977. *Memberships*: National Congress of American Indians (conference planning committee, 1983); Native American Press Association (Board of Directors, 1986-88). *Published works*: North America's Indian Country Gaming Guide & The Pow Wow Directory (Indian Country Communications); publisher of "News From Indian Country," a national twice-monthly newspaper located on the Lac Courte Oreilles Ojibway reservation of northern Wisconsin; also publishes, "Explore Indian Country" (Indian Country Communications) a monthly entertainment tabloid and distributes native language materials and books;

DE MALLIE, RAYMOND J.
(professor, author)
Address & Affiliation: Director, American Indian Studies Research Institute, Indiana University, Bloomington, IN 47405 (812) 855-1203. *Published works*: Editor - North American Indian Anthropology: Essays on Society & Culture (University of Oklahoma Press, 1994).

DEMARAY, ELIZABETH
(college president)
Affiliation: Fort Berthold Community College, P.O. Box 490, New Town, ND 58763 (701) 627-4738 Fax 627-3609.

DE MEYER, TRACE A. (*Winyan Ohmanisa waste la ke*) (Cherokee) 1956-
(journalist, editor, author, independent scholar)
Born in 1956, St. Paul, Minn. *Education*: University of Wisconsin-Superior, BFA (Communications/Theatre). *Principal occupation*: Journalist, editor, author, playwright, independent scholar. *Home address*: 21 Ramsdell St., Groton, CT 06340. *Office address*: P.O. Box 3130, Mashantucket, CT 06339 (860) 396-6572 Fax 396-6570. E-mail: tdemer@mptn-nsn.gov. Website: www.mashantucket.com. *Affiliations*: Editor, Ojibwe Akiing (regional newspaper started December, 1996; staff writer, News From Indian Country, 1996-1999; Native American Journalists Association, 1997-present; UW-Superior Chancellors Council of Advisors, 1996-99; Cable Hayward Area Regional Arts Council, 1996-99; Editor, The Pequot Times, Mashantucket Pequot Tribal Nation, Mashantucket, CT, 1999-present. *Community activities*: Interviews with Eastern Tribal leaders; independent research into Indian slavery; upcoming book on Native American Adoptees with Sandy White Hawk (2004); working with others that were adopted by non-Native families. *Memberships*: First Nations Orphans Association; National Coalition of Independent Scholars 2002; Mashantucket Pequot Museum & Research Center; National Museum of the American Indian; Native American Rights Fund; Association of Women in Radio & Television; International Women's Writers Guild; WOJB-FM radio; Native American Music Awards Board. *Awards, honors*: NAJA General Excellence Award: Honorable Mention - Pequot

TimesPresenter at the 2000 Native American Journalist Conference: on First Contact/Native American Slavery/The Unwritten History; Interviewed by Michael Kicking Bear on Native Opinion.com, 2001; Presenter at 6th Annual Drug Elimination Conference 2001: Communications, Efective News Writing' Wiping of the Tears Ceremony, PBS Documentary, Menominee Powwow, October 2001; Lecture on Native American Journalism, Gateway Community College, 2004. *Interests*: Native American history; research on First Contact & Indian slavery; film, theatre; music; travel; genealogy. *Published works*: Contributing author of "Honor Restored: Jim Thorpe's Olympic Medals" chapter 2 page 38-50 in the book, The Olympics at the Millennium: Power, Politics and the Olympic Games 2000, by Shaffer & Smith (Rutgers Press, 2001).

DEMIENTIEFF, SAMUEL S. (Eskimo)
(former BIA agency supt.)
Addresses & Affiliations: Supt., Fairbanks Agency, Bureau of Indian Affairs, Fairbanks, AK; executive director, Fairbanks Native Association, 310 1st Ave., 2nd Floor, Fairbanks, AK 99701 (907) 452-1648.

DEMMERT, ROSEANN (Eskimo)
(AK coop association president)
Affiliation: Klawock Cooperative Association, P.O. Box 112, Klawock, AK 99925 (907) 755-2265.

DEMPSEY, HUGH A. (*Potaina - Flying Chief*) 1929-
(historian)
Born November 7, 1929, Edgerton, Alberta, Can. *Principal occupation*: Historian. *Home address*: 95 Holmwood Ave., N.W., Calgary, AB T2K 2G7 (403) 289-8149. *Affiliations*: Reporter, Edmonton Bulletin; Publicity Bureau, Province of Alberta, Canada; Glenbow Alberta Institute, Calgary, Alberta (archivist, 1956-67; technical director, 1967-70; director of history, 1970-78; chief curator, 1978-91; associate director, Glenbow-Alberta Institute, 1980-91 {retired}). *Other professional posts*: Adjunct professor, University of Calgary, 1979-94; Editor, Alberta History, 1958-; editor, Canadian Archivist, 1963-66; editor, Glenbow, 1968-74; Canadian editor, Montana Magazine of History; editorial board, Royal Canadian Geographical Society; contributing editor, American West. *Community activities*: Alberta Indian Treaties Commemorative Program, 1976-78; Alberta Heritage Learning Resources Advisory Committee, 1978-79. *Memberships*: Historical Society of Alberta (executive committee, 1953; vice president, 1955-56; president, 1956-57); Canadian Historical Association (chairman, archives section, 1961-1962); Indian Association of Alberta (secretary, 1959-64; advisory board, 1959-68); Canadian Museums Association (executive committee, 1968-70); Indian -Eskimo Association of Canada (executive committee, 1960-65); International Council of Museums (Canadian committee, 1968-71). *Awards, honors*: Alberta Historian of the Year, 1962; honorary doctorate, University of Calgary, 1974; Order of Canada, 1975; Alberta Achievement Award, 1974-1975; honorary chief, Blood Tribe, 1967; winner of Alberta Non-Fiction Award, 1975. *Published works*: Crowfoot, Chief of the Blackfeet (University of Oklahoma Press, 1972); Charcoal's World (University of Nebraska Press, 1978); Red Crow, Warrior Chief (Prairie Books, 1980); History in Their Blood; The Indian Portraits of Nicholas De Grandmaison (Hudson Hill, 1982); Big Bear, The End of Freedom (Douglas & McIntyre, 1984); The Gentle Persuader, A Biography of James Gladstone, Indian Senator (Prairie Books, 1986); Bibliography of the Blackfeet (Scarecrow Press, 1989); Treasures of the Glenbow Museum, 1991; The Amazing Death of Calf Shirt and Other Blackfoot Stories (Fifth House, 1995); The Golden Age of the Canadian Cowboy (Fifth House, 1995); Tribal Honors (Kainai Chieftainship, 1997); Tom Three Persons, Legend of an Indian Cowboy (Purich Publishers, 1997); Indians of the Rocky Mountain Parks (Fifth House, 1998); co-authored with Colin Taylor, With Eagle Tail (Salamander Books, 1999). *Monographs*: A Blackfoot Winter Count, 1966; Tailfeathers, Indian Artist, 1970; Blackfoot Ghost Dance, 1968; Indian Names for Alberta Communities, 1969.

DEMPSEY, JAMES
(health clinic coordinator)
Affiliation: Native American Services Agency, Missoula Indian Center, 2300 Regent St. #A, Missoula, MT 59801 (406) 329-3373 fax 329-3398.

DEMPSEY, L. JAMES (*Kitsemonisi* - High Otter)
(Blood) 1958-
(historian)
Born September 20, 1958, Calgary, Alberta, Can. *Education*: University of Calgary, BA, 1985, MA, 1987; University of East Angelia (England), 1992- (PhD candidate). *Principal occupation*: Historian. *Home address*: 7944 - 85 Avenue, Edmonton, AB, Can. T6C 1C2 (403) 492-2991 (work). *Affiliation*: Director of the School of Native Studies, University of Alberta, Edmonton, AB, Can., 1992-; professor, Saskatchewan Indian Federated College, Saskatoon, SK, Can., 1987-92. *Interests*: As a member of the Blood tribe, my interests have centered on the Northern Plains culture & history with a particular emphasis on Blackfoot Indians & warfare. I have also studied the role of Canadian Indians in World War I & World War II. Currently, I am studying the significance of Blackfoot pictography to warfare. *Published works*: Problems of Western Canadian Indian War Veterans After World War I (Native Studies Review, 1989); editor, Treaty Days (Glenbow Museum, 1991).

DENAM, WILBUR
(Indian band chief)
Affiliation: Burnt Church Indian Band, RR 2, Lagaceville, New Brunswick, Canada E0C 1K0 (506) 776-8331.

DENET, DOROTHY KATHERINE (Pephise) (Hopi)
(lecturer, consultant, entrepreneur)
Born in Keams Canyon, Ariz. *Education*: Northland Pioneer Colege, AA, 1989. *Principal occupation*: Lecturer, consultant, entrepreneur. *Address*: P.O. Box 210, Polacca, AZ 86042 (602) 737-2534. *Affiliations*: General Manager, Hopi Cultural Center, Second Mesa, AZ; vice-president, Secakuku Enterprises, Second Mesa, AZ; president, Polingyami, Inc., Polacca, AZ, 1992-. *Other professional posts*: lecturer, Northern Arizona University, Elder Hostel Program, Flagstaff, AZ, 1990-; lecturer, Yavapai College Elder Hostel Program, Prescott, AZ, 1990-. *Community activities*: Arizona State Tourism Advisory Council (appointed by Governor, 1988-94); Arizona State Employment & Training Advisory Council (appointed by Governor, 1989-94); Applied Economics/Junior Achievement, Hopi Jr.-Sr. High School (busines consultant, 1990-); Arizona Strategic Planning for Economic Development, Native American Coalition and Tourism Cluster, member, 1989-92. *Memberships*: Arizona Coalition for Displaced Homemakers, Governor's Office for Women, 1989-94; Arizona Tribal Private Industry Council (chairperson-member, 1987-89); Hostelling International (Ameriac Youth Hostel), Arizona Chapter, Board of Dirctors, member, 1992-). *Interests*: "Tourism, particularly as related to Indian reservations; economics-cultural compatibility; employment & training - Job Training Partnership Act on tribal reservations and their congruence with the states including women in non-traditional training, jobs; women's issues - cultural impact and changes." *Biographical sources*: Junior Achievement Partners, "Applied Economics in Hopiland, Fall 1991, Vol. 7, No. 4; Indian Business and Management, March/April 1992, Vol. 3, No. 2.

DENETDEAL, DONALD
(Indian center instructor)
Affiliation: Center for Dine Studies, Dine (Navajo) College, P.O. Box 126, Tsaile, AZ 86556 (520) 724-6671 Fax 724-3327.

DENNEY, ARTHUR (Butch) (Santee Sioux)
(tribal council chairperson)
Affiliation: Santee Sioux Tribal Council, Route 2, Niobrara, NE 68760 (402) 857-3302.

DENNING, SHARILYN
(health director)
Affiliations: Milwaukee Indian Health Center, 930 North 27th St., Milwaukee, WI 53208 (414) 931-8111; chairperson, American Indian Chamber of Commerce, P.O. Box 775, Milwaukee, WI 53201 (414) 221-9858.

DENNIS, HERMAN W.
(Indian band chief)
Affiliation: Chawathil (Hope) Indian Band, Box 1659, Hope, British Columbia, Canada V0X 1L0 (604) 869-9994.

DENNIS, PHILBERT
(school chairperson)
Affiliation: Hotevilla Bacavi Community School, P.O. Box 48, Hotevilla, AZ 86030 (602) 734-2462.

DENNY, AVERY
(Indian center instructor)
Affiliation: Center for Dine Studies, Dine (Navajo) College, P.O. Box 126, Tsaile, AZ 86556 (520) 724-6671 Fax 724-3327.

DENNY, ROSS
(BIA-agency supt.)
Affiliation: Blackfeet Agency, Bureau of Indian Affairs, P.O. Box 880, Browning, MT 59417 (406) 338-7544 Fax 338-7761.

DENNY, RUTH (Zibiquah) (Potawatomi/Winnebago/Oneida) 1957-
(newspaper editor)
Born November 11, 1957, Milwaukee, Wisc. *Education*: Uiversity of California, Berkeley. *Principal occupation*: Newspaper editor. *Address & Affiliation*: The Circle, Minneapolis American Indian Center, 1530 E. Franklin Ave., Minneapolis, MN 55404 (612) 871-4749. *Membership*: Native American Journalists Association.

DE ROCHE, TROY (Blackfeet)
(craftsperson)
Affiliation: Owner, Song Stick, P.O. Box 490, Chimacum, WA 98325 (360) 732-4279. *Products*: Traditional handcrafted Native American flutes and accessories.

DeROIN, DEEANN, MD (Iowa of Kansas & Nebraska)
(member-board of directors)
Affiliation: Member-Board of Directors, Association on American Indian Affairs, P.O. Box 268, Sisseton, SD 57262 (605) 698-3998.

DeROIN, LOUIS (Iowa Kansas & Nebraska)
(tribal chairperson)
Affiliation: Iowa Tribe of Kansas & Nebraska, 2340 - 330th St., White Cloud, KS 66094 (785) 595-3258.

DEROUEN, ELIZABETH ELGIN (Eh'La Puti'A - Fying Feather) (Pomo) 1964-
(rancheria band chairperson; ICWA advocate)
Born February 12, 1964, Santa Rosa, Calif. *Education*: AS/Juvenile Corrections; Court Reporting Graduate. *Principal occupation*: Rancheria Band chairperson; ICWA advocate. *Address*: P.O. Box 607, Geyserville, CA 95441 (707) 431-2388 Fax 431-2615. E-mail: Liz@dry-creek-rancheria.com. *Affiliation*: Dry Creek Rancheria Band of Pomo Indians, Geyserville, CA (vice chair, 1996-2000; chair, 2000-present). *Other professional post*: ICWA advocate, 1994-present; Statewide Tribal Steering Committee member, CNIGA. *Memberships*: NAIC; CNIGA, NIGA. *Interests*: Athletics, music, traditional wellness ceremonies.

DERRICK, ELMER
(Indian band chief)
Affiliation: Kitwancool Indian Band, Box 340, Kitwanga, B.C., Canada V0J 2A0 (604) 849-5222.

DERRIKSAN, NOEL C.
(president-Indian society)
Affiliation: Indian Arts & Crafts Society of British Columbia, 540 Burrard St., Suite 505, Vancouver, British Columbia, Canada V6C 2K1 (604) 682-8988.

DERWIN, TIMOTHY (Sault Ste. Marie Ojibwe)
(Indian youth activities director)
Address: Sault Ste. Marie Tribe JTPA, 1919 14th Ave. N., Escanaba, MI 49829.

DESBIEN, NINA
(health center director)
Affiliation: Cibecue PHS Indian Health Center, Cibecue, AZ 85941 (602) 332-2560.

DESCHAMPE, NORMAN (Ojibwe)
(tribal president)
Affiliations: President, Minnesota Chippewa Tribal Executive Committee, P.O. Box 217, Cass Lake, MN 56633 (218) 335-8581; chairperson, Grand Portage Reservation Business Committee, P.O. Box 428, Grand Portage, MN 55605 (218) 475-2277.

DESCHEENY-JOE, ELEANOR
(executive director)
Affiliation: Arizona Commission of Indian Affairs, 1400 W. Washington St. #300, Phoenix, AZ 85007 (602) 542-3123.

DESJARLAIT, GEORGE
(Indian band chief)
Affiliation: West Moberly Indian Band, General Delivery, Moberly Lake, BC, Can. V0C 1X0 (604) 788-3663.

DESJARLAIT, ROBERT (Akoongiss)
(Red Lake Ojibway) 1946-
(artist, writer)
Born November 18, 1946, Redlake, Minn. *Principal occupation*: Artist, writer. *Home address*: 5901 Rhode Island Ave., N., Minneapolis, MN 55428 (612) 535-0091. *Art/cultural consultant*: Minnesota Center for Arts Education, Minneapolis, 1993; Four Winds Ojibwe/French Language School, Minneapolis, MN, 1993; Saturn School of Tomorrow, St. Paul, 1994; Minneapolis Institute of Arts, 1994; American Indian Movement, Minneapolis, 1994; University of Minnesota, - Weisman Gallery, Minneapolis, 1995; Minnesota Historical Society, St. Paul, 1995; Migizi Communications, Side-by-Side Program, Minneapolis, 1996. *Other professional posts*: Art instructor, Heart of the Earth Survival School, Minneapolis, MN, 1989-90; art director/curriculum developer, Northern Winds Community Arts Project, Minneapolis, 1992-95; Native arts history teacher, NAES College, Minneapolis, 1996; traditional arts teacher, American Indian OIC, Minneapolis, 1996; Native arts history teacher, Lac Courte Orielles Community College, Minneapolis, 1996. *Commissions*: Minnesota Indian Women's Resource Center, Minneapolis, 1991; Minnesota Museum of American Art, St. Paul, 1992; Phillips Gateway Project, Minneapolis, 1993-95; Philips Neighborhood Safe Arts Project, Minneapolis, 1995; Minneapolis Indian Education Program, Minneapolis, 1996. *Community activities*: Minneapolis Institute of Arts Advisory Panel on Art of the Americas, 1993; "Promoting Social Change Through the Arts: A Conference for Activists and Artists in Grass Roots Community Organizations," Headwaters Fund, Minneapolis, 1994; Native Arts Circle Advisory Panel on Artists in Education, Minneapolis, 1995. *Awards, honors*: Ojibwe Art Expo, 1985 2nd Place - Drawing, 1987 2nd Place - Painting, 1988 1st Place - Drawing; 1988 Percy Fearing Award - Illustration, Minnesota Council on the Teaching of Foreign Languages; CUE Award, Minneapolis Commission on the Arts, 1995. *Biographical sources*: "DesJarlait Depicts Ojibwe Vision," Red Lake Times, Nov. 1987; "Minnesotan Culturally Diverse Artists," Minnesota Monthly, July 1992; "Interview - Robert DesJarlait," Northern Light and Insights (Video), Minneapolis Public Library Artist/Author Series, 1992; "Patrick DesJarlait & Family: Red Lake Ojibway Tradition," Resources for Indian Schools: Minnesota Indian Artists, Internet (http://indy4.fdl.cc. mn.us/~isk/art/art), 1996. *Published works*: Author - O-do-i-daym Ojibway: Clans of The Ojibway Coloring Book (Minnesota Indian Women's Resource Center Press, 1989); Nimiwin: A History of Ojibway Dance (Anoka-Hennepin Press, 1991). Illustrator - Sparrow Hawk, by Meridel Le Seur (Holy Cow Press, 1987); Cherish The Children (MIWRC Press, 1987); Young Child, Old Spirit (MIWRC, 1990); The Spirit Within - Encouraging Harmony and Health in American Indian Children (Minnesota Indian Women's Resource Center Press, 1992); Rethinking Stereotypes: Native American Imagery in European & Euro-American Art (Anoka-Hennepin Press, 1993); "No-ko-miss Wa-kaigan," essay in Ojibway Family Life in Minnesota: 20th Century Sketches (Anoka-Hennepin Press, 1993); "Patrick DesJarlait: Art of Tribe & Culture," exhibition catalog, "Patrick DesJarlait and the Ojibwe Tradition), Minnesota Museum of American Art, St. Paul, 1994; Art of the Ojibway: Traditional to Contemporary (Northern Winds Desktop Press, 1996); "Niimiwin: An Ojibway Dance Curriculum Coloring Book (Northern Winds Desktop Press, 1996); "Contest Powwow Vs. Traditional Powwow and the Role of the Native American Community," article in Wicazo Sa Review, University of Minnesota Press, 1997.

DeVAULT, PENNY
(dean of student services)
Affiliation: Leech Lake Tribal College, 6530 U.S. Hwy. 2 NW, Cass Lake, MN 56633 (218) 335-4220 Fax 335-4209. E-mail: penny@lltc.org.

DeVERNEY, TED
(executive officer)
Affiliation: Organization of North American Indian Students, P.O. Box 26, University Center, Northern Michigan University, Marquette, MI 49855 (906) 227-2138.

DEVERS, CHRISTOBAL C., SR. (Luiseno)
(tribal council chairperson)
Affiliation: Pauma-Yuima Band of Mission Indians, P.O. Box 369, Pauma Valley, CA 92061 (760) 742-1289.

DEW, WILLIAM K.
(IHS-tribal activities)
Affiliation: Nashville Area IHS, 711 Stewarts Ferry Pike, Nashville, TN 37214 (615) 736-2478.

DeWALL, ROBB
(editor)
Affiliation: "Crazy Horse Progress," Crazy Horse Memorial Foundation, Ave. of the Chiefs, Black Hills, Crazy Horse, SD 57730-9988 (605) 673-4681.

DIAMOND, ARTHUR
(Indian school principal)
Affiliation: Shonto Boarding School, P.O. Box 7900, Shonto, AZ 86054 (520) 672-2652 Fax 672-2849.

DIAMOND, BILLY (Cree) 1949-
(politician)
Born May 17, 1949, at Waskaganish, Quebec, Can. *Education*: Bawating Collegiate & Vocational High School (5 year arts & science program, graduated in June 1968). *Principal occupation*: Politician. *Address*: P.O. Box 9, Waskaganish, Quebec, Can. J0M 1R0 (819) 895-8971. *Affiliations*: On-the-job-training, Dept. of Indian Affairs and Northern Development, Val D'or, Quebec; band manager, 1969-71; chief, 1970-76, Rupert House Band, Rupert House, Quebec; communications worker, 1972, regional chief, 1972-74, Indians of Quebec Association, Huron Village, Quebec; grand chief, Grand Council of the Crees (of Quebec), Rupert House, Quebec, 1974-84; chairman & school commissioner for Cree Regional Authority, 1976-88; chairman/grand chief, Cree Regional Authority, Val D'or, Quebec, 1978-84; chairman & president, Cree Housing Corporation, 1984-87; president, Air Creebec, Inc., 1982-; proprietor, Diamond Brothers Enterprises Registered, 1983-; chief Waskaganish Band Council, James Bay, Quebec, re-elected 1988-. *Other professional posts*: Member, Board of Directors, Creeco (Cree Regional Economic Enterprises Co.) and Cree Construction Co., 1980-; president, Native Peoples Television Network, 1982-; chairman, Board of Advisors, National Native Bible College, 1984-; Band councillor, Waskaganish Band Council, P.O. Box 60, Waskaganish, P.Q., James Bay J0M 1R0, 1984-; president, Waskaganish Enterprises Development Corporation (WEDCO), 1985-; member, Board of Directors, Construction Regional Authority, Northern Flood Committee, Manitoba, 1985-; chairman, Cree-Yamaha Motor Enterprises Ltd., 1986-; member, Board of Directors of the Grand Council of the Crees and the Council of the Cree Regional Authority, 1984-. *Awards, honors*: Inducted as a Knight in the Order of Quebec, Jan. 15, 1987.

DIAMOND, CLIFFORD
(Indian band chief)
Affiliation: Wahgoshig Indian Band, Box 722, Matheson, Ontario, Canada P0K 3C0 (705) 567-4891.

DIAMOND, GERALD B. (*Zeemucka*)
(Chippewa) 1938-
(business owner)
Born January 10, 1938, Hayward, Wisc. *Education*: Mt. Senario College (Ladysmith, WI), BA, 1982. *Principal occupation*: Business owner. *Home address*: Rt. 2, Box 2330, Hayward, WI 54843 (715) 634-2655; 634-4499 (work). *Affiliation*: President, American Indian Gift Store, Hayward, WI, 1988-. *Military service*: U.S. Army, 1957-77 SFC National Defenses (Good Conduct Awards; Meritorious Service Medal). *Community activities*: Governors Council on Tourism. *Awards, honors*: National Honor Society (college); Past Master in the Masons. *Interests*: "I spent four years in Italy, 3 years in Germany, and 2 years in Korea. I had tours of duty in IL, CO, VA, MO, TX, GA, & FL."

DIAMOND, MARGARET
(Lac Courte Oreilles Chippewa)
(tribal chairperson)
Affiliation: Lac Courte Oreilles Tribal Governing Board, Route 2, Box 2700, Hayward, WI 54843 (715) 634-8934.

DICK, ERNEST W. (Navajo)
(Indian school chairperson)
Affiliation: Rough Rock Community School, RRDS, Box 217, Rough Rock, AZ 86501 (602) 728-3311.

DICK, GEORGIA (Oklahoma Cherokee)
(director of Indian education)
Address & Affiliation: Director of Indian Education, Tahlequah Public Schools, District I-35, P.O. Box 517, Tahlequah, OK 74465 (918) 458-4162 Fax 458-4103, 1990-present. *Community activities*: Sponsor of "Native Reflections," a youth group focused on performing community projects and addressing community needs. Students utilize classroom skills in all their activities; Briggs Community Organization, Tahlequah, OK. *Memberships*: National Indian Education Association; National Coalition for Indian Education; Oklahoma Council of Indian Education; national Drop-out Prevention Network; National Johnson O'Malley Association; National Service-Learning Association; Tahlequah Parent-Teacher Association.

DICK, LEROY S. (Navajo) 1943-
(health systems administrator)
Born December 15, 1943, Shiprock, N.M. *Education*: Loretto Heights College, Denver, BA, 1975; Leslie Graduate School, MA, 1984. *Principal occupation*: Health systems administrator. *Address*: P.O. Box 836, Shiprock, NM 87420 (505) 632-1801 (work). *Affiliation*: Vice-president of Management Board, Navajo Tribal Utility Authority, Ft. Defiance, AZ; director, Dzilth-Na-O-Dith-Hle PHS Indian Health Center, Bloomfield, NM. *Other professional post*: Counseling psychologist. *Military service*: U.S. Army, 1965-67 (E-5 Sergeant, 7th Division; Outstanding Leadership Award, 12/66 while serving in Korea). *Community activities*: Vice-president, School Board, Central School District 22, 1981-; board member, Four Winds Alcoholic Treatment Center. *Memberships*: National Institute of Business Management, Inc.; National Rural Electric Co-op Association; American Public Power Association. *Awards, honors*: "I am the only American Indian to receive a 7th Division Outstanding Leadership Award for Outstanding Performance"; Recognition of High Quality of Performance, PHS - Shiprock, NM, 1973; Letter of Commendation for Outstanding Performance, PHS - Shiprock, 1974; Recognition of Appreciation for Outstanding Services in EEO Program by Marlene E. Haffner, M.D., NAIHS, Window Rock, AZ, 1975. *Interests*: "I enjoy outdoor activities, hiking, hunting, and picnics with family. This is probably due to my Native American up-bringing. In my spare time, the family will travel to Rock Point, AZ where we manage a small herd of cattle, which takes up alot of our time and something I enjoy doing."

DICK, MATTHEW, Jr. (Colville)
(tribal business committee chairperson)
Affiliation: Colville Tribal Business Committee, P.O. Box 150, Nespelem, WA 99155 (509) 634-4711.

DICK, RALPH, Sr.
(Indian band chief)
Affiliation: Cape Mudge Indian Band, P.O. Box 220, Quathiaski Cove, British Columbia, Canada V0P 1N0 (604) 285-3316.

DICK, ROBBIE
(Indian band chief)
Affiliation: Whapmagoostui (Cree) Indian Band, Box 390, Great White River, Hudson Bay, Quebec J0M 1G0 (819) 929-3384.

DICK, STEPHEN GEORGE
(Indian band chief)
Affiliation: Kwiakah Indian Band, 1440 Island Highway, Campbell River, British Columbia, Canada V9W 2E3 (604) 286-1295.

DICKERSON, ANN
(librarian)
Affiliation: Nisqually Tribal Library, 4814 She-Nah-Num Dr., SE. Olympia, WA 98513 (206) 456-5221.

DICKMAN, DAVID
(BIA special education coordinator)
Affiliation: Fort Apache Agency, Bureau of Indian Affairs, P.O. Box 560, White River, AZ (520) 338-5441 Fax 338-1944; Pima Agency, BIA, c/o Western Regional Office, P.O. Box 10, Phoenix, AZ 85001 (602) 379-3944.

DIEBEL, JERRY E.
(Indian school principal)
Affiliation: Tuba City Boarding School, P.O. Box 187, Tuba City, NM 86045 (520) 283-2330 Fax 283-2265.

DIEGUEZ, LORENE
(BIA agency supt.)
Affiliation: Ramah-Navajo Agency, BIA, Rt. 2, Box 14, Ramah, NM 87321 (505) 775-3235.

DIETZ, ELISABETH (*Miigiisdeahkwe*)
(Sault Ste. Marie Chippewa) 1941-
(art gallery manager)
Born February 16, 1941, Sault Ste. Marie, Mich. *Education*: College. *Principal occupation*: Art gallery manager. *Address & Affiliation*: Manager/resident artist, Bawating Native Art Gallery, 558 East Spruce St., Sault Ste. Marie, MI 49783 (906) 632-0530 ext. 53529. *Community activities & Interests*: Help with elders and volunteer with the local Anishnabe (Chippewa) School. "I teach herb gathering and pipe-carving to young people. I am what you call a medicine woman, an artist and a pipe-maker. a published author, and a tribal elder/pipe carrier. *Published works*: Star of Bethlehem (American Federation of Astrologers {Tempe, AZ}); Now Is the Hour (native prophecies) (Blue Dolphin Press {CA}).

DIETZ, JERRY
(editor)
Affiliation: Susquehanna Valley Native American Eagle, P.O. Box 99, Walnut Valley Farm, Loganville, PA 17342 (717) 428-1440.

DIETZ-BELL, ELISABETH (*Miigesiiahkwe*) (Sault Chippewa)
(traditional medicine; pipe-maker)
Address: P.O. Box 1685, Sault Ste. Marie, MI 49783. *Community activities*: Teach traditional arts & crafts in Bawating Art Gallery; storyteller; work with children and elders. *Published work*: Star of Bethlehem; Now Is the Hour: Native Prophecies (Blue Dolphin).

DILLION, HERMAN, SR. (Puyallup)
(tribal chairperson)
Affiliation: Puyallup Tribal Council, 2002 East 28th St., Tacoma, WA 98404 (360) 597-6200.

DILLNER, JERRY R. (Seneca-Cayuga)
(tribal chief)
Address & Affiliation: Seneca-Cayuga Tribes, P.O. Box 1283, Miami, OK 74355 (918) 542-6609 Fax 542-3684.

DIONNE, JACKIE
(radio producer)
Affiliation: Migizi Communications, Inc., 3123 E. Lake St., Suite 200, Minneapolis, MN 55406 (612) 721-6631.

DITTBENNER, CAROL
(Indian education program director)
Affiliation: Puget Sound Educational Service District, Indian Education Program, 400 S.W. 152nd St., Burien, WA 98166 (206) 439-3636 Fax 439-3961.

DITMANSON, PAUL, M.D.
(clinical director)
Affiliation: Red Lake PHS Indian Hospital, Red Lake, MN 56671 (218) 679-3912.

DITMAR, SELENA ELL (*Brown Owl Woman*)
(Assiniboine) 1927-
(nurse, teacher-language)
Born December 2, 1927, Fort Belknap, Mont. *Education*: GED Certificate - Class 7 Certification. *Principal occupation*: Nurse, teacher-language. *Address*: Rte. 1 Box 42, Harlem, MT 59526 (406) 353-2676. *Affiliations*: Public Health - Indian Health Sertvice (IHS), 1963-87; Fort Belknap Community College, 1994-2003. Other professional post: Councilperson, Fort Belknap Indian Community Council, 1991-93, 2003-present. *Awards, honors*: Superior Rating Service Award, IHS. *Community activities*: Language, cultural;

oversight on natural resource programs (land, forestry and buffalo). *Interests*: Working on land and water issues; beading; saving our language and culture; youth. Ms. Ditmar writes, "I am an active Native American elder who keeps involved in all aspects of Native American government. I have worked as an Assiniboine language and cultural teacher at our tribal college for seven years and they have been the most gratifying years. I have been trying to incorporate our language into the curriculum. I encourage our youth to pursue their education and return home to work with our people. I worked with two linguists from Indiana University on our language. As a consultant, I helped them with language lessons and work sheets. We also produced a 250-word verb book. In the summertime, I am involved in language camps, working with young people with presentations and stories."

DIXON, LARRY
(Indian center director)
Affiliation: Kitsap County Indian Center, 3337 N.W. Byron St., Silverdale, WA 98383 (206) 692-7460.

DIXON, PATRICIA
(Indian program chairperson)
Affiliation: American Indian Studies Program, Palomar Community College, 1140 W. Mission Rd., San Marcos, CA 92069 (619) 744-1150 Fax 744-8123.

DIXON, SUSAN
(managing editor)
Affiliation: Akwe:kon Journal, Akwe:kon Press, Cornell University, 300 Caldwell Hall, Ithaca, NY 14850 (607) 255-4308.

DOBYNS, HENRY F. 1925-
(consultant; adjunct professor)
Born July 3, 1925, Tucson, Ariz. *Education*: University of Arizona, B.A., 1949, M.A., 1956; Cornell University, Ph.D., 1960. *Principal occupation*: Consultant, adjunct professor. *Affiliations*: Research associate, Cornell University, 1960-66; professor, University of Kentucky, 1966-70; professor, Prescott College, AZ, 1970-73; visiting professor, University of Wisconsin, Parkside, 1974-75; visiting professor, University of Florida, 1977-79; director, Native American Historical Demography Project, D'Arcy McNickle Center for the History of the American Indian, The Newberry Library, Chicago, 1979-86; adjunct professor, Dept. of Anthropology, University of Oklahoma, Norman, 1987-. *Military service*: U.S. Army, 1943. *Memberships*: American Association for the Advancement of Science (Fellow); American Anthropological Association; American Society for Ethnohistory (former president). *Awards, honors*: Shared Anisfield-Wolf Award, 1968; Malinowski Award, Society for Applied Anthropology, 1952. *Published works*: The Apache People (Coyotero) (Indian Tribal Series, 1971); The Papago People (Indian Tribal Series, 1972); The Mescalero Apache People (Indian Tribal Series, 1973); Prehistoric Indian Occupation Within the Eastern Area of the Yuman Complex: A Study in Applied Archaeology (Garland, 1974); Spanish Colonial Tucson (University of Arizona Press, 1976); Native American Historical Demography (Indiana University Press, 1976); From Fire to Flood (Ballena Press, 1981); Their Number Become Thinned (University of Tennessee Press, 1983).

DOCKSTADER, FREDERICK J. 1919-
(museum consultant)
Born February 3, 1919, Los Angeles, Calif. *Education*: Arizona State College, BA, MA; Western Reserve University, PhD, 1951. *Principal occupation*: Museum consultant. *Home address*: 165 W. 66 St., New York, NY 10023. *Affiliations*: Teacher, Flagstaff, Arizona schools, 1942-50; staff ethnologist, Cranbrook Institute of Science, 1950-52; faculty member and curator of anthropology, Dartmouth College, 1952-55; assistant director, director, Museum of the American Indian, Heye Foundation, 1955-75. *Other professional posts*: Advisory editor, Encyclopedia Americana, 1957-; U.S. Indian Arts & Crafts Board (commissioner, 1955-64; chairman, 1964-67; visiting professor of art and archaeology, Columbia University, 1961-; member, New York State Museum Advisory Council; trustee, Huntington Free Library. *Memberships*: American Association for the Advancement of Science (Fellow); Cranbrook Institute of Science (Fellow); American Anthropological Association (Fellow); Society for American Archaeology; New York Academy of Sci-

ences; Cosmos Club; Century Club. *Awards, honors*: First Prize (silversmithing), Cleveland Museum of Art, 1950; Fellow, Rochester Museum of Arts and Sciences; Honorary D.F.A. Degree, Hartwick College, Oneonta, NY, 1991; Honorary D.H.L. Degree, University of South Dakota, Vermillion, SD, 1992. *Biographical sources*: Who's Who in America; Who's Who in Art; American Men of Science; Who's Who in the East; American Indian Authors; Who's Who in the World. *Published works*: The Kachina and the White Man (Cranbrook Institute of Sciences, 1954; revised edition, University of New Mexico Press, 1985); The American Indian in Graduate Studies (Museum of the American Indian, 1957, revised in two volumes, 1974); Indian Art in America (New York Graphic Society, 1960); Indian Art in Middle America (New York Graphic Society, 1964); Indian Art in South America (New York Graphic Society, 1966); Pre-Columbian and Later Tribal Arts (Abrams, 1968); Indian Art of the Americas (New York, 1973); Great North American Indians: Profiles of Life & Leadership (New York, 1977); Weaving Arts of the North American Indian, 1978, revised edition of Weaving Arts of the North American Indian (HarperCollins, 1993); Song of the Loom (Hudson Hills, 1987).

DOCKTER-PINNICK, LYNN
(college president)
Affiliation: Fort Berthold Community College, P.O. Box 490, New Town, ND 58763 (701) 627-3665.

DODGE, DONALD (Navajo) 1929-
(BIA agency supt.-retired)
Born July 15, 1929, Crystal, N.M. *Education*: University of New Mexico. *Principal occupation*: BIA agency supt.-retired. *Address*: Shiprock Agency, BIA, Box 966, Shiprock, NM 87420 (505) 368-4427. *Affiliation*: Director, Navajo Tribe's Public Service Division, 1969-70; supt., BIA, Fort Defiance Agency, AZ, 1972-76; director, BIA, Navajo Area Office, Window Rock, AZ, 1977-86; supt., Shiprock Agency, Shiprock, NM, 1987-92. *Military service*: U.S. Army - Korean War. *Awards, honors*: Grandson of famous Navajo leader, Chee Dodge, first chairman of Navajo Tribal Council. *Interests*: Mr. Dodge sees the Bureau's relationship to the Tribe as government-to-government. "We have our government structure and the Tribe has its structure. We need to get together and compare the two and see where the relationship can be improved. Most of our programs are contractible except those involving areas of trust responsibility." Mr. Dodge concludes, "My main objective is to get a good organization going, one that can coordinate and communicate with the Tribe, so that the best interests of the individual will be served."

DODGE, HENRY
(BIA agency supt.)
Affiliation: San Carlos Irrigation Project, BIA, P.O. Box 209, Coolidge, AZ 85228 (602) 723-5439.

DOERING, MAVIS V. (Cherokee)
(craftsperson)
Address: 211 W. Tierra Buena, Phoenix, AZ 85023 (602) 375-2110.

DOLCHOK, LISA
(AK village council director)
Affiliation: Cook Inlet Tribal Council, 670 W. Fireweed Lane, Anchorage, AK 99503 (907) 276-3343.

DOLSON, LEROY
(Indian band chief)
Affiliation: Munsee-Delaware Nation Indian Band, RR #1, Muncey, ON, Canada N0L 1Y0 (519) 289-5396.

DOMINGUEZ, DAVID (Chumash)
(tribal chairperson)
Affiliation: Santa Ynez Band of Mission Indians, P.O. Box 317, Santa Ynez, CA 93460 (805) 688-7997.

DONAHUE, KATHIE M. (*Apv-Whilt-Tin-Toom*)
(Spokane) 1946-
(professional genealogist)
Born in 1946, in Spokane, Wash. *Education*: College & professional training. *Principal occupation*: Professional genealogist for American Indian Research. *Address*: 4516 E. Sixth Ave., Spokane, WA 99212 (509) 535-6821 Fax 333-3797. E-mail: bkdonahue@ ieehouse.net. *Memberships*: International Commission for the Accreditation of Professional Genealogists;

Board for Certification of Genealogist. *Published works*: American Indian Genealogy Help Center; Website: www.amerindgenhelp.homestead.com/ index.html.

DONALD, GARY W. (Chippewa)
(tribal committee chairperson)
Affiliation: Nett Lake Reservation, Bois Forte Tribal Business Committee, P.O. Box 16, Nett Lake, MN 55772 (218) 757-3261.

DONELSON, FRANCES A.
(librarian)
Affiliation: Bacone College Library, 2299 Old Bacone Rd., Muskogee, OK 74403 (918) 683-4581 ext. 263.

DONEY, TENNEYSON
(director-Indian hospital)
Affiliation: Crow Agency PHS Indian Hospital, Crow Agency, MT 59022 (406) 638-2624.

DONGOSKE, KURT E. 1952-
(Hopi Tribal archaeologist)
Born November 24, 1952, Mineapolis, Minn. *Education*: University of Minnesota, BA, 1976; University of Arizona, MA, 1984. *Principal occupation*: Hopi Tribal archaeologist. *Home address*: 104 N. Maricopa Dr., Winslow, AZ 86047 (602) 734-2441 (work). *Affiliation*: The Hopi Tribe, Kykotsmovi, AZ. *Memberships*: American Anthropological Association; American Association of Physical Anthropologists; Society for American Archaeology; Society of Professional Archaeologists; Arizona Archaeological Council; Arizona Archaeological & Historical Society. *Interests*: "Cultural resource management, human osteology, faunal analysis, archaeology & Native American concerns, laser mapping instruments & AutoCad, geographic information systems, and Western US archaeology, and Native American oral tradition, and the Archaeological Record."

DONHAUSER, NATTIE
(AK village president)
Affiliation: Native Village of Stoney River, P.O. Box SRV, Stoney River, AK 99557 (907) 537-3214.

DONICA, RILEY (Cherokee) 1933-
(minister)
Born April 19, 1933, Nashoba, Okla. *Education*: Dallas Christian College, BA, 1954. *Principal occupation*: Minister. *Address*: Box 70, Honobia, OK 74549 (918) 755-4462. *Affiliation*: Director, Nations Ministries, Honobia, OK, 1981- (editor, "The Nation News"). *Other professional post*: Supt., Kiamichi Mountains Mission. *Community activities*: Board of Regents, Dallas Christian College. *Memberships*: North American Christian Convention; World Evangelism Conference. *Interests*: "Firearms collector; trail rider - owns & directs "The Wild Horse Trail Ride"; travel - Canada, Mexico, England, Africa." *Biographical sources*: Daily Oklahoman - Tulsa World; Lone Star Horse Report - The Trail Rider. *Published works*: "Stomp'n Snakes" (Standard, 1964); "Farther We Go" (Star, 1973); "Mountain Time" (Star, 1974).

DONNELL, VERN
(hospital director)
Affiliation: Wagner PHS Indian Hospital, 110 Washington St., Wagner, SD 57380 (605) 384-3621.

DOONKEEN, EULA NARCOMEY (Seminole) 1931-
(artist)
Born December 12, 1931, Oklahoma City, Okla. *Education*: Central State College, BA (Eduction), 1965. *Principal occupation*: Artist. *Home address*: 1608 N.W. 35th, Oklahoma City, OK 73118. *Affiliation*: Co-owner, Alco Printing Co., Oklahoma City, OK. *Military service*: U.S.A.F. Women's Reserve, 1951-55. *Community activities*: Shawnee Area Health Advisory Board; Neighborhood Services Organization, Oklahoma City (secretary, 1972); Oklahoma City Community Council; Oklahoma City Area Health Advisory Board; West Central Neighborhood All Sports Association (vice president). *Memberships*: Seminole General Tribal Council (member; assistant chief); Five Civilized Tribes Inter-Tribal Council (sergeant-at-arms); National Congress of American Indians (area vice president, 1967-68); Kappa Pi; Bacone Alumni Association; Oklahoma Federation of Indian Women; American Indian Center (secretary, 1968); Feathers and Buckskin Society;

American Indian Press Association; Indian Development Center, Inc.; Universal Link, Plains Center, Oklahoma City (vice president). Awards, honors: Several awards for painting in acrylics. Exhibits: Mrs. Doonkeen writes, "I have exhibited at the Smithsonian Institution (but) I paint mainly on commission and rarely enter competitions because I feel most competitions are based on bias and inherent traditional favoritism, and not on realistic approaches." Interests: "I am very interested in athletic events, both as a participant and (an) observer. In 1965, I captured the women's collegiate fencing championship of Oklahoma in the novice division. I have traveled extensively over the U.S. on business for Indian organizations and my own Seminole Nation's business. I also travel extensively for my own business, the Alco Printing Co. I am well known all over the country for my greeting card and stationery designs."

DOR, CLIV (Passamaquoddy)
(tribal governor)
Affiliation: Pleasant Point Passamaquoddy Tribal Council, P.O. Box 343, Perry, ME 04667 (207) 853-2551.

DORAK, ROBERT M.
(college president)
Affiliation: Crownpoint Institute of Technology, P.O. Box 849, Crownspoint, NM 87313 (505) 786-5851 Fax 786-5644.

DORAME, CHARLIE
(BIA education chairperson)
Affiliation: Northern Pueblos Agency, Bureau of Indian Affairs, P.O. Box 4269, Fairview Station, Espanola, NM 87533 (505) 753-1465; Tesuque Day School, Route 5, Box 360-T, Santa Fe, NM 87501 (505) 983-2667.

DORE, CLIV (Passamaquoddy)
(tribal governor)
Affiliation: Pleasant Point Passamaquoddy Tribal Council, P.O. Box 343, Perry, ME 04667 (207) 853-2600.

DOTEN, HARRY (Havasupai)
(school principal)
Affiliation: Havasupai School, P.O. Box 40, Supai, AZ 86435 (602) 448-2901.

DOUGLAS, GARY (Saginaw Swan Creek Chippewa)
(learning resource assistant)
Address: 307 Russel St., Winters, CA 95694 (916) 758-0470 Fax 758-4891 (work). Affiliation: Learning Resource Assistant, D-Q University, Davis, CA, 1990-. Membership: Saginaw Swan Creek Chippewa Tribe.

DOUGLAS, LARRY
(editor)
Affiliation: "Honoring the Children," National Indian Child Welfare Association, 3611 SW Hood St. #201, Portland, OR 97201 (503) 222-4044.

DOUGLAS, THEODORE (SAM)
(Indian band chief)
Affiliation: Cheam Indian Band, 379 - 10704 No. 9 Highway, Rosedale, B.C., Canada V0X 1X0 (604) 794-7924.

DOUPHINAIS, LOUIS (Chippewa)
(school principal)
Affiliation: Turtle Mountain Middle School, P.O. Box 440, Belcourt, ND 58316 (701) 477-6471.

DOUVILLE, VICTOR
(museum chairperson; dept. head; editor)
Affiliation: Buechel Memorial Lakota Museum, St. Francis Indian Mission, 350 South Oak St., Box 149, St. Francis, SD 57572 (605) 747-2828; Dept Head, Lakota Studies/Creative Writing Program & editor, "Wanbliho: A Literary Arts Journal," Lakota Studies/Creative Writing Program, Sinte Gleska College, P.O. Box 8, Mission, SD 57555.

DOVE, DAWN (Niantic Narragansett)
(cultural center director)
Address & Affiliation: Director, Dovecrest Indian Cultural Center, 390 Summit Rd., Arcadia Village, Exter, RI 02822 (401) 539-7795.

DOWNING, CARL
(executive director)
Affiliation: Oklahoma Native American Language Development Institute, P.O. Box 963, Choctaw, OK 73020 (405) 454-2158.

DOWNES, BRADLEY G. BLEDSOE (Chickasaw)
(attorney)
Address & Affiliation: Dorsey & Whitney LLP, Center Tower, 650 Town Center Dr, Suite 1850, Costa Mesa, CA 92626-1925 (714) 662-7300 Fax 662-5576. E-mail: Downes.Bradley@dorseylaw.com. Attorney in the Indian Law practice group since 1999. Practices in the areas of Federal Indian law, gaming law, business law, civil litigation, Indian Child Welfare and Federal Government relations..

DOWNWIND, FRANCIS (Ojibwe)
(radio project director)
Affiliation: Red Lake Chippewa Tribal Council Radio Project, Red Lake, MN 56671 (218) 679-3331.

DOVLAN, REV. JOHN M., S.J.
(museum curator)
Affiliation: Kateri Galeries, The National Shrine of N.A. Martyrs, Auriesville, NY 12016 (518) 853-3033.

DOYLE, RICHARD M. (Passamaquoddy)
(tribal governor)
Affiliation: Pleasant Point Passamaquoddy Tribe, P.O. Box 343, Perry, ME 04667 (207) 853-2600.

DOXTATOR, DEBORAH (Oneida)
(tribal chairperson)
Affiliation: Oneida Business Committee, P.O. Box 365, Oneida, WI 54155 (414) 869-2214 Fax 869-2194.

DOXTATOR, TERRY
(executive director)
Affiliation: Can Am Indian Friendship Centre, P.O. Box 441, Station "A", Windsor, Ontario, Canada N9A 6L7 (519) 252-8331.

DOYLE, RICHARD M. (Passamaquoddy)
(tribal lt. governor)
Affiliation: Pleasant Point Passamaquoddy Tribal Council, P.O. Box 343, Perry, ME 04667 (207) 853-2600.

DRABENT, BETH, M.D.
(IHS-health programs)
Affiliation: Nashville Area IHS, 711 Stewarts Ferry Pike, Nashville, TN 37214 (615) 736-2400.

DRAKE, ELIZABETH (Ojibwe)
(tribal chairperson)
Affiliation: Bad River Band of Lake Superior Ojibwe (Chippewa), P.O. Box 39, Odanah, WI 54861 (715) 682-7111.

DRAKE, ELROY (Navajo) 1942-
(financial manager)
Born March 20, 1942, Tuba City, Ariz. Education: Northern Arizona University, BS, 1972. Principal occupation: Financial manager. Home address: P.O. Box 805, Window Rock, AZ 86515 (602) 871-4705. Affiliation: Manager, Navajo Savings Branch of First Federal Savings, Phoenix, AZ, 1975-85; manager, part owner, Window Rock Travel Services, Inc., 1986-. Other professional post: College instructor. Military service: U.S. Army, 1964-66 (Vietnam Service Medal; SP/4 Class-Military Police). Community activities: VFW; helped establish United Way organization on the Navajo reservation (Navajo Way). Memberships: Northern Arizona University Indian Club (social manager). Awards, honors: 1977 Young Navajo of Year, The Navajo Tribe. Interests: Established first Savings & Loan Association on Indian Reservation to promote housing; calligraphy, woodworking, astronomy, restoring VW "bug" sedans, traveling, golfing.

DRAKE, MICHAEL (United Lumbee) 1954-
(publisher)
Born July 30, 1954, Miami, Okla. Education: Washburn University, BBA, 1977. Principal occupation: Publisher. Affiliation: Owner, Talking Drum Publications, Goldendale, WA, 1991-. Memberships: (Shago) High Eagle Warrior Society of United Lumbee Nation; Oregon Natural Resources Council; Friends of Enola Hill. Interests: "My primary interests include writing, pub-

lishing, and drummaking. The drum is the heart of my life & work. I travel throughout the Pacific Northwest presenting lectures & workshops on drumming. I also support the preservation of Native American sacred sites through lectures & articles that raise people's awareness of their cultural & religious significance. Biographical source: "Drumming Our Way to Balance" by Robert Mann (The New York Times, July 1993). Published work: The Shamanic Drum (Talking Drum Publications, 1991).

DRAPEAU, DARRELL (Yankton Sioux)
(tribal chairperson)
Affiliation: Yankton Sioux Tribal Business & Claims Committee, Box 248, Marty, SD 57361 (605) 384-3804.

DRAPER, LENA M.
(school principal)
Affiliation: Kinlichee Boarding School, Hwy. 264, Ganado, AZ 86505 (520) 755-3430 Fax 755-3448.

DRAPER, WILLIAM H.
(Indian school principal)
Affiliation: Nazlini Boarding School, Ganado, AZ 86505 (602) 755-6125

DRAUGHON, SCOTT (Oklahoma Cherokee) 1952-
(social worker, attorney)
Born June 17, 1952, Muskogee, Okla. Education: Oklahoma State University, B.A., 1974; University of Tulsa Law School, J.D., 1977; University of Oklahoma, MSW, 1992. Principal occupation: Attorney. Address: Cushing Regional Hospital, 1023 E. Cherry, Tulsa, OK 74129. Affiliation: Director of Research/Information, Oklahoma Credit Union, Tulsa, OK, 1990-91; social worker, Tulsa Boys' Home (Aftercare Dept. Coordinator, 1992-94); medical social worker, Olsten Kimberly Quality Care, Tulsa, OK, 1995-; legal counsel, Tulsa City-County Health Department, Tulsa, OK, 1996-; clinical social worker, Cushing Regional Hospital, Cushing, OK, 1996-. Other professional post: Attorney in Private Practice, Tulsa, OK, 1979-; Director of Research/Information, Oklahoma Credit Union League, Tulsa, OK, 1988-91; stockbroker, 1983-93. Community activities: alumnus, Leadership Oklahoma, Inc.; Leadership Tulsa (lifetime member); Phi Delta Phi (lifetime member); Cushing Care Clinic (volunteer); Master Mason, Petroleum Lodge #474; Tulsa Human Rights Commission (past executive board); Indian Affairs Commission of the City of Tulsa (past board); International Council of Tulsa (past Board); Tulsa Senior Services, Inc. (past board). Memberships: National Association of Social Workers (past treasurer, executive board - Oklahoma Chapter); Oklahoma Association of Municipal Attorneys; Tulsa Area Human Resources Association (past vice president of Community Relations); Oklahoma Bar Association. Awards, honors: Graduate College Fee Waiver Scholarship, University of Oklahoma, Fall 1991; Regional Finalist, White House Fellowship; Leadership Oklahoma, Inc. 1993-94 Class; 1994 nominee, Friends of Children Award, Oklahoma Institute for Child Advocacy. Interests: Traveled widely throughout the U.S., including Alaska (prior to statehood) and Hawaii; Western Europe, Canada, Mexico, Australia, New Zealand, and Russia. Hobbies - golf, biking, fishing, reading, arts. Biographical sources: Oklahoma Observer (Jan. 25, 1994); Tulsa Tribune (Aug. 26, 1992; Tulsa World Newspaper (Dec. 22, 1993; Cherokee Advocate Newspaper (Sept. 1993); Who's Who in Human Service Professionals; Who's Who in American Law; Who's Who in Finance and Industry; Who's Who in America, 1997.

DREADFULWATER, SHIRLEY A.
(IHS-executive officer)
Affiliation: Nashville Area IHS, 711 Stewarts Ferry Pike, Nashville, TN 37214 (615) 736-2400.

DREADFULWATER, SHIRLEY A.
(IHS-operations services specialist)
Affiliation: Nashville Area IHS, 711 Stewarts Ferry Pike, Nashville, TN 37214 (615) 736-2400.

DRESSLER, THOMAS
(health director)
Affiliation: Reno Tribal Health Station, 34 Reservation Rd., Reno, NV 89502 (702) 329-5162.

DRIBEN, PAUL 1946-
(anthropologist)
Born May 4, 1946, St. Boniface, Manitoba, Can. *Education*: University of Manitoba, MA, 1969; University of Minnesota, PhD, 1976. *Principal occupation*: Anthropologist. *Home address*: 166 College St., Thunder Bay, Ontario, Can. P7A 5J7 (807) 343-8568 (work). *Affiliation*: Professor of anthropology, Lakehead University, Thunder Bay, Ontario, Can. *Interests*: Ethnohistory & ethnography of the Ojibway Indians and the Metis. *Published works*: When Freedom Is Lost: The Dark Side of the Relationship Between Government and the Fort Hope and the Fort Hope Band (University of Toronto Press, 1983; We Are Metis: The Ethnography of a Halfbreed Community in Northern Alberta (AMS Press, 1985; Aroland Is Our Home: An Incomplete Victory in Applied Anthropology (AMS Press, 1986; Portrait of Humankind: An Introduction to Human Biology & Prehistoric Culture (Prentice Hall, 1994); Grand Portage Chippewa: Stories and Experiences of Grand Portage Band Members (Grand Portage Tribal Council, 2000).

DROMEY, JOY E. (Yavapai)
(tribal library director)
Affiliation: Yavapai-Prescott Tribal Library,
530 E. Merritt, Prescott, AZ 86301 (602) 445-8790.

DuBRAY, DONNA (Cheyenne River Sioux)
(museum chairperson)
Affiliation: Buechel Memorial Lakota Museum, 350 S. Oak St., Box 499, St. Francis, SD 57572 (605) 747-2745.

DuBRAY, FRED (Cheyenne River Sioux) 1950-
(rancher)
Born July 16, 1950, Cheyenne Agency, S.D. *Education*: Black Hills State University, B.S., 1990. *Principal occupation*: Rancher (buffalo, horses & cattle). *Home address*: HCR 30 Box 32, Mobridge, SD 57601 (605) 733-2387. *Affiliations*: Director, Bison Enhancement Project, Cheyenne River Sioux Tribe (5 years); founder & president, Inter-Tribal Bison Cooperative, 1560 Concourse Dr., Rapid City, SD 57703 (605) 394-9730 Fax 394-7742. *Military service*: U.S. Marine Corps, 1968-71 LCpl (Vietnam Campaign Ribbons; Combat Action Ribbon). *Interests*: Mr. DuBray has made several presentations & speeches about the benefits of buffalo re-introduction to tribes & the environment. *Biographical sources*: "Tatanka Returns," by Richard Simonelli in Winds of Change (Vol. 8, No. 4 Autumn 1993); "Where the Buffalo Roam," by Andrew Nikiforuk in Harrowsmith Country Life (August 1993); articles in New York Times (Sunday, July 5, 1994) & National Geographic (Nov. 1994).

DUCHENEAUX, FRANKLIN D.
(Cheyenne River Sioux) 1940-
(attorney)
Born January 30, 1940, Cheyenne Agency, S.D. *Education*: University of South Dakota, BS, 1963; University of South Dakota Law School, JD, 1965. *Principal occupation*: Attorney. *Affiliation*: Special Counsel on Indian Affairs, Committee on Interior & Insular Affairs, U.S. House of Reps., Washington, DC, 1973-.

DUCHENEAUX, WAYNE (Cheyenne River Sioux)
(tribal council chairperson)
Affiliations: Cheyenne River Sioux Tribal Council, P.O. Box 590, Eagle Butte, SD 57625 (605) 964-4155; president, National Congress of American Indians, 900 Pennsylvania Ave., SE, Washington, DC 20003 (202) 546-9404.

DUCKEY, DONNA (Paiute-Shoshone)
(tribal chairperson)
Affiliation: Chairperson, Big Pine Reservation, P.O. Box 700, Big Pine, CA 93513 (619) 938-2003.

DUDGEON, PAUL J.
(college vice president)
Affiliation: Saskatchewan Indian Federated College, University of Regina, 118 College West, Regina, Sask. Canada S4S 0A2 (306) 584-8333.

DUFF, DIANA
(achives director)
Affiliation: National Archives-Central Plains Region, 2312 E. Bannister Rd., Kansas City, MO 64131 (816) 823-5029 Fax 926-6982. E-mail: diana.duff@nara.gov.

DUFF, JUDY
(Indian education program coordinator)
Affiliation: Longview School District #122, Indian Education Program, 1410 8th Ave. #14, Longview, WA 98632 (360) 575-7437 Fax 575-7429. E-mail: jduff@longview.k12.wa.us.

DUFFEK, KAREN
(curator of art)
Affiliation: Curator of Art, University of British Columbia Museum of Anthropology, Vancouver, BC, Canada. *Published works*: Bill Reid: Beyond the Essential Form & The Transforming Image: Painted Arts of Northwest Coast First Nations; Bill Reid & Beyond: Expanding Native Art (University of Washington Press, 2004).

DUFFIELD, LATHAL
(BIA branch chief)
Affiliation: Bureau of Indian Affairs, Chief-Branch of Tribal Enrollment, Div. of Tribal Government Services, MS4641-MIB, 1849 C St., NW, Washington, DC 20240 (202) 208-2472.

DUGAN, JOYCE C. (Eastern Cherokee)
(school director; former tribal chief)
Born August 25, 1948, Cherokee, N.C. *Education*: Bacone Jr. College, 1965-66; Western Carolina University, BS, 1975, MA, 1981. *Principal occupation*: School director; former tribal chief. *Address & Affiliation*: Director, Cherokee Elementary School & Central High School, P.O. Box 134, Cherokee, NC 28719 (704) 497-6370 Fax 497-4373. *Past professional post*: Principal Chief, Eastern Band of Cherokee Tribal Council, Cherokee, NC. *Community activities*: Cheokee Boy's Club Board of Directors; member of Parent Advisory Board for Special Education; served on United South & Eastern Tribes, Inc. *Awards, honors*: Selected a member of the White House Conference on Indian Education, 1992 (appointed to a task force to study & develop improved procedures and forms for special education); was nominated for Citizen of the Year by the Asheville Times - was selected as one of three finalists; selected as one of North Carolina's Most Distinguished Women in Education, 1994. *Interests*: "Great supporter of special programs for special students."

DUKEPOO, FRANK C. (Hopi-Laguna) 1945-
(geneticist)
Born in 1945 on the Mohave Reservation. *Education*: Arizona State University (BS in Biology, 1966; MS in Zoology, 1968; and PhD in Zoology, 1973). *Principal occupation*: Geneticist. *Address*: Dept. of Biological Sciences, Northern Arizona University, Flagstaff, AZ (602) 523-7227. *Affiliations*: Assistant professor of biology, San Diego State University, 1973-77; program manager, National Science Foundation, Washington, DC, 1977-78; executive secretary, National Cancer Institute, NIH, Washington, DC, 1978-80; special assistant to the academic vice president (1980-94) & senior lecturer in the Dept. of Biological Sciences (1990-present), Northern Arizona University, Flagstaff, AZ. *Other professional posts*: Founder & current director, National Native American Honor Society; director, Center for Indian Education, Northern Arizona University, 1980-84; consultant to the BIA, Dept. of Education, NIH, NSF, Southwest Development lab and the Far West Lab; served as consultant to the production of the film, "The Four Corners: A National Sacrifice Area," 1987; served as consultant and featured in the film, The River That Harms," 1988; served as advisor, consultant and starred in "the Frank Duckepoo Story," film was produced as part of the Whizkids Project in 1993. *Memberships*: SACNAS (Society for the Advance of Chicanos & Native Americans in Science (founding member); AISES (founding member); *Awards, honors*: John Hay Whitney & Ford Foundation Fellowships; Bo Jack Humanitarian Award; Iron Eyes Cody Medal of Freedom Award; Outstanding Educator of the Year Award from the National Coalition of Indian Education; 1995 Indian Man of the Year; inducted into the Indian Hall of Fame; listed in "Past & Present Indian leaders" and selected for inclusion in "Bibliographies of Outstanding Native Americans"; 1996 Hopi of the Year and received the "Lifetime Achievement Award" for service to Indian people. He is the first Hopi to have earned a doctorate and one of six Indians nationally who hold earned doctorates in the sciences. He is one of only two Native American geneticists in the country. *Interests*: For the past ten

years he has expanded his interest in the area of retention and motivation. In recent years he has gained considerable reputation as on eof the country's outstanding motivators of Indian students. In addition to retention and motivation studies, his other research interests include the study of birth defects in Southwest Native Americans and albinism and inbreeding among the Hopi Indians of northern Arizona. He is attempting to map the albino gene and has made two films pertaining to his research. The Whizkids production has received the ABC Excellence Award in Children's Programming, Telly Award and the School Library Journal Award. In 1995, the production was accepted for airing by the Minnesota Public Television. Currently, he is developing culturally-relevant science material, science modules and science kits for elementary students. As an amateur magician he gives "Mind, Magic and Motivation" shows to Indian youth. *Published works*: Numerous articles.

DuMARCE, HARVEY W.
(Sisseton-Wahpeton Sioux) 1946-
(attorney)
Born September 5, 1946, Sisseton, S.D. *Education*: University of California, Berkeley, BA, 1976; University of Iowa, College of Law, JD, 1994. *Principal occupation*: Law student. *Address*: P.O. Box 164, Sisseton, SD 57262-0164. *Community activities*: Tribal court, Sissteon-Wahpeton Sioux Reservation (7 years). *Memberships*: Native American Law Student Association; Disabled Law Student Society. *Interests*: "I am interested in American Indian law, voting rights. I would like to work for a tribe as a judge or legal counsel when I am finished with law school. I have always been active in the field of voting rights for Indian people. I was one of the plaintiffs in a landmark voting rights case in South Dakota captioned Buckanaga v. Sissteon School District. We were the first group of American Indians to file a voting rights act complaint in the U.S.After seven years of litigation, we were able to settle our case out of court, and as a result of our long struggle, we had the old at-large voting system in the Sissteon School District replaced by a cumulative voting scheme. Now for the first time i the history of the Sissteon-Wahpeton Sioux Tribe, Indian parents were able to elect candidates of their choice to sit on the Sissteon School Board. I envision a day soon when an Indian will win an election in South Dakota to the U.S. Senate on the strength of Indian votes."

DUMONTIER, GREG (Salish-Kootenai)
(health director)
Affiliation: Flathead PHS Indian Health Center, P.O. Box 280, St. Ignatius, MT 59865 (406) 745-2411.

DUNCAN, CLIFFORD (Ute)
(museum director)
Affiliation: Ute Tribal Museum, P.O. Box 190, Hwy. 40, Fort Duchesne, UT 84026 (801) 722-4992.

DUNCAN, DOUGLAS (Pomo)
(rancheria chairperson)
Affiliation: Robinson Rancheria, P.O. Box 1119, Nice, CA 95464 (707) 275-0527.

DUNCAN, LENA
(administrative director)
Affiliation: National American Indian Housing Council, 900 Second St., NE #305, Washington, DC 20002 (800) 284-9165; (202) 789-1754 Fax 789-1758.

DUNKEN, VICKIE
(gallery & center director)
Affiliation: Oglewanagi Gallery & Center, 842b N. Highland Ave., Atlanta, GA 30306 (404) 872-4213.

DUNLAP, GJRJLE (Chemehuevi)
(former tribal chairperson)
Affiliation: Chemehuevi Tribal Council, P.O. Box 1976, Havasu Lake, CA 92363 (760) 858-4301.

DUNN, CAROLYN (Lower Creek,)
(poet, writer)
Address: 2231 Grenadier Dr., San Pedro, CA 90732 (310) 833-6621.

DUNN, KENNETH E. (Half Eagle)
(Creek/United Lumbee) 1956-
(writer, researcher, book reviewer, historian)
Born December 17, 1956, Santa Barbara, Calif. *Edu-*

cation: Grossmont Community College (San Diego, CA), GPA. *Principal occupation*: Writer, researcher, book reviewer, historian. *Address*: 10151 Sierra Madre Rd., Spring Valley, CA 91977 (619) 670-3396. *Affiliations*: Pan American Indian Association News (Contributing reporter, 1990-94; staff writer, 1995-98); contributor, United Lumbee Nation Times, 1995-. *Memberships*: Pan American Indian Association; United Lumbee Council member, Red Tailed Hawk Band of Southern California. *Award*: 1975 Cal Expo Award for racing photo entitled "CMC Shot of Top Southern California Professional IMX Racers at Continial Motor Sports Club Event", Carlsbad, CA. *Interests*: Politics, civil rights, film, literature, writing, motor cross/supercross racing. *Unpublished works*: "Tusten - nuggee," "Cry of the Mountain," "Autumn Winds," "Season of the Wolf," (history of the Eastern (U.S.) American Indian); book reviews, essays, historical semigenealogical work.

DUNNINGTON, JEAN
(editor)
Affiliation: Tsa'Aszi' (The Yucca) Magazine of Navajo Culture, Tsa'Aszi Graphics Center, Ramah Navajo School Board, CPO Box 12, Pine Hill, NM 87321 (505) 783-5503.

DUNSTAN, GUY
(Indian band chief)
Affiliation: Siska Indian Band, Box 358, Lytton, British Columbia, Canada V0K 1Z0 (604) 455-2219.

DuPREE, DOROTHY
(associate director)
Affiliation: Albuquerque Area Indian Health Services, 505 Marquette Ave., NW, Suite 1502, Albuquerque, NM 87102 (505) 766-2151.

DURHAM, BARBARA (Timbisha Shoshone) 1955-
(tribal administrator)
Born September 23, 1955, Lone Pine, Calif. *Principal occupation*: Tribal administrator. *Address*: P.O. Box 206, Death Valley, CA 92328 (760) 786-2374 Fax 786-2376. E-mail: timbisha@aol.com. *Affiliation*: Timbisha Shoshone Tribe. *Community activities*: Land restoration team member; chairperson of tribal non-profit center; represents tribe on Toiyabe Indian Health Project. *Membership*: National Congress of American Indians.

DURO, HENRY (Serrano)
(Indian band chairperson)
Affiliation: San Manuel Band of Mission Indians, P.O. Box 266, Patton, CA 92369 (909) 864-8933.

DUTHU, N. BRUCE (Houma) 1958-
(vice dean, professor of law)
Born December 30, 1958, Houma, La. Education: DartmouthCollege, BA; Loyola University School of Law, JD. *Home address*: P.O. Box 96, Chelsea St., South Royalton, VT 05068 (802) 831-1285 Fax 763-2663 (work); E-Mail: bduthu@vermontlaw.edu. *Affiliations*: Vice Dean for Academic Affairs and Professor of Law, Vermont Law School, So. Royalton, VT, 1991-present; Adjunct Professor in Native American Studies, Dartmouth College, Hanover, NH. Other professional post: Board of Trustees for Earthjustice, one of the leading environmental non-profit litigation firms in the country. *Past professional posts*: Visiting Professor of Law, Harvard Law School, University of Trento (Italy),, University of Wollongong (Australia), and University of Sydney (Australia). *Community activities*: Board member, Native American Program, Brown School of Social Work, Washington University; advisory committee, Hood Museum Repatriation Project, Dartmouth College. *Memberships*: Association of American Law Schools; Louisiana Bar Association; Federal Indian Bar Association; Tucker Foundation of Dartmouth College (board of visitors); Native American Alumni Association of Dartmouth College (National Steering Committee); American Indian Program, Brown School of Social Work, Washington University, St. Louis, MO (board of visitors).

DYE, SARA
(clinical director)
Affiliation: Carl Albert Indian Hospital, 1001 North Country Club Rd., Ada, OK 74820 (405) 436-3980.

DYER, PATRICIA (Mukwa Odae Kwa)
(Little Traverse Bay Bands of Odawa-Mississippi Choctaw) 1953-
(admissions counselor)
Born February 14, 1953, Charlevoix, Mich. *Education*: Northern Michigan University, B.S.W., 1981; Michigan State University, M.A., 1997. *Principal occupation*: Admissions counselor. *Home address*: 3572 Annis Rd., Mason, MI 48854 (517) 589-5065. *Affiliation*: Michigan Association of College Admissions Counselors, 1990-. *Other professional post*: American Indian historian. *Community activities*: Little Traverse Bay Band of Odawa Tribal Council (Eagle President). *Memberships*: Ethnohistory Association; Native American Indian Higher Education Council; Eagle President, an American Indian faculty & staff association at Michigan State University. *Interests*: "I make Michigan Native American art - porcupine quillwork, beadwork, leatherwork." *Published works*: Native American Experience (Michigan Dept. of Education, 1989); WPA Arts & Crafts Project (Michigan History Magazine, 1995); The Northern Michigan Ottawa Association, (MSU, 1997).

DYSON, PEGGY
(museum president)
Affiliation: Baranov Museum, Erskine House, 101 Marine Way, Kodiak, AK 99615 (907) 486-5920.

E

EADIE, BETTY J. (Rosebud Lakota)
(writer)
Address: P.O. Box 25490, Seattle, WA 98109. *Published work*: "Embraced by the Light."

EAGLE, CHARLES R.
(Indian band chief)
Affiliation: Moose Woods Indian Band, Box 149, RR 5, Saskatoon, Saskatchewan, Canada S7K 3J8 (306) 477-0908.

EAGLE, TOM
(Indian council president)
Affiliation: N.W.T. Council of Friendship Centres, P.O. Box 2859, Yellowknife, Northwest Territories, Canada X1A 2R2 (403) 920-2288; director, Tree of Peace Friendship Centre, P.O. Box 2667, Yellowknife, N.W.T., Canada X1A 1H0.

EAGLEMAN, MARJORIE
(BIA agency supt.)
Affiliation: Northern Cheyenne Agency, Bureau of Indian Affairs, P.O. Box 40, Lame Deer, MT 59043 (406) 477-8242 Fax 477-6636.

EAGLESTAFF, ROBERT (To Wakanhi Wamblee-Blue Lighting Eagle) (Lakota) 1952-
(educator)
Born December 20, 1952, Dupree, S.D. *Education*: University of South Dakota, B.S., M.S.; University of Washington, 1991- (doctoral candidate). *Principal occupation*: Educator. *Home Address*: American Indian Heritage School, 9600 College Way N., Seattle, WA 98103 (206) 298-7895. *Affiliation*: Principal, Seattle Public Schools, Seattle, WA, 1989-present (206) 298-7801; American Indian Heritage School, Seattle, WA. *Other professional posts*: Teacher, consultant, engineering assistant. *Community activities*: Enrolled at the Cheyenne River Sioux Reservation. *Memberships*: National Association of Secondary School Principals; Association of Washington School Principals; Principals Association of Seattle Schools; Lakota Sundancer Society, 1978-. *Awards, honors*: Numerous athletic awards, especially in basketball; numerous academic awards as well. *Interests*: "I am interested in researching the history of my family at various sites throughout the U.S. I would like to go back thousands of years and document those years."

EAR, JOHNNY
(Indian band chief)
Affiliation: Bearspaw Group (Stoney) Indian Band, Box 40, Morley, Alberta, Canada T0L 1N0 (403) 881-3770.

EARLY, HARRY D. (Laguna Pueblo)
(pueblo governor)
Affiliation: Pueblo of Laguna, P.O. Box 194, Laguna, NM 87026 (505) 552-6654.

EARRING, LYNDA
(supt. for education)
Affiliation: Little Wound Day School, P.O. Box 500, Kyle, SD 57752 (605) 455-2461.

EASTERDAY, ADEL (Nodiwayqua) (Seneca) 1954-
(teacher)
Born Sept. 30, 1954, Hillsdale, Mich. *Education*: Western Michigan University, BS (History), MA (Educational Leadership). *Principal occupation*: Teacher. *Address*: 6439 Nicolet Rd., Sault Ste. Marie, MI 49783 (906) 632-8611. E-mail: ayooper2@yahoo.com. *Affiliation*: Sault Ste. Marie Public Schools, Dept. of Indian Education, 1980-96; Bahweting Tribal School, Sault Ste. Marie, MI, 1997-. *Other professional posts*: Guest lecturer, speaker, and storyteller presenting various workshops, inservices and addresses on education, curriculum and topics relative to American Indian history and culture to public schools, colleges and universities, and professional organizations and conferences. *Membership*: American Legion Auxilary, Unit Number 0053. *Interests*: Writing, fishing, old movies, history, finger weaving, music, beadwork and world politics.

EASTES, FRANK, JJ.
(executive director)
Affiliation: Native American Indian Media Corporation, P.O. Box 59, Strawberry Plains, TN 37871 (615) 933-6246.

EASTMAN, CLARENCE (Sioux)
(Indian band chief)
Affiliation: Oak Lake Sioux Indian Band, P.O. Box 146, Pipestone, Manitoba, Canada R0M 1T0 (204) 854-2261.

EBBERT, PAUL, MD
(clinical director)
Affiliation: Fort Duchesne PHS Indian Health Center, P.O. Box 160, Roosevelt, UT 84026 (801) 722-5122.

EBERHARD, ERIC D. 1945-
(attorney-Indian affairs law)
Education: Western Reserve University, BA, 1967; University of Cincinnati, School of Law, JD, 1970; George Washington University, LLM, 1972. *Principal occupation*: Attorney-Indian affairs law. *Address*: Senate Select Committee on Indian Affairs, Room SH 838, Hart Senate Office Bldg., Washington, DC 20510. *Affiliations*: Deputy Attorney General, Navajo Nation, 1983-85; executive director, Navajo Nation, Washington office, 1985-87; Minority Staff Director and Counsel, Senate Select Committee on Indian Affairs, Washington, D.C., 1987-. Mr. Eberhard has been actively engaged in the practice of Indian affairs law since 1973. His practice has involved all aspects of the representations of Indian tribes and individuals in federal, state, and tribal forums. As Deputy General of the Navajo Nation and Executive Director of the Navajo Nation, Washington Office, he was involved in the development and passage of federal legislation relating to all aspects of tribal self-governance and development.

EBY, RICHARD L. 1953-
(producer/publisher)
Born December 26, 1953, Cheboygan, Mich. *Education*: High school. *Principal occupation*: Producer/publisher). *Home address*: Unknown. *Affiliations*: Co-owner/general manager/producer, Lane Audio Productions, 1988-93; president/recordist/producer, VIP Publishing, Fayetteville, AR, 1990-. *Membership*: National Museum of the American Indian (charter member). *Awards, honors*: Produced "When the Century Was Young" audio autobiographical sketch of Dee Brown, published by August House of Little Rock, AR, and selected in top 3 historical audio programs by Publishers Weekly. *Interests*: "I have been interested in Native American cultures since childhood, and I'm happy that saving some of their heritage is part of our common purpose in this life. Since joining with Gregg Howard to form Various Indian Peoples Publishing, Inc. (VIP Publishing) in 1989, we have worked with elders of several Native Nations to develop language learning programs which are helping to preserve and strengthen Native cultures. It is well known that a language holds the essence of a culture. Respect for a people begins with respect for their beliefs, and their language. We first created programs for self-instruction and now offer classroom teaching materials as well. It is our firm belief that people should be able to

hear Native Speakers of Native American languages in their libaries and other educational facilities around the world, as they can now hear English, Spanish, and French, etc. We wish to restore proper respect for their cultures, languages, and teachings of all Native Americn Nations."*Published works*: Book and Audiotape Sets - Introduction to Cherokee, 1990; Choctaw Language Sampler, 1992; Introduction to Choctaw, 1992; Choctaw Legends with Charley Jones, 1992; Choctaw Singing With Charley Jones, 1993; Chickasaw Language Sampler, 1993; Introduction to Chickasaw, 1994; Western Cherokee Language Sampler, 1994; Eastern Cherokee (Kituwah) Language Sampler, 1995; The Choctaw Language Awareness Teacher's Manual (K-3), 1995; Chickasaw/Choctaw Singing, Vls. 1 & 2, 1996 (all published by VIP Publishing). "Sequoyah, the Cherokee Syllabary Teacher" (Multimedia Interactive Windows program), 1996. Audiotapes only - Cherokee Legends with Sam Hider, 1990; Kiowa Language Sampler, 1991; Kiowa Eagle Legend with Evalu Ware Russell, 1991; American Indian Music, 1991.

ECHOHAWK, BRUMMETT (Pawnee) 1922-
(artist, writer, actor)
Born March 3, 1922, Pawnee, Okla. *Education*: Detroit School of Arts and Crafts, 1945; Art Institute of Chicago, 1945-48; studied creative writing at the university of Tulsa. *Principal occupation*: Artist, writer, actor. *Home address*: P.O. Box 1922, Tulsa, OK 74101. *Affiliations*: Staff artist, Chicago Daily Times and Chicago Sun Times; artist, Bluebook, McCall's Magazine Corp., New York. *Military service*: U.S. Army, 1940-45 (Purple Heart with oak-leaf cluster; did Combat sketches published in the Army's Yank Magazine, and 88 newspapers by N.E.A. News Syndicate). *Community activities*: Gilcrease Museum, Tulsa, OK (board member). *Exhibitions*: Paintings shown in Pakistan & India, through the Art in the Embassies Program, State Department; other works shown at the De Young Museum, San Francisco; Amon Carter Museum, Fort Worth, Texas; Gilcrease Museum; Imperial War Museum. London; Bad Segeberg, Hamburg, West Germany. *Acting*: As stage actor, Mr. Echohawk has appeared in the role of Sitting Bull in Kopit's play Indians in Tulsa, Fort Worth, and Lincoln, Neb. Also played at the Virginia Museum Theater, Richmond, Questor's Theater, London, and Karl May Theater, Bad Segeberg, West Germany; he did a TV film in Hamburg, W. Germany. *Awards, honors*: Assisted Thomas Hart Benton with one of the greatest mural in America: The Truman Memorial Library mural called Independence and the Opening of the West, at Independence, MO; commissioned by the Aluminum Co. of America for a painting depicting early American history of the Tennessee Valley; commissioned by Leaning Tree Publishing Co., Boulder, CO for paintings to be reproduced as Christmas cards; Mr. Echohawk's paintings are of a classic and representational style, which cover the subjects of the Indian and the American West. *Biographical sources*: Encyclopedia of the American Indian; Indians of Today; Dictionary of International Biography; National Geographic's American Indians. *Published works*: Writings, with illustrations, have appeared in the Tulsa Sunday World, Oklahoma Today Magazine, The Western Horseman Magazine, and others.

ECHOHAWK, JOHN E. (Pawnee) 1945-
(attorney)
Born August 11, 1945, Albuquerque, N.M. *Education*: University of New Mexico, BA, 1967; University of New Mexico, School of Law, JD, 1970. *Principal Occupation*: Attorney. *Address & Affiliation*: Native American Rights Fund, 1506 Broadway, Boulder, CO 80302 (303) 447-8760 (research associate, 1970-1972; deputy director, 1972-73, 1975-77; executive director, 1973-75, 1977-). *Community activities*: Association on American Indian Affairs (member-board of directors); American Indian Lawyer Training Program (board of directors); National Committee on Responsive Philanthropy (member-board of directors). *Memberships*: American Indian Bar Association; American Bar Association. *Awards, Honors*: Assisted in forming the American Indian Law Student's Association; Americans for Indian Opportunity, Distinguished Service Award; White Buffalo Council, Friendship Award; 1987 National Indian Achievement Award from the Indian Council Fires; National Congress of American Indians, President's Indian Service Award; appointed to the Wayne Morse

Chair of Law and Politics at the University of Oregon. *Interests*: Indian law.

ECHOHAWK, LARRY (Pawnee) 1948-
(politician)
Born in Wyo. *Education*: Brigham Young University, BA, 1970; University of Utah Law School, J.D., 1973. *Principal occupation*: Politician; Idaho state attorney general. *Address*: Unknown. *Affiliation*: Idaho State Attorney General, Boise, ID, 1990-94. *Interests*: Politics.

ECHOHAWK, WALTER (Pawnee)
(senior staff attorney)
Affiliations: Senior staff attorney, Native American Rights Fund, 1506 Broadway, Boulder, CO 80302; a national coordinator for American India Religious Freedom Act Coalition; member, Board of Trustees, American Indian Ritual Object Repatriation Foundation, 463 East 57th St., New York, NY 10022 (212) 980-9441.

ECOFFEY, ROBERT (Oglala Lakota)
(BIA deputy regional director)
Born on the Pine Ridge Reservation, S.D. *Address & Affiliation*: Deputy Regional Director, Great Plains Regional Office, Bureau of Indian Affairs, 115 4th Ave., SE, Federal Bldg., Aberdeen, SD 57401 (605) 226-7416 (2004-present). Mr. Ecoffey oversees BIA programs for North & South Dakota, and Nebraska, including social services, transportation, law enforcement and child welfare. *Past professional posts*: Appointed to U.S. Marshall from SD, 1994-96 (first Native American to ever hold that post); Supt., BIA Pine Ridge Agency, Pine Ridge, SD, 1996-2001; Deputy Director of BIA Office of Law Enforcement Services, Albuquerque, NM, 2001-2004.

EDDY, DANIEL, Jr. (Navajo)
(tribal chairperson)
Affiliation: Colorado River Indian Tribal Council, Route 1, Box 23-B, Parker, AZ 85344 (928) 669-9211.

EDDY, FRANK W. 1930-
(archaeologist/anthropologist)
Born May 7 1930, Roanoke, Va. *Education*: University of New Mexico, BA, 1952; University of Arizona, MA, 1958; University of Colorado, PhD, 1968. *Principal occupation*: Archaeologist-anthropologist. *Address*: Dept. of Anthropology, CB 233, University of Colorado, Boulder, CO 80309 (303) 492-7947. *Affiliations*: Curator, Museum of New Mexico, researcher and director of the Navajo Reservoir Salvage Archaeological Project, 1959-65; research assistant at the University of Colorado Museum—dig foreman at Yellow Jacket and Jurgens Site excavations, 1965-68; executive director, Texas, Archaeological Salvage Project, University of Texas, Austin, 1968-70; director, Chimney Rock Archaeological Project, University of Colorado, 1970-73; associate professor, professor of anthropology, University of Colorado, 1970-present. *Other professional posts*: Director and principal investigator, Two Forks Archaeological Project, University of Colorado, 1974-75; intern, Interagency Archaeological Services, Denver, National Park Service, 1975-76; co-director and principal investigator of the Bisti-Star Lake Cultural Resource Inventory, Archaeological Associates, Inc., summer, 1977. *Military service*: U.S. Army, 1952-54. *Memberships*: Society for American Archaeology, 1953-; Society for the Sigma Xi, 1965—73; American Quaternary Association, 1970-; Colorado Archaeological Society, 1970-; Society of Professional Archaeologists, 1976- (counselor, standards board); Association of Field Archaeologists, 1977-. *Interests*: Cultural ecology; prehistoric settlement studies; cultural change as revealed by archaeology; technology of primitive societies. *Published works*: An Archaeological Survey of the Navajo Reservoir District, Northwestern New Mexico, with Alfred E. Dittert, Jr., and James J. Hester (Monograph, School of American Research, Museum of New Mexico, 1961); Excavations at Los Pinos Phase Sites in the Navajo Reservoir District (Museum of New Mexico, 1961); Excavations at the Candelaria Site, LA 4406, chapter II in Pueblo Period Sites in the Piedra River Section, Navajo Reservoir District, assembled with A.E. Dittert, Jr. (Museum of New Mexico, 1963); Prehistory in the Navajo Reservoir District, Northwestern New Mexico (Museum of New Mexico, 1966); Archaeological Investigations at Chimney Rock Mesa: 1970-1972 (Memoirs of the Colorado Archaeological Society, 1977); An Archaeological Study of Indian

Settlements and Land Use in the Colorado Foothills, with Ric Windmiller (Memoirs of Southwestern Lore, Colorado Archaeological Society). Several articles in journals, and papers delivered at regional meetings and national conferences.

EDDY, PHYLLIS
(special assistant)
Affiliation: Office of the Director, Indian Health Service, Rm. 6-22 Parklawn Bldg., 5600 Fishers Lane, Rockville, MD 20857 (301) 443-7261.

EDER, JEANNE (Dakota Sioux)
(associate professor)
Affiliation: Director of Alaska Native Studies Program and Associate Professor of History, University of Alaska, Anchorage, AK. *Published works*: The Dakota Sioux & the Makah; American Indian Education: A History, with Jon Reyhner (University of Oklahoma Press, 2004).

EDERER, CHARLES J.
(executive director)
Affiliation: Urban Indian Health & Human Services, Inc., 4100 Silver, SE, Suite B, Albuquerque, NM 87108 (505) 262-2481.

EDEVOLD, MARVIN
(IHS-tribal activities)
Affiliation: Office of Tribal Activities, Bemidji Area Office, Indian Health Service, 127 Federal Bldg., Bemidji, MN 56601 (218) 759-3424.

EDGAR, M.J. YVONNE
(Indian band chief)
Affiliation: Mississaugas of Scugog Indian Band, RR #5, Port Perry, Ontario, Canada L0B 1N0 (416) 985-3337.

EDGE, JAMES E. 1948-
(health administrator)
Born April 29, 1948, Anacortes, Wash. *Education*: University of Washington, BS, 1971; University of Hawaii, MPH, 1979. *Principal occupation*: Health administrator. *Home address*: 1580 Rio Vista Way S., Salem, OR 97302 (503) 399-5937. *Affiliation*: Service Unit Director, Western Oregon Service Unit, Indian Health Service, Salem, OR, 1980-. *Other professional post*: Chairperson, Service Unit Directors' Steering Committee on Health Care Reform, Portland Area Indian Health Service, 1993-. *Military service*: Commissioned Officer, 18 years, USPHS, (Captain). *Memberships*: American College of Healthcare Executives; Association of Military Surgeons of the U.S.; Reserve Officers Association; American Academy of Medical Administrators; Commissioned Officers Association of the U.S. Public Health Service; American Public Health Association; Washington State Pharmaceutical Association. *Awards, honors*: Indian Health Service Long Term Training, 1978-79; USPHS Citation and Ribbon, 1984; USPHS Commendation Medal, 1986; USPHS Outstanding Unit Citation, 1988; USPHS Unit Commendation, 1989; USPHS Outstanding Service Medal, 1991). *Interests*: "Special interest in rural and minority health care. Eighteen years broad based experience in American Indian health care. Extensive travel & consultation in Pacific Island health care; running, skiing, fishing, antique cars." *Biographical sources*: The National Dean's List, 1979-80; Outstanding Young Men of American, 1980; Marquis Who's Who in Finance and Industry, 1992-93.

EDMO, ED, Jr. (Shoshoni-Bannock) 1944-
(consultant, poet)
Address: 9430 N.E. Prescott, Portland, OR 97220 (503) 256-2257. *Interests*: Professional Native American story teller who visits schools, libraries, colleges, and museums to present a program of arts and crafts, story telling of legends and myths of various Native American tribes. He is a crafts artist with shows held periodically in cities and towns of the Northwest. He has many published poems and is author of book and magazine materials.

EDMO, KESLEY (Shoshone-Bannock)
(board member)
Affiliation: National Indian Youth Council, Albuquerque, NM.

EDMO-SUPPAH, LORI
(Shoshone-Bannock) 1959-
(editor)
Born September 30, 1959, Blackfoot, Idaho. *Education*: University of Montana, BA, 1980. *Principal occupation*: Editor. *Address*: P.O. Box 900, Fort Hall, ID 83203 (208) 478-3701 Fax 478-3702; E-mail: edmosup @ida.net. *Community activities*: Board member, Shoshone-Bannock Jr./Sr. High School. *Memberships*: Native American Journalists Association (NAJA); Idaho Press Club (IPC); Inland Press Association. *Published work*: "From the Frontlines," essay.

EDMO-SUPPAH, LORRAINE P.
(Shoshone-Bannock) 1948-
(journalist, program administrator)
Born October 26, 1948, Blackfoot, Idaho. *Education*: University of Montana, BA (Journalism), 1970; University of New Mexico, MA, 1982; University of Missouri, Multi-Cultural Management Program; University of Idaho, School of Communications (Journalist in Residence 2001-2002 through a grant from the Freedom Forum). *Principal occupation*: Journalist, program administrator. *Home address*: Resides in Fort Hall, Idaho. *Address*: c/o Native American Journalists Association (NAJA), 3359 36th Ave. So., Minneapolis, MN 55406 (612) 729-9244 Fax 729-9373. E-mail: edmo-suppah @naja.com. *Affiliations*: TV News Reporter, 1970-72; resource development specialist, 1972-73, executive director, 1973-75, Idaho Inter-Tribal Board, Inc., Boise, Idaho; technical writer, 1976-79, development officer, 1979-80, Native American Rights Fund, Boulder, CO; executive director, American Indian Graduate Center, Albuquerque, NM, 1984-93; editor, Sho-Ban News (weekly tribal newspaper), 1993-present. *Other professional post*: Treasurer, Native American Journalists Association. *Community activities*: Warden & treasurer, Episcopal Urban Indian Ministry, Albuquerque, NM, 1986-93; board of directors, UNITY: Journalists of Color, Inc. *Memberships*: National Indian Education Association (executive committee-board of directors, 1989-92; executive director, 1993-99); National Organization of Native American Women (former president); National Congress of American Indians. *Awards, honors*: Selected by the Albuquerque Tribune as one of 12 "Rising Stars" in the education field for 1988; selected as a 1989 Outstanding Young Woman of American, Boulder, CO; 1995 Wassaja Award from NAJA Board of Directors for excellence in Native journalism; numerous awards from NAJA and the Idaho Press Club for her photography and writing. NAJA named the Sho-Ban News the Best Native Weekly in 2000, and honorable mention for General Excellence in 2001. *Interests*: "I am interested in working for the betterment of Indian tribal governments and American Indian people. I attempt to do this through advocacy; service on Board and commissions, writing, etc. I have travelled extensively to visit and work with tribes and Indian organizations throughout the country."

EDMUND, RICK
(editor)
Affiliation: Susquehanna Valley Native American Eagle, Box 99, Walnut Valley Farm, Loganville, PA 17342 (717) 428-1440.

EDMUNDS, JUDITH A. 1943-
(dealer-American Indian jewelry)
Born September 8, 1943, Waltham, Mass. *Education*: Massachusetts College of Pharmacy. *Principal occupation*: Dealer of fine American Indian jewelry and related items. *Home address*: Box 788, West Yarmouth, MA 02673. *Affiliation*: President-treasurer, Edmonds of Yarmouth, Inc., 1973-. *Other professional posts*: State chairperson, Indian Arts & Crafts Association (served on Education & Public Relations Committee; currently chairperson for Massachusetts). *Interests*: Ms. Edmunds writes, "My business is a retail outlet, but my greatest pleasure is educating the general public on the different Indian tribes and their style of work and their living conditions, and to create collectors of fine Indian art.By educating these people - those dealers that are selling fakes and misrepresenting their wares will soon be out of business, I travel to reservations a couple of times a year and spend time in the Hopi Mesas and San Domingo Pueblos, as well as on the Navajo Reservation, as we have Indian friends spread out through the various reservations, as well as Anglo friends. My interests outside of the Indian field is fine American antiques."

EDWARDS, DAVID (Tyme Maidu)
(rancheria chairperson)
Affiliation: Berry Creek Rancheria, 5 Tyme Way, Oroville, CA 95966 (530) 534-3859.

EDWARDS, EDDIE V. (Oklahoma Choctaw) 1930-
(BIA-government service manager)
Born October 7, 1930, Kingfisher, Okla. *Education*: Oklahoma City University, BA, 1960; Oklahoma University Engineering Graduate School, 1962-64; Oklahoma City University, School of Law, JD, 1969. *Principal occupation*: BIA-government service manager. *Home address*: 2114 Mistletoe Lane, Edmond, OK 73034. *Affiliation*: U.S. Dept. of the Interior, BIA, Real Estate Services, 1849 C St., NW, MS: 4522-MIB, Washington, DC 20240 (202) 208-5474. *Other profesional post*: Oklahoma Highway Design Engineer, Oklahoma State Capital, 1960-69. *Military service*: U.S. Navy (Korean Service, 1950-54; six campaign medals, Korean Service medal w/6 Battlestars). *Memberships*: Oklahoma Bar Association, Federal Bar Association, and American Indian Bar Association. *Interests*: Indian law.

EDWARDS, JAMES (Tyme Maidu)
(rancheria chairperson)
Affiliation: Berry Creek Rancheria, 5 Tyme Way, Oroville, CA 95966 (530) 534-3859.

EDWARDS, JAMES LEE (Absentee Shawnee)
(tribal governor)
Address & Affiliation: Absentee Shawnee Tribe, 2025 S. Gordon Cooper, Shawnee, OK 74801 (405) 275-4030 Fax 275-5637.

EDWARDS, JANE
(museum director/curator)
Affiliation: Mitchell Indian Museum, Kendall College, 2408 Orrington Ave., Evanston, IL 60201 (708) 866-1395.

EDWARDS, KENNETH LEE (*Rainbow Cougar*)
(Colville) 1956-
(artist, storyteller/speaker/comedian)
Born February 8, 1956, Greenville, S.C. *Education*: Institute of American Indian Arts, AFA, 1977. *Principal occupation*: Artist-painter; storyteller/speaker/comedian. *Address*: 287-H Omak Riverside Eastside Dr., Omak, WA 98841 (509) 826-4744. *Membership*: Indian Arts & Crafts Association, 1984-present. Ken resides on the Colville Indian Reservation and works in a wide variety of media: predominantly watercolor, oil, acrylic, and pen and ink. He is experienced in silversmithing, welding, drafting, photography and beadwork. An additional talent is that of storyteller and oral historian. Ken has traveled to about 100 Indian reservations and memorized more than one thousand stories from many tribes. *Awards, honors*: Participated in the First National Indian Art Show, Nov. 1985, held in Washington, DC; did the painting which was made into a Porter-Print announcing the first Miss Indian U.S.A. Pageant; his painting, "First Love" was part of a Native American Art Show at the December 1987 International Friendship House, Moscow, USSR. His artwork has been exhibited and sold in fine art shows and galleries across the U.S. He has received several top awards at major shows. His ink drawings and poetry have been published in ten Indian newspapers. *Published works*: Illustrated five children's books - How the Animals Got Their Names, How Food Was Given, Neekna and Chemai, and Turtle and the Eagle - published by Theytus Books, Penticton, B.C., Canada; Wintercount Card Co., Newcastle, CO has purchased 15 of Ken's watercolors and added them to their series of cards by Native American artists.

EDWARDS, LEONARD
(Indian band chief)
Affiliation: Nanoose Indian Band, RR #1, Box 124, Lantzville, BC, Canada V0R 2H0 (604) 390-3661.

EDWARDS, TRACY (Pit River)
(rancheria chairperson)
Affiliation: Redding Rancheria, 2000 Rancheria Rd., Redding, CA 96001 (530) 225-8979.

EDWARDSON, GEORGE (Inupiat)
(AK village president)
Affiliation: Inupiat Community of the Arctic Slope, P.O. Box 1232, Barrow, AK 99723 (907) 825-6907.

EGAN, EILEEN
(Indian program coordinator)
Affiliation: Native American Program, Read House, Appian Way, Harvard University, Cambridge, MA 02138 (617) 495-4923 Fax 496-3312.

EGER, LESLIE
(editor)
Affiliation: Win-Awaenen-Nisitotung, Sault Ste. Marie Tribe of Chippewa Indians, 2218 Shunk Rd., Sault Ste. Marie, MI 49783-9326 (906) 635-6050.

EID, LEROY V. 1932-
(professor of history)
Born December 22, 1932, Cincinnati, Ohio. *Education*: University of Dayton, BS (Education), 1953; St. John's University, MS, 1958, PhD (History), 1961; University of Toronto, MA (Philosophy), 1968. *Principal occupation*: Professor of history. *Home address*: 1181 Kentshire Dr., Centerville, OH 45459 (937) 229-2825 (office). *Affiliation*: Professor, Dept. of History, University of Dayton, 300 College Park, Dayton, OH, 1961- (chairman of dept. 1969-83). *Interests*: Teaching history of American Indians. *Published works*: Articles: "National War Among Indians of Northeastern North America" (Canadian Review of American Studies, Summer, 1985); The Ojibwa-Iroquois War, (Ethnohistory, 1979); "Their Rules of War": The Validity of James Smith's Analysis of Indian War," The Register of the Kentucky Historical Society (Winter, 1988); "A Kind of Running Fight" Indian Battlefield Tactics in the Late Eighteenth Century," The Western Pennsylvania Historical Magazine (April, 1988); :The Slaughter Was Reciprocal" Josiah Harmar's Two Defeats, 1790 (Northwst Ohio Quarterly, Spring, 1993); "American Indian Military Leadership" (Journal of Military History, Jan. 1993).

EISENBERGER, VELMA
(Indian school principal)
Affiliation: Dennehotso Boarding School, P.O. Box LL, Dennehotso, AZ 86535 (520) 658-3201.

ELAM, EARL H. 1934-
(professor of history)
Born December 7, 1934, Wichita Falls, Tex. *Education*: Midwestern University, B.A., 1961; Texas Tech University, MA, 1967, PhD, 1971. *Principal occupation*: Professor of history. *Home address*: Resides in Texas. *Affiliations*: Instructor, Texas Tech University, 1967-71; professor of history, Sul Ross State University, Alpine, TX, 1971-; director, Center for Big Bend Studies, Sul Ross State University, 1987-. *Other professional post*: Editor, Journal of Big Bend Studies, an annual publication dedicated to the history and culture of the Southwest with emphasis on the Big Bend of Texas. *Military service*: U.S. Navy, 1953-57 (Radioman). *Memberships*: Western History Association; West Texas Historical Association (president, 1991-92); Texas State Historical Association. *Interests*: American Indian history; Indian land claims; American Indian ethnology and archaeology; Texas history, Southwestern American history, Spanish borderland history. *Published works*: Several articles and reports; thesis, dissertation, and reports on Wichita Indian history and ethnology.

ELBERT, HAZEL E.
(executive director)
Affiliation: ARROW, Inc., 1000 Connecticut Ave., NW, Suite 1206, Washington, DC 20036 (888) ARROW10; (202) 296-0685 Fax 659-4377.

ELDRIDGE, NEIL
(BIA field rep.)
Affiliation: Taholah Field Office, Bureau of Indian Affairs, P.O. Box 39, Taholah, WA 98587 (360) 276-4850 Fax 276-4853.

ELEAZER, JAMES, JR. (Shinnecock)
(tribal trustee)
Affiliation: Shinnecock Tribe, P.O. Box 59, Southampton, NY 11968 (516) 283-1643.

ELEAZER, KEVIN (Shinnecock)
(tribal trustee)
Affiliation: Shinnecock Tribe, P.O. Box 59, Southampton, NY 11968 (516) 283-1643.

ELGIN, DR. CAROLYN
(college president)
Affiliation: Southwestern Indian Polytechnic Institute,
P.O. Box 10146, 9169 Coors Rd., NW, Albuquerque,
NM 87184 (505) 897-5347 Fax 897-5343.

ELKHART-NAKAI, ANNO
(prevention projects manager)
Affiliation: National Native American AIDS Prevention
Center, 436 14th St., Suite 1020, Oakland, CA 94609
(510) 444-2051 Fax 444-1593.

ELKINS, BRYAN
(health center director)
Affiliation: Fallon Tribal Health Center, P.O. Box 1980,
Fallon, NV 89406 (702) 423-3634.

ELLIOTT, JERRY C. (*High Eagle*) (Osage/Cherokee)
(physicist, author, composer, musician, actor)
Born February 6, 1943, Oklahoma City, Okla. *Education*: BS in Physics, Mathematics. *Principal occupation*: Physicist, author, composer, musician, actor. *Address & Affiliation*: High Eagle Productions, Inc., P.O.
Box 58182, Houston, TX 77258 (281) 483-0819; *E-
mail*: higheagle@ghg.net; *Website*: www.ghgcorp.com/
higheagl. *Other professional posts*: Deputy chief technologist. NASA Johnson Space Center, Houston, TX.
Awards, honors: Presdiential Medal of Freedom; Medal
of Honor from the National Society of Daughters of
the American Revolution; Bronze Halo Award for Outstanding Contributions to Humanity, presented by the
Southern California Motion Picture Council. *Memberships*: American Society of Composers; Authors & Publishers (ASCAP) American Indian Science & Engineering Society, Inc. (AISES); Sigma Xi, Scientific Research
Society. *Interests*: Music, writing, acting, seminar
presenting.*Published works*: Campfire Stories & Legends, Vol. I & II; Soul Fire Odyssey; Lovebeams; Mystic Moods of Love and Life.

ELLIOTT, LEROY J. (Diegueno)
(tribal council chairperson)
Affiliation: Manzanita Band of Mission Indians,
P.O. Box 1302, Boulevard, CA 91905 (619) 766-4930.

ELLIS, RICHARD N. 1939-
(professor)
Born June 6, 1939. *Principal occupation*: Professor.
Address & Affiliation: Director, Institute of Southwest
Studies (1987-present), Fort Lewis College, Durango,
CO 81301 (970) 247-7590. E-Mail: ellis_r@fortlewis.
edu. *Other professional posts*: Consultant, Navajo In-
dian Water Rights in the San Juan Basin; consultant,
"Geronimo and the Apache Resistance," National Ex-
perience Series, PBS; professor, University of New
Mexico, Albuquerque, NM, 1968-86; consultant for
Southern Ute Cultural Center, National Endowment for
the Humanities Grant, 1993-94; Colorado Historical
Fund grant to work with Cheyennes and Arapahos on
Sand Creek Massacre Project, 1995; Colorado His-
torical Fund Grant to Search for the Site of the Sand
Creek Massacre, 1996-97; consultant and research
director, Southern Ute Archives Project; consultant on
Taos Pueblo Water Rights for Historical Research As-
sociates and the Bureau of Indian Affairs, 1996-97;
Expert Witness. *Awards, honors*: Villagra Award for
Teaching, Historial Society of New Mexico; Teacher of
the Year Award, Univesity of New Mexico. *Community
activities*: Southern Ute Museum (board of directors);
Resource Advisory Council, Bureau of Land Management; University Press of Colorado (chairperson, board
of directors); Colorado Historical Records Advisory
Board - expert witness for Cuthair et al v. Cortez/
Montezuma Co. School Board. *Memberships*: Western History Association; Organization of American Historians; Historical Society of New Mexico. *Published
works*: General Pope and U.S. Indian Policy; A Forest
in Trust: Three Quarters of a Century of Indian Forestry (co-author); Colorado: A History in Photographs
(co-author); Cheyenne Dog Soldiers: A Ledgerbook
History of Coups and Combat (co-author, 3/97).

ELLISON, CARL, M.D.
(clinical director)
Affiliation: Claremore PHS Indian Hospital, Will Rogers
& Moore, Claremore, OK 74017 (918) 342-6200.

ELLISON, ROSEMARY
(museum curator)
Affiliations: Curator, Southern Plains Indian Museum,

715 E. Central Blvd., P.O. Box 749 Anadarko,
OK 73005 (405) 247-6221 Fax 247-7593

ELROD, SAM
(IHS-director of administrative services)
Affiliation: Division of Administrative Services, Office
of Administration & Management, Indian Health Service, 5600 Fishers Lane, Room 4B-42, Rockville, MD
20857 (301) 443-0815.

ELUSKA, STEVE
(AK village council chief)
Affiliation: Telida Village Council, P.O. Box 217,
Telida, AK 99629 (907) 843-8115.

ELVASAAS, FRED H.
(AK village council president)
Affiliation: Native Village of Seldova, P.O.
Drawer L, Seldova, AK 99770 (907) 234-7625.

EMANUEL, H. RAY
(executive director)
Affiliation: Native American Indian Association of Tennessee, 932 Stahlman Bldg., 211 Union St., Nashville,
TN 37201 (615) 726-0806 Fax 726-0810.

EMERSON, PAM
(school principal)
Affiliation: Rocky Ridge Boarding School, P.O. Box 299,
Kykotsmovi, AZ 86039 (520) 725-3415. Fax 652-3252.

**EMERY, STEVEN CHARLES (*Mato Tanka*)
(Cheyenne River Sioux) 1958-**
(tribal attorney)
Born November 14, 1958, in S.D. *Education*: Univer-
sity of South Dakota, BA, 1986; Harvard Law School,
JD, 1989. *Principal occupation*: Tribal attorney. *Ad-
dress*: P.O. Box 190, White River, SD 57579 (605) 964-
6686 (office). *Affiliations*: Attorney, Cheyenne River
Sioux Tribe, Eagle Butte, SD, 1989-; partner, Van
Norman & Emery, Eagle Butte, SD, 1989-. *Other pro-
fessional post*: General counsel, Mart Indian School,
Marty, SD, 1990-. *Community activities*: Cheyenne
River Sioux Tribal Police Commission (chairperson,
1989-91); Dakota Plains Legal Services Board of Di-
rectors, 1989-91; Cheyenne River Community College
Board of Directors (vice-chairperson), 1990-. *Member-
ships*: South Dakota Bar Association; Federal Bar As-
sociation; American Bar Association; Eighth Circuit
Court of Appeals, U.S. *Awards, honors*: McGovern-
Abourezk Human Rights Award, USD Political Science/
Criminal Justice Dept., 1985; Phi Beta Kappa (Alpha
Chapter, USD, 1986); Faculty Appreciation Award,
USD Political Science/Criminal Justice Dept., 1986;
Who's Who in American Universities & Colleges (1985-
86 Edition); Massachusetts Indian Association Fellow
(1986-89); U.S. Dept. of Education American Indian
Fellowship Recipient (1986-89). *Interests*: "Traditional
singer (Itazipco Hoka); singer/songwriter; guitarist;
lectures on topics such as: federal Indian law, Lakota/
Dakota culture and language." *Published work*: Musical album - Dakota Wakan Cekiye Odowan (collection
of ten hymns played and sung by Steve Emery in the
Dakota language, June 1986.

EMM, ELWOOD L., JR. (Yerrington Paiute)
(tribal chairperson)
Affiliation: Yerrington Paiute Tribal Council, 171
Campbell Lane, Yerrington, NV 89447 (775) 463-3301.

EMMERT, REG
(archive director)
Affiliation: Alaska's Motion Picture Film Archive Center, P.O. Box 95203, University of Alaska, Fairbanks,
AK 99701 (907) 479-7296.

ENDREZZE ANITA (Yaqui) 1952-
(writer, artist, professor)
Born March 15, 1952, Long Beach, Calif. *Education*:
BA in English & Secondary Education; MA in Creative
Writing. *Principal occupation*: Writer, artist, professor.
Address: Unknown. *Affiliations*: Teach part time in area
universities. *Community activities*: Volunteer art
teacher for daughter's school. *Published works*: The
Mountain and the Guardian Spirit (CDR Forlag, Den-
mark, 1986); At the Helm of Twilight (Broken Moon
Press, 1992); The Humming of Stars and Bees and
Waves (Making Waves Press, 1998); Throwing Fire
at the Sun, Water at the Moon (University of Arizona
Press, 2000).

ENEAS, ADAM
(Indian band chief)
Affiliation: Penticton Indian Band, R.R. #2, Site 80,
Comp. 19, Penticton, British Columbia, Canada V2A
6J7 (604) 493-0048.

ENGELSTAD, KURT (Eskimo-Inupiaq) 1937-
(business executive, attorney)
Born October 3, 1937, Corvallis, Ore. *Education*: Oregon State University, BS, 1960; Northwest School of
Law, Lewis & Clark College, JD, 1972. *Principal occupation*: Business executive, attorney. *Address*: Unknown. E-mail: kinupiaq@aol.com. *Affiliations*: Chairperson of the Board of Directors, The 13th Regional
Corporation, Seattle, WA, 1983-. *Other professional
posts*: Managing member, NW Business Services
Group LLC, of Seattle, WA. *Military service*: U.S. Air
Force (active duty), 1960-61; active Air Force reserve,
1961-; (Lt. Colonel; Air Force Longevity Service Ribbon with hour glass device; Air Force Reserve Medal
with 4 oak leaves; Small Arms Marksmanship Medal);
retired Air Force Reserve. *Community activities*:
Former Boy Scout troop leader; former director and
board chairman, Multnomah County, Oregon legal
services. *Memberships*: Oregon State Bar, 1972-;
Multnomah Bar, 1972-; District Court Bar, 1972-; joint
committee of Oregon Bar with Press and Broadcasters (1974-77 member and chairman). *Awards, honors*: Chief Frank White Buffaloman award for Outstanding Service to the Native American community of Portland, Oregon by Portland Urban Indian Council; Outstanding Journalism graduate for 1960 bestowed by
Sigma Delta Chi honorary, Oregon State University
chapter; appointed by the Governor of Oregon as a
member of the State of Oregon's Workforce Quality
Council; Mail Boxes Etc. Domestic Area Franchisee
of the Year for 1997; Pacific Northwest Franchise Executive of the Year for 1998. *Interests*: Vocational: Indian law, business management and finance;
Avocational: Writing, photography, philately. *Biographical source*: "Natives Without a Land Base," by Elizabeth Roderick, October, 1983 edition Alaska Native
News Magazine; "Between Worlds. How the Alaska
Native Claims Settlement Act Reshaped the Destinies
of Alaska's Native People," 1998, Juneau Empire. *Published works*: Editorial staff, Environmental Law Review of Northwest School of Law of Lewis & Clark College, 1972.

ENGEN, LISA M.
(museum curator)
Affiliation: Wickliffe Mounds Research Center Museum,
P.O. Box 155, Wickliffe, KY 42087 (502) 335-3681.

ENGLEHARDT, KEN
(school supt.)
Affiliation: Takini School, HC77, Box 537,
Howes, SD 57748 (605) 538-4399.

ENGLES, WILLIAM LYNN (Oneida) 1935-
(BIA agency supt.)
Born September 29, 1935, Poplar, Mont. *Education*:
The Evergreen State College, BA, 1974. *Principal occupation*: BIA agency supt. *Address*: Resides in Montana. *Affiliations*: Public information officer, BIA, Washington, DC, 1975-1980; Intergovernmental affairs officer, BIA, Portland, OR, 1980-84; commissioner, Administration for Native Americans, Dept. of Health &
Human Services, Washington, DC, 1984-89; supt.,
Flathead Agency, BIA, Pablo, MT, 1989-. *Other professional posts*: Reporter & Bureau Chief, United Press
International. *Military service*: U.S. Army, 1955-57 (SP-
4). *Community activities*: Indian advisory Council, Boy
Scouts of America.

ENGLISH, SAMUEL F. (Chippewa) 1942-
(artist)
Born June 2, 1942, Phoenix, Ariz. *Education*: Bacone
College, 1960-62; University of San Francisco, 1967-
68. *Principal occupation*: Artist. *Home address*: Resides in Albuquerque, NM. *Affiliation*: Owner, Native
American Art Gallery, Albuquerque, NM, 1982-.

ENGLISH, SHIRLEY (Potawatomi)
(former tribal chairperson)
Affiliation: Huron Potawatomi Indian Council, Pine
Creek Reservation, 2221 1.5 Mile Rd., Fulton, MI
49052 (616) 729-5151.

ENINGOWUK, LUCI (Eskimo)
(AK village president)
Affiliation: Native Village of Shishmaref, P.O. Box 72110, Shishmaref, AK 99772 (907) 649-3751.

ENNO, DARLENE (Turtle Mountain Chippewa)
(college instructor)
Affiliation: Leech Lake Tribal College, 6530 U.S. Hwy. 2 NW, Cass Lake, MN 56633 (218) 335-4220 Fax 335-4209.

ENOS, AMELIA (Pima-Papago)
(director of human services)
Affiliation: American Indian Community House, Human Service Resource Dept., 404 Lafayette St., New York, NY 10003.

ENOS, JERRY O. (Pima-Papago)
(tribal chairperson)
Affiliation: Chairperson, Ak Chin Indian Community Council, 42507 W. Peters & Nall Rd., Maricopa, AZ 85239 (520) 568-2227.

ENYART, CHARLES D. (Eastern Shawnee)
(tribal chief)
Address & Affiliation: Eastern Shawnee Tribe, P.O. Box 350, Seneca, MO 64865 (918) 666-2435 Fax 666-3325.

EPOO, JOHNNY
(president-Indian organization)
Affiliation: Avataq Cultural Institute, Inc., Inukjuak, Quebec; office - 294 Carre St. Louis, Montreal, Quebec H2X 1A4 (514) 844-0109.

ERASMUS, BILLY (Dene)
(president-Dene Nation)
Affiliation: Dene Nation, Denedeh National Office, P.O. Box 2338, Yellowknife, Northwest Territories, Canada Y1A 2P7 (403) 873-4081.

ERASMUS, GEORGES HENRY (Dene) 1948-
(administration)
Born August 8, 1948, Fort Rae, N.W.T., Can. *Education*: High school, Yellowknife, NWT. *Principal occupation*: Co-chair, Royal Commission on Aboriginal Peoples. *Address*: unknown. *Affiliations*: Secretary, Indian Band Council, Yellowknife, NWT, Can., 1969-71; Organizer & chairman, Community Housing Association, Yellowknife, 1969-72; advisor to president, Indian Brotherhood of NWT, 1970-71; fieldworker and regional staff director, Company of Young Canadians, 1970-73; chairman, University Canada North, 1971-75; director, Community Development Program, Indian Brotherhood of Northwest Territories (later the Dene Nation) (director, Community Development Program, 1973-76; president, 1976-83); president, Denedeh Development Corporation, 1976-83; elected Northern vice-chief, Assembly of First Nations, 1983; elected National Chief, Assembly of First Nations, Ottawa, Canada, 1985, re-elected 1988-91; co-chair, Royal Commission on Aboriginal Peoples, Ottawa, ON, 1991-99. *Membership*: Honorary member, Ontario Historical Society, 1990. *Awards, honors*: Representative for Canada on Indigenous Survival International, 1983; Canadian delegate to World Council of Indigenous Peoples International Conferences, 1984-85; appointed director of the World Wildlife Fund of Canada, 1987; appointed to the Order of Canada, 1987; appointed to the Board of the Canadian Tribute to Human Rights, 1987; board member, Energy Probe Research Foundation, Operation Dismantle, 1988; honorary committee member, International Youth for Peace and Justice, 1988; advisory council member, The Earth Circle Foundation, 1988; Honorary Degree of Doctorate of Laws, Queen's University, 1989; board of directors, Earth Day 1990; Board of Directors, SAVE Tour, 1990; art, school, athletic awards. *Interests*: Reading, travel, outdoors, canoeing and art. *Biographical sources*: New Canadian Encyclopedia; Who's Who in Canada. *Published work*: co-author, Drumbeat: Anger and Renewal in Indian Country (Summer Hill Publishers, 1990).

ERDOES, RICHARD
(historian, ethnographer, photographer, author)
Born in Austria. *Address*: unknown. *Published works*: Lame Deer: Seeker of Visions; American Indian Myths & Legends; A.D. 1000: Living on the Brink of Apocalypse; A Sound of Flutes; co-author of Lakota Woman

(made into a movie by Turner Broadcasting); Gift of Power, with Archie Fire Lame Deer & Crying for a Dream (Bear & Co.).

ERDRICH, HEID (Turtle Mountain Chippewa)
(poet)
Address & Affiliation: University of St. Thomas, English Dept. - 30F, St. Paul, MN 55105 (612) 962-5626.

ERDRICH, LOUISE (Turtle Mountain Chippewa)
(writer)
Address: c/o Harper Collins Publishing, 10 E. 53 St., New York, NY 10022 (800) 242-7737.

ERIACHO, DONALD (Zuni)
(pueblo council governor)
Affiliation: Zuni Pueblo Tribal Council, P.O. Box 339, Zuni, NM 87327 (505) 782-4481.

ERIACHO, OLA (Zuni)
(craftsperson)
Affiliation: Co-owner, Eriacho Arts & Crafts, P.O. Box 912, Zuni, NM 87327. *Memberships*: Council for Indigenous Arts & Culture; Indian Arts & Crafts Association.

ERIACHO, TONY (Zuni)
(craftsperson)
Affiliation: Co-owner, Eriacho Arts & Crafts, P.O. Box 912, Zuni, NM 87327. *Memberships*: Council for Indigenous Arts & Culture (vice-president); Indian Arts & Crafts Association.

ERICKSON, VINCENT O. 1936-
(professor of anthropology)
Born January 17, 1936, Mount Vernon, Wash. *Education*: University of Washington, BA, 1958, MA, 1961, PhD, 1968. *Principal occupation*: Professor of anthropology. *Home address*: 175 Southampton Dr., Fredericton, New Brunswick, Can. E3B 4T5. *Affiliation*: University of New Brunswick, Fredericton, Can., 1966-. *Memberships*: American Anthropological Association; American Ethnological Society; Canadian Ethnology Society; American Folklore Society; Canadian Folklore Society. *Interests*: Ethnohistory, ethnolinguistics, ethnography and folklore of the Eastern Algonkians, especially of the Indians of New Brunswick. Indian agent to the Passamaquoddy, 1965-; fieldwork among Passamaquoddy, 1967-, and among the Coast Salish Indians of Washington and British Columbia, 1960-62.

ERMELOFF, LEONTE (Kenaitse)
(AK village council president)
Affiliation: Native Village of Nikolski, Nikolski, AK 99638 (907) 576-2225.

ERNST, CLYDE
(museum director/curator)
Affiliation: Coronado-Quivira Museum, 221 E Ave. So., Lyons, KS 67554 (316) 257-3941.

ERVIN, CAROL (Yurok)
(rancheria chairperson; director-Indian health program)
Affiliation: Trinidad Rancheria, P.O. Box 630, Trinidad, CA 95570 (707) 677-0211; director, Chapa-De (Auburn) Indian Health Program, Auburn, CA; Northern Valley Indian Health Program, 827-A S. Tehama St., Willows, CA 95988.

ERWIN, SARAH
(curator of archival collections)
Affiliation: Thomas Gilcrease Institute of American History & Art Library, 1400 Gilcrease Museum Rd., Tulsa, OK 74127 (918) 596-2700.

ESBER, JR., GEORGE S. (Tchuggi) 1939-
(ethnographer)
Born July 10, 1939, Canton, Ohio. *Education*: Western Reserve University, MA, 1964; University of Arizona, MA, 1976, PhD, 1977; University of Cincinnati, MSW, 1985. *Principal occupation*. Ethnographer. *Home address*: U.S. Dept. of the Interior, National Park Service, P.O. Box 728, Santa Fe, NM 87501 (505) 988-6777 (work). *Affiliations*: Ethnographer, Office of American Indian Programs, National Park Service, Santa Fe, NM, 1991-; professor of anthropology, Earlham College, Richmond, IN, 1988-91; professor of anthropology, Miami University, Oxford, OH, 1979-88. *Com-

munity activities: Secretary of the Board for Extended Total Curriculum (Gifted Program), Oxford, OH. *Memberships*: Native American Rights Fund; Society for Applied Anthropology; National Association of Practicing Anthropologists; American Anthropological Association; Society of Sigma Xi; Central States Anthropological Association; National Geographic Society. *Awards, honors*: Archaeological expeditions at San Xavier del Bac, Tucson, and a Yana village site, Northern California. Field research on the Tonto Apache Reservation in Payson, Arizona. *Published works*: Numerous articles in journals, and edited volumes.

ESCUDERO, GARY, M.D.
(clinical director)
Affiliation: Gallup Indian Medical Center, P.O. Box 1337, Gallup, NM 87305 (505) 722-1000.

ESKEET, EDISON
(organization executive director)
Affiliation: Executive director, Wings of America, The Earth Circle Foundation, Inc., 1601 Cerrillos Rd., Santa Fe, NM 87505 (505) 982-6761 Fax 988-3879.

ESKILIDA, KAREN (Athapascan)
(AK village president)
Affiliation: Native Village of Chitina, P.O. Box 241, Gakona, AK 99586 (907) 822-3503.

ESKOFSKI, M. LOLLIE (New York Oneida) 1949-
(Indian education program coordinator)
Born January 22, 1949, Waukegan, Ill. *Education*: Associates Degree in Communications/English. *Principal occupation*: Indian education program coordinator. *Address & Affiliation*: Title VII coordinator (1991-present), Rapid River Public Schools, P.O. Box 68, Rapid River, MI 49878 (906) 474-6411 ext. 572 Fax 474-9883. E-Mail: leskofski@rapidriver.k12.mi.us. *Other professional posts*: Senior class advisor; Yearbook advisor. *Community activities*: Eucharistic minister; lector @ church. *Interests*: Gardening, photography, camping, baseball, football, animals, Chicago Cubs.

ESPARZA, TONSASHAY (Eskimo)
(AK village president)
Affiliation: Chinick Eskimo Community (aka Golovin), P.O. Box 62020, Golovin, AK 99762 (907) 779-3521.

ESQUERRA, L. FLINT
(filmmaker)
Address: P.O. Box 1753, Salt Lake City, UT 84110-1753.

ESQUERRA, RALPH
(BIA-project engineer)
Affiliation: San Carlos Irrigation Project, BIA, P.O. Box 250, Coolidge, AZ 85228 (520) 723-5439..

ESQUIRO, PETE
(village council president)
Affiliation: Sitka Community Association, 456 Katlian St., Sitka, AK 99835 (907) 747-3207.

ESTEVES, PAULINE (Timbisha Shoshone)
(tribal chairperson)
Address & Affiliation: Chairperson, Historic Preservation Committee and Tribal Council, Timbisha Shoshone Tribe, P.O. Box 206, Death Valley, CA 92328 (760) 786-2374 Fax 786-2375; E-mail: timbisha@aol.com. *Community activities*: Alliance to Protect Native Rights in National Parks Historic Preservation Committee; enrollment committee for Timbisha Shoshone Tribe. *Memberships*: National Congress of American Indians; Toiyabe Indian Health Project, Inc.; California Indian Manpower Consortium. *Published work*: The Timbisha Shoshone Tribe and Their Living Valley, written by the Timbisha Historic Preservation Committee.

ETTAWAGESHIK, FRANK (Odawa)
(tribal president)
Affiliation: Little Traverse Bay Bands of Odawa Indians, P.O. Box 246, 915 Emmet St., Petoskey, MI 49770 (616) 439-3836.

ETTER, PATRICIA A.
(librarian/archivist)
Born in Winnipeg, Manitoba, Can. *Education*: California State University, Long Beach, BA (Anthropology), 1979; University of Arizona, MLS, 1986. *Principal oc-

cupation: Librarian, archivist. *Home address*: 1051 S. Dobson Rd. #218, Mesa, AZ 85202 (480) 965-0270 (work) Fax 965-0776; E-Mail: patricia.etter@asu.edu. Web site: www.asu.edu/lib/archives/labriola.htm. *Affiliations*: Curator, Labriola National American Indian Data Center & Archivist for Information Services, Dept. of Archives & Manuscripts, Arizona State University, Tempe, AZ, 1988-. *Memberships*: Western History Association, 1986-; Dwight Smith Award Committee for WHA, 1993-96; past sheriff, Scottsdale Corral, Westerners International and current member of Posse 1986-; member, editorial advisory board, "Overland Journal; Society of Southwestern Archivist; Society of Southwestern Authors; Arizona & California Historical Societies. *Awards, honors*: Outstanding Alumna, Anthropology, California State University, Long Beach, 1992; Beta Pi Mu International Library Honor Society, 1986; elected Phi Kappa Phi Honor Society, 1979; and recipient of two Coke Wood Awards from Westerners International for best article on American history published in a journal, 1993 & 1995. *Interests*: "Major area of research & publication is the history of Southwestern trails in Arizona, New Mexico and California in the mid to late 1800s. I don't claim any tribal affiliation though my great, great grandmother was Cree." *Published works*: Editor, American Odyssey (University of Arkansas Press, 1986; numerous journal articles & book reviews dealing with Southwestern topics including Native Americans; author, The Southern Route 1849: An Annotated History & Bibliography (The Arthur H. Clark Co., 1998).

ETTINGER, RICHARD PRENTICE 1922-
(school president)
Born September 27, 1922, New York, N.Y. *Education*: Dartmouth College, AB, 1947. *Principal occupation*: School president. *Address*: Resides in Santa Fe, NM (505) 989-3511 (work). *Affiliation*: President, Native American Preparatory School, Santa Fe, NM. *Community activities*: Board of Directors, Native American Preparatory School; President's Circle, National Academy of Sciences; Board of Advisors, Whittier School of Law. *Interests*: Environmental to Native American affairs. Ettinger Scholarships - provides educational grants—scholarships to Native American students.

EULER, ROBERT C. 1924-
(tribal anthropologist)
Born August 8, 1924, New York, N.Y. *Education*: Arizona State College, BA, 1947, MA, 1948; University of New Mexico, PhD (Anthropology), 1958. *Principal occupation*: Consulting anthropologist. *Home address*: 724 W. Pine Knoll Dr., Prescott, AZ 86303 (520) 445-8863. *Affiliations*: Ranger, National Park Service, Wupatki National Monument, 1948-49; anthropological consultant, Albuquerque Area Office, BIA, 1950-51; instructor, associate professor, Arizona State College, 1952-64; curator of anthropology, Museum of Northern Arizona, 1952-56; research associate, Museum of Northern Arizona, 1956-; associate professor, professor and chairman, Dept. of Anthropology, University of Utah, 1964-79; adjunct professor, Dept. of Anthropology, Arizona State University, 1979-94; tribal anthropologist, Yavapai-Prescott Indian Tribe. *Other professional posts*: Anthropological consultant, Hualapai Tribe, land claim litigation, 1953-57; member, board of trustees, Museum of Navajo Ceremonial Art, 1954-64; anthropological consultant, U.S. Department of Justice, Southern Paiute land claim litigation, 1956; consultant in cross-cultural education, Phoenix, AZ, public school system, 1961, '64; ethnohistorian, Upper Colorado River Basin Archaeological Salvage Project, University of Utah, 1962; Arizona Governor's Historical Advisory Committee, 1961-64; ethnohistorical consultant, Arizona Commission on Indian Affairs, 1962-64; anthropological consultant, Operation Headstart, U.S. Office of Economic Opportunity, involving Navajo, Paiute, Mojave, and Chemehuevi participation, 1965. *Memberships*: American Anthropological Association (Fellow); American Ethnological Society; Society for Applied Anthropology (Fellow); Society for American Archaeology; Current Anthropology (associate); American Association for the Advancement of Science (Fellow); American Indian Ethnohistoric Conference; The Society for Sigma Xi; The Western History Association; Arizona Academy of Science (charter member; president, 1962-1963); Arizona Archaeological & Historical Society; New Mexico Historical Society; New Mexico Archaeological Society; Utah Historical Society. *Awards, honors*: Society for Ameri-

can Archaeology 50th Anniversary Award, for Outstanding Contributions to American Archaeology, 1985; Fellow, Museum of Northern Arizona, Flagstaff, 1985. *Interests*: Ethnographic fieldwork involving historical ethnography, ethnohistory and applied anthropology among the Navajo, Hopi, Walapai, Havasupai, Yavapai, Chemehuevi, Southern Paiute, Southern Ute, Isleta Pueblo, and Zia Pueblo; historical archaeological research in Walapai, Havasupai, Yavapai, and Southern Paiute sites. *Published works*: Editor, Woodchuck Cave, A Basketmaker II Site in Tsegi Canyon, Arizona, with H.S. Colton (Museum of Northern Arizona, 1953); Walapai Culture History (University of New Mexico, doctoral dissertation, University Microfilms, 1958); Southern Paiute Archaeology in the Glen Canyon Drainage: A Preliminary Report (Nevada State Museum, 1963); Havasupai Religion & Mythology (Anthropological Papers, University of Utah, 1964); with Henry F. Dobyns: The Havasupai People, The Hopi People, The Paiute People, The Navajo People; The Walapai People (Indian Tribal Series, 1971, 72, 76); Havasupai of Arizona, 1150-1890 (Clearwater, 1974); Havasupai Historical Data (Garland Publishing, 1974); with Dobyns: Indians of the Southwest: A Critical Bibliography (Indiana University Press, 1980); The Grand Canyon: Intimate Views, with Frank Tikalsky, editor (University of Arizona Press, 1993); Havasupai Legends: Religion & Mythology of the Indians of Grand Canyon (University of Utah Press, 1994); numerous articles, reviews and monographs.

EVANOFF, LARRY (Eskimo)
(former village president)
Affiliation: Native Village of Chanega Council, P.O. Box 8079, Chanega Bay, AK 99574 (907) 573-5132.

EVANS, ANITA
(Indian education program director)
Affiliation: Royal Valley Unified School District #337, Indian Education Program, P.O. Box 155, Mayetta, KS 66509 (913) 966-2251 Fax 966-2253.

EVANS, MICHAEL C. (Snohomish)
(former tribal vice-chairperson)
Affiliation: Snohomish Tribe, 18933 59th Ave., NE, Arlington, WA 98223.

EVANS, RALPH
(council chairperson)
Affiliation: North Carolina Advisory Council on Indian Education, c/o Hope County Schools, P.O. Box 468, Halifax, NC 27839.

EVANS, WAYNE H. (*Wokopacola*) (Rosebud Sioux) 1938-
(associate professor of education)
Born April 19, 1938, Rosebud, S.D. *Education*: Black Hills State College, BS, 1962; University of South Dakota, EdD, 1976. *Principal occupation*: Associate professor of education. *Home address*: 24 S. Pine, Vermillion, SD, 57069 (605) 677-5808 (work). *Affiliation*: Associate Professor of Education, University of South Dakota, Vermillion, 1969-. *Other professional post*: Drum keeper, lead singer on drum. *Community activities*: Evening study time lab for Native American children - facilitator. *Memberships*: South Dakota Indian Education Association (former president); South Dakota Indian Counselor's Association. *Awards, honors*: Outstanding Young Man of America. *Interests*: Counseling, guidance; family therapy; values - value orientation. *Biographical sources*: Who's Who Among the Sioux (Institute of Indian Studies, University of South Dakota, 1987). *Published work*: Indian Student Counseling Handbook (Black Hills State College, 1977); Bicultural Teaching Method & Materials (University of South Dakota, 1987); Issues in Undergraduate Education - chapter on: Native Americans in Undergraduate Education (Univ. of South Dakota, 1988).

EVANS-WIDENHOUSE, JOY
(editor)
Affiliations: Cherokee Voice," Cherokee Boy's Club, Cherokee Center for Family Services, P.O. Box 507, Cherokee, NC 28719 (704) 497-5001.

EVELYN, DOUGLAS
(museum director of public affairs)
Affiliation: National Museum of the American Indian, Smithsonian Institution, 470 L'Enfant Plaza, SW,#7103, Washington, DC 20560 (202) 287-2525 Fax 287-3369.

EVENINGTHUNDER, L. DAVID (Shoshone) 1947-
(owner/manager, artist)
Born May 3, 1947, Western Shoshone Hospital, Idaho/Nevada border. *Education*: Lee College, A.A., A.S.T., AGS, 1986; Sam Houston State University, B.A., 1989. *Principal occupation*: Owner/manager, artist. *Address*: 5926 Indian Springs, Livingston, TX 77351-9524 (936) 563-3200. *Affiliation*: Owner, Contemporary Native American Art, Coldspring, TX, 1989-. *Military service*: U.S. Strategic Air Command, 1966-67 Sgt. *Community activities*: Member, Shoshone-Bannock Tribe & San Jacinto Historical Society; alumnus, Sam Houston State University.

EVERETT, BETTY JOE (KERR) (Choctaw) 1926-
(civil engineer)
Born August 21, 1926, Oklahoma City, Okla. *Education*: University of Oklahoma, BS (Civil Engineering), 1946; Louisiana State University, MS (Civil Enginnering-Transportation & Planning), 1969. *Principal occupation*: Civil engineer. *Home address*: 6507 Vickburg St., New Orleans, LA 70124 (504) 486-3923. *Affiliations*: Design construction and supervision on various engineering projects, 1946-69; civil engineer, City of New Orleans, 1969-78; owner/president, Chatah, Inc., New Orleans, 1978-86; director, Department of Streets, City of New Orleans, 1986-91; consultant to engineering firms (C&S Engineering, Perrin & Associates, Moreland & Altobelli, New Orleans), 1991-. *Community activities*: Gulf South Minority Purchasing Council (board of directors); Louisiana Institute for Indian Development (board of directors); American Career Council for Women; Munholland United Methodist Church (board of trustees). *Memberships*: American Public Works; National Society of Professional Engineers; Society of Women Engineers; American Indian Science and Engineering Society. *Awards, honors*: Supplier of the Year Award, NMSDC, 1980; Achievers Awards 1983, New Orleans; Distinguished Engineer Award, University of Oklahoma, 1991. *Interests*: "I have always been interested in the problems of opening engineering schools in the metro New Orleans area to women and minorities who might be interested in engineering careers. Working closely with Tulane University and University of New Orleans Engineering Departments and Xavier Uiversity, Dominican College and Delagdo Community College, we created a new five-year engineering curriculum. One of my goals in life has been to ease the road into engineering for women and minorities who come after me. I feel that we have created a model program in New orleans that will help make that possible."

EVERETT, LESTER OLIVER
(Indian band chief)
Affiliation: Berens River Indian Band, Berens River, Manitoba, Canada R0B 0A0 (204) 382-2161.

EVERS, LARRY
(professor)
Education: University of Nebraska, PhD, 1972. *Affiliation*: Professor, American Indian Studies Program, The University of Arizona, Harvill Bldg., Rm. 430, P.O. Box 210076, Tucson, AZ 85721 (520) 621-7108 Fax 621-7952. E-mail: aisp@email.arizona.edu. *Interests*: American Indian Literature.

EWAN, G. GLENDA (Athapascan)
(AK village council president)
Affiliation: Gulkana Village Council, P.O. Box 254, Gakona, AK 99586 (907) 822-5213.

EWAN, NORMAN (Athapascan)
(ex-AK village first chief)
Affiliation: Mentasta Lake Village, P.O. Box 6019, Mentasta Lake, AK 99780 (907) 291-2319

EWAN, ROY S. (Athabascan) 1935-
(corporate president)
Born February 2, 1935, Copper Center, Alaska. *Education*: High school. *Principal occupation*: Corporate president. *Home address*: P.O. Box 242, Gakona, AK 99586 (907) 822-3476 (office). *Affiliations*: President, Ahtna, Inc., Drawer G, Copper Center, AK; board member, Grandmet/Ahtna; board member, Ahtna Development Corporation. *Other professional posts*: Serves as ex-officio member on all corporate committees, and shareholder committees and subsidiary boards. *Military service*: U.S. Army, 1953-55 (Corporal). *Community activities*: Gulkana Village Council (Indian educa-

tion, past president). *Memberships*: Alaska Federation of Natives (board member); Alaska Native Federation; The Alliance. *Awards, honors*: 1985 AFN Citizen of the Year, Alaska Federation of Natives.

EWEN, ALEX
(editor)
Affiliation: "Native Nations," (magazine), Solidarity Foundation, 310 W. 52nd St., New York, NY 10019 (212) 765-9731 Fax 956-4211

EWERS, JOHN CANFIELD
***(Little Chief-Blackfeet)*1909-**
(anthropologist/ethnologist)
Born July 21, 1909, Cleveland, Ohio. *Education*: Dartmouth College, BA, 1931, DSc, 1968; Yale University, MA (Anthropology), 1934; University of Montana, LLD, 1966. *Principal occupation*: Anthropologist/ethnologist. *Home address*: 4432 - 26th Rd. N., Arlington, VA 22207 (703) 524-1775. Affiliations: Field curator, Museum Division, National Park Service, 1935-40; curator, Museum of the Plains Indian, 1941-44; associate curator of ethnology, planning officer, U.S. National Museum, Smithsonian Institution, 1946-59; director, Museum of History and Technology, Smithsonian, 1959-65; senior scientist, Office of Anthropology, 1965-79, now ethnologist emeritus, Department of Anthropology, Smithsonian Institution, Washington, D.C. *Other professional posts*: Museum planning consultant, Bureau of Indian Affairs, 1948-49; Montana Historical Society, 1950-54; editor, Journal of the Washington Academy of Sciences, 1955; member, editorial board, The American West, Western Historical Quarterly, and Great Plains Quarterly, 1979-; consultant, American Heritage, 1959; research associate, Museum of the American Indian, Heye Foundation, 1979-. Military service: U.S. Navy, 1944-46 (Lieutenant). *Memberships*: American Indian Ethnohistoric Conference (president, 1961); Rochester Museum of Arts and Science (Fellow); Sigma Xi (president, D.C., chapter); Western History Association (honorary life member). *Awards, honors*: Recipient First Exceptional Service Award for contributions to American history and ethnology, Smithsonian Institution, 1965; Oscar O. Winthor Award, Western History Association, 1976; Distinguished Published Writings in the Field of American Western History, 1985, Western History Association; Honor Award of Native American Arts Studies Association for contribution to the field, 1989; Gold Medal, Buffalo Bill Historical Center, Cody, WY, for contributions to western history and ethnology, 1991. *Interests*: Field research in ethnology and ethnohistory conducted among the Blackfeet tribes of Montana and Alberta (Canada), the Assiniboine of Montana, the Flathead of Montana, the Sioux of South Dakota, and the Kiowa of Oklahoma; studies of Indian art since 1932. Biographical sources: Who's Who in America; The Reader's Encyclopedia of the American West, 1977, by Howard Lamar, editor; Plains Indian Studies, Douglas H. Ubelaker and Herman J. Viola, editors (Smithsonian Contribution to Anthropology) - a collection of essays in honor of John C. Ewers and Waldo R. Wedel (includes a complete list of John C. Ewer's approximately 163 publications through 1981; Fifth Annual Plains Indian Seminar in Honor of Dr. John C. Ewers, George Horse Capture and Gene Ball, editors (Buffalo Bill Historical Center, 1984); Western Historical Quarterly (April, 1986). *Published works*: Mr. Ewers writes, "My research and publications over a period of more than fifty years have been primarily on the history, art, and culture of the Plains Indians, the work of non-Indian artists who pictured those Indians, and on the museum interpretation of American Indians' art and culture." Among authored books — Plains Indian Painting (Stanford University Press, 1940); The Horse in Blackfeet Indian Culture (Smithsonian Institution, 1955; reprinted in Classics of Smithsonian Anthropology Series, 1980); The Blackfeet: Raiders on the Northwestern Plains (University of Oklahoma Press, 1958); Artists of the Old West (Doubleday, 1965); Indian Life on the Upper Missouri (University of Oklahoma Press, 1968); Murals in the Round: Painted Tipis of the Kiowa and Kiowa-Apache Indians, 1978; Plains Indian Sculpture, Traditional Art from America's Heartland (Smithsonian Institution, 1986); Plains Indian History and Culture (University of Oklahoma Press, 1997). *Editor*: Adventures of Zenas Leonard, Fur Trader, 1959; Crow Indian Medicine Bundles, 1960; Five Indian Tribes of the Upper Missouri by Edwin Thompson Denig (University of Oklahoma Press, 1961); O-Kee-pa: A Religious Ceremony and Other Customs of the Mandans, (George Catlin), 1967; Indians of Texas in 1830 (Smithsonian Institution, 1969); Indian Art in Pipestone, George Catlin's Portfolio in the British Museum, 1979. In addition, published chapters in more than 20 books and more than 150 articles in some 40 journals of anthopology, art or history.

EXENDINE, LEAH
(health center director)
Affiliation: Lassen Indian Health Center, Susanville Indian Rancheria, 745 Joaquin St., Susanville, CA 96130 (916) 257-2542.

EXENDINE, PEGGY
(BIA field rep.)
Affiliation: West-Central Alaska Field Office, Bureau of Indian Affairs, 3601 C St., Suite 1100, Anchorage, AK 99503 (907) 271-4088 Fax 271-4083.

EYAHPAISE, DON
(Indian band chief)
Affiliation: Okemasis Indian Band, Box 312, Duck Lake, Saskatchewan, Canada S0J 1J0 (306) 466-4959.

EYRAUD, COLBERT H.
(museum director)
Affiliation: Cabot's Old Indian Pueblo Museum, 67-616 E. Desert View Ave., Desert Hot Springs, CA 92240 (619) 329-7610.

EZOLD, JUNE O. (*Migizi Manitou Equay*) (Brothertown Indians of Wisconsin) 1922-
(retired-ad counselor; tribal chairperson)
Born August 20, 1922, Fond du Lac, Wisc. *Education*: High school. *Principal occupation*: Ad Counselor-retired. *Home address*: 2848 Witches Lake Rd., Arbor Vitae, WI 54568 (715) 542-3913 Fax 542-3269. E-mail: jezold@nnex.net. *Affiliations*: Senior Clerk, MONY, Milwaukee, WI, 1939-47; Ad Counselor, Milwaukee Journal/Sentinel, 1964-81, Marian College Library, Fond du Lac, WI, 1981-96. *Other professional post*: Chairperson, Brothertown Indians of Wisconsin. *Community activities*: PTA (president & city council secretary); Cub Scout Den Mother Instructor; Girl Scout Leader; Deacon Calvary Lutheran Church (council member, lay reader); Task Force for Ministry with Native Americans, Evangelical Lutheran Church. *Memberships*: HONOR-AARP, Smithsonian Institute; Fond du Lac Historical Society.

F

FADDEN, JOHN (*Kahionhes*) (Mohawk-Turtle Clan) 1938-
(painter, illustrator; museum director)
Born December 26, 1938, Massena, N.Y. (near Akwesasne, St. Regis Indian Reservation). *Education*: Rochester Institute of Technology, BFA, 1961. *Principal occupation*: Art teacher, artist, illustrator. *Address*: Six Nations Indian Museum, HCR 1, Box 10, Onchiota, NY 12989 (518) 891-2299. *Affiliations*: Art teacher, Saranac Central School District, Saranac, NY, 1961-94; staff curator & director, Six Nations Indian Museum, Onchiota, NY, 1954-present. *Other professional posts*: Museum curator; illustrator, consultant. *Exhibitions*: Six National Indian Museum, 1954-present; Penn State Museum, Harrisburg, 1962; "Art of the Iroquois," Erie County Savings Bank, Buffalo, 1974; New York State Fair, Syracuse, 1977; The Woodland Indian Cultural - Educational Centre, Brantford, Ontario, 1977, '80, '84; American Indian Community House Gallery, New York City, 1977, '80, '82, '84; Akwesasne Museum, Hogansburg, NY, 1980; Schoharie Museum of the Iroquois Indian, 1981-85; Iroquois Indian Festival II, feature artist, Cobleskill, NY 1983; Akwesasne: Our Strength, Our Spirit, World Trade Center, New York City, 1984; "The Iroquois Experience: A Festival of the Arts," North Country Community College, Saranac Lake, NY, 1993; among others. Also numerous illustrations in periodicals, cover illustrations, calendar illustrations, and posters. *Community activities*: Advisory Committee, North American Indian Traveling College, Akwesasne Mohawk Territory; Akwesasne Mohawk Board of Education; Cornell University, Ithaca, NY, American Indian Program Advisory Committee; Round Dance Productions, Inc., Thirty Two Acres Oneida Territory, board of directors. *Memberships*: NY State Education Dept. (Native American Social Studies Writers Committee); NY State Museum (Native Peoples of New York Exhibition Advisory Committee); Round Dance Productions (Board of Directors); Tree of Peace Society (Board of Directors); Iroquois Indian Museum; and Viola White Water Foundation (Board of Directors). *Interests*: As John looks back over the years, he sees the 1961-68 period as one of experimentation in which he worked with pen and ink and painted in tempera, selling a few of his works at the family museum (Six Nations Indian Museum), and giving away others. As became more aware of the political changes taking place at Akwesasne, and throughout Native America, he began to make more political statements through his art, mainly through drawings and cover illustrations for Akwesasne Notes, a newspaper published by the Mohawk Nation at Akwesasne. The details of his work typically show native nationalism and political assertiveness based on the traditions of the native peoples. He has illustrated many books and periodicals, and has done cover art for many books; also, calendar art for Akwesasne Notes Calendar, 1972-. He has produced art for films/video: Who Were the Ones (National Film Board of Canada, 1970); Hodenosaunee: People of the Longhouse (Stiles-Akin Films, 1981); The Iroquois Creation Myth (video tape, Image Film, 1982); Why the Bear Clan Know Medicine (Quinn-Sturgeon, 1990); Moyers-Oren Lyons the Faithkeeper (Public Affairs Television, 1991).

FADDEN, RAY
(museum owner)
Affiliation: Six Nations Indian Museum, Onchiota, NY 12968 (518) 891-0769.

FADDEN, STEPHEN
(editor)
Affiliation: The Web, Indigenous Communications Resource Center, American Indian Program, 400 Caldwell Hall, Cornell University, Ithaca, NY 14853 (602) 255-6587.

FAHRER, MARTHA
(cultural center director)
Affiliation: Native American Cultural Center, 1344 University Ave., Suite 230, Rochester, NY 14607 (716) 482-1100 Fax 482-1304.

FAIRBANKS, DEANNA L.
(Chippewa-Ojibway) 1949-
(tribal consultant)
Born May 15, 1949, Leech Lake Reservation, Cass Lake, Minn. *Education*: Bemidji State University, B.A., 1985; University of Minnesota, J.D., 1988. *Principal occupation*: Tribal consultant. *Address*: The Leech Lake Reservation, RR 2, Box 227, Cass Lake, MN 56633 (218) 335-6767. *Affiliation*: Self-employed - consultant in specific federal areas, to tribes only. *Other professional posts*: Special Magistrate for the Court of Central Jurisdiction, the Mille Lacs Band of Ojibwe. *Community activities*: Minnesota Environmental Quality Board & the Minnesota Arts Task Force; committee member, American Indigenous Games to be held in Bemidji, MN in 1995. *Awards, honors*: Minnesota Woman of the Year, 1993 - decreed by Governor Arne Carlson. *Interests*: Tribal sovereignty & jurisdiction. The Self-Governance Act, interpretation & implementation; environmental issues, the arts. "I'm an active Democrat and Politics consumes me."

FAIRBANKS, DEVERY J. (*Ma in ga nens*) (Anishinaabe-White Earth Chippewa) 1957-
(educator)
Born May 24, 1957, Minneapolis, Minn. *Education*: Minneapolis Community College, AA, 1984; University of Minnesota, BA, 1988. *Principal occupation*: Educator. *Address*: Resides in Minnesota *Affiliation*: Admissions officer, American Indian Student Recruiter, University of Minnesota, Minneapolis, MN, 1989-93; Minority Student Services Director, Rainy River Community College, International Falls, MN, 1993-. *Other professional posts*: Free-lance writer, painter, graphic illustrator. *Community activities*: Board member of five American Indian organizations & institutions: Alcohol & Drug treatment Center, Indian Parent Committee, et al. *Memberships*: Minnesota Indian Education Association; National Indian Education Association; American Indian Higher Education Consortium; American Indian Science & Engineering Society; UNITY. *Interests*: "Principal American Indian student recruiter for the University of Minnesota; job requires extensive

travel—numerous friendships and acquaintances nationwide in fields of art, publications, powwows, sports, and chemical dependency. Art and literature: wrote and produced one play, "A Long Road for Milo," reviews favorably on both coasts (by Vizenor & Bruchac). Trade, collect, and volunteer at Indian Art Shows in the Southwest, Midwest & Ontario, Canada. Visited over 30 states in the U.S. & Canada; mostly Indian reservations and reserves. Also visited major urban Indian communities." *Biographical source*: Article in the University of Minnesota Counselors Quarterly magazine, March 1992. *Published works*: Articles published in the following periodicals: The Circle (Minneapolis, MN), Anishnabe-Oyate Newsletter (University of Minnesota), the NIEA News (Washington, D.C.), and The Journal (Hayward, WI).

FAIRBANKS, FRANCES
(executive director)
Affiliation: Minneapolis American Indian Center, 1530 E. Franklin Ave., Minneapolis, MN 55404 (612) 871-4555.

FALCON, AUDREY (*Algunkwe*)
(Saginaw Chippewa/Grand River Ottawa) 1953-
(employee relations manager)
Born January 18, 1953, Detroit, Mich. *Education*: Ferris State University (Big Rapids, MI) 1972-74, Registered Nurse, Associate Degree, Health Services Management, 1980-84. *Home address*: 7580 Ogemaw Dr., Mt. Pleasant, MI 48858 (517) 775-4034 (phone & fax). E-mail: afalcon@sagchip.org, *Affiliations*: Health administrator, Nimkee Memorial Wellness Center, Mt. Pleasant, MI, 1977-94; Saginaw Chippewa Indian Tribe, Mt. Pleasant, MI (tribal operations personnel manager, 1994-96, employee relations manager, 1996-). *Community activities*: Saginaw Chippewa Tribal Council (member/treasurer 1990-) Ziibiiwing Cultural Society-Repatriation (board of directors); museum/cultural center planning committee, 1999. *Memberships*: Society for Human Resource Management; Mid Michigan Human Resource Association; American Public Health Association; Michigan Public Health Association; American Red Cross-Local Chapter. *Award*: Indian Health Service, U.S. Public Health Service, Exceptional Performance Award, Nov. 1988.

FALCON, RON
(health center director)
Affiliation: Trenton-Williston Tribal Health Services, P.O. Box 210 Trenton, ND 58853 (701) 774-0461.

FALLEY, NANCI (*Many Spirits Woman*) 1938-
(rancher)
Born October 19, 1938, San Angelo, Tex. *Education*: California Polytechnic Institute (Certificate in Horse Management), 1960. *Principal occupation*: Rancher. *Address & Affiliation*: President, American Indian Horse Registry & Museum, 9028 State Park Rd., Lockhart, TX 78644 (512) 398-6642. *Other professional posts*: President, Indian Horse Hall of Fame, Lockhart, TX; editor, American Indian Horse News.

FAMILIO, DORSIE
(branch library supervisor)
Affiliation: The Seneca Nation Library, Allegany Reservation Branch, P.O. Box 231, Salamanca, NY 14779 (716) 945-3157.

FARIS, JAMES C.
(professor emeritus; author)
Address: Resides in Santa Fe, NM. *Affiliation*: Emeritus Professor of Anthropology, University of Connecticut, Storrs, CT. *Published works*: The Nightway: A History of Documentation of a Navajo Ceremonial; Navajo & Photography: A Critical History of the Representation of an American People (University of New Mexico Press (hardcover), University of Utah Press (paperback), 2003).

FARLEE, CHERIE
(BIA education administrator)
Affiliation: Cheyenne River Agency, Bureau of Indian Affairs, P.O. Box 2020, Eagle Butte, SD 57625 (605) 964-8722; supt., Cheyenne-Eagle Butte School, Eagle Butte, SD 57625 (605) 964-8772 Fax 964-1155.

FARLEE, DONALD
(high school principal)
Affiliation: Tiospaye Topa School, P.O. Box 537, Howes, SD 57652 (605) 733-2290.

FARMER, DELBERT (Shoshone-Bannock)
(tribal chairperson)
Affiliation: Fort Hall Business Council, P.O. Box 306, Fort Hall, ID 83203 (208) 238-3700.

FARMER, GARY (Cayuga)
(editor & publisher)
Affiliation: The Runner, Native Magazine for the Communicative Arts, c/o ANDPVA, 39 Spadina Rd., 2nd Floor, Toronto, ON M5R 2S9 (416) 972-0871 Fax 972-0892. Quarterly magazine.

FARMER, TINA
(head teacher)
Affiliation: Promise Day School, HCR 30, Box 10, Mobridge, SD 57601.

FARR, FONDA
(museum director)
Affiliation: Last Indian Raid Museum, 258 S. Penn Ave., Oberlin, KS 67749 (913) 475-2712.

FARR, WILLIAM
(associate director of humanities & culture)
Address & Affiliation: Center of the Rocky Mountain West, University of Montana, Missoula, MT 59812. *Published works*: The Reservation Blackfeet, 1885-1945.

FARRELL, MARY ANNE, M.D.
(health center director)
Affiliation: United Regional Youth Treatment Center, P.O. Box C-201, Cherokee, NC 28719 (704) 497-3958.

FARRER, CLAIRE R. 1936-
(professor of anthropology)
Born December 26, 1936, New York, N.Y. *Education*: University of California, Berkeley, BA, 1970; University of Texas, Austin, MA (Anthropology/Folklore; Thesis: Performances of Mescalero Apache Clowns), 1974, PhD (Anthropology/Folklore; Dissertation: Play & InterEthnic Communication: A Practical Ethnography of the Mescalero Apache), 1977. *Principal occupation*: Professor of anthropology. *Home address*: 2170 Alicia Point #201, Colorado Springs, CO 80919-5103. *Affiliations*: Weatherford Resident Fellow, School of American Research, Santa Fe, NM, 1977-78; assistant professor of anthropology, University of Illinois - Urbana/Champaign, IL, 1978-85; Dept. of Anthropology, California State University, Chico, CA 95929 (associate professor, 1985-89, professor of anthropology, 89-01; professor emerita, 2001-); visiting professor, Southwest Studies, The Colorado College, Colorado Springs, CO, 2002-. *Other professional posts*: Western Folklore, California Folklore Society (book review editor, 1985-89; executive editor, 1994-99); consulting editor for Archaeoastronomy, 1984-; Anthropology & Humanism, ed. board member; reader for refereed journals; guest lecturer. *Field research*: Individual work with Mescalero Apache Singers of Ceremonies on ritual, religion, medicine, and healing, 1997-; Mescalero Apache Indian Reservation - ethnographic investigation with tribal consent and support, 1975-76; focus on children's free play. Also participant-observation of daily life and ritual activities as well as some linguistic fieldwork, 1974-75; Mescalero Apache Indian Reservation - focused research on ethnoastronomy (summer) with astronomers, 1984 & 1986; general ethnography and ethnoastronomy with Mescalero Apache Indians, 1976-88. Whiteriver, AZ Apache medicine man, 1996-; Also minor, a periodic work on the Warm Springs Confederated Tribe in Oregon in the 1960's and 1970s, and minor work in 1970s and 1980s at various sites in New Mexico including the pueblos of Laguna, San Juan, Santo Domingo, Tesuque, and Zuni. "I also work with Whiteriver, AZ Apaches since 1996." *Memberships*: American Anthropological Association; American Ethnological Society; American Folklore Society; American Society for Ethnohistory; California Folklore Society; Society for Cultural Anthropology; Traditional Cosmology Society (United Kingdom). *Honors, Awards*: Whitney M. Young, Jr. Memorial Foundation Academic Fellow while doing dissertation fieldwork, 1974-75; invited participant for Southwestern Indian Ritual Drama by School of

American Research, Santa Fe, NM; American Philosophical Society, Phillips Fund and University of Illinois-Urbana, $2,500 for transcription/translation of wax cylinders recorded in 1931 at Mescalero, 1982; outstanding teacher at University of Illinois-Urbana, 1985; American Council of Learned Societies grant for ethnoastronomy of the Mescalero Apache; Professional Promise Award and Professional Achievement Award, California State University, Chico, 1987; Student Internship Service Grant to support powwow and other Indian songs taping, California State University, Chico, 1989; private donor grant to work on Southwestern Indian basketry at the Pitt Rivers Museum, University of Oxford, England (summer), 1990; Outstanding Professor, California State University, Chico, 1993-94; Master Teacher, CSU-Chico, 1999-2000; Living Life's Circle (book) chosen as Outstanding Book by CHOICE; also 1st Honorable Mention in Victor Turner Prize for Ethnographic writing; grants also from Thanks Be To Grandmother Winifred Foundation in 1995; and The American Philosophical Society in 1996. *Interests*: Language, travel. *Published works*: Books: editor, Women and Folklore (University of Texas Press, 1976; reissue, Waveland Press, 1986); co-editor, with Edward Norbeck, Forms of Play of Native North Americans (West Publishing, 1979); editor, Play and Inter-Ethnic Communications: A Practical Ethnography of the Mescalero Apache, 31 volume series of outstanding dissertations (Garland, 1990); Living Life's Circle: Mescalero Apache Cosmovision, 8 chapters (University of New Mexico Press, 1991); co-editor, with Ray Williamson, 14 chapters, Earth and Sky: Visions of the Cosmos in Native American Folklore (University of New Mexico Press, 1992); Thunder Rides a Black Horse: Mescalero, Apaches & the Mythic Present (Waveland Press, 1994; 2nd Ed. 1996); Folklore! In Celebration of Ourselves, and Addressing The Divine: Religion in Anthropological Perspective (both undercontract at time of publication). *Books in preparation*: Kaleidoscope Vision & the Rope of Experience (on shamanism); & Reflections: Words to Live By (While Having Cancer). Numerous book chapters; monographs; journal, encyclopedic, newspaper & magazine articles; book reviews; books & articles refereed.

FARRIS, GARY D.
(organization director)
Affiliation: Indians Into Medicine, University of North Dakota, School of Medicine, 501 N. Columbia Rd., Grand Forks, ND 58201 (701) 777-3037.

FARVE, EMIL (Chickasaw)
(editor & publisher)
Affiliation: Chickasaw Times, Chickasaw Nation Tribal Government, P.O. Box 1548, Ada, OK 74820 (405) 436-2603.

FARWELL, ROBERT D.
(museum director)
Affiliation: Fruitlands Museum, 102 Prospect Hill Rd., Harvard, MA 01451 (508) 456-3924.

FAST, DR. PHYLLIS
(professor of anthropology)
Affiliation: Dept. of Anthropology, University of Alaska, 3211 Providence Dr., Anchorage, AK 99508 (907) 786-6840 Fax 786-6850. *Interests*: Alaska Native studies; Athabaskan, Cross-cultural gender. E-mail: ffpaf@uaa.alaska.edu.

FAST HORSE, JOSEPH (Kickapoo)
(school principal.)
Affiliation: Loneman Day School, P.O. Box 50, Oglala, SD 57764 (605) 867-5633.

FAT, MARY WEASEL (*Diving Around Woman*)
(Blood) 1955-
(journalist)
Born December 12, 1955, Cardston, Alberta, Canada. *Education*: Grant McEwan Community College, Edmonton, Alberta (1 Yr. Certificate, Native Communications Program), 1980. *Principal occupation*: Journalist. *Address*: Box 181, Cardston, Alberta T0K 0K0 (403) 737-2854.

FAULKNER, TIM
(Indian education program director)
Affiliation: Los Angeles Unified School District, Indian Education Program, P.O. Box 513307, Los Angeles, CA 90051 (213) 229-2043 Fax 687-7482.

FAVELL, GENE H.
(museum director/president)
Born May 2, 1926, San Francisco, Calif. *Education*: Stanford University, BA. *Affiliation*: Owner, Favell Museum of Western Art and Indian Artifacts, 125 W. Main St., Klamath Falls, OR 97601 (541) 882-9996. *Military service*: U.S. Navy, 1944-47. *Membership*: Kiwanis International. Awards, honors: Honorary Chairman, National Western Art Show; Ace Powell Award, National Western Art Show; Polly Mosby Award; Governor's Art Award & State of Oregon Medal; Environmental Improvement Award, City of Klamath; Best Room Display, National Western Art Show; 1990 Klamath Co. Retailer of the Year.

FAVRHOLDT, KEN
(museum director/curator)
Affiliation: Kamloops Museum & Archives, 207 Seymour St., Kamloops, B.C., Canada V2C 2E7 (604) 828-3576,

FAWCETT, JAYNE GRANDCHAMP
(Mohegan of Connecticut) 1936-
(teacher, assistant curator)
Born January 6, 1936, New London, Conn. *Education*: University of Connecticut, BA, 1957. *Principal occupation*: Teacher, assistant curator. *Affiliations*: Teacher, Ledyard Junior High School, Gales Gerry, CT, 1972-; assistant curator, Tantaquidgeon Indian Museum. *Other professional posts*: Lecturer, American Field Studies. *Interests*: Inspired by the travels of my Aunt, Gladys Tantaquidgeon, my family and I have traveled extensively throughout the western part of America, visiting as many groups of native American as we were able.

FAY, NICK
(health center director)
Affiliation: Indian Health Center of Santa Clara Valley, 1333 Meridian Ave., San Jose, CA 95125 (408) 294-7553.

FEATHER, WALTER
(Indian center operations manager)
Affiliation: Southern California Indian Center, P.O. Box 2550, Garden Grove, CA 92642 (714) 530-0221.

FEHER-ELSTON, CATHERINE (*Kateri*) (Mohawk) 1953-
(historian, author)
Born July 20, 1953. *Education*: Washington State University; University of Texas at Austin, BA (History/Anthropology); MA (History); PhD candidate (American History/Middle East/Energy Resource Development). *Principal occupation*: Historian, author. *Address*: Unknown. E-mail: ravenfair@aol.com or raven@mail.utexas.edu. *Affiliations*: Media Specialist, Navajo-Hopi Task Force, Navajo Tribe, 1982-83; Editor, Navajo-Hopi Observer, 1983-86; founding editor, Hopi Tutu-veh-ni, The Hopi Tribe, 1986-93; instructor of history, Northern Arizona University, History Dept., Flagstaff, AZ, 1990-. *Other professional posts*: Director of Southwest Information (an investigative news and resource agency), 1983-93; news director of the Navajo-Hopi Observer, 1983-85. *Community activities*: Working on building models of sustainable development for the living future of the Colorado Plateau through Canyon Forest Village, 3/97-present; DNA Legal Services, Window Rock, AZ; editor, DNA newsletter; grant proposal writer; Rio Puerco Nuclear Study coordinator. *Awards, honors*: Her book, "Ravensong," won Best Book of 1992 Award from the Rocky Mountain Publishers Association; selected Outstanding Young Woman of America, 1984, for news work with the Navajo-Hopi Observer; selected as an Arizona Humanities Council Scholar, 4/97; selected to present paper at the "Seventh Tampere Conference on North American Studies"; selected to address the "Sixth Maple Leaf and Eagle American Studies Conference" at Helsinki, Finland in May, 1996 - presentation title, "Indians of the Imagination, New Age Hucksterism and Cosmic Profits"; recipient of Southwest Thematic Fellowship for 1997-98; recipient of Graduate Opportunity Fellowship from the University of Texas, 1993-97; recipient of University of Texas Graduate Opportunities Summer Research Award, 1995. *Memberships*: Native American Journalists' Association; Renvall Institute of the University of Helsinki, Finland; American Historical Association; Organization of American Historians; Wildlife Rehabilitation Association; Phi Alpha Theta. *Interests*:

"My interests revolve around cultural diversity, imperialism, ethnohistory, understanding changes in lands and peoples as a result of resource development and colonization; environmental history, law and politics. I am interested in cross-cultural conflict resolution and the interface between people, cultures and their governments. Teaching, writing, research, editing and communication are my strong areas. I have been honored by the friendship, trust and confidence of many tribal leaders and friends among the Navajo, Hopi and Apache, and it is my wish to be a bridge between worlds, tribal worlds, international worlds, corporate worlds and the world of man and nature." *Published works*: Children of Sacred Ground (Northland, 1988); Ravensong: A Natural and Fabulous History of Ravens and Crows (Northland, 1992); The Navajo Cookbook (1982, '83, '84); Comanche History (1997) in progress; Seeds of Empowerment, Seeds of Divisiveness: Indian Organization, Resource Development and the Transformation of the Colorado Plateau.

FELIX, KITTY
(outreach worker)
Affiliation: Native American Services Agency, Missoula Indian Center, 2300 Regent St. #A, Missoula, MT 59801 (406) 329-3373.

FELLER, JOHN (Tlingit)
(AK coop. association president)
Affiliation: Wrangell Cooperative Association, P.O. Box 1198, Wrangell, AK 99929 (907) 874-3482.

FELTY, NORMA L.
(editor)
Affiliation: Anishnabe Dee-Bah-Gee-Mo-Win, White Earth Reservation Tribal Council, P.O. Box 418, White Earth, MN 56591 (218) 983-3285.

FENELON, JAMES
(BIA area director)
Affiliation: Sac & Fox Area Field Office, Bureau of Indian Affairs, 1657 320th St., Tama, IA 52339 (515) 484-4041.

FENTON, WILLIAM NELSON 1908-
(anthropologist)
Born December 15, 1908, New Rochelle, N.Y. *Education*: Dartmouth College, BA, 1931; Yale University, PhD, 1937; Hartwick College, LLD, 1968. *Principal occupation*: Anthropologist. *Home address*: 7 N. Helderberg Parkway, Slingerlands, NY 12159 (518) 439-4385. *Affiliations*: Community worker, U.S. Indian Service, in charge of Tuscarora and Tonawanda Reservations, 1935-37; ethnologist, Smithsonian Institution, Bureau of American Ethnology, 1939-51; executive secretary for anthropology & psychology, National Academy of Sciences, National Research Council, 1952-54; assistant commissioner, State Museum and Science Service, New York State Education Department, 1954-68; research professor of anthropology, SUNY at Albany, 1968-74; distinguished professor emeritus, 1974-79. *Military service*: Research associate, Ethnogeographic Board, 1942-45. *Memberships*: American Anthropological Association (executive board); American Folklore Society (Fellow; past president); American Society for Ethnohistory (past president); American Ethnological Society (past president); American Association for the Advancement of Science (Fellow); Museum of the American Indian (trustee, 1976-89). *Awards, honors*: Adopted Seneca (Iroquois); Peter Doctor Award, Seneca Nation of Indians, 1958, for outstanding service to Iroquoian peoples; Cornplanter Medal for Iroquois Research, Cayuga County Historical Society, 1965; Hon. LLD., Hartwick College, 1968; Dartmouth College Class of 1930 Award, 1979; named Dean in Perpetuum of Iroquoian Studies, 30th Conference on Iroquois Research, 1979; Fulbright-Hays research fellow to New Zealand, 1975; National Endowment for the Humanities fellow, Huntington Library, 1977-1979; member, Iroquois Documentary History Project, Newberry Library, 1979-81. *Published works*: The Iroquois Eagle Dance (Bureau of American Ethnology, 1953); editor, Symposium on Local Diversity in Iroquois Culture (Bureau of American Ethnology, 1955); editor, Symposium on Cherokee and Iroquois Culture (Bureau of American Ethnology, 1961); American Indian & White Relations to 1830 (Institute of Early American History and Culture, University of North Carolina, 1957); Parker on the Iroquois (Syracuse University Press, 1968); editor & translated

with E.L. Moore, Lafitan's Customs of the American Indian (1724) (The Champlain Society, 1974, 1977); The False Faces of the Iroquois (University of Oklahoma Press, 1987).

FERGUSON, BOB (Choctaw)
(museum director)
Affiliation: Choctaw Museum of the Southern Indian, P.O. Box 6010, Philadelphia, MS 39350 (601) 650-1685 Fax 656-6696

FERGUSON, JOHN P.
(editor)
Affiliation: "Museum Notes," Iroquois Indian Museum, P.O. Box 7, Howes Cave, NY 12092 (518) 296-8949.

FERNANDEZ, ARNE G. (Laguna Pueblo) 1953-
(storekeeper)
Born June 2, 1953, Albuquerque, N.M. *Education*: University of New Mexico (5 years). *Principal occupation*: Storekeeper, Laguna Pueblo. *Home address*: 212 Carlisle, NE, Albuquerque, NM 87106 (505) 268-2662. *Membership*: Indian Arts and Crafts Association, 1986-. *Interests*: "I specialize in finding traditional pottery for clients - top museums and collectors. I was a judge for the 1991 & 1992 Gallup Ceremonials. I have dealt with most major potters and their work from a first name basis for over 20 years."

FERREIRA, NANCY
(professor of Native American studies)
Affiliation: Native American Studies Dept., College of St. Scolastica, Duluth, MN 55811 (218) 723-6046.

FICKEL, VIOLET M.
(executive director)
Affiliation: American Native Corporation, 2451 St. Mary's St., Omaha, NE 68102 (402) 341-8471.

FIDDLER, JONAS
(Indian band chief)
Affiliation: Sandy Lake Indian Band, via Favourable Lake, Ontario, Canada P0V 1V0 (807) 774-3421.

FIDDLER, TANYA (Cheyenne River Lakota)
(executive director)
Affiliation: Four Bands Community Fund, P.O. Box 932, Eagle Butte, SD 57625 (605) 964-3687 Fax 964-3689.

FIELD, CAROL
(project director)
Affiliation: Native American Recruitment, National Marrow Donor Program, 7910 Woodmont Ave., Bethesda, MD 20814 (800) 627-7693.

FIELD, RAYMOND
(executive director)
Affiliation: National Tribal Chairman's Association, Washington, DC (202) 293-0031.

FIELDS, JAMES E.
(BIA acting area director)
Affiliation: Muskogee Area Office, Bureau of Indian Affairs, , 101 N. 5th St., Muskogee, OK 74401 (918) 687-2296; supt., Wewoka Agency, Bureau of Indian Affairs, Wewoka, OK.

FIELDS, MIKE
(executive director)
Affiliation: Southwest Missouri Indian Center, 543 S. Scenic Ave., Springfield, MO 65802 (417) 869-9550.

FIFE, BILL S. (Creek)
(tribal chairperson)
Affiliation: Creek Nation of Oklahoma, P.O. Box 580, Okmulgee, OK 74447 (918) 756-8700.

FIFE, GARY D. (Creek, Cherokee) 1950-
(producer/host)
Born September 21, 1950, Tulsa, Okla. *Education*: North East State College, Tahlequah, OK, 1968-72 (Journalism; University Without Walls (Westminster College), B.A., 1974. *Principal occupation*: Producer/ host. *Address*: Unknown. *Affiliation*: One Sky Productions, Ltd., Anchorage, AK 99503 (907) 272-8111, 1993-. *Past professional post*: Producer/host, Alaska Public Radio Network, Anchorage, AK, 1986-93. *Memberships*: Native American Public Broadcasting Consortium (Board member); Alaska Press Club; Native

American Press Association. *Awards, honors*: 1983 Nominee for Outstanding Achievement in Radio, by Native American Public Broadcasting Consortium; 1984 Outstanding Young Men of America; 1988 Men of Achievement by International Biographical Center; 1988 National Public Radio Resident in News & Information by National Public Radio. *Interests*: Traveled to Honduras & Nicaragua to cover refugees' stories; also traveled above Arctic Circle to cover Alaska Native issues. *Biographical sources*: We Alaskans (1/4/87); Daily Courier, Grants Pass, OR (2/19/87); Tulsa World (2/20/87); Olympian (WA) (2/22/87; Tulsa Tribune (2/25/87); Anchorage Daily News; The Arctic Sounder (11/3/89).

FIGHTING BEAR (Navajo/Cherokee)
(teacher supervisor & student counselor)
Education: G.E.D . High School Diploma. *Principal occupation*: Teaching supervisor & student counselor with the public schools. *Address*: 1300 S. Fairview Rd., Columbia, MO 65203. *Affiliation*: Aurora Public Schools-Continuing Education, Aurora, CO ("I teach students 14 years old and up). *Other professional posts*: Owner, Fighting Bear Enterprises (American Indian arts & crafts, stained glass, and cultural presentations), Denver, CO. "I give presentations on American Indian history, culture and art to schools, colleges, corporations, recreation and senior centers, private organizations, government agencies, and the public at large." " I have had professionally paid parts in the following: "The Marz Project" a made for TV movie in 1999; "Larger Than Life" with Bill Murray, released in 1997; "Deep Grease" a comedy spoof on contemporary society" "One on One" with Robbi Benson; and "The Mayor." Had roles in various theatrical productions. *Community activities*: Member, Thunderbird Society ('my Aunt Red Squirrel is the founder and chief elder"); member, Cheery Creek School's, Hope of Our People (H.O.O.P.) Program; member, The Denver Indian Center; member, Native American Multicultural Education School (N.A.M.E.S.). *Awards, honors*: 1980 "One of the Outstanding Young Men in America" by the National Jaycees; 1991 Nominated by Aurora Public Schools for National Teacher of the Year; 1995 Nominated for the national, "Cornelius P. Turner Award, sponsored by the American Council on Education, GED office; 1995 voted by "my people" as the most frequently published American Indian in the greater Denver metro area. *Interests*: " I like to help coordinate powwows; I like to draw; I enjoy visiting other reservations/pueblos during the summer months; I really enjoy and feel honored in being able to spend time with my Aunt Red Quirrel. I get such a great feeling each time I am invited to be a guest speaker at an elementary or high school, a business luncheon or an organizatyional meeting, so, I do it a lot." Published works: Author, The Proud People (an overview of American Indians in the U.S.); poetry in the book, "Suede Milk"; "I won a national poetry writing contest and appear in the book, "The Lasting Joy," published by the National Library of Poetry. Further examples of my poetry can be viewed on the Internet at www.poets.com. I have a picture story in the book, "Algo Dicho, Something Said." I also have picture stories in three national magazines, La Luz, Sports Karate, & Tac Kwon Do Digest."

FIKES, JAY COURTNEY 1951-
(writer/researcher of Native American issues)
Born June 14, 1951, San Luis Obispo, Calif. *Education*: University of California, Irvine, BA, 1973; University of San Diego, MEd, 1974; University of Michigan, MA, 1977, PhD (Anthropology), 1985. *Principal occupation*: Writer -researcher of Native American issues. *Address*: P.O. Box 517, Carlsbad, CA 92018. E-mail: jayfikes@sbcglobal.net. *Affiliations*: Owner of Cuatro Esquinas Traders (Mexican Indian art), 1979-84; land use planner & housing consultant to Navajo Nation, 1983; professor of Social Science Research Methods, Marmara University, Istanbul, Turkey, 1985-87; independent writer, Las Vegas, N.M., 1987-89; legislative secretary specializing in Native American issues, Friends Committee on National Legislation, Washington, DC, 1990-91; post-doctoral fellow, Smithsonian Institution, 1991-92; president, Institute of Investigation of Inter-Cultural Issues, Carlsbad, CA, 1993-; professor, Dept. of Anthropology, Yeditepe University, Istanbul, Turkey, 1999-2004. *Memberships*: Religious Society of Friends. *Awards, honors*: Two academic scholarships from University of Michigan; graduate

cum laude from University of California, Irvine; graduated with honors from the University of San Diego in 1974; awarded Smithsonian fellowship, 1988; Smithsonian Post-Doctoral Fellow in Anthropology, 1991-93. *Interests*: "Translating & interpreting songs & "myths" of the Huichol Indians of Mexico; debunking the books of Carlos Castaneda and his academic allies. I am planning to write more autobiographical and biographical works on Native Americans of today. I am learning how to produce documentary films, including one on the Huichol Indian ritual cycle circa 1934." *Biographical sources*: Who's Who in California; Who's Who in Education, 6th Ed. *Published works*: Huichol Indian Identity and Adaptation (University of Michigan microfilms, 1985); Step Inside the Sacred Circle (Wyndham Hall Press, 1989); Carlos Castaneda, Academic Opportunism, and the Psychedelic Sixties (Millenia Press, 1993); Reuben Snake, Your Humble Serpent (Clear Light Publishers, 1996); Huichol Indian Ceremonial Cycle - film available from Pennsylvania State University, 1997; La Mitologia de los Huicholes (Colegio de Michoacan, 1998); The Man Who Ate Honey (Ambrosia Books, 2003); Huichol Mythology, edited with Phil Weigand and Acelia Garcia de Weigand (University of Arizona Press, 2004).

FINEDAY, MIKE
(Indian band chief)
Affiliation: Witchekan Lake Indian Band, Box 27, Spiritwood, SK, Can. S0J 2M0 (306) 883-2787.

FINLAYSON, WILLIAM D.
(museum executive director)
Affiliation: Museum of Indian Archaeology, University of Western Ontario, Lawson-Jury Bldg., London, ON, Can. N6G 3M6 (519) 473-1360.

FISCUS, CAROLYN K.
(program director)
Affiliation: Native American Student Services, Colorado State University, 312 Student Services Bldg., Fort Collins, CO 80523 (303) 491-1332.

FISHER, JOE (Blackfeet) 1943-
(photographer/filmmaker)
November 19, 1943, Santa Monica, Calif. *Education*: Haskell Indian Jr. College, AA, 1964; Northern Montana College, 1964-66; University of Montana, 1973-74; Montana State University, Film/TV Production, 1994. *Principal occupation*: Photographer/filmmaker *Home address*: P.O. Box 944, Browning, MT 59417 (406) 338-7869. *Affiliation*: Historical documenter, photographer, Blackfeet Tribe, Browning, MT. *Community activities*: American Legion; Blackfeet Societies: Rough Rides, Slickfoot, and Crazy Dog. *Military service*: U.S. Army (Sp-5 Engs.) (Vietnam Service Unit Commendation). *Membership*: VFW. *Award*: The Montana State Alumni Award of Excellence in Film & TV Production, Oct. 1993. *Interests*: Photographic showing, Indian Pride on the Move, in Browning, Missoula, Helena; Blackfeet art slide presentation. Presently working on TV documentaries on the Blackfeet & a Crow Indian elder. *Published work*: Blackfeet Nation, 1977. *Video*: Produced & directed with D. Kipp, "Transitions," 1992.

FISHER, LLEVANDO (*Cowboy*)
(Northern Cheyenne)
(tribal council president)
Affiliation: Northern Cheyenne Tribal Council, P.O. Box 128, Lame Deer, MT 59043 (406) 477-8284.

FISHER, REIS
(administrative officer)
Affiliation: Blackfeet PHS Indian Hospital, Browning, MT 59417 (406) 338-6153.

FISHER, SAM
(Indian center chairperson)
Affiliation: Genessee Indian Center, 609 W. Court St., Flint, MI 48503 (313) 239-6621.

FITZSIMMONS, GENEVA (Luiseno)
(ex-tribal chairperson)
Affiliation: La Jolla Band of Mission Indians, Star Route, Box 158, Valley Center, CA 92082 (619) 742-3771.

FIXICO, DONALD L.
(profesor of history)
Affiliation: History Dept., Western Michigan University, Kalamazoo, MI 49008 (616) 387-4650.

FIXICO, JUNE (Creek)
(town king)
Affiliation: Kialagee Tribal Town, 318 S. Washila, Box 332, Wetumpka, OK 74883 (405) 452-3263.

FLAIG, EVETTE NICKELL (*Snowolf*)
(Cherokee) 1930-
(artisan)
Born January 18, 1930. *Education*: University of Louisville, LBST. *Principal occupation*: Artisan, all media. *Address*: Wooden Nickell & Phoenix Enterprises, P.O. Box 9662, Panama City, FL 32417 (850) 234-5467. *Affiliations*: Writer for Beach Bay News Weekly, P.C. Beach Florida (three years); pow-wows, AZ, TX, OK (six years). *Membership*: American Indian Federation (Intertribal). *Interests*: All things of nature and the environment, etc. for my photo graphic posters; photography; designing jewelry, aintings, etc. for judged museum shows and art shows. Writing book with Paul William Flaig (White Bear).

FLAIG, PAUL WILLIAM (*White Bear*)
(Cherokee) 1941-
(retired detective, NYPD)
Born January 18, 1941, Brooklyn, NY. *Eduaction*: Columbia University. *Principal occupation*: Retired Detective, NYPD. *Address*: Wooden Nickell & Phoenix Enterprises, P.O. Box 9662, Panama City, FL 32417 (850) 234-5467. *Affiliation*: Vice president, American Indian Federation, Inc., Panama City, FL. *Other professional post*: Pow wow honor guard - opening ceremonies. *Miltary service*: U.S. Army, 1969-71 (1st Air Calvery-helicopter pilot). *Community activities*: Traveling with our small business to powwows and other educational events. Interest: Nature and the environment. *Published works*: Dawn Comes Early (Nam' stories); Travels With the Wind (police stories); Powwow & Indian Philosophies.

FLEMING, CANDACE
(association president)
Affiliation: National Association for Native American Children of Alcoholics, 130 Andover Park E. #230, Seattle, WA 98188 (800) 322-5601; (206) 467-7686 Fax 467-7689. E-mail: nanacoa@aol.com.

FLEMING, DALE
(Indian center director)
Affiliation: Native American Indian Center, Stockton U.S.D., 1425 S. Center, Stockton, CA 95206 (209) 953-4803 Fax 953-4261. E-mail: dfleming @telis.org.

FLEMING, ELAINE (Leech Lake Ojibwe)
(college instructor)
Affiliation: Leech Lake Tribal College, 6530 U.S. Hwy. 2 NW, Cass Lake, MN 56633 (218) 335-4220 Fax 335-4209.

FLEMING, DR. WALTER C.
(college professor)
Affiliation: Native American Studies Dept., Montana State University, 2-179 Wilson Hall, P.O. Box 172340, Bozeman, MT 59717 (406) 994-3881 Fax 994-6879. *Interests*: Native American literature; Montana Indians.

FLEMMING, JOSEPH
(health director)
Affiliation: Shakopee Mdweakanton Health Council, 2320 Sioux Trail, NW, Prior Lake, MN 55372 (612) 445-8900.

FLEMMING, TIMOTHY, M.D.
(medical center director)
Affiliation: Gallup Indian Medical Center, P.O. Box 1337, Gallup, NM 87301 (505) 722-1000.

FLESHER, ELSIE
(school principal)
Affiliation: San Simon School, P.O. Box 8292, Sells, AZ 85634 (520) 362-2331 Fax 362-2405.

FLETT, FRANCIS
(Indian band chief)
Affiliation: The Pas Indian Band, Box 297, The Pas, Manitoba, Canada R9A 1K4 (204) 623-5483.

FLETT, JACK
(Indian band chief)
Affiliation: St. Theresa Point Indian Band, St. Theresa Point, MB, Canada R0B 1J0 (204) 462-2106.

FLETT, NORMAN
(Indian band chief)
Affiliation: Split Lake Cree Indian Band, Split Lake, Manitoba, Canada R0B 1P0 (204) 342-2045.

FLEURY, KATHLEEN M.
(Indian affairs coordinator)
Affiliation: State Coordinator of Indian Affairs, Governor's Office of Indian Affairs, Rm. 202, State Capitol Bldg., Box 200801, Helena, MT 59620 (406) 444-3702.

FLICK, SHIRLEY
(Indian education program coordinator)
Affiliation: Warroad Public Schools - ISD #690, Indian Education Dept., 510 Cedar Ave., Warroad, MN 56763 (218) 386-1820 Fax 386-1909.

FLOCKEN, HENRY (White Earth Ojibwe)
(college instructor)
Affiliation: Leech Lake Tribal College, 6530 U.S. Hwy. 2 NW, Cass Lake, MN 56633 (218) 335-4220 Fax 335-4209.

FLORES, AMELIA
(library director)
Affiliation: Colorado River Indian Tribes Public Library/ Archives, Tribal Administration Center, Rte. 1, Box 23-B, Parker, AZ 85344 (602) 669-9211.

FLOWERS, GARY
(council director)
Affiliation: Virginia Council on Indians, P.O. Box 1475, Richmond, VA 23219 (804) 786-7765.

FLOYD, JAMES R.
(IHS area director)
Affiliation: Portland Area Office IHS, 1220 S.W. Third Ave., Rm. 476, Portland, OR 97204 (503) 326-2020.

FLUTE, JERRY
(executive director)
Affiliation: Executive Director, Association on American Indian Affairs, Inc., P.O. Box 268, Tekakwitha Complex, Agency Rd. #7, Sisseton, SD 57262 (605) 698-3998.

FOGELMAN, GARY L. 1950-
(editor/publisher)
Born January 1, 1950, Muncy, Pa. *Education*: Lock Haven State University, BS, 1972; West Chester State University (2 years). *Principal occupation*: Editor/publisher. *Home address*: RD 1, Box 240, Turbotville, PA 17772. *Affiliation*: Editor/publisher, Indian-Artifact Magazine. *Memberships*: Local, state and northeastern archaeological societies; SPA (Chapter No. 8, vice president); IACAP (vice president). *Awards, honors*: Catlin Peace Pipe Award. *Interests*: Collecting Indian artifacts; hunting and fishing. *Published works*: The Muncy Indians (Grit Publishing, 1976); The Pennsylvania Artifact Series (in progress).

FOGELSON, RAYMOND D. (*Talageesi*) 1933-
(professor of anthropology)
Born August 23, 1933, Red Bank, N.J. *Education*: Wesleyan University, BA, 1955; University of Pennsylvania, MA, 1958, PhD, 1962. *Principal occupation*: Professor of anthropology. *Home address*: 1761 N. Sedgwick, Chicago, IL 60614 (312) 642-7693. *Affiliations*: Assistant professor, University of Washington, Seattle, 1962-65; Department of Anthropology, University of Chicago, 1965-. *Other professional posts*: Book review editor, "American Anthropologist". *Memberships*: American Ethnological Society; American Society for Ethnohistory (president); Central State Anthropological Society (president); Society for Psychological Anthropology; Society for Medical Anthropology. *Interests*: Southeastern Indians, Plateau. *Biographical sources*: Who's Who in America. *Published works*: The Cherokees: An Annotated Bibliography (Indiana University Press); editor: A.I. Hallowell, Contributions to Anthropology (University of Chicago Press); editor (with R.N. Adams): The Anthropology of Power (Academic Press).

FOGHORN, CARMEN A.
(Indian program coordinator)
Affiliation: Coordinator, American Indian Graduate Program, University of California, 316 Sproul Hall #5900, Berkeley, CA 94720 (510) 642-3228 Fax 642-8909.

FOLLETTI, SUSAN (Tlingit)
(art studio owner)
Affiliation: Chilkat Valley Arts, P.O. Box 145, Haines, AK 99827 (907) 766-2990 Fax 766-3090.

FOLLIS, BILL GENE (Modoc)
(tribal chief)
Address & Affiliation: Modoc Tribe of Oklahoma, 515 "G" St. SE, Miami, OK 74354 (918) 542-1190 Fax 542-5415.

FONSECO, NICK (Me-wuk)
(rancheria chairperson)
Affiliation: Shingle Springs Rancheria, P.O. Box 1340, Shingle Springs, CA 95682 (530) 676-8010.

FONTAINE, JERRY
(Indian band chief)
Affiliation: Fort Alexander Indian Band, Box 280, Fort Alexander, Manitoba, Canada R0E 0P6 (204) 367-2287.

FOOTE, JAMES
(health center director)
Affiliation: McLaughlin PHS Indian Health Center, P.O. Box 879, McLaughlin, SD 57642 (605) 823-4459.

FORBES, JACK D. (Powhatan-Renape, Delaware-Lenape) 1934-
(professor of Native American studies)
Born January 7, 1934, Long Beach, Calif. *Education*: University of Southern California, BA, 1953; MA, 1955, PhD, 1959. *Principal occupation*: Professor of Native American studies. *Address*: Native American Studies Dept., College of Letters & Science, 2401 Hart Hall, University of California, Davis, CA 95616 (530) 752-3237 Fax 752-7097. *Affiliations*: Assistant professor, San Fernando Valley State College, 1960-64; associate professor & acting director, Center for Western North American Studies, University of Nevada, 1964-67; research program director, Far West Laboratory, Berkeley, CA, 1967-69; professor/department head, Native American Studies Dept., University of California, Davis, 1969-. *Other professional post*: Co-editor, Attan-Akamik. *Awards, honors*: Phi Beta Kappa; Social Science Research Council Fellow, 1957-58; Guggenheim Fellow, 1963-64; Fulbright Visiting Professor, University of Warwick, 1981-82; Tinbergan Chair, Erasmus University, Rotterdam, 1983-84; Visitor Scholar, Institute of Social Anthropology, Oxford University, 1986-87; Visiting Professor, University of Essex, U.K., 1993; American Book Award-Lifetime Achievement, 1997. *Community activities*: Powhatan Confederation (Chief's Council), 1969-79; California Indian Legal Services, Inc. (board of directors), 1969-79; Member, D-Q University National Advisory Committee, 1981-present. *Membership*: California Indian Education Association; Native Writer's Circle of the Americas. *Interests*: Founder, Native American Movement (chairman, 1961-1962); co-founder of Coalition of Eastern Native Americans; co-founder of the United Native Americans, 1968; co-founder, D-Q University (volunteer instructor); working with Renape, Lenape, and other related languages; . *Biographical sources*: Who's Who; Who's Who in the West; Contemporary Authors; Native American Almanac. *Published works*: Apache, Navajo & Spaniard (University of Oklahoma Press, 1960, paperback, 1980; reprinted by Greenwood Press, 1980; revised edition, 1994); Editor, The Indian in America's Past (Prentice-Hall, 1964); Warriors of the Colorado (University of Oklahoma Press, 1965); Editor, Nevada Indians Speak (University of Nevada Press, 1967); Afro-Americans in the Far West (U.S.G.P.O., 1967); Native Americans of California & Nevada (Naturegraph, 1969; revised edition, 1982); Handbook of Native American Studies (Tecumseh Center, 1971); Aztecas del Norte: The Chicanos of Aztlan (Fawcett, 1973); The Wapanamikok Languages (Tecumseh Center, 1976); American Words (Tecumseh Center, 1979); Native American languages (Tecumseh Center, 1979); Attan-Akamik Powhatan-Renape Guide to the Washington, DC Region (Native American Studies, UC-Davis, 1979); Atlas of Native History (D-Q University Press, 1981); Native Americans & Nixon: Presidential Policy & Minority Self-Determination (UCLA American Indian Studies Center, 1982); Editor, Native American Higher Education: The Struggle for the Creation of D-Q University, 1960-71 (D-Q University Press, 1985); Black Africans & Native Americans: Race, Caste & Color in the Evolution of Red-Black Peoples (Blackwell, 1988; paper, University of Illinois Press, 1993); Columbus and Other Cannibals (Autonomedia, 1992); Only Approved Indians (University of Oklahoma Press, 1995); Red Blood (Theytus Books, 1997); Proposition 209 (Kahonkok Press, 1998, revised 1999); What Is Time? (Kahonkok Press, 1999); What Is Space? (Kahonkok Press, 2001); Atta! And Other Poems on 9-11, War and Peace (Kahonkok Press, 2002); numerous monographs, articles and book reviews

FORCE, ROLAND W. 1924-
(anthropologist)
Born December 30, 1924, Omaha, Neb. *Education*: Stanford University, BA, 1950, MA, 1951, MA,1952, PhD (Anthropology), 1958. *Principal occupation*: Anthropologist. *Residence*: Honolulu, Hawaii. *Affiliations*: Lecturer, Dept. of Anthropology, University of Chicago, 1956-61; curator of Oceanic Archaeology and Ethnology, Chicago Natural History Museum (Field Museum of Natural History), Chicago, 1956-61; member, Graduate Affiliate Faculty, University of Hawaii, 1962-77; director, B.P. Bishop Museum, 1962-76; holder, Charles Reed Bishop Distinguished Chair in Pacific Studies (1976-77), director emeritus, B.P. Bishop Museum, 1976-91; director & secretary, board of trustees, Museum of the American Indian, Heye Foundation, New York City, 1977-91. *Other professional posts*: Honorary consultant, B.P. Bishop Museum, 1977-91; trustee, W.T. Yoshimoto Foundation, Hawaii, 1979-. *Military service*: U.S. Army, 1943-46 (sergeant; Corps of Engineers; combat duty, European Theatre of Operations). *Community services*: Member, advisory board, State-based Humanities Program, Hawaii, 1972-75; member, Distribution Committees, Sophie Russell Testamentary Trust & Jessie Ann Chalmers Charitable Trust, Honolulu, 1972-77; member, Barstow Foundation Committee (Samoan Education), Hawaii, 1963-. *Memberships*: Pacific Club, Honolulu, 1962-; Social Science Association, Honolulu, 1962-; American Anthropological Association; American Association for the Advancement of Science; American Association of Museums; International Council of Museums; National Trust for Historic Preservation; Pacific Science Association. *Awards, honors*: Selected by Chicago Junior Chamber of Commerce as one of Chicago's ten outstanding young men, 1958; Honorary Member, Association of Hawaiian Civic Clubs, 1967; Honorary Doctor of Science, Hawaii Loa College, 1973; Honorary Life Member, Bishop Museum Association, 1976; commendation, Senate Concurrent Resolution, Hawaii, 1976; Honorary Life Fellow, Pacific Science Association. *Biographical sources*: Who's Who in America; American Men of Science. *Published works*: Many articles in the Museum of the American Indian Newsletter, and other periodicals, including: Arctic Art: Eskimo Ivory, American Indian Art Magazine, 1981); A Common Misperception, (MAI Newsletter, 1984); That Without Which Nothing, (MAI Newsletter, 1984); Beacons in the Night, (MAI Newsletter, 1984); The Owls' Eyes Obsession, (MAI Newsletter, 1984); Solving the Puzzle of the Past, (MAI Newsletter, 1985); among others.

FORD, RICHARD IRVING 1941-
(curator of ethnology)
Born June 27, 1941, Harrisburg, Pa. *Education*: Oberlin College, Ohio, MA, 1963; University of Michigan, MA, 1965, PhD, 1968. *Principal occupation*: Curator of ethnology. *Home address*: 227 Valle Del Sol Dr., Santa Fe, NM 87501-1178. *Affiliation*: Assistant professor of anthropology, University of Cincinnati, 1967-69; Curator of ethnology and director, Museum of Anthropology, University of Michigan, Ann Arbor, 1970-. *Other professional post*: Professor of anthropology and botany, University of Michigan. *Memberships*: Conference of Native American Studies (national advisory committee); American Anthropological Association; Society for American Archaeology (executive committee); Society for Economic Botany (editorial board); The Archaeological Conservancy (secretary); American Association for Advancement of Science (section H, chairperson). *Interests*: Expert witness, Zuni Pueblo, N.M.; consultant to San Juan Pueblo, N.M.; North American ethnobotany; origins of American Indian agriculture; excavations, Jemez Cave and Bat Cove, N.M., and Cloudspitter, Ky. *Awards, honors*: Distinguished Service Award, University of Michigan, 1971; National Science Foundation grantee, 1970-73, 1975-76, 1978-79; Weatherhead scholar, School of Ameri-

can Research, 1978-79; *Biographical source*: Who's Who in America. *Published works*: co-author, Paleoethnobotany of the Koster Site (Illinois State Museum, 1972); editor, The Nature and Status of Ethnobotany (University of Michigan, 1978); editor, Prehistoric Food Production in North America (University of Michigan, 1985).

FOREMAN, ALLEN (Klamath)
(tribal chairperson)
Affiliation: Klamath General Council, P.O. Box 436, Chiloquin, OR 97624 (541) 783-2219.

FOREMAN, EDWARD R. (Pit River)
(former rancheria chairperson)
Affiliation: Redding Rancheria, 2000 Rancheria Rd., Redding, CA 96001 (530) 225-8979.

FORQUERA, RALPH (Juaneno Band of California Mission Indians) 1948-
(health care administrator)
Born July 7, 1948, Delano, Calif. *Education*: MPH. *Principal occupation*: Health care administrator. *Address*: Seattle Indian Health Board, 606 - 12th Ave. S., Seattle, WA 98144 (206) 324-9360 Fax 324-8910: E-Mail: ralphf@sihb.org. *Affiliations*: San Diego County Dept. of Public Health, 1979-82; San Diego American Health Center, 1982-89; executive director, Seattle Indian Health Board, Seattle, WA, 1990-present. *Other professional posts*: Clinical faculty, University of Washington School of Public Health. *Community activities*: Visiting committee-Master's Program in non-profit leadership, Seattle University; advisory board, King County Health Systems/Health Status Committee; commissioner, American Indian Health Commission for Washington State. *Memberships*: American Public Health Association; American Indian, Alaska Native & Native Hawaiian Caucus (chair); Society of Non-Profit Agencies. *Published works*: Health Status of Urban American Indians & Alaska Natives.

FORSMAN, LEONARD (Suquamish) 1962-
(museum director)
Born January 25, 1962, Bremerton, Wash. *Education*: University of Southern California, 1979-81; University of Washington, BA (Anthropology), 1987. *Principal occupation*: Museum director. *Address*: P.O. Box 654, Suquamish, WA 98392 (206) 598-3311. *Affiliations*: Researcher, Suquamish Tribal Cultural Center, Suquamish, WA, 1981-85; director, Suquamish Museum, 1985-. *Other professional post*: Editor of museum newsletter. *Community activities*: Secretary, Suquamish Tribal Council; member, Kitsap County Council on Human Rights. *Published works*: Eyes of Chief Seattle (Suquamish Museum, 1984); A Time of Gathering (Burke Museum/University of Washington Press, 1990).

FORTIN, CLAUDETTE
(executive director; editor)
Affiliation: The National Indian Arts and Crafts Corporation, 1 Nicholas St., Suite 1106, Ottawa, Ontario, Canada K1N 7B6 (613) 232-2436. *Other professional post*: Editor, Artscraft.

FORTUNE, JUDY
(dance team coordinator)
Affiliation: Rappahannock-Mattaponi Dancers, Route 1, Box 522, Tappahannock, VA 23023 (804) 769-4205.

FOSDICK, ROSE ATUK
(services director)
Affiliation: Journal of Alaska Native Arts, Institute of Alaska Native Arts, P.O. Box 80583, Fairbanks, AK 99708 (907) 456-7491.

FOSS, PHILIP, Jr.
(editor)
Affiliation: Institute of American Indian Arts (IAIA) Museum, P.O. Box 20007, Santa Fe, NM 87504 (505) 988-6463.

FOSTER, JEFF
(executive director)
Affiliation: Four Tribes Consortium of Oklahoma, P.O. Box 1193, Anadarko, OK 73005 (405) 247-9711.

FOSTER, KARIN L.
Address: 151 Shearer Lane, Toppenish, WA 98948 (509) 865-2880.

FOSTER, MORRIS W.
(professor of anthropology)
Born January 28, 1960, Alva, Okla. *Education*: University of Oklahoma, BA, 1981; Yale University, MPhil, 1984, PhD, 1988. *Principal occupation*: Assistant professor of anthropology. *Home address*: 819 W. Brooks, Norman, OK 73069 (405) 325-2491 (work). *Affiliation*: Native American Studies Program, Dept. of Anthropology, University of Oklahoma, Norman, OK, 1988-. *Other professional post*: Editor, American Indian Quarterly (University of Nebraska Press), 1993-. *Memberships*: Society for Linguistic Anthropology, American Anthropological Association; American Society for Ethnohistory. *Awards*: 1992 Erminie Wheeler Voegelin Prize for best book in ethnohistory, the American Society for Ethnohistory. *Interests*: Anthropology, Native American studies, ethnohistory, sociolinguistics, specializing in the people of the Native Plains and Native Southwest. *Published work*: Being Comanche: The Social History of an American Indian Community (University of Arizona Press, 1991).

FOSTER, MELVIN "TIM" (Yakama) 1938-
(rancher)
Born November 11, 1938 in Toppenish, Wash. *Principal occupation*: Rancher. *Address*: 1541 Foster Rd., Toppenish, WA 98948 (309) 854-1329. *Affiliations*: Pine Springs Cattlemen's Association (1957-; sec./treas. 1957-65; president, 1966-); president, National American Indian Cattleman's Association, 1978-; Yakama Nation Housing Authority, 1970-94; chairman, 1971-94; National American Indian Housing Council, 1973-93; secretary, HUD's National Advisory Committee on Indian Housing, 1983-87; *Community activities*: School District Director, Granger, WA, 1973-93; board director, Central Memorial Hospital, Toppenish, WA, 1973-81; board chairman, Mt. Adams Furniture Factory, 1973-81; assistant basketball coach, Sunnyside Christian High School, 1994-96. *Other professional post*: Editor & publisher of newsletter and yearbook of the National American Indian Cattleman's Association. *Memberships*: Association of Governing Boards of Universities and Colleges; American Hereford Association (lifetime); American Quarter Horse Association. *Awards, honors*: Recipient of "Individual Recognition Outstanding Community Leader Award" HUD, 1992; honored by Yakima Nation for 25 years service in Indian housing by naming of new elderly building "Tim Foster Retirement Center," dedicated July 1994.

FOUGNIER, RAY
(periodical director)
Affiliation: "Indian Studies Quarterly," 400 Caldwell Hall, Cornell University, Ithaca, NY 14853 (607) 256-8402.

FOWLER, CHUCK
(health program director)
Affiliation: Central Valley Indian Health Program, 20 N. Dewitt, Clovis, CA 93482 (209) 299-2578.

FOWLER, LORETTA
(professor)
Affiliation: Dept. of Anthropology, Indiana University, Rawles Hall 108, Bloomington, IN 47405 (812) 855-1203.

FOWLER, VERNA M. (Menominee) 1942-
(educational administrator)
Born July 1, 1942, Keshena, Wisc. *Education*: PhD in Educational Administration. *Principal occupation*: Educational administrator. *Address & Affiliations*: Founding President, College of the Menominee Nation, P.O. Box 1179, Keshena, WI 54135 (800) 567-2344; (715) 799-4921 Fax 799-1308. E-mail: vfowler@menominee.edu. Website: www.menominee.edu. *Other professional posts*: Executive director, National Indian Gaming & Hospitality Institute, College of the Menominee Nation, Keshena, WI; Supt. for Education, Menominee Tribal School, Neopit, WI. *Awards, honors*: Honorary Doctorate from the University of Wisconsin, Oshkosh. *Memberships*: Menominee Indian Tribe of Wisconsin; American Indian College Fund (board member); Ameriacn Indian Higher Education Consortium. Published work: The Menominee (book).

FOWLER-OTTO, CLARA (Menominee)
(head start director)
Affiliation & Address: Menominee Tribe, P.O. Box 910, Keshena, WI 54135 (715) 799-5100 Fax 799-3373.

FOWLER, VERNA
(institute director)
Affiliation: National Indian Gaming & Hospitality Institute, College of the Menominee Nation, P.O. Box 1179, Keshena, WI 54135 (715) 799-5600 Fax 799-1308.

FOX, CHARLES D. (Mole Lake Chippewa)
(former tribal chairperson)
Affiliation: Sokaogon (Mole Lake) Chippewa Community, 3086 State Hwy. 55, Crandon, WI 54520 (715) 478-7500.

FOX, DENNIS R. (Mandan-Hidatsa) 1943-
(BIA-chief, Div. of Education)
Born September 8, 1943, Elbowoods, N.D. *Education*: Dickinson State College, BS, 1966; Penn State University, MEd, 1971, DEd, 1977. *Principal occupation*: Assistant director of education, BIA. *Address*: Dept. of the Interior, Bureau of Indian Affairs, Rm. 3517 MS-3512-MIB, 1849 C St., NW, Washington, DC 20240 (202) 208-7388. *Affiliations*: Education program administrator, Johnson O'Malley Program, BIA, Cheyenne River Agency and Aberdeen Area Office, SD, 1975-83; assistant director of education, BIA, Washington, DC, 1983-. *Other professional post*: Teacher, worked in BIA higher education grant program. *Memberships*: National Indian Education Association; Phi Delta Kappa. *Awards, honors*: Gave presentation at National School Administration Conference. *Interests*: Educational administration. *Biographical source*: Indians of Today, 1970 edition.

FOX, JOHN, M.D.
(clinical director)
Affiliation: Rocky Boy's PHS Indian Health Center, P.O. Box 664, Box Elder, MT 59521 (406) 395-4489.

FOX, JOSEPH B. (Gros Ventre)
(tribal council member)
Address & Affiliation: Fort Belknap Community Council, P.O. Box 1019, Harlem, MT 59526.

FOX, PAULA LONG
(Indian foundation chairperson)
Born and raised in rural South Dakota. *Education*: University of South Dakota, BA (History), MA (School Administration and Counseling). *Principal occupation*: Indian foundation chairperson. *Address & Affiliation*: Chairperson, American Indian Education Foundation, P.O. Box 27491, Albuquerque, NM 87125 (800) 881-8694. *Past professional posts*: Teacher and guidance counselor since 1980, primarily in schools with majority-American Indian enrollment.

FOX, ROY
(Indian band chief)
Affiliation: Blood Indian Band, Box 60, Standoff, AB, Canada T0L 1Y0 (403) 737-3753.

FOX, SANDRA J. (HARRELL)
(Oglala/Cheyenne River Sioux) 1944-
(BIA education specialist)
Born December 9, 1944, Kadoka, S.D. *Education*: Dickinson State College, BS, 1966; Penn State University, MEd, 1971, DEd, 1976. *Principal occupation*: Education specialist. *Address*: Bureau of Indian Affairs, Office of Indian Education Programs, MS: 3512-MIB, 1849 C St., NW, Washington, DC 20240 (202) 273-2382. *Affiliations*: Education specialist, Bureau of Indian Affairs, Aberdeen Area Office, SD; education specialist-curriculum, ORBIS, Inc., Washington, D.C., 1985-. *Other professional post*: Education specialist and consultant, B.I.A. *Memberships*: International Reading Association; National Indian Education Association; North American Indian Women's Association. *Awards, honors*: North Dakota Indian Scholarship; invited to join Pi Lambda Theta; given presentations at National Council of Teachers of English Convention, National Reading Conference, and International Reading Association Convention. *Interests*: Elementary and secondary education reading improvement. *Published work*: An Annotated Bibliography of Young People's Books on American Indians (Bureau of Indian Affairs, 1973).

FOX, TAMMY, P.A.
(clinical director)
Affiliation: Oneida Community Health Center, P.O. Box 365, Oneida, WI 54155 (414) 869-2711.

FRAGUA, MARISHA (Paiute)
(rancheria chairperson)
Affiliation: Cedarville Rancheria, 200 N. Howard St., Cedarville, CA 96101 (530) 2333-3969.

FRANCIS, LEE, III (Laguna Pueblo) 1945-
(organization director; author, associate professor, poet)
Born May 21, 1945, Albuquerque, N.M. *Education*: San Francisco State University, B.A., 1983, M.A., 1984; Western Institute for Social Research, PhD, 1991. *Principal occupation*: Director-Indian organization; author, associate professor, poet. *Address*: Wordcraft Circle of native Writers & Storytellers, 4905 El Aguila Place, NW, Albuquerque, NM 87120-1009 (505) 352-9118 Fax 817-3244; E-mail: wordcraft@sockets.net. Website: www.wordcraftcircle.org. *Affiliations*: Sr. Partner, Associated Businesses, Albuquerque, NM, 1978-81; San Francisco State University (Administrative coordinator, Student Affirmative Action Program, 1981-83; associate director, Educational Opportunity Program, 1983-84; senior faculty, Meta-Life Adult Professional Training Institute, Washington, DC, 1984-88; core faculty, Western Institute for Social Research, Berkeley, CA, 1989-90; 1991-93; vice president, First Americans Research, Washington, DC, 1993-95; national director, Wordcraft Circle of Native Writers & Storytellers, Columbia, MO, 1992-; editor, "Moccasin Telegraph, Columbia, MO, 1992-; Associate Professor of Native American Studies (tenured), The University of New Mexico, Native American Studies Dept., Mesa Vista Hall Room 3080, Albuquerque, NM 87131 (505) 277-3917 Fax 277-1818, 2002-. *Current professional posts*: Currently on the board of directors of American Indian Broadcasting, Inc., Broken Bow, OK; the First Book Award (for poetry and prose)Selection Committee for the Native Writers' Circle of the Americas; Trustee and secretary of the board, Laguna Pueblo Education Foundation, Laguna, NM; board of directors, Native Writers' Circle of the Americas & The Greenfield Literary Review Center; member of the editorial board of Contemporary Native American Communities book series of AltaMira Press (a division of Sage Publications); member of the editorial board for Michigan State University Press - American Indian Literature Series. *Past professional posts*: consultant, Indian Youth Specialist, U.S. Dept. of the Interior, BIA, Office of Alcohol & Substance Abuse Prevention, and editor, "Prevention Quarterly", 1994. *Community activities*: advisory boards of the Minority Opportunities in Science Teaching (MOST) at California State University, Long Beach & The Children's Foundation; chair, Education Committee, American Indian Inter-Tribal Cultural Organizations, Rockville, MD, 1992-93; task force member, Research & Rehabilitation Institute (RRI), Huntington Beach, CA, 1992-93. *Memberships*: National Psychiatric Association (life member); National Coalition for Indian Education; National Indian Education Association; Native Writers Circle of the Americas (board of directors, 1992-). *Awards, honors*: Certificate of Appreciation, Student Affirmative Action Program, San Francisco State University, 1981-82; AILOTT (American Indian Leaders of Today & Tomorrow) California State University, Long Beach, 1990; American Indian Student Council, California State University, Long Beach, 1990. *Interests*: Dr. Francis is actively engaged in a number of research projects-currently focusing on studying the interrelationship of PTSD (Post Traumatic Stress Disorder) as applied to particular Native Cultural groups and intertribal social change dynamics; he enjoys speaking to large & small groups on a variety of topics. He is regularly invited too speak to organizations throughout the country. His areas of expertise are social policy, multicultural communication and organizational development. Dr. Francis has made numerous keynote addresses and lectures. "Other interests include writing poetry, Native-centered science fiction, and plays...traveling on the Internet superhighway...participating in pow wows all across Indian Country...composing music/songs and playing them on my guitar." *Published works*: Books: BEST Course: A Cultural Communications Handbook (Met-Life Publishing, 1986); Native Time: A Historical Time Line of Native America (St. Martin's Press, 1996); Reclaiming the Vision — Past, Present and Future: Native Voices for the Eighth Generation, edited with James Bruchac (Greenfield Review Press, 1996; On the Good Red Interstate: Truck Stop Tellings and Other Poems (Taurean Horn Press, 2002). Short stories & essays: "This Business of Columbus" (with Paul Gunn Allen) in, Columbus and Beyond: Views from Native Americans, edited by Randolph Jorgen (SPMA Publishing, 1992); "Elder Wisdom: Native American Culture Studies," in, English Studies/Culture Studies: Institutionalizing Dissent (University of Illinois Press, 1994); "Keresian Dawn," in, Callaloo: Native Literatures Special Issue, edited by Charles H. Rowell (Johns Hopkins University Press, 1994; "The Atsye Parallel", in, Blue Dawn, Red Earth: New Native American Storytellers, an anthology edited by Clifford Trafzer (Doubleday, 1996); "Child of the Sun", in, The Telling of the World: Native American Legends and Stories, edited by W.S. Penn (Stewart, Tabori & Cheng, 1997).

FRANCIS, RODERICK P.
(Indian band chief)
Affiliation: Pictou Landing Indian Band, Box 249, Trenton, Nova Scotia, Canada B0K 1X0 (902) 752-4912.

FRANCIS-BEGAY, KAREN
(educator)
Affiliation: College of Education, University of Arizona, Tucson, AZ 85721 (602) 621-1311.

FRANK, BILLY, JR. (Nisqually) 1931-
(commission chairperson)
Affiliation: Co-founder & chairperson (25 years), Northwest Indian Fisheries Commission, 6730 Martin Way E., Olympia, WA 98506 (360) 438-1180 Fax 754-8659. *Past affiliation*: Helped to found the Northwest Renewable Resources Center in 1984. *Awards, honors*: 1992 Albert Schweitzer Award for his "achievements as a mediator between opposing interest groups and as a protector of the fragile cultural & environmental heritage that all humanity share"; 2004 Indian Country Today 's first, "American Indian Visionary Award."

FRANK, EDDIE (Athapascan)
(AK village council president)
Affiliation: Venetie Village Council, P.O. Box 99, Arctic Village, AK 99781 (907) 849-8212.

FRANK, FRANCIS F.
(Indian band chief)
Affiliation: Yia-O-Qui-Aht First Nations, Box 18, Tolfino, British Columbia, Canada V0R 2Z0 (604) 725-3233.

FRANK, HAROLD (Forest County Potawatomi)
(tribal chairperson)
Affiliation: Forest County Potawatomi Community Executive Council, P.O. Box 340, Crandon, WI 54520 (715) 478-2903.

FRANK, JAMES
(Indian band chief)
Affiliation: Kanaka Bar Indian Band, Box 210, Lytton, British Columbia, Canada V0K 1Z0 (604) 455-2279.

FRANK, JOYCE (Eskimo)
(ex-AK village council president)
Affiliation: Organized Village of Saxman, Route 2, Ketchikan, AK 99901 (907) 225-5163.

FRANK, NOAH (Caddo)
(tribal chairperson)
Affiliation: Caddo Tribal Council, P.O. Box 487, Binger, OK 73009 (405) 656-2344.

FRANK, NORMAN
(Indian band chief)
Affiliation: Comox Indian Band, 3320 Comox Rd., Courtenay, British Columbia, Canada V9N 3P8 (604) 339-7122.

FRANK, WALLY
(AK village president)
Affiliation: Angoon Community Association, P.O. Box 188, Angoon, AK 99820 (907) 788-3411.

FRANKE, JUDITH A.
(museum director)
Affiliation: Dickson Mounds Museum, Lewiston, IL 61542 (309) 547-3721.

FRANKS, JEANNIE (*Shinning Star*)
(United Lumbee)
(chief of United Lumbee Black Bear Clan)
Address: 2510 Markwardt, Joplin, MO 64801 (417) 781-0213. *Principal occupation*: Chief of United Lumbee Black Bear Clan. *Home address*: 13159 Oakwood Trail, Neosho, MO 64850. *Affiliations*: Manager, Crossways, 1960-65; manager, Steak & Grape, 1965-70; manager, Colony Inn, 1970-74; manager, Howard Johnsons, 1974-80; domestic engineer, 1980-present. *Community activities*: Athletic Boosters; B.P.O. Elks USA; fund raising for various organizations. *Memberships*: United Lumbee Black Bear Clan; B.P.O. Elks USA; Loma Linda Country Club; Golden Hawk Society.

FRANKSON, ERNIE (Eskimo)
(AK village council president)
Affiliation: Point Hope Village Council, P.O. Box 91, Point Hope, AK 99766 (907) 368-2453.

FRANTZ, DONALD G. (Omahkokoyaato'si) 1934-
(linguistic research & consultation; professor emeritus)
Born January 20, 1934, Oakland, Calif. *Education*: University of California, Berkeley, BA, 1960. *Principal occupation*: Linguistic research & consultation; professor emeritus. *Home address*: 9 Lafayette Crescent, Lethbridge, Alberta, Canada T1K 4B5 (403) 381-0302; E-Mail: frantzn@hg.uleth.ca. *Affiliation*: Professor emeritus, University of Lethbridge, AB, Canada. *Military service*: U.S. Coast Guard, 1953-57 (1st Class P.O.). *Community activities*: Zone representative, Board of Directors, Alberta Triathlon Association. *Memberships*: Linguistics Society of America; Society for the Study of Indigenous Languages of the Americas. *Interests*: Native language research; triathlon participation. *Published works*: "Blackfoot Dictionary," 1989 & 1995, and "Blackfoot Grammar," 1991 (University of Toronto Press)

FRAZIER, GREGORY W. (Crow)1947-
(writer/adventurer)
Born September 5, 1947, Richmond, Ind. Education: Earlham College, 1965-67; Temple University, BA, 1972; University of Puget Sound, MBA, 1978, PhD, 1988. *Principal occupation*: Writer/adventurer. *Address*: P.O. Box 427, Englewood, CO 80151. E-mail: gregfrazier@yahoo.com. Website: www.horizons unlimited.com/gregfrazier. *Affiliations*: Instructor/consultant, American Indian Management Institute, Albuquerque, N.M., 1972-74; executive director, Seattle Indian Center, Inc., 1974-77; executive director, AL-IND-ESK-A (The 13th Regional Corp.), Seattle, 1977-79; chairman, Absarokee Investments, Seattle, 1977-; president National Urban Indian Council, Denver, CO, 1979-; president, National Indian Business Council, Englewood, CO, 1977-89; owner, Intracity Properties, Englewood, CO; president/chairman, Indians for United Social Action; president, GAMA, Englewood, CO; chairman, Arrowstar, Yellowtail, MT; Current: President, Whole Earth Motorcycle Center, P.O. Box 102125, Denver, CO 80250. *Community activities*: Indians for United Social Action (member); National Low Income Housing Coalition (member). *Memberships*: Indian Motorcycle Owners Association (vice president); American Motorcyclists Association; America Film Producers Association; America Writers Guild. *Awards, honors*: Outstanding Contribution Award, CETA Coalition; Individual Personal Achievement Award, IHRC, Inc.; Outstanding Minority Writer, 1985, U.S. Writers Association; Best Business Efforts, Community Chamber of Commerce, 1985; Outstanding Minority Writer of the Year, 1988; Presidential appointee, National Advisory Council on Indian Education; appointee, Secretary's Advisory Group, Department of HUD; appointee, Department of Labor Ad Hoc Advisory Committee. *Interests*: Business and economic development; international economic development; developing countries; political & bureaucratic abuses of authority; fundraising. "Dr. Frazier is a professional motorcycle adventurer, having traveled around the world by motorcycle. He has written extensively about his travel adventures. He has won professional events throughout the U.S. as a BMW and Indian racer. Dr. Frazier is a well known figure in the motorcycle industry both in Europe and the U.S. Dr. Frazier has long been an advocate for the rights of American Indians and Alaska Natives, having served as president of the National Urban Indian Council from 1977-89. As a registered lobbyist in the U.S. House & Senate, he lobbied for Native rights and funding and is a noted expert on urban Indian policy in America. Dr. Frazier has spent 30 years exposing government abuses, discrimination, and bureaucratic malfeasance in federal agencies. As an Indian activist, he has been responsible

for changes in federal laws and regulations that have benefited American Indians & Alaska Natives." *Published works*: While We're At It, Let's Get You a Job (NCIB Press, 1984); American Indian Index (Arrowstar Publishing, 1987); Smoke Signals (Arrowstar Publishing, 1989); American Indian/Alaska Native Higher Education Funding Guild (Arrowstar Publishing, 1989); Urban Indians: Drums from the Cities (Arrowstar); Motorcycle Sex, Or Freud Would Never Understand the Relationship Between Me and My Motorcycle (Arrowstar); Urban Indian Profile in America (Arrowstar); Alaska by Motorcycle, Europe by MotorcyIce, Riding South-Mexico, Central America and South America by Motorcycle, and New Zealand by Motorcycle; (Whole Earth Motorcycle Center); BMW GSing Around the World (Whole Earth Motorcycle Center) Indian International Motorcycle Directory (Whole Earth Motorcycle Center).

FRAZIER, HAROLD (Cheyenne River Lakota) 1966-
(tribal chairperson)
Born November 23, 1966 in White Horse, S.D. *Education*: White Horse Day School, 1981; Cheyenne River Butte High School, 1985; Chadron State College, Chadron, Neb; Eastern Wyoming College, AA, 1989. *Principal occupation*: Tribal chairperson. *Affiliation*: Chairperson, Cheyenne River Sioux Tribe, P.O. Box 590, Eagle Butte, SD 57625 (605) 964-4155. *Past professional posts*: Cheyenne River Gas & CATV Co., 1990-98; elected as a District 4 Council Representative representing the communities of White Horse, Timber Lake, Green Grass, and West Eagle Butte. *Memberships*: Great Plains Tribal Chairman's Association (chair); Intertribal Monitoring Association (chair); National Congress of American Indians (Great Plains Regional Vice-President). *Interests*: Riding and raising horses; singing at the drum with his relatives and friends; and researching the treaties and the history of the Great Sioux Nation.

FRAZIER, JEFF
(seminary director)
Affiliation: Carter Seminary, 2400 Chickasaw Blvd., Ardmore, OK 73401 (405) 223-8547.

FRAZIER, JOE
(BIA education administrator)
Affiliation: Papago Agency, Bureau of Indian Affairs, P.O. Box 490, Sells, AZ 85634 (520) 383-3292 Fax 383-2399.

FRAZIER, KATHY (Tyme Maidu)
(rancheria vice-chair)
Affiliation: Vice-Chairperson, Berry Creek Rancheria, 5 Tyme Way, Oroville, CA 95966 (916) 534-3859.

FRAZIER, RUTH T.
(organization president)
Affiliation: Futures for Children, 805 Tijeras, NW, Albuquerque, NM 87102 (505) 247-4700.

FRED, JENNIFER (Mono)
(rancheria vice-chair)
Affiliation: Cold Springs Rancheria, P.O. Box 209, Tollhouse, CA 93667 (209) 855-5043.

FREDERICK, CLARENCE
(director-Indian hospital)
Affiliation: Turtle Mountain PHS Indian Hospital, Belcourt, ND 58316 (701) 477-6112.

FREDERICKS, GLENN (Eskimo)
(village president)
Affiliation: Native Village of Georgetown, 1400 Virginia Court, Georgetown, AK 99501 (907) 274-2194.

FREDERICKS, MICHELLE CATHERINE
(Pinto Horse Woman) **(Mandan, Hidatsa & Arikara) 1966-**
(administrative director)
Born October 21, 1966, Fort Yates, N.D. *Education*: University of Colorado, BA, 1989. *Principal occupation*: Administrative director. *Home address*: Resides in Rapid City, SD (605) 394-9730 (work). *Affiliation*: Administrative director, InterTribal Bison Cooperative, Rapid City, SD, 1983-. *Community activities*: American Indian Ambassador Class of 1994 for Americans for Indian Opportunity. *Interests*: "I am entering into the field of fund raising through my work with the InterTribal Bison Cooperative. In February (1994), I

attended a course offered by the Fund Raising School of Indian University's Center on Philanthropy." *Biographical source*: "Tatanka Returns," by Richard Simonelli, in Winds of Change, Vol. 8, No. 4, Autumn 1993.

FREDERICKSON, CHARLES
(high school principal)
Affiliation: Takini School, HC 77, Box 537, Howes, SD 57652 (605) 538-4399.

FREDERIKSEN, ROBERT DOUGLAS
(Tzuscum Doogie) **(Tsimshian) 1967-**
(storyteller)
Born April 17, 1967, Seattle, Wash. *Education*: Seattle Pacific University, 1985-86; University of Washington, 1992-. *Principal occupation*: Storyteller (ancient Tsimshian legends & parables). *Address*: Resides in Seattle, WA (206) 587-3415. *Affiliations*: Raven Speaks Productions, Seattle, WA, 1988-. *Other professional post*: Secretary, Tsimshian Tribal Association of Washington; former vice-chairperson & choreographer of Alaska Native Cultural Heritage Association in Washington. *Community activities*: Currently organizing two related organizations, Wisdom, a social research organization dedicated to change, and F.E.E.D. (Foundation for Educational & Economic Development), a trust fund for self-help & education programs. *Interests*: "Pan American Native history; development of self-sustaining solutions to problems facing Natives and other disadvantaged peoples; reading historical fiction, writing; revitalizing hope in an increasingly disenchanted urban youth; constitutional study; economics, market theory. I love to dance, travel & debate."

FREED, STANLEY A.
(museum curator)
Affiliation: American Museum of Natural History, 79th & Central Park West, New York, NY 10024 (212) 769-5375.

FREELAND, FRANKLIN
(director-Indian hospital)
Affiliation: Ft. Defiance PHS Indian Hospital, P.O. Box 649, Ft. Defiance, AZ 86504 (602) 729-5741.

FREEMAN, CLIFFORD
(Indian band chief)
Affiliation: Drift Indian Band, General Delivery, Driftpile, AB, Canada T0G 0V0 (403) 355-3868.

FREEMAN, CYNDEE
(dancer)
Cyndee is a women's Fancy Dancer and a traditional singer. She is co-director of the Native American Awareness program which provides educational performances with dances and singers. Additionally skilled in beadwork, poetry and writing. She can be reached at (203) 720-1685.

FREEMAN, DOUGLAS
(Indian education program coordinator)
Affiliation: Cut Bank Public Schools, Indian Education Program, 101 Third Ave. S.E., Cut bank, MT 59427 (406) 873-4421 Fax 873-4691.

FREEMAN, EVERETT (Nomlaki)
(tribal chairperson)
Affiliation: Paskenta Band of Nomlaki Indians, P.O. Box 398, Orland, CA 95963 (530) 865-3119.

FREEMAN, JOAN
(executive director)
Affiliations: American Indian Free Clinic, 1330 S. Long Beach Blvd., Compton, CA 90221 (213) 537-0103; American Indian Free Clinic, 9500 Artesia Blvd., Bellflower, CA 90706 (310) 920-7227.

FREEMAN, ROBERT LEE (Dakota-Luiseno) 1939-
(artist, cartoonist, muralist, printmaker)
Born January 14, 1939, Rincon Indian Reservation, Calif. *Education*: Palomar College, AA, 1976. *Principal occupation*: Artist, cartoonist, muralist, printmaker. Resides in San Marcos, CA. *Affiliation*: Art instructor, Palomar College. *Military service*: U.S. Army, 1957-60 (E-2 Korea, 1959). *Exhibitions*: One-man shows: Schiver Gallery, St. Louis, Mo.; Sioux Museum, Rapid City, S.D.; Turtle Mountain Gallery, Philadelphia, Pa.; Gallery of the American Indian, Sedona, Ariz; among

others. *Group shows*: U.S. Department of the Interior, Washington, DC; Heard Museum, Phoenix, Ariz.; Scottsdale National Indian Art Exhibit, Ariz.; among others. Murals: Los Angeles Public Library (45 ft.) and five private murals in homes. Numerous selected public & private collections. *Awards, honors*: 150 national Indian art awards from the following: Scottsdale National Indian Art Exhibit, Heard Museum, Red Cloud Art Show, Southern California Exposition, Gallup Ceremonial, and California State Fair. *Interests*: Mr. Freeman works in several media and has won awards in oil, watercolor, woodcarving, etching, pen and ink, bronze, airbrush and drawing, acrylic & lithography. He has instructed the course Native American Art at Grossmont College, San Diego, and Palomar College, San Marcos, Calif. Travel. *Biographical sources*: Who's Who in Indian Art; International Artists & Writers (Cambridge, England). *Published works*: Mr. Freeman's work has appeared in such periodicals as Ford Times, Western Horseman, Southwest Art Scene, Indian Voices, Genie, North County Living, Westerner, and Artist of the Rockies. Paintings included in two books, I Am These People, and Contemporary Sioux Paintings. Mr. Freeman has illustrated two books: The Layman's Typology Handbook, and The Luiseno People. He is author and publisher of two cartoon books, For Indians Only, 1971, and War Whoops and All That Jazz, 1973; Robert Freeman Drawings, 1985.

FREESE, ALISON 1951-
(educator, information specialist)
Born August 13, 1951, Washington, DC. *Education*: University of Wisconsin, BA, 1974; University of New Mexico, MA, 1986, PhD, 1991. *Home address*: Unknown. *Affiliation*: Information Specialist, Native American Studies Dept., University of New Mexico, Albuquerque, NM, 1991-98. *Community activities*: Organize speakers series, liaison with Native American organizations; editor of monthly newsletter; computer networking with tribal libraries. Memberships: America Society for Ethnohistory; American Historical Association; American Library Association, New Mexico Library Association, Phi Kappa Phi Honorary Society. *Interests*: "Pueblo/Spanish relations in 17th century New Mexico; cultural resistance strategies implemented by Native American groups in response to European colonization, particularly in the Pueblo Southwest; ethical issues relating to scholarship in Native American studies. Also interested in facilitating Native American students at UNM and encouraging them to pursue a career in Native American studies through research and writing." *Published works*: UNM Dissertation - "Sacred Clowns" Role in Cultural Boundary maintenance Among the Pueblo Indians; editor, et al, By Force of Arms: The Journals of don Diego de Vargas, New Mexico, 1691-93 (UNM Press, 1992); chapter, "Send in the Clowns: Resistance Strategies Among the Pueblo Indians in 17th Century New Mexico," in The Spanish Missions of New Mexico: A Sourcebook, Vol. 2, by David Hurst Thomas, et al, Editors (Garland Press, 1991).

FRENCH, A. LEVON
(education administrator)
Affiliation: Billings Area Office, Bureau of Indian Affairs, 316 N. 26th St., Billings, MT 59101 (406) 247-7953 Fax 247-7965.

FRENCH, LA WANDA
(museum director)
Affiliation: Ponca City Cultural Center and Museum, 1000 East Grant, Ponca City, OK 74601 (405) 765-5268.

FRENCH, ROY
(Indian band chief)
Affiliation: Takla Lake Indian Band, Takla Landing, British Columbia, Canada V0J 2T0.

FRICHNER, TONYA GONNELLA
(attorney)
Affiliation: Director, American Indian Law Alliance, 708 Broadway, 8th Floor, New York, NY 10003 (212) 598-0100 x 257.

FRICK, KATHY
(Indian organization president)
Affiliation: American Indian Intertribal Cultural Organization, P.O. Box 775, Rockville, MD 20848 (301) 869-9381.

FRIDLEY, LaMERLE
(IHS-health programs administrator)
Affiliation: Office of Health Programs, California Area IHS, 1825 Bell St., Suite 200, Sacramento, CA 95825 (916) 978-4202.

FRIED, RONALD, D.O.
(clinical director)
Affiliation: Shawnee Indian Health Center, 2001 S. Gordon Cooper Dr., Shawnee, OK 74801 (405) 275-4270.

FRITZ, LINDA
(native law centre instructor)
Affiliation: University of Saskatchewan, Native Law Centre, Diefenbaker Centre, Saskatoon, SK, Canada S7N 0W0 (306) 966-6189.

FROMAN, RONALD (*Hon-Wat-We-Se-Mo*)
(Peoria, Miami) 1940-
(tribal chief)
Born June 29, 1940, Miami, OKla. *Education*: Oklahoma State University, BS. *Principal occupation*: Chief of the Peoria Tribe of Indian of Oklahoma. *Address*: Peoria Tribal Office, P.O. Box 1527, 118 S. Eight Tribes Trail, Miami, OK 74355 (918) 540-2535 Fax 540-2538. E-mail: rfroman@peoriatribe.com. *Affiliations*: Staff CPA, Hurst Thomas & Co., 1969-72; executive director, Creek Housing Authority, 1972-84; athletic business manager, O.S.U., 1984-89; consultant, Indian House, 1992-98; chief, Peoria Tribe, Miami, OK, 1993-. *Military service*: U.S. Army, 1962-65.

FROST, CLEMENT J. (Southern Ute)
(former tribal chairperson)
Affiliation: Southern Ute Tribe, P.O. Box 737, Ignacio, CO 81137 (970) 563-0100.

FROST, RICHARD D.
(executive officer)
Affiliation: Alaska Area Native Health Services, Indian Health Service, 250 Gambell St., Third & Gambell St., Anchorage, AK 99510 (907) 257-1155.

FRY, JACK
(school principal)
Affiliation: Paschal Sherman Indian School, Omak Lake Rd., Omak, WA 98841 (509) 826-2097.

FULLER, J.B. (BUTCH), JR., (Creek) 1952-
(cultural educator)
Born August 5, 1952, Wetumpka, Alaska. *Education*: University of Montevallo (AL), 1971-72. *Principal occupation*: Cultural educator. *Home address*: 705 Cornelia Rd., Brierfield, AL 35035 (205) 665-5137. *Affiliation*: Alabama Power Co., Birmingham, AL, 1974-96; cultural educator (specializing in Creek Indian history & culture), 1996-present. *Membership*: Founder & president, Southeastern Indian Heritage Association; Native American Resource Center, University of Alabama (advisory board member); Baha's Faith; Native American Teaching Committee. *Awards, honors*: Outstanding Young Men of America, 1981. *Interests*: Reproducing early Southeastern Indian material culture pieces for collectors and museums. "(I'm a)maker of museum-quality Southeastern Indian bows, arrows & tools; (I'm a) demonstrator at museums and educational events; and a freelance magazine writer." *Publication*: Creek Indians of the Early 1800's: A Coloring Book for All Ages.

FULTON, NOLAN, M.D.
(chief of staff)
Affiliation: Choctaw Health Center, Route 7, Box R-50, Philadelphia, MS 39350 (601) 656-2211.

FUNMAKER, KENNETH, SR. (Ho-Chunk)
(tribal enterprise manager)
Affiliation: Hocak Wazijaci Language & Culture Program (Ho-Chunk Tribe), P.O. Box 390, N4845 Hwy. 58, Mauston, WI 53948 (800) 492-5745; (608) 847-5694 Fax 847-7203.

G

GACHUPIN, EARL (Pueblo)
(former pueblo governor)
Affiliation: Pueblo of Zia Council, General Delivery, San Ysidro, NM 87053.

GADWA, GORDON
(Indian band chief)
Affiliation: Kehewin Indian Band, Box 6218, Bonnyville, Alberta, Canada T0A 0L0 (403) 826-3333.

GAFFNEY, PAT
(school principal)
Affiliation: Ahfachkee Day School, Star Route, Box 40, Clewiston, FL 33440 (813) 983-6348.

GAHBOW, ARTHUR (Chippewa)
(ex-tribal chairperson)
Affiliation: Mille Lacs Reservation Business Committee, Star Route, Onamia, MN 56359 (612) 532-4181.

GAIASHKIBOS (Lac Courte Oreilles Ojibwe)
(tribal chairperson)
Affiliations: Lac Courte Oreilles Tribal Governing Board, Route 2, Box 2700, Hayward, WI 54843 (715) 634-8934.

GAINES-GRAY, ELIZABETH (Cherokee/Shawnee)
(magazine publisher)
Affiliation: Co-publisher, Native American Times, Oklahoma Indian Times, Inc., P.O. Box 6920050, Tulsa, OK 74169 (918) 438-6548 Fax 438-6545. E-mail: liz@okit.com.

GAJAR, DR. ANNA H. 1943-
(associate professor)
Education: Hunter College, BA, 1964; University of Virginia, MEd, 1973, PhD, 1977. *Principal occupation*: Associate professor of special education. *Home address*: 272 Spring St., State College, PA 16801 (814) 237-5473; 863-2284 (work). *Affiliations*: Assistant professor (1977-84), associate professor of special education (1984-), Dept. of Special Education, Penn State University, 226B Moore Bldg., University Park, PA 16802. Teaches a seminar on Issues in American Indian Special Education. *Other professional posts*: Consulting - evaluation of the American Indian Professional Training Program of the Dept. of Speech & Hearing Sciences, University of Arizona, Tucson, AZ, 1985; external evaluation of a professional degree training program entitled American Indian Professional Training in Speech-Language Pathology and Audiology at the University of Arizona, 1985. *Interests*: Improvement of graduate and undergraduate teacher education in special education (American Indian projects.) *Published works*: American Indian personnel preparation in special education: Needs, program components, programs (refereed) "Journal of American Indian Education," 1985; American Indian Special Education Teacher Training Program (U.S. Dept. of Education, Personnel Preparation report); American Indian Special Education Personnel Preparation (presentation before CEC International Convention); A Model Program for American Indian Special Education Teacher Training at The Pennsylvania State University (presentation at NIEA Convention).

GALBAVY, STEVE
(college president)
Affiliation: Stone Child Community College, RR 1, Box 1082, Box Elder, MT 59521 (406) 395-4313 Fax 395-4836.

GALE, NANCY
(editor)
Affiliation: "Linkages," TCI, Inc., 3410 Garfield St., NW, Washington, DC 20007 (202) 333-6350.

GALER, PAUL
(Indian school administrator)
Affiliation: Sac & Fox Settlement School, 1349 Meskwakie Rd., Tama, IA 52339 (515) 484-4990 Fax 484-3265.

GALLAGER, CATHERINE
(education coordinator)
Affiliation: Crow Creek/Lower Brule Agency, Bureau of Indian Affairs, P.O. Box 139, Fort Thompson, SD 57339 (605) 245-2398.

GALLEGOS, ANDREW (Pueblo)
(former pueblo governor)
Affiliation: Pueblo of Santa Ana, 2 Dove Rd., Bernalillo, NM 87004 (505) 867-3301.

GALLEGOS, BENNY (Pueblo)
(Indian school principal)
Affiliation: Tesuque Day School, Route 11, Box 2 Santa Fe, NM 87501 (505) 982-1516 Fax 982-2331.

GALLEGOS, DENNIS (Pueblo)
(Indian school principal)
Affiliation: Zia Day School, 350 Riverside Dr., San Ysidro, NM 87053 (505) 867-3553 Fax 867-5079.

GALLI, MARCIA
(board chairperson)
Affiliation: Utah Board of Indian Affairs, 144 N. Pinewood Cir., Layton, UT 84041 (801) 626-6818.

GALLOWAY, BRENT
(college department head)
Affiliation: Indian Languages, Literature and Linguistics, Saskatchewan Indian Federated College, University of Regina, 118 College West, Regina, SK, Canada S4S 0A2 (306) 584-8333.

GALLOWAY, DAVE
(health director)
Affiliation: Choctaw Nation Indian Health Center, 903 E. Monroe, McAlester, OK 74501 (918) 423-8440.

GALLOWAY, JAMES, MD
(clinical director-Indian hospital)
Affiliation: Whiteriver Indian Hospital, Whiteriver, AZ 85941 (602) 338-4911.

GAMBARO, RETHA WALDEN
(Muscogee-Creek) 1917-
(sculptor)
Born December 9, 1917, Lenna, Okla. *Education*: Corcoran School of Art, 1969. *Principal occupation*: Sculptor. *Home address*: 74 Dishpan Lane, Stafford, VA 22554 (540) 659-0130 Fax 720-0153. E-mail: viagambaro1@aol.com. *Arts specialization*: sculpture wall hangings. *Medium or media*: sculpture in bronze, stone, and wood. Mixed media sculpture. Wall hangings of mixed media only. Conferences attended or lectures presented: Galludet College, Washington, DC; Eugene O'Neill Center, Waterford, CT; Slater Memorial Museum, Norwich, CT; Williams School, New London, CT; Haverford College, Haverford, PA; Haskell Indian Jr. College, Lawrence, KS; Marywash College. *Exhibitions*: Smithsonian Institution-Museum of Natural History, Kennedy Center (Night of the First Americans), National Cathedral, Howard University, Folger Shakespeare Library, Trinity Episcopal Church, American Spirit Gallery, Art Barn, St. Augustine Chapel, People Life Insurance, Midtown Gallery, and U.S. Safe Deposit (all in Washington, D.C.); Art Institute of Philadelphia; Slater Museum, Norwich, CT; Coast Guard Academy & Yah Ta Hey Gallery (both in New London, CT); Peabody Museum (Cambriidge, MA); Hampton Museum (Hampton, VA); among others. *Major Collections*: U.S. Dept. of Parks, VA; National Aboretum, Galludet College, Washington, DC; B'Nai B'Rith Museum, Church of the Reformation, Native American Research, Howard University, and the Convention Center (all in Washington, D.C.); Daybreak Art Center, Seattle, WA; among others. *Memberships*: Artists Equity; Indian Arts and Crafts Association; National Museum of Women in the Arts (charter member); National Museum of the American Indian (charter member). *Awards, honors*: Best in Show at the Art League of Northern Virginia, and Best in Sculpture at the Mystic Harbour Invitational in Connecticut. *Biographical sources*: In publications - "Art Business News, Vol. 9 Issue 3, March 1982; "National American Indian Women's Art Show"; American Artists of Renown, 1981-82; Women At Work; Contemporary American Women Sculptors; Art and the Animal. Video - Born of Fire (28 minute educational film by White Light Productions); catalog - Attitude of Prayer.

GAMBLE, RICHARD
(Indian band chief)
Affiliation: Beardys Indian Band, Box 340, Duck Lake, SK, Canada S0K 1J0 (306) 467-4523.

GANIS, EVERETT
(school chairperson)
Affiliation: Little Wound Day School, P.O. Box 500, Kyle, SD 57752 (605) 455-2461.

GANJE, LUCY ANNIS 1949-
(professor of graphic arts)
Born December 14, 1949, Eagle Butte, S.D. *Education*: Black Hills State University, BS, 1983; Academy of Art College, MFA, 1984. *Principal occupation*: Professor of graphic arts. *Home address*: 419 Princeton St., Grand Forks, ND 58203 (701) 772-9259. *Affiliations*: Instructor, Cheyenne River Sioux Tribe Community College, 1985-86; Assistant professor of graphic arts, Native American Media Center Committee, Indian Programs Committee, University of North Dakota, School of Communication, Grand Forks, ND, 1988-. *Other professional posts*: Manager, Printing Division, Cheyenne River Sioux Tribe Telephone Authority, 1984-88; design consulting. *Professional activities*: Presenter, "Publication Design" Native American Journalists Association, Annual Convention, March 1991; Coordinator, North Dakota Indian Youth Leadership Institute, ND Dept. of Public Instruction, Indian Programs Division, Grand Forks, ND, June 1991; "Press Freedom in Indian Country" panel for Editors-Broadcasters Day, Oct. 1991; among others. *Memberships*: Association for Education In Journalism and Mass Communication; American Advertising Federation; Native American Journalists Association. *Awards, honors*: Invited and designed material for Native American Manufacturers Marketing Conference, Feb. 1989; Curriculum Development Grant for attendance at Native American Journalists Conference, Denver, CO, March 1991. Creative activity: Videos - "Rock Art at Pinon Canyon Maneuver Site," Southeastern Colorado, March 1990, produced by the National Rock Art Research Foundation; "Cultural Resources at Pinon Canyon," produced for the National Park Service, Summer 1991-.

GARCIA, CAROLE J. (Tohono O'Odham)
(craftsperson, store owner)
Affiliation: Reservation Creations, 2000 W. San Xavier Loop Rd., P.O. Box 27626, Tucson, AZ 85726 (602) 622-4900. *Other professional post*: Co-director, National Native American Cooperative, P.O. Box 1000, San Carlos, NM 85550.

GARCIA, CHARLOTTE (Pueblo)
(school principal)
Affiliation: Sky City Community School, P.O. Box 349, Acoma, NM 87034 (505) 552-6671 Fax 552-6672.

GARCIA, JOE
(NCAI vice president)
Affiliations: Vice President, National Congress of American Indians (NCAI), 1301 Connecticut Ave., NW #200, Washington, DC 20036 (202) 466-7767 Fax 466-7797.

GARCIA, LAURA V. (Navajo)
(school principal)
Affiliation: Crownpoint Community School, P.O. Box 178, Crownpoint, NM 87313 (505) 786-6160.

GARCIA, LEONARD D. (Santa Ana Pueblo)
(pueblo council governor)
Affiliation: Santa Ana Pueblo Council, 2 Dove Rd., Bernalillo, NM 87004 (505) 867-3301.

GARCIA, MARCELINO (Tewa Pueblo) 1932-
(instructional aid worker)
Born June 2, 1932, San Juan Pueblo, N.M. *Education*: U.S. Indian School, Santa Fe. *Principal occupation*: Instructional aid worker, B.I.A. *Home address*: P.O. Box 854, San Juan Pueblo, N.M. *Community Activities*: San Juan Pueblo Church (chairman). *Awards, honors*: Prize for Indian ceremonial sash belt, New Mexico State Fair.

GARCIA, MARTHA (Ramah Navajo)
(former tribal president)
Affiliation: Ramah Navajo Chapter Council, Rt. 2 Box 13, Ramah, NM 87321 (505) 775-7130.

GARCIA, MARVIN (Klamath)
(former tribal chairperson)
Affiliation: Klamath General Council, P.O. Box 436, Chiloquin, OR 97624 (503) 783-2219.

GARCIA, RAMON (Santo Domingo Pueblo)
(pueblo governor)
Affiliation: Pueblo of Santo Domingo, Box 99, Santo Domingo Pueblo, NM 87052 (505) 465-2214.

GARCIA, TONY (Yankton Sioux) 1951-
(educational administration/Indian education)
Born October 7, 1951, Pierre, S.D. *Education*: University of South Dakota, Ed.D., 1991. *Principal occupation*: Educational administration/Indian education. *Address*: unknown. *Affiliation*: Director of Indian Education, Rapid City School District, 1991-. *Other professional posts*: Assistant principal; teacher; director of child protection services; director of juvenile prevention; high school counselor; community educator. *Military service*: U.S. Army, 1970-72 (Spec. 4th class; Vietnam Veteran). *Community activities*: Board Member, Big Brothers & Big Sisters. *Memberships*: National Indian Education Association; South Dakota Indian Education Association; National Association of Bilingual Education; South Dakota Bilingual-Bicultural Association. *Awards, honors*: 1993 Dakota Wesleyan Indian Alumna of the Year. *Interests*: Founder of Ateyapi (Fatherhood) Society for Lakota People, Rapid City, SD. *Published works*: Dissertation - Attitude Difference As Seen by Indian and Non-Indian students Towards Their Teachers, 1991.

GARCIA, VINCE
(Te-Moak Band of Western Shoshone)
(tribal council chairperson)
Affiliation: South Fork Band Council, Box B-13, Lee, NV 89829 (702) 744-4273.

GARCIA, WILFRED (Pueblo)
(pueblo governor)
Affiliation: San Juan Pueblo Council, Box 1099, San Juan Pueblo, NM 87566 (505) 852-4400.

GARDNER, ARNOLD
(Indian band chief)
Affiliation: Eagle Lake #27 Indian Band, Box 27, Eagle River, Ontario, Canada P0V 1S0 (807) 755-5526.

GARDNER, GLENN, Jr. (Aleut)
(former AK village president)
Affiliation: Native Village of Sand Point, P.O. Box 447, Sand Point, AK 99661 (907) 383-3525.

GARDNER, LAURIE
(health administrator)
Affiliation: Upper Sioux Board of Trustees, P.O. Box 147, Granite Falls, MN 56241 (612) 564-2360.

GARDNER, LINDA N. (*Talking Bear*)
(United Lumbee) 1948-
(business owner)
Born August 1, 1948 in Amazonia, Mo. *Address*: Unknown. *Affiliations*: Co-owner, Moon & Stars Farm-Dolls, Falcon, MO, 1991-present. *Community activities*: United Lumbee Nation's Black Bear Clan; United Lumbee Nation's Black Bear Clan (council member, secretary/treasurer; newsletter editor); chief, Golden Hawk Society. *Memberships*: Black Bear Clan's Golden Hawk Society; Good Medicine Society (Wyota Council leader & philosophy teacher). *Interests*: "Since the mid-1980's, I have become more deeply involved in historical, philosophical and spiritual studies. In the past few years, I have devoted the majority of my time to learning (and sharing with others) the beliefs and traditions of our ancestors. I believe it is our sacred duty to pass on the ancient wisdom to future generations, so that the people might live."

GARFIELD, CATHI
(editor)
Affiliation: Southern California Indian Center News, P.O. Box 2550, Garden Grove, CA 92746 (213) 977-1366.

GARFIELD, DUANE (Yokut)
(tribal chairperson)
Affiliation: Tule River Tribal Council, P.O. Box 589, Porterville, CA 93258 (559) 781-4271.

GARNETTE, SHIRLEY (Sioux)
(school principal)
Affiliations: Wounded Knee School District, P.O. Box 350, Manderson, SD 57756 (605) 867-5433; Loneman Day School, Box 50, Oglala, SD 57764 (605) 867-5633.

GARRETT, THOMAS E.
(BIA director)
Affiliation: Congressional & Legislative Affairs, Bureau of Indian Affairs, Dept. of the Interior, 1849 C St., NW, Washington, DC 20240 (202) 208-5706.

GARRIOCH, SYDNEY
(Indian band chief)
Affiliation: Cross Lake Indian Band, Cross Lake, Manitoba, Canada R0B 0J0 (204) 676-2218.

GARZA, JOSE L. (*Aztatl*) (Coahuilteca/Lipan Apache) 1942-
(free lance writer, lecturer, workshops)
Born November 24, 1941, San Antonio, Tex. *Education*: Wayne State University, 1970-72. *Principal occupation*: Free lance writer, lecturer, workshops. *Home address*: 4643 6th St., Ecorse, MI 48229 (313) 388-6933. *Military service*: U.S. Air Force. *Memberships*: Casa De Unidad Cultural & Media Arts Center, 1980-; Latino Poets Association, 1985-; Native Writers Circle of the Americas, 1992-; Wordcraft Circle of Native Writers, 1992-. *Awards, honors*: Michigan Council for the Arts, 1989 Individual Artists Grant. *Interests*: Lectures and workshops on Native writing and culture. "Two hour workshops help dispel the stereotypes attributed to the many Native cultures of the Americas; focus is on reading and discussing works by contemporary Native writers that express a wide range of human emotions, experiences and current trends in writing." *Published works*: Masks, Folk Dances & Whole Bunch More (Ridgeway Press, 1989); Kamikazi (Edinboro Book Arts, 1992); Apple Comes Home (Red Age Unlimited, 1994).

GARZA, RAUL (Kickapoo of Texas)
(tribal chairperson)
Affiliation: Kickapoo Traditional Tribe of Texas, HC 1, Box 9700, Eagle Pass, TX 78853 (210) 773-2105.

GASPAR, DENNIS
(Indian education program director)
Affiliation: Todd County School District, Indian Education Program, P.O. Box 87, Mission, SD 57555 (605) 856-4869 Fax 856-2449.

GASSNEY, DR. PATRICK
(Indian school principal)
Affiliation: Ahfachkee Day School, Star Route, Box 40, Clewiston, FL 33440 (941) 983-6348 Fax 983-6535.

GASTELUM, ARCADIO (Pascua-Yaqui)
(former tribal chairperson)
Affiliation: Pascua-Yaqui Tribal Council, 7474 S. Camino De Oeste, Tucson, AZ 85746 (602) 883-2838.

GAYNOR, BASIL M.
(president; editor)
Affiliation: President, American Indian Liberation Crusade, Inc., 4009 S. Hallday Ave., Los Angeles, CA 90062 (323) 299-1810. *Other professional post*: Editor, "Indian Crusader," quarterly newsletter of the American Indian Liberation Crusade.

GEACI, ROBERT
(site director)
Affiliation: Ste. Marie Among the Iroquois, P.O. Box 146, Onondaga Lake Park, Liverpool, NY 13088 (315) 457-2990.

GEARY, MAUREEN
(attorney)
Affiliation: California Indian Legal Services, P.O. Box 488, Ukiah, CA 95482 (707) 462-3825.

GEBOE, CHARLES
(Indian education)
Affiliation: Chief, Branch of Elementary & Secondary Education, Office of Indian Education Programs, Bureau of Indian Affairs, Dept. of the Interior, MS-4140-MIB, 1849 C St., NW, Washington, DC 20240 (202) 208-1129.

GEDNALSKI, BOB
(elementary school principal)
Affiliation: St. Francis Indian School, P.O. Box 379, St. Francis, SD 57572 (605) 747-2299.

GEHMAN, R. DALE (Poarch Band Creek) 1957-
(radio broadcaster, consulting engineer)
Born June 16, 1957, Carlisle, Penn. *Education*: Alabama Aviation and Technical College, AB, 1976; Jefferson Davis College (Brewton, AL), AAS (Indus-

trial Electronics), 1993; Atmore State Tech. College, 1991-93 (General Electronics). *Principal occupation*: Radio broadcasting, consulting engineer. *Address*: Resides in Pennsylvania. *Affiliations*: President, chief engineer, Digital Engineering Service, Ephrata, PA, 1992-; chief engineer, WIOV AM/FM, Ephrata, PA, 1993-. *Past professional posts*: Broadcaster, consulting engineer, WASG Radio, Atmore, AL, 1981-92; board member, Alabama Broadcasters Association; board member, Creek Indian Enterprises (The economic development arm of the Poarch Band of Creek Indians). *Community activities*: Atmore Chamber of Commerce (director, 1984-90); Gospel Light Church, Inc. (board member, secretary); Creek Indian Arts Council (board member). *Memberships*: Certified Senior Broadcast Engineer by the Society of Broadcast Engineers, 1993-; Alabama Broadcasters Association, 1987-93; Alabama Emergency Broadcasting System (chairperson, 1993); Poarch Band of Creek Indians Tribal Council (member, 1977-90); Atmore Civitan Club (past president). *Awards, honors*: "Outstanding Young Men of America" 1987. *Interests*: Private pilot at age 16; first class FCC Radiotelephone license at age 16; outdoor camping, skiing; electronics; public service for my community and tribe.

GEIOGAMAH, HANAY
(director/writer)
Affiliation: American Indian Dance Theatre, 223 East 61st St., New York, NY 10021. *Address*: 1750 Wilcox St. #223, Los Angeles, CA 90028 (213) 463-8535.

GELPIN, OLLIE
(school principal)
Affiliation: Toadlena Boarding School, P.O. Box 857, Toadlena, NM 87324 (505) 789-3201.

GENDAR, JEANNINE
(editor)
Affiliation: "News From Native California," Heyday Books, P.O. Box 9145, Berkeley, CA 94709 (510) 549-3564.

GENE, DAVID
(AK village council president)
Affiliation: Native Village of Gakona, P.O. Box 124, Gakona, AK 99586 (907) 822-3497.

GENERAL, GAIL (Mohawk)
(artist; store co-owner/manager)
Affiliation: Mohawk Impressions, Mohawk Nation, P.O. Box 20, Hogansburg, NY 13655 (518) 358-2467.

GENETT, WARREN DEAN
(Potawatomi/Menominee) 1957-
(U.S. Geological Survey)
Born August 20, 1957, Menominee Indian Reservation, Keshena, WI. *Education*: Georgia State University, B.A., 1987. *Principal occupation*: U.S. Geological Survey, Water Resources Division. *Home address*: 228 Valleybrook Dr., Woodstock, GA 30188 (404) 926-4531. *Affiliation*: Chairperson, The Native American Center of Georgia, 110 S. Main St., Suite 203, Woodstock, GA 30188 (404) 924-3738, 1993-. *Military service*: U.S. Air Force, 1977-81. *Community activities*: Chair, Atlanta Couples Together, 1987-89; Atlanta Regional Commission, Diversity Collaborative, 1994. *Membership*: American Society for Quality Control, 1993-. *Awards, honors*: Emory University, for Native American History Month, 1994; United Way (Atlanta, GA) for V.I.P. Selection Committee, 1994; U.S. Geological Survey, WRD for Total Quality Management. *Interests*: "Primary focus is to develop a sound organizational structure for the Native American Center of Georgia (formed in 1993) and to promote the organizational success of the Center throughout the state of Georgia."

GENTRY, BARBARA (Wampanoag) 1948-
(Native American education)
Born October 21, 1948, Utica, N.Y. *Education*: Utah State University, BS, 1974; University of Wyoming, MA, 1975. *Principal occupation*: Native American education. *Affiliations*: Counselor, Union High School, West Jr. High School and Ute Tribe, Fort Duchesne, UT, 1974-76; head counselor/director of paraprofessional counseling program, University of Wyoming, 1976-77; education unit director, Boston Indian Council, 1977-83; entrepreneur, partnership in family-owned business, 1983-90; multicultural coordinator, Eastern Michi-

gan University, Ypsilanti, MI, 1990-. *Other professional posts*: Consulting in Indian education. *Memberships*: National Indian Education Association, 1974-86; National Indian Adult Education (Northeast Representative, 1982). *Honors, awards*: 1991 Gold Medallion Award, Eastern Michigan University; "Oustanding Young Woman of America," 1982; "Successful Indian Education Program," by Office of Indian Education, U.S. Dept. of Education, 1980.

GENTRY, BEATRICE (Wampanoag) 1910-
(teacher)
Born August 31, 1910, Aquinnah (Gay Head), Mass. *Education*: Framingham State College, BS, 1932; Bureau of Indian Affairs Summer Institute, Pine Ridge, SD, summer, 1935; Tulsa University, Teacher Certificate, 1962; Bridgewater State College, Hyannis, MA, 1967-1968. *Principal occupation*: Teacher. *Home address*: State Road, Box 72, Aquinnah, MA 02535 (508) 645-9900. *Affiliations*: Teacher, Fort Sill Indian School, Lawton, OK, 1934-41; teacher, Wagoner Elementary School, OK, 1960-64; teacher, Chilmark Elementary School, MA, 1964-74. *Other professional posts*: President, Wampanoag Tribal Council of Gay Head, 1972-76 (helped establish modern organizational structure of tribal government, first governing officer); member, Massachusetts Commission on Indian Affairs, 1974-76 (helped establish and organize the first Massachusetts Indian Commission in the 20th century, and whose membership was all Native Americans of MA). *Community activities*: Town of Gay Head (zoning committee; Gay head Public Library (trustee); Gay Head Community Council (charter member); Wagoner School Band (president); Officers' Wives' Club (member, 1943-1958; secretary, 1947-1948; Griffith Air Force Base, Rome, N.Y.). *Memberships*: OK Education Association, 1934-42, 1961-64; MA Teachers Association, 1964-75; National Indian Education Association, 1972-75; National Retired Teachers' Association, 1975-. *Awards, honors*: Alumni Achievement Award, 1982, from Framingham State College Alumni Association at 50th anniversary of graduating class; Ancient Aquinnah (Gay Head) Indian Cemetery on behalf of the Wampanoag Tribal Council of Gay Head; speaker at dedication ceremonies of Gay Head Cliffs as National Landmark, centennial celebration of Town of Gay Head, OK Education Association Conference, and J.F. Kennedy Bicentennial Memorial Dinner, Natick Democratic Town Committee. *Interests*: "As an Air Force officer's wife, I have had the opportunity to live and travel to all parts of the continental U.S. & Europe. As a Native American educator with experience providing direct services to Native American children from different tribes, and experience working within the public school system in different parts of the country, I have learned that the only way for Native American people to determine their own destiny economically and politically among the dominant white society is to make the necessary demands upon the educational system of Indians and non-Indians alike: to provide an avenue to attain the goals that each society deems essential and demand respect for those values and cultures. The educational system's complete disregard and disrespect for Native American values and culture along with lack of Native American input in education programs, communication, counseling and advisement, and lack of role models result in not only inadequate preparation for college, but inadequate for life. I feel it is only through those demands on the educational system for all Americans (including Native Americans) that Native American people will be able to realize our basic needs: the preservation of our lands, the preservation of our religion, culture, and history, and the preservation of our families; that is the sacred rights of our people."

GENTRY, JO LYNN
(editor)
Affiliation: Business Alert, First Nations Financial Report, 69 Kelly Rd., Falmouth, VA 22405 (703) 371-5615.

GENTRY-LEWIS, JO LYNN (Dine-Navajo)
(board president)
Address & Affiliation: President, Phoenix Indian Center, 2601 North 3rd St. #100, Phoenix, AZ 85004 (602) 264-6768 Fax 263-7822

GEOIGAMAH, HANAY (Kiowa)
(playwright, movie producer)
Address: 1750 N. Wilcox #223, Los Angeles, CA 90028 (213) 463-8535. Founder of the American Indian Dance Theatre.

GEORGE, ART (Nooksack)
(tribal chairperson)
Affiliation: Nooksack Indian Tribe, P.O. Box 157, Deming, WA 98244 (360) 592-5176.

GEORGE, DOUGLAS M. *(Kanentiio)*
(Mohawk) 1955-
(writer; journalist)
Born February 1, 1955, Akwesasne Mohawk Reservation, N.Y. *Education*: Syracuse University, 1977-80; Antioch School of Law (Washington, DC), 1980-83. *Principal occupation*: Writer; journalist. *Home address*: Box 450, Oneida Iroquois Territory, Oneida Castle, NY 13421 (315) 363-1655 (work-phone & fax). E-mail: kanentiio@aol.com. *Affiliations*: Editor, Akwesasne Notes, Mohawk Nation, Rooseveltown, NY, 1986-92; columnist, Syracuse Newspapers, 1993-94; chairperson, Round Dance Productions, 1992-; Trustee, National Museum of the American Indian, 1996-2002. *Other professional posts*: Chairperson, Round Dance Productions, Inc. (non-profit educational & cultural organization formed for the preservation of Native American culture), 1991-; editor, Indian Time newspaper, 1986-90; in the process of writing for film & book publishers. *Community activities*: Mohawk Nation Land Claims Committee, 1984-91; Mohawk Nation Business Committee, 1984-90; Member of the volunteer Akwesasne emergency team, 1983-91. *Membership*: Akwesasne Communications Society - Radio CKON (board member). *Awards, honors*: D'Arcy McNickle Fellowship Recipient, 1979, Newberry Library, Chicago, IL; Wassaja Award for Journalism Excellence from the Native American Journalists Association, 1994. *Interests*: Creative writing; travels to Europe, Mid-East, China, India, Thailand, Korea, and extensive travel throughout North America - historical research and writing. *Biographical sources*: Articles - Los Angeles Times, Oct. 1991; Syracuse (NY) Herald Journal, July 1990; Now Magazine (Toronto, ON), May 1990; Gentlemen's Quarterly, Nov. 1993. *Published works*: Skywoman (Clear Lighr Press, 1999); Syracuse herald columnist - over 40 articles; numerous stories printed in Akwesasne Notes, 1986-.

GEORGE, LYLE EMERSON (Suquamish)
(tribal chairperson)
Affiliation: Suquamish Tribal Council, P.O. Box 498, Suquamish, WA 98392 (206) 598-3311.

GEORGE, EVANS McCLURE, JR. (Catawba) 1932-
(textile worker)
Born January 26, 1932, Rock Hill, S.C. *Education*: Clemson University, 1952-56. *Principal occupation*: Textile worker. *Home address*: 1119 McDow Dr., Rock Hill, SC 29730. *Affiliation*: Celanese Corporation, Celriver Plant, Rock Hill, SC, 1958-. *Community activities*: Member, Rock Hill Parks & Recreation Commission; member, Catawba Indian Tribe; York County IPTAY Club (past president); Church Youth leader, 1968-. *Awards, honors*: Captain of 1950 South Carolina Shrine Bowl team; Clemson University Football team (captain, 1955); drafted by Washington Redskins, 1955; outstanding volunteer, American Cancer Society. *Interests*: Lifelong vocational interest in the American textile industry; coaching football; carpentry; fishing. *Biographical source*: Red Carolinian - Where Are They Now? and People of the River, Evening Herald articles.

GEORGE, GAIL (Saginaw-Chippewa)
(former tribal chief)
Affiliation: Saginaw-Chippewa Tribal Council, 7070 E. Broadway Rd., Mt. Pleasant, MI 48858 (517) 772-5700.

GEORGE, GEORGIA C. (Suquamish)
(tribal chairperson)
Affiliation: Suquamish Tribal Council, P.O. Box 498, Suquamish, WA 98392 (206) 598-3311.

GEORGE, LEONARD
(Indian band chief)
Affiliation: Burrard Indian Band, 3082 Chum-Iye Dr., N. Vancouver, B.C., Canada V7H 1B3 (604) 929-3455.

GEORGE, LEVI (Yakima)
(school chairperson)
Affiliation: Yakima Tribal School, P.O. Box 151, Toppenish, WA 98948 (509) 865-5121.

GEORGE, LYLE EMERSON (Suquamish)
(tribal council chairperson)
Affiliation: Suquamish Tribal Council, P.O. Box 498, Suquamish, WA 98392 (360) 598-3311.

GEORGE, LOUIS, JR.
(Indian band chief)
Affiliation: English River Indian Band, General Delivery, Patunak, Saskatchewan, Canada S0M 2H0 (306) 396-2055.

GEORGE, MERVIN, JR. (Hoopa)
(former tribal chairperson)
Affiliation: Hooppa Valley Tribal Council, P.o. Box 1348, Hoopa, CA 95546 (530) 625-4211.

GEORGE, NORMAN
(Indian band chief)
Affiliation: Mowachtaht Indian Band, P.O. Box 459, Gold River, B.C., Canada V0P 1G0 (604) 283-2532.

GEORGE, OSWALD C. (Coeur D'Alene) 1917-
(tribal official)
Born May 22, 1917, De Smet, Idaho. *Education*: Gonzaga University, 1936-37. *Principal occupation*: Tribal official. *Home address*: P.O. Box 155, Plummer, ID 83851. *Affiliation*: Coeur D'Alene Tribal Council. *Military service*: U.S. Army Infantry, 1940-45. *Community activities*: Boy Scouts of America (institutional representative); Veterans of Foreign Wars. *Memberships*: Affiliated Tribes of Northwest Indians (past president); National Congress of American Indians (vice president, Portland area); Pacific Northwest Indian Center, Inc., Spokane, Wash. (board of trustees). *Interests*: "My interest lies in the youth of our nation; promoting citizenship, and training the future leaders of our country. I'm also very much interested in the preservation of our Indian culture and heritage; preservation of our treaty rights and the perpetual retention of our land base — these to me are sacred rights and should be respected."

GEORGE, SAM (Athapascan)
(former AK village president)
Affiliation: Native Village of Kluti-Kaah (aka Copper Center), P.O. Box 68, Copper Center, AK 99573 (907) 822-5541.

GESSAY, GREGORY, MD
(clinical director)
Affiliation: Phoenix, Indian Medical Center, 4212 North 16th St., Phoenix, AZ 85016 (602) 263-1200.

GETCHES, DAVID
(attorney-professor)
Affiliation: University of Colorado School of Law, 404 UCB - Fleming Law Bldg., Rm. 080, Boulder, CO 80309 (303) 492-0966.

GETTCHELL, RICHARD (Micmac)
(former tribal chief)
Affiliation: Arrostook Band of Micmac Indians, P.O. Box 772, Preque Island, ME 04769 (207) 764-1972.

GETTY, IAN
(director-Indian Institute)
Affiliation: Nakoda Institute, Stoney Tribal Administration, P.O. Box 120, Morley, Alberta, Canada T0L 1N0 (403) 881-3770.

GETZWILLER, STEVE
(craftsperson)
Address: Spear G Ranch, Benson, AZ 85602 (520) 586-2579 Fax 586-2960. E-mail: getzwiller@theriver. com. Website: www.navajorug.com. Steve is a leading authority on Navajo textiles. He has been a collector, trader, and collaborative-innovator of Navajo weaving for over 25 years. He frequently exhibits his textiles in museum exhibits.

GEVING, RENEE
(museum manager)
Affiliation: Walker Wildlife & Indian Artifacts Museum, State Hwy. 200, Box 336, Walker, MN 56484 (218) 547-1257.

GHOST BEAR, GEORGE (Oglala Sioux)
(education committee chair)
Affiliation: Chairperson, Education Committee, Oglala Lakotah Tribe, P.O. Box H, Pine Ridge, SD 57770 (605) 867-2244 Fax 867-2609.

GIAGO, TIM (*Nanwica Kciji*) (Oglala Sioux) 1934-
(journalist, editor & publisher)
Born July 12, 1934, Pine Ridge Reservation, S.D. *Education*: San Jose Junior College; University of Nevada, Reno; Harvard University (Nieman Fellowship, 1990-91). *Principal occupation*: Publisher. *Address*: Unknown. *Affiliation*: Publisher/owner, Indian Country Today, P.O. Box 2180, Rapid City, SD 57709 (605) 341-0011 Fax 341-6940, 1981-. *Community activities*: U.S. West Communications (state executive board); Multi-Cultural Management Training Program - University of Missouri, Columbia (board of directors); Native Peoples (editorial board). *Awards, honors*: 1985 - H.L. Menkin Award from the Baltimore Sun for Best Column; Civil & Human Rights Award from the National Education Association in 1988; Harvard University Award for Contributions to Minority Journalism in 1990; University of Missouri School of Journalism, Medal of Honor for Distinguished Journalism; inducted into the South Dakota Hall of Fame in 1995; Distinguished Service Award from the Washington Times, and has been Publisher while his newspaper, "Indian Country Today," has received more than 70 awards for excellence; articles featured in "People" magazine, "Denver Post" magazine, "Minnesota Monthly," "Chicago Tribune" magazine; and has appeared on CBS Nightwatch, the Oprah Winfrey Show, and the NBC Nightly News. *Published works*: The Aboriginal Sin (Historian Press, 1978); Notes From Indian Country, Volume I, 1978-82; editor, The American Indian and the Media; write a weekly column syndicated by Knight Ridder Tribune Service; articles in various magazines.

GIAMMARINO, BARBARA
(*Mi Ma Ku-Berry Woman*)
(storyteller)
Address: 24 Burt Rd., Springfield, MA 01118 (413) 783-1665. Barbara presents history and culture of American Indian people in a unique program of singing, drumming, dancing, and storytelling. An artistically organized performance to present her collection of authentic Native American articles.

GIBBS, BONNIE
(museum director)
Affiliation: School of Nations Museum, Principia College, Elsah, IL 62028 (618) 374-2131 ext. 312.

GIBBS, HUGH (Etowah Cherokee)
(tribal chief)
Affiliation: Etowah Cherokee Nation, Cleveland, TN.

GIBBS, JAMES
(school supt.)
Affiliation: Fort Towson Schools, Indian Education Program, P.O. Box 39, Fort Towson, OK 74735 (405) 873-2712.

GIBSON, JIMMY L.
(BIA agency supt.)
Affiliation: Okmulgee Agency, Bureau of Indian Affairs, P.O. Box 370, Okmulgee, OK 74447 (918) 756-3950 Fax 756-9626.

GIBSON, WILLIAM (*Wassaja*) (Onondaga) 1932-
(retired account technician)
Born January 20, 1932, Yonkers, N.Y. *Education*: Manhattan College, 1956-58. *Principal occupation*: Retired account technician - municipal housing authority *Home address*: 66 Washington St. #12B, Poughkeepsie, NY 12601. *Affiliation*: Principal Chief & President, Northeastern Native American Association (845) 473-2833 Fax 471-7106. *Other professional posts*: Editor/Publisher, Smoke Signals; editor, Common Ground; editor, Westchester Advocate; security supervisor, Sentry Investigations; security director & account technician, Municipal Housing Authority; *Military service*: U.S. Marine Corps, 1950-52. *Community activities*: Labor & Industry chairman (C.A.C.) NYS Urban Development Commission; labor chairman & national board member of Negro Labor Council, Yonkers Human Rights Commission; chairman, Yonkers Community Action Program; commissioner of deeds, Westchester County, NY; coordinator of 1963 March on Washing-

ton. *Membership*: Native American Writers & Artists Association (secretary); Pan American Indian Association; American Indian Community House. *Awards, honors*: 1982 Golden Globe for Poetry; Even Eleven-Man of the Year, 1965; 1986 Silver Scribe (Native American Writers/Artists). *Interests*: Chief Wassaja is also an ordained minister in the Native American Church - ordained 1995. "Goal in life: To be an instrument of peace, to lead, walk beside or follow those who still follow the path of our fathers into the 7th generation. To be loved, respected and needed;" guest columnist with several Native American newspapers. *Biographical sources*: Who's Who in Poetry (World of Poetry); 1989 American Anthology of Contemporary Poetry.

GIBSON, WILLIAM
(monument supt.)
Affiliation: Mound City Group National Monument, 16062 State Route 104, Chillicothe, OH 45601 (614) 774-1125.

GILBERT, ERIC MICHAEL
(Indian band chief)
Affiliation: Williams Lake Indian Band, RR #3, Box 4, Williams Lake, British Columbia, Canada V2G 1M3 (604) 296-3507.

GILBERT, NINA, MD
(clinical director)
Affiliation: Lac Courte Oreilles Tribal Clinic, Route 2, Box 2750, Hayward, WI 54843 (715) 634-4153.

GILBERT, TRIMBLE (Gwitch'in Athapascan)
(village council chief)
Affiliation: Arctic Village Traditional Council, P.O. Box 22050, Arctic Village, AK 99722 (907) 587-5320.

GILBERT, WILLARD S., JR.
(board president)
Affiliation: Native Americans for Community Action, Inc., Flagstaff Indian Center, 2717 N. Steves Blvd., Suite 11, Flagstaff, AZ 86004 (520) 526-2968.

GILES, DONALD E. (Peoria)
(tribal chief)
Affiliation: Peoria Indian Tribe of Oklahoma, P.O. Box 1527, Miami, OK 74355 (918) 540-2535.

GILES, MARCELLA (Creek)
(attorney)
Address: 926 Ridge Dr., McLean, VA 22101 (202) 208-6050. *Affiliation*: Delegate, Muskogee Creek National Tribal Bar Association.

GILES, SHARON
(Indian education program director)
Affiliation: Newcastle Public Schools I-1, Indian Education Program, 101 N. Main St., Newcastle, OK 73065 (405) 387-4304 Fax 387-2891.

GILKEY, JESSIE M. (Maidu)
(tribal chairperson)
Affiliation: Mooretown Rancheria, P.O. Box 1842, Oroville, CA 95965 (916) 533-3625.

GILLENWATER, STEVE
(BIA special education coordinator)
Affiliation: Shiprock Agency, Bureau of Indian Affairs, P.O. Box 3239, Shiprock, NM 87420 (505) 368-4427 ext. 5 Fax 368-4427 ext. 300.

GILLILAND, RICHARD M. (*Ne Mook Na Na*) 1937-
(artist & craftsman)
Born October 9, 1937, Detroit, Mich. *Education*: Michigan State University (2 years). *Principal occupation*: Artist & craftsman. *Home address*: Rt. 1, Box 836, Interlochen, MI 49643 (616) 275-6476. *Affiliations*: Ward & Eis Art Gallery, Petoskey, MI (major outlet); Minnetrista Council for Great Lakes Native American Studies, Muncie, IN (recently commissioned for museum work). *Military service*: U.S. Army, 1958-60 (E-5; 82nd Airborne Div.; Military Intelligence Det.) *Community activities*: Lecture to schools and scouting activities on Native American arts and crafts. *Memberships*: Liberty Tree (Black Powder Club) (president, 1981-88); Grand Traverse Metis, 1983-. *Interests*: "My main vocational interests are birch bark ma kuks, quill boxes, medicine drums, trade silver work, flint lock rifles, and any area of arts and crafts of the Eastern

Woodland people. Most of my avocational interests are in the same vane; I attend many rondezvous gaining any expertise of brain tanning, etc. and meeting and talking with people with like interests. I spent 18 years living in the Alaskan bush. Halibut fishing, horse wrangling, guiding, log cabin building were but a few of my activities. I was closely associated with Indian and Eskimo people in my life there. Currently, I have about 100 pages written on my life there. Also, I'm currently writing for grants to work on book devoted to bark ma kuks and quill boxes and the people doing them."

GILLIHAN, JAMES EDWARD (Eastern Cherokee) 1935-
(personal property appraiser)
Born May 25, 1935, Wabash County, Ill. *Education*: Southern Illinous University, BS, 1957; Sussex College (England), LHD, 1971. *Principal occupation*: Personal property appraiser. *Address*: Resides in Illinois. *Affiliations*: Senior Appraiser, Gillihan & Associates, DeKalb, IL, 1964-; instructor in anthropology, Northern Illinois University, DeKalb, IL, 1989-. *Other professional post*: Guest curator & chairperson of the Advisory Board, Indian Museum of North America, Crazy Horse Memorial, Crazy Horse, SD. *Community activities*: Rotary Club of DeKalb, IL; lecturer in Native American philosophy and religion, The Theosophical Society, Wheaton, IL; Keeper of the Pipe of Sitting Bull (noted Lakota religious leader); guest lecturer in public schools. *Memberships*: International Society of Appraisers; Art Appraisers of America, Ltd.; New England Appraiser's Association. *Awards, honors*: Has served on advisory boards of the following organizations: The Illinois Historic Preservation Commission; The SD Committee on the Humanities; The Grant Review Committee of the IL Arts Council and the National Trust for Historic Preservation; he was the IL State Historic Preservation Officer and the Cultural Preservation Director for the State of SD; and has been vice president at both Wabash College and Yankton College. *Interests*: "I have great interest in preserving Native American religion & philosophy. I give many lectures both in North America and in Europe to promote understanding of these beliefs." *Biographical sources*: International Who's Who in Art & Antiques; Who's Who in the West and Southwest; Illinois Lives; Dictionary of International Biography. *Published works*: Barbizon Art, 1966; Primitive Art, 1967; The American West, 1968 (all published by Lakeview Center, Peoria, IL)

GILLILAND, HAP *(Splits the Rock)* 1918-
(professor emeritus)
Born August 26, 1918, Willard, Colo. *Education*: Western State College, BA, 1949, MA, 1950; University of Northern Colorado, EdD, 1958. *Principal occupation*: Professor emeritus of education & Native American studies . *Home address*: 2032 Woody Dr., Billings, MT 59102 (406) 652-7598 Fax 248-3465. E-mail: hapcie@aol.com. *Affiliations*: Professor of education and Native American studies, Montana State University, Billings, 1960-88, emeritus, 1989-present. *Other professional post*: President & editor, The Council for Indian Education, Billings, MT, 1972-present; speaker on Indian education, and conducts teacher training workshops on reservations throughout the U.S. teaching teachers how to adapt to the Native American cultures, 1988-present; speaker on education of Native people at conferences. *Past professional posts*: Director, Northern Cheyenne Campus Experience Project, 1965; director, Crow Indian Reservation Educational Survey, 1966-67; director, Remedial Reading, Northern Cheyenne Reservation, 1965-68; director, Indian Upward Bound Project, 1966-69; director, EPDA and NDEA in Remedial Reading for Indian students, 1967, 1969-70; reading specialist, Lake Penn Schools, Alaska (14 Indian and Eskimo villages), Fall 1980, '81, '83. *Military service*: U.S. Army Air Corps, 1941-46. Past *community activities*: Directed remedial reading program in 4 schools serving Northern Cheyenne reservation, 1965-68; director, Upward Bound Project, 1966-69; Northern Cheyenne Tribal Scholarship Committee (chairman, 1969-72); Northern Cheyenne Education Planning Committee, 1968-75; National Indian Education Committee of the Association on American Indian Affairs, 1965-85. *Memberships*: Committee on Native Americans and Reading, International Reading Association (chairman, 1979-1980). *Awards, honors*: Outstanding Alumnus Award, Western State College, 1979; Bronz Plaque in recognition of Outstanding Contributions to Child's Rights & Education," Billings Committee for International Year of the Child, 1978; $1000 Merit Award for Research & Creative Endeavor, Committee on Evaluation of Faculty, Montana State University-Billings. *Interests*: Study of native cultures; traveling, photography; and writing in relation to that interest. Three extended trips to South America to live with Yanoamo Indians; two trips to New Zealand to conduct teacher training for teachers of Maori students. *Published works*: Textbooks: Indian Children's Books (Council for Indian Education, 1976), Chant of the Red Man (Council for Indian Education, 1976); Teaching the Native American (Kendall-Hunt, 1988; revised edition, 1992, 1995 & 1999); Drums of the Headhunters (Winston, 1988); Mystery Tracks in the Snow: A Guide to Animal Tracks & Tracking (Naturegraph, 1990); Flint's Rock (Roberts Rinehart, 1994); Voices of Native America (Kendall Hunt, 1997); Alone in the Wilderness (Naturegraph, 2001); Wolf River (Council for Indian Education, 2001); Two novels and 19 children's book on Indian life & culture; edited 120 children's books published by the Council for Indian Education; Standardized Tests: Red Cloud Diagnostic Reading Test (Council for Indian Education; journal articles: "The New View of Native Americans in Children's Books," The Reading Teacher.

GILLIS, KAREN
(school principal)
Affiliation: Dunseith Day School, P.O. Box 759, Dunseith, ND 58371 (701) 263-4636.

GILMAN, DAVID R. *(Gney Ottah)* (Abenaki of Mazipskwik) 1938-
(retired-social scientist, U.S. Forest Service)
Born October 12, 1938. *Principal occupation*: Retired-social scientist, U.S. Forest Service. *Address*: Unknown. *Affiliations*: Sawtooth National Forest, Twin Falls, ID, retired 1994. "Since retirement, I've done soil consulting work, but have spent most of my time volunteering for the Abenaki of Mazpskwik." *Community service*: Tribal council financial officer, Abenaki of Mazipskwik; local and statewide environmental projects.

GILMORE, KEN
(Indian center director)
Affiliation: Lone Pine Indian Education Center, 1120 Goodwin St., Lone Pine, CA 93545 (760) 876-5394.

GIPP, DAVID M.
(college president)
Affiliation: United Tribes Technical College, 3315 University Dr., Bismarck, ND 58501 (701) 255-3285 ext. 293.

GIPP, GERALD E.
(executive director)
Affiliation: Executive director, American Indian Higher Education Consortium (AIHEC), 121 Oronoco St., Alexandria, VA 22314 (703) 838-0400 Fax 838-0388. E-mail: ggipp@aihec.org. *Past professional post*: president, Haskell Indian Nations University, Lawrence, KS.

GIPP, WILLIAM C. (Standing Rock Sioux) 1940-
(BIA agency supt.)
Born November 11, 1940, Fort Yates, N.D. (Standing Rock Sioux Reservation). *Education*: Black Hills State College, BS, 1968; South Dakota State University, MA, 1973. *Principal occupation*: BIA agency supt. *Address*: Blackfeet Agency, BIA, Browning, MT 59417 (406) 338-7544. *Affiliation*: Supt., Rosebud Sioux Agency, Rosebud, SD, 1984-87; supt., Blackfeet Agency, BIA, Browning, MT, 1987-. *Other professional post*: Board of directors, Boy Scouts of America, Minnesota. *Military service*: U.S. Army, 1963-67 (Sergeant E-5, Special Forces, Vietnam Vet). *Memberships*: American Legion; Veterans of Foreign Wars; National Congress of American Indians; South Dakota Teachers Association.

GIRTY, FLOSSIE I.
(BIA field rep.)
Affiliation: Southern Paiute Field Station, BIA, P.O. Box 720, St. George, UT 84771 (435) 674-9720.

GISH, ROBERT FRANKLIN (Cherokee of Oklahoma) 1940-
(writer, professor emeritus)
Born April 1, 1940, Albuquerque, N.M. *Education*: University of New Mexico, MA, 1967, PhD, 1972. *Principal occupation*: Writer, emeritus professor. *Address*: P.O. Box 12562, Albuquerque, NM 87195. E-mail: robert.gish@uni.edu. *Affiliations*: Distinguished Scholar & Professor of English, University of Northern Iowa, 1967-91; Director, Ethnic Studies Program, Professor of English, English Dept., California Polytechnic State University, San Luis Obispo, CA, 1991-2000; visiting NM writer, University of New Mexico, 2001-present. *Other professional post*: Contributing editor, "The Bloomsbury Review." *Memberships*: Authors Guild; Pen West; Western Writers of America. *Award*: Distinguished Alumni Award, University of New Mexico. *Biographical sources*: Who's Who in America; Who's Who in the West. *Published works*: First Horses: Stories of the New West (University of Nevada Press, 1993); Songs of My Hunter Heart (University of New Mexico Press, 1994); When Coyote Howls (University of New Mexico Press, 1994); Bad Boys and Black Sheep (University of Nevada Press, 1996); Beyond Bounds (University of New Mexico Press, 1997; Dreams of Quivira (Clear Light Publishers, 1998); Beautiful Swift Fox: Erna Ferguson's Southwest (Texas A&M University Press, 1998).

GISHEY, LAWRENCE
(college president)
Affiliation: Navajo Community College, Tsaile Rural Post Office, Tsaile, AZ 86556 (602) 724-3311.

GISHIE, LEO T. (Navajo) 1941-
(educational administration)
Born April 26, 1941, Tees To Community, Ariz. *Education*: Northern Arizona University, BS, 1973; University of New Mexico, MA, 1984. *Principal occupation*: Educational administration. *Home address*: Resides in Arizona. *Affiliations*: Assistant to Dean of Instruction, Navajo Community College, Tsaile, AZ (5 years); principal, BIA School, Holbrook, AZ, 1987-90; principal, Wide Ruins Boarding School, Chambers, AZ, 1991-93; principal, Lukachukai Boarding School, Lukachukai, AZ, 1993-. *Other professional posts*: AIRCA (president, 4; years personnel director, 4 years). *Military service*: U.S. Army (Staff Sgt. or E-5, 1963-66; Expert Medal). *Community activities*: Local board member (8 years). *Awards, honors*: Outstanding Award for BIA Service. *Interests*: Administration; rodeo competition; public work, public speaking; some travel.

GIVENS, MARY (Kialegee)
(former tribal mekko)
Affiliation: Kialegee Tribal Town, P.O. Box 332, Wetumka, OK 74883 (405) 452-3262 Fax 452-3413.

GIVIN, LEWIS B. (Manadan)
(professor)
Affiliation: University of Massachusetts, Room 217, New Africa House, Amherst, MA 01003 (413) 545-5103.

GLANCY, DIANE (Cherokee) 1941-
(professor of English, writer)
Born March 18, 1941, Kansas City, Mo. *Education*: University of Missouri, BA (English Literature), 1964; University of Central Oklahoma, MA (English),1983; University of Iowa, MFA, 1988. *Principal occupation*: Professor of English, writer. *Home address*: 261 Brimhall, St. Paul, MN 55105 (651) 690-2174 Fax 696-6430. E-mail: glancy@macalester.edu. *Affiliation*: Professor of English, Macalester College, St. Paul, MN, 1988-present. *Membership*: Wordcraft Circle of Native Writers and Storytellers. *Awards, honors*: Received the 1986 Lakes and Prairies Prize for "One Age in a Dream," poetry book; received the 1988 Capricorn Prize from the Writer's Voice, New York, for "Iron Woman"; received the 1992 Minnesota Book Award for Poetry; 2001 Cherokee Medal of Honor; 2003 National Endowment for the Arts. *Published works*: "Brown Wolf Leaves the Res," poetry book (Blue Cloud Quarterly, 1984); "One Age in a Dream," poetry book (Milkweed Edition, Minneapolis, MN, 1986; "Offering," poetry book (Holy Cow! Press, 1988); "Iron Woman," poetry book (New Rivers Press, Minneapolis, 1990); "Lone Dog's Winter Count," poetry book (West End Press, 1991); "Coyote's Quodlibet," poetry book (Chax Press, 1995); "Boom Town," poetry book (Black Hat Press, 1995); "The Only Piece of Furniture in the House," poetry book (Moyer Bell, Wakefield, RI, 1996); "Pushing the Bear," a novel of the Trail of Tears

(Harcourt Brace, 1996); "War Cries," a collection of nine plays (Holy Cow! Press, Duluth, MN, 1996); "A Primer of the Obsolete," poetry book (Chax Press, 1998); "Flutie," poetry book (Moyer Bell, Wakefield, RI, 1998); "(Ado) ration," poetry book (Chax Press, 1999); "The Closets of Heaven," poetry book (Chax Press, Tucson, 1999); "Fuller Man," poetry book (Moyer Bell, Wakefield, RI, 1999); "Cold-and-Hunger Dance," essay (University of Nebraska Press, 2000); "The Mask Maker," novel (University of Oklahoma Press, 2001); "Designs of the Night Sky," novel (University of Nebraska Press, 2002); "The Man Who Heard the Land," novel (Minnesota Historical Society, 2002); "American Gypsy," play (University of Oklahoma Press, 2002); "Stone Heart: A Novel of Sacajawea" (Overlook Press, 2003); "The Shadow's Horse," poetry book (University of Arizona Press, 2003); "In-Between Places," essay (University of Arizona Press, 2004).

GLATKE, THEODORE
(Indian program director)
Affiliation: American Indian Professional Training Program in Speech-Language Pathology & Audiology, University of Arizona, Dept. of Speech & Hearing Sciences, Tucson, AZ 85721 (520) 621-1969.

GLAZIER, HERB (Paiute)
(tribal council chairperson)
Affiliation: Bridgeport Indian Colony, P.O. Box 37, Bridgeport, CA 93517 (760) 932-7083.

GLEASON, JEAN
(organization coordinator)
Affiliation: Yukon Indian Cultural Education Society, 22 Nisutlin Dr., Whitehorse, Yukon, Canada Y1A 1K1 (403) 667-2779.

GLOADE, CLARA
(president-native women's association)
Affiliation: Nova Scotia Native Women's Association, P.O. Box 805, Truro, Nova Scotia, Canada B2N 5E8 (902) 893-7402.

GLORY, TRAILE G.
(BIA agency supt.)
Affiliation: Chickasaw Agency, Bureau of Indian Affairs, 1500 N. Country Club Rd., P.O. Box 2240, Ada, OK 74821 (580) 436-0784 Fax 436-3215.

GO FORTH, APRIL
(Indian education center director)
Affiliation: Resources for Indian Student Education, 109 North St., Alturas, CA 96101 (916) 233-2226.

GOATSON, ERNEST
(school chairperson)
Affiliation: Kaibeto Boarding School, Kaibeto, AZ 86053 (602) 673-3480.

GOBERT, W. JOHN
(health director)
Affiliation: Fort Totten PHS Indian Health Center, P.O. Box 200, Fort Totten, ND 58335 (701) 766-4291.

GOBIN, HENRY
(speaker)
A cultural and historical speaker, Henry is a specialist in languages of the Native American people with background in Museum Studies. He can be reached at (206) 653-4585 ext. 365.

GOEHRING, SUSAN
(site manager)
Affiliation: Schoenbrunn Village State Memorial, P.O. Box 129, East High Ave., New Philadelphia, OH 44663 (216) 339-3636.

GOFF, RALPH (Diegueno)
(tribal chairperson)
Affiliation: Campo Band of Mission Indians, 36190 Church Rd., Suite 1, Campo, CA 91906 (619) 478-9046.

GOGGLEYE, JENEAL
(health director)
Affiliation: Bois Fort Tribal Clinic, P.O. Box 15, Nett Lake, MN 55772 (218) 757-3296.

GOGOL, JOHN M. 1938-
(professor; publisher; institute president)
Born August 15, 1938, Westfield, Mass. *Education*: Clark University, BA, 1960; University of Washington, MA, 1965, ABD Doctoral Candidacy, 1969. *Principal occupation*: University professor, publisher. *Address*: P.O. Box 66124, Portland, OR 97266 (503) 233-8131. *Affiliations*: Instructor, Colorado State University, 1965-68; assistant professor of humanities, Pacific University, Forest Grove, Oreg., 1970-74; publisher, Mr. Cogito Press, Pacific University, 1973-; publisher, American Indian Basketry and Other Native Arts, 1979-; director, Institute for the Study of Traditional American Indian Arts, Portland, OR, 1979-. *Memberships*: Oregon Archaeological Society; Oregon Historical Society; Central States Archaeological Society; Coordinating Council of Literary Magazines; COSMEP. *Awards, honors*: Graves Prize Award in the Humanities, 1971. *Interests*: "In a long teaching career (I) taught German, Russian, comparative literature, American Indian studies, American history, European history, mathematics, physics, and humanities; poet and translator of German, Russian and Polish poetry." *Biographical sources*: Poetic Justice, by Walt Curtis (Willamette Week, Oct.-Nov., 1985); Basketry and Reservation of Culture, by Paul Pintarich (Northwest Magazine, The Oregonian, June, 1983); among others. *Published works*: Native American Words (Tahmahnawi's Publishers, 1973); Columbus Names the Flowers (Mr. Cogito Press, 1984); articles and other publications in numerous periodicals.

GOHDES, DOROTHY, M.D.
(IHS-program director)
Affiliation: Diabetes Program, Indian Health Service, 5300 Homestead Rd., NE, Albuquerque, NM 87110 (505) 837-4182.

GOINGS, JULIE
(BIA special education coordinator)
Affiliation: Pine Ridge Agency, Bureau of Indian Affairs, P.O. Box 333, Pine Ridge, SD 57770 (605) 867-1306 Fax 867-5610.

GOINS, WILL MOREAU (Tsiyohi-Uhayli: Do)
(Eastern Cherokee/Lumbee) 1961-
(executive/artistic director)
Born December 2, 1961, Washington, D.C. *Education*: The George Washington University, BA, 1983; The Pennsylvania State University, MEd, 1989, PhD, 1994. *Principal occupation*: Executive/artistic director. *Home address*: Unknown. *Affiliations*: CEO, Executive/artistic director, National Native Network of Talent/The Washington's First Americans Theater, Washington, DC, 1982-. *Other professional posts*: Co-editor/contributing writer, Indian Youth Magazine, 1981-83; free-lance communications specialist for various private & governmental agencies developing educational, public informational & industrial films, videos, brochures & media, 1984-; free-lance writer-correspondent (journalistic articles), 1981-; producer-director, U.S. Indian Health Service, video series for health professionals, 1984-85; professor, The Pennsylvania State University, Dept. of Educational Administration, Policy, Foundations, and Comparative-International Education, "American Indian, Education & Media," 1992-93. *Community activities*: Class Agent for The Columbian College Alumni Association, The George Washington University, 1990-; Officer, Native American Student Association of Penn State, 1989-93. *Memberships*: American Anthropological Association; National Education Association; American Educational Research Association; ; National Indian Educational Association; AERA-SIG American Indian Sig (Special Interest Group), American Alliance of Health Education, Physical Fitness, Recreation & Dance; American Indian Registry of Performing Arts; National Association for the Advancement of Colored People; National Eagle Scout Association; North Carolina Historical Society; The Gonzaga Dramatics Association. *Awards, honors*: Award of Excellence, Rackley Scholarship, Penn State University, 1988-94; American Indian Leadership Program Fellow, 1988-92; Commendation for Outstanding Service, U.S. Surgeon General, Dr. Everett Rhodes, U.S. Public Health Service, 1984; Outstanding Service Award, Indian Health Service, 1984; Outstanding & Dedicated Service Award, Penn State University, Native American Indian Student Association, 1993. AFTRA-SAG, 1984-; ASCAP; Native American Journalists Association, 1983-; American Film Institute,

1980-. *Interests*: Founder, executive artistic director of "The Free Spirit Players," a non-profit collective of Native performing and creative artists and production technicians for the region east of the Mississippi. Biographical source: 1980 article in "Indian Youth Magazine," called a Profile. *Published works*: Co-author of play, "Feather in the Wind" (NNT Publishing, 1984); author, "Feathers" the musical (NNT Publishing, 1989; Administering Culturally Specific Health Educational Programs and Curriculum (Penn State, 1989); The Perceptions of Native American Alumni of Graduate Level Educational Degree Programs at the Penn State University (UMI Publishing, 1994).

GOLDBERG-AMBROSE, CAROLE 1947-
(law professor)
Born September 3, 1947, Chicago, Ill. *Education*: Smith College, BA, 1968; Stanford Law School, JD, 1971. *Principal occupation*: Law professor & director of Joint Degree Program in Law & American Indian Studies. *Address*: UCLA School of Law & American Indian Studies Center, P.O. Box 951476, Los Angeles, CA 90095 (310) 825-4429 Fax 206-6489 (office). E-mail: goldberg@law.ucla.edu. *Affiliation*: Professor, UCLA Law School, 1972-; director of Joint Degree Program in Law & American Indian Studies, American Indian Studies Center, UCLA. *Interests*: "I teach courses in American Indian law and tribal legal systems." *Published work*: Co-editor & co-author, Felix Cohen's Handbook of Federal Indian Law (Michie Co., 1982); Planting Tail Feathers: Tribal Survival and Public Law 280, 1997.

GOLDFEIN, ROANNE P.
(editor)
Affiliation: American Indian Art Magazine, 7314 E. Osborn Dr., Scottsdale, AZ 85251 (602) 994-5445.

GOLDMAN, LAWRENCE
(Cherokee/Choctaw/Apache)
(business owner/operator)
Address: P.O. Box 465, Mackinaw City, MI 49701 (616) 436-5158. *Affiliations*: President/CEO, Monadnock Trading Co., Inc., 1975-present; president/CEO, Sticks N Stones, Inc., 1984-present. *Community activities*: Chairman, Mackinaw City Downtown Development Authority, 1984-present. *Memberships*: Indian Arts & Crafts Association; Michigan Retailers Association; Mackinac Associates. *Published work*: Field Guide to Geology of the Eastern Upper Peninsula of Michigan.

GOLDOFF, RAYMOND (Eskimo)
(AK village council president)
Affiliation: Atka Village Council, P.O. Box 47030, Atka, AK 99574 (907) 767-8001.

GOLDTOOTH, ADELBERT (Navajo)
(school administrator)
Affiliation: Hotevilla Bacavi Community School, P.O. Box 48, Hotevilla, AZ 86030 (520) 734-2462 Fax 734-2225.

GOLDTOOTH, ANTHONY (Navajo)
(college instructor)
Affiliation: Navajo Community College, P.O. Box 580, Shiprock, NM 87420 (505) 368-5291.

GOLDTOOTH, THOMAS
(director-Indian organizations)
Affiliation: Indigenous Environmental Network, P.O. Box 485, Bemidji, MN 56601 (218) 679-3959.

GOLLA, VICTOR
(organization secretary)
Affiliations: Secretary, Society for the Study of the Indigenous languages of the Americas (SSILA), Box 555, Arcata, CA 95518. E-mail: golla@ssila.org; American Indian Languages & Literature Program, Humboldt State University, The Center for Community Development, Arcata, CA 95521 (707) 826-3711.

GON HENRY
(Indian band chief)
Affiliation: Rae Lakes Dene Indian Band, Rae Lakes, Northwest Territories, Canada X0E 1R0 (403) 997-3441.

GONZALES, ANGELA ANN (Hopi) 1964-
(assistant profesor)
Born June 3, 1964, San Bernardino, Calif. *Education*:

University of California, Riverside, B.A., 1990; Harvard University, MA in Education., 1994, MA in Sociology, 1996, PhD, 2001. Dissertation title: American Indian Identity Matters: The Political Economy of Ethnic Boundaries. *Address*: Cornell University, 320 Warren Hall, Dept. of Development Sociology, Ithaca, NY 14853 (607) 255-1795 Fax 254-2896; E-Mail: aag27@cornell.edu. *Affiliations*: Social Analyst (provided information to congressional staffers on issues concerning Native Americans; and assisted the Senate Select Committee on Indian Affairs in the evaluation of material presented as testimony before the committee), Teaching Fellow, Harvard University, Dept. of Religious Studies, 1991-95; director, Grants & Scholarship Program, Hopi Tribe, Kykotsmovi, AZ, 1994-95; Department of American Indian Studies, San Francisco State University (lecturer, assistant professor, 1996-; chair of American Indian Studies, 1997-98). *Other professional posts*: External Reviewer, American Indian Culture & Research Journal, 1996-; external reviewer, SIGNS: Journal of Women in Culture and Society, 1998-; Development Commitee, American Indian Museum and Culture Center, 1998-. *Selected Conference Presentations*: Annual National Indian Educators Association Conferences, Nov. 1991-93; panelist at the Leading Ideas in American Indian Studies Conference, University of Wisconsin, Madison, Sept. 1993; Papers given at the American Indian Graduate Student Conference, U of California, Berkeley, April 1996, American Indian Research Forum, Stanford, Palo Alto, CA, April 1996, the National Academy of Science, Ford Conference of Fellows, U. of California, Irvine, Oct. 1996; and a panelist at the American Academy of Religion, Annual Conference, New Orleans, LA, Nov. 1996; among others. *Awards, honors*: UCR Alumni Award, 1990; Rupert Costo Scholarship, 1990; Hopi Tribal Scholarship, 1988-present; Harvard Prize Fellowship, 1995-present; Ford Foundation, Pre-Doctoral Fellowship, 1992-95; SFSU grants, 1997-99. *Memberships*: American Sociological Association; Association of American Indian and Alaskan Native Professors; National Congress of American Indians; American Studies Association.

GONZALES, ANNE WHEELOCK
(executive director)
Affiliation: Wings of America, 1601 Cerrillos Rd., Santa Fe, NM 87505 (505) 982-6761 Fax 988-3879.

GONZALES, MARIO
(tribal attorney)
Affiliation: Attorney, Oglala Sioux Tribe, P.O. Box H, Pine Ridge, SD 57770 (605) 867-2244.

GONZALES, RALPH
(BIA director of public affairs)
Affiliation: Bureau of Indian Affairs, Office of Public Affairs, 1849 C St., NW, Washington, DC 20240 (202) 219-4150.

GONZALES, RAYMOND (Te-Moak Shoshone)
(tribal council chief)
Affiliation: Elko Band Council, P.O. Box 748, Elko, NV 89801 (702) 738-8889.

GONZALES, REBECCA
(director of operations)
Affiliations: Seattle Indian Health Board, 606 - 12th Ave. S., Seattle, WA 98144 (206) 324-9360 Fax 324-8910.

GONZALES, VERONICA
(organization director)
Affiliation: American Indian Higher Education Consortium (AIHEC), 121 Oronoco St., Alexandria, VA 22314 (703) 838-0400.

GONZALEZ, BOBBY (Taino) 1951-
(storyteller, lecturer, poet)
Born September 22, 1951, New York, N.Y. *Education*: Manhattan College. *Principal occupation*: Storyteller, lecturer, poet. *Home address*: 3215 Hull Ave. #5C, Bronx, NY 10467 (212) 459-4753 (work). E-mail: bobbyguno@aol.com. Website: www.bobbygonzalez.com. *Community activities*: Master of Ceremonies and Event Coordinator for annual Native Harvest Festival held in Riverdale, NY. *Memberships*: Taino Del Norte, 1989-; Native American Heritage Committee, 1990-. *Interests*: (I) "write a monthly column for the publication, "Latino Village News"; (I) "have given presenta-

tions on the history and culture of the Taino at the American Museum of Natural History, S.U.N.Y. at Binghamton, the Waterloo Indian Village Museum, Carnegie Hall, the National Museum of the American Indian, and the University of New Mexico." *Published works*: Puerto Rican Indian Wars: Part Two; Song of the American Holocaust: Native Poetry from the South Bronx Reservation.

GOODEAGLE, GRACE (Quapaw)
(former tribal chairperson)
Affiliation: Quapaw Tribe of Oklahoma, P.O. Box 765, Quapaw, OK 74363 (918) 542-1853.

GOODFOX, JR., LAWRENCE (Pawnee)
(advisor)
Affiliation: Council of Advisors, American Indian Heritage Foundation, 6051 Arlington Blvd., Falls Church, VA 22044-2788 (703) 237-7500.

GOODMAN, LINDA J.
(professor)
Born in Denver, Colo. *Education*: University of Colorado, Boulder, BA, 1966; Wesleyan University, MA, 1968; Washington State University, Pullman, PhD, 1978. *Principal occupation*: Professor. *Home address*: 4135 Dover St., Wheat Ridge, CO 80033. *Affiliation*: Assistant professor, Dept. of Music, Colorado College, Colorado Springs, CO, 1979-. *Other professional posts*: Advisor of Native American students at Colorado College; director of tribes program for pre-college Native American students. *Community activities*: Talks on Native American music and culture to various museum groups, tour groups, and Native American groups; have organized various Native American music and dance performances for non-Indian audiences; consultant for Native American music education programs, District II public schools, Colorado Springs, Colo.; member, Colorado Springs Native Americans Women's Association; organized Native American symposia, art shows, and guest speakers at Colorado College. *Memberships*: American Anthropological Association, 1975-; American Folklore Society, 1975-; American Ethnological Society, 1975-; Society for Ethnomusicology, 1975-; Native American Women's Association, Colorado College, 1977-. *Awards, honors*: American Philosophical Society grant, 1967, to work on Pueblo Indian music; 1979 Humanities Division Research Grant from Colorado College, to work on life history of Makah Indian singer; 1980 Mellon Grant, to work on Southwest Indian music, to teach as a new course; 1983 American Council of Learned Societies Fellowship for work on life history of a Northwest Coast musician. *Interests*: "Native American music and culture, especially Northwest Coast and American Southwest. "(I) have spent much time traveling and living on reservations in both areas, studying music and culture, attending ceremonies, learning from the people in those areas. Have lead many field trips of college students to various reservations in the Southwest so that they could see and talk to the people living there and learn from them firsthand. Have lead a tour group of older people to the Makah Reservation for the same purpose. I am writing books and articles on Native American music and culture. I am very interested in teaching, counseling, and advising Native American young people, helping them find a way to fit into two worlds. Have worked with a number of Native American students over the years, and I'm interested in Indian singing and dancing, and participate on the few occasions when it is appropriate." *Published works*: Music and Dance in Northwest Coast Indian Life (Navajo Community College Press, 1977); A Makah Biography, in Dalmoma: Digging for Roots (Empty Bowl Press, 1985); Nootka Indian Music, in New Grove Dictionary of Music in the U.S. (Macmillan, 1986).

GOODNER, GEORGE
(BIA agency supt.)
Affiliation: Fort Defiance Agency, Bureau of Indian Affairs, P.O. Box 619, Fort Defiance, AZ 86504 (602) 729-5041.

GOODRIDGE, EDWARD L., SR. (Stillaguamish)
(tribal chairperson)
Affiliation: Stillaguamish Board of Directors, P.O. Box 277, Arlington, WA 98223 (360) 652-7362.

GOODTHUNDER, JOSEPH (Mdewakanton Sioux)
(former tribal chairperson)
Affiliation: Lower Sioux Indan Community Council, RR 1, Box 308, Morton, MN 56270 (507) 697-6185.

GOODTRACK, WILLIAM
(Indian band chief)
Affiliation: Wood Mountain Indian Band, Box 104, Wood Mountain, Sask., Canada S0H 4L0 (306) 266-4422.

GOODWIN, DUANE (White Earth Ojibwe)
(college instructor)
Affiliation: Leech Lake Tribal College, 6530 U.S. Hwy. 2 NW, Cass Lake, MN 56633 (218) 335-4220 Fax 335-4209.

GOODYEAR, JR., FRANK H.
(museum director)
Affiliations: The Heard Museum, 2301 N. Central Ave., Phoenix, AZ 85004 (602) 252-8840;

GOOGOO, RODERICK A.
(Indian band chief)
Affiliation: Whycocomagh Indian Band, Box 149, Whycocomagh, Nova Scotia, Canada B0E 3M0 (902) 756-2337.

GOOMBI, JOSEPH (Kiowa)
(tribal chairperson)
Affiliation: Kiowa Business Committee, P.O. Box 369, Carnegie, OK 73015 (405) 654-2300.

GOPHER, FRANCES M.
(administrative officer)
Affiliation: Northern Idaho PHS Indian Health Center, P.O. Drawer 367, Lapwai, ID 83540 (208) 843-2271.

GORDON, GARY L. (Mohawk)
(executive director)
Affiliation: Executive Director, National American Indian Housing Council, 900 Second St., NE #305, Washington, DC 20002 (800) 284-9165; (202) 789-1754 Fax 789-1758.

GORDON, JEROME
(BIA-health programs)
Affilistion: Office of Health Programs, California Area Office, Bureau of Indian Affairs, 1825 Bell St., Suite 200, Sacramento, CA 95825 (916) 978-4202.

GORDON, MARK R.
(corporation president)
Affiliation: Makivik Corporation, 4898 Maisonneuve West, Montreal, Quebec, Canada H3Z 1M8 (514) 483-2780.

GORDON, PATRICIA TRUDELL
(Santee Sioux-Mdewakanton Band) 1943-
(foundation president)
Born August 24, 1943, Woodbury County, Iowa. *Education*: Morningside College, BA, 1977; Boalt Hall School of Law, University of California, Berkeley, JD, 1992. *Principal Occupation*: Executive Director, Indian Youth of America, Inc. *Address*: P.O. Box 2786, Sioux City, IA 51106 (712) 276-0794 (work). *Affiliations*: Camp Director, Indian Youth Camps in Oregon, Arizona, Idaho, and South Dakota, summer of 1976-90; assistant director, Indian Studies Program, Morningside College, 1977-84; Indian Student Advisor, Student Services, Morningside College, 1975-77; executive director, Indian Youth of America, Sioux City, Iowa, 1978-; president, George Bird Grinnell American Indian Children's Education Foundation, Dover Plains, NY, 1991-. *Community Activities*: Iowa Supreme Court Commission on Continuing Legal Education (commissioner, 1984-89); Sioux City Human Rights Commission (commissioner & chairperson, 1982-89); United Way of Siouxland Agency Relations Committee (panel chair, 1981-86, board of directors, 1987-89); Native American Child Care Center, Sioux City, IA, (Co-founder & president, 1980-89); George Bird Grinnell American Indian Children's Educational Foundation, Dover Plains, NY, (co-founder & president, 1988-); Edwin Gould Foundation for Children, New York, NY (trustee & charter member, 1987-). *Memberships*: American Indian Law Students Association, 1989-91. *Awards, Honors*: Participant for the Community International Fellows, a program of the International Leadership Development Institute; Robert F.

Kennedy Memorial Fellow, 1977-80; Sertoma Service to Mankind Award, 1983; appointed, in 1984, by the Iowa Supreme Court to serve on the State Commission on Continuing Legal Education; Distinguished Alumni Award, Morningside College, 1987; Soroptimist International of Berkeley Award, 1991-92; recently completed an internship at the U.S. Senate Select Committee on Indian Affairs in Washington, D.C. where she reviewed and drafted legislation. *Interests*: "My main concern and interest at this time is working with Indian young people and improving there lives. I am also very interested in the law especially pertaining to American Indians. Women's issues will always be one of my concerns. My work has taken me throughout the U.S. giving lectures and presentations. I have very little time for hobbies, however, I make time for racquetball, bicycling and reading."

GORDON, PAUL (Lake Superior Chippewa)
(tribal council vice-chairperson)
Affiliation: Bad River Tribal Council, P.O. Box 39, Odanah, WI 54861 (715) 682-7111.

GORDON, ROXY (Choctaw)
(poet, writer)
Address: 5476 Oram, Dallas, TX 75206 (214) 827-9309.

GORMAN, CLARENCE N. (Navajo) 1931-
(monument supt.)
Born May 28, 1931, Chinle, Ariz. *Education*: Northern Arizona University. *Principal occupation*: Monument supt. *Address*: Unknown. *Affiliations*: Maintenance foreman, park ranger, Canyon de Chelly National Monument, Chinle, AZ; park ranger, Mesa Verde National Park, CO; park ranger, White Sands National Monument, Alamagordo, NM; supt., Wupatki-Sunset Crater National Monument, Flagstaff, AZ; supt., Pipestone National Monument, Pipestone, MM; supt., Aztec National Monument, Aztec, NM *Other professional posts*: Navajo Tribal Ranger, 1958; teacher, Bureau of Indian Affairs, 1959. *Military service*: U.S. Marine Corps, 1951-54 (Good Conduct Medal, U.S. Service Medal, National Defense Medal, Presidential Unit Citation, Korean Presidential Unit Citation, Korean Service Medal with three Battle Stars). *Memberships*: National Riflemen's Association; Southwest Parks and Monuments Association, Inc.; Parks & Recreation Association; Pipestone Shrine Association.

GORMAN, R.C. (Navajo) 1931-
(artist)
Born July 26, 1931, Chinle, Ariz. *Education*: Northern Arizona University, Honorary Doctorate of Fine Arts; Mexico City College. *Principal occupation*: Artist. *Address*: Navajo Gallery, P.O. Box 1756, Taos, NM 87571 (505) 758-3250. Affiliation: Owner, Navajo Gallery, Taos, NM, 1979-. *Military service*: U.S. Navy, 1952-56. *Memberships*: Pacific Northwest Indian Center, Gonzaga University (board member); Wheelwright Museum, Santa Fe, NM (board member); Kellogg Fellowship Screening Committee, Navajo Health Authority, Window Rock, AZ (Fellow); Four Corner State Art Conference; NM Arts and Crafts Fair (standards committee, juror). *Exhibitions*: Mr. Gorman's work has appeared in numerous one-man and group shows and is part of public and private collections. *Awards, honors*: Numerous awards and prizes for art from the following exhibitions and shows: All American Indian Days Art Exhibition; American Indian Artists Exhibitions; Center for Arts for Indian America; Heard Museum; National Cowboy Hall of Fame; Philbrook Indian Art Exhibitions; Scottsdale National Indian Arts Exhibition. In the Fall of 1973, Mr. Gorman was the only living artist to be included in the show, Masterworks of the Museum of the American Indian, held at the Metropolitan Museum in New York City. Two of his drawings were selected for the cover of the show's catalog. In 1975, he was honored by being the first artist chosen for a series of one-man exhibitions of contemporary Indian artists held at the Museum of the American Indian. Interests: Mexican art and artists; lithography; cave painting and petroglyphs. *Biographical sources*: A Taos Mosaic (University of New Mexico Press); American Indian Painter; Arrow III (Pacific Grove Press); Art and Indian Individuals (Northland Press); Dictionary of International Biography; Indian Painter and White Patrons, J.J. Brody; Indians of Today; Masterworks from the Museum of the American Indian (Metropolitan Museum of Art); Register of U.S. Living

Artists; Who's Who in America; Who's Who in the West; Who's Who in American Art. *Published works*: Mr. Gorman's works appear in the following books: American Indian Painters (Museum of the American Indian); Great American Deserts (National Geographic Society, 1972); Southwest Indian Painting (University of Arizona Press, 1973); The Man Who Sent the Rain Clouds (Viking Press, 1974); Gorman Goes Gourmet; The Lithographs of R.C. Gorman (Northland Press); Graphics: A Self Portrait of America.

GORMAN. ZONNIE M. (Navajo) 1963-
(special events coordinator)
Born May 15, 1963. *Education*: University of Redlands (CA), 1981-82; University of Arizona, 1982-83; Navajo Community College, Spring 1984; University of New Mexico (Gallup), AA (Elementary Education), 1986, AA (Secondary Education), 1987; University of Arizona, BA, 1992. *Principal occupation*: Special events coordinator. *Address*: unknown. *Affiliation*: Program coordinator, Gallup Inter-Tribal Indian Ceremonial Association, Church Rock, NM, 1997-present. *Other professional posts*: Indian Country Tour Guide (self-employed) on Amtrak's Southwest Chief, round trips, Gallup-Albuquerque; Sundance Tours, Albuquerque, NM; 2-day Navajo Reservation tour; Gallup (NM) Film Festival (associate producer, 1993, 1994; program coordinator, 1995, 1996, 1997). *Community activities*: 1996 UNM Gallup Ambassador, University of New Mexico-Gallup Campus. *Memberships*: Navajo Education & Scholarship Foundation, Window Rock, AZ (member, board of directors, 1995-present); Golden Key National Honor Society (University of Arizona). *Awards, honors*: Certificate of Recognition for contribution to the success of Amtrak's Southwest Chief Enhancement Program during the year of introduction, 1985-86; Certificate of Recognition for Indian Country guide service, 1986-89, presented by the Inter-Tribal Indian Ceremonial Association; Award of Excellence, Student Art Exhibition of Northern Arizona, 1989; poetry awards, 1997. *Video produced*: Co-produced, and main researcher for 16 minute video, "Navajo Code Talkers: The First Twenty-nine," 1992.

GOROSPE, GEORGE E. (Pueblo)
(owner/publisher-Indian newspaper)
Affiliation: Pueblo Times, Pueblo Times Publishing Co., 1860 Dom Pasqual Rd., Los Lunas, NM 87031 (505) 865-4508.

GOROSPE, KATHY
(director-Indian commission)
Affiliation: Commission on Indian Services, 454 State Capitol, Salem, OR 97310 (503) 378-5481.

GOSHORN, SHAN (Eastern Band Cherokee)
(artist, studio owner)
Address: 1637 S. Delaware Ave., Tulsa, OK 74104 (918) 744-0698. *Products*: Hand-colored black-and-white photographs featuring contemporary native images; large abstract acrylic paintings; posters, etc.

GORSUCH, EDWARD L.
(institute director)
Affiliation: Institute of Social & Economic Research, University of Alaska, 3211 Providence Dr., Anchorage, AK 99508 (907) 786-7710.

GOSS, JAMES ARTHUR 1934-
(professor emeritus)
Born September 14, 1934, Marion County, Ore. *Education*: University of Oregon, BA, 1960; University of Chicago, MA, 1962, PhD, 1972. *Principal occupation*: Professor emeritus. *Address*: Dept. of Anthropology, Texas Tech University, Lubbock, TX 79409 (806) 742-2228; E-mail: jgoss@ttac.ttu.edu. *Affiliations*: Visiting lecturer in anthropology and linguistics, UCLA, 1964-66; assistant-associate professor of anthropology, Washington State University, 1966-79; professor/director, Ethnic Studies Program, Texas Tech University, Lubbock, TX , 1979-. *Other professional post*: Chair, Council for American Indian Interpretation. *Military service*: U.S. Air Force, 1954. *Community activities*: Consultant on problems of Nez Perce children learning English, Nez Perce Headstart Program. *Memberships*: American Anthropological Association; Linguistic Society of America; Society for American Archaeology; Society of Sigma Xi; Northwest Anthropological Conference; Great Basin Anthropological Conference; International Salish Conference. *Awards, honors*: NDEA

Title IV Fellowship in Anthropology, University of Chicago, 1960-63; research assistantship and linguistic research grant, Tri-Ethnic Project, University of Colorado, 1961, '62; Dept. of the Interior, National Geographic Society Research Grant, Wetherill Mesa Verde National Park, CO, 1961-63; UCLA Academic Senate Grant for A Pilot Demographic Study of the American Indian Community of the Greater Los Angeles Area, 1965; WSU Grant-in-Aid for A Survey of Interior Salish Languages, 1967; consultant grant, Nez Perce Headstart Program, 1971; NEH Postdoctoral Fellowship in American Indian Studies, Indiana University, 1972-73. *Interests*: Linguistic anthropology; ethnosemantics; culture-historical reconstruction. *Published works*: Various technical articles in professional journals.

GOUDIE, JOSEPH
(association president)
Affiliation: Labrador Metis Association, P.O. Box 599, Station "B", Happy Valley/Goose Bay, Labrador, Canada A0P 1E0 (709) 896-5431.

GOUGE, LORRAINE (Santee Sioux)
(former tribal chairperson)
Affiliation: Upper Sioux Indian Community, P.O. Box 147, Granite Falls, MN 56241 (612) 564-2360.

GOULAIS, PHIL
(Indian band chief)
Affiliation: Nipissing Indian Band, RR 1, Sturgeon Falls, Ontario, Canada P0H 2G0 (705) 753-2050.

GOULD, CYNTHIA
(museum curator)
Affiliation: Tonkawa Tribal Museum, P.O. Box 70, Tonkawa, OK 74653 (405) 628-5301.

GOULD, GARY
(president-Indian council)
Affiliation: New Brunswick Aboriginal Peoples Council, 320 St. Mary's St., Fredericton, New Brunswick, Canada E3A 2S5 (506) 458-8422/3.

GOULD, JANICE (Maidu)
(poet, writer)
Address: 515 Fitzpatrick Rd., NW, Albuquerque, NM 87107 (505) 344-7570.

GOULD, MARK M. (Lenni-Lenape)
(tribal chairperson)
Affiliation: Chairperson, Nanticoke Lenni-Lenape Indians of NJ, Inc., 18 E. Commerce St., Bridgeton, NJ 08302 (609) 455-8210.

GOULD, RICHARD
(historic site curator)
Affiliation: Curator, Pawnee Indian Village State Historic Site, Kansas State Historical Society, RR 1 Box 475, Republic, KS 66964 (913) 361-2255.

GOULD, ROY
(publisher)
Affiliation: Micmac News, Nova Scotia Native Communications Society, P.O. Box 344, Sydney, Nova Scotia, Canada B1P 6H2 (902) 539-0045.

GOURD, CHARLES A. (Cherokee of OK) 1948-
(administrator)
Born December 2, 1948, Miami, Okla. *Education*: University of Oklahoma, M.A., 1976; University of Kansas, Ph.D., 1984. *Principal occupation*: Administrator. *Address & Affiliations*: Keys Elementary School, HC 69 Box 151, Park Hill, OK 74451 (918) 456-4501 Fax 456-7559,1992-present. *Other professional post*: Private consulting services, 1982-present. *Past professional post*: Ex-director, Oklahoma Indian Affairs Commission. *Award*: Independent Filmmakers Award, American Film Institute. *Interests*: Tribal sovereignty; Indian self-government; tribal courts; language preservation; rural development. *Published works*: No Contest: Dependent Sovereign-From Tribe to Nation (Univ. Micro, 1984); Sovereignty Symposium Series (Sovereign Symposium, 1988-).

GOURNEAU, DR. WILLIAM
(college academic dean)
Affiliation: Turtle Mountain Community College, P.O. Box 340, Belcourt, ND 58316 (701) 477-5605 Fax 477-5028.

GOVER, KEVIN
(Ass't Secretary-Indian Affairs)
Affiliation: Assistant Secretary-Indian Affairs, Dept. of the Interior, Bureau of Indian Affairs, 1849 C St., NW, MS 4140-MIB, Washington, DC 20240 (202) 208-7163.

GOWAN, RAY
(editor/publisher)
Affiliation: Indian Books from the Four Winds, P.O. Box 3300, Rapid City, SD 57709 (605) 343-6064.

GRADY, GLENN
(Indian band chief)
Affiliation: Ta'an Kwach'an Council, 22 Niutlin Dr., Whitehorse, Yukon, Canada Y1A 3S5 (403) 668-3613.

GRAF, TIM
(Indian education program director)
Affiliation: Wilmot School District 54-7, Indian Education Program, P.O. Box 100, Wilmot, SD 57279 (605) 938-4647 Fax 938-4185.

GRAHAM, BOYD (Duckwater Shoshone)
(former tribal chairperson)
Affiliation: Duckwater Shoshone Tribal Council, P.O. Box 140068, Duckwater, NV 89314 (702) 738-0569.

GRAHAM, LAURA
(project director)
Affiliation: National Indian Council on Aging, 10501 Montgomery Blvd. NE #210, Albuquerque, NM 87111 (505) 888-3302.

GRAHAM, STEPHEN B.
(museum chairperson)
Affiliation: Blackbird Museum, P.O. Box 192, Harbor Springs, MI 49740 (616) 526-2104.

GRANADOS, ALFRED C.
(BIA area health administrator)
Affiliation: Office of Administration, California Area Office, Bureau of Indian Affairs, 1825 Bell St., Suite 200, Sacramento, CA 95825 (916) 978-4202.

GRANNING, GEORGE, M.D.
(clinical director-Indian hospital)
Affiliation: Cherokee PHS Indian Hospital, Cherokee, NC 28719 (704) 497-9163.

GRANT, JANELLE
(Indian school principal)
Affiliation: Loneman Day School, P.O. Box 50, Oglala, SD 57764 (605) 867-5633.

GRANT, JAMES E. (Otoe-Missouria)
(tribal chairperson)
Address & Affiliation: Otoe-Missouia Tribe, 8151 Hwy. 77, Red Rock, OK 74651 (580) 723-4434 Fax 723-4273.

GRANT, LANA SUE (Sac & Fox-Shawnee) 1942-
(library director & newspaper editor)
Born November 25, 1942, Pawnee, Okla. *Education*: El Reno Junior College, AA, 1968; University of Oklahoma, BS, 1970; University of Oklahoma, MLS, 1977. *Principal occupation*: Library director and newspaper editor. *Home address*: 1401 Abbey Dr., Norman, OK 73071 (918) 968-3526 (office). *Affiliations*: Director, Sac and Fox National Public Library, and editor of the "Sac and Fox News", Route 2, Box 246, Stroud, OK 74079, 1982-.

GRANT, KENNETH
(AK Indian association president)
Affiliation: Hoonah Indian Association, P.O. Box 402, Hoonah, AK 99829 (907) 945-3549.

GRANT, WENDY
(Indian band chief)
Affiliation: Musqueam Indian Band, 6370 Salish Dr., Vancouver, B.C., Canada V6N 2C6 (604) 263-3261.

GRANT, WILLIAM L. (Otoe-Missouria)
(tribal council chair)
Affiliation: Otoe-Missouria Tribal Council, P.O. Box 68, Red Rock, OK 74058 (405) 723-4434.

GRANT-KOTA, SHARON LEONA (Ojibwae) 1946-
(coordinator for Indian education)
Born December 16, 1946, St. Clair County, Mich. *Edu-*cation: Wayne State University, B.S., 1973. *Principal occupation*: Coordinator for Indian education. *Home address*: 5315 Ravenswood Rd., Kimball, MI 48074 (810) 989-2727 Fax 984-6624. *Affiliations*: Coordinator for Indian Education and assistant director of gifted & talented program, coordinates gifted and talented parent meeting, Destination Imagination and Chess Club, Quiz Bowl and gifted & talented Summer Enrichment School, Port Huron Area School District, Port Huron, MI, 1977-. *Other professional posts*: Indian Education Program, Grant Application Panelist - reader for American Indian Fellowships; reader for Discretionary Proposals. *Community activities*: Chair, American Indian Communities Leadership Council; board member, Southeastern Michigan Indian Center; chair, Michigan Indian Education Association; conference committee, St. Clair County Preschool Group; minority board, St. Clair County Community College; co-chair & treasurer, Blue Water Indian Pow-wow. *Memberships*: Michigan Association for the Education of Young Children; Blue Water Association for the Education of Young Children (newsletter chairperson); Blue Water Native American Indians; New Detroit, Inc. (race relations committee); Wayne State University Alumni Association. *Awards, honors*: Selected as Michigan Urban Delegate to White House Conference on Indian Education; scholarship recipient, North American Indian Association, 1971-73. *Interests*: "I coordinate a full-time Title IX Indian Education Program for eligible American Indian students. The main aspects of the program are cultural classes, tutoring, counseling and home visits. Conferences, career days, field trips, parent committee meetings and a monthly newsletter are also included in this position. Culture and self-determination are the program's major goals." Attend workshops. Other interests include sports, American Indian literature and professional readings, music, powwows and good friends.

GRANTHAM, LARRY
(historic site manager)
Affiliation: Osage Village Historic Site, P.O. Box 176, Jefferson City, MO 65102 (314) 751-8363.

GRAVES, DARLA F.
(executive director)
Affiliation: Executive Director, Alabama Indian Affairs Commission, One Court Sq., Suite 106, Montgomery, AL 36104 (800) 436-8261; (334) 242-2831 Fax 240-3408.

GRAVETT, FRANKLIN
(BIA agency supt.)
Affiliation: Crow Creek Afency, Bureau of Indian Affairs, P.O. Box 616, Fort Thompson, SD 57339 (605) 245-2311.

GRAY, ALLEN
(school chairperson)
Affiliation: Dennehotso Boarding School, P.O. Box LL, Dennehotso, AZ 86535 (602) 658-3201.

GRAY, ELMER (*Shorty - Little Scout*)
(United Lumbee/Cherokee) 1934-
(log scaler)
Born November 2, 1934, Los Angeles, Calif. *Education*: Modesto City Schools, CA; Lassen Junior College (out reach), 1986 & 1989. *Principal occupation*: Log scaler. *Home address*: 651-970 Lumbee Dr., Little Valley, CA 96056. *Affiliation*: United Lumbee Nation (secretary, 1988-; Deer Clan chief, 1989-). *Community activities*: Inter-Mountain Horseman's Association (vice president, 1984; president, 1985). *Memberships*: United Lumbee Nation's Deer Clan (vice-chief, 1984; chief, 1985-); United Lumbee Nation Mantoac Medicine Society, 1984-93; High Eagle Warrior Society 1984-93; keeper of the pipe, 1985-88); Fire Fighting Tree Falling Team, 1989-. *Awards, honors*: California State Horseman's Association (Region 18 High Point Champion Gymkhana Rider, 1983 & 1984; 1983 & 1985 High Point Rider, Inter-Mountain Horseman's Association; 1989 Silver Eagle Award, given each year by the United Lumbee nation for outstanding work for the Nation/Band/Clan; Senior Volunteer Service Award, May 5, 1990, in recognition for countless hours of volunteer service to Lassen County, CA USDA program. *Interests*: "Signing for the deaf; signing exact English and Using it with Indian heritage lore; putting on programs about Indian lore for school children. *Traditional skills*: hunting, fishing, scouting; fur training, bow hunt-ing, horse-raising; shelter building, survival living." *Biographical source*: Section in United Lumbee's Deer Clan Cook Book.

GRAY, GERALD J.
(school principal)
Affiliation: Chemawa Indian School, 3700 Chemawa Rd., NE, Salem, OR 97303 (503) 399-5721.

GRAY, GREGORY GRAYSON (*Mah-She-Hop-Pee*)
(Osage) 1947-
(silversmith, business owner)
Born April 4, 1947, Muskogee, Okla. *Education*: Central State University (Edmond, OK), BA, 1991. *Principal occupation*: Silversmith, business owner. *Address*: Unknown. *Affiliation*: Owner, Gray Deer Arts, Edmond, OK, 1990- (production and distribution of Native American recordings). *Other professional post*: State trooper, Oklahoma Highway Patrol (retired). *Military service*: U.S. Army Reserve, 1967-75 (Sergeant E-5; National Service Award and Certificate of Commendation for Outstanding Performance of Duty). *Community activities*: Civil Air Patrol; Little League Coach; Art Judge, 1991 Oklahoma Native American High School Art Competition; Red Earth Art Competition Committee, 1992. *Memberships*: Indian Arts & Crafts Association; Gallup Inter-Tribal Association; Celebrations of the American Indian, Ormand Beach, FL (board of directors). *Awards, honors*: Awards won in the following: Tulsa Indian Art Festival; Indian Summer, Bartlesville, OK; Edmond (OK) Art Show; Canterbury Art Show, Edmond, OK; Okmulgee (OK) Indian Art Market; Chism Trail Art Show, Yukon, OK. *Interests*: "History of Indian jewelry, gems and stones used in jewelry and legends and lore of Native Americans. Due to the extensive traveling I have done in the past five years throughout the U.S., I have developed an insatiable desire to learn all that I can about my heritage." *Biographical source*: The Source Directory (Indian Arts and Crafts Board, U.S. Dept. of the Interior. *Published works*: Currently writing a book on the history of Southwest jewelry; completed a recording entitled, The History of Southwest Jewelry.

GRAY, JIM (Osage)
(magazine pubisher)
Affiliation: Co-publisher, Native American Times, Oklahoma Indian Times, Inc., P.O. Box 6920050, Tulsa, OK 74169 (918) 438-6548 Fax 438-6545. E-mail: admin@nativetimes.com; Website: nativetimes.com

GRAY, JOHN
(B.I.A. agency supt.)
Affiliation: Mescalero Agency, Bureau of Indian Affairs, P.O. Box 189, Mescalero, NM 88340 (505) 671-4423.

GRAY, LYNNE CATHERINE (*Migizi Wi Quay & Ukchevwhoosh*) (Yaqui) 1951-
(tv producer/director, president; business consultant)
Born August 21, 1951, Los Angeles, Calif. *Education*: Cypress College, AA, 1973; California State University, Long Beach, BA, 1982, Field Work/Internship, 1982, Gerontology Certificate, 1983, Basic Education/Social Science Credentials, 1989. *Principal occupation*: Television producer/director and president; business consultant. *Address*: Unknown. *Affiliations*: Veterinary manager, Bristol Veterinary Clinic, Santa Ana, CA, 1971-77; partner, franchise, L&W Service Co., Norwalk, CA, 1976-83; associate practitioner, Developmental Guidance Services, Inc., Long Beach, CA, 1984-89; assistant director, National Conference of Christians & Jews, Minneapolis, MN, 1990-92; Native American Television, St. Cloud, MN (television producer," First Americans Journal," 1991-; president, 1991-). *Professional activities*: Member, American Indian Media Image Task Force, 1990-; professional member, Women in Broadcast Technology. *Published works*: "Broadcast Media: Indian Access & Careers," feature articles in Winds of Change, publication of the American Indian Science & Engineering Society, Summer 1991; managing editor, *The American Indian & the Media*, a publication of the American Indian Media Image Task Force, Jan. 1992. *Published works*: Stars in the Mouth (children's book).

GRAYEYES, WILLIE
(school chairperson)
Affiliation: Navajo Mountain Boarding School, P.O. Box 787, Tonalea, AZ 86044 (602) 672-2851.

GRAYMOUNTAIN, ROBERT (Navajo)
(school chairperson)
Affiliation: Navajo Mountain Boarding School, P.O. Box 10010, Tonalea, AZ 86044 (602) 672-2851.

GRAYSON, NOLAN
(Indian center director)
Affiliation: American Indian Center of Santa Clara Valley, 919 The Alameda, San Jose, CA 95126 (408) 971-9622.

GREEN, BETTY
(executive director)
Affiliation: Indian Family Services, Inc., 1315 Penn Ave. North, Minneapolis, MN 55411 (612) 348-5788.

GREEN, CANDACE
(anthropologist)
Education: University of Oklahoma, PhD. *Principal occupation*: Anthropologist. *Address & Affiliation*: Specialist for North American Ethnology, Dept. of Anthropology, Smithsonian's National Museum of Natural History, NHB 112, Washington, DC 20560. *Interests*: Specializes in the art and culture of the Southern Plains. She has published widely on Kiowa and Cheyenne drawings. She is now directing a major project for the preservation of 20,000 pieces of artwork in the National Anthropological Archives, including 2,700 Plains drawings. *Publication*: Silver Horn: Master Illustrator of the Kiowa (University of Oklahoma Press, 1999).

GREEN, CAROL
(school principal)
Affiliation: Cottonwood Day School, Chinle, AZ 86503 (602) 725-3256.

GREEN, ELWOOD
(museum director/curator)
Affiliation: Native American Center for the Living Arts, 25 Rainbow Blvd., Niagara Falls, NY 14303 (716) 284-2427.

GREEN, JESS (Chickasaw)
(attorney)
Address: 301 E. Main St., Ada, OK 74820 (405) 436-1946 Fax 332-5180. *Affiliation*: Chairperson, Family Law Section, Oklahoma Bar Association, 1989-. *Memberships*: Oklahoma Bar Association; American Bar Association (Judiciary Committee Vice Chair, General Practice Section, 1995-96). *Community activities*: Pontotoc Co. March of Dimes Council, 1986-; National Organization for Victim Assistance Racial Minority Committee; Vice President of TELL, Child Abuse Prevention Organization.

GREEN, JOHN D. (Yurok)
(tribal chairperson)
Affiliation: Chairman, Elk Valley Tribal Council, P.O. Box 1042, Crescent City, CA 95531 (707) 464-4680 Fax 464-4519. *Other professional post*: Intertribal Bison Cooperative (policy council).

GREEN, JOSEPH V.
(school principal)
Affiliations: Jemez Day School, P.O. Box 139, Jemez Pueblo, NM 87024 (505) 834-7304 Fax 834-7081.

GREEN, MARGARET (Samish)
(tribal chairperson)
Affiliation: Samish Tribe, P.O. Box 217, Anacortes, WA 98221 (360) 293-6404.

GREEN, MICHAEL DAVID 1941-
(associate professor)
Born February 17, 1941, Cedar Rapids, IA. *Education*: Cornell College, BA, 1963; University of Iowa, MA, 1965, PhD, 1973. *Principal occupation*: Associate professor. *Affiliations*: Assistant professor, West Texas State University, 1970-74; assistant professor, 1977-83, associate professor, 1983-92, Dartmouth College. *Other professional post*: Fellow, D'Arcy McNickle Center for the History of the American Indian, The Newberry Library, Chicago, IL. *Memberships*: Western History Association; Organization of American Historians; American Society for Ethnohistory (executive committee, 1985-87). *Published works*: The Creeks: A Critical Bibliography (University of Indiana Press, 1979); The Politics of Indian Removal: Creek

Government and Society in Crisis (University of Nebraska Press, 1982); The Creeks (Chelsea House, 1990).

GREEN, PAT
(museum director/curator)
Affiliation: Wrangell Museum, Box 2050, 1126 Second St., Wrangell, AK 99929 (907) 874-3770.

GREEN, RAYNA (Cherokee) 1942-
(museum administrator/program manager)
Born July 18, 1942, Dallas, Tex. *Education*: Southern Methodist University, Dallas, BA, 1963, MA, 1966; Indiana University, Bloomington, Ph.D. (Folklore, American Studies), 1974. *Principal occupation*: Museum administrator/program manager. *Home address*: 814 G St., SE, Washington, DC 20003 (202) 357-2071. *Affiliations*: Program director, American Association for the Advancement of Science, 1975-80; program director, Dartmouth College, Hanover, NH, 1980-83; planner, 1983-85, director, American Indian Program, National Museum of American History, 1985-, Smithsonian Institution, Washington, DC,1983-. *Other professional posts*: Visiting professor, University of Massachusetts, and Yale University; consultant to numerous federal agencies, tribes, tribal/Indian organizations, institutions, museums, and universities. *Community activities*: Ms. Foundation for Women (board member); Indian Law Resource Center, Fund for the Improvement of Post-Secondary Education (board member); Phelps-Stokes Fund (Indian advisory board); American Indian Society of Washington; American Indian Intertribal Cultural Organization. *Memberships*: American Folklore Society (president); American Engineering Society; Society for the Advancement of Native Americans and Chicano Scientists; American Anthropological Association. *Awards, honors*: Smithsonian Fellow, 1970; Ford Foundation, National Research Council Fellow, 1983; Distinguished Service Award, American Indian Society of Washington. *Interests*: "American folklorist; research on Native American women; Southern women; American material culture; Indian traditional science, technology, and medicine; relations between Indians & museums; Indian energy/minerals development; poetry/short fiction; film/ TV script writing; exhibit production." *Published works*: Native American Women: A Contextual Bibliography (Indiana University Press, 1982); That's What She Said: Contemporary Poetry and Fiction by Native American Women (Indiana University Press, 1984); Introduction to Pissing in the Snow: Other Ozark Folktales; Handicrafts in the Southern Highlands; articles and essays in Ms. Magazine, Southern Exposure, Science, Handbook of American Folklore, Handbook of North American Indians, and Signs.

GREEN, ROBERTA
(editor & publisher)
Affiliation: Tekawennake Six Nations - New Credit Reporter, Woodland Indian Cultural Education Center, 184 Mohawk St., Box 1506, Brantford, Ontario Canada N3T 5V6 (519) 753-5531.

GREEN, ROBIN
(grand chief)
Affiliation: Grand Council Treaty No. 3, P.O. Box 1720, Kenora, Ontario, Canada P7N 3X7 (807) 548-4215.

GREENE, DANIEL P. (Makah)
(tribal council chief)
Affiliation: Makah Tribal Council, P.O. Box 115, Neah Bay, WA 98357 (206) 645-2205 Ext. 36.

GREENE, JEANIE (Upayok) (Inupiat Eskimo) 1951-
(television host, director, producer)
Born August 31, 1951, Sitka, Alaska. *Education*: University of Alaska, Anchorage, B.A., 1990. *Principal occupation*: Television host, director, producer. *Address*: Unknown. *Affiliation*: Executive producer, One Sky Productions, Ltd., "Heartbeat Alaska", Anchorage, AK (907) 272-8111 Fax 272-7007. *Memberships*: Native American Journalists Association; Alaska Press Club; Alaska Press Women. *Awards, honors*: Alaska Press Club Awards (1993-3rd Place, "Best Public Affairs"; 1994-2nd Place, "Best Feature Story," and 2nd Place, "Best Public Affairs. *Interests*: "Heartbeat Alaska," focuses on the life and times of rural Alaska residents; "One Sky," which is a discussion style forum for rural issues, gets its name from the philosophy that all people are all members of the family of man and share

the same hopes and dreams." Greene, an award-winning journalist and producer, distributes the show herself.

GREENE, JEROME A.
(research historian, author-editor)
Affiliation: National Park Service, Denver, CO. *Published works*: Slim Buttes, 1876: An Episode of the Great Sioux War (University of Oklahoma Press); Battles & Skirmishes of the Great Sioux War, 1876-1877: The Military View (University of Oklahoma Press, 1993); Lakota & Cheyenne: Indian Views of the Great Sioux War, 1876-1877 (University of Oklahoma Press, 1994); Morning Star Dawn: The Powder River Expedition and the Northern Cheyennes, 1876 (University of Oklahoma Press, 2003); Washita: The U.S. Army & the Southern Cheyennes, 1867-1869 (University of Oklahoma Press, 2004).

GREENE, JUDITH (Seneca-Deer Clan) 1940-
(museum director)
Born January 2, 1940, Buffalo, N.Y. *Education*: Alfred University, BFA, 1984; University of Massachusetts at Dartmouth, MA, MFA, 1990. *Principal occupation*: Museum director. *Address & Affiliation*: Seneca-Iroquois National Museum, Allegany Indian Reservation, P.O. Box 442, Broad St. Extension, Salamanca, NY 14779 (716) 945-1738. *Other professional post*: Grant reviewer, New York State Foundation for the Arts. *Community activities*: Member, (Seneca Nation) Human Resource Oversight Committee, Higher Education Committee & the Bingo Advisory Committee.

GREENE, MARIE N. (Eskimo)
(association president)
Affiliation: Maniilaq Association, P.O. Box 256, Kotzebue, AK 99752 (907) 442-3311.

GREENE, MONICA
(Indian art gallery manager)
Affiliation: American Indian Community House Gallery, 404 Lafayette St., New York, NY 10003 (212) 598-0100.

GREENER, SHARON
(curator)
Affiliation: Effigy Mounds National Monument, RR 1, Box 25A, Harpers Ferry, IA 52146 (319) 873-3491.

GREENFEATHER, DON (Loyal Shawnee)
(tribal chairperson)
Address & Affiliation: Loyal Shawnee Tribe, P.O. Box 893, Tahlequah, OK 74465 (918) 456-0671 ext. 333 Fax 456-6485.

GREENHAGEN, EDNA
(school principal)
Affiliation: Enemy Swim Day School, R.R. 1, Box 87, Waubay, SD 57273 (605) 947-4605.

GREENHALG, KATHLEEN
(librarian)
Affiliation: Indian & Colonial Research Center, Eva Butler Library, P.O. Box 525, Old Mystic, CT 06372 (203) 536-9771.

GREENWOOD, BRENDA
(editor)
Affiliation: "Turtle Mountain Times," Turtle Mountain Tribe, Belcourt, ND 58316 (701) 477-6451.

GREENWOOD, DONALD EARL (Little Boy)
(Oklahoma Cherokee) 1935-
(craftsman)
Born July 5, 1935, Dewey, Okla. *Education*: West Texas Barber College (Amarillo, TX) Master Barber, 1971. *Principal occupation*: Craftsman. *Home address*: 10414 Autumn Meadow Lane, Houston, TX 77064-5035 (918) 866-2653. *Professional posts*: Owner, Barber Shop, Borger, TX, 1971-; craftsman, 1992-. *Military service*: U.S. Army (PFC), 1959-61. *Membership*: Indian Arts & Crafts Association, 1994-. *Interests*: "I am presently making the Indian dream catcher into intricate jewelry. I enjoy working with feathers, making the Indian fans. I also enjoy working with leather and specialize in the dream catcher necklaces & earrings covered with leather with leather fringe. Even though I earn my living from the sale of my jewelry, I consider them an art form. I look at each piece as a piece of art instead of a commercial item. At a later date, I plan to

use my ability as an artist in Indian & biblical drawings. I also plan to add photography. It is my desire to travel to different reservations for my photography & also to get any unusual shots in my travels. I, of course, love to capture any of God's beauty on canvas or on film. I like to read, walk & travel. In the summer of 1992, I worked many of the powwows in Oklahoma. I have taken my jewelry into Oklahoma, almost all of Texas, New Mexico, Missouri, Arkansas, Tennessee and Arizona. I have added photography and now making rings with turquoise and precious gems. My work will soon be found in the gift store of Palo Duro Canyon State Park in Amarillo, Texas."

GREGOIRE, RAPHAEL
(executive director-friendship centre)
Affiliation: St. John's Native Friendship Centre, P.O. Box 2414, Station "C", St. John's, Newfoundland, Canada A1C 6E7 (709) 726-5902.

GREGOR, GAIL (Stillaguamish)
(tribal chairperson)
Affiliation: Stillaguamish Board of Directors, P.O. Box 277, Arlington, WA 98223 (206) 652-7362.

GREGORY, JACK (Cherokee)
(craftsperson)
Address: Rt. 1, Box 79, Watts, OK 74964 (918) 723-5408. *Products*: Contemporary wooden laminated Indian corn bowls from native woods, wooden jewelry.

GREY, ANDREW J., SR. (Sisseton-Wahpeton Dakota)
(former tribal chairperson)
Affiliation: Sisseton-Wahpeton Dakota Tribal Council, P.O. Box 509, Agency Village, SD 57262 (605) 698-3911.

GREY, STEVEN (Navajo)
(Indian program head)
Affiliation: Lawrence Livermore National Laboratory, American Indian Program, 1994; manager, Field Office, Navajo Community College, Shiprock, NM, 1988-94.

GREYBEAR, LORRAINE
(school chairperson)
Affiliation: Four Winds Commuity School, P.O. Box 199, Fort Totten, ND 58335 (701) 766-4161.

GREYEYES, ALEX
(publisher; president of Indian centre)
Affiliation: Saskatchewan Indian, Saskatchewan Indian Media Corporation, 2121 Airport Dr. #201A, Saskatoon, Saskatchewan, Canada S7L 6W5 (306) 665-2175; Saskatchewan Indian Cultural Centre, Saskatoon.

GRIECO, VIRGINIA
(Indian education center director)
Affiliation: Osa/Fresno-Clovis Indian Education Center, 2236 N. Fine, Suite 103, Fresno, CA 93727 (209) 252-8659 Fax 252-3824.

GRIFFIN, LOUIE (Keetowah Cherokee) 1914-
(loan officer, live stock farming)
Born October 5, 1914, Cookson, Okla. *Education*: Chilocco Indian School; Oklahoma State University, BS, 1940. *Principal occupation*: Loan officer, live stock farming. *Home address*: 909 S. State, Tahlequah, OK 74464 (918) 456-9678. *Affiliation*: Loan officer, Tahlequah and Wewoka, Okla. (16 years); past vice chief, Keetowah Cherokee. *Military service*: U.S. Army, 1942-46; Army Reserve, 1940-67. *Community activities*: Kiwanis (past Lt. Governor); FRU Board of Trustees, Stilwell, OK (chairperson).

GRIFFIS, STEVE
(casino/bingo general manager)
Affiliation: Tulalip Casino & Bingo, 6330 33rd Ave. NE, Marysville, WA 98271 (206) 653-7395.

GRIFFITH, MALINDA
(program coordinator)
Affiliation: American Indian Education Foundation, P.O. Box 27491, Albuquerque, NM87125 (866) 866-8642 Fax (505) 641-0495. E-mail: info@aiefprograms.org.

GRIMES, BARBARA FORNASERO (Cherokee) 1930-
(editor)
Born August 19, 1930, San Diego, Calif. *Education*: Wheaton College, BA, 1952, Litt.D., 1993. *Principal occupation*: Editor. *Home address*: 84-664 Ala Mahiku, 191-B, Waianae, HI 96792 (808) 695-8402. *Affiliations*: Summer Institute of Linguistics, 7500 W. Camp Wisdom Rd., Dallas, TX 75236 (member, 1951-; field investigator, Huichol language project, Mexico, 1952-67, 1979-80; field investigator, Hawaii Creole English (Pidgin) language project, 1987-). *Other professional post*: Editor, Ethnologue: Languages of the World, 1971-2000. *Awards, honors*: Scholastic Honor Society, Wheaton College. *Interests*: "Participated in linguistic workshops in 23 countries, from 2-6 months in each." *Published works*: Hawaii Pidgin New Testament, with Joseph E. Grimes, 2000; numerous articles.

GRINDE, DONALD ANDREW, JR. (Yamasee) 1946-
(professor of American history)
Born August 23, 1946, Savannah, Ga. *Education*: Georgia Southern College, Statesboro, BA, 1966; University of Delaware, MA, 1968, PhD (History), 1974. *Principal occupation*: Professor of American history. *Address*: Unknown. *Affiliations*: Assistant professor, Mercyhurst College, Erie, PA, 1971-73; assistant professor, SUNY at Buffalo, 1973-77; associate professor of history, California Polytechnic State University, San Luis Obispo, 1977-78, 1979-81, 1984-1998; visiting associate professor, UCLA, 1978-79; director, Native American Studies, University of Utah, Salt Lake City, 1981-84. *Other professional posts*: Instructor in Native American history, United Southeastern Tribes, Inc., and SUNY, College at Buffalo, Program for Indian Teacher Education at Allegany and Cattaraugus (Seneca) Reservations, 1974-75; Native American consultant, Buffalo City Schools, 1974-75; consultant, Smithsonian Institution, 1977; Native American consultant, Salt Lake City Schools, 1982-83; editor, Journal of Erie Studies, 1971-1973; editorial board, Indian Historian, 1976-. *Community activities*: Buffalo North American Indian Culture Center (corresponding secretary and board member, 1974-77); American Indian Historical Society (board member, 1976-); Central Coast Indian Council, Calif. (vice chairman, 1979-80); Salt Lake Indian Center (chairman of board, 1983-84). *Memberships*: National Indian Education Association (member of Resolutions Committee, 1981-83); American Indian Historian's Association (charter member); American Indian Historical Society; Organization of American Historians (charter member); National Association of American Indian Professors; American Indian Scholars Association; Phi Alpha Theta; Smithsonian Institution. *Awards, honors*: Hagley Fellow, University of Delaware, 1966-70; Grant-in-Aid Scholar, Eleutherian Mills Historical Library, 1970-71; project historian and conservation consultant, Southern Railroad Restoration Project, National Park Service; Faculty Seed Grant, UCLA, American Indian Studies Center, 1978-79; Outstanding Professional Award (Education), 1984, from Wasatch Regional Minority Business and Professional Directory (Salt Lake City, Utah); Eugene Crawford Memorial Fellow, 1987-88; Rupert Costo Professor of American Indian History, University of California, Riverside, 1989-91. *Interests*: American Indian history including: 20th century Indian policy, Native American science, American Indian political theory, history of American technology, museum administration; published testimony, "The Iroquois Roots of American Democracy," U.S. Senate Select Committee on Indian Affairs, Dec. 2, 1987. *Biographical sources*: Wasatch Regional Minority Business and Professional Directory (Salt Lake City, Utah, 1984); Resource Directory of American Indian Professionals, 1987. *Published works*: Contributing editor, Readings in American History: Bicentennial Edition, II (Guilford, Conn., Dushkin Publishing, 1975); The Iroquois and the Founding of the American Indian (Indian Historian Press, 1977); Exemplar of Liberty: Native American and the Evolution of American Democracy, with Bruce E. Johansen (UCLA American Indian Studies, 1991).

GRINNELL, RANDY
(BIA-environmental health)
Affiliation: Office of Environmental Health, Oklahoma Area Office, Bureau of Indian Affairs, 215 Dean A. McGee St., NW, Room 409, Oklahoma City, OK 73102 (405) 231-4796.

GRITZBAUGH, GARY S., D.D.S.
(IHS-director, dental services)
Affiliation: Dental Special Services Branch, Indian Health Service (headquarters West), 300 San Mateo, NE, Suite 500, Albuquerque, NM 87102 (505) 766-6319.

GROBE, MARY LOU
(museum president)
Affiliation: Pueblo Grande Museum, 4619 E. Washington St., Phoenix, AZ 85034 (602) 275-3452.

GROBSMITH, ELIZABETH S. (*Anpo wicahpi*) 1946-
(professor of anthropology)
Born May 27, 1946, Brooklyn, N.Y. *Education*: Ohio State University, BMus, 1968; University of Arizona, MA, 1970, PhD (Anthropology), 1976. *Principal occupation*: Assistant Vice Chancellor for Academic Affairs, Director of Summer Sessions, University of Nebraska. *Address*: Unknown. *Affiliations*: Professor of anthropology, Dept. of Anthropology, University of Nebraska, Lincoln, NE, 1975-; Assistant Vice Chancellor for Academic Affairs, Office of Academic Affairs, University of Nebraska, Lincoln, NE, 1992-; *Other professional posts*: Consultant, Association on American Indian Affairs, 1984-85; consultant, Indian Club, Nebraska State Penitentiary, and American Anthropological Association lecture series. *Memberships*: Plains Anthropological Society (board of directors, 1979-81; vice president, 1980-81); American Anthropological Association; University of Nebraska Graduate Faculty; Sigma Delta , Iota Chapter (Graduate Women's Scientific Fraternity); Association on American Indian Affairs; Society for Applied Anthropology. *Interests*: "My major professional interests are in studying and working with American Indian communities, with specific interests in helping them to design strategies and programs which alleviate reservation problems, be they juvenile justice concerns, alcoholism, curriculum development, legal or economic. When possible, I enjoy traveling to observe indigenous peoples to achieve a better understanding of native cultures (e.g. Alaska, Guatemala). Interested in Indian prisoners and their struggle to obtain religious freedom rights behind the walls. Serve as consultant/expert witness in numerous court cases involving Indian prisoners' efforts to practice their native culture and religion despite their incarceration. Served as expert witness for Northern Ponca tribal restoration, 1990. (I) Enjoy travel, particularly in Indian country and especially in Southwest U.S. Hobbies: choral music." *Published works*: Books: Lakota of the Rosebud, A Contemporary Ethnography (Holt, Rinehart and Winston, 1981); Indians in Prison: A Study of Incarcerated Native Americans in Nebraska (University of Nebraska Press, 1994). Chapters in books: "The Plains Culture Area", chapter in Native North Americans: An Ethnohistorical Approach, edited by Daniel Boxberger (Kendall/Hunt, 1990); "Indian Prisoners", to appear in Encyclopedia on Native Americans in the 20th Century, Museum of the American Indian (Garland, 1992). Articles: "The Relationship Between Substance Abuse and Crime Among Native Americans in the Nebraska Department of Corrections", Human Organization, Vol. 48, No. 4, Winter 1989; "The Impact of Litigation on the Religious Revitalization of Native American Inmates in the Nebraska Department of Corrections", Plains Anthropologist, Vol. 34, No. 124, Part I, 1989; "The Revolving Door: Substance Abuse Treatment and Criminal Sanctions for Native American Offenders", co-authored with Jennifer Dam, Journal of Substance Abuse, Vol. 2, No. 4, 1990; "Termination and Restoration of American Indian Tribes: The Northern Ponca Case", with Beth R. Ritter, Human Organization, Spring, 1992; "Inmates & Anthropologists: The Impact of Advocacy on the Expression of Native American Culture in Prison", High Plains Applied Anthropologist, Vol. II, No. 1, Spring, 1992. Numerous book reviews

GROS-LOUIS, MAX (MAGELLA)
(Indian band grand chief)
Affiliation: Bande Indienne de la Nation Huronne-Wendat, 255, Place Chef Michel Laveau, Wendake, Quebec, Canada G0A 4V0 (418) 843-3767.

GROSDIDIER, KATHERINE
(executive director)
Affiliation: Southcentral Foundation, 670 Fireweed Lane, Suite 123, Anchorage, AK 99503 (907) 276-3343.

GROSPE, LARRY
(executive director)
Affiliation: American Indian Center of Dallas, Inc., 1314 Munger Blvd., Dallas, TX 75206 (214) 826-8856.

GROSS, GLEN
(museum director)
Affiliation: Ute Indian Museum - Puray Memorial Park, P.O. Box 1736, Montrose, CO 81402 (303) 249-3098.

GROSS, SHIRLEY
(Indian center program coordinator)
Affiliation: Pierre Indian Learning Center, Star Route 3, Pierre, SD 57501 (605) 224-8661.

GROSSMAN, DAVID, MD, MPH
(Native American committee chairperson)
Affiliation: Chairperson, Committee on Native American Child Health, American Academy of Pediatrics, 141 Northwest Point Blvd., Elk Grove Village, IL 60007 (800) 433-9016 ext. 4739; (847) 981-4739. E-mail: nativeamerican@aap.org.

GROUNDS, RICHARD (Yuchi)
(assistant professor)
Address & Affiliation: Assistant Professor of Anthropology, University of Tulsa, Tulsa, OK 74104.

GRUBS, RUBY (Yurok)
(tribal clerk)
Affiliation: Yurok Tribe, P.O. Box 1027, Klamath, CA 95548 (707) 482-1350 ext. 396 Fax 482-1377.

GRUMMER, BRENDA KENNEDY
(Citizen Band Potawatomi)
(professional artist)
Born in El Reno, Okla. *Principal occupation:* Professional artist. *Home address:* 11105 Coachman's Rd., Yukon, OK 73099. *Affiliation:* Grummer Art Studio, Yukon, OK, 1980-. *Memberships:* National League of American Pen Women; National Cowboy Hall of Fame; American Indian Arts and Crafts Association. *Awards, honors:* Grand Award, Philbrook National India Artists Exhibition; First Place painting awards at Trail of Tears National Exhbition & Gallup Inter-Tribal Ceremoial; shown at Kennedy Center, Smithsonian Institution; Franco-American Union, Rennes, France, dozens of museums shows and awards. *Interests:* Professional writer as well as artist. *Biographical sources:* Mentioned in articles in "Southwest Art," "Art of the West," "Oklahoma Today," "Oklahoma Home and Garden."

GRUNERT, CLEMENS
(former AK village president)
Affiliation: Native Village of Chignik Lagoon, General Delivery, Chignik Lagoon, AK 99565 (907) 840-2206.

GUAFFAC, CARLOS (Diegueno)
(tribal chairperson)
Affiliation: Mesa Grande Band of Mission Indians, P.O. Box 270, Santa Ysabel, CA 92070 (619) 282-9650.

GUARDIPEE, FRED (Blackfeet)
(school chairperson)
Affiliation: Blackfeet Dormitory, Blackfeet Agency, P.O. Box 880, Browning, MT 59417 (406) 338-7441 Fax 338-5725.

GUARDIPEE, LEONARD L. (Blackfeet)
(school counselor)
Affiliation: Blackfeet Dormitory, Blackfeet Agency, P.O. Box 880, Browning, MT 59417 (406) 338-7441 Fax 338-5725.

GUASSAC, CARLOS (Diegueno)
(tribal chairperson)
Affiliation: Chairperson, Mesa Grande Band of Mission Indians, P.O. Box 270, Santa Ysabel, CA 92070 (619) 282-9650.

GUENTHARDT, BOB (Ottawa)
(tribal chairperson)
Affiliation: Little River Band of Ottawa Indians, 375 River St., Manistee, MI 49660 (616) 723-8288.

GUIMARES, PAULO, M.D.
(clinical director)
Affiliation: PHS Indian Hospital, P.O. Box 60, Cass Lake, MN 56633 (218) 335-2293.

GUITIERREZ, DENNY (Santa Clara Pueblo)
(pueblo governor)
Affiliation: Santa Clara Pueblo Council, P.O. Box 580, Espanola, NM 87532 (505) 753-7330.

GUMLIKPUK, PETER (Athapascan)
(former AK village president)
Affiliation: New Stuyahok Village Council, General Delivery, New Stuyahok, AK 99636 (907) 693-8002.

GUN SHOWS, DAN
(administrative officer)
Affiliation: Lodge Grass PHS Indian Health Center, Lodge Grass, MT 59050 (406) 639-2317.

GUNDERSON, PAUL
(AK village council president)
Affiliation: Native Village of Nelson Lagoon, P.O. Box 13, Nelson Lagoon, AK 99571 (907) 989-2204.

GUNN, BRIAN (Colville)
(attorney)
Address & Affiliation: Dorsey & Whitney LLP, 1001 Pennsylvania Ave., NW, Suite 300 So., Washington, DC 20004 (202) 824-8863. E-mail: gunn.brian@ dorseylaw. com. Associate since 1999. Practices in the areas of Federal Indian law and general litigation.

GUNN, VIRGIL L.
(clinic director)
Affiliation: David C. Wynecoop Memorial Clinic, P.O. Box 357, Wellpinit, WA 99040 (509) 258-4517.

GUNYAH, EDWARD W.
(BIA field rep.)
Affiliation: Metlakatla Field Office, Bureau of Indian Affairs, P.O. Box 450, Metlakatla, AK 99926 (907) 886-3791 Fax 886-7738.

GURNOE, ROSE (Red Cliff Chippewa)
(tribal chairperson)
Affiliation: Red Cliff Tribal Council, P.O. Box 529, Bayfield, WI 54814 (715) 779-3700.

GUS, LARRY (Hopi-Navajo) 1954-
(photographer)
Born August 12, 1954, Keams Canyon, Ariz. *Education:* California Institute of the Arts (2 years). *Principal occupation:* Photographer (self-employed). *Memberships:* Native American Journalists Association; Native Indian/Inuit Photographer's Association; national Press Photographer's Association; Advertising Photographers of America (APA) Crew Director, 1992/17th Ed.; ATLATL; Committee to Protect Journalists. *Awards, honors:* Finalist-Western Region-Leica Medal of Excellence, 1987. *Interests:* News photographer. "I try to photograph Indian people as they are in everyday life, not the way foreigners have convinced themselves that Indians should look and behave. As a photojournalist, my responsibility and obligation will remain with the subject being photographed—not with any organization or individual that has hired my services or which expects me to produce images for their use and/or viewing."

GUST, WALLY (Athapascan)(
(AK village council president)
Affiliation: New Stuyahok Village Council, General Delivery, New Stuyahok, AK 99636 (907) 693-8002.

GUSTAFSON, CHARLES
(BIA education coordinator)
Affiliation: Aberdeen Area Office, Bureau of Indian Affairs, 115 4th Ave., SE, Federal Bldg., Aberdeen, SD 57401 (605) 226-7416. Other professional posts: Education coordinator, Fort Berthold Agency, New Town, ND, and Standing Rock Agency, Fort Yates, SD.

GUSTIN, WILLIAM E.
(museum manager)
Affiliation: Serpent Mound Museum, State Route 73, Box 234, Peebles, OH 45660 (513) 587-2796.

GUTIERREZ, DOROTHY (Navajo)
(craftsperson)
Address: P.O. Box 1441, Espanola, NM 87532 (505) 753-2890. *Products:* Pottery animals, mudheads, storytellers, mudhead storyteller, nativity sets.

GUTIERREZ, FLORENCE
(BIA agency supt.)
Affiliation: Southern Pueblos Agency, Bureau of Indian Affairs, P.O. Box 1667, Albuquerque, NM 87103 (505) 346-2423 Fax 346-2426.

GUTIERREZ, GIL
(school principal)
Affiliation: Akiachak IRA Contract School, General Delivery, Akiachak, AK 99551 (907) 825-4428.

GUTIERREZ, PAUL (Santa Clara)
(craftsperson)
Address: P.O. Box 1441, Espanola, NM 87532 (505) 753-2890. *Products:* Pottery animals, mudheads, storytellers, mudhead storyteller, nativity sets.

GUTIERREZ, RAFAEL
(executive director)
Affiliation: Indian Pueblo Cultural Center, 2401 12th St., NW, Albuquerque, NM 87104 (505) 843-7270.

GUTSHALL, SANDY
(foundation president)
Affiliation: Viola White Water Foundation, 4225 Concord St., Harrisburg, PA 17109 (717) 652-2040.

GUY, JOSEPH
(AK village council president)
Affiliation: Kwethluk Village, P.O. Box 84, Kwethluk, AK 99621 (907) 757-6714.

GUY, PAUL (Eskimo)
(former AK village president)
Affiliation: Napaskiak Village Council, General Delivery, Napaskiak, AK 99559 (907) 737-7626.

GUYER, DAVID L.
(foundation president)
Affiliation: Save the Children Federation, 54 Wilton Rd., Westport, CT 06880 (203) 226-7271.

H

HAAG, MARCIA (Choctaw)
(professor of Native American studies)
Affiliation: Native American Studies Program, University of Oklahoma, 455 W. Lindsey, Rm. 804, Norman, OK 73019 (405) 325-2312.

HAAS, LAUREN
(executive director)
Affiliation: American Indian Youth Running Strong, 8815 Telegraph Rd., Lorton, VA 22079 (703) 550-2123 Fax 550-2473. E-mail: info@indianyouth.org.

HACKER, PAUL (Choctaw-Cherokee) 1948-
(knife & flutemaker/player-recording artist, writer)
Born August 4, 1948, Oklahoma City, Okla. *Principal occupation:* Knife & flutemaker/player-recording artist, writer. *Home address:* Resides in Oklahoma (405) 787-8600. *Affiliation:* Owner, Paul Hacker Knives & Flutes, Bethany, OK. *Memberships:* Choctaw Tribe of Oklahoma; Kituwah; Indian Arts & Crafts Association; Gallup Intertribal Ceremonial; Southern Plains Association. *Awards, honors:* Over 80 awards in 15 years, including the 1992 2nd place and 1993 1st place Smithsonian Celebration of the American Indian. *Interests:* "My intention is to promote traditional and contemporary art. Most of my demonstration are with young people and elementary schools. I enjoy doing concerts and lectures. I attend and show at Native American & Western Shows." *Published works:* Tapes: "Winds of the Past" Volumes I & II; "To Those Who've Gone Before Us," and "The Horses Still Cry" - flute music on cassette & compact discs - music composed and played by Paul Hacker. He's recorded music for several videos on domestic violence and recently "LaCrosse, the Creator's Game" by Ken Murch Productions (won 1st place Native American Film Festival for Documentarys. His music also on videos: "The Basketweavers" and The Woodcarvers" (available from Qualla Arts & Crafts, Cherokee, NC). He is currently working on a gospel album, "Healing Spirit."

HACKETT, DAVID KRAMER (Woktela) (Yuchi) 1948-
(professional engineer, writer)
Born November 11, 1948, Frankfort, Ind. *Education:* University of Tennessee, BS, 1972. *Principal occupa-*

tion: Professional engineer, writer. *Home address*: 6500 Trousdale Rd., Knoxville, TN 37921 (615) 691-7835 (work). *Affiliations*: Engineer, Aztech Research Services, Knoxville, TN, 1975-77; welding engineer, Nuclear Div., Union Carbide, Oak Ridge, TN, 1977-81; owner, Aztech Research Services, Knoxville, TN, 1981-; CEO, Science Advocacy Pellissippi Science Enrichment Programs, Knoxville, TN, 1989-; consultant, Oak Ridge National Laboratory, Oak Ridge, TN, 1990-. *Community activities*: Science programs for the public: I.D. Day, Spaceweek, Astroweek, Earth Day, Science & Technician Week, Science Olympiad. *Memberships*: American Indian Science & Engineering Society; American Society for Metals; Dinosaur Society. *Awards, honors*: Numerous awards for photo documentation; Museum Replica Grants, 1987-89 for stone carving, American Indian Pipes; "Recently it has been my honor to rediscover the origin of the state name, Tennessee, in my Native tongue." *Interests*: "Forensic & failure science, science education, trickster path, critical thinking, paleontology, stone carver." *Biographical source*: Who's Who in the World (Marquis, 12th Ed.). *Published works*: Editor: Spruce Pine Mineral District (Aztech, 1979); Ambient Lighting Extremes (Aztech, 1984); Tales From the Red Earth & A Blue Planet (pending); numerous articles in professional journals.

HACKETT, MICHAEL
(BIA agency supt.)
Affiliation: Winnebago Agency, Bureau of Indian Affairs, P.O. Box 18, Winnebago, NE 68071 (402) 878-2502 Fax 878-2943..

HAGAN, WILLIAM T.
(professor of Native American studies)
Address: Unknown. *Affiliation*: Native American Studies Program, University of Oklahoma, Norman, OK. *Published works*: Quanah Parker, Comanche Chief, The Sac & Fox Indians, and United States-Comanche Relations (all published by University of Oklahoma Press).

HAGER, CLAY STEVEN (Cherokee) 1958-
(attorney)
Born February 25, 1958, Enid, Okla. *Education*: Phillips University, B.A., 1981; University of Oklahoma, J.D., 1987. *Principal occupation*: Attorney. *Home address*: 2307 Ripple Creek Lane, Edmond, OK 73034 (405) 840-5255 (work). *Affiliation*: Oklahoma Indian Legal Services, Oklahoma City, OK, 1990-. *Other professional post*: Professor, American Institute of Paralegal Studies, Oklahoma City, OK. *Memberships*: Oklahoma Bar Association (Indian Law Section); Oklahoma Indian Bar Association; various tribal bar associations. *Awards, honors*: Guest lecturer, "Indian Housing Into the 90's" seminar, and "Sovereignty Symposium V - The Year of the Indian;" Who's Who in American Law. *Interests*: Indian Child Welfare Act expert. "I am currently rewriting our handbook on the subject." *Published works*: Editor, Oklahoma Indian Child Welfare Act Handbook (Oklahoma Indian Legal Services, 1991); Prodigal Son: The Existing Indian Family Exception (Clearinghouse Law Review, 1993); contributor, Sovereign Symposium VII (Oklahoma Sup. Ct., 1994).

HAIL, BARBARA A. 1930-
(museum administrator)
Born November 2, 1930, Philadelphia, Penna. *Education*: Brown University, 1948-51; Cornell University, BA, 1952, MA, 1953. *Principal occupation*: Museum administrator. *Home address*: 300 Tower St., Bristol, RI 02809 (401) 253-8388 Fax 253-1198. *Affiliations*: Deputy director/curator, Haffenreffer Museum of Anthropology, Brown University, Providence, RI, 1973-. *Other professional posts*: Wampanoag Indian Program, Plimoth Plantation (board, 1996-2002); American and world history teacher, Ithaca (NY) High School, and White Plains (NY) High School. *Memberships*: American Association of Museums (curator's committee); New England Museum Association (board, 1988-94); Association of College & University Museums & Galleries; American Anthropological Association; Native American Art Studies Association (board, 1997-2001). *Awards, honors*: Elisha Benjamin Andrews Scholar, Pembroke College; Phi Beta Kappa, Brown University, 1950; Danforth Graduate Fellowship for Women, Columbia University, 1965-67; National Endowment of the Arts Fellowship for Museum Profes-

sionals, 1976, 1985. *Interests*: "History, ethnohistory, ethnology; museology, stylistic and technical aspects of material culture of North America; Peru; Africa; Nepal; current research is in the art & material culture of the Subarctic." *Published works*: Hau, Kola! The Plains Indian Collection of the Haffenreffer Museum of Anthropology (Haffenreffer Museum of Anthropology, 1983); Out of the North, with Kate Duncan (Haffenreffer Museum of Anthropology, 1988); Collecting Native America, edited with Shepard Krech, III (Smithsonian Press, 1999); editor, Gifts of Pride and Love; Kiowa and Comanche Cradles (Heffenreffer Museum of Anthropology and University of Oklahoma Press, 2000, 2004).

HAIL, RAVEN *(Golanun)*
(Cherokee of Oklahoma) 1921-
(writer, speaker, singer)
Born January 27, 1921, Dewey, Okla. *Education*: Oklahoma State University, BA, 1946; Southern Methodist University, (2 years). *Principal occupation*: Writer. *Address & Affiliation*: Owner, Raven Hail Books, P.O. Box 543, Asheville, NC 28802 (828) 254-0548. Website: www.hanksville.org/storytellers/hail/order_form.html. *Awards, honors*: Medallion presented to Ms. Hail by United Poets Laureate International for exemplary service for world brotherhood & peace, 1992; Certificate of Award by 13th World Congress of Poets, 1992. *Memberships*: Wordcraft Circle of Native Writers & Storytellers; Asheville Storytelling Circle; National Storytelling Association; Arizona State Poetry Society. *Interests*: "I have traveled all over the U.S. for most of my adult life, collecting Native American lore and artifacts. Writer, performer, speaker, teacher of Native American subjects. Google me at "Raven Hail" for a list of 150 websites mentioning me." Hail also lectures on many aspects of Cherokee culture and is an instructor of such traditional skills as beadwork, basketry, singing, dancing, and folklore. *Biographical source*: Native American Women: A Biographical Dictionary, by G.M. Betaile, Editor (Garland Publishing, 1993). *Published works*: "Native American Foods" (Children's Coloring Book, 1979). Novels: "Windsong: Texas Cherokee Princess," 1986; "The Raven Speaks, 1987; "The Raven's Tales" (Cherokee legends), 1987; & "The Pleiades Stones," 1987. "Ravensong" (book and audiocassette - poetry). Recording: The Raven Sings (Native American Songs). Play: "The Raven & the Redbird: The Indian Life of Sam Houston & His Cherokee Wife" a play in three acts, 1965, reissued in 1993. "The Raven Speaks" (originally published as monthly newsletters written from 1968-72), 1988; The Cherokee Sacred Calendar (Inner Traditions, 2000); The Cherokee Path Cards (a deck of 40 cards and an instruction book with spreads—to be used with the book, The Cherokee Sacred Calendar.

HAIRE, WENONAH GEORGE (Catawba) 1953-
(dentist)
Born November 27, 1953, York County, Rock Hill, S.C. *Education*: Clemson University, BS, 1976; Medical University of SC, Charleston, D.MD, 1979. *Principal occupation*: Dentist. *Address*: Unknown. *Community activities*: Education committee, Career Development Center; chairman, Dental Health Month, 1985; Girl Scout Aid. *Memberships*: Tri-County Dental Society, Rock Hill, SC (secretary, 1985); U.S. Public Health Service (Lt., inactive reserve); Medical University Alumni Association; First Baptist Church. *Interests*: Enjoys travel vacations (Mexico and U.S.); collects Indian jewelry, paintings and pottery; enjoys pottery making (Catawba traditional coil method); enjoys canning. Only female dentist in Rock Hill, S.C.; just had her first child. *Biographical source*: Charlotte Observer article entitled Rock Hill Dentist Drills by Day, Fills by Night.

HALBRITTER, RAY (Oneida) 1953-
(newspaper publisher, tribal representative)
Born July 17, 1953, Oneida, N.Y. *Education*: Syracuse University, BA, 1985; Harvard University, JD, 1990. *Principal occupation*: Newspaper publisher, tribal representative. *Home address*: P.O. Box 1, West Rd., Vernon, NY 13476 (315) 361-6300 (work). *Affiliations*: Representative & CEO, Oneida Indian Nation, Oneida, NY; president & CEO, Four Directions Media, Inc., Indian Country Today (newspaper), Canastota, NY. *Other professional post*: Adjunct assistant professor, New York University, New York, NY. *Community activities*: Lecturer. *Memberships*: National Congress of Ameri-

can Indian; USET. *Awards, honors*: Man of the Year, by the Leatherstocking Country, NY; Grand Marshal, Rome (NY) America Days. *Biographical sources*: "Ray Halbritter," Central New Yorker Magazine, Nov. 12, 1993; "The Man Behind the Casino," Business Journal, Nov. 29 - Dec. 12, 1993; "A Salute to Those Who Came Before Us," Rome Observer, July 20, 1993; "Ray Halbritter," Syracuse New Times, June 9-June l6, 1993.

HALE, ALBERT (Navajo)
(attorney; AZ State Senator)
Adddress & Affiliation: AZ State Senate, Capitol Complex, Rm. 313, 1700 West Washington, Phoenix, AZ 85007; or P.O. Box 4468, Window Rock, AZ 86515. Website: www.arizonasenate.org. Mr. Hale rep[resents District 2 which spans a 300-mile width of Arizona from New mexico to Nevada, including Flagstaff and the counties of Navajo, Apache, Coconino and Mohave with a population of 70,000 people and includes the navajo, Hopi, Hualapai and Havasupai Nations. *Past professional posts*: Mr. Hale has been an attorney for 27 years specializing in federal Indian law and natural resource issues; president, Navajo Nation, Window Rock, AZ, 1994-98; served as assistant attorney general for the Navajo Nation; special counsel to the Navajo Nation Council. *Memberships*: Navajo Nation Bar Association (past president).

HALE, BENNY
(school principal)
Affiliation: Nazlini Boarding School, HC 58 Box 35, Ganado, AZ 86505 (520) 755-6125 Fax 755-3729.

HALE, PHIL
(education director)
Affiliation: Southern California Indian Center, 6055 E. Washington Blvd. #700, Commerce, CA 90040 (323) 728-8844 Fax 728-9834.

HALFTOWN, ELDENA
(editor)
Affiliation: O-He-Yoy-Noh, Seneca Nation, Plummer Bldg., Box 231, Salamanca, NY 14779.

HALL, CALVIN S. (Meherrin)
(tribal chief)
Affiliation: Meherrin Indian Tribe, P.O. Box 508, Winton, NC 27986 (252) 398-3321.

HALL, LESLIE
(tribal health director)
Affiliation: Greenville Rancheria Tribal Health, P.O. Box 279, Greenville, CA 95947 (916) 284-6135.

HALL, PATRICIA A. 1945-
(attorney)
Born November 18, 1945, Oak Park, Ill. *Education*: Arizona State University, BA, 1970; Arizona State University College of Law, JD, 1976. *Principal occupation*: Attorney. *Home address*: 7859 County Road 203, Durango, CO 81301 (970) 247-1755 Fax 247-8827 (work). *Affiliation*: Partner, Maynes, Bradford, Shipps & Sheftel, Durango, CO, 1991-; General Counsel for the Southern Ute Indian Tribe. *Community activities*: La Plata County Judge, 1982-89; Southern Ute, Chief Judge, 1980-82; Ute Mountain Ute Judge, 1980-82; Jicarilla Apache Alt. Judge, 1982; Domestic Violence Prevention Coalition. Memberships: Colorado Bar Association; Arizona State Bar; Navajo Nation Bar Association. *Awards, honors*: 1986 Judge of the Year, Colorado Dept. of Heath; 1988 Excellence in Criminal Justice Award, La Plata County Sheriff's Department. *Interests*: Indian law, criminal law; travel, music concerts, independent film, organic gardening.

HALL, ROBERT
(school administrator)
Affiliation: Wahpeton Indian School, 832 8th St. North, Wahpeton, ND 58075 (701) 642-3796.

HALL, TEX (Hidatsa) 1956-
(NCAI president; tribal chairperson)
Born September 18, 1956, Watford, N.D. *Education*: University of South Dakota, MA, 1980. *Address*: Box 488, Mandaree, ND 58757 (701) 759-3311. *Affiliations*: President, National Congress of American Indians (NCAI), 1301 Connecticut Ave., NW #200, Washington, DC 20036 (202) 466-7767 Fax 466-7797; Chairperson, Three Affiliated Tribes, HC 3, Box 2, New Town, ND 58763 (701) 627-4781 Fax 627-3805. *Oher pro-

fessional posts: Chairerson, Mandaree Day School, Mandaree, ND; chairperson, Native American Bancorporation Co. *Memberships*: North Dakota Indian Education Association; North Dakota Stockman's Association; National Indian Athletic Association; North Dakota & National Principals Association. *Awards, honors*: Outstanding Young Men of America, 1983, '86, '87. *Interests*: "Traveled to Europe, Canada, Soviet Union, Mexico, Puerto Rico & Western U.S., and most Indian reservations, instructing at basketball camps & playing basketball tournaments."

HALLER, ROSEMARIE
(Indian band chief)
Affiliation: High Bar Indian Band, c/o Fraser Canyon Indian Administration, Box 400, Lytton, BC, Canada, V0K 1Z0 (604) 455-2279.

HALLIGAN, PHYLLIS
(enterprise development specialist)
Affiliation: Sicangu Enterprise Center, P.O. Box 205, Mission, SD 57555 (605) 856-2955 Fax 856-4671.

HALOTE, OLIVIA (Zuni)
(craftsperson; studio owner)
Address: Me'shiwi, 544 Harrell Dr., Orlando, FL 32828 (407) 568-5162.

HALOTE, TERENCE (Zuni)
(craftsperson; studio owner)
Address: Me'shiwi, 544 Harrell Dr., Orlando, FL 32828 (407) 568-5162.

HALSEY, THERESA
(radio host/producer)
Affiliation: "Indian Voices," KGNU 88.5 FM - Public Radio, P.o. Box 885, Boulder, CO 80306 (800) 737-3030.

HALVORSON, ELMER
(museum curator)
Affiliation: Buffalo Trails Museum, Box 22, Epping, ND 58843 (701) 859-3512.

HALVORSON, VINCENT J.
(monument supt.)
Affiliation: Pipestone National Monument, P.O. Box 727, Pipestone, MN 56164 (507) 825-5464.

HAMILTON, ANGE (*Aunko*) (Kiowa)
(attorney)
Born in Lawton, Okla. *Education*: University of Oklahoma, BA, 1980; Oklahoma City University School of Law, JD, 1991. *Home address*: 1326 S. 5th St., Aberdeen, SD 57401-6810. *Affiliation*: Staff Attorney, Oklahoma Indian Legal Services, Oklahoma City, OK, 1992-. *Other professional posts*: General Counsel, Wichita & Affiliated Tribes, Anadarko, OK, 1991-. *Community activities*: Children's Review Board Commission; Campaign for Justice & Human Development (board of directors); Oklahoma City Archdiocese. *Memberships*: Oklahoma Bar Association; American Bar Association; Oklahoma Indian Bar Association; Native American Indian Bar Association. *Awards, honors*: American Association of University Women Fellow, 1990-91; recipient of Oklahoma Bar Foundation Scholarship, 1990; Association of Business & Professional Women Scholarship, 1989-90; Daughters of American Revolution Scholarship. *Interests*: Federal Indian law; tribal court development; Indian child welfare.

HAMILTON, CLEO
(BIA agency supt.)
Affiliation: Fort Belknap Agency, Bureau of Indian Affairs, RR 1, Box 980, Harlem, MT 59526 (406) 353-2901 ext. 23 Fax 353-2886.

HAMILTON, D'ANNE MARIE (*Paaniikaaluk*)
(Inupiat Eskimo) 1959-
(producer, host)
Born July 12, 1957, Kotzebue, Alaska. *Education*: Kauai Community College, 1978; University of Alaska, Fairbanks, 1979; Arizona State University, 1979-81. *Principal occupation*: Producer/host. *Address*: Alaska Public Radio Network, 810 E. Ninth Ave., Anchorage, AK 99501 (907) 277-2776. *Affiliations*: Production assistant, Northwest Arctic Instructional Television Center, Kotzebue (1 year); reporter, K.O.T.Z. Radio Station, Kotzebue (1 year); producer-reporter, Alaska

Public Radio Network, Anchorage, 1989-; producer-reporter, National Native News, Anchorage, 1989-94; producer/host, National Native News, 1994-. *Community activities*: Rural Alaska Television Network Board, 1983; Inupiat Ilitqusiat Committee, 1983. *Membership*: Alaska Press Club; Native American Journalists Association. *Awards, honors*: Alaska Native Fellowship, Grotto Foundation. *Interests*: "I am interested in increasing coverage of Native issues, particularly in the state of Alaska. I am also interested in steps by Inuit towards political unity, and was part of a three-person reporting team covering the Inuit Circumpolar Conference in July of 1989 in Greenland. I lived in Germany for nearly four years, and did a bit of traveling in Europe. I speak some German and Spanish, and hope to begin learning Russian this year." *Biographical sources*: Anchorage Daily News; Tundra Times; Arctic Sounder.

HAMILTON, HAMILTON, Sr. (Athapascan)
(AK village chief)
Affiliation: Native Village of Shagelkuk, Shageluk, AK 99665 (907) 473-8239.

HAMILTON, JONATHAN S. (Mohegan)
(editor of tribal newspaper)
Affiliation: Ni Ya Yo, Mohegan Tribe, 5 Crow Hill Rd., Uncasville, CT 06382 (800) MOHEGAN; Fax (860) 862-6115. *Membership*: Native American Journalist Association.

HAMILTON, JOSEPH (Cahuilla)
(Indian band representative)
Affiliation: Ramona Band of Cahuilla Indians, P.O. Box 391670, Anza, CA 92539 (909) 763-4105.

HAMILTON, MANUEL (Cahuilla)
(tribal representative)
Affiliation: Ramona Band of Mission Indians, P.O. Box 391670, Anza, CA 92539 (909) 763-4105.

HAMILTON, MARY G.
(publisher)
Affiliation: American Indian Art Magazine, 7314 East Osborn Dr., Scottsdale, AZ 85251 (602) 994-5445.

HAMILTON, RICHARD H. (Penobscot)
(tribal governor)
Affiliation: Penobscot Nation Tribal Council, Community Bldg., Indian Island, 6 River Rd., Old Town, ME 04468 (207) 827-7776.

HAMLEY, JEFFREY (Turtle Mountain Ojibwe)
(program director)
Born in North Dakota. *Education*: Western Washington University, BA; Harvard University, MA, PhD candidate. *Address & Affiliation*: Harvard Native American Program, Graduate School of Education, Read House, Appian Way, Cambridge, MA 02138 (617) 495-4923.

HAMMEREN, PATSY (Sioux)
(elementary school principal)
Affiliation: Mandaree Day School, P.O. Box 488, Mandaree, ND 58757 (701) 759-3311.

HAMMERSMITH, BERNICE
(director-Indian council)
Affiliation: Aboriginal Women's Council of SK, 62-17th St. West, Prince Albert, SK, Canada S6V 3X3 (306) 763-6005.

HAMMETT, BRIAN (Gros Ventre)
(radio announcer, language instructor)
Affiliation: Announcer, KGVA 88.1 FM Radio, Fort Belknap Reservation, RR 1, Box 66, Harlem, MT 59526; certified language instructor of White Clay language and gives a daily language lesson on 88.1 FM radio.

HAMMETT, PAULA
(editor)
Affiliation: Native Self-Sufficiency, Seventh Generation Fund, P.O. Box 10, Forestville, CA 95436 (707) 887-1559.

HAMMOND, DICK
(Indian band chief)
Affiliation: Ross River Indian Band, Ross River, Yukon, Canada Y0B 1S0 (403) 969-2278.

HAMMOND, WYLIE
(Indian center director)
Affiliation: Director, Native American Cultural Center, Minot State University, 500 University Ave. West, Minot, ND 58707 (701) 858-3112.

HAMNER, DOROTHY (Colville)
(Indian education program director)
Address: Okanogan School District #105, P.O. Box 592, Okanogan, WA 98840 (509) 422-3770 Fax 422-1525. *Affiliation*: Director, J.O.M./Title IX Native American Program (serves the unique needs of federally recognized Indian students, Okanogan School District #105, Okanogan, WA. *Community activities*: Inter-tribal student club (parent committee).

HAMP, ERIC P. 1920-
(professor emeritus)
Born November 16, 1920, London, England. *Education*: Amherst College, BA, 1942; Harvard University, MA, 1948, PhD, 1954. *Principal occupation*: Professor emeritus of linguistics & behavioral science, University of Chicago, 1950-. *Home address*: 5200 So. Greenwood Ave., Chicago, IL 60615 (773) 324-9170 Fax 834-0924. *Affiliation*: University of Chicago (instructor-professor, 1950-91; Robert Maynard Hutchins Distinguished Service Professor of Linguistics, Psychology, 1973-91). *Military service*: U.S. Army, 1946-47 (Sgt.). *Community activities*: IL Place-Name Survey (chairman, 1966-); consultant U.S. Office of Education, NEH, NSF; Council on International Exchange of Scholars (advisory committee, 1966-); UNESCO (U.S. National Commission, 1972-); International English Braille: Linguistics (committee, 1994-); among others. *Memberships*: American Association for the Advancement of Science (Fellow); American Anthropological Association; American Philosophical Society (Phillips Fund Committee, 1977-); Linguistic Society of America (president, 1971); Society for the Study of Indigenous Languages of the Americas (president, 1986-87); Modern Language Association (appointed to various committees); member of many other societies. *Awards, honors*: Linguistic Society of America; hon. LHD, Amherst College, 1972; Guggenheim Fellow, 1973-74; Fellow, American Academy of Arts & Sciences, 1976; Robert Maynard Hutchins Distinguished Service Professor, University of Chicago; various guest professorships. *Interests*: Languages and cultures of the American Indian, the Balkans, and the Celts; travel and fieldwork: Ojibwa, Cheyenne, Quileute, several Salishan, Eskimo, Otomanguean of Oaxaca. "I have worked principally in Ojibwa, as well as other Algonquian; Quileute; Otomanguean languages of Mexico; and on problems of North American language classification." *Biographical sources*: Who's Who in America; Who's Who in the World; Directory of American Scholars; Dictionary of International Biography; American Men & Women of Science; Men of Achievement; The Blue Book. *Published works*: Associate editor, 1966-92, emeritus editor, 1992- (devoted to Native American languages), International Journal of American Linguistics (University of Chicago Press); editor, Native American Text Series (University of Chicago Press, 1974-); chapters: "Native American Languages," "Chimakuan Languages," and U.S.A.: Language Situation," in The Encyclopedia of Language & Linguistics (Pergamon Press, 1993-94); author of publications on Ojibwa, Narragansett, Algonquian, Wiyot, Yurok, Quileute, Upper Chehalis, Comox, Kwakwala, Karok, Miwok, Zuni, Crow, Eskimo, etc. Contributed over 1,400 publications (articles, chapters, books).

HAMPTON, CAROL CUSSEN McDONALD (Caddo) 1935-
(clergy)
Born September 18, 1935, Oklahoma City, Okla. *Education*: H. Sophie Newcomb College, New Orleans, LA, 1953-54; University of Oklahoma, BA, 1957, MA, 1973, PhD, 1984; Certificate of Individual Theological Studies, Episcopal Theological Seminary of the Southwest, 1998; Master of Divinity, Phillips Theological Seminary, summa cum laude, 1999. *Principal occupation*: Clergy - ordained to priesthood (Episcopal Church) Dec. 1999, curate, 1999-2001; appointed Canon of St. Pauls Cathedral (Episcopal) Dec. 2001. *Home address*: 1414 N. Hudson, Oklahoma City, OK 73103 (405) 235-1905 Fax 235-2257. E-mail: hampton 918@aol.com. *Affiliations*: Teaching assistant, University of Oklahoma, Norman, 1973-84; associate director and coordinator, Consortium for Graduate Oppor-

tunities for American Indians, University of California, Berkeley; Field Officer for Native American Ministry of the Episcopal Church, 1986-94; officer for multicultural ministry, 1994-98; ordained to diaconate (Episcopal Church) June, 1999; ordained to priesthood, Dec. 1999. curate, St. .Pauls' Episcopal Church. *Community activities*: Caddo Indian Tribe of Oklahoma (tribal council, 1976-); Caddo Tribal Constitution Committee, 1975-76; Oklahoma City Area Indian Health Service (advisory board); Junior League of Oklahoma City, 1965-; National Committee on Indian Work, Episcopal Church (Co-chair, 1986); World Council of Churches (commissioner, Program to Combat Racism, 1985-91); Oklahoma State Regents for Higher Education on Social Justice (member, advisory board, 1984-86); Council of Native American Ministries (vice-chair, 1988-97); National Council of Church's (Racial Justice Working Group Co-convenor, 1991-94); Oklahoma Conference of Churches (board member); Indigenous Theological Training Institute (board member). Central Oklahoma Human Rights Alliance; American Indian Graduate Center (Honorary Advisory Council of 100). *Memberships*: National Indian Education Association; National Historical Society; Oklahoma Historical Society; Western Historical Association; Organization of American Historians; American Historical Association; Oklahoma Foundation for the Humanities (Trustee, 1983-86). *Awards, honors*: Francis C. Allen Fellowship, D'Arcy McNickle Center for the History of the American Indian, Newberry Library, 1983; State of Oklahoma Human Rights Award, 1987; attendee, United Nations 4th World Conference on Women, Beijing, 1995. *Interests*: My interests are in history, philosophy and theology of American Indians as well as social and racial justice. *Biographical sources*: Who's Who Among American Women; Who's Who in the World; etc. *Published work*: Indian Colonization in the Cherokee Outlet & Western Indian Territory (Chronicles of Oklahoma, 1976). *Articles*: "Peyote and the Law", Between Two Worlds, Oklahoma Series, 1986; "Why Write History? A Caddo Grandmother's Perspective", The Creative Woman, Fall, 1987; "Opposition to Indian Diversity in the 20th Century", American Indian Policy and Cultural Values, UCLA, 1987; "Tribal Esteem and the American Idian Historian", An American Indian Identity, San Diego State University Publications, 1988; "A Heritage Denied: Racial Justice for American Indians", Sojourners, Jan. 1991; "Native American Church", Encyclopedia of North American Indian, 1996; editor, "When Caddos Came Upon the Earth," First Peoples Theology Journal, Vol. 2 No. 1, Sept. 2001.

HAMPTON, JAMES WILBURN, M.D.
(*Sheko Okti Onna*) (Chickasaw/Choctaw) 1931-
(physician & educator)
Born September 15, 1931, Durant, Okla. *Education*: University of Oklahoma, BA, 1952; University of Oklahoma, School of Medicine, MD, 1956. *Principal occupation*: Physician & educator. *Home address*: 1414 N. Hudson, Oklahoma City, OK 73103. E-mail: james. hampton@usoncology.com. *Affiliations*: Medical Director, Troy and Dollie Smith Cancer Center, Baptist Medical Center, Oklahoma City; Clinical Professor of Medicine, University of Oklahoma Medical School, 1956-; member, Cancer Core Associates (U.S. Oncology). *Other professional posts*: Professor and head, Hematology-Oncology, University of Oklahoma Medical School, 1971-77; head Hematology Research Laboratories, Oklahoma Medical Research Foundation, 1971-77; National Cancer Institute, Chairperson, Network for Cancer Control in American Indians/Alaska Natives, 1990-2000. *Community activities*: Oklahoma Indian Tumor Registry (Initiator); Oklahoma County Medical Society (member, board of directors, 1979-82, 1989-92; editor, The Bulletin, 1983-); Heritage Hills, Inc. (member, board of directors, 1973-90); Central Oklahoma American Indian Health Council (board member, 1974-90); Faculty House (board member, 1974-75); Frontiers of Science Foundation of Oklahoma, Inc. (board member, 1974-78). *Memberships*: American Association for the Advancement of Science; American Association for Cancer Research, Southwest Section; American Association of Pathologists and Bacteriologist; American Association of University Professors; American Federation for Clinical Research; American Genetic Association; American Medical Association; American Physiological Society; American Psychosomatic Society; American Society for Clinical Pharmacology and Therapeutics; American Society for

Clinical Oncology; American Society of Angiology; American Society of Hematology; Central Society for Clinical Research; International Society on Thrombosis and Haemostasis; New York Academy of Sciences; Oklahoma County Medical Society; Oklahoma State Medical Association; Sigma Xi; Southern Society for Clinical Investigation; Southwest Oncology (Chemotherapy Study) Group; Association of American Indian Physicians (president, 1979-80, 1989-90); National Hemophilia Foundation; National Institutes of Health; American Heart Association; American Cancer Society (member of Committee on Cancer in the Socioeconomically Disadvantaged, Medicine & Scientific Committee; member at large, Board of Directors, 1990-95). *Consultations*: Consultant in Medicine, Tinker Air Force Base Hospital, Oklahoma City, Okla., 1965-; consultant for National Institutes of Health, National Cancer Institute, 1973-76, 1989-; National Heart & Lung Institute, 1971-92; consultant for Navajo Health Authority, 1974-76; consultant for Regional Breast Cancer Detection and Treatment Center, 1974-79. *Awards, honors*: NIH Career Development Award, 1965-75; Angiology Research Foundation Honors Achievement Award, 1967-68; Preservation and Restoration Award, Heritage Hills Association, 1973; chairman, Planning Committee for Native American Medical School, sponsored by the Navajo Health Authority, 1974-76; associate editor, Journal of Laboratory and Clinical Medicine, 1974-76; member, Blue Cord, 1974; Indian Physician of the Year Award, 1987 & 2000; Special Certificate of Appreciation from the National Cancer Prevention and Control Intervention Research Program for Special Populations, 1990; Special Recognition from National Indian Health Board; member, Minority Affairs Consortium, AMA, 1998-2000; member, Dialog on Concern (American Cancer Society), 1998-; The Humanitarian Award of the American Cancer Society, 1999. *Interests*: Cancer in American Indians/Alaska Natives. *Biographical sources*: Who's Who in America; Who's Who in the South and Southwest; American Men of Science; The International Registry of Who's Who. *Published works*: Experimental articles, non-experimental articles, books, pamphlets, editorials in journal "Cancer in Minorities" ed. L. Jones, Ph.D., 1989; abstracts presented at national or international meetings; lectures.

HANE, MARIANNA (Choctaw)
(health director)
Affiliation: Choctaw Health Center, Route 7, Box R-50, Philadelphia, MS 39350 (601) 656-2211.

HANES, TERI (*Tey'rille Nashta Na*)
(United Lumbee) 1949-
(financial systems analyst)
Born April 5, 1949, Wolfpoint, Mont. *Principal occupation*: Financial systems analyst. *Home address*: Unknown. E-mail: retro02@airmail.net or lumbeecougar band@netscape.net. *Community activities*: Goodwill ambassador for United Lumbee of N.C. & America when called on; blood donor for American Cancer Society. *Memberships*: United Lumbee Nation of N.C. & America-Cougar Band (secretary/treasurer); American Management Association: *Biographical sources*: Who's Who in Professional Management, 1997; Who's Who of American Women, 1986, 1987; Women in Computing, Dallas Chapter, 1985; Executive Female Association, 1990. *Interests*: "I originated "Toys for Tots" at 7 years of age. (I'm) currently doing college course work in computer science."

HANEY, JERRY G. (Seminole of Oklahoma)
(tribal chief)
Affiliation: Seminole Nation of Oklahoma, P.O. Box 1498, Wewoka, OK 74884 (405) 257-6287 Fax 257-6205.

HANEY, ENOCH KELLY (Seminole-Creek)
(artist, art gallery owner)
Address: Kelly Haney Art Gallery, P.O. Box 3817, 723 E. Independence, Shawnee, OK 74801 (405) 275-2270. *Products*: Original Indian paintings, sculpture, jewelry, baskets, pottery.

HANEY, MICHAEL (Seminole/Sioux)
(consultant, foundation chair)
Affiliations: Consultant, American Indian Arbitration Association, Minneapolis, MN; chairman, Board of Directors, American Indian Ritual Object Repatriation Foundation, 463 East 57th St., New York, NY 10022

(212) 980-9441; vice-chairman of the Newcomer Band of the Seminole Nation of Oklahoma.

HANITCHAK, MICHAEL S. (Choctaw)
(Indian studies program director)
Affiliation: Dartmouth College, Native American Studies Center, 37 N. Main St., The Sherman House, Hanover, NH 03755 (603) 646-2110. *Other professional post*: Director of Native American Program, Dartmouth College. E-mail: native.american.program @dartmouth.edu.

HANLEY, JOY J. (Navajo)
(executive director; treasurer-board of directors)
Affiliations: Executive Director, Arizona Indian Centers, Inc., 2400 N. Central Ave. #301, Phoenix, AZ 85004 (602) 252-9040; Treasurer-Board of Directors, Association on American Indian Affairs, Sisseton, SD.

HANLEY, BETTY
(radio station manager)
Affiliation: KEYA - 88.5 FM, Turtle Mountain Chippewa Tribe, P.O. Box 190, Belcourt, ND 58316 (701) 477-5686.

HANNA, AUGUSTINE (Havasupai)
(tribal chairperson)
Affiliation: Havasupai Tribal Council, P.O. Box 10, Supai, AZ 86435 (928) 448-2961.

HANNA, DANA
(tribal attorney general)
Affiliation: Attorney General, Rosebud Sioux Tribe, P.O. Box 430, Rosebud, SD 57570 (605) 747-2381 Fax 747-2243

HANNA, JEANETTE
(BIA acting area director)
Affiliation: Phoenix Area Office, BIA, P.O. Box 10, Phoenix, AZ 85001 (602) 379-6600.

HANRAHAN, GENE
(radio station manager)
Affiliation: WYRU - 1160 AM, Lumbee Tribe, P.O. Box 0711, Red Springs, NC 28377 (919) 843-5946.

HANSEN, CECILE (Duwamish)
(tribal chairperson)
Affiliation: Duwamish Tribe, Renton, WA 98055 (206) 226-5185.

HANSEN, ED
(VP hospital operations)
Affiliation: Yukon-Kuskokwim Hospital, Pouch 3000, Bethel, AK 99559 (907) 543-3711.

HANSEN, ELIZABETH (Pomo)
(rancheria chairperson)
Affiliation: Redwood Valley Pomo Tribe, 3250 Road I, Redwood Valley, CA 95470 (707) 485-0361.

HANSEN, EMMA I. (Pawnee)
(museum curator)
Born March 5, 1947, Oklahoma City, Okla. *Education*: Oklahoma State University, BA; University of Oklahoma, MAs (Sociology & Anthropology), A.B.D. - Anthropology. *Principal occupation*: Museum curator. *Address*: 720 Sheridan Ave., Cody, WY 82414 (307) 587-4771 Fax 587-5714 (work). E-mail: emmah@ blohc.org. *Affiliations*: Anthropology Dept., University of Oklahoma, Norman, OK, 1978-80, 1985-89; Stovall Museum, University of Oklahoma, Norman, OK, 1978-84; Oklahoma Museums Association, Oklahoma City, OK, 1990-91; curator, Plains Indian Museum, Buffalo Bill Historical Center, Cody, WY, 1991-; visiting curator, Hood Museum of Art, and Assistant Professor, Native American Studies, Dartmouth College, 1997; Associate Curator of Ethnology, Glenbow Museum, Calgary, Alberta, Canada, 1994-. *Other professional post*: Board member, Wyoming Council for the Humanities, 2003-2006. *Community activities*: Programs presented at numerous museums and organizations, nationally and internationally; Powerful Images: Portrayals of Native America - exhibition touring major museums, 1998-2000; organizes annual Plains Indian Museum Powwow in Cody and Plains Indian Seminar. *Membership*: American Anthropological Association; American Association of Museums (board of curator's committee); Council for Museum Anthropology (officer); Native American Art Studies Association (board

member, 1999-2006). *Awards, honors*: AASLH Award of Merit; Ford Foundation Fellowship; Newberry Library - Resident Research Fellowship; Sequoyah Graduate Award; American Philosophical Society, Phillips Fund Grant; several NEA and NEH grants, as well as grants from private foudnations. *Interests*: Plains Indian culture and ethnohistory; Pawnee history, contemporary art. *Published work*: The Artist and the Missionary - Into. & edited, 1994; Powerful Images: Portrayals of Native America (University of Washington Press, 1998); Article, "People Without Borders: Natives of the North American Plains," in Voices from the West (Gibbs Smith Publishers, 1999); over 30 articles in journals.

HANSEN, JOAN LOUISE (Cherokee) 1945-
(reporter, photographer)
Born February 2, 1945, New Orleans, La. *Education*: Bacone College. *Principal occupation*: Reporter, photographer. Resides in Muskogee, OK. *Affiliation*: Reporter, photographer, Muskogee Daily Phoenix & Times Democrat. *Awards, honors*: Paintings shown at Philbrook Indian Annual, Tulsa; paintings shown at Department of the Interior, Washington, DC; numerous awards at local fairs. *Interests*: Reading of Plains Indian traditions and legends; art.

HANSEN, TERRI C. (Nebraska Winnebago) 1953-
(journalist)
Born October 18, 1953, Portland, Oreg. *Education*: Clark College (Vancouver, WA), 1990-92. *Principal occupation*: Journalist. *Address*: Address unknown. E-Mail: reporter@aman.com. *Affiliations*: Bureau Chief, Pacific NW Bureau (OR, WA, ID, northern CA, B.C.), News From Indian Country, Hayward, WI, 1992. *Other professional post*: Correspondent, Native American Smoke Signals, Meyer, AZ, 1993-96. *Community activities*: Local Indian Child Welfare Advisory Council; Council of Better Business Bureau's National Panel of Consumer Arbitrators. *Memberships*: Winnebago Tribe of Nebraska; Native American Journalist's Association, 1990-; Wordcraft Circle of Native Writers, 1993-; Society of Environmental Journalists (Fellow, 1993); National American Indian Environmental Illness Foundation. *Award*: The Oregonian Publisher's Award of Excellence, 1990. *Interests*: "Vocational - As a reporter of regional and national Indian issues for several regional and national Indian newspapers, I am particularly concerned with environmental and health issues as they pertain to American Indians. Avocational - mountaineering (member of Mazama's Mountaineering Club, Portland, OR); white water kayaking, hiking, backpacking."

HANSON, BETH ROSE (Eastern Cherokee) 1957-
(administrator)
Born December 14, 1957, Biloxi, Miss. *Education*: University of Wisconsin, Stevens Point, BS, 1989; University of Wisconsin, Oshkosh, MBA (current). *Principal occupation*: Administrator. *Home address*: 425 Front St., Stevens Point, WI 54481 (715) 342-1444 (work). *Affiliations*: Program Manager, Las Vegas Indian Center, Las Vegas, NV, 1989-90; Coordinator, Weekend College Program for Native Americans, University of Wisconsin-Stevens Point, 1991-. *Other professional post*: Benefits administrator for Command Technologies of Virginia, 1993-. *Military service*: U.S. Army Journalist (enlisted member serving in Washington, DC). *Awards, honors*: Graduate Cum Laude from UW-SP; awarded the Chancellor's Leadership Award upon graduation in May 1989; State of Wisconsin Native American Leadership Award recipient; 1992 Mrs. North Carolina; 1992 National Mrs. U.S. Photogenic Winner, Las Vegas, NV. *Interests*: "Current primary career focus is developing education programs for Native Americans and transitional housing projects for homeless Native American families."

HANSON, CECILE M. (Duwamish)
(tribal council chairperson)
Affiliation: Duwamish Tribe, 140 Rainier Ave. S. #7, Renton, WA 98055 (206) 226-5185.

HANSON, CHARLES E., Jr. 1917-
(museum director)
Born April 4, 1917, Holdredge, Neb. *Education*: Kearney State College (1 year); University of Colorado (2 years); Chadron State College, Honorary Doctorate of Letters. *Principal occupation*: Museum director. *Address*: 6321 Hwy. 20, Chadron, NE 69337 (308) 432-3843. *Affiliation*: Museum of the Fur Trade,

Chadron, NE, 1978-. *Other professional post*: Editor, Museum of the Fur Trade Quarterly, 1964-; Industrial engineer. *Military service*: Civilian engineer, U.S. Air Force, 1942-44, 1952 (Post Citation Liberal AAF). *Community activities*: Member, Dawes County (NE) Travel Board. *Memberships*: American Association of Museums; Nebraska State Historical Society (life); Company of Military Historians (fellow); American Society of Arms Collectors. *Awards, honors*: Henry Fonda Tourism Award, 1985; Chamber of Commerce Ambassador, Magic Key Award, 1989. *Interests*: Hobbies - travel & hunting; museum oriented travel all over U.S., Canada, Alaska, and Europe. *Biographical source*: Who's Who in the World. *Published works*: The North West Gun (Nebraska State Historical Society, 1955); The Plains Rifle (Stackpole, 1960); The Hawken Rifle, Its Place in History (The Fur Press, 1979); The David Adams Journals (Museum of the Fur Trade, 1994).

HANSON, ED (Eastern Cherokee)
(executive director)
Affiliation: Cherokee Historical Association, P.O. Box 398, Cherokee, NC 28719 (704) 497-2111.

HANSON, FRANKLIN S.
(school supt.)
Affiliation: Quileute Tribal School, P.O. Box 39, LaPush, WA 98350 (206) 374-2061.

HARVEY, DONALD
(Indian school principal)
Affiliation: Leupp Boarding School, P.O. Box HC61, Winslow, AZ 86047 (520) 686-6211 Fax 686-6216.

HENSON, KEN (Samish)
(tribal chairperson)
Affiliation: Samish Indian Nation, P.O. Box 217, Anacortes, WA 98221

HAOZOUS, BOB (Chiricahua Apache-Navajo) 1943-
(artist)
Born April 1, 1943, Los Angeles, Calif. *Education*: Utah State University; California College of Arts and Crafts. *Principal occupation*: Artist. Resides in Santa Fe, NM. *Exhibitions*: Scottsdale National Indian Art Exhibition; Philbrook Art Center American Indian Artists Exhibitions; Oakland Museum Indian Show; Southwest Fine Arts Biennial-Museum of New Mexico. *Permanent collections*: Heard Museum; Southern Plains Indian Museum; Crafts Center, Anadarko, OK. *Awards*: First Prize, Sante Fe Indian Market, 1971; Gold Medal, Wood Sculpture I and II, Heard Museum, 1973, 1974; Grand Prize, Heard Museum National Sculpture Competition, 1975; among others.

HAPPYJACK, ALLAN
(Indian band chief)
Affiliation: Waswanipi (Cree) Indian Band, Waswanipi River, Waswanipi, QB, Canada J0Y 3C0 (819) 753-2587.

HARASICK
(health center director)
Affiliation: Chief Andrew Isaac Health Center, 1638 Cowles St., Fairbanks, AK 99701 (907) 451-6682.

HARDEN, PHYLLIS (Pomo)
(tribal vice-chairperson)
Affiliation: Upper Lake Pomo Tribal Council, P.O. Box 245272, Sacramento, CA 95820 (916) 371-2576.

HARDING, SHIRLEY
(museum curator)
Affiliation: Hubbell Trading Post, National Historic Site, P.O. Box 150, Ganado, AZ 86505 (602) 755-3475.

HARDMAN, MARY GEORGE
(executive director)
Affiliation: Survival International, U.S.A., Washington, DC 20008 (202) 265-1077.

HARDWICK, FRANK
(editor)
Affiliation: Navajo Area Newsletter, BIA, Box M, Window Rock, AZ 86515 (602) 871-5156.

HARDWICK, SHEILAH
(foundation director)
Affiliation: 4 Directions Foundation, 23431 130th Ave., SE, Kent, WA 98031 (206) 854-1611.

HARDY, DAN
(Indian band chief)
Affiliation: Lake Helen First Nation (Red Rock) Indian Band, Box 1030, Nipigon, Ontario, Canada P0T 2J0 (807) 887-2510.

HARDY, JAMES
(Indian band chief)
Affiliation: Rocky Bay Indian Band, MacDiamond, Ontario, Canada P0T 2P0 (807) 885-3401.

HARDY, JOE C.
(school principal)
Affiliation: Low Mountain Boarding School, Chinle, AZ 86503 (602) 725-3308.

HARE, JOSEPH F.
(Indian band chief)
Affiliation: West Bay Indian Band, Excelsior P.O., West Bay, Ontario, Canada P0P 1G0 (705) 377-5362.

HARJO, ALAN (Creek)
(hospital director)
Affiliation: Creek Nation Community Hospital, P.O. Box 228, Okemah, OK 74859 (918) 623-1424.

HARJO, DUKE (Creek)
(former tribal chief)
Affiliation: Alabama-Quassarte Tribal Town, P.O. Box 537, Henryetta, OK 74437 (918) 652-8708.

HARJO, JOY (Muscogee Creek) 1951-
(professor, writer, musician)
Born in 1951, Tulsa, Okla. *Education*: Institute of American Indian Arts, 1968; University of New Mexico, BA, 1976; University of Iowa, MFA (Creative Writing), 1978; Anthropology Film Center (Santa Fe, NM). *Principal occupation*: Professor, writer, musician. *Address*: Resides in Albuquerque, NM area. *Affiliations*: Lecturer, Arizona State University, 1980-81; instructor, Santa Fe Community College, 1983-84; instructor, Institute of American Indian Arts, 1983-84 & 1978-79; assistant professor, University of Colorado, Boulder, 1985-88; associate professor, University of Arizona, Tucson, 1988-90; professor, Creative Writing Program, Dept. of English, University of New Mexico, Albuquerque, 1991-present. *Other professional posts*: Editor, Americans Before Columbus, 1979-80; contributing editor, Contact II, 1984-; contributing editor, Tyuonyi, 1985-; High Plains Literary Review (poetry editor, 1986-89; poetry advisor, 1989-). *Community activities*: Advisory Committee, Spirits of the Present, Native American Public Broadcasting Consortium and the Smithsonian; "High Plains Review" Poetry Advisor; Steering Committee of the En'owkin Centre International School of Writing (for Native American writers). *Membership*: Muscogee Tribe. *Awards, honors*: Academy of American Poetry Award, University of New Mexico, 1st Place in Poetry, 1976; Writers Forum, University of Colorado, 1st Place in Poetry, 1977; National Endowment for the Arts Creative Writing Fellowship, 1978 & 1992; Santa Fe Festival for the Arts, 1st Place Poetry, 1980; Outstanding Young Women of America, 1978 & 1984; Pushcart Prize Poetry, 1988 & 1990; Recipient of 1989 Arizona Commission on the Arts - Creative Writing Fellowship, and two NEA Creative Writing Fellowships; 1990 American Indian Distinguished Achievement Award; 1991 William Carlos Williams Award from the Poetry Society of America; the Delmore Schwartz Award from New York University; The American Book Award, 1991; Poetry Award from the Mountains and Plains Booksellers Association, 1991; one of the winners of the Josephine Miles Award for Excellence in Literature from PEN Oakland, 1991; Delmore Schwartz Memorial Award, NYU, 1991; Honorary Doctorate, Benedictine College, 1992; Woodrow Wilson Fellowship, Green Mountain College, Poultney, VT, 1993; Witter Bynner Poetry Fellowship, 1994. *Interests*: Travels extensively around the country giving readings & workshops; plays saxophone with her band, "Poetic Justice." *Screen writing experience*: Co-writer with Henry Greenberg, "The Gaan Story," one-hour dramatic story, produced by Silvercloud Video Productions; assistant screenwriter with Henry Greenberg, "The Beginning," half-hour dramatic story, produced by Native American Public Broadcasting Consortium (NAPBC), 1983-84; producer, "We Are One, Umonho," a series of eight 20-minute scripts for Nebraska Educational Television (NET), 1984; "Maiden of Deception Pass," a one-hour dramatic screenplay for NAPBC,

1984-85; "I Am Different From My Brother," rewrite of six half-hour scripts, NAPBC, 1986; "The Runaway," half-hour teleplay, NET, 1986; "Indians & AIDS," 20 & 30 second public service announcements for national television, Powhatan Renape Nation, 1988; "When We Used to Be Humans," in development (American Film Foundation); co-producer & writer, "The Sacred Revolt: The Red Sticks' Wars," full-length dramatic story. *Other film experience*: "American Indian Artist Series II" (composed poetry for narration & worked as production assistant, PBS, 1986); appeared on "Wildflowers," with Helen Hayes (KERA-TV documentary as a storyteller, PBS, 1992); reader for audio library recording, Circle of Nations, Voices & Visions of American Indians, edited by John Gattuso (Beyond Words, 1993); narrator, "Sand Creek," dramatic on-hour movie for Deborah Dennison (Santa Fe, 1994); narrator, the "Native Americans" 6-part series (Turner Broadcasting, 1994). *Biographical sources*: International Authors & Writers Who's Who; International Who's Who of Authors; World Who's Who of Women; Personalities of the West & Midwest; Foremost Women of the 20th Century; 5,00 Personalities of the World; The International Directory of Distinguished Leadership; Who's Who in U.S. Writers, Editors, & poets; Contemporary American Writers; Poets & Writers. *Published works*: She has published four books of poetry including, She Had Some Horses (Thunder's Mouth Press, New York, NY); In Mad Love and War (Wesleyan University Press, 1990); anthology, Talking Leaves, Contemporary Native American Short Stories (Dell, 1991); collaborated with photographer/astronomer Stephen Strom to produce, Secrets From the Center of the World (University of Arizona Press); The Woman Who Fell From the Sky (W.W. Norton, 1994); also, an anthology of Native women's writing, Reinventing the Enemy's Language (University of Arizona Press, 1994); A Love Supreme (W.W. Norton, 1996); children's book, The GoodLuck Cat (Harcourt Brace, 1996). Released CD with her band "Poetic Justice," Letter From the End of the 20th Century (Red Horses Records, 1996).

HARJO, LISA
(Indian center director)
Affiliation: Denver Native Americans United, Denver Indian Center, 4407 Morrison Rd., Denver, CO 80219 (303) 937-0401.

HARJO, SUZAN SHOWN (Cheyenne, Hodulgee Muscogee) 1945-
(writer, lecturer, curator, policy analyst)
Born June 2, 1945, El Reno, Okla. *Principal occupation*: Writer, poet, policy analyst, arts curator. *Address & Affiliation*: President & Executive Director, The Morning Star Institute, 611 Pennsylvania Ave., SE #377, Washington, DC 20003 (202) 547-5531 Fax 546-6724 (work), 1984-present. Website: www.morning stararts.com (a non-profit organization for Native American cultural rights and arts advocacy). *Other professional posts*: Founding Co-chair, Howard Simons Fund for Indian Journalists, 1989-; columnist for Indian Country Today. *Past professional posts*: Special assistant for Indian Legislation, Carter Administration, 1978-79; co-founder & vice-president, Native Children's Survival; executive director, National Congress of American Indians, 1984-89; news director, American Indian Press Association; drama & literatur director and "Seeing Red" producer for WBAI-FM Radio in New York City. *Community activities*: Common Cause (national governing board, 1982-88); National Museum of the American Indian, 1990-96 (Founding Trustee; member, executive committee, and collections committee; chair, program planning committee); lead negotiator of both the 1989 agreement with the Smithsonian Institution that led to the first repatriation law & the later agreement with the national museum community which resulted in the Native American Grave Protection & Repatriation Act of 1990, and was key to the development of the 1991 NMAI Trustees Policy Statement on Repatriation; Ms. Harjo served on the steering committee and as advocacy committee co-chair of a broad-based national coalition of Indian nations and organizations & environmental, human rights & religious groups to secure legal protections for Native Peoples' sacred places and passage of the Native American Free Exercise of Religion Act of 1993. She served as co-chair of the Indian organizing committee for the 1993 March on Washington, and is a charter member and organizer of Artists in Support of American Indian Religious Freedom, formed in

1992. She has helped Indian nations to recover nearly a million acres of land and to achieve appropriations & protections for sacred sites, natural resources, child welfare, health and other social services programs, hospitals, schools and cultural concerns. She has championed treaty rights and individual civil liberties cases, and has developed key federal Indian policy in Washington, DC for nearly two decades, conducting more than 350 successful legislative and appropriation efforts. On December 29, 1990, she participated in the 100-year commemoration of the Massacre of Lakota people at Wounded Knee. At the end of 1990, Congress passed a formal resolution apologizing tot he descendants of the victims of the 1890 Massacre. At the end of 1991, the legislation to establish a Little Big Horn Indian Memorial and to drop the name of Custer from the National Monument was signed into law; she curated three journal gallery exhibits for the Cornell-based *Native Americas*: "Native Images in American Editorial Cartoons" (2001); "New Native Warrior Images in Art" (2001); and "Identity Perspectives by Native Artists" (2002). *Memberships*: Cheyenne-Arapaho Tribes of Oklahoma; American Association of Museums (Committee on Museum & Native American Collaboration); Museum of the American Indian Heye Foundation (Trustee, 1983-90); National Congress of American Indians (executive director, 1984-89); The Association of American Cultures (board member, 1990-); National Commission on Libraries & Information Services Native American Task Force (board member, 1990-); American Indian Press Association (former news director). *Awards, honors*: The Keynote Speaker for the following events: California Indian Education Annual Conference, the University of South Dakota Law School's Indian Law Symposium on Sovereignty, the Ohio Arts Council's Native American Regional Conference, the Native North American Indian Women's Association's Annual Conference, the Federal Communication's Commission Heritage Symposium, the Tourism Conference of the Affiliated Tribes of Northwest Indians, and the Journalism & Women Symposium; Guest Speaker in the Getty Center for the History of Art in Los Angeles, at the "Red Nations Celebration of Native American Women" in Santa Fe, as well as the benefit concert for the "Sacred Run," introduced by Sacred Run Coordinator, Dennis Banks, at the El Ray Theatre in Albuquerque; 1998-99 Brain Trust Member for UNITY; Journalists of Color and a presenter at UNITY '99 in Seattle and UNITY '94 in Atlanta; the 1996 Stanford University Visiting Mentor; Special Guest Speaker at the 1995 All Apache Summit in Albuquerque; and 1992 Dartmouth Collect Montgomery Fellow...she was the first Native American selected for the honor by Stanford's Haas Center for Public Policy, and the first Native woman chosen for the Montgomery Fellowship Award. In 1993, she presented poetry readings at the Denver Art Museum, the Cleveland Public Theatre, and the Roxy Theatre in Los Angeles. She has appeared in poetry readings with Native American poets Joy Harjo & John Trudell, and with 20 American women writers including Nikki Giovanni and Alice Walker. She was a National Coordinator of the 1992 Alliance, which was the focal point for Native voices on the Columbus Quincentenary, and was co-chair and coordinator of "Our Visions: The Next 500 Years," the historic gathering of Native artists, writers and wisdomkeepers (Taos Pueblo, 1992). Her policy & political writings have appeared in many magazines, journals, and newspapers. She has helped Native Peoples' recover more than one million acres of land. She also has developed the most important national policy advances in the modern era for the protection of Native American cultures and arts, including the 1996 Executive Order on Indian Sacred Sites, the 1990 Native American Graves Protection and Repatriation Act, the 1989 National Museum of the American Indian Act, and special assistant for Indian Legislation & Liaison in the Carter Administration and principal author of the 1979 President's Report to Congress on American Indian Religious Freedom. She has been profiled in the NY Times, Lear's, Fortune, High Times, UNITY Magazine, Glamour, Rocky Mountain News, and The Plains Dealer, and has been featured on the Oprah Winfrey Show, Larry King Live, CNN's World Day, Crier & Co., and Sonya Live, among others. In 1993, she wrote the Foreword for George Cantor's North American Indian Landmarks (Visible Ink Press, 1993). Ms. Harjo lectures throughout the U.S., including speeches for the past decade at the Harvard Law School, the Nieman Foundation for Jour-

nalism, and the Principal's Institute. She has presented poetry and/or lectures at various other universities and colleges. In 1991, she read with author, Michael Dorris from "The Crown of Columbus," at Chapters in Washington, DC. In 1992, she keynoted with Rev. Jesse Jackson the Multicultural Leadership Summit in January in Washington, DC, and shared a keynote address with California State Assemblyman Tom Hayden to open the "Seeds of Change" Conference in Sept. in Santa Fe, NM. *Interests*: At present, Ms. Harjo is developing Native Peoples' cultural property rights policy .. for the protection of such cultural property as tribal names, symbols, history and music...building on the cultural patrimony provisions of the repatriation laws and policies. At the same time, she is addressing the issues of stereotyping, name-calling and the use of Indian imagery in popular culture through broad public awareness campaign, focusing on the sports world. *Published works*: Ms. Harjo's poetry has been published in journals, anthologies & textbooks. Her policy writings, arts criticism and social commentary have appeared in numerous newspapers and magazines. She has authored entries on Contemporary Native American arts: 1960-1995 for the "Encyclopedia of American Indians" (1996), and on the U.S. Senate Committee on Indian Affairs for "Native America in the Twentieth Century: An Encyclopedia." Her work is included in such books as "American Voices"; "Cast a Cold Eye: American Opinion Writing, 1990-91; "The Concise Guide to Writing"; "Elements of Writing"; "Exploring Ancient Native America"; "Family Ethnicity"; Native America: Portrait of the Peoples'; "Native North American Voices"; Rethinking Schools" among others.

HARLOW, FRANCIS H. 1928-
(physicist)
Born January 22, 1928, Seattle, Wash. *Education*: University of Washington, BS, 1949, PhD, 1953. *Principal occupation*: Theoretical physicist. *Home address*: 1407 11th St., Los Alamos, NM 87544. *Affiliations*: Staff member, Los Alamos Scientific Laboratory, 1953-; research associate, Museum of New Mexico, 1965-; research associate, School of American Research, 1999-. *Military service*: U.S. Army, 1946-47. *Interests*: Theoretical fluid dynamics and numerical analysis; Pueblo Indian pottery, history, technology, and artistry. *Published works*: Contemporary Pueblo Indian Pottery (Museum of New Mexico, 1965); Historic Pueblo Indian Pottery (Museum of New Mexico, 1967; reprinted 1968, '70); The Pottery of San Ildefonso, with Kenneth Chapman (School of American Research, 1970); Mattepaint Pottery of the Tewa, Keres and Zuni Pueblos (Museum of New Mexico Press, 1973); Historic Pottery of the Pueblo Indians, 1600-1880, with Larry Frank (New York Graphic Society, 1974); Modern Pueblo Pottery, 1880-1960 (Northland Press, 1977); Glazed Pottery of the Southwest Indians (American Indian Art Magazine, Nov. 1976); Pueblo Indian Pottery Traditions (VILTIS, 1978); Pueblo Art: Southwestern Indian Pottery (The Somesuch Press, Dallas, TX, 1983); Two Hundred Years of Pueblo Pottery: The Gallegos Collection (Morningstar Gallery, Santa Fe, NM, 1990); Pueblo Indian Pottery, with Jack Silverman (Silverman Museum, Santa Fe, NM, 2001); The Pottery of Zia Pueblo, with Dwight Lanmon (Museum of New Mexico Press, Santa Fe, NM, 2003); The Pottery of Santa Ana Pueblo, with Duane Anderson & Dwight Lanmon (Museum of New Mexico Press, Santa Fe, NM, 2004).

HARMON, PAT
(museum docent)
Affiliation: Nanticoke Indian Museum, Rt. 13, Box 170A, Millsboro, DE 19966.

HARPER, CHARLES (Cree)
(member-board of directors)
Affiliation: Intertribal Christian Comunications, P.O. Box 3765, Station B, Winnipeg, Manitoba, Canada R2W 3R6 (204) 661-9333.

HARPER, FRED
(Indian band chief)
Affiliation: Red Sucker Lake Indian Band, Red Sucker Lake, Manitoba, Canada R0B 1H0 (204) 469-5041.

HARPER, HENRY S.
(executive director)
Affiliation: National Indian Athletic Association, P.O. Box 295, Cass Lake, MN 56633 (218) 335-8289.

HARPOLE, JACKIE (Choctaw)
(school principal)
Affiliation: Standing Pine Elementary School, 538 Hwy. 487 East, Carthage, MS 39051 (601) 267-9225 Fax 267-9129.

HARRAGARRA-WATERS, DEANNA J.
(library director)
Affiliation: National Indian Law Library, Native American Rights Fund, 1522 Broadway, Boulder, CO 80302 (303) 447-8760.

HARRELL, BEATRICE ORCUTT
(Ohoyo Oti) (Choctaw/Creek)
(tutor)
Address: 13962 Hickory Place, Glenpool, OK 74033 (918) 291-3014. *Affiliation*: Indian education tutor, Sapupla Public Schools, Sapulpa, OK. *Community activities*: Cultural & fund raising activities for the Indian education program. *Membership*: Wordcraft Circle of Native American Writers & Storytellers. *Published work*: How Thunder & Lightning Came to Be.

HARRELL, RAY EVANS (*Nudvwiv Ani-noquisi*)
(Keetoowah) 1941-
(artistic director, conductor, master teacher, performing artist)
Born December 3, 1941, Ada, Okla. *Education*: University of Tulsa, B. Mus., 1972; Manhattan School of Music, M. Mus., 1973; The Ilana Rubenfeld Center (New York, NY), RSM Certification, 1979. *Principal occupation*: Artistic director, conductor, master teacher, performing artist. *Home address*: 200 West 70th St., #6C, New York, NY 10023 (212) 724-2398 (work). *Affiliations*: Teacher, Manhattan School of Music, New York, NY, 1979-86; artistic director & developer of the Magic Circle Opera Repertory Ensemble, Inc. of New York, and the Magic Circle Training, New York, NY, 1978-. Harrell conducts the Magic Circle Ensemble in world premiere recordings of operas by Ned Rorem, "A Childhood Miracle & Three Sisters Who Are Not Sisters," as well as the Kurt Vonnegut/Edgar D. Grana Humanist Requiem, "Stones, Times and Elements." He is producer/artistic director/conductor for works like LaMama E.T.C.'s revolutionary "Flamenco Carmen" in New York City. A veteran performer and Metropolitan Opera Regional semi-finalist, Mr. Harrell is known for critically acclaimed performances and recitals across America in such venues as New York City's Weill Recital Hall and Lincoln Center's Alice Tully Hall, Carnegie Hall Main Stage and Avery Fisher Hall at Lincoln Center, Wolf Trap, and Constitution Hall in the Nation's Capital, among others. *Other professional posts*: Mr. Harrell writes, "a private teacher of illustrious singers in classical, contemporary and popular music, my students have performed in every major venue in New York City, across America, as well as in Europe and the Far East." Institutional Teaching and Lecture credentials include commissioned piano teacher and educational research (4 years), University of Tulsa, OK; teacher of voice, Singers and Composer's Workshop and Vocal Anatomy at Manhattan School of Music, New York City (7 years); director of summer opera productions at Mannes College (2 summers), New York City; guest lecturer on "Learning Organizations & Donald Schon" in Columbia U. Teacher's College PhD program (2 years); lecturer on Somantics, the Arts and the Future of Work, Arts Economics, Culture and Diversity, e.g. at various schools and companies in the New York City area, Auburn and Union Theological Seminary, Adelphi U., Manhattan School of Music, Mannes College, Lucent Technologies, New York City's Museum of Natural History, and conferences here and in Canada, and on the Internet. Opera singer in New York City & on London Records with Antol Dorati; conductor, MCORE Opera & Concert & Newport Classics Recordings; private voice teacher; former editor, The New York Singing Teacher's Bulletin; columnist, "Nuyagi Keetoowah Journal." *Military service*: U.S. Army Chorus, 1966-70 (staff sgt.); soloist, U.S. Army Field Band (touring) Fort Meade, Md., 1965-66. *Community activities*: Harrell is the Traditional Cherokee Proest (Didahnvwisgi) in New York's traditional Keetoowah community and speaks regularly on American Indian subjects in schools and companies as well as at the United Nations. *Membership*: Nuyagi Keetoowah Society (council & columnist); New York Singing Teacher's Association (former editor & board of directors); Screen Actor's Guild; The American Guild of Musical Artists. *Awards, honors*: His curiosity and interests have taken him from directing religious music both in church, school, synagogue and Native American Ceremonials to soloing in both of the top choruses for the U.S. Army where he toured extensively and sang regularly in the nation's capital and at the White House. In the Army Chorus he welcomed the Astronauts home from the moon and opened the St. Louis Gateway Arch. Harrell has convened a Blue Ribbon Roundtable of International Arts and Economics Experts on the Internet. In 2003, he will produce the Ned Rorem International Festival in New York City hosting performances of Rorem's work nationwide and in Europe. *Featured performances*: Recently featured in the premiere of both production and recording of composer David Friedman's prizewinning Broadway Christmas Oratorio "King Island Christmas" produced by 12-time Grammy winner Thomas Z. Shepard. He has performed King Island Christmas at the "Lamb's Theater," the Houseman and Fairbanks theaters in New York and at the Papermill Playhouse. He sang for the upcoming film by Godfrey Reggio & Philip Glass, Naqoyqatsi; Native soloist in "Making Music" world music project for Pearson Entertainment. He has been placed on the performer's list for Native American soloists for an upcoming Cirque Du Soleil production. *Interests*: Harrell's goal is to develop a self-sustaining Chamber Opera Arts Center in every city of 100,000 or more across America thus stimulating work opportunities for American Indian Artists in the Vocal Arts. To this end his company, the Magic Circle Opera Repetory Ensemble, Inc. gives each year $130,000 in fellowships, scholarships and project grants. *Biographical source*: The International Who's Who in Music & Musicians' Directory, 11th (1988) and 20th (1996) editions.

HARRINGTON, SOPHIA (Creek)
(publisher)
Address & Affiliation: Owner, Semihoye-Shawnee Publishing, P.O. Box 5595, Norman, OK 73070 (405) 321-0900 Fax 321-7245.

HARRIS, GENEVA
(health systems administrator)
Affiliation: Okemah Indian Health Center, P.O. Box 429, Okemah, OK 74859 (918) 623-0555.

HARRIS, JULIE
(Indian education program director)
Affiliation: Eau Claire School District, Indian Education Program, 500 Main St., Eau Claire, WI 54701 (715) 833-3491.

HARRIS, LaDONNA (Comanche) 1931-
(organization founder/president)
Born February 15, 1931, Temple, Okla. *Education*: High school. *Address & Affiliation*: Founder/President, Americans for Indian Opportunity (1971-), 681 Juniper Hill Rd., Bernalillo, NM 87004 (505) 867-0278 Fax 867-0441 (work); E-Mail: aio@aio.org. *Select Lectureships*: Woodrow Wilson Fellow, 1982-; Aspen Institute; America Program Institute; Washington School of the Institute for Policy Studies. *Networking experience*: Launched a National American Indian leadership Program: The American Indian Ambassador's Program: "Medicine Pathways for the Future"; created the first Indian-owned & operated National Computer Network dedicated to provide information of interest to Native Americans & access to the National Information Highway; developed & implemented a series of four regional issue management forums for Indian tribes in overcoming barriers to working with environment protection agency; facilitated a series of governance forums with Poarch Creek, Winnebago, Comanche, Cheyenne-Arapaho, Pawnee, Apache & Menominee tribes; among others. *Community activities*: Oklahomans for Indian Opportunity, Inc. (founder/past president, 1965-70); founder, Council for Energy Resource Tribes, 1976. *Memberships*: Haskell Indian Junior College Foundation; National Indian Business Association; National Institute for Women of Color (advisory council); National Institute for the Environment (advisory council); Jacobson Foundation (honorary board); Native American Public Broadcasting Consortium; among others. *Awards, honors*: Outstanding American Citizen of 1965, Anadarko (OK) American Indian Exposition and the Tulsa Indian Council, 1965; Woman of the Year, 1979, Ladies Home Journal; Lucy Covington Award for a Life of Leadership; Human Rights Award: Delta Sigma Theta Society, National Education Association; Outstanding Leadership in Advancing Public Support: 1990 Census; Honorary Doctor of Law, Dartmouth College; Honorary Doctor of Humanities, Marymount College; Honorary Doctor of Public Service, Westfield State College, MA; Honorary Doctor of Humanities, Northern Michigan University. *Interests*: Traveled extensively through Latin America, Russia & the former Soviet Union & Greece. Harris has spent many years training the executive branch of the federal government that tribes are an integral part of the political fabric of the U.S. She has held hundreds of forum on the issues surrounding the interaction between tribes & federal agencies. She applies much of her energy in reinforcing & strengthening tribal government. She has encouraged tribes to reweave traditional value based methods of consensus building into their governance systems. Harris was instrumental in the adoption of official Indian policies by the EPA, the Dept. of Energy, and most recently the Dept. of Agriculture. She still advocates for every federal department to create Indian policies that reaffirm a government to government relationship. In recent years, Harris has devoted much of her energies to her newest initiatives, the Americans for Indian Opportunity Ambassadors Program, which researches and demonstrates the innovations of Indigenous leadership development and identity. She believes that part of her own work as a leader must be mentoring and cultivating new leaders to take her place and the places of others like her. Consequently, the Ambassadors Program was designed to facilitate this trans-generational transition of leadership in Indian Country. This award-winning initiative is the only leadership program in the U.S. that encourages its participants to weave their respective traditional tribal values into a contemporary reality. *Published works*: LaDonna Harris: A Comanche Life, book edited by Henrietta Stockel (University of Nebraska Press, 2000); numerous books & pamphlets published by the Americans for Indian Opportunity, including: A Resource Bibliography for Tribal Participation in Environmental Protection Activities, 1990; Tribal Governments in the U.S. Federal System, 1990; Designing the Future of the Comanche Tribe, 1990; To All My Comanche Relatives, 1990; Tribal Governments As Rural Health Providers; Designing the Economic Future of the Menominee People, 1991; Partnerships for the Protection of Tribal Environments, 1991; significant papers include: "To Govern or Be Governed: Indian Tribes at a Crossroads"; "Partnerships for the Protection of Tribal Environments"; "Indian Business Opportunities and the Defense Sector"; "Alternatives for Agriculture: Successful Tribal Farms"; "Hard Choices: Development of Non-Energy Non-Replenishable Resources"; and "Tribal Governments in the U.S. Federal System"; among others.

HARRIS, NICKY
(Indian education program coordinator)
Affiliation: Chelsea Public Schools, Indian Education Program, 508 Vine, Chelsea, OK 74016 (918) 789-2528 Fax 789-3271.

HARRIS, RAYMOND
(Indian band chief)
Affiliation: Chemainus Indian Band, R.R. #1, Ladysmith, British Columbia, Canada V0R 2E0 (604) 245-7155.

HARRIS, ROLAND (Mohegan)
(former tribal chairperson)
Affiliation: Mohegan Tribe, P.O. Box 488, Uncasville, CT 06382 (860) 204-6100.

HARRIS, REBECCA MEANS
(historic site director)
Affiliation: Angel Mounds State Historic Site, 8215 Pollack Ave., Evansville, IN 47715 (812) 853-3956.

HARRIS-TAYLOR, RHONDA LYNETTE
(Choctaw of Oklahoma) 1951-
(library science educator)
Born April 24, 1951, Hugo, Okla. Education: North Texas State University, BS, 1974; Baylor University, Certificate for School Librarian, 1978; Texas Woman's University, MLS, 1980, PhD, 1985. *Address & Affiliations*: School of Library & Information Science, 401 W. Brooks, Room 120, University of Oklahoma, Norman, OK 73019 (405) 325-3921 Fax 325-7648, assistant professor, 1992-99, associate professor, 1999-. *Other professional posts*: American Indian Li-

brary Association (AILA) (past president, 1984-90; editor, AILA Newsletter). *Academic service activities*: Member, Office of Admissions native American Appeals Committee, 1995-; member, Planning & Budget Committee, College of Arts & Sciences, University of Oklahoma, 1999-2001. *Memberships*: American Indian Library Association; American Library Association; Association for Library & Information Science Education; Association of American Indian/Alaska Native Professors; Oklahoma Library Association; Popular Culture Association (area co-chair-with Judith Overmier-Libraries and Popular Culture (panel), 1995-). *Awards, honors*: Beta Phi Mu; Beta Lambda Chapter; Delta Kappa Gamma; Phi Kappa Phi.

HARRISON, DAVID C. (Osage-Cherokee) 1945-
(attorney; Indian program director)
Born July 28, 1945, Pawhuska, Okla. *Education*: Grinnell College, BA, 1967; Harvard Law School, JD, 1975. *Principal occupation*: Federal Indian service. *Address*: Unknown. *Affiliations*: Rights Protection Officer, Bureau of Indian Affairs, Washington, DC, 1975-. *Other professional post*: Director, Native American National Intern Program, American University, Washington, DC. *Military service*: U.S. Marine Corps, 1967-71 (Captain, Vietnamese Cross of Gallantry, Bronze Star, Purple Heart). *Memberships*: Osage Heloshka Society; Harvard Law School Association. *Awards, honors*: "I served as senior investigator and authored several chapters of report called by New York Times editorial, a magnificent document, sweeping in scope, meticulous in detail, unsparing in assessing blame." *Published work*: Attica, Official Report of the New York State Special Commission on Attica (Bantam, paper, Praeger, hardcover, 1972).

HARRISON, GARY (Aleut)
(village president)
Affiliation: Native Village of Chickaloon, P.O. Box 1105, Chickaloon, AK 99674 (907) 745-0707.

HARRISON, KATHRYN (Confederated Tribes)
(former tribal chairperson)
Affiliation: Confederated Tribes of the Grand Ronde Tribe, 9615 Grand Ronde Rd., Grand Ronde, OR 97347 (503) 879-5211.

HARRISON, LYNN
(museum curator)
Affiliation: Museum of Native American Cultures, Eastern Washington State Historical Society, 2316 West 1st Ave., Spokane, WA 99204 (509) 456-3931.

HARRY, ANDREW
(Indian band chief)
Affiliation: Anaheim Indian Band, Alexis Creek, British Columbia, Canada V0L 1A0 (604) 393-4342.

HARRY, LILLIEN
(Indian band chief)
Affiliation: Canoe Creek Indian Band, Dog Creek, British Columbia, Canada V0L 1J0 (604) 440-5645.

HARRY, NORMAN (Paiute)
(tribal council chairperson)
Affiliation: Pyamid Lake Paiute Tribal Council, P.O. Box 256, Nixon, NV 89424 (702) 574-1000.

HARRY, RICHARD
(Indian band chief)
Affiliation: Homalco Indian Band, P.O. Box 789, Campbell River, British Columbia, Canada V9W 6Y4 (604) 287-4922.

HARRY, ROBERT H., D.D.S.
(IHS area director)
Affiliation: Oklahoma Area Indian Health Service, 5 Corporate Plaza, 3625 NW 56th St., Oklahoma City, OK 73112 (405) 945-6820.

HARRY, WILLIAM
(Indian band chief)
Affiliation: Canoe Creek Indian Band, General Delivery, Dog Creek, British Columbia, Canada V0L 1J0 (604) 440-5645.

HART, ROBERT G. 1921-
(government official-retired)
Born December 28, 1921, San Francisco, Calif. *Education*: American Institute for Banking, 1939-41. *Prin-*

cipal occupation: Governmental official-retired. *Home address*: Unknown. *Affiliations*: Manager, Southern Highlanders, Inc., New York, NY, 1946-52; Southwestern representative, Indian Arts & Crafts Board, Santa Fe, NM, 1954-57; treasurer, Westbury Music Fair, 1957; director, public relations, Constructive Research Foundation, New York, NY, 1958-59; editor, director of publications, Brooklyn Museum, 1959-61; general manager, Indian Arts & Crafts Board, Dept. of the Interior, Washington, DC, 1961-93. *Other professional posts*: Chairman, Federal Inter-Departmental Agency for Arts & Crafts, 1963-93; member, National Advisory Board, Foxfire Fund, 1981-93. *Military service*: U.S. Army, 1943-45. *Memberships*: Conseil Internationale des Musees; American Association of Museums; American Craftsmen's Council; World Crafts Council; American Political Science Association. *Awards, honors*: N.Y. State Governor's Award for Outstanding Service, 1951. *Interests*: Folk art. *Published works*: How to Sell Your Handicrafts (David McKay, 1953); Guide to Alaska (David McKay, 1959); editor, Masters of Contemporary American Crafts (Brooklyn Museum Press, 1960); among others.

HARTMAN, RUSSELL P.
(museum director/curator)
Affiliation: Navajo Tribal Museum, P.O. Box 308, Highway 264, Window Rock, AZ 86515 (602) 871-6673.

HARVEY, DONALD (Navajo)
(school principal)
Affiliation: Leupp Boarding School, P.O. Box HC-61, Winslow, AZ 86047 (602) 686-6211.

HASKIE, LILLIE M. (Navajo)
(health administrator)
Affiliation: Tsaile PHS Indian Health Center, P.O. Box 467, Tsaile, AZ 86556 (602) 724-3391.

HASKEW, DENNY (Citizen Band Potawatomi) 1948-
(artist/bronze sculptor)
Born March 15, 1949, Denver, Colo. *Education*: University of Utah, BA, 1971. *Principal occupation*: Artist/bronze sculptor. *Home address*: 540 N. Grant, Loveland, CO 80537 (970) 663-6375. *Affiliation*: Owner, Haskew Studio's, Loveland, CO, 1986-. *Other professional posts*: Rafting guide - Idaho/Arizona; ski instructor - Utah/Idaho. *Military service*: U.S. Army, 1971-73 (PFC-4; Markmanship, Leadership, Honorable Discharge). *Memberships*: Indian Arts & Crafts Association; American Indian Cowboy Association. *Awards, honors*: Cheyenne Frontier Museum Regional Shows, Cheyenne, WY: 1987 & 1989 Sculpture Awards for, "Robed in Indigo" & "Courage to Lead" respectively; Red Earth Invitational, Oklahoma City, OK: 1988, 1990, 1992 & 1993 Sculpture Awards for, "Ancient Defender," "Moulding Our Future" monument; "Strength of the Maker," & "Courage to Lead" monument; Colorado Indian Market, Denver, CO: 1988 & 1989 Best of Class for "Trail of Prayers" & "At Eagles Glance"; Santa Fe Indian Market: 1989 1st Place Sculpture for, "At Eagles Glance"; 1989 presentation of "Courage to Lead" to W.K. Kellogg Foundation by the National Fellowship Program, Battlecreek, MI; Indian Arts & Crafts Association: "1991 Artist of the Year" Award for "Courage to Lead"; 1991 Judges Merit Award for "Trail of Prayers" from Wildlife and Western Art Exhibition; 1991, 1st, 2nd & 3rd Place for "Trail of Prayers," "He Who Fights With a Feather," & "Committed" from Odham Tosh, Casa Grande, AZ; 1991, 1st & 2nd Place for "Strength of the Maker" & "Committed;" 1s & 2nd Place, 1991 & 1992 Gallup Ceremonial Show; Smithsonian Institute (1992 Best of Show, 1st & 3rd Place, 1st Place Sculpture Award, "Courage to Lead" monument1992 Santa Fe Indian Market; 1993 "Wester Heritage Award," Festival of Western Art. Finalist, Holocaust Memorial, Palm Desert, CA; finalist, City of Redwood, Public Art Competition pending. *Public Commissions*: Life Size Relief "John Yoder" - Minnoite School, 1987; "Youth in Crisis" - Dr. Thomas Barrett Counselor, 1987; "Judge Hatfield Chilson" Loveland, CO, 1988; "Crawford Follmer" Life Size - McKee Medical Center, Loveland, CO, 1990. *Shows*: 1989 Oklahoma Indian Artist Show, House of Representatives, Washington, DC; 1989 Kennedy Center for Performing Arts, Washington, DC, "Colorado Living Artists"; 1989 & 1990 Allied Artist of America Shows, New York, NY; 1991 Potawatomi Museum, Shawnee, OK, Permanent Display, "Trail of Prayers"; Franco American Exhibit at Rennes Institute, Paris France,

1992. *Permanent Exhibit*: National Museum of the American Indian. *Biographical source*: "Art of the West," May/June, 1992.

HASKIE, JEANNIE G. (Navajo)
(school principal)
Affiliation: Sanostee Day School, P.O. Box 159, Sanostee, NM 87461 (505) 723-2476 Fax 723-2425.

HASKIE, LILLIE M. (Navajo) 1946-
(nurse)
Born February 21, 1946, Chinle, Ariz. *Education*: Navajo Community College, ADN, 1983. *Principal occupation*: Nurse. *Address*: P.O. Box 293, Lukachukai, AZ 86507 (602) 787-2335. *Affiliation*: Administrative Nurse, Tsaile PHS-IHC, Tsaile, AZ, 1984-.

HASSETT, JOHN D., SR. (Peewee)
(Powhatan) 1946-
(retired; chief)
Born in 1946, Healdsburg, Calif. *Address*: P.O. Box 4879, Salinas, CA 93912 (831) 751-9885 (phone & fax). *E-mail*: powhatanorg@earthlink.net. *Website*: powhatangov.org. *Affiliation*: Chief, The Powhatan Nation, Salinas, CA. *Military service*: U.S. Marines, 1970. *Community activities*: Computers. *Interests*: Electronics. *Published works*: The Powhatan Nation, The Real Hell; Powhatan Winchester E-Power Electric Rotary Electric Injection Engine, 2001.

HASSRICK, PETER H.
(center & museum director)
Affiliation: Buffalo Bill Historical Center & Plains Indian Museum, P.O. Box 1000, Cody, WY 82414 (307) 587-4771.

HASTINGS, JIM
(Indian school principal)
Affiliation: Sherman Indian School, 9010 Magnolia Ave., Riverside, CA 92503 (888) 584-4004; (909) 276-6327 Fax 276-6336.

HASTINGS, WILLIAM
(school principal)
Affiliation: Theodore Roosevelt School, P.O. Box 567, Fort Apache, AZ 85926 (602) 338-4464.

HATCH, NANCY
(Indian school administrator)
Affiliation: Bahweting Anishnabe School, 1301 Marquette Ave., Sault Ste. Marie, MI 49783 (906) 635-5055 Fax 635-3805.

HATCH, VIOLA (Arapahoe)
(tribal chairperson)
Affiliation: Cheyenne-Arapaho Tribal Business Committee, P.O. Box 38, Concho, OK 73022 (405) 262-0345. *Other professional post*: Member, Board of Directors, National Indian Youth Council, Albuquerque, NM.

HATFIELD, RAYMOND ESPANIEL
(director-association)
Affiliation: National Association of Friendship Centres, 251 Laurier Ave., West, Suite 600, Ottawa, Ontario, Canada K1P 5J6 (613) 563-4844.

HAUXWELL, JON 1948-
(physician)
Born July 31, 1948, Marysville, Kans. *Education*: University of Kansas, BA, 1970; University of Kansas, School of Medicine, Kansas City, MD, 1974. *Principal occupation*: Physician. *Address*: Unknown. *Affiliation*: Clinical director, medical officer, Northern Cheyenne Service Unit, Indian Health Service, Lame Deer, MT, 1977-. *Other professional posts*: Associate clinical professor, Family Medicine, University of Washington, School of Medicine; family nurse practitioner preceptor, University of North Dakota. *Military service*: Commissioned Corps, USPHS, 1977- (Outstanding Service Medal, 1989). *Community activities*: Member, Northern Cheyenne Gourd Dance Society; honorary member, Kit Fox Society (traditional Cheyenne military society). *Memberships*: American College of Surgeons (Advanced Trauma Life Support Instructor, 1981-); Northern Cheyenne Multidisciplinary Chemical Dependence Team (chairman, 1986-). *Awards, honors*: National Indian Health Board, Certificate of Appreciation, 1982; National Outstanding Clinician Award - 1985, by National Council of Clinical Direc-

tors. *Interests*: Powwow-ing ("every member of family has been on pow wow head staff and hosted giveaways on numerous occasions"). Photography; music (piano & vocal) gardening; teaching medical students; hiking; cooking; cross-cultural activities; track and field; football; reading; history; Native American art, especially beadwork. Iroquois ancestry, non-registered. *Published work*: The Cheyenne (Children's Press, 1988).

HAVATON, EARL (Hualapai)
(tribal chairperson)
Affiliation: Hualapai Tribal Council, P.O. Box 179, Peach Springs, AZ 86434 (520) 769-2216.

HAVERKATE, RICK (Sault Ste. Marie Chippewa) 1965-
(university faculty)
Born October 2, 1965, Elmhurst, Ill. *Education*: Northern Michigan University, B.S., 1989; University of Hawaii-Manoa, MPH, 1993. *Principal occupation*: University faculty. *Home address*: 1890 East West Rd., Moore Hall 405, Honolulu, HI 96822 (808) 956-6234. *Affiliations*: Coordinator, American Indian Recruitment Program, University of Hawaii, Honolulu, 1992-; health education consultant, Inter Tribal Council of Michigan, Sault Ste. Marie, MI, 1991-. *Other professional post*: Community health educator, Sault Ste. Marie Tribe of Chippewa Indians. *Community activities*: V.P. American Heart Association, Upper Peninsula, 1991-92; Chippewa County AIDS Task Force, 1990-92; LifeGuard Hawaii — AIDS Prevention/Education Peer Program. *Memberships*: Society of Public Health Educators of Hawaii, 1992-; American Public Health Association, 1993-. *Awards, honors*: Health Educator of the Year, Bemidji Area IHS; Michigan Competitive Scholarship (4 years); Mortar Board Honor Society: Outstanding College Student of the Year; Student Commencement Speaker, 1989, Northern Michigan University. *Interests*: "Spent 8 weeks exploring the public health systems throughout Thailand during summer of 1993, Included Bangkok Metro area as well as Hill Tribe areas in extreme northern Thailand and rural farming regions. I am interested in community development issues and how health care and politics relate. Exploring a developing country helped me gain important insight in to our own country."

HAWK, JOHNNY T.
(executive director)
Affiliation: Calista Corporation, 601 W. 5th Ave. #200, Anchorage, AK 99501 (907) 279-5516 Fax 272-5060.

HAWK, RAY (Chippewa)
(clinical director)
Affiliation: Bois Fort Tribal Clinic, P.O. Box 15, Nett Lake, MN 55772 (218) 757-3296.

HAWK, ROBIN
(school principal)
Affiliation: Crow Creek Sioux Tribal Elementary School, P.O. Box 469, Fort Thompson, SD 57339 (605) 245-2373.

HAWK, WARREN
(executive director)
Affiliation: Cherokee Initiative, 1106 S. Muskogee Ave., Suite A, Tahlequah, OK 74464.

HAWKINS, MEL
(foundation director)
Affiliation: Georgia Cherokee Heritage Foundation, Rt. 3, Box 750, Dahlonega, GA 30533 (706) 864-6010.

HAWKINS, RUSSELL (Sisseton-Wahpeton Sioux)
(tribal chairperson)
Affiliation: Sisseton Wahpeton Sioux Tribal Council, Route 2, Agency Village, Sisseton, SD 57262 (605) 698-3911.

HAWORTH, JOHN
(museum director)
Affiliation: National Museum of the American Indian, Smithsonian Institution, George Gustav Heye Center, New York, NY 10004 (212) 514-3772

HAWLEY, HERBERT W. (Burns Paiute)
(tribal chairperson)
Affiliation: Burns Paiute General Council, HC 71, 100 Pa Si Go St., Burns, OR 97720 (503) 573-2088.

HAYDEN, IOLA (Comanche)
(executive director)
Affiliation: Oklahomans for Indian Opportunity, 3001 S. Berry Rd., Norman, OK 73069 (405) 329-3737.

HAYES, CHARLES H. "Pete" (Nez Perce)
(tribal chairperson)
Affiliation: Nez Perce Tribal Executive Committee, P.O. Box 305, Lapwai, ID 83540 (208) 843-2253.

HAYES, ELLEN
(executive director)
Affiliation: Southeast Alaska Indian Cultural Center, 106 Metlakatla St., Sitka, AK 99835 (907) 747-8061.

HAYES, HOWARD, M.D.
(clinical director)
Affiliation: White Earth PHS Indian Health Center, White Earth, MN 56591 (218) 983-3221.

HAYES, LEE ANN Pala Band of Mission Indians) 1939-
(tutorial aide)
Born November 29, 1939, Soboba Indian Reservation, Soboba, Calif. *Principal occupation*: Tuturial aide. *Address*: P.O. Box 80, Pala, CA 92059 (760) 742-3300 Fax 742-3102. E-mail: vbpala@juno.com. *Community activities*: Tribal council memeber; Chairperson, Boys & Girls Club of Pala; J.O.M. Committee; Tekakwitha Council; California Manpower Consortium; and Pala Indian Education Committee.

HAYS, ELLEN
(executive director)
Affiliation: Southeast Alaska Indian Cultural Center, 106 Metlakatla St., Sitka, AK 99835 (907) 747-8061.

HAYS, PATRICK
(BIA director)
Affiliation: Director, Office of Trust Responsibilities, Bureau of Indian Affairs, DOI, MS-4513-MIB, 1849 C St., NW, Washington, DC 20240 (202) 208-5831.

HAYWARD, GLEN (Wintun)
(rancheria chairperson)
Affiliation: Redding Rancheria, 2000 Rancheria Rd., Redding, CA 96001 (916) 225-8979.

HAYWARD, RICHARD A. "SKIP"
(Mashantucket Pequot) 1948-
(tribal vice-chairman)
Born November 28, 1948, Groton, Conn. *Address & Affiliation*: Mashantucket Pequot Tribal Council (Chairperson, 1975-98; vice-chairpeson, 1998-), P.O. Box 160, Ledyard, CT 06339 (203) 536-2681. *Other professional posts*: Chairman, Board of Directors, Native American Rights Fund, Boulder, CO, 1988-94 (continues to serve on the executive board); chairman, Mashantucket Pequot Gaming Enterprise, 1991-; member, board of directors of Foxwoods Management Co. *Community activities*: Chairman, Mashantucket Pequot Indian Housing Authority; chairman, Economic Development & Planning Committee; member-Board of Directors, Mashantucket Pequot Museum & Research Center, set to open in late 1997; committee member, 1995 Special Olympics World Games, held in Connecticut, and to which the tribe donated $2 million (the largest single donation received by that organization). *Awards, honors*: Appointee of the Governor of Connecticut to the Legislative Task Force on Indian Affairs; received the National Historic Preservation Award, 1988; The Mashantucket reservation is designated a National Historic Landmark; honorary doctorate degrees (in 1994) from The University of Connecticut, Eastern Connecticut State University, and Roger Williams College in Rhode Island. In Sept. 1995, Mr. Hayward received the Jay Silverheels Award from the National Center for American Indian Enterprise Development in Los Angeles.

HAZELTON, HANK
(director-Indian organization)
Affiliation: Rights for All Indigenous Nations, Inc. (R.A.I.N.), R.D. 1, Box 308A, Petersburg, NY 12138 (518) 658-3055.

HEAD, PHILIP
(Indian band chief)
Affiliation: Red Earth Indian Band, Red Earth, Saskatchewan, Canada S0E 1K0 (306) 768-3640.

HEAD, ROGER
(executive director)
Affiliation: Minnesota Indian Affairs Council, 1819 Bemidji Ave., Bemidji, MN 56601 (218) 755-3825.

HEADLEY, LOUIS R. (Arapahoe) 1948-
(Indian school supt.)
Born February 25, 1948, Fort Washakie, Wyo. *Education*: University of Montana, Missoula, BA, 1974; University of South Dakota, Vermillion, MA, 1977; University of Wyoming, Laramie, EdS, 1986. *Principal occupation*: Indian school supt. *Home address*: Box 344, St. Stephens, WY 82524 (307) 856-4147. *Affiliations*: Teacher, Principal, St. Stephens Indian School, 1977-; minority counselor, special services, University of Wyoming, Laramie, 1984-. *Other professional posts*: Home-school coordinator, Lander (WY) Valley High School; field coordinator, Tri-State Tribes, Inc., Billings, MT. *Community activities*: Wind River Indian Education Association, Wind River, Wyo. (past chairman); Keepers of the Fire Indian Club, University of Wyoming (advisor); Cub Scout volunteer, St. Stephens, WY; Head Start Policy Council, Ethete, WY (vice-chairman). *Memberships*: Phi Delta Kappa; National Association of Elementary School Principals; National Indian Education Association (treasurer); Wyoming Association for Bilingual-Bicultural Education (treasurer). *Awards, honors*: Wyoming Golden Gloves Championship Scholarship Award; Korean Temple Band, Casper, Wyo; Outstanding Young Men of America, U.S. Jaycees, 1978. *Interests*: "I was a member of the Arapahoe and Shoshone Indian Dance Troupe that danced in Switzerland. I was also selected to dance in Washington, D.C. during the 1976 Bicentennial. I have been chosen to be the head dancer in Denver, Steamboat Spring, Colorado and Rocky Boy Reservation."

HEADDRESS, ARLYN (Assiniboine & Sioux)
(tribal chairperson)
Affiliation: Fort Peck Tribal Executive Board, P.O. Box 1027, Poplar, MT 59255 (406) 768-5155.

HEAPE, STEVEN R.
(executive producer)
Address & Affiliation: Executive Producer, Rich-Heape Films, Inc., 5952 Royal Lane, Suite 254, Dallas, TX 75230 (888) 600-2922; (214) 696-6916. E-mail: steven@richheape.com. *Professional activities*: Producing Native American videos, films and movies dedicated to inform, educate and encourage the awareness of the history, cultures, languages, traditions and aspirations of Native Americans and other Native Peoples. Rich-Heape Films has been recognized as 1999 & 2003 American Indian Business of the Year by the American Indian Chamber of Commerce of Texas, and has reeceived numerous awards. *Published works*: Videos: "Black Indians: An American Story," 60 mins. VHS & DVD; "How to Trace Your Native American Heritage," 35 mins. VHS & DVD; Tales of Wonder I & II, 60 mins. each. VHS & DVD, CD soundtrack; "Native American Healing in the 21st Century," 40 mins. VHS & DVD; "Walela-Live in Concert," DVD, VHS & audio CD (2004). *Book*: "American Indian Directory" - 1999 (national listing of over 500 federally-recognized American Indian nations & tribes.

HEAPE, TOYE
(executive director)
Affiliation: Tennessee Commission on Indian Affairs, 401 Church St., L&C Annex, 7th Floor, Nashville, TN 37243-0459 (615) 532-0745 Fax 532-0732; E-mail: theape@mail.state.tn.us. Web site: www.state.tn.us/environment/cia/index/hml

HEARN, EARNEST R. (Tohono O'odham)
(BIA acting supt.)
Affiliation: Papago Agency, BIA, P.O. Box 578, Sells, AZ 85634 (520) 383-3286.

HEATH, MARGARET A. 1947-
(education program manager)
Born October 24, 1947, Boulder, Colo. *Education*: University of Colorado, BA, 1972, MA, 1979. *Principal occupation*: Manager of education program. *Work address*: P.O. Box 758, Dolores, CO 81323 (970) 882-5637 Fax 882-7035; E-mail: megg_heath@co.blm.gov. *Website*: www.blm.gov/heritage/. *Affiliations*: Administrator & teacher, Adams County School District No. 50, Westminster, CO, 1972-79; director, Ute Mountain Ute Tribal Youth Shelter, Towaoc, CO, 1988-; director

of education, Crow Canyon Archaeological Center, Cortez, CO, 1986-92; manager, Heritage Education Program, Bureau of Land Management, Dolores, CO, 1992-. *Community activities*: Galloping Goose Historical Society. *Memberships*: Society for American Archaeology (Public Education Committee); National Council for the Social Studies; National Council for History Education. *Interests*: "Heritage education and interesting the public in preserving and protecting historical places and cultural resources; K-112 education; experiential education, especially archaeology for all ages and designing curriculum about the Anasazi; curriculum development; motivating students; Native American crafts, past and present - learning how to do them; hiking and rafting canyons of the Southwest; writing." *Published works*: Co-authored, Crow Canyon Archaeological Center: Teacher's Guide to Archaeological Activities (Crow Canyon Archaeological Center, 1989); co-authored with Lewis Matis, Crow Canyon Archaeological Center: Windows Into the Past & Inquiries Into the Past (Crow Canyon Archaeological Center, 1989); "Why Archaeology" in Whole Language Catalog (McGraw-Hill, 1990); Editor of series: Discovering Archaeology in: Arizona (1994), Alaska (1996), Wyoming (1997), New Mexico (1998), Colorado (1999); History Mystery Series: The Mystery of Butch Cassidy and the Sundance Kid," (2003); Art & Archaeology: Conflict and Interpretation in a Museum Setting," in Ancient Muses: Archaeology and the Arts (University of Alabama Press, 2003).

HEAVY HEAD, MARTIN
(Native student services officer)
Affiliation: Dept. of Native American Studies, The University of Lethbridge, 4401 University Dr., Lethbridge, Alberta, Canada T1K 3M4 (403) 329-2635.

HEAVY RUNNER, GEORGE
(communications)
Affiliation: Blackfeet Indian Telecommunications, P.O. Box 819, Browning, MT 59417.

HEBBRING, MARGE (*Bibogonikwe*)
(Lac Courte Oreilles Ojibwe) 1948-
(grant director)
Born January 13, 1948, Winter, Wisc. *Education*: MA (Educational Professional Development); Ed.D in progress. *Principal occupation*: Grant director. *Home address*: 7361 203rd St., Chippewa Falls, WI 54729 (715) 723-5278 Fax 836-5021. E-mail: hebbrima@uwec.edu. Website: www.uwec.edu/gearup. *Affiliations*: Title IX Coordinator, Eau Claire Area School District, Eau Claire, WI, 1995-99; coordinator, American Indian Academic & Student Services; grant director, UW-Eau Claire, Eau Claire, WI, 1999-present. *Other professional posts*: Gear Up director, UW-Eau Claire & Lac du Flambeau Reservation; instructor, Wisconsin Indian Curriculum Development. *Membership*: Wisconsin Indian Education Association (board member); Wisconsin Charter Schools Association; Wisconsin Women in Higher Education Leadership. *Interests*: Fur trade re-enacting, American Indian history and culture; charter schools, education and learning. Presently writing historic novel on fur trade history in Wisconsin.

HECKERT, MARK
(executive director)
Affiliation: Intertribal Bison Cooperative, 1560 Concourse Dr., Rapid City, SD 57703 (605) 394-9730 Fax 394-7742.

HECOMOVICH, BILL
(Indian center director)
Affiliation: Director, Lake County Citizens Committee, P.O. Box 90, Cobb, CA 95426 (707) 928-5591 Fax 928-6128.

HEDGE COKE, ALLISON
(Indian education)
Affiliation: Edison Middle School, Indian Education Program, 2101 S. West, Sioux Falls, SD 57103.

HEDGPETH, DANA (Haliwa-Saponi)
(journalist-business reporter)
Born in Halifax, NC. *Education*: University of Maryland - College Park, BA (journalism). *Address*: c/o Native American Journalists Association (NAJA), 3359 36th Ave. South, Minneapolis, MN 55406 (612) 729-9244 Fax 729-9373. E-mail: hedgpeth@naja.com. *Affiliation*: Currently, Business Reporter, Washington

Post, Washington, DC. *Other professional posts*: Member-board of directors, Native American Journalists Association; writing mentor for NAJA's Project Phoenix, which is a week-long journalism boot camp for Native American youth.

HEDRICK, HENRY E.
(organization president; editor)
Affiliation: American Indian Liberation Crusade, Inc., 4009 S. Halliday Ave., Los Angeles, CA 90062 (213) 299-1810. *Other professional post*: Editor, Indian Crusader.

HEFFINGTON, DENNIS
(IHS-tribal activities)
Affiliation: Office of Tribal Activities, California Area IHS, 1825 Bell St., Suite 200, Sacramento, CA 95825 (916) 978-4202.

HEFLIN, DONNA JO
(museum curator)
Affiliation: Choctaw Nation Museum, HC 64, Box 3270, Tuskahoma, OK 74574 (918) 569-4465.

HEIDE, SUSAN
(executive director)
Affiliation: United American Indians of the Delaware Valley, 225 Chestnut St., Philadelphia, PA 19106 (215) 574-9020.

HEIDENREICH, DR. C. ADRIAN
(college instructor)
Affiliation: Dept. of Native American Studies, Montana State University, 1500 North 30th St., Billings, MT 59101 (406) 657-2311 Fax 657-2187.

HEINRICH, ALBERT C. 1922-
(professor of anthropology)
Born February 2, 1922, Ill. *Education*: New School for Social Research, BA; University of Alaska, MEd; University of Washington, PhD, 1960. *Principal occupation*: Professor of anthropology & linguistics (retired). *Home address*: 29605 N.E. Pheasant Ave., Corvallis, OR 97333 (503) 752-8089. *Affiliation*: Retired professor of anthropology & linguistics, University of Calgary, Alberta, Canada. *Memberships*: American Association for the Advancement of Science. *Awards, honors*: Seattle Anthropological Society Prize, 1962. *Interests*: Linguistics; social structure; arctic; Indians of North America; South Asia; Have spent extended periods of time in Alaska, Arctic Canada, The Labrador, South America, India, Europe. Have written numerous articles on Athabascans, Eskimos.

HEINZ, JOHN R.
(health director)
Affiliation: Sophie Trettevick Indian Health Center, P.O. Box 410, Neah Bay, WA 98357 (206) 645-2233.

HEISLER, FRANKLIN
(health director)
Affiliation: White Earth PHS Indian Health Center, White Earth, MN 56591 (218) 983-3221.

HELFIN, DONNA JOE (Choctaw)
(museum curator)
Affiliation: Choctaw Nation Museum, Route 1, Box 105 AAA, Tuskahoma, OK 74574 (918) 569-4465.

HELIN, LAWRENCE
(Indian band chief)
Affiliation: Lax-Kw'alaams Indian Band, 206 Shashaak St., Port Simpson, British Columbia, Canada V0V 1H0 (604) 625-3474.

HELM, JUNE
(program director)
Affiliation: American Indian & Native Studies Program, University of Iowa, 113 Macbride Hall, Iowa City, IA 52242 (319) 335-0539.

HELTON, LESTER
(Indian school principal)
Affiliation: Greyhills High School, P.O. Box 160, Tuba City, AZ 86045 (520) 283-6271 Fax 283-6604.

HELTON, NORA (Mojave)
(former tribal chairperson)
Affiliation: Fort Mojave Tribal Council, 500 Merriman Ave., Needles, CA 92363 (760) 629-4591.

HEMAURER, Fr. GILBERT F.
(executive director)
Affiliation: Tekakwitha Conference National Center, P.O. Box 6759, Great Falls, MT 59406 (406) 727-0147.

HEMMY, PATRICK J.
(BIA agency supt.)
Affiliation: Turtle Mountain Agency, Bureau of Indian Affairs, P.O. Box 60, Belcourt, ND 58316 (701) 477-3191 Fax 477-6628.

HENA, JAMES (Pueblo Tesuque-Zuni)
(member-board of directors)
Affiliation: Member-Board of Directors, Association on American Indian Affairs, P.O. Box 268, Sisseton, SD 57262 (605) 698-3998. *Past professional post*: Chairperson, All Indian Pueblo Council, Albuquerque, NM.

HENDERSON, EDWARD
(Indian band chief)
Affiliation: William Charles Indian Band, Box 106, Montreal Lake, Saskatchewan, Canada S0J 1Y0 (306) 663-5349.

HENDERSON, GLEN E.
(national monument supt.)
Affiliations: Tuzigoot National Monument, P.O. Box 68, Clarkdale, AZ 86324 (602) 634-5564; Montezuma Castle National Monument, P.O. Box 219, Camp Verde, AZ 86322.

HENDERSON, JANICE
(Indian band chief)
Affiliation: Stangecoming Indian Band, Box 609, Fort Frances, Ontario, Canada P9A 3M6 (807) 274-2188.

HENDERSON, SAM R.
(national monument supt.)
Affiliation: Casa Grande Ruins National Monument, 1100 N. Ruins Dr., Coolidge, AZ 85228 (602) 723-3172; Walnut Canyon National Monument, Flagstaff, AZ.

HENDRICKS, SONNY (Miwok)
(rancheria chairperson; health director)
Affiliations: Tuolumne Me-Wuk Rancheria, P.O. Box 699, Tuolumne, CA 95379 (209) 928-3475; director, Tuolumne River Indian Health Program.

HENDRICKSON, DAVID
(BIA agency supt.)
Affiliation: Bethel Agency, Bureau of Indian Affairs, 1675 C St., Anchorage, AK 99501 (907) 271-4088.

HENERICKSON, LINDA J.E.
(association president)
Affiliation: Association of Alaska Native Contractors, 700 W. 58th, Unit F, Anchorage, AK 99518 (907) 562-1866.

HENRICHS, ROBERT (Eskimo)
(village president)
Affiliation: Native Village of Eyak, P.O. Box 1388, Cordova, AK 99574 (907) 424-7738.

HENRY, EARL (Athapascan)
(AK village council president
Affiliation: Venetie Village Council, P.O. Box 99, Arctic Village, AK 99781 (907) 849-8212.

HENRY, GORDON D., JR.
(White Earth Chippewa) 1955-
(ass't. professor, poet, short fiction writer)
Born October 19, 1955, Philadelphia, Penna. *Education*: Michigan State University, MA, 1983; University of North Dakota, PhD, 1992. *Principal occupation*: Assistant professor of English. *Address*: Unknown. *Affiliation*: Assistant professor, Dept. of English, Michigan State University, E. Lansing, MI, 1992-95. *Other professional posts*: Artist in the schools; North Dakota Arts Council, 1984-86; lecturer-storyteller, West Central Michigan Humanities Council. *Memberships*: Wordcraft Writing Circle; North American Native Writers Circle. *Award*: Thomas McGrath Award for Poetry, University of North Dakota. *Interests*: Fulbright, Lecture Award for Spain, 1995. *Biographical source*: Article in "Genre," by Kim Blaeser, 1994. *Published works*: Outside White Earth (Blue Cloud, 1985); The Light People (University of Oklahoma Press, 1994).

HENRY, HAROLD
(Indian band chief)
Affiliation: Kwaw-Kwaw-A-Pilt Indian Band, Box 412, Chilliwack, British Columbia, Canada (604) 858-0662.

HENRY, JEANETTE
(director-Indian society; editor)
Affiliation: American Indian Historical Society, 1451 Masonic Ave., San Francisco, CA 94117 (415) 626-5235. *Other professional post*: Editor, The Indian Historian.

HENRY, LAWRENCE
(Indian band chief)
Affiliation: Roseau River First Nation, Box 30, Ginew, MB, Canada R0A 2R0 (204) 427-2312.

HENRY, LEO R. (Haudenosaunee)
(tribal chief)
Affiliation: Tuscarora Indian Nation, 2006 Mt. Hope Rd., Lewiston, NY 14092 (716) 622-7061.

HENRY, PHILIP NATHANIEL (Saginaw Chippewa)
(Indian outreach worker)
Born June 7, 1933, Saginaw, Mich. *Education*: St. Clair Co. Community College. *Principal occupation*: Indian outreach worker. *Home address*: 715 Summer St., Algonac, MI 48001 (810) 794-5413 fax 975-4910. *Affiliation*: Oakland Co. Family Independence Agency, Pontiac, MI, 1994-. *Other professional posts*: Home health care primary case manager; commissioner Region I, Michigan Commission on Indian Affairs. *Past professional posts*: Building Trades Roofer Local 149 (25 years); JTPA Indian Employment & Service Counselor (7 years); director of Indian education, Algonac Community Schools, Port Huron, MI, 1976-80. *Membership*: Saginaw Chippewa Indian Tribe of Michigan. *Community activities*: Board member, Down River Nutrition Center, Marine City, MI; past board member, Down River Community Services, Algonac, MI. *Military service*: U.S. Marine Corps, 1953-54. *Awards, honors*: Certificate of Recognition & Appointed by Governor Engler to Region I, Michigan Commission on Indian Affairs (Aug. 1992, reappointed, 1994-97); recognized as elder and Indian leader for Michigan Indian community; brother of Thelma Henry Shipman, former director of Urban Indian Affairs, Wayne County Mich. Dept. of Social Services.

HENRY, VIRGINIA
(Indian center director)
Affiliation: American Indian Center of Arkansas, 235 N. Greenwood, Fort Smith, AR 72901 (501) 785-5149.

HENSLEY, WILLIAM L. (Eskimo) 1941-
(state senator)
Born 1941, Kotzebue, Alaska. *Education*: University of Alaska, 1960-1961; George Washington University, BA, 1966; University of Alaska, 1966; University of New Mexico Law School, 1967; UCLA Law School, 1968. *Principal occupation*: State Senator. *Home address*: Kotzebue, Alaska. *Affiliations*: Alaska House of Representatives, 1966-70; Alaska State Senate, 1970-. *Community activities*: Rural Affairs Commission, 1968-1972 (chairman, 1972); Land Claims Task Force (chairman, 1968); Northwest Regional Educational Laboratory (board of directors, 1968-1969); Northwest Alaska Native Association Regional Corporation (board of directors). *Memberships*: Alaska Federation of Natives, 1966- (organizer, 1966; president, 1972); Northwest Alaska Native Association (organizer, 1966); National Council on Indian Opportunity, 1968-70. *Interests*: Land claims implementation; rural economic development; education facilities in the bush; old-age centers; bilingual programs.

HENSON, C.L.
(BIA administrator)
Affiliation: Chief, Division of Administrative Services, Office of Indian Education Programs, Bureau of Indian Affairs, Dept, of the Interior, MS-3530-MIB, 249 C St., NW, Washington, DC 20240 (202) 208-4234.

HENSON, ED
(executive director)
Affiliation: Cherokee Historical Association, P.O. Box 398, Cherokee, NC 28719 (704) 497-2111.

HENSON, JIM (United Keetoowah Cherokee)
(tribal chief)
Address & Affiliation: United Keetoowah Band of Cherokees, P.O. Box 746, Tahlequak, OK 74465 (918) 456-5491 Fax 456-9601.

HENSON, RICHARD ALLEN (Comanche) 1942-
(BIA employment assistance officer)
Born January 26, 1942, Pawnee, Okla. *Education*: Oklahoma State Tech, 1960-62; Minot State College, BA, 1976. *Principal occupation*: BIA employment assistance director. *Address*: Bureau of Indian Affairs, 1951 Constitution Ave., NW, Rm. 331S, MS: 331SIB, Washington, DC 20245 (202) 343-1780. *Affiliations*: Metropolitan Life Insurance Co., Ardmore, OK, 1967-71; guidance counselor, United Tribes Employment Training Center, Bismarck, ND, equal employment opportunity counselor, job developer and employment assistance officer, United Tribes Employment Training Center, Minot, ND, 1971-74, Fort Berthold Agency, BIA, New Town, N.D., 1974-76; area equal employment opportunity officer, BIA, Albuquerque, NM, 1976-77; director, equal employment opportunity, Indian Health Service, Rockville, MD; employment assistance officer, BIA, Washington, DC. *Military service*: U.S. Air Force, 1963-67. *Community activities*: Minot Indian Club (president, 1974); Minot Mayor's Human Rights Committee (member); Minot's Mental Health & Retardation Board (member). *Interests*: "To continue to work with Indian people in Indian affairs and to return to school to earn my master's degree in public health."

HEPFER, RUSSELL J. (Lower Elwha S'Klallam)
(tribal chairperson)
Affiliation: Lower Elwha Band of of S'Klallam Indians Tribal Council, 2851 Lower Elwha Rd., Port Angeles, WA 98362 (360) 452-8471 Fax 452-3428

HER MANY HORSES, CLEVE
(BIA agency supt.)
Affiliation: Lower Brule Agency, Bureau of Indian Affairs, P.O. Box 190, Lower Brule, SD 57548 (605) 473-5512 Fax 473-5491.

HERIARD, JACK B. 1948-
(editor/publisher)
Born July 26, 1948, New Orleans, LA. *Principal occupation*: Editor/publisher. *Home address*: 53236 Old Uneedus Rd., Folsom, LA 70437 (504) 796-5433 (work/home). *Affiliation*: Editor/publisher, "Crafts: American Indian Past & Present," Written Heritage, Inc., Folsom, LA, 1967-. *Other professional post*: Managing editor, "Whispering Wind," Folsom, LA , 1967-. *Military service*: U.S. Air Force, 1969-72 (E7). *Memberships*: Louisiana Indian Heritage Association (president, 1967-72, 1978; secretary/treasurer, 1987-89, 1990-92). *Interests*: "American Indian culture; attending numerous powwows; dancing and singing."

HERMAN, JEFFREY
(attorney)
Affiliation: Partner, Herman & Mermelstein, 3230 Stirling Rd., Suite One, Hollywood, FL 33021 (800) 686-9921; (954) 962-2200 Fax 962-4292. Website: www.hermanlaw.com

HERMOSILLO, PATRICIA (Pomo)
(rancheria chairperson)
Affiliation: Cloverdale Rancheria Council, 555 S. Cloverdale Blvd. #1, Cloverdale, CA 95425 (707) 894-5775.

HERNANDEZ-AVILA, INEZ (Nez Perce/Chicana) 1948-
(assistant professor)
Born in Texas, 1948. *Education*: University of Houston, BA, 1970, MA, 1972, PhD (English), 1984. *Principal occupation*: Assistant professor. *Address & Affiliation*: Dept. of Native American Studies, 2401 Hart Hall, University of California, One Shields Ave., Davis, CA 95616 (530) 752-4394 Fax 752-7097 (work). *Other professional post*: Editorial Advisory Board, "Hurricane Alice: A Feminist Quarterly." *Memberships*: Modern Language Association; MALCS (Mujeres Activas en Letras y Cambio Social); National Association of Chicano Studies; California Indian Education Association. *Awards, honors*: Phi Kappa Phi Honor Society; Outstanding Chicana in the Arts (Literature) for the Austin community, 1977, award presented by the Mexican American Professional and Business Women of Austin; Outstanding Chicana faculty, 1977, award presented by the Minority Student Services, University of Texas, Austin; Outstanding Chicana faculty, 1978, award presented by the Center for Mexican American Studies, University of Texas, Austin; elected to Board of Directors of D-Q University, Davis, CA, June 1983, served through April 1986. *Interests*: "My mother is Nimipu (known as Nez Perce) Indian; I am an enrolled member of the Colville Confederated Tribes of Nespelem, Washington. My father is Texas-Mexican. I am Nimipu and Chicana. I am fluent in English and Spanish (reading, writing, speaking, translating)." Writer & director of the dramatic work "El Dia de Guadalupe," which featured eight women players focusing on the different forms of abuse that Chicanas encounter in contemporary society. *Published works*: Article - "Finding Our Way Back Home: Native American Women Writers," Dictionary of Native American Literature, edited by Andrew Wiget (Greenwood Press, 1991); "Open Letter to Chicanas: The Power and Politics of Origin," for Changing Our Power: An Introduction to Women's Studies, eds. Jo Whitehorse Cochran, et al (Kendall-Hunt, 1991); "Sara Estela Ramirez," bio-bibliographical essay, The Longman Anthology of World Literature by Women, 1895-1975, eds. Barbara Shollar and Marian Arkin (Longman Press, 1989); "Body of Mine, Body Be Mine," Blue Mesa Review, No. 4 (Spring 1992); among other articles and chapters. Collections of poetry: Con Razon, Corazon (Caracol Publications, 1977; second edition, M&A Editions, 1987); Abrecaminos: Collected Poems, 1978-1990 (unpublished manuscript); and numerous individual poems in various publications. Recordings of poetry: "Para Teresa," for the Houghton-Mifflin Secondary Education Audiocassette Series, 1991.

HERNANDEZ, GLORIA (Paiute)
(tribal chairperson)
Affiliation: Las Vegas Indian Colony, One Paiute Dr., Las Vegas, NV 89106 (702) 386-3926.

HERNANDEZ, SALLY A. (Laguna Pueblo)
(attorney)
Address: Address unknown. *Affiliation*: University of New Mexico School of Law, Albuquerque, NM. *Memberships*: Native American Bar Association (Native American Legal Resource Center representative); American Bar Association.

HERNASY, KEN
(hospital director)
Affiliation: Fort Yuma PHS Indian Hospital, P.O. Box 1368, Yuma, AZ 85364 (602) 572-0217.

HERNE, SUSAN (Mohawk)
(museum giftshop manager)
Address & Affiliation: Akwesasne Cultural Center - Akwesasne Library & Museum, St. Regis Mohawk Nation, Rt. 37 RR 1, Box 14C, Hogansburg, NY 13655 (518) 358-2240.

HERRERA, J. MARVIN (Pueblo)
(former pueblo governor)
Affiliation: Pueblo of Tesuque, Rt. 11, Box 1, \Santa Fe, NM 87501.

HERRERA, JOHN R. (Leech Lake Chippewa) 1952-
(company president)
Born June 4, 1952, Milwaukee, Wisc. *Education*: University of Wisconsin, Milwaukee, BA, 1976; University of Minnesota, MBA, 1986; William Mitchell College of Law (St.Paul, MN), JD, 1992. *Principal occupation*: Company president. *Address*: Unknown. *Affiliations*: Div. director, economic development, Minnesota Chippewa Tribe, Cass Lake, MN,1978-80; director of business enterprises, Leech Lake Reservation, Cass Lake, MN, 1980-82; business finance representative, State of Minnesota, Prior lake, MN, 1983-85; area credit officer/Indian services branch chief, Bureau of Indian Affairs, Minneapolis, MN, 1985-88 (managed implementation of Indian Finance Act for federally recognized Indian reservations in the four state area - provided loans & loan guarantees for business development); finance & planning consultant, Shakopee Sioux Community, Prior Lake, MN, 1988-90 (provided financial & developmental direction for the community which owns one of the largest and most successful Native American gaming ventures in the U.S.; president, First American Companies; Equipment Leasing & Securities, Minneapolis, MN, 1991- (provides con-

sultant & equipment leasing services to a client base of Native American Tribes. *Other professional posts*: Judge, Leech Lake Reservation; associate judge, Minnesota Chippewa Tribe Appeals Court. *Membership*: Minnesota Indian Chamber of Commerce (founder/ member).

HERROD, RANDALL
(association director)
Affiliation: National Commander, Vietnam Era Veterans Inter-Tribal Association, 805 Rosa, Shawnee, OK 74801 (405) 382-3128.

HERSCH, ROBERT C.
(librarian)
Affiliation: Native American Resource Center Library, Pembroke State University, College Rd., Pembroke, NC 28372 (919) 521-4214.

HERSHEY, ROBERT ALAN
(professor of Indian law)
Education: The University of Arizona, J.D., 1972. *Affiliation*: American Indian Studies Program, The University of Arizona, Harvill Bldg., Rm. 430, P.O. Box 210076, Tucson, AZ 85721 (520) 621-7108 Fax 621-7952. E-mail: aisp@email.arizona.edu.

HESS, MERVIN (Paiute-Shoshoni)
(former tribal chairperson)
Affiliation: Bishop Indian Tribal Council, 50 Tu Su Lane, Bishop, CA 93514 (760) 873-3584.

HESS, FELIX P.
(corporate chairperson)
Affiliation: Calista Corporation, 601 W. 5th Ave. #200, Anchorage, AK 99501 (907) 279-5516 Fax 272-5060.

HESSE, CURTIS
(health program director)
Affiliation: Riverside/San Bernardino Indian Health Program, 11555 1/2 Potrero Rd., Banning, CA 92220 (714) 849-4761.

HESTER, JAMES J. 1931-
(professor emeritus; senior consulting archaeologist)
Born September 21, 1931, Anthony, Kans. *Education*: University of New Mexico, BA, 1953; University of Arizona, PhD (Anthropology), 1961. *Principal occupation*: Anthropologist. *Address*: Dept. of Anthropology, CB233 University of Colorado, Boulder, CO 80309 (303) 492-7419. E-mail: james.hester@colorado.edu. *Affiliations*: Department of Anthropology, University of Colorado, Boulder (professor, 1975-99; professor emeritus, 2000-present). *Other professional post*: Consulting Archaeologist, Walker Research Group, Ltd., Boulder, CO. *Past professional posts*: Assistant curator, Museum of New Mexico, 1959-64; adjunct professor, Southern Methodist University, 1964-65; scientist administrator, National Institute of Health, 1965-75; consultant, U.S. Army Corp. of Engineers, 1985-88 (directed a nationwide program in "in situ" site preservation). *Military service*: U.S. Air Force, 1954-56. *Awards, honors*: Served as Chief Archaeologist for the President's Advisory Council on Historic Preservation from 1978-79. *Memberships*: American Anthropological Association (Fellow); Society for American Archaeology; Sigma Xi; American Society of Naturalists; Current Anthropology. *Interests*: "Archaeology of Navajo Indians; prehistory of Sahara desert; directed culture change; relationship of man to his environment. Currently writing fiction based on contemporary Native American issues - Sioux, Tlingit, Navajo, Hopi, Comanche. *Published works*: An Archaeological Survey of the Navajo Reservoir District, Northwestern New Mexico, with A.E. Dittert, Jr. & Frank W. Eddy (Museum of New Mexico, 1961); Early Navajo Migrations and Acculturation in the Southwest (Museum of New Mexico, 1962); Studies at Navajo Period Sites in the Navajo Reservoir District, with Joel Shiner (Museum of New Mexico, 1963); Rance Hood, Comanche Mystic Painter, to be published by (University of New Mexico Press, 2005).

HESTER, THURMAN LEE, JR. (Oklahoma Choctaw) 1961-
(director of Native American studies)
Born June 23, 1961, Oklahoma City, OK. *Education*: BS (History); MS & PhD (Philosophy). *Principal occupation*: Director of Native American Studies. *Home address*: 1353 Dorchester Dr., Norman, OK 73069;

Office address: University of Science & Arts of Oklahoma, Chickasaha, OK 73018 (405) 574-1289 Fax 521-1220. E-mail: pachesterl@usao.edu. Website: www.usao.edu. *Affiliations*: University of Oklahoma, 1988-94; Lakeland University, Thunder Bay, ON, Canada (visiting appointment in philosophy), 1995; Oklahoma City University, 1994-99; The University of Science & Arts of Oklahoma, Chickasha, OK, 2000-present. *Other professional post*: Founding editor (along with Dennis McPherson) of Ayaangwagmizin: The International Journal of Indigenous Philosophy. *Community activities*: Cultural Chairman, Oklahoma Choctaw Tribal Alliance. *Memberships*: American Philosophical Association, American Indian Philosophical Association, APA Committee on the Status of American Indians. *Interests*: Indian law, philosophy. *Published work*: Political Principles and Indian Sovereignty (Routledge Press, 2001).

HESTER, JOE
(director-Indian centre)
Affiliation: Niagara Regional Native Centre, R.R. #4, Queenston & Taylor Rd., Niagara-on-the-Lake, Ontario, Canada L0S 1H0 (705) 472-2811.

HESTER, DR. LEE
(American Indian studies dept. chairperson)
Affiliation: Dept. of American Indian Studies, University of Science & Arts of Oklahoma, 17th & Grand, Chickasha, OK73018 (405) 574-1289 Fax 521-1220.

HETH, CHARLOTTE WILSON
(Oklahoma Cherokee) 1937-
(museum professional)
Born October 29, 1937, Muskogee, Okla. Education: Oklahoma Baptist University, 1955-56; University of Tulsa, BA, 1959, MM, 1960; University of California, Los Angeles, PhD, 1975. *Principal occupation*: Museum professional. *Address*: Unknown. *Affiliations*: The National Museum of the American Indian, Smithsonian, Washington, DC, 1995-2000; American Indian Studies Center, University of California, Los Angeles (Professor of ethnomusicology, 1974-87, 1989-95; director, 1976-87); director American Indian Program, Cornell University, Ithaca, NY, 1987-89. *Community activities*: Panel chair, Folk Arts Program, National Endowment for the Arts, 1981-83; Indian Centers, Inc., Los Angeles (board member). *Memberships*: Society for Ethnomusicology (council chair, 1981-82; president, 1993-95); National Indian Education Association; American Indian Historians' Association. *Awards, honors*: Senior Postdoctoral Fellowship, Center for the History of the American Indian, The Newberry Library, 1978-79; Southern Fellowships Fund, Post-doctoral Fellowship, 1978-79; National Research Council senior postdoctoral fellowship, 1984-85 (Ford Foundation Minority Fellowship). *Interests*: "American Indian music and dance; Cherokee language and culture; previously I was a Peace Corps volunteer in Ethiopia (1962-64) teaching English as a second language. I also was a high school teacher in OK, NM, and CA from 1960-72. I have traveled to Europe, the Middle East, East Africa, Mexico, Latin America, and Canada." *Published works*: General editor, "The Music of the American Indians", (Selected Reports in Ethnomusicology, 1982); general editor, "Music and the Expressive Arts", (American Indian Culture and Research Journal, 1982); Issues for the Future of American Indian Studies: A Needs Assessment and Program Guide, co-authored with Susan Guyette (American Indian Studies Center, UCLA, 1985); general editor, organizer, and contributor, Sharing a Heritage: American Indian Arts Conference, No. 3 in the Contemporary American Indian Issues Series (American Indian Studies Center, UCLA, 1984); general editor & contributor, Native American Dance: Ceremonies and Social Traditions (American Indian Studies Center, UCLA, 1994).

HEWITT, ARNOLD (Tuscarora)
(tribal head chief)
Affiliation: Chief (lifetime), Tuscarora Indian Nation, 2006 Mt. Hope Rd., Lewiston, NY 14092 (716) 297-3995.

HEWITT, CHAR
(director-IHS field office)
Affiliation: Indian Health Service Field Office, Kincheloe, MI 49788 (906) 495-2289.

HEYANO, ROBERT (Eskimo)
(AK village council president)
Affiliation: Native Village of Ekuk, General Delivery, Ekuk, AK 99576 (907) 842-5937.

HIBBELER, TED (Rosebud Lakota) 1951-
(director of Native American education)
Born July 9, 1951, Rosebud, S.D. *Education*: Hastings College (Neb), MA, 1973. *Principal occupation*: Director of Native American education. *Address & Affiliation*: Phoenix Union High School District, 4502 N. Central Ave., Phoenix, AZ 85012 (602) 271-3514 Fax 271-3204. E-mail: ted.hibbeler@qm.phxhs.k12.az.us. *Community activities*: Hoop of Learning Program - early bridge college program with Phoenix College, Phoenix, Ariz. *Interests*: "I am just a humble Native....trying to help our own young Native people live in balance with the world around them...Are we not all trying to do the same thing?"

HICKS, CHERYL
(Indian education program director)
Affiliation: Washoe County School District, P.O. Box 30425, Reno, NV 89520 (775) 850-8017 Fax 851-5649.

HICKS, MITCHELL (Eastern Cherokee)
(tribal chairperson)
Affiliation: Chairperson, Eastern Band Cherokee Tribal Council, Qualla Boundary, P.O. Box 455, Cherokee, NC 28719 (828) 497-2771 Fax 497-7007.

HICKS, PHYLLIS (Monacan)
(tribal representative)
Affiliation: Monacan Indian Tribe, P.O. Box 112, Monroe, VA 24574 (804) 946-2431.

HIGDON, HELEN C.
(Indian school principal)
Affiliation: Winslow Dormitory, 600 N. Alfred Ave., Winslow, AZ 86047 (520) 829-4483 Fax 829-2821.

HIGGINS, SUSAN
(Indian school principal)
Affiliation: John F. Kennedy School, P.O. Box 130, White River, AZ 85941 (520) 338-4593 Fax 338-4592.

HIGH TOWER, VALERIE (Mohawk)
(writer-children's literature)
Address: 430 S. Muskogee Ave., Tahlequah, OK 74464 (918) 456-7195.

HIGHWATER, JAMAKE
(Blackfeet/Eastern Cherokee) 1942-
(author, lecturer)
Born February 14, 1942, Glacier County, Mont. *Education*: Holds degrees in music, comparative literature, and cultural anthropology. *Principal occupation*: Author, lecturer. *Address*: Unknown. *Affiliations*: Lecturer, Indian culture, various Universities in U.S. & Canada; founding member, Indian Art Foundation, Santa Fe, NM. *Community activities*: Cultural Council of American Indian Community House, New York, N.Y. (past president & founding member); NY State Council on the Arts (member, task force on individual artist). *Memberships*: National Congress of American Indians; White Buffalo Society of American Indians, Denver, CO; Dramatists Guild; Authors Guild; American Federation of Radio and Television Artists (AFTRA); BMI; League of American Authors. *Awards, honors*: Appointed Honorary Citizen by Governor of Oklahoma; appointed Colonel aid-de-camp on the Staff of the Governor of NM; 1978 Newberry Honor Award for novel Anpao by the American Library Association; Jane Addams Peace Book Award, 1978, for Many Smokes, Many Moons; Anisfield-Wolf Award in race relations, 1980, for Song From the Earth: American Indian Painting; interviews with Mr. Highwater have appeared in most major American, European, Latin American and Near Eastern newspapers and magazines. *Interests*: Travels extensively and does fieldwork in North and Central Africa, most American Indian communities and reservations in the U.S.; travels to Central America and Mexico, Europe and the Near East; written and presented talks about American Indian studies for th BBC, Radio Three in London, Radio Pacifica, CBS-Radio, WMCA-Radio, and numerous other radio and television networks and stations. *Biographical sources*: Who's Who in America; Directory of American Poetry; Directory of American Fiction Writers; International

Who's Who; Dance World; Theatre World; Pop Bibliography; Who's Who in the East. *Published works*: Fodor's Indian American (David McKay, 1975); Song From the Earth: American Indian Painting (New York Graphic Society, Little Brown, 1976); Ritual of the Wind: American Indian Ceremonies, Music and Dances (Viking Press, 1977); Anpao: An American Indian Odyssey (J.B. Lippincott, 1977); Dance: Rituals of Experience (A & W Visual Library, 1978); Many Smokes, Many Moons: American Indian History Thru Indian Arts (J.B. Lippincott, 1978); Journey to the Sky: In Search of the Lost World of the Maya (T.Y. Crowell, 1979); The Sweet Grass Lives On: 50 Contemporary North American Indian Artists (Viking Press, 1980); Masterpieces of American Indian Painting, 8 Vols., 1978-1980; The Sun, He Dies: The End of the Aztec World, 1980; The Primal Mind: Vision and Reality in Indian America, 1981; among others (nothing added since 1981). Mr. Highwater has written numerous introductions for other books; also many articles in journals and magazines.

HILDEN, PATRICIA PENN (Nez Perce) 1944-
(professor)
Born May 31, 1944, Burbank, Calif. *Education*: University of California, Berkeley, BA, 1965; University of Cambridge (England), MA, 1979, PhD, 1981. *Principal occupation*: Professor. *Home address*: unknown. *Affiliation*: Associate professor, Emory University, Atlanta, GA, 1982-. *Other professional posts*: Fellow in History, Trinity Hall, Cambridge, England; coordinator, Special Action Tutoring Program, University of California, Davis (Office of Economic Opportunity). *Community activities*: New York University Talking Circle; Emory University Native America Awareness Month; Advisory Board, Mohawk Valley Project, 1993-94. *Memberships*: Wordcraft Circle of Native American Mentor & Apprentice Writers (regional coordinator, Northeast, 1992-93, board member, 1994-); American Historical Association, 1982-. *Awards, honors*: Best Article Prize, Berkshire Conference of Women Historians, 1992; Research awards from Fulbright Foundation, American Council of Learned Societies, National Endowment for the Humanities, British Academy, and Social Science Research Council. *Interests*: "History of France, Belgium, the Netherlands, especially labor history and the history of women. Currently working on a book about Europeans' fascination with Native Americans from the 19th century." *Biographical sources*: Who's Who in the South & Southeast; Dictionary of International Biography; The Word Who's Who of Women. *Published works*: Working Women & Socialist Politics in France (Oxford University Press, 1986); Women, Work & Politics; Belgium 1830-1914 (Oxford University Press, 1993); When Nickels Were Indians: Growing Up Mixed Blood (Smithsonian Press).

HILDERBRAND, LOUIS
(BIA agency supt.)
Affiliation: Wapato Irrigation Project, Bureau of Indian Affairs, P.O. Box 220, Wapato, WA 98951 (509) 877-3155.

HILDERMAN-SMITH, MARY
(museum executive director)
Affiliation: Marin Museum of the American Indian, P.O. Box 864, 2200 Novato Blvd., Novato, CA 94947 (510) 897-4064.

HILFIKER, MARY
(BIA special education coordinator)
Affiliation: Minneapolis Area Office, Bureau of Indian Affairs, 331 S. Second Ave., Minneapolis, MN 55401 (612) 373-1000 Fax 373-1065.

HILL, CHARLENE
(IHS-FAS project coordinator)
Affiliation: Indian Health Service, 5300 Homestead Rd., NE, Albuquerque, NM 87110 (505) 837-4228.

HILL, DANIEL C. (Cayuga)
(craftsperson)
Address: P.O. Box 22, Akron, NY 14001 (716) 542-3637. *Products*: Traditional carved flutes, Iroquois silverwork.

HILL, EARL
(Indian band chief)
Affiliation: Mohawks of the Bay of Quinte Indian Band, RR #1, Deseronto, Ontario, Canada K0K 1X0 (613) 396-3424.

HILL, GERALD, MD
(Indian center director)
Affiliation: Center of American Indian and Minority Health, School of Medicine, 10 University Dr., Duluth, MN 55812-2487 (218) 726-7235 Fax 726-6235.

HILL, GERALD L.
(attorney, tribal judge)
Affiliation: Oneida Tribe of Wisconsin, P.O. Box 365, Oneida, WI 54155 (414) 869-2345; Prairie Band Potawatomi Nation Tribal Court, 15498 K Rd., Mayetta, KS 66509 (866) 966-2242 or (785) 966-2242 Fax 966-2662. E-mail: tribalcourt@pbpnation.org. Website: www.pbpnation.org/tribalcourt. *Membership*: Wisconsin Indian Lawyers League.

HILL, GWENDOLYN A. (Chippewa/Cree) 1952-
(higher education administrator)
Born October 31, 1952, Ft. Belknap, Mont. *Education*: Northern Montana College, BS, 1976; University of South Dakota, MPA, 1989. *Principal occupation*: Higher education administrator. *Home address*: RR 1, Box 1, Sisseton, SD 57262 (605) 698-3331; 698-3966 (work). *Affiliations*: Teacher, BIA, Stewart Indian School, Stewart, NV, 1975-80; dean/president, Sisseton-Wahpeton Community College, Sisseton, SD, 1981-. *Community activities*: Sisseton Public Schools (Parent Advisory Committee, Title IV, 1984-88); Native American Student Advisory Council, University of Minnesota, Morris, 1988-89. *Memberships*: American Indian Higher Education Consortium, 1988-; AACJC, 1989; National Association of Women Deans, Administrators and Counselors, 1987-89. *Interests*: "Extremely interested in promoting Indian higher education on the national, state and local level. As an administrator of a tribal college located on Lake Traverse Reservation where unemployment reaches 80%, it is imperative to ensure that our institution meets the unique educational needs of the Sisseton-Wahpeton Sioux Tribe." *Biographical source*: Carnegie Foundation for the Advancement of Teaching: Report on Tribal Colleges, 1989.

HILL, DR. JANE H.
(professor of anthropology)
Affiliation: Dept. of Anthropology, Emil Haury Anthropology Bldg., Rm. 221A, University of Arizona, Tucson, AZ 85721 (520) 621-2585 Fax 621-2088. E-mail: jhill@u.arizona.edu. Interests: Sociolinguistics of Native American languages.

HILL, JANICE
(foundation president)
Affiliation: Klukwan Heritage Foundation, P.O. Box 972, Haines, AK 99827 (907) 465-4700.

HILL, JAY (Seneca)
(organization president)
Affiliation: American Indian Society of Washington, DC, P.O. Box 6431, Falls Church, VA 22040 (804) 448-3707.

HILL, MARGO (Spokane)
(attorney)
Affiliation: Attorney, Spokane Tribe, P.O. Box 100, Wellpinit, WA 99040 (509) 258-4581 Fax 258-9243.

HILL, MAXINE
(museum general manager)
Affiliation: Museum of the Cherokee Indian, U.S. Hwy. 441 North, Box 770-A, Cherokee, NC 18719 (704) 497-3481.

HILL, NORBERT S., JR. (Oneida) 1946-
(executive director)
Born November 26, 1946, Detroit, Mich. *Education*: University of Wisconsin, B.S., 1969, M.S., 1971; Cumberland College (Williamsburg, KY), Honorary Doctorate, 1994. *Home address*: P.O. Box 769, Algodones, NM 87001-0769. *Affiliations*: Assistant Dean of Students, University of Wisconsin, Green Bay, 1972-77; director, Native American Educational Opportunity Program, University of Colorado, Boulder, 1977-83; executive director, American Indian Science & Engineering Society, Albuquerque, NM, 1983-. *Other professional posts*: Chairman, Oneida Tribal Education Committee, 1970-74; Chairman, Oneida Film Project, 1976; Chairman, Native American Career Exposition, Denver, CO, 1978-79; president, Dr. Rosa Minoka Hill Foundation, 1982-; publisher, "Winds of

Change" magazine, 1986-; Chairman, Smithsonian Institution's National Museum of the American Indian, 1991-. *Community activities*: Colorado Endowment for the Humanities (board of directors, 1993-); "Technos Quarterly," Editorial Advisory Board, 1993-); Environmental Defense Fund (board of directors, 1992-); Women & Foundations/Corporate Philanthropy (board of directors, 1992-); National Science Foundation's "Project Mosaic," Advisory Committee, 1992-; George Bird Grinnell American Indian Children's Education Foundation (board of directors, 1990-); National Action Council for Minorities in Engineering (NACME), 1986-. *Memberships*: American Chemical Society (member, Blue Ribbon Advisory Panel, 1993-); American Association for the Advancement of Science. *Awards, honors*: Indian Grant Scholarship, 1964-68; Education Policy Fellow, Institute for Educational Leadership, Washington, DC, 1980-81; Reginald H. Jones Distinguished Service Award, National Action Council for Minorities in Engineering, 1988; Chancellor's Award, University of Wisconsin, Oshkosh, 1988; member, Council of Advisors to President-Elect Clinton's Transition Team for Education, Dec. 1992; Honorary Doctorate, Cumberland College, 1994. *Published works*: Articles in "Smithsonian Handbook of American Indians," 1978; article in "The Indian Historian," Vol. II, No. 4, Dec. 1978; editor, "Changing America: The New Face to Science & Engineering," report (National Science Foundation, 1989); editor, "Education That Works: An Action Plan for the Education of Minorities," report (Quality Education for Minorities Project, 1990); editor, "Our Voices, Our Vision," report (The College Board/Charles Stewart Mott Foundation, 1990); editor, "Native American Repatriation of Cultural Patrimony Act & The Native American Grave & Burial Protection Act," testimony (AISES, 1990); publisher, "Winds of Change," magazine, 1985-; editor, "The Demographics of American Indians: One Percent of the People: Fifty Percent of the Diversity," report (Institute for Educational Leadership, Inc./Center for Demographic Study, 1990); Words of Power—Voices From Indian America (Fulcrum, 1994).

HILL, RICHARD G., Sr. (Tuscarora-Oneida)
(tribal chairperson)
Affiliations: Special assistant, National Museum of the American Indian, Smithsonian Institution; co-chair, Committee on Museum-Native American Collaboration, American Association of Museums; chairman, Oneida Tribal Business Committee, P.O. Box 365, Oneida, WI 54155 (414) 869-2772; chairperson, National Indian Gaming Association, Washington, DC.

HILL, SID (Onondaga)
(former chief)
Affiliation: Chief, Onondaga Nation, RR 1 Box 270-A, Nedrow, NY 13120.

HILL, THOMAS VERNON (Seneca) 1943-
(museum director)
Born May 9, 1943, Ohsweken, Six Nations Reserve. *Education*: Ontario College of Art, Toronto, 1964-67 - A.O.C.A.; Carleton University, Ottawa, 1968; currently completing Ontario Museums Studies, Ontario Museums Association, 1985-89. *Principal occupation*: Museum director. *Address*: Box 129, Ohsweken P.O., Ontario, Canada N0A 1M0 (519) 759-2650. *Affiliations*: Director, Cultural Development, Indian & Northern Affairs, Ottawa, 1968-78; social development officer, 1979-81, native policy advisory, 1981-82, Secretary of State, Toronto, 1979-81; museum director, Woodland Cultural Centre, Brantford, 1982-. *Other professional post*: Vice-president, Visual Arts Ontario, Toronto, 1988-; chairman, Task Force on First Nations and Museums, Canadian Museums Association, 1989-; Editor, MUSE Magazine (Canadian Museums Association, 1989). *Community activities*: Six Nations Tourism; H.M. Chapel of the Mohawks Restoration; Ad Hoc Museum Committee, Brant County. *Memberships*: Visual Arts Ontario (vice-president); Canadian Museums Association; Ontario Museums Association; Ontario Genealogical Association; Society of Canadian Artists of Native Ancestry; Royal Ontario Museum; Ontario Association of Art Galleries; Canadian Native Arts Foundation; Native Canadian Centre of Toronto; The Association of Cultural Executives; National Indian Arts Council. *Awards, honors*: H.R. Majesty Service Award, 1978; Certificate of Merit, Art Director, 1976; Public Service Commission Merit Award, 1974. *Interests*: Vocational: First Nations and museums; Avocational:

Film-making, painting, pottery, theatre and print-making; Eskaneh singing. Published works: Editor, Indian Art in Canada (Government of Canada, 1972); Norval Morrisseau and the Emergence of the Image-Makers (Methuen Art Gallery of Ontario, 1984); Canadian Native Peoples, Vol. II (Heirloom Publishing, 1988); Beyond History (Vancouver Art Gallery, 1989).

HILLABRANT, WALTER JOHN
(Citizen Band Potawatomi) 1942-
(psychologist)
Born December 17, 1942, Corsicana, Tex. *Education*: University of California, Berkeley, AB, 1965; University of California, Riverside, PhD, 1972. *Principal occupation*: Psychologist. *Home address*: 1927 38th St., NW, Washington, DC 20007. *Affiliations*: Assistant professor, Howard University, Washington, DC, 1971-80; psychologist, president, Support Services, Inc., Silver Spring, MD, 1980-. *Memberships*: American Psychological Association; Washington Academy of Sciences; National Indian Education Association. *Interests*: Indian education; cross-cultural psychology; application of computer and telecommunication technology to social problems. *Published work*: The Future Is Now (Peacock Press, 1974).

HILLER, JOE (Lakota)
(professor)
Education: University of Wyoming, PhD, 2000. *Affiliation*: American Indian Studies Program, The University of Arizona, Harvill Bldg., Rm. 430, P.O. Box 210076, Tucson, AZ 85721 (520) 621-7108 Fax 621-7952. E-mail: aisp@email.arizona.edu. *Interests*: Agriculture and natural resources technical and policy issues, especially water, in Indian country.

HILLSMAN, MATTHEW J.
(Pequewas-Silver Dog) 1935-
(museum curator/archaeologist-physicists)
Born on October 1, 1935 in Crucible, Penn. *Education*: Penn State University, BS, 1961; Eastern New Mexico University, MA (Anthropology), 1992. *Address & Affiliation*: Curator, Blackwater Draw Museum (1986-present), Eastern New Mexico University, Station 3, Portales, NM 88130 (505) 562-2202 Fax 562-2291; E-Mail: matthew.hillsman@enmu.edu. *Military service*: U.S. Air Force, 1953-57. Interests: Amateur Radio-KD5GTH; astronomy and classical music.

HILPERT, BRUCE
(professor of anthropology)
Affiliation: Dept. of Anthropology, Emil Haury Anthropology Bldg., Rm. 221A, University of Arizona, Tucson, AZ 85721 (520) 621-2585 Fax 621-2088. E-mail: bhilpert.@u.arizona.edu. *Interests*: American Indians of the Southwest.

HINES, MIFAUNWY SHUNTONA
(Indian center director)
Affiliation: American Indian Information Center, 139-11 87th Ave., Briarwood, NY 11435 (718) 291-7732.

HINKLEY, EDWARD C. 1934-
(educator)
Born December 16, 1934, Bridgewater, Mass. *Education*: Harvard University, BA, 1955, MEd, 1959. *Principal occupation*: Educator. *Home address*: P.O. Box 101, Vienna, ME 04360. *Affiliations*: Elementary school teacher, Bureau of Indian Affairs, UT and AZ, 1959-61; educational specialist, U.S. Public Health Service, Division of Indian Health, AZ and NV, 1961-65; Commissioner of Indian Affairs, State of Maine, 1965-69; education and management consultant, T.R.I.B.E., Inc. (Teaching and Research in Bicultural Education), Maine and Canada, 1969-. *Interests*: "Indian affairs of Canada and the U.S. on a contemporary level; bicultural education; community development; leadership training and counseling."

HINKSMAN, IAN
(association president)
Affiliation: B.C. Association of Indian Friendship Centres, 533 Yates St., Penthouse, Victoria, British Columbia, Canada V8W 1K7 (604) 384-3211.

HINTON, CHERYL M. 1953-
(museum director)
Born October 24, 1953, New York, N.Y. *Education*: San Diego State University, BA & MA in Anthropology. *Principal occupation*: Museum director. *Address*: Barona Cultural Center & Museum, 1095 Barona Rd., Lakeside, CA 92040 (619) 443-7003 ext. 2 Fax 443-0173. E-mail: chinton@barona.org. *Affiliations*: Anthropologist, Palm Springs Desert Museum, 1988-92; Curator, Agua Caliente (Band of Cahuilla Indians) Cultural Museum, 1992-96; Southwest Curator, Southwest Collections & NAGPRA (Repatriation) Coordinator, San Diego Museum of Man, 1996-99; director/first curator of the Barona Cultural Center & Museum, Lakeside, CA, 1999-present. *Other professional posts*: Adjunct Professor of Anthropology, University of San Diego, 1999-present; editor, Barona Spirits Speak, 2001-present. *Community activities*: Community liaison for local tribes for USD Indian Market & Festival; representative for Barona to Tribal Digital Village; Special Events Chair for Self Realization Fellowship, San Diego Temple; Indian Heritage Festival, Education Coordinator, 1993-96. *Memberships*: American Association of Museums: Tribal Museums Branch/Diversity Coalition; Western Museums Association; Society for Applied Anthropology; American Anthropology Association. Honors: *Interests*: Self-Image of stereotypes among Indians; NAGPRA (Native American Graves Protection & Repatriation; Yoga and Eastern religious philosophies. *Publications*: The Bear Shaman Tradition of Southern California Indians (Barona Cultural Center & Museum, Publication 01-2002).

HIPPS, BARRY (Eastern Cherokee)
(general manager)
Affiliation: Cherokee Historical Association, P.O. Box 398, Cherokee, NC 28719 (704) 497-2111.

HIRSCH, DEBORAH
(editor)
Affiliation: "The Native Magazine," Tod Bedrosian, Publisher, 7427 Braeridge Way, Sacramento, CA 95831 (916) 421-5121.

HIRSCHFELDER, ARLENE
(scholarship program contact)
Affiliation: Association on American Indian Affairs, 245 Fifth Ave., Suite 1801, New York, NY 10016 (212) 689-8720.

HIRST, STEPHEN MICHAEL 1939-
(writer)
Born December 20, 1939, Dayton, Ohio. *Education*: Miami University (Oxford, Ohio), BA, 1962; Johns Hopkins School of Advanced International Studies (Washington, DC), MA, 1966. *Principal occupation*: Writer. Resides in Marquette, MI. *Affiliations*: Preschool director, Havasupai Tribe, 1967-68, 1970-73; planner, Havasupai Tribe, 1975-76. *Memberships*: The Authors Guild, 1976-. *Awards, honors*: 1961 Best Columnist Award of Ohio Collegiate Newspaper Association; 1962 Greer-Hepburn Fiction Award; 1966 U.S. Commerce Department Service Award; 1976 Havasupai Tribe Service Award; 1979 Cincinnati Arts Consortium Writing Award; 1981 Ohio Arts Council Fiction Award; finalist for 1982 Arizona Commission on the Arts fiction award. *Published works*: Life In a Narrow Place: The Havasupai of the Grand Canyon (David McKay Co., 1976); Havsuw'Baaja (Havasupai Tribe, 1985).

HOAG, DEBBIE (Seneca)
(editor)
Affiliation: Seneca Tribal Nesletter, Cattaraugus Indian Reservation, 1490 Route 438, Irving, NY 14081.

HOBBS, CHARLES A.
(attorney)
Education: Yale University, BA, 1950; George Washington University, JD, 1957. *Principal occupation*: Attorney. *Address & Affiliation*: Senior Partner, Hobbs, Straus, Dean & Walker, LLP, 2120 L St., NW, Suite 700, Washington, DC 20037 (202) 822-8282 Fax 296-8834. E-mail: chobbs@hsdwdc.com. *Past professional posts*: Clerk, Judge Warren F. Burger, U.S. Court of Appeals, DC Circuit, 1958-65; Wilkinson, Cragun & Barker, Washington, DC, 1968-82 (assisted tribal governments in all areas of Indian law, and prosecuted a large number of tribal land claims under the Indian Claims Commission Act; past chairperson, Committee on Indian Affairs, Administrative law Section, American Bar Association. In 1982 when Wilkinson, Cragun & Barker dissolved, Mr. Hobbs, along with Jerry Straus and Bobo Dean, formed the present firm, dedicated to advising and representing Indian tribes and Indian people. Mr. Hobbs has been a named attorney in over 100 litigations resulting in written decisions on Indian rights. He has argued five Indian cases before the U.S. Supreme Court, including *United States v. Mitchell*, 463 U.S. 206 (1983), which established that the U.S. must pay money damages when it breaches its trust duties to Indians, and *Menominee Tribe v. United States*, 391 U.S. 404 (1968), which held that when Congress terminates Indian tribes, the tribes retain their treaty rights unless specifically nullified. He also handled *Rhode Island v. Narragansett Tribe*, 19 F.3d 685 (1994), in which the First Circuit Court of Appeals held that the Tribe was entitled to operate gaming under the Indian Gaming Regulatory Act. Mr,. Hobbs and William Norman were the drafters of Chapter 2 of "Empowerment of Tribal Governments: Final Workgroup Report," developed by the Tribal Workgroup on Tribal Needs Assessments, May 1999. Mr. Hobbs' entire career has been spent working for Indian tribes and organizations, and individual Indians. He was honored in 1993 at the National Congress of American Indians' national convention for distinguished service to the Indian community.

HOBSON, ARTHUR K.
(school principal)
Affiliations: Many Farms High School, P.O. Box 307, Many Farms, AZ 86532 (520) 781-6226

HOBSON, BARBARA (Torralba) (Comanche) 1951-
(educator)
Born May 26, 1951, Lawton, Okla. *Education*: Oklahoma State University, BA, 1973; University of New Mexico, MA, 1978; University of Oklahoma, PhD, 1994. *Home address*: adress unknown. *Affiliations*: Counselor, Southwestern Indian Polytechnic Institute, Albuquerque, NM, 1973-77; minority counselor, University of Albuquerque, 1978-80; counselor, Native American Program, College of Engineering, University of Oklahoma, 1985-88; Native American Studies Program, University of Oklahoma, Norman, OK, 1994-. *Other professional post*: Returning the Gift Native Writers Project, 1990-92. *Awards, honors*: Foundations in Native Education Fellow, 1989-93, University of Oklahoma, College of Education; American Indian Education Fellow, Dept. of Indian Education, Washington, DC, 1990-93. *Interests*: "Special area of interests - American Indian retention." *Unpublished dissertation*: Cultural Values & Persistence Among Comanche College Students, University of Oklahoma, 1994. *Published work*: "Tribally Controlled Colleges: Meeting the Needs of American Indian Adults," monograph (Office of Indian Affairs, State of Oklahoma, 1991);

HOBSON, DOTTIE F. (Navaho) 1945-
(school principal)
Born March 9, 1945, Tohatchi, N.M. *Education*: University of Arizona, BA, 1972; University of New Mexico, MA, 1977; Northern Arizona University, MA, 1977. *Principal occupation*: School princpal. *Address & Affiliation*: Dilcon Boarding School, HC63, Box G, Winslow, AZ 86047 (602) 657-3211. *Other professional post*: Supt. for education, Chinle Agency, BIA, Chinle, AZ, 1978-90. *Community activities*: Boy Scouts of America (institutional representative); Gyro Scouts; Federal Women's Program Coordinator, Chinle Agency. *Memberships*: Navaho School Administrators Association; National Indian Education Association. *Published works*: Kee's Grandfather (Rough Rock Demonstration School, Chinle, AZ, 1970).

HOBSON, GEARY (Cherokee-Quapaw/Chickasaw) 1941-
(professor, poet, writer/editor)
Born June 12, 1941, Chicot County, Ark. *Education*: Arizona State University, BA, 1968, MA, 1969; University of New Mexico, PhD, 1986. *Principal occupation*: Professor. *Address & Affiliation*: Dept. of English, University of Oklahoma, 760 Van Vliet Oval, Room 113, Norman, OK 73019 (405) 325-6231 (work), 1988-. *Military service*: U.S. Marine Corps, 1959-65. *Community activities*: Project Director of Returning the Gift (now called Native Writers Circle of the Americas); co-organizer of the Arkansas Band of Quapaw Indians. *Awards, honors*: Rockefeller Fellowship for Minority Scholars, 1981-82; National Endowment of the Arts grant, 1982-83; Lifetime Achievement Award from the Native Writers' Circle of the Americas in 2003. *Biographical source*: Contemporary Authors, Vol. 122. *Published works*: Editor, The Remembered Earth: An

Anthology of Contemporary Native American Literature (University of New Mexico Press, 1979); Deer Hunting & Other Poems (Point Riders Press, 1990); The Last of the Ofos (University of Arizona Press, 2000).

HODGE, FELICIA SCHANCHE (Wailaki) 1949-
(scientist)
Born January 3, 1949, Garberville, Calif. *Education*: University of California, Berkeley, MPH, 1976, Dr.P.H., 1987. *Principal occupation*: Scientist. *Home address*: 608 Adams St., Albany, CA 94706 (510) 843-8661 (work). *Affiliations*: Northwest Portland Area Indian Health Board, Portland, OR (evaluation coordinator, 1976-77; executive director, 1977-82; student research assistant, UC-Berkeley (while working on a doctoral degree); principal investigator, American Indian Cancer Control Project, Berkeley, CA, 1990-; principal investigator, American Indian Women's Talking Circle, Berkeley, CA, 1993-; director, Center for American Indian Research & Education, Western Consortium for Public Health, Berkeley, CA, 1994-. *Other professional posts*: Consultant to agencies/projects; lecturer, School of Social Welfare, UC-Berkeley; director, American Indian Graduate Program, UC-Berkeley, 1989-present. *Community activities*: Chairman-Board of Directors, American Indian Child Resource Center, 1990-91, 1994; trustee, Administrative Board of the California Teen Nutritional & Fitness Program, Western Consortium for Public Health, Berkeley), 1993; Advisory Board, Rural Institute on Disabilities, University of Montana, 1994. *Membership*: National Network for Cancer Control Research Among American Indians & Alaska Native Populations. *Awards, honors*: Duncan Neuhauser Award, UC-Berkeley, 1984; Kaiser Award, Golden State Minority Foundation, Los Angeles, 1984 & 1985; IHS Scholarship, 1985 & 1986; Ruth Muscrat Bronson Memorial Scholarship, Save the Children, Westport, CT, 1986; post-doctoral Fellowship, Alcohol Research Group, UC-Berkeley, 1987. *Published works*: Graduate Education & Employment, A Study of American Indian & Non-Indians in the School of Public Health, UC-Berkeley, 1971-85 (UC-Berkeley, 1986); The Socio-Cultural Aspects of Disability: A Survey of Disabled Adult American Indians, monograph, with R. Edmonds (University of Arizona, 1987); Creating an Agenda for American Indian Health in the Year 2000, monograph, with A. Williams & W. Whitehorse (State of California, 1992); "Contemporary U.S. Indian Health Care," in The Native North American Almanac (Gale Research, 1994); Papers submitted & accepted for publication: "Smoking Cessation for American Indians in Northern California," & "Tobacco Use Policies & Practices in Diverse Indian Settings" (Preventive Medicine, 1994); among other articles, and professional papers.

HODGES, RANDY
(Indian high school principal)
Affiliations: Choctaw Central High School, 150 Recreation Rd., Philadelphia, MS 39350 (601) 656-8938 Fax 656-7077.

HOERIG, KARL A.
(museum director)
Affiliation: White Mountain Apache Cultural Center & Museum, P.O. Box 507, Fort Apache, AZ 85926 (928) 338-4625 Fax 338-1716 E-mail: fortapachemuseum@ hotmail.com. Website: www.wmat.nsn.us

HOFFER, JEFF 1972-
(park historian)
Born May 28, 1972, Fargo, N.D. *Education*: B.S. (in History). *Principal occupation*: Park historian. *Home address*: 4480 Fort Lincoln Rd., Mandan, ND 58554 (701) 667-6350 Fax 667-6349. E-mail: jhoffer@state. nd.us. *Affiliations*: North Dakota Parks ^ recreation Dept. (since inception) Fort Abraham Lincoln State Park, Mandan, ND.; Fort Abraham Lincoln Foundation (1996-present). *Military service*: U.S. Navy, 1991-95; ND Army National Guard, 1995-2000; Minnesota Air National Guard, 2000-2004. *Awards, honors*: Commissioned as a Second Lieutenant in 2nd Battalion, 156th Infantry Mechanized, 2004, Golden Shellback, 1994; Enlisted Aviation Warfare Specialist, 1994. *Community activities*: Serving my country in the military. *Membership*: Frontier Army of the Dakota, 17th U.S. Infantry Regiman (reenactors). *Interests*: Military & Native American History, Aviation, Architecture, firearms; swimming, reading, writing, music.

HOFFMAN, MICHAEL P. 1937-
(anthropologist, professor, museum curator)
Born September 15, 1937, Council Bluffs, Iowa. *Education*: University of Illinois, BA, 1959; Harvard University, PhD, 1971. *Principal occupation*: Anthropologist, professor, museum curator. *Home address*: 409 N. Washington, Fayetteville, AR 72701. *Affiliations*: Professor of anthropology, museum curator, University of Arkansas, Fayetteville, 1964-. *Community activities*: Arkansas Folklore Society (board of directors); ANL Research Laboratory (board of directors); Arkansas Preservation Program (past member, State Review Committee); *Memberships*: Society for American Archaeology, 1960-; American Anthropological Association (Fellow) 1961-; Caddo Conference, 1964-; Southeastern Archaeological Conference, 1975-; Current Anthropology (Associate); American Indian Historical Society; Association for American Indian Affairs; Arkansas Archaeological Society. *Awards, honors*: Phi Beta Kappa. *Interests*: Southeastern Indians, past & present; Caddo, Quapaw, and Cherokee ethnology and contemporary life; avocational interests—running, fishing; expeditions: archaeological fieldwork in Arkansas, Missouri, Illinois, Arizona, Massachusetts, and Guatemala. *Published works*: Three Sites in Millwood Reservoir (Arkansas Archaeological Survey, 1970); The Kinkaid-Mainard Site, 3PU2 (Arkansas Archaeologist, 1977); Ozark Reservoir Papers (Arkansas Archaeological Survey, 1978); Prehistoric Ecological Crises (Kennikat Press, 1980); Arkansas Indians, (Arkansas Naturalist, 1984).

HOGAN, LINDA (Chickasaw) 1947-
(professor-retired; writer)
Born July 16, 1947, Denver, Colo. *Education*: MA in English/Creative Writing. *Principal occupation*: Professor-retired, writer. *Address*: P.O. Box 141, Idledale, CO 80453 (303) 697-9097. *Affiliation*: Retired professor, University of Colorado, Boulder. *Awards, honors*: Native Writers Circle Lifetime Achievement Award; National Endowment for the Arts; Before Columbus American Book Award; Pulitzer Finalist; National Book Writers Finalist; Oklahoma Book Award; Colorado Book Award (2); Wordcraft Circle Lifetime Achievement Award. *Community activities*: Colorado Chickasaw Council. *Memberships*: Writers Guild; Authors Guild; PEN. *Interests*: Horses, chorus member, Native science and indigenous knowledge. *Published works*: The Book of Medicines; Power; Solar Storms; Mean Spirit; Dwellings; Red Clay; Seeing Through the Sun; Savings; Co-edit: Intimate Nature: The Bond between Woman and Animals (Farrar, Straus & Giroux); The Sweet Breathing of Plants: Women & The Green World (Farrar, Straus & Giroux); The Mysterious Journey of the Gray Whale (National Geographic); Woman Who Watches Over the World: A Native Memoir (Norton, 2001).

HOGAN, PHYLLIS
(Arizona Indian herbology)
Affiliation: Northern Arizona University, Native American Indian Studies, Dept. of Anthropology, Box 15200, Flagstaff, AZ 86011 (520) 523-3180.

HOGGATT, ARDELLE COLES (LYNCH)
(*Calm Water*) (United Lumbee) 1939-
(data entry acquisitions & procurer; nurse's aide)
Born December 31, 1939, Montebello, Calif. *Principal occupation*: Data entry acquisitions & procurer; nurse's aide. *Education*: High school, some college. *Address*: P.O. Box 160, Bieber, CA 96009 (530) 294-5817. *Community activities*: United Lumbee Deer Clan (councilperson, 2000-present; treasurer, 2001); Big Valley Art League, 1995-present; Big Valley Days Committee (treasurer, 2001-present); Chapel of Our Lord Jesus (councilperson, 2001-present). *Membership*: American Miniature Hereford Association. *Interests*: Oil painting, crafts, cross stitch, crochet, flying; learning about and making Native American crafts and memorabilia.

HOGGATT, HENRY F. (*Standing Strong*)
(United Lumbee) 1932-
(construction, rancher, plumber)
Born May 18, 1932, Hastings, Neb. *Principal occupation*: Construction, rancher, plumber. *Education*: High school, some college. *Address*: P.O. Box 160, Bieber, CA 96009 (530) 294-5817. *Affiliations*: U.S. Forestry Service USDA; B Lazy Y Ranch Miniature Hereford Cattle. *Other professional posts*: Educator/instructor;

life teaching credentials, State of California. *Military service*: U.S. Navy, 1950's (civil ammunition inspector). *Community activities*: Vice-president, senior adults 50+ program; member, Big Valley Days Committee; Chapel of Our Lord Jesus, councilperson, 2001-present; Native American Wolf Clan; vice chief, Golden Hawk Society, 2001-present). *Membership*: United Lumbee Nation (Chief, Deer Clan, 2001-present); American Hereford Association. *Interests*: Genealogy; animals (livestock); ranching, handcrafts. "Represent the Native American at community functions whenever possible and every time the opportunity comes ...leading my people to our betterment."

HOIG, STAN
(professor emeritus)
Affiliation: Professor Emeritus of Journalism, University of Central Oklahoma, Edmond, OK. *Published works*: The Sand Creek Massacre (University of Oklahoma Press, 1961); The Peace Chiefs of the Cheyennes (University of Oklahoma Press, 1980); Tribal Wars of the Southern Plains (University of Oklahoma Press, 1993); Beyond the Frontier: Exploring the Indian Country (University of Oklahoma Press, 1998); The Western Odyssey of John Simpson Smith: Frontiersman & Indian Interpreter (University of Oklahoma Press, 2004).

HOKANSEN, SHERRY (Yakama)
(librarian)
Affiliation: Yakima Cultural Heritage Library, P.O. Box 151, Yakima Nation Cultural Center, Toppenish, WA 98948 (509) 865-2800.

HOLFORD, CLARENCE "TURK"
(former BIA agency supt.)
Affiliation: Yakama Agency, Bureau of Indian Affairs, P.O. Box 632, Toppenish, WA 98948.

HOLLAND, ERIK L.
(historic site interpretive supervisor)
Address: Jamestown Settlement, Powhatan Village, Box 1607, Williamsburg, VA 23187 (757) 253-7311 Fax 253-7350; E-Mail: esholland@aol.com. *Affiliations*: Fort Clark State Historic Site, ND, 1975-84; Knife River Indian Village, National Historic Site, ND, 1984-90; Milwaukee Public Museum, 1992-93; Interpretive Supervisor of Native American Culture, Jamestown-Yorktown Foundation, 1993-present. *Memberships*: Native American and Museum Collaborative Network (AAM) (education committee); American Association of Museums; American Association for State & Local History; Williamsburg Garden History Society.

HOLLISTER, GEOFF
(organization chairperson)
Affiliation: Wings of America, The Earth Circle Foundation, Inc., 1601 Cerrillos Rd., Santa Fe, NM 87505 (505) 982-6761 Fax 988-3879.

HOLLOWBREAST, DONALD (*Box Elder*)
(Northern Cheyenne) 1919-
(retired newspaper columnist, artist)
Born May 17, 1919, Birney, Mont. *Address*: P.O. Box 126 - Apt. 28, Lame Deer, MT 59043-0126 (406) 477-8707. *Affiliation*: Owner, Great Plains Gallery, Lame Deer, MT. *Memberships*: National Mustang Association; Intertribal Agriculture Council. *Interests*: Writing newspaper columns: Birney Arrow, Northern Cheyenne Tribal News, and Lame Deer News (Rosebud County Press.)

HOLM, MICHAEL
(historic site manager)
Affiliation: Knife River Indian Villages National Historic Site, RR 1 Box 168, Stanton, ND 58571 (701) 745-3300.

HOLM, TOM (Cherokee/Creek)
(writer, professor)
Education: University of Oklahoma, PhD, 1978. *Affiliation*: American Indian Studies Program, The University of Arizona, Harvill Bldg., Rm. 430, P.O. Box 210076, Tucson, AZ 85721 (520) 621-7108 Fax 621-7952. E-mail: aisp@email.arizona.edu. *Interests*: Federal Indian policy, colonization of Native peoples. *Published work*: Strong Hearts, Wounded Souls: Native American Veterans of the Vietnam War (University of Texas Press).

HOLM, WILLIAM
(museum curator)
Affiliation: Washington State Museum, Thomas Burke Memorial, University of Washington, Seattle, WA 98195 (206) 543-5590.

HOLMAN, LARRY D.
(BIA education administrator)
Affiliation: Eastern Navajo Agency, Bureau of Indian Affairs, P.O. Box 328, Crownpoint, NM 87313 (505) 786-6150 Fax 786-6112.

HOLMAN, WILLIAM
(health director)
Affiliation: Sonoma County Indian Health Program, P.O. Box 7308, Santa Rosa, CA 95407 (707) 544-4056.

HOLMES, WALTER F. (Crow)
(consultant, paralegal)
Address & Affiliation: Consultant and paralegal, Albietz Law Corporation, 2001 N St., Suite 100, Sacramento, CA 95814 (916) 442-4241 Fax 444-5494. Mr. Holmes was former chief of Lands and Minerals for the State of California's Bureau of Land management (BLM). He has 36 years of experience in minerals and lands adjudication with the BLM, and was responsible for program implementation as well as policy determination. *Awards, honors*: In 1983, Mr. Holmes received the U.S. Dept. of the Interior's highest honor for "Superior Service."

HOLT, RONALD (Nez Perce) 1944-
(TV station director)
Born November 26, 1944, Orifino, Idaho. *Education*: Los Angeles Community College, 1970-72; Columbia College of Fine Arts, 1972-75. *Principal occupation*: TV station director. *Address & Affiliation*: Principal, KHMT - Channel 4, 445 S. 24th St. W., Suite 404, Billings, MT 59102 (406) 652-7366 Fax 652-6963. *Past professional posts*: TV producer, National Education Association, Washington, DC; KOBL-TV, Dull Knife Memorial College, Lame Deer, MT. *Other professional post*: TV-host, TV writer; editorial board, "Native People" Magazine. *Memberships*: National Press Club; Native American Press Association; National Association of Broadcasters.

HOLTSOI-ROBBINS, EUNICE (Navajo)
(registrar/student affairs)
Address & Affiliation: Cook College & Theological School, 708 S. Lindon Lane, Tempe, AZ 85281 (602) 968-9354 Fax 968-9357. *Interests*: Give Native American presentation especially about the Navajo Tribe.

HOLY EAGLE, CLEM (Wanbli Wakan) (Oglala Lakota) 1969-
(dancer)
Born July 24, 1969, Pine Ridge, S.D. *Address*: P.O. Box 167, Wanblee, SD 57577 (605) 462-6724. Clem is a Hoop Dance performer, and a known expert on Lakota culture and heritage. Holy Eagle focuses on the deepening of Lakota values and Lakota customs in his performances.

HOMAN, PAUL
(BIA-special trustee)
Affiliation: Bureau of Indian Affairs, Office of Special Trustee for American Indians, MS: 5140-MIB, 1849 C St., NW, Washington, DC 20240 (202) 208-4866.

HOMER, DARVIN E.
(school principal)
Affiliation: Herfano Dormitory, P.O. Box 639, Bloomfield, NM 87413 (505) 786-6160.

HOMER, DENISE
(BIA acting area director)
Affiliation: Minneapolis Area Office, Bureau of Indian Affairs, 331 S. Second Ave., Minneapolis, MN 55401 (612) 373-1000.

HOMER, ELIZABETH
(BIA-director)
Affiliation: Bureau of Indian Affairs, Director-Office of American Indian Trust, MS: 2471-MIB, 1849 C St., NW, Washington, DC 20240 (202) 208-3338.

HOMER, PETE, JR.
(government agency director)
Affiliation: Office of Native American Affairs, Small Business Administration, 409 3rd St., SW, Washington, DC 20416 (202) 205-6421.

HOMER, VERONICA L.
(BIA field rep.)
Affiliation: Salt River Field Office, Bureau of Indian Affairs, 10000 E. McDowell Rd., Scottsdale, AZ 85256 (480) 421-0807 Fax 421-0814.

HONAHNI, BRANT
(school chairperson)
Affiliation: Moencopi Day School, P.O. Box 185, Tuba City, AZ 86045 (602) 283-5361.

HONAKER, KEITH (Shoshone)
(tribal chairperson)
Affiliation: Duckwater Shoshone Tribal Council, P.O. Box 140068, Duckwater, NV 89314 (702) 738-8889.

HONANIE, GILBERT, JR. (Hopi) 1941-
(architect, planning)
Born April 11, 1941, Tuba City, Ariz. *Education*: Pasadena City College, AA, 1969; Arizona State University, BA (Architecture), 1972. *Principal occupation*: Architect, planning. Resides in Phoenix, AZ (602) 277-6844. *Affiliation*: President, owner, architect, Gilbert Honanie, Jr., Inc., Phoenix, AZ, 1975-. *Other professional posts*: National Council of Architectural Registration Board; American Indian Council of Architects & Engineers; Western & Arizona Society of Architects. *Community activities*: Member of Hopi Tribe; member, Arizona Indian Chamber of Commerce; member. Central Arizona Chapter of Architects. *Biographical sources*: Articles in the Arizona Republic & Gazette, Arizona Builder, Progressive Architecture, and Architectural Journal.

HONANI, KING, SR. (Hopi)
(crafts/art gallery owner)
Affiliation: Honani Crafts-Gallery, P.O. Box 221, Second Mesa, AZ 86043 (520) 737-2238.

HONANIE, WENDELL
(BIA agency supt.)
Affiliation: Hopi Agency, Bureau of Indian Affairs, P.O. Box 158, Keams Canyon, AZ 86034 (928) 738-2228 Fax 738-5187.

HONEA, DONALD, SR. (Athapascan)
(AK village president)
Affiliation: Native Village of Ruby, P.O. Box 21, Ruby, AK 99768 (907) 468-4406.

HONER, JANELLE A. (Seminole) 1954-
(artist, gardener)
Born February 28, 1954, Hayward, Calif. *Education*: Humboldt State University, BA (Art, Native American Studies), 1976; Anderson Ranch, Snowmass Village, CO (seminars & workshops), 1978-82. *Principal occupation*: Artist, gardener. *Affiliations*: Owner operator, Doug & Janella's Garden, El Jebel, CO, 1981-; gallery artist, Janie Beggs Fine Arts Ltd., Aspen, Colo., 1986-. *Community activities*: Advisor, Aspen Dance Connection. *Memberships*: National Gardening Association; American Crafts Council; Aspen Art Museum; Colorado Council on the Arts; Carbondale Council on the Arts & Humanities. *Art exhibitions & shows*: Featured artist, Cohen Gallery, Denver, Colo., 1985; Roaring Fork Annual, Aspen Art Museum, 1985; Colorado Artists-Craftsmen Exhibit, Boulder, Colo., 1984; one-person show, Sioux National Museum, 1981; Roaring Fork Valley Art Show, Aspen Center for the Visual Arts, 1981. *Awards, honors*: Magna Cum Laude, Humboldt State University, Arcata, Calif., 1976; first & second place prizes, Women Art West, Grand Junction, Colo., 1982-1983; Craft Range Magazine award for Buy the Heartland, 1982; first place sculpture, Woman Art West, 1980; inclusion in Northern Plains, Southern Plains Indian Museum art collections; among others. *Interests*: Vocational: "We are organic farmers with a gourmet produce market garden. We teach people basic skills and give garden tours, sell produce. We educate about wild edibles, food storage; we both are chefs. I also do mixed media sculpture and ceramic sculpture, that is the art I show. We travel extensively. My goal is to help feed the hungry."

HONYOUTI, HARVEY A. (Loma'oo yee) (Hopi)
(teacher/coach)
Address: P.O. Box 998, Keams Canyon, AZ 86034 (520) 738-5285 Fax 738-5333. *Affiliations*: Arizona Coaches Association, 1986-; Arizona Track Coaches Association, 1986-. *Community activities*: Local youth projects.

HOOBAN, HOMER, II "LOUIS" (Flying Eagle) (Bannock) 1943-
(publisher, writer, educator)
Born June 21, 1943, Coeur d'Alene, Idaho. *Education*: Idaho State University, BA, 1966, MEd, 1969; University of Wyoming, Ed.S, PhD (Psychology), 1971. *Principal occupation*: Publisher, public speaker, educator. *Address*: P.O. Box 752, McCall, ID 83638 (423) 277-1103. *Affiliations*: CEO, Indian Heritage Council, McCall, ID. *Other professional posts*: Publisher, Native American Publishing, 1990-; board of directors, Native American University. *Community activities*: CEO, Books to Reservations; CEO, Plants to Reservations; CEO, Herbs to Reservations; sponsor of boy scout groups - national dance champions; B.P.O.E. - youth director; coach of all sports (25 years-never had a losing season as a head coach); sponsored first national pow-wows (1989-93) at Pigeon Forge, TN. Also sponsored numerous Native American events; involved in kayak and canoe instruction. *Awards, honors*: Poet Laureate of the Native Americans, 1988 - World's Fair Site of National Pow-wow - Knoxville, TN; Poet of the Year, Writer of the Year, Publisher of the Year; Indian Heritage Council Award for Literature; Eagle Award from Aniyonwiya Nation, a Native American think tank. *Community activities*: Director of the Youth Indian League; National Pow-Wow Coordinator. *Membership*: Native American Guild; Indian Heritage Council; Native American Poets Association; National Education Association; Boy Scouts (sponsor); National Psychological Association; Native American Consortium of CEOs. *Interests*: Writing, reading, environment, poetry, hiking, kayaking, adventure travel, pow-wows; "have traveled around the world, to all major landmarks"; healing arts; "have always coached winning teams (all sports)." *Biographical sources*: Who's Who; Dictionary Biography of the West; Who's Who International Biography. *Published works*: Native American Play; The Vision Quest; Native American Drug Usage; Native American Coloring Book (Indian Heritage Publishing); The Scorched Earth (Scotway Press, 1988); editor - Great American Indian Bible (Indian Heritage Publishing, 1990); Indian Nation (a 3 act play) (Indian Heritage Publishing, 1991); The Indian Anthology of Poetry (Indian Heritage Publishing, 1993); Poetry of Native Americans (Indian Heritage Publishing, 2000); Crazy Horse's Philosophy of Riding Rainbows (Indian Heritage Publishing, 2001); The Vision: Native American Predictions (Indian Heritage Publishing, 2002).

HOOD, RANCE (Comanche)
(artist)
Affiliation: Rance Hood Studio, P.O. Box 73, Denison, TX 75021 (903) 463-6020. *Products*: Original paintings, limited edition offset prints, serigraphs, and Giclee prints; posters and note cards.

HOOPER, BOB G.
(school principal)
Affiliation: Pine Springs Boarding School, P.O. Box 4198, Houck, AZ 86506 (520) 871-4311 Fax 871-4341.

HOOVER, HERBERT T. (Ta Chanunpa Ska) 1930-
(professor of history)
Born March 9, 1930, Oakwood Township, Wabasha County, Minn. *Education*: New Mexico State University, BA, 1960, MA, 1961; University of Oklahoma, Norman, PhD, 1966. *Principal occupation*: Professor of history. *Home address*: 401 Sunset Dr., Beresford, SD 57004 (605) 763-5323. *Office address*: Dept. of History, 414 E. Clark St., Dakota Hall, University of South Dakota, Vermillion, SD 57069 (605) 677-5218. E-mail: hhoover@usd.edu. Website: www.usd.edu/nplhist. *Affiliations*: Assistant professor of history, East Texas State University, 1965-67; professor of history, University of South Dakota, Vermillion, 1967-. *Other professional posts*: Director, Newberry Library Center for the History of the American Indian, Chicago, IL, 1981-83; director, South Dakota Oral History Center, 1967-; director, South Dakota Oral History Center, 1977-present; director, Indian Studies program, 1985-

91. *Military service*: U.S. Navy, 1951-55 (Fleet Marine Corpsman with First Marine Division in Korean War). *Community activities*: SD Council of Humanists; SD Committee on the Humanities; National Endowment for the Humanities (review panels); SD Historical Society (board of trustees); SD Fairview Township Board of Control; SD Historical Publications & Records Commission; Augustana College, Center for Western Studies, National Council, 1984-present; Rhodes Scholar, SD State Selection Committee, 1991-96; chair, 1996-). *Memberships*: Western History Association, 1962- (chair, nominating board; local arrangements committee; program committee; membership committee; board of editors); Organization of American Historians, 1970- (nominating board; membership committee); Phi Alpha Theta, 1960- (international councillor; international board of advisors); SD Historical Society; Missouri Historical Society; Minnesota Wabasha County Historical Society. *Awards, honors*: Outstanding Educator of America Award, Washington, DC, 1975; Augustana College Center for Western Studies, 1985 Achievement Award, National Board of Advisors; National Endowment for the Humanities, Research Grant Award, 1978-81; Western America Award, 1984; National Teacher of the Year Award, 1985; 1990 Governor's Award for History (South Dakota); Professor of the Year, 2003, University of South Dakota Student Association. *Interests*: "Travel and recreation is tied to principal occupational interests: the history of Indian-white relations, and the preservation of natural life." *Biographical sources*: Who's Who in the Midwest, 1984; Who's Who in Science and Engineering, 1996; Who's Who Among America's Teachers, 1998; Who's Who in American Education, 2003. *Published works*: To Be An Indian (Holt, Rinehart & Winston, 1971); The Practice of Oral History (Microfilming Corp. of America, 1975); The Chitimacha People (Indian Tribal Series, 1975); The Sioux: A Critical Bibliography (Indiana University, 1979); Bibliography of the Sioux (Scarecrow Press, 1980); The Yankton Sioux (Chelsea House Publishers, 1988); Wildlife on the Cheyenne River and Lower Brule Reservations (University of South Dakota Press, 1992); co-author, Yanktonai Sioux Images; The Watercolors of John Saul (Center for Western Studies, Augustana College, 1993); co-author, South Dakota History: An Annotated Bibliography (Greenwood Press, 1993); The Sioux and Other Native American Cultures of the Dakotas: An Annotated Bibliography (Greenwood Press, 1993); co-author, Bon Homme County History (Pine Hill Press, 1994; co-author, U.S. History from Colonial Times to the Civil War, with carol Goss Hoover and Elizabeth Simmons (Houghton Mifflin/Burgess International Custom Publication, Prentice Hall, 1995-); U.S. History From the Civil War (Houghton Mifflin/Burgess International Custom Publication, Prentice Hall, 1995-); Sioux Country: A History of Indian-White Relations, with Carol Goss Hoover (Center for Western Studies, Augustana College, 2000); numerous articles, book chapters, book reviews, and consultations on publications.

HOOVER, JAY BRUCE
(school principal)
Affiliation: Wingate High School, P.O. Box 2, Fort Wingate, NM 87316 (505) 488-6400.

HOPAHNIS, BRANT (Hopi)
(BIA education chairperson)
Affiliation: Hopi Agency, Bureau of Indian Affairs, P.O. Box 568, Keams Canyon, AZ 86034 (602) 738-2262.

HOPE, ARLENE
(Indian band chief)
Affiliation: Klahoose Indian Band, Box 9, Squirrel Cove, British Columbia, Canada V0P 1T0 (604) 935-6650.

HOPE, EVE
(museum director/curator)
Affiliation: Ksan Museum, P.O. Box 333, Hazelton, British Columbia, Canada V0J 1Y0 (604) 842-9723.

HOPE, GERALD E.
(corp. president)
Affiliation: Ketchikan Indian Corporation, 429 Deermount Ave., Ketchikan, AK 99901 (907) 225-5158.

HOPKINS, GEORGE H. (Narragansett)
(tribal chief)
Affiliation: Narragansett Indian Tribal Council, P.O. Box 268, Charleston, RI 02813 (401) 364-1100.

HOPKINS, JOHN CHRISTIAN (*Paukunnawaw Neepoush - Standing Bear*) (Narragansett)1960-
(journalist/author)
Born July 6, 1960, Westerly, RI. *Education*: University of Rhode island, BA. *Principal occupation*: Journalist/author. *Address*: 59 John St., Westerly, RI 02891. E-mail: kngauthor@aol.com; Website: www.jchopkins.homestead.com. *Membership*: Native American Journalist Association (NAJA). *Interest*: Old West, Native Americana. *Awards*: Won four 2003 NAJA awards: 1st newswriting, 1st feature writing, 2nd column writing, 3rd sports writing; 2000 RI Press Association, 3rd column writing. *Published articles*: "Carlomagno" (2003, Iunivese); "Nacogdoches", 2004, PublishAmerica.

HOPKINS, SUE (*Jowanna*) (Cherokee-OK) 1940-
(school secretary)
Born December 10, 1940, Durant, Okla. *Education*: High school. *Principal occupation*: School secretary. *Address*: Silo School, HC-62, Box 227, Durant, OK 74701 (405) 924-7000 (work). *Affiliation*: School secretary, Indian Education Director, Title V-C, JOM, Silo, OK, 1970-; pianist, Silo Baptist Church, 1970-. *Other professional post*: Piano teacher, 1964-. *Community activities*: Pianist for Memorial Day Services, Contatas, Plays, Rest Homes, Senior Citizens, Funerals, Weddings. *Memberships*: NAFIS, OASIS. *Interests*: "As Indian Education director, I travel to Washington, DC each year for meetings and visits with White House officials; JOM Meetings in Tulsa, OK, NAFIS Meetings in Yakima, WA. I am in the process of completing a journal which I am planning to put into a short story."

HOPSON, BARBARA
(program interim director)
Affiliation: Native American Studies Program, University of Oklahoma, 455 W. Lindsay, Rm. 804, Norman, OK 73019 (405) 325-2312.

HORACE, EMERSON, Jr.
(Indian school principal)
Affiliation: Hoteville Bacavi Community School, P.O. Box 48, Hoteville, AZ 86030 (602) 734-2462.

HOREJSI, RICK (Hoh)
(former tribal chairperson)
Affiliation: Hoh Tribal Business Committee, 2464 Lower Hoh Rd., Forks, WA 98331 (360) 374-6582.

HORLAN, THERESA
(museum curator)
Affiliation: Carl Nelson Gorman Museum, Native American Studies, 2401 Hart Hall, Davis, CA 95616 (916) 752-6567.

HORNBACHER, HARLAN
(school prinicpal)
Affiliation: Red Lake Day School, P.O. Box 39, Tonalea, AZ 86044 (602) 283-6325.

HORNBROOK, JOHN R. (*Anumpuli Shall Ossi*) (Choctaw of Oklahoma) 1943-
(associate professor)
Born May 17, 1943 in Lawton, Okla. *Education*: Oakland City University, B.A., 1964; B.S., 1965; M.A. (Teaching), 1968; Oklahoma City University, M.A.T., 1969; Nova University, D.Ed (Early Childhood Administration), 1986. *Principal occupation*: Associate professor. *Home address*: R1 Box 264EE, Francisco, IN 47149 (812) 782-9047. E-mail: hornbrook@oak.edu. *Affiliations*: Assistant director, Educational Extension Center, Evansville, IN, 1974-85; special concerns counselor, Student Services, E-VSC, 1985-88; assistant principal, Glenwood Middle School, Evansville, IN, 1988-89; principal, Howard Roosa Elementary School, Evansville, IN, 1989-2000; Associate Professor, Oakland City University, Oakland City, IN, 2000-. *Other professional post*: Director of Student Teaching, Oakland City University, 2000-. *Military service*: U.S. Army, 1959-61. *Community activities*: Indiana Native American Council Board Member, 1992-present. *Memberships*: Choctaw Nation of Oklahoma; National Congress of American Indians; National Indian Education Association; Society for Early Childhood Development; Indiana Association for Counseling and Development; National Association for Counseling and Development; National Elementary School Principals Association; Native American Indian Association; Native American Law Enforcement Association; Indians State Dept. of Education, Native American Curriculum Committee,

1993-present; Indiana American Indian Movement (state education director); Native American Inter-Tribal Council (president). *Awards, honors*: Indiana's Delegate - White House Conference on Indian Education, 1992; Awarded Sagamore of the Wabash by Indian's Governor, 1992; Who's Who Among Outstanding Americans, 1994-present; University of Evansville's Outstanding Administrator Award, 1995. *Interests*: "To educate the public about respect for all people and providing accurate information about American Indians. Indian storytelling and sharing about the Choctaw people to numerous civic groups as well as public and private schools. I feel honored along with my friend Nick Mejia to have been instrumental in changing the history of the U.S. through education.We started an educational process which eventually enlisted 125 Indian nations, the most profitable company in the U.S., and a vast general public audience. Through television and printed news medias, we presented the American Indian religious beliefs concerning respect for Indian graves and culture. After eight years of educating the public, the General Electric Corp. allowed Native Americans the honor of reburying our dead ancestors along with the funerary objects with which they were buried. This was the first time in the history of this country that valuable grave items were returned to graves instead of placing them in institutions. Through education, a precedence has been established that is changing the mentality of citizens about reburial issues for all races; especially Native Americans. We have changed one Indiana textbook which was insultive to Native Americans. By educating the editors of Silver-Burdette-Ginn, the company was apologetic and has revised the book. Thousands of students will benefit from this correction." *Published works*: You Are Somebody Special (Zoe Publications, 1980; The Miracle of Touching (Huntington House, 1985).

HORSE, ANTHONY WHIRLWIND (Sioux)
(school chairperson)
Affiliation: Pine Ridge School, P.O. Box 1202, Pine Ridge, SD 57770 (605) 867-5198.

HORSE, BILLY EVANS (Kiowa)
(tribal chairperson)
Affiliation: Kiowa Indian Tribe Business Committee, P.O. Box 369, Carnegie, OK 73015 (580) 654-2300.

HORSE CAPTURE, GEORGE P. (*Spotted Otter*) (A'ani Gros Ventre) 1937-
(museum curator-administrator)
Born October 20, 1937, Fort Belknap, Mont. *Education*: University of California, Berkeley, BA, 1974; Montana State University, MA (History), 1979; Honorary Doctorate of Letters, Montana State University, Bozeman, 1996. *Principal occupation*: Museum curator and administrator. *Home Address*: 11207 Mitscher St., Kensington, MD 20895 (301) 962-7304 Fax 238-3202 E-mail: ghc@ic.si.edu. *Affiliations*: Curator, Plains Indian Museum, Buffalo Bill Historical Center, Cody, WY, 1979-91; currently, special assistant and (senior counselor to the director, 1999), National Museum of the American Indian, Smithsonian Institution, Cultural Resources Center. 4220 Silver Hill Rd., Suitland, MD 20746, 1995-. *Other professional posts*: Assistant professor, Montana State University; curriculum researcher, College of Great Falls, MT. *Military service*: U.S. Navy, 1957-61 (2nd class ship fitter; Good Conduct, China Service Medal). *Community activities*: Founding member and Presidential appointment to Institute of Museum Services Board; Governor's appointment to Wyoming Travel Commission; and others. *Awards, honors*: The 1983 W.E. Cody Motion Picture Award for "I'd Rather Be Powwowing." Several grants from various organizations. *Interests*: Participate in powwows and ceremonies; have researched museums in U.S., Canada and Europe; interested in Indian music and artwork, culture and history. *Published works*: Editor, "The Seven Visions of Bull Lodge"; exhibition catalogs.

HORSE, IMOGENE (Sioux)
(school principal)
Affiliation: Pine Ridge School, P.O. Box 1202, Pine Ridge, SD 57770 (605) 867-5198.

HORSE, PERRY G. (Kiowa)
(college president)
Born in Carnegie, Okla. *Education*: Harvard Univer-

sity Graduate School of Education, MEd; University of Arizona, PhD. *Principal occupation*: College president. *Address & Affiliation*: Institute of American Indian Arts, 83 Avan Nu Po Rd., Santa Fe, NM 87508 (505) 988-6463 Fax 988-6446. *Past professional activities*: Has worked in Indian post secondary education for the past 24 years including managment of community college development programs; has consulted on strategic & institutional planning & staff development for a number of tribal colleges across the country; was instrumental in developing the American Indian Higher Education Consortium; was an advisor to The MacArthur Foundation on funding for tribal colleges and the Albuquerque Public Schools on developing an American Indian cultural curriculum; has taught tribal government and Federal Indian Law for the Institute for Development of Indian Law, Oklahoma City, OK; and most recently, has been in charge of leadership and management development at Sandia National Laboratories in Albuquerque, NM.

HORSEMAN, DALE ROBERT
(Indian band chief)
Affiliation: Horse Lake Indian Band, P.O. Box 303, Hythe, Alberta, Canada T0H 2C0 (403) 356-2248.

HORSMAN, REGINALD 1931-
(retired-professor emeritus)
Born October 24, 1931, Leeds (Yorkshire) England. *Education*: University of Birmingham, England, BA, 1952, MA, 1955; Indiana University, PhD, 1958. *Principal occupation*: Retired. Professor Emeritus. *Home address*: Astor Hotel, 924 E. Juneau Ave. #623, Milwaukee, WI 53202; E-mail: horsmans@juno.com. *Affiliations*: Instructor, 1958-59, professor, 1959-73, distinguished professor of history, 1973-99; professor emeritus, 1999-, University of Wisconsin-Milwaukee. *Memberships*: D'Arcy McNickle Center for the History of the American Indian, Newberry Library (member, Advisory Council, 1988-93); Organization of American Historians; Society of American Historians; Society for Historians of the Early Republic; State Historical Society of Wisconsin; Phi Beta Kappa (honorary member); Phi Kappa Phi (honorary member); Phi Eta Sigma (honorary member); Phi Alpha Theta. *Awards, honors*: University of Wisconsin Kiehofer Award for Excellence in Teaching, 1961; Alumni Award for Teaching Excellence, 1995 from University of Wisconsin-Milwaukee; Guggenheim Fellowship, 1965. *Interests*: "Research on race and expansion in American history; shaping of American Indian policy; early American foreign policy; Wisconsin Oneida." *Biographical source*: Who's Who in America. *Published works*: The Causes of the War of 1812 (University of Pennsylvania Press, 1962); Matthew Elliott: British Indian Agent (Wayne State University Press, 1964); Expansion and American Indian Policy, 1783-1812 (Michigan State University Press, 1967); Napolean's Europe; The New America (Paul Hamlyn, London, 1970) The Frontier in the Formative Years, 1783-1815 (Holt, Rinehart, 1970) Race and Manifest Destiny: The Origins of American Racial Anglo-Saxonism (Harvard University Press, 1981); The Diplomacy of the New Republic, 1776-1815 (Harlan Davidson, 1985); Dr. Nott of Mobile: Southerner, Physician, and Racial Theorist (LSU Press, 1987); Frontier Doctor: William Beaumont, America's First Great Medical Scientist (University of Missouri Press, 1996); The New Republic: The United States of America, 1789-1815 (Longman, 2000)

HOSICK, H. CLARK
(executive director)
Affiliation: North American Indian Cultural Center, 1062 Triplett Blvd., Akron, OH 44306 (216) 724-1280.

HOSKINS, HELEN (Southern Ute)
(cultural center director)
Affiliation: Southern Ute Cultural Center, P.O. Box 737, Ignacio, CO 81137 (970) 563-4649.

HOSMER, BRIAN
(Indian center director)
Affiliation: Director, D'Arcy McNickle Center for American Indian History, Newberry Library, 60 W. Walton, Chicago, IL 60610 (312) 255-3564 Fax 255-3696.

HOSTLER, DAVID E.
(museum curator)
Affiliation: Hoopa Tribal Museum, P.O. Box 1348, Hoopa, CA 95546 (916) 625-4110.

HOTCH, JOE
(AK village council president)
Affiliation: Chilkat Indian Village of Klikwan, P.O. Box 219, Haines, AK 99827 (907) 767-5505.

HOULIHAN, PATRICK T. 1942-
(anthropologist)
Born June 22, 1942, New Haven, Conn. *Education*: Georgetown University, BS, 1964; University of Minnesota, MA, 1969; University of Wisconsin, PhD, 1972. *Principal occupation*: Anthropologist. *Address*: Unknown. *Affiliations*: Instructor, University of Wisconsin, Oshkosh, 1969-71; director, Anthropology Museum, University of Wisconsin, Oshkosh, 1969-71; museum intern, Milwaukee Public Museum, 1971-72; adjunct professor, Arizona State University, 1972-80; director, The Heard Museum, Phoenix, 1972-80; director, New York State Museum, Albany, 1980-81; instructor, American Indian art, UCLA, Extension Division. 1981-87; director, Southwest Museum, Los Angeles, Calif., 1981-87; director, Milicent Rogers Museum, Taos, NM, 1987-92. *Memberships*: American Association of Museums (first vice president, Western Regional Conference); American Anthropological Association (council on museum education). *Field work*: Urban Indian research for the Indian employment service (BIA sponsored), Minneapolis, 1967. *Awards, honors*: Honorary PhD, Occidental College, Los Angeles, CA. Interests: American Indian art. *Published works*: Museums & Indian Education, (Journal of Indian Education, Oct., 1973) Southwest Pottery Today, (Arizona Highways, May, 1974); The Hopi Kachinas, (Image Roche Magazine, No. 63, 1974); Indian Art: Fads and Paradoxes, (Phoenix Magazine, Feb., 1975); Basketry Designs in the Greater Southwest, (Exhibit Catalog, Utah Fine Arts Museum, Salt lake City, April, 1976); Contemporary Indian Art, (Exhibit Catalog, Mid-America Arts Association, Spring, 1979); Prints and the American Indian Artist, (American Indian Arts Magazine, Spring, 1979); Indians of the Northwest Coast, (Reader's Digest, 1980); various articles in Masterkey, a quarterly publication of the Southwest Museum, 1981-. Editorial director for the following Heard *Museum publications*: Kachinas: A Hopi Artist's Documentary, 1973; Pueblo Shields, April, 1976; The Other Southwest: Indian Arts and Crafts of Northeastern Mexico, April, 1977. Editorial director for the following Southwest Museum publications: Native Faces: Indian Cultures in American Art, co-author with Patricia Trenton, 1984; Kachinas of the Zuni (Northland Press, 1985); Lummis in the Pueblos (Northland Press, 1985); Native Americans: Five Centuries of Changing Images (Harry Abrams, 1989). *Television programs*: Script author for six one-half hour television programs, Indian Art at the Heard, produced by KAET, 1975; script researcher/writer for five one-half hour television programs titles, American Indian Artists, produced by KAET, 1976; script author for a one-half hour television program on The Craft Arts of Northwestern Mexico, produced by KAET, 1977; guest curator, Generation in Clay, traveling exhibit of Pueblo Pottery, the American Federation of Art, New York, 1980-83; principal investigator (1977-80), Navajo Film Project, KAET, Tempe, AZ.

HOUSE, CARRIE H. (Navajo/Oneida) 1965-
(freelance film/video productions)
Born March 19, 1965, Winslow, Ariz. *Education*: Navajo Community College, 1982-83; University of Montana, BS (Natural Resource Conservation(, 1987. *Principal occupation*: Freelance film/video productions. Resides in Santa Fe, NM. *Affiliations*: Native American Public Broadcasting Consortium, Lincoln, NE, 1985-90; National Center for Production of Native Images, Santa Fe, NM, 1991-. *Other professional post*: Engine Forepoerson-fire fighter, USDA Coconino National Forest, Peaks Ranger District. *Community activities*: Navajo Nation, voluntarily assist in acquire/document history of our Oaksprings community for the Oaksprings Chapter House; presentations for educational institutions; presentations of Fire Behavior with Bureau of Land Management, USDI in Farmington, NM. *Awards, honors*: Public Affairs Production at the WGBH Educational Foundation as a WGBH - CPB Fellow in Feb. 1992; Award Fellow Recipient of Native American Public Broadcasting Consortium for Robert McKee's Story Structure Course in April 1991. *Interests*: Infinite travels for research/development of film/video and personal initiatives; yearly participant of the International Wildlife Film Festival in Missoula, MT, since 1985 to present. *Biographical sources*: Articles:

"D-5 Sweeps CHIPA Muster," The Coconino Forest Pine Log, Sept. 1990; "Its a Jungle Out There," Los Angeles Times, Sect. F, April 11, 1991; and "House Completes Boston Workshop," Navajo Times, Vol. 23, No. 10, March 5, 1992.

HOUSE, CONRAD (Navajo)
(artist)
Address: P.O. Box 70, St. Michaels, AZ 86511. *Membership*: Indian Arts & Crafts Association.

HOUSE, ERNEST (Ute Mountain Ute)
(tribal chairperson)
Affiliation: Ute Mountain Ute Tribe, General Delivery, Towaoc, CO 81334 (970) 565-3751.

HOUSEMAN-WHITEHAWK, LAURIE (Winnebago)
(artist)
Address: RR#3, Box 155-B, Lawrence, KS 66044 (913) 842-1948.

HOUSER, SCHUYLER "SKY"
(college president)
Affiliation: Nebraska Indian Community College, P.O. Box 428, Macy, NE 68039 (402) 837-5078 Fax 837-4183.

HOUSTON, MARGARET
(museum director)
Affiliation: Indian Museum of the Carolinas, 607 Turnpike Rd., Laurinburg, NC 28352 (919) 276-5880.

HOUTEN, MARGARET (Paiute) 1946-
(court administration)
Born October 2, 1946, Schurz, Nev. *Education*: High school. *Principal occupation*: Clerical. *Home address*: 14 Waterline Rd., P.O. Box 265, Nixon, NV 89424 (702) 574-0205. *Professional posts*: Court clerk; vice-president, National American Indian Court Clerks Association, Washington, DC. Community activities: Not as active as before, due to kidney failure. Assist with donation for fundraising such as Veteran's Memorial, church, senior citizens, when possible. *Memberships*: National American Indian Court Clerks Association, 1979-; National Notary Public Association. *Interests*: "Vocation mostly geared toward legal matters, plan to do more traveling with arts & craft after retirement, possibly after a kidney transplant. Would like to get more into the legal aspect of Indian law in the future. I have had a lot of contact with Indian lawyers and judges, men and women, and it is exciting."

HOWARD, CARYN (Sault Ste. Marie Chippewa) 1960-
(business owner)
Born September 13, 1960, Lansing, Mich. *Education*: University of Michigan, BA, 1982. *Principal occupation*: Business owner. *Address*: P.O. Box 326, Brooklyn, MI 49230 (517) 592-3439. *Affiliation*: Owner, Bear Tracks DBA Bundy's Bungalow, Brooklyn, MI. *Community activities*: Member, Chamber of Commerce, Brooklyn, MI; ex Peace Corps Volunteer.

HOWARD, DAVID (Eskimo)
(AK village first chief)
Affiliation: Village of Eagle, P.O. Box 19, Eagle, AK 99738 (907) 547-2271.

HOWARD, GREGG (Cherokee/Powhatan) 1934-
(writer, narrator, storyteller)
Born May 5, 1934, Central City, Kentucky. *Education*: Ohio State University, 1956-58. *Principal occupation*: Writer, narrator, Cherokee storyteller. *Address & Affiliations*: Executive Producer, V.I.P. (Various Indian Peoples) Publishing Co., 301 N. St. John's Dr., Richardson, TX 75081 (972) 671-3525 Fax 671-3529; E-mail: VIPublish@aol.com., 1987-. *Military service*: U.S. Marine Corps (Sgt.), 1953-57 (Korean Network). *Memberships*: Oklahoma Native Language Association; Wordcraft Circle of Native Writers & Storytellers; Texas Storytelling Association; Oklahoma Native Language Association; Cherokee Honor Society (spokesman); National Storytelling Association. *Awards, honors*: Wrangler Award, Cowboy Hall of Fame, 1966; IABC Golden Quill Award, 1984; Silver Mike Award, 1990; Native American Music Awards - Spoken Word Category, for "Tales of Wonder" - CD version. *Interests*: Formed Various Indian Peoples (V.I.P.) Publishing Co. in 1988 with Alfred Houser (brother of Alan Houser - the late Apache sculptor from Santa Fe, NM),

and Rick Eby of Fayetteville, AR. The company is now owned by Lari Howard of Dallas, TX. VIP's mission was, and is, to record and publish American Indian language, legends, and cultural programs. They have produced language and legends programs for the Cherokee, Choctaw, Chickasaw, Muskogee (Creek), Kiowa and Western Delaware peoples. All of their language programs employ speakers who spoke their language first - English being their second language. A portion of every program is returned to the nation, Tribe or individual who assisted in developing the program. Gregg has taught the Cherokee language since 1992 in and around Dallas at various colleges and through the continuing education program at Texas A&M in Commerce, Texas. He also teaches a weekly class at Stringbean Restaurant in Dallas. He is continuing to work with Indian Nations and Tribes as they work to reclaim their language and cultural past. *Published works*: Audio tapes: Authentic Indian Music of the Apache, Sioux, Navajo (Dine), Crow, Ute, and Shawnee; Cherokee, Choctaw, and Kiowa legend tapes; Introduction programs include Cherokee, Choctaw, Chickasaw, Muskogee (Creek), and Western Delaware. Language Samplers in Cherokee, Choctaw, Chickasaw, Muskogee (Creek), and Kiowa, Caddo; Cheyenne Legends (in English & Cheyenne); Cherokee Scary Stories - CD; Life With Little People - (Creek) in association with book, "Life With Little People." "Tales of Wonder" video & CD (winner of five awards), and "Tales of Wonder II" video (both now on DVD. A 9,500 word English to Cherokee/Cherokee to English glossary is currently a "work-in-progress."

HOWARD, LYNN (Cherokee)
(editor)
Affiliation: Cherokee Advocate, Cherokee Nation of Oklahoma, Communications Department, P.O. Box 948, Tahlequah, OK 74465 (918) 456-0671.

HOWE, CRAIG (Oglala Lakota)
(deputy assistant director for cultural resources)
Education: University of Nebraska, MA; University of Michigan, PhD (Architecture & Anthropology). Address: Cultural Resources Center, 4220 Silver Hill Rd., Suitland, MD 20746 (301) 238-6624 Fax 238-3202. *Affiliations*: Director, D'Arcy McNickle Center for American Indian History, Chicago, IL, 1995-98; deputy assistant director for cultural resources, National Museum of the American Indian, 1999-present.

HOWE, LEANNE (Anolitubbee)
(Choctaw of Oklahoma) 1951-
(professor, writer)
Born April 29, 1951, Edmond, Okla. *Education*: Vermont College, MFA (Creative Writing), 2000. *Principal occupation*: Professor, writer. *Home address*: 601 Main St. SE #516, Minneapolis, MN 55414. E-mail: lhowe1@aol.com. *Affiliations*: Lecturer, American Indian & Native Studies Program, University of Iowa, Iowa City, IA, 1992, 1994, 1995; visiting faculty, American Studies, English, Carleton College, Northfield, MN, 1996-97; Grinnell College, Grinnell, IA (visiting lecturer, 1997; assistant professor, 1997-2000); University of Cincinnati (OH) (visiting lecturer, Spring 2002; visiting professor, Fall 2002; Louis D. Rubin Writer-in-Residence, MFA graduate program, Hollins University, Roanoke, VA, 2003; Loft Mentor Series in Creative Prose & Poetry, Minneapolis, MN, 6/2003; Professor, Dept. of American Indian Studies, University of Minnesota, Minneapolis, MN, 2003-present. *Awards, honors*: 2002 American Book Award from the Before Columbus Foundation for "Shell Shaker." *Memberships*: AWP, Associated Writing Programs; American Studies Association; Native American Women's Playwrights Association (Miami University, Oxford, OH); Association of American Indian & Alaska Professors; American Society for Ethnohistory; Choctaw Code Talkers Association (Chickasha, OK); Wordcraft Circle, Native Writer Mentoring Program, Native Writers Circle of the Americas (an organization of North & South American indigenous writers, including the Arctic; formerly part of *Returning the Gift*). *Interests*: Gormet cooking, American Indian history, chess, dove hunting. *Published works*: Shell Shaker, novel (Aunt Lute Books); Coyote Papers (Wowapi Press).

HOWE, RAYMOND
(school principal)
Affiliation: Loneman Day School, P.O. Box 50, Oglala, SD 57764 (605) 867-5633.

HOWELL, FARRELL
(Indian program director)
Affiliation: American Indian Studies Program, University of Denver, University College, Liberal Studies Dept., 2211 S. Josephine St., Denver, CO 80208 (303) 871-3381 Fax 871-4877. fhowell@du.edu.

HOWELL, GEORGE E. (Pawnee-Cheyenne) 1935-
(health systems administrator)
Born December 30, 1935, Pawnee, Okla. *Education*: Westminster College, Salt Lake City, BS, 1978; University of Utah, MSW, 1980. *Principal occupation*: Health systems administrator. *Address*: Lawton PHS Indian Health Center, Lawton, OK 73501 (405) 353-0350. *Affiliations*: Health systems administrator, PHS Indian Health Center, Fort Thompson, SD, 1983-85; health systems administrator, PHS Indian Health Hospital, Wagner, SD, 1985-88; service unit director, PHS Indian Hospital, Pine Ridge, SD, 1988-92; director, Lawton PHS Indian Health Center, Lawton, OK, 1993-. *Other professional posts*: Director, Mental Health/Social Services, social worker, clinical instructor, University of Utah; division manager, data processing firm. *Military service*: U.S. Air Force, 1954-58 (A/1c). *Community activities*: Four Corners Gourd Dance Society (president); Alcohol Treatment Program (chairman, board of directors); UNAC (chairman, board of directors). *Memberships*: National Association of Social Workers; Native American-Alaska Native Social Workers Association. *Awards, honors*: CSWE Scholarship Grant; 4 consecutive years - "Outstanding Performance Awards" as Service Unit Director, for Indian Health Service. *Interests*: Accounting-computer programming; alcohol counseling, clinical instructor, social worker; administration, community planning; health systems administrator. Golfing, Indian dancing - Gourd dancer.

HOWELL, KEN
(director)
Affiliation: Smoki People, 145 N. Arizona Ave., P.O. Box 10224, Prescott, AZ 86304 (928) 445-1230.

HOWELL, PATTIE
(project director)
Affiliation: American Indian Head Start Quality Improvement Center, American Indian Institute, College of Continuing Education, University of Oklahoma, 555 Constitution St., Suite 228, Norman, OK 73072 (405) 325-4129 Fax 325-7319. E-mail: phowell@ou.edu.

HOWELL, PATRICIA
(health center director)
Affiliation: Lower Brule PHS Indian Health Center, P.O. Box 248, Lower Brule, SD 57548 (605) 473-5544.

HOWLETT, DANA
(museum curator)
Affiliation: Aztec Ruins National Monument, P.O. Box 640, Ruins Rd., Aztec, NM 87410 (505) 334-6174.

HOXIE, FREDERICK E. 1947-
(teacher)
Born April 22, 1947, Hoolehua, Molokai. *Education*: Amherst College, BA, 1969; Brandeis University, PhD, 1977. *Principal occupation*: Teacher. *Home address*: 2717 Lincolnwood Ave., Evanston, IL 60201 (217) 333-8660 (work). *Affiliation*: Director, D'Arcy McNickle Center for the History of the American Indian, Newberry Library, Chicago, IL, 1983-93; Academic Vice President, The Newberry Library, Chicago, IL, 1994-; Swanlund Professor, University of Illinois, Urbana Champaign, 1998-.. *Other professional posts*: Adjunct professor of history, Northwestern University; Trustee, National Museum of the American Indian, 1990-95; Trustee, Amherst College, 2001-. *Memberships*: American Historical Association; Organization of American Historians; American Society of Ethnohistory. *Awards, honors*: Rockefeller Foundation Humanities Fellowship, 1983-84; NEH Fellowship, 1990-91; Doctor of Humane Letters, Amherst College, 1994. *Biographical source*: Who's Who in America; Who's Who in the Midwest. *Published works*: Editor, With the Nez Perces (University of Nebraska Press, 1981); author, A Final Promise (University of Nebraska Press, 1984); editor, Indians in American History (Harlan Davidson, 1988); author, The Crow (Chelsea House, 1989); author, Parading Through History: The Making of the Crow Nation in America, 1805-1935 (Cambridge Press, 1995); editor, Encyclopedia of the North American Indians

(Houghton Mifflin, 1996); editor, Talking Back to Civilization: Indian Voices From the Progressive Era (Bedford Books (Boston), 2001); co-editor (with James Merrell and Peter Mancall) American Nations: Encounters in Indian Country, 1850-2000 (Routledge, 2001).

HUBBARD, FREDERICK L.
(hospital director)
Affiliation: San Carlos PHS Indian Hospital, P.O. Box 208, San Carlos, AZ 85550 (602) 475-2371.

HUBBARD, GALEN
(BIA field rep.)
Affiliation: Horton Field Office, Bureau of Indian Affairs, P.O. Box 31, Horton, KS 66439 (785) 486-2161 Fax 486-2515.

HUBBARD, JOHN, JR.
(IHS area director)
Affiliation: Navajo Area IHS, P.O. Box 9020, Window Rock, AZ 86515 (602) 871-5811.

HUBBELL, CLARENCE
(Indian education program coordinator)
Affiliation: Smokey Mountain Elementary School, Indian Education Program, Rt. 1, Box 242 Whittier, NC 28789 (704) 586-2334 Fax 586-5450.

HUBBELL, ROY
(radio station manager)
Affiliation: KTNN-660 AM, Navajo Nation, P.O. Box 2569, Window Rock, AZ 86515 (602) 871-2582.

HUBER, DENNIS
(Indian center director)
Affiliation: North Dakota/South Dakota Native American Business Development Center, 3315 University Dr., Bismarck, ND 58504 (701) 255-3285 Fax 530-0607.

HUDSON, CHARLES M., JR. 1932-
(professor)
Born December 24, 1932, Monterey, Ky. *Education*: University of Kentucky, BA, 1959; University of North Carolina, PhD, 1964. *Principal occupation*: Professor. *Home address*: 740 Floyd Rd., Danielsville, GA 30633 (706) 789-3329. *Affiliation*: Professor of anthropology, 1964-2000, Franklin professor emeritus, 2000-present, University of Georgia, Athens. *Military service*: U.S. Air Force, 1950-53 (Staff Sergeant). *Memberships*: American Anthropological Association; Southern Anthropological Society (president, 1973-74); American Society for Ethnohistory (president, 1992-93). *Awards, honors*: Woodrow Wilson Fellow, 1959-60; senior fellow, Newberry Library, 1977-78; 1991 & 1995 James Mooney Prize, Southern Anthropological Society; Rembert W. Patrick Book Award, Florida Historical Society, 1994. *Interests*: "My primary interest is in the historical anthropology of the Indians of the Southeastern U.S." *Biographical sources*: Joyce Rockwood Hudson, Looking for DeSoto (University of Georgia Press, 1993; Who's Who in the Southeast. *Published works*: The Catawba Nation (University of Georgia Press, 1970); editor, Four Centuries of Southern Indians (University of Georgia Press, 1975); The Southeastern Indians (University of Tennessee Press, 1976; editor, Black Drink: A Native American Tea (University of Georgia Press, 1978); editor, Ethnology of the Southeastern Indians (Garland Publishig, 1985); The Juan Pardo Expeditions (Smithsonian Institution Press, 1990); with Gerald Milanich, Hernando DeSoto and the Indians of Florida (University of Florida Press, 1993); co-editor, with Carmen Tesser, The Forgotten Centuries (University of Georgia Press, 1994); Knights of Spain, Warriors of the Sun (University of Georgia Press, 1997); co-editor, with Robbie Ethridge, The Transformation of the Southeastern Indians, 1540-1760 (University Press of Mississippi, 2002); co-editor, with John C. Guilds, An Early and Strong Sympathy: The Indian Writings of William Gilmore Simms (University of South Carolina Press, 2003); Conversations with the High Priest of Coosa (University of North Carolina Press, 2003).

HUDSON, GAYLA
(Indian education program director)
Affiliation: Allen Public Schools, Indian Education Program, P.O. Box 430, Allen, OK 74825 (405) 857-2419 Fax 857-2636.

HUDSON, LESTER
(BIA education administrator)
Affiliation: Shiprock Agency, Bureau of Indian Affairs,
P.O. Box 3239, Shiprock, NM 87420 (505) 368-4427
ext. 5 Fax 368-4427 ext. 300.

**HUERTA, C. LAWRENCE (Yaqui Pasqua Pueblo)
1924-**
(chancellor emeritus)
Born August 16, 1924, Nogales, Ariz. *Education*: University of Arizona, LLB & JD, 1953. *Principal occupation*: Chancellor emeritus. Resides in Arizona. *Affiliations*: President, United Services of America, Washington, DC, 1962-74; holder of the Chair of Economic
Development, Navajo Community College, Tsaile, AZ,
1974-; Chancellor Emeritus, Navajo Community College, 1975-90. *Other professional posts*: Associate
(Navajo) Tribal attorney; special assistant, Attorney
General (AZ); Commissioner, AZ Industrial Commis-
sion; Judge, Maricopa Superior Court, Phoenix; con-
tract management specialist, U.S. Dept. of Commerce,
Washington, DC. *Community activities*: Founder, Na-
vajo Judicial Systems; founder, American Indian
School of Medicine; U.S. Dept. of State, Washington,
DC (Foreign Service Evaluation/Selection Board).
Memberships: American Indian Society, Washington,
DC; Phi Delta Pi; International Legal Fraternity; AZ
State Bar; NM State Bar; Bar of the DC; U.S. Supreme
Court; Pasqua Yaqui Association; Tsaile Kiwanis Na-
vajo Reservation. *Awards, honors*: Founder, American
Coordinating Council on Political Education; Casey
Club (businessmen) Vesta Club; 3rd Degree Knights
of Columbus. *Interests*: Copyrights, trademarks; stu-
dent of Panama and U.S. Canal Zone; lecturer on
American Indians (North and South America); Indian
law, religion, government; student of Latin American
affairs. *Published works*: Enriquezca Su Vida (self,
1968); Arizona Law & Order (self, 1968).

HUFF, RICHARD
(hospital director)
Affiliation: Sisseton PHS Indian Hospital, P.O.
Box 189, Sisseton, SD 57262 (605) 698-7606.

HUGHBOY, WALTER
(Indian band chief)
Affiliation: Wemindji (Cree) Indian Band, James
Bay, Quebec, Canada J0M 1L0 (819) 978-0254.

HUGHES, JUANITA
(museum curator)
Affiliation: Museum of the Cherokee Indian, U.S. Hwy.
441 North, Box 770-A, Cherokee, NC 18719 (704) 497-
3481.

HUGHES, LANCE
(director)
Affiliation: Native Americans for a Clean Environment,
P.O. Box 1671, Tahlequah, OK 74465 (918) 458-4322.

**HUGHES, LITTLETREE ELIZABETH (Mohawk)
1953-**
(company owner)
Born January 27, 1953, in Onondaga, N.Y. *Address*:
Unknown. *Affiliations*: Owner, The Indian Connection,
Glen Burnie, MD; co-owner, Different (Jewelry Co.),
Baltimore, MD, 1993-. *Other professional post*: Member-Board of Directors, Mid-Atlantic Great Dane Rescue League. *Community activities*: American Indian
Hope Foundation, 1988-; Animal rescue worker for
several local organizations. *Interests*: "Volunteer for
25 years for local humane groups: Bowie SPCA, Mid-
Atlantic Great Dane Rescue League, and Baltimore
Great Dane Rescue League, handling adoptions, rescue work, housechecks, and fundraising.

HUGHTE, PHIL (Zuni) 1954-
(artist - painter)
Born April 27, 1954, Zuni, N.M. *Education*: Northern
Arizona University, BFA, 1980. *Principal occupation*:
Artist - painter. *Address*: P.O. Box 151, Zuni, NM 87327
(505) 782-4920. *Affiliation*: Member, Pueblo of Zuni
Higher Education Committee. *Membership*: Indian Arts
& Crafts Association. *Award*: 1990 Best of Show, The
Zuni Show, Flagstaff, AZ. *Biographical source*: Zuni
Artist Looks At Frank Hamilton Cushing, 43 cartoons
which is a traveling exhibition.

HULETT, TROWEN (Navajo)
(radio station owner)
Affiliation: KABR - 1500 AM, Alamo Navajo School
Board, P.O. Box 907, Magdalena, NM 87825 (505) 854-
2632.

HULL, CHARLES E.
(Indian middle school principal)
Affiliations: Choctaw Central Middle School, 150 Rec-
reation Rd., Philadelphia, MS 39350 (601) 656-8938
Fax 656-7077.

HUME, GAYE (Potawatomi)
(attorney)
Address: 130 S. Woodrow St., Arlington, VA 22204.
Memberships: Native American Bar Association (treasurer); American Bar Association.

**HUMMINGBIRD, JESSE T. (Oklahoma Cherokee)
1952-**
(fine artist)
Born February 12, 1952, Tahlequah, Okla. *Education*:
Middle Tennessee State University, 1970-71; Univer-
sity of Tennessee, 1971-77; The American Academy
of Art in Chicago. *Principal occupation*: Fine artist.
Address: 102 Silver St., Bisbee, AZ 85603 (520) 432-
7305 Fax 432-4306. *Affiliations*: Printer, Peabody College, Nashville, TN, 1975-77; printer, FISI (Banking
Institute), 1977-79; graphic artist, DLM (Chicago &
Dallas), 1979-83; self-employed, 1983-. *Memberships*:
Indian Arts & Crafts Association; Inter-tribal Indian
Ceremonial Association; Southwestern Association for
Indian Arts. *Interests*: As a successful printer, graphic
artist, and commercial illustrator, Jesse pursues both
Cherokee and Native American themes, especially
legends of both Cherokee and other tribes passed to
him. In addition to his original works, he has three full-
color prints and publishes a new notecard/holiday card
annually. "I am a traditionalist-both in spirit and art.
I'm influenced by the nature that's around me. No
matter how difficult, I want people to know I'm proud
of my culture and traditions. I want to preserve what
we have left as I create the new." *Published work*: Pow
Wow Activity Book.

HUNDLEY, DAN
(school principal)
Affiliation: Low Mountain Boarding School, Navajo
Route 65, Chinle, AZ 86503 (520) 725-3308 Fax 725-
3306 Fax 652-3252.

**HUNGRY WOLF, ADOLPH (Natosina-Sun Chief)
(Blackfoot) 1944-**
(writer)
Born February 16, 1944, Southern Germany. *Educa-
tion*: California State University, Long Beach, BA. *Ad-
dress*: Box 844, Skookumchuck, BC V0B 2E0, Canada.
Membership: Blackfoot Crazy Dogs Society. *Published
works*: Good Medicine book series; The Blood People
- A Division of the Blackfoot Confederacy (Harper &
Row, 1977); Shadows of the Buffalo - A Family Odys-
sey Among the Indians, with Beverly Hungry Wolf
(William Morrow & Co., 1983); Canadian Railway
Scenes, 5 Vols. (Canadian Caboose Press, 1983, '85,
'86, '91, '97); Children of the Sun - Stories By and
About Indian Kids, with Beverly Hungry Wolf (William
Morrow & Co., 1987); Indian Tribes of the Northern
Rockies, with Beverly Hungry Wolf (William Morrow &
Co., 1987); Children of the Circle, with Star Hungry
Wolf (Good Medicine Books, 1992); et al.

HUNGRY WOLF, BEVERLY
(writer)
Address: Box 844, Skookumchuck, BC V0B 2E0,
Canada. *Published works*: The Ways of My Grand-
mother (William Morrow & Co., 1980); Shadows of the
Buffalo - A Family Odyssey Among the Indians, with
Adolph Hungry Wolf (William Morrow & Co., 1983);
Children of the Sun - Stories by and about Indian Kids,
with Adolph Hungry Wolf (William Morrow & Co., 1987).

HUNKLER, SAM, M.D.
(clinical director)
Affiliation: Metlakatla Indian Community Health Center, P.O. Box 439, Metlakatla, AK 99926 (907) 886-
4741.

HUNN, EUGENE S. 1943-
(professor of anthropology)
Born April 23, 1943, Louisville, KY. *Education*: Stanford

University, BA, 1964; University of California, Berkeley, MA, 1970, PhD, 1973. *Principal occupation*: Professor of anthropology. *Home address*: 1816 N. 57th
St., Seattle, WA 98103 (206) 524-8112. *Affiliation*:
Dept. of Anthropology, University of Washington, Seattle, WA 1972-. *Memberships*: American Anthropological Association; Society of Ethnobiology. *Awards,
honors*: Fellow, American Association for the Advancement of Science. *Interests*: Mayan Indian ethnobiology;
Sahaptin (Columbia River Plateau) Indian Ethno-biol-
ogy, language and culture, history, and ecology; Alaskan Native subsistence and national parks. *Published
works*: Tzeltal Folk Zoology: The Classification of
Discontinuities in Nature (Academic Press, 1977); co-
edited with Nancy M. Williams, Resource Managers:
North American & Australian Hunter-Gatherers
(Westview/Australian Institute of Aboriginal Studies,
1982, '86); Nch'i-Wana 'The Big River': with James
Selam, Mid-Columbia Indians & Their Land (University of Washington Press, 1990)

HUNT, ALFRED (Kwakiutl)
(Indian band chief)
Affiliation: Kwakiutl Indian Band, 395A Kinchant St.,
Box 1440, Port Hardy, British Columbia, Canada V0N
2P0 (604) 949-6012.

HUNT, ELI O. (Chippewa)
(tribal chairperson)
Affiliation: Leech Lake Reservation Business Committee, Route 3, Box 100, Cass Lake, MN 56633 (218)
335-8200.

HUNT, KATHERINE
(program director)
Affiliation: Institute of Alaska Native Arts, P.O. Box
70769, Fairbanks, AK 99707 (907) 456-7491 Fax 451-
7268.

HUNT, MARK A.
(museum/mission director)
Affiliations: Kansas Museum of History, Kansas State
Historical Society, 6425 SW 6th, Topeka, KS 66615;
Shawnee Methodist Mission, 3403 West 53rd,
Shawnee Mission, KS 66205 (913) 262-0867; Iowa,
Sac and Fox Presbyterian Mission, Route 1, Box 152C,
Highland, KS 66035 (913) 442-3304.

HUNT, MICHAEL (Eskimo)
(AK village president)
Affiliation: Native Village of Kotlik, P.O. Box 20096,
Larsen Bay, AK 99620 (907) 899-4326.

HUNT, TERRY (Sunboy) (Laguna-Acoma)
(craftsperson)
Address: Sunboy Gallery, 708 Canyon Rd. #3, Santa
Fe, NM 87501 (505) 983-3042 or 266-8900. *Products*:
Pueblo Indian jewelry and wood sculpture.

HUNTER, ALICE
(director-Indian centre)
Affiliation: Port Alberni Friendship Centre, 3178 - 2nd
Ave., Box 23, Port Alberni, B.C., Canada V9Y 4C3
(604) 723-8281.

HUNTER, ANTHONY (Shinnecock) 1959-
(registered nurse)
Born June 28, 1959, Queens, N.Y. *Education*:
LaGuardia Commuity College, AAS, 1986; Hunter
College, BSN, 1989. *Principal occupation*: Registered
nurse. *Address & Affiliation*: American Indian Commu-
nity House, 404 Lafayette St., 2nd Floor, New York,
NY 10003 (212) 598-0100 (director, health program,
1992-). *Community activities*: Board of Directors,
American Indian Community House, 1982-. *Awards,
honors*: Member of the United Nations NGO Commit-
tee for the 1993 International Year of Indigenous
People. *Interests*: "Certified in psychiatric and mental
health nursing by the American Nurses Association.
Currently pursuing Master of Public Health (MPH)
Degree in Intenational Commuity Helth Education at
NYU. Hobby - genealogical research."

HUNTER, GERRY
(Indian band chief)
Affiliation: Halfway River Indian Band, P.O. Box 59,
Wonowon, British Columbia, Canada V0C 2N0 (604)
787-4452.

HUNTER, HENRY (Eskimo)
(native council president)
Affiliation: Orutsaramuit Native Council (aka Bethel), 835 Ridgecrest Dr., Bethel, AK 99559 (907) 543-2608.

HUNTER, IRMA (Yokut)
(former tribal chairperson)
Affiliation: Tule River Reservation, P.O. Box 589, Porterville, CA 93258 (209) 781-4271.

HUNTER, JOHN D.
(monument supt.)
Affiliation: Bandelier National Monument, HCR 1 Box 1, Rte. 4, Suite 15, Los Alamos, NM 87544 (505) 672-3861.

HUNTER, JULIUS ANDREW (*EagleHawk*)
(Meherren) 1947-
(mortician)
Born December 25, 1947, Ahoskie, N.C. *Education*: North Carolina Central University, B.Sc., 1969; American Academy McAllister (New York City), MS, 1971. *Principal occupation*: Mortician. *Home address*: P.O. Box 973, Ahoskie, NC 27910 (919) 332-4923 Fax 332-7580. *Affiliations*: Owner, Hunter's Funeral Home, Ahoskie, NC & Rich Square, NC, 1974-; owner, Meherrin/Shinnecock Traders, Ahoskie, NC, 1992-. *Community activities*: Council Chairman, Meherrin Indian Tribe; Councilman, Town of Ahoskie; member, Board of Directors, United Tribes of North Carolina. *Memberships*: National Funeral Directors & Embalmers Association; North Carolina & Virginia Funeral Directors & Embalmers Association; Kappa Alpha Psi Frat. *Biographical sources*: Who's Who Among Outstanding Professionals; 2000 Notable American Men.

HUNTER, MICHAEL (Delaware)
(tribal vice president)
Affiliation: Delaware Executive Committee, P.O. Box 825, Anadarko, OK 73005 (405) 247-2448.

HUNTER, PRISCILLA (Pomo)
(tribal chairperson)
Affiliation: Coyote Valley Reservation, P.O. Box 39, Redwood Valley, CA 95470 (707) 485-8723.

HUNTER, RAYMOND, (Dieguено)
(tribal chairperson)
Affiliation: Jamul Band of Mission Indians, P.O. Box 612, Jamul, CA 91935 (619) 669-4785.

HUNTER, ROBERT L.
(BIA agency supt.)
Affiliation: Western Nevada Agency, Bureau of Indian Affairs, 1677 Hot Springs Rd., Carson City, NV 89706 (775) 887-3500 Fax 702-3531.

HUNTER, TERRY
(chief executive officer)
Address & Affiliation: Oklahoma City Indian Health Clinic, 4913 W. Reno, Oklahoma City, OK 73127 (405) 948-4900. *Past professional post*: Executive director, Association of American Indian Physicians, Oklahoma City, OK.

HURD, LAURA I.
(Indian education program director)
Affiliation: Sapulpa Public Schools, Indian Education Program, 3 So. Mission, Sapulpa, OK 74066 (918) 224-9322 Fax 224-0174.

HURLBERT, CHARLES
(BIA agency supt.)
Affiliation: Osage Agency, Bureau of Indian Affairs, P.O. Box 1539, Pawhuska, OK 74056 (918) 287-1032 Fax 287-4320

HURLEY, MARIANNE (Coeur d' Alene)
(storyteller)
Address: P.O. Box 8, Worley, ID 83876 (208) 274-5050. Marianne is a storyteller and performer of traditional songs of the Coeur d' Alene people of Northern Utah. She is an educator specializing in Native American arts & crafts, and focuses on Native American cultural values.

HURTADO, DENNY (Skokomish)
(tribal chairperson)
Affiliation: Skokomish Tribal Council, N. 80 Tribal Center Rd., Shelton, WA 98584 (360) 426-4232.

HUSSION, JOSEPH
(health center director)
Affiliation: Dulce PHS Indian Health Center, P.O. Box 187, Dulce, NM 87528 (505) 759-3291.

HUTCHINS, DEAN K. (*Yansv Gvnage-Black Buffalo*)
(Cherokee-Keetoowah) 1951-
(writer, poet, videographer)
Born November 1, 1951, Bronx, N.Y. *Education*: Queens College (Queens, NY); Manhattan College (New York, NY). *Principal occupation*: Writer, poet, videographer. *Address*: P.O. Box 462, Nyack, NY 10960 (914) 582-4020 Fax (845) 352-2648. E-mail: yansvgvnage@aol.com. Website: www.deanhutchins productions.com. *Affiliations*: President, Nighthawk Communications (video production company). *Other professional posts*: Freelance videographer and writer. *Community activities*: Served on the Board of the Native American Education Program of New York City, including two years as Chairperson; member, Rockland Coalition for Undoing Racism. He is active in New York's traditional Keetoowah community and produces television programs of interest to the Native community for cable television. *Memberships*: Wordcraft Circle; Native American Journalists Association; Fellowship of Reconciliation. *Interests*: Hutchins worked in the computer industry for over 30 years, developing computer systems and methodologies for both government agencies and Fortune 500 corporations. He was the prime architect of systems methodologies for such companies as IBM and McDonald's. He has taught technical seminars at NYU and for companies all over the U.S., Canada, Mexico and Europe. His interest in communications gave him a second career as a writer. His poetry has been published in "Talking Stick" and "Native Realities." He has appeared at the biannual People's Poetry Gathering in New York City and has been a featured speaker at the American Museum of Natural History, the Native American Video Cultural Festival, The Nuyorican Poets Cafe, the American Indian Community House in New York City, Queens (NY) Public Television, and Pacifica Radio, and the United Nations.

HUTCHINS, JEANETTE L.
(museum director/curator)
Affiliation: Chief Oshkosh Museum, 7631 Egg Harbor Rd., Egg Harbor, WI 54209 (414) 868-3240.

HUTCHINSON, DOUGLAS W.
(executive director)
Affiliation: Oregon Commission on Indian Services, 454 State Capitol, Salem, OR 97310 (503) 986-1067.

HUTCHISON, DAALBAALEH (Navajo)
(health director)
Affiliation: Shiprock PHS Indian Hospital, P.O. Box 160, Shiprock, NM 87420 (505) 368-4971.

HUTCHISON, SARAH (Oklahoma Cherokee)
(professor emeritus; marriage & family counselor)
Affiliation: Native American Studies Program, University of California, Davis, 2401 Hart Hall, Davis, CA 95616 (916) 752-3237.

I

IGNACE, RONALD ERIC
(Indian band chief)
Affiliations: Skeetchestn Indian Band, Box 178, Savona, B.C. Can. V0K 3J0 (604) 373-2493; co-chair, Simon Fraser University, The Secwepeme Cultural Education Society, 345 Yellowhead Hwy., Kamloops, B.C., Can. V2H 1H1 (604) 374-0616.

IKE, FELIX (Te-Moak Shoshone)
(tribal chairperson)
Affiliation: Te-Moak Tribe of Western Shoshone, 525 Sunset St., Elko, NV 89801 (775) 738-9251.

IMOTICHEY, PAUL
(association director)
Affiliation: Native American Indian Association of Tennessee, 932 Stahlman Bldg., 211 Union St., Nashville, TN 37201 (615) 726-0806.

IMPSON, ROBERT
(BIA agency supt.)
Affiliation: Chickasaw Agency, Bureau of Indian Affairs, P.O. Box 2240, Ada, OK 74821 (405) 436-0784 Fax 436-3215.

INCOGUITO, ELAINE (Sioux)
(school administrator)
Affiliation: Twin Buttes Day School, Route 1, Box 65, Halliday, ND 58636 (701) 938-4396.

INMAN, ESTELLE
(museum director)
Affiliation: Kwagiulth Museum, P.O. Box 8, Quathiaski Cove, BC, Canada V0P 1N0.

INNES, PAM (Creek)
(professor of Native American studies)
Affiliation: Native American Studies Program, University of Oklahoma, 455 W. Lindsey, Rm. 804, Norman, OK 73019 (405) 325-2312.

INNUKSUK, RHONDA
(association president)
Affiliation: Inuit Tapirisat of Canada, 176 Gloucester St., 3rd Floor, Ottawa, Ontario, Canada K2P 0A6 (613) 238-8181.

INOUYE, DANIEL (Hawaiian)
(U.S. Senator, D-HI)
Affiliation: Vice-chairperson (former chairperson), Senate Select Committee on Indian Affairs, 838 Hart Senate Office Bldg., Washington, DC 20510 (202) 224-2251.

INTERPRETER, RAY
(BIA education administrator)
Affiliation: Fort Apache Agency, Bureau of Indian Affairs, P.O. Box 560, White River, AZ (520) 338-5441 Fax 338-1944.

IRON, FRANK
(Indian band chief)
Affiliation: Canoe Lake Indian Band, Canoe Narrows, Saskatchewan, Canada S0M 0K0 (306) 829-2150.

IRWIN, KENNETH D., SR. (*Two Mans*)
(Mandan, Hidatsa, Arikara)
(Indian center chairperson)
Born on the Fort Berthold Reservation, N.D. *Education*: Standing Rock Indian School, Wahpeton Indian School, White Shield Indian School, Flandreau Indian School. *Principal occupation*: CEO/Chair, OCNAA. *Home address*: Ohio Center for Native Americans, 7916 Braun Rd., Groveport, OH 43125-9405. *Affiliations*: CEO/Chair, Ohio Center for Native American Affairs (OCNAA), Columbus, OH; president, Ohio Council for Native American Burial Rights - Ohio Indian Movement, Columbus, OH. *Other professional post*: Irwin-Ruffini Committee (drafting bill for Ohio to coincide with Federal-Native American Grave Protection & Repatriation Act. *Community activities*: Coorinator of the Eastern Region of the American Indian Movement. Has hosted the last two Eastern Regional AIM Conferences in Columbus, OH. *Awards, honors*: Appointed by the Ohio Supreme Court and has served on the Ohio Commission on Racial Fairness as a Commission member. *Interests*: "Indian rights activist including protection of Indian religious freedom, Indian grave protection and repatriation, cultural protection and education. Reburial of ancient ancestors; spiritual rights of prisoners; Indian Child Welfare Act issues; sports mascot issue; issues relating to alcohol/substance abuse prevention/treatment, *Published works*: Contributed as a consultant to the development of a handbook used by the Ohio Dept. of Corrections in dealing with various religious issues relating to the prisoner population.

IRWIN, MICHAEL
(special staff assistant)
Affiliation: Alaska Office of the Governor, P.O. Box A, Juneau, AK 99811 (907) 465-3500.

ISAAC, CALVIN JAMES (Choctaw) 1933-
(Indian school principal)
Born December 5, 1933, Philadelphia, Miss. *Education*: Delta State University, BA (Music Education), 1954. *Principal occupation*: Education. *Address*: Conehatta Elementary School, 851 Tushka Dr.,

Conehatta, MS 39057 (601) 775-8254 Fax 775-9229. *Affiliations*: Education specialist, Title I, BIA, Philadelphia, MS, 1972-75; former tribal chief, Mississippi Band of Choctaw Indians, Philadelphia, MS, 1975-80; principal, Bogue Chitto Day School, Philadelphia, MS, 1980-94; principal, Conehatta Elementary School, Conehatta, MS, 1994-present. *Other professional posts*: Director, Choctaw Head Start Program, Service Unit director; teacher supervisor (elementary), BIA; education specialist (fine arts). *Military service*: U.S. Dept. of Defense, Army. *Community activities*: Choctaw Housing Authority (chairman); Choctaw Advisory School Board (chairman); Policy Advisory Council (tribal representative). *Memberships*: Mississippi State Advisory Committee, 1975-; United Southeastern Tribes, Inc., 1975-; National Tribal Chairman's Association, 1975-; Governor's Colonel Staff, 1976-; Governors Multicultural Advisory Council, 1976-. *Awards, honors*: John Hay Whitney Fellowship Scholar, 1967-68; Phi Delta Kappa, Mississippi State University, 1976; Omicron Delta Kappa, Delta State University, 1975.

ISAAC, NICK (Athapascan)
(AK village council president)
Affiliation: Native Village of Ohogamiut, Fortuna Ledge, AK 99585 (907) 679-6740.

ISAAC, VERNON (Cayuga)
(tribal chief)
Affiliation: Cayuga Indian Nation, P.O. Box 11, Versailles, NY 14168 (716) 532-4847.

ISNANA, MELVIN
(Indian band chief)
Affiliation: Standing Buffalo Indian Band, Box 128, Fort Qu-Appelle, SK, Canada S0G 1S0 (306) 332-4685.

IVAN, IVAN M. (Yup'ik Eskimo)
(state legislator)
Affiliation: Alaska State Legislature, Pouch V, Juneau, AK 99801.

IVAN, OWEN (Yup'ik Eskimo)
(AK village president)
Affiliation: Akiak Native Village, P.O. Box 52165, Akiak, AK 99552 (907) 765-7112.

IVANOFF, HENRY
(radio station manager)
Affiliation: KNSA-AM, P.O. Box 178, Unalakleet, AK 99684 (907) 624-3101.

IVERSON, PETER 1944-
(professor of history)
Born April 4, 1944, Whittier, Calif. *Education*: Carleton College, BA, 1967; University of Wisconsin-Madison, MA, 1969, PhD, 1975. *Principal occupation*: Professor of history. *Affiliation & Address*: Dept. of History, Arizona State University (1988-present), Box 872501, Tempe, AZ 85287-2501 (480) 965-0032 Fax 965-0310; E-mail: peter.iverson@asu.edu. *Community activities*: Advisory Board, American Indian Studies, Arizona State University; member of Heard Museum (Phoenix) and Museum of Northern Arizona (Flagstaff). *Memberships*: Western History Association; American Society for Ethnohistory; Organization of American Historians. *Fellowships*: NEH Fellowship for Research, 1999-2000; Johnn Simon Guggenheim Memorial Foundation for Research, May 2000 to Jan. 2001. *Awards, prizes*: Chief Manuelito Award for Contribution to Navajo Education, 1984; Carleton College Alumni Association Award for Distinguished Achievement, 1992. *Published works*: The Navajos: A Critical Bibliography (Indiana University Press, 1976); Carlos Montezuma and the Changing World of American Indians (University of New Mexico Press, 1982); The Navajo Nation (University of New Mexico, 1983); edited, The Plains Indians of the 20th Century (University of Oklahoma Press, 1985); The Navajos (Chelsea House, 1990); The Plains Indians of the Twentieth Century (University of Oklahoma Press, 1992); When Indians Became Cowboys: Native Peoples & Cattle Ranching in the American West (University of Oklahoma Press, 1994); edited with Albert Hurtado, Major Problems in American Indian History (D.C. Heath, 1994); We Are Still Here: American Indians in the 20th Century (Harlan Davidson, 1998); edited with Frederick Hoxie, Indians in American History, 2nd Ed. (Harlan Davidson, 1998); Riders of the West: Portraits From Indian Rodeo (University of Washington Press, 1999).

IVEY, G.H.
(health services director)
Affiliation: Alaska Area Native Health Services, Indian Health Service, 250 Gambell St., Third & Gambell St., Anchorage, AK 99510 (907) 257-1153.

J

JABBOUR, ALAN ALBERT 1942-
(archivist)
Born June 21, 1942, Jacksonville, Fla. *Education*: University of Miami, BA, 1963; Duke University, MA, 1966, PhD, 1968. *Principal occupation*: Archivist. *Home address*: 3107 Cathedral Ave., NW, Washington, DC 20540 (202) 707-6590 (office). *Affiliations*: Head, Archive of Folk Song, Library of Congress, 1969-74; head, Folk Arts Program, National Endowment for the Arts, Washington, DC, 1974-76; director, The American Folklife Center, Library of Congress, Washington, DC, 1976- (the Center engages in the preservation, presentation & dissemination of American folk cultural traditions, and contributes to the cultural planning & programming of the Library, federal government and the nation); chairperson, Fund for Folk Culture, 1991-. *Memberships*: American Folklore Society; Society for Ethnomusicology; John Edwards Memorial Foundation (advisor); American Folklife Center (member, board of trustees). *Awards, honors*: Phi Beta Kappa; University of Miami Music Scholarship, 1959-62; Woodrow Wilson Fellowship, 1963; Duke University Scholarship, 1964-66; Danforth Teaching Fellowship, 1966-68; responsible for the initiation of one of the Library's American Revolution Bicentennial projects, an anthology of 15 long-playing records containing examples of major folk music traditions of the U.S. — Anglo-American, Afro-American, American Indian, and other rural and urban ethnic groups. The series is called, Folk Music in America. *Interests*: Folk music & song; folklore; medieval English literature; musicology; American studies. *Published works*: Numerous papers presented & published.

JACK, AMBROSE (Yakima)
(former BIA agency supt.)
Affiliation: Yakima Agency, BIA, P.O. Box 632, Toppenish, WA 98948 (509) 865-2255.

JACK, ANTHONY (Pomo)
(rancheria chairperson)
Affiliation: Big Valley Rancheria, 2726 Mission Rancheria Rd., Lakeport, CA 95453 (707) 263-3924.

JACK, ARCHIE
(Indian band chief)
Affiliation: Penticton Indian Band, RR 2, Site 80, Comp. 19, Penticton, BC, Canada V2A 6J7 (604) 493-0048.

JACK, EARL WILBUR
(Indian band chief)
Affiliation: Penelakut Indian Band, Box 360, Chemainus, BC, Canada V0K 1K0 (604) 246-2321.

JACK, KATHERINE (Ojibway)
(Indian band chief)
Affiliation: Ojibways of Onegaming Band, Box 160, Nestor Falls, ON, Canada P0X 1N0 (807) 484-2162.

JACK, PIUS
(Indian band chief)
Affiliation: Nee-Tahi-Buhn Indian Band, RR 2, Box 28, Burns Lake, BC, Canada V0J 1E0 (604) 694-3301.

JACK, SYLVESTER, Sr. (Tlingit)
(Indian band chief)
Affiliation: Taku River Tlingit Indian Band, Box 132, Atlin, B.C., Canada V0W 1A0 (403) 651-7615.

JACK, VALENTINO (Pomo)
(tribal council chairperson)
Affiliation: Big Valley Rancheria, P.O. Box 430, Lakeport, CA 95453 (707) 263-3924.

JACKA, JERRY
(photographer, illustrator)
Born and raised on ranches north of Phoenix, Ariz. *Address*: c/o Northland Publishing, P.O. Box 1389, Flagstaff, AZ 86002. *Awards*: Western Heritage Award, best art book for 1988, "Beyond Traditions"; and, Emmy Award in Cultural Documentary for video version of "Beyond Traditions". *Published works*: Photographs

for: "Beyond Tradition: Contemporary Indian Art and Its Evolution," with Lois Jacka (Northland Publishing, 1988); "David Johns; on the Trail of Beauty" (Snailspace Publication, 1991); "Enduring Traditions: Art of the Navajo," with Lois Jacka (Northland Publishing, 1994); "Navajo Jewelry: A Legacy of Silver & Stone" (Northland Publishing, 1995). Illustrated seven books and four special issues of "Arizona Highway" on Native American art.

JACKA, LOIS
(writer)
Born and raised on ranches north of Phoenix, Ariz. *Address*: c/o Northland Publishing, P.O. Box 1389, Flagstaff, AZ 86002. *Awards*: Western Heritage Award, best art book for 1988, "Beyond Traditions"; and, Emmy Award in Cultural Documentary for video version of "Beyond Traditions." *Published works*: "Beyond Tradition: Contemporary Indian Art and Its Evolution," with Jerry Jacka (Northland Publishing, 1988); David Johns: On the Trail of Beauty (Snailspace Publication, 1991); Enduring Traditions: Art of the Navajo (with Jerry Jacka) (Northland Publishing, 1994); "Navajo Jewelry: A Legacy of Silver & Stone" (Northland Publishing, 1995). Articles for "Arizona Highway" and other magazines.

JACKSON, CRAIG (Tlingit)
(craftsperson)
Affiliation: Owner, Indian Arts, P.O. Box 85273, Las Vegas, NV 89185. *Products*: Jewelry with semi-precious stones, dream catcher necklaces; baskets.

JACKSON, DIXIE (Chukchansi)
(rancheria chairperson)
Affiliation: Picayune Rancheria of Chukchansi, 46575 Road 417, Coarsegold, CA 93614 (559) 683-6633.

JACKSON, EDGAR (Eskimo)
(AK village council president)
Affiliation: Shaktoolik Native Village, P.O. Box 100, Shaktoolik, AK 99771 (907) 955-3701.

JACKSON, FRANCES
(historic site president)
Affiliation: The Chief John Ross House, P.O. Box 863, Rossville, GA 30741 (404) 861-3954.

JACKSON, GALILA
(BIA field rep.)
Affiliation: Concho Field Office, Bureau of Indian Affairs, P.O. Box 68, El Reno, OK 73005 (405) 262-7481 Fax 262-3140.

JACKSON, GORDON
(BIA agency supt.)
Affiliation: Crow Agency, Bureau of Indian Affairs, Crow Agency, MT 59022 (406) 638-2672.

JACKSON, HARRY
(school chairperson)
Affiliation: Mariano Lake Community School, P.O. Box 787, Crownpoint, NM 87313 (505) 786-5265 Fax 786-5203.

JACKSON, JERRY (Choctaw)
(tribal chief)
Affiliation: Jena Band of Choctaws, P.O. Box 14, Jena, LA 71342 (318) 992-2717.

JACKSON, KEN (*Grey Eagle*)
(storyteller)
Address: Sacred Circle Storytellers, 3810 Hubble Ct., Clinton, WA 98236 (206) 324-0071. He provides educational storytelling, cultural workshops and sharing circle ceremonies. Ken has performed in many countries and contexts. He also offers training in storytelling and theatre.

JACKSON, LOIS
(BIA agency supt.)
Affiliation: Sisseton Agency, Bureau of Indian Affairs, P.O. Box 688, Agency Village, SD 57262 (605) 698-3001 Fax 698-7784.

JACKSON, LOOMIS (Pit River)
(tribal chairperson)
Affiliation: Pit River Tribal Council, P.O Drawer 70, Burney, CA 96013 (916) 335-5421.

JACKSON, LOUIE
(counselor)
Affiliation: Bacone College, 2299 Old Bacone Rd., Muskogee, OK 74403 (918) 683-4581.

JACKSON, MARTHA
(Indian center instructor)
Affiliation: Center for Dine Studies, Dine (Navajo) College, P.O. Box 126, Tsaile, AZ 86556 (520) 724-6671 Fax 724-3327.

JACKSON, MIKE, JR. (Quechen)
(tribal president)
Affiliation: Quechen Tribal Council, Fort Yuma Reservation, P.O. Box 1899, Yuma, AZ 85366 (760) 572-0213.

JACKSON, WILLIAM R. *(Rattlesnake)*
(Cherokee) 1928-
(retired principal chief)
Born December 23, 1928, Moultrie, GA. *Principal occupation*: Retired principal chief of American Cherokee Confederacy (formerly Southeastern Cherokee Confederacy). *Address*: American Cherokee Confederacy, 619 Pine Cone Rd., Albany, GA 31705-6906 (229) 787-5722 (phone & fax). *Affiliations*: Retired Marine Corps Logistics, Albany, GA, 1964-89; principal chief, American Cherokee Confederacy, Albany, GA, 1976-. *Military service*: U.S. Army, 1950-52 (Korean War Medal); retired Marine Corps Logistics Base, Albany, GA 1964-89. *Community activities*: Hold monthly clan meetings for local members of the Rattlesnake Clan (formerly the Eagle Clan) in Albany, GA and surrounding area; two meetings each year for all members. *Memberships*: American Legion; VFW; American Cherokee Confederacy, 1976-. *Awards, honors*: Letter of Appreciation, 25-Year Service Awards with Civil Service; Safety Awards. "I have personally received a Proclamation from ex-governor of Georgia, George Busbee." *Interests*: Fishing and raising chickens, annual meetings, and pow-wows. *Publication*: Ex-editor of the American Cherokee Confederacy Newsletter.

JACOB, IGNATI (Eskimo)
(AK council president)
Affiliation: Oscarville Traditional Council, P.O. Box 1554, Oscarville, AK 99559 (907) 737-7321.

JACOBS, ADRIAN
(director)
Affiliation: Wesleyan Native American Ministries, P.O. Box 7038, Rapid City, SD 57709 (605) 343-9054.

JACOBS, ALEX A. *(Karoniaktatie)* **(Mohawk) 1953-**
(writer, artist, editor)
Born February 28, 1953, Akwesasne Reservation, via Rooseveltown, N.Y. *Education*: Institute of American Indian Arts, Santa Fe, N.M., AFA (sculpture, creative writing), 1977; Kansas City Art Institute, BFA (sculpture, creative writing), 1979. *Address*: Resides in Albuquerque, NM. *Affiliations*: Editor, Akwesasne Notes, via Rooseveltown, N.Y., 1979-1985; editor, Akwekon Literary Journal, Akwesasne Notes, Hogansburg, N.Y., 1985-91; instructor, University of New Mexico, Albuquerque, 1991-. *Other professional posts*: Board of directors, CKON-F, Radio Station, Mohawk Nation. *Awards, honors*: 1975 poetry award, Scottsdale National Indian Art Exhibit; 1979 honorable mention, Society of Western Art, Kansas City, Mo. *Interests*: Poetry, prose, short stories; graphic arts; sculpture; painting, printmaking; ceramics; video/audio/performance art; editor of Native American literature and journalism; networking national and international native peoples; poetry readings and workshops; travel U.S.A. with White Roots of Peace, 1973-74 (native touring group/communications). Published works: Native Colours (Akwesasne Notes, 1974); Landscape: Old & New Poems (Blue Cloud Quarterly, 1984); Anthologies: Come to Power, The Remembered Earth, The Next World, 3rd World Writers, and Songs From the Earth on Turtle's Back, in various literary magazines, 1972-1985; editor, Akwekon Literary Journal, 1985-91.

JACOBS, CARMEN
(BIA agency supt.)
Affiliation: Standing Rock Agency, Bureau of Indian Affairs, P.O. Box E, Fort Yates, ND 58538 (701) 854-3433 Fax 854-7184.

JACOBS, JOSEPH (Mohawk/Cherokee) 1947-
(NIH program director)
Born in 1947. Resides in Guilford, CT. *Education*: Yale Medical School, MD, 1974; Wharton School of Business, University of Pennsylvania, MBA, 1985. *Address & Affiliation*: Director, Office of Alternative Medicine, National Institutes of Health, Bethesda, MD, 1992-. *Past professional posts*: Pediatrician, Indian Medical Center, Gallup, NM; U.S. Public Health Service, Rockville, MD; Aetna Life Insurance Co., Hartford, CT.

JACOBS, L. DAVID (Mohawk)
(tribal chief)
Affiliation: St. Regis Mohawk Council Chiefs, Akwesasne-Community Bldg., Hogansburg, NY 13655 (518) 358-2272.

JACOBSEN, REMONIIA I. (Iowa-Otoe-Missouria)
(craftsperson; company owner)
Affiliation: Monkapeme, P.O. Box 457, Perkins, OK 74059 (405) 547-2948. *Products*: Custom-made contemporary fashions featuring Native Ameican mootifs.

JACOBSEN, WILLIAM H., JR. 1931-
(professor of linguistics)
Born November 15, 1931, San Diego, Calif. *Education*: Harvard University, AB, 1953; University of California, Berkeley, PhD, 1964. *Principal occupation*: Professor of linguistics, University of Nevada, 1965-. *Home address*: 1411 Samuel Way, Reno, NV 89509. *Memberships*: Linguistic Society of America; International Linguistic Association; Society for the Study of the Indigenous Languages of the Americas (vice-president, 1991, president, 1992); American Anthropological Association; Society for Linguistic Anthropology; Great Basin Anthropological Conference. *Awards, honors*: Outstanding Researcher Award, University of Nevada, Reno, 1983. *Interests*: American Indian languages, primarily Washo and Makah, and the Hokan and Wakashan families; also, fieldwork or publication on Salinan, Yana, Nootka, Nez Perce, Numic, and Chimakuan. *Published works*: First Lessons in Makah (Makah Cultural & Research Center, revised ed. 1999); Beginning Washo (Nevada State Museum, 1996).

JACOBSON, CRAIG A.
(attorney)
Education: University of oregon, BA; Northwestern School of Law of Lewis & Clark College, J.D., 1995; Certificate in Environmental & Natural Resources Law. *Principal occupation*: Attorney. *Address & Affiliation*: Hobbs, Straus, Dean & Walker, LLP, 851 S.W. Sixth Ave., Suite 1650, Portland, OR 97204 (503) 242-1745 Fax 242-1072, 1998-present. E-mail: caj_hsdwor@hotmail.com. *Past professional post*: Prior to joining HSDW, Mr. Jacobson was a sole practitioner focusing on environmental issues in Indian country, Title IV Self-governance (both BIA and non-BIA), and Indian Health Service related issues. Presently, he specializes in environmental and natural resources law and policy issues in Indian country.

JACOX, SHARON
(executive director)
Affiliation: National Native American Purchasing Association, P.O. Box 309, Willamina, OR 97396 (503) 876-3307.

JACQUES, RONALD
(Indian band chief)
Affiliation: Restigouche Indian Band, 17 Riverside W., Restigouche, QB, Can G0C 2R0 (418) 788-2136.

JAEGER, JERRY L.
(BIA area director)
Affiliation: Aberdeen Area Office, Bureau of Indian Affairs, Federal Bldg., 115 Fourth Ave., SE, Aberdeen, SD 57401 (605) 226-7343.

JAEGER, ROBERT R.
(BIA agency supt.)
Affiliation: Great Lakes Agency, Bureau of Indian Affairs, 615 Main St. W., Ashland, WI 54806 (715) 682-4527. E-mail: robertjaeger@bia.gov.

JAEGER, RONALD M.
(BIA regional director)
Affiliation: Pacific Regional Office, Bureau of Indian Affairs, Federal Office Bldg., 2800 Cottage Way, Sacramento, CA 95825 (916) 978-6000 Fax 978-6099.

JAENEN, CORNELIUS J. 1927-
(professor emeritus)
Born February 21, 1927, Cannington Manor, Saskatchewan, Canada. *Education*: University of Manitoba, Winnipeg, BA, 1947, MA, 1950, BEd, 1958; University of Ottawa, Ontario, PhD, 1963; University of Winnipeg, LLD, 1982. *Principal occupation*: Professor emeritus. *Home address*: 9 Elma St., Gloucester, ON K1T 3W8 (613) 521-0167. *Affiliations*: Assistant & associate professor of history, United College (now University of Winnipeg), 1959-67; Associate and full professor of history, 1967-92, professor emeritus, 1992-present, University of Ottawa. *Community activities*: Canadian Consultative Council on Multiculturalism; Native Awareness Program of Department of External Affairs (Ottawa). *Memberships*: American Society for Ethnohistory; Canadian Historical Association, 1952- (council member, 1987-91; vice-president, 1987-88; president, 1988-89); Social Science Federation of Canada (council member, 1987-90); Institut d'histoire de l'Amerique francaise, 1952- (council member, 1979-81); French Colonial Historical Society (vice president; president, 1986-89); Canadian Ethnic Studies Association (founding president, 1971-73, councilor, 1971-); Royal Society of Canada (secretary); (board of directors-Historica Foundation. *Awards, honors*: Ste. Marie Prize in Canadian History , 1974, for Friend and Foe, awarded by Ministry of Culture, Government of Ontario; also Book Prize of the French Colonial Historical Society in 1976. LLD honoris causa from University of Winnipeg, 1981, in recognition of work on minorities, ethnic groups, Native peoples; J.B. Tyrell Medal in History, Royal Society of Canada, 1994; Distinguished Professor Award, Canadian Historical Association, 1996; Officer of the Order of Leopold II (Belgium); Lifetime Achievement Award, Canadian Ethnic Studies Association, 2003. *Interests*: Visiting professor in Canada, India, France, Belgium, and Italy dealing with French colonization, Native peoples, ethnicity. Participant in international congresses in Paris, Bucharest, Budapest, Fort-de-France, Pondichery, Taipai, Bordeaux, Toulouse, and Brussels dealing with North American Indian issues. *Biographical sources*: Dictionary of International Biography; International Who's Who in Community Service; International Who's Who in Education; A Bibliographical Directory of Canadian Scholars; International Book of Honor; Who Who in Canada. *Published works*: Friend and Foe: Aspects of French-Amerindian Cultural Contact in the Sixteenth and Seventeenth Centuries (Columbia University Press, 1976); The Role of the Church in New France (McGraw-Hill - Ryerson, Ltd., 1976); The French Relationship With the Native Peoples of New France (Indian & Northern Affairs, Canada, 1984); (in collaboration) Emerging Identities, Selected Problems and Interpretations in Canadian History (Prentice-Hall, Canada, 1986); (in collaboration) The American Indian and the problem of History (1987); (in collaboration) Readings in Canadian Native History (1988); (in collaboration) Canada, A North American Nation (McGraw-Hill-Ryerson, 1989); (in collaboration) Sweet promises: A Reader on Indian-White Relations (1991); (in collaboration) Les Hurons de Lorette (1996) The French Regime in the Upper Country in the Seventeenth Century (Toronto: Champlain Society, 1996); Material Memory: Vol. I (Addison Wesley, 1998); (in collaboration) American Encounters. Natives and Newcomers (2000); (in collaboration) The native North American Almanac (2001); First Contacts (Markham & Fitzhenry & Whiteside, 2002); also, chapters in books & articles in refereed journals on Canadian Indians.

JAFFE, A.J. 1912-
(retired statistician)
Born February 28, 1912, in Mass. *Education*: University of Chicago, PhD, 1941. *Principal occupation*: Statistician (retired). *Home address*: 314 Allaire Ave., Leonia, NJ 07605 (201) 944-1364. *Affiliations*: Senior research scholar (retired), Columbia University, New York, N.Y. *Other professional posts*: Research associate, National Museum of the American Indian, New York, N.Y. *Memberships*: American Statistical Association; American Association for the Advancement of Science. *Interests*: Indians of North America; U.S. Labor Force; social and demographic change. *Published works*: People, Jobs, and Economic Development (Free Press, 1959); Changing Demography of Spanish Americans (Academic Press, 1980); Misuse of Statistics (Marcel Dekker, Inc., 1987); The First Im-

migrants From Asia: A Population History of the North American Indians (Plenum Press, 1992).

JAMES, ALBERT
(Indian band chief)
Affiliation: McDowell Lake Indian Band, Box 740, Red Lake, ON, Canada P0V 2M0 (807) 727-2803.

JAMES, ALBERT E. (Wiyot)
(rancheria chairperson)
Affiliation: Table Bluff Rancheria, P.O. Box 519, Loleta, CA 95551 (707) 733-5055.

JAMES, ALVIN R. (Paiute)
(former tribal chairperson)
Affiliation: Pyramid Lake Paiute Tribal Council, P.O. Box 256, Nixon, NV 89424 (702) 574-1000.

JAMES, CHEEWA (Modoc)
(speaker, corporate trainer, author)
Address & Affiliation: Horizons, 3330 Union Springs Way, Sacramento, CA 95827 (916) 369-6616 Fax 369-5664. E-mail: cheewa@cheewa.com. *Published work*: Catch the Whisper of the Wind: Inspiring Stories and Proverbs from Native Americans, revised edition. 1994.

JAMES, EVELYN (Paiute)
(tribal vice president)
Affiliation: San Juan Southern Paiute Council, P.O. Box 1989, Tuba City, AZ 86045 (928) 283-4589.

JAMES, GORDON (Skokomish)
(former tribal chairperson)
Affiliation: Skokomish Tribal Council, N. 80 Tribal Center Rd., Shelton, WA 98584 (360) 426-4232.

JAMES, JOHN A. (Cahuilla)
(tribal chairperson)
Affiliation: Cabazon General Council, 84-245 Indio Spring Dr., Indio, CA 92203 (760) 342-2593.

JAMES, LORIE (Wintun)
(rancheria chairperson)
Affiliation: Greenville Rancheria, P.O. Box 279, Greenville, CA 95947 (530) 284-7990.

JAMES, OVERTON
(foundation chairperson)
Affiliation: Five Civilized Tribes Foundation, c/o Chickasaw Nation, P.O. Box 1548, Ada, OK 74820 (405) 436-2603.

JAMES, WABUN 1945-
(writer, lecturer, teacher)
Born April 5, 1945, Newark, N.J. *Education*: George Washington University, BA, 1967; Columbia University, MA, 1968. *Principal occupation*: Writer, lecturer, teacher. *Address*: 3750A Airport Blvd. #223, Mobile, AL 36608 (509) 326-6561. *Affiliation*: Executive director, The Bear Tribe Medicine Society, Mobile, AL, 1972-. *Published works*: The People's Lawyers (Holt, Rinehart & Winston, 1973); The Bear Tribe's Self-Reliance Book (Bear Tribe Publishing, 1977); The Medicine Wheel Book (Prentice-Hall, 1980); Sun Bear: The Path to Power (Bear Tribe Publishing, 1983).

JAMES, WALTER S., JR.
(executive director)
Affiliation: Council for Native American Indians, 280 Broadway, Suite 316, New York, NY 10007 (212) 732-0485.

JANDREAU, MICHAEL B. (Lower Brule Sioux)
(tribal chairperson)
Affiliation: Lower Brule Sioux Tribal Council, P.O. Box 187, Lower Brule, SD 57548 (605) 473-5561.

JANVIER, WALTER
(Indian band chief)
Affiliation: Janvier Indian Band, Chard, Alberta, Canada T0P 1G0 (403) 559-2259.

JANZ, PAM
(department head-Indian college)
Affiliation: Department of Indian Education, Saskatchewan Indian Federated College, University of Regina, 118 College West, Regina, Saskatchewan, Canada S4S 0A2 (306) 584-8333.

JARAMILLO, ERNEST CHARLES
***(Eagle Feather)* (Isleta Pueblo) 1936-**
(USAF-retired; farmer/rancher)
Born May 15, 1936, Isleta Pueblo, N.M. *Education*: University of New Mexico, 1983-84. *Principal occupation*: USAF-retired; farmer-rancher. *Home address*: P.O. Box 543, Isleta, NM 87022 (505) 869-9284. *Military service*: U.S. Air Force, 1954-74 (Technical Sergeant; received the Air Force Commendation Medal for meritourious service in support of Southeast Asia while stationed in Taiwan in 1966). *Memberships*: American Indian Veterans Association, Albuquerque, NM (chairperson).

JARBOE, MARK A.
(attorney)
Born August 19, 1951, Flint, Mich. *Education*: University of Michigan, BA, 1972; Harvard University Law School, JD, 1975. *Principal occupation*: Attorney. *Address*: Dorsey & Whitney, LLP, Minneapolis, MN. E-Mail: jarboe.mark@dorseylaw.com. *Affiliation*: Dorsey & Whitney, LLP, Minneapolis, MN, 1976-. *Memberships*: Native American Bar Association; Minnesota American Indian Bar Association; Federal Bar Association. *Awards, honors*: Phi Beta Kappa. *Interests*: "Chairman of Indian Law Dept. at Dorsey & Whitney; represents tribes across the country in matters of finance and development, business diversification, governmental regulation and other areas. Speaker at various conferences and workshops on the subject of business transactions in Indian country." *Biographical sources*: Who's Who in America; Who's Who in American Law; Who's Who in the Midwest. *Published works*: Regulating Indian Gaming; Fairness or Finagling? (Bench & Bar of Minnesota, 1993); The Nature of Tribal Sovereignty (The Legend, 1994); Fundamental Legal Principles Affecting Business Transactions in Indian Country (Hamline Law Review, 1994); Lending in Indian Country - The Principal Legal Issues (ABA Bank Compliance, 1995).

JARIS, BEN (Lower Brule Sioux)
(BIA education chairperson)
Affiliation: Bureau of Indian Affairs, Crow Creek/Lower Brule Agency, P.O. Box 139, Fort Thompson, SD 57339 (605) 245-2398.

JAROS, ROSEMARY (Chippewa)
(school principal)
(school principal)
Affiliation: Turtle Mountain High School, P.O. Box 440, Belcourt, ND 58316 (701) 477-6471 Fax 477-6470.

JAURE, RUTH A.
(executive director)
Affiliation: National American Indian Housing Council, 900 2nd St., NE, Suite 007, Washington, DC 20002 (202) 789-1754.

JEANNOTTE, PLACIDE
(Indian band chief)
Affiliation: Gaspe (Micmac) Indian Band, Box 69, Fontenelle, Gaspe, Quebec G0E 1H0 (418) 368-6005.

JEANOTTE, DARRELL (Sioux)
(supt. of education)
Affiliation: Pierre Indian Learning Center, HC 31, Box 148, Pierre, SD 57501 (605) 224-8661.

JEANOTTE, DUANE L.
(IHS area director)
Affiliation: Billings Area Office, Indian Health Service, P.O. Box 2143, Billings, MT 59103 (406) 657-6403.

JEANOTTE, LEIGH D. (Turtle Mountain Chippewa) 1948-
(higher education administrator)
Born November 1, 1948, Rolette, N.D. *Education*: University of North Dakota, Ed.D. *Principal occupation*: Higher education administrator. *Address*: Box 8274, University of North Dakota, Grand Forks, ND 58202 (701) 777-4291 Fax 777-3282. E-mail: leigh.jeanotte@und.nodak.edu. Affiliation: American Indian Student Services, University of North Dakota, Grand Forks, ND (1972-present). *Other professional posts*: Treasurer, North Dakota Indian Education Association; Vice President, Higher Education Resource Organization for Students. *Awards, honors*: 1987 North Dakota Indian Educator of the Year; University of North Dakota Outstanding Meritorious Service, 1986; 1998

Friend of ASPIRE Award; 1999 International Honorary for Leaders in University Communities. *Community activities*: Evaluator of several tribal/federal education projects; Northeast Human Services Advisory Board. *Memberships*: North Dakota Indian Education Association; Higher Education Resource Organization for Students; North Dakota College Personnel Association; American College Personnel Association. *Interests*: "Promotion of cultural sensitivity, educational evaluation and assessment, higher education, student support services."

JEMISON, G. PETER (Seneca) 1945-
(historic site manager)
Born January 18, 1945, Silver Creek, N.Y. *Education*: Buffalo State College, University of Buffalo. *Principal occupation*: Historic site manager. *Address*: P.O. Box 239, Victor, NY 14564 (585) 924-5848 Fax 742-2353, E-mail: pjemison@frontiernet.net. *Affiliation*: Ganondagan State Historic Site, Victor, N.Y. *Other professional post*: Curator of Native American art exhibits consultant and lecturer on history and art. *Community activities*: Board of Trustees, Memorial Art Gallery of Rochester, NY; Native American Graves, Protection and Repatriation Act representative for the Seneca Nation of Indians. *Interests*: "I am a professional artist." *Published work*: Treaty of Canandaigua 1794: 200 Years of Treaty Relations Between the Iroquois Confederacy and the U.S. (Clear Light Publishers).

JEMISON, NANCY L.
(BIA office director)
Affiliation: Office of Economic Development, Bureau of Indian Affairs, Dept. of the Interior, MS-2061-MIB, Rm. 2529, 1849 C St., NW, Washington, DC 20240 (202) 208-5324.

JENKS, PEGGY
(administrative officer)
Affiliation: Cherokee PHS Indian Hospital, Cherokee, NC 28719 (704) 497-9163.

JENSEN, CARL (Athapascan)
(AK village council president)
Affiliation: Pedro Bay Village, P.O. Box 4720, Pedro Bay, AK 99647 (907) 850-2225.

JENTOFF-NILSEN, LYNETTE
(museum director)
Affiliation: Sheldon Museum & Cultural Center, P.O. Box 269, Haines, AK 99827 (907) 766-2366.

JEROME, BERNARD (Maria Band of Micmacs)
(tribal cultural director)
Address: 50 Micmac Dr., Presque Isle, ME 04769; E-mail: bjerome@micmac.org. *Affiliation*: Cultural director, Aroostook Band of Micmacs, Presque Isle, ME. *Past professional post*: Former chief, Maria Band of Micmac, Quebec, Canada.

JEROME, LOUIS
(Indian band chief)
Affiliation: Bande Indienne du Lac Simon, Lac Simon, Canada J0Y 3M0 (819) 736-2351.

JERRALL, CATHERINE
(association coordinator)
Affiliation: Canadian Alliance in Solidarity with the Native Peoples, 16 Spadina Rd., Suite 302, Toronto, Ontario, Canada M5R 2S7 (416) 964-0169.

JILEK, WOLFGANG GEORGE (*Kas'lidi*) 1930-
(psychiatrist, anthropologist)
Born November 25, 1930, Tetschen, Bohemia. *Education*: Medical schools of the universities of Munich, W. Germany, Innsbruck, Austria, and Vienna, Austria, MD, 1956; McGill University, Montreal, Quebec, Canada, MSc, 1966; University of British Columbia, Vancouver, Canada, MA (Anthropology), 1972. *Principal occupation*: Psychiatrist, anthropologist. *Home address*: 571 English Bluff Rd., Delta, B.C. Canada V4M 2M9 (604) 940-8574. *Affiliations*: Dept. of Anthropology & Sociology, 1974-80; clinical professor of psychiatry, Dept. of Psychiatry, 1980-96, University of British Columbia, Vancouver; affiliate professor, University of Washington, Seattle, 1986-96; clinical professor emeritus of psychiatry, University of British Columbia, Vancouver, B.C., 1996-present; guest professor in transcultural and ethno-psychiatry, Univer-

sity of Vienna, Vienna, Austria. *Other professional posts*: Consultant psychiatrist, Greater Vancouver Mental Health Service; consultant in mental health, World Health Organization, 1984-85; refuge mental health coordinator, United Nations H.C.R., Bangkok, Thailand, 1988-89. *Memberships*: Canadian Psychiatric Association (organizer & chairman of the Task Force, later Section, on Native People's Mental Health, 1970-80); American Psychiatric Association (member, Task Force on American Indians, 1971-77); World Psychiatric Association (Transcultural Psychiatry section, secretary, 1983-92, chairman, 1993-99; honorary advisor, 1999-present); Native Mental Health Association of Canada; Canadian Medical Association; Fellow, Royal College of Physicians and Surgeons of Canada; editorial advisor, "Transcultural Psychiatry," McGill University, Montreal, Canada; editorial advisor, Curare-Journal of Ethnomedicine & Transcultural Psychiatry, Heidelberg, W. Germany. *Interests*: "Transcultural psychiatry; traditional medicine and ceremonialism, especially of aboriginal North & South American peoples; ethnomedical & ethnopsychiatric research among aboriginal people of Canada, U.S. (especially Northwest Pacific culture area), and South America; Haiti; East Africa; Southeast Asia; Papua, New Guinea, 1963)." *Published works*: Salish Indian Mental Health and Culture Change (Holt, Rinehart & Winston, Toronto, 1974); Indian Healing-Shamanic Ceremonialism in the Pacific Northwest Today (Hancock House, 1982); Traditional Medicine and Primary Health Care in Papua, New Guinea (WHO & Papua, New Guinea University Press, 1985); numerous chapters in books and articles which deal with North American Indians; "The Therapeutic Aspects of Salish Spirit Dance Ceremonials" in Handbook of Culture, Therapy and Healing, edited by U.P. Giellen, Fish & J. Draguns, 2004.

JILEK-AALL, LOUISE M. 1931-
(psychiatrist, anthropologist)
Born April 21, 1931, Oslo, Norway. *Education*: University of Oslo, Norway, 1949-50; University of Tuebingen, Germany, 1951-55; University of Zurich, Switzerland, MD, 1958, Dipl. of Trop. Med., 1959; University of Basel, Switzerland, 1959; McGill University, Montreal, Canada, Dipl. of Psychiatry, 1965; University of British Columbia, Vancouver, Canada, MA (Social Anthropology), 1972. *Principal occupation*: Psychiatrist, anthropologist. *Home address*: 571 English Bluff Rd., Delta, British Columbia V4M 2M9 (604) 940-8574. *Affiliations*: Clinical professor of psychiatry, University of British Columbia, Vancouver, B.C. (member, faculty of medicine, 1975-97; clinical professor emerita, 1997-present). *Other professional posts*: Consultant psychiatrist, Greater Vancouver Mental Health Service; consultant psychiatrist, University Hospital, Vancouver, B.C. *Military service*: Medical officer, U.N. Congo Mission, 1960-61 (Citation and Congo Medal of the League of Red Cross Societies, 1961). *Memberships*: Canadian Psychiatric Association (vice chairperson, Section on Native Mental Health); Canadian Psychiatric Association (member, Task Force/Section on Native Mental Health, 1970-); Native Mental Health Association of Canada; Royal College of Physicians and Surgeons of Canada, 1966- (Fellow); World Psychiatric Association, 1974- (member, Transcultural Section); International Congresses on Circumpolar Health (contributor). *Interests*: Transcultural psychiatry; ethnomedicine; Canadian, American and Alaskan Native mental health; Native therapeutic resources; alcohol abuse prevention and rehabilitation. Fieldwork and research in transcultural psychiatry and ethnomedicine in North and South America, the Caribbean, Asia, Africa, Oceania; neurological research in epilepsy. *Biographical sources*: Who's Who of American Women (10th Ed., 1977-78 p. 446); The World Who's Who of Women (4th Ed., International Biographical Centre, Cambridge, Eng. 1978 p. 583). *Published works*: Call Mama Doctor (Hancock House, 1978); Working with Dr. Schweitzer (Hancock House, 1990); "The Woman Who Could Not escape Her Spirit Song," in Culture and Psychotherapy; Articles dealing with North American Indian matters.

JIM, GELFORD (Te-Moak Band of Western Shoshone)
(tribal chairperson)
Affiliation: Battle Mountain Band Council, 37 Mt. View Dr. #1040-09, Battle Mountain, NV 89820 (702) 635-2004.

JIMENEZ, DR. JENNY D.
(school principal)
Affiliation: Kayenta Boarding School, P.O. Box 188, Kayenta, AZ 86033 (520) 697-3439 Fax 697-3490; Dilcon Boarding School, HC63 Box G, Winslow, AZ 86047 (520) 657-3211 Fax 657-3370.

JIMENEZ, MORRIE
(chairperson)
Affiliation: Oregon Indian Coalition on Post Secondary Education, 2708 Shelly Ann Way, NE, Salem, OR 97305.

JIMMIE, ROBERT B.
(Indian band chief)
Affiliation: Squiala Indian Band, Box 392, Chilliwack, B.C., Canada V2P 6J7 (604) 792-8300.

JIMMY, ROGER (Kluskus)
(Indian band chief)
Affiliation: Kluskus Indian Band, 395 A Kinchant St., Quesnel, B.C., Canada V2J 3J8 (604) 992-8186.

JINKS-WEIDNER, JANIE
(editor)
Affiliation: The Indian Relic Trader, P.O Box 88, Sunbury, OH 43074.

JOBE, BARBARA
(executive director)
Affiliation: Red Earth Indian Center, 2100 NE 52 St., Oklahoma City, OK 73111 (405) 427-4228.

JOCKS, CHRISTOPHER P. (*Ronwanien:te*) (Kahnawake Mohawk) 1954-
(assistant professor)
Born February 11, 1954, Omaha, Neb. *Education*: Lewis & Clark College, BA, 1985; University of California, Santa Barbara, MA, 1990; PhD, 1994. *Principal occupation*: Assistant Professor of Native American Studies and Religion. *Address*: Unknown. *Affiliations*: University of California, Santa Barbara, CA, 1988-93; Assistant Professor of Native American Studies and Religion, Dartmouth College, Hanover, NH, 1993-2000. *Community activities*: Faculty advisor, Native American House at Dartmouth College. *Memberships*: American Academy of Religion; Society for the Study of Native American Religious Traditions. *Awards, honors*: Recipient of first annual (1993-94) Native American Dissertation Fellowship, Dartmouth College. *Interests*: "My academic work aims at describing & interpreting American Indian religious life in ways that do not intrude upon or exploit Indian communities; that use Indians' own languages and categories; and that expand our understanding of religion itself." *Published works*: "Native North American Environments as Webs of Relationship," chapter in book on World Religions and the Environment (Quo Vadis, 1994).

JOE, CINDY
(school principal)
Affiliation: Second Mesa Day School, P.O. Box 98, Second Mesa, AZ 86043 (520) 737-2571 Fax 737-2470.

JOE, DONALD (Athapascan)
(AK village council vice president)
Affiliation: Tetlin Village Council, P.O. Box 520, Tetlin, AK 99780 (907) 883-2321.

JOE, JASPER (Navajo)
(college PR director)
Affiliation: Director of Public Relations, Navajo Community College, P.O. Box 580, Shiprock, NM 87420 (505) 368-5291.

JOE, JENNIE R. (Navajo)
(professor)
Born in New Mexico. *Education*: University of New Mexico, BS; University of California, Berkeley, MA, MPH, PhD. *Principal occupation*: Professor. *Home address*: 5625 E. Rosewood St., Tucson, AZ 85711 (602) 621-5075 (work). *Affiliations*: American Indian Studies Center & Dept. of Anthropology, UCLA, 1981-85; Professor of Family & Community Medicine, University of Arizona, Tucson, AZ; 1985-present. *Other professional post*: Director, Native American Research & Training Center, Tucson, AZ. *Military service*: U.S. Navy - Lt. *Community activities*: National Museum of

the American Indian (Board of Trustees-Smithsonian Institution. *Memberships*: American Anthropological Association; American Public Health Association; Society for Medical Anthropology; The Congress of the Americanist. *Awards, honors*: 1994 National Katrin Lamon Scholar, Santa Fe, NM; 1995 Switzer Scholar, Washington, DC. Interests: American Indian health issues. *Published works*: Too numerous to list.

JOE, ROBERT, SR. (*Wa Walton*) (Swinomish)
(tribal chairperson)
Affiliation: Swinomish Indian Senate, P.O. Box 817, LaConner, WA 98257 (360) 466-3163.

JOEST, PATTA LT (Choctaw)
(artist, designer)
Education: University of Oklahoma, BA (Fashion Arts, Clothing and Textiles), 1982. *Principal occupation*: Artist, designer of original contemporary Native influence clothing. *Address*: 814 N. Jones, Norman, OK 73069 (405) 360-0512. *Affiliations*: Owner, The Dancing Rabbit, Norman, OK. *Shows*: Heard Museum, Phoenix, AZ; The Living Desert Museum, Palm Desert, CA; The Indian Art Market, Denver, CO; Indian Land, Scottsdale, AZ; The Inter-Tribal Indian Ceremonial in Gallup, NM; The Red earth Festival, Oklahoma City, OK; the Mulvane Museum of Fine Arts, Kansas City, MO. *Awards, honors*: Commissioned by Chief Wilma Mankiller of the Cherokee Nation of Oklahoma to create an ensemble for her and her Chief of Staff to wear to the Presidential Inaugural Gala in Washington, DC in January 1992; One of eight Native American artists selected to be highlighted in the "Goldbook," a nationally published book featuring the "Best of the Best"; honored by the Oklahoma Hospitality Club as one of eighteen "Ladies in the News"; special commission project to design Joseph's coat in the musical "Joseph and the Amazing Technicolor Dreamcoat," performed by a local company; 1993 "Best of Show" Artwear '93, Ft. Collins, CO; 1994 & 1995 "Best of Show" Embellishments IV & V, University of Tulsa School of Art; 1995. *Interests*: Patta frequently lectures around the country on how to design modern clothing using ancient tribal themes. "My artistic goal is to reach another dimension by using all elements of fiber, art, and textiles to develop my idea into wearable art."

JOHANNSEN-HANKS, CHRISTINA B. 1950-
(anthropologist)
Born October 29, 1950, Rahway, N.J. *Education*: Beloit College, BA, 1972; Brown University, PhD, 1984. *Principal occupation*: Museum director. *Home address*: 139 Van Farm Rd., Warnerville, NY 12187 (518) 234-2841 (work). E-mail: hankaero@midtel.net. *Affiliation*: Trustee, Iroquois Indian Museum, Howes Cave, NY, 1980-present (vice-president & research associate, 1995-present). *Other professional post*: Lecturer, State University of New York at Albany. *Interests*: "Research and promotion of contemporary Iroquois art. Actively involved in educating the public about the contributions of Iroquois peoples today and to an understanding of their past. Concern in maintaining professional museological standards in small museums and delineating a museum's purposes and goals. Continued field research in Iroquois communities throughout the U.S. and Canada. Special interest in creatively photographing museum objects. Living part-time in South Africa. New interest in contemporary southern African arts." *Published works*: European Trade Goods and Wampanoag Culture in the Seventeenth Century in Burr's Hill: A 17th Century Wampanoag Burial Ground in Warren, Rhode Island (Haffenreffer Museum of Anthropology, Brown University, 1980); Iroquois Arts: A Directory of a People and Their Work, co-edited with Dr. John P. Ferguson (Association for the Advancement of Native North American Arts and Crafts, 1984); Efflorescence and Identity in Iroquois Art, Ph.D. Dissertation, Brown University, 1984.

JOHN, ALLEN
(AK village chief)
Affiliation: Native Village of Clark's Point, P.O. Box 16, Clark's Point, AK 99569 (907) 236-1221.

JOHN, GENEVIEVE
(health director)
Affiliation: Pyramid Lake Health Dept., P.O. Box 227, Nixon, NV 89424 (702) 574-0107.

JOHN, JOHNNIE, Jr. (Eskimo)
(AK village council president)
Affiliation: Native Village of Crooked Creek Council, P.O. Box 69, Crooked Creek, AK 99575 (907) 432-2227.

JOHN, LIONEL
(executive director)
Affiliation: United South & Eastern Tribes, 711 Stewarts Ferry Pike #100, Nashville, TN 37214 (615) 361-8700.

JOHN, RICHARD
(Indian band chief)
Affiliation: One Arrow Indian Band, Box 1, RR 1, Wakaw, Saskatchewan, Canada S0K 4P0 (306) 423-5900.

JOHN, ROBERTA (Navajo) 1960-
(administrative service officer; writer)
Born May 26, 1960, Monticello, Utah. *Education*: Arizona State University, BS, 1982; Brigham Young University, MA (Communications), 1987. *Principal occupation*: Administrative service officer; writer. *Home address*: P.O. Box 2978, Window Rock, AZ 86515 (928) 871-7375 Fax 871-7381 (work). *Affiliation*: Administrative service officer, Navajo Nation Division of Economic Development, Window Rock, AZ, 1989-. "I send out press releases regarding economic development projects and activities within the Navajo Nation. I also send out an economic development newsletter." *Other professional post*: New Mexico Quincentennial Commissioner. *Community activities*: Publicity coordinator, Navajo Nation Fair and Fourth of July PRCA Rodeo & Pow Wow Celebration. *Membership*: New Mexico Indian Tourism Association (board member). *Interests*: "I handle and coordinate the overall promotion, advertising and marketing of the Navajo Nation. I am in the process of writing and editing a major Navajo Tourism strategy for the Navajo Nation. This master plan will be used to help plan, develop and create more jobs for the Navajo people - developing the tourism industry on North America's largest reservation, Navajoland. I was part of a ten-member New Mexico, German Sales Mission Delegation - I promoted New Mexico tribes, mainly the Navajo Nation. I enjoy writing feature stories. I also would like to produce and write a video about the Navajo Nation." *Published work*: Navajoland Tourism Brochure, 1990; Red is Beautiful, 2003, children's book (viewed & ordered on www.salina bookshelf.com).

JOHN, WILLIAM (Eskimo)
(AK village council president)
Affiliation: Native Village of Pitka's Point, P.O. Box 127, St. Mary's, AK 99658 (907) 438-2833.

JOHNNY, RONALD EAGLEYE
(Indian organization president)
Affiliation: President, Native American Law Students Association, American Indian Law Center, University of New Mexico School of Law, P.O. Box 4456, 1117 Stanford NE, Albuquerque, NM 87196.

JOHNNY, WILLIE (Te-Moak Shoshone)
(tribal chairperson)
Affiliation: Wells Indian Colony, P.O. Box 809, Wells, NV 89835 (775) 752-3045.

JOHNS, BOBBY THOMAS (Lower Muskogee Creek) 1936-
(artist/craftsman)
Born March 24, 1936, Dodge County, Ga. *Education*: College courses; Graphic Arts Certificate. *Principal occupation*: Artist/craftsman. *Home address*: 12533 Polonious Pkwy., Pensacola, FL 32506 (904) 492-3593. *Affiliation*: Instructor and technical advisor for military training films & communications operations in a civilian capacity at Fort Gordon, GA (20 years). Disability retirement. *Military service*: U.S. navy (4 years) (Airman, sea/air rescue). *Community activities*: Museum of Commerce (volunteer); Northwest Florida Arts Council (Arts in Education Committee); Indian culture demonstrations for many events. *Memberships*: Pensacola Historical Society; National Woodcarvers Association; Arts Council of Northwest Florida; Historic Pensacola Village. *Awards, honors*: Artist Fellowship for folk art - Secretary of State, Cultural Affairs; Master Artist & Apprentice Program, Florida Folklife Division, Secretary of State. *Interests*: "Helping to keep alive the traditional attitudes and crafts/art of our Na-

tive American peoples. Visiting schools and public powwows where interaction with others can take place to foster a better understanding of our people."

JOHNS, JOSEPH F. (*Cayoni*) (Eastern Creek) 1928-
(museum manager, artist)
Born January 31, 1928, Okefenokee Swamp, Ga. *Education*: High school (U.S. Armed Forces Institute). *Principal occupation*: Museum manager, artist. *Home address*: 7 Russell St., West Peabody, MA 01960 (508) 535-2426. *Affiliation*: Indian Artist in Residence (sculpture and carving in any medium) & Building Manager, Peabody Museum Peabody Museum, Harvard University, Cambridge, MA, 1974-. "I maintain a small studio, at my home, for carving the eight traditional masks of the Creek people." *Military service*: U.S. Naval Amphibious Forces (Sniper), 1944-1946 (U.S. Navy P.O. 3; Asiatic Pacific Medal, Silver Star Medal); U.S. Coast Guard (retired), 1947-1965 (U.S.C.G. P.O. 1; Silver Life Saving Medal presented by President Harry S. Truman in Washington, D.C., 1947). *Community activities*: Masonic Shriner at Alleppo Temple, Wilmington, Mass. *Membership*: Boston Indian Council; Peabody Museum (Associate; member, Repatriation Committee). *Awards, honors*: "I was a crew member of the Coast Guard Cutter Westwind Expedition to the North Pole (Dew Line), 1953-1954; and a crew member of the Coast Guard's Cutter, Eastwind Expedition to the South Pole (Operation Deep Freeze, 1961-1962); (I am) holder of Antarctica Service Medal. A book about my life is now being written by Mitchell Wade."

JOHNS, KEN
(executive director)
Affiliation: Copper River Native Association, Drawer H, Copper Center, AK 99573 (907) 822-5241.

JOHNS, MARY FRANCES (Florida Seminole) 1944-
(craft artist; shop owner)
Born October 7, 1944, Miami, Fla. *Education*: Edison Community College (Ft. Myers, FL), Nursing, 1979-1983. *Principal occupation*: Craft artist; shop owner. *Home address*: Rt. 6, Box 595, Brighton Seminole Reservation, Okeechobee, FL 34974 (813) 467-7312. *Affiliation*: Owner, Arts & Crafts Shop, Brighton Reservation, 1984-. *Other professional posts*: Resource person for museums as arts & crafts demonstrator, storytelling & history of the Seminoles & Southeastern Indians. *Interests*: "I have demonstrated basketry, patchwork, doll making and Indian foods all over the State of Florida. I have given talks on our culture and its history throughout North & Central Florida. I was hired by the Tallahassee Junior Museum thru a State Dept. grant to be artist in resident. This is how I got started in this field. I am presently helping Charles Daniels with his Creek language classes and am studying the Muskogean & Southeastern Indian culture thru Mr. Daniels classes. I speak Miccosukee, Creek and English fluently, and some Spanish. My hobbies are painting, crafts, and artifacts making." *Published works*: Co-author, with D. Alderson, "Muskogee Fires" (Muskogee Press, 1994); Muskogee Words & Ways-also Dictionary III, a Southeastern Reader V (7 part series).

JOHNS, SHAWN
(research director)
Affiliation: National Indian Gaming Association, 224 2nd St., SE, Washington, DC 20003 (202) 546-7711 Fax 546-1755. E-mail: sjohns@indiangaming.org.

JOHNS, WILLIE (Seminole) 1951-
(tribal director of education)
Born March 23, 1951, Okeechobee, Fla. *Education*: B.B.S. *Principal occupation*: Director of Education - Seminole Tribe. *Address*: Rt. 6, Box 750, Okeechobee, FL 34974 (941) 763-4483. E-mail: wmjohns@ictransnet.com. *Affiliations*: Seminole Tribe, Okeechobee, FL; United South & Eastern Tribes. *Community activities*: President, E.I.R.A.; community adult education director. *Membership*: Eastern Indian Rodeo Association (commissioner-Indian national finals).

JOHNSON, ALVIS (Karuk)
(tribal chairperson; health program director)
Affiliation: Karuk Tribe of California, P.O. Box 1016, Happy Camp, CA 96039 (530) 493-5305. *Other professional post*: Director, Karuk Tribal Health Program.

JOHNSON, BEN, JR. (Makah)
(former tribal chairperson)
Affiliation: Makah Indian Tribal Council, P.O. Box 115, Neah Bay, WA 98357 (360) 645-2201.

JOHNSON, CHARLES E.
(BIA education administrator)
Affiliation: Fort Defiance Agency, Bureau of Indian Affairs, P.O. Box 110, Fort Defiance, AZ 86504 (602) 729-7251 Fax 729-7286.

JOHNSON, CHARLIE
(AK village council president)
Affiliation: Portage Creek Village, P.O. Box 1031, Portage Creek, AK 99576 (907) 842-5218.

JOHNSON, CHERYL
(secondary school administrator)
Affiliation: Enemy Swim Day School, RR 1, Box 87, Waubay, SD 57273 (605) 947-4605.

JOHNSON, DONNA
(high school principal)
Affiliation: Tate Topa Tribal School (Four Winds), P.O. Box 199, Fort Totten, ND 58335 (701) 766-4161 Fax 766-4766. *Membership*: North Dakota Indian Education Association.

JOHNSON, FRANK
(Indian band chief)
Affiliation: Oweekeno Indian Band, Box 3500, Port Hardy, British Columbia, Canada V0N 2P0.

JOHNSON, FREDERICK M.
(Indian school principal)
Affiliation: Rocky Ridge Boarding School, P.O. Box 299, Kykotsmovi, AZ 86039 (602) 725-3415.

JOHNSON, GARY C.
(Indian education program director)
Affiliation: South Bend Schools, Indian Education Program, P.O. Box 437, South Bend, WA 98586 (360) 875-5707.

JOHNSON, GEORGE W.
(Indian band chief)
Affiliation: Chapel Island Indian Band, RR #1, St. Peters, Nova Scotia, Canada B0A 1J0 (902) 535-3317.

JOHNSON, GLENN
(Indian center director)
Affiliation: American Indian Graduate Student Center, Office of Indian Programs, University of Arizona, Tucson, AZ 85721 (602) 621-2794.

JOHNSON, JACQUELINE L. (*Kus ees*) (Tlingit)
(NCAI executive director)
Affiliations: Executive director, National Congress of American Indians (NCAI), 1301 Connecticut Ave., NW #200, Washington, DC 20036 (202) 466-7767 Fax 466-7797. *Past professional posts*: Executive director, Oneida Riders Association, Seymour, WI; chairperson, National American Indian Housing Council, Washington, DC 20002; liaison to Native America for the Clinton Administration.

JOHNSON, JAMES
(Indian band chief)
Affiliation: Spuzzum Indian Band, RR 1, Yale, BC, Canada V0K 2S0 (604) 863-2205.

JOHNSON, JERI (Tonto Apache)
(former tribal chairperson)
Affiliation: Tonto Apache Tribal Council, Tonto Reservation #30, Payson, AZ 85541 (602) 474-5000.

JOHNSON, JOAN
(editor)
Affiliation: Micmac News, Nova Scotia Native Communications Society, P.O. Box 344, Sydney, Nova Scotia, Canada B1P 6H2 (902) 539-0045.

JOHNSON, JOE (Creek) 1950-
(mayor, chief justice)
Born August 24, 1950, Council Hill, Okla. *Education*: Eastern Oklahoma State College (Wilburton, OK), AA; Oklahoma State University (2 years). *Principal occupation*: Mayor, chief justice. *Address*: Unknown. *Affiliations*: Mayor, City of Eufaula, OK, 1975-; chief justice, Muscogee Creek Nation, 1987-93; director, Na-

tive American Studies Program, Rose State College, Midwest City, OK 73110 (405) 733-7308. *Community activities*: Eastern OK Development District Board of Directors (3 terms); Eufaula Municipal Hospital Board of Directors (chairperson, 1976-86); OK Municipal League (president, vice-president & currently past president); McIntosh County Democratic Central Committee (past secretary-treasurer); OK Police Pension & Retirement Board (6 years); State Higher Education Alumni of ESC. *Memberships*: National American Indian Court Judges Association; OK Conference of Mayors; OK Conference of Regional Councils; Lions Club; Greater Eufaula Chamber of Commerce; Lake Eufaula Association (board member); serves on Development Council of Connors State College; serves on the Domestic Violence and Substance Abuse PAC Board; serves on the Board of Directors for Literacy Council, and OK Travel Industry Association. *Awards, honors*: Elected in 1975 as the youngest mayor in the state, at age of 24 years; selected to Who's Who in the South and Outstanding Young Men of America; George Nigh Mayor's Award. *Interests*: "Developed the local Posey Park, named after Alexander Posey, the most recognized Indian poet in Oklahoma's history; developed the Eufaula Community Center and the Eufaula Memorial Library; instrumental in the development and implementation of the Eufaula Main Street Program."

JOHNSON, JOSEPH (Nooksack)
(tribal council chairperson)
Affiliation: Nooksack Tribal Council, P.O. Box 157, Deming, WA 98244 (206) 592-5176.

JOHNSON, LARRY
(Indian band chief)
Affiliation: Caldwell Indian Band, Box 163215 Main St., Bothwell, Ontario, Canada N0P 1C0 (519) 695-3642.

JOHNSON, LEWIS (*Micco*) (Seminole)
(assistant curator, historian)
Address: 524 S. Wewoka, P.O. Box 1532, Wewoka, OK 74884 (405) 257-5580 Fax 257-6205. *Affiliation*: Seminole Nation Museum, Wewoka, OK. *Other professional post*: Representative on Tourism, Seminole Nation of Oklahoma. *Community activities*: Sorghum Day Festival grounds coordinator; Seminole Nation Day living history director; consultant for the National Park Service on Native American Projects. *Memberships*: Oklahoma Museum Association; Oklahoma Historical Association; Seminole Nation Historical Society. *Interests*: "I'm a Seminole Indian who makes and plays the Native flute. I also have an audio and video tape with recordings of Native flute music. I have worked with the Discovery Channel with the "How the West Was Lost" series. Time-Life magazine "The Southeastern Woodland Indians" project. Also made an appearance at the 1996 Olympic games in Atlanta."

JOHNSON, MADELINE
(clinic director)
Affiliation: Ardmore Chickasaw Health Clinic, 2510 Chickasaw Blvd., Ardmore, OK 73401 (405) 226-8181.

JOHNSON, PATRICIA LUCILLE PADDLETY (Kiowa) 1938-
(attorney)
Born October 22, 1938, Mountain View, Okla. *Education*: Oklahoma College of Liberal Arts, Chickasaw, BS, 1971; University of Oklahoma School of Law, JD, 1975. *Principal occupation*: Attorney. *Address*: Unknown. *Affiliation*: Associate Magistrate, Bureau of Indian Affairs, Code of Indian Offenses, Court, Anadarko, OK. *Community activities*: Indian Capital Baptist Church (member and teacher); Oklahoma Indian Rights Association; OK Indian Women Association. *Memberships*: OK Bar Association, 1975- (Minorities Law Committee, 1976); Federal Bar for the Western District of OK, 1975-. *Interests*: "I am interested in assisting young Indian people to achieve their life's goals, whether in Law or in any other field of training. I work extensively with our church in attempting to inspire and inform Indians in this area of the opportunities available to them. Alcoholism and drug related offenders make up the majority of my clients, and when I have the time, I counsel and encourage them."

JOHNSON, RENO, SR. (Apache)
(former tribal chairperson)
Affiliation: White Mountain Apache Tribal Council, P.O.

Box 700, Whiteriver, AZ 85941 (602) 338-4346. *Other professional post*: Member, Council of Advisors, American Indian Heritage Foundation, Falls Church, VA.

JOHNSON, ROLAND E. (Laguna Pueblo)
(pueblo governor)
Affiliation: Laguna Pueblo Councl, P.O. Box 194, Laguna, NM 87026 (505) 552-6654.

JOHNSON, ROY S. (Crazy Horse) (Rappahannock) 1928-
(research writer, lecturer, educator)
Born December 7, 1928, Caroline County, Va. *Education*: Temple University, 1947-49; University of Pennsylvania, BA, 1951; College of Metaphysics, PsD, 1972. *Principal occupation*: Research writer, lecturer on Indian affairs, educator. *Military service*: U.S. Army, 1943-46 (1st Lt.; 6 major campaigns—Pacific Theatre Medal, Silver Star, Bronze Star, Purple Heart, Presidential Unit Citation, Good Conduct Medal). *Community activities*: Coalition of Native Americans. Memberships: Rappahannock Tribe, State of Virginia (field chief); Powhatan Indians of Delaware Valley (chairman). *Interests*: Mr. Johnson teaches basic adult education to Native Americans; teaches self-defense and the Powhatan language. *Published work*: East Coast Indian Tribes, with Jack D. Forbes.

JOHNSON, SAM 1938-
(Indian village president)
Born August 14, 1938, Ashdown, Ark. *Education*: University of Arkansas, Fayetteville, BA *Principal occupation*: President/director, Ka-do-ha Indian Village, P.O. Box 669, Route 1, Murfressboro, AR 71958 (501) 285-3736, 1978-. *Military service*: U.S. Army (4 years).

JOHNSON, SHEILA MEADOWS (*Tsula Atsila*) (Southeastern Cherokee) 1949-
(arts-in-education teacher)
Born December 5, 1949, Collinsville, AL. *Education*: Jacksonville State University (AL), 1967-70 (major in art). *Principal occupation*: Arts-in-education teacher. *Address*: P.O. Box 227, Collinsville, AL 35961 (205) 524-2218. *Affiliation*: Alabama Arts Council, Dekalb County School System, Collinsville, AL. *Community activities*: North Alabama Cherokees (first vice-chief; tribal information & enrollment director; pow wow & event coordinator); past president, Collinsville Business & Professional Association. *Memberships*: Indian Arts & Crafts Association (member, Education & Enrollment Committee); Atlatl Native Arts Registry; Smithsonian National Museum of the American Indian (charter member). *Awards, honors*: Beloved Woman of the North Alabama Cherokees. *Interests*: "Serve as emcee of all tribal pow wows and events, and also emcee pow wows for other tribes and groups in the Southeast. Coordinate may local festivals and school programs." *Biographical source*: Featured articles in "People and Places," published by the Gadsden Times.

JOHNSON, TADD
(U.S. government agency staff director)
Affiliation: Majority Staff Director, Native American Affairs Subcommittee, U.S. House Committee on Interior & Insular Affairs, 1522 Longworth House Office Bldg., Washington, DC 20515 (202) 226-7736.

JOHNSON, TIFFANY
(school principal)
Affiliation: Wa He Lut Indian School, 11110 Connie Ave. SE, Olympia, WA 98513 (360) 456-1311.

JOHNSON, TROY R.
(professor, historian)
Born February 29, 1940, Wichita Falls, Tex. *Education*: San Diego State University, BA, 1986; UCLA, MA, 1989, PhD, 1993. *Principal occupation*: Professor, historian. *Home address*: 555 Main Ave. #420, Long Beach, CA 90802 (310) 432-8721; 985-8703 (work). *Affiliation*: Visiting professor, Native American Studies Program, University of California, Davis, Davis, CA, 1993-94; visiting research scholar, American Indian Studies Center, UCLA, Los Angeles, CA, 3/94-8/94; assistant professor, American Indian Studies Center, Dept. of History, California State University, Long Beach, CA, 1994-. *Military service*: U.S. Navy Retired (Lt. Commander), 1957-80 (Combat Action Ribbon, Vietnam Service Medal; Vietnam Presidential Citation; Navy Expeditionary Medal (Cuba). *Membership*: American Historical Society. *Interests*: American

Indian history & culture, history of the American West, history of the 1960s. *Published works*: Master's Thesis, "Status of Adoption & Foster Home Placement of Indian Children Under the Indian Child Welfare Act (UCLA, 1988); book reviews, "American Indian Culture & Research Journal (UCLA, 1990-92); "Depression, Despair, and Death; Indian Youth Suicide," Looking Glass edited by Clifford Trafzer (San Diego University Press, 1991); editor, Proceedings of the First & Second Annual National Conference on Indian Child Welfare, "Indian Homes for Indian Children," and "Unto the Seventh Generation" (UCLA, 1991 & 1993); editor, Activism Poetry & Political Statements from Alcatraz: The Indian Voice (American Indian Studies Center, UCLA, 1994); associate editor, Native North American Almanac (Gale Research, 1993); associate editor, Chronology of the North American Indian (Gale Research, 1994); associate editor, Native American: A Portrait of a People (Visible Ink Press, 1994); article, with Joane Nagel, "The Indian Occupation of Alcatraz Island: Twenty-Five Years Later," in American Indian Culture & Research Journal, Nov. 1994); The Indian Occupation of Alcatraz Island and the Rise of Indian Activism (University of Illinois Press, 1995); editor, American Indian Activism: Alcatraz to the Longest Walk; editor, Contemporary Native American Political Issues; Red Power: The American Indians' Fight for Freedom, Second Edition, edited with Alvin M. Josephy, Jr. and Joane Nagel (University of Nebraska Press, 1999).

JOHNSON, VIOLA
(hospital director)
Affiliation: Huhukam Memorial Hospital, P.O. Box 38, Sacaton, AZ 85247 (602) 562-3321.

JOHNSON, WANDA (Paiute)
(tribal chairperson)
Affiliation: Burns Paiute General Council, HC 71, 100 Pa Si Go St., Burns, OR 97720 (541) 573-2088.

JOHNSTON, BASIL H. (Ojibway) 1929-
(author)
Born July 13, 1929, Parry Island Reserve, Ontario, Can. *Education*: Loyola College, Montreal, BA, 1954; Ontario College of Education, Secondary School Teaching Certificate, 1962. *Principal occupation*: Author. *Home address*: 253 Ashlar Rd., Richmond Hill, ON L4C 2W7 (416) 884-9375 (home) 586-5538 (work). *Affiliations*: Assistant manager, 1957-59, manager, 1959-61, Toronto Board of Trade; teacher, Earl Haig Secondary School, 1962-69; lecturer, Ethnology Department, Royal Ontario Museum, 100 Queen's Park, Toronto, 1969-; teacher, private language teacher of Ojibway Indians, Toronto, 1974-. *Other professional posts*: Academic lectures and keynote addresses or major presentations at universities and conferences across the U.S. & Canada; media consultant, narrator on films; script writer-reviewer. *Community activities*: Toronto Indian Club; Canadian Indian Centre of Toronto (executive and vice president, 1963-69); Indian Eskimo Association (executive, legal committee, speakers committee, 1965-68); Union of Ontario Indians; Federal Indian Consultations, Toronto; Indian Hall of Fame (committee member, 1968-70); Wigwamen Inc., 1974-75; Ontario Geographic Names Board, 1977-87. *Awards, honors*: Centennial Medal in recognition of work on behalf of Native community, 1967; 1976 Samuel S. Fells Literary Award for first publication "Zhowmin and Mandamin"; Order of Ontario - for service of the greatest distinction and of singular excellence...benefiting society in Ontario and elsewhere, April 1989. *Published works*: Ojibway Language Course Outline (Education Division, Indian Affairs Branch, 1979); Ojibway Language Lexicon for Beginners and Others (Education Division, Indian Affairs Branch, 1979); Ojibwa Heritage (University of Columbia Press, 1976); How the Birds Got Their Colours (Kids Can Press, Toronto, 1978); Tales Our Elders Told (Royal Ontario Museum, Toronto, 1981); Ojibway Ceremonies (McClelland and Stewart, Toronto, 1983); By Canoe and Moccasin (Waapoone Publishing, Lakefield, ON, 1986); Moose Meat and Wild Rice (McClelland and Stewart, Toronto, 1978); Indian School Days (University of Oklahoma Press, 1989); Numerous stories, essays, articles and poems in various publications.

JOHNSTON, ROBERT (Comanche) 1953-
(lawyer)
Born January 28, 1953, Little Rock, Ark. *Education*: Wichita State University, BA, 1975; University of Oklahoma, College of Law, JD, 1978. *Principal occupation*: Lawyer. *Home address*: 1330 Dorchester Dr., Norman, OK 73069. *Interests*: Indian law; oil and gas law; natural resources law. *Published work*: Whitehorn v. State: Peyote and Religious Freedom in Oklahoma (American Indian Law Review, Vol. V, No. 1, winter, 1977).

JOJOLA, JOSEPH R. *(White Snow)*
(Isleta Pueblo) 1945-
(electronics technician; craftsperson)
Born September 18, 1945, Albuquerque, N.M. *Education*: New Mexico State University, 1986-89; New York Regeants (New York, NY), BS, 1993. *Principal occupation*: Electronics technician. *Address*: Unknown. *Affiliation*: Electronics technician, Army Research Laboratory, White Sands M.R., NM, 1989-. *Other professional posts*: Ammunition/explosives handler; owner of White Sands Photography; & craftsman of silversmithing & repair. *Military service*: U.S. Army Retired Master Sergeant/E-8 - 21 years active duty)12 years in Germany (Meritorious Service Medal; 7 Good Conduct Medals; 2 Army Commendation Medals; German & American Expert Marksmanship Badges; among others). *Community activities*: Mayor of White Sands Missile Range for two years. *Memberships*: Indian Arts & Crafts Association. *Awards, honors*: "I was honored in a Purification Ceremony in Dec. 1994 in the "Black Eye" clan. This consists of 4 days & 3 nights of total prayer & singing, no sleeping or eating (can drink). *Interests*: "I have traveled to approximately 14 countries in Europe and the Far East. I attend tribal functions when duty allows me to. I enjoy silversmithing and have taught all 5 of my children how to make Indian jewelry and they have successfully made themselves jewelry."

JOJOLA, TED (Isleta Pueblo) 1951-
(educator, administrator)
Born November 19, 1951, Isleta Pueblo, N.M. *Education*: University of New Mexico, BA; Massachusetts Institute of Technology, MA; University of Hawaii-Manoa, PhD (Political Science), 1982; University of Strasbourg, France, Certificate of International Human Rights Law, 1985. *Principal occupation*: Educator, administrator. *Home address*: Route 6, Box 578, Albuquerque, NM 87105 (505) 277-3917 (work). *Affiliations*: Internal planner, National Capital Planning Commission, Washington, DC, 1973; legal/historical researcher, Institute for the Development of Indian Law, Washington, DC, 1976; visiting research associate, Institute of Philippine Culture, Manila, 1977-78; visiting professor of urban planning, UCLA, 1984; professor of planning, University of New Mexico, Albuquerque, 1982-; director, Institute for Native American Development (INAD), Native American Studies Department, University of New Mexico, Albuquerque, 1982-95; Architecture Dept., University of New Mexico, Albuquerque, 1997-. *Other professional posts*: Consultant, Thurshun Consultants, Albuquerque, NM, 1980-; coordinator, Ethnic/Minority Directors' Coalition, 1983-; Apple Computer Corporation (Education Grants Program, 1986-); Museum of the American Indian Arts & Culture, State Museum of New Mexico, (Advisory Board, 1987-); New Mexico Architecture Foundation (advisory board, 1988-). *Major research*: Cohort Retention Study of Indian Students at UNM, 1973-84, 1985-; Preschool Computer Program in an Isolated American Indian Community, Education Grants Program, Apple Computer Corp., 1985-; On-site coordinator: "Headstart Classroom of the Future", U.S. Dept. of Health & Human Services, 1989 research involving the Isleta Pueblo Head Start Program along with two other sites in Michigan; Ethnographic Undercounts - 1990 Census, 1989, U.S. Census Bureau. *Community activities*: 9th Inter-American Indian Congress, Santa Fe, N.M. (U.S. organizing committee, 1985-); Zuni Tribal Museum, Zuni, N.M. (advisory board, 1985-); JOM/Indian Education Parent's Committee, Isleta Pueblo, N.M. (chair). *Memberships*: Native American Studies Association. *Awards, honors*: Postdoctoral Fellow, American Indian Studies, UCLA, 1984; public grantee, Atherton Trust, Honolulu, 1976; recipient of Participant Award, East-West Center, Honolulu. *Interests*: My main interest lay in the notion of continued tribal survival, and the various and varying strategies that have ensued in the course of this struggle. Currently, I have been doing research in the notion of tribal (traditional) consensus making and its theoretical modeling toward the idea of using this mechanism for the integration of tribal policy in the regional development process. *Biographical source*: Who's Who in the West (Marquis, 1985-); (Marquis; Who's Who Among Young Emerging Leaders (Marquis, 1987). *Published works*: Memoirs of an American Indian House: The Impact of a Cross-National Housing Program on Two Reservations, 1976; Foreword and series editor, Irredeemable America: The Indians' Estate and Land Claims, Edited by Imre Sutton; Contributing editor, Wicazo sa Review (Eastern Washington University, 1988-); foreword and series editor, Public Policy Impacts on American Indian Development; Modernization & Pueblo Lifeways: Isleta Pueblo, chapter in Pueblo Style & Regional Architecture (Van Nostrand Reinhold, 1989); many articles in various publications.

JOJOLA, TONY *(Thur-shun - Sunrise)*
(Isleta Pueblo) 1958-
(artist, craftsperson)
Born August 11, 1958, Albuquerque, N.M. *Education*: Institute of American Indian Arts, AA, 1978; College of Santa Fe, BFA, 1983. *Principal occupation*: Artist, craftsperson. *Address*: P.O. Box 725, El Prado, NM 87529 (505) 776-9657. *Other professional posts*: One/ two day lectures/symposiums. *Exhibitions*: Indian Pueblo Cultural Center, Albuquerque, NM, 1979; Southern Plains Indian Museum, Anadarko, OK, 1988; Indian Pueblo Cultural Center, Albuquerque, NM, 1990; Milicent Rogers Museum, Taos, NM, 1993; numerous selected group exhibitions. *Awards, honors*: Most Innovative Artist, Red Cloud Indian Art Show, Browning, MT, 1984; Indian Market—SWAIA, Santa Fe, NM (Misc. Contemporary, 1985; Misc. Contemporary, 1st & 2nd Place, 1986; Misc. Contemporary, 3rd Place, 1988; Misc. Contemporary, 1989, Creative Excellence Award, 1991; 1st Place & Honorable Mention, 1992; 1st Place, Diversified Art Forms, 1993); among others. *Membership*: Southwestern Association of American Indian Affairs. *Interests*: Free-blown glass and cast sculptural work. *Biographical sources*: "Anthony Jojola," by Gail Bird, in Indian Market Magazine, August-1988; "Tony Jojola," by Suzanne Carmichael, in The Travelers Guide to American Craft, 1990; "Glass Artist Tony Jojola Looking for a Niche," by John Villani, in Pasa Tempo, Aug. 16, 1991; "Award Winning Glass Sculpture," by Irvin Borowsky, in Artists Confronting the Inconceivable, 1992; among others. *Film*: "Indian Market—A Winter Event," by Ms. Lena Carr, a SWAIA-sponsored Symposium filmed Dec. 9, 1988 (K-Karr Productions, Albuquerque, NM).

JOKA, GARY (Navajo)
(school principal)
Affiliation: Holbrook Dormitory, P.O. Box 758, Holbrook, AZ 86025 (602) 524-6222.

JONAITIS, ALDONA 1948-
(museum director)
Born Nov. 27, 1948. *Principal occupation*: Museum director. *Address & Affiliation*: Director, University of Alaska Museum (1993-present), 907 Yukon Dr., Fairbanks, AK 99775 (907) 474-7505 Fax 474-5469; E-Mail: ffaj@uaf.edu.; American Museum of Natural History, 1989-93; SUNY, Stony Brook, NY, 1977-89. *Memberships*: American Association of Museum, American Anthropological Association, NAASA. *Published works*: Art of the Northern Tlingit, 1986; From the Land of the Totem Poles, 1988; Chiefly Feasts: The Enduring Kwakiutl Potlatch, 1991; A Wealth of Thought: Franz Boas on Native American Art, 1995; Looking North, Art from the University of Alaska Museum, 1998; The Yuquot Whalers' Shrine, 1999.

JONES, A. BRUCE
(executive director)
Affiliation: North Carolina Commission on Indian Affairs, 325 N. Salisbury St., Suite 579, Raleigh, NC 27603 (919) 733-5998.

JONES, CHARLENE
(tribal librarian)
Affiliation: Mashantucket Pequot Research Library, P.O. Box 3060, Indiantown Rd., Ledyard, CT 06339 (203) 536-7200.

JONES, CORA L.
(BIA regional director)
Affiliation: Great Plains Regional Office, BIA, Federal Bldg., 115 4th Ave. SE, Aberdeen, SD 57401 (605) 226-7943.

JONES, CYNTHIA
(museum curator)
Affiliation: Sheldon Museum, P.O. Box 269, Haines, AK 99827 (907) 766-2366.

JONES, DAN
(film producer)
Address: P.O. Box 421, Stillwater, OK 74076 (405) 372-8859 Fax 372-7571.

JONES, DAVID S. (Choctaw) 1928-
(educator)
Born July 24, 1928, Boswell, Okla. *Education*: Eastern A & M College, 1950-51; East Central State College, 1951-52; Central State University (Edmonds, OK), 1955-63, BA, MA. *Principal occupation*: Educator. *Affiliation*: Principal, Crystal Boarding School, Navajo, NM, 1983-92. *Other professional post*: Council for Exceptional Children, Navajo Area (vice president). *Military service*: U.S. Navy, 1945-47; U.S. Naval Reserve (18 years); U.S. Army Reserve (Staff Sergeant, 12 years); (Meritorious Service Medal, World War II Victory Medal, Asiatic Pacific Medal, Armed Forces Reserve Medal, Marksman. *Community activities*: El Reno Lions Club, Okla. (past president); Methodist Church (chairman, official board); Methodist Mens Club; Church School (superintendent). *Memberships*: National Indian Education Association (life member); Elementary School Principals Association; Oklahoma Governor's Council for Vocational Education; National Indian Scouting Association. *Awards, honors*: Masonic Teacher of Today Award; American Legions Award for Achievement; GrayWolf Award for Outstanding Indian Scouter, Boy Scouts of America. *Interests*: Travels with Naval and Army Reserve trainings. *Published work*: Co-author, A Guide for Teachers of Indian Students (OK Dept. of Education, 1972).

JONES, DORA ANN
(special collections librarian)
Affiliation: E.Y. Berry Library-Learning Center, Black Hills State University, 1200 University, Spearfish, SD 57799 (605) 642-6833.

JONES, GERALD J. (Port Gamble S'Klallam)
(tribal chairperson)
Affiliation: Port Gamble Business Committee, 31912 Little Boston Rd., NE, Kingston, WA 98346 (360) 297-2646.

JONES, HENRY L.
(monument supt.)
Affiliation: Wupatki and Sunset Crater National Monument, HC 33, Box 444A, Flagstaff, AZ 86001 (602) 527-7152.

JONES, MRS. JAMES L.
(museum director)
Affiliation: Caddo Indian Museum, 701 Hardy St., Longview, TX 75604 (214) 759-5739.

JONES, KATE
(historic site curator)
Affiliation: Angel Mounds State Historic Site, 8215 Pollack Ave., Evansville, IN 47715 (812) 853-3956.

JONES, KENNETH
(Indian band chief)
Affiliation: Pacheenaht Indian Band, General Delivery, Port Renfrew, BC, Canada V0S 1K0 (604) 647-5521.

JONES, LEON (Eastern Cherokee)
(tribal chief)
Affiliation: Eastern Band of Cherokee Tribal Council, Qualla Boundary, P.O. Box 455, Cherokee, NC 28719 (828) 497-2771.

JONES, MATTHEW
(Native American film producer/consultant)
Affiliation: Native American Public Broadcasting Consortium, P.O Box 83111, Lincoln, NE 68501 (402) 472-3522; editor, Newsletter.

JONES, MIKE (Zuni)
(tribal enterprise manager)
Affiliation: Pueblo fo Zuni Arts & Crafts, P.O. Box 425, Zuni, NM 87327 (505) 782-5531 Fax 782-2136. *Products*: Zuni jewelry, pottery, fetishes; contemporary art.

JONES, PATRICK STANFIELD (Tsalagi {Cherokee}) 1957-
(musician, singer/songwriter, arranger/composer)
Born March 23, 1957, Teaneck, NJ. *Principal occupation*: Musician, singer/songwriter, arranger/composer. *Address*: 35 Main St., Nyack, NY 10960 (914) 348-0446. *Affiliation*: Performs with Sylvester Brothers and solo compositions. *Membership*: Nuyagi Keetoowah Society.

JONES, PETER B. (Onondaga-Seneca) 1947-
(potter/sculptor)
Born June 8, 1947, Cattaraugus Indian Reservation, N.Y. *Education*: Institute of American Indian Arts; Archie Bray Foundation (Helena, MT). *Principal occupation*: Potter/sculptor. *Address*: P.O. Box 174, Versailles-Plank Rd., Versailles, NY 14168 (716) 532-5993. *Exhibitions*: Peter B. Jones Retrospective Exhibition (1965-90), Iroquois Indian Museum, Schoharie, NY, 1990; Pottery Through the Ages: Traditions in Clay, Pueblo Grande Museum, Phoenix, AZ, 1990; Contemporary Native Ceramics, CN Gorman Museum, University of California, Davis, 1991; New Works in Ancient Traditions, Shoestring gallery, Rochester, NY, 1991; Creativity in Our Tradition: Three Decades of Contemporary Indian Art, Institute of American Indian Arts, Santa Fe, NM, 1992: Reflecting Contemporary Realities, Los Angeles, County Folk Art & Craft Museum, 1993; Art of First Nations, Brantford, Ontario, 1993; Area Artists Collection 1993 Members Gallery, Albright-Knox Art Gallery, Buffalo, NY, 1993. *Permanent collections*: Indian Arts & Crafts Board, U.S. Dept. of the Interior, Washington, DC; Institute of American Indian Arts, Santa Fe, NM; Heard Museum, Phoenix, AZ; Everson Museum, Syracuse, NY; Iroquois Indian Museum, Howes Cave, NY; Southern Plains Indian Museum, Anadarko, OK; Rochester Museum & Science Center, Rochester, NY; New York State Museum, Albany; Museum of Fine Arts Boston, MA. *Awards, honors*: Div. Award, Best of Class, Scottsdale (AZ) Native American Cultural Foundation, 1987 & 1988; Best of Show, Festival of Iroquois Arts, Cattaraugus Indian Reservation, NY, 1989; Excellence in Iroquois Arts, Iroquois Indian Museum, Howes Cave, NY, 1990; Best of Show, Quinnehtukqut Native American Festival, E. Hartford, CT, 1992. *Works featured in the books & periodicals*: Southwest Art, Sept. 1988, Vol. 18 No. 4, "Contemporary Native American Ceramics"; Beyond Tradition-Contemporary Indian Art and Its Evolution by Jerry & Lois Jacka (Northland Press, 1988); Peter B. Jones, Iroquois Art, Retrospective Catalogue, Iroquois Indian Museum, Howes Cave, NY; Winds of Change, Fall 1991, Vol. 6 No. 4, "Reflections of a Native Vision: American Indian Contemporary Art" by Ray Moisa.

JONES, PETER L.
(museum director)
Affiliation: Owasco Teyetasta, Rt. 38A Emerson Park, 203 Genessee St., Auburn, NY 13021 (315) 253-8051.

JONES, ROBERT
(BIA agency supt.)
Affiliation: Shawnee Field Office, Bureau of Indian Affairs, 824 W. Independence, #114, Shawnee, OK 74801 (405) 273-0317.

JONES, ROBERTA (Seneca)
(artist, craftsperson)
Address: P.O. Box 174, Versailles, NY 14168 (716) 532-5993. *Interest*: Beadwork.

JONES, ROGER
(Indian band chief)
Affiliation: Shawanaga Indian Band, RR 1, Nobel, Ontario, Canada P0G 1G0 (705) 366-2526.

JONES, ROY, Jr. (Eskimo)
(AK village council president)
Affiliation: Native Village of Larsen Bay, P.O. Box 35, Larsen Bay, AK 99624 (907) 847-2207.

JONES, SCOTT 1959-
(primitive technology/outdoor skills instructor)
Born December 25, 1959, Canton, Ga. *Education*: Community College of the Air Force, AAS, 1985; University of Georgia, AB, 1990. *Principal occupation*: Primitive technology/outdoor skills instructor. *Address & Affiliation*: Director, Hofunee Programs - Prehistoric Living Skills, The Woods, Rt. 1, Box 182-A, Carlton, GA 30627 (706) 743-5144, 1987-. *Other professional posts*: Instructor, Continuing Education instructor, University of Georgia, Athens, 1988-; Dept. of Anthropology, Departmental Affiliate, 1993-. *Military service*: U.S. Air Force, 1982-85; Georgia Air National Guard, 1986-90 (Sergeant; Marksman Award). *Memberships*: Society of Primitive Technology (regional organizing coordinator); Society for Georgia Archaeology (Northeast Georgia Chapter President, 1992). *Interests*: "Attend courses in outdoor skills at the Boulder Outdoor Survival School in Rexburg, Idaho, and worked with many outstanding instructors in the field of primitive skills since 1987; instructed and co-instructed courses in aboriginal/outdoor skills at state parks in Georgia and South Carolina, the National Park Service, the South Carolina Institute of Archaeology and Anthropology, as well as for colleges, schools, museums, and wilderness camps throughout the Southeast; monthly aboriginal skills workshops, Hofunee Programs, Oglethorpe County, GA; and primitive skills demonstrations at Pow wows throughout the Southeastern U.S. I'm currently working on some projects relating to old world (European & African) prehistory. I'm also very interested & involved in sustainable low-impact lifestyles including organic farming, log home building (from raw timber), and making use of abundant local resources. I now live in a small log house I built. While it was under construction, I lived in my tipi (for about one year." *Biographical sources*: Athens Banner Herald, June 1993; CNN: July 1993 - filmed segment for character profile on "Earthnet" and Earth-Matters" programs. *Published work*: Contributing author, "The Profile," 1993, "Early Georgia," 1994 (periodicals for The Society for Georgia Archaeology); "Features & Profiles", (periodical of the Archaeological Society of South Carolina, 1994); Handbook of Primitive Gourdcraft (University of Georgia Press, Athens, 1995).

JONES, STANLEY G., SR. *(Scho Hallem)*
(Snohomish-Klallam) 1926-
(commercial fisherman; tribal vice chairperson)
Born July 10, 1926, Monroe, Wash. *Principal occupation*: Commercial fisherman; tribal chairperson. *Home address*: 5327 7th Ave. NE, Tulalip, WA 98271 (360) 659-6052. *Affiliations*: Owner, Jones Trucking, 1987-; owner, High Liner Fishing Supply, 1985-; *Other professional posts*: Tulalip Tribe of Washington (fishing committee, 1954-; board of directors, 1966-, chairperson, 1981-); member, Board of Directors of 1st Heritage Bank. *Military service*: U.S. Marine Corp, 1944-46. *Community activities*: Active in all tribal social services. *Memberships*: National Congress of American Indians, 1966-; Affiliated Tribes of the Northwest. *Awards, honors*: Appreciation Award, Tulalip Housing Authority, 1984; Helped secure tribal fishing rights, 1988; appointed by B.I.A., Dept. of the Interior, one of four member National Gaming Commission; received the 2001 Wendell Chino Humanitarian Award from the National Indian Gaming Association. *Interests*: National tribal timber delegation to China; travel; trade commission major timber tribes in U.S.; commercial fishing in Alaska, Canada and most of the states; will be writing book on years of establishing treaty fishing rights pre-1974 U.S. Supreme Court decision to 1989. *Biographical sources*: Guide to the Indian Tribes of the Northwest (University of Oklahoma Press); Paddle to Seattle 1989 Washington State Centennial.

JONES, STEPHEN S. *(Red Dawn)* (Santee Sioux) 1921-
(lecturer, educator, folklorist, anthropologist)
Born June 1, 1921, Flandreau, S.D. *Education*: Sioux Falls College, S.D., B.A., 1948; California State University, Fullerton, M.A., 1978. *Principal occupation*: Lecturer, educator, folklorist, anthropologist, American Indian Programs, Anaheim, CA. Resides in southern California. *Affiliations*: Curator of anthropology, Science Museum of Natural History, Gastonia, N.C. (6 years); *Other professional post*: Registered medical technologist. *Military service*: U.S. Army, 1942-45 (Staff Sergeant). *Memberships*: American Indian Lore Association (director); Continental Confederation of Adopted

Indians (director); American Anthropological Association; Southwest Museum; Minnesota Historical Society. *Awards, honors*: 1973 Catlin Peace Pipe Award, American Indian Lore Association. *Interests*: Field of American Indian dance, ethnology, history and folklore. Lifelong avocation in interpreting Indian lifeways (traveling extensively throughout the nation presenting Indian programs for schools and civil groups). Tour master for college groups into the Southwest; major field of interest—customs and traditions of Southwest Indians. Traveled nationally lecturing and researching, 1976-. *Published work*: Editor, Great on the Mountain: The Spiritual Life of Crazy Horse (Naturegraph, 1971); editor, Master Key (Southwest Museum, 1972-1982.

JONES, WILLIAM E. (Lummi)
(tribal chairperson)
Affiliation: Lummi Indian Business Council, 2616 Kwina Rd., Bellingham, WA 98226 (360) 384-1489.

JORDAN, DILLARD (Oklahoma Cherokee)
(historic site curator)
Affiliation: Sequoyah Home Site, Route 1, Box 141, Sallisaw, OK 74955 (918) 775-2413.

JORDAN, LAWRENCE
(hospital director)
Affiliation: Santa Fe PHS Indian Hospital, 1700 Cerrillos Rd., Santa Fe, NM 87501 (505) 988-9821.

JORDAN, SUE ZANN (Mescalero Apache) 1959-
(teacher)
Born December 17, 1959. *Education*: University of Illinois, BA, 1979; Sangamon State University, MA, 1983. *Principal occupation*: Teacher, Chapter I Coordinator. *Address*: Cibecue Community School, Cibecue, AZ 85911 (602) 332-2444/2480. *Affiliation*: Teacher, Chapter I Coordinator, Cibecue Community School, Cibecue, AZ, 1984-. *Other professional post*: Part-time teacher, Northern Pioneer College. *Membership*: Arizona Media Association. *Awards, honors*: State of South Dakota Poetry Award and money certificate; Golden Poet Award, World of Poetry. *Interests*: General: Poetry, art, music, education, earth science, and literature. Vocational: Woodworking, graphic arts, ceramics, weaving, and horticulture. *Travels*: "(I) traveled extensively in North and South America and less extensively overseas." *Published works*: Poetry, too numerous to list.

JORGENSEN, JOSEPH GILBERT 1934-
(professor of anthropology)
Born April 15, 1934, Salt Lake City, Utah. *Education*: University of Utah, BS, 1956; Indiana University, PhD, 1964. *Principal occupation*: Professor of anthropology. *Home address*: 1517 Highland Dr., Newport Beach, CA 92660 (714) 824-5894 (work); E-Mail: jjorgens@orion.oac.ucc.edu. *Affiliations*: Assistant professor, Antioch College, 1964-65, University of Oregon, 1965-68; professor of anthropology, University of Michigan, Ann Arbor, 1968-74; professor of anthropology and social sciences, School of Social Sciences, University of California, Irvine, Calif., 1974-. *Other professional posts*: Coordinator, Northern Ute Tribe (Unitah and Ouray Ute Indian Reservation, Fort Duchesne, Utah), 1960, '62; research associate, John Muir Institute, 1970-; research consultant to the following: Soboba Band of Indians, Louis Berger and Associates, Human Relations Area Files, and the Senate Select Committee on Indian Affairs. *Community activities*: Mariners Community Association (president); Society to Preserve Our Newport (board member); Newport Beach Aquatics Support Group (president). *Memberships*: Human Relations Area Files (board of directors); Native Struggles Support Group (board of directors and co-chair); Anthropology Resource Center (board of directors); American Association for the Advancement of Science (Fellow); American Anthropological Association (member of Ethics Committee, 1969-71); Society for Applied Anthropology (associate editor of Human Organizations, 1986-89); American Indian Historical Society (editorial advisory board, 1974-80); Sigma Xi. *Awards, honors*: John Simon Guggenheim Fellow, 1974-75; C. Wright Mills Book Award for Sun Dance Religion, 1972; F.O. Butler Lecturer at South Dakota State University, 1976; M. Crawford Lectures at the University of Kansas, 1980; Rufus Wood Leigh Lecture at the University of Utah, 1982; Ford Lecturer, Brazilian Anthropological Association, San Paulo. Interests: "Research into the rela-

tions among environment, language and culture in aboriginal western North America; analysis of the consequences to North American Indian, Eskimo, and Aleut societies from the nation's political economy." *Published works*: Salish Language and Culture (Indiana University, 1969); Sun Dance Religion (University of Chicago Press, 1972); Native Americans and Energy Development, I and II (Anthropology Resource Center, 1978 & 1984); Western Indians (W.H. Freeman, 1980); Oil Age Eskimos (University of California Press, 1990). Editorial board: Behavioral Science Research, 1973-; The Indian Historian, 1974-; Southwest Economy and Society, 1976-; Social Science Journal, 1978-; Environmental Ethics, 1978-; Social Policy Revue, 1981-; contributing articles to New York Review of Books, and to professional journals.

JOSEPH, ANDREW C.
(museum director/curator)
Affiliation: Colville Confederated Tribes Museum, P.O. Box 233, Coulee Dam, WA 99116 (509) 633-0751.

JOSEPH, ANGIE
(Indian band chief)
Affiliation: Dawson Indian Band, P.O. Box 599, Dawson City, Yukon, Canada Y0B 1G0 (403) 993-5387.

JOSEPH, FRANK A.
(BIA agency supt.)
Affiliation: Crow Creek Agency, Bureau of Indian Affairs, P.O. Box 139, Fort Thompson, SD 57339 (605) 245-2311.

JOSEPH, JASON L. (Sauk-Suiattle)
(tribal chairperson)
Affiliation: Sauk-Suiattle Tribal Council, 5318 Chief Brown Lane, Darrington, WA 98241 (360) 436-0131.

JOSEPH, JUDY
(BIA field rep.)
Affiliation: Puget Sound Field Office, Bureau of Indian Affairs, 2707 Colby Ave., Suite 1101, Everett, WA 98201 (425) 258-2651 Fax 258-1254.

JOSEPH, LOREN (Navajo)
(school principal)
Affiliation: Kayenta Boarding School, P.O Box 188, Kayenta, AZ 86033 (602) 697-3439.

JOSEPH, MICHAEL
(IHS-director of tribal activities)
Affiliation: Phoenix Area Office, 3738 N. 16th St., Suite A, Phoenix, AZ 85016 (602) 640-2106.

JOSEPH, NORMAN (Suquamish)
(Indian band vice-chief)
Affiliation: Suquamish Indian Band, P.O. Box 86131, N. Vancouver, BC, Canada V7L 4J5 (604) 985-7711.

JOSEPH, RACHEAL (Paiute-Shoshone)
(rancheria chairperson)
Affiliation: Lone Pine Paiute-Shoshone Tribe, P.O. Box 747, Lone Pine, CA 93545 (760) 876-1034.

JOSEPHY, ALVIN M., JR. 1915-
(author, historian)
Born May 18, 1915, Woodmere, N.Y. *Education*: Harvard College, 1932-34. *Principal occupation*: Author, historian. *Home address*: 4 Kinsman Lane, Greenwich, CT 06830 (203) 869-4953 Fax 625-0339; E-mail: ajosephy@discovernet.net. *Affiliations*: Associate editor, Time Magazine, 1951-60; editor-in-chief, American Heritage Publishing Co., Inc., New York, N.Y., 1960-79. *Other professional posts*: Consultant, Secretary of the Interior, 1963; commissioner and vice chairman, Indian Arts and Crafts Board, Dept. of the Interior, Washington, DC, 1966-70; president, National Council, Institute of the American West, Sun Valley, Idaho, 1976-83; contributing editor, American West Magazine, Tucson, Ariz., 1983-89; Board of Trustees, National Museum of the American Indian, Smithsonian Institution, 1990-96. *Military service*: U.S. Marine Corps, 1943-45 (Master Technical Sergeant; Bronze Star). *Memberships*: Association on American Indian Affairs (director, 1961-95); Museum of the American Indian (trustee, 1976-90; president, National Council, 1978-90); Western History Association; Society of American Historians; American Antiquarian Society. *Awards, honors*: Western Heritage Award, National Cowboy Hall of Fame, 1962, '65; Eagle Feather Award,

National Congress of American Indians, 1964; Award for Merit, American Association on State & Local History, 1965; Golden Spur, Golden Saddleman and Buffalo Awards, Western Writers of America, 1965; Guggenheim Fellowship, 1966-67; National Book Award nominee, 1968; Doctor of Humanities, Albertson College, Idaho, 1987; Charles Erskine & Scott Wood Award, Oregon Institute of Literary Arts, 1993; Wallace Stegner Award, Center of the American West, Boulder, Colorado, Govewrnor's Arts Award, Oregon, 1996; Red Earth Award, OKlahoma, 1997. *Interests*: History, culture and concerns of the American Indians; western American history; conservation; extensive western travel. *Biographical source*: Who's Who in America. *Published works*: American Heritage Book of the Pioneer Spirit, co-author (Simon & Schuster, 1959); The American Heritage Book of Indians (Simon & Schuster, 1961); The Patriot Chiefs (Viking Press, 1961); The Nez Perce Indians and the Opening of the Northwest (Yale University Press, 1965); editor, The American Heritage History of the Great West (Simon & Schuster, 1965); The Indian Heritage of America (Knopf, 1968); Red Power (McGraw-Hill, 1971); Now That the Buffalo's Gone (Knopf, 1982); War on the Frontier (Time-Life Books, 1986); The Civil War in the American West (Knopf, 1991); America in 1492 (Knopf, 1992); 500 nations (Knopf, 1994); among others.

JOURDAIN, JOSEPH (Couchiching First Nations)
(college instructor)
Affiliation: Leech Lake Tribal College, 6530 U.S. Hwy. 2 NW, Cass Lake, MN 56633 (218) 335-4220 Fax 335-4209.

JOURDAIN, STEVE
(Indian band chief)
Affiliation: Lac La Croix Indian Band, Box 640, Fort Frances, Ontario, Canada P9A 3N9 (807) 485-2431.

JOYCE, DEE DEE
(museum director/curator)
Affiliation: Catawba Museum of Anthropology, 2113 Brenner Ave., Salisbury, NC 28144 (704) 637-4111.

JUANCITO, CHARLES H. (Tall Dog)
(Rappahannock) 1909-
(educator)
Born January 30, 1909, Philadelphia, Penna. *Education*: University of Pennsylvania, Doctorate of Vocational Industrial Arts Education-Indian Studies, 1958; Messiah College, University of State of New York; Howard University. *Principal occupation*: Educator. *Address*: Native American Cultural Center, 927 N. 6th St., Philadelphia, PA 19123 (215) 627-7304. *Affiliations*: Teacher, Chester-Upland School District, Chester, PA; director, Native American Cultural Center. *Other professional posts*: Engineering technician, draftsman. *Community activities*: Native American Cultural Center of Delaware Valley (ex-director). *Memberships*: Rappahannock Tribe of Powhatan-Renape Nation (elder); National Education Association (secretary, First American Task Force); Pennsylvania Education Association; American Vocational Education Association; Pennsylvania Industrial Arts Association; Coalition of Eastern Native Americans. *Awards, honors*; Commendation for work as a teacher of adult basic education and English as a second language, State of Pennsylvania Adult Education Dept., Harrisburg, PA; Teacher of the Year, Vocational & Industrial Arts-Indian Studies; only Indian on Bicentennial 1976 Committee; the only American Indian in North America with degrees in Vocational-Industrial Arts Education; only American Indian guest at a reception of Mapuche Indians of Chile, and speaker honored by Government of Chile & Chamber of Commerce of Chile; speak, read & write four languages; East Coast activist *Interests*: Education; ethnology & anthropology; geology. English as a second language; Indian studies; adult basic education; master printer, master machinist.

JUANICO, JUAN S. (Acoma Pueblo)
(museum director)
Affiliation: Acoma Museum, P.O. Box 309, Pueblo of Acoma, Acomita, NM 87034 (505) 552-6606.

JUAREZ, DEBORA
(executive director)
Affiliation: Governor's Office of Indian Affairs, 1515 S. Cherry St., Box 40909, Olympia, WA 98504 (360) 753-2411 Fax 586-3653.

JUDD, CYNTHIA 1952-
(business owner)
Born August 19, 1952, Roswell, N.M. *Education*: Southwestern Business College, 1986. *Principal occupation*: Business owner. *Home address*: Resides in Albuquerque, NM (505) 271-1981 (work). *Affiliation*: American Heritage Indian Arts, Albuquerque, NM, 1990- (owner of authentic Indian-made warbonnet factory). *Membership*: Indian Arts and Crafts Association. *Awards, honors*: "Warbonnets took 1st, 3rd & 4th prizes at the New Mexico State Fair - under Indian art. All of my employees are Native Amercians."

JUDKINS, RUSSELL ALAN 1944-
(anthropologist)
Born August 8, 1944, Salt Lake City, Utah. *Education*: Brigham Young University, BS, 1966; Cornell University, PhD, 1973. *Principal occupation*: Anthropologist. *Home address*: 142 W. Buffalo St., Warsaw, NY 14569 (716) 245-5277. *Affiliation*: Associate professor, Department of Anthropology (1972-), State University of New York, College, Geneseo, NY 14454 (716) 245-5277. *Memberships*: American Anthropological Association (Fellow); Northeastern Anthropological Association; Society for Medical Anthropology; American Folklife Society; New York Folklore Society; Rochester Academy of Science. *Interests*: Social & cultural anthropology; symbolism; medical anthropology; American Indians (Iroquois and Catawba); migration and resettlement; folklore and mythology; American Indian world view; American Indian intellectuals. *Biographical source*: American Men and Women of Science. *Published works*: Iroquois Studies, 1987; First International Scholars Conference on Cambodia, 1988; Handbook for Archival Research in the Dr. Charles Bartlett Iroquois Collection, 1989. All published by Papers in Anthropology, SUNY College at Geneseo).

JULES, CLARENCE THOMAS (Kamloops)
(Indian band chief)
Affiliation: Kamloops Indian Band, 315 Yellowhead Highway, Kamloops, British Columbia, Canada V2H 1H1 (604) 828-9700.

JULES, HARVEY
(Indian band chief)
Affiliation: Adams Lake Indian Band, Box 588, Chase, British Columbia, Canada V0E 1M0 (604) 679-8841.

JULES, LINDA (Kamloops)
(museum curator)
Affiliation: Secwepemc Cultural Education Society, 345 Yellowhead Highway, Kamloops, British Columbia, Canada V2H 1H1 (604) 374-1096.

JULES, RAY (Kyuquot)
(Indian band chief)
Affiliation: Kyuquot Indian Band, Kyuquot, B.C., Canada V0P 1J0 (604) 332-5259.

JULIAN, BRENDA (Jicarilla Apache)
(tribal enterprise director)
Affiliation: Jicarilla Arts & Crafts & Museum, P.O. Box 507, Dulce, NM 87528 (505) 759-3242 ext. 274. *Products*: Jicarilla Apache beadwork, baskets, and paintings.

JUMBO, VIRGINIA
(Indian school principal)
Affiliation: Crownpoint Community School, P.O. Box 178, Crownpoint, NM 87313 (505) 786-6159 Fax 786-6163.

JUMPER, BETTY MAE (Seminole) 1927-
(director-Seminole communications)
Born April 27, 1927, Indiantown, Fla. *Education*: Cherokee (NC) Indian School, 1949 (first Seminole Indian to receive a high school diploma). *Principal occupation*: Director-Seminole communications. *Address*: Seminole Tribe, 6333 Forrest (N.W. 30th) St., Hollywood, FL 33024 (305) 962-4853. *Affiliation*: Chairperson, Seminole Tribe, 1967-71; director of communications and editor-in-chief of the Seminole Tribune (the newspaper of the Seminole Tribe), Seminole Tribe of Florida, 6333 Forrest (N.W. 30th) St., Hollywood, Fla. 33024. *Community activities*: Speaker at schools throughout Florida about Seminole Tribe; advisor, Manpower Development and Training Committee for the State of Florida; member, Independent Bible Baptist Church. *Memberships*: Native American Press As-

sociation; Florida Press Association. *Awards, honors*: Served on first tribal council as secretary-treasurer, and later resigned to serve as vice chairperson. In 1967, Betty Mae was the first woman elected as chairperson of the Seminole Tribe, serving four years. In 1968, Betty joined three Southeastern Tribes in signing a Declaration of Unity in Cherokee, N.C. The declaration implemented the Inter-Tribal Council, United Southeastern Tribes. While serving as chairperson of the Seminole Tribe, she was appointed by the President of the U.S. to become one of eight Indian members to work with Vice President Agnew. Only two women were chosen to serve on the committee, the National Congress on Indian Opportunity under President Nixon. She was chosen Woman of the Year by the Department of Florida Ladies Auxiliary of Jewish War Veterans of the U.S. for her outstanding contributions in the field of humanities. Betty Mae received a medicine peace pipe and a gold pin from the United Southeastern Tribes. *Interests*: Betty did much to improve the health, education and social conditions of the Seminole people. Through her efforts, the Tribe was one of the first tribes to obtain the CHR (Community Health Representative) Program. She was also effective in her concerns for Indian people on regional, national and state levels. *Published work*: ...And With the Wagon - Came God's Word (Seminole Print Shop, 1984); Legends of the Seminoles.

JUMPER, MOSES, Jr. *(Shem pa he gee)*
(Florida Seminole) 1950-
   (recreation director, coach, poet)
Born January 9, 1950, Fort Lauderdale, Fla. *Education*: Haskell Indian Jr. College, AA, 1971. *Principal occupation*: Recreation director, coach. *Address*: 6073 Stirling Rd., Hollywood, FL 33021 (813) 983-9234. *Affiliation*: Recreation director, Seminole Tribe of Florida, Hollywood, FL. *Other professional posts*: Cattleman & writer. *Community activities*: Chairman, Education Board of Florida. *Memberships*: President, Native American Sports Association; Native American Youth Organization. *Awards, honors*: Writers Award in Kansas from writers organization; Photo Award in Hollywood; Best Poem Award in Hollywood, FL; Who's Who in Poetry Award - numerous films & documentaries. *Biographical source*: Seminole Tribune. *Published work*: Echoes in the Wind (Pineapple Press, 1991).

JUNEAU, ALFRED LeROY *(Mutsah-Wanna-Kuhpi)*
(Blackfeet) 1919-
   (accountant)
Born August 21, 1919, Browning, Mt. *Education*: Southwestern University, BS, 1951. *Principal occupation*: Public accounting. *Home address*: 539 Crane Blvd., Los Angeles, CA 90065 (213) 225-8787. *Affiliations*: Fiscal Officer & Comptroller, Los Angeles Indian Center, 1971-75; Associate consultant, Los Angeles Regional Manager, Vice President, United Indian Development Association, 1975-80 (Native Indian Urban Business Development); United American Indian Council (Indian socio-economic concerns) Chairman of the Board & Treasurer, 1976-81; commissioner (appointed by Mayor Tom Bradley), Los Angeles City-County Native American Indian Commission, 1977-83. *Other professional posts*: Comptroller & Secretary-treasurer, U.S. Steel Buildings Co., Los Angeles, 1963-. *Military service*: U.S. Army Signal Corps, 1941-45 (Sergeant; two Bronze Stars, Good Conduct Medal, Europe-Africa-Middle Eastern Theatre Service Medal, Meritorious Unit Award). *Memberships*: California Public Accountants, 1951-81; Loyal Order of Moose, 1973-; National Congress of American Indians; Parent Teachers Association, Los Angeles; Smithsonian Institution; Blackfeet Indian Tribe, Browning, MT. (enrolled member); Veterans of Foreign Wars (VFW), 1996. *Interests*: General accounting and related financial matters; continuing interest in socio-economic betterment of American Indians in urban areas and on reservations; invited and attended, Feb. 2, 1978, President and Mrs. Carter's prayer breakfast in Washington, DC; and an All-Indian prayer breakfast at the U.S. Capitol in Washington, DC; have played professionally a trumpet in the U.S. and Europe. *Biographical source*: Vida Reporter (Los Angeles, April, 1977), a short biographical article with photo.

JUNEAU, CAROL (Blackfeet)
   (association president; state representative)
Affiliation: President, Montana Indian Education Association, P.O. Box 848, Harlem, MT 59526 (406) 353-

2205. *Other professional post*: Montana State Representative (D-Browning).

JUNEAU, DENISE (Hidatsa-Mandan/Blackfeet)
   (Indian education specialist)
Born April 5th in Oakland, Calif. *Education*: Montana State University, BA; Harvard Graduate School of Education, EdM. *Principal occupation*: Indian education specialist. *Address & Affiliation*: Office of Public Instruction, P.O. Box 202501, Helena, MT 59620 (406) 444-3013 Fax 444-1373. E-mail: djuneau@state.mt.us. *Memberships*: National Indian Education Association; Montana Indian Education Association; Montana Association of Teachers of English and Language Arts; American Education Research Association.

JUSTIN, WILSON
   (association president)
Affiliation: Ahtna, Inc., P.O. Box 649, Glennallen, AK 99588 (907) 822-3476.

JUSTUS, CYNDEE
   (editor)
Affiliation: Ak-Chin O'odham Runner, Ak Chin Indian Reservation, 42507 Peters & Nall Rd., Maricopa, AZ 85239 (602) 568-2095.

K

KAAPANA, DOUG (Hawaiian)
   (club president)
Affiliation: c/o Tukwila Sr. Club, Seattle, WA 98168 (206) 776-9420.

KADAKE, HENRICH (Eskimo)
   (AK village council president)
Affiliation: Organized Village of Kake Council, P.O. Box 316, Kake, AK 99830 (907) 758-6471.

KAGANAK, TIMOTHY (Athapascan)
   (AK village council president)
Affiliation: Native Village of Scammon Bay, P.O. Box 126, Scammon Bay, AK 99662 (907) 558-5113.

KAGAWA, SIEGFRIED S.
   (museum president)
Affiliation: Bernice Pauahi Bishop Museum, P.O. Box 19000-A, Honolulu, HI 96817 (808) 847-3511.

KAHKLEN, ALBERT
   (BIA agency supt.)
Affiliation: Anchorage Agency, Bureau of Indian Affairs, 1675 C St., Anchorage, AK 99501 (907) 271-4088 Fax 271-4083.

KAHKLEN, JOSEPH
   (Alaska liaison officer-BIA)
Affiliation: Bureau of Indian Affairs, Dept. of the Interior, MS-4140-MIB, 1849 C St., NW, Washington, DC 20240 (202) 208-5819.

KAHN, FRANKLIN (Navajo) 1934-
   (artist)
Born May 25, 1934, Pine Springs, Ariz. *Education*: Stewart Indian School. *Principal occupation*: Artist. *Address*: 4 N. Leroux St., Flagstaff, AZ 86001 (602) 774-0174. *Affiliation*: Sketch artist and sign painter, Federal Sign and Signal Corp., Flagstaff; co-owner with Mary Jane Kahn, Turquoise Hogan, Flagstaff, AZ. *Membership*: American Indian Service Committee. *Awards, honors*: Second Prize, Scottsdale National Indian Art Show. Interests: Watercolor and oil painting; Indian designs and symbols. *Published work*: Illustrator, Going Away to School (Bureau of Indian Affairs, 1951).

KAIGLER, DR. ANQUANITA
   (Indian education program director)
Affiliation: Lawton Public Schools, Indian Education Program, 753 Fort Sill Blvd., Lawton, OK 73502 (580) 357-6900 ext. 279 Fax 585-6473.

KAIRAIUAK, LARRY
   (project coordinator)
Affiliation: Two Spirits Project, National Native American AIDS Prevention Center, 436 14th St., Suite 1020, Oakland, CA 94609 (510) 444-2051 Fax 444-1593.

KAISWATUM, ART
   (Indian band chief)
Affiliation: Piapot Indian Band, Box 4, Craven, Saskatchewan, Canada S0G 0W0 (306) 781-4848.

KAKAR, LEONA M. (Papago & Pima)
   (former tribal chairperson)
Affiliation: Ak Chin Indian Community Council, 42507 W.Peters & Nail Rd., Maricopa, AZ 85239 (520) 568-2227.

KAKEWAY, GEORGE
   (Indian band chief)
Affiliation: Wauzhushk Onigum Indian Band, Box 1850, Kenora, Ontario P9N 3X7 (807) 548-5663.

KAKUM, JOHNSON
   (Indian band chief)
Affiliation: Little Pine Indian Band, Box 70, Paynton, Saskatchewan, Canada S0M 2J0 (306) 398-4942.

KALMAKOFF, ARCHIE (Eskimo)
   (AK village council president)
Affiliation: Ivanoff Bay Village Council, P.O. Box K1B, Ivanoff Bay, AK 99502 (907) 699-2204.

KAMINE, MARGIE
   (administrative director)
Affiliation: Wings of America, 801-J Griffin St., Santa Fe, NM 87501 (505) 982-6761.

KAMKOFF, WILLIE
   (AK village council president)
Affiliation: Native Village of Hamilton Council, P.O. Box 21030, Koatlik, AK 99620 (907) 899-4313.

KAMPESKA, GABE
   (elementary school principal)
Affiliation: Tiospa Zina Tribal School, Box 719, Agency Village, SD 57262 (605) 698-3953 Fax 698-7686.

KAN, SERGEI *(Shaakunastoo & Gunaak'w)* **1953-**
   (professor of anthro. & Native American Studies)
Born March 31, 1953, Moscow, Russia. *Education*: Boston University, BA, 1976; University of Chicago, MA, 1978, PhD, 1982. *Principal occupation*: Professor of anthropology and Native American Studies. *Home address*: 18 Wellington Cir., Lebanon, NH 03766 (603) 646-2550. E-mail: sergei.a.kan@dartmouth.edu *Affiliations*: Assistant professor of anthropology, University of Michigan, Ann Arbor, 1983-89; associate professor & chairperson, Dept. of Anthropology & Native American Studies Program, Dartmouth College, Hanover, NH 1989-. *Other professional post*: Editorial Board, "Journal of Ethnohistory." *Community activities*: Native American Council, 1989-; Hood Museum of Art (acquisitions committee, 1989-93; director's advisory council, 1990-91; faculty advisory committee, Institute of Arctic Studies, 1989-; Dartmouth Fellow, Research Program for the Comparative Study of Intergroup Conflict in Multinational States, 1991-94; faculty representative, Foundation for Jewish Life at Dartmouth, 1992-; Alaska Native Brotherhood, 1979-. *Memberships*: American Anthropological Association; American Ethnological Society; American Society for Ethnohistory; Alaska Anthropological Association; American Association for the Advancement of Slavic Studies; International Arctic Social Science Association. *Awards, honors*: Heizer Award for the Best Article in Ethnohistory by the American Society for Ethnohistory, 1987; American Book Award for "Symbolic Immortality," awarded by the Before Columbus Foundation, 1990. *Interests*: Ethnographic field research in southeastern Alaska since 1979 (intermittent); extensive archival research on Tlingit history & culture, since 1979; history of American and Russian anthropology; Russian anthropologists and the indigenous peoples of Siberia. *Biographical source*: "Death & Dying," Dartmouth Alumni Magazine, Sept. 1992. *Published works*: Translated & edited, Tlingit Indians of Alaska, by Fr. A. Kamenskii (University of Alaska Press, 1985); Symbolic Immortality: Tlingit Potlatch of the 19th Century (Smithsonian Press, 1989); Memory Eternal: Tlingit Culture and Russian Orthodox Christianity Through Two Centuries (University of Washington Press, 1999); edited volume (which includes Dr. Kan's essay): Strangers to Relatives: Adoption and Naming of Anthropologists in Native North America (University of Nebraska Press, 2001); numerous articles.

KANE EDWIN (White Mountain Apache)
(finance director)
Affiliations: Finance Director, Yavapai-Apache Nation, Camp Verde, AZ (520) 567-1007 Fax 567-3994. E-mail: ya125@yavapai-apache-nation.com; First V.P.-Board of Directors, Native American Finance Officers Association, P.O. Box 12743, Green Bay, WI 54307.

KAPASHESIT, RANDY
(Indian band chief)
Affiliation: Mocreebec Indian Government, Box 4, Moose Factory, Ontario, Canada (705) 658-4769.

KAPAYOU, EVERETT (Mesquakie)
(singer)
Address: 713-320th St., Tama, IA 52339 (515) 484-2453. A member of the Mesquakie tribe in Iowa, Everett is respected as a distinguished tribal elder and religious devotee and for his commanding knowledge of Mesquakie history. He is a singer of traditional Mesquakie songs and a 1993 recipient of the National Heritage Fellowship from the Folk Arts Program of the National Endowment for the Arts.

KAPLAN, DIANE
(radio network president)
Affiliation: Native Broadcast Center, Alaska Public Radio Network, 810 E. Ninth Ave., Anchorage, AK 99501 (907) 277-2776.

KAQUATOSH-ARAGON, YVONNE M.
(editor)
Affiliation: Menominee Tribal News, Menominee Indian Tribe, P.O. Box 397, Keshena, WI 54135 (715) 799-5168.

KAR, DANA WILSON
(Indian center director)
Affiliation: Center for American Indian Studies in Social Services, Washington University, Campus Box 1196, St. Louis, MO 63130 (314) 889-6288.

KARMUN, WILBUR, Sr. (Eskimo)
(AK village council president)
Affiliation: Native Village of Deering Council, P.O. Box 89, Ekwok, AK 99736 (907) 363-2145.

KARNES, CHRISTOPHER A. (Tuscarora of NY)
(attorney)
Born in 1969, Maryland. *Education*: Dartmouth College, BA, 1991; American University, JD, 1994. *Office Address*: Dorsey & Whitney LLP, 1001 Pennsylvania Ave., NW, Suite 300 South, Washington, DC 20004 (202) 824-8800 Fax 824-8990; E-mail: karns.christopher@dorseylaw.com. *Affiliations*: U.S. Dept. of the Interior, Office of the Solicitor, Division of Indian Affairs, 1994-98; Attorney, Dorsey & Whitney LLP, 1998-. Associate in the Indian and Gaming Law practice group at Dorsey & Whitney since 1998. Practices in the areas of federal Indian law, and gaming law.

KASANOUKWAS-SUNDHEIM, JOYCE (Penobscot-Mohawk)
(craftsperson)
Address: Indian Sun, Inc., 3831 Monica Parkway, Sarasota, FL 34235 (941) 366-0023.

KASAYULIE, JAMES T. (Yup'ik Eskimo)
(AK village council president)
Affiliation: Platinum Village Council, Platinum, AK 99651 (907) 979-8126.

KASAYULIE, WILLIE (Akiachak Yup'ik Eskimo)
1951-
(administrator)
Born June 1, 1951, Fairbanks, Alaska. *Education*: High school. *Principal occupation*: Council chairperson. *Address*: P.O. Box 70, Akiachak, AK 99551 (907) 825-4813 (home). *Affiliations*: Chairperson & CEO, Akiachak IRA Council, Akiachak, AK, 1984-; chairperson, Association of Village Council Presidents (AVCP, Inc.), Box 219, Bethel, AK, 1985-. *Other professional posts*: Chairperson, Akiachak Limited, 1989-90; member, BIA Tribal Task Force, 1990-. *Military service*: Alaska Army National Guard (discharged in 1990 with the rank of 1st Lt.). *Community activities*: Chairperson, Yupiit School District, 1985-; Alaska Federation of Natives (Board member, 1991-). *Memberships*: Alaska Native Coalition (chairperson, 1985-); board member, Native American Rights Fund, 1990-. *Awards, honors*: 1985 AFN Citizen of the Year; 1987 CEDC Tribal Leadership Award. *Interests*: "I travel promoting self-sufficiency and self-determination for the Yup'ik Eskimo on local, national and international levels opf policy development effecting indigenous peoples." *Biographical sources*: Life Magazine (Feb. 1986); Who's Who Among American High School Students, 1969/71 edition; The Wake of An Unseen Object, by Tom Kizzia.

KASHEVAROF, GILBERT G. (Aleut)
(AK village council president)
Affiliation: St. George Island Council, P.O. Box 940, St George Island, AK 99660 (907) 859-2205.

KASKALLA, LELA (Nambe Pueblo)
(pueblo governor)
Affiliation: Nambe Pueblo Council, Rt. 1, Box 117-BB, Santa Fe, NM 87501 (505) 455-2036.

KASKASKE, DANNY (Kickapoo of Oklahoma)
(tribal chairperson)
Affiliation: Kickapoo of Oklahoma Business Committee, P.O. Box 70, McLoud, OK 74851 (405) 964-2075.

KAST, SHERRY
(communications specialist)
Affiliation: United National Indian Tribal Youth, Inc., 4010 Lincoln Blvd., Suite 202, P.O. Box 25042, Oklahoma City, OK 73125 (405) 424-3010.

KATCHATAG, STANTON (Eskimo)
(AK village president)
Affiliation: Unalakleet Village Council, P.O. Box 270, Unalakleet, AK 99684 (907) 624-3622.

KATO, BRUCE
(museum curator)
Affiliation: Sheldon Jackson Museum, 104 College Dr., Sitka, AK 99835 (907) 747-8981.

KATZEEK, DAVID G.
(executive director)
Affiliation: Sealaska Heritage Foundation, 1 Sealaska Plaza, Suite 201, Juneau, AK 99801 (907) 463-4844.

KAUFFMAN, CARLOTTA (*According to Coyote*)
(actress)
Address: P.O. Box 3085, Payson, AZ 85547. She tells Plains Indian Coyote stories in theatrical form...a combination of traditional storytelling and modern drama suitable for all ages. A one-person, one act play.

KAULEY, MATTHEW
(executive director)
Affiliation: Association of American Indian Physicians, 1235 Sovereign Row, Suite C-7, Oklahoma City, OK 73108 (405) 946-7072 Fax 946-7651.

KAULEY, RALPH, JR.
(health center director)
Affiliation: Carnegie PHS Indian Health Center, P.O. Box 1120, Carnegie, OK 73105 (405) 654-1100.

KAVALSKY, MAGGIE (Athapascan)
(AK village mayor)
Affiliation: Native Village of Nuiqsut, Nuiqsut, AK 99723 (907) 480-6714.

KAVANAGH, THOMAS W.
(museum curator)
Address & Affiliation: Curator of Collections, William Hammond Mathers Museum, Indiana University, Bloomington, IN. *Published work*: The Comanches: A History, 1706-1875.

KAVASCH, MS. E. BARRIE (Cherokee/Creek/Powhatan)1942-
(author, artist, ethnobotanist, food historian)
Born December 31, 1942, Springfield, Ohio. *Education*: Western Connecticut University. *Principal occupation*: Author, artist, ethnobotanist, food historian. *Address*: 324 Main St. South, P.O. Box 239, Bridgewater, CT 06752 (860) 354-3128 Fax 868-1649. *Affiliations*: President, Native Harvests, Inc. (food business), Bridgewater, CT, 1987-present; Trustee & Research Associate, Institute of American Indian Studies, 1990-present; *Other professional posts*: Guest lecturer on numerous college campuses and at museums; curator of the "Native Harvests: Plants in American Indian Life" Exhibition for SITES-Smithsonian, 1984-87. *Community activities*: Bridgewater Historical Society (Trustee); curator of American Indian Visions 1992 at the Silo Gallery at Ruth & Skitch Henderson's Silo in New Milford, CT. *Memberships*: Association on American Indian Affairs; Native American Rights Fund; Byelorussia American Society. *Awards, honors*: O'Connor Lecturer at Cornell Plantations, Cornell University, Ithaca, NY, Oct. 1992; Cullum Lecturer at Augusta College, Augusta, GA, Oct. 1992. *Interests*: Ms. Kavasch has traveled, researched, and lectured through much of North & Central America, and has worked with and written about numerous Native American Indian tribes and interest groups. She has done extensive ethnobotanical research, especially food & medicinal documentation. She writes, photographs & illustrates, as well as collects & presses plant specimens, while documenting diverse herbal/healing knowledge. "I am working on a new book on Native American Healing for a major publisher, as well as a book on American Indian plants and people, along with several children's books for young readers. I will also be curating another fine gallery show of select American Indian art. Planning committee for the 1991 & 1992 American Indian Thanksgiving & Feast of Reconciliation at the Cathedral of St. John the Devine in New York City." *Biographical sources*: "American Indian Foods: A Harvest of American Indian Specialties" in Bon Appetite, Nov. 1987; "A Native Thanksgiving: American Indian Cooking" in Cooks Magazine, Nov. 1984; "My Grandmother's Hands" in Through the Kitchen Window (Beacon, 1997); and "Wild Things: Wild Foods" in Martha Stewart Living, March 1996. *Published works*: Native Harvests: Recipes & Botanicals of the American Indians (Random House, 1979); Herbal Traditions: Medicinal Plants in American Indian Life (SITES: Smithsonian Institution, 1984); Botanical Tapestry (Gunn Historical Museum, 1979); Guide to Eastern Mushrooms, 1982, Introducing Eastern Wildflowers, 1982, and Guide to Northeastern Wild Edibles, 1981 - full color photographic guide books - (Hancock House/Big Country Books); American Indian Cooking (Native Harvests, 1991); Earthmaker's Lodge: Native American Folklore, Activities, Foods (Cobblestone Press, 1994);Enduring Harvests: Native American Foods & Festivals for Every Season (Globe Pequot Press, 1995); "Native Northeastern Foods & Healing" (chapter) in Enduring Traditions (Greenwood Press, 1995); A Student's Guide to Native American Genealogy (Oryx Press, 1996); American Indian Earthsense: Herbaria, Ethnobotany & Ethnomycology (IAIS, 1996).

KAWENNIIOSTA BOOTS (Onondaga-Iroquois)
(museum intern)
Address & Affiliation: School of American Research, P.O. Box 2188, Santa Fe, NM 87504 (505) 995-1924; E-Mail: Boots@sar. *Other professional posts*: Intern, Iroquois Indian Museum, 1995; Carnegie Museum (Pittsburgh), 1995. *Memberships*: American Association of Museums; AIES; SWAIA.

KAY, JIM (Miccosukee)
(tribal enterprise manager)
Affiliation: Miccosukee Gift Shop & Cultural Center, P.O. Box 440021, Tamiami Station, Miami, FL 33144 (305) 223-8380.

KAYE, ROGER
(Indian band chief)
Affiliation: Vuntut Gwitchen (Old Crow) Indian Band, Old Crow, Yukon, Canada Y0B 1N0 (403) 966-3261.

KEAHNA, SAMSON
(Indian center director)
Affiliation: American Indian Center, 1630 West Wilson, Chicago, IL 60640 (312) 275-5871.

KEALIINOHOMOKU, JOANN WHEELER 1930-
(anthropologist, independent scholar)
Born May 20, 1930, Kansas City, Mo. *Education*: Northwestern University, BS, 1955, MA, 1965; Indiana University, PhD, 1976. *Home address*: 518 S. Agassiz St., Flagstaff, AZ 86001 (520) 774-8108; E-Mail: jwk3@jan.ucc.nau.edu. Website: www.ccdr.org. *Principal affiliation*: Director of Collections, Cross-Cultural Dance Resources, Inc., Flagstaff, AZ (a non-profit organization - a living museum for scholars & performers to talk, study, consult). *Other professional posts*: Faculty, Semester at Sea, Institute for Shipboard Edu-

cators, University of Pittsburgh; visiting professor for University of Hawaii, Manoa Campus; University of Hawaii, Hilo Campus; New York University; World Campus Afloat. *Community activities*: Native American for Community Action (board of directors, 1977-82; secretary of board, 1979-82). *Memberships*: American Anthropological Association (Fellow); American Ethnological Society; American Folklore Society; Association for the Study of Play; Bishop Museum Association, CORD (Congress on Research in Dance) (board of directors, 1974-77); Cross-Cultural Dance Resources (founder & director); Society for Ethnomusicology (council member, 1967-70, 1980-83). *Awards, honors*: Weatherhead Resident Scholar, School of American Research, Santa Fe, 1974-75; Research Fellow, East-West Center, Honolulu, Hawaii, 1981; Dedicatee for Tenth Annual Flagstaff Indian Center's Basketball Tournament, 1983; 1996 "Distinguished Public Scholar" Award from Arizona Humanities Council; "Outstanding Contribution to Dance Research" award by Congress on Research in Dance. *Interests*: "Performance arts, especially dance; cultural dynamics; field work in Southwest U.S., especially with Hopi and other Pueblos." *Biographical sources*: Dictionary of International Biography; The World Who's Who of Women; Who's Who in Oceania; Who's Who of American Women. *Published works*: Hopi and Polynesian Dance: A Study in Cross-Cultural Comparison (Ethnomusicology, 1967); with Frank Gillis, Special Bibliography: Gertrude Prokosch Kurath (Ethnomusicology, 1970); Dance Culture as a Microcosm of Holistic Culture (New Dimensions in Dance Research: Anthropology and Dance—The American Indian, 1974); Theory and Methods for an Anthropological Study of Dance, Ph.D. dissertation, anthropology (University Microfilms, 1976); The Drama of the Hopi Ogres, chapter in Southwestern Indian Ritual Drama, edited by Charlotte Frisbie, (University of New Mexico Press, 1980); Music and Dance of the Hawaiian and Hopi Peoples, chapter in Becoming Human Through Music (Music Educators National Conference, 1985); "The Would-Be Indian", chapter in Anthropology and Music: Essays in Honor of David P. McAllester, edited by Charlotte Frisbie (University of Michigan Press, 1985); "The Hopi Katsina Dance Event 'Doings'", chapter in Seasons of the Kachina, edited by Lowell J. Bean (Ballena Press, 1989); among other articles, reviews and chapters in various publications.

KEAMS, GERALDINE (GERI) *(Yithaazbah')* (Navajo) 1951-
(actress, storyteller, writer)
Born August 19, 1951, Winslow, Ariz. *Education*: University of Arizona, BFA, 1978. *Principal occupation*: Actress, storyteller, writer. *Home address*: 2767 Butter Creek Dr., Pasadena, CA 91107. *Affiliation*: President, Hozhoni Productions, Hollywood, CA (film, video, theatre productions). *Other professional posts*: Navajo storyteller presents songs and stories of her people. Dramatizes legends and myths. She's on tour with Los Angeles Music Center on Tour. *Community activities*: Board of Advisors, ATLATL, a Native American arts organization, Native American Television; promoted Native Americans in film, video, media. *Memberships*: National Association for the Preservation & Perpetuation of Storytelling (NAPPS), 1989-; Screen Actors Guild, 1970-; American Indian Registry for the Performing Arts (board member, 1988-90; president, board of directors, 1990-91). *Awards, honors*: Bahti Award - Outstanding American Indian Student, University of Arizona; recipient of a Los Angeles Cultural Affairs Traditional Arts Grant. *Interests*: "Began performing at 7 years old; co-starred in, "Outaw Josie Wales," with Clint Eastwood; appearances in "Northern Exposure," "Twin Peaks." Storyteller featured at the National Storytelling Festival in Jonesborough, Tenn, St. Louis, Miami, and Smithsonian Discovery Theatre for Children Institute's, Washington, DC; San Francisco Storytellers on Tape Series, 1993. Featured on television shows, "Nickelodeon," & "Sesame Street": traveled as a storyteller throughout he U.S., Canada & Europe." *Published works*: Children's book - Grandmother Spider Steals the Sun (Northland Press, 1995); Poet Anthologies - "A Gathering of Spirits," 1985, "When Clouds Threw This Light," 1983, "Circle of the Moon."

KEDELTY, THERESA A.
(school supervisor)
Affiliation: Cottonwood Day School, Navajo Route 4, Chinle, AZ 86503 (520) 725-3256 Fax 725-3255.

KEEL, FRANKLIN
(BIA regional director)
Affiliation: Eastern Regional Office, BIA, 711 Stewarts Ferry Pike, Nashville, TN 37214 (615) 467-1700 Fax 467-1701.

KEEL, LELAND
(BIA agency supt.)
Affiliation: Seminole Agency, Bureau of Indian Affairs, 6075 Stirling Rd., Hollywood, FL 33024 (954) 581-7050 Fax 792-7340.

KEELER, BRAD (Cherokee of Oklahoma)
(president, board of directors)
Affiliation: President, Board of Directors, Association on American Indian Affairs, P.O. Box 268, Sisseton, SD 57262 (605) 698-3998.

KEENAN, DAVID
(Indian band chief)
Affiliation: Teslin Tlingit, Teslin, Yukon, Canada Y0A 1B0 (403) 390-2532.

KEENATCH, JOHN
(Indian band chief)
Affiliation: Big River Indian Band, Box 519, Debden, Saskatchewan, Canada S0J 0S0 (306) 724-4216.

KEENE, TRACY (Black Eyes) (Comanche) 1966-
(MIS coordinator, office manager)
Born Oct. 1, 1966. *Address*: 1100 N. University, Suite 133, Little Rock, AR 72207 (501) 666-9032 Fax 666-5875.

KEESWOOD, LARRY (Dine-Navajo) 1954-
(silversmith)
Born January 26, 1954, Shiprock, N.M. *Education*: High school. *Principal occupation*: Silversmith. *Address*: P.O. Box 210, Kingston, MA 02364 (508) 830-1256. *Affiliation*: Native Expressions (Native fine arts store-jewlery smithing), Plymouth, MA. *Other professional post*: Machinist. *Interests*: Attends powwows; rodeos, basketball, fishing, reading, creating dream catchers, antique jewelry, Native American music, horses, dancing, and singing at the drum when invited to do so

KEGG, MATTHEW M. (Chippewa) 1953-
(teacher)
Born October 5, 1953, Brainerd, Minn. *Education*: Bemidji State University, BA, 1976. *Principal occupation*: Teacher. *Address*: Star Route Resides in Minnesota. *Affiliations*: Graduate assistant, Indian Studies Program, Bemidji State University, 1980-81; teacher, Mille Lacs Indian Reservation, Onamia, MN, 1981-. *Awards, honors*: Recipient of Certificate of Appreciation from State Dept. of Education of Minnesota, 1980, for contributions to Indian education; Most Valuable Player award from hockey team, Bemidji Northland Icers, 1980. *Interests*: "Hockey; published several articles in magazines; poetry; outdoor activities - camping, backpacking, canoeing, biking."

KEHOE, ALICE BECK 1934-
(professor of anthropology)
Born September 18, 1934, New York, N.Y. *Education*: Barnard College, BA, 1956; Harvard University, PhD, 1964. *Principal occupation*: Professor of anthropology. *Home address*: 3014 N. Shepard Ave., Milwaukee, WI 53211 (414) 962-5937 Fax 229-5848. *Affiliations*: Assistant professor of anthropology, University of Nebraska, 1965-68; professor of anthropology, Marquette University, Milwaukee, WI, 1968-99. *Memberships*: American Anthropological Association; Society for American Archaeology; American Society for Ethnohistory. *Interests*: Cultural anthropology and archaeology; fieldwork among Blackfoot, Cree and Dakota tribes in the U.S. & Canada; archaeological fieldwork in Montana & Saskatchewan; ethnographic fieldwork in Montana, Alberta, Saskatchewan, and Bolivia. *Published works*: Hunters of the Buried Years (Regina, Sask. School Aids & Text Book Co., 1962); North American Indians (Prentice-Hall, 1981; 2nd ed. 1992); The Ghost Dance (Holt, Rinehart & Winston, 1989); Humans: An Introduction to Four-field Anthropology (Routledge, 1998); The Land of Prehistory: A Critical History of American Archaeology (Routledge, 1998); Shamans and Religion: An Anthropological Exploration in Critical Thinking (Waveland, 2000); America Before the European Invasions (Longman, 2002).

KECKLER, KENTON (Cheyenne River Sioux)
(CPA, NAFOA secretary)
Affiliation: CPA, Kenton Keckler & Co., P.C., Santa Fe, ,NM 87505 (505) 955-0747 Fax 955-0795. E-mail: cpaskk@cs.com. *Other professional post*: Secretary, Native American Finance Officers Association, P.O. Box 12743, Green Bay, WI 54307.

KEDELTY, STANLEY
(school principal)
Affiliation: Chilchinbeto Day School, P.O. Box 740, Kayenta, AZ 86033 (520) 697-3448 (phone & fax).

KELLAR, DAVID
(radio program director)
Affiliation: WOJB - 88.9 FM, Lac Courte Oreilles Ojibwe Broadcasting Corp., Route 2, Box 2788, Hayward, WI 54843 (715) 634-2100.

KELLEY, BEATRICE
(health administrator)
Affiliation: Lac Vieux Desert Band Health Clinic, P.O. Box 446, Watersmeet, MI 49969 (906) 358-4457.

KELLY, AUDREY DIANA
(Indian band chief)
Affiliation: Ohamil Indian Band, C4, Site 22, RR 2, Hope, B.C., Canada V0X 1L0 (604) 869-2627.

KELSEY, JULIE
(editor)
Affiliation: Choctaw Community News, Mississippi Band of Choctaw Indians, Route 7, Box 21, Philadelphia, MS 39350 (601) 656-5251.

KENDALL, H. KEITH
(organization executive secretary)
Affiliation: Executive secretary, Associated Committee of Friends on Indian Affairs, P.O. Box 2326, Richmond,, IN 47375 (765) 935-0801.

KENNEDY, CHERYL (Confederated Tribes of Grand Ronde)
(tribal chairperson)
Affiliation: Confederated Tribes of the Grand Ronde Tribal Council, 9615 Grand Ronde Rd., Grand Ronde, OR 97347 (503) 879-5211.

KENNEDY, ROY (Shoshone)
(former tribal chairperson)
Affiliation: Timbisha Shoshone Tribe, P.O. Box 206, Death Valley, CA 92328 (619) 786-2374.

KENNAN, LAUREL
(health clinic director)
Affiliation: Bay Mills Indian Commuity Health Clinic, Route 1, Box 313, Brimley, MI 49715 (906) 248-3204.

KENNELLY, MICHAEL E.
(chief)
Affiliation: Smoki People, 145 N. Arizona Ave., P.O. Box 10224, Prescott, AZ 86304 (928) 445-1230.

KENNY, MAURICE (Mohawk)
(short fiction editor & publisher, poet)
Address: 15 Lake St., Box 1029, Saranac Lake, NY 12983 (518) 891-5865.

KEO, SANDRA (Sac & Fox of Missouri)
(tribal chairperson)
Affiliation: Sac & Fox of Missouri Tribal Council, 305 N. Main St., Reserve, KS 66434 (785) 742-7471.

KEPLIN, DEBBIE L. (Turtle Mountain Chippewa) 1956-
(general manager-radio station)
Born February 28, 1956, Belcourt, N.D. *Education*: Flandreau Indian School, 1974; University of North Dakota (2 years liberal arts instruction). *Principal occupation*: Public radio station general manager. *Home address*: P.O. Box 236, Belcourt, ND 58316. *Affiliation*: General manager, KEYA Radio Station, Belcourt, ND. *Other professional posts*: Occupied positions at KEYA radio of program director, news director, music director, and executive secretary. *Community activities*: Member, St. Ann's Society, Belcourt, ND; assistant-religious education, St. Anthony's Catholic Church, Belcourt; member, Turtle Mountain Musicians; member, Turtle Mountain Historical Society. *Memberships*: National Association of Female Executives, 1985-;

Corporation for Public Broadcasting-National Public Radio (authorized representative). *Awards, honors*: Certificate of Native American Leadership Training by the Community Council of the Northern Plains Teacher Corps, Nov. 1979 & Feb. & April, 1980; Certificate of Training-Explosive Devices Training by the U.S. Dept. of the Interior, Sept., 1984; dedicated service to the KEYA Radio Station and the Belcourt community by Turtle Mountain Community School, Nov., 1985; for community service by Turtle Mountain Band of Chippewa Indians, Feb., 1985. *Interests*: "To promote and educate the local community and surrounding communities on the history and culture of the Turtle Mountain Band of Chippewa through the use of radio. To develop programs focusing on problems affecting the local community, such as alcoholism, unemployment, housing, recreation, etc. To encourage the training of high school students in the operation of broadcast facilities-radio." *Programs produced*: All Nations Music, 1980- (features traditional and contemporary Native American music, legends and stories); Memorial to James Henry, former chairman of Turtle Mountain Band of Chippewa, 5-minute piece aired nationally on radio series First Person Radio of Minn. in Sept., 1983; Music of the Turtle Mountains, 1985- (program features the talents and biographies of local artists, musicians and poets); the music of Floyd Westerman, Sr. Mary Anthony Rogers, many local fiddlers, Adella and Gilbert Kills Pretty Enemy, 1985- (program features biographical sketches of artists through interview and music selections).

KERKMAN, MARCEL (Navajo)
(school principal)
Affiliation: Alamo Navajo School, P.O. Box 907, Magdalena, NM 87825 (505) 854-2543.

KERNAK, ALBERT (Eskimo)
(AK village council president)
Affiliation: Napakiak Native Village, Napakiak, AK 99634 (907) 589-2227.

KERR, THOMAS
(museum CEO)
Affiliation: The Mitchell Indian Museum, Kendall College, 2408 Orrington Ave., Evanston, IL 60201 (708) 866-1395.

KESSELER, DAVID, M.D.
(clinical director)
Affiliation: Zuni PHS Indian Hospital, P.O. Box 467, Zuni, NM 87327 (505) 782-4431.

KETCHER, JOHN
(health center director)
Affiliation: Washoe Tribal Health Center, 950 Hwy. 395 S., Gardnerville, NY 89410 (702) 883-4137.

KETCHUM, DEE (Delaware)
(tribal chief & chairperson)
Address & Affiliation: Delaware Tribe of Indians, 220 NW Virginia Ave., Bartlesville, OK 74003 (918) 336-5272 Fax 336-5513.

KETZLER, ALFRED R., SR. (Athabascan)
(vice-president, board of directors)
Affiliation: Vice-President, Board of Directors, Association on American Indian Affairs, P.O. Box 268, Sisseton, SD 57262 (605) 698-3998.

KEWAYGOSHKUM, ROBERT (Ottawa)
(tribal chairperson)
Affiliation: Grand Traverse Band of Ottawa & Chippewa Indians, Peshawbestown Community Center, 2605 N.W. Bayshore Dr., Suttons Bay, MI 49682 (231) 271-3538.

KHERA, SUSHEILA
(executive director)
Affiliations: Fairbanks Native Assn., Fairbanks, AK, 1983-92; executive director, Institute of Alaska Native Arts, P.O. Box 70769, Fairbanks, AK 99707 (907) 456-7491 Fax 451-7268, 1996-. *Community activities*: Fairbanks North Star Borough Commission on Historic Preservation. *Membership*: Fairbanks Arts Association.

KHOW, VIDA
(health center director)
Affiliation: Winslow PHS Indian Health Center, P.O. Drawer 40, Winslow, AZ 86047 (602) 289-4646.

KIBBLE, JOHN F.
(Indian center director)
Affiliation: Native American Center, Lake Superior State University, 1000 College Dr., Sault Ste. Marie, MI 49783 (906) 635-2223.

KICKINGBIRD, K. KIRKE (Kiowa)
(attorney, law professor)
Address: Institute for the Development of Indian Law, 2501 N. Blackwelder, Oklahoma City, OK 73106 (405) 521-5188 Fax 521-5185; E-Mail: kkbird@frodo.okcu.edu. *Affiliations*: Executive Director, Institute for the Development of Indian Law, Oklahoma City, OK, 1971-present; law professor, Oklahoma City University, School of Law, 1988-present. *Community activities*: Native American Asset Advisers - board member. *Memberships*: American Bar Association; Federal Bar Association; Native American Bar Association; Oklahoma Indian Bar Association. *Published works*: "One Hundred Million Acres," and "Indians and the U.S. Constitution: A Forgotten Legacy.".

KICKINGBIRD, LYNN
(editor)
Affiliation: American Indian Journal, Institute for the Development of Indian Law, 2600 Summit Dr., Edmond, OK 73034

KICKINGBIRD, ROBIN (Kiowa)
Has been involved in tribal libraries for several years and is currently working to set up a Tribal Library Association in Oklahoma. She published "The Directory of Tribal Libraries" in 1991. She has worked in the Metropolitan Library System of Oklahoma City & in the Archives of the Oklahoma Historical Society, which is known for its extensive collection of documents related to Native American history. She was awarded the first Minority Fellowship for Librarian at the American Library Association in 1991. She has worked as a law librarian and is now attending law school at the University of Oklahoma - College of Law.

KIDD, SAM (Cherokee)
(artist)
Address: Sam Kid Originals, Rt. 2 Box 66-4, Muldrow, OK 74948 (918) 427-3793. *Products*: original artwork; limited edition prints.

KIDWELL, CLARA SUE (Choctaw/Chippewa/Creek) 1941-
(college professor)
Born July 8, 1941, Tahlequah, Okla. *Education*: University of Oklahoma, BA, 1962; MA, 1966, PhD, 1970. *Principal occupation*: College professor. *Address*: University of Oklahoma, Native American Studies Program, 455 W. Lindsey, Rm. 805, Norman, OK 73019 (405) 325-2312 Fax 325-0842. *Affiliations*: Lecturer, Kansas City Art Institute, 1966-68; instructor, Haskell Indian Junior College, 1970-72; assistant professor, American Indian Studies Department, University of Minnesota, 1972-74; associate professor, Native American Studies, University of California, Berkeley, 1974-; assistant director of cultural resources, National Museum of the American Indian, Smithsonian Institution, Washington, DC, 1993-95; director, Native American Studies, University of Oklahoma, OK, 1995-present. *Memberships*: American Historical Association; Western History Association; American Society for Ethnohistory (president, 1991); History of Science Society; American Indian Science and Engineering Society. *Awards, honors*: Rockefeller Foundation Humanities Fellowship, 1976-77. *Published work*: The Choctaws: A Critical Bibliography (University of Indiana Press, 1981); Choctaws & Missionaries in Mississippi, 1818-1918 (University of Oklahoma Press, 1994).

KIE, GERALD
(school principal)
Affiliation: Laguna Elementary School, P.O. Box 191, Laguna, NM 87026 (505) 552-9200 Fax 552-7294.

KIGER, LOUISE, R.N.
(director)
Affiliation: Nursing Education Center for Indians, Indian Health Service, 5600 Fishers Lane, Rockville, MD 20857 (301) 443-1840.

KIHEGA, MARY
(association secretary-treasurer)
Affiliation: National Indian Social Workers Association, P.O. Box 45, Valentine, AZ 86437-0045.

KILLER, GRACE FOUR
(head counselor-Indian organization)
Affiliation: Navajo Nation Higher Education, P.O. Drawer S, Window Rock, AZ 86515 (800) 223-7133 (in AZ); (800) 243-2956, elsewhere.

KILLS PRETTY ENEMY, MICHAEL
(school principal)
Affiliation: Rock Creek Day School, P.O. Box 127, Bullhead, SD 57621 (605) 823-4971.

KILPATRICK, JACQUELYN (Choctaw-Cherokee)
(professor of English)
Affiliations: Professor of English, Governor's State University, University Park, IL; Professor of English, California State University, Channel Islands. *Published works*: Celluloid Indians: Native Americans & Film (University of Nebraska Press, 1999) Louis Owens: Literary Reflections on His Life & Work (University of Oklahoma Press, 2004).

KIMBALL, CARLA REICHERT (Ottowah) 1949-
(Native American cultural heritage instructor)
Born May 8, 1949, Muskegon, Mich. *Education*: University of Alabama, MEd, 1987. *Principal occupation*: Native American cultural heritage instructor. *Address*: Resides in Alabama. *Affiliation*: Curriculum planning/teacher, Scottsboro City Schools, Scottsboro, AL, 1983-. *Memberships*: National Indian Education Association; Alabama Indian Education Association. *Awards, honors*: Basic Education Grant Award, 1989 for research on Cherokee Treaties; resolution from Alabama Governor Guy Hunt - outstanding program. *Interests*: Native American studies; Native American art studies. Presentations at Anniston Army Depot (Anniston, AL), Birmingham Museum (Birmingham, AL), Russell Cave National Monument (Bridgeport, AL), Burritt Museum (Huntsville, AL); and Gadsden Graduate Center, University of Alabama (Gadsden, AL).

KIMBALL, ERNEST H.
(health center director)
Affiliation: Puget Sound PHS Indian Health Station, 2201 6th Ave., Rm. 300, Seattle, WA 98121 (206) 615-2781.

KIMBLE, GARY NILES (Gros Ventre)
(commissioner)
Born in 1944, Mont. *Education*: University of Montana, BA, 1966; University of Montana-College of Law, JD, 1972. *Principal occupation*: Commissioner. *Address*: Administration for Native Americans, U.S. Dept. of Health & Human Services, Humphrey Bldg., 200 Independence Ave., SW, Washington, DC 20201 (202) 690-7776. *Affiliations*: Partner & General Counsel for Fort Belknap Indian Community, Kimble, Smith & Connors, Missoula, MT, 1972-75; assistant professor, Native American Studies, University of Montana, Missoula, 1974-79; Chief Counsel, U.S. Senate Select Committee on Indian Affairs, Washington, DC, 1979; delegate to U.S.-Canada Treaty Negotiations, U.S. Dept. of State, 1979-82; Executive Director, Columbia River InterTribal Fish Commission, 1979-82; Advisor on Indian Affairs, State of Montana, Office of the Governor, 1983-89; adjunct professor of Federal Indian Law & director of Affirmative Action Program, Northwestern School of Law, Lewis & Clark College, 1987-89; executive director, Association on American Indian Affairs, New York, NY, 1989-93; commissioner Administration for Native Americans, U.S. Dept. of Health & Human Services, Washington, DC, 1994-. *Other professional posts (legal & consultation)*: Kimball & Associates (consulting & economic development firm, 1982-) Major clients included: Qua-Qui Corp., Missoula, MT, 1982-84; Fort Peck Tribe, NAES College, Poplar, MT, 1984-87; Valley Industrial Park, Glasgow, MT, 1985-86; American Training & Technical Assistance, Albuquerque, NM, 1987-88; Tulalip Tribe, Marysville, WA, 1988; Multnomah Co. Risk Management Team, Portland, OR, 1988-90; Health & Human Services, Public Health Indian Health, Portland, OR, 1988-89. Aboriginal Public Policy Institute (member, Board of Directors & Advisory Board), 1990-. *Public service*: Northwest Communities Project, Port-

land, OR (chairperson, Board of Directors), 1986-89; Minority Education, Research & Training Institute, New York Medical College, New York, NY (co-principal investigator), 1990-93.

KIMERY, JAMES
(school director/counselor)
Affiliation: Flagstaff Dormitory, P.O. Box 609, Flagstaff, AZ 86002 (520) 774-5270.

KINDLE, WILLIAM (Rosebud Sioux)
(tribal council president)
Affiliation: Rosebud Sioux Tribal Council, P.O. Box 430, Rosebud, SD 57570 (605) 747-2381.

KING, ANDREW
(Indian band chief)
Affiliation: Lucky Man Indian Band, 401 Packham Place, Saskatoon, Saskatchewan, Canada S7N 2T 7 (306) 374-2828.

KING, CLARICE
(school chairperson)
Affiliation: Two Eagle River School, Flathead Indian Reservation, P.O. Box 160, Pablo, MT 59855 (406) 675-0292 Fax 674-0294.

KING, DUANE H.
(museum director)
Affiliation & Address: National Museum of the American Indian, Smithsonian Institution, George Gustav Heye Center, One Bowling Green, New York, NY 10002 (212) 283-2420 Fax 491-9302. *Past affiliations*: Director, Cherokee National Historical Society, Tahlequah, OK; director, Cherokee National Museum (TSA-LA-GI), Cherokee Heritage Center, Tahlequah, OK; editor, "Journal of Cherokee Studies, Museum of the Cherokee Indian, Cherokee, NC.

KING, GWEN G.
(museum director)
Affiliation: Indian Museum of Lake County, Ohio, c/o Lake Erie College, 391 W. Washington, Painesville, OH 44077 (216) 352-3361.

KING, HAROLD (Navajo)
(school principal)
Affiliation: Many Farms High School, P.O. Box 307, Many Farms, AZ 86538 (602) 781-6226.

KING, MARTIN J.
(organization chairperson)
Affiliation: Committee for Action for Rural Indians, 1235 Hazelton, Petoskey, MI 49770 (616) 347-0059.

KING, PATRICIA L.
(commission director)
Affiliation: Maryland Commission on Indian Affairs, 100 Community Place, Crownsville, MD 21032 (410) 514-7651.

KING, RICHARD L.
(executive director)
Affiliation: Cross & Feather News, Tekkakwitha Conference National Center, P.O. Box 6768, Great Falls, MT 59406 (406) 727-0147.

KING, ROSS
(radio program director)
Affiliation: "South Dakota Forum," & "Voices of the Plains," South Dakota Public Radio Network, P.O. Box 5000, Vermillion, SD 57069 (605) 677-5861.

KING, THOMAS
(Indian studies dept. chairperson)
Affiliation: American Indian Studies Dept., University of Minnesota, 102 Scott Hall, 72 Pleasant St. SE, Minneapolis, MN 55455 (612) 624-1338 Fax 624-3858.

KING, TRACY C. (Gros Ventre & Assiniboine)
(tribal council president)
Affiliation: Fort Belknap Community Council, Rt. 1, Box 66, Harlem, MT 59526 (406) 353-2205.

KING, WINDELL R. (Mohawk) 1960-
(tribal research & development coordinator)
Born in 1960, Massena, N.Y. *Affiliation & Address*: Hercules Development, P.O. Box 6, Hogansburg, NY 13655 (619) 653-1012.

KING-TANTTU, MARGARET
(college dept. director)
Affiliation: Indian/Minority Services Dept., Mesabi Range Community & Technical College, 1001 Chestnut St. W., Virginia, MN 55792 (218) 749-7727 Fax 749-0318. E-mail: m.king-tanttu@mailmr.mnscu.edu.

KINGEEKUK, KENNETH (Eskimo)
(AK village council president)
Affiliation: Native Village of Savoonga, P.O. Box 129, Savoonga, AK 99769 (907) 984-6414.

KINGERY, JAMES
(site manager)
Affiliation: Moundbuilders State Memorial, 7091 Brownsville Rd., SE, Glenford, OH 43739 (614) 787-2476; The Ohio Indian Art Museum, 99 Cooper Ave., Newark, OH 43055 (614) 344-1920.

KINNEY, RODNEY P. (Half Moon)
(Yup'ik Eskimo) 1932-
(engineer)
Born September 11, 1932, Nome, Alaska. Education: University of California, San Jose, B.S. (Civil Engineering), 1960; graduate studies at University of California, Berkeley & San Jose, and University of Alaska, Anchorage. *Principal occupation*: Engineer. *Address*: P.O. Box 771102, Eagle River, AK 99577 (907) 694-2332 (work). *Professional posts*: Geotechnical consultant, Woodward Clyde Consultants, Anchorage, AK, 1961-75; engineering coordinator, Alyeska Pipeline Service Co., 1975-79; manager of Engineering & Planning Division, Anchorage Water & Wastewater Utility, 1979-1980; principal engineer, Rodney P. Kinney Associates, Eagle River, Alaska, 1980-. *Military service*: U.S. Navy, 1951-59. *Community activities*: Local Chamber of Commerce; Municipal Advisory Commission for Water & Wastewater; Founding Trustee of Alaska Southcentral Museum of Natural History; Vice-chair of Youth Club of Anchorage. *Memberships*: American Society of Civil Engineers; Bering Straits Native Association; American Indian Science and Engineering Society; American Water Works Association; American Public Works Association. *Interests*: Rodney P. Kinney Associates, a qualified Eskimo firm, was established October 2, 1980. The firm emphasizes consultation and services in general civil engineering, including roads & drainage, water and sewer, as well as soil testing & data collection. We also offer geophysical (seismic refraction and resistivity) and slope inclinometer services, water resource development services, and consultation for private and public systems. "I am currently studying Russian and preparing for my 6th visit to Russia and the Republics. Expert at current Russian affairs and of eastern Siberian anthropology. Plan a mutual "dig" in near future. Have flown my Cessna to Russia last June (1991) across the Diomedes to Provedinya and back. Have received an honorary PhD of highest order from MCA Riga Latvia for special recognitions. Am being considered as Latvia Ambassador Counsel for Alaska." *Biographical sources*: Who's Who in the West; Who's Who in Technology Today; International Men of Distinction; many scientific/geographical papers.

KINSEY, DANNA NICOLE (Axteca) 1970-
(historian, museum curator)
Born April 25, 1970, Santa Barbara, Calif. *Education*: BA in U.S. History, Native American Studies & Geography; Masters (in progress), Landscape Architecture. *Principal occupation*: Historian, museum curator. *Address*: P.O. Drawer 170, Moose, WY 83012 (307) 739-3591 Fax 739-3504. *Affiliation*: National Park Service Historian; Curator, Colter Bay Indian Arts Museum, Grand Teton National Park, Moose, WY. *Community activities*: Grand Teton National Park Cultural Rendezvous, 1999; Mexican Independence Fiesta, 1999.

KIPP, WOODROW LOUIS (Sun Chief)
(Blackfeet) 1945-
(guidance counselor; journalism instructor; columnist)
Born October 5, 1945, Browning, Mont. (Blackfeet Reservation). *Education*: University of Montana, BA (Journalism), 1991. *Principal occupation*: Guidance counselor; journalism instructor & columnist. Resides in Missoula, MT (406) 243-5834 (work). *Affiliation*: Guidance counselor & journalism instructor, University of Montana, Missoula, MT, 1991-. *Other professional posts*: Columnist, Lakota Times (SD), Great

Falls Tribune (MT), and Missoula Independent. *Military service*: U.S. Marine Corps, 1964-68 (Vietnam, 1965-67); Trail of Broken Treaties, Wounded Knee occupation. *Commuity activities*: Lecturer at school and civic organizations. *Memberships*: Native American Journalists Association; Blackfeet Medicine Pipe Society; Magpie Society. *Awards, honors*: Great Falls Tribune, Native American Scholarship Award. *Interests*: Pow-wow dancer; grass dance.

KIRBY, MARY M.
(project director)
Affiliation: MacArthur Foundation Library Video Project, P.O. Box 409113, Chicago, IL 60640 (800) 847-3671.

KITCHEYAN, KATHLEEN W. (San Carlos Apache)
(tribal chairperson)
Affiliation: San Carlos Apache Tribe, P.O. Box 0, San Carlos, AZ 85550 (928) 475-2361 Fax 475-2567

KITKA, JULIA E.
(association president; editor)
Affiliation: Alaska Federation of Natives, 1577 C St. #300, Anchorage, AK 99501 (907) 276-7989. *Other professional post*: Editor, "AFN News," monthly newsletter.

KITO, LEILANI
(AK Indian association president)
Affiliation: Petersburg Indian Association, P.O. Box 1418, Petersburg, AK 99833 (907) 772-3636.

KITTO, RICHARD (Santee Sioux)
(tribal chairperson)
Affiliation: Santee Sioux Tribal Council, Route 2, Niobrara, NE 68760 (402) 857-3302.

KITTREDGE, JOHN, M.D.
(chief medical officer)
Affiliation: IHS Office of Health Program Research & Development, 7900 South "J" Stock Rd., Tucson, AZ 85746 (520) 295-2406.

KITZES, JUDITH A., M.D.
(IHS-chief medical officer)
Affiliation: Albuquerque Area Office, Indian Health Service, 505 Marquette Ave., NW, Suite 1502, Albuquerque, NM 87102 (505) 766-2151.

KIZER, DARRELL (Washoe)
(tribal chairperson)
Affiliation: Stewart Community Council, 5258 Snyder Ave., Carson City, NV 89701 (702) 885-9115.

KIZER, LENORA (Washoe)
(tribal vice-chairperson)
Address: 854 Amador Cr., Carson City, NV 89705 (702) 687-3111 (office). *Affiliation*: Washoe Tribal Council.

KLEIN, BONITA
(school administrator)
Affiliation: Menominee Tribal School, P.O. Box 39, Neopit, WI 54150 (715) 756-2354 Fax 756-2364.

KLENITZ, BETTY
(commission director)
Affiliation: Michigan Commission on Indian Affairs, P.O. Box 30026, Lansing, MI 48909 (517) 373-0654.

KLESERT, DR. ANTHONY L.
(dept. director)
Affiliation: Navajo Nation Archaeology Dept., Northern Arizona University, P.O. Box 6013, Flagstaff, AZ 86011 (520) 523-7428.

KLIMIADES, MARIO NICK
(museum librarian/archivist)
Affiliation: The Heard Museum, 22 E. Monte Vista Rd., Phoeniz, AZ 85004 (602) 252-8840.

KNACK, MARTHA C. 1948-
(professor, anthropologist)
Born January 27, 1948, Orange, N.J. *Education*: University of Michigan, BA, 1969, PhD, 1975. *Principal occupation*: Professor, anthropologist. *Address & Affiliation*: Dept. of Anthropology & Ethnic Studies, University of Nevada, 4505 Maryland Pkwy., Las Vegas, NV 89154-5003 (702) 895-3590 Fax 895-4823 (1977-present; chairperson, 1983-86). *Other professional posts*: Consulting for Native American Rights Fund,

1986-88; Pyramid Lake Paiute Tribe, 1984-87; Walker River Paiute Tribe & U.S. Dept. of Justice, 1994-present; adjunct professor, Boyd School of Law, 2002. *Awards, honors:* Distinguished Professor, 2002; John C. Ewers Award for Ethnohistory, 2002. *Memberships:* American Anthropological Association; American Ethnological Society; American Society for Ethnohistory; Southwestern Anthropological Association; Great Basin Anthropological Conference. *Awards, honors:* Barrick (University of Nevada) Distinguished Research Scholar, 1991; Rockefeller Fellow, 1989-90. *Interests:* Great Basin Native American culture & history, Native American water rights & legal history, Native American women & social structures. *Published works:* "Life Is With People: Household Organization of the Contemporary Southern Paiute Indians of Utah" (Ballena Press, 1980); "Contemporary Southern Paiute Household Structure & Bilateral Kinship Clusters" (HRAF, 1982); "As Long As the River Shall Run: An Ethnohistory of Pyramid Lake Reservation, Nevada," with Omer C. Stewart (University of California Press, 1984); "Native Americans & Wage Labor: Ethnohistorical Perspective," edited with Alice Littlefield (University of Oklahoma Press, 1996); Boundaries Between: Southern Paiutes, 1775-1995 (University of Nebraska Press, 2001).

KNAPP, MILLICENT
(editor)
Affiliation: Turtle Quarterly," Native American Center for the Living Arts, 25 Rainbow Blvd., S., Niagara Falls, NY 14303 (716) 284-2427.

KNICK, STANLEY
(museum director/curator)
Affiliation: Native American Resource Center, Pembroke State University, Pembroke, NC 28372 (919) 521-4214.

KNIGHT, HALE P. (Pomo)
(former tribal chairperson)
Affiliation: Hopland Band of Pomo Indians, P.O. Box 610, Hopland, CA 95449 (707) 744-1647.

KNIGHT, MIKE (Pomo)
(rancheria chairperson)
Affiliation: Sherwood Valley Rancheria, 190 Sherwood Hill Dr., Willits, CA 95490 (707) 459-9690.

KNIGHT, STANFORD (Te-Moak Shoshone)
(tribal chairperson)
Affiliation: Battle Mountain Band Council, 37 Mountain View Dr. #C, Battle Mountain, NV 89820 (775) 635-2004.

KNIGHT, STILLMAN, Jr. (Te-Moak Western Shoshone)
(tribal council chairperson)
Affiliation: South Fork Band Council, Box B-13, Lee, NV 89829 (702) 744-4273.

KNIGHT, TED
(company president)
Address & Affiliation: President, Washington Consulting & Management Associates, Inc., P.O. Box 5169, Arlington, VA 22205 (703) 532-2210 Fax 532-0704.

KNIGHT, YVONNE T. (Ponca) 1942-
(attorney)
Born December 19, 1942, Pawnee, Okla. *Education:* University of Kansas, BS, 1965; University of New Mexico, School of Law, JD, 1971. *Principal occupation:* Attorney. *Home address:* 1268 Westview Dr., Boulder, CO 80303 (303) 447-8760 (office). *Affiliation:* Native American Rights Fund, Boulder, CO (staff attorney and member, Litigation Management Committee), 1972-. *Memberships:* Colorado Indian Bar Association; American Indian Bar Association; American Indian Policy Review Commission (Task Force on Law Consolidation, Revision, and Codification, 1975-76). *Awards, honors:* Pioneer Minority Women's Attorneys Award by Colorado Women's Bar Association, 1992; Reginald Haber Smith Fellowship, 1971-74.

KNIGHT-FRANK, JUDY (Ute)
(tribal chairperson)
Affiliation: Ute Mountain Ute Tribal Council, General Delivery, Towaoc, CO 81334 (970) 565-3751.

KNOCKWOOD, B.A. (Micmac) 1932-
(director-Indian center)
Born July 18, 1932, Micmac Reservation, Nova Scotia, Canada. *Education:* St. Mary's University, 1977-84. *Principal occupation:* Director-Indian center. *Home address:* 2158 Goffingen St., Halifax, Nova Scotia, Canada B3K 3B4 (902) 420-0686 (office). *Affiliations:* Instructor, Cambrian College, Sudbury, Dalhousie University; director, Micmac Learning Center, Halifax, N.S., 1988-. *Other professional posts:* Spiritual Indian Medicine Man. *Military service:* Royal Canadian Artillery; served in Canada, USA, Japan and Korea (awarded the Korean Medal and U.N. Service Medal). *Community activities:* Involved in human rights at both provincial and national level; public speaker on native rights and native spirituality. *Memberships:* National Native Advisory Council, Connections Canada of the Solicitor General's Department; Spiritual Science fellowship; Assembly of First Nations; National Native Veterans Association; Canadian Legion; Korean Veterans Association. *Awards, honors:* Received a lifetime appointment to the Micmac Nation's Grand Council; given the title of the Micmac Spiritual Medicine Man by the Grand Chief. *Interests:* "I re-introduced the traditional Native beliefs, philosophy , holy ritual, and sacred ceremonies to Native Micmacs and others who are interested in traditional Indian beliefs. Teach and assist Native people in sacred fasting to receive a "vision" and spiritual purification through the Sweat Lodge Ceremony."

KNOTT, ELIJAH
(Indian band chief)
Affiliation: Wasagamack Indian band, Wasagamack, Manitoba, Canada R0B 1Z0 (204) 457-2337.

KNOWS GUN, ELLIS "RABBIT"
(Ba Sa' Goshe)(Crow) 1948-
(administration , fine arts)
Born in Crow Agency, Mont. *Education:* Little Big Horn College (Crow Agency, MT), AA, 1988. *Principal occupation:* Administration, fine arts. *Address:* Box 133, Crow Agency, MT 59022 (406) 638-2922 (work). *Affiliation:* Crow Tribe, Crow Agency, MT. *Other professional post:* Fine Arts & Advisory Board, Native American Cultural Institute, Billings, MT. *Military service:* U.S. Army, 1968-71; U.S. Army Reserves (Billings, MT), 1983-86. His paintings portray Native American themes in an abstract manner. Knows Gun has been exhibiting his works since 1973, when he received the M.L. Woodrow Award at the 6th annual Red Cloud Indian Art Show in Pine Ridge, South Dakota. *Community activities:* Parish Council vice-president, St Dennis Parish, Crow Agency, MT; PAC Committee Chairman, School District 17H, Hardin, MT; Crow Tribe (secretary, 1976-78; chairman, Crow Air Quality Commission, 1992); past speaker on environmental issues affecting Crow Tribe; Carbon County Arts Guild, 1992. *Awards, honors:* Fine Arts awards; 1986 AIHEC basketball champs (Nationals.) *Biographical source:* Montana's Indians Yesterday & Today.

KNOWS-HIS-GUN, JOYCE (Northern Cheyenne)
(board member)
Affiliation: National Indian Youth Council, 318 Elm SE, Albuquerque, NM 87102.

KOCH, ELIZABETH, M.D.
(clinical director)
Affiliation: Sophie Trettevick Indian Health Center, P.O. Box 410, Neah Bay, WA 98357 (206) 645-2233.

KOESTER, DR. DAVID C.
(Alaskan Native studies instructor)
Affiliation: Dept. of Alaskan Native Studies, Dept. of Anthropology, Box 757720, 310 Eielson Bldg., Fairbanks, AK 99775 (907) 474-7288 Fax 474-7453.

KOEZLINA-IRELAN, MARILYN (Eskimo)
(AK community council president)
Affiliation: King Island Native Community Council, P.O. Box 992, Nome, AK 99762 (907) 443-5494.

KOHNEN, AUDREY (Mdewakanton Sioux)
(tribal president)
Affiliation: Prairie Island Indian Community, 5636 Sturgeon Lake Rd., Welch, MN 55089 (651) 388-2554.

KOLB, ADELA
(Indian education center director)
Affiliation: Director, Rincon Indian Education Center, P.O. Box 1147, Valley Center, CA 92082 (760) 749-1386 Fax 749-8838.

KOMONASEAK, LUTHER (Eskimo)
(AK village council president)
Affiliation: Native Village of Wales, P.O. Box 549, Wales, AK 99783 (907) 664-3511.

KOMPKOFF, GARY (Aleut)
(AK village council president)
Affiliation: Native Village of Tatitlek, P.O. Box 171, Tatitlek, AK 99677 (907) 325-2311.

KONICEK, STEVEN, M.D.
(clinical director)
Affiliation: Kayenta PHS Indian Health Center, P.O. Box 368, Kayenta, AZ 86033 (602) 697-3211.

KOONOOKA, GERRARD
(AK village council president)
Affiliation: Gambell Village Council, P.O. Box 99, Gambell, AK 99742 (907) 985-5346.

KOOSEES, DAN
(Indian band chief)
Affiliation: Kashechewan Indian Band, General Delivery, Kashechewan, Ontario, Canada P0L 1S0 (705) 275-4440.

KOOSHET, JOHN
(Indian band chief)
Affiliation: Wabigoon Indian Band, Box 41, Dinorwic, ON, Canada P0V 1P0 (807) 938-6684.

KORTLEVER, RON
(BIA field rep.)
Affiliation: Siletz Field Office, Bureau of Indian Affairs, P.O. Box 569, Siletz, OR 97380 (541) 444-2679 Fax 444-2513.

KOSBRUK, HARRY W. (Eskimo)
(AK village council president)
Affiliation: Perryville Village, P.O. Box 101, Perryville, AK 99648 (907) 853-2203.

KOSKI, RENEE M.
(Indian education program director)
Affiliation: Mt. Iron/Buhl High School, Indian Education Program, 5720 Mineral Ave., Mt. iron, MN 55768 (218) 735-8216.

KOSTURA, JOHN
E-mail: jkostura@nartnatam.com

KOSTZUTA, HENRY (Apache)
(tribal chairperson)
Affiliation: Apache Tribal Business Committee, P.O. Box 1220, Anadarko, OK 73005 (405) 247-9493 Fax 247-7617.

KOTA, SHARON L.
(Indian education program coordinator)
Affiliation: Port Huron Area School District, Indian Education Program, 1320 Washington St., Port Huron, MI 48061 (810) 989-2727 Fax 984-6624.

KOZEVNIKOFF, EILEEN (Athapascan)
(AK village council director)
Affiliations: Native Village of Tanacross, P.O. Box 77130, Tanacross, AK 99776 (907) 366-7160; health service director, Tanana Chiefs Conference Health Center, 122 First Ave., Fairbanks, AK 99701 (907) 452-8251.

KOZLOWSKI, GERALDINE
(Indian education program director)
Affiliation: Duluth Public Schools, Indian Education Program, 215 N. 1st Ave., Duluth, MN 55802 (218) 723-4150 Fax 723-4194.

KRAFT, HERBERT C. 1927-
(professor of anthropology, museum director)
Born June 1, 1927, Elizabeth, N.J. *Education:* Seton Hall University, 1947-50, MA, 1961; Hunter College, C.U.N.Y., MA, 1969. *Principal occupation:* Professor of anthropology & director of University Museum, Seton

Hall University, South Orange, NJ, 1960-97. *Address*: Unknown. *Other professional posts*: Archaeological consultant for cultural resources surveys. *Military service*: U.S. Merchant Marines, 1945-47. *Community activities*: New Jersey Historic Sites (member, State Review Board). *Memberships*: Archaeological Society of Staten Island (member, Executive Board); Society of Professional Archaeologists; Archaeological Society of New Jersey (president, 1974-78, 1986-90; editor of Bulletin; honorary member); Eastern States Archaeological Federation; New York State Archaeological Association (Fellow; president, 1982-84); New Jersey Academy of Sciences (Fellow); Society for Pennsylvania Archaeology; Middle Atlantic Archaeological Conference (president, 1985-87); Middle States Archaeological Conference. *Awards, honors*: Archie Award, Society for Pennsylvania Archaeology; recipient of two grants from the New Jersey Historical Commission; ten grants from the National Park Service, for excavations of prehistoric sites in New Jersey; John Alden Mason Award, Society for Pennsylvania Archaeology, 1980; Litt. D., Kean College of New Jersey, 1981; John A. Booth Prize, New Jersey Historical Society, 1986; McQuaid Medal, Seton Hall University, 1987; Achievment Award, New York State Archaeological Association, 1989; 1991 Governor Richard J. Hughes Award, New Jersey Historical Commission. *Interests*: "(My) primary interest is the prehistoric and contact period archaeology of New Jersey, and the Northeast and Middle Atlantic States generally. Since 1964, I have conducted archaeological excavations for the National Park Service, and for Seton Hall University sponsored research in the Upper Delaware Valley, N.J., and on several sites in northeastern New Jersey and Staten Island, N.Y. These excavations have encompassed the entire span from Paleo-Indian to the Historic Contact Period. Extensive travel to areas of archaeoogical or natural interst: Meso-America, Peru, Egypt, the Serengetti; Europe and China (taught at Wuhan Uiversity in 1990)." *Biographical sources*: Dictionary of International Biography; American Men and Women of Science; Current Biographies of Leading Archaeologists; Outstanding Educators of America, 1971; Who's Who in American Education; Who's Who in therEast. *Published works*: The Miller Field Site (Seton Hall University Press, 1970); Archaeology in the Upper Delaware Valley (Pennsylvania Historic and Museum Commission, 1972); A Delaware Indian Symposium (Pennsylvania Historic and Museum Commission, 1974); The Archaeology of the Tocks Island Area (Archaeological Research Center, Seton Hall University, 1975); The Minisink Site: A Re-evaluation of a Late Prehistoric and Early Historic Contact Site in Sussex County, New Jersey (Archaeological Research Center, Seton Hall University, 1978); (Film) "Lenape," 30 minutes, color. (Humanities on Film Project, William Paterson College of New Jersey, 1981); The Lenape: A Symposium (Archaeological Research Center, Seton Hall University Museum, 1984); The Indians of Lenapehoking & Supplement - Resources and Activities (Seton Hall University Museum, 1985); The Lenape: Archaeology, History and Ethnography (New Jersey Historical Society, 1986); The Lenape Indians of New Jersey (supplementary text for fourth grades) (Seton Hall University Museum, 1987); "Evidence of Contact and Trade in the Middle Atlantic and Northeast Regions," in Archaeology of Eastern North America, Vol. 17, 1989 pp. 1-29; "The Minisink Indians," in The People of the Minisink, edited by David G. Orr and Douglas V. Campana (National Park Service, 1990); editor of The Arachaeology and Ethnohistory of the Lower Hudson Valley & Neighboring Regions: essays in Honor of Louis A. Brennan (Occasional Publications in Northern Anthropology, 1992); numerous articles on the Lenape-Delaware Indians in the Bulletin of the Archaeological Society of New Jersey, and other publications.

KRAFT, JOHN T.
(museum curator)
Affiliation: The Lenape Indian Museum & Village, Waterloo Village, Stanhope, NJ 07874 (201) 347-0900.

KRAUSS, MICHAEL
(center director)
Affiliation: Alaska Native Language Center, University of Alaska, Eielson Bldg., 2nd Floor, Fairbanks, AK 99775 (907) 474-7874.

KRECH, SHEPARD, III
(museum director)
Affiliation: Haffenreffer Museum of Anthropology, Brown University, Mt. Hope Grant, Bristol, RI 02809 (401) 253-8388.

KREIN, DR. HARLAN
(school chairperson)
Affiliation: Northern Cheyenne Tribal School (Busby School), P.O. Box 150, Busby, MT 59016 (406) 592-3646 Fax 592-3645.

KREIPE de MONTANO, MARTHA
(Prairie Band Potawatomi) 1944-
(museum professional)
Born November 9, 1944, Topeka, Kan. *Education*: Haskell Indian Junior College (Certificate, Welding), 1975; University of Kansas, Lawrence, BFA (Painting), 1978, MA (Special Studies-Anthropology-History). *Principal occupation*: Museum professional. *Work address*: National Museum of the American Indian/CRC, 4220 Silver Hill Rd., Suitland, MD 20746 (301) 238-6624 ext. 6422. E-mail: demontanom@si.edu. Website: www.conexus.si.edu. *Affiliation*: Manager, Indian Information Center, National Museum of the American Indian, New York, NY, 1984-. *Community activities*: Indian Center, Lawrence, KS (board of directors); Circle of Red Nations, New York, N.Y. (president, board of directors); Native American Education Program, New York, NY (parent's committee); Grupo Aymara Productions (board of directors); New York City Native American Heritage Month (committee). *Awards, honors*: HUD Minority Fellowship, University of Kansas. *Interests*: Vocational interests: Contemporary North American Indian activities—cultural, social, artistic; Andean Indian life and music; Mayor's Ethnic New Yorker Award, 1986. *Published works*: 49's, A Pan Indian Mechanism for Boundary Maintenance and Social Cohesion (AAA meeting, 1980); Native American Conceptions of Time (Manhattan Laboratory Museum Symposium, 1983); Teacher's Kit: The Parfleche (Museum of the American Indian, Heye Foundation, 1985); Diplomacy In New England (Indians, Promises & Us, 1987); editor, Pachamama Project (Grupo Aymara, Inc., 1988); The Native American Almanac, with Arlene Hirschfelder (Macmillan, 1993); Coyote In Love With a Star; Harvest Ceremony, a play (George Gustav Heye Center, NY, 1996).

KREPPS, ETHEL CONSTANCE *(Kontameah)*
(Kiowa/Miami) 1941-
(public health nurse III - R.N.; attorney)
Born October 31, 1941, Mt. View, Okla. *Education*: St. John's Medical Center, Tulsa, RN, 1971; University of Tulsa, BS, 1974; University of Tulsa, College of Law, JD, 1979. *Principal occupation*: Public Health Nurse III - R.N.; attorney. *Home address*: 3000 N.W. 12th, Oklahoma City, OK 73107 (405) 942-7203. *Affiliations*: Lawyer, Native American Coalition of Tulsa, Inc., Tulsa, OK 74107, 1981-88; Public Health Nurse III - R.N., Attorney, OK State Dept. of Health, Oklahoma City, OK, 1989-. *Other professional post*: Director, Oklahoma Indian Affairs Commission, Oklahoma City, OK, 1991-. *Community activities*: Kiowa Tribe of OK (secretary); Native American Chamber of Commerce (secretary); Tulsa Indian Affairs Commission; American Indian Toastmasters. *Memberships*: National Trial Lawyers Association; American Bar Association; Federal Bar Association; OK Bar Association; OK Indian Attorney's Association; Tulsa County Bar Association; Tulsa Women Lawyers Association; Women Lawyers Association of OK; Phi Alpha Delta Legal Fraternity; National Indian Social Workers Association (past president); Oklahoma Indian Child Welfare Association (past president); American Indian/Alaskan Native Nurses Association (past national vice-president); OK Indian Legal Association (past board secretary) . *Awards, honors*: Indian Business Person of the Year Award, 1984; Outstanding Leadership Award, 1985, from International Indian Child Conference; Trial Lawyers Association National Essay Award; Tulsa Mayor's Appreciation Award. Interests: "Domestic law; Indian law; Writing, painting, photography; lap quilting; collection of unique indigenous cultural items from around the world; travel." *Biographical sources*: Who's Who in Finance and Industry; Who's Who in the South and Southwest; Who's Who of American Law; Who's Who of American Women; Who's Who in the World of Women; Who's Who in Society; 1,000 Personalities of the World. *Published works*: A Strong Medicine Wind

(Western Publications, 1981); Oklahoma Memories, chapter (University of Oklahoma Press, 1982); Oklahoma Images, chapter (U. of Oklahoma Press, 1983).

KROSKRITTY, PAUL V.
(professor)
Affiliation: Chairperson (MA Program), American Indian Studies Center, UCLA, 3220 Campbell Hall, P.O. BOX 951548, Los Angeles, CA 90095 (310) 825-7315.

KRUPAT, ARNOLD
(professor of literature)
Affiliation: Sarah Lawrence College, Bronxville, NY. *Published work*: Woodsmen, or Thoreau & the Indians: A Novel (University of Oklahoma Press, 1994).

KRUSE, CAROL
(national monument supt.)
Affiliation: Tonto National Monument, P.O. Box 707, Roosevelt, AZ 85545 (602) 467-2241.

KUCATE, ARDEN
(radio station manager)
Affiliation: KSHI - 90.0 FM, Zuni Pueblo, P.O. Box 339, Zuni, NM 87327 (505) 782-4811.

KUDRIN, RENA J. (Aleut)
(AK village council president)
Affiliation: Aleut Community of St. Paul Island, P.O. Box 35, Larsen Bay, AK 99660 (907) 546-2211.

KUENZIL, SARAH
(conference director)
Affiliation: Tanana Chiefs Conference, 122 1st Ave., Fairbanks, AK 99701 (907) 452-8251.

KUHL, ELEANOR K.
(librarian)
Affiliation: Dine College East, P.O. Box 580, Shiprock, NM 87420 (520) 368-3501 Fax 368-3519.

KUKA, KING D. (Blackfeet) 1946-
(professional artist)
Born August 13, 1946, Blackfeet Reservation, Browning, Mt. *Education*: Institute of American Indian Arts, Diploma, 1965; University of Montana, BFA, 1973; Montana State University, M.A. *Principal occupation*: Artist (sculpture and painting); owner-operator, Blackwolf Gallery. *Home address*: 907 Ave. C, NW, Great Falls, MT 59404 (406) 452-4449. *Military service*: U.S. Army, 1965-67. *Exhibits*: One-man shows: Reeder's Alley, Helena; University of Montana Center, Missoula; Museum of the Plains Indian, Browning; Rainbow Gallery, Great Falls; Flathead Lake Lookout, Lakeside. Painting and sculpture exhibits at Riverside Museum, New York, N.Y.; San Francisco; Philbrook Art Center, Tulsa, Okla.; Gallery of Indian Arts, Washington, D.C. *Awards, honors*: Numerous awards for art and creative writing; selected to exhibit and demonstrate in Kumamoto, Japan in 1992. *Membership*: Indian Arts & Crafts Association. *Interests*: Mr. Kuka's main interest is in the arts, Indian culture & outdoor life. *Published works*: Poetry: The Whispering Wind (Doubleday); Voices of the Rainbow (Viking Press); Anthologies: The First Skin Around Me (Territorial Press); The Remembered Earth (Red Earth Press); among others.

KULAS, CHERYL M.
(Indian education office director)
Affiliation: North Dakota Dept. of Public Instruction, Indian Education Office, 600 E. Blvd., 9th Floor, Bismarck, ND 58505 (701) 224-2250 Fax 328-4770.

KUNESH, PATRICE
(attorney)
Address: Native American Rights Fund, 1506 Broadway, Boulder, CO 80302 (303) 447-8760. *Memberships*: Native American Bar Association; Colorado Indian Bar Association (secretary-treasurer).

KURIP, CARLEEN
(editor)
Affiliation: Ute Bulletin, Ute Indian Tribe, P.O. Box 220, Fort Duchesne, UT 84026 (801) 722-5141.

KURTH, REV. E.J., S.J.
(school supt.)
Affiliation: Red Cloud Indian School, Holy Rosary Mission, Pine Ridge, SD 57770 (605) 867-5491.

KURTNESS, REMI
(Indian band chief)
Affiliation: Montagnais Du Lac St-Jean Indian Band, Reserve Indienne de Mashteuiatsh, 151, rue Quiatchouan, Pointe-Bleue, Quebec, Canada G0W 2H0 (418) 585-3744.

KUSSY, JAMES C., M.D.
(clinical director)
Affiliation: Barrow PHS Alaska Native Hospital, Barrow, AK 99723 (907) 852-4611.

KUTSCHE, PAUL 1927-
(cultural anthropologist)
Born January 3, 1927, Grand Rapids, Mich. *Education*: Harvard College, BA, 1949; University of Michigan, MA, 1955; University of Pennsylvania, PhD, 1961. *Principal occupation*: Cultural anthropologist. *Home address*: 220 Paris Ave., S.E., Grand Rapids, MI 49503 (616) 459-4442. *Affiliations*: Dept. of Anthropology, Colorado College, Colorado Springs, CO, (professor of anthropology, 1959-93; professor emeritus, 1993-present). *Military service*: U.S. Army, 1945-46. *Community activities*: Member, Grand Rapids Historical Commission, 2000-present. *Memberships*: American Anthropological Association (Fellow); Western Social Science Association (executive council, 1969-1972); Association of Borderland Scholars, 1976- 85 (executive council, 1977-83); American Ethnological Society; Anthropology Research Group on Homosexuality (co-chair, 1984-87); Association of Senior Anthropologists. *Interests*: Cherokee Indians, especially ethnohistory; New Mexico Hispanic village structure; rural-urban migration; local history; Hispanic cultures; gender issues. *Published works*: Survival of Spanish American Villages (Colorado College Studies, 1979); Canones: Values, Crisis and Survival (University of New Mexico Press, 1981); A Guide to Cherokee Documents in the Northeastern U.S. (Scarecrow Press, 1986); Voices of Migrants (University Press of Florida, 1994); Field Ethnography: A Manual for Doing Cultural Anthropology (Prentice Hall, 1998).

KUWANWISIWMA, LEIGH (Hopi)
(tribal office director)
Affiliation: Cultural Preservation Office, Hopi Tribe, P.O. Box 123, Kykotsmovi, AZ 86039 (928) 734-2441 Fax 734-6665

KUZCHIKIN, SIMEON
(AK village president)
Affiliation: Native Village of Belkofsky, P.O. Box 57, King Cove, AK 99612 (907) 497-2304.

KVASNIKOFF, VINCENT (Eskimo)
(AK village council president)
Affiliation: Nanwalek Village Council (aka English Bay), Homer, AK 99603 (907) 281-9219.

KWACHKA, PAT
(editor)
Affiliation: Theata," Cross Cultural Communications Dept., Alaskan Native Program, University of Alaska, Fairbanks, AK 99708 (907) 474-7181.

KWAIL, DAVID (Yavapai-Apache)
(tribal chairperson)
Affiliation: Yavapai-Apache Community Council, P.O. Box 1188, Camp Verde, AZ 86322 (520) 567-3649.

KWAS, MARY L.
(area supervisor)
Affiliations: Pinson Mounds State Archaeological Area, Ozier Rd., Rt. 1, Box 316, Pinson, TN 38366 (901) 988-5614; curator of education, Chucalissa Archaeological Museum-Library, 1987 Indian Village Dr., Memphis, TN 38109 (901) 785-3160.

L

LaBATTE, ROBERT (*Woableza*)
(institute director)
Affiliation: Institute for Native American News & TV, P.O. Box 77, Fairfax, CA 94930 (414) 459-0321.

LaBELLE, GEORGE
(Indian band chief)
Affiliation: Goodstoney (Wesley Group) Indian Band, Box 40, Morley, Alberta, Canada T0L 1N0 (403) 881-3770.

LaBELLE, MICHAEL JAMES (Sisseton-Wahpeton Sioux/Turtle Mountain Chippewa) 1961-
(radio station manager)
Born July, 16, 1961, Chicago, Ill. *Address & Affiliation*: Station Manager, Dakota Nation Broadcasting Corp., KSWS 89.3 FM, P.O. Box 142, Sisseton, SD 57262 (605) 698-7972 Fax 698-7897.

LABILLOIS, ROMEY
(director-Indian institute)
Affiliation: Restigouche Institute of Cultural Education, Restigouche Indian Band, 2 Riverside West, Restigouche, QB, Canada G0C 2R0 (418) 788-5336.

LABOUCAN, EUGENE
(Indian band chief)
Affiliation: Driftpile Indian Band, General Delivery, Driftpile, Alberta, Canada T0G 0V0 (403) 355-3868.

LACAPA-MORRISON, CAMILLE
(Lac Courte Oreilles Ojibwe)
(radio station general manager)
Affiliation: WOJB-FM, Lac Courte Orielles Ojibwe Broadcasting Corp., Route 2, Box 2700 Hayward, Wisconsin 54843 (715) 634-2100.

LACHAPPA, CLIFFORD M., SR. (Diegueno)
(tribal chairperson)
Affiliation: Barona General Business Council, 1095 Barona Rd., Lakeside, CA 92040 (619) 443-6612.

LACROIX, NOBLE
(BIA agency supt.)
Affiliation: Lower Brule Agency, Bureau of Indian Affairs, P.O. Box 190, Lower Brule, SD 57548 (605) 473-5512.

LADD, EDMUND JAMES (Zuni) 1926-
(Pacific archaeologist-retired; museum curator)
Born January 4, 1926, Fort Yuma, Calif. *Education*: University of New Mexico, Albuquerque, B.S., 1955, M.A., 1964. *Principal occupation*: Pacific archaeologist-retired; museum curator. *Home address*: 2016 Conejo Dr., Santa Fe, NM 87505. *Affiliations*: Pacific archaeologist, USDI, National Park Service, Honaunau, Kona, Hawaii, (23 years); curator of ethnology, Museum of Indian Arts & Culture, Santa Fe, NM. *Other professional post*: Consultant to Smithsonian Institution as Tribal translator & interpreter. *Military service*: U.S. Army, 1944-46. *Memberships*: American Anthropological Association; Society for American Archaeology; Archaeological Conservancy (board member).

LADUCER, WANDA
(financial aid director)
Affiliation: Turtle Mountain Community College, P.O. Box 340, Belcourt, ND 58316 (701) 477-5605 Fax 477-5028.

LaDUKE, WINONA (White Earth Chippewa)
(environmentalist)
Affiliations: Founder, White Earth Land Recovery Project, White Earth Reservation, Hwy. 224, P.O. Box 418, White Earth, MN 56591 (218) 983-3285. She founded the Recovery Project in 1989 with a $20,000 human-rights award from Reebok. *Other professional post*: President, Indigenous Women's Network, Lake Elmo, MN. *Past professional post*: Ran for Vice President of the U.S. with Ralph Nader on the Green Party in 1996. *Interests*: She has quietly been buying back reservation land owned by non-Indians. The land is held in a conservation trust by the project, with the eventual goal of ceding the property to the tribal government. Winona supervises maple sugar and wild-rice processing operations, a stable of horses, an Anishinaabe language program, a wind-energy project, and a herd of buffalo. She is a devotee of coffee and imports beans harvested by peasants in Mexico. She's considering running for Governor of Minnesota.

LaFOND, HARRY
(Indian band chief)
Affiliation: Muskeg Lake India Band, Box 248, Marcelin, Saskatchewan, Canada S0J 1R0 (306) 466-4959.

LaFONTAINE, CATHIE (Turtle Mountain Chippewa) 1957-
(school principal)
Born January 14, 1957, Rolla, N.D. *Education*: University of North Dakota, MA, 1983. *Principal occupation*: Indian school principal. *Address*: P.O. Box 564, Belcourt, ND 58316 (701) 477-3378. *Affiliation*: Ojibwa Indian School, Belcourt, ND, 1990-. *Community activities*: Chairperson for Twila Martin-Kekakbah - Tribal Council Campaign. *Memberships*: National Association of Elementary School Principals; North Dakota Association of Elementary School Principals. *Awards, honors*: Ojibwa Indian School - Service Award.

LaFORME, HARRY S.
(chief commissioner)
Affiliation: Canadian Indian Claims Commission, P.O. Box 1750, Station B, Ottawa, ON K1P 1A2 (613) 943-2737.

LaFORME, MAURICE
(Indian band chief)
Affiliation: Mississauga Indian Band, RR 6, Hagersville, Ontario, Canada N0A 1H0 (416) 768-1133.

LaFORTUNE, RICHARD (*Angukcuaq*) (Yup'ik) 1960-
(restaurant owner)
Born November 25, 1960, Bethel, Alaska. *Education*: Moravian College, 1978-79; St. Olaf College, 1980. *Principal occupation*: Restaurant owner. Resides in Minneapolis, MN *Affiliations*: Worker-owner, The New Riverside Cafe Collective, Minneapolis, MN (612) 333-4814 (work), 1988-. *Other professional post*: Task force member, Native American Cultural Arts Program, Minneapolis, MN, 1988-. *Community activities*: North American Native Gay and Lesbian organizer, and Native community organizer; co-founder, American Indian Gays & Lesbians, 1987-. *Interests*: "Classically-trained musician; traditional eco-culture; traditional Native Arts, Western fine arts; lived/traveled in Southeast Asia, South Pacific, Caribbean; language student, literature studies, indigenous peoples' studies." *Published work*: Poem printed in: Living the Spirit, a Gay American Indian Anthology (St. Martin's Press, 1988).

LaFRANCE, GREG
(BIA field rep.)
Affiliation: Chiloquin Sub-Agency, Bureau of Indian Affairs, P.O. Box 360, Chiloquin, OR 97624 (503) 783-2189.

LaFRANCE, RON
(program director)
Affiliation: American Indian Program, Cornell University, 300 Caldwell Hall, Ithaca, NY 14853 (607) 255-4308.

LaFROMBOISE, GENE
(school supt.)
Affiliation: White Shield School, HC 1, Box 45, Roseglen, ND 58775 (701) 743-4355.

LaFROMBOIS, MARY ELLEN
(hospital director)
Affiliation: Blackfeet PHS Indian Hospital, Browning, MT 59417 (406) 338-6153.

LaFROMBOISE, RICHARD (Turtle Mountain Sioux)
(tribal chairperson)
Affiliation: Turtle Mountain Tribal Council, P.O. Box 900, Belcourt, ND 58316 (701) 477-0470.

LAGO, EDUARDO, M.D.
(clinical director)
Affiliation: Fort Yates PHS Indian Hospital, Box J, Fort Yates, ND 58538 (701) 854-3831.

LAHREN, SYLVESTER (BUS)
(consultant in applied anthropology)
Education: University of Colorado, PhD (Anthropology). *Affiliation*: Research associate, Walker Research Group, Ltd., P.O. Box 4147, Boulder, CO 80306 (303) 492-6719. Website: www.walkerresearchgroup.com. Dr. Lahren has conducted applied research projects with American Indians, Hispanic populations, and Anglo-American populations of the Plains and Northwest in both Canada and the U.S. He is also trained and experienced in various aspects of cultural resource management throughout Western North America.

LAIWA, SHIRLEY (Miwok)
(rancheria representative)
Affiliation: Potter Valley Rancheria, P.O. Box 2273, West Sacramento, CA 95619 (916) 467-3307.

LAKE, ARTHUR
(former BIA agency supt.)
Affiliation: Bethel Agency, Bureau of Indian Affairs,
P.O. Box 347, Bethel, AK 99559 (907) 543-2727.

LAKE, TIMOTHY C. (Lakotah)
(BIA agency supt.)
Affiliation: Yankton Agency, Bureau of Indian Affairs,
P.O. Box 577, Wagner, SD 57380 (605) 384-3651.

LAKE, WILLIAM W., JR.
(Indian education program coordinator)
Affiliation: Bark River-Harris School District, Indian
Education Program, P.O. Box 350, Harris, MI 49845
(906) 466-9981 Fax 466-2925. E-mail: blake@dsisd.
k12.mi.us.

LAKSHMAN, JAI
(executive director)
Address & Affiliation: Southwestern Association for
Indian Arts (SWAIA), P.O. Box 969, Santa Fe, NM
87504-0969 (505) 983-5220 Fax 983-7647. E-mail:
jlakshman@swaia.org

LAKTONEN, JERRY (Alutiiq, Koniag)
(artist; studio owner)
Affiliation: Whale Dreams Studio, P.O. Box 635,
Carlsborg, WA 98324 (360) 582-0961. *Products*: Alutiiq
(Sugpiaq) masks and paddles.

LA MARR, CINDY
(Indian center director)
Affiliation: Director, Capitol Area Indian Resources,
Inc., 2701 Cottage Way, Suite 9, Sacramento, CA
95825 (916) 971-9190 Fax 971-0480.

LAMB, JEFF (Gros Ventre)
(association president)
Affiliation: Native American Finance Officers Assn., P.O.
Box 12743, Green Bay, WI 54307 (480) 704-1769 Fax
704-1780. E-mail: jlamb@millerschroeder. com.

LAMBERT, MARILYN
(director-Indian center)
Affiliation: Sault Ste. Marie Indian Friendship Centre,
29 Wellington St., Sault Ste. Marie, ON, Can. P6A 2K9
(705) 256-5634.

LAMEBULL, CINDY
(clinic director)
Affiliation: Warner Mountain Indian Health, P.O.
Box 127, Fort Bidwell, CA 96112 (918) 279-6194.

LAMEMAN, ALPHONSE
(Indian band chief)
Affiliation: Beaver Lake Indian Band, Box 960, Lac La
Biche, Alberta, Canada T0A 2C0 (403) 623-4549.

LAMENTI, EVELYN (Navajo) 1937-
(administration)
Born November 18, 1937, Albuquerque, N.M. *Education*: University of Massachusetts, BS; San Francisco
State University, MA. *Principal occupation*: Administration; *Home address*: 1437 Janet Lane, Concord, CA
94521 (510) 836-8209 (work). *Affiliation*: Program
manager, teacher on special assignment, resource
teacher, Oakland Unified School District, 1975-. *Community activities*: Cultural Arts, City of Oakland; Dance
for Power (executive board member); Bay Area American Indian Education Council. *Memberships*: California Indian Education Association (vice-president);
National Indian Education Association.

LAMENTI, JIM
(executive director)
Affiliation: Intertribal Friendship House, 523 East 14th
St., Oakland, CA 94606 (510) 452-1235.

LA MERE, FRANK DEAN (Winnebago) 1950-
(executive director)
Born March 1, 1950, Sioux City, Iowa. *Education*: Nebraska Indian Community College, AA, 1989; Bellevue
(NE) College, BS (Professional Studies), 1992. *Principal occupation*: Executive director-Indian organization, *Home address*: 600 Pioneer Place, So. Sioux City,
NE 68776 (402) 878-2242 (work). *Affiliation*: Executive Director, Nebraska Indian Inter-Tribal Development
Corp., Rt. 1, Box 66A, Winnebago, NE 68071. *Other
professional posts*: Chairperson, Nebraska Indian
Commission; Board of Trustees of Nebraska Indian

Community College, JTPA Indian & National Native
American Advisory Commission; NE State Job Train-
ing Coordinating Council; NE Rural Development Com-
mission; Board Member, National Rainbow Coalition;
member, Winnebago Health Planning Committee.
Community activities: Chairperson of National Indian
Democrats; Associate Chairperson of NE Democratic
Party; member of Democratic National Committee;
Board of NE Wildlife Federation; Parents Advisory
Council of University of Nebraska; Board of Counselors, NE Medical Center; Core Planning Committee-
Dakota County Law Enforcement. *Interests*: Experienced motivational speaker and political activist. Also,
founder of the NO Americans, the International Indian
fast pitch softball team headquartered in Neb., 1991.

LANE, JOHN
(professor of English)
Address & Affiliation: Dept. of English, 429 N. Church
St., Wofford College, Spartanburg, SC 29303.

LANG, RICHARD W.
(museum director)
Affiliation: The Wheelwright Museum of the American
Indian, P.O. Box 5153, 704 Camino Lejo, Santa Fe,
NM 87502 (505) 982-4636.

LANGAN, JULIA M.
(BIA agency supt.)
Affiliation: Pawnee Agency, Bureau of Indian Affairs,
P.O. Box 440, Pawnee, OK 74058 (918) 762-2585.

LANGLEY, BERTNEY (Coushatta)
(Indian enterprise owner)
Affiliation: Bayou Indian Enterprises, P.O.
Box 668, Elton, LA 70532 (318) 584-2653.

LANGREN, CLINT (Chippewa)
(tribal chairperson)
Affiliation: Bois Forte Tribal Business Committee,
P.O. Box 16, Nett Lake, MN 55772 (218) 757-3261.

LANGSTON, WILLIAM K. (*Strong Bear*)
(Nansemond)
(tribal assistant chief)
Affiliation: Nansemond Indian Tribal Association, P.O.
Box 9293, Chesapeake, VA 23321 (804) 487-5116.

LAPAZ EMMA L. (Mescalero Apache) 1961-
(criminal court clerk)
Born August 7, 1961, Mescalero, N.M. *Principal occupation*: Criminal court clerk. *Address*: P.O. Box 747,
Mescalero, NM 88340 (505) 671-4489 (work). *Affiliation*: Court clerk, Mescalero Apache Tribal Court,
Mescalero, NM, 1987-. *Memberships*: National American Indian Court Clerks Association, 1989-.

LAPENA, FRANK (*Tauhindauli*) (Wintu-Nomtipom)
1937-
(teacher)
Born October 5, 1937, San Francisco, Calif. *Educa-
tion*: Chico State College, BA; San Francisco State
University, Secondary Life Credential; California State
University, Sacramento, MA. *Prinicpal occupation*:
Teacher. *Home address*: 1531 42nd St., Sacramento,
CA 95819 (916) 278-6645. *Affiliation*: Professor, California State University, Sacramento, CA. *Other professional post*: Commissioner of California State Capitol. *Awards, honors*: 1988 Meritorious Performance &
Profesional Promise Awad, California State University,
Sacramento. *Interests*: Native American art: traditional
and contemporary - emphasis on California; traditional
dance and ceremony. *Published work*: World Is a Gift
(Limestone Press, 1987).

LAPLANTE, JOE
(BIA agency supt.)
Affiliation: San Carlos Agency, BIA, P.O. Box 209,
San Carlos, AZ 85550 (520) 475-2321.

LAPOINTE, DARYL (Winnebago)
(former tribal chairperson)
Affiliation: Winnebago Tribal Council, P.O. Box 687,
Winnebago, NE 68071 (402) 878-3100.

LAPOINTE, ERIC J.
(BIA agency supt.)
Affiliation: Fort Hall Agency, Bureau of Indian Affairs,
P.O. Box 220, Fort Hall, ID 83203 (208) 238-2301 Fax
237-0466.

LAPOINTE, JEROME (Winnebago)
(tribal newspaper editor)
Affiliation: Winnebago Indian News, Winnebago Indian
Tribe of Nebraska, P.O. Box 687, Winnebago, NE
68071 (402) 878-3220 Fax 878-2632.

LAPOINTE,, LAWRENCE (Puyallup)
(former tribal chairperson)
Affiliation: Puyallup Tribal Council, 2002 East 28th St.,
Tacoma, WA 98404 (253) 597-6200.

LAPOINT, ERIC (Blackfeet)
(BIA agency supt.)
Affiliation: Fort Hall Agency, Bureau of Indian Affairs,
P.O. Box 220, Fort Hall, ID 83203 (208) 238-2301 Fax
237-0466.

LAPOINT, OREN
(editor)
Affiliation: American Indian Graduate Record, 4520
Montgomery Blvd., NE, Suite 1-B, Albuquerque, NM
87109 (505) 881-4584.

LARGO, ANTHONY (Cahuilla)
(tribal spokesperson)
Affiliation: Santa Rosa Rancheria, 325 N. Western
Ave., Hemet, CA 92343 (909) 849-4761.

LARIMORE, COLLEEN K. (Comanche) 1963-
(student support services)
Born March 3, 1963, Lakewood, N.J. *Education*:
Dartmouth College, AB, 1985; Harvard University,
EdM, 1990. *Principal occupation*: Director, Native
American program. *Address*: Dartmouth College, Stu-
dent Support Services, First Year Office, Hanover, NH
03755. *Affiliations*: Dartmouth College, Hanover, NH
(assistant director, Native American Recruiter, 1985-
88; Office of Admissions, acting director of Minority
Recruitment, 1988-89; director, Native American Pro-
gram, 1990-93; student support services, First Year
Office, 2002-present); Harvard University, Cambridge,
MA (administrative intern, American Indian Program,
1989-90). *Memberships*: National Indian Education
Association, 1985-; National Association of Women
Deans and Counselors, 1990-. *Interests*: "As a
Comanche Indian and a first-generation college graduate, my interest in teaching and minority education
stems from my own odyssey through the educational
system and the history of my family, my tribe and Native peoples in general. My research interests include:
cultural styles of learning evinced among Native American students; the diversification of teaching methods
to address learning differences; the advent of the tribally controlled community colleges, and these institutions' growing success in establishing tribal culture as
a viable and effective curriculum base for their students and the communities they serve."

LARIMORE, JAMES (Comanche)
(college dean)
Affiliation: Dean, Dartmouth College,
Hanover, NH 03755

LARSEN, TERI (Lower Sioux)
(health director)
Affiliation: Lower Sioux Community Council,
P.O. Box 308, Morton, MN 56270 (612) 564-2360.

LARSON, ALAN
(village president)
Affiliation: Native Village of Chickaloon, P.O.
Box 1105, Chickaloon, AK 99674 (907) 746-0505.

LASH, VIRGINIA (Paiute)
(rancheria chairperson)
Affiliation: Cedarville Rancheria, 200 S. Howard St.,
Altura, CA 96101 (530) 233-3969.

LASLEY, GARY (Omaha)
(tribal chairperson)
Affiliation: Omaha Tribal Council, P.O. Box 368,
Macy, NE 68039 (402) 837-5391.

LATHLIN, OSCAR (The Pas)
(legislator)
Affiliation: Manitoba Legislative Assembly, Legislative
Bldg., Regina, MB Canada R3C 0V8 (204) 945-6487.
Past professional post: Chief, The Pas Indian Band,
The Pas, Manitoba.

LAUBIN, GLADYS W.
(lecturer, entertainer)
Home address: Grand Teton National Park, Moose, WY 83012. *Principal occupation*: Lecturer & entertainer (presentation of Indian dances on the concert stage). *Memberships*: Association on American Indian Affairs; National Congress of American Indians; Chicago Indian Center; Jackson Hole Fine Arts Foundation. *Awards, honors*: Adopted member of Sioux Tribe; dance prizes, Standing Rock and Crow Reservations; Capezio Dance Award, 1972; Catlin Peace Pipe Award, Special Literary Award, American Indian Lore Association, 1976. *Interests*: Research among Sioux, Crow, Blackfeet, Cherokee, Kiowa, and other American Indian tribes related to dance, customs, Indian lore, music; photography; painting; costume making; woodcraft. *Published works*: Co-author, The Indian Tipi (University of Oklahoma Press, 1957); documentary art films, produced with Reginald Laubin: Old Chiefs Dance, Talking Hands, War Dance, Indian Musical Instruments, Ceremonial Pipes and Tipi How (University of Oklahoma Press, 1951-58); Indian Dances of North America and Their Importance to Indian Life (University of Oklahoma Press, 1977); The Indian Tipi, 2nd Edition (University of Oklahoma Press, 1977); American Indian Archery (University of Oklahoma Press, 1978).

LAUBIN, REGINALD K.
(lecturer, entertainer)
Home address: Grand Teton National Park, Moose, WY 83012. *Education*: Hartford Art School; Norwich Art School. *Principal occupation*: Lecturer and entertainer (presentation of American Indian dances and lore on the concert stage). *Memberships*: Association on American Indian Affairs; National Congress of American Indians; Chicago Indian Center; Jackson Hole Fine Arts Foundation. *Awards, honors*: Guggenheim Fellowship, 1951; adopted son of Chief One Bull, nephew of Sitting Bull; dance prizes, Standing Rock and Crow Reservations; Capezio Dance Award, 1972; Catlin Peace Pipe Award, Special Literary Award, American Indian Lore Association, 1976. *Interests*: Research among Sioux, Crow, Blackfeet, Cherokee, Kiowa and other tribes on dance, custom, lore, music and general anthropology; archery; photography; duplication of Indian craft techniques; primitive camping and cooking; woodcraft. *Published works*: The Indian Tipi (University of Oklahoma Press, 1957); series in Boy's Life on Indian crafts; six documentary films on Indian dance and culture, produced with Gladys Laubin; Indian Dances of North America, and Their Importance to Indian Life (University of Oklahoma Press, 1978).

LAUGHLIN, DON (Mojave)
(casino operator)
Affiliation: Mojave Casino, 500 Merriman Ave., Needles, CA 92363 (619) 326-4591.

LAUGHLIN, SARAH
(Indian program coordinator)
Affiliation: Portal Program of the Palace of the Governors, P.O. Box 2087, Santa Fe, NM 87504 (505) 827-6474. *Products*: Traditional crafts of the 22 recognized New Mexico tribes and pueblos.

LAUTANEN-RALEIGH, MARCIA
(center director)
Affiliation: Schlingoethe Center for Native American Cultures, Aurora University, 347 S. Gladstone, Dunham Hall, Aurora, IL 60506 (708) 844-5402

LAVAN, DOUGLAS PAUL (Kikiallus)
(tribal chief)
Affiliation: Kikiallus Indian Nation, 3933 Bagley Ave. N., Seattle, WA 98103.

LAVELL, WILLIAM G.
(BIA office director)
Affiliation: Bureau of Indian Affairs, Office of Self-Governance, Dept. of the Interior, MS: 2253-MIB, 1849 C St., NW, Washington, DC 20240 (202) 219-0240.

LAVELLE, JOHN (Santee Sioux)
(organization director)
Affiliation: Center for Support & Protection of Indian Religions & Indigenous Traditions, National Congress of American Indians, 900 Pennsylvania Ave., SW, Washington, DC 20003 (202) 546-9404.

LAWRENCE, ELDEN
(college president)
Affiliation: Sisseton-Wahpeton Community College, Agency Village CPO, Box 689, Sisseton, SD 57262 (605) 698-3966 Fax 698-3132.

LAWRENCE, LINDA (Sioux)
(elementary school administrator)
Affiliation: Duckwater Shoshone Elementary School, P.O. Box 140038, Duckwater, NV 89314 (702) 863-0242 Fax 863-0157.

LAWRENCE, WILLIAM J. (Red Lake Chippewa)
1939-
(publisher)
Born August 31, 1939, Red Lake Chippewa Reservation, Minn. *Education*: BA in Business Administration & JD. *Principal occupation*: Publisher. *Address*: 3501 Lakeside Dr. #2 NE, Bemidji, MN 56601 (218) 444-7800 Fax 444-7320. E-mail: presson@isd.net. *Affiliation*: Publisher of the weekly newspaper Native American Press/Ojibwe News. *Community activities*: President, Minnesota Minority Media Coalition. *Military service*: U.S. Marine Corps, 1962-66 (Commissioned Officer; served in Vietnam). *Membership*: National Rifle Association. *Published works*: "Tribal Justice: Red Lake Court of Indian Offenses," in the North Dakota Law Review, summer, 1972 (vol. 48, no. 4); "In Defense of Indian Right," essay in book on race entitled, Beyond Victimization (Hoover Institution Press, 2000).

LAWSON, MICHAEL
(historian)
Affiliations: Presently manages the office of Historical Research Associates (a consulting firm specializing in cultural and environmental resource management and litigation support) in Washington, DC; formerly the senior historian for the Bureau of Indian Affairs. *Published works*: Dammed Indians: The Pick-Sloan Plan and the Missorui River Sioux, 1944-1980 (University of Oklahoma Press, 1982).

LAWSON, RAYMOND R. *(Grey Wolf)*
(Melundgeon Cherokee) 1923-
(auto mechanic)
Born February 10, 1923, Claiborne Co., Tenn. *Education*: U.S. Army, GED. *Principal occcupation*: Auto mechanic. *Address*: P.O. Box 1784, Thomasville, GA 31799 (912) 226-0717 (work). *Affiliation*: Manager, Carroll Hill Auto Electric, Thomasville, GA, 1970-. *Other professional post*: Principal Chief, Deer Clan, Inc., Valdosta, GA. *Military service*: U.S. Army (22 years) (served in 3 wars, WWII, Korean & Vietnam-2 Combat Stars, American Defense Medal, Pacific Theatre Medal, & Commendation Service Medal for 22 years of duty). *Community activities*: Steering Committee, Cherokee Unity Council, Jasper, TN; Masonic Lodge; VFW Post 165, Ochlocknee, GA. *Memberships*: Southeastern Cherokee Confederacy (vice-chief, 1989-93). *Interests*: "My main desire is to go to the Midwest and study all Native American cultures and religions; horticulture & electronics." *Biographical source*: Article, "To Guard Against Invading Indians: Struggling for Native Community in the Southeast," in American Indian Culture & Research Journal, Fall 1994.

LEACH, MICHAEL P. (Lillooet)
(Indian band chief)
Affiliation: Lillooet Indian Band, P.O. Box 615, Lillooet, B.C., Canada V0K 1V0 (604) 256-7613.

LEAFFE, JAMES (Cayuga)
(tribal chief)
Affiliation: Chief (lifetime), Cayuga Nation, P.O. Box 11, Versailles, NY 14168 (716) 532-4847.

LEAMING, JUDY (Catawba/Cherokee)
(attorney)
Address: Resides in Charlotte, NC. *Membership*: Native American Bar Association (past president).

LEAP, WILLIAM L. 1946-
(anthropologist)
Born November 28, 1946, Philadelphia, Pa. *Education*: Florida State University, BA, 1967; Southern Methodist University, PhD (Anthropology), 1970. *Principal occupation*: Anthropologist. *Address & Affiliation*: Professor of anthropology , Dept. of Anthropology, American University, 4400 Massachusetts Ave., NW, Washington, DC 20016 (202) 885-1830 (work), 1970-

Other professional post: Director, Indian Education Program, Center for Applied Linguistics, Arlington, VA, 1974-79; director, Indian Education, National Congress of American Indians, Washington DC, 1980-83. *Awards, honors*: 1986 Finalist, Washington Association of Practicing Anthropologists' PRAXIS Award for outstanding achievement in anthropological problem-solving. *Interests*: "My vocational interests center on Indian self-determination through education. A major component of such a strategy is relevant education, and that means addressing the Indian (e.g. tribal or traditional) as well as the mainstream cultural components of the students interests, lifestyle, and life-options. My work in the field has centered on assisting Tribal governments and Tribal agencies develop programs to provide Tribal members to take charge of and manage such programs without reliance on outside sources of support." *Published works*: Language Policies in Indian Education: Recommendations, 1973, and Handbook for Staff Development in Indian Education, 1976 (Center for Applied Linguistics); Studies in Southwestern Indian English (Trinity University Press, 1977); American Indian Language Education (National Bilingual Research Center, 1980); American Indian Language Renewal in Annual Review of Anthropology, 1981; Assumptions and strategies in Mathematics Problem-Solving by Ute Indian students in Linguistic and Cultural Factors in Mathematics Education, edited by Rodney Cocking and Jose Metre (Erlbaum Press, 1987); Applied Linguistics and American Indian Language Renewal (Human Organization - Journal of the Society for Applied Anthropology, 1989); Pathways and Barriers to Indian Language Literacy - Building on the Northern Ute Reservation (Anthropology & Education Quarterly, 1991); American Indian English (University of Utah Press, 1993).

LEASK, JANIE (Haida/Tsimshean) 1948-
(organization president)
Born September 17, 1948, Seattle, Wash. *Education*: East Anchorage High School, 1966. *Principal occupation*: Alaska Federation of Natives, 411 W. 4th Ave., Suite 301, Anchorage, 1974- (vice president, 1977-82; president, 1982-). *Home address*: 7021 Hunt Ave., Anchorage, AK 99504 (907) 274-3611 (work). *Community activities*: Enrolled in Cook Inlet Region (one of the 12 in-state Alaska Native Regional corporations; The State Board of Education; the Anchorage Organizing Committee for the 1992 Olympics; the Alaska Land Use Council; the ARCO Scholarship Committee. *Awards, honors*: Governor's Award in 1983 for work on behalf of Alaska Native people.

LeBEAU, BARRY (Dakota)
(professional stage actor)
Address: P.O. Box 1037, Pierre, SD 57501. Has experience in musical comedy, comedy, drama, and Shakespeare.

LeBEAU, EDWARD A. (Cheyenne River Sioux)
1941-
(contracting specialist, public health advisor)
Born June 14, 1941, Cheyenne Agency, S.D. *Education*: Minot State University, BA, 1965. *Principal occupation*: Contracting specialist, public health advisor. *Home address*: 1323 Minnesota Ave., Bemidji, MN 56601 (218) 751-7701. *Affiliations*: Tribal projects coordinator, Indian Health Service, Bemidji, MN, 1981-. *Military service*: U.S. Army, 1985-87. Northern Minnesota Indian Athletic Assn. (charter member, 1973).

LeBEAU, MARCELLA
(association president)
Affiliation: North American Indian Women's Association, P.O. Box 805, Eagle Butte, SD 57625 (605) 964-2136.

LeBEAU, WARREN D.
(BIA agency supt.)
Affiliation: Fort Totten Agency, Bureau of Indian Affairs, P.O. Box 270, Fort Totten, ND 58335 (701) 766-4545 Fax 766-4117.

LeBLANC, ALTON (Chitimacha)
(tribal chairperson)
Affiliation: Chitimacha Tribal Council, P.O. Box 661, Charenton, LA 70523 (337) 923-7215.

LeBOURDAIS, RICHARD
(Indian band chief)
Affiliation: Whispering Pines Indian Band, RR 1, Site 8, Comp. 4, Kamloops, British Columbia, Canada V2Z 1Z3 (604) 579-5772.

LECAM, MICHAEL J.
(school principal)
Affiliation: Zia Day School, San Ysidro, NM 87053 (505) 867-3553.

LeCLAIR, LIONEL (Ponca)
(former tribal chairperson)
Address & Affiliation: Ponca Tribe, 20 White Eagle Dr., Ponca City, OK 74601 (580) 762-8104 Fax 762-2743.

LECOMPTE, CLARA (Maidu)
(tribal chairperson)
Affiliation: United Maidu Nation, P.O. Box 204, Susanville, CA 96130 (916) 257-9691.

LEDBETTER, GARY ALLEN (*Bear Paw*) (United Lumbee/Cherokee/Choctaw) 1949-
(ceramic artist, teacher)
Born June 4, 1949, Los Angeles, Calif. *Education*: High school. *Principal occupation*: Ceramic artist, teacher. *Home address*: P.O. Box 271, McArthur, CA 96056. *Membership*: United Lumbee Nation's Beaver Clan (vice-chief, 1991-95); member, Native American Wolf Clan, 1993-; councilperson, Chapter NC001, 1995-; member, United Lumbee Nation's Grand Council, 1995-; United Lumbee Nation's Hawk Society, 1999- (The Nation's Society of Tradition Keepers); United Lumbee Nation's Deer Clan's Golden Hawk Society Chief, 1999-; Chapel of Our Lord Jesus, minister & council member, 2001-. *Interests*: "Indian heritage, ceramic art, jazz music; helping my Indian people."

LEDBETTER, PATTY DEEANNE REED (*Flaming Star*) (United Lumbee/Cherokee/ Choctaw) 1943-
(sales clerk)
Born July 30, 1943, in Calif. *Education*: High school. *Principal occupation*: Sales clerk. *Home address*: P.O. Box 271, McArthur, CA 96056. *Community activities*: Police Reserve, Linn and Desshutes Counties, OR, 1984-95. *Memberships*: Native American Wolf Clan, 1978- - Chapter NC001 Chief, 1995-; United Lumbee Nation's Beaver Clan Chief, 1988-95; United Lumbee Nation's Hawk Society, 1999- (The Nation's Society of Tradition Keepers); Chapel of Our Lord Jesus, minister and council member, 2001-present. *Interests*: "Indian heritage; ceramic art, jazz music; helping my Indian people."

LEE, ANTHONY J.
(legal counsel)
Affiliation: Legal counsel, Foxwoods Resort Casino, P.O. Box 3777, Mashantucket, CT 06338. E-mail: alee@mptn-nsn.gov.

LEE, ISAIAH
(school principal)
Affiliation: Cibecue Community School, P.O. Box 80068, Cibecue, AZ 85911 (520) 332-2480 Fax 332-3241.

LEE, DR. MOLLY
(professor of anthropology)
Affiliation: Dept. of Anthropology, University of Alaska, 3211 Providence Dr., Anchorage, AK 99508 (907) 786-6840 Fax 786-6850. *Interests*: Alaska Native and Inuit art of the historical and contemporary periods. E-mail: ffmcl@uaa.alaska.edu.

LEE, PATRICK (Oglala Sioux)
(chief judge)
Affiliation: Oglala Sioux Tribe, 203 E. Oakland St., Rapid City, SD 57701.

LEE, RON S.
(executive director)
Affiliation: Arizona Commission on Indian Affairs, 1400 W. Washington St. #300, Phoenix, AZ 85007 (602) 542-3123 Fax 542-3223.

LEE, STEPHANIE
(Indian education program coordinator)
Affiliation: Mt. Morris Central Schools, Indian Education Program, 1000 Genesee St., Mt. Morris, MI 48458 (810) 591-5740 Fax 687-8052.

LEE, VIVIAN (Hoh)
(tribal chairperson)
Affiliation: Hoh Tribal Business Committee, 2464 Lower Hoh Rd., Forks, WA 98531 (360) 374-6582.

LEE, WAYNE (Bois Forte Ojibwe)
(college instructor)
Affiliation: Leech Lake Tribal College, 6530 U.S. Hwy. 2 NW, Cass Lake, MN 56633 (218) 335-4220 Fax 335-4209.

LEEDS, WILLIAM P.
(BIA agency supt.)
Affiliation: Ramah-Navajo Agency, Bureau of Indian Affairs, RR 2, Box 14, Ramah, NM 87321 (505) 775-7130.

LEEDS, YAMIE (Laguna Pueblo)
(BIA agency supt.)
Affiliation: Laguna Agency, Bureau of Indian Affairs, P.O. Box 1448, Laguna, NM 87026 (505) 552-6001 Fax 552-7497.

LEFFUE, JOHN C.
(school principal)
Affiliation: Santa Rosa Boarding School, Sells, AZ 85634 (602) 361-2331.

LEFTHAND, JOSEPHINE (Jicarilla Apache)
(supervisor)
Affiliation: Jicarilla Apache Higher Education Program, P.O. Box 507, Dulce, NM 87528 (505) 759-3615/6.

LEHI, JOHNNY, SR. (Southern Paiute)
(tribal president)
Affiliation: San Juan Southern Paiute Council, P.O. Box 1989, Tuba City, AZ 86045 (928) 283-4589.

LEHMAN, KENNETH (Menominee)
(school administrator)
Affiliation: Menominee Tribal School, Menominee Indian Tribe of Wisconsin, P.O. Box 910, Kehena, WI 54135 (715) 756-2354.

LEIGHTON, DANNY VICTOR (Metlakatla)
(Indian band chief)
Affiliation: Metlakatla Indian Band, Box 459, Prince Rupert, BC, Canada V8J 3R1 (604) 628-9294.

LEIGHTON, DAWN
(Indian education program coordinator)
Affiliation: Lewiston Independent School District #1, Indian Education Program, 3317 12th St., T-12 South, Lewiston, ID 83501 (208) 748-3000 Fax 748-3059. E-mail: dleighton@mail.lewiston.k12.id.us.

LEIGHTON, RONALD W.
(corporation president)
Affiliation: Ketchikan Indian Corp., 429 Deermount Ave., Ketchikan, AK 99901 (907) 225-5158.

LEITKA, MARY K. (Hoh)
(tribal chairperson)
Affiliation: Hoh Tribal Business Committee, HC 80, Box 917, Forks, WA 98331 (206) 374-6582.

LEMAR, WALTER
(deputy director-BIA)
Address & Affiliation: Deputy Director, Bureau of Indian Affairs, Office of Law Enforcement Services, P.O. Box 66, Albuquerque, NM 87103.

LEMON, BECKY
(editor)
Affiliation: "The Native Nevadan," Reno-Sparks Indian Colony, 98 Colony Rd., Sparks, NV 89502 (702) 359-9449.

LEMONS, NOKOMIS
(Indian dance team coordinator)
Affiliation: Rising Water Dancers, Route 2, Box 107-B, Bruington, VA 23023.

LENDS HIS HORSE, JOSEPH
(college president)
Affiliation: Cheyenne River Community College, P.O. Box 220, Eagle Butte, SD 57625 (605) 964-8635.

LENO-GRANT, JACKIE
(Native American program chairperson)
Affiliation: Native American Program, Eastern Oregon University, 1410 "L" Ave., La Grange, OR 97850 (541) 962-3741 Fax 962-3849.

LENT, DAVID
(health director)
Affiliation: Toiyabe Indian Health Council, P.O. Box 1296, Bishop, CA 93515 (619) 873-8464.

LENT, JOSEPH (Paiute-Mono)
(store owner)
Affiliation: Eastern Sierra Trading Co., P.O. Box 731, Bridgeport, CA 93517 (619) 932-7231.

LENT, MARY (Laguna-Tewa Pueblo)
(store owner)
Affiliation: Eastern Sierra Trading Co., P.O. Box 731, Bridgeport, CA 93517 (619) 932-7231.

LENZ, MONSIGNOR PAUL A. (*Thunder Cloud*) 1925-
(executive director - Roman Catholic Priest)
Born December 15, 1925, Gallitzin, Penna. *Education*: St. Vincent College & Seminary (Latrobe, PA); Penn State University. *Principal occupation*: Executive director, The Bureau of Catholic Indian Missions, Washington, DC, 1977-. *Home address*: 2021 H St., NW, Washington, DC 20006 (202) 331-8542. *Other professional posts*: Board of trustees: The Catholic University of America, Washington, DC; Xavier University, New Orleans; St. Vincent Seminary, Latrobe; National Catholic Indian Tekakwitha Conference, and The National Catholic Development Conference, Washington, DC. *Awards, honors*: Alumnus of Distinction, St. Vincent College, Latrobe, PA; Doctor of Divinity, St. Vincent Seminary, Latrobe, PA. *Interests*: "Travel constantly to Indian reservations and American Indian rural areas in the U.S." *Published work*: Newsletter - Bureau of Catholic Indian Missions, Washington, DC (published ten times per year.)

LEO, RICHARD
(Indian band chief)
Affiliation: Kyuquot Indian Band, General Delivery, Kyuquot, BC, Canada V0P 1J0 (604) 332-5259.

LEONARD, FLOYD E. (*Waw-paw-waw-quah - White Loon*) (Miami) 1925-
(tribal chief)
Born September 19, 1925, Picher, Okla. *Education*: Pittsburg State University (KS), BS, 1951, MS, 1952, EdS, 1971. *Principal occupation*: Chief, Miami Nation of Oklahoma. *Address & Affiliation*: Miami Nation of Oklahoma, P.O. Box 1326, Miami, OK 74355 (918) 542-1445 Fax 542-7260. E-mail: fleonard@miami nation.com. Website: www.miaminaton.com. *Military service*: U.S. Coast Guard, 1943-46. *Community activities*: Northeast Inter-Tribal Council, Miami, OK (president); Claremore Indian Hospital Board (member); U.S. Bishops Advisory Council (former member). *Awards, honors*: Honorary Alumnus, Miami University, Oxford, OH.

LEONARD, LELAND (Dine-Navajo)
(program administrator)
Born in Chinle, Ariz. *Education*: MA in Education. *Principal occupation*: Program administrator. *Affiliation*: Executive Director, Division of Dine Education (2004-present), P.O. Box 9000, Window Rock, AZ 86515 (928) 871-6352 Fax 871-4025. *Past professional post*: Executive Director, Phoenix Indian Center, Inc., Phoenix, AZ, 1998-2003.

LEONARD, MICHELE TINSLEY (Shinnecock) 1956-
(administrator)
Born October 26, 1956 in Southampton, N.Y. *Education*: Wellesley College, BA, 1977. *Principal occupation*: Administrator. *Address & Affiliation*: Executive director, United American Indians of Delaware Valley, 225 Chestnut St., Philadelphia, PA 19106 (215) 574-9020 Fax 574-9024. *Other professional posts*: Assistant executive director, Council of Three Rivers American Indian Center, Pittsburgh (responsible for the Native American Elders Program, the Speaker's Bureau, and the Youth Group); coordinator of the Western Pennsylvania Native American Advisory Committee to the Carnegie Museum's new American Indian Hall that opened in 1996; developer and propri-

etor of a consulting firm called Spirit Guides (offers information on American Indian educational and cultural issues and is active in research and curriculum writing.) *Community activities*: Board of directors, Pennsylvania Small Business Education Scholarship Fund. Interests: She is a writer of American Indian curriculum and contemporary articles and is doing research with oral histories.

LEOTSAKOS, LINDA (Passamaquoddy)
(school principal)
Affiliation: Indian Township School, Peter Dana Point, Princeton, ME 04668 (207) 796-2362.

LEPINE, MATTHEW (Cree)
(Indian band chief)
Affiliation: Cree Indian Band, P.O. Box 90, Fort Chipewyan, Alberta, Canada T0P 1B0 (403) 697-3740.

LeROY, FRED (Ponca)
(tribal chairperson)
Affiliation: Ponca Tribe of Nebraska, P.O. Box 288, Niobrara, NE 68760 (402) 857-3391.

LeROY, LYNN R. (Serrano)
(rancheria chairperson)
Affiliation: San Manuel Band of Mission Indians, P.O Box 266, Patton, CA 92369 (909) 864-8933.

LESTER, A. DAVID (Muscogee-Creek) 1941-
(executive director; co-publisher & writer)
Born September 25, 1941, Claremore, Okla. *Education*: Brigham Young University, Provo, Utah, BA (Political Science), 1967. *Principal occupation*: Executive director. *Home address*: 8688 E. Otero Circle, Centennial, CO 80112. *Affiliations*: Council of Energy Resource Tribes (CERT), 695 S. Colorado Blvd. #10, Denver, CO 80246 (303) 282-7576 Fax 282-7584. E-mail: cert1975@aol.com. Website: www.certredearth.com. Co-publisher & writer, with Kenneth Robbins, of "RedEarth" Magazine, Council Publications, Denver, CO. *Past affiliations*: Vice-chairman, American Indian Scholarships, Inc., Taos, NM (2 years); president, United Indian Development Association, Los Angeles (7 years); economic development specialist, National Congress of American Indians, Washington, DC. *Other professional posts*: Board of Trustees, Institute of American Indian Arts, Santa Fe, NM; Commissioner, Administration for Native Americans, U.S. Dept. of Health & Human Services, Washington, DC; Boards of Directors: American Indian National Bank, Washington, DC; Americans for Indian Opportunity, Albuquerque; American Indian Scholarships, Inc., Taos, NM; National Area Development Institute, and Los Angeles (CA) Indian Center. *Community activities*: Served as a Presidential appointee to the National Advisory Council on Minority Enterprise, which advised cabinet-level officials on strategies to stimulate minority business ownership, and to the National Council on Indian Opportunity, devoted to improving social & economic opportunities for American Indians; served as Human Relations Commissioner for the City of Los Angeles and as Chairman of the Los Angeles County American Indian Commission. *Awards, honors*: Received the Indian Council First Indian Achievement Award; the Americans for Indian Opportunity's Distinguished Services Peace Pipe Award; a proclamation of David Lester Day by the Governor of Oklahoma; recognition by the California State Assembly for contributions to Indian-State relations; the United Indian Development Association's Jay Silverheels Achievement Award; the White Buffalo Council of American Indians' National-Level Award for Outstanding Service to American Indians; created a self-supporting management institute which trained 2,000 Indian businessmen and women; received the National Communicator Awards 2001 Crystal Award of Excellence for "RedEarth" Magazine; presented a wide variety of Indian and Native American issues before conferences, conventions, and other meetings and on radio and television; received the Dept. of Commerce, Minority Business Development, 2003 National Legacy Award for Lifetime Achievement. *Interests*: "Indian affairs; powwows; Indian cultures; Indian economic progress is my vocational goal."

LESTER, JOAN 1937-
(museum curator)
Born July 4, 1937, New York, N.Y. *Education*: Brown University, BA, 1959; Sorbonne, Paris, France, Certificate of Studies, 1958; UCLA, MA (Primitive Art/American Indian Art), 1963; Union Institute for Graduate Study, PhD (Native American Art), 1998. *Principal occupation*: Museum curator. *Home address*: 2 Muster Ct., Lexington, MA 02173. *Affiliations*: Boston Children's Museum; coordinator of North American Indian resources & workshop (courses & workshops presenting Indian people in southern New England), co-developer of American Indian programs in Greater Boston area, 1971-74; museum assistant, 1963-70, museum coordinator-Native American Advisory Board, 1973-, developer/curator, American Indian Collections and Programs, 1976-, associate curator, 1975-78, curator of collections, 1978-85, chief curator, 1985-; lecturer, Indian Studies, Tufts University, 1987. *Other professional posts*: Chair, National Curator's Committee, 1982-; member-at-large, Council for Museum Anthropology, 1983-; principal investigator, American Indian Games, National Endowment for the Humanities Planning Grant, 1983-. *Community activities*: Member, advisory boards: Phoenix School, Cambridge, Mass.; MIT Museum; Native American Studies Department of Plimoth Plantation, Mass.; Tomaquag Indian Memorial Museum, Exeter, R.I. MAP assessor, Museum Assessment Program. *Memberships*: American Association of Museums (curator's committee); International Council of Museums; New England Museum Association; Native American Art Studies Association; Council for Museum Anthropology; Peabody Museum Association. *Awards, honors*: Boston Indian Council Certificate of Merit, 1975; Bay State Historical League Award of Excellence, for Indians Who Met the Pilgrims, June, 1975; Award of Distinction, A.A.M. for "We're Still Here", catalog, 1987. *Interests*: "American Indian art; American Indian arts in New England as they continue today; cooking, bicycling, cross country skiing, theater, classical music, folk dancing, reading." *Published works*: The American Indian, A Museum's Eye View, in Indian Historian, summer, 1972; Indians Who Met the Pilgrims, the Match Program, American Science and Engineering, Boston, 1974; A Code of Ethics for Curator's, in Museum News, Jan/Feb., 1983; chapter I - The Production of Fancy Baskets in Maine (American Indian Archaeological Institute, 1986); American Indian Art in New England (Boston Children's Museum, 1986); The Art of Tomah Joseph, Passamaquoddy Artist (Turtle Quarterly, Spring 1988). Reports: American Indian Art Association, Tomah Joseph, Passamaquoddy Artist, Sept., 1983; Metropolitan Museum of Art, The Northeast Native American Program at the Children's Museum, April, 1983; York Institute, Saco, Maine, Northeast Native American Baskets: A Continuing Tradition, Oct., 1982); Massachusetts Indian Association, The Significance of the Katherine Hall Newall Collection, Oct., 1982; American Indian Art Association, They're Still Here, Native American Art in New England, March, 1982; Institute for Contemporary Art, Native American Ash Splint Basketry in New England, Feb., 1982.

LEUTHEN, PAM
(Indian education program counselor)
Affiliation: Claremoire Public Schools, Indian Education Program, P.O. Box 907, Claremore, OK 74018 (918) 341-5270 Fax 341-8447.

LEVALDO, ANITA
(health center director)
Affiliation: Crownpoint PHS Indian Hospital, Crownpoint, NM 87313 (505) 786-5291.

LEVI, ALBERT
(Indian band chief)
Affiliation: Big Cove Indian Band, Box 1, RR 1, Site 11, Rexton, NB, Canada E0A 2L0 (506) 523-9183.

LEVI, CARL
(school director/supt.)
Affiliation: Rough Rock Demonstration School, RRDS, Box 217, Chinle, AZ 86503 (602) 728-3311.

LEVI, CORRINE L.
(organization director)
Affiliation: TCI, Inc., 2126 Connecticut Ave., NW, Suite 52, Washington, DC 20008.

LEVIAS, MATTHEW, Sr. (Chemehuevi)
(tribal chairperson)
Affiliation: Chemehuevi Reservation, P.O. Box 1976, Havasu Lake, CA 92363 (619) 858-4301.

LEVIER, FRANCIS ANDREW
(Citizen Band Potawatomi) 1950-
(tribal administrator, business committeeman)
Born November 13, 1950, Topeka, Kan. *Education*: Hofstra University, BA, 1973; University of Kansas, MS, 1975, EdD, 1979. *Principal occupation*: Tribal administrator & business committeeman. *Address*: Citizen Band Potowatomi Tribe, 1901 S. Gordon Cooper Dr., Shawnee, OK 74801 (405) 275-3121. *Affiliations*: Acting director, Supportive Educational Services, 1975-76, instructor, School of Social Welfare, 1977-79, assistant director of Minority Affairs, 1974-80, University of Kansas, Lawrence; director, Health Programs, Prairie Band Potawatomi Tribe, 1980-81; acting executive director, Prairie Band Potawatomi Tribe of Kansas, 1980-81; executive director, Region VI Indian Alcoholism Training Program, 1982-83; executive director, A proposal, Evaluation, Research, and Training consulting firm (P.E.R.T., Inc.), 1982-; director of economic development, Citizen Band Potawatomi Tribe, 1983-85; tribal administrator and business committeeman, Citizen Band Potawatomi Tribe, Shawnee, OK, 1983. *Other professional post*: Member of the Board of Regents, Haskell Indian Jr. College, 1979-83; consultant, Rockefeller Foundation, 1979; consultant, instructor, Leavenworth Federal Penitentiary, KS, 1978-80; consultant, Kickapoo Tribe of Kansas, 1978; consultant, Powhatten School District, KS, 1978; assistant director, Topeka (KS) Indian Center, 1977-78. *Community activities*: Affirmative Action, University of Kansas (board member, 1976-80); United Indian Recovery Association (board member, 1980-81); Emergency Services Council, City of Lawrence, KS (chairman, 1977-80). *Awards, honors*: Recipient of Ford Foundation Fellowship for American Indians, 1973-76; Elected to five-member Business Committee (governing body) of the Citizen Band Potawatomi Tribe in June, 1985. Was first business committee member ever named to the position of tribal administrator in the history of the 12,000 member tribe. *Published works*: A Brief History of the Pedigree Papers, 1983; editor, Using Indian Culture to Develop Alcohol & Drug Materials for Indian Adults and Youth, 1983; Overview of Inhalent Abuse Among American Indian Youth, 1981; An Attitude Survey of Urban Indians in N.E. Kansas Toward Higher Education, 1979; all published by the American Indian Institute, University of Oklahoma, 1983. The Need for Indian Student Organizations in Large Institutions of Higher Education, N.E.C.C.A. Conference Article, K.C., MO, 1979.

LEVINE, CHERYL (Paiute)
(rancheria chairperson)
Affiliation: Big Pine Reservation, P.O. Drawer 3060, Trinidad, CA 95570 (707) 938-2003.

LEVINE, VICTORIA LINDSAY 1954-
(ethnomusicologist; college professor)
Born September 8, 1954, Palo Alto, Calif. *Education*: San Francisco State University, BA (Anthropology), 1977, MA (Music History), 1980; University of Illinois at Urbana-Champaign, PhD (Musicology), 1990. *Principal occupation*: Ethnomusicologist; college professor. *Home address*: 6265 Savannah Way, Colorado Springs, CO 80919. *Affiliation*: Colorado College, 14 E. Cache la Poudre St., Colorado Springs, CO 80903 (719) 389-6183 Fax 389-6650 (assistant professor, 1988-94; associate professor of ethnomusicology, 1994-present). *Other professional post*: W.M. Keck Foundation Director of the Hulbert Center for Southwestern Studies at Colorado Colorado, 1999-present *Memberships*: Society for Ethnomusicology; College Music Society; Society for American Music; The International Council for Traditional Music. *Awards, honors*: John D. & Catherine T. MacArthur Professor, 1991-93, Colorado College; Jackson Fellow, 1991-92 (Colorado College); Ingolf Dahl Award in Musicology, 1979 (USC); Jackson Fellow, 19991-92, 1995-96, 1998-99; American Council of Learned Societies, Senior Fellowships, 1994-95; Ida Halpern Fellowship & Award, Society for Ethnomusicology, 1999. *Interests*: "Choctaw musical culture; musical cultures of Louisiana tribes; southeast & southwest Native American ethnomusicology." *Published work*: Choctaw Music and Dance (U. of Oklahoma Press, 1990); Music in the Ruben Cobos Collection of Spanish New Mexican Folklore: A Descriptive Catalogue (Hulbert Center Press, 1999); Writing American Indian Music: Historic Transcriptions, Notations, and Arrangements (A-R Editions, American Musicology Society, 2002).

LEVY, CARMELLA
(health director)
Affiliation: Indian Health Center of Santa Clara Valley, 1333 Meridian Ave., San Jose, CA 95125 (408) 294-7553.

LEWEY, ALISON (Passamaquoddy-Maliseet)
(company president, inventor)
Address: Lewey's Eco-Blends, Inc., 176 Amsden Rd., Corrina, ME 04928 (207) 278-5504. *Professional activities*: Started Lewey's Eco-Blends, Inc. and created a natural insect repellent, "Buzz-Off"...a soybean-based blend of natural oils that penetrates the skin and provides protection against more than 20 different kinds of insects. Ms. Lewey states, "...as a company we're committed to developing safe, natural products that people enjoy using." Lewey's other business focus is to expand on her company's mission of providing jobs and opportunity to Native people. She is currently working with groups in Maine and in Alaska to create economic opportunities.

LEWIS, CHUCK (Blackfeet)
(artist)
Address: Chuck Lewis Editions, P.O. Box 917, Questa, NM 87556 (505) 751-2158. *Products*: Monoprints, etchings, paper casts, lithographs, and original art.

LEWIS, FRANCIS
(Indian band chief)
Affiliation: Kitkatla Indian Band, Kitkatla, British Columbia, Canada V0V 1C0 (604) 628-9305.

LEWIS, GEORGE R. (Ho-Chunk)
(tribal president)
Education: BS in Public Administration. *Affiliation*: Presient, Ho-Chunk Nation, P.O. Box 667, Black River Falls, WI 54615 (715) 284-9343. *Past professional posts*: Former Personal Director, District V Legislator, Ho-Chunk Nation; employed with Jackson County for 28 years; former Union President of American Federation of State, County and Municipal Employees (AFSCME).

LEWIS (MYRICK), JOAN
(Grand Traverse Ottawa & Chippewa) 1951-
(health project director)
Born June 30, 1951, Traverse City, Mich. *Education*: Western Michigan University, BS, 1973; University of Houston, 1981-83; Trinity University (San Antonio, TX), MS, 1987. *Principal occupation*: Health project director. *Home address*: Resides in Minneapolis-St. Paul, MN area. *Affiliations*: Medical technologist, Hospital Laboratory, Kalamazoo, MI, 1974-80; chief medical technologist, Physician Clinical Laboratory, Houston, TX, 1981-87; AIDS Project Director, American Indian Health Care Association, St. Paul, MN, 1988-. *Community activities*: Community advisors to the Executive Planning Committee for the National Minority AIDS Conference, Census Awareness Committee, Minority Recruitment Committee, and University of Minnesota. *Memberships*: National Minority AIDS Council; National AIDS Network. *Interests*: Culturally Sensitive AIDS presentations at regional and national meetings.

LEWIS, JUDY (Onondaga)
(attorney)
Address: Unknown. *Memberships*: Court of Indian Appeals Bar Association (president); Oklahoma Indian Bar Association; Native American Bar Association.

LEWIS, ROBERT (Zuni Pueblo)
(pueblo governor)
Affiliation: Pueblo of Zuni, P.O. Box 339, Zuni, NM 87327 (505) 782-4481.

LEWIS, ROBERT W. 1930-
(professor & editor)
Born December 15, 1930, Elrama, Penna. *Education*: University of Pittsburgh, BA; Columbia University, MA; University of Illinois, PhD. *Principal occupation*: Professor & editor. *Address*: Dept.of English, University of North Dakota, Grand Forks, ND 58202 (701) 777-3321 Fax 777-3650. E-mail: robert_lewis@und.nodak. edu. *Affiliation*: Professor, University of North Dakota, Grand Forks, ND. *Other professional post*: Editor, North Dakota Quarterly. *Military service*: U.S. Army, 1952-54. *Published works*: Hemingway on Love (University of Texas Press, 1965; reprinted by Haskell House, 1973); Hemingway in Italy and Other Essays (Praeger, 1990); Hemingway's A Farewell to Arms: The War of the Words (Twayne, 1992); pamphlet, American Indian Literature, with Joseph DeFlyer, edited by Elaine Benally (Educational Resources Information Center, 1983); articles and chapters in books.

LEWIS, ROD (Navajo)
(attorney)
Address: Arizona Bar Association (Indian Law Section-chairperson), P.O. Box 400, Sacaton, AZ 85247 (520) 562-3611. *Membership*: Native American Bar Assn.

LEWIS, S. JO (Navajo)
(school principal)
Affiliation: Blackwater Community School, Route 1, Box 95, Coolidge, AZ 85228 (520) 215-5859 Fax 215-5862.

LEWIS, DR. TOMMY H., JR. (Navajo)
(college president)
Affiliation: Dine (Navajo) College, P.O. Box 126, Tsaile, AZ 86556 (520) 724-6671 Fax 724-3327.

LIBERTY, ADRIAN (Leech Lake Ojibwe)
(college instructor)
Affiliation: Leech Lake Tribal College, 6530 U.S. Hwy. 2 NW, Cass Lake, MN 56633 (218) 335-4220 Fax 335-4209.

LIDMAN, ROGER W.
(museum director)
Born in Norfolk, Va. *Education*: Arizona State University, BA (Anthropology). *Principal occupation*: Museum director. *Affiliation*: Pueblo Grande Museum & Cultural Park, 4619 E Washington St., Phoenix, AZ 85034 (602) 495-0901. *Community activities*: Board Member, Artability; Papago Salado Association; State Library Advisory Council. *Memberships*: American Association of Museums; Western Museums Association (V.P.); Museum Association of Arizona (former president). *Interests*: Guitar, natural history.

LIDOT, TOM
(executive director)
Affiliation: National Native American Aids Task Force, c/o Indian Health Council, P.O. Box 406, Pauma Valley, CA 92061 (619) 749-1410.

LIGHTNING, GEORGINA LYNN (Cree)
(actor/singer & lyricist)
Born July 4 in Edmonton, Alberta, Can. *Education*: Concordia College (Edmonton, AB); American Academy of Dramatic Arts & UCLA. *Principal occupation*: Actor/singer & lyricist. *Home address*: Resides in Calif. *Community activities*: Volunteer to operations of American Indians in film and American Indian recognition of entertainers in media honored by the annual Kokopeli Awards and Concert Benefit. *Membership*: American Academy Alumni/Repertory Company. *Awards, honors*: Michael Toma Award by Concordia College for most progressed actor, first time ever awarded to a Canadian, not to mention first for an Indian graduate from the Academy; and first to be invited as a repertory actor. *Interests*: Performing arts/entertainment (music, 1977-; acting, 1988-); political activist willing to give her life for the rights and obligations the government owes to her people, the natives of this country. "I wish to travel the world as a performer who earns the public's appreciation and support for a native American point of view and deserved acceptance as an equal in art. I have written several songs which I hope to record soon." *Biographical source*: "Stars in the Desert," Navajo newspaper.

LILLY, DEBORAH
(editor)
Affiliation: Editor, Indian Progress, Associated Committee of Friends on Indian Affairs, P.O. Box 2326, Richmond, IN 47375. Website: www.acfiaquaker.org.

LINCOLN, MICHEL E. (Navajo/Cherokee)
(IHS-acting director)
Affiliation: Indian Health Service, Office of the Director, 5600 Fishers Lane, Rm. 6-05, Rockville, MD 20857 (301) 443-1083.

LINCOLN, ROY (Karuk)
(tribal chairperson)
Affiliation: Quartz Valley Indian Community, P.O. Box 24, Fort Jones, CA 96032 (530) 468-5907.

LIND, PATRICK WILLIAM (Aleut)
(artist, art studio owner)
Affiliation: Small Treasures, 8851 Cordell Circle #5, Anchorage, AK 99502 (907) 248-9639.

LINDLEY, BRENDA (*Mahkoonsahkwa*) (Wea)
(herbalist, homeopathic practitioner, tribal administrator)
Affiliation: Wea Indian Tribe and Herbal Remedy Clinic, 715 Park Ave., Lafayette, IN 47904; E-mail: weatribe @wea-indian-tribe.com, or apilitasremedy@aol.com Website: www.wea-indian-tribe.com, or www.angelfire. com/in4/herbalremedies. *Activities*: She specializes in Western & Native American Herbology, with knowledge in aromatherapy, homeopathy, surgical technology, and conventional medicines with over 16 years of experience. She studied under Master Herbalist, Michael Tierra, and is a licensed/certified herbalist. She also has 30 years of genealogical research experience. *Other professional post*: Administrator, genealogist & historian for the Wea Indian Tribe, and owns a Genealogy Service wih an e-mail address, bloodlngenealogy @aol.com

LINFORD, LAURANCE D.
(executive director)
Affiliation: Inter-Tribal Indian Ceremonial Association, 226 W. Coal Ave., Gallup, NM 87301 (800) 233-4528; (505) 863-3896 FAX 722-5158.

LINGERFELT, WILLIAM D. (*Chief Medicine Wolf*)
(Eastern Cherokee) 1949-
(construction contractor)
Born July 20, 1949, Atlanta, Ga. *Education*: High school. *Principal occupation*: Construction contractor. Resides in Canton, GA (404) 479-4627. *Military service*: U.S. Army, 1969-71 (Specialist 4th Class; Vietnam Vet - 1 Bronze Star, Vietnam Campaign Medal, Good Conduct Badge, several others). *Community service*: VFW member. *Interests*: "I am a lecturer and the voice of my people in the northern Georgia area. My family and I are active in the powwow trail. We are dancers and make Native American jewelry, costumes, beadwork, etc. I m chief medicine man for the Southeastern Cherokee Confederacy. I am a chief and sit on the Chief's Council. My wife "Snow Deer" is chief of the Wolf Clan." *Biographical sources*: Paper which have done stories on Mr. Lingerfelt: The Atlanta Journal Constitution; The Cherokee Tribune; The Cleveland; Georgia Telegraph; Gainesville, GA Newspaper; The Indian Trader Magazine.

LINK, MARTIN A. 1934-
(publisher)
Born September 26, 1934, Madison, Wisc. *Education*: University of Arizona, BA, 1959. *Principal occupation*: Publisher. *Home address*: 2302 Mariyana Dr., Gallup, NM 87301 (505) 863-6459. *Affiliations*: Former director, Navajo Tribal Museum, Window Rock, AZ; publisher, The Indian Trader, Gallup, N.M., 1985-. *Other professional post*: Anthropology & history instructor, University of New Mexico-Gallup Branch Campus. *Military service*: U.S. Army, 1961-63. *Community activities*: Kiwanis Club; Knights of Columbus; Gallup-McKinley Co. Chamber of Commerce. *Memberships*: Plateau Sciences Society, 1959-; Inter-Tribal Indian Ceremonial Association, 1963-; Archaeological Society of New Mexico, 1965-83; Indian Arts & Crafts Association, 1985-. *Awards, honors*: Navajo Nation Achievement Award in Science - 1976; Navajo Code Talker's Medal of Merit - 1986. *Interests*: "Writing, research and photography, especially throughout the Southwest. Have traveled throughout the Southwest, Grand Canyon, northern Mexico. Present research focuses on Indian-Spanish Inter-Relationships." *Published works*: Navajo: A Century of Progress (K.C. Publications, 1968); A Goat in the Rug (McMillian & Co., 1975); The Beauty of Shalako (The Indian Trader, 1985); Early Franciscan Missions (The Indian Trader, 1989).

LINKLATER, NORMAN
(Indian band chief)
Affiliation: Nelson House Indian Band, Nelson House, Manitoba, Canada R0B 1A0 (204) 484-2332.

LINZER, ANNA (Lenape) 1950-
(writer)
Born February 10, 1950, Seattle, Wash. *Education*: University of Washington, Lewis & Clark College,

Southern Oregon State College. *Principal occupation*: Writer. *Address*: P.O. Box 374, Indianola, WA 98342 (360) 297-8331 Fax 297-8254; E-mail: rslinzer@earthlink.net. *Affiliation*: Richard & Anna Linzer, Facilitation & Consultation. *Memberships*: Native Writers Circle of the Americas; NW Native Writers Circle. *Awards, prizes*: 1999 American Book Award for "Ghost Dancing." *Published works*: Ghost Dancing (Picador of St. Martin's Press, 1998); numerous works of fiction, poetry & essays in literary magazines.

LISA, SUZI (Apache)
(trading post manager)
Affiliation: Stewart Indian Museum Trading Post, 5366 Snyder Ave., Carson City, NV 89701.

LIPOVAC, PETE A.
(school supt.)
Affiliation: Sho'ban School District #512, P.O Box 306, Fort Hall, ID 83203 (208) 238-3975.

LISTO, SYLVESTER (Tohono O'odham)
(former tribal chairperson)
Affiliation: Tohono O'odham Council, Sells Reservation, P.O. Box 837, Sells, AZ 85634 (602) 388-2221.

LITTLE, ANTHONY F. (Rosebud Sioux)
(attorney)
Address: P.O. Box 817, Bernalillo, NM 87004 (505) 867-3391 (office). *Membership*: Native American Bar Association (board member).

LITTLE, JOSEPH D.
(former BIA area director)
Affiliation: Bureau of Indian Affairs, Albuquerque Area Office, P.O. Box 26567, Albuquerque, NM 87125 (505) 766-3170.

LITTLE, PETE
(administrative officer)
Affiliation: Acoma-Canoncito Laguna PHS Indian Hospital, P.O. Box 130, San Fidel, NM 87049.

LITTLE BEAR, LEROY ROBERT (Blackfoot) 1941-
(professor-Native American studies)
Born November 11, 1941, Alberta, Can. *Education*: Wenatchee (WA) Valley College, AA, 1966; University of Lethbridge (Alberta, Can.), BA, 1971; University of Utah, School of Law, JD, 1975. *Principal occupation*: Professor of Native American studies. *Affiliations*: Native American Studies Department, University of Lethbridge, Alberta, Canada (associate professor, 1975-; chairperson, 1975-81) (403) 329-2733. *Other professional posts*: Consultant: National Indian Brotherhood, Lethbridge, AB, 1976-78; Department of Indian Affairs, Lethbridge, 1980-81; Blood Indian Tribe, Cardston, AB, 1980-; Indian Association of Alberta, Lethbridge, 1983-. *Community activities*: Blood Tribe Police Commission (volunteer), 1980-; Legal Aid Society of Alberta, Lethbridge (volunteer), 1981-82; Lethbridge Friendship Centre (volunteer), 1969-71. Conferences: Subcommission of Human Rights Commission (representative), 1984; United Nations' Conference (representative), 1984; attended Constitutional conventions on Native Rights, 1983, 1984 and 1985) as a legal advisor for Indian Association of Alberta. Memberships: Canadian Lawyers' Association; Indian Association of Alberta. Interests: Indian law; Native Canadian Government issues. Speak, read and write English & Blackfoot. *Published works*: Books: Pathways to Self-Determination: Native Indian Leaders' Perspectives on Self-Government, and Quest for Justice: Aboriginal Rights in Canada, both with Nenno Boldt and J. Anthony Long. Articles: "Dispute Settlement Among the Nacirema," Journal of Contemporary Law; "A Concept of Native Title," presentation to MacKenzie Valley Pipeline Inquiry (Thomas Berger Commission Chairman).

LITTLE CHIEF, BARTHELL (Kiowa-Comanche)
(artist)
Address: Rt. 3, Box 109A, Anadarko, OK 73005 (405) 464-2564. *Products*: Original sculpture in alabaster and bronze reproductions; original paintings in gouache; limited edition prints.

LITTLE DEAR, KIMBERLY (Blackfoot)
(writer)
Address: 15150 S. Golden Rd. #1002, Golden, CO 80401 (303) 271-9223.

LITTLE DOG, ADELE F.
(school principal)
Affiliation: Little Eagle Day School, P.O. Box 26, Little Eagle, SD 57639 (605) 823-4235.

LITTLE FINGER, LEONARD
(cultural resource educator)
Affiliations: Cultural resource educator, Loneman Day School P.O. Box 50, Oglala, SD 57764 (605) 867-5633 Fax 867-5109

LITTLE HAWK, KENNETH (Micmac/Mohawk)
(educator, lecturer, storyteller,
musician, composer)
Address: P.O. Box 107, Whiting, NJ 08759 (732) 716-0456 Fax 716-1752; E-mail: littlehawk@kennethlittle hawk.com. Website: www.kennethlittlehawk.com. *Professional skills*: Little Hawk shares Native American culture, traditions, and musical instruments in a lecture, storytelling, and muscial demonstration format. Little Hawk performs for a wide variety of audiences. His themes include Native American culture, cultural diversity, self-esteem, and respect for others and our environment. As a recording artist, Little Hawk composes, sings and plays Native American music on flutes, drums, rattles, and other traditional instruments for moviews, plays, television, radio, and concerts. His music and singing are heard in the films, "The West," and "Lewis and Clark," both produced by Ken Burns. The soundtrack for "The West," produced by SONY, includes Little Hawk's original music and singing. "Wind, Sun and Stars," Helicon Records, was nominated for Best Children's Recording of 1998 by Native American Music Awards. Little Hawk's recordings include "First Light," "The Hawk Project," "From the Heart of Little Hawk," "In a Very Real Way," "In a Good Way," and "Brothers of the Wind." He has composed and performed music with the Westchester Philharmonic, New York. As an actor, Little Hawk appeared in "Black Elk Speaks" at the Denver Center Theatre Company and at the Mark Taper Forum in Los Angeles. He played Chief Joseph in "Indians" at the McCarter Theater Company in Princeton, NJ. He portrayed a Native American elder in "The Inheritance," a film directed by Mark Williams, NYU Dept. of Film & TV. He played an attorney in the film, "Petty Crimes," directed by Michael Ferry, and a storyteller in the film, "Campfire Stories," directed by Andrzej Krakowski and Jeff Mazzola. *Military service*: U.S. Army Paratrooper (honorable discharge-Good Conduct Medal. *Awards, honors*: Nominated twice by Native American Music Awards for "Best Storyteller" and "Best Spoken Word;" Has been on TV-PBS (Ken Burns' documentaries; Lewis & Clark, and Land of the Eagle. *Community activities*: Lecture and perform in public libraries and schools, colleges and universities, senior citizens' homes, and Veterans' hospitals. *Memberships*: Screen Actors Guild, Actors' Equity, Project Impact, BOCES, The Hawk Project, The Gatherers' Institute. *Interests*: Teaching respect for our Earth and all living things. Composing and playing Native music on traditional, natural instruments. *Published CD's*: "The Great Mystery," "In a Very Real Way," "In a Good Way," and "Wind, Sunn, and Storm."

LITTLE LIGHT, CLOYCE (Crow)
(editor)
Affiliation: "Hunter," North American Indian League P.O. Box 7, Deer Lodge, MT 59731.

LITTLE LIGHT, GARFIELD (Crow)
(IHS-administrative support)
Affiliation: Indian Health Service, Billings Area Office, P.O. Box 2143, Billings, MT 59103 (406) 657-6403.

LITTLE LIGHT, MARLA (Crow)
(craftsperson)
Affiliation: Bison Specialties, 9230 Pryor Rd., Billings, MT 59101 (406) 259-6342. E-mail: bison@mch.net.

LITTLE HAWK, KENNETH (Micmac/Mohawk) 1936-
(educator/lecturer/musician/storyteller)
Born January 14, 1936, in New Jersey. *Principal occupation*: Educator, lecturer, musician, composer, and storyteller. *Address*: P.O. Box 107, Whiting, NJ08759. Website: www.kennethlittlehawk.com.

LITTLE THUNDER, KAREN
(general manager)
Affiliation: "The Lakota Times," 1920 Lombardy Dr., Box 2180, Rapid City, SD 57709 (605) 341-0011.

LITTLE WOUNDED, CAROLE (Rosebud Lakota)
(secondary school administrator)
Affiliation: Secondary School Administrator, Sicangu Oyate Ho., Inc., St. Francis Indian School, P.O. Box 379, St. Francis, SD 57572 (605) 747-2299.

LITTLEBEAR, DR. RICHARD
(Native American studies program coordinator)
Affiliation: Dull Knife Memorial College, P.O. Box 98, 1 College Dr., Lame Deer, MT 59043 (406) 477-6215 Fax 477-6219. *Past professional post*: Director, Multi-functional Resource Center, Anchorage, AK.

LITTLEBIRD, LARRY
(writer)
Address: P.O. Box 2900, Santa Fe, NM 87501 (505) 455-3196.

LITTLEBREN, THOMAS, JR.
(Indian center instructor)
Affiliation: Center for Dine Studies, Dine (Navajo) College, P.O. Box 126, Tsaile, AZ 86556 (520) 724-6671 Fax 724-3327.

LITTLECHIEF, BARTHELL (*White Horse*)
(Kiowa-Comanche) 1941-
(self-employed artist-sculptor/painter)
Born October 14, 1941, Kiowa Indian Hospital, Lawton, Okla. *Education*: Cameron University, 1964-65; University of Oklahoma, 1966-67. *Principal occupation*: Artist-sculptor/painter. *Home address*: Route 3, Box 109A, Anadarko, OK 73005 (405) 464-2564. *Military service*: U.S. Army National Guard, 1966-71 (SP/4). *Memberships*: Kiowa TIA-PAIH Society of Oklahoma; Native American Church. *Awards, honors*: 1988 Colorado Indian Market - "Best Traditional Painting"; 1989 Red Earth Indian Market - "3rd Graphics"; 1990 Santa Fe Indian Market "3rd Place - Painting"; 1991 Trail of Tears Art Show - "Grand Award"; 1991 American Indian Exposition - "1st Place Painting." *Biographical sources*: Who's Who in North American Indian Art; Who's Who in American Art; American Artists; Kiowa Voices; feature article in Santa Fean magazine; and articles in Southern Living magazine, and Texhoma Monthly magazine.

LITTLECHILD, WILLIE (*Wetaskiwin*)
(Canadian parliament member)
Address: Parliament Bldgs., Ottawa, ON K1A 0A4 (613) 995-9364.

LITTLEFIELD, DAN
(editor)
Affiliation: American Native Press, 2801 S. University, Little Rock, AR 72204 (501) 569-3160.

LITTLEMAN, JUDY
(BIA special education coordinator)
Affiliation: Oklahoma Education Office, Bureau of Indian Affairs, 4149 Highline Blvd., Suite 380, Oklahoma City, OK 73180 (405) 945-6051 Fax 945-6057.

LITZAU, KEN
(Indian school administrator)
Affiliation: Circle of Life Survival School, P.O. Box 447, White Earth, MN 56591 (218) 983-3285 ext. 269 Fax 983-3767.

LIVERMORE, EARL (Blackfeet)
(artist)
Address: Livermore Fine Arts & Design, P.O. Box 2173, Bellingham, WA 98227 (360) 647-9137. *Products*: Original artwork and limited edition prints.

LIVINGSTONE, E. CYRIL
(Indian band chief)
Affiliation: Cowichan Lake Indian Band, Box 1376, Lake Cowichan, British Columbia, Canada V0R 2G0 (604) 745-3548.

LIVINGSTON, ROBBIE
(school principal)
Affiliation: Dibe Yazhi Habitiin Olta, Inc., Borrego Pass School, P.O. Box 679, Crownpoint, NM 87313 (505) 786-5392 Fax 786-5956.

LOCKE, KEVIN (*Tokeya Inajin*) (Standing Rock Lakota-Hunkpapa Sioux)
(educator/performer)
Born in Calif., raised in SD. *Principal occupation*: Edu-

cator/performer (traditional Northern Plains flute player & hoop dancer) dba Lakota Performing Arts. *Address*: P.O. Box 2525, Redway, CA 95560; E-mail: klocke@btigate.com. *Awards & honors*: NEA National Heritage Award, 1990; delegate & featured performer at Earth Summit (Brazil 1992); 1993 Parent's Choice Gold Award, 1993 for "Wopila - A Giveaway," for outstanding material for children ages 4-9; United Nations Habitat II Conference (Turkey 1996). *Interests*: Kevin not only performs and lectures in schools al accross the Plains states, he has toured the world, appearing in Canada, China, Spain, Australia, and Africa. *Published works*: Open Circle, 1996; Keepers of the Dream, 1994; Wopila-A Giveaway, 1993; Flash of the Mirror, 1992; Dream Catcher, 1992; The Flash of the Mirror, 1992; Make Me a Hollow Reed, 1990; Lakota Love Songs & Stories, 1990; The Seventh Direction, 1990; Love Songs of the Lakota, 1982. All cassettes & CDs produced & recorded at Meyer Creative Productions for Makoche Records (Bismarck), EarthBeat! Records (Redway), and Indian House Recordings (Taos).

LOCKE, PATRICIA
(institute director)
Affiliation: Native American Language Institute, P.O. Box 963, Choctaw, OK 73020 (405) 769-4650.

LOCKHART, GEMMA
(film producer)
Affiliation: Whirlwind Soldier, P.O. Box 154, Rosebud, SD 57570 (605) 747-2835.

LOCKLEAR, JUANITA O. (Lumbee)
(center director)
Affiliation: Native American Resource Center, Pembroke State University, Pembroke, NC 28372 (919) 521-4214.

LOCKLEAR, PATRICIA (Lumbee)
(playwright)
Address: P.O. Box 68-P, Pembroke, NC 28372 (910) 521-8602.

LOETHER, CHRISTOPHER
(Indian studies program director)
Affiliation: Indian Studies Program, Dept. of Sociology, Anthropology, Social Work, Idaho State University, P.O. Box 8005, Pocatello, ID 83209 (208) 236-2629. Interests: Linguistics, language; Indians of California.

LOEW, PATTY *(Waswaganokwe)*
(Bad River Band-Ojibwe) 1952-
(assistant professor; public TV host)
Born May 15, 1952, Milwaukee, Wisc. *Education*: University of Wisconsin, LaCrosse, BS (Mass Communications), 1974; University of Wisconsin, Madison, MA (Broadcast Journalism), 1992, PhD in Mass Communications, 1998. *Principal occupation*: Assistant professor, UW-Madison Dept. of Life Sciences Communication and Journalist, Wisconsin Public Television. *Home address*: 7788 W. Old Sauk Rd., Verona, WI 53593. *Office address*: University of Wisconsin, Madison, Dept. of Life Sciences Communication, Rm. 224A Ag Journalism, 440 Henry Mall, Madison, WI 53706 (608) 262-0654 Fax 265-3042 (office); E-Mail: paloew@wisc.edu. Website: www.lsc.wisc.edu/pattyloew.htm. *Affiliations*: Wisconsin Public Television, madison, Wisc, 1993-present. WKOW-TV Madison, WI, 1975-79 and 1985-96. KHQ-TV, Spokane, WA, 1979-81. KATU-TV, Portland, OR, 1981-85. *Other professional posts*: Affiliated Faculty, UW-Madison, American Indian Studies, UW-Madison School of Human Ecology, and UW-Madison Dept. of Family & Consumer Science. *Awards, honors*: Honorary Doctorate, Doctor of Humane Letters, Edgewood College, 2003; Women of Achievement Award, Wisconsin Woman of Color Network, 2003; Friend of Education, Wisconsin State School Superintendent's Award, 2003; Honorary Doctorate, Doctor of Public Service, Northland College, 2002; Outstanding Book Award, Wisconsin Library Association, 2001; Outstanding Service Award, Great Lakes Inter-Tribal Council, 1998; Frances C. Allen Fellowship, D'Arcy McNickle Center for American Indian History, Newberry Library, Chicago, IL, 1997; Anna Julia Cooper Fellow, UW History, 1996; Howard Simons Fellow, 1992. *Community activities*: UW Committee on Gender and Diversity, Wisc.; Advisory Board, Logan Museum of Anthropology, Beloit College; Advisory Board, Sequoyah Research Center, University of Arkansas at Little Rock. membership: Native American Journalists Association (former board member); Native American Public Televcommunications (former board member: Wisconsin Historical Society. *Interests*: American Indian treaty rights, Origin Stories, environmental justice issues, tribal and mainstream media. *Published work*: Books: Indian Nations of Wisconsin (Wisconsin Historical Society Press, 2001); Native people of Wisconsin (Wisconsin Historical Society Press, 2003); book chapter in A Wisconsin Fifteen (Wisconsin Historical Society Press, 1998) .

LOHMAN, CHERYL
(BIA agency supt.)
Affiliation: Warm Springs Agency, Bureau of Indian Affairs, P.O. Box 1239, Warm Springs, OR 97761 (541) 553-2411 Fax 553-2426.

LOMAHAFTEWA, LINDA (Hopi) 1947-
(teacher, artist)
Born July 3, 1947, Phoenix, Ariz. *Education*: San Francisco Art Institute, BFA, 1970, MFA, 1971. *Principal occupation*: Teacher, artist. *Home address*: Route 11, Box 20 SP 59, Santa Fe, N.M. 87501. *Affiliation*: Assistant professor of Native American Art, California State College, Rohnert Park, 1971-73; teacher, painting and drawing, Native American Studies, University of California, Berkeley, 1974-76; drawing and painting instructor, Institute of American Indian Arts, Santa Fe, 1976-. *Exhibitions*: Festival of Native American Art, Aspen Institute at Baca, 1982; Contemporary Native American Art, Gardiner Art Gallery, Oklahoma State University, Stillwater, Okla., 1983; Contemporary Native American Photography, Southern Plains Indian Museum, Anadarko, Okla., 1984; Shadows Caught Images of Native Americans, Gilcrease Museum, Tulsa, 1984; 2nd Annual Heard Invitational, Heard Museum, Phoenix, 1985; One Woman Exhibit, American Indian Contemporary Arts, San Francisco, 1985; Women of Sweetgrass, Cedar and Sage, Gallery of the American Indian Community House, New York, N.Y., 1985; The Art of the Native American, Owensboro Museum of Fine Arts, KY, 1985; Native to Native, Alchemie Gallery, Boston, 1986. *Community activities*: City of Santa Fe Arts Board. *Memberships*: San Francisco Art Institute Alumni Association; Institute of American Indian Arts Alumni Association. *Awards, honors*: Indian Festival of Arts - First Place Painting, La Grande, Oreg., 1974; 61st Annual Indian Market - Third Place Painting, Santa Fe, 1982. *Interests*: "Art—displayed at the following permanent collections: Southern Plains Indian Museum, Anadarko, Okla.; Millicent Rogers Museum, Taos, N.M.; University of Lethbridge, Native American Studies Department, Alberta, Canada; Native American Center for the Living Arts, Inc., Niagara Falls, NY; American Indian Historical Society, San Francisco; Center for the Arts of Indian America, Washington, DC." *Biographical sources*: Who's Who in American Art, 1976; The Sweet Grass Lives on 50 Contemporary Native American Indian Artists, by Jamake Highwater (Lippincott, 1980); American Women Artists, by Charlotte Streifer Rubinstein (Avon, 1982); The World Who's Who of Women, Eighth Edition, 1984; Bearing Witness Sobreviviendo, An Anthology of Writing and Art by Native American/Latina Women (Calyx: A Journal of Art and Literature by Women, Corvallis, Ore., 1984); The American West, The Modern Vision, by Patricia Janis Broder (Little, Brown, 1984).

LOMAKEMA, MILLAND, SR. (Hopi)
(Hopi craftsmen's coop guild manager)
Affiliation: Hopi Arts & Crafts/Silvercraft Cooperative Guild, P.O. Box 37, Second Mesa, AZ 86043 (520) 734-2463 Fax 734-6647

LOMAWAIMA, HARTMAN H. (Hopi)
(associate director-museum)
Education: Harvard University, EdM, 1972. *Address & Affiliation*: Associate Director, Arizona State Museum, University of Arizona, Tucson, AZ 85721 (520) 621-6281 Fax 621-2976; E-Mail: hartman@u.arizona.edu. Other professional post: American Indian Studies Program, University of Arizona, Harvill Bldg., Rm. 430, P.O. Box 210076, Tucson, AZ 85721. *Affiliations*: Hearst Museum of Anthropology, UC Berkeley, CA, 1980-88; University of Washington, Seattle, 1988-94; Arizona State Museum, Tucson, AZ, 1994-present. *Community activities*: President, Hopi Foundation, Hotevilla, AZ; Council, Adult Literacy Initiative, University of Arizona Press. *Memberships*: National Indian Education Association; American Association for State & Local History (National Council); American Association of Museums. *Interests*: Museology, ethnology. *Published works*: "I have authored articles and chapters that have been published in journals, readers and encyclopedias."

LOMAWAIMA, K. TSIANINA (Creek) 1955-
(professor of American Indian studies)
Born March 30, 1955, in Kansas. *Education*: Stanford University, MA, 1979, PhD, 1987. *Principal occupation*: Professor of American Indian studies. *Address*: American Indian Studies, Harvill 430, University of Arizona, Box 210076, Tucson, AZ 85721 (520) 621-2269 Fax 621-7952. E-mail: lomawaim@email.arizona.edu. *Affiliation*: Assistant Professor, Dept. of Anthropology, American Indian Studies, University of Washington, Seattle, 1988-94; University of Arizona, American Indian Studies, Tucson, AZ (associate professor, 1994-98; professor, 1998-present). *Memberships*: American Society for Ethnohistory, 1987-present; American Anthropological Association, 1990-present; American Educational Research Association, 1997-present. *Awards, honors*: Ford Doctoral Fellow, 1977-79; Dorothy Danforth Compton Fellow, 1984; 1994 Native North American Prose Award; 1994 University of Washington Distinguished Teaching Award; 2003 University of Arizona Alumni Association Extraordinary Faculty Award. *Interests*: History of American Indian education, especially experiences of native people in federal boarding schools. Federal policy and practice to transform Native homes, and Native response. *Published works*: They Called It Prairie Light: The Story of Chilocco Indian School (University of Nebraska Press, 1994); Away From Home: American Indian Boarding School Experiences, 1878-2000, with M. Archuleta & B. Child (Heard Museum, 2000); Uneven Ground: American Indian Sovereignty and Federal Law, with D. Wilkins (University of Oklahoma Press, 2001); articles.

LONE FIGHT, EDWARD (Mandan-Hidatsa) 1939-
(school supt.)
Born May 28, 1939, Elbowoods, N.D. *Education*: Dickinson State College, BS, 1964; Arizona State University, MA, 1970. *Principal occupation*: BIA Indian education. *Address*: Mandaree Day School, P.O. Box 488, Mandaree, ND 58636 (701) 759-3311 Fax 759-3493. *Affiliations*: Supt., Riverside Indian School, Anadarko, OK; Indian education, BIA, Washington, DC; chairperson of education, BIA, Fort Berthold Agency, New Town, ND; former tribal chairperson, Three Affiliated Tribes of the Fort Berthold Reservation, New Town, ND; Supt., BIA, Mandaree Day School, Mandaree, ND, 1991-93; Supt., Mandaree Public School, 1993-present. *Community activities*: Jaycees; Kiwanis Club. *Membership*: National Education Association.

LONEFIGHT, TONY
(journalist)
Affiliation: Grand Forks Herald, P.O. Box 6008, Grand Forks, ND 58206 (701) 780-1228.

LONETREE, JACOB (Ho Chunk)
(tribal president)
Affiliation: Ho Chunk (Winnebago) Nation, P.O. Box 667, Black River Falls, WI 54615 (715) 284-9343.

LONEWOLF, PECITA M. (NORWOOD) (Nanticoke/Delaware) 1936-
(retired-federal service)
Born January 17, 1936. *Education*: Haskell Institute, 1949-55. *Principal occupation*: Retired-with 32 years of Federal Service - curently volunteering in Nanticoke tribal operations. *Address*: Rt. 4, Box 1150, Millsboro, DE 19966 (302) 945-3052 Fax 945-7187; E-mail: LW1of3@aol.com. *Affiliations*: Guidance counselor, Bureau of Indian Affairs' Employment Assistance and Training programs for Indian families or individuals relocating to Los Angeles, CA, 1955-70; supervisor, Indian Head Starts on Indian Reservations, 1970-80, 1986-90; supervisor, Administration for Native Americans' (ANA) Social/Economic Development Programs for tribes, 1980-85, 1990-91. *Community activities*: VP-Tourism/Events, Greater Millsboro Chamber of Commerce; board member, Southern Delaware Tourism; member, Delaware State Historic Preservation review team; community services director/communications

representative, Millsboro 7th Day Adventist Church; marketing/media director, Nanticoke Tribe. *Memberships*: Nanticoke Indian Tribe of Delaware; Haskell Alumni Association, Lawrence, KS and OK chapters. *Interests*: "Using my talents, resources and experience to help others and writing weekly in local newspapers."

LONG, ALBERT (Blackfeet-Navajo) 1919-
(trader/craftsman)
Born September 9, 1919, Billings, Mont. *Education*: Los Angeles Art Center, 1946-48; received Graduate Gemologist diploma, 1967. *Principal occupation*: Trader/craftsman. *Address*: P.O. Box 40, Lake Havasu City, AZ 86405 (602) 453-5929. *Military service*: U.S. Marine Corps, 1941-45 (First Marine Division-Communications Specialist; Guadalcanal and New Britain campaigns). *Membership*: Master Gemology Association. *Interests*: "Having worked both silver and gold, many times using non-traditional gemstones such as opals & diamonds, his work has appeared in "Arizona Highways" magazine & in numerous juried shows including the Scottsdale National & the Inter-Tribal Ceremonial in Gallup. Now, semi-retired, he plans to work on shows for his many trader friends & be involved with organizations such as the Inter-Tribal Ceremonial Association as well as other museums & foundations showing exclusive Native American arts & crafts. He is available for craft judging in juried shows of Native American crafts. He is no longer accepting commissions on his jewelry, though still offers his assistance to former customers & serious collectors."

LONG, JON (Pima-Maricopa)
(arts & crafts center manager)
Affiliation: Gila River Arts & Crafts Center, Box 457, Sacaton, AZ 85247 (602) 963-3981.

LONG SOLDIER, HELEN
(association contact)
Affiliation: National Indian Counselor's Association, University of Nebraska, 223 Administration-M.C.A., Lincoln, NE 68588 (402) 472-2027.

LONG STANDING BEAR CHIEF
(editor)
Affiliation: "Spirit Talk," P.O. Box 430, Blackfoot Nation, Browning, MT 59417 (406) 338-2882.

LONG, SUSIE (Yurok)
(tribal chairperson)
Affiliation: Yurok Tribal Council, 1034 6th St., Eureka, CA 95501 (707) 444-0433.

LONGBOW, CARL WATSON (Cherokee of NJ)
(principal chief)
Affiliation: Cherokee Nation of New Jersey, 1164 Stuyvesant Ave., Irvington, NJ 07111 (973) 351-1210.

LONGBRAKE, FAYE
(school principal)
Affiliations: Cherry Creek Day School, Cherry Creek, SD 57622 (605) 538-4238.

LONGCROW, BARBARA
(school principal/teacher)
Affiliation: White Horse Day School, P.O. Box 7, White Horse, SD 57661 (605) 733-2183.

LONGFISH, GEORGE C.
(Iroquois-Seneca/Tuscarora) 1942-
(professor/artist)
Born August 22, 1942, Oshweken, Ontario, Can. *Education*: School of the Art Institute of Chicago, BFA (Painting, Sculpture), 1970; and MFA (Filmmaking), 1972. *Principal occupation*: Professor/artist. *Address*: Native American Studies Dept., College of Letters & Science, 2401 Hart Hall, University of California, Davis, CA 95616 (530) 752-3237 Fax 752-7097. *Affiliations*: Director of the graduate program in American Indian Art, University of Montana, Missoula, 1972-73; professor in Native American Studies, University of California, Davis, 1973-. *Other professional post*: Director, Carl Nelson Gorman Museum, 2401 Hart Hall, Native American Studies, University of California, Davis, CA. *Awards, honors*: Numerous awards and prizes throughout the years for his work. *Interests*: Contemporary Native American art; attended over 170 art exhibitions exhibiting paintings, sculpture & film; art lectures. *Biographical sources*: Cited in Jamake Highwater (Ed.) The Sweet Grass Lives On: Fifty Con-

temporary North American Indian Artists (Lippincott & Crowell); cited in "Horizon", Sept. 1980; *Publications*: Numerous articles; Book: with J. Smith - Personal Symbols: Recent Paintings and Works on Paper (University of Northern Iowa, 1986).

LONGIE, ERICH
(college president)
Affiliation: Cankdeska Cikana Comunity College (Little Hoop), P.O. Box 269, Fort Totten, ND 58335 (701) 766-4415 Fax 766-4077.

LONGIE, PHILLIP "SKIP"
(Sisseton-Wahpeton Sioux)
(tribal chairperson)
Affiliation: Spirit Lake Sioux Tribal Council, P.O. Box 359, Fort Totten, ND 58335 (701) 766-4221.

LONSDALE, RICK
(art coop manager)
Affiliation: Taheta Arts & Cultural Group (Eskimo, Indian & Aleut nonprofit cooperative), 605 "A" St., Anchorage, AK 99501 (907) 272-5829.

LOOKING ELK, ALEX (Standing Rock Sioux)
(radio project manager)
Affiliation: KAEN - 89.5 FM, Standing Rock Sioux Radio Project, P.O. Box D, Fort Yates, ND 58538 (701) 854-7226.

LOPEMAN, DAVID (Squaxin Island)
(tribal chairperson)
Affiliation: Squaxin Island Tribal Council, S.E. 70, Squaxin Lane, Shelton, WA 98584 (360) 426-9781.

LOPEZ, ART (Cahuilla)
(former rancheria chairperson)
Affiliation: Torres-Martinez Desert Cahuilla Indians, P.O. Box 1160, Thermal, CA 92274 (760) 397-8144.

LOPEZ, ARTHUR (Pomo)
(rancheria chairperson)
Affiliation: Manchester/Port Arena Rancheria, P.O. Box 623, Point Arena, CA 95468 (707) 882-2788.

LOPEZ, DAYNE E.
(editor)
Affiliation: "Native American Connections," Gloria J. Davis, Publisher, P.O. Box 579, Winchester, CA 92596 (909) 926-1728.

LOPEZ, ELEANOR (Yurok)
(rancheria chairperson)
Affiliation: Lytton Rancheria, P.O. Box 7882, Santa Rosa, CA 95407 (707) 537-1655.

LOPEZ, MARIAN M. (Tolowa)
(tribal chairperson)
Affiliation: Smith River Rancheria Tribal Council, 250 N. Indian Rd., Smith River, CA 95567 (707) 487-9255.

LOPEZ, NORMAN (Mountain Ute)
(traditional flute player)
Address: Ute Mountain Ute Tribe, Towaoc, CO 81334 (970) 565-3751. Lopez incorporates stories about the flute and his tribe during his performances.

LORAN, JOHN (St. Regis Mohawk)
(tribal head chief)
Affiliation: St. Regis Mohawk Council Chiefs, RR 1, Box 14C, Hogansburg, NY 13655 (518) 358-2272.

LORENCE, DR. ROBERT J.
(college president)
Affiliation: Northwest Indian College, 2522 Kwina Rd., Bellingham, WA 98226 (206) 676-2772 Fax 738-0136.

LORING, DONNA M. (Penobscot)
(tribal representative/coordinator)
Education: University of Maine at Orono, BA (Political Science); graduate of Maine Criminal Justice Academy; graduated Fleming Fellows Leadership Institute-Center for Policy Alternatives, 2001; recent graduate of the Eleanor Roosevelt Global Leadership Institute (leadership program). *Address*: 174 River Rd., Richmond, ME 04357 (207) 737-2608. E-mail: dmldab@wiscasset.net. *Affiliation*: Penobscot Nation's Representative to the Maine State Legislature, 10/97 to present. Note: Maine is the only state that has tribal representatives seated in it's legislature, representing

tribal governments not districts; Penobscot Nation's Coordinator of Tribal, State and International Relations; president, Four Directions Development Corporation. *Military service*: U.S. Army, 1966-69 (Vietnam Veteran, 1967-68 - served in the communications center at Long Binh Army Base during the TET Offensive). *Past professional posts*: Police Chief for the Penobscot Nation, 1984-90; director of security, Bowdoin College, 1992-97. *Community activities*: Member and former chair, Commission on Women Veterans; member, Maine Advisory Committee to the U.S. Commission on Civil Rights; Joint Legislative standing committee on Judiciary; member, Chancellor's Diversity Task Force; member, Maine Community Foundation Board of Directors; Northeast Historic Film Board of Directors; Advisor to the Governor Angus King on woman veteran affairs; member, Coastal Enterprises, Inc. Capital Management LLC Advisory Board. *Honors/awards*: She was the first woman police academy graduate to become police chief in the State of Maine; appointed Aide de Camp to former Governor Angus King, March 1999; received the Mary Ann Hartman Award from the University of Maine's Women in Curriculum & Women's Studies Program; appointed House Chair of the Casino Study Task Force by the former Speaker of the House, Michael Saxl, Aug. 2002 (the first tribal representative to be appointed as the House Chair of any committee); as a recent graduate of the Eleanor Roosevelt Global Leadership Institute, she was one of 14 state legislators, selected from among more than 7,000 eligible state legislators from across the nation, to be sent to Chile to learn about the Chilean development process in the areas of social and economic development, and foreign trade; recently appointed by Governor Baldacci to serve on the New England Board of Higher Education. *Membership*: Maine Chiefs of Police (eleven years); Commission on Women Veterans (former chair); Joint Legislative Standing Committee on the Judiciary; Chancellor's Diversity Task Force; Maine Community Foundation Board of Directors; Northeast Historic Film Board of Directors; Coastal Enterprises, Inc. Capital Management LLC Advisory Board.

LORENZO, PAULA (Wintun)
(rancheria chairperson)
Affiliation: Rumsey Rancheria, P.O. Box 18, Brooks, CA 95606 (530) 796-3400.

LORING, DONNA M. (Penobscot)
(tribal representative)
Education: University of Maine at Orono, BA (Political Science); Maine Criminal Justice Academy. *Principal occupation*: Tribal representative. *Address*: 174 River Rd., Richmond, ME 04357 (207) 737-2608. *Affiliations*: Police Chief of Penobscot Nation, 1984-90 (first woman police academy graduate to become police chief in the State of Maine); director of security, Bowdoin College, 1992-97; Penobscot Nation's Representative to the Maine State Legislature. *Other professional post*: Penobscot Nation's Coordinator of Tribal, State and International Relations. *Military service*: U.S. Army (Vietnam Veteran-Communications Center at Long Binh Army Base processing all casualty reports), 1967-68. *Memberships*: Maine Chiefs of Police (member for 11 years). *Awards, honors*: Appointed Aide de Camp to former Governor Angus King on march 17, 1999 and was commssioned with the rank of Colonel by the Governor. Advisor to Governor King on women veteran affairs.

LOUDNER, GODFREY, Jr. (Crow Creek Sioux) 1946-
(mathematics instructor)
Born September 30, 1946, Fort Thompson, S.D. *Education*: Black Hills State College, BS; South Dakota School of Mines and Technology, MS; University of Notre Dame, PhD (Mathematics), 1974. *Principal occupation*: Mathematics instructor, Sinte Gleska College, Rosebud, S.D. *Home address*: Box 432, Mission, SD 57555. *Memberships*: American Mathematics Society. *Interests*: Professional: "lie groups, differential geometry, harmonic analysis; mountain climbing, cave exploration. Working on monograph about Automonophic Forms With Applications."

LOUIE, GENE
(Indian band chief)
Affiliation: Sliammon Indian Band, RR 2, Sliammon Rd., Powell River, B.C., Canada V8A 4Z3 (604) 483-9646.

LOUIE, LOUIS
(Indian band chief)
Affiliation: Iskut Indian Band, General Delivery, Iskut, B.C., Canada V0J 1K0 (604) 234-3331.

LOUIE, ROBERT
(Indian band chief)
Affiliation: Westbank Indian Band, 515 Highway 97 South, Kelowna, BC, Canada V1Z 3J2 (604) 769-5666.

LOUIE, WAYNE
(Indian band chief)
Affiliation: Lower Kootenay Indian band, Box 1107, Creston, BC, Canada V0B 1G0 (604) 428-4428.

LOUIS, ROY
(association president)
Affiliation: Indian Association of Alberta, P.O. Box 516, Winterburn, AB, Canada T0E 2N0 (403) 470-5751.

LOUTTIT, REG
(Indian band chief)
Affiliation: Attawapiskat Indian Band, Box 248, Attawapiskat, ON, Canada P0L 2H0 (705) 997-2166.

LOVATO, ERNEST (Santo Domingo Pueblo)
(Pueblo governor)
Affiliation: Santo Domingo Pueblo Council, P.O. Box 99, Santo Domingo, NM 87052 (505) 465-2214.

LOVATO, MANUELITA
(museum curator)
Affiliation: Institute of American Indian Arts Museum, 83 Avon Nu Po, Santa Fe, NM 87508 (505) 988-6463.

LOW, DENISE 1949-
(professor & administrator)
Born May 9, 1949, Emporia, Kans. *Education*: University of Kansas, PhD (English). Principal occupation: Professor & administrator. *Address & Affiliation*: Professor, English Dept. & American Indian Studies Dept., Haskell Indian Nations University, Lawrence, KS 66046 (785) 749-8431, 1984-present. E-mail: dlow@haskell. edu. *Memberships*: SAIL; Assoc. Writing Programs. *Interests*: American Indian literature; Cheyenne ledger art. *Published works*: New and Sel;ected Poems, 1980-1999 (Lawrence: Penthe, 1999); Thailand Journal (Topeka-Woodley/Washburn University Press, 2003); articles and reviews.

LOWE, CHLORIS, JR. (Wisconsin Ho Chunk)
(tribal committee president)
Affiliation: Ho Chunk Nationof Wisconsin Business Committee, P.O. Box 667, Black River Falls, WI 54615 (715) 284-9343.

LOWE, LINDA
(health clinic administrator)
Affiliation: Eufaula Indian Health Clinic, 800 Forest Ave., Eufaula, OK 7432 (918) 689-2547.

LOWE, PATRICIA
(librarian)
Affiliation: Will Rogers Memorial Library, P.O. Box 157, Claremore, OK 74018 (918) 341-0719.

LOWE, PHYLLIS
(health services director)
Affiliation: St. Croix Health Services, P.O. Box 287, Hertel, WI 54845 (715) 349-2195.

LOWE, SHELLY (Navajo)
(graduate education program facilitator)
Affiliation: American Indian Studies Program, The University of Arizona, Harvill Bldg., Rm 430, P.O. Box 210076, Tucson, AZ 85721 (520) 621-7108 Fax 621-7952. E-mail: aisp@email.arizona.edu.

LOWERY, JINNIE (Lumbee) 1953-
(health administrator)
Born February 21, 1953, Robeson County, N.C. *Education*: Pembroke State University, Pembroke, NC, B.A., 1978; UNC-Chapel Hill, NC, MSPH, 1982. *Principal occupation*: Health administrator. *Home address*: Resides in Lumberton, NC. *Affiliations*: Associate director, 1986-91, executive director, 1991-, Robeson Health Care Corporation, Pembroke, NC; business manager, Lumbee Medical Center, Pembroke, NC, 1989-. *Community activities*: Founding member and past secretary of the Robeson County Dispute Reso-

lution Center, 1988-; founding member and past president of the Robeson County Rape Crisis Center; past board member of the Lumbee Regional Development Association's Head Start Policy Council; member of Harper's Ferry Baptist Church; member of Steering Committee of the Health Access Coalition. *Memberships*: American Public Health Association; North Carolina Primary Health Care Association (past secretary, current vice-president of board of directors); National Association of Community Health Centers; National Association for Female Executives; National Geographic Society. *Awards, honors*: Graduated Magna Cum Laude - Pembroke State University, 1978; Recognized by Robeson County Rural Development Panel for Volunteer Service and Leadership in development of the Rape Crisis Center; Invited to be listed in the The World Who's Who of Women; member of North Carolina Kappa Chapter of Alpha Chi Honor Society; recipient of the Indian Health Scholarship.

LOWRY, DWIGHT (Paiute)
(rancheria chairperson)
Affiliation: Susanville Indian Rancheria, P.O. Drawer U, Susanville, CA 06130 (530) 257-6264.

LOWRY, IRENE
(association director)
Affiliation: North American Indian Association of Detroit, Inc., 22720 Plymouth Rd., Detroit, MI 48239 (313) 535-2966.

LOWRY, SANDRA
(Indian center director)
Affiliation: Lassen County American Indian Organization, P.O. Box 1549, Susanville, CA 96130 (916) 257-2687 Fax 257-9071.

LUCAS, MERLE R. (Sioux) 1944-
(administrator)
Born June 9, 1944, Vanport City, Ore. *Education*: Northern Montana College, 1963-64. *Principal occupation*: Administrator. *Address*: Montana Inter-Tribal Policy Board, P.O. Box 850, Browning, MT 59417 (406) 652-3113. *Affiliations*: Director, Native American Studies, Carroll College, Helena, MT (1 year); associate professor, Native American Studies, Blackfeet Community College, Browning, MT (2 years); coordinator of Indian affairs, State of Montana, State Capitol, Helena, MT (9 years); associate planner, Dept.of Planning & Economic Development, State of MT (3 years); executive director, Montana Inter-Tribal Policy Board, Browning, MT, 1983-. *Military service*: U.S. Army Airborne, 1965-68 (E-5; Bronze Star; Army Commendation Medal with one Oak Leaf; Purple Heart; National Defense Service Medal; Vietnam Service Medal with 3 Bronze Service Stars; Republic of Vietnam Campaign Medal). *Community activities*: Helena Indian Center (president, 3 years); MT United Indian Association, Helena (treasurer, 2 years). *Memberships*: Governors Inter-State Indian Council, 1973-82; MT Indian Education Association; MT Indian Education Advisory Board, 1985-. *Awards, honors*: Outstanding Vietnam Era Veteran (1977) of the Nation for outstanding contributions shown to the community, state, and nation since returning to civilian life, No Greater Love Organization, Washington, D.C. *Biographical sources*: Western Business Magazine article concerning economic development for Montana reservations; periodic news articles concerning Indian issues relating to Native Americans in Montana. *Published works*: Profile of Montana Native American (State of Montana, 1974); Annual Report of the Governors' Interstate Indian Council Conference, 1979.

LUCAS, PHIL (Choctaw)
(film/video producer)
Affiliation: Institute of American Indian Arts, Communications Arts Department, CSF Campus, St. Michael's Dr., Santa Fe, NM 87501 (505) 984-2365. An independent film/video producer for mor than two decades, established his own production company in 1980. He has worked on productions with many tribes. His classic "Images of Indians" television series (1979) called to detailed account the damning misrepresentations of Indian character & tradition in American popular culture. He was honored for Lifetime Achievement at the October 1991 Two Rivers Native Film & Video Festival.

LUCAS, STEVE (*Koyemsi*) (Hopi-Tewa)
(craftsperson)
Address: 301 Calle Pinon, Gallup, NM 87301.
Product: Traditional and contemporary Hopi pottery.

LUCERO, ALVINO (Isleta Pueblo)
(pueblo governor)
Affiliation: Isleta Pueblo Council, P.O. Box 1270, Isleta, NM 87022 (505) 869-3111.

LUCERO, KEITH (Pueblo)
(cultural center manager)
Affiliation: Indian Pueblo Cultural Center, 2401 12th St., NW, Albuquerque, NM 87104 (800) 766-4405; (505) 843-7270.

LUCERO, LUCILLE (Miwok)
(tribal representative)
Affiliation: Buena Vista Rancheria, 4650 Coalmine Rd., Ione, CA 95640.

LUCERO, RICHARD, JR. (*Morning Star*)
(Mescalero Apache-Seminole) 1944-
(administration)
Born September 24, 1944, Billings, Mont. *Education*: University of Wyoming, 1963-66; Eastern Montana College, 1966-67; Rocky Mountain College (Billings), BA (Psychology), 1968. *Principal occupation*: Entrepreneur; minority business consultant. *Home address*: 3733 Magnolia Dr., Grand Prairie, TX 75052 (972) 262-0939 Fax 262-0998. E-mail: hungryhoss@aol.com. *Affiliations*: Executive director, Dallas Inter-Tribal Center, Dallas, TX 1980-89; director of Minority Affairs, Greater Dallas Chamber of Commerce, 1990-92; president, CEO, American International Materials (distribution for metal welding supplies), 1992-; vice-president, Capital Concepts (financial management/college scholarships), 1992-; president/CEO, Dialogue Resources (marketing-advertising-consulting to health care professionals attorneys), 1994-; president, Morning Star Consulting Services (develop contracts for small minority businesses with corporations in; provide diversity seminars to state institutions & businesses; help develop minority employment & minority vendor contracts for public & private businesses), 1994-; president/CEO, Finite Ventures Unlimited (marketing, product development, distribution, consulting services), 1994-98; director of Winfree Academy Alternative School in Dallas (services to high school students - academic, counseling, social, emotional, family counseling), 1998-present. *Other professional posts*: Currently on contract to Dallas Cowboys as consultant on minority contracting (developing Cowboy minority contracting & employment program), 1996-present; consultant to Elite Care Care Clinic, marketing concepts for car cleaning and waxing products, 1996-present. *Community activities*: Board member, Irving Together Town Organization, 1996-present; NAACP branches in Irving & Dallas, 1996-98; moderator, Black/Brown Dialogue in Dallas, 1995-96; consultant to Ross Perot and the John Sarota Group on Education issues at Dallas Independent School District, June 1998 to Nov. 1998. *Memberships*: American Indian Health Care Association (chairman, Region VII, Health Directors Board, 1982-84; treasurer, 1983-84; president, 1984-); Dallas Council on Alcoholism and Drug Abuse (board member, 1988-); Greater Dallas Community Relations Commission (board of directors, 1989, 1st vice-chair, chairperson-Health and Human Services Committee); Society for Advancement of Chicanos and Native Americans in Science; Texas American Indian Chamber of Commerce; National Minority Contractors Association (charter board member, 1994); New Image Business Associates (advisory member). *Awards, honors*: Appointed by President Gerald Ford to serve on National Drug Abuse and Adolescents Task Force, 1977; "Leadership Dallas" Graduate 1988 - Dallas Chamber of Commerce Program for Selected Community Leaders; "Dallas Together" - committee member, selected by Dallas Mayor to recommend ways to diffuse racial tensions in Dallas, 1988-89; Outstanding Board Member Award for community contributions; 1989 Greater Dallas Community Relations Commission for "Outstanding Leadership"; 1989 1st Annual Leadership Awards sponsored by Dallas Chapter of American Muslim Commission; recipient, Community Service Award, 1991, Senator Eddie Bernice Johnson. *Interests*: "Minority business development, minority employment; political and economic enfranchisement in Dallas metro area;

enhanced police/community relationship, access to college education for capable students of color; avocational interests include: music, tennis, coaching baseball, and reading." *Published works*: Minority Business Development Handbook, 1991 and Minority Personnel Enhancement Handbook, 1992 (Greater Dallas Chamber of Commerce).

LUCERO-GACHUPIN, CAROL G. (Jemez)
(artist, craftsperson)
Address: P.O. Box 210, Jemez Pueblo, NM 87024 (505) 834-7757.

LUHMAN, FRED
(associate commissioner)
Affiliation: Office of the American Indian, Alaskan Native & Native Hawaiian Programs, U.S. Dept. of Health & Human Servics, Humphrey Bldg., 330 Independence Ave., SW, Washington, DC 20201 (202) 619-2957.

LUJAN, ALEX (Sandia Pueblo)
(pueblo governor)
Affiliation: Sandia Pueblo Council, P.O. Box 6008, Bernalillo, NM 87004 (505) 867-3317.

LUJAN, FRED R. (Pueblo)
(Pueblo governor)
Affiliation: Isleta Pueblo Council, P.O. Box 1270, Isleta, NM 87022 (505) 869-3111.

LUJAN, J.P. (Pueblo)
(Indian school director)
Affiliation: San Juan School, P.O. Box 1077, San Juan Pueblo, NM 87566 (505) 852-2154 Fax 852-4305.

LUJAN, JOE M. (Sandia Pueblo)
(Pueblo governor)
Affiliation: Sandia Pueblo Tribal Council, P.O. Box 6008, Bernalillo, NM 87004 (505) 867-3317.

LUJAN, LANCE (Pueblo)
(college dept. director)
Affiliation: Indian Resource Development Dept., New Mexico University, Box 30001, Dept. MSC, Las Cruces, NM 88003 (505) 646-1347 Fax 646-5975.

LUJAN, PHIL
(professor)
Affiliation: Native American Studies Program, University of Oklahoma, 455 W. Lindsey, Rm. 804, Norman, OK 73019 (405) 325-2312.

LUKE, CHRIS (Kootenay)
(Indian band chief)
Affiliation: Lower Kootenay Indian Band, Box 1107, Creston, British Columbia, Canada V0B 1G0 (604) 428-4428.

LUKE, GERALD
(Indian band chief)
Affiliation: Mattagami Indian Band, Box 99, Gogama, ON, Canada P0M 1W0 (705) 894-2072.

LUMSDEN, JOSEPH K. (Chippewa) 1934-
(educational administration)
Born October 10, 1934, Sault Ste. Marie, Mich. *Education*: Michigan Technological University, BS, 1967; Northern Michigan University, Teaching Certificate, 1969. *Principal occupation*: Educational administration. *Home address*: 1101 Johnston St., Sault Ste. Marie, MI 49783. *Affiliation*: Sault Ste Marie Tribe of Chippewa Indians, 1973-. *Military service*: U.S. Marine Corps, 1953-56 (Corporal). *Community activities*: Michigan Fishery Advisory Committee (chairman); Chippewa-Ottawa Fishery Management Authority. *Memberships*: National Congress of American Indians; National Tribal Chairman's Association. *Awards, honors*: Recognition of Leadership & Achievement, Bureau of Indian Affairs, 1984.

LUNA, EILEEN (Choctaw/Cherokee)
(professor)
Education: University of San Diego, J.D., 1978; Harvard University, MPA, 1996. *Affiliation*: American Indian Studies Program, The University of Arizona, Harvill Bldg., Rm 430, P.O. Box 210076, Tucson, AZ 85721 (520) 621-7108 Fax 621-7952. E-mail: aisp@email.arizona.edu. *Interests*: Tribal governments; law enforcements on reservations; federal Indian policy.

LUNDERMAN, EILEEN
(center director)
Affiliation: Sicangu Enterprise Center, P.O. Box 205, Mission, SD 57555 (605) 856-2955.

LUNDY, PAUL A. (Lakota-Mniconjou (Cheyenne River Sioux) 1944-
(licensed professional engineer)
Born August 30, 1944, Sioux Falls, S.D. *Education*: South Dakota School of Mines & Technology, BS, 1967. *Principal occupation*: Licensed professional engineer. *Home address*: 4316 Phoenix St., Ames, IA 50014-3626 (515) 292-5255 Fax 281-8895. *Affiliations*: Project engineer, Iowa Dept. of Transportation, Ames, 1967-80; Environmental engineer, Iowa Dept. of Natural Resources, Des Moines, 1980-. *Military service*: U.S. Army, 1967-69; U.S. Army Reserve, 1969-87 (retired as Major; Humanitarian Service Medal, 1980; Army Achievement Medal, 1986). *Community activities*: Ames Council of PTAs (president, 1978); Ames Municipal Band, 1973-present (vice-president, 1987-); Boy Scouts of America, 1967- (assistant District Commissioner, Broken Arrow District, Mid-Iowa Council). *Memerbship*: American Indian Science & Engineering Society, 1982-; United Methodist Church, 1963-present (Lay Speaker, 1995-; candidate, Diaconal Ministry, 1996-); Certified Church Business Administrator, 2000-. *Awards, honors*: Distinguished Toastmaster, Toastmaster International, in 1974; Public Service Award by American Radio Relay League in 1972 & '79 for emergency communications handled. *Interests*: Amateur Radio; music (play sax and clarinet); railroading/model railroading (charter member of the Kate Shelley Division, 1992) of the National Model Railroad Association; history/genealogy. *Vocational*: Transportation and environmental engineering. *Biographical source*: Article in American Indian Scientist & Engineers, Vol. I, 1985.

LUPE, RONNIE (Apache)
(tribal chairperson)
Affiliations: White Mountain Apache Tribal Council, P.O. Box 700, Whiteriver, AZ 85941 (520) 338-4346; chairperson, Theodore Roosevelt School, Fort Apache, AZ.

LURIE, NANCY OESTREICH 1924-
(anthropologist)
Born January 29, 1924, Milwaukee, Wisc. *Education*: University of Wisconsin, Madison, BA, 1945; University of Chicago, MA, 1947; Northwestern University, PhD, 1952. *Principal occupation*: Anthropology Curator (Retired), Milwaukee Public Museum. *Address*: Unknown. *Affiliations*: Instructor, anthropology and sociology, University of Wisconsin, Milwaukee, 1947-49, 1951-53; research associate, North American ethnology, Peabody Museum, Harvard University, 1954-56; consultant and expert witness for law firms representing tribal clients before the U.S. Indian Claims Commission, 1954-; lecturer in anthropology, Rackham School of Graduate Studies Extension Service, University of Michigan, 1956-61; lecturer in anthropology, School of Public Health, University of Michigan, 1959-61; assistant coordinator, American Indian Chicago Conference, University of Chicago, 1960-61; associate professor of anthropology, University of Wisconsin, Milwaukee, 1963; Fulbright appointment (lectureship, University of Aarhus, Denmark) involved teaching a course on the American Indian and a course on applied anthropology, 1964-65; professor, 1965-, dept. chair, 1967-70, adjunct professor, 1973-, Dept. of Anthropology, University of Wisconsin, Milwaukee; Curator of Anthropology, Milwaukee Public Museum, 1972-1992. *Community activities*: Wisconsin Historic Sites Preservation Board, 1972-79; Wisconsin Humanities Committee, NEH, 1981-83; served on various review panels for National Endowments for the Humanities and Arts; Action Anthropology projects with Wisconsin tribes and Milwaukee intertribal community. *Memberships*: American Anthropological Association (president, 1983-85); American Ethnological Society; American Society for Ethnohistory; Wisconsin Archaeological Society; Central States Anthropological Society (president, 1967); Council for Museum Anthropology; American Association of Museums; Sigma Xi; Society for Applied Anthropology; Wisconsin Academy of Science, Arts, and Letters; American Association for the Advancement of Science; International Congress of Anthropological and Ethnological Sciences; member of editorial board of Northeast Vol. 15 of Handbook of North American Indians. *Awards, honors*:

Award of Merit for Mountain Wolf Woman, American Society for State and Local History, 1962; Saturday Review Anisfield Wolf Award with co-editor for The American Indian Today, 1968; Woman of the Year, Milwaukee Municipal Women's Club, 1975; Honorary Doctorate of Letters, Northland College, Ashland, Wis., 1976; Increase Lapham Medal, Wisconsin Archaeological Society, 1977; Merit Award, Northwestern University Alumni Association, 1982; several awards for publications, including A Special Style: The Milwaukee Public Museum 1882-1982, from Wisconsin State Historical Society, 1985, and from Milwaukee County Historical Society, 1984; Award of Merit, Wisconsin Academy of Sciences, Arts, & Letters, 1984, Fellow, 1987; Wisconsin Winnebago for writings on tribal history and culture; Honorary Doctorate, Northland College. *Interests*: Ethnological research Wisconsin and Nebraska Winnebago; Dogrib Indians (Northwest Territory, Canada), Menominee; Consultant and Expert Witness, U.S. Indian Claims Commission, Court of Claims, and lower courts for eight different tribes; lecturer on museology, 6 weeks, Norway; attended international anthropology meetings USSR, Japan, Mexico, etc. *Biographical sources*: Marquis Who's Who; Women Anthropologists (University of Illinois Press). *Published works*: Editor, Mountain Wolf Woman, Sister of Crashing Thunder (University of Michigan Press, 1961); The Subsistence Economy of the Dogrib Indians of Lac La Marte, Canadian Northwest Territories, with June Helm (Northern Research and Coordination Centre, Ottawa, 1961); editor, with Stuart Levine, The American Indian Today (Everett/Edwards Press, 1968; Penguin, 1970); editor, with Eleanor B. Leacock, The North American Indian in Historical Perspective (Random House, 1971, Waveland Press reprint, 1988); Wisconsin Indians (State Historical Society of Wisconsin, 1980); A Special Style: The Milwaukee Public Museum, 1882-1982 (Milwaukee Public Museum, 1982); North American Indian Lives (Milwaukee Public Museum, 1985); co-editor and contributed chapter, North American Indians in Historical Perspective (Waveland Press, 1988).

LUTHER, MIKE
(school principal)
Affiliation: Red Rock Day School, P.O. Box 2007, Red Valley, AZ 86544 (520) 653-4456 Fax 653-5711.

LUTZ, DIXON
(Indian band chief)
Affiliation: Liard River Indian Band, Box 328, Watson Lake, Yukon, Canada Y1A 1C0 (403) 536-2131.

LYALL, PAT
(Indian corporation president)
Affiliation: Nunasi Corporation, 280 Albert St., #902, Ottawa, ON, Can K1A 5G8 (613) 238-4981

LYLES, RAY
(health center director)
Affiliation: Hugo Health Center, P.O. Box 340, Hugo, OK 74743 (405) 326-7561.

LYNCH, ARCHIE
(editor)
Affiliation: "Smoke Signals," Baltimore American Indian Center, 113 S. Broadway, Baltimore, MD 21231 (410) 675-3535.

LYNCH, MARLENE
(association president)
Affiliation: Native American Finance Officers Assn, P.O. Box 170, Fort Defiance, AZ 86504 (520) 729-6218.

LYNN, SHARON
(BIA Indian education)
Affiliation: Branch of Supplemental Services, Bureau of Indian Affairs, MS: 3512-MIB, 1849 C St., NW, Washington, DC 20240 (202) 208-6364.

LYONS, JACK (*Little Eagle*)
(Indian center founder)
Affiliation: Native American Center & Veterans Center, P.O. Box 1319, Norton, OH 44203 (330) 825-7796.

LYONS, SCOTT (Leech Lake Ojibwe)
(college instructor)
Affiliation: Leech Lake Tribal College, 6530 U.S. Hwy. 2 NW, Cass Lake, MN 56633 (218) 335-4220 Fax 335-4209.

Mc

McADAMS, GARY (Wichita)
(tribal president)
Affiliation: Wichita & Affiliated Tribes, P.O. Box 729, Anadarko, OK 73005 (405) 247-2425 Fax 247-2430.

McALISTER, DIANE
(editor)
Affiliation: "Native American Connection," Spotted Horse Tribal Gifts, P.O. Box 414, Coos Bay, OR 97420.

McALLESTER, DAVID P. (Narragansett) 1916-
(professor-retired)
Born August 6, 1916, Everett, Mass. *Education*: Harvard University, BA, 1938; Columbia University, PhD, 1949. *Principal occupation*: Professor-retired. *Home address*: Star Route 62, Box 40, Monterey, MA 01245. *Affiliations*: Professor of anthropology and music, Wesleyan University, Middletown, CT, 1947-86 (retired). *Other professional posts*: Visiting professor, Yale University, University of Hawaii; University of Sydney and University of Queensland, Australia; consultant, American Folklife Festival, Smithsonian Institution, Washington, DC, 1975-76; one of the founders and secretary-treasurer, editor, and president of Society for Ethnomusicology. *Community activities*: Valley View Hospital (advisory board); a founder of Middletown Friends Meeting and South Berkshire Friends Meeting. *Memberships*: Society for Ethnomusicology (secretary-treasurer, editor, president, 1953-); American Anthropological Association (Fellow), 1949-1976; American Academy of Arts and Sciences, 1968-; Institute of American Indian Archaeology, Washington, Conn. (trustee, 1976-). Awards, honors: Social Science Research Council Grant, 1950; Guggenheim Foundation Fellowship, 1957-58 (study Navajo religion); National Science Foundation Grants, 1963-65 (study Navajo religion); J.D.R. III Foundation Grant, 1971; National Endowment for the Humanities Grant, 1976; Fulbright Foundation (senior lecturer in Australia), 1978; Tokyo National Research Institute of Cultural Properties (lecture), 1980. *Interests*: Studies of American Indian ceremonialism, music, folklore, mythology, religious literature. Field work with Navajos, Apaches, Zunis, Passamaquoddies, Penobscots, Comanches, Hopis. Canoeing, hiking, mountain-climbing, camping. Musical performance of Native American songs. *Biographical source*: Autobiographical sketch in a Festschrift, "Explorations in Ethnomusicology, edited by Charlotte Frisbie (Detroit, 1986). *Published works*: Peyote Music (Viking Fund, 1949); Enemy Way Music (Peabody Museum, 1954); Myth & Prayers of the Great Star Chant (Wheelwright Museum, 1956); Indian Music of the Southwest (Taylor Museum, 1961); Reader in Ethnomusicology (Johnson Reprint, 1971); Navajo Blessingway Singer, with Charlotte Frisbie (University of Arizona, 1978); Hogans: Navajo Houses & House Songs, with Susan McAllester, (Wesleyan University, 1980); other monographs and pamphlets; about sixty articles and other contributions. Recordings: Music of the American Indian, 12 LP with pamphlet (Litton Educational Publishing, 1978); Music of the Pueblos, Apache, and Navajo, with Don N. Brown, 12 LP with 7-page pamphlet, texts, photographs (Taylor Museum, 1962); Navajo Creation Chants, five 10 78 rpm records, with pamphlet (Peabody Museum, 1952).

McARTHUR, EUGENE, JR. (Chippewa)
(tribal chairperson)
Affiliation: White Earth Reservation Tribal Council, P.O. Box 418, White Earth, MN 56591 (218) 983-3285.

McBRIDE, BUNNY 1950-
(writer)
Born April 9, 1950, Washington, D.C. *Education*: Michigan State University, BA, 1972; Boston University, MFA courses, 1973-75; Columbia University, MA (Anthropology), 1980. *Principal occupation*: Writer. *Address*: 3301 Buffalo, Manhattan, KS 66503 (785) 776-3876. E-mail: bmcb@ksu.edu. Website: www.personal.ksu.edu/~bmcb/. *Affiliations*: Adjunct lecturer in anthropology, Prncipia College, Elsah, IL, 1981-; Adjunct lecturer in anthropology, Kansas State University, Manhattan, KS, 1996-. *Other professional posts*: Consultant, Aroostook Band of Micmacs, Presque Isle, ME, 1982-91; Member, Advisory Committee on Exhibits & Programming, Abbe Museum, Bar Harbor, ME, 1998-present; Curator of the Abbe's 2002 exhibit, "Four Mollys: Women of the Dawn," chronicling the lives of four Native American women whose combined lives spanned four centuries. *Community activities*: Manhattan Habitat for Humanity (Development Board), 1996-; Martin Luther King Task Force, Manhattan, KS, 1997-; Oral History Advisor, Kansas Humanities Council, 1997-; Reader, Christian Science Church, Manhattan, KS, 1997-. *Awards, honors*: Pulitzer nominee for Molly Spotted Elk: A Penobscot in Paris; Friends of American Writers Literary Award in 2000; special commendation from Maine State Legislature for "tremendous contribution" as the first author to research and write books about the history of Native American women in Maine — initiated by the Penobscot and Passamaquoddy tribal representative to the legislature. *Biographical sources*: Contemporary Authors; Globe Sunday Magazine 6/3/01. *Selected published works*: Our Lives in Our Hands: Micmac Indian Basketmakers (photos by Donald Sanipass, Aroostook Mimac); National Audubon Society Field Guide to African Wildlife, with Peter Alden, Richard Estes & Donald Schlitter (Knopf, 1995); Molly Spotted Elk: A Penobscot in Paris (University of Oklahoma Press, 1995); Women of the Dawn (University of Nebraska Press, 1999); Lucy Nicolar: The Artful Activism of a Penobscot Performer" in Sifters: Native American Women's Lives, ed. by Theda Perdue (Oxford University Press, 2001).

McBRIDE, CAROL
(Indian band chief)
Affiliation: Temiskaming (Algonquin) Indian Band, Box 336, Notre-Dame du Nord, Quebec, Canada J0Z 3B0 (819) 723-2335.

McBRIDE, MARY (San Felipe Pueblo) 1948-
(high school principal)
Born June 3, 1948, Albuquerque, N.M. *Education*: Eastern New Mexico University, Portales, BS, 1971; New Mexico Highlands University, Las Vegas, MA, 1982. *Principal occupation*: High school principal, BIA, Isleta Pueblo, NM, 1984-. *Home address*: P.O. Box 751, Algodones, NM 87001 (505) 867-4766; 867-2388 (work). *Affiliations*: Elementary school principal, B.I.A., Isleta Pueblo, NM, 1984-86; high school principal, Bernalillo School District, Bernalillo, NM, 1986-. *Memberships*: Phi Delta Kappa, 1987-; Delta Kappa Gamma Society International, 1988-; National Education Association, 1990-. *Awards, honors*: Graduate Professional Opportunity Program. *Interests*: "I will be on leave of absence for a year to work on a MA in counseling for AT RISK youth."

McCAIN, JOHN
(U.S. Senator, R-AZ)
Affiliation: Chairperson, Senate Select Committee on Indian Affairs, 838 Hart Senate Office Bldg., Washington, DC 20510 (202) 224-2251.

McCAFFERTY, MICHAEL
(college president)
Affiliation: Cheyenne River Community College, P.O. Box 220, Eagle Butte, SD 57625 (605) 964-8635 Fax 964-1144.

McCALEB, NEAL
(assistant secretary-BIA)
Affiliation: Assistant Secretary, Bureau of Indian Affairs, Dept. of the Interior, 1849 C St., NW - MS 4140-MIB, Washington, DC 20240 (202) 208-7163 Fax 208-5320.

McCARTAN, KATHLEEN (Mohawk/Oneida) 1963-
(naval flight officer)
Born in 1963, Clarence, N.Y. *Education*: U.S. Naval Academy, BS, 1985. *Principal occupation*: Naval flight officer, U.S. Navy. At the Acadmy, she was editor of a literary magazine, president of the Bicycle Racing Club; san in the Glee Club and Choir and the Messiah Church group; she rowed on the crew team for two years. She is a qualified navigator and an Airborne Communications Officer. She has flown the T-34 C, and T-43. She currently flies the EC-130, an aircraft from Oahu, Hawaii.

McCARTHY, JOAN DOLORES (Sun Dancer)
(Blackfoot-Bear Clan) 1935-
(shop owner)
Born January 14, 1935, Easton, Penna. Education: Churchman's Business College (Easton, PA). *Principal occupation*: Reservation trader. *Home address*: 1500 Eddy St., Merritt Island, FL 32952 (407) 631-0092 (work). *Affiliation*: Family owns four shops: "This N' That," Cocoa Village, FL, 1975-; "Rags to Riches," Cocoa Village, FL—authentic Native American jewelry and crafts; "Sundancer Gallery, Cocoa Village, FL; and "Spare Time Hobby Shop," Cocoa Village, FL. "I'm known as Sun Dancer woman who keeps spirits together and bright, and bringer of light (lightening the soul or spiritual healing). (I) started business on my own as a single parent with three children to raise—no outside help or child support." *Community activities*: Counsel Native Americans on their rights, on or off the reservation, the business or schooling open to them, water rights, etc.; give speeches to youth groups, all sorts of organizations; display in libraries, schools, and banks; guidance counselor - troubled teens of Brevard County; swimming instructor for handicapped and retarded citizens; and water safety instructor for American Red Cross, Miami, FL; crisis home/assisted Brevard Sheriff Rollin Zimmerman with benefits for teens, runaways-delinquents, etc.; assisted aid to several emergency charities. *Memberships*: Brevard County, Merritt Island, FL Chamber of Commerce; Big Mountain Legal Fund, Flagstaff, AZ; Kuwaiti Legal Fund, Cocoa Village, FL; Pioneer Women of Brevard Co. *Awards, honors*: Art awards in silversmithing, pen and ink, watercolors, copper and enamel work, and sketching; Pioneer Women of Brevard - Entrepreneur in 6 businesses; Brevard County Board of Education Award for donations to local high schools. *Interests*: "Native American Rights including helping young artists to merchandise their products; helping young artists to seek grants; water rights on several reserves: Taos, Zuni, Ft. McDowell Apache Reservation; Big Mountain Legal Aid for displaced Native Americans (land disputes-Navajo, Mohawk). My desire is to give back the pride to the Native American encouraging them to protect their culture; travel to all the Southwestern reservations." *Biographical source*: The Department of Interior Source Directory; American Indian Index; article in Warpath, monthly newsletter, 1988-89; Who's Who in the Indian World; Today newspaper; Tribune; Larry King Show; Brevard Pioneer Women..

McCAULEY, CECE
(Indian band chief)
Affiliation: Inuvik Native Indian band, Box 2570, Inuvik, Northwest Territories, Canada X0E 0T0 (403) 979-3344.

McCAULIFFE, DENNIS (Osage of Oklahoma)
(journalist recruiter)
Born in Oklahoma. *Address*: c/o Native American Journalists Association (NAJA), 3359 36th Ave. South, Minneapolis, MN 55406 (612) 729-9244 Fax 729-9373. E-mail: talahongva@naja.com. *Affiliations*: One of four Freedom Forum Diversity Fellows, who travel across the country to colleges, universities and junior colleges with high minority enrollments to identify talented students of color for creers in print journalism. The position is a key part of the Freedom Forum's national effort to increase diversity in newspaper newsrooms. He focuses on recruitment of Native Americans. A Freedom Forum grant brought him to the University of Montana School of Journalism in Spring Semester 1999 as the Native American Journalist-in-Residence to direct the school's American Indian program. *Other professional post*: Secretary, Native American Journalists Association. *Past professional post*: The night Foreign Editor of The Washington Post, Washington, DC (16 years). At The Post, he also reported on Native American issues and, for a while, was the Foreign Desk's Africa Editor and area specialist; write sports for the Washington (D.C.) Daily News. *Military service*: U.S. Army. *Awards, honors*: 1968 Grantland Rice Memorial Scholarship for Sportswriting; 1995 Oklahoma Book Award for Non-Fiction. *Published work*: "The Deaths of Sybil Bolton: An American History," an account of the murder of his Osage grandmother during the Reign of Terror against the Osage Indians in the 1920s (republished in paperback as "Bloodland: A Family Story of Oil, Greed and Murder on the Osage Reservation").

McCAY, WILLIAM JAMES (Irontail) (Cherokee)
1925-
(master electrician)
Born October 1, 1925, Pensacola, Fla. *Education*: High

school. *Address & Affiliation*: Executive director, Intertribal Council of American Indians, Inc., 1765 Woodchuck Ave., Pensacola, FL 32504 (904) 484-9282. E-mail: cherokeeirontail@aol.com. *Military service*: U.S. Army, 1944-1949. *Interests*: Fishing, Indian crafts, camping, RVing.

McCLANAHAN, ALEXANDRA
(editor & pblisher)
Affiliation: The Tundra Times, Eskimo, Indian, Aleut Publishing Co., P.O. Box 92247, Anchorage, AK 99509 (907) 274-2512.

McLAUGHLIN STEVEN
(BIA agency supt.)
Affiliation: Crow Creek Agency, Bureau of Indian Affairs, P.O. Box 139, Fort Thompson, SD 57339 (605) 245-2311 Fax 245-2343.

McCLEARY, TIMOTHY (Crow)
(speaker, teacher, author)
Address: Box 2116, Star Route, Hardin, MT 59034. *Interests*: Crow speaker; teacher at Crow Community College; active in Native American church.

McCLELLAND. JOHN
(organization chairperson)
Affiliation: Native Amerian Coalition of Tulsa, Inc., 1740 West 41st St., Tulsa, OK 74107 (918) 446-8432.

McCLELLAND, ROBERT
(Indian school principal)
Affiliations: Pearl River Elementary School, Philadelphia, MS 39350 (601) 656-9051 Fax 656-3054.

McLEOD, LINDA
(Indian school principal)
Affiliation: Indian Island School, Indian Education Program, 1 River Rd., Old Town, ME 04468 (207) 827-4285 Fax 827-3599. E-mail: lmcleod@iis.bia.edu.

McLEMORE, LAURIE, M.D.
(association director)
Affiliation: Association of Native American Medical Students, 1235 Sovereign Row, Suite C7, Oklahoma City, OK 73159 (405) 677-1468.

McCLINTOCK, CAROLYN
(hospital director)
Affiliation: Barrow PHS Alaska Native Hospital, Barrow, AK 99723 (907) 852-4611.

McCLOUD, JANET
(Indian center director)
Affiliation: Northwest Indian Women's Circle, P.O. Box 8279, Tacoma, WA 98408 (206) 458-7610.

McDOWELL, NORA (Mojave)
(tribal chairperson)
Affiliation: Fort Mojave Tribal Council, 500 Merriman Ave., Needles, CA 92363 (760) 629-4591. E-mail: gjsrecordings@ftmojave.com.

McLOUD, MARTHA A.
(college president)
Affiliation: Bay Mills Community College, Rt. 1, Box 315A, Brimley, MI 49715 (906) 248-3354 Fax 248-3351.

McCLURE, ELMIRA
(center director)
Affiliation: St. Augustine's Center, 4512 N. Sheridan Rd., Chicago, IL 60640 (312) 784-1050.

McCLURE, MIKE (Paiute)
(tribal enterprise manager)
Affiliation: Moapa Tribal Enterprises, P.O. Box 340, Moapa, NV 89025 (702) 864-2600.

McCLURE, RUSSELL J. (Sioux)
(BIA agency supt.)
Affiliation: Cheyenne River Agency, Bureau of Indian Affairs, P.O. Box 325, Eagle Butte, SD 57625 (605) 964-6611.

McCOMBS, SOLOMON (Creek) 1913-
(artist)
Born May 17, 1913, Eufaula, Okla. *Education*: Bacone College, 1931-37; Tulsa University, 1943. *Principal occupation*: Artist. *Home address*: 3238 East 3rd St.,

Tulsa, OK 74104. *Affiliation*: Foreign service reserve officer, U.S. Dept. of State, Washington, DC, 1966-73; former vice-chief, Creek Nation of Oklahoma. *Other professional posts*: Board of directors, American Indian National Bank, Washington, DC, 1973-75; lifetime member of board of directors, designed bank logo. Served as a member of the Subcommittee on Indian participation during President Johnson's and President Nixon's Inaugural parades—supervised the construction of four American Indian floats. *Memberships*: National Congress of American Indians, 1965-; Five Civilized Tribes (council member, Inter-Tribal Council; chaplain, 1976-); National Council of the Creek Nation (speaker, 1976-); CWYW Club of Tulsa (lifetime member, 1977-). *Awards, honors*: Five Civilized Tribes Museum Seal, 1955; Waite Phillips Special Indian Artists Award for contributions in Indian Art over a period of five years, Philbrook Art Center, Tulsa, 1965; Grand Award, Philbrook Art Center, 1965; Grand and Gran Masters Award, 1965, '70, '73, '77; Army Award (commissioned to paint depicting one of the American Indian Congressional Medal of Honor recipients of World War II in battle), Washington, DC, 1976; First Prize Awards, All American Indian Days, Sheridan, Wyo., and Pawnee (OK) Bill Museum, 1970; Bacone College Distinguished Service Award, 1972; Heritage Award, Five Civilized Tribes Museum, Muskogee, OK, 1977; Grand Prize of $1,000 at Central Washington State College; among others. *Interests*: "Graphics, architectural design; lecturing on American Indian art; Indian painting (traditional); tours of paintings; exhibits and lectures throughout the Middle East, Africa, India, and Burma, sponsored by the U.S. Department of State, Washington, DC." *Biographical sources*: Indians of Today, 1960-70; Who's Who in the South & Southwest; Register of U.S. Living Artists, 1968; Personalities of the South; Dictionary of International Biography; Notable Americans, 1976-77. *Published works*: McCombs Indian Art Calendar, 1978; White Eagle-Green Corn, 1979.

McCONNELL, JOSEPH F. (Gros Ventre)
(tribal president)
Address & Affiliation: Fort Belknap Community Council, RR 1, Box 66, Harlem, MT 59526 (406) 353-2205.

McCOOL, DANIEL
(center director)
Education: University of Arizona, PhD, 1983. *Address & Affiliation*: Director, The American West Cemter, University of Utah, 1901 E. South Campus Dr., Rm. 1023, Salt Lake City, UT 84112-8922 (801) 581-7611 Fax 581-7612. Publications: Command of the Waters: Iron Triangles, Federal Water Development, and Indian Water Rights (University of California Press, 1987; University of Arizona Press, 1994); Waters of Good Faith: Indian Water Settlements and the Second Treaty Era (University of Arizona Press, 2001).

McCOVEY, DONALD (Yurok)
(rancheria chairperson)
Affiliation: Coast Indian Community of the Resighini Rancheria, P.O. Box 529, Klamath, CA 95548 (707) 482-2431.

McCOY, MELODY
(attorney)
Affiliation: Native American Rights Fund, 1506 Broadway, Boulder, CO 80302 (303) 447-8760. *Membership*: Colorado Indian Bar Association (president).

McCREA, CYNTHIA
(school principal)
Affiliation: Cheyenne-Eagle Butte School, P.O. Box 672, Eagle Butte, SD 57625 (605) 964-8744.

McCULLY, SHARON
(executive director)
Affiliation: Intra-Departmental Council on Indian Affairs, U.S. Dept. of Health & Human Services, Humphrey Bldg., 200 Independence Ave., SW, Washington, DC 20201 (202) 245-6546.

McDADE, MARVIN (Te-Moak Western Shoshone)
(former Indian colony chairperson)
Affiliation: South Fork Band Council, Box B-13, Lee, NV 89829 (702) 744-4273.

McDANIEL, SHANNON
(health clinic director)
Affiliation: Choctaw Nation Health Clinic, 205 E. 3rd St., Broken Bow, OK 74728 (405) 584-2740.

McDERMOTT, BILL (Sault Ste. Marie Chippewa)
(program director)
Affiliation & Address: Indian youth education & activities program director, Sault Ste. Marie Tribe of Chippewa Indians, 174 Zhigag, Manistique, MI 49854.

McDONALD, ARTHUR LEROY (Sioux) 1934-
(research consultant)
Born December 26, 1934, Martin, S.D. *Education*: University of South Dakota, AB, 1962, MA, 1963, PhD, 1966. *Principal occupation*: Research consultant. *Home address*: Box 326, Lame Deer, MT 59043. *Affiliation*: Owner, Cheyenne Consulting Service. *Other professional posts*: Acting head, Psychology Dept., Central College, 1963-64; head, Psychology Dept., Montana State University, 1968-71. *Military service*: U.S. Marine Corps, 1953-56 (Sergeant). *Memberships*: Pine Ridge Sioux Tribe; American Psychological Association; Sigma Xi; American Association for the Advancement of Science; American Quarter Horse Association. *Interests*: Indian research in mental health, education, alcohol, and evaluation; raising quality American quarter horses. *Published works*: Psychology and Contemporary Problems (Brooks-Cole, 1974); co-authored, Schooling of Native America, 1977; Cheyenne Journey, 1977; numerous articles in scientific journals.

McDONALD, JOHN
(radio station manager)
Affiliation: KYUK - 640 AM, Bethel Broadcasting, Inc., P.O. Box 468, Bethel, AK 99559 (907) 543-3131.

McDONALD, JOSEPH
(college president)
Affiliation: Salish-Kootenai College, P.O. Box 117, Pablo, MT 59855 (406) 675-4800 Fax 675-4801.

McDONALD, ROY
(Indian band chief)
Affiliation: Islington Indian Band, Whitedog, Ontario, Canada P0X 1P0 (807) 927-2068.

McDOUGALL, HARRY
(Indian band chief)
Affiliation: Abitibiwinni (Algonquin) Indian Band, Box 36 Pikogan, Amos, Quebec, Canada J9T 3A3 (819) 732-6591.

McELROY, DAVID W. (Oklahoma Choctaw)
(attorney)
Address & Affiliation: Dorsey & Whitney LLP, 50 S. Sixth St., Suite 1500, Minneapolis, MN 55492-1498. E-mail: mcelroy.david@dorseylaw.com.

McGEE, HAROLD FRANKLIN, JR. 1945-
(professor of anthropology)
Born June 5, 1945, Miami, Fla. *Education*: Florida State University, BA, 1966, MA, 1967; Southern Illinois University, PhD, 1974. *Principal occupation*: Professor of anthropology. *Address*: Dept. of Anthropology, Saint Mary's University, Halifax, Nova Scotia, Can. B3H 3C3 (902) 420-5628. *Affiliations*: Professor, Dept. of Anthropology, Saint Mary's University, Halifax, Nova Scotia, Can. *Other professional post*: Consultant to museums and other institutions. *Memberships*: Royal Anthropological Institute of Great Britain and Ireland (Fellow). *Interests*: Mr. McGee writes, "(My) major area of interest and expertise is with contemporary and historic Micmac and Malecite peoples of Atlantic Canada. In addition to standard ethnological concerns as an academic, I am interested in getting the non-native population to understand the reasons for similarity and difference of the native peoples' life ways to their own so that they will encourage governments to allow for greater local autonomy by the native people. Academically, I am particularly interested in native world view, politics, aesthetics, and reconstruction of aboriginal society and culture." *Published works*: Native Peoples of Atlantic Canada (McClelland and Stewart, 1974); The Micmac Indians: The First Migrants in Banked Fires-The Ethnics of Nova Scotia, edited by D. Campbell (Scribbler's Prss, 1978); journal articles and papers.

McGERTT, CHARLIE (Creek)
(tribal town king)
Affiliation: Thlopthlocco Tribal Town, Box 706, Okemah, OK 74859 (918) 623-2620.

McGESHICK, JOHN (Chippewa)
(tribal chairperson)
Affiliation: Lac Vieux Desert Band of Chippewa Indians, P.O. Box 249, Choate Rd., Watersmeet, MI 49969 (906) 358-4577.

McGINNIS, HELEN
(museum director)
Affiliation: Tsut'ina K'osa (Sarcee), 3700 Anderson Rd., S.W., P.O. Box 67, Calgary, Alberta, Canada T2W 3C4 (403) 238-2676/7.

McGREEVY, SUSAN BROWN 1934-
(anthropologist)
Born January 28, 1934, Chicago, Ill. *Education*: Mt. Holyoke College (2 years); Roosevelt University, BA, 1969; Northwestern University, MA, 1971. *Principal occupation*: Anthropologist. *Home address*: 704 Camino Lejo, Box 5153, Santa Fe, NM 87502. *Affiliation*: Director, 1978-82, research associate, 1983-, The Wheelwright Museum, Santa Fe, NM. *Other professional posts*: Curator of North American Ethnology, Kansas City Museum, 1974-77. *Memberships*: American Anthropological Association; Society for American Archaeology; American Society for Ethnohistory; Society for Applied Anthropology; American Ethnological Society; Council for Museum Anthropology; American Association of Museums; Native American Art Studies Association. *Interests*: Research and exhibit curator, Southwest Indian arts and cultures; hiking, camping, rafting, SCUBA diving. *Published work*: The Dyer Collection, (American Indian Art Magazine, 1978); Lullabies From the Earth: Cradles of Native North America, 1980; Translating Tradition: Basketry Arts of the San Juan Paiutes, with Andrew Hunter Whiteford (Wheelwright Museum, 1985); Anii Anaadaalyaa'igii: Continuity and Innovation in Recent Navajo Art, with Bruce Bernstein (Wheelwright Museum, 1988); contributing articles to professional publications.

McGUIRE, BETSY (Athabascan)
(radio station manager)
Affiliation: KSKO - 870 AM, P.O. Box 195, McGrath, AK 99627 (907) 524-3001.

McGUIRE, DR. THOMAS R.
(professor of anthropology)
Affiliation: Dept. of Anthropology, Emil Haury Anthropology Bldg., Rm. 221A, University of Arizona, Tucson, AZ 85721 (520) 621-2585 Fax 621-2088. E-mail: tmcguire@u.arizona.edu. *Interests*: Native American economic development.

McGUIREAKIS, DAN
(Indian band chief)
Affiliation: Sand Point Indian Band, 921 Athabasca St., Thunder Bay, Ontario, Canada P7C 3E5 (807) 632-4227.

McHALE, PHILIP A.
(consortium director)
Affiliation: Native American Center of Excellence Consortium, College of Medicine, P.O. Box 26901, Oklahoma City, OK 73190 (405) 271-2316.

McHENRY, DELORES
(former rancheria chairperson)
Affiliation: Chico Rancheria, 3006 Esplanade St., Chico, CA 95926 (916) 899-8922.

McHORSE, CHRISTINE C. (Navajo)
(craftsperson)
Address: P.O. Box 1711, Santa Fe, NM 87504 (505) 989-7716. E-mail: mchorse@ix.netcom.com. *Products*: Taos style, Navajo handbuilt micaceous pottery and silverwork.

McHORSE, JOEL C. (Navajo-Taos)
(craftsperson)
Address: P.O. Box 1711, Santa Fe, NM 87504 (505) 989-7716. E-mail: mchorse@ix.netcom.com. *Products*: Micaceous pottery, and silver jewelry and silverwork.

McINTYRE, ALLAN J.
(museum curator)
Affiliation: The Amerind Foundation Museum, P.O. Box 248, Dragoon, AZ 86509 (602) 586-3666.

McKAY, GINA
(program centre head)
Affiliation: West Region Tribal Council, Indian Cultural Education Program, 21-4th Ave., N.W., Dauphin, Manitoba, Canada R7N 1H9 (204) 638-8225.

McKAY, WALLY (Ojibwe)
(member-board of directors)
Affiliation: Intertribal Christian Comunications, P.O. Box 3765, Station B, Winnipeg, Manitoba, Canada R2W 3R6 (204) 661-9333.

McKEE, RICHARD
(Indian education program counselor)
Affiliation: Milburn Public School, Indian Education Program, P.O. Box 429, Milburn, OK 73450 (405) 443-5522 Fax 443-5303.

McKEE, WILLIAM
(administrative officer)
Affiliation: Clinton PHS Indian Hospital, Route 4, Box 213, Clinton, OK 73601 (405) 323-2884.

McKENZIE, ALEXANDRE
(Indian band chief)
Affiliation: Montagnais de Schefferville, Quebec, Canada G0G 2T0 (418) 585-2601.

McKENZIE, WILLIAM
(Indian band chief)
Affiliation: Tanakteuk Indian Band, Box 327, Alert Bay, British Columbia, Canada V0N 1A0 (604) 974-5489.

McKEVITT, GERALD 1939-
(professor of history)
Born July 3, 1939, Longview, Wash. *Education*: University of San Francisco, BA, 1961; University of Southern California, MA, 1964; UCLA, PhD, 1972; Pontifical Gregorian University, Rome, Italy, BST, 1975. *Principal occupation*: Professor of history. *Address*: Nobili Hall, Santa Clara University, Santa Clara, CA 95053 (408) 554-4124. *Affiliations*: Director, Santa Clara University Archives, 1975-85; professor, History Department, Santa Clara University, 1975-. *Other professional posts*: Member, Board of Trustees, Gonzaga University, 1989-97; member, National Seminar for Jesuit Higher Education, 1990-94. *Memberships*: Western History Association; California Historical Society; American Historical Association; American Society of Church History, American Catholic Historical Association. *Awards, honors*: 1991 Oscar O. Winther Award by Western Historical Association for "Jesuit Missionary Linguistics in the Pacific Northwest: A Comparative Study," best article appearing in "The Western Historical Quarterly. *Interests*: "Teach courses on university level on California history, American Far West, Native American History, U.S. Catholicism, Historical Methodology. Current research interests: Jesuits in the American Far West, missionaries to Native Americans in the 19th century." *Published works*: The University of Santa Clara, A History, 1851-1977 (Stanford University Press, 1979); Serving the Intellect, Touching the Heart: A Portrait of Santa Clara University, 1851-2001, with George F. Giacomi, Jr. (Hong Kong: Santa Clara University, 2000); numerous articles and book reviews.

McKINLEY, FRANCIS
(executive director)
Affiliation: National Indian Training & Research Center, 2113 S. 48th St., Suite 102, Tempe, AZ 85282 (602) 967-9484.

McKINLEY, THOMAS R.
(museum director)
Affiliation: Ataloa Lodge Museum, Bacone College, 2299 Old Bacone Rd., Muskogee, OK 74403 (918) 683-4581 ext. 283.

McKINNEY, ROGER (Sinnagwin) (Kickapoo) 1957-
(educator)
Born Febrary 24, 1957, Kansas City, Mo. *Education*: Graceland College (Lamoni, IA), BA, 1982; The American University (Washington, DC), MFA (Painting), 1986. *Principal occupation*: Educator. *Home address*:

Resides in the Phoenix, AZ area. *Affiliations*: Art instructor/guidance counselor, Kickapoo Nation School, Horton, KS (acting supt./prinicpal), 1982-83; associate/trainer, ORBIS Associates, Washington, DC, 1986-88; coordinator, Youth Leadership Program, Zuni School District, Zuni, NM, 1988-89; program management and design specialist, Southwest Resoiurce and Evaluation Center IV, Tempe, AZ, 1989-91; educator, The Heard Museum, Phoenix, AZ, 1991-. *Other profssional post*: Professional artist. *Exhibitions*: Ha-Pa-Nyi Fine Arts Gallery, Santa Barbara, CA, 1988; Native American Arts Exhibition, UCSB, 1988; 68th Inter-Tribal Indian Ceremonial, Gallup, NM, 1989; Second Annual Lawrence Indian Arts Show, University of Kansas, 1990; Cultural Reality or Cultural Fantasy, Institute of American Indian Arts, Santa Fe, NM, 1991-92; Santa Fe Indian Market, 1991; among others. *Works in Public Collection/Places*: Graceland College Art Collection, Lamoni, IA; Kickapoo Nation School, Powhattan, KS; Watkins Gallery Colection, The American University, Washington, DC; among others. *Awards, honors*: Guitano Capasso Award, All Dept. Shoe, Graceland College, 1982; Second Premium Watercolor, Fairfax Co. Parks, Burke, VA, 1984; Wolpoff Award, Works on Paper, The American University, Watkins Collection, 1986; Honorable Mention, 68th Annual Inter-Tribal Indian Ceremonial, 1989; DeGrazia, Artist in Residence, The Heard Museum, 1990; Merit Award, Lawrence Indian Arts Show, 1990. *Biographical sources*: Public TV Broadcasring - Kickapoo Nation, Return to Sovergnty (University of Kansas, PBS, 1983); Twenty First Century Native American (CBS, Phoenix, AZ).

McKINNEY, THOMAS R., Sr. (Gentgeen-Dancer) (Seneca) 1951-
(fire fighter, museum director)
Born October 27, 1951, Butler Co., Penna. *Education*: Bacone Junior College, AA, 1974. *Principal occupation*: Fire fighter, museum director. *Home address*: 323 Lawrence St., Muskogee, OK 74403 (918) 682-9138. *Affiliations*: Museum director, Bacone College, Muskogee, OK, 1990-; fire fighter, Muskogee Fire Dept., Muskogee, OK, 1979-. *Other professional posts*: Dancer of traditional Native American origin; Post Master of Boy Scouts, explorer post, specializing in Native American culture. *Community activities*: Inspector for district election board, member, Chamber of Commerce; member, Muskogee antique collector's guild. *Membership*: Muskogee Fire Fighters local #57. *Awards, honors*: Instructor I professional Fire Fighters; Honorable mention and work in the permanent collection of the Black Hills art competition; Eagle Scout; Vigil member of The Order of the Arrow; DAR achievement award. *Interests*: Native American studies, professional fire fighting skills, anthropology & ethnology; Native American dancing & the making of traditional clothing.

McKNIGHT, CINDY
(editor)
Affiliation: "Smoke Signals," Dallas Inter-Tribal Center, 209 E. Jefferson Blvd., Dallas, TX 75203 (214) 941-1050.

McLAREN, DALE (Fire Eagle) (Lumbee) 1935-
(investment banker)
Born March 25, 1935, in Illinois. *Education*: Southern Illinois University, BA, MA. *Address*: P.O. Box 2704, Huntington Beach, CA 92647 (714) 840-2400 Fax 840-3444. E-mail: dalemcl@aol.com. *Principal occupation*: Investment banker. *Affiliation*: Chairman/CEO, Allied Eurasian Co. Pte. Ltd., Republic of Singapore. *Other professional post*: Planning consultant, Dale McLaren. Consultant (regional & urban planning venture into planning consultation; zoning maps, zoning ordinances, professional advice, and lobbying); financial consultant, Allied Eurasian Co. (USA), Ltd. (facilitates and syndicates international loans for qualified applicants), 1982-. *Memberships*: American Academy of Political and Social Science; Illinois Railroad User's Association (executive secretary); United Lumbee Nation's Golden Hawk Warrior Society Chief, 1990-; vice chief, United Lumbee Nation's Red Tail Hawk Clan, 1992-. *Awards, honors*: Governor's Task Force for Economic Alternatives for Illinois; United Lumbee Nation's Silver Eagle Award 1993 (given each year to a tribal member that has done outstanding work for the Nation and the Indian community." *Biographical source*: Who's Who in North America, 1976.

McLAUGHLIN, MICHAEL (*Kaga shoga*)
(Winnebago of Nebraska) 1951-
(Indian center librarian)
Born in 1951, Sioux City, Iowa. *Education*: University of California, Los Angeles, MLIS, 1995, MA (American Indian Studies-History & Law), 1999. *Principal occupation*: Indian center librarian, American Indian subject specialist. *Address*: American Indian Resource Center, Los Angeles County Public Library, 6518 Miles Ave., Huntington Park, CA 90255 (323) 583-2794 Fax 587-2061. E-mail: airc90255@yahoo.com. *Affiliations*: Los Angeles Public Library Municipal Reference, 1989-95; UCLA-American Indiann Studies Center - Americann Indian Terminology Project, 1995-99; American Indian Resource Center, Huntington Park, CA, 1999-present. *Community activities*: Member, American Indian Children's Council (Los Angeles County). *Membership*: American Indian Library Association. *Interests*: Urban American Indian topics; tribal sovereignty and relations with U.S. Government; developing library materials on American Indian subjects beyond standard library classification practices and systems.

McLAUGHLIN, STEVE
(BIA agency supt.)
Affiliation: Crow Creek Agency, BIA, P.O. Box 616, Ft. Thompson, SD 57339 (605) 245-2311.

McLEAN, DORIS
(Indian band chief)
Affiliation: Carcross/Tagish Indian Band, Box 130, Carcross, Yukon, Canada Y0B 1B0 (403) 821-4251.

McLEOD, LINDA
(Indian school principal)
Affiliation: Indian Island School, 1 River Rd., Old Town, ME 04468 (207) 827-4285 Fax 827-3599. E-mail: lmcleod@iis.bia.edu.

McLEOD, MARTHA
(college president)
Affiliation: Bay Mills Community College, Route 1, Box 315A, Brimley, MI 49715 (906) 248-3354.

McMANUS, JILL
(freelance writer, composer, jazz pianist, teacher)
Born in N.J. *Education*: Wellesley College, BA. *Principal occupation*: Freelance writer, composer, jazz pianist, teacher. *Home address*: 401 East 81st St., New York, NY 10028. *Affiliation*: Staff, Mannes College of Music, 1981-92. *Other professional posts*: Freelance writer, reporter, researcher, Time Magazine, 1963-71; jazz pianist performing with top jazz artists in the U.S. and Europe, 1973-. *Membership*: American Association on Indian Affairs. *Awards, honors*: Grants, Sandoval County Human Services to continue research & develop support for project to produce educational videotapes on diabetes prevention for Pueblos & Navajo Nation, and write proposal (March 1986); Health & Human Services to produce a culturally appropriate pilot video for Navajo youth on nutrition, exercise & diabetes prevention, "Children of Long Life," now in use by health educators and teachers; grants towards completion and teacher's guide (Dec. 1993). *Interests*: Teaching jazz theory and piano; travel. *Published/produced works*: Produced album "Symbols of Hopi" (Concord Jazz, 1984) containing four Hopi songs adapted for jazz quintet plus cottonwood drum & percussion (played by Louis Mofsie & Alan Brown), as tribute to Hopi song-poets & Native American music (5 stars in Down Beat). *Articles*: "Women Jazz Composers and Arrangers" for Greenwood Press series, "Diabetes in Indian America," profiles of musicians.

McMASTER, GERALD R. (Plains Cree-Nehiyawuk)
1953-
(deputy assistant director for cultural resources)
Born March 9, 1953, North Battleford, Saskatchewan, Can. *Education*: Institute of American Indian Art (Santa Fe, 1973-75); Minneapolis College of Art & Design, BFA, 1977; Banff School of Fine Arts (Banff, Alberta), 1986; Carleton University (Ottawa, ON), MA, 1994. *Principal occupation*: Deputy Assistant Director for Cultural Resources. *Address*: National Museum of the American Indian, Smithsonian Institution, 470 L'Enfant Plaza, SW, Suite 7103, Washington, DC 20560 (202) 287-2525 Fax 287-3369. *Affiliations*: Head of the Indian Art Program, Saskatchewan Indian Federated College, Regina, Sask., 1977-81; curator, Canadian

Museum of Civilization, Ottawa, Ont., 1981-2001; Deputy Assistant Director for Cultural Resources, National Museum of the American Indian, New York, NY, 2001-present. *Other professional posts*: Adjunct Research Professor, Carleton University, 1992-95; self-employed visual artist, 1977-; artistic coordinator for Plains Indian Dancers & Singers, the Holland Festival, Amsterdam, the Netherlands, 1984-85; program coordinator, Native Art Studies Group of Ottawa, 1984-85. *Solo exhibitions*: The Cowboy/Indian Show - Ufundi Gallery, Ottawa, Ontario, 1990; McMichael Canadian Gallery, Kleinburg, Ontario, 1991. Savage Graces: "afterimages by Gerald McMaster - UBC-Museum of Anthropology, Vancouver, BC, 1992; Winnipeg Art Gallery, 12/94-1/95; Windsor Art Gallery, 1994; Southern Alberta Art Gallery, 1994; Ottawa Art Gallery, 1994; Edmonton Art Gallery, 1995; Memorial Art Gallery, St. Johns, Newfoundland, 1995; numerous group exhibitions. *Collections represented*: Carleton University, Canadian Museum of Civilization, Dept. of Indian Affairs (Ottawa, ON), University of Regina, Canada Council Art Bank, City of Ottawa, City of Regina, Institute of American Indian Arts (Santa Fe, NM), Gettysburg College (Gettysburg, PA), Guilford Native American Art Gallery (Greensboro, NC). *Commissions*: Metro-Toronto, 1992; City of Ottawa, 1991; Canadian Museum of Civilization, Ottawa, 1988; among others. *Membership*: Native Art Studies Association of Canada (vice-president, 1987, president, 1988-92; editor, NASAC Newsletter); Ontario Arts Council (board member, 1991-); ICOM Canada (board member, 1992-). *Awards, honors*: Canada Council Travel Grants, to travel and present papers at various conference and workshops, 1989, '90, '93; Honorable Mention, National Educational Film Festival/Certificate for Creative Excellence, U.S. Industrial Film Festival, Firearms Safety Series, Indian Hunting Traditions, 1983; First Prize, "Byron and His Balloon, La Roche, Saskatchewan, 1981; Second Prize, wood sculpture, Scottsdale Annual Indian Art Competition, 1976. *Interests*: Travel; art exhibitions. From 1986 to 1989 developed concept for a National Indian & Inuit Art Gallery in the new Canadian Museum of Civilization. *Reviews on artist*: "Punning Artist Uses Native Wit," by Robin Laurence (The Georgia Straight, Aug 14-21, 1992); "Native Painter's Criticism Packs Strong Punchline," by Christopher Hume (The Toronto Star, Feb. 8, 1991); "Native Artist Throws Comic Curves But With a Serious Twist," by Nancy Baele (Ottawa Citizen, Feb. 24, 1991); "Indian Lore," by Nancy Baele (Ottawa Citizen, June 15, 1989); "Public Servant-Painter Wants to Help Native Artists," by Nancy Baele (Ottawa Citizen, Nov. 11, 1988); "Teacher-Artist's Commitment Extends Beyond Work As Curator," by Bill White (Echo-National Museums of Canada, Vol. 4, No. 7, Oct/Nov., 1984); among others. *Biographical source*: Savage Graces: 'After-Images," Harbor Magazine of Art & Everyday Life, Montreal, 1994. *Published works*: Indigena: Contemporary Native Perspectives, edited with Lee-Ann Martin (Douglas & McIntyre, Vancouver, 1992); First American Art: The Charles & Valerie Diker Collection of American Indian Art (University of Washington Press, 2004); Native Universe:Voices of Indian America, edited with Clifford Trafzer (National Geographic Books, 2004); numerous articles. *Recordings*: "Songs from Bismarck," Indian Records, Taos, N.M (sang with the Red Earth Singers), 1976.

McNEELY, KATHLEEN (Sault Ste. Marie Chippewa)
1951-
(librarian-director of library services)
Born February 19, 1951, Petoskey, Mich. *Education*: Lake Superior University, Sault Ste. Marie, MI (4 years); University of Southwestern Louisiana, Lafayette (1 year). *Principal occupation*: Librarian-Director of Library Services, Hannahville School-Community Library (Nah Tah Wahsh Library), Hannahville Reservation, Wilson, MI, 1985-. *Address*: W1971 Isaacson Dr., Menominee, MI 49858 (906) 466-2556 (work). *Other professional posts*: Lifestyle editor, Sault Evening News, Sault Ste Marie, MI; managing editor, Franklin Banner, Franklin, LA. *Community activities*: St. Ignace Pow Wow Committee, St. Ignace, MI; Menominee County Library (board of trustees); Michinemackinong Pow Wow Committee (chairperson). *Memberships*: Bay De Noc Culture Association (board of directors); American Library Association (Minorities Round Table). *Awards, honors*: 1980 Outstanding Citizens of the Year - West St. Mary Parish Chamber of Commerce, Franklin, LA; 1991 Candidate for

Medal of Honor, Michigan Daughters of the American Revolution. *Interests*: "Traditional & jingle dress dancer promoting traditional ways to our youth as alternatives to substance abuse."

McNEIL, RONALD S. (*His Horse Is Thunder*)
(Hunkpapa Lakota) 1958-
(college president)
Born March 19, 1958, Rapid City, S.D. *Education*: Standing Rock College, AA, 1982; Black Hills State College, BS, 1985; University of South Dakota Law School, JD, 1988. *Address*: P.O. Box 67, Fort Yates, ND 58538 (701) 854-3861 Fax 854-3403 (work). *Affiliations*: Indian Law Instructor & Federal Grants Administrator, University of South Dakota Law School, 1989-91; President, Sitting Bull College (Standing Rock College), 1341 92nd St., Fort Yates, ND 58538, 1991-; President, American Indian College Fund, 21 West 68 St., #1F, New York, NY 10023 (212) 787-6312, 1993-. *Community activities*: Participates in tribal government and cultural activities. *Memberships*: SD Indian Education Association; American Indian Higher Education Consortium. *Interests*: Vocational: Native American higher education. In his two-year term as president of the American Indian College Fund, he hopes to help the Fund broaden its outreach and greatly increase its funding. "This is a very exciting time in the Indian-college movement. The older colleges are maturing and starting to offer bachelor's and master's programs, while new colleges are emerging all the time. Indian colleges are vital to the cultural survival of our people. I want to do all I can to help them grow." *Avocational*: Fishing & hunting.

McNELEY, DR. JAMES K.
(college vice president)
Affiliation: Dine (Navajo) College, P.O. Box 126, Tsaile, AZ 86556 (520) 724-6671 Fax 724-3327.

McNICHOLS, ROBERT R.
(Indian affairs)
Born October 16, 1950, Columbus, Ohio. *Education*: BS (Gneral Studies/Forestry). *Principal occupation*: Indian affairs. *Home address*: 7175 Seneca St., Kingman, AZ 86401. E-mail: bobmcnichols@yahoo. com. *Affiliation*: Superintendent, Truxton Canon Agency, Bureau of Indian Affairs, P.O. Box 37, Valentine, AZ 86437 (928) 769-2286 Fax 769-2444. *Other professional post*: Certified Economic Developer. *Memberships*: American Economic Development Council; Society of American Foresters. *Interests*: Native American economic and community development

McPEEK, GEORGE
(director-organization)
Affiliation: Intertribal Christian Communications, P.O. Box 3765, Station B, Winnipeg, Manitoba, Canada R2W 3R6 (204) 661-9333.

McPETERS, ANTHONY STEPHEN
(*Walks in Two Worlds*) (Lumbee) 1944-
(drum builder)
Born July 26, 1944, Griffin, GA. *Address*: 117 Milling Rd., Poulan, GA 31781-2020 (912) 776-4292. *Affiliation*: Owner, Two Worlds Arts & Crafts, Poulan, GA, 1986-. *Military service*: U.S. Navy, 1959-63.

McTAGGART, FRED
(author)
McTaggart was a postdoctoral fellow in the Newberry Library's Center for the History of the American Indian, Chicago. *Published works*: Wolf That I Am: In Search of the Red Earth People (University of Oklahoma Press, 1985.

M

MAAS, GARY (Iroquois/Ojibwe)
(stuntman, script-writer, film-maker)
Address: c/o Dreamcatcher Films, Inc., 8251 Continental, Warren, MI 48089 (810) 756-6007.

MACARRO, MARK A. (Luiseno)
(tribal spokesperson)
Affiliation: Pechanga Band of Mission Indians, P.O. Box 1477, Temecula, CA 92593 (909) 676-2768.

MACARTNEY, KATE
(Indian education center director)
Affiliation: Woodfords Indian Education Center, 96-B

Washo Blvd., Markleeville, CA 96120 (916) 694-2964 Fax 694-2739. E-mail: kmacartney@telis.org.

MacDONALD, ARTHUR
(college president)
Affiliation: Dull Knife Memorial College, P.O. Box 98, Lame Deer, MT 59043 (406) 477-6219.

MacDONALD, GEORGE F. 1938-
(archaeologist)
Born July 4, 1938, Galt, Ontario, Can. *Education*: University of Toronto, BA, 1961; Yale University, PhD, 1966. *Principal occupation*: Archaeologist. *Address*: Resides in Quebec Province, Can. *Affiliations*: Atlantic Provinces Archaeologist, 1964-1966, head-Western Canada Section, 1966-69, National Museums of Canada; chief, Archaeology Division, 1969-71; chief, Archaeological Survey of Canada, 1971-77, senior archaeologist, Office of the Director, 1977-, National Museum of Man. *Other professional post*: Conjunct professor, Dept. of Anthropology, Trent University, 1974-. *Memberships*: Canadian Archaeological Association (president, 1969-70); American Association for the Advancement of Science (Fellow); American Anthrological Association (Fellow); Archaeological Institute of America, Ottawa Chapter (vice president, 1976-77); Society for American Archaeology (first positions, executive committee, 1977-78); International Quarternary Association (head, working group for Eastern North America-Commission for the Paleo-Ecology of Early Man, 1976-77); Council for Canadian Archaeology; International Union of Prehistoric and Protohistoric Sciences. *Awards, honors*: Numerous awards and research grants. *Interests*: "Native peoples of North and South America; prehistory, field research, Atlantic and Pacific Coast of Canada, Ontario and Yukon Territories; traditional Native American arts and crafts; Northwest Coast Indian print-making, scultpure, Ojibwa print-making; assembled and wrote catalogues for numerous exhibitions of contemporary and traditional Native American art that traveled in Europe, North America, Asia, New Zealand; study travel." *Published works*: Numerous articles, papers, reports, and reviews, 1965-; directed the prodcution of 45 short study 16mm, color films on West Coast art and technology; production of gallery films and study video tapes and public release films such as To Know the Hurons, 1977.

MacDONALD, PETER, Sr. (Navajo) 1928-
(former tribal chairman)
Born December 16, 1928, Teec Nos Pos, Ariz. *Education*: Bacone Junior College, AA, 1951; University of Oklahoma, BS, 1957; UCLA, graduate studies, 1958-62. *Affiliations*: Project engineer, member of technical staff, Hughes Aircarfts Co., El Segundo, Calif., 1957-63; director, Management, Methods & Procedures, 1963-65; Office of Navajo Economic Opportunity, 1965-70, The Navajo Tribe, Window Rock, AZ; chairman, Navajo Tribal Council, 1970-88. *Military service*: U.S. Marine Corps, 1944-46 (Corporal; member, Navajo Code Talkers in the South Pacific). *Community activities*: New Mexico Governor's Economic Development Advisory Group, 1963-67; New Mexico State Planning Commission, 1963-67; Navajo Community College, Tsaile, AZ (board of regents, 1971-); Antioch School of Law, Washington, D.C. (board of visitors); Patagonia Corporation, Tucson (board of directors); Navajo Agricultural Products Industry, Farmington, NM (board of directors, 1972-); NM Governor's Energy Task Force, Santa Fe; NM Commission, Regional Housing Authority, Santa Fe; Non-Profit Housing/Community Development Corp., Shiprock, NM, 1972; Arizona State Justice Planning Agency Governing Board; Arizona Advisory Committee of U.S. Commission on Civil Rights, Washington, DC, 1970-74. *Memberships*: University of Oklahoma Alumni Association; National Association of Community Development (board of directors, 1968-70; National Tribal Chairman's Association; American Indian National Bank, Washington, D.C. (board of directors). *Awards, honors*: Appointed by President Nixon to the National Center for Voluntary Action, 1970-74; Presidential Commendation for exceptional services to others, 1970; Citation, Distinguished American, National Institute for Economic Development, 1970; Citation, Distinguished Baconian, Bacone Junior College, OK, 1971; Arizona Indian of the Year, 1971; Good Citizenship Medal, National Society of Sons of the American Revolution, 1972; Silver Beaver Award, Boy Scouts Of America, Kit Carson

Council, 1973l member (appointed by Secretary of Commerce), National Public Advisory Committee on Regional Economic Development, U.S. Department of Comerce, Washington, DC, 1973-77; Citation, One of the 200 Rising American Leaders by Time Magazine, 1974; inducted into Engineering Hall of Fame, University of Oklahoma, 1975. *Biographical sources*: Who's Who in America; Who's Who in the West; Mr. MacDonald has been written about in magazines and newspapers, such as: Newsweek; Time; U.S. News & World Report; Signature; People; Washington Post; New York Times; Chicago Times; Los Angeles Times, etc.

MacEEACHEM, ZONDRA
(editor)
Affiliation: Canadian Native Law Reporter, Native Law Centre, University of Saskatchewan, Room 141, Diefenbaker Centre, Saskatoon, Saskatchewan, Canada S7N 0W0 (306) 966-6189.

MACHELL, WILLIAM
(Indian band chief)
Affiliation: Lillooet Indian Band, Box 615, Lillooet, B.C., Canada V0K 1V0 (604) 256-4118.

MACHIMITY, EDWARD
(Indian band chief)
Affiliation: Saugeen Indian band, Savant Lake, Ontario, Canada P0V 2S0 (807) 584-2989.

MACHUKAY, TONY
(executive director)
Affiliation: Arizona Commission on Indian Affairs, 1645 W. Jefferson, Suite 127, Phoenix, AZ 85007 (602) 542-3123.

MacKENZIE, ELEANOR DOVE
(Naintic Narragansett)
(cultural center host)
Address & Affiliation: Dovecrest Indian Cultural Center, 390 Summit Rd., Arcadia Village, Exter, RI 02822 (401) 539-7795.

MacNABB, ALEXANDER S. (Micmac) 1929-
(attorney)
Born August 24, 1929, Bay Shore, N.Y. *Education*: Colgate University, AB, 1956; Washington and Lee University Law School, JD, 1959; NYU Law School, postgraduate, 1960-61. *Principal occupation*: Attorney. *Home address*: 10600 Sunlit Rd., P.O. Box 86, Oakton, VA 22124. *Affiliations*: President, Alexander MacNabb Associates, Bay Shore, NY, 1960-67; president, Town Almanac Publishing Co., Bay Shore, N.Y., 1960-67; member, President's Comittee on Manpower, U.S. Office of Economic Opportunity, 1966-67, special assistant to director, Community Action Program, 1967-69; OEO representative to Presidentially established National Program for Voluntary Action, Washington, DC, 1969-70; director, Office of Operating Services, U.S. Dept. of the Interior, BIA, Washington, DC, 1970-72, director, Office of Engineering, 1972-73; director, Office of Indian & Territorial Development, U.S. Dept. of the Interior, 1973-74; deputy director, Office of Federal Contract Compliance, Empoyment Standards Administration, Dept. of Labor, 1974-75; director, Indian & Native American Programs, Employment and Training Administration, Washington, DC, 1975-80; National Alliance of Business, 1980-81; MacNabb, Preston & Waxman, Attorneys at Law, 1981-86; Alexander MacNabb, Attorney-at-Law, 1986-. *Military service*: U.S. Navy, 1950-54 - Korean War, Task Force 95 of the 7th Fleet in Korea (Presidential Unit Citation, Presidential Unit Citation Republic of Korea; Korean Medal; the UN Medal; the China Service Medal & the American Defense Medal). *Community activities*: National Council of the Boy Scouts of America (25+ years) (Chairperson of the National American Indian Committee on Scouting, the National Advisory Committee on Scouting for the Handicapped); National Board of the American Red Cross. *Memberships*: American Political Science Association; American Academy of Political and Social Sciences; National Congress of American Indian (Micmac Tribe); National Indian Youth Council; MENSA.

MACRI, MARTHA JANE MITCHELL (*Tsoee*)
(Oklahoma Cherokee) 1945-
(professor of Native American studies)
Born March 10, 1945, Lansing, Mich. *Education*: Cali-

fornia State University, Fullerton, BA, 1968; University of California, Berkeley, MA (Linguistics), 1982, Ph.D. (Linguistics), 1988. *Principal occupation*: Professor of Native American studies. *Home address*: 2212 Whittier Dr., Davis, CA 95616 (916) 752-7086 (work). *Affiliations*: Dept. of Anthropology & Native American Studies, University of California, Davis, 1985- (postgraduate researcher, 1985-88; lecturer, 1988-90; Postdoctoral Fellow, 1990-91; assistant professor, 1991-). *Other professional posts*: Project coordinator, Art & Archaeology Database Project, Pre-Columbian Art Research Institute, San Francisco, CA, 1988-91; instructor, D-Q University, Davis, CA, 1990; New Faculty Research Grants, Tzeltal Language Project, 1991-94; Sr. Investigator, Maya Archival Database Project, Merle Greene Robertson, principal investigator, National Endowment for the Humanities, Reference Materials-Access, through the Pre-Columbian Art Research, San Francisco, CA; principal investigator, Maya Hieroglyphic Database Project, National Endowment for the Humanities, Reference Materials-Tools, 1992-94, 1994-96. *Community activities*: Group leader, La Leche League International (board of directors, N. Calif.); assistant chairperson, Leader Applicants for Northern California, 1976-78; volunteer teacher's aid, in programs for Gifted and Talented, ESL, and regular classroom, Fitch Mtn. Elem. School, Healdsburg, CA, 1978-80; volunteer caregiver, Home Hospice of Sonoma County, CA, 1990-91. *Memberships*: Pre-Columbian Art Research Institute (research associate); American Anthropological Association; California Indian Education Association; Linguistic Society of America; Society for the Study of the Indigenous Languages of the Americas. *Interests*: "I am committed to research and teaching about the world views of indigenous peoples of the Americas through study of their own writing systems. Areas of emphasis include Maya Hieroglyphic writing, Epi-Olmec writing and Micmac hieroglyphic writing (Canada), linguistic prehistory of the Americas, Native American language instruction, computers in linguistic research and electronic data archiving." *Published works*: Numerous articles; *in press*: A Glyphic Text from Naranjo, in Native American Text Series, Louanna Furbee, editor (Mouton, The Hague); among others; *in preparation*: with James Brooks, The Maya Graphene Codes & Reference File (book) (University of Oklahoma Press); Teaching & Learning Indian Languages; numerous articles in journals, and chapters in books.

MADALENA, REYES (Jemez Pueblo)
(craftsperson)
Address: 1070 Wagner, Moab, UT 84532 (801) 259-8419. *Product*: Authentic Pueblo Indian pottery.

MADDOX, GREG
(BIA agency supt.)
Affiliation: Seminole Agency, Bureau of Indian Affairs, 6075 Stirling Rd., Hollywood, FL 33024 (954) 581-7050 Fax 792-7340.

MADDUX, MICHAEL THOMAS (*Red Hawk*) (N. Alabama Cherokee) 1955-
(tribal officer)
Born July 12, 1955, Albertville, Ala. *Education*: High school. *Home address*: 203 West Don's Ave., Albertville, AL 35950 (205) 878-9602. *Affiliation*: Autorized tribal officer, Dist. #2 North Alabama Cherokees. "We have seven districts with enrollment of nearly 1,000 people. *Awards, honors*: Golden Arrowhead Society, North Alabama Cherokees, Creek Path-Williston Dist. *Interests*: Native American pow wows in TN, GA, and AL.

MADINA, NANCY
(Indian education center director)
Affiliation: Big Pine Indian Education Center, P.O. Box 684, Big Pine, CA 93513 (760) 938-2530.

MADISON, CURT 1949-
(video documentary producer)
Born September 9, 1949, St. Paul, Minn. *Education*: Stanford University, BA, 1971; University of Hawaii, MA (Political Science, Communications), 1976; East-West Center (Communications Institute Certificate), 1976. *Address*: Unknown. *Video Productions*: Director/editor, Profiles of Alaskans, Thelma Saunders-Kaltag, Emmitt Peters-Ruby, Catherine Attla-Huslia, 1982 (State of Alaska Instructional TV Network) 39

minutes, documentary of three rural Alaskans; director/editor, Huteetl: Koyukon Memorial Potlatch, 1983 (Yukon-Koyukuk School District) 55 minutes, documentary of the Memorial Potlatch festival; director/editor, Songs in Minto Life, 1986 (National Endowment for the Arts and Yukon-Koyukuk School District) 28 minutes, documentary of four important music categories in Minto-dance songs, hunting songs, songs of remembrance, and a potlatch song sung directly to the spirit; director/writer/editor, Tanana River Rat, 1989 (National Endowment for the Arts and KUAC-TV Fairbanks) 52 minutes, narrative drama depicting the crisis of young men in rural Alaska and village cohesiveness; producer/director, Bedrock Pay, 1991 - documentary of historic placer gold mining around Hot Springs-Rampart District, 1890-1940; producer/director, Hitting Sticks, Healing Hearts, 1991 (with KUAC-TV Fairbanks) documentary of the most important Native ceremony in Minto. Early Documentaries on Film: Director/camera/editor, Subsistence Fishing on the Tanana River, 1972 - 22 minutes (University of Alaska Media Dept.); writer, Athapaskan Art: Where Two Rivers Meet, 1973 - 30 minutes (University of Alaska Media Dept.); Ka'apuni Kakou, 1975 - 20 minutes (University of Hawaii); sound recordist, Inuit, 1978 (documentary of first Inuit Circumpolar Conference in Barrow). Slide/Tape Programs: photographer/writer, Morris Gundrum: Professional Woodsman, 1972 (Alaska Native Language Center; photographer/writer, A Haida Chief, 1977; photographer/writer, People and Places, 1979 - filmstrip (Yukon-Koyukuk School District). Still Photography: Point Lay Ethography, Point Lay, AK (U.S. Dept. of the Interior, 1990); Genieve Nahulu: Nanakuli, HI (Dept. of Education, Honolulu, HI), 1991; Ines Cayaban: A Filipina Woman (Dept. of Education, Honolulu, HI, 1991; among others. Writings: Writer/photographer, "Alaska Biography Series," 21 book series for use in Alaska schools - oral history of Native and White elders in rural Interior Alaska, 70-150 pages per book, 1978-87; writer/photographer, Walter Northway - oral history with the oldest Native of the Tanana Valley (Alaska Native Language Center, 1988); writer/photographer, Andrew Isaac - oral history of Interior Alaska's traditional chief (Central Alaska Curriculum Consortium, 1989). Awards, honors: Fellowships and Prizes - National Endowment for the Arts-Documentary Production, 1985, '87, '89; Rocky Mountain Film Center-Documentary Production, 1989, '90; Alaska State Council on the Arts-Writing, 1988; Alaska State Humanities Forum-Documentary Production, 1991; Red Ribbon, American Film and Video Festival, New York, 1984, '87; Museum of the American Indian Festival, 1984, '89; New Works Feature, National Video Festival AFI, Hollywood, 1984, '89; Arctic Film Festival, Finland, curated, 1986; Best Documentary, Northwest Film and Video Festival, Oregon Art Institute, 1989; Best Documentary, Atlanta Film and Video Festival, 1989; Premier Program, National Broadcast Spirit of Place, 1989.

MADSEN, LOIS
(Indian education program coordinator)
Affiliation: Capistrano Unified School District, Indian Education Program, 24242 La Cresta Dr., Dana Point, CA 92629 (714) 248—7037.

MADUENO, PATRICIA (Mojave)
(tribal chairperson)
Affiliation: Fort Mojave Tribal Council, 500 Merriman Ave., Needles, CA 92363 (619) 326-4591.

MAESTAS, JOHN R. (Pueblo)
(advisor)
Affiliation: Council of Advisors, American Indian Heritage Foundation, 6051 Arlington Blvd., Falls Church, VA 22044 (703) 237-7500.

MAESTAS, MARJORIE (Pueblo)
(school principal)
Affiliation: Tesuque Day School, Route 11, Box 2, Santa Fe, NM 87501 (505) 982-1516.

MAGANTE, BENJAMIN, SR. (Luiseno)
(tribal chairperson)
Affiliation: Pauma Band of Mission Indians, P.O. Box 369, Pauma Valley, CA 92061 (760) 742-1289.

MAGEE, DENNIS (Luiseno Band Mission Indians) 1937-
(health administration)
Born October 9, 1937, Pala Indian Reservation, Calif. Education: San Diego City College, GE, 1957; San Diego State University, BS, 1962. Principal occupation: Health administration. Home address: Pala Mission Rd., P.O. Box 86, Pala, CA 92059 (619) 749-1410 (work). Affiliation: Administrator, Indian Health Council, Inc., Pauma Valley, CA, 1970-. Community activities: Board of Directors, San Diego Council of Community Clinics; Citizens Equal Opportunity Commission, City of San Diego; United Way of San Diego (board of directors); Advisory policy panel, Indian Health Branmch, State Department of Health Services; board of directors, Comprehensive Health Planning Association of San Diego, Riverside and Imperial Counties; among others. Memberships: Native American Training Associates Institute (board chairman); National Social Workers Techni-Culture Coalition (vice-president); Pauma Valley Community Association; California Association for Indian Health Administrators; Mental Health Association in California (board member); National Indian Health Board (board of directors); California Rural Indian Health Board (chairman, board of directors); Masters in Public Health Program for Native Americans, University of California, Berkeley (advisory board). Awards, honors: Recipient of Robert F. Kennedy Memorial Fellowship, 1970; selected as one of the "Ten Outstanding Young Men of San Diego" by the San Diego Junior Chamber of Commerce, 1971; selected as "San Diego North County Man of the Year" by the Northern San Diego County Associated Chamber of Commerce, 1971; awarded a "Resolution of Commendation" for outstanding community service by the California State Senate, 1972; awarded the "National Distiguished Community Service Award by the National Social Workers Techni-Culture Coalition, 1973; Dedication by Indian Health Center, 1976; Letter of Commendation, 1980, by President Jimmy Carter; Luna Wessel Distinguished Service Award, Californoa Rural Indian Health Board, 1986; Official Commendation, U.S. Senator Daniel K. Inouye, Chairperson of the Senate Select Committee on Indian Affairs, 1989. Interests: Testified before the Senate and House subcommittees on appropriations, Washington, D.C., 1971-. Biographical sources: Who's Who in California (California Historical Society); Who's Who in Human Service Professionals (National Reference Institute, Washington, D.C.); Who's Who in U.S. Executives.

MAGEE, DON (Luiseno)
(BIA field ofice director)
Affiliation: Palm Springs Field Office, Bureau of Indian Affairs, P.O. Box 2245, Palm Springs, CA 92263 (760) 416-2133 Fax 416-2687.

MAGISKAN, WILLIAM, JR.
(Indian band chief)
Affiliation: Aroland Indian band, Box 390, Nakina, Ontario, Canada P0T 2H0 (807) 329-5970.

MAGNAM, DR. VERONICA
(Indian school principal)
Affiliation: Beatrice Rafferty School, Pleasant Point Reservation, RR 1, Box 338, Perry, ME 04667 (207) 853-6085 Fax 853-6210.

MAHIEU, REGINA M.
(organization director)
Affiliation: Quad City League of Native Americans, 418 19th St., Rock Island, IL 61201.

MAHSETKY, MIKE
(director of legislative affairs-IHS)
Address & Affiliation: Director of Legislative Affairs, Indian Health Service, 5600 Fishers Lane, Rm. 6-22, Rockville, MD 20857.

MAIER, GARY E.
(Indian council commissioner)
Affiliation: Commissioner, Wyoming Indian Affairs Council, Community Services, U.S. West Bldg., Rm. 259B, 6101 Yellowstone, Cheyenne, WY 82002 (307) 777-6779 Fax 777-6779.

MAINES, BILL J. (Aleut) 1954-
(radio station general manager)
Born October 30, 1954, Anchorage, AK. Education:

Electronic Institute, Pittsburgh, AA, 1974. Principal occupation: General Manager. Home address: P.O. Box 109, 4667 Okakok St., Barrow, AK 99723 (907) 852-6046 (work). Affiliations: KDLG-AM, Dillingham, AK, 1977-88; KBRW-AM, Barrow, AK, 1988-. Other professional posts: Alaska Public Radio Network (board of directors); Alaska Native Communications Society (co-chair). Community activities: Choggiung Ltd. - Dillingham Village corporation. Memberships: Bristol Bay Native Corporation - regional corp.; Alaska Federation of Natives.

MAINVILLE, JOAN
(Indian band chief)
Affiliation: Couchiching Indian band, Box 723, Fort Frances, Ontario, Canada P9A 3N1 (807) 274-3228.

MAKIL, IVAN (Pima-Maricopa)
(tribal council president)
Affiliation: Salt River Pima-Maricopa Indian Community Council, 10005 E. Osborn, Scottsdale, AZ 85256 (480) 874-8000 Fax 874-8014.

MALA, CYNTHIA A. (Pretty, Good Talk Woman)
(Spirit Lake Nation) 1951-
(public administration)
Born June 28, 1951, St. Paul, Minn. Education: University of North Dakota, BA, 1981; University of South Dakota, 1988; PhD candidate - working on doctorate in educational leadership from UND. Principal occupation: Public administration. Address: Unknown. Affiliations: ProfessionalServices Director, Aberdeen Area Indian Health Service, Aberdeen, SD, 1987-89; Assistant Professor, Community Medicine and Rural Health and Associate Director, Center for Rural Health, University of North Dakota School of Medicine, Grand Forks, ND, 1989-91; executive director, Northern Plains Healthy Start, Aberdeen, SD, 1991-92; wrote and developed the Northern Plains Healthy Start Initiative; associate director, University of North Dakota's Center for Rural Health; Senior advisor to the Director, Indian Health Service, Rockville, MD, 1994-96; coordinator, Grand Forks Historic Preservation Commission, Grand Forks, ND 1997-98; executive director, North Dakota Indian Affairs Commission, Bismarck, ND, 1998-present. Other professional posts: Adjunct, Assistant Professor of Community Medicine and Rural Health with UND School of Medicine, 1989-; consultant & advisor to the Kaiser Family Foundation. Community activities: Indian Women's Health Steering Comittee; Foster parents Advisory Board. Awards, honors: Service/Appreciation Award, National Indian Health Board, 1995; TRIO Achiever Award for ASPIRE, University of North Dakota, 1995; Certificate of Appreciation, American Association of Indian Physicians, 1995; National TRIO Achiever Award, NCEOA, Washington, DC, 1996; Service Appreciation Award, IHS, 1996; Notable North Dakotan, Bismarck Tribune, 1998; Bush Leadership Fellowship, 1999; Good Housekeeping Award for Women in Government, 1999.

MALCOLM, JAN (Oneida)
(museum director)
Affiliation: Oneida Nation Museum, P.O. Box 365, Oneida, WI 54155 (414) 869-2768.

MALDONADO, RAYMOND
(BIA agency supt.)
Affiliation: Olympic Penninsula Agency, Bureau of Indian Affairs, P.O. Box 48, Aberdeen, WA 98550 (360) 533-9100.

MALLOTT, BYRON (Tlingit) 1943-
(chief executive officer)
Born April 6, 1943, Yakutat, Alaska. Education: Western Washington State College, 1961-64. Principal occupation: Chief executive officer. Resides in Juneau, AK. Address: Sealaska Corporation, One Sealaska Plaza, Suite 400, Juneau, AK 99801 (907) 586-1512 (work). Affiliations: Mayor, City of Yakutat, 1965; elected to City Council, City of Yakutat, 1968; local government specialist, Office of the Governor, Juneau, 1966-1967; special assistant to U.S. Senator Mike Gravel, Washington, DC, 1969; executive director, Rural Alaska Community Action Program, Inc., Anchorage, 1970; director, Local Affairs Agency, Office of the Governor, 1971-72; commissioner, Dept. of Community & Regional Affairs, State of Alaska, 1972-74; consultant, Alaska Natives Resources, Inc., 1974-78; president, Alaska Federation of Natives, Inc., 1977-

78; chairman of the board, Sealaska Corporation, Juneau, 1976-84; chief executive officer, Sealaska Corporation, Juneau, 1982-. *Other professional posts*: Owner Yakutat Bay Adventures (commercial fishing), 1974-; director, Alaska Airlines, 1982-; board member, Alaska United Drilling, Inc., 1982-; director, Federal Reserve Bank, Seattle Branch, 1982-; board member, United Bank of Alaska, 1984-; board member, Colville Tribal Enterprise Corp., 1985-; board member, The Mediation Institute, 1985-. *Community activities*: Rural Affairs Commission, State of Alaska, 1972-76; Alaska Native Foundation (vice chairman, 1975-79); Yak-Tat Kwaan, Inc. (Yakutat Village Corp.) (board of directors, 1974-78; chairman, 1976-77); B.M. Behrends Bank (director, 1975-84); Capital Site Planning Commission, State of Alaska, 1977-79; Governor's Rapportionment Board, State of Alaska (chairman, 1979-80); White House Fellowship Selection Commission-Western Region, 1978-83; Commercial Fisheries & Agricultural Bank, State of Alaska (director, 1979); University of Alaska Foundation (director, 1980-85). *Awards, honors*: Governor's Award for Service to Alaska, 1982; recipient of the Alaska Native Citizen of the Year Award from the Alaska Federation of Natives, 1982; Honorary Doctorate Degree in the Humanities by the University of Alaska, 1984. *Published works*: Several recent articles are One Day in the Life of a Native Chief Executive, in 2 parts, Alaska Native Magazine, Sept. & Oct., 1985; Byron's Brew, Alaska Business Monthly, Oct., 1985; Sealaska: Soon to Rival Oil Companies in Power? an interview with Byron Mallott, Alaska Industry, Sept., 1981.

MALOTKI, EKKEHART
(professor of languages)
Affiliation & Address: Dept. of Linguistics, Northern Arizona University, Flagstaff, AZ 86011. *Publications*: The Bedbugs' Night Dance and Other Hopi Tales of Sexual Encounter (University of Nebraska Press); Hopi Tales of Destruction (University of Nebraska Press); Kokopelli: The Making of an Icon (University of Nebraska Press, 2000).

MALOTTE, DALE S. (Te-Moak Western Shoshone)
(former tribal chairperson)
Affiliation: Tribal Council of the Te-Moak Western Shoshone Indians of Nevada, 525 Sinset St., Elko, NV 89801 (702) 738-9251.

MANAKAJA, LINCOLN (Havasupai)
(former tribal chairperson)
Affiliation: Havasupai Tribal Council, P.O. Box 10, Supai, AZ 86435 (520) 448-2961.

MAMAKWA, JAMES
(Indian band chief)
Affiliation: Kingfisher Lake Indian Band, Kingfisher Lake, Ontario, Canada P0V 1Z0 (807) 536-0067.

MANATOWA, ELMER, JR. (Sac & Fox)
(tribal chairperson)
Affiliation: Sac & Fox of Oklahoma Business Committee, Route 2, Box 246, Stroud, OK 74079 (918) 968-3526.

MANDAMIN, ELI
(Indian band chief)
Affiliation: Shoal Lake #39 Indian band, Kejick P.O., Shoal Lake, Ontario, Canada P0X 1E0 (807) 733-2560.

MANDAN, ROSELLA
(administrative officer-Indian health center)
Affiliation: Fort Berthold PHS Indian Health Center, New Town, ND 58763 (701) 627-4701.

MANDELL, KEITH ALAN (Paiute)
(tribal chairperson)
Affiliation: Pyramid Lake Paiute Tribal Council, P.O. Box 256, Nixon, NV 89424 (775) 574-1000.

MANDSAGER, RICHARD, M.D.
(health director)
Affiliation: Alaska Native Health Center, 255 Gambel St., Anchorage, AK 99501 (907) 279-6661.

MANESS, KATHRYN G. (*Starbright*)
(United Lumbee) 1931-
(retired)
Born February 19, 1931. *Address*: 2828 State Rte. NN, Centertown, MO 65023 (573) 584-3696. *Community*

activities: Missouri River Quilters Guild; United Lumbee, Black Bear Clan Council Person; Golden Hawk Society; Phoenix Society.

MANESS, PHILLIP
(Indian band chief)
Affiliation: Chippewas of Sarina, 93 Tashmoo Ave., Sarnia, Ontario, Canada N7T 7H5 (519) 336-8410.

MANESS, RAYMOND E. (*Tall Horse*)
(United Lumbee) 1928-
(retired)
Born September 23, 1928, Republic, Mo. *Education*: Some college. *Home address*: 2828 State Rte. NN, Centertown, MO 65023 (573) 584-3696. *Military service*: U.S. Navy 1948-52. *Community activities*: American Legion; Disabled American Veterans; United Lumbee - Black Bear Clan Council Person; Golden Hawk Society, vice-chief, assistant firekeeper, pipe carrier; Phoenix Society.

MANESS, SHERMAN
(organization president)
Affiliation: Ontario Federation of Indian Friendship Centres, 234 Eglinton Ave. East, Suite 207, Toronto, Ontario, Canada M4P 1K5 (416) 484-1411.

MANGUM, BETTY OXENDINE
(education director)
Affiliation: North Carolina State Dept. of Public Instruction, Division of Indian Education, 301 N. Wilmington St., Raleigh, NC 27601 (919) 715-1000.

MANKILLER, WILMA P. (Oklahoma Cherokee)
(former principal chief-Cherokee Nation of OK)
Born in northeastern Oklahoma. *Address & Affiliation*: Principal Chief (acting, 1985-87; elected, 1987-94), Cherokee Nation of Oklahoma, P.O. Box 948, Tahlequah, OK 74465 (918) 456-0671. *Interests*: Native rights issues; writing, reading, history; spending time with grandchildren (family). "I will continue to be involved. I'm going to try to organize rural Cherokee communities into doing Saturday academics... language, films, dinners, sharing cultural and historical issues. I've always been involved in these issues." *Published work*: Autobiography, "Mankiller: A Chief and Her People, by Wilma Mankiller & Michael Wallis (St. Martins Press, 1993)

MANN, CHERYL J. (Cheyenne River Sioux)
(administrator)
Born January 17, 1945, Cheyenne Agency, S.D. *Education*: Western State College of Engineering (Los Angeles, CA), ASEE, 1971; UCLA, 1971-73; University of New Mexico (Non-Profit Management), 1987. *Home address*: Resides in the Albuquerque, NM area. *Affiliation*: National Indian Youth Council, Albuquerque, NM (associate director, 1974-88; executive director, 1989-95). *Other professional post*: Editor, Americans Before Columbus, NIYC newspaper published 6x/year. *Community activities*: Youth athletic groups. *Membership*: Indian Executive Directors, Networking (chairperson-3 years). *Interests*: "Very active in youth athletics and Indian cultural activities - pow wows, etc."

MANN, DR. HENRIETTA
(Southern Cheyenne/Arapaho)
(college professor)
Affiliation: Native American Studies Dept., Montana State University, 2-179 Wilson Hall, P.O. Box 172340, Bozeman, MT 59717 (406) 994-3881 Fax 994-6879. Interests: American Indian religion.

MANNES, MARC
(editor)
Affiliation: American Indian Law Newsleter, American Indian Law Center, P.O. Box 4456, Station A, Albuquerque, NM 87196 (505) 277-5462.

MANNING, JOHN W. "JACK" (Fort Peck Sioux)
1950-
(attorney)
Born March 8, 1950, Miles City, Mont. *Education*: Dartmouth College, AB, 1972; Stanford University Law School, JD, 1975. *Principal occupation*: Attorney. *Home address*: 211 3rd Ave. N., Great Falls, MT 59401 (406) 727-3632 (work) *Affiliations*: Associate, Davis Polk & Wardwell, New York, NY 1975-80; Dorsey & Whitney Law Firm, Great Falls, MT (associate 1980-84; partner, 1984-) *Community activities*: Board mem-

ber of Neighborhood Housing Services & Great Falls Native American Center at various times.

MANNING, LINDSEY
(tribal chairperson)
Affiliation: Shoshone Paiute Business Council, Duck Valley Reservation, P.O. Box 219, Owyhee, NV 89832 (702) 757-3161.

MANOOK, RON
(institute president)
Affiliation: Institute of Alaska Native Arts, Fairbanks, AK 99707 (907) 456-7491 Fax 451-7268.

MANOR, PATRICIA K.
(administrator)
Affiliation: Native American Fish & Wildlife Society, 750 Burbank St., Boulder, CO 80020 (303) 466-1725.

MANSON, SPERO M. (Pembina Chippewa) 1950-
(medical anthropologist)
Born May 2, 1950, Everett, Wash. *Education*: University of Washington, BA, 1972; University of Minnesota, MA, 1975, PhD (Anthropology), 1978. *Principal occupation*: Mental health researcher. *Address*: Dept. of Psychiatry, UCHSC, Box A011-13, Denver, CO 80220 (303) 315-9232. *Affiliations*: Professor and director, Institute on Aging, School of Urban and Public Affairs, Portland State University, 1982-86; associate professor and director, Social Psychiatric Research, Dept. of Psychiatry, School of Medicine, Oregon Health Sciences University, 1982-86; adjunct associate professor of anthropology, Portland State University, 1982-86; director, National Center for American Indian & Alaska Native Mental Health Research, University of Colorado Health Sciences Center, Denver, 1986-; associate professor, Dept. of Psychiatry, University of Colorado Health Sciences Center, Denver, 1986-; editor-in-chief, American Indian and Alaska Native Mental Health Research. *Other professional posts*: Program co-director, Robert Wood Johnson Foundation's Healthy Nations Initiative, a six-year, $16 million effort to assist 15 Indian and Native communities in their struggle to reduce harm due to substance abuse by promoting comprehensive intervention strategies that integrates resources across formal and informal sectors of the local citizenry; recently awarded a $1.2 million grant by the Administration on Aging to establish and direct the Native Elder Health Care Resource Center (NEHCRC). *Consultant ships*: Billings Area Office, Indian Health Service, MT, 1984-; Northwest Portland Area Indian Health Board, 1985-; Alaska Native Health Board, 1985-. *Community activities*: National Institute of Mental Health Epidemiology & Services Research Review Committee, 1983-87; NIDA Advisory Committee on Prevention, 1983-85; Oregon State Governor's Task Force on Alcohol & Drug Abuse, 1984-86; vice-chair, Denver Indian Health & Family Services; board of directors, CO Gerontological Society. *Memberships*: American Anthropological Association; Gerontological Society of America; Society for Applied Anthropology (Fellow); Society for Medical Anthropology. *Awards, honors*: 1984 Oregon State System of Higher Education, Faculty Excellence Award; Phi Beta Kappa; State of Oregon Excellence Award in Higher Education (1985); Fulbright-Hays Scholar; CIC Traveling Scholar; National Science Foundation Scholarship; 1994 Researcher of the Year, The Colorado Public Health Association; 1995 Beverly Visiting Professor at the University of Toronto (a national award honoring significant contributions to the mental health field); received the Indian Health Service's Distinguished Service Award, July, 1996. *Interests*: Vocational - Diagnosis, epidemiology, treatment and prevention of serious psychological dysfunction and major mental illness across the developmental life span among American Indians & Alaska Natives. Avocational - Hunting, flyfishing, skiing, photography. *Published works*: Co-editor, books in preparation: American Indian Youth: Seventy-five Years of Psychosocial Research (Greenwood Press); New Directions in Prevention (Oregon Health Sciences University, 1982); Psychosocial Research with American Indian and Alaska Native Youth (Greenwood Press, 1984); Health and Behavior: A Research Agenda for American Indians (University of Colorado Health Sciences Center, 1988); editor, Medical Anthropology: Implications for Stress Prevention Across Cultures (National Institute of Mental Health, Government Printing Office). Numerous articles in professional journals.

MANUAL, HILDA
(BIA depty commissioner)
Affiliation: Deputy Commissioner of Indian Affairs, Bureau of Indian Affairs, 1849 C St., NW, MS: 4140-MIB, Washington, DC 20240 (202) 208-5116 (1993-).

MANUEL, EDWARD (Tohono O'odham)
(tribal chairperson)
Affiliation: Tohono O'odham Council, Sells, AZ 85634 (520) 383-2028.

MANUELITO, ETHEL M. (Navajo) 1954-
(associate director; consultant)
Born July 6, 1954, Fort Defiance, Ariz. *Education*: University of New Mexico, BS, 1977, MA, 1982; Western New Mexico University (Silver City), 3 years. *Principal occupation*: Associate director; consultant. *Home address*: P.O. Box 51, Tohatchi, NM 87325 (505) 733-2200 (work). *Affiliation*: Associate director for Direct Services, Tohatchi Special Education & Training Center, 1978-. *Other professional post*: Consultant to Navajo Initiative Project. *Community activities*: Gallup McKinley County Schools (Board of Education, secretary); University of New Mexico-Gallup Branch (Advisory Board Member); New Mexico School Board (Region I President). *Memberships*: Council for Exceptional Children; National School Board Association; Navajo Nation Public School Board Association. *Awards, honors*: Navajo Tribal Scholarships. *Interests*: "Travel to various parts of the U.S.; beadwork, crochet, sewing Native American clothes."

MANYARROWS, VICTORIA LENA
(Eastern Cherokee) 1956-
(social service/arts administrator; writer)
Born Aril 10, 1956, Des Moines, Iowa. *Education*: San Francisco State University, MSW, 1993. *Principal occupation*: Social service/arts administrator; writer. *Address*: Unknown. *Affiliation*: Support Service for the Arts, San Francisco, CA (administrator; co-director, 1981-). *Other professional post*: Counselor/administrator in various alcohol, substance abuse & homeless programs. Youth Empowerment Council member, United Indian Nations, Oakland, CA; volunteer, American Indian Contemporary Arts, San Francisco, & Indian Education Center, Oakland; volunteer, Brava! for Women in the Arts & Casa El Salvador (both in San Francisco). *Memberships*: ATLATL; National Service Organization for Native American Artists; Native Writer's Circle of the Americas; Wordcraft Circle of Native Writers & Apprentices; Indigenous Women's Network. *Awards, honors*: Graduate Honor Fellowship, San Francisco State University, 1991-92; Featured Poet (Summer, 1993), "Orphic Lute" journal, Seattle, WA. *Interests*: "Creative writing (especially poetry and essays) and teaching creative writing to Native women and youth. Have traveled extensively in Mexico & Central America (speak Spanish) and speak out on international Indian issues. Other interests: public health, environmental, and social psychological needs of Native women, children and communities; photography, video, and mixed media (poetry and visual art collaborative pieces)." *Published work*: Poetry, Songs From the Native Lands (Turtleland/Pajarta Press, 1995). *Poems & essays published in various journals & anthologies in the U.S. and Canada, including*: Without Discovery: A Native Response to Columbus (Broken Moon Press, 1992); The Colour of Resistance: A Contemporary Collection of Writing by Aboriginal Women (Sister Vision Press, Canada, 1993); Looking At the Words of Our People (Theytus Books, Canada, 1993); The Worlds Walking (New Rivers Press, 1994); Unsettling America: Race & Ethnicity in Contemporary American Poetry (Viking Penguin Press, 1994).

MANYBEADS, NORA
(school chairperson)
Affiliation: Aneth Community School, P.O. Box 600, Montezuma Creek, UT 84534 (801) 651-3271.

MAR, JOSE MATOS
(director of Inter-American Indian Institute)
Born November 1, Peru. *Education*: Universidad Nacional Mayor de San Marcos-Lima, Peru (Anthropology); Universidad de Paris (Ethnology), Post-graduate. *Principal occupation*: Director, Inter-American Indian Institute, #232, Colonia Pedregal de San Angel, Delegacion Alvaro Obregon C.P.01900, Mexico D.F. *Home address*: Popo No. 20-3 Col. Florida, Mexico, D.F. 01030 (6672724).

MARACLE, SYLVIA
(executive director)
Affiliation: Ontario Federation of Indian Friendship Centres, 234 Eglinton Ave. East, Suite 207, Toronto, Ontario, Canada M4P 1K5 (416) 484-1411.

MARCANO-QUINONES, MR. RENE
(Cibanacan) (Taino) 1941-
(tribal organizer)
Born September 16, 1941, Santurce, San Juan, P.R. *Education*: High school. *Home address*: 174 W. 107 St. #3E, New York, NY 10025 (212) 866-4573 (phone & fax). *Affiliation*: Principal Cacike, Taino Nation of the Antilles (more than 4,000), P.O. Box 883, New York, NY 10025, Puerto Rico & abroad. *Other professional posts*: Editor of bimonthly, bilingual tribal newsletter, the "Boletin Informativo de la Nacion Taina de las Antillas"; lecturer on Taino history, culture, heritage an restoration. *Interests*: "Impart conferences regarding Taino restoration efforts regarding culture, history, music and art." Principal organizer of the Taino restoration movement which began in the late 1980s. 1990 organized the Taino Indigenous Association which gave way in 1992 to the Taino Nation of the Antilles found in Puerto Rico, eastern Cuba and U.S. diaspora. One of the Natiuve American leaders and consultants advising the national Museum of the American Indian on the propriety of exhibiting and publishing objects of great cultural and spiritual sensitivity, and a source of information on Taino people in the Smithsonian's publication, "Creation's Journey: Native American Identity and Belief," (October 1994-Feb. 1997). *Biographical sources*: "The Native American Response to the Columbus Quincentenary," Multi-Cultural Review magazine, Jan. 1992, Vol. 1 No. 1, pp. 20-22.

MARCEL, PATRICK
(Indian band chief)
Affiliation: Athabasca Chipewyan Indian Band, Box 366, Fort Chipewyan, Alberta, Canada (403) 697-3730.

MARCELLAIS, ROMAN
(school principal)
Affiliation: Turtle Mountain Elementary School, P.O. Box 440, Belcourt, ND 58316 (701) 477-6471 Fax 477-6470.

MARCHAND, ARNOLD N. (Colville)
(museum director)
Affiliation: Colville Confederated Tribes Museum, Box 150, Nespelem, WA 99155 (509) 634-4711.

MARCHAND, DOROTHY
(school principal)
Affiliation: Paschal Sherman Indian School, Omak Lake Rd., Omak, WA 98841 (509) 826-2097.

MARCHAND, THELMA (Colville) 1932-
(tribal officer)
Born April 17, 1932, Okanogan County, Wash. *Education*: Wenatchee Junior College. *Principal occupation*: Secretary, Colville Business (Tribal) Council. *Home address*: 320 Columbia St., Omak, Wash. 98841.

MARCY, HOWARD K. (Diegueno)
(tribal council chairperson)
Affiliation: Mesa Grande Band of Mission Indians, P.O. Box 270, Santa Ysabel, CA 92070 (760) 782-3818.

MARGOLIN, MALCOLM 1940-
(publisher, writer)
Born October 27, 1940, Boston, Mass. *Education*: Harvard University, BA, 1964. *Principal occupation*: Publisher, writer. *Address*: P.O. Box 9145, Berkeley, CA 94709 (510) 549-3564 (office). *Affiliation*: News From Native California, Berkeley, CA, 1987-; publisher, Heyday Books, Berkeley, CA, 1975-. *Interests*: "Writing and publishing has focused on the history and ongoing cultures of California Indian people. A major commitment of both Heyday Books & "News from Native California" has been to provide a vehicle by which Native Californians can describe their history and culture in their own voices." *Published works*: Ohlone Way: Indian Life in San Francisco Area (Heyday Books, 1978); Way We Lived: Reminiscence, Stories, Songs (Heyday Books, 1981).

MARION-KULAS, CHERYL
(Oglala Lakota-Turtle Mountain Chippewa)
(director of Indian education)
Address: 325 Willow Lane, Bismarck, ND 58505-0440 (701) 328-2250 Fax 328-4770; E-mail: ckulas@maihi dpi.state.nd.us. *Affiliation*: Director of Indian Education, State Dept. of Public Instruction. Prior to current position, served as state's coordinator for Race & National Origin Equity; and Education Specialist to United Tribes Technical College. *Memberships*: National Indian Education Association; University of Arizona Alumni; University of North Dakota Alumni.

MARK, CHARLES
(Indian band chief)
Affiliation: Montagnais de Pakua Shipi Indian Band, St-Augustin, Quebec G0G 2R0 (418) 947-2253.

MARKISHTUM, HUBERT (Makah)
(tribal chairperson)
Affiliation: Makah Tribal Council, P.O. Box 115, Neah Bay, WA 98357 (360) 645-2201.

MARKOWITZ, HARVEY
(acting director-Indian center)
Affiliation: D'Arcy McNickle Center for American Indian History, 60 W. Walton St., Chicago, IL 60610 (312) 255-3564 Fax 255-3513. E-mail: mcnickle@newberry. org.

MARKS, C. HARDAWAY
(council chairperson)
Affiliation: Virginia Council on Indians, 8007 Discovery Dr., Richmond, VA 23229-8699 (804) 662-9285.

MARKS, COLEEN KELLEY (Susquahana) 1951-
(museum curator, arts consultant)
Born January 12, 1951, Altoona, Pa. *Education*: College of the Redwoods (Eureka, CA), AA, 1978; Humboldt State University (Arcata, CA), two BA's, 1988. *Principal occupation*: Museum curator, American Indian arts consultant. *Address*: P.O. Box 295, Orick, CA 95555 (707) 488-3545. *Affiliations*: Curator, End of the Trail Museum, Klamath, CA, 1993-98; consultant of Native American arts, Orick, CA, 1979-. *Other professional posts*: Assistant director of California Indian Project, Lowie Museum of Anthropology (Berkeley, CA), 1988-89; director/curator, Clarke Memorial Museum, Eureka, CA (7 years); Redwood National Park, Patrick's Point State Park, and Del Norte County Historical Society - curated all collections (2 1/2 years). *Community activities*: Past vice president, YWCA; past member of Humboldt County Status of Women Commission; past president of Humboldt Open Door Clinic; past chair of Women's History Month for Humboldt County; past member, City of Arcata Design Assistance Committee; current member, Alice Spinas Basketry Collection Committee; board member, SPPLIA, Sumeg Yurok Indian Village. *Membership*: Phi Kappa Phi. *Interests*: "Collecting American Indian art & books; have traveled in Europe, Canada, Mexico, Caribbean & the USA. Have made numerous trips to Europe to view & study American Indian art in museum collections." *Curated Exhibits*: "Elizabeth Conrad Hickox: Baskets From the Center of the World," Reese Bullen Gallery, Humboldt State University, 1/90; "From Classic to Contemporary: The Basketry of Northwestern California," Muckenthaler Cultural Center, Fullerton, CA, 5-7/91; "From Women's Hands: The Basketry of Lena Reed McCovey and Ethel Jones Williams" Reese Bullen Gallery, Humboldt State University, 11/92; "Her Mind Made Up: Weaving Caps the Indian Way", Reese Bullen Gallery, Humboldt State University 4/97; among others. *Published works*: Editor, The Hover Collection of Karuk Baskets (Clarke Memorial Museum, 1985); co-authored with Ron Johnson, "From Women's Hands: The Basketry of Lena Reed McCovey and Ethel Jones Williams," (Humboldt State University, 1992); Her Mind Made Up: Weaving Caps the Indian Way," with Ron Johnson (Humboldt State University, 1997).

MARKS, PATRICIA ANN 1954-
(attorney, lobbyist, consultant)
Born March 2, 1954, Brockport, N.Y. *Education*: S.U.N.Y. at Brockport, BS, 1976; Georgetown University Law Center, JD, 1987. *Principal occupation*: Attorney, lobbyist, consultant. *Home address*: 15992 AE Mullinix Rd., Woodbine, MD 21797. *Affiliations*: Personal staff member, U.S. Senator James Abourezk, Washington, DC, 1975-76 (during this period, Sen.

Abourezk was chairman of the Senate Indian Affairs Subcommittee of the Senate Interior and Insular Affairs Committee); professional staff member, American Indian Policy Review Commission, Washington, DC, 1976-77; legislative assistant, U.S. Senate Select Committee on Indian Affairs, Washington, DC, 1977-79; vice president and co-founder, Karl A. Funke & Associates, Inc., Washington, DC, 1979- (a lobbying & consulting firm which represents Indian tribes, national Indian organizations, business and local governments). *Other professional post*: Co-founder and officer, AAA Roofing Co. *Memberships*: National Congress of American Indians; ABA Student Bar Association. *Awards, honors*: National Indian Health Board Award for Service, 1983. *Interests*: "Indian health; Indian legislative specialist; Indian Child Welfare Act; national Indian budget issues; Indian economic development." *Published work*: American Indian Policy Review Commission Final Report, U.S. Congress.

MARKWARDT, HOLLY JEAN (Ojibway) 1970-
(American Indian admissions counselor)
Born October 27, 1970, Virginia, Minn. *Education*: St. Cloud State University, B.A., 1994; University of Minnesota, M.A., 1994. *Principal occupation*: American Indian admissions counselor. *Home address*: 8748 Kilbirnie Ter., Brooklyn Park, MN 55443. *Affiliation*: University of Minnesota, Minneapolis, MN.

MARKUSSUN, BERNADETTE (Washoe)
(tribal chairperson)
Affiliation: Carson Colony Community Council, 400 Shoshone St., Carson City, NV 89702 (702) 883-6431.

MARNEY, MARGIE E. (Cherokee) 1948-
(educator)
Born February 25, 1948, Alva, Okla. *Education*: Phillips University (Enid, OK), B.S., 1970; University of Northwestern Oklahoma (Alva, OK), Masters of Reading & L.D. Educ., 1983; Oklahoma State University, Admin. Cert., 1990. *Principal occupation*: Educator. *Address*: Enid Public Schools, 2102 Beverly Dr., Enid, OK 73703 (580) 242-7185 Fax 242-6177; E-mail: mmarney@ionet.net. *Affiliation*: Elementary Principal & Director of Indian Education, Enid Public Schools, Enid, OK, 1970-present. *Other professional posts*: Professor, Phillips University; Enid higher education instructor. *Community activities*: "Keeper of the Plains" scholarship officer & board member; president & board member, Cherokee Reading Council; Intertribal Club member. *Memberships*: National Education Association; Oklahoma Education Association; International Reading Association; Oklahoma Reading Association; Cherokee Strip Reading Council (president, 1985-); National Council on Indian Education; NIEA member; Oklahoma Indian Education Association. *Interests*: "Avid reader and learner; parent of four active children in education; educator of kindergarten to college level."

MAROQUIN, GENE (Apache of Oklahoma)
(tribal chairperson)
Affiliation: Apache Tribe of Oklahoma Business Committee, P.O. Box 1220, Anadarko, OK 73005 (405) 247-9493.

MARQUARDT, GENE
(executive director)
Affiliation: Southwestern Association for Indian Arts, P.O. Box 31066, Santa Fe, NM 87594 (505) 983-5220 Fax 983-7647.

MARQUAT, CLARK, M.D.
(chief medical officer)
Affiliation: Oklahoma Area Office, Indian Health Service, Five Corporate Plaza, 3625 NW 56th St., Oklahoma City, OK 73102 (405) 231-4796.

MARQUES, SALLY (Shoshone)
(tribal chairperson)
Affiliation: Ely Colony Council, 16 Shoshone Cir., Ely, NV 89301 (702) 289-3013.

MARQUEZ-BAINES, CAROL
(center director)
Affiliation: Urban Indian Child Resource Center, Oakland, CA 94610 (510) 832-2386.

MARQUEZ, DERON (Serrano)
(tribal council chairperson)
Affiliation: San Manuel Band of Mission Indians, P.O. Box 266, Patton, CA 92369 (909) 864-8933.

MARQUEZ, JAMES
(Indian education center director)
Affiliation: Foothill Indian Education Alliance, P.O. Box 1418, El Dorado, CA 95623 (916) 621-3096 Fax 621-3097.

MARSH, DR. CAROLYN
(school director)
Affiliation: Muckleshoot Tribal School, 39015 172nd Ave. SE, Auburn, WA 98002 (253) 931-6709 Fax 939-2922.

MARSH, LORNA (Nez Perce)
(trading post owner)
Affiliation: Marsh's Trading Post, 1105 36th St. N., Lewiston, ID 83501 (208) 743-5778.

MARSHALL, CHRISTOPHER
(museum director)
Affiliation: Maine Tribal Unity Museum, Quaker Hill Rd., Unity, ME 04988 (207) 948-3131.

MARSHALL-BRINGS PLENTY, CARLA RAE *(Oyate Wowakiye Wi)* (Cheyenne River Sioux) 1966-
(education, graphics)
Born May 7, 1966, Bitberg, Germany (USAF). *Education*: Black Hills State College (Spearfish, SD), Associate of Science, 1987. *Principal occupation*: Education, graphics. *Home address*: Address unknown. *Affiliation*: HP/DP Task Force Coordinator, Cheyenne River Sioux Tribe, Eagle Butte, SD, 1990-91; Indian Country Today/Lakota Times, Rapid City, SD (classified advertising representative, 1992-93; advertising sales director, 1993); administrative assistant, editor, education coordinator, InterTribal Bison Cooperative, Rapid City, SD, 1993-. *Other professional posts*: Write monthly and annual reports along with articles and ads. *Awards, honors*: YMCA Scholarship; Crazy Horse Memorial Scholarship; Kevin Whirlwind Horse Memorial. *Community activities*: "I was YMCA Chapter Coordinator for the Iron Lightning Community, located on the Cheyenne River Sioux Reservation. This volunteer work involved planning and coordinating activities for the youth in the community; also I was secretary for the two powwow committees, the Iron Lighting Community and Lakota Ominiciya at Black Hills State."

MARTEL, PAT
(Indian band chief)
Affiliation: Hat River Dene Indian Band, Box 1638, Hay River, Northwest Territory X0E 0R0 (403) 874-6701.

MARTELL, PAM
(education coordinator)
Affiliation: Michigan Indian Education Office, Dept. of Education, P.O. Box 30008, Lansing, MI 48909 (517) 373-6059.

MARTGAN, REBECCA
(BIA supt. for education)
Affiliation: Standing Rock Agency, Bureau of Indian Affairs, Fort Yates, ND 58538 (701) 854-3497.

MARTIN, ALBERT (Tyne Maidu)
(rancheria chairperson)
Affiliation: Berry Creek Rancheria Tribal Council, 5 Tyme Way., Oroville, CA 95966 (916) 534-3859.

MARTIN, AMY (Pomo)
(rancheria chairperson)
Affiliation: Dry Creek Rancheria, P.O. Box 607, Geyserville, CA 95441 (707) 857-3045.

MARTIN, ANNIE (Eskimo)
(village coordinator)
Affiliation: Point Lay Native Village, P.O. Box 101, Point Lay, AK 99759 (907) 833-2428.

MARTIN, BONNIE
(BIA education administrator)
Affiliation: Choctaw Field Office, Bureau of Indian Affairs, 421 Powell St., Philadelphia, MS 39350 (601) 656-1521.

MARTIN, BRUCE W. (*Ta-ma-tet*)
(Delaware of Oklahoma) 1962-
(Indian center executive director)
Born August 15, 1962, Webb City, Mo. *Education*: College High School, Bartlesville, OK. *Principal occupation*: Indian center executive director. *Address*: 1423 Haskell Ave., Lawrence, KS 66046 (785) 841-7202 Fax 841-7255. E-mail: bmartin@pelathe.org. Website: www.pelathe.org. *Affiliation*: Executive director, Pelathe Community Resources Center, Lawrence, KS. *Other professional posts*: Director, Haskell Indian Nations University Upward Bound; director, New Dawn Native Dancers. *Awards, honors*: 1997 & 1999 Arena Director (3rd Favorite) in Oklahoma by Oklahoma Indian Times; 1999 Native American Parent of the Year (KANAE). *Community activities*: Co-sponsor, Lawrence High School, Native American Club; co-dirctor, "Battle of the Plains" Youth Pow-Wow Contest. *Memberships*: New Dawn Native Dancers; Intertribal Indian Club of Tulsa; Lenape Gourd Dance Society. *Interests*: "I have served on several pow-wow committees and enjoy traveling to pow-wow and stomp dances."

MARTIN, DOUGLAS
(Indian band chief)
Affiliation: Micmacs of Gesgapegiag Indian Band, Maria Indan Reserve, Box 1280, Maria, Quebec, Canada G0C 1Y0 (418) 759-3441.

MARTIN, JACK B.
(associate professor)
Affiliation: Director of Linguistics & Associate Professor of English, College of William & Mary, VA. *Published works*: A Dictionary of Creek/Muskogee, co-author with Margaret Mauldin; Totkv Mocvse/New Fire: Creek Folktales, edited and trans. with Margaret Mauldin & Juanita McGirt.

MARTIN, JAMES T. (Poarch Creek)
(executive director)
Address: 711 Stewarts Ferry Pike, Suite 100, Nashville, TN 37214 (615) 872-7900 Fax 872-7417; E-Mail: 102414.1756@compuserve.com. *Affiliation*: Executive Director, United South & Eastern Tribes (USET), Inc., Nashville, TN; president, Calumet Development Corp., Nashville, TN. *Other professional posts*: Tribal administrator, Poarch Creek Indians, Atmore, AL, 1986-95; served for 8 years as a member of the USET Board of Directors, representing the Poarch Creek Indians; current member of the Federal Advisory Committee for HHS/DOI; current member of Indian Health Service, Contract Support Work Group; current member of the 638 Re-Invention Lab for Self-Determination Contracts under both the Indian Health Service and the Bureau of Indian Affairs.

MARTIN, JERRY
(museum director)
Affiliation: Mid-America All-Indian Center Museum, 650 N. Seneca, Wichita, KS 67203 (316) 262-5221 ext. 41 Fax 262-4216.

MARTIN, JOY
(BIA Indian education)
Affiliation: Oklahoma Education Office, Bureau of Indian Affairs, 4149 Highline Blvd., Suite 380, Oklahoma City, OK 73180 (405) 945-6051 Fax 945-6057.

MARTIN, KALLEN M. (Mohawk)
(radio station manager)
Affiliation: CKON - 97.3 FM, Akwesasne Communications Society, P.O. Box 140, Rooseveltown, NY 13683 (518) 358-3426.

MARTIN, LEO
(commission director)
Affiliation: Maine Indian Affairs Commission, State House Sta. #38, Augusta, ME 04333 (207) 287-5800.

MARTIN, MARY ANN (Cahuilla)
(Indian band chairperson)
Affiliation: Augustine Band of Mission Indians, P.O. Box 846, Coachella, CA 92236 (760) 398-4722.

MARTIN, MICHAEL (Mohaw/Onondaga)
(student; national rep-AISES)
Education: Major in Economics, Buffalo State College. *Principal occupation*: Student. *Address*: Buffalo State College, P.O. Box 136, Buffalo, NY 14213. *Affiliation*: National representative, AISES, Boulder, CO.

MARTIN, PATRICIA L.
(Indian education supervisor)
Affiliation: Supervisor, Indian Education Office, Washington State Dept. of Public Instruction, Old Capitol Bldg., P.O. Box 47200, Olympia, WA 98504 (360) 753-3635.

MARTIN, PETER J. (White Earth Chippewa) 1937-
(federal government administrator)
Born July 21, 1937, White Earth Indian Reservation, White Earth, Minn. *Education*: University of New Mexico, BA, 1967. *Principal occupation*: Federal government administrator-Indian affairs. Resides in White Earth, MN. *Affiliations*: Administrative manager, Albuquerque Indian School, 1966-1969; administrative director, Institute of American Indian Arts, Santa Fe, 1969-70; executive assistant, 1970, chief, 1970-72, Plant Management Engineering Center, B.I.A., Denver, CO; chief, Indian Technical Assistance Center, Denver, 1972-77; program specialist, Muskogee Area Office, BIA, 1977-80; owner, Indian consultant business, American Indian Programs, White Earth, MN, 1980-. *Memberships*: Anishnabe Akeeng (The People's Land); National Congress of American Indians; Minnesota Indian Contactor's Association; Minnesota Democratic Farm Labor Party - National Roster of Buy Indian Contractor's. *Awards, honors*: Certificate of Superior Performance, Dept. of the Interior, BIA (for service in connection with the placement of 220 Job Corps employees, July, 1969); Dept. of the Interior, Bureau of Indian Affairs, 20-year Service Pin, April, 1978. *Interests*: Interested in and work for betterment of all American Indians; presently engaged as nationwide consultant in American Indian Programs (sole proprietorship enterprise); have visited over 200 Indian reservations and worked with respective tribal councils and program heads; research, writing articles and books, and study of American Indian tribes and involvement with Indian-Federal-State-Municipal programs and relationships.

MARTIN, PHILLIP (*Tulliokchiishko*)
(Mississippi Choctaw) 1926-
(tribal chief)
Born March 13, 1926, Philadelphia, Miss. *Education*: Cherokee (NC) High School, 1945; Meridian (MS) Junior College, 1955-57. *Principal Occupation*: Chief, Mississippi Band of Choctaw Indians. *Address*: P. O. Box 6010 - Choctaw Branch, Philadelphia, MS 39350 (601) 656-5251. *Affiliations*: Mississippi Band of Choctaw Indians (chief, 1959-65, 1971-75, 1979-; president, National Indian Management Service, Philadelphia, MS, 1975-). *Other Professional Posts*: Founder & past president, United South & Eastern Tribes, 1968-1969, 1971-72; president, National Tribal Chairmen's Association, 1981-83. *Military Service*: U.S. Air Force, 1945-55. *Community Activities*: Mississippi Band of Choctaw Indians (councilman, 1957-66, 1971-75, 1977-79); Choctaw Housing Authority (chairman of board, 1964-1971); Choctaw Community Action Agency (executive director, 1966-71); Chata Development Company (president-board of directors, 1969-75); Haskell Indian Junior College (president-board of regents, and board member, 1970-76); Chahta Enterprise, Choctaw Greetings Enterprise, and Choctaw Electronics Enterprise (chairman). *Memberships*: National Tribal Chairmen's Association; National Congress of American Indians; United South and Eastern Tribes; Americans for Indian Opportunity; American Indian Policy Review Commission (member, Task Force 7); Master's in Public Health for Native Americans Program, University of California at Berkeley (advisory committee); Neshoba County Chamber of Commerce. *Awards, Honors*: Indian Council Fire, Indian Achievement Award; United South and Eastern Tribes Leadership Award, 1984; American Vocational Association's 1987 Award of Merit for the successful work of the tribe's Vocational Education program; the 1988 statewide Employer Support of the Guard and Reserve Outstanding Employer award; the 1988 HUD Certificate of National Merit in the National Recognition Program for Urban Development Excellence for the tribe's innovative Early Childhood Education Center; the United Indian Development Association's Jay Silverheels Award; the Minority Supplier/Distributor of the Year award from the Small Business Administration and the Minority Business Administration; the "Soar Like an Eagle" achievement award from the United Indian Youth Organization (UNITY), and an economic achievement award from the U.S. Department of Housing and Urban Develop-

ment (HUD). *Interests*: Indian tribal government development and economic development. During his most recent tenure as Chief (since 1979), reservation unemployment rates have declined from around 50% to their current level of about 20%. He has been responsible for establishment of an industrial park, a tribally-owned construction company, and several public service enterprises, such as the Choctaw Transit Authority, and Choctaw Utility Commission. Most importantly, though, he has developed the Chahta Enterprise, which assembles automotive wiring harnesses in three plants for the Ford Motor Company and small motors for United Technologies. In addition, he created the Choctaw Greetings Enterprise, which handfinishes greeting cards for the American Greetings Corporation of Cleveland, Ohio — the first plant built on an Indian reservation through use of state industrial revenue bonds. *Biographical sources*: Books - Tribal Assets: The Rebirth of Native America, by Robert White; The Choctaws, by Emilie U. Lepthien; Providence, by Will Campbell. Articles - "Reader's Digest," Nov. 1984; "Fortune" Magazine, April 19, 1993.

MARTIN, RENEE (Turtle Mountain Chippewa)
(college instructor)
Affiliation: Leech Lake Tribal College, 6530 U.S. Hwy. 2 NW, Cass Lake, MN 56633 (218) 335-4220 Fax 335-4209.

MARTIN, ROBERT G.
(college president)
Affiliation: Haskell Indian Nations University, 155 Indian Ave. #1305, Lawrence, KS 66046 (785) 749-8404 Fax 749-8406.

MARTIN, THOMAS EVERETT
(Indian band chief)
Affiliation: Eel River Bar Indian band, Box 1444, Dalhousie, NB, Canada E0K 1B0 (506) 684-2366.

MARTIN, TONY
(tribal town king)
Affiliation: Kialagee Tribal Town, 318 S. Washla, Box 332, Wetumka, OK 74883 (405) 452-3413.

MARTIN-KEKABAH, TWILA (Chippewa)
(tribal chairperson)
Affiliation: Turtle Mountain Tribal Council, P.O. Box 900, Belcourt, ND 58316 (701) 477-5198.

MARTINE, CYNTHIA "CINDY"
(Jicarilla Apache/Navajo) 1964-
(manufacturing engineer)
Born November 3, 1964, Gallup, N.M. *Education*: New Mexico State University, BS, 1987. *Principal occupation*: Manufacturing engineer. *Home address*: 685 N. Greece Rd., Rochester, NY 14626 (716) 392-8397. *Affiliation*: Eastman Kodak Co., Rochester, NY 1988-. *Community activities*: spokesman, Native American Council at Kodak; Native American Cultural Center, Rochester, NY; Friends of Ganodogan, Victor, NY (Board of Trustee member); co-chair, Native American Women's Recognition Event 1994. *Membership*: American Indian Science & Engineering Society (AISES) (board member, treasurer). *Interests*: "Very interested in helping young Indian students become interested in science, math, engineering. Have done numerous workshops on science projects for young students (grades K-8). Recently (I) did a workshop for young women (grades 6-8) in expanding Your Horizons in Science & Math. I strongly believe that our Indian people are becoming more prominent in their communities; reaching out to the young people and introducing opportunities for our young people in all arenas. I truly enjoy speaking to young people about opportunities in science & engineering and doing science projects with young students. I believe our young people can make great strides in any fields they choose because they have support systems in place to help them, such as AISES." *Biographical sources*: "Minority Programs & Mentoring," (biography) in Chemical & Engineering News 2/8/93; "Corporate Role Model," in Patriots Magazine - 1992 Native American Heritage Issue.

MARTINE, DAVID BUNN (*Chee/Waukus*)
(Shinnecock/Montauk (Algonquian)-
Chiricahua Apache) 1960-
(museum director-curator)
Born June 11, 1960, Southampton, N.Y. *Education*:

University of Oklahoma, BFA, 1982; Institute of American Indian Arts, 1983; Central State University, MEd, 1984. *Principal occupation*: Artist, museum director. *Address*: P.O. Box 1285, Shinnecock Reservation, Southamtpon, NY 11969 (631) 287-6931 (phone & fax). E-mail: cswmartine@hotmail.com. Website: www.amerinda.org. *Affiliation*: Director, Shinnecock Nation Museum Cultural Center Complex; director, Channel 25 Cable Vision, "Voices of Native America," Shinnecock Indian Tribe, Southampton, NY. *Other professional posts*: Professional artist - oil paintings - wood carvings; board member, American Indian Artiosts (Amerinda), New York, NY; Museum curator/exhibit designer, Shinnecock Nation Cultural Center & Museum, 2001; Book Illustrations: The Montaukett Indians of Eastern Long Island, Syracuse University, 2001; Fine artist; lecturer, Cooper Union, New York, NY, 1989-92. *Exhibits*: Rogers Memorial Library, Southampton, NY, 2001; "Whaling: A Cultural Odyssey", Sag Harbor Whaling & Historical Museum, NY, 2001; "Rider With No Horse," Artists Collective, Native Americans of New York City Area; The Native American Experience: Long Island, New York & Beyond, "We Are All Connected" - New York, NY, 1997. Selected Commissions: Children's Mural, Challenge America Grant joint project, Family Preservation Center, Shinnecockk Reservation, Southampton, NY 2002; "The Peaceful People and the First Nations Mural," American Friends Service Committee, c/o Amerinda, Inc., New York, NY 2001; Shinnecock Indian Wigwam Replica, full-size scale exhibit, "Treasures of Long Island" exhibition, Museums at Stony Brook, NY, 1998. *Community activities*: member, Governance Committee of the Shinnecock Indian Nation Tribal Council; *Membership*: North Sea Poetry Scene (poetry club); Suffolk County Archaeological Association. *Interests*: Playing piano; writing poetry; teaching; environmental preservation movement; civil rights issues of Native American community; host, "Voices of Native America" Cablevision, Channel 25, Riverhead, NY; proposal reader, evaluator, Administration for Native Americans, Dept. of HHS, Washington, DC, 1991. *Biographical source*: "The Shinnecock Indians: A Culture History," (Ginn, 1984).

MARTINEZ, ALFRED G.
(school principal)
Affiliation: Casa Blanca Day School, P.O. Box 940, Bapchule, AZ 85221 (602) 315-3489.

MARTINEZ, CAMERON (Pueblo)
(BIA agency supt.)
Affiliation: Northern Pueblos Agency, Bureau of Indian Affairs, Box 4269, Fairview Station, Espanola, NM 87533 (505) 753-1400.

MARTINEZ, LEE, Jr. (Jicarilla Apache)
(radio station manager)
Affiliation: KCIE - 90.5 FM, Jicarilla Apache Tribe, P.O. Box 603, Dulce, NM 87528 (505) 759-3681.

MARTINEZ, PERRY (San Ildefonso Tewa)
(pueblo governor)
Affiliation: San Ildefonso Pueblo Tribal Council, Rt. 5, Box 315-A, Santa Fe, NM 87501 (505) 455-2273.

MARTINEZ, REYES (Picuris Pueblo)
(pueblo governor)
Affiliation: Picuris Pueblo Council, P.O. Box 127, Penasco, NM 87553 (505) 587-2519.

MARTINEZ, ROBERT C.
(school principal)
Affiliation: Taos Day School, P.O. Drawer X, Taos, NM 87571 (505) 758-3652.

MARTZ, MICHAEL
(TV executive producer)
Affiliation: Bethel Broadcasting, Inc., Yup'ik Eskimo Station, P.O. Box 468, Bethel, AK 99559 (907) 543-3131.

MASAYESVA, VERNON (Hopi)
(tribal chairperson)
Affiliation: Hopi Tribal Council, P.O. Box 123, Kykotsmovi, AZ 86039 (602) 734-2445.

MASAYESVA, VICTOR, Jr. (Hopi)
(film producer/director)
Born in 1951 in Hotevilla, Ariz. *Education*: Princeton University, BA, 1973; University of Arizona (graduate

studies). *Principal occupation*: Film producer/director. *Address*: P.O. Box 747, Hotevilla, AZ 86030. He has created a body of video & photographic work that represents the culture & traditions of Native Americans - particularly the Hopi of Southwest Arizona - through poetic visualizations. Masayesva employs high tech computer animation & graphics in lyrical translations of Hopi myths, rituals & history. Articulating the richness of his heritage in his own language, he allows the Hopi voice to be heard. *Videos produced, directed & photographed*: "Hopiit" (lyrical work observing Hopi cultural activities through the cycle of the seasons), 15 minutes, color, 1982; "Itam Hakim, Hopiit" (poetic visualization of Hopi philosophy & prophesy - myths, religion, legends & history of the Hopi people), 58 minutes, color, 1985; "Ritual Clowns" (the traditions & myths of their emergence in the plazas of Southwest Native American communities), 18 minutes, color, 1988; "Pot Starr" (addresses ceramic designs, computer analysis & interpretation), 6 minutes, color, 1990; "Siskyavi - The Place of Chasms" (presents the ceramic traditions of Native Americans), 28 minutes, color, 1991. *Awards, honors*: His numerous awards include fellowships from the Ford Foundation, the Rockefeller Foundation, and the Southwest Association on Indian Affairs; and grants from the National Endowment for the Arts, and the Arizona Commission on the Arts; he was guest artist and artist-in-residence at the School of the Art Institute of Chicago, Princeton University, & the Yellowstone Summer Film/Video Institute, Montana State University. His videotapes have been exhibited internationally at festivals and institutions including the Native American Film & Video Festival, New York; the Museum of Modern Art, New York; World Wide Video Festival, The Hague, Netherlands; Whitney Museum of American Art Biennial, New York; San Francisco Art Institute; and the American Indian Contemporary Arts "Festival 2000," San Francisco.

MASON, GLENN
(museum director)
Affiliation: Cheney Cowles Museum, Eastern Washington State Historical Society, West 2316 First Ave., Spokane, WA 99204 (509) 456-3931.

MASON, K. GAYLE
(executive director)
Affiliation: Union of Ontario Indians, 27 Queen St. East, 2nd Floor, Toronto, Ontario, Canada M5C 1R2 (416) 366-3527.

MASON, RUSSELL "BUD", Sr. (Mandan/Hidatsa)
(tribal chairperson)
Affiliation: Three Affiliated Tribes Business Council, HC 3, Box 2, Administration Bldg., New Town, ND 58763 (701) 627-4781.

MASON, VELMA
(BIA office director)
Affiliation: Bureau of Indian Affairs, Office of Alcohol & Substance Abuse Prevention, 1849 C St., NW, MS: 4140-MIB, Washington, DC 20240 (202) 208-6179.

MASSA, JOSEPH (Santee Sioux)
(casino general manager)
Affiliation: Royal River Casino, Santee Sioux Tribe, P.O. Box 283, Flandreau, South Dakota 57028 (605) 997-3891.

MASSEY, DALLAS, SR. (White Mountain Apache)
(tribal chairperson)
Affiliation: White Mountain Apache Tribal Council, P.O. Box 700, Whiteriver, AZ 85941 (928) 338-4346.

MASTEN, SUSAN M. (Yurok)
(tribal chairperson)
Affiliation: Yurok Tribe, 1034 Sixth St., Eureka, CA 95501 (707) 444-0433.

MATCHEWAN, JEAN-MAURICE
(Indian band chief)
Affiliation: Barriere Lake (Algonquin) Indian Band, Rapid Lake, Parc de la Verendrye, Quebec, Canada J0W 2C0 (819) 824-1734.

MATHESON, WILLIAM E. (Snohomish)
(tribal chairperson)
Affiliation: Snohomish Tribal Council, Arlington, WA.

MATHEWS, DEREK (Cherokee) 1951-
(educator; events promoter; media specialist)
Born September 10, 1951, Chicago, Ill. *Education*: College of Santa Fe, BA, 1974; Governors State University, MA, 1977; University of New Mexico (Graduate work)1979-85. *Principal occupation*: Educator; events promoter; media specialist. *Address & Affiliation*: Director, Gathering of Nations, 3301 Coors Rd., NW, Suite R-300, Albuquerque, NM 87120 (505) 836-2810 Fax 839-0475. E-mail: derekmathews@gathering ofnations.com; Website: www.gatheringofnations.com (work). *Other professional post*: Dean of Students, University of New Mexico, Albuquerque, NM. *Awards, honors*: Recipient of Media Grant, National Endowment for the Humanities, 1980. *Interests*: Traveled Europe, South Central America, Canada, and Asia.

MATHIAS, ISAAC
(Indian band chief)
Affiliation: Beaverhouse Indian Band, Box 1022, Kirkland Lake, Ontario, Canada P2N 3L4 (705) 567-4713.

MATHIAS, JOE
(Indian band chief)
Affiliation: Squamish Indian band, Box 86131, North Vancouver, B.C., Canada V7L 4J5 (604) 985-7711.

MATHIESON, LLOYD
(rancheria chairperson)
Affiliation: Chicken Ranch Rancheria, P.O. Box 1159, Jamestown, CA 95327 (209) 984-3057.

MATHIS, AMY W.
(school principal)
Affiliation: Dlo'ay Azhi Community School, P.O. Box 789, Thoreau, NM 87323 (505) 862-7525 Fax 862-7910.

MATRIOUS, SUSAN (Ojibwe)
(editor)
Affiliation: "Win-Awaenen-Nisitotung," Saulte Ste. Marie Tribe of Chippewa Indians, 2218 Shunk Rd., Saulte Ste. Marie, MI 49783 (906) 635-6050.

MATT, FRED (Confederated Salish & Kootenai)
(tribal chairperson)
Affiliation: Tribal Council of the Confederated Salish & Kootenai Tribes, P.O. Box 278, Pablo, MT 59855 (406) 675-2700.

MATTERN, PHYLLIS (Brotherton)
(tribal vice chairperson)
Affiliation: Brotherton Indians of Wisconsin, AV2848 Witches Lake Rd., Woodruff, WI 54568 (715) 542-3913.

MATTHEWS, ALEX
(former tribal chairperson)
Affiliation: Pawnee Business Committee, P.O. Box 470, White Eagle, Pawnee, OK 74058 (405) 762-3624.

MATTWAOSHSHE, GALILA
(BIA agency supt.)
Affiliation: Concho Agency, Bureau of Indian Affairs, P.O. Box 68, El Reno, OK 73005 (405) 262-7481.

MAUCHAHTY-WARE, TOM (Kiowa/Comanche) 1949-
(musician, entertainer, educator)
Born March 21, 1949, Lawton, Okla. *Education*: Brookhaven College, Farmers Branch, TX (2 years); UCLA (30 hours). *Principal occupation*: Musician, entertainer, educator. *Address*: 101 Mollie Lane, P.O. Box 1771, Anadarko, OK 73005 (405) 588-2392 (home) 247-9494 Fax 247-5571 (work). *Titles*: Indian Flute Player; Lead Singer of the all Indian Blues Band, "Tom Ware and Blues Nation"; Indian Dance Champion; Traditional and Contemporary Vocalist; Accomplished Public Speaker and educator; traditional artist (painter, sculptor, flute maker, beadworker and featherworker). Shows: Colorado Indian Market - Western Art Roundup, Annual in Jan.; Texas Indian Market & Southwest Showcase, Annual in March; Kansas City Indian market & Southwest Showcase, Annual in April; Native American Days - Angel Mounds Historical Site, Evansville, IN, Annual in September; Inter-tribal Indian Ceremonials, Gallup, NM, Annual in August. *Other professional post*: Arts & crafts dealer. *Community

activities*: Charter member, Optimist International; member, Toastmasters International. *Membership*: Kiowa Tribal Employment Association (vice-president, 1983-84). *Awards, honors*: "Best Counselor Award," National Indian Youth Vocational Association, *Interests*: Former Oklahoma Friendship Force Ambassador to Ireland and Wales, Oct. 1979. *Biographical sources*: Listed in numerous newspapers, magazines, etc. Three movie soundtracks: "Last of the Caddos," HBO - 1980; "Son of the Morning Star," 1991 ABC Mini-Series; "Circle of Life, American Cancer Society - 1992.

MAUDLIN, REV. STANISLAUS
(*Wambdi Wicasa - Eagle Man*)1916-
(Catholic priest)
Born December 16, 1916, Greensburg, Ind. *Education*: St. Meinrad College, B.A., 1936; Collegio di St. Anselmo, Rome, S.T.L., 1939; Institute of Alcoholism Studies, NDSU, 1966. *Principal occupation*: Catholic Priest. *Address*: P.O. Box 98, Marvin, SD 57251 (605) 398-9200 Fax 398-9201; E-mail: indian@bluecloud. org. Website: www.bluecloud.org. *Affiliation*: Founder & Executive Director, American Indian Culture Research Center, Blue Cloud Abbey, Marvin, SD, 1968-. *Other Professional posts*: Associate pastor, work in adolescent and adult education, Liaison with Turtle Mountain Chippewa Tribe, Belcourt, ND, 1941-50; supt. of schools, St. Michael, ND, 1950-56; fundraising for St. Michael School on the Fort Totten Indian Reservation, 1950-56; member of Industrial Development Committee, Devils Lake, ND, 1954-56; president of five state Tekakwitha Indian Missionary Conference, 1955-1956; founder and pastor of St. John Indian Mission, Pierre, SD, 1955-66; Counselor, summer camp director, Pierre Indian School, Belcourt, ND, 1957-66; president, Five State Tekakwitha Indian Missionary Conference, 1967-68; broadcasting on radio, 1973-2000. *Community activities*: South Dakota Committee for the Humanities (executive committee, 1970-79); lecturer on cross cultural understanding to numerous groups, especially to college and university audiences, as well as state and national Church conferences; director of workshops on Indian culture, religion and education; member of evaluation board for Methodist Fund for Reconciliation (South Dakota region). *Membership*: South Dakota Historical Society (Life member). *Awards, honors*: Adopted into the Yankton Band, Dakota Tribe, 1941 (name-*Wambdi Wicasa*); 1954 (name-*Tikdisni*) adopted into Fort Totten Band, Dakota Tribe; adopted into Crow Creek Band, Dakota Tribe, 1961 (name-*Nasdad Mani*); adopted into the Turtle Mountain Tribe, 1966 (name-*Mahcheekwaneeyash*); Invited to Washington, DC, as advisor to Senator McGovern and the late Senator Humphrey, in first anti-poverty legislation, 1964; Citation from South Dakota Association of Counselors & Student Personnel Service Directors for Outstanding Service to Youth, 1971; Citation from South Dakota Social Welfare Conference for services to the social, cultural and humanitarian development of individuals in our State, 1972; adopted into the Blackfeet Tribe, 1973 (name-*Yellow Medicine*); South Dakota Historian of the Year, 1994 by the South Dakota History Conference; 20th Century Benedictine Award, SD History Conference, 1999; received the Journalism Award from the Catholic Diocese of Sioux Falls, SD, 2003; elected to the South Dakota Hall of Fame, 2003.

MAULSON, THOMAS (Lake Superior Ojibwe)
(tribal president)
Affiliation: Lac du Flambeau Tribal Council, P.O. Box 67, Lac du Flambeau, WI 54538 (715) 588-3303.

MAXCY, HOWARD (*Kayetanto*)
(Mesa Grande Band of Mission Indians)
(fire chief)
Born August 22, 1945. *Education*: AA Fire Science. *Principal occupation*: Fire chief. *Address*: P.O. Box 270, Santa Ysabel, CA 92070 (760) 782-3818 Fax 782-9029. *Affiliation*: Fire Captain, California Dept. of Forestry & Fire (30 years). *Other professional post*: Consultant to reservation fire service. *Membership*: Southern California Tribal Chairmans Association.

MAXCY, REBECCA (Diegueno)
(tribal chairperson)
Affiliation: Inaja-Cosmit Band of Mission Indians, 1040 E. Valley Pkwy., Unit A, Escondido, CA 92025 (760) 747-8581.

MAY, CHERYL (Oklahoma Cherokee) 1949-
(journalism)
Born February 22, 1949, Kansas City, Mo. *Education*: University of Missouri, BA, 1974; Kansas State University, MS, 1985. *Principal occupation*: Journalism. *Home address*: 2005 Somerset Square, Manhattan, KS 66503 (785) 532-6415 Fax 532-6418 (office); E-Mail: news1@ksu.edu. *Affiliations*: Communications director, American Maine-Anjou Association, Kansas City, MO, 1975-; deputy managing editor/research editor, University Relations, 1979-87, general news editor, 1987-88, director, Media Relations and Marketing, 1988-, Kansas State University (KSU), Manhattan, KS. *Other professional post*: Elected to KSU Faculty Senate, 1991-97. *Community activities*: United Way, KSU publicity chair, 1985; Riley County Historical Society volunteer (organized Celebrate American Indian Heritage); 4-H project leader; helped organize Kansas State's first Native American Heritage Month activities for March 1990; panel moderator, "People Making a Difference: People Keeping the King Tradition Alive," KSU Martin Luther King Week, Jan. 24, 1991; served on several search committees; volunteer with Flint Hills Breadbasket; co-founder & president, two terms, Heartland Dog Training Club. *Memberships*: Phi Kappa Phi; National Association of Science Writers; Council for Advancement and Support of Education (CASE); Kansas Association for Native American Education. *Awards, honors*: Grants and gifts for Native American Heritage Month, 1990-91; Best in Show photography award, K-State Union Program Council, 1990; Award of Excellence for "Perspectives" magazine, CASE, editor, 1987; Special Merit Award for Cattle Research in Kansas, Council for Advancement and Support of Education CASE, writer, 1984; scholarship winner, Communicating University Research, CASE, 1983; selected for listing in Ohoyo 1000, 1982, and for the Resource Directory of Alaskan and Native American Indian Women, 1980; Award for Merit for Artificial Insemination of Beef and Dairy Cattle, slide script, Society for Technical Communication, 1980; Award for Achievement for Safety in Handling Livestock, slide script, Society for Technical Communication, 1980; Award for Outstanding News Reporting, Carlsbad, Calif. Chamber of Commerce, 1969. *Interests*: "Since I have been director of News Services at Kansas State University. I supervise science reporting; radio-television news; and campus news as well as the faculty-staff newsletter. I am interested in photography and use it in my professional and private life. I have won numerous awards for photography and for writing." *Published works*: Cattle Management (Reston-Prentice-Hall, 1981); Legacy, Engineering at Kansas State University (KSU Press, 1983).

MAY, JAMES HARVEY (United Keetoowah Cherokee) 1937-
(university dean & professor)
Born August 30, 1937, Trenton, Mo. *Education*: Stanford Uiversity, BS, 1958; Harvard University, MBA, 1964; Columbia University, DLS, 1978. *Principal occupation*: University dean & professor of computer science. *Home address*: 1505 Devers Ct., Marina, CA 93933. *Affiliations*: Vice-president, co-founder, Pandex, Inc. (subsidiary of Macmillan Publishing Co.), New York, NY, 1966-72; director, Center for Communication and Information Research, and Assistant Professor, Graduate School of Librarianship, Uiversity of Denver, Denver, CO, 1972-74; Associate Library Director, Sonoma State University, CA, 1974-83; Vice Provost for Information Resources and Professor of Computer Science, California State University, Chico, CA, 1983-. *Other professional posts*: Consulting - on collections and use of technology for the Smithsonian Institution on its planned National Museum of the American Indian, 1991-92, and with the National Indian Policy Center to create a national Indian information clearinghouse, 1991-92; lectures on information technology for American Indians and on European contact and tribal conflict: the Cherokee experience; Scarecrow Press, Advisory Board Member for Native American Bibliographic Series (current). *Military service*: U.S. Navy, 1959-62. *Community activities*: Official representative and advisor to the United Keetoowah Band of Cherokee Tribe; recently designed the tribal seal and flag for his tribe; California State University-Academic Information Resources Council (Executive Committee, 1992-). *Memberships*: United Keetoowah Cherokke Tribe; Society for Computer Simulation, International (Official Historian, 1991-); and American Library Association (Institutional representative to EDUCOM and CAUSE, 1983-). *Awards, honors*: President Bush appointed him to the first White House Conference on Indian Education which was held in January, 1992. commissioned to do a paper on "Technological Needs: Joining the Information Age" for its Native American Pre-Conference to the White House Conference on Library and Information Services, 1991; chosen to be a witness before the U.S. Senate Select Committee on Indian Affairs in May, 1992, on information technology for Native Americans. participated in the White House Conference on Library and Information Services & led a successful petition drive for support of American Indian libraries, against considerable opposition. *Published works*: Numerous articles & papers on library & information science.

MAYER, TERRY "HAWK"
(school administrator)
Affiliation: Lac Courte Oreilles Ojibwa School, P.O. Box 2800, Hayward, WI 54843 (715) 634-1442.

MAYNOR, GERALD
(Indian education)
Affiliation: North Carolina Advisory Council on Indian Education, NC Dept. of Public Instruction, c/o Pembroke State University, Pembroke, NC 28372.

MAYTUBBIE, DONNA (Choctaw)
(artist, craftsperson)
Address: 200 E. Lockheed Dr., Midwest City, OK 73110 (405) 733-8534. *Products*: Terra cotta sculpture & bowls.

MAYTUBBIE, DOUG (Choctaw)
(artist, craftsperson)
Address: 200 E. Lockheed Dr., Midwest City, OK 73110 (405) 733-8534. *Products*: Original paintings, drawings, graphics, and sculpture.

MAYO, WILL
(center president)
Affiliation: Tanana Chiefs Conference Health Center, 12 First Ave., Fairbanks, AK 99701 (907) 452-8251.

MAZZA, PAMELA J.
(attorney)
Education: Indiana University of Pennsylvania, BA, 1980; George Washington University National Law Center, JD, 1984. *Affiliation*: Senior partner, Piliero, Mazza & Pargament, PLLC, Farragut Square, 888 17th St., NW, Suite 1100, Washington, DC 20005 (202) 857-1000 Fax 857-0200. E-mail: pmazza@pmplawfirm.com. Ms. Mazza practices in the areas of corporate counseling, government contracts, government relations and Native American law. She represents Indian tribes and Alaska Native Corporations and related entities on a variety of issues pertaining to sovereignty, economic development, land issues, housing and establishing tribal enterprises and subsidiaries to participate in commercial business and government contracts. She is an editor of the firm's newsletters, "Legal Advisor," and "Tribal Advocate," and a guest columnist for the "Government Contract Audit Report."

MEANS, DAVID
(health director)
Affiliation: Northern Cheyenne PHS Indian Health Center, P.O. Box 70, Lame Deer, MT 59043 (406) 477-6201.

MEANS, RUSSELL (Oglala Sioux)
(speaker; activist, actor)
Affiliation: Chairperson, American Indian Anti-Defamation Council, 215 W. Fifth Ave., Denver, CO 80204 (303) 892-7011. Recently had roles in The Last of the Mohicans, and other films.

MECHELS, DONALD (Chinook)
(tribal chairperson)
Affiliation: Chinook Indian Tribe, P.O. Box 228, Chinook, WA 98614 (360) 777-8303.

MEDFORD, CLAUDE, JR. (Choctaw) 1941-
(artist)
Born April 14, 1941, Lufkin, Tex. *Education*: University of New Mexico, BA, 1964; Oklahoma State University, 1969. *Principal occupation*: Artist. *Address*: Coushatta Indian Tribe, P.O. Box 818, Elton, LA 70532 (318) 584-2261. *Affiliations*: Museum director, Alabama-Coushatta Indian Reservation; manager of the Coushatta Cultural Center, Elton, LA; taught classes and workshops at the American Indian Archaeological Institute in Washington, CT in 1979, and the Clifton Choctaw Indian Community west of Alexandria, LA, in 1981; received a folk arts apprenticeship fellowship from the Louisiana State Arts Council, Division of the Arts, and now teachers basketry to any interested Indian among the five surviving tribes of Louisiana. Mr. Medford is a gifted craftsman and practitioner of Southeast Indian arts, including basketry, pottery, wood working, shell working, metalworking, fingerweaving, beadwork, featherwork, horn and hoofwork, brain tanning of deer hides, leatherworking and gourd work. His baskets are in numerous private collections as well as several public collections, that of the Southern Plains Indian Museum, the Museum of the Red River in Idabel, OK, Tantaquidgeon Mohegan Museum in Uncasville, CT and a traveling exhibit to be circulated by the Smithsonian Institution Traveling Exhibition Service. Since 1972, he has show his work each year at the New Orleans Jazz and Heritage Festival. *Interests*: To perpetuate the arts and culture of the Southeastern Indian tribes. *Published works*: numerous articles for various publications.

MEDICINE, BEATRICE (Sihasapa Lakota-Standing Rock Sioux) 1923-
(research anthropologist)
Born August 1, 1923, near Wakpala, S.D. *Education*: South Dakota State University, BS, 1945; Michigan State University, MA, 1954; University of Wisconsin, Madison, PhD, 1982. *Principal occupation*: Research anthropologist. *Home address*: Box 80, Wakpala, SD 57658 (605) 845-7970. *Affiliations*: Associate professor emeritus, California State University, Northridge, 1982-88; professor, University of Calgary, Alberta, 1985-88; president, Warrior Women, Inc. *Other professional posts*: Visiting Professor (Dartmouth College, Stanford University, University of Washington, University of Toronto, University of New Brunswick, South Dakota State University); Professor, University of South Dakota & University of Montana; Research Coordinator, Women's Perspectives, Royal Commission on Aboriginal Peoples, Ottawa, Canada, 1993-95; visiting professor, University of Illinois, Champaign-Urbana, 2004-. *Community activities*: Expert witness (five tribal/human rights cases) San Francisco Status of Women Committee; Board-Indian centers-Seattle, Vancouver, BC, and Calgary, Canada; school board, Wakpala Public School; board member, Pardon Board-Standing Rock Sioux Tribe; treasurer, Elder's Council of Wakpala District. *Memberships*: American Anthropological Association, 1966- (Minority Education Committee; Fellow); Society for Applied Anthropology, 1966- (Fellow); Canadian Anthropology Association, 1963-; National Congress of American Indians, 1969- (education & cultural consultant); Native American Women's Association; American Ethnohistory Society; Museum and Anthropology Association. *Awards, honors*: Standing Rock Reservation, Sacred Pipe Woman, Sun Dance, 1977; Oustanding Alumni - South Dakota State University, 1977; Honorary Doctorate of Humane Letters, Northern Michigan University, 1979; "Outstanding Woman of Color, National Institute of Women of Color, Washington, DC, 1983; "Outstanding Minority Researcher," 1983, American Education Research Association; CHOICE Award for Outstanding Academic book, 1983 for "The Hidden Half - Studies of Indian Women in the Northern Plains, with Patricia Albers"; 1984 Faculty Award for Meritorious Service, California State University, Northridge; "Martin Luther King Outstanding Minority Professor," University of Michigan, 1987, Wayne State University, 1988; Distinguished Service Award, American Anthropological Association, 1991; 1993 "Ohana Award," American Counseling Association; 1995 "Malinowski Award," Society for Applied Anthropology; Adjunct Professor, University of Alberta, Edmonton, 1995-present; Honorary Doctorate of Humanities, Michigan State University, 1998; Stanley Knowles Distonguished Research Professor, 1998 Brandon University, Manitoba; Distinguished Minority Research Career, AERA, 1999. *Interests*: "Travels to visit indigenous peoples and read invited papers: Mexico, 1955, '65, '67; Moscow, 1984; Darwin, Australia, 1988; Canberra, Australia, 1986; New Zealand, 1986-88; Lithuania, 1989; Sweden and Yugoslavia, 1988; researching pow wows held in Russia, 1991-94; currently: research - gender issues, children's health, alcoholism, Native education; pow

wows. *Published works*: Native American Women: A Perspective - ERK Press, San Antonio, TX, 1978); The Hidden Half - Studies of Indian Women in the Northern Plains, with Patricia Albers (University Press of America, 1982); An Ethnography of Drinking & Sobriety Among the Lakota (In Press); produced, Seeking the Spirit - Plains Indians in Russia, 1997; 2001 - Learning to be an Anthropologist and Remaining "Native" (University of Illinois Press, 2001); and more than 100 articles and book chapters; poetry; prose.

MEDICINE-EAGLE, BROOKE *(Daughter of the Rainbow)* **(Crow/Lakota/Nez Perce) 1943-**
(international educator-catalyst for wholeness)
Born April 24, 1943, Crow Reservation, Mont. *Education*: University of Denver, BA; Mankato State University, MS; Humanistic Pschology Institute, ABD in Body Therapy and Native American Systems of Wholeness. *Address*: P.O. Box C401, One 2nd Ave. E., Polson, MT 59860 (406) 883-4686 Fax 883-6629. E-mail: brooke@medicine-eagle.com. Website: www.medicine -eagle.com. *Affiliations*: Self-employed via Earth Mages, Unlimited; Singing Eagle Music; Eagle Song Camps; also teaching affiliate with Feathered Pipe Foundation. *Community activities*: Serves a global community of those interested in healing themselves and Mother Earth. *Interests*: Her dedication is to bring forward the ancient truths concerning how to live a fully human life in harmony with All Our Relations. Brooke's primary interest is in the renewal of ancient ritual forms for creating a beautiful path upon Mother Earth, today and for the future. To this end she is creating an in-depth training, *Wakantia*, to awaken and challenge participants to the next level of being human, as Earth Mages living in harmony and grace upopn a renewed Earth. She and Feathered Pipe Foundation produce "Song of the Nations" — a blending of the finest teachers of Celtic, native and other traditions to open a path of beauty into the future. *Published works*: Buffalo Woman Comes Singing, a spiritual autobiography, 1991; The Last Ghost Dance: A Guide for Earth Mages 2000.

MEDICINEBULL, ORIE *(Hugaitha)* **(Western Mono)**
(executive director)
Born December 6 in Madera County, Calif. *Education*: UCLA, MFA, 1981; UC-Berkeley, MPH, 1983. *Principal occupation*: Administrator, artist-filmmaker, professor. *Address*: American Indian Center of Central California, P.O. Box 607, Auberry, CA 93602 (209) 855-2705 Fax 855-2695 (work); E-Mail: omedicinebull@ telis.org. *Affiliations*: Executive director, American Indian Center of Central California, Auberry, CA; professor, Fresno City College, Fresno, CA. *Other professional posts*: Coordinator, Indian Education, Title V, Oakhurst, CA; coordinator, Sierra Children's Center, Oakhurst, CA. *Community activities*: Fresno American Indian Council (manpower director); Communication Committee (chairperson). *Memberships*: American Indian Women's Association (chairperson); Sierra Mono Museum; American Film Institute; UCLA & UC-Berkeley Alumni. *Awards, honors*: American Independent Filmmaker Award-Best Documentary, American Indian Film Festival; Best Documentary, Brockman International Gallery; Best Documentary Short, People's Film Festival (Italy); Carny Award, Golden Hills School District. *Interests*: "Major area of interest is outdoor, physical endurance hiking workout in Sierra Nevada Mountains as a team, ethnographic film study of Central California Indians of Central California (Numa)." *Published works*: Documentaries: "Colliding Worlds," 1980); Visions of Youth," 1991; and Success for American Indian Children," 1993 (all produced by Hugaitha Productions).

MEDINA, MAGDALENA "MENA" (Chehalis)
(former tribal chairperson)
Affiliation: Chehalis Community Council, P.O. Box 536, Oakville, WA 98568 (206) 273-5911.

MEEKIS, FRED
(Indian band chief)
Affiliation: Deer Lake Indian Band, Box 335, Deer Lake, Ontario, Canada P0V 1N0 (705) 775-2141.

MEEKS, ELSIE (Lakota Sioux)
(fund raising)
Affiliation: Executive director, The Lakota Fund, P.O. Box 340, Kyle, SD 57752 (605) 455-2500. *Other professional post*: Editor of newsletter.

MEINERS, PHYLLIS A. 1940-
(publisher, consultant)
Born November 8, 1940, Boston, Mass. *Education*: University of California, Berkeley, BA, 1962; Mass. Institute of Technology, 1969. *Principal occupation*: Publishing. *Address*: P.O. Box 22583, Kansas City, MO 64113 (800) 268-2059; (913) 385-9707 Fax 361-2115 (work); E-Mail: books@crcpub.com; Website: www. crcpub.com. *Affiliation*: President, CRC Publishing Co.- EagleRock Books, Kansas City, MO, 1982-. *Other professional posts*: Founding director, Corporate Resource Center Library & Corporate Resource Consultants, Kansas City, MO, 1992-present. *Community activities*: Philanthro-Net Committee (Corporate Database); Chamber of Commerce Entrepreneur's Council; Democratic Committee; Center for Management Assistance volunteer consultant. *Memberships*: National Society of Fund Raising Executives, Native Americans in Philanthropy; American Prospect Research Association; Publishers Marketing Association; Association of American Publishing; Mid America Publishers Association; Greater Kansas City Council of Philanthropy; National Center for Black Philanthropy. *Interests*: Non-profit management & fund development; travel throughout Latin America, South America, Europe, and U.S.; economic development on American Indian reservations; antiques and collectibles. *Biographical sources*: Marquis Who's Who in the Midwest; Marquis Who's Who in Finance & Industry; Marquis Who's Who in the World; Who's Who in American Women. *Published works*: National Directory of Philanthropy for Native Americans (Corporate Resource Consultants, 1992); Church Philanthropy for Native Americans and Other Minorities: A Guide to Multicultural Funding from Religious Sources (CRC Publishing Co., 1995); Corporate & Foundation Fundraising Manual for Native Americans (CRC Publishing, 1996); National Directory of Foundation Grants for Native Americans.

MEISTER, MARK
(executive director)
Affiliation: Archaeological Institute of America, 675 Commonwealth Ave., Boston, MA 02215 (617) 353-9361.

MEJIA, MARJORIE (Yurok)
(rancheria chairperson)
Affiliation: Lytton Rancheria, 1250 Coddingtown Center #1, Santa Rosa, CA 95401 (707) 575-5917.

MELENDEZ, ARLAN (Paiute)
(tribal chairperson)
Affiliation: Reno-Sparks Tribal Council, 98 Colony Rd., Reno, NV 89502 (775) 329-2936.

MELENDEZ, RANDY
(Indian school principal)
Affiliation: Pyramid Lake High School, P.O. Box 256, Nixon, NV 89424 (702) 574-1016 Fax 574-1037.

MELKILD, MARTIN A.
(museum curator)
Affiliation: Indian Drum Lodge Museum, 2308 North U.S. 31, Traverse City, MI 49684.

MELODY, MICHAEL E. 1947-
(professor)
Born October 14, 1947, Philadelphia, Penn. *Education*: University of Notre Dame, PhD, 1976. *Principal occupation*: Professor. *Address*: Barry University, 11300 N.E. 2nd Ave, Miami Shores, FL 33161 (305) 758-3391 (work). *Affiliation*: Professor, Barry University, Miami, FL, 1979-. *Other professional post*: Director & editor, Native American Policy Network & Newsletter.

MELONI, ALBERTO C. 1946-
(executive director-Indian organization)
Born July 14, 1946, Lucca, Italy. *Education*: Marquette University, BA, MA; Harvard University, MA; University of Minnesota, Ph.D. *Principal occupation*: Executive director-Indian organization. *Address*: The Institute for American Indian Studies, P.O. Box 1260, Washington, CT 06793 (203) 868-0518. *Affiliation*: Executive Director, The Institute for American Indian Studies, Washington, CT, 1991-. *Other professional posts*: Chief curator of collections and research; director of education; chief development officer, university instructor. *Community activities*: Hospice volunteer.

MENARD, ROBIN (Ojibway-Canada)
(coordinator, tutor)
Education: Bay de Noc Community College; Northern Michigan University. *Address*: 1919 14th Ave. North, Escanaba, MI 49829 (906) 786-8615 Fax 786-0106; E-Mail: escindiand@bresnanlink.net. *Affiliations*: Equity in Education Committee, 1980-81; 1993-present; Central Upper Peninsula Indian Education Network Team, 1994-present; Big Brothers/Big Sisters of Delta County, 1996-present. *Community activities*: Advisor, Escanaba Schools Student Club - N.A.K.K. (Native Amrican Kids Who Kare, 1994-present; Network Team Mini Powwow; tax assistance for senior citizens; MMAP volunteer. *Membership*: Phi Theta Kappa Alumni; Bay de Noc Community College Alumni.

MENDOZA, LARRY
(school director)
Affiliation: Red Scaffold Indian School, P.O. Box 168, Howes, SD 57748 (605) 538-4317.

MENEED, BERNARD
(Indian band chief)
Affiliation: Tallcree Idian Band, Box 367, Fort Vermillion, Alberta, Canada T0H 1N0 (403) 927-3727.

MENESS, CLIFFORD
(Indian band chief)
Affiliation: Algonquin (Golden Lake) Indian Band, Box 100, Golden Lake, Ontario, Canada K0J 1X0 (613) 625-2800.

MENINICK, JERRY (Yakima)
(tribal chairperson)
Affiliation: Yakima Tribal Council, P.O. Box 151, Toppenish, WA 98948 (509) 865-5121.

MENUSAN, FRANC *(Nookoosilichapko)* **(Creek/Metis) 1954-**
(educator-special education; musician)
Born May 17, 1954, New York, N.Y. *Education*: New York University, MA, 1984. *Principal occupation*: Educator-special education teacher. *Home address*: Address unknown. *Affiliation*: Board of Education of the City of New York, 1982-; Museum of Natural History, New York, NY (Museum Teacher Associate Program); National Museum of the American Indian, Smithsonian, New York, NY (cultural interpreter, artist in residence). *Other professional posts*: Musician (Native American Flutes); composer of music (using Native American instruments of MesoAmerica); speaker & consultant on Native American cultures; writer. *Community activities*: "I work with the American Indian Community House (New York City) as one of their artists on file," co-producing "Giving of Thanks to the First Peoples" Cathedral of St. John the Divine (Ann Rockefeller Roberts, 11/93); Committee (working/advisory), "Cry of the Earth-Legacy of the First Nations" (United Nations, 11/ 93); board trustee of the American Indian Ritual Object Repatriation Foundation. *Membership*: New York University Alumni. *Interests*: "Travels to collect indigenous musical instruments from Mexico, USA, and Canada. I share Native stories and music" *Biographical source*: April 27, 1994 - Part 2 New York Newsday "Home on the Urban Range" - The Indian Nation in New York is a Microcosm of the Gorgeous Mosaic. pp. 84-5. *Performances*: "Native American Music and Dance," Dept. of Education/Special Education Progam - American Museum of Natural History, NYC, Dec. 10, 1996; Songs and Flutes for the Navajo Exhibitions, National Museum of the American Indian, NYC, Oct. 4, 1996; Flute/Song/Storytelling for the Visiting Peace Corps, American Indian Community House, NYC, June 27, 1994...among others; numerous concerts and workshops. *Published works*: Two curriculum guides for the Westchester Philharmonic, "Native American Music" and "Native Iroquois Culture", both for elementary and secondary schools; Fiddlesticks "Pre Columbian Music of the Americas - What Columbus Might Have Heard," 1992; New Orchestra of Westchester - "American Indigenous People - Contact Period to Present," 1992-93; Cobblestones "Rock of the Ages PreColumbian American Music" p. 24 (Vol. 14) 1993.

MEQUISH, PAUL
(Indian band chief)
Affiliation: Conseil Des Attikameks D'Obedjiwan Indian band, Reserve Indienne d'Obedjiwan, Via Roberval, Quebec, Can. G0W 3B0 (819) 974-8837.

MERCER, BILL 1960-
(museum curator)
Born May 14, 1960, Anaheim, Calif. *Education*: Texas Tech University, M.A., 1986; University of New Mexico (Ph.D. candidate). *Principal occupation*: Museum curator for the Art of Africa and the Americas. *Home address*: 4324 Watterson St., Cincinnati, OH 45227-2931 (513) 721-5204 x 297 Fax 721-0129 (work). *Affiliations*: Texas Tech University Museum, Lubbock, TX, 1984-85; Plains Indian Museum, Cody, WY, 1985-86; National Park Service, 1988-93; curator, Cincinnati Art Museum, Cincinnati, OH, 1993-. *Memberships*: American Association of Museums; Midwest Museums Association; Ohio Museums Association; Native American Art Studies Association (secretary/treasurer, 1995-97). *Interests*: "I am especially interested in pow wows and contemporary traditional Native American art. My Ph.D. dissertation is a study of contemporary pow wow clothing and how it communicates the identity of the wearer. I am currently developing a traveling exhibition of Pueblo pottery entitles, "Singing the Clay: Pueblo Pottery of the Southwest Yesterday and Today." *Published work*: "Singing the Clay: Pueblo Pottery of the Southwest Yesterday and Today," exhibition catalog (Cincinnati Art Museum, 1995).

MERCIER, MARK (Confederated Tribes)
(tribal chairperson)
Affiliation: Confederated Tribe of the Grande Ronde Tribal Council, 9615 Grand Ronde Rd., Grande Ronde, OR 97347 (503) 879-5211.

MERCREDI, NAPOLEAN
(Indian band chief)
Affiliation: Fond du Lac Indian Band, Fond du Lac, SK., Canada S0G 0W0 (306) 686-2102.

MERICLE, MIKE
(health director)
Affiliation: Ignacio PHS Indian Health Center, P.O. Box 899, Ignacio, CO 81137 (303) 563-4581.

MEREDITH, HOWARD L. (Cherokee/Akokisa) 1938-
(college professor)
Born May 25, 1938, Galveston, Tex. *Education*: University of Texas, BS, 1961; S.F. Austin State University, MA, 1963; University of Oklahoma, PhD, 1970. *Principal occupation*: College professor. *Address*: American Indian Studies, University of Science & Arts of Oklahoma, Chickasha, OK 73018 (405) 224-3140 Fax 521-6244 (work). *Affiliations*: Cookson Institute, Oklahoma City, OK (chairman, 1974-79; research associate, 1979-) ; professor, American Indian Studies, University of Science & Arts of Oklahoma, Chickasha, OK, 1985-. *Community activities*: Board, National American Indian Hall of Fame, Anadarko, OK; board member, Jacobson House Foundation; board member, Oklahoma Center for the Book. *Memberships*: Western Writers of America; Native American Circle of Writers; Western Historical Association; Oklahoma Historical Society ; Cherokee National Historical Society; Oklahoma Heritage Association. *Awards, honors*: Muriel Wright Heritage Award for Writing Oklahoma History, 1980, by Oklahoma Historical Society; Westerners' International Award for the Best Book on the West, 1989; McCasslin Award (Teaching), Oklahoma Heritage Association, 1994; Regents Award for Superior Teaching, 1995 & 1998; Regents Award for Superior Research, 1996; Coke Wood Award for Best Monograph, 1998. *Interests*: American Indian thought; cross cultural communication; American Indian tribal government; Southwestern heritage. *Biographical source*: Oklahoma Monthly (June, 1977); The Trend (Oct. 26, 1989); Chickasha Sunday Express (Oct. 29, 1989); Trend (Chickasaw), Feb. 1994; Who's Who in the Southwest, 1994-95; Who's Who in America, 1999-2000. *Published works*: "The Native American Factor" (Seabury Press, 1973); "Native Response...Rural Oklahoma" (Oklahoma Historical Society, 1977); "Of the Earth," with M.E. Meredith (Oklahoma Historical Society, 1980; "Bacone Indian University," with J. Williams (Oklahoma Heritage Society, 1980; "DCWY," with V. Milam (Indian University Press, 1981); "Bartley Milam: Principal Chief of the Cherokee Nation" (Indian University Press, 1985); "Hasinai," with V. Newkumet (Texas A&M University Press, 1989); Modern American Indian Tribal Government (Navajo College Press, 1993); Dancing on Common Ground (University Press of Kansas, 1995).

MEREDITH, MARY ELLEN (MILAM) (Cherokee of Oklahoma) 1946-
(society board president)
Born October 3, 1946. *Principal occupation*: Society board president. *Address*: 623 Culbertson Dr., Suite A, Oklahoma City, OK 73105 (405) 524-2615. E-mail: noksi@aol.com. *Affiliation*: Board President, Cherokee National Historical Society; Interim Executive Director, Cherokee Heritage Center, 1999-2003. Other professional posts: Cherokee Nation Enterprises (secretary of board);Noksi Press, Oklahoma City, OK (present). *Community activities*: Board member, Red Earth, Inc.; member, Junior League of Oklahoma City; Trail of Tears Advisory Commission, National Park Service. *Membership*: Pocahontas Club. *Interests*: Fiction writing. *Published work*: Edited with Howard Meredith, "Of the Earth: Oklahoma Architectural History" (Oklahoma Historical Society, 1980); B.D. Eddie (Bio); George Shirk (Bio); Cherokee Humanities Course Text; Cherokee Literary Perspectives (2003).

MERICLE, MICHAEL N.
(health center director)
Affiliation: Ignacio PHS Indian Health Center, P.O. Box 889, Ignacio, CO 81137 (303) 563-4581.

MERRELL, JAMES H. 1953-
(professor of history)
Born October 19, 1953, Minneapolis, Minn. *Education*: Lawrence University, BA, 1975; Oxford University, England, BA, 1977; Johns Hopkins University, MA, 1979, PhD, 1982. *Address*: Vassar College, Poughkeepsie, NY 12604-0432. *Affiliation*: Professor of History, Vassar College, Poughkeepsie, NY, 1984-. *Memberships*: American Historical Association; Organization of American Historians; Society of American Historians; Omohundro Institute of Early American History & Culture. *Awards, honors*: Rhodes Scholarship; Danforth Fellowship; Predoctoral Fellowship, Newberry Library; Postdoctoral Fellowship, Institute of Early American History & Culture; America: History & Life Award; Robert F. Heizer Award, Douglass Adair Prize, Frederick Jackson Turner Award, Merle Curti Award, and Bancroft Prize for book, "The Indians' New World"; Fellowships from American Council of Learned Societies, Guggenheim Foundation, and National Endowment for the Humanities; Bancroft Prize for "Into the American Woods". *Published works*: Co-editor, Beyond the Covenant Chain, and book, The Iroquois & Their Neighbors in Indian North America, 1600-1800 (Syracuse University Press, 1987); The Indians' New World: Catawbas and Their Neighbors from European Contact Through the Era of Removal (University of North Carolina Press, 1989); The Catawbas (Chelsea House, 1989); Into the American Woods (W.W. Norton, 1999).

MERRILL, DAVID (St. Croix Chippewa)
(tribal chairperson)
Affiliation: St. Croix Chippewa Indians, P.O. Box 287, Hertel, WI 54845 (715) 349-2195.

MERRILL, HAMP
(American Indian studies)
Affiliation: Special assistant to the Director, American Indian Studies Program, Harvill Bldg., Rm. 430, P.O. Box 210076, University of Arizona, Tucson, AZ 85721 (520) 621-7108 Fax 621-7952. E-mail: hmerrill@u.arizona.edu.

MESHIGUAD, KENNETH (Potawatomi)
(tribal chairperson)
Affiliation: Hannahville Indian Community Council, N14910 Hannahville Blvd, Rd., Wilson, MI 49896 (906) 466-2342.

MESHORER, HANK
(chief-Indian resources)
Affiliation: U.S. Dept. of Justice, Indian Resources Section, Land & Natural Resources Division, Rm. 624, 10th & Constitution Ave., NW, Washington, DC 20530 (202) 724-7156.

MESSINGER, CARLA J.S. (Lenni Lenape Delaware) 1949-
(teacher)
Born May 20, 1949, Allentown, Pa. *Education*: Lehigh County Community College, AA, 1969; Kutztown University, BA, 1971; Lehigh University, MA (Elementary/Special Education), 1973. *Principal occupation*: Teacher. *Home address*: 1819 1/2 Linden St., Allentown, PA 18104 (610) 434-6819. *Past professional posts*: Substitute teacher of elementary education & special education (12 years); special consultant, presents multi-media programs on Lenape culture to other organizations, such as Philadelphia school district; leads in service programs on "Unstereotyping Indians" for school districts, colleges, and church groups; consultant & speaker for "Native Culture for Senior Citizens," St. Francis de Salles College, and Agape project "Leni Lenape Indians, 1981-84; Founder & executive director, Lenni Lenape Historical Society & Museum, Allentown, PA. *Memberships*: Pennsylvania Federation of Museums & Historical Societies. *Awards, honors*: 1985 President's Volunteer Action Award, Citation by the House of Representatives, PA; Keystone Award of Merit, Governor's Private Sector Initiatives Task Force for Lenni Lenape Historical Society; 1986 Award of Merit to the Society from the Pennsylvania Federation of Historical Societies for "Continuing Achievement in Public Education under Carla Messinger"; 1987 Jefferson Award from KYW-TV3; 1989 Letter of Commendation to the Society from the Pennsylvania Federation of Historical Societies for the publication of a new flyer (editor, Susanne Jeffries-Fox); 1989 Allentown Human Relations Award for creating and operating the Lenni Lenape Historical Society/Museum; appointed to the Advisory Council for constructing and Institute for Native American Studies at Mansfield University, 1990; 1991 Executive Leadership Award for two weeks at the Smithsonian Institution; chosen to participate in the 1991, two-week "Archaeology and Ethnography Collection Care and Maintenance Course" offered through the U.S. Dept. of the Interior, National Park Service; provided Lenape cultural programs to audiences in Scotland and England through the British North American Indian Association (Scotland in 1992 & 1996); in July 1993, she was a representative to the 9th European Conference on Indian Questions held in Trondheim, Norway, and then went to Stockholm, Sweden to meet with support groups and museum representatives; The Museum of Indian Culture/Lenni Lenape Historical Society was one of ten American organizations chosen to exhibit its crafts at the National Crafts Center in Washington, DC for 1993, International Year of the Indigenous People & the American Year of Handicrafts; provided educational, multi-media cultural programs in former East Germany in 1994, and the United Kingdom in 1996; received a scholarship from the Yakima Nation to attend the American Association of State & Local Historical Societies conference in Denver, Sept. 30 to Oct. 5, 1997; panelist for the Smithsonian Institutions workshop titled, "Making a Difference in American Indian/Museum Relationships in Rochester, NY, Nov. 13-16, 1997; attended the ATLATL conference in San Francisco, Oct. 6-11, 1998; attended the Smithsonian Institution's Exhibits Development for Tribal Museums Conference in Ft. Lauderdale, FL, Feb. 23-26, 1999; received a scholarship to participate in the American Association for State and Local History and Mid-Atlantic Association of Museums' Annual Meeting from Sept. 29th through October 2nd, 1999; scholarship to attend National Trust for Historic Preservation Conference, Oct. 19th - 24th, 1999, in Washington, DC; scholarship, American Indian Women with Disabilities Conference, Mohave Reservation, Nev., Feb. 29th to March 2nd, 2000; scholarship, Pennsylvania Federation of Museums and Historical Societies Conference, Penn State, State College, PA, April 5th to 8th, 2000; Carla was a representative to the United Kingdom in July, 2001, presenting Lenape cultural programs and environmental programs in England. *Interests*: Lenni Lenape history & culture. *Biographical sources*: International Leaders in Achievement & Who's Who in International Women Leaders, 1990-2001 editions (International Biographical Center, London, England).

MESTES, BEVERLY
(BIA supt. for education)
Affiliation: Pima Agency, Bureau of Indian Affairs, P.O. Box 8, Sacaton, AZ 85247 (602) 562-3557.

METATAWABIN, EDWARD
(Indian band chief)
Affiliation: Fort Albany Indian band, Fort Albany, Ontario, Canada P0L 1H0 (705) 278-1044.

METCALF, EDWARD L. (Coquille)
(tribal chairperson)
Affiliation: Coquille Indian Tribe, P.O. Box 783, North Bend, OR 97549 (541) 756-0904.

METOXEN, LORETTA
(organization president)
Affiliation: Coalition for Indian Education, 8200 Mountain Rd., NE, Suite 203, Albuquerque, NM 87110 (505) 262-2351.

METOYER, CHERYL A. (Cherokee) 1947-
(professor; director of information resources)
Born February 18, 1947, Los Angeles, Calif. *Education*: Indiana University, PhD in Library and Information Science, 1976. *Address*: Mashantucket Pequot Tribal Nation, 110 Pequot Trail, Mashantucket, CT 06339 (860) 396-6952 Fax 396-6874. E-mail: cmetoyer @mptn.org. *Affiliations*: Graduate School of Library & Information Science, University of California, Los Angeles, CA, 1977-81, 1988-93, Assistant Dean, 1989-92; Rupert Costo Professor in American Indian History, University of California, 1993-97; Director of Information Resources, Mashantucket Pequot Museum & Research Center, Mashantucket, CT, 1997-present. *Community activities*: Lector, St. Eugene Catholic Church, Southwest Museum. *Memberships*: American Indian & Alaska Native Professors Association; American Library Association (Library Research Round Table, Subcommittee on Library Services to American Indian People, Minority Recruitment Subcommittee); American Society for Information Science; Association of College & Research Libraries; Native American Professors Association; Kateri Circle. *Awards, honors*: Rupert Costo Professor in American Indian History, University of California, Riverside, 1993-97; "American Indian Research Literature as Reflected through Citation Analysis." Paper selcted for presentation at the ALA, LRRT Research Forums, Miami, Florida, June 26, 1994; Honoree, Assocaition of College & Research Libraries, Racial & Ethnic Diversity Committee. Honored for research monograph, "Gatekeepers in Ethnolinguistic Communities"; K.G. Saur Award for Best Article in College & Research Libraries in 1992. Article: "Literature Reviews & Innacurate Referencing: An Exploratory Study of Academic Librarians." *Published work*: Gatekeepers in Ethnolinguistic Communities (Ablex Publishing Corp., 1993).

MEWBORN, FRANKIE
(site supt.)
Affiliation: New Echota Historic Site, 1211 Chatsworth Hwy. N.E.Calhoun, GA 30701 (404) 629-8151.

MEYER, WILLIAM H. (Chickamauga Cherokee/ Creek) 1938-
(artist, publisher, farmer)
Born October 19, 1938. *Principal occupation*: Artist, publisher, farmer. *Address*: P.O. Box 729, Tellico Plains, TN 37385 (423) 253-3680. *Affiliations*: Information officer, Young American Indian Council, New York, NY , 1967-70; co-founder, American Indian News Team, NYC, Indian Press Service; The American Indian Historical Society, San Francisco, CA, 1973-74; editor, Indigena, Inc., Berkeley, CA, 1974-76; owner, Orange Bear Trading Co. (art), and Snowbird Publishing Co., Tellico Plains, TN, 1987-present. *Other professional posts*: Co-editor (with Joanna Meyers) "The Four Directions: American Indian Literary Magazine." *Community activities*: Community organization advisor. *Published works*: Native Americans: The New Indian Resistance, 1969; The History of Suppression of Native American Religions (unpublished); The Huerfano Butcher Shop (novel-unpublished)

MEYERS, JOSEPH
(executive director)
Affiliation: National Indian Justice Center, 7 Fourth St., Suite 46, Petaluma, CA 94952 (707) 762-8113.

MEZA, KENNETH A. (*Misquish*) (Kumeyaay) 1945-
(tribal chairperson)
Born December 3, 1945, Monte Vista Ranch, Calif. *Address & Affiliation*: Chairperson, Jamul Indian Village, P.O. Box 612, Jamul, CA 91935 (619) 669-4785 Fax 669-4817. *Military service*: U.S. Marines (Vietnam Vet). *Memberships*: National Indian Gaming Association; National Congress of American Indians; California Nations Indian Gaming Association; California Indian Manpower Consortium.

MIANSCUM, HENRY
(Indian band chief)
Affiliation: Mistassini (Cree) Indian Band, Mistassini Lake, Via Chibougamau, Quebec, Canada G0W 1C0 (819) 923-3523

MICHAELS, MARK A. 1959-
(lawyer/writer)
Born August 2, 1959, New York, N.Y. *Education*: University of Michigan, BA, 1980; New York University School of Law, JD, 1985. *Principal occupation*: Lawyer/writer. *Address*: 708 Broadway, 8th Floor, New York, NY 10003 (212) 598-0100. *Affiliations*: Staff attorney, American Indian Alliance, New York, NY 1990- (established to address all issues affecting Indian survival); deputy director, Native American Council of New York City for 1992, New York, NY , 1991- (administrator for and advisor to a coalition of the three most active Native American organizations in New York City). *Other professional posts*: Literary manager, Roundabout Theatre, 1988-90, and Double Image Theatre, 1989-91. Speeches, Lectures & Panels: Native American Council Summit, Jan. 1991; Columbus Indians and 1992, The Learning Alliance, Columbia University School of Law, Dec. 1991; The Impact of the James Bay II Hydropower Project on Indigenous People, Sarah Lawrence College, Dec. 1991; The Contiuing Impact of Columbus' Arrival on Native Americans, Northern Westchester Society for Ethical Culture, Dec. 1991. *Memberships*: American Bar Association; Dramatist Guild. *Published works*: Articles - "Native American Council Update," American Indian Community House Bulletin, regular column in newsletter; "Native Americans and Free Exercise: Double Standard at Work," with Tonya Gonnella Frichner, National Bar Association Magazine, Vol. 8, No. 1, Jan, 1991; "War Decalred on Religious Freedom," with Tonya Gonnella Frichner, Native Nations, Vol. 1, No. 2, Feb. 1991.

MICHANO, ROY
(Indian band chief)
Affiliation: Ojibways of Pic River (Heron Bay) Indian band, Heron Bay, ON, Can. P0T 1R0 (807) 229-1749.

MICHEL, KAREN LINCOLN (Wisconsin Winnebago)
(journalist; association president)
Education: Marquette University, MA. *Address & Affiliation*: President, Native American Journalists Association (NAJA), 1433 E. Franklin Ave., Suite 11, Minneapolis, MN 55404 (612) 874-8833. *Other professional posts*: Reporter, LaCross Tribune & Dallas Morning News; business partner & board member of Indian Country Communications, Hayward, WI, publishers of News From Indian Country. *Awards/Honors*: Ms. Michel is the first woman to head NAJA.

MICHELS, CAROLYN
(exeutive director)
Affiliation: Norton Sound Health Corp., P.O. Box 966, Nome, AK 99762 (907) 443-3311.

MIHESUAH, DEVON A. (Choctaw of Oklahoma) 1957-
(professor of history, editor, writer)
Born June 6, 1957, Wichita Falls, Tex. Education: Texas Christian University, BS, 1981, MEd, 1982, MA, 1986, PhD (History), 1989. Dissertation: "History of the Cherokee Female Seminary: 1851-1909." *Address & Affiliations*: Professor of Applied Indigenous Studies & History, College of Social & Behavioral Sciences (2000-present), Northern Arizona University, P.O. Box 15020, Flagstaff, AZ 86011 (928) 523-5159. E-mail: devon.mihesuah@nau.edu. Website: www.jan.ucc. nau.edu/~mihesuah; Professor of History, College of Arts & Sciences, Northern Arizona University, Flagstaff, AZ, 1999-present Other *professional posts*: "American Indian Quarterly" (associate editor of history, 1993-98; editor, 1998-present); Editor, University of Nebraska Press Book Series: Contemporary American Indigenous Issues, 2000-2005; member, Board of Trustees, Museum of Northern Arizona, Flagstaff, AZ, 1999-2003; consultant and reviewer: "Western Social Science Journal," "American Indian Culture & Research Journal," "Choice," "The Historian," "Frontiers," "Signs," 1990-present. *Awards, honors*: Won Phi Alpha Theta/Westerners International Award for Best Dissertation in Western History, directed by Donald E. Worcester; Winner of the 1995 & 1998 American Educational Studies Association Critics' Choice Awards for "Cultivating the Rosebuds: The Education of Women

at the Cherokee Female Seminary, 1851-1909" & "Natives and Academics: Researching and Writing About American Indians" respectively; 1996-97 Ford Foundation Postdoctoral Fellowship; Winner of the The Oklahoma Writers' Federation Trophy Award for the Best Fiction Book of 2000 for "The Roads of My Relations"; Wordcraft Circle of Native Writers' 2001 Journal Editing Award for the "American Indian Quarterly," 2001. *Membership*: American Indian & Alaskan Native Professors' Association; American Society for Ethnohistory; Oklahoma Historical Society; Phi Alpha Theta; Western History Association; Wordcraft Circle of Native Writers. *Interests*: Recovering indigenous knowledge; methodologies of studying Natives; activism. *Publications*: Cultivating the Rosebuds: The Education of Women at the Cherokee Female Seminary, 1851-1909 (University of Illinois Press, 1993, 1996); American Indians: Stereotypes and Realities (Clarity Press, 1996/1997); Natives and Academics: Researching and Writing About American Indians (University of Nebraska Press, 1998); Editor, Repatriation: Social and Political Dialogues (University oif Nebraska Press, 1999); The Roads of My Relations (University of Arizona Press, 2000); "First to Fight": Henry Mihesuah, NU MU NUU (Comanche) (University of Nebraska Press, 2002); American Indigenous Women: Decolonization, Empowerment, Activism (University of Nebraska Press, 2003); Indigenizing the Academy: Native Academics Sharpening the Edge (the sequel to "Natives and Academics: Researching and Writing About American Indians") with Angela Cavender Wilson (University of Nebraska Press, 2004).

MIKE, DEAN (Luiseno)
(Indian band chairperson)
Affiliation: Twenty-Nine Palms Band of Luiseno Indians, 46-200 Harrison St., Coachella, CA 92236 (760) 775-5566.

MIKE, JUNE (Luiseno)
(tribal chairperson)
Address: 555 Sunrise Hwy. #200, Palm Springs, CA 92264. *Affiliation*: Twenty Nine Palms Band of Mission Indians, Palm Springs, CA (619) 322-0559.

MIKE, LORNA J. (Elwha S'Klallam)
(former tribal chairperson)
Affiliation: Elwha S'Klallam Tribe, 2851 Lower Elwha Rd., Port Angeles, WA 98362 (360) 452-8471.

MIKE, RICHARD (Navajo)
(association president)
Affiliation: Navajo Nation Business Association, P.O. Box 1217, Kayenta, AZ 86033 (520) 697-3534.

MIKE, RODNEY (Shoshone)
(former tribal chairperson)
Affiliation: Duckwater Shoshone Tribal Council, P.O. Box 140068, Duckwater, NV 89832 (702) 863-0227.

MIKE, ROSALYN (Southern Paiute)
(tribal chairperson)
Affiliation: Moapa Business Council, P.O. Box 340, Las Vegas, NV 89025 (702) 865-2787.

MIKKANEN, ARVO Q. (Kiowa/Comanche)
(attorney)
Address & Affiliation: Assistant U.S. Attorney, 210 W. Park Ave., Suite 400, Oklahoma City, OK 73102 (405) 879-5924. *Memberships*: Native American Bar Association (past president); Oklahoma Indian Bar Association, P.O. Box 1062, Oklahoma City, OK 73101 (president); Native American Alumni Association of Dartmouth College (president).

MILANOVICH, RICHARD M. (Cahuilla)
(tribal chairperson)
Affiliation: Agua Caliente Tribal Council, 600 E. Tahquitz Canyon Way, Palm Springs, CA 92262 (760) 325-3400 Fax 325-0593. His service on the tribal council began in 1978, serving as secretary from 1981 until 1984 when he was elected chairperson. *Community activities*: In 1990, appointed to the State Historical Resources Commission; honorary member of the Desert Riders, Coachella Valley Mountains Conservancy; founding member of the Santa Rosa & San Jacinto National Monument; serves on the Rupert Costo Advisory Committee at UC, Riverside; represents the tribe as their voting member on the Coachella Valley Assn. of Governments Executive Committee.

MILBRIDGE, DAN
(commission of health/human services)
Affiliation: Mill Lacs Ne0la0Shing Clinic, HCR 67, Box 241, Onamia, MN 56359 (615) 532-4163.

MILES, MARILYN
(attorney)
Affiliation: California Indian Legal Services, 324 F St., Suite A, Eureka, CA 95501 (707) 443-8397.

MILES, WILLIAM P. *(Swift Water)*
(Pamunkey of Virginia) 1943-
(director of administration)
Born November 28, 1943, New Jersey. *Education*: Central University (Pella, IA), 1 year. *Principal occupation*: Director of administration. *Address*: Rt. 1, Box 987, King William, VA 23086 (804) 843-2851. *Affiliation*: Director of Administration, U.S. Dept. of HUD, Richmond, VA, 1985-. *Other professional posts*: Chief of Pamunkey Indian Tribe, King William, VA, 1993-. *Military service*: U.S. Army, 1962-65 (E-4).*Community activities*: Vice chairman, United Indians of Virginia; boar member, Mattaponi, Pamunkey, Monacan, Inc.; member, King William Agricultural Committee. *Interests*: Fishing, hunting, gardening.

MILK, THERESA M. (Cheyenne River Sioux) 1960-
(student; assistant college instructor)
Born May 1, 1960, Rapid City, S.D. *Education*: Haskell Indian Nations University, BA (American Indian Studies; University of Kansas (currently working on MA in Higher Education Administration). *Principal occupation*: Student; assistant instructor at Haskell Indian Nations University. *Home address*: 1603 W. 21st Ter., Lawrence, KS 66046 (785) 843-4564. E-mail: tmilk@ku.edu. *Memberships*: Higher Education Student Association; First Nations Student Association. *Interests*: Writing, sewing, spending time with family.

MILLER, ANDREW, JR. (Eskimo)
(village president)
Affiliation: Nome Eskimo Community, P.O. Box 1090, Nome, AK 99762 (907) 443-2246.

MILLER, CAROL
(elementary school principal)
Affiliation: Lower Brule Day School, P.O. Box 245, Lower Brule, SD 57546 (605) 473-5382.

MILLER, DONNA
(Indian education program director)
Affiliation: Bowler Public Schools, Indian Education Program, P.O. Box 8, Bowler, WI 54416 (715) 793-4101 Fax 793-1302. E-mail: millerd@bowler.k12.wi.us.

MILLER, GLENN (Menominee)
(tribal chairperson)
Affiliation: Menominee Indian Tribe of Wisconsin, P.O. Box 910, Keshena, WI 54135 (715) 799-5100.

MILLER, HAROLD (Crow Creek Sioux)
(tribal chairperson)
Affiliation: Crow Creek Sioux Tribal Council, P.O. Box 50, Fort Thompson, SD 57339 (605) 245-2221.

MILLER, JAY (Delaware) 1947-
(Native Americanist)
Born April 7, 1947. *Education*: University of New Mexico, BA, 1969; Rutgers University, PhD, 1972. *Principal occupation*: Native Americanist. *Address*: Indian Studies Program, University of Washington, Seattle, WA 98195. *Affiliations*: Teaching assistant, lecturer, instructor of anthropology, Rutgers University at Livingston and Newark, 1969-72; assistant professor of anthropology, Montclair State College; executive committee, Indian Studies Program, University of Washington, 1975-. *Other professional posts*: Adjunct curator, North American Ethnology, Washington State Memorial Thomas Burke Museum; consultant, San Juan County Archaeological Research Project, 1973-; contributor, Smithsonian Handbook of North American Indians. *Memberships*: American Anthropological Association (Fellow); Society for American Archaeology. *Awards, honors*: National Science Foundation Predoctoral Fellowship, 1969; grant-in-aid for research in New Jersey history from the New Jersey Historical Commission, 1973; Summer Salary Award, University of Washington Graduate Research Fund, 1974; Delaware Indian Music, University of Washington Graduate Research Fund, Interdisciplinary Grant, 1975-76;

Social Context of Southern Tsimshian, Jacobs Research Fund, Whatcom County Museum, 1977; among others. Field research: Archaeology, Anasazi Origins Project (summers, 1966-67); ethnography, Southwestern Pueblos, 1966-69; ethnography, Unami Delaware, 1972-; Southern Tsimshian: new language & ethnography at Hartley Bay, 1976 and Kelmtu, 1977, British Columbia; Colville Reservation: conceptual landscape, 1977-. Dissertation: The Anthropology of Keres Identity (A Structural Study of the Ethnographic and Archaeological Record of the Keres Pueblos). *Published works*: Shamanic Odyssey, Mourning Dove, Tsimshian and Their Neighbors. Numerous papers and articles.

MILLER, JEANETTE
(Indian education program director)
Affiliation: Rush-Henrietta Central School District, Indian Education Project, 2034 Lehigh Station Rd., Henrietta, NY 14467 (716) 359-5047.

MILLER, JOHN (Potawatomi)
(tribal chairperson)
Affiliation: Pokagon Band of Potawatomi Indians, P.O. Box 180, Dowagiac, MI 49047 (616) 782-8998.

MILLER, KAREN L. (Tolowa)
(rancheria chairperson)
Affiliation: Smith River Rancheria, 250 N. Indian Rd., Smith River, CA 95567 (707) 487-9255.

MILLER, LESLIE (Pomo)
(tribal co-chairperson)
Affiliation: Scotts Valley Band of Pomo Indians, 149 N. Main #200, Lakeport, CA 95453 (707) 263-4771.

MILLER, MICHAEL R. (Chippewa-Stockbridge Munsee) 1946-
(Native American programs director)
Born April 26, 1946, Minneapolis, Minn. *Education*: Appalachian State University, Boone, N.C., BS, 1968; University of Minnesota, Duluth, MSW, 1984. *Principal occupation*: Native American programs director. *Address*: University of Wisconsin, River Falls, WI 54022. *Affiliations*: Indian education coordinator-supervisor, Title IV-A, Superior Public Schools, WI, 1974-81; Native American Outreach Coordinator, Northland College, 1981-84; director of Native American programs, international student advisor, University of Wisconsin, River Falls, WI, 1984-. *Memberships*: Wisconsin Indian Education Association, 1985-; National Association for Foreign Student Affairs, 1985-. *Interests*: My main areas of interest include Indian education, the social aspects of education, improving the image of Native Americans as this image relates to alcoholism, and learning more about international problems and how they relate to the U.S. and Native American experience.

MILLER, NANCY
(health center director)
Affiliation: Fort Thompson PHS Indian Health Center, P.O. Box 200, Fort Thompson, SD 57339 (605) 245-2285.

MILLER, ROBERT
(council president)
Affiliation: Intertribal Agricultural Council, 100 North 27th St. #500, Billings, MT 59101 (406) 259-3525.

MILLER, STEPHEN
(monument supt.)
Affiliation: Navajo National Monument, Tonalea, AZ 86044 (602) 672-2366.

MILLER, THOMAS G.
(school administrator)
Affiliation: Hannahville Indian School, N14911 Hannahville B1 Rd., Wilson, MI 49896 (906) 466-2952 Fax 466-2556.

MILLER, VERNON (Paiute)
(tribal council chairperson)
Affiliation: Fort Independence Paiute Tribal Council, P.O. Box 67, Independence, CA 93526 (760) 878-2126.

MILLER, VIRGINIA P. 1940-
(professor of anthropology)
Born October 28, 1940, Paterson, N.J. *Education*: Smith College, 1958-60; University of California, Ber-

keley, BA, 1962; University of California, Davis, MA, 1970, PhD, 1973. *Address & Affiliation*: Professor of anthropology, Dept. of Sociology & Anthropology, Dalhousie University, Halifax, Nova Scotia B3H 1T2, Can., 1974-. E-mail: vpmiller@ns.sympatico.ca. *Memberships*: American Anthropological Association; American Society for Ethnohistory; Canadian Anthropology Society; Canadian Historical Association (Native History Study Group, 1989-). *Interests*: Ethno-history of North America, especially California and Eastern Canada; historical demography. *Published work*: Ukomno'm: The Yuki Indians of Northern California (Ballena Press, 1979); various articles on Micmac & Yuki ethnohistory and demography.

MILLS, BARBARA
(professor)
Education: University of New Mexico, PhD, 1989. *Affiliation*: American Indian Studies Program, University of Arizona, Harvill Bldg., Rm 430, Box 210076, Tucson, AZ 85721 (520) 621-7108 Fax 621-7952. E-mail: aisp@email.arizona.edu. *Interests*: Southwestern archaeology; archaeology of Native Americans; Native American gender & archaeology; materials culture.

MILLS, JEANETTE
(editor)
Affiliation: Kumtux," Native American Task Force, Church Council of Greater Seattle, 4759 15th Ave. NE, Seattle, WA 98105.

MILLS, SIDNEY L.
(BIA area director)
Affiliation: Albuquerque Area Office, Bureau of Indian Affairs, P.O. Box 26567, Albuquerque, NM 87125 (505) 766-3754.

MILLS, WALTER R.
(BIA area director)
Affiliation: Phoenix Area Office, Bureau of Indian Affairs, P.O. Box 10, Phoenix, AZ 85001 (602) 379-6600.

MILROY, JAMES L.
(association president)
Affiliation: Creek Indian Memorial Association, Town Square, Okmulgee, OK 74447 (918) 756-2324.

MINGS, LARRY W.
(BIA agency acting supt.)
Affiliation: Talihini Agency, Bureau of Indian Affairs, P.O. Drawer H, Talihini, OK 74571 (918) 567-2207.

MINER, MARCELLA HIGH BEAR
(Cheyenne River Sioux) 1935-
(tribal official)
Born July 31, 1935, Cheyenne Agency, S.D. *Education*: Cheyenne River Boarding School; Aberdeen School of Commerce. *Principal occupation*: Tribal official. *Home address*: Eagle Butte, SD 57625. *Affiliations*: Tribal treasurer, 1962-66, assistant finance officer, 1968-69, bookkeeper, 1969-, Cheyenne River Sioux Tribal Council. Community activities: Cheyenne River Mission, Episcopal Church (treasurer, 1963-66).

MINGS, LARRY W.
(BIA field rep.)
Affiliation: Talihina Agency, Bureau of Indian Affairs, P.O. Drawer H, Talihina, OK 74561 (918) 567-2207.

MINHAS, JASJIT
(college president)
Affiliation: Lac Courte Oreilles Ojibwa Community College, RR 2, Box 2357, Hayward, WI 54843 (715) 634-4790 Fax 634-5049.

MINTHORN, ANTONE C. (Umatilla)
(tribal chairperson)
Affiliation: Umatilla Board of Trustees, P.O. Box 638, Pendleton, OR 97801 (541) 276-3165.

MINTZIES, PAULA
(organization president)
Affiliation: George Bird Grinnell American Indian Children's Fund, 11602 Montague Court, Potomac, MD 20854 (301) 424-2440 Fax 424-8281.

MIRANDA, JENNIE (Luiseno)
(tribal spokesperson)
Affiliation: Pechanga Band of Mission Indians, P.O. Box 1477, Temecula, CA 92390 (714) 676-2768.

MISIKIN, ALICIA (Aleut)
(radio station manager)
Affiliation: KUHB - FM, Pribiloff School District, St. Paul, AK 99660 (907) 546-2254.

MISQUEZ, SARA (Mescalero Apache)
(tribal president)
Affiliation: Mescalero Apache Tribal Council, P.O. Box 227, Mescalero, NM 88340 (505) 464-4494.

MITCHELL, FRANCIS (Penobscot)
(former tribal governor)
Affiliation: Penobscot Indian Nation, Community Bldg., Indian Island, 6 River Rd., Old Town, ME 04468 (207) 827-7776.

MITCHELL, GARY E. (Prairie Potawatomi)
(former tribal chairperson)
Affiliation: Prairie Band Potawatomi Trbal Council, 14880 K. Rd., Mayetta, KS 66509 (913) 966-2255.

MITCHELL, JEFF (Klamath)
(tribal chairperson)
Affiliation: Klamath General Council, P.O. Box 436, Chiloquin, OR 97624 (541) 783-2219.

MITCHELL, SR. KATERI
(center director)
Affiliation & address: Tekakwitha Conference National Center, P.O. Box 6768, Great Falls, MT 59406-6768 (800) 842-9635; (406) 727-0147 Fax 452-9845. E-mail: sisterkateri@worldnet.att.net.

MITCHELL, MICHAEL (Mohawk)
(Indian band chief)
Affiliation: Mohawks of Akwesasne, Box 579, Cornwall, Ontario, Canada K6H 5T3 (613) 575-2348.

MITCHELL, RON (Cherokee)
(artist; gallery owner)
Affiliation: Cherokee Artist Studio-Gallery, Rt. 1, Box 263, Prague, OK 74864 (405) 567-2856.

MITCHELL, RUDI L., DR. (Omaha)
(former tribal chairperson)
Affiliation: Omaha Tribal Council, P.O. Box 368, Macy, NE 68039 (402) 837-5391.

MITCHELL, THEDIS
(hospital director)
Affiliation: Clinton PHS Indian Hospital, P.O. Box 279, Clinton, OK 73601 (405) 323-2884.

MITCHELL, THEODORE N.
(Indian center director)
Address & Affiliation: Director, Wabanaki Center, University of Maine, Rm. 314, 5724 Dunn Hall, Orono, ME 04469 (207) 581-1417 Fax 581-4760; E-mail: tedm@maine.maine.edu

MITCHELL, WAYNE LEE
(Santee Sioux-Mandan) 1937-
(health administrator)
Born March 25, 1937, Rapid City, S.D. *Education*: University of Redlands, BA, 1960; Arizona State University, MSW, 1970, EdD, 1979. *Principal occupation*: Health administrator. *Address*: P.O. Box 9592, Phoenix, AZ 85068. *Affiliations*: Professional social worker, various county, state and federal agencies, 1962-70; social worker, BIA, Phoenix, AZ, 1970-77; assistant professoor, Arizona State University, Tempe, AZ, 1977-84; supervisor, 1984-88, program director of social services, 1988-2003, U.S. Public Health Service, Indian Health Service, Phoenix, AZ. *Other professional post*: Assistant professor, Arizona State University. *Military service*: U.S. Coast Guard, 1960-66. *Community activities*: Phoenix Indian Community School (board of directors); Phoenix Indian Center (board of directors); Phoenix Area Health Advisory Board, 1975; Community Behavioral Mental Health Board, 1976; Council on Foreign Relations; Heard Museum (board of trustees). *Memberships*: National Congress of American Indians; National Association of Social Workers; Association of American Indian Social Workers; American Orthopsychiatric Association; Nucleus Club; Arizona Town Hall; Phi Delta Kappa; Kappa Delta Pi; Chi Sigma Chi. *Awards, honors*: Delegate to White House Conference on Poverty, 1964; nominated, Outstanding Young Men of America, 1977; Phoenix Indian Center: Community Service Award, 1977; Temple

of Islam Community Service Award, 1980; Arizona State University: Community Service Award, 1996; Phoenix Area Indian Health Service: Professional Employee of the Year Award, 2000; NASW: Lifetime Achievement Award, 2003; Arizona State University: Outstanding Native American Alumnus, 2003; Combined Federal Campaign Award: Oustanding Volunteer, 2003. *Interests*: World traveler. *Biographical sources*: Who's Who in the West; Who's Who in America; Men of Achievement. *Published works*: The Inside-Outside School Concept As Observed in Educational Institutions in the People's Republic of China; A Study of Cultural Identification on the Educational Objectives of Hopi Indian High School Seniors (master's thesis), (Arizona State University, 1970); Native American Substance Abuse (Arizona State University Press, 1983); American Indian Families: Developmental Strategies and Community Health (Arizona State University Press, 1983).

MITCHUM, MARIA (Maidu)
(study skills specialist)
Affiliation: Learning Skills Center, University of California, Davis, Basement, South Hall, Davis, CA 95616 (916) 752-2013.

MITCHUM, WAYNE (Wintun)
(rancheria chairperson)
Affiliation: Colusa Rancheria, 50 Wintun Rd., Colusa, CA 95932 (530) 458-8231.

MITHUN, MARIANNE 1946-
(linguist, professor of linguistics)
Born April 8, 1946, Bremerton, Wash. *Education*: Pomona College, BA, 1969; Yale University, MA, M.Phil., PhD, 1969-1974. *Principal occupation*: Linguist, professor of linguistics. *Address*: Dept. of Linguistics, University of California, Santa Barbara, CA 93106; E-Mail: mithun@linguistics.ucsb.edu. *Affiliations*: Assistant/associate professor of linguistics, SUNY at Albany, 1973-81; professor of linguistics, University of California, Berkeley, 1981-86; professor of linguistics, University of California, Santa Barbara, 1986-. *Community activities*: Organizer, Iroquois Conference, 1973-85. *Memberships*: Society for Linguistic Anthropology (president); American Anthropological Association (executive committee, board of directors, administrative advisory committee); Society for the Study of the Indigenous Languages of the Americas (president, vice-president, executive board); Linguistics Society of America (executive board). *Interests*: American Indian languages and linguistics, especially Iroquoian (Mohawk, Oneida, Onondaga, Cayuga, Seneca, Tuscarora, Huron), Pomo (Central Pomo), Siouan (Dakota, Lakota, Tutelo), Algonquian (Cree); Yu'pik Eskimo; Navajo. *Published works*: A Grammar of Tuscarora (Garland Press, 1976); Kanien'keha'Okara'shon:'a (Mohawk Stories) and Iontenwennaweienstahkhwa' (Mohawk Spelling Dictionary) (New York State Museum Bulletin, 1976,1977); The Languages of Native America (University of Texas Press, 1979); Watewayestanih: A Grammar of Cayuga (Woodland Indian Culture & Education Centre, 1982); Extending the Rafters: An Interdisciplinary Approach to the Iroquois (SUNY Press, 1984); The Native Languages of North America (Cambridge University Press, 1999); numerous articles in "International Journal of American Linguistics."

MITRE, ALFREDA (Paiute)
(tribal chairperson)
Affiliation: Las Vegas Tribal Council, One Paiute Dr., Las Vegas, NV 89106 (702) 386-3926.

MITTEN, LISA A. (Mohawk)
(librarian)
Education: University of Pittsburgh, BA, MLS. *Address & Affiliation*: G20-U Hillman Library, University of Pittsburgh, Pittsburgh, PA 15260 (412) 648-7780 Fax 648-7798; E-Mail: lmitten@vms.cis.pitt.edu. Web site: www.pitt.edu/~lmitten/indians.html. *Community activities*: Consultant, Alcoa Hall of Native Americans, Carnegie Museum of Natural History, Pittsburgh, PA; board member, Oyate, Berkeley, CA; Board of Directors, Council of Three Rivers American Indian Center, Pittsburgh, PA, 1998-. *Memberships*: American Library Association; American Indian Library Association; National Museum of the American Indian. *Published work*: Assistant editor, "Native America in the Twentieth Century: An Encyclopedia" (Garland Publishing, 1994).

MODUGNO, REV. THOMAS A.
(director)
Affiliation: Marquette League for Catholic Indian Missions, 1011 First Ave., New York, NY 10022 (212) 371-1000.

MOFFETT, ELLIOT (Nez Perce)
(BIA agency supt.)
Affiliation: Northern Idaho Agency, BIA, P.O. Box 277, Lapwai, ID 83540 (208) 843-2300 Fax 843-7142.

MOFFETT, WALTER L. (Nez Perce) 1927-
(pastor)
Born June 23, 1927, Kamiah, Idaho. *Education*: College of Idaho, BA, 1955. *Principal occupation*: Pastor. *Home address*: P.O. Box 668, Kamiah, ID 83536. *Affiliations*: Clerk-stenographer, U.S. Dept. of the Interior, Standing Rock Reservation, ND, 1949-50; intern pastor, Brigham City, UT, 1955-58; clerk and sanitarian, USPHS, Indian Health Service, Idaho & Washington, 1958-62; pastor, Kamiah-Kooshia United Presbyterian Churches, Kamiah, ID, 1964-; council member, Nez Perce Tribal Executive Committee, 1970-. *Other professional posts*: Guidance counselor, Kamiah Public Schools (2 years); member, Council of Advisors, American Indian Heritage Foundation, Falls Church, VA. *Military service*: 1945-47 (Corporal). *Community activities*: Northwest Regional Eductional Laboratory (past member, board of directors); Small Business Administration (advisory council); State Advisory Council, Title III ESEA, Idaho; Idaho Historic Sites Review Board; Community Relations Council, Cedar Flats Job Corps Center, Kooshia, Idaho (past chairman). *Memberships*: Affiliated Tribes of Northwest Indians (president); National Congress of American Indians (area vice president); National Indian Council on Aging. *Interests*: Politics—1974 Republican candidate for State Senator; held pastorate fourteen years. *Biographical source*: Personalities of the West and Midwest, 1971.

MOFSIE, LOUIS (*Greenrainbow*) (Hopi/Winnebago) 1936-
(teacher)
Born May 3, 1936, Brooklyn, N.Y. *Education*: Buffalo State Teachers College, BS, 1958; Hofstra University, MA, 1973. *Principal occupation*: Teacher. *Home address*: 204 W. Central Ave., Maywood, NJ 07607 (201) 587-9633. *Affiliation*: Director, Thunderbird American Indian Dancers, New York, NY; *Other professional post*: Art teacher, East Meadow Board of Education, East Meadow, NY (36 years); consultant, National Museum of the American Indian, 1991. *Community activities*: Chairman of the Board, American Indian Community House, New York, NY; president, International Council of McBurney YMCA. *Memberships*: New York State Art Teachers Association; Classroom Teachers Association. *Awards, honors*: Association of Southwestern Indians Award for painting submitted to the Annual Indian Artists Exhibition, Santa Fe Art Museum; New York City Indian of the Year, 1984; 1986 Calumet Award for Outstanding Achievement by the American Indian Community House, New York, NY; 1987 Ethnic New York Award; 1990 Outstanding Achievement Award by the New York State Council of the Disabled; 1991 Outstanding Achievement Award by the New York City Lawyers Local; Ellis Island Congressional Medal of Honor, 1993. *Interests*: American Indian dance - "as a dance company, we have traveled all over the U.S., Canada, Israel and Mexico. I am currently teaching dance at Brooklyn College and the YMCA." *Biographical sources*: "Indians of Today," by Marion Gridley; "American Indian Painters," by Joanne Snodgrass; "Dance Annuals," by John Mills. *Published work*: Co-author & illustrator, The Hopi Way (J.B. Lippincott, 1970); illustrator, Coyote Tales, and Teepee Tales (Holt, Rinehart & Winston).

MOHAWK, JOHN C. (Seneca) 1945-
(professor of American Indian studies; editor)
Born August 30, 1945, Buffalo, N.Y. *Education*: Hartwick College, BA, 1968; SUNY at Buffalo. *Principal Occupation*: Professor of American Studies at SUNY Buffalo. *Affiliations*: Professor of American Studies, Center for the Americas, SUNY at Buffalo, Buffalo, NY; Indigenous People's Network, 226 Blackman Hill Rd., Berkshire, NY 13736 (607) 657-8413; former editor, Akwesasne Notes, 1976-1983; editor, Daybreak Magazine. *Other Professional Post*: Writer, "Native Americas", magazine; columnist for "Indian Country

Today", weekly newspaper. *Community Activities*: Seventh Generation Fund (chairperson); Indian Law Resource Center (board member). *Published Work*: A Basic Call to Consciousness (Akwesasne Notes, 1978).

MOLASH, CHARLENE
(IHS-executive officer)
Affiliation: Bemidji IHS Area Office, 127 Federal Bldg., Bemidji, MN 56601 (218) 759-3413.

MOLIN, PAULETTE FAIRBANKS
(White Earth Chippewa)
(educator, writer)
Address: 102 Willis Church Yar, Hampton, VA 23669. E-Mail: pfmolin@aol.com. *Affiliations*: Director, American Indian Educational Opportunities Program, Hampton University, Hampton, VA , 1991-99; assistant dean, Graduate College, Hampton University, 1991-94; director, Indian Elementary Curriculum Project, Minneapolis Public Schools. *Memberships*: American Indian Science & Engineering Society; Indigenous Women's Network; National Indian Education Association; Wordcraft Circle of Native Writers & Storytellers (board officer). *Published works*: Co-author, "To Lead and To Serve: American Indian Education at Hampton Institute, 1878-1923" (Hampton University & Virginia Foundation for the Humanities and Public Policy, 1989); co-author, "Unanswered Questions: Native Americans and Euro-Americans in Minnesota" for an exhibition and publication entitled "Minnesota 1900: Art & Life on the Upper Mississippi 1890-1915" (Associated University Press, 1994); Additional writings have included co-authorship of biographical booklets (historic Hampton students from Fort Berthold and Standing Rock), co-authorship of an encyclopedia; authorship of encyclopedia entries, curricula units, journal articles, and other publications. Guest co-editor of "Callaloo" (a special issue, Native American Literature, Winter, 1994); co-edited, American Indian Stereotypes in the World of Children, 2nd Ed. (Scarecrow Press, 1999).

MOLLENHOFF, LORI
(board president)
Affiliation: Migizi Communications, Inc., 3123 E. Lake St., Suite 200, Minneapolis, MN 55406 (612) 721-6631.

MOMADAY, NAVARRE SCOTT (Kiowa, Cherokee)
1934-
(writer, painter, educator)
Born February 27, 1934, Lawton, Okla. *Education*: University of New Mexico, BA, 1958; Stanford University, MA, 1960, PhD, 1963. *Principal occupation*: Writer, educator, painter. *Address*: The University of Arizona, American Indian Studies Program, Harvill Bldg., Rm. 430, P.O. Box 210076, Tucson, AZ 85721 (520) 621-7108 Fax 621-7952. *Affiliations*: Assistant professor, associate professor of English, University of California, Santa Barbara, 1962-69; professor of English and Comparative Literature, University of California, Berkeley, 1969-72; professor of English, Stanford University, 1972-80; professor of English & American Literature, University of Arizona, Tucson, AZ, 1981-. *Other professional posts*: Consultant, National Endowment for the Humanities, 1970-; trustee, Museum of the American Indian, 1978-; currently Regents Professor of the Humanities, University of Arizona, he directs projects which focus upon Native American oral tradition and Native American concepts of the sacred. *Memberships*: American Studies Association; MLA. *Awards, honors*: Guggenheim Fellowship, 1966; Recipient of the Pulitzer Prize for fiction, 1969; an award from the National Institute of Arts & Letters; the Golden Plate Award from the American Academy of Achievement; and the Premio Letterario Internazionale Mondello, Italy, 1979 (Italy's highest literary award); Fellow of the American Academy of Arts & Sciences; his paintings, drawings, and prints have been exhibited in the U.S. and abroad. A one-man, 20-year retrospective was mounted at the Wheelwright, Santa Fe, NM, in 1992-93. He holds 12 honorary degrees fro American colleges & universities, including Yale, University of Massachusetts, and the University of Wisconsin. *Biographical source*: Who's Who in America. *Published works*: The Complete Poems of Frederick Goddard Tuckerman (Oxford University Press, 1965); House Made of Dawn (Harper & Row, 1968); The Way to Rainy Mountain (University of New Mexico Press, 1969); Angle of Geese and Other Poems (David R. Godine, 1973); The Gourd Dancer (Harper & Row,

1976); The Names (Harper & Row, 1976); The Ancient Child (Doubleday); In the Presence of the Sun (St. Martin's Press); Circle of Wonder (St. Martin's Press; The Storyteller and His Art (Oxford University Press); A Dark, Indifferent Rage (Doubleday); and The Blind Astrologers (St. Martin's Press); his play "The Indolent Boys," which was given staged readings to full houses at Harvard in Feb. 1993, had its world premiere at the Syracuse Stage in Feb. 1994; his articles have appeared in "Natural History," "American West," "The New York Review of Books," "New York Newsday," "The New York Times Book Review," "The New York Times Magazine," etc..

MONETTE, GERALD
(college president)
Affiliation: Turtle Mountain Community College, P.O. Box 340, Belcourt, ND 58316 (701) 477-5605 Fax 477-5028.

MONETTE, RICHARD A, (Chippewa)
(tribal chairperson)
Affiliation: Turtle Mountain Tribal Council, P.O. Box 900, Belcoirt, ND 58316 (701) 477-0470.

MONIAS, EUGENE
(Indian band chief)
Affiliation: Heart Lake Indian Band, Box 447, Lac La Biche, Alberta, Canada T0A 2C0 (403) 623-2130.

MONONGYE, JESSE L. (Navajo)
(artist/jeweler)
Address: 6102 E. Charter Oak Rd., Scottsdale, AZ 85254 (602) 991-8159. *Membership*: Indian Arts & Crafts Association.

MONSEN, MARIE A. 1939-
(federal government program analyst)
Born October 18, 1939, New York, N.Y. *Education*: Bucknell University, BA, 1961; East-West Center, Honolulu, HI, MA, 1963. *Principal occupation*: Federal government program analyst. *Home address*: 6807 Hopewell Ave., Springfield, VA 22151. *Affiliations*: Training officer, Peace Corps, Thailand Program, 1964-70; evaluation specialist, Dept. of the Interior, Washington, DC, 1971-79; chief, Local & Indian Affairs, Dept. of Energy, Washington, DC, 1979-. *Community activities*: Annandale Christian Community for Action (vice president); Shelter House, Fairfax County (board of directors); elder in Presbyterian Church. *Membership*: Women's Council on Energy and the Environment, 1983-. *Awards, honors*: Certificate of Special Achievement, Bureau of Indian Affairs, 1979; Outstanding Achievement Award, 1984, Americans for Indian Opportunity; Superior Job Performance Awards, 1984-1985, Dept. of Energy. *Interests*: Indian energy; tribal government.

MONTAGUE, FELIX J.
(BIA agency supt.)
Affiliation: Fort Yuma Agency, Bureau of Indian Affairs, P.O. Box 1591, Yuma, AZ 85364 (619) 572-0248.

MONTALVO, PILAR
(program coordinator)
Affiliation: American Indian Ritual Object Repatriation Foundation, 463 E. 57th St., New York, NY 10128 (212) 980-9441 Fax 421-2746.

MONTANA, ALEX
(council chairperson)
Affiliation: American Indian Religious Rights (AIRR), 1017 Lincoln Ave., College Station, TX 77840 (409) 268-9008 Fax 758-1187.

MONTANO, FRANCIS (Ojibwe)
(museum director)
Affiliation: Red Cliff Tribal Museum, Arts & Crafts Cultural Center, P.o. Box 529, Bayfield, WI 54814 (715) 779-5609.

MONTEAU, CYNTHIA (Standing Rock Sioux)
(office manager)
Affiliation: National Indian Health Board, 1385 S. Colorado Blvd., Suite A708, Denver, CO 80221 (303) 759-3075.

MONTEAU, HAROLD A. (Chippewa-Cree)
(attorney)
Affiliation: Monteau Guenther & Decker, 410 Central

Ave., Suite 522, Great Falls, MT 59401 (406) 452-9955/9787. *Membership*: Native American Bar Association (board member).

MONTES, JAMES (Chippewa Cree)
(BIA field rep.)
Affiliation: Rocky Boy's Agency Rep., Bureau of Indian Affairs, RR 1 Box 542, Box Elder, MT 59521 (406) 395-4476 Fax 395-4382.

MONTGOMERY, JANNEY
(executive officer)
Affiliation: Indian Rights Association, 1801 Market St., 10th Floor, Philadelphia, PA 19103 (215) 665-4523. *Other professional post*: Editor, Indian Truth," bionthly news journal of the Indian Rights Association.

MONTOUR, WILLIAM
(Indian band chief)
Affiliation: Six Nations of the Grand River Indian Band, Box 1, Ohsweken, Ontario, Canada N0A 1M0 (519) 445-2201.

MONTOYA, GERONIMA CRUZ (*P'otsunu*) (Pueblo)
1915-
(retired artist, teacher)
Born September 22, 1915, San Juan Pueblo, N.M. *Education*: St. Joseph's College, BS, 1958; University of New Mexico; Claremont College. *Principal occupation*: Art teacher, Santa Fe, NM. *Home address*: 1008 Calle de Suenos, Santa Fe, NM 87505 (505) 471-5480 (home). *Affiliation*: Co-founder, lifetime board chairperson, San Juan Pueblo Arts & Crafts Cooperative, 1973-. *Community activities*: Community Concert Association (captain); San Juan Pueblo Choir (secretary-treasurer); SWAIA _ Southwest American Indian Arts (board member); on Advisory Panel with Indian Art & Culture Museum. *Awards, honors*: School of American Research Purchase Award; Museum of New Mexico Special Category Prize, Inter-Tribal Indian Ceremonial, Gallup, N.M.; Special Prize, Philbrook Art Center, Tulsa, Okla.; DeYoung Museum Purchase Prize; among others.

MONTOYA, JOSEPH
(administrative officer)
Affiliation: Santa Fe PHS Indian Hospital, 1700 Cerrillos Rd., Santa Fe, NM 87501 (505) 988-9821.

MONTOYA, RON (Santa Ana Pueblo)
(former Pueblo governor)
Affiliation: Santa Ana Pueblo Council, 2 Dove Rd., Bernalillo, NM 87004 (505) 867-3301.

MONTOYA, VINCE (*Pubsay*) (Isleta Pueblo) 1939-
(civil engineer)
Born July 19, 1939, Tohatchi, N.M. (Navajo Reservation). *Education*: University of New Mexico, BS, 1964; St. Mary's University (San Antonio, TX), MA, 1978. *Principal occupation*: Civil engineer. *Home address*: 9208 Northridge Dr., NE, Albuquerque, NM 87111 (505) 291-8402; 846-7904 (work). *Affiliations*: Project Manager, 542d Civil Engineering Squadron, Kirtland AFB, NM, 1986-. *Other professional post*: American Indian Employment Programs Manager, Kitland AFB, NM, 1986-. *Military service*: U.S. Air Force, 1964-84 (Major {0-4}-retired; Missile Engineer (Minuteman) at Vandenburg AFB, CA; Site Civil Engineer at Hopedale Air Station, Labrador; Civil Engineering Chief of Operations at Torrejon AB & Zaragoza AB, Spain; and Korat Royal Thai Air Base, Thailand; Chief Civil Engineer Inspector, HQ 9th Air Force, Shaw AFB, SC; Chief Maintenance Management Division, DCS Engineering & Services, HQ Air Training Command, Randolph AFB, TX; and as Base Civil Engineer, Zaragoza AB, Spain & RAF Chicksands, U.K.). *Community activities*: Persian Gulf Support Groups at various Indian commuities; work with all Indian organizations in the Albuquerque area; conduct various activities at annual American Indian Heritage Week, Kitland, NM. *Memberships*: Air Force Association; Disabled American Veterans Association; Society of American Military Engineers. *Awards, honors*: His military decorations and awards include: the Meritorious Service Medal with four oak leaf clusters; the Air Force Commendation Medal; the Air Force Outstanding Unit Award with Valor; Small Arms Markmanship Ribbon; National Defense Service Tibbon; Republic of Vietnam Gallantry Cross with Palm; and the USAF Missileman Badge. His civilian awards include the USAF Performance Award

for each year he has been assigned at Kitland. He was awarded a Quality Step Increase for 1991. He also received the Air Force Distinguished Equal Employment Opportunity Award for the American Indian/Alaskan Native Employment Program for 1991.

MOODY, EDWARD
(Indian band chief)
Affiliation: Bella Coola Indian Band, Box 65, Bella Coola, BC, Can. V1C 1C0 (604) 799-5613.

MOODY, ROBERT, JR. (Potawatomi)
(former tribal chairperson)
Affiliation: Pokagon Band of Potawatomi Indians, P.O. Box 180, Dowagiac, MI 49047 (616) 782-8998.

MOON, JAMES W., JR. (Wiyot)
(rancheria chairperson)
Affiliation: Bear River Band of Rohnerville Rancheria, 32 Bear River Dr., Loleta, CA 95551 (888) 733-1900.

MOORE, ARDINA REVARD
(*Ma-shro-gita*) (Quapaw-Osage) 1930-
(business owner; designer-Indian clothes; teacher)
Born December 1, 1930, Belton, Tex. *Education*: Oklahoma State University, 1952-53; Northeastern State University (Tahlequah, OK), BS (Education), 1957. *Principal occupation*: Business owner; designer-Indian clothing; teacher. *Home address*: 1204 Sky Lane, Miami, OK 74354; *Office address*: P.O. Box 1556, Miami, OK 74355 (918) 542-8870 (office). *Affiliations*: Owner, Buffalo Sun, Miami, OK, 1982- (specialty Indian clothing business); instructor, Indian Studies Program, Northeastern Oklahoma Jr. College, Miami, OK, 1989-. *Community activities*: Chamber of Commerce, Miami, OK; Promenade India Club (president, 1992); Keepers of the Treasures; Quapaw Tribal Business Committee (secretary-treasurer (2 years). *Memberships*: Okalhoma State Medical Auxiliary; Oklahoma Education Association; Quapaw Tribe of Oklahoma; Osage Tribe of Oklahoma; Oklahoma Federation of Indian Women; \National Congress of American Indians; Indian and Western Arts Association; American Indian Designers Association (president, 1989). *Awards, honors*: Mother of the Year, 1992, Oklahoma Federation of Indian Women; Artistic Awards - 2nd Place, Creek Council House, Okmulgee, OK, 1989; 1st & 2nd Place, Indian Summer Art Show, Bartlesville, OK, 1990, 1991. *Interests*: Genealogy research, Federal Archives; Indian Dance Troupe and fashion shows around the country. *Biographical sources*: Facets Magazine (American Medical Association Auxiliary, Spring & Winter 1978); in Joplin Magazine, Business Profiles, Feb. 1986; Math America text book series (Houghton Mifflin, 1992. *Published works*: Editor, Auxiliary Page, Oklahoma State Medical Journal, 1965-66; editor, Montana Medical Auxiliary Newsletter, 1970-71; editor, Genealogy Society, Miami, OK Newsletter, 1979-80.

MOORE, DAISY POCAHONTAS (Wampanoag) 1931-
(director-Wampanoag Indian program)
Born July 6, 1931, Mashpee, Mass. *Education*: Boston University, BA, 1958. *Principal occupation*: Director, Wampanoag Indian Program, Living History Museum, Plimoth Plantation, Plymouth, MA, 1983-. *Home address*: P.O. Box 4462, Washington, DC 20017. *Other professional post*: Member, Mashpee Tribal Council (Wampanoag). *Membership*: American Museum Association. *Interest*: "Primary area of interest—museum; have traveled throughout Africa; taught school in Africa for three years under the auspices of the Methodist Church; limited travel to Europe; attended the University of Grenoble, France for one year." *Biographical sources*: Articles in local newspapers: In Harmony With Nature, Cape Cod Times, June 13, 1985; Collection at Mashpee Wampanoag Museum Enhanced by Plimoth Plantation Loan, The Enterprise (Falmouth, Mass., May 24, 1985).

MOORE, DONALD W., SR.
(Bad River Band of Lake Superior Ojibwe)
(former tribal chairperson)
Affiliation: Bad River Tribal Council, P.O. Box 39, Odanah, WI 54861 (715) 682-7111.

MOORE, GENE
(museum manager)
Affiliation: Kotzebue Museum, P.O. Box 46, Kotzebue, AK 99752 (907) 442-3401.

MOORE, JOHN H. (*Nokoshutke-Muskogee Creek*) 1939-
(anthropologist)
Born February 27, 1939, Williston, N.D. *Education*: New York University, PhD, 1974. *Principal occupation*: Anthropologist. Home address: 3328 NW 18th Ave., Gainesville, FL 32605 (352) 846-0263 (work). *Affiliations*: Chair & professor, Dept. of Anthropology, University of Oklahoma, Norman, OK, 1977-93; chair & professor, University of Florida, Gainesville, FL, 1993-98. *Past professional post*: Consultant, Sand Creek Descendants Association, Muskogee Creek Tribal Towns, Inc. *Military service*: U.S. Army, 1962-64 (lieutenant). *Memberships*: American Anthropological Association; American Ethnological Society; American Association for the Advancement of Science. *Awards, honors*: Received title of Emafanaka from Muskogee Tribal Towns Organization; Certificate of Achievement from Cheyenne Sand Creek Descendants, "Most Helpful Faculty Member, American Indian Students Association, University of Oklahoma; Oklahoma Governor's Community Service Award for work with Creek communities; Fellow, American Association for the Advancement of Science. *Interests*: Treaty rights; health; demography. Presently working on Sand Creek Massacre Claim, the Twinn case in Canada involving band sovereignty. *Biographical source*: Search for the Sand Creek Descendants, Sooner Magazine, Spring, 1983; Who's Who in the South & Southwest, 1985-; Who's Who in America, 2003. *Published works*: Ethnology in Oklahoma (Papers in Anthropology, 1980); The Cheyennes in Moxtavhohona (Northern Cheyenne Tribe, Inc., 1981); The Cheyenne Nation (University of Nebraska Press, 1986); Political Economy of North American Indians (University of Oklahoma Press, 1993); The Cheyenne (Blackwell, 1996).

MOORE, KELLY R. (Creek) 1955-
(physician)
Born May 24, 1955, Tahlequah, Okla. *Education*: University of Oklahoma, BA, 1977; University of Oklahoma, Tulsa Medical School, MD, 1983, Pediatric residency, 1986. *Principal occupation*: Physician. *Address*: Unknown. *Affiliations*: Women's counselor, University of Oklahoma Health Sciences Center, Headlands Indian Health Careers Program, Mackinac City, MI, 1978-80; clinical director, Kayenta PHS, Indian Health Center, Kayenta, AZ on Navajo Reservation, 1987-89; clinical director, USPHS, Indian Health Service Clinic, Taholah, WA, 1989-91; clinical director, Sacaton PHS Indian Hospital, Sacaton, AZ, 1991-95; clinical director, PHS-Indian Health Service, Fort Duchesne, UT, 1995-. *Military service*: Commissioned Officer, USPHS, 1987- (Commander; received Isolated Hardship Duty Ribbon and Achievement Medal. *Memberships*: American Academy of Pediatrics (Fellow); Association of American Indian Physicians; Commissioned Officers Association. *Awards, honors*: Ungerman Scholarship Recipient, University of Oklahoma Health Sciences Center, 1982-83; University Scholar, U. of Oklahoma, 1973-74. *Interests*: Child advocacy issues - child sexual/physical abuse; sex/AIDS education; fetal alcohol syndrome prevention; children's diabetes.

MOORE, MARIJO (Eastern Cherokee) 1952-
(writer, lecturer, publisher, artist)
Born August 24, 1952, Tenn. *Education*: Tennesee State University; Lancashire Polytechnic (Preston, England) BA Literature. *Principal occupation*: Writer, lecturer, publisher, artist. *Address*: P.O. Box 2493, Candler, NC 28715 (828) 665-7630 Fax 670-6347. E-mail: marijo@aol.com. Website: www.marijomoore.com. *Affiliation*: Owner, Renegade Planets Publishing, NC (only American Indian-owned publishing co. in NC). *Other professional posts*: Contributing editor to An Anthology of 20th Century North Carolina Poets, Points of Entry: Cross-Currents in Storytelling; she has presented over 300 literary readings/lectures and creative writing workshops at numerous literary gatherings and educational institutions. *Community activities*: Board member, North Carolina Humanities Council. *Membership*: Wordcraft Circle of Native American Writers & Storytellers (National Caucus). *Awards, honors*: North Carolina's Distinguished Woman of the Year in the Arts in 1998; Ms. Moore was chosen by "Native Peoples" magazine as one of the top five American Indian writers of the new century (June/July 2000 issue). *Interests*: Working with unpublished Native authors. *Published/produced works*: Play, "Your Story," was produced at Lancashire Community Theatre in Preston, England, in 1991; *books*: Crow Quotes, Desert Quotes, Spirit Voices of Bones, Tree Quotes, Feeding the Ancient Fires: A Collection of Writings by North Carolina American Indians (editor), Ice Man, The First Fire, Red Woman with Backward Eyes & Other Stories (all published by Renegade Planets Publishing); The Cherokee Little People (children's books, published by Rigby Education); a bilingual edition (Dutch/English) Woestijnwoorden ("Desert Words" published by Uitgeverij, Kamat, Belgium); The Diamond Door Knob, a novel (Renegade Planet, Publishing); editor, Genocide of the Mind (Nation Books/Thunder's Mouth Press); her work has appeared in numerous publications

MOORE, PATRICK EDWARD (*Totkv Vfvstv*) (Creek) 1942-
(attorney)
Born May 16, 1942, Wewoka, Okla. *Education*: University of Oklahoma, BS, 1972; Oklahoma City University School of Law, JD, 1977; University of Houston (Post Graduate Law); National Judicial College, University of Nevada. *Principal occupation*: Attorney. *Home address*: 1 Edgevale Rd., Okmulgee, OK 74447 (918) 756-3391 Fax 758-0019 (office). *Affiliations*: Moore & Moore (law firm), Okmulgee, OK, 1975-; Assistant District Attorney, Okmulgee, OK, 1983-1995. *Other professional posts*: District Judge, Muscogee (Creek) Nation; District Judge, Devils Lake Sioux Nation; Board of Directors, CASA; instructor, Oklahoma Council on Law Enforcement & Training; member, State-Federal-Tribal Judicial Council, Five Civilized Tribes Council. *Military service*: U.S. Air Force, 1963-67 (E-5; Presidential Unit Citation, DSM, Good Conduct, Fairchild Trophy, Standboard). *Community activities*: President, Okmulgee County Shrine Bedovin A.A.N.O.M.S. *Memberships*: Oklahoma Tribal Judges Association (president); Okmulgee County Bar Association (past president); Creek Indian Memorial Association (Board of Trustees; U.S. Supreme Court, 10th Circuit Court of Appeals; U.S. District Courts for Western, Northern & Eastern Districts of Oklahoma; Supreme Court of Oklahoma; Supreme Court of the Muscogee (Creek) Nation; National Association of District Attorneys; Federal Bar Association; Oklahoma Association of District Attorneys; National Association of Tribal Court Judges; American Judicature Society. *Awards, honors*: Graduate, National Judicial College; U.S. Inspector General-Outstanding Prosecution Award; Governor's Commission on Law Enforcement.

MOORE, TRACEY ANN (*E-ne-opp-e -Protected One*) (Pawnee/Otoe-Missouria/Osage/Sac & Fox) 1964-
(office clerk)
Born August 14, 1964, Fairfax, Okla. *Education*: Northern Oklahoma College, 1982-84; University of Oklahoma, 1984-87. *Principal occupation*: Office clerk. *Home address*: 511 Mason, Fairfax, OK 74637 (918) 287-4491 (work). *Affiliations*: American Indian Student Service, University of Oklahoma, Norman, 1986-88; Claremore Indian Hospital, Claremore, OK, 1988-89; . *Other professional posts*: CETA Summer Youth Program, The Osage Nation, 1981-. *Awards, honors*: Nominated twice for Outstanding Young Women of America, 1985; Osage Nation representative for Miss National Congress of American Indians Pageant, 1985; University of Oklahoma, American Indian Student Association Princess, 1985-1986; Tulsa Powwow Princess, 1984; Miss Indian Oklahoma, 1st runner-up-most talented; National Viet Nam Veterans Powwow Princess & Association Princess, 1982-84; Osage Tribal Princess, 1980 & 1983; 1st Place Women's Fancy Shawl, University of Oklahoma, American Indian Student Association Pow wow, March 19, 1994; 2nd Place Women's Fancy Shawl, Red Earth Celebration, Oklahoma City, June 1994; 4th Place Gathering of Nations, Albuquerque; 5th Place Women's Fancy Shawl, 1993, Denver March Powwow; 1st Place Women's Fancy Shawl, Potawatomi Days Powwow, June 1993 in Shawnee, OK; 2nd Place Women's Fancy Shawl, Aspen, CO, July 1993 powwow to benefit the new Smithsonian Institution, National Museum of the American Indian; "I danced at the National Governors Association Convention in Sand Springs, OK, Aug. 1993 -

President Clinton was an honored guest"; "Me and my gramma, Mary Osage Green (full blooded Osage) are painted in the Osage Council Chambers with other prominent Osages." *Interests*: "I am applying for IHS scholarship to further my education in business and/ or public administration. I plan to document the elders of my tribe. I feel my elders are cherishable because they are our history, they lived in the beginning of the 1900's. There stories are true compared to history books. I want to preserve our heritage. I enjoy traveling across the U.S. to Native American celebrations of every kind. I have represented my tribe at powwows, state and national organizations which involved me traveling to all 4 directions. My parents are Ted Moore, Sr., a former world champion fancy dancer for a number of consecutive years at the American Indian Exposition in Anadarko, Okla., and Thomasine Moore, a former Osage princess and current Osage Tribal Director at the American Indian Exposition. My greatgrandfather was See-Haw, a great leader of the Osage Nation."

MOORE, WILMA
(school principal/teacher)
Affiliation: Toksook Bay Day School, Toksook, AK 99637 (907) 543-2746.

MOOREHEAD, VIRGIL (Yurok)
(rancheria chairperson)
Affiliation: Big Lagoon Rancheria, P.O. Drawer 3060, Trinidad, CA 95570 (707) 826-2079.

MOQUINO, JOSEPH
(health center director)
Affiliation: Northern Idaho PHS Indian Health Center, P.O. Drawer 367, Lapwai, ID 83540 (208) 843-2271.

MORAN, ERNEST T. "BUD" (Confederated Salish & Kootenai/Chippewa Cree) 1939-
(BIA supt.)
Born August 27, 1939, Harlem, Mont. *Education*: Oceanside Junior College, 1960; Santa Ana Junior College, 1962-63; completed numerous training courses in administration and management while in the USMC and working for the government. *Principal occupation*: BIA supt. *Address*: Flathead Agency, Bureau of Indian Affairs, P.O. Box A, Pablo, MT 59855 (406) 675-2700 Fax 675-2805. *Affiliations*: Credit and business development officer, director of economic development program, Confederated Salish & Kootenai Tribes; Indian Community Action Program, University of Montana, Missoula; Bureau of Indian Affairs: housing officer, Rocky Boy, MT; reservation programs officer, Lame Deer, MT; credit and business development, Jicarilla Agency, Dulce, NM; tribal operations officer, Western Nevada Agency, Stewart, NV; field representative in Klamath, CA; supt., Northern Cheyenne Agency, Lame Deer, MT, 1980-85; supt., Northern Idaho Agency, Lapwai, ID, 1985-86; supt., Crow Agency, MT, 1986-89; supt., Colorado River Agency, Parker, AZ, 1989-91; supt., Flathead Agency, Pablo, MT, 1991-. *Other professional posts*: President, Indian American Foundation; past president, NFFE Union, Jicarilla Apache Agency Post, NM. *Military service*: U.S. Marine Corps, 1958-67 (Navy Unit Citation; Vietnam Unit Citation with Star; Vietnam Service Medal with Star; National Defense Service Medal with Star; Armed Forces Expeditionary Medal with 2 Stars). *Community activities*: Active Corps of Executives (member); Aide de Camp to Governor of New Mexico; Toastmasters Club, Lame Deer, MT (past president); coached four years of Little League, Lame Deer, MT. *Memberships*: Confederated Salish & Kootenai Tribe; tribal affiliations with Chippewa Cree Tribe and Rocky Boy Tribe. *Awards, honors*: Special Achievement Award from Bureau of Indian Affairs; Letter of Appreciation from Jicarilla Apache Tribe and Northern Cheyenne Tribe; guest speaker (at Dull Knife Memorial College on numerous occasions) on government and their relations with tribes.

MORAN, GEORGE F.
(museum director & executive V.P.)
Affiliation: Indian City, U.S.A., P.O. Box 695, Anadarko, OK 73005 (405) 247-5661 Fax 247-2467. E-mail: indianncity@aol.com.

MORAZA, ELENA (Chichimeca of Mexico)
(dancer)
Address: 11 Esta Rd., Plymouth, MA 02360 (508) 830-

1256. Elena is a Northern traditional woman dancer who specializes in dance demonstrations with lecture/ discussions. Proficient in various art forms including beadwork, jewelry, ribbon applique and dance outfits. Performances presented in full dance regalia to educate others about Native American culture.

MORGAN, DAVE
(hospital director)
Affiliation: Parker PHS Indian Hospital, Rt. 1, Box 12, Parker, AZ 85344 (602) 669-2137.

MORGAN, DONALD I. (Blackfeet) 1934-
(BIA official)
Born June 12, 1934, Browning, Mont. *Education*: College of Great Falls; University of New Mexico; Central Washington University. *Principal occupation*: BIA official. *Address*: Fort Toten Agency, BIA P.O. Box 270, Fort Totten, ND 58335 (701) 766-4545. *Affiliations*: Administrator, Wind River Agency, BIA, Fort Washakie, Wyo.; administrator, vocational training and job placement worker, Los Angeles Field Employment Office; vocational counselor, Blackfeet Agency, Browning, MT, Northern Cheyenne Agency, Lame Deer, MT, Yakima Agency, Toppenish, WA; administrator, Crow Creek Agency, BIA, Fort Thompson, S.D.; supt., Fort Totten Agency, BIA, P.O. Box 270, Fort Totten, ND. *Military service*: U.S. Army, 1957-59.

MORGAN, JUDI
(executive director)
Affiliation: Nebraska Commission on Indian Affairs, State Capitol Bldg., 6th Floor, Box 94981, Lincoln, NE 68509 (402) 471-3475 Fax 471-3392.

MORGAN, MARILYN ELIZABETH 1944-
(technical editor)
Born June 30, 1944, Bremerton, Wash. *Education*: California State University, San Francisco, BA, 1972. *Principal occupation*: Technical editor. *Home address*: 2858 North Highview Ave., Altadena, CA 91001. *Affiliations*: Technical editor, Jet Propulsion Laboratory, California Institute of Technology, Pasadena. *Other professional post*: Editor, Native American Annual. *Memberships*: Society for Technical Communication (audio-visual committee); Astronomical Society of the Pacific. *Interests*: Technical communiction; astronomy and science in general; Native American progress and cultural integrity. *Published work*: Editor, Native American Annual (Native American Publishing Co., Margaret Clark-Price, Publisher, 1985).

MORGAN, RONALD J. (*Whitewolf*) (Blackfoot) 1940-
(writer, photographer, jeweler)
Born October 4, 1940, Seattle, Wash. *Education*: Universal Life Church (Modesto, CA), BA (History), 1974; McGraw-Hill Paralegal School, Washington, DC, 1990. *Principal occupation*: Writer, photographer, jeweler. *Home address*: P.O. Box 297, Redwater, TX 75573. *Occupational activities*: "I'm a public speaker, lecturer and dancer. I give talks on the Old West and Indians, also have slide shows and video displays using artifacts from my collections. As a dancer, I've demonstrated Indian dances for tourists, school and youth groups. I have appeared in three video movies, filmed on the Alabama-Coushatta Reservation, Livingston, Texas. I speak the Dakota Sioux language, sign language and Spanish." *Memberships*: Smithsonian Institution; National Archives. *Awards, honors*: Awarded honorary title, Special Consultant-American Indian Affairs, 1969; "I have been consulted by writers, U.S. Senators and many Indian organizations over the years. *Interests*: "Research is one of my main interests. I'm an Indian historian and always try to learn the old ways. My interests are many: archaeology, linguistics, publishing and law. I'm especially interested in state and federal law books relating Indian court cases. Collecting Indian artifacts; documents, photographs and original historical newspapers are just some of my interests, As a professional photographer, I'm busy recording western and Indian historical sites, graves of famous Indians and Indian powwows. My photographs are now in the permanent collections of three major museums: U.S. Dept. of the Interior, National Park Service, Fort Bowie, AZ; North American Indian Heritage Center, in WY; and the Amon Carter Museum, Fort Worth, TX. I'm a part-time jeweler, casting in both gold and silver. My future plans are to produce video movie documentaries pertaining to Indian

ceremonies and wild life. I'm currently working on fictional book about intertribal wars. The University of South Dakota, Institute of Indian Studies, has expressed an interest in using my photographs in a future publication, Who's Who Among the Sioux; I now paint acrylic and oil paintings of my Indian people; I have made over 30 Indian videos (Indian dancing), filmed all over Texas and Tulsa, OK; I am learning to speak the Kiowa language, because of my close association with them." *Biographical sources*: Source Directory (U.S. Dept. of the Interior, BIA, 1985-87); The American Indian Index: A Directory of Indian Country (Arrowstar Publishing, 1986-87). *Published works*: Articles: I Fought With Geronimo by Jason Betzinez as told to Ronald Morgan (The Westerner, Stagecoach Publishing, 1971); series, The Indian Side, in The Frontier, Real West, True West, and American West Magazines; among others.

MORGAN, VANESSA (*Paukeigope*) (Cherokee)
(dancer, traditional crafts demonstrator)
Address: P.O. Box 1101, Anadarko, OK 73005 (405) 643-5075. Vanessa is a traditional Southern Plains dancer and performs in cloth or buckskin regalia. She lectures and provides slide presentations, and has a strong background as a cultural arts demonstrator.

MORGAN-GIBSON, REGLA (*Winter Flower*)
(Ramapough-Mohawk) 1951-
(computer specialist, health educator)
Born November 23, 1951, Bronx, N.Y. *Education*: York College, B.S. (Community Health Education, Summa Cum Laude). *Home address*: 198-04 120th Ave. St. Albans, NY 11412 (718) 978-7057 Fax 978-7200. *Affiliations*: Clanmother of the Northeastern Native American Association, P.O. Box 266, Hollis, NY 11423. Community health educator; HIV/AIDS educator; primary care consultant; counselor. *Community activities*: AIDS Center of Queens County; American Red Cross; American Indian Community House; Planned Parenthood; emergency medical services; Mary Immaculate Hospital; St. Albans Extended Care Facility; Queen of Peace Nursing Home. *Memberships*: Pan-American India Association; American Indian Community House; Native American Leadership Commission on Health and AIDS. Native American Writers & Artists Association. *Awards, honors*: American Red Cross; AIDS Center for Queens County. *Interests*: "Educate the health care sector that Native American people are still here. Because Native Americans are usually racially mixed, they suffer two fold when it comes to health issues, I want to come up with a program that addresses their specific needs. Implement a comprehensive health program for my organization (Northeastern Native American Association). It's mission is to reach out into the Native American community and provide social services. Promote cultural programs and educate the public about Native American issues and concerns. I want to follow the spiritual path of my ancestors in a humble and quiet way. To counsel, to teach, to grow." *Biographical source*: Who's Who in Poetry (World of Poetry, 1985). *Published works*: Notes; Pan-American Indian Newspaper; Mary Immaculate Newsletter; Smoke Signals.

MORIGEAU, MICHAEL A.
(BIA field representative)
Affiliation: Plummer Field Office, Bureau of Indian Affairs, c/o Coeur D'Alene Tribe, P.O. Box 408, Plummer, ID 83851 (208) 686-1887.

MORIN, LYMAN
(school principal/supt.)
Affiliation: Cheyenne-Eagle Butte School, P.O. Box 672, Eagle Butte, SD 57625 (605) 964-8744.

MORRIN, LARRY
(BIA regional director)
Affiliation: Midwest Regional Office, BIA, One Federal Dr., Rm. 550, Fort Snelling, MN 55111 (612) 713-4400 Fax 713-4401.

MORRIS, DORAN L., SR. (Omaha)
(tribal chairperson)
Affiliation: Omaha Tribal Council, P.O. Box 368, Macy, NE 68039 (402) 837-5391.

MORRIS, ELIZABETH (Athabascan) 1933-
(former director-Indian organization)
Born February 16, 1933, Holikachuk, Alaska. *Educa-*

tion: Seattle Community College, 1969-70. *Principal occupation*: Former executive director, Seattle Indian Center. Resides in Seattle, WA. *Community activities*: Candidate for Washington State Legislature, 1970; Seattle Community Council (advertising screening committee). *Interests*: Ms. Morris writes, "(I am) interested in the welfare of my people, and devote most of my time toward improving the quality of (their) lives. Because of my own experiences and difficulties, I am interested in helping (my people) maintain their identity and unique culture, (while) at the same time adapt(ing) to the urban scene."

MORRIS, C. PATRICK 1938-
(professor of Native American studies)
Born December 5, 1938, Watsonville, Calif. *Education*: Arizona State University, BA, 1964, MA, 1970, PhD (Anthropology), 1974. *Principal occupation*: Professor of Native American Studies. *Address & Affiliation*: Center for Native American Studies, Montana State University, Bozeman, MT 59717 (406) 994-4201. *Community activities*: Assist tribal colleges organize International Exchange Program for 23 Indian tribes with Norway & France. *Memberships*: National Indian Education Association; Montana Indian Education Association. *Awards, honors*: Marshall Fellowship, Norway; Fulbright Award, Norway, University of Oslo; Goodwill Award for International Understanding, Norway. *Interests*: Indian law and policy; international human rights and indigenous people; Indian reservation economies; tribally controlled colleges; American Indian religious thought; Indian literature—oral and written. *Published works*: As Long As the Water Flows: Indian Water Rights, A Growing National Conflict in the U.S., in Native Power, edited by J. Brosted, et al (University of Oslo, 1985); The Hill of Sorrow: Ethnohistory of the Little Shell Chippewa (in press).

MORRIS, DORAN L., SR. (Omaha)
(former tribal chairperson)
Affiliation: Omaha Tribal Council, P.O. Box 368, Macy, NE 68039 (402) 837-5391.

MORRIS, GLENN T.
(executive director)
Affiliation: Fourth World Center for the Study of Indigenous Law & Politics, University of Colorado, Dept. of Political Science, Campus Box 190, P.O. Box 173364, Denver, CO 80217 (303) 556-2850.

MORRIS, JOANN SEBASTIAN
(BIA office director)
Affiliation: Director, Office of Indian Education Programs, Bureau of Indian Affairs, 1849 C St., NW, Rm. 3510, MS:3512-MIB, Washington, DC 20240 (202) 208-6123.

MORRISON, DENNIS
(executive director)
Affiliation: Upper Midwest American Indian Center, 1113 W. Broadway, Minneapolis, MN 55411 (612) 522-4436.

MORRISON, EDDIE (Oklahoma Cherokee) 1946-
(artist-sculptor)
Born September 29, 1946, Claremore, Okla. *Education*: Northeastern State College (4 years); Institute of American Indian Art (2 years). *Principal occupation*: Artist-sculptor. *Home address*: Caldwell, KS 67022-0148 (316) 845-2355; 845-2259 (work). *Affiliation*: Owner, Eddie Morrison Studio & Gallery, Caldwell, KS. Specializes with wood and stone sculpture in a contemporary traditional style. "Besides my own feelings and interpretations, my ideas and themes come from the philosophies of Indians about life, spirituality, respect for life, animals, and all that is around us, and the Great Creator." *Exhibits*: Annual Santa Fe Indian Market; Red Cloud Art Show, Pine Ridge, SD; Trail of Tears Art Show, Tahlequah, OK; Museum of the Cherokee, Cherokee, NC; America Indian Arts Council Art Show, Dallas, TX; Annual Indian Arts & Crafts Association, Denver, CO; Lawrence Indian Arts Show, Lawrence, KS; The Five Civilized Tribes Museum Show, Muskogee, OK; Scottsdale (AZ) Native American Indian Cultural Foundation; and Southwest American Indian Annual Indian Market, Santa Fe, NM. *Military service*: U.S. Army Reserve, 1964-69. *Community activities*: Caldwell Chamber of Commerce. *Memberships*: Indian Arts & Crafts Association; Southwest Association on Indian Affairs; Art Student League of

Denver. *Awards, honors*: Faculty Departmental Award for Outstanding Student in 3 Dimensional Arts, Institute of American Indian Art; 2 Honorable Mention Awards for wood sculpture at Santa Fe Indian Market, 1991; Best of Wood & Stone Category, 1st Place, 1994 Indian Arts & Crafts Association, Phoenix, AZ; his work has been featured in: Contemporary Native American Art in Kansas" Show; Smokey Hill Museum, Salina, KS, 1990; also numerous private collections and several galleries throughout the U.S.

MORRISON, ROBERT (North Alabama Cherokees) 1938-
(maintenance)
Born October 27, 1938 in Alabama. *Affiliation*: Owner, Cherokee Indian Records, P.O. Box 41, Boaz, AL 35957 (205) 593-7336. Cherokee national Indian search; some Seminole, Choctaw & Chickasaw research; individual and family charts. *Charges*: $10/name, $20/family.

MORRISSEY, LAVERNE
(Indian center president)
Affiliation: American Indian Alliance of Santa Clara Valley, 2114 Senter Rd. #8, San Jose, CA 95112 (408) 350-3531 Fax 277-0291.

MORROW, PHYLLIS 1950-
(professor of anthropology &
cross-cultural communications)
Education: Harvard University, BA (summa cum laude, Social/Cultural Anthropology)1972; Cornell University, MA, 1976, PhD, 1987. *Principal occupation*: Associate professor of anthropology of anthropology & cross-cultural communications. *Address*: Dept. of Alaskan Native Studies, Dept. of Anthropology, Box 757720, 310 Eielson Bldg.,University of Alaska, Fairbanks, AK 99775 (907) 474-6608 (office), (907) 479-5911 (home). E-mail: ffpm@uaf.edu. *Affiliations*: Graduate teaching assistant, Cornell University, 1973-76; courses/workshops in Yup'ik Eskimo culture/history and language/linguistics, Kuskokwim College, Bethel (University of Alaska), 1977-86; director, Yup'ik Eskimo Language Center, Kuskokwim College, 1979-81; assistant professor of anthropology and cross-cultural communications, University of Alaska, Fairbanks, 1987-. *Other professional posts*: Field coordinator for cross-cultural Education Development Program teaching B.Ed. students in rural Alaskan village sites, 1978; material development and teacher training for the Lower Kuskokwim School District in Bethel, AK, 1981-86; consulting services-law, education, and oral history/literature' conference/workshop presentations, 1981- *Community activities*: Museum Collections Advisory Committee, Alaska State Museums (vice-chair); Alaska Organizing Committee member and conference chair, 1990 Conference on Hunting & Gathering Societies. *Memberships*: American Anthropological Association; Alaska Anthropological Association; Commission on Folk Law and Legal Pluralism; Society for Applied Anthropology. *Awards, honors*: Phi Beta Kappa (Harvard-Radcliffe), 1971; Andrew White Graduate Fellowship, 1973-74; National Institute of Mental Health Predoctoral Fellowship for ethnographic fieldwork in Southwestern Alaska, 1976; Alaska Historical Commission Grant for publication of Cauyarnariuq, 1985; Alaska Humanities Forum Grant for "The Writing of Cultural and Culture of Writing," 1988; Spencer Foundation Grant for "Yup'ik Eskimo Ceremonialism: Traditional Religion in Contemporary Education, 1989. *Published works*: Co-author, Qaneryaurci Yup'igtun: Learn to Speak Yup'ik, 1981; "It Is Time for Drumming: A Summary of Recent Research on Traditional Yup'ik Ceremonies," Etudes/Inuit/Studies, Vol. 8 The Central Yup'ik Eskimos, 1984; editor, Cauyarnariuq ('it is time for drumming", high school text: reconstructs and discusses the traditional ceremonial round of Yup'ik Eskimos In Yup'ik Eskimo (author, Elsie P. Mather); co-author, Teacher's Guide: Secondary Yup'ik Language and Culture Program for the Lower Kuskokwim School District (LKSD, Bethel), 1987; "Competing Realities: The Negotiation of Ethnic Identity and Public Plicy in Rural Alaska" in Cross-Cultural Issues in Alaskan Education, V. III, Ray Barnhardt, Ed. (Center for Cross-cultural Studies, Fairbanks, AK, 1989; "Oral Literature of the Alaskan Inuit," in Dictionary of Native North American Literature, Andrew Wiget, Ed. (Greenwood Press, 1990); "The Woman Who Returned from the Dead," in Coming to Light (Brian Swam, ed. Random House); National Science Foundation 1991 cross-cul-

tural legal encounters in western Alaska; When Our Words Return: Hearing, Writing, & Remembering Oral Traditions of Alaska & the Yukon (Utah State U Press, 1995); "Yup'ik Eskimo Agents & American Legal Agencies: Perspectives on Compliance & Resistance (Journal of the Royal Anthropology Institute, 1996).

MORTON, DR. NEIL
(center director)
Affiliation: Native American Center for Excellence, Center for Tribal Studies, Tahlequah, OK 74464 (918) 456-5511 ext. 3690 Fax 458-2193.

MOSE, ELWOOD (Te-Moak Shoshone)
(tribal chairperson)
Affiliation: Te-Moak Band of Western Shoshone Indians of Nevada, 525 Sunset St., Elko, NV 89801 (775) 738-9251.

MOSELY, MARY JEAN
(program director)
Affiliation: Fort Lewis College, Division of Intercultural Studies, 120 Miller Student Center, Durango, CO 81301.

MOSES, CAROL
(club manager)
Affiliation: North American Indian Club, P.O. Box 851, Syracuse, NY 13201 (315) 476-7425.

MOSES, DARRYL CYRIL
(Indian band chief)
Affiliation: Lower Nicola Indian Band, RR 1, Site 17, Comp. 18, Keremeos, British Columbia, Canada V0K 2B0 (604) 378-5157.

MOSES, JOHNNY
(storyteller)
Address: 6515 15th Ave., NE, Seattle, WA 98115 (206) 325-4280. Johnny is a traditional Northwest Coast storyteller in eight Native languages, English, and sign language.

MOSES, LILLY L. (Nez Perce) 1949-
(economic development planner)
Born November 8, 1949, Seattle, Wash. *Education*: Oregon State University, BS (Education), 1976; University of Idaho, College of Law, 1979-80. *Principal occupation*: Economic development planner. *Address*: Nez Perce Tribe, P.O. Box 365, Lapwai, ID 83540. *Affiliations*: Cooperative education coordinator, American Indian Higher Education Consortium, Denver, CO, 1973-74; teacher intern, Madras Public Schools, Madras, OR, 1975-76; grants/contracts specialist, Planning Department, Warm Springs Confederated Tribes, Warm Springs, OR, 1976-77; community service manager, Nez Perce Tribe, Lapwai, Idaho, 1977-79; researcher, Cobe Consultants, Portland, OR, 1980-81; economic development planner/manager, Limestone Enterprise, Nez Perce Tribe, Lapwai, ID 83540. *Community activities*: Kamiah Revitalization Committee, Kamiah, ID (member, 1983-); elected to Housing Board of Commissioners, Nez Perce Tribal Housing Authority, 1985-89. *Memberships*: Assn. for the Humanities in Idaho , 1978-81. *Awards, honors*: 1971 After Dinner Speech Award; All-Indian Debate Tournament, Dartmouth College. *Interests*: "To gain a professionally gratifying position in the federal government that assists American Indian tribes in achieving self-sufficiency; camping, hunting, fishing, beadwork, dancing."

MOSES, SHARON (Apache)
(administrator, part-time college faculty)
Address & Affiliations: Coordinator, Native American/ Multicultural Affairs Department, Flathead Valley Community College, 777 Grandview Dr., Kalispel, MT 59901 (406) 756-3945 Fax 756-3815. *Community activities*: Native American cultural liaison for Montana State Dept. of Commerce and state: Kumamoto, Japan and Taiwan. *Membership*: Native American Journalist's Association.

MOSES, TED
(Indian band chief)
Affiliation: Eastman (Cree) Indian Band, Eastman, Quebec, Canada J0M 1W0 (819) 977-0211.

MOSS, MYRNA
(executive director)
Affiliation: Cherokee National Historical Society, P.O.

Box 515, Tahlequah, OK 74465 (918) 456-6007. *Other professional post*: Editor, "The Columns," quarterly newsletter.

MOTLOW, SHIRLEY M. (Seminole)
(Indian store owner)
Address: North American Native Arts & Crafts, P.O. Box 15112, Baton Rouge, LA 70895.

MOUNT, HARLAN K. (Gros Ventre)
(former tribal chairperson)
Affiliation: Fort Belknap Community Council, RR 1, Box 66, Harlam, MT 59526 (406) 353-2205.

MOUSSEAU, SHARON A. (Oneida)
(school administrator)
Affiliation: Oneida Tribal School, P.O. Box 365, Oneida, WI 54155 (414) 869-2795.

MOWRER, JEFFREY (Cheyenne River Sioux) 1957-
(mental health counselor)
Born March 25, 1957, Mobridge, S.D. *Education*: South Dakota State University, BS, 1979; University of Wyoming, MS, 1987. *Principal occupation*: Mental health counselor. *Address*: Resides in Oklahoma City, OK (405) 232-0736 (office). *Affiliation*: Counseling psychologist, Oklahoma City Indian Clinic, Oklahoma City, OK, 1990-. *Awards, honors*: Indian Education Fellowship, U.S. Dept. of Education. *Interests*: "To professionally integrate mental health concerns and issues, in a culturally sensitive manner to our Indian people."

MOYLE, ALVIN (Paiute)
(tribal chairperson)
Affiliation: Fallon Business Council, 8955 Mission Rd., Fallon, NV 89406 (775) 423-6075.

MULL, CHESTER M., Sr. (Cherokee) 1938-
(company owner/president)
Born May 18, 1938, Harrison, Tenn. *Education*: High school. *Principal occupation*: Ironworker. *Home address*: 10 Mull Dr., Rittman, OH 44270-9777 (216) 927-5098 (home) 927-6855 (office). *Affiliations*: President, Rittman, Inc., Rittman, OH,1981-; president, Chippewa Steel Fabricating, Rittman, OH, 1982-; president, Marbri Engineering, Cleveland, OH,1989-. *Other professional posts*: president, John's Steel Service, Rittman, OH, 1990-; Summit Committee for Ohio Department of Economic Development, Columbus, OH (board member). *Community activities*: School board; president of Athletic Club; Junior Improvement League. *Memberships*: Grotto; Masons; Shrine 32nd Degree; Norh American Cultural Center; Night Templar; Eastern Stars; Medina Country Club; member of South Akron Board of Trade. *Awards, honors*: 1991 "Minority Manufacturer of the Year," by the City of Cleveland, Mayor's Office of Equal Opportunity; The Ohio Humanitarian Award for Heritage Preservation, Jan. 16, 1992 by the State of Ohio; Rittman Chamber of Commerce, "Member Award," 1993; other awards from U.S. Chamber of Commerce, North American Indian Center, Akron, OH; American Builders Exchange, et al.

MULL, RAQUEL (Dine') 1953-
(ordained deacon-pastor)
Education: University of New Mexico; Perkins School of Theology, Southern Methodist University, Duke University (seminary work completed in 2000). *Principal occupation*: Ordained deacon-pastor in the United Methodist Church (UMC). *Address*: 2220 Utah St. NE, Albuquerque, NM 87110 (505) 298-5138. *E-mail*: bideezhi1@aol.com. *Affiliations*: Co-pastor (with Craig Mull), Grandfalls Union Church, Grandfalls, TX, and Imperial UMC, Imperial, TX, 1996-2002; Appointed as Funding pastor of First nations UMC (a church for urban Native Americans), Albuquerque, NM, 2002-present. Ordained deacon in the UMC, under appointment in the New Mexico Conference for eight years. Currently, a probationary member, anticipating ordination as Elder, May, 2005. *Community activities*: Within the UMC - Chair for the Conference Ethnic Minority Local Church Task Force; member, South Central Jurisdiction American Indian Ministries; past chair of the South Central Region, Native American Intenational Caucus of the UMC (NAIC); board member, General Commissionn on Role and Status of Women. Locally - President, Albuquerque Indian Center, Community Development Board; member, Albuquerque Navajo Club; member, Trustees, University Heights UMC; member, Albuquerque Indian Chamber of Commerce. *Membership*: National American Indian Women's Association.

MULLEN, DOUGLAS
(rancheria chairperson)
Affiliation: Greenville Rancheria, 645 Antelope Blvd. #15, Red Bluff, CA 96080 (916) 528-9000.

MULLEN, JOSEPH (Snoqualmie)
(tribal chairperson)
Affiliation: Snoqualmie Tribal Organization, P.O. Box 670, Fall City, WA 98024 (425) 222-6900.

MUNDY, ERMA
(executive director)
Affiliation: Indian Community Health Service, 3008 N. 3rd St., Phoenix, AZ 850012 (602) 263-8094.

MUNETA, ANITA
(health director)
Affiliation: Crownpoint Comprehensive Health Care Facility, P.O. Box 358, Crownpoint, NM 87313 (505) 786-5291.

MUNOZ, VINCE, JR. (Ysleta Del Sur Pueblo)
(former Pueblo governor)
Affiliation: Ysleta Del Sur Pueblo, P.O. Box 17579, Ysleta Sta., El Paso, TX 79917 (915) 859-7913.

MUNRO, PAMELA
(professor of linguistics)
Affiliation: Dept. of Linguistics, University of California, Los Angeles. *Published works*: Chickasaw: An Analytical Dictionary (University of Oklahoma Press, 1994); Mojave Syntax

MUNSON, THOMAS A.
(monument supt.)
Affiliation: Effigy Mounds National Monument, RR 1, Box 25A, Harpers Ferry, IA 52146 (319) 873-3491.

MUNYAN, GEORGE F. *(Little Turtle)* (Nipmuc)
(author-illustrator; medicine person)
Born July 23rd in Putnam, Conn. *Education*: High school; various courses in art and related subjects, University of Connecticut, Worcester Art Museum, et al. *Principal occupation*: Author-illustrator-Indian subjects. *Home address*: Resides in East Douglas, MA. *Community activities*: Medicine person, past secretary, and tribal roll genealogist, Chaubunagungamaug Nipmuck Tribal Council. *Memberships*: New England Antiquities Research Association (contributing writer, Native American consultant). *Awards, honors*: Several awards from Nipmuck and other tribal groups for educational and cultural projects contributed to or participated in. *Interests*: "Pre-Columbian American history, Native American and primitive art particularly in a spiritual context, herbal medicinal uses and propagation, environmental issues, inter-cultural understanding." *Published works*: Contributing writer/illustrator, Native American Sourcebook (Concord Museum, 1987); resource person, Legends of the New England Indians (Mohawk Arts, 1988); contributor-poetry: The Coming of Dawn (National Library of Poetry, Oct. 1993); All My Tomorrows (Quill Books, Feb. 1994).

MURDOCK, DON
(BIA field representative)
Affiliation: Tribal Operations: Minnesota Sioux Field Representative, Minneapolis Area Office, Bureau of Indian Affairs, 331 Second Ave., South, 6th Floor, Minneapolis, MN 55402 (612) 349-3382.

MURDOCK, VERONICA L.
(BIA agency supt.)
Affiliation: Salt River Agency, Bureau of Indian Affairs, 10000 E. McDowell Rd., Scottsdale, AZ 85256 (602) 640-2168 Fax 640-2809.

MURPHEY, BARBRA
(BIA special education coordinator)
Affiliation: Idaho Education Field Office, Bureau of Indian Affairs, P.O. Box 277, Lapwai, ID 83540 (202) 843-5025 Fax 843-7412.

MURPHY, CHARLES W. (Standing Rock Sioux) 1948-
(tribal chairperson)
Born December 27, 1948, Fort Yates, N.D. *Education*: Saint Benedict College, 1968-69. *Principal occupation*: Former tribal chairperson. *Address*: P.O. Box D, Fort Yates, ND 58538 (701) 854-7202. *Affiliations*: Police officer, BIA, Fort Yates, ND, 1970-72; range technician, BIA, Standing Rock Sioux Tribe, 1972-76; agricultural director, 1976-79, economic development planner, 1979-81, vice chairman & councilman, 1981-83, chairperson, 1983-95; 1999-2001, Standing Rock Sioux Tribe, Fort Yates, ND. *Military service*: U.S. Army, 1969-70 (Vietnam Veteran; Army Commendation Medal; Bronze Star). *Community activities*: Standing Rock Irrigation Board, Standing Rock Sioux Tribe (chairman, 1981-); United Tribes Educational Technical Center, Bismarck, ND (board of directors, 1983-); Aberdeen Area Roads Commission (chairman, 1985-); Aberdeen Tribal Chairman's Association (chairman, 1986-); Theodore Jamerson Elementary School, Bismarck, ND (school board, 1984-); Saint Alexius Medical Center, Bismarck, ND (board of directors, 1985-). *Memberships*: National Tribal Chairman's Association, 1983-; United Sioux Tribes, Pierre, SD (chairman, 1985-). *Awards, honors*: Certificate of Special Achievement, Dept.of the Interior, 1980. *Interests*: "Elected by the enrolled members of the Tribe (Standing Rock Sioux), (I) serve as the chair of the Tribal Council & the chief executive officer of the tribal government. Specialized experience or other related background in personnel management, administration, planning and budgeting, & land & resource management. Responsible for implementation of tribal law; & represent the Tribe before Congress & government agencies."

MURPHY, PATT (Iowa/Sauk)
(Indian art center owner)
Affiliation: Owner, American Indian Art Center, 206 S. Buckeye Ave., Abilene, KS 67410 (913) 263-0090. Specializes in Woodland and Prairie Indian items

MURPHY, RACHEL
(storyteller)
Address: 7 Hilda Rd., Bedford, MA 01730 (617) 275-6824. Rachel is a Native American storyteller and educator, and focuses on the importance of Native American awareness. Presentations include stories about the circle, the four directions, and dispelling the myths and misconceptions of Native American people. Rachel has performed in elementary schools, churches, civic organizations as well as ethnic folk festivals.

MURPHY, VIRGIL (Stockbridge-Munsee Mohican)
(tribal chairperson)
Affiliation: Stockbridge-Munsee Tribal Council, N 8476 Mo He Con Nuck Rd., Bowler, WI 54416 (715) 793-4111.

MURR, LINDA
(Indian education center director)
Affiliation: Towanits Indian Education Center, P.O. Box 589, Porterville, CA 93258 (209) 784-6135 Fax 784-1351.

MURRAY, ARTHUR E. (Kaweah)
(mayor)
Home address: 28 Sunnydell, South Hutchinson, KS 67505 (316) 662-7410. *Affiliations*: Mayor, South Hutchinson, KS; National Tribal Chairman, Kaweah Indian Nation of Western USA & Mexico. *Other professional post*: Deacon in local Southern Baptist Church.

MURRAY, DONALD CLYDE (Micmac-Algonquian) 1932-
(engineering manager)
Born April 11, 1932, Bayside, N.Y. *Education*: University of Louisville, BA, 1952; University of Southern California, MA, 1965; U.C.L.A., PhD (Psychology), 1973. *Principal occupation*: Engineering manager, Hughes Aircrafts Co., Los Angeles, CA, 1953-. *Home address*: 2106 West Willow Ave., Anaheim, Calif. 92804. *Other professional posts*: Licensed psychologist, State of California; senior associate, Al. J. Murray & Associates (mechanical consultants). *Military service*: U.S. Marine Corps, 1952-54 (Captain; Reserves-retired). *Memberships*: American Association for the Advancement of Science; American Physical Society. *Awards, honors*: Howard Hughes Doctoral Fellowships, 1968-73; Order of the Chevalier, Cross of Honor, and Legion of Honor recipient, International Order of DeMolay. *Interests*: Consultant and lecturer; management psychology; executive counseling. *Biographcial source*: Registry of Native American Professionals.

MURRAY, FRANK (Iowa)
(tribal enterprise manager)
Affiliation: Bah-Kho-Je Art Gallery (Iowa Tribe of Oklahoma enterprise), 103 S. 2nd St., Guthrie, OK 73044 (405) 282-7282.

MURRAY, L. ROBERT (Shoshone)
(attorney)
Affiliation: Holland & Hart, 2515 Warren Ave., Suite 450, Cheyenne, WY 82001 (307) 778-4225. *Membership*: Native American Bar Association (board member).

MURRAY, LAWRENCE P. (Ioway)
(tribal chairperson)
Affiliation: Iowa Tribe of Oklahoma Business Committee, Rt. 1, Box 721, Perkins, OK 74059 (405) 547-2402 Fax 547-5294.

MURRAY, ROBERT T. (Metis Cherokee)
(tribal chief)
Affiliation: Tennessee River Band of Chickamauga Cherokee located near Flintstone, GA.

MURRY, LARRY (Shoshone)
(association president)
Affiliation: Wyoming Indian Education Association, P.O. Box 248, Fort Washakie, WY 82514 (307) 332-2681.

MURRY, W. DAVID (Mewuk)
(rancheria chairperson)
Affiliation: Shingle Springs Rancheria, P.O. Box 1340, Shingle Springs, CA 95682 (619) 676-8010.

MUSHKOOUB
(commissioner of education)
Affiliation: Nay Ah Shing School, HC 67, Box 242, Onamia, MN 56359 (612) 532-4181.

MUSICK, JACK (Luiseno)
(former tribal chairperson)
Affiliation: La Jolla Band of Luiseno Indians, 22000 Hwy. 76, Pauma Valley, CA 92061 (760) 742-3771.

MUSTUS, HOWARD
(Indian band chief)
Affiliation: Alexis Indian Band, Box 7, Glenevis, Alberta, Canada T0E 0X0 (403) 967-2225.

MYERS, BRANDY (*Weeasayha*) (Cherokee)
(chaplain, councilor)
Affiliation: Native American Indian Community, Rd. 2 Box 247A, Kittanning, PA 16201-9332 (724) 548-7335.

MYERS, JOSEPH
(executive director)
Affiliation: National Indian Justice Center, 5250 Aero Dr., Santa Rosa, CA 95403 (800) 966-0662; (707) 762-8113 Fax 762-7681.

MYERS, LARRY
(executive secretary)
Affiliation: Native American Heritage Commission, 915 Capitol Mall, Rm. 364, Sacramento, CA 95814 (916) 653-4082.

MYERS, THOMAS P.
(museum curator, professor)
Education: PhD. *Address & Affiliation*: University of Nebraska State Museum (curator/professor), W436 Nebraska Hall, Lincoln, NE 68588 (402) 472-5044 Fax 472-8949; E-Mail: tmyers1@unl.edu. *Memberships*: American Anthropological Association (Fellow); Society for American Archaeology; Plains Anthropological Society; Council for Museum Anthropology. *Interests*: Archaeology, ethnohistory, Native American art. *Published works*: Magic in Clay (editor); Birth and Rebirth of the Omaha; Sarayacu: Ethnohistorical and Archaeological Investigations at a Nineteenth Century Franciscan Mission in the Peruvian Montana.

MYLER, MICHAEL (Waccamaw-Siouan)
(tribal chairperson)
Affiliation: Waccamaw-Siouan Indians of SC, Gallivant's Ferry, SC 29544 (803) 248-9843.

N

NABOKOV, PETER 1940-
(professor of anthropology)
Born October 11, 1940. *Education*: Columbia University, BS, 1965; Goddard College, MA (Ethnic Studies & Language Arts), 1972; University of California, Berkeley, PhD (Anthropology), 1988. *Principal occupation*: Professor of anthropology. *Address*: Dept. of World Arts & Cultures, UCLA, 124 Dance Bldg., Box 951608, Los Angeles, CA 90095-1608. *Affiliations*: Research associate, Museum of the American Indian, Heye Foundation, New York, NY, 1962-85; University of California, Dept. of Native American Studies (instructor, Fall 1979 & 1980, Winter 1981, Spring 1982, Spring/Fall 1984, Spring 1985; lecturer, Fall 1989); lecturer, American Studies, University of California, Santa Cruz, Fall/Winter, 1987-88, Winter/Spring, 1988-89; Resident Fellow, D'Arcy McNickle Center for the History of the American Indian, Newberry Library, Chicago, IL, 1986-87; Dept. of Anthropology, University of Wisconsin-Madison, 1991-96; Professor, University of California, Los Angeles, World Arts & Cultures, 1997-. *Other professional posts*: Consulting and lecturing; manuscript and grant reviewing. Workshop Developer & Coordinator: The Blood of Things: American Indian Culture and History, D'Arcy McNickle Center Workshop series, Aug. 1991; consultant, Educational Broadcasting Corp./WNET-Thirteen. script critique for series on American environmental history entitled Nature: Land of the Eagle, 1989-91; member, The National Faculty of Humanities, Arts and Sciences, 1990-; member, Little Big Horn College Library & Advisory Board, 1987-; principal consultant, Native American Architecture, exhibit at the Festival of American Folklife, Smithsonian Institution, Summer/Fall, 1979; delivered Native American architecture slide lectures to departments of architecture, art, and anthropology at various universities & museums, 1977-82; among others. Activities in Native American Communities: Summers 1963-66: Museum of American Indian fieldworker-Crow Indian Agency, Pryor, Lodge Grass, MT (for book, "Two Leggings"); Summer/Fall 1972: Adult Education Consultant-Indian Island, Penobscot Nation, Maine; Spring 1973/Fall 1974/Winter 1975: Alabama-Coushatta Indian Reservation, Livingston, TX (for book profiling four contemporary Native American communities); Summer 1985-87: Three Affiliated Tribes, Newtown, ND (for film, "Peoples of the Earthlodge"); Winter/Summer 1985-86: Crow Indian Reservation (conducting field research on history of the Crow Tobacco Society toward PhD dissertation, "Cultivating Themselves: The Inter-Play of Crow Indian Religion and History." *Awards, honors*: Awards for Native American Testimony: American Library Association Best Book for Young Adults, 1978; Library School Journal Best Book, 1978; National Council for the Social Studies, Carter G. Woodson Book Award, 1979. Awards for Native American Architecture: 9th Annual Bay Area Book Reviewers Association Awards, 1989; The American Institute of Architects, "Institute Honor" award, AIA National Annual Convention, Washington, DC, 1991. *Published works*: Two Leggings: The Making of a Crow Warrior (Thomas Y. Crowell, 1967; Apollo Books (paperback), 1970; University of Nebraska Press, Bison Books, 1981); Native American Testimony: An Anthology of Indian and White Relations, Vol. I: First Encounter to Dispossession (Thomas Y. Crowell, 1978; Harper & Row (paperback), 1979); Indian Running (Capra Press, 1981; Ancient City Press edition, 1987); Architecture of Acoma Pueblo (Ancient City Press, 1986); Native American Architecture, with Robert Easton (Oxford University Press, 1989); Native American Testimony: From Prophecy to the Present, 1492-1992 (including complete text of Native American Testimony, 1978, plus second unpublished sequel volume, "Reservation to Resurgence" (Viking Penguin, 1991); among others, as well as book chapters, introductions, research reports, papers, lectures and numerous articles and reviews.

NAGANASHE, PATRICK
(organization president)
Affiliation: South Eastern Michigan Indians, Inc., 26641 Lawrence St., Center Line, MI 48090 (810) 956-1350.

NAGARUK, LUTHER (Eskimo)
(village president)
Affiliation: Native Village of Elim, P.O. Box 39070, Elim, AK 99739 (907) 890-3741.

NAGEL, JOANE
(professor of sociology)
Address & Affiliation: Chairperson, Dept. of Sociology, University of Kansas, Lawrence, KS. *Published works*: American Indian Ethnic Renewal: Red Power and the Resurgence of Identity & Culture; Red Power: The American Indians' Fight for Freedom, Second Edition, edited with Alvin M. Josephy, Jr. and Troy Johnson (University of Nebraska Press, 1999).

NAGEL, PEGGY
(college president)
Affiliation: Stone Child College, Rocky Boy Route, Box 1082, Box Elder, MT 59521 (406) 395-4313.

NAHWEGAHBOW, BARBARA
(director-Indian centre)
Affiliation: Native Canadian Centre of Toronto, 16 Spadina Rd., Toronto, Ontario, Canada (416) 964-9087.

NAILOR, GERALD (Picuris Pueblo)
(pueblo council governor)
Affiliation: Picuris Pueblo Council, P.O. Box 127, Penasco, NM 87553 (505) 587-2519.

NAKAI, RAYMOND CARLOS (Navajo-Ute) 1946-
(artisan, musician, lecturer)
Born April 16, 1946, Flagstaff, Ariz. *Education*: Northern Arizona University, BS, 1979; University of Arizona, 1987-92. *Principal occupation*: Artisan, musician, lecturer. *Home address*: Resides in Tucson, AZ (602) 743-9902 (work). *Affiliations*: Canyon Records Productions, Phoenix, AZ (artist, 1984-); Arizona Commission on the Arts, Phoenix, AZ (artist/consultant, 1982-). *Other professional posts*: Touring Artist, Western States Arts Foundation, 1991-93; Certified Secondary teacher in Graphic Communications, State of Arizona; co-founder of the ethnic jazz ensemble Jackalope. Jackalope has released two albums, Jackalope and Weavings. History: In 1973, after earlier music studies on the classical trumpet at Northern Arizona University, Nakai began playing the wooden Native American flute. He learned the traditional flute melodies and music forms of the Plains and Woodlands peoples and soon began to adapt these ideas to fit a style of his own. Nakai has recorded 12 albums for Canyon Records, including Earth Spirit, Canyon Trilogy, Carry the Gift, and most recently, Spirit Horses, a classically-oriented release featuring a concerto written for Nakai's Native American flute and chamber ensemble. Spirit Horses was chosen by Pulse music magazine as one of the top albums of 1991. Nakai's albums of solo flute music on the Canyon Records label include Changes, Journeys, Earth Spirit & Canyon Trilogy. On Cycles, Nakai uses the traitional flute with synthesizer accompaniment to create a dramatic work that serves as the music track for the multimedia presentation "Our Voices, Our Land" at The Heard Museum in Phoenix, AZ. Nakai has brought the Native American flute, traditionally a solo instrument used for courting and healing, into the realm of ensemble performance. In March 1993, he will appear as a soloist with the Phoenix Symphony in the world premiere of a new concerto for the cedar flute and orchestra composed by James DeMars. Nakai has collaborated with guitarist and luthier William Eaton on two albums, Carry the Gift and Winter Dreams. A new album by the duo will be released in 1992. Naka has performed at the World Music Seminar in Woodstock, NY, in concert, at schools, and at music festivals including the Telluride Bluegrass Festival, the Magic Flute Festival and throughout Europe & Japan. He has written & performed scores for film and TV, including selections for WGBH-TV, the National Park Service, the National Geographic Society, Fox TV, as well as many commercial productions. In October 1988, the Martha Graham Dance Co. premiered a dance set to five selections from nakai's album, Cycles. Since 1990, Nakai has collaborated and toured with pianist Peter Kater. Together they've recorded two albums, Natives and Migration. He has recorded Sundance Season and Desert Dance for the Celestial Harmonies label. Nakai continues to tour extensively throughout the U.S., Canada, Europe and Japanm, performing and lecturing on Native American culture and philosophy. *Military service*: U.S. Navy, 1966-71 (E-4, Radioman). *Community activities*: Panelist, The National Endowment for the Arts, Tucson Community Foundation, Phoenix Arts Commission; director, Arts Genesis, Ari-

zona Ethnobotanical Research Association. *Memberships*: Cheyenne-Arapaho Gourd Society; National Flute Association; Blue Star Society. *Awards, honors*: Arizona State Governor's Arts Award, 1992, for individual achievement. *Interests*: "While I am engaged in the study of indigenous North American native culture and music, my goals will include but are not limited to the following: research the historical traditions and technology of Native American music and oral traditions; compose, arrange and perform new music for the Native American flute; demonstrate and lecture on aboriginal and contemporary Native American culture, music, spirituality and philosophies of self-awareness and survival, and most importantly, to express ideas, observations, and thoughts in a positive, non-rhetorical and unbiased manner, to educate rather than castigate. My objective is to communicate a perspective based upon the future oriented and on-going, living oral traditions of the Dine' and other aboriginal native peoples of North America that are uncoached in romantic and/or stereotypical idealism. I will utilize contemporary teaching methods to develop a creative learning atmosphere in which to share awareness." *Biographical sources*: European Review of Native American Studies, 2:2: 1988; "It's Not Just Music: An Interview...R. Carlos Nakai, Native American Flutist, David P. McAllester. Numerous performances. Published works: "Living Voices: R. Carlos Nakai," an article on Native American music for Inside Performance magazine, 1989; "Native American Music," an article for New-Age Music Guide, edited by P.J. Birosek (Macmillan, 1990).

NAKOGEE, JOANNE
(Indian band chief)
Affiliation: Chapleau Ojibway Indian Band, Box 279, Chapleau, Ontario, Canada P0M 1K0 (705) 864-2213.

NANENG, MYRON P.
(association president)
Affiliation: Association of Village Council Presidents, Inc., P.O. Box 219, Bethel, AK 99559 (907) 543-3521.

NANEPASHEMET
(program manager)
Affiliation: Plimoth Plantation, Wampanoag Indian Program, P.O. Box 1620, Plymouth, MA 02360 (617) 746-1622.

NAPIER, L.A.
(center director)
Affiliation: American Indian Education Policy Center, Pennsylvania State University, 320 Rackley Bldg., University Park, PA 16803 (814) 865-1489.

NAPONSE, LARRY
(Indian band chief)
Affiliation: Whitefish Lake (Naughton) Indian Band, Box 39, Naughton, Ontario, Canada P0M 2M0 (705) 692-3423.

NARANJO, MARY L. (Pueblo)
(school principal/teacher)
Affiliation: San Ildefonso Day School, Route 5, Box 308, Santa Fe, NM 87501 (505) 455-2366 Fax 455-7351.

NARANJO, MICHAEL A. *(Mountain Meadows)*
(Tewa-Santa Clara Pueblo) 1944-
(sculptor)
Born August 28, 1944, Santa Fe, N.M. *Education*: Highlands University (2 years). *Principal occupation*. Sculptor. *Address*: P.O. Box 5803, Santa Fe, NM 87502. E-mail: naranjostudio@hotmail.com. *Military service*: U.S. Army, 1967-68 (PFC; Accommodation Medal; Purple Heart in Vietnam). *Exhibits*: "My work has been shown in both one-man and group shows across the country, one of the latest being, "Miniatures," The Albuquerque Museum, Group Show, Oct. 1996 to Jan. 1997. *Permanent collections*: Albuquerque Museum; Museum of Fine Arts, Santa Fe, NM; State Capitol, Santa Fe, NM; Heard Museum, Phoenix, AZ; The White House, Washington, DC; Magee Women's Hospital, Pittsburgh, PA; The Vatican, Italy; among other places. *Commissions*: "Kokopelli," custom estate home, "Indian Springs Estates, Chatsworth, CA, 1985; "Yes, I Can" Award, Foundation for Exceptional Children, Reston, VA, 1988; "The Dancer," The Albuquerque Museum, 1989; "Justice," the Dennis Chavez Federal Bldg., Albuquerque, NM, 1993; "Spirit Mother," Yale

Park, University of New Mexico, Albuquerque, 1996; "Emergence" monumental, Capitol Arts Board, State Capitol, Santa Fe, NM, 2000; "The Gift" - New Mexico State Library, Records & Archives, Santa Fe, NM; "Inner Visions - The Sculpture of Michael Naranjo," one person show at the Heard Museum, Phoenix, AZ, 9/00 to 2/01. *Awards, honors*: Appointed board member of the New Mexico State Arts Commission, 1971; Catlin Peace Pipe Award, 1973; "Governor's Award" for sculpture by Governor of New Mexico, Jerry Apodaca, 1976; presented with the 1982 "Profiles in Courage Award," by the New Mexico Vietnam Veteran's Association; presented sculpture to Pope John Paul II, at papal audience, Vatican City, Italy, 1983; chosen as "New Mexico Veteran of the Year,", 1986; 1990 "Distinguished Achievement Award," by the American Indian Resources Institute, National Press Club, Washington, DC; 1991 recipient of the 1st Clinton King Purchase Award, Museum of Fine Arts, Santa Fe, NM; First prize, Southwest Art Exhibition '92, Del Rio Council of the Arts, Del Rio, TX; numerous prizes and medals at exhibits and shows. Nominated in 1996 by President Bill Clinton to serve on the Board of Trustees of the Institute of American Indian & Alaskan Native Culture and Arts Development. 1999 "Outstanding Disabled Veteran of the Year," by the Disabled American Veterans and LIFE Foundation"; "Presidential Unsung Hero Award". *Interests*: Sculpturing mainly in bronze, but has begun experimenting in stone. *Biographical sources*: Michael Naranjo, The Story of an American Indian (Dillon Press, 1975); Art and Indian Individualists (Northland Press, 1976);The Sweet Grass Lives On - 36 Contemporary American Indian Artists, by Jamake Highwater (Thomas Crowell, Co., 1980); Contemporary Western Artists (Southwest Art Publishing, 1982; In Pursuit of the American Dream (Atheneum, 1985; "The Spirit of Michael Naranjo," a biographical short story by Mary Carroll Nelson, in Time Was (Scott, Forsman Reading, 1986); featured in Beyond Tradition: Contemporary Indian Art and Its Evolution (Northland Press, 1988); featured in the 1988 CBS's Special, "Bodywatching", produced by New Screen Concepts, Louis H. Gorfain, Producer; feature article in "Southwest Art Magazine", Oct. 1989 issue; featured on PBS's "Colores" in 1992; "Motion in Bronze and Stone: The Sculpture of Michael Naranjo," in Kaleidoscope Magazine (Summer/Fall Issue, 1992); "A very Special Arts Story...Freedom of Expression," a syndicated television special, produced by Very Special Arts Production, Washington, DC, 1992 - Kara Kennedy, Producer; Santa Fe Indian Market: Showcase of Native American Art, by Sheila Tryk (Tierra Publications, 1993); "Michael Naranjo: An Evolving Union," in Pasatiempo magazine of Santa Fe, NM, by Gussie Fauntleroy, Sept. 13, 1996; "A Touch of Genius," by Patricia Millman (Highlights for Children Magazine, 11/00); "An Artist's Visions," by David Kirby, (Modern maturity Magazine, March-April, 2000 issue; The Price of Their Blood, by Jesse Brown & Daniel Paisner (Bonus Books). Michael is currently listed in Who's Who in the West, and Who's Who in American Art.

NARANJO, TESSIE
(Tewa-Santa Clara Pueblo) 1941-
(cultural preservationist/consultant,
Pueblo culture)
Born January 16, 1941, Santa Clara Pueblo, N.M. *Education*: Loma Linda (CA) University, MPH, 1977; University of New Mexico, PhD, 1992. *Principal occupation*: Cultural preservationist/consultant, Pueblo culture. *Address*: P.O. Box 1807, Espanola, NM 87532 (505) 753-3736. *Affiliation*: Santa Clara Pueblo, Espanola, NM, 1990-. *Memberships*: Rio Grande Institute, 1982- (vice-president); chairperson, Native American Graves Protection & Repatriation Act. *Interests*: Culture of the Southwest Pueblos. PhD Dissertation: Social Change and Pottery-Making at Santa Clara Pueblo, 1992.

NARANJO, TITO E. *(T'amu P'iin-Morning Mountain)*
(Tewa-Santa Clara Pueblo) 1937-
(professor emeritus, sculptor, writer, consultant)
Born August 6, 1937, Santa Clara Pueblo, N.M. *Education*: Baylor University, 1956-58; Hardin-Simmons University, 1958-59; New Mexico Highlands University, BA, 1962, MA, 1963; University of Utah, MSW, 1967. *Principal occupation*: Professor emeritus, sculptor, writer, consultant. *Home address*: P.O. Box 516, Mora, NM 87732 (505) 387-5658 (home). *Affiliations*: Community organizer, State of New Mexico, Taos, NM,

1964-65, 1967-69; State of Alaska director, Bristol Bay Social Services, Dillingham, AK, 1969-70; director of social services, Mora County, N.M., 1970-71; assistant professor, College of Santa Fe, NM, 1972-75; New Mexico Highlands University, Las Vegas, NM (associate professor of social work, 1976-90, professor emeritus-part time professor, writer, sculptor, 1990-). *Other professional posts*: Sculptor, writer, consultant; Mora Valley Health Services, Inc. (board of directors). *Community activities*: Intermountain Centers for Human Development (board member); tribal secretary for Santa Clara Pueblo, 1976. *Memberships*: American Indian Higher Education (board of directors). *Interests*: "I am a part time rancher, part-time artist and writer. I enjoy hunting, fishing and photography. I am a distance runner in the masters category and I also love to canoe, hike and adventure in Alaska and Mexico." *Biographical source*: A Conversation With Tito Naranjo, in (Confluencia, summer, 1980); "Running on the Edge of Time," in Early Winters 10th Anniversary Catalogue, 1982. Published work: Native Americans of the Southwest - A Journey of Discovery (Running Press, 1993)

NARCHO, JOHN B.
(IHS-executive officer)
Affiliation: Tucson IHS Office of Health Program Reserch & Development, 7900 South "J" Stock Rd., Tucson, AZ 85746 (602) 295-2406.

NARSISIAN, MARK
(publisher)
Affiliation: Akwesasne Notes, P.O. Box 196, Mohawk Nation, Rooseveltown, NY 13655 (518) 358-9531.

NASH, GARY B. 1933-
(historian)
Born July 27, 1933, Philadelphia, Pa. *Education*: Princeton University, BA, 1955, PhD, 1964. *Principal occupation*: Historian. *Home address*: 16174 Alcima Ave., Pacific Palisades, CA 90272. *Affiliations*: Assistant to the Dean of the Graduate School, 1959-61, assistant professor, Dept. of History, 1964-66, Princeton University; Professor, Dept. of History, UCLA, 1966-. *Other professional posts*: Dean, Council on Educational Development, UCLA, 1980-84; dean of Undergraduate and Intercollege Curricula Development, UCLA, 1984-; faculty advisory committee, American Indian Studies Center, UCLA, 1973-92; editorial board, American Indian Culture & Research Journal, 1980-. *Memberships*: American Historical Association; Institute of Early American History and Culture; Organization of American Historians (nominating committee, 1980-83; president, 1994-95); American Antiquarian Society; American Academy of Arts & Sciences. *Awards, honors*: Research grants from University of California Institute of Humanities and Research Committee, UCLA, 1966-83; Prize from the American Historical Association, Pacific Coast Branch, 1970, for best book, Quakers and Politics: Pennsylvania, 1681-1726; runner-up Pulitzer Prize in History for The Urban Crucible, 1979; 1980 Commonwealth Club of California, Silver Prize in Literature for The Urban Crucible. *Published works*: Co-edited, Struggle & Survival in Colonial America (University of California Press, 1981); Red, White and Black: The Peoples of Early America (Prentice-Hall, 1974; 2nd Ed., 1982; 3rd Ed., 1991; 4th Ed., 1999); The American People: Creating a Nation and a Society (Harper and Row, 1986); Retracing the Past: Readings in the History of the American People 2 volumes (Harper & Row, 1986); Forbidden Love: The Secret History of Mixed-Race America (Harper & Row, 1999); among others. Numerous articles in various professional journals.

NASON, JAMES D. (Comanche) 1942-
(museum curator, social anthropologist)
Born July 19, 1942, Los Angeles, Calif. Education: University of California, Riverside, BA, 1964; University of Washington, MA, 1967, PhD, 1970. *Principal occupation*: Museum curator, social anthropologist. *Address*: Thomas Burke Memorial Washington State Museum, Box 353010, University of Washington, Seattle, WA 98195 (206) 543-9680 Fax 685-3039. E-mail: jnason@u.washington.edu. *Affiliations*: Professor, Dept. of Anthropology, Curator of New World Ethnology, 1991-; Acting Curator of Archaeology, Thomas Burke Memorial Washington State Museum, 1999-2000; director of Museology Program, Graduate School, 1993-; faculty associate, American Indian Studies Center, 1995-; faculty associate, Canadian

Studies Program, Jackson School of International Studies, 1989-; University of Washington, Seattle, WA. *Other professional posts*: Member, Ethics and Standards Committee, American Association for State and Local History, 1997-; co-founder and member, Executive Committee, American Indian Museum Association, 1997-. Community activities: People's Lodge design and EIS work, United Indians of All Tribes, Seattle, WA, 1994-; member, Circle of Advisors, National Museum of the American Indian Master Exhibition Plan, the Mall and New York, Phase 1, Smithsonian Institution, 1997-. *Memberships*: American Anthropological Association, 1970 (Fellow); American Association for the Advancement of Science, 1970- (Fellow); American Ethnological Society, 1970- (Fellow); Royal Anthropological Institute (Fellow); International Council of Museums; Association for Social Anthropology in Oceana, 1971- (Fellow); American Association of Museums (member); Canadian Museums Association (member); Western Museums Association; Washington State Museums Association; British Columbia Museums Association; Council for Museum Anthropology; International Council of Museums; Pacific Conservation Group. *Interests*: Museology; cultural heritage policy and law; intellectual property rights; socioculture change; curatorial conservation; museum architectural and operational design; Native North America; Micronesia. *Published works*: Edited with Mac Marshall, Micronesia, 1944-1974 (Human Relations Area Files Press, 1976); Museums and Indians. In, "Native American in the Twentieth Century: An Encyclopedia," ed. by Mary Davis (Garland, 1994); Beyond Repatriation: Issues of Cultural Policy and Practice for the 21st Century. In, "Borrowed Power: Essyas on Cultural Appropriation," Part 5, ed. by Bruce Ziff and P.V. Rao (Rutgers University Press, 1997); Native American Intellectual Property Rights: Issues in the Control of Esoteric Knowledge. In, "Borrowed Power: Essyas on Cultural Appropriation," Part 6, ed. by Bruce Ziff and P.V. Rao (Rutgers University Press, 1997); Our Indians: The Unidimensional Indian in the Disembodied Local Past. In, "Changing Presentations of the American Indian in Exhibits," ed. by George Horse Capture (Smithsonian Institution Press, 1999).

NATALIA, AILEEN (Navajo)
(dancer)
Address: 701 Airport Rd. #3, Santa Fe, NM 87505 (505) 473-4346. Aileen has over 20 years of dance experience. A former junior soloist with the Los Angeles Ballet, Aileen was granted a full scholarship to study with the Joffrey Ballet in New York City. She has won the Best of New Mexico dance choreographers showcase and has eprformed in several major productions.

NATAY, ED LEE (Navajo)
(singer)
Address: c/o Canyon Records Productions, 4143 North 16th St., Suite 6, Phoenix, AZ 85016 (602) 266-7835.

NATHANIEL, JAMES, Sr.
(village first chief)
Affiliation: Chalkyitsik Village, P.O. Box 57, Chalkyitsik, AK 99788 (907) 848-8893.

NATHANSON, JULIA
(association contact)
Affiliation: New Mexico Indian Education Association, P.O. Box 16356, Santa Fe, NM 87506 (505) 989-5569.

NATIVIDAD, RAY (Diegueno)
(former rancheria chairperson)
Affiliation: San Pasqual General Council, P.O. Box 365, Valley Center, CA 92082 (619) 749-3200.

NATSEWAY, THOMAS (Laguna Pueblo)
(craftsperson)
Address: P.O. Box 15, Acoma Pueblo, NM 87034 (505) 552-7225. Products: Traditional miniatures and replicas of old pottery circa late 1700s and earlier Mimbres.

NAUMAN, H. JANE 1929-
(filmmaker)
Born May 4, 1929, Grinnell, Iowa. *Education*: University of Iowa, BA, 1950; University of Heidelberg, Germany, advanced studies, 1955-56. *Principal occupation*: Filmmaker. *Home address*: Box 232, Custer, SD 57730 (605) 673-4065 (home & office); E-mail: hjane232@aol.com. *Affiliations*: Executive vice-president, producer-editor, Nauman Films, Custer, SD,

1955-89; president, Sun Dog Films, Custer, SD, 1989- *Other professional posts*: Free-lance photo journalist specializing in articles on Native American culture (published in Indian Trader, Native Peoples magazine, Dakota Heritage Magazine, Four Winds, and many others), 1955-; location manager for NBC's "Chi Chi Hoo Hoo Bogey Man," a film based on a story written by Sioux author Virginia Driving Hawk Sneve; location manager, Kevin Costner 1989 film "Dances With Wolves" about the Sioux in 1860; Indian historian & location manager for "Son of the Morning Star," an ABC-TV Special Feature (1990) regarding Native American involvement in the last ten years of General Custer's life; location manager for "Thunderheart," a Tri-Star Tribecca Production feature film filmed ion Pine Ridge Reservation & S.D. Badlands, involving Indians and the FBI; screenwriter of historic feature "Jesse Moran." including the first Native American graduate of Harvard in a major role; research, historian & set decorator coordinator for "Lakota Woman," a TV Feature Special for TBS, based on book by Mary Crow Dog, regarding the AIM uprising at Wounded Knee, 1972; humanities lectures on the seven Indian reservations in South Dakota on films dealing with Plains Indians, as well as at Harvard, Dartmouth, University of South Dakota, and many other universities, museums, etc.; 1998-2000, Regional Technician for the U.S. Census Bureau with primary emphasis to ensure an exact count of First Americans in the 92 tribal governments in the 2000 Census in the ten states of the Denver Regional Census Center. *Awards, honors*: Fulbright Scholarship Award; Cine "Golden Eagle" Award (twice); American Film Festival Blue Ribbon (three times); American Indian Film Festival; UCLA Film & Folklore (best film on folklore); Governor's Award in the Arts, 1989; Festival of American Folklife Ethnographic Film; (all of the above awards for films on Native Americans); . *Interests*: Native American Indian Culture; travel; interested in any world travel involving filmmaking or other positive involvement with cultures; expedition into canyons of Sierra Madre Occidental of Mexico to film Tarahumara Indian culture and Easter festival; have planned and executed many film festivals dealing with Native American films. *Films produced*: Johnny Vik, 35mm full length feature film, 1971; produced and edited Sioux Legends (16mm documentary of Plains Indians culture, 1972 (Cine Golden Eagle Award; Martin Luther King, Jr. Award); wrote, directed, produced, edited and narrated, "Lakota Quillwork-Art & Legend" (honored at the 10th Annual American Indian Film Festival, San Francisco; best film on folklore in the UCLA Film & Folklore Festival; honored at the Smithsonian Institution's Festival of American Folklife Ethnographic Film; among other honors; assistant director, editor and producer of "Tahtonka," (a Cine "Golden Eagle" award winner; among 100 best educational films; best film of the week on BBC; Brussells International Film Festival, San Francisco International Festival, American Film Festival award winners, among many others); produced and edited "They Are Coming to Norogachic" about the Tarahumara Indians of the Sierra Madre canyons in Mexico. *Published works*: Have written more than 300 stories about Native Americans and Native American culture, published in national and regional publications, such as Native Arts West, American West, The Homemaker Magazine, Dakota West, etc.; and written and produced educational slide films about Hopi, Navajo, Southwest Pueblos, and Plains Indians, Mandans, and Cliff Dwellers, and the Sioux sweat lodge and Sioux women.

NAVA, DOUGLAS A. (Taos-Apache) 1951-
(gold & silversmith; jewelry designer)
Born July 14, 1951, Montrose, Colo. *Education*: University of Colorado, 1969-71; Western State College (Gunnison, CO), BA, 1978. P*rincipal occupation*: Gold & silversmith; jewelry designer. *Home address*: 61336 Highway 90, Montrose, CO 81401 (303) 249-8131. Affiliation: Owner, Nava Southwest, Ouray, CO, 1979- (retail-Native American arts). *Other professional posts*: Board member & chairperson, Atlatl, 1982-84; appointed to State Arts Agency Panel, National Endowment for the Arts, 1985-88. *Community activities*: Appointed to Goernor's Colorado Council on the Arts & Humanities, 1979-83. *Memberships*: Indian Arts & Crafts Association; Friends of the Ute Indian Museum. *Awards, honors*: Appointed to Who's Who in American Colleges and Uiversities, 1978; 1985 - 2nd Place Ribbon, Lapidary, Gallup Indian Intertribal Ceremonials; 1986 - Ribbon for Jewelry at Pasadena

(CA) American Indian & Western Relic Show; 1987 - 1st, 2nd & 3rd Place Ribbons for jewelry, O'Odham Tash Indian Festival, Casa Grande, AZ; 1988 - 1st Place Ribbons for necklace and bracelet, Lapidary, Gallup Intertribal Ceremonials. *Interests*: "Jewelry design, painting (both oil and acrylic), sculpture-alabaster, marble, fiberglass resin. Also own and operate Nava Southwest, Ouray, Colo."

NAYLOR, JACK C.
(BIA agency supt.)
Affiliation: Miami Agency, Bureau of Indian Affairs, P.O. Box 391, Miami, OK 74354 (918) 542-3396.

NEAMAN, BRYCENE
(museum curator)
Affiliation: Yakima Nation Museum, Yakima Nation Cultural Center, P.O. Box 151, Toppenish, WA 98948 (509) 865-2800 Ext. 720.

NEELY, SHARLOTTE 1948-
(professor of anthropology)
Born August 13, 1948, Savannah, Ga. *Education*: Georgia State University, BA, 1970; University of North Carolina, MA, 1971, PhD, 1976. *Principal occupation*: Professor of anthropology. *Home address*: 632 Riddle Rd., Cincinnati, Ohio 45220 (606) 572-5259 (work). *Affiliation*: Professor of anthropology & coordinator of anthropology, Northern Kentucky University, Highland Heights, KY, 1974-. *Community activities*: City of Cincinnati's Environmental Advisory Council; Sierra Club. *Memberships*: American Anthropological Association (Fellow); Southern Anthropological Association; Anthropologists & Sociologists of Kentucky (past president); American Society for Ethnohistory. *Awards, honors*: Predoctoral Research Fellowship, National Institutes of Mental Health, 1974; Alternate for Post-doctoral Fellowship, (D'Arcy McNickle) Center for the History of the American Indian, Newberry Library, Chicago, Ill., 1974; Certificate of Appreciation, NKU Student Government; NKU Outstanding Professor Award, 1994. *Interests*: Current & historical research with Southeastern Indians, especially the Eastern Band of Cherokee Indians of North Carolina and Ohio's Shawnee Nation United Remnant Band; revising Wendell Oswalt's Indians textbook, "This Land Was Theirs," with addition of Navajo chapter; environmental issues. Unpublished PhD dissertation, "Ethnicity in a Native American Community," and unpublished MA thesis, "The Role of Formal Education Among the Eastern Cherokee Indians, 1880-1971," University of North Carolina, Chapel Hill. *Published works*: Snowbird Cherokees (University of Georgia Press, 1991); numerous articles & papers.

NEGONSOTT, EMERY (Kickapoo)
(former tribal chairperson)
Affiliation: Kickapoo of Kansas Tribal Council, P.O. Box 271, Horton, KS 66439 (913) 486-2131.

NELSON, CAPTAIN (Chaawanta) (Rappahannock)
(tribal chief)
Affiliation: United Rappahannock Tribe, Indian Neck, VA 23077 (804) 769-3128.

NELSON, CASEY
(community mayor)
Affiliation: Metlakatla Indian Community Council, P.O. Box 8, Metlakatla, AK 99926 (907) 886-4441.

NELSON, HERMAN (Athapascan)
(village president)
Affiliation: New Koliganek Village Council, P.O. Box 5057, Kaliganek, AK 99576 (907) 593-3434.

NELSON, IRVING
(library system manager)
Affiliation: Navajo Nation Library System, Window Rock Public Library, P.O. Box 9040, Window Rock, AZ 86515 (520) 871-6376.

NELSON, MICHAEL (Navajo) 1941-
(corporate president)
Born February 2, 1941, Whitecone (Navajo Nation), Ariz. *Education*: Fort Lewis College, BA., 1966. *Principal occupation*: President, Michael Nelson & Associates, Inc., Window Rock, AZ. *Home address*: P.O. Box 614, Window Rock, AZ 86515. *Affiliation*: Michael Nelson & Associates, Inc. maintains retail outlets in Teesto, Tuba City and Kayenta, AZ. *Memberships*:

Navajo Business Association (president, 1974-78). *Awards, honors*: National Indian Businessperson of the Year, 1983; Minority Retail Firm of the Year, 1985; other local awards. *Interests*: Travels to other parts of the world; recent travels to Hawaii, Hong Kong, Bahamas, and all the small islands in the Caribbean, Mexico. *Biographical source*: The Maazo Magazine, Vol. 1, No. 3, entitled Business on the Navajo Reservation, The Maazo Interview with Michael Nelson a Successful Navajo Businessman. *Published work*: Publisher and editor of 1979 & 1980, Airca Rodeo Championship Edition (All Indian Rodeo Cowboy Association).

NELSON, ROBERT M.
(association director; editor)
Affiliation: Association for the Study of American Indian Literatures, Box 112, University of Richmond, Richmond, VA 23173 (804) 289-8311 Fax 289-8313; editor, "Studies in American Indian Literatures."

NELSON, SCOTT H. 1940-
(psychiatrist)
Born July 31, 1940, Cleveland, Ohio. *Education*: Yale University, BA, 1962; Harvard University, MD, 1966; Harvard School of Public Health, M.P.H., 1970. *Principal occupation*: Psychiatrist. *Address*: Box 6081, Santa Fe, NM 87502 (505) 766-2873 (work). Chief of Mental Health Programs, Indian Health Service, Albuquerque, NM, 1987-. *Other professional post*: Psychiatric consultant, Santa Fe Indian Hospital. *Military service*: U.SPHS (Captain, 1970-). *Membership*: American Psychiatric Association (Fellow, 1970-); National Association of State Mental Health Program Directors, (president & chairperson of the board,1981-83); American Art Pottery Association (president, 1983-85). *Interests*: "Extensive travel to Indian tribes as part of work responsibility; interested in tribal arts." *Published works*: More than 30 publications in various mental health and government journals/documents.

CHIEF NEMATTANEW (ROY CRAZY HORSE)
(Powhatan Renape)
(tribal chief)
Affiliation: Powhatan Renape Nation, P.O. Box 225, Roincocas, NJ 08073 (609) 261-4747.

NEMECEK, DIANE (Choctaw/Cherokee)
(educator)
Principal occupation: Educator - Title IX tutor. *Address*: P.O. Box 430, Allen, OK 74825 (405) 857-2419 Fax 857-2636.

NENEMA, GLEN (Kalispel)
(tribal chairperson)
Affiliation: Kalispel Business Committee, P.O. Box 39, Usk, WA 99180 (509) 445-1147.

NEPTUNE, STAN (Penobscot) 1949-
(master woodcarver, artist)
Born April 1, 1949, Indian Island, ME. *Education*: Old Town High School. *Principal occupation*: Master woodcarver, artist. *Address*: P.O. Box 128, Old Town, ME 04468 (207) 827-28847. *Affiliation*: Traditional Native American woodcarver, 1972-present. *Other professional post*: Indian arts and crafts director, Indian Island, ME. *Military service*: U.S. Army, 1969-71 (SP-5; Honorable Discharge). *Awards, honors*: Connecticut River Pow Wow & Rendezvous, 1990 & 1991, and 1st Annual Indian Market, Dayton, OH, 1990; He and his son, Petakisis ("Little Thunder') are the 1997 recipients of the Maine Arts Commission Apprenticeship Training Award as well as numerous awards of excellence for Stan's 25 years of carving. *Annual Demonstrations/Presentations*: Indian Summer Festival, Milwaukee, WI (Sept.); Boston Children's Museum (April); Tufts University, Medford, MA (April); Common Ground Fair, Unity, ME (Sept.); various Indian powwows - east and midwest U.S. *Interests*: Traditional Penobscot woodcarver, Stan specializes in hand carved ceremonial war clubs and walking sticks from birch, poplar and cedar, while some may be inlaid with various stones. This traditional art form is being done only by the Wabanaki people of the northeast woodlands. He also carves totem poles from poplar and cedar. Most of his carvings are in private collections, but some go to galleries, gift shops, and museums all over the country, such as the Abbe Museum, Bar Harbor, ME; Mashantucket Pequot Museum, Ledyard, CT; Penobscot nation Museum, Indian Island, ME; Boston Children's Museum; and American Indian Archaeo-

logical Institution. Stan is available for carving demonstrations. He is a private pilot, currently working on a commercial/instrument rating. *Awards, honors*: Received Letter of Recognition from the Maine State House of Representatives and the members of the Senate for his work as a master artist in the preservation of the Penobscot Indian practice of carving traditional birch root clubs (Augusta, ME, April 7, 1997); among others. *Artist/Work in Publications*: We're Still Here, Joan A. Lester (Children's Museum, Boston, 1987); Turtle Quarterly, Native American Center for the Living Arts, Spring, 1988; Artists of the Dawn, Lee Ann Konrad with Christine Nicholas (Northeast Folklore Society, 1987); ATLATL Directory of Native American Performing Artists (ATLATL, Phoenix, AZ, 1990); Eagle Wing Press, Winter 1984; March-April 1991; Colonial Homes, Hearst Corp. (Vol. 15, No. 5, Oct. 1989); American Indian Healing Arts, by E. Barrie Kavasch & Karen Baat, 1999; Stanley Neptune - Penobscot Artist/Carver, by Henry Bird, "The Northeast," Vol. 126, No. 9 (Advent, 1998); Spirits in the Wood, by Joyce Butler (Maine Historical Society, Portland, ME), 1997; Artifacts, The American Indian Archaeological Institute (various issues); A Wabanaki Guide to Maine (Maine Indian Basketmakers Alliance, 2001); among others.

NERBURN, KENT
(author)
Resides in Bemidji, Minn. *Address*: c/o New World Library, 14 Pamaron Way, Novato, CA 94949-6215 (415) 472-2100. *Professional posts*: Directed "Project Preserve", an award-winning education program in oral history onthe Red Lake Ojibwe Reservation. *Published works*: Neither Wolf Nor Dog: On Forgotten Roads With an Indian Elder, 1994; Native American Wisdom, book and audiocassette; The Wisdom of the Chief (all published by New World Library).

NETZ, TOM (*Soft Shell Turtle*) (*Ah-koot-yah*)
(United Lumbee Nation-Great Lakes Band) 1960-
(pebbles oxide operator)
Born August 15, 1960, Elmore, Ohio. *Education*: High school. *Principal occupation*: Metal casting operator. *Home address*: 201 Harrison St., Walbridge, OH 43465 (419) 666-3257. E-mail: ahkootyah@aol.com. *Affiliations*: Museum consultant, president, Woodland Indian Alliance, 1989-96; pebbles oxide operator, Brush Wellman Engineering Materials, Elmore, OH, 1986-. *Other professional posts*: United Lumbee Nation (clan chief, traditional storyteller & spiritual leader); lead singer-pow-wow drum, Blue Heron Singers. *Memberships*: United Lumbee Nation of N.C. & America; NRA, Sandusky Co. Sportsmans Club, National Gourd Society. *Interests*: "I teach educational programs on Native American culture from pre-contact to removal period; instructor on many types of traditional work shops, flintknapping, basketry, rattles, drums, traditional clothing, beading, Native herbs. (I) enjoy Native flute, old songs, dancing and being with all my Native brothers & sisters from the Four Winds."

NEW, LLOYD H. (*professional name-Lloyd Kiva*) (Cherokee) 1916-
(arts educator, artist, designer)
Born February 18, 1916, Fairland, Okla. *Education*: Oklahoma State University, 1933-34; Art Institute of Chicago, 1934-35; University of New Mexico, 1937; University of Chicago, 1938; School of the Arts Institute of Chicago, BAE, 1938; Laboratory of Anthropology, Santa Fe, NM, 1939; graduated from 6-week Arts Management Institute, MBA Division, Harvard University, 1973. *Principal occupation*: Arts educator, artist, designer. *Home address*: 706 Calle Vibora, Santa Fe, NM 87501 (505) 989-7333 Fax 988-5260. *Affiliations*: Director, Indian Exhibit, Arizona State Fair, 1939-50; instructor in arts & crafts, U.S. Indian School, Phoenix, AA, 1938-41; owner, Lloyd Kiva, Inc. (fashion fabric designer) and Kiva Craft Center, 1946-61; president, Institute of American Indian Arts, 1961-78; consultant, Indian art, 1978-present. *Other professional posts*: instructor in art education, U.S. Indian summer schools for teachers, 1949-51; co-director, Southwest Indian Arts Project (sponsored by the Rockefeller Foundation), University of Arizona, 1959-61; 1995 served as project consultant to Redevelopment of Corte Madera Village, Marin County, Calif. *Military service*: U.S. Naval Reserve, 1941-46 (Deck Officer Amphibious Corps.) *Awards, honors*: 1973 Speaker: Unesco Conference; Lifetime Honorary Fellow in the American Crafts Council; 1990 President Emeritus, In-

stitute of American Indian Art; 1990 honored as "Living Treasure of Santa Fe."; The theme room of the Institute of American Indian Arts Museum, Santa Fe, named in honor of Lloyd New, 1991; 1994 received annual "Indian of the Year Award," Red Earth Indian Organization, Oklahoma City; 1996 "Visionary Award," IAIA Foundation. *Interests*: Mr. New writes, referring to the period during which he established the Lloyd Kiva Studios in Scottsdale, AZ, "During this period (I) was devoted to the problem: Can Indian craftsmen produce contemporary craft items for general use, enabling the craftsmen to earn a living, pursuing their crafts in a general society? This implies some understanding of design inspiration from Indian tradition, careful craftsmanship, fashion, and marketing. (My) 'Kiva Bags' (a craft item Mr. New created) have been marketed by outstanding fashion stores throughout the country. Top fashion publications have featured these and other Kiva fashions from time to time." Mr. New has attended various conferences relating to indigenous arts and crafts forms in the U.S. and Mexico. *Published work*: Using Cultural Differences as a Basis for Creative Expression (Institute of American Indian Arts, 1964).

NEW HOLY, DR. ANDREA
(college professor)
Affiliation: Native American Studies Dept., Montana State University, 2-179 Wilson Hall, P.O. Box 172340, Bozeman, MT 59717 (406) 994-3881 Fax 994-6879. *Interests*: Fedeal Indian policy & law; Native Americans and the cinema.

NEWAGO, GEORGE P.
(Red Cliff Lake Superior Ojibwe)
(former tribal chairperson)
Affiliation: Red Cliff Tribal Council, P.O. Box 529, Bayfield, WI 54814 (715) 779-3700.

NEWCOMB, STEVEN
(research coordinator)
Affiliation: Indigenous Law Research Coordinator, Kumeyaay Community College, Sycuan Band of Kumeyaay Nation, 5459 Dehesa Rd., El Cajon, CA 92021 (619) 445-2613 Fax 445-1927; co-founder & co-dirctor, Indigenous Law Institute, Kumeyaay Community College; columnist, Indian Country Today.

NEWCOMB, WILLIAM W., JR. 1921-
(professor emeritus)
Born October 30, 1921, Detroit, Mich. *Education*: University of Michigan, BA, 1943, MA, 1946, PhD, 1953. *Principal occupation*: Professor emeritus. *Home address*: 6206 Shoal Creek Blvd., Austin, TX 78757. *Affiliation*: Professor of anthropology, 1962-87; professor emeritus, 1987-, University of Texas, Austin, TX. *Past professional post*: Director, Texas Memorial Museum, 1957-78. *Military service*: U.S. Army Infantry, 1943-46. *Memberships*: American Anthropological Association (Fellow); Texas Archaeological Society. *Awards, honors*: Awards for Indians of Texas, Texas Institute of Letters, Dallas Public Library; 1998 4th Annual White Shaman Award, The Rock Art Foundation, for "The Rock Art of Texas." *Interests*: "American Indian ethnology, particularly Plains and Texas; culture change; primitive art; ethnographic field work with Delaware Indians; archaeological field work in Arkansas and Texas; rock art of the Texas Indians; ethnohistory of Wichita." *Biographical sources*: Who's Who in America; Contemporary Authors. *Published works*: The Culture and Acculturation of the Delaware Indians (University of Michigan Press, 1956); The Indians of Texas (University of Texas Press, 1961); The Rock Art of Texas (University of Texas Press, 1967); A Lipan Apache Mission, San Lorenzo de la Santa Cruz, 1762-1771, with Curtis Tunnell (Texas Memorial Museum, 1969); North American Indians: Anthropological Perspective (Goodyear Publishing, 1974); The People Called Wichita (Indian Tribal Series, 1976); German Artist of the Texas Frontier, Richard Friedrich Petri (University of Texas Press, 1978).

NEWCOMBE, ROBERT
(health director)
Affiliation: Pine Hill PHS Indian Health Center, P.O. Box 310, Pine Hill, NM 87357 (505) 775-3271.

NEWELL, WAYNE (Passamaquoddy)
(educator)
Address: P.O. Box 271, Princeton, ME 04668.

NEWLIN, GORDON (Eskimo)
(village president)
Affiliation: Noorvik Native Community, P.O. Box 71, Noorvik, AK 99763 (907) 636-2144.

NEWTON, WAYNE
(singer, entertainer)
Address: 6629 S. Pecos, Las Vegas, NV 89120.

NEZ, PHOEBE (White Mountain Apache)
(radio station manager)
Affiliation: KNNB - 88.1 FM, White Mountain Apache Tribe, P.O. Box 310, Whiteriver, AZ 85941 (602) 338-5229.

NICHOLAS, GRAYDON
(association president)
Affiliation: Union of New Brunswick Indians, 35 Dedam St., Fredericton, NB, Canada E3A 2V2 (506) 458-9444.

NICHOLAS, JOHN C.
(BIA office director)
Affiliation: Office of Equal Opportunity Programs, Bureau of Indian Affairs, MS-4559-MIB, Rm. 4561, 1849 C St., NW, Washington, DC 20240 (202) 208-3600.

NICHOLAS, SHEILAH (Hopi)
(Indian program coordinator)
Affiliations: Program coordinator, American Indian Language & Development Institute, American Indian Studies Program, The University of Arizona, Harvill Bldg., Rm 430, P.O. Box 210076, Tucson, AZ 85721 (520) 621-7108 Fax 621-7952. E-mail: aisp@email.arizona. edu.

NICHOLS, ROGER L. 1933-
(professor of history)
Born June 13, 1933, Racine Wisc. *Education*: Wisconsin State College, BS, 1956; University of Wisconsin, Madison, MS, 1959, PhD, 1964. *Principal occupation*: Professor of history. *Address*: Dept. of History, 215 Social Science, University of Arizona, Tucson, AZ 85721 (520) 621-4684 Fax 621-2422; E-mail: roger-nichols@ns.arizona.edu. *Affiliations*: Professor, History Department, Wisconsin State University, Oshkosh, 1963-65; Professor, History Department, University of Georgia, Athens, 1965-69; Professor, History Department, University of Arizona, Tucson, 1969-. *Community activities*: Board of Directors, Arizona Humanities Council. *Memberships*: American Society for Ethnohistory; Immigration & Ethnic History Society; American Historical Association; Organization of American Historians; Western History Association; Society for Historians of the Early Republic. *Awards, honors*: Huntington Library Fellowship; director, National Endowment for the Humanities, Summer Seminar for College Teachers, 1981, 1988, 1993; Fulbright Senior Lecturer, Martin Luther University, Germany, 1996-97; Senior Fulbright Scholar, University of Cologne, germany, 2003-04. *Interests*: "History of the American frontier and West; American Indian relations; comparative history — U.S.A. & Canada. *Biographical sources*: Contemporary Authors; Directory of American Scholars — History. *Published works*: General Henry Atkinson (University of Oklahoma Press, 1965); editor, The Missouri Expedition (University of Oklahoma Press, 1969); Stephen Long & American Frontier Exploration (University of Delaware, 1980); editor, American Frontier & Western Issues (Greenwood Press, 1986);editor, The American Indian: Past & Present (Alfred Knopf, 1986, '81, '71); co-author, Natives and Strangers (Oxford University Press, 2003, 1996, '90, '79); Black Hawk and the Warrior's Path (Harlan Davidson, 1992); Indians in the U.S. & Canada: A Comparative History (University of Nebraska, 1998); editor, The American Indian: Past & Present (McGraw-Hill, 5th Ed., 1999); Black Hawk's Autobiography (Iowa State University Press, 1999); American Indians in U.S. History (University of Oklahoma Press, 2003).

NICHOLSON, KEN
(health center director)
Affiliation: Wind River PHS Indian Health Center, Fort Washakie, WY 82514 (307) 332-9416.

NICHOLSON, MARY EILEEN (Colville) 1924-
(tribal official)
Born March 1, 1924, Okanogan County, Wash. *Education*: St. Mary's Mission. *Principal occupation*: Member, Colville Business (Tribal) Council, Nespelem,

Wash. *Home address*: Route 1, Box 90, Tonasket, WA 98855. *Community activities*: Western Farmers Association; Agricultural Stabilization Conservation Service (committee member).

NICHOLSON, WILLIAM E.
(BIA agency supt.)
Affiliation: Colville Agency, Bureau of Indian Affairs, P.O. Box 111, Nespelem, WA 99155 (509) 634-2316 Fax 634-2355.

NICK, OSCAR
(AK village president)
Affiliation: Village of Atmautluak, P.O. Box ATT, Atmautluak, AK 99559 (907) 553-5610.

NICKERSON, TEK
(organization director)
Affiliation: S.H.A.R.E. (Sacred Hoop of American Resource Exchange), 114 Cat Rock Rd., Cos Cob, CT 06807 (203) 622-6525.

NICKLASON, FRED 1931-
(historian)
Born May 5, 1931, Swatara, Minn. *Education*: Gustavus Adolphus College, BS, 1953; University of Pennsylvania, MA, 1955; Yale University, PhD, 1967. *Principal occupation*: Historian. *Home address*: 6323 Utah Ave., NW, Washington, DC 20015. *Affiliations*: Assistant professor, University of Maryland, College Park, MD, 1967-; director, Nicklason Research Associates, Washington, DC, 1971-. *Military service*: U.S. Army, 1955-57 (Research Analyst). *Memberships*: American Historical Association; Western Historical Association; Southern Historical Association; American Studies Association; American Ethnohistorical Association. *Awards, honors*: American Philosophical Society Grant. *Interests*: American Indian policy; American Southwest travel.

NICKLIE, DAVID (Athapascan)
(AK village president)
Affiliation: Native Village of Cantwell, P.O. Box 94, Cantwell, AK 99729 (907) 768-2151.

NICOLL, MICHAEL
(Indian band chief)
Affiliation: Masset Indian Band, Box 189, Masset, British Columbia, Canada V0T 1M0 (604) 626-3337.

NIELSEN, ANITA G. (*Mishanagwus*) (Wampanoag) 1922-
(lecturer/teacher)
Born June 21, 1922, Mashpee, Mass. *Education*: Massasoit Community College, MA, 1975; Bridgewater State College, MA, 1989. *Principal occupation*: Lecturer/teacher, Wampanoag culture; retired from full-time job. *Address*: P.O. Box 402, Middleboro, MA 02346 (508) 947-4159 (home). *Affiliation*: Teacher, Middleboro, MA, 1986-92; lecturer/teacher, Wampanoag culture presentations, Plimoth Plantation, Living Museum, Plymouth, MA, schools by appointment - New England, 1983-present; honorary lecturer at Lesley College (once a year since 1994), other colleges include Harvard University, Wellsley College, Brown University, and University of massachusetts, Amherst, MA. *Community activities*: Middleboro-Robbins Museum of Archaeology/Mashpee Wampanoag Tribal Council - Mashpee Archives Loaned Artifact for Exhibition. *Membership*: Wampanoag Tribal Council (life membership); Smithsonian Institution; Massachusetts Archaeology. *Awards, Honors*: Received Recognition, March 1995, by the State of Massachusetts, House of Representatives - for outstanding efforts educating the public on Wampanoag cultures and lifestyles...presented personally by the Speaker of the House; Honorable Mention, Heard Museum; National Competition, Contemporary Craft - Finger-Twined Bag - purchased by Dept. of Interior, Bureau of Indian Affairs crafts - displayed in resource directory. *Interests*: To keep the younger generation involved; demonstrate the uses of natural resources and the importance of respecting all of mother earth's resources. Work with museums on children's workshops; travel to Europe; teacher's conferences; presentations (curriculum). *Biographical sources*: "Personalities of America" (The American Biographical Institute); cover picture, "Plymouth Guide"; photographed for Indian documentation, by Jay Stock; "Career Close Up", by Boston Herald News.

NIELSEN, TIM
(organization director)
Affiliation: Indian Life Ministries, Intertribal Christian Communications, P.O. Box 32, Pembina, ND 58271 (204) 661-9333. *Other professional post*: Editor, "Indian Life: Christian Media for Native North Americans."

NIGHT PIPE, ORVILLE
(hospital director)
Affiliation: Eagle Butte PHS Indian Hospital, P.O. Box 1012, Eagle Butte, SD 57625 (605) 964-7030.

NIGHT SHIELD, EUSTACE
(home living specialist)
Affiliation: Rosebud Dormitories, P.O. Box 669, Mission, SD 57555 (605) 856-4486.

NINKE, BETH
(health director)
Affiliation: Sacramento Urban Indian Health, 801 Broadway, Suite B, Sacramento, CA 95818 (916) 441-0918.

NOGANOSH, JOAN
(Indian band chief)
Affiliation: Magnetawan Indian Band, Box 15, RR 1, Britt, Ontario, Canada P0G 1A0 (705) 383-2477.

NOLAN, DAVID
(Indian program director)
Affiliation: Escambia County Middle School, Indian Education Program, P.O. Drawer 1236, Atmore, AL 36504 (205) 368-9105.

NOLAN-RENDE, HELEN (*Kanaiehson*)
(Kahnawake Mohawk)
(administrator & lecturer)
Born on Kahnawake Mohawk Reserve, Canada. *Education*: Rutgers University, Newark, MA in Public Administration; Kennedy-Western University (WY), PhD in Public Administration. Certificates in Gerontology and Volunteer Management, pursuing certifcates in Human Service Management & Train the Trainer from Rutgers School of Social Work. Continuing Education in Piscataway, NJ.*Principal occupation*: Director of social services. *Home address*: 21 Village Rd., Morganville, NJ 07751. *Affiliations*: Assistant Director of Social Services & Director, Office on Aging, Township of Old Bridge, Old Bridge, NJ, 1982-; Commissioner, New Jersey State Commission on American Indian Affairs, 1996-present. *Community activities*: Old Bridge Community School Advisory Board (past member); Old Bridge Management Association; Old Bridge Emergency Food Bank Coordinator; Old Bridge Employee Trip Reduction Coordinator; Inter-Tribal American Indians of New Jersey (council member, past president); Middlesex County Older Adult Service Providers; Notary Public of New Jersey; New Jersey Affirmative Action Referral Contact. *Memberships*: New Jersey Association of Senior Citizen Center Directors; American Society on Aging; National American Indian Council on Aging; National Council on Aging; National Institute of Senior Centers; American Association of Public Administrators; National Honor Society, Pi Alpha Alpha. *Awards, honors*: Honorary member - National React/Pacers (police activated citizens Emergency Response Service) NJ Council; New Jersey Division on Civil Rights, 1986 Award for Outstanding Contribution; "Sentinel Newspaper, East Brunswick, NJ, 1987 Outstanding People Award; Society of St. Anthony of Padua, 1990 Padua Award; New Jersey General Assembly Citation 1990, Outstanding Commitment to Community; appointed (by Governor Whitman) commissioner of newly created New Jersey State Commission on American Indian Affairs, 1996; Indo-American Senior Citizens of New Jersey, 2000 Certificate of Commendation; United Way of Central New Jersey, 2000 Hometown Hero Nominee.. *Interests*: "Advocate for problems and concerns of aging population, accomplished lecturer & published writer on American Indian issues and concerns. Appeared on New Jersey network & radio stations on interviews regarding these issues."

NOLEY, GRAYSON (Choctaw) 1943-
(tribal education administrator)
Born September 4, 1943, Talihina, Okla. *Education*: Southeastern Oklahoma State University, BA, 1969; Penn State University, University Park, MEd, 1975, PhD, 1979. *Principal occupation*: Tribal education ad-

ministrator. *Address*: Sequoyah High School, P.O. Box 558, Tahlequah, OK 74464 (918) 456-0671. *Affiliations*: Director, American Indian Leadership Program, Penn State University, Education Policy Studies, University Park, PA, 1979-88; administrator, Sequoyah High School, Tahlequah, OK, 1988-. *Other professional posts*: Assistant professor of education; assistant director, American Indian Special Education Teacher Training Program; director, American Indian Education Policy Center, Penn State University. *Military service*: U.S. Army, 1961-64. *Community activities*: Partnership Coordinating Committee; Committee for Understanding Others (local school district); Minorities Committee (graduate record examination board), *Memberships*: American Educational Research Association; Comparative and International Education Society; National Indian Education Association. *Awards, honors*: Kellogg Foundation, National Fellowship Program, 1984-87; participant, Phoenix Seminar, Penn State University, 1975; American Indian Leadership Program Fellowship, Penn State University, 1974-79; Music Scholarship, Southeastern State University, Durant, OK. *Interests*: Federal policies on Native American education; drug and alcohol abuse in adolescent Native Americans; travel. *Published work*: Two chapters in The Choctaw Before Removal (Mississippi University Press, 1985); articles in various education journals and American Indian journals.

NOLLNER, PADDY (Athapascan)
(village chief)
Affiliation: Galena Village Council, P.O. Box 182, Galena, AK 99741 (907) 656-1366.

NOMEE, ALFRED
(tribal school chairperson)
Affiliation: Coeur d'Alene Tribal School, P.O. Box A, DeSmet, ID 83824 (208) 274-6921.

NOMEE, CLARA (Crow)
(tribal chairperson)
Affiliation: Crow Tribal Council, P.O. Box 159, Crow Agency, MT 59022 (406) 638-2601.

NORDSTRAND, POLLYANNA
(education & repatriation coordinator)
Affiliations: American Indian Ritual Object Repatriation Foundation, 463 East 57 St., New York, NY 10128 (212) 980-9441 Fax 421-2746.

NORDSTRUM, FRANK
(school principal)
Affiliation: Santa Clara Day School, P.O. Box 2183, Espanola, NM 87532 (505) 753-4406 Fax 753-8866.

NORDWALL, WAYNE
(BIA regional director)
Affiliation: Western Regional Office, Bureau of Indian Affairs, P.O. Box 10, Phoenix, AZ 85001 (602) 379-6600 Fax 379-4413.

NORGREN, JILL
(professor emerita, author)
Affiliations: Professor Emerita of Government & Legal Studies, John Jay College of Criminal Justice and the Graduate Center, The City University of New York. *Published works*: Coauthor of "Partial Justice: Federal Indian Law in a Liberal-Constitutional System," and "American Cultural Pluralism and Law"; The Cherokee Cases: Two Landmark Federal Decisions in the Fight for Sovereignty (University of Oklahoma Press, 2004); forthcoming biography of Belva Lockwood.

NORMAN, MARGARET JANE (Oklahoma Seminole)
(museum curator)
Affiliation: Seminole Nation Museum, 524 S. Wewoka, Box 1532, Wewoka, OK 74884 (405) 257-5580.

NORMAN, WILLIAM R., JR. (Muscogee Creek)
(attorney)
Education: University of Central Oklahoma, BBA, 1989; University of Oklahoma, J.D., 1992. *Principal occupation*: Attorney. *Address & Affiliation*: Hobbs, Straus, Dean & Walker, LLP, 117 Park Ave., 2nd Floor, Oklahoma City, OK 73102 (405) 602-9425 Fax 602-9426. E-mail: william@hsdwok.com. Mr. Norman joined the Washington, DC office in 1994 and in 1996 opened the Oklahoma office; Partner, 2000-present. *Memberships*: American Bar Association; Oklahoma Bar Association; District of Columbia Bar. *Areas of concen-

tration: Indian Self-Determination and Education Assistance Act; taxation, transportation, gaming, tribal sovereignty, and adminsitrative and federal litigation resulting from disputes in such matters. Mr. Norman was primary author of Chapter 2 of "Empowerment of Tribal Governments: Final Workgroup Report" developed by the Tribal Workgroup on Tribal Needs Assessments in May 1999. *Awards, honors*: Received the Salem Civil Rights Award for the note entitled, "Native American Inmates and Prison Grooming Regulations: Today's Justified Scalps," *18 Am. Indian L. Rev. 191 (1993)*.

NORRGARD, PHILIP
(health director)
Affiliation: Min-No-Aya-Win Human Service Center, 927 Trettel Lane, Cloquet, MN 55720 (218) 879-1227.

NORRIS, LEONARD
(organization director)
Affiliation: Organization of the Forgotten American, P.O. Box 1257, Klamath Falls, OR 97601 (503) 882-4441.

NORTH, CHARLES, M.D.
(clinical director)
Affiliation: Albuquerque PHS Indian Hospital, 801 Vassar Dr, NE, Albuquerque, NM 87106 (505) 254-4000.

NORTHBIRD, LOUIS (Leech Lake Ojibwe)
(college instructor)
Affiliation: Leech Lake Tribal College, 6530 U.S. Hwy. 2 NW, Cass Lake, MN 56633 (218) 335-4220 Fax 335-4209.

NORTHRUP, JIM (Gi Gi Kunaw a magawinini)
(Fond du Lac Lake Superior Chippewa) 1943-
(writer, basketmaker)
Born April 28, 1943, Fond du Lac Reservation, Minn. *Principal occupation*: Writer, basketmaker. *Home address*: 266 Northrup Rd., Sawyer, MN 55780 (218) 879-1691. Professional posts: Writes a syndicated columns, "Fond du Lac Follies" in three Indian newspapers, 1989-; and "Commentaries," in Duluth News Tribune, 1993-. *Military service*: U.S. Marine Corps, 1961-66 (Sgt. - Vietnam Campaign). *Video accomplishments*: Warriors (PPTV - Fargo, ND, 1988); Diaries (KTCA - St. Paul, MN, 1991); Zero Street (Weapon of Choice, 1993); With Reservations (C.I.E., St. Paul,MN, 1994). *Radio accomplishments*: Commentaries - Superior Radio Network, 1992; Fresh Air Radio - NPR, 1994. *Awards, honors*: Lake Superior Contemporary Writers, 1986; Best Feature Story, Native American Journalists Association, 1987; Minnesota Book Award, Augsburg College, 1993; Northeast Minnesota Book Award 1994, University of Minnesota, Duluth. *Biographical sources*: Lake Superior Magazine, Oct. 1993; St. Paul Pioneer Press, 1993. *Published works*: "Touchwood" (New Rivers Press, 1987); "Stillers Pond" (New Rivers Press, 1988); "North Writers" (University of Minnesota Press, 1990); "Frags & Fragments"- Vietnam poetry (self published, 1990); "Three More" (Minnesota Center for the Book Arts, 1992); "Walking the Rez Road" (Voyageur Press, 1993); "Days of Obsidian, Days of Grace" (Poetry Harbor, 1994).

NORTON, GREGORY (Umpqua & Suislaw)
(former tribal chairperson)
Affiliation: Confederated Tribes of Coos Lower Umpqua & Suislaw Indians, 338 Wallace Ave., Coos Bay, OR 97420 (503) 267-5454.

NORTON, JOSEPH TOKWIRO
(Indian band chief)
Affiliation: Mohawk Nation, Box 720, Kahnawake, Quebec, Canada J01 1B0 (514) 638-6790.

NORTON, MARY (Wintun)
(rancheria chairperson)
Affiliation: Cortina Rancheria, P.O. Box 1630, Williams, CA 95987 (916) 726-7118.

NOSIE, WENDSLER, Sr.
(co-chairperson)
Affiliation: Apaches for Cultural Preservation, San Carlos Apache Reservation, P.O. Box 249, San Carlos, AZ 85550 (520) 475-2494.

NOTAH, GLORIA (San Carlos Apache)
(tribal department director)
Affiliation: San Carlos Recreation & Wildlife Dept., P.O. Box 97, San Carlos, AZ 85550 (520) 475-2343.

NOVAK, YVONNE
(association president)
Affiliation: National Indian Education Association, 121 Oronoco St., Alexandria, VA 22314 (703) 838-2870 Fax 838-1620.

NOVAS, AMERICA
(Indian school principal)
Affiliation: Miccosukee Indian School, Box 440021, Tamiami Station, Miami, FL 33144 (305) 223-8380 Fax 223-1011.

NUCKOLLS, LARRY (Absentee-Shawnee)
(tribal governor)
Affiliation: Absentee-Shawnee Executive Committee, 2025 S. Gordon Cooper Dr., Shawnee, OK 74801 (405) 275-4030.

NUMKENA, WILFRED (Tsung-Aya) (Hopi) 1943-
(education)
Born December 24, 1943, Moencopi, Ariz. *Education*: Brigham Young University, BS, 1973; Pennsylvania State University, MEd., 1979. *Principal occupation*: Education. *Home address*: Resides in Flagstaff, AZ area. *Affiliation*: Executive director, Utah Division of Indian Affairs, Salt Lake City, UT, 1991-98. *Military service*: U.S. Army, 1965-67 (Sergeant E-5; Honorable Discharge). *Community activities*: Utah Columbus Quincentennial Commission; Utah Interagency Task Force. *Memberships*: National Indian Education Association; Natioal Congress of American Indians; Utah Federation for Indian Education. *Awards, honors*: Ute Indian Education Award; University of Utah Intertribal Student Association Leadership Recognition.

NUNLEY, JOHN W.
(museum curator)
Affiliation: Curator, St. Louis Art Museum, Forest Park, St. Louis, MO 63110 (314) 721-0067; curator of the "Art of the Osage" exhibit. *Published work*: Art of the Osage, with Garrick Bailey, Daniel C. Swan, & E. Sean StandingBear (university of Washington Press, 2004).

NUNNERY, BETTY D.
(program coordinator)
Affiliation: American Indian Professional Training Program in Speech-Language Pathology & Audiology, University of Arizona, Dept. of Speech & Hearing Sciences, Tucson, AZ 85721 (520) 621-1969. *Published works*: Editor, "Desert Connections"; Directory of Native Americans in Speech-Language Pathology & Audiology.

NUSKE, VIRGINIA (Menominee)
(association director)
Affiliation: Wisconsin Indian Education Association, Menominee Indian Tribe, P.O. Box 910, Keshena, WI 54135 (715) 799-5110.

NUSS, BOB 1941-
(business owner)
Born in 1941, Ohio. *Education*: Marietta (OH) College, BA, 1963; University of Arizona, 1963-65, 1969-71. *Principal occupation*: Owner, Drumbeat Indian Arts, Inc. *Address & Affiliation*: Drumbeat Indian Arts, 4143 N. 16th St., Phoenix, AZ 85016 (602) 266-4823 Fax 265-2402 (manager, 1972-83; owner, 1984-). *Military service*: U.S. Army, 1966-68. *Community activities*: Board of Directors, ATLATL & Pueblo Grande Museum; Phoenix Indian Center (benefit dinner committee); Sun-N-Sand Model Railroad Club. *Awards, honors*: Outstanding Business for Service to the American Indian Community, Phoenix Indian Center, 1993. *Interests*: Drumbeat Indian Arts (until 1997 it was named Canyon Records & Indian Arts) is the largest distributors of American Indian recordings (cassettes, CDs, videos) - over 2,500 titles.

NUTTER, DELBERT
(health director)
Affiliation: W.W. Hastings Indian Hospital, 100 S. Bliss, Tahlequah, OK 74464 (918) 458-3100.

NUVAMSA, BENJAMIN H.
(BIA agency supt.)
Affiliation: Fort Apache Agency, Bureau of Indian Affairs, P.O. Box 560, Whiteriver, AZ 85941 (928) 338-5353 Fax 338-5383.

NUVAYESTEWA, EVANGELINE
(Taskya-Kyaaro-Yellow Parrot) (Hopi-Tewa) 1940-
(elementary-primary teacher)
Born February 17, 1940, Keams Canyon, Ariz. *Education*: Phoenix Junior College, AA, 1961; Northern Arizona University, BS, 1972, MA, 1980. *Principal occupation*: Elementary-primary teacher. *Home address*: P.O. Box 637, Polacca, AZ 86042 (602) 737-2272; 737-2581 (work). *Affiliations*: K-2 teacher, Polacca Day & Second Mesa School , 1971-; Headstart teacher, 4 schools on the Hopi Reservation (6 years). *Other professional post*: Education specialist, NFFE Secretary, Hopi Jr./Sr. High School treasurer. *Community activities*: Save the Children Federation (advisor-secretary); Elderly Committee (secretary). *Memberships*: International Reading Association. *Awards, honors*: Outstanding Teachers of America, awarded by Gilbert Beers, Ph.D., director; Outstanding Dedication Award, Hopi Tribal Follow Through Program; Special Education Dedication Award, Polacca Day School. Interests: "I enjoy going to professional workshops to enhance my teaching skills in any area offered. I am also dedicated to participating in all our Hopi Religious Ceremonies on the mesa in our villages."

NUVAYESTEWA, LEON
(school principal)
Affiliation: Hopi High School, P.O. Box 37, Keams Canyon, AZ 86034 (602) 738-5111.

NYE, DORIS R.
(council president)
Affiliation: National Urban Indian Council, 100068 University Park Station, Denver, CO 80210 (303) 750-2695.

NYGAARD, ROBERT WAYNE
(Sault Ste. Marie Chippewa) 1953-
(director-planning & development)
Born September 5, 1953, Gaylord, Mich. *Education*: Bay de Noc Community College (Escanaba, MI), AA, 1972; Central Michigan University, BA, 1974. *Principal occupation*: Director-planning & development. *Home address*: 1829 Chestnut, Sault Ste. Marie, MI 49783. *Office address*: 5232 Ashmun, Sault Ste. Marie, MI 49783 (906) 635-6050 Fax 635-4969 (work). *Affiliation*: Director-Planning & Development, Sault Ste. Marie Tribe of Chippewa Indians, Sault Ste. Marie, MI, 1978-. *Other professional posts*: Adjunct professor, Bay Mills (MI) Community College 1991-present; member, Management Board, Kentwood Holdings (L.L.C.), 1996-present. *Community activities*: member, Census Advisory Committee on the African American, American Indian & Alaskan Native, Pacific Islander, and Hispanic Populations, Washington, DC, 1994-; board of directors, Inter-tribal Bison Cooperative, Rapid City, SD, 1995-. *Membership*: Sault Ste. Marie Tribe of Chippewa Indians. *Awards, honors*: 15 Year Service Award, Sault Ste. Marie Tribe, 1993; Outstanding State Leadership Recognition Award, Circle of Life Conference, 1984.

O

OAKES, GORDON
(Indian band chief)
Affiliation: Nekaneet Indian Band, Box 548, Maple Creek, Saskatchewan, Canada S0N 1N0 (306) 662-3660.

OBAGO-NICOLAR, LINDA (Lakota)
(chief finanial officer)
Affiliation: CFO, Sisseton Wahpeton College, P.O. Box 689, Agency Village, SD 57262 (605) 698-3966 Fax 698-3132.

OBERLY, ACEY, JR. (Yakama)
(BIA agency supt.)
Affiliation: Yakama Agency, Bureau of Indian Affairs, P.O. Box 632, Toppenish, WA 98948 (509) 865-2255 FAX 865-3636.

OBERLY, JOHN
(administrative officer)
Affiliation: Wind River PHS Indian Health Center, Fort Washakie, WY 82514 (307) 332-9416; Arapaho PHS Indian health Center, Arapaho, WY 82510 (307) 856-9281.

OBOMSAWIN, TOMAS (Abenaki)
(musician)
Address: c/o Abenaki Tribal Office, P.O. Box 276, Missisquoi, VT 05488 (802) 868-7146. Tomas plays contemporary and traditional Native American theme music. Lyrics are of American Indian struggles and situations.

O'BRIEN, IRMA
(museum coordinator)
Affiliation: Dillingham Heritage Museum, Pouch 202, Dillingham, AK 99576 (907) 842-5601.

OCHOA, CARMEN (Cahto-Pomo)
(rancheria chairperson)
Affiliation: Laytonville Rancheria, P.O. Box 1102, Laytonville, CA 95454 (707) 984-6197.

O'CONNELL, STEVE
(Indian center director)
Affiliation: Director, Roundhouse Council, Inc., P.O.Box 217, Greenville, CA 95947 (916) 284-6866 Fax 284-6714.

O'DONNELL, JIM
(museum director)
Affiliation: Akta Lakota Museum, St. Joseph Indian School, P.O. Box 89, Chamberlain, SD 57325 (605) 734-3455.

OESTREICHER, DAVID M. 1959-
(anthropologist, writer, teacher)
Born December 5, 1959, New York, N.Y. Education: SUNY at Purchase, BA, 1981; New York University, MA, 1985. *Principal occupation*: Anthropologist, writer, teacher. *Home address*: 19 Forbes Blvd., Eastchester, NY 10709 (914) 632-1295. *Affiliations*: Speaker for schools, New York Botanical Garden; consultant for Native American Heritage Committee of New York; Scarsdale Audubon Society (board of directors). *Other professional posts*: Consultant for four books, a number of articles, and two films on the Lenape, including Lenape: The Original People, by Thomas Agnello, which he helped conceive and produce. Mr. Oestreicher is recognized as a leading authority on the Lenape and related Algonkian tribes. His research has taken him from remote areas of Wisconsin and Canada to Oklahoma. For seven years until her death in November of 1984, much of his research work was conducted with the late "Touching Leaves Woman", or Nora Thompson Dean, one of the few remaining full blooded Lenape, one of the last speakers of her language and the last person fully raised in the traditions of her ancestors. Much of this information is recorded on tapes, notes and video and is a major contribution to the Delaware Indian Resource Center at Ward Pound Ridge Reservation, Cross River, N.Y. Mr. Ostreicher organized and is principal curator of the traveling exhibit "Touching Leaves and Her People: The Lenape", initially funded in part by a grant from the New York Council for the Humanities. He has appeared as a guest on WOR radio in New York with Ed and Pegeen Fitzgerald; has taught government sponsored Title IV (Native American Indian Education) programs (his students, members of the Ramapo Mountain Indian Tribe, studied Delaware language and culture with him) and has taken part in and helped arrange various Delaware Indian symposiums and programs at Yale University, Tulsa University, Seton Hall University, SUNY Purchase, Kent State University, New York City Hall, the New Jersey Highlands Historical Society, the Archaeological Society of New Jersey, and elsewhere. Oestreicher has also been a consultant for films and book in connection with the Delaware Indians. *Other interests include*: ancient Near Eastern and Jewish history, poetry, classical and folk music, art, conservation, canoeing and the outdoors. *Published works*: Surviving Historic Traditions of the Unami Delaware and The Munsee and Northern Unami Today: A Study of Traditional Ways at Moraviantown to be published by the New York Historical Society; under preparation is a biography of Nora Thompson Dean.

OFFICER, JAMES E. 1924-
(retired-professor of anthropology)
Born July 28, 1924, Boulder, Colo. *Education*: University of Kansas, 1942-43; University of Arizona, AB, 1950, PhD, 1964. *Principal occupation*: Retired professor of anthropology, University of Arizona. *Home address*: 621 N. Sawtelle Ave., Tucson, AZ 85716 (602) 795-4043. *Affiliations*: Information officer, Dept. of State, 1950-53; instructor, University of Arizona, 1957-60; associate commissioner, Bureau of Indian Affairs, 1961-67; assistant to the Secretary of the Interior, 1967-69; coordinator of international programs, University of Arizona, 1969-76; professor of anthropology, University of Arizona, Tucson, 1969-89. *Community activities*: U.S. Representative, Interamerican Indian Institute (Mexico City), 1968-78; Democratic Precinct Committeeman, 1970-76. *Memberships*: Arizona Historical Society (board of directors, 1986-92); American Anthropological Association (Fellow), 1956-; Society for Applied Anthropology (Fellow), 1956-; Southwestern Mission Research Center (board of directors, 1986); Southwest Park and Monuments Association (board of directors, 1989-). *Awards, honors*: Distinguished Service Award, Department of the Interior, 1968; Quill and Scroll National Journalism Scholarship, 1942; Tucson-Mexico Goodwill Award, Tucson Trade Bureau, 1982; Creative Teaching Award, University of Arizona Foundation, 1983; Southwest Book Award, 1988; AZ Historical Foundation Prize, 1988; AZ Historical Society Prize, 1988. *Interests*: "Primary activities at present involve speaking on subjects related to Native American and Hispanic Americans, and doing research and writing on the same topics." *Biographical sources*: Who's Who in the West. *Published works*: Indians in School (University of Arizona Press, 1955); Anthropology and the American Indian (Indian Historian Press, 1973); The Hodge's Site (University of Arizona Press, 1978); Arizona's Hispanic Perspective (Arizona Academy, Phoenix, 1981); Hispanic Arizona, 1536-1956 (University of Arizona Press, 1987).

O'JAY, BETTY (Navajo)
(school director)
Affiliation: Navajo Preparatory School, 1200 W. Apache, Farmington, NM 87401 (505) 326-6571 Fax 326-2155.

OJIBWAY, FR. PAUL
(commissioner)
Affiliation: Los Angeles City/County Native American Indian Commission, 500 W. Temple St., Room 780, Los Angeles, CA 90012 (213) 974-7554.

OKITKUN, MARK
(tribal chairperson)
Affiliation: Native Village of Bill Moore's Slough, P.O. Box 20037, Kotlik, AK 99620 (907) 899-4712.

OKLEASIK, M. LaVONNE 1936-
(clerk, teacher)
Born July 4, 1936, Iowa. *Education*: Luther College, BA, 1960. *Principal occupation*: Clerk, teacher. *Home address*: Box 356, Nome, AK 99762. *Affiliations*: Clerk, City of Nome, Alaska; financial secretary, education chairman, bible study teacher, Our Savior's Lutheran Church, Nome. *Other professional post*: Private piano teacher. *Community activities*: Community alcohol program in Nome since 1980. "These activities have been with the Eskimo people. My husband is an Eskimo from Teller, Alaska. My desire for the people in this area is for them to be confident, to be happy about themselves and able to look at problems realistically and try to solve them in a satisfying manner. This I have tried to do in a volunteer basis through the church and the community alcohol program, working with all ages—children and elderly."

OLD BEAR, DAVID, SR. (Sac & Fox)
(former tribal chief)
Affiliation: Sac & Fox Tribe of the Mississippi in Iowa, 349 Meskwaki Rd., Tama, IA 52339 (515) 484-4678

OLD COYOTE, BARNEY (Crow) 1923-
(government official, professor)
Born April 10, 1923, St. Xavier, Mont. *Education*: Morningside College, 1945-47. *Principal occupation*: Government official, professor. *Address*: Montana State University, Bozeman, MT 59717. *Affiliations*: National Park Service, Crow Agency, MT; Bureau of Indian Affairs: Fort Yates, N.D., Crow Agency, MT,

Aberdeen, SD, Rocky Boys, MT, Rosebud, SD; special assistant to the secretary, U.S. Dept. of the Interior, 1964-69; assistant area director, BIA, Sacramento, CA, 1969-70; professor and director, American Indian Studies, Montana State University, Bozeman, MT, 1970-. Military service: U.S. Army Air Corps, 1941-45. *Community activities*: American Legion (post commander); Knights of Columbus (grand knight). *Memberships*: National Federation of Federal Employees (president, credit union; chairman, board of directors). Awards, honors: Special Achievement Award and Management Training Intern, Bureau of Indian Affairs; Doctor of Humane Letters (honor), Montana State University, 1968; Distinguished Service Award, U.S. Department of the Interior, 1968. *Interests*: Mr. Coyote writes, "General interest is in the welfare of Indians and youth of all races, particularly in the education and general participation in the American way of life of all citizens during formative years; conservation of natural and human resources and the general appreciation of the aesthetic values of the American way of life."

OLD PERSON, CHIEF EARL (Blackfeet)
 (tribal chief)
Affiliation: Blackfeet Tribal Business Council, P.O. Box 850, Browning, MT 59417 (406) 338-7276. *Other professional post*: Member, Board of Regents, American Indian Heritage Foundation, Falls Church, VA.

OLDMAN, GERALD (Athapascan)
 (AK village chief)
Affiliation: Hughes Village Council, P.O. Box 45010, Hughes, AK 99745 (907) 899-2206.

OLIVER, ELEANOR J. (Navajo)
 (craftsperson)
Address: Ellie's Southwestern Arts & Crafts, 32 Sisson Dr., Rochester, NY 14623 (716) 334-5335.

OLSON, BEVERLY
 (outreach)
Affiliation: Native American Coalition of Programs, P.O. Box 1914, Fargo, ND 58107 (701) 235-3124.

OLSON, MS. JOEL C.
 (Indian organization president)
Affiliation: President, American Indian Arts Council, 725 Preston Forest Shopping Center, Suite B Dallas, TX 75230 (214) 891-9640 Fax 891-0221

OLSON, MARTIN L., Sr. (Ipaloluk) (Eskimo) 1927-
 (commercial pilot, merchant)
Born June 24, 1927, White Mountain, Alaska. *Education*: Spartan School of Aeronautics, Tulsa, OK (aircraft and engine mechanic license, commercial pilot license). *Principal occupation*: Commercial pilot, merchant. *Home address*: P.O. Box 62100, Golovin, AK 99762 (907) 779-3071. *Affiliations*: President, Olson Air Service, Golovin, Alaska. *Military service*: U.S. Navy, 1946-47 (Mate 3rd Class; Aviation Machinist). *Community activities*: Bering Straits Native Assn., Nome, Alaska (first vice president); Golovin Village Council (past president); Golovin Native Corp. (president); Alaska Federation of Natives (board member).

OLSON, TRACY
 (newsletter director)
Affiliation: "Smoke Signals," Confederated Tribes of the Grand Ronde Community of Oregon, 9615 Grand Ronde Rd., Grand Ronde, OR 97347 (503) 879-5211.

OLSON, DR. WALLACE
 (professor emeritus of anthropology)
Affiliation: Dept. of Anthropology, University of Alaska, 3211 Providence Dr., Anchorage, AK 99508 (907) 786-6840 Fax 786-6850. *Interests*: Alaska natives, culture history, modernization.

OMINAYAK, BERNARD
 (Indian band chief)
Affiliation: Lubicon Lake Indian Band, Box 6731, Peace River, Alberta, Canada T8S 1S5 (403) 629-3945.

OMOTTO, LOREN
 (executive director)
Affiliation: Native American Journalists Association, 3359 36th Ave. S., Minneapolis, MN 55406 (612) 729-9244 Fax 729-9373. E-Mail: omotto@naja.com; Web site: www.naja.com

ONDOLA, GEORGE (Athapascan)
 (AK village president)
Affiliation: Eklutna Native Village, 26339 Eklutna Village Rd., Chugiak, AK 99567 (907) 688-6020.

ONE BEAR-HOLT, MURIEL (Crow & Northern Cheyenne)
 (TV station principal)
Address & Affiliation: Principal, KHMT-Channel 4 (American Indian-owned TV station), 445 S. 24th St. W., Suite 404, Billings, MT 59102 (406) 652-7366 Fax 652-6963.

ONETTA, KATHRYN
 (editorial director)
Affiliation: "Daybreak Star Indian Reader," Bernie Whitebear, P.O. Box 99100, Seattle, WA 98199 (206) 285-4425.

ONEY, RAYMOND D.
 (AK village president)
Affiliation: Village of Alakanuk, P.O. Box 167, Alakanuk, AK 99554 (907) 238-3313.

OPIKOKEW, BRIAN
 (dean of students)
Affiliation: Saskatchewan Indian Federated College, University of Regina, 118 College West, Regina, Saskatchewan, Canada S4S 0A2 (306) 584-8333.

OPLER, MORRIS EDWARD 1907-
 (professor emeritus)
Born May 16, 1907, Buffalo, N.Y. *Education*: University of Buffalo, BA, 1929, MA, 1930; University of Chicago, Ph.D, 1933. *Principal occupation*: Professor emeritus. *Home address*: 4006 Brookhollow Rd., Norman, OK 73069. *Affiliations*: Research assistant and associate, Dept. of Anthropology, University of Chicago, 1933-35; assistant anthropologist, Bureau of Indian Affairs, 1936-37; assistant professor of anthropology, Claremont College, 1938-42; visiting and assistant professor, Howard University, 1945-48; professor of anthropology and Asian studies, Cornell University, Ithaca, N.Y., 1948-79; director, Cornell University American Indian Program, 1948-79; professor emeritus, Dept. of Anthropology, Cornell University. *Other professional post*: Associate editor, Journal of American Folklore, 1959-79. *Memberships*: Sigma Xi; Phi Delta Kappa; Phi Beta Kappa; Alpha Kappa Delta; American Association of University Professors; American Sociological Association; American Anthropological Association (Fellow; executive board, 1949-52; president-elect, 1961-62; president, 1962-63); Society for Applied Anthropology; American Ethnological Society; American Folklore Society (Fellow; first vice president, 1946-47; executive committee, 1950; council member, 1957-60). **Published works**: The Ethnobiology of the Chiricahua and Mescalero Apache, with E.F. Castetter (Bulletin, University of New Mexico Press, 1936); Dirty Boy: A Jicarilla Tale of Raid and War (American Anthropological Association, Memoirs No. 52, 1938); Myths and Tales of the Jicarilla Apache Indians (Stechert, 1938); Myths and Legends of the Lipan Apache Indians (J.J. Augustin, 1940); An Apache Life-Way: The Economic, Social, and Religious Institutions of the Chiricahua Indians (University of Chicago Press, 1941; University Microfilms; Cooper Square Publishers, 1966); Myths and Tales of the Chiricahua Apache Indians (Banta, 1942); The Character and Derivation of the Jicarilla Holiness Rite (University of Ne Mexico, 1943); Childhood and Youth in Jicarilla Apache Society (The Southwest Museum, 1946); among others.

ORECHIA, GWEN
 (association president)
Affiliation: New Brunswick Native Indian Women's Council, 65 Brunswick St., Rm. 258, Fredericton, New Brunswick, Canada E3B 1G5 (506) 458-1114.

OROPEZA, JOSE (Pomo)
 (rancheria chairperson)
Affiliation: Manchester - Port Arena Rancheria, P.O. Box 623, Point Arena, CA 95468 (707) 882-2788.

OROPEZA, LAURA
 (deputy director)
Affiliations: National Native American AIDS Prevwention Center, 436 14th St., Suite 1020, Oakland, CA 94609 (510) 444-2051 Fax 444-1593.

ORR, DELILAH (Navajo)
 (professor)
Address: English Dept., Fort Lewis College, Durango, CO 81301 (970) 247-7627. *Affiliations*: Navajo Community College, Tsaile, AZ, 1980-90; Fort Lewis College, CO, 1990-present. *Awards, honors*: Newberry Library Summer Fellow, 1990, 1991; Ford Fellowship Recipient, 1993-present.

ORTEGA, A. PAUL (Mescalero Apache)
 (tribal president; singer, songwriter)
Affiliation & Address: Mescalero Apache Tribal Council, P.O. Box 176, Mescalero, NM 88340 (505) 671-4494. *Other professional posts*: Singer & songwriter for Canyon Records Productions, Phoenix, AZ. *Awards, honors*: Lifetime Achievment Award from the First Americans in the Arts for Outstanding Musical Achievement, February 1996.

ORTEZ, JOAN K. (Steilacoom)
 (tribal chairperson)
Affiliation: Steilacoom Indian Tribe, P.O. Box 419, Steilacoom, WA 98388 (206) 584-6308; director, Steilacoom Tribal Cultural Center & Museum.

ORTIZ, JOHN A.
 (executive director)
Affiliation: Mid-America All-Indian Center, Inc., 650 N. Seneca, Wichita, KS 67203 (316) 262-5221 Fax 262-4216.

ORTIZ, JUAN
 (Indian education program director)
Affiliation: Mt. Baker School District, Indian Education Program, P.O. Box 45, Deming, WA 98244 (360) 383-2015 ext. 4511 Fax 383-2029.

ORTIZ, ROXANNE DUNBAR (Southern Cheyenne) 1938-
 (professor of Native American studies)
Born September 10, 1938, Oklahoma. *Education*: San Francisco State University, BA, 1963; UCLA, MA, 1965, PhD (History), 1974. *Principal occupation*: Professor of Native American studies. *Address & Affiliation*: Dept. of Ethnic Studies. California State University, Hayward, 1974-present. *Community activities*: Staff member, International Indian Treaty Council (non-governmental organization in consultative status with U.N.). *Published work*: The Great Sioux Nation (Random House, 1977).

ORTIZ, SIMON J. (Acoma Pueblo) 1941-
 (writer, poet, teacher)
Born May 27, 1941, Albuquerque, N.M. *Education*: Fort Lewis College, 1961-62; University of New Mexico, Albuquerque, 1966-68; University of Iowa, Iowa City, 1968-69. *Principal occupation*: Writer, poet, teacher. *Home address*: 4 Devonshire Pl., Massey College, Toronto, ON M5S 2E1, Canada. *Affiliation*: Instructor and co-director, Creative Writing Program, Sinte Gleska College, Mission, SD. *Other professional posts*: Consulting editor to Pueblo of Acoma, Institute of American Indian Arts Press, and Navajo Community College Press. *Military service*: U.S. Army, 1963-66. *Community activities*: National Indian Youth Council (community organizer, 1970-73); Adult Community Education, Acoma Pueblo, N.M. (director, 1975); AIM House, Oakland, Calif. (member of board, 1977-79). *Memberships*: Americans Before Columbus Foundation (board of directors, 1978-); American PEN, 1980-. *Awards, honors*: Discovery Award (Creative Writing, 1970), Fellowship (Creative Writing, 1981), National Endowment for the Arts. *Interests*: "Avocational interests include listening to music, long distance running, travel. Places I've traveled include all of the areas of the U.S., including Alaska in 1979, 1981, and 1984; I traveled to Europe, including Holland, Belgium, and Germany." *Biographical sources*: This Song Remembers (article-interview)(Macmillan, 1980); Coyote Said This (biographical article)(University of Aarhus, Denmark, 1984); I Tell You Now (autobiographical article)(University of Nebraska Press, 1986). *Published works*: Naked In The Wind (Quetzal-Vihio Press, 1971); Going For The Rain (Harper & Row, 1976); A Good Journey (Turtle Island Press, 1977); Howbah Indians (Blue Moon Press, 1978); The People Shall Continue (Children's Press Books, 1978); Fight Back (INAD-University of New Mexico, 1980); From Sand Creek (Thunder's Mouth Press, 1981); A Poem Is A Journey (Pternandon Press, 1982); Fightin' (Thunder's Mouth

Press, 1983); Blue and Red (Acoma Pueblo Press, 1983); The Importance of Childhood (Acoma Pueblo Press, 1983); Woven Stone (University of Arizona Press, 1992); After and Before the Lightning (University of Arizona Press, 1994); Speaking for the Generations (University of Arizona Press, 1998); Men on the Moon (University of Arizona Press, 1999); From Sand Creek (University of Arizona Press, 2000); Out There Somewhere (University of Arizona Press, 2002); The Good Rainbow Road (University of Arizona Press, 2004);.

OSAWA, SANDY
(film producer/director)
Affiliation: Upstream Productions, 420 First Ave. W., Seattle, WA 98119 (206) 524-8879.

OSBORNE, LOIS I.
(park manager)
Affiliation: Red Clay State Historic Park, 1140 Red Clay Park Rd., S.W., Cleveland, TN 37311 (615) 478-0339.

OSBORNE, MARVIN
(tribal chairperson)
Affiliation: Fort Hall Business Council, P.O. Box 306, Fort Hall, ID 83203 (208) 238-3700.

OSBURN-BIGFEATHER, JOANNA
(Western Cherokee)
(artist, curator)
Address & Affiliation: Director/Curator of Exhibitions, American Indian Community House Gallery & Museum, 708 Broadway, 2nd Floor, New York, NY 10003 (212) 598-0100.

OSCEOLA-BRANCH, MARIE
(Miccosukee/Seminole)
(legislative specialist)
Education: University of Miami, BA (Elementary Education), 1975. Florida International University, MS (Educational Leadership), 1988. *Principal occupation*: Legislative specialist. *Address & Affiliation*: Hobbs, Straus, Dean & Walker, LLP, 2120 L St., NW, Suite 700, Washington, DC 20037 (202) 822-8282 Fax 296-8834, 1994-present. E-mail: mosceola-branch@ hsdwdc.com. *Past professional post*: Miccosukee Tribe, 1980-94, as health education coordinator, tribal school principal, and government programs manager. *Firm responsibilities*: Monitoring and advocacy on various legislative and appropriations issues, including Indian Self-Determination and housing as well as the BIA and HUD budgets. She closely follows legislation related to gaming and transportation.

OSKOLKOFF, D.L. (Kenaitse)
(executive director)
Affiliation: Ninilchik Traditional Council Health Clinic, P.O. Box 39070, Ninilchik, AK 99762 (907) 567-3313.

OSKOLKOFF, GASSIM (Kenaitse)
(association president)
Affiliation: Ninilchik Native Association, Inc., P.O. Box 282, Ninilchik, AK 99639 (907) 567-3313.

OSKOLKOFF, PAT
(health director)
Affiliation: Ninilchik Traditional Council Health Clinic, P.O. Box 39070, Ninilchik, AK 99762 (907) 567-3313.

OTHOLE, JEAN
(hospital director)
Affiliation: Zuni PHS Indian Hospital, P.O. Box 467, Zuni, NM 87327 (505) 782-4431.

OTIS, DR. MORGAN G.
(Indian college president)
Affiliation: D-Q University, P.O. Box 409, Davis, CA 95617 (530) 758-0470 Fax 758-4891.

OTT, BILLIE D.
(BIA area director)
Affiliation: Eastern Area Office, Bureau of Indian Affairs, 3701 N. Fairfax Dr., MS: 260, Arlington, VA 22203 (703) 235-3006.

OVERBERG, KAROLE
(BIA agency supt.)
Affiliation: Northern Idaho Agency, Bureau of Indian Affairs, P.O. Box 227, Lapwai, ID 83540 (208) 843-2300.

OVERFIELD, THERESA 1935-
(consultant, professor emeritus)
Born July 22, 1935, Buffalo, N.Y. *Education*: D'Youville College, BS, 1958; Columbia University, MPH, 1962; University of Colorado, MA, 1972, PhD, 1975. *Principal occupation*: Professor emeritus of nursing, research professor of anthropology. *Home address*: 172 Braewick Rd., Salt Lake City, UT 84103 (801) 359-6274. *Affiliations*: Itinerant public health nurse, AK Dept. of Health, Bethel, AK, 1959-61; nurse epidemiologist, Arctic Health Research Center, USPHS, Anchorage, AK, 1962-65; nursing consultant, Colorado Dept. of Public Health, Denver, 1966-69; research assistant professor, 1975-76, assistant professor of nursing, 1976-78, College of Nursing, University of Utah, Salt Lake City; associate professor, College of Nursing, Brigham Young University, Salt Lake City, 1978-84; adjunct assistant and associate professor, 1976-85, research professor, 1985-, Dept. of Anthropology, University of Utah, Salt Lake City; director of research, 1979-, professor, 1984-92, College of Nursing, professor emeritus, 1992-, Brigham Young University, Salt Lake City. *Other professional posts*: Advisory board, 1978-82, reviewer, 1979-, Western Journal of Nursing; reviewer, Research in Nursing and Health. *Community activities*: Western Commission on Higher Education in Nursing, Boulder, CO (research steering committee member, 1978-82); Transcultural Nursing Conference Group, Utah Nurses Association, Salt Lake City (chairperson, 1978-80); Salt Lake Indian Health Center, Inc. (advisory committee member and board of directors, 1981-82); Veterans Administration Medical Center, Salt Lake City (nursing research committee member, 1982-; member, Health Services Research and Development Review Board, 1983-). *Awards, honors*: USPHS, Special Nurse Predoctoral Fellowships, 1969-74; American Nurses Foundation, Inc. Grant for Pseudo cholinesterase Silent Allele in Alaskan Eskimos, 1974; University of Utah, Demography Study Group, Grant for computer use on Eskimo data for fertility study, 1976-77; American Journal of Nursing, Excellence in Writing Award, 1981. *Interests*: "Racial variation; biomedical research; Eskimos—western Alaska; papers, lectures, workshops and conferences presented on the Alaskan Eskimo and the American Indian, too numerous to mention." *Published works*: "Biological Variation in Health & Illness: Race, Age & Sex Differences," 2nd Ed. (CRC Press, 1995); numerous articles in professional journals.

OWEN, GARY
(Indian band chief)
Affiliation: Poplar Hill Indian Band, Box 5004, Poplar Hill, ON, Canada P0V 2M0 (807) 772-8838.

OWENS, LOUIS (Choctaw/Cherokee)
(writer, professor of literature)
Born July 18, 1948, Lompoc, Calif. *Education*: University of California, Santa Barbara, BA, 1971, MA, 1974; University of California, Davis, PhD, 1981. *Principal occupation*: Writer, professor of literature. *Home address*: 9 Campo Rd., Tijeras, NM 87059 (505) 277-6347 (work). *Affiliation*: University of New Mexico, Albuquerque, NM, 1984-89; Professor of Literature, University of California, Santa Cruz (professor of literature), 1989-94; Professor of English and Native American Studies, University of California, Davis, 1994-present. *Other professional post*: Co-editor, American Indian Literature & Critical Studies Series, University of Oklahoma Press. *Community activities*: Board member, American Indian Literature Prize; board member, North American Indian Prose Award. *Memberships*: Choctaw Writers Guild; Modern Literature Association; American Studies Association; PEN International; American Literature Association. *Awards, honors*: Fulbright Scholarship, 1981; National Endowment for the Humanities Fellowship, 1987; National Endowment for the Arts Fellowship, 1989. *Interests*: "My major interest is in literature by Native American Indian authors. I spent seven years working with the U.S. Forest Service as wilderness ranger & fire fighter. I backpack and flyfish with my daughters. I write." *Published works*: American Indian Novelists: An Annotated Critical Bibliography, with Tom Colonnese (Garland Press, 1985); John Steinbeck's Re-Vision of America (University of Georgia Press, 1985); Trouble in the Promised Land: Steinbeck's The grapes of Wrath (G.K. Hall, 1989); editor, American Literary Scholarship (Duke University Press, 1990); Wolfsong (West End Press, 1990; University of Oklahoma Press, 1994);

Other Destinies: Understanding the American Indian Novel (University of Oklahoma Press, 1992); The Sharpest Sight (University of Oklahoma Press, 1992; Bone Game (University of Oklahoma Press, 1994); Nightland (Dutton Signet, 1996); Mixedblood Messages: Literature, Film, Family, Place (University of Oklahoma Press, 1998); Dark River (University of Oklahoma Press, 1999); I Hear the Train (University of Oklahoma Press, 2001).

OWEN, ROGER C. 1928-
(anthropologist, professor emeritus)
Born September 14, 1928, Port Arthur, Tex. *Education*: Michigan State University, BA, 1953; University of Arizona, MA, 1957; UCLA, PhD (Anthropology), 1962. *Principal occupation*: Anthropologist, professor emeritus. *Address*: Unknown. *Affiliations*: Instructor & professor of anthropology, University of California, Santa Barbara, 1959-67; professor of anthropology, 1967-92, professor emeritus, 1992-, Queens College, Flushing, NY. *Other professional post*: Curriculum development consultant, Holt, Rinehart & Winston, Inc., 1968-77. *Military service*: U.S. Army, 1946-47. *Memberships*: American Anthropological Association (Life Fellow); Current Anthropology (Associate); Sigma Xi (Fellow); numerous nonprofessional organizations devoted to topics in anthropology and Native American affairs. *Awards, honors*: National Science Foundation Undergraduate Research Participation Award, 1961-63; Research Grants, University of California, Santa Barbara, 1961-66; Grant-in-aid, Holt, Rinehart & Winston, 1969-71; Distinguished Teacher of the Year, Queens College, 1983-84; Mellon Foundation Fellowship, Queens College, 1983-84. *Interests*: American Indians; Latin America. *Biographical source*: Who's Who in the East. *Published works*: Senior editor, North American Indians: A Sourcebook (Macmillan, 1967); The Contemporary Ethnography of Baja, California, Mexico, chapter in Handbook of Middle American Indians (Tulane University Press, 1969); American Indian Society and Culture: A Conspectus, in Encyclopedia of Indians of the Americas, Vol. 1 (Scholarly Press, 1974); Native North Americans: The Anthropology of Americans Original Inhabitants (Queens College Reprographics, 1977); Indians, American, in Academic American Encyclopedia (Arete Publishing Co., 1980); The Mountain Pai; An Ethnography of the Indians of Baja, California, Mexico (typescript, 1984); among others; numerous papers on the American Indian read at meetings.

OWENS, DIANNE T.
(school principal)
Affiliation: Wingate Elementary School, P.O. Box 1, Fort Wingate, NM 87316 (505) 488-6400 Fax 488-6444.

OWL BOY, LILLIE
(administrative officer)
Affiliation: Fort Totten PHS Indian Health Center, Fort Totten, ND 58335 (701) 766-4291.

OWLIJOOT, THOMAS (Inuit)
(director-Institute)
Affiliation: Inuit Cultural Institute, Eskimo Point, N.W.T., Canada X0C 0E0 (819) 857-2803.

OXENDINE, DARLENE (Lumbee)
(BIA area office director)
Affiliation: Director, Minneapolis Area Office, Bureau of Indian Affairs, 331 Second Ave. S., Minneapolis, MN 55401 (612) 373-1000 Fax 373-1186.

OXENDINE, DR. LINDA
(Indian studies dept. chairperson)
Affiliation: American Indian Studies Dept., Univesity of North carolina at Pembroke, P.O. Box 1510, Pembroke, NC 28372 (910) 521-6266. E-mail: linda@papa. uncp.edu.

OXENDINE, LLOYD E. (Lumbee)
(museum curator)
Affiliation: The American Indian Community House Gallery/Museum, 708 Broadway at Waverly Place, New York, NY 10003.

OXENDINE, THOMAS (Lumbee) 1921-
(naval officer, government information officer, consultant)
Born December 23, 1921, Pembroke, N.C. *Education*: Pembroke State College, BA, 1948; Armed Forces In

formation School, 1966. *Principal Occupation*: Naval Officer and Government Information Officer. *Home Address*: 1141 N. Harrison St., Arlington, VA 22205 (703) 536-4877. *Affiliations*: U.S. Navy, Naval Aviator, 1942-47, Commander, 1951-70; Public Affairs Officer, Bureau of Indian Affairs, Washington, DC, 1970-87; Census Promotion Officer, Bureau of Census, Washington, DC, 1988-90; American Indian Consultant, Multimedia Business Services, Washington, DC, 1990-92; American Indian Consultant, E.O.P. Group, 1992-. *Military Service*: Naval Aviator-World War II, United States Navy, 1942-47 (Distinguished Flying Cross-Air Medal); Navy Jet Fighter Pilot, 1951-60; Commanding Officer, Training Squadron Two, Naval Air Basic Training Command, Pensacola, Florida, 1960-62; Deputy Fleet Information Officer, Staff of the Commander-in-Chief, U.S. Pacific Fleet, 1962-65; Public Affairs Officer, Commander Task Force 77, Gulf of Tonkin, 1965; Aviation Plans Officer/Director, Plans Division, Office of Information, Department of Navy, The Pentagon, Washington, DC, 1965-68; Public Affairs Officer, Naval Air Systems Command, Dept. of Navy, Washington, DC, 1968-70. *Memberships*: National Congress of American Indians; National Aviation Club; National Press Club; Native American Journalist Association. *Awards, Honors*: First Distinguished Alumnus Award, 1967, Pembroke State College; Athletic Hall of Fame, 1980, Pembroke State University; extensive press coverage as First American Indian to complete Naval Aviation Cadet Flight Program. *Biographical Sources*: Who's Who in Government; Who's Who in the East.

P

PABLO, FRED
(Indian school chairperson)
Affiliation: San Simon School, P.O. Box 8292, Sells, AZ 85634 (520) 362-2331 Fax 362-2405.

PABLO, MATT
(museum director/curator)
Affiliation: Malki Museum, Inc., 11-795 Fields Rd., Morongo Indian Reservation, Banning, CA 92220 (714) 849-7289.

PABLO, MICHAEL T. (Confederated Salish/Navajo)
Affiliation: Confederated Salish & Kootenai Tribal Council, P.O. Box 278, Pablo, MT 59855 (406) 675-2700.

PACE, ROSA
(health director)
Affiliation: Santa Ynez Indian Health Program, Santa Ynez Reservation, P.O. Box 539, Santa Ynez, CA 93460 (805) 688-4886.

PACHANO, JANE (Cree)
(director-Indian centre)
Affiliation: Cree Cultural Education Centre, Box 291, Chisasibi, Quebec, Canada J0M 1E0 (819) 855-2821.

PACHANO, VIOLET (Cree)
(Indian band chief)
Affiliation: Chisasibi (Cree) Indian Band, James Bay, Quebec, Canada J0M 1E0 (819) 855-2878.

PACHECO, TOMMY (Shoshoni)
(tribal chairperson)
Affiliation: Northwestern Band of Shoshoni Nation, P.O. Box 637, Blackfoot, ID 83221 (208) 785-7401.

PADDOCK, CHARLES (Chilkoot)
(AK association president)
Affiliation: Chilkoot Indian Association of Haines, P.O. Box 490, Haines, AK 99827 (907) 766-2310.

PADDYAKER, DAREN (Comanche-Cherokee) 1964-
(adolescent counselor)
Born November 18, 1964, Oklahoma City, Okla. *Education*: University of Oklahoma, BA (Psychology), 1989. *Principal occupation*: Adolescent counselor. *Home address*: 14301 S. Rockwell, Oklahoma City, OK 73173 (405) 232-0736 (work). Oklahoma City Indian Clinic, Oklahoma City, OK (Adolescent Counselor, 1991-). *Other professional post*: worked with repeat juvenile offenders for 3 years in an inpatient setting. *Community activities*: Member, Oklahoma City Public Schools Task Force on Reducing Gang Involvement in Oklahoma City Public Schools; speak with public school Title V programs and parent committees about street gangs and gang-related activities in the urban Indian community. *Membership*: University of Oklahoma American Indian Alumni Society. *Interests*: "My major area of vocational interest includes working with "at-risk" urban Indian youth and helping them to find traditional as well as non-traditional support bases. My avocational interests include historical tribal research, traveling, hunting, and fishing."

PADILLA, FERNANDO, JR.
(San Felipe Pueblo-Navajo) 1958-
(artist-painter)
Born July 29, 1958, Los Angeles, Calif. *Education*: Indian Bible College, Albuquerque; Bethany (OK) Southern Nazarene University. *Principal occupation*: Artist-painter. *Home address*: 4632 SE 20th, Del City, OK 73115 (405) 672-9724. *Membership*: Indian Arts & Crafts Association. *Awards, honors*: "Judges Best of Show," 1981-OK Indian Youth Art Festival; "Second Place - Sculpture," 1985-Native American Art and Craft Show, Rose State Colege, Midwest City, OK; Annual Trail of Tears Art Show, Tahlequah, OK (1985-"Newcomers Award,"; 1986-"Special Merit Award"; and 1989-"Special Merit Award"); Intertribal Ceremonial, Gallup, NM (1987-"First Place-Painting" and First Place-Miniatures; 1988-"Second Place-Watercolors; 1990-First Place-Watercolors; 1991-"First Place-Mixed Media and "Third Place-Acrylics"; among others.

PADILLA, JERRY (Penobscot)
(former tribal governor)
Affiliation: Penobscot Tribal Council, Community Bldg., Indian Island, Old Town, ME 04468 (207) 827-7776.

PADILLA, NICOLAS J.
(rancheria chairperson)
Affiliation: Susanville Rancheria, P.O. Drawer U, Susanville, CA 96130 (916) 257-6264.

PADILLA, RANDOLPH (Jemez Pueblo)
(former pueblo governor)
Affiliation: Jemez Pueblo Council, P.O. Box 100, Jemez, NM 87024 (505) 834-7359.

PADILLA, SOLOMON, Jr. (Pueblo)
(school principal)
Affiliation: Santa Clara Day School, P.O. Box HHH, Espanola, NM 87532 (505) 753-4406.

PAHDOPONY, JUANITA (Puh-Nah-Vet-Tha - the only daughter) (Comanche) 1947-
(professor)
Born January 18, 1947, Portland, Oreg. *Education*: Southwest Oklahoma State University, BA, 1970; Oklahoma City University, M.Ed., 1989. *Principal occupation*: Professor. Address unknown. *Affiliation*: Dept. of Education, Cameron University, Lawton, OK, 1994-. *Other professional post*: National Advisory Board of Native Writers, Wordcraft Circle; professional artist; gifted & talented education. *Community activities*: Board member, Institute of the Great Plains; board member, Jacobson Foundation; Comanche Gourd Dancer. *Memberships*: Oklahoma Art Therapists Association; Word craft Circle (National Advisory Board, 1992-96). *Awards, honors*: McMahon Foundation, 1985; "Outstanding Teacher of the Gifted" Jolene Grantham Award, Oklahoma City University, 1989;"Moving Murals" 2 year traveling tip show (State Arts Council, Jacobson Foundation), 1994. *Interests*: Professional painter, published poet. *Biographical sources*: Artist cover: Callaloo, Vol. 17 #1, by Native American Literatures, Johns Hopkins University Press); designed logo of the National Indian Policy Center, Washington, DC. *Published works*: 2 poems in - "Poetry Nebraska English Journal," 1994, & Returning the Gift, 1994; 2 published scholarly papers - "Creative Perspectives," 1990, & "Native American Art Therapy," 1985.

PAHMAHMIE, ZACH (Prairie Band Potawatomi)
(tribal council chairperson)
Affiliation: Prairie Band Potawatomi Tribal Council, 16281 Q Rd., Mayetta, KS 66509 (785) 966-4000.

PAILES, RICHARD
(instructor-Native American studies)
Affiliation: Native American Studies Program, University of Oklahoma, 455 W. Lindsey, Rm. 804, Norman, OK 73019 (405) 325-2312.

PAINTE, DEBORAH A. (Red Prairie Rose)
(Arikara, Hidatsa)
(executive director)
Born in Stanley, N.D. *Education*: Haskell Indian Jr. College, AA, 1977, AAS, 1978; Central State University (Edmond, OK), BBA, 1984; Montana State University, MPA, 1992. *Principal occupation*: Executive director-Indian commission. *Address & Affiliation*: North Dakota Indian Affairs Commission, 600 E. Blvd., 1st Fl., State Capitol, Bismarck, ND 58505 (701) 224-2428, 1991-; Fort Berthold Community College, New-town, ND (3 years). *Other professional post*: Chairperson-Board of Directors, Three Affiliated Tribes Museum.

PAINTER, ROBERT
(author)
Address & Affiliation: First Nations Art, P.O. Box 7596, Albuquerque, NM 87194 (505) 836-2960. E-mail: indianart@painter.net. *Publication*: The Native American Indian Artist Directory, 1998.

PAISANO, EDNA
(liaison)
Affiliation: Liaison for American Indian & Alaska Natives, Bureau of the Census, Federal Center, Suitland, MD 20233 (301) 763-2607.

PAISANO, STUART (Pueblo)
(Pueblo governor)
Affiliation: Sandia Pueblo Tribal Council, P.O. Box 6008, Bernalillo, NM 87004 (505) 867-3317.

PAISANO, WALLY (Western Shoshone)
(health director)
Affiliation: Owyhee Community Health Facility, P.O. Box 364, Owyhee, NV 89832 (702) 757-2415.

PAIVA, JAMES (Shoshone)
(tribal chairperson)
Affiliation: Shoshone Paiute Business Council, Duck Valley Reservation, P.O. Box 219, Owyhee, NV 89832 (775) 757-3161.

PAKOOTAS, JOSEPH (Confederated Tribes)
(former tribal chairperson)
Affiliation: Colville Business Committee, P.O. Box 150, Nespelem, WA 98568 (360) 273-5911.

PALE MOON, PRINCESS (Win Yon Sa Han We)
(Cherokee/Ojibwa)
(performing author, concert recording artist; foundation executive)
Born April 15th in Asheville, N.C. *Education*: Sonoma State College, Sonoma, CA (Liberal Arts). *Principal occupation*: Performing author, concert recording artist; and foundation executive. *Address*: 6051 Arlington Blvd., Falls Church, VA 22044 (703) 237-7500 (work). *Affiliation*, Founder-president & chairman of the Board, American Indian Heritage Foundation, Falls Church, VA, 1973-. *Memberships*: National Congress of American Indians (life member); Native American Advisory Committee; Boy Scouts of America; American Pen Women; Business and Professional Women's Association; International Platform Assn. *Awards, honors*: Many outstanding achievement awards and other awards from colleges, independent organizations and service clubs, including: Sertoma International, "Humanitarian of the Year"; American Hostess at the International Olympics; concert performer at the Kennedy Center; featured on four vocal albums; Ambassador of Friendship representative for USO shows in Europe; hostess of annual Children's Shows at the Kennedy Center. *Interests*: Has represented the U.S. & the American Indian people in numerous countries, both as spokesperson & as a performing artist. Has special interest in building better understanding between the tribes & people of the world. Many articles have been written about Pale Moon, & the Foundation, including the Style Section of the Washington Post, Decision Magazine, the Los Angeles, Times, the Fairfax Journal & many radio & TV interviews. *Biographical source & Published work*: Pale Moon: The Story of an Indian Princess (Tyndale, 1975).

PALMENTEER, EDDIE, Jr. (Colville)
(former tribal chairperson)
Affiliation: Colville Business Committee, P.O. Box 150, Nespelem, WA 99155 (509) 634-4711.

PALMER, DIXON (Kiowa)
(craftsperson)
Affiliation: Dixon Palmer Headdresses and Tipis, Rt. 3 Box 189, Anadarko, OK 73005 (405) 247-3983.

PALMER, JIM L. (Miam/Peoria of Oklahoma) 1943-
(founder/director-cultural center)
Born July 29, 1943, Oklahoma City, Okla. *Education*: Oklahoma University (2 years); Tulsa Technical College. *Principal occupation*: Founder-director-cultural center. *Address & Affiliation*: Founder-director, Native American Cultural Center, Fort Dodge, IA (515) 576-3867. *Military service*: U.S. Marine Corps (Cpl. - Received Heroism Award, 1983, Kiwanis-Las Vegas, NV). *Community activities*: Protection Advocacy Program of Iowa (board member), Des Moines; Pilot Parents of Iowa, Fort Dodge; Iowa Job Service, Fort Dodge; teach classes to college, high school & elementary levels, on culture, language & legends at request of teachers. *Interests*: "We research Indian languages on the verge of extinction (to reproduce, teach & put in libraries for posterity). We educate the general public about Native peoples customs, legends, languages, etc. We have craft classes for the general public, and had our 1st Annual Indian Powwow in Aug. 1994." *Biographical source*: "Fort Dodge Messenger," front page articles, Dec., 1993 & May, 1994.

PALMER, TRACY L. (Creek/Seminole/Cherokee) 1958-
(director of Indian education)
Born December 31, 1958, Tulsa, Okla. *Education*: University of Tulsa, BFA, 1983, Oklahoma City University, MEd, 1991. *Principal occupation*: Training specialist/Indian educator. *Home address*: 1558 E. 41 St., Tulsa, OK 74105 (918) 747-1488; (405) 399-9118 (work). *Affiliation*: American Indian Research & Development, Inc., Norman, OK, 1991-95; director, Indian Education Program, Jones Public Schools, Jones, OK, 1995-present. *Community activities*: Educational and Cultural Association for Indian Youth; volunteer, Democratic Party of Oklahoma. *Memberships*: National Association for Gifted Children; Oklahoma Federation of Indian Women. *Awards, honors*: Nominee for Leadership Tulsa, 1988; selected to do a presentation in Kansas City, MO, at the National Convention for Gifted Children, November, 1991; also gave same presentation at the State of Oklahoma Association for Gifted & Talented Children on cross-cultural development integrating art into mathematics for gofted and talented Native American students. *Interests*: "I have traveled throughout Oklahoma giving presentations on self-esteem and motivation along with leadership, primarily targeting junior and senior high Indian students."

PALMER, VERA B.
(native American studies instructor)
Affiliation: Dartmouth College, Native American Studies Dept., Hanover, NH 03755 (603) 646-3530.

PANEAK, RAYMOND (Eskimo)
(village council president)
Affiliation: Village of Anaktuvuk Pass, Anaktuvuk, AK 99721 (907) 661-3113.

PAPATISSE, HENRI
(Indian band chief)
Affiliation: Grand Lac Victoria (Algonquin) Indian Band, Louvicourt, Quebec, Canada J0Y 1Y0 (819) 824-1914.

PAPINEAU, IRVING
(school principal)
Affiliation: St. Regis Mohawk School, Gowanda Central School District, Hogansburg, NY 13655.

PAQUIN, DANIEL GERARD (Chippewa) 1953-
(mechanical engineer)
Born January 4, 1953, Grand Rapids, Mich. *Education*: University of Hawaii, BS, 1980, MS, 1984. *Principal occupation*: Mechanical engineer. *Home address*: 650 Ainapo St., Honolulu, HI 96825 (808) 395-2175. Affiliation: Dept. of Agricultural Engineering, University of Hawaii, Honolulu, 1986-. *Other professional post*: President, American Society of Agricultural Engineers, Hawaii Section. *Military service*: U.S. Navy, 1972-75; Reserves, 1976-80 (E-4). *Memberships*: American Indian Science and Engineering Society; Sierra Club. *Interests*: "Science-by-mail "scientist" for Museum of the Rockies; enjoy hiking, surfing, listening and watching "Rainbow Warrior" baseball for the University of Hawaii."

PAQUIN, RONALD J. (Sault Ste. Marie Chippewa)
(self-employed artist)
Born September 4, 1942, St. Ignace, Mich. *Address*: 1200 E. 11th Ave., Sault Ste. Marie, MI 49783 (906) 635-8158. *Affiliation*: Marquette Mission Park & Museum of Ojibwa Culture, St. Ignace, MI, 1985-2001. *Awards, honors*: 2003 Michigan Heritage Award. *Membership*: Sault Ste. Marie Tribe of Chippewa Indians. *Interests*: Birch bark canoe maker. *Published work*: Not First In Nobody's Heart: The Life Story of a Contemporary Chippewa, with Robert Doherty (RJP Press, St. Ignace, MI).

PARADA, GWENDOLYN (Diegueno)
(tribal chairperson)
Affiliation: La Posta Band of Mission Indians, P.O. Box 1048, Boulevard, CA 91905 (619) 478-2113.

PARASHOUTS, TRAVIS N. (Southern Paiute) 1953-
(director-Utah Indian affairs)
Born October 10, 1953, Cedar City, Utah. *Education*: Southern Utah State College, BA, 1979; University of Utah (Masters of Social Work candidate). *Principal occupation*: Director, Utah Division of Indian Affairs, 6220 State Office Bldg., Salt Lake City, Utah. *Address*: Resides in Salt Lake City, Utah (801) 533-5334 (work). *Other professional posts*: Former tribal chairman, Paiute Tribe; American Indian Service, Brigham Young University, Provo, Utah (board member); American Indian Cultural Foundation, Page, AZ (board member); Indian Affiliates, Orem, UT (board member). *Awards, honors*: Spencer W. Kimball Award for working with Indian people; Paiute Tribal Award for service as tribal chairman; Cedar City Chamber of Commerce Award. *Interests*: "I assisted the Paiute Tribe in getting federal recognition in 1980 and helped them get back 5,000 acres of land and established a 2.5 million dollar irrevocable trust fund for economic development." *Published work*: Paiute Language—For Beginner (Southern Utah State College, 1980).

PARCEAUD, JUDY
(director-Indian centre)
Affiliation: Cree Indian Centre, 95 rue Jaculet, Chibougamau, Quebec, Canada G8P 2G1 (418) 748-7667.

PARDILLA, JERRY
(executive director)
Affiliation: National Tribal Environmental Council, 2221 Rio Grande NW, Albuquerque, NM 87104 (505) 242-2175.

PARDUE, DIANA
(museum curator)
Affiliation: Curator of Collections, The Heard Museum, 2301 N. Central Ave., Phoenix, AZ 85004 (602) 252-8840.

PAREDES, J. ANTHONY 1939-
(professor of anthropology)
Born September 29, 1939, New York, N.Y. *Education*: Oglethorpe University (Atlanta, GA) , AB, 1961; University of New Mexico, MA, 1964, PhD, 1969. *Principal occupation*: Professor of anthropology. *Home address*: Resides in Tallahassee, Fla. (904) 644-4281 (work). *Affiliations*: Upper Mississippi Mental Health Center, Bemidji, MN, 1964-66; Bemidji State College (acting director, American Indian Studies), University of Minnesota, Bemidji, MN, 1967-68; Professor of anthropology, Department of Anthropology, Florida State University, Tallahassee, FL, 1969-. *Other professional posts*: Consultants to various federal and state agencies and private firms; editorial board, American Indian Culture and Research Journal. *Community activities*: Member, Scientific and Statistical Committee, Gulf of Mexico Fishery Management Council (1978-88; task force on Federal Recognition, Association on American Indian Affairs, 1987-88. *Memberships*: Society for Applied Anthropology (president, 1993-95); Southern Anthropological Society (president, 1988-89);

American Anthropological Association (Fellow); Sigma XI, the Scientific Research Society. *Awards, honors*: Woodrow Wilson Fellow, 1961-62; National Institute of Mental Health Predoctoral Fellow, 1968-69; Poarch Creek Indian Service Award, 1990. *Interests*: Ethnographic field work in Minnesota (non-Indians and Chippewa), Alabama (Creek Indians), Mexico (small town residents); Florida (commercial fisherman); travel in Southwestern U.S. and Spain. *Biographical sources*: American Men and Women of Science, Social and Behavioral Sciences (12th Edition); Who's Who in America, 48th Ed. *Published works*: Anishinabe: Six Studies of Modern Chippewa (University Presses of Florida, 1980); editor, Indians of the Southeastern U.S. in the Late 20th Century (Alabama University Press, 1992); Indios de los Estados Unidos Anglosajones (Fundacion Mapfre America, Madrid, 1992); 55+ articles, chapters, reviews, etc. in scholarly books and journals.

**PARENT, ELIZABETH ANNE *(Wa Su Win)*
(Athabascan) 1941-**
(professor of Native American studies)
Born January 12, 1941, Bethel, Alaska. *Education*: University of Alaska, BA (Anthropology); Harvard Graduate School of Education, MEd & CAS, 1973; Stanford University, PhD, 1984. *Principal occupation*: Professor of American Indian Studies. *Home address*: 715-13 One Appian Way, So. San Francisco, CA 94080 (650) 589-4041. *Affiliation*: San Francisco State University, 1600 Holloway Ave., San Francisco, CA 94132, 1980-. *Other professional post*: Information & Technology Committee, National Museum of the American Indian, Smithsonian Institution. *Memberships*: American Indian Science & Engineering Society; Stanford Indian Alumni Association; American Indian Education Association. *Awards, honors*: Postdoctoral Fellow, American Indian Studies Center, U.C.L.A., 1985-1986; Ford Fellow; Danforth Fellow; Meritorious Professional Promise Awards, San Francisco State Uiversity, 1987 & 1989. *Interests*: American Indian education, and women's rights. *Published work*: The Educational Experiences of the Residents of Bethel, Alaska, Ph.D. dissertation (Stanford University); "Betty Parent - Woman With a Mission" in Winds of Change; and "Native Ability" in Spring Alumni SFSU, 1991.

PAREZO, NANCY J.
(professor)
Education: University of Arizona, PhD, 1981. *Affiliation*: American Indian Studies Program, The University of Arizona, Harvill Bldg., Rm 430, P.O. Box 210076, Tucson, AZ 85721 (520) 621-7108 Fax 621-7952. E-mail: aisp@email.arizona.edu. *Interests*: Cultural/social anthropology; ethno-history southwest, especially Navajo.

PARISH, WAYNE
(health clinic director)
Affiliation: El Reno PHS Indian Health Clinic, 1631A E. Hwy. 66, El Reno, OK 73036 (405) 262-7631.

PARISIAN, DEAN T. (White Earth Chippewa) 1953-
(investment management)
Born December 20, 1953, Morris, Minn. *Education*: University of Minnesota, Morris, BA, 1976. *Principal occupation*: Investment management. *Address & Affiliation*: Chairperson, Native American Advisors, Inc., 801 N. Brookshade Pkwy., Alpharetta, GA 30004 (770) 772-1621 Fax 772-0102. E-Mail: thechippewafund@aol.com. *Memberships*: Association of Investment Management and Research; Atlanta Society of Financial Analysts; President's Club of the University of Minnesota; Georgia Ornithological Society; Southeastern Hedge Fund Association. *Awards, honors*: While living on the Yankton Sioux Reservation, he received the South Dakota Outstanding Indian Athlete Award. After receiving an appointment to West Point and playing football there for a year, Dean transferred to the University of Minnesota. He has funded a $25,000 scholarship for Native American students for the President's Club of the University of Minnesota. Mr. Parisian was named one of the 1996 "Top Alumni Entrepreneurs" from the University of Minnesota. *Interests*: His avocational hobbies are hunting, trapping, and bird watching.

PARK, DAVID L.
(museum director)
Affiliation: Hershey Museum, 170 W. Hersheypark Dr., Hershey, PA 17033 (717) 534-3439.

PARK, ROBERT
(clinic director)
Affiliation: Salina Community Clinic, P.O. Box 936, Salina, OK 74365 (918) 434-5397.

PARKER, ANGELA K. (Mandan-Hidatsa)
(admissions recruiter for Native American students)
Affiliations: Dartmouth College, Admissions Office, Hanover, NH 03755

PARKER, BERNIE (Seneca)
(tribal chief)
Affiliation: Chief (lifetime), Tonawanda Band of Senecas Council of Chiefs, 7027 Meadville Rd., Basom, NY 14013 (716) 542-4244.

PARKER, JEFFREY D. (Chippewa)
(tribal chairperson)
Affiliation: Bay Mills Executive Council, 12140 W. Lakeshore Dr., Brimley, MI 49715 (906) 248-3241.

PARKER, LARRY
(education administrator)
Affiliation: Billings Area Office, Bureau of Indian Affairs, 316 North 26th St., Billings, MT 59101 (406) 657-6375.

PARKER, LaRUE (Caddo)
(tribal chairperson)
Address & Affiliation: Caddo Tribe, P.O. Box 487, Binger, OK 73009 (405) 656-2344 Fax 656-2892.

PARKER, PAULINE A. (Pechanga Luiseno) 1947-
(Indian education)
Born May 23, 1947, Escondido, Calif. *Education*: Palomar College (2 years). *Principal occupation*: Indian education. *Home address*: 842 B St., Ramona, CA 92065 (619) 789-1624. *Affiliation*: Project coordinator, Indian Education, Ramona Unified Schools, Ramona, CA (619) 788-5010, 1982-present. *Other professional post*: Member, American Indian Education Council, Escondido, CA. *Community activities*: No. County American Indian Education Council; Ramona Unified School District (district advisory committee); past president, Chapter One Parent's Council. *Memberships*: San Diego No. County American Indian Education Council; League of American Pen Women. *Awards, honors*: Showcase Writers Guild Awards (1st Place - Poetry, 1991; 1st Place - Short Story, 1992 & 1993; 2nd Place Children's Story, 1992; 1st Place Article, 1993; 2nd Place - Short Story, 1993); National League of American Pen Women, 1992; San Diego Writer's Showcase, 1994-95 (fiction, non-fiction, poetry). *Interests*: "My main goal is to instill in my students a sense of pride and honor in their heritage. Each and every child should know their history, learn from it and grow into adulthood strong, proud men and women who will face the future with dignity and hope."

PARKER, WAYNE (Comanche) 1938-
(farmer and rancher)
Born September 23, 1938, Spur, Texas. *Education*: West Texas State University, BS, 1961. *Principal occupation*: Farmer and rancher. *Home address*: P.O. Box 845, Ralls, TX 79357-0845. *Affiliations*: Archaeological curator, Pioneer Memorial Museum, Crosbyton, Texas, and Ralls Historical Museum, Ralls, TX; editorial staff for Artifacts Society of Ohio, and La Tierra archaeological journal. *Community activities*: Cotton Gin Board (member); Museum Board (member); Boy Scout Commission; Crosby County Historical Commission. *Memberships*: Texas Archaeological Society; Central States Archaeological Society; South Plains Archaeological Society; Artifacts Society; Southern Texas Archaeological Society (editorial board, Journal). *Awards, honors*: Life Saving Award signed by President Eisenhower; Best Committee Member, Texas Historical Commission, 1971; guest speaker at History Day at the Ranch, Matador Ranch, 1984 and 1985; 4th cousin to Chief Quanah Parker (Kwahadi Comanches). *Interests*: "I have written over 95 articles concerning Indian artifacts which have been published throughout the U.S. (I) hunted bull elk in Colorado for

20 years." *Biographical sources*: Arrowheads and Projectile Points; North American Indian Artifacts; Selected Preforms, Points and Knives of the North American Indians. *Published works*: The Bridwell Site and The Roberson Site (Crosby County Museum Association, 1982 & 1986.

PARKHURST, HURLEY (Oneida) 1934-
(consultant)
Born July 1, 1934, Wisconsin. *Education*: Brigham Young University, BS, 1969; University of Arizona, MLS (Library Science), 1974. *Principal occupation*: Consultant. *Military service*: U.S. Navy, 1953-57. *Interests*: Amateur astronomy; ballet; crystal detectors (expect to publish a book soon); ethnobotany (American Indian uses of plants for food, fiber, medicine); outdoor survival skills; amateur radio.

PARKS, DOUGLAS R.
(Kaakaataaka-White Crow) 1942-
(linguist)
Born August 28, 1942, Long Beach, Calif. *Education*: University of California, Berkeley, BA, 1964, PhD, 1972. *Principal occupation*: Linguist. *Home address*: 8275 East State Road 46, Bloomington, IN 47401. *Affiliations*: Director, Title VII Program, White Shield School District, Roseglen, N.D. (3 years); research associate, Dept. of Anthropology, Indiana University, Bloomington, 1983-. *Other professional post*: Editor, "Anthropological Linguistics"; Associate director, American Indian Studies Research Institute, Indiana University. *Memberships*: Plains Anthropological Society (board of directors, 1980-82; president, 1982); American Anthropological Association; American Society for Ethnohistory. *Awards, honors*: American Council of Learned Societies Fellow, 1982-83; Smithsonian Fellow (Smithsonian Institution, 1973-74). *Published works*: A Grammar of Pawnee (Garland Publishing, 1976); An Introduction to the Arikara Language (Title VII Materials Development Center, Anchorage, Alaska, 1979); Ceremonies of the Pawnee, 2 Vols. (Smithsonian Institution Press, 1981); Arikara Coyote Tales: A Bilingual Reader (White Shield School, 1984); An English-Arikara Student Dictionary (White Shield School, 1986); Traditional Narratives of the Arikara Indians, 4 Vols. (University of Nebraska Press, 1991).

PARKS, RON
(site director)
Affiliation: Kaw Indian Mission, 500 North Mission, Council Grove, KS 66846 (316) 767-5410.

PARMAN, DONALD L. 1932-
(retired historian)
Born October 10, 1932, New Point, MO. *Education*: Central Missouri State College, BS, 1958; Ohio University, MA, 1963; University of Oklahoma, PhD, 1967. *Principal occupation*: Historian. *Home address*: 614 Rose St., West Lafayette, IN 47906 (317) 743-3514. *Affiliation*: Dept. of History, Purdue University, West Lafayette, IN, 1966-2001. *Military service*: U.S. Army, 1953-55 (Corporal). *Memberships*: Indiana Historical Society; Western History Association; Indiana Association of Historians. *Interests*: Main research interests are Navajo Indian history and twentieth century Indian affairs; main travels are in the Southwest and elsewhere in "Indian Country." *Biographical sources*: Directory of American Scholars, Vol. 1; Dictionary of International Biography; Contemporary Authors. *Published works*: Co-editor, American Search, 2 Vols. (Forum Press, 1974); Navajos and the New Deal (Yale University Press, 1976); Indians and the American West in the Twentieth Century (Indiana University Press, 1994); editor - Window to a Changed World: The Personal Memoirs of William Graham (Indiana Historical Society, 1998).

PARR, DIANE
(center administrator)
Affiliation: Sycuan Medical/Dental Cener, 5442 Dehesa Rd., El Cajon, CA 92019 (619) 445-0707.

PARRA, DONNA C. (Navajo) 1941-
(counseling services)
Born September 7, 1941, Rehoboth, N.M. *Education*: University of New Mexico, BA, 1970, MA, 1974. *Principal occupation*: Counseling services. *Home address*: 819 Gonzales Rd., Santa Fe, NM 87501. *Affiliations*: Medical secretary, USPHS Indian Hospital, Gallup,

NM, 1961-63, 1965; research assistant, National Institutes of Mental Health (Alcoholism Project: A Community Treatment Plan for Navajo Problem Drinkers), Family Service Agency, 1966-68; director of counseling services, Institute of American Indian Arts, Sante Fe, NM, 1976-. *Other professional posts*: Instructor of English, counselor, Gallup High School, 1970-75; consultant to teach workshops on ethnic literature, 1973-75, consultant, Curriculum Development, Native American Literature, 1974-75, Gallup-McKinley County Schools; consultant, University of New Mexico Cultural Awareness Center, Albuquerque, NM, 1975. *Community activities*: Santa Fe Public Schools Title IV Indian Education Parent Committee (officer); New Mexico Human Rights Commission Film Project (scholar and advisor); Ford Canyon Youth Center, Gallup, N.M. (advisory board); Gallup Inter-Agency Alcoholism Coordinating Committee (member); New Mexico International Women's Year Convention, June, 1977 (workshop leader on Indian Women). *Memberships*: League of Women Voters; New Mexico Association of Women Deans and Counselors; National Indian Education Association. *Awards, honors*: Four-year Navajo Tribal Scholarship recipient; Charles S. Owens Future Teachers of America Scholarship (Gallup High School, 1959); Sequoyah Indian Fellowship, University of New Mexico, 1970. *Interests*: Ms. Parra writes, "I have great interest in the field of human rights, specifically issues of Indian sovereignty, because I feel that this whole issue relates directly to the survival of the American Indian as a group. I also have great interest in Native American literature and have developed a curriculum on this which has been adopted by the Gallup-McKinley County School district. I have been involved in alcohol research among the American Indian in a National Institutes of Mental Health Project in Gallup, A Community Treatment Plan for Indian Problem Drinkers (1966-68), and am presently directing a program I designed with students and staff of our educational facility."

PARRIS, JIM (Cherokee/Osage)
(CPA, treasurer)
Affiliation: Treasurer, Native American Finance Officers Association, P.O. Box 12743, Green Bay, WI 54307 (505) 998-3245 Fax 998-3333. E-mail: jimparris@aol.com.

PARRISH, EUPHEMA 'SUE'
(executive director)
Affiliation: North American Indian Association of Detroit, Inc., 22720 Plymouth Rd., Detroit, MI 48239 (313) 535-2966 Fax 535-8060.

PARRISH, RAIN (Navajo) 1944-
(museum curator)
Born February 8, 1944, Tuba City, Ariz. *Education*: University of Arizona, BA (Anthropology), 1967. *Principal occupation*: Museum curator. *Home address*: 704 Kathryn Ave., Santa Fe, NM 87501 (505) 982-4636. *Affiliation*: Curator of American Indian Collections, Wheelwright Museum of the American Indian, Santa Fe, 1979-. *Membership*: New Mexico Museum Association. *Awards, honors*: Navajo Woman of the Year in the Arts, 1985; 10 Who Made a Difference, 1985 The New Mexican Newspaper). *Interests*: Travel, art history, anthropology, sports, skiing, hiking, reading, writing. *Published works*: The Stylistic Development of Navajo Jewelry (Minneapolis Institute of the Arts, 1982); Woven Holy People (Wheelwright Museum, 1983); The Pottery of Margaret Tafoya (Wheelwright Museum, 1984).

PARSLEY, ROBERT
(Indian education specialist)
Affiliation: Montana State Office of Public Instruction, State Capitol, Rm. 106, Helena, MT 59620 (406) 444-3031.

PARSONS, JACKIE (Blackfeet)
(crafts association manager)
Affiliation: Northern Plains Indian Crafts Association, P.O. Box E, Browning, MT 59417 (406) 338-5661.

PASHE, DENNIS
(Indian band chief)
Affiliation: Dakota Tipi Indian Band, Box 1569, Pontage La Prairie, Manitoba, Canada R1N 3P1 (204) 857-4381.

PASQUAL, REGINALD T. (Pueblo)
(pueblo governor)
Affiliation: Pueblo of Acoma, P.O. Box 309, Acomita, NM 87034 (505) 552-6604.

PATAWA, ELWOOD H. (Umatilla)
(former tribal chairperson)
Affiliations: U.S. Dept. of Agriculture, Office of Intergovernmental Affairs, Washington, DC 20250; former tribal chairperson, Umatilla Board of Trustees, Pendleton, OR.

PATT, OLNEY, JR. (Confederated Tribes of Warm Springs)
(executive director, tribal chairperson)
Affiliations: Chairperson, Confederated Tribes of Warm Springs, P.O. Box C, Warm Springs, OR 97761 (541) 553-1161; executive director, Columbia River Inter-Tribal Fish Commission, 729- NE Oregon St., Suite 200, Portland, OR 97232 (503) 238-3561 Fax 235-4228. E-mail: patto@critfc.org.

PATTEA, CLINTON (Mohave-Apache)
(tribal council president)
Affiliations: Mohave-Apache Community Council, P.O Box 17779, Fountain Hills, AZ 85268 (480) 837-5121; chairperson, Arizona Commission on Indian Affairs, 1645 W. Jefferson, Suite 433, Phoenix, AZ 85007.

PATTERSON, DONALD (Tonkawa)
(tribal president)
Address & Affiliation: Tonkawa Tribe, P.O. Box 70, Tonkawa, OK 74653 (580) 628-2561 Fax 628-3375.

PATTERSON, ELAINE
(rancheria chairperson)
Affiliation: Cortina Rancheria, P.O. Box 1630, Williams, CA 95987 (530) 473-3274.

PATTERSON, ELMA (JONES) (Tuscarora) 1926-
(social worker-retired)
Born August 13, 1926, Lockport, N.Y. *Education*: Cornell University, BS, 1949; SUNY at Buffalo, MSW, 1963. *Principal occupation*: Social worker. *Home address*: 1162 Ridge Rd., Lewiston, NY 14092. *Affiliations*: Supervisor of Field Services for Indians...A State Agency (retired). *Community activities*: New York Iroquois Conference, Inc. (founder; past chairman; board of directors); Seneca Nation Educational Foundation, Inc. (trustee); Americans for Indian Opportunity (AIO)(past vice chairman & secretary-treasurer); Governor's Interstate Indian Council (chairman); New York State Library Services for Indians (advisory committee). *Membership*: American Indian Social Workers Association (charter member).

PATTERSON, JESSICA
(museum director/curator)
Affiliation: Sac & Fox Tribal RV Park and Museum/ Cultural Center, Rte. 2, Box 246, Stroud, OK 74079 (918) 968-3526.

PATTERSON, KENNETH (Tuscarora)
(tribal chief)
Affiliation: Tuscarora Indian Nation, 2006 Mt. Hope Rd., Lewiston, NY 14092 (716) 297-3995.

PATTERSON, LOTSEE (Comanche) 1931-
(professor of library & information studies)
Born December 3, 1931, Indian land near Apache, Okla. *Education*: Oklahoma College for Women, BS, 1959; University of Oklahoma, MLS, 1969, PhD, 1979. *Principal occupation*: Professor of library & information studies. *Home address*: 1705 Pembroke Dr., Norman, OK 73072 (405) 325-3921. *Affiliations*: University of New Mexico, Albuquerque, 1972-78; Texas Woman's University, Denton, TX, 1978-85; director, Trails (Training & Assistance for Indian Library Service, University of Oklahoma, Norman, OK, 1985-87; director, Library Media Services, Oklahoma City Public Schools, 1989-91; associate professor, University of Oklahoma, School of Library & Information Studies, 1991-; editor, American Indian Libraries Newsletter, American Indian Library Association, 1992-97. *Other professional posts*: Advisory Committee, Brodart Foundation, Williamsport, PA, 1971-; White House Conference on Libraries & Information Services Taskforce, 1982- (Awards Committee, 1992-); National Archives & Records Administration, National Historical Publications & Records Commission (field advisory committee; review grant proposals under the Native American Institute), 1985-; National Commission on Libraries & Information Science (consultant to the Commission's Native American Task Force, Washington, DC, 1989-93); Admission Committee, School of Library & Information Studies, University of Oklahoma, 1991-; Western History Associates, University of Oklahoma, Board of Trustees (vice president, 1992-; chair, Acquisitions Committee, 1990-); member, Board of Directors, Native American Library & Museum Project, Washington, DC, 1994-; numerous conference presentations and invited formal lectures, 1985-. *Memberships*: American Library Association (council member, 1984-88); American Indian Library Association (president, 1981-84, 1984-87, 1991-); American Association of School Librarians (board member, 1980-83); Oklahoma Library Association. *Awards, honors*: Expert witness, Senate Select Committee on Indian Affairs: Hearing; Equality Award 1994, American Library Association; Silver Award 1996, National Commission on Libraries and Information Science; Beta Phi Mu Award, American Library Association, 2001. *Published works*: Contributor to Pathways to Excellence: A Report on Improving Library & Information Services for Native American Peoples (USGPO, 1992); "History and Status of Native Americans in Librarianship." Library Trends 49(1) 182-193; Comanche," in Native America in the Twentieth Century: An Encyclopedia, edited by Mary B. Davis (Garland Publishing, 1994); co-authored with Mary Ellen Snodgrass, Indian Terms of the Americas (Libraries Unlimited, 1994); Native Americans and Native American Resources, Guide to Multicultural Resources, 1995-96, 1997-98, edited with Alex Boyd (Highsmith Press, 1997); Native American Videos - Culturally Diverse Media Collections for Youth, 1997, edited with Irene Wood (Neal-Schuman, 1997); "Historical Overview of Tribal Libraries in the Lower Forty Eight States." in Bringing Libraries to People (McFarland, 2002).

PATTERSON, WES
(association president)
Affiliation: Oregon Native American Business & Entrepreneurial Network, P.O. Box 1359, Warm Springs, OR 97761.

PAUKAN, MOSES, Sr. (eskimo)
(village council president)
Affiliation: Native Village of Algaaciq, P.O. Box 48, St. Mary's, AK 99658 (907) 438-2932.

PAUL, ALICE (Tohono O'odham)
(professor emeritus)
Education: University of Arizona, PhD, 1978. *Affiliation*: American Indian Studies Program, The University of Arizona, Harvill Bldg., Rm 430, P.O. Box 210076, Tucson, AZ 85721 (520) 621-7108 Fax 621-7952. E-mail: aisp@email.arizona.edu.

PAUL, ARVADA
(health director)
Affiliation: Redding Rancheria, 3184 Chum Creek Rd., Redding, CA 96002 (916) 224-2700.

PAUL, BENJAMIN PETER
(Indian band chief)
Affiliation: Pabineau Indian Band, RR 5, Site 26, Box 1, Bathurst, New Brunswick, Canada E2A 3Y8 (506) 548-9211.

PAUL, BENOIT (Pabineau)
(chief/director-Indian band/centre)
Affiliation: Pabineau Indian Band, Cultural/Educational Centre, R.R. #5, Box 1, Site 26, Bathurst, New Brunswick, Can. E2A 3Y8 (506) 548-9211.

PAUL, BLAIR F. (Tlingit) 1943-
(attorney)
Born July 5, 1943, Juneau, Alaska. *Education*: Western Washington State College, BA, 1966; University of Washington Law School, JD, 1970. *Principal occupation*: Attorney. Resides in Seattle, Wash. *Community activities*: Pioneer Square Historic Preservation Board, 1974-; Washington Trust for Historic Preservation (president, 1976-77); United Indians of All Tribes (board member, 1969-71): Seattle Indian Health Board, 1970-73; Seattle Indian Services Commission, 1972-73. *Memberships*: American Trial Lawyers; Washington Trial Lawyers; Seattle-Kings County Bar.

PAUL, DAVID
(association president)
Affiliation: New Brunswick Indian Arts & Crafts Association, 212 Queen St., Suite 402, Fredericton, New Brunswick, Can. E3V 1A7 (506) 459-7312.

PAUL, JOHNNIE
(village president)
Affiliation: Native Village of Kipnuk, P.O. Box 57, Kipnuk, AK 99614 (907) 896-5515.

PAUL, LAWRENCE ALEXANDER
(Indian band chief)
Affiliation: Millbrook Indian Band, Box 634, Truro, Nova Scotia, Canada B2N 5E5 (902) 895-4365.

PAUL, LEONARD
(Indian band chief)
Affiliation: Eskasoni Indian Band, Eskasoni, Nova Scotia, Canada B0A 1J0 (902) 379-2800.

PAUL, MONICA (Kahen Ten Hawi)
(Kahnawake Mohawk)
(educator, council member)
Born in Kahnawake, Canada. *Home address*: 21 Village Rd., Morganville, NJ 07751. *Community activities*: After retiring from NJ Bell, Monica has been working as a crossing guard since 1986. She is an active member of the Old Bridge Senior Choral Group which travels extensively throughout the area performing; she also volunteers for the Old Bridge Office on Aging as a commodity distribution helper. *Membership*: Inter-Tribal Indians of New Jersey (heads the Sunshine Committee), a non-profit cultural and educational organization dedicated to preserving and continuing American Indian heritage. Monica is one of the organization's educators that provides cultural/educational services at various institutions, such as the New Jersey State Museum, Newark Museum, schools and colleges. *Awards, honors*: Winner of the "Young at Heart" Award from the U.S. Health Core; elected as one of seven council members of the Inter-Tribal Indians of New Jersey; an award recognizing people who inspire community by activities and attitude. *Interests*: Ms. Paul instructs Mohawk language classes and traditional clothing and beadwork; she is a member of the Inter-Tribal Dance Group, and participates in all performances, explaining her regalia; writing - Monica compiled a book of memoirs for her family and is writing a second book that will contain the family tree with historical sketches on some of her ancestors.

PAUL, MOSES (Athapascan)
(village chief)
Affiliation: Nenana Native Association, P.O. Box 356, Nenana, AK 99760 (907) 832-5662.

PAUL, PATRICK (Cree-Kootnay) 1942-
(educator; consultant-human development)
Born January 24, 1942, Cranbrook, B.C. Can. *Education*: The Evergreen State College (Olympia, WA), MA, 1980; Antioch University (Seattle, WA), MA, 1984. *Principal occupation*: Educator; consultant-human development. *Home address*: Resides in Bellingham, WA. *Affiliation*: Assistant professor and coordinator, Native American Chemical Dependency Studies, Northwest Indian College, Bellingham, WA, 1984-; youth and family counselor, Chemical Dependency, United Indians, Seattle, 1984-88. *Other professional posts*: Trainer and consultant, 1982-; secretary/treasurer of the Northwest Indian Council on Chemical Depedency and the Northwest Indian Alcohol/Drug Specialist Certification Board. *Awards, honors*: National Indian Board on Alcoholism and Drug Abuse, for providing excellent Alcohol/drug education to the Indian people of the Pacific Northwest, 1980-90.

PAUL, TERRANCE
(Indian band chief)
Affiliation: Membertou India Band, 111 Membertou St., Sydney, Nova Scotia, Canada B1S 2N9 (902) 539-6688.

PAUL, WILBUR
(BIA agency supt.)
Affiliation: Cherokee Agency, Bureau of Indian Affairs, Cherokee, NC 28719 (704) 497-9131 Fax 497-6715.

PAULETTE, MIKE (Metis)
(president-Metis association)
Affiliation: Metis Association of the NWT, P.O. Box 1375, Yellowknife, N.W.T. X1A 2P1 (403) 873-3505.

PAYMELLA, BETTY
(school principal)
Affiliation: Second Mesa Day School, P.O. Box 98, Second Mesa, AZ 86043 (602) 737-2571.

PAYNE, SUSAN
(institute director)
Affiliation: American Indian Studies Institute, Curtis Rd., Box 1260, Washington, CT 06793 (203) 868-0518.

PEACHES, DANIEL (Navajo) 1940-
(administrator, cultural consultant)
Born September 2, 1940, Kayenta (Navajo County) Ariz. *Education*: Northern Arizona University, BS, 1967; University of New Mexico, 1968-69 (Indian Law); American University, 1969 (Internship). *Principal occupation*: Navajo Tribal Administrator. *Address*: P.O. Box 1801, Kayenta, AZ 86033 (928) 697-5523 Fax 697-5524 (work). *Affiliations*: Navajo Peace Maker Court, 1990-; Dineh Spiritual & Cultural Society, 1985-; Board of Regents, Northland Pioneer College, Holbrook, AZ, 1985-; Board of Regents, Navajo Community College, Tsaile, AZ, 1988-. *Other professional posts*: Elected, Navajo Nation Council, 1998-2003; member, Ethics & Rules Committee, Navajo Nation, 1999-2003; Navajo Mountain Soil & Water Conservation District, 1984-; Arizona Townhall Council, 1974-; National Indian Education Advisory Council, 1972-76. *Community activities*: Navajo Environmental Protection Commission, 1976-85; Governor's Commission on Arizona Indian Affairs, 1974; Kayenta Boarding School, 1985-; Arizona Town Hall. *Memberships*: Native American Grant School Association; Navajo Area School Board Association. *Awards, honors*: Presidential appointment to National Indian Education Advisory Council, 1972 by President Nixon; Honorary Degree in Law, Navajo Community College, 1978; Council Delegate of the Year, 2000. *Interests*: Elected to Arizona State Legislature, House of Representatives from Legislative Dist. 3, 1974-85. Biographical sources: Newsweek Magazine, 1981; Arizona Republic, Sunday Magazine, 1982; Time Magazine, 1984; Who's Who in the West, 1985-; Who's Who in America, 1986-

PEACOCK, HOWARD
(Indian band chief)
Affiliation: Enoch Indian Band, Box 2, Site 2, RR 1, Winterburn, Alberta, Canada T0E 2N0 (403) 470-4505.

PEACOCK, MICHAEL D. (*Milky Way*)
(Pueblo of Laguna/Seneca/Mohawk) 1957-
(business consultant)
Born March 27, 1957, Albuquerque, N.M. *Education*: University of New Mexico, AAS, 1986; College of Santa Fe, BA, 1989. *Principal occupation*: Business consultant. *Address*: Unknown. *Affiliation*: Consultant, New Mexico Indian Business Development Center, Albuquerque, NM, 1992-. *Other Professional post*: Board of Directors, Laguna Commercial Enterprises.

PEACOCK, ROBERT "SONNY"
(Lake Superior Chippewa)
(tribal chairperson)
Affiliation: Fond du Lac Reservation Business Committee, 105 University Rd., Cloquet, MN 55720 (218) 879-4593.

PEACOCK, THOMAS D. (Chippewa)
(school supt.)
Affiliation: Fond du Lac Ojibway School, 105 University Rd., Cloquet, MN 55720 (218) 879-0241.

PEAKE-RAYMOND, MARGARET (Chippewa)
(executive director)
Address & Affiliation: Minnesota Indian Women's Resource Center, 2300 15th Ave. S., Minneapolis, MN 55404 (612) 728-2000 Fax 728-2039.

PEARCE, CRAIG
(organization chairperson)
Affiliation: Antelope Indian Circle Religious Group, P.O. Box 790, Susanville, CA 96130 (916) 257-2181 ext. 468.

PEARCE, EILEEN (*Little Axe*) (Absentee Shawnee) 1961-
(journalism, mid-management)
Born June 8, 1961, Oklahoma City, Okla. *Education*: Rose State College (Midwest City, OK), AA, 1982, AAS, 1993; Central State University (Edmond, OK), BA, 1984. *Principal occupation*: Journalism, Mid-Management. *Home address*: 5225 S. Foster Rd., Oklahoma City, OK 73129 (405) 677-2560 (phone & fax); E-mail: lapearce@aol.com. *Affiliation*: Former Treasurer, Shawnee Tribe of Oklahoma, 1988-2000. *Community activities*: Member of Gloneta Indian Baptist Church; former member of Miss Indian Oklahoma Pageant. *Membership*: Native American Journalists Association. *Awards, honors*: Golden Touch Award, Wix/Dana Corp., 1993, 1994; wona a Supreme Court deceision in tribal court, Assc 1999-01 Pearce vs. Nuckolls, et al. *Published work*: Author of a small pamphlet, "Consumer Over-the-Counter Drug Pocketbook" (1997).

PEARSON, M. PAT (*Blue Feather*)
(United Lumbee/Cherokee/Choctaw) 1942-
(carpenter; silversmith, saddle maker, rock carver)
Born October 16, 1942, Broken Arrow, Okla. *Education*: High school. *Principal occupation*: Carpenter; silversmith, saddle maker, rock carver. *Address*: Resides in Fresno, CA. *Affiliation*: Indian Traders Guild (silversmith, saddle maker, rock carver). *Community activities*: Counseling & referral, Alcoholics & Drugs Anonymous; work with Special Olympics kids. *Memberships*: United Lumbee Nation's Bear Clan (vice-chief, 1993-); Fresno Gem & Mineral Society. *Awards, honors*: 1987-91 Fresno Fair (10-1st Places, 2-2nd Places, 1 Honorable Mention; Sept., 1993 Pasadena Indian Show, 1st Place. All awards for - Open Class Indian Jewelry & Art. *Interests*: Researching Indian languages & traditional arts & crafts; customs, etc. (Cherokee, Choctaw, Lenape, Mohawk, etc.; traveling. *Published work*: Learn to Speak Cherokee, Jan. 1993.

PEARSON, MARIA D. (Hamichia Ianko-Running Moccasins) (Yankton Sioux) 1932-
(consultant-Indian affairs)
Born July 12, 1932, Springfield, S.D. *Education*: Marty Indian School, Marty, SD, 1938-49; Iowa Western Community College, Council Bluffs, IA. *Principal occupation*: Consultant-Indian affairs. *Address*: Resides in Ames, Iowa. *Affiliation*: Owner, Maria Pearson, Consultant, Ames, IA. *Community activities*: Commissioner, Iowa Substance Abuse Commission; chair, State Archaeologist's Advisory Committee; chair, Iowa Governors Indian Advisory Council. *Awards, honors*: Governor's Award for Volunteer Work, Iowa Governor. *Membership*: Native American Advisory Council on Substance Abuse (treasurer). *Interests*: "Maria Pearson is generally regarded as the person who initiated the movement for protection of Indian burials and reburial of remains in universities, museums and private collections. Got first law on this subject passed in this area; initiated substance abuse treatment for Indians in Omaha, Neb. (CARE Program), one of the first such treatment programs. Funding member of Indian substance abuse group which got national programs initiated on reservations and in cities though Indian Health Service; has given many talks on both these subjects to professional society groups and national or state conferences. Very active as advisor to Iowa Governor and Iowa government agencies on these and other topics." *Biographical sources*: Many magazine & newspaper articles: Newsweek, Time, Wall Street Journal, Chicago Tribune, Des Moines Register, Omaha World Herald, etc.

PEARSON, MYRA S. (Sisseton-Wahpeton Sioux)
(former tribal chairperson)
Affiliation: Spirit Lake Sioux Tribal Council, P.O. Box 359, Fort Totten, ND 58335 (701) 766-4221.

PEASE-PRETTY ON TOP, JANINE
(college president)
Affiliation: Little Big Horn Community College, P.O. Box 370, Crow Agency, MT 59022 (406) 638-7211 Fax 638-2229.

PECOS, JOSE L. (Jemez Pueblo)
(former pueblo governor)
Affiliation: Jemez Pueblo Council, P.O. Box 100, Jemez, NM 87024 (505) 834-7359.

PECOS, REGIS (Cochiti Pueblo)
(pueblo governor)
Affiliations: Governor, Cochiti Pueblo Council, P.O. Box 70, Cochiti, NM 87072 (505) 465-2244; executive director, New Mexico Office on Indian Affairs, La Villa Rivera Bldg., 228 E. Palace Ave., Santa Fe, NM 87501 (505) 827-6440.

PECOTTE, JEFF
(health director)
Affiliation: Hannahville Indian Community Health Clinic, N14911 Hannahville B1. Rd., Wilson, MI 49896 (906) 466-2782.

PECUSA, DAVIS F.
(BIA agency supt.)
Affiliation: Pima Agency, Bureau of Indian Affairs, P.O. Box 8, Sacaton, AZ 85247 (520) 562-3326 Fax 562-3543.

PEDRO, JAMES (Cheyenne-Arapaho)
(former tribal chairperson)
Affiliation: Cheyenne-Arapaho Tribe, P.O. Box 38, Concho, OK 73022 (405) 262-0345 Fax 262-0745.

PEEBLES, JOHN
(tribal lawyer)
Affiliation: Santee Sioux Tribe, P.O. Box 283, Flandreau, SD 57028 (605) 997-3891.

PEGO, DAVID PAUL (*Anungons - Little Star*)
(Saginaw Chippewa) 1954-
(journalist, writer)
Born February 1, 1954, Mt. Pleasant, Mich. *Education*: Central Oklahoma State University, 1972-74. *Principal occupation*: Journalist. *Home address*: 1103 Hatteras, Austin, TX 78753 (512) 990-1472; E-mail: NIE77@aol.com. *Work address*: P.O. Box 670, Austin, TX 78767 (512) 445-3590 Fax 912-2919. *Affiliations*: The Daily Oklahoman & The Oklahoma City Times, 1974-84; The Dallas Times Herald, 1984-88; The Associated Press, Dallas, TX, 1988-90; Journalist, writer, The Austin American Statesman, Austin, TX, 1990-. *Other professional posts*: Founded Great Promise, 1992- (a non-profit organization that publishes educational materials for young American Indians). *Community activities*: Founding co-chair of the Austin Powwow and American Indian Art Festival; founding co-chair, First Americans of Central Texas; member, Texas Education Agency Technology Task Force; Rising Star Foundation Board; chair, Austin Independent School District's Community Involvement and Parenting Committee; workshop panelist, 1992 & 1993, Austin Women in Media seminar for non-profit organizations; workshop panelist, 1992 Texas Conference on Indian Education; Austin Independent School District's Native American Parents Committee (founding chairman); Conference on Minority Health (organizing committee for 1994); member of the Greater Austin Chamber of Commerce (community issues & action committee - wrote special section on crime); presented more than 200 school lectures and performances on American Indians, and about 40 lectures on journalis; served on leadership Austin communications and diversity committees; performed storytelling and poetry, Texas Culture Bash, 1996; performer, Texas Minority Health Conference, 1996. *Awards, honors*: Oklahoma City YMCA Service Awards in 1982, 1983; 1988 minority fellowships for American Newspapers Publishers Workshop for Editors; 1991 University of Oklahoma Visiting Professor in Residence; guest lecturer at various colleges & universities; selected by President Bush in 1992 as delegate to the White House Conference on Indian Education; invited to appear on local television and radio shows; designed and coordinated production of special newspaper on AIDS that was approved for use by the Dallas Independent School District; appointed by Gov. George W. Bush as member of Goals 2000 Committee for Texas; Texas State Indian Education Conference Award, 1996; NIE Infor-

mation Service Bright Ideas Award. *Memberships*: Leadership Austin, Native American Journalists Association; Southern Newspaper Publishers Association (literacy committee member); Texas Newspapers in Education (board member); Wordcraft Circle of Native Writers and Storytellers (national caucus member, 1996); Capital Area Social Studies Council; American Indian Resources and Educational Coalition. *Published work*: Short story, "Indian Medicine" in literacy quarterly published by Johns Hopkins University in 1994.)

PELTIER, JERRY
(Indian band chief)
Affiliation: Kanesatake (Mohawk) Indian Band, Box 607, Kanesatake, Quebec, Canada J0N 1E0 (514) 479-8373.

PELTIER, LEONARD (*Gwarth-ee-las*) (Anishinabe - Turtle Mountain) 1944-
(artist, human rights worker)
Born September 12, 1944, Grand Forks, N.D. *Education*: St. Mary;s (Leavenworth, KS), 1990-91. *Principal occupation*: Activist, artist. *Address*: Prisoner #89637-132, USP Box 1000, Leavenworth, KS 66048. *Affiliation*: Leonard Peltier Defense Committee, P.O. Box 583, Lawrence, KS 66044 (785) 842-5774, 1976-. E-mail: lpdc@idir.net *Military service*: U.S. Marine Corps, 1960. *Community activities*: AIM activist; food & clothing drives for reservations and public awareness regarding issues facing prisoners, Native peoples, and basic civil/human rights. *Memberships*: Leonard Peltier Defense Committee, 1977-; Rosenburg Fund for Children; Walk Across Europe (1994). *Awards, honors*: Frederick Douglas Award, Spanish Human Rights Award; Sacco & Vanzetti Award; Humanitarian Award; Nobel Prize nominee. *Interests*: Art, specifically oil painting; working on cars, gardening. *Biographical sources*: Spirit of Crazy Horse, by Peter Matthiessen; Agents of Repression, by Ward Churchill; Trial of Leonard Peltier, by Jim Messerschmidt; (documentary) "Incident at Oglala," by Robert Redford; (video) Freedom by Rage Against the Machine, MTI. *Published work*: Prison Writings: My Life Is My Sundance (St. Martin's Press).

PEMBER, MARY ANNETTE (Red Cliff Ojibwe)
(freelance photojournalist, writer)
Education: University of Wisconsin-Madison, School of Journalism. *Principal occupation*: Freelance photojournalist, writer. *Address*: Resides in Cincinnati, Ohio. *Affiliations*: Past professional post: President, Board of Directors, Native American Journalists Association (NAJA) (retired); coordinates NAJA's annual Photo-Shoot-out competition sponsored by The New York Times, USA Today; staff photojournalist at the Green Bay Press-Gazette, The Oregonian and the Arizona Republic; photo editor of the The Lexington Heald-Leader. Her photojournalism has dealt primarily with social issues, such as homelessness, drug abuse, youth gangs, as well as women's and indigenous people's issues in the U.S., Nepal and India. Currently, she is focusing exclusively on Native topics. *Awards, honors*: In 1995 traveled to Beijing as a representative of both NAJA and UNITY: Journalists of Color, Inc., as part of the United Nations' World Conference on Women; served on the Visual Task Forceof UNITY '99; won several awards from the National Press Photographers Association, The Kentucky Newspaper Association, The Ohio Press Photographers Association; The Arizona Press Club; The Associated Press, and the Oregon Newspaper Association, as well as the Ralph Nafsiger Alumni Achievement Award from the University of Wisconsin-Madison School of Journalism; NAJA names her Best Photographer in 2000; she is a current recipient of a University of Maryland Child and Family Policy Journalism Fellowship. *Memberships*: National Press Photographers Association; Ohio Press Photographers Association; Native American Journalists Association. *Published works*: She has been published in Life, Time, Newsweek, The New York Times, USA Today, Ms., Indian Country Today, Aboriginal Voices, Winds of Change, News From Indian Country, Native Peoples, Indigenous Woman, The Discover Channel.com, The National Museum of the American Indian Magazine, and others. Her essays on Native American history and culture have just been published in the book, "America, The Complete Story."

PEMBERTON, ALFRED "TIG" (Chippewa)
(tribal chairperson)
Affiliation: Leech Lake Reservation Business Committee, Route 3, Box 100, Cass Lake, MN 56633 (218) 335-8200.

PENCILLE, HERBERT W. (Chemehuevi) 1927-
(businessman)
Born January 29, 1927, Los Angeles, Calif. *Education*: Los Angeles Valley College (Business Law). *Principal occupation*: Businessman. *Home address*: 12243 Hartland St., N. Hollywood, CA 91605. *Affiliations*: General manager, Hydrex Termite Control Co. of Southern California, 1969-; chairman, Chemehuevi Indian Tribal Council, 1972-; Owner, Hydrex Pest Control Co., East San Fernando Valley, 1975-. *Military service*: U.S. Army Air Corps, 1946-47. *Memberships*: National Pest Control Association, 1949- (director, 1962); Pest Control Operators of California, Inc. (president, 1959; director, 1959, 1960). *Awards, honors*: Man of the Year Award, Pest Control Operators of California, Inc., 1968. *Interests*: Private pilot license.

PENN, ALVIN (Hoh)
(tribal chairperson)
Affiliation: Hoh Tribal Business Committee, 2464 Lower Hoh Rd., Forks, WA 98331 (360) 374-6582.

PENN, W.S. (Nez Perce/Osage) 1949-
(writer, teacher)
Born March 21, 1949, Los Angeles, Calif. *Education*: University of California, Davis, AB, 1970; Syracuse University, DArts, 1979. *Principal occupation*: Writer, teacher. *Home address*: 963 Lantern Hill Dr., East Lansing, MI 48823-2831 (517) 337-7313 Fax 337-0418; E-mail: penn@pilot.msu.edu. *Affiliations*: Professor, Michigan State University (MSU), E. Lansing, MI, 1986-; Wordcraft Circle of Native Writers & Storytellers, Albuquerque, NM (mentor, 8 years). *Other professional post*: Director, Creative Writing Program, MSU (2004-present). *Memberships*: Wordcraft Circle (regional coordinator, member of National Advisory Council on Native American Writing); Associated Writing Programs; Modern Language Association. *Awards, honors*: 1994 North American Indian Prose Award for "All My Sins are Relatives" (narrative essays) from the University of Nebraska Press; Michigan Council on the Arts Award & New York Foundation on the Arts Grant for "The Absence of Angels" (novel); American Book Award, 2001 for "Killing Time With Strangers (novel); Choice Award for Most Significant Books, 2001, for "This Is the World (stories); Distinguisged Faculty Award, MSU (2003). *Interests*: Writing (novels, essays); teaching/mentoring; giving back to the community; travel; reading. *Published works*: Novel - "The Absence of Angels" (The Permanent Press - hardcover edition, 1994); The Absence of Angels (University of Oklahoma American Indian Lit. Series - paperback edition, 1995); Killing Time With Strangers (University of Arizona Press, 2000); narrative essays "All My Sins Are Relatives" (University of Nebraska Press, 1995); The Telling of the World; As We Are Now: Essays on Race and Identity; editor, Native American Literatures (The Johns Hopkins University Press, 1994) a special anthology; Feathering Custer - essays (University of Arizona Press, 2000); This Is the World - stories (Michigan State University Press, 2000); editor, Michigan State University Press, American Indian Literature Series.

PENNEY, DAVID
(association president)
Affiliation: President, Native American Arts Studies Association, Detroit Institute of the Arts, 5200 Woodward Ave., Detroit, MI 48202 (313) 833-7900.

PENNEY, SAMUEL N. (Nez Perce)
(tribal chairperson)
Affiliation: Nez Perce Tribal Executive Committee, P.O. Box 305, Lapwai, ID 83540 (208) 843-2253.

PENOI, CHARLES R. (Laguna Pueblo/Oklahoma Cherokee) 1911-
(publisher; consultant)
Born September 23, 1911, Kiowa Agency, Anadarko, Okla. *Education*: University of Oklahoma, BS, MEd, DEd, 1956. *Principal occupation*: Publisher; consultant. *Home address*: 704 Neal Circle, El Reno, OK

73036 (405) 262-2013. *Affiliations*: Teacher, 1947- 67, Bureau of Indian Affairs' schools: Rosebud Boarding School, Fort Wingate Indian School, Sequoyah Indian School, Pawnee Indian School, and Riverside Indian School; employment assistance officer, Cheyenne & Arapaho Agency, Concho, OK (1967-retired -1973); owner, Pueblo Publishing Press, Yukon, OK, 1974-. *Other professional post*: After retirement he established his counseling service in Yukon, Okla. He was certified as a school counselor and as a school psychologist. *Military service*: U.S. Army, 1941-45 (45th Infantry-500 days of combat in the European theatre-EAME Service Ribbon with One Silver Star, One Bronze Service Star and One Bronze Arrowhead, Good Conduct Medal; American Defense Service Ribbon). *Community activities*: Established the El Reno School of Continuing Education which has been in session for 18 years. It is a school for all races, both male and female; member, Rotary International. *Awards, honors*: 30 Years Length of Service Award from the Bureau of Indian Affairs. *Interests*: "I have seen and visited all of the major cities in the Western Hemisphere." *Biographical sources*: The Daily Oklahoman. *Published works*: No More Buffalos, The Cheyenne & Arapaho Tribes of Oklahoma (Pueblo Publishing Press, 1991); Indian Time (Pueblo Publishing Press, 1984) and about 15 other books published by the Press.

PENOLI, NEVADA P. (Te-Moak Western Shoshone)
(former tribal chairperson)
Affiliation: Wells Indian Colony Band Council, P.O. Box 809, Wells, NV 89835 (702) 752-3045.

PENSONEAU, RALPH R.
(BIA agency supt.)
Affiliation: Southern Ute Agency, Bureau of Indian Affairs, P.O. Box 315, Ignacio, CO 81137 (303) 563-4511.

PEONE, ALFRED (Spokane)
(tribal chairperson)
Affiliation: Spokane Business Council, P.O. Box 100, Wellpinit, WA 99040 (509) 258-4581.

PEPION, LORETTA F. (Blackfeet) 1942-
(museum curator)
Born May 11, 1942, Mont. *Address & Affiliation*: Museum of the Plains Indian, Box 398, Browning, MT 59417 (406) 338-2230.

PERALA, RENEE
(Title V coordinator)
Affiliation: Native American Coalition of Programs, P.O. Box 1914, Fargo, ND 58107 (701) 235-3124.

PERATROVICH, ROY Jr. (Tlingit) 1934-
(consulting engineer)
Born May 17, 1934, Klawock, Alaska. *Education*: University of Washington, BS, 1957. *Principal occupation*: Civil engineer. *Address*: Resides in Anchorage, AK 99515. *Affiliations*: Engineer, Seattle Engineering Dept., 1957-61; bridge engineer, AK Dept. of Highways, 1961-72; supervisor of activities, R&M Consultants, Inc., 1972-77; first director, State of Alaska, Div. of Facility Procurement Policy, 1977-79; president, Peratrovich Consultants, Inc., Anchorage, 1979-; Sr. Vice President, Peratrovich, Nottingham & Drage, Inc. - Consulting Engineers, Anchorage, 1979-. *Other professional post*: Founder & member of board, Architects and Engineers Insurance Co." a nationwide company formed in 1987 to sell liability insurance; member of School of Engineering Advisory Committee, University of Alaska; former BIA agency supt. *Memberships*: State of AK Board of Registration for Engineers, Architects, and Land Surveyors; American Society of Civil Engineers; The Society of American Military Engineers. *Awards, honors*: Five awards from James & Lincoln Arc Welding Foundation for design of welded structures; and numerous awards from Municipality of Anchorage Urban Design Awards Program, among others; first Alaska Native to become licensed as a professional engineer in the state of Alaska. *Interests*: "Son of prominent Alaskan civil rights activists, Roy and Elizabeth Peratrovich. Over 30 years experience in structural and civil engineering, facility planning, and engineering management, working in both government and private sector. Primary work emphasis has been in the fields of bridge and marine structural design and management of major planning agencies.

One of my goals has been to be the very best civil engineer I can be and to provide an example for other Indian boys and girls to follow. Now that I can afford it, I enjoy traveling to see other ports of the world; enjoy sports and my family." *Published work*: Co-author, Guide to Maintenance and Operations of Small Craft Harbors, 1988, the first manual of its kind in the U.S.; articles on bridge design and construction, with Dennis Nottingham.

PERDASOFPY, ROGER V. (Kiowa, Apache, Comanche) 1959-
(drum maker, singer)
Born November 1, 1959, Lawton, Okla. *Principal occupation*: Drum maker. *Address*: P.O. Box 932, Midlothian, TX 76065 (972) 723-2984. E-mail: perdasofpy@cnbcom.net. *Affiliation*: Perdasofpy Crafts, 1990-present. *Other professional posts*: Employed as tour guide, singer, dancer, Village builder, Indian City U.S.A., Anadarko, OK, 1984-present. He has run dance shows, sung and danced professionally since the age of 10. *Military service*: U.S. Army, 1977-81 (Corporal or E-4). *Memberships*: Indian Arts & Crafts Association, IACA (Albuquerque); American Indian Art Council (Dallas); American Indian Chamber of Commerce of Texas; Native American Church. *Awards, honors*: He's won numerous First Place awards in national competition for his drums at Indian Markets around the country and National Champion Fancy Dancer; he has appeared on television and in many newspaper articles. *Interests*: He creates men's dance regalia and other cultural items, as well as jewelry and beadwork, along with his wife, Sharon. Roger is primarily a drum maker, in the Southern Plains Tradition. He is a southern singer and it is from his traditional background he creates hand drums to large pow wow drums, using cedar and a variety of other wood and hide. Roger has lectured on his culture, hide and drum making at various art councils, and the Native American educational organization JOM (Johnson O'Malley), also included in some of this lecture is demonstrations. He makes other cultural items but drum making is his specialty. He runs dance shows, teepee exhibitions, lectures, workshops, demonstrations & cultural programs. He enjoys fishing, being around water, camping, their many dogs and cats, watching wrestling, sports, movies & visiting with friends. "It's my wish that people when they hear the drum (the heartbeat of Mother Earth) that they feel good." *Biographical sources*: Texas Touring Arts Program Company & Artist Roster for the Texas Commission on the Arts.

PERDASOFPY, SHARON (Comanche, Cherokee)
(jeweler)
Born in Santonio, Tex. *Principal occupation*: Jeweler. *Address*: P.O. Box 932, Midlothian, TX 76065 (972) 723-2984. E-mail: perdasofpy@flash.net. *Affiliation*: Perdasofpy Crafts, 1990-present. *Memberships*: Indian Arts & Crafts Association, IACA (Albuquerque); American Indian Chamber of Commerce of Texas; American Indian Art Council, Inc. (Dallas); Arlington (TX) Gem & Mineral Club; Native American Church; American Indian Methodist Church. *Awards, honors*: Numerous awards for her jewelry. Her award winning jewelry is with collectors internationally, including Loretta Lynn & Family, Dr. menninger, The Art Institute of Chicago & about 40 other museums around the country. Featured artist at Macy's, set an emerald from the Nuestra de Atocha (which sank in 1617). *Interests*: Sharon, besides beadworking, making small shields and a variety of jewelry, specializes in custom work, hand-sculptured wire jewelry (a 3,300 year old art form), silversmithing & repairs. "I love making jewelry with gifts from Mother Earth. It's my wish that people feel this flow from these gifts and that of The Creator. I love working with stones hand-sculpting them with sterling silver wire, or gold wire; with fossils, with carvings and sometimes in combination with woods, bone, etc. I love the the outdoors: hiking, camping, working in the yeard, our dogs & cats, visiting with friends, and watching true story movies and comedy. My wish is that people feel the flow of the Creator (thru my created jewelry pieces, know how loved we are, and how we are all inter-related brothers and sisters.)" *Biographical sources*: Texas Touring Arts Program Company & Artist Roster for the Texas Commission on the Arts.

PERDUE, THEDA
(professor of history)
Address & Affiliation: Professor of History, University of North Carolina, Chapel Hill, NC. *Published works*: Slavery and the Evolution of Cherokee Society, 1540-1866 (University of Tennessee Press, 1979); Native Carolinians: The Indians of North Carolina (North Carolina Division of Archives & Cherokee Publications, 1985); Cherokee Women (University of Nebraska Press, 1988); The Cherokee (Chelsea House, 1988); The Columbia Guide to American Indians in the Southeast (Columbia University Press, 2001); Mixed Blood Indians: Racial Construction in the Early South (University of Georgia Press, 2002).

PEREA, JACOB (Mescalero Apache)
(college dean)
Education: PhD. *Affiliation*: Dean, College of Education, San Francisco State University, 1600 Holloway, San Francisco, CA 94132.

PEREA, JOHN-CARLOS (Mescalero Apache) 1975-
(musician)
Born March 7, 1975, Dulce, N.M. *Education*: San Francisco State University, BA (Music). *Principal occupation*: Musician. *Home address*: 149 Gonzalez Dr., San Francisco, CA 94132 (415) 452-8421. E-mail: pereajc@yahoo.com. *Community activities*: Co-leader, Sweetwater Singers, pow-wow drum. *Membership*: Wordcraft Circle of Native Writers and Storytellers. *Interests*: "Finding a musical language where pow-wow music and jazz can co-exist respectfully." *Published works*: Jazz CDs: Gathering of Ancestors (Asian Improv Arts, 1999); First Dance (Aerep Music, 2001).

PEREAU, JOHN J.V.
(BIA agency supt.)
Affiliation: Crow Agency, Bureau of Indian Affairs, Crow Agency, MT 59022 (406) 638-2672.

PEREZ, DAVID A. (Nambe Pueblo)
(Pueblo governor)
Affiliation: Nambe Pueblo Council, Rt. 1 Box 117-BB, Santa Fe, NM 87501 (505) 455-2036.

PEREZ, MARGARET C. (Assiniboine Sioux)
(college president)
Affiliation: Fort Belknap Community College, P.O. Box 159, Harlem, MT 59526-0159 (406) 353-2578.

PERKINS, DOROTHY ALLEEN (*Fallen Leaf*) (Texas Lumbee) 1926-
(retired librarian, tribal chief)
Born September 21, 1926, Franklin, Tex. *Education*: High school. *Address*: & *Affiliation*: Texas Lumbee Tribe, 104 Holly St., Franklin, TX 77856 (979) 828-4977. *Past professional post*: Retired librarian, Franklin Carnegie Library, 1990-2000. *Awards, honors*: A street named after me (South Perkins St.). *Community activities*: Volunteer to help "Our Open Hands," Inc. that help the poor with their needs; member of the Mt. Pleasant Southern Baptist Church. Planning our annual, non-profit, Intertribal Native American gathering, a pow-wow. *Memberships*: Daughter's of Republic of Texas' Ladies VFW Auxiliary, since 1947; Brazos Valley Retired & Senior Volunteer Program. *Interests*: Teaching my grand children about their Native American heritage, crafts, and dances, pow-wow style; going to my church, the Mt. Pleasant Southern Baptist Church. Ms. Perkins writes, "I'm an historian for this band, helping Native Americans to trace their roots; and I'm the "Beloved Woman" of this band, a great honor bestowed on me. I am of Lumbee and Cherokee blood. I write news items for our newspaper on Native Americans; was in a movie as an extra, "No Turning Back" (aired the Fall of 1996) on Native Americans. (I) retired as librarian at Carnegie Library in 1998. (I) work full time as chief of 170 members (Intertribal) of the Texas Lumbe Tribe, a tribe formed in 1997, in Robertson Co., Franklin, Texas." *Published works*: Oral History on the Odyssey and Making of the Texas Lumbee, by Dr. Raeschelle Potter-Deimel (2003)

PERKINS, TWILA
(editor)
Affiliation: "The Seminole Tribune," Seminole Tribe of Florida, 6333 N.W. 30th St., Hollywood, FL 33024 (305) 964-4853.

PERVAIS, CHRISTI
(Indian band chief)
Affiliation: Fort William Indian Band, Box 786, Station F, Thunder Bay, Ontario, Canada P7C 4W6 (807) 623-9543.

PESHEWA, MACAKI (Shawnee; Shaman) 1941-
(priest-Native American Church)
Born May 23, 1941, Spartanburg, S.C. *Education*: Spartanburg Junior College, AA, 1966; Wofford College, BA, 1968; Furman University, 1969; University of South Carolina, 1971-73; University of Tennessee, Knoxville, MS, 1974, 1976-77); Auburn University, 1974-75; Native Americas University (Doctorate-Human Development, 1975; Doctorate-System Theory of Life Science, 1976). *Principal occupation*: Priest-Native American Church, Knoxville, TN. *Address*: Native American Church, P.O. Box 53, Strawberry Plains, TN 37871. *Affiliations*: Regional coordinator, Catawba Labor Program; Chairman, Tennessee Indian Council, Knoxville, TN; chairman and founder, Native American Indians in Media Corporation, Knoxville, TN; chairman, Indian Historical Society of the Americas, Knoxville, Tenn. *Other professional post*: Founder & publisher of the National Indian Reader Newspaper; founder of the Peace Park-Valley of the Totems; business developer in Idian Bingo. *Military service*: U.S. Air Force. *Community activities*: Work with off-reservation Indians; Tennessee Band of Cherokees (medicine man, business advisor); The American Indian Movement (urban Indian, Shawnee Nation); Native American Church of the Southeast (incorporator and head); National Lenape Band of Indians (medicine man); Consciousness Expansion Movement of Native Americans (president, chairman of the board); Tuskegee Alumni Foundation, Knoxville, Tenn. (advisory board); Knoxville Communications Cooperative (advisory board); Native Americas University (Southeast regional coordinator; board of regents; Indian Voters League. *Memberships*: Association of Humanistic Psychology; XAT-American Indian Medicine Society; International Minority Business Council/Association; Phi Delta Kappa; Alpha Delta Omega. *Awards, honors*: Notary-at-Large, Tennessee; Key-to-City Certificate of Appreciation, Knoxville, Tenn.; Governor Recognitions: Appreciation Certificate, and Colonel-past and present administration. *Interests*: Archives of living elders in America today; art collector for Native American Church collection. Parapsychology; existential philosophy; existential phenomenology; altered states of consciousness and metaphysics; herbal medicine; yoga; handball; travel. *Published work*: Film produced: Amonita Sequoyah (Native American Media, 1982); Archives: Longest Walk for Survival, 1981; Archives: Black Elk, Sun Bear, AmyLee, Simon Brasquepe.

PESULCH, SCOTT
(health director)
Affiliation: Fresno Indian Health Association, 4991 E. McKinley, Suite 109, Fresno, CA 93727 (209) 255-0261.

PETE, FRED, Sr. (Eskimo)
(association president)
Affiliation: Stebbins Community Association, P.O. Box 2, Stebbins, AK 99671 (907) 934-3561.

PETE, HARLEN (Goshute)
(tribal chairperson)
Affiliation: Goshute Business Council, P.O. Box 6104, Ibapah, UT 84034 (801) 234-1136.

PETE, JAMES E.
(office director)
Affiliation: IHS-Rhinelander Field Office, P.O. Box 537, Rhinelander, WI 54501 (715) 362-5145.

PETER, DOUGLAS G., M.D.
(IHS-chief medical officer)
Affiliation: Navajo Area Office, IHS, P.O. Box 9020, Window Rock, AZ 86515 (520) 871-5813.

PETERS, CHRIS
(executive director)
Affiliation: Seventh Generation Fund for Indian Development, Inc., P.O. Box 4569, Arcata, CA 95518 (707) 825-7640 Fax 825-7639.

PETERS, ELAINE F.
(museum director)
Affiliation: Ak Chin Indian Him-Dak Museum/
Archives, 42507 W. Peters & Nall Rd., Maricopa, AZ
85239 (520) 568-9480 Fax 568-9557.

PETERS, JIM
(executive director)
Affiliation: Massachusetts Commission on Indian Affairs, One Congress St., 10th Floor, Boston, MA 02114
(617) 727-6394 Fax 727-4938. E-mail: jim.peters@
state.ma.us. Website: www.state.ma.us/dhcd/compo-
nents/ind_affairs.

PETERS, PHILLIP G., SR. (Saginaw-Chippewa)
(tribal chief)
Affiliation: Saginaw-Chippewa Tribal Council, Isabella
Reservation, 7070 E. Broadway, Mt. Pleasant, MI
48858 (517) 772-5700.

PETERS, RAMONA (Nosapocket)
(Mashpee Wampanoag) 1952-
(repatriation consultant, artist)
Born July 22, 1952. *Principal occupation*: Wampanoag
Confederation Repatriation Project consultant, artist.
Address: P.O. Box 244, Mashpee, MA 02649 (508)
477-1361; E-Mail: nosap@cape.com. Web site re-
sume: http://www.realbodies.com/rpeters. *Community
activities*: Mentor for Tribal Girls (28 girls), teach
Wampanoag traditional pottery to interested tribal
members, conduct cultural sensitivity workshops, some
ceremonial duties/responsibilities. *Memberships*:
Mashpee Women's Medicine Society (board member);
Mashpee Domestic Violence Prevention Project;
Wampanoag Nation Singers and Dancers Troupe.

PETERS, CHIEF RUSSELL (Mashpee Wampanoag)
(tribal chief)
Affiliation: Mashpee Wampanoag Indian Tribal
Council, P.O. Box 1048, Mashpee, MA 02649.

PETERS, STAN (Eskimo)
(village chief)
Affiliation: Holy Cross Village Council, P.O.
Box 203, Holy Cross, AK 99602 (907) 476-7134.

PETERS, VAN A.
(education administrator)
Affiliation: Portland Area Office, Bureau of Indian
Affairs, 911 N.E. 11th Ave., Portland, OR 97232
(503) 230-5682.

PETERS, WINIFRED
(school principal)
Affiliation: Hunters Point Boarding School,
zP.O. Box 99, St. Michaels, AZ 86511 (520) 871-4439.

PETERSON, GARY W.
(board president)
Affiliation: National Indian Child Welfare Association,
5100 SW Macadam Ave., Suite 300, Portland, OR
97201 (503) 222-4044. Website: www.nicwa.org.

PETERSON, JAMES E.
(IHS-executive officer)
Affiliation: Bemidji Area Office, Indian Health Service,
203 Federal Bldg., Bemidji, MN 56601 (218) 751-7701.

PETERSON, KENNETH
(BIA agency education chairperson)
Affiliation: Dlo'ay Azhi Community School, P.O.
Box 789, Thoreau, NM 87323 (505) 862-7525.

PETERSON, MARY
(school administrator)
Affiliation: Oneida Turtle School, P.O. Box 365,
Oneida, WI 54155 (920) 869-4364.

PETERSON, NICK, Sr. (Eskimo)
(village president)
Affiliation: Akhiok Native Village, P.O. Box 5072,
Akhiok, AK 99615 (907) 836-2229.

PETERSON, PAT
(executive director)
Affiliation: American Indian Arts Council, 725 Preston
Forest Shopping Center, Suite B, Dallas, TX 75230
(214) 891-9640 Fax 891-0221

PETERSON, TONY
(IHS-executive officer)
Affiliation: Aberdeen IHSArea Office, Federal Bldg., 115
Fourth Ave., SE, Aberdeen, SD 57401 (605) 226-7581.

PETIQUAN, BARNEY
(Indian band chief)
Affiliation: Wabauskang Indian Band, Box 1730,
Kenora, Ontario P9N 3X7 (807) 547-2555.

PETRIVELLI, PATRICIA
(executive director)
Affiliation: Institute of Alaska Native Arts Information
Center, P.O. Box 70769, Fairbanks, AK 99707 (907)
456-7491.

PETTIGREW, DAWN KARIMA
(Creek/Chickasaw/Cherokee) 1970-
(author & novelist)
Born May 13, 1970, Columbus, Ohio. *Education*:
Harvard University, BA, 1992; Ohio State University,
MFA, 1996. *Principal occupation*: Author & novelist.
Address: P.O. Box 1748, Qualla Boundary Reserva-
tion, Cherokee, NC 28719. *Affiliation*: Writer, 1979-
present; instructor/researcher, Ohio State University,
Columbus, OH, 1993-96; freelance correspondent for
News from Indian Country, 1995-present; correspon-
dent, "Whispering Wind" Magazine (current); writer-
in-residence, Western Carolina University (current).
Community activities: The Northeasterners, Inc.; Mem-
ber, Cherokee United Methodist Church; singing, po-
etry and literary readings, mentoring. *Memberships*:
Wordcraft Circle of Native Writers & Storytellers; Na-
tive American Journalists' Association; Native Writers
Circle of the Americs. *Awards, honors*: Her novel, "The
Way We Make Sense, was a finalist for the North
American Native First Book Award; a first runner-up in
Kent State'sSouthern Regional Education Board Doc-
toral Scholar, 1998-2001; 2000-2001, Miss Native
American Worldwide Achievement; finalist - Woodford
Reserve Literary Competition. *Interests*: Beadwork, tra-
ditional arts and dance, film. *Published works*: The
Way We Make Sense (Aunt Lute Books-San Francisco,
2002) Website: www.auntlute.com; The Marriage of
Saints (play).

PETTIGREW, JACKSON D. (Chickasaw) 1942-
(artist, business manager)
Born July 2, 1942, Ada, Okla. *Education*: East Central
University, BA, 1973. Principal occupation: Artist, business manager. *Home address*: 3727 Governor Harris
Dr., Ada, OK 74820. *Affiliations*: Owner, Native American Arts (retail/wholesale), Ada, OK, 1984-. *Other professional post*: Chairman of the board, First American
Foundry Arts, Inc. (art bronze), Ada, Okla. *Community
activities*: Teach art classes for young people, J.O.M.
Indian program. *Membership*: Southern Oklahoma
Artist Association. *Interests*: "Artistic growth and sharing concepts with young people who are interested in
art as a career. Also interested in civil rights. I was an
equal opportunity specialist at the Dallas Regional
Office of Civil Rights, Dallas, TX, 1973-79. I was also
vice chairperson for the Regional Indian Affairs Council from 1974-78. We served as an advocate for Native Americans in Region VI and the nation. Other interests include: silversmithing, painting and sculpturing. I have competed in various national juried art
shows."

PEWEWARDY, DR. CORNEL (Oyate Omp Moni)
(Comanche/Kiowa) 1952-
(school principal)
Born Jañary 20, 1952, Lawton, Okla. *Education*: Northeastern State University, BS, 1976, MEd, 1977; University of New Mexico, EdS, 1986; Penn State Uni-
versity, DEd, 1989. *Principal occupation*: Indian school
principal. *Address & Affiliation*: Principal, Mounds Park
All-Nations Magnet School, 1075 E. 3rd St., St. Paul,
MN 55106 (612) 293-5938. *Other professional posts*:
Postdoctoral Fellow, University of Oklahoma, 1989-
91. *Community activities*: Board Director, Dayton's
Bluff/Dist. 4; Afrocentric Academy; Minnesota Institute
of Arts; St. Paul Indians in Unity; Kirkpatrick Center;
Minnesota Technical College System. *Memberships*:
National Association for Multicultural Education (found-
ing member); St. Paul Principals Association; Ameri-
can Education Research Association; Association of
Teacher Education; National Association of American

Indian Professors; PDK; Pi Lambda Theta; National
Council of Teachers of English; National Indian Education Association; Oklahoma Council for Indian Education; Association of Institute Research. *Awards, honors*: John C. Rouillard Scholarship; Outstanding Young
Men of America, 1988; Kozak Memorial Award, 1989;
1991 National "Indian Educator of the Year," by the
National Indian Education Association; Minnesota
Transformational Leadership Award, 1991; served on
tribal advisory councils, state textbook review committees, and national special interest groups in
multicultural education. *Interests*: Director of research
and development, Southwestern Indian Polytechnic
Institute, Albuquerque, NM; performing artist who continues to promote and perpetuate the songs & dances
of the Southern Plains' tribes; singing and playing the
American Indian flute; teaches Native American song
and dance. Dr. Cornel is a descendent of Chief Wild
Horse. *Biographical sources*: Native American Mascots and Imagery; Struggle of Unlearning Indian Stereotypes; Medicine Wheel Circle; Indian Aerobics;
Perceptions of American Indian High School Students
Attending Public School. *Published works*: Culturally
Responsible Pedagogy (National Education Services,
1992); American Indian Stereotypes in the World of
Children (Scarecrow, 1992); Spirit Journey - cassette,
CD (Meyer Creative Productions, 1993).

PFEFFER, MICHAEL S. 1949-
(attorney)
Born October 14, 1949, New York, N.Y. *Education*:
Cornell University, BA, 1971; University of California,
Berkeley, JD, 1979. *Affiliations*: Executive director,
California Indian Legal Services, 510 16th St., 4th
Floor, Oakland, CA 94612 (510) 835-0284 Fax 835-
8045, 1982-. E-mail: mikepfeffer@calindian.org.
Website: www.calindian.org. *Membership*: State Bar
of California.

PFLUG, MELISSA A.
(professor of anthropology)
Address: Dept. of Anthropology, Wayne State University, Detroit, MI 48202 (313) 577-2935. *Affiliations*:
Wayne State University, Detroit, MI, 1985-92, 1996-
present; University of Wisconsin, Eau Claire, 1993-
96. *Community activities*: Working with a committee
to develop an American Indian studies program at
Wayne State University. *Memberships*: Society for the
Study of Native American Religious Traditions; American Academy of Religion; American Anthropological
Association; American Society for Ethnohistory. *Published works*: Rural Criminal Justice: Conditions, Con-
straints and Challenges, with T. MacDonald & R. Wood
(Sheffield Publishing Co., 1996); Civilization of the
American Indian Series (University of Oklahoma Press,
1997).

PHELAN, BERTHA
(centre director)
Affiliation: United Native Friendship Centre, 2902 - 29th
Ave., Vernon, B.C., Canada V1T 5E6 (604) 542-1247.

PHELPS, REBECCA BERMAN
(attorney)
Education: Brandeis University, BA, 1989; University
of Colorado School of Law, JD, 1992. *Principal occupation*: Attorney. *Address & Affiliation*: Albietz Law
Corporation, 2001 N St. #100, Sacramento, CA 95814-
4222 (916) 442-4241 Fax 444-5494. Ms. Phelps practices in American Indian law and civil rights, among
other areas.

PHELPS, RICHARD
(executive director)
Affiliation: The Falmouth Institute, Inc., 3702 Pender
Dr. #300, Fairfax, VA 22030 (703) 352-2250 Fax 352-
2323.

PHILBRICK, DOUGLAS R.
(school principal)
Affiliation: Keams Canyon Boarding School, P.O.
Box 397, Keams Canyon, AZ 86034 (520) 738-2385.

PHILBROOK, MARY (Micmac)
(tribal president)
Affiliation: Aroostook Band of Micmac Indians, P.O.
Box 772, Presque Island, ME 04769 (207) 764-1972.

PHILEMONOF, DEMITRI
(executive director)
Affiliation: Aleutian Islands Association, 401 E. Fireweed Lane, Suite 201, Anchorage, AK 99503 (907) 276-2700.

PHILIPS, JIM
(Indian school principal)
Affiliation: Sho'Ban School District #512, P.O. Box 790, Fort Hall, ID 83203 (208) 238-4300 Fax 238-2629. E-mail: jphilips@shoban.com

PHILLIPS, MABEL ANN
(organization chairperson)
Affiliation: Dakota Women of All Red Nations, P.O. Box 69, Fort Yates, ND 58538 (701) 854-7592.

PHILLIPS, MELVINA PRITCHETT
(Echota Cherokee) 1948-
(literacy practitioner)
Born September 1, 1948, New Hope, Ala. *Education*: University of Montevallo (AL), BS, 1970; Alabama A&M University (Huntsville), MEd., 1976; UAB/VA, Ed.D. *Principal occupation*: Resource specialist; educator. *Home address*: 2279 Oak Grove Rd., New Hope, AL 35760 (256) 723-2256 Fax 723-2464. E-mail: phillipsm@principals.org. Website: www.principals.org. *Affiliations*: Madison County Board of Education, Huntsville, AL (teacher/principal, 1982-2003; Indian education, Title IX coordinator, 1989-2003; Literacy Practitioner, NASSP, Reston, VA. *Other professional post*: Board member, North Alabama Education Credit Union; Board member, FEMA (distribute funds to organizations that work with needy individuals). *Community activities*: Burritt Museum; Early Works Children's Museum; Education Committee, Huntsville Botanical Gardens. *Memberships*: Alabama Indian Education Association (secretary); National Indian Education Association; Alabama Environmental Education Association; Tennessee Valley Genealogical Association. *Awards, honors*: Madison County Title IV/IX Projects recognized as Exemplary Projects by USDOE, was selected as Showcase Project by the U.S. Dept of Education in 1987 & 1993; Outstanding Governor's Awards (two); Exemplary School Recognition; delegate to the White House Conference on Indian Education; education consultant to the Smithsonian's new Museum of the American Indian; Certificate of Recognition from Gov. Guy Hunt and the Alabama Environmental Education Association for Best Environmental Education Curriculum Guide for 1991. *Interests*: "Literacy, native American education, and historical preservation of historical sites, environmental issues. Established two science camps for minority students. Involved with environmental concerns and organizations; serves as consultant to various local museums; consultant and demonstrator at Burritt Museum's Annual Indian Festival and Russell Cave National Monument's Indian Day Historian; favorite pastimes are reading and art." *Published works*: Several journal articles.

PHILLIPS, NATHAN (Omaha)
(executive director)
Affiliation: Native Youth Alliance, 1711 Kenyon St., NW, Washington, DC 20010 (202) 328-9060.

PHILLIPS, NEIL
(Indian band chief)
Affiliation: Douglas Indian Band, Box 339, Harrison Hot Springs, BC, Canada V0M 1K0 (604) 820-3082.

PHILLIPS, PAM 1947-
(retail gallery owner)
Born December 4, 1947, Chicago, Ill. *Education*: Indiana University, R.N., 1968. *Principal occupation*: Retail gallery owner. *Home address*: 103 E. 173rd Ave., Lowell, IN 46342 (219) 942-9022. *Affiliation*: Owner, Skystone N'Silver, Hobart, IN, 1979-. *Community activities*: Southlake Mental Health Center (past president & board of directors, 1989-); "I organize an annual Indian Arts Expo featuring Native American artists, working demonstrations, and a live auction to raise money for the Council for Indigenous Arts & Culture. *Other professional post*: Board of Directors, Indian Arts Foundation, Albuquerque, NM, 1992-. *Memberships*: Gallup InterTribal Indian Ceremonial Association; Indian Arts & Crafts Association (past president); Council for Indigenous Arts & Culture (treasurer, 1998-

present); Indian Art Foundation. *Award*: Best in Category, Inlay Jewelry Award, Gallup InterTribal Indian Ceremony Association. *Interests*: Photography, writing, collecting Native American arts. "Travel six times a year throughout the West and Southwest buying from reservation artists for the gallery; provide educational programs to schools and Indiana University; Northwest Native American culture & arts. I am a silver and gold smith and also do lapidary & jewelry design. I enjoy doing lectures, radio interviews, TV interviews about Native American culture & arts. (My gallery) Skystone N'Silver is committed to selling only Native American handmade art; rugs, pottery, jewelry, kachinas, baskets, quillboxes and many items too numerous to list. *Published works*: authored the Jewelry section of the book "Collecting Authentic Indian Arts & Crafts (Book Publishing Co., 1999); currently writing a book on Pueblo artists to be completed and published by Book Publishing Co. in 2002.

PHILLIPS, ROBIN (Pomo)
(former chairperson)
Affiliation: Sherwood Valley Rancheria, 190 Sherwood Hill Dr., Willits, CA 95490 (707) 459-9690.

PHILLIPS, WILLIAM (Micmac)
(tribal chief)
Affiliation: Aroostook Band of Micmac Indians, P.O. Box 772, Presque Island, ME 04769 (207) 764-1972.

PHILP, KENNETH R. 1941-
(professor of history)
Born December 6, 1941, Pontiac, Mich. *Education*: Michigan State University, BA, 1963, PhD, 1968; University of Michigan, MA, 1964. *Principal occupation*: Professor of History, University of Texas, Arlington, 1968-. *Home address*: 2801 Greenbrook, Arlington, TX 76016 (817) 451-8315; 273-2864 (work). *Memberships*: American Historical Association; Western History Association; Organization of American Historians. *Awards, honors*: Oscar Winther Award for the best article in the 1988 volume of the Western Historical Quarterly. *Interests*: American Indian history; federal Indian policy. *Published works*: Co-editor, Essays on Walter Prescott Webb (University of Texas Press, 1976); John Collier's Crusade for Indian Reform (University of Arizona Press, 1977); editor, Indian Self-Rule: From Roosevelt to Reagan (Howe Brothers, 1986); Termination Revisited: American Indians On the Trail to Self-Determination (University of Nebraska Press, 1999).

PICKERING, GWEN
(health director)
Affiliation: White Eagle PHS Indian Health Center, P.O. Box 2071, Ponca City, OK 74601 (405) 765-2501.

PICKETT, EVELYN
(BIA-public information officer)
Affiliation: Office of Tribal Services, Bureau of Indian Affairs, Dept. of the Interior, MS-2620-MIB, 1849 C St., NW, Washington, DC 20240 (202) 208-3710.

PICO, ANTHONY (Diegueno)
(tribal chairperson)
Affiliation: Viejas Tribal Council, P.O. Box 908, Alpine, CA 91903 (619) 445-3810.

PICOTEE, WILLIAM H.
(health center director)
Affiliation: Yakima PHS Indian Health Center, 401 Buster Rd., Toppenish, WA 98948 (509) 865-2102.

PICOU, GERALD
(Indian education program director)
Affiliation: Terrebonne Parish School District, Indian Education Program, 301 Academy St., Houma, LA 70360 (504) 851-1553 Fax 868-6278.

PICTOU, ROGER (Micmac)
(former tribal president)
Affiliation: Aroostook Band of Micmac Indians, P.O. Box 772, Presque Island, ME 04769 (207) 764-1972.

PIERCE, GEORGE EARL (Meherrin)
(tribal chief)
Affiliation: Meherrin Indian Tribe, P.O. Box 508, Winton, NC 27986 (919) 358-4375.

PIERCE, LARRY
(school principal)
Affiliation: Wa He Lut School, 11110 Conine Ave., SE, Olympia, WA 98503 (206) 456-1311.

PIERCING EYES, CHIEF
(executive director)
Affiliation: Pan-American Indian Association, P.O. Box 244, Nocatee, FL 33864 (813) 494-6930.

PIERRE, ED
(Indian band chief)
Affiliation: Katzie Indian Band, 10946 Katzie Rd., Pitt Meadows, British Columbia, Canada V3Y 1Z3 (604) 465-8961.

PIETACHO, PHILIPPE
(Indian band chief)
Affiliation: Montagnais de Mingan Indian Band, Box 319, Mingan, PQ, Canada G0G 1V0 (418) 949-2234.

PIGEON, BERNICE MILLER (Stockbridge-Munsee)
(library/museum director)
Affiliation: Stockbridge-Munsee Historical Library and Museum, Route 1, Box 300, Bowler, WI 54416 (715) 793-4270.

PIGSLEY, DELORES (Siletz)
(tribal chairperson)
Affiliation: Siletz Tribal Council, P.O. Box 549, Siletz, OR 97380 (541) 444-2532.

PIKE, KEITH R. (Pomo)
(rancheria chairperson)
Affiliation: Guidiville Rancheria, Box 339, Talmadge, CA 95481 (707) 462-3682.

PIKE, STEWART
(former tribal chairperson)
Affiliation: Uintah & Ouray Tribal Business Council, P.O. Box 190, Fort Duchesne, UT 84026 (801) 722-2406.

PINO, LEO L. (Navajo)
(tribal president)
Affiliation: Ramah Navajo Chapter Council, Rt. 2, Box 13, Ramah, NM87321 (505) 775-7130.

PINO, STANLEY (Zia Pueblo)
(former pueblo governor)
Affiliation: Zia Pueblo Tribal Council, 135 Capitol Sq. Dr., Zia Pueblo, NM 87053 (505) 867-3304.

PINOLA, LESTER (Kashia Pomo)
(rancheria chairperson)
Affiliation: Kashia Business Committee, 1420 Guerneville Rd., Suite 3, Santa Rosa, CA 95403 (707) 591-0580.

PINTO, JOHN (Pueblo)
(chairperson)
Affiliation: New Mexico Senate Standing Committee on Indian Affairs, State Capitol, Santa Fe, NM 87503 (505) 986-4314.

PINTO, JUDY (Laguna Pueblo) 1953-
(substance abuse counselor)
Born June 6, 1953, Springs, Colo. *Education*: GED, Grants Branch College, 1979. *Principal occupation*: Substance abuse counselor. *Address*: Southwest Indian Polytechnic Institute, Albuquerque, NM (505) 766-8418. *Affiliations*: Counselor, Santa Clara Rehabilitation Center, Santa Clara Pueblo, NM, 1980-84; counselor, 1984-88; supervisor, 1987-88; substance abuse counselor, Southwest Indian Polytechnic Institute, Albuquerque, NM, 1989-. *Membership*: New Mexico Alcohol and Drug Counseling Association.

PINTO, TONY J. (Diegueno)
(tribal chairperson)
Affiliation: Cuyapaipe General Council, P.O. Box 2250, Alpine, CA 91901 (619) 455-6315.

PIPE, ROBERT W.
(health center director)
Affiliation: Peach Springs PHS Indian Health Center, P.O. Box 190, Peach Springs, AZ 86434 (520) 769-2204.

PIPER, AURELIUS H. PIPER, SR. *(Chief Big Eagle)*
(Golden Hill Paugussett)
  (tribal chief)
Born August 31, 1916, Bridgeport, Conn. *Principal occupation*: Owner/operator of trucking company. *Home address*: 427 Shelton Rd., Golden Hill Indian Reservation, Trumbull, CT 06411 (203) 377-4410. *Affiliation*: Chief of Golden Hill Band of Paugussett Indians, Golden Hill Indian Reservation, Trumbull, CT. *Community activities*: Founder of the Spiritual Circle in Connecticut State prisons. *Military service*: U.S. Navy, 1942-45. *Awards, honors*: Member of Indian Affairs Council, State of Connecticut; founder/president of the White Buffalo Society. *Interests*: Eastern tribes. *Published works*: Quarter Acre of Heartache, by Claude C. Smith (Pocahontas Press, 1985); Chief Big Eagle... Red Man in Red Square, by Claude C. Smith (Pocahontas Press, 1994).

PIPER, AURELIUS H., JR. *(Chief Quiet Hawk)*
(Golden Hill Paugussett)
  (tribal council chief)
Affiliation: Golden Hill Indian Reservation, 95 Stanavage Rd., Trumbull, CT 06611 (203) 377-4410.

PIPER, KENNETH *(Moonface Bear)*
(Golden Hill Paugussett) 1960-
  (warchief)
Born September 9, 1960, Bridgeport, Conn. *Principal occupation*: Warchief of the Golden Hill Paugussetts. *Address*: Golden Hill Reservation, Trumbull, CT 06415 (203) 537-0390. *Community activities*: American Indians for Development (ex-Board member); Connecticut Indian Task Force of the Legislature Sovereignty Committee; Native American Heritage Advisory Council on Reburrials. *Membership*: Connecticut Indian Affairs Council.

PITKA, ARLENE
  (village chief)
Affiliation: Beaver Village, P.O. Box 24029, Beaver, AK 99724 (907) 628-6126.

PITMAN, WILLARD (Creek) 1927-
  (Indian Supreme Court Justice)
Born June 17, 1927, Stidham, Okla. *Education*: Muskogee (OK) Jr. College (2 years). *Principal occupation*: Indian Supreme Court Justice. *Home address*: 2209 Nebraska St., Muskogee, OK 74403 (918) 682-1975. *Affiliations*: Credit sales manager, Sears, Roebuck & Co., Chicago, IL (30 years-retired); Finance Dept., Veterans Administration Regional Office, Muskogee, OK, 1986-; Supreme Court Justice, Muscogee Creek Nation, Muskogee, OK, 1984-. *Military service*: U.S. Marine Corps, 1945-46. *Community activities*: President & vice-president, Muscogee Indian Community, Muskogee, OK.

PITTSLEY, RICH
  (museum director)
Affiliation: Chief Plenty Coups State Park & Museum, P.O. Box 100, Pryor, MT 59066 (406) 252-1287.

PLAINFEATHER, MARDELL HOGAN
(Baahin'naaje) (Crow) 1945-
  (park ranger, Plains Indian historian)
Born September 28, 1945, Billings, Mont. *Education*: Maricopa County Junior College, 1967-68; Rocky Mountain College, BA, 1979. *Principal occupation*: Park Ranger, Plains Indian historian. *Affiliation*: Plains Indian historian, Little Bighorn National Monument, P.O. Box 38, Crow Agency, MT 59022 (406) 638-2621, 1980-. *Other professional post*: Part-time instructor (U.S. History & Montana State History): Crow Tribal Junior College, Little Big Horn College, Crow Agency, MT. *Community activities*: Fort Phil Kearny/Bozeman Trail History Association (board member); Crow Tribal Archives (board member). *Memberships*: Custer Battlefield Historical & Museum Association; Jailhouse Gallery; Big Horn County Historical Association; Montana State Oral History Association; Montana Committee for the Humanities (speaker's bureau); Yellowstone County History Association (honorary member); Yellowstone Coral of Westerners. *Awards, honors*: History Department Award, Rocky Mountain College, 1979; prize for Performance Achievement, Custer Battlefield National Monument, 1982; award from St. Augustine Preservation of Indian Culture, Chicago, IL in 1987. *Interests*: "My interest is in the

cultural history of the Plains Indians, specifically from prehistory to 1880's. I enjoy visiting battlefields and making sure that the history is told correctly from the Indian viewpoint. I am also interested in exhibits in museums and their labelling. I am interested in oral history and the preservation of all sacred sites of Native peoples." *Biographical sources*: Mentioned in Dec.,1986 National Geographic article; interviewed by KUED, Salt Lake City in a documentary "Dreams Along the Little Big Horn" by Ed Nelson. *Published works*: A Personal Look at Curly After the Little Big Horn (Custer Battlefield Historical & Museum Association, in The Greasy Grass, annual publication, 1987); The Apsaalooke: Warriors of the Big Horns (Fort Phil Kearny/Bozeman Trail History Association, 1989).

PLATERIO, DAVID LOUIS *(Tosa-Wi-e)*
(Shoshone) 1960-
  (Native American consultant)
Born January 24, 1960, Elko, Nev. *Principal occupation*: Native American consultant. *Home address*: P.O. Box 822, Elko, NV 89803 (702) 738-3618 (work). *Affiliations*: Native American Consultant, Shoshone Information Network, Elko, NV, 1992-; political consultant for the European Parliament, 1992-; *Other professional posts*: Historian, Native American Consultant, Western Shoshoni National Council, Elko, NV. *Community activities*: Founding member, Western Shsohone Historic Preservation Society; board member, Citizen's Alert (environmental watchdog for Nevada); member, Cultural Commission of Northern Nevada; member, Alliance of Native Americans; citizen/lobbyist training from Military Production Network; registered researcher, National Archives & Library of Congress. *Memberships*: National Environmental Coalition of Native Americans; member of the Congress of the Global Anti-Nuclear Alliance (International); Rural Alliance for Military Accountability (SkyGuard); The International Declaration & Inquiry Commission. *Awards, honors*: Received diploma on completion of training in reading of nuclear waste documents from the "Institute for Energy & Environmental Research." *Interests*: "I take a real hard stand on cultural protection, burial grounds, culturally significant sites, battlegrounds, white chart quarries (Tosa-Wi) across our aboriginal territory. I'm also an alternate for the Western Shoshone National Council, which I speak on behalf of Western Shoshones. I'm currently in the process of (working on) a chronology of events concerning the Western Shoshoni - fur trapper, expeditions, explorations, wars & depredations, conditions, placement of names on a map, etc. (I was) a featured speaker at the 1991 Indian Survival Summit held at California State University, Los Angeles; speaker at 9th annual European Meeting of Indian Support Group in Trondheim, Norway, July, 1993; speaker at the National Lawyers Committee on Civil Rights Under Law, March, 1993; among other events.

PLUMAGE, CHARLES J.
  (hospital director)
Affiliation: Fort Belknap PHS Indian Hospital, Harlem, MT 59526 (406) 353-2651.

PLUMMER, LA NITA
  (legal services)
Affiliation: Four Rivers Indian Legal Services, P.O. Box 68, Sacaton, AZ 85247 (520) 263-8094.

POCHOP, VIRGIL
  (BIA agency supt.)
Affiliation: Office of Facilities Management, Bureau of Indian Affairs, P.O. Box 1248, 500 Gold Ave., SW, 8th Floor, Albuquerque, NM 87103 (505) 766-2825.

POE, WILLIAM (Navajo)
  (school principal)
Affiliation: Ojo Encino Day School, HCR 79, Box 7, Cuba, NM 87013 (505) 731-2333 Fax 731-2361.

POFF, WILLIAM
  (health director)
Affiliation: San Diego American Indian Helth, 2561 First Ave., San Diego, CA 92103 (619) 234-2158.

POKER, PROTE
  (Indian band chief)
Affiliation: First Nation Council of Davis Ilet, Davis Inlet, Labrador, NF, Canada A0P 1A0 (709) 478-8827.

POLACCA, SYLVIA (Tewa)
  (Indian program facilitator)
Affiliation: Program Facilitator for Community Development, American Indian Studies Program, The University of Arizona, Harvill Bldg., Rm 430, P.O. Box 210076, Tucson, AZ 85721 (520) 621-7108 Fax 621-7952. E-mail: aisp@email.arizona.edu.

POLANCO, MARY F.
  (editor)
Affiliation: Jicarilla Chieftain, Jicarilla Apache Tribe, P.O. Box 507, Dulce, NM 87528-0507 (505) 759-3242.

POLCHIES, RICHARD
  (Indian band chief)
Affiliation: St. Mary's Indian Band, 247 Paul St., Fredericton, New Brunswick, Canada E3A 2V7 (506) 458-9511.

POLESE, RICHARD 1941-
  (editor)
Born November 16, 1941, Berkeley, Calif. *Education*: San Jose State College, 1959-61; Hanover College (IN), BA, 1962. *Principal occupation*: Editor. *Home address*: P.O. Box 1295, Santa Fe, NM 87501. *Affiliations*: Editor, El Palacio, Southwestern Quarterly; book editor, Museum of New Mexico Press, 1969-. *Other professional posts*: Columnist for the Santa Fe Reporter. *Awards, honors*: Edited and designed the award-winning book, Music and Dance of the Tewa Pueblos, by Dr. Gertrude Kurath. *Interests*: Mr. Polese has written and edited publications on the Southwest and its people since 1962. These include several articles in El Palacio magazine, and editing and designing of several books and is recognized as an authority on the New Mexico Zia sun symbols, its origins and variations. *Published works*: Original New Mexico Cookery, 1965; editor, Pueblo Pottery of New Mexico Indians, 1977; editor, Music and Dance of the Tewa Pueblos, 1969; editor, In Search of Maya Glyphs, 1970; editor, Navajo Weaving Handbook, 1977. All published by Museum of New Mexico Press.

POLLAK, GENEVIEVE (Ponca)
  (former tribal chairperson)
Affiliation: Ponca Business Committee, P.O. Box 2, White Eagle, Ponca City, OK 74601 (405) 762-8104.

POLLARD, DENISE (Paiute)
  (tribal council chairperson)
Affiliation: Fort Bidwell Community Council, P.O. Box 129, Fort Bidwell, CA 96112 (530) 279-6310.

POLSON, JERRY
  (Indian band chief)
Affiliation: Long Point (Algonquin) Indian Band, Box 1, Winneway River, Quebec J0Z 2J0 (819) 722-2441.

PONCHO, LOVELIN (Coushatta)
  (tribal chairperson)
Affiliation: Coushatta Tribal Council, P.O. Box 818, Elton, LA 70523 (337) 584-2261.

PONCHO, ROLAND (Alabama-Coushatta of Texas)
  (tribal enterprise manager)
Affiliation: Alabama-Coushatta Tribal Enterprise, Rt. 3, Box 640, Livingston, TX 77351 (800) 392-4794; (409) 563-4391. *Past professional post*: Former tribal chairperson, Alabama-Coushatta Tribe, Livingston, TX.

POND, RONALD JAMES *(Itxutwin)*
(Umatilla, Palouse) 1939-
  (cultural consultant)
Born December 6, 1939, McKay Creek, Oreg. *Education*: Blue Mountain Community College, Pendleton, OR, 1966-67; Eastern Oregon State College, BA, 1974; Oregon State University, Teaching Certificate, 1977, MA, 1992. *Principal occupation*: Cultural consultant. *Home address*: Route 3, Box 110, Pendleton, OR 97801. *Affiliation*: Teacher, School District 16-R, Pendleton, OR, 1977-79; elected leader/education director, Umatilla Tribe, Mission, OR, 1981; archaeology technician/assistant., U.S. Forest Service, Pendleton, 1985-; co-curator, "Plateau Exhibit," Washington State University, Pullman, WA. *Other professional posts*: Firefighter, U.S. Forest Service, 1963-69; general council chairperson, governing body member, 1979-80, education director, 1981, Umatilla Confederated Tribes, Pendleton, OR; research consultant,

elder/oral traditions. *Community activities*: Umatilla Tribe Cultural Committee, 1968-; Blue Mountain Equestrian Trail Ride, 1992-93. *Awards, honors*: Best All Around Indian Dancer/Indian Festival of Arts, LaGrange, OR, 1970; Smoke Jumper: Silver Wings, 1966; Seven Drums Religion, 1974-94; Annual Spring "First Food Feast": Singer, Lead Hunter, Lead Server; coordinator: 1976 Bi-Centennial Exposition, Umatilla cultural group to Washington, DC. *Biographical source*: Local paper, "East Oregonian," covers cultural activities on the Umatilla Reservation.

PONDER, ROBERT EARL *(Silver Badger)*
(Sioux/Cherokee/Choctaw) 1944-
(executive director/principal chief)
Born September 18, 1944, Carnegie, Okla. *Education*: North American Trade School, Newport Beach, CA, 1978-81. *Principal occupation*: Executive director, principal chief, Northwest Cherokee Wolf Band, Talent, OR, 1980-. *Address*: Unknown. *Other professional posts*: Oregon Economic Development Program (Native American Representative & board member). *Military service*: U.S. Navy, 1960-62 (Seaman Apprentice). *Community activities*: Jackson County Consortium Member, Southern Oregon/Rogue Valley Area. *Awards, honors*: Certificate of Appreciation from the Indian Education Title IV Program for eight years of dedicated service in Jackson County as a District Representative to the Oregon Indian Education Association. *Interests*: Gunsmithing; police science; Native American drumming.

POOLAW, LINDA S. *(Lees-seet-teen)*
(Delaware-Kiowa) 1942-
(health research)
Born April 8, 1942, Lawton, Okla. *Education*: University of Sciences and Arts of Oklahoma, BA, 1974; University of Oklahoma, Masters work in Communications (2 years). *Principal occupation*: Tribal cultural consultant, Delaware Tribe of Western Oklahoma, Anadarko, OK. *Home address*: P.O. Box 986, Anadarko, OK 73005 (405) 247-7059. *Other professional post*: Playwrite. *Community activities*: Salvation Army, Caddo County (chairperson); Delaware Tribe of Western Oklahoma (treasurer); Riverside Indian School Board (vice president); American Indian Exposition (vice president). *Memberships*: Indian and Western Arts Association (vice president). *Interests*: "Writing fiction and history about American Indians. (I) have traveled coast to coast to develop relationships with tribes. In 1986, I plan to research and write a book on my deceased father's work in photography, 50 Years of Life on the Southern Plains, (Horace Poolaw)." *Plays*: "Skins", 1974; "Happiness Is Being Married to a White Woman", and "Written, Spoken and Unspoken Word" (University of Oklahoma Press, 1982); "The Day the Tree Fell", children's play (American Indian Institute, Norman, Okla., 1983).

POOLHECO, WALTER L. (Southern Ute)
(health director)
Affiliation: Southern Colorado Ute Health Center, P.O. Box 778, Ignacio, CO 81137 (303) 563-9443.

POORMAN, RICHARD
(Indian band chief)
Affiliation: Kawacatoose Indian Band, Box 10, Quinton, Saskatchewan, Canada S0A 3G0 (306) 835-2125.

POPE, JERRY L. (Shawnee) 1941-
(artist)
Born April 26, 1941, Greenfield, Ind. *Education*: John Heron School of Art; Indiana University, B.F.A., 1964. *Principal occupation*: Artist. *Affiliations*: Curator, American Indian People's Museum, Indianapolis, IN; editor, Tosan, American Indian People's News, Indianapolis, IN; principal chief, United Remnant Band, Shawnee nation of Indiana, Ohio, Kentucky and Pennsylvania; director, Three Feather Society (Native-professional-social organization). *Other professional post*: Assisted in the compilation of Smithsonian Institution's list of native publications. *Memberships*: League of Nations, Pan-American Indians; National Association of Metis Indians; Three Feather Society (director); Mide Widjig, Grand Medicine Lodge Brotherhood, Albuquerque, NM. *Awards, honors*: First Prize, national Exhibition of Small Paintings; selected to preside over and organize dedication of world's largest collection of Cuna Indian art, Dennison University, Granville, OH, 1972;

among others. *Interests*: Mr. Pope writes, "1. Professional Native artist, by vocation; 2. editing and publishing of the Inter-Tribal Native publication, Tosan; 3. rebuilding the United Remnant Band of the Shawnee Nation, beginning in 1970 with seven persons; we now have re-established all twelve clans; 4. re-education of my people in traditional ways, instilling due pride in knowledge of their birthright; 5. work with in-prison Native groups." *Published work*: Native Publications in the United States & Canada (Smithsonian Institution, 1972).

PORTER, FRANK W., III
(institute director)
Affiliation: American Indian Research and Resource Institute, Gettysburg College, P.O. Box 576, Gettysburg, PA 17325 (717) 337-6265.

PORTRA, TERRY
(BIA education administrator)
Affiliation: Minneapolis Area Office, Bureau of Indian Affairs, 331 S. Second Ave., Minneapolis, MN 55401 (612) 373-1000 Fax 373-1065.

PORVAZNIK, JOHN, M.D.
(associate director-IHS)
Affiliation: Indian Health Service, Parklawn Bldg., 5600 Fishers Lane, Rockville, MD 20857 (301) 443-1083.

POSEY, IVAN (Shoshone)
(tribal chairperson)
Affiliation: Wind River Shoshone Tribal Business Council, P.O. Box217, Fort Washakie, WY 82514 (307) 332-3532.

POTTS, DONNA MARIE (Mewuk)
(rancheria spokesperson)
Affiliation: Buena Vista Rancheria, 4650 Coalmine Rd., Ione, CA 95640 (209) 274-6512.

POUIER, TERRY
(hospital director)
Affiliation: Fort Yates PHS Indian Hospital, P.O. Box J, Fort Yates, ND 58538 (701) 854-3831.

POWELL, MALEA (Indiana Miami/
Eastern Shawnee) 1962-
(associate professor)
Born December 7, 1962, Kokomo, Ind. *Education*: Indiana University, BA, 1992; Miami University, MA, 1994; PhD, 1998. *Principal occupation*: Associate Professor of American Thought & Language. *Address*: American Thought & Language, Michigan State University, 273 Bessey Hall, East Lansing, MI 48824-1033 (517) 432-2577 Fax 353-5250. E-mail: powell37@msu. edu; sail2@msu.edu. *Affiliations*: Miami University (Ohio), 1992-98; University of Nebraska, 1998-2002; Michigan State University, 2002-present. *Other professional post*: Editor, Studies in American Indian Literatures. *Community activities*: Member, Board of Directors, Center for the Study of Great Lakes Native American Culture. *Memberships*: American Association of University Professors, American Association of University Women, American Literature Association, American Studies Association, Association for American Indian & Alaskan Native Professors, Association for Studies in American Indian Literatures, Coalition of Women Scholars in the History of Rhetoric, International Society for the History of Rhetoric, MLA Division on American Indian Literatures, National Association for Native American Studies, National Indian Education Association, Wordcraft Circle of Native Writers, Native Writers Circle of the Americas, et al. *Grants & Awards*: Recipient, National Council for Teachers of English Scholars for the Dream Award Recipient, 1994; Certificate of Recognition for Contributions to Students, The Parents' Association and the Teaching Council of the University of Nebraska, January 2000; Recipient, University of Nebraska Research Council Grant-in-Aid, January 2001; Nominee, University of Nebraska College of Arts & Sciences Distinguished Teaching Award, 2001-2002; Wordcraft Circle Writer's Award (Scholarly Editing), 2002. *Interests*: American Indian rhetoric and literature. *Articles Published*: "Imagining a New Indian: Listening to the Rhetoric of Survivance in Charles Eastman's From the Deep Woods to Civilization." (Paradoxa, August 2001); "Rhetoric of Survivance: How American Indians Use Writing." (College Composition and Communication 53.3 February 2002;

"Real Indians," (Native Realities 3:2 Spring, 2003); "Extending the Hand of Empire: Women and Indians in the Indian Reform Movement, a Beginning," (American Ethnic Rhetorics, march 2003); Princess Sarah, the Civilized Indian: The Rhetoric of Cultural Literacies in Sarah Minnemucca-Hopkins' Life Among th4e paiutes," in book, Rhetorical "Woman:" Fragmented Traces, Roles, Representations, edited by Bridwell-Bowles & Miller (University of Alabama Press, 2004); "Dear Simon, A Response to Simon Ortiz," in Writing Environments: Rhetoric, Texts, and the Construction of Nature, by Dobrin & Keller (SUNY Press, 2005). *Projects in Process*: Editor, Of Color: Native American Literature, an anthology with a rhetoric apparatus, under contract with Prentice Hall; critical book project in progress.

POWER, SUSAN (Standing Rock Sioux)
(writer)
Address: c/o G.P. Putnam's Sons, 200 Madison Ave, New York, NY 10016. *Published work*: The Grass Dancer.

POWERS, MARLA N. 1938-
(anthropologist)
Born January 8, 1938, Cranston, R.I. *Education*: Brooklyn College, C.U.N.Y., BA, 1973; Rutgers University, MA, 1979, PhD (Anthropology; dissertation: Oglala Women in Myth, Ritual, and Reality), 1982. *Principal occupation*: Anthropologist. *Home address*: 74 Stillwell Rd., Kendall Park, NJ 08824. *Affiliation*: Visiting research associate, Institute for Research on Women, Rutgers University, New Brunswick, N.J., 1983-. *Other professional posts*: Associate editor, Powwow Trails: American Indians, Past and Present, Somerset, NJ, 1964-66; consultant, Title IV Bilingual Health Program, Pine Ridge Indian Reservation, Summer, 1976; consultant, Psychiatric Nursing Program, University of South Dakota and USPHS satellite program, Oglala Sioux Community, Pine Ridge Reservation, Summer, 1976; consultant, Lakota Culture Camp (program evaluation for Dept. of Special Education, State of SD), Pine Ridge Indian Reservation, Summer, 1980; member of thesis committee in Psychiatric Nursing, Rutgers University—thesis title: An Exploratory Study of Mentoring Relationships Among Indian Women in the Profession of Nursing, 1982; also thesis committee in anthropology—Ph.D. thesis entitled: Comanche Belief and Ritual, 1985. *Memberships*: American Anthropological Association; Society for Medical Anthropology; Society for Visual Anthropology; American Folklore Society; American Ethnological Society; Philadelphia Anthropological Society; Society for Ethnomusicology; Nebraska State Historical Society; American Dance Therapist Association; American Craftsman's Council; Actor's Equity; American Federation of Television and Radio Artists. *Fieldwork*: Pine Ridge, South Dakota, Oglala (Sioux), also various tribes of New Mexico, Arizona, Oklahoma and Wyoming; urban U.S. "I have done extensive anthropological research among the Oglala Lakota on the Pine Ridge Indian Reservation in South Dakota. A major part of the research focused on Native subsistence, food procurement, preparation, storage, distribution, and nutrition. I also studied Native therapeutic techniques, particularly treatment of psychosomatic disorders." *Awards, honors*: Wenner-Gren Foundation Grant-in-aid, Summer, 1980 (field research on the relationship of Oglala traditional women's roles to social structure); National Endowment for the Humanities, Research Assistant on Oglala Music and Dance, Sept. 1980 - Aug. 1982, Jan. 1983 - Dec. 1983; Douglass Fellows Grant for Research on photographs of American Indian women, Spring, 1983 & 1984; National Endowment for the Humanities, Planning Grant: principal investigator, Lakota Women: A Photographic Retrospective, Jan. 1985 - Dec. 1985; Minnesota Historical Society, grant for field research on Lakota medicine, Summer, 1985. *Interests*: "American Indians, particularly Northern Plains, urban U.S.; intercultural health care systems; anthropology of gender, medicine, art, and dance. Dance: have appeared in numerous Broadway and off-Broadway shows; on major network television shows; taught dance. American Indian art: have studied traditional crafts among the Sioux and Comanches and am proficient in various techniques of American Indian beadwork, quillwork, and ribbonwork." Papers presented: Images of American Indian Women: Myth and Reality, Rome, Italy, 1984, tour in West Germany-1985;

Symbols in Contemporary Oglala Art, Vienna, Austria; Workshop on American Indian Music and Dance (with William K. Powers), Budapest, Hungary, 1985; Stereotyping American Indians, Cologne, West Germany, 1985; Native American Motherhood: A View From the Plains, Rutgers University, 1985; among others. *Published works*: Co-editor, Lakota Wicozanni-Ehank'ehan na Lehanl (Lakota Health Traditional and Modern), three volumes plus teacher's guide (Oglala Sioux Community College, 1977); Metaphysical Aspects of an Oglala Food System, in Food and the Social Order (Russell Sage Foundation, 1984); Oglala Women: Myth, Ritual, and Reality (University of Chicago Press, 1986); Putting on the Dog: Ceremoniousness in an Oglala Stew, with William K. Powers, in Natural History (American Museum of Natural History-in press); Lakota Foods, with William K. Powers (in preparation); Lakota Medicine (Minnesota Historical Society Press-in preparation).

POWERS, W. ROGERS
(professor, dept. head)
Affiliation: Dept. of Alaskan native Studies, University of Alaska, Dept. of Anthropology, 310 Eielson Bldg., Fairbanks, AK 99775 (907) 474-7288.

POWERS, WILLIAM K. 1934-
(professor of anthropology, journalist)
Born July 31, 1934, St. Louis, Mo. *Education*: Brooklyn College, BA, 1971; Wesleyan University, MA (Anthropology; thesis: Yuwipi Music in Cultural Context), 1972; University of Pennsylvania, PhD (Anthropology; dissertation: Continuity and Change in Oglala Religion). *Principal occupation*: Professor of anthropology, journalist. *Home address*: 74 Stillwell Rd., Kendall Park, NJ 08824. *Affiliations*: Associate editor, American Indian Tradition, 1960-62; editor and publisher, Powwow Trails, 1964-66; consulting editor, American Indians Then and Now Series (G.P. Putnam's Sons), 1968-; instructor, North American Indian music and dance, Wesleyan University, 1971-72; teaching fellow, 1972-73, lecturer, 1973-77, (North American Indians),University of Pennsylvania; visiting lecturer, assistant professor, Dept. of Anthropology, Rutgers University, New Brunswick, NJ, 1974-. *Fieldwork*: Primarily among the Oglala Sioux, Pine Ridge, South Dakota, 1966-; also various tribes in NM, AZ, OK and WY. Grants and fellowships: Research in American Indian religion, linguistics, and music, American Philosophical Society, 1966, '67, '77; among others. *Awards, honors*: Award of Excellence in Juvenile Literature, NJ State Teachers of English, 1972, '73; Faculty Merit Award, Rutgers University, 1977; among others. *Memberships*: American Anthropological Association; Society for Applied Anthropology; Washington Anthropological Society; Philadelphia Anthropological Society; Society for Ethnomusicology; Indian Rights Association. Interests: "North American Indian studies—historical and contemporary Indian affairs; urban U.S.; social organization; comparative religion; history of anthropology; sociolinguistics; ethnomusicology; culture change." *Published works*: Indian Dancing and Costumes (G.P. Putnam's Sons, 1966); Young Brave (For Children, Inc., 1967); Crazy Horse and Custer (For Children, Inc., 1968); Indians of the Northern Plains (G.P. Putnam's Sons, 1969); The Modern Sioux: Reservation Systems and Social Change (University of Nebraska Press, 1970); Indians of the Southern Plains (G.P. Putnam's Sons, 1971); Continuity and Change in the American Family, with Marla N. Powers (Dept. of HEW); Indians of the Great Lakes (G.P. Putnam's Sons, 1976); co-author, Lakota Wicozani - Ehank'ehan na Lehanl (Indian Health- Traditional and Modern), 1976; Oglala Religion (University of Nebraska Press, 1977); Lakota Foods, with Marla N. Powers (in preparation); numerous papers, articles in scholarly journals, notes, book reviews, abstracts, etc.

POWLESS, DAVID (*Lani Kuhlaha'wis*)
(Oneida) 1943-
(business executive)
Born May 29, 1943, Ottawa, Ill. *Education*: University of Oklahoma, 1961-62; University of Illinois, BS, 1966. *Principal occupation*: Business executive. *Home address*: 161 Sagebrush Dr., Corrales, NM 87048 (505) 897-9445. *Affiliations*: Owner & founder, Oneida Materials Co., Colorado Springs, CO., 1976-85; president & founder, ORTEK (Environmental Laboratory), Oneida Tribe, Green Bay, WI, 1987-92; V.P. Market-

ing-Western Regional, Arctic Slope Regional Corp., 1992- (owned by Inupiat Eskimos); also maintains a business interest in Bear Paw, Inc. which provides insurance benefits to tribes. Bear Paw is a joint venture with Dick Butkis (NFL Hall of Fame and former football team mate). *Memberships*: Oneida Tribe; American Indian Science & Engineering Society (board of directors, 1986-90). *Awards, honors*: University of Illinois Rose Bowl Team, 1963; professional football, NY Giants, 1965, Washington Redskins, 1966; National Science grant in 1977 to research, at the Colorado School of Mines, methods for recycling iron oxide wastes produced by steel mills. This was the first NSF Grant given to an individual Native American; 1981 - SBA Award "National Innovation Advocate of the Year". *Interests*: "Training Indians to be scientists to work in tribally-owned environmental laboratories; mediation training of groups. He is committed to caring for the environment. It is his belief that this commitment is one of the duties the creator has given to all Native Americans. Currently involved with tribal economic development with Arctic Slope Joint Ventures With Tribes."

POWLESS, IRVING, JR. (Oneida)
(tribal chief)
Affiliation: Onondaga Nation Tribal Council, RR 1, Box 319-B, Nedrow, NY 13120 (716) 469-8507.

POWVAL, SAMUEL (Luiseno)
(former tribal chairperson)
Affiliation: Pauma Band of Mission Indians, P.O. Box 86, Pauma Valley, CA 92061 (619) 742-1289.

POYNTER, KEN
(executive director)
Affiliation: Native American Fish & Wildlife Society, 750 Burbank St., Broomfield, CO 80020 (303) 466-1725 Fax 466-5414.

PRATT, MICHAEL E. (*Wat-Si-Mori*) (Osage) 1947-
(professor/administrator)
Born March 3, 1947, Hominy, Okla. *Education*: Utah State University, Logan, BS, 1971, MS, 1977; University of Oklahoma, PhD, 1986. *Principal occupation*: Professor/administrator. *Home address*: 702 N. Katy Ave., Hominy, OK 74035-1028 (918) 287-2587. *Affiliations*: Coach/Instructor, Pratt College, KS; instructor, University of Oklahoma, 1982-. *Community activities*: Arkansas Museum of Natural History & Science (advisor, Indians of Arkansas exhibit). *Awards, honors*: Award from Administration for Native Americans. *Interests*: "White Hair Memorial, Oklahoma Historical Society; developed curriculum for preservation of Osage language, cultural retention courses for Osage people." *Published works*: Stenotyping of the American Indian (Utah State, 1978); Osage Kinship (University of Oklahoma Press, 1986).

PREGO, DAVID
(editor)
Affiliation: "Great Promise Magazine," 1103 Hatteras, Austin, TX 78753 (512) 480-9922. A quarterly journal for and about Native American children.

PRESCOTT, LEONARD (Mdewakanton Sioux)
(casino/bingo hall CEO)
Affiliation: Mystic Lake Casino & Bingo Hall, 2400 Mystic Lake Blvd., Prior Lake, MN 55372 (800) 262-7799.

PRESCOTT, ROGER (Mdewakanton Sioux)
(tribal chairperson)
Affiliation: Lower Sioux Indian Community Council, Rt. 1, Box 308, Morton, MN 56270 (507) 697-6185.

PRESTON, VICTOR (Paiute)
(former rancheria chairperson)
Affiliation: Susanville Indian Rancheria, P.O. Drawer U, Susanville, CA 06130 (530) 257-6264.

PRETTY ON TOP, BURTON, Sr. (*Flirts With Women/ Two Mornings*) (Crow) 1946-
(spiritual leader; public speaker, teacher)
Born September 17, 1946, Crow Agency, Mont. *Education*: Rocky Mt. College (Billings, MT), 1965-67; Eastern Mt. College (Billings, MT), 1969-70. *Principal occupation*: Native American spiritual leader; public speaker, teacher). *Address*: Unknown. *Affiliation*: Crow

Tribal Council Public Relations Director, Crow Agency, MT, 1991-97; *Other professional post*: Spiritual leader for Crow Catholic Parishes, 1991-. *Community activities*: Traveled for 13 years giving talks & presentations on Native spirituality, nationally & internationally; involved with social justice issues, and protection of human rights. *Memberships*: Tekakwitha Conference (board of directors, 1988-93); Thanksgiving Square (Dallas, TX). *Awards, honors*: "I was one of two Native American spiritual leaders selected to represent the Native American traditions from the Western Hemisphere, at the "World Day of Prayer for Peace" held at Assisi, Italy (October, 1986); I was asked to sign a World Thanksgiving Document along with 11 other religious leaders from across the world, in 1987, at Dallas, TX; I was among 100 religious leaders honored at the "Thanksgiving Square" in Dallas (Sept., 1989); I was one of seven Native spiritual leaders asked to attend & give a presentation at the "Parliament of Worlds Religions" gathering in Chicago, IL (Sept./Oct., 1993)." *Interests*: "I am a member of the Whistling Water and Bad War Deed Clans of the Crow Nation. I am a child of the Big Lodge Clan. Among the Crow people today, we are blessed by our Creator "Akbaadaadia" in a way that is very unique; we all speak the Crow language, practice our Native spirituality, customs and traditions. We still follow and respect the 'clan' system." *Biographical sources*: Magazine articles: Theosophical Link, Sept/Dec. 1993, Vol. 5 No. 3; Time Magazine, May 10, 1993; Lily of the Mohawks magazine, Fall/Winter 1993; among others. Newspaper articles: The New York Times - Sunday, Aug. 9, 1992; The Dallas Morning News - Sunday, Oct. 4, 1992; Billings Gazette - Saturday, April 17, 1993; among others.

PRINGLE, ROBERT
(education administrator)
Affiliation: Anchorage Education Field Office, Bureau of Indian Affairs, 3601 C St., Suite 1100, Anchorage, AK 99503 (907) 271-4115 Fax 271-3678.

PRINS, HARALD E.L. 1951-
(professor)
Born September 7, 1951, Alphen a/d Rijn, The Netherlands. *Education*: University of Nijmegen, The Netherlands, 1971-76 (Doctoral-Anthropology/History); New School for Social Research (New York, NY), PhD, 1988. *Principal occupation*: Professor. *Home address*: 3301 Buffalo Rd., Manhattan, KS 66502 (785) 776-3876; 532-6865 (office); E-mail: prins@ksu.edu. *Affiliations*: Tribal Researcher, Aroostook Band of Micmacs, Presque Island, ME, 1981-; Professor of Cultural Anthropology & American Ethnic Studies, Kansas State University, Manhattan, KS, 1990-; Miawpukek First Nation of Mi'kmaqs, Newfoundland, Canada, 1996-; guest curator, National Museum of Natural History, Smithsonian Institution, Washington, DC, 2003-2005; principal investigator, Acadia National Parks Ethnographic Research, national parks Services, 2003-2005. *Other professional post*: Consultant on ethnohistory, ethnographic film, native rights; Visual Anthropology Editor, American Anthropologist, 1998-2002. *Community activities*: Aroostook Micmac Indian Community; Apache Tribe of Oklahoma (Culture Committee); Miawpukek Band of Micmacs, Newfoundland (Land Claims Team); Amnesty International. *Memberships*: American Anthropological Association; American Society for Ethnohistory; Society for Visual Anthropology (board of directors; president, 1999-2001); Society for Latin American Anthropology; Native American Rights Fund; National Museum of the American Indian (charter member); Current Anthropologist (Associate, 2002-). *Awards, honors*: Aroostook Micmac Council Service Award, 1982; Conoco Prize for Outstanding Undergraduate Teaching, 1993; International Observer in Paraguay, 1993; Expert Witness on Tribal Rights, U.S. Congress, 1990; Jury Baxter Aawrd, Maine Historical Society, 1991-; Margaret Mead Award Finalist, 1992 & 1997; Program Chair, Visual Anthropology, 1996; Honorable mention, Society for Visual Anthropology for film, "Wabanaki: A New Dawn, 1996; Vera G. List Fellowship; Criterion Foundation Award; Maine Humanities Council Film Award; Maine Arts Commission Award; National Endowment for the Humanities Award; Columbian Quincentennial Fellowship; Presidential Award for Outstanding Teaching, KSU, 1999; Distinguished Lecturer & Keynote Speaker, 2002-2003; University Chair of Distinguished Teach-

ing Scholars, Kansas State University, 2004-2005. *Interests*: Canadian Maritimes, New England, Great Plains, Argentine Pampas, Paraguayan Chaco, Upper Amazon, Andean Highlands, Patagonia. "As a cultural anthropologist/ethno-historian/filmmaker, I have served the Aroostook Band of Micmacs in their quest for native rights in Maine since 1981. In 1990, I testified as expert witness in U.S. Congress, and November 26, 1991, the Band was officially recognized by the Federal Government and was awarded funding to purchase 5,000 acres of land which will serve as a landbase. The federal recognition was based on ethnographic and historical documentation which I researched and presented as tribal anthropologist for the Micmacs. My documentary film "Our Lives in Our Hands," which aired on public television and featured at numerous national and international film festivals, portrays this Micmac Indian community in northern Maine in their quest for survival." *Biographical sources*: Articles - "Anthropologist Aids Micmacs in Fight for Federal Recognition," in Bangor Daily News, Dec. 21, 1987; "The Micmacs of Maine: A Continuing Struggle," (by B. McBride), in R.G. Carlson, ed., "Rooted Like the Ash Trees: New England Indians and the Land," (Eagle Wing Press, 1987); "Anthropologist Believes Cultures Should Be Helped...," in Kennebec Journal, Sept. 20, 1989; Who's Who Among America's Teachers, 1996; Contemporary Authors (Gale, Vol. 164, 1998); Who's Who in the Midwest (Marquis, 1998); Who's Who in America (Marquis, 2000). *Published works*: "Our Lives in Our Hands," 49 min., color 16mm/video (Documentary Educational Resources, 1985); Tribulations of a Border Tribe (University of Michigan Press, 1989); American Beginnings: Exploration, Culture, and Cartography in the Land of Norumbega, co-edited with E Baker et al. (U of Nebraska Press, 1994); The Mi'kmaq: Resistance, Accommodation, and Cultural Survival (Harcourt Brace, 1996).

PRITCHARD, EVAN (*Abachbahamedtch - chipmunk*) (Micmac)
(professor of Native American history, speaker/lecturer)
Affiliations: Founder, The Center for Algonquin Culture, P.O. Box 1028, Woodstock, NY 12498; Resonance Communications (212) 714-7151; Council Oaks Books (800) 247-8850; E-mail: rezman@ulster.net. Website: www.algonquinculture.org; professor of Native American history, Marist College, Poughkeepsie, NY. *Community activities*: "Native New Yorker" walking tours of lower Manhattan for the Smithsonian Institution, The Open Center, South Street Seaport, and other institutions; shared his findings on Native American life in manhattann on Leonard Lopate's "New York and Company" show, on WBAI/Pacific Radio, ABC news, etc. He was the organizer of the North American Friendship Circle gathering on Columbus Day, 1992; also the founder of the Red Willow Society, Resonance Communications, and Roads to Awareness Seminars. *Interests*: His work helping Algonquin elders and brining their message to the media has helped thousands of people gain a better understanding of Native American civilization and its teachings. He lectures frequently around the U.S., sharing storytelling, traditional and contemporary songs, and bilingual poetry. *Biographical sources*: Feature article on Native New Yorkers in the November/December 2002 issue of Native Peoples Magazine; cover article in 2003 in the "Village Voice" by Erik Baard. *Published works*: Native New Yorkers, The Legacy of the Algonquin People of New York, No Word for Time; The Way of the Algonquin People; Introductory Guide to Micmac Words & Phrases; Aunt Helens Little Herb Book (A Miramichi Indian Woman's World of Herbs); Secrets of Wholehearted Thinking; Take the Red Road (poetry); Eagle Song: An Honor Roll of Great Algonquins. *In the works*: A Lenape Phrase Book is nearing completion, and Penobscot & Shinnecock language projects are being planned.

PRITCHARD, LARRY
(anthropologist, research associate)
Education: University of Colorado, MA (Anthropology), 1995. *Affiliation*: Research associate, Walker Research Group, Ltd., P.O. Box 4147, Boulder, CO 80306 (303) 492-6719. Website: www.walkerresearchgroup.com. Mr. Pritchard has worked with Dr. Deward Walker of Walker Research Group since 2000 and has been an integral part of a variety of research projects including

an assessment of socioeconomic and housing conditions for the Rosebud Sioux Tribe, analysis of census methodology on Native American reservations, and socioeconomic & demographic analyses for a number of other Native American tribes. Also, he conducts research in the area of human health & the environment.

PROCTOR, J. HUGH
(organization president)
Affiliation: Maryland Indian Heritage Society, P.O. Box 905, Waldorf, MD 20601 (301) 888-1566.

PROPHET, SU ZANNA K. (Shawnee/Delaware) 1951-
(city management)
Born in 1951 in Tulsa, Okla. *Education*: Oklahoma State University, BA, 1973; Haskell Indian Junior College, AA (Art), 1978; University of Kansas, MA, 1979, MPA, 1985; University of Bridgeport, CT, BFA (Painting), 1981. *Principal occupation*: City management. *Home address*: RR 1, Box 137, Firth, NE 68358 (402) 791-5898. *Affiliations*: Budget Research Analyst, Odessa, TX, 1983-89; Administrative Assistant to City Manager, Urbandale, IA, 1989-98; Assistant City Manager, Urbandale, IA, 1998-.

PROULX, JOANNE
(IHS-chief)
Affiliation: Nutrition & Dietetics Training Branch, Indian Health Service, P.O. Box 5558, 1700 Cerillos Rd., Bldg. #5, Santa Fe, NM 87502 (505) 262-1232.

PROVO, DAN
(museum curator)
Affiliation: Museum of the Great Plains, P.O. Box 68, 601 Ferris Ave., Lawton, OK 73502.

PRUCHA, FRANCIS PAUL 1921
(professor of history emeritus)
Born January 4, 1921, River Falls, Wis. *Education*: River Falls State College, BS, 1941; University of Minnesota, MA, 1947; Harvard University, PhD, 1950; St. Louis University, 1952-54; St. Mary's College, STL, 1958. *Principal occupation*: Professor of history emeritus. *Address*: Dept. of History, Marquette University, Milwaukee, WI 53233 (414) 288-5000 Fax 288-1758. *Affiliations*: Society of Jesus, 1950; ordained priest, 1957; professor of history, 1960-88, professor emeritus, 1988-, Marquette University, Milwaukee, WI. *Military service*: U.S. Army Air Force, 1942-46. *Memberships*: American Historical Association; Organization of American Historians; State Historical Society of Wisconsin (board of curators, 1971-78); Western History Association (council, 1972-78, 1983-85, president, 1983); Milwaukee County Historical Society (board of directors, 1964-81, president, 1976-78). *Published works*: Broadax and Bayonet (State Historical Society of Wisconsin, 1953); Army Life on the Western Frontier (University of Oklahoma Press, 1958); American Indian Policy in the Formative Years (Harvard University Press, 1962); Guide to Military Posts of the U.S., 1789-1895 (State Historical Society of Wisconsin, 1964); The Sword of the Republic (Macmillan, 1969); Indian Peace Medals in American History (State Historical Society of Wisconsin, 1971); The Indians in American History (Holt, Rinehart & Winston, 1971); Americanizing the American Indians: Writings by the Friends of the Indians 1880-1900 (Harvard University Press, 1973); Documents of the United States Indian Policy (University of Nebraska Press, 1975; rev. eds. 1990, 2000); American Indian Policy in Crisis: Christian Reformers and the Indian, 1865-1900 (University of Oklahoma Press, 1976); A Bibliographical Guide to the History of Indian-White Relations in the U.S. (University of Chicago Press, 1977); United States Indian Policy: A Critical Bibliography (Indiana University Press, 1977); The Churches and the Indian Schools, 1888-1912 (University of Nebraska Press, 1979); editor, Cherokee Removal: The William Penn Essays and Other Writings, by Jeremiah Evarts (University of Tennessee Press, 1981); Indian Policy in the United States: Historical Essays (University of Nebraska Press, 1981); Indian-White Relations in the United States: A Bibliography of Works Published, 1975-1980 (University of Nebraska Press, 1982); The Great Father: The United States Government and the American Indians, 2 vols. (University of Nebraska Press, 1984); The Indians in American Society: From the Revolutionary War to the Present (University of Cali-

fornia Press, 1985); Handbook for Research in American History (University of Nebraska Press, 1987; rev. ed. 1994); Atlas of American Indian Affairs (University of Nebraska Press, 1990); American Indian Treaties: The History of a Political Anomaly (University of California Press, 1994).

PRUSIA, SHIRLEY (Concow Maidu)
(rancheria chairperson)
Affiliation: Mooretown Rancheria, 1 Alverda Dr., Oroville, CA 95966 (530) 533-3625.

PUCKETT, AL (Cherokee) 1926-
(farmer)
Born July 15, 1926, Cunningham, Ky. *Home address*: 6365 Bethel Ch. Rd., Kevil, KY 42053 (502) 462-3210. *Other professional post*: Private contractor, Union Carbide, Atomic Enrichment Electrical Energy, Inc. *Military service*: U.S. Navy 1941-45, Shipfitter, 3rd Class (Atlantic Campaign, Pacific Campaign Medal, Victory Medal). *Community activities*: Snake River Alliance; Coalition for Health Concern; Military Production Network. *Interests*: Environmental concerns. "(I) participated in production of television program "nuclear shame"; featured in TV program, "Protest at Paducah Gaseous Defusion Plant"; featured in TV program, "Back to Basics."

PUEBLA, MARGARET J.
(school supt.)
Affiliation: St. Stephens Indian School, P.O. Box 345, St. Stephen, WY 82524 (307) 856-4147.

PULLAR, GORDON L. (Koniag) 1944-
(association president)
Born January 22, 1944, Bellingham, Wash. *Education*: Western Washington University, BA, 1973; University of Washington, MPA (Tribal Administration Program - course of study designed to meet the contemporary management needs of Native American corporations, organizations, and tribal governments as well as federal and state agencies dealing with Native American issues and programs), 1983. *Principal occupation*: Association president. *Address*: Kodiak Area Native Association, 3449 E. Rezanos Dr., Kodiak, AK 99901 (907) 486-5725. *Affiliations*: Rewind operator/supervisor, Georgia Pacific Corp., Bellingham, WA, 1963-79; business analyst/marketing specialist, Small Tribes Organization of Western Washington, Sumner, 1979-81; associate editor, Nations magazine (National Communications, Inc., Seattle, 1981; owner/publisher, Kodiak Times, Kodiak, AK 1983-85; president/executive director, Kodiak Area Native Association, 1983-. *Other professional post*: Assistant editor, business editor, The Indian Voice (Small Tribes Organization of Western Wash.), 1979-81. *Community activities*: Volunteer work in social programs involving Native Americans: Washington State Dept. of Social and Health Services, Whatcom County Detoxification Center, and Whatcom County Juvenile Probation Dept.; Northwest Indian News Association (board of directors, 1979-81); Governor's Minority and Women's Business Development Advisory Council (appointed by Governor of State of Washington, 1980-81); Native American Business Alliance (board of directors, vice president-publicity chairman, 1981-83); Alaska Regional Energy Association (board of directors, 1984-85); Kodiak Area State Parks Advisory Board, 1983; Alaska Federation of Natives, Inc. (board of directors, 1983-). *Memberships*: Koniag, Inc. (regional Native corporation); Leisnoi, Inc, Woody Island ANCSA Corp.; National Congress of American Indians; American Society for Public Administration (South Central Alaska Chapter).

PURDY, JOHN 1949-
(university professor)
Born January 6, 1949, Salem, Oreg. *Education*: Western Oregon State College (Monmouth, OR), BA, 1978; University of Idaho, MA, 1980; Arizona State University, PhD, 1986. *Principal occupation*: University professor. *Home address*: 5334 Mosquito Lake Rd., Deming, WA 98244 (206) 650-3243 (work). *Affiliation*: Western Washington University, Bellingham, WA, 1991-. *Other professional post*: Associate editor (for fiction and Native American poetry) from Calapooya College, 1988-. *Military service*: U.S. Naval Air, 1968-72. *Memberships*: Association for the Study of American Indian Literatures (editor of newsletter, 1988-; executive board, 1990-); American Literature Associa-

tion; Modern Language Association. *Awards, honors*: Fulbright Lecturer, Universitat Mannheim, West Germany, 1989-90; Fulbright Lecturer, University of Canterbury, New Zealand, Fall 1993; Director, National Endowment for the Humanities, Summer Seminar for School Teachers, 1993. *Interests*: Degrees in American Literature, with emphasis in Native American Literatures. *Biographical source*: Word Ways: The Novels of D'Arcy McNickle (University of Arizona Press, 1990).

PURICH, DONALD J.
(centre director/instructor)
Affiliation: University of Saskatchewan, Native Law Centre, Diefenbaker Centre, Saskatoon, Sask., Canada S7N 3S9 (306) 966-6189.

PYEATTE, SHARON 1949-
(Indian education program director)
Born March 11, 1949, Fayette, Mo. *Education*: University of Missouri, BS, 1972; University of Colorado, MA, 1987. *Principal occupation*: Counselor; Indian education program director. *Home address*: 9352 E. Arbor Dr., Englewood, CO 80111-5263. *Affiliations*: Assistant program director, College Board, Denver, CO, 1989-91; Director, Indian Education Program, Jenks Public School, 205 East "B" St., Jenks, OK 74037, 1993-present. *Military service*: U.S. Naval Reserve, 1967-71.

PYLE, GREGORY E. (Choctaw of Oklahoma)
(tribal chief)
Affiliation: Choctaw Nation of Oklahoma, P.O. Drawer 1210, Durant, OK 74701 (580) 924-8280 Fax 924-1150.

Q

QITSUALIK, RACHEL A. (Inuit)
(columnist)
Address & Affiliation: Columnist, Indian Country Today, 3059 Seneca Turnpike, Canastota, NY 13032 (315) 829-8355. Website: www.indiancountry.com. Rachel was born into a traditional Igloolik Inuit lifestyle. She has worked in Inuit sociopolitical issues for the last 25 years, and has witnessed the full transition of her culture into the modern world.

QOYAWAYMA, AL (HOPI) 1938-
(consultant/artist)
Born in 1938, Los Angeles, Calif. *Education*: California State Polytechnic University, BSME, 1961; University of Southern California, MSME, 1966; Arizona State University, 1979-85 (Graduate Studies in archaeological ceramic materials, painting passim); Scottsdale Artists School, 1990 & 1991 (Sculptural Studies); Scottsdale Community College, 1981-91 (Studies in Drawing, passim). *Principal occupation*: Potter & sculptor. Address unknown . *Affiliations*: Project engineer, Litton Systems, Woodland Hills, CA, 1961-71; Manager, Environmental Services Dept., Salt River Project, Phoenix, AZ, 1971-90; investigator, Smithsonian Institute, 1982-present (with a 4-man research group identifying original clay sources and pottery migration for ancient Hopi Sikyatki potter); political and technical consultant, Hopi Tribe, Kykotsmovi, AZ, 1989-91. *Community activities*: Board of Directors, The Heard Museum, Phoenix, AZ; Publication Board of Directors, "Winds of Change," American Indian Science & Engineering Society, 1986-; judge at various art shows. *Memberships*: American Indian Science & Engineering Society (co-founder & first chairperson); Institute of American Indian & Alaska Native Culture & Arts (Board of Trustees, 1988-; vice-chairperson of the Board; chairperson, Presidential Search Committee, 1989; member, Developmental Committee); Institute of Electrical & Electronic Engineers. *Awards, honors*: Popovi Da Award, Memorial Award, Scottsdale National Indian Arts Exhibition, 1976; recipient, AISES, Ely S. Parker Award for Engineering Achievement & Service to the American Indian Community, 1986; University of Colorado, Regents' Honorary Degree of Doctor of Humane Letters, Boulder, May 1986; California Polytechnic University, San Luis Obispo, Alumnus of the Year, 1989; G.B. Grinnell American Indian Children's Education Foundation: Annual Al Qoyawayma Award for Excellence in Science and Engineering and the Arts or Cultural Contribution, established 1990; One of twenty "vision makers" invited, "A

Vision for the Third Millennium," United Nations-The Club of Rome and UN Environmental Program, New York, NY 1991; appointed (by the Arizona Governor) Commissioner, Arizona Commission on the Arts, 1991; chairperson - Arizona Design/Public Art Panel, 1991. *Interests*: Al is an artist-potter in the tradition of his Hopi culture. He attributes his pottery training to working with his aunt Polingaysi E. Qoyawayma (aka Elizabeth Q. White), a noted Hopi potter, educator, and writer, who died in 1990. His pottery is known and collected throughout the U.S. Since 1989, he has produced five bronze sculpture series. In June of 1990, Al left his management position in the utility industry to pursue his art career full time. Enjoys travel & research. *Selected Exhibits*: ACA American Indian Art, New York, One-Man Show, 1982; "Night of the First Americans," Kennedy Center, Washington, DC, 1982; Smithsonian Institute of Natural History, Washington, DC, First Showing of Contemporary American Indian Art, 1982-83; Gallery 10, Scottsdale, annual exhibits, 1980-88; "Al Qoyawayma: A Retrospective," Taylor Museum, Colorado Springs, CO, Feb.-April 1985; Santa Fe Indian Market, 1978-93; Arizona State Museum, University of Arizona, Tucson, "Yellow Ware Road," 1990-94. *Selected Publications*: Generations in Clay - Pueblo Pottery of the American Southwest, by Dittert & Plog (Northlands Press, 1980); Santa Fe Design, by Baca & Deats (Crown Publishing, 1990 (3 color photos & story); "Recipient of Tradition," by Barbara Cortright, in Southwest Profile, Aug. 1985 (critical essay, photos); Art of Clay, by Lee M. Cohen, pp. 78-85 (Clearlight Publishers, 1993). *Selected Videos*: 1980 - Generations in Clay - Pueblo Pottery of the American Southwest, voice-over by Al Qoyawayma; 1985 - 30 minute Interview, Charles Loloma & Al Qoyawayma, PBS, Santa Fe, NM; 1988 - "Taking Tradition to Tomorrow," segment, in AISES Video; 1988 - Victor Masayesva, director & producer: Hopi film on ancient Hopi ceramics project, Smithsonian Institute, Washington, DC; 1989 - Jerry and Lois Jacka, "Beyond Tradition," four segments (video won two Rocky Mountain Emmy Awards); 1991 - contract for video consulting: Media Resource Associates; future video segment on "Indian America," PBS TV, Washington, DC, anticipated release, 1992. *Lectures*: Phoenix Art Museum, 1981; Arizona State University, 1985; Taylor Museum, 1985; University of Colorado, 1987; Scottsdale Historic Society, 1987; Museum of Northern Arizona, Flagstaff, 1988; Heard Museum, Phoenix, AZ ("Between Two Worlds: Native American Professional Today,", 1991; Maori and South Pacific Arts Commission, Fullbright Fellowship, cultural exchange (one month), New Zealand, May 1991.

QUARTZ, KATHERINE MARIE *(Cloud Woman)*
(Walker River Paiute) 1963-
(writer, volunteer, floral designer)
Born January 14, 1963, Portland, Ore. *Education*: Western Nevada Community College (Fallon, NV) (2 years); Clackamas Community College (Oregon City, OR) (1 year). *Principal occupation*: Writer, volunteer, floral designer. *Address*: Resides in OR. *Community activities*: Chairperson, Native American Intergroup, Schurz, NV, 1992-; volunteer, Native American Youth Conference, Portland State University, 1994; volunteer, Clackamas County Gang Task Force, 1994. *Memberships*: Native Writers Circle; National Alcoholic Anonymous for Native Americans, Las Vegas, NV (committee). *Awards, honors*: Award from Canada Drug Strategy , Nechi Institute for campaign in U.S. for National Addictions Awareness Week; speaker/presentation on cultural roots and adoption search at the 1992 Healing Our Spirit Worldwide Conference for Indigenous People, Edmonton, Alberta, Canada; speaker on cultural values, presentation entitled, "The Healing Journey Within," at the Women's InterTribal Conference, Reno, NV, 1993. *Interests*: "I feel by volunteering I can devote my time and services to the youth, and also be a role model so they may follow. Speaking and giving presentations at various events. *Work in progress*: The Secret of Rose (expected 1995).

QUASULA, TED
(BIA division director)
Affiliation: Bureau of Indian Affairs, Division of Law Enforcement, 1849 C St., NW, MS: 4140-MIB, Washington, DC 20240 (202) 208-5786.

QUERRY, RON (Choctaw of Oklahoma) 1943-
(writer/novelist)
Born March 22, 1943, Washington, D.C. *Education*: University of New Mexico PhD, 1975. *Principal occupation*: Writer. *Address*: PMB 76-A, 2415 E. Musser, Laredo, TX 78043-2434 (524) 152-3524 (Mexico). E-mail: ronquerry@mpsnet.com.mx. *Past professional post*: Former professor, University of Oklahoma. *Military service*: U.S. Marine Corps, 1961-63. *Memberships*: Native Writers Circle of the Americas; PEN; Tucson Pima County Arts Commission (board of directors, 1994-97). *Awards, honors*: Mountains & Plains Booksellers Award & Border Regional Library Association Southwest Book Award (both for The Death of Bernadette Lefthand); Writer-in-Residence, Amerind Foundation (Dragoon, AZ). *Published works*: Growing Old At Willie Nelson's Picnic (Texas A&M University Press, 1987); Native Americans Struggle for Equality (Rourke, 1993); I See By My Get-Up (University of Oklahoma Press, 1994); The Death of Bernadette Lefthand (Bantam Books, 1995; German translation, Kruger Verlag, 1996); Le Dernier Powwow (Editions du Rocher, France, 1996); Bad Medicine (Bantam Books, 1997).

QUETONE, JIM
(school administrator)
Affiliation: Sequoyah High School, P.O. Box 948, Tahlequah, OK 74464 (918) 456-0631 Fax 456-0634.

QUETONE, JOE A.
(executive director)
Affiliation: Florida Governor's Council on Indian Affairs, Inc., 1341 Cross Creek Cir., Tallahassee, FL 32301 (850) 488-0730 Fax 488-5875.

QUINONES, RENE CIBANAKAN MARCANO (Taino)
(tribal chief)
Affiliation: Taino Nation of the Antilles, P.O. Box 883, New York, NY 10025 (212) 866-4573.

QUINONEZ, JUDITH
(attorney)
Affiliation: Director, The Native American Legal Service Program of New York City, American Indian Law Alliance, The American Indian Community House, 708 Broadway, 8th Floor, New York, NY 10003.

QUINTANA, JOSEPH C. (Cochiti Pueblo)
(Pueblo governor)
Affiliation: Cochiti Pueblo Council, P.O. Box 70, Cochiti, NM 87072 (505) 465-2244.

QUINTANILLA, OSCAR ARZE
(institute director)
Affiliation: Inter-American Indian Institute, Av. Insurgentes Sur 1690, Col. Florida, Mexico D.F. 01030 Mexico (905) 660-0007.

QUINTERO, ROBERT W. (Paiute)
(tribal chairperson)
Affiliation: Walker River paiute Tribal Council, P.O. Box 220, Schurz, NV 89427 (775) 773-2306.

QUIRK, PAT
(director-Indian health center)
Affiliation: Lower Brule PHS Indian Health Center, Lower Brule, SD 57548 (605) 473-5544.

QUIROGA, WILLIAM
(executive director)
Affiliation: Tucson Indian Center, Tucon, AZ 85702 (520) 884-7131 Fax 884-0240.

QUISNO, PATRICIA
(administrative officer-Indian hospital)
Affiliation: Fort Belknap PHS Indian Hospital, Harlem, MT 59526 (406) 353-2651.

QUISTGAARD, JOHN
(director)
Affiliation: Native American Studies Dept., Bemidji State University, Bemidji, MN 56601 (218) 755-2032.

QUITITQUIT, LUWANA
(executive director)
Affiliation: Ya-Ka-Ama Indian Education & Development, Inc., 6215 Eastside Rd., Forestville, CA 95436 (707) 887-1541.

R

RABBIT, BILL (Cherokee)
(artist; gallery co-owner)
Affiliation: Rabbit Studio Gallery, P.O. Box 34, 583 S. Mill, Pryor, OK 74362 (800) 613-3716; (918) 825-3788 or 825-3716. *Products*: Original paintings, limited edition prints and posters; sculpture, knives, baskets, pottery.

RABBIT, TRACI (Cherokee)
(artist; gallery co-owner)
Affiliation: Rabbit Studio Gallery, P.O. Box 34, 583 S. Mill, Pryor, OK 74362 (800) 613-3716; (918) 825-3788 or 825-3716.

RABIDEAUX, MICHAEL
(Indian education program director)
Affiliation: Fond du Lac Ojibway School, 105 University Rd., Cloquet, MN 55720 (218) 878-4648 Fax 878-4687.

RACHAL, SANDRA L. (Mole Lake Chippewa)
(tribal chairperson)
Affiliation: Sokaogon (Mole Lake) Chippewa Community, 3086 State Hwy. 55, Crandon, WI 54520 (715) 478-7500.

RACHO, MICHAEL (Pomo)
(rancheria chairperson)
Affiliation: Dry Creek Rancheria, P.O. Box 607, Geyserville, CA 95441 (707) 431-2388.

RADFORD, ROBIN (Cherokee)
(craftsperson)
Address: Radford Bead Co., 11451 Old Kings Rd., Jacksonville, FL 32219 (904) 765-4886.

RADULOVICH, MARY LOU FOX
(foundation director)
Affiliation: Ojibwe Cultural Foundation, Excelsior Post Office, West Bay, Ontario, Canada P0P 1G0 (705) 377-4902.

RAGSDALE, NANCY
(organization director)
Affiliation: South Eastern Michigan Indians, Inc., 26641 Lawrence St., Center Line, MI 48090 (810) 956-1350.

RAIN, WALTER
(Indian band chief)
Affiliation: Paul Indian Band, Box 89, Duffield, Alberta, Canada T0E 0N0 (403) 892-2691.

RAMBEAU, DAVID L.
(executive director)
Affiliation: United American Indian Involvement, 1614 W. Temple St., Los Angeles, CA 90013 (213) 625-2565.

RAMEY, KATHY (Miwok)
(tribal band chairperson)
Affiliation: Ione Band of Miwok Indians, P.O. Box 1190, Ione, CA 95640 (209) 274-6753.

RAMIREZ, RION (Turtle Mountain Chippewa)
(attorney)
Address & Affiliation: Dorsey & Whitney LLP, Dorsey & Whitney LLP, U.S. Bank Centre, 1420 Fifth Ave., Suite 3400, Seattle, WA 98101. E-mail: ramirez.rion@dorseylaw.com.

RAMIRIZ, RAYMOND
(museum supt.)
Affiliation: Ysleta Del Sur Pueblo Museum, P.O. Box 17579, Tigua Indian Reservation, El Paso, TX 79917 (915) 859-7913.

RAMOS, DIANA S. (Yaqui/Cherokee) 1949-
(secretary)
Born June 5, 1949, Corpus Christi, Tex. *Principal occupation*: Secretary. *Home address*: 6407 Starstreak Dr., Austin, TX 78745 (512) 444-6451. *Community activities*: American Indian Resource & Education Coalition (treasurer); Native American Parent Committee; Boy Scouts of America; Girl Scouts of America; PTA.

RAMSEY, ANDREW (Florida Eastern Creek)
(tribal chief)
Affiliation: Florida Tribe of Eastern Creek, P.O. Box 3028, Bruce, FL 32455 (904) 835-2078.

RANDALL, VINCENT (Yavapai-Apache)
(tribal chief)
Affiliation: Yavapai-Apache Community Council, Camp Verde, AZ 86322 (520) 567-3649.

RANFRANZ, THOMAS (Santee Sioux)
(tribal president)
Affiliation: Flandeau Sante Sioux Exec. Committee, P.O. Box 283, Flandreau, SD 57028 (605) 997-3891.

RANGEN, NEIL
(museum supt.)
Affiliation: Hauberg Indian Museum, Black Hawk State Park, 1510 46th Ave., Rock Island, IL 61201 (309) 788-9536.

RANIIREZ-SHLWEGNAABI, BEN
(center director)
Affiliation: Native American Center, 012 Old Main, UW-Stevens Point, Stevens Point, WI 54481 (715) 346-2004.

RANSOM, JAY ELLIS 1914-
(author, teacher, technical writer, editor)
Born April 12, 1914, Missoula, Mont. *Education*: University of Washington, BA, 1935; University of Washington Graduate School, 1936-41 (PhD level, Anthropology); UCLA, MA (Education), PhD level Psychology, 1949. *Principal occupation*: Author, teacher, technical writer, editor. *Home address*: 1901 East 19th St., The Dalles, OR 97058 (541) 296-9414. *Affiliation*: President & executive secretary, Western America Institute for Exploration, Inc., The Dalles, OR, 1954-. *Other professional posts*: Chief technical writer/editor, aerospace industry, 1949-70; freelance magazine feature writer, 1936-; news correspondent for various newspapers, 1936-; occasional lecturer to organizations. *Field linguistics researches*: Flathead Salish, Western Montana, summer of 1934; Duwamish Salish, Western Washington, 1936; other Northwest languages & cultures between 1934-41 include Chinook jargon, Sahaptin, Chinook-Kwakiutl, Tlingit; Fox Island Aleut. Taught four years, 1936-40, in the Alaskan Indian Service schools;1936-37 at Nikolski, Umnak, Alaska. In 1974, Dr. Michael Krauss, chairman of the linguistics department at the University of Alaska, requested Ransom's Aleut materials to assist them and the Alaska State Department of Education in developing native Aleut teaching materials comparable to what they had initiated two years earlier for Eskimo native schools; Kutchin Dene Acculturation: Between 1938 & 1940 the Indian Service assigned me to teach in the native school at Stevens Village, on the central Yukon River 100 miles north of Fairbanks; Paleo-Indian Studies, 1975-91, extensively worked on studies of the Bighorn Medicine Wheel in the northern Wyoming Bighorn Mountains. *Awards, honors*: Blood Brother, Flathead Tribe. *Interests*: Photography, writing, educating. *Biographical sources*: Contemporary Authors; Who's Who in America. *Published works*: "A bibliography of 76 papers (16 university research journals) and in popular, general distribution magazines illustrated with my own photography, 1935-84. All in some way incorporate aspects of anthropology, Native American linguistics, primitive folklore, ethnology, or Indian education and are extracted from a more complete bibliography of some 400 titles archived in the Suzzallo Library, University of Washington. Not included are an estimated 3,000 news stories, editorials, and features under my byline written in my journalism career." Also many books & monographs, including: Morphology of Fox Island Aleut; Phonology & Morphology of Duwamish Salish; Notes & Morphology of Flathead Salish; Aleut Gossip Texts; Fox Island Aleut Diaries & Literature; Duwamish Mythological Texts; Anthropology & Native American Linguistics at the University of Washington, 1934-41 (Suzzalo Library, U of WA, Seattle, 1982); Archaeolinguistics & Paleoethnography of Ancient Rock Structures in Western North America (Western America Institute for Exploration, 1984); Big Horn Medicine Wheel—The Birth and Death of Humanity (Yellowstone Printing & Publishing, Cody, WY, 1992); Collected Writings About the Fox Island Aleut Peoples of Alaska, 1993.

RANSOM, JOSEPHINE
(museum director)
Affiliation: Chieftains Museum, 501 Riverside Parkway, Rome, GA 30162 (404) 291-9494.

RANVILLE, STIRLING
(director-Indian centre)
Affiliation: Indian & Metis Friendship Centre, 239 Magnus Ave., Winnipeg, Manitoba, Canada R2W 2B6.

RAPHAEL, JOSEPH C. (Chippewa)
(tribal chairperson)
Affiliation: Grand Traverse Band Tribal Council, P.O. Box 118, Suttons Bay, MI 49682 (616) 271-3538.

RATION, NORMAN (Laguna-Navajo)
(president-board of directors)
Affiliation: National Indian Youth Council, 318 Elm, SE, Albuquerque, NM 87102 (505) 247-2251 Fax 247-4251.

RAVE, AUSTIN JERALD (Minneconjou Sioux) 1946-
(artist)
Born August 5, 1946, Cheyenne River Sioux Reservation, S.D. *Education*: Institute of American Indian Arts, Santa Fe, NM, 1964-66; San Francisco Art Institute, 1966-67; Engineering Drafting School, Denver, CO, 1970-72. *Principal occupation*: Artist. *Home address*: P.O. Box 356, Eagle Butte, SD 57625. *Other professional posts*: Draftsman, technical illustrator. *Awards, honor*: Numerous awards for art. *Biographical source*: Dictionary of International Biography.

RAVEN, FRED TIDEWATERS
(association director)
Affiliation: Indigenous Tribes Association, 1030 S. 317th St., Federal Way, WA 98003 (206) 839-5635.

RAWLS, ROB (Inupiaq Eskimo)
(radio station manager)
Affiliation: KOTZ - 720 AM, P.O. Box 78, Kotzebue, AK 99752 (907) 442-3435.

RAY, DONALD (Pomo) 1951-
(senior vice president)
Born February 27, 1951, Ukiah, Calif. *Education*: Mendocino Community College, 1972-73; American River College, 1974; Sacramento State University; Sacramento State University (2 years). *Principal occupation*: Gaming accountant at local casino. *Home address*: 12900 S. Hiway 101, Hopland, CA 95449 (707) 744-2040 Fax 744-9610; E-Mail: donr@pacific.net. *Website*: www.shokawah.com. *Affiliations*: Payroll clerk, Inter Tribal Council of California, Sacramento, CA, 1973-78; controller/director, Eagle Child, Indian Child Welfare Project, 1978-81; executive director, "Six Tribal Nations" (Indian child welfare program), Mendocino County, CA, 1981-82; Hopland Band of Pomo Indians, CA (tribal council, 1982-92; chair, 1984-92; rep. for California tribes on the BIA, Tribal Reorganization Act, 1988-92); consultant - advised tribes on gaming contracts and found investors for gaming and/or other economic development ventures, 1992-94; accountant, Shodakai Coyote Valley Casino, Redwood Valley, CA, 1994-99; senior vice president, Hopland Tribe Economic Development Corp., 1999-present; worked on (Proposition 5) legislation to approve gaming in California; also worked on Proposition 1-A until passed by the voters of California and amended to the California State Constitution. Presently working on new casino expansion for Hopland Tribe, to be completed in 2003. *Other professional posts*: Central California Policy Committee, BIA, Sacramento, CA, 1976-80; Consolidated Tribal Health, Inc., Ukiah, CA, 1980-84; finance officer, Lake County Tribal Health, Inc. (first health clinic in lake County for Indian people), 1981-82; regional rep to the Central California Advisory Board for BIA services and Health Care Services), 1981-82; chairman, Mendocino County Tribal Chairman's Association, 1988-92; League of Indian Voters, 1990-92 (wrote the overall plan and design of this organization for the Indian people within California. *Military service*: U.S. Army, 1970-72 (Sergeant, Vietnam Era Veteran; Service Medal, Marksman Award-Firearms, Missile Special Training Award). *Community activities*: Board member on the Regional and Statewide "Indian Health Services" policy committee, 1986-91; Mendocino County Development Corporation, 1988-91; board

member of Northern Circle Indian Housing Authority, 1985-91; chairman of board for Consolidated Tribal Health Clinic, Inc., 1985-92; 1990-92 implemented the area wide policy committee of the BIA.membership: Chamber of Commerce (Ukiah) Mendocino County. *Membership:* Shanel Pomo Hopland. *Interests:* "I travel extensively throughout the U.S. on tribal business and representing California tribes in congressional hearings and other representatives as appropriate for Indian people. Now, I am working fulltime and helping local Indian people understand how the gaming business can be a benefit for their future, but not the answer to all." Also, computer programming. *Biographical sources:* "Modern Day Warrior," 1985 (local newsletter publication about his life).

RAY, DUANE J. (Seneca)
(former tribal president)
Affiliation: Seneca Nation Tribal Council, P.O. Box 231, Salamanca, NY 14479 (716) 945-1790.

RAY, FRANCES
(Indian band chief)
Affiliation: Flying Post Indian Band, Box 937, Nipigon, Ontario, Canada P0T 2J0 (807) 886-2443.

RAYMOND, MARGARET PEAKE
(Oklahoma Cherokee) 1941-
(planning consultant; executive director)
Born June 22, 1941, Tahlequah, Okla. *Education:* Northeastern State College (Tahlequah, OK), BS, 1963; University of Oklahoma, MSW, 1974. *Principal occupation:* Planning consultant. *Address:* 2520 E. 22 St., Minneapolis, MN 55406 (612) 343-0363; E-Mail: margray@gold.tc.umn.edu. *Affiliations:* Owner, First Phoenix American Corp., Minneapolis, 1978-84; founder, Minnesota Indian Women's Resource Center, 2300 15th Ave. S., Minneapolis, MN 55404 (612) 728-2000, 1984-present. *Other professional posts:* Special assistant to the director, Minnesota Alcohol & Drug Authority, St. Paul, MN, 1974-77; tribal planner, Cherokee Nation of Oklahoma, 1976-77; National Advisory Council on Drug Abuse, 1980-84; field instructor, University of Minnesota, School of Social Work, 1990-. *Community activities:* United Way of Minneapolis Area. *Memberships:* Child Welfare League of America (Chemical Dependency Commission); Minnesota Board of Social Workers; American Indian Business Development Corporation; Hennepin County Foster Care Re-Design Commission; Healthy Nations Advisory Committee to Robert Woods Johnson Foundation; Minnesota Women's Economic Roundtable, 1994; Governor's Task Force on Housing, 1994. *Awards, honors:* "Resourceful Women's Award 1992; Jesse Bernard Award, Center for Women Policy Studies, 1992; Minneapolis Leadership Award, 1992; People of Phillips Leadership, 1994."

RAYMOND, THOMAS
(education management)
Affiliation: Crazy Horse School, P.O. Box 260, Wanblee, SD 57577 (605) 462-6511.

REAL BIRD, HENRY LEE *(Timber Leader)*
(Crow) 1948-
(educator)
Born July 24, 1948, Crow Agency, Mont. *Education:* Montana State University, BS, 1971; Eastern Montana College, MEd. *Principal occupation:* Educator. *Address:* P.O. Box 5, Garryowen, MT 59031 (406) 638-7211 (work). *Other professional post:* Boss of a cow camp. *Memberships:* American Indian Higher Education Consortium; Crow Tobacco Society; Native American Church. *Interests:* "I've taught on the Navajo, Cheyenne, and Crow Reservations. I've been asked to read my poetry from Texas, New Mexico, Colorado, Nevada & Montana. I rodeoed when I was young from amateur-pro." *Published work:* Where Shadows Are Born (Guildhall, 1990).

REASON, JAMIE (Southeastern Cherokee) 1947-
(traditional carver)
Born March 11, 1947, Muncie, Ind. *Principal occupation:* Owner/manager, Sacred Earth Studio, Mastic Beach, NY, 1980- (Native American art studio). *Home address:* 197 Longfellow Dr., Mastic Beach, NY 11951 (516) 399-4539. Affiliation: Journeys Into American Indian Territory, Fall 2003 to present. *Military service:* U.S. Air Force, 1966 (A/3/C; Vietnam Era Veteran;

National Defense Expert Marksman; Air Police). *Memberships:* Indian Arts & Crafts Association; Vietnam Era Veterans Inter-Tribal Association; Ani-Yvwiya Association of New York. *Awards, honors:* 1988 Gallup Inter-Tribal 1st & 3rd prizes), 1989 Gallup Inter-Tribal (best in category peyote box); first place-Div. II Carved Cedar Box, Sinte Gleska Native American Art Show, 1987; 1987 Recipient of the "Elkus Award" at Gallup; designated "Master Artist" of the Southeastern Cherokee Confederacy 1992. *Interests:* "Even though I am self taught, I attribute my ability to my grandfather, George Reason, who was a carver. He has been an inspiration and great influence on my art and in my life. Mr. Reason is probably best known for his solid carved cedar feather boxes. Since 1990, "most of my production of carvings were decoys, a traditional Native American art form indigenous to the Americas. Also, since 1990, "have operated Seatuck Gallery (for 14 years) in Eastport, NY (since 1995, formerly in Moriches, NY)." *Exhibitions:* Art work exhibited at the Museum of the American Indian, The Gallery of the American Indian Community House (New York City), Red Cloud Indian Art Show, Dartmouth College; Native American Symposium at Old Westbury College (N.Y.); Rhode Island Indian Council; Red Earth, Oklahoma City; The Ceremonial, Gallup Inter-Tribal, 1986-89; Sinte Gleska Native American Art Show (Tahlequah, OK); Scottsdale All-Indian Art Show (Scottsdale, AZ); and many galleries. *Biographical sources:* The Museum of the American Indian News, Sept. 24, 1983; Suffolk Life, 1983-84; Southeastern Cherokee News; American Indian Community House Newsletter, 1984; The Knoxville Journal, April 7, 1984; Daily News, April 4, 1984; New York Times, August 18, 1985, August 8, 2003; Three Village Herald, Long Island, Oct. 7, 1987 & Aug. 9, 1989; American Indian Collectibles - First Ed. 1988, by Reno; The Day, New London, CT, Jan. 29, 1988; Mandan News, Mandan, ND, Oct. 1988; Long Island Advance, April 16, 1989; Manchester Journal, Manchester Center, VT, Sept. 20, 1989; The Travelers Guide to American Crafts East of the Mississippi, by Suzanne Carmichael; Southeastern Native American Arts Directory, by Nadema Agard-Smith; "Jamie Reason, Born to Carve," in Decoy Magazine, Jan-Feb. 1999, May-June 1999, July-Aug. 2000, March-April 2002, Nov. Dec. 2003, and Jan. Feb. 2004;" Suffolk Life, April 1999; Southampton Press, Oct. 21, 1999, Sept. 27, 2001, April 18, 2002, & Nov. 21, 2002; New York Times Metro, Feb. 24, 2001, & Aug. 8, 2003.

REBAR, JOAN (Sac & Fox of Missouri)
(former tribal chairperson)
Affiliation: Sac & Fox of Missouri Tribe, Rte. 1, Box 60, Reserve, KS 66434 (913) 742-7471.

RECK, PAT (Pueblo)
(museum curator)
Affiliation: Indian Pueblo Cultural Center, 2401 12th St., NW, Albuquerque, NM 87102 (505) 843-7270.

RED BEAR, CHARLES (Sioux)
(school chairperson)
Affiliation: Rock Creek Day School, Bullhead, SD 57621 (605) 823-4971.

RED ELK, BONNIE
(editor)
Affiliation: Wotanin Wowapi, Fort Peck Assiniboine & Sioux Tribes, P.O. Box 1027, Poplar, MT 59255 (406) 768-5155 Ext. 2370.

RED ELK, LOIS (Yankton Sioux)
(poet)
Address: P.O. Box 371, Wolf Point, MT 59201 (406) 653-3300.

RED HORSE, JOHN
(professor & director of Indian center)
Affiliation: American Indian Studies Center, University of California, Los Angeles, 3220 Campbell Hall, Los Angeles, CA 90024 (213) 825-7315.

RED-HORSE, VALERIE (Eastern Cherokee/
Cheyenne River Sioux) 1959-
(actress, writer, spokesperson)
Born August 24, 1959, in Calif. Education: UCLA, BA - Theater Arts (cum laude), 1981; Lee Strasberg Theater Institute/Professional Master Class (acting). *Principal occupation:* Actress, writer, spokesperson. *Home*

address: 6028 Calvin Ave., Tarzana, CA 91356 (818) 705-6972; 705-4905 (work). *Television credits:* The Dennis Miller Show; Unsolved Mysteries, Anything But Love; Santa Barbara; Divorce Court; Perry Mason; Buck James; Murder, She Wrote; among others. *Film credits:* Pow Wow Highway (voiceover); First & Ten (choreography); Return to the Country (lead dancer). *Talk show hosting/spokesperson:* First Americans (talk show hostess); Walking In Both Worlds (keynote speaker & featured performer); Trail of Tears Youth Conference (keynote speaker & featured performer); Native Americans in the Media (celebrity panelist); Women of Color: Invisible On Screen)celebrity panelist). *Theater:* Love's Labour's Lost (Rosaline-lead); Uncommon Women & Others (Kate-lead); Dreams (Lisa-lead); A Hotel Chain (Rose-lead); From Broadway With Love (lead dancer/singer). *Other professional posts:* Co-owner (with husband, Curt Mohl), Executive Specialties (a promotional advertising retail business) and Maverick Outdoor Media Group, Inc. (a corporation specializing in outdoor signage for real estate developers); lead dancer & choreographer for the Bel Air Presbyterian Liturgical Dance Co. *Community activities:* Bel Air Presbyterian Church; Youth for Christ Mentor Mom Program; The Sylmar Juvenile Hall Prison Task Force; Los Angeles Mission "City Light" (women's rehabilitation program). *Memberships:* Women in Film; Sacred Dance Guild; First Americans In the Arts; Native Writers Circle: Multicultural Minority Motion Picture Awards Board. *Awards, honors:* Keynote addresses to such organizations as The California Indian Manpower Association, and the California American Indian Women's Association; Honoring voting committee member of the Minority Motion Picture Awards Association; recently selected to testify for a Senate Committee reviewing minorities & females in the Film & Television industry. *Interests:* Writing - recently completed original screenplay, "Lozen," which chronicles the life of a historical Apache woman warrior and the women who fought alongside her. Valerie hopes that her script will, "dispel some of the stereotypical images of the Native American female which television and film have created. As a Native American actress & writer, I am dedicated to improving and furthering the portrayal of Native American women in the media." *Biographical source:* Featured article in "Today's Christian Woman (July/Aug. 1993 issue).

RED SHE BEAR (DEANNA BARNES) (Ute) 1938-
(teacher, craftswoman)
Born June 25, 1938, Boise, Idaho. *Education:* College of the Redwoods; Humboldt State University. *Principal occupation:* Founder/manager, Red Bear Creations, Bandon, OR. *Home address:* 358 N. Lexington Ave., Bandon, OR 97411 (541) 347-9560. *Affiliations:* Founder, Indian Survival Society, Brandon, OR; founder and president, Women's Center. *Community activities:* American Red Cross (provider and secretary); Coos and Curry Area Agency on Aging (provider); Intertribal Sweat Lodge Board (officer); District 7 Sub-Area Health Advisory Council (provider); Women's Crisis Service (advisory board). *Membership:* National Indian Health Care Association (spokeswoman). *Interests:* "Making traditional quilts and blankets. Preserving our old culture and traditions is very important to me. I am an elder, pipecarrier, sweatleader, storyteller in the winter, tech survival skills in the woods, lecture on traditional uses of indigenous plants as food and medicine, and on Indian women's roles in society. I'm currently writing book, Crystal Wind Warrior, about a crystal who became a human to help the people (manuscript, 1986)."

RED SHIRT, DELPHINE (Lakota)
(writer)
Publications: Bead on the Anthill: A Lakota Childhood (U. of Nebraska Press, 1997); Turtle Lung Woman's Granddaughter (U. of Nebraska Press, 2002);

REDAN, PERRY
(Indian band chief)
Affiliation: Cayoose Creek Indian Band, Box 484, Lillooet, BC, Can. V0K 1V0 (604) 256-4136.

REDDICK, GINGER (Comanche)
(craftsperson, shop owner)
Address & Affiliation: Owner (with husband, Rex Reddick), Crazy Crow Trading Post, P.O. Box 847, 1801 N. Airport Rd., Pottsboro, TX 75076 (800) 786-

6210; (903) 786-2287 Fax 786-9059; E-Mail: crazy crow@texoma.com; Web site: www.crazycrow.com.

REDDING, THEODORE, M.D.
(chief medical officer)
Affiliation: Phoenix Area Office, Indian Health Service, 3738 M. 16th St., Suite A, Phoenix, AZ 85016 (602) 640-2052.

REDEAGLE, ANITA
(administrative officer)
Affiliation: Pawnee PHS Indian Health Center, RR 2, Box 1, Pawnee, OK 74058 (918) 762-2517.

REDEAGEL, J. PAUL
(IHS-area deputy director)
Affiliation: Indian Health Service, California Area Office, 1825 Bell St., Suite 200, Sacramento, CA 95825 (916) 978-4202.

REDSKY, LLOYD
(Indian band chief)
Affiliation: Shoal Lake #40 Indian Band, Kejick P.O. , Shoal Lake, Ontario, Canada P0X 1E0 (807) 733-2315.

REED, EVA SILVER STAR (United Lumbee/ Cherokee/Choctaw) 1929-
(homemaker, national chieftain)
Born November 29, 1929, Vanita, Okla. *Principal occupation*: Home maker. *Home address*: P.O. Box 512, Fall River Mills, CA 96028 (530) 336-6701. *Affiliation*: National Chieftain, United Lumbee Nation of N.C. and America, 1983-. *Other professional posts*: Parent committee of Title IV and Johnson O'Malley Indian Education Program, Tulare-Kings Counties, CA; National Secretary , 1979-82, Head Chief, 1982-, and Grand Council member, 1979-, United Lumbee Nation of N.C. and America. *Memberships*: Native American Wolf Clan (secretary, 1977-); Chapel of Our Lord Jesus (church) (secretary, 1974-2001; president, 2001-present); United Lumbee Nation's Hawk Society, 1996-. *Awards, honors*: Numerous 1st & 2nd prizes for Indian bead work at the Inter-Mountain Fair, McArthur, CA; 1991 Silver Eagle Award, United Lumbee Nation. *Interests*: "I teach an Indian Beading Class each year since 1980 — I am editor of the United Lumbee Nation Times since 1981. I do sewing, leather crafts, painting, and bead work, and write articles for the paper and books. Caring for my people the United Lumbees." *Biographical sources*: Articles in the United Lumbee Nation Times. *Published works*: Compiler, Over the Cooking Fires, featuring traditional Lumbee recipes (United Lumbee Nation, 1982); Lumbee Indian Ceremonies (United Lumbee Nation, 1982); United Lumbee Nation's Deer Clan Cook Book (United Lumbee Nation, 1988); co-author with Frank Chilcote, A Message to Our People (United Lumbee Nation, 1989).

REED, MARY BETH
(school principal)
Affiliation: Ojibwa Indian School, P.O. Box 600, Belcourt, ND 58316 (701) 477-3108.

REED-CRUM, ANNETTE
(Native American Studies instructor)
Affiliation: Native American Studies Dept., College of Letters & Science, 2401 Hart Hall, University of California, Davis, CA 95616 (530) 752-3237 Fax 752-7097.

REELS, KENNETH M. (Mashantucket Pequot)
(tribal chairperson)
Address: Mashantucket Pequot Tribal Nation, P.O. Box 3060, 1 Matts Path, Mashantucket, CT 06339 (860) 396-6572 Fax 396-6570. *Affiliations*: Mashantucket Pequot Tribe (member, tribal council, 1991-; vice chairperson (3 terms); chairperson, 1999-present). *Other professional posts*: Mashantucket Pequot Tribe (property purchasing & contracting officer, 1987-95; director, Centralization Project, 1995-98. *Military service*: U.S. Army.

REESE, WILLIAM
(director of education)
Affiliation: Pine Hill Schools, CPO Drawer H, Pine Hills, NM 87357 (505) 775-3242.

REESER, RALPH R. 1932-
(research)
Born November 26, 1932, Fairbanks, Alaska. *Education*: Seattle University, 1952-55; University of Washington, BA, 1956; George Washington University Law School, JD, 1960. *Principal occupation*: Research. *Home address*: 3702 Spruell Dr., Wheaton, MD 20902; E-Mail: r.reeser@comcast.net. *Affiliations*: Attorney-advisor, Public Housing Administration, Washington, DC, 1961-66; director, Housing Development, B.I.A., Washington, DC, 1966-70; deputy director, Publicly Financed Housing, Dept. of HUD, Washington, DC, 1970-72; director, Congressional & Legislative Affairs, B.I.A., Washington, DC, 1972-89; consultant, 1989-. *Other professional post*: Teaching course on "Indian Land & the Law" for Falmouth Institute, 1991-92. *Military service*: U.S. Air Force, 1951-52 (S/Sgt.). *Community activities*: Montgomery County, MD Advisory Committee on Cable Communications (member, 1991-96). *Membership*: D.C. Bar Association. *Published work*: Manual of Indian Gaming Law (Falmouth Institute, 1992); A Complete Guide to P.L. 93-638: Contracting Through the Indian Self-Determination Act (Native American Technologies, 1996).

REEVES, JANET
(executive director)
Affiliation: Nevada Urban Indians, 1190 Bible Way, Reno, NV 89502 (775) 788-7600 Fax 788-7611.

REFT, ALICIA (Aleut)
(village president)
Affiliation: Native Village of Karluk, P.O. Box 22, Karluk, AK 99608 (907) 241-2218.

REGGUINTI, GORDON (Ojibway) 1954-
(company president)
Born February 10, 1954, in Minnesota. *Education*: University of Minnesota, BA (Indian Studies), 1987. *Principal occupation*: Company president. *Home address*: 1008 Russell Ave. No., Minneapolis, MN 55411 (612) 287-9104 Fax 287-9106. *Affiliations*: Currently, President, Native News & Entertainment Television, Minneapolis, MN; former executive director, Native American Journalists Association, Minneapolis, MN. *Other professional posts*: Newsletter instructor, Migizi Communications, Minneapolis, MN, 1988-; series editor, Lerner Publications, Minneapolis, MN, 1990-. *Published work*: The Sacred Harvest, Ojibway Wild Rice Gathering (Lerner Publications, 1992).

REID, MARY
(education director)
Affiliation: Oklahoma Department of Indian Education, 2500 N. Lincoln Blvd., Oklahoma City, OK 73105 (405) 521-3311.

REID-ALANIZ, MICHELLE (Raven Moon) (Wampanoag/Mic Mac) 1954-
(native village director)
Born October 27, 1954, Taunton, Mass. *Education*: Johnson & Wales, Providence, RI, Fashion Merchandising (2 years). *Principal occupation*: Native village director. *Address*: P.O. Box 296, Grantham, NH 03753-0296. *Affiliation*: Director, Moon Shadow Native Village, Lowell, VT. *Other professional post*: La Leche League leader; childbirth educator. *Community activities*: Birthright counselor/teen pregnancy; Coalition for Teen Pregnancy, Falmouth, MA; volunteer in public schools; help single moms. *Memberships*: Pan American Indians, 1991; Connecticut River Pow wow Society, 1992-; Seneca Wolf Clan, 1991-; Indigenous Women's Network, 1992-; Good Medicine Society, 1993-. *Award*: Merit Award for work in public schools in Falmouth, MA. *Interests*: "My work involves sending boxes to those in need on the reservations. I have visited Akwesasne Reservation in New York, and Rosebud Reservation in South Dakota. (I am) presently helping two Navajo elders through Adopt a Native Elder Program. I have studied with Grandmother Alloday of the Good Medicine Society; studying with Spider about Moon Lodge Women's Cycle. Spider is of Seneca Wolf Clan; I use herbs for healing, making medicines & salves. Also homeopathy." *Biographical sources*: Articles have appeared in Pan American newsletter, prison newsletters, and Shadowlight newsletter.

REILING, DENNIS L.
(tribal special judge)
Affiliation: Prairie Band Potawatomi Nation Tribal Court, 15498 K Rd., Mayetta, KS 66509 (866) 966-2242 or (785) 966-2242 Fax 966-2662. E-mail: tribalcourt@pbpnation.org. Website: www.pbpnation. org/tribalcourt

REIMER, JOHN
(BIA education administrator)
Affiliation: Portland Area Office, Bureau of Indian Affairs, 911 N.E. 11th Ave., Portland, OR 97232 (503) 872-2743 Fax 231-6219.

RENDON, ANDREW
(school principal)
Affiliation: Porcupine Day School, P.O. Box 180, Porcupine, SD 57772 (605) 867-5336.

RENICK, DORIS (Pomo)
(tribal chairperson)
Affiliation: Coyote Valley Reservation, P.O. Box 39, Redwood Valley, CA 95470-0039 (707) 485-8723.

RENTERIA, JOE (Cherokee)
(Indian center chairperson)
Affiliation: Indian Human Resource Center, 4040 30th St., Suite A, San Diego, CA 92104 (619) 281-5964 Fax 281-1466.

RENVILLE, ROBIN
(elementary school principal)
Affiliation: Wounded Knee District School, P.O. Box 350, Manderson, SD 57756 (605) 867-5433.

RESTOULE, TIM
(Indian band chief)
Affiliation: Dokis Indian Band, Dokis Bay, Monteville, Ontario, Canada P0M 2K0 (705) 763-2200.

REVARD, CARTER C. (Nompewathe) (Osage) 1931-
(professor emeritus, writer)
Born March 25, 1931, Pawhuska, Okla. *Education*: University of Tulsa, BA, 1952; University of Oxford, BA/MA, 1958; Yale University, PhD, 1959. *Principal occupation*: Professor emeritus, writer. *Home address*: 6638 Pershing Ave., St. Louis, MO 63130 (314) 727-9358. E-mail: ccrevard@artsci.wustl.edu. *Affiliations*: Washington University, St. Louis, MO, 1961-97; professor emeritus, 1997-). *Memberships*: Modern Language Association; Association of American Rhodes Scholars; American Indian Center of Mid-America. *Interests*: Writing, gourd dancing, medieval research and writing, poetry readings, talks. *Published works*: Ponca War Dancers! (poems) (Point Riders Press-Norman, OK, 1980); Cowboys and Indians, Christmas Shopping (poems) (Point Riders Press, 1992); An Eagle Nation (poems) (University of Arizona Press, 1993); Family Matters, Tribal Affairs (prose-scholarly essays and autobiography) (University of Arizona Press, 1998); Winning the Dust Bowl (poems & memoirs) (University of Arizona Press, 2001).

REYHNER, JON ALLAN 1944-
(professor of education)
Born April 29, 1944, Fountain Hill, Penna. *Education*: University of California, Davis, BA, 1966, MA, 1967; Northern Arizona University, MA, 1973, EdS, 1977; Montana State University, Bozeman, EdD, 1984. *Principal occupation*: Associate professor of education, Eastern Montana College. *Address*: Department of Education, Northern Arizona University, Flagstaff, AZ. *Affiliations*: Principal, Rocky Boy Public School, Box Elder, MT, 1978-80; university supervisor of professional & student teachers, Dept. of Elementary Education, Montana State University, Bozeman, 1980-81; principal/federal projects director, Heart Butte Public School, MT, 1982-84; administrator/principal, Havasupai School, Supai, AZ, 1984-85; academic coordinator & school administrator, Cibecue Community School, Cibecue, AZ, 1984-85; associate professor of education, Eastern Montana College, Billings, 1985-97; professor of education, Northern Arizona University, Flagstaff, AZ, 1997-present. *Memberships*: National Association for Bilingual Education; American Educational Research Association; International Reading Association; American Association of School Administrators; National Indian Education Association;

Council for Indian Education; Phi Delta Kappa; Phi Alpha Theta. *Interests*: Bilingual education; Indian education; photography; historical research on Western America. *Published works*: Heart Butte: A Blackfeet Indian Community, 1984; editor, Stories of Our Blackfeet Grandmothers, 1984; editor, The Story of Running Eagle, by James Willard Schultz, 1984; editor, Famine Winter, by James Willard Schultz, 1984; editor, The Loud Mouthed Gun, by James Willard Schultz, 1984; all published by Council for Indian Education; A History of Indian Education (Eastern Montana College, 1989); Effective Language Education Practices (NALI, 1990); Teaching American Indian Students (University of Oklahoma Press, 1992); American Indian Education: A History, with Jeanne Eder (Univ. of Oklahoma Press, 2004); numerous articles.

REYNA, SHARON *(Dryflower)* (Taos Pueblo) 1949-
(artist-clay)
Born August 20, 1949, Taos, N.M. *Education*: Institute of American Indian Art, AFA (Museum Studies /3 Dimensional Art), 1987. Santa Fe Community College (Painting/Business). *Principal occupation*: Artist-clay. *Home address*: P.O. Box 3031, Taos, NM 87571 (505) 758-3790. 1991 *Open Shows*: Denver Indian Market; Native American Art Festival; Heard Museum; Scottsdale Native American Culture Foundation; Retrospective of Taos, 4-Man Show, Sables Art Center; Red Earth Fine Art Show; Eight Northern Indian Pueblos Art Show; Indian Market, Santa Fe. Collections: Denver Natural History Museum-Vernon Rickmeyer Collection; Millicent Rogers Museum; Institute of American Indian Arts, Santa Fe; Alll Indian Pueblo Culture Center, Albuquerque; Tony Reyna (private collection); Chicago Natural History Museum; Red Cloud Heritage Center, Rapid City, SD; among others. *Memberships*: Indian Arts and Crafts Association; The National Museum of Women in the Arts, Washington, DC; Stables Art Association; Spring Arts Board; TAA - Visual Arts Committee. *Awards, honors*: Best of Class, Ceramic Sculpture - 4th Annual Fine Art Show, Scottsdale Native American Indian Cultural Foundation; 1st, Pottery Division - Heard Museum Student Show; 2nd, Ceramic Division - Red Earth Fine Arts Show, Oklahoma City, OK; Thunderbird Scholarship, Hinsel Award & Purchase Award from the Red Cloud Heritage Center, Pine Ridge, SD; Gallup Ceremoial; Artist of the Year, Native American Fish & Wildlife Society. *Published works*: Taos Pueblo (Nancy Wood, 1988-89); Gold Book (Gold Book Publishers, 1992).

REYNA, TONY (Taos Pueblo)
(Indian shop owner)
Address: Tony Reyna Indian Shop, P.O. Box 1892, Taos Indian Pueblo, Taos, NM 87571 (505) 758-3835.

REYNOLDS, ALLIE
(organization president)
Affiliation: The National Hall of Fame for Famous American Indians, Highway 62, Box 808, Anadarko, OK 73005 (405) 247-5795.

REYNOLDS, PAUL
(school principal)
Affiliation: Hopi Middle/High School, P.O. Box 337, Keams Canyon, AZ 86034 (520) 738-5111 Fax 738-5266.

REYNOLDS, STEPHANIE
(professor of anthropology)
Address & Affiliation: School of Social Sciences, 3151 Social Science Plaza, University of California, Irvine, Irvine, CA 92697-5100 (714) 824-5894. *Activities*: Teaches lower and upper division social sceince courses pertaining to the Indians, Aleuts, and Eskimos of North America)past and present). Dr. Reynolds is a foremost authority on Native American dance; she offers a course on comparisons of dance among urban and reservation Utes, Shoshoes, Eastern Pueblos, and Mixtecans, all groups among whom she has conducted field research.

RHINE, GARY 1951-
(film & video producer/director)
Born June 26, 1951, San Francisco, Calif. *Principal occupation*: Film & video producer/director. *Address & Affiliation*: Kifaru Productions (president, 1987-present), 23852 Pacific Coast Hwy. Suite 766, Malibu, CA 90265 (310) 457-1617 Fax 457-2688; E-Mail: rhino@kifaru.com. *Other professional post*: CEO, Dreamcatchers, Inc., 1994-present). *Awards, honors*: For "Wiping the Tears of Seven Generations": American Indian Film Festival's, "Best Video" award; National Educational Film Festival's, "Best Native American" Gold Apple; New York Festival's "Silver Medal" award; Munich International Film Festival, "One Future Prize." For "The Peyote Road": Chicago International Film Festival's "Silver Plaque" award; National Education Film & Video Festival's "Silver Apple" award," The C.I.N.E. "Golden Eagle" award; and the Great Plains Film Festival's "Best Documentary' award. For "The Red Road to Sobriety": the National Educational Media Network "Silver Apple" award; and CINE "Golden Eagle" award. For Follow Me Home": The San Francisco International Film Festival's "Audience Award for Best Feature Film" award. *Interests*: "Committed to amplifying the efforts of Native American spiritual leaders through the use of film & video documentaries. *Films produced & directed*: "Wiping the Tears of Seven Generations," 1992; "The Peyote Road," 1993; "Understanding A.I.R.F.A.," 1993; The Red Road to Sobriety, 1995; Your Humble Serpent: The Wisdom of Reuben Snake, 1996; Follow Me Home, 1997; "Rezrobics," 2002; "First Peoples TV," 2002; "A Seat at the Table; Struggling for American Indian Religious Freedom," 2003.

RHINES-LAWSON, VIVIAN L. (*Panther*)
(Southeastern Cherokee) 1940-
(accountant)
Born April 25, 1940, Knoxville, Tenn. *Education*: Adult Education Night School (Columbus, GA) , Accounting. *Principal occupation*: Accountant. *Address*: P.O Box 1784, Thomasville, GA 31799 (912) 574-5497; 226-0717 (work). *Affiliation*: Owner/president, Carroll Hill Auto Electronics, Inc., Thomasville, GA, 1974-. *Other professional posts*: Principal Chief, Southeastern Cherokee Confederacy Steering Committee. *Community activities*: Teacher & lecturer of Cherokee history & culture in area schools. *Memberships*: Southeastern Cherokee Confederacy; Cherokee Unity Council; Council of Clan Mothers; Deer Clan, Inc. *Awards, honors*: A plaque for my six years of video taping & showing to the students at Central High School Band, so they can improve their performance - half-time shows, concerts and competitions. *Interests*: "My main avocational interests are: genealogy, Native American history & culture, geology, painting of portraits & Native American bead work. My vocational interests are the personal computer & word processing." *Biographical source*: Article, "To Guard Against Invading Indians: Struggling for Native Community in the Southeast," in American Indian Culture & Research Journal, Fall 1994.

RHOADES, EVERETT RONALD, M.D. (Kiowa) 1931-
(physician)
Born October 24, 1931, Lawton, Okla. *Education*: Lafayette College, 1949-1952; University of Oklahoma, College of Medicine, MD, 1956. *Principal occupation*: Physician. *Home address*: 1808 Dorchester Dr., Oklahoma City, OK 73120 (405) 271-1417 Fax 271-3032. *Affiliations*: Chief, Infectious Diseases, Wilford Hall, U.S. Air Force Hospital, 1961-66; assistant professor of microbiology and associate professor of medicine, University of Oklahoma Medical Center, 1966-72; professor of medicine, Chief, Infectious Diseases, University of Oklahoma College of Medicine, Oklahoma City, OK, 1968-82; professor of medicine & adjunct professor of microbiology, University of Oklahoma, Health Sciences Center, 1972-82; Chief, Infectious Diseases Service University Hospital, 1975-82; director, Indian Health, Rockville, MD, 1982-93; Assistant Surgeon General, USPHS, 1982-93; associate dean, University of Oklahoma College of Medicine, 1993-; director of Education Initiatives, Center for American Indian/Alaska Native Health, Johns Hopkins School of Public Health, 1993-; director, Native American Prevention Research Center, University of Oklahoma College of Public Health, 1998-. *Military service*: U.S. Air Force, 1957-66 (Major; Certificate of Merit, 1967). *Community activities*: Oklahoma Lung Association (board of directors); Task Force on Health of American Indian Policy Review Commission (chairman, 1975); National Advisory Allergy and Infectious Disease Council (NIH), 1971-75; Central Oklahoma Indian Health Project (board of directors; chairman, 1976); Kiowa Tribal Business Committee (1967-70, 1979-81; vice chairman, 1974-76); Kiowa Tribal Land Management Committee, 1967-70; National Congress of American Indians (health committee); founder & donor, Dorothy Rowell Rhoades Prize to outstanding graduating Indian student, Elgin High School, Okla. *Memberships*: American Thoracic Society, 1963-82; American Federation for Clinical Research, 1960-; American College of Physicians, 1963- (Fellow); American Society for Microbiology, 1970-; Association on American Indian Affairs (board of directors, 1967-82; vice president, 1978-82); Association of American Indian Physicians (founder, 1971; president, 1972, 1976); Sigma Xi; Phi Beta Kappa; Kiowa Gourd Clan, 1970-; Association of Military Surgeons, 1982-; Infectious Disease Society of America, 1974-. *Awards, honors*: Markle Scholar, Academic Medicine, 1967-72; John Hay Whitney Opportunity Fellow, 1952-56; Student Research Achievement Award, 1956; Outstanding Achievement, Veterans Administration Hospital, 1960, 1961; Recognition Award, Association of American Indian Physicians, 1973, 1976; Breath of Life Award, Oklahoma Lung Association, 1977; Public Health Service Recognition Award, 1977; National Honor Lecturer, Mid-America State Universities Association, 1979; Association of American Indian Physicians Award of Excellence, 1980; PHS Meritorious Service Medal, 1985; Richard Kern Lecture Award, 1988; Kiowa Tribe of Oklahoma, "Exemplary Contributions to Health of Native Americans, 1988; Kiowa Veterans Association and Auxiliary, " In Appreciation for Dedicated Service to the American Indian Health Service, 1988; PHS Chief of Staff's Special Commendation Award, 1989. *Interests*: Internal medicine; infectious diseases; Kiowa Gourd Clan; Kiowa Blacklegging Society; dancing and powwows; amateau archaeology; history of medicine and Indians; travel. *Biographical sources*: Directory of Medical Specialists; Dictionary of International Biography, 1973; Who's Who in the South and Southwest; American Men & Women of Science; Indians of Today; Contemporary American Indian Leaders; Voices: A History of the Kiowa Tribe. Published works: Numerous articles in scientific journals relating to infectious diseases, microbiology, and Indian life; author of Kiowa Tribe for World Book Encyclopedia; edited Task Force Report to American Indian Policy Review Commission (Health), U.S. Government Printing Office, 1975.

RHOADES, KAREN A.
(school principal)
Affiliation: Kasigluk Day School, Kasigluk, AK 99609 (907) 477-6714.

RHOADS, KAY
(college president)
Affiliation: Medicine Creek Tribal College, 2002 E. 28th St., tacoma, WA 98404 (253) 593-7950 Fax 593-7895.

RHODD, DOUGLAS G. (Ponca)
(former tribal chairperson)
Affiliation: Ponca Tribe of Oklahoma, Business Committee, 20 White Eagle Dr., Box 2, Ponca City, OK 74601 (405) 762-8104.

RICE, ALEX (Mohawk of Quebec, Can.)
(actress)
Contact: Imparato Fay Management, Los Angeles, CA (3100 557-2112; Website: www.alexrice.biz. *Credits*: *Films*: "The Doe Boy," 2001; "Chasing Indigo," "The War Bride," "Thunderbird," and in "Lewis & Clark: Great Journey West." *TV Guest Star appearances*: "Spin City" (ABC); "Strong Medicine" (Lifetime); "CSI: Crime Scene Investigation" (CBS; "The Sopranos" (HBO); PBS mysteries, "Skinwalker," (2002); "Coyote Waits," (2003); and "Thief of Time," (2004); based on Tony Hillerman's novels; ABC miniseries, "Dreamkeeper." Awards: Nominated for Best Actress for, "Skinwalkers," 2002, and won Best Actress for "Coyote Waits," 2003, American Indian Motion Picture Awards.

RICE, G. WILLIAM (United Keetoowah Cherokee) 1951-
(associate professor of law)
Born August 3, 1951, Anadarko, Okla. *Education*: Phillips University (Enid, OK), BA, 1973; Lowell (MA) Technological Institute (MS degree program), 1973-75; University of Oklahoma College of Law, JD, 1978. *Principal occupation*: Associate professor of law. *Address*: University of Tulsa College of Law, 3120 E. 4th

Place, Tulsa, OK 74104 (918) 631-2439. *Affiliations*: Instructor, Antioch School of Law, Washington, DC, 1978-79; visiting assistant professor, Dept. of Political Science, University of Oklahoma, Norman, 1988-94; faculty member and first director of the Northern Plains Tribal Judicial Training Institute, University of North Dakota School of Law, Grand Forks, ND, 1994-95; adjunct professor of law, Cornell Law School, Ithaca, NY, 1995-96; associate professor of law, University of Tulsa School of Law, 1995-. *Areas of Teaching Specialization*: Federal Indian Law, Tribal Indian Law, Tribal Government, Jurisprudence, Constitutional Law, Criminal Law, Appellate Advocacy. *Other professional posts*: Sr. Attorney & President, G. William Rice, P.C., Norman, OK, 1979-88; Chairman of the Board of the Keetoowah Tribal Loan Fund, Tahlequah, OK, 1990-92; Attorney General for Sac & Fox Nation, Stroud, OK, 1985-95; general law practice, Rice & Bigler, Cushing, OK, 1988-95. *Community activities*: Chief Justice of Supreme Court of the Citizen Band Potawatomi Tribe, Shawnee, OK, 1986-; Court of Indian Offenses Bar Association (First President & Executive Director, 1979-83, 1986-88); Oklahoma Indian Legal Services Corp. (board of directors, 1981-82); Kiowa Tribal Tax Commission, Carnegie, OK, 1985-87); Absentee Shawnee Business Development Commission (Commissioner, 1987-88). *Memberships*: American Bar Association; Native American Bar Association; Oklahoma Indian Bar Association; Federal Bar Association. *Awards, honors*: Dannenburg Memorial Scholarship, University of Oklahoma College of Law; Martin Luther King Teaching Fellowship, Lowell Technological Institute; Phillips University Scholarship; Phi Delta Phi Honorary Legal Fraternity, University of Oklahoma College of Law; Honorary Mayor-President, City of Baton Rouge, Parish of East Baton Rouge, 1987. *Interests*: Powwows and other Indian social functions, hunting, fishing. *Published works*: Cases and Material on Indian Property Law (Antioch School of Law, 1978); Court Rules of the Court of Indian Offenses (BIA, Anadarko Area Office, 1979); Cases and Materials on the Impact of the Indian Child Welfare Act in Oklahoma (Indian Legal Resource Center, 1980); Indian Children, State Laws, and the Indian Child Welfare Act of 1978 (Indian Legal Resource Center, 1980); Oklahoma Indian Law (Indian Legal Resource Center, 1980); Materials on the Impact of the Indian Child Welfare Act in Nebraska (Indian Legal Resource Center, 1980); Indian Child Welfare Act Handbook for Tribes in Oklahoma (OK Indian Affairs Commission, 1980); Handbook of Federal Indian Law (Michie, Bobbs-Merrill, 1982) contributing author for revision of Felix Cohen's 1942 edition. *Articles*: "The Mythology of the Oklahoma Indians: A Survey of Legal Status of Indian Tribes in Oklahoma" (American Indian Law Review, 259, 1979); "The End of Indian Sovereignty or a Self-limitation of Contractual Ability?" (American Indian Law Review, 239, 1977); "The Journey from Ex Parte Crow Dog to Littlechief: A Survey of Tribal Civil and Criminal Jurisdiction in Western Oklahoma" (American Indian Law Review, 1, 1979). Authored and edited many contributions, federal charters, ordinances and complete law and order codes for various tribes which are too numerous to list.

RICE, JOHN
(Indian band chief)
Affiliation: Wasauksin (Parry Island) Indian Band, Box 253, Parry Sound, Ontario, Canada P0P 2X4 (705) 746-2531.

RICE, STAN, JR. (Yavapai)
(tribal president)
Affiliation: Yavapai-Prescott Board of Directors, 530 E. Merritt St., Prescott, AZ 86301 (928) 445-8790.

RICE, WILLIAM
(Indian program co-director)
Affiliation: Native American Law Certificate Program, University of Tulsa College of Law, 3120 E. 4th Pl., Tulsa, OK 74104 (918) 631-3139 Fax 631-2194.

RICEHILL, ERNEST (Winnebago/Omaha) 1948-
(administrator)
Born November 29, 1948, Winnebago, Neb. *Education*: Briar Cliff College (Sioux City, IA), 1976. *Principal occupation*: Administrator. *Home address*: Resides in NE. *Affiliations*: Curator, Sioux City Art Center, 1973-79; director, Office of Indian Education, Sioux City

Community Public Schools, 1979-84; personnel administrator, Omaha Tribe of Nebraska, 1984-88; executive director, Sioux City American Indian Center, Sioux City, IA, 1991-95. *Community activities*: Sioux City Community Schools (member of Project Awareness, the Curriculum Committee, Multicultural Committee, and Committee on Formulating Policy on Chronic Absenteeism); chairman of Sioux City Minority Coalition; board member, Native American Alcoholic Treatment Center; chairman of Siouxland Council of Agency Executives; member of Winnebago Tribe's Healthy Start Planning Committee; member of the Siouxland Housing Corporation; among others. *Memberships*: National Indian Education Association; National Indian Media Association; Iowa Museum Association. *Awards, honors*: Elected Delegate to the precinct, county, and state Democratic Conventions, 1972-80, 1984-85; appointed Chairman of Precinct 16, Democratic Party; elected National Delegate to the 1972, 1988 & 1992 National Democratic Conventions; appointed Iowa State Coordinator of the Native Americans for Clinton-Gore National Election Committee, Aug. 1992; member of the President Clinton's transition team of the Native Americans for Clinton-Gore National Election Committee, Nov. 1992; appointed member of the White House/Robert Wood Johnson Foundation panel on "Conversations on Health: A Dialogue with the American People, Amkeny, Iowa, March 1993; member/representative to the National Native American Listening Conference sponsored by the Dept. of Justice & Interior, Albuquerque, May 1994.

RICHARD, ORIE
(editor)
Affiliation: "Turtle Mountain Times," Turtle Mountain Tribe, Belcourt, ND 58316 (701) 477-6451.

RICHARDS, RICK
(clinic director)
Affiliation: Sam Hider Jay Community Clinic, P.O. Box 350, Jay, OK 74346 (918) 253-4271.

RICHARDS, THOMAS, JR. (Aviaq) (Inupiat Eskimo) 1949-
(writer/planner)
Born September 27, 1949, Kotzebue, Alaska. *Education*: University of Denver, 1967-68; University of Alaska, 1968; Armed Forces Air Intelligence Training Center, CO, 1969. *Principal occupation*: Writer/planner. *Home address*: Unknown. *Affiliations*: Editor/publisher, Tundra Times (newspaper), 1973, 1977-80; vice-president, Association of Village Council Presidents, Bethel, AK, 1981-86; owner/operator, Thomas Richards, Jr. & Associates, Bethel, AK (current). *Other professional post*: Author. *Military service*: U.S. Navy, 1969-73 (Vietnam Service Vet, E-5; Photo-Intelligence Specialist. *Community activities*: Founding director, Institute of Alaska Native Arts (board of directors, 1975-76); member, Inuit Circumpolar Conference Communications & Broadasting Commission, 1979-84. *Memberships*: Alaska Federation of Natives (Human Resources Board, 1980-86); American Legion, Post No. 11. *Awards, honors*: Congressional Intern, 1970-72, office of U.S. Rep. Nick Begich; Governor's Representative, State Committee, Alaska Humanities Forum (Chairperson & member, 1975-82); Committee on Arctic Cultural Development, UNESCO, United Nations (U.S. Representative, 1979-80, appointed by U.S. Dept. of State);Oustading Young Man of America, U.S. Jaycees, nominated by the Office of the Governor, 1979; Howard Rock Award for Native community service, presented by the Board of Directors, Tundra Times, 1980. *Interests*: "After 20 years as a writer and an administrator for Alaska Native organizations, my primary career interest now centers on economic and business development. Although I still write (mostly histories), most of my current work is in entrepreneurship training. I help rural Alaskans research and write business plans and start-up their own business ventures." *Published works*: Alaska Native Claims-Unit 4 (Alaska Native Foundation, 1976); Pribilof Progress... PribilofPace (Aleutian/Pibilof Islands Association, 1979); ANCSA and Related Studies - textbook history of Alaska Native land claims for Lower Kuskokwim School District, Bethel, AK (Lower Kuskokwim School District, 1992).

RICHARDS, WILLIAM H., Sr. (Xus-x'a-yo)
(Smith River Rancheria-Tolowa)
(tribal chairperson)
Born March 17, 1936, Del Norte, Calif. *Education*: College of the Redwoods (2 years). *Home address*: 301 N. Indian Rd., Smith River, CA 95567 (707) 487-9255 (work). *Affiliation*: Chairman, Smith River Rancheria, Smith River, CA , 1978-. *Military service*: 1955-58 (Sp. 4). *Community activities*: State Committee on Indian Juvenile Justice (member).

RICHARDSON, BARRY (Haliwa-Saponi) 1954-
(tribal administrator)
Born August 13, 1954, Warren County, N.C. *Education*: Pembroke State University, BA (Political Science), 1976. *Principal occupation*: Tribal administrator. *Home address*: P.O. Box 609, Hollister, NC 27844 (919) 586-4017 (work). *Affiliations*: Executive director, Baltimore American Indian Center, Baltimore, MD; president, Pow-Wow, Hollister, NC, 1990-. *Other professional posts*: Founder & treasurer of the National American Indian Council. *Community activities*: Preserve Haliwa Now, Bethlehem Recreation, Inc. *Membership*: National Congress of American Indians. *Interest*: Coin collecting.

RICHARDSON, BILL
(U.S. Congressman)
Affiliation: Chairperson, House Committee on Interior & Insular Affairs, Subcommittee on Native American Affairs, U.S. House of Representatives, 1522 Longworth House Office Bldg., New Jersey & Independence Ave., SE, Washington, DC 20515 (202) 226-7736 Fax 226-0522.

RICHARDSON, JEFFREY
(executive director)
Affiliation: Nevada Urban Indians, 1190 Bible Way, Reno, NV 89502.

RICHARDSON, JOSEPH (Haliwa-Saponi)
(tribal chairperson)
Affiliation: Haliwa-Saponi Tribe, P.O. Box 99, Hollister, NC 27844 (919) 586-4017.

RICHARDSON, KENNETH
(health center director)
Affiliation: Walker River Paiute Tribal health Center, P.O. Drawer C, Schurz, NV 89427 (702) 773-2005.

RICHARDSON, LINDA
(BIA assistant director)
Affiliation: Bureau of Indian Affairs, Office of Financial Management, 1849 C St., NW, MS: 4140-MIB, Washington, DC 20240 (202) 208-6342.

RICHARDSON, PATRICIA ROSE (BREWINGTON)
(Coharie-Cherokee) 1933-
(crafts consultant)
Born July 21, 1933, Clinton, N.C. *Education*: East Carolina Indian School, 1952; Nash Technical College, AA, 1986. *Principal occupation*: American Indian crafts consultant/pottery and beadwork. *Home address*: P.O. Box 130, Hollister, NC 27844. *Affiliations*: Instructor, Title IV Indian Education, Halifax Board of Education, N.C. (six years); crafts instructor, Haliwa-Supai Indian Tribe, Hollister, N.C. (5 years). *Memberships*: North Carolina Crafts Association (board member); American Indian Heritage Foundation. *Awards, honors*: First Place Awards—Excellence in Beadwork, Schiele Museum Indian Festival, 1978/1986; Good Medicine Crafts Award, 1980/1986. *Interests*: Exhibitions at major Indian festivals: Grand Prairie, TX, Hunter Mountain, NY, Palm Beach, FL, NC Indian festivals, National Indian Festival, Washington, DC.

RICHARDSON, W.R. (Haliwa-Saponi)
(tribal chief)
Affiliation: Haliwa-Saponi Tribe, P.O. Box 99, Hollister, NC 27844 (919) 586-4017.

RICHIE, CHIP
(film director; co-owner)
Address & Affiliation: Director, Rich-Heape Films, Inc., 5952 Royal Lane, Suite 254, Dallas, TX 75230 (888) 600-2922; (214) 696-6916. E-mail: chip@richheape.com; Website: www.richheape.com *Professional activities*: Director of Native American videos, films and movies dedicated to inform, educate and encourage

the awareness of the history, cultures, languages, traditions and aspirations of Native Americans and other Native Peoples. Rich-Heape Films has been recognized as 1999 & 2003 American Indian Business of the Year by the American Indian Chamber of Commerce of Texas, and has reeceived numerous awards. *Published works*: *Videos*: "Black Indians: An American Story," 60 mins. VHS & DVD; "How to Trace Your Native American Heritage," 35 mins. VHS & DVD; Tales of Wonder I & II, 60 mins. each. VHS & DVD, CD soundtrack; "Native American Healing in the 21st Century," 40 mins. VHS & DVD; "Walela-Live in Concert," DVD, VHS & audio CD (2004). *Book*: "American Indian Directory" -1999 (national listing of over 500 federally-recognized American Indian nations & tribes.

RICHMOND, ROSEMARY (Akwesasne Mohawk) 1937-
(executive director, administrator)
Born December, 19, 1937, White Plains, NY. *Address & Affiliations*: Executive Director, American Indian Community House (AICH), 708 Broadway, 8th Floor, New York, NY 10003 (212) 598-0100 Fax 598-4909. E-mail: rrichmond@aich.org. Website: www.aich.org. *Other professional posts*: Board member, Spiderwoman Theatre Company, 1990-present; founding board member, Flying Eagle Woman Fund for Peace, Justice & Sovereignty, 1990-present. *Community activities*: Founding member, Thunderbird American Indian Dancers, NYC; member, New York City Work Force Investment Board (past officer), 2000-present; member, Statewide Advisory Committee, American Indian Program, Cornell University, Ithaca, NY; member of the Native American Council of NYC, an organization formed to bring Native social issues to the attention of the general public; served on the Board of Directors of the American Indian Health Care Association for Region I, 1988-94. *Interests*: Ms. Richmond has been associated with the American Indian Community House in administrative capacities since 1975, and has been its executive director since 1987. Under her leadership, AICH has grown from a loose consortium of groups and individuals into its present status as a multi-faceted social support and cultural center. AICH serves the Native American community of New York City with health counseling and referral programs, job training, alcoholism and substance abuse counseling, and the first American Indian HIV/AIDS project in the Northeast. In addition to these social services, AICH houses an off-off Broadway theater, a performing arts program for Native artists of any media, and a 1,600 square foot art gallery which presents exhibitions of both contemporary and traditional Native American visual artists. and is a founding member of the Thunderbird American Indian Dancers, who, since 1963, have raised funds through educational performance for scholarships for Indian college and vocational students.

RICKER, BERNADINE R.
(administrative officer)
Affiliation: Not-Tsoo Gah-Nee Indian Health Center, P.O. Box 117, Fort Hall, ID 83203 (208) 238-2400.

RIDDLES, LEONARD *(Black Moon)* (Comanche) 1919-
(artist, rancher/farmer)
Born June 28, 1919, Walters, Okla. *Education*: Fort Sill Indian School (Valedictorian, 1941). *Principal occupation*: Artist, farmer/rancher. *Home address*: Route #1, Box 89, Walter, OK 73572 (405) 281-3623. *Professional posts*: Elected as tribal officer for the Kiowa, Comanche and Apache Tribal Council, and later tribal officer on the Comanche Tribal Council. *Military service*: U.S. Army, 1941-45 (Pfc; Sharp Shooter, 8P Service Ribbon, American Defense Ribbon, two bronze stars). *Community activities*: Comanche Tribal Council (former officer); Masons. *Membership*: American Indian Artists Association; Cotton County Art Council; Comanche Little Pony War Society. *Awards, honors*: He has been the recipient of awards and honors in regional shows and exhibits throughout the U.S. His paintings are included in permanent public collections at the Lyman Allen Museum, New London, CT; Dept. of the Interior, Washington, DC; and Southern Plains Indian Museum, Anadarko, OK. His work is included in numerous private collections in the U.S. and foreign countries. He was commissioned by the Indian Arts & Crafts Board, Dept. of the Interior, in 1968 to

create a series of hide paintings which include "Comanche Medicine Shield" and Battle of Adobe Walls". *Exhibitions*: Philbrook Art Center, Inter-Tribal Indian Ceremonial; Museum of New Mexico; U.S. Department of the Interior Gallery; among others. *Interests*: Art work. Mr. Riddles writes, "I am interested in the history of the American Indian and in any phase of archaeological study. We do research on the Comanche Tribe, so (I) find all expeditions of real interest. Museums are also of great interest to me." He has mastered the medium of watercolor with paintings that reflect narrative portrayals of Comanche Tribal heritage. One of his paintings, "Eagle Dancer', was featured in the Oklahoma India Artists Calendar, 1976. Mr. Riddles illustrated the book Storms Brewed in Other Men's Worlds; and the jacket for Buried Colts, by Harley Smith.

RIDESHORSE, SAMUEL (Cocopah)
(BIA agency supt.)
Affiliation: Fort Yuma Agency, Bureau of Indian Affairs, P.O. Box 11000, Fort Yuma, AZ 85366 (928) 782-1202 Fax 782-1266.

RIDGELY, EUGENE, JR. (Arapaho)
(language professor)
Affiliation: Director, Bilingual Education Program, Wind River Tribal College, Ethete, WY.

RIDINGTON, ROBIN 1939-
(anthropologist)
Born November 1, 1939, Camden, N.J. *Education*: Swarthmore, BA, 1962; Harvard University, Ph.D., 1968. *Principal occupation*: Anthropologist. *Home address*: RR 2, Site 44 C-16, Galiano, BC V0N 1P0 Canada (250) 539-3095 Fax 539-3096; E-mail: ridington@gulfislands.com. Website: www.retreat.com. *Affiliations*: Professor of anthropology, University of British Columbia, Vancouver, BC, 1967-95, professor emeritus, 1995-present; associate dean of graduate studies, University of Retreat Island. *Memberships*: Society for Humanistic Anthropology (Canadian representative); Canadian Ethnology Society; American Anthropological Association. *Award*: 1989 Hubert Evans Non-Fiction Book Prize of British Columbia. *Interests*: Field research among Beaver Indians, 1964-; writing about Omaha ceremony, 1985-. *Biographical source*: "A Sacred Object as Text: Reclaiming the Sacred Pole of the Omaha Tribe," American Indian Quarterly, 1993. *Published works*: Articles: "From Artifice to Artifact: Stages in the Industrialization of a Northern Native Community" (Journal of Canadian Studies, 1983); "Stories of the Vision Quest Among Dunne-za Women" (Atlantis, 1983); "Beaver Indians" (The Canadian Encyclopedia, Hurtig, 1985); "Native People, Subarctic" (The Canadian Encyclopedia, Hurtig, 1985); "Fox and Chicadee: The Writing of Indian White History" in volume edited by Calvin Martin; "The Northern Hunters" (Newberry Library volume, America in 1492, Alvin Josephy, Editor, 1990); among others. *Books*: Swan People: A Study of the Dunne-za Prophet Dance (National Museums of Canada, 1978); co-author, People of the Trail: How the Northern Forest Indians Lived (Douglas & McIntyre, 1978); co-author, People of the Longhouse: How the Iroquoian People Lived (Douglas & McIntyre, 1982; Trail to Heaven: Knowledge & Narrative in a Northern Native Community (University of Iowa Press, 1988); Little Bit Know Something: Stories in a Language of Anthropology (University of Iowa Press, 1990); Blessing for a Long Time: The Sacred Pole of the Omaha Tribe, with Dennis Hastings (University of Nebraska Press, 1997).

RIDLEY, PATRICIA L. (Poarch Creek)
(library curator)
Affiliation: Poarch Creek Indian Heritage Center, P.O. Box 633, Wetumpka, AL 36092 (205) 368-9136.

RIDLEY, SANDRA L.
(curator)
Affiliation: Poarch Creek Indian Heritage Center, HCR69A, Box 85B, Atmore AL 36502 (205) 368-9136.

RIDLING, DANA
(board president)
Affiliation: National Native American AIDS Prevention Center, 436 14th St., Suite 1020, Oakland, CA 94609 (510) 444-2051 Fax 444-1593.

RIDOLFI, JOAN
(museum docent)
Affiliation: Nanticoke Indian Museum, Rt. 13, Box 107A, Millsboro, DE 19966 (302) 945-7022.

RIGGS, JIM W. 1945-
(primitive technologist instructor; writer, photographer, illustrator)
Born February 17, 1945, Portland, Oreg. *Education*: Oregon State University, BA, 1968. *Principal occupation*: Primitive technologist instructor; writer, photographer, illustrator. *Home address*: P.O. Box 627, Wallowa, OR 97885 (541) 437-1895. *Affiliations*: Instructor of ethnobotany & aboriginal life skills courses, Maheur Field Station, Princeton, OR (Summers, 1974-89). *Other professional posts*: Board member, International Society of Primitive Technology; archaeologist, Forest Service, Hells Canyon NRA and private groups. As a freelance writer, photographer & illustrator, he has contributed to numerous periodicals and books and written his own treatise, Blue Mountain Buckskin (self-published, 1980), " the most in-depth how-to book available on brain-tanning. He was informational consultant for book series, "Clan of the Cave Bear." His replications of Great Basin material culture components comprise several exhibits at the High Desert Museum in Bend, OR. *Interests*: Specializing in prehistoric cultural ecology and environmental adaptations of aboriginal peoples of the Northern Great Basin & Columbia Plateau regions, he continues to research & practice primitive skills & technologies how to instruct workshops & intensive field courses covering these subjects. Biographical source: Chapter in "Footprints Across Oregon," by Mike Thoele. *Published works*: Blue Mountain Buckskin (self-published, 1980); several chapters in "Best of Woodsmoke," "Primitive Outdoor Skills," & "Woodsmoke," edited by Richard & Linda Jamison.

RILEY, CHARLES W., II
(school principal)
Affiliation: Pine Springs Boarding School, P.O. Box 198, Houck, AZ 86506 (602) 871-4311.

RILEY, DELBERT
(Indian band chief)
Affiliation: Chippewas of the Thames, RR 1, Muncey, ON, Canada N0L 1Y0 (519) 264-1528.

RINER, REED D. 1941-
(anthropologist/futurist)
Born December 22, 1941, Mentone, Ind. *Education*: University of Colorado, Ph.D., 1977 (dissertation: A Study of Attitudes Toward Formal Education Among Indian Parents and Students in Six Communities. *Principal occupation*: Professor of anthropology, Northern Arizona State University, Flagstaff, 1975-. *Home address*: 506 Charles Rd., Flagstaff, AZ 86001. *Military service*: U.S. Naval Reserve, 1963-68. *Memberships*: American Anthropological Association; Society for Applied Anthropology; High Plains Society for Applied Anthropology (past president); World Future Studies Federation; World Future Society - Professional Section; Contact Cultures of the Imagination (board of directors). *Interests*: "My primary professional interests are applied futures research; Native American Indian studies, especially Indian education; and the application of anthropology in the solution of—especially institutional—organizational problems such as the future of Native American Indians." *Published works*: Numerous articles in professional journals.

RIOS, MICHAEL (O'Odham)
(association board member)
Affiliation: National Indian Youth Council, 318 Elm, SE, Albuquerque, NM 87102.

RISLING, DALE, SR. (Hoopa)
(BIA agency supt.)
Affiliation: Central California Agency, Bureau of Indian Affairs, 1824 Tribute Rd., Suite J, Sacramento, CA 95815 (916) 566-7121 Fax 566-7510.

RISLING, DAVID (Hoopa-Yurok/Karok) 1921-
(professor emeritus; volunteer work)
Born April 10, 1921, Weitchpec (Hoopa Reservation Ext.), Calif. *Education*: California Polytechnic University, BS, 1948, MA, 1953. *Principal occupation*: Retired-doing volunteer work for American Indians

throughout North America. *Home address*: 2403 Catalina Dr., Davis, CA 95616 (530) 756-7085 Fax 752-7097. *Affiliations*: President and chairman of Board of Trustees of DQ University, Davis, CA; professor emeritus, Native American Studies Department, University of California, Davis, 1970-. *Past professional posts*: Agricultural instructor, 1951-70 & counselor, 1962-70, Modesto Jr. College, Modesto, CA; *Military service*: U.S. Navy, 1942-45 (Commanding Officer of an anti-submarine ship, 1945). *Community activities*: In 1967, Risling organized the first statewide conference on Indian education at Stanislaus State College. He helped organize the first Indian-controlled conference on education in the U.S. which conference led to the founding of the California Indian Education Association; chairperson, D-Q University Board of Trustees; speaker at many universities regarding lives of American Indians; one of the leaders of the Traditional Circle Indian Elder and Youth; coordinator, Tecumseh Center, University of California, Davis; former chairperson of: California Indian Legal Services, Native America Rights Fund, American Indian Higher Education Consortium, and several other Indian and non-Indian organizations. *Memberships*: Association on American Indian Affairs (member-board of directors); California Indian Education Association, 1968- (cofounder and past president, 1968-70); American Indian Institute; American Friends Service Committee; United Native Nations; National Indian Education Association (co-founder and board of directors for several years); Hoopa Tribe. *Awards, honors*: Outstanding agricultural teacher in central California, 1963; from 1973-81, Risling served on the National Advisory Commission on Indian Education, appointed to the post by Presidents Nixon, Ford and Carter; "Outstanding Indian Educator of the Year," by the State Dept. of Education & State Senate, 1990; The Native American Elders Award, 1990, by the State Dept. of Education and the California Indian Education Association; 1992 UC Davis "Distinguished Public Service Award." David was the first Native American known to have graduated a university. *Interests*: Indian rights, spirituality, sovereignty, Indian education, self-determination, Indian history; "helping our Indian people, participating in our Indian ceremonials"; fishing and sports; travel in Europe, New Zealand, Australia, and South America. *Biographical sources*: Book - The Lives of Ethnic Amerians (Kendall-Hunt, 1991); Articles - "Risling Legacy," Sacramento Magazine, June 1990; "Native Son," Sattert Town News, May 1991; "From All Four Directions," Pacific Discovery, Winter 1992.

RISLING, DOUGLAS
(center director)
Affiliation: Northern California Indian Development Center, 241 F St., Eureka, CA 95501 (707) 445-8451.

RISLING, LOIS
(center director)
Affiliation: Center for Indian Community Development, Humboldt University, Brero House 93, Arcata, CA 95521 (707) 826-3711.

RISLING, MARY
(attorney)
Affiliation: California Indian Legal Services, 324 F St., Suite A, Eureka, CA 95501 (707) 443-8397.

RITTER, BETH R. 1961-
(anthropologist, geographer)
Born June 21, 1961, Kearney, Neb. *Education*: University of Nebraska, MA, 1990, PhD (expected 1996). *Principal occupation*: Anthropologist, geographer. *Home address*: 2725 S. 16th, Lincoln, NE 68502 (402) 472-9677 (work). *Affiliations*: Anthropologist, National Park Service, Lincoln, NE, 1993-94; instructor, University of Nebraska, Lincoln, 1992-. *Other professional post*: Consultant, Ponca Tribe of Nebraska & Black Eagle Corp. *Memberships*: American Anthropological Association; Society for Applied Anthropology. *Interests*: "Primary interest is the Plains Indians & contemporary issues; Federal Indian policy; Native American political & legal systems; Indian gaming (consultant to Ponca Tribe of Nebraska during recent (1990) restoration of their federally-terminated status)." *Published works*: Articles: "The Ponca Tribe of Nebraska: The Process of Restoration of a Federally-Terminated Tribe," in Human Organization, 1992; "The Politics of Retribalization: The Northern Ponca Case," in Great

Plains Research, 1994; "Will the House Win: Does Sovereignty Rule in Indian Casinos," in Great Plains Research, 1994.

RITTER, GLADINE
(editor)
Affiliation: "Oregon Directory of American Indian Resources," Commission on Indian Services, 454 State Capitol, Salem, OR 97310 (503) 986-1067.

RITZ, LAN BROOKES
(writer/filmmaker)
Principal occupation: Writer/filmmaker, Brown Bird Productions, 1971 N. Curson Ave., Hollywood, CA 90046 (213) 851-8928. *Film produced*: Annie Mae — Brave Hearted Woman (written, produced, and directed by Lan Brookes Ritz) this film is an account of recent Native American history told from the intimate perspective of a dedicated young Indian woman killed on a reservation in the aftermath of the human rights stand at Wounded Knee (16mm, 80 minutes, color). *Awards, honors*: Best Motion Picture, American Indian Film Festival; Award of Excellence, Film Advisory Board; Best in Category, San Francisco International Film Festival. *Featured screenings*: Museum of Modern Art, New York, NY; Kennedy Center, Washington, DC; London and Melbourn Film Festivals; Cinema du reel, France; etc. *Interest*: Visual design.

RIVERA, BARRY L. (Lenni Lenape)
(historical society secretary)
Address & Affiliation: Secretary, Lenni Lenape Historical Society, 2825 Fish Hatchery Rd., Allentown, PA 18103 (610) 797-2121 Fax 797-2801. E-mail: lenape@lenape.org.

ROACH, MILBURN H.
(IHS-executive assistant)
Affiliation: Office of the Director, Indian Health Service, Room 6-05, 5600 Fishers Lane, Rockville, MD 20857 (301) 443-1083.

ROACH-WHEELER, MARGARET
(Chickasaw-Choctaw)
(designer-craftsperson)
Affiliation: Owner, Mahota Handwovens, 67 Horseshoe Dr., Joplin, MO 64804 (417) 782-7036. *Products*: American Indian clothing adapted for contemporary wear.

ROBBINS, EARL (Catawba)
(craftsperson)
Address: 1599 Hagler Dr., Rock Hill, SC 29730 (803) 324-0204. *Products*: Traditional Catawba pottery.

ROBBINS, KENNETH (Standing Rock Sioux)
(organization president; co-publisher & writer)
Affiliations: National Center for American Indian Enterprise Development, 953 E. Juanita Ave., Mesa, AZ 85204 (800) 462-2433; (480) 545-1298 Fax 545-4208. Co-publisher & writer, with A. David Lester, of "RedEarth" Magazine, Council Publications, Denver, CO.

ROBBINS, REBECCA (Standing Rock Sioux)
(writer)
Education: PhD. *Affiliation*: Writer, "RedEarth" Magazine, Council Publications, 695 S. Colorado Blvd., Suite 10, Denver, CO 80246 (303) 282-7576 Fax 282-7584.

ROBERTS, BARBARA (Lummi) 1955-
(college administrator)
Born June 14, 1955, Bellingham, Wash. *Education*: Walla Walla College, BA, 1977; University of Hawaii, MPH, 1980. *Principal occupation*: College administrator. *Home address*: 2730 Cagey Rd., Bellingham, WA 98226-9287 (206) 676-2772 (work). *Affiliations*: Dept. Head, Lummi Health & Human Services, Bellingham (10 years); Title III Director, Personnel Officer, Northwest Indian College, Bellingham, 1990-. *Interests*: Development of culturally relevant curriculum for college courses.

ROBERTS, BILL (Cherokee)
(artist, craftsperson)
Affiliation: Owner, Brad Hawiyeh-Ehi, 4399 E. Moores Pike, Bloomington, IN 47401 (812) 335-1240. *Membership*: Indian Arts & Crafts Association.

ROBERTS, CARLA A. (Delaware) 1957-
(administrator; consultant)
Born in 1957. *Education*: University of Alaska, Fairbanks, BFA, 1979; University of Iowa, MFA, 1981. *Principal occupation*: Administrator; consultant. *Address*: ATLATL, P.O.Box 34090, Phoenix, AZ 85067 (602) 277-3711 Fax 277-3690 (office). *Affiliations*: Coordinator, Univerity of Alaska, Rural Education, Fairbanks, AK, 1976-79; assistant director, Intermedia Arts-Minnesota, University of Minnesota, Minneapolis, 1982-86; executive director, Boston Film/Videl Foundation, Boston, MA, 1986-87; consultant, Art Management for Boston Conservatory, Indian Hill Arts, University of Lowell, Center for Native American Awareness, 1988-91; executive director, ATLATL, Phoenix, AZ. *Other professional posts*: Consultant, Tribal Museum Program, Arizona Commission on the Arts, Phoenix, AZ, 1991-; speaking engagements: "The Ethics of Celebration & De-Celebration," University of Florida, Gainesville, Dec. 1991; "Indian smoking Museums," Arizona State University, Tempe, Nov. 1991; "Native American Storytelling" & "Multi-Cultural Literature, University of Lowell (MA), March-April, 1991. *Community activities*: National Endowment for the Arts (panelist, Jan. 1992; advisory group, 1991-93) panelist, Arizona Commission on the Arts, Phoenix, AZ, 1991-; board member, Indian Hill Arts, Littleton, MA, 1991. *Published works*: ATLATL: Serving the Needs of Native American Artists, Art View (National Assembly of State Arts Agencies, Washington, DC, 1991).

ROBERTS, CHRIS 1948-
(photographer/writer; video/book distributor)
Born March 29, 1948, London, England. *Education*: Masters Degree in Interpersonal Communications. *Principal occupation*: Photographer/writer; video/book distributor. *Affiliation & Address*: Meadowlark Media, P.O. Box 7218, Missoula, MT 59807 (888) 728-2180. (406) 728-2180 Fax 549-3090. *Military service*: U.S. Army, 1966-70. *Community activities*: Powwow Committee; Boy Scouts of America. *Published works*: Powwow Country, 1993; People of the Circle, 1998.

ROBERTS, DELORES (Mono)
(rancheria chairperson)
Affiliation: North Fork Rancheria, P.O. Box 929, North Fork, CA 93643 (559) 877-2461.

ROBERTS, HOLLIS E. (Choctaw)
(tribal chief)
Affiliation: Choctaw Tribal Council, P.O. Drawer 1210, Durant, OK 74702 (405) 924-8280.

ROBERTS, ISAAC (Sac & Fox)
(former tribal chief)
Affiliation: Sac & Fox Tribe of the Mississippi Reservation, Sac & Fox Tribal Council, 3137 F Ave., Tama, IA 52339 (515) 484-4678.

ROBERTS, JAMES D. (Sauk-Suiattle)
(former tribal chairperson)
Affiliation: Sauk-Suiattle Tribal Council, 5318 Chief Brown Lane, Darrington, WA 98241 (360) 435-8366.

ROBERTS, MICHAEL E.
(institute director)
Affiliation: First Nations Development Institute, The Stores Bldg., 11917 Main St., Fredericksburg, VA 22408 (703) 371-5615.

ROBERTS, ROY
(Indian band chief)
Affiliation: Campbell River Indian Band, 1400 Weiwaikum Rd., Campbell River, British Columbia, Canada V9W 5W8 (604) 286-6949.

ROBERTSON, ELEANOR
(IHS-program director)
Affiliations: Indian Health Service, 300 Mateo, NE, Suite 500, Albuquerque, NM 87102 (505) 766-6215; director, Tucson Office of Health Program Development, 7900 So. JJ Stock Rd., Tucson, AZ 85746 (602) 670-5010.

ROBERTSON, ELLEN (Oklahoma Cherokee) 1945-
(reference librarian)
Born March 7, 1945, Washington, D.C. *Education*: University of California, Berkeley, B.A., 1973, M.L.S., 1974. *Principal occupation*: Reference librarian. *Home*

address: 3000 18th St., Boulder, CO 80304 (303) 939-9003. *Affiliations*: Librarian, American Indian Law Center, University of New Mexico School of Law, Albuquerque, N.M., 1975-77; reference librarian, University of New Mexico General Libraries, 1977-84; reference librarian & online search service coordinator, University of Colorado, University Libraries, Boulder, 1984-. *Memberships*: American Library Association, 1985-; Colorao Library Association, 1985-. *Interests*: Reading, hiking, travel (Peace Corps, 1966-1968 - Tunisia; Europe, Australia.)

ROBERTSON, SIGRUN C.
(Alaska Native coop manager)
Affiliation: "Oomingmak" Musk Ox Producers' Cooperative (Yup'ik and Inupiat), 604 H St., Anchorage, AK 99501 (907) 272-9225.

ROBERTSON, WILBERT (Sioux)
(board member)
Affiliation: Intertribal Christian Comunications, P.O. Box 3765, Station B, Winnipeg, Manitoba, Canada R2W 3R6 (204) 661-9333.

ROBICHAUX, BRENDA DARDAR (Houma)
(tribal chairperson)
Affiliation: United Houma Nation, 20986 Hwy. 1, Golden Meadow, LA 70357 (504) 475-6640.

ROBINSON, D. DWANE
(school principal)
Affiliation: Dzilth-Na-O-Dith-Hle Community School, P.O. Box 5003, Bloomfield, NM 87413 (505) 632-1697 Fax 632-8563.

ROBINSON, DIANA D.
(Indian band chief)
Affiliation: Acadia Indian Band, RR 4, Box 5914C, Yarmouth, NS, Canada B5A 4A8 (902) 742-0257.

ROBINSON, GAIL S.
(museum director)
Affiliation: Woodruff Museum of Indian Artifacts, Bridgeton Public Library, 150 E. Commerce St., Bridgeton, NJ 08302 (856) 451-2620.

ROBINSON, GARY
(Cherokee-Mississippi Choctaw) 1950-
(filmmaker, writer, media consultant)
Born January 12, 1950, Dallas, Tex. *Education*: University of Texas, Austin, BS, 1973; MA (Radio, TV, Film), 1978. *Principal occupation*: Filmmaker, writer, media consultant. *Address*: Unknown. *Affiliations*: Production assistant, Instructional Media Department, Tulsa Public Schools, Tulsa, OK 1973-74; media specialist, Texas Department of Mental Health/Mental Retardation, Austin, TX 1975-78; branch sales manager, Magnetic Media Corp., Austin, TX, 1978-1979; Writer, producer, director of video programs about the history, culture and current affairs of the Muscogee (Creek) Indian Nation, Okmulgee, OK, 1981-90; owner-producer, Pathfinder Communications (produced programs for other Indian organizations and clients), Okmulgee, OK, 1981-90; vice president, American Indian Media Services (planned and supervised projects, produced media programs for Indian tribal governments, Indian-owned businesses and Indian organizations; developed Oklahoma statewide American Indian newspaper called "Intertribal."); independent writer/producer/media consultant, Spirit World Productions, Santa Fe, NM, 1992-present. *Awards, honors*: "Dances for the New Generations" (director of photography) Emmy-nominated documentary and "Best Documentary" awards at film festivals - on the American Indian Dance Theater and the tribal roots of these dances. *Interests*: Robinson has been working on several film and video projects with his partner and wife Joanelle Nadine Romero (Apache) with their company "Spirit World Productions. He is co-creator and co-producer of "The Red Nation Celebration, an annual live performance of contemporary and traditional Native American Entertainment, and co-creator of "Red Blanket," a contemporary Native American TV series, which is currently being pitched to TV executives in Hollywood. He has also written two feature film screenplays which are available for production and is currently writing a novel. Robinson writes, "Throughout my adult life, one of my over-riding interests has always been, and continues to be, the promotion of understanding

between diverse cultural and ethnic groups, to promote a better understanding of the roles that culture, history and the arts play in our daily lives, and to promote an ethnic and cultural diversity within the arts." Avocational interests include: music, religion, movies, travel. *Video productions*: He has produced and directed over 50 film and video programs about Native American history, culture, health, education, economic development and other contemporary issues affecting Native peoples. Recent project credits include: director of "Allan Houser: A Listing Vision"; writer/director, "Home, Home On the Rez"; a demo episode of "Red Blanket" series; director of photography on an international co-production, "Storytellers of the Pacific" for PBS; co-producer and director of photographer on Melvin & John, 1994, a segment on American Indians with AIDS for a PBS documentary series; and director of "Where the Red Road Meets the Information Superhighway, 1994, an introduction to telecommunications technologies for tribal communities.

ROBINSON, NATHAN WINFIELD
(Eastern Band Cherokee) 1938-
(motel/restaurant owner)
Born October 29, 1938, Ashland, Wis. *Education*: Southern Tech, Atlanta, Ga., 1957-58. *Principal occupation*: Owner/operator, El Camino Motel, and El Camino Craft Gallery, 1960-. *Home address*: P.O. Box 482, Cherokee, NC 28719. *Military service*: U.S. Army, 1961-62. *Community activities*: Cherokee (Tribal) Health Board (vice chairman & chairman, 1974-76); Cherokee Sheltered Workshop (board of directors); Cherokee Baptist Church (youth committee). *Interests*: Own and operate El Camino Motel; own restaurant, but have leased to another party; own & operate El Camino Craft Gallery, dealing in hand made crafts from all over the U.S. Hobbies: gardening, vintage cars, photography, racing karts.

ROBINSON, PRENTICE (Cherokee) 1932-
(teacher; business owner)
Born September 25, 1932, Hominy, Okla. *Education*: Masters Degree in Education. *Home address*: 4158 E. 48 Place, Tulsa, OK 74135 (918) 749-3082. E-mail: prenticewillena@aol.com. Website: www.cherokee madeeasy.com. *Affiliation*: Owner (with wife Willena), Cherokee Language & Culture; president & secretary, Cherokee Heritage Indian Education Foundation (C.H.I.E.F.) (purpose is to preserve Cherokee history on video). *Military service*: U.S. Army, 1954-56. *Community activities*: Active in Church; on call for questions on Cherokee history and language. At present, working on a major monument/memorial for Cherokee history. *Interests*: Recording & preserving Cherokee language. *Memberships*: First Methodist Church; National Woodcarvers Association. *Published works*: Cherokee Made Easy (booklet with tapes); Cherokee Language Workbook with tape; Out of the Flame (beliefs and practices of the ancients).

ROBINSON, RICHARD DUANE (Choctaw)
(artist, company owner)
Affiliation: Wak Bok Ola Intannap (This Side of Beef Creek), P.O. Box 23, Maysville, OK 73057 (405) 867-5330. *Products*: Abstract American Indian paintings, ceramics, prints and drawings.

ROBINSON, VIOLA
(council president)
Affiliation: Native Council of Nova Scotia, P.O. Box 1320, Truro, NS, Canada B2N 5N2 (902) 895-1523.

ROBINSON, WILLENA (Cherokee) 1938-
(teacher; business owner)
Born February 13, 1938, Peggs, Okla. *Education*: Teacher's Degree. *Home address*: 4158 E. 48 Place, Tulsa, OK 74135 (918) 749-3082. E-mail: prentice willena@aol.com. Website: www.cherokeemadeeasy. com. *Affiliation*: Owner (with husband Prentice), Cherokee Language & Culture, 1974-present; Cherokee Heritage Indian Education Foundation (C.H.I.E.F.), 1991-present. The purpose of the Foundation is to preserve Cherokee history on video. *Community activities*: Active in Church; on call for questions on Cherokee history and language. At present, working on a major monument/memorial for Cherokee history. *Interests*: Designing, writing, painting, Cherokee history and research. *Memberships*: First Methodist Church; C.H.I.E.F. *Published works*: Design artist and

proof writer - Cherokee Made Easy (booklet with tapes); Cherokee Language Workbook with tape; Out of the Flame (beliefs and practices of the ancients).

ROCHA, FELIX, JR. (United Lumbee) 1945-
(criminal investigator)
Born March 24, 1945, San Antonio, Tex. *Education*: Golden West College, 1999). *Principal occupation*: Criminal Investigator. *Home address*: 9867 Sturgeon Ave., Fountain Valley, CA 92708 (714) 964-3939 (phone & fax). *Affiliation*: U.S. Dept. of Justice/Immigration & Naturalization Service (primarily in the Investigation Division/Organized Crime Unit), 1967-. *Military service*: U.S. Air Force, 1966. *Community activities*: Elected to the Orange Co. Board of Education, 1992 & 1996 (4 year terms); currently President of the Board of Education. *Interests*: Currently working on a sitcom. *Memberships*: American Legion, 1972- (formerly post commander; currently Commissioner for Boys State). *Published screenplays*: Snakeheads; For the Greater Good; & Diary of a Special Agent.

ROCHE, BOB
(Indian center chairperson)
Affiliations: American Indian Education Center, Cleveland, OH 44102; director, AIM (Cleveland office), 5075 E. 86th St., Cleveland, OH 44125.

ROCKEFELLER, DR. DOROTHY
(Indian education program director)
Affiliation: Unified School District #321, Kaw Valley Special Services, Indian Education Program, P.O. Box 578, Rossville, KS 66533 (913) 584-6731 Fax 584-6720.

ROCKMAN, JEREMY
(health director)
Affiliation: Wisconsin Winnebago Health Dept., P.O. Box 636, Black River Falls, WI 54615 (715) 284-7548.

RODEE, MARIAN E. 1940-
(museum curator; consultant
on Native American art)
Born March 13, 1940, Philadelphia, Penna. *Education*: University of Pennsylvania, BA, 1961; Columbia University, MA, 1965. *Principal occupation*: Museum curator; consultant on Native American art. *Home address*: 413 Camino de la Sierra N.E., Albuquerque, NM 87123 (505) 298-3105. *Affiliations*: Research assistant, Brooklyn Museum, 1968-69; Maxwell Museum of Anthropology, University of New Mexico, Albuquerque, NM (registrar, 1970-73; associate curator, 1975-76; curator, 1977-. *Other professional posts*: Shows & brochures for Museum, 1972-; lecturer, Art Department, College of Fine Arts, University of New Mexico; seminars, exhibits and classes. *Memberships*: Smithsonian Institution; Textile Museum; Textile Society; New Mexico Association of Museums. *Awards, honors*: Smithsonian Fellowship for Studies in Conservation, 1978-79, 1981-82; Pasold Fellowship, 1982; Smithsonian Institution Visiting Fellowship, 1987 (study of the 19th century Zuni fetishes); New Mexico Humanities Council grant, 1989 (visit Zuni and do study of fetish carvers. *Interests*: "In the past 15 years, I have examined the collections of Native American & Spanish American weaving along with the storage, exhibition & conservation techniques of various museums." *Biographical sources*: Who's Who in American Women. *Published works*: Numerous articles and book reviews.

RODEWALD, ROYETTA
(judicial administrator)
Affiliation: Prairie Band Potawatomi Nation Tribal Court, 15498 K Rd., Mayetta, KS 66509 (866) 966-2242 or (785) 966-2242 Fax 966-2662. E-mail: tribal court@pbpnation.org. Website: www.pbpnation.org/ tribalcourt

RODGERS, ED (Quapaw)
(tribal chairperson)
Address & Affiliation: Delaware Executive Committee, P.O. Box 765, Quapaw, OK 74363 (918) 542-1853 Fax 542-4694.

RODGERS, RAYMOND
(hospital director)
Affiliation: Albuquerque PHS Indian Hospital, 801 Vassar Dr., NE, Albuquerque, NM 87106 (505) 254-4000.

RODGERS, WAYNE "GUARDIAN BEAR"
(New River Metis)
(tribal chief)
Affiliation: New River Tribe of Metis, P.O. Box 1126, Laurel Springs, NC 28644 (910) 657-8891.

RODRIGUEZ-SELLAS, JOSE E. 1954-
(information & resources developer)
Born May 4, 1954, Ponce, Puerto Rico. *Education*: University of New Haven (Conn.), B.A. (History), 1978; University of Puerto Rico/Rio Piedras, Labor Relations Institute, 1979-1981; Labor Education Institute, Santurce, PR, 1981. *Principal occupation*: Information and resources developer. *Address*: Resides in Hartford, CT (203) 238-4009 (work). *Affiliation*: Information & resources developer, Chemical Abuse Services Agency (CASA), Bridgeport, CT, 1988-. *Other professional posts*: Co-editor of American Indians for Development Newsletter, and director of May Wutche Aque'ne (journal). *Community activities*: President of Latin Student Organization (1978), University of New Haven, West Haven, CT; spokesperson and coordinator of Brother/Sisterhood of Caribbean and Latin American People , 1983-85; secretary, Hispanic Historical Society of Connecticut (present); Latinos Against AIDS (board of directors, coordinator of the personnel committee). *Awards, honors*: Certificate for Services rendered to the members of the Brotherhood of Social Services Workers of Puerto Rico by the National Leadership of said organization. *Interests*: "My main interests at present are: journalism, graphic arts, photography and writing in general and poems in particular (both English and Spanish. I am very concerned about the status of the so-called "minorities" and the particular behavior exhibited by the people of European descent who are racist in the U.S. The civil rights, the economic justice and the struggle for self-determination of all the people of Latin America and the Caribbean are the tour of duty by which I live. It is the main demand that the Latin American Mother Land imposes on her sons and daughters."

ROE, CHUCK
(BIA agency supt.)
Affiliation: Employee Data & Compensation, Bureau of Indian Affairs, P.O. Box 2026, Albuquerque, NM 87103 (505) 766-2336.

ROEHL, IDA (Athapascan)
(village president)
Affiliation: Dillingham Village Council, P.O. Box 216, Dillingham, AK 99576 (907) 842-2384.

ROEHL, PAT
(Indian education program director)
Affiliation: Fresno Unified School District, Indian Education Program, 2348 Mariposa St., Fresno, CA 93726 (559) 457-3634.

ROELS, STARLA K.
(attorney)
Education: Arizona State University, BA, 1992; Northwestern School of Law of Lewis & Clark College, J.D., 1996. *Address & Affiliation*: Associate, Hobbs, Straus, Dean & Walker, LLP (1999-present), 851 S.W. Sixth Ave., Suite 1650, Portland, OR 97204 (503) 242-1745 Fax 242-1072. E-mail: starla.roels@hsdwor.com. *Professional activities*: Her work includes a wide range of issues, including salmon and natural resources, health care, employment and personnel, and matters under the Indian Self-Determination and Education Assistance Act. She also was actively involved in the reauthorization of the Indian Health Care Improvement Act by assisting the national Steering Committee of tribal leaders in developing legislative language and exploring policy issues relating to health facilities. Starla has made numerous presentations on tribal rights and the ESA. She also participated in a national dialog on HCPs (Habitat Conservation Plans) to address tribal participation in such ESA planning processes. *Past professional post*: Policy analyst with the Columbia River Inter-Tribal Fish Commission, focusing on treaty-reserved fishing rights and the impacts on those rights caused by hydroelectric dams. *Memberships*: Oreegon State Bar Association (member, Environmental & Natural Resources Section; Chair, Executive Committee, Indian Section; editor, "The Arrow's Edge," newsletter).

ROESSEL, DR. ROBERT
(school principal)
Affiliation: Rough Rock Community School, Hwy. 59, RRDS, Box 217, Chinle, AZ 86503 (520) 728-3500 Fax 728-3502.

ROFKAR, TERI (Tlingit)
(craftsperson, art studio owner)
Affiliation: Raven Art Studio, 820 Charles St., Sitka, AK 99835 (907) 747-3641; E-mail: cuthbert@ptialaska.net

ROGERS, ED (Quapaw)
(ex-tribal chairperson)
Affiliation: Quapaw Tribal Business Committee, P.O.Box 765, Quapaw, OK 74363 (918) 542-1853.

ROGERS, EDWARD S. 1923-
(ethnologist)
Born May 2, 1923, Lee, Mass. *Education*: Massachusetts Institute of Technology, 1942-44; 1946-47; Middlebury College, B.A., 1951; University of New Mexico, MA, 1953, PhD, 1958. *Principal occupation*: Curator, Dept. of Ethnology, Royal Ontario Museum, 100 Queen's Park, Toronto, ON, Can. M5S 2C6. *Other professional post*: Part-time professor of anthropology, McMaster University, Hamilton, Ontario, Can. *Military service*: U.S. Army, 1943-46 (Army Specialized Training Program, 1943-44; Infantry, 1944-45). *Memberships*: Arctic Institute of North America; American Anthropological Association. *Interests*: Consultation on contemporary matters concerning North American Indians. *Published works*: The Round Lake Ojibwa (Royal Ontario Museum, 1962); The Hunting Group-Hunting Territory Complex Among the Mistassini Indians (National Museums of Canada, 1963); An Athapaskan Type of Knife (National Museums of Canada, 1965); Subsistence Areas of the Cree-Ojibwa of the Eastern Subarctic: A Preliminary Study, two parts (National Museums of Canada, 1963-66); North Pacific Coast Indians (Canadian Antiques Collector, 1967); The Material Culture of the Mistassini (National Museums of Canada, 1967); Indian Farmers of Parry Island (Royal Ontario Museum, 1967); Canadian Indians (Swan Publishing, 1967); Indians of Canada (Clarke, Irwin, 1969); Forgotten Peoples (Royal Ontario Museum, 1969); Band Organization Among the Indians of Eastern Subarctic Canada (National Museums of Canada, 1969); Natural Environment-Social Organization-Witchcraft: Cree Versus Ojibwa-A Test Case (National Museums of Canada, 1969); Indians of the North Pacific Coast (Royal Ontario Museum, 1970); Iroquoians of the Eastern Woodlands (Royal Ontario Museums, 1970); Indians of th Subarctic (Royal Ontario Museum, 1970); Indians of the Plains (Royal Ontario Museum, 1970); Algonkians of the Eastern Woodlands (Royal Ontario Museum, 1970); The Indians of Canada/A Survey (Royal Ontario Museum, 1970); The Quest Food and Furs-The Mistassini Cree, 1953-1954 (National Museums of Canada, 1973); Parry Island Farmers: A Period of Change in the Way of Life of the Algonkians of Southern Ontario, with Flora Tobobondung (National Museum of Man, 1975); and others; also numerous papers, reviews, and articles in scholarly journals.

ROGERS, KAREN D.
(executive secretary)
Affiliation: Colorado Commission on Indian Affairs, 130 State Capitol, Denver, CO 80203 (303) 866-3027.

ROGERS, STEVE
(library curator)
Affiliation: The Wheelwright of the American Indian, Mary Cabot Wheelwright Research Library, P.O. Box 5153, 704 Camino Lejo, Santa Fe, NM 87501 (505) 982-4636.

ROGERS, WILL, JR. (Cherokee) 1911-
(publisher, journalist)
Born October 20, 1911, New York, N.Y. *Education*: Stanford University, B.A., 1935. *Principal occupation*: Publisher, journalist. *Home address*: Santos Ranch, Tubac, AZ 85646. *Affiliations*: Publisher/journalist, Beverly Hills Citizen, newspaper, 1935-53; U.S. Congressman, 16th District, California, 1942-1944; special assistant to the Commissioner of Indian Affairs, 1967-1969; creative consultant, George Spota Theatre Production of Will Rogers, U.S.A. starring James Whitmore, 1968-. *Other professional posts*: Motion picture actor, television commentator, lecturer. *Military service*: U.S. Army, 1944-45 (Bronze Star). *Community activities*: Beverly Hills Chamber of Commerce; chairman, Southern California Truman campaign committee, 1948; Will Rogers Memorial Commission, State of Oklahoma (member); California State Parks Commission (chairman). *Memberships*: Arrow, Inc. (founder and honorary president); National Congress of American Indians, 1946-; Oklahoma Cherokee Tribe. *Interests*: In recent years he has divided his energies between his real estate business in Beverly Hills and his ranch in Tubac, Arizona. He continues to be active in Indian affairs, making occasional trips for the Bureau of Indian Affairs. A well known lecturer, he continues active in this field. He has worked with the Alaskan Federation of Natives. *Theatrical activities*: Movies: Star in The Will Rogers Story, (Warner Brothers, 1951); The Boy From Oklahoma, and Wild Heritage. Plays: Ah, Wilderness, and Street Scene (Pasadena Playhouse). *Radio*: Rogers of the Gazette. Television: Good Morning Show, CBS.

ROHRER, BARBARA
(Indian education program director)
Affiliation: Vivian Banks Charter School, Pala Band of Mission Indians, P.O. Box 80, Pala, CA 92059 (760) 742-3300 Fax 742-3102.

ROKWAHO (DAN THOMPSON) (Mohawk) 1953-
(publications & graphic design consultant)
Born November 7, 1953, Akwesasne Territory. *Education*: High school. *Principal occupation*: Publications and graphic design consultant. *Home address*: P.O. Box 166, Rooseveltown, NY 13683. *Affiliations*: Media specialist, St. Regis Mohawk Language Program, 1980-82; co-founder (with John Fadden) and production manager, Pictographics, P.O. Box 166, Rooseveltown, NY, 1977-. *Other professional posts*: Literary editor, artist and photographer, Akwesasne Notes, 1982-83; founding editor, Indian Time, an Akwesasne biweekly newspaper, 1983; art director for Indian Studies, Cornell University, Ithaca, N.Y., 1984; editor, Akwesasne Notes and Indian Time, 1984-85; co-founder of Akwekon, a literary and arts quarterly published by Akwekon/Akwesasne Notes; co-founder of Suntracks, a tracking and nature observation school in the Adirondack Mountains near Ochiota, N.Y. *Membership*: Association for the Advancement of Native North American Arts and Crafts (administrative executive; project, Iroquois Arts: A Directory of a People and Their Work, published, 1984). *Interests*: Music, literature, theatre, computer science, electronic and mechanical gaggetry, the sciences, and archaic Mohawk words and semantics (compiling a dictionary of terms). *Published works*: Editor & designer, Trail of Broken Treaties. B.I.A. I'm Not Your Indian Anymore (Akwesasne Notes, 1974); translator & illustrator, Teiohakwente, a Mohawk language textbook (Dept. of Indian Affairs, Ottawa, Can., 1977); author and artist, Covers (poetry, illustrations) (Strawberry Press, 1982); contributor of poetry to numerous anthologies; cover art and illustrations for many publications, as well as design production for Akwesasne Notes Calendars.

ROLATOR, FRED S. 1938-
(professor of history)
Born July 22, 1938, McKinney, Tex. *Education*: Wake Forest University, B.A., 1960; University of Southern California, M.A., Ph.D., 1960-1963. *Principal occupation*: Professor of history, Middle Tennessee State University, Murfreesboro, 1967-. *Home address*: Resides in Murfressboro, Tenn. (615) 898-2639 (work). *Other professional post*: Associate professor of history & chairman of the History & Social Sciences Dept., Grand Canyon College, Phoenix, AZ, 1964-67. *Community activities*: Frequent speaker on Indian matters for civic organizations and school in area; co-director, The American Indian and the Jacksonian Era: The Impact of Removal: A Sequi-Centennial Symposium (The national symposium on the adoption of the Indian Removal Bill of 1830) held Feb., 1980; Rutherford County Heritage Commission (member, 1978-80). *Memberships*: Tennessee Baptist Historical Society (former president); Southern Baptist Historical Commission; Baptist History & Heritage (board of directors); Organization of American Historians; The Western Historical Association; Tennessee Historical Society; The Southern Historical Society. *Awards, honors*:

National Merit Scholar, Wake Forest, 1956-1960; National Defense and Haynes Fellow, USC, 1960-1963; Tennessee Baptist Convention, Heritage Award, 1984; Fulbright Professor, Japan, 1987. *Interests*: History of the American Indian, especially previous to 1492; American church history; director of Historic Preservation effort, Camp Palma, located near Tupa, Sao Paulo state, Brazil (1976). *Biographical sources*: Directory of American Scholars; Dictionary of International Biography; Who's Who in the South and Southwest. *Published works*: The Continental Congress: A Study in the Origins of American Public Administration (Xerox, 1971); Charles Thompson (Harrington Associates, 1977); Japanese Americans (Rourke, 1991). Article: "The Time They Cried", Journal of American Studies (Japan) 1988 (no. 4) - an article concerning the Trail of Tears in Japanese and is one of the first articles in Japanese concerning the American Indian; article, "The American Indian & the Origin of the Second American Party System," in the Wisconsin Magazine of History (Spring, 1993).

ROLLER, TONI (Santa Clara Pueblo)
(craftsperson)
Address: Toni Roller Indian Pottery Studio & Gallery, Box 171, Santa Clara Pueblo, Espanola, NM 87532 (505) 753-3003. *Product*: Handmade traditional Santa Clara pottery of natural materials.

ROLLINS, DOUGLAS J.
(BIA agency supt.)
Affiliation: Central California Agency, BIA, 1824 Tribute Rd., Suite J, Sacramento, CA 95815 (916) 566-7121.

ROMANO, SHARON
(student services director)
Affiliation: American Indian Student Services, Anoka Ramsey Community College, 11200 Mississippi Blvd., N.W., Coon Rapids, MN 55433 (612) 422-3470.

ROMERO, JOHN, JR. (*Blue Lake Night Dancer*) (Taos Pueblo)
(Indian education coordinator)
Address: Taos Municipal Schools, 213 Paseo del Canon, Taos, NM 87571 (505) 758-3884 ext 49 Fax 758-5298. *Affiliations*: Santa Fe Indian School, 1978-91; Taos Municipal Schools, Taos, NM, 1992-present. *Military service*: U.S. Army, 1968-72 (Vietnam, 1969-70). *Community activities*: Member, Community Education Program; member, Indian Education Committee. *Memberships*: National Coalition for Indian Education; National Indian Education Association.

ROMERO, JOANELLE NADINE (*Redhawk*) (Apache-Cheyenne)
(film-maker, director, singer, actress)
Born in Albuquerque, N.M. *Address*: Resides in Santa Fe, NM. *Affiliations*: Founder, Spirit World Productions, Santa Fe, NM, 1992-. *Film & Video credits*: Romero, with seventeen films to her credit as a lead actress, is perhaps best known for her leading roles in such films as "A Girl Called Hatter Fox" and "Pow Wow Highway," a winner at a previous Sundance Film Festival. In 1992, she founded Spirit World Productions, an American Indian production company, dedicated to supporting Native American music, film and television projects. Spirit World's introductory project was Michael Jackson's Black or White music video. Then Romero began producing, directing, and writing her own film and video projects, the first of which was a documentary short film, "The Third Verse, 500 Years, Land of the Children. This film won a merit award at the Columbus International Film Festival in 1993, a first place trophy at the Red Earth Film Festival in 1994, and shown two years in a row at the American Indian Film Festival in San Francisco. In 1994, she produced an informational video for U.S. West Communications, "Where the Red Road Meets the Information Super Highway," 1st Place award winner at the Red Earth Film Festival in 1995. Also in 1994, she directed "Melvin and John," a documentary segment for a PBS series about people living with HIV/AIDS all across America...won 1st Place at Red Earth in 1995. In 1995, she co-created and co-produced the first "Red Nation Celebration" (contemporary Native American entertainment to Santa Fe's Indian Art Market each year) and was one of the featured performers. In 1996, Romero produced "Allan Houser: A Lasting Vision," a documen-

tary on the early life of world renowned Apache Indian sculptor Allan Houser. Recently, she co-created and produced a contemporary American Indian dramatic TV series, "Red Blanket," currently being pitched to major networks and studios. She also produced "Home, Home on the Rez," a demo episode of this series. As a direct result of the demo, she and her production company were written up in Newsweek, appeared on the cover of the LA Times. Romero believes that the TV series, "Red Blanket" will begin shooting in 1997. Most recently, Romero co-created and co-wrote an American Indian children's program which will be produced in 1997. Currently, Romero is in production on a documentary feature film, "When It's All Over, I'll Still Be Indian. *Interests*: Ms. Romero has been a true activist against Alcoholism among her American Indian people. Romero, fifteen years sober, promotes sobriety and healthy lifestyles within the American Indian community. She has traveled from reservation to reservation to speak with youth and racism, alcoholism, and encouraging them to "Live Their Dream." She is writing her autobiography: Maybe I'm Not Crazy. She believes that there should be more stories by and about American Indian women.

ROMERO, M. SUE (Hidatsa/Creek) 1955-
(administrative assistant)
Born August 11, 1955, Claremore, Okla. *Education*: University of New Mexico, 1985-86. *Principal occupation*: Administrative assistant. *Home address*: Resides in Albuquerque, NM (505) 766-8418 (office). *Affiliations*: Clerical specialist, Albuquerque Public Schools, Indian Education Dept., 1977; administrative assistant: Santa Fe Indian School, 1977-85; All Indian Pueblo Council, Albuquerque, 1985-87; SW Indian Polytechnic Institute, Albuquerque, 1988-. *Community activities*: SW Indian Personnel Management, 1983-85. *Memberships*: Santa Fe Indian School Alumni Association; NONAW - National Organization of Native American Women, 1989-; Indian Bowling Association, 1989-. *Awards, honors*: Nominated to Outstanding Women in America, 1984; SW Region Personnel Management Training Intern, 1984; 1985 Santa Fe Indian School Employee of the Year. *Interests*: "Over 12 years of extensive experience working with Native American Programs from a boarding school situation to a political entity to a substance abuse program."

ROMERO, MICHAEL
(school principal)
Affiliation: Isleta Elementary School, P.O. Box 550, Isleta, NM 87022 (505) 869-2321 Fax 869-1625.

ROMERO, RAMOS (Tesuque Pueblo)
(former Pueblo governor)
Affiliation: Tesuque Pueblo Council, Rt. 5 Box 360-T, Santa Fe, NM 87501 (505) 983-2667.

ROMERO, RUBEN (Taos Pueblo)
(former Pueblo governor)
Affiliation: Taos Pueblo Council, P.O. Box 1846, Taos, NM 87571 (505) 758-9593.

ROOD, DAVID S. (kiic'akwakhariw) 1940-
(professor of linguistics)
Born in 1940, Albany, N.Y. *Education*: University of California, Berkeley, PhD, 1969. *Principal occupation*: Professor of linguistics. *Address & Affiliation*: 295 UCB, Dept. of Linguistics, University of Colorado, Boulder, CO 80309-0295 (303) 492-2747 Fax 492-4416. E-mail: rood@colorado.edu. *Published works*: Beginning Lahkota, 4 vols. with Allan R. Taylor, 1972 (Garland, 1972); Wichita Grammar (Garland, 1976).

ROOTE, VERNON
(Indian band chief)
Affiliation: Chippewas of Saugeen, RR 1, Southampton, Ontario, Canada N0H 2L0 (519) 797-2218.

ROSALES, SALVADOR (Pomo)
(rancheria chairperson)
Affiliation: Potter Valley Rancheria, 112 N. School St., Ukiah, CA 95482 (707) 485-5115.

ROSE, DONALD (Eastern Cherokee) 1932-
(engineer; president & CEO)
Born in 1932 on the Cherokee Reservation, N.C. *Education*: University of Nebraska, BA (Political Science).

Principal occupation: Engineer; president & CEO. *Address & Affiliation*: President & CEO, Command Technologies, P.O. Box 670, Warrenton, VA 22186. Their work - primarily software creation & consulting - includes development of computer-based learning systems, artificial intelligence applications in education, logistics support for F-15 testing equipment and a study of missile theatre defense tactics and equipment. *Military service*: U.S. Air Force, 1949-74 (Radar officer & instructor). *Awards, honors*: The "Washington Technology" newspaper names Rose's, Command Technologies one of region's 50 fastest growing high-tech firms.

ROSE, JOHN S.
(library director)
Affiliation: Dorothy Cummings Memorial Library, Americn Indian Bible College, 10020 N. 15th Ave., Phoenix, AZ 85021 (602) 944-3335.

ROSE, MICHAEL "FLYING EAGLE" (Cherokee)
(member-board of regents)
Affiliation: Member, Board of Regents, American Indian Heritage Foundation, 6051 Arlington Blvd., Falls Church, VA 22044-2788 (703) 237-7500.

ROSE, PHYLLIS
(art/media consultant; business owner)
Education: California State University, Los Angeles, BA in Broadcast Communications. *Principal occupation*: Art/media consultant; business owner. *Address*: 47080 Pala Rd., Temecula, CA 92592. *Affiliations*: Photojournalist for "The Talking Leaf Publication; hosted two radio shows while working as an independent radio producer for National Public Radio. Some of her interviews include: Native American political prisoner Leonard Peltier, U.S. Senator Ben Nighthorse Campbell, Rita Coolidge and Connie Stevens; Presently, she is owner of First People Communications so she could assist individuals and organizations as an art/media consultant in various aspects needed to obtain their goals. Most of Phyllis's experience has been working in film and television. She has worked in various aspects of production from on camera shows such as, "Crazy Horse," "Dances With Wolves," "Ninja Kids Knucke Up," and the children's show, "Romper Room." *Community activities*: California Indian Legal Services (committee member, board of directors); Pechanga Tribe (councilperson, youth program volunteer); speaker, Cal State Northridge Native American Student Group. *Memberships*: SAG, AFTRA. *Interests*: Phyllis says her legacy is to follow her grandmother's commitments for Native Ameican concerns and love for their culture.

ROSE, ROBERT "SWIFT ARROW" (Cherokee)
(advisor)
Affiliation: Council of Advisors, American Indian Heritage Foundation, 6051 Arlington Blvd., Falls Church, VA 22044 (703) 237-7500.

ROSE, WIL (Dr.) 1931-
(foundation executive)
Born September 13, 1931, in Ohio. *Education*: Santa Monica City College; Ashland University, Litt.D. *Principal occupation*: Foundation executive. *Home address*: 6555 Dearborn Dr., Falls Church, VA 22044 (703) 354-2270. *Affiliations*: President, People to People, Inc., 1966-67; founder & president, Involvement, Inc. (developed non-profit service organization designed to mobilize and utilize voluntary resources of America), 1967-76; national director, United Way of America - Volunteer Mobilization Project, 1976-77; president, National Leadership Institute, Washington, D.C., 1979-80; president, National Foundation for Philanthropy, 1979-81; co-founder & president, National Heritage Foundation, 1968-81; chief executive officer, American Indian Heritage Foundation, 1973-present; founder/president, PlanAmerica (full service master planning firm), 1981-. *Other professional posts*: Serve on several boards of non-profit organizations. *Military service*: U.S. Marine Corps, 1950-54 (Korean conflict; Staff NCO with Purple Heart Award). *Community activities*: Rotary International. *Memberships*: Society for International Development; the Sacred Concert Society; Outstanding Americans Foundation. *Awards, honors*: For activities with DATA International and People-to-People, was selected by the U.S. Jaycees and featured in "Look Magazine" as one of the

Ten Outstanding Young Men in the U.S.; selected by the California Jaycees as one of Five Outstanding Young Men in California; featured in the "People On the Way Up" section of the Saturday Evening Post; Sertoma International conveyed their Service to Mankind Award; married to Princess Pale Moon, Cherokee/Ojibwa concert and recording artist and president of the American Indian Heritage Foundation.

ROSEN, LAWRENCE 1941-
(professor of anthropology)
Born December 9, 1941, Cincinnati, Ohio. *Education*: Brandeis University, BA, 1963; University of Chicago, MA, 1965, PhD, 1968, JD, 1974. *Principal occupation*: Professor of anthropology. *Home address*: 435 Alexander St., Princeton, NJ 08540 (609) 258-5535 (work). E-mail: lrosen@princeton.edu. *Affiliations*: Professor, 1977-, dept. chairperson, 1989-2001, Dept. of Anthropology, Princeton University, Princeton, NJ; adjunct professor of law, Columbia Law School, New York, NY, 1979-. *Community activities*: Volunteer legal work for the Native American Rights Fund. *Memberships*: American Anthropological Association; Law and Society Association (board of directors). *Awards, honors*: John D. & Catherine T. MacArthur Foundation Award; John Simon Guggenheim Foundation Fellow; National Science Foundation Fellow, 1990-92; Phi Beta Kappa Visiting Scholar. *Interests*: "Research on American Indian legal problems, especially the return of Indian skeletal remains, the furtherance of Indian religious rights, and the rights of indigenous peoples in international law; extensive research in North Africa, particularly on Islamic law." *Biographical source*: American Men and Women of Science. *Published work*: Editor, The American Indian and the Law (Transaction Books, 1976); Bargaining for Reality (University of Chicago Press, 1984); The Anthropology of Justice (Cambridge University Press, 1989); Other Intentions (School of American Research Press, 1994); The Justice of Islam (Oxford University Press, 2000); The Culture of Islam (University of Chicago Press, 2002); Law as Culture (Oxford University Press, 2004); The Rights of Indigenous Peoples (Oxford University Press, 2005).

ROSS, A. CHUCK *(Ehanamani-Walks Among)* (Santee Sioux) 1940-
(educational administration, writer)
Born October 25, 1940, Pipestone, Minn. *Education*: Black Hills State College, BS, 1967; Arizona State University, MA, 1971; University of Minnesota, ABD, 1973; Western Colorado University, Ed.D., 1980. *Principal occupation*: Educational administration. *Home address*: 7892 W. 1st Place, Lakewood, CO 80226 (303) 238-3420. *Affiliations*: Instructor (contract), Native American Studies, University of Colorado, Boulder, 1977-80; health & education consultant, Edgewater, CO, 1980-83; instructor (contract) - Native American Studies, Standing Rock College, Fort Yates, ND; Oglala Lakota College, Kyle, SD, & Fort Peck Community College, Poplar, MT, 1983-90; Agency Supt. for Education, Bureau of Indian Affairs, Fort Yates, ND; supt., Little Wound School, Kyle, SD, 1990-91; author, publisher, international consultant (Bear Publishing),1991-. *Other professional posts*: Lecturer, 'In Search of the Origins of the Red Man,' presented in 44 state & 6 Canadian provinces, 1975-; lecturer on topics including Lakota history & culture, psychology, wholistic health & education, 1975-; primary investigator for various publications; and technical advisor for various film/TV broadcast. *Military service*: U.S. Army Airborne, 1962-65. *Memberships*: Dakota Astronomical Society; National Indian Education Association. *Awards, honors*: Friendship Award, White Buffalo Council, 1977; nominee, National Indian Educator of the Year, National Indian Education Association, 1980; Outstanding Volunteer Service Award, U.S. Dept. of Health & Human Services, 1982; Gubernatorial Appointment, North Dakota Teacher's Professional Practices Commission, 1985; Who's Who Among the Sioux - University of South Dakota, 1986; Participant, Effective Schools Team for BIA, 1988; Honoree, 'Top 50' Selection at International Book Fair, Frankfurt, Germany, recognition for "Mitakuye Oyasin," 1992; Special Recognition Award for Contribution to Indian Education, National Indian Education Association, 1992; Mitakuye Oyasin approved for cinema film production by Osmond Productions (Pleasant Grove, UT), 1994. *Interests*: Lectures & presentations; Dr. Ross

has worked for 25 years in the field of education as a teacher, principal, superintendent, college professor, and college department chairman. He has lectured on cultural understanding in 44 states in the U.S., 6 Canadian provinces, and 8 European countries and Japan. His book Mitakuye Oyasin was a best-seller. *Published work*: Biographies of Spotted Tail & Crow Dog for the Encyclopedia of the Indians of the Americas, 1975; Mitakuye Oyasin: We Are All Related (Bear Publishing, 1989); Ehanamani: Walks Among (Bear Publishing, 1992), a book that compares customs, languages, and spiritual beliefs of Indians with other peoples; Keeper of the Female Medicine Bundle (Bear Publishing, 1998).

ROSS, DALLAS (Dakota)
(tribal chairperson)
Affiliation: Upper Sioux Board of Trustees, P.O. Box 147, Granite Falls, MN 56241 (320) 564-2360 Fax 564-3264.

ROSS, DENIS
(Indian band chief)
Affiliation: Montagnais de les Escoumins, 27, rue de la Reserve, Box 820, Les Escoumins, Quebec, Canada G0G 1V0 (418) 233-2509.

ROSS, JACQUELYN (Pomo/Coast Mewuk)
(outreach coordinator)
Affiliation: Relations with Schools/EOP Outreach Services, 2828 Chiles Rd. Hall, Davis, CA 95616 (916) 752-3124.

ROSS, JOHN (Cherokee)
(tribal chairperson)
Affiliation: United Keetoowah Band of Cherokee Indians, P. O. Box 746, Tahlequah, OK 74465 (918) 456-5491.

ROSS, DR. KENNETH
(BIA administrator)
Affiliation: Office of Indian Education Programs, Bureau of Indian Affairs, Albuquerque Area Office, P.O. Box 26567, Albuquerque, NM 87125 (505) 766-3170.

ROUBIDOUX, JAMES
(BIA agency supt.)
Affiliation: Bureau of Indian Affairs, OIRM, 2051 Mercator Dr., Reston, VA 20191.

ROUBIDEAUX, NANETTE S.
(Ioway of Kansas/Nebraska) 1940-
(museum professional)
Born July 20, 1940, Porcupine, S.D. *Education*: Haskell Indian Junior College, AAS, 1975; University of Kansas, B.A. (Honors), 1977, PhD candidate. *Principal occupation*: Museum professional. *Address*: The Gustav Heye Center, Museum of the American Indian, Smithsonian Institution, One Bowling Green, New York, NY 10004. *Affiliations*: Teaching assistant, research assistant, assistant instructor, graduate assistant, University of Kansas, Lawrence, Kan., 1977-83; co-director, Kansas Committee for the Humanities Project Change, Continuities, and Challenges, Haskell Indian Junior College, 1984-85; intern fellowship, Museum of the American Indian, New York, N.Y., 1985-. *Other professional posts*: Consultant: KANU Radio, University of Kansas, 1981-; Women's Transitional Care, Lawrence, KS, 1982-; Haskell Indian Junior College, 1984-; Museum of the American Indian, 1985-; chairperson, Grand Review Committee for Dept. of Health and Human Services, Office of Human Development Services, 1985-. *Memberships*: American Historical Association; American Anthropological Association; Phi Alpha Theta; Society for Values in Higher Education. *Awards, honors*: Danforth Foundation Fellowship, 1979-1982; Outstanding Americans Program, listed in Outstanding Young Women in America, 1977; American Indian Scholarship Program, 1977-80; Lawrence Professional and Business Women's Outstanding Haskel Indian Junior College Student, 1975; Merwlyn Foundation Research Grant, 1976; Commission of the Status for Women, Outstanding Student in Contributions to a Minority Culture, 1976; Minority Affairs Teaching Assistant Award, 1977; Graduate School, Dissertation Fellowship, 1984-85. *Interests*: Contemporary Native American activities. *Biographical source*: Outstanding Young Women in America, 1977. *Published works*: The Native American Woman: A Cross-Disci-

plinary Bibliography (in preparation); Up Before Dawn: A Study of the Family Farm, paper given at regional meeting of American Anthropological Association, Memphis, Tenn., 1979.

ROUBIDEAUX, RAMON ARTHUR *(Wanblee Ohitika-Brave Eagle)* (Rosebud Sioux) 1924-
(lawyer-private practice)
Born November 15, 1924, Rosebud, S.D. *Education*: Haskell Institute, 1942; George Washington Uiversity, AA, 1948, LLB, 1950. *Principal occupation*: Lawyer-private practice. *Home address*: 2620 Holiday Ln., Apt. 118, Rapid City, SD 57702-5361 (605) 348-0122. *Military service*: U.S. Air Force, 1942-46 (1st Lt.; Air Medal with Oak Leaf Cluster and three battle stars). *Community activities*: South Dakota Assistant Attorney General; State's Attorney; Tribal Court Judge; Tribal Attorney for various tribes. Chairperson of various political and Indian groups and associations through the years. Member of State Commission on Indian Affairs; chairperson of State Bar Civil Rights Committee; member of State Bar Criminal Law Committee. *Memberships*: Sixth Judicial Circuit Bar Association (president); American Bar Association (Civil Rights Committee); National Congress of American Indians; American Legion (Post and Couty Commander); V.F.W. *Interests*: Formed partnership with Charles Poches and Gerald L. Reade, specializing in criminal and personal injury actions. Partnership dissolved Jan. 1, 1968. Formed partnership with David Bergren in Fall of 1971. Active in Indian affairs generally. Advocate of State Jurisdiction on Indian Reservations. *Biographical sources*: Who's Who in the Midwest.

ROUFS, TIMOTHY G. 1943-
(professor)
Born August 30, 1943, Cokato, Minn. *Education*: University of Notre Dame, A.B., 1965; University of Minnesota, Ph.D., 1971. *Principal occupation*: Professor, Dept. of Sociology, Anthropology, Geography, University of Minnesota, Duluth, 1970-. *Community activities*: A.M. Chisholm Museum, Duluth, MN (board of directors). *Memberships*: American Ethnological Society; Society for Applied Anthropology (Fellow); American Anthropological Association (Fellow); The Royal Anthropological Association of Great Britain and Ireland (Fellow); Current Anthropology (Associate); Sigma Xi, 1980-. *Awards, honors*: 1973 Service Award from Anishnabe, University of Minnesota-Duluth, American Indian Student Association; 1976 City of Duluth Bicentennial Award; 1980 Outstanding Young Men of America. *Interests*: Anishnabe, Chippewa, and Ojibwa ethnohistory; culture and personality studies. *Biographical source*: Who's Who in the Midwest. *Published works*: The Anishnabe of the Minnesota Chippewa Tribe (Indian Tribal Series, Phoenix, 1975); Working Bibliography of the Anishnabe & Selected Related Works (Lake Superior Basin Studies Center, Duluth, 1981, 1984); editor, with Larry P. Atkins, Information Relating to Chippewa Peoples (from the Handbook of American Indians North of Mexico, 1907-1910) (Lake Superior Basin Studies Center, Duluth, 1984).

ROUNTREE, HELEN C. 1944-
(anthropologist)
Born October 8, 1944, Camp Le Jeune, N.C. *Education*: College of William & Mary, AB, 1966; University of Utah, MA, 1968; University of Wisconsin, Milwaukee, PhD, 1973. *Principal occupation*: Anthropologist. *Home address*: 268 Harris Creek Rd., Hampton, VA 23669 (804) 683-3812 (work). *Affiliation*: Professor, Old Dominion University, Norfolk, VA, 1968-. *Memberships*: American Anthropological Association, 1968-; Royal Anthropological Institute of Great Britain & Ireland, 1969-; Society for Applied Anthropology, 1981-; American Society for Ethnohistory, 1988-. *Interests*: Professional interests: North American Indian ethnology, especially Virginia Algonquians; ecological anthropology; political anthropology; anthropology of gender; Middle Eastern ethnology (ancient & modern), ethnicity. *Avocations*: music, textiles, embroidery-designing. *Published works*: The Powhatan Indians of Virginia: Their Traditional Culture (University of Oklahoma Press, 1989); Pocahontas' People: The Powhatan Indians of Virginia Through Four Centuries (University of Oklahoma Press, 1990); editor, Powhatan Foreign Relations, 1500-1722 (University Press of Virginia - forthcoming).

ROUWALK, ALYCE
(BIA agency supt.)
Affiliation: Shiprock Agency, Bureau of Indian Affairs, P.O. Box 966, Shiprock, NM 87420 (505) 368-4301.

ROWELL, RONALD
(center director)
Affiliation: National Native American AIDS Prevention Center, 134 Linden St., Oakland, CA 94607 (510) 444-2051.

ROWLAND, TED
(school supt.)
Affiliation: Busby School, P.O. Box 38, Busby, MT 59016 (406) 592-3646.

ROWLEN, SHALAH (Sac & Fox-Pawnee)
(craftsperson; store owner)
Affiliation: American Indian Handicrafts, P.O. Box 358, Meeker, OK 74855 (405) 279-2896. *Products*: Ribbonwork blankets and apparel, beadwork and featherwork.

ROY, LORIENE (Minnesota Chippewa-Pembina Band) 1954-
(associate professor)
Born June 12, 1954. *Education*: Oregon Institute of Technology, AS, BT, 1977; University of Arizona, MLS, 1980; University of Illinois at Urbana-Champaign, PhD, 1987. *Principal occupation*: Associate professor. *Address & Affiliation*: Graduate School of Library and Information Science, SZB 564, University of Texas at Austin, Austin, TX 78712-1276 (1987-present) (512) 471-3959 Fax 471-3971; E-Mail: loriene@uts.cc.utexas.edu. *Community activities*: Austin Free Net volunteer. *Memberships*: American Library Association; American Indian Library Association (president, 1995-present); Public Library Association; Library & Information Science Education; National Trust for Historic Preservation; Oral History Association; Popular Culture Association; Texas Library Association. *Interests*: "Current writing interest areas include: library service to Native American populations; collection management; progressive era librarian education; creative fiction." *Published works*: Over 40 professional papers, reports, chapters; over 60 presentations at professional conferences.

ROY, STEWART
(Indian band chief)
Affiliation: West Bay Indian Band, Box 2, West Bay, Ontario, Canada P0P 1G0 (705) 377-5362.

ROYBAL, LOUIS (Piro/Manso/Tiwa) 1927-
(retired-aerospace logistics specialist; former tribal governor)
Born August 14, 1927, Las Cruces, N.M. *Education*: California Western University (San Diego), B.A., 1955; San Diego Miramar College, A.S. (Criminal Justice), 1977; University of San Diego (Paralegal), 1981. *Address & Affiliation*: Governor, Piro/Manso/Tiwa Indian Tribe, Pueblo of San Juan de Guadalupe, P.O. Box 16243, Las Cruces, NM 88004 (505) 647-5372 (phone & fax), 1991-2001 (administered tribal governmental affairs for the tribe). *Other professional post*: Director, Turtle River Nation, Inc., Las Cruces, NM. *Past professional posts*: Teledyne Ryan Aeronautical Co., San Diego, CA, 1952-55, 1966-1981; General Dynamics/Convair & Space Systems, San Diego, CA, 1955-62, 1982-92; The Boeing Co., Seattle, WA, 1962-66. *Military service*: U.S. Navy (1944-46) World War II Veteran. *Awards, honors*: "During the second session of the 106th Congress, I was invited by Senator Ben Nighthorse Campbell, Chairman of the Senate Select Committee on Indian Affairs to a Committee Hearing on May 24, 2000 in Washington DC to testify on Senate Bill S.611, a Bill to provide administrative procedures to extend Federal recognition to certain Indian groups. The Tribe advocated passage of Senate Bill S.611, which would have established a Congressional Commission on Indian recognition in lieu of 25CFR83, the Bureau of Indian Affairs process." *Interests*: Advocacy by the people and the tribal council for federal acknowledgement. "Cultural anthropological research establishes that the "ROYBAL" family have in succession carried the Spiritual and Ceremonial Office of "Casique" in the Pueblo for over three (3) hundred years. During the early 1800's, my Grandfather, Casique Felipe Roybal, Sr., was instrumental in re-settlement of the present Tribe, consisting of twenty-two Indian families from the Piro Pueblos of Senecu del Sur, Socorro del sur, Tiwa Indians from Ysleta del Sur and MANSO Indians from El Paso del Norte to the Las Cruces area of southern New Mexico."

ROYER, BARBARA
(tribal library director)
Affiliations: Yavapai-Prescott Tribal Library, 530 E. Merritt, Prescott, AZ 86301 (928) 445-8790 Fax 778-9445.

ROYSTER, JUDITH
(Indian program co-director)
Affiliation: Native American Law Certificate Program, University of Tulsa College of Law, 3120 E. 4th Pl., Tulsa, OK 74104 (918) 631-3139 Fax 631-2194. E-mail: judith-royster@utulsa.edu.

ROZIE, LEE *(Mixashawn)* (Mohegan)
(musickeeper)
Born in Hartford, Conn. *Principal occupation*: Musickeeper. *Home address*: 108 Sisson St., E. Hartford, CT 06118 (800) 949-MIXA. *Membership*: Executive Director, Pequonawonk Canoe Society, E. Hartford, CT. *Interests*: "The musical trio, "Afro-Algonquin" which derives its name from the ethnic background of its two co-leaders, Rick & Lee Rozie. The idea behind the group is to integrate American Indian folk music themes into modern Afro-American jazz. Lee plays tenor and soprano saxophones, flutes, percussion, vocals. "Maheekanew," is the traditional name of our people." *Records & CDs*: "Word, Out" Music for the Next Century," "Plastic Champions," & "Maheekanew View of Mixashawn," all produced by (Indian Runs Records, 1991-93).

RUBEL, PAULA G. 1933-
(professor emerita of anthropology)
Born March 13, 1933, New York, N.Y. *Education*: Hunter College, A.B., 1953; Columbia University, Ph.D., 1963. *Principal occupation*: Professor of anthropology. *Home address*: 560 Riverside Dr., Apt. 18D, New York, NY 10027 (212) 663-3694. *Affiliations*: Department of Anthropology, Barnard College, Columbia University, New York, NY (lecturer, 1965-66; assistant professor, 1966-70; associate professor, 1970-74; professor, 1974-98; professor emerita, 1998-). *Fellowships and grants*: SSRC Faculty Research Grant, summer 1968 (research on potlatch-type societies; NSF Research Grants, 1969-70, 1971-72, 1974-75, 1986-87; Barnard Faculty Research Grants, 1972-73, 1978-81; Guggenheim Fellowship, 1986-87. *Interests*: "I teach courses at the graduate and undergraduate level on Native American cultures." *Published works*: Co-author, with Rosman: Feasting With Mine Enemy: Rank and Exchange Among Northwest Coast Societies (Columbia University Press, 1971; paperback edition, Waveland Press, 1986); The Tapestry of Culture, 8th Ed. (McGraw-Hill, 2003); edited with Abraham Rosman, Translating Cultres: Persepctives on Translation and Anthropology (Oxford: Berg Press, 2003). *Articles*: "Potlatch and Sagali: The Structure of Exchange in Trobriand and Haida Societies," in Transactions of the New York Academy of Sciences, June 1970; "Potlatch and Hakari: An Analysis of Maori Society in Terms of the Potlatch Model," in Man, Vol. 6, No. 4, Dec. 1971; "The Potlatch: A Structural Analysis," in American Anthropologist 74, 1972; among others. Conference papers: "West Coast Tribes and Their Social Structural Transformations" presented at the American Association for the Advancement of Science, Los Angeles, CA, May 1985; "The Kwakiutl Potlatch: A Sacred or Secular Ritual?" presented at Seminar on the Role of Ritual in the System of Culture, Jagiellonian University, Poland, Sept. 1985; "Structural Patterning in Kwakiutl Art, Symbol and Ritual" presented at 12th International Congress of Anthropological & Ethnological Sciences, Zagreb, July 1988; "The Material Culture of the 'Noble Savage': Artifact Collecting and Images of Other" presented at the Dept. of Anthropology, University of Chicago, Feb. 1992.

RUBY, ROBERT H. (Soo-huk-min)1921-
(physician and surgeon)
Education: Whitworth College, B.A., 1942; Washington University, M.D., 1945. *Principal occupation*: Physician and surgeon. *Home address*: 4535 W. Peninsula Dr., Moses Lake, WA 98837. *Affiliation*: Currently on the staff of five hospitals in the Columbia Basin area; Instructor (course, "Indians of the Pacific Northwest), Big Bend Community College, Moses Lake, WA, 1986-present. *Military service*: U.S. Army Air Corps, 1946-47 (in Japan; Public Health Service, with service served on the Pine Ridge Indian Reservation, 1953-54. *Past professional post*: Consultant to the Confederated Tribes of the Umatilla Indian Reservation, 2001 & 2002. *Community activities*: Dr. Ruby has served on numerous civic and state and local committees. *Memberships*: American College of Surgeons (Fellow); Grant County Medical Society; Washington State Historical Society (board of curators, 1984); Adam East Museum, Moses Lake, WA (museum development committee, 1990). *Awards, honors*: Papers presented: "Indian Shaker John Slocum's 'Death,' a Reappraisal," at the 44th Annual Pacific Northwest History Conference, April 4, 1991; and "Esther Ross and the Resurrection of the Stillaguamish Tribe," at the 6th Annual Conference of the American Society for Ethnohistory, Nov. 8, 1996; honored, June 21, 2003 by the Okanagon Tribe, in a name giving ceremony with the name Soo-huk-min, translated "Caretaker (of the history)." *Published works*: The Oglala Sioux Warriors in Transition (Vantage Press, 1955); Half-Sun on the Columbia: A Biography of Chief Moses (University of Oklahoma Press, 1965); The Spokane Indians: Children of the Sun (University of Oklahoma Press, 1970); The Cayuse Indians: Imperial Tribesmen of Old Oregon (University of Oklahoma Press, 1972); Myron Eells and the Puget Sound Indians (Superior Publishing, 1976); The Chinook Indians: Traders on the Lower Columbia River (University of Oklahoma Press, 1976); Indians of the Pacific Northwest: A History (University of Oklahoma Press, 1981); A Guide to the Indian Tribes of the Pacific Northwest (University of Oklahoma Press, 1986); Dreamer Prophets of the Columbia Plateau (University of Oklahoma Press, 1989); Indian Slavery in the Pacific Northwest (Arthur H. Clark Co., 1993); John Slocum and the Indian Shaker Church (University of Oklahoma Press, 1996); Esther Ross: Stilliguamish Champion (University of Oklahoma Press, 2001); numerous articles in magazines and journals; book reviews.

RUDOLPH, LINDA
(school supt.)
Affiliation: Puyallup Nation Education System, Chief Leschi School System, 2002 East 28th St., Tacoma, WA 98404 (206) 593-0218.

RUEGAMER, JOHN A.
(school principal)
Affiliation: Coeur D'Alene Tribal School, P.O. Box 338, DeSmet, ID 83824 (208) 274-6921.

RUNDSTROM, ROBERT
(instructor-Native American studies)
Affiliation: Native American Studies Program, University of Oklahoma, 455 W. Lindsey, Rm. 804, Norman, OK 73019 (405) 325-2312.

RUNNELS, DENNIS M.
(Colville Confederated Tribes) 1941-
(college instructor)
Born March 29, 1941, Bremerton, Wash. *Education*: University of Washington, PhD Candidate in Romance Language. *Principal occupation*: College instructor. *Home address*: RR 1 Box 576, Sharon, VT 05065 (802) 763-7554 Fax 646-0333; E-mail: dennis.runnels@dartmouth.edu. *Affiliation*: Instructor, Native American Studies program, Dartmouth College, 1990-present (teaches courses on American Indian Autobiography, Native American Languages, American Indian Identity, Spanish, and Latin American Studies. *Military service*: U.S. Marine Military Academy, King's Point, 1959-63. *Published works*: Journal articles.

RUOFF, A. LaVONNE BROWN 1930-
(professor emerita of English)
Born April 10, 1930, Charleston, IL. *Education*: Northwestern University, B.S., 1953, M.A., 1954, Ph.D., 1966. *Principal occupation*: Professor Emerita of English; Interim director, D'Arcy McNickle Center for American Indian History, Newberry Library. *Home address*: 300 Forest Ave., Oak Park, IL 60302 (708) 848-9292 Fax 848-9308; E-Mail: lruoff@uic.edu. *Affiliation*: Dept. of English, University of Illinois, Chicago, 1966-94. *Community activities*: Chicago Indian Council Fire,

1980-89; Indian Business Associate Advisory Board, 1977-84. *Memberships*: Modern Language Association, 1966-; Association for the Study of Amerian Indian Literature, 1977-; Discussion Group on American Indian Literature (MLA, 1978-; chair, 1978, 1990); Society for the Study of Multi-Ethnic Literature in the U.S., 1978-; American Studies Association; Native American Literature Symposium. *Awards, honors*: Achievement Award, Indian Council Fire, 1989; Distinguished Contribution to Ethnic Studies, Society for the Study of Multi-Ethnic Literature in the U.S., 1986; director, Summer Seminars for College Teachers on American Indian Literatures, 1979, 1983, 1989, 1994; National Endowment for the Humanities Fellowship, 1992-93; honored for contributions to American Indian literature by the Division of American Indian Literatures, Modern Language Association, and Association for Study of American Indian Literatures, 1993; American Book Awards, Before Columbus Association, 1998; Writer of the Year for Bibliography, Wordcraft Circle of Native Writers & Storytellers, 1998; Writer of the Year for Series Editing, Wordcraft Circle of Native Writers & Storytellers, 2002; Lifetime Scholarly Achievement Award, Modern Language Association, 2002. *Interests*: History of American Indian literature written in English. *Biographical source*: Directory of American Scholars; Who's Who in the Midwest; Who's Who in America (millenium edition); Writer's Directory. *Published works*: The Mocassin Maker, by E. Pauline Johnson, edited with intro. by Ruoff (University of Arizona Press, 1987; reprinted by University of Oklahoma Press, 1998); co-editor, Redefining American Literary History, with Jerry Ward (Modern Language Association, 1990; American Indian Literatures (Modern Language Association, 1990); Literatures of the American Indian (Chelsea House, 1990); Wynema: A Child of the Forest, by S. Alice Callahan, edited with intro. by Ruoff (University of Nebraska Press, 1997); Life Letters and Speeches, edited with intro. by Ruoff and biography by Donald Smith (University of Nebraska Press, 1997); editor, American Indian Lives Series (University of Nebraska Press); From the Deep Woods to Civilization with Excerpts from Indian Boyhood, by Charles A. Eastman, edited with an intro. by Ruoff, Lakeside Classic Series (Donnelley Press, 2001).

RUPERT, RHONDA (Maidu)
(tribal councilmember)
Affiliation: United Maidu Nation, P.O. Box 204, Susanville, CA 96130 (916) 257-9691.

RUPNICKI, MAMIE (Prairie Band Potawatomi)
(tribal chairperson)
Affiliation: Prairie Band Potawatomi Tribal Council, 16277 Q Rd., Mayetta, KS 66509 (785) 966-2255.

RUSS, JAMES
(Indian education center director)
Affiliation: Round Valley Indian Tribes Education Center, P.O. Box 448, Covelo, CA 95428 (707) 983-1062 Fax 983-1073.

RUSS, JOSEPH A., Sr.
(tribal president)
Affiliation: Covelo Indian Community Council, Round Valley Reservation, P.O. Box 448, Covelo, CA 95428 (707) 983-6126.

RUSSELL, JERRY L. (Cherokee) 1933-
(communications executive)
Born July 21, 1933, Little Rock, Ark. *Education*: University of Arkansas, B.A., 1958. *Principal occupation*: Communications executive. *Home address*: 9 Lefever Lane, Little Rock, AR 72207 (501) 225-3996. *Affiliations*: Owner, Campaign Consultants, Little Rock, AR 1971-; owner, River City Public Relations, Little Rock, AR, 1971-; national chairman, Order of the Indian Wars, Little Rock, AR, 1980-. *Other professional posts*: National chairman, Civil War Round Table Associates; national chairman, Confederate Historical Institute. *Military service*: U.S. Army, 1953-56. *Community activities*: Friends of the Library (past president). *Memberships*: American Association of Political Consultants; Western Historical Association; Little Big Horn Associates; Custer Battlefield Historical & Museum Association (director); Custer Battlefield Preservation Committee (director); Westerners International. *Awards, honors*: Past president, Arkansas Advertising Federation; past president, Arkansas Chapter,

Public Relations Society of America. *Interests*: Military history; political campaigning; travel. *Biographical source*: Who's Who in the South & Southwest.

RUSSELL, JIM *(Chief Badger)* (Kaweah)
(vice principal chief, publisher)
Address: 2220 E 4500 S. Apt. 1, Salt Lake City, UT 84117. *Affiliations*: Vice principal chief, Kaweah Indian Nation of Western USA & Mexico; tribal chief, Kayenta Kaweah Tribe. *Other professional post*: Member, American Indian Defense of Americas.

RUSSELL, LUVETTE
(BIA special education coordinator)
Affiliation: Papago Agency, Bureau of Indian Affairs, P.O. Box 490, Sells, AZ 85634 (520) 383-3292 Fax 383-2399.

RUSSELL, NEIL (Sioux)
(secondary school principal)
Affiliation: Lower Brule Day School, P.O. Box 245, Lower Brule, SD 57548 (605) 473-5510.

RUSSELL, NORMAN H. (Cherokee) 1921-
(retired university professor)
Born November 29, 1921. *Education*: PhD. *Address*: P.O. Box 3714, Edmond, OK 73083-3714 (405) 341-5447. *Military service*: AAF, 1942-46. *Published works*: 28 books; latest being (poetry), "From Star to Leaf."

RUSSELL, DR. SCOTT C.
(professor of anthropology)
Affiliation: Dept. of Anthropology, Box 872402, Arizona State University, Tempe, AZ 85287 (480) 965-6213 Fax 965-7671. *Interests*: Native American studies. E-mail: scott.russell@asu.edu.

RUSSELL, SIERA (Yavapai)
(program director)
Affiliation: Indian Legal Program, Arizona State University College of Law, Box 877906, Tempe, AZ 85287 (480) 965-6204.

RUSSELL, JUDGE STEVE
(Oklahoma Cherokee) 1947-
(associate professor of criminal justice)
Born February 10, 1947, Bristow, Okla. *Education*: University of Texas, B.S.Ed. (magna cum laude), 1972, J.D., 1975; University of Nevada, Reno, Masters of Judicial Studies, 1993. *Thesis*: "Ethnic Cleansing and Land Ownership: Why the Native American Graves Protection & Repatriation Act Does Not Protect Native American Graves in Texas." *Principal occupation*: Associate professor of criminal justice. *Address & Affiliation*: Associate professor, Dept. of Criminal Justice, 1033 E. 3rd St., 302 Sycamore Hall, Indiana University, Bloomington, IN (812) 855-2601 Fax 855-5522. E-mail: swrussell@indiana.edu. *Other professional post*: Visiting Judge, State of Texas, 1995-present. *Past professional posts*: Teaching - Instructor, University of Texas School of Law, 1985-90, 1992-93; Assistant Professor, Division of Social & Policy Sciences, The University of Texas at San Antonio, 1995-2000; Assistant Professor, Division of Criminal Justice, The University of Texas at San Antonio, 2000-2001; *Professional* - Simons, Cunningham, Coleman, Nelson & Howard, law clerk, 1974-75, associate, 1975-76; partner, Russell & Mahlab, 1976-78; Austin Municipal Court, Associate Judge, 1978-80, Presiding Judge, 1980-82; Judge, Travis County Court at Law No. Two, 1982-94. *Military service*: U.S. Air Force, 1964-68 (Top Secret Security Clearance). *Professional Training*: Numerous workshops, symposiums and seminars, including: "Sovereignty and the Right to Death," Cleveland-Marshall College of Law, Cleveland, OH, 2003; "International Indian Treaty Council Conference," Sac & Fox Nation, 2003; "Decolonizing American Indian Studies," The Newberry Library, Chicago, IL, 2003; "Honoring Nations," The Harvard Project on American Indian Economic Development, Santa Fe, NM 2002 (invited). *Memberships*: Academy of Criminal Justice Sciences (life); American Association of University Professors; American Society of Criminology (life); American Society of Criminology (life); American Indian Philosophy Association; Association of Trial Lawyers of America; Bristow Historical Society; Cherokee National Historical Society; Law & Society Association; Native Writers Circle of the Americas; Ninth Circuit Historical Society; State Bar of Texas; Texas Indian Bar Association

(two term president); U.S. District Court Bar (Western District of Texas); U.S. Supreme Court Bar; Wordcraft Circle of Native American Writers & Storytellers. *Published works*: Numerous book chapters, book & film reviews; refereed & law review artciles; non-refereed articles; poetry &fiction; & paper presentations.

RUSSONIELLO-DAMASKOS, RUBY K.
(Gros Ventre/Assiniboine) 1963-
(teacher; Indian education facilitator)
Born June 19, 1963, Havre, Mont. *Education*: University of Montana, BA (Elementary Education), 1985; University of Washington (Med-At Risk Education). *Principal occupation*: Teacher; Indian education facilitator. *Address & Affiliation*: Tacoma Public Schools District #10 (special education teacher; Dept. Chair, 1990-2001; Indian education facilitator, 2001-present), 601 S. 8th St., P.O. Box 1357, Tacoma, WA 98401 (253) 571-1139 Fax 571-2637. E-mail: ruby_russoniello@hotmail.com or E-mail: rdamask@tacoma.k12.wa.us. *Past professional posts*: Chapter 1/special education teacher, Woodman School District #18, Lolo Creek, MT, 1987-89; special education teacher, Bonner, MT, 1989-90. *Community activities*: Parent Advisory Committee - Indian Education; Pow wow Planning Committee - UPS - Tacoma, WA. *Memberships*: National Indian Education Association; Phi Delta Kappa; Teaching Tolerance; Council of Exceptional Children Foundation; National Education Assn. *Interests*: History, ancestry, reading, poetry, animals, movies, hiking.

RYAN, ARNOLD R. (Sisseton-Wahpeton Sioux)
(former tribal chairperson)
Affiliation: Sisseton-Wahpeton Sioux Tribe, Rt. 2 - Agency Village, Sisseton, SD 57262 (605) 698-3911.

RYAN, IRENE (Washoe)
(Indian store owner)
Affiliation: The Teepee, 2500 E. 2nd St., Suite #38, Reno, NV 89595 (702) 322-5599.

S

SABATTIS, MR. CLAIR (Maliset)
(tribal chairperson)
Affiliation: Houlton Band of Maliset Indians, Rt. 3, Box 450, Houlton, ME 04730 (207) 532-4273.

SACKLER, ELIZABETH
(foundation founder/president)
Affiliations: American Indian Ritual Object Repatriation Foundation, 463 East 57 St., New York, NY 10128 (212) 980-9441 Fax 421-2746; president, Board of Directors, Arthur M. Sackler Foundation, New York, NY.

SACOBIE, RUPERT
(Indian band chief)
Affiliation: Oromocto Idian Band, Box 417, Oromocto, Manitoba, Canada E2V 2J2 (506) 357-2083.

SACOBIE, STEPHEN
(Indian band chief)
Affiliation: Kingsclear Indian Band, RR 6, Box 6, Comp. 19, Fredericton, New Brunswick, Canada E3B 4X7 (506) 363-3028.

SADDLEMAN, ALBERT
(Indian band chief)
Affiliation: Okanagan Indian Band, Siye 8, Comp. 20, RR 7, Vernon, B.C., Canada V1T 7Z3 (604) 542-4328.

SADDLEMAN, GEORGE
(Indian band chief)
Affiliation: Upper Nicola Indian Band, Box 3700, Merritt, B.C., Canada V0K 2B0 (604) 350-3342.

SAFFORD, GLEN
(administrative officer)
Affiliation: Peter Christiansen Health Center, 450 Old Abe Rd., Lac du Flambeau, WI 54538 (715) 588-3371.

SAINTE-MARIE, BUFFY (Cree) 1942-
(folksinger, poet, author)
Born February 20, 1942, Craven, SK, Can. *Education*: University of Massachusetts, BA (Philosophy), 1963. *Principal occupation*: Folksinger, poet. *Address*: Unknown. *Affiliations*: Recording artist, Vanguard Record-

ing Society; president, Cradleboard Teaching Project (promotes multicultural education programs to grade schools around North America). *Other occupation*: Free-lance writer on Indian culture and affairs; associate editor, The Native Voice (Vancouver, B.C., Can.); teaches at York University, Indian Federated College in Saskatchewan, Evergreen State College in Washington State, and the Institute for American Indian Arts in Santa Fe, NM. *Awards, honors*: Wrote song, "Up Where We Belong," recorded by Joe Cocker and Jennifer Warnes for the film, An Officer and a Gentleman, won an Academy Award in 1982; Lifetime Musical Achievement by the First Americans in the Arts. *Interests*: Lecturing on Indian affairs; composing, singing. Miss Sainte-Marie writes, "I am best known for songs and poems directly related to past and present American Indian affairs. (I have contributed) to The Native Voice, Thunderbird, American Indian Horizons, and Boston Broadside in the fields of North American Indian music and Indian affairs. Have lived on and visited reserves (reservations) in fifteen states and four provinces; have traveled, lectured and sung in England, France, Canada, Italy, and Mexico, and have given performances in concert and on television internationally and in all major American cities." *Published works*: She has contributed writings to "The Native Voice," "Thunderbird," "American Indian Horizons," and "Boston Broadside," in the field of North American Indian music and Indian affairs. Sainte-Marie is the author of *Nokosis and the Magic Hat* (1986), a children's adventure book set on an Indian reservation. *Recordings*: Confidence & Likely Stories (CD), 1993; Up Where We Belong, collection of new songs (CD), 1996.

ST. CLAIR, KATHLEEN INEZ McATEE *(Oanther Walker)* **(United Lumbee) 1952-**
   (artist-craftsperson)
Born June 27, 1952, Los Angeles, Calif. *Education*: High school. Principal occupation: Artist-craftsperson. *Address*: Resides in California. *Affiliation*: Owner of Kat's Creations Somewhere in Time, Shingletown, CA; make handmade items, specializing in Native American traditional crafts, customs, moccasins, jewelry, leather goods, etc., 1989-. *Community activities*: Shasta Wildlife Rescue-Rehab Trainee, Educational Trainee, 1992 - Shasta County, CA. *Membership*: United Lumbee Nation's Deer Clan. *Interests*: "Rehabing and training wild & domestic animals. Working with children & adults, teaching traditional crafts & ways of our Native people, sharing spiritual beliefs & traditional dances."

ST. CLAIR, ROBERT N.
   (professor of linguistics)
Born April 24, 1934, Honolulu, Hawaii. *Education*: University of Hawaii, BA, 1963; University of Kansas, PhD (Eskimo Language), 1974. *Principal occupation*: Professor of linguistics, *Home address*: 4404 Brownhurst Way, Louisville, KY 40241 (502) 429-8574 Fax 852-4182 (work); E-Mail: rnstcl01 @ulkyvm.louisville.edu.com. *Affiliation*: Professor of linguistics, Dept. of English, University of Louisville, Louisville, KY, 1973-. *Other professional posts*: Consultant on language renewal - Yakima, Wanapam, Nez Perce, Eskimo; grant evaluator; member, Institute for Communication Studies (San Antonio, TX). *Military service*: U.S. Army, 1957-60 (Sgt., instructor-Nike Ajax Guided Missile). *Professional activities*: Xth International Conference on Salish Languages (chairperson); editor, Lektos; editor, Language Today; editorial board: language problems and language planning, invisible speech, Annuario (Santo Domingo); co-editor, Philosophical Linguistics; chairman, Commission on Academic Excellence. *Memberships*: National Council of Teachers of English; Modern Language Association; International Conference on Salishan Languages; Linguistics Society of America; American Association for the Advancement of Science. *Awards, honors*: Outstanding Educator Award, 1975; Distinguished Visiting Professor (New Mexico State University), 1977; 1996 Distinguished Professor of Research & Scholarship, University of Louisville; adjunct professor of linguistics, Josai International University, Chiba, Japan, 1996. *Field work*: Salishan languages: Skagit, Lummi; Sahaptian languages: Yakima, Wanapam; Eskimo: Yupik Eskimo. *Interests*: Bilingual education; sociolinguistics; political linguistics; travel. Dissertation - Theoretical Aspects of Eskimo Phonology, University of Kansas, Dept. of Linguistics. *Biographical*

sources: Who's Who in the South and Southwest; Who's Who International, 1994. Dictionary of International Biography. *Published works*: Languages of the World (Hanshin Publishers, S. Korea, 1992) Social Metaphors (University Press of America, 1994); Language, Culture, and Societal Transformations, with J. Busch (Social Systems Press, 1999); numerous articles, papers, monographs, and book reviews in scholarly journals.

ST. CYR, WEHNONA *(Mi'-texi-Sacred Moon, Buffalo Clan)* **(Omaha) 1957-**
   (health systems administrator)
Born December 6, 1957, Wichita, Kans. *Education*: High school (Riverside Indian School, Anadarko, OK); Morningside College, BS, 1981; University of Hawaii, MPH, 1987. *Principal occupation*: Health systems administrator. *Home address*: Resides in NE. *Affiliations*: Omaha Tribe of Nebraska, Macy, NE (social worker-2 years; nursing home administrator-3 years; health systems administrator-2 years); currently employed by the Public Health Service, U.S. Government, Indian Health Service as a Service Unit Director at the Winnebago Indian Hospital in Winnebago, NE. *Community activities*: Member of the Dr. Susan Picotte Hospital restoration Committee in Walthill, NE. Dr. Picotte was the first Native American woman physician in the U.S. *Memberships*: American College of Healthcare Executives; Nebraska State Historical Foundation (board of trustees); "I am also the Service Unit Director Chairperson for 1990 in the Aberdeen Area." *Awards, honors*: Received an "Outstanding" EPMS rating for 1989 thru Indian Health Service, and was also nominated by the Winnebago Hospital staff for outstanding employee in the area of Administration for 1989. *Interests*: "I continue to be involved in the Native Hawaiian Rights issues, specifically in the area of Health Care. I did receive my MPH from the University of Hawaii in 1987 and have traveled there again in 1989 to try and keep current and lend my expertise to their struggle. I also am active in my culture and dance in the traditional style."

ST-DENIS, HAROLD
   (Indian band chief)
Affiliation: Wolf Lake (Algonquin) Indian Band, Box 1060, Temiscaminque, Quebec, Canada J0Z 3R0 (819) 627-3628.

ST. FRANCIS, HOMER (Abenaki)
   (tribal chief)
Affiliation: Abenaki Tribal Council, P.O. Box 276, Swanton, VT 05488 (802) 868-7146.

ST. GERMAINE, HENRY, SR.
(Lake Superior Chippewa)
   (tribal chairperson)
Affiliation: Lac du Flambeau Tribal Council, P.O. Box 67, Lac du Flambeau, WI 54538 (715) 588-3303.

ST. GERMAINE, RICHARD *(Migisi)*
(Lac Courte Oreilles Ojibwa) 1947-
   (associate professor)
Born March 4, 1947, Idabel, Okla. *Education*: University of Wisconsin, Eau Claire, BA, 1969; Arizona State University, MA (Education), 1972, PhD, 1975. *Principal occupation*: Associate professor. *Address*: Foundations of Education Dept., University of Wisconsin, Eau Claire, WI 54701. *Affiliations*: Tribal chairperson, Lac Courte Oreilles Tribe, Hayward, WI, 1977-86; director of the American Indian Graduate Studies Program & lecturer, University of California, Berkeley, 1986-88; associate professor, University of Wisconsin, Eau Claire, 1989-. *Other professional posts*: President, American Indian Graduate Center, Albuquerque, NM; (appointed by President Clinton) member of the National Advisory Council on Indian Education, 1994- *Memberships*: National Indian Education Assn (president,1975-77); National Tribal Chairmen's Assn (treasurer, 1978-80). *Awards, honors*: Ford Foundation Fellowship, 1971-75.

ST. PIERRE, MARK
   (executive director; adjunct professor)
Affiliations: Executive Director, Pine Ridge Chamber of Commerce, Pine Ridge, SD; adjunct professor of sociology, anthropology, and creative writing at Regis University, Steamboat Springs, CO. He has lived among the Lakota people since 1971, both as a edu-

cator and as an encourager of American Indian art. *Published works*: Madonna Swann: A Lakota Woman's Story (University of Oklahoma Press, 1992).

ST. PIERRE, NATE (Chippewa/Cree) 1962-
   (faculty, administrator)
Born December 28, 1962, Fort Belknap, Mont. *Education*: Montana State University, MEd., 1989, EdD in progress. *Principal occupation*: Faculty, administrator. *Address*: P.O. Box 6773, Bozeman, MT 59771 (406) 994-3992 (work). *Affiliations*: Acting director, Office of Tribal Service, Rocky Boy's Reservation, Chippewa-Cree Tribe, Box Elder, MT; faculty, administrator, Montana State University, Bozeman, MT, 1992-president. *Interests*: Adult education; Indian health education. *Published works*: "Educational Issues in Montana's Tribal Colleges," in Adult Literacy & Basic Education, 1990; "Multiculturalism: A Native American Perspective," in Journal of Lifelong Learning, 1993.

SAKAR, SOPHIE
   (village chief)
Affiliation: Native Village of Chuathbaluk, P.O. Box 31, Chuathbaluk, AK 99557 (907) 467-4313.

SAKIESTEWA, NOREEN
   (Indian school principal)
Affiliation: Moencopi Day School, P.O. Box 185, Tuba City, AZ 86045 (520) 283-5361 Fax 283-4662.

SAKIM (Alleghenny Lenape)
   (tribal chief)
Affiliation: Chief (lifetime), Alleghenny Tribal Council, Canton, OH 44705 (216) 453-6224.

SALAS, JOSEPH
   (health center director)
Affiliation: Ysleta Del Sur Servie Unit, P.O. Box 17579, El Paso, TX 79907 (915) 859-7913.

SALAZAR, EARL (San Juan Pueblo)
   (pueblo council governor)
Affiliation: San Juan Pueblo Council, P.O. Box 1099, San Juan Pueblo, NM 87566 (505) 852-4400.

SALGADO, ERNIE
   (Indian education director)
Affiliation: Ahmium Education, Inc., 701 Esplanade St., Suite H, San Jacinto, CA 92582 (909) 654-2781 Fax 654-3089. E-mail: ernie@ivic.net.

SALGADO, LEE ANN (Cahuilla)
   (tribal spokesperson)
Affiliation: Cahuilla Band of Mission Indians, P.O. Box 391760, Anza, CA 92539 (909) 763-5549.

SALGADO, ROBERT J., SR. (Luiseno)
   (tribal spokesman)
Affiliation: Soboba Band of Luiseno Indians, P.O. Box 487, San Jacinto, CA 92381 (909) 654-2765 Fax 654-4198.

SALISBURY, NEAL 1940-
   (historian)
Born May 7, 1940, Los Angeles, Calif. *Education*: University of California, Los Angeles, BA, 1963, MA, 1966, PhD, 1972. *Principal occupation*: Historian. *Address & Affiliation*: Professor, Dept. of History, Smith College, Northampton, MA 01063 (413) 585-3726, 1973-. *Memberships*: American Historical Association; American Society for Ethnohistory; Organization of American Historians. *Awards, honors*: Fellow, Smithsonian Institution, 1972-73; Fellow, Newberry Library Center for History of the American Indian, 1977-78; Fellow, National Endowment for the Humanities, 1984-85; Fellow, Charles Warren Center for Studies in American History, 1989; Fellow, National Humanities Center, 1991-92; Fellow, American Antiquarian Society, 1995-96; Fellow, American Council of Learned Societies, 2000-2001. *Published works*: Manitou and Providence: Indians, Europeans, and the Beginnings of New England, 1500-1643 (Oxford University Press, 1982); The Indians of New England: A Critical Bibliography (Indiana University Press, 1982); The Sovereignty and Goodness of God, by Mary Rowlandson, and Related Documents (1997); A Companion to American Indian History, with Philip J. Deloria (2002); The Enduring Vision: A History of the American People, 2nd Ed., with Paul S. Boyer, et al (D.C. Heath, 2002).

SALISBURY, RALPH (Eastern Cherokee) 1926-
(writer, professor)
Born January 24, 1926, Arlington, Iowa. *Education*: University of Iowa, MFA, 1951. *Home address*: 2377 Charnelton, Eugene, OR 97405 (541) 343-5101. *Affiliation*: Professor (1960-), English Dept., University of Oregon, Eugene, OR. *Military service*: U.S. Air Force, 1944-46. *Awards, honors*: Rockefeller Bellagio Award for novel; Chapelbrook Award, Short Story & Poetry. *Interests*: Writing fiction & poetry. *Published works*: Pointing At the Rainbow (Blue Cloud, 1980); Spirit Beast Chant (Blue Cloud, 1982); A Nation Within (Outrigger, 1983); Going to the Water (Pacific House, 1983); A White Rainbow (Blue Cloud, 1985); One Indian, Two Chiefs (Navajo Community College Press, 1993); Trekways of the Wind (University of Arizona, 1994); The Last Rattlesnake Throw (stories) (University of Oklahoma Press, 1997; Rainbows of Stone (University of Arizona Press, 1999).

SALLEE, JACLYN (Inupiat Eskimo) 1964-
(director-Native broadcast center)
Born November 15, 1964, Anchorage, Alaska. *Education*: Western Washington University, 1983-85; University of Alaska, Anchorage, BA, 1988. *Principal occupation*: Director-Native broadast center. *Address*: Unknown. *Affiliation*: Native Broadcast Center, Anchorage, AK, 1988-. *Other professional post*: Task Force Chairperson, Native Broadcast Center, 1991-. *Community activities*: United Way (member, Allocation Committee). *Memberships*: Alaska Press Club (board member, 1989-91); Alaska Native Communications Society (Steering Committee, 1988-). *Interests*: Art, Alaska Native issues, skiing.

SALOIS, CHANE (Chippewa of Montana) 1947-
(civil engineer)
Born February 20, 1947, Kalispel, Mont. *Education*: Montana State University, BS (Math), 1970, BS (Civil Engineering), 1974. *Principal occupation*: Civil engineer. *Address*: Unknown. *Affiliations*: Manager, Bureau of Indian Affairs (Roads Branch Manager, Lame Deer, MT, 2 years; Colville Agency, Nespelem, WA, 6 years; Flathead Agency, Pablo, MT, 9 years; Flathead Agency, Irrigation Division, St. Ignatius, MT, , 1992-. *Community activities*: Little Shell Tribe of Chippewa Indians of Montana (secretary/treasurer). *Membership*: Association of County Engineers, 1988-. *Interests*: Vocational - road & bridge construction, pavements, concrete construction, irrigation facilities. Avocational - hunting, snowmobiling, all terrain vehicles, traveling.

SALSEDO, RAY
(chairperson)
Affiliation: Antelope Indian Circle Religious Culture Group, P.O. Box 790, Susanville, CA 96130 (916) 257-2181 ext. 1534.

SALTER, JOHN L., JR.
(department of Indian studies chairperson)
Affiliation: University of North Dakota, Department of Indian Studies, Grand Forks, ND 58202 (701) 777-4314.

SALTZEN, JOAN
(Indian education program director)
Affiliation: Colusa County School District, Indian Education Program, 345-5th St., Suite C, Colusa, CA 95932 (916) 458-0305.

SALVADOR, MARIA "LILLY" (Dzaisratyaitsa)
(Acoma Pueblo) 1944-
(craftsperson, potter, gallery owner/manager)
Born April 6, 1944, McCartys Village, Acoma Pueblo, N.M. *Education*: New Mexico State (1 year). *Principal occupation*: Traditional Native American potter; craftsperson. *Address*: P.O. Box 342, 505 Acoma Rd., Acoma, NM 87034 (505) 552-9501. *Affiliations*: Pottery is displayed at the following museums and galleries: Boston Museum of Fine Arts; The Heard Museum, Phoenix; The Museum of Man, San Diego; Museum of Natural History, Los Angeles; The Whitehorse Gallery, Boulder, CO; Museum of Arizona, Tucson, AZ; Elitejorge Museum, Indiana. *Other institutional affiliation*: National Indian Council on Aging Catalogue. *Awards, honors*: 1st & 2nd Prize Awards for handcrafted pottery from Whitehorse Gallery, Boulder, CO; 1st & 3rd Prize Award Ribbons from New Mexico State Fair; 1st, 2nd & 3rd Prize Awards for handcrafted/

hand painted pottery from the Southwest American Indian Arts Association, 1st, Honorable Mention Awards from the Gallup InterTribal Indian Ceremonial; 1st, Special Award Ribbon from the Heard Museum, Phoenix, AZ; Southwestern Association on Indian Affairs, 1st Prize Ribbon for finest of Acoma Pueblo pottery; 1st, 2nd & 3rd Prize Ribbons from Elitejorge Museum, Indiana. *Community activities*: Native needle embroidery instructor, Acoma Adult Education Programs; secretary, Sky City Community School; member, parent-student association of Saint Joseph School, San Fidel, NM; demonstrate pottery making to Acoma Sky City Elementary School and Cubero Elementary School. *Memberships*: Gallup Intertribal Ceremonial Association; Southwest American Indian Arts Association; National Indian Arts & Crafts Association; Southwestern Association on Indian Affairs; AICA; Smithsonian Institution. *Interests*: "To develop and expand my present pottery gallery (the first at the Pueblo Acoma) into a major showcase for collectors, tourists (who visit, annually, the oldest inhabited village in the U.S.) and discriminating curators of various museums throughout the U.S. With the private invitations extended by the above mentioned museums and galleries, I have traversed the southwest and northwest region of the U.S. exhibiting my traditional hand-crafted/hand painted Acoma Pueblo pottery and figurines. I started working with oil paints. My gallery is open by appointment only." *Biographical sources*: American Indian Pottery, 2nd Edition; Amerika newsletter, Chicago, Ill.; National Indian Council on Aging Catalogue; Talking With Clay - Pueblo Storytellers, by Barbara Babcock.

SALVIS, CATHLEEN
(Indian school principal)
Affiliation: Noli School, P.O. Box 487, San Jacinto, CA 92581 (909) 654-5596 Fax 654-4198.

SALWAY, HAROLD D. (Oglala Lakotah)
(former tribal president)
Affiliation: Oglala Lakotah Tribal Council, P.O. Box H #468, Pine Ridge, SD 57770 (605) 867-5821.

SALWAY-BLACK, SHERRY
(institute vice president)
Affiliation: First Nations Development Institute, The Stores Bldg., 11917 Main St., Fredericksburg, VA 22408 (703) 371-5615.

SALZANO, JOSEPH (Choctaw)
(musician)
Born in 1958, Biloxi, Miss. and raised in Rochester, NY on Lake Ontario. *Address*: c/o Morning Star Music, 7-B Park Lane, Lansing, NY 14882 (607) 533-8867. Trained in the clarinet, sax and composition since age 8 and American Indian flute since 1985—on flute, Joe has studied with R. Carlos Nakai and Eddie Box, Sr. and learned from Kevin Locke and Tom Ware. He has performed live, and on radio & TV throughout the U.S. including schools, concerts and clubs. *Recordings*: "Turtle Island Flute, " & "Four Winds." Both distributed by Morning Star Music. A collection of traditional and contemporary Native American flute music. *Quote*: "Being half Italian and half Choctaw, a soxophonist and flute player, a performer of Jazz and Indian music, I seek to use my music as a way of bridging differences and affirming that we are all children of Mother Earth."

SALZMANN, ZDENEK 1925-
(anthropologist)
Born October 18, 1925, Prague, Czech Republic. *Education*: Caroline University, Prague, 1945-47 (Absolutorium, 1948); Indiana University, MA, 1949, PhD, 1963. *Principal occupation*: Visiting professor of anthropology. *Home address*: 120 Highland Dr. So., Sedona, AZ 86351 (928) 284-0344. E-mail: dennysalz@aol.com. *Affiliations*: Professor of anthropology emeritus, University of Massachusetts, Amherst, 1968-89; adjunct professor of anthropology, Northern Arizona University, Flagstaff, 1990-. *Other professional posts*: Visiting professor, Yale University; consultant to Wind River Reservation schools on Arapaho language and culture curriculum, 1979-; visiting professor, Charles University, Prague, Czech Republic. *Memberships*: Linguistic Society of America, 1949-; American Anthropological Association, 1954-. *Awards, honors*: Research grants from the following:

American Philosophical Society; National Endowment for the Humanities; Senior Fulbright-Hays Scholar; International Research and Exchanges Board; American Council of Learned Societies. Given in a public ceremony and with the approval of Arapaho elders, the name hinono 'ei neecee (Arapaho Chief). *Interests*: Fieldwork among Northern Arapaho Indians, 1949-; numerous trips to the Wind River Reservation under various auspices. *Biographical sources*: American Men and Women of Science; Contemporary Authors; Who's Who in America; Directory of American Scholars. *Published works*: Dictionary of Contemporary Arapaho Usage (Arapaho Language & Culture Commission, 1983); The Arapaho Indians: A Research Guide and Bibliography (Greenwood Press, 1988); Language, Culture & Society: An Introduction to Linguistic Anthropology, 1st Ed. 1993, 2nd Ed. 1998, 3rd Ed. 2004 (Westview Press); Guide to Native Americans of the Southwest (Westview Press, 1997); among others; numerous articles in various scholarly journals.

SAM, GERALD
(village chief)
Affiliation: Alatna Village, Alatna, AK 99720 (907) 968-2241.

SAM, GEORGE (Eskimo)
(village president)
Affiliation: Lower Kalskag Village, P.O. Box 27, Lower Kalskag, AK 99626 (907) 471-2307.

SAM, JIMMY L.
(executive director)
Affiliation: Boston Indian Council, Inc., 105 S. Huntington, Jamaica Plain, MA 02130 (617) 232-0343.

SAM, PAUL IGNATIUS
(Indian band chief)
Affiliation: Shuswap Indian Band, Box 790, Invermere, B.C., Canada V0A 1K0 (604) 342-6361.

SAM, ROBERT (Paiute)
(tribal chairperson)
Affiliation: Summit Lake Paiute Council, 655 Anderson St., Winnemucca, NV 89445 (702) 623-5151.

SAMPLE, JEANETTE
(rancheria chairperson)
Affiliation: Big Sandy Rancheria, P.o. Box 337, Auberry, CA 93602 (209) 855-4003.

SAMPSON, DONALD (Umatilla)
(tribal chairperson)
Affiliation: Umatilla Board of Trustees, P.O. Box 638, Pendleton, OR 97801 (541) 276-3165.

SAMUEL, ELIZABETH
(school supt.)
Affiliation: Crow Creek Reservation High School, P.O. Box 12, Stephan, SD 57346 (605) 852-2455.

SAMUELSON, LILLIAN THOMPSON 1926-
(former owner/manager-Indian shop)
Born July 13, 1926, Mecklenburg County, Va. *Education*: Virginia Polytechnic Institute, 1945-1947; Illinois Institute of Technology, BS, 1949. *Principal occupation*: Retired-owner/manager, American Indian Treasures, Inc., Guilderland, NY, 1968-91. *Home address*: P.O. Box 579, Guilderland, NY 12084. *Community activities*: Sponsored Native American art show at Siena College, Loudonville, N.Y. each Spring for 13 years. *Memberships*: National Congress of American Indians; Association on American Indian Affairs, Inc.; Indian Arts and Crafts Association (board of directors, 1976-91; vice president, 1978; president, 1982; member of the year, 1983). *Interests*: Ms. Samuelson writes, "My interest in the American Indian goes back to early childhood, with serious studies of the arts and crafts of living Indians having been pursued the last 20 years, Travel has been extensive during this time, and I've come to know the products of most reservations in the U.S. (I) worked as a consultant on Indian education for the New York State Education Dept. I started American Indian Treasures in 1967, selling only handmade Indian crafts from a broad range of tribes and cultures. Items sold are personally collected to assure authenticity, with buying trips made regularly throughout the year." *Published works*: Articles about American Indian artists.

SANCHEZ, BRUCE (Santa Ana Pueblo)
(Pueblo governor)
Affiliation: Santa Ana Pueblo Council, 2 Dove Rd., Bernalillo, NM 87004 (505) 867-3301.

SANCHEZ, CARMEN
(public affairs specialist)
Affiliation: George Gustav Heye Center, National Museum of the American Indian, Smithsonian Institution, 1 Bowling Green, New York, NY 10004 (212) 283-2420.

SANCHEZ, FRED (Yavapai-Apache)
(tribal vice-chairperson)
Affiliation: Yavapai-Apache Community Council, 2400 Datsi, Camp Verde, AZ 86322 (520) 567-3649.

SANCHEZ, DORIAN (Nisqually)
(tribal chairperson)
Affiliation: Nisqually Indian Community Council, 4820 She-Na-Num Dr., S.E., Olympia, WA 98503 (206) 456-5221.

SANCHEZ, JOSEPH (San Felipe Pueblo)
(former tribal chairperson)
Affiliation: San Felipe Pueblo Council, P.O. Box A, San Felipe, NM 87001 (505) 867-3381.

SANCHEZ, MERLENE (Pomo)
(rancheria chairperson)
Affiliation: Guidiville Rancheria, P.O. Box 339, Talmadge, CA 95481 (707) 462-3682.

SANCHEZ, PHILIP
(BIA agency supt.)
Affiliation: Umatilla Agency, Bureau of Indian Affairs, P.O. Box 520, Pendleton, OR 97801 (541) 278-3786 Fax 278-3791.

SANDERS, CAROLEEN (Catawba)
(craftsperson; company owner)
Affiliation: Creations from the Good Earth, 2253 Indian Trail, Catawba Indian Nation, Rock Hill, SC 29730 (803) 329-2707. *Products*: Catawba Indian ceremonial pottery with ancient catawba designs and motifs.

SANDERS, CHERYL (Catawba)
(craftsperson; company owner)
Affiliation: Catawba Arts, 1822 Indian Trail, Rock Hill, SC 29730 (803) 325-2012. *Products*: Catawba pottery.

SANDERS, E. FRED (Catawba) 1926-
(machinist, assistant chief)
Born April 9, 1926, Catawba Indian Reservation, York County, S.C. *Education*: Catawba Indian School; vocational and technical school—machinist courses. *Principal occupation*: Maintenance machinist, General Tire Corp, Charlotte, N.C., 1967-. *Home address*: 2053 Reservation Rd., Rock Hill, SC 29730. *Other professional post*: Master barber. *Military service*: U.S. Army, 1944-50 (1st Sergeant; Infantry, World War II: Combat Infantry Badge; Bronze Star; 2 Campaign Battle Stars; V.E. Ribbon; Army Occupation Award-Austria). *Community activities*: Assistant chief, Catawba Nation, S.C., 1975-; Charlotte-Mecklenburg Public School System—Indian Education (chairperson-Title IV Program). *Memberships*: National Congress of American Indians; Veterans of Foreign Wars, Rock Hill, S.C.; American Legion, Rock Hill, S.C. *Interests*: Travel as official tribal delegate to many National Congress of American Indians' conferences and conventions in various states. Support tribal leaders with positive attitude and assurance that Native Americans will continue to have a voice and input concerning the future destiny of tribal government and its people.

SANDERS, DR. JEFFREY
(Native American studies dept. director)
Affiliation: Dept. of Native American Studies, Montana State University, 1500 North 30th St., Billings, MT 59101 (406) 657-2311 Fax 657-2187.

SANDERS, WARREN (Catawba)
(craftsperson; company owner)
Affiliation: Catawba Arts, 1822 Indian Trail, Rock Hill, SC 29730 (803) 325-2012. *Products*: Catawba pottery.

SANDERSON, PRISCILLA LANSING (Navajo) 1959-
(vocational rehabilitation)
Born November 26, 1959, Shiprock, N.M. *Education*: Southwestern College (Winfield, KS), BA, 1983; Oklahoma State University, MS, 1984. *Principal occupation*: Vocational rehabilitation. *Address*: P.O Box 247, Flagstaff, AZ 86002 (602) 523-5581 (work). *Affiliations*: Director, American Indian Rehabilitation Research & Training Center, Northern Arizona University, Flagstaff, AZ, 1991-; vocational rehabilitation services specialist, Arizona Rehabilitation Services Administration, Flagstaff, 1986-. *Community activities*: American Indian Disability Legislation Advisory Panel, 1993-. *Community activities*: Flagstaff Mayor's Committee on Disability Awareness, 1990-92; northern Arizona FAS/FAE Task Force, 1993-94; Statewide Independent Living Council, AZ, 1993-. *Memberships*: Consortia of Administrators for Native American Rehabilitation & Research (chairman, 1993-); National Congress of American Indians, 1994-; Rehabilitation Leadership Council, 1994- *Awards, honors*: Outstanding Young Women of America, Sonoma Club, 1984; Professional Worker of the Year," Flagstaff Mayor;s Committee on Disability Awareness, 1989; "In recognition for your leadership in providing service to American Indians," Texas Rehabilitation Commission, 1994. *Interests*: "American Indian & Alaska Native vocational rehabilitation & independent living; reading about different American Indian cultures & values; enjoy watching traditional American Indian dances & pow-wows." *Published works*: "Needs of American Indians with Disabilities" (American Indian Rehabilitation Research & Training Center, 1993); "Response to Perspectives" (The Leading Edge...Focusing on Rehabilitation's Human Resources, 1993); "Needs Assessment Survey to the State Vocational Rehabilitation Agencies" (American Indian Rehabilitation Research & Training Center, 1994).

SANDO, JOE SIMON (Paa Peh) (Jemez Pueblo) 1923-
(teacher, writer)
Born August 1, 1923, Jemez Pueblo, N.M. *Education*: Eastern New Mexico State University, Portales, BA, 1949; University of New Mexico, 1950-51, 1973; Vanderbilt University, 1959-60. Resided in Albuquerque, NM. *Affiliations*: Instructor emeritus in ethnohistory, Institute of American Indian Arts, Santa Fe, NM; director, Institute for Pueblo Indian Studies, Indian Pueblo Cultural Center, Albuquerque, NM. *Other professional posts*: Lecturer on history, Pueblo Indian Cultural Center; education specialist and teacher of Pueblo Indian history, University of New Mexico. *Military service*: U.S. Navy, 1943-46 (Yeoman 2nd; World War II; Pacific Campaign Ribbon with four stars). *Community activities*: All Indian Pueblo Council (chairman of education, 1970); New Mexico State Judicial Council (chairman, 1970); American Indian Scholarships (sec./treas.- 14 years); Ancient City Toastmasters Club, Santa Fe, NM (president, 1968); Diocese of Santa Fe "Cuarto Centennial (1598-1998)" committee; City of Albuquerque "Cuarto Centennial (1598-1998)" committee. *Memberships*: New Mexico Historical Records Advisory Board; New Mexico Statuary Hall Commission; Chamiza Foundation Board. *Awards, honors*: Alumnus of the Year, 1970, Eastern New Mexico University; Recipient of 1993 State of New Mexico Heritage Presentation Award. *Interests*: "Gardening with numerous blue ribbons for garden crops from New Mexico State Fair; woodworking; writing for publication on Indian history and education; lecture tour of New Zealand Maori area in 1979; lecture tour of Switzerland and West Germany in 1981; lecture tours - Italy, 1991 & Spain, 1993, 1999; lecturing to civic groups on Indian history. *Biographical sources*: Personalities of the West and Midwest, 1971; Indians of Today, Fourth Edition, 1971. *Published works*: "Pope" in the (World Book Encyclopedia, 1970); The Pueblo Indians (Indian Historian Press, 1976, 1982); Pueblo Indian Biographies (S.I.P.I. Press, Albuquerque, 1976); Nee Hemish, The History of Jemez Pueblo (University of New Mexico Press, 1982); Pueblo Indians: Eight Centuries of Pueblo Indian History (Clear Light Publishers, 1992); "Pope" in the Encyclopedia of the American Indian (Houghton-Mifflin, 1996); Pueblo Profiles: Cultural Identity Through Centuries of Change (Clear Light Publishers, 1998); columnist, "The Albuquerque Tribune"; many articles in "New Mexico" Magazine, "The Indian Historian", "HUD" Magazine.

SANDS, DR. KATHLEEN M.
(professor of English)
Affiliation: Dept. of English, Arizona State University, Tempe, AZ 85287 (480) 965-6213 Fax 965-7671. *Interests*: American Indian literature. E-mail: kathleen.sands@asu.edu.

SANDSTROM, ALAN R. 1945-
(anthropologist)
Born July 2, 1945, Springfield, Mas. *Education*: American International College, BA; Indiana University, MA, PhD. *Principal occupation*: Anthropologist. *Home address*: 2828 N. Anthony Blvd., Ft. Wayne, IN 46805 (219) 471-3216; E-mail: sandstro@ipfn.edu. *Memberships*: American Anthropological Association (Fellow); Central States Anthropological Society. *Interests*: "Have conducted ethnographic field research since the early 1970s in northern Veracruz, Mexico among Nahua Indians (Nahuatl speakers). *Published works*: Traditional Papermaking & Paper Cult Figura of Mexico, with Pamela E. Sandstrom (University of Oklahoma Press, 1986; Corn Is Our Blood (University of Oklahoma Press, 1991).

SANGRIS, JONAS
(Indian band chief)
Affiliation: Yellowknife "B" (Dettah) Indian Band, Box 2514, Yellowknife, Northwest Territories, Canada X1A 2P8 (403) 873-4307.

SANIPASS, WILLIAM
(Indian band chief)
Affiliation: Bouctouche Indian Band, RR 2, Kent County, Bouctouche, New Brunswick, Canada E0A 1G0 (506) 743-6493.

SANTOS, STEVE C. (Mechoopda) 1957-
(tribal chairperson)
Born May 11, 1957, Chico, Calif. *Education*: Butte Community College, A.A. *Address & Affiliation*: Chairperson, Mechoopda Indian Tribe of the Chico Rancheria, 125 Mission Ranch Blvd., Chico, CA 95926 (530) 899-8922 Fax 899-8517. E-mail: ssantos@mechoopda.nsn.us. *Military service*: U.S. Air Force, 1975-99 (Honorable Discharge).

SANYAL, GOVINDA
(Creek/Seminole & Asian Indian) 1947-
(psychotherapist, special educator, Southeastern Native American historian, genealogist)
Born August 12, 1947. *Education*: Manhattan Community College, AAS, 1971; Hunter College (NY), BA, 1975; Long Island University, MS (Special Education), 1982, New York University, PD, 1984; MS (Educational Psychology), 1997; California Institute of Integral Studies, current PhD (Native Studies). *Principal occupation*: Special educator, New York City Board of Education. *Home address*: 85 Regis Dr., Staten Island, NY 10314 (718) 761-5436. *Community activities*: Director of Mandala Nataka, a cultural center of Native American and Asian Indian philosophy and art. Presently serving as a researcher, historian and genealogist for Southeastern Native communities specializing in the Carolinas, Georgia and Florida. *Awards, honors*: Ford Foundation Award, 1982 - Social Studies. *Interests*: "My ambition is to assist in restoring the ancient historical tradition and knowledge of those descendants of indigenous populations of the Southeast."

SARABIA, EDWARD W., JR. (*Stockk-Waan*) (Tlingit) 1948-
(Indian affairs coordinator)
Born November 11, 1948. *Education*: Seattle University, BA in Rehabilitation. *Principal occupation*: Indian affirs coordinator. *Address & Affiliations*: Connecticut Office of Indian Affairs, 79 Elm St., Hartford, CT 06106 (860) 424-3066 fax 424-4058. E-mail: edward.sarabia@po.state.ct.us. *Other professional posts*: Board member, Institute for American Indian Studies, Washington, CT; board member, Institute for Community Research, Hartford, CT; liaison between Connecticut Indian Affairs Council and Connecticut Dept. of Environmental Protection, the tribes and tribal members. *Community activities*: Volunteer for the Connecticut Dept. of Corrections, Native American religious services.

SARAYDAR, DR. STEPHEN C.
(professor of anthropology)
Affiliation: Native American Studies Program, Dept. of Anthropology & Sociology, SUNY, Oswego, NY 13126 (315) 341-4190.

SARGENT, ELVERA (*Konwanaktotani*)
(Akwesasne Mohawk)
(manager)
Address: P.O. Box 290, Rooseveltown, NY 13683 (518) 358-2073 Fax 358-2081. E-mail: bela@westelcom.com. *Affiliations*: Director, Native American Travelling College; director, Akwesasne Area Management Board. *Interests*: Native American education, language, and culture.

SARK, GEORGE JAMES
(Indian band chief)
Affiliation: Abegweit Indian Band, Box 220, Cornwall, PEI, Canada C0A 1H0 (902) 675-3842.

SARK, JACK J.T.
(Indian band chief)
Affiliation: Lennox Island Indian Band, Lennox Island, PEI, Canada C0B 1P0 (902) 831-2779.

SASAKAMOOSE, MURIEL
(museum director)
Affiliation: Secwepemc Cultural Education Society, 345 Yellowhead Hwy., Kamloops, BC, Canada V2H 1H1 (604) 374-1096.

SATALA, TAYLOR J. (Yavapai-Apache/Hopi) 1945-
(health systems administrator)
Born August 25, 1945, Prescott, Ariz. *Education*: San Francisco City College, AA, 1966; Arizona State University, BS, 1976, MSW, 1978. *Principal occupation*: Health systems administrator. *Address*: Keams Canyon PHS-IHS Hospital, P.O. Box 98, Keams Canyon, AZ 86034 (602) 738-2211 (work). *Affiliation*: Service unit director, USPHS, Indian Health Service, Keams Canyon, AZ, 1989-. *Other professional posts*: Health Center Director, IHS, Peach Springs, AZ; extension associate, University of Kansas, Lawrence, KS; social worker, MCH, Rapid City, SD. *Military service*: U.S. Air Force, 1966-70 (E-4 Sgt.; Vietnam Era Veteran-stationed at DaNang Air Base); USPHS Commission Corps, National Health Service, 1978-80. National Association of Social Workers (vice president, 1978-84); Black Hills Region of South Dakota State Chapter; Council on Social Work Education (member, House of Delegates, 1982-83); American Indian/Alaska Native Association of Social Workers, 1978-84. *Awards, honors*: Exceptional Performance Award, 1989, for Effective Management. *Published works*: Multi-Cultural Development in the Aging Network: "An Indian Perspective" "A Forgotten People" (University of Kansas, 1981); The Indian Experience: Special Topics in Social Welfare (University of Kansas, 1983).

SATTER, MICHELLE
(institute director)
Affiliation: The Sundance Institute, c/o S.P.E., 10202 W. Washington Blvd., Culver City, CA 90232 (310) 204-2091.

SATZ, RONALD N. (*Wasbishka Ogitchida*) 1944-
(university provost/vice chancellor & professor of history)
Born February 8, 1944, Chicago, Ill. *Education*: Illinois Institute of Technology, BS, 1965; Illinois State University, MA, 1967; University of Maryland, PhD, 1972 (Dissertation: Federal Indian Policy, 1829-1849). *Principal occupation*: University provost/chancellor & professor of American Indian history. *Home address*: 4015 White Pine Dr., East, Eau Claire, WI 54701 (715) 836-2320 Fax 836-2902 (work); *E-Mail*: rsatz@uwec.edu. Website: www.uwec.edu/admin/provost. *Affiliations*: Assistant professor, 1971-75, associate professor with tenure, 1977-80, dean of graduate studies, 1976-83, dean of research, 1977-83, professor with tenure, 1980-83, University of Tennessee at Martin; dean, School of Graduate Studies, director, Office of University Research, and professor of history, 1983-95, director, Center of Excellence for Faculty and Undergraduate Student Research Collaboration, 1988-95, director, Wisconsin Indian History, Culture, and Tribal Sovereignty Project, 1991-, Founding Dean, School of Human Sciences and Services, 1994-95, Founding Dean, College of Professional Studies & Office of University Research, 1995-99, Provost & Vice Chancellor, Office of Academic Affairs, 1999-, The University of Wisconsin, Eau Claire, WI. *Other professional posts*: Editorial board member, Maryland Historian, 1970-71, University of Tennessee Press, 1975-78, 1981-83, American Indian Quarterly, 1977-82, and National Forum, 1994-98; consultant, Native American Rights Fund, 1977-80; Chippewa Valley Museum, 1990-98; Wisconsin Dept. of Public Instruction, 1991-99, Council of Graduate Schools, 1992, and Fond du Lac Band of Chippewa Indians, 1993-96; proposal reviewer, National Endowment for the Humanities, 1978-; board of directors, Chippewa Valley Museum, 1992-98, and Cray Academy, 1995-99; advisory committee on minority student affairs, and undergraduate teaching improvement council, University of Wisconsin, Madison, 1984-86, 1991-92; campus liaison, University of Wisconsin System Committee on University/Industry Cooperation, 1985-; publications committee, Midwestern Association of Graduate Schools, 1985-90; Distinguished Master's Thesis Award Committee, 1993-96; chair, Western History Association Walter Rundell Graduate Student Award Committee, 1986; President's Select Committee on the Status of Minority Faculty and Staff, University of Wisconsin System, 1987-88; and University of Wisconsin System and State Historical Society of Wisconsin Joint Planning Committee for the National Conference on American Indian History & Culture, 1990-91; editor, Proceedings of the Midwestern Association of Graduate Schools, 1988-89; editor, Issues in Teaching and Learning, 1989-92, editor, Humanity, 1996-99; featured speaker, Wisconsin Humanities Council Speakers Bureau, 1992-99; consultant, Great Lakes Indian Fish & Wildlife Commission; consultant, WDSE-TV, PBS 8, Duluth-Superior Area. *Community activities*: Ad Hoc Commission on Racism of the Lac Courte Oreilles Lake Superior Ojibwa Tribal Governing Board (member); Parent-Teacher Organization, Manz Elementary School and South Junior High School, Eau Claire, WI (member); The Heritage Club of the Chippewa Valley Museum, Eau Claire (member); Planning Committee, Chippewa Valley Technology Charter School and Health Occupation Charter Academy (member). *Memberships*: American Association for Higher Education; American Association of University Administrators; American Historical Association; Minnetrista Council for Great Lakes Native American Studies; National Museum of the American Indian (charter member); Native American Rights Fund; State Historical Society of Wisconsin; Organization of American Historians; Society for American Indian Studies and Research; Western History Association; Southern Historical Association; Wisconsin Academy of Sciences, Arts, and Letters; Sigma Xi; Pi Gamma Mu; Phi Alpha Theta; Phi Kappa Phi; Delta Tau Kappa; Omicron Delta Kappa; among others. *Award, honors*: Fellow in Ethnic Studies, Ford Foundation, 1971; Younger Humanist Research Fellow, National Endowment for the Humanities, 1974; Title III Grant, U.S. Office of Education, University of Tennessee at Martin, 1978, '81, '82, University of Wisconsin-Eau Claire, 1991; Wisconsin Dept. of Public Education Grant for Chippewa Treaty Rights Project, 1991, and grant for Indian Treaties and Tribal Sovereignty Project, 1992; Merit Award for Distinguished Service to History, State Historical Society of Wisconsin; Excellence in Public Service Award, University of Wisconsin, Eau Claire Foundation, 1995; 1996 Distinguished Document of the Year Award, Wisconsin Library Association; recipient of Ojibwe name, Wasbishka Ogitchida ("The White Warrior for Treaty Rights and Earth Protector"), 1999. *Interests*: "Indian-white relations, especially the 19th century; American Indian policy; Indian sovereignty and treaty rights; tribal history; Indian-black relations; Indian religious beliefs and the impact of Christian missionary efforts on Indian religions." *Biographical sources*: Outstanding American Educators, 1974-75; Directory of American Scholars, 6th-8th eds.; Contemporary Authors, 1982; Dictionary of International Biography, 1976-77; Who's Who in the South and Southwest, 16th-18th eds.; Personalities of the South, 1978-79, 1979-80 Eds.; International Who's Who in Education, 1980 ed.; Who's Who in the Midwest, 20th ed., 23rd ed. ; Men of Achievement, 16th International ed.; Who's Who in American Education, 4th ed.; Who's Who in America, Vol. 3, 48th ed.; Who's Who in the World, 12th ed. *Published works*: American Indian Policy in the Jacksonian Era (University of Nebraska Press, 1975; reprint revised, University of Oklahoma Press, 2002); Tennessee's Indian Peoples: From White Contact to Removal, 1540-1840 (University of Tennessee Press, 1979); Chippewa Treaty Rights: The Reserved Rights of Wisconsin's Chippewa Indians in Historical Perspective (Wisconsin Academy of Sciences, Arts, and Letters, 1991; rev. ed. 1994); co-author: America: Changing Times, textbook (John Wiley & Sons, 1979-1st Ed.; Random House, 1984-2nd Ed.-1984); and Classroom Activities on Chippewa Treaty Rights (Wisconsin Dept. of Public Instruction, 1991); contributor: Heroes of Tennessee (Memphis State University Press, 1979); The Commissioners of Indian Affairs, 1824-1977 (University of Nebraska Press, 1979); American Vistas, 1607-1877, 3rd-7th eds. (Oxford University Press, 1979, '84, '87, '91, '95); Wisconsin's Educational Imperative: Indian-White Relations (Lac Courte Oreilles Ojibwa Community College, 1984); After Removal: The Choctaw in Mississippi (University Press of Mississippi, 1986); An Anthology of Western Great Lakes Indian History (University of Wisconsin-Milwaukee, 1987); Enhancing Educational Diversity Through Professional Diversity (University of Wisconsin System President's Select Committee on the Status of Minority Faculty and Staff, 1988); History of Indian-White Relations vol. 4 of Handbook of North American Indians (Smithsonian Institution Press, 1988); The Susquicentennial of Cherokee Removal, 1838-1839 (Special issue of the Georgia Historical Quarterly, Fall 1989); Cherokee Removal: Before and After (University of Georgia Press, 1991); compiler, Lucretia Caldwell Twentieth Century Menominee Newspaper Collection (Menominee Tribal Library, 1993); Proceedings of the Hayward Indian Congress of 1934 (State Historical Society of Wisonsin, 1994); editor: Proceedings of the University of Wisconsin System and State Historical Society of Wisconsin National Committee on American Indian History & Culture, 1991, and Classroom Activities on Wisconsin Indians: Treaties and Tribal Sovereignty (Wisconsin Dept. of Public Instruction, 1996); The Lac Courte Oreilles Ojibwe Indians and the Chippewa Flowage (Great Lakes Indian Fish & Wildlife Commission, 1997); and author of numerous articles & book reviews in scholarly journals.

SAUBEL, CATHERINE (Luiseno)
(Indianband spokesperson)
Affiliation: Los Coyotes band of Mission Indians, P.O. Box 189, Warner Springs, CA 92086 (760) 782-0711.

SAUBEL, KATHERINE SIVA (Cahuilla) 1920-
(museum trustee)
Born March 7, 1920, Los Coyotes Reservation, Calif. *Principal occupation*: Trustee & president, Malki Museum, Inc. *Address*: 11-795 Fields Rd., Morongo Indian Reservation, Banning, CA 92220 (714) 849-7289 (work). *Other professional posts*: Advisory representative, County of Riverside, CA, Historical Commission; consultan/lecturer, California State College at Hayward, CA, University of Colorado, and University of California. *Community activities*: Los Coyotes Tribal Council; Mothers Club, Morongo Indian Reservation. *Interests*: Ms. Saubel participated in the Indian Leadership Training Program at the University of California; other interests are Indian history and ethnography, and linguistics. She writes, "I have traveled extensively in the Southwest & California, visiting reservations and museums which display Indian history and culture." *Published works*: Cahuilla Ethnobotanical Notes: Oak, and Mesquite and Screwbean, both with Lowell J. Bean (University of California, Archaeological Survey Annual Report, 1962, 1968); Temalpah: Economic Botany of the Cahuilla Indians, with Lowell J. Bean (Malki Museum, 1969); Kunvachmal, A Cahuilla Tale (The Indian Historian, 1969).

SAULQUE, JOSEPH C. (Paiute) 1942-
(administration/planning; college instructor)
Born October 20, 1942, Bishop, Calif. *Education*: West Valley Community College, Campbell, Calif., AA, 1970; Brigham Young University, BA, 1973; University of California, Davis, 1978-80 (Graduate work on MA). *Principal occupation*: Administration/planning; college instructor. *Address*: Benton Paiute Reservation, Rt. 4, Box 56-A, Benton, CA 93512 (619) 933-2321. *Affiliation*: Instructor, Cerro Coso Community College, Bishop, CA (current). *Other professional posts*: Utu Utu Gwaitu Paiute Tribe, Benton Paiute Reservation,

Benton, CA (chairperon, 1973-90; vice-chairperson, 1991-); chairperson, Toiyabe Indian Health Project (board of directors, 1977-); chairperson, California Rural Indian Health Board (board of directors, 1978-). *Military service*: U.S. Army, 1961-64 (E-4/Sp-4, 101st Airborne Division). *Community activities*: Grand Jury, County of Mono, CA; Tri-Valley Regional Planning and Advisory Commission to the Tri-Valley Water District, County of Mono, CA; Owens Valley Indian Water Commission (member). *Memberships*: National Congress of American Indians, 1974-; California Tribal Chairman's Association, Sacramento, Calif. (secretary-three years); California Indian Manpower Consortium, Inc. (past vice-chairperson, 1988-90). *Interests*: "Indian affairs, especially tribal government concepts; Amerian Indian history; Indian health issues and operations; college instructor on American Indian studies; history and career opportunities."

SAULQUE, ROSE MARIE (Utu Utu Gwaitu Paiute)
(tribal council chairperson)
Affiliation: Utu Utu Gwaitu Paiute Tribal Council, Benton Paiute Reservation, 167 Yellow Jacket Rd., Benton, CA 93512 (760) 933-2321.

SAUNDERS, ERIC
(Indian band chief)
Affiliation: York Factory Indian Band, York Landing, Manitoba, Canada R0B 2B0 (204) 341-2180.

SAUNDERS, FERRELL
(monument supt.)
Affiliation: Russell Cave National Monument, Rte. 1, Box 175, Bridgeport, AL 35740 (205) 495-2672.

SAUNDERS, LINDA
(BIA agency supt.)
Affiliation: Horton Agency, Bureau of Indian Affairs, P.O. Box 31, Horton, KS 66439 (913) 486-2161.

SAUNOOKE, OSLEY BIRD, JR.
(Eastern Cherokee) 1943-
(attorney, business consultant)
Born April 6, 1943, Jacksonville, Fla. *Education*: East Tennessee State University, 1962-63; Brigham Young University, BS, 1965; University of New Mexico Law School, JD, 1972. *Principal occupation*: Attorney, business consultant. *Home address*: 2435 Gulf Gate Dr., Sarasota, FL 34231 (813) 921-3297. *Affiliations*: Teacher-guidance counselor, Cleveland, Ohio, Chicago, Ill., 1965-69; executive director, United Southeastern Tribes, Inc., 1972-73; executive director, Florida Governor's Council on Indian Affairs, 1973-74. *Awards, honors*: 1987 Regional Minority Entrepreneur of the Year - Atlanta Region OMBE. *Memberships*: National Congress of American Indians (Southeast area vice president, 1972-73; first vice president, 1973-74; board member, American Indian Scholarships, 1974-.

SAVAGE, JEFF (Lake Superior Ojibwe-Anishinabe) 1950-
(artist)
Born November 28, 1950, Duluth, Minn. *Education*: College of St. Scholastica, 1974-76. *Principal occupation*: Artist. *Home address*: 1780 Blue Spruce Dr., Cloquet, MN 55720 (218) 879-0157. *Affiliation*: Artist and Public Informatiom Specialist, Fond du Lac Reservation, Cloquet, MN. *Other professional posts*: "Have also worked in many local schools and tribal colleges doing Native Amerian art workshops specializing in pipe stone sculpture and traditional pipes. *Community activities*: Currently vice-chairperson, Indian Advisory Board, Minnesota Historical Society; former tribal election judge for Fond du Lac Reservation. *Memberships*: Minnesota Historical Society (chairperson of local Indian Education Committee). *Awards, honors*: 1981 Gallup Intertribal, Certificate of Merit, Blue Ribbon, and special exhibit awards; 1985 1st Place Sculpture Award in Ojibwe Art Expo. *Interests*: "Personal interest in pursuing the perpetuating of endangered Ojibwe art forms, i.e., pipestone quarrying, pipe making, traditional Ojibwe sweet grass baskets and birch bark baskets, moccasins and beadwork of floral Ojibwe design done in hand tanned leather."

SAVAGE, MARILYN (Athabascan)
(radio station manager)
Affiliation: KZPA-AM, P.O. Box 126, Fort Yukon, AK 99740 (907) 662-2587.

SAYERS, ANN-MARIE (Costanoan)
(tribal chairperson)
Affiliation: Indian Canyon Mutsun Band of Costanoan Indians, P.O. Box 28, Hollister, CA 95024.

SAYLER, HAROLD
(school principal)
Affiliation: Pyramid Lake High School, P.O. Box 256, Nixon, NV 89424 (702) 574-0142.

SAZUE, ROXANNE (Crow Creek Sioux)
(tribal chairperson)
Affiliation: Crow Creek Sioux Tribal Council, P.O. Box 50, Fort Thompson, SD 57339 (605) 245-2221.

SCERATO, BEN (Diegueno)
(former tribal chairperson)
Affiliation: Santa Ysabel Band of Mission Indians, P.O. Box 130, Santa Ysabel, CA 92070 (760) 765-0846.

SCHAAF, GREGORY (Northern Cherokee) 1953-
(author; organization director)
Born July 24, 1953, Kansas City, MO. *Education*: University of California, Santa Barbara, BA, MA, PhD. *Principal occupation*: Author; organization director. *Address & Affiliation*: CIAC-Center for Indigenous Arts & Culture (director, 1994-present), P.O. Box 8627, Santa Fe, NM 87504 (505) 473-5375 Fax 424-1025. E-mail: greg@indianartbooks.com. Website: www.indianart books.com, or www.indianartforsale.com. *Other professional posts*: Co-founder, executive director and vice-chair, Tree of Peace Society, Inc., Washington, DC, 1984-present; secretary, Southwest Learning Center, Santa Fe, N, 1995-present; co-founder, Indian Art Collectors Circle, Santa Fe. *Past professional posts*: Visiting lecturer, Native American Studies, Dept. of ABS, University of California, Davis, 1986-87; assistant professor and acting coordinator of American Indian Studies, Dept. of Ethnic & Women's Studies, California State University, Chico, CA, 1988-90; associate professor and coordinator of American Indian Studies, Dept. of Ethnic Studies, Minnesota State University, Mankato, MN, 1990-93; Native American consultant, The Last of His Tribe, a movie for HBO starring John Voight and Graham Greene, 1992; over-all contributing script consultant, 500 Nations (8-hour TV mini-series for CBS, produced by Kevin Costner, 1995). *Community activities*: "Southwest Indian Curricula: Our Visions for the 21st Century," World Conference on Indigenous Peoples Education, Albuquerque, NM 1996; "Symbols in Indian Art," Children's Indian Art Camp, Santa Fe, 1997; "Evaluating Indian Art," Elder Hostel, College of Santa Fe, 1998; "Preserving Indian Baskets," Museum of Indian Arts & Cultures, 1999; "Mesa Verde: Clan Stories Leading to Living Pueblo Descendants," Americas Quest for a million school children via www.classroom.com, 2000. *Published works*: The Iroquois Great Law of Peace and the U.S. Constitution (Canal Press, New York, 1987); Wampum Belts and Peace Trees: George Morgan, Native Americans and Revolutionary Diplomacy (Fulcrum, Inc., 1990); Ancient Ancestors of the Southwest (Graphic Arts Center Publishing Co., Portland, OR, 1996); Honoring the Weavers (Kiva Press, Santa Fe, 1996); Hopi-Tewa Pottery: 500 Artist Biographies (CIAC Press, Santa Fe, 1998); Pueblo Indian Pottery: 750 Artist Biographies (CIAC Press, Santa Fe, 2000); American Indian Textiles: 2,000 Artist Biographies (CIAC Press, Santa Fe, 2001); Southern Pueblo Pottery: 2,000 Artist Biographies (CIAC Press, Santa Fe, 2002); American Indian Jewelry: 1,200 Artist Biographies (CIAC Press, Santa Fe, 2003); American Indian Baskets: 1,200 Artist Biographies (CIAC Press, Santa Fe, 2004); Franklin, Jefferson, & Madison: On Religion & the State (CIAC Press, Santa Fe, 2004);

SCHAAFSMA, POLLY
(author)
Affiliation: Museum of New Mexico, Santa Fe, NM. *Interests*: Southwestern rock art. *Published works*: Images in Stone; Indian Rock Art of the Southwest; Rock Art in New Mexico (Museum of New Mexico

Press, 2002).

SCHAEFFER, PETER (Eskimo)
(AK village chairperson)
Affiliation: Native Village of Kotzebue, P.O. Box 296, Kotzebue, AK 99752 (907) 442-3467.

SCHAFER, LORNA
(publisher)
Affiliation: Tsa'Aszi (The Yucca) Magazine of Navajo Culture, Tsa'Aszi Graphics Center, Ramah Navajo School Board, CPO Box 12, Pine Hill, NM 87321 (505) 783-5503.

SCHEETZ, ANITA
(library director)
Affiliations: Fort Peck Community College Library, P.O. Box 398, Poplar, MT 59255 (406) 768-5551 Fax 768-5552.

SCHEIRBECK, HELEN MAYNOR (Lumbee) 1935-
(human resources administrator)
Born August 21, 1935, Lamberton, N.C. *Education*: Berea (KY) College, BA, 1957; VPI - SU, (Blacksburg, VA), EdD, 1980. *Principal occupation*: Human resources administrator. *Address & Affiliation*: Director, American Indian Programs, Save the Children Federation, 54 Wilton Rd., Westport, CT 06880 (1983-). *Other professional posts*: Chairperson, Indian Education Task Force, American Indian Policy Review Commission, U.S. Congress; director, Office of Indian Affairs, U.S. Office of Education, Dept. of HEW; professional staff, U.S. Senate Subcommittee on Constitutional Rights. *Memberships*: United Indians of America (project advisor); National Indian Education Association (vice president). *Awards, honors*: John Hay Whitney Foundation, Opportunity Award; Outstanding Lumbee Award; Outstanding American Indian Award; Pepsi People Pour It On Award. *Interests*: Dr. Scheirbeck has traveled and worked throughout the U.S. She has worked with the majority of Indian tribes in the U.S. She has served on Legislature and Executive Task Forces investigating various issues affecting Indian people. Her hobbies include photography, writing, collecting legends, and swimming. *Biographical sources*: Outstanding Indians in USA; Indians of the Southwest; Outstanding Minority Women; Biographies of Outstanding American Indian Women. *Published works*: Indian Education: Tool for Cultural Politics (Harvard Center for Law & Education, Dec., 1970); The First Americans (American Red Cross Youth News, Nov., 1972); The History of Federal Indian Education Policy (American Indian Policy Review Commission, 1976); A Study of Three Selected Laws & Their Impact on American Indian Education (House of Interior & Insular Affairs, Oct., 1976); Public Policy and Contemporary Education of the American Indian (Ph.D. Dissertation, 1980).

SCHELL, LAWRENCE M. 1948-
(professor)
Born November 7, 1948, Boston, Mass. *Education*: Oberlin College, BA, 1970; Temple University, MA, 1974; University of Pennsylvania, PhD, 1980. *Principal occupation*: Professor of anthropology. *Address*: Dept. of Anthropology, SS-263 , SUNY, Albany, NY 12222 (518) 442-4714 Fax 442-5710 (work); E-Mail: lmschell@albany.edu. *Affiliations*: Clinical associate professor, Albany Medical College, 1983-; professor of anthropology and epidemiology, SUNY, Albany, 1994-; associate dean of research, SUNY, Albany, 2003-. *Memberships*: European Anthropological Association (treasurer); American Association of Physical Anthropologists; Human Biology Association; Society for Pediatric and Perinatal Epidemiology. *Awards, honors*: Ales Hrdlicka Prize awarded by the American Association of Physical Anthropologists. *Published works*: Articles: co-author, "Distribution of Albumin Variants Naskapi and Mexico Among Aleuts, Frobisher Bay Eskimos, and Micmac, Naskapi, Mohawk, Omaha, and Apache Indians" in American Journal of Physical Anthropologists, Vol. 49:111-119, 1978; "Anthropometric Variation in Native American Children and Adults" in Origins and Affinities of the First Americans, W.S. Laughlin and A.B. Harper, Eds., 1979; "Alloabuminemia and the Migrations of Native Americans" in Yearbook of Physical Anthropology Vol. 31:1-13, 1988; "Physical Growth and Development of American Indian and Eskimo Children and Youth" in Handbook of

North American Indians, Vol. 3, Environment, Origins, and Population, R. Ford, editor; "A Partnership Study of PCBs and the Health of Mohawk Youth: Lessons From Our Past, Guidelines for Our Future in Environmental Health Perspectives," Vol. 106 (Supp 13) 833-840, 1998; "Polychlorinated Biphenyls (PCBs) and Thyroid Function in Adolescents of the Mohawk Nation at Akwesasne," in Human Growth from Birth to Maturity, G. Gilli, L. Benso and L. Schell, Eds., 2002; "Environmental Contaminants and Growth of Mohawk Adolescents at Akwesasne," in Human Growth from Birth to Maturity, G. Gilli, L. Benso and L. Schell, Eds., 2002; "Organochlorines, Lead and Mercury in Akwesasne," in Environmental Health Perspectives, Vol. 111:954-961, 2003. *Book*: Urban Ecology and Health in the Third World, Schell, Smith & Bilsborough, eds. (Cambridge University Press, 1993);

SCHEMMEL, TERI
(health director)
Affiliation: Lower Sioux Community Council, P.O. Box 308, Morton, MN 56270 (507) 697-6185.

SCHERER, MARK R.
(attorney, adjunct instructor of history)
Address & Affiliation: Dept. of History, University of Nebraska, Lincoln, NE; instructor of law, College of St. Mary, Lincoln, NE; practicing attorney. *Published work*: Imperfect Victories: The Legal Tenacity of the Omaha Tribe, 1945-1995 (University of Nebraska Press, 1999).

SCHILL, VICTOR
(association president)
Affiliation: American Indian Library Association (AILA), 620-U Hillman Library, University of Pittsburgh, Pittsburgh, PA 15260 (412) 648-7780. vschill@stic.lib.tx.us

SCHINDLER, CYRUS (Seneca)
(tribal council president)
Affiliation: Seneca Nation Tribal Council, 1490 Rt. 438, Irving, NY 14081 (716) 532-4900.

SCHINDLER, DUANE E. (Turtle Mountain Chippewa) 1944-
(educational administration)
Born April 22, 1944, Turtle Mountain Indian Reservation, Belcourt, N.D. *Education*: University of North Dakota; Valley City State College, ND; University of Wisconsin, Eau Claire; Arizona State University; University of South Dakota. *Affiliations*: Program development specialist, Eastern Montana State College, Billings (2 years); program specialist, University of New Mexico (1 year); instructor, Adult Programs, Wenatchee Valley College, Omak, WA (2 years); director, Adult Education, Colville Confederated Tribes, Nespelem, WA (1 year); director, American Indian Student Division, University of Washington, Seattle, WA (1 year); principal, Turtle Mountain Chippewa High School, Belcourt, ND. *Other professional posts*: Field reader, consultant: Logo language; computer applications, computer literacy, computer office systems; curriculum development; school board training; program evaluation management. *Community activities*: American Indian Center, Spokane, WA (chairperson). *Memberships*: National Association of Secondary School Principals; National Indian Education Association; ASCD, NABE. *Awards, honors*: Outstanding Teacher, Oglala Community Schools, Pine Ridge, SD. *Interests*: Computers in the classroom; research in mathematics. *Biographical source*: Outstanding Young Men of America, 1973. *Published works*: Concepts of American Indian Learners (Education, Tempe, Ariz.); Language, Culture and the Mathematics (Journal of the American Indian, 1986).

SCHINDLER, MICHAEL W. (Seneca)
(tribal council president)
Affiliation: Seneca Nation Tribal Council, P.O. Box 231, Salamanca, NY 14479 (716) 945-1790.

SCHLENDER, JAMES H.
(executive director)
Affiliation: Great Lakes Indian Fish & Wildlife Commission, P.O. Box 9, Odanah, WI 54861 (715) 682-6619.

SCHMELZ-KEIL, LYNNE M.
(librarian)
Affiliation: Tozzer Library, Harvard University, 21 Divinity Ave., Cambridge, MA 02138 (617) 495-2248.

SCHMIDT, MARSHA KOSTURA
(attorney)
Education: University of Pittsburgh, BA, 1981; George Washington University, J.D., 1984. *Address & Affiliation*: Hobbs, Straus, Dean & Walker, LLP (Associate, 1984-93; Partner, 1994-present), 2120 L St., NW, Suite 700, Washington, DC 20037 (202) 822-8282. E-mail: mkschmidt@hsdwdc.com. She represents tribal clients in diverse matters including gaming, contract disputes, tax, land acquisition, and the Indian Health Care Improvement Act. She also played a major role in Menominee Tribe v. United States, a case before the U.S. Court of Federal Claims which successfully sought money damages for the wrongful termination of the Tribe and mismanagement of tribal timber resources by the federal government.

SCHNEBERK-KING, KATHRYN
(attorney)
Affiliation: New Jersey Governor's Office, Ethnic Advisory Council, State House CN001, 125 W. State St., Trenton, NJ 08625 (609) 292-6000.

SCHNEIDER, DR. MARY JANE
(Indian studies dept. chairperson)
Affiliation: Indian Studies Dept., University of North Dakota, Campus Box 7103, Grand Forks, ND 58202 (701) 777-4314 Fax 777-4145.

SCHNEIDER, THERESA E.
(Indian education program coordinator)
Affiliation: North Syracuse Central Schools, Native American Education Program, 5355 W. Taft Rd., No. Syracuse, NY 13212 (315) 452-3189 Fax 452-3055.

SCHOENECKE, CINDY
(health center director)
Affiliation: Black Hawk Health Center, Sac & Fox Nation, Rte. 2, Box 246, Stroud, OK 73079 (918) 968-9531.

SCHOENFELD, MICHAEL
(school principal)
Affiliation: Isleta Elementary School, P.O. Box 550, Isleta, NM 87022 (505) 869-2321.

SCHOENHUT, ROBERT JOHN (Holy Bear)
(Standing Rock Uncpapa Lakota) 1940-
(writer, cinematographer, photographer)
Born December 27, 1940, Fort Yates, N.D. *Education*: University of Portland, 1958-61; Naval Photo School, 1961-62; Brooks Institute of Photography (Santa Barbara, CA), BFA, 1971-74; American Film Institute (Los Angeles), MFA, 1976; U.S. Naval Photographic School, 1961-62. *Principal occupation*: Writer, cinematographer, photographer. *Address*: Unknown. *Affiliations*: Cinematographer, various studios, Hollywood, 1974-2000; producer/director, PBS, 1974-2000; currently writing and correlating photographs for publication. *Other professional posts*: Camera operator: "Dances With Wolves" 1989; "Quantum Leap," 1990; "Dinosaurs," 1991-93; "Ellen;" "Mystery Men;" "To Sell a Child," NBC movie 1994; director of photography: "The Trial of Standing Bear," 1987-88 NETV/PBS; "I'd Rather Be Powwowing, Europe; producer/director, "Standing Rock: A Vision," 1979 AFI grant; "Fanfare for the Common Man;" Cinematographer for German TV WDR, Cologne; writer, "Endangered Species," BBC/WDR Cologne. *Military service*: U.S. Marine Corps, 1961-63 (Photo Reconnaissance; Good Conduct Medal). *Memberships*: International Alliance of Theatrical Stage Employees; Hollywood Cinematographers (only Native American member), 1975-; International Photographers Guild, Local 600, Hollywood (only Native American member). *Interests*: "The myths and stereotypes perpetuated by Kevin Costner in "Dances With Wolves" continue to plague contemporary Native Americans in this country and abroad and will continue to do so until a large scale film is made that addresses what the Native American is today. Americans by-and-large wish to keep Indians in their historical past so they don't have to deal with them today, much like the aborigines in Australia and the

Aussie's embarrassment about their mistreatment of them. Anybody who doesn't see this is casting a blind eye to the truth and is a coward. It will take a brave person to address this in film or television since corporate America doesn't want to know unless they can make lots of money from it. Why does it have to be about money? A reader may think me naive but to them I say we must and can do this for the benefit of our children and all non-Indian people who seek the truth."

SCHOLDER, FRITZ (Mission) 1937-
(artist)
Born October 6, 1937, Breckenridge, Minn. *Education*: Sacramento State College, BA, 1960; University of Arizona, MFA, 1964. *Principal occupation*: Artist. Resides in Santa Fe. *Other professional posts*: Participant, Southwest Indian Art Project, Rockefeller Foundation, 1961-63; chairman, Fine Arts Committee, First Convocation of American Indian Scholars, Princeton University, 1970. *Awards, honors*: Numerous awards for painting at the following exhibitions: Southwestern Drawing and Print Exhibition, Dallas Museum of Fine Arts; Mid-America Exhibition, Nelson Gallery of Art, Kansas City, Mo.; National Indian Exhibition, Scottsdale, AZ; among others. *Biographical sources*: Who's Who in the West; Who's Who in American Art; Dictionary of International Biography.

SCHREIBER, GEORGE
(school principal/teacher)
Affiliation: Swift Bird Day School, HCR 3, Box 119, Gettysburg, SD 57442 (605) 733-2143.

SCHROYER, DAN
(BIA education administrator)
Affiliation: Crow Creek/Lower Brule Agency, BIA, P.O. Box 139, Fort Thompson, SD 57339 (605) 245-2398.

SCHUCKER, ALBERT E. *(Al Red Oak)*
(Nanticoke) 1922-
(construction company owner)
Born September 1, 1922, Reading, Penna. *Education*: Chicago Tech, 1941 - Construction Efficiency; University of Pennsylvania, 1950-56. *Principal occupation*: Owner/president, Schucker Construction Company, Reading, PA (47 years). *Home address*: 1510 Greenview Ave., Reading, PA 19601 (610) 373-4046; *Office address*: Luzerne & Warren St., Reading, PA 19601 376-8046 (work) Fax 376-0211. *Other professional posts*: Served as expert witness & did some government intelligence work. *Military service*: U.S. Army, 1943 (Corporal). *Community activities*: Member, City Council, Reading, PA; County Comprehensive Water-Sewer Committee (chairperson); Industrial Waste Regulation Committee (chairperson); Church Consistory. *Memberships*: Eastern Delaware Nations (past vice president & president; now an elder); American Concrete Institute; American Building Contractors; Masons; Rotary Club (past president); American Legion; Penwriters Club; Masons; Shrine; United American Indians of the Delaware Valley. *Awards, honors*: Paul Harris Award in Rotary; Certificate of Merit by President Reagan, and various other awards; Business Weekly stated that Schucker Construction is the 5th largest Minority Business Enterprise (MBE) in eastern Pennsylvania. *Interests*: "Traveled extensively, including Mexican jungles; experienced with herbs and the healing arts; helped many people to heal themselves mentally and physically." *Biographical sources*: Articles in the local and state news media. *Published works*: Few articles published in trade journals.

SCHULTZ, MARILOU (Navajo)
(craftsperson)
Address: P.O. Box 882, Mesa, AZ 85211 (602) 964-3566.

SCHUMACHER, WILLIAM (Flandreau Santee Sioux)
(tribal executive committee president)
Affiliation: Flandreau Santee Sioux Executive Committee, P.O. Box 283, Flandreau, SD 57028 (605) 997-3891.

SCHUTT, DENNIS
(school supt.)
Affiliation: Marty Indian School, P.O. Box 187, Marty, SD 57361 (605) 384-5431.

SCHUTT, AARON M. (Athabaskan) 1973-
(attorney)
Born March 28, 1973, Anchorage, Alaska. *Education*: Washington State University, BS, 1996; Stanford University, MS, 1997, Stanford Law School, JD, 2000. *Principal occupation*: Attorney. *Address*: Unknown. *Affiliations*: Judicial law clerk, Alaska Supreme Court - Juneau, AK, 2000-2001; Associate Attorney, Heller, Ehrman White & McAuliffe, Anchorage, AK, 2001-. *Community activities*: Covenant House Alaska (board of directors). *Membership*: Alaska Bar Association; Alaska Bar Examiners Committee.

SCHUTT, ETHAN G. (Athabaskan) 1973-
(attorney)
Born March 28, 1973, Anchorage, Alaska. *Education*: Washington State University, BS, Mathematics; Stanford Law School, JD. *Principal occupation*: Attorney. *Address*: Unknown. *Affiliations*: Judicial law clerk, Alaska Supreme Court - Justice Walter Carpeneti - Juneau, AK, 1999-2000; Associate Attorney, Dorsey & Whitney LLP, Anchorage, AK, 2000-present. *Community activities*: Covenant House Alaska (board of directors). *Membership*: Alaska Bar Association. *Interests*: Native American higher education; rural economic development; basketball, ice hockey; outdoor recreation; hunting & fishing.

SCHWARTZ, DR. DOUGLAS W.
(college president)
Affiliation: School of American Research, Indian Arts Research Center, P.O. Box 2188, Santa Fe, NM 87504 (505) 982-3584 Fax 989-9809.

SCHWEI, BARBARA
(foundation president; dance producer)
Born in Wisc. *Education*: Carnegie Tech (studied drama); New York University, BFA. *Principal occupation*: dance producer, foundation president. *Home address*: 223 East 61st St., New York, NY 10022 (212) 308-9555. *Affiliations*: Founder/producer, American Indian Dance Theater (dancers, singers and drummers representing tribes from across the nation and Canada), 1986-; founder/president, Native American Performing Arts Foundation (to develop and expand projects by Native Americans in the performing arts, and on Native American themes), 1988-.

SCOTT, DR. COLIN (Kaa-uumaakiimishit) 1952-
(professor of anthropology)
Born June 1, 1952, Indian Head, Sask. Can. *Education*: University of Regina, BA, 1972; McGill University (Montreal), MA, 1983, PhD, 1983. *Principal occupation*: Professor. *Address*: Resides in Montreal, Quebec, Canada. *Affiliation*: Assistant professor of anthropology, McGill University, Montreal. *Other professional post*: Consultant to aboriginal and regional governments. *Memberships*: Canadian Anthropological Society; American Anthropological Association. *Awards, honors*: Social Sciences and Humanities Research Council of Canada, Strategic Research Grant, "Aboriginal Government, Resources and Development"; Australian National University, Visiting Fellowship, 1991. *Interests*: Knowledge construction among Cree hunters of James Bay; political discourse of aboriginal rights; development in the Subarctic. *Published works*: Books - section, "Ideology of Reciprocity Between the James Bay Cree and the Whiteman State" in P. Skalnik, ed. Outwitting the State (Transaction Publishers, 1989); Income Security for Cree Hunters, with H. Feit (M.A.S., 1992); article - "Knowledge Construction Among Cree Hunters" Journal de la Societe des Americanistes (LXXV: 193-208, 1989).

SCOTT, GEORGE
(BIA supt. for education)
Affiliation: Papago Agency, Bureau of Indian Affairs, P.O. Box 38, Sells, AZ 85634 (602) 383-3292.

SCOTT, KENDALL (Kickapoo)
(tribal chairperson)
Address & Affiliation: Kickapoo Tribe, P.O. Box 70, McLoud, OK 74851 (405) 964-2075 Fax 964-2745.

SCOTT, LARRY
(health director)
Affiliation: Watonga PHS Indian Health Center, P.O. Box 878, Watonga, OK 73772 (405) 623-4991.

SCOTT, MARILYN M. (Skagit)
(health center director, tribal chairperson)
Affiliations: Lummi PHS Indian Health Center, 2592 Kwina Rd., Bellingham, WA 98226 (360) 676-8373; Upper Skagit Tribal Council, 25944 Community Plaza, Sedro Wooley, WA 98284 (360) 856-5501.

SCOTT, STEPHANIE (Nisqually)
(former tribal chairperson)
Affiliation: Nisqually Indian Community, 4820 She-Nah-Num Dr. SE, Olympia, WA 98513 (360) 456-5221.

SCOTT, WILLIAM J. (Yurok)
(rancheria chairperson)
Affiliation: Resighini Rancheria, Coast Indian Community Council, P.O. Box 529, Klamath, CA 95548 (707) 482-2431.

SCRIBNER, PRINCESS ROSE (Penobscot) 1940-
(president/founder, Indian center)
Born April 3, 1940, Gardiner, Maine. *Education*: Mohegan Community College, Norwich, CT, AA, 1978. *Principal occupation*: President/founder, White Cloud Cultural Center, Norwich, CT, 1975-. *Memberships*: National Historic Preservation Society; National Indian Education Association; Indian Rights Association. *Awards, honors*: Outstanding Minority Award, Mohegan Community College; American Education Award, University of Connecticut. *Interests*: "My main goal in life (vocational) is to become a good Indian leader in serving our Native American people. I've traveled throughout the U.S. in observing model education programs much needed for Indian people. I hope to be appointed by the President of the U.S. in serving on the National Indian Education Advisory Board, Washington, D.C. I feel by this appointment, I can have the opportunity of getting more school books portraying Indian children properly, so that other children can read and learn what Indian people are all about. To wipe out the present stereotype Indian. Any expeditions I plan for the future will be one of taking a canoe trip down the Allegash, this area is one in which my famous grandfather guided many famous authors, Lord's of England, Countess's of Canada, on many a trip or expedition." *Published work*: Ethnic People of Connecticut (University of Connecticut, 1979).

SCRIBNER, VIVIAN (Cahuilla)
(tribal spokesperson)
Affiliation: Santa Rosa Band of Mission Indians, P.O. Box 390611, Anza, CA 92539 (909) 849-4761.

SCUDERO, JIM (Eskimo)
(mayor)
Affiliation: Metlakatla Indian Community Council, P.O. Box 8, Metlakatla, AK 99926 (907) 886-4441.

SCULLY, DIANA C.
(executive director)
Affiliation: Maine Indian Tribal State Commission, P.O. Box 87, Hallowell, ME 04347 (207) 622-4815.

SCHWARTZ, E.A.
(professor, writer)
Education: University of Missouri, Columbia, PhD in history. *Affiliation*: Assistant professor of history, California State University at San Marcos. Assigned as a reporter at the 1985 trial of two Siletz Indians accused of murdering a grave robber. That experience inspired him to write a "brief account" of the Siletz Indians and subsequently to acquire a doctorate in Indian history. *Published works*: The Rogue River Indian War and Its Aftermath, 1850-1980 (University of Oklahoma Press, 1997).

SEABOURN, BERT D. (Cherokee-Chickasaw) 1931-
(artist)
Born July 9, 1931, Iraann, Tex. *Education*: Oklahoma City University, MFA, 1963; Central State University, Edmond, OK, 1973; University of Oklahoma, 1976. *Principal occupation*: Artist. *Home address*: 6105 Covington Lane, Oklahoma City, OK 73132 (405) 722-1631. *Military service*: U.S. Navy (Journalist, Third Class, 1951-55). *Community activities*: Oklahoma State Arts Council; Oklahoma City Arts Council. *Memberships*: Oklahoma Art Guild (past president); Oklahoma Art Directors Club (past president); Oklahoma Watercolor Association (past treasurer). *Awards, honors*: Best of Show (oil), Oklahoma Art Guild Annual,

Oklahoma City, OK, 1966; Grand Award (acrylic), Five Civilized Tribes Museum, Muskogee, OK, 1973; Best of Show (watercolor), Red Cloud National Indian Art Exhibition, Pine Ridge, SD, 1974; Governor's Award, presented by Governor George Nigh, Oklahoma State Capitol, Oklahoma City, OK 1981; Sculpture Commission (23' bronze), Southwestern Bell Corporate Headquarters, Oklahoma City, OK, 1986; Best of Show (watercolor), Master Artist Show, Five Civilized Tribes Museum, 1988; numerous First Prizes in watercolor, oil, graphics, acrylics, and drawings at above shows, et al. *Interests*: "In 1989, I had art shows in Taiwan in March, and in July shows in Singapore; two art shows in Germany, one in the 60's and one in the 70's. Works are exhibited in The Heard Museum, Phoenix; The Five Civilized Tribes Museum, Muskoge, OK; Oklahoma Art Center, Oklahoma City, OK; Red Cloud Indian School, Pine Ridge, SD; The Vatican Museum of Modern Religious Art, Italy; Inter-Tribal Indian Ceremonial Association, Gallup, NM; among others. *Biographical sources*: Who's Who in America; Who's Who in American Art; Who's Who in American Indian Art; Who's Who in the South and Southwest; Dictionary of International Biography; Artists of Reknown; Contemporary Southwest Painters. *Published works*: Master Artists of the Five Civilized Tribes, 1976; Cherokee Artist, 1981; and Vanishing Americans, 1984 - all published by Seabourn Graphics.

SEABOURN, CONNIE (Cherokee) 1951-
(painter, printmaker)
Born Seoptember 20, 1951, Purcell, Okla. *Education*: University of Oklahoma, BFA, 1980. *Principal occupation*: Painter, printmaker. *Home address*: P.O. Box 23795, Oklahoma City, OK 73123 (405) 728-3903. *Selected Exhibitions*: 1990: New Watercolors, Chrysallis Art Gallery, Denver, CO; Masters of the Southwest, Adagio Gallery, Palm Springs, CA; Connie Seabourn, Carnegie Library Town Hal, Lawton, OK; Three Female Painters, Oklahoma Indian Art Gallery, Oklahoma City, OK. 1991: Internationally Known Southwest Artists, Tradewind Wildlife Art Gallery, Kansas City, MO; An Important Art/Expression, Christian Wolf Gallery, Albuquerque, NM: Vision Makers/Connie and Bert Seabourne, Oklahoma Indian Art Gallery; Premier Art Event: New Originals, Impressions, Ltd. Estes Park, CO; L.A. Art Expo, Los Angeles, CA; Annual Colorado Indian Market and Western Art Roundup, Boulder/Denver, CO; Five Civilized Tribes Museum Annual Competitive Show, Muskogee, OK. 1992: People, Places & Spirits, Adagio Gallery; Red Earth, Oklahoma City; Winter Art Show, Indian Paintbrush Gallery, Siloam Springs, AR; Color-Culture-Creed: Multi-Culturism in Oklahoma, City Arts Center, Oklahoma City; Connie & Bert Seabourne, El Taller, Austin, TX; Joan Cawley Gallery, Santa Fe, NM. Numerous other exhibitions from 1969-89. *Collections*: Museum of the American Indian, New York City; The Heard Museum, Phoenix; Center for Cherokee Heritage Museum, Cherokee, NC; Southern Plains India Museum, Anadarko, OK; Gilcrease Museum, Tulsa, OK; among many others. *Recent Lectures & Public Speaking Engagements*: Blind Embossment Printmaking Workshop, Johnson Atelier, Tulsa, OK, 1992; Demonstration, Bartlesville Art Guild, Bartlesville, OK, 1992; Demonstration, Mid-Del Art Guild, Midwest City, OK, 1992; Demonstration, Central Oklahoma Art Guild, Oklahoma City, OK, 1991; Lecture and Demonstration, Southeastern State College, Wilburton, OK, 1990; among many others. *Recent Awards*: Third Place, Watercolor, Gallup Intertribal Ceremonial, Gallup, NM, 1990; Third Place, Watercolor, Layers of Stories, Chisholm Trail Art Show, El Reno, OK, 1990; Special Merit Award, Painting, Annual Trail of Tears Show, Trail of Tears Museum, Tahlequah, OK, 1989; First Place, Graphics, Little Clasic Art Show, for Winter Vision, Guthrie, OK, 1988; among many others. *Recent Honors*: Commission to do signed reproduction/poster, One Voice for Children, for SACUS (Southern Association of Children Under Six) for national conference meeting in Tulsa, OK, 1992; 1991 Indian Images Calendar, Layers of Stories, used for May, published by Indian Images Productions, Evansville, IN; 1991 American Indian Art Calendar, Gentle Guardian used for August (Semihoye Publications, Norman, OK; Commission to do Limited Edition Reproduction, Tribal Renewal for Drug Recovery, Inc., Oklahoma City, 1990; Judge for Miss Indian Oklahoma Pageant, 1990; among others. *Biographi-*

cal sources: Who's Who in American Art, 1984; International Who's Who of Contemporary Achievement, 1984; Directory of Distinguished Americans, 3rd Ed.; Community Leaders of the World, 1984; Personalities of the South, 1985; International Directory of Distinguished Leadership, 1986; The Artist As Printmaker: Connie Seabourne, 1986; Personalities of America, 4th Ed., 1987; Foremost Women of the 20th Century, 1987.

SEAMAN, P. DAVID 1932-
(professor of linguistics)
Born January 31, 1932, Connellsville, PA. *Education*: Asbury College, AB, 1957; University of Kentucky, MA, 1958; Indiana University, PhD (Linguistics), 1965. *Principal occupation*: Professor of Linguistics, Dept. of Anthropology, Northern Arizona University, Flagstaff, AZ (1967-94; consultant, researcher, author, and professor emeritus, 1994-present). *Home address*: 4221 E. White Aster St., Phoenix, AZ 85044 (480) 759-0969. E-mail: pdseaman@asu.edu. *Past professional posts*: Bilingual/bicultural consulting for Zuni Tribal Council, 1970-72; linguistic consulting for Bureau of Indian Affairs, 1968-69, 1970-76; cross-cultural management consulting for Hopi Tribal Council, 1974-79; accounting and management consulting for Fort Mojave Tribal Council, 1977-80. *Military service*: U.S. Army, 1951-54 (Sergeant; U.S. Army Commendation Medal for efficient administration of U.S. Army field hospital in Korea, 1953). *Community activities*: University Heights Corporation, Flagstaff (director and corporate secretary, 1972-); Flagstaff Medical Center (finance committee, 1980-). *Memberships*: Linguistic Society of America; Society for Study of Indigenous Languages in America; Society for Linguistic Anthropology; Friends of Uto-Aztecan. *Awards, honors*: Distinguished Faculty Award, Northern Arizona University, 1980; among others. *Research*: Hopi dictionary project; traditional Havasupai culture; American Indian languages/cultures; H.C. Diehl Hopi Archives, 1976; Hopi Linguistics Articles - compiled by Mary & Dave Seaman in 1977; Helen M. Greene Indian Archives in 1985; Alfred F. Whiting Ethnographic Notes and Papers: Southwest Indian tribes, 1993; P. David Seaman Hopi Archives (Hopi language materials relating to Seaman's 1974-1985 Hopi Dictionary project), 1993. *Interests*: American Indian languages and culture; Greek language and culture. Paper delivered: "Hopi Dictionary and Computers," joint meeting, Arizona Humanities Association & Arizona Alliance for Arts Education, Scottsdale Community College, 1983 (article—Arizona Humanities Association Journal, Feb., 1984). Presently collaborating with another author on a screenplay for my book, *Born a Chief*. *Published works*: Co-editor, Havasupai Habitat: A.F. Whiting's Ethnography of a Traditional Indian Culture (University of Arizona Press, 1985); Hopi Dictionary: Hopi-English, English-Hopi (Northern Arizona University, Anthropological Paper, 1985; revised edition 1996); Born a Chief: The Nineteenth Century Hopi Boyhood of Edmund Nequatewa (U. of Arizona Press, 1993). Article: "Hopi Linguistics: An Annotated Bibliography" (Anthropological Linguistics, 1977).

SEBASTIAN, JACK
(Indian band chief)
Affiliation: Hagwilget Indian Band, Box 460, New Hazelton, B.C., Canada V0J 2J0 (604) 842-6258.

SEBASTIAN, ROY (Chief Hockeo) (Pequot)
(tribal chairperson)
Affiliation: Eastern Pequot Reservation, North Stonington, CT 06359.

SECAKUKU, FERRELL (Hopi)
(tribal chairperson)
Affiliation: Hopi Tribal Council, P.O. Box 123, Kykotsmovi, AZ 86039 (520) 734-2441.

SEETOT, ELMER
(AK village president)
Affiliation: Native Village of Brevig Mission, Brevig Mission, AK 99785 (907) 642-3851.

SEGEL, NORMAN
(executive director)
Affiliation: The Education for Parents of Indian Children With Special Needs Project, Southwest Communication Resources, P.O. Box 788, Bernalillo, NM 87004 (800) 765-7320; (505) 867-3396.

SEHOM, RODNEY
(school principal)
Affiliation: Newtok Day School, Newtok, AK 99559 (907) 237-2328.

SEIDNER, CHERYL (Wiyot)
(rancheria chairperson)
Affiliation: Table Bluff Rancheria, 1000 Wiyot Dr., Loleta, CA 95551 (707) 733-5055.

SEKAQUAPTEWA, EMORY (Hopi)
(attorney, educator)
Education: University of Arizona, J.D., 1970. *Affiliation*: The Tribal Law & Policy Program, American Indian Studies Program, The University of Arizona, Harvill Bldg., Rm 430, Box 210076, Tucson, AZ 85721 (520) 621-7108 Fax 621-7952. E-mail: aisp@email.arizona.edu. *Interests*: Hopi language/lexography/culture; dictionary of Hopi.

SEKAQUAPTEWA, KEN
(publisher)
Affiliation: Eagle's Eye, Brigham Young University, Office of Student Programs, 4th Floor, ELWC, Provo, UT 84602 (801) 378-6263.

SELAM, LONNIE, SR. (Yakima)
(tribal chairperson)
Affiliation: Yakima Tribal Council, P.O. Box 151, Toppenish, WA 98948 (509) 865-5121.

SELF, GEORGE WESLEY *(Twin Eagles)*
(Comanche, Cherokee-Ouachita Indian Confederation) 1941-
(swap meet dealer)
Born April 1, 1941, Los Angeles, Calif. *Education*: San Diego State University, BA, 1977. *Principal occupation*: Swap meet dealer (sell crystals). *Home address*: 7561 El Cajon Blvd., Apt. 14, La Mesa, CA 91941 (619) 298-5248. *Military service*: U.S. Army (PFC). *Memberships*: San Diego Museum of Man (life member); Vice-President, San Diego Lapidary Society, 1993-; San Diego State University Alumni Association. *Honor*: Council member, Ouachita Indian Confederation; *Interests*: "I enjoy gems & minerals (rockhounding). I was an archaeologist."

SELSOR, DONALD
(spiritual leader)
Affiliation: Antelope Indian Circle Religious Culture Group, P.O. Box 790, Susanville, CA 96130 (916) 257-2181 ext. 1534.

SEMINOLE, LYNETTE
(N.A. ecumenical ministry)
Affiliation: Native American Coalition of Programs, P.O. Box 1914, Fargo, ND 58107 (701) 235-3124.

SENA, CARLOS (Southern Ute)
(radio station manager)
Affiliation: KSUT - 91.3 FM, Southern Ute Tribe, P.O. Box 737, Ignacio, CO 81137 (303) 563-0255.

SEOUTEWA, CLAYTON
(BIA agency supt.)
Affiliation: Zuni Agency, Bureau of Indian Affairs, P.O. Box 369, Zuni, NM 87327 (505) 782-5591 Fax 782-5715

SEPPANEN, JOHN (Chippewa)
(health director)
Affiliation: Keweenaw Bay Indian Community Health Clilc, Route 1, Baraga, MI 49908 (906) 353-6671.

SERO, THOMAS (Mohawk)
(board member)
Affiliation: Intertribal Christian Comunications, P.O. Box 3765, Station B, Winnipeg, Manitoba, Canada R2W 3R6 (204) 661-9333.

SETH, LEROY L. (*Pe-Nock-We-Ya-Tillupt*) (Nez Perce) 1936-
(patient advocate)
Born December 23, 1936, Lewiston, Idaho. *Education*: University of Montana, MA. *Principal occupation*: Patient advocate. *Address*: P.O. Box 396, Lapwai, ID (208) 843-7303 Fax 843-7387. E-mail: leroys@enterprise.nezperce.org. *Affiliation*: Indian Health Service, Lapwai, Idaho, Nez Pece Tribe. *Other professional*

posts: Consultant, painter and dancer. *Military service*: U.S. Army (Paratrooper). *Community activities*: Works with Indian basketball tournaments; assist pow-wow committees; Indian advisory boards. *Interests*: Art, photography, old cars, Indian rugs.

SETTEE, PIERRE
(Indian band chief)
Affiliation: Cumberland Indian Band, Box 220, Cumberland House, SK, Canada S0E 0S0 (306) 888-2152.

SEVIER, JACKIE (Northern Arapaho) 1953-
(artist)
Born July 30, 1953, Riverton, Wyo. *Education*: Casper (WY) College, 1971-72. *Principal occupation*: Artist. *Address & Affiliation*: Northern Plains Studio, P.O. Box 86, Seneca, NE 69161 (308) 639-3227. *Membership*: Indian Arts & Crafts Association. *Awards, honors*: Red Earth, Oklahoma City; Northern Plains Tribal Arts, Sioux Falls, SD; Aspen Celebration for the American Indian; Smithsonian Institution, Museum of Anthropology; Twin Cities Indian Market, Minneapolis; Aspen Award & Diederich Award at Red Cloud Art Show, Pine Ridge, SD; Lawrence Indian Art Festival, Lawrence, KS. *Exhibits*: Stuhr Museum, Grand Island, NE; Sioux Indian Museum, Rapid City, SD; Buffalo Bill Historical Society, Cody, WY; and 1989 World Expo in Shizouka, Japan.

SEWEPAGAHAM, A.J.
(Indian band chief)
Affiliation: Little Red River Indian Band, Box 1165, High Level, Alberta, Canada T0H 1Z0 (403) 759-3912.

SEXTON, LINDA
(foundation administrator)
Affiliation: The Jacobson Foundation, 609 Chautauqua, Norman, OK 73071 (405) 329-3012.

SEYLER, BERTHA
(editor)
Affiliation: The Rawhide Press, Spokane Tribal Business Council, P.O. Box 359, Wellpinit, WA 99040 (509) 258-7320.

SEYLER, WARREN (Spokane)
(tribal chairperson)
Affiliation: Spokane Business Council, P.O. Box 100, Wellpinit, WA 99040 (509) 258-4581.

SEYMOUR, TRYNTJE VAN NESS 1956-
(writer, lecturer)
Born July 2, 1956, New York, N.Y. *Education*: Smith College, BA, 1978. *Principal occupation*: Writer, lecturer. *Home address*: P.O. Box 363, Salisbury, CT 06068 (203) 435-2236. *Affiliation*: Guest curator, The Heard Museum, Phoenix, 1985-87. *Membership*: The Author's Guild. *Interests*: Extensive travels in the Southwest since 1970. Conducted in-depth interviews of Native American artists. Served as assistant boatman and, recently, as archaeology guide on raft trips through the Grand Canyon. Judge of paintings at Santa Fe Indian Market, 1987. *Biographical source*: "Traditional India Art," by Paula Panich in Southwest Profile, Feb. 1987. *Published works*: Acoma (Lime Rock Press, 1980); When the Rainbow Touches Down: The Artists and Stories Behind the Apache, Navajo, Rio Grande Pueblo and Hopi Paintings in the William and Leslie Van Ness Denman Collection (The Heard Museum-Dist. by University of Washington Press, 1989); The Gift of Changing Woman (Henry Holt & Co., 1993).

SHACKLEFORD, BRUCE M. (Creek)
(museum director)
Affiliation: Creek Council House Museum, Okmulgee, OK 74447 (918) 756-2324.

SHADE, HASTINGS (Cherokee of Oklahoma)
(deputy principal chief)
Affiliation: Deputy Principal Chief, Cherokee Nation of Oklahoma, P.O. Box 948, Tahlequah, OK 74465 (918) 456-0671. E-mail: hshade@cherokee.org

SHAFFER, SUSAN M. (Umpqua)
(tribal chairperson)
Affiliation: Cow Creek Band of Umpqua Indians, 2371 N.E. Stevens, Suite 100, Roseburg, OR 97470 (541) 672-9405.

SHAHROKH, RENEE
(college instructor)
Principal occupation: College instructor. *Address & Affiliation*: D-Q University, P.O. Box 409, Davis, CA 95617 (916) 758-0470 Fax 758-4891. *Affiliations*: D-Q University, 1995-present; American River College, 1991-present. *Memberships*: California Native Plant Society (hike leader); Lichenology Society.

SHAKESPEARE, JUNE (*Singing Pipe*) (Arapaho)
(Indian education director, home school coordinator)
Address: Riverton High School, 2001 W. Sunset, Riverton, WY 82501 (307) 856-9491 ext. 13 Fax 856-2333. *Affiliations*: Chair, Wind River Reservation Health Promotion Board of Directors, 1995-present. *Other professional posts*: Coalition of Families and Youth member, 1992-present; Wind River Reservation Youth Council Board member, 1996-present. *Community activities*: Region VI-HIV/AIDS Committee member; Region VI - Peer Mentors Advisor, 1995-present; Wind River Chapter, Ameriacn Red Cross, 1995-present. *Memberships*: National Indian Education Association; American Indian Education Advisory Committee, Central Wyoming College (Riverton, WY); Institute of American Indian Arts Alumni Association (Santa Fe, NM).

SHALIFOE, RICHARD (Chippewa)
(tribal president(
Affiliation: L'Anse Reservation, Keweenaw Bay Indian Community of Michigan, 107 Beartown Rd., Baraga, MI 49908 (906) 353-6623.

SHANIGAN, MARIANE (Kanatak)
(village president)
Affiliation: Native Village of Kanatak, P.O. Box 693, Dillingham, AK 99576 (907) 842-4004.

SHANKS, LAURENCE "SWIFT TIDE" (Schagticoke)
(tribal chief)
Affiliation: New England Coastal Schagticoke Indian Association, P.O. Box 551, Avon, MA 02322 (617) 961-1346.

SHANLEY, DR. JAMES
(college president)
Affiliation: Fort Peck Community College, P.O. Box 398, Poplar, MT 59255 (406) 768-5551 Fax 768-5552.

SHANNON, LEE K. (Cowichan of B.C., Can.)
(attorney)
Education: Seattle University, BS, 1986; University of Washington, J.D., 1993, MBA, 1994. *Affiliation & Address*: Associate, Hobbs, Straus, Dean & Walker, LLP, (2001-present), 851 S.W. Sixth Ave., Suite 1650, Portland, OR 97204 (503) 242-1745 Fax 242-1072. E-mail: lshannon@hsdwor.com. Mr. Shannon focuses on finance, tax, tribal gaming, tribal sovereignty, and economic development for Indian tribes. *Past professional posts*: Staff attorney and acting executive director of the Native American Program of Oregon Legal Services where he concentrated on commercial, corporate, gaming, finance and tax issues on behalf of Oregon tribes, tribal enterprises and Indian non-profit corporations. *Community activities*: Board of directors, Legal Aid Services of Oregon; board of directors, Oregon Law Center; board of directors, Affiliated Tribes of Northwest Indians. *Memberships*: Oregon State Bar Association (member and former chair of the Indian Law Section); Washington State Bar Association (member and former secretary-treasurer of the Indian law Section); Northwest Indian Bar Association; Federal Bar Association; National Association of Bond Lawyers; National Indian Gaming Association.

SHANNON, RALPH
(Indian school principal)
Affiliation: Indian Township School, Peter Dana Point, HC78, Box 1A, Princeton, ME 04668 (207) 796-2362 Fax 796-2726.

SHAW, CARL F.
(BIA-director of public affairs)
Affiliation: Office of Public Affairs, Bureau of Indian Affairs, Dept. of the Interior, MS-4140-MIB, 1849 C St., NW, Washington, DC 20240 (202) 208-7315.

SHAW, FRANCES (Diegueno)
(tribal chairperson)
Affiliation: Manzanita General Council, P.O. Box 1302, Boulevard, CA 91905 (619) 766-4930; chairperson, Southern Indian Health Council, P.O. Box 20889, El Cajon, CA 92021.

SHECANAPISH, GEORGE
(Indian band chief)
Affiliation: Naskapi of Quebec, Box 970, Kawawachikamach Indian Reserve, Schefferville, QB, Canada G0G 2T0 (418) 585-2370.

SHEDD, AARON
(educational administrator)
Affiliation: Director, Office of Indian Education, U.S. Dept of Education, Rm. 2177, Federal Office Bldg. 6, 400 Maryland Ave., Washington, DC 20202 (202) 401-1887.

SHEEK, JOHN
(program administrator)
Address & Affiliation: Executive Director, National Indian Education Association, 700 N. Fairfax St., Suite 210, Alexandria, VA 22314 (703) 838-2870.

SHEGONEE, HARTFORD (Potawatomi) 1943-
(administrator; former tribal chairperson)
Born October 27, 1943, Hayward, Wisc. *Education*: Nicolet College (Vocational Diploma-Auto Mechanics, 1986); Mt. Scenario College,1987-88. *Principal occupation*: Administrator. Resides in Crandon, WI. *Affiliation*: Former tribal chairperson, Forest County Potawatomi Executive Council, Crandon, WI, 1987-91. *Community activities*: Great Lakes Inter-Tribal Council (sec/treas, 1987-); Inter-Tribal Timber Council, 1987-; also active in local chapter of Headstart program. National Congress of American Indians. *Awards, honors*: Honored with Plaque by the Canadian Potawatomi for assistance in quest for federal (U.S.) recognition of treaty. *Interests*: "Anything that will improve the lifestyle of the Forest County Potawatomi people. Instrumental in the Potawatomi having land in the City of Milwaukee placed into Trust for the Tribe in 1990. Restored political stability after BIA shutdown operations of the tribe in 1987."

SHELDON, LINDA
(health director)
Affiliation: Yerington Health Dept., 171 Campbell Lane, Yerington, NV 89447 (702) 463-3301.

SHELTON, M.L. "PETE" (Oglala Sioux) 1936-
(business owner)
Born July 29, 1936, Martin, S.D. *Education*: Scottsdale Junior College; Chadron State College. *Principal occupation*: Business owner. *Address & Affiliations*: Owner, Native American Office Products Supplies, P.O. Box 1360, Rapid City, SD 57709 (605) 343-7464, 1979-; owner, Native American Originals, Rapid City, SD, 1986-. *Community activities*: Minority Relations Chairperson, 1983-84. Membership: BPOE, 1964-.

SHEMICK, H. "MISSY"
(RN-health director)
Affiliation: Health Director, Nevada Urban Indians, 2100 Capurro Way #C, Sparks, NV 89431 (702) 329-2573; exeutive director, College Career & Vocational Resoure Library, Nevada Urban Indians, Sparks, NV.

SHENANDOAH, ADE (Onondaga) 1950-
(catering/food service)
Born April 28, 1950, Syracuse, N.Y. *Principal occupation*: Catering/food service. *Home address*: P.O. Box 450, Oneida, NY 13421-0450 (315) 363-6248. *Affiliation*: Shenandoah Sandwiches, Oneida, NY, 1986-. *Other professional post*: Alcohol-prevention counselor. *Community actvities*: Alcohol youth prevention programs.

SHENANDOAH, DIANE (Oneida) 1958-
(catering/food service)
Born October 21, 1958, Syracuse, N.Y. *Principal occupation*: Catering/food service. *Home address*: Box 10, Oneida, NY 13421 (315) 363-6248. *Affiliation*: Shenandoah Sandwiches, Oneida, NY, 1986-. *Other professional post*: Artist/writer. *Award, honors*: Indian Market, Santa Fe, NM. "Shenandoah Sandwich," First

Place, Native American Cuisine, Connecticut River Society. *Interests*: Traveled extensively along the East Coast from Maine to Florida. *Biographical sources*: "The Clouds Threw This Light," and "Spaning the Medicine River."

SHENANDOAH, JOANNE (*Tekalihwakwa-She Sings*) (Oneida-Iroquois) 1957-
(musician-composer)
Born June 23, 1957, Syracuse, N.Y. *Education*: Andrews University, 1975-76; Columbia Union College, 1976-78. *Principal occupation*: Musician-composer. *Home address*: Oneida Nation Territory, P.O. Box 450, Oneida, NY 13421 (315) 363-1655. E-mail: shesings@borg.com. Web site: www.joanneshenandoah.com. *Affiliations*: Systems engineer, Inforex, Inc., Rockville, MD, 1976-81; business development manager, Computer Science Corp., Falls Church, VA, 1986-87; president, Red Line Computers, 1987-90; president, Round Dance Productions, Inc., Oneida, NY, 1991-. *Memberships*: ASCAP; ACTRA; National Congress of American Indians; National American Indian Women's Association. *Interests*: "Music writing, performing, producing, composing; travels to Europe, throughout North America; sailing, canoeing; historical research. Round Dance Productions is a non-for-profit corporation formed specifically to assist in the preservation and development of indigenous North American language, history, music and art. Primary focus is on the Haudenosaunee (Oneida, Mohawk, Onondaga, Seneca, Cayuga and Tuscarora Nations) although it encompasses other aboriginal cultures as well." *Awards, honors*: 1992 Special Award for dedicated service to Oneida Nation from U.S. Indian Health Service; "1993 Native Musician of the Year"; performed for first lady Hillary Clinton & V.P.'s wife, Tipper Gore in Washington, DC; 1994 & 1997 Outstanding Musical Achievement Awards; Native American Woman's Recognition Award, 1996; Native American Record of the Year, NAIRD 1997 INDIE Award; Native American Woman of Hope Award, 1997; 1998 Best Female Artist and Best Children's Album, Native American Music Awards; 1998 ASCAP, Popular Awards Recipient; 1998 Grammy Nominations for 2 albums: World Music - Matriarch and Children's Music - All Spirits Sing. *Biographical source*: Who's Who in the East, 1991-92; feature story in, "The Turtle" magazine, Winter 1993. 1994 Who's Who Among Native Americans; Joanne has appeared on numerous television shows, radio broadcasts, and video documentaries. *Produced works*: She released her first album with Canyon Records in September 1989. She also recorded with NATO Records in France for the 2-CD album "Oyate" produced by Tony Hymas. Two of her compositions are featured on the Leonard Peltier album, "In the Spirit of Crazy Horse." "Loving Ways" is co-produced with a A. Paul Ortega, Canyon Records, Phoenix, AZ. "Nature Dance" with Sun Child Productions, distributed by Eye-Q Records, Warner of Germany was released June 1991 and made "Record of the Month." "Orenda" Native American Songs of Life, "Matriarch" Iroquois Women's Songs, and "Life Blood" all by Silver Wave Records. *Performances*: Shenandoah has performed thousands of concerts throughout North America and Europe. Some of the more recent include: Indian Time II, Winnipeg, Canada, - American Indian Music Festival, San Francisco, June 1991; National Canadian TV, Toronto Harbourfront Festival, July 1991; Earth Day, Washington, DC, May 1991; Woodstock 94, Spoecial Olympics, 1996; 1997 Presidential Innaugural in Washington, DC; among others. Future Projects: TV Mini Series - Wampum Belts and Peace Trees, Author, Dr. Gregory Schaaf, Executive Producer, Sam Bottoms; European Tour, 1992 Spring "Indian Saga"; Planet Live - Earth Day, 1992. *Published work*: Skywoman - Legends of the Iroquois with co-writer Doug George (Clearlight Publishers).

SHEPHERD, ALEX (Paiute)
(tribal chairperson)
Affiliation: Paiute Indian Tribe of Utah Tribal Council, 600 N. 100 E. Paiute Dr., Cedar City, UT 84720 (801) 586-1121.

SHEPHERD, BERNARD
(Indian band chief)
Affiliation: Whitebear Indian Band, Box 700, Carlyle, Sask., Canada S0C 0R0 (306) 577-2461.

SHEPPARD, LAVERNE (Shoshone-Bannock) 1960-
(executive director)
Born April 17, 1960, Blackfoot, Idaho. *Education*: University of Arizona, 1982; Idaho State University, BA (Journalism), 1984. *Principal occupation*: Executive director. *Affiliations*: Editor, Sho-Ban News, Fort Hall, ID, 1984-89, National American Indian/Alaska Native Media Specialist, U.S. Census Bureau, Seattle, 1989-90; Executive Director, Native American Journalism Association, University of Colorado School of Journalism, Campus Box 287, Boulder, CO 80309 (303) 492-7397, 1990-. *Other professional post*: Co-chairperson, Native Communications Group, Lincoln, NE, 1990-.

SHERIDAN, MATTHEW, SR.
(health project officer)
Affiliation: Carl T. Curtis Health Center, P.O. Box 250, Macy, NE 68039 (402) 837-5381.

SHERLOCK, LONNIE
(Indian education program coordinator)
Affiliation: Alliance Public Schools, Indian Education Program, 1604 Sweetwater, Alliance, NE 69301 (308) 762-1580 Fax 762-8249.

SHERMAN, DUANE, SR. (Hoopa)
(tribal chairperson)
Affiliation: Hoopa Valley Tribal Council, P.O. Box 1348, Hoopa, CA 95546 (530) 625-4211.

SHERMAN, GERALD J. (Oglala Sioux) 1949-
(bank manager)
Born July 17, 1949, Kyle, S.D. *Education*: Oglala Lakota College, BS, 1987. *Principal occupation*: Bank manager. *Address*: Resides in SD (605) 473-9280 (work). *Affiliations*: Founding chairman of the board & executive director. The Lakota Fund, Kyle, SD, 1987-91 (a community loan fund on the Pine Ridge Indian Reservation); Pine Ridge Area Director, Native American Economic Development Project, Business Opportunity Center - University of South Dakota , 1991-93 (provided business technical assistance to tribal members at Pine Ridge); manager, Norwest Bank Lower Brule (a new bank on the Lower Brule Indian Reservation), Lower Brule, SD, 1993-. *Community activities*: Board member, Habitat for Humanity, Ft. Thompson, SD; board member, Food Services of South Dakota. *Membership*: North Plains Tribal Arts Council. *Awards, honors*: Minority Small Business Advocate of the Year, 1993, for South Dakota & SBA Region VIII. *Interests*: Indian economic development, finance. As founding chairman of the board & executive director of the Lakota Fund, Mr. Sherman played a principal role in developing the Fund and forging the relationships between the fund, its investors, funders, and clients. He traveled to Canada and Bangladesh to study the peer group lending method now in use by the Lakota Fund to make micro enterprise loans. Gerald has several years experience in television production but has been active in Indian economic development since 1986.

SHERMAN, GERALDINE (Sioux)
(craftsperson)
Affiliations: Contemporary Lakota Fashions by Geraldine Sherman, 714 Wambli Dr., Rapid City, SD 57701 (605) 341-7560

SHERRILL, NANCY
(Indian education program coordinator)
Affiliation: Smokey Mountain High School, Indian Education Program, 505 E. Main St., Sylvia, NC 28779 (704) 586-2311 Fax 586-5450.

SHERWOOD, NEVA
(BIA education administrator)
Affiliation: Rosebud Agency, Bureau of Indian Affairs, P.O. Box 669 (605) 856-4478 Fax 856-4487.

SHEWANO, DON
(health director)
Affiliation: Forest Co. Potawatomi Community Clinic, P.O. Box 346, Crandon, WI 54520 (715) 478-3471.

SHEWISH, ADAM
(Indian band chief)
Affiliation: Sheshaht Indian Band, Box 1218, Port Alberni, B.C., Canada V9Y 7M1 (604) 724-1225.

SHIELDS, CALEB (Assiniboine Sioux)
(tribal chairperson)
Affiliation: Fort Peck Tribal Executive Board, P.O. Box 1027, Poplar, MT 59255 (406) 768-5155.

SHIJE, AMADEO (Zia Pueblo)
(council chairperson)
Affiliation: All Indian Pueblo Council, P.O. Box 400, Albuquerque, NM 87190 (505) 881-1992 Fax 883-7682.

SHIJE, HENRY (Zia Pueblo)
(former pueblo governor)
Affiliation: Zia Pueblo Tribal Council, 135 Capital Square Dr., Zia Pueblo, NM 87053 (505) 867-3304.

SHINGOITEWA, LEROY N. (*Dawa yes va*) (Hopi) 1942-
(tribal administrator)
Born August 4, 1942, Keams Canyon, Ariz. *Education*: Northern Arizona University, BS, 1969; Pennsylvania State University, MEd, 1972. *Principal occupation*: Tribal administrator. *Home address*: P.O. Box 1258, Tuba City, AZ 86045 (602) 283-5623. *Affiliation*: Hotevilla Bacavi Community School, Hotevilla, AZ, 1990-93; executive assistant, Office of Hopi Tribal Chairman, Hopi Indian Tribe, Kykotsmovi, AZ, 1993-. *Other professional post*: Executive assistant, Navajo Nation Division of Health. *Community activities*: Member of Tuba City School Board; Arizona School Board Association (Legislative Committee, Resolution Committee, Chapter I Committee); White House Delegate for Indian Education; Indian Education Graduate Advisory Board, Berkeley, CA. *Memberships*: National Indian Education Association; Curriculum and Supervision Association; National School Board Association. *Awards, honors*: National Civic Award - Supermarkets Association; President Bush 1000 Points-of-Light Award; Hopi Man-of-the-Year (Hopi-Navajo Observer). *Interests*: "Work to help all Indian people throughout the U.S. in education and management areas."

SHIPLEY, PRISCILLA (Stillaguamish)
(former tribal chairperson)
Affiliation: Stillaguamish Board of Directors, P.O. Box 277, Arlington, WA 98223 (360) 652-7362.

SHIPPS, THOMAS H. 1953-
(tribal attorney)
Born February 13, 1953, Hyannis, Mass. *Education*: Fort Lewis College, BA, 1976; University of Houston Law School, JD, 1979. *Principal occupation*: Attorney. *Home address*: P.O. Box 2717, Durango, CO 81302 (970) 247-1755. *Affiliation*: Tribal attorney, Southern Ute Indian Tribe, Ignacio, CO, 1980-. *Memberships*: American Bar Association; Colorado Bar Association; Colorado Indian Bar Association; National Indian Law Support Center (board of directors); Rocky Mountain Mineral Law Foundation. *Published works*: The American Indian and the Constitution (University of Houston Law Center, 1979); "Oil and Gas Lease Operation and Royalty Valuation on Indian Lands," Rocky Mountain Mineral Law Foundation, 1991.

SHOEMAKE, BEN
(coalition chairperson)
Affiliation: Native American Coalition of Tulsa, 1740 West 41st, Tulsa, OK 74107 (918) 446-8432.

SHOEMAKER, EDWARD C.
(Cherokee of Oklahoma) 1943-
(director of research management)
Born July 20, 1943, Nowata, Okla. *Education*: Oklahoma State University, BA; University of Oklahoma, MLS. *Principal occupation*: Director of research management. *Home address*: 2331 Rockwood Lane, Norman, OK 73071. *Affiliation*: Director, Research Division (1980-present), Oklahoma Historical Society, 2100 North Lincoln Blvd., Oklahoma City, OK 73105 (405) 522-4025. E-mail: edshoemaker@ok-history.mus.ok.us. Website: www.ok-history.mus.ok.us. *Military service*: U.S. Navy, 1967-69 (Mobile Riverine Forces). *Military awards, honors*: Combat Action Ribbon, Good Conduct, Vietnam Campaign Medal, Republic of Vietnam Medal. *Community activities*: Member of Canticle Singers & Chair of Library Council, McFarlin Memorial United Methodist Church, Norman, OK. *memberships*: Mobile Riverine Forces Association; Navy MSO Association.

SHOEMAKER, MARY J.
(school principal)
Affiliation: San Juan Day School, P.O. Box 1077, San Juan Pueblo, NM 87566 (505) 852-2154.

SHOPODOCK, PHIL (Forest County Potawatomi)
(tribal chairperson)
Affiliation: Forest County Potawatomi Executive Council, P.O. Box 340, Crandon, WI 54520 (715) 478-2903.

SHOPTEESE, JOHN T. (*Washah*)
(Prairie Band Potawatomi) 1938-
(freelance jeweler, designer, artist; photographer; tribal consultant)
Born February 28, 1938, Mayetta, Kan. *Education*: Haskell Indian Junior College, 1956-58. *Principal occupation*: freelance jeweler, designer, artist; photographer; tribal economic development consultant. *Home address*: 14471 Kipling Ave. S., Savage, MN 55378 (612) 895-5207; E-mail: johnshop@gold.tc.umn.edu. *Affiliations*: Indian Health Service, Rockville, MD, 1958-86; National Indian Health Board, Denver, CO, 1992-94. *Military service*: U.S. Army Medical Corps, 1961-62. *Memberships*: Native Arts Circle, Minneapolis, MN; Southwest Association on Indian Affairs, Santa Fe, NM, 1980-. Community activities: Indian Parents Committee, School District 191, MN. *Awards, honors*: Several awards for achievement in the arts (I am a jeweler—gold/silver smith); sculpture in bronze, pewter, clay; received several juried art show awards throughout the Southwest; 1994 fellowship from the Jerome Foundation of Minnesota. *Interests*: Pursuing excellence in Native arts; to enhance cultural awareness and enact the trends of art through significant application of contemporary overtones. (I) "have displayed my arts/crafts at major art shows of Native American artists."

SHORE, NANCY (*Sos'setv*) (Creek/Seminole) 1947-
(education)
Born April 6, 1947, Glades County, Fla. *Education*: Barry University (Miami, FL), MSW, 1982. *Principal occupation*: Education. *Affiliation*: Seminole Tribe of Florida, Hollywood, FL, 1973-. *Community activities*: Seminole Higher Education Committee; Seminole Womens Club; Parent Advisory Committee; Okee Parent/Teacher; Seminole Education Advisory.

SHORT, PHYLLIS
(museum director)
Affiliation: Nana Museum of the Arctic, P.O. Box 40, Kotzebue, AK 99752 (907) 442-3301.

SHORTBULL, THOMAS
(college president)
Affiliation: Oglala Lakota Community College, P.O. Box 490, Kyle, SD 57752 (605) 455-2321 Fax 455-2787.

SHORTING, HECTOR
(Indian band chief)
Affiliation: Little Saskatchewan Indian Band, Gypsumville, Manitoba, Canada R0C 1J0 (204) 659-4584.

SHORTMAN, PHILLIP
(college professor)
Affiliation: Fort Belknap Community College, P.O. Box 159, Harlem, MT 59526 (406) 353-2607 Fax 353-2898.

SHROLL, WILLIAM
(school principal/supt.)
Affiliation: Crow Creek High School, P.O. Box 12, Stephan, SD 57346 (605) 852-2255.

SHUCKAHOSEE, CORBIN (Sac & Fox of Missouri)
(tribal chairperson)
Affiliation: Sac & Fox of Missouri Tribal Council, Rt. 1, Box 60, Reserve, KS 66434 (913) 742-7471.

SHULTES, STEPHANIE E. (Iroquois)
(museum curator)
Affiliation: Iroquois Indian Museum, Box 7, Caverns Rd., Howes Cave, NY 12092 (518) 296-8949.

SHUNATONA, GWEN
(executive director)
Affiliation: Orbis Associates, P.O. Box 39335, Washington, DC 20016-9335 (202) 628-4444.

SHURR, JOHN CARTER
(Oklahoma Cherokee) 1947-
(journalist, bureau chief-Associated Press)
Born March 15, 1947, Muskogee, Okla. *Education*:
University of Oklahoma, BA (Journalism), 1973. *Principal occupation*: Bureau chief, Associated Press.
Home address: 116 Shallow Brook Dr., Columbia, SC
29223 (803) 788-1077; E-Mail: jshurr@ap.org. *Affiliation*: Chief of Bureau, The Associated Press, Columbia, SC, 1984-. *Other professional post*: Curriculum
Advisory Committee, University of South Carolina,
College of Journalism. *Military service*: U.S. Navy,
1966-70 (2nd Class Radioman, E-5; Vietnam, 1967-68; Vietnam Service Medal, Vietnam Campaign Medal-3 Bronze Stars; Presidential Unit Citation, Navy Unit
Commendation, Combat Action Ribbon). *Memberships*: Reporters Committee for Freedom of the Press,
1991- (Steering Committee); First Amendment Congress (Trustee & Vice President, 1980-88); South
Carolina Press Association Freedom of Information
Committee, 1986-, Chairperson; Society of Professional Journalists; Native American Journalists Association. *Awards, honors*: American Bar Association
Gavel Award, 1981; SC Press Association Award, 1987
& 1994; several Associated Press Managing Editors
Awards. *Interests*: Avid sailboat racer; tennis. *Published work*: Freedom of Information Guide (SC Press
Association, 1987-93).

SHUTIVA, RONALD (Acoma Pueblo)
(pueblo council governor)
Affiliation: Acoma Pueblo Council, P.O. Box 309,
Acomita, NM 87034 (505) 552-6604.

SICKEY, ERNEST
(health center director)
Affiliation: Dallas Inter-Tribal Council Health Center,
209 E. Jefferson, Dallas, TX 75203 (214) 941-1050.

SIDNEY, IVAN (Hopi)
(former tribal chairperson)
Affiliation: Hopi Tribal Council, P.O. Box 123,
Kykotsmovi, AZ 86039 (602) 734-2445.

SIGALA, SANDRA (Pomo)
(tribal chairperson)
Affiliation: Hopland Tribal Council, P.O. Box 610,
Hopland, CA 95449 (707) 744-1647.

SIGO, CHARLES (Suquamish)
(museum curator)
Affiliation: Suquamish Museum, P.O. Box 498,
Suquamish, WA 98392 (206) 598-3311.

SILAS, BERKMAN (Athapascan)
(village chief)
Affiliation: Minto Village Council, P.O. Box 26,
Minto, AK 99758 (907) 798-7112.

SILEX, EDGAR (Tiqua del Sur) 1958-
(creative writing instructor/poet, author)
Born March 31, 1958, El Paso, Tex. *Education*: University of Maryland, MFA, 1994. *Affiliation*: The Cafe
Workshops, Baltimore, MD. *Membership*: Native
American Student Union of University Maryland. *Biographical source*: Washington Post article, 6/15/93.
Published works: Even the Dead Have Memories (New
Sins Press); Through All the Displacements (Curbstone
Press, 1995).

SILHANEK, BETH
(school administrator)
Affiliation: Sac & Fox Settlement School,
1657 320th St., Tama, IA 52339 (515) 484-4990.

SILLIBOY, ROSELLA (Micmac)
(craftsperson)
Affiliation: Owner, Three Feathers Native baskets, P.O.
Box 644, Houlton, ME 04730 (207) 532-0862. *Products*: Traditional brown ash utility and work baskets
made by Micmac tribal members.

SILVERBIRD, J. REUBEN (Navajo/Apache) 1940-
(storyteller, actor, screen writer, film producer)
Born July 27, 1940, Placentia, Calif. *Education*: St.
Michaels College (2 years). *Principal occupation*: story
teller, actor, screen writer, film producer. *Address*:
Unknown. *Affiliation*: President, Silverbird Productions
(Music, Film, Stage & TV), Orlando, FL, 1984-. *Other*

professional post: Trying to help finance "Iroquois
National Lacrosse Team for England tour & documentary. *Military service*: U.S. Army (2 years) Special Services (Master Sergeant) taught electronics (produced
& appeared in show that toured for Special Services).
Certificate of Achievement for teaching electronics.
Community activities: Association on American Indian
Affairs, NYC; American Indian College Fund, NYC;
American Indian Community House, NYC. *Memberships*: American Society of Composers & Publishers;
Screen Actors Guild; Actor's Equity Association; New
York Screen Writer's Association. *Awards, honors*:
Owned & operated NYC 1st Native American restaurant, 1984-87. *Interests*: Singing tour of Asia (3 times);
lectures on behalf of Native America.

SILVERMAN, RICHARD
(museum president)
Affiliation: The Heard Museum, 2301 N. Central Ave.,
Phoenix, AZ 85004 (602) 252-8840.

SILVERTHORNE, JOYCE
(Confederated Salish & Kootenai)
(education coordinator)
Affiliation: Education Coordinator, Confederated Salish
& Kootenai Tribes, P.O. Box 278, Pablo, MT 59855
(406) 675-2700 Fax 675-2806.

SILVESTER, JOHN
(program director)
Affiliation: Native American Studies Program,
Scottsdale Community College, 9000 E. Chaparral St.,
Scottsdale, AZ 85256 (602) 423-6139.

SILVEY, LEANNE E.
(executive director)
Affiliation: Michigan Indian Child Welfare Agency, 405
E. Easterday Ave., Sault Ste. Marie, MI 49783 (906)
635-9400.

SIMEONOFF, HELEN J. (Aleut)
(artist; art studio owner)
Affiliation: Alonda Studio, 3212 West 30th Ave.,
Anchorage, AK 99517 (907) 248-0454.

SIMEONOFF, KELLY, JR.
(association president)
Affiliation: Kodiak Area Native Association Health Center, 402 Center Ave., Kodiak, AK 99615 (907) 486-5725.

SIMMONS, DOUGLAS V.
(school principal)
Affiliation: Mariano Lake Community School, P.O.
Box 498, Crownpoint, NM 87313 (505) 786-5265.

SIMMONS, JOHN (Nisqually)
(tribal chairperson)
Affiliation: Nisqually Indian Community, 4820 She-Nah-
Num Dr. SE, Olympia, WA 98513 (360) 456-5221.

SIMMS, DON
(school supt.)
Affiliation: Riverside Indian School, Route 1,
Anadarko, OK 73005 (405) 247-6670 Fax 247-5529.

SIMMS, RUSSELL
(executive director)
Affiliation: Council of Three Rivers American Indian
Center, Inc., Rt. 2, Box 247-A, Dorseyville, PA 15238
(412) 782-4457. *Other professional post*: Editor, The
Singing Winds Newsletter.

SIMON, BROTHER, S.J.
(museum director/curator)
Affiliation: The Heritage Center, Red Cloud Indian
School, Hwy. 18W, Pine Ridge, SD 57770 (605) 867-5491.

SIMON, FRANKLIN (Huslia Athabascan)
(AK village council chief)
Affiliation: Huslia Village Council, P.O. Box 45010,
Hughes, AK 99745 (907) 899-2206.

SIMON III, JOSE (Pomo)
(rancheria chairperson)
Affiliation: Middletown Rancheria, P.O. Box 1035,
Middletown, CA 95461 (707) 987-3670.

SIMON, LUCAS (Pomo)
(tribal chairperson)
Affiliation: Middletown Rancheria,
P.O. Box 292, Middletown, CA 95461.

SIMON, LINCOLN (Eskimo)
(village president)
Affiliation: Native Village of White Mountain, P.O. Box
84082, White Mountain, AK 99784 (907) 638-3651.

SIMON, MARCEL (Pomo)
(tribal chairperson)
Affiliation: Middletown Rancheria, P.O. Box 1035,
Middletown, CA 95461 (707) 987-3670.

SIMON, MIKE (Sisseton Wahpeton Sioux)
(radio station manager)
Affiliation: KSWS - 89.3 FM, Sisseton Wahpeton Sioux
tribe, P.O. Box 268, Sisseton, SD 57262 (605) 698-7972.

SIMONE, JEROME J.
(health services director)
Affiliation: United Indian Health Services, P.O. Box 420,
Trinidad, CA 95570 (707) 677-3693.

SIMPSON, JR., H.B.
(BIA agency supt.)
Affiliation: Zuni Agency, Bureau of Indian Affairs,
P.O. Box 369, Zuni, NM 87327 (505) 782-5591.

SIMS, RUSSELL
(executive director)
Affiliation: Council of Three Rivers American Indian
Center, Rt. 2, Box 247-A, Dorseyville, PA 15238 (412)
782-4457.

SINCLAIR, ALFRED
(Indian band chief)
Affiliation: Washagamis Bay (McKenzie Portage) Indian Band, Box 625, Keewatin, Ontario, Canada P0X
1C0 (807) 543-2532.

SINCLAIR, WENDELL
(Indian band chief)
Affiliation: Brokenhead Ojibway Nation, Scanterbury,
Manitoba, Canada R0E 1Wo (204) 766-2494.

SINCLAIR, WILLIAM
(BIA officer)
Address & Affiliation: Director of Office of Self
Governance, Bureau of Indian Affairs, Room 2550;
MS: 2548-MIB, 1849 C St., NW, Washington, DC
20240 (202) 219-0240.

SINEWAY, CARLA
(Indian education program director)
Affiliation: Mt. Pleasant Public Schools, Saginaw
Chippewa Education Dept., 770 E. Broadway, Mt.
Pleasant, MI 48858 (517) 775-3672 Fax 772-0672.

SINQUAH, ALBERT T.
(school principal)
Affiliation: Keams Canyon Boarding School, P.O. Box
397, Keams Canyon, AZ 86034 (520) 738-2385 Fax
738-2385.

SINOWAY, DOUG
(Indian band chief)
Affiliation: Whitesand Indian Band, Box 68,
Armstrong, Ontario, Canada P0T 1A0 (807) 583-2177.

SINYELLA, WAYNE (Havasupai)
(tribal chairperson)
Affiliation: Havasupai Tribal Council,
P.O. Box 10, Supai, AZ 86435 (520) 448-2961.

SIOUI, RICHARD HENRY (Huron) 1937-
(chemical engineer)
Born September 25, 1937, Brooklyn, N.Y. *Education*:
Northeastern University, BS, 1964; University of Massachusetts, PhD, 1968; Worcester Polytechnic Institute, Graduate in 1976 of School of Industrial Management; 1986 Graduate of the Tuck Executive Program at Dartmouth College. *Principal occupation*:
Chemical engineer. *Home address*: 22 Streeter Rd.,
Hubbardston, MA 01452 (508) 795-5507 (work); E-Mail: tsi8i@aol.com. *Affiliation*: Norton Co.,
Superabrasives Division, Worcester, MA, 1968- (se-

nior research engineer, 1968-71; research supervisor, 1971-78; technical manager, 1978-83; research director, 1983-87, director of technology, 1987-present). *Other professional post*: Member of Safety, Standards & Health Committee, Diamond Wheel Manufacturers Institute, 1994-present). *Military service*: U.S. Air Force, 1955-59. *Community activities*: Committee chairperson, Boy Scouts of America, Holden, MA, 1981-86. *Memberships*: American Institute of Chemical Engineers; American Indian Science and Engineering Society; Sigma Xi Research Society; Tau Beta Pi Engineering Society. *Awards, honors*: Outstanding Engineering Alumnus (1995), University of Massachusetts. *Interests*: "Expert in the qualification and application of industrial diamond. Numerous U.S. and foreign patents relative to the manufacture and composition of abrasive products in which diamond or cubic boron nitride is the abrasive."

SIQUIEROS, NINA (Tohono O'Odham)
(BIA supt.)
Affiliation: Papago Agency, Bureau of Indian Affairs, P.O. Box 578, Sells, AZ 85634 (520) 383-3286 Fax 383-2087.

SISCO, DENNIS
(BIA agency supt.)
Affiliation: Miami Agency, Bureau of Indian Affairs, P.O. Box 391, Miami, OK 74355 (918) 542-3396 Fax 542-7202.

SISCO, MICHAEL (Yokut)
(rancheria chairperson)
Affiliation: Santa Rosa Rancheria, P.O. Box 8, Lemoore, CA 93245 (559) 924-1278.

SISK, CALEEN
(Indian education center director)
Affiliation: Director, Four Winds of Indian Education, 1388 Longfellow, Suite M, Chico, CA 95926 (916) 895-4212 Fax 895-6569. E-mail: csisk@csu.oa.vax.edu.

SISTO, EARL DEAN (San Carlos Apache)
(education, artist)
Address & Affiliation: Native American Student Programs, 224 Costo Hall, University of California, Riverside, CA 92521, 1977-present (909) 787-4143 Fax 787-2221; *E-Mail*: sisto@ucracl.ucr.edu. *Other professional post*: Na Chee, 1995-present. *Community activities*: San Bernardino/Riverside American Indian Council.

SKAGGS, JOANNE
(center director)
Affiliation: Haskell Indian Health Center, 2415 Massachusetts Ave., Lawrence, KS 66044 (913) 843-3750.

SKEETER, ANDREW (Yuchi)
(tribal chairperson)
Address & Affiliation: Yuchi Tribe, P.O. Box 10, Sapulpa, OK 74067 (918) 224-3605 Fax 224-3140.

SKEETER, CARMELITA
(executive director)
Affiliation: Tulsa Urban Health Clinic, Indian Health Care Resource Center of Tulsa, 550 S. Peoria Ave., Tulsa, OK 74120 (918) 582-7230.

SKENANDORE, FRANCIS R.
(attorney)
Affiliation: Oneida Tribe, P.O. Box 129, Oneida, WI 54155; Associate Justice, Prairie Band Potawatomi Nation Appelate Court, 15498 K Rd., Mayetta, KS 66509 (866) 966-2242 or (785) 966-2242 Fax 966-2662. E-mail: tribalcourt@pbpnation.org.

SKENANDORE, JUDY (Oneida)
(health center director)
Affiliation: Oneida Comunity Health Center, P.O. Box 365, Oneida, WI 54155 (414) 869-2711.

SKENANDORE, KEVIN (Navajo)
(BIA education administrator)
Affiliation: Northern Pueblos Agency, Bureau of Indian Affairs, P.O. Box 4269, Fairview Station, Espanola, NM 87533 (505) 753-1465 Fax 753-1475.

SKENANDORE, PAUL A. (Shenandoah) (Scan doa) (Oneida) 1939-
(editor/publisher, bookstore owner)
Born January 21, 1939, Kaukauna, Wisc. *Education*: High school. *Principal occupation*: Editor/publisher, bookstore owner. *Home address*: 736 W. Oklahoma St., Appleton, WI 54914 (414) 832-9525 (office). *Affiliations*: Editor/publisher of "Shenandoah," the monthly Oneida newsletter, 1973-; owner/operator, Shenandoah Bookstore, Appleton, WI, 1983-. *Military service*: U.S. Army, 1962-1964 (E-4 Sergeant). *Interests*: "To educate Native peoples on their rights as independent nations and peoples; to educate all peoples of the world on the spiritual existence of all societies and our responsibility to said; to take the U.S. (Government) to World Court and charging them with trespass and genocide, and to have aboriginal nations assume their correct place on Great Turtle Island." *Published works*: Newsletter - Shenandoah; and other native newsletters. I have written by the name of Skenandoah, Shenandoah, or Scan doa."

SKIBINE, ALEX TALLCHIEF (Osage)
(attorney)
Affiliation: University of Utah College of Law, Salt Lake City, UT 84112 (801) 581-4177. *Membership*: Native American Bar Association (secretary).

SKIBINE, GEORGE (Osage)
(BIA office director)
Affiliation: Bureau of Indian Affairs, Officeof Indian Gaming Management Staff, MS:2070-MIB, 1849 C St., NW, Washington, DC 20240 (202) 219-4066.

SKYE, HARRIETT (Marphia Tko-Blue Sky) (Standing Rock Sioux) 1931-
(scholarship coordinator)
Born December 6, 1931, Rosebud, S.D. *Education*: Northern Virginia Community College, AA (cum laude), 1991; New York University, BA (cum laude) (Film & Television Production), 1993, MA, 1995. *Principal occupation*: Scholarship coordinator. *Affiliations*: Producer, director, moderator, "Indian Country Today" Television Show, KFYR-TV Channel 5, Bismarck, ND (12 years); Scholarship coordinator (part time), Association on American Indian Affairs, New York, NY, 1991-95. *Community activities*: North Dakota Social Services Board of Directors (secretary-6 years); North Dakota Advisory Committee to the U.S. Civil Rights Commission (board member & chairperson-8 years). *Memberships*: Talking Circle; New York University Alumni Association *Awards, honors*: "Outstanding Adult Learner of the Year, 1991, Northern Virginia Community College; Pioneer Award from Native American Association; 1993 Key Pin Award, Outstanding Scholastic Achievement & Honors Scholar, New York University; Wind & Glacier Voices Filmmakers Award for 27-minute documentary, "The Right to Be (May, 1994); The Distinguished Recent Alumni Award, NYU, in recognition of contributions as an advocate of the rights & culture of Native Americans, 1994; United Nations Environmental Programme Award, (UNEP), 1994. *Interests*: "I completed "The Right To Be," a documentary film in Jan. 1994, which was premiered at Sundance Film Festival, Park City, UT. In a collaborative effort, we just completed a one-minute Public Service Announcement for the Association on American Indian Affairs. Throughout the years, I have traveled and lived on many Indian reservations. I have always found this experience to be exciting and extremely stimulating for this reason. The reservations I have lived on were cultures that were ageless. Many still have practices and belief systems that are intact despite cultural genocide & interference from outside sources." *Biographical source*: The Greeter, "Harriett Skye - The Voice of North Dakota Indians." *Published work*: The Legacy of Indian Women (Dickinson Press, 1982).

SKYHAWK, SONNY
(executive director)
Affiliation: American Indians in Film, 65 N. Alien Ave., Suite 105, Pasadena, CA 91106 (818) 578-0344.

SKYWATER, HENRY
(Indian band chief)
Affiliation: Birdtail Sioux Indian Band, Box 22, Beulah, Manitoba, Canada R0M 0B0 (204) 568-4540.

SLACK, JOAN
(health director)
Affiliation: Red Cliff Health Services, P.O. Box 529, Bayfield, WI 54814 (715) 779-5801.

SLADE, LYNN H. 1948-
(attorney)
Born January 29, 1948, Santa Fe, N.M. *Education*: University of New Mexico, BA, 1973, Law School, JD, 1976. *Principal occupation*: Attorney with substantial experience in American Indian law. *Address*: P.O. Box 2168, Albuquerque, NM 87103 (505) 848-1800. *Community activities*: Chairperson, Committee on Native American Natural Resources, American Bar Association, 1991-92. *Memberships*: American Bar Association; American Indian Bar Association; State Bar of New Mexico (Natural Resource Section Chair); Indian Law Section (Board of Directors). *Awards, honors*: Best Lawyers in America, 1989-90, 1991-92 Editions. *Interests*: "Representation of businesses doing business on Indian lands; litigation and advice concerning Indian law and Indian lands law." *Published work*: article, "Coal Surface Mining on Indian Lands: Checkerboard or Crazy Quilt," (Rocky Mountain Mineral Law Foundation, 1989); article, "Puzzling Powers: Overlapping Jurisdictions of Indian Tribes, the Federal, State, and Local Governments in Development of Natural Resources in Indian Country," (42 Rocky Mountain Mineral Law Inst. 11-1 (1996).

SLICKPOO, ALLEN P., Sr. (Nez Perce-Walla Walla-Cayuse) 1929-
(administration; tribal councilman)
Born May 5, 1929, Slickpoo Mission, Culdesac, Idaho. *Education*: Chemawa Indian School, 1945-48; University of Idaho, 1953-55. *Principal occupation*: Tribal historian, councilman, administrator, Nez Perce Tribal Executive Committee, Lapwai, Idaho. *Home address*: 809 Nez Perce Lane, Box 311, Kamiah, ID 83536 (208) 843-2253 (work). *Affiliation*: Nez Perce Tribe, Lapwai, ID, 1955- (chairperson, General Council, 1961-63, 1986-88; chairperson, Resolutions Committee, 1988-89; secretary, vice-chairperson, and chairperson, Executive Committee, 1955-86). *Other professional posts*: Tribal historian and cultural consultant; consultant to the Northwest Regional Educational Laboratory on Indian education and curriculum; consultant to documentary movies including, "I'll Fight No More Forever" about Nez Perce War of 1877, etc. *Military service*: U.S. Army, 1948-1952 (Japanese Occupation/Korea/UN Service). *Community activities*: Served on the Governor's Indian Advisory Council, Idaho; Veterans of Foreign Wars (Kamiah, Idaho); 2nd Presbyterian Church of Kamiah; Mat'alym'a (Up-river Nez Perce) Culture Club. *Awards, honors*: Outstanding Achievement Award, Indian Child Welfare, 1983; Governor of Idaho Award for Promoter of the Week, 1961. *Interests*: "Have traveled to Mexico City and Canada to participate and/or speak at conference relating to the Indian of North America; also to Tokyo, Japan, to lecture on Native American history and culture; bilingual/bicultural activities; consultant on historical and cultural concerns (recognized as authority on the history and culture of the Nez Perce people); have lectured at major institutions, including Newberry Library, Chicago, University of Colorado, Oregon State University, Dartmouth College, University of Washington, Navajo Community College, etc.; has lectured in public schools, to students and organizations relative to American Indian history, culture, government, education, and economic status; has been a reader and/or panelist for the National Endowment for the Humanities; have participated on many panels, workshops, and conferences. Advocate to promote tribally-sponsored projects relating to the preservation of the knowledge and identity of the Nez Perce history and culture; developing plans for tribal archives." *Published works*: NuMeePoom Tit-Wah-tit (Pruitt Press, 1973); Noon Nee MePoo (Pruitt Press, 1974); Nez Perce Attitude Toward the Missionary Experience (Pruitt Press, 1987); wrote a paper for the Northwest Quarterly on Anthropology, relating to Indian fishing rights controversy; articles for World Book Encyclopedia, 1983-.

SMAGGE, RITA
(executive director)
Affiliation: Kenaitze Indian Tribe Health Center, P.O. Box 988, Kenai, AK 99611 (907) 283-3633.

SMALL, JERRI (Northern Cheyenne)
(tribal president)
Affiliation: Northern Cheyenne Tribal Council, P.O. Box 128, Lame Deer, MT 59043 (406) 477-6284.

SMART, JOSEPH (Eskimo)
(village president)
Affiliation: Native Village of Hooper Bay, P.O. Box 2193, Hooper Bay, AK 99604 (907) 758-4915.

SMARTT, DENNIS (Shoshone-Paiute)
(tribal council chairperson)
Affiliation: Fort McDermitt Tribal Council, P.O. Box 457, McDermitt, NV 89421 (702) 532-8259.

SMILEY-MARQUEZ, CAROLYNA
(San Juan Pueblo) 1946-
(consultant)
Born in 1946 in N.M. *Education*: Indiana University, BA, 1973, MA, 1974; University of Colorado, PhD (Social and Multicultural Foundations of Education), 1985. *Principal occupation*: Consultant. *Address*: P.O. Box 211, Hygiene, CO 80533 (303) 772-1714; E-Mail: carolyna@uconsultus.com. *Affiliations*: New Mexico State Dept. of Education (Cross Cultural, Title IX Education Specialist), 1974-79; Washington State University (Minority Recruitment Officer, Interim Assistant Director, Instructor-Bilingual Education Institute), 1976-81; University of Colorado, Health Sciences Center (Chief Curriculum Development Liaison, 1981-83; Director for Affirmative Action and Coordinator for Staff Development and Guest Relation, 1986-90); , University of Colorado (Instructor & Lecturer), 1982-; professional consultant, C. Smiley-Marquez, dba, Smiley & Co., 1988-. *Other professional posts*: Adjunct professor, University of Northern Colorado, Greeley, 1992-. *Community activities*: Hope for the Children, Kempe National Center for the Prevention and Treatment to Child Abuse and Neglect (board member). *Awards, honors*: Outstanding Young Women of America, 1982-84; Outstanding Young Women in Colorado, 1986; President's Award, EEO/Affirmative Action Coalition (Regional Professional Association), 1991. *Membership*: National Association for Human Rights Workers (board member , 1988-90). *Biographical source*: Directory of American Indian & Native American Women, 1985-. *Published works*: Monographs, brochures & bibliographies published by the State Dept. of Education, State of New Mexico, 1975-80. Videotapes: Pieces of Life - Profiles of Minority Women in Longmont (documentary), 1982; New Indian Wars (documentary of the conflict for American Indians and those seeking rights over natural resources on reservations), 1983; Storyteller (video presenting Anah Nahtanaba, American Indian Storyteller maker in the tradition of the Cochiti), 1985; Know It When You See It: Sexual Harassment for Supervisors and Managers and the Rights and Responsibilities of Employees (sexual harassment training), 1986; Cultural Awareness: Introduction, 1990; Mentoring: Special Issues of Women and Minorities in Organizations, 1990. Education training kits: Diversity Training Kit for Managers and Employees, and Diversity Training for Law Enforcement Officers.

SMITH, ANN
(Indian band chief)
Affiliation: Kwanlin Dun Indian Band, 154 Tlingit St., Whitehorse, Yukon, Canada Y1A 2Z1 (403) 667-6465.

SMITH, ARCHIE C.
(site manager)
Affiliation: Town Creek Indian Mound State Historic Site, Route 3, Box 50, Mt. Gilead, NC 27306 (919) 439-6802.

SMITH, BEVERLY S. (Choctaw)
(tribal chief)
Affiliation: Jena Band of Choctaw Indians, P.O. Box 14, Jena, LA 71342 (318) 992-2717.

SMITH, BOB A. (Chickasaw)
(attorney)
Affiliation: Oklahoma Indian Bar Association, P.O. Box 1062, Oklahoma City, OK 73101 (405) 521-5277.

SMITH, BRAD (Shinnecock)
(tribal trustee)
Affiliation: Shinnecock Tribe, P.O. Box 59, Southampton, NY 11968 (516) 283-1643.

SMITH, CALVIN H., Sr. (Kashia Pomo)
(rancheria chairperson)
Affiliation: Kashia Business Committee, Stewarts Point Rancheria, P.O. Box 3854, Stewarts Point, CA 95480 (707) 725-0721.

SMITH, CURT
(health center director)
Affiliation: Rocky Boy's PHS Indian Health Center, Rocky Boy Rt., P.O. Box 664, Box Elder, MT 59521 (406) 395-4489.

SMITH, CARLTON R. *(Shanak'w Uwaa)*
(Tlingit) 1950-
(associate broker of real estate)
Born June 22, 1950, Seattle, Wash. *Education*: Stanford University, BA, 1973. *Principal occupation*: Associate broker of real estate. *Home address*: P.O. Box 33765, Juneau, AK 99803. *Affiliations*: Associate broker, Re-Max Properties, Inc., Anchorage, AK 1985-93; associate broker, Bond, Stephens & Johnson, Inc., Anchorage, 1993-. *Other professional posts*: Vice president, secretary/treasurer & trustee, Sealaska Heritage Foundation; director, Sealaska Corp. (An Alaska Regional for Profit Corp.) *Community activities*: Statewide co-chairperson of the Alaska Native Hire Network, sponsored by the Federal Executive Association founding officer, Alaska Association of Alaska Native Real Estate Professionals. *Memberships*: National Association of Realtors; Anchorage, Board of Realtors; Commonwealth North, Inc.; Certified Commercial Investment Managers Association. *Awards, honors*: American Academy of Achievement, 1969; Re-Max Executive Club; Re-Max International, 1987-89. This designation places individuals in the top 1% of Real Estate Professionals nationwide with an excess of $2 million in sales per year. *Interests*: "My principal interest outside of developing my own brokerage business is corporate fund-raising in the area of scholarships for Native American students. At present, I am working with other trustees to build a $3.2 million endowment for our 501(C) (3) to a $10 million fund by the year 2000." *Published work*: Local Government Encyclopedia (State of Alaska, 1979).

SMITH, CHADWICK *(Ugisata - Corntassel)*
(Oklahoma Cherokee) 1950-
(principal chief)
Born December 17, 1950, Pontiac, Mich. *Education*: University of Georgia, BA (Education), 1973; University of Wisconsin, Madison, MS, 1975; University of Tulsa Law School, JD, 1980. *Principal occupation*: Attorney. *Address*: Cherokee Nation, P.O. Box 948, Tahlequah, OK 74465 (918) 456-0671; in OK (800) 256-0671. E-mail: csmith@cherokee.org. *Affiliations*: Private practice, Tulsa, OK, 1982-; Cherokee Nation, Tahlequah, OK (director of tribal planning, legal historian, tribal attorney, prosecutor, director of justice and advisor to the tribal tax commission, 1984-99; principal chief, 1999-present). *Other professional posts*: Speaker, educator and constitutional scholar; taught college courses in Indian law and history around the country including Indian law as a visiting professor at Dartmouth College. *Memberships*: Oklahoma Bar Association; American Bar Association; 10th Circuit Federal District Court; Cherokee Nation; Creek Nation. *Interests*: Indian law; Cherokee legal history. *Published works*: Cherokee Nation Course Work (Cherokee Nation Press, 1993); Cherokee Case Book (Cherokee Nation Press, 1993).

SMITH, CHARLES E.
(museum manager)
Affiliation: Syms-Eaton Museum, 418 W. Mercury Blvd., Hampton, VA 23666 (804) 727-6248.

SMITH, CRAIG (Chippewa)
(member-board of directors)
Affiliation: Intertribal Christian Communications, P.O. Box 3765, Station B, Winnipeg, Manitoba, Canada R2W 3R6 (204) 661-9333.

SMITH, DENNIS J. (Assiniboine) 1950-
(educator)
Born July 23, 1950, Helena, Mont. *Education*: Montana State University, B.S., 1972; University of Iowa, Certificate Physical Therapy), 1974; University of Montana, M.A., 1983. *Principal occupation*: Educator. *Home address*: 3134 Virginia St., Sioux City, IA 51104

(712) 274-5105 Fax 274-5101; E-Mail: djs001@alpha.morningside.edu. *Affiliations*: Instructor/Dean of Instruction, Fort Peck Community College, Poplar, MT, 1981-85; director of Indian Studies, Morningside College, Sioux City, IA, 1989-. *Community activities*: Guest speaker on tribal cultures, Sioux City and surrounding area. *Membership*: National Indian Education Association; Western Historical Association. *Interests*: "Indian issues (contemporary), national political affairs, environmental issues - particularly energy related impacts; travelled through U.S., Canada, Mexico, Europe & Japan."

SMITH, DON
(health director)
Affiliation: Lac Courte Oreilles Tribal Clinic, Route 2, Box 2750, Hayward, WI 54843 (715) 634-4153.

SMITH, DON LELOOSKA (Cherokee) 1933-
(woodcarver)
Born August 31, 1933, Sonora, Calif. *Principal occupation*: Woodcarver. Resides in Ariel, Wash. *Affiliation*: Lecturer, dance programmer, Oregon Museum of Science & Industry. *Award*: Inter-Tribal Indian Ceremonial, Gallup, N.M., 1966. *Interests*: Woodcarving, Northwest Coast styles; Indian dance and drama; Indian music; various forms of Indian arts and crafts.

SMITH, EDWARD (Chemehuevi)
(tribal chairperson)
Affiliation: Chemehuevi Reservation, P.O. Box 1976, Havasu lake, CA 92363 (760) 858-4301.

SMITH, FAITH (Chippewa)
(college president)
Affiliation: President, NAES (Native American Educational Services) College, 2838 W. Peterson Ave., Chicago, IL 60659 (773) 761-5000 Fax 761-3808. *Other professional posts*: Chairperson, Native American Public Telecommunications, Lincoln, NE; editor, "Inter-Com Newsletter, NAES College, Chicago, IL.

SMITH, GRACE A. (Muscogee Creek)
(adjunct professor of flute; musician/composer)
Affiliation: Adjunct professor of flute, Dept. of Music, University of Central Oklahoma, Edmond, OK, 1993-present. *Community activities*: Henderson Hills Baptist Church Orchestra; Oklahoma Iris Society. *Memberships*: National Flute Association; Oklahoma Flute Society; Edmond Sigma Alpha Iota Alumnae. *Published compositions*: "Whisper on the Land" for flute & piano (Medici Music Press) included in the National Flute Association Collection at the University of Arizona's Library & the "New Plains Review," University of Central Oklahoma, 1986; "A Distant Dream" for flute & piano (Harmon Richard Music) included in the Contemporary Anthology of Music by Women (Indiana University Press, 1996); "Legende" for alto flute (Harmon Richard Music) included in "New Plains Review," University of Central Oklahoma, 1989.

SMITH, GREGG
(association president)
Affiliation: Indian Association of Alberta, 11630 Kingsway Ave., Edmonton, Alberta, Canada T5G 0X5 (403) 452-4330.

SMITH, JAMES M.
(village president)
Affiliation: Native Village of Goodnews Bay, P.O. Box 3, Goodnews Bay, AK 99589 (907) 697-8629.

SMITH, JANE M. (Colville) 1954-
(court administrator/magistrate)
Born April 9, 1954, Colville, Wash. *Education*: Inchelium High School, WA, 1972; University of Washington (2 years). *Principal occupation*: Tribal court administrator. *Home address*: P.O. Box 665, Nespelem, WA 99155 (509) 634-8846 Fax 634-8566 (office). *Affiliation*: Colville Tribal Court, Nespelem, WA, 1981-. *Other professional posts*: Instructor with DCI out of Albuquerque, NM, 1993-; Chairperson, CCT Safety Committee, 1990-91; member, Joint Safety Committee, 1990-91. *Military service*: U.S. Naval Reserve (Legalman Second Class),1987-91). *Community activities*: On committee that designed and contributed photos for the "Time for Gathering" exhibit honoring Indian tribes in the State of Washington for Centennial in 1989; junior rodeo timer; tribal exhibit

committee; University of Washington museum exhibit. *Membership*: Women's International Bowling Congress, 1977-; Women of the Moose, 1985-; National Indian Court Clerks' Association (president, 1986-88; member, 1985-); Fraternal Order of Eagles Auxiliary, 1987-. *Interests*: "On team which evaluated the Hopi Tribal Court in November, 1991. Traveled to the Hopi Reservation, interviewed tribal members and staff, made an evaluation with recommendations. It was very interesting to see the differences and similarities between the Hopi and the Colville Tribal Courts. Photography is my first love. I Take extensive outdoor and recreational pictures. I love to fish and hike. I enjoy watching most sports. I'm very interested in wildlife matters and concerns. I read extensively and have a large private library."

SMITH, JANET "NANCY" (Cherokee)
(artist; art studio owner)
Affiliation: Turtle Woman Studio, 1106 SE 7th St., Wagoner, OK 74467 (918) 485-5878. *Products*: Traditional and contemporary Cherokee water colors, original oils and acrylics paintings.

SMITH, JEFF
(association president)
Affiliation: HONOR, Inc., 6435 Wiesner Rd., Omro, WI 54963 (414) 582-7142.

SMITH, JOEL D.
(BIA agency supt.)
Affiliation: Minnesota Agency, Bureau of Indian Affairs, Federal Bldg., Rm. 418, 522 Minnesota Ave., NW, Bemidji, MN 56633 (218) 751-2011 Fax 751-4367.

SMITH, JOSEPH
(health systems administrator)
Affiliation: Kyle PHS Indian Health Center, P.O. Box 540, Kyle, SD 57752 (605) 455-2451.

SMITH, KATHERIN JANE *(Laughing Water)* **1916-**
(librarian)
Born October 11, 1916, Saugatuck, Conn. *Education*: Wells College (Aurora, NY), BA, 1938. *Principal occupation*: Librarian. *Home address*: 3530 Schrock St., Sarasota, FL 34239 (813) 365-6054. *Affiliations*: Librarian/contract coordinator, McDonnell Douglas Corp., St. Louis, MO (12 years); St. Louis County Library, St. Louis, MO (8 years); research associate, Johnson O'Connor Research Foundation. *Community activities*: Elected Elder, Southeastern Cherokee Confederacy (SCCI). *Membership*: Phi Beta Kappa, 1938-. *Interests*: "Researching Native American (especially Cherokee) history, customs & genealogy for the SCCI, building its library & assisting and participating, as possible; gardening, travel (three trips to Yucatan, one to Guatemala and Peru), reading, archaeology, aircraft engineering & development, civic affairs."

SMITH, KENT
(Indian studies program director)
Affiliation: Indian Studies Program, Bemidji State University, 1500 Birchmont Dr. NE, Bemidji, MN 56601 (218) 755-3977.

SMITH, LaMARR
(museum director)
Affiliation: Memorial Indian Museum, P.O. Box 483, Broken Bow, OK 74728 (405) 584-6531.

SMITH, LESLIE
(school principal)
Affiliation: Kipnuk Day School, Kipnuk, AK 99614 (907) 896-5513.

SMITH, LEONARD (Quapaw)
(tribal chairperson)
Affiliation: Quapaw Tribal Business Committee, P.O. Box 765, Quapaw, OK 74363 (918) 542-1853.

SMITH, MARLENE
(director-Indian group)
Affiliation: Indian Choir, Bacone College, Muskogee, OK 74401 (918) 683-4581.

SMITH, MARY HILDERMAN
(museum director)
Affiliation: Marin Miwok, P.O. Box 864, Novato, CA 94947 (510) 897-4064.

SMITH, MELANIE M. (Dakota (Santee)-Mdewankanton Band) 1943-
(alcohol/drug program director)
Born August 17, 1943, Wisconsin Rapids, Wisc. *Education*: Blackhawk College (Moline, IL), 1972-74. *Principal occupation*: Alcohol/drug program director. *Home address*: 2350 Wallace Rd. NW, Salem, OR 97304 (503) 585-0564 Fax 585-3302 (work); E-Mail: tahana@open.org. *Affiliations*: Director, Tahana Whitecrow Foundation, Salem, OR, 1987-; Mid-Willamette Behavioral Care Network, Salem, OR, 1995-. *Community activities*: Prach sustainable development; client advocate; sustainable development; POW/MIA Float - Albany Vets Day Parade; member, Ladies Auxiliary Military Order of Purple Heart. *Memberships*: American Correctional Association; National Alcohol/Drug Counselors Association; AARP; Salem Chamber of Commerce; Greater Area Veterans Association; Native American Counselor II. *Interests*: Journalism, grant writing, substance abuse. *Published works*: Reflections; The Wall.

SMITH, MICHAEL
(resource centre chairperson)
Affiliation: Yukon Indian Cultural-Education Society Resource Centre, Council of Yukon Indians, 22 Bisutlin Dr., Whitehorse, Yukon, Canada Y1A 3S5 (403) 667-7631.

SMITH, MICHAEL
(institute director)
Affiliation: American Indian Film Institute, 333 Valencia St., Suite 322, San Francisco, CA 94103 (415) 554-0525 Fax 554-0542.

SMITH, MICHAEL R.
(BIA regional director)
Affiliation: Eastern Oklahoma Regional Office, Bureau of Indian Affairs, 101 N. 5th St., Muskogee, OK 74401 (918) 687-2296 Fax 687-2571.

SMITH, MONA
(Native American film producer)
Address: 2116 16th Ave., So., Minneapolis, MN 55404 (612) 872-7886.

SMITH, NOREEN
(family services director)
Affiliation: Indian Health Board of Minneapolis, 1315 East 24th St., Minneapolis, MN 55404 (612) 721-7425.

SMITH, PAUL
(BIA agency supt.)
Affiliation: Pima Agency, Bureau of Indian Affairs, P.O. Box 8, Sacaton, AZ 85247 (520) 562-3326.

SMITH, RAY (Chippewa)
(board member)
Affiliation: Member, Board of Directors, Intertribal Christian Comunications, P.O. Box 3765, Station B, Winnipeg, Manitoba, Canada R2W 3R6 (204) 661-9333.

SMITH, RAYMOND R. (Navajo)
(Navajo tribal enterprise manager)
Affiliation: Navajo Arts & Crafts Enterprise, P.O. Box 160, Window Rock, AZ 86515 (520) 871- 4090 Fax 871-3340.

SMITH, RICK J.
(Indian center director)
Affiliation: American Indian Learning Resource Center, University of Minnesota, Duluth, 114 Cina Hall, 10 University Dr., Duluth, MN 55812 (218) 726-6379.

SMITH, ROBERT (Cupa)
(tribal chairperson)
Affiliation: Pala Band of Mission Indians, P.O. Box 50, Pala, CA 92059 (760) 742-3784.

SMITH, ROSE MARY
(school director)
Affiliation: Pinon Dormitory, P.O. Box 159, Pinon, AZ 86510 (520) 725-3250.

SMITH, SHEILA S. (Oneida of Wisconsin) 1962-
(artist)
Born September 19, 1962, Green Bay, Wisc. *Education*: University of Wisconsin, La Crosse. *Principal*

occupation: Artist. *Address & Affiliation*: Volunteer, Oneida (WI) Nation Museum, 1980-. *Awards, honors*: 1st Place, University of Wisconsin, Stevens Point, 1985 Woodlands Indian Arts Festival; proclaimed a master of my art by the U.S. Dept. of the Interior and the Wisconsin Arts Board. *Interests*: "I have brought back the last art of the Iroquois costume designs. I have sold four costumes to the U.S. Dept. of the Interior for their permanent collection of Indian artifacts. I had two costumes worn during President Reagan's Inaugural Festivities. I was also a selected artist from Wisconsin to be videotaped and exhibited by the National Endowment of the Arts and Wisconsin Arts Council as a national traveling exhibit. I have also had a cover of the Stevens Point Magazine published in Stevens Point, Wisconsin."

SMITH, THEODORE, SR. (Yavapal Apache)
(spiritual leader)
Affiliation: Yavapai-Apache Tribe, 2400 W. Datsi, Camp Verde, AZ 86322 (520) 567-3649. *Past professional post*: Former chairperson, Yavapai-Apache Tribal Council, Camp Verde, AZ.

SMITH, WILLIAM C. (Red Bear) (Cherokee) 1923-
(retired aeronautical engineer)
Born March 30, 1923, Ada, Okla. *Education*: University of Missouri, St. Louis, EE, 1962. *Principal occupation*: Aeronautical engineer (retired). *Home address*: 1400 Montego, Apt. 440, Walnut Creek, CA 94598. *Affiliation*: McDonnell Douglas Corp., St. Louis, MO (production supervisor-aircraft, 1941-64, engineer, 1964-79). *Community activities*: United National Association, Florida Division (newsletter editor, 1987-90; vice president, 1979-); Southeastern Cherokee Confederacy, 1971- (band chief, 1981-4; assistant principal chief, 1985-91; principal chief, 1991-93; assistant principal chief, 1993-).

SMITMAN, GREG
(executive director)
Affiliation: Intertribal Agricultural Council, 100 North 27th St., Suite 500, Billings, MT 59101 (406) 259-3525.

SMOKE, BARBARA (Mohawk)
(Indian center director)
Affiliation: Rochester City School Dostrict, Native American Resource Center, 200 University Ave., Rochester, NY 14605 (716) 262-8970 Fax 262-8963.

SMOKE, EDWARD (St. Regis Mohawk)
(former tribal chief)
Affiliation: St. Regis Mohawk Council, Akwesasne Community Bldg., Rt. 37, Hogansburg, NY 13655 (518) 358-2272.

SMOKE, ERNIE
(Indian band chief)
Affiliation: Dakota Plains Tribal Council, Box 110, Portage La Prairie, MB, Canada R1N 3B2 (204) 252-2288.

SMOKE, HILDA (St. Regis Mohawk)
(tribal chief)
Affiliation: St. Regis Mohawk Indian Council, Akwesasne Community Bldg., Rt. 37, Box 8A, Hogansburg, NY 13655 (518) 358-2272.

SMOKER, KENNETH, JR. (Assiniboine-Sioux)
(health director)
Affiliation: Fort Peck PHS Indian Health Center, Poplar, MT 59255 (406) 768-3491.

SMOKEY, ANTHONY (Washoe)
(tribal chairperson)
Affiliation: Dresslerville Community Council, Washoe Tribe, 919 Hwy. 395 South, Gardnerville, NV 89410 (775) 883-1446.

SMOKEY, ROMAINE, Jr. (Washoe)
(former tribal chairperson)
Affiliation: Dresslerville Community Council, 1585 Watasheamu Rd., Gardnerville, NV 89410 (702) 265-5845.

SMUCK, HAROLD
(director/editor)
Affiliation: Associated Committee of Friends on Indian Affairs, P.O. Box 2326, Richmond, IN 47375 (317) 962-9169; editor, "Indian Progress."

SNAKE, ALFRED
(Indian band chief)
Affiliation: Young Chippewayan Indian Band, 409-19th St. E., Prince Albert, SK, Canada S6V 4A1 (306) 486-2326.

SNAKE, LAWRENCE F. (Delaware)
(tribal president)
Affiliation: Delaware Nation Executive Committee, P.O. Box 825, Anadarko, OK 73005 (405) 247-2448.

SNAKE, RICHARD
(Indian band chief)
Affiliation: Delaware of the Thames (Moraviantown) Indian Band, RR 3, Thamesville, Ontario, Canada N0P 2K0 (519) 692-3936.

SNAPP, HELEN (Shoshone)
(tribal chairperson)
Affiliation: Fort McDermitt Tribal Council, P.O. Box 457, McDermitt, NV 89421 (702) 532-8259.

SNEVE, SHIRLEY K. (Rosebud Sioux) 1956-
(education)
Born July 14, 1956, Rapid City, S.D. *Education*: South Dakota State University, BA, (Journalism) 1978; University of South Dakota & University of Massachusetts, Amherst (graduate work in public and arts administration), 1984-86. *Principal occupation*: Education. *Office address*: The Arts Extension Service, Contuing Education Bldg., University of Massachusetts, 358 N. Pleasant St., Amherst, MA 01003-9296 (413) 545-5240 Fax 577-3838. E-Mail: sksneve@yahoo.com. *Affiliations*: Minority Affairs Producer, South Dakota Public Broadcasting, Vermillion, SD, 1981-87; Executive director, Alliance of Tribal Tourism Advocates, a consortium of the nine tribes in South Dakota, 1995-97; contractual services for Native American Public Telecommunications, Lincoln NE, 1996-98; director, Visual Arts Center at the Washington Pavilion of Arts & Science, Sioux Falls, SD, 1998-2000; consultant services, Technical Assistance Consultant Group, South Dakotans for the Arts, Sioux Falls, SD, 2000-2001; director, Arts Extension Service, Amherst, MA, 2001-present. *Community activities*: Project director, Native Arts Planning Effort, funded by NEA Locals program, 1991-present. Native American Advisory Committees, State Historical Society, Pierre, SD, 1993, and Siouxland Heritage Museums, Sioux Falls, 1992-present; University of Massachusetts Fine Arts Center Strategic Planning Committee, 2001-present; Steering Committee, Western Massachusetts Arts Alliance, 2001-present; Five College Native American Studies Committee. *Memberships*: New England Region of University Continuing Education Association (vice president); The National Community Arts Network (vice president).

SNEVE, VIRGINIA DRIVING HAWK (Rosebud Sioux) 1933-
(guidance counselor, writer)
Born February 21, 1933, Rosebud, S.D. *Education*: South Dakota State University, BS, 1954, MEd, 1969. *Principal occupation*: Counselor-Indian students; writer. *Home address*: Unknown. *Affiliations*: Teacher-counselor, Flandreau Indian School, Flandreau, SD, 1966-70; editor, Brevet Press, Sioux Falls, SD, 1970-72; consultant, producer-writer, SD Public TV, Brooking, 1973-80; educational counselor, Flandreau Indian School, 1981-85; guidance counselor, Rapid City Central High School, 1986-present. *Other professional posts*: Part time English instructor, Oglala Community College, Rapid City Extension. *Community activities*: Rapid City Project 2,000 (drop out prevention coalition) Emanual Episcopal Church, Episcopal Diocese Commission on Racism. *Memberships*: SD Press Women (secretary, 1976-78); National Federation Press Women; SD Diocese of the Episcopal Church (historiographer, 1977-85); SD State University, Foundation Board, 1990-; enrolled member of Rosebud Sioux Tribe. *Awards, honors*: Council on Interracial Book Award for Jimmy Yellow Hawk, 1972; Western Writers of America Award for Betrayed, 1974; SDPress Woman of the Year, 1974; National Federation Press Alumnus Women, Achievement, 1974; Distinguished Alumnus Award, SD State University, 1974; Special Contribution to Education, SD Indian Education Association, 1975; Honorary Doctorate of Letters, Dakota Wesleyan University, 1979; Distinguished Contribution

to SD History, Dakota History Conference, 1982; 2nd Annual Native American Prose Award, University of Nebraska Press, 1992, for ms. "Completing the Circle. *Interests*: Indian education, art and literature. *Biographical source*: Who's Who of American Women. *Published works*: Jimmy Yellow Hawk (Holiday House, 1972); High Elk's Treasure (Holiday House, 1972); editor, South Dakota Geographic Names (Brevet Press, 1973); Betrayed (Holiday House, 1974); When Thunders Spoke (Holiday House, 1974); The Dakota's Heritage (Brevet Press, 1974); The Chichi Hoohoo Bogeyman, Ms. Sneve wrote the script for the screen play of the same title for the Vegetable Soup Children's TV series (Holiday House, 1975); They Led a Nation (Brevet Press, 1975); That They May Have Life: The Episcopal Church in South Dakota, 1859-1976 (Brevet Press, 1981); Dancing Teepees (Holiday House, 1989); The Navajos (Holiday House, 1993); When Thunders Spoke (University of Nebraska Press, 1993); The Nez Perce (Holiday House, 1994); The Seminoles (Holiday House, 1994); The Sioux (Holiday House, 1994); Completing the Circle (University of Nebraska Press, 1995); The Trickster and the Troll (University of Nebraska Press, 1997); Grandpa Was a Cowboy and an Indian & Other Stories (University of Nebraska Press, 2000); short stories & non-fiction articles.

SNIPP, C. MATTHEW
(program director)
Affiliation: American Indian Studies Program, University of Wisconsin, 1188 Educational Sciences, 1025 W. Johnson St., Madison, WI 53706 (608) 263-5501 Fax 263-6448.

SNOOKS, PAUL (Te-Moak Western Shoshone)
(tribal chairperson)
Affiliation: Battle Mountain Band Council, 35 Mountain View Dr., #138-13, Battle Mountain, NV 89820 (702) 635-2004.

SNOW, VIVIAN
(administrative officer-Indian hospital)
Affiliation: Omaha-Winnebago PHS Indian Hospital, Winnebago, NE 68071 (402) 878-2231.

SNYDER, BARRY (Seneca)
(tribal council president)
Affiliation: Seneca Nation Tribal Council, 1490 Rt. 438, Irving, NY 14081 (716) 532-4900.

SNYDER, MICHAEL C.
(executive director)
Affiliation: Oklahoma Indian Legal Services, Inc., Founders Tower, 5900 Mosteller Dr. #610, Oklahoma City, OK 73112 (800) 658-1497; (405) 840-5255 Fax 840-7060.

SOBOTTA, BOB
(coordinator, elementary & Indian education)
Address & Affiliation: Coordinator, Elementary & Indian Education, Idaho Dept. of Education, P.O. Box 83720, Boise, ID 83720-0027 (208) 332-6942 Fax 334-4664; E-Mail: bsobott@sde.state.id.us. *Past affiliations*: Supt.of Schools, Lapwai School District, Lapwai, ID; Assistant Supt. of Schools, Wapato School District, Wapato, WA.

SOCKYMA, MICHAEL C., SR.
(Mong-eu-ma-Young Corn) (Hopi) 1942-
(Hopi silver/gold smith)
Born June 4, 1942, Hotevilla, Ariz. *Education*: Phoenix Indian High School. *Principal occupation*: Hopi silver/gold smith. *Address*: P.O. Box 96, Kykotsmovi, AZ 86039 (928) 734-1050. *Affiliations*: Hopi Kiva Arts & Craft Shop (Sockyma's Hopicrafts),Kykotsmovi, AZ, 1975-. *Community activities*: Member of Hopi Tribal Council. *Awards, honors*: "(I) have won ribbons for jewelry at Jemez Indian Art Shows, and Gallup Indian Art Shows, New Mexico; Red Earth Art Craft Show, Oklahoma; Houston and Dallas Art Craft Shows, Texas; and Sedona, Arizona Art Craft Show." *Interests*: "35 years in making Hopi overlay jewelry in silver and gold; custom jewelry in precious stones; artist in oil and acrylic; specialize in both men and women concho belts; council member for the Hopi Tribe; active in traditional cultural activities." *Biographical source*: Government Directory of Indian Arts; Hopi Silver I & II, by Margaret Wright.

SOCKYMA, THEODORA (Hopi)
(store manager)
Affiliation: Sockyma's Hopicrafts, P.O. Box 96, Kykotsmovi, AZ 86039 (928) 734-6607 or 734-6667.

SOCTOMAH, DONALD (Passamaquoddy)
(tribal historian)
E-mail: soctomah@ainop.com. *Affiliation*: Historian, Passamaquoddy Tribe. *Past professional post*: Tribal representative in the Maine State Legislature for the Passamaquoddy Tribe. He has authored several books.

SOEDER, PAMELA (Muscogee Creek) 1953-
(associate professor)
Born December 8, 1953. *Education*: Mt. Senario College, BS, 1977; University of Wisconsin, MA, 1981, PhD, 1985. *Principal occupation*: Associate professor. *Address*: Slippery Rock University, Early Childhood Education Dept., 112 McKay Education Bldg., Slippery Rock, PA 16057 (412) 738-2864 Fax 738-2880; E-Mail: pamela.soeder@sru.edu. *Affiliations*: Madison Metropolitan School District, Madison, Wi (Elementary teacher, 1977-81; coordinator, American Indian Program, 1987-90); associate professor, Slippery Rock University, Slippery Rock, PA, 1990-present.

SOHOLT, DONALD (Stillaguamish)
(tribal chairperson)
Affiliation: Stillaguamish Board of Directors, P.O. Box 277, Arlington, WA 98223 (360) 652-7362.

SOLDIER, KENNETH
(Indian band chief)
Affiliation: Chiniki Group (Stoney) Indian Band, Box 40, Morley, Alberta, Canada T0L 1N0 (403) 881-3770.

SOLDIER, LARRY
(executive director-Indian centre)
Affiliation: Ma-Mow-We-Tak Friendship Centre, Inc., 122 Hemlock Crescent, Thompson, Manitoba, Canada R8N 0R6 (204) 778-7337.

SOLOMON, CORA NICHOLASA (NICKY)
(Victory Walker or War Path Woman)
(Winnebago of Nebraska) 1933-
(former national director , CHR program)
Born February 11, 1933, Winnebago, Neb. *Education*: High school. *Affiliation*: Former national director, Community Health Representatives (CHR)) Program, Indian Health Service, Rockville, MD, 1983-95. Mrs. Solomon was the first national director of the CHR program. *Home address*: P.O. Box 596, Winnebago, NE 68071 (402) 878-2521. *Other professional post*: Director, Winnebago Tribe of Nebraska Health Department; IHS Aberdeen Area Alcoholism Program Coordinator; Business Representative, Northwestern Bell Telephone Co.; former business partner in a trading post. *Community activities*: Former secretary, Winnebago Tribal Council; Winnebago Public School Board; Nebraska Indian Commission; Nebraska Indian Inter-Tribal Development Corporation; Goldenrod Hills Community Action Agency; Seven States Indian Health Association; American Indian Human Resource Center Board (Alcohol Program). *Membership*: National Association of Community Health Representatives; National Congress of American Indians. *Awards, honors*: Membership in the California Scholarship Federation; Woman Pioneer Award (social services) from the Governor of Nebraska, Charles Thone; awards received from the Lakota Health Association and the CHR organizations throughout Indian country. In 1994, the Office of Inspector General presented their "Integrity" Award for work done for the CHR program. Mrs. Solomon is the first person in the history of Indian Health Service to receive this award. *Interests*: "Since 1969, my interest and occupation has been in tribal health. The CHR program was the forerunner to the concept of Indian self-determination. Tribes began to provide services of CHRs through contractual agreements with IHS in 1968. Since that time, the CHRs have distinguished themselves as a different type of health care provider; they live in their communities and are on-call 24 hours a day, 365 days a year and are oftentimes the only health care provider immediately available in crisis situations. They are providers of health promotion and disease prevention services, as well as health care outreach workers, and are the epitome of commitment and dedication to serving

American Indians and Alaska Natives. I am proud to be a part of this great movement and become filled with emotion just thinking of the great sacrifices CHRs make on a daily basis." Co-authored paper, "A Population-Based Assessment of Alcohol Abuse Using a Community Panel."

SOLOMON, GLENN W. (Oklahoma Cherokee) 1945-
(professor of research)
Born in 1945, Ochelata, Okla. *Education*: University of Oklahoma, BA, 1967, MA, 1972; U of OK Health Sciences Center, MPH, 1981, PhD, 1990. *Principal occupation*: Professor of research. *Home address*: 1033 Leslie Lane, Norman, OK 73069 (405) 364-0308. *Affiliation*: University of Oklahoma Health Sciences Center, Dept. of Pediatrics, Adolescent Medicine, Oklahoma City, OK. *Other professional posts*: Editor, "Wassaja," (American Indian Historical Society, San Francisco, CA) the national newspaper of Indian America, 1971-86; founding member, Advisory Board, Jacobson Foundation for American Indian Art, Norman, OK, 1986-; health careers consultant, Northeastern State University, Tahlequah, OK, 1988-; Urban Indian Health Forum, Health Concerns, Oklahoma City, OK, 1990-; visiting assistant professor, University of Oklahoma, Human Relations, Norman, OK, 1992-. *Research activities*: Minority recruitment & retention policy development for State Regents of Higher Education & State Supt. of Instruction, 1971-; development of criteria & analysis of minority students in higher education including health professionals, 1971-; quality assurance for field aid stations - combat & non-combat conditions, U.S. Army Special Forces, Worldwide Multi-National Scope of Service, 1980-; cultural assessment in adolescent health behaviors, Oklahoma Youth Health Risks (funded), 1990-; women, infant & children nutritional program, State Health Dept., Wichita, Caddo, & Delaware WIC, Cherokee Nations, WIC, 1990-; Cherokee Nation baseline study of substance abuse (funded), Evaluator for Substance Abuse Program in Cherokee Nation, 1992-; Cheyenne & Arapaho Health Needs Assessment (funded), 1993-. *Community activities*: Advisor to Executive Council, American Indian Training & Employment Program, Oklahoma City, OK, 1980-; member, Board of Directors, Native American Center, Oklahoma City, 1978-81; member, Advisory Board, Central Tribes Health Manpower Project, IHS, Shawnee, OK, 1979-82; member, Advisory Board, State Dept. of Public Health, Child & Maternal Care, Oklahoma City, OK, 1979-85; Native American Center for Excellence, University of Oklahoma Health Sciences Center, College of Medicine, 1991-93; producer & host, American Indian Magazine (weekly television program), 1984-89; president, American Indian/Alaskan Native Staff & Faculty, University of Oklahoma Health Sciences Center, Oklahoma City, 1989-90; sponsor, American Indian Science & Engineering Students, University of Oklahoma, Health Sciences Center, 1989-91. *Membership*: National Indian Education Association (presidential search committee, 1988). *Awards, honors*: Public Health Fellow, University of Oklahoma Health Sciences Center, Oklahoma City, 1976-77; Fellowship, U.S. Office of Indian Education, 1977-80; Outstanding Staff & Faculty Award, American Indian Women's Association, University of Oklahoma, Norman, 1984; Oklahoma Human Rights Award, Oklahoma City, OK, 1986; American Indian Scholarships, Albuquerque, NM, 1988-90; Oklahoma State Regents of Higher Education, Minority Doctoral Scholar, Oklahoma City, OK, 1988-90; Major Bass Academic Scholarship, University of Oklahoma Health Sciences Center, Oklahoma City, 1988. *Published works*: The Odyssey of Wassaja: Carlos Montezuma, MD; First American Indian Physician (1972 master's thesis - University of Oklahoma), currently being revised for submission to a university press; "American Indian Studies: A Status Report," paper presented at the Organization of American Historians, New Orleans, LA, 1974; "American Indian Advocate for the Campus," National Indian Education Association, 1980; "Status of American Indian Studies & Students," National Indian Education Association, 1982; AIDS: Prevention for Life Saving, a 1 hour video, Ft. Bragg, ND, 1987; "Cultural Involvements & Substance Abuse of Oklahoma Cherokee Adolescents," American Federation for Clinical Research, Carmel, CA, 1993; editor, et al, "Complexities of Ethnicity Among Oklahoma Native Americans: Health Behaviors of Rural Adolescents," in The Culture of

Oklahoma (University of Oklahoma Press, 1993); "Nutritional Status of Obesity in Oklahoma Indians" (current).

SOOTKIS, RUBIE
(Native American film producer/writer)
Affiliation: Morning Star Productions, P.O. Box 671, Lame Deer, MT 59043 (406) 477-8315.

SORENSON, MARK
(school principal)
Affiliation: Little Singer Community School, Star Route, Box 239, Winslow, AZ 86047 (520) 774-7456.

SORENSON, TOM
(radio news director/host)
Affiliation: South Dakota Public Broadcasting, South Dakota Public Radio Network, P.O. Box 5000, Vermillion, SD 57069 (605) 677-5861.

SORENSON, WANDA
(school principal)
Affiliation: Chilchinbeto Day School, P.O. Box 547, Kayenta, AZ 86033 (520) 697-3448.

SORRELL, DARLENE A., DDS (Navajo)
(dentist)
Address: 704 Rio Vista Dr., Rio Rancho, NM 87144 (505) 892-3124. *Principal occupation*: Dentist. *Affiliations*: Clinical Director, Albuquerque Indian Health Service Dental Clinic, 1994-present; vice-president, Society of American Indian Dentists, 1991-present. *Military service*: Indian Health Service - Commissioned Officer, 1985-present). *Awards, honors*: First Navajo dentist. *Community activities*: High School Principal Selection Committee, 1996, Rio Rancho, NM, 1996; Board member of the Circle of Light, Navajo Educational Project, 2002-present. *Memberships*: American Dental Association (1985-present); Commissioned Officers Association (1985-present); Oregon Health Sciences, University Alumni Association, 1985-present); national Society of American Indian Dentists (1990-present); Association of Military Surgeons of the U.S. (1995-present); University of Arizona, American Indian Alumni Association (1997-present); North American Indian Women's Association (2000-present).

SOSNOWSKI, DANIEL
(school principal)
Affiliation: Beclabito Day School, P.O. Box 1146, Shiprock, NM 87420 (505) 656-3555.

SOTO, CYNTHIA
(Indian education program director)
Affiliation: Audubon Elementary School, Indian Education Program, 3500 N. Hoyne, Chicago, IL 60618 (773) 534-5709 Fax 534-5785.

SOTO, PETER
(tribal chairperson)
Affiliation: Cocopah Tribal Council, P.O. Bin G, Somerton, AZ 85350 (520) 627-2102.

SOUERS, TWILA
(association president; editor)
Affiliations: Editor, "Native News," School Dist. 4J Indian Education Program, 3411-A Willamette St., Eugene, OR 97405; Oregon Indian Education Association (president), 720 Nantucket, Eugene, OR 97404 (541) 687-3489.

SOUKUP, LEO
(BIA project supt.)
Affiliation: Navajo Irrigation Project, Bureau of Indian Affairs, New Energy Bldg., Room 103, Farmington, NM 87401 (505) 325-1864.

SOUTHARD, PEGGY ANN (DEE) (Starfire)
(United Lumbee) 1969-
(sociologist & anthropologist)
Education: Central Oregon Community College, AA, 1989; Southern Oregon State College, BA, 1991; University of Oregon, MS (Sociology), 1993, PhD (Sociology), 1997. *Dissertation*: "Looking for Sanctuary: Staying on Publicly-Owned Lands as a Response to Homelessness." *Address*: Unknown; *E-Mail*: southard@oregon.uoregon.edu. *Web site*: www.oregon.uoregon.edu/~southard/southard.htm. *Tribal affiliation*: Head Chief of the Beaver Clan of the

United Lumbee Nation. *Affiliations*: Administrative analyst, Proteus Adult Training, Visalia, CA, 1975-83; business consultant/owner, Yesterday's Gone Bookstore, Bend, OR, 1983-89, and Pageantry Book Co. (mail order), 1989-96; professor's assistant, Southern Oregon State College, Ashland, OR, 1989-91; administrative assistant and assistant editor, University of Colorado, Boulder, CO, 1991-92; National Science Foundation Research Fellow, University of Oregon, Eugene, OR, 1992-95; sociology instructor, University of Oregon, Eugene, OR, 1993-present; sociology instructor, Central Oregon Community College, Bend, OR, 1995-present. *Community activities*: Oregon Council for the Humanities, Chautauqua Lecture Series Presenter, 1994-98; member of the Homeless Leadership Council, Deschutes County, Bend, OR, 1995-present; director, Low Income Families Together (LIFT) for Central and Southern Oregon, 1995-present; coordinator of the Global Homeless Discussion List and Electronic Archives, 1994-present, located at: http://csf.colorado.edu/homeless. *Memberships*: Beaver Clan of the United Lumbee Nation (head chief); American Sociological Association; Pacific Sociological Association; International Association of Visual Sociologists for Women in Society; Central Oregon Archaeological Society; Sociologists for Women in Society; Qualitative Researchers Association; National Coalition for the Homeless; Phi Kappa Phi; Omicron Delta Kappa. *Published works*: Shelters are for Scum, and I Ain't No Bum!: Homeless People Who Avoid the Shelters (California Anthropology Press, 1992).

SOUTHWIND, ROGER
(Indian band chief)
Affiliation: Lac Seul Indian Band, General Delivery, Lac Seul, Canada P0V 2A0 (807) 582-3211.

SPAIN, DR. FRANNIE L.
(school supervisor)
Affiliation: Chinle Boarding School, P.O. Box 70, Many Farms, AZ 86538 (520) 781-6221 Fax 781-6376.

SPANG, ALONZO, SR.
(college president)
Affiliation: Dull Knife Memorial College, P.O. Box 98, 1 College Dr., Lame Deer, MT 59043 (406) 477-6215 Fax 477-6219. *Past professional post*: Rosebud Agency, Bureau of Indian Affairs, Rosebud, SD.

SPANIOLA, CHERYL L. (*Ikwe Awesii Salagliwed*)
(Eastern Cherokee) 1954-
(Indian education program director)
Born October 2, 1954, Flint, Mich. *Education*: Bay Mills Community College, Native Language & Instructors Institute, 1999. *Address*: 2166 S. Elms Rd./8354 Cappy Lane, Swartz Creek, MI 48473 (810) 591-2312 ext. 252 Fax 635-3921. E-mail: ikweawesii@juno.com. *Affiliations*: Director, Swartz Creek Indian Education Program, 1980-present; Native Language Instructors Institute, Bay Mills College, MI, 1994-present. *Community activities*: University of Michigan, Flint, Native American Indian Student Organization (annual powwow committee member, secretary, chair, 1983-95). *Memberships*: Genesee Valley Indian Association (powwow committee member - secretary, chair, 1983-95; board of directors - secretary, vice-chair, chair, 1989-95); Genesee County Indian Education Committee; National Indian Education Association; Michigan Indian Education Association; Anishinaabemowin Teg, Inc., 1998-.

SPARKMAN, RON (Shawnee)
(tribal chairperson)
Affiliation: Shawnee Tribe, P.O. Box 189, Miami, OK 74355 (918) 542-2441.

SPEAKS, STANLEY M. (Oklahoma Chickasaw) 1933-
(BIA regional director)
Born November 2, 1933, Tishomingo, Okla. *Education*: Northeastern State College, Tahlequah, OK, BS, 1959, MEd, 1962. *Principal occupation*: B.I.A. area director. *Address*: Northwst Regional Office, Bureau of Indian Affairs, 911 NE 11th Ave., Portland, OR 97232 (503) 231-6702 Fax 231-2201. *Affiliations*: supt., Anadarko Agency, BIA, 1975-77; area director, Anadarko Area Office, BIA, Anadarko, OK, 1976-80; director, Portland Area Office, BIA, Portland, OR, 1980 *Community activities*: Boy Scouts of America (mem-

ber-American Indian Relations Committee); 16th American Indian Tribal Leader's Seminar on Scouting (chairman, 1972-73); Rotary International (member); Oklahoma Governor's Committee on Small Business (member). *Interests*: Boating, fishing, hunting, golf; Boy Scouts of America.

SPEAKTHUNDER, BENJAMIN (Gros Ventre)
  (former tribal vice president)
Address & Affiliation: Fort Belknap Community Council, P.O. Box 1019, Harlem, MT 59526.

SPEAKTHUNDER, RONALD G. (Gros Ventre)
  (tribal council member)
Address & Affiliation: Fort Belknap Community Council, P.O. Box 871, Harlem, MT 59526.

SPEARMAN, GRANT (*Avingaluk*-Inupiaq name) 1951-
  (museum curator)
Born April 24, 1951, Seattle, Wash. *Education*: University of Washington, BA, 1975. *Principal occupation*: Museum curator. *Home address*: 3022 Main St., Anaktuvuk Pass, AK 99721 (907) 661-3413 (work). *Affiliation*: Curator, Simon Paneak Memorial Museum, Anaktuvuk Pass, AK, 1986-. *Memberships*: Museums Alaska; Alaska Anthropological Association; International Association of Arctic Social Scientists. *Interests*: Archaeology, ethnography, ethnology, oral history, aviation history.

SPEARS, ERICA (Omaha)
  (executive director)
Affiliation: Executive Director, Omaha Tribal Housing Authority, P.O. Box 150, Macy, NE 68039 (402) 837-5728.

SPENCE, CYRIL HENRY
  (Indian band chief)
Affiliation: Nicomen Indian Band, Box 328, Lytton, B.C., Canada V0K 1Z0 (604) 455-2279.

SPENCER, BUFORD MARYLAND, Jr.
(Curly) **(United Lumbee/Cherokee) 1943-**
  (logger, long haul truck driver)
Born July 5, 1943, Mt. Airy, N.C. *Education*: Chemekgta Community College (Salem, OR), AS (Forest Technology), 1989. *Principal occupation*: Logger, long haul truck driver. *Home address*: 1458 SW Hill St., Dallas, OR 97338 (503) 623-8971. *Military service*: U.S. Army, 1962-654. *Community activities*: Honorary honor guard of the Confederated Tribes of Grand Ronde; board member & chief of safety & security of the United InterTribal Dancing Club of Salem. *Membership*: Northwest Indian Veterans Association. *Awards, honors*: President of Forestry Club at college, 1988-89. *Interests*: "My interests are to learn as much as I can about my people, to live the best way I can by following the "Red Road," to be of service to all Indian people in whatever way "Grandfather" directs me; to be proud of my heritage, respect my elders. *Published songs*: "Truckers Hall of Fame," & "Thank You Lord," both published in 1980.

SPEPETIN, MIKE (Nisqually)
  (tribal chairperson)
Affiliation: Nisqually Indian Community Council, 4820 She-Nah-Num Dr. SE, Olympia, WA 98503 (360) 456-5221.

SPIELMANN, ROGER *(Shaganash)* 1951-
  (associate professor)
Born April 13, 1951, Chicago, Ill. *Education*: University of Texas, Arlington, MA, 1978; University of British Columbia, PhD, 1984. *Principal occupation*: Associate professor. *Home address*: address unknown. E-mail: rspielma@nickel.laurentian.ca. *Affiliation*: Associate professor, Dept. of Native Studies, Laurentian University, Sudbury, ON, 1990-. *Other professional post*: Algonquian language consultant. *Community activities*: board of directors, University of Sudbury. *Memberships*: American Anthropological Association; Survival International. *Interests*: Algonquian languages & cultures; Native education; Algonquian Discourse Analysis; sociolinguistics, ethnomethodology. *Published works*: Numerous articles on the Algonquian language in journals & books.

SPILBURY, DELAINE (Western Shoshone) 1937-
  (owner-Indian shop)
Born September 21, 1937, Ely, Nev. *Address & Affiliation*: Owner, Ms. Squaw Indian Handcrafts, 2429 Salt Lake St., N. Las Vegas, NV, 1972-. *Community activities*: Director, Pow Wow of the 4 Winds. *Membership*: National Bowhunting Rights Organization. *Awards, honors*: National Field Archery Association - Big Game Awards. *Interests*: Bowhunting; traveling the West to promote Native craftsmen. *Biographical sources*: National Bowhunter magazine; Native Nevadan magazine; Indian Trader magazine.

SPINKS, BRIAN JAMES
  (Indian band chief)
Affiliation: Lytton Indian Band, Box 20, Lytton, British Columbia, Canada V0K 1Z0 (604) 455-2304.

SPITZ, KATHY
  (BIA special education coordinator)
Affiliation: Eastern Navajo Agency, Bureau of Indian Affairs, P.O. Box 328, Crownpoint, NM 87313 (505) 786-6150 Fax 786-6112.

SPIVEY, TOWANA (Chickasaw) 1943-
  (curator, archaeologist)
Born November 8, 1943, Madill, Okla. *Education*: Southeastern State University, BA, 1968; University of Oklahoma, 1970-71. *Principal occupation*: Curator, archaeologist. *Home address*: 2101 Oak St., Duncan, OK 73533. *Affiliation*: Curator of anthropology, Museum of the Great Plains, Lawton, OK, 1974-. *Other professional posts*: Curator-archaeologist, Oklahoma Historical Society, 1974-; archaeologist, Oklahoma Archaeological Survey (2 years). *Military service*: Army National Guard, 1960-68. *Memberships*: Oklahoma Anthropological Society, 1963- (board member); Oklahoma Museums Association, 1973- (council member); Society for Historic Archaeology, 1973-; Council on Abandoned Military Posts (vice president of Oklahoma Department, 1975-). *Interests*: Historic sites-restoration, archaeology, etc.; 19th century military forts and camps; fur trade and exploration of the Trans-Mississippi West; conservation of cultural material or artifacts; wagon restoration. *Published works*: Co-author, An Archaeological Reconnaissance of the Salt Plains Areas of Northwest Oklahoma (Museum of the Great Plains, 1976); co-author, Archaeological Investigations Along the Waurika Pipeline (Museum of the Great Plains, 1977).

SPOONHUNTER, HARVEY, SR. (Arapahoe)
  (tribal chairperson)
Affiliation: Shoshone & Arapahoe Joint Tribal Business Council, P.O. Box 217, Fort Washakie, WY 82514 (307) 332-6120.

SPOTTED BEAR, ALYCE (Mandan/Hidatsa)
  (educator)
Education: Dickinson State College (ND), BS, 1970; Penn State University, MA in Education, 1978; Cornell University, PhD Candidate in Education. *Home address*: P.O. Box 86, Halliday, ND 58636. *Office address*: Native American Studies, Dartmouth College, 37 N. Main St., Hanover, NH 03755 (603) 646-3530 Fax 646-0333. *Affiliations*: Supt., Twin Buttes School District #37, 1993-96; President, Fort Berthold Community College, 1997; Visiting Instructor, Native American Studies, Dartmouth College, Hanover, NH, 1998-present (teaches course entitled, "American Indian Women of the Plains: A Social History." *Community activities*: North Dakota Committee to Prevent Child Abuse Advisory Committee, 1994-present. *Honors, awards*: Native American Women of Upstate NY Recognition "Hall of Fame," 1990-91; Anonymous Donor Fellowship, Cornell University, 1992-93; Educational; Leadership Award, TAT Tribal Education Dept., 1993; Educator of the Year, TAT Tribal Government, 1994; New York State Minority Fellowship, Cornell University, 1997-98; David L. Call Achievement Award, Cornell Universty, 1997.

SPOTTED EAGLE, CHRIS
  (president-Indian society)
Address: 2524 Hennepin Ave., Minneapolis, MN 55401 (612) 377-4212. *Affiliation*: American Indian Talent Society, 2225 Cavell Ave. North, Golden Valley, MN 55427.

SPOTTEDBIRD, LAWRENCE
  (executive director)
Affiliation: Lincoln Indian Center, 1100 Military Rd., Lincoln, NE 68508 (402) 474-5231.

SPRAGUE, DAVID K. (Pottawatomi)
  (tribal chairperson)
Affiliation: Match-e-be-nash-she-wish Band of Pottawatomi Indians, P.O. Box 218, Dorr, MI 49323 (616) 681-8830.

SPRAGUE, DONOVIN (Minnicoujou Lakota)
  (university instructor, author,
  director of cultural center,)
Born on the Cheyenne River Sioux Reservation, Dupree, S.D. *Education*: Black Hills State University, BS; University of South Dakota, MA. *Principal occupation*: University instructor and education director at Crazy Horse Memorial. *Address*: Crazy Horse Memorial, Ave. of the Chiefs, Rapid City, SD (605) 673-4681 Fax 673-2185. E-mail: memorial@crazy horse.org. Website: www.crazyhorsememorial. org. *Affiliations*: University instructor at the Indian University of North America, Crazy Horse Memorial, 1996-present; director, Native American Educational & Cultural Center, and assistant director of Indian Museum of North America, 1996-present. *Other professional posts*: Owner, Rock-N-Records, 1985-present; part-time lecturer in Lakota Studies, Oglala Lakota College, 1988-; part-time instructor in American Indian Studies, Black Hills State University, 1990-; Past professional posts: General manager-Lakota Radio (100,000 watts), KILI-FM, 1995-96; American Indian coordinator, Iowa Universities (Iowa State, University of Iowa, and University of Northern Iowa), 1994-95. Credited on several major artist's CD recordings. *Community activities*: Rapid City (SD) Indian/White Relations Committee (10 year member & chairperson); Rapid City Human Relations Commission; Rapid City Minority Relations Committee; Rapid City Area Schools-Indian Education; Board President of Rapid City American Indian Development Corporation; Rapid City Office Manager of United Sioux Tribes, Choctaw Nation of Oklahoma, Citizen Potawatomi Nation, Oklahoma. *Memberships*: Cheyenne River Sioux Tribe (enrolled member); Wounded Knee Survivors Association; American Indian Science & Engineering Society (AISES); National Indian Education Association (NIEA). *Awards, honors*: Donovin Sprague Day, March 23, 1994, proclaimed by Mayor of Rapid City, SD; received grandfather's name, "Hump," on Wounded Knee Day, Dec. 29, 2001, in a ceremony; award winning flutes in art shows; movie extra in the movie, "Lakota Woman." *Interests*: Musician: guitar/vocals - music productions; artist: Lakota flute maker; instructor in Lakota arts & crafts; historical field research. Mr. Sprague writes, "Lecturer in American Indian studies (throughout the U.S. and Canada), such as the warrior, Crazy Horse and the Battle of the Little Bighorn, Fetterman Fight, and Wagonbox Fight in which my Great, Great Grandfather, Chief Hump led his warriors. Hump's father was also named Hump and was the uncle of Chief Crazy Horse." *Published works*: Books: "Images of America, Cheyenne River Sioux," 2003; and "Images of America, Standing Rock Sioux," 2004. Music: CD producer of the band "Shakedown," 2002.

SPRAGUE, RODERICK
  (senior historical archaeologist, ethnohistorian)
Education: PhD. *Affiliation*: Research associate, Walker Research Group, Ltd., P.O. Box 4147, Boulder, CO 80306 (303) 492-6719. Website: www.walker researchgroup.com. Dr. Sprague is a senior historical archaeologist and ethnohistorian with extensive experience in environmental impact research and mitigation. He is experienced in both Canada and the U.S., and especially in the Columbia Basin.

SPRINGER, HOWARD (Iowa of Oklahoma)
  (former tribal chairperson)
Affiliation: Iowa of Oklahoma Business Committee, Iowa Veterans Hall, P.O. Box 190, Perkins, OK 74059 (405) 547-2403.

SPURR, LAURA (Huron Potawatomi)
  (tribal chairperson)
Affiliation: Nottawaseppi Band of Huron Potawatomi, 2221 - 1.5 Mile Rd., Fulton, MI 49052 (616) 729-5151.

SPYBUCK, GLORIA
(BIA agency supt.)
Affiliation: Wewoka Agency, Bureau of Indian Affairs, P.O. Box 1060, Wewoka, OK 74884 (405) 257-6259 Fax 257-6748.

STACHELRODT, MARY (Yup'ik Eskimo)
(museum director)
Affiliation: Yupiit Piciryarait Cultural Center & Museum, Association of Village Council Presidents, P.O. Box 219, Bethel, AK 99559 (907) 543-3521.

STAGSDILL, WILLIAM (Lummi)
(school system director)
Affiliation: Lummi Tribal School System, 2530 Kwina Rd., Bellingham, WA 98225 (206) 647-6251.

STAHL, STACY L. (Yerington Paiute)
(tribal chairperson)
Affiliation: Yerington Paiute Tribal Council, 171 Campbell Lane, Yerington, NV 89447 (702) 463-3301.

STALLING, STEVEN L.A. (San Luiseno-Mission Indians-Rincon Reservation) 1951-
(association president)
Born May 12, 1951, San Diego, Calif. *Education*: California State University, Long Beach, BS; University of Southern California, MBA. *Principal occupation*: Association president. *Address*: National Center for American Indian Enterprise Development, 953 E. Juanita Ave., Mesa, AZ 85204 (800) 423-0452, or (602) 831-7524. *Affiliations*: Prior to joining the National Center, Mr. Stalling was executive director of a consulting firm in San Francisco and supervised a job creation program which trained 300 American Indians; National Center for American Indian Enterprise Development, Mesa, AZ, 1976- . *Other professional posts*: Session chairman, Fifth International Symposium on Small Business, 1978; delegate to the White House Conference on Small Business, 1978. *Community activities*: Coordinator for the National Congress of American Indians, a lobbying group; former member of the steering committee for the National Indian Education Association; member of Board of Directors for a beginning Development Band directed at solving the domestic financing needs of American Indians; member of Advisory Committee for 1984 Olympics; served on Los Angeles Bicentennial Commission and the Los Angeles Private Industry Council; appointed to the Los Angeles City/County Indian Commission by Republican Supervisor Dean Dana. *Awards, honors*: Cited and recognized by the State Assembly of California for his contributions and efforts in small business and economic development. *Interests*: The National Center assists over 600 businesses annually and has secured over $200 million in financing and contracts for its clients. Long interested in developing American Indian talent, an interest that has accelerated since the formation of UIDA's Management Institute which trains Indian managers, Mr. Stallings has conducted dozens of workshops and seminars. Two of his training books are used throughout America by Indians learning planning and management. *Biographical sources*: Who's Who in Finance and Industry, 1982-1983; Who's Who in the West, 1982-1983. *Published work*: Directory of American Indian Businesses (National Center for American Indian Enterprise Development).

STANCAMPIANO, MICHAEL
(BIA agency supt.)
Affiliation: Southern Ute Agency, Bureau of Indian Affairs, P.O. Box 315, Ignacio, CO 81137 (970) 563-4511 Fax 563-9321

STANDING BEAR, ZUG G. *(Kompau*skwe)* (Kanienkehaka/Abenaki/Wampanoag/Metis) 1941-
(professor)
Born January 10, 1941, Boston, Mass. *Education*: University of Nebraska, BS; The George Washington University, MSFS; University of Southern California, MSEd; Jacksonville (AL) State University, MPA; Florida State University, PhD; Fellow in Forensic Medicine, The Armed Forces Institute of Pathology, Washington, DC. *Principal occupation*: Professor. *Home address*: 514 Hopi Circle, Divide, CO 80814 (719) 687-8087 Fax 687-8082. E-mail: mgspikers@aol.com. *Affiliation*: Valdosta State University, Dept. of Sociology, Valdosta, GA, 10986-95; Colorado State University, Dept. of Sociology, Fort Collins, CO, 1995-2001; Associate pro-

fessor & coordinator of Forensic Health Science Programs, University of Colorado, Colorado Springs,, CO, 2001-present. *Other professional posts*: Secretary (1987-88), chairman (1988-90), program co-chair (1995-96), General Section, American Academy of Forensic Sciences; program committee member, Academy of Criminal Justice Sciences (1996-97); chairman, Ethics Committee, International Association of Forensic Nurses (1995-present); member, Commission on Gender Equality, Colorado State University (1997-2000); consultant in criminal justice, criminal investigation, and forensic science administration, organization, management, and curriculum design, 1981-; member, Governor's Criminal Justice Coordinating Council (State of Georgia, 1988-92). *Military service*: U.S. Army, 1958-81 - Special Agent, U.S. Army Criminal Investigation Command (Bronze Star, Vietnam, 1970; Meritorious Service Medals, oak leaf cluster; Army Commendation Medals, oak leaf cluster). *Community activities*: Lowndes Drug Action Council (member, Board of Directors, 1992-95); Valdosta Symphony Orchestra (member, Board of Directors, 1993-95); Black on Black Crime Committee, Valdosta (member); Community Policing Transition Project, Valdosta Police Dept. (member, Leadership Council, 1994-95); Readership Board, The Valdosta Daily Times, 1994-95; treasurer, Wolves Offered Life & Friendship, Inc., LaPorte, Co., 1995-2000; administrator, The Flash & Thelma Memorial Hedgehog Rescue, Inc., Divide, Co., 1997-present. *Memberships*: American Academy of Forensic Sciences (Fellow); American College of Forensic Examiners (Life Fellow); American Sociological Association; American Society of Criminology; Academy of Criminal Justice Sciences (Life Member); Southern Criminal Justice Association (Life Member); Institute of Criminal Justice Ethics; National Congress of American Indians; Association on American Indian Affairs; Vietnam Veterans of America; Veterans for Peace; National Organization for Women; American Association of University Professors; International Association of Forensic Nurses (Distinguished Fellow). *Awards, honors*: Service Award and Distinguished Fellow Award, International Association of Forensic Nurses, 1994, 1995; Meritorious Service Award, American Academy of Forensic Sciences, 1996; numerous military awards, 1960-81. *Biographical sources*: Who's Who in the South & Southeast (1991-94); Who's Who in American Education (1992-97); Who's Who in the World (1993-97); Who's Who in the West (1997-98); Who's Who in America (1996-2002). *Published works*: Books: Law Enforcement (U. of Florida, Dept. of Continuing Education, 1985); Criminology (U. of Florida, Dept. of Continuing Education, 1985). *Articles*: "Crime Statistics in Nursing" (Journal of Psychosocial Nursing and Mental Health Services, Oct. 1996); "Will the Vision be Co-Opted: Forensic Nursing and Death Investigation (Journal of Psychosocial Nursing and Mental Health Services, Sept. 1995); "To Guard Against Invading Indians: Struggling for Native Community in the Southeast" (American Indian Culture & Research Journal, Nov. 1994); "Crime Scene Responders: The Imperative Sequential Steps (Critical Care Nursing Quarterly, May 1999); numerous other articles in various journals.

STANDINGBEAR, E. SEAN (Osage)
(oral historian, artist)
Affiliation: Osage Tribal Council, P.O. Box 779, Pawhuska, OK 74056 (918) 287-1085 Fax 287-2257.
Published work: "Art of the Osage," with Garrick Bailey, Daniel C. Swan, and John W. Nunley (University of Washington Press, 2004).

STANDING ELK, DON (Sioux)
(school principal)
Affiliation: American Horse School, P.O Box 660, Allen, SD 57714 (605) 455-2480.

STANDING, NETTIE
(cooperative manager)
Affiliation: Oklahoma Indian Arts & Crafts Cooperative, P.O. Box 966, Anadarko, OK 73005 (405) 247-3486.

STANDING-CAPES, LAVERNA
(coop manager)
Affiliation: Oklahoma Indian Arts & Crafts Cooperative, P.O. Box 966, Anadarko, OK 73005 (888) 405-4963; (405) 247-3486.

STANDINGHORN, EDWARD
(Indian band chief)
Affiliation: Sweetgrass Indian band, Box 147, Gallivan, Saskatchewan, Canada S0M 0X0 (306) 937-3555.

STANGEL, CAROLINE
(Indian education program coordinator)
Affiliation: Grand Rapids ISD #318, Indian Education Program, 820 N. Pokegama Ave., Grand Rapids, MN 55744 (218) 326-1409 Fax 327-2269.

STANLEY, BURNE
(center director)
Affiliation: Massachusetts Center for Native American Awareness, Inc., P.O. Box 5885, Boston, MA 02114 (617) 884-4227; editor, "Turtletalk."

STANLEY, NATALIE T. 1963-
(museum interpreter)
Born December 4, 1963, Fort Riley, Kans. *Education*: Christopher Newport College, BA , 1985; William and Mary (continuing education courses in archaeology and Virginia Native American culture.) *Principal occupation*: Museum interpreter. *Home address*: 81 Robinson Dr., Newport News, VA 23601 (804) 595-4931. *Affiliation*: Interpreter (conduct tours through Indian Village; presents slide show on the Eastern Woodland Indian culture), Syms-Eaton Museum and Kecoughtan Indian History Center, Hampton, VA, 1985-91. *Memberships*: The Lower James Chapter of the Archaeological Society of Virginia, (founder and president, 1988-; 1984-88 Kicotah Chapter of ASV (vice-president, 1986-87). *Interests*: "Apart from interpreter, I'm an active researcher of Native American cultures; work with Virginia and North Carolina tribal members. Assist other researchers; research and reconstruct native dwellings and implements; have working knowledge of native American domestic skills; participate and attend Native American festivals; work with archaeologists - research and site work."

STANLEY, RAYMOND (San Carlos Apache)
(former tribal chairperson)
Affiliation: San Carlos Apache Tribe, P.O. Box 0, San Carlos, AZ 85550 (520) 475-2361 Fax 475-2567.

STANTON, ALFRED (Shoshone)
(tribal chairperson)
Affiliation: Ely Colony Tribal Council, 16 Shoshone Circle, Ely, NV 89301 (775) 289-3013.

STANTON, MEREDITH
(director-BIA Arts & Crafts Board)
Affiliation: Indian Arts & Crafts Board, Dept. of the Interior, MS: 4004-MIB, 1849 C St., NW, Washington, DC 20240 (202) 208-3773 Fax 208-5196.

STAR, APRIL CRANE (San Juan Pueblo)
(arts & crafts coop manager)
Affiliation: Oke Oweenge Arts & Crafts, P.O. Box 1095, San Juan Pueblo, NM 87566 (505) 852-2372.

STARNA, DR. WILLIAM A.
(professor of anthropology)
Affiliations: Dept. of Anthropology, SUNY, Oneonta, NY 13820 (607) 431-3345. *Interests*: Eastern Woodlands, Iroquoians, Algonquians.

STARR, IRVIN
(Indian band chief)
Affiliation: Starblanket Indian Band, Box 456, Balcarres, SK, Canada S0G 0C0 (306) 334-2206.

STATELY, JOANNE
(Indian council director)
Affiliation: Minnesota Indian Affairs Council, 127 University Ave., St. Paul, MN 55155 (612) 296-3611.

STAUDIE, JANICE
(BIA agency supt.)
Affiliation: San Carlos Agency, Bureau of Indian Affairs, P.O. Box 209, San Carlos, AZ 85550 (928) 475-2321 Fax 475-2783.

STAUSS, DR. JOSEPH H. "JAY"
(Jamestown Band S'Klallam)
(program director)
Education: Washington State University, PhD, 1972. *Affiliation*: American Indian Studies Program, The Uni-

versity of Arizona, Harvill Bldg., Rm. 430, P.O. Box 210076, Tucson, AZ 85721 (520) 621-7108 Fax 621-7952. E-mail: aisp@email.arizona.edu. *Interests*: American Indian studies program development; Pacific Northwest tribes.

STEARNS, CHRISTOPHER T. (Navajo) 1964- (attorney)
Born December 13, 1964 in Los Angeles, Calif. *Education*: Williams College, BA, 1986; Cornell Law School, JD, 1989. *Address & Affiliation*: Hobbs, Straus, Dean & Walker, LLP (Associate, 1989-94; Partner, 2001-present), 2120 L St., NW, Suite 700, Washington, DC 20037 (202) 822-8282. E-mail: cstearns@hsdwdc.com. He specializes in the practice of energy, health care, self-determination and self-governance, education, campaign and election law, and matters involving the U.S. Congress and federal agencies. *Past professional posts*: In 1994, Mr. Stearns worked as Counsel to the House of Representatives Sub-committee on Native American Affairs for then Chairman, Bill Richardson (D-NM) where he helped secure passage of the 1994 Indian Self-Determination Act Amendments; from 1995-98, he served as Democratic Counsel to the U.S. House Committee on Resources where he handled Native American issues for Ranking Member, George Miller (D-CA). Among the issues for which he had direct oversight were Indian gaming, labor relations, health care, federal recognition, the original Title V Self-Governance legislation, amendments to the Indian Child Welfare Act, and California Indian Policy; between 1998 and 2000, he served as Director of Indian Affairs at the U.S. Dept. of Energy under Secretary Bill Richardson. He oversaw all national DOE tribal relations and policy initiatives; Mr. Stearns served as the North Dakota state campaign director for former Vice-Presdient Al Gore's campaign in the 2000 presidential campaign. He is the first Native American appointed to the position of state director in presidential campaign history. *Membership*: Native American Bar Association (board member); District of Columbia Bar Association.

STEBBINS, SUSAN ANN (Mohawk/Metis) 1951- (associate professor)
Born March 15, 1951, Springfield, Mass. *Education*: Florida Atlantic University, BA; VCU, MA. Education; SUNY Albany, Doctor of Arts. *Address*: 119 MacVicar Hall, SUNY Potsdam, 44 Pierre Point Ave., Potsdam, NY 13676 (315) 267-2047 Fax 267-3176; E-mail: stebbisa@potsdam.edu. *Affiliations*: Richmond Public Schools, Richmond, VA, 1972-82; Girls Incorporated, Schenectady, NY, 1988-92; Associate Professor, SUNY College at Potsdam, Potsdam, NY, 1992-present. Other professional post: Director of Native American Studies, SUNY, Potsdam. *Community activities*: North Country Public Radio Advisory Board. *Membership*: American Society for Ethnohistory.

STEELE, BRUCE O. (school principal)
Affiliation: Polacca Day School, P.O. Box 750, Polacca, AZ 86042 (520) 737-2581 Fax 737-2323.

STEELE, JACQUELINE (Washoe) (tribal chairperson)
Affiliation: Stewart Indian Community Council, 5352 Dat-So-La-Lee Way, Carson City, NV 89701 (775) 883-1446.

STEELE, JOHN (*Yellow Bird*) (Oglala Sioux) (tribal council president)
Affiliation: Oglala Lakotah Tribal Council, Pine Ridge Reservation, P.O. Box H, No. 468, Pine Ridge, SD 57770 (605) 867-2244.

STEELE, LOIS (Fort Peck Assiniboine) 1939- (physician)
Born November 27, 1939, Washington, D.C. *Education*: Colorado College, BA, 1961; University of Montana, MS, 1969; University of Minnesota Medical School, Duluth & Minneapolis, MD, 1978. *Principal occupation*: Physician. *Home address*: 2360 W. Canada, Tucson, AZ 85746 (520) 578-0644; (520) 383-7211 (work). *Affiliation*: Clinical Director, Sells Service Unit, USPHS-Indian Health Service, Tucson, AZ, 1980-. *Other professional posts*: Clinical Director, Pascua Yaqui Health Dept., 1986-91; director, Indians Into Medicine Program (INMED), University of New Mexico. *Community activities*: Assistant Cub Scout Master, 1986, 1988-89; PTA, 1986-90; United Way, Tucson (board member); Holy Way Presbyterian Church, Tucson (Deacon, 1991); Theodore & Vivian Johnson Foundation (board member). *Memberships*: Association of American Indian Physicians; American Academy of Family Physicians; American Medical Association; Commissioned Officers of America; Arizona Academy of Family Physicians. *Awards, honors*: Faculty President, Dawson College, 1972; Outstanding Woman Medical Student, Lampson Award, University of Minnesota Medical School, Duluth, 1976; Distinguished Achievement Award, Rocky Mountain College Alumni Association, 1981; National Indian Health Board - Honoree, 1982; selected as Advisory Committee Member, FDA - Consumer Status, 1982-83; University of North Dakota Indian Students Association, Time-Out Award, 1983; Wonder Women Foundation - Finalist, 1983; USPHS Unit Commendation, April 1988; American Indian Science and Engineering Society Eli Parker Award, 1989; Indian Health Service Award for Health Promotion, Disease Prevention Work, 1989; Pascua Yaqui Project Head Start Volunteer Award, 1991; AMA Physicians Recognition Award, 1991-1993; among others. *Interests*: Member, "Saturay Group" Sophisticated Dancers of Tucson - woman's tap dance performing group. Numerous presentations, workshops, field readings and consulting positions over the years. Research and Publications: "(AIDS) Education Among Native Americans in Arizona: The Pascua Yaqui, Navajo Nation and Urban Indian Experience". May 1990; Stone and Steele. Presented at the International AIDS Conference in Puerto Rico; "Leading Causes of Death Among Yaqui Indians, 1970-90" Sept. 1990 - Presented at American Public Health Associations Annual Meeting, New York; "Cardiovascular Risk Among the Pascua Yaqui" April 1991. Presented at the IHS National Research Conference, Tucson; among others.

STEELE, RUPERT (Goshute) (tribal chairperson)
Affiliation: Goshute Business Council, P.O. Box 6104, Ibapah, UT 84034 (435) 234-1138.

STEIN, WAYNE J. (Turtle Mountain Chippewa) 1950- (professor/administrator)
Born September 17, 1950, Wolf Point, Mont. *Education*: Montana State University, BS, 1973; Penn State University, MEd., 1977; Washington State University, EdD, 1988. *Principal occupation*: Professor-administrator. *Home address*: 515 N. 20th, Bozeman, MT 59715 (406) 994-3881 (work). *Affiliation*: Dept. chairperson, Native American Studies Dept., Montana State University, 2-17 Wilson Hall, P.O. Box 172340, Bozeman, MT 59717, 1991-. *Other professional posts*: Vice President, International College; President, Standing Rock College, AZ. *Memberships*: Montana Indian Education Association; National Indian Education Association. *Awards, honors*: Bush Leadership Award, 1985; Community College Educator of the Year, WSU, 1986. *Interests*: Rights and needs of the poor and working people of U.S.; rights of indigenous people of the world; world environment issues; economic development of State of Montana and its Indian reservations; reading, writing, fishing. *Published work*: Tribally Controlled College (Peter Lang, 1992).

STEINBRIGHT, JAN (editor)
Affiliation: Journal of Alaska Native Arts, Institute of Alaska Native Arts, P.O. Box 70769, Fairbanks, AK 99707 (907) 456-7491.

STEINBRING, JOHN H. (JACK) 1929- (anthropologist)
Born July 1, 1929, Oshkosh, Wisc. *Education*: University of Wisconsin, Oshkosh, BA, 1955, Madison, MA, 1959; University of Minnesota, PhD, 1975. *Principal occupation*: Anthropologist. *Home address*: 18 Browning Blvd., Winnipeg, Manitoba R3K 0L4 (204) 832-0326 (home) 786-9719 (office). *Affiliation*: Professor & senior scholar, Dept. of Anthropology, University of Winnipeg, Manitoba, 1963-. *Military service*: Wisconsin National Guard/U.S. Army Reserve, 1949-62 (1st Lt.; Expert Rifle, Pistol, Carbine). *Community activities*: President, Assiniboine Senior Rifle Club, 1978-90. *Memberships*: American Anthropological Association (Foreign Fellow); Society for American Archaeology; Society of Professional Archaeologists; Rock Art Association of Canada (president, 1990); Rock Art Association of Manitoba (president, 1993-); Australian Rock Art Research Association (vice president, 1988-92. *Interests*: "Extensive research into the impact of television among Algonkian populations resulting in several books, 1974-81; studies of alcohol among the Northern Ojibwa, 1964-82, resulting in one book and one professional paper; general ethnographic studies among the North Ojibwa, 1963-, resulting in numerous papers and a chapter in the Handbook of North American Indians (Vol. 6, Smithsonian); many years of research into Native North American rock art leading to many professional papers and the identification of two rock art styles and the discovery of Canada's oldest dated rock art; further rock art research in Hawaii, Australia, England, Scotland, and the American Southwest." *Published works*: Television and the Canadian Indian (University of Winnipeg Press, 1979); Alcohol and the Native Peoples of the North (University Press of America, 1980); An Introduction to Archaeology on the Winnipeg River (Manitoba Historic Resources Branch, 1980); Communications in Cross-Cultural Perspective (University of Winnipeg Press, 1980); General Guidelines in the Development of Native Television Programming (University of Winnipeg Press, 1981); The Impact & Meaning of Television Among Native Communities in Northern Manitoba (Canadian Commission for UNESCO, 1984); numerous articles on rock art & archaeology.

STEINDORF, HARRY J. (*Keddy-Ju-Sa-Skagga, White Blackhawk*) (Ho-Chunk Nation) 1946- (educational administrator)
Born February 20, 1946, Black River Falls, Wisc. *Education*: University of Wisconsin, Whitewater, BBA, 1973; University of Wisconsin, Madison Law School, 1973-75. *Principal occupation*: Educational administrator. *Home address*: 460 Bonnie Rd., Cottage Grove, WI 53527 (608) 262-0314 Fax 265-4593 (work); E-mail: hsteindorf@hotmail.com. *Affiliation*: University of Wisconsin-Madison, Art Dept., 1988-present; Academic Advancement Program, 1974-80. *Past professional posts*: Vice-Chairman, Wisconsin Winnebago Business Committee, 1978-79; director of planning & economic development for Wisconsin Winnebago Tribe, 1980-83; Winnebago Research Center, Inc. (board of directors, 1980-83; sec/treas. of Wisconsin Winnebago Enterprises, Inc. (founding board of directors, 1980-83); executive director, Ho-Chunk Nation Business Dept., 1995; DJ Hosts Corp. (President & CEO, 1995-98). *Military service*: U.S. Marine Corps, 1964-70; Aviator, Captain (Distinguished Flying Cross; Sixteen Strike/Flight Air Medals; Vietnam Gallantry Cross; Vietnam Service Medal; Vietnam Campaign Medal; Naval Unit Citation; Meritorious Unit Citation). *Community activities*: Veterans of Foreign Wars #7591, Madison, WI; Disabled American Veterans, Post #2, Madison, WI; American Legion Post #442, Wisconsin Rapids, WI; Wisconsin Aviation Hall of Fame, Waunakee, WI, 1995-present. *Awards, honors*: "Top Gun" Award from 2nd Marine Air Wing, 1968, MCAS Cherry Point, NC; Outstanding Young Alumnus Award, University of Wisconsin, Whitewater, 1978; Outstanding Young Men of America, 1979; Commander VFW Post #7591, Madison, WI, 1996-97; Keynote Address Speaker, Veterans Day Ceremony, State Capitol Rotunda, Madison, WI, 1996. *Interests*: Fiction writing, pleasure flying, hunting & camping. *Published works*: In progress: "Seaworthy Injun."

STEINHAUSER, JAN (program director)
Affiliation: American Indian Studies Program, University of Denver, 2211 S. Josephne St., Denver, CO 80208 (303) 871-3155 ext. 254.

STEINSIEK, TOMMY A. (curator)
Affiliation: Creek Indian Memorial Association, Creek Council House Museum, Town Square, Okmulgee, OK 74447 (918) 756-2324.

STENSGAR, ERNEST L. (Coeur d'Alene) 1947- (tribal chairperson)
Born on the Coeur d'Alene Indian Reservation. *Education*: Chilocco Indian School in Oklahoma, 1965. *Affiliation*: Chairperson (1986-present), Coeur d'Alene Tribal Council, P.O. Box 408, Plummer, ID 83851 (208) 686-1800. Website: www.cdatribe-nsn.gov. *Other pro-*

fessional posts: President, Affiliated Tribes of Northwest Indians (rpresenting 55 tribes), 1996-present; Chairperson, Alliance of Idaho Tribes; Portland Area Vice President for the National Congress of American Indians. **Military service**: U.S. Marine Corps, 1965-67 (Vietnam-Purple Heart). **Community activities**: Representative, Tribal Leaders Task Force; member, Tribal School Board; co-chair, Idaho Centennial Committee; Commander, Joseph R. Garry American Legion Post #5, Plummer, ID; also District Commander; created the Coeur d'Alene Warrior Society (veterans on the Coeur d'Alene Reservation). **Awards, honors**: First tribal leader to be listed among Idaho's 100 most influential people; first tribal leader named to the Idaho Hall of Fame; first tribal leader to be honored with the Byard Rustin Award, for the advancement of human rights; first tribal leader to be awarded an honorary Doctor of Laws Degree from Gonzaga University, Spokane, WA.

STEORTS, DENNIS, DR. *(Chief Red Eagle)*
(Kaweah)
(principal chief, minister)
Address & Affiliation: Principal chief, Kaweah Indian Nation of Western USA & Mexico, P.O. Box 642, Abilene, KS 67410. *Other professional posts*: Co-national chairman, American Indian Defense of the Americas, Hutchinson, KS; general secretary, Native American Church, P.O. Box 265, Hutchinson, KS 67501. *Community activities*: Board member, Congregational Bible Churches International; Minister of Native American Church/CBC Division.

STEPETIN, JACOB
(village president)
Affiliation: Native Village of Akutan, P.O. Box 89, Akutan, AK 99553 (907) 698-2301.

STEPHENSON, DAVID
(attorney, consultant)
Education: University of Colorado, PhD (Anthropology), 1982; University of Denver, J.D., 1984. *Principal occupation*: Attorney, consultant. *Affiliations*: Attorney, Brauchli-Snyder, LLC (law firm); research associate, Walker Research Group, Ltd., P.O. Box 4147, Boulder, CO 80306 (303) 492-6719. Website: www.walkerresearchgroup.com. Mr. Stephenson performs consulting and legal work in areas of American Indian economic and business development, housing, complex business litigation, and American Indian intellectual property rights and licensing.

STEPHENSON, MICHAEL LYNN *(Cloud Walker)*
(Cherokee/Kickapoo/Osage/French) 1965-
(caregiver)
Born January 12, 1965, Phoenix Ariz. *Education*: High school. *Principal occupation*: Caregiver (caring for disabled persons). *Home address*: 5356 Border Ave., Joshua Tree, CA 92252 (760) 366-2875. *Community activities*: Landers (CA) Breakfast Club Volunteer, 1983-. *Memberships*: United Lumbee Nation Desert Sage Band (Black Hawk Warrior Society, Keeper of the Fire, 1992; council person, 1992-). *Award*: Landers (CA) Breakfast Club, 10 Year Service Award, Dec. 1993. *Interests*: Indian beadwork, carving, gardening; specializing in Gourd growing, student of Indian history & ceremonies.

STEVENS, BRIAN *(Tyo'glo'ta'kwa)*
(Oneida of Wisc.) 1954-
(Native American education coordinator)
Born April 25, 1954, Detroit, Mich. *Education*: University of Wisconsin, Oshkosh, BS (Social Work), 1976. *Principal occupation*: Native American education coordinator. *Address & Affiliation*: Pupil Services Dept., Howard/Suamico School District, 1935 Cardinal Lane, Green Bay, WI 54313 (920) 662-7886 Fax 662-7900. E-mail: briastev@hssd.k12.wi.us. *Other professional post*: Vice-chairperson, United American Indian Center, Green Bay, WI, 2002-present. *Awards, honors*: Received the Dutch Uncle Award from the Big Brothers organization while attending college; numerous youth awards for outstanding leadership. *Community activities*: Mr. Stevens writes, "Provides instructional activities within school systems and participates in ongoing cultural workshops to share knowledge." *Interests*: he also writes, "Active in ceremonies within our Longhouse and spending quality time instructing my three children in traditional values."

STEVENS, BRUCE (Te-Moak Western Shoshone)
(tribal chairperson)
Affiliation: Wells Indian Colony Band Council, P.O. Box 809, Wells, NV 89835 (702) 752-3045.

STEVENS, CONNIE (Iroquois-Cherokee) 1938-
(actress; executive director-foundation)
Born August 8, 1938, Brooklyn, N.Y. *Principal occupation*: Actress (25 years). Resides in Beverly Hills, CA. *Affiliation*: Founder, president, executive director, Windfeather Foundation. *Memberships*: Screen Actors Guild, AFTRA, Actors Equity.

STEVENS, ERNIE, JR. (Oneida of Wisconsin)
(association chairperson)
Affiliation: National Indian Gaming Association, 224 2nd St., SE, Washington, DC 20003 (202) 546-7711 Fax 546-1755. E-mail: estevens@indiangaming.org.

STEVENS, ESSIMAE
(hospital director)
Affiliation: Red Lake Comprehensive Health Service, Red Lake, MN 56671 (218) 679-3912.

STEVENS, FERMINA (Te-Moak Shoshone)
(tribal chairperson)
Affiliation: Elko Band Council, 511 Sunset St., Elko, NV 89803 (775) 738-8889.

STEVENS, JOHN W. (Passamaquoddy) 1933-
(tribal governor)
Born August 11, 1933, Washington Co., Maine. *Education*: High school. *Principal occupation*: Tribal governor, Indian Township—Passamaquoddy Tribal Council, Princeton, ME. *Address*: P.O. Box 301, Princeton, ME 04668 (207) 796-2301. *Military service*: U.S. Marines, 1951-54 (Presidential Unit Citation; Korean Presidential Unit Citation; United Nations Medal). *Interests*: Mr. Stevens writes, "Being the chief of an Indian tribe of about a thousand members who are struggling in court and on all fronts to overcome local discrimination and poverty and to have our reservation treaty rights respected by the State of Maine is enough of a task, & doesn't leave much time for anything else."

STEVENS, KATHRYN
(education director)
Affiliation: Arizona Dept. of Education, Indian Education Unit, 1535 W. Jefferson St., Phoenix, AZ 85007 (602) 542-4391.

STEVENS, RICHARD (Passamaquoddy)
(tribal chairperson)
Affiliation: Indian Township Passamaquoddy Tribal Council, P.O. Box 301, Princeton, ME 04668 (207) 796-2301.

STEVENSON, GELVIN (OK Cherokee) 1944-
(writer, consultant, teacher, mediator)
Born November 6, 1944, Chelsea, Okla. *Education*: Carleton College, BA; Washington University, MA, PhD. *Address*: 2160 Bolton St., Bronx, NY 10462 (718) 863-4156. E-mail: gelvins@earthlink.net. *Affiliations*: Investment consultant for Oneida Trust Committee; Adjunct professor, Urban Environmental Policy, New School University; independent writer & consultant. *Community activities*: Member, Board of Directors of American Indian Community House (NYC), First Nations Development Institute, & Cherokee National Historical Society. *Memberships*: Nuyagi Keetowah Society; Social Investment Forum; International String Figure Association. *Published work*: Indigenous Economics, co-authored with Rebecca Adamson (forthcoming).

STEVENSON, LOUIE J.
(Indian band chief)
Affiliation: Peguis Indian Band, Box 219, Hodgson, Manitoba, Canada R0C 1N0 (204) 645-2359.

STEVENSON, SCOTTIE
(museum curator)
Affiliation: American Indian Horse Museum, Rt. 3, Box 64, Lockhart, TX 78644 (512) 398-6642.

STEWART, JOHN R.
(credit union director)
Affiliation: Sisseton-Wahpeton Federal Credit Union, P.O. Box 627, Agency Village, SD 57262 (605) 698-3462 Fax 698-3907.

STILLWELL, LUCILLE
(executive director)
Affiliation: Kiva Club, University of New Mexico, Mesa Vista Hall #1117-A, Albuquerque, NM 87131 (505) 277-8259.

STINE, WENDY (Paiute)
(former tribal chairperson)
Affiliation: Fort Independence Tribal Council, P.O. Box 67, Independence, CA 93526 (760) 878-2126.

STIVER, LOUISE
(museum collections)
Affiliation: Museum of Indian Arts and Culture, Laboratory of Anthropology, P.O. Box 2087, 708 Camino Lejo, Santa Fe, NM 87504 (505) 827-6344.

STOCK, MICHELE DEAN (Seneca-Iroquois)
(museum director)
Affiliation: Seneca-Iroquois National Museum, Allegany Indian Reservation, 794-814 Broad St., Salamanca, NY 14779 (716) 945-1738/3895 Fax 945-1760

STOCK, STEPHEN
(Indian band chief)
Affiliation: Mohawks of Gibson, Box 327, Bala, Ontario, Canada P0C 1A0 (613) 762-3343.

STOFFLE, RICHARD
(professor)
Education: University of Kentucky, PhD, 1972. *Affiliation*: American Indian Studies Program, The University of Arizona, Harvill Bldg., Rm 430, P.O. Box 210076, Tucson, AZ 85721 (520) 621-7108 Fax 621-7952. E-mail: aisp@email.arizona.edu. *Interests*: American Indian social impact assessment; American Indian natural resource policy.

STOGAN, WALKER (Salish)
(spiritual leader)
Address: 4035 Thallaiwhaltum Ave., Musqueam Reserve, Vancouver, B.C., Canada V6H 3V1. *Interests*: Salish elder/spiritual leader of Winter Spirit Dance ceremonial.

STOGSDILL, WILLIAM
(school system director)
Affiliation: Lummi Tribal School System, 2530 Kwina Rd., Bellingham, WA 98225 (206) 647-6251.

STOLTZ, JOHN (Warm Springs Confederated)
(radio station manager)
Affiliation: KTWI-KTWS - 96.5 FM, Warm Springs Confederated Tribes, Bend, OR 97701 (541) 389-9500.

STONE, BEVERLY
(health director)
Affiliation: Cherokee Nation Health Clinic, 1311 W. Locust St., Stilwell, OK 74960 (918) 696-6911.

STONE, EVELYN
(Indian band chief)
Affiliation: Michipicoten Indian Band, Site 7, RR 1, Box 26, Wawa, Ontario, Canada P0S 1K0 (705) 856-4455.

STONE, NATHAN
(monument manager)
Affiliation: Coronado State Monument, P.O. Box 95, Bernalillo, NM 87004 (505) 867-5351.

STONE, WANDA (Kaw)
(tribal chairperson)
Affiliation: Kaw Nation of Oklahoma, Drawer 50, Kaw City, OK 74641 (580) 269-2552 Fax 269-2301.

STONES, CHRISTINE (Shoshone)
(former tribal chairperson)
Affiliation: Ely Colony Tribal Council, 16 Shoshone Cir., Ely, NV 89301 (702) 289-3013.

STORHOLM, TERRY (Cheyenne)
(advertising sales manager)
Education: Cardinal Stritch (WI), Business. *Principal occupation*: American Indian tribal consultant. *Office address*: 620 Opperman Dr., Eagan, MN 55123 (612) 687-7327 (work). *Affiliation*: West Publishing, Eagan, MN, 1989-.

STORY, CHARLENE TUCKALEECHE
(Northeast Alabama Cherokee) 1939-
(medical communications director)
Born May 29, 1939, Moorpark, Calif. *Education*: Ventura (CA) College. *Principal occupation*: Customer relations manager. *Home address*: 53 Buckworth Cir., Trafford, AL 35172 (205) 681-0080; 856-2544 (work). *Affiliation*: Commissioner for Alabama Indian Affairs, 1995-2001. *Community activities*: Principal Chief, Northeast Alabama Cherokee Tribe, 1998-present; representing Native Americans thru churches, schools, parades, and at powwows. *Interests*: Indian festivals, powwows, traditional southern cloth dancer, head lady dancer at pow wows; collect Native American artist plates. *Biographical sources*: "I have been subject of several articles in "The Blount Countian" regarding tribal activities."

STORY, JUDY BIVENS
(Indian education program director)
Affiliation: Fort Smith School District, Indian Education Program, P.O. Box 1948, Fort Smith, AR 72902 (501) 783-1202. E-mail: jstory@rogers.fssc.k12.ar.us.

STOTT, MARGARET 1945-
(museum curator)
Born September 25, 1945, Vancouver, Can. *Education*: University of British Columbia, BA, 1966; McGill University, MA, 1969; University of London (England), PhD, 1982. *Principal occupation & Address*: Museum curator of ethnology, Museum of Anthropology, University of British Columbia, Vancouver, 1979-. *Memberships*: British Columbia Museums Association; Canadian Museums Association; American Association of Museums; Canadian Ethnology Society; Canadian Anthropology and Sociology Association; Mediterranean Institute; Modern Greek Studies Association; Council for Museum Anthropology. *Interests*: Northwest Coast Indian material culture and art with particular emphasis on the Bella Coola Indians; material culture studies; museum studies; Mediterranean ethnography with particular emphasis on modern Greece; tourism studies, particularly in the Mediterranean. *Published works*: Bella Coola Ceremony and Art (National Museums of Canada, 1975); Material Anthropology: Contemporary Approaches to Material Culture (University Press of America, in press). *Exhibitions*: Northwest Coast Indian Art, exhibition of contemporary Indian art (20 pieces), displayed in four cases at Air Canada Maple Leaf Lounge, Vancouver International Airport, 1980-; numerous other exhibitions in the past. Audio-visual productions: The Raven and the First Man, visuals of the sculpture carved by Haida artist Bill Reid, with the artist narrating the Haida origin myth depicted in the carvings; Salish Art and Culture, an interview with an anthropologist in the Museum exhibition Visions of Power, Symbols and Wealth; among others.

STRAIT, DOROTHY MAY (Doe-Kwo te.-Ha-Na)
(Cherokee) 1935-
(artist)
Born September 6, 1935, Phoenix, Ariz. *Education*: Scottsdale Community College (2 years). *Principal occupation*: Artist. *Home address*: 1299 E. Canyon, Apache Junction, AZ 85217 (602) 983-4545. *Memberships*: Indian Arts and Crafts Association; High Country Art & Craft Guild; Southwestern Association on Indian Affairs. *Awards, honors*: 1982 Art Show, John F. Kennedy Center-Night of the First American, Washington, DC; 1983 One Woman Show - Gambaro Studio Gallery, Washington, DC; 1984 Museum of Natural History - Smithsonian Institution, Washington, DC; 1988 Inter-Tribal Indian Ceremonial Poster Award, Gallup, NM; 1992 & 1993 Multicultural Calendar, Christopher Columbus and the Native Americans. *Interests*: Attend large Native American art shows icluding: Denver Art Show, CO; Gallup Art Show, NM; Red Earth Art Show, OK; High Country Art and Craft Guild Show, Asheville, NC. *Biographical sources*: 1982 OHOYO - A Resource Guide of American Indian Alaska Native Women; California Art Review, Les Krantz; Arizona Arts Magazine, Vol. I, II, III.

STRANGE OWL, ANN (Medicine Eagle Feather Woman) (Northern Cheyenne) 1936-
(gallery owner)
Born June 1, 1936, Birney Village, Mont. *Education*: University of Alaska (2 years); Ames College, Greeley,

CO (2 years). *Principal occupation*: Store owner. *Address*: 9853 Hwy. 7, Allenspark, CO 80510 (303) 747-2861 (work) Website: www.eagleplume.com. *Affiliation*: Owner/partner, Eagle Plume's, Allenspark, CO, 1976-.

STRANGE OWL, NICO (Buffalo Appearing Woman) (Northern Cheyenne) 1963-
(gallery owner; American Indian art appraiser)
Born June 28, 1963, Bakersfield, Calif. *Education*: Colorado State University (5 years). *Principal occupation*: Store owner; appraiser, consultant. *Address*: 9853 Hwy. 7, Allenspark, CO 80510 (303) 747-2861 (work) E-mail:strangeowl@aol.com; Web site: www.eagleplume.com. *Affiliations*: Manager, Squash Blossom, Vail. CO, 1986-89; managing director, Lone Mountain Gallery, Vail, CO; consultant, Denver Art Museum, 1991-93; partner, Eagle Plume's, Allenspark, 1993-. *Community activities*: Various lectures regarding American Indian art & culture; member, Douglas Society. *Memberships*: American Society of Appraisers (candidate member); Indian Arts & Crafts Association; Antique Tribal Arts Dealers Association; Southwestern Association on Indian Affairs; Douglas Society (Denver Art Museum). *Published work*: Four Great Rivers to Cross.

STRAUS, JERRY C.
(attorney)
Education: Columbia University, BA, 1958, LL.B., 1961; U.S. Attoney General's Honors Program. *Address & Present Affiliation*: Co-founder (with Chalres Hobbs and Bobo Dean in 1982), Hobbs, Straus, Dean & Walker, LLP (1988-present), 2120 L St., NW, Suite 700, Washington, DC 20037 (202) 822-8282. E-mail: hwalker@hsdwdc.com. E-mail: jstraus@hsdwdc.com. *Past professional posts*: Dept. of Justice, Washington, DC, 1961-63; Wilkinson, Cragun & Barker, Washington, DC, 1963-82. Mr. Straus has worked in the field of Indian law since 1963. He led the successful legislative efforts to return the 48,000-acre Blue Lake land to the Taos Pueblo in 1970, and the 26,000-acre Santa Cruz Spring Tract to the Pueblo de Cochiti in 1984. He assisted the Seminole Tribe of Florida in successfully negotiating a landmark water rights compact with the State of Florida. He led the firm's legislative efforts to secure congressional approval of a $32 million award to the menominee Tribe of Wisconsin for damages the Tribe suffered as a result of the termination of its federal trust status in 1961. Presently, Mr. Straus specializes in representing tribes who conduct high stakes gaming, and assists those tribes in defining their rights under the Indian Gaming Regulatory Act (IGRA). He represented the Mohegan Tribe of Connecticut in its successful efforts to establish a major casino in that state. He was also co-counsel to the Seminole Tribe in the 1996 case of Seminole Tribe of Florida v. State of Florida, the first IGRA case to reach the U.S. Supreme Court. Mr. Straus is a major strategist in tribal opposition to federal legislation that would curtail Indian gaming rights.

STRICKLAND, CALEB
(museum director)
Affiliations: Community Services Dept., National Museum of the American Indian, Smithsonian Institution, 4220 Silver Hill Rd., Suitland, MD 20746 (301) 238-6624.

STRICKLAND, JOHNYE E.
(secretary/treasurer)
Affiliation: American Native Press Archives and Research Association, American Indian & Alaska Native Periodicals, Research Clearinghouse, 502 Stabler Hall, University of Arkansas, 33rd & University Ave., Little Rock, AR 72204 (501) 569-3160.

STRICKLAND, RENNARD JAMES (Osage-Cherokee) 1940-
(law professor; law center director)
Born September 26, 1940, St. Louis, Mo. *Education*: Northeastern State College, BA, 1962; University of Virginia, JD, 1965, SJD, 1970; University of Arkansas, MA, 1966. *Principal occupation*: Professor of law. *Address*: Center for the Study of American Indian Law, University of Oklahoma School of Law, 300 Timberdell Rd., Norman, OK 73019 (405) 325-4676. *Affiliations*: Professor, University of Arkansas, 1965-69; professor of law, University of Tulsa, 1972-74; Acting Dean,

School of Law, University of Tulsa, 1974-75; associate professor, University of Washington, 1975-76; supervising director, Shleppey Native American Collections, University of Tulsa, 1976-85; John W. Shleppey Research Professor of Law & History, University of Tulsa, 1976-85; dean & professor, School of Law, Southern Illinois University, 1985-88; professor of law, University of Wisconsin, Madison, 1988-90; professor of law & director, Center for the Study of American Indian Law, The University of Oklahoma, College of Law, Norman, OK, 1990-. *Other professional posts*: Director, Indian Heritage Association, Muskogee, Okla., 1966-84; director, Oral History Project, University of Florida, 1969-1971; Site Inspector, American Bar Association, Section on Legal Education and Admission to the Bar, 1974-; chair, Indian Advisory Board, Philbrook Art Center, 1979-83; editor-in-chief, revision of Handbook of Federal Indian Law, Solicitor's Office, Dept. of the Interior, 1975-82; member, National Museum Advisory Board, Heard Museum, 1986-; board of directors, ATLATL, Native American Arts Service Organization, 1988-90; consultant, Panel for National Dialogue on Museums — Native American Relations, Center for Cross-Cultural Communications, 1989-90; Law School Admissions Council, 1988-90; Smithsonian Institution, Planning Committee, 1990-91; American Bar Association, Affirmative Action Committee, 1988-91. *Visiting professor at the following*: Sylvan Lange Distinguished Visiting Professor, St. Mary's University, Summer 1973, University of New Mexico, Fall 1976, Summer, 1975-79, University of West Virginia (Reyer Distinguished), October 1982, University of Florida, Spring, 1983; University of Kansas (Langston Hughes Distinguished); Heard Museum of Native American and Primitive Art (Scholar-in-Residence), 1988-89; Arizona State University, 1988-89; public lectures. *Memberships*: Association of American Law Schools (Accreditation Committee, 1990-92; president, 1994); American Society of Legal History; Selden Society; Communications Association of America; Oklahoma Historical Society; American Society for Ethnohistory; American Association of Museums (member, Task Force-Reparations of Ceremonial Objects and Human Remains, 1987-88; American Bar Association (co-chair, Section on Legal Education and Admission to the Bar, Bicentennial Committee on the U.S. Constitution, 1984-87; member, Task Force on Minorities in the Legal Profession, 1987-89). *Awards, honors*: Sacred Sash of the Creeks for Preservation Tribal History; Fellow in Legal History, American Bar Association, 1970-1971; Fellow, American Council of Learned societies, 1972; Fellow, Doris Duke Foundation, 1970-73; Distinguished Service Award, Creek Indian Nation, 1972; Outstanding Faculty member, School of Law, University of Tulsa, 1975; Distinguished Alumnus Award, Northeastern State College, 1976; Society of American Law Teachers Annual Award for Outstanding Teaching and Contribution to Law Reform, 1978; Award of Merit, Association for State and Local History, 1981 (editorial board member); Award of Excellence, Western Book Association, for A Trumpet of Out Own, 1982; Distinguished Service Citation, American Indian Coalition, Tulsa, OK, 1985; Chairman's Award, Contribution to Development of Indian Law in Oklahoma, presented by Chief Claude Cox, Chairman, Oklahoma Indian Affairs Commission, Tribal Summit, 1990. *Interests*: Indian law, Indian art, film & filmmaking. Mr. Strickland writes, "Primary interest (is in) law and the American Indian, including programs to attract Indian students to the law as a profession, and programs to make the law responsive to the needs of Indian citizens; culture of the American Indian, with primary emphasis upon myths and legends and upon the arts and crafts of native tribes; contemporary American Indian paintings, and the evolution of Indian culture as reflected in evolving styles; ethnohistory of specific tribes—the Cherokee, Creek. Seminole, Choctaw and Chickasaw; development of traditional legal systems among the tribes." *Published works*: Sam Houston With the Cherokees, 1829-1833, with Jack Gregory (University of Texas Press, 1967); Starr's History of the Cherokees (1968); Cherokee Spirit Tales (1969); Cherokee Cook Book (1969); Creek-Seminole Spirit Tales (1971); Choctaw Spirit Tales (1972); Hell on the Border (1971); Adventures of an Indian Boy (1973); American Indian Spirit Tales (1973); all with Jack Gregory, published by Indian Heritage Association; Cherokee Law Ways (University of Oklahoma Press, 1972); with Earl Boyd Pierce - The Cherokee People (Indian

Tribal Series, 1973; How to Get Into Law School (Hawthorne Books, Inc, 1974, revised editions, 1975-77-79-82); Fire and Spirits: Cherokee Law From Clan to Court (University of Oklahoma Press, 1975); with William & Janet Phillips - Avoiding Teacher Malpractice (Hawthorne Books, 1976); The Prelaw Handbook (Assn. of American Law Schools, 1975, rev. eds. 1976-79); The Indians in Oklahoma (University of Oklahoma Press & Oklahoma Images Project, 1980); A Trumpet of Our Own: Yellow Bird on the American Indian (Book Club of California, 1981); Handbook of Federal Indian Law (Michie-Bobbs-Merrill, 3rd Ed., 1982); Magic Images: Contemporary Native American Art (University of Oklahoma Press, 1982); As In a Vision: Masterworks of American Indian Art (University of Oklahoma Press, 1983); Arizona Memories (University of Arizona Press, 1984: The Right Law School for You (Law School Admission Council, Newtown, PA, 1986, 1987); "Keeping Our Word: Indian Treaty Rights & Public Responsibilities," a report (with S.J. Herzberg & S.R. Owens) for the Senate Select Committee on Indian Affairs, 1990; Shared Visions: Native American Painting & Sculpture (The Heard Museum, 1991); Trying a New Way: An Assessment of the Indian Self-Governance Demonstration Project, an analysis prepared for the BIA & Self-Governance Demonstration Tribes, 1992; Savages, Sinners, and Redskinned Redeemers: Images of the Native American (University of New Mexico Press); Indian Dilemma: Rhetoric and Reality of Cherokee Removal (University of Oklahoma Press); numerous edited books/studies, & articles/chapters/essays.

STROMMER, GEOFFREY D.
(attorney)
Education: University of California, Berkeley, BA, 1986; Georgetown University Law Center, J.D., 1990. *Address & Affiliation*: Managing Partner, Hobbs, Straus, Dean & Walker, LLP (1992-present), 851 S.W. Sixth Ave., Suite 1650, Portland, OR 97204 (503) 242-1745. E-mail: gstrommer@hsdwor.com. . Represents tribal clients on a wide range of issues, specializing in the Indian Self-Determination and Education Assistance Act (ISDEAA). He was actively involved with the development of regulations to implement Title IV of the ISDEAA, and was a key member of the tribal team that drafted and successfully lobbied for the enactment of the Self-Governance Amendments of 2000. He's also an active participant in the negotiated rulemaking process to develop a new formula and regulations for the Indian Reservation Roads Program as well as the negotiated rulemaking process under Title V of the ISDEAA. *Past professional posts*: Adjunct professor of law, Northwestern School of Law at Lewis & Clark College, 1997, where he taught a course on federal Indian law. instructor, Dept. of Health & Human Services Executive Leadership Program. Geoffrey has written several larticles for legal publications on Indian law issues. He co-authored a law review article (with Craig Jacobson), "Indian Tribes and the Base Realignment & Closure Act: Recommendations for Future Trust Land Acquisitions," North Dakota Law Review, Sept. 1999.

STULL, DONALD D.
(professor of anthropology)
Education: University of Colorado, PhD, 1973; University of California-Berkeley, MPH, 1975. *Affiliation*: University of Kansas, Dept. of Anthropology, 622 Fraser Hall, Lawrence, KS 66045 (785) 864-4103 Fax 864-5224. E-mail: stull@ku.edu. Dr. Stull works closely with the Kansas Kickapoo.

STURGES, RALPH W. *(Chief G'tine'mong)* (Mohegan) 1918-
(marble sculptor; tribal chief)
Born December 25, 1918, New London, Conn. *Education*: Penn Institute of Criminology (Philadelphia), Diploma, 1947. *Principal occupation*: Marble sculptor; tribal chief. *Home address*: 97 Raymond St., New London, CT 06320 (860) 442-8005. *Affiliation*: Marble sculpturing -many of which are placed in state and city buildings and private places; Lifetime Chief of the Mohegan Tribe, Uncasville, CT; camera clubs, Waterford, CT and Westerly, RI. *Other professional post*: Owned and operated my own distribution company. *Military service*: U.S. Army, 1940-45 (Intelligence; served in Pacific Theater). *Community activities*: Salvation Army. *Awards, honors*: Katherine Duggan Award for encouraging others to become interested in the arts, Marlborough (CT) Community Art Council. *Interests*: Sports, photography, arts.

STURTEVANT, MARGARET
(museum president)
Affiliation: Tribal House of the Bear, Box 868, Wrangell, AK 99929 (907) 874-3505.

SUAGEE, DEAN B. (Cherokee of Oklahoma)
(attorney)
Education: University of Arizona, BA, 1972; University of North Carolina, J.D., 1976; American University, LL.M., 1989. *Principal occupation*: Attorney. *Affiliations*: Attorney Of Counsel, Hobbs, Straus, Dean & Walker, LLP, 2120 L St., NW, Suite 700, Washington, DC 20037 (202) 822-8282 (Associate, 1988-93; Of Counsel, 1993-present); Director of the First Nations Environmental Law Program, Vermont Law School (VLS) (802) 763-8303, 1998-present, E-mail: dsuagee@vermontlaw.edu; also serves as the Director of VLS Indian Country Environmental Justice Clinic. Mr. Suagee specializes in environmental and natural resources law and cultural heritage preservation. He has taught courses in Indian country environmental law and federal Indian law at VLS and the Washington College of Law, American University. He frequently speaks at seminars on environmental law and federal Indian law, and has authored many law journal articles in these fields.

SUDDUTH, LEONARD
(school principal)
Affiliation: Chitimacha Day School, Route 2, Box 222, Jeanerette, LA 70544 (318) 923-4921.

SUINA, HENRY (Pueblo)
(former Pueblo governor)
Affiliation: Cochiti Pueblo Council, P.O. Box 70, Cochiti, NM 87072 (505) 465-2244.

SULCER, PATRICIA
(editor)
Affiliation: How Ni Kan, Citizen Band Potawatomi Tribe, Route 5, Box 151, Shawnee, OK 74801 (405) 275-3121.

SULLIVAN, DOROTHY (Oklahoma Cherokee) 1939-
(artist)
Born January 8, 1939, Seminole, Okla. *Education*: East Central University, Ada, OK, BA in Art Education & History. *Principal occupation*: Artist. *Address & Affiliation*: Owner & Cherokee Master Artist, Memory Circle Studio, P.O. Box 732, Norman, OK 73070 (405) 360-0751 Fax 579-3244. *Awards, honors*: Numerous awards fro her art. *Interests*: Exhibitions and One Woman Shows. Collections: Dorothy's art work is in the Museum of the Cherokee Indian and Cherokee Heritage Museum in Cherokee, NC; and in private art collections including Wilma Mankiller, Betty Ford, Wes Strudi, John Quinn, III, etc. *Memberships*: Indian Arts & crafts Association; National Penn Women (Artists, Writers, Musicians) for Art & Letters; Cherokee Historical Society. *Published work*: Cherokee Heritage Collection, 1994 (sold out edition) "seven years of my art and research;" Biographical Directory of Native American Painters (Oklahoma University Press, 1995); Illustrator, Winter Story Time (Children's Press, 1994); Illustrator, The Man Hunting for the Sun (McMillan Spotlight Books, 1996; The Woman's Way - She Speaks for Her Clan (Time Life Books, 1995). Calendars: Cherokee Heritage 1999; Native American People's 1997; American Indian Artists, 1995-92; Dorothy's Cherokee Heritage Collection, 1994.

SUMMERFIELD, HARRY B., JR. (Paiute)
(former tribal chairperson)
Affiliation: Lovelock Tribal Council, P.O. Box 878, Lovelock, NV 89419 (702) 273-7861.

SUMMERFIELD, TAMARA R. (Quapaw)
(tribal chairperson)
Affiliation: Quapaw Tribal Business Committee, P.O.Box 765, Quapaw, OK 74363 (918) 542-1853 Fax 542-4694. E-mail: tsummerfield@chek.com.

SUMMERS, ALLEN (Paiute)
(tribal chairperson)
Affiliation: Bishop Indian Tribal Council, P.O. Box 548, Bishop, CA 93514 (619) 873-3584.

SUMMERS-FITZGERALD, DIOSA (Mississippi Choctaw) 1945-
(director of education, artist)
Born December 23, 1945, New York, N.Y. *Education*: State University College at Buffalo, BA, 1977; Northwestern University Archaeological Center, Kampsville, IL (Certificate), 1981; Harvard University Graduate School of Education, EdM, 1983. *Principal occupation*: Director of education, artist. *Home address*: Resides on Staten Island, NY. *Affiliations*: Instructor, History Dept. and Continuing Education Dept., State University College at Buffalo, NY, 1975-77; instructor, Haffenreffer Museum of Anthropology, Bristol, RI, 1979-80; acting tribal coordinator, Narragansett Tribal Education Project, Inc., 1980; administration, instructor, proposal writer, program coordinator, 1980-81, education director, instructor, 1982-85, Tomaquag Indian Memorial Museum, Exeter, RI; Native American historical and educational consultant, Plimoth Plantation, Plymouth, MA, 1981-82; artist in residence, Folk Arts Program, RI State Council on the Arts, Providence, 1982-85; artist, Native American Art Forms Nishnabeykwa Productions, Charlestown, RI, 1982-85; education director, Jamaica Arts Center, Jamaica, NY, 1985-. *Other professional post*: Owner, artist, consultant, Nishnabeykwa Productions, Staten Island, N.Y., 1982-. *Memberships*: Harvard Club of RI. *Awards, honors*: 1st Prize, Photography, Thomas Indian School Exhibit; Kappa Delta Pi, national Undergraduate Honor Society; Phi Alpha Theta, International History Honor Society. *Interests*: "Over the years, I have devoted most of life to Native American art, and a clear understanding of the roots of Native American tradition through art. I have also sought to develop a better understanding of the Native American through art as well as in the classroom initially as a teacher, and more recently a curriculum developer, and program developer. Other expertise: Cultural consultant and educational consultant; craft demonstrations; curator of exhibitions." *Published works*: Native American Foods; Fingerweaving, narrative and instruction; Ash Splint Basketry; Tomaquag Indian Museum brochures.

SUMNER, DELORES TITCHYWY *(Toos-z)* (Comanche) 1931-
(special collections librarian)
Born May 11, 1931, Lawton, Okla. *Education*: Northeastern State University, BS, 1964, MEd, 1967; University of Oklahoma, MLS, 1981. *Principal occupation*: Special collections librarian; assistant professor. *Home address*: 405 N. Bliss, Tahlequah, OK 74464 (918) 456-5511, Ext. 3252 (office); Fax 458-2197; E-Mail: sumner@cherokee.nsuok.edu. *Affiliations*: Special Collections Librarian, John Vaughn Library, and assistant professor of Library Services, Northeastern State University, Tahlequah, OK, 1982-present; coordinator/director, Comanche Cultural Center, Comanche Complex, Lawton, OK. *Community activities*: Northeastern State University Symposium on the American Indian (appointed member, 1982-). *Memberships*: North American Indian Women's Association (president, Northeastern Oklahoma chapter, 1989-92); American Indian Libraries Association; Association of College and Research Libraries; Tahlequah Area Arts and Humanities Council; Philbrook Museum Association; Gilcrease Museum Association; North American Indian Museum Association; Oklahoma Historical Society; Oklahoma Library Association; American Library Association; Delta Kappa Gamma (Research Committee Chairperson). *Awards, honors*: Certificate of Appreciation, Oklahoma Library Association . *Interests*: "Supporting the traditional artists in Native American art by traveling to exhibits, showings, and galleries is one of my main interests. I am very much interested in the preservation of Native American culture and tradition through oral history, genealogy, art work, and the retention of the native language, of which I have accomplished only a small portion while working for my tribe as their cultural director. Today, I am still working toward this goal by personally contacting elders to record their songs, stories, and memories. I also record Comanche hymns whenever possible." *Published works*: Numa-Nu: The Fort Sill Indian School Experience (Oklahoma Humanities Committee, 1980); Descendants of Titchywy, 2001; Descendants of Wis-sis-che, 2001.

SUN BEAR *(Gheezis Mokwa)* **(Chippewa) 1929-**
(author, lecturer)
Born August 31, 1929, White Earth Reservation, Bemidji, Minn. *Education*: LA Duke School, White Earth Reservation, MN (8 years). *Principal occupation*: Author, lecturer. *Address*: Bear Tribe Medicine Society, 3750A Airport Blvd #223, Mobile, AL 36608. *Affiliation*: Founder/president, The Bear Tribe Medicine Society, Spokane, WA, 1966-. *Other professional* posts: Editor/publisher, Many Smokes magazine; motion picture actor and extra, 1955-65; technical director, Wagon Train, Bonanza, and Wild, Wild West, television series. *Membership*: Midiwidin Society; National Congress of American Indians. *Interests*: "I have been involved in Indian affairs most of my life, and I've spent some time teaching survival living to Indian and non-Indian people. I'm concerned with our Indian people, and other people, becoming more self-sufficient on the land, and learning a better balance with each other, and the Earth Mother; teaching, lecturing, writing; ceremonial leader of pilgrimages to sacred sites on the globe; businessman. Primary interest is to bridge Native and non-native cultures, sharing knowledge to help heal people and the earth during the time of global changes." Sun Bear is a world traveler and lecturer, his travels have taken him to Europe, Australia, and India. *Biographical sources*: Mother Earth News, Sept.-Oct. 1988; Visions and Revisions, Winter 1988; New Realities, Spring 1988; Joy of Life, Spring, 1989; Guide to New Age Living, 1989; Sacred Earth News, Spring, 1989; The Light Connection, Oct. 1989; Wholistic Living News, Oct. 1989. *Published works*: At Home in the Wilderness (Naturegraph, 1968); Buffalo Hearts (Bear Tribe Publishing, 1970); Walk in Balance (Prentice-Hall); The Bear Tribe's Self-Reliance Book (Bear Tribe Publishing, 1977); The Medicine Wheel Book (Prentice-Hall, 1980); Sun Bear: The Path of Power (Bear Tribe Publishing, 1983); Black Dawn, Bright Day (Simon & Schuster, 1991); Dancing the Wheel (Simon & Schuster, 1991).

SUNCHILD, JOHN (Chippewa-Cree)
(tribal chairperson)
Affiliation: Chippewa-Cree Business Committee, Rocky Boy's Reservation, Rocky Boy Route, Box 544, Box Elder, MT 59521 (406) 395-4282.

SUNDSTROM, LINEA
(consultant, author)
Affiliation: Private consultant in archaeology, historic resource management, and ethnohistory. *Published works*: Rock Art of the Southern Black Hills: A Contextual Approach; coauthor, Rock Art of Western South Dakota; Storied Stone: Indian Rock Art in the Black Hills Country (University of Oklahoma Press, 2004).

SUNSHINE, RON
(Indian band chief)
Affiliation: Sturgeon Lake Indian Band, Box 757, Valleyview, Alberta, Canada T0H 3N0 (403) 524-3307.

SUPAHAN, SARAH
(Indian education program director)
Affiliation: Klamath-Trinity Joint Unified School District, Indian Education Program, P.O. Box 1308, Hoopa, CA 95546 (916) 625-4412 (phone & fax).

SUPERNAW, KATHLEEN RAE (Creek/Munsee) 1949-
(attorney)
Born October 15, 1949, Hominy, Okla. *Education*: Northeastern Oklahoma A & M College, AA, 1969; Central State University, BS, 1971; Antioch University, MA, 1986; University of Oklahoma Law School, JD, 1992. *Principal occupation*: Attorney. *Home address*: 7906 E. 33rd St., Tulsa, OK 74145 (918) 669-7730. *Affiliations*: Indian Tribes Community Development Association (past president), Oklahoma City, 1984-88; American Indian Law Review (editor-in-chief), Norman, OK, 1991-92; U.S. Dept. of the Interior, Office of the Field Solicitor, Tulsa, OK, 1993-. *Other professional posts*: Attorney, Pitchlynn, Odom, Morse & Ritter; Research Associate, University of Oklahoma - Center for American Indian Law & Policy; Rural Development Fellow, University of California, Davis, CA, 1985-86. *Community activities*: Recruitment of Indians to go to law school; work in Indian communities to encourage Indian kids to complete education and establish goals; support Indian arts and crafts fairs and promotions.

Memberships: Oklahoma Indian Bar Association; American Indian Bar Association; American Indian Heritage Center. *Awards, honors*: Outstanding Second Year Editor, American Indian Law Review; recipient of the Gretchen Harris, Dean's, and Jones-Givens Scholarships; Joseph Rarick Outstanding Native American Student Award. *Interests*: Environmental and Indian law; Indian history and Indian studies; education in general; Indian tribal planning and development. Major employment before law school was working for several Indian tribes as the drafter of planning. *Published work*: Co-authored with Rennard Strickland, "Back to the Future: A Proposed Model Tribal Act to Protect Native Cultural Heritage (Arkansas Law Review, 1993).

SUPERNAW, KUGEE (Quapaw-Osage)
(craftsperson; Indian company owner)
Affiliation: Supernaw's Oklahoma Indian Supply, 303 East WC Rogers Blvd., P.O. Box 216, Skiatook, OK 74070 (918) 396-1713.

SURIANO, PATRICK
(school principal)
Affiliation: Kaibeto Boarding School, East Hwy. 160, Kaibeto, AZ 86053 (520) 673-3480 Fax 673-3489.

SURVEYOR, CHARLES (Cheyenne-Arapaho)
(tribal chairperson)
Affiliation: Cheyenne-Arapaho Business Committee, 100 Red Moon Cir., Box 38, Concho, OK 73022 (405) 262-0345.

SUTEER-FENTON, BEVERLY S. (Ojibwe) 1950-
(American Indian advisor)
Born April 16, 1950, Cape Girardeau, Mo. *Education*: University of Illinois, 1968-69; Eastern Illinois University, BA, 1989, MS, 1991. *Principal occupation*: American Indian advisor. *Home address*: 4130 Granby Ct., Fort Collins, CO 80526. *Affiliation*: University of Utah, Salt Lake City, UT, 1991-97. *Community activities*: Board of Directors, Indian Walk-In Center, Salt Lake City; Utah InterTribal Veterans Association Auxiliary; Heber Valley Pow Wow Committee. *Memberships*: Utah Coalition for the Advancement of Minorities in Higher Education; National Indian Education Society; American College Personnel Association; Phi Delta Kappa Honorary Education Society. *Awards, honors*: Outstanding Community Service Award, Salt Lake City Indian Community, 1992. *Interests*: "Have participated in numerous workshops & presentations which address the recruitment & retention of American Indians in higher education."

SUTTEER, BARBARA A. (Northern Ute, Cherokee) 1940-
(American Indian liaison)
Born December 9, 1940, Roosevelt, Utah. Education: University of Utah, 1959-60. *Principal occupation*: American Indian lisiason. *Address & Affiliation*: Liaison, Office of American Indian Trust Responsibility, National Park Service, Rm. 550 (Rocky Mountain System Support Office), P.O. Box 25287, Lakewood, CO 80225 (303) 969-2511 Fax 969-2063; E-mail: barbara_sutteer@nps.gov. 1993-. *Other professional posts*: Supt., Little Bighorn Battlefield National Monument, Crow Agency, MT; Indian Allotment Coordinator, Bureau of Indian Affairs (Alaska). *Community activities*: Serves on the American Indian Task Force, Denver Art Museum & Colorado History Museum. *Awards, honors*: Special Achievement, Bureau of Indian Affairs (Alaska). *Interests*: Federal Indian Policy; interpretation of American Indian cultures/histories. *Biographical sources*: Chapter on Little Bighorn Battlefield (Name Change/Indian Memorial) in biography, "Ben Nighthorse Campbell."

SWAIN, PHILIBERT (Moapa Paiute)
(tribal chairperson)
Affiliation: Moapa Business Council, P.O. Box 340, Moapa, NV 89025 (702) 865-2787.

SWALLEY, LARRY (Oglala Lakota Sioux)
(radio station program director)
Affiliation: KILI - 90.1 FM, Oglala Lakota Sioux Tribe, P.O. Box 150, Porcupine, SD 57772 (605) 867-5002.

SWAN, ANITA L. (Yakima)
(school supt.)
Affiliation: Yakima Tribal School, P.O. Box 151, Toppenish, WA 98948 (509) 865-5121.

SWAN, CLAIRE (Kenaitze)
(tribal chairperson; health director)
Affiliation: Kenaitze Indian Tribe Executive Committee/Tribal Council & Health Center, P.O. Box 988, Kenai, AK 99611 (907) 283-3633.

SWAN, DAVID (Inupiat)
(AK village council president)
Affiliation: Native Village of Kivalina Council, P.O. Box 50051, Kivalina, AK 99750 (907) 645-2153.

SWAN, JAMES A. (Canadian Metis) 1943-
(author/events producer)
Born February 25, 1943, Trenton, Mich. *Education*: University of Michigan, BS, 1965; MS (Resource Planning), 1967; 1967-69 (Environmental Psychology). *Principal occupation*: Author/events producer. *Address*: P.O. Box 637, Mill Valley, CA 94942 (415) 383-5064. *Affiliations*: President, Institute for the Study of Natural Systems, Mill Valley, 1987-; associate professor, California Institute of Integrated Studies, San Francisco, CA, 1987-. *Membership*: American Bison Association. *Awards, honors*: Homer N. Calver Lecturer for American Public Health Association; California State Assembly Award of Recognition; Xi Sigma Forestry Honorary; Phi Sigma Biological Sciences Honorary. *Interests*: Cross-cultural psychology and applications to ecology; producer of concerts, symposiums, and conferences; actor/musician. *Biographical sources*: Who's Who in the West; "James Swan: On Aligning Oneself With Sacred Places" Wingspan. *Published works*: Sacred Places (Bear & Co., 1990); The Power of Place (Quest, 1991); Nature As Teacher and Healer (Villard-Random House, 1992).

SWAN, JOSEPH, SR. (Inupiat)
(village president)
Affiliation: Native Village of Kivalina, P.O. Box 50051, Kivalina, AK 99750 (907) 645-2153.

SWAN, RAYMOND
(Indian band chief)
Affiliation: Lake Manitoba Indian Band, Vogar, MB, Can. R0C 3C0 (204) 768-3492.

SWANBERG, KIM *(Bboon kwe)* **(Sault Chippewa) 1953-**
(Indian education program director)
Born July 4, 1953, Munising, Mich. *Principal occupation*: Coordinator/director-Indian education program. *Address*: 411 Elm St., Munising, MI 49862 (906) 387-3861 Fax 387-5311. E-mail: kimswanberg@hotmail. com. *Community activities*: Powwow annual presentations. *Awards, honors*: AIGER County's "Women of Honor" Award of 1996.

SWANEY, RHONDA R. (Confederated Salish & Kootenai) 1952-
(tribal chairperson)
Born May 15, 1952, in St. Ignatius, Mont. *Education*: University of Montana, B.A. (Political Science, Honors), 1984. *Address*: P.O. Box 278, Pablo, MT 59855 (406) 675-2700 Fax 675-2806; E-Mail: csktadmn@ronan.net. *Affiliations*: Bureau of Indian Affairs, Flathead Agency, Ronan, MT, 1974-80 (clerk typist, 1974-79, Rights of Way Specialist, 1979-80); Bureau of Indian Affairs, Portland Area Office, Portland, OR, 1984-87 (natural resources specialist, 1984-85; realty specialist, 1985-87); Chairperson, Tribal Council of the Confederated Salish & Kootenai Tribes, Pablo, MT, 1987-present (natural resources department head, 1987-94; vice-chairperson of tribal council, St. Ignatius District Rep., 1994-96, chairperson, St. Ignatius District Rep., 1996-present. *Community activities*: Self-governance and environmental protection committees. *Awards, honors*: Ms. Swaney became the first ever tribal chairwoman in 1996.

SWANSON, JOANNE (Inupiaq Eskimo)
(artist)
Born July 7, 1952, in Shaktoolik, Alaska (Norton Sound Village). *Education*: Alaska Pacific University, BA (Elemenatry Education), 1985 *Address*: P.O. Box 53027, Koyuk, AK 99753 (907) 963-2450; E-mail:

swanson@artnatam.com. *Awards, honors*: Honorable Mention, Inuit Circumpolar Conferences Logo Contest, 2002. *Professional interests*: Painting in watercolor of contemporary and traditional Eskimo village scenes, activities, and portraits. *Personal interests*: Reading, studying, beading, camping, berry picking, some travel.

SWEENEY, THOMAS W. (Citizen Potawatomi)
(director of public affairs)
Affiliation: Director of Public Affairs, Smithsonian National Museum of the American Indian, 470 L'Enfant Plaza Sw, Suite 7103, Washington, DC 20560 (202) 287-2525 ext. 142 Fax 357-3369. E-mail: sweeneyt@nmai.si.edu.

SWENTZELL, ROXANNE (Santa Clara Pueblo)
(artist)
Address: P.O. Box 4154, Fairview, NM 87533 (505) 753-6590. *Product*: Contemporary and traditional pottery and clay sculpture.

SWIFT ARROW, BERNADINE
(Indian education director)
Affiliation: Director, Quechan Indian Tribe Education Dept., P.O. Box 1446, Winterhaven, CA 92283 (760) 572-0603 Fax 572-2102

SWIFTWOLF, GERALD
(Indian band chief)
Affiliation: Moosomin Indian Band, Box 45, Cochin, Saskatchewan, Canada S0M 0L0 (306) 386-2014.

SWIMMER, ROSS O. (Oklahoma Cherokee) 1943-
(president/CEO-Cherokee Nation Industries)
Born October 26, 1943, Oklahoma City, Okla. *Education*: University of Oklahoma, BA, 1965; University of Oklahoma School of Law, J.D., 1967. *Principal occupation*: President & CEO of Cherokee Nation Industries. *Affiliations*: Law partner, Hansen, Peterson and Thompkins, Oklahoma City, Okla., 1967-72; general counsel, 1972-75, principal chief, 1975-85, Cherokee Nation of Oklahoma, Tahlequah, OK; executive vice president, 1974-75, president, 1975-85, First National Bank in Tahlequah, OK; Co-chairman, Presidential Commission on Indian Reservation Economies (a panel of tribal leaders appointed to seek ways to help tribes improve economic conditions), 1983-84; assistant secretary, U.S. Department of the Interior, Bureau of Indian Affairs, 1951 Constitution Ave., NW, Washington, DC, 1985-89; developed an Indian law practice for law firm of Hall, Estill, Harswick, Gale, Golden and Nelson, Tulsa, OK, 1989-92; president/CEO of Cherokee Nation Industries, Inc., Stillwell, OK, 1992-. *Other professional posts*: Director on several boards, including the University of Tulsa, Gilcrease Museum and the Oklahoma Medical Research Foundation; counsel to Hall, Estill, Hardwick, Gable, Golden and Nelson. *Community activities*: Boy Scouts of America in Eastern Oklahoma (executive committee); Cherokee National Historical Society (past president); Tahlequah Planning and Zoning Commission (former chairman); Eastern Oklahoma Indian Health Advisory Board (secretary-treasurer); Inter-Tribal Council of the Five Civilized Tribes (advisory board, director). *Memberships*: Oklahoma Bar Association; American Bar Association; Oklahoma Historical Society; Oklahoma Industrial Development Commission. *Awards, honors*: Honorary Doctoral Degree, Phillips University, Enid, OK; Distinguished Service Award, University of Oklahoma, Norman; Distinguished Service Citation, U.S. Dept. of Interior, 1989. *Interests*: USIA sponsored speaking tour of 14 cities in Germany to discuss issues related to the American Indian. Interior Secretary Donald Hodel said of Swimmer, "He combines a solid knowledge of tribal and Indian affairs with understanding and skill in modern business management. Swimmer has frequently expressed his views that Indian tribes should be less dependent on the federal government." When nominated for the position of Assistant Secretary, Swimmer said of President Reagan: "I know he is committed to an Indian policy that supports tribal self-determination, which is something I have worked for during my ten years at the Cherokee Nation."

SWINNEY, GORMAN
(Indian school principal)
Affiliation: Mescalero Apache School, P.O. Box 230, Mescalero, NM 88340 (505) 671-4431 Fax 671-4822.

SWISHER, KAREN GAYTON (Standing Rock Sioux)
1943-
(Indian college president.)
Born April 3, 1943, Fort Yates, N.D. *Education*: Northern State University, BS, 1964, MS, 1974; University of North Dakota, EdD, 1981. *Principal occupation*: College president. *Address*: Haskell Indian Nations University, 155 Indian Ave. #1305, Lawrence, KS 66046 (875) 749-8404 Fax 749-8406; E-Mail: kswisher@ross1.cc.haskell.edu. *Affiliations*: Teacher & principal, Bureau of Indian Affairs, 1967-77; assistant professor of education, University of Utah, Salt Lake City, 1982-85; associate professor/director of CIE, Arizona State University, Tempe, AZ, 1985-96; editor, "Journal of American Indian Education," Center for Indian Education, Arizona State University, Tempe, AZ, 1990-96; Chairperson, Teacher Education Department, 1996-2002; President, 2003-; Haskell Indian Nations University, Lawrence, KS. *Memberships*: American Educational Research Association (American Indian/Alaska Native Education Special Interest Group Chair, 1984-86, 1987-89); National Indian Education Association; Association for Supervision & Curriculum Development; American Anthropological Association; Council on Anthropology & Education. *Awards, honors*: Sioux Award, highest honor of University of North Dakota Alumni Association for professional career accomplishments, 1989; Early Contribution Award, AERA Committee on the Role and Status of Minorities in Educational Research & Development, 1990. *Interests*: "Enjoy travels to American Indian reservations in lower 48 states and desire to travel to other countries to study indigenous people's participation in educational systems." *Published works*: Co-editor, Special Issues on Learning Styles (Center for Indian Education, Arizona State University, 1989); co-editor, First American Firsts (Gale Research, 1997).

SYLVIA, TONY J. (Yurok/Narragansett)
(artist)
Address: Teewood Designs, P.O. Box 1409, Hoopa, CA 95546 (707) 499-1922.

SYNDER, FRED (Chippewa/Colville) 1951-
(director/consultant, editor/publisher)
Born March 8, 1951, Pennsylvania. *Education*: Rutgers University (2 years). *Principal occupation*: Director/consultant, National Native American Co-Operative, San Carlos, AZ. *Address*: P.O. Box 27626, Tucson, AZ 85726 (520) 622-4900. *Other professional posts*: Editor/publisher, Native American Directory—Alaska, Canada, U.S.; educator. *Community activities*: American Indian Market, monthly, Phoenix, Ariz. (sponsor); Pow Wow Attender for North America. *Awards, honors*: Blue Ribbon (3 years), Beadwork Competition, Heard Museum of Anthropology, Phoenix, AZ; numerous awards from Indian cultural programs, Title IV, Indian education, ethnic fairs. *Interests*: "Most of all my time is shared between directing the Co-Op (2,700 artisan members), distribution of Native American Directory (40,000 copies), traveling extensively throughout North America to Indian powwows, rodeos, craft shows and conventions, and establishing the first Watts Line American Indian Information Center and Chamber of Commerce." *Biographical sources*: Arizona Republic, Close Up feature article (May, 1984); Intertribal Enterprise, Close Up feature article (April, 1985); Navajo Times Today (May, 1985). *Published work*: Native American Directory—Alaska, Canada, U.S. (National Native American Co-Op, 1982 & 1996); On the Red Road: Powwows (National Native American Co-Op, 1993).

SZABO, LINDA (Sicangu Lakota)
(craftsperson)
Affiliations: Co-owner (with paul Szabo), Szabo Studio, P.O. Box 906, Mission, SD 57555 (605) 856-4548. *Product*: Handmade Northern Plains style jewelry.

SZABO, PAUL (Rosebud Sioux) 1947-
(high school art teacher)
Born December 26, 1947, Burke, S.D. *Education*: Southern State, 1966-70; Dakota State College, Madison, SD, 1970-71. *Principal occupation*: High school art teacher. *Address*: P.O. Box 906, Mission, SD 57555 (605) 856-4548. *Affiliations*: Art teacher, Todd County High School, Mission, SD, 1985-; owner, Szabo Studio, Mission, SD, 1975-. *Community activities*: Church leader; Boy Scouts. *Memberships*: National Education

Association; South Dakota Education Association; TCEA. *Awards, honors*: Northern Plains Art Show - 2nd place, 2 years, honorable mention; Cultural Heritage Art Show - 1st place, metal work; Renwick Collection at the Smithsonian, Washington, D.C. *Interests*: "Metalworking and selling; travel. *Biographical sources*: Numerous newspaper articles.

T

TABLOS, DERENTY
(executive director)
Affiliation: Chugachmiut, 4201 Tudor Centre, Suite 210, Anchorage, AK 99508 (907) 562-4155.

TABOR, ROBERT (Cheyenne-Arapaho)
(tribal chairperson)
Affiliation: Cheyenne-Arapaho Tribal Business Committee, P.O. Box 38, Concho, OK 73022 (405) 262-0345.

TAFOYA, PATRICK (Navajo)
(communications coordinator)
Born in Albuquerque, N.M. *Education*: BA (Classics), University of New Mexico; Harvard University (3 years in Divinity School). *Address & Affiliation*: Communications Coordinator, HIV/AIDS Project, American Indian Community House, 708 Broadway, 8th Floor, New York, NY 10003 (212) 598-0100.

TAH, ANDREW M. (Navajo)
(BIA agency supt. for education)
Affiliation: Chinle Agency, Bureau of Indian Affairs, P.O. Box 6003, Chinle, AZ 86503 (520) 674-5201 ext. 201.

TAH-BONE, GEORGE (Kiowa)
(attorney)
Affiliation: Oklahoma Indian Bar Association, P.O. Box 1062, Oklahoma City, OK 73101 (405) 521-5277. *Membership*: Oklahoma Indian Bar Association (committee chairperson-tribal courts).

TAHSUDA, MAX
(IHS-area tribal development)
Affiliation: Office of Tribal Development, Indian Health Service, Oklahoma Area Office, Indian Health Service, Five Corporate Plaza, 3625 NW 56th St., Oklahoma City, OK 73102 (405) 231-4796.

TAKEN ALIVE, JESSE "JAY" (Standing Rock Sioux)
(tribal chairperson)
Affiliation: Standing Rock Sioux Tribe, P.O. Box D, Fort Yates, ND 58538 (701) 854-7202.

TALACHY, PEARL (Nambe Tewa)
(potter)
Address: Rt. 1 Box 114-M, Nambe Pueblo, NM 87501 (505) 455-3429. *Product*: Pottery.

TALAHONGVA, PATTY (Hopi)
(multi-media journalist)
Born in Polacca (First Mesa), Ariz. *Principal occupation*: Independent multi-media journalist based in Tempe, AZ. *Address*: c/o Native American Journalists Association (NAJA), 3359 36th Ave. South, Minneapolis, MN 55406 (612) 729-9244 Fax 729-9373. E-mail: talahongva@naja.com. She is a former television news producer and has produced newscasts, special projects, and documentaries. Currently, she writes for several national magazines and newspapers. In addition, she is producing video documentaries on Native people. *Other professional posts*: Vice President, Board of Directors, Native American Journalists Association (NAJA);board of directors, Radio and Television News Directors Association as an Ex-Officio representative for NAJA through the RTNDA/UNITY Covenant. Since 1994 she has been the lead mentor for NAJA students in the summer broadcast project, NAJA News 4; she also contributes to the national radio talkshow, "Native America Calling." *Interests*: Her goal is to bring more Native and Aboriginal people into careers with mainstream television news.

TALAMANES, FRANK
(executive director)
Affiliation: Society for the Advancement of Chicanos & Native Americans in Science, Sinsheimer Labs, University of California, Santa Cruz, CA 95064 (408) 459-4272.

TALAMANTEZ, INES M. (Mescalero Apache)
(associate professor)
Address & Affiliation: Associate Professor of Religious Studies, University of California at Santa Barbara, Santa Barbara, CA 93106.

TALAMINI, THOMAS
(health director)
Affiliation: Claremore PHS Indian Hospital, W. Wil Rogers & Moore, Claremore, OK 74017 (918) 341-8430.

TALBOT, F. MEDICINE STORY (Manitonquat)
(Wampanoag) 1929-
(storyteller, teacher, author, lecturer)
Born July 17, 1929, Salem, Mass. *Education:* Cornell University, BA, 1954; MEd, 1974, PhD, 2002. *Principal occupation:* Storyteller, teacher, author, lecturer. *Address:* 167 Merriam Hill Rd., Greenville, NH 03048 (603) 878-3201 Fax 878-2310. E-mail: medicine story@yahoo.com. Website: www.circleway.org. *Affiliation:* Co-director, Another Place, Inc., Greenville, NH, 1980- ; Mettanokit Outreach, Greenville, NH. *Other professional post:* Editor, Native Liberation Journal: Heritage. *Military service:* U.S. Army, 1951-53 (PFC). *Community activities:* Elder & spiritual/ceremonial leader of Assonet Wampanoag; Liberation Reference Person for Native American Counselors (Eastern Canada & U.S.); spiritual advisor to Native Prison Programs in New England (re-evaluation counselor & counseling teacher); Tribal Healing Council (co-founder); Massachusetts Center for Native American Awareness; Watuppa Wampanoag Reservation Improvement Committee; Indian Spiritual & Cultural Training Council, Inc. *Interests:* "Counselor & spiritual advisor to six Native Prison Circles in New England; storyteller; author/lecturer/workshop & seminar leader at schools, universities, religious, cultural, environmental, health, peace and other organizations throughout North America & Europe; former writer-poetry editor-illustrator-cartoonist with Akwesasne Notes; now edits The Talking Stick, newsletter of activities of Mettanokit Outreach, Prison Program & Assonet Wampanoag activities. *Biographical sources:* Profiles in Wisdom by Stephen McFadden; numerous articles in newspapers and magazines. *Published works:* Manitonquat (Medicine Story): Return to Creation (Bear Tribe, 1991); story in "Spinning Tales, Weaving Hope" (New Society, 1991); The Children of the Morning Light (Macmillan, 1994); Ending Violent Crime, a Report on a Prison Program That Is Working (Story Stone 1996); The Circle Way (Story Stone, 1997).

TALGO, HARRISON, Sr. (Apache)
(former tribal chairperson)
Affiliation: San Carlos Apache Tribal Council, P.O. Box 0, San Carlos, AZ 85550 (602) 475-2361.

TALLCHIEF, GEORGE EVES (Sa-toa-enza) (Osage)
1916-
(president of Osage Nation)
Born November 16, 1916, Arkansas City, Kans. *Education:* Central State College (Edmond, OK), BA, 1952; Pacific University (Forest Grove, OR), MA, 1957. *Principal occupation:* President of the Osage Nation. *Home address:* P.O. Box 14, Fairfax, OK 74637 (918) 642-5642. *Affiliations:* President of the Osage Nation (former chief); president of State Indian Health Board; president of the United Tribes of kansas, Texas & Oklahoma; Board of Standing Bear Foundation*posts:* Supt. of Lodge Pole Schools, Hayes, MT; principal of Crescent & Fairfax Schools in Oklahoma; president, Indian Festival of Arts; coach & teacher (45 years in the field of education). *Community activities:* Rotary Club; Chamber of Commerce; Quarterback Club; volunteer fireman. *Membership:* National Tribal Chairman's Association (chairman, 1982; vice president-Sergeant at Arms, 1990). *Awards, honors:* Iron Eyes Cody Peace Medal; Golden Glove Champion of Oklahoma (in college); Little All-American Coach of the Year in Pacific Coast Wrestling Conference. *Interests:* "My interests at the present time is to better the lot of the American Indian; sports; raise cattle, Appaloosa Show horses, karakul sheep & Yorkshire Terrier dogs since retirement. In earlier years, I rodeoed - riding bulls & horses; roughnecked in the oil fields."

TALLMADGE, BERNADINE W. MINER
(Sitting in the Moonlight) (Wisconsin Winnebago)
1920-
(owner/curator-Indian museum)
Born April 6, 1920, Necedah, Wisc. *Education:* High school. *Principal occupation:* Owner/curator-Indian museum. *Address:* P.O. Box 441, 3889 N. River Rd., Wisconsin Dells, WI 53965 (608) 254-4006 or 254-2268. *Affiliation:* Owner/curator, Winnebago Indian Museum, Wisconsin Dells, WI, 1953-. *Community activities:* Organized Dells Area Indian Club; presently on State Council on Aging, Tribal Council on Aging, and Tribal Personnel Committee, Wisconsin Winnebago Tribe. *Awards, honors:* Attended Presidential Inaugural Parade in 1952 in full regalia; Mrs. Congeniality during competition in Mrs. Wisconsin Pageant, 1961. *Interests:* Master weaver of "needle loom," sash weaving and appliqué.

TALLMADGE-JOHNSON, ROXANNE
(museum manager)
Affiliation: Winnebago Indian Museum, P.O. Box 441, 3889 N. River, Wisconsin Dells, WI 53965 (608) 254-2268.

TANNER, CAROLYN
(school principal)
Affiliation: Salt River Day School, 10000 E. McDowell Rd., Scottsdale, AZ 85256 (602) 850-2900 Fax 850-2921.

TANNER HELEN HORNBECK 1916-
(consultant historian, expert witness)
Born July 5, 1916, Northfield, Minn. *Education:* Swarthmore College, BA, 1937; University of Florida, MA, 1949; University of Michigan, PhD, 1961. *Principal occupation:* Consultant historian, expert witness. *Home address:* 5178 Crystal Dr. Beulah, MI 49617 (616) 882-4969 Fax (312) 255-3513; E-Mail: hhtanner@aol.com. *Affiliations:* Lecturer in Extension Service, University of Michigan, 1961-74; director, Atlas of Great Lakes Indian History Project, 1976-81, research associate, 1981-95; senior research fellow, 1996-, The Newberry Library, 60 W. Walton St., Chicago, IL 60610. *Other professional posts:* Expert witness in cases before the Indian Claims Commission, and Court of Claims, as well as state & federal courts, 1962-82; assistant director, Center for Continuing Education of Women, The University of Michigan, 1965-68; consultant historian for legal cases involving Indian treaties, consultant for historical, archaeological exhibits and documentary films. *Community activities:* Commission on Indian Affairs, State of Michigan, (member, 1965-69). *Memberships:* American Historical Association; Society for the History of Discoveries; Chicago Map Society Conference on Latin American History; American Society for Ethnohistory (president, 1983-84); Minnesota Historical Society; Historical Society of Michigan; Florida Historical Society. *Awards, honors:* Grantee, 1976, National Endowment for the Humanities (for Atlas of Great Lakes Indian History project); Wheeler-Voegelin Book Award, American Society for Ethnohistory, 1988; NEH Independent Scholars, Fellowship, 1989; ACLS Grant, 1990; Tecumseh Award, State Bar Association of Michigan, 2001. *Interests:* "Special interest in mapping & geographic background of Indian history-location of towns, hunting camps, fishing stations, canoe and travel routes; inter-tribal contacts." *Biographical sources:* Who's Who in America; Directory of American Scholars; Who's Who of American Women; Who's Who of the Midwest; Historians of Latin America in the U.S.; Contemporary Authors, Vol. 61-64. *Published works:* Zespedes in East Florida, 1784-1790 (University of Miami Press, 1963; U. of Florida Press, 1989); Territory of the Caddo Tribe of Oklahoma. Caddo Indians IV (Garland Publishing, 1974); The Ojibwas: A Critical Bibliography (Indiana University Press, 1976); editor, Atlas of Great Lakes Indian History (University of Oklahoma Press, 1987); The Ojibwas (Chelsea House, 1992); editor, The Settling of North America, 1995.

TANTAQUIDGEON, GLADYS (Mohegan) 1899-
(tribal medicine woman; author)
Address: Uncasville, CT. *Affiliation:* Medicine Woman, Mohegan Tribe, Uncasville, CT; co-founder, Tantaquidgeon Museum, Uncasville, CT. *Published works:* Author of numerous publications on natural healing and tribal medicine.

TAPAHE, LOREN (Navajo) 1953-
(publishing)
Born September 17, 1953, Fort Defiance, Ariz. *Education:* Brigham Young University, AA, 1974. *Principal occupation:* General manager, Navajo Time Publishing, Window Rock, AZ, 1977-. *Home address:* P.O. Box 481, Window Rock, AZ 86515. *Other professional post:* Assistant director, Office of Business Management, The Navajo Tribe, Window Rock, AZ. *Interests:* Journalism; advertising; photography; travel—Northwestern tribes of North America, Southwestern tribes, Europe.

TAPAHONSO, LUCI (Navajo)
(instructor)
Education: University of New Mexico, MA, 1983. *Affiliation:* American Indian Studies Program, The University of Arizona, Harvill Bldg., Rm 430, P.O. Box 210076, Tucson, AZ 85721 (520) 621-7108 Fax 621-7952. E-mail: aisp@email.arizona.edu. *Interests:* Conteporary poetry in American Indian literature.

TARBELL, NORMAN (St. Regis Mohawk)
(tribal chief)
Affiliation: St. Regis Mohawk Council, Akwesasne Community Bldg., Rt. 37, RR 1, Box 8A, Hogansburg, NY 13655 (518) 358-2272.

TATE, CHARLES
(BIA agency supt.)
Affiliation: Ute Mountain Ute Agency, BIA, P.O. Box KK, Towaoc, CO 81334 (970) 565-8473 Fax 565-8906.

TATEM, ALEX
(school principal)
Affiliation: Chevak IRA Contract School, Chevak, AK 99563 (907) 858-7713.

TATSEY, DEBBIE
(health coordinator)
Affiliation: Native American Services Agency, Missoula Indian Center, 2300 Regent St. #A, Missoula, MT 59801 (406) 329-3373.

TATSEY-MURRAY, CAROL
(college president)
Affiliation: Blackfeet Community College, P.O. Box 819, Browning, MT 59417 (406) 338-7755 Fax 338-3272.

TAVARES, JESSICA (Miwok)
(rancheria chairperson)
Affiliation: United Auburn Rancheria, 616 Newcastle Rd. #1, Newcastle, CA 95658 (916) 663-3720.

TAVENNER, TERRI (Wabgoneese)1947-
(cultural curriculum developer)
Born January 23, 1947, Seattle, Wash. *Education:* Antioch University, BA, 1979. *Principal occupation:* Cultural curriculum developer. *Address:* 20532 S. Riverside Dr., Pickford, MI 49774 (906) 647-5807. *Affiliation:* Coordinate Language & Culture Program Development, Quileute Tribal School, LaPush, WA, 1974-95. *Community activities:* Various Indian education curriculum advisory boards, projects; Clallam County Heritage Advisory Board. *Membership:* Washington State Indian Education Assn. *Awards, honors:* Indian Education Showcase of Excellence Award, U.S. Dept. of Education, 1989. *Interests:* "Personally and professionally committed to preservation and protection of indigenous sacred site & practices; and revival of the Northwest tribes; canoe tradition-embarked on a cedar dugout canoe journey from LaPush, WA to Bella Bela, B.C., Canada in 1993. *Published works:* Editor, Manual for Building a Big House & Canoes, 1990, by David Forlines; co-authored with David Forlines & Joe Karchsey, Medicinal Plants of Northwest Indigenous Peoples (OSU Dept. of Forestry, 1992).

TAVUI, DOROTHY (Diegueno)
(tribal chairperson)
Affiliation: San Pasqual General Council, P.O. Box 365, Valley Center, CA 92082 (619) 749-3200.

TAYLOR, ALLEN R.
(center director)
Affiliation: Center for the Study of Native Languages of the Plains & Southwest, University of Colorado, Dept. of Linguistics, Campus Box 295, Boulder, CO 80309 (303) 492-2748.

TAYLOR, BANNING (Luiseno)
(tribal chairperson)
Affiliation: Los Coyotes Band of Mission Indians, P.O. Box 249, Warner Springs, CA 92086 (619) 782-3269.

TAYLOR, CHARLES (United Lumbee) 1917-
(furniture repairer, toy maker)
Born August 31, 1917, Brockton, Mass. *Education*: High school. *Address & Affiliation*: The Amber Lantern-Antiques, 545-205 Old Highway Rd., McArthur, CA 96056-8614 (916) 336-6656. *Community activities*: Board of Directors, Fort Crook Historical Society, Fall River Mills, CA; treasurer, Fall River Chamber of Commerce; Holds United Lumbee Tribal beading classes 12 weeks each year since 1985; Charles makes adjustable beading looms for the students on order. *Membership*: United Lumbee nation's Deer Clan. *Awards, honors*: Nominated Citizen of the Year, 1993, Fall River Mills, CA.

TAYLOR, CHIEF LONGHAIR
(Mowa Band of Choctaw)
(tribal chief)
Affiliation: Mowa Band of Choctaw Indians, 1080-A W. Red Fox Rd., Mount Vernon, AL 36560 (251) 829-5500.

TAYLOR, DAVE
(Indian band chief)
Affiliation: Hornepayne Indian Band, Box 465, Spruce St., Homepayne, ON P0M 1Z0 (807) 868-2039.

TAYLOR, FRANK (Luiseno)
(school principal)
Affiliation: Shiprock Northwest High School, Shiprock Alternative Schools, P.O. Box 1799, Shiprock, NM 87420 (505) 368-2070 Fax 368-5102.

TAYLOR , GERALD W.
(BIA agency supt.)
Affiliation: Seattle Support Center, Bureau of Indian Affairs, P.O. Box 80947, Seattle, WA 98104 (206) 764-3328.

TAYLOR, JOHN L.
(school principal)
Affiliation: Chi-Ch'il-Tah/Jones Ranch Community School, P.O. Box 278, Vanderwagen, NM 87326 (505) 778-5573.

TAYLOR, JONATHAN L. (Eastern Cherokee)
(tribal chief)
Affiliation: Eastern Band of Cherokee Indians, P.O. Box 455, Cherokee, NC 28719 (704) 497-2771.

TAYLOR, LEWIS (St. Croix Chippewa)
(tribal chairperson)
Affiliation: St. Croix Council, P.O. Box 287, Hertel, WI 54845 (715) 349-2195.

TAYLOR, LINDA (Cherokee)
(tribal enterprise manager)
Affiliation: Cherokee Nation Gift Shops, P.O. Box 948, Tahlequah, OK 74465 (800) 256-2123, (918) 456-2793

TAYLOR, PETER S. 1937-
(lawyer)
Born June 9, 1937, St. Paul, Minn. *Education*: Washburn University, BA, 1959; George Washington University, School of Law, LLB, 1963. *Principal occupation*: Lawyer. *Home address*: 1819 N. Lincoln St., Arlington, VA 22207. *Affiliations*: Co-director, Indian Civil Rights Task Force, Office of the Solicitor, Dept. of the Interior, 1971-75 (projects were the compilation of the Opinions of the Solicitor on Indian affairs; updating Kappler's, Indian Affairs, Laws & Treaties; development of a Model Procedural Code for use in courts of Indian offenses; and revision of Felix Cohen's, Handbook of Federal Indian Law); chairman, Task Force on Revision and Codification of Federal Indian Law, with the American Indian Policy Review Commission, 1975-77 (upon completion of the Task Force report, served on the editorial board of the Commission in preparation of the AIPRC report; special counsel, 1977-80, general counsel, 1981-85, staff director, 1985-86; senior counsel, 1987-, Senate Select Committee on Indian Affairs. *Memberships*: District of Columbia Bar Association; Virginia State Bar Association. *Published works*: Opinions of the Solicitor, Dept. of the Interior, Indian Affairs (U.S. Government, 1976);

editor, Kappler's, Indian Affairs, Laws and Treaties (revision, U.S. Government, 1976); Development of Tripartite Jurisdiction in Indian Country (Kansas Law Review, 1974).

TAYLOR, REBECCA T. (*Clear Sky*)
(Lac Courte Oreilles Ojibwe)
(educator)
Born May 2, 1960, Chicago, Ill. *Education*: Lac Courte Oreilles Ojibwe Community College, Hayward, WI, A.A. Native American Studies. *Home address*: 9664 N. County Rd., N., Hayward, WI 54843 (715) 634-8401. *Membership*: Honor the Earth Education Foundation (Board of Directors, 1980). *Awards, honors*: Inward Journey for Outstanding Service from L.C.D. College, 1991; Cultural Award in recognition of cultural contribution as a role model. *Biographical source*: "The Color of Our Song," educational video, 28 minutes, University of Eau Claire, WI.

TAYLOR, RHONDA
(editor)
Affiliation: American Indian Library Association, c/o SLIS, 401 W. Brooks, University of Okalhoma, Norman, OK 73019 (405) 325-3921.

TAYLOR, SARAH
(Indian education program director)
Affiliation: Washington Unified School District, Indian Education Program, 930 West Acres Rd., Rm. 17, West Sacramento, CA 95691 (916) 371-9300 ext. 70 Fax 371-8319.

TAYLOR, URSHEL (*Owl Ear*) (Pima-Ute) 1937-
(artist)
Born May 31, 1937, Phoenix, Ariz. *Education*: High school. *Principal occupation*: Artist. *Address*: 2901 W. Sahuaro Divide, Tucson, AZ 85742 (800) 487-0180 (orders only); (520) 297-4456; E-Mail: urshel@ artnatam.com; Website: http://www.artnatam.com/ utaylor. *Affiliation*: Former owner, The Owl Ear Gallery, Tucson, AZ, 1990-95. *Other professional posts*: Consultant to Tucson Indian Center & LFC, Inc. *Past professional posts*: Bureau of Indian Affairs, Intermountain Inter-Tribal School (art teacher), 1963-79 (Director of Cultural Arts Program, 1971-79); art teacher, Utah State University; owner, Indian Craft Shop, Brigham City, Utah, 1979-89. *Military service*: U.S. Marine Corps (Sgt.) 1956-63. *Community activities*: Tucson International Mariachi Conference. *Memberships*: Pima Salt River Community Indian Tribe; Indian Arts & Crafts Association. *Awards, honors*: 9 first place awards from 1984-90, then stopped entering contests. *Interests*: Urshel's years of study & research into historical Indian culture & crafts has served to reinforce his dedication to the authentic presentation of the American Indian. He says, "I always try to capture the dignity & majesty of what my people have been and what they continue to be today." *Published works*: Writes a column for Smoke Signals, Native American paper; working on children's book, "The Weasel Clan."

TAYLOR, VIRGINIA (Cherokee) 1922-
(graphic & commercial artist)
Born September 15, 1922, Los Angeles, Calif. *Education*: Art Center School (Los Angeles, CA). *Principal occupation*: Graphic and commercial artist. *Home address*: 4754 Hwy. 20 NW, Albany, OR 97321. *Affiliation*: Staff artist, Office of Publications, Oregon State University, art coordinator & designer, Oregon State University Press, 1963-67; assistant professor of art, Oregon State University, 1966, 1976; graphic designer and assistant to museum coordinator, Marine Science Laboratory, Dept. of Oceanography, Oregon State University, Corvallis, 1969-. *Other professional posts*: Taught Indian history and crafts, Linn Benton Community College; taught basic design, Oregon State University, 1975. *Interests*: Jury Indian art exhibitions; (I) frequently speak to civic, school and other organizations on Indian art. Numerous awards, joint and one-man exhibitions; work in private and public collections.

TAYLOR, WAYNE, JR. (Hopi)
(tribal chairperson)
Affiliation: Hopi Tribal Council, P.O.Box 123, Kykotsmovi, AZ 86039 (928) 734-2441.

TAYLOR, WILFORD (*Longhair*)
(Choctaw/Chickasaw) 1946-
(air conditioning & regrigerator technician)
Born October 31, 1946, McIntosh, Ala. *Education*: A.A. degree. *Principal occupation*: Air condition & refrigerator technician. *Address & Affiliation*: Chief, Mowa Band of Choctaw Indians, 1080 West Red Fox Rd., Mt. Vernon, AL 36560 (251) 829-5500 Fax 829-6328. E-mail: chieftaylor@mowachoctaw.com. *Other professional post*: Commissioner of Alabama Indian Affairs Commission. *Military service*: U.S. Army, 1967-68; Vietnam War Veteran. *Community activities*: Museum/Library Board of Advisory; Mowa Choctaw Housing Authority Commissioner; Chairman of Alabama Intertribal Council. *Interests*: "To eliminate poverty and substance abuse, and to provide sanitary living conditions for my people."

TAYLOR, WILLIAM E., Jr. (Tunikshiuti) 1927-
(archaeologist; museum director)
Born November 21, 1927, Toronto, Ontario, Can. *Education*: University of Illinois, MA, 1954; University of Michigan, PhD, 1956. *Principal occupation*: Archaeologist; museum director. *Home address*: 509 Piccadilly Ave., Ottawa, ON K1Y 0H7 (613) 729-7488. *Affiliation*: Archaeological Survey of Canada, Canadian Museum of Civilization, 100 Laurier St., Box 3100, Hill, PQ J8X 42.

TCHIN (Blackfoot-Narragansett)
(musician, storyteller)
Born in New England. *Education*: Rhode Island School of Design. Address unknown. Tchin's performances illustrate the significance of music and dance in the lives of Native Americans. He has performed extensively throughout the U.S.

TEEMAN, ALBERT (Burns Paiute)
(tribal chairperson)
Affiliation: Burns Paiute General Council, HC 71, 100 PaSiGo St., Burns, OR 97720 (541) 573-2088.

TEEPLE, SHARON L.
(executive director)
Affiliation: Inter-Tribal Council of Michigan, 405 E. Easterday Ave., Sault Ste. Marie, MI 49783 (906) 632-6896.

TELLER, JOANNE (Navajo)
(company owner)
Address & Affiliation: Infinity Horn Publishing, P.O. Box 1999, Chinle, AZ 86503 (520) 674-5259.

TELLER, JOHN H. (Menominee)
(tribal chairperson)
Affiliation: Menominee Tribal Legislature, P.O. Box 910, Keshena, WI 54135 (715) 799-5100.

TELLER, RENA L.
(school principal)
Affiliation: Tohaali' (Toadlena) Community School, P.O. Box 9857, Newcomb, NM 87455 (505) 789-3201 Fax 789-3203.

TEMPLE, JOHN (*di de yos gi*) (Cherokee) 1929-
(retired teacher; consultant)
Born August 7, 1929, Norwood, Ohio. *Education*: Salmon P. Chase (Cincinnati, OH), BS, 1955; University of Cincinnati, MEd., 1969. *Principal occupation*: Retired teacher; consultant. *Home address*: 2565 Villa Lane, Cincinnati, OH 45208 (513) 871-8886. E-mail: jctemple@eos.net *Affiliation*: Teacher of vocational education, Cincinnati Public Schools (30 years). *Other professional post*: Consultant, The Learning Center, Communications for Teachers & Education, Cincinnati (current). *Military service*: U.S. Air Force, 1946-49. *Community activities*: Charter member, North American Indian Council of Greater Cincinnati, 1970- (past chairman & editor of its monthly newsletter "Talking Leaves"); current project, "Electronic Bulletin Board Service for Educators in Greater Cincinnati," (promoting technology in communications for teachers & education). *Interests*: "Native American (indigenous) Indian research; Cherokee language, cultural & ceremonial. and development of curriculum for students to appreciate the vast expanse of our American cultural diversity. To network Native American Indian organizations so that they may share language, arts, cultural and events with each other or educators."

TERRANCE, CINDY (St. Regis Mohawk)
(editor)
Affiliation: "The People's Voice," Kanienkehaka Territory, P.o. Box 216, Hogansburg, NY 13655 (518) 358-3022.

TeSAM, STEVEN (Diegueno)
(tribal chairperson)
Affiliation: Viejas Baron Long Capitan Grande Band of Mission Indians, P.O. Box 908, Alpine, CA 91903 (619) 445-3810.

TESTAWICH, DON
(Indian band chief)
Affiliation: Duncan's Indian Band, Box 148, Brownvale, Alberta, Canada T0H 0H0 (403) 597-3777.

TETERS, MARCELLA L.
(BIA agency supt.)
Affiliation: Spokane Agency, Bureau of Indian Affairs, P.O. Box 389, Wellpinit, WA 99040 (509) 258-4561 Fax 258-7542.

TETREAULT, TERRY A.
(editor)
Affiliation: Sho-Ban News, Shoshone-Bannock Tribal Council, P.O. Box 900, Fort Hall, ID 83203 (208) 238-3887/8.

TEVIS, SANDY LUCAS
(Indian education program director)
Affiliation: Sunnyside Unified School District, Indian Education Program, 2238 E. Ginter Rd., Tucson, AZ 85706 (520) 741-2500 ext. 573.

TEWA, RICK, JR.
(executive director)
Affiliation: Native Americans for Community Action, Inc., Flagstaff Indian Center, 2717 N. Steves Blvd., Suite 11, Flagstaff, AZ 86004 (520) 526-2968.

TEYSEN, KENNETH
(museum CEO)
Affiliation: Teysen's Woodland Indian Museum, PO. Box 399, Mackinaw City, MI 49701 (616) 436-7011.

THEISZ, R.D. (Wicuwa) 1941-
(professor)
Born May 4, 1941, Yugoslavia. *Education*: Queens College, B.A., 1964; Middlebury College, MA, 1965; New York University, PhD, 1972. *Principal occupation*: Professor. *Address*: Box 9033, Black Hills State University, Spearfish, SD 57799-9033 (605) 642-6247 Fax 642-6762 (work); E-Mail: ronniethiesz@bhsu.edu. *Affiliations*: Professor, Sinte Gleska College, Rosebud, SD, 1972-77; Center of Indian Studies, Black Hills State University, Spearfish, SD (associate professor, 1977-83, director, 1983-88); chair, Division of Humanities, Black Hills State University, Spearfish, SD, 1988-, . *Memberships*: South Dakota Indian Education Association; MELUS (Multi-Ethnic Literary Society of the U.S.); Porcupine Singers (traditional Lakota singing group). *Awards, honors*: 1972 Excellence in Scholarship Award, NYU; 1981 Special Contribution to Education, South Dakota Indian Education Association. *Interests*: Comparative literature and education; Native American cultural history, especially Lakota culture: literature, music, dance, and art; cross cultural education. *Published works*: Buckskin Tokens (Sinte Gleska College, 1974); Songs & Dances of the Lakota, with B. Black Bear (Sinte Gleska College, 1976); Perspectives on Teaching Indian Literature (Black Hills State University, 1977); Lakota Art Is An American Art: Readings in Traditional & Contemporary Sioux Art (Black Hills State University, 1985); Standing in the Light, with S. Young Bear (University of Nebraska Press, 1994); Raising Their Voices: Essays in Lakota Ethnomusicology, 1996.

THIEL, MARK G. 1950-
(archivist)
Born July 10, 1950, Milwaukee, Wisc. *Education*: University of Wisconsin, Stevens Point, MA in History, 1980. *Principal occupation*: Archivist. *Home address*: 1500 Michigan Ave., Waukesha, WI 53188-4253. *Work address*: Marquette University, Raynor memorial Libraries, 1355 W. Wisconsin Ave., P.O. Box 3141, Milwaukee, WI 53201-3141 (414) 288-5904 Fax 288-6709. E-mail: mark.thiel@marquette.edu. *Affiliations*:

Oglala Lakota College, Kyle, Pine Ridge Reservation, SD, 1983-86; archivist, Marquette University Libraries, Dept. of Special Collections, Milwaukee, WI, 1986-present. *Awards, honors*: Certified Archivist, 2002-present. Community activities: Reviewer of Native American Library Enhancement Grants for the Institute of Museum & Library Services (U.S. Federal Agency. *Membership*: Society of American Archivists, 1981-; Academy of Certified Archivists, 1989-; International Council on Archives, 1995-; Midwest Archives Conference. *Interests*: Manages collections on Catholic Church-Native American relationships from throughout North America, 16th century to present. A leading proponent/supporter of Native American archives. *Published works*: Co-author with Philip C. Bantin, "Guide to Catholic Indian Missions and School Records in Midwest Repositories," Marquette University, 1984) revised online, 2003, www.marquette.edu/library/collections/archives/index.html, as "Guide to Catholic-Related Native American Records in Midwest Repositories;" "Indian Way," an illustrated reference guide (Noc Bay Publishing, 2001, CD-ROM); co-editor with Christopher Vecsey and Sr. Marie Therese Archambault, OSF, The Crossing of Two Roads, Being Catholic and Native in the U.S.," (Orbis Books, 2003).

THOMAS, ANDREW BENEDICT
(Indian band chief)
Affiliation: Esquimalt Indian Band, 1113A Admirals Rd., Victoria, British Columbia, Canada (604) 381-7861.

THOMAS, BERNIE
(school system chairperson)
Affiliation: Lummi Tribal School System, 2530 Kwina Rd., Bellingham, WA 98225 (206) 647-6251.

THOMAS, EDWARD K. (Tlingit & Haida) 1941-
(council president)
Born September 21, 1941, Craig, Alaska. *Education*: University of Alaska, Fairbanks, B.S., 1963; Penn State University, M.A. Educational Administration, 1965. *Principal occupation*: Council president. *Home address*: 3450 Meander Way, Juneau, AK 99801 (907) 789-2929; 585-1432 (work). *Affiliation*: Tlingit/Haida Central Council, Juneau, AK, 1984-. *Other professional post*: Education counselor, teacher. *Community activities*: Former chairperson, president, member of various Indian corporations in Alaska; delegate, National Congress of American Indians (National Tribal Advocacy Organization); delegate, Alaska Federation of Natives (State-wide Native Representative Organization). *Awards, honors*: Alaska Teaching Certificate, Type A; Alaska School Administrator's Certificate; Ketchikan Native Citizen of the Year, 1978; T&H Citizen of the Year, 1991.

THOMAS, FREDERICK R. (Kickapoo) 1946-
(tribal chairperson)
Born February 21, 1946, Horton, Kan. *Education*: Haskell Indian Junior College, AA, 1966. *Principal occupation*: Tribal chairperson. *Address &Affiliation*: Kickapoo of Kansas Tribal Council, P.O. Box 271, Horton, KS 66439 (785) 486-2131. *Other professional post*: Chairperson, Kansas Service Unit, Health Advisory Board. *Military service*: U.S. Army, 1966-68. *Community activities*: Powhattan Precinct (past board member); Kickapoo Housing Authority (past president); community fundraising projects; community food and clothing bank (founding member); Horton Chamber of Commerce; Horton City Commissioner for Economic Development. *Memberships*: National Tribal Chairman's Association; American Legion; Kickapoo Chapter, Lions International; National Indian Gaming Association (treasurer). *Awards, honors*: Goodyear—Tire Builder of the Year. *Interests*: Member of Delaware Singers; enjoys hunting and fishing, farming, traveling.

THOMAS, JACOB E. (Ha dajihgrenitha')
(Cayuga) 1922-
(consultant)
Born January 6, 1922, Six Nations Reserve-Grand River Territory. *Education*: Native Language Instructors Diploma, 1982. *Home address*: Six Nations Reserve, R.R. #1, Wilsonville, Ontario N0E 1Z0, Canada. *Affiliations*: Trent University, Peterborough, Ontario (assistant professor on Iroquois Culture, Dept. of Native Studies, 1975-91; professor emeritus, 1991-); in-

structor on Iroquois Culture & Traditions, Mohawk College (Hagersville, ON), 1985-91; founder & vice chair, Iroquoian Institute, Wilsonville, ON, 1986-93; founder, Jake Thomas Learning Centre, Wilsonville, ON, 1993-. *Other professional posts*: Condoled Cayuga Chief, Sandpiper Clan; Board of Governors, McMaster University, Hamilton, ON, 1992-96. *Interests*: Writes & speaks fluent Cayuga, Onondaga, Mohawk and understands Oneida & Seneca. Preservation of the North American Indian culture; instructs singing & dancing. Mr. Thomas is a foremost authority on Iroquoian culture, and is an Iroquois elder.

THOMAS, JAMES, JR., MD
(clinical director)
Affiliation: Inscription House PHS Indian Health Center, Inscription House, AZ 86054 (520) 672-2611.

THOMAS, JERRY
(BIA agency supt.)
Affiliation: Shiprock Agency, BIA, P.O. Box 966, Shiprock, NM 87420 (505) 368-4427 Fax 368-4321.

THOMAS, JOHN C.B. (Eastern Creek)
(tribal chairperson)
Affiliation: Florida Tribe of Eastern Creek Indians, P.O. Box 3028, Bruce, FL 32455 (904) 835-2078.

THOMAS, JOHN G., JR.
(director-IHS center)
Affiliation: Ketchikan PHS Alaska Native Health Center, 3289 Tongass Ave., Ketchikan, AK 99901 (907) 225-6135.

THOMAS, DR. JOHN L.
(school principal)
Affiliation: Hopi Day School, P.O. Box 42, Kykotsmovi, AZ 86039 (520) 734-2468 Fax 734-2470.

THOMAS, KIM M.
(Native American affairs specialist)
Affiliation: New York State Office of Children & Family Services, Native American Services, General Donovan State Office Bldg., 125 Main St., Rm. 475, Buffalo, NY 14203 (716) 847-3123.

THOMAS, LEO
(Indian band chief)
Affiliation: Pelican Lake Indian Band, Box 9, Leoville, Sask., Canada S0J 1N0 (306) 984-2313.

THOMAS, MARY V. (Pima-Maricopa)
(tribal council governor)
Affiliation: Gila River Indian Community Council, P.O. Box 97, Sacaton, AZ 85247 (520) 562-6000.

THOMAS, MATTHEW (Narragansett)
(chief sachem)
Affiliation: Chief Sachem, Narragansett Indian Tribal Council, P.O. Box 268, Charleston, RI 02813 (401) 364-1100 Fax 364-1104.

THOMAS, RAY (Mississippi Choctaw)
(BIA field rep.)
Affiliation: Choctaw Indian Agency, Bureau of Indian Affairs, 421 Powell St., Philadelphia, MS 39350 (601) 656-1521 Fax 656-2350.

THOMAS, ROBERT E.
(Indian band chief)
Affiliation: Nanaimo Indian Band, 1145 Totem Rd., Nanaimo, BC, Canada V9R 1H1 (604) 753-3481.

THOMAS, RONALD D
(health director)
Affiliation: Towaoc PHS Indian Health Center, Towaoc, CO 81334 (303) 565-4441.

THOMAS, THELMA
(college president)
Affiliation: Nebraska Indian Community College, P.O. Box 752, Winnebago, NE 68071 (402) 878-2414.

THOMAS, WESLEY K. (Dine-Navajo)
(assistant professor)
Born in Crownpoint, NM. *Education*: AA, 1975; BA, 1994; MA, 1996; PhD, 1999. *Principal occupation*: Assistant professor. *Office address*: Indiana University, Dept. of Anthropology, SB-130, Bloomington, IN

47405 (812) 855-3862 Fax 855-4358. E-mail: thomasw@indiana.edu. *Affiliations*: University of Washington, Seattle, 1991-99; Idaho State University, Pocatello, ID, 1999-2001; Indiana University, Bloomington, IN, 2001-present. *Community activities*: Annual Indian University Pow wows; IU's First Nations Speaker Series. *Memberships*: American Anthropological Association (life member); American Ethnological Society; Anthropology Museum Society. *Interests*: Social-cultural anthropology; gender and ethnic identities; American Indian studies, Navajo culture and language.

THOMASON, DOVIE M.
(Oglala Sioux-Kiowa Apache) 1948-
(lecturer, storyteller; art gallery owner)
Born August 14, 1948, Chicago, Ill. *Education*: Rockford College, BA, 1970; Cleveland State University, Teachers Certification, 1980. *Principal occupation*: Lecturer, storyteller; art gallery owner. Resides in Hartford, CT. *Affiliations*: Owner, Skystone & Silver, American Indian Art Gallery, Hartford, CT; chairperson, Native American Advisory Committee, 1987-, board of directors, 1989-, American Indian Archaeological Institute, Washington, CT. *Other professional post*: Secretary, board of directors, American Indians for Development, Meriden, CT. *Community activities*: Frequent lecturer/performer with youth groups. *Awards, honors*: Certificate of Excellence in Teaching. Cleveland State University, 1980. *Interests*: "I travel extensively to find new artists for my gallery - to meet with Indian people through the continent; gathering stories from our oral tradition which I share with thousands of children and adult annually; currently interviewing and researching for a biography of Red Thunder Cloud, Catawba herbalist, dancer, lecturer and healer; I hope to create children's books, illustrating stories from the American Indian oral tradition." *Biographical sources*: Hartford Courant (June 1986; Jan. & Nov., 1989).

THOMASON, TIMOTHY
(institute director)
Affiliation: American Indian Rehabilitation Research & Training, Institute for Human Development, Northern Arizona University, CU Box 5630, Flagstaff, AZ 86011 (520) 523-4791 Fax 523-9127.

THOMPSON, BETTY (Cherokee)
(artist, craftsperson)
Affiliation: Co-owner, Tah-Mels, P.O. Box 1123, Tahlequah, OK 74465 (918) 456-5461.

THOMPSON, CHAD (Xodaaw' Chwang' - Hupa) 1953-
(assistant professor of linguistics)
Education: University of Alaska, BA, 1975, MA, 1977; University of Oregon, PhD, 1989. *Principal occupation*: Assistant professor of linguistics. *Home address*: 6108 Old Brook Dr., Fort Wayne, IN 46835 (219) 485-6775. *Affiliation*: Indiana University/Purdue University, Fort Wayne, IN, 1991-. *Memberships*: Society for the Study of Indigenous Languages of the Americas; Linguistic Society of America; Hoosier Folklore Society. *Awards, honors*: 1990 Distinguished Service Award for dedication to and support of the teaching of Native American languages, Center for Community Development, Humboldt State University, Arcata, CA. *Interests*: Native American languages, literatures, and folklore, particularly those of Alaskan & Pacific Coast Athabaskan. *Published works*: 21 readers in the Alaskan Athabaskan Languages - Holikachuk & Deg Hit'an, mostly traditional stories (Yukon Koyukuk School District, 1983-87); co-author, "Dinaakk'a I" - Koyukon language for students in secondary grades & adults (Yukon Koyukuk School District, 1983); co-author, "Scope & Sequence for Teaching Koyukon Athabaskan" (Yukon Koyukuk School District, 1983); "Dinaakk'a for Children," Koyukon Athabaskan language for elementary grades (Yukon Koyukuk School District, 1984); "Athabaskan Languages & the Schools: A Handbook for Teachers" (Alaska Dept. of Education, 1984); "Denakenaga' for Children" - Tanana Athabaskan language for elementary grades (Yukon Koyukuk School District, 1987); "Dinaakk'a II" Second year Koyukon for secondary grades & adults (Yukon Koyukuk School District, 1987); "An Introduction to Athabaskan Languages" (Yukon Koyukuk School District, 1987); co-author, "Teachers Guide to Baakk'aatEgh Ts'EhEniy" (Alaska Native Language Center, 1989); co-editor, "Baakk'aatEgh Ts'EhEniy:

Stories We Live By" (Alaska Native Language Center, 1989); "An Analysis of K'etetaalkkaanee" (Alaska Native Language Center, 1990).

THOMPSON, CHARMAYNE
(elementary school principal)
Affiliation: Takini School, HC 77, Box 537, Howes, SD 57652 (605) 538-4399.

THOMPSON, DAVID
(IHS-EEO manager)
Affiliation: Indian Health Service, Oklahoma Area Office, 215 Dean A. McGee St., N.W., Rm. 409, Oklahoma City, OK 73102 (405) 231-4796.

THOMPSON, DONA K. (Caddo-Wichita) 1949-
(counselor/administrator)
Born August 31, 1949, Lawton, Okla. *Affiliations*: Counselor/Recrutier, University of Oklahoma Health Sciences Center, Oklahoma City, OK, 1981-87; Counselor for Native American Students, 1987-, Associate Director-Minority Affairs, 1991-, Washington State University, Pullman, WA. *Memberships*: National Indian Counselor's Association (president, 1987-89; treasurer, 1980-85, 1990-); Association of Faculty Women; National Association of Student Personnel Administrators; National Indian Education Association.

THOMPSON, DORA K.
(association president)
Affiliation: National Indian Counselor's Association, Washington State University, Wilson Hall, Room 104, Pullman, WA 99164 (509) 335-8676.

THOMPSON, DORIS W.
(health director)
Affiliation: Yellowhawk PHS Indian Health Center, P.O. Box 160, Pendleton, OR 97801 (541) 278-3870.

THOMPSON, DOROTHY
(Indian school principal)
Affiliation: Chitimacha Day School, 3613 Chitimacha Trail, Jeanerette, LA 70544 (318) 923-9960 Fax 923-7346.

THOMPSON, HARRY F.
(director of research collections and publications)
Affiliations: The Center for Western Studies Library, Augustana College, P.O. Box 727, Sioux Falls, SD 57197 (605) 274-4007.

THOMPSON, JOHN MASON, III 1941-
(consultant)
Born December 20, 1941, Alton, Ill. *Education*: Texas Christian University, BS, 1963, MBA, 1969. *Principal occupation*: Consultant. *Address*: Unknown. Office: (817) 740-0000 Fax 740-9600. E-mail: westart@guildhall.com. Website: www.guildhall.com. *Affiliations*: President, Loucks, Thompson, Starling & Associates, Fort Worth, TX, 1978-; president, Guildhall, Inc., Fort Worth, TX 1982-. *Other professional post*: Marketing and management departments faculty, Texas Christian University. *Military service*: U.S. Air Force, 1963-68 (Captain). *Community activities*: Board of Directors: Camp Fire (U.S.); Texas Boys Choir. *Memberships*: American Marketing Association; American Management Association; Indian Arts & Crafts Association; American Craft Council; National Trust for Historic Preservation; Southern Plains Indian Museum Association; National Cowboy Hall of Fame; Thomas Gilcrease Museum Association; Japan Society. *Interests*: "Through LTS (consulting) concerned with developing economic opportunities on reservations. Through Guildhall (art publishing and distribution) concerned with developing Indian arts and crafts, preserving traditions and marketing works of art."

THOMPSON, JOSEPH
(Indian band chief)
Affiliation: Nipigon Ojibway First Nation, Rocky Bay Reserve, Box 241, Beardman, Ontario, Canada O0T 2G0 (807) 885-5441.

THOMPSON, PHILIP M.
(museum president/CEO)
Affiliation: Eiteljorg Museum of Ameriacn Indians & Western Art, 500 W. Washington St., Indianapolis, IN 46204 (317) 636-9378.

THOMPSON, RAYMOND H.
(museum director)
Affiliation: Arizona State Museum, University of Arizona, Tucson, AZ 85721 (520) 621-6281.

THOMPSON, ROBERT
(BIA agency supt.)
Affiliation: Standing Rock Agency, Bureau of Indian Affairs, P.O. Box E, Fort Yates, ND 58538 (701) 854-3433 Fax 854-7541.

THOMPSON, TOMMY
(BIA agency supt.)
Affiliation: Fort Belknap Agency, BIA, RR 1 Box 980, Harlem, MT 59526 (406) 353-2901.

THOMS, ALSTON V. 1948-
(archaeologist/anthropologist)
Born June 18, 1948, Canyon, Tex. *Education*: PhD in Anthropology. *Principal occupation*: Archaeologist/anthropologist. *Address*: Dept. of Anthropology, Texas A&M University, College Station, TX 77843-4352 (979) 862-8541 Fax 845-4070. E-mail: a-thoms@tamu.edu. *Affiliations*: Senior archaeologist, Center for Northwest Anthropology, Washington State University, Pullman, WA, 1985-90; Associate Director, Archaeological Research Laboratory, Dept. of Anthropology, Texas A&M University, 1990-95; Director & Senior Lecturer, Center for Ecological Archaeology, Texas A&M University, 1995-2001; Assistant Professor, Dept. of Anthropology, Texas A&M University, College Station, TX, 2001-present. Community activities: Board Member, Cultural Preservation and Graves Protection Association; active in working toward passage of unmarked graves protection legislation in Texas. *Memberships*: Society for American Archaeology; Council of Texas Archaeologists. *Interests*: Working relationships between archaeolgoists and American Indians; NAGPRA implementation, past land-use studies (archaeology). *Published works*: Reassessing Cultural Extinction: Change and Survival at Mission San Juan Capistrano, Texas (editor & prinicpal author), 2001, San Antonio Missions National Historic Parks and Center for Ecological Archaeology, Texas A&M, a joint publication.

THORASSIE, PETER
(Indian band chief)
Affiliation: Churchill Indian Band, Tadoule Lake, Manitoba, Canada R0B 2C0 (204) 684-2022.

THORNE, WILLIAM, Jr.
(executive director)
Affiliation: Phoenix Indian Center, 2601 North 3rd St., Suite 100, Phoenix, AZ 85004 (602) 263-1017.

THORNLEY, LYNN HART
(museum director)
Affiliation: Five Civilized Tribes Museum, Agency Hill on Honor Heights, Muskogee, OK 74401 (918) 683-1701.

THORNTON, DIANE FRAHER
(artistic director)
Affiliation: American Indian Artists (Amerinda), Inc., c/o AFSC, 15 Rutherford Pl., New York, NY 10003 (212) 598-0968 Fax 529-4603. E-mail: amerinda@amerinda.org.

THRASHER, MICHAEL (*Ka-Whywa-Weet*) (Metis)
(teacher & consultant)
Address: 5470 Fowler Rd., Saanich, B.C. Canada V8Y 1Y3 (250) 658-6717 Fax 658-6747. E-mail: turtleshell@telus.net. *Affiliation*: Turtle Island Intercultural Consulting - provides consulting services to First Nations, governments, industry, community organizations and educational institutions since 1977. He is a nationally recognized Metis teacher of Anishinabi First Nation's philosophy, tradition and culture. He uses traditional knowledge and viewpoints to address contemporary issues. *Awards, honors*: Michael was one of four traditional teachers and elders invited to conduct the sacred pipe ceremony at the opening of the Royal Commission on Aboriginal People. In addition, he was co-chair of the first Round Table Hearings for the Royal Commission in Edmonton.

THUEMLER, DONNA
(Indian council director)

Affiliations: Director, Indian Action Council of Northwest California, P.O. Box 1287, Eureka, CA 95501 (707) 443-8401 Fax 9281.

THUNDER, GORDON (Winnebago)
(tribal chairperson)
Affiliation: Wisconsin Winnebago Business Committee, P.O. Box 667, Black River Falls, WI 54615 (715) 284-9343.

THUNDER, JAMES
(Indian band chief)
Affiliation: Buffalo Point Indian Band, Box 37, Middlebro, MB, Canada R0A 1B0 (204) 437-2133.

THUNDERHAWK, MADONNA
(field coordinator)
Affiliations: Dakota Women of All Red Nations, P.O. Box 69, Fort Yates, ND 58538; Women of All Red Nations, P.O. Box 2508, Rapid City, SD 57709.

THUNDERHORSE, IRON (*Kanatisoquili*)
(Algonquin/Cherokee/Delaware) 1950-
(author, craftsman, artist)
Born January 29, 1950, New Haven, Conn. *Education*: Lee College (TX) (1 year). *Principal occupation*: Author, craftsman, artist. *Home address*: Resides in New Haven, CT (203) 782-9715. *Affiliation*: Columnist, Indian Country Communications, Hayward, WI. *Memberships*: Thunderbird Alliance (grand peacekeeper); Algonquin Confederacy of the Quinnipiac Tribal Council (founder & member); member of about six traditional Medicine Societies. *Interests*: "Specialize in Native American symbolism culture and traditional teachings. Traveled all over Canada, Mexico, S. America and every state in U.S., except Alaska. *Biographical sources*: Writer's Digest Bookclub Newsletter, Dec. 1986. *Published works*: Paradox, A Psychic Journey (Abbetira Publishing, 1984); Medicine Visions - Poetry Chapbook (Thunderbird Free Press, 1985); Relocation, Crimes Against Nature (Thunderbird Free Press, 1986); Thunderbird Voices Speaking (Thunderbird Free Press, 1987); Return of the Thunderbeings (Bear & Co., 1990).

TIBBITTS, NORMA
(BIA education administrator)
Affiliation: Pine Ridge Agency, Bureau of Indian Affairs, P.O. Box 333, Pine Ridge, SD 57770 (605) 867-1306 Fax 867-5610.

TIBBETTS, STEVEN
(BIA agency supt.)
Affiliation: Eastern Nevada Agency, Bureau of Indian Affairs, 1555 Shoshone Cir., Elko, NV 89801 (702) 738-0569 Fax 738-4710.

TICKNER, RAY
(health director)
Affiliation: Shasta-Trinity Indian Health Program, P.O. Box 1603, Weaverville, CA 96093 (916) 365-0125.

TIDRICK, DOLORES BRONSON
(organization president)
Affiliation: ARROW, Inc., 1000 Connecticut Ave., NW, Suite 1206, Washington, DC 20036 (888) ARROW10; (202) 296-0685 Fax 659-4377.

TIGER, BUFFALO (Creek)
(BIA agency supt.)
Affiliation: Miccosukee Agency, Bureau of Indian Affairs, P.O. Box 44021, Tamiami Station, FL 33144 (305) 323-8380.

TIGER, DANA (Creek/Seminole-Cherokee) 1961-
(artist)
Born in 1961. *Address*: 26467 S. Peaceful Valley Lane, Park Hill, OK 74451 (918) 457-6035. *Awards, honors*: Served as the featured artist for the Indians in Medicine project, a scholarship program, in 1992; Selected nationally as one of nine women to serve as a committee member for the national Organization for Women in the planning of the National Racial & Ethnic Diversity Conference. *Interests*: Painting in acrylics, watercolors and gouche.

TIGER, CYNTHIA (Creek)
(health systems administrator)
Affiliation: Indian Health Service, Billings Area Office, P.O. Box 2143, Billings, MT 59103 (406) 657-6403.

TIGER, GEORGE (Creek)
(tribal communications coordinator)
Affiliation: Muscogee (Creek) Nation, P.O. Box 580, Okmulgee, OK 74447 (918) 756-8700 Ext. 312.

TIGER, JOHNNY, JR. (Tony) (Creek-Seminole) 1940-
(artist, sculptor; gallery owner)
Born February 13, 1940, Tahlequah, Okla. *Education*: Bacone College, 1959-60; Chilocco Indian School, 1960-61. *Principal occupation*: Artist-sculptor; gallery owner. *Address*: P.O. Box C, Muskogee, OK 74402 (918) 687-3505. *Affiliation*: Co-owner, Tiger Art Gallery, 2110 E. Shawnee St., Muskogee, OK 74403, 1982-. *Other professional post*: Design T-shirts for the Tiger Gallery (Indian themes). *Military service*: U.S. Air Force, 1963-65 (E-4). *Memberships*: Creek Tribe; Indian Arts & Crafts Association; Five Civilized Tribes Museum (Master Artist). *Awards, honors*: "I've won over 100 major awards all over the country (USA) in my 30 year span in painting & sculpture." *Interests*: "I've had art shows all over the country, and also London, England in 1987 (one man art shows)." Currently, Johnny's paintings and prints are in galleries across the nation. He has paintings on permanent display a the Russian Cultural Museum, Togliatle, Russia. *Biographical source*: Southwest Art magazine.

TIGER, MICHAEL D. (Creek)
(IHS-area deputy director)
Affiliation: Nashville Area IHS Office, 711 Stewarts Ferry Pike, Nashville, TN 37214 (615) 736-2400.

TIGER, PEGGY (Cherokee)
(artist; gallery owner)
Affiliation: Co-owner, Tiger Art Gallery, 2110 E. Shawnee St., Muskogee, OK 74403.

TIGERT, SCOTT
(curator)
Affiliation: Red Earth Indian Center, 2100 NE 52 St., Oklahoma City, OK 73111 (405) 427-4228.

TIJERINA, KATHRYN HARRIS
(association president)
Affiliation: Institute of American Indian Arts, P.O. Box 20007, Santa Fe, NM 87504 (505) 988-6463.

TIKIUN, THADEUS, JR.
(council chairperson)
Affiliation: Orutsararmuit Native Council, Box 927, 835 Ridgecrest Dr., Bethel, AK 99559 (907) 543-2608.

TILLMAN, CHARLES O., JR. (Osage)
(tribal chief)
Address & Affiliation: Osage Nation, P.O. Box 779, Pawhuska, OK 74056 (918) 287-1128 Fax 287-1259.

TILOUSI, REX (Havasupai)
(former tribal chairperson)
Affiliation: Havasupai Tribal Council, P.O. Box 10, Supai, AZ 86435 (602) 448-2961.

TIMOTHY, JOHN, II (*Yafke - Evening*)
(Muscogee Creek)
(artist)
Address & Affiliation: Staff artist, Five Civilized Tribes Museum, Agency Hill on Honor Heights Dr., Muskogee, OK 74401 (918) 683-1701 Fax 683-3070. Resident artist and tour guide for the museum. *Interests*: Traditional Indian art and history; study of traditional Southeasten cultures, symbolism and religious rites. Member of the Cherokee Dancers of Fire (Tommy Wildcat). Available for oral storytelling, flute playing, blow gun demonstrations & stickball demonstrations.

TINGLE, TRICIA A. (Oklahoma Choctaw) 1955-
(attorney)
Born May 1, 1955, Wharton, Tex. *Education*: Southwest Texas State University (San Marcos), BS, 1978, Post-Graduate-Paralegal Certificate, 1985; Oklahoma City University School of Law, JD, 1990. *Principal occupation*: Attorney. *Address*: Unknown. *Affiliations*: Teacher, Brazosport Independent School District, Freeport, TX, 1978-84; paralegal, Texas Railroad Commission, Austin, TX, 1985-87; paralegal, Cox & Smith, Inc., San Antonio, TX, 1987; Clinic Legal Aid for Native American Indians, Oklahoma Indian Legal Services, 1989; law clerk for Judge Tom Brett, Oklahoma Court of Criminal Appeals, Oklahoma City, 1989; General Practice, Leon Breeden & Associates, San Marcos, TX, 1990; self-employed, Law Office of Tricia A. Tingle, San Antonio, San Marcos, TX, 1990-. *Other professional posts*: Legal counsel to: American Indian Resource and Education Coalition, Inc., Austin, TX; Redwood Community Center, Inc., Hays County, TX; Program Director and original Board Member of Great Promises, Inc. (children's newspaper dealing with Indian issues). *Memberships*: Texas Bar Association; Texas Indian Bar Assn. (president & original Boiard Member); Association of Trial Lawyers of America; Hays County Bar Assn. (director); Oklahoma Indian Bar Assn.; Native American Bar Assn. (president-elect). *Awards, honors*: Presidential Delegate to White House Conference on Indian Education, 1992.

TINKER, GEORGE (Osage)
(associate professor)
Born in 1945. *Education*: New Mexico Highlands University, BA, 1967; Pacific Lutheran Theological Seminary (Berkeley, CA), M.Div., 1972; Graduate Theological Union (Berkeley, CA), PhD, 1983. *Principal occupation*: Associate professor of Cross-Cultural Ministries. *Address & Affiliation*: Iliff School of Theology, 2201 S. University Blvd., Denver, CO 80210 (303) 744-1283, 1985-. *Other professional post*: Pastor (part-time), Living Waters Indian Church, Denver, CO. *Community activities*: Director, Bay Area Native American Ministry (3 years). *Memberships*: American Academy of Religion (co-chair, Native American Religious Traditions Group, 1991-93); American Indian Scholars Association (corresponding secretary, 1991-); Native American Theological Association (chairperson, 1985-87). *Awards, honors*: Recipient of a Lutheran Brotherhood Award for doctoral work & two Bacon Fellowships at the Graduate Theological Union. *Interests*: Native American studies; Native American Mission history; cross-cultural studies, including the study of "racism." *Published work*: Missionary Conquest & the Cultural Genocide of Native Americans (Fortress Press, 1993); numerous papers & articles in journals.

TINKER, GEORGE (Eskimo)
(village president)
Affiliation: Native Village of Chignik, P.O. Box 11, Chignik Lake, AK 99563 (907) 749-2285.

TINNO, KEITH (Shoshone-Bannock)
(former tribal chairperson)
Affiliation: Fort Hall Business Council, P.O. Box 306, Fort Hall, ID 83203 (208) 238-3700.

TIPPECONNIC, JOHN W.
(BIA office director)
Affiliation: Office of Indian Education Programs, Bureau of Indian Affairs, U.S. Dept. of the Interior, MS: 3530-MIB, 1849 C St., NW, Washington, DC 20240 (202) 208-6123. *Past professional post*: Instructor/Editor (Journal of American Indian Education), Center for Indian Education, Arizona State Univ., Tempe, AZ.

TIPPECONNIE, BETTY
(BIA agency supt.)
Affiliation: Anadarko Agency, Bureau of Indian Affairs, P.O. Box 309, Anadarko, OK 73005 (405) 247-6677 Fax 247-9232.

TIPPECONNIC FOX, MARY JO
(Comanche/Cherokee)
(professor)
Education: University of Arizona, PhD, 1982. *Affiliation*: American Indian Studies Program, The University of Arizona, Harvill Bldg., Rm 430, Box 210076, Tucson, AZ 85721 (520) 621-7108 Fax 621-7952. E-mail: aisp@email.arizona.edu. *Interests*: American Indian higher education; American Indian women's issues.

TITLA, PHILLIP, Sr. (San Carlos Apache) 1943-
(artist)
Born September 17, 1943, Miami, Ariz. *Education*: Eastern Arizona College, AA, 1979. *Principal occupation*: Artist. *Address*: P.O. Box 497, San Carlos, AZ 85550. *Affiliations*: Director of development, San

Carlos (AZ) Apache Tribe, 1967-81; director, Phillip Titla Apache Galleria, San Carlos, Ariz., 1981-. *Other professional post*: Board member, San Carlos Arts and Crafts Association, 1981-. *Community activities*: Bylas Recreation Program (chairman); San Carlos Powwow Association, 1980-; San Carlos Pageant Committee, 1978-; Cobke Valley Fine Arts Guild, Inc., 1985-86. *Awards, honors*: Sculpture Award, Best of Show, Pasadena (CA) Art Show. Interests: "My interest is to continue to grow in the art field; presently doing some gallery shows and lecture at various clubs on Apache culture; also sing Apache songs; shows at colleges, high schools and elementary schools of my work—for education." B*iographical source*: Art West, Sept./Oct., 1984.

TITUS, LEE (Athapascan)
  (village president)
Affiliation: Northway Village Council, P.O. Box 516, Northway, AK 99764 (907) 778-2250.

TITUS, ROBERT J. (*Whitefeather*) (Cherokee) 1938-
  (merchant; shaman)
Born December 17, 1938, Helena, Ark. *Education*: Phillips College, AA, 1969; Southern University, 1974-75 (Counselor - Alcohol). *Principal occupation*: Merchant, shaman. *Home address* : 311 Walnut St., Helena, AR 72342 (501) 338-7966. Affiliations: Helena Pawnshop, Helena, AR, 1978-; project director, Mid Delta Community Services, Helena, AR. *Other professional post*: Shaman, Circle of the Whitefeather, Helena, AR; regional chief, Free Cherokees. *Goals*: "To revive universal natural shamanism the world's original & true religious practice." *Community activities*: State Elector for Arkansas Green Party (environment); member of DEEP (Delta Environmental Ecology Project); advisor to USDA Forest Management - Ozark: St. Francis National Forests; storyteller for local schools and library; Blues Festival volunteer. *Memberships*: Arkansas Travelers Story Tellers Association; local library association & museum; Good Medicine Society of Arkansas; National Pawnbrokers Association (local board member). *Awards, honors*: Academic Excellence, Phi Theta Kappa (president); guest speaker, Lion's Club. *Interests*: Studied Obeah - drums & customs on remote islands in Caribbean; Mescalero customs; alcohol/drugs/crime problems of Sioux, Cheyenne & Navajo; spirituality of Hopi; "seek balance & harmony in confused, disharmonious persons; hiking, swimming, nature observation; social & economic education. Maintain a private collection of some spiritual artifacts: shaman's staffs, shaman's "Medicine Hats" & healing sticks & stones. *Published works*: Miser's Muniment (Pine Hill Press, 1985); Book of Shaman (Conservatory of American Letters, 1988); The Complete Book of Natural Shamanism (Snowbird Publishing, 1993); articles for various magazines.

TOBACCO, JIM
  (Indian band chief)
Affiliation: Moose Lake Indian Band, Moose Lake, Manitoba, Canada R0B 0Y0 (204) 678-2113.

TOCCO, MARIA
  (managing director)
Affiliation: Cultural Survival, 96 Mt. Auburn St., Cambridge, MA 02138 (617) 441-5400 Fax 441-5417. E-mail: csinc@cs.org. Website: www.cs.org.

TODACHEENEY, THOMAS
  (administrative officer)
Affiliation: Gallup Indian Medical Center, P.O. Box 1337, Gallup, NM 87305 (505) 722-1000.

TOFOYA, GILBERT (Santa Clara Pueblo)
  (pueblo governor)
Affiliation: Santa Clara Pueblo Council, P.O. Box 580, Espanola, NM 87532 (505) 753-7300.

TOHE, LAURA (Dine-Navajo) 1952-
  (associate professor, writer)
Born October 5, 1952, Fort Defiance, Ariz. *Education*: University of New Mexico, BA, 1975; University of Nebraska, MA, 1985, PhD, 1993. *Principal occupation*: Associate professor, writer. *Address & Affiliation*: Dept. of English, P.O. Box 870302, Arizona State University, Tempe, AZ 85287 (480) 965-5553 Fax 965-3451 (work), 1994-present. E-mail: l.tohe@asu.edu. Website: www.public.asu.edu/~ltohe. *Other professional*

posts: Affiliate faculty, ASU Women's Studies and American Indian Studies; writer. Community activities: Board member, Dine College, Dine Teacher Education Program, Tsaile, AZ; consultant, ACT (American College Testing). *Memberships*: Wordcraft Circle (National Caucus Member); MLA (Modern Language Association); American Poetry Association. *Awards, honors*: Blue Mesa Review Poetry Prize Winner, University of New Mexico; Regents Fellowship & Minority Fellowship, University of Nebraska; Outstanding Young Women of America; University of Nebraska Teaching Assistantship & Reading Assistantship; University of Nebraska, Omaha Goodrich Program Award; National Sports Academy Prize Winner; 1999 Poetry of the Year, Wordcraft Circle; 2003 Book Award nomination, Minnesota Book Award. *Interests*: Photography, film, poetry, travel, physical fitness training. *Published works*: Making Friends With Water (Nosila Press, 1986); coeditor, Nebraska Humanities (Nebraska Humanities Council, 1994); No Parole Today; Sister Nations.

TOINTIGH, JACKIE DALE (*Blackhorse*)
(Kiowa-Apache of Oklahoma) 1949-
  (artist)
Address: 511 E. Colorado, Anadarko, OK 73005 (405) 247-7695 Fax 247-7617; Website: www.geocities.com/paris/8300. *Principal occupation*: Artist. *Community activities*: Culture program director, Apache Tribe of Oklahoma; chair, Cultural and Community Enrichment Task Force; Native American Graves Protection & Repatriation Act, and State Historical Preservation Office representative; Nine Nations of Apache, delegate from Oklahoma. *Awards, honors*: Mr. Tointigh has won numerous awards and his paintings and his works are in permanent collections of Oklahoma University's Stovall Museum of Natural History, the Shoshone Warm Springs Tribal Museum, Wichita Tribal Museum, Apache Tribal Museum, the Mid-America All-Indian Center Museum (Wichita, KS), as well as private collectors. *Interests*: He also makes presentations of his art and lectures at high schools and universities on the history and culture of his tribal background which is the Kiowa and Apache Tribe of Oklahoma.

TOLEDO, RICHARD (Navajo)
  (school principal)
Born March 21, 1951, Crownpoint, N.M. *Education*: University of New Mexico, MEd (Administration, 1980 & MEd (Elementary Education, 1985). *Principal occupation*: School principal. *Address*: *Affiliation*: Bread Springs Day School (grades K-3), P.O. Box 1117, Gallup, NM 87305 (505) 778-5665 Fax 778-5692.

TOM, EUGENE (Moapa Paiute)
  (tribal chairperson)
Affiliation: Moapa Business Council, P.O. Box 340, Moapa, NV 89025 (7092) 865-2787.

TOM, EVELYN
  (health director)
Affiliation: Santa Rosa PHS Indian Health Center, Star Route, Box 71, Sells, AZ 85634 (602) 383-2261.

TOM, LORA E. (Paiute of Utah)
  (tribal chairperson)
Affiliation: Paiute Indian Tribe of Utah Tribal Council, 440 N. Paiute Dr., Cedar City, UT 84720 (435) 586-1112.

TOMAH, LEN
  (Indian band chief)
Affiliation: Woodstock Indian Band, RR 1, Box 8, Site 1, Woodstock, New Brunswick, Canada E0J 2B0 (506) 328-3304.

TOME, HARRY
  (BIA agency education chairperson)
Affiliation: Shiprock Agency, Bureau of Indian Affairs, P.O. Box 3239, Shiprock, NM 87420 (505) 368-4427 ext. 370; Red Rock Day School, P.O. Drawer 10, Red Valley, AZ 86544 (602) 653-4456.

TOMPKINS, JILL E. (Penobscot)
  (clinical professor of law)
Born June 20, 1963, Kingston, N.Y. Education: The King's College (NY) , BA (magna cum laude); University of Maine School of Law, J.D. *Address & Affiliation*: Director & Clinical Professor of Law (Dec. 2001-present), Indian Law Clinic, University of Colorado

School of Law, 404 UCB, Boulder, CO 80309-0404 (303) 735-2194 Fax 492-4587. E-mail: jill.tompkins@colorado.edu. Website: www.colorado.edu/law *Other professional posts*: President, Eastern Tribal Court Judges Association, 1997-present; Appellate Justice, Pokagon Band of Potawatomi Indians Court of Appeals, Dowagic, MI, 2003-present; Appellate Justice, Mashuntucket Pequot Court of Appeals, Mashantucket, CT, 2000-present; Appellate Justice, Passamaquoddy Appellate Court, Sipayik & Motakmikut, ME, 1999-present. *Past professional posts*: Executive director, National Tribal Justice Resource Center, Boulder, CO, Sept. 2000 to Nov. 2001; chief judge, Mashuntucket Pequot Tribal Court, 1994-2000; faculty, National Judicial College, Tribal Court Jurisdiction Course, 1993-97; chief judge, Passamaquoddy Tribal Court, 1992-95; Justice of the Peace, State of maine, 1992-97; director, Penobscot Nation Judicial System, Indian Island, ME, 1990-94. Awards, honors: First woman to serve as president of Region 7 Northeast, 1997-99; national coordinator for the annual National Tribal Judicial Conference, 1995-99; represented the NAICJA on national tribal justice issues, including testifying before the U.S. Senate Committee on Indian Affairs and meetings with members of Congress and Attorney General, Janet Reno. *Community activities*: Penobscot Nation Election Appeals Commission, 1994-present; secretary & treasurer, Board of Director, Maine Indian Basketmakers Alliance, 1993-present; founding member, Connecticut Tribal Coordinating Council for State & Tribal Courts, 1996-present; *Memberships*: Penobscot Indian Nation; National American Indian Court Judges Association (NAICJA), 1994-present; Maine Bar Association, Colorado Indian Bar Association; Connecticut Bar Association. *Interests*: Traditional Penobscot baskets; numerous presentation and papers on tribal sovereignty and Indian law. *Published works*: A Summary of Income Tax and Other Reporting Requirements for Investors Doing Busness in Maine (KPMG Peat Marwick, Portland, ME), 1989; Answers to Frequently Asked Questions About Native Americans in Maine (pamphlet), 2000; Handbook of Tribal Courts, with Alivina Lee (Navajo), in progress.

TONASKET, MEL
  (health center director)
Affiliation: Colville PHS Indian Health Center, P.O. Box 71, Nespelem, WA 99155 (509) 634-4771.

TONEMAH, STUART A.
  (association president)
Affiliation: American Indian Research and Development, 2233 W. Lindsey St., Suite 118, Norman, OK 73069 (405) 364-0656 Fax 364-5464.

TORIBIO, WILLIAM (Zia Pueblo)
  (pueblo governor)
Affiliation: Zia Pueblo Tribal Council, 135 Capitol Square Dr., Zia Pueblo, NM 87053 (505) 867-3304.

TORRALBA, RICHARD (Comanche)
  (school principal)
Affiliation: San Felipe Day School, P.O. Box E, San Felipe Pueblo, NM 87001 (505) 867-3364.

TORRES, ELIAS (Tigua)
  (pueblo governor)
Affiliation: Ysleta Del Sur Pueblo Council, Box 17579, Ysleta Sta., El Paso, TX 79917 (915) 859-7913.

TORRES, ELMER C. (San Ildefonso Pueblo)
  (pueblo governor)
Affiliation: San Ildefonso Tribal Council, Rte. 5, Box 315-A, Santa Fe, NM 87501 (505) 455-2273.

TORRES, GUADALUPE "LOU"
(White Mountain Apache)
  (engineer; corp. president/owner)
Principal occupation: Engineer; copr. president/owner. *Affiliations*: Field engineer, Lockheed Corp., 1968-1986; president/owner, Systems Integration & Research, Inc., 6800 Versar Center, Suite 300, Springfield, VA 22151 (703) 486-7933, 1986-. *Description*: The company's primary business is analyzing the life cycles of computer and technology systems and providing program management. A majority of its contract are with the Navy. Employs 150 people at eight offices across the country with two more planned for Sacramento and San Diego, California. *Award*: "Out-

standing National Technologies Firm of the Year," by the U.S. Small Administration, Office of Native American Affairs.

TORRES, REBECCA (Alabama-Quassarte)
(tribal chief)
Address & Affiliation: Alabama-Quassarte Tribal Town, 323 W. Broadway #300 • Muskogee, OK 74401 (918) 683-2388 Fax 683-3818

TORTALITA, TONY (Santo Domingo Pueblo)
(former Pueblo governor)
Affiliation: Santo Domingo Pueblo Council, P.O. Box 99, Santo Domingo, NM 87052 (505) 465-2214.

TOULOUSE, NELSON
(Indian band chief)
Affiliation: Sagamock Anishawbek Indian Band, Box 610, Massey, Ontario, Canada P0P 1P0 (705) 865-5421.

TOUSEY, LU ANN
(health director)
Affiliation: Stockbridge-Munsee Health Center, P.O. Box 86, Bowler, WI 54416 (715) 793-4144.

TOWNSEND, JOAN B. 1933-
(professor emeritus of anthropology)
Born July 9, 1933, Dallas, Tex. *Education*: UCLA, BA, 1959, PhD, 1965 (Dissertation: Ethnohistory and Culture Change of the Iliamna Tanaina). *Principal occupation*: Professor emeritus of anthropology. *Home address*: 85 Tunis Bay, Winnipeg, Manitoba, Can. R3T 2X2; *E-Mail*: townsnd@cc.umanitoba.ca. *Affiliation*: Professor emeritus, Dept. of Anthropology, University of Manitoba, Winnipeg, Manitoba R3T 2N2, 1964-. *Other professional posts*: Consultation and assistance in gathering data on Tanaina society and archaeological sites; for Cook Inlet Region, Inc. (Alaskan Native organization). *Field research*: Archival and ethnohistoric research of the 18th-20th centuries of southern Alaska with special emphasis on social, political, and economic conditions of Native Americans, Yup'ik Eskimos and Aleuts. *Memberships*: American Anthropological Association (Fellow); Society for the Scientific Study of Religion; Society for the Anthropology of Consciousness; Royal Anthropological Institute (Fellow). *Interests*: "Ethnohistory and socio-cultural change: North American indigenous people—Athapaskans; primary focus on Tanaina; Alaskan Pacific Rim ranked societies (Aleuts, Koniag and Chugach Eskimo; Tanaina, Ahtna, Eyak, and Tlingit Indians; (I) work with graduate students and conduct research in Shamanism and new religious movements; western society and modern religious movements; Shamanism—especially Nepal; core and neo-shamanism among non-Westerners and "Westerners"; traditional trading systems and alliances; mercantile and the fur trade in Alaska; political evolution; new religions and revitalization movements." *Published works*: Monograph: "Kijik: An Historic Tanaina Settlement" (Field Museum of Natural History, 1970); several works on Shamanism, core and neo-shamanism, and on Southwest Alaskan peoples in edited books; numerous articles, papers and book reviews.

TOWNSEND, RANDOLPH (Paiute)
(former tribal chairperson)
Affiliation: Fort Bidwell Community Council, P.O.Box 129, Fort Bidwell, CA 96112 (530) 279-6310 Fax 279-2233.

TOWNSEND, VIRGIL
(BIA agency supt.)
Affiliation: Southern California Agency, Bureau of Indian Affairs, 2038 Iowa Ave., Suite 101, Riverside, CA 92507 (909) 276-6624 Fax 276-6641.

TOYA, RONALD GEORGE (Jemez) 1948-
(BIA agency supt.)
Born March 8, 1948, Albuquerque, N.M. *Education*: Westmont College, BA (Economics), BS (Psychology), 1970. *Principal occupation*: B.I.A. agency supt. *Address*: BIA, P.O. Box 189, Mescalero, NM 88340 (505) 464-4202 Fax 464-4215. *Affiliations*: Chief, Branch of Reservation Programs, Southern Pueblos Agency, BIA, Albuquerque, NM; chief, Branch of Self-Determination Services, assistant area director, BIA, Albuquerque Area Office; supt., Mescalero Agency, BIA, Mescalero,

NM; supt., Southern Ute Agency, BIA, Ignacio, CO; special assistant to the Assistant Secretary of the Interior for Indian Affairs, Washington, DC; special assistant to the Commissioner of Indian Affairs; chief, Branch of Tribal Government Services, U.S. Dept. of Interior, BIA, Albuquerque Area Office. *Other professional post*: Executive director & chairman of the board, Tribal Government Institute; Chairman of the Board, New Mexico Commission on Higher Education. *Community activities*: Conduct radio show on Indian affairs entitled Native American Perspective; involved in youth activities, including baseball & special olympics. *Memberships*: New Mexico Industrial Development (board of directors, 1975-1981; CEDAM - international scuba & archaeological association; Society for American Baseball Research. *Awards, honors*: Special and Superior Achievement Awards, BIA 1972, 1979, 1981, 1982; various letters and citations. *Interests*: "Interested in the management of tribal governments; economic development & preservation of Indian culture; travel; baseball; scuba diving; car racing; hang gliding; dancing." *Published work*: Pueblo Management Development (Southwest Indian Polytechnic Institute, 1976).

TOYA, VINCENT (Jemez Pueblo)
(former Pueblo governor)
Affiliation: Jemez Pueblo Council, P.O.Box 100, Jemez, NM 87024 (505) 834-7359.

TRACK, JOANN SOGIE (Sioux-Tiwa) 1949-
(clay artist/poet)
Born June 26, 1949, Taos, N.M. *Home address*: P.O. Box 992, Taos, NM 87571. *Affiliation*: Assistant curator, Millicent Rogers Museum, Taos, NM, 1990-. *Other professional post*: Instructor in micaceous clay, Taos Institute of Art. *Membership*: American Association of Museums. *Published work*: Spider Woman's Granddaughters (Beacon Press, 1989).

TRACK, ROY *(Flyng Hawk)* **(Assiniboine-Sioux)**
1941-
(audio visual)
Born December 14, 1941, Owyhee, Nev. *Address*: P.O. Box 645, Phoenix, AZ 85001 (602) 207-3850 (work). *Affiliation*: Vice-president, New Mountain II Broadcasting, Phoenix, AZ, 1984-. *Other professional post*: TV host & executive producer, "21st Century native American," KTVK - Channel 3 (ABC), Phoenix. *Memberships*: Native American Broadcasting Consortium; Fort Peck (MT) Assiniboine-Sioux Tribe. *Interests*: Pow wows.

TRAFZER, CLIFFORD E. (Wyandot) 1949-
(professor)
Born March 1, 1949, Mansfield, Ohio. *Education*: Northern Arizona University, BA, 1970, MA, 1971; Oklahoma State University, PhD (History), 1973. *Principal occupation*: Professor of history and American Indian studies. *Home address*: 34815 Olive Tree Lane, Yucaipa, CA 92399 (909) 787-5401 ext. 11974 (work) E-Mail: cetrafzer@aol.com. *Affiliations*: Archivist of Special Collections, Northern Arizona University Library, 1969-70; museum curator, The Arizona Historical Society, 1973-76; instructor of history, Northern Arizona University, 1974-77; instructor, Navajo Community College, Tsaile, AZ, 1977-78; associate professor of history & Native American Studies, Washington State University, Pullman, 1977-82; professor & chair, Dept. of American Indian Studies, San Diego State University, 1982-91; professor of history, Dept. of History & Ethnic Studies, Director of Native American Studies (1991-2003), Dept. of History, University of California, Riverside, 1991-present; director, Costo Native American Research Center, Riverside, CA, 1993-2003. *Other professional post*: Commissioner, California State Native American Heritage Commission. *Community activities*: California Indian Days Celebration, San Diego Committee, 1984-91; vice-chair, Native American Heritage Commission, 1988-; San Diego American Indian Health Center Board, 1987-89; Native American Land Conservancy Board. *Memberships*: American Historical Association; Organization of American Historians; Wordcraft Circle of Native American Writers; Phi Kappa Phi; California Indian Education Association; American & Canadian Association for the History of Medicine; Sierra Club. *Awards, honors*: Oklahoma Heritage Association Doctoral Scholarship, $5,000; appointment by Gov. Raul

Castro to the Arizona Historical Records Advisory Board, 1976-77; Eagle Feather Award for teaching Excellence and service to the American Indian community by the American Indian Student Organizations of Washington State University and San Diego State University, 1982 & 1986; Research and Teaching Awards, San Diego State University, 1984, '85, '88 & '89; 1986 Governor's Book Award for "Renegade Tribe: The Palouse Indians and the Invasion of the Inland Pacific Northwest," and for "Washington's Native American Communities, Peoples of Washington," 1991 - best historical works in Northwestern history; Penn Oakland Literature Award, 1994, for "Earth Song, Sky Spirit"; Wordcraft Circle of native Writers Book Award for "Death Stalks the Yakama"; appointment by Gov. George Deukmajian to the California Native American Heritage Commission, 1988; Outstanding Faculty Award, Associated Students of San Diego State University, 1989-90; Academic Specialist Program Fellow, U.S. Information Agency, Sept. 1991, to Sweden lecturing on Native American History & Literature. *Interests*: Native American history, literature, and religion; writing, hiking, fishing, and camping. *Published works*: The Judge: The Life of Robert A. Hefner (University of Oklahoma Press, 1975); The Volga Germans: Pioneers of the Pacific Northwest, with Richard Scheuerman (University Press of Idaho, 1980); Yuma: Frontier Crossing of the Far Southwest (Western Heritage Press, 1980); The Kit Carson Campaign: The Last Navajo War (University of Oklahoma Press, 1982); editor, American Indian Identity: Todays Changing Perspectives (American Indian Studies, San Diego State, 1985); Northwestern Indians in Exile: Removal of the Modocs, Palouses and Nez Perces to the Indian Territory (Sierra Oaks Publishing Co., 1986); editor, Indians, Superintendents, and Councils: Northwestern Indian Policy, 1850-1855 (University Press of America, 1986); editor, Indian Prophets and Prophecy: An American Indian Tradition (Sierra Oaks Publishing Co., 1986 - reprint of special issue of American Indian Quarterly, Summer 1985); The Renegade Tribe: The Palouse Indians and the Invasion of the Inland Pacific Northwest, with Richard Scheuerman (Washington State University Press, 1986); Creation of a California Tribe: Grandfather's Maidu Indian Tales, 1988; California's Indians and the Gold Rush, 1989; American Indians as Cowboys, 1992; Chief Joseph's Allies, 1992 (all published by Sierra Oaks Publishing); also, The Chinook & The Nez Perce (Chelsea House, 1990 & 1992); editor, Looking Glass (San Diego State University Press, 1991); Yakima, Palouse, Cayuse, Umatilla, Walla Walla, and Wanapum Indians: An Historical Bibliography (Scarecrow Press, 1992); Earth Song, Sky Spirit: Short Stories of the Contemporary Native American Experience (Anchor/Doubleday, 1993). *Anthologies*: editor, Mourning Dove's Stories, with Richard Scheuerman (San Diego State University Press, 1991); editor, Looking Glass (San Diego State University Press, 1991); Death Stalks the Yakima: Epidemiological Transitions and Mortality on the Yakima Indian Reservation, 1888-1964, (Michigan State University Press, 1996); editor, Blue Dawn, Red Earth, (Anchor/Doubleday, 1996); Grandmother, Grandfather, and Old Wolf (Michigan State University Press, 1997); Chemehuevi People of the Coachilla Valley, with T. Madrigal and L. Madrigal (Chemehuevi Press, 1997); Exterminate Them!: Written Accounts of Murder, Rape, and Enslavement, with Joel Joel Hyer (Michigan State University, 1998); As Long As the Grass Shall Grow and Rivers Flow: A History of Native Americans (Harcourt, 2000); The People of San Manuel, with Gerald McMaster (San Manuel Tribe, 2003); The Native Universe (National Museum of the American Indian, 2004).

TRAHANT, MARK N. (Shoshone-Bannock) 1957-
(journalist, editor)
Born August 13, 1957, Fort Hall, Idaho. *Education*: Pasadena City College; Idaho State University. *Principal occupation*: Journalist, editor. *Home address*: 101 Elliott Ave. West, Seattle, WA 98110 (206) 448-8387. E-Mail: marktrahant@seattlepi.com. *Affiliations*: Editor-in-chief, The Sho-Ban News, Fort Hall, ID, 1976-86; editor & publisher, Navajo Nation Today, Window Rock, AZ, 1986-93; executive news editor, The Salt Lake Tribune, Salt Lake City, UT, 1993-95; editor & publisher, Moscow-Pullman Daily News, Moscow, ID, 1995-2002; Editor, Editorial pages, Seattle Post-Intelligencer, Seattle, WA, 2002-present. *Community*

activities: Chairperson, Maynard Institute for Journalism Education; Trustee, The Freedom Forum. *Membership*: Native American Journalists Association (past president); American Society of Newspaper Editors. *Published works*: "Pictures of Our Nobler Selves," 1995; "The Whole Salmon," 2002.

TRAVARES, JESSICA (Miwok, Maidu)
(rancheria chairperson)
Affiliation: United Auburn Indian Community, 661 New Castle Rd. #1, New Castle, CA 95658 (916)663-3720.

TREADWELL, HOWARD E. (Poospatuck)
(tribal chief)
Affiliation: Poospetuck Reservation, 198 Poospetuck Lane, Mastic, NY 11950 (516) 399-3843.

TREBIAN, CAROL A. (*Daat-Khu-Teez*)
(Tlingit-Haida) 1933-
(Native American studies-retired)
Born October 26, 1933, Juneau, Alaska. *Education*: CMC of Roosevelt University, B.Mus., 1957; University of Wisconsin, Stout, MS Ed., 1990. *Principal occupation*: Program director. *Address*: Unknown. *Past affiliations*: Supervisor, General Music, Ladysmith Schools, Ladysmith, WI, 1970-75; Administrative Assistant, MSC, Ladysmith, WI, 1976-86; director, Native American Studies Program, Mount Senario College, Ladysmith, WI, 1990-2001. *Other professional post*: Executive secretary, American Dental Association, Chicago, IL. *Membership*: Human Relations Committee, MSC, Ladysmith, WI, 1976-86, 1991-2001. *Awards, honors*: Sears Foundation for Teaching Excellence, 1991, MSC. *Interests*: School psyhcology/ counseling; writing; composing music. *Published works*: Short story, and several short poems for The Circle, Minneapolis, MN, 1978-79.

TREPANIA, ALFRED (Lake Superior Chippewa)
(tribal chairperson)
Affiliation: Lac Courte Oreilles Tribal Governing Board, 13394 W. Trapania Rd., Bldg. No. 1, Hayward, WI 54843 (715) 634-8934.

TREPPA-DIEGO, LEORA J. (Pomo)
(rancheria chairperson)
Affiliation: Upper Lake Rancheria (Habematolel), P.O. Box 516, Upper lake, CA 95485 (707) 275-0737.

TREUER, MARGARET SEELYE
(executive director)
Affiliation: Anishinabe Legal Services, P.O. Box 157, Cass lake, MN 56633 (218) 335-2223 Fax 335-7988.

TREVELYAN, AMELIA M. 1946-
(professor of art history)
Born July 21, 1946, Marshall, Mich. *Education*: University of Michigan, BA, 1968, MA, 1970; University of California, Los Angeles, PhD, 1987. *Principal occupation*: Professor of art history. *Home address*: 13547 Halliday Ave., St. Louis, MO 63118. *E-mail*: at@prin. edu. *Affiliations*: Instructor of art history, Rhode Island College, 1970-73; assistant professor of art history, Center for Creative Studies, Detroit, MI, 1981-84; assistant professor of art history, 1985-90, associate professor & Art Dept. Chair, 1990-2003, Gettysburg College; Professor & Chair of Art History, Principia College, Elsah, IL, 2003-. *Other professional post*: Free lance critic, Los Angeles Herald Examiner & New Worlds Magazine. *Memberships*: Native American Art Studies Association; Native Arts Studies Association of Canada - USA Area Rep.; College Art Association. *Awards, honors*: PEW Foundation grants 1993-96 to fund research & travel; Pennsylvania Council on the Humanities Grant for Exhibition, "Seeing a New World: The Art of Carl Beam and Frederic Remington;" Gettysburg College Research & Professional Grants to fund research & travel annualy, 1986-96; Canadian Embassy Cultural Programme Grants, 1990-91; Maryland Council of the Arts Grant, 1991; National Endowment for the Humanities, Summer Institute 1997; ELCA Research Grant, 1997. *Interests*: "Prehistoric cultures in the Eastern Woodlands of North America metallurgy, shellwork, ceramics; arts of Native North America; cross-cultural studies in prehistoric ritual symbolism and metallurgy; extensive travel and research in Greece; women's issues in art history." *Publications*: Contributor: The Grove Dictionary of Art, 1996; contributor: St. James Guide to Native North American

Artists, 1998; contributor: Celebration of Indigenous Thought of Expression, 1998; editor, The Art of Mary Beth Edelson (Durografiska, Malmo, Sweden, 2002); Iconography of the Southeastern Ceremonial Complex, 2003; contributing editor, Miskwabik: Metal of Ritual (University Presses of kentucky, 2003); co-editor, Ancient Mayan Gender Relating (Greenwood Publishing, 2003).

TREVATHAN, LOUIS "BUZZ", Jr. 1944-
(gallery owner)
Born October 9, 1944, in N.C. *Education*: U.S. Military Academy (West Point), BS, 1967. *Principal occupation*: Gallery owner. *Home address*: 420 Old Santa Fe Trail, Santa Fe, NM 87501 (505) 985-1417; 988-9881 (work). *Affiliation*: Co-owner, Cristof's, Santa Fe, NM 87501. *Military service*: U.S. Army, Captain-Vietnam Vet (Flying Cross, Bronze Star, Air Medals, etc.). *Published works*: Several magazine articles (1993-96) on contemporary Navajo weaving, in "Focus/Santa Fe."

TRIBBETT, NORMAN HENRY
(Forest County Potawatomi) 1948-
(tribal librarian)
Born November 5, 1948, Hayward, Wisc. *Education*: University of Wisconsin, Oshkosh, BA, 1981; University of Wisconsin, Madison, MLS, 1983. *Principal occupation*: Librarian. *Home address*: 801 Chelsee Way, Lake Placid, FL 33852. *E-mail*: nokmes@strat0.net. *Affiliation*: Library Director, Seminole Tribe of Florida, Rt. 6, Box 668, Okeechobee, FL 34974 (941) 763-4236 Fax 763-0679, 1986-. *Memberships*: American Indian Library Association; National Congress of Native Americans. *Military service*: U.S. Army (pvt.), 1969-70. *Interests*: Forest County Potawatomi history; history of the treaties for Potawatomi, & history of the natives who relocated to Canada.

TRIMBLE, CHARLES E. (Oglala Lakota)
(organization president)
Affiliation: Red Willow Institute, Omaha, NE. *Past professional posts*: Principal founder, American Indian Press Association, 1970; executive director, National Congress of Americn Indians, 1972-78.

TRIPP, CHARLES H.
(tribal special judge)
Affiliation: Prairie Band Potawatomi Nation Tribal Court, 15498 K Rd., Mayetta, KS 66509 (866) 966-2242 or (785) 966-2242 Fax 966-2662. *E-mail*: tribalcourt@pbpnation.org. *Website*: www.pbpnation. org/tribalcourt

TRITT, LINCOLN (*Shigin*) (Gwich'in Athabaskan)
1946-
(writer, speaker, musician)
Born October 18, 1946, Salmon River, AK. *Education*: Mt. Edgecumbe High School; University of Alaska, Fairbanks, 1984-86. *Principal occupation*: Writer, speaker. *Home address*: P.O. Box 22016, Arctic Village, AK 99722 (907) 587-5010 (messages only). *Affiliation*: 2nd Chief, Arctic Village Traditional Council, Arctic Village, AK. *Other professional posts*: Write articles for local newspapers; lobbyist, tribal judge. *Past professional posts*: Instructor, College of Rural Alaska, Interior Campus, Fort Yukon Center, Fort Yukon, AK; consulting in education, alcohol & drugs; teach Native pre-contact history in psychology, sociology, philosophy, spirituality, etc. *Military service*: U.S. Navy, 1966-70 (Radioman 3rd Class; Vietnam Vet). *Community activities*: Native Village of Venetie Tribal Government; Neets'aii Corp.; Arctic Village School Advisory Committee' Tanana Chiefs Conference; Interior Education Committee; Council for Athabaskan Tribal Government; Gwich'in Niintsyaa Coordinator. *Interests*: "Teach Native pre-contact human value system and why they lived the way they did and still do." *Biographical source*: "The County's Monthly" in Santa Cruz Magazine, Dec. 1991. *Published works*: Raven Tell Stories (Anthology) (The Greenfield Review Literary Center, 1991); Coyote Bark/Poetic Art (Harrison Publishers, 1991).

TRONCOSA, LAWRENCE (San Felipe Pueblo)
(pueblo governor)
Affiliation: San Felipe Pueblo Council, P.O. Box 4339, San Felipe, NM 87001 (505) 867-3381.

TROPE, JACK F.
(executive director)
Education: Harvard Law School. *Affiliation*: Executive Director, Association on American Indian Affairs, 966 Hungerford Dr., Suite 12-B, Rockville, MD 20850 (240) 314-7155 Fax 314-7159. *E-mail*: general.aaia@ verizon.net. *Website*: www.indian-affairs.org.

TROTTLER, DR. WAYNE
(school principal)
Affiliation: Ojibwa Indian School, P.O. Box 600, Belcourt, ND 58316 (701) 477-3108 Fax 477-6039.

TRUDELL, ROGER (Santee Sioux)
(tribal chairperson)
Affiliation: Santee Sioux Tribal Council, Route 2, Niobrara, NE 68760 (402) 857-2302.

TRUJILLO, EVELYN C. (Acoma)
(IHS-administrative officer)
Affiliation: Indian Health Service (Headquarters West), 300 San Mateo, NE, Suite 500, Albuquerque, NM 87102 (505) 766-6215.

TRUJILLO, JIM (Taos)
(Indian arts & gallery co-owner)
Affiliation: Bear Paw Indian Arts & Galery, 326 San Felipe, NW, Historic Old Town, Albuquerque, NM 87104 (505) 843-9337.

TRUJILLO, JOSEPH G. (Taos)
(IHS-property management chief)
Affiliation: Indian Health Service (Headquarters West), 2401 12th St., NW, Albuquerque, NM 87102 (505) 766-5557.

TRUJILLO, MARIAN (Taos-Acoma)
(Indian arts & gallery co-owner)
Affiliation: Bear Paw Indian Arts & Galery, 326 San Felipe, NW, Historic Old Town, Albuquerque, NM 87104 (505) 843-9337.

TRUJILLO, MARY A. (Acoma)
(Indian arts & gallery co-owner)
Affiliation: Bear Paw Indian Arts & Galery, 326 San Felipe, NW, Historic Old Town, Albuquerque, NM 87104 (505) 843-9337.

TRUJILLO, MICHAEL H., MD (Laguna Pueblo)
(associate professor)
Education: University of New Mexico Medical School, MD. *Address & Affiliation*: Associate Professor of Family & Community Medicine, University of New Mexico, School of Medicine, Albuquerque, NM. *Past professional post*: Former Director & Assistant Surgeon General, Indian Health Service (IHS), U.S. Dept. of Health & Human Services, Rockville, MD. Mr. Trujillo had a 30-year career in IHS, and he was the first full-blooded American Indian to have served as Director of the IHS.

TRUJILLO, PATRICK S. (Cochiti Pueblo) 1954-
(substance abuse counselor)
Born March 5, 1954, Albuquerque, N.M. *Education*: University of New Mexico Continuing Education (1 year), Certificate of Completion (288 hours of Alcohol & Drug Abuse Studies Institute). *Principal occupation*: Substance abuse counselor. *Address*: P.O. Box 1500, Pena Blanca, NM 87041 (505) 766-8418 (office) 465-9992 (home). *Affiliations*: Alcohol Counselor, Five Sandoval Indian Pueblos, Inc., Bernalillo, NM, 1985-88; substance abuse counselor, Southwestern Indian Polytechnic Institute, Albuquerque, NM, 1989-92; counselor, All Indian Pueblo Council, Inc., Albuquerque, NM, 1992-. *Memberships*: New Mexico Alcoholism & Drug Abuse Counselors Association. *Awards, honors*: Outstanding Academic Achievement - Drug/ Alcohol Studies; Certified Alcoholism Counselor. *Interests*: "Enjoy working with youths in prevention and I like to implement seminars/training for communities, public service agencies. I have great interest in implementing cultural awareness, a wholistic spiritual approach to wellness for both youths and adults. I am also a trainer for fetal alcohol syndrome prevention."

TRUJILLO, RAYMOND H. (Pueblo)
(tribal scholarship officer)
Affiliation: Zuni Scholarship Program, P.O. Box 339, Zuni, NM 87327 (505) 782-4481 Ext. 482/9.

TSABETSAYE, ROGER JOHN (*Eagle's Tail*) (Zuni) 1941-
(artist, jeweler & businessman)
Born October 29, 1941, Zuni Pueblo, N.M. *Education*: Institute of American Indian Arts, 1962-63; School for American Craftsmen, Rochester Institute of Technology, 1963-65; University of Arizona, 1960-63. *Principal occupation*: Artist, jeweler and businessman. *Address*: Unknown. *Affiliation*: Owner-founder, Tsabetsaye Enterprises, Zuni, NM (Zuni jewelry—wholesale/retail), 1970-88; Santa Ana Casino, Santa Ana Pueblo, NM. Self-employed artist-designed and produced original pieces of jewelry in gold, silver, precious and semi-precious gems to create both traditional and contemporary style pieces. *Community activities*: Zuni Pueblo (head councilman, tribal treasurer); board of directors, New Mexico State Office of Indian Affairs. *Membership*: Zuni Craftsmen's Coop Association. *Awards, honors*: Numerous awards from various exhibitions and shows, 1968-.

TSO, EMMETT (Navajo)
(school chairperson)
Affiliation: Greyhills High School, P.O. Box 160, Tuba City, AZ 86045 (602) 283-6271.

TSO, RON (Navajo)
(health director)
Affiliation: Chinle Comprehensive Health Care Facility, P.O. Drawer PH, Chinle, AZ 86503 (602) 674-5282.

TSO, SAMUEL (Navajo)
(school chairperson)
Affiliation: Lukachukai Boarding School, Navajo Route 12, Lukachukai, AZ 86507 (520) 787-2301 Fax 787-2311; Many Farms High School, P.O. Box 307, Many Farms, AZ 86532 (520) 781-6226.

TSO, WILLIAM (Navajo)
(school chairperson)
Affiliation: Navajo Preparatory School, 1200 West Apache, Farmington, NM 87401 (505) 326-6571.

TSOSIE, CALVIN (Navajo)
(school chairperson)
Affiliation: Chinle Boarding School, P.O. Box 70, Many Farms, AZ 86538 (520) 781-6221 Fax 781-6376.

TSOSIE, DEBRA (Navajo)
(director)
Affiliation: Winds of Change, P.O. Box 1213, Middlebury, CT 06762.

TSOSIE, KENNETH (Navajo)
(executive director)
Affiliation: National Indian Youth Council, 318 Elm St., S.E., Albuquerque, NM 87102 (505) 247-2251 fax 247-4251.

TSOSIE, LARRY, SR. (Navajo)
(school principal)
Affiliation: Shiprock Reservation Dormitory, Shiprock, NM 87420 (505) 368-5070.

TSOSIE, LORETTA A.W. (*Ke'hanibaa'*) (Navajo) 1943-
(administration)
Born March 13, 1943, Morenci, Ariz. *Education*: University of New Mexico, BS, 1971, MA (Educational Administration), 1976. *Principal occupation*: Administration. *Home address*: P.O. Box 112, Window Rock, AZ 86515 (520) 831-3957. *Affiliations*: Instructor, Navajo Community College, Tsaile, AZ, 1972-86; special liaison officer, Alamo-Canoncito Liaison Office, Bureau of Indian Affairs, Canoncito, NM, 1987-. *Other professional post*: Chairperson, Career Education Division, Navajo Community College.

TSOSIE, NELSON (Navajo-Dineh) 1961-
(stone & bronze sculptor, painter)
Born July 1, 1961, Shiprock, N.M. *Education*: Yavapai Community College (Prescott, AZ), AA, 1981; University of Arizona, Studio Arts major, 1981-82. *Principal occupation*: Stone & bronze sculptor, painter. *Address*: Resides in Santa Fe, NM. "Nelson's work remains steep in tradition, with a historical accuracy that can only come from a comprehensive love of one's own culture, and the people that represent it with such pride and dignity. He places great emphasis on his desire to portray the positive aspects of Navajo life rather than the harsher, more negative aspects that are so often over-exploited." *Professional post*: Co-owner, Free A.I.R. Fine Art, a Santa Fe-based promotional private art business that aids other artists as well. *Memberships*: Indian Arts & Crafts Association; Gallup Inter-Tribal Ceremonial Association (contributing member). *Awards, honors*: Numerous shows & awards, including: Santa Fe Indian Market, Inter-Tribal Indian Ceremonial (Church Rock, NM); Lovena Ohl Gallery, Scottsdale, AZ; Navajo Nation Fair Fine Art Show, Red Earth Art Show, Indian Arts & Crafts Association Show & Sale. *Interests*: "Travels frequently, participating in community activities, and works with his wife to promote the talents of other promising artists as well." *Biographical source*: Enduring Traditions, by Jerry & Lois Jacka.

TSOSIE, RAYMOND (Navajo)
(employment supervisor)
Affiliation: BHP Minerals, P.O. Box 155, Fruitland, NM 87416.

TSOSIE, REBECCA (Navajo)
(law professor)
Affiliation: Arizona State University, School of Law, Tempe, AZ 85287 (480) 965-2714

TSOSIE, WALLACE (Navajo)
(BIA agency chairperson)
Affiliation: Fort Defiance Agency, BIA, P.O. Box 110, Fort Defiance, NM 86504 (602) 729-5041.

TSOUHLARAKIS, KAY
(health director)
Affiliation: Taos PHS Indian Health Center, P.O. Box 1956, Taos, NM 87571 (505) 758-4224.

TUBBY, SHERRY
(Indian school principal)
Affiliation: Red Water Elementary School, 555 Red Water Rd., Carthage, MS 39051 (601) 267-8500 Fax 267-5193.

TUCCIARONE, ALEXANDER J. (A:rek) (Blackfoot)
(chief plumbing inspector)
Address: P.O. Box 662, Old Bridge, NJ 08857 (908) 591-8335. *Affiliations*: Chair, New Jersey Commission on Plumbing - Sub Code Committee; certified instructor in plumbing & pipe fitting. *Community activities*: Inter-tribal advisor on Native Affairs. *Awards, honors*: 1996 New Jersey Plumbing Inspector of the Year. *Membership*: New Jersey State Plumbing Inspectors Association (president).

TUCKER, DANIEL (Diegueno)
(former tribal spokesperson)
Affiliation: Sycuan Business Committee, 5459 Dehesa Rd., El Cajon, CA 92021 (619) 445-2613.

TUCKER, GEORGIA (Diegueno)
(tribal spokesperson)
Affiliation: Sycuan Reservation, 5459 Dehesa Rd., El Cajon, CA 92021 (619) 445-2613.

TUCKER, LIBBY (Cherokee)
(professor)
Born Nov. 29, 1948, Bethesda, Md. *Education*: Indiana University, PhD. Principal occupation: Professor of English. *Home address*: 500 Magnolia Dr., Vestal, NY 13850. *Affiliation*: Dept. of English, Binghamton University, Binghamton, NY 13902, 1977-present (607) 777-6402 (office). E-mail: ltucker@binghamton.edu. *Other professional post*: Editorial Board of "Voices: Journal of the New York Folklore Society." *Military service*: Peace Corps, 1972-74. *Community activities*: Vestal High School Parent-Teacher Association; speaker at community events related to folklore; organizer of poetry readings. Memberships: Wordcraft Circle of native Writers & Storytellers; American Folklore Society; New York Folklore Society; Hoosier Folklore Society; International Society for Folk Narrative Research. *Interests*: Children's and college students' folklore; ghost stories; Natuve American literature; poetry and memoir. *Published works*: "Campus Legends" (Greenwood Press, 2005); poetry and memoir pieces in Long Shot and Paterson Literary Review; folklore articles in Children's Folklore Review, International Folklore Review, Western Folklore, others.

TUCKER, MICHAEL
(museum manager)
Affiliation: California State Indian Museum, 2618 K St., Sacramento, CA 95816 (916) 324-0971.

TULEE, MIKE (*Koosheyi*) (Yakama) 1961-
(Indian education program manager)
Born April 11, 1961, Grand Coulee Dam, Wash. *Education*: University of Washington, BA, 1991, MEd, 1993. *Address & Affiliation*: Indian education program manager, Seattle School District, 1330 N. 90th St., Seattle, WA 98103 (206) 298-7945 Fax 298-7946. E-mail: mtulee@is.ssd.k12.wa.us. *Military service*: U.S. Air Force, 1983-87. *Membership*: Yakama Nation.

TULLIS, EDDIE (Creek)
(tribal chairperson)
Affiliation: Poarch Band of Creek Indians, 5811 Jack Springs Rd., Atmore, AL 36502 (251) 368-9136.

TUPAZ, PAUL A.
(recruitment, social relations)
Principal occupation: Director of recruitment & school relations. *Address & Affiliation*: D-Q University, P.O. Box 409, Davis, CA 95617 (916) 758-0470 Fax 758-4891. *Community activities*: Hermanos Macehual, Quetzalcoatl Citlalli, advisor to M.E.X.A. Chapter at D-Q University.

TURNBULL, DAVID J. (*Chief Piercing Eyes*) (Susquehannock/Conastoga) 1930-
(Indian chief, publisher, pastor)
Born May 18, 1930, Hornell, N.Y. *Education*: Elim Bible College, Ministerial Certificate, 1964. *Principal occupation*: Indian chief, publisher, pastor. *Address*: P.O. Box 244, Nocatee, FL 33864 (813) 494-6930. *Affiliations*: Chief of Indian organization with 3,300 members. *Other professional posts*: Publisher; paster of Cherokee Baptist Church. *Community activities*: Cherokee Unity Council; Habitat; HUGS (Hands United in Good Spirit). *Memberships*: Wiccan/Pagan Press Association; DeSoto County Ministerial Association; DeSoto County Chamber of Commerce; Universal Pagan Federation. *Awards, honors*: District 7 HRS - for donation of clothes and other items for their clients, 1991; numerous certificates, awards, etc. *Interests*: "Much concern about hype concerning the Indian Revival. I write articles and give lectures in my own organization and churches, societies, etc. Much travel to pow wows, Indian groups, and individuals interested in in Indians. We also help to organize revival groups. We gather clothes and emergency supplies to send to Indian reservations, revival groups, and local charities & individuals in need. Interested in genealogy and the official cover-up of records to disclaim Indian heritage in the general population and confine it to official enclaves. Also much concerned by criminal and "official" sale of babies and consequent loss of records of genetic heritage causing emotional distress and lack of medical aid such as organ transplants that require knowledge of actual kinfolk." *Published works*: Reviving Your Heritage (self-published, 1984).

TURNER, DALE A. (Teme-Augama Anishnabai) 1960-
(professor)
Born December 22, 1960, Sept-Iles, Quebec. *Education*: PhD in Philosophy. *Principal occupation*: Professor. *Home address*: 135 Drum Heller, Sharon, VT 05175 (603) 646-0324 Fax 646-0333; E-mail: dale.turner@dartmouth.edu. *Affiliations*: Professor, McGill University, 1992-97; Dartmouth College, 1997-. *Military service*: Canadian Navy, 1979-85. *Memberships*: American Philosophical Assn; American Political Science Assn; Canadian Philosophical Assn.

TURNER, DOYLE I. (Ojibwe)
(tribal chairperson)
Affiliation: White Earth Reservation Business Committee, P.O. Box 418, White Earth, MN 56591 (218) 983-3285.

TURNER, ELIZABETH ROBERTS 1957-
(gallery owner)
Born September 1, 1957, Newark, OH. *Education*: Ohio Wesleyan University, 1975-76; Denison University, BA, 1980. *Principal occupation*: Art gallery owner. *Home address*: Resides in Vermont (802) 645-9975.

Affiliation: Owner, Long Ago & Far Away (Native American art gallery), Manchester Center, VT, 1986-. *Memberships*: Indian Arts & Crafts Association; Southwestern Association of Indian Affairs; Manchester and the Mountains Chamber of Commerce.

TURNER, HAROLD
(Indian band chief)
Affiliation: Grand Rapids Indian Band, Box 500, Grand Rapids, Manitoba, Canada R0C 1E0 (204) 639-2219.

TURNER, LOWELL KEVIN *(Skypainter)* **(Choctaw) 1958-**
(sign painter, designer)
Born October 1, 1958, St. Louis, Mo. *Education*: National Beauty Academy, St. Louis, MO (Diploma-Manicuring & Nail Sculpturing), 1992. *Principal occupation*: Sign painter & designer. *Home address*: P.O. Box 166, Valles Mines, MO 63087-0166 (636) 337-4105. E-mail: skypntr58@aol.com. Website: www.profiles.yahoo.com/librame58. *Affiliation*: Self-employed, Lowell Turner & Son Sign Co., De Soto, MO, 1973-. *Other professional posts*: Native American Indian painter & jeweler; historian & archivist on family genealogy, public speaker; licensed manicurist. *Community activities*: Mastodon Museum, Imperial, MO; Jefferson Memorial History Museum, St. Louis, MO. *Memberships*: S.A.R. Sons of the American Revolution, Delaware Chapter), Jefferson Co., MO; St. Louis Hobby Association; Warbirds of the Royal Air Force, West Palm Beach, FL. *Awards, honors*: Honorable Mention Certificate, and 3 Master Division Award Plaques for (my) model making realism. *Biographical source*: U.S. Dept. of the Interior, Indian Arts & Crafts Board, Washington, DC; Voices From Spirit Magazine, Ellsworth, ME; and The Genealogical Helper Magazine. *Published work*: Mail order brochure, Turner Artworks, since 1987; artwork in "Native American Art & Folklore, edited by David Campbell (Crescent Books, 1993) and in Contemporary Native American Artists," by Dawn E. Reno (Alliance Publishing, 1995).

TUTHILL, STEVEN
(museum director)
Affiliation: Indian Temple Mound Museum, Box 4009, 139 Miracle Strip Parkway, Fort Walton Beach, FL 32549 (904) 243-6521.

TUTT, LOUIS
(health director)
Affiliation: Winslow PHS Indian Health Center, P.O. Drawer 40, Winslow, AZ 86047 (520) 289-4646.

TWIDDY, FRANCIS (Skokomish)
(former tribal chairperson)
Affiliation: Skokomish Tribal Council, N. 80 Tribal Center Rd., Shelton, WA 98584 (206) 426-4232.

TWISS, GAYLA
(hospital director)
Affiliation: Rosebud PHS Indian Hospital, Rosebud, SD 57570 (605) 747-2231.

TWITCHELL, JERRY
(school principal)
Affiliation: Chefornak IRA Contract School, Chefornak, AK 99561 (907) 867-8707.

TWO EAGLES, ROBERT (Oglala Lakota)
(poet, author)
Address: 15150 S. Golden Rd. #1002, Golden, CO 80401 (303) 271-9233.

TWO EAGLES, VINCE *(Choka Opi)* **(Yankton Sioux) 1953-**
(entertainer, songwriter, recording artist)
Born January 26, 1953, Yankton, S.D. *Education*: Dakota State College (2 years); Black Hills State College (1 year). *Principal occupation*: Entertainer, writer, recording artist. *Home address*: P.O. Box 9, Wagner, SD 57380 (605) 384-3814. *Affiliation*: Trainer, Institute of Reality Therapy, Los Angeles, CA (10 years). *Other professional posts*: Entertainer, songwriter, recording artist, lecturer on traditional Dakota culture and the impact of alcoholism/drug abuse. Trainer - intervention teams, protective services programs (tribal); co-ordinator, Yankton Sioux Tribe Radio Project, KONA, Inc., Marty School, Marty, SD. *Community activities*: Marty Indian School's Advisory Committee on Alcohol

and Drug Free Policy to the school's Board of Directors; member, Action Committee (designed to intervene in sexual, physical and emotional abuse of children); Yankton Sioux Tribe's representative on the "Lakota Camp Courage" Planning Board; Ad-Hoc Committee, Yankton Sioux Tribe's General Council. *Membership*: South Dakota Indian Counselors Association. *Awards, honors*: Currently an applicant for a Touring Arts and Artists Fellowship grant from SD Arts Council. *Interests*: "I have traveled throughout the U.S., Canada and Italy along with my backup musical group called, "People of the Earth," spreading a message of healing and support for local sobriety efforts and environmental issues and calling attention to the need for all races of people to come together in a spiritual manner toward reconciliation between the Native and non-Native communities as a means to fulfill the true teachings of our traditional elders and spiritual leaders." *Published songs*: "People of the Earth," 1990 & "In the Night," 1992 by Max Records; "In America," 1994 & 1996 by Sound of America Records.

TWO HAWKS, WEBSTER
(IHS-tribal health management)
Affiliation: Indian Health Service, Aberdeen Area Office, Federal Bldg., 115 4th Ave., S.E., Aberdeen, SD 57401 (605) 226-7591.

TWO RIVERS/BROEFFLE, E. DONALD
(performer)
Two-Rivers specializes in performance poetry relating to the urban experience of many Native Americans. He has appeared at the Center Theatre in Chicago as well as other area community theatres. He can be contacted at phone number 1-312-728-6756.

TYNDELL, WAYNE
(director-Indian center)
Affiliation: American Indian Center of Omaha, 3610 Dodge St., #2078, Omaha, NE 68131-3207.

TYNER, JAMES W. (Cherokee) 1911-
(historian)
Born September 13, 1911, Tahlequah, Okla. *Education*: Haskell Institute. *Principal occupation*: Historian. *Home address*: P.O. Box 881, Chouteau, OK 74337. *Affiliation*: Historian for Indian history project, American Indian Institute, University of Oklahoma, Norman. *Military service*: U.S. Navy, 1942-45 (Chief Petty Officer, World War II). *Awards, honors*: National Certificate of Commendation for published work, Our People and Where They Rest (Hooper Publishing, 1969-72), American Association for State and Local History. *Interests*: Indian history, including research and recording old cemeteries; woodcarving; cartridge collecting.

TYNES, ALICE W.
(school principal)
Affiliation: Teecnospos Boarding School, Teecnospos, AZ 86514 (520) 656-3451.

TYRO, FRANK
(film producer)
Affiliation: Salish Kootenai College, P.O. Box 117, Pablo, MT 59855 (406) 675-4800.

TYSON, JEAN
(Indian school principal)
Affiliation: Santa Rosa Ranch School, Sells Star Route, Box 230, Tucson, AZ 85735 (520) 383-2359.

TYZ, JEAN E.
(Indian education program director)
Affiliation: Greenway Schools ISD #316/319 Coleraine/Mashwauk, Office of Indian Education, P.O. Box 520, Coleraine, MN 55722 (218) 295-1287 Fax 245-2019.

U

ULMER, JOE
(director)
Affiliation: Ya-Ka-Ama, 6215 Eastside Rd., Forestville, CA 95448 (707) 887-1541.

UNGOTT, CLEMENT (Eskimo)
(Eskimo coop manager)
Affiliation: St. lawrence Island Original Ivory Cooperative, Ltd., P.O. Box 189, Gambell, AK 99742 (907) 985-5112 Fax 985-5927

USKAVITCH, ROBERT
(chief-information services)
Affiliation: U.S. Dept. of the Interior Library, 18th & C Sts., NW, Washington, DC 20240 (202) 343-5810.

USNER, DANIEL H., JR.
(Indian program director)
Affiliation: American Indian Program, Cornell University, 450 Caldwell Hall, Ithaca, NY 14853 (607) 255-8402 Fax 255-6246.

UTTLEY, JIM
(editor)
Affiliation: Indian Life Magazine, Intertribal Christian Communications, Box 3765 Station B, Winnipeg, Manitoba, Canada R2W 3R6 (204) 661-9333.

UTLEY, ROBERT M.
(writer)
Published works: The Lance and the Shield: The Life and Times of Sitting Bull; Cavalier in Buckskin: George Armstrong Custer & the Western Military Frontier.

V

VALDEZ, ROBERT (Pueblo)
(advisor)
Affiliation: Council of Advisors, American Indian Heritage Foundation, 6051 Arlington Blvd., Falls Church, VA 22044 (703) 237-7500.

VALENCIA, ROBERT (Pascua Yaqui)
(tribal chairperson)
Affiliation: Pascua Yaqui Tribal Council, 7474 S. Camino De Oeste, Tucson, AZ 85746 (520) 883-5000.

VALENCIA-WEBER, GLORIA
(attorney)
Affiliation: University of Tulsa College of Law, 3120 E. 4th Place, Tulsa, OK 74104 (918) 631-2439.

VALLE, FELIX (Diegueno)
(tribal chairperson)
Affiliation: Santa Ysabel General Council, P.O. Box 126, Santa Ysabel, CA 92070 (619) 765-0845.

VALLIE, LAURA (Chippewa)
(craftsperson; company co-owner)
Affiliation: La Ray Turquoise Co., P.O. Box 83, Cody, WY 82414 (307) 587-9564. *Products*: Navajo, Zuni, Chippewa, Hopi, and Santo Domingo silver and beadwork; Navajo rugs.

VALLIE, RAY (Chippewa)
(craftsperson; company co-owner)
Affiliation: La Ray Turquoise Co., P.O. Box 83, Cody, WY 82414 (307) 587-9564. *Products*: Navajo, Zuni, Chippewa, Hopi, and Santo Domingo silver and beadwork; Navajo rugs.

VAN CASTER, ROBERT (Sandia Pueblo)
(Pueblo enterprise manager)
Affiliation: Bien Mur Indian Arts & Crafts, P.O. Box 91148, Albuquerque, NM 87199 (800) 365-5400.

VAN MECHELEN, NADINE (Yurok-Karok-Tolowa)
(craftswoman; gallery owner)
Address: Rt. 1, Box 270, Pendleton, OR 97801 (503) 276-2566. *Affiliation*: Owner, Wind Song Gallery, 7 SE Court, Pendleton, OR 97801 (541) 276-7993. *Product*: Native dolls dressed in authentic Indian clothing, for collectors.

VAN NORMAN, TOM
(tribal attorney)
Affiliation: Tribal attorney, Cheyenne River Sioux Tribal Council, P.O. Box 590, Eagle Butte, SD 57625 (605) 964-4155.

VANDERHOOP, DAVID (Wampanoag)
(tribal council vice president)
Affiliation: Wampanoag Tribal Council of Gay Head, RFD Box 137, Gay Head, MA 02535 (508) 645-9265.

VANDERWAGEN, W. CRAIG, M.D.
(IHS-director/clinical services)
Affiliation: Office of Health Programs, Div. of Clinical Services, Indian Health Service, Rm. 6A-55, 5600 Fishers Lane, Rockville, MD 20857 (301) 443-4644.

VANN, DONALD *(Q-A Na Da-Ga-Do-Ga)*
(Oklahoma Cherokee) 1949-
(artist, publisher)
Born October 22, 1949, Adar County, Okla. *Education*: High school. *Principal occupation*: Artist, publisher. *Address & Affiliation*: Partner, Native American Images (a publishing co. that has worked with many renowned artists over the past 20 years), P.O. Box 746, Austin, TX 78767 (512) 472-3049 (work). *Military service*: U.S. Army, 1969-71 (First Calvary in Vietnam, helicopter gunman). *Awards, honors*: His original watercolors have won scores of ribbons across the country. Includes a half-dozen First Place & Grand Awards from th Five Civilized Tribes Museum; his paintings, lithographs & prints have been featured at exhibits across the U.S. More than 50 limited edition releases of his works have sold out and now command collector values many times their original issue price. The Smithsonian Institution's Museum of the American Indian has presented him with their highest honor. He has also been proclaimed "on of the best known Indian artists working in this century" by the Cherokee Historical Society. His paintings have been exhibited at the Smithsonian. *Interests*: Back-packing, camping, canoeing, skiing, heli-skiing, running, and video-photography.

VANN, MICHAEL V. (Turtle Mountain Chippewa)
(radio station president)
Affiliation: KEYA - 88.5 FM, Turtle Mountain Chippewa Tribe, P.O. Box 190, Belcourt, ND 58316 (701) 477-5686.

VANWINKLE, LORETTA
(executive secretary)
Affiliation: Intertribal Friendship House, 523 East 14th St., Oakland, CA 94606 (510) 452-1235.

VARESE, STEFANO 1939-
(professor of Native American studies)
Born July 27, 1939, Genova, Italy. *Education*: Catholic University (Lima, Peru) Diplomas (History & Anthropology), 1963 & 1964, BS (Ethnology), 1966, PhD (Anthropology), 1967. *Principal occupation*: Professor of Native American studies. *Home address*: 1309 Monarch Lane, Davis, CA 95616 (916) 753-9508; 752-0357 (work). *Affiliations*: Director, Unidad Regional de Oaxaca, Direccion General de Culturas Populares, Secretaria de Educacion Publica de Mexico, 1981-86; Native American Studies, University of California, Davis (visiting professor, 1988-90, professor, 1990-). *Other professional posts*: Consultant for United Nations agencies on indigenous peoples of the Americas. *Community activities*: Director of Unit of Indigenous Popular Cultures, Oaxaca, Mexico, 1979-87. *Memberships*: American Anthropological Association; Latin American Studies Association; Society for Applied Anthropology; Cultural Survival, Cambridge, MA (Advisory Board). *Awards, honors*: Tinker Visiting Scholar, Stanford University, 1986-87; Ford Foundation Fellow at the Humanities Center, Stanford University, 1987-88; Co-Chair-elect of Society for Latin American Anthropology (American Anthropological Association), 1989-90. *Interests*: Indians of the Americas. *Published works*: Numerous books and monographs, and chapters in edited books; official reports and articles.

VASKA, RUTH B. (Eskimo)
(AK village president)
Affiliation: Village of Aniak, P.O. Box 176, Aniak, AK 99557 (907) 675-4349.

VASSAR, JAN 1940-
(free lance journalist)
Born June 19, 1940. *Education*: Tulsa University, BA, 1962; University of Oklahoma, 1962-64. *Principal occupation*: Free lance journalist. *Home address*: P.O. Box 454, Chandler, OK 74834 (405) 258-1219 Fax 258-1412. *E-mail*: jvassar@aol.com. *Affiliations*: Sac & Fox Nation, Stroud, OK (reporter & editorial supervisor, 1985-89; historical researcher, 1986-92; editor of publications & library director, 1989-92; Sauk language presentation director, 1996-97; Sauk exhibit coordinator-fabricator, 1995-97); feature reporter-photographer, Stroud American, 1999-. *Community activities*: Lincoln County Arts & Humanities Council (board of directors); Sac & Fox National Public Library (board member); Sac & Fox Nation Tax Commission

(member, 1998-). *Memberships*: Native American Press Association; Oklahoma Historical Society; Lincoln County Historical Society (board member, president, curator). *Awards, honors*: Best Feature Photo, Native American Press Association. *Publication*: Handbook of American Women's History, 2nd Ed.

VATTER, ANTOINETTE
(organization director)
Affiliation: American Indian Service Corp., 1007 Dillingham St. #102, Honolulu, HI 96817 (808) 847-2511.

VAUGHAN, TOM
(park supt.)
Affiliation: Chaco Culture National Historical Park, Star Route 4, Box 6500, Bloomfield, NM 87413 (505) 786-5384.

VAUGHN, MARCELLA B.
(school principal)
Affiliation: Red Water Elementary School, Rte. 4, Box 30, Carthage, MS 39051 (601) 267-8500.

VECSEY, CHRISTOPHER 1948-
(professor)
Born December 7, 1948, New York, N.Y. *Education*: Hunter College, B.A.; Northwestern University, MA, PhD (Religion), 1977. Principal: Professor of Native American Studies. *Address*: Colgate University, Dept. of Philosophy & Religion, 13 Oak Dr., Hamilton, NY 13346 (315) 228-7277 Fax 228-7998. E-mail: cvecsey@mail.colgate.edu. *Affiliations*: Professor, Hobart & William Smith Colleges (1976-1982); Professor of Native American Studies, Colgate University, Hamilton, NY (1982-present). *Published works*: Traditional Ojibwa Religion and Its Historical Changes (American Philosophical Society, 1983); Imagine Ourselves Richly: Mythic Narratives of North American Indians (Crossroad/Continuum, 1988; Harper, San Francisco, 1991); On the Padres' Trail (Notre Dame, 1996); The Paths of Kateri's Kin (Notre Dame, 1997); Where the Roads Meet (Notre Dame, 1999); seven books edited or co-edited..

VEDOLLA, EDDIE, Sr. (Pomo)
(rancheria chairperson)
Affiliation: Guidiville Rancheria, P.O. Box 339, Talmadge, CA 95481 (707) 462-3682.

VEEDER, VOLKERT
(museum curator)
Affiliation: The Mohawk-Caughnawaga Museum, Route 5, Box 554, Fonda, NY 12068 (518) 853-3678.

VEGA, DOUG (Paiute)
(tribal council vice chairperson)
Affiliation: Bishop Indian Tribal Council, 50 Tu Su Lane, Bishop. CA 93514 (760) 873-3584.

VEGA, PEGGY
(Indian education center director)
Affiliation: Owens Valley Indian Education Center, P.O. Box 1648, Bishop, CA 93514 (760) 873-5740 Fax 873-4143.

VEILEUX, FRED (Ojibwe)
(social worker)
Address: 3624 - 13th Ave. So., Minneapolis, MN 55407 (612) 729-0850. *Affiliation*: Concerned American Indian Parents, CUHCC Clinic, Minneapolis, MN. *Membership*: Leech Lake (Reservation) Ojibwe.

VELASQUEZ, ROBERT (San Felipe Pueblo)
(former Pueblo governor)
Affiliation: San Felipe Pueblo Council, P.O. Box A4339, San Felipe Pueblo, NM 87001 (505) 867-3381.

VELKY, RICHARD (Schaghticoke)
(tribal chairperson)
Affiliation: Schaghticoke Tribal Council, 605 Main St., Monroe, CT 06468 (860) 459-2531.

VENDIOLA, MICHELE "SHELLY"
(Swinomish-Visayan)
(mediator, peacemaker consultant)
Address & Affiliation: Indian Dispute Resolution Services, Sacramento, CA 95814 (916) 447-4800 Fax 447-4808; E-Mail: idrs@tomatoweb.net. *Other profes-*

sional post: Adjunct Professor, D-Q University. *Community activities*: Community Boards Peacemaker Program; Student Council of Intertribal Nations, SFSU; American Indian Education Conference Planning Committee. *Memberships*: California Association of Community Mediation Program; National Association of Dispute Resolution Programs; Indigenous Women's Network; Greenpeace.

VENT, GILBERT (Athapascan)
(village first chief)
Affiliation: Allakaket Community, P.O. Box 30, Allakaket, AK 99720 (907) 968-2241.

VENT, WARNER (Athapascan)
(village chief)
Affiliation: Huslia Village Council, P.O. Box 32, Huslia, AK 99746 (907) 829-2202.

VERRET, C.A. KIRBY (Houma) 1947-
(supportive coordinator of Indian education)
Born June 26, 1947, Duharge, La. *Education*: College. *Principal occupation*: Supportive coordinator of Indian education. *Address*: Terrebonne Parish School District, Indian Education Program, 301 Academy St., Houma, LA 70360 (504) 851-1553 Fax 868-6278. *Affiliations*: Terrebonne Parish Indian Education, 1980-; pastor, Native American United Methodist Church. *Community activities*: Member & past chair of United Houma Nation Tribal Council; vice-chair, Salvation Army; member, Coastal Zone management Committee; member, Alcohol Drug Abuse Council Advisory Committee.

VERMILLION, EDWARD (Hopi)
(school principal)
Affiliation: Hopi Day School, P.O. Box 42, Kykotsmovi, AZ 86039 (520) 734-2468.

VESCEY, CHRISTOPHER
(professor)
Address & Affiliation: Colgate University, Hamilton, NY 13346 (315) 228-7276. E-mail: cvescey@mail.colgate. edu.

VETTESE, DENNIS
(health director)
Affiliation: Elko Southern Band Clinic, 515 Shoshone Cir., Elko, NV 89801 (702) 738-2252.

VIARIAL, JACOB (Pojoaque Pueblo)
(Pueblo governor)
Affiliation: Pueblo of Pojoaque, 39 Camino del Rincon #1, Santa Fe, NM 87501 (505) 455-2278.

VIGIL, B. THOMAS
(institute chairperson)
Affiliation: First Nations Development Institute, The Stores Bldg., 11917 Main St., Fredericksburg, VA 22408 (703) 371-5615.

VIGIL, FREDERICK (Tesuque Pueblo)
(association chairperson)
Affiliation: Chairperson, All Indian Pueblo Council, Tesuque Pueblo Council, Rt. 5, Box 360-T, Santa Fe, NM 87501 (505) 983-2667.

VIGIL, JOYCE
(Indian education program coordinator)
Affiliation: Adams-Arapahoe School District, Indian Education Program, 15700 East 1st Ave., Aurora, CO 8011 (303) 340-0510 ext. 302 Fax 343-7064.

VIGIL, SHERRYL J. (Jicarilla Apache)
(BIA agency supt.)
Affiliation: Jicarilla Agency, Bureau of Indian Affairs, P.O. Box 167, Dulce, NM 87528 (505) 759-3951 Fax 759-3948.

VIGIL, VIDA L. (Jicarilla Apache)
(editor)
Affiliation: Jicarilla Chieftain, Jicarilla Apache Tribe, P.O. Box 507, Dulce, NM 87528 (505) 759-3242.

VIGIL-MUNIZ, CLAUDIA J. (Jicarilla Apache)
(tribal president; education program counselor)
Affiliations: President, Jicarilla Apache Tribal Council, P.O. Box 507, Dulce, NM 87528 (505) 759-3242; counselor, Jicarilla Apache Higher Education Program, P.O. Box 507, Dulce, NM 87528 (505) 759-3615.

VILLA, NICOLAS, JR. (Miwok)
(tribal chairperson)
Affiliation: Ione Band of Miwok Indians, 2919
Jackson Valley Rd., Ione, CA 95640 (916) 566-7121.

VILLALOBOS, MIKE (Warm Springs Confederated)
(radio station manager)
Affiliation: KWSO - 91.9 FM, Warm Springs Confederated Tribes, P.O. Box 489, Warm Springs, OR 97761
(541) 553-1968.

VINEYARD, JOYCE L. (Chickasaw)
(craftsperson)
Address: 330 1/2 W. Main, Anadarko, OK 73005
(405) 247-9770. *Products:* Shawls and banners.

VIOLA, HERMAN J. 1938-
(historian)
Born February 24, 1938, Chicago, Ill. *Education:*
Marquette University, BA, 1962, MA, 1964; Indiana
University, PhD, 1970. *Principal occupation:* Historian-
specially American Indian history. *Home address:* 7307
Pinewood St., Falls Church, VA 22046. *Affiliations:*
Staff, National Archives, 1968-72; director, National
Anthropological Archives, Smithsonian Institution,
Washington, DC, 1972-87. *Other professional posts:*
Founder and first editor of Prologue, The Journal of
the National Archives, 1968-72; consultant to numer-
ous scholarly and educational organizations, including, the Galef Institute, Randam House, The Library
of the American West, and the Library of the American
Indian. *Military service:* U.S. Navy, 1960-62. *Memberships:* Society of American Archivists; Western History Association; Organization of American Historians;
Phi Beta Kappa. *Awards, honors:* 1984 Merit Award
for "Distinguished Professional Achievement," from
Marquette University; in 1987, he was one of three
finalists for the position of Archivist of the U.S., which
is a presidential appointment; in June 1988, he received an honorary doctor of letters degree from
Wittenberg University. *Interests:* Research specialties
are the American West and the American Indian. *Biographical source:* Who's Who in America. *Published
works:* Thomas L. McKinney, Architect of America's
Early Indian Policy, 1816-1830 (Swallow Press, 1972);
The Indian Legacy of Charles Bird King (Smithsonian
Institution Press & Doubleday, 1976); Diplomats in
Buckskin (Smithsonian Institution Press, 1981); The
National Archives of the U.S. (Harry N. Abrams, 1984);
Magnificent Voyagers: The U.S. Exploring Expedition,
1838-1841 (Smithsonian Institution Press, 1986); Ex-
ploring the West (Smithsonian Exposition Books,
1987); After Columbus: The Smithsonian's Chronicle
of the Indians of North America Since 1492
(Smithsonian Institution Press, 1990); and editor of
Seeds of Change, A Quincentennial Commemoration
(Smithsonian Institution Press, 1991).

VIRGIL, DALE Jicarilla Apache)
(former tribal chairperson)
Affiliation: Jicarilla Apache Tribal Council,
P.O. Box 147, Dulce, NM 87528 (505) 759-3242.

VIT, LINDA C. (Karuk/Cree) 1947-
(jewelry designer-traditional)
Born November 28, 1947, Yreka, Calif. *Principal occupation:* Jewelry designer-traditional. *Home address:*
326 2nd St., Eureka, CA 95501 (707) 442-3042 Fax
445-0745. E-mail: indianwest@yahoo.com. *Website:*
www.indianwest.com. *Affiliation:* Karuk Originals by Vit,
Eureka, CA, 1977-present. *Other professional post:*
Marketing developer, Northern California Development
Council. *Membership:* Indian Arts and Crafts Association (1980-present). Interests: Owner of two retail
American Indian and special occasion clothing boutique; fictional writing.

VIZENOR, ERMA (White Earth Chippewa)
(tribal chairperson)
Affiliation: White Earth Chippewa Tribe, P.O. Box 418,
White Earth, MN 56591 (218) 983-3285 Fax 983-3641

VIZENOR, GERALD
(Native American studies instructor)
Affiliation: Professor, Native American Studies Department, University of California, Dwinelle Hall, Suite
3415, Berkeley, CA 94720 (510) 642-6717.

VIZINA, RUSSELL (Chippewa)
(health director)
Affiliation: Sault Ste. Marie Tribal Clinic, Wilson Rd.,
Bldg. 312, Kincheloe, MI 49788 (906) 495-5615.

VOGT, DAVID, D.O.
(clinical director)
Affiliation: Sault Ste. Marie Tribal Clinic, 312 Water
Tower Dr., Kincheloe, MI 49788 (906) 495-5615.

VOIGHT, THOMAS F. 1947-
(publisher)
Born March 8, 1947, Milwaukee, Wisc. *Education:*
University of Wisconsin, Milwaukee, BA, 1972, MA,
1976. *Principal occupation:* Publisher. *Home address:*
P.O. Box 889, New Castle, CO 81647 (303) 984-3685.
Affiliation: President (owner/founder), Wintercount (art,
prose & poetry of the American Indian), New Castle,
CO, 1984-. *Other professional post:* Instructor, Colo-
rado Mountain College, Glenwood Springs, CO. *Com-
munity activities:* Member, Chamber of Commerce,
New Castle; member & volunteer, Public Radio Sta-
tion, KDNK, Carbondale, CO; board member, Rural
Fire District; sponsor Ute Legacy Juried Art Show.
Memberships: National Indian Youth Council; American Indian Arts & Crafts Association; National Museum
of the American Indian (charter member); National
Stuntman Hall of Fame, Moab, UT (charter member);
Appaloosa Horse Club. *Awards, honors:* Certificate of
Excellence, Colorado Mountain College. *Interests:*
"Extensive art collection of American Indian paintings
and crafts. Have traveled to numerous Indian reser-
vations and archaeological sites and have participated
in the discovery & restoration of archaeological areas."

VOISEY, EVA
(association president)
Affiliation: Inuit Women's Association, 200 Elgin St.,
Suite 804, Ottawa, ON, Can. K2P 1L5 (613) 238-3977.

VOLBORTH, JUDITH ANN
(Mountain-Leaf) (Blackfeet) 1956-
(writer, poet, speaker)
Born October 23, 1956, New York, N.Y. *Education:* Los
Angeles Pierce College, AA, 1975; University of California, Los Angeles, BA, 1986. *Principal occupation:*
Writer, poet. *Home address:* 1032B - 3rd St., Santa
Monica, CA 90403 (310) 395-5923. *Other professional
posts:* Educator, public speaker. *Community activities:*
Emergency medical technician (volunteer); Commu-
nity Emergency Response Team (search & rescue,
firefighting, triage); Disaster Service Worker (volun-
teer); volunteer working with homeless & mentally ill
adults. *Memberships:* Native Writer's Circle of the
Americas; Wordcraft: Circle of Native American Mentor & Apprentice Writers; Association for the Study of
American Indian Literature. *Awards, honors:* Ina
Coolbrith Memorial Prize for Poetry; Shirley Dorothy
Robbins Creative Writing Award; The May Merrill Miller
Award for Poetry; Academy of American Poets Award
(honorable mention). *Biographical sources:* "Portrait
of a Mentor," by Lee Francis, in Native American Renaissance, by Ken Lincoln; Indian Humor: Bicultural
Play in Native America, by Ken Lincoln; Native American Lesbian & Gay Literature, by Will Roscoe. *Published work:* Thunder-Root: Traditional & Contemporary Native American Verse (American Indian Studies
Center, UCLA, 1978).

VOLK, JOSEPH E.
(executive director)
Affiliation: Friends Committee on National Legislation,
245 Second St., NE, Washington, DC 20010 (202) 547-
6000 Fax 547-6019. E-mail: indian@fcnl.org. *Website:*
www.fcnl.org.

VOLZ, KATHARINE J.
(executive director)
Affiliation: Marin Museum of the American Indian Library, P.O. Box 864, 2200 Novato Blvd., Novato, CA
94948 (415) 897-4064.

VON FICKENSTEIN, MARIA 1942-
(curator of Inuit art)
Born March 10, 1942, in Germany. *Education:* BA in
Art History; MA in Art Therapy. *Principal occupation:*
Curator of Inuit art. *Home address:* 521 Chapel St.,
Ottawa, ON K1N 8A1, Canada (819) 776-8433 Fax
776-8429. E-mail: maria.vonfinckenstein@civilization.

ca. *Affiliations:* Indian and Northern Affairs Canada,
Ottawa, ON, 1980-93; curator of Inuit art, Canadian
Museum of Civilization, Hull, ON, 1997-present. *Inter-
ests:* Gardening, yoga, reading, films, meditation. *Pub-
lished works:* Celebrating Inuit Art, 1948-1970 (Key
Porter Books, 1999); Nuvisavik: The Place Where We
Weave (McGill/Queen's University Press, 2002).

VOSBERG, RICHARD
(Indian school superintendent)
Affiliation: Crazy Horse School, P.O. Box 260,
Wanblee, SD 57577 (605) 462-6511.

W

WABAUNSEE, JOHN (Potawatomi)
(tribal chief justice)
Affiliation: Prairie Band Potawatomi Nation Appelate
Court, 15498 K Rd., Mayetta, KS 66509 (866) 966-
2242 or (785) 966-2242 Fax 966-2662. E-mail: tribal
court@pbpnation.org. Website: www.pbpnation.org/
tribalcourt

WABNUM, FREDA F.
(BIA agency supt.)
Affiliation: Laguna Agency, Bureau of Indian Affairs,
P.O. Box 1448, Laguna, NM 87026 (505) 552-6001.

WACHACHA, MARY G.
(health education coordinator)
Affiliation: Cherokee Technical Support Center, P.O.
Box 429, Butler Bldg., Rt. 1, Sequoyah Trail, Cherokee, NC 28719 (704) 497-5030.

WACONDA, JOSEPHINE T.
(IHS area director)
Affiliation: Albuquerque Area Office, Indian Health
Service, 505 Marquette Ave., NW, Albuquerque, NM
87102 (505) 766-2151.

WADE, BEN
(school principal)
Affiliation: Greasewood Springs Community School,
HC 58, Box 60, Ganado, AZ 86505 (520) 654-3331 Fax
654-3384.

WADE, CLAUDIA ANN (Washoe)
(tribal chairperson)
Affiliation: Woodfords Washoe Community Council,
Alpine Washoe Reservation, 2111 Carson River Rd.,
Markleeville, CA 96120.

WADE, JACQUELINE N.
(school principal)
Affiliation: Holbrook Dormitory, 1100 W. Buffalo,
Holbrook, AZ 86025 (520) 524-6222 Fax 524-2231.

WADE, KEN
(librarian)
Affiliation: UCLA American Indian Studies Center Library, 3220 Campbell Hall, Box 951548, Los Angeles,
CA 90095-1548 (310) 206-7510 Fax 206-7060.

WADENA, DARRELL (Chippewa)
(tribal president/chairperson)
Affiliation: President, Minnesota Chippewa Tribal Executive Committee, P.O. Box 217C, Cass Lake, MN
56633 (218) 335-2252; chairperson, White Earth Reservation Business Committee, P.O. Box 418, White
Earth, MN 56591 (218) 983-3285; Circle of Life Survival School, White Earth, MN.

WADITAKA, LORNE
(Indian band chief)
Affiliation: Wahpeton Indian Band, Box 128, Prince
Albert, Saskatchewan, Canada S6V 5R4 (306) 764-
6649.

WADZINSKI, KEVIN J.
(Stockbridge/Munsee-Mohican) 1966-
(attorney)
Born May 3, 1966, Oconto Falls, Wisc. *Education:*
University of Wisconsin, BA, 1988; University of
Wisconsin Law School, JD, 1993. *Principal occupa-
tion:* Attorney. *Address & Affiliation:* Dorsey & Whitney
LLP, Indian Law Dept., 1001 Pennsylvania Ave., NW,
Suite 300 So., Washington, DC 20004 (202) 824-8863,

1993-. *Memberships*: Minnesota American Indian Bar Association; Native American Bar Association; Wisconsin Bar Association - Indian Law Section.

WAHLBERG, RON, M.D.
(IHS-chief medical officer)
Affiliation: Bemidji Area IHS, 127 Federal Bldg., Bemidji, MN 56601 (218) 759-3414.

WAHNEE, BEVERLY (Hopi)
(BIA special education coordinator)
Affiliation: Hopi Agency, Bureau of Indian Affairs, P.O. Box 568, Keams Canyon, AZ 86034 (520) 738-2262 Fax 738-5139.

WAHNEE, JOHN D. (Hopi)
(BIA education administrator)
Affiliation: Hopi Agency, Bureau of Indian Affairs, P.O. Box 568, Keams Canyon, AZ 86034 (520) 738-2262 Fax 738-5139.

WAHPEPAH, CAROL
(Indian center director)
Affiliation: American Indian Child Resource Center, 600 Grand Ave., Suite 308, Oakland, CA 94610 (510) 208-1877 Fax 208-1886.

WAHPEPAH, WILDA (Winnebago-Hoh Chunk)
(attorney)
Address & Affiliation: Dorsey & Whitney LLP, 50 S. Sixth St., #1500, Minneapolis, MN 55402-1498 (612) 340-2600. E-mail: wahpepah.wilda@dorseylaw. com.

WAHQUAHBOSHKUK, GEORGE
(Prairie Potawatomi)
(tribal chairperson)
Affiliation: Prairie Potawatomi Tribal Council, P.O. Box 97, Mayetta, KS 66509 (913) 966-2255.

WAHWASUCK, BADGER
(Prairie Band Potawatomi)
(former tribal council chairperson)
Affiliation: Prairie Band Potawatomi Tribal Council, 16281 Q Rd., Mayetta, KS 66509 (785) 966-4000.

WAKEMAN, RICHARD K.
(Flandreau Santee Sioux) 1923-
(tribal officer)
Born February 9, 1923, Flandreau, S.D. *Education*: Haskell Institute. *Principal occupation*: Tribal officer. *Address*: R.R. 1, Box 59A, Flandreau, SD 57028. *Affiliation*: Former president, Flandreau Santee Sioux Business Council. *Military service*: U.S. Marine Corps, 1942-45; U.S. Army, 1951-53 (Presidential Unit Citation; Commendation; Asiatic Pacific Award). *Community activities*: South Dakota Indian Commission; South Dakota Letter Carriers (president); Dakota Presbytery (moderator); Masonic Lodge. *Interests*: Tribal history.

WALCOTT, PETER, Sr.
(village president)
Affiliation: Ekwok Village Council, P.O. Box 70, Ekwok, AK 99580 (907) 464-3311.

WALDEN, HENRY ALTON, JR. (Pima) 1950-
(health systems management)
Born November 29, 1950, Albuquerque, N.M. *Education*: Phoenix City College, AA, 1976; Arizona State University, BS, 1978; University of Hawaii, MPH, 1982. *Principal occupation*: Health systems management). *Address*: Resides in Arizona. *Affiliations*: Community Health Education, Scottsdale, AZ, 1982-84; Public Health Education, Parker, AZ, 1984-88; hospital administrator, Indian Health Service, USPHS, Fort Yuma, AZ, 1988-. *Military service*: U.S. Navy, Dental Corps. (Petty Officer-Third Class, National Defense, Viet Nam Service, Viet Nam Campaign Good Conduct); Lt. Commissioned Corps, U.S. Public Health Service. *Community activities*: Board of directors, Behavioral Health Agency of Central Arizona. *Interests*: "Native American culture, social inter-actions between Native peoples and mainstream America, health and social problems and their resolutions. *Hobbies*: Automobile restoration, silversmithing, painting, musical instruments and my children." *Published works*: "A Second Opinion on Zuni Diabetes" (U.S. Public Health Reports, April 1983); "Are We Overlooking Some Winning Strategies (IHS Provider, June 1988).

WALDRAM, JAMES B. 1955-
(professor)
Born August 20, 1955, Oshawa, Ontario, Can. *Education*: University of Waterloo, BA, 1978; University of Manitoba, MA, 1980; University of Connecticut, PhD, 1983. *Principal occupation*: Professor. *Home address*: 247 Sylvian Way, Saskatoon, Saskatchewan, Can. *Affiliation*: Assistant professor, Dept. of Native American Studies, University of Saskatchewan, Saskatoon, Sask., Can., 1983-. *Other professional post*: Associate editor, Native Studies Review. *Memberships*: Canadian Ethnology Society; Canadian Indian/Native Studies Association; Canadian Association for Medical Anthropology; American Anthropological Association; Society for Applied Anthropology. *Awards, honors*: Social Sciences and Humanities Research Council of Canada Doctoral Fellowship. *Interests*: "The impact of hydroelectric development of northern Canadian Native communities. Dietary change in the Canadian north; education needs assessment of urban Native people; health and health care delivery of urban Native people." *Published work*: 1885 and After: Native Society in Transition (Canadian Plains Research Center, Regina, 1986).

WALDRON, DARRELL
(president-board of directors)
Affiliation: Rhode Island Indian Council, Inc., 444 Friendship St., Providence, RI 02907 (401) 331-4440.

WALKER, BETTY
(BIA area education administrator)
Affiliation: Minneapolis Area Office, Bureau of Indian Affairs, 331 Second Ave. South, Minneapolis, MN 55401 (612) 373-1090.

WALKER, CHRISTINE (Chemehuevi)
(tribal chairperson)
Affiliation: Chemehuevi Tribal Council, P.O. Box 1976, Chemehuevi Valley, CA 92363 (619) 858-4531.

WALKER, DARLENE
(health center director)
Affiliation: Inscription House PHS Indian Health Center, Inscription House, AZ 86054 (520) 672-2611.

WALKER, DEWARD, JR.
(research associate, anthropologist)
Born August 3, 1935, Johnson, Tenn. *Education*: University of Oregon, BA, 1961, PhD (Anthropology), 1964. *Principal occupation*: Research associate, anthropologist. *Address & Affiliation*: Walker Research Group, Ltd., P.O. Box 4147, Boulder, CO 80306 (303) 492-6719 Fax 492-7970. E-mail: walkerde@colorado. edu. Website: www.walkerresearchgroup.com. Mr. Walker has conducted research among tribal and non-tribal populations of the Columbia Basin, Western Plains, Northern Great Basin and Southwest. He is frequently retained by tribal governments and agencies to conduct demographics, legal, housing, health, education, and economic research relating to planning, program development, risk assessment, legal defense of treaty rights, and various tribal environmental initiatives concerning water, fish, mining, nuclear waste, logging, etc. *Community activities*: Advisory Board member, High Desert Museum Fellowship Program. *Awards, honors*: Invited Keynote Addresses: "The American Indian in Transition—Past as Prologue," Idaho State University, Pocatello, 1972; "Legal & Political History of the Indians of Idaho," Idaho State legislature, Boise, 1982; Northwestern Anthropoogical Conference, "Anthropology and the Law: American Indians & Cultural Resource Management," Moscow, Idaho, 1986; Newberry Library Conference on American Indian Religious Freedom, Chicago, 1988. Invited Testimony on "Amending the American Indian Religious Freedom Act," before the U.S. Senate Select Committee on Indian Affairs, Washington, DC, 1988. Nomination for various teaching awards at the University of Colorado, Boulder, 1989-1995. Acknowledgement by the Nez Perce Tribal Executive Committee for Successful Efforts to Protect and Preserve the Sacred Sovereignty of the Nez Perce Tribe, 2001. Invited member of EPA Region's 8 October Native American Sacred Lands Forum, 2001. Nomination for membership to the Technical Recovery Team for the Interior Columbia Basin Salmon Recovery Domain by the Shoshone-Paiute Tribes of the Duck Valley Indian Reservation, 2001. Invited Presenter at session

"Trouble in Paradise: Violence and Conflict Among the Indigenous Peoples of the Americas" at the AAA meeting in Chicago, Nov. 19-23, 2003. *Memberships*: American Anthropological Association, 1966-present; Society for Applied Anthropology, 1965-present; American Indian Development, 1969-present (Academic advisor, 1980-82); Northwest Anthropological Conference, 1970-present; High Plains Society for Applied Anthropology, Albuquerque, 1980-present. *Interests*: Acculturation and cultural change; natural and cultural resources; applied anthropology; ethnographic reconstruction and description; ethnography & ethnology of Northwestern North America; ethnohistory; religion, folklore, and language; cultures of the Southwest: Hispanic, Hopi, and Navajo. *Published works*: The Chinook Indians; Nez Perce Coyote Tales, 2nd Ed. (University of Oklahoma Press, 1998; "The Nez Perce," in American Indians of the Pacific Northwest Website (University of Washington & Library of Congress, 2000); Sacred Geography in Native North America (Encyclopedia of Religion & Nature, 2003); Paiute Culture, Religion & Nature (Encyclopedia of Religion & Nature, 2003); Western Shoshone Culture, Religion & Nature (Encyclopedia of Religion & Nature, 2003; Nez Perce (The Greenwood Encyclopedia of World Folklore, 2005); numerous articles and reviews.

WALKER, FRANKLIN
(park & museum supt.)
Affiliation: Nez Perce National Historical Park & Museum, P.O. Box 93, Spalding, ID 83551.

WALKER, HANS, JR. (Mandan/Hidatsa) 1936-
(attorney)
Education: University of North Dakota, Ph.B., 1957, LL.B., 1960. *Address & Affiliation*: Partner, Hobbs, Straus, Dean & Walker, LLP (1988-present), 2120 L St., NW, Suite 700, Washington, DC 20037 (202) 822-8282. E-mail: hwalker@hsdwdc.com. *Past professional posts*: General counsel for the Three Affiliated Tribes of the Fort Berthold Reservation of North Dakota, 1960-65; U.S. Dept. of the Interior (Assistant & Associate Solicitor for Indian Affairs, Director of the Office of Indian Water Rights), 1965-82. Presently, Mr. Walker is counsel for the St. Regis Mohawk Tribe in its suit for the return of thousands of acres of land taken by the State of New York early in the last century in violation of the Non-Intercourse Act. He has prepared manuals on taxation and gaming that are widely used in Indian country. *Areas of concentration*: Tribal sovereignty, taxation, Indian gaming, jurisdiction, trust and restricted Indian lands, water rights.

WALKER, JANA LYNN
(Cherokee/Delaware/Shawnee) 1954-
(attorney)
Born October 2, 1954, Tulsa, Okla. *Education*: University of Oklahoma, BS, 1977; University of New Mexico School of Law, JD, 1987. *Principal occupation*: Attorney. *Address*: P.O. Box 121, Placitas, NM 87043 (505) 867-0579. *Affiliation*: Formerly, Junior partner, Gover, Stetson & Williams (an Indian-owned law firm), Albuquerque, NM, 1989-93; solo practitioner, Placitas, NM, 1993-. *Memberships*: American Bar Association - Section of Natural Resources, Energy & Environmental Law (council member, 1991-94; secretary, 1994-96); Committee on Native American Natural Resources (chair, 1991-92, vice-chair, 1988-90); Standing Committee on Environmental Law (member, 1992-95);Section on General Practice, Solo, and Small Firms, Indian Law Committee (vice-chair, 1996); New Mexico Bar Association - Indian Law Section (chair, 1992-93; board member, 1989-94); Indian Bar Association of New Mexico; Arizona Bar Association - Indian Law Section; Native American Bar Association. *Biographical sources*: Who's Who Among Rising Young Americans, 1992; Who's Who in American Law, 1992-93, 7th Ed, 1993-94, 8th Ed. *Published works*: Articles - "On-Reservation Treaty Hunting Rights" (26 Natural Resources Journal 187, 1986); "Tribal Environmental Regulation" with B. Kevin Gover (36 Federal Bar Journal No. 9, Nov. 1989); " Tribal Civil Regulatory Jurisdiction to Enforce Environemtal Laws" with B. Kevin Gover (Institute on Mineral Development on Indian Lands, Paper No. 14, Rocky Mountain Mineral Law Foundation, 1989); "Native American Study Draws Poor Conclusions From Poor Conditions" with W. Richard West, Jr. (Legal Times, June 4, 1990; Texas Lawyer, July 2, 1990); "Indian Reserved Water Rights" with

Susan M. Williams (5 Natural Resources & Environment No. 4, Spring 1991); "Escaping Environmental Paternalism," with Kevin Gover (63 U. of Colorado Law Review. 933 (1992); "Commercial Solid & Hazardous Waste Disposal Projects on Indian Lands," (10 Yale J. on Reg. 229 (Winter 1993), with Kevin Gover; "Tribal Jurisdiction Over Reservation Water Quality and Quantity," (43 S.D. L. Rev. 315, 1998), with Jane Marx and Susan M. Williams; "A Closer Look at Environmental Injustice in Indian Country," with Jennifer Bradley & Timothy Humphrey, Sr. (Seattle Journal for Social Justice 379, 2002).

WALKER, MARIE-ANN DAY
(Indian band chief)
Affiliation: Okanese Indian Band, Box 759, Balcarres, Sask., Canada S0G 0C0 (306) 334-2532.

WALKER, RICKEY BUTCH
(Indian program director)
Affiliation: Lawrence County Schools, Indian Education Program, Oakville Indian Mounds park & Museum, 1219 County Rd. 187, Danville, AL 35619 (205) 905-2494.

WALKER, WILLARD 1926-
(professor emeritus-anthropology)
Born July 29, 1926, Boston, Mass. *Education*: Harvard College, BA, 1950; University of Arizona, MA, 1953; Cornell University, PhD, 1964. *Principal occupation*: Professor emeritus-anthropology, Wesleyan University, Middletown, CT, 1966-. *Home address*: 19 Battle Ridge Rd., Canaan, ME 04924 (207) 474-5316. E-mail: wbwalker@rynd.com. *Memberships*: American Society for Ethnohistory; Southern Anthropological Association; Northeastern Anthropological Association; Museum of the Cherokee Indian Association. *Military service*: American Field Service (British 8th Army), 1945-45. *Interests*: "Indian American languages, cultures, ethnohistory. Particular interest in Creeks and Cherokees in the Southeast, the Zuni, Hopi and Yaqui pueblos in the Southwest, and the Algonquian peoples of the Maine-Maritime area." *Published works*: Cherokee Primer (Carnegie Corp. Cross-Cultural Education Project, University of Chicago, 1965); co-author, Cherokee Stories (Laboratory of Anthropology, Wesleyan University, 1966); "Cherokee" in Studies in Southeastern Indian Languages (University of Georgia Press, 1975); The Proto-Algonquians" in Linguistics and Anthropology in Honor of C.F. Voegelin (Peter de Ridder Press, Lisse, 1975); "Zuni Semantic Categories" in Handbook of North American Indian, vol. 9 (Smithsonian Institution Press, 1979); Natchez Transcription, Sound System, Kinship Terminology and Kinship System" in The Natchez Annotated Translations from Antoine Simon le Page du Pratz's Histoire de la Louisiane (Oklahoma Historical Society, 1979); co-author, A Chronological Account of the Wabanaki Confederacy" in Political Organization of Native North Americans (University Press of America, 1980); "Native American Writing Systems" in Language in the U.S.A. (Cambridge University Press, 1981) and in Handbook of North American Indians, vol. 17 (Smithsonian Institution Press, 1996); Cherokee Curing and Conjuring, Identity, and the Southeastern Co-tradition" in Persistent Peoples Cultural Enclaves in Perspective (University of Arizona Press, 1981); The Hopis & the Tewas" in Hopis, Tewas, and the American Road (Wesleyan University, 1983); co-editor, Hopis, Tewas & the American Road (University of New Mexico Press, 1986); "What Zuni Is Really Like" in Essays in Honor of Charles F. Hockett (E.J. Brill, Leiden, 1983); "Wabanaki Wampum Protocol", Papers of the Fifteenth Algonquian Conference (Carleton University, 1984); "Creek Curing in Academe" in General and Amerindian Ethnolinguistics in Remembrance of Stanley Newman (Mouton de Gruyter, 1989); "The Responses of Bilingual and Monolingual Zunis to a Zuni Language Questionnaire" in The Content of Culture: Constants and Variants Studies in Honor of John M. Roberts (HRAF Press, 1989); numerous articles and papers.

WALKER, WILLIAM D.
(school supt.)
Affiliation: Labre Indian School, P.O. Box 406, Ashland, MT 59003 (406) 784-2347.

WALKER-GRANT, LEANNE (Yokut)
(rancheria chairperson)
Affiliation: Table Mountain Rancheria, P.O. Box 410, Friant, CA 93626 (559) 822-2587.

WALKING BULL, GILBERT C. (Oglala Sioux) 1930-
(spiritual teacher, artist)
Born June 18, 1930, Hot Springs, S.D. *Education*: Oregon College of Education (2 years). *Principal occupation*: Spiritual teacher. *Address*: P.O. Box 200, Wanblee, SD 57577 (605) 462-6544. *Affiliation*: Co-director, Ti Ospaye, Wanblee, SD, 1991-; editor, "Wolf Songs (quarterly newsletter). *Community activities*: Member, Pine Ridge Reservation, Oglala Sioux Tribe; Gilbert, while residing in Oregon from the early 1970s through 1990, was instrumental in starting Native American clubs, and played an important role in bringing pow wows to the Pacific Northwest. *Memberships*: Inter-Tribal Council, Portland, OR; National Indian Education Association (Project Media evaluation team); Independent Indian Arts & Crafts Persons Association (helped to organize). *Awards, honors*: Award for Distinction for Art, La Grande Indian Arts Festival, 1974; First Prize Award for Traditional Sioux Fancy Dance, Siletz, OR, 1973; First Prize Award for Traditional Sioux Painting, 1976, '77, La Grande Indian Arts Festival. *Interests*: "Do traditional Sioux geometrical designs on canvas in oil and acrylics; do Sioux crafts in beadwork & leather. (I am a) soloist, singing in the Lakota language with guitar and drum in public performance. Fancy dancer and participator in Indian gatherings since youth, winning many awards. At present, I am concentrating on traditional Sioux art, translating the legends of my people. I am traditional & bilingual. In my books, I am recording tales from the reservation, writing original poetry, translating songs and scoring songs." His grandfather was Move Camp (spiritual leader), his great grandfather was the prophet, Sitting Bull, and his great uncle was Crazy Horse. *Biographical source*: Who's Who Among the Lakotas. *Published works*: O-hu-kah-kan (Poetry, Songs, Legends, Stories), 1975; Wo ya-ka-pi (Telling Stories of the Past and Present), 1976; Mi ta-ku-ye (About Our People), 1977; all books co-authored with Montana H.R. Walking Bull, printed by the Itemizer Observer, Dallas, OR, and may be purchased from the Walking Bulls at their home address.

WALKING EAGLE, CARL
(Sisseton-Wahpeton Sioux)
(former tribal chairperson)
Affiliation: Spirit Lake Sioux Tribal Council, P.O. Box 359, Fort Totten, ND 58335 (701) 766-4221.

WALKING EAGLE, PATRICIA
(elementary school principal)
Affiliation: Tate Topa Tribal School (Four Winds), P.O. Box 199, Fort Totten, ND 58335 (701) 766-4161 Fax 766-4766. *Membership*: North Dakota Indian Education Association

WALKSALONG, WILLIAM (Northern Cheyenne)
(former tribal chairperson)
Affiliation: Northern Cheyenne Tribal Council, P.O. Box 128, Lame Deer, MT 59043 (406) 477-6284.

WALLACE, A. BRIAN (Washoe)
(tribal chairperson)
Affiliation: Washoe Tribal Council, 919 Highway 395 So., Gardnerville, NV 89410 (775) 883-1446.

WALLACE, ALBERT
(council chief)
Affiliation: Aukquan Traditional Council, 9296 Stephen Richards Memorial Dr., Junea, AK 99801 (907) 465-4120.

WALLACE, ANTHONY F.C. 1923-
(professor emeritus-anthropology)
Born April 15, 1923, Toronto, Can. *Education*: University of Pennsylvania, BA, 1947, MA, 1949, PhD, 1950. *Principal occupation*: Professor of anthropology. *Home address*: 614 Convent Rd., Chester, PA 19014. *Affiliations*: Professor of anthropology, University of Pennsylvania, 1961-; medical research scientist, Eastern Pennsylvania Psychiatric Institute, 1961-. *Other professional posts*: Member, National Research Council, Division of Behavioral Sciences; U.S. Office of Education, Research Advisory Committee; member, Behavioral Science Study Section, National Institute of Mental Health. *Military service*: U.S. Army, 1942-45. *Memberships*: American Anthropological Association (Fellow); American Association for the Advancement of Science (Fellow; chairman, Section H); American Sociological Association (Fellow); Sigma Xi; Philadelphia Anthropological Society. *Published works*: The Modal Personality Structure of the Tuscarora Indians, as Revealed by the Rorschach Bureau of American Ethnology, 1952); editor and author of introduction, The Ghost-Dance Religion and the Sioux Outbreak of 1890 (University of Chicago Press, 1965); The Death and Rebirth of the Seneca (Knopf, 1970); other books and numerous articles in professional journals.

WALLACE, BONNIE (*Gida-gaa-bines-ikwe*)
(Lake Superior Chippewa) 1946-
(program administrator)
Born December 4, 1946, Fond du Lac Reservation, Cloquet, Minn. *Education*: University of Minnesota, BA, 1974, graduate work, 1982. *Principal occupation*: Program administrator. *Address*: 2211 Riverside Ave., Minneapolis, MN 55454 (612) 330-1138 (work). *Affiliations*: Community program assistant, University of Minnesota, 1970-74; education specialist, Minnesota Chippewa Tribe, 1974-78; program administrator, Augsburg College, Minneapolis, MN, 1978- (director, American Indian Support Program, Minnesota Indian Teacher Training Project, American Indian Studies Minor, Woodland Anishinabe Library). *Other professional posts*: Fond du Lac Urban Representative; Minnesota Chippewa Tribe's Executive Committee; Fond du Lac Tribal College, Cloquet, MN (chair, board of regents); planner, Annual Ojibwe Art Expo; grants evaluator; advisory board of numerous organizations, including: American Indian Business Development Corp. *Community activities*: Grants reviewer, Minnesota State Department of Corrections; Victim Services Programs; member, Minnesota Indian State Scholarship Committee; member, Mixed Blood Theatre; member, Urban Advisory Council-State of Minnesota; member, Minnesota Minority Education Partnership; former chairperson, American Indian Business Development Corp. *Memberships*: Minnesota Chippewa Tribe; Minnesota Indian Education Association (advisory board); National Indian Education Association; Museum of the American Indian/Smithsonian. *Awards, honors*: Contributions to Community United Way of Minneapolis, 1984; Contributions to Elders Award, American Indian Family Services, 1986; Contributions to Youth Award, Minneapolis Youth Diversion Project, 1986; Counselor of the Year, Minnesota Indian Education Association, 1987; Award of Merit, National Women of Color Day, 1990. *Published works*: Battering and the Indian Women, State Dept. of Corrections, 1980); Case Study, Ojibwe Women, Minority Women (Women's Institute of S.E. Atlanta, 1981); Touchwood, A Collection of Ojibwe Prose (Two Rivers Press, 1987); article - "Great Strides, Great Strides" in Private College Magazine, 1988).

WALLACE, DOUGLAS
(AK Indian association president)
Affiliation: Douglas Indian Association, P.O. Box 020478, Juneau, AK 99802 (907) 586-1798.

WALLACE, MARLEITA (Tlingit-Tsimshian)
(craftsperson)
Address: Mardina Dolls, P.O. Box 611, Wrangell, AK 99929 (907) 874-3854

WALLACE, SR. MAUREEN
(school principal)
Affiliation: Beatrice Rafferty School, Pleasant Point Reservation, Perry, ME 04667 (207) 853-6085.

WALLS, BILL (Gros Ventre)
(executive director)
Affiliation: Executive Director, Missoula Indian Center, Missoula, MT (406) 329-3373 Fax 329-3398; E-Mail: mic@ism.net.

WALSTEDTER, ELAYNE (Navajo) 1959-
(academic librarian, assistant professor)
Born July 1, 1959. *Address*: Reed Library Fort Lewis College, 1000 Rim Dr., Durango, CO 81301 (970) 247-7662 Fax 247-7149; E-Mail: walstedter_e@fortlewis.edu. *Affiliations*: Education program liaison, Futures for Children, Albuquerque, NM, 1989-90; information

specialist, Native American Studies, University of New Mexico, Albuquerque, 1990-91; homemaker & school/community library volunteer, Chuska School, Tohatchi, NM, 1991-96; librarian & assistant professor, Reed Library, Fort Lewis College, 1996-present. *Memberships*: American Indian Library Association; Taa Dine (Navajo) Library Association; American Library Association; Association of College and Research Libraries, New Mexico & Colorado Library Association.

WALTER, MARY JO
(school principal)
Affiliation: Gila Crossing Day School, P.O. Box 10, Laveen, AZ 85339 (520) 237-4834.

WALTERS, ANNA LEE (Pawnee/Otoe)
(English teacher; writer-editor)
Address: P.O. Box 276, Tsaile, AZ 86566. *Affiliation*: Navajo Community College, Tsaile, AZ. *Other professional post*: National Advisory Caucus for Wordcraft Circle of Native American Mentor & Apprentice Writers. *Published works*: Talking Indian: Reflections on Writing and Survival; Neon Powwow: New Native American Voices of the Southwest.

WALTERS, BILL
(school principal)
Affiliation: Gila Crossing Day School, P.O. Box 10, Cibecue, AZ 85339 (520) 550-4834 Fax 550-4252.

WALTERS, TERRANCE C.
(BIA agency director)
Affiliation: Fort Berthold Agency, Bureau of Indian Affairs, P.O. Box 370, New Town, ND 58763 (701) 627-4707.

WANASSAY, VINCENT (Umatilla)
(poet)
Address: 1828 SE Tibbets, Portland, OR 97202 (503) 236-3029.

WANATEE, GAILEY
(former tribal chief)
Affiliation: Sac & Fox Tribal Council, 3137 F Ave., Tama, IA 52339 (515) 484-4678.

WANCHENA, MATTHEW JOHN
(Yakima-Blackfeet) 1951-
(building code consultant)
Born March 9, 1951, Tacoma, Wash. *Education*: Washington State University, BS (Architecture), 1974; City University (Bellevue, WA), 1984-89, MBA, MPA. *Principal occupation*: Building code consultant. *Home address*: 4529 Tacoma Ave. South, Tacoma, WA 98408 (253) 472-4011 (phone & fax); E-mail: tacbac2380@aol.com. *Affiliations*: Self employed building code consultant, Tacoma, WA. 1993-; building inspector/plans examiner for different local governments, 1979-. *Military service*: U.S. Army (Army Commendation, National Defense Army Reserves Overseas Medal, Army Reserve Components Achievement Medal, Overseas Service Medal, Army Service Medal, Southwest Asia Service Medal); rank currently LTC in U.S. Army Reserves, Corps of Engineers. *Community activities*: Currently helping with establishing WSU ROTC Alumni Association & Steering Committee member; Co-chairperson of Pierce County Native American Indian Advisory Council for Minority Commission; Pierce County Ethnic Commission (vice president, 1993); vice-president of the "Arts Together," an ethnic association in the Pierce County & Tacoma area; do job fairs at local schools. *Memberships*: American Institute of Architects, Tacoma, WA; International Conference of Building Officials, Whittier, CA; American Indian Science & Engineering Society; National Fire Protection Assn; Society of American Military Engineers. *Awards, honors*: Saudi Arabia Joint Support Medal from the Saudi Government for Desert Storm, 1991-92. *Interests*: "Architectural history, Native American architecture in the U.S.; visited Italy, Yugoslavia, Portugal and Spain. Have been through the Southwest & in my own Northwest to see the types of architecture that is out there. Currently helping the University of Puget Sound with setting up an American Indian Association, mentoring to junior high school & college students in the Tacoma & Pierce County area. Knowledgeable in computers & helping the local school districts with Indian students that need help." *Biographical source*: American Association of the Army, 1982 article by a soldier on me.

WAPATO, S. TIMOTHY
(executive director)
Affiliation: Columbia River Inter-tribal Fish Commission, 729 N.E. Oregon, Suite 200, Portland, OR 97232 (503) 238-0667 Fax 235-4228. *Past professional posts*: Commissioner, Administration for Native Americans, Dept. of Health & Human Services, Washington, DC, 1990-92; executive director, National Indian Gaming Association, Washington, DC.

WAQUAN, ARCHIE
(Indian band chief)
Affiliation: Cree Indian Band, Box 90, Fort Chipewyan, Alberta, Canada T0P 1B0 (403) 697-3740.

WAR BONNETT, AMANDA
(editor)
Affiliation: Lakota Times, Native American Publishing, 1920 Lombardy Dr., Rapid City, SD 57701 (605) 341-0011.

WARBURTON, MIRANDA
(dept. manager)
Affiliation: Navajo Nation Archaeology Dept. Northern Arizona University, P.O. Box 6013, Flagstaff, AZ 86011 (520) 523-7428.

WARD, ALFRED (Shoshone)
(tribal chairperson)
Affiliation: Shoshone Business Council, P.O. Box 217, Fort Washakie, WY 82514 (307) 332-3532.

WARD, JOHN A.
(museum president)
Affiliation: Sonotabac Prehistoric Indian Mound & Museum, P.O. Box 941, Vincennes, IN 47591 (812) 885-4330.

WARD, MICHAEL
(Indian band chief)
Affiliation: Red Bank Indian Band, Box 120, Red Bank, New Brunswick, Canada E0C 1W0 (506) 836-2366.

WARE, JAMIE M. (*White Feather*) (Rappahannock)
(society president)
Address: Unknown. *Affiliations*: President, Powhatan Society (address unknown); scholarship coordinator, United Indians of Virginia; job developer/counselor, Mattaponi-Pamunkey-Monacan, Inc., King William, VA. *Community activities*: Virginia Dept. of Minority Health Advisor; member/facilitator, Virginia Collaborative Leadership; member, United Rappahonnock Dance Troupe. *Memberships*: United Rappahonnock Tribe; American Indian Science & Engineering Program; Word Craft Circle intern; United Indians of Virginia; Virginia Council on Indians. *Interests*: To build a museum on Powhatan people and to build cultural healing program; to provide scholarships to Virginia Indian youth; doing job placement/counseling to Indian youth.

WARE, JOHN A.
(foundation director)
Affiliation: The Amerind Foundation, P.O. Box 400, Dragoon, AZ 85609 (520) 586-3666 Fax 586-4679.

WARE, SUE (Modoc) 1944-
(forensic anthropologist, teacher)
Born September 24, 1994, St. Joseph, Mo. *Education*: University of Northern Colorado, MA, 1977; University of Colorado, MA, 1990. *Principal occupation*: Forensic anthropologist, teacher. *Home address*: 307 Clermont St., Denver, CO 80202 (303) 322-8309 (work). *Affiliation*: Earth Gypsy, Denver, CO, 1990-; Denver Museum of Natural History (part time), 1981-. *Memberships*: American Institute of Archaeology; American Association of Physical Anthropology; Egyptian Study Society; Western Interior Paleontological Society; American Research Center in Egypt; American Indian Science & Engineering Society; Friends of Earth Sciences. *Interests*: "I travel extensively throughout the U.S., Egypt, and pursue an avid paraprofessional paleontology area of study interest."

WARNE, JIM E. (Oglala Lakota) 1964-
(human resource specialist)
Born November 27, 1964, Phoenix, Ariz. *Education*: Arizona State University, BS, 1987; San Diego State University, MS, 1993. *Principal occupation*: Human resource specialist. *Address & Affiliation*: San Diego

State University Foundation, 5850 Hardy Ave. #112, San Diego, CA 92182 (619) 594-6163, 1993-. *Other professional post*: Vice President, Southern California Chapter, California Indian Education Association, San Diego, CA, 1994-. *Past professional posts*: Football player, National Football League (Cincinnati Bengals, Detroit Lions, Tampa Bay Buccaneers, San Francisco 49ers), 1987-89; football player, World League of American Football, New York, NY, 1991; football player, Arena Football League, Albany, NY, 1992; extra/actor, Segal Productions, "Silk Stalkings" and "Renegade," one episode each. *Community activities*: Member, Consortium of Administrators for Native American Rehabilitation (chair, Professional Standards Committee), 1993-; member, San Diego East County Native American Education Council, San Diego, CA, 1993-; board member, American Indian Health Council, San Diego, CA, 1993-. *Awards, honors*: Keynote speaker, American Indian Empowerment Conference, San Diego State University, Nov. 1994; nominated for vice president for the Southern Chapter of the California Indian Education Association, San Diego, May 1994; conducted Cultural Diversity Training for various groups in 1994; keynote speaker, Arizona State University, American Indian Institute "Feast-n-Fest celebration for Native American students, Tempe, AZ, Nov. 1993; speaker at numerous other events. *Interests*: Rehabilitation counseling with an emphasis on education enhancement of Native American youth, multicultural issues, and Native American health, social, and rehabilitation issues.

WARNER, BARBARA A. (*The-Za'Teh*) (Ponca) 1949-
(executive director)
Born January 3, 1949,, Pawnee, Okla. *Education*: BA in Sociology & English; MBA in Management. *Address*: Oklahoma Indian Affairs Commission, 4545 N. Lincoln Blvd., Suite 282, Oklahoma City, OK 73105 (405) 521-3828 Fax 522-4427. E-mail: bwarner@oklaosf.state.ok.us. *Affiliations*: Cheyenne-Arapaho Tribe Manpower Program, Concho, OK, 1979-83; American Indian Institute, College of Continuing Education, U. of Oklahoma, Norman, OK 1987-91, 92-93; executive director, Oklahoma Indian Affairs Commission, Oklahoma City, OK, 1993-. *Community activities*: American Indian Business Legislative Day; Sovereignty Symposium (co-sponsor). *Memberships*: National Congress of American Indians; Governors' Interstate Indian Council; National Indian Education Assn; Haskell Indian Nations U.; Native American Preparatory School.

WARNER, LINDA
(program director)
Affiliation: American Indian Leadership Program, Penn State University, 320 Rackley Bldg., University Park, PA 16802 (814) 865-1489.

WARNER, RICHARD (Tolowa-Yurok)
(rancheria vice chairperson)
Affiliation: Elk Valley Rancheria Tribal Council, P.O. Box 1042, Crescent City, CA 95531 (707) 464-4680.

WARRIOR, DELLA C. (Otoe-Missouria)
(organization president)
Affiliation: Institute of American Indian Arts, 83 Avan Nu Po Rd., Santa Fe, NM 87505 (800) 804-6422; (505) 424-2300 Fax 424-4500. E-mail: dwarrior@iaiancad.org. Website: www.iaiancad.org.

WARRIOR, EMMA LEE (Peigan)
(poet)
Address: 17110 Cottonwood Canyon Rd., Yakama, WA 98908 (509) 575-2416.

WARRIOR, ROBERT ALLEN (Osage) 1963-
(professor of American Indian literature)
Born July 25, 1963, Marion County, Kans. *Education*: Yale University, MA, 1988, Union Theological Seminary (New York, NY), PhD, 1992. *Principal occupation*: Professor. *Address & Affiliation*: Dept. of English, Stanford University, Stanford, CA (415) 723-4592, 1992-present. *Memberships*: American Studies Assn; Native American Journalists Assn. *Awards, honors*: Anneberg Fellowship for outstanding junior faculty, Stanford University, 1993-95. *Published works*: Coauthor, "Like a Hurricane: How Wounded Knee II Changed Indian America," 1994; author, "Tribal Secrets; Recovering American Indian Intellectual Traditions" (University of Minnesota Press, 1995).

WASHAKIE, JOHN (Shoshone)
(former tribal chairperson)
Affiliation: Wind River Shoshone Tribal Business Council, P.O. Box217, Fort Washakie, WY 82514 (307) 332-3532.

WASHINES, RONNIE L. (Yakima)
(managing editor)
Affiliation: Yakima Nation Review, Yakama Indian Nation, P.O. Box 310, Toppenish, WA 98948-031 (509) 865-5121 Fax 865-2794.

WASHINGTON, PAULA S. (*Elewei Ditlihi Agehya*)
(Cherokee) 1952-
(teacher of orchestral music)
Born March 2, 1952, Frankfurt, Germany. *Education:* Smith College, BA, 1974; New York University, MA, 1976, PhD, 1993. *Principal occupation:* Teacher of orchestral music. *Home address:* 9 Oak Ridge Rd., Pomona, NY 10970 (914) 354-7452. *Affiliation:* Fiorello H. La Guardia High School of Music & Art and Performing Arts, New York, NY, 1981-. *Community activities:* Nuyagi Keetoowah Society/Cherokee Scribe Society. *Memberships:* Phi Delta Kappa; New York Viola Society; The Broadway Bach Ensemble; The Bergen Philharmonic.

WASSILLIE, RAYMOND (Aleut)
(village president)
Affiliation: Newhalen Village Council, P.O. Box 165, Iliamna, AK 99606 (907) 571-1226.

WASSON, GLENN (Southern Palute)
(tribal chairperson)
Affiliation: Winnemucca Indian Colony, P.O. Box 1370, Winnemucca, NV 89446.

WATAHOMIGIE, DON (Havasupai)
(tribal chairperson)
Affiliation: Havasupai Tribal Council, P.O. Box 10, Supai, AZ 86435 (602) 448-2961.

WATAN, STERLING (Cheyenee-Arapaho)
(broadcaster; co-chair, AIM)
Affiliation: Crow Tribal Council, Crow Agency, MT 59022 (406) 638-2316. *Other professional post:* Co-chair, American Indian Movement; owner, former KKUL-AM, Hardin, MT.

WATERS, KAREN K.
(principal/teacher)
Affiliation: Nunapitchuk Day School, Nunapitchuk, AK 99641 (907) 527-5711.

WATERS, MICHAEL
(editorial advisor)
Affiliation: American Indian Law Review, University of Oklahoma Law Center, 300 Timberdell Rd., Rm. 378, Norman, OK 73019 (405) 325-2840.

WATKINS, GORDON
(health clinic director)
Affiliation: Nowata Indian Health Clinic, Cherokee Nation, 507 E. Redwood, Nowata, OK 74048 (918) 273-0192.

WATKINS, MARY BETH OZMUN (Creek)
(library director)
Education: University of Oklahoma, BS, 1959, MLS, 1968, post-graduate, 1968-71. *Principal occupation:* Library director. *Address:* Unknown. *Affiliations:* Elementary field librarian, 1968-70, media consultant, 1970-71, Oklahoma City Public Schools; associate director, Eastern Oklahoma District Library, Muskogee, 1971-77; director of libraries, Bacone College, Muskogee, Okla. 1977-. *Memberships:* Oklahoma Library Association, 1968- (secretary, 1972-73; chairperson, membership committee, 1972-76; chairperson, publicity committee, 1972-73; chairperson, Sequoyah Children's Book Award, 1971-72; chairperson, intellectual freedom committee, 1976-77; co-chairperson, ad hoc committee serving as Humanities Council Project liaison, 1976-77, chairperson, 1977-78); Southwest Library Association, 1968- (SWLA membership chairperson for OLA, 1975-76, 1977-78); Oklahoma Education Association; National Education Association; Oklahoma Association of School Librarians (district chairperson, 1969-71); American Library Association, 1971- (member, Membership Task Force; chair-

person, Southwest Region, 1976-78); Oklahoma Association for Educational Communication and Technology, 1975-; Bacone Professional Association, 1977- (program committee; by-laws committee; vice president); Oklahoma Humanities Committee, 1977-80; American Association of University Women (treasurer, 1976-78; first vice president, program chairperson, 1978-80). *Awards, honors:* Outstanding Young Women of America, 1970. *Published works:* Articles in "Oklahoma Librarian."

WATKINS, SHERRIN (Shawnee/Cherokee)
(attorney)
Address: Unknown. *Affiliations:* Attorney, Muscogee (Creek) Nation, 1983-88; private practice, 1988-present; D.C. Phillips & Associates, P.C.; Loyal Shawnee Business Committee, 1995-present; Sac & Fox Supreme Court (Justice), 1995-present. *Community activities:* Haskell Pa-a-linn, General Federation of Women's Clubs. *Memberships:* Oklahoma Bar Association; U.S. District Court Northern District of Oklahoma and Eastern District of Oklahoma; U.S. Court of Appeals, 10th Circuit and D.C. Circuit; Cherokee Nation Bar; Creek Nation Bar. *Published works:* Native American History (Myles Publishing, Los Angeles, CA, 1992); White Bead Ceremony (Council Oak Books, Tulsa, OK, 1994); Green Snake Ceremony (Council Oak Books, Tulsa, OK, 1995); Headstart (Council Oaks Books, Tulsa, OK, 1997); Different Prayers (Council Oaks Books, Tulsa, OK, 1997).

WATSO (Wabanaki, Odanak Band) 1954-
(financial services)
Born May 4, 1954, Buffalo, N.Y. *Education:* Concordia Univesity, BA-Business. *Principal occupation:* Investment executive for Dain Rauscher Financial Services, Minneapolis, MN (working with Native bands, tribes and organizations. *Home address:* P.O. Box 7103, Minneapolis, MN 55407 (612) 371-7964 (work); E-mail: watso@dainrauscher.com. *Affiliations:* Owner "Singing Spirit", Native American Works, Dayton, OH, 1985-88; cultural director, Minneapolis American Indian Center, & curator, Two Rivers Gallery, Minneapolis, MN, 1988-99; planning consultant, National Indian AIDS Media Consortium & National Native American AIDS Prevention, Oakland, CA, 1993-; AFTRA (on camera print and voice overs). *Other professional posts:* National Advisor, Shooting Back Project, Washington, DC, 1991-; author of "Artline," in Circle Newspaper; curator for various art exhibits. *Community activities:* Public speaker - art, culture, issues; design consultant; actor; Metropolitan Regional Arts Council (board member, 1990-91); review panel, 93-94); Northern Plains Tribal Arts (advisory committee, 1990-91); Minneapolis American Red Cross (board member, 1989-91). *Membership:* Minnesota Association of Museums (steering committee, 1990-91); AFTRA. *Awards, honors:* Recipient of 1991-92 Arts Midwest Arts Administrative Fellowship. *Interests:* "To utilize resources, skills and experience to help Native people achieve financial security and growth."

WATSON, DONALD EVERT (*Walking Hawk*)
(United Lumbee/Cherokee) 1925-
(chemist)
Born October 16, 1925, Whittier, Calif. *Education:* BS & MS degrees. *Principal occupation:* Chemist. *Home address:* 5356 Border Ave., Joshua Tree, CA 92252 (619) 366-2875. *Community activities:* United Lumbee Nation's historian. *Memberships:* United Lumbee Nation's Desert Sage Band Chief, 1991-. *Awards, honors:* 1st Place Solar House design, CT A.I.A.; 2nd Place Award for Large Size Rugs and Blankets, Northern California Hand Weavers Association. *Interests:* Native American history; orchard grower; also plant breeding using Native American vegetables as subjects; weaver." *Published works:* Indians of the Mesa Verde (Mesa Verde Museum Association, 1961); Designing and Building a Solar House (Garden Way Publishing, 1977).

WATSON, GLEN (Maidu)
(rancheria spokesperson)
Affiliation: Enterprise Rancheria, 7470 Feather Falls Star Route, Oroville, CA 95965 (916) 589-0652.

WATSON, LARRY S. 1941-
(editor, writer)
Born May 3, 1941, Oklahoma City, Okla. *Education:*

Oklahoma State University, BA, 1963; Central Missouri State University, MA, 1964. *Principal occupation:* Editor, writer. *Home address:* Resides in Calif. *Affiliation:* Co-owner, Histree (genealogical research & publishing organization), Laguna Hills, CA, 1978-. *Other professional posts:* Active genealogical researcher for better than 40 years: Southern States & Native American; genealogical teacher for 20+ years; consultant: Riverside Indian Center, Saddleback College, Sac River Cherokee Indians & several other genealogical & Native American groups; editor of The Journal of American Indian Research (monthly nesletter of Histree). *Military service:* U.S. Army, 1959-78. *Community activities:* Organizing President of Southwest Oklahoma Genealogical Society; charter member, Stars & Bars, Lawton, OK. *Memberships:* California Genealogical Alliance. *Speaker at:* World Conference on Genealogical Research, New Orleans, LA, 1975, 1976, 1977; Cherokee Indian Descendants of the A-niyun-wiya, Inc., 1992; and numerous other genealogical & historical societies, 1974-. *Awards, honors:* Named Fellow of the Ark-La-Tex Genealogical Society, Shreveport, LA, 1976; Certificate of Acknowledge from The Richstone Family Center, Hawthorne, CA for "his time & expertise, assisting our Native American clients research their heritage," 1994. *Published works:* General editor of a reprint of Senate Document 512, 23rd Cong. 1st Sess. concerning Indian removal with comments and index; general editor of Series on Indian Treaties (28 volumes plus guide book); author/editor of several other records on Indians & books of historical & genealogical importance about Indian Territory & Oklahoma; numerous articles in various journal publications.

WATSON, MARY JO
(instructor-Native American studies)
Affiliation: Native American Studies Program, University of Oklahoma, 455 W. Lindsey, Rm. 804, Norman, OK 73019 (405) 325-2312.

WATT, CHARLIE
(parliament senator)
Affiliation: Canadian Parliament, Parliament Bldgs., Ottawa, ON K1A 0A4 (613) 992-2981.

WATTS, DANIEL
(Indian band chief)
Affiliation: Opetchesaht Indian Band, Box 211, Port Alberni, B.C., Canada V9Y 7M7 (604) 724-4041.

WATTS, STEVEN M. 1947-
(museum educator)
Born July 25, 1947, Lincoln County, N.C. *Education:* Appalachian State University, Boone, NC, BA, 1969; Duke University, M.Div., 1972. *Principal occupation:* Museum educator. *Home address:* 207 W. Fourth Ave., Gastonia, NC 28052 (704) 866-6912 (office). *Affiliation:* Director, Southeastern Native American Studies Program, Schiele Museum, Gastonia, NC, 1984-. *Other professional posts:* Director, "Abo-Tech," providing instruction in aboriginal/primitive skills and prehistoric tool replicas for museums and functional experiments. *Past work experience:* Minister, school counselor, classroom teacher, camp director, and substance abuse educator. *Community activities:* Commission on the Status of Women; Southeastern Indian Culture Study Group (director); American Indian Cultural Association (past director); Mental Health Association; volunteer work with schools, churches, scout groups, etc. *Memberships:* Center for the Study of Early Man; The Archaeological Society of North Carolina; Society of Prehistoric Technology; International ATLATL Association. *Awards, honors:* Statewide speaker for N.C. Mental Health Association (1984); Master of ceremonies, NC Commission of Indian Affairs—Unity Conference Intertribal Dance (1981); Outstanding Service Award, Mental Health Association, 1985. *Interests:* "Major interests is replication and experimental use of Native American tools, weapons, utensils, etc.—with the goal of (through educational programs) increasing the appreciation of primitive survival/subsistence skills and lifestyles among participants—helping to rediscover and preserve native technologies for generations to come; ethnology, archaeology. Most spare time is spent visiting native communities in the Southeast and historic and prehistoric native sites to increase the understanding and collection of knowledge." *Biographical sources:* Approximately a dozen newspaper

articles in local and statewide newspapers (copies available upon request). *Published works*: The Old Bearskin Report, journal (Schiele Museum, 1985); Southeastern Craft Articles, series (The Backwoodsman, Tex., 1984 & 1985).

WAUKAU, JERRY L. (*Keneahetim*) (Menominee) 1956-
(health administrator)
Education: Ripon College, 1974-78; University of Minnesota, Independent Study Program for Ambulatory Care Administration, 1987-88. *Address*: P.O. Box 970, W3275 Wolf River Dr., Keshena, WI 54135 (715) 799-5482 Fax 799-3099. *Affiliation*: Administrator, Menominee Indian Tribe of Wisconsin, Keshena, WI, 1981-85; health Administrator, Menominee Tribal Center, Keshena, WI, 1985-present. *Community activities*: Council on American Indian Health, Chairperson, 1994-97; secretary, Northern Wisconsin Area Health Education Center, Inc., 1990-96; St. Anthony's Parish Council, 2001-present. *Memberships*: Wisconsin Tribal Health Director's Association (1991-present); Red Cross, Lakeland Chapter (board of directors, 1987-92); American College of Healthcare Executives. *Awards, honors*: American Heart Association of Wisconsin Volunteer Recognition Award, 1987; Indian Health Service (IHS) Exceptional Performance Award, 1988; IHS Citation for Exemplary Group Performance, Menominee Tribal Clinic Management Team, 1990; IHS Citation for Exemplary Group Performance, Wisconsin Health Director's Association (chairperson, 1991-2004); Great Lakers Inter-Tribal Council, Inc. Award in recognition of Outstanding Service & Commitment, 1996 & 2003; Bemidji Area Director's Outstanding Health Administrator Award, Sept. 1998; Minority Health Leadership 2003. *Interests*: Enjoys fishing, committed to providing quality patient care to the Menominee people and reducing health disparities in the State and Indian Country.

WAUKAZOO, MARTIN
(health director)
Affiliation: Urban Indian Health Board, 3124 East 14th St., Oakland, CA 94601 (510) 261-0524; Native American Health Clinic, 56 Julian Ave., San Francisco, CA (415) 621-8051.

WAUNEKA, ANNIE DODGE (Navajo) 1910-
(tribal council member)
Born April 10, 1910, Old Sawmill, Ariz. *Education*: High school, B.I.A., Albuquerque, NM. *Principal occupation*: Tribal council member, Navajo Tribal Government, Window Rock, AZ, 1951-. *Home address*: Box 629, Ganado, AZ 86505. *Other professional posts*: Lecturer; member of Navajo Area health board representing U.S. Indian Health Services at Window Rock, AZ (current). *Community activities*: President, School For Me, Navajo Project Concern, Project Hope; Navajo Nation School Board Association (board member); Navajo Tribal Utility Authority (board member); Navajo Health Authority (board member); health educator in Navajo Way. *Memberships*: National Public Health Education; American Public Health Association; National TB Association; Society for Public Health (honorary lifetime member). *Awards, honors*: President's Freedom Medal Award, from President John F. Kennedy, 1963; Woman of the Year in Arizona; Honorary Doctor of Humanities Degree, University of Albuquerque, N.M., 1972; Woman of the Year, 1976, Ladies Home Journal. *Interests*: "Main interest is in health of American Indians, primarily Navajo; education and tribal government." *Biographical sources*: Indian Women of Today; Navajo Biography.

WAUPOOSE, JANET
(association president)
Affiliation: National Tribal Court Clerks Association, 1000 Connecticut Ave., NW, Suite 1206, Washington, DC 20036 (202) 296-0685.

WAUQUA, JOHNNY C. (Comanche)
(tribal chairperson)
Affiliation: Comanche Tribe, P.O. Box 908, Lawton, OK 73502 (580) 492-4988 Fax 492-3796.

WAX, MURRAY L. 1922-
(professor)
Born November 23, 1922, St. Louis, Mo. *Education*: University of Chicago, BS, 1942, PhD, 1959; University of Pennsylvania, 1947. *Principal occupation*: Professor. *Home address*: 572 Stratford Ave., University City, St. Louis, MO 63130. *Affiliations*: Professor of Sociology & Anthropology, University of Kansas, Lawrence, KS, 1964-73, Washington University, St. Louis, MO, 1973-. *Other professional posts*: Executive associate, Workshop on American Indian Affairs, University of Colorado, Boulder, 1959-60; director, Oglala Sioux Education Research Project (Emory University), 1962-63; director, Indian Education Research Project (University of Kansas), 1965-68. *Memberships*: American Anthropological Association (Fellow); American Association for the Advancement of Science (Fellow); American Sociological Association (Fellow); Current Anthropology (Associate); Royal Anthropological Institute of Great Britain and Ireland (Fellow); Society for Applied Anthropology (Fellow); Society for the Study of Religion; Society for the Study of Social Problems; American Educational Research Association; Midwest Sociological Society; Council on Anthropology and Education. *Awards, honors*: Adopted by Oglala Sioux Tribe; Phi Beta Kappa; Sigma Xi; National Institute of Education Grants, 1973-74, 1978-79; National Science Foundation Grant, 1978-1981; grants from: U.S. Office of Economic Opportunity, U.S. Office of Education, Wenner-Gren Foundation. Editorial boards, advisory editor: Human Organization (editorial board, 1966-); Journal of Cultural & Educational Futures (1979-); Phylon (1973-); Qualitative Sociology (1982-); Symbolic Interaction (1983-). *Published works*: Formal Education in an American Indian Community (Monograph 1, Society for the Study of Social Problems, 1964); co-editor, Indian Education in Eastern Oklahoma: A Report of Fieldwork Among the Cherokee (U.S. Office of Education, 1969); Indian Americans: Unity and Diversity (Prentice-Hall, 1971); Solving The Indian Problem (New Viewpoints/Franklin Watts, 1975); Formal Education in an American Indian Community (Waveland Press, 1989); numerous articles and essays in professional journals.

WAX, ROSALIE
(professor emerita)
Affiliation: Department of Anthropology, Washington University, St. Louis, MO 63130 (314) 889-5252.

WAY, J. EDSON 1947-
(museum administration)
Born May 18, 1947, Chicago, Ill. *Education*: Beloit College, BA, 1968; University of Toronto, M.A., 1970, PhD, 1972. *Principal occupation*: Museum administration. *Address*: Resides in NM. *Affiliations*: Associate professor of anthropology, Beloit College, 1972-85; director, Logan Museum of Anthropology, Beloit, WI, 1980-85; director, Wheelwright Museum of the American Indian, 1985-89; acting director, New Mexico Museum of Natural History, Albuquerque, 1990-91; executive director, International Space Hall of Fame, Alamogordo, NM, 1991-. *Community activities*: Public speaker, Native American arts and history; Society of Friends (Quakers); Southeast Asian Refugee Resettlement; Rotary; chair, Tourism Committee, Alamogordo (NM) Chamber of Commerce; vice-president, Apache Trails Tourism Promotions, Ruidoso, NM. *Memberships*: American Association of Museums; New Mexico Museum Association; American Association of Physical Anthropologists; Society for American Archaeology; Plains Anthropological Society. *Interests*: Archaeological fieldwork in Labrador, and Ellesmere Island, N.W.T., Canada; northern Wisconsin; northeast New Mexico; Native American arts; music; horsemanship; cross-country skiing; camping; fishing; Western history; and cattleranching. *Biographical source*: Who's Who in America.

WAYNEE, ROBERT (*Lone Eagle*)
(Saginaw Chippewa) 1939-
(sculptor in wood)
Born July 8, 1939, Bay City, Mich. *Address*: P.O. Box 15313, Santa Fe, NM 87506 (505) 466-3456 Fax 466-1248. *Principal occupation*: Sculptor in wood. *Other professional posts*: Carpenter, photographer, welder, furniture maker, artist. *Memberships*: Southwest Association for Indian Arts (Santa Fe Indian Market). *Awards, honors*: "Gate Keepers" Award by Country Home Magazine, held at the National Christmas Show, Washington, DC; a pictorial in the early American Home Magazine Directory, Aug. 1996; received first place and division awards at Santa Fe Indian

Market, 1995 & 1996; solo exhibit at the Southern Plains Indian Museum, Anadarko, OK, 1996; numerous other awards. He is featured in galleries and collections throughout the U.S.

WEAHKEE, FRED FIDEL (*Morning Star*-Jemez; *Rainbow*-Zuni) (Pueblo-Jemez/Zuni) 1926-
(electrical contractor, journeyman electrician)
Born September 1, 1926, Jemez Pueblo, N.M. *Education*: John Brown University (Siloam Springs, AR), 1947-50; International Correspondence School (Scranton, PA), Electrical Engineering Certificate, 1978; Electrical Contractor's School, 1979-80. *Principal occupation*: Electrical contractor, journeyman electrician. *Home address*: 24 Sandhill Rd., Lunas, NM 87031 (505) 865-5653. *Affiliations*: Facility manager, Albuquerque Indian School, 1977-81; facility manager, Jicarilla Agency, BIA, 1981-86; facility manager, Eastern Navajo Agency, BIA (maintenance of 21 different schools), 1986-88; electrical contractor, Fred's Electric, Los Lunas, NM, 1988-. *Military service*: U.S. Marine Corps, 1943-46 (Fleet Marine Force Scout; Purple Heart). *Memberships*: International Association of Electrical Inspectors; Electrical Contractors Assn. *Awards, honors*: Three Special Achievement Awards from the Bureau of Indian Affairs, 1976, 1977, 1981; served as chief informer for a linguist from the University of New Mexico. *Interests*: "Carpentry, plumbing, and electrical work; exercise (cross-country skiing and apparatus), swimming, bowling, daily Bible reading!" *Published work*: Dictionary - Jemez Language (Towa), 1963-64.

WEAHKEE, WILLIAM F. (Pueblo)
(executive director)
Affiliation: Five Sandoval Indian Pueblos, Inc., 1043 Hwy. 313, Bernalillo, NM 87004 (505) 867-3351.

WEASEL FAT, MARY
(editor)
Affiliation: Kainai News, Indian News Media, P.O. Box 120, Stand Off, Alberta, Can. T0K 0K0 (403) 653-3301.

WEATHERFORD, ELIZABETH 1945-
(head of film & video center)
Born July 30, 1945, Anson County, N.C. *Education*: Duke University, BA, 1966; The New School for Social Research, MA, 1970. *Principal occupation*: Head of film & video center. *Address*: National Museum of the American Indian-Smithsonian Institution, George Gustav Heye Center, One Bowling Green, New York, NY 10004 (212) 514-3730 Fax 514-3725. E-mail: wford@ic.si.edu. *Affiliations*: Research Associate, Dept. of Anthropology, New York University, New York, NY; department head, Film & Video Center, National Museum of the American Indian, New York, NY, 1981-. *Community activities*: Board Member, Human Studies Film Archives; Media Alliance. *Memberships*: National ASssociation for Media Culture; Association of Moving Image Archivists; American Anthropological Association; Association for Independent Video and Film Makers; Media Alliance; Society on Visual Anthropology; Cultural Survival. *Interests*: Recent and archival films and videotapes about Native Americans. *Published works*: Native Americans on Film & Video (Museum of the American Indian, 1981); Native Americans on Film and Video II (Museum of the American Indians, 1986); "Starting Fire with Gunpowder" in Film Comment (June 1992); To End & Begin Again: Victor Masayesva in Art Journal (Winter 1995).

WEAVER, FRAMON (Mowa Choctaw)
(tribal chief)
Affiliation: Mowa Band of Choctaw Indians, Rte. 1, Box 330-A, Reservation Rd., Mt. Vernon, AL 36560 (205) 829-5500 Fax 829-5580.

WEAVER, KESLER (Mowa Choctaw)
(tribal council chairperson)
Affiliation: Council Chairperson, Mowa Band of Choctaw Indians, 1080 West Red Fox Rd., Mt. Vernon, AL 36560 (251) 829-5500 Fax 829-6328. E-mail: kweaver@mowachoctaw.com

WEAVER, LAUREL
(school administrator)
Affiliation: Duckwater Shoshone Elementary School, P.O. Box 140038, Duckwater, NV 89314 (702) 863-0242 Fax 863-0301.

WEAVER, TIM
(tribal litigation attorney)
Education: University of Washington, BA, 1967; Williamette University, JD, 1970. *Principal occupation*: Tribal litigation attorney. *Address*: c/o Yakama Tribal Council, P.O. Box 151, Toppenish, WA 98948 (509) 575-1500. E-mail: weavertr@yakima-wa.org *Affiliations*: Of Counsel, Hobbs, Straus, Dean & Walker, LLP, 851 S.W. Sixth Ave., Suite 1650, Portland, OR 97204 (503) 242-1745 Fax 242-1072. *Other professional posts*: Tribal attorney, Yakama Nation, Toppenish, WA, 1971-present, handling all aspects of their legal matters & currently holds the title of litigation attorney. He is the former president of the Litigation Section Executive Committee of the Washington State Bar Association.

WEBBEC, GEORGE
(Indian school administrator)
Affiliation: Nay Ah Shing Schools, Mille Lacs Band of Ojibwe, HC67, Box 242, Onamia, MN 56359 (320) 532-4695 Fax 532-4675.

WEBBER, THUNDERBIRD (Kaweah)
(tribal chief)
Affiliation: Kaweah Indian Nation of Western USA & Mexico, Hutchinson, KS (316) 665-3614.

WEBSTER, EMERSON (Tonawanda Seneca)
(tribal chief)
Affiliation: Tonawanda Band of Senecas Council, 7027 Meadville Rd., Basom, NY 14013 (716) 542-4244.

WEBSTER, STELLA
(administrative officer)
Affiliation: Chinle PHS Indian Hospital, P.O. Drawer PH, Chinle, AZ 86503 (520) 674-5282.

WECKEAH (BILL BRADLEY) (Comanche)
(storyteller)
Address: Bill Bradley, Rt. 1, Box 128-A, Lawton, OK 73501. Weckeah tells traditional Comanche stories, Comanche oral history, original oral tales and original literary tales.

WEDDLE, STAR TEHEE (Oklahoma Cherokee)
(artist)
Born February 24 in Okla. *Education*: Southern Methodist University, 1973-75; Trinity University (San Antonio, TX), BA, 1977. *Principal occupation*: Artist. *Home address*: P.O. Box 1269, Bastrop, TX 78602 (512) 321-3733. *Affiliation*: Full time artist, 1984- (emphasis on easel art with Indian subject matter). *Community activities*: Judge of student art; art committee of Houston Livestock Show & Rodeo; office & director of InterTribal Council. *Memberships*: Indian Arts & Crafts Association; Southwestern Association for Indian Arts; Descendants of Cherokee Seminaries' Students; National Museum of the American Indian, Smithsonian Institution. *Awards, honors*: Santa Fe Indian Market: First Place in Painting, 1990; Third Place in Miniature Paintings, 1990; Honorable Mention, Contemporary Painting, 1990 & 1991; Third Place in Drawing, 1991; First Place in Miniature Paintings, 1991 & 1992. Gallup Inter-Tribal Ceremonial: Second Place in Miniature Painting, 1990. Ohio Inter-Tribal Experience: Honorable Mention in Painting, 1991. *Interest*: Featured artist at the State Capitol of Texas; participant in juried & invitational shows; numerous gallery exhibits and shows. Co-author of educational book in progress.

WEEDEN, ANNAWON S., SR.
(Mashpee Wampanoag) 1973-
(museum Native American program developer)
Born October 19, 1973, Westerly, R.I. *Education*. GED. *Principal occupation*. Museum Native American program developer. *Home address*: 99 David St., Apt. 1E, New Bedford, MA 02744 (508) 979-4171. E-mail: weeden@bostonkids.org. *Affiliations*: Museum teacher/artisan/speaker/interpreter, Plimoth Plantation, 1992-99; Native American program developer, The Children's Museum, Boston, MA, 1999-present. *Other professional posts*: Lectures, school visits (programs); wood/carving demonstrations; curriculum consultant; actor. *Community activities*: Helped develop a seven house village for Mashpee Wampanoag Tribe; American Indian Day Coordinator, Boston Pow-wow, 2002;

drummer & singer, public speaker; mentor. *Membership*: Mashpee Wampanoag Tribe (Mashpee, MA). *Interests*: Preservation of Wampanoag culture, heritage, traditions, oral history, songs, language, society, youth, etc.

WEEDEN, EVERETT G., JR. (*Tall Oak*)
(Mashantucket Pequot, Wampanoag) 1936-
(educational consultant; storyteller)
Born September 4, 1936, Providence, R.I. *Education*: Rhode Island School of Design, 1955-56. *Principal occupation*: Educational consultant. *Address*: 4600 S. County Trail, Charlestown, RI 02813-3426 (401) 364-8859. *Affiliations*: Boston Children's Museum, Boston, Mass., 1973-; Haffenreffer Museum of Anthropology, Brown University, Bristol, RI, 1992-. *Military service*: U.S. Army Reserves, 1957-63. *Memberships*: Charlestown Historical Society (charter member since 1970); Connecticut Society of Genealogists, 1981-; Indian & Colonial Research Center, Old Mystic, CT, 1992-; Rhode Island Historical Society; Mashantucket Pequot Museum Research Center (charter member); American Indian Friends Coalition (advisory board). *Awards, honors*: Helped develop the concept of the "National Day of Mourning" Observance at Plymouth Rock on Thanksgiving Day 1970. *Interests*: Tall Oak is a specialist in New England Native American historys and traditions. His lecture/demonstration programs are available using songs and dance of the New England Native Americans. "Always seeking to generate a more accurate and honest image of our people has led to my participation in several videos including Kevin Kostner's, "500 Nations" production in 1994, and "Mystic Voices" a documentary video on the Pequot War, now in production.

WEEKS, JANE L.
(executive director)
Affiliation: Alabama Indian Affairs Commission, 669 S. Lawrence St., Montgomery, AL 36104 (205) 261-2831.

WEEKS, JANET (Luiseno)
(tribal chairperson)
Affiliation: La Jolla Band of Mission Indians, HC 1, Box 158, Pauma Valley, CA 92061 (760) 742-3771.

WEIDNER, KEZBAH (Navajo)
(actress, playwright)
Address: Resides in Minneapolis, MN. Ms. Weidner is owner of production company, KEZ Productions. She has also written and produced short plays and children's programs. She has appeared in numerous movies and has been a Navajo language consultant to various projects.

WEIGAND, PHIL C. 1937-
(archaeology)
Born December 3, 1937, Omaha, Neb. *Education*: Indiana University, BA, 1962; Southern Illinois University, PhD, 1970. *Principal occupation*: Archaeology. Address unknown. *Affiliations*: Archaeologist, Museum of Northern Arizona, Flagstaff; professor, Northern Arizona University, Flagstaff; profesor de Investigaciones, Colegio de Michoacan. *Other professional post*: Research collaborator, Brookhaven National Laboratory. *Memberships*: Sociedad Mexicana de Antropologia; Society for American Archaeology; American Anthropological Association; American Society for Ethnohistory; American Association for the Advancement of Science. *Awards, honors*: Recipient of grants from the National Science Foundation, Wenner-Gren, etc. *Interests*: Expeditions - "The Ancient Mining Project "Currently focusing on Arizona); "The Teuchittan Mapping Project" currently focusing on the Atoyac Valley of Jalisco, Mexico); and "The Huichol Ethnohistory Project." Avocations - hiking and photography. *Published works*: co-author with M. Foster, Archaeology of West & Northwest Mesoamerica (Westview/Praeger, 1985); Ensayos Sobre El Gran Nayar: Entre Coras, Huicholes, y Tepehuanes (Instituto Nacional Indigenists, 1992); Origines y Desarrollo de la Civilizacion del Occidente de Mexico (co-edited with Brigitte Boehm, Colegio de Michoacan, 1992); and Arqueologia de Jalisco, Nayarit y Zacatecas: Evolucion de una Civilizacion (Colegio de Michoacan, 1992); and about 100 articles, book reviews and monographs.

WEILER, ROMAN
(high school principal)
Affiliation: Standing Rock Community High School, P.O. Box 377, Fort Yates, ND 58538 (701) 854-3461.

WEINERT, COLLEEN
(Indian education program coordinator)
Affiliation: Big Bay de Noc School, Indian Education Program, HC 01, Box 62, Cooks, MI 49817 (906) 644-2773 ext. 120 Fax 644-2615.

WEINROTH, ORNA
(information specialist)
Affiliation: Nationl Indian Policy Center, The George Washington University, 2101 F St., NW, Washington, DC 20052 (202) 994-1446.

WEISS, NICHOLAS, REV.
(museum chairperson)
Affiliations: The Mohawk-Caughnawaga Museum, Route 5, Box 554, Fonda, NY 12068 (518) 853-3678; director, Tekakwitha Shrine, Fonda, NY.

WELBURN, RON (Gingaskin Assateague/Cherokee)
(university faculty)
Born April 30, 1944, Berwyn, Penna. *Education*: Lincoln University (PA), BA; University of Arizona, MA; New York University, PhD in American Studies. *Principal occupation*: University faculty. *Address & Affiliation*: English Department, University of Massachusetts, Bartlett Hall, Amherst, MA 01003 (413) 545-5518, 577-1607 Fax 545-3880. E-mail: rwelburn@english.umass.edu. 1992-present. *Community activities*: Massachusetts Foundation for the Humanities; Southern Connecticut Library Council; consultant and discussion leader, Five Colleges Public School Partnership, Amherst, MA 1995-; Massachusetts Foundation for the Humanities *Memberships*: Association for American Indian & Alaskan Professors; Greenfield Review Literary Center (Board of Directors); Wordcraft Circle of Native Writers & Storytellers (Mentor). *Interests*: Hiking; "attending selected pow wows with my wife where we occasionally vend for the Native Authors Project and/or dance." *Published works*: Poetry: Peripheries, 1972; Heartland; The Look in the Night Sky; Brownup; Council Decision, 1990; Roanoke and Wampum: Topics in Native American Heritage and Literatures, 2001; Coming Through Smoke and the Dreaming: Selected Poems, 2001.

WELCH, JAMES (Blackfeet)
(poet, writer)
Address: 2321 Wylie St., Missoula, MT 59802 (406) 549-6713.

WELCH, KAMAILI (*Smiles*) (Mohawk)
(special education teacher)
Education: Western Maryland College, BA in Psychology; Johns Hopkins University, MS in Special Education. *Principal occupation*: Special education teacher. *Home address*: 4911 42nd Ave., Hyattsville, MD 20781. E-mail: kamaili_welch@fc.mcpps.k12.md.us. *Community activities*: Volunteer with animal rescue organizations.

WELCH, RICHARD (Eastern Cherokee)
(editor)
Affiliation: Cherokee One Feather, Eastern Band of Cherokee Indians, P.O. Box 501, Cherokee, NC 28719 (704) 497-5513.

WELLER, LAVONNA
(BIA agency supt.)
Affiliation: Eastern & Southern States Agency, Bureau of Indian Affairs, 3701 N. Fairfax Dr., Suite 260, Arlington, VA 22203 (703) 235-3233 Fax 235-3351.

WELLS, ELIZABETH A. (*Sh-ush*) (Mescalero Apache) 1940-
(program director/founder)
Born March 12, 1940, Mescalero, N.M. *Education*: High school. *Principal occupation*: Director/founder-Indian program. *Home address*: 6541 Baby Bear Dr., Anchorage, AK 99507 (907) 243-5561. *Affiliation*: Director & founder, Orre Drumrite Walking Heritage, Anchorage, AK (non-profit program to contact the Indian nation, thus to dedicate annually, an additional; thousand drums to sound at the same moment across all time

zones. 1991: 1,000 drums; 1992: 2,000 drums; 1993: 3,000 drums, etc.) *Other professional post*: Editor, "Dancing Prayers," quarterly publication of Orre Drumrite Walking Heritage. *Community activities*: Coordinating international drum ceremonies, "Parade of the Spirits," "World Drum: Secretts of Life," "Drums of the Whispering Moon," "Standing Sun-calls-drums." *Interests*: "To meet with and visit all indigenous people around the world."

WELLS, LYNDEE (Gros Ventre/Chippewa Cree)
(attorney)
Address & Affiliation: Dorsey & Whitney LLP, U.S. Bank Centre, 1420 Fifth Ave., Suite 3400, Seattle, WA 98101. E-mail: wells.lyndee@dorseylaw.com.

WELLS, SALLY
(association president)
Affiliation: Native American Indian Association of Tennessee, 932 Stahlman Bldg., 211 Union St., Nashville, TN 37201 (615) 726-0806 Fax 726-0810.

WELSH, CAROL L. (*Zitkana Ho Waste Wi*)
(Sisseton-Wahpeton) 1957-
(Indian center director)
Born April 5, 1957, Calif. *Education*: BS degree. *Principal occupation*: Executive director-Indian center. *Address & Affiliation*: Native American Indian Center of Central Ohio, 67 E. Innis Ave., P.O. Box 07705, Columbus, OH 43207-0705 (614) 443-6120 Fax 443-2651. E-mail: naicco@aol.com. *Interests*: Traditional music, dance, and crafts.

WELSH, DR. PETER H.
(professor of anthropology)
Affiliation: Dept. of Anthropology, Box 872402, Arizona State University, Tempe, AZ 85287 (480) 965-6213 Fax 965-7671. *Interests*: Native American studies. E-mail: peter.welsh@asu.edu. *Past professional post*: Curator, The Heard Museum, Phoenix, AZ 85004.

WELSH, RUSSELL (Mohave)
(tribal vice chairperson)
Affiliation: Colorado River Indian Tribal Council, Route 1, Box 23-B, Parker, AZ 85344 (928) 669-9211.

WESLER, KIT W.
(center director)
Affiliation: Wickliff Mounds Research Center, P.O. Box 155, Wickliff, KY 42087 (502) 335-3681.

WESLEY, ESTHER
(director-cultural centre)
Affiliation: Ojibway & Cree Cultural Centre, 84 Elm St. So., Timmins, Ontario, Can. P4N 1W6 (705) 267-7911.

WESLEY, LOWELL (Kialagee)
(tribal town king)
Affiliation: Kialagee Tribal Town, P.O. Box 332, Wetumka, OK 74883 (405) 452-3262.

WESLEY, NORMAN F.
(Indian band chief)
Affiliation: Moose Factory Indian Band, Box 190, Moose Factory, ON, Canada P0L 1W0 (705) 658-4619.

WESO, THOMAS F. (Menominee) 1953-
(instructor)
Born July 16, 1953, Keshena, Wisc. *Education*: University of Kansas, Bachelor's of General Studies. *Principal occupation*: Instructor. *Address*: 1916 Stratford Rd., Lawrence, KS 66044 (913) 841-5757. *Affiliations*: University of Missouri, Kansas City - U.S. Archives Research Project, 1994-95; Instructor, Avila College, 1997; G.T.A., University of Kansas Dept. of Biological Science, 1998-99; temporary instructor, Haskell Indian Nations University, 2001-03. *Membership*: Kansas Folklore Society; Native American Rights Fund..

WESSELS, WILLIAM (Chippewa)
(school administrator)
Affiliation: Circle of Life Survival School, P.O. Box 447, White Earth, MN 56591 (218) 983-3285 ext. 269.

WEST, W. RICHARD, Jr. (Cheyenne-Arapaho) 1943-
(museum director)
Born January 6, 1943, San Bernardino, Calif. *Education*: University of Redlands (CA), BA, 1965 (Magna Cum Laude-Phi Beta Kappa); Harvard University, MA,

1968; Stanford University Law School, JD, 1971. *Principal occupation*: Director, National Museum of the American Indian, Smithsonian Institution. *Address*: 470 L'Enfant Plaza, Suite 7102, Washington, DC 20560 (202) 357-3164 Fax 357-3369. *Affiliations*: Formerly a partner in the Washington, DC law firm of Fried, Frank, Harris, Shriver & Jacobson, and the Indian-owned, Albuquerque, NM law firm of Gover, Stetson, Williams & West, P.C. He served as general counsel and special counsel to numerous Indian tribes and organizations. *Community activities*: Member and treasurer, American Indian Lawyer Training Program, Inc., 1973-; member, National Support Committee, Native American Rights Fund, 1990-; board member, National Support Committee of the Native American Rights Fund, 1990-; board member, Bush Foundation, 1991-; board member, Redland, 1993-; board member, National Trust for Historic Preservation, 1994-; member, Committee on Conscience of National Advisory Forum of the U.S. Holocaust Memorial Museum, 1996-. *Memberships*: Cheyenne-Arapaho Tribe of Oklahoma; Bar of the State of California; Bar of the District of Columbia; Bar of the U.S. Supreme Court; Bar of the U.S. Court of Appeals for Eighth District; American Bar Association (former chairperson, Committee on Problems of the American Indian, Section of Individual Rights and Responsibilities); Federal Bar Association (Indian Section); Indian Bar Association of New Mexico; American Association of Museums (chair of the Board of Directors). *Awards, honors*: Recipient, Career Achievement Award, University of Redlands, 1987; Hilmer Oehlmann, Jr. Prize for excellence in legal writing at Stanford University Law School and served as an officer of the Stanford Law Review. *Interests*: As director of the National Museum of the American Indian, West is responsible for guiding the successful opening of the three facilities that will comprise the museum. He oversaw the completion of the George Gustav Heye Center, the museum's exhibition facility which opened in New York City on October 30, 1994, and continues to supervise the overall planning of the museum's Cultural Resources Center, which will house the NMAI's vast one-million object collection, scheduled to be completed in Suitland, MD, in 1999. West's philosophy and vision for the museum have been critical in guiding the architectural planning of the Mall museum, which is scheduled to open on the last available site on the National Mall in Washington, DC, in 2002. West has devoted his professional life and much of his personal life to working with American Indians on cultural, educational, legal, and governmental issues. West will continue to oversee the fund-raising campaign of the museum, which will provide for an endowment and ongoing educational and outreach programs. *Published works*: Articles - "Chief Justice Traynor and the Parol Evidence Rule (22 Stanford Law Review 547, 1970); co-author, "Healing v. Jones: Mandate for Another Trail of Tears" (N.D. Law Review 73, 1974); co-author, "The Alaska Native Claims Settlement Act: A Flawed Victory" (40 Law & Contemporary Problems 132, 1976); author, "The Source and Soopo of Tribal Powers" (Manual of Indian Law, 1977); co-author, "The Struggle for Indian Civil Rights" (Indians in American History, 1988).

WESTERMAN, FLOYD (*Red Crow*)
(actor)
Movies: "Dances With Wolves;" and "The Doors."

WESTERMEYER, JOSEPH JOHN, MD 1937-
(psychiatrist)
Born April 8, 1937, Chicago, Ill. *Education*: University of Minnesota, BS, 1959, MD, 1961; MA, 1969, MPH & PhD, 1970. *Principal occupation*: Psychiatrist. *Address*: VAMC, 1 Veterans Dr., Minneapolis, MN 55417 (612) 725-2037 Fax 467-5971. E-mail: weste010@umn.edu. *Affiliations*: University of Minnesota Hospitals & Clinics (UMHC), Minneapolis, MN, 1967-89, 1992-99; director of Mental & Behavioral Health Patient Service Line at Minneapolis VAMC, 1999-. *Other professional posts*: Director, Alcohol-Drug Dependence Program, (UMHC), 1982-; director, International Clinic (UMHC), 1984-. *Community activities*: Indian Guest House (halfway house for Indian alcoholics), Minneapolis, MN (board member, 1969-72); Juel Fairbanks House (halfway house for Indian alcoholics), St. Paul, Minn. (board member, 1970-73); South Side Receiving Center (a detoxification unit for American Indian alcoholics), Minneapolis, Minn. (consultant, 1974-75); Association of

American Indian Affairs, including Senate subcommittee hearing on American Indian child welfare, 1973-76. *Memberships*: American Psychiatric Association (Fellow); American Anthropological Association (Fellow); American Public Health Association; American Association of Family Practice (Fellow); Association of Academic Psychiatrists; Minnesota Psychiatric Society (president); National Association of V.A. Psychiatric Administrators & Leaders (past president) Society for the Study of Psychiatry & Culture; American Association of Addiction Psychiatry; et al. *Biographical sources*: Who's Who in America, 1985-; International Who's Who in Medicine (Cambridge, UK, 1994-); International Who's Who of Professionals (Jacksonville, NC, 1995-.; *Awards, honors*: Meritorious Service Award, U.S. Agency for International Development, 1966; Ginzburg Fellow, Group for the Advancement of Psychiatry, 1969-70; Annual Award for Distinguished Contributions to the Field, by AMERSA), 1987; The Best Doctors in America, Alcoholism-Addictions Psychiatry, 1993 & 1998; numerous research grants. *Published works*: Chapters in books & monographs: "The Ravage of Indian Families in Crisis," in The Destruction of Indian Family Life, S. Unger, ed. (Association of American Indian Affairs, 1976); edited with J. Baker, "Alcoholism and American Indian Alcoholism," in Alcoholism Development, Intervention and Consequences (E. Heinman, 1986); numerous journal articles, chapters in books and monographs; book reviews.

WESTHOVEN, THOMAS
(publishing)
Affiliation: Tipi Press, St. Joseph's Indian School, P.O. Box 89, Chamberlain, SD 57325 (605) 734-6021.

WESTON-BEN, WENDY
(editor)
Affiliation: ATLATL, P.O. Box 34090, Phoenix, AZ 85067 (602) 253-2731. Editor of the Directory of Native American Performing Artists,

WETMORE, RUTH L. 1934-
(museum curator)
Born 1934 in Nebraska. *Education*: Park College, BA, 1956; University of Kansas, MA, 1959. *Principal occupation & Address*: Curator, Indian Museum of the Carolinas, 607 Turnpike Rd., Laurinburg, NC 28352 (919) 276-5880, 1974-. *Memberships*: Archaeological Society of North Carolina; Oklahoma Anthropological Society; North Carolina Museums Council; Phi Beta Kappa; Pi Sigma Alpha. *Interests*: Philatelic writing and exhibiting. *Published work*: First on the Land: The North Carolina Indians (John F. Blair, Publisher, 1975).

WETSIT, DEBORAH
(dean of instruction)
Education: Ed.D. *Affiliation*: Haskell Indian Nations University, 155 Indian Ave. #1305, Lawrence, KS 66046 (875) 749-8404 Fax 749-8406. E-Mail: dwetsit@rossl.cc.haskell.edu

WETTENGEL, JACK
(public information director)
Affiliation: Oklahoma Historical Society, Indian Archives Division, 2100 N. Lincoln Blvd., Oklahoma City, OK 73105 (405) 521-2481.

WETZEL, DON (Flying Eagle) (Blackfeet) 1948-
(administrator)
Born August 1, 1948, Cut Bank, Mont. *Education*: University of Montana, BA, 1972, MA, 1981. *Principal occupation*: Administrator. *Address*: Governor's Office of Indian Affairs, 1218 E. 6th Ave., Helena, MT 59620 (406) 444-3702 (office). *Affiliation*: Coordinator, Governor's Office, Helena, MT, 1989-. *Other professional posts*: Teacher/coach in Browning, MT (8 years); High School Principal in Browning, MT (3 years); Supt. of Schools, Corvallis, MT (4 years); teacher/coach, Haskell Indian Junior College, 1982-83. *Awards, honors*: Nominated National Coach of the Year, 1980; Coach of the Year, Blackfeet Reservation, 1980; Jefferson Award-outstanding public service Administrator of the Year, State of Montana Library Association, 1988. *Interests*: "All on my own time - used vacation time and received the Jefferson Award for my crusade against drug and alcohol use among our young Indian People. I traveled 12,000 miles and talked with 10,000 students in Montana in a 2 1/2 year

span." *Biographical sources*: Article on crusade, "Indian Life"; Missoula and Great Falls Tribune, and Billings Gazette.

WHEELER, J. WAGNER
(executive director)
Affiliation: Michigan Indian Press, 45 Lexington, NW, Grand Rapids, MI 49504 (616) 774-8331.

WHEELOCK, RICHARD M. (Oneida of Wisconsin) 1950-
(associate professor)
Born April 30, 1950, Yakima, Wash. *Education*: Fort Lewis College, BA (English and teaching certification); University of Arizona, MA (American Indian Studies); University of New Mexico, PhD (American Studies). *Home address*: P.O. Box 524, Ignacio, CO 81137. *Office address*: 284 Center of Southwest Studies, Fort Lewis College, Durango, CO 81301 (970) 247-7227 Fax 274-7686; E-Mail: wheelock_r@fortlewis.edu. *Affiliation*: Associate Professor, Dept. of Southwest Studies, Fort Lewis College, Durango, CO. *Other professional post*: Faculty sponsor for the "Intertribal News," a bi-weekly student publication of Fort Lewis College. *Memberships*: Native American Journalists Association; Western Social Sciences Association (executive board member). *Interests*: Comunications issues in Indian country; tribal sovereignty issues; tribal-state relations; Indian education issues. *Published works*: The Ute Legacy: A Study Guide, with Farren Webb, provides activities for public high schools in their classes about the Ute Indian Tribe (Southern Ute Tribe, 1989); The Ute Circle of Life, edited with Farren Webb, an elementary school teaching unit (includes over 20 activities, and many games and photographs for classroom use) about the history and modern culture of the Southern Ute Tribe (Southern Ute Tribe, 1990); "Indian Self-Determination: The Charge to Indian Journalists," article in The Social Science Journal, Vol. 32, No. 3, 1995); "The Value of the Concepts of 'Tribalism' and 'Mass Society' in Tribal Communications Research," section in A Good Cherokee, A Good Anthropologist: Papers in Honor of Robert K. Thomas, ed. by Steve Pavlik (American Indian Studies Center, UCLA, 1998).

WHIPPLE, NORMAN (Pomo)
(former tribal chairperson)
Affiliation: Covelo Indian Community Council, P.O. Box 448, Covelo, CA 95428 (707) 983-6126.

WHITAKER, KATHLEEN 1945-
(research center director)
Born October 10, 1945, Los Angeles, Calif. *Education*: Northern Arizona University, BA, 1976; University of California, Los Angeles, MA, 1982, PhD, 1986. *Principal occupation*: Research center director. *Office Address*: 2501 Kerwin Pl., Los Angeles, CA 90065. E-mail: whitaker@sarsf.org. *Affiliations*: San Diego Museum of Man, 1976-79; chief curator, Southwest Museum, Los Angeles, CA, 1979-98; director, Indian Arts Research Center, School of American Research, Santa Fe, NM, 1998-present. *Other professional posts*: Former editor, Council for Museum of Anthropology; Research Associate, Los Angeles County Museum of Natural History. *Membership*: American Association of Museums; New Mexico Association of Museums; Native American Arts Studies Association; American Anthropological Association. *Published works*: Common Threads: Navajo & Pueblo Textiles in the Southwest Museum; Southwest Textiles: Weavings of the Navajo & Pueblo.

WHITE, ALBERT (Mohawk) 1950-
(artist)
Born January 25, 1950, Binghamton, N.Y. *Education*: Maryland Art Institute (Baltimore, MD), BA; attended San Francisco Institute of Art; post graduate student of Master Ann Schuler, disciple of the maroger technique. *Principal occupation*: Artist. *Home address*: 386 Loughlin Rd., Binghamton, NY 13904 (607) 775-2453 Fax 729-1858. E-mail: familycs@spectra.net. *Affiliations*: Otsiningo Pow Wow, Binghamton, NY, 1980-; affiliate artist, The Iroquois Museum, Howes Cave, NY, 1985-. *Other professional posts*: Commissioned portrait artist; consultant for A&E presentation, "How the West Was Lost," 1995. *Community activities*: teacher and storyteller in the Iroquois tradition; school presentations. *Memberships*: A.I.M.; World Wildlife Founda-

tion. *Published works*: Skunnywundy Stories, 1996; The Albert White Cookbook: YoWago "It Tastes Good!" 1999.

WHITE, BETTY JANE (*Usdi agehya*)
(Oklahoma Cherokee) 1943-
(professional nurse)
Born July 2, 1943, Holton, Kans. *Education*: Haskell Indian Jr. College, AA, 1991; Baker University/Stormont Vail School of Nursing (Baldwin City, KS), BS (Nursing), 1993; University of Kansas (currently working towards MS-Nursing); *Principal occupation*: Professional nurse. *Home address*: P.O. Box 906, Wagner, SD 57380-0906. *Affiliation*: St. Francis Hospital & Medical Center, Topeka, KS (Oncology Nursing; Clinical Caring for AIDS patients and other acute medical disease/illnesses), 1989-. *Community activities*: Topeka Railroad Days (chairperson for Native Americans); director of Native American Dance Troupe; lecturer of Native American history & legends. *Memberships*: American Nurses Association; Kansas Student Nurses Association; Native American Journalism Society; American Indian Science & Engineering Society (vice-president, local chapter, 1990-91; member, 1992-); Native American Cultural Society (chairperson, 1992). *Awards, honors*: Haskell Scholastic Excellence Award from Bess Spiva Timmons Foundation; Darby Scholarship Award for most active in Native American culture; Scholastic Excellence Award, Haskill Indian Jr. College; Selectee for Truman Award, Baker University; Kansas Nurse Foundation Award. *Interests*: "Areas I am most interested in are the protection & rights of children from all forms of abuse & neglect. I am involved in the beginning stages of organizing a chapter in Jefferson County for the prevention of child abuse. Health care to the elderly & disabled - longterm care facilities are needed on our reservations, run by the tribal members, for tribal members. Educating the public regarding misconceived ideas about Native Americans. Until the schools and media begin educating the public of the true history of the U.S., the public will always need educating. Holistic healing - the body, mind, and spirit needs to be in balance for healing to occur. If one is ill, the other two will be affected also. I have initiated and started up a Native American Dance Troupe to perform at various functions. The goal for this troupe is to perform nationwide and in foreign countries. Telling a story while the dancing is taking place and the dancing tells the story, is another way to educate the public about Native Americans." *Biographical sources*: Numerous articles relating to health care in "Nursing News," "Sunflower Times," & "Professional Journal"; and a weekly article entitled, "The Fun Side of Life," in Oskaloosa Independent Newspaper.

WHITE, BONNIE L. 1953-
(Indian education program director)
Born October 31, 1953, Tampa, Fla. *Education*: BA in Secondary Education & Foreign Languages (French & German). *Principal occupation*: Indian education program director. *Home address*: 312 Oswego St., Syracuse, NY 13204 (315) 435-4288 Fax 435-6553 (work); E-mail: blwhite315@aol.com. *Affiliations*: Syracuse City School District (Substance Abuse Prevention Counselor/Educator, 1988-95; Title IX Indian Education Program Director, 1995-present); Consultant & Interpreter, Ste. Marie Among the Iroquois Living History Museum, 1995-present. *Community activities*: Board member, North American Indian Project; Trainer & Facilitator for Community-Wide Dialogue on Race & Racism; advisory board member, AICH Outreach programs - WISH, GENERATIONS. *Memberships*: National Indian Education Association; NANACOA.

WHITE, CALVIN
(association president)
Affiliation: Federation of Newfoundland Indians, P.O. Box 275, St. George's, Newfoundland, Canada A0N 1Z0 (709) 647-3733.

WHITE, CAROL
(cultural center director)
Address & Affiliation: Akwesasne Cultural Center - Akwesasne Library & Museum, St. Regis Mohawk Nation, Rt. 37 RR 1, Box 14C, Hogansburg, NY 13655 (518) 358-2240. *Other professional post*: Editor, "Kariwenhawi Newsletter," St. Regis Mohawk Reservation, Hogansburg, NY.

WHITE, DEAN A.
(BIA field rep.)
Affiliation: New York Field Office, Bureau of Indian Affairs, P.O. Box 7366, 100 S. Clinton St., Room 523, Syracuse, NY 13261 (315) 448-0620 Fax 448-0624.

WHITE, JAMES M. (Mdewakanton Sioux)
(tribal council president)
Affiliation: Prairie Island Community Council, 5750 Sturgeon Lake Rd., Welch, MN 55089 (612) 385-2536.

WHITE, KALVIN (Dine-Navajo)
(CEO & founder)
Education: University of Utah, PhD in Counseling Psychology. *Address & Affiliation*: CEO & Founder, Native Wholistic Specialists, Inc., P.O. Box 3297, Window Rock, AZ 86515 (928) 871-5726 Fax 871-4598. Website: www.goodmedicine12.com.

WHITE, LINCOLN C. (Mohawk)
(tribal chief)
Affiliation: St. Regis Mohawk Council Chiefs, Akwesasne-Community Bldg., Hogansburg, NY 13655 (518) 358-2272. *Past professional post*: Director, National Advisory Council on Indian Education, Washington, DC.

WHITE, LINDA R.
(health director)
Affiliation: Kayenta PHS Indian Health Center, P.O. Box 368, Kayenta, AZ 86033 (520) 697-3211.

WHITE, LONNIE J. 1931-
(professor of history)
Born February 12, 1931, Haskell County, Tex. *Education*: West Texas State College, BA, 1950; Texas Tech University, MA, 1955, University of Texas, PhD, 1961. *Principal occupation*: Professor of history. *Home address*: 4272 Rhodes Ave., Memphis, TN 38111. *Affiliation*: Professor of history, Memphis State University, Memphis, TN, 1961-. *Military service*: U.S. Army, 1951-1953 (Sergeant). *Memberships*: Western History Association; Southern Historical Association; American Military Institute; American Historical Association; Journal of the West (editorial advisory board). *Interests*: Teach courses on history of American Indians at Memphis State University from 1968 to the present. *Biographical source*: Who's Who in the South and Southwest. *Published works*: Editor, co-author, Hostiles and Horse Soldiers: Indian Battles and Campaigns in the West (Pruett Press, 1972); editor, The Miles Expedition of 1874-1875: An Eyewitness Account of the Red River War, by Scout J.T. Marshall (Encino Press, 1971); editor, Chronicle of a Congressional Journey: The Doolittle Committee in the Southwest, 1865 (Pruett Press, 1975); Panthers to Arrowheads: The 36th (Texas-Oklahoma) Division in World War I (Presidial Press, 1984); Politics on the Southwestern Frontier: Arkansas Territory, 1819-1836 (Memphis State University Press, 1964); numerous articles in professional journals.

WHITE, MARILYN J. (Dine-Navajo)
(storyteller, writer, poet)
Address: 3023 W. Brenda Loop, Flagstaff, AZ 86001 (520) 774-2613.

WHITE, MINERVA
(program coordinator)
Affiliation: New York State Education Dept., Native American Program, 543 Education Bldg. Annex, Washington Ave., Albany, NY 12234 (518) 474-0537.

WHITE, SAMMY (*Tone-kei*) (Kiowa)
(storyteller, advisor)
Tone-kei has had extensive experience sharing traditional stories of his people with many groups of people including school age children and tour groups in the Southwest. He can be contacted at 1-602-946-7407 or the Arizona Commission on the Arts at 1-602-255-5882. *Affiliation*: Council of Advisors, American Indian Heritage Foundation, Falls Church, VA .

WHITE, THOMAS
(school principal)
Affiliation: St. Francis Indian School, P.O. Box 379, St, Francis, SD 57572 (605) 747-2299.

WHITE, THOMAS R., Sr. (Pima-Maricopa)
(tribal governor)
Affiliation: Gila River Indian Community Council, P.O. Box 97, Sacaton, AZ 85247 (520) 562-3311.

WHITE, TRAVIS, M.D.
(health director)
Affiliation: Cibecue Indian Health Center, Cibecue, AZ 85941 (520) 332-2560.

WHITE CLOUD XOCHIPILLICUEPONI
(executive director)
Affiliation: Natives of the Four Directions Cultural Center, P.O. Box 12301, Berkeley, CA 94712 (510) 724-2032.

WHITE EAGLE, CATHY (Eastern Cherokee) 1960-
(executive director)
Born July 14, 1960, Merced, Calif. *Education*: Santa Clara University, BS, 1982. *Principal occupation*: Executive director. *Address*: Unknown. *Affiliation*: Eagle Vision, Granite Bay, CA (916) 791-7910, 1992-. *Other professional posts*: Director, AIM, Sacramento Region; committee member, Multicultural Affairs, Sacramento Access. *Memberships*: American Indian Women's Association; National Organization for Women; American Indian Movement (AIM); Multi-Cultural Women's Network. *Awards, honors*: Honorary Award for community service, Sacramento State University; delegate to the United Nation on behalf of the American Indian Movement for the purpose of working on the basic human rights issues for American Indian people & children. *Interests*: "Sovereignty & treaty rights; currently working on the Native American Biography Series for Paramount's Modern Press, a series of six books for teachers to be released for 1995 school year.

WHITE EAGLE, GLENN C.
(school principal)
Affiliation: Tonalea (Red Lake) Day School, P.O. Box 39, Tonalea, AZ 86044 (520) 283-6325 Fax 283-6326.

WHITE EAGLE, LARRY (Nez Perce)
(craftsperson)
Address: Co-owner, White Eagle's Nez Perce Indian Arts, P.O. Box 4, Orofino, ID 83544 (208) 476-7753.

WHITE EAGLE, PAM (Nez Perce)
(craftsperson)
Address: Co-owner, White Eagle's Nez Perce Indian Arts, P.O. Box 4, Orofino, ID 83544 (208) 476-7753.

WHITE EAGLE, TOM (Oglala-Hunkpapa Sioux) 1941-
(artist)
Born October 26, 1941, Rapid City, S.D. *Education*: California Polytechnic University, BA; University of California, Davis, MS. *Principal occupation*: Artist. *Address & Affiliation*: Owner/curator, White Eagle Creations, P.O. Box 615, Elkron, OR 97436 (541) 584-2176. *Military service*: U.S. Air Force. *Interests*: "Restoration & study of Plains artifacts, primarily Lakota; work with youths & adults to promote Native culture; traditional dancer."

WHITE FEATHER, LARRY J.
(college counselor)
Affiliation: Madison Area Technical College, 3550 Anderson St., Rm. 171, Madison, WI 53704 (608) 246-6109.

WHITE HAT, ALBERT H. (Rosebud Sioux) 1938-
(Lakota studies instructor)
Born November 18, 1938, St. Francis, S.D. *Education*: Sinte Gleska College, AA (Lakota Studies), 1986. *Principal occupation*: Lakota studies instructor. *Home address*: P.O. Box 168, St. Francis, SD 57572 (605) 747-2711. *Affiliations*: Teacher, Indian Studies Program, St. Francis Indian School, 1974-80; part-time teacher, Lakota Medicine, 1979-85, Lakota studies instructor, Sinte Gleska College, Rosebud, SD, 1983-. *Other professional posts*: Tribal council (Rosebud Sioux) representative and committee work, 1979-81; president, Board of Directors, Sinte Gleska College, 1981-83. *Community activities*: Rosebud Community Action Program, 1967-70; Rosebud Ambulance Service, 1970-72; St. Francis Indian School (chairman of the board). Memberships: National Association for Bi-

lingual Education; SD Association for Bilingual Education; SD Indian Education Association. *Awards, honors*: Fellowship Award in 1978 to research Native American History for high school history course at Newberry Library, Chicago, IL; Voted in to serve on the Board of Trustees at Proctor Academy in Andover, NH (trustee, 3 years; corporate member, 5 years). *Interests*: "Carpentry, woodwork and construction; horse training; cultural and traditional activities. Presently, I am coordinating three instructional pamphlets in the areas of Lakota kinship—early childhood development, bilingual science, and bilingual language arts; I have done lectures on the philosophy of the Lakota, oral history and traditions in different colleges and organization, civic groups, pastoral groups, and church organizations." *Published work*: Co-editor, Lakota Ceremonial Songs (song book with cassette tape) (Sinte Gleska College).

WHITE OWL LAVADOUR, MARLENE (Navajo)
(craftsperson; art gallery co-owner)
Affiliation: Cayuse Gallery, 37 SE Court, Pendleton, OR 97801 (541) 966-1191.

WHITE OWL LAVADOUR, MAYNARD (Cayuse)
(craftsperson; art gallery co-owner)
Affiliation: Cayuse Gallery, 37 SE Court, Pendleton, OR 97801 (541) 966-1191.

WHITE TEMPLE, EMMET
(BIA education administrator)
Affiliation: Standing Rock Agency, Bureau of Indian Affairs, Agency Ave., P.O. Box E, Fort Yates, ND 58538 (701) 854-3497 Fax 854-7280.

WHITE TEMPLE, LILLIAN
(school chairperson)
Affiliation: Rock Creek Day School, P.O. Box 127, Bullhead, SD 57621 (605) 823-4971.

WHITEBIRD, DENNIS
(Indian band chief)
Affiliation: Rolling River Indian Band, Box 145, Erickson, Manitoba, Canada R0J 0P0 (204) 636-2211.

WHITEBIRD, FRANCIS
(Indian affairs coordinator)
Affiliation: South Dakota Indian Affairs Office, 118 W. Capitol, Rm. 300, Pierre, SD 57501 (605) 773-3415.

WHITECROW, JAKE L. (Quapaw-Seneca-Cayuga) 1928-
(health administrator)
Born July 2, 1928, Miami, Okla. *Education*: Oklahoma State University, BS, 1951. *Principal occupation*: Health administrator. Resides in Denver, CO (303) 394-3500 (office). *Affiliation*: Health administrator, National Indian Health Board, Denver, CO. *Other professional posts*: Health committee chairman, National Congress of American Indians; founder, Native American Free Loan Society, Denver, CO. *Military service*: U.S. Army, 1951-78 (Major-U.S. Army Reserve-retired; U.N. Medal; Korean War Medal with two Battle Stars; National Defense Medal; Army Reserve Medal). *Community activities*: Quapaw Tribe (chairman); Americans for Indian Opportunity, Washington, DC (board member, 7 years); American Indian Heritage Foundation, Washington, DC (board member, Advisory Council, 2 years); Native American Cattle Co. of OK (president). *Memberships*: OK State Historical Society (listed speaker); Thomas Jefferson Forum of Washington, DC (listed speaker); American Legion (precinct co-chairman, post commander). *Awards, honors*: Honorary member of 4-H Clubs of OK; "I was the only Oklahoma Indian to serve as a commissioner with the American Policy Review Commission (U.S. Congress, 1975-77)." *Interests*: "My avocational interests are: sport of rodeo, Indian customs and history, football, basketball, Indian dice, horse training, dog training." *Biographical source*: Indians of Oklahoma (University of Oklahoma Press). *Published work*: American Indian Policy Review Commission Final Report (USGPO, 1977).

WHITEDUCK, JEAN-GUY
(Indian band chief)
Affiliation: River Desert (Algonquin) Indian Band, Box 309, Maniwaki, Quebec, Canada J9E 3C9 (819) 449-5170.

WHITEEAGLE, CHIEF
(Indian center co-president)
Affiliation: Indian Awareness Center, Fulton County Historical Society, 37 E 375 N, Rochester, IN 46975 (574) 223-4436.

WHITEFEATHER, BOBBY (Red Lake Chippewa)
(tribal chairperson)
Affiliation: Red Lake Band of Chippewa Indians of Minnesota, P.O. Box 550, Red Lake, MN 56671 (218) 679-3341 Fax 679-3691 (employment and training program, 1975-86; tribal treasurer, 1986-90; tribal secretary, 1990-94, chairperson, 1994-),

WHITEFORD, ANDREW HUNTER 1913-
(anthropologist-retired)
Born September 1, 1913, Winnipeg, Can. *Education*: Beloit (WI) College, BA, 1937; University of Chicago, MA, 1943, PhD, 1950. *Principal occupation*: Research, teaching. *Home address*: 4000 E. Fletcher Ave., Tampa, FL 33613 (813) 977-9817. *Affiliations*: Director, Logan Museum, Beloit, WI, 1951-74; administrative director, School of American Research, Santa Fe, NM, 1981-84; research associate, Museum of Indian Arts & Culture, Santa Fe, NM, 1987-. *Other professional posts*: Professor emeritus, Beloit College. *Community activities*: Editorial board, "American Indian Art Magazine." *Memberships*: American Anthropological Association (Fellow); Native American Art Studies Assn. *Awards, honors*: LLD, Beloit College; Society of the Sigma Xi (science); Phi Beta Kappa; grants from the National Science Foundation, National Foundation for the Arts, American Philosophical Society; Career Award from Native American Art Studies Assn. *Interests*: Research on museums, here & abroad, also on reservation in the Southwest and western Great Lake. Interested in basketry of Southwestern tribes; beadwork of Lakes & Eastern tribes; non-loom weaving. *Biographical source*: Who's Who in the U.S. *Published works*: North American Indian Arts (Western Publishing, 1970); Southwestern Indian Baskets (School of American Research, 1988); Translating Tradition: Basketry Arts of the San Juan Paiutes, with S.B. McGreevy; Heritage, with D. Anderson, et al.

WHITEHAIR, KEN
(service unit director)
Affiliation: Annette Isalnd Servie Unit, Metlakatla Indian Community, P.O. Box 439, Metlakatla, AK 99926 (907) 886-4741.

WHITEHAWK, JOE
(cultural specialist)
Affiliation: Native American Services Agency, Missoula Indian Center, 2300 Regent St. #A, Missoula, MT 59801 (406) 329-3373.

WHITELAW, MICHAEL
(BIA agency director)
Affiliation: Spokane Agency, Bureau of Indian Affairs, P.O. Box 389, Wellpinit, WA 99040 (509) 258-4561.

WHITELAW, SHEILA (Colville)
(editor)
Affiliation: "Tribal Tribune," Colville Confederated Tribes, P.O. Box 150, Nespelem, WA 99155 (509) 634-8835.

WHITEMAN, DENNIS T.
(BIA agency supt.)
Affiliation: Fort Peck Agency, Bureau of Indian Affairs, P.O. Box 637, Poplar, MT 59255 (406) 768-5312 Fax 768-3405.

WHITENER, DAVE, SR. (Nisqually)
(tribal chairperson)
Affiliation: Squaxin Island Tribal Council, SE 70, Squaxin Lane, Shelton, WA 98584 (360) 426-9781.

WHITESELL, DAVE
(high school principal)
Affiliation: Pine Hill School, P.O. Box 220, Pine Hill, NM 87357 (505) 775-3243 Fax 775-3241.

WHITESELL, RICHARD
(BIA area director)
Affiliation: Billings Area Office, Bureau of Indian Affairs, 316 North 26th St., Billings, MT 59101 (406) 657-6315.

WHITETREE, TERRY L. (Seneca-Cayuga)
(tribal chief)
Affiliation: Seneca-Cayuga Tribe of Oklahoma, P.O. Box 1283, Miami, OK 74355 (918) 542-6609.

WHITFORD, THOMAS C., SR. (Blackfeet)1930-
(tribal business council chairman)
Born January 2, 1930, Browning, Mont. *Education*: City College of San Francisco, 1959-62; Eastern Montana College, 1970-71; University of Idaho, 1973-75. *Principal occupation*: Blackfeet Tribal Council, Chairman. *Address*: Resides in Browning, Mont. (406) 338-7276 (work). *Affiliation*: Director, Montana Inter-Tribal Policy Board, Billings, MT, 1977-80; deputy area director, BIA, Billings, MT, 1980-82; supt., BIA (Montana, Nevada, and California tribes), 1982-86; chairperson, Blackfeet Tribal Business Council and business owner, Browning, MT, 1986-. *Community activities*: Initiated the reorganization and revitalization of the Blackfeet Senior Citizens Organization and regularly assists needy families with food and holiday gifts for children. *Memberships*: Montana-Wyoming Tribal Chairman's Association (chairman, 1988-); National Congress of American Indians (Billings Area Vice-President, 1988-); Montana Democratic Committee on Policymaking, 1988-; Northwest Affiliated Tribes, 1989-; Concerned Reservation Indians, 1989-. *Awards, honors*: Outstanding performances and achievement, Bureau of Indian Affairs; Montana Inter-Tribal Policy Board Honors for Leadership; appearances on "Face the State" (Montana) and "Indians in Progress" to discuss Indian issues. *Interests*: "Member of the Blackfeet delegation who first successfully returned Indian skeletal remains collected by the Smithsonian Institute, Washington, D.C. to native people. The remains are those of fifteen people who had died during the "Starvation Winter" of 1883-84; established a nation-to-nation "open door" relationship between the Montana Tribes and the State of Montana, County and local representatives to achieve a more effective working relationship; initiated a market study to determine the potential for tourism and development of an enterprise zone on the Blackfeet reservation to attract investment for tourism."

WHITING, BERNARD (Rosebud Lakota Sioux)
(radio station manager)
Affiliation: KINI - 96.1 FM, Rosebud Lakota Sioux Tribe, P.O. Box 146, St. Francis, SD 57572 (605) 747-2291.

WHITING, PAUL J.
(museum director)
Affiliation: Buechel Memorial Lakota Museum, St. Francis Indian Mission, 350 S. Oka St., Box 149, St. Francis, SD 57572 (605) 747-2828.

WHITING-SORRELL, ANNA
(association president)
Affiliation: National Association for Native American Children of Alcoholics, 1402 3rd Ave. #1110, Seattle, WA 98118 (206) 322-5601.

WHITISH, HERBERT "IKE" (Shoalwater)
(tribal chairperson)
Affiliation: Shoalwater Bay Tribal Council, P.O. Box 130, Tokeland, WA 98590 (360) 267-6766.

WHITMAN, CARL, Jr. (*Black Fox*)
(Mandan/Hidatsa/Arikara) 1913-
(program director; university instructor)
Born March 6, 1913, Elbowoods, N.D. *Education*: ND State School of Science, 1934-36. *Principal occupation*: Director-Indian programs; university instructor. *Home address*: P.O. Box 203, Parshall, ND 58770 (701) 862-3260. *Afiliations*: Chairperson, Three Affiliated Tribes, New Town, ND (6 years); chairperson, ND Legal Services, New Town, ND (20 years). *Awards, honors*: Outstanding Senior North Dakotan, 1987; Recognition for 20 years as Chairperson of the Board of ND Legal Services. *Interests*: "Introducing cross-breeding of cattle as a way of increasing weight. Directing a laboratory studying alternative source of energy. (I did) a comprehensive renovation of the educational program for Indians of the Low Mountain School on the Navajo Reservation, 1964, which was rejected but was used by Dr. Robert Roessel of Arizona State University. It made a heavy impact in the Indian education field. Vernacular language was included in the curriculum program. Other relevant disciplines were included such as Indian history, community

problems, parapsychology at an applied level and sex education."

WHITMAN, KATHY (*Elk Woman*)
(Manadan-Hidatsa-Arikara) 1952-
(artist, sculptor, painter)
Born August 12, 1952, Bismarck, N.D. *Education*: University of South Dakota; Sinte Gleska College, Rosebud, SD; Standing Rock Community College, Ft. Yates, ND. *Principal occupation*: Artist, sculptor, painter. *Address*: Resides in Arizona. *Affiliations*: Owner, Nux-Baga Lodge, New Town, N.D., 1981-1985; owner, Recreation Center, New Town, N.D., 1985. *Other professional post*: Art instructor, Standing Rock Community College and Sinte Gleska College. *Community activities*: Parent representative-Headstart, Ft. Yates, N.D.; Ft. Berthold Community College, New Town, N.D. (board of directors); Pow-Wow, Canonball, N.D. (president, committee member). *Memberships*: Indian Arts and Crafts Association; Gallup Intertribal Ceremonial; Southwest Association on Indian Affairs. *Awards, honors*: Best Craftsman/Special Award, Bukllock's Santa Monica Indian Ceremonial, 1986; 1st Place, San Juan Bautista Indian Arts and Crafts Show, 1986; 1st Place, 1986, 2nd Place, 1987, 1st Place, 1990, Eight Northern Pueblos Arts and Crafts Show; Special Merit Award, Trail of Tears Arts Show, 1987; 3rd Place, Gallup Indian Ceremonial; Best of Fine Arts/Split Best of Show, Northern Plains Tribal Arts Show, 1988; 1989 Poster Artist, Southwest Association on Indian Affairs; 1990 One Woman Exhibition in Nurnberg, Germany; 1991 Best of Show, Pasadena Western Relic & Indian Arts and Crafts Show; Governors Award, Directors and Choice Merit Award, United Tribes Educational Training Center, Bismarck, N.D. *Interests*: "Demonstrated and exhibited paintings and sculpture in numerous galleries; danced and exhibited artwork in Charleroi, Belgium, Dijon, France, anmd Nurnberg, Germany; started a recreation center on Ft. Berthold Reservation for the youth and sponsored an alternative camp for youth. I believe that all things of the Sacred Mother Earth are special and holy. I want people to see and feel, the pride, the unity, the happiness, and the spiritual strength that is so close to us. There is serenity in having a strong relationship with the Great Spirit and all His Sacred Veings." *Biographical sources*: Article - "People, Faces of the 90's: A Closeup Look at Valley Newsmakers," Valley of the Sun Times, June 1991; articles in The Desert Leaf, July 1989; Antiques & the Arts Weekly, Sept. 1989; Santa Fe Reporter, Aug. 1990; Indian Trader, Aug. 1990; New York Times, Sept. 1991 ad. 1989 Video - Beyond Tradition, by Jerry and Lois Jacka (one of featured artists).

WHITMAN, ROBERT K. (Navajo) 1954-
(electrical engineer)
Born February 25, 1954, Fort Defiance, Ariz. *Education*: University of New Mexico, BS, 1977; Colorado State University, MS, 1986; University of Colorado, PhD (Electrical Engineering), 1990. *Principal occupation*: Electrical engineer. *Home address*: Unknown. *Affiliations*: Engineer, IBM Corp., San Jose, CA & Boulder, CO, 1977-90; deputy director, American Indian Science & Engineering Society, Boulder, CO, 1991-. *Other professional post*: Industrial Development Specialist, Navajo Nation Economic Development Dept., Window Rock, AZ, (3 months) 1987-88. *Community activities*: AISES student chapter advisor at University of Colorado, Boulder; member, University of Colorado Graduate School Advisory Council; member, Science Service International, Science & Engineering Fair Advisory Council; member, Committee on Feasibility of a National Scholars Program, National Research Council. *Memberships*: Institute of Electrical and Electronics Engineers (IEEE); American Indian Science & Engineering Society (AISES) (board of directors, 1983-87, board secretary, 1984-85, board chairperson, 1985-87, chair of Scholarship Committee, 1988-92). *Awards, honors*: NASA Minority Fellowship, 1975-77; Outstanding Achievement Award, Navajo Nation, 1980; Information Systems Division Achievement Award, IBM Corp., 1981; Information Products Division Achievement Award, IBM Corp., 1984; AISES/GE Fellowship, 1993. *Interests*: "Doctoral dissertation on human speech synthesis, non-linear methods of sound reconstruction. Outside activities include: reading history of American Indians, learning about Navajo traditional ways and about my ancestors; giving presentations to

high school and college students on technical careers and importance of traditions. Judge science fair projects at high school level; traveled to Europe 4 times." *Biographical source*: "New Mexico Professional Engineer," 9/78; "Graduate Engineer," 10/81; "Minority Engineer," Summer 1984; "Winds of Change," 2/86.

WICKLIFFE, DENNIS
(BIA agency supt.)
Affiliation: Tahlequah Agency, Bureau of Indian Affairs, P.O. Box 828, Tahlequah, OK 74465 (918) 456-6146.

WIDDISS, DONALD A. (Wampanoag)
(tribal president)
Affiliation: Wampanoag Tribal Council of Gay Head, State Rd., RFD Box 137, Gay Head, MA 02535 (508) 645-9265.

WIDMARK, LAWRENCE, Jr. (Sitka)
(tribal president)
Affiliation: Sitka Tribe of Alaska, 456 Katlian St., Sitka, AK 99835 (907) 747-3207.

WIESEN, DON
(school administrator)
Affiliation: Lac Courte Oreilles Ojibwa School, Route 2, Box 2800, Hayward, WI 54843 (715) 634-8924.

WILBANKS, BILLY M.
(school principal)
Affiliation: Pearl RiverSchool, Route 7, Box 19-H, Philadelphia, MS 39350 (601) 656-9051.

WILCOX, DR. DAVID R.
(museum curator; Indian studies instructor)
Affiliation: Museum of Northern Arizona, 3101 N. Fort Valley Rd., Flagstaff 86001 (520) 774-5211 Fax 779-1527; instructor, Native American Studies, Northern Arizona University, Flagstaff, AZ.

WILCOX, DEE
(BIA agency director)
Affiliation: Southern Paiute Field Station, Bureau of Indian Affairs, P.O. Box 986, Cedar City, UT 84720 (801) 586-1121.

WILDCATT, DR. LISA ANNE FRANCESCHINI
(Choctaw of Oklahoma) 1970 -
(pediatrician)
Born August 5, 1970, Fort Lauderdale, Fla. *Education*: University of North Dakota, BS, 1995, MD, 2000; Medical College of Georgia, Pediatric Residency. *Principal occupation*: Pediatrician. *Address & Affiliation*: Cherokee Hospital, Box C-268, Hospital Rd., Cherokee, NC 28719 (828) 497-9163 Fax 497-5343. E-mail: lisa.wildcatt@mail.ihs.gov. "I chose University of North Dakota because of the Native American Program (NAP) and the Indians Into Medicine Program (InMed)." *Memberships*: American Medical Association; Academy of American Family Physicians; American Academy of Pediatrics. *Interests*: Family; outdoors; biking, computers, reading, cooking, photography.

WILDER, DONI
(executive director)
Affiliation: Northwest Portland Area Indian HealthBoard, 527 SW Hall, Suite 300, Portland, OR 97201 (503) 228-4185 Fax 228-8182.

WILDER, RICHARD (Palute)
(tribal chairperson)
Affiliation: Fort Independence Reservation, P.O. Box 67, Independence, CA 93526 (619) 878-2126.

WILKINS, DAVID E. (Lumbee) 1954-
(assistant professor)
Born September 18, 1954, Fort Bragg, N.C. *Education*: Pembroke State University, BA, 1976; University of Arizona, MA, 1982; University of North Carolina, Chapel Hill, PhD, 1990. *Principal occupation*: Assistant professor. *Address*: American Indian Studies Dept., University of Minnesota, 102 Scott Hall, 72 Pleasant St. SE, Minneapolis, MN 55455 (612) 624-1338; 624-3858. *Affiliation*: Assistant Professor of Political Science & Indian Law & Policy, University of Arizona, Tucson, AZ, 1990-93; Assistant Professor of Political Science & American Indian Studies, University of Colorado, Boulder, CO., 1993-99; professor of

American Indian Studies, University of Minnesota, Minneapolis, MN, 2000 to present. *Other professional post*: Columnist, Indian Country Today, Canastota, NY. *Membership*: American Political Science Association. *Award*: Ford Foundation Dissertation Fellowship, 1989-90; Ford Foundation Post-Doctoral Fellowship, 1993-94; Center for Advanced Study in the Behavioral Sciences Post Doctoral Fellowship. *Published work*: Dine Bib eehaz'aanii: A Handbook of Navajo Government (Navajo Community College Press, 1987); numerous academic journal articles.

WILKINSON, CHARLES
(law professor)
Affiliation: University of Colorado, School of Law, Boulder, CO 80309. E-mail: wilkinson@colorado.edu

WILLARD, SHIRLEY
(writer, editor, museum work)
Born September 28, 1936, in Indiana. *Education*: Manchester College, BA; Ball State University, MA. principal occupation: Writer, editor, museum work. *Home address*: 3063 S 425 E, Rochester, IN 46975 (574) 223-2352. E-mail: wwillard@rtcol.com. *Affiliation*: Indian Awareness Center, Fulton County Historical Society, 37 E 375 N, Rochester, IN 46975 (574) 223-4436; editor, Awareness Center Newsletter. *Other professional posts*: Historian, Fulton County Historian, 1980s - present; "I write a history column for Rochester Sentinel and other area newspapers." *Awards, honors*: Sagamore of the Wabash, 2001. *Community activities*: Coordinator for placing of Trail of Death Regional Historic Trail historical markers-there are 74 now (over 660 miles from north central Indiana to eastern Kansas, commemorating the forced removal of the Potawatomi in 1838), making this the best marked American Indian historic trail; Trail of Death Commemorative Caravan every five years. The next one is scheduled for 2008. *Memberships*: Fulton County Historical Society (Genealogy Section); Indian Awareness Center; Fulton County Historical Power Association; Indiana Historical Society. *Interests*: History. *Published works*: Trail of Death Diary, 1988; Trail of Death Regional Historical Trail, 1998; Potawatomi Trail of Death, 2003, co—authored with Susan Campbell.

WILLIAMS, ANNIE LOU (Eskimo)
(village president)
Affiliation: Native Village of Kalskag, Kalskag, AK 99607 (907) 471-2248.

WILLIAMS, BETTY LOU
(organization director)
Affiliation: World Vision International, 919 W. Huntington Dr., Monrovia, CA 91016 (818) 303-8811.

WILLIAMS, CASSIDY (Paiute)
(tribal chairperson)
Affiliation: Walker River Paiute Tribal Council, P.O. Box 220, Schurz, NV 89427 (702) 773-2306.

WILLIAMS, CINDY (Duwamish)
(tribal secretary/treasurer)
Affiliation: Duwamish Tribal Council, 15616 First Ave. South, Seattle, WA 98148 (206) 244-0606.

WILLIAMS, DAVID EMMETT (*Tosque*)
(Kiowa/Apache/Tonkawa) 1933-
(artist)
Born August 20, 1933, Redstone, Okla. *Education*: Bacone College. *Principal occupation*: Artist. *Membership*: American Tribal Dancers and Singers Club, 1963- (head drummer and singer). *Awards, honors, exhibits*: Numerous art awards and one-man shows; work represented in permanent collections of several museums.

WILLIAMS, DELLA R. (SAM) (Papago) 1936-
(school principal)
Born February 13, 1936, Ventana Village, Papago Reservation, Ariz. *Education*: Phoenix Junior College, AA, 1958; Arizona State University, BA, 1962. *Principal occupation*: School principal. *Address*: San Simeon School, HC01, Box 8292, , Sells, AZ 85634 (602) 362-2231. *Affiliations*: Teacher, Santa Rosa Boarding School, BIA, 1962-75; principal, San Simeon School, Sells, AZ, 1977-. *Community activities*: Papago Tribal Education Committee (chairperson, 1965-70); OEO's Community Action Program; tribal representative at

various state and national conferences and workshops, as well as at congressional hearings. *Honor*: Inducted into the Phoenix Indian High School Hall of Fame as a charter member, 1977. *Interests*: "Consulting with students, teachers and administrators concerning grades and adjustment; higher education students, consultant and advisor; directed Tribal Education Grants and assisted with other financial needs of higher education; monthly reports to the General Council; participated and assisted in the introduction, planning and development of the first poverty program on the Papago Reservation; participated in supervising and hiring the first Head-Start school teachers, evaluated and made recommendations; participated as guest speaker in Indian education conferences in Tempe, Indian Clubs, The Papago Council, Phoenix Indian High School, Tucson Indian Center, and Papago District Councils."

WILLIAMS, EDWARD
(Indian band chief)
Affiliation: Moose Deer Point Indian Band, Box 119, Mactier, Ontario, Canada P0C 1H0.

WILLIAMS, FRANK
(IHS-director of support services)
Affiliation: Director of Support Services, Alaska Native Health Center, 250 Gambel St., Anchorage, AK 99501 (907) 279-6661.

WILLIAMS, HERMAN A., JR. (Tulalip)
(tribal chairperson)
Affiliation: Tulalip Board of Directors, 6700 Totem Beach Rd., Marysville, WA 98271 (360) 651-4000.

WILLIAMS, HUBERT (Nooksack)
(former tribal chairperson)
Affiliation: Nooksack Tribal Council, P.O. Box 157, Deming, WA 98244 (206) 592-5176.

WILLIAMS, IDA
(director-friendship centre)
Affiliation: Native Friendship Centre, 3730 Cote Des Neiges Rd., Montreal, Quebec, Canada H3H 1V6 (514) 937-5338.

WILLIAMS, JAMES L. (Paucatuck Eastern Pequot)
(grand chief sachem)
Affiliation: Paucatuck Eastern Pequot Indian Reservation, 640-A Lantern Hill Rd., No. Stonington, CT 06359 (860) 572-9899.

WILLIAMS, JOHN R.
(health director)
Affiliation: Mescalero PHS Indian Hospital, P.O. Box 210, Mescalero, NM 88340 (505) 671-4441.

WILLIAMS, JOHN W.
(health director)
Affiliation: Pawhuska PHS Indian health Center, 715 Grandview, Pawhuska, OK 74056 (918) 287-4491.

WILLIAMS, JUANITA (Paiute)
(rancheria spokesperson)
Affiliation: North Fork Rancheria, P.O. Box 120, North Fork, CA 93643.

WILLIAMS, LEONA (Pomo)
(rancheria chairperson)
Affiliation: Pinoleville Rancheria, 367 N. State St. #204, Ukiah, CA 95482 (707) 463-1454.

WILLIAMS, LEONARD (Caddo)
(tribal chairperson)
Affiliation: Caddo Tribal Council, P.O. Box 487, Binger, OK 73009 (405) 656-2344.

WILLIAMS, MARILYN
(health director)
Affiliation: N.W. Washington PHS Lummi PHS Health Center, 2592 Kwina Rd., Bellingham, WA 98226 (206) 676-8373.

WILLIAMS, MOGAN
(editor)
Affiliation: Wawatay News, Wawatay Native Communications Society, P.O. Box 1180, Sioux Lookout, Ontario, Canada P0V 2T0 (807) 737-2951.

WILLIAMS, PERRY (Alabama-Coushatta of Texas)
(tribal chairperson)
Affiliation: Alabama-Coushatta Tribe of Texas, Route 3, Box 659, Livingston, TX 77351 (409) 563-4391.

WILLIAMS, RICHARD B. (Oglala Lakota Sioux)
(educator, advocate, historian)
Born in Crawford, Neb. *Education*: University of Nebraska, Lincoln, BA (University Studies); University of Wyoming, MA (Education Administration). *Address*: 13028 Julian Court, Denver, CO 80221 (303) 492-5474. *Affiliations*: University of Denver, Denver, CO (teaches American Indian history for the graduate program in Indian Studies); executive director, American Indian College Fund, Denver, CO., 1997-present. The College Fund raises private support for scholarships, endowments, programs, and public awareness efforts on behalf of 32 tribally chartered colleges. *Other professional post*: Lecturer and presenter on Native American history and education. *Past professional posts*: Director, Student Academic Service Center, University of Colorado, Boulder, CO; director of Minority Student Affairs and director of the American Indian Upward Bound Program; consulting editor for the Discovery Channel series, "How the West Was Lost"; also worked with other programs targeting Indian youth and serving Indian reservation populations. *Awards, honors*: 1999 University of Nebraska-Distinguished Alumni Award; Mr. Williams was the first American Indian student ever to have earned a bachelor's degree from University of Nebraska, Lincoln. *Interests*: Working with American Indian and other youth promoting Indian education and the success of tribal peoples, and furthering the public's understanding of contemporary and historical Indian issues.

WILLIAMS, RICHARD (Chippewa)
(former rancheria chairperson)
Affiliation: Lac Vieux Desert Band of Lake Superior Chippewa, P.O. Box 249, Watersmeet, MI 49969 (906) 358-4577.

WILLIAMS, ROBERT, JR. (Lumbee)
(attorney, educator)
Education: Harvard Law School, J.D., 1980. *Affiliation*: The Tribal Law & Policy Program, American Indian Studies Program, The University of Arizona, Harvill Bldg., Rm 430, P.O. Box 210076, Tucson, AZ 85721 (520) 621-7108 Fax 621-7952. E-mail: aisp@email. arizona.edu. *Interests*: Energy/natural resource management; Indian law and policy.

WILLIAMS, ROBERT L. (Ojibway)
(Indian band chief)
Affiliation: Ojibways of Walpole Island, RR 3, Wallaceburg, ON, Canada B8A 1R0 (519) 627-1481.

WILLIAMS, SOLOMON (Eskimo)
(village president)
Affiliation: Mekoryuk Native Village, P.O. Box 66, Mekoryuk, AK 99630 (907) 827-8828.

WILLIAMS, WALTER L. 1948-
(professor)
Born November 3, 1948, Durham, N.C. *Education*: Georgia State University, BA, 1970; University of North Carolina, Chapel Hill, MA, 1972, PhD, 1974. *Principal occupation*: Associate professor, Anthropology Dept., University of Southern California, Los Angeles, CA, 1985-. *Home address*: 2319 Portland St., Los Angeles, CA 90007. *Other professional post*: Consultant, American Indian Studies Center, UCLA. *Community activities*: Gay American Indians, Inc. (consultant); Museum of the Cherokee Indians (consultant); International Gay and Lesbian Archives (president, board of directors). *Military service*: U.S. Army, 1973 (Captain). *Memberships*: American Anthropological Association; Society of Lesbian and Gay Anthropologists (chair, Ruth Benedict Prize Committee); Sociologists Lesbian and Gay Caucus; Committee on Lesbian and Gay History. *Awards, honors*: Woodrow Wilson Fellow, 1970; American Council of Learned Societies grant awards, 1977, 1983; UCLA American Indian Studies Center Fellow, 1980, 1982; Newberry Library Fellow, 1978; Ruth Benedict Prize Book Award, 1986, for The Spirit and the Flesh; . *Interests*: "Homosexuality and gender variance in American Indian cultures; Indian sexuality; 19th century Indian legal status; Southeastern Indian ethnohistory, 1830-present." *Published*

works: Editor, Southeastern Indians Since the Removal Era (University of Georgia Press, 1979); editor, Indian Leadership (Sunflower University Press, 1984); The Spirit and the Flesh: American Indian Androgyny and Male Sexuality (Beacon Press, 1986). Articles: Detour Down the Trail of Tears: Southern Indians and the Land (Southern Exposure, Fall, 1974); The Proposed Merger of Apaches with Eastern Cherokees in 1893 (Journal of Cherokee Studies, Spring, 1977); editor, Southeastern Indians Since the Removal Era (University of Georgia Press, 1979); editor, Indian Leadership (Sunflower University Press, 1984); author, The Spirit and the Flesh: Sexual Diversity in American Indian Culture (Beacon Press, 1986).book reviews on Southeastern Indians in: Ethnohistory, North Carolina Historical Review, American Indian Journal, & Journal of Southern History.

WILLIAMSON, BILLY TALAKO (Grey Eagle)
(Oklahoma Choctaw) 1948-
(film director/producer)
Born February 2, 1948, Okla. Education: CSU (Edmond, OK), BA, 1973; UCLA, MFA (Film), 1977. Principal occupation: Film director/producer. Address unknown. Affiliation: Director, I.T.I. Film & Video, Oklahoma City, OK, 1980-. Memberships: National Association of Amerian Indian Social Workers; Directors Guild of America; Screen Actors Guild; A.C.S. Awards, honors: 4 ADDY Awards; 6 Telly Awards. Interests: Zuni Pueblo.

WILLIAMSON, DIANA S.
(executive director)
Affiliation: Governor's Commission on Indian Affairs, 1885 Wooddale Blvd., Suite 111, Baton Rouge, LA 70806 (504) 925-4509.

WILLIAMSON, JIM (Chippewa) 1949-
(energy research management)
Born November 30, 1949, Williston, N.D. Education: Montana State University, BS, 1971; University of California, Berkeley, MS (Math), 1974. Principal occupation: Energy research management. Home address: 5025 Garton Rd., Castle Rock, CO 80104. Affiliation: Project Manager, U.S. Atomic Energy Commission, Oakland, CA (7 years); Director-International Solar Programs, Midwest Research Institute, Kansas City, MO (8 years); Associate Partner, Meridian Corporation, Alexandria, VA, 1988-; Manager, National Renewable Energy Laboratory, Washington, DC, 1989-. Community activities: Colorado Youth Soccer Association; Alexandria City Energy Commission; Colorado Alliance for Science. Memberships: American Indian Science & Engineering Society; Institute of Electrical & Electronic Engineers; American Solar Energy Society; American Management Association. Awards, honors: Project Achievement, King Abdul-Aziz Center for Science & Technology; Project Management, Atomic Energy Commission; Spacecraft Support Team Award, Energy Research & Development Administration. Interests: "Extensive international travel to energy research centers including an around-the-world trip in 1987. Raising horses in Virginia." Biographical sources: Who's Who in Colleges & Universities, 1971; American Indian Science & Engineering Society Mentor Calendar, 1983; Biographical Review in College Chemistry, Sept. 1990. Published works: Co-editor - Solar Cooling, April 1980; Solar Water Desalination, March 1981; Solar Storage, April, 1982; Solar Thermal Collectors, April 1983; Solar Buildings, May 1984; Solar for Remote Applications, April 1985 (all published by U.S. Dept. of Energy).

WILLIAMSON, LYNN
(museum curator)
Affiliation: The Institute for American Indian Studies, P.O. Box 1260, Washington, CT 06793 (203) 868-0518.

WILLIAMSON, VERNA (Pueblo)
(pueblo governor)
Affiliation: Isleta Pueblo Council, P.O. Box 317, Isleta, NM 87022 (505) 869-3111.

WILLIAMSON, WILLIAM P. (Choctaw)
(school principal)
Affiliation: Conehatta Elementary School, Route 1, Box 343, Conehatta, MS 39057 (601) 775-8254.

WILLIE, ELVIN (Paiute)
(Indian trading company owner)
Affiliation: Winter Moon Trading Co., P.O. Box 189, Schurz, NV 89427 (702) 773-2088.

WILLIE, FRITZ (Eskimo)
(village president)
Affiliation: Native Village of Eek, P.O. Box 87, Eek, AK 99579 (907) 233-2211.

WILLIE, JAMES Eskimo
(village president)
Affiliation: Napakiak Native Village, Napakiak, AK 99634 (907) 589-2227.

WILLIE, MARY ANN (Navajo)
(professor)
Education: University of Arizona, PhD, 1991. Affiliation: The American Indian Language Development Institute, American Indian Studies Program, The University of Arizona, Harvill Bldg., Rm 430, P.O. Box 210076, Tucson, AZ 85721 (520) 621-7108 Fax 621-7952. E-mail: aisp@email.arizona.edu. Interests: Navajo syntax; Athabaskan linguistics.

WILLIS, GEORGE "SHUKATA"
(executive director)
Affiliation: Executive Director, Indian Arts & Crafts Association, 4010 Carlisle NE, Suite C, Albuquerque, NM 87107 (505) 265-9149 Fax 265-8251. E-mail: info@iaca.com; Website: www.iaca.com.

WILLIS, NORMA (Navajo)
(financial aid director)
Affiliation: Navajo Community College, P.O. Box 580, Shiprock, NM 87420 (505) 368-5291.

WILLIS, ROY A.
(BIA agency supt.)
Affiliation: Wewoka Agency, BIA, P.O. Box 1060, Wewoka, OK 74884 (405) 257-6259 Fax 257-6748.

WILLMAN, ARTHUR
(director-SEARHC hospital)
Affiliation: Mt. Edgecumbe SEARHC Regional Health Hospital, 222 Tongass Dr., Sitka, AK 99835 (907) 966-8310.

WILLYARD, ANN
(Indian school principal)
Affiliation: T'iis Nazbas Community School, P.O. Box 102, Teecnospos, AZ 86514 (520) 656-3486 Fax 656-3252.

WILNOTY, JOHN JULIUS (Cherokee) 1940-
(stone carver)
Born April 10, 1940, Cherokee, N.C. Principal occupation: Stone carver. Home address: P.O. Box 517, Cherokee, NC 28719. Membership: The Qualla Indian Arts and Crafts Cooperative. Interests: "Building toys for children; rebuilding and designing machinery." Mr. Wilnoty's work is displayed at the Smithsonian Institution and the Museum of the American Indian.

WILSON, CATHERINE E. (Nez Perce)
(attorney)
Membership: Native American Bar Association; Native American Alumni Association of Dartmouth College.

WILSON, CHESLEY GOSEYUN (White Eagle)
(San Carlos Apache) 1932-
(musician, author, storyteller, actor, model)
Born July 31, 1932, Bylas, Ariz. Education: Carson City (NV) Community College (1 year). Principal occupation: Musician, author, storyteller, actor, model. Home address: 333 S. Alvernon Way, #60, Tucson, AZ 85711 (520) 881-4842. Affiliations: Comstock Silversmiths, Carson City, NV1960-80; artist, San Carlos Apache Tribe Cultural Center; Pinkerton Security Corp., Tucson, AZ, 1987-. Other professional posts: Various TV, film, stage and music productions; numerous television appearances over the years as free lance performer in the arts, music and dance; numerous live performances throughout the U.S. Military service: U.S. Army, 1950-52 (Corporal; Korea). Community activities: Tucson Indian Center - Powwow; president, Arco-Iris (Indian arts organization), Tucson, AZ. Memberships: San Carlos Apache Tribe; Gene Autry Western Heritage Museum (Los Angeles, CA). Awards, honors: 1st Place Award for silver work at the Tohono O'odham Spring Fair, 1987; 1989 Heritage Fellowship Award, National Endowment for the Arts-Folk Arts for his traditional Apache violin; An Apache violin made by Chesley is in the musical instruments collection of the Smithsonian Institution, Washington, DC; Chesley was commissioned by the Arizona Commission on the Arts to make a traditional Apache violin for the Governor's Arts Awards in March 1991; he played the role of "Singer of Songs" in the TNT production of Geronimo. Interests: Chesley is a singer, maker and player of traditional Apache violins and flutes which he handcrafts, woodcarver, storyteller and silversmith. He is the great-grandson of Aravaipa Apache Chief Eskiminzin and the great-great grandson of White Mountain Apache Chiefs Hashkedasila and Santo as well as the famous Chiricahua Apache Chief Cochise. He learned the arts of Apache musical instruments making from his uncles Albert Goseyun and Amos Gustina. He is considered an authority on Ga'an (Mountain Spirit or Crown Dancers) ceremonies. He regularly takes part in religious ceremonies on Apache reservations in Arizona as singer. Published work: When the Earth Was Like New, with CD & cassette tape (songs and stories of the Apache, with Ruth Longcor Harnisch Wilson; edited/published by Judith Cook Tucker; CD & cassette by World Music Press, Danbury, CT, 1994). Roles in Films: Buffalo Soldiers (role: Chief Nana), 1997; South of Heaven West of Hell (role: Chief Nathan), 1999.

WILSON, CLARA (Pomo)
(rancheria chairperson)
Affiliation: Robinson Rancheria, 1545 E. Hwy. 20, Nice, CA 95464 (707) 275-0527.

WILSON, DUFFY
(museum director)
Affiliation: Native American Centre for the Living Arts, Inc., 25 Rainbow Mall, Niagara Falls, NY 14303 (716) 284-2427.

WILSON, EDWARD P. (White bear)
(Southern Cheyenne)
(economic development specialist, administrator)
Born August 2, 1943, Clinton, Okla. Education: Haskell Institute, Northern Oklahoma College, Oklahoma State University. Principal occupation: economic development specialist, administrator. Home address: 1811 Shelby Court, Norman, OK 73071 (405) 329-4597. Affiliation: Chairman, Cheyenne-Arapaho Tribe, 1980-81. Other professional posts: Vice-president & secretary of Reserve Industrial Authority; director, Citizen Band Potawatomi's Tax Program; administrator, Sac & Fox Tribe of Missouri; director, National Indian Activities Association. Military service: U.S. Army Airborne, 1965-67, E-4 (Vietnam-Bronze Star & Purple Heart). Community activities: Parent Teachers Organization; Vietnam Era Veterans Organization; active in support of tribal ceremonial preservation; NAC (Church). Memberships: Board Member, Native Americans Veterans Services Access (model since mid 1993); board member, Oklahoma Indian Affairs Commission (appointed by Governor, 1992, re-appointed 1993 to full term. Interests: "Reservation/tribal economies; financing for individuals, groups, tribes, corporations; develop sources of capital to enhance development & employment; raise educational levels of groups or communities; develop entrepreneurship."

WILSON, ERIC
(BIA-Indian youth program specialist)
Affiliation: Office of Tribal Services, Bureau of Indian Affairs, Dept. of the Interior, MS-4603-MIB, 1849 C St., NW, Washington, DC 20240 (202) 3463.

WILSON, FRED
(school principal)
Affiliation: Phoenix Indian School, P.O. Box 10, Phoenix, AZ 85001 (602) 241-2126.

WILSON, GLORIA
(BIA field rep.)
Affiliation: Miami Field Office, Bureau of Indian Affairs, P.O. Box 391, Miami, OK 74355 (918) 542-2396 Fax 542-7202.

WILSON, JOHN
(school director)
Affiliation: Shiprock Reservation Dormitory,
P.O. Box 1180, Shiprock, NM 87420 (505) 368-5113.

WILSON, JOYCE
(Indian education program director)
Affiliation: Grand Traverse Band Tribal School, 2605
N. West Bay Shore Dr., Suttons Bay, MI 49682 (231)
271-7505 Fax 271-7510.

WILSON, KATHY B.
(BIA field rep.)
Addresses & Affiliations: Field Rep., Bureau of Indian
Affairs, Fairbanks Field Office, 101 12th Ave., Box 16,
Fairbanks, AK 99701 (907) 456-0522 Fax 456-0225.

WILSON, LARRY (Cree)
(member-board of directors)
Affiliation: Intertribal Christian Comunications, P.O. Box
3765, Station B, Winnipeg, Manitoba, Canada R2W
3R6 (204) 661-9333.

WILSON, LENA R. (Navajo)
(school principal)
Affiliation: Crystal Boarding School,
Navajo, NM 887328 (505) 777-2385.

WILSON, LINDA (*Poha Ma Hepi*)
(United Lumbee-Ute-Shoshoni)
(speaker, teacher, craftsperson)
Address: Unknown. *Principal occupation*: Speaker &
teacher of Native American ways; traditional Native
craftsperson. *Affiliations*: Secretary/treasurer, United
Lumbee Nation Eagle Clan, Arizona, 1995-; Mountain
Medicine Leather, Tubac, AZ, 1994-; Arivaca Merc.,
Arivaca, AZ, 1995-; freelance writer, Connection Newspaper, Arivaca, AZ, 1996-; Black Hawk Warrior Society Chief, United Lumbee Nation's Desert Sage Band,
San Bernardino, CA, 1990-94. *Community activities*:
Parks and Recreation Community Center (teacher of
Indian lore and crafts); Arivaca Library; Human Resources, Arivaca, AZ. *Memberships*: ATTRA Native
Seed/Search of Arizona, 1995-; Eagle Clan Growers
of Arivaca, AZ, 1994-. *Published works*: Vision of Reality (manuscript); many individual poetry pieces published in Arizona & California.

WILSON. NORMAN G. (Rosebud Sioux)
(former tribal president)
Affiliation: Rosebud Sioux Tribal Council, P.O.
Box 430, Rosebud, SD 57570 (605) 747-2381.

WILSON, RAYMOND 1945-
(professor of history)
Born April 11, 1945, New Kensington, Penna. *Education*: Fort Lewis College, BA, 1967; University of Nebraska, Omaha, MA, 1972; University of New Mexico,
PhD, 1977. *Principal occupation*: Professor of history,
Fort Hays State University, Hays, KS, 1979-. *Home
address*: 500 W. 30th, Hays, KS 67601. *Other professional post*: History instructor, Sam Houston State University, 1977-79. *Memberships*: Western History Association; Indian Rights Association; Kansas Council
for the Social Studies; Kansas Corral of the Westerners; Phi Alpha Theta; Pi Gamma Mu; Phi Delta Kappa;
Phi Kappa Phi. *Interests*: "My major area of study is
the American West with an emphasis on 19th & 20th
century American Indian history. I enjoy playing the
guitar, playing golf and traveling throughout western
America." *Published works*: Administrative History,
Canyon de Chelly National Monument, Arizona, co-
authored with David M. Brugge (U.S. Dept. of the In-
terior/National Park Service, 1976); Ohiyesa: Charles
A. Eastman, Santee Sioux (University of Illinois Press,
1983, paperback edition, 1999); Native Americans in
the Twentieth Century (Brigham Young University
Press, 1984), co-author, James S. Olson; Indian Lives:
Essays on 19th & 20th Century Native American Lead-
ers (University of New Mexico Press, 1985; Second
Edition, 1993), co-author, L.G. Moses; Kansas Land
(Gibbs M. Smith, Publisher, 1988; Second Edition,
1993), co-author, Thomas D. Isern.

WILSON, TERRY P.
(professor of Native American studies)
Affiliation: Professor, Native American Studies Department, University of California, Dwinelle Hall, Suite
3415, Berkeley, CA 94720 (510) 642-6717.

WILSON, TIMOTHY
(development director)
Affiliation: Sealaska Heritage Foundation, 1 Sealaska
Plaza, Suite 201, Juneau, AK 99801 (907) 463-4844.

WILSON, WILLIE
(Indian band chief)
Affiliation: Rainy River (Manitou) Indian Band, Box 450,
Emo, Ontario, Canada P0W 1E0 (807) 482-2479.

WINCE, DONALD R.
(school principal)
Affiliation: Manderson Day School,
Manderson, SD 57756 (605) 867-5433.

WINDCHIEF, ROBERTA DENNY
(*Black Hawk Woman*) (Assiniboine) 1941-
(health administrator)
Born January 16, 1941, Fort Belknap, Mont. *Education*: College of Great Falls, MT, BS; University of Oklahoma, MPH; University of Minnesota (Amb. Care).
Principal occupation: Health administrator. *Address*:
P.O. Box 118, Neola, UT 84053. *Affiliations*: Public
health educator, 1973-83, health systems administrator, 1983-85, Rocky Boy, MT; health system administrator, Fort Duchesne PHS Indian Health Center, Ft.
Duchesne, UT, 1985-. *Membership*: American College
of Health Care Professionals. *Interests*: Beading; traveling; intercultural communications.

WINDER, NATHAN W., JR. (*Strong Elk, Blue Fox*)
(Southern Ute) 1960-
(training coordinator)
Born October 2, 1960, Albuquerque, N.M. *Education*:
Stanford University, BA, 1983; University of Oregon,
School of Law, 1984-1985, 1986. *Principal occupa-
tion*: Training coordinator. *Address*: P.O. Box 227,
Ignacio, CO 81137 (800) 262-7623 (work). *Affiliations*:
Counselor, Nevada Urban Indians, Inc., Reno; counselor, grants/contracts administrator, Pyramid Lake
Paiute Tribal Council, Nixon, Nev., 1985-88; planning
director, Southern Ute Indian Tribe, Ignacio, CO, 1988-
; training coordinator, Colorado State University, Fort
Collins, CO, 1993-. *Other professional posts*: South-
ern Ute Indian Tribal Council; 190 Tribal Liaison Representative, U.S. Department of Commerce, Bureau
of Census, Economic Development Administrator;
Housing and Urban Development, Office of Indian Pro-
grams, Region VIII; *Community activities*: Colorado
Association of Non-Profit Organizations; Native Ameri-
can Church (vice president, Pyramid Lake chapter);
Save the Children Committee (chairman); chairman,
Southern Ute Indian Housing Authority, 1989-91 (term);
Leadership la Plata (participant); Southern Ute Lan-
guage & Cultural Committee; Community Development
Block Grant Administrator, Southern Ute Indian Tribe.
Membership: InterTribal Transportation Association
(Albuquerque Area Representative). *Awards, honors*:
Housing & Urban Development, Office of Indian Pro-
grams, Region VIII, Excellence in Maintenance; certi-
fied as an Economic Development Finance Profes-
sional by the National Development Council, Oct. 1990;
Merit Award from Southern Ute Indian Tribe recognizing dedication and commitment to tribe. *Interests*: Administration for Native Americans Grant Reader; Colorado Dept. of Corrections, Native American Spiritual
Facilitator; Western Colorado Grassroots Leadership
Development Program, 1992, Community Resources
Center, Denver, CO. "I am interested in traveling to
historical and spiritual areas across the Western Hemisphere. I would like to find an American Indian woman
who is interested and will participate in Sweat Lodge
ceremonies and spiritually support me and my family
during Sun Dance." *Published works*: Narrow Gauge
Scenic Road "HNTB Corp., Dec. 1993; Southern Ute
Transportation Study Update (Nurwoso, Dec. 1993).

WINDY BOY, ALVIN, SR. (Chippewa-Cree)
(tribal chairperson)
Affiliations: Rocky Boy's Reservation, Chippewa-Cree
Business Committee, RR 1, Box 544, Box Elder, MT
59521 (406) 395-4282. *Other professional posts*:
Chairperson of the following organizations: Montana-
Wyoming Area Indian Health Board, Rocky Boy's
Health Board, National Tribal Leaders Diabetes Com-
mittee, & National Tribal Diabetes Council; Vice-chair,
National Tribal Self-Governance Advisory Committee;
president, Montana-Wyoming Indian Stockgrowers
Assn; secretary, Intertribal Agriculture Council.

WINFREE, ROSA
(organization president)
Affiliation: Catching the Dream, 8200 Mountai Rd.,
NE, Albuqueruque, NM87110 (505) 262-2351.

WING, RANDALL E. (Gros Ventre)
(tribal council member)
Address & Affiliation: Fort Belknap Community
Council, P.O. Box 1019, Harlem, MT 59526.

WINN, ANGEL (Pit River)
(tribal council chairperson)
Affiliation: Pit River Tribal Council, 37014 Main St.,
Burney, CA 96013 (530) 335-5421.

WINNE, BRUCE (Spokane)
(former tribal chairperson)
Affiliation: Spokane Business Council, P.O.
Box 100, Wellpinit, WA 99040 (509) 258-4581.

WINTERS, CARL (Standing Rock Sioux)
(artist)
Born in S.D. Well-known Lakota artist, Mr. Winters has
won many awards for hist paintings on canvas, drums
& hides. His works are in numerous galleries & private collections worldwide, and a commissioned mural of his work is in the Denver International Airport,
CNN's "Across America" and Southwest Art Magazine
have featured him. "I strive to communicate the validity of the Indian experience," Wintes has said, "in hopes
that my work will serve as a vehicle for cross-cultural
understanding and respect."

WINTON, BEN (Yaqui)
(editor)
Address & Affiliation: Editor, Native Peoples Magazine,
5333 N. 7th St. #224C, Phoenix, AZ 85014 (602) 265-
4855 Fax 265-3113.

WIRICK, NOWETAH (*Nowetah*)
(Abenaki-Paugussett) 1947-
(owner/curator of store & museum; teacher,
craftswoman; Indian dancer; author)
Born February 21, 1947, New Haven, Conn. *Education*: High school. *Address & Affiliation*: Founder/owner/
curator, Nowetah's Indian Museum & Store (1969-
present), 2 Colegrove Rd. (Route 27), New Portland,
ME 04961-3821 (207) 628-4981. Website: www.maine
museums.org (then click on American Indian). *Other
professional posts*: "Currently teaching American Indian history, Indian dancing, and Indian crafts to school
children; as a museum curator - researching, cataloging & labeling museum pieces I purchase." *Memberships*: Connecticut Archaeological Society; Audubon;
National & International Wildlife Federation; Connecticut Herpetological Society; Maine Archives & Museums; Maine Tourism Association. *Awards, honors*:
Community Leaders & Noteworthy Americans Award,
1975-76, by the American Biographical Institute. *Interests*: "To start my museum and store, I traveled all
over the U.S. & Canada to make contacts with other
Indian people, so I could purchase direct from them
instead of buying crafts through big companies. I would
be called an amateur archaeologist. Of course my
major interest is naturally American Indian culture &
writing about it. But, another interest is herpetology
(giving nature talks on frogs, toads, salamanders,
snakes & an interest in birds. Have done nature studies in remote Ontario, Canada & Everglades Park in
Florida for Audubon & Wildlife (photographing & studies of habitat). Also, I teach classes on wild plants/
herbs as medicine & food. I'm a glass blower and make
glass animal figurines, hand weaving wool Indian rugs,
hand crafting Indian beadwork, porcupine quill jewelry,
fancy dream catchers, dolls, leather products, bone
jewelry, birchbark products; also, basketry, pottery,
etc." Mail order available. *Biographical source*:
"Nowetah's Indian Museum & Store," chapter in Profiles: Directory of Women Entrepreneurs (Wind River
Publishing, 1991). *Published works*: Writer of small
booklets with illustrations on past Indian life including,
"History of Indian Wampum" (shell beads), "Brain Tanning Hides & Pelts," How to Weave an Indian Rug,"
"The Drum," "The Sacred Pipe," The Ancient Wisdoms
& Knowledge of the Abenaki Indians"; The Medicine
Wheel; The Abenaki Indian Massacree with Fr. Rasle
at Narrantsauak (Aug. 23, 1724); Indian Legends,
Recipes & Names.

WIRTH, ROBERT, M.D.
(chief medical officer)
Affiliation: Indian Health Service, Tucson Office of Health Program Research & Development, 7900 South "J" Stock Rd., Tucson, AZ 85746 (520) 670-6600.

WISE OWL, CHIEF (Tuscarora)
(tribal chief)
Affiliation: Tuscarora Indian Tribe, Drowning Creek Reservation, Maxton, NC 28364 (919) 844-3827.

WITTSTOCK, LAURA WATERMAN (Seneca) 1937-
(administrator)
Born September 11, 1937, Cattaraugus Indian Reservation, N.Y. *Education*: University of Minnesota, BS. *Principal occupation*: Non-profit administrator. *Address*: Migizi Communications, Inc., 3123 E. Lake St., Suite 200, Minneapolis, MN 55406 (612) 721-6631. E-mail: wittstock@migizi.org. Website: www.migizi.org. *Affiliations*: independent education consultant, 1976-; Migizi Communications, Inc., Minneapolis, MN (director, curriculum project, 1985-99; president, 2000-present). *Past professional posts*: Editor, Legislative Review, 1971-73; executive director, American Indian Press Association, Washington, DC, 1975; associate director, Red School House, St. Paul, MN, 1975-77; director, Project Media, National Indian Education, Minneapolis, 1973-75; office manager, Native American Research Institute, Minneapolis, 1981; administrator, Heart of the Earth Survival School, Minneapolis, 1982-85. *Community activities*: Minnesota Governor's Job Training Council (vice chair, 1983-); Minneapolis Community Business Employment Alliance (vice chair, 1983-); United Way Planning & Priorities Committee (member); Christian Sharing Fund, Minneapolis-St. Paul Archdiocese (chair, 1981-86); Minnesota Women's Fund (executive committee, 1983-); Children's Theatre and School, Minneapolis (board member, 1984-). *Interests*: "Journalism, writing; American Indian education—program designer, evaluator, administrator; American Indian alcoholism and related problems; employment-program designer, board member, policy-maker; American Indian urban studies." *Biographical sources*: Let My People Know: American Indian Journalism, James E. and Sharon M. Murphy (University of Oklahoma Press, 1981); I Am the Fire of Time: The Voices of Native American Women, Jane Katz, editor (E.P. Dutton, 1977); Minnesota Women's Yearbook, 1978, 1984; Who's Who in the Midwest; Who's Who of American Women; Contemporary Native American Address (Brigham Young University, 1977; Women of Color poster series (St. Paul Public Schools, 1980). *Published works*: Indian Alcoholism in St. Paul, study with Michael Miller (University of Minnesota, 1981); Native American Women: Twilight of a Long Maidenhood, Comparative Perspectives of Third World Women, Beverly Lindsay, editor (Praeger, 1980); On Women's Rights for Native Peoples (Akwesasne Notes, 1975); editor, Indian Education, National Indian Education Association, 1973-74; The Federal Indian Relationship, Civil Rights Digest, Oct., 1973; editor, Legislative Review, 1971-73.

WOLF, CHIPA & RUBY (Chipa, Cherokee; Ruby, Rosebud Lakota)
(cultural affairs producer)
Affiliation & Address: Rolling Thunder Enterprise & The H.O.M.E. Organization, 34 Rolling Thunder Dr., Jasper, GA 30143 (770) 735-6275. E-mail: rte@rthunder. com; Website: www.rthunder.com. Producers of the annual Cherokee County Mother's Day Pow Wow in Canton, GA (The H.O.M.E. Organization); producers of special events - pow wows, rodeos, environmental expo's, wildlife rehab-animal handler; casting agents for motion pictures/television (Rolling Thunder Enterprise); Native American and Indigenous Peoples Talent Network. *Community activities*: School Program - dance, primitive skills, etc.; also H.O.M.E. Help Our Mother Earth (Stewardship Development Program). *Interests*: Bringing a better understanding between humans and those they share the Earth with. Wildlife rehabilitation and education - diversity programming.

WOLF, JAMES H. (Hidatsa)
(trading post owner)
Affiliation: Wolf's Trading Post, P.O. Box 877, New Town, ND 58763 (800) 735-6957; (701) 627-3393.

WOLF, LIZA
(Indian band chief)
Affiliation: Prophet River Indian Band, Box 3250, Fort Nelson, B.C., Canada V0C 1R0 (604) 774-1025.

WOLF, PATRICIA
(museum director)
Affiliation: Anchorage Museum of History & Art, 121 W. 7th Ave., Anchorage, AK 99501 (907) 343-4326.

WOLF EAGLE, ROBERT (Waccamaw)
(principal chief)
Affiliation: Waccamaw-Siouan Indians of South Carolina, Galivant's Ferry, SC 29544.

WOLFE, DAVID MICHAEL (*Wahya*) (Eastern Cherokee) 1948-
(administrator officer)
Born August 27, 1948, Huntington, W.V. *Education*: School of Visual Arts (New York, NY), 1968-70; Art Institute of Pittsburgh, 1978-79; LaRoche College, 1993-94. *Principal occupation*: Administrator officer; artist, historian, cultural consultant. *Home address*: 4-G Breeze Branch Ct., Timonium, MD 21093 (410) 683-8895; E—mail: aniwahya1@earthlink.net. *Affiliations*: Administrative officer, Maryland Dept. of Health & Mental Hygiene; American Indian artist & historian; cultural consultant; Kalahnu - Nuyagi Keetoowah Society; instructor of American Indian history, Goucher College, Towson, MD. *Past professional posts*: Young American Indian Council, New York, NY, 1968-70 (investigated racial & legal problems affecting urban & rural Indigenous communities nationally; participated in the establishment of the American Indian Community House in New York City; advocate for self-reliant & traditional governance); coordinator, American Indian Movement, South Eastern Community, Robeson County, NC, 1972-74 (Tuscarora Indian community of Robeson County); The American Indian Community House, New York, NY, 1974-76 (involved with the development of community based & oriented programs such as vocational counseling & programs, job training programs, cultural programs, summer youth-adult activities, and development of the Art Gallery); Veterans Administration Hospital, East Orange, NJ, 1976-77 (contract from New Jersey American Indian Center to the Visual Media Dept. - VA Hospital, 1978-79; consultant, Long Island Affirmative Action Program, Melville, NY (established Native American liaison within L.I.A.A.P); Snelling & Snelling, Melville, NY, 1980-82; Ewing Technical Designs, Melville, NY, 1982-83; Huntington Personnel, Huntington, NY, 1983-84; Wolfe Consultants, Long Island, NY & Pittsburgh, PA, 1984-91; cultural consultant to original indigenous communities of the Virginia's and Carolina's; co-operated in cross cultural-historic exchange with the Tirona of Columbia, S.A., 1997. *Exhibits* (for contemporary & traditional, fine art & illustration): Five Civilized Tribes Gallery/Museum, Muskogee, OK (awarded prize in graphics), 1990; U.S. Postage Stamp Commission - Regional Contest (awarded 2nd Place), 1991; Cherokee National Museum, Tahlequah, OK, annual Trail of Tears Art Show (awarded prize in graphics), 1992; among others. *Community activities*: Consultant/historian of Eastern Indigenous communities. *Memberships*: Eastern Cherokee Georgia Tribe - Echota Fire; Indian Nationalist Movement of North America; Nuyagi Keetoowah Society; Nuyagi Keetoowah Council (Chairperson). *Interests*: Traditional indigenous history/iconography. "As an advocate for the survival of traditional Indigenous people of the Americas since 1968, my primary involvement addresses social, legal and cultural concerns of rural and urban Indigenous communities. I have researched and documented a variety of previously ignored original eastern tribal histories and addresses their cultural, legal & social issues within public and secular forums. As an artist, I continue to produce contemporary wildlife, country and rural community life as well as, traditional Indigenous Iconography of the AniYunwiya. My mediums are oil and canvas, with additional work in Acrylic, water color and pen & ink." *Published works*: The People of the Red Bird; Daksi; Appalachian Mountain AniYunwiya (updated 2nd ed.); The Original Cherokee-Souian Alliance of the Central Appalachians and the Pocahontas Myth; People of the Red Bird, the Taeys Valley Cherokee; A Chronicle of the Cherokee and Souian Record of Ouscioto and Winginia; Daksi (in progress); Bibliographic-Iconographic Time Line of the Original People

with Cultural, Social, Traditional, Geologic, Scientific and Ethnologic Comparative Analysis.

WOLFE, JIM
(editor)
Affiliation: "The Muscogee Nation News," The Muscogee (Creek) Nation, P.O. Box 580, Okmulgee, OK 74447 (918) 756-8700.

WOLFEY, JEANETTE (Shoshone Bannock)
(attorney)
Address: P.O. Box 306, Fort Hall, ID 83203. *Membership*: American Bar Association (member, Committee on Opportunities for Minorities in the Profession).

WOMACK, JIM
(BIA-education)
Affiliation: Chief, Information Services, Office of Indian Education, Bureau of Indian Affairs, MS-3530-MIB, 1849 C St., NW, Washington, DC 20240 (202) 208-7111.

WONGAN, IVAN (Shoshoni)
(tribal chairperson)
Affiliation: Northwestern Band of Shoshoni Nation, Blackfoot, ID 83221 (208) 785-7401.

WOOD, ED (Ojibwe)
(board member)
Affiliation: Member, Board of Directors, Intertribal Christian Comunications, P.O. Box 3765, Station B, Winnipeg, Manitoba, Canada R2W 3R6 (204) 661-9333.

WOOD, MARGARET (Navajo/Seminole)
(craftsperson)
Affiliation: Owner, Native American Fashions, Inc., P.O. Box 44802, Phoenix, AZ 85064 (602) 956-7581. *Past affiliation*: Executive director, ATLATL, Phoenix, AZ.

WOOD, MARGUERITE L.
(museum manager)
Affiliation: Institute of American Indian Arts Museum, P.O. Box 20007, Cathedral Place, Santa Fe, NM 87504 (505) 988-6281.

WOOD, RON C.
(executive officer)
Affiliation: Navajo Area Office, Indian Health Service, P.O. Box 9020, Window Rock, AZ 86515 (520) 871-5813.

WOODALL, JOHN "LONE ELK" (Quachita)
(tribal chief)
Affiliation: Revised Quachita Indian Grand Council, Story, AR.

WOODALL, PHILIP, D.O.
(clinical director)
Affiliation: San Carlos PHS Indian Hospital, P.O. Box 208, San Carlos, AZ 85550 (520) 475-2371.

WOODARD, DON 1935-
(Indian arts & crafts dealer)
Born May 12, 1935, Gallup, N.M. *Education*: University of New Mexico, BA, 1958; Northern Arizona University, MA, 1968. *Principal occupation*: Indian arts & crafts dealer. *Address*: 120 S. Madison #122, Cortez, CO 81321 (303) 565-2563. *Affiliations*: Science teacher, Gallup High School Gallup, NM (7 years); owner, Woodard's Indian Arts, Gallup, N.M., 1952-72; owner, Don Woodard's Indian Trading Post, Cortez, CO, 1972-. *Other professional posts*: Land claims archaeologist for the Pueblos of Zia, Santa Anna, Jemez, Acoma & Laguna; group leader for Navajo Long Walk Re-enactment. *Community activities*: Director, Cortez Chamber of Commerce; Cortez Rotary Club (president, 1977 & 1978). *Memberships*: Inter-Tribal Indian Ceremonial, Gallup, N.M. (board member; program director; exhibition hall chairman); American Society of Appraisers; Indians Arts & Crafts Association (board member; ethics committee chairman). *Interests*: Indian arts & crafts; anthropology. *Biographical source*: Who's Who Worldwide, 1992-94.

WOODFIDE, SHERRY (Navajo)
(school principal)
Affiliation: Tse'll'Ahi' Community School, Drawer J, Crownpoint, NM 87313 (505) 786-5389.

WOODIS, PAMELA
(education program counselor)
Affiliation: Jicarilla Apache Higher Education Program, P.O. Box 507, Dulce, NM 87528 (505) 759-3615/6.

WOODRUFF, DOUGLAS (Quileute)
(tribal chairperson)
Affiliation: Quileute Tribal Council, P.O. Box 279, LaPush, WA 98350 (360) 374-6163.

WOODRUFF, RUSSELL, SR. (Quileute)
(tribal chairperson)
Affiliation: Quileute Tribal Council, P.O. Box 279, LaPush, WA 98350 (360) 374-6163.

WOODS, ANDREA R. (Te-Moak Western Shoshone)
(tribal chairperson)
Affiliation: Wells Indian Colony Band Council, P.O. Box 809, Wells, NV 89835 (702) 752-3045.

WOODS, DR. D.
(Indian education program director)
Affiliation: Adams-Arapahoe School District, Indian Education Program, 15700 East 1st Ave., Aurora, CO 8011 (303) 340-0510 ext. 302 Fax 343-7064.

WOODS, LONZO (Lower Creek Muscogee)
(tribal chairperson)
Affiliation: North Bay Clan of Lower Creek Muscogee Tribe, P.O. Box 687, Lynn Haven, FL 32444 (904) 265-3345.

WOODS, MURPHY
(director-Indian council)
Affiliation: Council of Native Americans of South Carolina, P.O. Box 21916, Columbia, SC 29221.

WOODS, WILBUR (Te-Moak Band of Western Shoshone)
(former tribal chairperson)
Affiliation: Elko Indian Colony Council, 511 Sunset St., Elko, NV 89803 (702) 738-8889.

WOODSIDE, SHERRY A. (Navajo)
(school principal)
Affiliation: Standing Rock Community School, P.O. Box 828, Crownpoint, NM 87313 (505) 786-5389 Fax 786-5635.

WOODWARD, BEATRICE L.
(school principal)
Affiliation: Baca Community School, P.O. Box 509, Prewitt, NM 87045 (505) 876-2310.

WOODWARD, DENNI DIANE
(Indian program adminsitrator)
Affiliation: American Indian & Alaska Native Program, Stanford University, Old Union Clubhouse #12, Stanford, CA 94305 (415) 725-6944 Fax 725-6900. E-mail: denni.woodward@forsyth.stanford.edu.

WOOSLEY, ANNE I.
(foundation director)
Affiliation: The Amerind Foundation, Inc., P.O. Box 400, Dragoon, AZ 85609 (520) 586-3666 Fax 586-3667.

WORDEMAN, JANICE
(school principal)
Affiliation: Promise Day School, Mobridge, SD 57601 (605) 733-2148.

WORKMAN DR. WILLIAM B.
(professor of anthropology)
Affiliation: Dept. of Anthropology, University of Alaska, 3211 Providence Dr., Anchorage, AK 99508 (907) 786-6840 Fax 786-6850. *Interests*: Archaeology and traditional cultures of northwest North America. E-mail: afwbw@uaa.alaska.edu.

WORKS, DAVID
(center chairperson)
Affiliation: American Indian Center for Central California, P.O. Box 607, 32980 Auberry Rd., Auberry, CA 93602 (209) 855-2705 Fax 855-2695.

WRIGHT, ALLEN (Pomo)
(rancheria chairperson)
Affiliation: Sherwood Valley Rancheria, 190 Sherwood Hill Dr., Willits, CA 95490 (707) 459-9690.

WRIGHT, BARTON A. 1920-
(museum curator-archaeologist; author-artist)
Born December 21, 1920, Bisbee, Ariz. *Education*: University of Arizona, BA, 1952, MA, 1954. *Principal occupation*: Museum curator-archaeologist; author-artist. *Home address*: 4143 W. Gelding Dr., Phoenix, AZ 85023 (602) 843-1362. *Affiliations*: Curator, assistant director, Museum of Northern Arizona, Flagstaff, AZ, 1955-77; scientific director, San Diego Museum of Man, 1978-82. *Other professional posts*: Archaeologist, Town Creek Indian Mound State Park, NC; artist/archaeologist, Amerind Foundation, Dragoon, AZ; artist, Arizona State Museum, Tucson, AZ. *Military service*: U.S. Army, 1943-45. *Community activities*: Indian Arts and Crafts Association (board of directors); Indian Art Foundation, Arizona State Rep. to W. Regional Museum; Indian Arts & Crafts Judge, Hopi Cultural Values Committee. *Memberships*: American Association of Museum (sr. accreditor); Arizona-Nevada Academy of Science (charter member); National Geographic Society (consultant); Western Regional History Association; Arizona Historical Association. *Awards, honors*: 1985 Southeastern Library Association, Southern Books Competition Award; 1986 Border Regional Library Association, Southwest Book Award; 1986 Anisfield-Wolf Award; all for Kachinas: A Hopi Artist's Documentary, 1973, and Kachinas of the Zuni, 1986. *Interests*: Kachinas of the Hopi, Zuni; material culture and religion of the Hopi; Indian arts and crafts; hallmarks of the Southwest. *Biographical sources*: Who's Who in American Art; Who's Who in the West; Men of Achievement; International Who's Who in American Art; Contemporary Authors. *Published works*: Kachinas: A Hopi Artist's Documentary (Northland Press, 1973); Kachinas: The Barry Goldwater Collection at the Heard Museum (Northland Press, 1975); Unchanging Hopi (Northland Press, 1975); Pueblo Shields from the Fred Harvey Collection (Northland Press, 1976); Hopi Kachina: The Complete Guide to Collecting Kachina Dolls (Northland Press, 1977); Hopi Material Culture (Northland Press, 1979); The Year of the Hopi, Paintings & Photographs by Joseph Mora, 1904-1906 (Smithsonian Institution, 1979); Kachinas of the Zuni (Northland Press, 1986); Pueblo Cultures (E.J. Brill, 1986); The Hopi Photographs of Kate Cory, 1905-12 (University of New Mexico Press, 1986); Patterns and Sources of Zuni Kachinas (Harmsgen, Tanner & Wright, 1987); The Mythic World of the Zuni (University of New Mexico Press, 1988); Who Made It? Trademarks of the Southwest (Schiffer Press, 1988); Hopi Clowns (Northland Publishing, 1994).

WRIGHT, BEVERLY M. (*Soaring Feather*)
(Wampanoag Aquinnah)
(tribal chairperson)
Born on Martha's Vineyard Island, Mass. Education: New York School of Design, 1962-65; Continuing Education, University of Massachusetts. *Home address*: 146 Lighthouse Rd., Aquinnah, MA 02535 (508) 645-2018 Fax 645-2026. *Office address*: Wampanoag Tribe of Gay Head/Aquinnah, 20 Black Brook Rd., Aquinnah, MA 02535 (508) 645-9265 Fax 645-3790. E-mail: chairprs@wampanoagtribe.net. *Affiliations*: Chairperson, Wampanoag Tribe of Gay Head/Aquinnah, Aquinnah, MA, 1991-present. *Past professional posts*: Owner of "The Wright Place" Restaurant, 1994-2001; administrative assistant, Dukes County Commissioners, 1982-91; treasurer, Town of Aquinnah, 1975-1982; office manager, Elder Services of Cape Cod & Islands, 1976-82. *Memberships*: United South & Eastern Tribes (USET) (vice-president & secretary); National Congress of American Indians (board member); BIA tribal Self-Govenance Advisory Council (board member); IHS Tribal Self-Governance Advisory Council (board member); Native Nations Institute (NNI), University of Arizona, Morris Udall Center (board member); Massachusetts Commission on Indian Affairs (board member); Female Tribal Leaders (board member); All Islands Selectmen Association (tribal representative); Harvard Project on American Indian Economic Development (board member); NCAI Chairman's Health Information Task Force (board member).

WRIGHT, BOBBY (Chippewa-Cree) 1950-
(research associate, assistant professor)
Born December 28, 1950, Tacoma, Wash. *Education*: University of San Francisco, BS, 1973; SUNY, Buffalo, MA, 1977; Montana State University, Bozeman,

EdD, 1985. *Principal occupation*: Research associate, assistant professor. *Address*: Resides in State College, PA (814) 865-6346 (office). *Affiliations*: Director, Montana State University, Bozeman, 1983-89; faculty, Penn State University, University Park, 1990-. *Memberships*: National Indian Education Association; American Society for Ethnohistory. *Awards, honors*: 1986 Distinguished Dissertation Award, Association for the Study of Higher Education; 1986 Montana State University Endowment and Alumni Foundation Award for Outstanding Graduate Performance.

WRIGHT, CATHY L.
(museum curator/director)
Affiliation: The Taylor Museum for Southwestern Studies, Colorado Springs Fine Arts Center, 30 West Dale St., Colorado Springs, CO 80903 (303) 634-5581.

WRIGHT, DEB (Ponca)
(former tribal chairperson)
Affiliation: Ponca Tribe of Nebraska, P.O. Box 288, Niobrara, NE 66760 (402) 857-3391.

WRIGHT, LEE
(curator)
Affiliation: Shawnee Methodist Mission, 3403 West 53rd, Shawnee Mission, KS 66205 (913) 262-0867.

WRIGHT, LAWRENCE
(school principal)
Affiliation: Wide Ruins Boarding School, P.O. Box 309, Chambers, AZ 86502 (520) 652-3251.

WRIGHT, MERVIN, JR. (Paiute)
(tribal chairperson)
Affiliation: Pyramid Lake Paiute Tribal Council, P.O. Box 256, Nixon, NV 89424 (702) 574-1000.

WRIGHT, MIKE
(editor)
Affiliation: "Nishnawbe News," Organization of North American Indian Students, Northern Michigan University, 140 University Center, Marquette, MI 49855.

WRIGHT, ROBIN K. 1949-
(curator & professor)
Born September 10, 1949, Mankato, Minn. *Education*: University of Washington, BA, 1971, MA, 1977, PhD (Art History), 1985. *Principal occupation*: Curator & professor. *Address & Affiliation*: Curator of Native American Art (1985-), Burke Museum, Box 353010, University of Washington, Seattle, WA 98195 (206) 543-5595 Fax 685-3039; E-mail: wright@u.washington.edu. *Other professional post*: Professor, School of Art, University of Washington, Seattle, 1990-present; director, Bill Holm Center for the Study of Northwest Coast Art. *Memberships*: American Association of Museums; College Art Association; Native American Art Studies Association (board member, 1989-93; president, 1999-2003). *Awards, honors*: Phi Beta Kappa. *Interests*: Northwest Coast Indian art: Haida art, specifically Haida argillite carving, and Washington State Native art. Travel to museums to do research in Canada, Europe and the U.S. *Published works*: A Time of Gathering - An Intertribal Welcome: Statements from 36 Washington Tribes, with Roberta Haines (eds.) (Burke Museum 1990); A Time for Gathering: Native Heritage in Washington State (Burke Museum & University of Washington Press, 1991); Northern Haida Master Carvers (University of Washington Press, 2001); and numerous articles in American Indian Art Magazine, and others.

WRIGHT, VICTORIA
(legislative associate)
Affiliation: National Congress of American Indians (NCAI), 1301 Connecticut Ave. NW, #200, Washington, DC 20036 (202) 466-7767 Fax 466-7797

WYACO, VIRGIL
(college chairperson)
Affiliation: Southwestern Indian Polytechnic Institute, P.O. Box 10146, Albuquerque, NM 87184 (505) 474-3197.

WYATT, BEVERLY J.
(museum curator)
Affiliation: Chickasaw Council House Museum, P.O. Box 717, Tishomingo, OK 73460 (405) 371-3351.

WYATT, CHARLES D.
(site supt.)
Affiliation: Hubbell Trading Post - National Historic Site, P.O. Box 150, Ganado, AZ 86505 (602) 755-3475.

WYATT, JANE E. (*Ishilee*) (Chuckchansi) 1943-
(tribal chairperson)
Born December 21, 1943, Madera, Calif. *Education*: Galen College (Fresno, CA), RDA, 1987. *Principal occupation*: Tribal chairperson. *Home adress*: P.O. Box 1661, Coarsegold, CA 93614 (559) 658-3951 Fax 822-3694 (office). *Affiliation*: Chairperson, Provisional Tribal Council, Picayune Rancheria, Coarsegold, CA, 1983-. *Other professional posts*: BIA Policy Task Force Representative; Sierra Tribal Consortium (board member); California Indian Manpower Co. (board member); CRIHB Representative; Central Valley Indian Health, Inc. (member-life); Table Mountain Rancheria (Special Player-life). *Community activities*: Master teacher, Chuckchansi Language; basket weaving classes; basket material gathering classes.

WYATT, KATHIE (Washoe)
(former tribal chairperson)
Affiliation: Dresslerville Indian Colony Community Council, 1585 Watasheamu Rd., Gardnerville, NV 89410 (702) 883-1446.

WYCKOFF, DON
(instructor-Native American studies)
Affiliation: Native American Studies Program, University of Oklahoma, 455 W. Lindsey, Rm. 804, Norman, OK 73019 (405) 325-2312.

WYNECOOP, JOSEPH A. (Spokane) 1919-
(teacher/librarian, Air Force Officer-intelligence)
Born March 22, 1919, Reardan, Wash. *Education*: Eastern Washington University, BA, 1946; Glendale University College of Law, BSL, 1971. *Principal occupation*: Manager, aerospace-information support. *Home address*: 2500 Honolulu Ave. Apt. 127, Montrose, CA 91020 (818) 248-7311. *Affiliation*: Manager, Jet Propulsion Laboratory, California Institute of Technology, Pasadena, 1968-81. *Other professional posts*: Library manager; Teacher, Oakland, CA secondary schools; Air Intelligence School, Defense Intelligence School. *Military service*: U.S. Air Force, 1942-68 (Lt. Colonel, retired; Air Force Outstanding Unit Award; Medal for Humane Action; Joint Chiefs of Staff Commendation Medal; Air Force Commendation Medal; Alexander the Great Medal (Greece); Greek Joint Chiefs Letter of Commendation). *Community activities*: Masonic Lodge, Scottish Rite, Shrine; All American Indian Celebration Corporation (vice president & director, 1969-70); Governor's (CA) Indian Assistance Project (representative, 1969-74); American Indian Enterprise (vice president, 1969-75); Pacific Northwest Indian Center (financial commissioner, 1971-73); Glendale Kiwanis, 1981-89; Glendale Chamber of Commerce, 1983-90; Sons of the Revolution, 1987-; director, Los Angeles, CA-Berlin, Germany Sister City Association, 1993-. *Memberships*: Indian Scholarship Fund Association (director and vice president, 1969-75); Urban Indian Development Association (vice president, 1969-75); Retired Officers Association; Air Force Association; National Congress of American Indians (member of board, Indian Scholarship Committee, 1977-); Aircraft Owners & Pilots Association. *Awards, Honors*: Outstanding Actor, Outstanding Speaker/Athletic Award, Air Force University; life membership in the Cal Tech Faculty Club "The Athenium;" Scotland Yard, London England - Honorary Member, Lynn Athletic Club, 1951-; Fellowship, British-American Comrades, sponsored by Gen. Eisenhower-Prime Minister Churchill; and The Honorable Artillery Co. (The Oldest active artillery company in Western Europe) and commanded by my ancestor in British Colonies "Sgt./Major/General, Thomas Dudley, Governor of Colonial Maryland, member 1951-. *Interests*: Private pilot; genealogy - "using my intelligence training, I was able to trace my Indian ancestors to Chief Kee Kee Nouskeen or Seoutkin (missionary name, Edwards) and my white ancestors back to the American Revolution, the Royals & to Emperor Charlemagne." *Biographical sources*: Who's Who in California, 1979; Who's Who in Library & Information Science. *Published works*: Co-author, editor of several scientific works by scientists & physicists at the Jet Propulsion Laboratory. "I was manager of the Tech-

nical Information & Documentation Division Support Section. My section edited & approved all books developed by scientific personnel."

WYNN, MARY
(attorney)
Affiliation: Yankton Sioux Tribe, P.O. Box 248, Marty, SD 57361 (509) 422-6267

WYNN, SAM
(executive director)
Affiliation: Native American International Caucus, United Methodist Church, 1503 Kimberly Rd., New Bern, NC 28562 (919) 424-0894. There are about 150 Native American congregations.

WYNNE, BRUCE (Spokane)
(former tribal chairperson)
Affiliation: Spokane Business Council, P.O. Box 100, Wellpinit, WA 99040 (509) 258-4581.

WYRICK, JAN
(museum director)
Affiliation: Seminole Nation Museum, 524 S. Wewoka Ave., Box 1532, Wewoka, OK 74880 (405) 257-5580.

WYSS, DIANNE
(organization director)
Affiliation: Indian Nation Network & Electronic Bulletin Board, Honor, Inc., Washington, DC (202) 338-7851.

Y

YALLUP, WILFORD (Yakima)
(former tribal chairperson)
Affiliation: Yakima Tribal Council, P.O. Box 151, Toppenish, WA 98948 (509) 865-5121.

YALLUP, WILLIAM "BILL" (Yakima)
(former tribal chairperson)
Affiliation: Yakima Tribal Council, P.O. Box 151, Toppenish, WA 98948 (509) 865-5121.

YARBROUGH, MARA
(librarian)
Affiliations: Laboratory of Anthropology Library, Museum of Indian Arts & Culture P.O. Box 2087, 708 Camino Lejo, Santa Fe, NM 87504 (505) 827-6344 Fax 827-6497.

YARDLEY, LINDA
(organization director)
Affiliation: National Indian Health Board, Campus Box A049, 4200 E. 9th Ave., Denver, CO 80262 (303) 315-5598.

YATES, HERBERT (Nambe Pueblo)
(former pueblo governor)
Affiliation: Nambe Pueblo Council, Rte. 1, Box 117-BB, Santa Fe, NM 87501 (505) 455-2036.

YATSATTIE, CLYDE
(administrative officer)
Affiliation: Zuni PHS Indian Hospital, P.O. Box 467, Zuni, NM 87327 (505) 782-4431.

YAZZI, ALBERT (Navajo)
(school principal)
Affiliation: Wide Ruins Boarding School, P.O. Box 309, Chambers, AZ 86502 (520) 652-3251 Fax 652-3252.

YAZZI, ANGEY (Navajo)
(BIA special education coordinator)
Affiliation: Fort Defiance Agency, Bureau of Indian Affairs, P.O. Box 110, Fort Defiance, AZ 86504 (602) 729-7251 Fax 729-7286.

YAZZI, BRUCE (Navajo)
(organization president)
Affiliation: Native American Business Coalition, 6025 N. Smokerise, Flagstaff, AZ 86004 (520) 526-0035.

YAZZIE, CALVIN (Navajo)
(school chairperson)
Affiliation: Nazlini Boarding School, Ganado, AZ 86505 (520) 755-6125.

YAZZIE, DOROTHY R. (Navajo)
(school director)
Affiliation: Black Mesa Community School, Star Route 1, Box 215, Rough Rock, AZ 86510 (520) 674-3632.

YAZZI, DUANE (Navajo)
(college chairperson)
Affiliation: Southwestern Indian Polytechnic Institute, P.O. Box 10146, Albuquerque, NM 87184 (505) 897-5347.

YAZZIE, EDWARD D. (Navajo)
(school chairperson)
Affiliation: Holbrook Dormitory, P.O. Box 758, Holbrook, AZ 86025 (520) 524-6222.

YAZZIE, ETHELOU (Navajo)
(school chairperson)
Affiliation: Cottonwood Day School, Navajo Route 4, Chinle, AZ 86503 (520) 725-3256 Fax 725-3255.

YAZZI, HERBERT (Navajo)
(attorney)
Address: Resides in Arizona. *Membership*: Navajo Nation Bar Association (president); Native American Bar Association.

YAZZI, JIMMIE (Navajo)
(school chairperson)
Affiliation: Bread Springs Day School, P.O. Box 1117, Gallup, NM 87305 (505) 778-5665.

YAZZI, LORENZO (Navajo)
(school chairperson)
Affiliation: Rocky Ridge Boarding School, P.O. Box 299, Kykotsmovi, AZ 86039 (520) 725-3415.

YAZZI, MELANIE (Navajo)
(assistant professor)
Education: University of Colorado, MFA, 1993. *Affiliation*: School of Art, c/o American Indian Studies Program, The University of Arizona, Harvill Bldg., Rm 430, P.O. Box 210076, Tucson, AZ 85721 (520) 621-7108 Fax 621-7952. E-mail: aisp@email.arizona.edu. *Interests*: Special focus in printmaking and contemporary indigenous artists.

YAZZIE, PAUL J. (Navajo)
(school principal)
Affiliation: Cove Day School, P.O. Box 190, Shiprock, NM 87420 (602) 653-4457.

YAZZI, RENA M. (Navajo)
(school principal)
Affiliation: Aneth Community School, P.O. Box 600, Montezuma Creek, UT 84534 (801) 651-3271.

YAZZIE, ROSEMARY (Navajo)
(vice president-board of directors)
Affiliation: National Indian Youth Council, 318 Elm, SE, Albuquerque, NM 87102.

YAZZI, STANLEY (Navajo)
(school chairperson)
Affiliation: Richfield Dormitory, P.O. Box 638, Richfield, UT 84701 (801) 896-5101.

YAZZIE, TOMMIE C. (Navajo)
(school director)
Affiliation: Leupp Boarding School, P.O. Box HC-61, Winslow, AZ 86047 (520) 686-6211.

YAZZIE-BALLENGER, VIRGINIA (Navajo)
(designer)
Affiliation: Owner, American Indian Fashions, 2407 E. Boyd, 11-B, Gallup, NM 87301 (505) 722-6837; (800) 377-6837. *Product*: "Navajo Spirit Southwestern Wear," women's clothing.

YAZZIE-KING, ELA M. (Navajo) 1955-
(rehabilitation specialist/counselor)
Born May 31m 1955, Fort Defiance, Ariz. *Education*: Virginia Intermount College (Bristol), BA, 1977; University of New Mexico, MA (Rehabilitation Counseling), 1981. *Principal occupation*: Rehabilitation counselor. *Address*: Unknown. *Affiliations*: Director, Spinal Cord Injury Follow-up Project, 1979-81; director, IHS Medical Management Project, 1981-82; director, Learn to Earn, Ltd., 1983-84; director, Navajo Undergradu-

ate Rehabilitation Training Project, 1984-86; Navajo Evaluation of Existing Disability Services, 1986-87; executive director, Chinle Valley School for Exceptional Children, 1988-90; coordinator, Indian Children's Program, Utah State University, Logan, UT, 1991-. *Professional presentations*: Multi-Cultural Successes: The Navajo Nation," at the National Association of Developmental Disabilities Councils, Orlando, FL, 1992; "Beyond Rhetoric-A Blueprint for Action" & "A Native American Perspective on Disability & Self-Determination," at the ADD Commissioner's Institute on Cultural Diversity, Washington, DC, 1992 & 1993; "Self-Determination-The Road to Personal Freedom," at NM Protection & Advocacy System Mini Conference, Albuquerque, 1993. *Other professional posts*: Adjunct Facility with Navajo Community College, 1984-87 (produced: "Rehabilitation Practicum Manual," 1984; "Job Development/Job Placement Manual," 1985; "Navajo Evaluation of Existing Disability Research Study" (unpublished), 1987. *Community activites*: Assistive technology; Independent Living Center. *Advisory/Council Membership*: Chairperson, Navajo Nation Advisory Council on the Handi-Capable, 1979-93; Native American Research & Training Center, Northern Arizona University, Flagstaff (advisory council, 1990-93; advisory board, 1987-); New Mexico Independent Living Advisory Council, 1990-; advisory council, American Indians with Disabilities Public Awareness Campaign, Anchorage, AK, 1991-93; Administration on Developmental Disabilities, Multi-Cultural Task Force, Washington, DC, 1992-; Developmental; Disabilities Advisory Council, Phoenix, AZ, 1992-95; National Council on Disabilities; Develoment Disabilities Advisory Council; Administration on Development Disabilities Advisory Council; Administration on Developmental Disabilities-Multi-Cultural Task Force; New Mexico Independent Living Advisory Council. *Awards, honors*: "Citizen of the Year," Arizona Governor's Council on Disabilities, Phoenix, 1985; "Outstanding Volunteer," Navajo Nation Council on the Handicapped, 1986.

YEAHQUO, EARL (Kiowa)
(tribal chairperson)
Affiliation: Kiowa Tribe, P.O. Box 369, Carnegie, OK 73015 (580) 654-2300 Fax 654-2188.

YELLOW ROBE, WILLIAM S., JR. (Assiniboine)
1960-
(playwright, director, actor, lecturer, instructor)
Born February 2, 1960, Poplar, MT. *Education*: High school. P*rincipal occupation*: Playwright, director, actor, lecturer, instructor. *Address*: Resides in Montana. *Affiliation*: Former literary manager of Seattle Group Theater; regional vice president, Literary Managers & Dramaturgs of America, New York, NY, 1990-91. *Works*: Plays: "The Council," for Honolulu Theater for Youth, 1992; "Taking Aunty to the Wake, Northern Montana College, Havre, MT, 1991; "The Independence of Eddie Rose," The Seattle Group Theater, 1990. *Directing*: "The Council," & "The Magic Flute," an opera, San Antonio (TX) Festival. *Acting*: Norman Bulanski, "The Boys Next Door"; and Donny Dubrow, "American Buffalo." *Lecturer*: 'Watermark reading series', University of Washington, Seattle; '10th Anniversary', New World Theater, University of Mass. *Instructor*: Playwrighting and writing, Fort Peck Community College, Poplar, MT; acting, St. Paul (MN) Central High School. *Community activities*: Advisory Board, Red Eagle Soaring Theater, Seattle, WA. *Membership*: Dramatists Guild of America (associate member, 1988-). *Awards, honors*: Jerome Fellowship, 1989; Princess Grace Fellowship, 1989; NEA Playwright's Fellowship, 1991; James Baldwin Honorable Mention. *Published works*: Sneaky, a one-act play, "SlantSix" an anthology (New Rivers Press, 1990); The Burning of Uncle, a short story, "Dancing on the Rim of the World," an anthology (University of Arizona Press, 1991).

YELLOWFAT, GAYLEEN
(elementary school principal)
Affiliation: Standing Rock Community School, P.O. Box 377, Fort Yates, ND 58538 (701) 854-3865 Fax 854-3461.

YELLOWHAWK, SANDRA
(health director)
Affiliation: Peach Springs PHS Indian Health Center, Peach Springs, AZ 86434 (520) 769-2204.

YELLOWTAIL, WILLIAM P. (Crow)
(EPA administrator)
Born in Crow Agency, Mont. *Education*: Dartmouth College, BA, 1971. *Principal occupation*: EPA administrator. *Home Address*: Resides in Colorado *Affiliations*: Wyoming State Senator, 1985-1993 (chairman-State Judiciary Committee and the Legislature's Environmental Quality Council); administrator, EPA Region 8, Denver, CO, 1994-. *Membership*: Native American Alumni Association of Dartmouth College (national steering committee).

YEPA, SHARON F.
(BIA agency supt.)
Affiliation: Spokane Agency, Bureau of Indian Affairs, P.O. Box 389, Wellpinit, WA 99040 (509) 258-4561.

YONGE, SANDRA JEFFERSON (Paiute)
(tribal chairperson)
Affiliation: Lone Pine Reservation, P.O. Box 747, Lone Pine, CA 93545 (619) 876-5414.

YORK, KEN
(Indian school principal)
Affiliation: Bogue Chitto Elementary School, Route 2, Box 274, Philadelphia, MS 39350 (601) 656-8611 Fax 656-8648.

YORK, LAURENE L.
(trading post owner)
Address & Affiliation: Owner, Mohawk Trading Post, 874 Mohawk Trail, Shelburne, MA 01370 (413) 625-2412 Fax 625-8134. E-mail: lyork@mohawk-trading-post.com. Web site: www.mohawk-trading-post.com. *Membership*: Indian Arts & Crafts Association.

YORK, STEVE
(BIA agency supt.)
Affiliation: Horton Agency, BIA, P.O. Box 31, Horton, KS 66439 (913) 486-2161 Fax 486-2515.

YOUCKTON, DAVID (Chehalis)
(tribal chairperson)
Affiliation: Chehalis Community Council, P.O. Box 536, Oakville, WA 98568 (360) 273-5911.

YOUNG, DAVID (Taos Pueblo)
(poet)
Address: P.O. Box 7523, Boulder, CO 80306 (303) 939-9021.

YOUNG, DORA (Sac & Fox of Oklahoma)
(principal chief)
Affiliation: Sac & Fox Business Committee, Rt. 2, Box 246, Stroud, OK 74079 (918) 968-3526.

YOUNG, ED 1906-
(Indian arts & crafts trader)
Born April 14, 1906, New York, N.Y. *Education*: City College of New York, BA, 1930. *Principal occupation*: Indian arts & crafts trader. *Address & Affiliation*: President, The Ed Young's, Inc., 2323 Krogh Ct. NW, Albuquerque, NM 87104-2508 (505) 864-1242 (1947-). *Interests*: "Trading & traveling the U.S." *Biographical source*: Indian Jewlery - Fact or Fantasy by Marsha Lund.

YOUNG, JOE
(associate justice)
Affiliation: Prairie Band Potawatomi Nation Appelate Court, 15498 K Rd., Mayetta, KS 66509 (866) 966-2242 or (785) 966-2242 Fax 966-2662. E-mail: tribalcourt@pbpnation.org.

YOUNG, JOANN
(BIA agency supt.)
Affiliation: Rosebud Agency, Bureau of Indian Affairs, P.O. Box 550, Rosebud, SD 57570 (605) 747-2224 Fax 747-2805.

YOUNG, PAUL
(BIA field rep.)
Affiliation: Eastern Nevada Field Office, Bureau of Indian Affairs, 1555 Shoshone Cir., Elko, NV 89801 (775) 738-0569 Fax 738-4710.

YOUNG, ROBERTA M. (Puyallup)
(former tribal chairperson)
Affiliation: Puyallup Tribal Council, 2002 East 28th St., Tacoma, WA 98404 (206) 597-6200.

YOUNG, THOMAS
(librarian)
Affiliation: Roberta Campbell Lawson Indian Library, Philbrook Museum of Art, P.O. Box 52510, Tulsa, OK 74125 (918) 748-5306.

YOUNG, WATHENE (Cherokee/Delaware)
(member-board of directors)
Affiliation: Member-Board of Directors, Association on American Indian Affairs, P.O. Box 268, Tekakwitha Complex Agency Rd. 7, Sisseton, SD 57262 (605) 698-3998.

YOUNG BEAR, RAY (Mesquakie)
(poet, writer)
Address: RR 2 Box 100-C, Tama, IA 52339 (515) 484-4678.

YOUNG MAN, ALFRED (*Eagle Chief*) (Cree) 1948-
(professor & chair of Native American studies)
Born in 1948, Browning, Montana on the Blackfeet Indian Reservation. Paternal and maternal Cree gandparent's were from the Duck Lake Reserve in Saskatchewan, the Erminiskin and Cold Lake reserves in Alberta, respectively. *Education*: Slade School of Fine Arts, University of London, England, BA, 1972; University of Montana, MA, 1974; Rutgers University, PhD (Anthropology), 1997. His thesis has been called "a history, an economic treatise, a political exercise, and cultural disquisition" - entitled, "The Socialization and Art-Politics of Native Art." *Principal occupation*: Professor & Chair of Native American Studies. *Address & Affiliation*: Professor & Chair, Native American Studies Dept., University of Lethbridge, 4401 University Dr., Lethbridge, Alberta, Can T1K 3M4 (403) 329-2635 (1977-). *Other professional posts*: Art instructor and reading specialist among his own people on the Chippewa-Cree reservation, Rocky Boy, and later on the Blackfeet reservation. In addition, he worked as media/TV specialist at Flathead Valley Community College in Kalispell, MT. He is writing a doctoral thesis on North American Indian Art for Rutgers University. *Memberships*: Member of the Chippewa/Cree Rocky Boy Indian Reservation, Box Elder, MT; Society of Canadian Artists of Native Ancestry, Dept of Indian & Northern Development, Ottawa, Ontario. *Awards, honors*: Numerous scholarships, fellowships, awards, contracts. *Biographical sources*: The Sweetgrass Lives On: 50 Contemporary North American Indian Artists, by Jamake Highwater (Lippincott & Crowell, 1980); Native Writers Circle of the Americas - A Directory 1993; American Indian Quarterly, Vol. 17, No. 4, by University of Nebraska Press, Fall 1993; *Published works*: "Token and Taboo - Academia vs. Native Art," (article) in Fuse Magazine, Vol. II, No. 6 (July, 1988); "Issues and Trends in Contemporary Indian Art," (article) in Parallelogram, Vol. 3, No. 3 (Feb./March, 1988); editor, Networking - National Native Indian Artists Symposium IV (Graphcom Printer, Lethbridge, 1988); "Visions of Power: Contemporary Art by First Nations, Inuit and Japanese Canadians," (article) in Earth Spirit Festival catalogue (Toronto, 1991); "The Metaphysics of North American Indian Art," (article) in Indigena: Contemporary Native Perspectives, Vancouver/Toronto: Douglas & McIntyre, 1992; "Kiskayetum: Allen Sapp, a Retrospective," Regina: The Mackenzie Art Gallery, 1994; "First Nations Art, 'Canada', and the CIA: A Short Non-Fiction Story," in Studies in Critical Practices, Calgary: Canadian/Communications Research Group, University of Calgary, 1994; "Native Arts in Canada: The State, Academia, and the Cultural Establishment," (article) in Beyond Quebec: Taking Stock of Canada, McGill-Queen's University Press, 1995; "Lawrence Abbot Interview with Alfred Young Man," co-authored and published by the Canadian Journal of Native Studies, Brandon, Manitoba, Spring 1997; North American Indian Art: It's a Question of Integrity, published by Kamloops Art Gallery, Kamloops, B.C., 1998; Indian Reality Today: Contemporary Indian Art of North America, published by the Westphalian State Museum of Natural History, Muenster, Germany, 1999. Latest manuscript: "You Are On Indian Land: A Native Perspective on Native Art/

Politics," a major critique of the issues and problems faced by Native artists today in North America; among many other published & unpublished articles, essays & books reviewed and published in many learned magazines, newspapers, and refereed journals over 25 years; also, produced and/or directed numerous videos.

YOUNGBEAR, JOANN
(health coordinator)
Affiliation: Native American Services Agency, Missoula Indian Center, 2300 Regent St. #A, Missoula, MT 59801 (406) 329-3373.

YOUNGDEER, MERRITT
(BIA area director)
Affiliation: Muskogee Area Office, Bureau of Indian Affairs, 101 N. 5th St., Muskogee, OK 74401 (918) 687-2296.

YOUNGE, SANDRA JEFFERSON (Paiute-Shoshini)
(former tribal chairperson)
Affiliation: Lone Pine Tribal Council, Star Route 1, 1101 S. Main St., Lone Pine, CA 93545 (619) 876-5414.

YUHAHA, MARCEL (Sioux)
(Indian band chief)
Affiliation: Oak Lake Sioux, Box 146, Pipestone, MB, Canada R0M 1T0 (204) 854-2261.

Z

ZAH, PETERSON (Navajo) 1937-
(advisor)
Born December 2, 1937, Low Mountain, Ariz. *Education*: Phoenix College, AA, 1960; Arizona State University, BA, 1963. *Home address*: Resides in Phoenix, Arizona area. *Affiliation*: Advisor to the president of Arizona State University, Tempe, AZ. *Past professional post*: Chairperson, Navajo Nation, Window Rock, AZ, 1983-94. *Community activities*: Wide Public School Association; Window Rock School Board (past president); National Association of the Indian Legal Services (founder); AZ State Advisory Committee to the U.S. Civil Rights Commission (member). *Memberships*: Navajo Education & Scholarship Foundation; National Tribal Chairmen's Association; Council of Energy Resource Tribes. *Awards, honors*: Humanitarian Award, City of Albuquerque, NM—Mayor Harry Kinney; Honorary Doctorate (Humanitarium), Santa Fe College.

ZAH-BAHE, LORENA (Navajo)
(former association president)
Affiliation: National Indian Education Association, 700 N. Fairfax, Suite 210, Alexandria, VA 22314 (703) 838-2870 fax 838-1620.

ZAHARLICK, ANN MARIE, 1947-
(professor of anthropology)
Born March 24, 1947, Scranton, Penna. *Education*: Cedar Crest College, BA, 1969; Lehigh University, MA, 1973; The American University, PhD, 1977 (Dissertation: Picuris Syntax). *Principal occupation*: Professor of anthropology. *Address*: Dept. of Anthropology, Ohio State University, 124 W. 17th Ave., Columbus, OH 43214 (614) 292-4149. *Affiliations*: Instructor and curriculum development specialist, Bilingual/Multicultural Teacher Training Program for Native Americans, The University of Albuquerque, NM, 1975-77; assistant professor and language development specialist, Native American Bilingual Teacher Education Program, The University of Albuquerque, 1977-79; professor, Dept. of Anthropology, The Ohio State University, Columbus, Ohio, 1979-. *Other professional posts*: Instructor, Acoma Pueblo Bilingual Education Program, 1978; instructor, Sandia Pueblo Language Program. *Research/fieldwork*: Research on the Picuris language, Picuris Pueblo, NM, 1973; research on Picuris syntax, Picuris and Taos, NM, 1974-76; development of Keresan language spoken by the pueblos of Acoma, Cochiti, Santo Domingo, Laguna, Zia, Santa Ana, and San Felipe, and development of curriculum guides and bilingual education materials in Keres and Picuris; analysis of Picuris syntax and semology—updating of John P. Harrington's Picuris Children's Stories and preparation of a dictionary and grammar for use in the Picuris bilingual education program, 1976-; linguistic research on passive construction and tone in Picuris,

Picuris, NM, 1980-81. *Community activities*: Assisted in the establishment of bilingual education programs at Acoma, Laguna, Cochiti, Santa Ana, and Picuris Pueblos, 1975-79; produced teaching guides and materials for the Picuris Bilingual Education Programs (10 stories and booklets in Picuris, 1975-); presentations on American Indians to 4th & 5th grade students in the Albuquerque and Columbus Public Schools, 1978-82. *Memberships*: American Anthropological Association (Fellow); American Association for the Advancement of Science; American Ethnological Society; Linguistic Association of the Southwest; Linguistic Society of America; New Mexico Association for Bilingual Education; New York Academy of Sciences; Society for Applied Anthropology (Fellow), Society for the Study of the Indigenous Languages of the Americas; Southwestern Anthropological Association; The Southwest Circle; Southwest Journal of Linguistics (editorial board, 1985-87); among others. *Awards, honors*: Distinction awarded for PhD comprehensive examination: Language Acculturation, 1974; The American University Dissertation Fellowship, 1974-75; The Honor Society pf Phi Kappa Phi; Edward Sapir Award in Linguistics (for Picuris Syntax), The New York Academy of Sciences, 1978; nominated for Outstanding Teaching Award, College of Arts and Sciences, The Ohio State University. *Interests*: Cultural and linguistic anthropology. *Biographical sources*: Outstanding Young Women of America; Who's Who in the Midwest; The International Directory of Distinguished Leadership; Personalities of America; The World Who's Who of Women. *Published works*: Picuris Syntax (University Microfilms, 1977); A Picuris/English Dictionary; Picuris Grammar; editor, Native Languages of the Americas (special issue of the Journal of the Linguistic Association of the Southwest, 1981); numerous book chapters, articles, book reviews, papers and presentation.

ZAUKAR, JANE (Athapascan)
(village president)
Affiliation: Native Village of Sleetmute, P.O. Box 21, Sleetmute, AK 99668 (907) 449-9901.

ZEDENO, MARIA NIEVES
(professor of anthropology)
Education: Southern Methodist University, PhD, 1995. *Affiliation*: Dept. of Anthropology, Emil Haury Anthropology Bldg., Rm. 221A, University of Arizona, Tucson, AZ 85721 (520) 621-2585 Fax 621-2088. E-mail: mzedeno@u.arizona.edu. *Interests*: American Indian cultural resource preservation.

ZEMAN, ALICE FITCH 1931-
(writer)
Born September 14, 1931, Yorkville, Ill. *Education*: College degree. Principal occupation: secretary/news reporter. *Address*: 3436 Chicago Rd., Paw Paw, IL 61353-0056 (815) 627-9027. E-mail: az@azeman.us. *Community activities*: Paw Paw Chamber of Commerce; United Presbyterian Church. *Published works*: "Wabansi: Fiend or Friend"; and "Chief Shabbona's Path of Peace."

ZEPEDA, GAYLE (Pomo)
(rancheria chairperson)
Affiliation: Redwood Valley Rancheria, P.O. Box 499, Redwood Valley, CA 95470 (707) 485-0361.

ZEPEDA, OFELIA (Tohono O'odham)
(educator, poet, editor)
Education: University of Arizona, PhD, 1984. *Address & Affiliation*: Dept. of Linguistics, Douglass 200 E, University of Arizona, Tucson, AZ 85721 (520) 621-8294/6897. Ofelia specializes in writing English and Tohono O'odham languages. Her writing is concerned with the American Southwest, environment, history, and culture. She is the editor of the Native American literacy publication series, Sun Tracks, in Tucson, AZ.

ZEPHIER, MITCHELL CHARLES (Cetan Ho Waste) (Lower Brule Lakota) 1952-
(Plains Indian jeweler)
Born July 5, 1952, Pine Ridge, S.D. *Education*: High school. *Principal occupation*: Plains Indian jeweler. *Address & Affiliation*: Whispering Thunder, 2107 Oak Ave., Rapid City, SD 57701 (605) 348-1695. *Exhibits/Shows*: Intertribal Missouri River Arts Festival, Lakota Council, Chamberlain, SD, July 1986 (won 1st Place

Ribbon and cash award); American Indian Gallery, Steamboat Springs, CO, Feb. 1987; Northern Plains Tribal Arts 88, Sioux Falls, SD, Sept. 1988 (won 1st Place; White Buffalo Winter—Opulence Jewelers, Breckenridge, CO, Feb. 1989; among others. *Interests*: "I've developed a singular and totally original style of jewelry that is a combination of artistry and craftmanship. I define my work as 'Lakota Jewelry Visions' because there is a visionary aspect to it as well as an expressionistic aspect which describes many ideas, legends, wintercounts, and Lakota cultural concepts. I work in sterling silver, brass, jeweler's gold, copper, Geman silver and have just recently begun to work in 14 karat gold. I encorporate stones and materials from the Northern Plains area . My work can be summed up as an honoring or a dedication to the heritage and spiritual values of my Lakota ancestors. My work is displayed in numerous private and public collections." *Biographical soures*: "Indian Trader" magazine article by Jane Nauman, Jan. 1980; "Dakota West" magazine article by James Aplan, Summer 1981; "Four Winds" magazine article by Rosemary Webb, Summer 1982; "Rapid City Journal" - two part article by Jane Nauman, Sept. 1984; Lost and Found Traditions, book by Ralph T. Coe (University of Washington Press, 1986); Crafts in America, book by Constance Stapleton (Harper & Row, 1988).

ZIBELL, WILLIAM (Eskimo)
(village president)
Affiliation: Noorvik Native Community, P.O. Box 71, Noorvik, AK 99763 (907) 636-2144.

ZILKA, CAROL L. (Cheyenne River Sioux) 1949-
(BIA special educator)
Born December 24, 1949, Sioux Falls, S.D. *Education*: Mankato State University, BS, 1972; Penn State University, MEd, 1984. *Principal occupation*: Special educator. *Home address*: 5781 Rayburn Ave., Apt. 163, Apt. 163, Alexandria, VA 22311-5726 (202) 343-6675 (office). *Affiliations*: Special education teacher, Hennepin Technical Centers, Hennepin, MN (2 years); educational case manager (seven years), special education coordinator, 1984-88, BIA, Office of Indian Education Programs, Eastern Area Office; early/childhood special education coordinator, Office of Indian Education, Central Office, BIA, 1951 Constitution Ave., NW, Washington, DC 20245. *Other professional posts*: Equal employment opportunities counselor for BIA, 1989-; Mountain Plains Regional Resource Center, Advisory Committee, 1989-. *Memberships*: Council for Exceptional Children, 1977- (MN board of directors, 1979-81; 1980 local arrangements chairperson for National Topical Conferences on seriously emotionally disturbed; 1978-81 Minnesota convention director; 1978 Minnesota chapter 32, president; 1977 Minnesota chapter 32 publicity and membership chairperson). *Awards, honors*: 1985, '86 & '87 Certificates of Special Achievement, Dept. of the Interior, BIA; 1983 Graduate Fellowship, Penn State University, American Indian Special Education Teacher Training Program (member of first graduating class); 1980 National Council for Exceptional Children, Certificate of Appreciation (served as local arrangements chairperson for national conference on seriously emotionally disturbed; 1980 MN Council for Exceptional Children, President's Award for Personal Contribution, dedicated effort and planning of Minnesota's first CEC Topical Conference; 1980 Hennepin Technical Center, Superintendent's Award for advancing professional development.

ZIMMERMAN, LARRY JOHN 1947-
(archaeologist)
Born May 24, 1947, Anamosa, Iowa. *Education*: University of Iowa, BA, 1969, MA, 1971; University of Kansas, PhD, 1976. *Principal occupation*: Archaeologist. *Address*: 3916 Freedoms Trail NE, Iowa City, IA 52240-7955. *Affiliations*: Professor of Anthropology, University of South Dakota, Vermillion, SD, 1974-96; University of Iowa, Iowa City (American Indian & Native Studies, 1996-2001; Dept. of Anthropology, 2002); Minnesota Historical Society, Dept. of Archaeology, 2003-. *Other professional post*: Editor, South Dakota Archaeology, 1977-79; editor, Plains Anthropologist, 1987-89; editor, World Archaeological Bulletin, 1990-94; secretary, World Archaeological Congress, 1990-94; chairman, Dept. of Social Behavior, 1988-. *Military service*: U.S. Air Force, 1965-69, 2nd Lt. *Community activities*: Vermillion Chamber of Commerce

(Board of Directors, 1983-84); Friends of the W.H. Over Museum (vice president, Board of Directors); consultant for Native American Rights Fund, American Indian Movement, American Indians Against Desecration, Pawnee Tribe of Oklahoma, and other groups; Friends of Grand Portage (director); Minnesota Archaeological Society (director). *Memberships*: Plains Anthropological Society (editor, 1987-89, member, 1971-); Fellow, American Anthropological Association; World Archaeological Congress (executive secretary, 1990-94; editor, 1990-94); Society for American Archaeology; Sigma Xi (scientific research society). *Awards, honors*: Phi Beta Kappa, Sigma Xi (national lecturer, 1991-92); USD Student Association Teacher of the Year, 1980; Danforth Association, 1981; Presidential Fellow (USD), 1985; Burlington Northern Award for Meritorious Teaching, 1986; Burlington Northern Award for Meritorious Scholar, 1990; Distinguished Regents Professor, 1990. *Interests*: "Primary interest is in the prehistory of North America, especially the Great Plains, others are ethical treatment of the dead, public education in archaeology, Native American rights; avocational interests are in racquetball, music (especially jazz)." *Published works*: Prehistoric Locational Behavior (University of Iowa Press, 1977); The Crow Creek Massacre (Corps of Engineers-Omaha, 1981); The Future of South Dakota's Past (South Dakota Archaeological Society, 1981); People of Prehistoric South Dakota (University of Nebraska Press, 1985); South Dakota Leaders (University of South Dakota Press, 1989); Idea to Institution: Higher Education in South Dakota (University of South Dakota Press, 1989); Native North America (Little Brown, 1996); Indians and Anthropology (University of Arizona Press, 1997); Ethical Issues in Archaeology (Alta Mira Press, 2003); The Archaeologist's Toolkit (Alta Mira Press, 2003); The American Indian/The First Nations: Native North American Myth, Life, 7 Art (Duncan Baird, 2003).

ZIOLKOWSKI, ANNE
(foundation/museum director)
Affiliation: Crazy Horse Memorial Foundation & Museum, Ave. of the Chiefs, The Black Hills, Crazy Horse, SD 57730 (605) 673-4681.

ZIOLKOWSKI, RUTH
(foundation chairperson)
Affiliation: Crazy Horse Memorial Foundation, Ave. of the Chiefs, The Black Hills, Crazy Horse, SD 57730 (605) 673-4681.

ZLOTKIN, NORMAN A.
(native law centre instructor)
Affiliations: University of Saskatchewan, Native Law Centre, Diefenbaker Centre, Saskatoon, SK, Canada S7N 0W0 (306) 966-6189; contributing editor, Canadian Native Law Reporter.

ZOBEL, MELISSA TANTAQUIDGEON (Mohegan)
(tribal historian)
Affiliation & Address: Trial Historian, Mohegan Tribe, 5 Crow Hill Rd., Uncasville, CT 06382 (860) 862-6100. *Community activities*: Editorial Board, NI Ya Yo (tribal newspaper).

ZONGOLOWICZ, HELEN
(school principal)
Affiliation: Chuska/Tohatchi Consolidated School, P.O. Box 321, Tohatchi, NM 87325 (505) 733-2280.

ZOTIGH, DENNIS W. (*T'don-say*) (Kiowa/ Santee Dakota/San Juan Pueblo)
(research historian)
Born in Lawton, Okla. *Education*: University of Oklahoma, BA (Journalism/Public Relations. *Principal occupation*: American Indian research historian. *Address & Affiliation*: Oklahoma Historical Society, 4901 N. Lincoln Blvd., Oklahoma City, OK 73105 (405) 843-5440. E-mail: dzotigh.ok-history.mus.ok.us. *Other professional posts*: National speaker on Indian culture and issues, American Speakers Bureau; Executive board of directors, American Indian Broadcasting, Inc.; Smithsonian Museum Affiliates Program, Washington, DC, 2002-present. *Awards, honors*: Powwow awards for powwow dancing and singing competition; emcee for the Miss Indian Woirld Pageant, Gathering of Nations, Albuquerque, NM, 1993, 1994, 1995; co-founder of the World Hoop Dance Championships, Heard Museum, Phoenix, AZ; consultant/cultural advisor for Hallmark Miniseries, "Dream Keepers," ABC TV, 2003; consultant/history advisor for "World of Americann Indian Dance," NBC TV, 2002. *Community activities*: Board member, Oklahoma Folk Life Council. *Memberships*: Mountain Plains Museums Association (Little, CO, 2001-present); Oklahoma Museums Association (Oklahoma City, 2001-present).

ZUMIGA, DR. ARTHUR W.
(Indian education program director)
Affiliation: Rapid City School District, Indian Education Program, 300 Sixth St., Rapid City, SD 57701 (605) 394-4071 Fax 394-4085. E-mail: arthur.zumiga@csac.rcas.org.

ZUNI, CHRISTINE (Pueblo)
(attorney)
Address: P.O. Box 402, Isleta Pueblo, NM 87022 (505) 869-3421. *Membership*: United Indian Pueblo Lawyers Association.

ZUNIGHA, MERLE
(BIA agency supt.)
Affiliation: Eastern Nevada Agency, BIA, 1555 Shoshone Cir., Elko, NV 89801 (702) 738-0569.

ZUNIGHA, WAYNE
(BIA agency supt.)
Affiliation: Salt River Agency, Bureau of Indian Affairs, Route 1, Box 117, Scottsdale, AZ 85256 (602) 640-2842.

INDIAN COUNTRY ADDRESS BOOK

Contains the names, addresses and phone numbers of about 15,000 Native American organizations, institutions, businesses and individuals arranged in about 60 categories, including: Artists & Craftspersons; Business Groups; Entertainment, Music, Dance; Environment & Natural Resources; Events; Foundations; Galleries & Craft Shops; Gaming; Government Agencies; Groups, Clubs, Associations; Health Organizations; Indian Centers; Indian Nations; Periodicals; Schools; Speakers, Storytellers; Travel &, Tourism; and more. Available on Diskette. 2005 - 5th Edition. 350 pages. ISBN 0-915344-65-3. $95.

NATIVE AMERICAN INTERNET GUIDE

Find interesting and useful Native American sites on the Web without having to waste hours searching for them. Native American Internet Guide puts information about Indian Country right at your fingertips. This book lists over 1,500 Native groups, organizations, nations, businesses and individuals and their web sites and e-mail addresses. Available on Diskette. 2005 - 3rd Edition. 96 pages. ISBN 0-915344-64-5. $50.

THE AMERICAN INDIAN CD-ROM

Contains the history of American Indians from 19th Century original source documents. A library of Indian resources. Includes extensive data on the Ojibwe (Chippewa), Cherokee, Sioux, Navajo and many other tribes. Linguistic coverage is broad; a full text of all treaties is included, and more. Available on Diskette. Hypertexted CD-ROM for IBM & Macintosh. $95.

THE CONCISE LAKHOTA DICTIONARY: ENGLISH TO LAKHOTA

Compiled by Cheyenne River Sioux tribal members. Features over 4,000 entries of words from the Lakhota dialect of the ancient Sioux language. 64 pages. $35.

THE BIG BOOK OF MINORITY OPPORTUNITIES: THE DIRECTORY OF SPECIAL PROGRAMS FOR MINORITY GROUP MEMBERS

Lists over 4,000 organizations that have established special programs to help African, Hispanic, Asian, and Native Americans meet their educational and career goals. Includes programs offered by public agencies, foundations, professional associations, community organizations, private industry, and colleges and universities. Lists scholarships, fellowships, grants, loans, employment programs, career training, summer employment, internships, and occupational information programs for minorities. 630 pages. $75.

NATIONAL DIRECTORY OF MINORITY-OWNED BUSINESS FIRMS

Lists more than 37,000 minority-owned businesses, organized by SIC code, alphabetically and geographically. Includes phone & fax numbers, contact names, number of employees, certification status, and start-up date. Key word business descriptions. 1,500 pages. $275.

NATIONAL DIRECTORY OF WOMEN-OWNED BUSINESSES

Lists more than 15,000 companies which are at least 50% women-owned, organized by SIC code, alphabetically & geographically. Includes phone & fax numbers, contact names, number of employees, certification status, and start-up date. Key word business descriptions. 1,100 pages. $275.